D1626895

Dictionary of Artists in Britain since 1945

Dictionary of Artists
in Britain since 1945

David Buckman

DICTIONARIES

First published in 1998 by Art Dictionaries Ltd.,
81g Pembroke Road, Bristol BS8 3EA.

ISBN 0 9532609 0 9

The publishers gratefully acknowledge the generous sponsorship support which they have received from Christie's International plc, Independent Art Promotions, Phillips Fine Art Auctioneers and Valuers, Sansom & Company Ltd., Sotheby's, Philippa Cooper and John Evans, and also the support of the galleries and other organisations which have taken advertising space in the dictionary.

SOTHEBY'S

Independent Art Promotions

BritArt.com

British Library Cataloguing in Publication Data
A catalogue record for this book is available from
The British Library.

Typeset by Inde-Dutch Systems (India) Ltd.
and printed by WBC Ltd., Bridgend, Mid Glamorgan

CONTENTS

INDEX OF ADVERTISERS

The advertisements appear on the pages indicated, and also throughout the dictionary.

ACKNOWLEDGEMENTS

Compiling a dictionary is impossible without the help of many others. First, my thanks go to John Sansom, of Art Dictionaries Ltd, who has enthusiastically overseen the complicated task of transforming a huge typescript into a finished book. Otherwise, my biggest "thank you" must go to John Kilgannon, without whose contribution the compilation might never have been accomplished and would certainly have taken much longer. He has offered continual encouragement from the start, and undertook much of the burden of mailing questionnaires and filing. Philippa Cooper put up with the project for several years, read the entries and made many useful suggestions. Alan Guest gave invaluable help with proofs.

Other special thanks go to Colin Ashford, for information on transport artists; Pat Bowring, of Woodlands Art Gallery, for background on its many exhibitions; Michael Canney, regarding Cornish artists; Alannah Coleman, for pointers to Australian artists who worked and showed in Britain; John Cranfield; Michael Daykin; Jane England and Peter Gordon-Stable, of England & Co; John Evans; Howard Goodall; Sue Graves, for information on Sheffield artists; the staff of Islington Libraries, especially the Central Reference Library; Waj and Edna Mirecki, of Chappel Galleries, for information on East Anglian artists; David Mitchell, of the Bankside Gallery archive; Richard Scott, for help with The Suffolk Group; University College, London, notably Joanna Shacklock and Carol Bowen, for information on Slade School students; the Welsh Arts Council/Arts Council of Wales staff, especially Rhian Basten, Linda Shakespeare and Valmai Ward, for details of Welsh artists; and Grant Waters, who worked with me to gather details on Ruth Doggett.

It would be impracticable to list the many hundreds of artists who have responded to my questionnaires; relations and friends of artists who have provided information; local newspapers, which in printing appeals for information have often proved a last resort in getting what was needed; and others who have put themselves out to assist. I have had endless help from commercial galleries, and have tried to include their names in artist entries, making further reader research possible. Numerous public galleries and museums also helped, and they and members of staff are in this list of organisations and individuals particularly useful to me:

Abbot Hall Art Gallery
Aberdeen Art Gallery
Aberdeen Artists' Society
Margaret Agnew
Ken Aitken
David Alston
Josephine Andersen
Emma Anderson
Antelope Productions Ltd
Michael Archer
Arnolfini
Tamar Arnon
Art Gallery of Western Australia
Art Matters
Art Workers' Guild
Arts Club
Arts Council of England
Arts Council of Ireland
Arts Council of Northern Ireland
Ashmolean Museum
Aspex Gallery
M V Attrill
Auckland City Art Gallery
Patricia Austin
Australian High Commission
Charles Baile de Laperriere
Anthony Bailey
Rupert Baker
J Baldry
Joan Banger
Bankfield Museum & Art Gallery
Barbican Centre

Barclays Bank PLC
Francis Bargman
Anne J Barlow
Andrew Barlow
J C S Barnes
Barnet Local History Archive
Bath College of Higher Education
Jeremy Beach
Anthony Beeson
Chris Beetles
Ben Uri Art Society
Jan Benington
Chloë Bennett
Janet Bennett
Susan Bennett
Jon Bennington
Bethnal Green Museum of Childhood
Jill Betts
Bryan Biggs
Birmingham Museums & Art Gallery
Birmingham Post
Eileen Black
Bluecoat Arts Centre
John Blundell
Bolton Museums and Art Gallery
Book Trust
Bea Bossom
Bournemouth & Poole College of Art & Design
Bournemouth Arts Club
Astrid Bowron
Bradford City Libraries
Fiona Bradley
Laurie Bray
Roger Breakwell
Brecknock Museum
D Bridge
David Briers
Brighton Area Libraries, Local Studies
Brighton Art Gallery and Museum
Brighton Polytechnic
Bristol Central Library
British Film Institute
British Library
British Medical Association
British Museum, Prints and Drawings
British Music Information Centre
British Olympic Association
British Society of Master Glass Painters
Anne Britton
Angela Broome
Sarah Brown
Lillian Browse
David C Bryan
Buckinghamshire College
George Bunting
The late Hazel Burston
Burstow & Hewitt
Bushey Museum
Buxton Museum & Art Gallery
Byam Shaw School of Art
Calderdale Central Library
Camberwell College of Arts
Cambridge Society of Painters and Sculptors
Camden Arts Centre
Camden Local Studies and Archives Centre
Irene Campbell
Paula Campbell
Vicki Campbell
Campden Hill Club
Jeannette Canavan
Canterbury City Council
Frances Carey
Colin Carlin
Gerry Carr
Cartwright Hall Art Gallery
Kate Carver
D M Catte
Amanda Catto
Central St Martins College of Art & Design
Stephen Chaplin
Chartered Society of Designers
Michael and Valerie Chase
Chelsea Arts Club
Chelsea College of Art & Design
Chelsea Library
Cheltenham & Gloucester College of Higher Education
Cheltenham Art Gallery and Museum
Cheltenham Ladies' College
Tessa Chester
Chevron UK Ltd
Christ's Hospital
Christchurch Mansion
Christie's South Kensington
Church House Inquiries Centre
Krzysztof Cieszkowski

R Aquila Clarke
Angela Clutterbuck
David Cobb
Harry Cobb
David Coke
Beverley Cole
Kathie Collins
Lisa Collins
Bill Connelly
Contemporary Art Society
Peter Cormack
Cornish Studies Library
Lesley Cornish
Coventry and Warwickshire Society of Artists
Coventry Art Guild
Coventry University
Alison Cowling
Crafts Council
Crawford Arts Centre
Wendy Crawford
Melva Croal
Croydon Art Society
Croydon College of Art & Design
Roger Cucksey
Maggie Cullen
Caroline da Costa
Susan Daniel
Darlington Museum
Peter Davies
Richard Davies
Judith Davis
Sarah Davy
Graham Day
De La Warr Pavilion
Raphaël De Smedt
Dean and Chapter of Canterbury
Debrett's Peerage
C Demeulemeester
Denbighshire Art Society
Derby Museum and Art Gallery
Derby Sketching Club
Design Museum Library
Christopher Di Rollo
Jo Digger
DLI Museum & Durham Art Gallery
Teresa Docherty
Patricia Dodsworth
Doncaster Museum and Art Gallery
Amanda-Jane Doran
Dulwich College
Sophie Duncan
Anne Dunlop
Philip Dunn
Ealing Art Club
East Kent Art Society
East Midlands Arts
Eastbourne Group
Eastern Arts
David Easton
Edinburgh City Art Centre
Mark Ellin
Hilda Elsmere
Janita Elton
Epping Forest District Museum
Eton College
Everard Read Gallery
Exeter Art School
Exeter Art Society
Falmouth Art Gallery
Federation of British Artists
Ferens Art Gallery
Alison Ferguson
James Fergusson
Fine Art Catalogues
Sarah Finlay
Fred Fleming
Ann Forsdyke
Stephen Foster
Ann Marie Fowles
Roger C C Frame
Jacci Fraser
Free Painters and Sculptors
Freud Museum
Fylingdales Group of Artists
Mireille Galinou
Gateshead Art Society
Peter Gauld
Rita Gibbs
Margaret Girvan
Christine Gist
Glasgow Art Club
Glasgow Museums & Art Galleries
Glasgow School of Art
Anne Gleave
Glenrothes Development Corporation
Glynn Vivian Art Gallery
Goethe-Institut
Anne Goodchild
Elizabeth Goudge

Barbara Graham
Graves Art Gallery
Gray's School of Art
Fleur Gray
Richard Green
Roger Green
Stephanie Green
Linda Greenlick
Greenwich Printmakers' Association
Pamela Griffin
Elyn Wyn Griffiths
Irving Grose
Grosvenor Art Society
The Guardian
Andrew Guest
Debbie Guest
Guild of Aviation Artists
Guild of Motoring Artists
Guild of Railway Artists
Guildford House Gallery
Guildhall Art Gallery
Richard Gundry
Mollie Haig
Ann Hall-Williams
Hampstead Garden Suburb Institute
Marcelle Hanselaar
Rosalind Hardiman
Dorothy Harding
Harris Museum & Art Gallery
Harrow School
Elaine Hart
Catherine Harvey
Haslemere Art Society
Hastings Museum and Art Gallery
P Hatfield
Hatton Gallery
Alasdair Hawkyard
Henry Moore Foundation
Henry Moore Sculpture Trust
Herbert Art Gallery and Museums
Nigel Herring
Alan Hibbs
Hilmarton Manor Press
Simon Hincks
Frank Hodges
Tony Hodges
Ann Holland
Malcolm Holmes
Juliet Hone
Hong Kong Government Office
Hong Kong Museum of Art
Bill Hopkins
Hove Museum & Art Gallery
Natasha Howes
Bill and Margaret Hume
Christopher Hunt
Peter Hunter
Elizabeth Hutchings
Sarah Hyde
Charlotte Ibbotson
Ikon Gallery
Illustrated London News
Imperial War Museum
Independent Art Promotions
The Independent
Institute of Contemporary Arts
Institute of International Visual Arts
Ipswich Art Club
Ipswich Museums & Galleries
Irish Museum of Modern Art
Vicki Irwin
Islington Art Circle
Sandra Jackaman
Zdzislaw Jagodzinski
Helen James
Jewish Chronicle
John Hansard Gallery
Penny Johnson
Isobel Johnstone
Barbara Jones
Paul Joyner
Valerie Kay
Brian Kennedy
Kent Institute of Art & Design
John R Kenyon
Alex Kidson
King's School, Canterbury
Monika Kinley
Terry Knight
Vivien Knight
Koninklijke Bibliotheek Albert I
I Lackajis
Laing Art Gallery
Lake Artists' Society
Pat Lambert
Ruth Lambert
Lancashire County Museum Service
Langham Sketch Club
Josephine Lanyon
Leamington Spa Museum & Art Gallery

Antonia Lean
Leeds Central Library
Leeds City Art Gallery
Leeds College of Art & Design
Leicester Museum and Art Gallery
Leicester Society of Artists
Leicestershire County Council Information Centre
Pauline Lellman
Leo Baeck Institute
Lewes Library
Lianne Jarrett Associates
Ivy Lin
David Linton
Liverpool Daily Post & Echo
Liverpool John Moores University
Liverpool Polytechnic
Livingstone Development Corporation
Karen Livingstone
Lloyd's Register of Shipping
London Group
London Press Club
London Sketch Club
London Transport Museum
Grant Longman
Louisiana Museum of Modern Art, Denmark
Rebecca Lowe
Patrick McCoy
Sarah Macdonald
Vicky Macdonald
Clare McGread
MacRobert Arts Centre
Eileen Maitland
Malvern Girls' College
Manchester Central Library
Manchester City Art Gallery
Manchester City Council Planning Department
Manchester Metropolitan University
Mander & Mitchenson Theatre Collection
Manor House Museum
Mansfield Society of Artists
Steve Manthorp
Mappin Art Gallery
Catherine Marshall
F Warren Marshall
Lesley Marshall
Sandra Martin
Medici Society
George Melly
Middlesex Polytechnic
Ariede Migliavacca
Malcolm Miles
Corinne Miller
Ministry of Defence
The Minories
Mold Library, Museum & Gallery
Michael Molnar
Michael Moody
Alan Moore
Lisa Moran
Patricia Moriarty
David Morris
Lynda Morris
Fiona Mosley
Mostyn Gallery
Museum of London
Museum of Modern Art, New York
Museum of Modern Art, Oxford
Museum of Reading
Pauline Mycock
Constance Nash
National Army Museum
National Art Library
National Gallery of Australia
National Gallery of Canada
National Gallery of Ireland
National Library of Wales
National Maritime Museum
National Museum of Labour History
National Museum of Wales
National Portrait Gallery Heinz Archive and Library
National Railway Museum
National Society of Painters, Sculptors and Printmakers
Rosemary Nattrass
New York Public Library
New Zealand High Commission
Susan Newell
Newlyn Art Gallery
Newport Museum and Art Gallery
NHS Estates
Norfolk and Norwich Art Circle
North West Arts Board
Northampton Museum and Art Gallery
Northern Arts
Norwich School of Art & Design

Nottingham Society of Artists
Sheila O'Hara
Ian O'Riordan
Österreichische Nationalbibliothek
Outsider Collection and Archive
Betty Owen
Emma Owen
Oxford Art Society
Pallant House
Rebecca Parkin
Linda Parry
Godfrey Omar Parsons
Anthony Parton
B Peckover
Lesley Pitman
Jonathan Platt
N M Plumley
Alison Plumridge
Plymouth City Museums and Gallery
Polish Library
B Pollak
Portsmouth City Museum and Art Gallery
Post Office Archives and Record Centre
Alan Powers
Susan M Preston
Prontaprint!, Holloway Road, Islington
Public Record Office
Publishers' Association
Punch
Eugene Rae
Denise Raine
Ravensbourne College of Design and Communication
Mark Read
Reading Guild of Artists
Chris Reeve
H C Reid
Ross Reyburn
Iris C Rhodes
Andrew F Richardson
Sarah Richardson
Ridley Art Society
Robert Gordon Institute of Technology
The Hon. Mrs Roberts
Fiona Robertson
Rowena Robertson
Sonia Robinson
Rochdale Art Gallery
Royal Academy of Arts
Royal Air Force, Air Historical Branch
Royal Air Force Museum, Hendon
Royal Albert Memorial Museum & Art Gallery
Royal Birmingham Society of Artists
Royal Cambrian Academy
Royal Collection Trust
Royal College of Art
Royal College of Surgeons of England
Royal Cornwall Museum Galleries, Truro
Royal Festival Hall
Royal Geographical Society
Royal Glasgow Institute of the Fine Arts
Royal Hibernian Academy
Royal Institute of British Architects
Royal Institute of Oil Painters
Royal Institution of Cornwall
Royal Marines Museum
Royal Photographic Society
Royal Scottish Academy
Royal Scottish Society of Painters in Water-Colours
Royal Society of Arts
Royal Society of British Sculptors
Royal Society of Marine Artists
Royal Society of Miniature Painters, Sculptors and Gravers
Royal Society of Painter-Printmakers
Royal Ulster Academy of Arts
Royal Watercolour Society
Royal West of England Academy
Rugby and District Art Society
Rural History Centre, University of Reading
Russell-Cotes Museum & Art Gallery
Josephine Ryan
Rye Art Gallery
Saatchi Gallery
Sabena
Salford Art Gallery
Judith Sandling
Angela Sansom
Clara Sansom
Fiona Sansom
Jessica Sansom
Pat Saunders
Gill Saunders
Doris Schneider-Wagenbichler
School of Oriental & African Studies
School of Slavonic and East European Studies

Alice Schwab
Walter Schwab
Science Museum
Duncan Scott
Scottish Arts Club
Scottish Arts Council
Scottish National Gallery of Modern Art
Scottish Sculpture Trust
John Seabrook
Victoria Searby
Julie Seddon Jones
Jane Sedge
Margaret Shaw
Irene Shawcock
Jim Shea
Sheeran Lock Fine Art Consultants
John Sheeran
Shipley Art Gallery
Ann Simpson
Colin Simpson
Sarah Simpson
Neil Sinclair
Victoria Slowe
Charles Smith
Donald Smith
Gaye Smith
Society of Authors
Society of Equestrian Artists
Society of Graphic Fine Art
Society of Scottish Artists
Society of Staffordshire Artists
Society of Wildlife Artists
Society of Women Artists
Joanna Soden
South African National Gallery
South Bank Centre
South East Arts
Southampton City Art Gallery
Southbourne Art Society
Gerald Southgate
Spacex Gallery
Margaret Spencer
Michael Spender
Jill Springall
St Bride Printing Library
St Ives School of Painting
Hugh Stevenson
Ann Stewart
Claire H Stewart
Tina Stiles
Stoke-on-Trent Museum and Art Gallery
Clare Storey
Judith Stringer
Eumie Imm Stroukoff
Alan Suddes
Sunderland Art Gallery
Sunderland University
Swiss Cottage Library
Tate at St Ives
Tate Gallery Library
Tate Gallery, Liverpool
A F Tatham
Alan Taylor
Pamela Taylor
Christine Thomas
Oscar Thompsett
Penny Thompson
Betty Thurston
The Times
Blair Todd
Cristina Tomas
Mike Tooby
Towneley Hall Art Gallery & Museum
Towner Art Gallery
David Tregunna
Hugo Trotter
Tunbridge Wells Art Club
Ulster Arts Club
Ulster Museum
United Society of Artists
University of Central England in Birmingham
University of Hertfordshire
University of Northumbria Gallery
University of the West of England
Usher Gallery
Nino Vella
Jo Velleman
Victoria & Albert Museum
Victoria Art Gallery, Bath
Carla Vigna
Maija Vilcins
Paul Vining
Eva and Zdenek Voráčkovi
Wakefield City Art Gallery
Walker Art Gallery
Rosemary Walker
Catherine Wallace
Jane Wallis
Walsall Museum & Art Gallery

Jean Walsh
Terry Walsh
Wansbeck District Council
Wapping Group of Artists
E V Watson
Rebecca Weaver
Ulla B Weinberg
Julia Weiner
Welwyn Garden City Art Club
West Derby Publishing
West Midlands Arts
Westminster Reference Library
Andrew Wheatley
Lucy Whetstone
John Whiddett
Marc Whiteside
Stephen Whittle
Whitworth Art Gallery
Timothy Wilcox
Alison Wild
Sandy Wilderspin
Stephen Wildman
John Willett
William Morris Gallery
Gower Williams
Williamson Art Gallery & Museum
David Williamson
Carolyn Wingfield
Thelma Winyard
Anne Wishart
Bryen Wood
Mara-Helen Wood
Richard Wood
Laura Woolley
Austin Wormleighton
Godfrey Worsdale
Worthing Museum & Art Gallery
Caroline Worthington
Michael Wright
Max Wykes-Joyce
Y Tabernacl
York City Art Gallery
Yorkshire Sculpture Park

INTRODUCTION

Although some dictionaries of British artists venture beyond 1945, there is nothing that attempts a comprehensive survey after that date to the present day. This book concentrates on the period which began with victory in Europe – VE-day was May 8, 1945 – in the belief that what went on before then has been fairly comprehensively covered by other dictionaries, and that the rebirth of the visual and other arts from the war's end demands a new approach. Inevitably, many artists included, as in previous surveys, started their careers before 1945, but thousands of new ones emerge who need recording.

The year 1945 proved an exciting one for a war-fatigued and -ravaged Britain. The Labour Party landslide election victory gave many new hope and shook up government and society. The country's six years of near-isolation culturally soon began to change, and there was a new confidence in the domestic product. In music, Benjamin Britten's opera *Peter Grimes* was a triumph for a British composer in a field where there was no tradition of achievement. Visits by such internationally distinguished performers as the composer Francis Poulenc, the cellist Pablo Casals and the violinist Ginette Neveu enhanced the concert scene. The 1945 drama season was, said *The Annual Register*, "one of the most remarkable in theatrical history … one of unbroken success", with outstanding performances by Ralph Richardson as Falstaff in Shakespeare's *King Henry IV* and by Laurence Olivier as Oedipus in Sophocles' *Oedipus*. Cinema, still dominated by American imports, saw a new interest in British films, such as *The Way to the Stars*, *Brief Encounter* and *Blithe Spirit*. In literature, George Orwell published *Animal Farm* and Evelyn Waugh *Brideshead Revisited*.

CEMA – the Council for Encouragement of Music and the Arts – was transformed into the Arts Council of Great Britain. It had been an important organiser of exhibitions during a war that had seen restricted showings for artists. Soon after hostilities ended, the dim, deprived art world of London began to come alive again. Just after VE-day, the National Gallery reopened with an exhibition of 50 masterpieces returned from storage in a Welsh slate quarry. The National Portrait Gallery reopened with Sir Godfrey Kneller's Kit-Cat Club portraits. The Royal Academy staged an important exhibition of Soviet graphic art, and one of more than 1,000 works out of the 5,000 commissioned or bought by the War Artists' Advisory Committee since 1940. Particularly enlightening at the end of 1945 were the Victoria & Albert Museum's exhibition of recent paintings by Pablo Picasso and a group of retrospective works by Henri Matisse, and the Tate Gallery's show at the National Gallery – the Tate was still closed for repairs – of pictures by Paul Klee. Such dazzling modern shows were still capable of creating controversy, but they would markedly influence British artists during the ensuing half-century.

This dictionary, which includes such artists, is designed to cover painters, sculptors, draughtsmen, teachers, video, film, installation and performance artists born in the United Kingdom. Foreign artists are included if they have a significant presence. Those who are primarily illustrators or craft workers, such as potters, are usually not included. I have endeavoured to avoid the scant entry often included in dictionaries, going for as reasonably comprehensive a listing as possible. Entries are designed to enlighten anyone spotting an unfamiliar name or canvas in the gallery or auction room, so working name is the principal guide. Therefore, L S Lowry appears as Laurence Stephen Lowry; Ferelyth, who signs thus, appears under that name, but is cross-referenced to Ferelyth Wills. Gilbert & George appear thus, with their full names within that entry. For groups such as the Situationists, Borough Group or New English Art Club there is no separate entry, as members showed under their own names. However, Art & Language and Fine Artz, where participants for a time exhibited jointly, have separate entries, with some individual entries in addition. Chinese names present a problem. The correct Chinese usage is surname first, but some artists adopt the Western practice of surname last, and I have tried to follow what the individual prefers.

Length of entry is not directly related to so-called importance. I hope that the listing for, say, Francis Bacon or Henry Moore supplies the basic facts; the reader can readily find more elsewhere. Entries for lesser-known artists – such as Oswell Blakeston, Louisa Hodgson, Humphrey Slater and William Lyons-Wilson – might be longer, as the published information on them has been hard to assemble, requiring time-consuming primary research. Some entries are not as complete as I would like and a few recommended names, such as Harry Belton, failed to yield essential facts sufficient to compile a satisfactory piece. If anyone can add to what a search of the literature, personal inquiries by phone and letter and letters to newspapers have failed to complete, I would like to hear. In a list of well over 10,000 names, mistakes will occur. Any constructive comment on an entry will be welcomed through the publisher (for reply, a stamped addressed envelope is necessary).

An aim has been to assemble entries mainly from primary sources, as experience shows that dependence on others' research too often leads to repeated mistakes (Mary Kessell is one artist who has suffered badly in this regard). I have found that catalogues put out by prestigious galleries and auction houses commonly have wrong years of birth and death (Ruth Doggett's dates in some published sources appeared to have been assembled by throwing dice). I have tried to update the long-outdated information which often is the only source available for some artists. Francis Butterfield is an example, where in previous sources the artist's entry usually ends in the late 1930s, even though he died in 1968 (the enterprising research of Ron Morley helped me here). Of more than 6,500 letters, cards and other communications sent out to gather information, over 1,500 were to confirm birth and death dates. Experience has shown that even family records may be inaccurate regarding dates, requiring independent checking. Hundreds of sources, ranging from museum and gallery officials in Britain and abroad to artists, their families, newspapers and even vicars checking gravestones have provided invaluable help. Some groups of artists have regularly assisted my researches freely. The insistence by a few on a quite high search fee has made the gathering of some information impracticable.

To give the dictionary a broad base, I have researched regional groups, notably Cornwall, Liverpool, the northeast and East Anglia, and specialists such as motoring, aviation, marine and equestrian artists. Non-inclusion of any artist does not mean he or she has been ignored. Persistent attempts to get some details have met with no response.

Art galleries listed are in London unless otherwise stated; sometimes location could not readily be determined. Where an autobiography has been published I try to mention this; biographies, because they are constantly appearing, are not usually cited in an entry, although some are listed in the bibliography. Entries adopt the past tense to avoid their being overtaken by events. Quotations are generally from the artists. County of birth is that current at the time, county of current residence usually using the terminology in vogue at time of writing. My use of descriptions such as abstract or Expressionist is a shorthand guide to an artist's style as I know it.

Such a book as this is inevitably work in progress. Its compilation has indicated to me how many fine and interesting artists remain little-known and need to have their details recorded for reference. Future editions will doubtless include more.

David Buckman

Keith Vaughan *Landscape*, c.1960s

England &co

14 Needham Road, London W11 2RP
Tel 0171-221 0417 Fax 0171-221 4499

The gallery opened in 1988 with a programme of retrospective exhibitions reassessing the work of British artists working in the 1940s, 50s and 60s, combined with a series of solo shows of contemporary art by both young and established artists. Survey exhibitions over the past ten years have included 'Art in Boxes', 'British Surrealism', 'The 1960s', 'The Collage Show', 'Reflections of the Fifties', 'Outsiders & Co' and 'Post War British Art'. Illustrated catalogues which have been produced to accompany many of these exhibitions are available from the gallery.

England & Co has sold works to many museums, public galleries and institutions, among them the Tate Gallery, the British Museum, the Imperial War Museum, The Arts Council of Great Britain, The Hunterian Gallery, The National Gallery of Ireland, the Whitworth Art Gallery, the Victoria & Albert Museum and the National Gallery of Australia. Significant corporate collections have purchased works from the gallery, as have many private collectors from Britain and abroad. The gallery always holds a selection of works by gallery artists together with a changing stock of works by modern British masters.

Early in 1999
the gallery will be moving to

216 Westbourne Grove, London W11 2RH
Tel 0171-221 0417 Fax 0171-221 4499

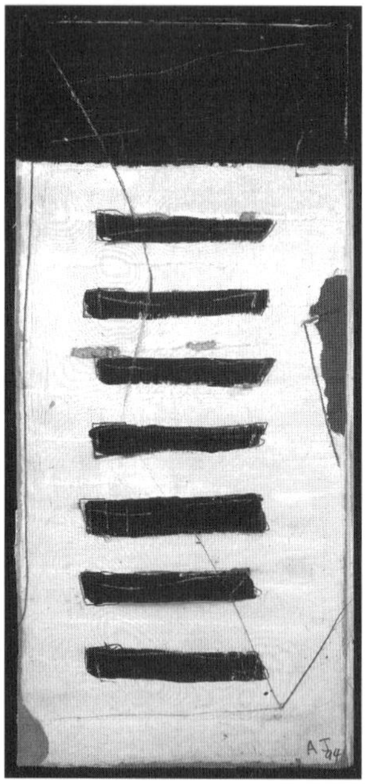

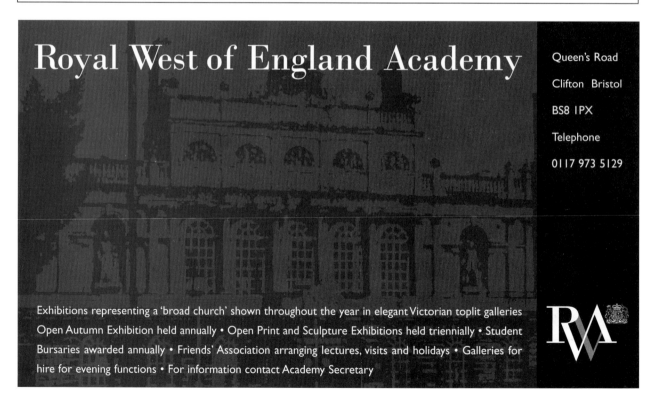

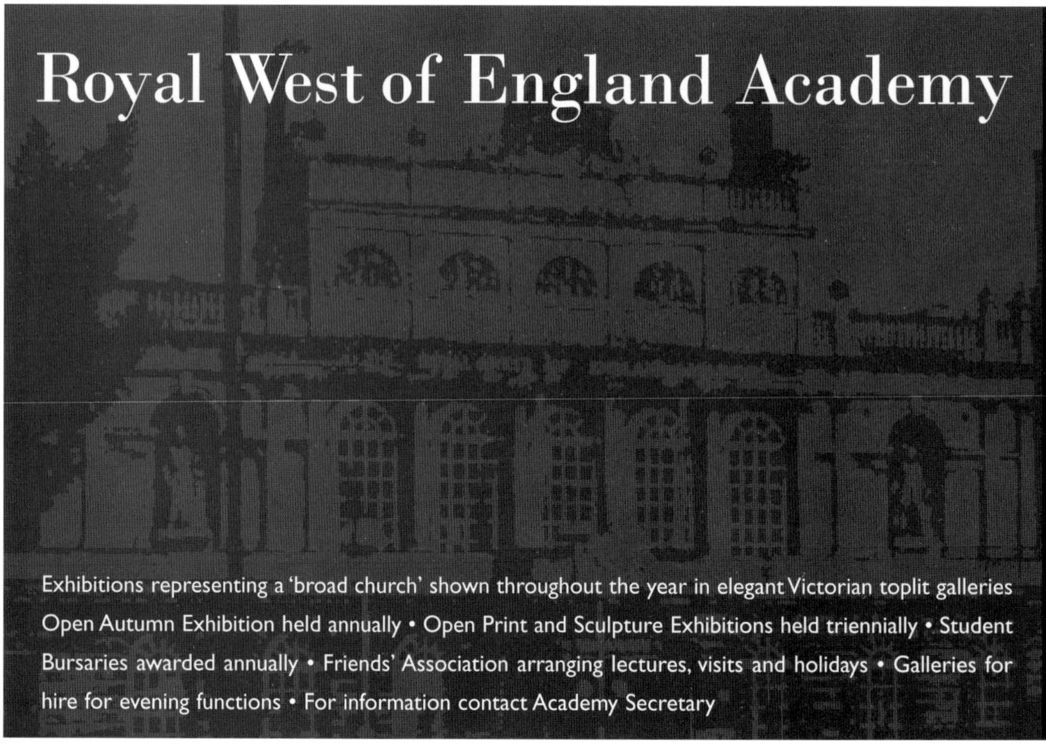

David Holmes in St Ives

DAVID HOLMES CHYWIDDEN, 6 CARNCROWS STREET, ST IVES, CORNWALL, TR26 1PJ • TEL: 01736 797068

DICTIONARY OF ARTISTS
in Britain since 1945

SYSTEM OF DATING

All reasonable effort has been made to establish correct years of birth and death. Where these are not obtainable, dates when an artist is believed to have flourished are used. The system followed is:

–c.1976	No birth year or time when started exhibiting known; year of death approximate
fl. c. 1908–1976	Exhibiting dates both approximate
fl. from c. 1908–1976	Death year firm only
1908–c.1976	Birth year firm; death approximate
–1976	No birth year or time when started exhibiting known; death year firm.
1908–	Artist alive at time of compilation; or known/believed to be dead, but year of death not yet available.

A dictionary of this nature will need periodic revision. Entries therefore adopt the past tense throughout to reflect the known circumstances at time of research and to facilitate updating for future editions.

ABBREVIATIONS

AAA	Allied Artists' Association
AEB	Art Exhibitions Bureau
AIA	Artists' International Association
BBC	British Broadcasting Corporation
BWS	British Water Colour Society
CASW	Contemporary Art Society for Wales
CEMA	Council for the Encouragement of Music and the Arts
HM	Her Majesty/His Majesty
HMS	Her Majesty's/His Majesty's Ship
HRH	Her/His Royal Highness
ICA	Institute of Contemporary Arts
IS	International Society of Sculptors, Painters and Gravers
LG	London Group
MAFA	Manchester Academy of Fine Arts
MP	Member of Parliament
NEAC	New English Art Club
NG	New Gallery
NPS	National Portrait Society
NS	National Society of Painters, Sculptors and Gravers/Printmakers
NWG	North Wales Group
OUP	Oxford University Press
PS	Pastel Society
RA	Royal Academy of Arts/Royal Academician
RBA	Royal Society of British Artists
RBC	Royal British Colonial Society of Artists
RBS	Royal Society of British Sculptors
RBSA	Royal Birmingham Society of Artists
RCamA	Royal Cambrian Academy
RE	Royal Society of Painter-Etchers and Engravers/Painter-Printmakers
RHA	Royal Hibernian Academy/Academician
RI	Royal Institute of Painters in Water Colours
RIBA	Royal Institute of British Architects
RMS	Royal Society of Miniature Painters, Sculptors and Gravers/Royal Mail Steamer
ROI	Royal Institute of Oil Painters
RP	Royal Society of Portrait Painters
RPS	Royal Photographic Society
RS	Royal Society
RSA	Royal Scottish Academy
RSMA	Royal Society of Marine Artists/Society of Marine Artists
RSW	Royal Scottish Society of Painters in Water-Colours/Royal Scottish Watercolour Society
RUA	Royal Ulster Academy of Arts/Academician
RWA	Royal West of England Academy/Academician

RWS	Royal Society of Painters in Water-Colours/Royal Watercolour Society
SBA	Society of British Artists
SEA	Society for Education in Art
SGA	Society of Graphic Art/Society of Graphic Artists/Society of Graphic Fine Art
SM	Society of Miniaturists
SPS	Society of Portrait Sculptors
SS	Screw Steamer/Steamship
SSA	Society of Scottish Artists
SSWA	Scottish Society of Women Artists/Scottish Artists and Artist Craftsmen
SWA	Society of Women Artists
SWAS	South Wales Art Society
SWE	Society of Wood Engravers
SWG	South Wales Group/The Welsh Group
SWLA	Society of Wildlife Artists
TRH	Their Royal Highnesses
UA	United Society of Artists
UNESCO	United Nations Educational, Scientific and Cultural Organization
USA	United States of America
WAC	Welsh Arts Council/The Arts Council of Wales
WIAC	Women's International Art Club
WSW	Watercolour Society of Wales

A

Andrew AARONS 1939– Painter, mostly in oil on canvas, and printmaker, mainly etching, born in London. He studied at Camberwell School of Art junior department, 1952, then between 1955–8 continued at Camberwell to gain his diploma, notable teachers being Gilbert Spencer and Joe Dixon. Aarons was a cricket enthusiast, played for Camberwell School and included sporting pictures in his shows. In 1959 Aarons did a Manchester University postgraduate course in textile design and technology, returning to Camberwell for a postgraduate diploma in printmaking, 1991. Among his awards were the Royal Manchester Institution's Haywood Prize and Silver Medal, both 1959, and several Canadian awards in the 1970s. Took part in many group shows in England and Canada, including South London Art Gallery, 1958; Art Gallery of Ontario, 1974; Castle Museum, Norwich, 1979; Churchill College, Cambridge, 1986; and Yarrow Gallery, Oundle, 1991. Later solo shows included Bodilly Gallery, Cambridge, where he lived, 1994. Canadian Broadcasting Corporation, Toronto; British Rail; and Berlin Museum hold examples.

Samira ABBASSY 1965– Painter and film-maker, born in Ahwaz, Iran. She moved to Britain in 1967 and completed a foundation studies diploma at Maidstone College of Art, 1983–4. An honours degree in fine art was achieved with studies at Birmingham Polytechnic, 1984–5, then Canterbury College of Art, 1985–7. From 1987 Abassy (pronounced Ab*bas*sy) was busy in group shows, work being included in Coast Lines, at Towner Art Gallery, Eastbourne, and Brilliant New Discoveries, at Drew Gallery, Canterbury, both in 1987; South East Young Painters, at Metropole, Folkestone, 1988, where she gained a first prizewinner purchase award; and at Mercury Gallery, where she had a solo show, 1993. Was art director for two short films in 1988–9: *Little Lotte* and *Peter and the Wolf*. Her work, often small and rather naive in appearance, was sometimes based on Iranian folk tales. South Eastern Arts Collection holds her work. Lived in Hastings, Sussex.

ABBOTT 1927– Printmaker, painter, designer and teacher, whose correct name was Barry Gordon Cope, born in Birmingham, where he attended art college, then studying at Royal College of Art with Robert Austin and Malcolm Osborne. He held a number of teaching posts, including Carmarthen School of Art and Yeovil School of Art, where he was head for some years. Exhibited widely and prepared official illuminated addresses for local authorities in Lichfield and Carmarthen. Lived in Yeovil, Somerset.

John ABBOTT 1884–1956 Painter in oil from his retirement as a member of the Indian Civil Service in the early 1930s. Studied with Francis Hodge. Exhibited RA, NEAC, ROI, provincial galleries and Paris Salon. Methuen published his book, *The Keys of Power*. Lived at Grasmere, Westmorland.

John ABBOTT 1948– Painter, draughtsman and teacher, born in Manchester, who attended Liverpool College of Art, 1965, West of England College of Art in Bristol, 1966, and Royal College of Art, 1969. From 1974 he taught at the school of art at South Devon Technical College. Abbott's figurative work has a slightly Surrealist quality, as shown in The British Art Show, Arts Council touring show in 1980, chosen by the critic William Packer. Solo shows included Bath Festival Gallery, 1978.

Faisal ABDU'ALLAH: *see* **FAISAL**

Roy ABELL 1931– Painter, printmaker and teacher, born in Birmingham, where he attended the College of Art, 1947–52, winning the Jackson Travelling Scholarship. Was then at Royal College of Art, 1954–7, obtaining first-class honours and a Silver Medal (Painting). In 1957 he was included in Jack Beddington's book *Young Artists of Promise*. Taught at Birmingham College of Art (Birmingham Polytechnic) from 1957–82, being made head of the painting school in 1974. Was on the West Midlands Arts fine art panel, 1975–8. His mixed shows included Young Contemporaries, 1956; RA; John Moores Liverpool Exhibition, 1958; Midland Art Now, Ikon Gallery, Birmingham, 1977; Tegfryn Art Gallery, Menai, 1984; and The Birmingham School, City Art Gallery, 1990. Was elected RBSA and had a series of solo shows there from 1961; others included Oriel Gallery, Cardiff, 1983; Keele University, National Museum of Wales, in Cardiff, and Christopher Hull Gallery, all 1985; and Birmingham Centenary Exhibition, 1989. Arts Council, Birmingham City Art Gallery and National Museum of Wales hold his work. Abell was notably a landscape painter, the oils tending more towards abstraction, built up with a heavy layering of paint. Lived at Sutton Coldfield, West Midlands.

Evelyn ABELSON 1886–1967 Painter in oil, born in London, who studied at Campden Hill School and Heatherley's School of Fine Art. Exhibited RA, NEAC, RBA, SWA and elsewhere. Lived in London.

Douglas ABERCROMBIE 1934– Abstract painter, born in Glasgow, where he studied at School of Art, 1952–6, in the latter year winning a RSA Carnegie Travelling Scholarship. In 1957 Abercrombie travelled with the Bertram Mills Circus, then for five years from 1958 was a painter-designer with Glasgow Citizens'

Theatre. In 1964 Abercrombie moved to London where he worked at the Royal Opera House, Covent Garden. After living and painting in Barcelona and Minorca for a couple of years from 1965 the artist returned to settle in London. He participated in many group shows and was included in British Painting 1952–1977 at RA in the latter year. His first one-man show was at 57 Gallery in Edinburgh in 1958, others including Citizens Theatre in 1961, Thames Gallery in Windsor in 1963, the Steuer Gallery in Lippstadt, Germany, in 1969 and a studio show at Bombay Wharf, in London, in 1977. Was included in a three-man show with Fred Pollock and Gabriel Flynn at The Living Room, Greenwich, 1995.

Anthony ABRAHAMS 1926– Artist who after gaining an arts degree from Cambridge University studied at the Anglo-French Art Centre. After concentrating on painting, he latterly turned to sculpting full-time, producing poised, enigmatic figures. Was included in Sixteen Sculptors at Sladmore Contemporary, 1997. Lived in Gloucestershire, with a studio in Cirencester.

Ivor ABRAHAMS 1935– Sculptor in a variety of materials, and teacher, born in Wigan, Lancashire. He studied at St Martin's School of Art, 1952–3; was in 1954–5 apprenticed to Fiorini Bronze Foundry; in 1954–7 studying with Karl Vogel at Camberwell School of Arts and Crafts. After several years as a display artist, from 1960–70 Abrahams taught sculpture as a visiting lecturer at Birmingham, Coventry, Hull and Goldsmiths' Colleges of Art. Having had a first solo show at Gallery One in 1962, Abrahams launched his international career in 1970 with an exhibition at Richard Feigen Gallery in New York. In London he showed with Felicity Samuel and Mayor Galleries and in 1995 was given a sixtieth birthday retrospective by Bernard Jacobson Gallery. Showed at RA Summer Exhibition and was elected RA in 1991. Working in such materials as flock fibre, latex and bronze, Abrahams focused his work on gardens in a way peculiarly his own, looking at how nature and the artificial coalesced. Arts Council holds his work. Lived in London.

Peter ABRAHAMS 1958– Abstract artist who worked in a wide range of media, including castings, computers and film. He was born in Liverpool, where he studied architecture at the University for a year before a foundation course at the Polytechnic; Camberwell School of Art, 1978–81; and Royal Academy Schools, 1981–4. Showed with The New Contemporaries at ICA, 1982; LG, Whitechapel Open and Beardsmore Gallery; and in the 1995–6 John Moores Liverpool Exhibition with a geometric acrylic and oil on canvas Caress of the Engineer. Later solo shows included Hanover Gallery, Liverpool, 1987; Creaser Gallery, 1988; and Morley Gallery, 1991. Lived in London.

Ruth ABRAHAMS 1931– Painter and teacher, born in London. She studied at St Martin's School of Art, 1951–5, notable teachers being Frederick Gore and Bateson Mason, then did postgraduate fine art at Royal Academy Schools, 1955–9, under Peter Greenham. Among her awards were the Landseer Medal for Drawing, David Murray Landscape Award and Leverhulme Award while at the Schools; in 1960 Abrahams gained the Harrogate Festival Painting Prize to the British School at Rome. In addition to teaching foundation studies at St Martin's, also taught at Trent Polytechnic, Derby Lonsdale College of Art and Loughborough College of Art & Design. Exhibitions included Young Contemporaries, LG and RA, and Singer & Friedlander/*Sunday Times* Watercolour Competition, 1990. In 1985 had a solo show at St Michael's Gallery, Derby. Durham University holds her work. Lived in Sedgebrook, Lincolnshire.

ACANTHUS 1909–1976 Cartoonist, architectural draughtsman, teacher and architect, born in India. His full name was Harold Frank Hoar. He went on a scholarship at 15 from Plymouth College to the Bartlett School of Architecture, London University, where he trained under Sir Albert Richardson. He was a fellow of the RIBA and a doctor of philosophy. He practised for some time as an architect, working on Gatwick Airport, churches in Hythe, Kent, and Woking, Surrey, where he lived, as well as on domestic and industrial buildings. Showed at RA but was mainly known as a cartoonist of architectural subjects with a great sense of fun and clarity of line. His best work was done for *Building* magazine in the 1960s; later he drew political cartoons for *The Sunday Telegraph.*

Anne ACHESON 1882–1962 Sculptor, born in Portadown, Craigavon, Northern Ireland. Attended Belfast School of Art and Royal College of Art, studying with Édouard Lantéri. Exhibited extensively in Britain and abroad, notably at RA, SWA, Paris Salon, in Italy, Belgium, Sweden, Canada, America and in New Zealand. In 1938 gained an award from the Feodora Gleichen Memorial Fund, administered by the RBS. Lived in London.

Joseph ACHESON 1918–1994 Painter, draughtsman and teacher, born in London. Acheson was educated in North America and England, studying art at Slade School of Fine Art and Courtauld Institute, 1946–50, subsequently in continental Europe and America. He became a member of Society of Industrial Artists. Teaching experience included Wimbledon School of Art; London, Surrey and Open Universities; and Workers' Educational Association. Showed with Leicester Galleries, RA, Arts Council and elsewhere and had work bought by The Football Association and Ministry of Works. Had a retrospective at The New Ashgate Gallery, Farnham, in 1996. Lived in Seale, Surrey.

Gerald ACKERMANN 1876–1960 Watercolourist, born in London, son of the art dealer Arthur Ackermann. After initial education in Eastbourne, he studied art at Heatherley's School of Fine Art, Westminster School of Art and the Royal Academy Schools, where he was a distinguished student. Ackermann painted widely in Britain, having a special affection for Sussex and Norfolk, where he settled at Blakeney. Although he worked on a fairly small scale he favoured big brushes; crisp detail, liquid washes, strong colours and careful delineation of architectural subjects are other features of his work. Exhibited extensively at Fine Art Society and Leicester Galleries, where he had one-man shows, also RA, Walker's Galleries, RI and RBA.

Judith ACKLAND 1892–1971 Watercolourist and artist in mixed media, born in Bideford, Devon. She studied at the Art School there, then at Regent Street Polytechnic School of Art, gaining a bronze medal for figure composition. There she met the artist Mary Stella Edwards, with whom she shared the rest of her life. They exhibited and painted landscapes together throughout Britain and worked jointly on historical models and dioramas, Ackland doing the figures, Edwards the settings. Windsor Guildhall holds examples. Ackland showed at RA, SWA and elsewhere and Victoria & Albert Museum holds her work. Lived in Bucks Mills in Devon and Staines, Middlesex.

Nicola ACKLAND-SNOW 1968– Artist in mixed media who studied at Bournemouth and Poole College of Art and Design and Bath College of Higher Education. Her assemblage Ark was included in Art in Boxes at England & Co, 1991. Ackland-Snow's work was used as a book cover by the publisher Longman Group UK and the artist Peter Blake, himself a box-maker, held an example. Lived in London.

Roger ACKLING 1947– Artist born in Isleworth, Middlesex, who studied at St Martin's School of Art after working as a gardener. He had many solo shows in Britain and abroad including LCF and Lisson Galleries from 1976; Amano Gallery, Osaka, from 1983; Juda Rowan Gallery, 1987; and Annely Juda Fine Art from 1990. His exhibition at Annely Juda in 1994 was largely of driftwood fragments taken from the beaches and foreshores of East Anglia which he then scored by using a burning glass, the ambiguous resulting objects often being quite small. Arts Council, British Council, Tate Gallery and many foreign collections hold his work, which was completed in Norfolk and London.

Jane ACKROYD 1957– Sculptor, notably in steel, born and lived in London. She gained a first-class honours degree in sculpture at St Martin's School of Art, 1979, then her master's degree at Royal College of Art, 1983. Among her awards were the Special Melchett Award for work in steel and a travel scholarship to Carrara, Italy. Her commissions included work at the Old Royal Free Hospital, Islington, and The Haymarket, London, wall sculpture. Showed at RA Summer Exhibitions from 1988 and was included in 1st RWA Open Sculpture Exhibition in 1993. Had a series of solo exhibitions at Anderson O'Day from 1988. Arts Council and Contemporary Art Society hold examples.

Norman ACKROYD 1938– Printmaker, painter and teacher, born in Leeds, Yorkshire. He studied at Leeds College of Art and Royal College of Art, 1961–4. Taught at Winchester College of Art and Central School of Art. Won a number of awards at Bradford International Print Biennale, 1972 and 1982; RE in 1984 and 1985; at Frechen Triennale, in Germany, in 1986. Was described by *Financial Times* critic William Packer as "by far our most adventurous and accomplished etcher." Ackroyd had several dozen solo shows, including Anderson O'Day; Aitken Dott, Edinburgh; Jersey Arts Centre, Channel Islands; Compass Gallery, Glasgow, and abroad. Victoria & Albert Museum, British Council and provincial British galleries hold his work. Lived in London and was made RA in 1991.

Stewart ACTON 1879–1960 Landscape painter, born in Brighton, Sussex, full name Walter Robert Stewart Acton. After education at the local Grammar School Acton became an antique dealer, like his father. Showed at RA, Brighton Arts Club and elsewhere and had several solo exhibitions in Sussex. In 1990 Canon Gallery, Chichester, held a retrospective. Brighton Museum and Art Gallery holds local views by Acton.

Bernard ADAMS fl. from 1916–1965 Portrait and landscape painter, son of the artist Robert Adams. Studied at Westminster School of Art, in Antwerp and with Philip de Laszlo, George Harcourt and Innes Fripp. Was a member of the Chelsea Arts Club and London Sketch Club. Exhibited RA, especially ROI, Chenil Galleries, Leicester Galleries and Paris Salon, where he won a silver medal in 1957. Lived in London.

Brian Lemesle ADAMS fl. from 1940s– Versatile artist in oil and watercolour, born in Wolverhampton, Staffordshire. After Bryanston School he studied at the Architectural Association, qualifying in 1949 after war service in the Army interrupted his education. Showed with the Soldier Artists' Exhibition in 1944. While working as an architect he continued to show pictures, including RA from 1947, RBA and NEAC. Had a solo show at Everyman Cinema, Hampstead, in 1957, with Sally Hunter Fine Art from 1986. Lived in London but painted widely in Britain.

Chris ADAMS 1867– Painter and miniaturist, born in Southampton, who studied at Reading University. Was married to the artist Minnie Walters Anson. Exhibited RA, RMS, in the provinces and abroad. Walker Art Gallery, Liverpool, holds his work. Finally lived at Parkstone, Dorset.

Danton ADAMS 1904– Painter, born in Eastbourne, Sussex. He studied at Putney and Chelsea Schools of Art and was for a time an advertisement manager. Produced the book *Musical Colour*, lectured and founded Wimbledon Art Group, becoming president. Showed with RA, RP, RBA, UA and at Paris Salon. Lived in New Malden, Surrey.

Elinor Proby ADAMS fl. from c. 1908–1945 Painter, teacher and writer, born in Sudbury, Suffolk, who studied at Slade School of Fine Art and won several awards. Showed at NEAC, Goupil Gallery, RA and elsewhere and lived at Sevenoaks, Kent.

Ernest D ADAMS 1884–1963 Painter, printmaker and draughtsman in pen and ink. Born in Margate, Kent, studied at Regent Street Polytechnic School of Art under Harry Watson and Harry Theaker. He did a variety of graphic work, ranging from posters and Christmas cards to illustrations in magazines such as *London Opinion* and *Bystander*. Exhibited RBA, NS, SGA, RA and RI. Lived in Folkestone, Kent.

Gilbert ADAMS 1906– Photographer, painter and teacher, brought up in Oxfordshire, who studied at Reading University's faculty of fine art, 1923–7, with Allen Seaby and Herbert Maryon. He was commissioned in 1945–51 by British Council to make series of photographs publicising Britain. From 1951–2 was technical advisor to Associated British Pathé Film, Coronation of H M Queen Elizabeth II. From 1951–77 Adams was visiting lecturer in photography and fine art at Berkshire and South Oxfordshire Colleges of Art. He showed with RBA, St Ives Society of Artists and Reading Guild of Artists. Was a noted photographer of children, work being published in many magazines. In 1985–6 his work was included in a Brotherhood of Ruralists and Friends show at Piccadilly Gallery. Imperial War Museum holds his work. Lived in St Ives, Cornwall.

Harry William ADAMS 1868–1947 Landscape painter, born in Worcester, where he was privately educated and made his career. Worked for Royal Worcester Porcelain Factory as decorator for eight years, then studied at Académie Julian, in Paris, 1895–6. Also worked in Switzerland on several occasions and became noted for mountain and winter scenes, such as his Winter's Sleep, owned by Tate Gallery. Showed for about 30 years from 1896 at RA, also extensively at RBA of which he was a member, RCamA and elsewhere.

Hervey ADAMS 1903–1996 Painter, teacher and writer who after Charterhouse School studied painting with Bernard Adams, 1928–30. Taught at Berkhamsted and Tonbridge Schools and wrote several books, including *The Student's Approach to Landscape Painting* and *The Adventure of Looking*. Showed with RBA of which he was a member, RA, Leicester Galleries and elsewhere. Lived at Houndscroft, Gloucestershire, but died at The Priory Nursing Home, Horsley. His wife Iris Adams, also an artist, predeceased him.

James Frederick ADAMS 1914–1984 Watercolour painter, born in Stoke-on-Trent; he studied at the local School of Art, at Burslem, 1930–4, under Harry Tittensor and Gordon Forsyth. Adams spent his career in the printing and advertising industry, working for many years with Purnell & Sons in Bristol. Exhibited widely, including RA, RWS, RI, RWA, in Canada and France. His work was reproduced in *The Studio* and *Staffordshire Life* magazines. Lived in Newcastle-under-Lyme, Staffordshire.

Joy ADAMS 1921– Painter, notably of flowers, born in Yorkshire, who settled from 1951 in Ealing, west London. Studied art at Ealing Technical College School of Art from 1963. In 1974 Adams won the open painting competition held by *The Artist* magazine; in the same year the Grenfell Silver Medal instituted by the Royal Horticultural Society, then went on to win the Silver-Gilt Medal in 1976 and 1979. Precision of detail and trueness of colour were a notable feature of her studies, shown at Medici Galleries in 1981.

Lindsey ADAMS 1951– Artist and teacher, born in London. Studied at Camberwell School of Arts and Crafts, 1969–74; won a David Murray Travelling Scholarship, 1974; then did postgraduate painting degree course at Royal Academy Schools, 1974–7. Went on to teach at Chelsea and Westminster, Clapham and Battersea and Southwark Adult Education Institutes and was included in Artists in Adult Education at Woodlands Art Gallery, 1982. Also showed at Stowells Trophy, Mall Galleries, 1971; Seven Dials Gallery and Ellingham Mill, Norfolk, both 1980; and in Three Women Painters at Norwich Castle Museum, 1982.

Marcus ADAMS 1875– Painter and professional photographer, born in Southampton, his father Walton Adams having the same interests. Adams went on to become a member of the London Salon of Photography, specialising in pictures of children. After studying at Reading University and in Paris, Marcus Adams exhibited his oils and watercolours with the St Ives Society of Artists and the Reading Guild of Artists. Lived in Wargrave, Berkshire.

Norman ADAMS 1927– Painter, stage and costume designer, mural and ceramics artist and teacher, born in London. He studied at Harrow School of Art, 1940–6, then Royal College of Art, 1948–51. Had first solo show at Gimpel Fils in 1952. Adams made an early name as a stage designer, in 1951 handling the Royal Ballet's *A Mirror of Witches* at Covent Garden, in 1953 the Sadler's Wells production *Saudades*. Murals were also a strong theme. In 1969 he gained an Abbey Major Award for the study of mural painting. He won a commission for a ceramic relief of the Stations of the Cross for the Roman Catholic church Our Lady of Lourdes, in Milton Keynes, Buckinghamshire in 1975–6. From 1962–70 Adams was head of the painting school of Manchester College of Art; he was professor of fine art at Newcastle University, 1981–6; then was professor of painting and keeper at Royal Academy, being elected RA in 1972. Adams said his work was concerned with his religious beliefs or the lack of them. Tate Gallery holds his work. Lived in Horton-in-Ribblesdale, Yorkshire.

Pauline ADAMS 1952– Sculptor using a wide range of materials to produce wall- and floor-mounted work, born and lived in London. She attended Barnet College, 1969–74. Group included ICA, 1974; Air Gallery Auction, 1980; and Berry Street Open Studios, 1984.

Richard ADAMS 1960– Painter and illustrator, born in Hampshire, who gained an honours degree in graphic design from Leicester Polytechnic, 1979–81. His extensive client list included Barclays Bank, Penguin Books, Saatchi & Saatchi, Royal Mail, *Cosmopolitan*, *Radio Times*, RA, Tesco and Nationwide Anglia. Adams won a series of awards in open competitions, including several first and second prizes, in the Benson & Hedges Gold and *Reader's Digest* Awards. His own pictures, which could be incident-packed and slightly jokey, were in chalk pastel on paper which was then varnished to give the rich colour and tonal effect of oils. Adams was a prolific artist, keeping copious sketch-books. English vernacular architecture, classic cars, animals and the countryside around Playden, Sussex, where he lived, were inspirations. As well as mixed exhibitions he had solo shows such as One Long Holiday, Hybrid Gallery, 1996. The Inkshed handled his illustration commissions.

Robert ADAMS 1917–1984 Sculptor of abstract and monumental works, designer and lithographer. Born in Northampton, Adams studied at the School of Art there in 1933, although later – 1938–44 – he had to make his living at various jobs while he studied part-time. At first influenced by Henry Moore, he later turned to non-figurative work, notably that of Brancusi and Gonzalez. Taught sculpture at the Central School of Arts and Crafts 1949–60. He exhibited widely internationally, including a number of International Biennales in the 1950s. Work in a series of important collections around the world, including the Tate Gallery, Arts Council, British Council and the Museum of Modern Art, New York. Retrospective Northampton Art Gallery, 1971. Lived at Great Maplestead, Halstead, Essex.

Will ADAMS 1951– Painter and muralist, born in Hunstanton, Norfolk. He studied at Reading University's fine art department, 1969–74. Among group shows he appeared in were a number of Whitechapel Opens; Whitechapel Art Gallery's Art for Society, in 1978; and John Moores Exhibition, Liverpool, 1991–2. Adams held a number of residencies as a community painter in London's East End and he painted a mural Conference of the Birds for a school in Bethnal Green. His solo exhibitions began with one at 57 Gallery, Edinburgh, in 1975, a later being at Camerawork, 1984. Lived in London.

William Dacres ADAMS 1864–1951 Painter who studied at Radley College and Oxford University and art at Sir Hubert Herkomer's Bushey School of Art and in Germany. Adams was a member of NPS and showed extensively at Fine Art Society as well as Leicester Galleries, with Ridley Art Club and RA. Lived in London, then Lewes, Sussex.

Crawfurd ADAMSON 1953– Painter, born in Edinburgh. He studied at Duncan of Jordanstone College of Art, Dundee, 1971–6. Became a full-time painter in 1983. Adamson's pictures explored relationships, real and abstract, through figures posed in interiors or on a seashore. He participated in many group shows and had solo exhibitions including Cylinder Gallery in 1984 and 1985, Thumb Gallery in 1988 and Scottish Gallery, 1989. Adamson's pictures are held by Metropolitan Museum of Art, New York; and Wiltshire Education Department. Lived in St Leonards-on-Sea, Sussex.

Edward ADAMSON 1911–1996 Art therapist and painter who studied at Bromley and Beckenham (later Ravensbourne College of Design and Communication) and took lessons in physiotherapy while working in his father's factory. During World War II he enlisted in the Royal Army Medical Corps, on demobilisation offered to work voluntarily for the Red Cross and for six months taught art to former soldiers suffering from tuberculosis. Was invited to join the staff of Netherne Hospital, a forbidding mental institution in Surrey, where he began innovative art lessons. He said that what he initiated was "less a question of treatment than of developing latent creativepossibilities." Adamson's work extended to pottery, woodworking and sculpture and the enhancement of the hospital, as well as the creation of a patients' gallery. After retirement in 1971 Adamson kept in touch with Netherne and when he heard it was to close set up The Adamson Collection, a charity trust, to prevent dispersal of patients' work. Part was housed in a barn on the Rothschild estate at Ashton with a view to a permanent site being obtained. Adamson's own work was exhibited in London and Paris.

George ADAMSON 1913– Humorous illustrator, artist in pen and ink and printmaker and teacher, born New York City. He studied at Wigan and Liverpool Schools of Art under "rigorous teachers" in the 1930s and went on to teach in art schools. During World War II was a Royal Air Force navigator, then was an official war artist with Coastal Command. Became a freelance humorist and illustrator, working 30 years for *Punch* and seven for *Private Eye* magazines and was designer and illustrator of 90 books, eight of them his own. Showed at RA, RE and had a solo exhibition in Exeter. Imperial War Museum, British Museum and Exeter and Ulster Museums hold his work. Lived at Countess Wear, Exeter, Devon.

H Leslie ADAMSON 1900– Painter, born in Bilston, Staffordshire. After attending Bishop Vesey's Grammar School in Sutton Coldfield and King Edward's Grammar School, Aston, Adamson served his engineering apprenticeship at Joseph Lucas Ltd and attended Harmondsworth Technical College. For 14 years from 1938 he studied part-time at Birmingham College of Art. Moved to Wales in 1955 and for some years was an evening class lecturer. Adamson was a member of RCamA, having a four-man show with it in 1971 and a solo exhibition in Llandudno the following year. Also showed with RBSA and RI.

Joy ADAMSON 1910–1980 Animal conservationist, painter, writer and lecturer, born Troppau, Austrian Silesia, into a comfortably off family. Her mother painted in oil and watercolour and Joy early developed an artistic talent. Settled in Kenya in 1938, between then and 1946 she became a skilled botanical artist, painting several hundred flower studies, in 1947 gaining the Royal Horticultural Society's Grenfell Gold Medal. For two terms in late-1946/early-1947 Joy attended the Slade School of Fine Art. In 1944 she had married her third husband, the Kenyan game warden George Adamson, and stemming from their life together published the international best-seller *Born Free*, about Elsa their lioness. It was successfully filmed and she wrote other books, including *Living Free*, her sketchbook *Joy Adamson's Africa* and *The Searching Spirit*, an autobiography, which fostered the cause of animal conservation. The Elsa Wild Animal Appeal and four game parks were among her other inspirations. She was a notable painter of African animal, bird and marine life and produced 600 tribal portraits, an invaluable record, now in the National Museums of Kenya. A temperamental, volatile woman, Adamson was murdered while camping.

Michael ADDISON 1957– Artist, notably a printmaker, and teacher, born in York. Studied at local School of Art, 1975–6, Manchester Polytechnic, 1976–9, Chelsea School of Art, 1979–80, and California College of Arts, 1981–2, as a Fulbright Scholar. Taught at Maidstone College of Art and Portsmouth Polytechnic. Addison showed in Britain, continental Europe and America and had work in Manchester Education Committee, Kent County Council and private collections. In 1996 he shared a show called Unreal Cities with Mark Davy at Kent Institute of Art & Design, Maidstone, where he lived.

John ADDYMAN 1929– Painter, ceramist, printmaker and teacher, born in Wallasey, Cheshire, attending the local School of Art, 1945–9. Was then at Royal College of Art, 1949–52, working for the advertising agency Colman, Prentis and Varley the following year. Then began teaching part-time at Swansea School of Art. Also taught Colchester School of Art, 1956–63; Nottingham College of Art and Design, 1963–7; University of Essex, 1969–70, Trent Polytechnic, 1974–8; and Norwich School of Art, 1978. He moved to Sudbury, Suffolk, in 1967 and was by then closely associated with the area, having a series of solo shows at the Minories, Colchester, starting in 1961; with a major exhibition at Oriel Bangor, 1976; others including Chappel Galleries, Chappel, 1977–8. Also showed with RA, New Grafton Gallery, Christchurch Mansion in Ipswich and was a major prize winner in Singer & Friedlander/*Sunday Times* Watercolour Competition, 1996. Was included in Artists in Residence Programme at British Embassy, Luxembourg, 1994–7, in 1996 was fellow of Ballinglen Arts Foundation, County Mayo, Irish Republic. WAC, National Museum of Wales in Cardiff, Government Art Collection and other notable collections hold examples.

Bernard ADENEY 1878–1966 Painter, mural artist, textile designer and teacher, born in London. He began his art training in St John's Wood when only nine, then studied at the Royal Academy Schools, 1892–7, Académie Julian, in Paris, 1897, Slade School of Fine Art, 1912, and Central School of Arts and Crafts for a year. Took part in the Second Post-Impressionist Exhibition in 1912, becoming a founder-member of LG the following year (he was subsequently president for a time). During World War I served in the Tank Corps painting camouflage, then became an official war artist. Married to the artist Noël Adeney. Founder-member of London Artists' Association, 1925, having three years before held a joint exhibition with Keith Baynes at the Independent Gallery. From 1903 taught at the Central School, where he was head of the textile school, 1930–47. Also taught at Putney School of Art and Blackheath School of Art. Painted murals for Plumstead Library and the Borough Polytechnic. Did textile designs for Allan Walton Textiles, Liberty's and Calico Printers' Association. Work held by Tate Gallery, Imperial War Museum and provincial galleries. Memorial exhibition at Woodlands Art Gallery, Blackheath, 1979. Lived in London.

Noël Gilford ADENEY 1890–1978 Painter, writer and dress designer, married to the painter Bernard Adeney. She studied at the Slade School of Fine Art, 1910–15. During her life she mixed dress designing and painting, one of her dresses being worn by the noted cellist Madame Suggia in Augustus John's portrait. Produced designs for Allan Walton Textiles. Exhibited regularly with LG, also with Cooling and Leicester Galleries and Goupil Gallery, and had memorial show at Woodlands Art Gallery in 1979. In the 1950s began writing and in 1956 published her novel *No Coward Soul*, based on the life of her friend the painter and writer Denton Welch. Lived in London and at Clavering, Essex.

Ivan Walter ADLER 1914–1989 Painter, born in Czechoslovakia, who graduated as a doctor of law at University of Prague, becoming resident in England in 1954. He was reluctant to show or sell his work which had a strong pattern quality with an erotic tinge and recurring themes such as dancing, nudes and cattle. He bred prizewinning pedigree cattle. During his life he had only one solo show, at Drian Galleries, a retrospective occurring at Adam Gallery, Bath, 1993.

Jankel ADLER 1895–1949 Painter, printmaker and teacher, born in Tuszyn, Poland, who attended Düsseldorf Academy, 1911–14. Conscripted into the Russian Army then taken prisoner by the Germans in World War I, he was released and returned to Warsaw, where he began to exhibit. During the 1920s he travelled widely in Europe, settling to teach in Düsseldorf in 1931, but fled to Paris in 1933 where in 1937, after a big retrospective in Warsaw in 1935, he worked with S W Hayter at Atelier 17. After a period in the Polish Army in World War II Adler settled and showed in Glasgow, where he was an influential figure, affecting the work of painters such as Benjamin Creme, then moved to London in 1943, where Robert Colquhoun was a friend. Had a series of shows with Lefevre Gallery, Gimpel Fils Gallery and Knoedler Galleries in New York. Arts Council gave Adler a memorial show in 1953; there was a major show in Düsseldorf, Tel-Aviv and Lodz in 1980; in 1993 his work was included in City Art Centre, Edinburgh, show Polish Roots – British Soil; and John Denham Gallery held a show of work of the 1930s and 1940s in 1996. Tate Gallery and major foreign galleries hold examples.

Valerie ADLER fl. from 1980s– Painter and designer, born in South Africa, who moved to London aged 17, studying at the Inchbald School of Interior Design. In late 1970s moved to Israel where, after studying art history at the Hebrew University, she was taught painting and drawing by Asher Rodnitsky, further studies taking place at Chelsea School of Art from early 1980s. After living in London she returned to Israel in the early 1990s. Exhibitions included Galleria Spania Nuova, Venice, 1986; Solomon Gallery, 1987; and Julius Gottlieb Gallery, Carmel College, Wallingford, 1989. Ben Uri Art Society holds her work.

Mark ADLINGTON 1965– Painter and draughtsman using a range of media and with a special interest in wildlife. He gained his master's degree at the University of Edinburgh, 1984–8; was at Sotheby's, 1989–91; then attended City and Guilds of London Art School, 1991–4. In 1994 he won The David Wolfers and Manya Igel Prizes and the City and Guilds Prize for Drawing. Mixed exhibitions included Tenterden Art Exhibition, from 1994; Highway House, 1995; and Young Masters Exhibition, Battersea Town Hall, 1996. Three-man exhibitions included Heron Pictures, Pangbourne, from 1995, and Arts Club, 1997. In that year he had a solo exhibition at New Grafton Gallery, much of the work inspired by a visit to Velavadar National Park, Gujarat, India.

Marion ADNAMS 1898–1995 Versatile artist and teacher, born and lived in Derby, notable for Surrealist works, influenced by René Magritte and Paul Nash. Trained as a teacher of modern languages, gaining an honours degree in 1919. Attended life classes at Derby School of Art; in 1936 began to paint with a view to getting her art teacher's diploma, gained in 1938; was appointed art mistress at Homelands Grammar School for Girls, Derby; in 1946 becoming senior lecturer and head of department in art at Derby Training College. She retired in 1960, then spent much time painting in France. Completed a series of murals for Immanuel Church, Stapenhill, Burton upon Trent, 1964–5, but had to cease painting in 1968 because of failing eyesight. From the end of the 1930s for about 30 years showed continuously in London and the provinces and had a retrospective exhibition at Midland Group Gallery, 1971. Public collections in Manchester, Salford, Nottingham, Leicester, Derby and Wolverhampton hold examples. Adnams was a singular woman, who had lived for years in the same tiny house which, even when she was old and blind, appeared as fresh as a St Ives studio of the 1930s. But she could be difficult to deal with, and among the people she fell out with was her mother, also an artist of talent.

ADRIAN: *see* **Adrian OFFICER**

Said ADRUS 1958– Painter and artist in mixed media, born in Kampala, Uganda. He studied at Stourbridge College of Technology and Art and Trent Polytechnic, Nottingham, where he remained to work. Adrus used self-portraits to discuss his political identity and previous status as a refugee, as shown in his contribution to the Norwich Gallery touring show History and Identity, 1991–2. Adrus took part in many mixed exhibitions in Nottingham and Leicester, in Artists Against Apartheid at Royal Festival Hall, 1985, and Black Art: Plotting the Course, at Oldham Art Gallery in 1988. In 1987 he gained a Gulbenkian Bursary in Community Arts.

Mary ADSHEAD 1904–1995 Artist, decorator, painter of murals and illustrator, born in London, her father an architect and good watercolourist, Stanley Adshead. For several years from 1921 attended Slade School of Fine Art, in 1924 being chosen by Henry Tonks to undertake a mural commission with Rex Whistler, a fellow-student, which led to several more commissions, including murals for Bank underground station, London. In 1929 married the artist and writer Stephen Bone. Following year had a one-man show at Goupil Gallery, also exhibiting at NEAC, RA, SWA and elsewhere. Retrospective at Sally Hunter Fine Art, 1986. Among other work completed by Mary Adshead from the early 1930s was a series of drawings and watercolours of Crystal Palace; London Underground posters; wall panels to decorate the restaurant of the British Pavilion at the 1937 Paris International Exhibition; stamp designs for the General Post Office in 1949; and the decoration of Selfridges' restaurant, in 1950, with jungle murals. In 1962 her growing interest in mosaic led her to study in Ravenna and Sicily and to take a course in Italian techniques at Kingston School of Art. A tireless worker whose illustrations and wall paintings contain much wit and charm. Graves Art Gallery, Sheffield, owns her 1931 self-portrait. Lived in London but travelled constantly, even into her eighties.

Idris AERON 1918– Horse artist and photographer, born in Birmingham, where she studied at St Agnes' Convent. Attended Birmingham College of Arts and Crafts, 1939–44, under Bernard Fleetwood-Walker and W F Colley and for some years worked under her actual name of Idris Elgina Williams, signing with initials, until adopting the signature Idris Aeron. Her work was widely used in equine publications and she also exhibited with Society of Equestrian Artists, at Mid-Wales Open and elsewhere and had solo shows backed by WAC. Lived in New Quay, Dyfed.

Eileen AGAR 1899–1991 Surrealist painter in oil and acrylic, collagist and object-maker. Born in Buenos Aires, Argentina, daughter of a businessman, she came to England in 1911. Studied part-time at the Byam Shaw School with Rex Vicat Cole, then with Leon Underwood at his Brook Green School and at the Slade School of Fine Art with Henry Tonks, Philip Wilson Steer and Walter Westley Russell. Married the artist Robin Bartlett and after divorce the Hungarian writer Joseph Bard. Studied for two years in Paris, where she became familiar with modern movements such as Surrealism. Became friendly with Ezra Pound, Evelyn Waugh, Pablo Picasso, Man Ray, Henry Moore and Paul Nash. Took part in the International Surrealist Exhibition in London, 1936. Began to show widely in London, having a first one-man exhibition at the Redfern Gallery in 1942. Retrospective at Birch and Conran 1988, the year she published her autobiography *A Look at my Life*. The Tate Gallery among others holds her work which has a strong jokey element. Shortly before she died, in London, she was elected RA.

Lionel AGGETT 1938– Landscape painter, muralist, architect and writer, born in Whiddon Down, Devon, and educated at Exeter School. Aggett studied part-time at Kingston School of Art and Architecture; he won two travelling scholarships, spent in Venice and Rome. Aggett was made a member of the RIBA in 1967 and gained six awards for architecture. Exhibited at PS, RWA, RI and South West Arts, where he won five awards. Solo exhibitions included A Spanish Daybook at The John Davies Gallery, Stow-on-the-Wold, 1997. Aggett's commissions included a number of murals and The Presentation of the New Colours by HRH The Duke of Kent to the 4th Battalion of the Devonshire and Dorset Regiment, 1992. His work hangs in public and private collections in Europe, Russia and North America. He published *Pastel Techniques and Acrylic Techniques*, 1992, and *Capturing the Light in Pastel*, 1995.

Christopher AGGS 1951– Painter, who studied fine art at the City & Guilds of London Art School, then the Royal Academy Schools. In 1976 he won the David Murray Award for Landscape Painting, in 1977 the Richard Ford Award for travel in Spain. Mixed shows included RA Summer Exhibition and Anna-Mei Chadwick, both 1997. Solo exhibitions included Arun Art Centre, Arundel Festival, 1983; Judd Street Gallery, 1989; and Terrace Gallery, Worthing, from 1990.

Patrice AGGS 1952– Painter, illustrator and printmaker, born in Detroit, Michigan, America. After studying at St John's College, Maryland, Aggs moved to Britain to attend the City & Guilds of London Art School. Illustration commissions included work on children's books for Methuen, 1979–89; for Simon & Schuster, 1989; Doubleday, 1990; Walker Books and ABC, both from 1991; Penguin Books, Frances Lincoln Publishing and Cambridge University Press, all 1995; and Hodder children's books, Orchard Books and *The Cricket Magazine* Group, all from 1996. Mixed shows included RA Summer Exhibition from 1980, Anna-Mei Chadwick, 1997, and elsewhere in London and Sussex.

Maurice AGIS 1931– Artist and teacher, born and lived in London, who studied painting and sculpture at St Martin's School of Art, 1958–62. He taught at Bath Academy of Art, 1962–4; between 1964–6 at St Martin's, London College of Design and Nottingham and Winchester Colleges of Art; and from 1967–73 at Goldsmiths' College. Agis (pronounced Aygis; hard g) won a series of awards and grants, including the Pratt Bequest for Sculpture, 1960; Sainsbury Award for Sculpture, 1961; a Netherlands Ministry of Education Scholarship, 1967–8; a Scottish Arts Council Award, 1968; and a string of Arts Council Awards, 1968–81. Among commissions received were Glasgow Garden Festival, 1988, and a Bedford Park Sculpture Commission, 1991. He showed at Young Contemporaries, 1960–2; at ICA, 1962; in Blow Up at Arts Council, 1970; and in Encounters at Atrium Gallery, 1994. Among his later solo shows was sculpture at Chelsea Arts Club, 1995. From 1972 evolved Colourspace, following on from Spaceplace. Colourspace was staged at numerous venues, including the 1995 Glasgow Mayfest and Cheltenham International Music Festival. Colourspace was made of many translucent, plastic ovoid units of various colours. A public-participation event, its aim was "to introduce people to their inner resources."

Michael AGNEW 1968– Printmaker, painter, draughtsman and teacher, born in Bellshill, Lanarkshire. He studied at Gray's School of Art in Aberdeen, the Royal College of Art and in Delphi, Greece. He was etching printer with Peacock Printers, 1992; lecturer in printmaking at Gray's in 1993; and was a visiting lecturer in printmaking at Duncan of Jordanstone College of Art, Dundee. Awards included George Davidson Scholarship to Ireland, 1990; a Fleur Cowles Award for Excellence and Atlantis Paper Purchase Prize, both 1992; and a Bob Bain Memorial Bursary, 1993. Showed at Aberdeen Artists' Annual Exhibition at Aberdeen Art Gallery from 1988; RSA from 1990; Scottish Prints & Monotypes, Lamont Gallery, 1993; and Royal Over-Seas League Open, 1994. Gray's School, Royal College of Art and Grampian Hospital Art Project hold examples.

John AIKEN 1950– Sculptor, installations artist and teacher, born in Belfast, Northern Ireland. He did a foundation course at Chelsea School of Art, 1968, remaining there until 1973 and gaining an honours degree in sculpture. From 1973–5 held a Rome Scholarship in Sculpture at British School, Rome, and while teaching at the University of Ulster returned to the Rome School's faculty, 1977–84. After lecturing part-time at Newport School of Art, 1980–2, Aiken joined the staff of the Slade School of Fine Art, in 1986 being appointed head of the sculpture department. He also taught widely abroad, including Canada, America and China, and in 1983 was artist-in-residence at the Henie Onstad Foundation, Oslo. Commissions included a 40-metre frieze in Purbeck stone for Belfast City Hospital, 1986; a steel sculpture for Arts Council of Northern Ireland headquarters, 1992; and in the same year two monumental sculptures in Portuguese granite, commissioned by the Department of the Environment. Fortifications were a key theme in the work of Aiken, as he explained in a BBC2 television programme on him in 1989, German fortifications in northern France being for him "the most impressive sculpture park in the world." Had a solo show at Arts Council Gallery in Belfast 1978, later ones including Orpheus Gallery, Belfast, 1991, and Centre for Contemporary Art, Gulbenkian Foundation, Lisbon, 1995. Arts Council of Ireland, University and Trinity Colleges in Dublin, National Museum of Contemporary Art in Oslo and other public collections hold examples.

John Macdonald AIKEN 1880–1963 Painter, stained glass artist and etcher. Born in Aberdeen, he studied at Gray's School of Art there, at the Royal College of Art under Gerald Moira and in Italy. He was head of Gray's School for three years immediately prior to World War I. Exhibited prolifically at RA, RSA, RE, RI, Royal Glasgow Institute of the Fine Arts and Paris Salon, where he won a silver medal, in 1928. Elected RSA in 1935. Several Scottish collections, including Aberdeen, Glasgow and Dundee, hold his work. Lived in Aberdeen.

John P AIKEN 1920– Painter and teacher, born in Dumbarton, where he lived for much of his life. After education at Dumbarton Academy he studied at Glasgow School of Art under Hugh Adam Crawford and W O Hutchison, then widely in Paris, including Atelier Colarossi. Taught at Glasgow School of Art. Exhibited RSA, SSA, Royal Glasgow Institute of the Fine Arts and on the continent and had several one-man shows in Glasgow and Edinburgh. New Museum and Art Gallery, Newport, holds his work.

David AINLEY 1943– Artist in a range of media and teacher, born in Derby, who settled in Matlock, Derbyshire. He studied at Derby and District College of Art, 1959–63, under Keith Richardson-Jones, then at Manchester College of Art and Design, 1963–4. From 1964 held a number of teaching posts, from 1983–93 being senior lecturer, art and art education, at Derbyshire College of Higher Education/University of Derby, then becoming a freelance artist, lecturer, writer and consultant in art education full-time. In 1995 Ainley said that his work had been concerned "with equivalents of processes of growth and change reflected in the 1960s in biomorphic images and in the 1970s in systems paintings related to the 'life game' of the mathematician John Horton Conway. More recent work has been gestural in character, embracing earlier interests and an exploration of perceptual responses to experience." Was at various times a member of Midland and Derby Groups and of National Society for Education in Art and Design. Had a series of solo shows including Ikon Gallery, Birmingham, 1966; St Michael's Gallery, Derby, 1971; and Derbyshire College of Higher Education, 1991. Lincolnshire & Humberside Arts Association; Trent University, Nottingham; and private collections hold examples.

John Anthony AINLEY 1931– Painter and teacher, born in Sheffield, Yorkshire. Educated at Chester College, Ainley went on to specialise in child development and the visual arts, being headmaster of St Philip's Special School, in Chessington, Surrey, for some years. Exhibited RCamA, Graves Art Gallery in Sheffield and elsewhere. Lived in Leatherhead, Surrey, where he was secretary of the Art Club.

George Frederick AINSCOW 1913– Painter and textile designer, born in Manchester, who attended Rochdale College of Art, 1929–33. Went on to show at RA, NEAC, RBA and Paris Salon, gaining gold and silver medals, 1980–1. Had a number of solo shows in Lancashire, including Rochdale Art Gallery and Museum, 1991. Royal Air Force Museum at Hendon holds his work. Lived at Castleton, Lancashire.

Sam AINSLIE 1950– Artist and teacher, born in North Shields, Northumberland. She did an arts foundation course at Jacob Kramer College of Art, Leeds, 1972–3, from 1974–7 studying art at Newcastle upon Tyne Polytechnic. The study of Sukiya architecture in Japan during 1975 proved a key influence. In 1977 she moved to Edinburgh to study tapestry at the College of Art, further influences being the adoption of abstract shapes and brighter colours. Ainslie sought in her wall hangings to create a new image of the female body, using a variety of materials. In 1983 she produced a large tapestry for Perth's General Accident headquarters, the year after making a series of banners for the inauguration of the Scottish National Gallery of Modern Art's new building in Edinburgh. Ainslie's Banner for Greenham, of 1985, indicated a move towards more politically engaged art. She went on to teach at Glasgow School of Art and in 1986 had a show at the city's Third Eye Centre.

Mark AINSWORTH 1954– Painter and teacher who said that "colour and all its magical properties is at the centre of my creative output," and who used a rich palette to create his shapes. He was born in Blackpool, Lancashire, where he attended the College of Art, 1972–3, then Ravensbourne College of Art, 1973–6, and Royal College of Art, 1977–80. His work appeared in John Moores Liverpool Exhibition in 1978 and 1995–6, Arts Council acquiring the acrylic on canvas Crag from the first show. Had solo shows at Moira Kelly Gallery and Grundy Art Gallery in Blackpool, 1980; Kerlin Gallery in Belfast and Dublin from 1986; The Sorcerer and the Apprentice, Belfast and Blackpool, 1993; and Art and Design Matters, Ulster Museum in Belfast, 1994. From 1982 taught at University of Ulster in Belfast, Northern Ireland, where he lived at Holywood.

Reginald AIRD 1890– Portrait and decorative artist and designer, born in London. Studied at Goldsmiths' College and in South Kensington with Arthur Cope and John Watson Nicol, also in France, Spain and Belgium. Aird was at various times consultant to the Calico Printers' Association, Manchester; taught at Salford School of Art, and at the Regional College of Art, Bradford. Exhibited RA, RP, NS, IS and widely in the provinces. Victoria & Albert Museum holds his work. Lived in Bradford.

Anna AIRY 1882–1964 Painter, draughtsman and printmaker, born in London, married to the painter Geoffrey Buckingham Pocock. Studied at Slade School of Fine Art, 1899–1903, under Henry Tonks, Fred Brown and Philip Wilson Steer; she won the Melville Nettleship Prize several times, the Slade Scholarship and all first prizes that could be won. Exhibited for first time at RA in 1905, for the last time in 1956. Also showed at Fine Art Society, RE, ROI, RI and Carfax Gallery extensively, and at many other venues. During World War I completed pictures in munitions factories for Imperial War Museum. In 1930 published *The Art of Pastel*, followed by *London Lyrics* in 1945 and *Making a Start in Art* in 1951. Anna Airy was an artist of great versatility whose work is in Victoria & Albert Museum, many provincial galleries as well as galleries in Australia, Canada and New Zealand. Retrospective at Christchurch Mansion, Ipswich, 1985. Lived at Playford, near Ipswich.

Craigie AITCHISON 1926– Painter, brought up in Scotland, full name John Ronald Craigie Aitchison. He adopted his father's name when he became an artist. Studied at Slade School of Fine Art, 1952–4, having rejected law as a career. In 1955 he received a British Council and Italian government scholarship to study in Italy, where the different light and landscape made a marked impression on his work. Aitchison's work took on a strong pastel colouring and he adopted a few simple shapes, such as a figure, a tree or a bird, which were to be his trademarks. His apparently simple pictures can be jokey or sad, but are always original. Had a series of shows at the

Beaux Arts Gallery, 1959–64, also showing with LG, Compass Gallery in Glasgow, Knoedler & Co and abroad. Notable exhibitions were held at Kettle's Yard, Cambridge, in 1979, and at the Serpentine Gallery in 1981, with a retrospective at Harewood House, Leeds, 1994, and a major show at the Gallery of Modern Art, Glasgow, in 1996. Was made an RA in 1988 and lived in London.

John Ernest AITKEN 1881–1957 Painter in watercolour, mainly of landscapes. Born in Liverpool, son of the artist James Aitken, with whom he studied. Also studied at Manchester, Liverpool and Wallasey Schools of Art. He exhibited widely, in Britain and abroad, river and marine views being favourite subjects, at RA, RWA, RI, RSA, Fine Art Society, Royal Glasgow Institute of the Fine Arts, as well as in Europe, India, Ceylon and North and South America. Wakefield City Art Gallery is one of several holding his work. Lived in Port St Mary, Isle of Man.

Kenneth AITKEN 1929– Artist in watercolour, charcoal, pen and wash and pencil, notable for aircraft and motoring subjects. He was born in Warwickshire and settled at Lillington, Leamington Spa. After leaving Leamington School of Art Aitken worked variously as an advertising agency visualiser; public house sign painter; had six years in the Royal Air Force; was a technical artist with Sir W G Armstrong Whitworth Aircraft; was a Rootes/Chrysler sales training and dealer development artist; then worked freelance. Aitken was chairman of the Guild of Motoring Artists and a member of the Guild of Aviation Artists and of the Coventry Society of Watercolour Artists. Royal Air Force Cosford and the Force's Museum at Hendon hold examples. Signed his cartoons Ken.

Manuel AJA-HERRERA 1955– Painter and printmaker, born in Spain. He did a foundation course at St Martin's School of Art, 1974–5, graduated with honours in painting, Birmingham Polytechnic, 1975–8, then obtained his master's degree at Manchester Polytechnic, 1978–9. Among his awards were the Sir Wallis Whitworth First Prize, 1977; Midland Open 25 (ATV Network Prize), 1978; and Midland Art 1978 First Prize. Showed in many group exhibitions, including Birmingham Institute, 1977 onwards; Stowells Trophy, 1979; and Air Gallery, 1983. Had a solo show at Midlands Art Centre in 1979, later ones including Woodlands Art Gallery, 1986, when Aja-Herrera's theme was man and the changing urban environment.

George Dixon AKED 1907–1989 Painter, draughtsman, photographer and traveller, born in Bingley, Yorkshire. After Skipton Grammar School he attended Skipton School of Art, Slade School of Fine Art and Central London Polytechnic, then moved to Paris and studied at Académie Julian. Although in the early 1930s he had begun showing at RA, NEAC and LG, a legacy enabled Aked – always known as Pat – to travel the world until World War II, when he served with ambulance units. Aked eventually settled in Barbados for some years, later sharing his time between England and stays overseas, often at others' expense, part of the time in a converted van. Aked had several solo exhibitions in Britain and abroad, a commemorative exhibition taking place at Sally Hunter Fine Art in 1991 which revealed Aked as a colourful painter. Aked's collection of paintings and photographs form part of the archive at the Pitt-Rivers Museum, Oxford.

Alexander ÅKERBLADH 1886– Painter, initially educated in Uppsala, Sweden. Studied architecture at Glasgow School of Art in 1900, after which he practised for a number of years. Later studied painting at St John's Wood School of Art, 1916, the following year in Munich. His work was featured in *The Studio* and *Colour* magazines and he showed at RA, Fine Art Society, ROI, RBA and in Paris. Huddersfield Art Gallery holds his work. Joined Art Workers' Guild in 1945. Lived in London.

Jeremy AKERMAN 1966– Artist using video, born in London, who gained a fine art degree at Goldsmiths' College, 1986–9, then did postgraduate studies at Jan van Eyck Academy in Maastricht, Netherlands, 1993–5. He took part in Foto 1 at 152c Brick Lane, 1994; in the Knokke Video Festival, Belgium, 1995; and was in New Contemporaries at Tate Gallery, Liverpool, and Camden Arts Centre, both 1996.

Alan ALBINSON 1915– Painter and advertising designer, born in Oldham, Lancashire. Attended Manchester School of Art, exhibiting at the City Art Gallery there, and at galleries in Oldham and Buxton. Completed poster work for Indian government. Lived at West Deeping, Northamptonshire.

Emma ALCOCK fl. from early 1990s– Painter whose work included atmospheric landscapes, as in her solo show at Cadogan Contemporary, 1998. She did an art and design foundation course at Trent Polytechnic, 1986–7; graduated with honours in fine art at Bristol Polytechnic, 1987–90; then studied visual Islamic and traditional arts for her master's at the Royal College of Art, 1990–2. Gained the John Hulla Award and The David Innes Wilkin Art in Architecture Award, Art in Architecture Society, both 1990; and The Kairos Education Trust Award, 1992. Exhibitions included Ibstock Design Centre, Bristol, and RWA, both 1990, and Alan Baxter Gallery and Goldmark Gallery, Uppingham, both 1997. Showed solo at Cadogan Contemporary from 1995.

Eva ALDBROOK 1925– Painter, designer and illustrator, born in Hamburg, Germany, whose family settled in London in 1938. After studying ballet Aldbrook danced until 1943. Following war work she worked for stage and screen and later as a fashion artist, having studied costume design at St Martin's School of Art. Later studied painting at Camden Arts Centre and was for a time vice-chairman of the Hampstead Artists' Council. Travelled widely. Her work was portraits, still life and flower paintings, usually done in Tuscany, Italy, where she settled. Had a solo show at Camden Arts Centre, 1975, with another in 1985, also Ben Uri Art Society, 1982, which holds her Portrait of Rosemary Friedman.

Eileen ALDRIDGE 1916–1990 Painter and restorer, born in Teddington, Middlesex, wife of the painter William Ware and mother of the artist Martin Ware. She studied at Kingston School of Art, 1933–8, and Regent Street Polytechnic School of Art. Exhibited RA, NEAC, WIAC, RP, Leger and Leicester Galleries and elsewhere. Despite severe arthritis she also wrote and illustrated children's books and published a volume on porcelain; with her husband she gained a high reputation for restoration of porcelain, paintings and frames, work being done for national galleries and museums. Lived in London for many years, then in Burwash, Sussex.

Frederick John ALDRIDGE 1909– Printmaker, born in Barnet, Hertfordshire, who attended Highgate School, followed by years in advertising. After World War II service, including photography in Royal Air Force, Aldridge did more advertising and editorial work, then 20 years in farming, and after retiring in 1974 took a course in decorating textiles, including Batik, lino-cut and screenprinting. He developed a print studio in the one-time farm office. Eventually concentrated on relief printing with lino-cuts. Showed in southern England and London galleries including Zella 9 and Graffiti. Lived at North Waltham, Hampshire.

James ALDRIDGE 1971– Abstract artist, born in Farnborough, Kent, who studied at Manchester Metropolitan University, 1990–3, then Royal College of Art, 1993–5. In 1994 he won a Paris Studio Award, Cité Internationale des Arts, and an IBM Direct Award; in 1995 a J Andrew Lloyd Scholarship. Group shows included Cooltan Arts, and Northern Graduates at New Academy Galleries, both 1993; Summer Profile at Paton Gallery, 1996; and, at that gallery, New Abstraction, 1997; and John Moores Liverpool Exhibition, 1997–8. Lived in London.

John ALDRIDGE 1905–1984 Painter, especially of the landscape of Essex, book illustrator, designer of wallpapers and textiles and enthusiastic gardener and plantsman. Born at Woolwich, Aldridge was a classical scholar at Oxford in the mid-1920s. Had drawn and painted since young, but never had any formal training. In 1933, the year of his first one-man exhibition at the Leicester Galleries, he settled at Great Bardfield, Essex, where he lived until he died. He had first exhibited with the 7 & 5 Society in 1931 at the Leicester Galleries, invited by Ben Nicholson. He became associated with East Anglian painters such as John Nash, Cedric Morris and Edward Bawden, with whom he began designing wallpapers, as Bardfield Wallpapers, in 1938. In 1949 William Coldstream invited him to teach at the Slade School, where he remained until 1970. Elected an RA in 1964. An excellent portrait painter, John Aldridge's portrait of his friend Robert Graves, the poet, is in the National Portrait Gallery, London. Although he began to establish an international reputation by exhibiting at the Venice Biennale in 1934, his work was shown mainly in London, especially at the Leicester Galleries. The Tate Gallery, Victoria & Albert Museum, Contemporary Art Society and many other public collections hold his work. A man of generous nature, Aldridge was a quintessentially English landscape painter, strong in design with often rich colours.

ALEXANDER 1927– Artist in a wide range of media, born in London, who preferred to be known only by his surname. Spent parts of his life in Britain, Australia and America, at Santa Monica, California. He studied at St Martin's School of Art until 1951, then for 20 years painted, for about another 20 was engaged in sculpture and holographic works, then in 1989 returned to painting. Had a first solo show at Artists' House, 1950, after which many one-man and mixed exhibition appearances followed, notably at Holdsworth Galleries, Sydney. In 1979, the year he had a solo show there, Alexander was commissioned to produce a monumental bronze, Jubilee Oracle, for South Bank and The Great Tower for Rutland Water, said to be the largest bronze sculpture of modern times. Some other notable events in Alexander's career were Festival of Perth, Western Australia, exhibition in 1982, including five monumental works mounted around festival theatres; holograms shown at Holdsworth Galleries, in Frankfurt, Tokyo and elsewhere, 1984; holograms chosen shown at Expo '85, Japan, and Pompidou Centre, Paris, 1985; in 1986 commissioned to make big musical sculpture with composer Moya Henderson and developed a new holographic movie process, making the art movie *Masks*, shown for first time at Stella Polaris Gallery, Beverly Hills; in 1987 was commissioned to make eight large holograms for Power House Museum, Sydney; 60 works shown at retrospective at Museum of Contemporary Art in São Paulo, Brazil, 1989; retrospective shown at The Modern Museum of Art, Santa Ana, California. Works by Alexander are held by many important collections around the world.

Catharine ALEXANDER 1904– Painter and draughtsman, married to the publisher and writer Noel Carrington. She was brought up in the village of Walberswick, Suffolk, where her father on retirement from teaching worked as a silversmith, her mother being a musician and painter. At 16 she followed her sister, the letterer Margaret Alexander, to the Slade School of Fine Art, studying under Henry Tonks, Philip Wilson Steer and Walter Russell. When she and Noel Carrington lived in Hampstead until World War II Alexander's circle of friends included the Carline family, the Spencers, Mark Gertler and his wife and Stephen and Mary Bone. After the war Alexander lived and painted at Lambourn, on the Berkshire Downs. She shared a show at New Grafton Gallery in 1976. Lived in Steyning, Sussex.

Christopher ALEXANDER 1926–1982 Artist and teacher, son of a window cleaner, he was born and lived in Margate, Kent. Alexander did military service with 3rd Polish Carpathian Regiment and graduated from Royal College of Art in 1951, his teachers including Robert Sargent Austin. He was described as "a natural and compulsive teacher", from graduation until his death. He served initially on the staff of Thanet School of Art, then at Canterbury College of Art and at other venues. Had a deep love of music. Alexander showed at RA Summer Exhibition. Before his death, with his sons Gregory and Matthew he had two shows in the Margate area, then in 1989 all their work was included in the Kent County Library three-man touring exhibition People and Places, in which Christopher's juicy use of oil paint was seen to good effect.

Elsie ALEXANDER 1912– Painter in oil who was by profession a businesswoman, born in Ware, Hertfordshire. She studied art with Hyman Warsager and Victor Askew, attending Montclair State College, New Jersey, 1958. Showed in the provinces, as a member of Buckingham Art Society, with Wine Trade Art Society and was granted freedom of the Worshipful Company of Painter-Stainers. Had a solo show in Mill Hill in 1971. Lived in Edgware, Middlesex.

Eugenie ALEXANDER 1919– Painter, fabric collagist, teacher and writer, born in Wallasey, Cheshire. She studied at Chelsea School of Art, 1936–9 and 1946–50, teachers including Graham Sutherland and Henry Moore, and Goldsmiths' College of Art, 1950–1. Presented radio and television programmes on her work; fabric collages filmed by Pathé Pictorial; and wrote *Fabric Pictures*. Showed with groups at Victoria & Albert Museum, Portal Gallery and Whitworth Art Gallery in Manchester, solo exhibitions including Arthur Jeffress, William Ware and Medici Galleries. Victoria & Albert Museum, National Museum of Wales in Cardiff and Embroiderers' Guild hold her work. She was married to the artist Bernard Carter and lived in London.

Gregory ALEXANDER 1960– Painter and teacher, born and lived in Ramsgate, Kent, son of the artist Christopher Alexander. He studied at Canterbury School of Art and West Surrey College of Art and Design, Farnham, graduating in 1981. At 23 he became one of the youngest-ever associate members of RWS, becoming a full member in 1987. Also exhibited at Athena Arts Awards, at Barbican Centre; RA Summer Exhibition; NEAC; and in 1989 shared a Kent County Library touring show with his father and brother Matthew. In 1992 shared a show with his brother at Catto Gallery which stemmed from extensive travels through Europe. In 1991 Catto had had an exhibition of Alexander's colourful pictures for an edition of Rudyard Kipling's *The Jungle Book*. He was noted for his vibrant, exotic landscapes.

Hazel ALEXANDER 1912– Sculptor in bronze, born in Newcastle upon Tyne, Northumberland. Although she early developed a talent for art and attended Luton Art School, 1936, further studies had to wait until 1970, under Joan Armitage at Camden Institute and privately with Fred Kormis. Showed at Royal Festival Hall, Ben Uri Gallery, Mall Galleries and permanently at Sharon Hotel, Herzliya, Israel. All England Lawn Tennis Club commissioned a sculpture of singles champion Kitty Godfree. The Crouching Child was inspired by the logo of the National Society for the Prevention of Cruelty to Children, and was produced in a limited edition; and Israeli Embassy selected sculpture of politician Golda Meir for the Hisdadrut Building, Tel-Aviv. Work was bought by private collectors around the world. Was the mother of the artist Naomi Alexander. Lived in London.

Herbert ALEXANDER 1874–1946 Painter, born in London, who travelled extensively, notably with the Army in World War I. He studied at Sir Hubert Herkomer's Bushey School of Art and at Slade School of Fine Art. He was a member of RWS and Royal British Colonial Society of Artists, also exhibiting at RA, ROI, Fine Art Society and elsewhere. Lived for a time at Cranbrook, Kent, and was a member of Chelsea Arts and Arts Clubs.

Isabel ALEXANDER 1910–1996 Painter, draughtsman, illustrator, lithographer and teacher, born in Edgbaston, Warwickshire. She studied at Birmingham School of Art, 1929–33, and at Slade School of Fine Art, 1934–5. After teaching, 1936–9, Alexander worked in documentary films (Paul Rotha Productions/Realist Films/Films of Fact), 1939–49, and was a freelance book illustrator during this period; was a lecturer/senior lecturer in art, Saffron Walden College of Education, 1949–70; then in retirement travelled and painted, 1970–95. Alexander illustrated B L Coombes' *Miner's Day* for Penguin, 1945, and wrote and illustrated *The Story of Plant Life*, Puffin, 1946. A number of themes ran through Alexander's work: Social Realism (for example the Rhondda works in Swansea), 1940s and 50s; portraits, 1940s–1960s; landscapes, 1950s; in the 1960s and 70s there was an abstract period grounded in landscape; and during the 1980s there were studies of sea, land and light, dominated by the Hebrides islands. Her many group exhibitions included Linton Festival and Walker's Galleries, both 1957; Saffron Walden Festival, 1958; Colchester Art Society and Phoenix Gallery, Lavenham, both 1960; Pictures for Schools, RA, from 1963; Pictures for Essex Hospitals, from 1968; Crescent Gallery, Scarborough, 1984; and Stonegate Gallery, York, 1989. Her later solo shows included a series there from 1987. Glynn Vivian Art Gallery, Swansea, holds examples. Died in Ilkley, Yorkshire.

James Stuart Carnegie ALEXANDER 1900–1952 Painter of flowers and landscape, his watercolours noted for their simplicity and sense of design. His wife Euphen Alexander was also an artist. He was born near Selkirk, son of a solicitor, and was educated at Haileybury College, spending six months at the Royal Field Artillery cadet school. His artistic career was encouraged by the artists Tom Scott and Robert and Edwin Alexander. From the late 1920s Alexander showed at RSW, RSA, RA, RI, Walker Art Gallery in Liverpool and Royal Glasgow Institute of the Fine Arts. An exhibition at Mainhill Gallery, Ancrum, in 1996 was the first since Alexander's memorial show in 1952.

Matthew ALEXANDER 1953– Landscape painter, printmaker and teacher, son of the artist Christopher Alexander and older brother of painter Gregory Alexander. He studied at Canterbury College of Art and in the graphic design department of Maidstone College of Art. With his brother also studied at evening classes run by his father at Hilderstone College of Further Education, formerly Thanet School of Art, eventually replacing his father as tutor in figure drawing. Took the post of art teacher at Hartsdown Secondary School in his home town of Margate, Kent, teaching his brother for a time. Matthew Alexander eventually combined travelling for landscape painting with running a business producing limited edition prints of his watercolours. He was elected an associate of ROI in 1982 and a member of RBA in 1984. Also showed at RA and in 1992 shared a show with Gregory at Catto Gallery which stemmed from extensive travels in Europe. The two sons and the father held three-man exhibitions in the Margate area and in 1989 there was a Kent County Library touring show of all their work. Matthew Alexander's work developed to become cooler, more detached and subtle-toned. Choice of subject was a key feature, as was the relationship of buildings to landscape.

Naomi ALEXANDER 1938– Artist and picture conservator, born in Harpenden, Hertfordshire, daughter of the sculptor Hazel Alexander. She studied at Hornsey College of Art, 1954–9, then Central School of Arts and Crafts, her teachers including Alfred Daniels. She was apprenticed to the chairman of the British Picture Restorers' Association, of which she became a member, for five years, and went on to do work for government and private Old Master galleries. Showed at RA, Mall Galleries, ROI of which she was a member, NEAC, RBA and RP plus provincial municipal galleries. Solo shows included Ben Uri and Seen Galleries and Paintings in Hospitals, The Sheridan Russell Gallery, 1997. Victoria & Albert Museum holds her work. Lived in London.

Robert ALEXANDER 1875–1945 Watercolourist who lived in Brentwood, Essex. The county, especially the barges, windmills and breakwaters around Frinton and Walton-on-the-Naze, featured in much of Alexander's prolific output. His wife was a pupil of Hercules Brabazon Brabazon, whose atmospheric, washy influence can be seen in Robert Alexander's work. Although his Presbyterian family urged him to make a career in an export merchant's office in the City, Alexander studied in the evening at Hornsey School of Art and the Slade School of Fine Art and received encouragement from Mark Fisher and George Clausen. Alexander showed his watercolours of England and continental Europe at RA, NEAC and Grosvenor Gallery. Later the Parkin Gallery had several exhibitions of his work, which is held by British Museum, Victoria & Albert and Fitzwilliam Museums.

Louis ALEXANDRE 1867– Painter and sculptor, son of the sculptor F A Alexandre. He was born in Paris, educated in Battersea, then studied art solo in Paris. He exhibited RA, Paris Salon and in the provinces and received a silver medal at the 1900 Paris Exhibition. Collected French and English pictures. Grundy Art Gallery, Blackpool, bought his work. Lived in Woodmansterne, Surrey.

Sara ALEXANDRI 1913– Painter, printmaker and teacher, born in Kherson, Russia. She was educated in Palestine and on the continent, studying art at the Royal Institute d'Arte and the Royal Academy of Fine Arts, Florence, 1936–40 and 1946–7. Showed at RA, RWA, Paris Salon and elsewhere. Lived in Bath, later in St Leonards-on-Sea, Sussex.

John ALFORD 1890– Painter and draughtsman, born Edward John Gregory Alford. He was educated at Tonbridge School and Cambridge University. He did graduate work at University College, University of London, and taught at the Courtauld Institute of Art. Alford became principal of the Ontario Department of Education summer school for teachers of art; special lecturer in art at McMaster University, Hamilton, Ontario; instructor at Queen's University, Kingston, Ontario, in the school of fine arts; then from 1934–45 was professor of fine art and head of the department at the University of Toronto. From 1945–54 he was on the staff of the Rhode Island School of Design as head of the department of art history. Exhibited LG and at several venues in Canada. Lived at East Chatham, NY, in America.

John ALFORD 1929– Painter of landscape, conversation and marine pictures, born in Tunbridge Wells, Kent. Studied at Camberwell School of Arts and Crafts, 1949–53, his teachers including Gilbert Spencer, Richard Eurich and Bernard Dunstan. Went on to become director of art at Shrewsbury School, retiring in 1989, then painting with studios in Shrewsbury, Shropshire, where he lived, and in Cornwall. Elected to NEAC and RBA, also showing at RSMA, RA and RWA. Had solo shows in England, South Africa, France and Canada. Reading Borough Council and Shropshire County Council hold his work, which became more complex when retired.

David ALISON 1882–1955 Teacher and painter, born in Dysart, Fifeshire. Studied at Kircaldy High School and Glasgow School of Art as well as on the continent. He became head of the drawing and painting school of Edinburgh College of Art, where he was nicknamed Bouff, being a gritty, strict traditionalist, an admirer of Raeburn, Velasquez, Ingres and Goya, but out of sympathy with modern art trends. His portraits of his many distinguished students were fine and he was elected RP and RSA. Showed widely in Scotland and abroad and is represented in many public collections. Lived in Edinburgh.

Hassan ALIYU 1964– Painter, illustrator and curator, born in Barnet, who continued to live in London. Graduated with honours, fine art, majoring in painting/mosaic and wall decoration, Ahmadu Bello University, Zaria, Nigeria, in 1986, gaining the Nigerian Arts Council Award for Best Final Year Student in Fine Art. Taught and conducted workshops in Britain and abroad, latterly being a tutor with Lewisham Social Services/Community Education. Took part in many group exhibitions, including Spring Salon, 198 Gallery, 1994; Anne Bellion Gallery, 1996; and Transforming the Crown, American tour 1997.Later solo exhibitions included Winds of Change: The Paintings of Hassan Aliyu, Russell-Cotes Art Gallery, Bournemouth, 1997.

Alexander ALLAN 1914–1972 Painter in gouache and of pastel portraits, pen and ink draughtsman. Born in Dundee,

Allan studied art at the College of Art there under the landscape painter James McIntosh Patrick. Allan later taught part-time there. He also studied at Reimann School, in London, and at Westminster School of Art under Mark Gertler. Work in the collections of the Scottish Arts Council, Nuffield Foundation and Dundee Corporation. Lived at Newport-on-Tay, Fifeshire.

Archibald Russell Watson ALLAN 1878–1959 Painter, born in Glasgow where he studied at the School of Art, then in Paris at Atelier Colarossi and Académie Julian. Allan was a member of Glasgow Art Club and showed extensively with Royal Glasgow Institute of the Fine Arts and RSA. Glasgow and Paisley Corporations bought examples. Lived in Stirling.

Eva Dorothy ALLAN: *see* **Julian Phelps ALLAN**

Griselda ALLAN 1905–1987 Painter and lithographer, born into a well-off shipping family in Sunderland, County Durham. She was a student at the local School of Art in the mid-1920s under Richard Ray, contributing three flower panels to the library frieze painted by the students in 1925. Her training was continued at the Royal College of Art and on the continent and she was at the Ruskin School of Drawing, Oxford, under Albert Rutherston, 1935–9. During World War II she taught drawing for several years at the evacuated Slade/Ruskin Schools, continuing after the war at the Ruskin. The 1940s saw her producing some notable pictures, such as New Shipyard at Southwick, 1944, held by Sunderland Museum and Art Gallery. War Artists' Advisory Committee bought Allan's work. Her later pictures, often featuring trees, were not so remarkable. By then she had returned to live in Sunderland.

Julian Phelps ALLAN 1892–1996 Sculptor, born in Millbrook, Southampton. Gave up training as a domestic science teacher to study at Westminster School of Art, then from 1922–5 at Royal Academy Schools. Among other awards won RA Gold Medal in 1925, the following year studying with Libero Andreotti in Florence. Three years later changed her name to Julian Phelps from Eva Dorothy. In World War II served in the Auxiliary Territorial Service, becoming a colonel and first president of its War Office Selection Board. Created reliefs at Lambeth and Maudsley Hospitals and elsewhere. Tate Gallery holds her bronze Marjorie and her Mother and Child is illustrated in the volume *RBS: Modern British Sculpture*, published in 1939. She was elected a fellow of the RBS in 1947. She was interested in Romanesque and Byzantine sculpture, travelling in France and Yugoslavia to study it, and these styles are apparent in her own output. Showed often at RA Summer Exhibition, 1925–49. For some years lived in Balerno, Midlothian, with a studio in Edinburgh which was taken over by the sculptor Michael Snowden. About 1970 Allan left Scotland, finally living in Henley-on-Thames, Oxfordshire, having for long been blind.

Mary Parsons Reid ALLAN 1917– Painter, draughtsman and teacher, born in Glasgow, who studied at the School of Art there, 1935–9. She retired in 1976 after a long teaching career, briefly in Aberdeen and for a long time at Laurel Bank, Glasgow. Was at various times a member of SSWA, Glasgow Society of Lady Artists and of its Society of Women Artists. Specialised in still life, especially flowers, landscape in Scotland and France and early on some portraits. Also showed with Royal Glasgow Institute of the Fine Arts and RSA. Had solo shows in Edinburgh and at Pitlochry Theatre and in 1983 at Broughton Gallery, by Biggar. Visited and studied pictures in many continental galleries and admired Bonnard, Morisot, early Chagall, Morandi and Cézanne; William and Ben Nicholson, David Donaldson, Duncan Shanks and Elizabeth Blackadder among modern British artists. Won the Lauder Award in 1951 and 1965 for oil paintings. Glasgow Museums & Art Galleries holds Miss Allan's Still Life with fish, 1955. Lived latterly in Helensburgh, Dunbartonshire.

Ronald ALLAN 1900– Painter and draughtsman most noted for portraits and figure studies, born at Cheadle Heath, Cheshire, son of Harry Allan, a shipper. Studied at Manchester School of Art and Slade School of Fine Art. Exhibitions included RSW, RA, RBSA, RCamA, Wertheim Gallery and Senefelder Club in London and Chicago. Solo shows included XXI Gallery, 1928; Salon Club in Manchester, 1930, and at Mid-Day Studios, 1947, where he was a member of the progressive Manchester Group encouraged by Margo Ingham. Salford Art Gallery and Manchester University hold his works as does Manchester City Art Gallery which has his portrait of Kenneth Russell Brady. In 1933, seeking to borrow it in a bid to get RBA membership, Allan wrote that he thought "it would open a new field of attack" as it was "perhaps the best portrait I have done so far." Lived for some years at Heaton Moor, Stockport, Cheshire.

Rosemary ALLAN 1911– Painter and draughtsman, born in Bromley, Kent, wife of the artist Allan Gwynne-Jones and mother of the painter Emily Gwynne-Jones. She studied at Central School of Arts and Crafts, 1928, then the Slade School of Fine Art, 1930–5, under Randolph Schwabe, gaining a Slade Scholarship in 1932. Showed at RA, LG, NEAC and Leicester, Wildenstein and Redfern Galleries. Solo exhibitions included Upper Grosvenor Galleries, 1971. In 1997 she was part of a Gwynne-Jones family exhibition at Sally Hunter Fine Art. Imperial War Museum holds her work. Lived in Eastleach, Gloucestershire.

Reginald Geoffrey ALLARD 1947– Painter, born in Chester, where he attended the School of Art, 1964–6, then studying at Liverpool Regional College of Art, 1966–9. Various shows including solo at Fine Art Society. First National City Bank of New York bought his work. Lived for some time at Upton-by-Chester, Cheshire.

Annette ALLCOCK 1923– Painter in oil or gouache, illustrator and animator, born in Bromley, Kent. In her teens she was a member of Clifton Arts Club, Bristol, where Kit Gunton and Mary Fairclough were influences; studied at West of England

College of Art, Bristol, 1941–3, also at other art colleges. Became a greetings card designer, illustrator of children's books and cartoon films animator. Her portraits were mostly of children. Showed at RWA, Beaux Arts Gallery in Bath and extensively around Britain. Admired the work, and was influenced by, Stanley Spencer, who was a distant cousin, visiting him many times at Cookham. Lived latterly in Corsham, Wiltshire.

Walter Herbert ALLCOTT 1880–1951 Painter and teacher, born in Birmingham, who studied at the School of Art there. Early in the 1920s he toured Italy extensively, painting townscapes and landscapes also visiting Spain and Majorca. Exhibited RSBA and Fine Art Society especially, also RA, RI and Walker Art Gallery, Liverpool. He taught in local authority schools and was art instructor, 1945–6, to the Women's Royal Naval Service. Birmingham City Museum and Art Gallery holds his work. Lived at Haslemere, Surrey.

Betty ALLEN fl. from 1970s– Printmaker and sculptor who studied at Centre for Arts and Crafts, Bromley. She showed with South London Artists, at RA and was included in Group '77 Printmakers at Woodlands Art Gallery, 1981. Work held in private collections worldwide and bought by Government of British Columbia, Canada.

Charles John ALLEN 1862–1956 Sculptor and teacher, born in Greenford, Middlesex. Studied at Lambeth School of Art under Edgar Silver Frith, then at Royal Academy Schools, gaining four silver medals. Went on to become vice-principal and teacher of sculpture at Liverpool City School of Art. Was a fellow of RBS and showed extensively at RA, Walker Art Gallery in Liverpool and Royal Glasgow Institute of the Fine Arts, winning a gold medal for sculpture at Paris International Exhibition in 1900. Major works included Florence Nightingale and Queen Victoria Memorials in Liverpool, Glasgow Corporation acquiring his marble The Woman Thou Gavest Me. Was a member of Art Workers' Guild from 1894, retiring in 1936. Lived latterly at Albury, near Guildford, Surrey.

Colin ALLEN 1926– Painter, designer, illustrator and teacher, born in Cardiff. He studied at the School of Art there, 1942–4, then was in His Majesty's forces until 1948, resuming studies at Royal College of Art, 1949–52, in 1952–3 taking up a Major Travelling Scholarship to Spain, France, Italy, Sicily and North Africa. From the early 1950s taught for many years at Carlisle College of Art and Design. As well as extensive group shows Allen had some solo exhibitions, starting in 1946 at the Chinese Art Gallery, Hong Kong, followed by Howard Roberts Gallery in Cardiff and Border Gallery, Carlisle. He provided illustrations for the publication *The Story of Carlisle*. His Landscape with Snow is in the collection of the Glynn Vivian Art Gallery and Museum, Swansea.

Daphne ALLEN 1899– Painter and illustrator, born in London. She studied art with her parents, her father being the painter Hugh Allen, and at life classes in Chelsea. As a child she had several shows at the Drummond Gallery, also showing at SWA, Burlington Gallery and in the provinces, notably in the Gloucestershire area, where she lived for many years at Chalford. Her work had a strong religious element and she completed pictures in a series of churches. Her picture The Kingdom was shown at Sir Edward Elgar's centenary exhibition. The Medici Society Ltd and A R Mowbray Ltd, the religious publishers, published her work. Victoria & Albert Museum holds early drawings by her, done about the same time as her two books *The Birth of the Opal* and *A Child's Visions* were published.

Frank Humphrey ALLEN 1896–1977 Painter in oil and gouache, draughtsman in ink. Born in London, he studied at Chelsea School of Art, 1933–5, under Graham Sutherland and Harold Sandys Williamson. Exhibited at LG, AIA, Leicester Galleries in the provinces and in Paris. The City of Birmingham Museum and Art Gallery holds his work. Lived in Norwich.

George Warner ALLEN 1916–1988 Painter, notably in tempera, and teacher who was born in Paris. He was educated at Lancing College, then studied at Byam Shaw School of Drawing and Painting under Ernest Jackson, eventually returning there to teach. During World War II he was engaged in camouflage work for the Ministry of Home Security. His exhibitions included solo shows at Walker's Galleries and Reading Museum and Art Gallery. That gallery, Tate Gallery and the public gallery in Nottingham hold his work. George Warner Allen was a disciple of the techniques of the Old Masters and regarded modern art as barbaric. In 1973 he was converted to the Roman Catholic faith, thereafter concentrating on religious subjects. Lived at Wallingford, Oxfordshire.

Georgina ALLEN 1954– Painter of abstracts who studied at University of St Andrews, Goldsmiths' College and Chelsea School of Art. Showed at Paton Gallery, Royal Festival Hall and with Contemporary Art Society at Smith's Galleries. In 1991–2 was included in the Spanish tour of Six Young British Painters.

Harry Epworth ALLEN 1894–1958 Painter, notably in tempera, especially of Derbyshire. Born in Sheffield, Allen attended King Edward VII School for boys, then became a clerk in the steel works of Arthur Balfour, in his spare time attending Sheffield Technical School of Art. Served in the Army in World War I, gaining the Military Medal for conspicuous gallantry. Although badly injured and having an artificial leg Allen continued to paint and became Balfour's confidential secretary until the slump made Allen redundant in 1931. He now painted full-time and joined the new Yorkshire Group of Artists. Began exhibiting RA. Also showed with RSBA and PS. Although Allen's early work is conventionally realistic he soon developed his distinctive style of simplified landscape and figure studies, which eventually were shown abroad in Canada and America. In the early 1940s Allen published a series of articles in *The Artist* on landscape painting in which he expounded his approach. His work is in a number of provincial galleries, notably Sheffield, Wakefield, Newcastle upon Tyne, and Newport, as well as in Australia and New Zealand. Memorial show at Graves Art Gallery, Sheffield, in 1959, which in 1986 held an exhibition of his decorative works, and tour. Lived in Ecclesall, Sheffield.

Heather ALLEN 1952– Sculptor born in Romford, Essex. She studied at University of Reading with Terry Pope. Her sisal and wood entry Plait was included in the 1992 East & South Norwich Gallery/Kent Institute of Art and Design show. Power, repression, containment and enclosure were features of her work. Lived in Norwich, Norfolk.

James ALLEN 1941– Painter, draughtsman, printmaker and teacher, born in Lurgan, Armagh, Northern Ireland, attending Belfast College of Art, 1961–5, then Brighton College of Art, 1965–7. Before returning to Northern Ireland, between 1965–76 he taught for periods at Goldsmiths' College School of Art and Ravensbourne College of Art. Ran a print workshop at Arts Council of Northern Ireland headquarters, Belfast. Exhibitions included Queen's University in Belfast, Serpentine Gallery, Upper Street Gallery, Arnolfini Gallery in Bristol and Tom Caldwell's Galleries in Belfast and Dublin. Queen's University and Ulster Museum hold examples. Lived in Belfast.

Joe ALLEN 1955– Painter and teacher, born in Airdrie, Lanarkshire. He studied at St Martin's School of Art, 1975–6; Camberwell School of Arts and Crafts, 1976–9; and Royal Academy Schools, 1979–82. From 1985 he divided his time between London and Germany, where he was a visiting teacher at the European Academy of Fine Art in Trier. From 1986–92 showed regularly with Gallery Ariadne, Vienna, later solo exhibitions including Cynthia Bourne Gallery, 1995. In 1995–6 John Moores Liverpool Exhibition Allen showed the oil on canvas Sea Barn.

Kathleen ALLEN 1906–1983 Artist, muralist, designer and teacher, born in Acton, west London, known to friends as Kay, who prior to 1938 exhibited as Saywell Allen. She was notable for her views of London, where she lived in Bloomsbury for many years. Educated initially at home because of illness, after Bromley County School for Girls, 1920–4, she studied at the Royal College of Art painting school, 1924–8, then taught in London and the Midlands until 1936, when she set up a studio in the City of London. The late 1930s included studies at the Slade School of Fine Art, 1936–7, painting murals at her old school and elsewhere and more teaching, from 1938 at Henrietta Barnett School. During World War II Allen was seconded by the City one day weekly to record war industries. A bomb in 1941 destroyed her early work. In 1946 Allen was appointed senior lecturer at Goldsmiths' College, from 1960 until retirement in 1966 being principal lecturer and head of art and design. Allen was a member of the central committee of the AIA, 1938–48; was involved in CEMA from 1940; was a member of the Society of Industrial Artists, 1945–9; and was made a member of the Worshipful Company of Painter-Stainers, 1954. A frequent group and solo exhibitor, she had a retrospective at South London Art Gallery, 1983. Tate Gallery archive holds her self-portrait of 1955; Arts Council, Imperial War Museum, Morley College, corporate and local education authority collections also hold examples.

Michael ALLEN 1925– Painter mainly of landscape and marine subjects who was also a commercial designer, Allen was born in Morecambe, Lancashire, and educated at the Friends School, Lancaster. Studied art at Lancaster and Morecambe College of Art 1943–9 with a break in 1944–5 as a prisoner of war. His teachers included Walter Bayes. Exhibited mainly in Lancashire. Lived for a time at Horsforth, Leeds, then later in Welwyn Garden City, Hertfordshire.

Ralph ALLEN 1926– Painter, sculptor and teacher, educated at Kimbolton School, Huntingdonshire. He attended Sir John Cass College of Art, 1948–50; Slade School of Fine Art, 1950–3, with a postgraduate year there, 1953–4. From 1955–7 Allen assisted Helen Lessore at Beaux Arts Gallery, then moved to Canada. He joined the staff of Queen's University, Kingston, Ontario, in 1958, being full-time professor of fine art from 1972, retiring in 1990. Allen was director of the Agnes Etherington Art Centre, 1963–73, where he had a touring show in 1990 after a long period of non-exhibiting. In 1968–9 Allen had a sabbatical year in England. Showed extensively in Canada, with work in collections of Art Gallery of Ontario, National Gallery of Canada, Art Collection of Kingston, Leeds University and elsewhere. Allen's later work had an icon-like quality, figurative and abstract. Earlier he had produced pictures described as "romantic Impressionism ranging to a modified realism". He lived in Kingston.

Richard ALLEN 1933– Abstract artist, teacher and exhibition consultant, born in Worcester. He attended the School of Art there, 1955–7, after National Service in the Far East, then was at Bath Academy of Art, Corsham, 1957–60. Allen was an Italian Government Scholarship winner, 1960–1, a Commonwealth Scholar, in art and architecture, India, 1966–7, an artist-in-residence with a fellowship at University of Sussex, 1967, then gained a Major Award for Painting from Arts Council, 1973. Allen had begun teaching two days a week at Croydon College of Art, 1962–7, and many appointments to London and provincial colleges followed. From 1973 he was appointed exhibition consultant to the Polytechnic of Central London, also lecturing in visual arts subjects. Allen participated in numerous group shows in Britain and abroad from 1964. His individual shows included University of Sussex, 1966, and Angela Flowers Gallery, 1971, later ones including shows in France, Japan and the Netherlands as well as University of Exeter, 1985, and Printworks Ltd, Chicago, 1987. Peter Stuyvesant Foundation, Arts Council, Museum of Modern Art in Rome and Chase Manhattan Bank hold his work. Lived at Whitney-on-Wye, Herefordshire.

Saywell ALLEN: *see* **Kathleen ALLEN**

Tim ALLEN 1950– Painter and teacher who spent his childhood in Durham. Gained a degree at department of fine art in Newcastle upon Tyne, 1968–72, and his master's at Goldsmiths' College, 1978–80. Went on to teach at St Martin's School of Art. Was a prizewinner in the Festival Hall Flag Competition, under auspices of Arts Council, 1977. Mixed exhibitions included Whitechapel Open at Whitechapel Art Gallery, from 1976; Artists for Nuclear Disarmament, Acme Gallery, 1981; Royal Academy Summer Exhibition, 1982; and Paint, Presence, Other Stories, Ikon Gallery, Birmingham, 1983. There his gestural work was described at "improvisatory and accretive". Solo exhibitions included Abbot Hall Art Gallery, Kendal, 1976.

John Ivor ALLENBY 1899–1950 Sculptor, born in Breslau, Poland. After studying at Strasbourg University, Allenby studied art at the Bauhaus, Weimar, under Walter Gropius, 1918–21, then in Paris, 1925–33. In England Allenby changed his name from Johannes Ilmari Allerbach; he was a son of the musician Max Allerbach. Exhibited Salon d'Automne and Salon des Tuileries, Paris, Leicester Galleries, AIA, RA, RIBA and elsewhere. Was a member of the AIA. After World War II Allenby taught at the Oxford School of Art. Signed work with monogram. Lived in Oxford.

Anthea ALLEY 1927–1993 Artist and teacher, whose work developed from figuration to abstraction and who used a variety of materials. Born in Seremban, Malaya, she attended Chelsea School of Art, 1948–51, then Royal College of Art, 1951–3, although as a sculptor she was self-taught. For several years she taught at Bath Academy of Art, Corsham. Mixed shows included Young Contemporaries in Manchester in 1954, RA Summer Exhibition and in 1961 she won a painting prize at John Moores Liverpool Exhibition. Her first solo show was at Molton Gallery in 1960. In 1964 solo exhibitions comprised Hamilton Gallery and Arts Council of Northern Ireland Gallery, Belfast; had a solo show at Arnolfini Gallery, Bristol, and Bradford City Art Gallery and tour, 1969; and shared several shows with Gillian Ayres. In 1990 Alley was Sandra Blow's choice as an Artist of the Day at Flowers East. Arts Council holds her Horse, in welded iron, 1960, and Rock, in steel, 1964. Lived in London.

Melissa ALLEY 1962– Painter and teacher, daughter of the curator and writer Ronald Alley and the artist Anthea Alley. She did a foundation course at Wimbledon School of Art, 1982–3; gained an honours degree in painting at Central School of Art, 1983–6; and studied with Cecil Collins, 1985–9. Between 1988–96 worked part-time at the England & Co gallery; she also taught part-time from her studio in Camberwell. Alley described her pictures as "orchestrated through concerns such as colour and line, masculine and feminine, figuration and abstraction, until a harmony is achieved". Mixed shows included Paperworks, Battersea Arts Centre, 1985; England & Co, Christmas Exhibition, 1996–7; and Benjamin Hargreaves, 1997. Solo shows included Putney Library, 1996, and ASC Studios, 1997.

Mabel ALLEYNE 1896–1961 Illustrator and printmaker, born in Southampton, Hampshire, who attended Goldsmiths' College School of Art and Royal Academy Schools. Among books illustrated were Shelley's *Adonais* and Emily Brontë's *Wuthering Heights*. She showed at RA, RHA, Redfern Gallery, SWA and NEAC and lived in London.

Nicola ALLFORD 1964– Sculptor in a variety of materials who did a foundation arts diploma at Weston-super-Mare College of Further Education, 1987–8, then an honours degree in ceramics at Bath College of Higher Education, 1988–91. She next spent some time on the continent. Among her exhibitions was 1st RWA Open Sculpture Exhibition, 1993. Lived in Bristol.

John ALLIN 1934–1991 Painter, born in London, who became famous for his simple and direct pictures of East End streets. Many of these depicted scenes he had known as a child. Allin was a fine natural draughtsman who joined prison art classes while serving a sentence for theft, and continued to work in the evenings later when employed as a lorry driver. In the late 1960s began showing at the Portal Gallery and in the 1970s won fame on the continent, in 1979 gaining the Prix Suisse Peinture Naive award. In 1974 his book *Say Goodbye* was published, with an accompanying text by the playwright Arnold Wesker, who had shared a similar childhood. A second book, *Circus Life*, followed after the artist spent two years with Gerry Cottle's circus.

Edward ALLINGTON 1951– Sculptor and draughtsman, working in ink and emulsion on used ledger paper, born in Westmorland. He studied at Lancaster School of Art, 1968–71, and Central School of Arts and Crafts, 1971–4. Had first solo show in 1981 and exhibited regularly at Lisson Gallery. Foreign one-man exhibitions included Diane Brown, New York, 1987, and Fuji TV Tokyo and Gallery Face Tokyo, 1988. Also took part in foreign group shows, including British Sculpture 1960–1988 in Antwerp, in 1988. Participated in John Moores Liverpool Exhibition from 1985, in 1989–90 gaining a prize. Arts Council holds his work. Lived in London.

Adrian ALLINSON 1890–1959 Painter, sculptor, draughtsman and poster designer. Born in London. He initially studied medicine, but gave this up to study art at the Slade School of Fine Art, 1910–12, where he was a member of a notable group of students working under Henry Tonks, Philip Wilson Steer, Fred Brown and Walter Westley Russell. Won a Slade Scholarship. Allinson was an athletic man, keen on skiing and climbing, a member of the Ski Club. At various times he taught drawing and painting at Westminster School of Art, designed posters for British Railways and was scenic designer for the Beecham Opera Company. Exhibited RA, NEAC, RBA, ROI, Leicester Galleries and Fine Art Society, which put on a retrospective in 1984. Allinson wrote an autobiography, *Painter's Pilgrimage*. Galleries in Manchester, Bradford and Rochdale hold his work. Although he was fond of travelling, Allinson finally lived in London.

Jane ALLISON 1959– Painter, notably of portraits, and designer, educated at Charterhouse, who studied painting at Chelsea School of Art and Slade School of Fine Art until 1982. Held an appointment as artist-in-residence at St Pancras Hospital. Designed book covers for Virago and Women's Press and showed regularly with Contemporary Portrait Society of which she was a member, RP, ROI and The Heifer Gallery.

Douglas ALLSOP 1943– Versatile artist and teacher, born in Watford, Hertfordshire, who attended St Albans School of Art, 1960–4. Allsop from 1995 was tutor in painting at the Royal College of Art, also director of studies at Byam Shaw School of Art. His first geometric colour studies/use of the square and its divisions took place in 1965; in 1970 he created his first objects and installations employing electronic and reflective light systems, and in 1974 his first systematic black objects. Allsop participated in many group shows internationally, especially in Germany. These included Kleine Formate, Galerie Wack, Kaiserslautern, Germany, 1985; Kapil Jariwala Gallery, 1987; Minimal Means, The Showroom/John Hansard Gallery, University of Southampton, 1989; Project 30 x 30, Wilhem-Hack-Museum, Ludwigshafen, Germany, 1994; and Repères, Musée des Ursulines, Mâcon, France, 1997. A steady stream of solo shows began with Maynard Gallery, Welwyn Garden City, 1965, later ones including Laure Genillard Gallery, 1994 and 1998. Tate Gallery, Victoria & Albert Museum (National Art Library), The British Library, Museum of Modern Art in New York, City Museum and Art Gallery in Portsmouth and many other British and foreign collections hold examples. Allsop lived and worked in London from 1975.

George ALLSOP 1911– Painter and teacher, born in Hay, Herefordshire. He attended Farnham Grammar School, Surrey, then studied at the School of Art there under Otway McCannell, 1931–3; Malvern School of Art with Victor Moody, 1935–8; and Birmingham School of Art, 1938–9. Showed at RA, RBA, NEAC and elsewhere and lived in Marple Bridge, Cheshire.

Bruce ALLSOPP 1912– Painter, teacher, writer and publisher, born in Oxford. Trained as an architect at Liverpool University's school of architecture, Allsopp went on to write a number of books about art, design and furniture, including *Style in the Visual Arts* and *A General History of Architecture*. He held several teaching posts, for some years lecturing at Durham University. Married to the painter Florence Woodroffe. He was a master of the Art Workers' Guild and was chairman of Oriel Press. Sometimes signed his work B A. Worthing Art Gallery holds his watercolour Bosham Harbour. Lived in Stocksfield, Northumberland.

Darren ALMOND 1971– Artist, born in Wigan, Lancashire, who graduated in fine art from Winchester School of Art, 1993. Group exhibitions included Southampton Quays, Southampton, 1992; Art & Innovation Prize (winner), ICA, and Something Else, Exmouth Market, both 1996; and Sensation, RA, 1997. Had a solo exhibition at Crawford Art College, Cork, Ireland, 1991; KNI20, at Great Western Studios, 1995; and in 1997 both ICA/Toshiba Art & Innovation Commission, at ICA, and a one-man show at Jay Jopling/White Cube. Saatchi Collection holds his work. Lived in London.

Will ALSOP 1947– Artist, architect and teacher, born in Northampton where he studied at the School of Art, 1967. As well as being a partner for a time in Will Alsop & John Lyall, architects, Alsop taught at the Architectural Association and in the sculpture department of St Martin's School of Art. He had a special interest in photography and video. Showed at Riverside Studios, Fruitmarket Gallery in Edinburgh and abroad. Lived in London.

Rowland Wright ALSTON 1895–1958 Oil and watercolour painter who was for many years curator of The Watts Gallery, established to commemorate the Victorian painter G F Watts, at Compton, Surrey. Alston studied at the Slade School of Fine Art. Showed at the RA and NEAC, sometimes signing work RWA. Lived at Compton.

Meyer Daniel ALTSON 1881–1965 Painter, decorative artist and printmaker, born in Middlesbrough, Yorkshire, who studied art at Melbourne National Gallery, gaining a scholarship at 16; and in Paris at Atelier Colarossi and L'École Nationale des Beaux-Arts. Showed a series of portraits at RA between 1925–41, also exhibiting in the provinces. His brother was the artist Abbey Altson. Lived in London.

ALVA 1901–1973 Artist, born in Berlin, Germany, as Siegfried Alweiss, to Austrian parents. At his Jewish school his art master, Otto Geismar, gave encouragement. After a poor academic start, in 1919 he entered Kern's Konservatorium to prepare for the State Academy to become a professional musician, but left the Academy to take over his father's raincoat factory. When it closed, he turned to commercial art for a living and in 1925 went to life classes run by the Freie Secession, signing his work Alva. In Paris in 1928 Alva attended the Atelier Colarossi, sold work and then between 1929–32 travelled through France, Switzerland and Italy. After selling works at Salon d'Automne in Paris in 1933, in 1934 travelled in Palestine, Syria and Greece, having a first solo show at Maskit Gallery, Tel-Aviv. In 1938 Alva settled in England, becoming a naturalised British citizen, but was interned in the Isle of Man in 1940. Had a solo show at Leger Gallery in 1943, after which he had numerous exhibitions internationally, sometimes working from a studio in Paris. In 1973, the year of his solo exhibition at Waddington Galleries, he published his autobiography *With Pen and Brush* which was liberally illustrated. Ben Uri Art Society holds examples of Alva's work, which could be formalised or calligraphic, then from 1969 was strong, based on the nude female figure. Lived in London.

Siegfried ALWEISS: *see* **ALVA**

Ray AMBROSE 1927–1989 Painter, draughtsman, printmaker and teacher, born in Grays, Essex, married to the artist Moyra

Gilchrist. He studied at South-East Essex Technical College and School of Art in Dagenham, 1955, teachers including John Wellings, then at Royal Academy Schools, 1955–6, under Peter Greenham. Taught in London and showed in mixed exhibitions with Young Contemporaries, Upper Street Gallery and Orion Gallery, Penzance, also having many solo shows. Sometimes signed work with initials. Nuffield Foundation and Copenhagen Institute hold examples. Lived in Newlyn, Cornwall, and died at Penzance railway station.

Victor AMBRUS 1935– Book illustrator, graphic designer and teacher, born in Budapest, Hungary, where he studied at the Academy of Fine Art. Arriving in England following the uprising of 1956, Ambrus further studied at Royal College of Art, 1957–60. He taught graphic design at West Surrey College of Art in Farnham. Although he showed at RA and RE, of which he was a fellow, Ambrus was mainly a book illustrator, with several hundred titles to his credit, some of them his own. Military and naval subjects were favoured by him. America's Library of Congress, Washington, holds his work. Lived in Fleet Hampshire, later in Farnham and Runfold, Surrey.

Shenda AMERY fl. from mid-1970s– Figurative sculptor, painter and draughtsman, brought up in Essex, who studied chemistry at college and married an architect who was a pupil of Frank Lloyd Wright in America. Amery studied there with a Japanese artist. Lived in the Middle East for 18 years, returning to London in 1978, sharing her time between a flat in Chelsea and an old mill-house in Cambridgeshire. Originally exhibited as a painter, group shows including Institute of Women Painters, Teheran, Iran, 1975; Loggia Gallery, 1978 (she was a member of the Society of Free Painters and Sculptors); and Trends, Mall Galleries, 1979. Later solo painting shows included Loggia, 1978. Turned to sculpture, mixed exhibitions including Chelsea Art Society, of which she was a member. Had a series of solo sculpture exhibitions at The Orangery, Holland Park. For the Chelsea Conservative Association made a portrait bust of prime minister Margaret Thatcher, presented to her at 10 Downing Street in 1981.

Paul AMEY 1957– Sculptor, born and lived in Oxford, who attended Oxford Polytechnic, 1975, then Hornsey College of Art, 1976–9. He was a founder-member of Oxford Artist Group, 1983–92; Oxford Sculpture Project, 1987; and Chiltern Sculpture Trust, 1990. Took part in many mixed exhibitions, including Camden Annual, 1983; Mappin Art Gallery, Sheffield, 1984; The Day Book Travelling Exhibition, 1988; Museum of Modern Art, Oxford, 1992; and Galerie Horst Dietrich, Berlin, 1995. Had a solo show at Oxford Gallery, Oxford, 1983, later ones including Galerie III, Nijmegen, Netherlands, 1994, and Beaux Arts, Bath, 1995. Installations/Projects included Artweek 83, Oxford, 1983, then subsequent Artweeks; Trustland Sculpture Project II, Oxford, 1989; and Europees Keramisch Werkcentrum, 's Hertogenbosch, Netherlands, artist-in-residence, 1994. Commissions included Wouthill Park Youth Centre, Bracknell, 1984; Basingstoke Hospital, 1988; and House & Smoke multiple for Living Stone Press, The Hague, Netherlands, and Galerie Horst Dietrich, 1994. In his work Amey took objects out of their everyday context: a snake becomes smoke out of a chimney; fish take the place of leaves on a tree; an aeroplane appears to fly out of a wooden head, attached by an umbilical cord. Identity and relationships were questioned.

Maria Ajike AMIDU 1967– Artist, notably in glass and ceramics, born in London, who did a foundation course at St Helens College of Art & Design, Merseyside, 1985–6; gained an honours degree in three-dimensional design at West Surrey College of Art, Farnham, 1986–9; then her master's in glass and ceramics at Royal College of Art, 1990–2. Among awards were the Wingate Scholarship and Eduardo Paolozzi Travel Bursary, both 1991; Prince's Youth Business Trust Award, 1995; and S G Warburg Grant, 1996. Exhibitions included Crafts Council Glass Show, 1993; New Light, Solomon Gallery, Dublin, 1996; Expo Gas International I, Tucson, Arizona, 1997; and 198 Gallery. Victoria & Albert Museum Pilkington Collection holds her work.

Blair ANDERSON 1967– Painter, born in Glasgow, who studied at Gray's School of Art in Aberdeen and who won an Elizabeth Greenshields Foundation Award, 1993. Group shows included New Generation at Compass Gallery, 1989; Olympia Art Fair, 1990; Trinity Gallery, 1991; and Royal Over-Seas League Open, 1995. Had a solo show at Byzantium Gallery, Edinburgh, 1990, later ones including Rendezvous Gallery, Aberdeen, 1995.

Christopher ANDERSON 1914– Sculptor, painter and teacher, born in Yorkley, Gloucestershire. Studied at Lydney School of Art, at Royal College of Art under Richard Garbe and at Goldsmiths' College School of Art. Taught sculpture at Hornsey School of Art and at Borough Polytechnic. Showed at RA, LG and in the provinces. Lived in London.

Douglas ANDERSON 1934– Portrait painter who studied with Pietro Annigoni in Florence. For a time Anderson lived in London, was a member of Chelsea Arts Club and ran Douglas Anderson Ltd, later moving to Pisa, Italy. Showed at RP and RA, in 1965 Summer Exhibition showing a portrait of HM The Queen.

Gary ANDERSON 1960– Painter and draughtsman, born in Baillieston, Glasgow. Anderson studied at Glasgow School of Art, 1980–4, gaining a fine art honours degree. He had early success, winning the John D Kelly Award at the Glasgow School in 1981. Further awards included D W T Cargill Award (under 30), in 1984, and Arthur Young Exhibitionship Prize, 1987, both at Royal Glasgow Institute of the Fine Arts; and in 1989 the Elizabeth Greenshields Foundation Award and the Arts in Fife Purchase Award, Fife House Collection. In 1984 Anderson showed in mixed exhibitions at Compass Gallery in Glasgow and Open Eye Gallery and Mercury, both in Edinburgh, and many other group shows soon followed. His first solo show was at Corners Gallery, Glasgow, 1985, then from the early 1990s Ewan Mundy Fine Art showed Anderson in Glasgow, London and New

York. Anderson's work showed fine draughtsmanship, rich colour in the Glasgow tradition and a quirky imaginative streak drawing on such sources as Chinese watercolours and the circus. Lived in Glasgow.

Harry ANDERSON 1923– Artist in various media and teacher, born in Selkirk, Selkirkshire. He studied at Edinburgh College of Art. Gained a post-diploma scholarship and a travelling scholarship to Europe. He taught for London County Council and Harlow Technical College. Showed with AIA Gallery from 1957; Douglas and Foulis Gallery, Edinburgh, 1964; and in 1965 he was included in The Visual Arts, Harlow Arts Festival. Glasgow University holds his work.

Janette ANDERSON 1938–1996 Painter of exuberant and colourful still lifes and landscapes in the Scottish Colourist tradition. Studied at Glasgow School of Art under William Drummond, Geoffrey Squire and David Donaldson, graduating with a diploma in drawing and painting, 1956–60, with a post-diploma, 1961. Exhibited at RSA, Royal Glasgow Institute of the Fine Arts, SSWA, and elsewhere in mixed shows. Later solo shows included Lillie Art Gallery, Milngavie, 1992; Torrance Gallery, Edinburgh, 1994; and Duncan Campbell Contemporary Art, 1996, this show finished two days before the artist's death. Many private collections in Britain and abroad hold her work, once described by a critic as "if painted at the wheel of a fast car, the paint flung on with impetuous abandon".

John ANDERSON 1926– Designer and painter, born in Borrowash, Derbyshire, who studied at Harrow School of Art, his teachers including Maurice de Sausmarez and Christopher Sanders, 1939–43 and 1947–9. Went on to run Anderson Art Studios. He showed at Young Contemporaries, RA and RBA. Lived for a time at Northwood, Middlesex.

Kay ANDERSON 1902– Painter and versatile printmaker who married the artist Thomas Clough. She was a qualified art teacher who studied at Liverpool School of Art and the Royal College of Art under William Rothenstein. Exhibited RA, NEAC, provincial galleries, in France and North America. British Museum holds her work. Lived in London.

Lindsay ANDERSON 1947– Artist, born in Edgbaston, Birmingham, who attended Sutton Coldfield School of Art, 1963–5, then gained a first-class honours degree in sculpture from Leeds College of Art, 1965–8. After a dozen years, Anderson returned to work as an artist in 1980, beginning with drawings and etchings, then in 1988 began to carve and paint simple boxes, which became more narrative and evolved into the panels for which she became known. These were in limewood, painted, and for her were "a kind of drawing with chisels". They expressed a semi-autobiographical narrative, involving mysterious dreaming women, standing winged guardian seraphim and strange, serene faces. Mixed shows included Scottish Gallery, Edinburgh, 1990; The Woodcarver's Art, Crafts Council tour, and Christmas Show, Ruskin Gallery in Sheffield, both 1993; and Fish, Hove Museum and Art Gallery, 1995. Had a solo show at England & Co, 1996. Contemporary Art Society; John Makepeace, at Parnham House and Gallery; and Hampshire Museums Service own examples. From 1995 Anderson lived in London.

Madeleine ANDERSON 1910–1976 Painter and printmaker, born in Belvedere, Kent. She studied at Airdrie Academy, in Lanarkshire, then art at Kingston School of Art, 1931–2, with James Anthony Betts and John Gerald Platt, and Royal College of Art, 1932–4, where her teachers included Gilbert Spencer. Showed at NEAC and elsewhere and had a studio at Lechlade, Gloucestershire. Notable flower painter. Ministry of Works and Cheltenham Art Gallery bought her work.

Margaret ANDERSON 1926– Portrait painter and miniaturist, born in Newport, Monmouthshire, also known as Margaret Anderson-Rees. She studied at Newport Polytechnic, 1944, and went on to exhibit with RMS, PS, RA and elsewhere. Lived in Everton, Hampshire.

Sally ANDERSON 1933– Abstract sculptor who studied at Edinburgh College of Art. Her first job was as a technical assistant at Central School of Arts and Crafts. She organised the First Group, five artists who exhibited at municipal galleries in England and gave talks on patronage at the towns visited; also helped to arrange the Resolution 42 exhibition following the Trades Union Congress decision to support the arts; and then Thesis 80, an organisation to promote the visual arts. She showed with 57 Gallery, Edinburgh, in 1959; AIA Gallery from 1961; and in 1965 was included in Harlow Arts Festival's The Visual Arts.

Stanley ANDERSON 1884–1966 Engraver and painter. Born in Bristol, the son of an engraver Alfred E Anderson, Stanley had his initial art education in the city, having been apprenticed to his father's business as an heraldic engraver at 15. He attended the Royal College of Art, 1909–11, and Goldsmiths' College School of Art, but insisted that he was greatly self-educated in art, especially in the British Museum and National Gallery. From the time he won a British Institution Engraving Scholarship in 1909 Anderson marked his course as an outstanding engraver. His delineation of several dozen country craft subjects, which occupied about 20 years from the early 1930s, is a remarkable record, the engravings being meticulously accurate and beautifully composed. Anderson was for many years a member of the engraving faculty at the British School at Rome and in 1938 was chosen by the British Council as the sole British representative of line engraving and drypoint at the Venice Biennale. Elected RA 1941. Anderson won many medals and other awards. His work has been bought widely by British Commonwealth and American galleries and museums. Abbott and Holder had the first show of Anderson's etchings for 60 years in 1995. Lived near Aylesbury, Buckinghamshire.

Margaret ANDERSON-REES: *see* **Margaret ANDERSON**

Eileen ANDERTON 1924– Artist in various media who was born and lived in Bradford, Yorkshire, her father being a teacher of art. Studied at local School of Art, 1939–44, her teachers including Vincent Lines. Showed at SWA, RWS, at City Art Gallery in Bradford and elsewhere in north of England, including Bradford Arts Club of which she was a member.

Athene ANDRADE 1908– Painter and printmaker who studied at Central School of Arts and Crafts and Bromley and Beckenham School of Art. She showed at RA, SWA, NS and elsewhere. Lived in Bromley, Kent.

Conrad R ANDREAE 1871–1956 Landscape watercolourist, born in London, who was educated at Osborne House in Margate and in Germany. Attended Slade School of Fine Art, where he won a first-class certificate in figure painting, and at Académie Julian, Paris. Exhibited at RA and Walker Art Gallery in Liverpool, being principally known for his views of England and France. Settled in Brighton, Sussex, where he was a member of the Arts Club and where the Museum and Art Gallery holds watercolours of the beach by him.

Margaret ANDRESEN 1951– Watercolourist and illustrator, born in Dunfermline, Fife. Studied at Duncan of Jordanstone College of Art in Dundee, 1969–75. Had one-man shows in Scotland, including Stirling Gallery. Lived in Glasgow.

Keith ANDREW 1947– Artist and designer, born in London. He studied at Ravensbourne College of Art & Design, Bromley, his teachers including Michael Tyzack. Worked as a graphic designer for eight years before returning to painting full-time in 1975. This coincided with his move to Holyhead, Anglesey. His exhibitions included RA Summer Exhibition, 1981; Bangor Art Gallery and National Eisteddfod, Swansea, 1982; Mid-Wales Open, 1984, where he won a prize; Prints from Wales, Wenniger Graphics, Boston, 1987; and Artists in the National Parks, Victoria & Albert Museum, 1988. In 1981 Andrew was elected a full member of RCA. CASW, University of Wales in Swansea and University of Wales print collection, Aberystwyth, hold his work.

Neale ANDREW 1958– Notably a portrait sculptor, born in Northampton. He trained at Blackpool College of Art and graduated with an honours degree in fine art from Trent Polytechnic, Nottingham, in 1980. His sporting portraits included the cricketer Geoff Boycott, the golfer Tony Jacklin and footballer Gary Lineker. Major commissions included a bronze for Newark town commemorating the Civil War and the D H Lawrence Memorial for the author's study centre in Nottingham. His work was cast by The Morris Singer Foundry.

Arthur Henry ANDREWS 1906–1966 Painter, printmaker and teacher, born in London, married to the artist Sushila Singh. They were fellow students at Hornsey School of Art and Royal College of Art under William Rothenstein, graduating in 1929. He held a number of teaching posts in Sheffield and Derby Colleges of Art and Batley School of Art, eventually being principal of Poole College of Further Education and art adviser to Dorset Education Committee. He showed at Foyles Gallery and at public galleries in Bradford and Leeds one-man, also in group exhibitions at RA, Grabowski and Redfern Galleries. He was made a member of Design and Industries Association in 1934, SWE in 1935. Sir Edward Marsh held his work, as did Victoria & Albert Museum and public galleries in Leeds, Bournemouth and Southport. Lived latterly in Bournemouth, Hampshire.

Christopher ANDREWS 1952– Artist in photography, film and video and teacher, born in Essex. He studied at Sir George Williams University, Montreal, and London College of Printing, going on to teach there and at Southend School of Art and Design. Andrews' exhibitions and screenings included the Arts Council travelling show New British Image; Acme Gallery; Tokyo Video Festival, Japan; Atelier St Anne, Brussels; The Basement, Newcastle; and in 1983 the Goldsmiths' show at Woodlands Art Gallery. ICA Video Library, London Video Arts Library and Sheffield City Polytechnic hold his work.

Edith Lovell ANDREWS 1886–1980 Painter and poster designer, born in Newport, Monmouthshire. She studied at Glasgow School of Art, 1908–10, under Fra Newbery, then with Gerald Massey at Heatherley's School of Fine Art, 1911–14. Miss Lovell Andrews showed extensively abroad as well as in Britain, notably in St Ives, Cornwall, where she lived and was a member of St Ives Arts Club, the Society of Artists and had a solo show in 1957. British Museum holds her work.

Eileen ANDREWS 1897– Painter, craft worker and teacher, notable for her watercolours, born in West Bridgford, Nottinghamshire, as Dorothy Eileen Andrews. She studied at Northampton School of Art, 1916–21, under Oswald Crompton, then with William Rothenstein at Royal College of Art, 1921–3. Then taught at Leyton School of Art and Borough Polytechnic until 1938, when she began 25 years at South-West Essex Technical College School of Art, Walthamstow. Showed at NS, ROI, Russell-Cotes Art Gallery, Bournemouth, and elsewhere. Lived in Woodford Green, Essex, for many years.

Florence Christine ANDREWS 1905– Decorative painter and artist in lacquer, born in Ipswich where she continued to live. She studied at the local Art School with the watercolourist George Rushton and showed in the Ipwich area.

Jane ANDREWS fl. from mid-1990s– Painter, whose figurative pictures could have an amusing-grotesque quality, as in her contribution to Eight by Eight, at Pallant House, Chichester, 1997. She obtained a fine art honours degree at West Surrey College of Art & Design, Farnham, 1991–4. Mixed exhibitions included Fresh Art, Islington, where she was shortlisted for a Space Award, 1994, and No Turkeys, Raw Gallery, 1995. Had solo exhibitions at Sadler's Wells, 1995 and 1996, with one titled Jamboree at Piano Nobile, 1997. Lived in Milford, Surrey.

Kerry ANDREWS 1956– Painter and draughtsman who studied at Ruskin School of Drawing, Oxford, 1976–9. Exhibitions included Ruskin Copies at Christ Church College, Oxford, 1977–8; Mostly Photographic Gallery, Essex, 1981; Drawing on Life, Battersea Arts Centre, 1982; and in 1983 Goldsmiths' show at Woodlands Art Gallery.

Lea ANDREWS 1958– Artist born in Sonning Common, Oxfordshire. He studied at Banbury School of Art, 1981–2, Brighton Polytechnic, 1982–5, then Slade School of Fine Art, 1985–7. In 1988 he was artist-in-residence at Tooting Bec Hospital. Also in 1988 he shared a show with Robert Mabb at Riverside Studios; in 1989 he was in Behold the Man, at Stills Gallery, Edinburgh, and tour; and 1990 was in The British Art Show, a South Bank Centre touring exhibition. The year before had had a solo show at Battersea Arts Centre called A Change in Thinking. Andrews' photographic prints focused on imaginary public sculptures to invent a history of where he had lived. Arts Council holds his work. Lived in London.

Leonard Gordon ANDREWS 1885–1960 Painter and designer, born at Lindfield, Sussex. Studied art at Battersea Polytechnic School of Art, 1900–03, under William Thomas; Clapham School of Art, 1903–4; Regent Street Polytechnic School of Art, 1906, under George Gaskell; Birmingham School of Art, 1908; and West Bromwich School of Art, 1909, under J A Pearce. Andrews held a number of art teaching positions in the West Midlands and London areas, finishing with the South-West Essex Technical College School of Art, 1938–50. He exhibited RA, RBA, ROI, NS and RSMA. Lived at Woodford Green, Essex.

Liam ANDREWS 1913– Painter in oil and watercolour who was brought up in Belfast, where he continued to live. Studied at Belfast College of Art, 1930–6, his teachers including the local artist Seamus Stoupe. Exhibited RUA.

Lilian ANDREWS 1878–c.1975 Watercolourist, notably of birds and animals, daughter of the inventor Stephen Rusbridge, born in Brighton where she studied at the School of Art. She gained a bronze medal and later taught there. Married the artist Douglas Sharpus Andrews, principal of Leeds School of Art, who predeceased her by about 30 years in 1944. She was a member of Leeds Art Club. Exhibited at RA, IS, RSA, Paris Salon and widely in the provinces. Nottingham Art Gallery holds her work and Leeds City Art Gallery holds Douglas' watercolour Ingleton and her Peahen and Chick. She lived latterly in London.

Marcia ANDREWS fl. from mid-1960s– Expressionist painter, born in London, who studied at Medway College of Art, 1960–4, with Eric Frankland. She was on the staff of the British Council. Exhibited abroad and with Free Painters and Sculptors of which she was a member, Medway Little Theatre, Corn Exchange in Chesterfield, Cockpit Theatre and Turret Gallery. University of Surrey holds her work, featured in a series of solo exhibitions. Lived in Chatham, Kent.

Michael ANDREWS 1928–1995 Painter and teacher, born in Norwich, Norfolk, attending City of Norwich School. He studied at Slade School of Fine Art, 1949–53, after part-time study at Norwich Art School. In 1953 won Rome Scholarship in painting and Abbey Scholarship. Showed at Beaux Arts Gallery and at ICA in 1952 and had first one-man show at Beaux Arts in 1958. About this time he decorated the Colony Room Club, and early work was concerned with Soho night-life and party-going, but he tired of these subjects. Taught at Norwich, Chelsea and the Slade Schools, 1959–66. Andrews' later work, mixed realism and fantasy, was often concerned with themes, such as balloons over landscapes, tropical fish and Ayers Rock, in Australia. A cerebral, technically accomplished painter highly regarded by his peers, Andrews latterly showed with Anthony d'Offay and hadretrospectives at Hayward Gallery in 1980, organised by Arts Council, and Whitechapel Art Gallery in 1991. Tate Gallery holds his work. Andrews returned to the Norwich area from 1977–92, settling finally in London where he died of cancer.

Sybil ANDREWS 1898–1992 Printmaker, painter and teacher, born in Bury St Edmunds, Suffolk, who began painting as a child. While working as a welder in an aircraft factory in 1918 she took John Hassall's art correspondence course, then went to Heatherley's School of Fine Art, taught by Henry Massey. With Cyril Power, the architect, she formed an artistic partnership which lasted until World War II, while serving as first secretary of Grosvenor School of Modern Art. There she met Claude Flight, pioneer Cubist/Futurist lino-cut artist, by whom she was influenced, and she exhibited reguarly between 1928–37 at Redfern and Ward Galleries. Shared a solo show with Power in 1933 at Redfern. During World War II she worked in boatbuilding at Hythe, near Southampton, and made sketches which formed the basis for seven canvases in collection of Royal Air Force Museum, Hendon. In 1947 she married Walter Morgan and they emigrated to Canada, settling in Campbell River, British Columbia, where Andrews painted and taught. She was a member of the Canadian Painter Etchers and the Print and Drawing Council of Canada. Andrews was included in Parkin Gallery's 1975 exhibition Claude Flight and his Circle and in another in 1978 which also toured Italy. In 1982–3 Glenbow Museum, Alberta, gave Andrews a retrospective which toured. Her work is in several Canadian galleries, Los Angeles Museum, Victoria & Albert Museum and British Museum.

Patricia ANGADI 1914– Painter, notable for her portraits, born and lived in London. She was married to the Indian writer and teacher Ayana Angadi in 1943. Helped with her money and support Ayana Angadi and friends in Hampstead in 1946 founded the Indian Music Circle, later renamed the Asian Music Circle, a principal promoter of Indian music and culture in the West. Patricia Angadi studied at Heatherley's School of Fine Art, 1933–7, her teachers including Frederic Whiting and Bernard Adams. She became chairman of the Hampstead Artists' Council. Showed at RP, SWA, NEAC, Paris Salon and elsewhere. Birkbeck College holds her portrait of the philosopher C E M Joad and the

Maxton Memorial Committee bought that of the Socialist Member of Parliament James Maxton for presentation to the City of Glasgow.

John ANGEL 1881–1960 Sculptor, born at Newton Abbot, Devon. Studied at Exeter College of Art, Lambeth School of Art and the Royal Academy Schools, where he gained several awards, followed by studies in Italy and Greece. Worked in the studio of Sir George Frampton for several years. Exhibited RA, RSA, Royal Glasgow Institute of the Fine Arts and overseas. In the mid-1920s went to live at Sandy Hook, Connecticut. Angel, who was elected a fellow of the RBS, did a volume of work in England and American churches.

Marie ANGEL 1923– Illustrator and calligrapher who studied at Croydon School of Art, 1940–5, then at Royal College of Art design school, 1945–8. Showed at RA, with Society of Designer Craftsmen and widely in America, where she had solo exhibitions. Illustrated a number of books, notably in America. Victoria & Albert Museum and Harvard College Library hold her work. Lived in Warlingham, Surrey.

Cristiana ANGELINI 1937– Painter in oil, draughtsman and teacher, born in Tuscany, Italy. She studied at the Scuola di Belle Arti in Carrara in 1952 and travelled widely through Africa in the late 1950s. Moved to England in 1963, becoming a British citizen. Settled in London. Figure compositions, townscapes and large interiors featured in her work, which had a strong sense of draughtsmanship and mood. From the early 1970s she appeared in many mixed shows, including South London Art Gallery from 1981, Whitechapel Art Gallery Open in 1984, Celebration of London at Smith's Gallery, 1988, and in 1990 she gained first prize for London and South-East Region in Laing Collection Exhibition. Had solo shows at Woodlands Art Gallery, 1978, Greenwich Theatre Gallery, 1982, and Sweet Waters Gallery, 1989. From 1985 taught in adult education.

Ethel Elizabeth ANGELL fl. from c.1930– Painter and teacher. Studied at Nuneaton Art School under John Park and Alfred Jones. Exhibited RA, RBSA, ROI and with Warwickshire Society of Artists. Lived at Nuneaton, Warwickshire.

Mea ANGERER 1905– Artist in pen and ink and gouache, but primarily a designer of textiles. Born in Vienna, where she studied at the Academy of Applied Art, Angerer in Britain worked for several bodies connected with textile production, as well as for the 1951 Festival of Britain. Signed work MEA. It is held by the Victoria & Albert Museum. Lived in London.

Christine ANGUS 1953– Sculptor, born in Grimsby, Lincolnshire. She worked for BMW from 1971–3, then in 1974–8 attended Brighton Polytechnic to study sculpture. From 1979 she was self-employed, taking part in a number of group exhibitions. These included Basingstoke Arts Festival, 1982 Serpentine Summer Show and in 1983 she participated in Welsh Sculpture Trust's Margam exhibition, Sculpture in a Country Park. Angus won a Major Bursary from Southern Arts in 1980 and held a solo show at Southampton Civic Centre. She worked in stone, carving objects of a contemplative disposition. Her earliest work was tightly designed geometric forms in which spacing and proportion were key elements; later the forms tended to suggest real objects. Arts Council holds her Bath stone carving Ophidia, of 1982, and in 1984 her Snail Block and Triangle was sited at Milton Keynes General Hospital, commissioned by the Development Corporation there. Lived in Hampshire.

Peggy ANGUS 1904–1993 Painter, draughtsman, designer and teacher, born in Chile, who was brought by her parents to England in 1909. She attended the North London Collegiate School, at 17 a scholarship taking her to the Royal College of Art where she became friends with Eric Ravilious and Edward Bawden. Taught in Nuneaton and Eastbourne, later at the North London Collegiate, after divorce from her husband James Richards, editor of *The Architectural Review*. Angus turned to designing tiles and wallpapers, being retained by Carter's of Poole, in Dorset. For many years Angus lived in a primitive shepherd's cottage in the Sussex Downs near Glynde which became the focus of artistic activity, commemorated in a show at Towner Art Gallery, Eastbourne, 1987. In 1992 she shared an exhibition at Sally Hunter Fine Art which covered her pre-World War II work. Died in London. North London Collegiate held a memorial show in 1994.

Kofi ANKOBRA 1954– Painter, born in Johannesburg, South Africa, who studied at the Ghanatta College of Art in Accra, Ghana, 1975–8. He had a first solo exhibition at Windsor Community Arts Centre in 1985, subsequently showing in London and Santa Fé, in America. He returned to Ghana to paint, one result being his colourful canvas Murokie outside Rasta Bar, shown in 1993–4 John Moores Liverpool Exhibition. Lived in London.

Dorothy ANNAN 1908–1983 Painter, mosaicist, mural artist, potter and teacher, born in Pará, Brazil. Annan's initial education and art tuition were obtained abroad. In 1949 she taught at Bath College of Art and she exhibited at RA, LG, NEAC and elsewhere. Manchester City Art Gallery holds her picture Christmas 1944, and she is also represented in public galleries in Brighton and Stoke-on-Trent. She completed a great deal of public work in the form of mosaic panels, tiled murals and painted murals in London and the provinces, including Ministry of Education, Durham University Library, Bank of England and 70 Farringdon Road. Known as Dodo or Dolly, Annan lived the artistic life in London with her sculptor husband Trevor Tennant. Died in the Sue Ryder Home, Snettisham, Norfolk.

Jeremy ANNEAR 1949– Painter and teacher whose work showed Cubist influences. He was born in Exeter and worked in Devon until the late 1980s, after which he was based in Cornwall, with periods working in Germany and Australia. From 1988, showed regularly with Newlyn Art Gallery and the

Penwith in St Ives, elsewhere widely and was included in Now and Then, David Messum Fine Art, 1997. He had solo exhibitions in France, Germany and Switzerland as well as Britain.

Richard ANNELY 1962– Sculptor, born in Plymouth, Devon, whose interactive work The Stone Scratcher, made from various materials and emitting a range of ringing tones, was part of the 1997 Lewes Sculpture Trail. After hotel and catering studies Annely worked as a chef and catering manager, and while he was in Germany attended Munich Art Academy, 1990, being a guest student of Tony Cragg at Düsseldorf Art Academy, 1992. Annely gained his master's degree from Chelsea College of Art & Design, 1994, from 1995 working there as masters' technician. Exhibitions included St Wendel, Town Museum, 1992; Neuhauser Strasse Project, Munich, 1993; Galery Annelie Brusten, Wuppertal, with Herbert Willems & five pigs, 1994; and Interface, Sackville Gallery, 1997.

David ANNESLEY 1936– Sculptor, painter and teacher, born and lived in London. From 1947–56 he was educated in England, Australia and Southern Rhodesia, then after two years in the Royal Air Force he was from 1958–61 at St Martin's School of Art. He was to have studied painting, but found sculpture more exciting. For a time Annesley was Anthony Caro's assistant. Spent six months in Majorca in 1962, then in 1963 began teaching at Central School of Art and Croydon College of Art, from 1964 at St Martin's. An important influence on Annesley was the American painter Kenneth Noland, with whom he stayed in 1966. Annesley's sculpture, which could be brightly painted, was abstract, light and lyrical in feeling. In 1969 Annesley resumed painting. Showed with LG from 1989 and RA Summer Exhibition from 1991. In 1993 he was included in 1st RWA Open Sculpture Exhibition. Later solo exhibitions included Anderson O'Day Gallery, 1989. Annesley was a prizewinner in BP Sculpture Competition, 1990, and he did work for Royal Hampshire County Hospital, Winchester, 1992. Tate Gallery in London and Liverpool, Arts and British Councils and Museum of Modern Art in New York hold examples.

Lady Mabel ANNESLEY 1881–1959 Printmaker and watercolourist, daughter of the 5th Earl of Annesley, of Castlewellan, County Down, Northern Ireland. She studied in mid-1890s at Frank Calderon's School of Animal Painting and early in 1920s with Noel Rooke at Central School, being elected to SWE in 1924. She was also a member of Belfast Art Society and showed wood engravings at Redfern Gallery, although arthritis later made working difficult. During World War II she left Belfast for New Zealand, returning to England in the early 1950s, settling at Clare, Suffolk. Illustrated several books and wrote a part-finished autobiography, *As the Sight is Bent*, published 1964. British Museum and Belfast Museum and Art Gallery hold examples.

Pietro ANNIGONI 1910–1988 Painter of portraits and frescoes, draughtsman and teacher, born in Milan, Italy. He studied at the Accademia delle Belle Arti, Florence. He emerged from obscurity in 1955 when his classically styled portrait of the young Queen Elizabeth II, commissioned by the Worshipful Company of Fishmongers, brought instant fame. Crowds went to London to see it and a limited-edition print published by *The Times* was fully subscribed. Former president of the RA, Sir Alfred Munnings, declared Annigoni "the greatest painter of the age". During the 1950s, with a studio in London, Annigoni painted the Duke of Edinburgh and Princess Margaret, other subjects being the ballerina Dame Margot Fonteyn and the Maharanee of Jaipur. A second portrait of the Queen, in 1970, was not so successful, made for the National Portrait Gallery. In 1958 Annigoni returned to Florence, continuing to visit London. In Italy he painted frescoes. Several Italian collections, including Milan's Gallery of Modern Art, hold examples, and the Tate Gallery's archive holds a self-portrait of 1953. *The Memoirs of Annigoni* appeared in 1956, a *Spanish Sketchbook* in 1957 and *An Artist's Life* in 1977.

Len ANNOIS 1906–1966 Painter, muralist and graphic artist, born in Malvern, Victoria, Australia, who studied during evening classes at the National Gallery of Victoria art school, 1930–2, and was inspired to concentrate on watercolour by James Flett. He showed with the Victorian Artists' Society, after World War II being on its board and helping to foster public interest in the National Gallery's work. During the war, Annois was production illustrator for the Commonwealth Aircraft Corporation, from 1946–50 serving as advertising manager for the firm G J Coles & Company while painting in his spare time and winning a number of notable watercolour prizes. Soon he could concentrate on painting full-time, and he furthered his education with trips to Europe in 1950–1 and 1952–3. Annois contributed to the first Australian Artists' Association show at the RWS' Conduit Street gallery in 1953; so accomplished was his work that he had been elected an associate of the RWS in 1952, being made full RWS in 1958. A further trip to Europe followed in 1962, the year he showed English watercolours in New York. After a visit to New Guinea in 1965, Annois died the following year in Melbourne. By then he had accomplished a number of murals in fresco and mosaic in public buildings, had achieved 23 solo shows across Australia and in London and had been widely featured in international travelling exhibitions. National Gallery of Victoria has a large collection of Annois' work, which is also held by HM Queen Elizabeth The Queen Mother.

Boris ANREP 1883–1969 Artist in mosaic, born in St Petersburg, Russia, where he first studied law but then Byzantine art. Travelled widely and from 1908 studied in Paris at Académies Julian and La Grande Chaumière and at Atelier La Palette. In 1910–11 he was at Edinburgh College of Art under Frank Morley Fletcher. He was associated with Roger Fry's Second Post-Impressionist Exhibition in 1912 and settled in England after World War I, although he later lived in Paris. Among his mosaics in public buildings are the National Gallery floors, Tate Gallery, Westminster Cathedral and Bank of England. Also showed oil paintings at LG in early 1920s. The Anrep family is the subject of a notable painting by Henry Lamb.

ANSCHLEE 1931– Painter and draughtsman, born in Shanghai, China, educated in America, her full name being Anne Schlee. She studied at International School, 1962–5, then Famous Artists' School, 1970–2, gaining her fine art certificate. Teachers included Chow Chian-Chui, Charles Reid and John Pellew. She was a leading member of NS, for a time being its president, also showing with Chelsea Art Society and elsewhere. Lived in Cranleigh, Surrey.

Norah ANSELL 1906– Sculptor who studied at Birmingham College of Arts and Crafts and part-time with William Bloye. Exhibited RA. Lived at Edgbaston, Birmingham.

William Henry ANSELL 1872–1959 Etcher who was by profession an architect. Born in Nottingham, he studied at the Architectural Association and etching at the Royal College of Art with Sir Frank Short. Became president of the Architectural Association in 1928 and was master of the Art Workers' Guild in 1944. Exhibited RA, RBA and RE. Lived at Sevenoaks, Kent.

Peter Frederick ANSON 1889–1975 Draughtsman, watercolourist and writer, christened Frederick Charles Anson when born in Portsmouth into a naval family. A weak heart prevented his going to Eton College. He studied art at the Architectural Association School, 1908–10, and briefly in 1918 with Frederick L Griggs which was "a turning point in my artistic career". Anson was a Roman Catholic convert and his twin interests were the religious life and maritime subjects. He spent much time in religious communities all over Europe, was an authority on them and eventually became a Cistercian. The name Peter was an adopted one. Anson led a roving life, reflected in such books as *A Pilgrim Artist in Palestine* and *A Roving Recluse*. Was a fine church architectural and marine draughtsman, was a founder member of RSMA and National Maritime Museum has much of his work. Showed with RA, RSA, RHA, Goupil Gallery and elsewhere. Lived much of his life in Scotland (see his book *Harbour Head*), latterly in Montrose, Angus. Died in Edinburgh.

Walters ANSON 1875– Portrait and miniature painter, born in London as Minnie Walters Anson. Studied at Lambeth School of Art, where she won a series of medals. Was married to the miniaturist Arthur Adams. She exhibited RA, Walker Art Gallery, Liverpool, RMS, Paris Salon and in Canada. Lived at Parkstone, Dorset.

ANTON 1912–70 Artist in pen and ink and wash, real name Antonia Yeoman, she was born in Brisbane, Queensland, Australia, but moved to England as a small girl. After private education she attended the Royal Academy Schools, 1928–30, taught by Steven Spurrier. In the mid-1930s she drew for magazines under her maiden name of Botterill, then from 1937 jointly with her brother Harold Thompson she began submitting humorous drawings under the name of Anton, for which she latterly was mainly responsible. They appeared in magazines such as *Punch* and *Lilliput* and Anton also illustrated a number of books in which her aristocratic, sharply delineated characters were instantly recognisable. Also exhibited at RSA, SGA and in cartoon shows. Lived in London.

Victor ANTON 1909–1980 Sculptor, born in Worthing, Sussex. Anton was a career journalist who worked for almost 30 years on the *Guardian-Gazette* series of newspapers in Chingford and Walthamstow. He took up sculpting untutored in 1949 and had solo shows at Gimpel Fils, 1953; Grabowski Gallery, 1963; Lords Gallery, 1965; and he had a retrospective at University Centre, Birmingham, 1974. In 1992 Belgrave Gallery included his Untitled Sculpture, 1962, in British abstract art of 50s and 60s. Anton worked in a variety of materials and experimented with light in his pursuit of the problems of equilibrium.

Myles ANTONY fl. from 1960s– Designer and watercolourist, born in Dublin, Ireland. He studied art under Fergus O'Ryan, then in 1960s was art director for John Stephen when the Carnaby Street craze was going strong. Further work included record covers, television logos and film posters in Britain, continental Europe and North America. Antony began to develop his watercolours in the early 1980s, concentrating on figures and portraits. Mixed shows included RHA, solo exhibitions being at The Other Gallery, in Edinburgh, in 1985; The Cathedral, Bury St Edmunds, Suffolk, in 1988; St Jude's, 1989 and 1991; and Lane Gallery Restaurant, Dublin, 1990–1.

Angela ANTRIM 1911–1984 Book illustrator, cartoonist and sculptor. Born at Sledmere, Malton, Yorkshire, she was educated privately and then studied art in Brussels and at the British School in Rome. One-man exhibitions included the Beaux Arts in 1937 and after World War II the Hamet Gallery and galleries in Belfast. The RA, RHA and RUA had mixed shows including her work. She illustrated several books, including *The Antrim McDonnells* and *Jam Tomorrow*, also magazines such as *Harpers, Queen* and *Vogue*. Signed work A A. She was Countess Antrim, was married to the Earl of Antrim and lived in County Antrim and London. Her son, The Honourable Hector McDonnell, was also an artist.

Sally APLIN fl. from 1980s– Sculptor, enameller and teacher, who gained a diploma in art education at Bristol Polytechnic, 1984; an honours degree in fine art there, 1992; then her master's degree in fine art at University of Wales, 1995. She was a part-time sculpture and drawing teacher at Filton College, Bristol, 1993, and a visiting lecturer at University of the West of England, 1994–5. In 1989 won a prize at International Enamel Biennale, Laval, Canada, having shown enamels since 1985 in international juried shows. Exhibitions included Senate House at University of Bristol, 1986; Women for Art, Bristol City Museum & Art Gallery, 1990; New Art in the South-West, Spacex Gallery, Exeter, 1995; and 2nd Open Sculpture Exhibition at RWA, 1996. Lived in Bristol.

Leonard APPELBEE 1914– Painter, printmaker, verse writer and teacher, born in London, married to the artist Frances

Macdonald. He studied at Goldsmiths' College, 1931–5, under Clive Gardiner, then at Royal College of Art with Barnett Freedman, 1935–8. Taught at Bournemouth College of Art. Appelbee showed at RA, RSA, Arts Council, British Council and in small group shows at Wildenstein, 1947, and Fine Art Society, 1968. His picture One-man Band was one of the 60 Paintings for '51 Festival of Britain show. Had a series of solo shows at Leicester Galleries from 1948 and a notable exhibition at City Museum and Art Gallery, Plymouth, 1977. Appelbee was a distinctive portrait painter, carrying out commissions for Sir Edward Marsh, Eton College, Corpus Christi College in Cambridge and other clients. He won a silver medal at Paris Salon in 1970. Published his book of verse *That Voice* in 1980. Tate Gallery, Arts Council, many provincial and foreign galleries hold his work. Appelbee (pronounced Ap*pel*bee) lived latterly at Kincardine-on-Forth, Fife, then Aberdeen.

Wynne APPERLEY 1884–1960 Painter and draughtsman whose full name was George Owen Wynne Apperley and who was born in Ventnor, Isle of Wight. Although mainly self-taught, he did study with the Herkomer School at Bushey. Lived for much of his life in Spain, where he worked and exhibited, and in Morocco, being honoured by the Spanish government. Exhibited extensively at Leicester and Walker's Galleries, RI and RSA. Apperley was adept in line and wash at catching the sun-filled landscapes of the Mediterranean area. His work is in the Victoria & Albert Museum.

Chris APPLEBY 1951– Painter, born in Birmingham, who studied at Wolverhampton College of Art, 1971–3, then Royal College of Art, 1975–8. Had a studio in east London, showing in East London Open Studios, Whitechapel Open and various gallery mixed exhibitions. His oil on panel Beauty and the Beast was in the 1995–6 John Moores Liverpool Exhibition.

Peter APPLETON 1955– Sculptor, born in Liverpool. He studied at Chester College of Art and Newcastle upon Tyne University, graduating in 1978 and gaining his master's degree in 1982. Appleton won a Yorkshire Arts Bursary in 1985. He took part in A Noise in Your Eye touring international exhibition of sound sculpture in 1985; in 1986 provided the soundtrack for *Children of A Lesser God*, Northcott Theatre, Exeter; and was one of six artists representing Britain at World Expo '88 in Brisbane. Triophonic Water Sculpture and Solar Device for Deep Field Noises were both commissioned by World Expo '88, the second being sponsored by BP Solar Australia.

Richard APPLETON 1909– Painter whose full-time occupation was as chief draughtsman with the Merseyside and North Wales Electricity Board. Born in Norwich, he later studied in the life class at Denbighshire Technical College, going on to exhibit RCamA, at the Atkinson Art Gallery, Southport, NWG, ROI, RWA and elsewhere. Lived in Wrexham, Denbighshire.

Fred APPLEYARD 1874–1963 Painter and mural decorator, born in Middlesbrough, Yorkshire. He studied at Scarborough School of Art, Royal College of Art and Royal Academy Schools, winning the Turner Gold Medal and several scholarships. Was a frequent exhibitor at RA and RWA, of which he was a member. Worked in South Africa, 1910–12. Tate Gallery holds his canvas A Secret and he carried out a number of murals in public places, including Royal Academy Burlington House restaurant and Nottingham General Hospital. Died at Alresford, Hampshire, his home for many years.

Joseph APPLEYARD 1908–1960 Painter and draughtsman specialising in sporting subjects. Studied during evenings, 1925–32, at Leeds College of Art. Exhibited widely in Yorkshire, having one-man shows in Leeds, where he lived at Far Headingley. Appleyard had his work reproduced in Yorkshire newspapers and magazines, gaining a reputation as a horse painter, and he became honorary secretary of the Yorkshire Group of Artists. Newcastle upon Tyne and Wakefield art galleries hold his work.

Vivien AP RHYS PRYCE 1937– Sculptor and teacher, born in Woking, Surrey, who studied at City & Guilds of London Art School, 1955–61. She gained the Beckwith Travelling Scholarship, 1957; Bronze Medal and Certificate of Merit, 1961; and Feodora Gleichen Award, 1964. Was elected a fellow-member of RBS, 1972. She taught at Elmhurst Ballet School, 1961–2; City & Guilds, 1964–74; and Twickenham College of Technology, 1970–2. Her exhibitions of work, notably in bronze, included RA from 1959; RSA, 1963; NEAC, 1965; Madame Tussauds; RWA from 1969; Marjorie Parr Gallery, 1968–75; Tib Lane Gallery, Manchester; and Bruton Gallery, Somerset. Among commissions were John Player League Cricket Trophy and Medals, 1969; John Pinches Ltd, 1972; and The Tower Mint, 1976. National Gallery of New Zealand, Wellington, holds her work. Lived in Calne, Wiltshire.

Rasheed ARAEEN 1935– Painter, sculptor, performance artist and polemicist, born in Karachi, Pakistan. After training as a civil engineer at University of Karachi, he travelled to England in 1964 and turned to sculpture full-time, being inspired by Anthony Caro's work at St Martin's School of Art. By this time Araeen had, in Pakistan, produced two seminal works, the painting Ham Raqs and the sculpture Burning Bicycle Tyres. He was concerned to remove gestural and pictorial allusions from his work. "Art should not only be manufactured but mass-produced to make it accessible to everybody." He wanted that "in the end art is no longer a sacred/precious object, but becomes an idea." Won a John Moores Exhibition, Liverpool, prize in 1969 and an Arts Council award, 1978. From 1970 staged a series of performances with public participation; became active in movements such as the Black Panthers and curated The Other Story exhibition at Hayward Gallery, 1989–90, with tour, which included his work; in 1996 had a show of sculpture in grounds of Serpentine Gallery. His autobiography, *Making Myself Visible*, was published in 1984. Arts Council and Walker Art Gallery in Liverpool hold examples.

Malcolm ARBUTHNOT 1874–1967 Painter, photographer and sculptor, born in Suffolk, his mother a dedicated amateur artist. Arbuthnot did not take up painting seriously until he was in his late thirties, but as a young man he was a keen photographer. After working as a clerk between 1893–1905 during which time he developed his photographic skills, from around 1906 he was able to set up his own studio. Worked freelance for papers such as *Illustrated London News* and *Sketch* and became a noted portrait photographer. Commissioned by the Goupil Gallery to photograph artists such as Sir Edward Poynter, James Pryde and William Nicholson, Arbuthnot came into contact with Wyndham Lewis and the Vorticists, who influenced his painting style. In 1926 he closed his London studio to concentrate on painting. Earlier he had been taught by C A Brindley, had attended a life class in Liverpool and was later to be instructed by J D Fergusson and W P Robins. While living in France he showed some bronzes at the Paris Salon, and he was also to show at the RA, ROI, Leicester Galleries and extensively elsewhere. One-man shows in London including Fine Art Society, and exhibitions after his death have been held by Grabowski Gallery and David Cross, Bristol. Arbuthnot's work is held by Victoria & Albert Museum and Salford Art Gallery. Finally lived at La Houle, Jersey.

Frank ARCHER 1912–1995 Printmaker, painter and teacher. Studied at Eastbourne School of Art in 1928–32, Royal College of Art, 1932–8, that year winning the Prix de Rome. Was only able to study at British School in Rome for a year due to the war. Later taught at Eastbourne School of Art and became head of fine art at Kingston College of Art. Despite teaching he was a prolific artist. His work, sometimes on themes such as music and musicians, was influenced by his ability as a draughtsman. The earlier work tends to be more architectural in construction, but later it became more personal, and looser. Exhibited RA, RE and RWS. In 1990 he had retrospectives at RWS, of which he was a fellow, and Catto Gallery, with another at Bankside Gallery, 1992. British Council and Walker Art Gallery in Liverpool own examples. Lived in Eastbourne, Sussex.

Michael ARCHER 1954– Artist and critic who studied natural sciences and the history of art at Cambridge University, 1973–6, then aesthetic education at Manchester University, 1980–1. He worked as a freelance critic and with William Furlong ran Audio Arts (see separate entries). Lived in London.

William ARCHER 1928– Sculptor, oil painter and draughtsman. Born at Thornley, County Durham, Archer studied art at Sunderland College of Art, 1946, then again from 1949–52, after which he was three years at the Royal College of Art. He began exhibiting at the RA in the mid-1950s, also showing with the RSA and Northern Artists. Northumberland Education Authority owns his work. Lived at Thornley.

Charlotte ARDIZZONE 1943– Painter and printmaker, born in London, where she lived for some time, later moving to Norfolk. She was the niece of the illustrator Edward Ardizzone. Artist friend Kathleen Allen initially encouraged Charlotte Ardizzone to paint, and she became the youngest ever exhibitor at the RA Summer Exhibition. Studied briefly at St Martin's School of Art, 1960, then at Byam Shaw School of Drawing and Painting, 1961, gaining an Ernest Jackson Scholarship. For periods worked as an art therapist, teacher and illustrator, as well as painting still life and landscape in Britain and on the continent in which a strong sense of light was evident. Showed in mixed exhibitions at NEAC, of which she was a member, RWA and elsewhere. From 1970 had several solo exhibitions at Drian Galleries, later shows including Christopher Hull, 1988, and Sally Hunter Fine Art, 1991. Nuffield Foundation, Dublin University and several overseas galleries hold her work.

Edward ARDIZZONE 1900–1979 Book illustrator, lithographer, watercolourist and writer for children. Born in Haiphong, Indo-China, Ardizzone – whose work was sometimes signed DIZ or E A – studied art under Bernard Meninsky and F J Porter at evening classes at Westminster School of Art in 1920–1. After working as a clerk, he decided in 1926 to pursue art full-time; five years later he had his first one-man show at the Leger Galleries. He was an official war artist during World War II, working widely in Europe and North Africa, and his illustrated war diaries are notable records. After the war he established a strong following as a book illustrator, titles ranging from Walter de la Mare's *Peacock Pie* and John Bunyan's *Pilgrim's Progress* to H E Bates' *Uncle Silas* stories and Maurice Gorham's *Back to the Local*. He also wrote and illustrated his own children's books, such as *Little Tim and the Brave Sea Captain*. Ardizzone's intimate scenes of bar-room and back-stage life and street life in London are drawn with a whimsicality and charm that are inimitable and unmistakeable. Retrospective show at the Victoria & Albert Museum, 1974. Lived at Rodmersham Green, Sittingbourne, Kent.

Antonio ARGENIO 1961– Painter, born in Bedford, whose figures had a tortured, Expressionist appearance, as in The Idiot, one of five pictures acquired by New York British art collectors Robert and Susan Summer at Argenio's 1988 sell-out graduation show at Royal College of Art. He had previously studied at Winchester School of Art and was a Delfina Studios Trust resident artist, 1988–90. Argenio also won a Basil H Alkazzi Foundation Award, Aaron Lane Penguin Book Prize and a Slotover Travelling Scholarship, all 1988. Group exhibitions included Mall Galleries, 1986; Paton Gallery, 1988; The Figure Laid Bare, Pomeroy-Purdy Gallery, 1992; and Summer Show at Purdy-Hicks Gallery and Royal Over-Seas League Open, both 1995.

Jeanne ARGENT 1944– Sculptor, painter, printmaker and writer, born in Hastings, Sussex, where she attended the School of Art, 1960–2, for the foundation course. Her career progressed through journalism and freelance writing of books and magazine articles until in the early 1980s, with children at school, she took up art again. She was a member of Surrey Sculpture Society, showing with it at Chilworth Manor Lodge, near Guildford. Shared a show at The Harvey Gallery, Guildford, 1993. As a result of a competition run by Guildford Borough Council Argent was commissioned to produce a sculpture of Alice, erected in 1990 in the Castle Grounds, near Chestnuts, where the author of *Alice Through the Looking-Glass*, Lewis Carroll, stayed just before he died. The sculpture shows Alice making her way through the glass. Argent lived nearby in Merrow, Surrey.

Paul ARGENT 1959– Mixed media/constructions artist and teacher, born in Southern Rhodesia. He studied at Colchester Institute, 1977–8, Chelsea School of Art, 1978–81, then Slade School of Fine Art, 1981–3, where he also taught. His exhibitions included Harrison McCann Show, 1982; City University Gallery, Cockpit Theatre Gallery and 15 British Contemporaries, in California, America, all 1983; Lyric Theatre, 1984; and in 1985 participated in four-man show at Woodlands Art Gallery.

Margarita ARGÜELLES 1941– Painter, born in Lisbon, Portugal, her parents being Spanish, her father in the diplomatic service. The family moved to London in 1945, Margarita attending the Convent of the Sacred Heart in Tunbridge Wells, Kent, until the age of 11, when her father was posted back to Spain. Although she showed an aptitude for art at school, she studied philosophy at Madrid University, studies interrupted by marriage. After dealing in antiques she returned to art, spending several years drawing before concentrating on oils. Her first solo exhibition was at Galeria Yguanzo in 1986, with a second at Caja de Madrid, 1989. In 1991 Sally Hunter Fine Art gave her a first exhibition outside Spain, showing Spanish and English landscapes and still life.

Saleem ARIF 1949– Painter and sculptor, born in Hyderabad, India, who moved to England aged 17. He studied sculpture and painting, attending Birmingham College of Art, 1969–70, and Royal College of Art, 1972–5. In the early 1980s won Arts Council and British Council awards, and an Italian Government Bursary enabled him to work in Florence, Italy. In a search for a cultural identity Arif travelled widely through India and studied Dante's *Inferno*, both of which experiences influenced his painting. Created his own symbolism, including birds, men and objects, which produced pictures often of great charm and subtlety. Took part in many group exhibitions in Britain and abroad. Solo shows included Art Heritage Gallery, New Delhi, and British Council Gallery, 1984, and Plymouth Arts Centre and Anderson O'Day Gallery, 1988. Participated in The Other Story, Hayward Gallery, 1989–90, and touring. Government Art Collection and Arts Council hold his work.

Ernest ARIS 1882–1963 Black-and-white artist, illustrator and watercolourist. Son of the artist Alfred Aris, Ernest studied at Bradford School of Art under Charles Stephenson, then at the Royal College of Art under Gerald Moira. Exhibited at the RA, RBA, RI, RWS and in the provinces. Aris started as a portrait painter, later taught for a while and was eventually illustrated in publications throughout the world. He illustrated many children's books, including *Tales for Tiny Tots* and *The Brambledown Tales*. Lived in London.

Lesley ARKLESS 1956– Painter, writer and illustrator, born in Northumberland, who after school in Newcastle upon Tyne graduated with honours at West Surrey College of Art and Design, Farnham, 1974–8. Wrote and illustrated *What Stanley Knew*. Showed at Ash Barn Gallery, Petersfield; National Museum of Wales, Cardiff; and at public gallery in Le Havre, Normandy. Lived in Winchester, Hampshire.

Don ARLETT 1937– Watercolourist, notable for his depictions of the Norfolk landscape, born in London. He attended Croydon School of Art, 1952–5, Norwich School of Art, 1955–7, then worked in advertising in London and Vienna from 1958, eventually retiring to concentrate on his own work. He gained many creative awards, from 1982–8 was director of the British Television Advertising Awards and in 1984 was one of the judges at Cannes Film Festival. Had a solo show at Mistral Galleries, 1994.

Frederick Marcus ARMAN 1908–1978 Sculptor in wood and metal, born in Ipswich, Suffolk. He retired in 1970 after a lifetime of work in the Post Office and was the first curator of the National Postal Museum. He wrote authoritatively in the Philatelic Bulletin on Victorian postage stamps and was a member of the Post Office Arts Club. Exhibited at Lincoln Cathedral, New Metropole Arts Centre in Folkestone, elsewhere in the provinces and in America. Lived in Bromley, Kent.

Thomas William ARMES 1894–1963 Artist and teacher, born in St Ives, Huntingdonshire, one of a large family of an innkeeper and farmer. Was encouraged by Walter Dendy Sadler and then studied at Cambridge School of Art, in 1913 being awarded a scholarship to study in The Hague. When World War I broke out Armes joined the Army, served at the front in France and was eventually invalided out. Poor health was to plague his career. Settled in Chelsea in the 1920s and befriended by George Clausen Armes became a prolific artist, showing at RA and RBA and taking private pupils. After a chest operation prior to World War II, during which Armes served in the Home Guard, he chose to settle with his wife Myra in Sheringham, Norfolk, where the climate was more congenial. He completed posters for British Railways and the local council and had three solo shows at Norwich Assembly House, in 1953, 1958 and 1960. In 1975 his widow showed Armes' work at the Little Gallery, which she had opened after his death. It became the Westcliffe Gallery and gave him a retrospective in 1990.

Diana M ARMFIELD 1920– Painter, designer and teacher, born in Ringwood, Hampshire, married to the artist Bernard Dunstan. She went to school at Bedales, then studied at Slade School of Fine Art and Central School of Arts and Crafts. From 1959 she taught at Byam Shaw School of Art. Was included in many mixed shows, including Festival of Britain, and was a member of RWA, RWS, NEAC and RA, 1991. After showing solo at Tegfryn Art Gallery, Anglesey, in 1975 and 1978, Armfield began a long association with Browse & Darby, also exhibiting in

America and Australia. In 1988 Oriel 31 Gallery in Newtown and Welshpool gave her and Dunstan a combined retrospective. Their work was similarly on a small scale, owing much to the Sickert tradition, Armfield being noted for her sensitive still lifes of flowers. Among her commissions was one from the National Trust in 1988, another from HRH The Prince of Wales in 1989. British Museum, Contemporary Art Society for Wales and Government Picture Collection hold her work, and Victoria & Albert Museum holds textile work. Signed work D M A. Lived in London and Wales.

Maxwell ARMFIELD 1882–1972 Painter and decorative artist, especially in tempera, and writer. Born in Ringwood, Hampshire, Armfield was educated at Birmingham School of Art – there is a Birmingham Arts and Crafts flavour in his pictures – then in Paris and Italy. Exhibited extensively, including RA, Fine Art Society, for long a noted dealer in his work, NEAC, Leicester Galleries and abroad. His work is held by the British Museum, provincial and overseas galleries. He illustrated about 20 books and wrote *A Manual of Tempera Painting*, *Tempera Painting Today*, *An Artist in America* and *An Artist in Italy*. Armfield was a painter of landscape and still life well crafted and full of detail. Lived in Bath, Somerset.

Stuart ARMFIELD 1916– Painter, notably in tempera, born in Sanderstead, Surrey. He studied at West of England College of Art, Bristol, and was from 1935–40 on the art staff of Ealing Studios. Wrote the manual *Tempera Painting*. Showed at RA, with St Ives Society of Artists of which he was a member, Arthur Jeffress Gallery, RWS and in America. Lived in Looe, Cornwall, later in Plymouth, Devon. James Colman Fine Art held an eightieth birthday retrospective in 1996.

Ann ARMITAGE 1959– Painter, muralist, therapist and teacher, born in Huddersfield, Yorkshire, who studied at Grimsby School of Art & Design and Canterbury College of Art & Design. In 1990 she taught in the London Borough of Hackney, working as an art therapist for Kent County Council, 1990–1. Commissions included a mural for the Barnaby Rudge public house in Broadstairs, and Kent Countryside Productions' *A Midsummer Night's Dream*, both 1989. Group shows included Portraits, Faversham Library, 1989; Pastels Today, Mall Galleries, and Royal Over-Seas League Open, both 1994. In that year Armitage gained an Elizabeth Foundation for the Arts, New York, Award.

Catharine ARMITAGE 1944– Painter and printmaker, born in Surbiton, Surrey, married to the painter Paul Feiler. She studied at Slade School of Fine Art, 1967–71, then as a postgraduate, 1971–3, under Anthony Gross and Bartolomeu Dos Santos. She showed in groups at Galerie 20, Paris, 1987, and Salthouse Gallery, St Ives, 1988, having solo exhibitions in Wiesbaden, Germany, 1979, and at Chapel Hill and Winston-Salem, North Carolina, 1984. University College London and St Thomas' Hospital hold her work. Lived near Penzance, Cornwall.

David ARMITAGE 1943– Painter, born in Tasmania, Australia. He studied at Royal Melbourne Institute of Technology, 1960–5, lived in New Zealand from 1967–73, then settled in Britain. He had many group shows throughout New Zealand, also appearing at Bonython Gallery, Sydney, in 1972, in Young Artists 75 in New York, 1975, and at Museum of Modern Art in Oxford, 1985, in an exhibition of children's book illustrations. Showed solo with Barry Lett Galleries, Auckland, from 1968, later shows including a shared one at Duncan Campbell Contemporary Art, 1993. All the major public galleries in New Zealand hold his work.

Joshua Charles ARMITAGE: *see* **IONICUS**

Kenneth ARMITAGE 1916– Sculptor and teacher, born in Leeds, where he studied at the College of Art, 1934–7, then at Slade School of Fine Art, 1937–9. He served in the Army, 1939–46, then taught sculpture at Bath Academy of Art until 1956, although he was a Gregory Fellow in Sculpture at Leeds University, 1953–5. Armitage had his first solo show at Gimpel Fils in 1952, two years later at Bertha Schaefer Gallery in New York. Was represented in British pavilion at Venice Biennale in 1952, where he showed People in a Wind, of 1950, a characteristic work of this period. Earlier Armitage had been a carver. From the end of the 1960s his technique changed again, figures of plaster, paper and wood being produced. Armitage represented Britain at the 1958 Venice Biennale, winning the David E Bright Sculpture Prize. By then Armitage was launched on an international exhibiting career. Armitage was guest artist in Caracas, Venezuela, in 1964; artist-in-residence at City of Berlin Kunstlerprogram, 1967–9; and guest teacher at centenary year, Boston University, 1970. He had retrospectives at Whitechapel Art Gallery in 1959, the Arts Council in 1972, and an eightieth birthday show at Yorkshire Sculpture Park, Bretton Hall, 1996. Tate Gallery, Victoria & Albert Museum and many other public collections hold examples. Armitage married the artist Joan Moore in 1940. Lived in London.

George Denholm ARMOUR 1864–1949 Painter and illustrator of sporting and military scenes, born in Waterside, Lanarkshire. He studied at St Andrews University, Edinburgh School of Art and Royal Scottish Academy Schools through much of the 1880s. Armour illustrated for magazines such as *Punch*, *The Tatler* and *The Graphic* and showed at RA, Royal Glasgow Institute of the Fine Arts and RSA. He illustrated many books, including his own *Pastime with Good Company*, 1914, *A Hunting Alphabet*, 1929, and *Bridle and Brush*, 1937. Armour's life was horses and hunting, and he hunted with the Beaufort, Sparkford Vale Harriers and the South Berks. In World War I he joined the Remount Service and ended as director of the Salonica Force. Victoria Art Gallery, Bath, holds his work. Lived for many years in Wiltshire.

Hazel ARMOUR 1894–1985 Sculptor and medallist, born in Edinburgh, where she studied at the College of Art, also in Paris, gaining bursaries, an honours diploma and a travelling scholarship. Also worked in southern Africa. Exhibited at RSA, Royal

Glasgow Institute of the Fine Arts, RA, SWA and Walker Art Gallery in Liverpool, as well as abroad. For many years she maintained studios in Edinburgh and London. Did work for the Scottish National War Memorial in Edinburgh, Scottish women's hospitals, Edinburgh University and Glasgow School of Architecture. Hunting was a favourite recreation, along with travel and music. Armour's head of the theatrical designer Leslie Hurry is included in Eric Newton's monograph *British Sculpture 1944–1946*, published in 1947. She had work in the collection of the artist Edward Le Bas and was included in the Fine Art Society's Sculpture in Britain Between The Wars, 1986. Died in Aldeburgh, Suffolk.

Heda ARMOUR 1916– Painter and etcher. After private education she attended Guildford School of Art, 1930–3, then for six years was at the Royal Academy Schools under Thomas Monnington and Sir Walter Westley Russell. Exhibited RA and in the provinces. British Museum holds an etching by her, but under her first married name of Heda Napper. Lived at Cranleigh, Surrey.

Keith ARMOUR 1931– Printmaker and teacher who studied at Leeds and Royal Colleges of Art. He was included in the British Printmakers exhibition in 1962–3 and in 1964 in The Teaching Image, work by staff of Leeds College of Art, 1964, at Leeds City Art Gallery. Had solo exhibitions in New York and Hong Kong. After the death of his wife in the early 1980s Armour went to the Far East and subsequently died.

Mary ARMOUR 1902– Painter, notably of flowers and landscapes in oil, using a rich palette, born in Blantyre, Lanarkshire, married to the artist William Armour. Like him she taught at Glasgow School of Art, having studied there, 1920–5, under Maurice Greiffenhagen and David Forrester Wilson. She showed with RSW, RSA and Royal Glasgow Institute of the Fine Arts, being a member of all, as well as SSA and Fine Art Society in Glasgow. She was honorary president of Glasgow School of Art in 1982. Collections at public galleries in Glasgow, Paisley, Aberdeen, Perth and Edinburgh hold her work. Lived in Kilbarchan, Renfrewshire.

William ARMOUR 1903–1979 Painter in oil and watercolour, draughtsman in pastel and wood engraver. Born at Paisley, Renfrewshire, Armour studied art at Glasgow School of Art 1918–23 under Maurice Greiffenhagen like his wife Mary Armour, whom he married in 1927. William Armour was for a time head of drawing and painting at the same school. Exhibited RSA, RSW and elsewhere. Painted a notable portrait of his wife as a young woman. Work held widely in public collections in Scotland, and elsewhere. Lived at Kilbarchan, Renfrewshire.

Ian ARMOUR-CHELU fl. from 1960s– Painter who studied with Vivian Pitchforth at Chelsea School of Art. He was the husband of the artist Angela Burfoot and father of the painter Louise Armour-Chelu. Began painting in 1968 and had the first of a series of solo shows in Britain and abroad in 1972. Showed with Agnew and took part in a family exhibition at Markswood Gallery, Great Bardfield, in 1990. Continental landscapes were a feature of his output. Lived at Wissett, near Halesworth, Suffolk.

Louise ARMOUR-CHELU 1960– Artist in pen and ink and coloured inks, born in London, daughter of the artists Ian Armour-Chelu and Angela Burfoot. She studied at Cambridge College of Arts and Technology under David Baxter, 1978–81, gaining an honours degree in English/History of Art. Worked intermittently as an archaeological illustrator, 1981–7, exhibiting drawings from 1982 and illustrating her first book in 1983. Drew for several publishers and admired the work of children's illustrators Peggy Fortnum, Victor Ambrus and Richard Kennedy. Appeared in mixed shows at Mercury Theatre, Colchester; Markswood Gallery, Great Bardfield; Peter Hedley Gallery, Wareham; and Phoenix Gallery, Lavenham. Had a solo show in 1990 with Max Bally. Lived at Hedenham, Suffolk.

Anthony ARMSTRONG 1935– Versatile artist, teacher and gallery director, born in Ireland, who studied at Glasgow School of Art, 1953–7, attending Jordanhill Training College, with a scholarship to Italy, in 1958. Armstrong taught art, 1958–60; engaged in full-time studio work as artist and designer, 1960–7; was part-time director of various galleries, 1967–79, then became a full-time painter. Armstrong exhibited with NEAC, Paisley Institute, RA, Royal Glasgow Institute of the Fine Arts and Flying Colours Gallery. Studied and worked in the Caribbean, France, Italy, the Sandwich Islands and America, with over a dozen solo shows in Britain and abroad. Portraits included the Earl and Countess of Stormont; ecclesiastical commissions a resurrection mural and Stations of the Cross; and corporate commissions included BBC Television; British Petroleum; Scottish Television; and the Royal Automobile Club. Glasgow Museum & Art Galleries; Hunterian Museum in Glasgow; Paisley Museum; Royal Concert Hall in Glasgow, and several overseas collections hold examples.

Arthur Charlton ARMSTRONG 1924– Artist in oil and mixed media, born in Carrickfergus, County Antrim, self-taught. He lived in London, 1956–61, with frequent periods in Spain, 1960–77. Appeared in travelling Irish Arts Council shows in Europe and America. Had a solo show at Avignon Gallery, 1974, and Kreisler Gallery, 1977, both in Madrid, having an Arts Council retrospective, 1950–80, in Belfast in 1981. Arts Councils in north and south of Ireland hold his work. Was a member of RHA. Lived in Dublin.

Helen ARMSTRONG 1938– Artist and illustrator in a range of media, and teacher, born in Bristol, wife of the artist John Armstrong, their son being the artist Joseph Armstrong. She studied at Chelsea and Brighton Schools of Art, 1954–9, teachers including Elizabeth Frink and George Hooper. Taught art in schools, 1960–2, then worked as a freelance illustrator while raising a family. Armstrong's work was "influenced by

Expressionist art, Kathe Köllwitz, Matisse and Georgia O'Keeffe". She was a member of the Society of Sussex Painters, Society of Catholic Artists and the International Society of Christian Artists and her work was included in Gerald Woods' 1996 books *Drawing with Pastels* and *The Artist's Studio*. Armstrong showed regularly in Brighton Festival exhibitions from 1976, and in 1996 at the Identity show at Towner Art Gallery in Eastbourne and the Sussex Open Exhibition at Brighton Art Gallery. The dealer Lucy Wertheim owned her work. Lived in Hove, Sussex.

John ARMSTRONG 1893–1973 Painter of imaginative and classical subjects in oil, tempera and gouache; mural painter; designer of film and stage sets; book illustrator and advertising designer. Born in Hastings, Sussex, after Oxford University Armstrong studied at St John's Wood School of Art, 1913–14, then after service in the Army in World War I returned to St John's Wood briefly. First one-man show at the Leicester Galleries in 1928, became a member of Unit One in 1933, exhibiting in a group show at the Mayor Gallery, 1934. After Unit One Armstrong's work took on a Surrealist character. In the 1930s Armstrong worked as a designer for the theatre and films, including the first performance of the ballet *Façade* and several films made by Sir Alexander Korda. He also did work for Shell-Mex and ICI. During World War II Armstrong was an official war artist. After it he continued to exhibit widely, including The Storm, for the Festival of Britain in 1951, and at the RA extensively from that year. He painted a ceiling for the Council Chamber, Bristol, in 1955 and a mural for the Royal Marsden Hospital, at Sutton, Surrey, six years later. Armstrong had strong left-wing political convictions and from the time of the Spanish Civil War, when he painted Pro Patria, his pictures occasionally reflected his views. Symbolism is also a feature of his work. Armstrong's pictures are fastidiously painted in muted colours and reflect his own dry wit and gentle nature. Memorial exhibition at RA in 1975, with tour. Lived in London.

John ARMSTRONG 1937– Artist, mainly in oil, and teacher, born in Mitcham, Surrey, husband of the artist Helen Armstrong, their artist son being Joseph Armstrong. John Armstrong studied at Swindon, Walthamstow and Brighton art schools, his teaching including University of Brighton. Armstrong was a painter of Christian and spiritual subjects, a member of the International Society of Christian Artists, Christian Arts UK and the Society of Catholic Artists. The Byzantine and Sienese Schools were an influence. Also showed with the Society of Sussex Painters, at RA and Mall Galleries, and had solo exhibitions at Hove Museum & Art Gallery, 1975, and Grange Art Gallery, Rottingdean, 1996. Gerald Woods' books *Art of Landscape and Seascape Painting* and *Practical Oil Painting* included Armstrong's work. Notable work for churches included altarpieces for St Mary's, Bath, and St Peter's, Brighton, 10 paintings for St George's, Hove, and a great crucifix for St Boniface, Tooting. Nuffield Foundation and East Sussex County Council hold examples. Lived in Hove, Sussex.

Joseph ARMSTRONG 1971– Artist and illustrator, using acrylic, gouache and lino-print, born in Brighton, Sussex, son of the artists John and Helen Armstrong. He studied at Norwich Institute of Art and Design, 1990–3, teachers including Robert Mason, then at University of Brighton, 1993–5, under John Lord. Was a member of the Brighton Illustrators Group and showed with the Society of Catholic Artists, 1995. Solo exhibitions included Terre à Terre, Brighton, and the town's Library Gallery, both 1996, and Duke of York's, Brighton, 1998. Lived in Hove, Sussex.

Shearer ARMSTRONG 1894–1983 Painter, printmaker and illuminator, born in Penge, southeast London, as Alixe, also known as Alice, Jean Shearer (her husband was a civil servant, Henry Armstrong). She studied at Slade School of Fine Art, 1912–14, also in Karlsruhe, Germany, and briefly with Stanhope Forbes in Newlyn, having moved to Cornwall in 1921. Armstrong showed with RA, RSA and Penwith Society of Arts of which she was a founder member, with St Ives Society of Arts and Taurus Artists as a member, elsewhere in the provinces and widely abroad. Had solo shows at Chiltern Gallery and Scottish Gallery, Edinburgh. She had a studio in St Ives for many years, living in Carbis Bay. The windswept romanticism of Cornwall was a key element in Armstrong's work. HRH The Duke of Edinburgh, Scottish Education Committee and Cornwall Education Authority hold examples.

Tim ARMSTRONG 1945– Painter, printmaker, artist in opto-kinetic construction and teacher, born in Cambridge. Studied at Cambridgeshire College of Arts and Technology, 1962–4, Nottingham College of Art and Design, 1964–7, where his work was influenced by the tuition of Bridget Riley, and at Slade School of Fine Art, 1967–9, under Robyn Denny. Went on to teach at Glasgow School of Art. Did some scientific book illustration. Showed widely in England and abroad. Work held by Doncaster Museum and Art Gallery, Scottish Arts Council and Cambridge University. Lived for some time at Kirkintilloch, Dunbartonshire.

Warwick ARMSTRONG 1919– Painter, designer and teacher, born in Melbourne, Victoria, Australia, a strong draughtsman and Colourist, influenced by Picasso. He attended the Royal Melbourne Institute of Technology, studying interior design, 1937–9, and stage design and painting, 1945–6. For several years he concentrated on theatre design in Melbourne, then moved to Britain, 1949–58, where he worked among others for the Mercury and Mermaid Theatres, Royal Shakespeare Theatre at Stratford-upon-Avon, Glyndebourne Opera, The Old Vic, in films for the J Arthur Rank Organisation, EMI Records and the Royal Opera House. He exhibited with the Australian Artists' Association in its first show at RWS' Conduit Street gallery, 1953. Back in Australia, Armstrong continued with stage work and taught extensively, took part in mixed and solo shows, and had a retrospective at Devise Gallery, Melbourne, 1987, of selected paintings, 1962–86. In 1978–9 he was granted leave by the

Chisholm Institute of Technology, where he taught art history, 1961–84, to research the work of several European painters including Picasso, and was for five months at the Michael Karolyi Foundation at Vence, southern France. Melbourne University, other Australian collections and the Royal Shakespeare Theatre Collection, Stratford, hold examples.

Sarah ARMSTRONG-JONES 1964– Painter, draughtsman and designer, born in London, daughter of HRH The Princess Margaret and the photographer the Earl of Snowdon. She did an art foundation course at Camberwell School of Arts and Crafts, 1982–3. Next at Middlesex Polytechnic she studied printed textiles, 1984–5, then at Royal Academy Schools, 1985–8, obtained an undergraduate diploma, in 1988–91 a postgraduate diploma. Gained the Winsor & Newton Drawing Prize in 1988, the Creswick Landscape Prize & Silver Medal in 1990. From 1987 showed at RA Summer Exhibition, taking part in Premium Show, RA, 1988–90. In 1995 had a solo show at Redfern Gallery. After much study of a place it was transformed into space and light in her work, with a strong underlying draughtsmanship and expressive brushstrokes.

Barbara ARNASON: *see* **Barbara Moray WILLIAMS**

Keith ARNATT 1930– Artist and teacher, born in Oxford. He studied at the School of Art there, 1951–5, then Royal Academy Schools, 1956–8. Arnatt used photographs and text, examples of which are held by Arts Council, parody and irony to comment on the state of art in his time. From the early 1960s he held several teaching posts, including Liverpool, Manchester and Newport Colleges of Art. Arnatt exhibited in a series of British and overseas mixed shows such as Environmental-Reversal, Camden Arts Centre, 1969; Seven Exhibitions at Tate Gallery and The New Art, Hayward Gallery, both in 1972; British Artists of the 60s at Tate Gallery in 1977; and Museum of Drawers at ICA in 1979. His one-man show at Whitechapel Art Gallery in 1977 was called Looking at Me. Arts Council holds works from his 1980s Pictures from a Rubbish Tip and Howlers Hill series. Lived in Llandogo, Gwent.

Raymond ARNATT 1934– Sculptor and teacher, born in Oxfordshire. He studied at Oxford School of Art, 1951–5, and Royal College of Art, 1957–61, in the latter year gaining the Sainsbury Award. During most of the 1960s he taught in art schools, in 1971 becoming senior lecturer in sculpture at Chelsea School of Art. Among Arnatt's commissions were one for Queen's College, Edgbaston, in 1966, and one for Milton Keynes in 1975. He received a prize in the Sir Joseph Swan Memorial Sculpture Competition in 1969 and the Herbert Baker Travelling Award from Royal Academy in 1974. In that year he had a one-man show at Park Square Gallery, Leeds. He also took part in Arts Council travelling show in 1967 and group exhibition at Serpentine Gallery in 1977.

Victoria ARNEY 1965– Abstract painter and teacher, born in Southampton, who studied at Winchester School of Art, 1984–5; gained a first-class honours degree from Wimbledon School of Art, 1985–8; then a higher diploma at Slade School of Fine Art, 1989–91. Among awards were selection from the Slade for the Trinity College Fellowship, 1991; Cheltenham Fellowship in Painting, 1991–2; and in 1992 she gained the Duveen Travel Scholarship to India and won the East & South Open at Norwich Gallery. From 1992 had considerable teaching experience, including Cheltenham & Gloucester College of Art; Nottingham, Northumberland, Staffordshire, Sunderland, Reading and Central England Universities; Wimbledon School of Art; and Birmingham Institute of Art & Design. In 1996 she held a residency at Casa Manilva, Spain. Group shows included Bernard Jacobson and New Academy Galleries, both 1992; Acme Open Studios, 1993; Paintscapes, Harewood House, Leeds, 1995; and Cross Currents, Reed's Wharf Gallery at Barbican Centre, 1996. Solo shows included Isis Gallery, Birmingham, 1993.

Marjorie ARNFIELD 1930– Artist, notably working in acrylic, and teacher, born in Sunderland, County Durham, who was struck by juvenile chronic arthritis aged four, and suffered from arthritis for much of her life. Despite the need for regular hospital treatment, she obtained her design and art teacher's diplomas studying at Sunderland College of Art and at the King Edward VII College of Art, Durham University, tutors including Lawrence Gowing, Harry Thubron, Quentin Bell and Victor Pasmore. She returned to teach at her old school in Sunderland, other experience including adult education departments of Nottingham and Stirling Universities; Cumbria and Nottinghamshire Education Authorities; Workers' Educational Association; King's College in Cambridge; and many painting schools in Britain and abroad. Took part in many mixed exhibitions, including Northern Young Artists Exhibition, touring; Huddersfield Art Gallery; RWS; Lake Artists, Grasmere; Castle Museum in Nottingham; and Laing Art Gallery, Newcastle upon Tyne. In the early 1990s, Arnfield was drawn to record the demise of the coal industry, in 1994 British Coal touring her show: Coal Mining in Nottinghamshire – a Tribute, for which she went underground, in a wheelchair, to see the industry first hand. Exhibitions at Renishaw Hall, seat of the Sitwell family, and at municipal art galleries and museums in Chesterfield, Mansfield and Ilkeston were followed in 1996–7 by a WAC-funded tour in south Wales. Arnfield had several dozen solo shows. Graves Art Gallery in Sheffield, Sunderland and Middlesbrough galleries and other mining museum and corporate collections hold examples. Lived in Westhorpe, Southwell, Nottinghamshire.

Ann ARNOLD 1936– Painter, born in Newcastle upon Tyne, Northumberland, married to the painter Graham Arnold. She studied at Epsom School of Art, 1956–9, working as an art therapist, 1959–69. Was one of the seven artists who formed The Brotherhood of Ruralists in 1975, which had its first exhibition in 1976. Apart from Ruralist shows she exhibited in mixed shows including Festival Gallery, Bath, 1974; Bristol City Art Gallery, 1975; and RA Summer Exhibition, from 1977. Had her first solo show at Festival Gallery, Bath, 1979, exhibiting with New

Grafton Gallery from 1981. She had a strong affinity with the poet John Clare and illustrated *Clares Countryside*, published in 1981.

Charles Geoffrey ARNOLD 1915– Painter, commercial artist and teacher, born in Clayton, Yorkshire, where he finally settled. After a period of initial study at Bradford College of Art, under Henry Butler, 1931–4, Arnold spent five years until early in World War II with the advertising agency Marshall Hardy as a studio artist. After the war he was from 1946–7 at Camberwell School of Arts and Crafts, then at Slade School of Fine Art, 1947–50, his teachers including William Coldstream. Arnold showed with RWA of which he was a member, LG and RA.

Graham ARNOLD 1932– Painter and teacher, born in Beckenham, Kent, married to the artist Ann Arnold. He was one of the seven founders of The Brotherhood of Ruralists, in 1975, which had its first show at RA in 1976. Arnold studied at Beckenham School of Art, 1947–52, and at Royal College of Art, 1955–8. He was awarded a painting scholarship to Italy, 1958–60. For a dozen years from 1961 he taught at Ravensbourne and Kingston Colleges of Art and the Royal Academy Schools. His group contributions included Gimpel Fils, 1955; LG, 1962; Chichester National Art Exhibition, 1975, where he gained major prize for painting; Fischer Fine Art, 1976. Solo shows included Brillig Arts Centre, 1979; David Paul Gallery, Chichester, 1982; Piccadilly Gallery, 1983; and a retrospective at The Tabernacle Cultural Centre, Machynlleth, 1992. Contemporary Art Society and provincial galleries hold his work.

Liz ARNOLD 1964– Painter, whose work included brightly coloured, slightly Surrealist pictures such as her Mythic Heaven, 1995, included in New Contempories, 1996, at Tate Gallery in Liverpool and at Camden Arts Centre. She was born in Perth, Scotland, and gained a degree in fine art at Middlesex Polytechnic, 1987–90, and her master's degree at Goldsmiths' College, 1992–4. Other exhibitions included Tinsel Adam Gallery, 1994; and Hard Work Shift One, at London's Exmouth Market, and Cocaine Orgasm, Bank, both 1995.

Phyllis Anne ARNOLD 1938– Painter and miniaturist, born in Belfast. Her father was an engineer and she worked for a time in the commercial art department of the aircraft makers Short Brothers and Harland, claiming to be self-taught as a painter. She was a Hunting Group competition finalist on several occasions in the early 1980s and showed RA, RMS, SM and widely in Northern Ireland, where she was for a time vice-president of the Ulster Society of Women Artists. Sometimes signed work only with initials. Lived in Bangor, County Down.

William Arthur ARNOLD 1909–1977 Commercial artist in scraperboard and watercolour, born in London. Attended Leyton School of Art. Exhibited at RA and Army Art Society and had a one-man show at the Towner Art Gallery, Eastbourne, in 1947. Sold a watercolour to the Pakistan government. Lived at Chalfont St Giles, Buckinghamshire, and in Bridport, Dorset.

Sally ARNUP 1930– Sculptor and teacher, married to the painter and potter Mick Arnup. From the age of five she wanted to sculpt, attending Kingston School of Art from 1943. Karel Vogel was an influence. From 1950–1 was at Camberwell School of Arts and Crafts, then for several years at Royal College of Art, where Frank Dobson and John Skeaping were important teachers. After marriage settled in Yorkshire and was head of sculpture at York Art School, 1958–72. Showed at RA, RSA, RBA, Paris Salon and John Davies Contemporary, Stow-on-the-Wold. Was made a fellow of RBS. Arnup's speciality was bronzes of animals, created with the live animal in front of her, with great attention to detail. In 1971 she made and cast a silver leopard, presented to HM The Queen by City of York.

Margaret ARRIDGE 1921– Painter and private art tutor, born in Salisbury, Wiltshire. After education in Croydon she attended Chelsea School of Art, where her teachers included Bernard Adams. She eventually settled in Johannesburg, South Africa, where she held a number of solo shows, but also exhibited in England at RA and elsewhere as well as at Paris Salon.

Sydney ARROBUS 1901–1990 Watercolourist, commercial painter and artist in collage, he studied at Heatherley's School of Fine Art. Showed widely, including RI, RWA, SGA and with Hampstead Artists' Council. Also had many one-man shows, including Woodstock Gallery, Cooling Gallery, several times in Everyman Foyer Gallery in Hampstead and Finsbury Library, Islington. Both the London Boroughs of Camden and Islington hold his work, which is notable for its light, often witty touch. Lived in London.

Sue ARROWSMITH 1950– Artist using photographs and mixed media, born in Lancashire. Symbols were a key element in her work. She studied at University of Nottingham, 1968–71, then Slade School of Fine Art, 1973–5. Was artist-in-residence at Wolfson College, Cambridge, 1986–7. Group shows included John Moores Liverpool Exhibition from 1987; she won a prize in 1989–90. Others were Excavations, Vienna and Southampton, 1988, and Photography Now, Victoria & Albert Museum and Tate Gallery, Liverpool, 1988–9. Her first solo show was at Matt's Gallery, 1982, after which she showed regularly with Anthony Reynolds Gallery. Arts Council holds her work.

Sue ARROWSMITH 1968– Artist producing abstract work, as in her ink and acrylic on fibreboard Forge, made of myriad vertical lines, which won her a prize in the 1997–8 John Moores Liverpool Exhibition. Born in Denton, Manchester, Arrowsmith did a foundation course at Thameside College of Technology, 1984–6, then gained an honours degree in textiles at Goldsmiths' College, 1987–90. Group exhibitions included Woodlands Art Gallery, 1990, and Archbishop Tenison's Grammar School, 1992. Had solo shows at Entwistle, 1994 and 1997. Arts Council holds her work. Lived in London.

ART & LANGUAGE Group of conceptual artists formed in 1968 by Terry Atkinson, David Bainbridge, Michael Baldwin and Harold Hurrell. Their aim was to produce the magazine *Art-Language*, which first appeared in 1969, and it was to analyse the relationship of the word and the image. Atkinson, Bainbridge and Baldwin were in close contact as they all taught the art theory course at Coventry College of Art from autumn 1969 to mid-1971, when it was terminated. Bainbridge, Baldwin and other staff members were dismissed, Atkinson remaining until the final intake of art theory students graduated in 1973. By then Bainbridge had parted company with Art & Language about two years, and Atkinson, after a period of gradual disenchantment, left in 1975. Eventually, the group would expand to include several dozen people, with an international membership. Their work was to appear under the common Art & Language label, breaking with the tradition of the personality artist. Texts, posters, paintings and other works were given an extensive worldwide showing, Lisson Gallery being a notable venue. Arts Council holds Art & Language productions.

ARTO 1940–1987 Painter and writer, full name Arto der Haroutunian, born in the Middle East of Armenian parents. Arrived in Britain in his early teens and qualified as an architect at Manchester University. As well as designing many restaurants, clubs and hotels, he became known as a cookery writer and broadcaster, an authority on the culinary cultures of the Middle East and North Africa, publishing many books. As a painter he was noted for landscapes which drew on Oriental sources and had strong abstract traits. He showed at Central Library, Manchester, 1964; Colin Jellicoe Gallery, Manchester, 1964–86; Manchester University, 1965; Langton Gallery, 1977; Stockport Art Gallery, 1982; and elsewhere. National Art Gallery of Armenia, Sarian Academy of Arts in Syria and several other foreign galleries hold his work.

James ARUNDEL 1875–1960 Painter, born in Bradford where he died, although he also lived for a time in Lincolnshire. By profession a lighthouse builder and refurbisher, Arundel did not begin painting seriously until shortly before World War II, studying part-time at Bradford Arts Club. Showed at RA, Beaux Arts Gallery, Paris Salon and extensively in the provinces. City Art Gallery, Bradford, holds his work and gave him a retrospective in 1959.

Marit Guinness ASCHAN 1919– Painter, enameller and writer who studied in Germany, Italy and France and with Barry Craig. Showed RA, Leicester Galleries, in public galleries in Exeter and Manchester and abroad. Had a solo exhibition at Beaux Arts Gallery in 1948, later ones including Saga Gallery, 1990. She was president of the Artist Enamellers from foundation in 1968 and among her books was *The Art of Jewellery*, published that year. Among her commissions was the focal point for the cross for the high altar in Exeter Cathedral. Victoria & Albert Museum, Royal Norwegian Embassy and Brooklyn Museum in New York hold examples. Chelsea Arts Club member who lived in London.

Pamela ASCHERSON: *see* **Pamela RACHET**

Roy ASCOTT 1934– Artist, theoretician and teacher, born in Bath, Somerset. He studied at department of fine art at King's College, Newcastle upon Tyne, 1955–9, graduating with an honours degree, teachers including Victor Pasmore and Richard Hamilton. From 1960–80 Ascott worked, exhibited and taught as a painter in England and America. From 1980 he worked in cyberspace, mostly with projects involving international telematic networks. He published over 50 theoretic texts. Ascott became director of the Centre for Advanced Inquiry in the Interactive Arts and head of the field of interactive arts at Newport School of Art & Design, Gwent College of Higher Education. He took part in numerous group shows, international and touring exhibitions, 1960–70. Had a solo exhibition at Univision Gallery, Newcastle, 1960, later one-man exhibitions including Dartington Hall, Totnes, 1980. Lived in Bristol.

Barbara ASH 1966– Sculptor in stone who was born and then settled in London. She studied at West Sussex College of Art & Design, 1983–5; Middlesex Polytechnic, 1985–9; and Royal College of Art under Glynn Williams, 1993–5. Group shows included Gloria Gallery in Nicosia, Cyprus; Clevedon Pier Gallery; Bristol Sculpture Shed; and Opus 39 Gallery, Nicosia. Had a solo show at Fallen Angel, Islington, and one in 1993 at Herbert Read Gallery, Kent Institute of Art & Design, Canterbury. She was Henry Moore Fellow, 1992–3. Middlesex Polytechnic, Lemba Pottery in Cyprus, J Sainsbury, and Horice Museum and Rabasova Gallery, both in the Czech Republic, hold her works.

Bernadette ASH 1934– Painter and draughtsman who was a professional radiographer until 1973. Then studied at Byam Shaw School of Painting, 1973–4, Camberwell School of Arts and Crafts, 1974–7. Showed with NEAC, at RA and RWA. Lived in the Exmoor National Park and featured the countryside in much of her work, which was given a solo show at Woodlands Art Gallery, 1982.

Derek ASHBY 1926– Painter, sculptor in steel and teacher, born in Chadderton, Lancashire. He studied at Edinburgh College of Art, 1948–51, teachers including William Gillies and Robert Henderson Blyth, then at Royal Academy Schools, 1953–6, with Henry Rushbury and Peter Greenham. Lecturer at Gray's School of Art, Aberdeen, 1960–87. Was a member of SSA and Aberdeen Artists' Society, also showing at RA and RSA. Scottish Arts Council, Keston Training College and galleries in Brighton and Dunfermline hold his work. Lived in Banchory, Kincardineshire.

Nigel ASHCROFT 1951– Painter, especially in watercolour, who was born in Heemstede, Holland, living in Sweden and Eire as a child before moving to England in 1965. After education at Berkhamsted School, spent a term at Gloucestershire College of Art & Design, 1969. Exhibited in mixed shows at RA, 1987, RWA 1981–2–4 and abroad, including the Dordogne, France, where he spent many summers painting. Solo shows at Frost &

Reed, subject matter "tending towards the familiar", notably buildings, landscapes and everyday objects. Lived near Stroud, Gloucestershire.

Faith ASHE: *see* **Faith WINTER**

Edward James ASHENDEN 1896– Watercolour painter, designer, model-maker and decorative artist. Born at Wandsworth Common, London, he studied at Putney School of Art just prior to World War I, then again 1919–22. Ashenden's designing and model-making skills were employed widely, including the Wellcome Historical Medical Museum and the Century of Progress Exhibition, in Chicago. During World War II he was a camouflage officer with the Air Ministry. Exhibited RA, RI and in the provinces. Lived in London.

Florence May ASHER 1888–1977 Painter and printmaker. She studied at the Royal Academy Schools 1913–18, where she won a silver medal and gained the Landseer Scholarship. She lived in a number of places in southern England and exhibited extensively at RBA, also at Goupil Gallery, RA, SWA and elsewhere. Finally lived in Reigate, Surrey, with the painter Rosalie Emslie.

Colin James ASHFORD 1919– Painter and illustrator in oil and watercolour, born in Ackworth, Yorkshire. He attended Wakefield School of Art, 1933–7, then Glasgow School of Art, 1937–9, under W O Hutchison and Tom Purvis. Ashford worked in advertising studios and magazine publishing before going free-lance as a painter and illustrator. He was a founder-member of the Guild of Aviation Artists and a fellow of the Central Institute of Art and Design. Ashford was "influenced by marine artists of the 1920s and 1930s, also poster illustrators of the same period". Took part in group exhibitions at RSMA and RI and had solo shows in Kent galleries. Historical marine and aviation subjects were a speciality. Royal Air Force Museum, Hendon, National Maritime Museum and Ashmolean Museum in Oxford are among collections holding examples. Lived in London.

ASHLEY 1903–1973 Industrial designer, commercial artist, designer and painter, full name Ashley Havinden. He had not received any formal art training when he joined one of London's largest advertising agencies, W S Crawford, in 1922. Influenced by the Bauhaus movement in Germany, he developed a bold, angular style with uncluttered typography. During the 1930s he handled several major advertising campaigns, including Drink Milk Daily. Humorous line drawings were a feature of his work, and he created the Ashley typeface. His skills were also used for the Paris Exhibition of 1937; by the Imperial War Museum for shows; in textile and rug designs, fabrics and posters. After World War II service he resumed his position with Crawford's and made a big contribution to the Britain Can Make It exhibition at the Victoria & Albert Museum in 1946. His paintings, abstract in style, were shown at Marlborough Fine Art, Reid and Lefevre and Leicester Galleries. Official positions included governor, Central School of Arts and Crafts, 1958–67, president of the Society of Industrial Artists, 1953, and president of the Double Crown Club, 1955–6. From 1967–9 Havinden was master of the exclusive Royal Designers of Industry, having been elected in 1947. Lived at Hertingfordbury, Hertfordshire for many years. In 1995 Hertford Museum held an exhibition.

ASHTOCK 1932– Interior decorator and painter in oil. His full name was David Ashton-Bostock, which he sometimes used on work. Born in London, he attended Wellington College, then studied at Maidstone College of Art, 1947–50, and Byam Shaw School of Art, 1953–4, under Patrick Phillips. Went on to establish his own interior decorating business in London, where he lived, also near Sittingbourne, Kent. Showed At UA, NEAC, ROI, Ridley Art Club of which he was a member, Paris Salon and elsewhere.

Audrey ASHTON 1892–1985 Painter in oil, born in Ben Rhydding, Yorkshire. She was educated partly in Paris, where she also studied art and at Central School of Arts and Crafts. Showed at RA, RBA, Leicester Galleries, LG and Young Contemporaries. Lived near Ashford, Kent.

Graham ASHTON 1948– Artist in mixed media, born Birkenhead, Cheshire. He studied at Manchester College of Art, 1966–7, Coventry College of Art, 1967–70, and University of Calgary, 1970–1. In 1983–4 Ashton was artist-in-residence at Walker Art Gallery and Bridewell Studios, Liverpool, his Dry Dock being commissioned for International Garden Festival. A dominant theme in his work for many years was the threat of global nuclear annihilation, as in his Is that Death? And are there Two? in John Moores Liverpool Exhibition, 1987. His work appeared in Images of War, at Chapter Art Gallery, Cardiff, 1985. His first solo show was in 1977, later ones including Museum of Modern Art, Oxford, 1985. Arts Council holds his work. Lived in London.

Raymond ASHTON 1929– Painter, poster designer and teacher. Attended Middlesbrough School of Art, 1946–50 then Leeds College of Art, 1950–1. Painted a number of posters and murals, some while serving in Egypt, others in Middlesbrough, where he lived.

Tony ASHTON 1948– Painter of geometrical abstracts who attended Bath Academy of Art, Corsham, Lincoln College of Art and West of England College of Art in Bristol, 1966–71. He took part in Coracle Press Miniatures show which toured Britain. Had solo shows at 5 Dryden Street Gallery and LYC Gallery, Cumbria, and in 1980 at Woodlands Art Gallery. Lived in Plumstead, south-east London.

Will ASHTON 1881–1963 Landscape and seascape painter, born in York, but early on educated in Adelaide, Australia, where he had gone with his family, his father being an artist, James Ashton. Back in Europe John William Ashton, to give him his full name, studied in Paris at the Académie Julian, also under Julius Olsson and Algernon Talmage. Painted widely in Europe and exhibited RA, Goupil Gallery, ROI, RBA and Paris Salon; also established a reputation in Australia, where his work is held in many public collections. He won a number of awards in Australia, such as the Wynne Art Prize, on several occasions, the Godfrey Rivers Prize and the Society of Artists Medal. Served on the Commonwealth Art Advisory Board, of which he was chairman in 1953. Was director of the National Art Gallery of New South Wales, Sydney, 1937–44; was knighted 1960. Lived at Mosman, New South Wales.

David ASHTON-BOSTOCK: *see* **ASHTOCK**

John Atkinson ASHWORTH 1915– Architect and artist, born in Rochdale, Lancashire, who worked in oil and watercolour. He studied at Liverpool University school of architecture, 1932–8, under Charles Reilly, becoming an associate of RIBA. Started in Liverpool Corporation Housing Department, 1938–9; then was with what became Building Design Partnership, Preston, 1939–45; was a principal in Ashworth & Fletcher, Rochdale, 1945–63; being a private consultant architect in Kendal, Cumbria, where he settled, 1963–78. Showed in group exhibitions at Walker Art Gallery in Liverpool and Rochdale Art Gallery, both holding examples.

Elaine ASK 1952– Painter and draughtsman, using a rich palette and with a strong feeling for paint. She worked a lot in Greece, being married to the artist Andreas Kouyioumtzis. She was born in Staffordshire and studied at Padgate College of Education, 1970–2. Group appearances included British Council, Athens, 1978; Batley Art Gallery, 1981; Harris Art Gallery, Preston, from 1982; and Art North Gallery, Huddersfield, 1983. Solo shows included Gallery Arsa from 1972; Citibank, 1975–9; Little Gallery, Diagonios, 1980; and Huddersfield Sports Centre, 1982. Leeds Educational Art Loans Services holds her work. Lived in Liversedge, West Yorkshire.

Victor ASKEW 1909– Artist in various media, born at Rotherham, Yorkshire. Studied part-time at Sheffield School of Art for three years in the mid-1920s. Exhibited RA, PS and ROI and is represented in several public collections including Harris Museum and Art Gallery, Preston, and Canadian galleries. Wrote *Painting for Everyone*. Lived at Bayford, Hertfordshire.

Ruth ASPDEN 1909– Painter and etcher who studied at Blackburn School of Art, 1927–33, with Arthur Jackson and George Reed, then at the Royal College of Art, 1933–7, under Percy Hague Jowett. During World War II she was employed for several years on camouflage design. Exhibited RA, RE, in the provinces and North America. Blackburn Museum and Art Gallery bought her work. Lived in London.

Sofy ASSCHER 1901– Painter, draughtsman and miniaturist who studied art at Girls' Art School, Amsterdam, where she became a certificated teacher of drawing, at Chelsea Polytechnic and privately. Showed at RA, UA, Leger and Tooth's Galleries and overseas. Solo shows included Foyles Gallery. Lived in London, then Seaford, East Sussex.

Christopher John ASSHETON-STONES 1947– Artist in pastel and writer, born in Ceylon. He did a pre-diploma course at Exeter College of Art, then did his diploma at Bournemouth and Poole College of Art. Was elected to PS aged 21, and became a council member. Signed his work CJA-Stones with year. Also exhibited at RWA, RSMA and Paris Salon and had regular solo shows in Britain and France. Assheton-Stones wrote several books: *Working with Pastel*, 1983; *Buildings and Towns in Pastel* and *Painting with Pastels*, both 1984; and he wrote occasionally for *Leisure Painter* magazine. He described his work as falling into two categories: fairly conventional landscapes and other pictures as an aid to teaching; and semi-figurative serious painting which developed year by year. Lived in Weasdale, Newbiggin on Lune, Kirkby Stephen, Cumbria.

Paul ASTBURY 1945– Ceramic sculptor and teacher, using a variety of materials including found objects. He was born in Cheshire and trained at Stoke-on-Trent College of Art, 1962–8, and Royal College of Art, 1968–71. Awards included Arts Council, 1977. Teaching included Brighton and Middlesex Polytechnics and Central School of Art. Commissions included Liberty's, 1971, and Crafts Advisory Committee, 1974. Mixed exhibitions included Clay Sculpture, Midland Group Gallery, Nottingham, 1972; New Ceramics, Arts Council of Northern Ireland tour, 1974; Clay Sculpture, Yorkshire Sculpture Park, 1980; and The Raw and the Cooked, Museum of Modern Art, Oxford, and tour, 1994. Solo shows included Enhanced Images, Aberystwyth Arts Centre, 1984. Astbury's work was held in many public collections in Britain and abroad, including Crafts Council, Ulster Museum in Belfast, Portsmouth City Museum and Art Gallery and North West Arts in Manchester. Lived in London.

Evelin Winifred ASTON fl. from c.1924–1975 Sculptor in wood, painter in oil. Studied at Birmingham School of Art under Bernard Fleetwood-Walker. Taught at a school for the blind, in Birmingham. Exhibited RSA, RBA, ROI and locally. Lived at Erdington, Birmingham.

Paul ASTON 1948– Sculptor and teacher, born in Awre, Gloucestershire. He studied at Gloucester College of Art, 1964–7, gained a first-class diploma from Leicester College of Art and Design, 1967–70, winning his higher diploma from Chelsea School of Art, 1970–1. In 1971–3 Aston was an Abbey Major Scholar at British School, Rome, then after extensive travel in Italy and the Mediterranean area taught painting at Aegean School of Fine Art, Paros, Greece, 1973–4. He supported his art with a variety of part-time work from then and exhibitions included Ikon Gallery, Birmingham, 1985; Royal Institute, Truro, 1992; and 1st RWA Open Sculpture Exhibition, 1993. In that year he shared a show at Gloucester City Museum and Art Gallery. Lived in Lydney, Gloucestershire.

George Thomas ATACK 1886– Watercolourist, born in London, who worked as a stockbroker's clerk. After attending the Borough Polytechnic, he studied art at Camberwell School of Arts and Crafts. Exhibited RI, Stock Exchange Art Society and City of London Art Exhibition, Guildhall, 1954. Lived in West Wickham, Kent.

John ATHERTON HAWKINS 1918– Painter and constructor in wood who also taught, born in Bristol where he attended the West of England College of Art under Donald Milner, 1936–9, then 1946–8. He held a number of teaching posts in the west of England, then at the County Grammar School for Boys in Barrow-in-Furness, Lancashire, where he lived. Showed with Barnstaple Art Club and elsewhere.

Kevin ATHERTON 1950– Sculptor and teacher, born in the Isle of Man, who attended the College of Art there, 1968–9, then studied fine art at Leeds Polytechnic, 1969–72. His teaching posts part-time included Chelsea and Winchester Schools of Art, Maidstone College of Art and Middlesex Polytechnic. Apart from work in various exhibitions Atherton did commissioned sculptures, such as the ankle and shoe disappearing into a wall at Langdon Park School in Poplar, completed 1983, and A Different Ball Game, at King's Hill business park, West Malling.

Peggy ATHERTON 1968– Artist, born in Nottingham, who studied at Harrow College of Art & Design, 1990–1 (later working there as a technician), then graduated from Bath College of Higher Education, 1991–4. Mixed shows included Heaven on Earth Gave Me a Migraine, Alternative Space, Bath, 1992; Fresh Art at Islington's Business Design Centre and Start 94, Plymouth Art Centre and tour, both 1994; and Selected Boiled Works, Riding House Street, 1995. Atherton gained national publicity in 1996 with her solo show Road Kills, at The Cut Gallery, in which dead animals scooped up from the road had been dipped in porcelain at her north London studio and fired in a kiln. For several years she had returned each animal so treated to where it was killed as a protest and "to give them their last rites. We are disgusting. I do want to shock people."

Rachel ATHERTON 1969– Painter who was born and lived in Birmingham. She studied at Bournville College of Art and Staffordshire Polytechnic and among her shows was East & South, Norwich Gallery/Kent Institute of Art and Design, 1992.

John ATKIN 1959– Artist working in various media, and teacher. He attended Teesside College of Art, 1977–8, and Leicester Polytechnic, 1978–81, where he graduated with honours in painting. After teaching at Teesside College, 1981–2, Atkin completed his master's degree in sculpture at Royal College of Art, 1982–5, then had a Picker Fellowship at Kingston Polytechnic, 1985–6. He won a string of awards, including a Major Award, Northern Arts, Newcastle, 1981–2, a Henry Moore Foundation Scholarship, 1982, and a drawing prize at Royal College, 1985. He was Grizedale Forest artist-in-residence, 1987, then was for some years in Australia, having residencies at Mildura Arts Centre, Victoria College in Melbourne and at Jam Factory Gallery, Adelaide. Among his group appearances were The Eighties, Juda Rowan Gallery, 1985; National Garden Festival 90, Gateshead; and Sculpture at Canterbury, 1991–2. Had a solo show at Hatton Gallery, Newcastle upon Tyne, 1985, one at Juda Rowan, 1986, later shows including Darlington Arts Centre, 1991–2. His commissions included Head of Mies van der Rohe, KIUK, 1984, and The Watcher, Marina Development, Cleveland, 1988–9.

Liz ATKIN 1951– Draughtsman in pencil, born in Stamford, Lincolnshire, daughter of the artist Peter Atkin. She studied at St Martin's School of Art, 1971–4. Solo shows included Laing Art Gallery, and touring, 1990–1. She also participated in mixed shows with Nicholas Treadwell Gallery in England and in continental Europe. *Liz Atkin, Drawings 1987–90* was published by Laing Art Gallery, funded by Northern Arts. Nicholas Treadwell Gallery and Cleveland Gallery, Middlesbrough, hold her work, which is often narrative in nature, on a large scale. Lived at Longbenton, Newcastle upon Tyne.

Peter ATKIN 1926– Watercolourist and teacher, born in Wallasey, Cheshire, father of the artist Liz Atkin. He had no formal training beyond instruction in watercolour by Wilfrid René Wood. Became a part-time art tutor for Northamptonshire County Council Education Department, 1970–91, and ran his own summer classes. Showed at Northampton Central Museum and Art Gallery, RI, RBA, UA of which he became a member in 1968, and NS, his main dealer being Savage Fine Art, Northampton, where he lived at Collingtree. Private collections in Britain and abroad held his work.

Ron ATKIN 1938– Painter and teacher, born in Leicestershire, who studied at Loughborough College of Art, 1954–7, then Royal Academy Schools, 1957–61. He taught at the Beaford Centre in north Devon, living in West Putford. Showed at RA; Plymouth City Museum and Art Gallery; Roland, Browse & Delbanco; and in the West Country. Plymouth City Museum and Dartington Hall hold his work.

Ray ATKINS 1937– Painter and teacher, born in Exeter, Devon. He studied at Bromley College of Art, 1954–6, then again, 1958–61, after National Service in the Army. Atkins was much influenced by the work of Frank Auerbach, and while at the Slade School of Fine Art doing postgraduate studies worked in Auerbach's studio. In 1965 Atkins taught at Bournemouth College of Art, from 1965–70 at Reading University's department of fine art under Claude Rogers and in 1971 at Epsom School of Art. After some adult education centre teaching in the early 1970s based in Reading, Atkins went on to teach at Falmouth School of Art. From the early 1970s he showed in many mixed shows, including LG. Had one-man show at Piers Morris Gallery in 1970, then showed regularly solo throughout Britain, with a series at Art Space Gallery from 1989. In 1996 there was a show there to complement Atkins' retrospective at RWA. Arts Council, South West Arts, the British Council and Somerset County Council hold examples. The catalogue for the retrospective traced developments from the dark London period of the 1960s to the mature paintings from Cornwall where Atkins developed "a unique and extraordinary method of working on a large scale from direct observation by erecting structures in the landscape and leaving the work on site until completed".

Anthony ATKINSON 1929– Painter, teacher and exhibition organiser, born in London, who worked in oil and gouache. He studied at Wimbledon School of Art and Royal College of Art, 1951–5, teachers including Rodrigo Moynihan and Carel Weight. He gained a silver medal and edited *Ark* magazine. Became head of Colchester School of Art, 1964–75, faculty head, 1975, and dean of art and music at Colchester Institute, 1986–9. Was organiser for Ernst & Young annual exhibitions from 1986. As a painter of architectural and landscape themes in East Anglia and Provence, Atkinson showed at RA from 1950; Victoria & Albert Museum; NEAC; New Grafton and Leicester Galleries; and elsewhere. His solo shows included Leighton House; Minories, Colchester; Gainsborough's House, Sudbury; Phoenix Gallery, Lavenham; and Coach House Gallery, Guernsey. Work was commissioned by the Post Office, Shell and London Transport. Minories, Essex County Council and Royal London Insurance hold his work. He was an honorary member of Colchester Art Society and a governor of Gainsborough's House Society. Lived in Great Horkesley, Essex.

Charles Gerard ATKINSON 1879–c.1957 Painter, born at Seaford, Sussex. Studied with Walter Hilton in Liverpool, where he exhibited, also at RWS, RCamA and RBSA. Lived at Grasmere, Westmorland.

Conrad ATKINSON 1940– Artist using variety of media, and teacher, born in Cumbria, whose work frequently had political and social implications and was on occasion controversial. He studied at Carlisle College of Art, 1957–61; Liverpool College of Art, 1961–2; then Royal Academy Schools, 1962–5. In the latter year he gained Leverhulme Award and Abbey Minor Scholarship, then in 1967 won a Granada Fellowship. As well as taking part in a number of important group exhibitions, Atkinson had solo shows; in 1972 his show Strike was held at ICA; the same venue being chosen for Work, Wages and Prices in 1974; then the year following his subject was Northern Ireland at Belfast Arts Council Gallery, this topic being repeated at Art Net in 1976; in 1977 his exhibition Approaching Reality was staged at Northern Arts Gallery, Newcastle upon Tyne. From 1974–6 Atkinson was fellow in fine arts at Northern Arts Association in Newcastle, 1976 onwards joining the staff of Slade School of Fine Art. His installation For Emily: Plus Equals, based on Emily Brontë, was held at Dean Clough, Halifax, 1992. Arts Council holds his work.

Dale ATKINSON 1962– Painter, born in Sunderland, who did a foundation course at the Art College there, 1981–2. From 1982–6 studied at Newcastle University for an honours degree in painting. In the latter year had a solo exhibition at Anne Berthoud Gallery of paintings, with another of works on paper also in 1986. Additional shows occurred at the same gallery, further showings taking place at Readheads, Newcastle upon Tyne, 1989–90, and at Newcastle Polytechnic Gallery, 1991. In the mid-1980s Atkinson had a studio in Bristol, in 1989 moving to Newcastle, where he exhibited at University of Northumbria in 1995 and 1997. Atkinson was a nonconformist as a student, producing visionary pictures based on stories his father had told him as a child. His later paintings were more pared down, but continued his interest in "the psychology of paint", the way a chance mark or colour change could alter identity and significance.

Eric ATKINSON 1928– Artist in mixed media and teacher, born in Hartlepool, County Durham. He said that his pictures were "records of journeys through the landscape ... and also explorations into the existence of possible bridges between the physical structure of man and his empathy for the environment". Atkinson studied at West Hartlepool College of Art, under Harry Thubron, 1943–7, then Royal Academy Schools, 1950–5, under Henry Rushbury. After teaching at Leeds College of Art, 1964–9, moved to Canada, settling in Ontario, where he was dean in the faculty of applied arts, Fanshawe College, London, 1972–82. Group shows included Tate Gallery, 1954–6; Richard Demarco, Edinburgh, 1967; British Council tour, Tel-Aviv, 1970; Museum of Art, Carnegie Institute, Pittsburgh, 1980; and Art Gallery of Ontario, Toronto, 1984. Had series of solo shows at Redfern Gallery from 1954, later ones including Mendel Art Gallery, retrospective, at Saskatoon, 1980, and Concept Gallery, Pittsburgh, 1987. Elected to NEAC, 1956, Royal Canadian Academy of Arts, 1978. Many public collections held his work, including Arts Council, Contemporary Art Society and provincial galleries.

Jane ATKINSON fl. from early 1970s– Painter, printmaker and teacher, born in London. She studied at Central School of Art and Design and Waltham Forest School of Art, 1964–8. Was an adult education tutor in Kent. Showed in groups at Blackheath Art Society and Rye Art Gallery. Took part in three-artist shows at Associate House, Ashford; Drew Gallery, Canterbury; New Metropole Arts Centre, Folkestone; and in 1989 at Woodlands Art Gallery. Had solo show in Washington with United States of America International Monetary Fund.

Marshall Forster ATKINSON 1913–1990 Artist in various media, born in Gateshead, County Durham, where he continued to live. He studied at King's College, Newcastle. Showed widely, including Royal Glasgow Institute of the Fine Arts of which he was a member, PS, UA, RBA, RWS, RCamA and Paris Salon. Was a member of Univision Group and Gateshead Art Society and was closely associated with Shipley Art Gallery, Gateshead, where he had a solo show in 1952; it holds his work and held a memorial exhibition of his Tyneside shipbuilding and other scenes in 1997.

Ted ATKINSON 1929– Sculptor, etcher and teacher, born in Liverpool. He studied at Liverpool College of Art, 1944–8, under Karel Vogel, then at Slade School of Fine Art, 1950–4, with Reg Butler and Henry Moore. Taught at Exeter and Leeds Colleges of Art, then was head of sculpture at Coventry Polytechnic, 1968–83. Atkinson concentrated on sculpture commissions. His work was "an attempt to crystallise a range of feelings, emotions, undercurrents, facts, conflicts and gestures of the psyche. It asserts that reality simply fails to live up to the demands of art." Major public sculptures were completed in Birmingham, Coventry, Düsseldorf and Hamburg. Atkinson was a member of RE and a fellow of RBS. Group shows included RA, RWA and LG. He was one of six artists representing Britain at World Expo '88 in Brisbane. He was awarded Barcham Prize at RE, 1987, etching prize in RA Summer Exhibition in 1988 and a similar prize at Artists in Essex show, 1990. Ashmolean Museum and Saatchi Collection hold his work. Lived in Wivenhoe, Essex.

Terry ATKINSON 1939– Painter, draughtsman, writer and polemicist, and teacher, born in Thurnscoe, Yorkshire. He attended school in Darlington, meeting Harold Hurrell; was at Barnsley School of Art, 1958–60, getting to know David Bainbridge; and was at Slade School of Fine Art, 1960–4. Atkinson felt that teaching there was not relevant to the society in which he lived. In 1962 he showed Dead Cat on a Runway, at Young Contemporaries, where his Postcard from Ypres won the Arts Council Prize in 1963. World War I was to remain a preoccupation as an artist. Taught part-time at Birmingham College of Art, 1965–7; at Coventry College of Art (later Lanchester Polytechnic), 1966–73, where he met Michael Baldwin; took up a Gulbenkian Foundation Fellowship in 1975, working at Sidney Stringer School, Coventry on the Community Education Video Project; and lectured in fine art at Leeds University from 1977. In 1964 Atkinson helped form the group Fine Artz with John Bowstead, Roger Jeffs and Bernard Jennings, but left it in 1966. In 1967 Atkinson and Baldwin produced a series of prints and texts together, including Notes on Time Show, Declaration Propositions and Types of quasi-intention. The group Art & Language was founded in 1968, the first issue of *Art-Language*, a conceptual art journal, appearing in 1969, edited by Atkinson, Bainbridge, Baldwin and Hurrell. Atkinson left the group in 1975, and the following year a show of his subsequent work was organised for Midland Group, Nottingham, with a tour. Atkinson showed at Sydney and Venice Biennales in 1984 and in 1985 at John Moores Liverpool Exhibition. Had a retrospective at Whitechapel Art Gallery, with tour, 1983–4; another key show, indicating how Atkinson had consistently examined the meaning and purpose of art, was toured from Norwich Gallery, Norwich School of Art and Design, 1996. Arts Council holds his work. Lived for a time in Leamington Spa, Warwickshire.

ATRI: *see* **Atri BROWN**

Mary ATTENBOROUGH: *see* **Mary POTTER**

Jake ATTREE 1950– Painter, notably of landscapes, born in York, who studied at the School of Art there, 1966–8, Liverpool College of Art, 1968–71 and Royal Academy Schools, 1974–7. Two years later Attree began painting full-time, although he did various other jobs such as scene painting at Theatre Royal in Norwich. Exhibitions included RA Summer Exhibition and Serpentine Gallery Summer Show 1 in 1982. Attree was later a resident artist at Dean Clough, Halifax, having a show of his New York drawings in 1996, when he also had an exhibition at Art Space Gallery. Nuffield Trust holds his work.

Norman Stewart ATTWELL 1921– Painter in oil, born in Hastings, Sussex. Studied at Richmond School of Art, afterwards at Royal College of Art with a break for war service. Exhibited RA, at other London and provincial galleries. Lived at Twickenham, Middlesex.

Clare ATWOOD 1866–1962 Painter, born at Richmond, Surrey, the daughter of an architect. Studied at Westminster School of Art and Slade School of Fine Art under Henry Tonks and Philip Wilson Steer. One-man show at Carfax Gallery, 1911, also showing at NEAC, RA, Ridley Art Club and many other venues. Did World War I paintings for the Canadian government, some of her work also going to Imperial War Museum. Tate Gallery holds her portrait of the actor Sir John Gielgud's room, in 1933. Lived at Smallhythe, Tenterden, Kent, where she was known as Tony, in a group which included Ellen Terry's daughter Edith and the woman writer Christopher St John.

John AUBREY 1939– Painter, sculptor and teacher, born in Pontyberem, Dyfed. After attending grammar school near Llanelli, in 1958 Aubrey studied at the department of fine art at King's College, Newcastle upon Tyne, until 1963 when he began lecturing in fine art at Wolverhampton College of Art, later being on the staff of Wolverhampton Polytechnic. Took part in many group shows including Bear Lane Gallery, Oxford; Howard Roberts Gallery, Cardiff; and John Moores Exhibition, Liverpool, at Walker Art Gallery. WAC holds his work and Royal Academy of Music has his portrait of Sir Thomas Armstrong, a former principal.

AUDIO ARTS Organisation run by artists Michael Archer and William Furlong (see separate entries). It participated in the Serpentine Gallery/South Bank Centre's The Sculpture Show, 1983, where it was declared to be "linked with work that is concerned with the urban media environment, with meaning, content and process in relation to electronic media, with the manipulation of such media and the implication of widespread dissemination through magnetic tape, broadcasting and satellite communications". Arts Council holds Audio Arts' Objects and Spaces, 1983, 90-minute sound tapes.

Mary AUDSLEY 1919– Artist working in a variety of media who entered Westminster School of Art, 1934, her teachers including the sculptor Eric Schilsky and painters Mark Gertler and Bernard Meninsky. She was to have taught at the School, but it closed with the onset of World War II. During the war Audsley served for a short time in the Women's Royal Air Force until she was invalided out. She did teach, but ill-health, family responsibilities and other problems hindered Audsley's artistic career, which she took up seriously again in the early 1970s, producing paintings, ceramics, carvings, prints and collages, her work showing a strong School of Paris influence. Showed RA, LG and in the provinces and in 1990 had solo show at Sally Hunter Fine Art.

Arnold AUERBACH 1898–1978 Sculptor, painter and etcher, born in Liverpool. He studied at its School of Art, in Paris and Switzerland. Was for a time a lecturer at Regent Street Polytechnic and Chelsea School of Art. Exhibited at RA, Goupil Gallery, Walker Art Gallery in Liverpool and in the provinces. Wrote a number of books on sculpture, such as *Sculpture, a History in Brief*. Work was illustrated in *British Sculpture, 1944–1946*, by Eric Newton, and William Aumonier's *Modern Architectural Sculpture*. Auerbach's work ranged in style from conventional torsos to his heavily stylized Vorticist Head and decorative panels, as at Davis Theatre, Croydon, in the manner of Eric Gill. Lived in London.

Erna AUERBACH 1897–1975 Artist, teacher and writer, born in Frankfurt-am-Main, Germany. She studied at the Art School there, 1917–22, in Paris in 1926, then again in Frankfurt, 1928–30. With the Nazi ascendancy in the early 1930s her ability to work was undermined, and in 1933 Auerbach moved to England, where she settled in London and reassembled her career. Had a first solo show in England at Brook Street Gallery in 1938 and during World War II completed pictures related to the war effort, but destruction of her studio during the Blitz prompted her to do more teaching and writing. Was included in Art in Exile in Great Britain 1933–45 at Camden Arts Centre, 1986.

Frank AUERBACH 1931– Painter, draughtsman, printmaker and teacher, born in Berlin. Settled in England in 1939 and studied at the Borough Polytechnic in 1948, St Martin's School of Art, 1948–52, Royal College of Art, 1952–5, and at evening classes under David Bomberg, 1948–53. Had the first of a series of solo exhibitions at Beaux Arts Gallery in 1956. From that year for about a dozen years he taught, being a visiting teacher for Kent and Middlesex County Councils and including sessions at Camberwell School of Arts and Crafts and Slade School of Fine Art. After an appearance in the Gulbenkian International Exhibition in 1964, in 1965 Auerbach joined Marlborough Fine Art and began to show globally. By 1978 he had a retrospective at Hayward Gallery. Tate Gallery and Saatchi Collection hold his work. From 1954 Auerbach worked in a run-down studio in Camden Town, one of the seedier areas he chose to paint. He also painted certain models obsessively. Their portraits could take 150 sittings and, like the townscapes, were created from a heavily reworked mass of pigment.

Eric AUMONIER 1899–1974 Sculptor, born in Northwood, Middlesex, full name Aubrey Eric Stacy Aumonier, one of a line of artists and writers (the author Stacy Aumonier was his uncle). Eric's grandfather, William, also a sculptor, founded William Aumonier & Son, which specialised in architectural work; William's son William, also a sculptor, was responsible for over 100 war memorials and wrote *Modern Architectural Sculpture*, 1930, in which his son Eric's work is featured. Eric studied at Central School of Arts and Crafts, joining the family business in the early 1920s, eventually working on his own. Notable among Aumonier's achievements were, in the late 1920s, a South Wind figure on the Underground Railway (later London Transport) building in Broadway; in 1930 two terracotta panels on East Sheen cinema; for the 1932 opening of the old *Daily Express* building in Fleet Street, two foyer panels: Industries of the British Isles and British Empire Industries; in 1939 Royal Arms for the British Pavilion at the New York World's Fair, and a striking figure of an archer outside East Finchley underground station; for the 1946 Powell and Pressburger film *A Matter of Life and Death* historical figures up the moving staircase to heaven (*Black Narcissus*, *Ivanhoe*, *Knights of the Round Table*, *Beau Brummell* and *Spring in Park Lane* also used Eric's talents); in 1951 the White Knight statue for the Festival of Britain; in 1960 giant nursery rhyme figures for the Food Fair, Olympia; and in 1964 work on the Fortnum & Mason clock, Piccadilly. In 1968 rheumatoid arthritis forced him to abandon sculpture, so Aumonier and his wife went to live in Ashburton, New Zealand, for his health's sake, and there he died.

David AUSTEN 1960– Artist in oil and mixed media, his pictures frequently containing an assemblage of objects, as in Story, 1996, included in About Vision, at Museum of Modern Art, 1996–7, and tour. Austen was born in Harlow, Essex, and attended Maidstone College of Art, 1978–81, then Royal College of Art, 1982–5. Group shows included Canvass: New British Painters, John Hansard Gallery, Southampton, and tour, 1986; New Editions, Cirrus, Los Angeles, 1991; and Take it From Here, Sunderland Museum and Art Gallery, 1996. Showed with Anthony Reynolds Gallery solo from 1986. Lived in London.

Winifred AUSTEN 1876–1964 Bird and animal painter and printmaker. Born in Ramsgate, Kent, she studied under Cuthbert Swan and Louise Jopling-Rowe. Made a point of visiting zoos to study animals on site. She was a prolific exhibitor, showing at the RA, Fine Art Society, Leicester Galleries, SWA, RE and elsewhere. Her pictures appeared in a number of books on birds and she is represented in several provincial collections in Britain, in Preston, Bradford and Ipswich, and in America. Lived at Orford, Suffolk.

Frederick AUSTIN 1902–1990 Printmaker and painter, born in Leicester, brother of the artist Robert Sargent Austin. He studied at Leicester School of Art and at Royal College of Art under Malcolm Osborne, William Rothenstein and Randolph Schwabe, 1924–7. Prix de Rome for engraving won in 1927. Exhibited RA, RE of which he was a member, and extensively abroad. British Museum, Graves Art Gallery in Sheffield and several foreign collections hold his work. Lived in London.

John Anthony AUSTIN 1949– Painter and designer, born in Birmingham, who worked in oil. After 15 years as a creative lighting designer he became a full-time artist, concentrating on trains, planes and automobiles. His main works were "large railway subjects and Severn Valley Railway publicity posters and leaflets". Was a member of the Guild of Railway Artists and showed with Halcyon Gallery, Birmingham, work also appearing in *Railway Magazine*. Lived at Bridgnorth, Shropshire.

Robert Sargent AUSTIN 1895–1973 Printmaker and draughtsman, born in Leicester. He studied at the School of Art there and at Royal College of Art, 1914–16 and 1919–22, winning the Rome Scholarship for engraving in the latter year. He taught engraving at Royal College of Art, 1927–44, becoming professor in the department of graphic design, 1948–55. Showed with RWS of which he was a member and president; RE of which he was a member; and RA, to which he was elected in 1949. Austin was a meticulous craftsman-engraver and a vigorous draughtsman, as his series of drawings of Women's Auxiliary Air Force and ballooning activities done during World War II shows. Tate Gallery holds his work.

Trish AUSTIN 1954– Abstract sculptor and teacher, born in Bristol. She studied at St Martin's School of Art, 1973–7, then for her master's degree on the fine art course at Goldsmiths' College School of Art. Did part-time teaching for Inner London Education Authority while maintaining a studio in the capital. Showed in New Contemporaries, 1976; St Martin's South Bank Show, 1977; Waterloo Gallery and New Gallery, Hornsey, both 1980; and in 1982 shared a show at Woodlands Art Gallery.

John AUSTIN-WILLIAMS 1947– Artist in mixed media, oil on canvas/board and charcoal, born in Kew, Surrey, who attended Exeter University, 1966–9. After brief art studies in Dorset, 1970–1, Austin-Williams was trained in the exacting disciplines of the Polish School of Art, 1976–80, under Marian Bohusz-Szyszko, being awarded the diploma of the Stefan Batory University, with distinction. Austin-Williams' work was influenced by music and the output of the Fauves: powerful, colourful landscapes, seascapes and still lifes. He said that one of his pictures was "not necessarily 'about' other things; it is about itself". Was a founder-member of Wessex Contemporary Artists, 1988. Solo exhibitions included POSK Gallery (Polish Cultural Institute), 1983; Alpha House Gallery, Sherborne, 1993; and Dillington House, near Ilminster, 1995. Austin-Williams' main works included the Kerry landscapes series, 1991–5, and Fountain study series, 1995. West Dorset Hospital, Dorchester, holds his work. Lived in Parkstone, Poole, Dorset.

Giles AUTY 1934– Art critic and painter, born in Kent, who studied art privately before National Service. He worked at various jobs before settling in west Cornwall in 1959 to paint full-time. He had a number of solo shows in London and exhibited at Belgrave Gallery in 1970s, when he was starting to write about art, from a conservative standpoint. In 1977–8 had solo show at Belgrave Gallery and in 1992 was included in a show of three critics at Cadogan Contemporary. Was art critic for *The Spectator*, in 1995 moving to Sydney where he wrote criticism for *The Australian*.

Josephine AVELINE 1914– Artist, notably in pastel, born in Carshalton, Surrey, who studied at Worthing College of Art under Charles Morris. She became a fellow of the Society of Botanical Artists and a member of PS and SWA. Also showed RP, carrying out a series of commissioned portraits, including work for The Clothworkers' Hall and Royal College of Surgeons of England. Lived in Littlehampton, Sussex.

Simon AVERILL 1961– Painter, printmaker and teacher, born in Brighton, Sussex, where he studied fine art at the Polytechnic, graduating with honours. After running the Balwest printmaking workshop, 1986–90, went on to teach printmaking and drawing part-time at Falmouth School of Art. His work showed essential elements rather than recognizable features in the Cornish landscape. He was included in Artists from Cornwall at RWA in 1992. Among other shows in which he participated were Newlyn Orion Gallery, Penzance, 1990, and Gordon Hepworth Gallery, Exeter, 1991.

Wilfred AVERY 1926– Artist using various media including collage, born in Devon, who trained as an art teacher in Cheltenham in World War II. In 1952 moved to London and showed work during late 1950s at Beaux Arts Gallery and at Gallery One. During 1963–4 worked in France. Returning to England, he settled in Blackheath, southeast London, in 1969. Showed occasionally, then had a major exhibition at Woodlands Art Gallery in 1977 covering 20 years, organised with the assistance of Greater London Arts Association. The work ranged from Cubist-influenced depictions of Devon coast to highly stylised work touching on "the myths, legends and archetypes that are so much part of our inner life".

Walter AWLSON 1949– Figurative sculptor and teacher who graduated from Edinburgh College of Art in furniture design and sculpture in 1971, in 1972 gaining the certificate in secondary education at Moray House, Edinburgh. He developed an interest in ceramics while teaching in secondary schools and further education, including Falkirk College of Technology, in 1991 resigning from full-time lecturing to develop his own work. Since 1985 he had run a workshop in Alloa, Clackmannanshire, where he produced slip-cast ceramic sculptures in limited editions, specializing in raku firing in two kilns, one gas- and one wood-fired. Awlson was winner of the SPA Alistair Dunn Award, 1990, and became a professional member of SSWA in 1991. Showed at RSA, Open

Eye Gallery in Edinburgh, Andrew Usiskin Contemporary Art, Rooksmoor Gallery in Bath and with Royal Glasgow Institute of the Fine Arts and elsewhere. Lidl UK Ltd's supermarket in Alloa has a ceramic mural by Awlson.

AYA: *see* **Aya BROUGHTON**

Duffy AYERS fl. from early 1930s– Painter and teacher, who studied at Central School of Arts and Crafts. She was married to the artist Michael Rothenstein, for a time being known as Betty Rothenstein, then to the designer Eric Ayers. The painter Anne Rothenstein was her daughter. Taught painting at the Women's Institute's Denman College for many years. Fry Art Gallery in Saffron Walden holds her portrait of the matron of Dr Barnardo's, Kitty Edwards. As well as being known for her portraits, Ayers produced small, richly coloured and darkish still lifes and genre scenes, a group being included in the Tenth Anniversary show at Cadogan Contemporary, 1996. She also exhibited at RA, SWA and elsewhere and lived in London.

Eric AYERS 1921– Designer, married to the artist Duffy Ayers. He studied at Beckenham School of Art and Royal College of Art. Became a member of the Society of Industrial Artists/Chartered Society of Designers. Showed with Council of Industrial Design, at 1951 Festival of Britain and in America. Lived in London.

Ulmen AYGIN 1959– Sculptor who was born in Limassol, Cyprus. Studied at Istanbul Academy of Fine Art, 1978–9, then St Martin's School of Art, 1980–3. Showed with groups in Kyrenia, Cyprus, in 1978; took part in Kornarija Symposium of Sculpture, Yugoslavia, 1981–3; showed with group at Marusici, Yugoslavia, 1983; and in that year participated in Have You Seen Sculpture from the Body? at Woodlands Art Gallery.

George AYLING 1887–1960 Marine and landscape painter and teacher, born in London. The Aylings were associated with sculling and paddlemaking and George pursued the business for some years before studying at Putney School of Art, 1912. He continued to live near the River Thames, was a member of Chelsea Arts Club and the Art Workers' Guild and taught in Middlesex. Exhibited RA, ROI, NEAC, New Grosvenor Gallery and at marine painting shows in France. Lived at Kew, Surrey.

Joan AYLING 1907–1993 Painter in oil and tempera, her married name being Joan Eleanor Rees, who was born in Edinburgh. She studied art at Kilburn Polytechnic, Birmingham School of Arts and Crafts under B J Fletcher and Slade School of Fine Art with Henry Tonks, finally learning etching techniques privately with F L Maur Griggs. She exhibited at RA, RBA, Walker Art Gallery in Liverpool, Birmingham's Arlington Gallery and at Paris Salon, where she gained a Silver Medal, 1952, and Gold Medal, 1957. Was included in the exhibition Sladey Ladies at Michael Parkin Gallery, 1986. Lived in London.

Richard AYLING 1950– Painter, influenced by Cubism, born in Middlesex, who gained a diploma with honours at Twickenham College of Technology, 1967–71. During the period 1971–5 Ayling did a series of art-related jobs, including mural painting and freelance illustration, then he moved to Cornwall in 1977. Exhibited with Camden Arts Centre, RI, Beaux Arts in Bath, Andrew Usiskin, and a number of Cornish galleries including Penwith and Wills Lane Galleries in St Ives and Newlyn Gallery in Newlyn.

AYNSCOMB 1937– Painter, sculptor and teacher, full name Martin Aynscomb-Harris, born in Farnham, Surrey. He attended Folkestone and Dover School of Art, 1953–5, Medway College of Art, 1955–6, Wimbledon College of Art, 1956–8, and Hornsey College of Art, 1958–9. Held several teaching appointments, including Nuneaton School of Art, 1961–3. Mixed show appearances included Phoenix Gallery, Lavenham; Nicholas Treadwell Gallery; Hilton Gallery; and abroad. Solo shows included Heal's Mansard Gallery; Woodstock Gallery; Seen Gallery; and overseas. Royle Publications and Frost & Reed published his work. Oxfordshire Education Committee, Marks & Spencer Ltd and British Airways owned examples. Lived in Sheerness, Kent.

Martin AYNSCOMB-HARRIS: *see* **AYNSCOMB**

Arthur James John AYRES 1902–1985 Sculptor and teacher, noted as a distinguished carver, who was married to the painter Elsa Gronvold who died shortly before him. He studied at the Royal Academy Schools under William McMillan and at the British School in Rome, having won the Prix de Rome in 1931. Ayres was elected a fellow of RBS and showed at RA, RSA, at Royal Glasgow Institute of the Fine Arts, in the provinces and in Rome. Ayres taught carving at the Royal Academy Schools for many years and part-time at City & Guilds of London Art School until he died. He and his wife were active members of the Reynolds Club, for former Royal Academy Schools students, founded in 1951. Bolton Art Gallery holds Ayres' work. His carved brick panel Power is illustrated in Eric Newton's monograph *British Sculpture 1944–1946*. Ayres had a memorial service in Westminster Abbey. Lived in London.

Gillian AYRES 1930– Painter, mural artist and teacher, born in London, where she mainly worked. Was married for a time to the painter Henry Mundy, having shared AIA Gallery administration with him after leaving Camberwell School of Art, where she studied 1946–50. Three years before she left AIA Gallery in 1959 Ayres had first solo show at Gallery One. As well as appearing in many key group shows – such as Tachist and Abstract Art at Redfern Gallery, in 1957; British Painting in the 60s, at the Whitechapel Art Gallery in 1965; and the Royal College of Art show Exhibition Road in 1988 – Ayres had important solo exhibitions at Museum of Modern Art, Oxford, in 1981; Serpentine Gallery, 1983; Gimpel Fils, 1996; and RA, 1997 (she had been made RA in 1991). Awards included an Arts Council

Award and Arts Council Bursary. Ayres taught at Bath Academy of Art, St Martin's School of Art, Winchester School of Art and Royal College of Art. Arts Council holds her work, richly coloured pictures in the Abstract Expressionist manner.

Roy AYRES 1945– Painter, born in Epping, Essex, who studied at South-West Essex Technical College and School of Art, Walthamstow, 1961–5, then at Royal Academy Schools, 1965–8, under Ken Howard, Peter Blake, Derek Hirst and Fred Dubery. Ayres continued painting in London until 1973, worked at other occupations until 1988, then moved from Sussex to Pembrokeshire. Early exhibitions included Young Contemporaries, 1968. Later group shows included Riverside Gallery, Crickhowell, 1992; New Gallery, Swansea, 1993; and in 1995 Mall Galleries for the Laing Competition, National Eisteddfod of Wales and Aberystwyth Art Centre. From 1989 he was gallery artist with West Wales Art Centre, Fishguard, where he had a solo show in 1995 and where he lived. Ayres had found there "an environment providing the impetus and inspiration to restart painting and develop my ideas about landscape". Later he explored the "same elemental forms in the broader landscape of Pembrokeshire's Preseli Hills and coastline".

Tim AYRES 1965– Artist working in variety of media, born in Hastings, Sussex. He studied at Loughborough College of Art, 1985–8, then Chelsea School of Art, 1988–9. Showed at Mall Galleries postgraduate show in 1989, Barclays Young Painters' Award exhibition at Royal College of Art Gallery in the same year and in John Moores Liverpool Exhibition 1989–90. Lived in London.

Michael AYRTON 1921–1975 Painter and sculptor of imaginative and mythological subjects, theatre designer, illustrator, broadcaster, writer and critic. He was born in London as Michael Ayrton Gould, son of the poet and critic Gerald Gould and Barbara Ayrton, feminist and prominent member of the Labour Party. Eventually Ayrton changed his name by deed poll. He was thus heir to a richly literate, articulate family tradition which became evident in his work. Illness interrupted his education but after wide European travel, where he first became interested in drawing, he attended Heatherley's and St John's Wood Schools of Art. Early influences were Pavel Tchelitchew, Henry Moore and Graham Sutherland, which led to Ayrton's identification with the English Neo-Romantics. He also shared a studio in Paris with John Minton in 1939, studying with the French Neo-Romantic Eugéne Berman. Ayrton taught drawing and theatre design – at 18 he was commissioned to design Gielgud's *Macbeth* – at Camberwell School of Art, 1942–4. His versatility is evident in his acting as art critic for the *Spectator*, 1944–6; serving as a member of the BBC Brains Trust; writing books such as *British Drawings*, 1946, and *Golden Sections*, 1957; and his pursuit of sculpture from the mid-1950s. Ayrton was obsessed by certain themes; the skull, the maze, the minotaur and Daedalus. His work can be disturbing, even sinister, but it has attracted a firm body of admirers. Represented in many public galleries, including the Tate. Retrospective exhibition at Whitechapel Art Gallery, 1955, Agnew 1984. Lived at Toppesfield, Essex.

Millicent AYRTON 1913– Painter whose work in oil was "largely Impressionist, semi-abstract in watercolour". She was born in Hoylake, Cheshire and attended Liverpool College of Art, 1930–5, teachers including Will C Penn. Taught privately and founded Deeside Art Group in 1945, being its chairman for 40 years. Also belonged to Liverpool Academy and RCamA and showed RWA, RA, RI and had a solo show in Hoylake. Williamson Art Gallery, Birkenhead, holds her work. Lived in West Kirby, Wirral, Merseyside.

Mary Anne AYTOUN-ELLIS 1965– Artist, notable as a printmaker, married to the sculptor Marcus Cornish. She did a foundation course at Brighton Polytechnic, 1983–4; studied for first year of a visual arts degree at Lancaster University, 1984–6; gained a fine art degree at Ruskin School of Drawing, Oxford, 1987–90; then her master's in printmaking, Royal College of Art 1990–2. Awards included Geoffrey Rhoades Commemorative Bursary; Egerton Coghill Landscape Prize; Senior Scholarship, St Hugh's College, Oxford; and Beck's Bier Award. In 1992–3 Aytoun-Ellis held an Erna Plachte Fine Art Fellowship at the Ruskin School, specialising in large experimental etching; in 1994–5 she held a residency at Frans Masereel International Printmaking Centre, Belgium. Group shows included Fifth Humberside Print Show, 1991; Flowers East, 1992; BP Portrait Award, National Portrait Gallery, 1994; and RP, Mall Galleries, 1996. Had a solo show at Dolphin Gallery, Oxford, 1990. Bodleian Library in Oxford and Museum of Modern Art in Wakayama, Japan, hold examples. Lived in Lewes, Sussex.

B

Maria Louise BABB 1893–1975 Painter and silversmith, born in Brussels, of Belgian parents. After a convent education she attended finishing school in England, aged 17. In 1914 was in England again as a refugee with her parents. In the 1920s, after a short first marriage, she attended art school in Chelsea and did a course in silverwork. After marrying Captain Babb in 1935 they lived in Cairo, then returned to Godmanstone, Dorset, where she remained, although her husband moved to west Somerset at the end of World War II. Maria Babb travelled abroad during the winter months. She became an accomplished artist in oil, watercolour and pastel, was a keen ornithologist, botanist and herbalist, member of the Buddhist Society and British Society of Dowsers.

Stanley Nicholson BABB 1873–1957 Sculptor, born in Plymouth, where he studied art, also at Royal Academy Schools. Won a gold medal and travelling scholarship, 1901–2, and studied and worked in Italy. Became a member of Art Workers' Guild in 1919, retiring in 1945. Exhibited at RA, RMS, RSA and elsewhere and was a fellow of RBS. Babb's war memorial is outside the civic centre in Tunbridge Wells, Kent. Two examples of his decorative style of sculpture are illustrated in the volume *RBS: Modern British Sculpture*, published in 1939.

Irene BACHE 1901– Watercolourist and teacher, born in London. She studied at Croydon College of Art, Central School of Arts and Crafts and Camberwell College of Art. Then taught in a series of schools until she was appointed head of the art department for Swansea College of Education, 1942–66. That College gave her a retrospective show in her final year. She had also had a solo exhibition at the Glynn Vivian Art Gallery, Swansea, in 1954 and showed in group shows with Howard Roberts Gallery, Cardiff; Swansea Art Society, of which she was a leading member; and Dillwyn Gallery, Swansea. On retirement she taught in her own studio, landscape being her speciality. In 1991 had ninetieth birthday shows at Glynn Vivian and Plantasia, Swansea, where she lived at Gower.

David BACHMANN 1964– Artist, who studied graphic design at Camberwell School of Art, then worked for the National Gallery as an exhibition and publicity designer. In 1989 went to study painting in Florence, Italy, at the Cecil Graves Academy. On his return to London worked for two years as a portrait painter, then settled in Seville, Spain. Exhibitions included a shared show with Romanos Moukarzel in 1997 at The Edith Grove Gallery.

Ken BACK 1944– Artist and teacher, born in Guildford, Surrey. He studied at Dover School of Art, 1959–60, Folkestone School of Art, 1960–2, Canterbury College of Art, receiving his diploma in painting and sculpture, 1962–4, then gained a painting certificate with distinction at Royal Academy Schools, 1964–7. He won several prizes at the Schools, including the Eric Kennington Prize for drawing in 1965–6, and Landseer Prize for painting in the same years. From 1963 taught, including Folkestone, Dover and Ipswich Art Schools, Open College of the Arts and Suffolk College of Art & Design, going part-time from 1985 to have more time for painting. Among his group appearances were Metropole Arts Centre, Folkestone, 1966; RA Summer Exhibitions from 1967; Piccadilly Gallery from 1983; and Continuing the Tradition, Chappel Galleries, Chappel, 1993. Nuffield Foundation, St John's College in Cambridge and Sir Brinsley Ford held examples. Lived at Dickleburgh, near Diss, Norfolk.

Robert BACK 1922– Painter with a strong interest in marine subjects, teacher, born in Adelaide, South Australia. His father, William Edward Back, as a young man sketched regularly in East Anglia with Sir Alfred Munnings, who gave him his first oil paint box, and he had his first solo show in Bond Street aged 18, but family refusal to let him take up art as a career led to his giving it up at 23. Robert himseslf attended Edinburgh College of Art in 1940 and 1946–9, teachers including William Gillies, Leonard Rosoman and John Maxwell. In World War II Back followed a family tradition and served at sea, participating in Russian and Atlantic convoys and the relief of Malta. He had four years in the merchant navy, taught in various schools and was a noted sailor, being Norfolk Broads dinghy champion three years and an Olympic trialist. A number of Back's works appeared as limited edition prints. Showed at Omell Gallery, RSMA, RSA and David Messum and Malcolcom Henderson Galleries. From 1983 had a series of solo shows at The Atlantic Gallery, Washington, America. Campbell College in Belfast, United States Naval Academy in Annapolis and New Orleans Academy hold examples. Lived in Seaford, East Sussex.

Daniel BACKHOUSE 1963– Painter and draughtsman in various media, born in Seal, Kent. He did a foundation course at Maidstone College in 1983, teachers including Arthur Neal; in 1984 moved to Norwich, painting at Ethelreda Studios, using the life room at Norwich School of Art, where John Lessore was an influence; then returned to Maidstone College, 1985, for an honours degree course. In 1988 Backhouse travelled in Europe, settling in West Berlin, where he set up a studio for five months; during 1986–7 he worked on various murals in London; then in 1989 moved to Wales, settling at Goodwick, Pembrokeshire.

Exhibitions included South East Painters, Maidstone, 1987; Le Weekend Gallery, Berlin, 1988; Mid-Wales Open, at Aberystwyth Arts Centre, 1990; and A Sense of Place, curated by Ian McKay, in association with Rebecca Hossack Gallery, 1985. In 1994 Backhouse shared a show at West Wales Arts Centre, Fishguard.

David BACKHOUSE 1941– Sculptor in bronze, born in Corsham, Wiltshire. Studied at West of England College of Art, Bristol, and became member of RWA. Backhouse taught sculpture in Bristol for a time, then worked extensively abroad: in 1971 in Luxembourg, portrait heads of Prince Charles of Luxembourg and family; in 1972 in Rome and Florence, bronze casting. Among assignments completed were portrait head of the conductor Colin Davis, collection of Royal Opera House, Covent Garden, 1974; sculpture for Mercantile and General Reinsurance Company, Cheltenham, 1977–8; and life-size, three-figure bronze fountain for John Perkins, 1979. Exhibitions included Lad Lane Gallery, Dublin, 1975; Alwin Gallery, 1979; retrospective at Century Galleries, Henley-on-Thames, 1980; and Orangery, Holland Park, 1981. RWA holds his work and included him in its 1st Open Sculpture Exhibition, 1993. Lived in Lullington, Somerset.

Sonia M BACKHOUSE 1926– Book illustrator, printmaker and watercolourist who studied at Willesden School of Art, 1940–4, and at the Royal College of Art, 1944–7, with Percy Hague Jowett and Ernest Tristram. She exhibited at RA and worked periodically as an illustrator for Folio Society books. Lived in London.

Cecil Walter BACON 1905–1992 Designer and illustrator, born in Battle, Sussex, educated at Sutton Valence School and St Lawrence College in Ramsgate. He attended Hastings School of Art, 1923–5, under Philip Cole, then joined a commercial studio and advertising agency in London in 1926, where he was soon noted for his incisive style. In 1929 Bacon – who signed his work C W B – went freelance, and began to design posters for London Underground and other organisations; these later included British Railways and the Post Office Savings Bank. He began contributing line drawings and scraperboard illustrations for *Radio Times* in 1935, an association which lasted until 1968. He did a number of outstanding covers for the periodical, notably his Festival of Britain, in 1951, and The Queen Returns, in 1953. His work was shown at Folio Society in 1957 and an exhibition was subsequently toured in America by the Arts Council. In 1981 he contributed to the Fifty Years of Design show at London Design Centre and the *Radio Times* show at the Victoria & Albert Museum. In 1984 he had a retrospective exhibition at Hastings Museum and Art Gallery with a memorial show in 1993. Lived at St Leonards-on-Sea, Sussex.

Francis BACON 1909–1992 Painter, by many considered the greatest British artist of his generation. He was born in Dublin of English parents. In the mid-1920s he lived in Berlin and Paris, in London in the 1930s having some success as an interior decorator and designer of rugs and furniture. Self-taught, he began painting in the late 1920s. At first he worked slowly and occasionally, destroying much of his output. In 1934 he had a solo show at Transition Gallery, three years later appearing at Agnew in Young British Painters. With a series of one-man exhibitions at the Hanover Gallery from 1949 – having spent the late 1940s in Monte Carlo – Bacon began to build a London reputation. This was reinforced from 1960 with an impressive series at Marlborough Fine Art. He had a first solo show at Durlacher Bros in New York in 1953 and in Paris at Galerie Rive Droite four years later. His painting was shown in the British pavilion at Venice Biennale in 1954. A series of international one-man shows followed, along with retrospectives. In Britain there was one at the ICA in 1955; one at the Tate Gallery, with a subsequent European and American tour, in 1962–4; and another at the Tate in 1985. The Tate Gallery in Liverpool held a show in 1990–1; there was a retrospective at Centre Georges Pompidou, Paris/Haus der Kunst, Munich, 1996; and a reappraisal at the Hayward Gallery, 1998. The Tate Gallery, like other international collections, holds examples of Bacon's work, including one of his long line of triptychs, the key Three Studies for Figures at the Base of a Crucifixion, of 1944, which made Bacon famous in the art world. Bacon's figure studies, such as Two Figures on a Bed; his portraits; and the series based on Velasquez's portrait of Pope Innocent X distort conventional appearances to raw, powerful effect, creating haunting images. He painted a stream of self-portraits plus others of friends such as George Dyer, Muriel Belcher and Isabel Rawsthorne. Bacon lived in London but died in Madrid, Spain, having consistently refused all official honours.

Peter James BACON 1951– Artist and designer creating entirely with materials such as rope and twine, the son of an architect, born in north London. Attended Hornsey School of Art. Showed at Mall Galleries and elsewhere in London and was a member of the Free Painters and Sculptors. Lived in Enfield, Middlesex.

Yehuda BACON 1929– Artist, illustrator and teacher, born in Ostrava, Czechoslovakia, who studied with various Jewish artists in Theresienstadt and Auschwitz camps, 1941–5. In 1945 Bacon (pronounced Bahcon) was a private student of Willi Nowak of the Prague Academy of Art, from 1946–51, with a scholarship, attending Bezalel Academy in Jerusalem under Mordecai Ardon. Further studies followed with work periods abroad; in 1956–7 Bacon studied etching with Merlyn Evans at Central School of Arts and Crafts, with a time on scholarship in Italy in 1956; was at École des Beaux-Arts in Paris, 1957–8; was a private student of Bernard Reder, in Florence in 1958; returned to study etching and lithography at Central School, 1963–4; did advanced studies and experimental work at Pratt Institute Graphics Center, New York, 1971–3; studied teaching methods in various Scandinavian art schools in 1973; then in 1983 had a sabbatical year studying widely on the continent. His own teaching experience began in 1951 in Jerusalem, at Brandeis and other schools; from 1959 he was on the staff of Bezalel Academy; and in 1976–7 lectured at

Haifa University. Bacon gained a number of awards and medals and took part in numerous group shows, including RA Summer Exhibition. Several dozen solo exhibitions included University of London Westfield College Library, 1978, and Arts 38 Gallery, 1980. Among many book covers and illustrations completed were Alan Sillitoe's *Out of the Fire*, 1979. Victoria & Albert Museum, British Museum and Ben Uri Art Society hold examples.

Pamela BACZKOWSKA 1938– Sculptor, born in Bradford, Yorkshire, married to the artist Henry Baczkowski. She worked in a variety of materials, figurative and abstract works. Studied at Regional College of Art, Bradford, and trained as a potter for 10 years, in 1963 starting to make ceramic sculpture, then bronzes and carvings, from 1967 working exclusively on sculpture. Travelled in Europe, America and North Africa. Was a member of Free Painters and Sculptors. Exhibitions included Woodstock Gallery; Mall Galleries; Sackville Gallery, East Grinstead; Rudolf Shaeffer Hause, Rotenberg; Riverside Gallery; and Galerie Angle Aigue, Brussels. Deutsche Bank, Heilbronn, Germany, owned her work, one influence on which was the painter Howard Hodgkin. Lived in East Grinstead, Sussex.

John Fanshawe BADELEY 1874–1951 Printmaker, born in Elswick, Lancashire. He was educated at Radley College and Oxford University. Henry John Fanshawe Badeley was in the Judicial Office of the House of Lords and from 1934 was Clerk of the Parliaments, being knighted in 1935. A member of RE, he was noted for his heraldic work, also showing at RA and RMS. Lived in London.

Stanley Roy BADMIN 1906–1989 Watercolourist, draughtsman and printmaker, born in London. Studied at Camberwell School of Arts and Crafts and Royal College of Art, which he left in 1928. Badmin soon established a reputation for his detailed, affectionate depictions of the English countryside and country life. He illustrated *Shell Guides*, Shell posters, produced over a hundred greetings card designs for Royle's the fine art publishers, produced covers for *Reader's Digest* and illustrated travel and topographical books. Aged 26, he became one of the youngest-ever members of RWS, also becoming a member of RE. Showed Fine Art Society, Leicester Galleries, Arts Council and abroad. In 1985 Chris Beetles Ltd held a major retrospective to coincide with Beetles' biography *S R Badmin and the English Landscape*. Victoria & Albert Museum and British Museum hold his work. Lived for many years in Bignor, Sussex.

Howard BAER 1906– Cartoonist, illustrator, painter and printmaker, born at Finleyville, in the Allegheny Mountain section of Pennsylvania, America, where his father ran a small department store. Settled in New York in 1930 after studying at Carnegie Tech, Pittsburgh. As a young man, apart from his own paintings and prints, Baer was drawing as many as 365 cartoons a year for a newspaper syndicate and magazines, for *Esquire* alone five a month. He became an artist-war correspondent for Abbott Laboratories in 1944 in China, Burma and India, completing paintings of the Medical Corps at the front. This work is now in the Pentagon's Archives of War. Travelled extensively in Europe from 1948, with time in London from 1960. Illustrated many books. He made his debut as an artist in 1941 with an exhibition of paintings at the New York gallery of Associated American Artists. Other shows included Ben Uri Art Society, 1965 and 1972, which holds several examples, as do the Metropolitan Museum in New York and the Butler Art Institute.

Jo BAER 1929– Artist who produced a large body of abstract work, born in Seattle, Washington, America, using oil, various contés, pencils and other media. She trained as a scientist at University of Washington and the graduate facility, New York School for Social Research. Baer's group shows included Kaymar Gallery, New York, 1964; Documenta IV, Museum Friedericianum, Kassel, 1968; Lisson Gallery from 1975; American Painting of the 1970s, Albright-Knox Art Gallery, Buffalo, 1979; and From Minimal to Conceptual Art, National Gallery of Art, Washington, 1994. Had a solo exhibition at Fischbach Gallery, New York, 1966, then showed prolifically, later shows including Rhona Hoffman Gallery, Chicago, 1989; Paul Andriesse Gallery, Amsterdam, 1990; and Paley/Levy Gallery, Moore College, Philadelphia, 1993. Starting in Ireland in 1978 Baer collaborated with Bruce Robbins until 1984, when she moved to the Netherlands, settling in Amsterdam. Their joint appearances included 112 Workshop, New York, 1980; Riverside Studios, 1982; and Oliver Dowling Gallery, Dublin, 1984.

Peter BAER 1924–1996 Printmaker, painter, draughtsman and teacher, born in Berlin, Germany, whose family emigrated to Spain in 1936, then London, where he eventually settled. In 1939 he was interned at Huyton and was a draughtsman in an aircraft factory, 1940–6, from 1947–50 studying at Central School of Arts and Crafts under Anthony Gross and Morris Kestelman. During following years he did many jobs, including printer and photographer. From 1960–5 Baer was a printer of artists' lithographs at Curwen Press, serving an apprenticeship with Stanley Jones which Baer said taught him much. He printed his own etchings in Birgit Skiöld's Print Workshop, 1967–75. Baer was lecturer in printmaking at Hammersmith School of Art, then at Chelsea, from 1970. His work ranged from large, dramatic black-and-white etchings to exuberant, Expressionistic landscapes, employing among other colours vibrant reds and brilliant blues. Mixed shows included RA, Whitechapel Art Gallery, Victoria & Albert Museum and international print exhibitions; he was in the 1986 Berlin show Art in Exile. Solo print exhibitions latterly included Camden Arts Centre, 1981, and University College, 1982; solo shows of paintings Amalgam Arts, 1992, and BBC White City, 1994. Ben Uri Art Society holds his work.

Pier Luigi BAFFONI 1932– Painter and draughtsman, born in Turin, Italy. His uncle, Achille Parachini, was a notable portrait painter. Baffoni studied at College of Art, Turin, 1954–8, with Luigi Guglielmino and privately with Alessandro Pomi, other artists who influenced him being Nino Springolo and Juti

Ravenna. In 1963 Baffoni won a prize at an international exhibition in Castelfranco Veneto. After moving to England Baffoni was elected to NS and ROI. He won the Scharf Prize for figure painting at ROI's annual show in 1983, two years later being made a Sociétaire of the Société des Artistes Indépendants after showing at the Grand Palais in Paris. Baffoni held one-man shows in Italy and in the English provinces. Used a rich palette for landscapes, portraits and still lifes. Several of his pictures were bought by the Bedfordshire Education Art Loan Service. Lived in Lower Stondon, Bedfordshire.

Alfred Charles BAILEY 1883– Watercolourist, born in Brighton, Sussex, who after private education attended Brighton School of Art under Louis Grier. Exhibited extensively at Goupil Gallery, RBA and Redfern Gallery. In the early part of the century he lived in St Ives, Cornwall, where he was a member of the Society of Artists, later residing in Richmond, Surrey.

Arthur BAILEY 1903– Architect and watercolourist, born in Alsager, Cheshire. Bailey was articled to a firm of architects for several years after World War I, eventually working in a practice known as Ansell and Bailey. He also studied, as an articled pupil, at the Central School of Arts and Crafts. He eventually became a fellow of the RIBA and showed at RA. Reform Club member. Lived in London.

Cecil Raymond BAILEY 1907–1973 Artist in charcoal, oil and watercolour, born and lived in London, who won a scholarship to Martin's School of Art, having shown promise as a portrait painter. Family circumstances forced him to leave and take up casual labour. Became a cleaner at Westminster Abbey in 1929, a verger in 1935 and from 1960 was canons verger until he retired in 1972. Art remained a consuming hobby for Bailey, who constantly sketched and studied part-time with David Bomberg at the Borough Polytechnic and also attended Morley College. Bomberg suggested that Bailey join him painting in Spain, but Bailey could not leave his family. He was a founder-member of the Borough Bottega in 1953 and took part in in its exhibitions as well as other mixed shows, and had two solo exhibitions at BH Corner Gallery, 1969 and 1970. Turner, Picasso, Henry Moore, the French Impressionists, the architecture of the Abbey and, latterly, the sombre London skyline were all influences. Bailey's final work was mainly abstract. After retirement Bailey had seven major operations. He was encouraged to jot down his memories which, as *A Verger's Diary*, his wife had published privately in a small edition after his death.

George William BAILEY 1880–1955 Landscape painter in oil and watercolour, born in Spalding, Lincolnshire. Studied at Chelsea School of Art, 1903–4, under Ernest Borough Johnson. Exhibited RWA, RSA, Foyles Gallery and provincial galleries including Usher Gallery, Lincoln, which holds his work. Signed pictures G W B. Was for many years closely associated with Spalding Gentlemen's Society. Lived at Spalding, Lincolnshire.

James BAILEY 1922– Stage designer and painter, born in London. He was initially educated in England and Switzerland, then studied art at the Byam Shaw School and Slade School of Fine Art, 1939–40, where his teachers included Vladimir Polunin. Although he had his first one-man show at Redfern Gallery in 1955, Bailey made his name as a stage designer. He designed for major productions at the Royal Opera House, Covent Garden; the Lyric Theatre, Hammersmith, for *The Way of the World* during a John Gielgud season; for the Old Vic; and for La Scala, Milan. Lived in London.

Julian BAILEY 1963– Painter and draughtsman, born in Cheshire. Bailey studied at Ruskin School of Art in Oxford and was a member of New College there, 1982–5, attending Royal Academy Schools, 1985–8. He was awarded the Egerton Coghill Landscape Prize (Oxford University), in 1984; the David Murray Landscape Award, in same year; the Turner Gold Medal at the Royal Academy Schools in 1986; and Landseer Scholarship in 1988. In 1989 Bailey visited Australia and the Far East, where the strength of light impressed him, as a painter whose debt was to the muted influences of Walter Sickert and the Camden Town Group. Mixed shows included RA, LG, Cadogan Contemporary and New Grafton Gallery, where he had his first solo show in 1991.

Keith BAILEY 1929– Sculptor in a variety of materials and teacher, born in St Helens, Lancashire. He attended Liverpool College of Art, 1946–8, Manchester College of Art, 1948–51, then City and Guilds School, 1953–4. Was for some time a visiting teacher at West Dean College, in Sussex. In 1967 had a solo show at Cambridge Building Centre and completed panels for churches and educational institutions in various parts of England. Lived for some years at Royston, Hertfordshire.

Peter BAILEY 1944– Sculptor and teacher, born near Wrexham, Denbighshire. He studied at University College of Wales, Aberystwyth, then at Bath Academy of Art, from 1969–73 being a part-time tutor in sculpture at the University College. In 1969–70 Bailey was part-time technical assistant to the sculptor and printmaker Michael Pennie, then in the early 1970s he took up a teaching fellowship in sculpture, again at University College of Wales. Bailey participated in many group shows, including Northern Young Contemporaries, Manchester; Laing Art Gallery, in Newcastle upon Tyne; and Arnolfini Gallery, Bristol. WAC and Victoria & Albert Museum hold his work.

Terry BAILEY 1937– Painter and teacher, born in Wolverhampton, Staffordshire. He studied at local Technical High School, then at Wolverhampton College of Art, 1954–8, and Bournemouth College of Art, 1962. Went on to teach at Northumberland College of Higher Education, 1962–79. Showed at RP, at RBSA where he was a prizewinner in the Open exhibition, 1986, and had several solo shows. National Library of Wales, Aberystwyth, holds his work. Lived in Aberdovey, Gwynedd.

William BAILLIE 1905– Painter, photographer and teacher, whose work embraced figurative, Surrealist and latterly entirely abstract pictures. By then, he felt that "the art of painting is not about other things, but has an independent existence of its own." Baillie was born in Larkhall, Lanarkshire, son of a coal miner, and gained his diploma from Glasgow School of Art in 1927, having studied with A E Haswell Miller. He had first exhibited at RSA in 1925 (at this time Baillie's works were mainly in transparent watercolour), and he was to show there regularly, also at the Royal Glasgow Institute of the Fine Arts. Baillie taught from 1928, and for this purpose made an extensive study of modern artistic trends. In 1931, Baillie had works bought to decorate the merchant ship *Monarch of Bermuda*. In the mid-1930s Baillie became interested in photography, in 1936 being elected a member of The Scottish Photographic Circle, at which he lectured and showed, also exhibiting with The Scottish National Salon and in 1938 at the British Empire Exhibition. In 1989 the Fine Art Society, Glasgow, had a show of work by Baillie and his pupil, William J Bunting. Latterly, Baillie lived in Hamilton, Lanarkshire, and was known as William Baillie of Hamilton. The museum there and Perth's art gallery hold examples.

William BAILLIE 1923– Painter and teacher, born in Edinburgh where he continued to live. He studied at Edinburgh College of Art and Moray House College of Education, 1941–51, although from 1942–7 served in Army, mainly in the Far East. In 1955 Baillie became resident tutor at the National Gallery of Canada Summer School, in Ottawa. Then from 1960–88 he taught at Edinburgh College of Art, finally as senior lecturer in the drawing and painting school. In 1980 the English Speaking Union sponsored Baillie to travel to India, Nepal and Sikkim; this resulted in a body of work. Baillie was president of RSW, 1974–88 and was elected RSA in 1979, becoming its president in 1990; he was made Hon. RA and Hon. RWA in 1991. After a one-man show at Saltire Society Festival Exhibition in 1961 Baillie went on to show extensively in Scotland and England, notably at Lower Loomshop Gallery, Lower Largo, Fife; Heal's Gallery; and retrospective at Kirkcaldy Art Gallery in 1977. RSA, Scottish Arts Council and Scottish National Gallery of Modern Art hold his work.

Donald BAIN 1904–1979 Painter, draughtsman and stage designer, born in Kilmacolm, Renfrewshire. After education at Moffat Academy, Bain studied art with W Y MacGregor, one of the Glasgow Boys, who introduced him to the work of S J Peploe and J D Fergusson, whose style is sometimes reflected in Bain's pictures. In the late 1920s Bain went to Paris, where Matisse's work further influenced him. Bain returned to Glasgow in 1940, working in the shipyards and with Fergusson became involved in the New Scottish Group from its formation in 1942. A further stay of several years in France in the period after World War II put him in touch with Cézannesque influences in contemporary French painting before he settled in Glasgow in 1948. There Fergusson's wife Margaret Morris commissioned Bain to design the scenery for a dance version of *A Midsummer Night's Dream*. Bain exhibited widely in France and a touring exhibition in major Scottish cities in 1972–3 revived interest in him, but at time of his death he was suffering neglect. Scottish Arts Council and Scottish National Gallery of Modern Art hold his work.

Peter BAIN 1927– Painter and draughtsman, born in London, who studied at Bath Academy of Art, Corsham, under William Scott and Bernard Meadows. As well as Army service Bain was a butcher, poultry farmer and a teacher. He showed in London and the provinces. Lived in Old Bosham, Sussex.

David BAINBRIDGE 1941– Conceptual artist and teacher who attended Barnsley Art School in the late 1950s, where he met Terry Atkinson, but left to be a bus conductor. Bainbridge then worked at a Sheffield steelworks, became a shop steward and joined the Communist Party of Great Britain. Bainbridge moved to London in 1963 and enrolled at St Martin's School of Art sculpture department. He began teaching at Coventry College of Art in 1967, the year that he and Harold Hurrell shared the Hardware Exhibition at the Architectural Association. In 1968, Bainbridge, Hurrell, Atkinson and Michael Baldwin formed the influential exhibiting and publishing group Art & Language, but Bainbridge chose to leave it in 1971. This was the year when with Baldwin he was dismissed from Coventry, as the art theory course, on which they and Atkinson had taught, was summarily ended. Settled in Old Swinford, West Midlands.

Eric BAINBRIDGE 1955– Sculptor and draughtsman, born in County Durham, who studied at Newcastle Polytechnic, 1974–7, then Royal College of Art, 1978–81. Bainbridge said that he needed to "play around with the size of objects – increasing them to above human scale – and also to remake them … into the world of sculpture", as in the giant spoons forming More Blancmange in the South Bank Centre's touring The British Art Show 1990. Bainbridge participated in many group shows from New Contemporaries, at ICA, in 1981. His solo exhibitions began with Ayton Basement, Newcastle, 1978, later ones including Salvatore Ala Gallery, New York, 1988, Stedelijk Museum, Amsterdam, 1989–90, and Cornerhouse, Manchester, 1997. Arts Council holds his work. Lived in London.

John BAINBRIDGE 1920– Painter, draughtsman and poster artist, born in Sydney, New South Wales. Studied at Swinbourne Technical College, Melbourne, and Melbourne Art Gallery. Exhibited in Australia, where he is represented in National Gallery of South Australia in Adelaide, also at London and Redfern Galleries. Did posters for Ealing Studios, London Underground and British European Airways. Lived for some years in London.

Kenneth BAINBRIDGE 1908– Printmaker, craftsman and teacher, born in Colne, Lancashire. He attended Burnley Municipal School of Art, 1929–34, then Royal College of Art, 1934–8, when Ernest Tristram and the calligrapher Edward

Johnston taught him, and simultaneously at Central School of Arts and Crafts. Showed in London and in the Burnley area, where he lived.

Dick BAINES 1940– Painter, printmaker and teacher, born in Hastings, Sussex. He studied at Regent Street Polytechnic School of Art, 1957–61, where his teachers included James Osborne, then at Goldsmiths' College School of Art where Paul Drury taught him. Design lecturer for some years at the London College of Fashion. For a period he was president of the East Sussex Arts Club. Showed NS and ROI of both of which he was a member, and RBA. Had solo show at Hastings Public Museum and Art Gallery; Borough of Hastings holds his work. Lived in London.

Glyn BAINES 1930– Influential teacher and painter in oil whose work included subtle abstracts. Born in Carrog, Merionethshire, Baines studied at Wrexham School of Art and Cardiff Teacher Training College. Until 1961 he worked at home on the farm, then was head of art at Bala Comprehensive School until 1989, latterly working in his own studio. Baines was a member of Gweled, The Welsh Society of Visual Arts. Group shows included numerous appearances at National Eisteddfod of Wales; Broekman Gallery, Chester; Mostyn Open, Llandudno; Y Tabernacl, Machynlleth; and and Invited Artists '96, at RCamA, Conwy. Solo shows included Plas-Glyn-y-Weddw, Llandbedrog; The Gallery at Mold, Clwyd; and Oriel Cantref Bala, Gwynedd, near to where he lived.

Harry BAINES 1910–1995 Realistic figurative painter and draughtsman, full name Frederick Harry Baines, born in Manchester, who attended the School of Art there, 1930–4, gaining a diploma in mural painting. During the next five years Baines completed several murals in the north of England, Timperley Church, Cheshire, and Longford Cinema, Manchester, being represented in the Tate Gallery show Contemporary British Mural Painting, 1938. Service in the Royal Engineers, 1941–6, introduced Baines to India; he was seconded to be design studio director for the Indian government's exhibitions division information department. On later visits Baines recorded impressions of a new steelworks; painted murals for the British pavilion at the Delhi Industrial Fair; with Richard Lannoy prepared the book *The Eye of Love* on temple sculpture, 1976; and produced drawings exhibited as part of the Festival of India, 1983. Baines' interest in Neo-Realism had been stimulated by meeting Italian artists such as Guttuso, Mucchi, Zigaina and Treccani, whose work dominated the Venice Biennale of 1951. Baines' "superb draughtsmanship" was praised by critic John Berger, who noted that "the weight of a stone that a woman carries on her head can be seen in her ankle." Mixed shows included RA, Whitechapel Art Gallery, Leicester Galleries and The Forgotten Fifties, Graves Art Gallery, Sheffield, and tour, 1984. Later solo shows included a series at Camden Arts Centre from 1980; Alpha House Gallery, Sherborne, 1992; and a memorial exhibition at Art Connoisseur Gallery, 1996. Lived in London.

Charlie BAIRD 1955– Painter and printmaker, born in Nairn, who studied lithography and screenprinting at the Instituto Allendes, San Miguel, Mexico; did an art course at Wimbledon; then was in residence at Cité Internationale des Arts, Paris, 1983–5. Mixed shows included Thumb Gallery, 1980; RA Summer Exhibition from 1989; Jonathan Clarke Gallery, 1991; Michael Parkin Gallery, 1994; and Tenth Anniversary show at Cadogan Contemporary Art, 1996. It gave Baird a solo exhibition in 1995, where a subtle colour sense and a wittily idiosyncratic style of landscape were evident.

Edward BAIRD 1904–1949 Painter and teacher, born in Montrose, Angus, where poor health confined him for most of his life. After education at Montrose Academy he attended Glasgow School of Art, 1923–7, winning the Newbery Medal as top student of his year. A travelling scholarship took him to Italy for a year, where the study of early Renaissance pictures influenced his own work. Meticulous detail, Hyper-Realist and Surrealistic elements all had a part in this. From 1938–40 Baird taught at Dundee College of Art. Much of his output was portraits, examples being in the Scottish Arts Council and Dundee Art Galleries and Museums collections. It was the Council's show of his work in 1968 which revived interest in Baird, then largely forgotten. Scottish National Gallery of Modern Art held a retrospective of Baird's small output – less than three dozen canvases – in 1992.

Nancy BAIRSTOW fl.c.1925–55 Miniaturist in watercolour, born in Wolstanton, Staffordshire. She was educated privately, then studied art with the miniaturist Edwin Morgan. Showed extensively at RI, also RA, RMS, Walker Art Gallery, Liverpool, and Paris Salon. Lived at Chorley Wood Common, Hertfordshire.

Alexandra BAKER 1947– Watercolourist, born in Southborough, Kent. She came from and was married into a military family and specialised in military subjects. Studied at Sir John Cass School of Arts and Crafts, 1964–5. Was a member of SGA where she showed, also elsewhere in London, and illustrated a number of books with military themes, such as *Gunners at Larkhill*. Was a member of the Society for Army Historical Research and had work in the collections of the National Army Museum as well as various regiments. Lived in Salisbury, Wiltshire.

Bobby BAKER 1950– Artist who was born Lindsey Baker in Sidcup, Kent, married to the photographer Andrew Whittuck. She employed the media of performance, painting, video and food. Studied painting at St Martin's School of Art, 1968–72, in the latter year starting to perform with food as a medium, venues including galleries, public and domestic spaces. Solo performances from this period included An Edible Family in a Mobile Home, Stepney, 1976; Art Supermarket, ICA, 1978; and Packed Lunch, Hayward Gallery, 1979. After doing no public work for eight years Baker resumed in 1988, selected performances including Drawing on a Mother's Experience, ICA with extensive national and international tour, 1989; Kitchen Show, London, with tour, 1991; How to Shop, London and tour, 1993; and Take a Peek!, South Bank Centre/Arnolfini Gallery, Bristol, 1995. Also took part in group events, including Food Art, Kettle's Yard, Cambridge, 1977; Sucre d'Art, Louvre, Paris, 1978; About Time, ICA/Arnolfini, 1980; and Food as Politics, Camerawork, 1985. Marina Warner, an enthusiast for Baker's work, wrote of her that "she could be called a hunger artist, working with her own cravings and the common needs of people for sustenance, for comfort, for nourishment, of which food is the chief sign ... She is the target of the laughter she provokes, but remains in control." Lived in London.

Charles Henry Collins BAKER 1880–1959 Painter, art historian and curator, born in Ilminster, Somerset. He was educated at Berkhamsted School and studied art at Royal Academy Schools. Was for a time keeper at the National Gallery, surveyor of the king's pictures and then on the research staff of the Huntingdon Library, California. He was art critic of *Outlook* and of the *Saturday Review* and wrote a series of books, including *Crome*, 1921, and *British Painting to 1900*, 1933. Showed at NEAC, RA, Goupil Gallery and elsewhere. Contemporary Art Society and public galleries in Manchester and Huddersfield bought his work. Lived latterly in London.

Chris BAKER 1944– Painter who was brought up in south London in a tough environment, was a motor mechanic for a decade and did not go to Camberwell School of Arts and Crafts until 1971. After four years there he was at Royal College of Art, 1975–8, in 1977 winning the Lubiam Award in Mantova, Italy. Baker's work reflected his experience of city life transformed on canvas into slowly formed but telling images. Baker had a key solo show at Warwick Arts Trust in 1983, also exhibiting at Paton Gallery. He was included in Exhibition Road in 1988 at Royal College, which holds his work, as does Arts Council.

Christopher BAKER 1956– Painter, printmaker, teacher and writer, born in Essex. He studied at West Surrey College of Art & Design, Farnham, 1974–5, then Gloucester College of Art & Design, 1975–8, under David Carpanini, and at University of Exeter School of Education. He was artist-in-residence at Oundle School, 1981–3, then a full-time art teacher at Kimbolton School, Cambridgeshire, 1983–6. Also taught at West Dean College in Sussex, where he settled at Arundel. From 1987 Baker wrote for *The Artist* magazine, carried out commissioned work and with two other painters ran Herringbroom Studios. Royal Mint commissioned his services. Baker was elected to RBA in 1984, also showing with RWA, Medici Galleries and Portsmouth and Brighton public galleries. Among his solo shows was Pallant House, Chichester, 1993, views of the Portsmouth area.

Ethelwyn BAKER fl. from c.1930– Sculptor, painter and commercial artist, born in Belfast, daughter of the artist A R Baker. Studied at Slade School of Fine Art and Royal Academy Schools. Exhibited RA, Cooling Galleries, Festival of Britain, AIA and Beaux Arts Gallery. Sometimes signed work E B. Lived in London.

Frederick William BAKER 1916– Stained and painted glass artist, born in London, where he was partly educated, also at technical school in Toronto, Canada. He studied at Blackheath School of Art and Royal College of Art, then went on to carry out many ecclesiastical commissions in England, West Africa, America and Canada. Lived finally in Exeter, Devon.

Geoff BAKER 1950– Architect and artist who gained a Bachelor of Science degree at London University, 1972, then his master's degree at Sheffield University, 1974, and worked as an architect. He exhibited at RA Summer Exhibitions, RCamA and was included in the Walker Art Gallery, Liverpool, 1986–7 touring show Merseyside Artists 3, with two etchings.

Geoffrey Alan BAKER 1881–1959 Painter and teacher, born in Faversham, Kent. He attended Canterbury Art School, 1898–1902, then the Royal College of Art, 1902–07. He became principal of Bournemouth College of Art, 1913–47, and exhibited RA and elsewhere. The Russell-Cotes Art Gallery and Museum, Bournemouth, holds his work. Lived at Christchurch, Hampshire, where he was a member of the Arts Guild.

Gladys BAKER 1889– Painter and draughtsman, notable for her portraits, born and lived in London. She was educated at Queen's College, St John's Wood Art School and Royal Academy Schools, winning a silver medal for composition there. Showed at RBA, RI, NPS, in the provinces and America and frequently at RA, finally in 1947.

Jo BAKER 1963– Painter, collagist and artist in mixed media, born in London. In 1980–1 she spent a period dancing in south of France and attended evening classes run by Bruce McLean at Croydon College of Art. In 1982 Baker studied at Staffordshire Polytechnic, graduating with an honours degree in fine art in 1985. While there she met Kelvin Bowers, with whom she lived in a converted cowshed in the Staffordshire countryside and collaborated on many projects. In 1985 they showed in Northern Young Contemporaries at Whitworth Art Gallery, Manchester, and two years later they held readings of Christopher Wood's unpublished letters for the Winifred Nicholson touring show Unknown Colour. The mid-1980s saw Baker and Bowers taking part in group shows at the City Museum and Art Gallery, Stoke-on-Trent, and after a trip to New York and New Mexico, in 1989, in 1990 Baker was commissioned to paint a large canvas for St Modwen Developments. In that year they shared a first London exhibition at England & Co. Baker's work mixed Expressionist colour, Primitivism, fantasy and Surrealism.

Joan Elizabeth BAKER 1922– Painter, born in Cardiff. She attended the College of Art there, 1939–44. Then taught briefly at Bath School of Art, taking up a position at Cardiff College of Art in 1945. In 1952 completed a mural in Heol Trelai School in the city. Took part in Six Cardiff Artists shows in Cardiff and at Glynn Vivian Museum and Art Gallery, Swansea, in 1953 and 1955 respectively, as well as in SEA, WAC and SWG shows. WAC and Glynn Vivian hold her work.

John BAKER 1922– Painter, draughtsman, illustrator, writer and lecturer, born in Birmingham, where he attended the School of Art, then Slade School of Fine Art. Worked under the guidance of the prolific newspaper draughtsman Hanslip Fletcher and free-lanced for various publications, also lecturing on anatomy at Sir John Cass School. During the 1970s showed at RP, portraying civic dignitaries and show business personalities, then developed towards animal painting, involved in the early days of the Society of Equestrian Artists. Baker from 1966 wrote and illustrated a series of articles in the *Surrey Advertiser* called The Seeing Eye, and gained a local reputation as a controversial critic on architecture. He published *A Picture of Surrey* in 1980. Latterly lived near Salisbury, Wiltshire. Guildford Borough collection holds his works.

Percy Bryant BAKER 1881–1970 Sculptor in the classical style, born in London, who studied at City and Guilds Technical Institute and graduated from the Royal Academy Schools. Awarded first medal for portraiture, first medal for design in sculpture and other awards. Showed Walker Art Gallery in Liverpool, London and Paris Salons, RA many times and elsewhere. Completed numerous marble busts of notabilities, including King Edward VII, executed for Queen Alexandra, with many replicas made for other members of the royal family; heroic statue of same king, Huddersfield, unveiled by King George V, 1912; Arthur Purey Cust, Dean of York; President Woodrow Wilson, in Boston, America; and General W C Gorgas, bronze bust, Panama City, and replica, Army Medical Museum, Washington. Corcoran Gallery of Art in Washington put on a special exhibition of Baker's works in 1923. Manchester City Art Gallery holds his marble Eros, Hull his marble Memory.

Rebecca BAKER 1972– Painter and teacher, born in Birmingham, who studied at Bournville School of Art and Falmouth College of Art. From 1996 taught art at Bromley College. Group exhibitions included NEAC, Mall Galleries, 1995, and in 1996 the autumn exhibition at Langham Fine Art, Bury St Edmunds, and Royal Over-Seas League Open Exhibition. Baker chose to paint "the ordinary; small, apparently insignificant objects, but obviously selected and very specifically depicted".

Robert BAKER 1909–1992 Painter, sculptor, potter, conservator and teacher, he was married to Eve Baker, the conservator who died in 1990. Baker trained as painter and sculptor at Royal College of Art. His murals at Coleg Harlech, Gwynedd, and in the village hall at Wood Green, Hampshire, where he finally lived, were notable. During World War II Baker ran the Rural Industries Bureau. He was director of the art college at Stoke-on-Trent, then from 1948–59 was professor of ceramics at Royal College of Art. From late 1950s to 1971 he was chief designer and art director of Royal Worcester, the porcelain company, remaining a consultant until 1982. He was for many years involved in conservation, on which he became a leading authority, at such venues as Winchester, Lincoln and especially Wells Cathedrals. At Wells he was responsible for the saving of almost 200 early sculpted masterpieces as chief conservator of the west front.

Roger BAKER 1935–1989 Sculptor in stone, wood and metals who studied at West of England College of Art, Bristol, and Slade School of Fine Art. Commissioned work included a crucifix for Blackburn Convent, 1958, and a font in Portland stone for Mercers Chapel, in London. Showed at RWA and was included in 19 Young Sculptors at Hillfield Gardens, Gloucester, 1962. Taught at West of England College of Art/Bristol Polytechnic until retirement in 1987. Last solo show was in late 1970s at Gillian Tucker Gallery, Bristol, where he lived.

Sadanand BAKRE 1920– Born in Baroda, India, he had early success as a sculptor, winning a number of prizes. He was not recognised as a painter until 1948, when Baroda Museum bought two of his pictures. Bakre was a founder member of the Progressive Arts Group with Ara, Gade, Hussain, Raza and Souza. Moved to Europe in 1951 and participated in many important group exhibitions there, in America and in the Far East. In Britain showed with Nicholas Treadwell Gallery, his solo exhibitions including Gallery One, 1959, and Centaur Gallery, 1962. Bakre, a Hindu, suffered from tinnitus which undermined his health, and he eventually returned to India.

Iwan BALA 1956– Painter, born at Sarnau, near Bala, Merionethshire. Studied at University of Wales, Aberystwyth, 1974, Chester College of Art, 1975–6, and Cardiff College of Art, 1976–8. Bala's work could be Expressionist, near-abstract using a rich palette. Mixed exhibitions included National Eisteddfod; Oriel Llangefrai, North Wales; Mid-Wales Open, Aberystwyth Arts Centre; Greenpeace Clean Irish Sea Exhibition; City of Birmingham Museum and Art Gallery; and Café Gallery. Solo shows included Sherman Theatre, Cardiff; Dolman Theatre, Newport; and National Gallery of Zimbabwe, Harare. Bala won the National Eisteddfod of Wales Gold Medal in Fine Art, 1997. Lived in Grangetown, Cardiff.

Suzanne BALCHIN 1963– Painter, born in Woking, Surrey. She studied at Camberwell School of Arts and Crafts, 1983–6, graduating with an honours degree in graphic design. Delicate flower studies were a feature of her work. She shared a first joint exhibition at Hyde Park Gallery in 1991 with George Popesco, another in 1992.

Frederick William BALDWIN 1899–1984 Watercolourist and draughtsman who after an elementary school education taught himself to paint. Exhibited RA, RBA and in the Ipswich area. Baldwin was noted for his studies of Suffolk churches and lived in the county at Stoven. The public galleries in Ipswich and Birmingham hold his work.

Gordon BALDWIN 1932– Ceramist and teacher, born in Lincoln, who studied at the College of Art there, 1949–51, then Central School of Art, 1951–4. He taught at Central and Eton College. Took part in numerous group exhibitions, including Primavera Gallery, 1961; New Directions, Oxford Gallery, Oxford, 1972; Clay Sculpture, Yorkshire Sculpture Park, 1980; Artist Potters Now, Museum of Oxford, and tour, 1984; The Raw and the Cooked, Barbican Centre and tour, 1993; and The Jerwood Prize for Applied Arts, Crafts Council, 1996. Later solo shows included Gordon Baldwin Ceramics, Crafts Council Shop at Victoria & Albert Museum, 1995. Many public collections in Britain and abroad hold examples, including Victoria & Albert Museum; Contemporary Art Society; Kettle's Yard, Cambridge; Paisley Museum and Art Gallery; and Usher Gallery, Lincoln. Lived in Market Drayton, Shropshire.

John BALDWIN 1937– Artist noted for his wood carvings, which featured grotesque and amusing characters. He was born in London and studied at Camberwell School of Arts and Crafts, 1962–5, after that working in commercial and visual arts. In 1982 he began carving and was involved in mixed shows including Oxford Gallery, 1985; Primavera, Cambridge, 1986; British Relief Carving, an Arts Council touring exhibition, 1988; and John Hunt Galleries, Brightling, 1992. Had a solo show at Centaur Gallery, Highgate, 1984, later ones including Metropole Arts Centre, Folkestone, 1991, and Sevenoaks Library Gallery, 1992.

Mervyn BALDWIN 1934– Sculptor, draughtsman, restorer and teacher, born in Immingham, Lincolnshire, full name Arthur Mervyn Baldwin. He studied at Grimsby School of Art, 1953–5, and Leicester College of Art, 1953–5. After working as a stonemason and at Leicester College as a caretaker/studio assistant, Baldwin gained the Prix de Rome in sculpture, 1960, then was for two years in Italy. Series of teaching appointments included principal lecturer, Newport College of Art. Was a member of 56 Group, also exhibiting at Ikon Gallery, Birmingham; Grabowski Gallery; Whitechapel Art Gallery; University College of Wales, Aberystwyth; and elsewhere, including abroad. WAC and National Museum of Wales, Cardiff, hold his work. Lived in Cardiff.

Michael BALDWIN 1945– Conceptual artist and teacher, born in Chipping Norton, Oxfordshire, one of several – the others being Terry Atkinson, David Bainbridge and Harold Hurrell – who formed the influential exhibiting and publishing group Art & Language in 1968. Atkinson in 1966 met Baldwin who was in the second year of his three-year course for a diploma in art and design at Coventry College of Art, where Atkinson was to join the staff. Atkinson and Baldwin collaborated for a time on several works, such as Air Show, Air Conditioning Show and Oxfordshire, the Maps. Early in 1967 Baldwin was expelled from Coventry and returned to Oxfordshire, but kept in touch with Atkinson, one outcome being Art & Language's creation. Baldwin returned to Coventry College periodically to teach on the art theory course, but when it was terminated in mid-1971 he, like Bainbridge, was dismissed. Although Atkinson and Bainbridge were to leave Art & Language, Baldwin continued and, with his collaborator Mel Ramsden, settled at Middleton Cheney, Northamptonshire. Art & Language staged numerous exhibitions internationally and published many texts, Lisson Gallery being a notable venue.

Nancy BALDWIN 1935– Painter, born in Sunderland, County Durham, husband of the artist Gordon Baldwin. Attended Lincoln School of Art, 1949–52, then Central School of Arts and Crafts, 1952–4. Showed at Ikon Gallery, Birmingham; Bohun Gallery, Henley-on-Thames; with the Midland Group, and elsewhere in the provinces. Ashmolean Museum in Oxford holds her work. Lived in Eton, Berkshire.

Rosalind BALDWIN fl. from early 1970s– Painter, draughtsman, teacher and book illustrator, born in Glasgow where she attended the School of Art, 1969–73. After teaching in Scotland she freelanced from 1979. She painted many animal portraits, and her wildlife designs were reproduced as calendars and cards by several publishers and Royal Society for the Protection of Birds. Showed with RSW, Royal Glasgow Institute of the Fine Arts, SSA, SSWA, Society of Equestrian Artists and Patricia Wells Gallery in Thornbury. Held solo shows in Britain and America. Lived for a time in Bourne, Lincolnshire.

Warren BALDWIN 1950– Painter who studied at Wimbledon School of Art and London College of Printing. Showed at RA Summer Exhibition and elsewhere and with the study Wilhelmine II gained a third prize in the 1990 Singer & Friedlander/*Sunday Times* Painting Competition. Was originally a graphic designer. Lived in Bournemouth, Dorset.

Maria BALFOUR 1934– Painter, born and lived in London, who studied art privately and was married to Lord Balfour of Inchaye. She was a member of Free Painters and Sculptors, also showing with Chelsea Art Society, Kensington and Chelsea Artists and at Paris Salon.

Michael BALFOUR 1918–1997 Character actor, clown, painter and sculptor, who appeared in over 250 films, notable for his good humour, craggy face and stocky figure. Although born in Kent, the son of an Army officer, and a public schoolboy, in 1947 Balfour broke into the professional theatre by assuming a Detroit accent, persuading Laurence Olivier that he was American and should be given a part in Garson Kanin's *Born Yesterday* at the Garrick Theatre. Balfour made his film debut in *Just William's Luck*, 1948; appeared in many British B-movies, commonly in Cockney parts; and went on to act in such notable films as *Reach for the Sky*, *Genevieve*, *Macbeth*, *Farenheit 451* and *The Canterbury Tales*. Balfour overcame many crises, such as a car accident in 1953 which killed his friend Bonar Colleano and left Balfour with almost 100 stitches in his face; a fight against alcoholism; and latterly cancer of the sinus, which necessitated painful, disfiguring operations. Illness at 77 ended his touring as a clown with Gerry Cottle's Circus. Clowns and fantasy were an important part of his prolific output as an artist. He established a gallery near his home in Spain to show his own and others' work. Died at Princess Alice Hospice, Esher, Surrey.

Vincent BALFOUR-BROWNE 1880–1963 Watercolourist who was a keen field sportsman, born and lived in London, although he spent much time in Scotland at Goldielea, by Dumfries, as he was a keen deer-stalker. He was educated at Radley and Oxford University. Showed extensively with the Fine Art Society.

Bernard BALL 1921– Sculptor in a wide range of materials, born in Brisbane, Queensland, Australia. Studied sculpture at Sir John Cass College, London, in 1946 with Bainbridge Copnall, then five years later in Paris at Académie Julian. Showed at RA, Loggia Gallery, Birmingham University and elsewhere. Lived in Whitstable, Kent.

Gerry BALL 1948– Painter, notably in tempera, born in Ashton-under-Lyne, Lancashire. He studied art at local College of Further Education. Showed at Agnew, RI, Manchester Academy and with RCamA, of which he was a member. Coleg Harlech, Wales, holds his work. Lived in Ludlow, Shropshire.

Julia BALL 1930– Artist and teacher who studied at Reading University's school of art as a printmaker. She lived in Cambridge from the early 1960s, taught in local schools and from the early 1970s–90 at Anglia University, painting, part-time. Ball's interest was the landscape of East Anglia, especially the Fens. She said that she was "working towards trying to sum up *place*, the place, a particular place, by colour alone … it should be possible to sum it up with one colour". Her subtly coloured, light-filled pictures had a strong abstract element. Exhibitions included Bluecoat Gallery, Liverpool, 1978; Kettle's Yard, Cambridge, from 1980; University of Nottingham, 1986; Lynne Strover Gallery, Fen Ditton, from 1992. Eastern Arts, Kettle's Yard Loan Collection, Fitzwilliam College in Cambridge and Towner Art Gallery, Eastbourne, hold examples. The North American artist Agnes Martin, given a 20-year retrospective at the Serpentine Gallery in 1993, was an artist admired by Ball.

Martin BALL 1948– Painter and teacher, born in Leicestershire. Studied at Central School, Royal College of Art and Ohio State University, in America. He later taught at Art Institute of Chicago while working in the city. Ball's work, which employed a limited range of primary colours, involved the creation of abstract designs of a gritty nature, reflecting the ambience of the urban areas around him. The artist was included in surveys such as The British Art Show of 1979 and the South Bank Centre's touring exhibition of 1988–9, The Presence of Painting. Ball's early work was shown in solo exhibitions at Ikon Gallery, Birmingham, and Sunderland Arts Centre. He was a member of LG and the Newcastle Group, taking part in its 1990 show The Northern Lights, DLI Museum & Arts Centre, Durham, and tour. Became senior lecturer in painting at Newcastle Polytechnic and visiting lecturer elsewhere. Ashmolean Museum, Oxford, holds his work. Lived in Newcastle.

Peter Eugene BALL 1943– Sculptor and teacher, whose figurative work in found materials, mainly driftwood, drew on ancient and modern mythologies. He was born in Coventry, Warwickshire, where, after comprehensive school, he studied at Coventry College of Art for his design diploma. Rather than sculpt and teach, he opted for labouring and factory jobs. In 1973, began lecturing part-time on sculpture at Lanchester Polytechnic, Coventry, becoming a full-time sculptor in 1975. In 1963, Ball's work had been included in a six-artists show at Herbert Art Gallery, Coventry, and in 1964 he was in mixed exhibitions at Midland Contemporaries, Nottingham, and Marjorie Parr Gallery, where he started to exhibit solo from 1970. His work began to be shown widely internationally. He made sculpture, armour and masks for Christopher Logue's adaptation of Homer, *War Music*, for the Prospect Theatre at the Old Vic, 1977. Ball's first church commission came in 1974, a crucifix for Westminister Cathedral. Others included a large crucifix and altarpieces at Birmingham Cathedral, 1983, and a crib for Winchester Cathedral, 1991. Later solo shows included Gallery Gilbert, Dorchester, 1997. Latterly lived in Newark, Nottinghamshire, spending summers in the Loire Valley, France.

Robert BALL 1918– Painter, draughtsman, printmaker and teacher, born in Birmingham, son of a silversmith. Attended Moseley Road Junior School of Arts and Crafts there, 1930–3, winning many prizes and a scholarship to Central School of Arts and Crafts/College of Art, 1933–40. Won an exhibition to Royal College of Art, 1941–2, where gained many prizes and scholarships. Held a series of teaching posts, including senior lecturer in drawing and painting at Gloucestershire College of Art, 1954–81. Showed with RA, RE, RBSA, RBA and RWA. Ashmolean Museum in Oxford, a number of other provincial galleries and Victoria & Albert Museum hold his work. Ball's etching Mr Everitt, a Birmingham Tram Conductor, of 1936, is in the collection of the City Museum and Art Gallery, was included in its 1990 show The Birmingham School and was praised by J B Priestley in his book *English Journey*. Ball latterly lived in Painswick, Gloucestershire.

Robin BALL 1910–1979 Painter, draughtsman and teacher, born in Battle, Sussex. He attended Hastings School of Art, then the Royal College of Art, becoming an associate in 1938. Ball won a travelling scholarship to Europe, but this opportunity was cut short by the declaration of war. During 1938–45 Ball served with the Royal Artillery, and while he was never an official war artist he did complete many sketches and pictures of service life, with a strong vein of humour which runs through much of his work. From 1946–75 Ball taught at West Surrey College of Art and Design, at Farnham, where he died. Ball's oils and watercolours reflect his interest in the daily life of ordinary people, busy with figures and alive with incident. Some are realistic, some more highly structured, reflecting such developments as

Cubism and Futurism. Ball showed in mixed exhibitions at RA, Whitechapel Art Gallery, Ashgate Gallery in Farnham and Roland, Browse & Delbanco, and there was a small retrospective at Connaught Brown in 1987. Imperial War Museum holds his work.

Sarah BALL 1965– Painter, designer and illustrator whose work included simplified images and contours abstracted from landscape. She was born in Rotherham, Yorkshire, gaining her diploma in art and design, 1981–3, with an honours degree in graphic design, 1983–6. Her work was widely illustrated in such publications as *Images* and the *European Illustration Annual* and clients included British Telecom, Morgan Grenfell, *Saturday Times Review*, Clydesdale Bank, Time-Life, Decca, EMI, *New Scientist* and Greenpeace. Co-operative Retail Services' headquarters in Rochdale has a large canvas by her. In 1993 she won W H Smith and Norwegian Gullblyanten awards for illustration. Exhibitions included Gwent Illustrators, AOI Gallery, 1986; Images, The Best of British Illustration, at Smith's Gallery, from 1987; Montpelier Gallery, Bath Contemporary Art Fair, 1993; and New Ashgate Gallery, Farnham, 1995. Solo exhibitions included Contours at Hybrid Gallery, 1996. Lived in south Wales.

Percy des Carrieres BALLANCE 1899–1971 Landscape painter, born in Birmingham, who studied at Slade School of Fine Art. He exhibited RA, Cooling Galleries, RI and Paris Salon, where he gained an Honourable Mention in 1925. Member of Chelsea Arts Club, also of Art Workers' Guild from 1968. Lived in Wells, Somerset.

Evelyn BALLANTINE 1931– Painter, draughtsman and teacher, born in London. She attended Beckenham School of Art, 1946–52, and Royal College of Art, 1952–5, her teachers including Carel Weight, Roger de Grey, John Minton, Ruskin Spear and Robert Buhler. She went on to teach part-time at Morley College for many years. Around 1970 Ballantine's work was transformed by the experience of motherhood, and when she had a solo show at Brighton Polytechnic in 1980 Dennis Creffield wrote that Ballantine's painting had "the same vivid physicality as Sylvia Plath's poetry ... Raw, and often awkward, it nevertheless rings with existence". David Bomberg was a strong influence, through Creffield. Christian and pagan subjects were key factors in her pictures. Ballantine was a member of LG, other group appearances including Towner Art Gallery, Eastbourne, and Morley Gallery. Also showed solo there and at Mario Flecha Gallery. Lived in Brighton, Sussex.

Gino BALLANTYNE fl. from early 1980s– Painter and draughtsman who obtained an honours degree from the Glasgow School of Art, 1983–7, specialising in drawing and painting. Soon went on to show in mixed and solo exhibitions in Edinburgh, Glasgow and London, including RSA. One-man show held at Sue Rankin Gallery, 1990.

Arthur BALLARD 1915–1994 Painter and teacher, born in Liverpool, where he spent most of his career. Studied at Liverpool College of Art, 1932–5, then in 1935–6 in Paris at Académie de la Grande Chaumière, and again in Paris in 1957–8 under a Liverpool Corporation release scheme for teachers. Ballard went on to become head of the department of foundation studies at Liverpool Polytechnic. Showed Arts Council, Liverpool Academy, John Moores Exhibition in Liverpool, at Roland, Browse and Delbanco and elsewhere. Ballard painted in a number of styles: abstract, in a Pop Art manner and figurative works recalling the heroes of his youth as a working-class boy in the city. Was president of the Liverpool Academy, 1964–8. Work held by Walker Art Gallery, Liverpool University and Atkinson Art Gallery, Southport. Later lived in Corwen, Clwyd, north Wales. Belgrave Gallery held a show after Ballard's death, in 1996.

Brian BALLARD 1943– Painter, born in Belfast, where he continued to live. He attended the College of Art there, followed by Liverpool College of Art. Ballard was a rich Colourist, in the tradition of the Scottish painters Peploe and Cadell, notable for his still lifes. His exhibitions included Butlin Foundation for Young Irish Artists, Arts Council, Belfast, 1967; Tom Caldwell Gallery, Belfast, from 1972; Main Fine Art, Glasgow, 1986; Mistral Galleries, 1990; and Waterman Fine Art Ltd, 1992. Ballard's work is held by Arts Council of Northern Ireland; Crawford Municipal Gallery, Cork; and Ulster Museum, Belfast.

Morag BALLARD 1961– Producer of abstract reliefs and boxed constructions, born in London. She attended Chelsea School of Art, 1981–2, then Bath Academy of Art, 1982–5. After a period in the southwest of Scotland from late in 1986, in the summer of 1991 Ballard moved to Penzance, Cornwall, important moves as landscape was her principal reference for work in the tradition of Naum Gabo, Peter Lanyon and Ben Nicholson. Group shows participated in included Boxes and Totems and Art in Boxes at England & Co respectively in 1990 and 1991, and in the latter year the gallery gave her the first of several solo shows.

Niel BALLY 1951– Artist and teacher, born in Wantage, Berkshire, who studied at the Ruskin School of Art in Oxford, 1969, and in the fine art department of West Surrey College of Art & Design, Farnham, 1969–74. Went on to teach between 1975–86 at Camden, Central and Putney Inner London Education Authority Institutes, Canterbury, Chelsea, City and Guilds, Kingston and Wimbledon Schools of Art. From 1986–7 lived and worked in Mexico and America; in London, 1987–92; South Africa, 1992–5; then in London and Talgarth, Powys. Exhibited in RA Summer Exhibition from 1975; Whitechapel Open, 1978; Artists in Adult Education, at Woodlands Art Gallery, 1982; England & Co, 1991; and Hunting Prize Awards, from 1996. Later solo exhibitions included Brian Sinfield Gallery, Burford, 1991; Canvas Gallery, 1993; and Great Western Studios, studio shows, from 1995. Sheffield City Art Galleries, Stellenbosch University Museum and a number of corporate collections hold examples.

Barbara BALMER 1929– Painter and teacher, born in Birmingham, who was married to the artist George Mackie. She studied at Coventry and Edinburgh Colleges of Art, 1946–51, at the latter with an Andrew Grant Scholarship, then in 1951–2 had a travelling scholarship which took her to Spain and France. Was a visiting lecturer at Grays School of Art, Aberdeen. Group showings included John Moores Exhibition, Liverpool, and Richard Demarco Gallery, Edinburgh; Richard Demarco gave her a one-man show in 1970 after one at the Traverse Theatre Gallery 14 years before, after which she had several at the Scottish Gallery in the city as well as an important one at Aberdeen Art Gallery, 1995–6. It holds her work, as do HM The Queen, Scottish Arts Council, Glasgow's Kelvingrove and Lillie Art Gallery, Milngavie. She lived and worked at various times in Aberdeen, Edinburgh and Lincolnshire.

Derek BALMER 1934– Painter and photographer. He was noted for his richly coloured, painterly landscapes of Britain and abroad. Balmer was born and lived in Bristol, where he became a noted photographer, closely associated with the Bristol Old Vic. John Boorman, later a Hollywood director, used Balmer as his photographer during the making of television documentaries. Aged 15 Balmer was accepted at West of England College of Art by Donald Milner, his teachers including Paul Feiler. He was offered a place at the Slade School of Fine Art, but his family could not afford the expense. Group exhibitions included RWA of which he was a member; Fimbarrus and Arnolfini Galleries, in Bath and Bristol; Bear Lane Gallery, Oxford; Louise Hallett Gallery; and New Art Centre. Had a first solo show at Fimbarrus Gallery in 1959, later ones including Gisela van Beers, 1991, and Anthony Hepworth, Bath, 1992. Balmer was represented in public and private collections in Britain and abroad.

Thomas BALSTON 1883–1967 Writer and painter in oil, born at Bearsted, Kent. Balston was educated at Eton College and Oxford University. During the 1930s he studied painting for a short period with Mark Gertler and he exhibited extensively at Redfern Gallery. He was a discriminating collector whose own pictures are held by Manchester City Art Gallery and the Ashmolean Museum, Oxford. Balston was a connoisseur who contributed to the specialist periodicals *Image* and *Signature* and who wrote several books on wood engraving, including a study of Robert Gibbings. Savile and Garrick Club member who lived in London.

Kathleen BAMFORD 1879– Oil and watercolour painter, born in Hull. Studied part-time at the School of Art there, in Finland and portrait painting in London with Arthur Hickman-Smith. Exhibited at Hull College of Art, SWA and Islington Art Circle. Lived in Greenford, Middlesex. Diabetes and poor sight prevented Bamford working in her later years.

William BANBURY 1871– Sculptor and craftsman in various materials, born in Leicester, to which he eventually returned, living at Newtown Linford. Studied at Leicester College of Art, the Royal College of Art and in Paris, winning a number of medals. He went on to become head of sculpture at Aberdeen College of Art. Banbury showed at RA, RSA, elsewhere in Scotland and in Leicester. Arbroath Public Library and Forfar Academy obtained his work. Banbury was an honorary member of RBS.

John BANGS 1949– Artist, teacher and administrator, born in Hendon, north London, who studied at Reading University's fine art department, 1969–71, then at Goldsmiths', 1971–2, teachers including Terry Frost, Claude Rogers and Roger Cook. Taught between 1972–89 at Bow Secondary School and Templars' Special School, then held several administrative positions with National Union of Teachers. Bangs worked especially in dry pastel, also oil pastel. He favoured "straight and strong drawing where the colour holds the meaning". Brittany, notably Finistère, and Greenwich, where he lived, were key inspirations, and Edward Hopper, Bonnard, Medardo Rosso and Cy Twombly were respected artists. Showed at Whitechapel Open from 1984, Greenwich Festival Open Studios from 1990, also at Woodlands Art Gallery, Café Gallery and Blackheath Concert Halls.

Shirley BANHAM 1942–1991 Draughtsman and painter, notably in egg tempera, born and lived in Chalfont St Peter, Buckinghamshire. Studied at High Wycombe Technical School of Art, 1977–9. Showed with SGA of which she was a member, at Mall Galleries and with local societies.

Brian BANKS 1939– Painter, born and lived in London, who studied at St Martin's School of Art, 1956–7, his teachers including James Dring and Edward Middleditch, and in private studios. Group exhibitions included William Ware, Lower, Ansdell and Obelisk Galleries in London; Colin Jellicoe Gallery, Manchester; Galerie Salammbo, Paris, from 1987; and Austen Hayes Gallery, York. Solo shows were held at Colin Jellicoe, Ansdell and Zaydler Galleries, Trinity Arts Centre in Tunbridge Wells and from 1984 at Leigh Gallery. British and foreign private collections held his work.

Harry BANKS 1869–1947 Printmaker and painter in watercolour, born in London. He attended Goldsmiths' College, later studying in Antwerp. Designed invitation card for coronation of Edward VII. In 1902 Banks moved to Thorncombe, Dorset, where he was a friend and neighbour of Lucien Pissarro. When the Banks' daughter Audrey was at school in Bristol they would live during term in Clifton, where Banks made prints of the city and docks. He also completed West Country views as well as continental scenes done on holiday. Showed with Bristol Savages, RWA, RI, RA, UA, Paris Salon and Print Makers' Society of California. Banks was unusual in printing his own plates, some in colour. Bristol City Art Gallery has his work. Banks was buried in Salcombe, Devon.

Lesley BANKS 1962– Painter and teacher, born in Oxford, who studied at Glasgow School of Art, 1980–4, gaining an honours degree in drawing and painting. In 1985–6 she won an Elizabeth

Greenshields Foundation, allowing European travel, with several months in Amsterdam. After a period working at Compass Gallery, Glasgow, 1987–9, she left to paint full-time, in 1990 being visiting artist on the Castle Toward, Strathclyde Education, art course. Further awards included Royal Glasgow Institute of the Fine Arts David Cargill Award in 1990; and in 1991 the Scottish Artist Prize at Royal Over-Seas League Open and the Scottish Amicable Award at the Royal Glasgow Institute. Banks took part in many group shows from 1984, where she appeared in New Generation Artists at Compass; also Paisley Drawing Competition, Paisley Museum, from 1989; Jobson's Choice, Jill George Gallery, 1992; and Royal Over-Seas League Open, 1995. Banks' work blended realistic and Surrealist elements. Aberdeen Art Gallery, Lillie Art Gallery in Milngavie, BBC Scotland and Motherwell District Libraries hold examples.

Peter BANKS 1950– Artist and teacher who employed photographs, wooden structures and ceramics to create works for galleries, outdoor walls and hoardings. He was born in Newcastle upon Tyne and studied at Leeds Polytechnic, 1969–72. Was a technician at Lincoln College of Art, 1972–3, teaching appointments including Salford and Southwark Colleges. Showed at ICA, Peterloo Gallery in Manchester and in Summer Show 3 at Serpentine Gallery, 1981. Had a solo show at Monks Hall, Eccles, in 1974, later ones including Whitworth Art Gallery in Manchester, 1980. Lived for a time in London.

Robert BANKS 1911– Watercolourist and architect, born in Cheltenham, Gloucestershire. He was a qualified architect who was professionally engaged in town planning until the late 1950s, when he had more time to paint. Showed at Trafford and Alwin Galleries and lived in London. Banks was a fellow of the RIBA.

Roger BANKS 1929– Artist in watercolour and oil and writer concentrating on botanical subjects. Spent 1952–5 with Falkland Islands Dependencies Survey on Antarctic service, married in 1964 and settled in Crail, Fife. From 1990–4 was chairman of the School of Scottish Artists in Malta. Among his books were *The Unrelenting Ice*, 1962; *Living in a Wild Garden*, 1980; and *Cottage Garden Flowers*, 1983. Showed with the Imperial Institute in 1955, then from 1970 with Oliver Swann Galleries, National Trust, National Trust for Scotland and Scottish Wildlife Trust. Was a member of the Botanical Society of the British Isles who specialised in painting wild flowers on site, especially Scottish arctic and alpine plants. British Museum botanical library and HM Queen Elizabeth The Queen Mother hold his work.

Delmar BANNER 1896–1983 Oil and watercolour painter specialising in portraits. Born at Freiburg-in-Breisgau, Germany, Banner studied at Cheltenham, Oxford and Regent Street Polytechnic. He married the sculptor Josephina de Vasconcellos, with whom he shared two shows. The Ashmolean, Fitzwilliam and Victoria & Albert Museums hold his work as do many other public galleries throughout Britain. Lived at Little Langdale, Ambleside, Cumbria, Lake District scenes being a feature of his work.

Fiona BANNER 1966– Artist in various media, born Merseyside, who gained her bachelor's degree at Kingston Polytechnic, 1986–9, and her master's at Goldsmiths' College, 1991–3. Group exhibitions included Artificial Eden, Camerawork Gallery, 1993; Drawings at Laure Genillard Gallery, BT New Contemporaries at Camden Arts Centre with tour, and The Antidote, Centre 181 Gallery, all 1994; 4 Projects, Frith Street Gallery, and Venice Biennale, both 1995. Had a solo show Pushing Back the Edge of the Envelope, at City Racing, 1994. Lived and worked in London.

Afrakuma BANNERMAN 1950– Painter in oil and enamel, born in Accra, Gold Coast, who was educated in England, including Malvern Girls' College. Studied art at Kingston Polytechnic, 1969–73, and London University Institute of Education, graduating with honours with an art teacher's certificate. Taught part-time at the Institute in mid-1970s. Showed Mall Galleries, Woodstock and Ibis Galleries and abroad. Lived in London.

Geoff BANNISTER 1924– Commercial artist, designer and teacher, born in Birmingham, not far from where he settled in Walsall, West Midlands. During World War II he served in the Royal Navy, in the mid-1940s teaching commercial art while still in uniform. He went on to form his own design consultancy while continuing to paint a variety of subjects.

Adrian BANNON 1959– Artist who studied at University of Reading. He took part in various group exhibitions, including Art in Boxes, England & Co, 1992. Was artist-in-residence at Goldsmiths' College, 1985–6, in 1987 having a solo show at Oriel Gallery in north Wales. England & Co gave Bannon another one-man exhibition in 1994 of works in the Arte Povera tradition, "using simple or 'poor' materials to create works that are rich in their power to evoke associations or ideas".

John BANTING 1902–1972 Surrealist painter and designer, born in London. Banting studied under Bernard Meninsky at evening classes at Westminster School of Art from 1921, going to Paris the following year for further studies. Returning to London in 1925 he became connected with the Bloomsbury Group painters, joined LG and showed with the 7 & 5 Society. At the beginning of the 1930s he again went to France where he met Breton, Creval, Giacometti, Duchamp and other artists. Further activities included designing for the Carmargo Society ballet *Pomona*; designing book jackets for Hogarth Press; in 1936 contributing pictures to the International Surrealist Exhibition, in London; and travelling to Madrid during the Spanish Civil War, where he met Ernest Hemingway, the writer. During World War II he was involved in Strand Films and was art editor of *Our Time*, a left-wing political monthly. After the war Banting published *A Blue Book of Conversation*. Lived in rural Ireland for a while, then settled near his friend Edward Burra at Hastings, Sussex, where he died. Since his death Banting has been included in many exhibitions connected with Surrealism, and he was given a retrospective at Oliver Bradbury and James Birch, 1983.

Cuillin BANTOCK 1935– Artist in a range of media, including oil pastel and lino-cut, born in Birmingham. He studied at the School of Art there, 1953–5; Oxford School of Art, 1955–61 (part-time while reading zoology and evolutionary ecology at the University), gaining his bachelor's degree in 1958, then his master's degree and doctorate in 1961; and at Camberwell College of Art, 1961–4. Important teachers were Robert Medley, Henry Inlander, Euan Uglow, Richard Eurich and Anthony Eyton, main influences being Lanyon, de Staël and Hofmann. Bantock spent two decades as a professional environmentalist, with several books and many scientific papers published, then returned to painting full-time in 1989. Bantock regarded himself "as a landscape painter, but I mostly work non-figuratively, as I believe that sensation and metaphor are more important than illusion and narrative ... My background in ecology indirectly informs all my work." Took part in numerous mixed and solo shows, main ones being Clevedon: Sharing a View, APT Gallery and tour, 1997–8; two-man shows at Woodlands Art Gallery in 1995 and Beardsmore Gallery, 1997; with a solo exhibition at Cut Gallery, 1994. Cuillin (pronounced Coolin) Bantock organised a number of exhibitions, such as the inaugural Made in Greenwich 1974–1994, in 1994 at The Living Room. He was also a director of The Art in Perpetuity Trust and helped to run The Bantock Society, the composer Granville Bantock being his grandfather. Lived in London.

Janina BARANOWSKA 1925– Painter, born in Grodno, Poland, where she stayed until World War II, in 1940 being deported to Russia. After leaving there with the Polish Army for the Middle East, she finished her education in Palestine and settled in Britain in 1945. Studied at Borough Polytechnic, 1946–9, Polish University in London, 1951–4, then Putney School of Art, 1955–9. She was a leading member of the Association of Polish Artists in Great Britain, being its chairman, 1980–91. Group shows included New Burlington Galleries, 1955; Grabowski Gallery from 1959; Westminster Cathedral, 1984; and in 1993 she was in Polish Roots – British Soil, at City Art Centre, Edinburgh. As well as a series of solo shows at Drian Gallery from 1958, latterly exhibited at Bloomsbury Gallery, London University, 1988, and Zacheta Gallery, Warsaw, 1991. Public and private collections in Britain and abroad hold her work. Lived in London.

Bruno BARBIER 1962– Sculptor and teacher of Swiss origin who completed a foundation course at Watford College of Art, 1980–1, then graduated with honours in sculpture at Canterbury College of Art, 1981–4. He was a part-time lecturer at South Kent College of Technology in Ashford, 1984–5, then had two visiting lectureships in architecture: 1989 at Polytechnic of East London, and 1991 at Oxford Polytechnic. Barbier's mixed shows included St Augustine's Abbey Gardens, Canterbury, 1983; The Festival of London, Alexandra Park, 1988; Swiss Artists in Britain 1991, *The Economist* Building, 1991; and Sculpture at Canterbury, 1992. He had a solo show at Trinity Arts Centre, Tunbridge Wells, 1985; another at Gallery 22, Forest Row, 1986; and Sculpture, Recent Works, at Crypt Gallery, 1991.

Colville BARCLAY 1913– Painter, born in London, son of Sir Colville Barclay. He was educated at Eton College and Oxford, obtaining a master's degree, studying art at Ruskin School of Art with Albert Rutherston. Showed in mixed exhibitions at RA, RBA, LG and at public galleries in Bradford, Brighton and Sheffield. Arts Council, Bradford City Art Gallery and the London County Council Pictures for Schools scheme held his work. Sir Colville lived near Petworth, Sussex.

John Rankine BARCLAY 1884–1964 Painter and etcher, born in Edinburgh, who studied there and on the continent. He won a Carnegie Travelling Scholarship and the Guthrie Award and showed at RSA Royal Glasgow Institute of the Fine Arts and elsewhere. Barclay was a member of the Edinburgh Group formed just before World War II and was represented in the exhibition covering it at City Art Centre, Edinburgh, and touring, 1983. He went on to paint in an often experimental style and lived for over 30 years in St Ives, Cornwall, where he was associated with such artists as Sven Berlin and Misomé Peile. Stoke-on-Trent City Museum and Art Gallery bought his picture The Pont Neuf.

Stephen BARCLAY 1961– Painter, born in Ayrshire, who did degree and postgraduate studies at Glasgow School of Art, 1980–5. He gained a Hospitalfield Summer Scholarship, 1983, and an Adam Bruce Thomson Award, 1984. His many group appearances included Royal Glasgow Institute of the Fine Arts, 1984; Compass Gallery, Glasgow, from 1984–5; Warwick Arts Trust, 1985; Clare Hall, Cambridge, New Art from Scotland, 1986; and Galerie Bureaux & Magasins, Oostende, 1991. Had a solo show at Paton Gallery, 1987, then a series at Raab Galerie, Berlin and London, from 1989. Contemporary Art Society, Metropolitan Museum of Modern Art in New York and provincial galleries hold his work. Lived near Arbroath, Angus.

Kenneth BARDEN 1924–1988 Architect, designer, teacher and painter, born in Huddersfield, Yorkshire. He took apprenticeship to a decorator, studying at Huddersfield School of Art, where his father Harry taught, then was at Royal College of Art, 1947, under Gilbert Spencer and Ernest Tristram. Taught at Croydon College of Art, then, although he wanted to paint full-time, joined George Wimpey & Company. As the firm's principal architect he designed several hundred murals worldwide. Was a member of RI and also showed at ROI, RA, at public galleries in Huddersfield and Winchester and in London. As well as large watercolour landscapes and still lifes, Barden in later years was a witty designer of figure pieces. His murals were in flats in Kingston upon Thames, factories in Sheffield and schools in Croydon. Lived latterly in Chiswick, west London.

Geoffrey BARGERY 1938– Painter and illustrator, born in Cardiff, South Wales. Attended Kingston School of Art, 1953–8, then Royal Academy Schools, 1958–61, when Peter Greenham taught him. Did a considerable amount of mural and other commissioned work for bodies such as the BBC and the Institute of Directors. Nuffield Foundation holds his work. Lived in Surbiton, Surrey.

Jean BARHAM 1924– Painter and printmaker, born and lived in London, whose main interest was depicting the River Thames. She studied at Camberwell School of Art, 1947–50, with Lawrence Gowing, Claude Rogers, Victor Pasmore and William Coldstream. Was a member of Greenwich Printmakers and was an award winner in the Spirit of London Competition at Royal Festival Hall in 1979. Also exhibited at Blackheath Concert Halls and Greenwich Theatre. Had a solo show at World Trade Centre, 1973, another at clipper *Cutty Sark*, Greenwich, 1979.

Allen BARKER 1937– Artist who was born in Australia, son of the artist Keith David, who studied at National Art School in Sydney, 1955–60. Showed at Lucy Milton Gallery; Ikon Gallery, Birmingham, ICA; Ferens Art Gallery, Hull; and abroad. British and foreign galleries hold his work. Lived in London.

Cecily Mary BARKER 1895–1973 Painter, illustrator and writer of children's books, born in Croydon. After private education she was largely self-taught as an artist, although she did study part-time at Croydon School of Art and she continued to live in the town for a while, then in Storrington, Sussex. Although she exhibited SWA, RI and elsewhere, she was principally known for her illustrations of fairy children, as in *Flower Fairies of the Spring*, 1923, and *Flower Fairies of the Wayside*, 1948. Also did stained glass windows, her work featuring in St Andrew's Church, Croydon, and St George's Church at Waddon. Signed work CMB.

Clive BARKER 1940– Sculptor in bronze, born in Luton, Bedfordshire. He studied at Luton College of Technology and Art, 1957–9. Mixed exhibitions included Young Contemporaries, RBA Galleries, 1962; New Idioms, Robert Fraser Gallery, 1966; Young British Artists, Museum of Modern Art, New York, 1968; Der Geist des Surrealismus, Baukunst-Galerie, Cologne, 1971; British Artists of the 60s, Tate Gallery, 1977; British Pop Art, Birch and Conran, 1987; and Serpentine Gallery, 1991. After a solo show at Robert Fraser Gallery, 1968, later ones included Boxes, Wolverhampton Art Gallery, 1985, and Portraits, National Portrait Gallery, 1987. Arts Council, British Council, Imperial War Museum and Smithsonian Institute in Washington hold his work. Lived in London.

Dale Devereux BARKER 1962– Versatile printmaker and lecturer, born in Leicester, who studied at Loughborough College of Art and Design, 1980–1; Leicester Polytechnic (travelling scholarship – award), 1981–4; and Slade School of Fine Art, 1984–6. In 1996 he was elected a fellow of RE. Teaching appointments included visiting lectureships at Leicester Polytechnic, 1986–92, and North Hertfordshire College, 1991–2, from 1991 lecturing at University College, Suffolk. Between 1992–6, Barker was workshop co-ordinator at Gainsborough's House, Sudbury. Group shows included The Eagle Gallery; National Print Exhibition, Mall Galleries (Robert Horne Award); 2nd Kochi International Print Biennale, Japan (Commended); 10th and 11th British International Print Biennale, Cartwright Hall, Bradford (Forbo-Nairn Prize for Best Linocut); and Barbican Centre. Had a solo show, Leaves to Find, Galerie Dusseldorf, Perth, Australia, 1989, later ones including a retrospective at The Fermoy Arts Centre, King's Lynn, 1995, and Come Upstairs and see my Etchings!, Christchurch Mansion, Ipswich, 1996–7. Commissions included Elton John Aids Foundation; Russell Davies (Container Freight); British Rail Freight; and Lloyds Building. Victoria & Albert Museum, Ipswich Museums and Galleries, Ashmolean Museum in Oxford, Wakefield Museum, a number of county council and corporate collections hold examples.

David BARKER 1945– A printmaker and teacher, Barker was born in Dorchester, Dorset. He studied at Goldsmiths' College School of Art, 1962–7, where Paul Drury was among his teachers. He was a member of the Printmakers' Council and worked on the printmaking side at the College of Art in Cambridge, where he lived, 1967–8, then moved to Northern Ireland where from 1974 he was senior lecturer at the school of fine art at Ulster College. His many exhibitions included Grabowski Gallery, Octagon Gallery in Belfast, Arts Council of Northern Ireland Gallery and Third Eye Centre in Glasgow. New University of Ulster, Southwark Print Collection and California College of Arts and Crafts in America hold examples.

John Edward BARKER 1889–1953 Painter in oil and watercolour, son of the artist John Joseph Barker. Studied at Bath School of Art, 1905–10, under Nathaniel Heard, and the Camden School of Art, in London, 1910–13. Exhibited at the City Art Gallery, Manchester, and elsewhere in the provinces. Was head of the art department at Bacup and Rawtenstall Grammar School, near where he lived in Rossendale, Lancashire.

John Rowland BARKER 1911–1959 Painter and draughtsman who taught for many years in Sussex and London. Studied at Leicester School of Art until 1932, then moved to London where he began a career as a graphic designer, producing stylised posters and magazine designs for companies such as Shell, Imperial Chemical Industries and British Railways, as well as fabrics for Sanderson. Showed widely in America and his work was reproduced in magazines such as *Graphis* and the *Architectural Review*, sometimes just signed JB. From the 1940s began a series of paintings with nautical links, a group of which was shown at Waterhouse and Dodd in 1991, providing comparisons with Edward Wadsworth or John Tunnard. Lived at Fordingbridge, Hampshire.

Kit BARKER 1916–1988 Painter and teacher, correct name Gordon Barker, he was born in London, the brother of the poet George Barker. He attended Northampton School of Art. In the mid-1940s Barker lived in Cornwall, at Newlyn and near Zennor, before going to America, where from 1949–53 he taught at Skidmore College, New York, and California School of Fine Arts. Many exhibitions included Waddington Galleries and his work is held by extensive collections including Arts Council and public galleries in Aberdeen, Bradford and Eastbourne. Barker's pictures are often of landscape with water in a near-abstract style. Settled in 1953 at Lodsworth, Sussex. Barker's War Composition, of 1944, was included in Messages from Nowhere at Austin/Desmond & Phipps, 1991.

Margaret BARKER 1907– Figure painter, born in London, who studied at Royal College of Art, 1925–9, under Randolph Schwabe. He pressed her to show her canvas Any Morning at NEAC in 1929, and through the Chantrey Bequest it found its way to Tate Gallery.

Patrick BARKER 1959– Figurative sculptor, creator of free-standing pieces and wall reliefs. He often used a soft limestone to produce amusing, rounded, tactile characters. Born in Shropshire, Barker studied at Bristol Polytechnic, 1978–9, Bath Academy of Art, 1979–82, then did a postgraduate course at Cyprus College of Art, 1984–5. Group shows included RWA, 1986; Millfield Open, Millfield School, 1990; and Ghent International Arts Fair, Belgium, 1992. His solo shows were Andrew Usiskin Contemporary Art, 1991, and Beaux Arts, Bath, 1992. In 1993 Barker shared a show at New Academy Gallery and Business Art Galleries. Lived in West Harptree, Somerset.

Peter BARKER-MILL 1908–1994 Mainly abstract artist in oil, gouache, wood engraving and sculpture, born in Italy. He was married for a time to the artist Elsa Vaudrey, their daughter being the painter Amanda Barker-Mill. Barker-Mill attended Sandhurst, spent several years abroad in the Army, then gave up his commission to attend the Grosvenor School of Modern Art under Iain Macnab for three years, followed by 18 months, from 1932, under André Lhote in Paris. Barker-Mill then showed with LG, NEAC and several London galleries; worked on settings and associated figures for the film *Paper People Land*; was commissioned by Golden Cockerel Press, 1937–55, to make wood engravings for four books; in World War II was in the Civil Defence Camouflage Unit; then in 1944 joined the Ministry of Town and Country Planning Model Unit. Mural materials research occupied him in the 1950s, then from 1961–81 Barker-Mill did commissioned work. He pursued "the communicative power and potential of colour, its organisation upon a surface and in space" in his own abstract pictures. Had an important show at Arnolfini Gallery, Bristol, 1989, another at The Minories, Colchester, in 1991. Lived at Wookey Hole, Somerset, and died from a stroke in hospital in Bristol.

Harold BARKLAM 1912– Painter in oil and watercolour, and teacher, born in Tipton, Staffordshire. He attended Ryland Memorial School of Art, West Bromwich, Royal College of Art under Gilbert Spencer, 1933–6, then Birmingham College of Arts and Crafts, 1936–7. Apart from Army service, 1940–6, taught at schools of art in West Bromwich, Kidderminster, Bilston and Lowestoft, 1937–50, finally at Derby School of Art, 1950–76. Completed a number of mural paintings as well as pictures of stately homes for English Life Publications, Derby. Showed at Derby and Birmingham Art Galleries and elsewhere in Midlands. Lived at Littleover, Derby.

Elsie BARLING 1883–1976 Teacher, painter and draughtsman, born in Newnham, Gloucestershire. Little is known of her early life or training, and she appears to have been largely self-taught. Her father died when she was young and, now living in Broadstairs, Kent, she supported the family by teaching in schools. At Queen Bertha's School, Birchington, she and the pupils made a mural of the landing of Queen Bertha. John Craxton, taught by her at Betteshanger School, Eastry, in the early 1930s, called her "an inspired teacher". Pupils' work was shown at Bloomsbury Gallery in 1933 opened by Slade principal Henry Tonks, to national press acclaim. The main influence on Barling was Frances Hodgkins, whom she met at her class at Burford in 1923 and with whom she painted abroad. When World War II broke out Barling moved to Studland, Dorset, teaching at Bryanston School, 1940–3. Barling was a fine draughtsman rather than a notable Colourist, and was fond of working in gouache, as seen in her memorial show at Dorset Country Museum, Dorchester, in 1977.

Bohuslav BARLOW 1947– Painter, born in Czechoslovakia, who moved to England aged eight. He eventually settled in Todmorden, Yorkshire. Gained honours degree from Central School of Art. Barlow's pictures featured situations such as playing, dreaming or floating, the characters in them being clowns and puppets based on real, life-size figures which he created. The world they inhabit is generally the stony architecture of the Pennines. He began showing with South-East London Art Group and RE in 1970 and went on to appear in numerous group exhibitions, including Hartnoll & Eyre, 1976; MAFA from 1982; Chalk Farm Gallery, 1984; and House of Commons, in a show of Calderdale Artists, 1987. Showed solo at Ginnel Gallery, Manchester, and Grundy Art Gallery, Blackpool, 1989. Rochdale Art Gallery and Museum and Leeds City Council hold his work.

Gillian BARLOW 1944– Watercolourist on paper and vellum, and teacher, noted for her paintings of flowers. She was born in Khartoum, Sudan, and gained a diploma in fine arts at Slade School of Fine Art, 1962–3, before studying with Quentin Bell and Hans Hess at University of Sussex, acquiring a bachelor's and master's degree in the history of art. Her work combined a personal freedom with scientific precision in the tradition of Bauer, Ehret and Redouté, the rose painter. She was sent to India by the British Council as visiting professor at Baroda University, also living in New York producing sets of flower paintings for interior decorators wanting the English look. Showed all over the world, with a solo exhibition, The Botanical Garden, at Spink & Son, 1995. The previous year Barlow had gained the Royal Horticultural Society Gold Medal for painting. British Council; Boscobel Restoration and Vassar College, both in New York; and The Hunt Institute, Carnegie-Mellon University, Pittsburgh, hold examples.

Jeremy BARLOW 1945– Painter, notably of landscapes and townscapes in oil, born in Kettering, Northamptonshire, who studied at Northampton School of Art, 1960. Worked in art studios in London and Midlands, then in 1977 moved to Düsseldorf, Germany, and showed extensively in Germany and Netherlands, returning to live in England in 1983, settling in Norfolk. Mixed exhibitions included RI, RA Summer Exhibition and ROI, of which he was elected a full member in 1993. Had first solo exhibition at Mistral Galleries in 1994, previous one-mans including Bourne Gallery, Reigate, 1991, and Llewellyn Alexander, 1992.

Phyllida BARLOW 1944– Sculptor in a variety of media, printmaker and teacher. She was born in Newcastle upon Tyne, Northumberland, and studied at Chelsea School of Art, 1960–3, and Slade School of Fine Art, 1963–6, then returning to Chelsea to teach. Early on she participated in group shows such as Young Contemporaries, LG, AIA and at Woodstock Gallery and Camden Arts Centre. In 1976 shared a two-man exhibition with Fabian Peake at St Catherine's College, Oxford.

Sid BARLOW 1952– Painter, stained glass artist and teacher, born in Chile. He studied at Wolverhampton College of Art, 1972–5, Manchester Polytechnic, 1976–7, and Glasgow School of Art, 1984–5. Went on to teach stained glass at W R Tuson College, Preston. His group shows included Royal Glasgow Institute of the Fine Arts, 1985, MAFA, 1988, and in 1989–90 John Moores Liverpool Exhibition. Had a solo exhibition at Rochdale College of Art in 1987. Lived in Bolton, Lancashire.

Yvonne BARLOW fl. from 1950s– Painter who studied at Central School of Arts and Crafts, Chelsea School of Art and London University. Her work appeared in many mixed shows including RA, Paris Salon, Whitechapel Art Gallery, LG and at Christopher Hull Gallery, where she was given a solo exhibition in 1989. Lived in London.

Gwen BARNARD 1912–1988 Painter and printmaker who studied at Chelsea School of Art. She was for some time chairman of WIAC. As well as group shows she had many solo exhibitions, including AIA, Drian Gallery, Camden Arts Centre, Upper Street Gallery and abroad. Lived for many years in the famous Mall Studios, Hampstead. Her history of them appeared in the *Camden History Review*, in 1980. Barnard's work was originally naturalistic, but under the influence of a Polish painter friend in the 1940s she turned more towards abstraction, being at various times concerned with themes such as river and rock shapes.

Margaret BARNARD 1898–1992 Painter, draughtsman, lino-cut artist and designer, born in India, but moved to Scotland aged seven for schooling. Attended Glasgow School of Art, winnin two travelling scholarships and the Guthrie Award. She journeyed to Italy where she married fellow-student Robert Mackechnie. She loved the light of Italy and they decided that they could live cheaply in a small coastal town not far from Florence. Landscapes, done in Italy and on the Scottish west coast, especially lona, were a key feature of her output, signed MB in monogram form. Her lino-prints typified British graphic work of the 1920s/1930s, with clean lines and subtle colouring. Winter Cavalcade, 1938, and Leisure Days in the Parks, 1939, were posters commissioned by London Underground. In 1994 there was a memorial show at Rye Art Gallery which holds her work. She lived in the Sussex town from 1934.

Roger BARNARD 1951– Artist in variety of media, including set-ups, some including video; mixed-media installations; painting; sculpture; drawing; photography; holography; writing; and teaching, who was born and lived in London. He attended West Sussex College of Design, 1970–1, then graduated in fine art from North Staffordshire Polytechnic, 1971–4. From 1971–2 was engaged in use of holograms; 1976–8 lectured occasionally at Maidstone College of Art and Lanchester Polytechnic and was founder-member and first chairman of London Video Arts (Access); from 1980 being involved in Video Artists on Tour. Took part in mixed shows at Tate Gallery, Serpentine Gallery, Hayward Gallery and in provincial events. Had solo shows at Tate, Air Gallery, Third Eye Centre in Edinburgh, Royal Cornwall Museum in Truro and elsewhere. That museum and Contemporary Art Centre in Osaka, Japan, hold his work.

Thomas Henslow BARNARD 1898– Painter, printmaker and teacher who studied at West of England College of Art, Bristol, having attended Malvern College. He was commissioned as a Sandhurst-trained officer in the Army in both World Wars. Showed at RA, RWA to which he was elected in 1972 and NEAC. Ministry of Works and public galleries in Cheltenham and Gloucester held his work. Was a member of Cheltenham Group of Artists. Lived at Leckhampton, Gloucestershire.

Hugh BARNDEN 1946– Designer and painter, born Oxfordshire, who studied at Royal College of Art, 1968–71. Mixed shows included Crafts Centre from 1964; Eroticism in Fashion at ICA, 1976; London Fashion Designers at Victoria & Albert Museum, which holds his work, 1979; Wapping Artists Open Studios from 1980. Solo exhibitions included Francis Kyle, 1983. Lived for some years in London.

Alfred Richard Innott BARNES: *see* **INNOTT**

Ann BARNES 1951– Botanical artist using airbrush, and teacher, born in London, daughter of the watercolourist William Barnes. Attended Stockwell College of Education, Bromley, and graduated with honours. Showed with Free Painters and Sculptors, to which she was elected in 1974, NS and Society of Botanical Artists. Had a series of solo shows in Home Counties galleries. Lived in Ewell, Surrey.

Desmond BARNES 1921– Painter, commercial artist and printmaker who after several years' initial art training in Birmingham attended the College of Art there, 1936–42, under Bernard Fleetwood-Walker. He went on to show at RA, ROI, RWA, NEAC, in the provinces and at the Paris Salon, where he gained an Honourable Mention and bronze medal in the 1940s. Lived at Handsworth, Birmingham, then in London.

Garlick BARNES 1891–1987 Artist in oil and watercolour, born in London, who showed an early talent but had to defer painting while she brought up four children. She then studied at Sidney Cooper School of Art in Canterbury, Heatherley's School of Fine Art and in 1936 became Walter Sickert's pupil when they were both living in Thanet. She showed a Sickert-influenced picture, La Ballerina, in an exhibition with him at E J Lovely & Sons Art Gallery, Margate. At the outbreak of World War II Barnes moved to Cornwall, where she became a member of the St Ives and Newlyn Societies and a founder-member of the Penwith Society of Arts. She continued to paint, garden and write poetry into her eighties. Barnes' twin sons John and Bill were keen filmmakers and students of the cinema, for over 20 years from the mid-1960s running a museum on the subject in St lves. John Barnes published several volumes on the history of the Victorian cinema.

George William BARNES 1909– Painter, sculptor, printmaker and designer, born in Boothstown, Lancashire. Studied at Huddersfield School of Art, 1925–36. Showed with Huddersfield Art Society, which gave him a one-man show, and with Saddleworth Art Club, being a member of both. Lived in Marsden, West Yorkshire.

Jeannette BARNES 1961– Draughtsman, painter and teacher, born in Great Harwood, Lancashire, and studied at Accrington and Rossendale Foundation College; Liverpool Polytechnic; Royal Academy Schools; and Royal College of Art. She taught at Liverpool Polytechnic, 1984–9; was artist-in-residence at Northampton School for Boys, 1990–1; then became outreach teacher for the RA's education department. Among her awards were a John Moores Scholarship, 1983; Armitage Prize, 1985; Richard Ford Spanish Scholarship, 1987; and she was a Drawing for All prizewinner in 1994. Mixed shows included RA Summer Exhibition from 1986; NEAC, 1991; and Royal Over-Seas League Open from 1992. Had a solo show at Blackburn College of Art, 1984.

Maurice BARNES 1911–1971 Painter, draughtsman and noted watercolourist, born in Swansea. He was educated in Newport, Monmouthshire, and spent his life there, studying at the local College of Art, Croydon School of Art and with William Watkins. His career was with British Rail, but his two main preoccupations were painting and the Church of Wales. Barnes was a founder-member, chairman and president of Newport Art and Crafts Society, also exhibiting at NEAC, RA, Royal National Eisteddfod, Paris Salon and elsewhere. CASW holds his work, also Newport Museum & Art Gallery, which in 1997 gave Barnes a retrospective, which concentrated on pictures of Newport, St Woolos' Cathedral and Christchurch and St John the Baptist, both severely damaged by fire in 1948.

Melanie BARNES 1966– Artist who worked in mixed media who studied at Leicester and Liverpool Polytechnics. She showed at Fouts and Fowler, Design Association, Association of Illustrators and was included in Art in Boxes at England & Co, 1991.

Pauline Margaret BARNES: *see* **Pauline Margaret BEILBY**

Robert Henry BARNES 1899–1979 Painter who spent much of his life in Surrey after living in London. He showed at Royal Glasgow Institute of the Fine Arts, RBA, Walker Art Gallery in Liverpool and from 1924–53 at RA, latterly having a studio at Bridgnorth, Shropshire. Simon Carter Gallery, Woodbridge, included a typical portrait, Jean, in a mixed show in April 1992.

Ross BARNES 1962– Constructionist/printmaker whose work displayed wit and social comment. He was born at Castallack, Lamorna, Cornwall, eventually having a studio at The Penwith Gallery, St Ives. Barnes began showing at Salt House Gallery in St Ives from 1990 and joined the Penwith Society of Arts as an associate member. Completed a two-year course in general art and design at Falmouth School of Art, 1991–3, then studied for honours degree in fine art at Canterbury. Further exhibitions included From Cornwall, Art and Inspiration, Anderson Gallery, Broadway, and self-portrait exhibition at Porthmeor Gallery, St Ives, both 1992; New Work, at Rainy Day Gallery, Penzance, 1993; and St Ives at David Holmes Contemporary Art, Peterborough, 1996. In 1993 shared an exhibition with David Pearce at Salt House Gallery.

William BARNES 1916– Watercolour artist and designer, he was born in London and studied art at Camberwell and Wimbledon Schools of Arts and Crafts. He took part in mixed shows at the RI, RWS, RBA, PS and NS and held one-man exhibitions in Croydon, Ealing, Guildford, Leatherhead and Richmond and elsewhere in southeast England. The City of London, Massey Fergusson and the London Goldhawk Building Society own his work and he illustrated *In Britain* for the British Tourist Authority. Lived in London.

Christine BARNETT 1963– Artist in gouache, pen and ink and watercolour. She studied at Gloucestershire College of Arts and

Technology, then at West Surrey College of Art and Design where she obtained an honours degree in fine art – painting, 1983–6, being a research fellow, 1987–8. She began to show in mixed exhibitions in 1985 at Whitworth Young Contemporaries, Manchester. After many more appearances she was shown at the Bath Contemporary Art Fair, the Glyndebourne Festival and the 20th Century British Art Fair in 1992, when Marsden Fine Art gave her a solo show at Smith's of Covent Garden. Work included still lifes, often using primary colours and introducing mystical elements, dancing figures and symbolic birds. Lived in Pershore, Worcestershire.

Henry BARNETT 1916– Landscape painter and illustrator who studied at Cheltenham Art School and at the Royal Academy Schools under Thomas Monnington and Walter Westley Russell. Exhibited at RA from mid-1930s. Lived at Isleworth, Middlesex.

John BARNETT 1914– Self-taught painter, born in Manchester, who attended evening classes at Heginbottom School of Art, Ashton-under-Lyne, in textile design. As a painter he was drawn "to the urban landscape of my childhood". Showed at MAFA and elsewhere in north of England. Manchester City Art Gallery holds his oil on canvas Old House, Cheltenham. Lived in Droylsden, Lancashire.

May BARNETT: *see* **Alice May COOK**

Olaf BARNETT 1911– Painter, art dealer and private teacher, born in London. He was educated at Oxford University, studying art at the Ruskin School of Drawing and at the Slade School of Fine Art, his teachers including Randolph Schwabe and Barnett Freedman. He ran the Collectors' Gallery in London and Drusilla's Collectors' Gallery at Alfriston, Sussex. Showed RA, RBA, NS of which he was a member, on the continent and in North America. Towner Art Gallery, Eastbourne, holds his work. Lived in London, then in Seaford, Sussex.

Walter Durac BARNETT 1876– Painter, born in Leeds, where he attended the School of Art, also Wrexham and Lambeth Schools of Art , the latter under Innes Fripp, 1896–1900, where he won a medal and scholarship. During World War I served in Artists' Rifles. Exhibited RA, RP, ROI, NS, Goupil Gallery and in the provinces. Was a member of the Artists of Chelsea, a group living in or connected with that part of London. Cartwright Hall Art Gallery, Bradford, holds his work. Lived in London.

Catherine BARNEZET fl. from 1980s– Painter, printmaker, sculptor, photographer and installations artist, educated in England and France, who during the 1970s trained in beadwork, metalwork and paintwork and black-and-white photography; in 1980 gaining a playleader certificate at the Camden Institute; a certificate in arts, education and artistic therapy at Rudolph Steiner College, Fair Oaks, California, 1989; did an access foundation in art and design at Falmouth School of Art, 1993; then gained an honours degree in fine art at Plymouth University, 1996. Exhibited at Summer Show, Cabrillo Arts Center, Santa Barbara, 1985; Annual Show, Sacramento Fine Art Center Gallery, California, 1989; Aspires, Sherwell Centre, Plymouth, 1995; and Unquiet Voices, Doncaster Museum & Art Gallery, 1997. Lived in Exminster, Devon.

Denis BARNHAM 1920– Painter, draughtsman, writer and teacher, born in Feltham, Middlesex. Studied at Royal Academy Schools with Sir Walter Westley Russell, 1936–9. At end of World War II showed with war artists at National Gallery; also showing at RA, RBA, Leicester Galleries, NEAC and elsewhere. Imperial War Museum holds his work. Taught art for some years at Epsom College, in Surrey, and had strong interest in Oriental art. Lived in Epsom.

Nicholas BARNHAM 1939– Artist in watercolour and relief printing, and teacher, born in Walsingham, Norfolk. He studied painting and stone carving at Norwich School of Art, 1954–60, teachers including Jeffrey Camp and Malcolm Andrews. At various times Barnham lived in Shetland (where he eventually settled at Uyeasound, Unst, from 1984), Essex, Norfolk and north Yorkshire, as he favoured the east coast for his on-the-spot landscapes. In 1967–73 Barnham taught at Cambridge School of Art. Boats and trees were key themes in Barnham's very linear work, with early Mondrian, Edward Bawden, William Blake and Samuel Palmer strong influences. Showed at RA, RE and in Germany and had series of shows at Thackeray Gallery, The Old Fire Engine House, Ely, and at The Shetland Museum Gallery, Lerwick. Collections including his work were those of Cambridgeshire County Council, the musicians Richard Rodney Bennett and Christopher Hogwood, Somerville College, Oxford, and Marks and Spencer.

John BARNICOAT 1924– Painter, administrator and teacher. After World War II service in the Navy, Barnicoat studied history at Oxford University. He was a student at Royal College of Art, 1952–5, then was senior tutor there in the painting school, 1976–80, where he was very influential. He had his first one-man show at Galerie Colette Allendy, in Paris, in 1959. Was included in the Royal College of Art Exhibition Road show in 1988. Lived in London.

Denis BARNS 1946– Mural painter, sculptor, teacher and town art adviser, born in Kirkcaldy, Fife. Studied at Glasgow School of Art for a diploma in mural design, 1964–8, then did a year's post-diploma course. Taught in secondary schools in Dunbartonshire until appointment as town artist to Livingston Development Corporation, 1974. A wide range of artists, including Ian Hamilton Finlay, William Tucker and Andrew Mylius, plus members of the community were engaged by Barns, who in 1979 had received so many offers of work that he resigned his post and set up Town Art & Design Ltd. Barns was then a consultant to many United Kingdom local authorities, also working for Middle Eastern municipalities. Barns' work was collected by Glasgow

University, Edinburgh Corporation, Girvan Town Council and private collections, documented work being held in the Tate Gallery and Victoria & Albert Museum.

Wilhelmina BARNS-GRAHAM 1912– Painter and teacher, born in St Andrews, Fife. She attended Edinburgh College of Art, 1932–7, having a studio in the Scottish capital, 1936–40. In the latter year Barns-Graham pursued an Andrew Grant post-graduate travelling scholarship and went to live in St Ives, Cornwall, which with St Andrews remained her base. There she joined the Newlyn Society of Artists, the St Ives Society of Artists and became a founder-member of the Penwith Society in 1949. She had known Margaret Mellis in Edinburgh and now became friends with Ben Nicholson, Barbara Hepworth and Naum Gabo. A key influence was a visit to Switzerland in 1948, where she fell in love with glaciers as a subject, their transparency combined with their roughness. Took up an Italian Government Travelling Scholarship in 1955 which produced another impressive body of work emphasising her incisive draughtsmanship. Taught at Leeds School of Art, 1956–7, then from 1961–3 had studio in London before returning to St Ives. At an early age she had drawn abstracts in coloured chalks, and during the 1960s and 1970s Barns-Graham's work became more conceptually abstract. She exhibited at Downing's Bookshop, St Ives, in a solo show in 1947 and 1949 and showed steadily after that, selected venues being Roland, Browse and Delbanco; Richard Demarco Gallery, Edinburgh; New Art Centre; and Pier Arts Centre, Stromness. The first major retrospective of her work was organised at Newlyn Art Gallery, 1989–90 and touring. Arts Council and Scottish National Gallery of Modern Art hold her work.

Ian BARR 1946– Painter and administrator, born in Glasgow, where he graduated from the School of Art and where he continued to live. He became director of the Scottish Consultative Council on the Curriculum. Barr showed widely in Scandinavia and Scotland, producing some abstract work. He had solo shows at Compass Gallery in 1973 and 1977 and his work is in Scottish Arts Council and other public and private collections.

Shona BARR 1965– Painter in oil and watercolour who employed brilliant colour and fluent handling of paint. Born in Glasgow, she graduated from the School of Art there, 1984–8; won a postgraduate scholarship, Statens Kunstakademi, Oslo, Norway, 1988–9; and obtained her master's in European fine art from Winchester School of Art (Barcelona) and Southampton University, 1991–2. Awards included Glasgow School Landscape Prize, 1987; Armour Prize for Still Life, 1988; and David Cargill Award at Royal Glasgow Institute of the Fine Arts, 1989. Took part in extensive group shows, including Compass Gallery, Glasgow, from 1988; RSW from 1989; RSA from 1990; and RA from 1995. Had a series of solo exhibitions with Flying Colours Gallery from 1989. Lillie Art Gallery in Milngavie and a number of corporate collections hold examples.

Steven Thomas BARRACLOUGH 1953–1987 Printmaker, born in Batley, Yorkshire, where he attended the School of Art, 1969–71; then Camberwell School of Arts and Crafts, 1971–4; and Slade School of Fine Arts, 1974–5. In 1981, Barraclough obtained a one-year fellowship, in etching and lithography, at Manchester Print Workshop, University of Salford; in 1983 was printmaker-in-residence, Arts Council of Northern Ireland; in 1985 being invited for a three-month visit to China by the Minister of Culture, attending Central Academy of Fine Arts Beijing, Hangzhou and Canton Academy. Group exhibitions included RA, from 1974; Leeds City Art Gallery, 1977; Whitworth Art Gallery, Manchester, 1982; Exhibition of Hand Made Paper, Thumb Gallery, 1985; and Dolan Maxwell Gallery, Philadelphia, 1988. Showed with Angela Flowers Gallery from 1979. Victoria & Albert Museum; Museum of Modern Art, New York; Arts Councils of Ireland and Northern Ireland; Leeds Education Authority, and other public and corporate collections hold examples.

Paul BARRAND 1959– Painter who was born in Chesterfield, Derbyshire. He studied at the Polytechnics of Sheffield, 1977–8, Liverpool, 1978–81 and Leicester, 1981–2. He appeared in the Night and Day show in Leicester, 1984, and Metroland, at Loseby Gallery in Leicester, the same year. In 1984–5 Barrand's work was included in Midland View 3, and his landscape canvas Goodbye appeared in the 1987 John Moores Liverpool Exhibition. Lived in Leicester.

Elizabeth BARRATT 1956– Painter and teacher, born in London. She studied at Byam Shaw School of Art, 1974–6, won a David Murray Studentship in 1978, did a postgraduate course at Royal Academy Schools, 1978–81, winning the Henfield Foundation Award in 1980, the Boise Travelling Scholarship, to Italy, in 1981. She taught under a fellowship at Gloucestershire College of Art and Design, 1981–2, then in the latter year the Elizabeth Greenshields Award took her to Italy again. From 1985 taught occasionally at Byam Shaw. Barratt showed in National Portrait Gallery John Player Exhibition in 1984, at the RA from the same year, and a group show at Argile Gallery in 1988, the year she shared an exhibition at Brunel Gallery.

Kenneth BARRATT 1924– Painter, sometimes in semi-abstract style, illustrator, printmaker and teacher. Born in London, he attended East Ham Grammar School, where he initially became interested in painting, then Sir John Cass School of Arts and Crafts under Bainbridge Copnall. Showed at RA, NS, SGA and RI. Lived in London.

Krome BARRATT 1924–1990 Painter, teacher and writer, full name Kenneth Krome Barratt, who signed some work Krome. He studied civil engineering at West Ham College of Technology and art at Sir John Cass College, 1947–51. Was principal lecturer at Polytechnic of North London, lectured on history and technology of painting and was also an engineering designer. Work included abstracts, seascapes and landscapes. Published *Logic and Design* in 1980. Barratt was president of NS and ROI, a member of RBA, showing also at RA and overseas galleries. Had solo shows at

Drian Galleries and AIA. Towner Art Gallery, Eastbourne, holds his work. Lived in Hockley, Essex.

Oliver BARRATT 1962– Sculptor, draughtsman and teacher who obtained his bachelor's degree with honours in sculpture at Falmouth School of Art, 1983–5. He then taught at a Care home for mentally handicapped adults from 1986, at Streete Court School in Surrey, 1988–90, pre-foundation sculpture at Canterbury College, 1991–2, then first-year sculpture at Kent Institute of Art and Design, Canterbury, from 1992. He was Henry Moore Fellow there in 1991–2 and had an exhibition of his work in 1992. Barratt had a two-man show at The Pine Gallery in Tunbridge Wells, 1988; at Winchester Cathedral, 1989, King's Walk Gallery, 1991; *Economist* Building Plaza in 1992, represented by the New Art Centre; and in the same year at Roche Court, Salisbury. His commissions included Fuller's Brewery at Russia Docks, 1988; Eastern Arts, a collaboration project, 1990; and National Power, a Landmark Sculpture Commission, in 1991. The artist wrote that the forms he made had "their origin in experience. They are deeply autobiographical and point to the undefined heart of an experience". Lived in Ightham, Kent.

Guitti BARRATT-DENYER 1942– Painter in oil, also known as Guitti, born in Paris. He studied at University of Western Australia, 1980–4, showed in Western Australia and returned to London in 1985. Also trained under William Ware while living at Burwash Common, East Sussex. Was a member of Ridley and Chelsea Art Societies and showed at Hurlingham, New King's Road and Edith Grove Galleries.

Ronald BARRAUD 1906– Painter and architect who studied at the Welsh School of Architecture, 1925–8. Exhibited RA, NEAC, UA and in the provinces. Lived at Wollaton, Nottinghamshire.

Christopher BARRETT 1954– Artist and teacher using oil for easel pictures, acrylic for murals, specialising in these for hospitals from 1987. He was born in London and graduated in fine art painting from Bath Academy of Art, 1972–5. He taught at Banbury School of Art, 1980–90, then Rycotewood College, Thame, 1986–90. Was artist-in-residence, Chastleton House, Oxfordshire, 1989, and in 1992–3 at Furness General Hospital, Barrow-in-Furness. Was a designer for Dunford Wood hand-painted silk, 1991–2. Group shows included A Century of Art in Oxford, Museum of Modern Art, Oxford, 1993, Christie's, 1994, and Banbury Museum and Woodstock Museum, 1996. Solo exhibitions included Manor House Gallery, Chipping Norton, 1989. Murals included Wokingham Hospital, Berkshire, 1987; John Radcliffe Hospital, Oxford, 1993; Royal Free Hospital, 1995–6; and Leeds General Infirmary, 1997. Institute of Education holds Barrett's work. Lived in Lower Brailes, Banbury, Oxfordshire.

Elsie May BARRETT 1913– Painter, born in Stoke-on-Trent, Staffordshire. After local education she attended St Martin's School of Art under Harold Workman and City & Guilds School of Art, her teachers including Bernard Adams and A R Middleton Todd. Was elected to Royal Glasgow Institute of the Fine Arts and belonged to Free Painters and Sculptors; showed with Harpenden Arts Club, St Albans Art Club; won a number of overseas awards. Lived in Harpenden, Hertfordshire.

Max BARRETT 1937–1997 Sculptor and carver who was born in Penzance, Cornwall. He worked as a steeplejack and as a steel erector, then began sculpting full-time in 1972. His Gentle Wave at Land's End was commissioned by the St Ives Festival Committee in 1982. Barrett's work was included in Artists from Cornwall at RWA in 1992. Later completed a large granite sculpture outside Sainsbury's store in Truro, Cornwall, and lived in the county at Hayle. Had a solo show at The Acorn Theatre, Penzance, 1996. Barrett, who came from old Cornish and gypsy stock, was an uncompromising character, scornful of the orthodox artistic community, its committees and organisations, and this meant his sculpting career was not always smooth. Yet he was a deeply spiritual man who, commonly inspired by music, and using often unpromising materials, strove "to channel the beauty of life through my work".

Oliver O'Connor BARRETT 1908–1987 Sculptor, teacher, poet and composer, born in London, brother of the artist Roderic Barrett. He was educated at the Royal Grammar School, Colchester, and Fircroft College, Birmingham. He showed at RA and had a solo show at Cooling Galleries prior to World War II, then moved to America, 1940–70, where he supported himself and his family as a freelance sculptor and part-time teacher. Teaching positions included Museum of Modern Art, Brooklyn Museum and Cooper Union, in New York, as well as Norton Museum, Palm Beach. He also wrote for and presented a series of programmes on art for the NBC television channel. Additional appearances at RA took place at Summer Exhibitions when he had returned to England from America. Also in his life he showed in Birmingham, Colchester, New Orleans, New York, Palm Beach and Potsdam. Among his notable works are Christ and the Money Changers, 1949; Don Quixote's Deathbed, 1952; and Madonna and Child, 1953. Colchester Public Library and Hudson Walker Gallery hold his work, which is in many private collections in Britain and America. In 1980 the artist published a photographic record of his work with accompanying poems called *Myself Emerging*. Lived for some years in Colchester, Essex, later at Cwm Prysor, Trawsfynydd, Gwynedd.

Roderic BARRETT 1920– Painter, draughtsman and teacher, brother of the sculptor Oliver O'Connor Barrett, born and lived in Colchester, Essex. He studied at Central School of Arts and Crafts, teachers including Bernard Meninsky, John Farleigh and William Roberts, 1936–40. Began teaching in 1947, from 1968 being tutor at Royal Academy Schools. As an artist Barrett strove "to make works which are well made and without false feeling". Barrett's pictures, using a muted palette, were sometimes completed over several years, could be subject to reworking and were notable for the meticulous placing of objects

The Museum Of Modern Art, Wales
Heol Penrallt
Machynlleth
Powys SY20 8AJ
Tel 01654 703355
Fax 01654 702160
Y TABERNACL

and people within them. Barrett was a member of Colchester Art Society and took part in its Fifty Years Anniversary Exhibition at Chappel Galleries, Chappel, in 1996. Other group shows included LG; Wildenstein; RA; Piccadilly and Mercury Galleries; Roland, Browse & Delbanco and widely overseas. Solo shows included Beaux Arts Gallery from 1954; Minories, Colchester, from 1962; Alwin Gallery from 1966; Oxford Gallery, Oxford, from 1971; Mansion House, Ipswich, 1987; and in 1996 there was a retrospective at Barbican Centre and Minories. Victoria & Albert Museum and many provincial galleries hold Barrett's work.

Tom BARRETT fl. from mid-1950s– Painter and teacher who studied at Norwich Art School, 1954–5, then at Reading University fine art department, 1955–9. After teaching in various colleges from 1959–62, Barrett was appointed lecturer in fine art at Reading University in 1963. In 1962 he had co-founded Gallery 5 in Reading, which mounted many exhibitions over three years. In 1975 Barrett moved to Dorset, where the area around Lulworth became a central feature of his work, which employed a light palette and often primary colours, while continuing to teach at Reading. Among Barrett's mixed exhibitions were Reading Museum and Art Gallery, AIA Gallery, LG and Graves Art Gallery, Sheffield. One-man shows included Centre for Visual Arts, Cheltenham, in 1981; and Austin/Desmond Fine Art, Sunninghill, 1990.

Alan BARRETT-DANES 1935– Ceramist, whose wife Ruth was also an artist. They created individual pieces hand-modelled and moulded in porcelain, sometimes with the addition of hand-thrown units. Limited editions of work were developed around a central theme. Examples were Cabbage Kingdoms III & IV, shown in Recent Purchases, for CASW, a WAC touring show, 1979. Exhibitions also included New Directions in Ceramics, Oxford Gallery, 1973; Newport Museum & Art Gallery, 1980; Westminster Gallery, Boston, America, 1982. National Museum of Wales, Cardiff; public galleries in Birmingham, Newport, Portsmouth and Southampton; Ulster Museum, Belfast; and Perth and Melbourne public galleries in Australia hold examples. Lived in Abergavenny, Gwent.

Mardie BARRIE 1931– Painter and teacher, born in Kirkcaldy, Fife. She studied at Edinburgh University and Edinburgh College of Art, 1948–53, and went on to teach at Broughton High School in Edinburgh, where she lived. Barrie, an exuberant painter and colourist, showed in many group exhibitions in Britain and abroad, notably in the Scottish Arts Council's show Painters in Parallel. In 1963 she had a solo show at Douglas and Foulis Gallery in Edinburgh, with another three years later. She then showed regularly, notably at Scottish Gallery in Edinburgh and Bruton Gallery, Somerset. Many public galleries hold her work, including Glasgow and Laing Art Gallery in Newcastle upon Tyne; a number of Scottish Education authorities; Scottish Arts Council; and HRH The Duke of Edinburgh. Was an RSW member.

Jim BARRINGTON *see* **Jim GILBERT**

John BARRINGTON 1920–1991 Sculptor, artist, photographer and writer, born as John Engljahringer in London, where he finally lived. Studied at St Martin's School of Art and École des Beaux-Arts, in Paris, where Barrington was friendly with Jean Cocteau. After World War II Barrington engaged in theatre and film journalism; mounted theatrical productions; wrote novels prompted by his friend the theatre critic James Agate; and began taking professional photographs of male nudes, the subjects of many of his sculptures. Barrington's interest in the nude evinced itself in books such as *Art and Anatomy* and *A Camera Life Class* and in contributions to magazines such as *Male Model Monthly.* His autobiography *Inside My Skull* was based on extensive diaries.

David BARRON 1938– Painter and teacher, born in London. After education at Wells House and Oundle Schools Barron attended St Martin's School of Art and Goldsmiths' College School of Art. He took up teaching in 1959 and during the 1960s was at Chester School of Art and Swansea College of Art, from the early 1970s taking over the foundation course at Swansea. Was a member of RCamA and frequent exhibitor there. Lived in Swansea.

Gladys BARRON fl. from c.1905–1967 Sculptor and painter, born in India, who initially showed under her maiden name Gladys Logan. She studied with the sculptor Gertrude Bayes and at St John's Wood Art School and became noted for her portrait busts. Showed at Walker Art Gallery in Liverpool, RSA and RA and lived in Inverness.

Howard BARRON 1900– Painter and draughtsman, born in Sidcup, Kent, who was educated at Christ's Hospital, Horsham. In Sydney, Australia, studied with Will Ashton, 1928–49, and is widely represented in Australian collections, including Imperial War Museum, Canberra. Back in England studied with Robin Guthrie and Ralph Middleton Todd at City and Guilds Art School, 1950–1, and showed at ROI, Fine Art Society and St Ives Society of Artists, of which he was a member. Lived for some years at Copthorne, Sussex.

Francis BARRY 1883–1970 Painter and printmaker whose full name was Sir Claude Francis Barry, Bart. Born in London, he was educated at Harrow School, then studied art in Newlyn, Cornwall, with Stanhope Forbes, also being a pupil of Sir Alfred East. Showed at RA, NEAC, RBA of which he was a member, Paris Salon and elsewhere. Sir Francis lived in St Ives, Cornwall, later in Val Plaisant, Jersey, in Channel Islands.

James BARTHOLOMEW fl. from early 1990s– Painter, son of a Lancashire mining surveyor, a background that prompted an early interest in industrial subjects, for which he won awards. Bartholomew gained an honours degree in graphic design from Leicester Polytechnic in 1992. In 1993, he won prizes in the

Laing Art and National Mining Art Competitions, in 1994 a prize in the MAFA Open Exhibition and the Sir Peter Scott Memorial Prize for a Young Artist Under 25, organised by *The Artist* magazine. From that show his gouache Farm Fence and Crows went on display at the Nature in Art Museum in Gloucestershire. Bartholomew was asked to illustrate British marine life for the Chevron U K Ltd 1995 calendar, prompting a second commission to portray the oil company's North Sea Britannia platform and appearance in its 1997 ICA show. Land- and seascapes of Scotland became a feature of Bartholomew's work. He showed at the Mall Galleries in 1996, had several solo shows in and around his home town of Wigan and commissions included one from West Lancashire District Council for large oil paintings for permanent exhibition.

Lindsay BARTHOLOMEW 1944– Watercolourist and teacher, born in Wirral, Cheshire. She studied at Ruskin School of Drawing, Oxford, 1961–4, in the latter year winning the Ruskin Prize for Portraiture. She taught in London for a dozen years, then in 1985 moved to Somerset. After she finished at the Ruskin Bartholomew became especially interested in painting the English landscape in watercolour, developing a technique which employed wet washes and dramatic skies. She took part in many group shows, including New Grafton Gallery, RWA, Maas Gallery and Roland, Browse & Delbanco, and was a frequent solo exhibitor from the mid-1970s. These included several at Austin/Desmond Fine Art, Sunninghill. Stirling University, Trust House Forte and Robert Fleming & Company hold her work.

Zou-zou Elise BARTHOLOMEW 1911– Miniaturist and watercolourist, who sometimes signed work ZEB, she was born in Hankow, China. Educated in England, she studied art at the Central School of Arts and Crafts, 1928–30, and at the St John's Wood School, 1930–3, where her teachers included Patrick Millard. She became a member of the SM and showed at RI, RA, RMS and in China. Lived in Worcester Park, Surrey.

Jill BARTHORPE 1961– Painter and draughtsman. Studied at Trent Polytechnic, Nottingham, 1980–81. She then completed studies at Slade School of Fine Art, 1981–5, a David Bayley Scholarship taking her to France in 1985–6. She was a busy exhibitor in group shows from mid-1980s, including Martin, Keville, Baily Gallery, in Washington, America, 1986; Six of the Best, at Cadogan Contemporary, 1988; Glittering Prizes, at Alton Gallery, 1989; Kingfisher Fine Art, Edinburgh, 1991; and Spring Show, Francis Iles Gallery, Kent, 1992. She had a solo show of drawings at L'Escargot, 1992, and in that year shared a show at Cadogan Contemporary. Painting in France was a feature of her output, working in the landscape of Quercy, east of Cahors.

Adrian BARTLETT 1939– Artist in oil, acrylic, etching and lithography, teacher and writer, married to the artist Victoria Bartlett, born and lived in London. He studied at Camberwell School of Art, 1958–61, under Frank Auerbach and Robert Medley. Went on to become head of printmaking at Morley College and visiting lecturer at Oxford University and Wimbledon School of Art. Bartlett was elected to LG in 1979, and in 1993 became its president and an honorary member of Printmakers' Council. Bartlett contributed to group shows in many countries, including representing Britain at the Florence Biennale, 1976, and RA Summer Exhibitions. Later solo shows included British Council, Athens, 1985; Oxford Gallery, 1987; Blenheim Gallery, 1988; and Tsikalioti Museum, Greece, 1989. Ashmolean Museum in Oxford, British Museum, British Council, provincial and overseas collections hold examples. Bartlett's publications include *Drawing and Painting the Landscape*, 1982, and *British Art in the Eighties*, 1983.

Charles BARTLETT 1921– Painter and printmaker, born in Grimsby, Lincolnshire. His full name was Henry Charles Bartlett and he was married to the artist Olwen Jones. Studied at Eastbourne School of Art, then Royal College of Art, 1946–50, his teachers including Ruskin Spear and Robert Austin. He was president of RWS and a member of RE, also showing regularly at RA. Had a first solo show in London, 1960, a dozen others following, his work mainly landscape, especially the coast of East Anglia. Victoria & Albert Museum, National Gallery of South Australia, Albertina in Vienna, Department of the Environment and several dozen municipal galleries hold his work. There was a major retrospective at Bankside Gallery, 1997. Lived at Fingringhoe, Essex.

John BARTLETT 1960– Figurative painter and teacher, who gained an honours degree in fine art, Maidstone College of Art, 1980–3; a postgraduate higher diploma in fine art, Byam Shaw School of Art, 1990–1; a postgraduate diploma in painting, Royal Academy Schools, 1991–4; then did an Acava digital art computer course, 1995. Bartlett's scholarships included the William Lake Beard Prize, 1979; Bird's Charity and Bernard Bershinger Bursary, both 1991; Edwin Landseer Scholarship and Eric Kennington Prize for Academic Drawing, both 1992; and in 1994 the Richard Jack Prize and Richard Ford Award. In 1994 he held a residency at Oundle School, including teaching, and in 1995 was commissioned for BAA Art Programme, Art at Heathrow. Exhibitions included Stowells Trophy, RA, 1983; Ways of Seeing, Braintree Arts Centre, Braintree, 1988; RA Summer Exhibition, from 1992; Cocktail, Raw Gallery, 1993; and Out of the Nineties, Mall Galleries, 1994. Bartlett's large History Painting, a depiction of the 1990 Trafalgar Square poll tax riot, sparked controversy and gained national newspaper coverage when shown at the Museum of London in 1997. It had Old Master and Socialist Realist overtones. Lived in London.

June Rosalyn BARTLETT 1947– Painter, notably of portraits, born in Barnet, Hertfordshire. She was educated at Holywell School for Girls, Folkestone. Bartlett earned her living as a portrait painter from 1970. In 1979 she left Britain to live and work in Dubai, having her first exhibition there as part of the British Trade Fair. After that she regularly visited the Middle East, to carry out commissions, and she showed at Mathaf Gallery and had further solo shows in the region. Also showed at UA of which she was a member and ROI. Her portrait of Earl Mountbatten of Burma is in the collection of Fleet Air Arm Museum, Yeovilton. Lived in London.

Nancy BARTLETT: *see* **Margaret Nancy ROBINSON**

Paul BARTLETT 1955– Painter, draughtsman, printmaker, photographer and teacher, born and lived in Birmingham. He studied at Moseley Road Secondary School of Art, Birmingham, 1966–73, under John Swift; Falmouth College of Art, 1973–6, gaining an honours degree in fine art, teachers including Francis Hewlett and Richard Platt; then did a Royal Academy Schools postgraduate course, 1977–80, under Peter Greenham and Margaret Green. From 1986–90 studied at Birmingham Polytechnic for teacher's certificate and further postgraduate work in history of art and design. Among Bartlett's awards were the Turner Gold Medal, 1978; Stowells Trophy overall winner, 1979; Elizabeth Greenshields Foundation Scholarship, 1981–2; and Daler-Rowney Prize at RBSA Open, 1996. Among his teaching appointments were visiting lectureships at Sutton Coldfield School of Art & Design, 1983–4, and Bournville College of Art, Birmingham, 1984–5. Wrote features for *Leisure Painter*. Group shows included Midland Printmakers, 1972–6; RA Summer Exhibition from 1978; and National Portrait Gallery from 1984. Was a member of RBA from 1981. Solo shows included RA, 1980.

Robin BARTLETT 1900–1976 Versatile painter, draughtsman, designer and illustrator, born in Brentford, Middlesex, full name Robert Arthur Bartlett, son of Arthur Edward Bartlett, an architect who exhibited at RA before World War I, and Ella Carlin. Robin was educated at Shrewsbury School, entered the Royal Navy as a cadet and was a midshipman from 1918 until late 1919, acting as a French interpreter. After graduating in history from Oxford University, 1921, worked in Paris, attending life classes in the evenings, then studied at the Slade School of Fine Art from 1922 under Henry Tonks (who in 1928 gave him a glowing reference), also history of art. Bartlett won several prizes, including a first for figure drawing and an Orpen Bursary, and did a little teaching. While at the Slade Bartlett began an affair with Eileen Agar, whom he married in 1925, but they divorced in 1929. Bartlett, a member of NS, travelled widely abroad, including California, Florida and New Mexico, where he painted D H Lawrence's widow Frieda, which she said was the "best portrait ever made" of her. Back in England, E McKnight Kauffer offered Bartlett a job with the W S Crawford advertising agency, which led to wide-ranging work and to Bartlett being called "a poster artist of the first rank". He also did freelance work for major railway, oil and telephone companies. In 1939 Bartlett volunteered for the Royal Navy, by 1941 attaining the rank of temporary acting lieutenant-commander, and served in the Intelligence Division. His time included four years at the Admiralty in the key Room 39 and in the underground bunker where he was in contact with Winston Churchill. After hostilities, Bartlett became art director with Erwin, Wasey and Company, where he designed the cupid tailor figure for Kayser Bondor; spent two years visiting America; then had several years as creative director with the Pictorial Publicity Company, while freelancing on book illustrations and covers. He retired in 1963 as a freelance consultant, in 1967 organising the first national anti-litter week. Bartlett's second wife, Peggy Nicoll, encouraged his advertising work and this and his wide range of styles undermined his being taken up by a major gallery. Bartlett's pictures (which included a fine portrait of his third wife, Georgette Holm, and her daughter) were shown at the RA and in a solo exhibition at Selfridges just after the war.

Thomas BARTLETT: *see* **THOMAS**

Victoria BARTLETT 1940– Artist in mixed-media sculpture, wall-hung relief collages, paper, silk and other materials, and teacher, wife of the artist Adrian Bartlett. She studied painting and sculpture at Camberwell School of Art, 1957–61, teachers including Karel Vogel and Frank Auerbach, then was at Reading University, 1961–2. Went on to teach at Morley College, also being a visiting lecturer at Ruskin School of Drawing, Oxford; Goldsmiths' College; and Middlesex Polytechnic. Group exhibitions included Picadilly Gallery, 1976–9; RA Summer Exhibition, from 1979; Edward Totah Gallery, 1984; Ikon Gallery touring show, Birmingham, 1988; and LG Open, Barbican Art Gallery, from 1992. Solo shows included Van Doren Gallery, San Francisco, 1975; Edward Totah and Camden Arts Centre, both 1981; and Benjamin Rhodes Gallery, from 1987. Lived in London.

Anthony BARTLEY 1964– Painter and participant in performance art who graduated from University of Ulster, 1985–9. He was involved in the art therapy movement and was a part-time instructor with the National Schizophrenia Fellowship. Took part in slide shows music and poetry readings in Antwerp in 1992 and Belfast, 1993, and exhibited widely in Irish Republic and Northern Ireland, including Works on Paper, Queen Street Studios, Belfast, 1994.

Glenys BARTON 1944– Sculptor and ceramist, born in Stoke-on-Trent, Staffordshire. She studied at Royal College of Art, 1968–71, winning a Travelling Scholarship in 1970. In 1971 she gained the Ruth Drew Prize for Design, in 1972 being British prizewinner in the International Ceramics Exhibition. Drew served on the Crafts Advisory Council Committee (later the Crafts Council), in 1974–8. The artist's total concern was with the human figure, her heads having a hieratic quality. She took part in many group exhibitions and had a long series of solo shows, from 1974 with the Angela Flowers Gallery. In 1977 Glenys Barton at Wedgwood, at the Crafts Council Gallery, contained 26 pieces of sculpture produced at the Josiah Wedgwood Factory, Barlaston, over 18 months. Later solo shows included Flowers East, 1996, and in 1997 National Portrait Gallery and Manchester City Art Gallery. Many public collections in Britain and abroad hold examples, including Birmingham, Leeds, Leicester, Manchester, Portsmouth and Southampton, WAC and Scottish National Portrait Gallery, Edinburgh.

Leonard BARTON 1893–1971 Painter and teacher, born in Manchester. He studied at Blackburn, Bury and Accrington Schools of Art, 1909–15, then at Royal College of Art, where his teachers included Robert Anning Bell, 1915–21. During World War I he was attached to the Air Ministry as an artist while serving in the Royal Air Force. Held a number of teaching posts, finally as principal of Lancaster and Morecambe College of Arts and Crafts from 1929. He was a member of MAFA, exhibited widely in Lancashire and has work in Lancaster Art Gallery. Lived in Lancaster.

Mary BARTON 1861–1949 Landscape painter, born at Farndreg, County Louth, Ireland. After initial education in England and France she studied art at Westminster School of Art and in Rome. She exhibited extensively at Fine Art Society and SWA, also at RHA, Ridley Art Club, in the provinces and widely abroad. Among her exhibiting venues was Mexico City, and she published *Impressions of Mexico with Brush and Pen.* Lived at Bracknell, Berkshire.

Saxon BARTON fl. c.1925–1960 Painter in oil who was by profession a medical consultant. Studied medicine at university in Scotland and Liverpool, where he then studied art privately with the painter James Watts. Exhibited RCamA and in Liverpool, where he lived.

Jordan BASEMAN 1960– Sculptor and teacher who studied at Temple University, Philadelphia, America, at its Tyler School of Art, gaining a bachelor's degree in fine art, 1979–83, obtaining his master's in fine art from Goldsmiths' College, 1986–8. He exhibited in the show East at Norwich Gallery, 1991; in East & South at same gallery in 1992; contributed artwork for Peter Gabriel's album *Us* show at Art 93; and was included in Young Artists VI at Saatchi Gallery, 1996. Was a visiting teacher at Byam Shaw School of Art and lived in London.

Mati BASIS 1932– Printmaker and painter, born in Tel-Aviv, Israel, where he studied art at the Avni Institute, 1956–8, before completing his studies at Hornsey and Chelsea Art Colleges in 1966–9. From 1960–4 he was under contract to the Israel Gallery, Tel-Aviv, but moved to London in 1966. Won several prizes at Tel-Aviv Museum and a scholarship prize at the Israel-America Foundation Competition in 1966. Group shows included Annely Juda Gallery, 1969; 2nd International Print Biennale, Paris and Lister Art Gallery, Johannesburg, both 1970; British International Print Biennale, Bradford, 1974; and Leinster Gallery, 1981. Later solo shows included National Theatre, 1982–3, and Crocodile Gallery, 1993. Israel Museum, Jerusalem; Museum of Modern Art, New York; Utrecht Museum, Netherlands; and Ben Uri Art Society hold examples.

Charles Henry BASKETT 1872–1953 Printmaker, born in Colchester, Essex, son of the artist Charles E Baskett. Studied at Colchester and Lambeth Schools of Art and with Frank Mura. Became principal of the Chelmsford School of Art and exhibited widely, including RE and Walker Art Gallery, Liverpool, especially, as well as Fine Art Society, Cooling Galleries, RA and RSA, signing his work CHB. Work reproduced in *Print Collectors' Quarterly*. Galleries in Liverpool and Manchester hold his work. Finally lived in Southampton.

Frank Greatorex BASS 1915– Painter, draughtsman and teacher, born in Southport, Lancashire. He studied at the School of Art there, 1932–6, his teachers including Ian Grant; at the Slade School of Fine Art, 1936–9, with Randolph Schwabe; then at the Institute of Education, in London, 1939–40. Bass returned to live in Southport in 1949, after a series of teaching posts, to become painting master at his old art school. He showed RBSA, with Southport Palette Club and widely in north of England.

George BASS 1920– Painter and printmaker, born in London. He studied at Blackheath School of Art, 1935–9, where his teachers included W L Clause and James Woodford, then at Royal College of Art, 1939 and 1946–8 interrupted by World War II, where Edward Bawden and John Nash taught him. He did a substantial amount of publicity and book work for clients such as British European Airways and the General Post Office and London Passenger Transport Board bought his work for its collection. Showed Leicester Galleries, NEAC, RI and with Blackheath Art Society of which he was a member, and had one-man shows at Walker's Galleries. Was latterly at Great Yarmouth College of Art.

Herbert Allen BASS 1897–1967 Painter, notably a watercolourist, born in Beckenham, Kent, who joined the Royal Marines in 1917, serving until 1947, when he requested retirement, as lieutenant-colonel. Took part in the North Russian Campaign, served in H M S *Warspite* and many other ships, was a signals instructor and during World War II spent several years in Colombo. He edited the Marines' *Globe and Laurel* magazine for some years. Bass studied with Percy Bradshaw at the Press Art School and with the marine artist W L Wyllie and exhibited with RI and RWS. He specialised in painting Marine uniforms, and much of his work is held by the Marines' Museum, Southsea, including a composite picture of uniforms from 1664–1964. Bass lived in London.

BASSETT 1888–1972 Painter and draughtsman, married to the artist Muriel Wilson. His full title was Brigadier Bassett Fitzgerald Wilson. He was a highly decorated soldier who served in the King's Royal Rifle Corps and the 4th American Corps in World War I and on Montgomery's staff and as provost-marshal of the 21st Army Group in World War II. He was educated at Rugby School, read law at Cambridge, was junior diplomat, then practised law in London before war broke out when, severely wounded in France, he was advised to take up art for convalescence. In 1917 had an exhibition of Western Front work at Walker's Galleries. During 1920s with his wife established reputation as a painter, being drawn into modern movement in 1930s after they moved to Paris and made friends with such artists as André Lhote. After successful shows with Knoedler in New York and Chicago at start of decade, Bassett – as he signed his work – showed widely in Paris and elsewhere alongside such artists as Dufy, Friesz, Miró, Kisling and Matisse. The Wilsons travelled extensively in Europe and elsewhere until the war intervened. In 1946 Bassett mounted a large retrospective at Galerie du Bac, Paris, from which the Musée National d'Art Moderne bought one of his chairs series. In 1981 Patrick Seale Gallery held a show of the Wilsons' work.

Vera BASSETT 1922–1997 Painter and draughtsman, full name Elizabeth Vera Bassett-Reynolds, born in Pontardulais, Glamorgan, where she lived until 1972, then moved a few miles to the coastal village of Burry Port. Bedridden while recovering from an accident, Bassett discovered a talent for art. Apart from a short time at Swansea College of Art, she was self-taught. Bassett became a sensitive draughtsman of figure subjects, who from the mid-1950s exhibited extensively, including Beaux Arts, Leicester and Zwemmer Galleries, Pictures from the Margaret Davies Collection at the National Museum of Wales in 1964, SWG, SWAS, Paris Salon, elsewhere on the continent and in America. Had regular solo shows including Howard Roberts Gallery in Cardiff, Stone Gallery in Newcastle upon Tyne, University College in Swansea and Bartley Drey Gallery, 1995. Her work is held by WAC, British Museum, National Museum of Wales, National Library of Wales in Aberystwyth and Glynn Vivian Museum and Art Gallery, Swansea.

Lewin BASSINGTHWAIGHTE 1928–1983 Painter, relief and printmaker. Born at Southminster, Essex, he studied art at South-West Essex Technical College, St Martin's School of Art and the Royal College of Art. Bassingthwaighte had a one-man show at the Leicester Galleries in 1957, then went on to show widely in London – a series of exhibitions at the Piccadilly Gallery, 1964–72 – as well as Oxford, Los Angeles, Venice and Stuttgart. "My work is about tenderness and humanity," Bassingthwaighte wrote, but an element of the strange is strong in his nudes and figure studies. "There is a sense of isolation, of the wonder of life," critic Terence Mullaly wrote about the 1968 show. Bassingthwaighte's work is in many public collections, including the Arts Council, Victoria & Albert Museum and Chantrey Bequest. Signed work with initials. Lived in London.

Paul BASSINGTHWAIGHTE 1963– Artist, born in London, who gained an honours degree in fine art, 1982–6. Group exhibitions included Spirit of London from 1981; Piccadilly Gallery from 1993; RWS from 1994; and City of London Art Fair with Flying Colours Gallery, 1997. Later solo shows included Bloomsbury Theatre and Mosaic Restaurant, both 1996. Leicester Museums Arts and Records Service holds his work.

Hella BASU 1924– Creative letterer, born at Kassel, Germany, and studied art at the art college there. Exhibited widely, including the Victoria & Albert Museum, Herbert Art Gallery and Museum, Coventry, with one-man shows with the British Council, Berlin, Klingspor Museum, Offenbach, the County Museum, Warwick, and Goethe Institute, Toronto. Was senior lecturer at the Regional College of Art in Hull, where she lived.

Bernard Philip BATCHELOR 1924– Painter, born in Teddington, Middlesex, where he settled at St Margaret's on Thames. Was the son of the artist Roland Batchelor. Studied, 1946–9, at St Martin's School of Art with H Andrew Freeth and Roland Pitchforth, and City and Guilds of London Art School with A R Middleton Todd. Went on to work in publicity department of Iliffe Press, commercial studios and for a construction company. Was elected RWS in 1976, also showing at Business Art Galleries, Wykeham Gallery, Catto Gallery and elsewhere.

Robert W BATCHELOR 1929– Painter, printmaker and teacher, born in Georgetown, British Guiana, where he attended Queen's College. Studied painting at Gray's School of Art, Aberdeen, 1946–50, going on to be head of art at various academies in Scotland. Later worked as a painter and printmaker and set up Peacock Printmakers' Workshop in 1974. Was a professional member of Aberdeen Artists' Society and showed with RA, RSA, RSW and SSA. Aberdeen Arts Centre gave him a solo show in 1978. Aberdeen Art Gallery, Grampian Television, Shell UK and Mobil North Sea hold his work.

Roland BATCHELOR 1889–1990 Painter, especially in watercolour, draughtsman and printmaker, born in London, father of the artist Bernard Batchelor. Born Bernard William Roland Batchelor, he started to paint as a child, but his father insisted that he pursue a steady career, so he worked in the Civil Service from 1905–49. In his spare time he studied and painted, learning from George Morrow at Putney School of Art and after World War I service from Harry Watson at Regent Street Polytechnic School of Art. After retirement he had invaluable tuition at the City and Guilds of London School with A R Middleton Todd. Was a regular exhibitor at RA and RWS, member 1966. Centenary show at Catto Gallery in 1989. Batchelor was a fluent French speaker who loved working in France. His watercolours, which commonly include shrewdly drawn figures, have great spontaneity and freedom. Victoria & Albert Museum holds his work. Lived in St Margaret's on Thames, Middlesex.

Valerie BATCHELOR 1932– Painter who studied at Salisbury School of Art. John Singer Sargent and Ken Howard influenced her landscapes, which sought to capture the diversity of light and its reflections, as in her work included in The Christmas Exhibition, The Jerram Gallery, Salisbury, 1997. She regularly showed with PS and RWA.

Francis BATE 1853–1950 Painter, studied at South Kensington Schools, where he won a scholarship, then at Antwerp Academy of Arts. Exhibited NEAC, Goupil Gallery, RBA, Royal Glasgow Institute of the Fine Arts and overseas. In 1887 published a book on *The Naturalistic School of Painting*. For many years he was honorary secretary and honorary treasurer of NEAC. Sometimes signed work with monogram. Lived at Bucklebury, Berkshire.

Howard Edward Davis BATE 1894–1974 Sculptor and teacher, son of the sculptor Adam Bate. Howard Bate studied in Plymouth, 1914, Torquay, 1915, at Regent Street Polytechnic School of Art, 1917, then at the Royal Academy Schools, 1920. Exhibited at RA, which bought his work. Taught at Hampstead Garden Suburb Institute for a time. Lived at Edgware, Middlesex, but retired to Bodmin, Cornwall, where he had originated.

Arthur BATEMAN 1883–1970 Versatile painter and art critic who was ordained in the Methodist ministry. Born in Nottingham, Bateman studied at Leeds University, Nottingham School of Art and in Paris. Held a number of church posts around the country, and while in Birmingham was art critic for the *Birmingham Post*. Lived latterly in the Bedale area of Yorkshire, serving as chaplain to the Royal Air Force Regiment at the nearby Catterick Camp. Showed at RA, RSA, Paris Salon and elsewhere.

Henry Mayo BATEMAN 1887–1970 Illustrator, designer and painter, born in Sutton Forest, New South Wales, Australia. He studied at Westminster School of Art, Goldsmiths' Institute and the studio of Charles van Havermaet for several years. By World War I he was established as a contributor of humorous drawings to magazines, becoming noted in *The Bystander*, *Pearson's Magazine*, *The Tatler* and *Punch*. His The Man who ... social clanger cartoons made him famous and have been much-copied. Book illustrations and advertising added to his considerable income between the wars. *The Man who ... and other drawings by H M Bateman*, 1975, was one of a long line of his books extending over about 60 years. On retirement in 1939 Bateman lived in North Tawton, Devon, spending much time in Malta when he could, dying nearby in Gozo. Latterly he concentrated on more serious painting. After he died the Fine Art Society had a memorial show, and in 1974 the Leicester Galleries held a retrospective. Bateman also exhibited at Brook Street and Chenil Galleries and RA.

James BATEMAN 1893–1959 Painter and wood engraver specialising in rural scenes and farm animals, pictures with a tight composition. Born in Kendal, Westmorland, Bateman came from a farming background. Started to study sculpture at Leeds College of Art, 1910–14, but World War I service injuries forced him to abandon sculpture for painting. Studied at the Slade School of Fine Art, 1919–21, Rome Scholarship finalist 1920. Taught Cheltenham School of Art, 1922–8, then at Hammersmith School of Art. While at Cheltenham exhibited with the Cheltenham Group and Cotswold Group, cycling out to paint the local countryside. Exhibited at the RA from 1924, being elected RA in 1942. Also showed Cooling Galleries, Fine Art Society, NEAC, RHA, RSA and extensively abroad. Many British provincial and Commonwealth galleries hold his work, as do the British Museum and Tate Gallery, which has several examples of cattle auction scenes, for which Bateman is especially noted. Lived in London.

Pete BATEMAN 1968– Artist and illustrator who studied at Staffordshire Polytechnic. He drew for publications such as *The Observer* and *New Statesman* and contributed mixed-media assemblages to Art in Boxes, 1992, at England & Co.

Vic BATEMAN 1950– Artist who was born in London, studying painting at Hornsey and Croydon Colleges of Art, 1968–75. Was visiting artist at Goldsmiths' College School of Art, 1978. His mixed show appearances included Brixton Art Gallery and Acme Gallery, both 1983; Nettlefold Gallery, 1984; and New Moon Group Show at Woodlands Art Gallery, 1986. Had solo show of paintings and drawings at Greenwich Theatre Gallery, 1982.

Denise BATES 1928– Painter, muralist and needlework designer who attended Liverpool College of Art, 1946–8, then Byam Shaw School, 1948–53, gaining Award of Merit, 1952. She showed in mixed exhibitions at RA, RCamA, NEAC, RMS, Patricia Wells Gallery in Thornbury, Paris Salon and elsewhere. Held a number of solo exhibitions in Cheshire, where she lived at Malpas. Carried out mural commissions for S S *Ivernia*, S S *Sylvania*, Imperial Institute and elsewhere; tempera commissions for Bunbury Church in Cheshire and Newport Church, Shropshire; and several church needlework designs. Lived at Haughton Thorn, near Tarporley, Cheshire.

Ken BATES 1927–1985 Portrait and figure painter in oil, pastel, charcoal and graphic media. Born in London, Bates studied at Willesden School of Art in the early 1940s under Maurice de Sausmarez, then for the later 1940s at Guildford College of Art with Maurice Wheatley. Exhibited at SGA, of which he was a council member, NS, RBA and PS. Lived at Earlswood, Redhill, Surrey.

Lynn BATES fl. from late 1970s– Painter and designer who worked in both Britain and South America, producing landscapes and comissioned portraits. Goya, Hogarth and other romantic artists were cited as influences. She studied at Byam Shaw School of Art, 1978–81, and Royal Academy Schools, 1983–6. From 1987–9 she trained as a scenic artist with BBC. Bates showed in mixed exhibitions with Cadogan Contemporary and had a solo show there in 1990.

Marjorie BATES 1883–1962 Painter and draughtsman, born in King's Newton, Derbyshire. Her family moved to Nottingham where she studied at the School of Art, 1902–13. She then travelled on the continent, where she had tuition from J P Laurens, in Paris. Most of her life was spent in Nottingham, although she travelled widely in England, drawing cottages and churches, reproduced as Christmas cards and calendars. Showed at RA, in provinces and at Paris Salon and was a regular exhibitor at Nottingham Castle Museum, which holds her work.

Robert BATES 1943– Artist and teacher, born in Wolverhampton, Staffordshire. He studied at Birmingham College of Art, 1960–5, and Royal College of Art, 1965–8. Taught printmaking at Medway College of Art. From 1970 had many solo shows at Lumley Cazalet as well as one at Hom Gallery, Washington, in 1982. Among the group exhibitions in which he participated was The Broad Horizon, Agnew, 1990. Bates' work was both colourful and precise, small and incorporating distinctive coloured borders. Lived for some years in Shropshire.

Trevor BATES 1921– Sculptor whose grandfather was the sculptor Harry Bates. Born in Eltham, Kent, he was educated at Harrow School, then studied at Slade School of Fine Art, 1947–51, and with Ossip Zadkine in Paris, in 1952, in his private studio at the Académie de la Grande Chaumière. Later taught at Hornsey College of Art. Bates exhibited at RBA and Salon de la Jeune Sculpture in Paris, having one-man show at Waddington Gallery in 1959. In addition to being awarded an Arts Council Prize in The Unknown Political Prisoner competition in 1953, he was granted a prize by the international jury when chosen to represent Great Britain. Bates' work is in the collections of the Arts Council, Victoria & Albert Museum and National Museum of Wales, Cardiff. His sculptures created powerful silhouettes rather than being three-dimensional objects, and Bates commented that it is "the unexpected and apparently illogical form in nature which concerns me". Lived in Sevenoaks, Kent.

Bath, MARQUESS of: *see* **Alexander THYNN**

Kevin BATKIN 1949– Painter brought up in East Anglia who, after Royal Air Force service 1965–7, attended North-East London Polytechnic in Dagenham. He had a background in electronics and computer systems and was "particularly interested in computer-aided design and technology". Studied at Norfolk College of Arts and Technology in King's Lynn, 1990–2, then De Montfort University, Leicester, 1992–5. Exhibitions included Lynn Sports Leisure Complex, King's Lynn, 1992; Peterborough Exhibitions Group, Peterborough Museum and Art Gallery, from 1994; and Towards an Abstraction, David Holmes Contemporary Art, Peterborough, 1995–6. Lived in Eastrea, Cambridgeshire.

Brian BATSFORD: *see* **Brian COOK**

Mark Wilfred BATTEN 1905–1993 Sculptor, draughtsman and painter, born in Kirkcaldy, Fife. He studied at Beckenham and Chelsea Schools of Art and gained Board of Education drawing and painting certificates. Batten was an advocate of direct carving of stone and published books on the subject: *Stone Sculpture by Direct Carving*, 1957, and *Direct Carving in Stone*, 1966. He gained experience of carving granite in Cornwall in the late 1920s. During World War II Batten served in the Life Guards, training armoured vehicle drivers. Showed with NEAC, Society of Present Day Artists, Royal Glasgow Institute of the Fine Arts and RBA, of which he was made a member in 1962. He was elected a fellow of RBS in 1953 and was its president, 1956–61. Bodleian Library in Oxford contains his work, as do British Museum and a number of provincial galleries. For many years lived a reclusive life at Dallington, Heathfield, Sussex.

Reg BATTERBURY 1928– Painter of landscapes and portraits, designer and teacher, born in east London. Trained locally at West Ham Municipal College of Art, St Martin's School of Art and West of England College of Art, Bristol. Became head of art department of Lockleaze Comprehensive School, retiring in 1978. Batterbury showed at RA from 1951, was a member of RWA and of the Bristol Savages, being president in 1980. American Museum in Bath and Longleat House hold his work. Lived in Bristol.

Elizabeth BATTERSBY 1946– Artist chiefly in oil and charcoal, born in Wiltshire. She did an external diploma London University, in the history of art, 1975–80; gained an honours degree in fine art and critical studies, St Martin's School of Art, 1983–8; and in 1982–4 attended Glamorgan Summer School, tutor Dennis Creffield. Mixed exhibitions included Whitechapel Open, 1983; LG Open, Royal College of Art, 1984; Alton Gallery, 1989; and Galerie Dagmar, 1991. Had a solo show at Morley College, 1987, later ones including The Wine Gallery, 1993. Lived in London.

Martin BATTERSBY 1914–1982 Painter, designer and decorator, printmaker, writer and collector, full name George Martin Battersby, born into a theatre- and cinema-loving family. From childhood, he was fascinated by painting and the decorative arts, spending many hours in museums and galleries. On leaving school, Battersby rejected university and the family law firm, studying architecture at Regent Street Polytechnic, spending five years in the design studio of Gill and Reigate and a year at the Royal Academy of Dramatic Art. After designing and painting scenery in repertory, he was commissioned to design settings for *Hamlet* at the Old Vic under Lilian Bayliss. There followed a string of Shakespeare commissions for Stratford-upon-Avon; modern plays; and operatic productions for Covent Garden and Glyndebourne. As a painter, Battersby specialised in trompe l'oeil, completing many rooms in England, France and America for private and business clients. His lithograph *Archaic Smile* was produced at Curwen Studio in 1981 and published by Ebury Gallery, which held a show of his pictures in 1982. He had first exhibited at Brook Street Gallery, 1948, with other shows at Arthur Jeffress, Redfern and Grosvenor Galleries and in America. Battersby revived interest in the collecting of Art Nouveau and Art Deco works, his books including *Art Nouveau* and *The Decorative Twenties*, both 1969; *The Decorative Thirties*, 1971; and *Trompe I'Oeil or The Eye Deceived*, 1974. Brighton Museum and Art Gallery and Southampton Art Gallery hold his work. Died from cancer in hospital at Lewes, Sussex.

Norman BATTERSHILL 1922– Painter, designer, writer and teacher, born in London, son of the artist Leslie Battershill. He studied at Twickenham College of Art and showed at RBA, ROI and PS of all of which he was a member, RA and NEAC. Was made a fellow of Society of Industrial Artists and Designers/Chartered Society of Designers in 1968 and won ROI's Stanley Grimm Award, 1989. Major companies held his work. Among Battershill's instructional books were *Painting and Drawing Water*, 1984, and *Learn to Paint Trees*, 1990. Lived in Woolland, Dorset.

John BAUM 1942– Painter and teacher, born in Wales. He studied at Slade School of Fine Art, then became a lecturer in foundation studies at the faculty of art and design at Liverpool Polytechnic. Took part in a number of group shows, including John Moores Exhibition in Liverpool, Ibis Gallery, WAC and Royal National Eisteddfod, in Wales. Both the Arts Council and WAC hold his work.

Lydia BAUMAN 1955– Painter, born in Warsaw, Poland. She graduated in fine art from the University of Newcastle upon Tyne, 1974–8, then obtained her master's degree in the history of art, graduating first-class with distinction, from the Courtauld Institute of Art, 1978–80. She won the John Christie Scholarship in 1976 and the Hatton Award in 1977. Bauman used a fresco-related technique in which pigments mixed with plaster were layered with resin and wax and then sanded down. After two solo shows at Leigh Gallery, 1985–6, she had many appearances in Britain and Poland, later solo exhibitions including several at Mistral Galleries from 1990 and Catto Gallery, 1993.

Pauline BAUMANN fl. from late 1920s– Painter, printmaker and teacher, full name Constance Amy Pauline Baumann. She attended St Martin's School of Art, studying under Frank Jones, then Royal College of Art, 1923–7, under William Rothenstein. Exhibited RA, Redfern Gallery, Senefelder Club and elsewhere, being especially noted for her etchings, engravings and lithographs. Lived in London.

Lewis BAUMER 1870–1963 Painter, printmaker and notable illustrator, born in London. He studied at St John's Wood Schools of Art, Royal College of Art and Royal Academy Schools. Exhibited extensively at Fine Art Society and RI, also at Cooling Galleries, ROI and Walker Art Gallery, Liverpool. From the 1920s Baumer concentrated on his illustrative work. He drew for many magazines, including Jerome K Jerome's *The Idler*, *Pick-Me-Up*, *Punch* and *The Strand Magazine*. Authors of books illustrated ranged from Ian Hay to Washington Irving and Mrs Molesworth. He was a light social commentator in his contemporary drawings, which have a fizzy charm. Arts Club member. Lived at Henley-on-Thames, Oxfordshire.

Charlotte BAWDEN 1902–1969 Painter, potter and teacher. She was born Charlotte Epton and met her future husband, the artist Edward Bawden, at Royal College of Art, marrying him in 1932. After College she studied pottery in St Ives, Cornwall, with Bernard Leach and Michael Cardew, and taught drawing at Cheltenham Ladies' College, Pate's Grammar School and helped found Denman College, the Women's Institute establishment. It and Victoria & Albert Museum hold her work.

Edward BAWDEN 1903–1989 Watercolourist, illustrator, designer, printmaker and teacher, born in Braintree, Essex, the county in which he spent much of his life, finally living in Saffron Walden. Studied at Cambridge School of Art from 1919, then at Royal College of Art, 1922–5, on a scholarship, in the design school being taught by Paul Nash. Soon began on commercial work for Poole Pottery and Curwen Press, then in 1928–9 with Eric Ravilious and Charles Mahoney did decorations for Morley College. Bawden went on studying engraving and bookbinding at Central School Arts and Crafts after leaving the Royal College and himself taught there, the Royal Academy Schools and Goldsmiths' College School of Art. First one-man show at Zwemmer Gallery in 1934, after which he showed extensively including RA, being elected RA in 1956. Work poured from Bawden's studio in the 1930s, for companies such as Shell-Mex; book illustrations such as *Good Food*, 1932, and *The Week-end Book*, 1939; and a mass of often ephemeral work which evinced a wonderful wit, economy and aptness to subject. Official War Artist in World War II, much of his output being in the Imperial War Museum. Tate Gallery and many other public collections hold his work. Bawden did decorations for the SS *Orcades* and *Oronsay* and for the Unicorn Pavilion for the Festival of Britain of 1951. His son was the artist Richard Bawden. Retrospective at Victoria & Albert Museum in 1989, with a tribute at Fine Art Society in 1992.

Richard BAWDEN 1936– Painter, printmaker, designer and illustrator, son of the artists Edward and Charlotte Bawden, married to the potter Hattie Bawden. He was born at Black Notley, near Braintree, Essex. Bawden attended Chelsea and St Martin's Schools of Art. During National Service he was able to attend Winchester School of Art, then became a student in the school of engraving and etching at Royal College of Art. As well as exhibiting in numerous mixed shows Bawden had several dozen solo exhibitions. He was a member of RE and of the Society of Designer-Craftsmen and was chairman of the Gainsborough's House Print Workshop in Sudbury, a group of printmakers. Bawden completed posters for the London Underground, a large mosaic for a swimming pool in Little Dunmow, murals for restaurants, book illustrations and editions of prints for Christie, Curwen and Editions Alecto, and he also decorated his wife's pottery. Bawden's work combined excellent draughtsmanship, a fine sense of colour and an eye for the unusual. It is in the collections of the Victoria & Albert Museum, the Tate Gallery and other public collections. Gainsborough's House gave Bawden a sixtieth birthday retrospective in 1996.

John BAWTREE 1952– Painter who qualified as an architect at Kingston Polytechnic School of Architecture, 1970–3 and

1975–7. He won Elizabeth Greenshields Foundation Awards, 1978–80, and the Foundation holds his work. Was elected RBA in 1984. Also showed in group exhibitions at RA and Richmond Gallery. Had several dozen solo shows including Piers Feetham Gallery; British Council, Muscat, Oman; and Caroline Hill Gallery, New York. Lived in Peasenhall, Suffolk.

Denis BAXTER 1936– Painter in oil, printmaker and lecturer, born in Southsea, Hampshire. After being a tea and rubber plantation manager in India for five years, Baxter was at Bournemouth and Poole College of Art, 1964–5, teachers including Sam Rabin and William Evans, then Stockwell College of Education, Bromley, 1965–6. Taught English in Bournemouth, 1968–87, then became an artist printmaker and lecturer. Was a member of NS and Printmakers' Council, also showing at RA, RWA, RBA, NEAC and RSMA. Had solo shows at Lyric and Mermaid Theatres and in Luxembourg. Baxter's main themes "concentrate around flowers and abandoned railway architectural subjects". Southampton General Hospital holds his work. Lived in Southbourne, Dorset.

Douglas BAXTER 1920– Painter and teacher, born in Kirkcaldy, Fife. Studied at Edinburgh College of Art under William Gillies and others, 1945–50, and at Patrick Allan-Fraser School of Art, Hospitalfield, with Ian Fleming; also won travelling scholarships to Scandinavia and Western Europe. He went on to teach at Loretto School in Musselburgh, Midlothian, where he lived, and was a lecturer at Edinburgh College of Art. Showed SSA of which he was a member, RSA, Royal Glasgow Institute of the Fine Arts, CEMA and elsewhere. Arts Council bought his work.

Glen BAXTER 1944– Artist, author, illustrator and teacher, born in Leeds, Yorkshire, where he studied at the College of Art, 1960–5. He taught at Victoria & Albert Museum, 1967–74, and was part-time lecturer in fine art at Goldsmiths' College School of Art, 1974–86. Was included in The Self-Portrait: a Modern View, an exhibition which toured widely from Artsite Gallery, Bath, 1987. Held a first solo show in New York in 1974 and subsequently had one-man shows in Venice, Cardiff, Bradford, Aberdeen and San Francisco, being represented for a time by Nigel Greenwood, then Richard Dennis Gallery in 1996. Baxter made a name for his artworks published as books, such as *The Billiard Table Murders*, 1990. Other books included *Atlas*, *The Impending Gleam*, *His Life: The Years of Struggle* and *Jodhpurs in the Quantocks*. Arts Council holds Baxter's work, which was figurative and abstract.

Robert BAXTER 1893– Painter, printmaker and teacher, born in Brighton, Sussex, full name Leslie Robert Baxter. He was apprenticed as an engraver, 1910–15, then studied under Louis Ginnett at Brighton School of Art, 1919–24. Held a series of teaching posts, latterly at Hammersmith College of Art and Building. Showed at RA, AIA, London Gallery and in Paris and had a one-man show at Mayor Gallery in 1948. Lived in London.

Lise Lotte BAYER 1931– Painter and teacher, born in Vienna. After initial education at Bradford Girls' Grammar School she studied art at Reading University with Anthony Betts, 1949–55. She showed at RA, RP, RBA, with the Young Contemporaries, and in the north of England. Member of Bradford Arts Club. Had a one-man show at Galerie Fuchs, in Vienna, 1959, and her work is held in several Austrian public collections. She returned to live in Vienna after a period in Shipley, Yorkshire, where her father, the painter Richard Franz Bayer, also lived. She sometimes signed her work L L B.

Richard Franz BAYER 1901– Painter and teacher at Bradford Grammar School, born in Vienna, Austria. He studied art in Vienna and showed there, in Bradford and elsewhere in the north of England. Member of Bradford Arts Club. Lived for some years in Shipley, Yorkshire, where his daughter the painter Lise Lotte Bayer also lived for a time. Sometimes signed his work R F B.

Gilbert BAYES 1872–1953 Sculptor of figures and monumental designer, born in London, son of the artist Alfred Walter Bayes and brother of the painter Walter Bayes. Studied at City and Guilds, Finsbury, classes and then, 1896–9, at the RA Schools, finally in Paris. He won an Honourable Mention at the Paris International Exhibition in 1900, a gold medal and diploma of honour at the Paris Exhibition of Decorative Art in 1925, as well as several medals at the Paris Salon and RBS. Was master of the Art Workers' Guild, 1925, and RBS president, 1939–44. Among his chief works are Selfridges' great clock, the great seal of HM King George V and the Seagrave Trophy. The Tate Gallery holds his work. He was married to the sculptor Gertrude Bayes and lived in London.

Jessie BAYES 1878–1970 Painter, illuminator and muralist who worked in the tradition of Walter Crane and the arts and crafts movement. Her father was the artist Afred Walter Bayes, her brothers the painter Walter Bayes and the sculptor Gilbert. She was made a member of RMS in 1906, becoming honorary RMS in 1935, also being a member of Arts and Crafts Exhibition Society, Society of Mural Decorators and Church Crafts League. Also showed at RA, Ridley Art Club, Baillie Gallery, Fine Art Society, Walker Art Gallery in Liverpool and elsewhere, including the continent and North America. Detroit Public Gallery had her work, and she completed the roll of honour for the King's Royal Rifles in Winchester Cathedral. Lived in London and Edinburgh.

Walter BAYES 1869–1956 Painter, writer, illustrator and teacher. Born in London, son of the artist Alfred Walter Bayes, brother of the sculptor Gilbert Bayes and of the artist Jessie Bayes. Studied between 1896–1902 variously at evening classes at the City and Guilds, Finsbury, Académie Julian, Paris, and Westminster School of Art, with Fred Brown. From early 1890s began exhibiting at RA and NEAC, his first work for a public collection, Top o' the Tide, being bought by the Walker Art Gallery, Liverpool, in 1900. Bayes was a founder-member of Frank Rutter's AAA in 1908, and thereafter was associated with

Walter Sickert and his friends at 19 Fitzroy Street, Camden Town Group and LG. One-man show at Carfax Gallery, 1913. In 1918 Bayes became head of Westminster School of Art, having previously taught at the City and Guilds, Bolt Court and Camberwell School of Arts and Crafts, and he held this post until 1934. From 1934–7 he was a visiting lecturer at Reading University, from 1944–9 being director of painting at Lancaster School of Art. Bayes was a painter of tonal subtlety, an intellectual who excelled at the science of picture-making. Among his grateful pupils was David Jones. At various times Bayes was critic for *Outlook*, *The Athenaeum*, *Saturday Review* and *Weekend Review*. He wrote a number of books, including one on *Turner*, 1931, *The Art of Decorative Painting*, 1927, and a delightful illustrated travel memoir, *A Painter's Baggage*, 1932. Tate Gallery holds his work. Retrospective at Michael Parkin Fine Art, 1978. Lived in London.

Thomas BAYLEY 1893–1966 Sculptor and teacher, also known as C Thomas Bayley, born in Willesden, London. Was educated at Chester School of Art and Royal College of Art, in 1922 gaining his diploma, in 1923 a travelling scholarship. During World War I Bayley had served with the Royal Field Artillery in France, Egypt and Palestine, producing panoramic drawings and maps. For the 1924 British Empire Exhibition Bayley modelled a map of the world. Showed at RA and in the provinces, notably Cheltenham, where he taught at the School of Arts and Crafts. Joined the Art Workers' Guild in 1931. Lived in Cheltenham, Gloucestershire, and in London.

Clifford BAYLY 1927– Painter, illustrator, writer and teacher, who studied at St Martin's and Camberwell Schools of Art, teachers including William Coldstream, Lawrence Gowing and John Minton. He taught at Margate, Canterbury and Maidstone Colleges of Art for 32 years, retiring early to concentrate on painting. Bayly was vice-president of RWS and president of Weald of Kent Art Group and showed at Piccadilly and Mall Galleries. Also showed extensively in Australia. He regarded his series of Alignment paintings as main works, "based on various forms of pathways and ancient sites". Wrote books on painting and drawing and for children. RWS Diploma Collection holds his work. Lived in Staplehurst, Kent.

Gertrude Emily BAYLY 1875– Painter, draughtsman and ivory miniaturist who studied at Margate School of Art, continuing to live in the town. Exhibited SWA, East Kent Art Society, widely in the provinces and in Paris.

Irene BAYMAN fl. from c. 1935– Painter, draughtsman, fabric printer and teacher. Educated in Wigan, Lancashire, she studied art at Wigan Technical College and went on to teach in Lancashire schools, including Eccles Grammar School. Exhibited in Preston and London. Lived in Wigan.

Keith BAYNES 1887–1977 Painter, mainly in oil. Born at Reigate, Surrey, Baynes went to Cambridge and then the Slade School, 1912–14. After World War I he became a member of the circle around the critic and painter Roger Fry and was strongly influenced by French Post-Impressionist artists. Showed with the London Artists' Association, encouraged and financed by Maynard Keynes and Samuel Courtauld from 1926 to the slump of 1931, which put a stop to the enterprise. Baynes also exhibited with Agnew, Adams Gallery and widely overseas. The British Council, Arts Council, provincial and foreign galleries own his pictures. *The Modern Movement in Art*, by R H Wilenski, features Baynes' work. For a time lived near Rye, Sussex. There was a show at The Bloomsbury Workshop in 1994.

Pauline BAYNES 1922– Book illustrator and designer, born in Brighton, Sussex, who studied at Farnham School of Art and Slade School of Fine Art after a childhood partly in India. Early in her career she was a member of WIAC. During World War II she was involved in Army camouflage, then worked for Admiralty Hydrographic Department. Illustrated many books, including *Chronicles of Narnia* and other titles in the series by C S Lewis; Enid Blyton's *The Land of Far Beyond*; and a *Dictionary of Chivalry*, which in 1968 gained her the Kate Greenaway Prize, for which she was runner-up in 1972. Sometimes signed work with a bird. Lived near Farnham, Surrey.

B B: *see* **Denys James WATKINS–PITCHFORD**

James Prinsep BEADLE 1863–1947 Painter, notably of military subjects, born in Calcutta, India, son of Major General James Beadle. He gained a scholarship to study under Alphonse Legros at Slade School of Fine Art and in Paris at École des Beaux-Arts. Won a bronze medal at Paris Universal Exhibition, 1889. Showed widely at Fine Art Society, RA, RBA, RHA and elsewhere, had much work reproduced and is represented in British and foreign public collections. Lived in London.

Edward BEALE 1950– Artist who studied at Camberwell School of Art, initially part-time, then full-time, 1968–72, finally at Royal Academy Schools, 1976–9. Beale showed in RA Summer Exhibition from 1977 and had a solo show in RA downstairs gallery in 1983. Among group exhibitions in which he participated was The Broad Horizon, Agnew, 1990, and Edward Beale's Choice, The Gallery at Architecture Ltd, 1996.

Helen BEALE 1946– Painter, draughtsman and teacher, born in Keighley, Yorkshire, the county where she made her career, settling in Knaresborough. Early work was signed with her maiden name, Elizabeth Helen Green. She studied at Harrogate School of Art, 1962–3, Brighton College of Art, 1963–4, and Liverpool College of Art, 1964–7. She was interested in decorative and design work and for a time directed a design company. Showed in mixed exhibitions in Yorkshire and London, notably with Free Painters and Sculptors and RA. Had several solo shows including Victoria Art Gallery, Harrogate. York Art Society member. Imperial Chemical Industries, Harrogate, holds her work.

Margaret BEALE 1886–1969 Painter in oil and watercolour, especially of seascapes and yachts, born at Yaldham, Kent. She studied art in London with William Orpen, 1906–8, then for two years in Paris under Percyval Tudor-Hart and with him in London, 1911–12. Exhibited frequently at RSMA of which she was a member, with Chichester Art Society and had a solo show in Chichester. Settled at Chidham, Sussex, had a studio overlooking the harbour and taught adults locally into her seventies until local authority discovered her age and would not let her continue. National Maritime Museum, Greenwich, holds her work.

Philippa BEALE 1946– Sculptor, painter and teacher, born in Winchester, Hampshire, where she attended the School of Art, 1961–5. After Goldsmiths' College, 1965–9, was at University of Reading. Went on to teach at Hornsey College of Art and was first artist-in-residence at City Art Gallery in Southampton, 1983. Among her mixed shows were Woolgate House, 1969; Annely Juda Fine Art and ICA, both 1970; Angela Flowers Gallery, 1972; Woodlands Art Gallery, 1973, in Space from the Quadrangle; and Berry Street Open Studios, 1984. Solo shows included Angela Flowers, 1982.

Nicola BEALING 1963– Painter, born in Hertford, who completed a foundation course at Herts College of Art and Design, St Albans, 1983, gaining a diploma in fine art from Byam Shaw School of Art from 1984. Group shows included Sue Williams Gallery, 1988; Six Painters from Porthleven, Porthmeor Gallery, St Ives, 1990; South-West Open Exhibition, Plymouth City Museum & Art Gallery and Plymouth Arts Centre, 1992, where she was first prizewinner; Peninsular Journeys, Coventry and Middlesex Universities' Art Galleries, 1993; and Royal Over-Seas League Open and Millfield Open, where she won a first prize, both 1995. Had a solo show at St Helier Galleries, Jersey, 1989, later ones including a shared exhibition at Cadogan Contemporary, 1993, and a one-man at Beaux Arts Gallery, Bath, 1994. Commissioned work included a mural at Quayside Fish Centre, Porthleven, 1988, and Embassy of Sultanate of Oman, 1989. Spanset International in Zürich and Unilever Corporate Collection hold examples.

Frederick Harold BEAMISS 1898–1979 Ink and scraperboard artist, born in Hornsey, Middlesex. Studied art at Cologne School of Art, Tottenham Polytechnic and elsewhere. Sometimes signed work Calbeam. Beamiss specialised in views of Devon and its churches, which he showed with Exeter Art Society. Lived in Exeter.

Anne BEAN 1950– Performance artist and teacher, born in Northern Rhodesia, who studied fine art at University of Cape Town and Reading University, 1968–73. Her first public performance was collaborative in the Piazza del Duomo, Florence, in 1970, after which, apart from many solo works, Bean initiated and participated in numerous joint projects, travelling throughout Britain, the continent, America, Mexico and Japan. The diverse venues included Imports, in the Kitchen Gallery, New York; Hayward Annual, at Hayward Gallery; Punk clubs in Hollywood; a zebra crossing outside Air Gallery; a disused fish factory in Norway; the foreshore on Sado Island, Japan; and the Museum of Modern Art in Oxford, Whitechapel Gallery and Pompidou Centre, Paris. Bean's video collaborations were shown on the BBC and commercial television. In 1983 she co-founded the Bow Gamelan Ensemble with Paul Burwell, the drummer, and sculptor Richard Wilson. In 1991, Bean was awarded, for the second time, the *Time Out* Dance and Performance Award for her long contribution to live arts. With the sculptor Peter Fink, in 1992 Bean realised Light Year, then the largest temporary art project in the United Kingdom, which took Canary Wharf as a canvas for a monumental light sculpture, seen over 40 kilometres by millions of Londoners. In 1993 Bean and Fink won a *Time Out* 25-year anniversary billboard. Later performances included Tribute to Yves Klein at Hayward Gallery, 1995, and Peace in rest, at St Thomas' Hospital, 1996. Bean taught regularly, especially at Middlesex University. Lived in London.

Frank BEANLAND 1936– Painter and designer in abstract, born in Bridlington, Yorkshire, who married the artist Emily Gwynne-Jones. He attended Hull College of Art, 1952–7, then Slade School of Fine Art, 1959–61, where his teachers included Claude Rogers. From 1961–2 a Boise Travelling Scholarship took him to Stockholm. Beanland began showing in mixed exhibitions in 1960 at Young Contemporaries, also exhibiting at Drian Galleries, LG and Gimpel Fils. Solo exhibitions included Smith's Gallery One, 1990, where the artist showed a series of decorated screens employing oil, aluminium and hardboard. Slade School, Paintings for Hospitals and Leverhulme Trust hold his work. Lived in Frostenden, Suffolk.

George Telfer BEAR 1874–c.1965 Artist in oil and pastel, born in Greenock, Renfrewshire. He studied at Glasgow School of Art under Fra Newbery and James Dunlop, then lived for a time in Canada. Exhibited extensively at Royal Glasgow Institute of the Fine Arts, also RSA, in London, the provinces and in Paris. Glasgow Museum and Art Galleries, the Scottish National Gallery of Modern Art and other galleries hold his work. Lived at Kilmacolm, Renfrewshire, then in Edinburgh.

John BEARD 1943– Painter of abstract works, designer and teacher, born in Aberdare, Glamorgan. He studied at Swansea College of Art, 1962–5, then University of London, 1965–6. Between 1968–70 Beard taught in various schools and universities in England and was a freelance design consultant, also producing and appearing in BBC television programmes. Was at London University, 1973–6, taught fine art for Milton Keynes College/Open University, 1974–9, then gained his master's degree at Royal College of Art, 1979–81. As well as part-time lecturing at Middlesex Polytechnic/Hornsey College of Art, 1979–83, Beard in 1981–2 co-founded the design-winning firm Artigiani before being appointed to Curtin University, Perth, Australia, in 1983, resigning in 1989 to paint full-time. Beard became a naturalised Australian citizen, although he travelled widely to paint, notably in Europe for a sustained period from 1991. As well as showing widely in group exhibitions in Britain and Australia Beard had many solo shows, starting with WAC in Cardiff, 1966. Later ones included William Jackson Gallery, 1993. National Library of Wales, Royal College of Art, Arts Council and many Australian galleries hold Beard's work.

Leonard BEARD 1942– Largely self-taught painter, apart from studies with a professional artist in Italy, Beard spent his career in the Merchant Navy, then moved to Wales in 1976 and decided to paint full-time. Mixed shows included National Museum of Wales, Cardiff, 1988, and Paris Salon, 1994. Had solo exhibitions at Martin Tinney Gallery, Cardiff, from 1993, that show a sell-out.

Josias Crocker BEARE 1881–1962 Landscape and architectural painter who practised as an architect. Born in Newton Abbot, Devon, Beare began practising in his home town in 1908 after initial studies in Torquay. Exhibited RA, RWA, RCamA, Walker Art Gallery, Liverpool, and BWS. Lived at Newton Abbot.

Karen L BEARE 1955– Painter and draughtsman who studied at the Art Students' League of New York, 1979–80. Went on to paint portraits, commissions including Anglo-Brazilian Society, 1996. Latterly turned to abstract works. An exhibition at The Gallery in Cork Street, 1997, contained abstracts painted with the left hand, a departure leading to colourful, more spontaneous pictures. Earlier in the year showed at Plazzotta Studio, Cathcart Road. Lived in London.

Cecil BEATON 1904–1980 Photographer, stage and film designer, draughtsman, painter and writer. Born in London, he was educated at Harrow – where he studied art under W Egerton Hine – and at St John's College, Cambridge. From the mid-1920s he fast established a reputation as a society photographer and arbiter of beauty, publishing his *Book of Beauty* and working for *Vogue*. First one-man show at Cooling Galleries in 1927, of photographs, drawings and stage designs. He was to hold a number of exhibitions, in Britain and abroad. Designed for C B Cochran, including Frederick Ashton's ballet *The Last Shoot*. During World War II worked for the Ministry of Information and travelled widely abroad, his *Indian Album* and *Chinese Album* resulting from the trips. Illustrated books such as *The School for Scandal* and *The Importance of Being Earnest*, designed book covers and notable stage and film successes such as *Lady Windermere's Fan* and *My Fair Lady*. Published six volumes of diaries, covering the period 1922–74. Knighted in 1972. Memorial exhibition at the Michael Parkin Gallery in 1983, with a sale at Christie's, London, in 1984. Lived at Broadchalke, Wiltshire.

Annette BEATTIE 1957– Artist/embroiderer, married to the etcher David Beattie, she signed her meticulously embroidered pictures of wildflowers and landscapes A L Beattie. She was born in the Vale of Belvoir, Nottinghamshire, and worked as a research technician, during which time she studied for an honours degree in biological sciences. Was taught needlework by her grandmother as a child and began to experiment with machine embroidery after the birth of her daughter in 1985. She prepared her canvas by creating a design in acrylic, then applied free machine stitching to give detail, depth of colour and perspective. Couching and appliqué was also used and some threads were hand-dyed to extend the colour range. Exhibited at studio gallery at Llandygwydd, Cardigan, Dyfed.

Basil BEATTIE 1935– Painter of abstract pictures, and teacher, born in West Hartlepool, County Durham. From 1950–5 he studied at West Hartlepool College of Art, moving to the Royal Academy Schools, 1957–61. The following year Beattie began teaching at Goldsmiths' College School of Art. Beattie showed in groups at John Moores Exhibition in Liverpool, in 1965; in 1971 at Museum of Modern Art, Oxford, in Four Painters; and in 1977 at RA in British Painting 1952–1977. In 1976 he won a Major Arts Council Award. His first one-man show was at Greenwich Theatre Art Gallery in 1968, after which he showed widely, including Minories, Colchester; and Bede Gallery, Jarrow; as well as several galleries in London. Beattie was second prizewinner in the 1989–90 John Moores Liverpool Exhibition. Arts Council holds several examples of his work. Lived in London.

David BEATTIE 1955– Etcher principally who also worked in carved wood, welded metal and ceramics, teacher, born in Nottingham. Studied at Loughborough College of Education, 1974–7, as an art and design student to become a teacher, but quit in his final term when early sales of prints made living as an artist seem feasible. Supported himself by working for HM Customs & Excise for several years, but set up his own studio and was able to etch full-time. Beattie was a keen conservationist and horseman whose subjects ranged from his cats to cockerels, farmyard doors, trees and countryside characters. Showed at RA Summer Exhibitions and with Christies' Contemporary Art. Established a studio gallery at Llandygwydd, Cardigan, Dyfed. His wife was the artist/embroiderer Annette Beattie.

Charles BEAUCHAMP 1949– Painter and printmaker, noted for his landscapes and figure subjects, some of whose work had a Surrealist element. He was born in London and attended Chelsea School of Art, 1967, travelled extensively in the Far East, 1968–9, then in 1971–2 studied etching and engraving at S W Hayter's Atelier 17 in Paris. From 1969 took part in many group shows, including Young & Fantastic, ICA and tour, 1969; Third British International Print Biennale, Bradford, 1972; Graves Art Gallery, Sheffield, 1986 in A Show of Hands; and Art into Ambit 2, Smith's Gallery, 1992. Among a series of awards were 1st prize, First Irish Miniprint Exhibition, Hendriks Gallery, Dublin 1986, and Openshaw Printmaking Residency Award, Cumbria, 1994. Had a series of solo shows at Gimpel Fils from 1974. Hirshhorn Museum and Sculpture Garden, Washington; National Gallery of Wales in Cardiff; and Winnipeg Art Gallery, Canada, are among many major collections holding examples. Settled in London with frequent visits to Colombia.

Paul BEAUCHAMP 1948– Artist, designer and teacher, born in Barrow-upon-Soar, Leicestershire. He studied at Loughborough College of Art from 1967, at Hornsey College of Art, 1968–71, then from 1971–3 was a postgraduate student at Slade School of Fine Art. Russian Constructivist art and the work of architects such as Frank Lloyd Wright and Le Corbusier were important influences. After creating a company called Aqua Designs with three other artists, in 1973 Beauchamp lectured part-time at the College of Art in Cardiff, where he settled, and helped turn twilight buildings into artists' studios. The following years saw Beauchamp using glass and silicone constructions, reflecting and refracting light; wall sculpture incorporating wood, paint and glass; cibachrome photographs and drawings; and laser as an art form. In 1983 he was chosen to redesign a room at Chapter Arts, Cardiff, his first commission working directly with an architect. Six years later he worked in Charleston, South Carolina, as an artist and lecturer, having a series of exhibitions. Also showed at Serpentine Gallery, Ian Birksted Gallery in London and New York, Ikon Gallery in Birmingham and National Museum of Wales, Cardiff. Doris and Charles Saatchi bought his work.

Basil BEAUMONT: *see* **Basil RÁKÓCZÍ**

Frederick Samuel BEAUMONT 1861– Painter and draughtsman in pastel. Studied art at the Royal Academy Schools and at the Académie Julian, Paris. Exhibited widely into his old age, including RA, RI, ROI and Walker's Gallery. Was a member of the Arts Club, London. Lived in London.

Leonard BEAUMONT 1891–1986 Painter, designer and printmaker, born and based in Sheffield, where he was honorary secretary of The Sheffield Print Club. He was associated with the Grosvenor School of Modern Art and his prints show an affinity with the work of Claude Flight. Exhibited at RA, SGA of which he was a member, Redfern Gallery, Walker Art Gallery in Liverpool and elsewhere in the provinces. Victoria & Albert Museum and Scottish National Gallery of Modern Art, Edinburgh, hold examples. Beaumont's work appeared in several art periodicals, including *The Studio* and *Fine Prints of the Year*.

Sharon BEAVAN 1956– Painter and teacher, born and lived in London. She had a great empathy with the city, tirelessly exploring the streets, absorbing and recording what she saw, which emerged in colourful panoramas which could take several years to complete. She studied at Hertfordshire College of Art and Design, 1974–6; Falmouth College of Art, 1976–9; and Royal College of Art, 1981–4. Teaching included Kingston University, Central St Martins School of Art and Hertfordshire College of Art and Design. Group exhibitions included RA Summer Exhibitions from 1985; South Bank Picture Show, Royal Festival Hall from 1987; and The Celebrated City, Barbican Art Gallery, 1992. Had a series of solo shows at Le Chat Noir Gallery from 1991. She was the subject of a London Weekend Television documentary. Guildhall Art Gallery and Museum of London hold examples.

Anton BEAVER 1965– Artist who studied at Liverpool Polytechnic from 1985. He was included in group shows at Acorn Gallery and Playhouse Theatre, Liverpool, in 1986, and in 1986–7 was included in Walker Art Gallery's touring show Merseyside Artists 3, where his acrylic Sunrise over the Mersey was exhibited.

Robert BEAVER 1906–1975 Painter in oil, born in Poole, Dorset, who was by profession a doctor. Educated at Winchester College, Oxford University and St Thomas' Hospital, Beaver studied art privately in Belgium. Exhibited, sometimes as R B, at RA, ROI, NEAC, NS and in Cornwall. Lived in London and then in Cowes, Isle of Wight, where he died.

Tessa BEAVER 1932– Printmaker, painter and teacher, born in London, who gained a fine art diploma from Slade School of Fine Art, 1953, then spent a year etching there under John Buckland-Wright. After six months in Italy and Greece she worked as a freelance illustrator, then as an art editor in publishing. In 1962 Beaver went with her husband to teach in western Kenya, began painting and taught herself woodblock printing, then for 10 years after returning to England showed seriously and in 1972 bought a press and began etching again. By 1977 big editions of her prints were being regularly published by Christie's Contemporary Art and Pallas Gallery. In 1978 she set up her own studio in Leamington Spa, Warwickshire. Took part in many mixed exhibitions in Britain and abroad, including RE, RA, ICA and RWA. Had a series of solo shows at University of Warwick from 1972, later ones including Church Street Gallery, Warwick, 1988. Birmingham City Museum and Art Gallery holds her work.

Ian BECK 1947– Printmaker, illustrator and painter, born in Brighton, Sussex. He studied at the College of Art there until 1968. Went on to work as a freelance illustrator, notably for *Radio Times*, Penguin Books and Conran Associates. His first illustrated children's book was published by Oxford University Press in 1983. Merivale Editions published his four-colour lithograph *Seaside Circus*, 1984. Beck showed paintings with Francis Kyle Gallery.

Paul BECK 1926– Painter, printmaker and teacher, born in Belvedere, Kent, who studied at Gravesend School of Art and Royal College of Art. Went on to teach at Cambridge College of Art. Work appeared in group shows, including RA, Cambridge Print Editions exhibitions, 1964–71, Brooklyn Museum, 1970, and elsewhere. One-man shows included Ludlow Craft Studio and Gallery, 1977, Malvern Festival, 1979, Graffiti Gallery, 1980, and a series at the Old Fire Engine House, Ely. His work is held in collections in continental Europe, Australia and America and in Britain, including Fry Art Gallery, Saffron Walden.

Stuart BECK 1903– Painter and writer, born in Barnes, south-west London, who began sea painting as a full-time career in 1968. Studied at Rochester School of Art, 1919–21. Was then 15 years a graphic designer with a London colour printing firm;

several years head of studio in a publishing company; in World War II did technical illustration for the Admiralty; and after demobilisation in 1946 did a variety of work from technical cutaways to posters and book jackets as a freelance. Was elected to RSMA in 1980. Also showed with RI, RBA, SGA and elsewhere. Had solo shows at Solent Gallery, Lymington, Hampshire, where he lived; and Skipwith Gallery, Winchester. RSMA holds work in its Diploma Collection as do Royal National Lifeboat Museum, Poole, and National Maritime Museum, Greenwich. Among his books were *How to Draw Fishing Craft* and *The Ship how she Works*.

Sarah BECKETT 1946– Painter, notable for rich palette. She studied at Byam Shaw School of Drawing and Painting, 1963–5, then Chelsea College of Art, 1977–80. From the early 1970s she appeared in many mixed exhibitions, including Six British Artists, Trinidad, 1971; San Patricio, Colombia, 1973; People's Gallery, 1982; NEAC, 1983; and Queen Elizabeth Hall, 1986. She had a solo exhibition at Bank of Nova Scotia, Trinidad, in 1971, then at The Gore Hotel, London, 1979. From 1985 showed one-man at Christopher Hull Gallery. National Labour Museum and several foreign public collections hold her work.

Janet BECKWITH 1956– Artist in a variety of media, and teacher, who did a foundation art and design course at Wakefield College, Wakefield, 1988–9, gaining an honours degree in fine art at Leeds Metropolitan University, 1989–92, attending a 1992 art therapy summer school at Leeds University. She lectured part-time at Wakefield College, art drama and independent learning skills for students with special needs. In 1997, Beckwith was artist-in-residence for DIVA (Development Initiatives for Voluntary Arts) and Yorkshire Art Circus. Mixed shows included Fresh Art at Business Design Centre, Islington, 1992; Bookies and Boxers, Manor House Gallery, Ilkley, 1993; and Brought to Book, Collins Gallery, Glasgow, and tour, 1996. Her solo show Ties, 1997–8, toured from the Art Gallery in Wakefield, Yorkshire, where she lived, to Hardware Gallery. This explored "ties that bind us together, make us feel safe and protected or tangle us in painful knots".

Roy BEDDINGTON 1910–1995 Painter, with a special interest in watercolours of natural history and the countryside, illustrator and author. Born in London, son of a barrister, he attended Rugby School, where he cultivated his lifelong passion for fishing; was then offered a place at Slade School of Fine Art by Henry Tonks, but spent only a few weeks there; opted instead to read law at Oxford University; then, after private lessons from Bernard Adams, returned to the Slade under Randolph Schwabe, also studying in Florence. His own books included *The Adventures of Thomas Trout*, 1939, and *A Countryman's Verse*, 1981. Among other books illustrated were a series by Stephen Gwynn, including *The Happy Fisherman*, 1936, and J W Walker's *Riverside Reflections*, 1947. Did posters for Shell encouraging travel through Britain. Showed in mixed exhibitions at RA, NEAC, RWS, Whitechapel Art Gallery and Fine Art Society. Ackermann's gave him his first solo pre-war show. He was an Arts Club member and for many years was a leading figure in the Salmon and Trout Association. His daughter Sarah Beddington was also a painter. Lived at Chute Cadley, Hampshire, and died in Salisbury, Wiltshire.

Sheila BEDELLS 1916– Painter, born in Duston, Northamptonshire, who studied at Epsom School of Art with David Birch, other teachers including Karl Hagedorn and Peter Oliver. Showed variously and did designs for Christmas and greetings cards. Lived in Betchworth, Surrey.

Celia BEDFORD 1904–1959 Portrait and figure painter, printmaker and draughtsman, born in London, daughter of the artist Francis Bedford. Studied at Chelsea School of Art under Percy Hague Jowett and John Revel. Exhibited WIAC, of which she was a member, RA, NEAC, LG and Leicester Galleries. Atkinson Art Gallery, Southport, and Birmingham City Museum and Art Gallery hold her work. Lived in London.

Francis Donkin BEDFORD 1864–1954 Illustrator and painter whose work reflected his architectural training. He was born and lived in London, studied at South Kensington and the Royal Academy architectural schools, then was articled to Sir Arthur Blomfield, the architect, for several years. His wife was the painter Helen Bedford. E V Lucas, W M Thackeray, Charles Dickens and Oliver Goldsmith were among the authors he illustrated. Bedford was a member of the Art Workers' Guild and showed at RA, Ridley Art Club and NEAC.

Helen BEDFORD 1874–1949 Portrait painter, daughter of the artist Hugh Carter and wife of the illustrator Francis Donkin Bedford. The family of the poet Sir Henry Newbolt and the architect Charles Voysey were among her subjects. She was a member of PS, Ridley Art Club and the Women's Guild of Arts, also showing at RA, NEAC and SWA. Lived in London.

Oliver Herbert BEDFORD 1902– Painter, teacher and printmaker, born in Boston Spa, Yorkshire, the son of an architect. Studied at the Royal Institute of Fine Arts in Rome, 1919–23, where he taught for a short time, then at the Courtauld Institute of Art, London, 1935–6. He went on to teach at Truro School of Art and elsewhere in Cornwall, which was the focus of his career, being closely associated with the St Ives Society of Artists and several other such societies within Cornwall. Showed extensively at Fine Art Society, also RI, SGA of which he was a member and NS. Lived in Truro.

Richard Perry BEDFORD 1883–1967 Sculptor in stone and marble, born in Torquay, Devon. Studied at Central School of Arts and Crafts and Chelsea School of Art. He was keeper at the the Victoria and Albert Museum, 1924–46, first of the Department of Sculpture, then of Circulation, and was then for two years curator of pictures for the Ministry of Works. Exhibited Cooling Galleries, Lefevre Gallery, RA, NS, LG, RWA and elsewhere in the provinces. The Victoria & Albert Museum and Bristol City Art Gallery hold his work. Bedford, who was son of the artist George Bedford, lived finally at West Mersea, Essex, and had a retrospective at The Minories, Colchester, in 1968.

Glynis BEECROFT 1945– Sculptor, teacher and writer who was educated at Portsmouth College of Art, 1962–6, then Goldsmiths' College School of Art, 1966–7. Teaching appointments included West Dean College, Sussex, and Southampton College of Art. Exhibitions included Southampton University, David Paul Gallery in Chichester, RBS and elsewhere. Her books *Carving Techniques* and *Casting Techniques* were acknowledged primers. Grantham Art Gallery holds her work and her limestone carving Family, 1983, was sited in Stevenage New Town. Lived in Clanfield, Hampshire.

Clem BEER 1931– Painter, printmaker, illustrator and teacher, born and lived in London. Studied at Slade School of Fine Art, 1949–52; lived in North Yorkshire for 10 years painting and teaching, having his first solo show at University of York, 1966; returned to Slade as a printmaking postgraduate, 1968–9, under Anthony Gross. In 1979 became chairman of Printmakers' Council. Showed with RWS, RA, Whitechapel Art Gallery, Woodlands Art Gallery and elsewhere, including Spirit of London Exhibition, Royal Festival Hall, 1982, where he was a prizewinner. Work was bought by RA under the Annie Hugill Trust. Beer was "interested in overturning the conventional viewpoint of perspective and allowing my work the freedom to find the new patterns and rhythms of a more personal vision". University College and Guildhall, British Museum and Arts Council plus several foreign collections hold examples.

Richard BEER 1928– Painter, draughtsman and designer, and teacher. He attended the Slade School of Fine Art, 1945–50. Won Robert Ross and Henriques Scholarships. Beer also studied at S W Hayter's Atelier 17, and École des Beaux-Arts, in Paris, under a French Government Scholarship. In 1955 Beer designed sets and costumes for John Cranko's *Lady and the Fool* at Royal Opera House, Covent Garden, later productions including *Change of Tune*, in 1958, at Strand Theatre, and in 1968 *Napoli*, also at Covent Garden. He taught at Slade, 1957–60, and later at Chelsea School of Art, in 1987 being engaged at the British School in Rome. Beer was especially interested in modest, quirky urban architecture, which found its outlet in a variety of printed work including some for Shell, Christie's Contemporary Art and magazine and book illustration. Had many mixed and one-man show appearances, the latter including Parkin Gallery, 1982, and Sally Hunter Fine Art, 1990–2. Tate Gallery, Victoria & Albert Museum and Arts Council hold his work.

Max BEERBOHM 1872–1956 Humorous caricaturist and writer, born in London, his half-brother being the actor-manager Sir Herbert Beerbohm-Tree. Educated at Charterhouse and Oxford University, Max was a leading figure in 1890s literary London. First published drawings appeared in *The Strand Magazine* in 1892 and he contributed to *The Yellow Book*. He succeeded Bernard Shaw as dramatic critic of the *Saturday Review*. First book of caricatures, *Caricatures of Twenty-Five Gentlemen*, was published in 1896 and he had his first one-man show at the Carfax Gallery eight years later. He was associated with the Leicester Galleries, NEAC, National Portrait Society and IS. From 1910, apart from the war years, he lived mainly in Rapallo, Italy. Tate Gallery holds his work. As well as his drawings Max was famous for his novel *Zuleika Dobson*, 1911, a fantastic picture of Oxford life, his essays and his broadcasts, all tinged with a dandyish flair. Tate Gallery holds his work. Knighted, 1939. Memorial exhibition Leicester Galleries, 1957.

Sue BEERE 1944– Artist and teacher who was for a time a research technician in the department of physiology at Oxford University, also working as personal assistant to the lung specialist Professor Ivan de Burgh Daly. Beere studied painting at Walthamstow School of Art, 1966–8, then taught at Royal College of Art, 1968–71. In 1974 she had a painting commissioned for Sir Robert McAlpine & Sons Ltd and taught part-time at the Central School. Was included in the 1978 Hayward Annual at Hayward Gallery, with four items; Installation Piece 1–4, slender geometrical abstracts in wood. Had a solo show at New 57 Gallery, 1973, with a studio exhibition at Butlers Wharf.

Jane BEESON 1930– Painter, born in Weybridge, Surrey, who studied at Kingston School of Art, 1949–51, then at École des Beaux-Arts, Paris, 1951–2, and at Slade School of Fine Art, 1953, with Lucien Freud. After having a family of four she began painting professionally in 1960, showing at John Moores Liverpool Exhibition, 1961, New Art Centre, Rowan Gallery and elsewhere. In 1963 she was a prizewinner at Arnolfini Open Competition, Bristol. Ferens Art Gallery, Hull, holds her work Mauve and Yellow, 1962. Beeson was a member of the St Ives art scene in the 1960s, although living in Devon. "My painting was Abstract Expressionist and was influenced by a period of four years when I was in Canada and America." Lived in Manaton, Devon.

David BEGBIE 1955– Sculptor, draughtsman and printmaker who was born in Edinburgh. He studied at Winchester School of Art, 1975–6, graduated with honours from Gloucestershire College of Art and Design, 1977–80, then was at Slade School of Sculpture, 1980–2. Among his awards was Gane Travel Scholarship, 1979, and Elizabeth Greenshields Award, Canada, 1980. Figurative steelmesh sculpture was a feature of Begbie's output, the results sometimes being hieratic, ambivalent, mysterious. His solo appearances included Brompton Gallery from 1984; Salama-Caro Gallery from 1987; and Catto Gallery, 1993. Group shows included Open Studios, Wapping, 1982; Young Variety Club of Great Britain, 1987; and International Art Fair, Miami, 1993. Lived in London.

Torie BEGG 1962– Artist, born in London, who studied graphic design at Richmond College, 1980; illustration at City and

Guilds of London Art School, 1984; and advanced printmaking at Central School of Art, 1987. Group exhibitions included Benson & Hedges Annual Gold Awards, Hamilton Gallery, 1985; Louise Hallett Gallery, 1987; Sue Williams Gallery, 1988; and Galerie Albrecht, Munich, and Real Art at Southampton City Art Gallery, both 1995. Solo exhibitions included *The Economist* Building, 1992, and Art & Public/Pierre Huber, Geneva, 1995.

Reinhard BEHRENS 1951– Artist and teacher, born in Scheeszel, West Germany, who attended Hamburg College of Art, 1971–9. After completing postgraduate studies at Edinburgh College of Art, 1979–80, he gained an Andrew Grant Scholarship (Major Award), 1980–1, from 1982 lecturing part-time there. Was included in Scottish Print Open Three, organised by Dundee Printmakers' Workshop, 1983. Behrens was a member of RSW, at one time president of SSA, also exhibiting at RSA. Lived in Pittenweem, Fife.

Romi BEHRENS 1939– Painter and printmaker, born in London, full name Rosemary Tunstall-Behrens. She had no formal training but was "'discovered' by Michael Canney in 1960". Her work was colourful, figurative but stylized and was shown at Newlyn Society of Artists of which she was a member; Brunswick Gallery; Judd Street Gallery; RA; Salt House Gallery, St Ives; and in 1993 she was included in Jeremy Le Grice's Cornwall: A Painter's Choice, at Cadogan Contemporary. Portraits of musicians were an important feature of her output. Lived at Rosudgeon, Penzance, Cornwall.

Timothy BEHRENS 1937– Painter, born in London, who studied at the Slade School of Fine Art, 1954–8. Showed at Young Contemporaries, 1955–8, was included in the Café Royal Memorial Exhibition, 1965, and in Helen Lessore and the Beaux Arts Gallery, Marlborough Fine Art, 1967. Behrens was one of a group of painters – including Auerbach, Andrews, Bacon and Freud – who frequented Muriel Belcher's Colony Room drinking club in Soho. He had three solo exhibitions at Beaux Arts from 1960; one at Upper Street Gallery, 1970; another toured from Galleria 88, Rome, 1973; and at William Darby, 1974. He travelled widely in Europe, settling in Italy in 1970. Arts Council has his oil on board A Lunch Party, 1961.

Pauline Margaret BEILBY 1927– Sculptor and textile designer, born in Bramcote, Nottinghamshire. Portrait busts and equine portraits were an important feature of her output. In 1947–51 studied at Nottingham School of Art. Was a part-time designer for George Pearson & Sons, of Basford, in mid-1950s. Showed at Gerald Anthony Fine Arts and Victoria Gallery, Nottingham. Lived at Woodthorpe, Nottinghamshire. Later showed under her married name Pauline Margaret Barnes.

George BELCHER 1875–1947 Cartoonist, painter and printmaker, born in London. He attended Gloucester School of Art, then gradually became known for his contributions to publications such as *Punch, The Tatler* and *Vanity Fair*. Showed extensively at RA, Fine Art Society and Leicester Galleries, where his shows such as London Types and Characters and London Life and Character before World War I were very successful. Died at Chiddingfold, Surrey, having a retrospective at Cranleigh Hall seven years later, with another at Marc Oxley Fine Art, Uppingham, 1995. Tate Gallery holds his work.

William BELCHER 1923– Painter and creator of boxes and mixed-media constructions. After service in World War II he studied at Worthing School of Art and Royal College of Art, gaining a travel bursary from Royal Society of Arts. He showed at RA Summer Exhibition, AIA and had several mixed-media constructions included in Art in Boxes at England & Co, 1991. Lived at Kew Gardens, Richmond, Surrey.

Betsy Tyler BELL fl.from 1980s– Painter, printmaker and teacher, born in Lancashire, who did a foundation course at Oxford Brooks University, then studying at Ruskin School of Art, 1984–8. She graduated in fine art, with her master's from St Edmund Hall. Tutors included Jean Lodge, Stan Smith and David Tindle. Bell was a visiting professor/artist-in-residence at Washington and Lee University, Virginia, also teaching at Sunningwell Art School, Oxford, at Abingdon College and Oxford Printmakers. Landscape, cycles of nature and the elements were key features of Bell's work. Although she might incorporate recognisable images, she preferred "to work in mainly abstract format using the textures of my own hand-made paper and the colour of pure pigments together with acrylic", inviting "the viewer to participate in a personal way without preconceptions". Pictures were built up "in layers over many weeks and sometimes months". Group shows included RE Open, Bankside Gallery, 1992; Place Juberon (Festival des Arts), Crest, France, 1994; and Templeton College, Oxford, 1997. Had a solo show at Templeton, 1994, later ones including Linacre College and Whistles Fashions, both in Oxford in 1997. Worked on a mural for children's ward in Westminster and Chelsea Hospital. Washington and Lee University, Southern Arts and Oxfordshire County Council also hold examples. Lived in Oxford, part of the year in Crest.

David BELL 1916–1959 Painter and curator, born in London, son of Sir Harold Bell who was keeper of manuscripts and Egerton librarian at the British Museum. David Bell attended Merchant Taylors' School, then studied art at Chelsea School of Art, 1933, and the Royal College of Art, 1933–7, where his teachers included Gilbert Spencer. Bell then spent two years as a draughtsman with the Egyptian Exploration Society. He was the Arts Council's assistant director for Wales, 1946–51, then until his death curator of the Glynn Vivian Art Gallery, Swansea. That gallery gave him a memorial show in 1960–1, and he had already exhibited widely in Wales. Bell was a prolific writer on art, his books including the notable *The Language of Pictures*, 1953, and *The Artist in Wales*, 1957. He lived in Cardiff and the National Museum of Wales there holds his work.

Eileen BELL 1907– Painter of figures, landscape and still life in a vigorous, Expressionist style. She studied at St John's Wood School of Art, 1939, under Patrick Millard, and at Anglo-French Art Centre, 1945. Other teachers included Kenneth Martin, Ernest Perry and Alfred Green. After the war Bell continued to paint but also worked freelance for the Council of Industrial Design on textiles and as an interior designer for exhibitions. She also painted furniture, designed sets and advertisements for magazines and potted. Was a member of AIA, showed by invitation with RBA and LG and exhibited at Leicester Galleries, Young Contemporaries and in the provinces. Later solo shows included Duncalfe Galleries, Harrogate, 1989, and Chappel Galleries, Chappel, 1992. Lived in Suffolk.

Harry BELL 1947– Painter, mainly in oil, also acrylic, largely self-taught. He was born and lived in Gateshead, County Durham. Attended local Boys' Grammar School, in 1972 studying art at night classes at Newcastle College of Art and Design. From 1989 he studied painting at Open College of the Arts based on Newcastle Polytechnic, with Liz Rowe and notably William Varley. Bell's interest was "in the forms and colour of the urban landscape, particularly that of Newcastle upon Tyne, and what it can say about its creators. The city is dark, sometimes bleak and unhappy, but it possesses an undercurrent of mystery and allure." He showed at Newcastle Polytechnic, 1991; Federation of Northern Art Societies, 1992; and in 1993 John Laing Exhibition, University of Northumbria and Open Door, at Halton House. University of Northumbria gave him a show in 1995. Bell's work is held by private collections in England and America.

Jean BELL 1923–1992 Painter in oil and teacher, born in Cheshire, married to the artist Tom Pemberton. She was the grand-daughter of the Liverpool portrait painter Mona Hopton Bell, 1867–1940. Studied at Liverpool School of Art, then taught at Wirral Grammar School for Girls, 1944–8; lectured at St Helens Municipal School of Art, 1948–50; joining City of Leeds College of Education, 1951–66, finally as senior lecturer. Showed in north of England in group shows, notably with Yorkshire Artists, and in Ashford, Kent, having a solo exhibition of work, 1950–80 at Associate House, Ashford, 1981. Her main works were the garden abstract series. Lived finally in Leeds, Yorkshire.

Judson BELL 1877– Watercolourist who was a professional businessman, born in Yeovil, Somerset, but educated in Shropshire. Studied at Welshpool School of Art, then later privately in London. Member of both the Langham Sketch Club and Wapping Group of Artists. Showed there, SMA and in the provinces. Lived at Pinner, Middlesex.

Laura Anning BELL 1867–1950 Portrait painter, notably in pastel, born in France of English parents. She studied in Paris and at the Slade School of Fine Art with Alphonse Legros. During her first marriage she exhibited under her married name of Laura Richard-Troncy, then after marrying the painter Robert Anning Bell used his surname, sometimes with a hyphen. Showed at RA from 1921, at Paris Salon where her awards included several medals, Fine Art Society, Ridley Art Society and elsewhere. Shared a show with Mary Davis at Fine Art Society in 1919. Tate Gallery has her portrait of Annie Horniman. Died in London.

Malcolm BELL 1963– Artist, born in Rothbury, Northumberland. He attended course at Newcastle, 1981–2, then Birmingham Polytechnic, 1982–3. Moved to Isle of Skye, in 1985 Bell began drawing with Hannah Horsfall, their works being joint efforts in which each had the right to make and obliterate marks. An example of their abstract work was Twentysixth Drawing, in 1992 East & South Norwich Gallery/Kent Institute of Art and Design show. Eventually worked in London.

Martin BELL 1907–1970 Painter and teacher, full name Norman Martin Bell, born in Great Meols, Cheshire. He was brought up in an artistic atmosphere and went on to train at Liverpool College of Art, 1925–30, Royal College of Art, 1931–3. Taught part-time at King's School, Chester, 1933–4, then returned to Liverpool College of Art, becoming head of the school of fine art, 1965–8, before retiring. Early influences on Bell's work were Puvis de Chavannes, the Post-Impressionists and Walter Sickert, but from the late 1950s it became more abstract, Nicolas de Staël's pictures becoming important to him. Recorded war bomb damage in Liverpool. Bell was long a member of the Liverpool Academy, being its president, 1957–60, and showed with Sandon Studios Society. In 1970 the Academy exhibition included a small memorial show of Bell's work, including a contribution from Walker Art Gallery, Liverpool. The rood screen at St Stephen's, Prenton, is a fine example of Bell's figurative work. Lived in Wallasey, Cheshire.

Norman Martin BELL: *see* **Martin BELL**

Ophelia Gordon BELL: *see* **Ophelia GORDON-BELL**

Quentin BELL 1910–1996 Painter, sculptor, potter, writer and teacher, son of the art critic Clive Bell and the artist Vanessa Bell. He went to Leighton School and with some help from Roger Fry studied painting in England and Paris. In World War II Bell was a member of the Political Warfare Executive. Among his teaching positions were Slade professor of fine art, Oxford University, 1964–5, Ferens professor of fine art, Hull University, 1965–6, and professor of history and theory of art, Sussex University, 1967–75, then being made emeritus professor. His books included *Ruskin*, 1963; *Bloomsbury*, 1968; *Virginia Woolf, a Biography*, 1972; a novel, *The Brandon Papers*, 1985; and his memoirs, *Elders and Betters*, 1995. Had a series of solo shows from 1935 as well as appearing in many mixed exhibitions. A number of public collections hold his work. With Duncan Grant and Vanessa Bell Quentin Bell painted extensive murals in Berwick Church, Sussex, near where he lived at Firle.

Richard BELL 1955– Creator of systematic paintings and reliefs, based in London. In 1977 he constructed a series of reliefs funded by Southern Arts Council. Bell was interested in structure, specifically relational qualities of colour, its grammar and figuration expressed within a practice of making paintings and related texts. As well as engaging in group theoretical work, Bell contributed to exhibitions including the 1979 Künstlerbücher show at Galerie Lydia Megert in Switzerland; The House Construction Show at House, 1981; Colour Presentations, Gardner Centre Gallery, Sussex University, and tour, 1986; and Complexions, at Galerie L'Idee, Zoetermeer, Netherlands, and Dean Clough, Halifax, 1989. Arts Council holds Bell's work.

Stan BELL 1928– Mural and relief artist and teacher, born and lived in Glasgow. Studied at local School of Art, 1966–70, where he later taught. His mural work was to be found around the city and he showed with Glasgow League of Artists, Scottish Young Contemporaries and The Clyde Group.

Trevor BELL 1930– Painter and teacher, born in Leeds, Yorkshire, where he attended the College of Art, 1947–52. For several years until mid-1950s he then taught at Harrogate College of Art. On the suggestion of the painter Terry Frost, Bell and his wife sold up their home and motorcycled to Cornwall to work in St Ives. In Yorkshire Bell had painted industrial landscapes, but in Cornwall his work took a new direction, and while still landscape-based he became concerned with land-shape and sea interactions which created abstract pictures. After short periods in Italy Bell took up a Gregory Fellowship at Leeds University in 1960. A number of teaching posts in Britain and America followed until in the mid-1970s he returned to Florida State University, Tallahassee. Bell showed with Penwith Society of Arts from 1956, at Tate Gallery and New Art Centre in group shows. In 1995 a group of his pictures was exhibited at Tate Gallery St Ives and in 1995–6 he was included in the John Moores Liverpool Exhibition. Had a series of solo exhibitions with Waddington Galleries from 1958; Whitechapel Art Gallery; Florida State University; and in 1998 The New Millennium Gallery, St Ives, celebrated Bell's return to Cornwall with his first major show at a private venue since his return to Britain. Arts Council holds his work.

Vanessa BELL 1879–1961 Painter, decorator and designer of textiles and ceramics, born in London. She was the daughter of the writer Sir Leslie Stephen, sister of the writer Virginia Woolf and married the art critic Clive Bell, all leading members of what became known as the Bloomsbury Group. She studied with Arthur Cope at the Royal Academy Schools. Worked in the Omega Workshops with Roger Fry and collaborated with Duncan Grant on various decorative projects, eventually living with Grant for many years at Charleston Farmhouse, Firle, Sussex. Was founder of Friday Club in 1910 and two years later participated in the Second Post-Impressionist Exhibition. Showed in groups at Leicester Galleries, NEAC, Lefevre and Redfern Galleries and elsewhere. Had first solo show at Independent Gallery in 1922. Memorial shows held by Adams Gallery in 1961 and Arts Council, with tour, in 1964. In 1996 there was a retrospective as part of Unione Donna's 7th Biennale in Ferrara, Italy, curated with Bloomsbury Gallery, where it was also shown.

Arthur Bell FOSTER 1900– Painter, designer and illustrator, born at Northallerton, Yorkshire. Attended Sheffield School of Art, 1924–9, under G Vernon Stokes. Exhibited RA, RI, RBA, UA, with AEB and widely in the provinces. Member of Midland Arts Club, Birmingham. Lived in Birmingham.

John BELLANY 1942– Painter, born into a fishing family at Port Seton, East Lothian. He attended Edinburgh College of Art, 1960–5. During his time there, in 1962, he won an Andrew Grant Scholarship, permitting travel to Paris; and for several years with Alexander Moffat he showed his pictures outside RSA, in opposition to the Establishment, work in the Northern European Expressionist-Realist tradition. Studied at Royal College of Art, 1965–8, where he continued to develop his personal symbolism, fed by travels to the Low Countries and Germany and the works and sights he saw there. A large number of watercolour portraits was completed in the 1980s, following a series of serious illnesses. By then Bellany was recognised as an artist of international stature. Had many solo shows, including The Dromidaris Gallery, Netherlands, 1965; a series at Drian Gallery in 1970s; Compass Gallery, Glasgow, 1987 and 1990; and abroad. His works are in principal public galleries in Britain, including Tate Gallery and Scottish National Gallery of Modern Art. Lived in London and was made RA in 1991.

William de BELLEROCHE 1912–1969 Painter, printmaker, collector and bohemian, born in London, but brought up in Sussex, where he finally lived in Brighton. His father was a painter, Albert, who died in 1944, and William – widely known as Count Willie – inherited the French title. Although he taught himself to paint, William was much influenced by the artist Frank Brangwyn, whom he met in 1934 and befriended for over 25 years. He wrote several books on Brangwyn, who encouraged William to take up printmaking. He was a great collector of objects such as shells, which appear in his paintings, and formed the largest private collection of Brangwyns in the world. Before World War II his initiative led to the foundation of the Brangwyn-de Belleroche Museum in Orange, France. He had a wide circle of friends, including the actresses Hermione Baddeley and Flora Robson, the artists Augustus John and James Fitton and Gwen, Lady Melchett, many of whom he painted. William was very fond of fish, and had a one-man show at Prunier's Restaurant in 1963, another being held in an interior design shop in Brighton the year following. Others followed annually at Upper Grosvenor Galleries. Fine Art Society held a show in 1989 which showed William to have been a witty, amusing Colourist. British Museum and many foreign collections hold his work.

Leslie BELLIN-CARTER 1878– Artist and teacher, born in London. He studied art with F G Stevens and at the Slade School of Fine Art, where he gained the Trevelyan Goodall Art

Scholarship, studying with Henry Tonks and Philip Wilson Steer. He published several books on drawing and was for many years a university board adjudicator, having taught at Eton College and while teaching at Wellington College. Exhibited RA, IS, Ridley Art Club and in the provinces. Lived at Woking, Surrey.

Elinor BELLINGHAM-SMITH 1906–1988 Painter and illustrator, born in London, daughter of the surgeon and art collector Guy Bellingham-Smith and niece of the painter Hugh Bellingham-Smith. Married the painter Rodrigo Moynihan in 1931, separating from him in 1957. Studied piano and dancing to advanced level, but eventually opted for painting, attending Slade School of Fine Art, 1928–31, where Henry Tonks regarded her highly. In 1930s she showed at LG and Leicester Galleries, having her first one-man show there in 1948, and also completed drawings and illustrations for Shell and *Harper's Bazaar*. Her painting The Island, done for the Festival of Britain in 1951, went into the Arts Council collection; the Tate Gallery and provincial collections also hold her work. Finally lived in Boxted, Suffolk, and died in Ipswich. Bellingham-Smith was noted for her sensitive pictures of figures in landscape, notably in her later years landscapes of East Anglia and the Fens. Memorial exhibition New Grafton Gallery in 1989.

Alan Waddington BELLIS 1883–1960 All-round architect, modeller, metal worker, painter and teacher, born in Manchester, who studied at Leeds College of Art and at the Royal College of Art, gaining his diploma in 1910. He won an RIBA Travelling Scholarship that took him to Italy, enhancing his architectural knowledge. Exhibited at RA, RWA and in the provinces, from 1921 being a member of Ipswich Art Club. Bellis lived in Ipswich, Suffolk, and taught at its Art School from 1914–48. He designed and made the diocesan crozier for the Bishop of St Edmundsbury and Ipswich when the See was created in 1916. He also carved the head of Sir Thomas Wolsey above the side door to the Wolsey Art Gallery at Christchurch Mansion, Ipswich, where a Bellis show was held in 1997. This included a drawing of Bellis by one of his pupils, Frank Ward, who remembered him as "a beautiful watercolourist who really knew his buildings". Leeds City Art Gallery also holds his work.

THE BELSIZE GROUP: *see* **Adèle REIFENBERG**

Franta BELSKY 1921– Sculptor, born in Brno, Czechoslovakia, who studied at Prague Academy of Fine Arts, Central School of Arts and Crafts, 1939, and Royal College of Art, 1950. After Army service, 1940–5, pursued career making portrait sculptures, figures and monuments. Commissions included Constellation, Colchester, 1953; Joy-Ride, Stevenage New Town, 1958; Fountains, Shell Centre, 1959–61; Mountbatten Memorial in Horse Guards Parade; Winston Churchill statue at Fulton, Missouri; and Lord Cottesloe, at National Theatre. Showed at RA from 1943 and he gained Jean Masson Davidson Award, 1978. Was included in British Sculpture in the Twentieth Century at Whitechapel Art Gallery, 1981–2. Was a fellow of RBS and president of SPS. Lived in Sutton Courtenay, Oxfordshire. In 1997 Belsky married the Czech Sculptor Irena Sedlecká.

Leslie Frederick BELTON 1912– Artist in various media, furniture maker and teacher, born and educated in Birmingham where he attended the College of Arts and Crafts, 1929–34. Showed at RA, PS, NS and widely in the provinces. Royal Air Force College in Cranwell and public galleries in Swindon and Reading hold his work. Lived in Reading, Berkshire, where he was a member of the Guild of Artists.

Geoffrey BEMROSE 1896–1974 Watercolour painter, born in Leicester, who studied art under B J Fletcher at the College of Arts and Crafts there. Bemrose, who became director of Stoke-on-Trent City Museum and Art Gallery, was a watercolour and ceramics specialist who wrote on the latter subject. He was finally at the Museum and Art Gallery, Leicester.

Zoë BENBOW 1963– Painter whose work included richly coloured abstract canvases, who studied at Berkshire College, Ravensbourne College and Royal College of Art. She was a British Institute Fund and Barclays Young Painter Finalist award winner. Took part in mixed shows at Long and Ryle, 1989; Sue Williams, 1990; Discerning Eye, at Mall Galleries and Galleria G, Madrid, both 1992; Salama-Caro Gallery, 1993; and Berkeley Square Gallery, 1994, plus regular appearances at LG and Contemporary Art Society Art Market. Later solo exhibitions include Delfina Studios Trust, 1995, and Christopher Hull Gallery, 1996. HRH The Prince of Wales, Arthur Andersen & Company and Unilever hold examples.

Mildred BENDALL 1891–1977 Painter of still life and landscape in a rich, Fauve-style manner and palette, born in Bordeaux, France, of Anglo-French parents. Their wealth enabled her to paint for her pleasure. She studied in atelier of Félix Carme, 1910–14, and had early success, the Union Feminine à Bordeaux and Musée des Beaux-Arts both acquiring works, as later did the Musée d'Art Moderne, Paris. In 1927–8 attended Académie de la Grande Chaumière, Paris, and worked closely with Matisse. When the Société des Artistes Indépendants was formed in Bordeaux in 1928 Bendall began a close association with it, holding several positions. She exhibited extensively in ensuing years until she died in Bordeaux, where she was buried in the Protestant cemetery. Large retrospective was held by Société Artistique de Mérignac in 1981. Another notable show was held at Whitford and Hughes, 1987, Whitford Fine Art adding a retrospective in 1996.

Zadok BEN-DAVID 1949– Artist in various materials and teacher, noted for abstract works in wood. Was born in Yemen, then emigrated to Israel. From 1971–3 studied at Bezalel Academy of Art and Design, Jerusalem. Moved to England as assistant to the sculptor N H Azaz in 1974 and became a student at Reading University fine art department. From 1975–6 studied on the advanced sculpture course at St Martin's School of Art, joining the staff there in 1977. In that year gained a commission for Runcorn Shopping City. Shows included Playhouse Gallery, Harlow, and Air Gallery, 1976; Vehicle Art, Montreal, 1979; and House Gallery, 1981. Had a solo show at Air Gallery, 1980, Woodlands Art Gallery, 1982, and Benjamin Rhodes Gallery, 1992. Arts Council holds his work.

Leslie Charlotte BENENSON 1941– Sculptor, printmaker, painter, illuminator and calligrapher, born in London, who studied at Regent Street Polytechnic, 1958–63, with Geoffrey Deeley and James Osborne, and manuscript illumination and calligraphy privately with Anthony Wood, 1962–4, during which she moved to Sussex, settling in Bexhill. Became a freelance artist from 1963, "tending to specialise in drawing animals and birds, also some landscape watercolours". Was elected a craft member of Society of Scribes and Illuminators, 1964, a fellow of RE, 1978. Was also a member of Guild of Sussex Craftsmen and the Eastbourne Group. Showed at RA from 1966, at Victoria & Albert Museum from 1971 and had solo shows with Rye Art Gallery, 1971, John Gage Gallery, Eastbourne, 1975, and elsewhere. In 1976 had 23 wood engravings published in *Coursing*. Ashmolean Museum in Oxford, Towner Art Gallery in Eastbourne and some churches hold her work.

Gordon BENINGFIELD 1936-1998 Creator of country books, painter, designer, artist on glass and broadcaster, born in London, his father a Thames lighterman. The family moved to Hertfordshire in the early 1940s, he settled after marriage near Hemel Hempstead and the county's countryside and that of Dorset were favourite subjects. Left school at 15, was apprenticed to Faithcraft, an ecclesiastical art firm in St Albans, then from 1968 freelanced, having had a successful London solo exhibition of wildlife pictures. Beningfield was a knowledgeable entomologist and conservationist. In 1981 the General Post Office commissioned a set of butterfly stamps, in 1985 a set of insects. He was made president of the British Butterfly Conservation Society in 1989, vice-chairman of the Countryside Restoration Trust in 1993 and in 1997 the British Naturalists' Association gave him the Peter Scott Memorial Award. Created a series of memorial windows for the Household Cavalry, Coldstream Guards and Parachute Regiment, in 1995 being elected a freeman of the City of London and a liveryman of the Glass Sellers' Company. He was best known for his many books, which included *Beningfield's Butterflies*, 1978; *Beningfield's Countryside*, 1980; and a pictorial autobiography, *Gordon Beningfield, The Artist and His Work*, 1994. Among his enthusiasms were field sports, cricket, steam trains, Spitfires and vintage cars. Died in London.

Ronald BENHAM 1915–1993 Painter, printmaker and teacher, born in London. He studied at Hornsey School of Art, teachers including John Moody, Robert Lyon and Russell Reeve. Became member of NEAC, 1972, and RBA, 1977, also showing at RA, RP, in the provinces and abroad. Taught at Epsom School of Art, lived in Cheam, Surrey, and died after a stroke.

John BENISON 1918– Advertising designer, artist in watercolour, chalk, pastel, pen and ink and pencil, and wood carver. Born in London, son of the artist Steven Spurrier, Benison went on to hold a number of positions in advertising agencies, with Kemsley Newspapers and as a teacher of advertising design. Studied art at the Central School of Arts and Crafts, teachers including Bernard Meninsky, John Skeaping and John Farleigh, and at the St John's Wood School under Patrick Ferguson Millard and Ernest Perry. Exhibited RA and RBA. Lived at Ashover, Chesterfield, Derbyshire.

Anthony BENJAMIN 1931– Painter, printmaker, sculptor and relief artist and teacher, born in Boarhunt, Hampshire. From 1946–9 Benjamin did a part-time engineering course at Southall Technical College, followed by four years at Regent Street Polytechnic, then several months studying drawing in Fernand Léger's Paris studio in 1951. Late in 1955 he moved to St Ives, Cornwall, where he divided his time between flower-growing and the painting of landscape-based abstracts. A French government award enabled him to study with S W Hayter the printmaker at Atelier 17 in Paris, 1958–9; this was followed by another year in Cornwall, 1959–60, then an Italian government award in 1960–1. After six years in London Benjamin taught in Canada and America until 1973, when he returned to London. He had had a solo show at Newlyn Art Gallery in 1958, and by the late 1960s he had embarked on an impressive series of international one-man exhibitions, including Gimpel Fils, 1994. Arts Council holds his work. Lived at Kelling Village, Holt, Norfolk.

William BENNER 1884–1964 Painter, black-and-white artist and teacher, born in Nottingham, where he settled at Sherwood. After education in Loughborough he studied at Nottingham School of Art, his teachers including Arthur Spooner and Herbert Wilson Foster. Showed at Nottingham Castle Art Gallery and Museum extensively, which acquired his work; also RBA and RI. Taught in Nottingham.

Brian BENNETT 1927– Painter in oil and teacher, who concentrated on the landscape of the Chilterns. He was born in Olney, Buckinghamshire. Bennett became director of art at Berkhamsted School. Obtained master's degree in history, 1954, at Oxford University. Although he had no full-time art tuition, "Peter Greenham taught me English at school" – he attended Magdelen College School – "and encouraged me." In addition, Bennett studied part-time at Ruskin School of Drawing, Oxford, 1950, and Regent Street Polytechnic, 1956. He was made a member of NS, 1985, and president of ROI, 1987, also being an honorary member of UA, and showed at RA, RP and NEAC. Lived in Berkhamsted, Hertfordshire.

Elizabeth BENNETT 1923– Woodcarver, illustrator and mural painter, born in London. She was educated at Cheltenham Ladies' College and studied art at the Slade School of Fine Art, 1940, under Randolph Schwabe, then in 1941 at the Art Students' League of New York. After war service she resumed her studies,

1946–9, at Regent Street Polytechnic School of Art with the sculptor Geoffrey Deeley. Exhibited SGA and was a member of ICA. Signed work E B. Lived in London.

Frank Moss BENNETT 1874–1953 Painter and designer of costume figures, born in Liverpool, who studied at Clifton College, then Slade School of Fine Art, St John's Wood Art School and Royal Academy Schools where he won a gold medal and travelling scholarship. Showed at Dudley Gallery, RA, RI and Paris Salon and lived in London.

Godwin BENNETT 1888– Painter and draughtsman in pen and ink, born in Brighton, Sussex. By profession an art dealer, he was a self-taught painter who exhibited at RA and elsewhere. Lived finally at Croydon, Surrey.

June BENNETT fl. from 1960s– Painter and artist/jeweller who returned to painting full-time in 1988. She was born in Grange-over-Sands, Lancashire, wife of Michael and mother of Justin Bennett, both artists. She studied at Lancaster and Leicester Colleges of Art. Showed at Goldsmiths' Hall; Midland Group Gallery, Nottingham; Park Square Gallery, Leeds; Mignon Gallery, Bath; and Ashgate Gallery, Farnham. Shared a four-man show at Linton Court, Gallery, Settle, 1992. Had a series of solo exhibitions at Castlegate House, Cockermouth, from 1988. Bennett's jewellery was held by Abbot Hall Art Gallery, Kendal, and Shipley Art Gallery, Gateshead. Her pictures were in the collections of Carlisle Museum and Art Gallery and Copeland Borough Council. The artist lived in Port Carlisle, Cumbria, on the Solway Firth, where the constantly changing light and shifting sands were sources of inspiration.

Justin BENNETT 1964– Artist and teacher, son of the painters Michael and June Bennett. He did a foundation course at Cumbria College of Art and Design, 1982–3; graduated in fine art at Sheffield City Polytechnic, 1983–6, studying sound, performance, sculpture and video; did a sonology course, Institute for Sonology, Koninklijk Conservatorium, Den Haag, 1988–90; then was at Jan van Eyck Akademie, Maastricht, 1991–2. From 1989 he taught there, having in 1987 been a visiting lecturer in the communications arts department, Sheffield City Polytechnic. Collaborative experience included working with a number of performance groups, later work including Frascati, Amsterdam, Action with human pendula, ultrasonics (with BMB con.), 1991, and Maasvlakte, Performance for video, 1992. Solo shows included Galerie Stroom, Den Haag (Dutch Arts Council), 1997.

Malcolm BENNETT 1942– Painter and teacher, born in Derby, many of whose canvases were abstracts from the Ulster landscape. After attending the Technical High School in Belfast, 1956–60, Bennett studied at Stranmillis College there. He then spent four years living in parts of Ireland, France and Switzerland before taking up a teaching appointment in County Down in 1970. Exhibitions included Queen's University in Belfast, Ulster Museum and Tom Caldwell Gallery in Belfast both as a member of Group 63 and solo and Barrenhill Gallery in Dublin. Arts Council of Northern Ireland, New University of Ulster and Allied Irish Banks hold examples. The Ards Peninsula, where Bennett lived for a time, was a favourite subject.

Michael BENNETT 1934– Painter and lecturer, born in Windermere, Westmorland, husband of June, father of Justin, both artists. He studied at Lancaster and Leicester Colleges of Art. From 1966–71 lectured in painting at Bretton Hall College of Education. In 1976 gained an Arts Council Grant, then in 1976–7 and 1979–80 Northern Arts Printmaking Bursaries. Bennett eventually settled at Port Carlisle, Cumbria, where he ran a successful specialist dealership in fine art books and catalogues, continuing to paint strongly atmospheric landscapes inspired by the Solway Firth area. Bennett showed in many group exhibitions, including Ulster Museum, Belfast; AIA Gallery; Bradford City Art Gallery; Usher Gallery, Lincoln; Colin Jellicoe Gallery, Manchester; and in America. His many solo shows began at Birmingham University, 1966, later ones including Leeds University, 1969; Gulbenkian Gallery, Newcastle upon Tyne, 1975; Bluecoat Gallery, Liverpool, 1976; and Castlegate House, Cockermouth, from 1990. Lancaster University, Kettle's Yard in Cambridge and Abbot Hall Art Gallery, Kendal, hold Bennett's work.

Michael BENNETT 1948– Painter and teacher, born in Manchester. He studied at Birmingham Polytechnic, 1967–70, Slade School of Fine Art, 1970–2, and had a fellowship at Cheltenham College of Art, 1972–3. He then went on to hold part-time teaching posts from 1974 at St Martin's and Winchester Schools of Art, Kingston Polytechnic and America's Syracuse University. Bennett was interested in "the metaphorical relationship of the materiality of paint to the materiality of earth". He was a rich Colourist, as in his prizewinning canvas Fertile Ground, at John Moores Liverpool Exhibition in 1989–90. Arts Council holds Crimson Lake, 1979, bought from Felicity Samuel Gallery, and Midnight Sonata, 1979–80, obtained by purchase award. Lived in London.

Terence BENNETT 1935– Painter and teacher, born and lived in Doncaster, Yorkshire. He attended the local School of Art, 1951–6, then after National Service taught, giving up teaching to paint full-time in a mining village near Rotherham, 1971. In 1973 gained a Yorkshire Fine Art Fellowship, not long after he had taken up up teaching part-time, eventually becoming head of art department, Thomas Rotherham College, Rotherham. Took part in many mixed exhibitions from series with Yorkshire Artists, Leeds, 1967; others including Park Square Gallery, Leeds from 1968; RA from 1974; and Anna-Mei Chadwick, 1987. Had solo show at Doncaster Museum and Art Gallery, 1967, later ones including Victoria Gallery, Harrogate, 1979. The Bank of England, Nuffield Foundation and Yorkshire Arts Association hold his work.

Violet BENNETT 1902– Painter, notably in tempera, born in London. She was privately educated and studied art privately with

Otto Flatter, 1946–7, and Ernest Perry, the year following, also receiving tempera instruction from Pietro Annigoni in Italy in the early 1950s. Showed at RA, UA and elsewhere, signing her work V B. Lived in London.

William BENNETT 1917– Painter, notably of miniatures, born in London, who studied art at Sir John Cass College. Showed at RA, Mall Galleries and was a member of RMS. Worked in Britain and Australia, collections there as well as that of HM The Queen holding his pictures. Lived in Sidmouth, Devon.

Ernest Alfred Sallis BENNEY 1894–1966 Painter, designer, teacher and administrator, born in Bradford where he attended the College of Art. Also studied at Royal College of Art. Was the father of the artist Derek Ward Sallis Benney. Sallis Benney went on to hold a series of posts at art schools throughout the country, ending up as principal of Brighton College of Art and director of art education there, 1934–58. Exhibited RA, RBA, Cooling Galleries, NEAC, ROI and provincial galleries. Work held by Victoria & Albert Museum, Towner Art Gallery, Eastbourne and in other provincial galleries. Member of Chelsea Arts Club. Lived in Brighton.

Gerald Sallis BENNEY 1930– Gold- and silversmith, painter and draughtsman, born in Hull, Yorkshire, son of E A Sallis Benney, brother of Derek Benney and father of Paul Benney, all artists. The female nude was a strong feature of Gerald's oils and acrylics, as in his solo exhibition at Century Galleries, Henley-on-Thames, 1998, where works by other members of the family were shown. Gerald was best known for his work in precious metals and jewels and was a Royal Designer of Industry. He held Royal Warrants of Appointment to HM The Queen and other members of the royal family; did commissions for governments and institutions and showed throughout the world; and had work in the collections of The Goldsmiths' Company, The Crafts Council and Victoria & Albert Museum.

Paul BENNEY 1959– Painter, notable for his portraits which while achieving a likeness tended to reveal personality as well. Benney was born and worked in London, but also spent many years in New York. Collaborated with poets and writers. Mixed exhibitions included Slick at Arts Club and Romanticism at New Math Gallery, both New York, 1984; Centre of Contemporary Art in Seattle, 1985; Artisan Space, New York, 1988; and Lamont Gallery, Art92, 1992. Had a series of solo shows at PPOW in New York from 1984, with Nigel Greenwood Gallery, 1992 and Long & Ryle from 1994. In 1994–5 his The Supreme Court, Jerusalem, was shown at National Portrait Gallery prior to display at the Supreme Court Building. It had been commissioned to commemorate its official opening. Sitters for Benney's portraits included Lords Sainsbury, Rothschild and Ashburton and Sir Reresby and Lady Sitwell.

Elspeth BENNIE 1962– Artist in sculpture and metalwork, born in Stirlingshire. She studied at Glasgow School of Art to gain a first-class honours degree in sculpture, 1979–83, then did an advanced sculpture course at St Martin's School of Art, 1983–5, teachers including Alan Gouk, Tim Scott and Katherine Gili. Became a member of British Artist Blacksmiths' Association and the Scottish Society of Artist Craftspeople. In 1985–6 Bennie was resident at the Scottish Sculpture Workshop, travelled in America and Canada, 1986–7, then began full-time as an artist blacksmith/sculptor in 1988. She won the RSA Benno Schotz Prize in 1987. Exhibitions included New Generation Artists at Compass Gallery, Glasgow, 1983; Scottish Drawing Biennial, Paisley Art Gallery, 1985; RSA from 1986; Scottish Sculpture Now, Aberdeen Art Gallery, 1989; Steel and Wood at Royal Exchange Theatre, Manchester, 1991; and The Bonhoga Gallery, Shetland, 1994. Commissions included Centenary Bell Tower, Baillieston Parish Church, in Glasgow where she lived, 1993; Roundabout Sculpture, East Kilbride Development Corporation, and Granite Gate, Fort William High Street, both 1994.

Nadia BENOIS 1896–1975 Painter, stage designer and writer, born near St Petersburg, Russia, into a cosmopolitan family that included a number of distinguished artists. Her father was Louis Benois, architect to the Tsar; her uncle, who taught her, was the great stage designer Alexandre Benois. She also studied at St Petersburg Academy. Was married to the journalist Iona Ustinov, their son being the actor-playwright Peter Ustinov. Nadia Benois settled in England with her family and had early successful shows at the Little Gallery, 1924, and with Tooth, 1929. Also showed with the Goupil, Leicester and Matthiesen Galleries and widely abroad. Tate Gallery and Manchester City Art Gallery hold her work, which like the painter was colourful, warm and impulsive. Nadia Benois was for many years an exhibitor and member of NEAC. Her designs for costumes and settings for *The Sleeping Beauty* ballet in London in 1939, at Sadler's Wells and Covent Garden, were a great success. She was included in Three Women Painters, 1975, at Michael Parkin Fine Art Ltd. From early years of World War II lived in Gloucestershire.

Lynn BENSON fl. from 1960s– Painter, printmaker and teacher who attended Wimbledon School of Art, 1963–5, Maidstone College of Art, 1965–8, and Brighton College of Art, gaining a teaching certificate, 1968–9. She taught part-time from 1969–79 at Abbey School, Reading, from 1980 at Caversham Art Centre. Noted for her landscapes, she showed at RA Summer Exhibition, NEAC, ROI, Charles Keyser Gallery, Thackeray Gallery, RBA and Patricia Wells Gallery, Thornbury. Had solo shows at Sadler's Wells Theatre and Century Galleries, Henley-on-Thames. Lived in Burghfield, Berkshire.

Susan BENSON 1931– Painter, illustrator and printmaker, born in Ruislip, Middlesex. Studied at Byam Shaw School of Drawing and Painting, 1947–50, her teachers including Peter Greenham; and at Slade School of Fine Art, 1950–3, with William Coldstream. She showed at Young Contemporaries, WIAC, Beaux Arts Gallery, Leicester Galleries and elsewhere. Her work also appeared in the Journal of the National Book League and in periodicals such as the *Illustrated London News* and *Radio Times*. Lived in London.

John BENSUSAN-BUTT 1911–1997 Artist, notable for landscapes, and writer on painting. He was born in Colchester, where he eventually settled, the family home, 1915–58, being The Minories, later a notable gallery. Bensusan-Butt was an exhibitioner in history at Oxford University, graduating in 1933. Began painting in 1934 and continued, apart from war service, until early 1960s. He studied as a pupil of Lucien Pissarro, 1935–9, his mother's brother-in-law, also etching at Royal College of Art, 1935, and lithography at Central School of Arts and Crafts, 1939. He had shows at French Gallery, 1937, Kensington Art Gallery, 1949, and Leicester Galleries, 1957, being elected RBA in that year; he resigned as inactive in 1975. He also exhibited at Minories Gallery from 1962 and was a member of Colchester Art Society from foundation after the war, usually on the hanging committee. In 1986 had retrospective at Eldon Gallery, Ashmolean Museum, Oxford. Bensusan-Butt was art critic to the *Essex County Standard*, 1950–66.

Margaret BENT 1917– Oil painter and teacher, born in London, she was married to the artist John Bent. She studied at Regent Street Polytechnic School of Art, 1936–9, at Bath School of Art, 1942–3, with Clifford Ellis, then in 1948 in Paris. Showed at RA, Victoria & Albert Museum, Tate Gallery and with the Bath Society of Artists. After World War II Margaret Bent taught for a time at Bath Academy of Art, having previously taught at Southlands Training College, London, for two years. Lived in London.

Medora Heather BENT 1901– Painter, notably of furniture, and potter, actual name Alannah Heather Bent. She was much influenced by the places where she lived, including Connemara, Sark and St Ives. Was born in North Kilworth, family home in Connemara, Ireland, being educated in England. Studied at Slade School of Fine Art, 1930–3, with Randolph Schwabe, and Central School of Arts and Crafts, including stained glass. She showed at LG, SGA, SWA and NS. In 1958 her *Paintings of Historical Houses of Purbeck* was published, in 1992 her autobiography. Lived in Wareham, Dorset.

Frank BENTLEY 1941– Untaught painter, particularly of marinescapes, of the naive school, born in Halifax, West Yorkshire, where he settled at Todmorden. His pictures were worked in acrylic with a mixed medium, giving a matt/chalk-like finish, and were from the imagination. Originally an electrician, then self-employed in the antiques trade, Bentley turned to painting in 1982. Group show appearances included Ferens Art Gallery, Hull, from 1984; RBA Open, 1988; MAFA Open, from 1989; Manchester Art Festival, 1993; and The Northern Art Show, Mall Galleries, 1994. Signed limited edition prints were published by Portfolio Fine Art, Failsworth, Manchester. Simpson Curtis Permanent Collection, Leeds, holds his work.

Lucy BENTLEY 1968– Figurative painter, born in West Germany, who studied at Salisbury College of Art; Bournemouth & Poole College of Art; and Norwich School of Art. In 1994 she was artist-in-residence, Godolphin School, Salisbury. Group shows included Erasmus Mixed Exhibition, Kunsthalle, Kiel, Germany, 1991; and Small Pictures at Salisbury Playhouse, Salisbury, and Royal Over-Seas League Open, both 1994. Her solo show Vision and Grace took place at Newhouse, Redlynch, Salisbury, 1993.

Nicolas BENTLEY 1907–1978 Illustrator and writer, born in London, son of EC Bentley, who invented the clerihew form of witty verse and wrote the classic detective novel *Trent's Last Case*. Nicolas Bentley attended Heatherley's School of Fine Art. In World War II he served in Home Intelligence and the Ministry of Information. By then he had begun to establish a solid reputation as a freelance writer and illustrator, consolidated after the war by his work for the *Daily Mail* and *Sunday Times* newspapers. Was also involved in publishing, with André Deutsch and Thomas Nelson. A witty, economical cartoonist and illustrator, his drawings graced many books, including clerihews and biographical writings by his father, Hilaire Belloc's *New Cautionary Tales*, 1930, and *Cautionary Verses*, 1940, and a string of volumes by the humorist George Mikes. Bentley's own book *A Version of the Truth* appeared in 1980. Cartoon Gallery, Chris Beetles and Abbott and Holder showed Bentley's work. Lived in London.

George Bernard BENTON 1872–1959 Painter, illustrator and teacher, born in Birmingham. He attended the College of of Arts and Crafts, later teaching there, and was president of the Art Circle in Birmingham, the city also buying his work. Exhibited RA, RBSA and elsewhere, his pictures often having historical themes. He had a strong interest in the early history of his locality, on which he wrote. Lived finally at Streetly, Warwickshire.

Pip BENVENISTE fl. from 1940s– Artist, designer and teacher, born in Newlyn, Cornwall, studying early with both parents who were artists, later with other Cornish painters. She moved to London in 1946 and from 1948–50 travelled extensively in France and Morocco, painting landscapes. Returned to England where she began exhibiting in many mixed shows in London and the provinces, including Nicholas Treadwell Galleries. In 1957 she spent some time in New York and made first experiments in abstract painting, and after returning to London from 1959 taught, designed fabrics and began working on pictures based on a controlled but intuitive delineation of energy in space. Lao Tzu and contemporary astro-physicists were influences. From 1990 had a series of solo shows at Primrose Hill Gallery.

Margaret BENYON 1940– Holographic artist, teacher and writer, born in Birmingham, who spent her childhood in Kenya, 1948–58. She studied painting at Birmingham College of Art, 1958–60; then was at Slade School, including a postgraduate year, 1961–6; her doctoral project at Royal College of Art, 1989–94,

How is Holography Art, being sponsored by Ilford Ltd. Held a number of fellowships, including Leverhulme Senior Art Fellow, University of Strathclyde, 1971–3, after being Fellow in Fine Art, University of Nottingham, 1968–71, also being Creative Arts Fellow, Australian National University, Canberra, 1978–9. Taught extensively, starting with silkscreen printing at Byam Shaw School, 1965–6, later appointments including visiting tutor to the holography unit, Royal College of Art, 1985–9. Benyon was a professional painter, 1965–70, then pioneered art holography in 1968. Took part in numerous group exhibitions, from Young Contemporaries, 1965, later shows including 4th International Symposium on Display Holography, Lake Forest, America, and Fiat Lux! Holography, at Asturias, Spain, both 1991, and 4 British Holographers, Smith's Gallery, 1992. In 1991 gained commission for Arts Council Award trophy. Had solo show at Nottingham University, 1969, later ones including Conjugal and Cosmetic Series, Interference Hologram Gallery, Toronto, 1987, and Cosmetic Series/Conjugal Series, Museum für Holographie & Neue Visuelle Medien, Pulheim, West Germany, 1990. Lived in Broadstone, Dorset.

Albert BERBANK 1896–1961 Painter in oil and watercolour, draughtsman in pen and ink and pencil, and wood engraver. Born in Nottingham, Berbank studied at the School of Art there, 1912–16; St Martin's School of Art, 1924–34; and at Westminster School of Art, 1934–6, under Walter Bayes and Bernard Meninsky. He exhibited at RA, NS, RI, SGA and abroad, one-man shows including New Vision Centre and elsewhere. Berbank, who taught and lectured, sold work to Leicestershire Education Committee. President of the London Sketch Club, 1960–1. Lived in London.

Otto BERCHEM 1967– Artist, born in Milford, Connecticut, America, who attended Yale Summer School of Music and Art, 1989; Parsons School of Design, New York, 1990; and the College of Art, Edinburgh, 1994. Exhibitions included several in that city, among them CD Show, Collective Gallery, 1992; Five, Wasps Gallery, 1993; and Aerial '94, 1994. Also in 1994 Berchem was in New Art in Scotland, at the Centre for Contemporary Arts, Glasgow, with installations which "tried to demystify certain notions of the Men's Room."

Alexander BERDYSHEFF 1964– Artist commonly working in mixed media on various supports, based in Tbilisi, Georgia. He graduated from Tbilisi Academy of Fine Arts in 1988 and produced highly personal work. This drew on Georgian and Russian influences, his father having been born in St Petersburg. Berdysheff developed contact with Scotland as a member of a graduate and postgraduate exchange programme permitting him to study at Glasgow School of Art in 1990. Four years later he revisited Scotland for six months, becoming better acquainted with the work of Western artists and taking advantage of materials and techniques unknown or unavailable in Georgia. Group exhibitions included Galeria Brik, Barcelona, Spain, 1990; Artbank Gallery, Glasgow, 1991; Roy Miles Gallery, 1995; Central House of Artists, Moscow, 1996; and in 1997 RSA Summer Exhibition and Midsummer Magic Exhibition at The Scottish Fine Art Group, Inverness. Solo exhibitions included The British Council, Edinburgh, 1994; Royal Concert Hall, Glasgow, 1995; and Edinburgh College of Art (part of the International Festival), 1997.

Frank Ernest BERESFORD 1881–1967 Painter, notably of horse subjects, and mural decorator. Born in Derby, he studied at the School of Art there, then St John's Wood School of Art and the Royal Academy Schools, where he finished in 1906. Exhibited RA, ROI, RI, RP and elsewhere. Beresford was a much-honoured painter. He won a British Institution Scholarship which took him on a world tour, as the result of which he gained the first award for art from the Imperial Japanese government, in 1909. For his work with the United States Air Force in World War II he won the Exceptional Service Award, only once before granted to a British subject. Lived at Northiam, Sussex.

Mary BERESFORD-WILLIAMS 1931– Painter, printmaker, draughtsman, photographer and teacher, born in London. She graduated with a class one honours degree at Reading University under J Anthony Betts. Taught mainly in the West Country, including Rolle College, Exmouth. In 1978 won a South West Arts Major Award. Took up photography in 1970, using it in conjunction with screenprinting; between 1985–8 photography became an interest in its own right, then returned to drawing and painting. Was a member of Newlyn Society of Artists and Devon Guild of Craftsmen, also showing at NEAC and RWA. In 1986 was photographer-in-residence for Television South-West. Devon Schools Museums Service holds her work. Lived in Galmpton, Brixham, Devon.

Adrian BERG 1929– Painter and teacher, born and lived in London. From 1949–53 he studied at Cambridge University, switching from medicine to English, and did a higher diploma in education at Trinity College, Dublin. Taught in schools, then studied at St Martin's and Chelsea Schools of Art, then Royal College of Art, 1955–61, his teachers including Ceri Richards. He was senior tutor at Royal College of Art, 1987–8. Showed in London regularly from 1964 as well as on continent and North America. He won a gold medal at Florence Biennale in 1973 and was a John Moores Liverpool Exhibition prizewinner in 1980. Exhibited often at Piccadilly Gallery. Later exhibitions included Serpentine Gallery, 1986, and tour, following a retrospective at Rochdale Art Gallery, 1980. Arts Council, British Museum, British Council and Tokyo Metropolitan Art Museum hold examples. Berg was a compulsive painter of landscape and foliage using a rich palette. He was made RA in 1992.

George BERGEN 1903–1984 Painter, notably of portraits and interiors, born in Minsk, Russia. The family settled in Brooklyn, in America, in 1909 and they were granted citizenship 10 years later. Bergen studied at various New York art schools, was then taught by George Bellows at the School of Fine Arts, Yale

University, and in 1925 crossed the Atlantic on a Yale travelling scholarship, having a first solo show at Goupil Gallery in the late 1920s. He had another in 1932 at Lefevre and also showed at Agnew and Leicester Galleries. Bergen was by then entangled artistically and emotionally with the Bloomsbury Group. In the 1930s Bergen spent part of each year in Spain and he lived for some time in California where he was friendly with stars such as Constance Collier and Charlie Chaplin, whom he painted. In 1939 he settled in New York, but his connections with Bloomsbury painters were renewed in the 1960s. In 1988 Sally Hunter Fine Art held a show, George Bergen and Bloomsbury.

BERGER: *see* **Margarete HAMERSCHLAG**

John BERGER 1926– Author, art critic, painter and teacher, born in London. He studied under Robert Kirkland Jamieson at Central School of Arts and Crafts, 1942–3, then at Chelsea School of Art, 1945–7, his teachers including Robert Medley. Exhibited Wildenstein, Lefevre, Leicester and St George's Galleries, Arts Council buying his work. Taught at St Mary's Training College, London, and wrote on art for *New Statesman* and *Tribune*. Berger became a controversial critic, advocating a Marxist approach to art. Later he established an international reputation as a writer of fiction, factual books, works of criticism and as a translator. Also appeared on television. Novels included *A Painter of Our Time*, 1958; *Corker's Freedom*, 1964; *Pig Earth*, 1979; and *G*, which won the Booker and James Tait Black Memorial Prizes. Non-fiction included *Permanent Red*, 1960; *Ways of Seeing*, 1972; and *Photocopies*, 1996. Lived in Taninges, France.

Joseph BERGER 1898–1989 Architect and watercolourist, born in Vienna, married to the artist Margarete Hamerschlag. Berger was a notable exponent of the Viennese modernist school of architecture who studied at the Technische Hochschule, Vienna, 1917–21, under Adolf Loos and Oskar Strnad. Worked in private practice, then when political situation darkened he lived for a period in the mid-1930s in Haifa, Palestine, moving to England with his wife in 1936. After internment as an enemy alien in the Isle of Man in World War II, Berger eventually joined the London County Council unit concerned with building schools, retiring in 1963. His wife having died in 1959, Berger spent his final years with Regina Gillinson-Schein, the cellist. Lived in London.

Margareta Livia BERGER: *see* **Margarete HAMERSCHLAG**

Sybille BERGER 1962– Artist whose work included brightly coloured geometrical abstracts, such as Without Title, 1994, included in New Contemporaries, 1996, at Tate Gallery in Liverpool and Camden Arts Centre. She was born in Stuttgart, West Germany, and gained both bachelor's and master's degrees in fine art in visual communication at Hochschule der Künste, Berlin, 1985–91, then her master's in fine art at Goldsmiths' College, 1993–5. Other exhibitions included Gallery Lasard, Berlin, 1993; Chisenhale Gallery, 1994; Exmouth Market, 1995; and John Moores Liverpool Exhibition, 1997–8. Lived in London.

Margarete BERGER-HAMERSCHLAG: *see* **Margarete HAMERSCHLAG**

Stephenie BERGMAN 1946– Painter who said that her pictures involved two processes: "The first is preparing material and the second is making something with it." Her entry to John Moores Liverpool Exhibition in 1985, Table, Vase and Fork, employed acrylic paint, canvas and mattress tacking. Bergman was born and lived in London and studied at St Martin's School of Art, 1963–7. After a first show at Garage Art in 1973 exhibited regularly in Britain and abroad. Had a solo show with Crafts Council Gallery in 1984 from which Arts Council bought her creation Thunderthighs.

Xenia BERKELEY 1915– Painter, draughtsman and commercial artist with strong interest in the theatre and ballet, born in London. She drew for magazines with women's interests prominent and illustrated several children's books. Educated in Teignmouth, Devon, she studied at Exeter School of Art. Exhibited NEAC, LG, NS, Arts Council and elsewhere. Sometimes signed work only as Xenia or X B. Lived in London.

Greta BERLIN 1942– Sculptor, ceramist, draughtsman and teacher, born in St Ives, Cornwall, daughter of the sculptor Sven Berlin, mother of the artist Zennor Witney. Berlin worked in bronze, plaster, clay, steel and stone. She described her sculptures as "Expressionist, figurative, an exploration of human forms alone and in relationship with each other". Berlin was a lecturer in ceramics at Brockenhurst Tertiary College, 1970–90; in the 1970s she was also engaged in archaelogical ceramic research at Butser Hill, Hampshire, in the 1980s working as a copyist at the Victoria & Albert Museum. Carried out many commissions, including a nine-foot bronze of Lord Mountbatten for Timberlaine, Grosvenor Square, Southampton, 1989; the comedian Max Wall, in Theatre Museum collection, 1992; and Birdman, Hampshire County Council, 1993. Group shows included Bristol Cathedral, 1979; RWA and Brighton Polytechnic, both 1985; Eye Gallery, Bristol, 1989; and Gordon Hepworth Gallery, Newton St Cyres, 1993. Had a solo show at Eccleston Square, 1983, later ones including Alton Museum, 1991. Lived in Wootton Fitzpaine, Bridport, Dorset.

Sven BERLIN 1911– Sculptor, painter, draughtsman and writer who led a bohemian, often controversial life. Born in London of an English mother and Swedish father, Berlin was apprenticed as a mechanical engineer, in 1928 enrolled at Beckenham School of Art, but decided instead to pursue a career as an adagio dancer in music halls. In 1934 and 1938 pursued art studies at Camborne-Redruth Schools of Art in Cornwall as well as other subjects such as poetry, philosophy and comparative religion. Had first one-man show at Camborne Community Centre in 1939, by which time he had begun sculpting. Although a conscientious objector at outset of World War II, he eventually joined the Army. Settled in St Ives, and was co-founder of Crypt Group in 1946 and a founder-member of Penwith Society in 1949, the year his book *Alfred Wallis, Primitive*, was published. Other books included *The Dark Monarch: A Portrait from Within*, about St Ives and its inhabitants; it led to several libel actions. His autobiography *A Coat of Many Colours*, 1994, contains chapters on fellow-artists in St Ives. After a few moves, partly by horse and gypsy waggon, Berlin eventually settled at Wimborne, Dorset. He was a regular exhibitor of work sometimes extremely strong, sometimes of variable quality. A notable show was at Belgrave Gallery, 1989. Victoria & Albert Museum, Tate Gallery, National Library of Scotland and other British and foreign collections hold his work. Sven Berlin's daughter Greta Berlin was a sculptor and his grand-daughter and her daughter the artist Zennor Witney.

BERNARD-BOWERMAN: *see* **Bernard BOWERMAN**

Lord BERNERS 1883–1950 Composer, painter, writer and eccentric, born at Apley Park, Bridgnorth, Shropshire. He was educated at Eton College and entered the diplomatic service, serving abroad in several posts, then inherited his titles in 1918. He was to become Sir Gerald Hugh Tyrwhitt-Wilson, 5th baronet and 14th Baron Berners. Bought Faringdon House, in Berkshire, where he then lived, although he spent some time in London and in Rome. His main interest was music, which he studied under Stravinsky and Casella. Berners composed orchestral and piano music and opera but was especially noted for his clever scores for Sadler's Wells Ballet and the 1926 success *The Triumph of Neptune* for the Diaghilev Ballet. Berners' playfulness and wit are best shown in his music, less in his landscape paintings, which were in the manner of Corot, whose work he collected along with that of Derain, Matisse, Sisley and Constable. Some of his pictures were in the style of the Douanier Rousseau. He had solo shows at Lefevre Galleries in 1931 and 1936, also exhibiting at Goupil Gallery. As a writer Berners was a satirist of social life, and he also penned two amusing autobiographical volumes, *First Childhood*, 1934, and *A Distant Prospect*, 1945, but failed to finish a third. He was noted for his practical jokes and eccentric behaviour. A centenary exhibition was held at Royal Festival Hall in 1983.

John Archibald Alexander BERRIE 1887–1962 Mainly a portrait painter, he was born near Manchester and studied at Bootle and Liverpool Schools of Art, at Hubert Herkomer's School at Bushey, then in Paris. Exhibited at RA, with RCamA of which he became a full member in 1923 and extensively with Walker Art Gallery in Liverpool, which holds portraits of local worthies by him. Had a solo exhibition at Walker's Galleries, 1936. Among his portraits were King George V and Winston Churchill. Lived in London, Harrogate and finally Johannesburg, South Africa.

Peter BERRISFORD 1932– Painter and lecturer, born in Northampton. He studied at Northampton and Chelsea Schools of Art and Bournemouth College of Art, gaining a travelling scholarship in 1953. Went on to lecture for bodies such as National Trust and Arts Council and was head of adult art studies at the College of Arts and Technology in Eastbourne, Sussex, where he lived. In 1957 was selected by Jack Beddington for inclusion in the book *Young Artists of Promise*. Showed RA, John Moores Liverpool Exhibition, Bear Lane Gallery in Oxford, Trafford Gallery, RBA and elsewhere. East Sussex County Council and galleries in Hull, Leicester and Northampton hold his work.

Arthur BERRY 1925–1994 Painter, teacher and writer, born in Smallthorne, Staffordshire, son of a bricklayer. At 13 Berry left council school to attend Junior Art School, at Queen Street, Burslem, in the Potteries. He became a student there in 1940, going to Royal College of Art in 1943. In 1946 Berry began part-time teaching at Manchester College of Art; in 1952 took on same role at Burslem College of Art and Chelsea School of Art, becoming full-time lecturer in Burslem in 1963. He was later principal lecturer in painting at North Staffordshire Polytechnic. In the mid-1940s Berry met Robert Colquhoun and Robert MacBryde, whose work had a great influence on him, and saw L S Lowry's paintings for the first time. In the mid-1970s Berry began writing stage plays, and in 1980 a talk broadcast on Radio Stoke won the Pye Award for the best scripted talk of the year. Berry's work reflects the primitive, gritty world of the pit village where he was born and reared. He was given a retrospective at Stoke-on-Trent City Museum and Art Gallery, 1984, another at The Gallery, Manchester, 1995.

Bill BERRY 1900–1971 Artist and designer, full name Charles William Berry. He trained as an artist at Camden, Bolt Court and at St Martin's School of Art, then was an apprentice at Stone Offset Lithography Works and worked at a process engraver's before joining the Winter Thomas advertising agency. After World War I service in the Royal Flying Corps and a period as art editor for the *Draper's Organiser* Berry between the wars served with various advertising agencies, settling with Lintas in 1933, where he stayed until retirement. He was included in the Lintas Beyond the Horizon exhibition at Agnew, 1988. Had a solo show of watercolours at Batsford Gallery in 1947, was elected RI in 1949 and showed with RSW.

Joanne BERRY 1966– Abstract artist and teacher, born in Bury, Lancashire, whose work explored the inner, subconscious self. She studied at Newcastle upon Tyne Polytechnic, Royal College of Art and Camberwell School of Art. In 1993 was artist-in-residence at Lowick House, Cumbria, from 1995 being a part-time art teacher at Loughborough College of Art & Design. Awards included Prince's Trust Business Award, 1990; Yorkshire Printmakers' Prize and Printmakers' Council Student Award, both 1996. Group exhibitions included Camden Arts Centre, 1991; 5 at Roupell Gallery, 1992; and in 1996 Redfern Gallery and Royal Over-Seas League Open. Had a solo exhibition at Gabriele Skelton Ltd, 1992. Victoria & Albert Museum holds Berry's work.

June BERRY 1924– Painter and printmaker, born in Melbourne, Derbyshire. She studied at Slade School of Fine Art, 1946–9. Exhibited RA. Lived in London.

Peter BERRY 1937– Sculptor and teacher who worked in a commercial art studio in Gloucester before studying at Gloucester College of Art, 1956–60, and Slade School of Fine Art, 1961–3. He taught sculpture at Gloucester, 1964, from 1965 lecturing in pre-diploma studies at Birmingham. Exhibited at John Walter Gallery, Upper Whitechapel Gallery and was included in 19 Young Sculptors at Hillfield Gardens, Gloucester, 1962. In 1966 had a solo show at Ikon Gallery, Birmingham.

Dave BERRY-HART 1940– Painter, teacher and sculptor using materials such as stone, wood, plastic and hessian. He was born in Trinidad and studied at St Martin's School of Art, 1959–61, his teachers including Frederick Gore, Joe Tilson and Derrick Greaves; then City of Birmingham Polytechnic, 1980–3, his master's degree dissertation being on Gauguin's colour. "Prehistoric and Neolithic art, traditions and folklore" were cited as influences on Berry-Hart's work, which was sometimes signed Jabir. Lectured at North Warwickshire College and elsewhere. Held a number of exhibitions with The Firm, 1983–7, open exhibitions including Liverpool Academy, Walker Art Gallery, 1960; Spectrum Central, 1971; and Mercia Artists, Herbert Art Gallery and Museum, Coventry, 1984. Had a solo show at AIA Gallery, 1969, later ones including Mid-Warwickshire College of Further Education, 1989, and Worcester Museum & Art Gallery, 1991. Imperial College holds his work. Lived in Nuneaton, Warwickshire.

Derek BERRYMAN 1926– Painter, printmaker, sculptor, designer and teacher, born in Chingford, Essex. He studied at Universities of Durham and Bristol, St Martin's School of Art, Sir John Cass College, City of London Polytechnic and in 1960 gained scholarship to Syracuse University, New York State. Held several teaching posts, including head of graphic design at Weston-super-Mare School of Art from 1968. Showed at RA, ROI, RWA and in America. Lived in Hutton, Avon.

Neville BERTRAM 1908– Sculptor and teacher, born in Cullercoats, Northumberland. Based in Newcastle, he studied at Durham University, 1926–9, gaining his diploma in fine art, in 1930 winning his Board of Education drawing and painting certificates, under Robert Lyon. He entered and submitted work for the Rome School, 1931. In 1932 Bertram taught part-time and studied modelling and pottery, also doing some stone carving. He moved to Liverpool in 1933, making commercial sculpture with Herbert Tyson Smith, marrying one of his daughters, in 1936 returning to Tyneside to work on further commercial projects. After six years with the Air Ministry, in 1945 Bertram took on part-time work at Liverpool College of Art, teaching full-time from 1950–73. Bertram joined Liverpool Academy in 1946, becoming honorary treasurer and secretary. About 1950 he was made an associate of RBS. Walker Art Gallery, Liverpool, holds Bertram's Quadripartite Form, of 1959. Lived in West Kirby, Cheshire.

Anna BEST 1965– Sculptor, born and lived in London, who was involved in installation/environmental/ collaboration/site-specific performance work. Her aim was "to make work, in whatever media are most appropriate, for a specific place and time". She did a Hounslow Borough College foundation course, 1983–4, with Clive Burton and Dave Smith; in 1984 was at Art Students' League of New York; in 1984–7, under Dick Whall, gained a first-class honours degree in fine art (sculpture) at Coventry Polytechnic. In 1991 Best won a British Council travel grant to America and had a Grizedale Forest Sculpture Residency, Cumbria; in 1992 was involved in Le Sens de la Mesure, European competition for residency and exhibition, Melun, France; in 1993 a Sculpture Space Inc., New York, funded residency; and in 1994–5 was a Rijksakademie van beeldende kunsten, Amsterdam, participating artist. She established the Red Cow Studios Co-operative in 1988; was involved in part-time lecturing at Chelsea School of Art and Hounslow Borough College foundation courses from 1989, plus additional teaching at Coventry Polytechnic, 1991. In that year was a participant at Triangle Artists' Workshop in New York, in 1992 being co-ordinator and participant in Shave Artists' Workshop, Somerset. Selected exhibitions included The McGrigor Donald Sculpture Prize Exhibition, with tour, 1990; Lockbund Sculpture Exhibition, Oxford Art Week, and On Site, Bermondsey, 1992; and Burning Toast, a collaborative work with Richard Reynolds, 1993. Leicestershire Education Authority holds her work.

Eleanor BEST fl. from c.1910–1958 Oil painter, born at Amport, Hampshire. Studied at the Slade School of Fine Art, 1909, with Henry Tonks and Walter Westley Russell. Exhibited RA, RSA, NEAC, NS, in the provinces and in America and Sweden. The Contemporary Art Society and a number of provincial galleries bought her work. Her work was included in Sladey Ladies at Parkin Gallery, 1986. Lived in London.

Gladys BEST 1898– Painter in oil and watercolour of landscapes and architectural subjects. Born in Chiswick, she studied at Exeter School of Art and was for a time on the staff of Cheltenham Ladies' College. She exhibited at the RA, RBA, RSA, RI, in the provinces and at the Paris Salon. The Victoria & Albert Museum and Ministry of Works bought her work and she participated in the Pilgrim Trust *Recording Britain* project. Lived at Topsham, Devon.

Alfred BESTALL 1892–1986 Although he worked as a painter in oil and watercolour, Alfred Bestall is best known as an illustrator whose most notable subject was Rupert Bear in the *Daily Express* newspaper and many annuals. After attending Rydal School, Bestall studied art in Birmingham and in classes run by London County Council and at the Central School. His teachers included A S Hartrick and Noel Rooke. He took part in exhibitions at the RA and RBA. He also worked for *Punch* and *Tatler* and illustrated several dozen books, including *The Spanish Goldfish, Myths and Legends of Many Lands* and *Folk Tales of Wales*. He finally lived at Beddgelert, Gwynedd, in Wales.

David BETHEL 1923– Painter, printmaker, designer and teacher, born in Bath, Somerset. He studied at Gloucester School of Arts and Crafts, 1946–8, and West of England Art College, Bristol, 1948–51, under Donald Milner. He went on to hold several art teaching appointments, including the directorship of Leicester Polytechnic. Showed at AIA, Kensington Gallery, SGA of which he was a member, and in the provinces, including RWA, which holds his work, as do galleries in Gloucester and Stafford. Lived at Stoneygate, Leicestershire.

Marion Ross BETHEL 1929– Illuminator, born in Wiesbaden, Germany. She studied with Daisy Alcock and Gladys Best. Worked as a map curator at Exeter University, illuminated books and showed at Salon de Société des Artistes Français. Lived in Topsham, Devon.

Peggie A E BETHEL: *see* **Peggie MARKS**

Noel BETOWSKI 1952– Painter and teacher, born in Tilbury, Essex, who gained a degree in fine art at Central School of Arts and Crafts, 1973–6, then his teacher's diploma at London University Institute of Education, 1976–7. For a decade he lived in north London, painting and teaching part-time in adult education, in 1987 moving to Penzance, where he ran The Betowski Gallery. Betowski's work was colourful, figurative-towards-abstract, a notable feature being a motif of tiny ships to form the sea in his seascapes. Group exhibitions included RA Summer Exhibition; Greater London Council's Spirit of London, Royal Festival Hall; New Grafton, Crane Kalman and Mercury Galleries; Camden Arts Centre John Constable Landscape Competition, where he won a third prize in 1987, second prize in 1988; and Islington and Edinburgh Art Fairs, both 1992. Had many solo exhibitions, including Salt House Gallery, St Ives, from 1982; Porthmeor Gallery there, from 1992; and Gallery Tresco, Tresco, Isles of Scilly, 1994.

Desmond BETTANY 1919– Painter, printmaker and teacher, born in Burnley, Lancashire. He studied art at Lancaster School of Art, where his teachers included Walter Bayes, then at Leeds College of Art. He went on to become, from 1950, acting principal of South Shields School of Art, in County Durham, where he finally lived. Bettany showed extensively in the Lancaster and South Shields areas with various clubs and groups.

Peter BETTANY 1945– Artist in a variety of media, born in Colwyn Bay, Denbighshire, who grew up on the coast of north Wales. Studied at Wimbledon Art School, Leicester College of Art and California College of Arts and Crafts, Oakland, America. Showed solo with JPL Fine Arts. Bettany's small sculpture Sinking, of 1974, is held by Arts Council and was included in its 1981–2 tour Fragments Against Ruin. Lived in London.

Anthony BETTS 1897–1980 Painter whose full name was James Anthony Betts, born in Skipton, Yorkshire. Studied at Bradford College of Art, Royal College of Art and overseas. In the 1920s and 1930s he was head of the school of painting at Sheffield College of Art, principal of Kingston School of Art and professor of fine art at Reading University. Exhibited in London, Paris and New York. Lived at Caversham, Berkshire.

Ida BETTS 1871–1951 Watercolour painter, especially of flowers, born in Chipperfield, Hertfordshire. She studied art in Bedford and St Ives and showed at the RA, RI, RBA and Paris Salon. Lived near Newbury, Berkshire.

Simon BETTS 1957– Painter, born in Peterborough, Huntingdonshire. He studied at Cambridge College of Arts and Technology, 1976–7; Sheffield Polytechnic, 1977–80; and Chelsea College of Art, 1991–2. Mixed exhibitions included Arte Viva, Senigaria, Italy, 1992; Post-Decadence at Café Gallery, 1994; and John Moores Liverpool Exhibition, 1995–6. Solo exhibitions included Peterborough City Museum and Art Gallery, 1983; Mappin Art Gallery, Sheffield, 1984; and Café Gallery, 1992. Lived in London.

Tadek BEUTLICH 1922– Printmaker, weaver of tapestries and teacher, born in Lwówek, Poland. He studied in Poland, elsewhere on the continent and in England. Victoria & Albert Museum, British Museum, other museums in Britain and in North America hold his work. Taught for a time at Camberwell School of Arts and Crafts. His work is in the Council for National Academic Awards collection. Beutlich was given a seventy-fifth birthday show at Hove Museum & Art Gallery in 1997, where he held master-classes. Lived nearby at Ditchling, Sussex.

David BEVAN 1915– Painter in oil, who was educated at Eton College. Showed at RA, other London and provincial galleries. Lived in London.

Graham BEVAN 1935– Painter and teacher, born in Pontypridd, Glamorgan. Attended Cardiff College of Art, 1951–3, then after National Service resumed studies at Slade School of Fine Art, 1956–9, followed in 1960 by a London University post-graduate studentship in fine art. Joined Sheffield College of Art Polytechnic as a lecturer in fine art. Participated in many group shows, including Young Contemporaries, 1958–60, LG and the 1964 show of Contemporary British Art in Bradford, having several one-man exhibitions at New Art Centre. Both Arts Council and WAC hold his work.

Oliver BEVAN 1941– Artist who as well as painting was involved in kinetics and light projects, collage and colour photography. He was born in Peterborough, Huntingdonshire, and studied at Royal College of Art, 1960–4. From an early stage he showed in mixed and held solo exhibitions internationally. Regarding group shows, in 1967 he was in Ornamentale Tendenzen, which toured West Germany; in 1971 in Jeux, Lumière et Animation, at Galerie Lacloche, in Paris, and in Play Orbit at ICA; in 1982 at Midland Group, Nottingham, Open Photography show; and in 1982–3 he was in Sainsbury's Images for Today, winning a Commendation Prize. Solo shows included Grabowski Gallery, 1965–7–9; Angela Flowers Gallery, 1981; Rochdale Art Gallery, and tour, 1983; Harlow Playhouse Gallery, Harlow, 1992; and in 1997 his Urban Mirror City Paintings, 1987–1997, was held at Royal National Theatre, revealing Bevan as a portrayer of the London landscape in rich colours. Bevan was married to the sculptor Pat Thornton. They used part of their west London house as Thornton Bevan Fine Arts to show other artists' works.

Peter BEVAN 1946– Painter, sculptor in various materials and ceramics artist, and teacher, born in the West Midlands. After studying at Gloucestershire College of Art and Royal College of Art, from 1973 Bevan lectured at Glasgow School of Art. He also had an exchange lectureship at Central Michigan University in 1986 and was a visiting artist in India. Among Bevan's mixed show appearances were John Moores Liverpool Exhibition; Smith Art Gallery, Stirling; and Germany. He was prizewinner in Cleveland Drawing Biennale in 1987. Solo exhibitions included Richard Demarco Gallery, Edinburgh, 1981, and Compass Gallery, Glasgow, 1986. Scottish Arts Council holds his work.

Tony BEVAN 1951– Figurative painter, born in Bradford, Yorkshire. He studied at the School of Art there, 1968–71, Goldsmiths' College School of Art, 1971–4, and Slade School of Fine Art, 1974–6. Bevan's work was included in The British Art Show, 1984–5, Human Interest at Cornerhouse in Manchester, 1985, Ikon Gallery in Birmingham, 1986, and John Moores Liverpool Exhibition, 1987, winning a prize there, 1997–8. He exhibited widely abroad. His first solo show was in 1976. There was a retrospective at ICA in 1988 and a major one at Whitechapel Art Gallery in 1993. This revealed Bevan as a singular painter of unsettling male figures and groups. Arts Council holds work. Lived in London.

Pamela Kathleen BEVES 1920– Illustrator and abstract painter, born in Brighton, Sussex. Studied at Brighton College of Art, 1945–7, her teachers including Dorothy Coke and Leslie Cole. Showed at Redfern, Leicester and Beaux Arts Galleries, NS, Heal's Mansard Gallery, SEA, in Stockholm and widely elsewhere. Had one-man shows at Archer Gallery in 1955 and Woodstock Gallery four years later. Lived in London.

Michael John Vaughan BEVIS 1948– Painter in oil and photographer, his photographic work being signed Vaughan. He was born in London and did a foundation course at Hornsey College of Art, 1966–7, then in 1967–70 Waltham Forest Technical College and School of Art, followed by North-East London Polytechnic, Barking, 1970–2, and London University Institute of Education, 1980–1. His teachers included Stuart Ray and Jack Smith. Went on to head the art and design department of St Peter's High School in Burnham-on-Crouch. Was a member of Free Painters and Sculptors, in 1980 having a solo show at Loggia Gallery, also exhibiting with LG. Bevis' work used bold and highly textured colours, was "preoccupied with structure and relates to a theory of the universe being like a doughnut, layered with endless passages", having "a dream-like quality". Lived in Maldon, Essex.

Pauline BEWICK 1935– Painter, illustrator and set designer, descended from the wood engraver Thomas Bewick. She was born in Corbridge, Northumberland. Had a bohemian, travelling childhood in England and Ireland, as described in her painter mother Harry Bewick's autobiography *A Wild Taste*, published in 1958. Pauline Bewick's prodigious ability as a decorative draughtsman developed in childhood. Aged 15 she was enrolled at the National College of Art, Dublin, but left before taking her teaching certificate examinations. Designed costumes and sets for Pike Theatre, Dublin; drew for Trinity College magazine *Icarus*; in 1954 contributed to the show Irish Living Art; in 1955 illustrated the cover for Thomas Kinsella's translation of *Thirty Three Triads*, part of *The Dolmen Chapbook*; in 1956 had pictures accepted accepted by the RHA; and in 1957 had a first solo show at Clog Gallery, Dublin. Two followed at Parkway Gallery, 1959–60, and there were many more in London, Dublin, Cork and Belfast. Bewick illustrated many books, notably *The Matchless Mice* series for children, did work for BBC Television and much periodical illustration. Arts Council of Northern Ireland, Arts Council of Ireland and many other public bodies hold her work. Bewick's daughter Poppy Melia was an artist.

Philip BEWS 1951– Figurative sculptor working in various materials who was included in Merseyside Artists 3, a Walker Art Gallery, Liverpool, touring show in 1986–7. Bews gained a diploma in landscape architecture from Manchester Polytechnic, 1970–4, then a first-class degree in fine art from Liverpool Polytechnic, 1983–6. Also exhibited at Norton Priory, Runcorn, May Day from 1984, and Bluecoat Gallery, Liverpool, 1986.

Steven BEWSHER 1964– Artist, born in Altrincham, Cheshire, educated at Sale Boys' Grammar School, who studied at Manchester and Wolverhampton, gaining an honours degree in fine art. Landscapes and the canal network in Cheshire were key themes in Bewsher's pictures. Showed at Mall Galleries and widely in the Cheshire and Manchester areas, including Colin Jellicoe Gallery. Lived in Manchester.

Janardan BHATT: *see* **JANARDAN**

Malgorzata BIALOKOZ SMITH 1937– Painter, printmaker, textile and photographic artist and teacher, born in Warsaw, Poland. After the German invasion, she remembered "being frightened and hungry and escaping into the unknown with my parents, through vast fields". Her mother's request for her to paint some Christmas cards started her interest in art, and she attended the Technical College of Art and the Academy of Art in Gdansk. Visited England in 1958 and was able to study at St Martin's School of Art, obtaining her further education teacher's certificate from Trent Polytechnic, Nottingham, 1973. Bringing up a family meant shelving her artistic interests, but on returning to them she became a frequent exhibitor. Later group shows included Ebury Gallery, 1982; Galleria el Talla, Lima, Peru, 1984; Pratt Manhattan Center Gallery, New York, and Brixton Art Gallery, both 1985; Open Print Exhibition, Bankside Gallery, 1988; and Oxford Art Society, Museum of Modern Art, Oxford, 1992. Later solo shows included Triada Gallery, Sopot, Poland, 1993, and Polish Cultural Institute, 1996, where Bialokoz Smith showed Expressionist works with a predominance of red. Ashmolean Museum, Macclesfield House and St Cross College, all in Oxford, where she had her studio, hold examples. Taught at various venues, including West of England College of Art, Bristol, 1987, and Bicester Community College, 1988.

Judy BIBBY fl.from 1970s– Painter and teacher, born in Liverpool. She studied at Southport, Liverpool and Royal College of Art. Went on to teach at St Martin's School of Art and Lanchester Polytechnic, Coventry. Bibby was included in the 1981–2 Woodlands Art Gallery touring show of Greater London Arts Association award winners. Also exhibited in 1980 Lina Garnard Memorial Prize and had a solo exhibition at Moira Kelly Fine Art.

André BICÂT 1909–1996 Artist, designer and teacher, working in a variety of media, born in Essex of French and Anglo-Irish parents. From 1947–85 he lived at Crays Pond, near Reading, where he worked in a converted barn, later living in London. Bicât was a Royal College of Art tutor, 1966–74. His varied career included much theatre work in the 1930s before war service, including Mercury Theatre productions from 1932; designing the setting for the New York production of *Murder in the Cathedral*, by T S Eliot, 1938; and designing for Windsor Repertory Theatre, 1939. Showed at RA; Redfern, Wildenstein, Leger and O'Hana Galleries; and with Sally Hunter & Patrick Seale Fine Art; also in Paris at Salon de la Jeune Sculpture and elsewhere widely overseas. Completed a ceramic mural for Hackney Downs School for Inner London Education Authority. Solo shows at Leicester Galleries were extensive, 1949–70, and Bohun Gallery, Henley-on-Thames, 1975–84; he had retrospectives at Reading Museum & Art Gallery, 1966, and Attic Gallery, Swansea, 1997. British Museum, Victoria & Albert Museum, Arts Council and provincial galleries hold examples.

Andrew BICK 1963– Artist producing geometrical abstractions, which could take a long time to complete and which might, like his 1997–8 John Moores Liverpool Exhibition entry For the Undecided, in wax and marker pen on wood, "exist as object (sculpture), drawing and painting at the same moment". Bick was born in Coleford, Gloucestershire, and studied at the University of Reading, 1982–6, and Chelsea College of Art, 1987–8. In 1992, he won a prize at the FIAR International Artists Under 30 show, held in several European and American cities. Had initial solo exhibitions at Todd Gallery and Cairn Gallery, Nailsworth, both 1989, later ones including Galerie Louise de Haan, Haarlem, Netherlands, 1996, and Eagle Gallery, 1998. Lived in London.

John BICKERDIKE 1895–1973 Sculptor and woodcarver, born near Bradford, Yorkshire. Apprenticed to a woodcarver when aged 14, Bickerdike attended evening classes at Bradford School of Art. After World War I, during which he served in Mesopotamia, Bickerdike returned to Bradford. He worked mainly for architects and for the brewing firm Watney. For the architect Clough Williams-Ellis he completed sculptures for his village Port Meirion, in Wales, and a large pair of lions at Stowe School. Watney commissions included work on Shakespeare's Head public house in London's Great Marlborough Street. With his wife the artist Rhoda Dawson, whom he married late in life, Bickerdike practised as a puppeteer and made large architectural models, including several for the Museum of Ghana. Was included in the show Sculpture in Britain Between The Wars at Fine Art Society, 1986. Lived in London.

Herbert BICKLE 1911– Painter, draughtsman, printmaker, designer and teacher, born in East Stanley, County Durham. After studying art at Durham University, 1932–6, with Robert Lyon, Bickle worked for much of the 1940s as aircraft design draughtsman, attending Southampton College of Art, 1948–50. Showed at RA, RBA and in the northeast of England. Lived in Southampton.

John BICKNELL 1958– Painter, printmaker and teacher, born in Surrey. He studied at West Surrey College of Art and Design, at Farnham, in 1975–7, at the North-East London Polytechnic, 1977–80, and Slade School of Fine Art, 1981–3. In the latter year he won a Slade Prize and a Boise Travelling Scholarship to Italy. Bicknell won a prize in the 1987 John Moores Exhibition, Liverpool, the same year that he had his first solo show in London at Carlile Gallery, after an earlier one at Eton College. Also showed solo at Pomeroy Purdy Gallery in 1990, and mixed exhibitions included The Last Wapping Show, 1985; Camden Annual, 1986; and XXV Joan Miró Drawing Prize Competition, Barcelona, 1986. In 1989–90 Bicknell was Henry Moore Printmaking Fellow at Leeds Polytechnic, where he went on to teach part-time. The expressive and emotional aspects of colour were important in Bicknell's abstract works. Lived in London.

Les BICKNELL 1943– Creator of bookworks, using a variety of materials ranging from chunks of wood to snail shells. They wittily commented on popular culture and family life, inviting the viewer to "Please touch". Did a foundation course at Lanchester Polytechnic, Coventry, 1981, then obtained an honours degree in graphic design at London College of Printing, 1982–5. Bicknell's residencies included Alnwick Fair, Camden Junior Arts Festival, Morton Hall Prison and Blackburn Museum. He carried out commissions for North Kesteven District Council and Scunthorpe Borough Council. Among positions held were part-time teaching at Lincolnshire College of Art and Humberside Art College. Took part in many group shows, including Arnolfini Gallery, Bristol, 1988, in Rubberstamps and Concrete Verse; and Small Presses, at New York Center for Book Arts, 1989. Had a solo show, from obscurity into oblivion, at London College of Printing, 1986, later ones including travelled books, Scunthorpe Museum & Art Gallery, 1991. Victoria & Albert Museum, Rijksmuseum in Amsterdam and New York Public Library hold examples. Lived at Sibton Green, Saxmundham, Suffolk.

Joyce BIDDER fl. from early 1930s– Sculptor in a variety of materials, notably of figures and animals. She studied at Wimbledon School of Art with Stanley Nicholson Babb, becoming one of his best pupils. In 1933 met Daisy Borne, whom she taught to carve. They worked in a studio in southwest London for many years and shared a liking for elegant, conservative sculpture tinged with modernism. Showed at SWA, RA and RMS and was a fellow of RBS. Her work was included in the Fine Art Society's Sculpture in Britain Between the Wars, 1986, and she shared a show there with Borne in 1987.

Winifred Percy BIDDLE 1878–1968 Watercolourist, born in Kingston upon Thames, who attended Lambeth School of Art, 1899–1910, under Innes Fripp, and Kingston Technical Institute. Exhibited RA, SWA, RI, NS and in the provinces. Lived in East Molesey, Surrey.

Elizabeth BIDDULPH 1927– Painter in oil, born in Port Elizabeth, South Africa. She studied at Wimbledon School of Art, 1944–7, with Gerald Cooper, then Slade School of Fine Art, 1949–51, under William Townsend. She was elected ROI in 1952, and an honorary senior member in 1982. Solo shows included Hornsey Library, 1971, Barclays Bank, Egham, 1973, Egham Library, 1985, then a shared show at Egham Literary Institute, 1991. Wrote for *Leisure Painter* magazine. Lived in Egham, Surrey.

Jon BIDDULPH 1958– Artist, born in Congleton, Cheshire, who was a member of TEA (see separate entry). He studied at Manchester Polytechnic, 1976–7, then three-dimensional design there, 1977–80; from 1980–81 was ceramics fellow at University of Salford. Lived in Manchester.

Peter BIEGEL 1913–1987 Painter of field sports subjects, born in Croxley Green, Hertfordshire. After Downside School and a period in business he studied at the Lucy Kemp-Welch School of Animal Painting, Bushey, at Bournemouth School of Art and worked with the sporting painter Lionel Edwards. The dealer J L W Bird and other galleries in Britain and in North America showed Biegel's work.

John BIGGE 1892–1973 Painter of abstracts who was briefly involved in Surrealism in the 1930s. Although he painted as John Bigge his full name was John Amherst Selby-Bigge (usually hyphenated); he was the son of Sir Amherst Selby-Bigge and was created 2nd Baronet in 1919. Born in Oxford, Bigge was educated at Winchester and Christ Church, Oxford, entered the Slade School of Fine Art briefly in 1914, but had his course "discontinued for military service" in World War I, partly spent with the Macedonian Mule Corps. (Bigge's first wife, Rachel Ruth Humphries, was also at the Slade.) After returning in 1919 Bigge worked as a chicken farmer, then as an estate agent, painting in his spare time. His friendship with Edward Wadsworth "opened my eyes to the various movements that were evolving in Paris" in the mid-1920s, and they shared an interest in the "aesthetic of machinery", Bigge relishing its forms in the Science Museum. Bigge's first solo show was at the Wertheim Gallery, 1931. Another took place at Galerie Vignon, Paris, 1932, a second London show at Lefevre, 1933. Latterly he was included in Unit I at Portsmouth City Museum and Art Gallery, 1978 (based on the 1934 Mayor Gallery show), and in Leeds City Art Gallery's Surrealist exhibition in 1986. Bigge travelled extensively in Europe from 1936, residing in Austria, France and Spain. During World War II he was a sub-editor with the BBC European News Service and worked with the British Red Cross. Finally lived at Le Bugue, Dordogne, and painted for his own pleasure. He wrote memoirs, unpublished at his death. Public galleries in Leeds and Hull hold Bigge's work.

BIGGLES 1959– Designer, artist, inventor and lecturer, actual name Stephen Riddle, whose nickname – which stemmed from the wearing of his father's flying jacket and a motorcycle helmet – was adopted professionally. He described himself as "a slightly eccentric English gentleman, going on polymorph", a common feature of whose work "has to be flexibility, wit and humour and a belief that all forms of art and design relate". After studying at New School, Kings Langley, founded by Rudolf Steiner, Biggles did a foundation course at Watford School of Art, 1976–7; gained a first-class honours degree in art and graphic design at The London College of Printing, 1977–80; and his master's in graphic design at the Royal College of Art, 1980–3. From mid-1980s was a visiting lecturer in graphic design at a number of colleges and schools of art, including Berkshire, Bath, Camberwell, Watford, Kensington and Chelsea and The London College of Printing. Simultaneously, he was a freelance designer, art director and design consultant. His extensive client list included Bethnal Green Museum of Childhood, British Airports Authority, British Telecom, Cabinet War Rooms, Imperial War Museum, The Open College, Serpentine Gallery, Victoria & Albert Museum and Workers Playtime Records. Events and exhibitions included Typos No 4, National Theatre, 1981; Blue Room Exhibition at Royal College of Art, 1982; Permanent Sand Castle Installations, Margate, 1992; and in 1993 Urban Art Attack I, Epping Forest, and 2, at Brixton. Lived in south London.

John R BIGGS 1909–1988 Painter, printmaker and illustrator born in Derby, where he initially studied art, followed by Central School of Arts and Crafts under John Skeaping, Bernard

Meninsky and Noel Rooke. Also studied at London University. He exhibited at RA, RCamA, Redfern Gallery, on the continent and in North America. Biggs, who was a specialist typographical designer, taught for many years, including overseas, being finally at Brighton Polytechnic, 1953–74. It published his *Autobiographica* in his final year there. He also illustrated a number of books; was at various times an art editor and production manager for publishing companies; and for many years ran the Hampden Press privately. Was master of the Art Workers' Guild in 1983 and has work in the British Museum. Lived in Brighton, Sussex.

Jessie P BIGNELL 1896–1992 Watercolourist and teacher, a native of Eltham, in southeast London. She was art and music mistress at the Gordon School, near where she lived. Showed at RI. Miss Bignell was noted for her watercolours of the English countryside, River Thames and old London, influenced by her many teachers. A memorial show was held at Holy Trinity Church, Eltham, in 1992.

Jack BILBO 1907–1967 Painter, sculptor, draughtsman and huger-than-life gallery owner, born in Berlin, Germany, as Hugo Baruch, of German-Jewish and English-Jewish parents. He led a peripatetic life on the continent in his early years and assumed the name Jack Bilbo in the early 1920s when he worked in films and journalism and wrote books, including *Carrying a Gun for Al Capone*. After his family was harried by the Nazis in the early 1930s, Bilbo settled in London in 1936 and began painting and sculpting. Had shows at Arlington and Zwemmer Galleries. After internment on the Isle of Man and brief Army service, Bilbo in 1941 founded the Modern Art Gallery in London and began writing books on art. His solo show at Lefevre in 1943 showed Bilbo as a strident Colourist. Bilbo's work mixed Expressionism, naivety, humour and the bizarre. In 1949 Bilbo moved the gallery to Weybridge and published his autobiography, *Jack Bilbo by Jack Bilbo*. The following year Bilbo left England on an old barge, settled to work in the south of France, then returned to Berlin in 1956, where he died. In 1988 England & Co held a retrospective, followed by one on his gallery in 1990.

John Gordon BILL 1915– Painter and teacher, born in London, married to the artist Coral Nerelle. After Radley College he studied art at Byam Shaw School with Bernard Dunstan and Charles Mahoney. Was elected RWA in 1978, also showing with RA, NEAC, and Cheltenham Group and had solo shows in Cotswolds area. RWA and Cheltenham Art Gallery hold his work, which went abstract from 1987. Lived in Northleach, Gloucestershire.

Simon BILL 1958– Painter, draughtsman and teacher who was born in Kingston upon Thames in Surrey. He studied at Epsom School of Art, 1976–7, St Martin's School of Art, 1977–80, and Royal College of Art, 1982–5. Went on to teach at St Martin's and Kingston Polytechnic. As well as showing with Anne Berthoud and Philip Solomon Galleries Bill exhibited at John Moores Liverpool Exhibition in 1980, with Still Life, and in 1989–90 with Jesus H Christ, one of a series related to the work of William Hogarth. Lived in London.

Edward S BILLIN 1911– Printmaker and painter who worked as a freelance commercial artist, born and lived in Sheffield, Yorkshire. Studied at Sheffield College of Art with Noel Spencer and Eric Jones. Wrote *Drawing on scraper board*. Showed with RA, SWE, RBA, RSA, BWS and in America, but in later years did not work owing to blindness. Graves Art Gallery, Sheffield, holds his work.

Richard BILLINGHAM 1970– Artist using photography, who grew up in Sunderland, County Durham, where he gained an honours degree in fine art at the University, 1991–4. He won the Prestige Photography Prize at the University, 1994; Felix H Man Memorial Prize, 1995; and The Citibank Private Bank Photography Prize, 1997. Group shows included Who's Looking at the Family?, Barbican Art Gallery, 1994; New Photography 12, Museum of Modern Art, New York, 1996; and the Saatchi Collection-related exhibition Sensation, at the RA, 1997. In that, Billingham recorded the grim squalor of his family's home life in the northeast. "British art has never been as scarily honest," commented critic Waldemar Januszczak. Solo exhibitions included Anthony Reynolds Gallery, the National Museum of Film and Photography, Bradford, and Portfolio Gallery, Edinburgh, all 1996; and a series in America, France and Italy in 1997.

Alfred John BILLINGHURST 1880–1963 Portrait, landscape and genre painter in oil and watercolour. Born at Blackheath, in southeast London, Billinghurst after initial education in England, Germany and Switzerland studied art at the Slade School of Fine Art, 1899–1902, with a period at the Goldsmiths' Institute, 1900, then a period in Paris which included time at Académie Julian and Atelier Cormon. Exhibited Paris Salon, ROI, RA, RI and a number of one-man shows. Billinghurst's work, which has about it the flavour of the 1920s and 1930s, is held by Plymouth Museum and Art Gallery. Was a member of the Ridley Art Club and lived at East Sheen, southwest London.

Bill BILLINGS 1938– Artist and teacher, born in London, who trained at the London School of Printing. He settled in Milton Keynes, Buckinghamshire, being involved in community arts there from 1974, was employed as community artist in 1978–80 and undertook two residencies in the city's schools. He was also a published poet, writer and playwright. His Triceratops, in concrete, was sited in 1979 at Peartree Bridge, Milton Keynes. Billings was a part-time lecturer in sculpture at Bletchley College and had an honorary master's degree from the Open University.

Stacy BILLUPS 1965– Painter, born in Surrey, whose work had a strong fantasy element. She studied at Reigate School of Art and Design, 1982–4, Wimbledon School of Art, 1984–7, and Chelsea School of Art, 1987–8. Her work was included in a number of group exhibitions including Young Painters South-

East, 1988; Cleveland Drawing Biennale, 1989; Royal Over-Seas League show in 1989 in which she was a prizewinner; and in 1989–90 John Moores Liverpool Exhibition. Had her first London solo show in 1991 at Christopher Hull Gallery. Lived in London.

Kenneth BILLYARD 1943–1976 Painter and teacher of art, born in Sale, Cheshire. He studied art at Newcastle University, 1962–6, under Kenneth Rowntree, Matt Rugg and Richard Hamilton. Showed at Chester Arts and Recreation Trust and at Portico Library, Manchester. His major work was the design for a huge mural on the side of the Museum of Science and Industry in Manchester which had to be executed by another artist as Billyard was killed in a car crash. He taught for several years at college in Salford and his own work, with abstract leanings and influenced by such artists as James Rosenquist, often featured canal boats. Had one-man show at Octagon Theatre, Bolton, in 1975. Lived in Withington, Manchester.

Pearl BINDER 1904–1990 Printmaker, illustrator, painter and writer, born in Fenton, Staffordshire, her father being a Jewish tailor. She arrived in London in 1925 and studied lithography, her favourite medium, at Central School of Arts and Crafts. Became involved in East End life, an active Socialist and member of AIA and freelance artist, writer, lecturer, designer of stained glass and crockery for Wedgwood. Was involved in government information service in World War II and married Elwyn Jones, later Lord Chancellor, when he was reading for the Bar. She was described as "a Bohemian in the heart of the Establishment". Although Lady Elwyn Jones, she remained a propagandist for many causes. Her son, Dan Jones, involved in social and youth work in London's East End, also painted.

Jack Armfield BINDON 1910–1985 Artist in a variety of styles, remembered in Hove, Sussex, where he had a studio, as a character and great self-publicist. Bindon worked variously as an undertaker, as a display artist and graphic designer for commercial enterprises in the Brighton area, as a sometimes cheeky muralist and teacher. He directed The Hove Art Club and conducted lively lecture tours in Europe and the Far East. Painted in Sussex and on the continent and Mediterranean area, in 1949 publishing *Diary of an Artist* about his travels. Showed locally, including Sussex County Arts Club and Hove Museum & Art Gallery, where he had a solo exhibition in 1950. Hove holds his atmospheric acrylic on board St John's Church, Palmeira Square, and an archive of material on Bindon's work and life.

Ginette BINGGUELY-LEJEUNE fl. from 1930s– Sculptor, initially educated in France and Belgium, studied art in Paris then with the sculptor Charles Doman in London. She exhibited RA, Fine Art Society, RBA, Royal Glasgow Institute of the Fine Arts, in the provinces and at Paris Salon. She completed a bust of Lord Nuffield for Nuffield College, Oxford, and her bust of the writer Rudyard Kipling is in the National Portrait Gallery. Lived for a time at Fairlight, Sussex.

Esmond BINGHAM 1948– Sculptor, draughtsman and teacher, born in Belfast, Northern Ireland. He attended Ulster College of Art & Design, 1968–9, Wolverhampton Polytechnic, 1969–72, and Goldsmiths' College School of Art, 1972–3. Went on to teach at Chelsea School of Art and Middlesex Polytechnic. Showed with Ikon Gallery, Birmingham; Camden Arts Centre; LG; Sir John Cass College; and Woodlands Art Gallery.

Dan BINNS 1896–1964 Artist, illustrator, craftsman and teacher, notable for his watercolours, father of the artist David Binns. He was born at Cowling, Yorkshire, and attended Skipton Art School. All his working life he taught at Skipton Secondary School, in the evening teaching bookbinding and lettering. For many years produced the cover for *The Yorkshire Dalesman* (later *The Dalesman*) magazine. Binns was president of Craven Art Club. Showed at RA, RI, RCamA, Royal Glasgow Institute of the Fine Arts and in Yorkshire. Died in the county at Sutton-in-Craven.

David BINNS 1935– Watercolourist, printmaker and teacher, born and lived in Sutton-in-Craven, Yorkshire. Binns worked "to convey the beauty and decorative qualities of wildlife and habitat", leading themes being foxes and ducks. He studied at Skipton Art School under his father Dan Binns, then at Leeds College of Art. Joseph Crawhall and C F Tunnicliffe were influences. Binns became head of art at Ermysted's Grammar School, Skipton, which he had attended, then became a freelance artist, running the Brent Gallery, Cowling. Was from 1968 a member of SWLA, also showing at RI, Manor House Gallery in Ilkley and Patricia Wells Gallery, Thornbury. Was also a member of BWS and Yorkshire Watercolour Society.

Lorna BINNS 1914– Watercolourist, born in Sheffield, Yorkshire, where she attended the College of Art under Maurice Wheatley, 1930–5, then Royal College of Art, 1935–9, under Ernest Tristram. Showed with RWS of which she became a member in 1977, also at RA and elsewhere. Lived in Surbiton, Surrey.

Helen BINYON 1904–1979 Watercolourist, illustrator, puppeteer and engraver. Born in London, daughter of the poet and writer on watercolour painting Laurence Binyon. Studied at the Royal College of Art, 1922–6, with Paul Nash, was at the Central School of Arts and Crafts, 1928–30. Exhibited at the Redfern Gallery with Edward Bawden and Eric Ravilious. She created Jiminy Puppets with her twin sister Margaret. Ran a travelling puppet theatre, performances in London including Harold Monro's Poetry Bookshop and the Mercury Theatre. Illustrated several books, including *Pride and Prejudice*, *Brief Candles* and the *Binyon Books*, with words by Margaret. Drew hydrographic charts for the Admiralty in World War II. In 1945–6 taught at Willesden School of Art, then at Bath Academy of Art 1949–65. In 1971 made a survey of professional puppetry in England, commissioned by the Arts Council, having written a standard work, *Puppetry Today*, in 1966. One-man show of watercolours at New Grafton Gallery in 1979. Lived at Chichester, Sussex.

BIRABONGSE Bhanudej Bhanubandh (Prince Birabongse) 1914–1985 Sculptor, racing driver and glider pilot, born in Burabhabiromse Palace, Bangkok, Thailand, son of HRH Phanurangsri Swangwongse. He was married to Ceril Birabongse, a painter. Educated at Eton College, Prince Bira studied at Byam Shaw School of Drawing and Painting. Wishing to become a sculptor he entered the studio of Charles Wheeler for three years, completing busts and animal sculptures, winning a first prize in a competition with Sealion Swallowing a Fish. Other work by him was bought by the singer Gracie Fields for her garden in Hampstead, made a fountain in Bangkok and a memorial to a car racing rival, Pat Fairfield, was designed by the Prince for Donington Racing Circuit. In his ERA racing car *Romulus* he won many prizes in the 1930s; he was a Grand Prix winner at Monaco. During World War II Prince Bira trained glider pilots for the Royal Air Force. He was known as the Gold Star Prince, whose life was commemorated by an exhibition at the National Gallery in Bangkok in 1989.

Ceril BIRABONGSE 1916– Painter who married Prince Birabongse of Thailand and became Princess Ceril. She studied at Byam Shaw School under Ernest Jackson, 1932–5, and exhibited at RA, ROI and RBA. Latterly lived at Verona, Italy. In 1992 she published *The Prince and I: Life with the Motor Racing Prince of Siam.*

Thomas Towning BIRBECK 1902–1982 Watercolourist, illustrator and writer who was by profession an officer with Chepstow Rural District Council for 40 years from 1927. He was born in Sunderland. In Chepstow he was largely responsible for turning Caldicot village, where he lived, into a Monmouthshire new town and for the purchase and restoration of the castle. He showed with Chepstow Art Society, Wye Valley Art Club and at the Cardiff and Swansea public galleries. He illustrated books, among them his own, published by the Chepstow Society and dealing with local history and issues.

David BIRCH 1895–1968 Landscape painter in oil, portrait painter and illustrator. Studied at Epsom School of Art and Goldsmiths' College School of Art. He became principal of Epsom and Ewell School of Art, 1930–61. He exhibited at the RA, ROI, RBA and Royal Glasgow Institute of the Fine Arts and his work was widely reproduced, notably by Royle Publications. Brighton Museum and Art Gallery and several other provincial galleries hold his work. Lived at Epsom, Surrey.

David BIRCH 1945– Painter and printmaker, born in Birmingham. Although early on interested in painting he went into farming, then for several years in the early 1970s worked in antiques in Broadway, Worcestershire. In 1974 became a full-time artist and five years later took up wood engraving guided by William Rawlinson. Showed at RA, RWA, RI and SWE. Also showed solo with John Noott Twentieth Century, in Broadway. Was commissioned by Confederation Life Insurance Company of Canada to produce views of Bristol.

John Anthony BIRCH 1946– Painter in acrylic with a special interest in audio-visual aids and multi-screen slide projection, born in Clevedon, Somerset. Studied at West of England College of Art, 1964–7. He settled in Bristol and showed at Arnolfini Gallery, Arnolfini Trust holding his work; and Bristol Arts Centre.

Samuel John Lamorna BIRCH 1869–1955 Landscape painter, principally of Cornwall, born in Egremont, Cheshire. Lamorna Birch's early youth was spent working in an office and in cotton mills, sometimes designing, in Lancashire, where he painted part-time. Mainly self-taught, apart from a short period at Atelier Colarossi, Paris, in 1895. From the late 1880s he visited the Penzance region. At this time Stanhope Forbes influenced his work. Eventually settled at Lamorna, adding this to his own name to avoid confusion with the painter Lionel Birch. Exhibited prolifically at Fine Art Society, where he had one-man shows, RWS, Walker's Galleries, RA, Walker Art Gallery, Liverpool, and elsewhere. In 1937 he painted in New Zealand. Elected RA, 1934. Tate Gallery holds his work, which found its way into many collections, and Falmouth Art Gallery gave him a retrospective in 1997, which toured to Plymouth.

Simon BIRCH 1921–1995 Stockbroker, watercolourist, architect and collector, born in London, who after Stowe School in 1938 enrolled at Westminster School of Art, in 1939 going up to Cambridge to read architecture. In 1941 was commissioned in the Coldstream Guards, on demobilisation in 1946 continuing architectural studies at Regent Street Polytechnic. On family advice, in 1950 became a stockbroker with Rowe Swann, retiring in 1983. Christie's approached him to set up a branch in the City, which closed in the early 1990s, although he remained a consultant. He was a keen clubman, a connoisseur of food and wine, an executive of the council of the City & Guilds of London Art School and was chairman of Minories Gallery, Colchester. Birch was a watercolourist of still life and hunting scenes who early in his career showed with Roland Ward Gallery. Died in Brantham, Suffolk.

Cyril Kenneth BIRD: *see* **FOUGASSE**

Gavin BIRD 1968– Artist, born in Chatham, Kent, who gained an honours degree in fine art at University of Leeds, 1987–91. Until early in 1993 Bird worked as a partnership with Graham Ramsay as Ramsay Bird. They gained the British Telecom Enabling Award, 1990, and in 1990–1 participated in British Telecom New Contemporaries, tour including Arnolfini Gallery, Bristol. Publications included *BLOC*, 1991. They had a solo show at Church View Gallery, Doncaster, 1989, later ones including Victoria Quarter, Leeds, and Orpheus Gallery, Belfast, both 1991; and Gimpel Fils, 1992, a show laced with humour and titled Post Neo Avant-Garde-ism.

Henry BIRD 1909– Painter, notably of murals and theatre scenery, draughtsman and teacher, born in Northampton, where he lived permanently from early 1950s. Bird did several menial jobs to pay his way through Northampton School of Art, and encouraged by the principal Lewis Duckett won a scholarship to Royal College of Art, gaining a number of awards there, including the Travelling Scholarship. In 1936 Bird was made a lecturer at University College, Aberystwyth, in 1937 marrying the actress Freda Jackson. He then became head scene-painter at the Old Vic and Sadler's Wells and by the end of World War II theatre designer for Embassy Theatre. He had done some church work in his home area, and now produced a large decoration for its Guildhall concurrently with a decorative scheme for London University Institute of Commonwealth Studies, in 1949. Took up teaching post at Northampton School of Art and continued with decorative schemes in the area, notably murals for Denton Church, 1974, included 35 life-size figures. Also painted safety curtain of Royal Theatre, Northampton. Bird was a brother of Art Workers' Guild and a member of the Tempera Society. His work was shown at Tate Gallery and Victoria & Albert Museum and he had solo shows in London and the provinces. At 73 Bird gained a Civil List pension for services to art. Several provincial collections hold Bird's work, including Northampton, Carlisle and Brighton.

Mary Holden BIRD fl.c.1920–1978 Painter and etcher, mainly of landscapes. Studied at Heatherley's School of Fine Art and went on to show at Fine Art Society, where she had frequent one-man exhibitions, RA, RSW, RBA and Paris Salon. Married to the cartoonist Cyril Kenneth Bird, who drew for *Punch* as Fougasse. Mary Holden Bird's work was widely reproduced by the Medici Society, in Britain and America. She was especially fond of the area around Morar, Scotland, and one of her typical transparent-washed watercolours is illustrated in Percy V Bradshaw's book *Water-Colour: A Truly English Art*. Mary Bird – known to her friends as Molly – lived in London for some time, then finally in Scotland.

Paul BIRD 1923–1993 Painter and teacher, born and lived in London, who studied at Bath School of Art under Clifford Ellis and was influenced by Walter Sickert and the colour theories of Peter Potworowski. After Royal Navy experience in India and the Far East in World War II, Bird studied at Institute of Education under Nikolaus Pevsner, returning to Bath to teach. Following a spell in the early 1950s teaching art at Bretton Hall Training College, in 1953 Bird – always interested in mysticism and religion – joined the Community of the Resurrection at Mirfield, where he stayed for eight years as a lay brother. After teaching at the Royal College of Art, Bird was appointed vice-principal at Central School of Art and Design, 1961–83. His summer school series of lectures The Art of Seeing, 1983–93, was influential.

Philip BIRD 1952– Painter and teacher, born in Bedford. He studied at Berkshire College of Art, 1972–3, and West Surrey College of Art at Farnham, 1975–8. In 1979 he set up a studio at Neatham Mill, near Alton, Hampshire. From 1980 Bird held a number of part-time teaching posts, including West Surrey College and Berkshire College of Art. He also taught mentally handicapped and children's classes. He won a number of Southern Arts Awards, including in 1981 artist-in-residence at Alton 6th Form College. Group shows included Wessex Artists, Southampton Art Gallery, 1980; Platform Four, at Reading Art Gallery and Museum, 1982; and Goldsmiths' show at Woodlands Art Gallery, 1983. Had series of solo shows, including Brillig Gallery, Bath, and Hexagon Art Centre, Reading, both 1979; and Southampton Art Gallery and West End Art Centre, Aldershot, both 1980.

Ramsay BIRD: *see* **Graham RAMSAY and Gavin BIRD**

Chris BIRD-JONES 1956– Artist specialising in glass constructions and teacher. She studied at Swansea College of Art and Royal College of Art. Went on to teach at schools, polytechnics and universities. As well as doing commissioned and collaborative work in Britain and abroad, she took part in many group shows, including Art in Boxes, 1992, at England & Co, where Nothing's Perfect and Blue were both made of glass. Completed Timepiece for WAC.

Geoffrey BIRKBECK 1875–1954 Watercolourist and muralist in the manner of John Singer Sargent, notable for Norfolk and Italian landscapes, born into a prominent Norfolk family at Stoke Holy Cross, Norwich, and educated at Eton College. His second wife, married in 1930, was Lady Maud Gundreda, daughter of the Earl of Cavan. In 1903 Birkbeck had a solo show at Carfax Gallery, after which he was showing at the New Dudley, Goupil and Walker's Galleries, Fine Art Society and abroad. He was a member of RBA and Norwich Art Circle. At Bracondale Woods he decorated a long room with murals for friend which contained views of lakeland scenery, Venetian lagoons and Italian gardens. Birkbeck is represented in Norwich Castle Museum, where he had exhibitions in 1940 and 1949 and a memorial show in 1954–5. In 1908 he published *Old Norfolk Houses*, containing 36 colour reproductions, which showed his feeling for the Baroque style.

Edith BIRKIN 1927– Painter in acrylic and teacher, born in Prague, Czechoslovakia. Birkin was deported to Lodz, Poland, in 1941, to Auschwitz in 1944 and then to a labour camp. January 1945 saw her on a death march through snow, then in March she was sent by cattle truck to Belsen. Upon being liberated in 1945 she returned to Prague, but finding no family or friend there joined her older sister in England, where she married and had children. She first studied painting in 1970s at Tetherdown Adult Education Centre, then at Camden Arts Centre. As a schoolteacher she was involved in remedial work. Moved to Hereford in 1980, three years later beginning a long series of works, Memories of the Holocaust. Anton Gill's *Journey Back from Hell*, the front cover of Ronnie Landau's *The Nazi Holocaust* and cover of *Voices from the Holocaust*, a British Library audio set, all featured Birkin's work. Was included in exhibitions at Birmingham and Hereford City Museums and Art Galleries. Solo shows included Coventry Cathedral, Ben Uri Art Society and Hanover Gallery in Liverpool. Ben Uri and Imperial War Museum hold examples.

Tony BIRKS: *see* **Tony BIRKS-HAY**

Tony BIRKS-HAY 1937– Artist in oil and clay (for bronze), graphic designer and teacher, who studied at Slade School of Fine Art under William Coldstream, Reg Butler and Henry Moore. Birks-Hay was an Oxford School of Art lecturer, 1959–63, was head of Art at Radley College, 1961–3, then freelanced. Group shows included RA, RWA and MAFA. Had solo exhibitions at Keble College, Oxford, 1961; Rotunda Gallery, 1970; and Alpha House Gallery, Sherborne, 1991. Portraits in oil or bronze and landscapes in oil were Birks-Hay's main works. St Edmund Hall, Oxford, and many private collections held examples. In 1973 he won the Westward Television Sculpture Award. Arts Club member who lived in Marston Magna, Yeovil, Somerset. Sometimes worked as Tony Birks. He was also a noted writer on ceramics.

Oswald BIRLEY 1880–1952 Portrait painter, born in Auckland, New Zealand, educated at Harrow School and Cambridge University. Also studied art in Dresden, Florence and in Paris at Académie Julian under Marcel Baschet. Birley served with a commission in the Intelligence Corps in France in World War I, gaining the Military Cross. He was a vice-president of RP, also being a member of ROI. Showed also at RA, Walker Art Gallery in Liverpool, RHA, RSA and elsewhere. Birley painted many distinguished figures, including Sir Edward Marsh the collector, the artist Glyn Philpot and the 1st Earl of Birkenhead in the National Portrait Gallery; portraits of King George VI for the Royal Agricultural Society and Royal Naval College, Greenwich; and for that collection a series of portraits of war admirals of World War II. He was knighted in 1949. Lived in London and in West Dean, Sussex.

William BIRNIE 1929– Painter in oil and watercolour, and teacher, married to the artist Cynthia Wall. He was born in Bathgate, West Lothian, and studied at Glasgow School of Art, 1946–51, teachers including William and Mary Armour, David Donaldson and Geoffrey Squire, and Hospitalfield House, Arbroath, 1950–1, with Ian Fleming. He painted extensively in Scotland and on the continent, mainly landscape, and preferred "complicated subjects". Birnie taught in west of Scotland schools, 1952–88 and was a principal examiner for the Scottish Examination Board, 1975–9. He was elected a member of RSW in 1964 and of the Royal Glasgow Institute of the Fine Arts, 1993, having been a founder-member of the Glasgow Group, 1958. Had a series of solo exhibitions with Open Eye Gallery, Edinburgh, from 1989. HRH The Duke of Edinburgh, Scottish Arts Council and Glasgow and Paisley Art Galleries hold examples. Lived in Kilbarchan, Renfrewshire.

Val BIRO 1921– Artist in pen and ink, scraperboard, watercolour, printmaker and writer, born in Budapest, Hungary. Aspired early to be an artist, then was sent by father in 1939 to England, where he studied until 1942 at Central School of Arts and Crafts, evacuated to Northampton. His main subject was illustration, his teachers including John Farleigh, Noel Rooke and Bernard Meninsky. In 1942 Biro joined Sylvan Press while working as a part-time fireman, then became art director for John Lehmann, the publisher. Had been freelancing on book jackets and advertising, and in 1953 went freelance full-time. Authors illustrated included C S Forester, Monica Dickens, Evelyn Waugh and Noël Coward. Drew for *Radio Times* for 21 years until 1972. Biro illustrated many children's books, then in 1966 published the first of his many Gumdrop stories, based on his ownership of a vintage car. He also retold traditional tales, with his own illustrations, such as *Hungarian Folk-Tales*, 1981. Also drew for *The Good Food Guide* and was a member of Chartered Society of Designers. Victoria & Albert Museum holds his work. His name was originally Bálint (translated Val(entine)) Stephen Biro and he settled in Bosham, Sussex.

Bill BIRRELL fl. from mid-1960s– Painter, graphic artist and teacher. After studying at Glasgow School of Art, 1964–6, Birrell worked in Canada and America as a graphic artist for two years, returning to Glasgow where he graduated in drawing and painting in 1970. He went on to teach in a secondary school in the city. Birrell's pictures were figurative, but had a Surrealist tinge. He showed at Royal Glasgow Institute of the Fine Arts, and in group shows in Markham Gallery in Toronto at Galerie d'Art Moderne in Geneva, in 1983, and at International Contemporary Art Fair at Olympia. He showed at Compass Gallery, Glasgow, in the New Generation Show in 1970, then participated in a three-man show there and had solo exhibitions in 1977 and 1988. His work is in extensive private collections in Britain and overseas.

Ronald BIRRELL fl. from 1970s– Artist who was born in Glasgow, where he studied at the School of Art, going on to Royal College of Art and Royal Academy of Fine Arts, Madrid. He won the Robert Hart Bursary, William Armour Prize and Torrance Award. He became a professional member of SSA, but his career hit a setback with the onset of multiple sclerosis in the late 1980s. A precision of statement marked Birrell's work, which is often tinged with a feeling of solitude. Was included in The Compass Contribution exhibition at Compass Gallery, Glasgow, 1990. Scottish Arts Council and Nuffield Foundation hold his work.

Cecil Harry BIRTWHISTLE 1910–1990 Artist in oil, pastel and watercolour, and teacher, son of the painter James Birtwhistle. Brought up in Sheffield, he began showing work as a child. Studied at the local College of Art, 1924–9, under Anthony Betts, then with Barnett Freedman and Gilbert Spencer at Royal College of Art, 1929–32. Birtwhistle later taught at Richmond School of Art. Exhibited RA, Royal Glasgow Institute of the Fine Arts, NEAC and in the north. In later years was a close friend of the artist Ottilie Tolansky, sharing exhibitions with her at Walker's Galleries. After Birtwhistle's death Piano Nobile Fine Paintings, of Richmond, showed fine examples of his Camden Town Group-influenced pictures in its Modern British Masters exhibitions, 1994–5. Lived in London.

Edward BISHOP 1902–1997 Painter, printmaker, designer, photographer and teacher who studied and taught at Central School of Arts and Crafts under A S Hartrick and Noel Rooke, 1920–6. In 1929 he joined the advertising agency Lintas, working there as a group art director until 1936, and he was included in Beyond the Horizon: Artists at Lintas 1930–1950 at Agnew, 1988. From Lintas he moved to S H Benson's before joining the Ministry of Information in 1941, where he designed propaganda material for neutral countries. During one night of the Blitz Bishop lost his mother, sister and one of his brothers, and his London flat, with all his completed paintings, was destroyed. In 1945, Bishop became a consultant advertising designer and painter, being particularly noted for his paintings of London. Bishop won the Lord Mayor of London's Art Award in 1975–6, and in 1978 won the first prize in the big Spirit of London competition. Was a member of RBA, 1950, and NEAC, 1960 (he was later appointed its first keeper, a post he held until 1990), was elected to and eventually became president of the London Sketch Club, and as chairman of the Chelsea Arts Club in the mid-1960s lobbied for admission of women. Showed extensively at RA, also at Leicester and Wildenstein Galleries. Nottingham Castle Museum, National Gallery of New South Wales, Sydney, Nottingham Castle Museum, National Gallery of New South Wales, in Sydney, and Department of the Environment hold examples. Bishop was married to the painter Celeste Radloff. Lived in London.

Molly BISHOP fl. from early 1930s– Painter, especially of portraits, and draughtsman, married to Lord George Scott. She studied at the Royal Academy Schools, 1930–2, under Walter Westley Russell. Exhibited RSA, RBA, Royal Glasgow Institute of the Fine Arts and elsewhere. Lived in Towcester, Northamptonshire, and London.

William Henry BISHOP 1942– Painter, especially of ships and the sea, who raced a Victory class one design yacht, born and brought up in Portsmouth area. As a boy he began drawing and modelling ships. With the help of marine artist W L Wyllie's daughter, who gave Bishop over 50 of her father's brushes, and that of marine artist Richard Joicey, Bishop showed successfully at RSMA. In 1980 the family firm was sold and Bishop began painting full-time, at first in watercolour. Early commissions came from naval officers needing portraits of their ships, and Bishop's pictures proved especially popular in America, where he supplied the Quester Gallery, Stonington, Connecticut. Bishop had a solo show at Royal Exchange Gallery, 1991. The *Mary Rose* Trust asked him to paint several versions of the ship; the Royal Naval Museum a scene from the Battle of Jutland; and he produced company calendars for John Courage Brewery and Chichester Press. Lived at Langstone, Havant, Hampshire.

Osmond Hick BISSELL 1906–1968 Painter, wood engraver and teacher, born at Harborne, Birmingham. Studied at Kidderminster School of Art under William Daly, 1924–8, then at Birmingham College of Art, 1928–9, with Harold Holden. Exhibited RA, NEAC, NS, PS, Paris Salon and elsewhere. He held the post of vice-principal at York School of Arts and Crafts from 1929. York and Kidderminster art galleries hold his work which was included in the *Recording Britain* exhibition at Victoria & Albert Museum in 1990. Lived in Kidderminster, Worcestershire.

Douglas BISSET 1908– Sculptor and teacher, born in Strichen, Aberdeenshire. He studied at Glasgow School of Art, 1930–3, with Archibald Dawson; at the Royal Danish Academy, 1933; then as a Rome Scholar attended the British School in Rome, 1934–5. Was then attached to the British School of Archaelogy in Athens for three years. Around the outbreak of World War II he returned to England and began teaching there for a number of years at Leeds College of Art after a short period at Brighton School of Art. Exhibited RA, Royal Glasgow Institute of the Fine Arts and elsewhere. Imperial War Museum holds his work. Lived in London.

George BISSILL 1896–1973 Painter, printmaker, draughtsman and furniture designer, born in Fairford, Gloucestershire. He was the son of a coal miner and was a miner himself for several years. Having been gassed during service in France during World War I Bissill studied at Nottingham School of Art, 1920–1. In the early 1920s he moved to London, working for a time as a pavement artist, but was given a solo show at Redfern Gallery in 1924. Also exhibited RA, NEAC, Maltzahn Gallery and Abbott and Holder. Although a landscape painter, Bissill is notable for his powerful images of miners at work. Tate Gallery holds his Landscape, Layton. Lived at Ashmansworth, near Newbury in Berkshire.

Roderick BISSON 1910–1987 Artist and art critic who worked extensively in gouache, born and based in Liverpool, son of a mariner, who was educated at Liverpool Institute. After working in the Picton Library Bisson joined the architectural practice Hinchliffe Davies. An admirer of Wyndham Lewis, Bisson developed an interest in Cubism and Surrealism and as early as 1932 a work of his caused a stir at the Sandon Studios (he became a member and was to publish the definitive account of *The Sandon Studios Society of the Arts* in 1965). Bisson during the 1930s was secretary of the Liverpool Young Communist League, was a conscientious objector early in World War II, but joined up when the Soviet Union was invaded by Germany. He became a cartographer with the 8th Army in the desert and in Italy, where the works of Masaccio and Piero della Francesca moved him. After the war Bisson worked as a design consultant for the local firm Lewis, from the 1950s serving as art critic of the *Liverpool Daily Post*, where he wrote perceptively for 25 years as Z. Unhappy about a possible conflict of interest and with developments in American art, in the late 1950s he gave up painting. Bisson was a reticent man, a rare exhibitor and a fluent French speaker who assembled an impressive library of French art publications. These were sold at Sotheby's shortly before his death, which coincided with a retrospective at Walker Art Gallery, Liverpool, which holds his work.

Bitte B-N 1917– Painter and illustrator, actual name Birgitte Brondum-Nielsen, who was born in Copenhagen, Denmark, where she was educated and studied art at the College of Arts and Crafts. As well as exhibiting in Denmark, showed with RA, RSA, SSA, with RI and SSWA, both of which she was a member, Brighton Art Gallery and Royal Glasgow Institute of the Fine Arts. Also had a series of solo exhibitions in Britain and Denmark. HRH The Duke of Edinburgh and Glasgow Art Gallery hold her work. Illustrated books for children. Lived for some years in Scotland, in Alloa and then Rannoch Station, Perthshire.

Edna BIZON 1929– Painter in oil on canvas, born in London, married to the artist Ken Bizon. She studied at Camberwell School of Arts and Crafts where her teachers included Claude Rogers, John Minton, Lawrence Gowing and Victor Pasmore. Bizon in her still lifes, genre and landscape scenes emulated painters of the Dutch and Norwich schools, believing that "skill in painting is very important to express ideas". She was a member of SWA and showed regularly at RA from 1973. Also exhibited at Thorndike Theatre, Leatherhead, 1971; Hal O'Nians, 1987–90; and she shared a show with Mary Carter at Llewellyn Alexander in 1991. Gulf International holds her work. Lived in North Creake, Norfolk.

Ken BIZON 1927– Painter in oil and watercolour of architectural themes as a background to human activity; teacher. Born in Warham, Norfolk, he studied at Norwich and Camberwell Schools of Art, his teachers including Joseph Dixon and William Townsend. For a time he was involved in exhibition and interior design work; was also senior lecturer in design at South Bank Polytechnic. Member of Royal Society of Arts. Bizon showed at RA; Thorndike Theatre, Leatherhead, 1979; and Llewellyn Alexander. Lived in North Creake, Norfolk, and was married to the painter Edna Bizon.

Dorothy BLACK 1963– Artist in various media who was particularly noted for her confident ability to make the line; her work had strong decorative and surreal elements and made much use of the human figure. Black was born in Forfar, Angus, and studied at Edinburgh College of Art, 1980–6. She lived and taught in Dunfermline, Fife. Her work was shown in solo and group shows in Britain and America, notably in Edinburgh City Art Centre's exhibition Through Women's Eyes, 1992–3. The Centre, Stirling University and BBC Scotland hold her work.

Dorrit BLACK 1891–1951 Painter and lino-cut artist, born Dorothea Black in Adelaide, Australia. After initial art education at Sydney Art School she moved to London to work under Iain Macnab and Claude Flight at the Grosvenor School of Modern Art, then went to Paris to study with André Lhote and Albert Gleizes. Eventually returned to Australia, where she settled in Magill, South Australia. Exhibited in Paris, Australia and in Britain at Redfern Gallery and WIAC. Victoria & Albert Museum holds her work.

Hamish BLACK 1948– Sculptor and teacher. Attended Eastbourne School of Art, 1965–7, North-East London Polytechnic, 1967–70, and Slade School of Fine Art, 1970–2. Had extensive teaching experience from 1973, including Workers' Educational Association, Brighton Polytechnic, West Sussex College of Art and Wimbledon School of Art. Took part in extensive group exhibitions, including Brighton Polytechnic Gallery, 1979; as artist-in-residence, Varndean College, Brighton, 1982; Sussex Artists, Brighton Festival, 1991; and Sculpture at Canterbury, 1992. From 1984 Black was in collaboration with the sculptor Anthony Caro. His solo shows included Southover Grange Gardens, Lewes, 1982, and Charleston Farmhouse, Firle, 1989. Black did a substantial amount of public work, including Maygrove Peace Park, Camden Council, 1985; a winning entry for Great Hurricane Sculpture Competition, American Express, Brighton Festival and South East Arts, 1989; and Tree House, Brighton Festival, 1990.

Ian BLACK 1929– Painter, draughtsman and teacher, born in Bury St Edmunds, Suffolk. He studied at Southampton College of Art, 1949, and Bath Academy of Art, Corsham, 1952–6, teachers including Peter Lanyon, William Scott and Martin Froy. Among mixed exhibitions were RWA of which he was a member, 1978, and RA, and he had a series of solo shows. Wadham and St Catherine's Colleges in Oxford as well as the New Zealand government hold his work. Became head of art at Bristol Cathedral School. Lived at Englishcombe, Bath, Avon.

John Frederick BLACK 1943– Painter, printmaker, textile designer and teacher, born in Appleby Magna, Leicestershire. He studied at Loughborough College of Art, 1960–4, his teachers including Edward Sharp; Brighton College of Art, 1965, under Ronald Horton; then in 1978–9 at Manchester Polytechnic for his master's degree. Went on to become a freelance designer; to operate The Gallery at his home in Wellingborough, Northamptonshire; and to teach at Bedford College of Higher Education. Showed in Britain and abroad.

Maureen BLACK 1926– Painter, printmaker, embroiderer and teacher who studied painting and embroidery at Goldsmiths' College School of Art and etching at Morley College. She was a founder-member of Greenwich Printmakers' Association, showed at RA Summer Exhibition, RE and had a solo show at Woodlands Art Gallery in 1980. Taught at Greenwich Adult Education Institute. In 1977–9 a hanging commissioned by the Ursuline Community to commemorate the centenary of St Ursula's High School, Greenwich, was designed and partly made by Black. Her work is also held by National Maritime Museum, Guildhall Art Gallery and other public collections in Britain and abroad. Lived in London.

Noël BLACK 1931– Sculptor in various materials, ceramist and teacher, born in Prescot, Lancashire. He studied at Loughborough College of Art, 1949–53, then Leicester College of Art, 1953–4. Went on to become senior lecturer in sculpture at

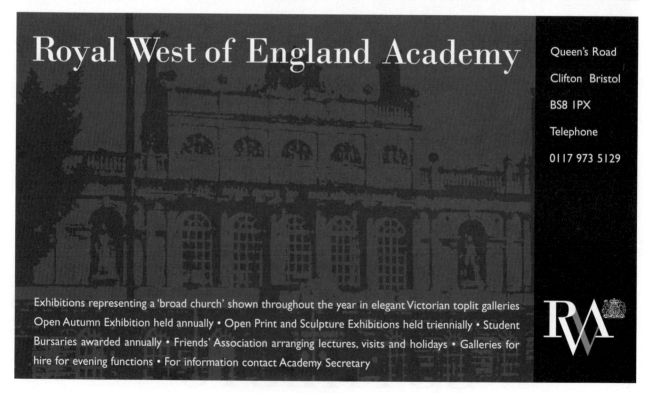

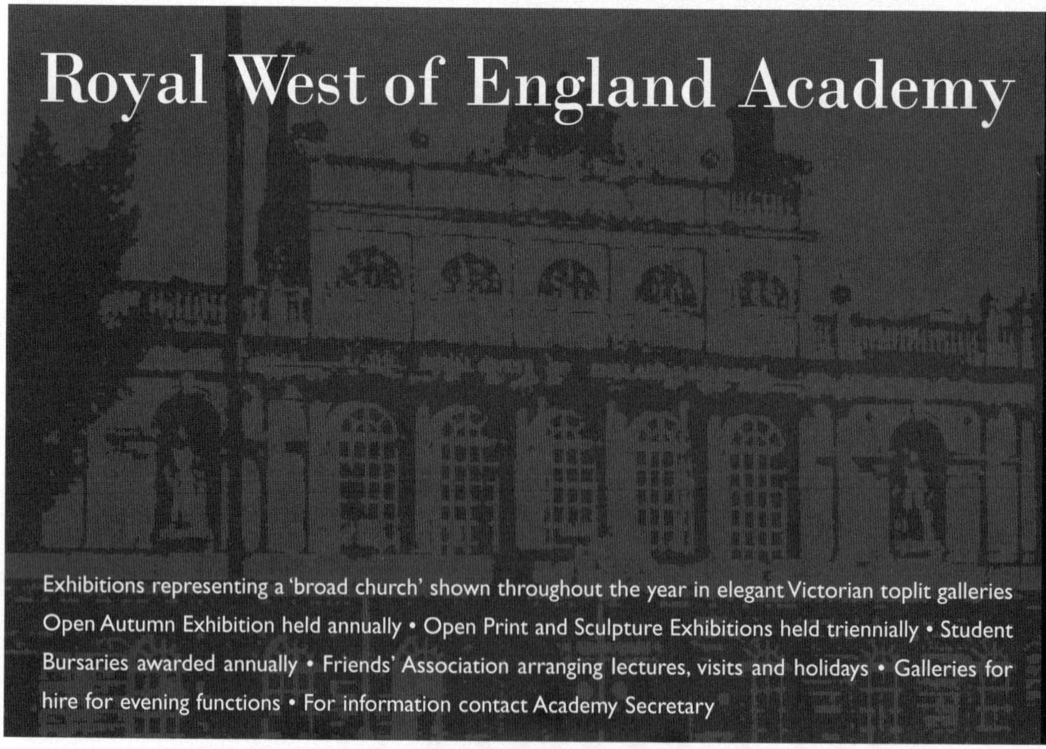

Kesteven College of Education and University of Evansville. Showed at Upstairs Gallery, Stamford, and handled public commissions. Lived in Skillington, Lincolnshire.

Roman BLACK 1915– Oil painter, mural and stained glass designer. Born in Poland, he studied at the Central School of Arts and Crafts and Brighton College of Art. Black, who lectured extensively, exhibited at the RA, LG, RBA, Wildenstein and the Paris Salon, where he was awarded a gold medal in 1968. He is represented in public national galleries in Ottawa, Melbourne, Dublin and elsewhere. Lived in London.

Sam BLACK 1913– Painter and teacher, born in Ardrossan, Ayrshire, where he attended the Academy. Attended Glasgow School of Art, 1932–6, then studied on the continent. Black was for a time principal lecturer in art at Jordanhill Training College, Glasgow, also an inspector of schools. During World War II his work was bought by the War Artists' Advisory Committee and Glasgow Museum and Art Galleries also hold a watercolour of St Enoch Square, in the city. Exhibited RSA and Royal Glasgow Institute of the Fine Arts. Lived at West Kilbride, Ayrshire.

Simon BLACK 1958– Artist born in Manchester, where he attended the Polytechnic, also Wolverhampton Polytechnic. He travelled on the continent and spent several periods in Israel, returning to England in 1983 and settling in London three years later. Showed with MAFA, where he won a prize in 1985; in 1986 at Ben Uri Art Society, which acquired his work, and at Leo Solomon Gallery in Rochdale; and in 1993 at Five Dryden Street Gallery.

Elizabeth BLACKADDER 1931– Watercolourist and teacher, born in Falkirk, Stirlingshire. She studied at Edinburgh University and Edinburgh College of Art, 1949–54, her teachers including Penelope Beaton, Robert Henderson Blyth and William Gillies. A Carnegie Travelling Scholarship in 1954 allowed her to visit several countries in southern Europe, a postgraduate scholarship in 1954–5 allowing further travels in Italy. In 1956 she married the painter John Houston and began teaching part-time at Edinburgh College of Art. Although she won commissions for stained glass, lithographs and tapestries, Blackadder was best known for her meticulous watercolours in which objects are carefully spaced on her studio table. Elected RSA in 1972 and RA in 1976. Showed regularly at Mercury Gallery, elsewhere in Britain and abroad. Scottish National Gallery of Modern Art holds her work. Lived in Edinburgh.

Christine BLACKBURN 1963– Artist, notably a printmaker, who studied at Wirral College of Art, 1981, Sheffield Polytechnic, 1982, San Jose State University, 1984, then Sheffield Polytechnic, 1985. She took part in Sheffield Open Art at Mappin Art at Mappin Art Gallery, 1985, Punchlines at Bluecoat Gallery in Liverpool, 1986, and was included in the Walker Art Gallery touring show Merseyside Artists 3, in 1986–7.

Clarence E BLACKBURN 1914– Painter, printmaker, commercial artist and potter, educated in Stoke-on-Trent, then studied at Burslem College of Art. Ran small pottery, 1944–59. Showed RA, RE and abroad. Lived in Hampton Wick, Surrey.

David BLACKBURN 1939– Artist in pastel, printmaker and teacher, born in Huddersfield, Yorkshire. His landscapes of England, North America and Australia had strong abstract and visionary qualities. Blackburn studied at Huddersfield School of Art, 1955–9, then Royal College of Art, 1959–62. He became a lecturer in 1966 at University of Manchester's school of architecture, other appointments including visiting lecturer at University of Melbourne, 1969–77; then he was visiting artist at Georgetown University, Washington, 1981, and Yale Center for British Art, 1989. Kenneth Clark and Humphrey Brooke were early supporters of Blackburn, who had his first solo show at Argus Gallery, Melbourne, in 1965. He had a retrospective at Mappin Art Gallery, Sheffield, 1970, others at University of York, 1978, and Huddersfield Art Gallery, 1979 and 1994. Showed at Hart Gallery, Nottingham, from 1989. Yale Center, the Museum of Modern Art in New York, several Australian galleries and Ashmolean Museum, Oxford, hold his work.

Mavis BLACKBURN 1923– Painter, earlier in oil, later in acrylic; teacher. She was born in Wallasey, Cheshire, and studied at Liverpool College of Art, 1942–8, teachers including Will C Penn, Martin Bell and Alfred Wiffen. Blackburn taught art at Holt Hill School, Birkenhead for two years; freelanced for two more; then taught until retirement in 1984, becoming department head at Upton Hall Convent, Birkenhead. Obtained bachelor's degree in 1980. Although she painted abstracts in 1960s and 1970s, the work of Bridget Riley and the floor of St Mark's in Venice being influences, Blackburn judged abstraction "to be a fascinating blind alley, and I reverted to a naturalistic style". Landscapes and buildings were key subjects. Became a member of RCamA, 1952, also being a member of Liverpool Academy, Wirral Society of Art and Deeside Art Group. Showed at RA, RBA and had a retrospective at Williamson Art Gallery, Birkenhead, which holds her work, in 1992. Lived at West Kirby, Wirral, Merseyside.

David BLACKER 1949– Sculptor of horses and trophy maker, born in Surrey and educated at Milton Abbey, Dorset. Blacker entered racing in 1967 and worked at the stables of trainer Tim Forster, beginning to ride as an amateur, then as a professional, 1969–82. Among his 327 winners were the Whitbread Gold Cup and *Daily Express* Triumph Hurdle and he rode in nine Grand Nationals. Retired from racing to concentrate on sculpture, taken up as a hobby in 1974. His most famous commission was Red Rum, in the grounds of Aintree racecourse. Other important ones included Aldaniti, another Grand National winner, and two Derby winners, Blakeney and Murston. The Hamilton Trophy, Kelso; the Dermot Daly Memorial Trophy, Cheltenham; and John Hughes Memorial Trophy, Liverpool, were made by Blacker, whose work was cast by The Morris Singer Foundry. Among his solo shows was Tryon & Moorland Gallery, 1988.

Doris May BLACKER 1905– Painter, potter and teacher, born in Dewsbury, Yorkshire. Brought up in Morecambe, Lancashire, where she eventually settled, she studied at Lancaster School of Art. For many years she taught at Skerton Girls' Modern School, in Lancaster, showing widely in Lancashire and Yorkshire. She was noted for her watercolours of the Lake District.

Harry BLACKER 1910– Versatile artist and writer, born into poor circumstances in London's East End. He was apprenticed to an engraver, attending Sir John Cass Technical Institute evening classes, taught by Frederick C Herrick and Robert Sargent Austin. He went on to work in advertising, clients including London Transport, Shell-Mex and BP and the Post Office. As a cartoonist he worked as Nero, in 1962 gaining joint first prize in a competition organised by the *Jewish Chronicle*. A dozen years later he published his illustrated autobiography, *Just Like it Was – Memoirs of the Mittel East*. Other books included *East Endings* and (as Nero), *Some of My Best Jokes are Jewish*, *With Laugh and Affection* and *By My Laugh it's Jewish*. Had a show at Lauderdale House, near where he lived in Highgate, north London, in 1981, another at Ben Uri Art Society, which holds his work, in 1986.

Kate BLACKER 1955– Artist who was born in Petersfield, Hampshire. She studied at Royal College of Art, 1979–81. Among her activities was work with performing artists, notably the dancer Gaby Agis. Had a first solo show in 1982 at Coracle Gallery, then widely in Britain and abroad, including Victoria Miro, 1989, Museum of Photography Charleroi, 1992, and in 1993 at John Hansard Gallery, Southampton. In 1993–4 she was included in the Arts Council tour Recent British Sculpture. Worked in Britain and France.

Dorothy BLACKHAM 1896–1975 Painter, artist in black-and-white and teacher, born in Dublin. Studied at Royal Hibernian Academy School with Dermod O'Brien, 1916–21, and at Goldsmiths' College School of Art, 1921–2, under Edmund J Sullivan and Frederick Marriott. Exhibited extensively in Ireland, including RHA, and LG, Tempera Society and SGA. Was an art teacher attached to the Ministry of Health just after World War II. Lived in London.

George BLACKLOCK 1952– Painter, draughtsman and teacher, born in Durham, who studied at Sunderland Polytechnic, 1970–1, Stourbridge College of Art, 1971–4, and Reading University, 1974–6. In 1976–8 he had a junior fellowship in painting at Cardiff College of Art, gained a WAC award and became senior lecturer at Wimbledon School of Art. Exhibitions included Whitechapel Open, Francis Graham-Dixon Gallery and he won a prize in John Moores Liverpool Exhibition, 1993–4. Had a solo show at Byam Shaw, 1993. Arts Council holds his work. Lived in London.

Audrey BLACKMAN 1907–1990 Sculptor, initially in bronze, then in ceramics, of figures; painter. She was born in London into an academic family and married Professor Geoffrey Blackman, who held the Sibthorpian chair in rural economy at Oxford. Having failed to obtain a place to study history at Oxford, Audrey Blackman went to the Kunstgewerbeschule, Graz, in Austria, and contemplated becoming a singer, but returned to her early love of art by studying at Goldsmiths' College School of Art 1926–30, and Reading University, 1931–5. Although her first sculptures were in bronze, she was persuaded by a visit to the Ashmolean Museum to turn to ceramics, learning the techniques at the Oxford School of Art under Gladys Grimshaw. In 1978 she published *Rolled Pottery Figures*. She became strongly involved in such bodies as the International Academy of Ceramics, Crafts Advisory Committee and Federation of British Crafts Societies. Showed RA, elsewhere in Britain and abroad. Work held by Fitzwilliam Museum, Cambridge; Oxfordshire County Museum; and Cecil Higgins Museum, Bedford. Lived at Boar's Hill, Oxford.

Clive BLACKMORE 1940– Painter in oil, watercolour and gouache, born in Kingston upon Thames, Surrey. He attended Twickenham and Kingston Schools of Art, then for many years was involved in pottery, stoneware and porcelain, having moved to Cornwall in 1960. As a full-time painter from 1984 Blackmore "worked mainly in Cornwall and Provence". His group appearances included Newlyn Orion and Penwith Gallery, St Ives; RA Summer Exhibition; NEAC; The Discerning Eye, at Mall Galleries; and in 1992 he was included in Artists from Cornwall at RWA. Had solo shows at Nevill Gallery, Bath, and New Academy Gallery. Lived at Rinsey, near Helston, Cornwall.

Basil BLACKSHAW 1932– Abstract painter, born in Glengormley, County Antrim, Northern Ireland. He studied at Belfast College of Art and in Paris. Among his mixed exhibitions were Belfast Museum and Art Gallery, 1958; Four Ulster Painters, at Arnolfini Gallery, Bristol, 1965; Watergate Gallery, Washington, in America, 1974; Arts Council of Northern Ireland, 1979, Major Award; Rosc '88, Dublin, 1988; and Contemporary Artists from Ireland, at Austin/Desmond Fine Art, 1990. Blackshaw showed solo at CEMA Gallery, Belfast, in 1961. Later shows included Tom Caldwell Gallery, Belfast, from 1973, and in 1974 he had a retrospective in the city at Arts Council of Northern Ireland. Lived in Antrim.

Simon BLACKWOOD 1948– Painter who was born in Colchester, Essex. Studied at Coventry School of Art under Michael Sandle and worked for a time in the restoration department of the Ashmolean Museum. Blackwood painted at Hawick, Roxburghshire, and had a studio on the Bosporus. His great interest in light led to his being termed a Romantic Luminist. Showed in Japan and North America and had a solo show at Michael Parkin Fine Art, 1991.

Alfred BLADEN fl.c.1925–1965 Painter, sculptor and teacher, born in Oldham, Lancashire. He studied at Wolverhampton

School of Art and the Royal College of Art. Was for a time attached to Derby School of Art. Showed at RA, RI, Wertheim and Storran Galleries and elsewhere and had solo shows at Wolverhampton Art Gallery and Museum and in Birmingham. The Wolverhampton gallery holds his work. Lived for a time in Derby, then in Shardlow, Derbyshire.

Peter BLAGG 1937– Versatile, innovative artist and teacher, born in Finchley, north London, married to the painter Linda Sutton. Blagg attended St Albans School of Art on a foundation course, 1954; went into the Royal Air Force for National Service in 1955, gaining early release in 1957; then completed his design diploma at St Albans. Teachers included Mary Hoad, Norman Adams, Anthony Blunt, William Scott, Anthony Fry, Carel Weight and Elizabeth Frink. He later obtained his teaching diploma and taught up to graduate level. In 1961 Blagg moved to Cornwall, and had a first solo exhibition at Newlyn Art Gallery in 1963 (a second followed at the Piccadilly Gallery), pictures of the semi-industrial landscape around Redruth. Blagg's writer friend John Branfield based his novel *In The Country* on the painter's experiences. After returning to Hertfordshire in 1964, Blagg's work became more hard-edged, showing Pop influences. Other activities included Jonathan Cape's *Jackdaw* resource series and work on an environmental design programme with Marcello Salvadori. Disenchanted with painting in the early 1970s, Blagg pioneered the application of multi-imaging (electronic media, installations, audio-visuals, live performances, and so on), devised a multimedia imaging course and founded Multivisual. This was a creative consultancy and production centre handling corporate and government presentations and involving work on the world tour of Frankie Goes to Hollywood. Blagg returned to painting in tandem with the multimedia work for rock shows, including Status Quo and Shakin' Stevens. Later exhibitions included a mixed show at Belgrave Gallery, 1996; a retrospective at Boxfield Gallery, Stevenage Arts Centre, and a further show at Stevenage Museum, both 1997.

Ernest BLAIKLEY 1885–1965 Painter in watercolour and etcher of figure studies and portraits. Born in London, he studied art at University College School, London, and the Slade School of Fine Art. He was Keeper of pictures at the Imperial War Museum from 1919 and deputy director, 1950–1. Had articles in *The Times*, *The Studio* and *John O'London's Weekly*. Exhibited RA, RBA, RP, IS and NEAC and his own Museum holds World War I drawings by him. Lived in London.

Iris BLAIN 1918– Artist and teacher, born in London, working in oil, acrylic, ceramic and etching. She studied at Regent Street Polytechnic School of Art, Royal Academy Schools and Anglo-French Art Centre, her teachers including Norman Blamey, Tom Monnington and Ruskin Spear. She practised theatre design with Tavistock Repertory Company, later becoming a professional stage and costume designer. Taught in Cheshire. Had a number of solo shows and group appearances included RA, LG, RBA, RWA, Arnolfini Gallery in Bristol, MAFA, Ben Uri Gallery and elsewhere. Was a member of Hampstead Artists' Council and Ridley Art Society. Hertfordshire County Council holds her work. In 1987 published her autobiographical *Recollections of a Jewish Childhood*. Lived in Kew, Surrey.

Doris V BLAIR: *see* **Doris BOURGUIGNON**

Louise BLAIR 1958– Painter, born in Kent, where she attended Canterbury College of Art, 1975–6; then Hornsey School of Art, 1976–9, and Chelsea School of Art, 1979–80. Her many group shows included Young Contemporaries at ICA, from 1977; RA Summer Exhibition, 1980; Sets for Station House Opera, Waterloo Gallery, 1982; Animals, Edward Totah Gallery, 1985; and Figure II: Naked, Aberystwyth Arts Centre and tour, 1988–9. Had a solo show at Cockpit Theatre, 1981, then a series at Nicola Jacobs Gallery from 1983. Although objects in the natural world might be the starting point for Blair's powerfully emotional works, the final pictures can be ambiguous, ghostly, virtually abstract. Contemporary Art Society holds work by Blair.

Eileen Mary BLAKE 1878– Watercolourist and black-and-white artist, born at Moseley, Birmingham. She studied at Birmingham College of Art and continued to live in Birmingham, where she belonged to leading art groups. Exhibited RBSA, SWA, ROI, RCamA and RI.

Frederick Donald BLAKE 1908–1997 Artist and designer, born in Greenock, Renfrewshire. After two years his parents moved to London, where he continued to live. Aged 13, Blake was funded by his amateur artist father to attend Camberwell School of Arts and Crafts for 18 months. At 15 went into a building trade drawing office, but for 10 years three nights a week attended such schools as Goldsmiths' College and Brixton School of Building. Became head of a drawing office, doing working drawings for swimming baths, pub fronts and cinemas; worked for a luxury bathroom maker; then in World War II drew for Ministry of Information; followed by work for the *Daily Express* and freelancing for 20 years, clients including *Reader's Digest*. Gave up commercial work to paint full-time. Was elected RI, RSMA, was president of the Wapping Group, and a member of London Sketch Club and Chelsea Arts Club. Showed in many London galleries as well as extensively abroad, being noted for his fluid, deft watercolours of ships and the sea and the use of clay-coated paper which allowed novel techniques, especially in the portrayal of textures. Had eightieth birthday show at Linda Blackstone Gallery, Pinner, in 1988.

Martin BLAKE 1955– Painter of abstracts, printmaker and teacher who studied at St Martin's School of Art, 1974–8. Was artist-in-residence at Felsted School, Essex, 1979–81, then went on to teach at Alleyn's School, Dulwich. Blake showed with London Art Schools at Air Gallery, 1978; Minories, Colchester, 1981; Bakehouse Gallery, 1982; and Gainsborough's House, Sudbury, 1983. In 1984 he had a solo show at Woodlands Art Gallery.

Michael BLAKE 1951– Artist in various media and teacher, born in Cheshire. Studied at Jacob Kramer College, Leeds, 1970–1, then Canterbury College of Art, 1971–4. He taught there, National School of Art in Dublin and on the postgraduate course at Cyprus College of Art. Blake took part in the Cyprus College show at Woodlands Art Gallery in 1983. Other exhibitions included Stockwell Depot, 1979, and Pennies Gallery, Greenwich, 1982. Lived in Kent.

Naomi BLAKE 1924– Sculptor, born in Czechoslovakia, a survivor of Auschwitz concentration camp. She trained at Hornsey School of Art, 1955–60, and worked in Milan, Rome and Jerusalem, eventually being based in London. Showed extensively in Britain and abroad, including SPS from 1962; Woodstock Gallery, 1972; Magdalene Street Gallery, 1976; Embankment Gallery, 1980; Norwich Cathedral, 1987; RWA, 1989; and Chelmsford Cathedral Festival, 1991. Several dozen works by her were permanently sited in public places, including North London Collegiate School, 1972; Bournemouth Synagogue, 1975; Bristol Cathedral, 1980; St Botolph's Church, Aldgate, 1985; Walsingham Parish Church, 1988; and Hospital for Sick Children, Great Ormond Street, 1990. Blake's work was figurative, with a clean and simple outline.

Peter BLAKE 1932– Painter, creator of collage and boxes, draughtsman and teacher, born in Dartford, Kent. He attended Gravesend Technical College and School of Art junior department 1946–9, then Gravesend School of Art, 1949–51. After National Service in Royal Air Force went to Royal College of Art, 1953–6, where he won a first-class diploma. A Leverhulme Research Award enabled him to study popular art on the continent in several countries, 1956–7. He taught at St Martin's, Harrow and Walthamstow Schools of Art in the early 1960s, then Royal College of Art, 1964–76. In 1961 he was featured in a BBC Monitor programme *Pop Goes the Easel*. By then he was associated with art concerned with popular images: picture postcards, children's games and magazine covers. A year after he won a junior prize at the John Moores Liverpool Exhibition, in 1961, he had a one-man show at the Portal Gallery. By 1969 he was having a retrospective show at the City Art Gallery, Bristol; others followed in the early 1970s on the continent; and his retrospective at the Tate Gallery in 1983, which travelled to Hanover, was the most successful ever there for a living artist. Blake also designed record covers and pop concert posters. Strongly associated with the Swinging Sixties, his art mixes fantasy with reality and associative references. Another aspect of his work was his founder-membership of the Brotherhood of Ruralists in 1975. Elected RA in 1981. Blake was married for a time to the artist Jann Haworth, then to Chrissy Wilson. Lived in London.

Quentin BLAKE 1932– Painter, illustrator and teacher, born in Sidcup, Kent, adept at pen, ink and watercolour work. He was educated at Cambridge University, attending part-time life classes at Chelsea School of Art. From 1957 was a freelance. Was tutor in illustration at Royal College of Art, 1965–78, head of illustration department from 1978, and was made senior fellow, 1988. Exhibitions of his watercolours were held from 1972 at Workshop Gallery, and he had a retrospective at National Theatre, 1983. Blake was noted for his deft, witty book illustrations. Among the many dozens of volumes illustrated were works by Patrick Campbell, Lewis Carroll, Roald Dahl, Michael Rosen and Evelyn Waugh. His own book *Mister Magnolia* won the Kate Greenaway Medal in 1980. He also drew for magazines such as *Punch* and *The Spectator* and for the BBC *Jackanory* television programme. Lived in London.

John BLAKELEY 1946– Sculptor and teacher, born in Blackpool, Lancashire. He studied at the local School of Art, 1962–5, St Martin's School of Art, 1965–6, and City & Guilds of London Art School, 1966–70, with periods in Greece and Italy. Blakeley was a member of SPS and an associate of RBS and was noted for his work in stone and clay. Showed at Guildhall, Royal Exchange, Mall Galleries, and Harris Museum and Art Gallery in Preston. Taught at Sir John Cass College. Lived in Welwyn Garden City, Hertfordshire.

Zelma BLAKELY 1927–1978 Printmaker, illustrator and teacher, born in London, was married to the artist Keith Mackenzie. She studied at Kingston School of Art, 1939–42, her teachers including Wilfred Fairclough, then at Slade School of Fine Art, 1945–8, with William Coldstream, Norman Janes and John Buckland Wright. She went on to teach at Heatherley's School of Fine Art and was elected a member of RE in 1966. Among books illustrated were André Simon's *English Fare and French Wines*, 1958, and the *Reader's Digest Bedside Book of Nature*, 1959. Lived at Pin Mill, Suffolk, where she was a member of the sailing club.

Michael BLAKER 1928– Painter, printmaker and writer on art, born in Hove, Sussex, studying at Brighton School of Art. Was elected RE in 1975 and RWA in 1987, also showing at RA and RP. Contributed to art magazines, edited RE's *Journal* and published several books, including *The Autobiography of a Painter-Etcher*, 1986, the year after he founded Beresford House Press. Victoria & Albert Museum holds his work. Lived in Rochester, Kent.

Oswell BLAKESTON 1907–1985 Painter, draughtsman, writer, lecturer and film maker. (His real name was Henry Hasslacher, the family of Austrian origin, connected with the Deinhard and Company wine importing business. The name Oswell was derived from that of the writer *Os*bert Sit*well*. The mother's surname was Blak*i*ston, which he modified.) Blakeston ran away from a Roman Catholic school and a bourgeois home in 1923. He became conjuror's assistant, a cinema organist and then a clapper boy with David Lean at Gaumont film studios. Began writing film criticism and became associate editor of the influential magazine *Close Up*. With Francis Brugiere he pioneered abstract films in Britain. Blakeston was also a novelist, poet and writer of film scripts, plays and travel books. His collaborator and companion of many years, Max Chapman, noted Blakeston's "quick eye for the bizarre and the outrageous". A large selection of Blakeston's books was shown at Haringey Central Library, 1980, previous to acquisition by Texas University. Blakeston was a witty artist and illustrator. Almost 100 mixed shows included Leicester and Mercury Galleries, and he had over 40 solo exhibitions, including Drian and Grabowski Galleries, New Vision Centre and Nicholas Treadwell Gallery, Croydon. In 1981 he shared a show with Chapman at Middlesbrough Art Gallery and in 1986 there was a memorial show at Camden Arts Centre. Victoria & Albert Museum, Ulster Museum in Belfast and the national galleries of Finland, Poland and Portugal hold examples. Lived in London.

Norman BLAMEY 1914– Painter, draughtsman, muralist and teacher, born in London, where he continued to work. He studied at Regent Street Polytechnic School of Art, 1931–7, his teachers including Harry Watson and A R Middleton Todd. From 1936–7 did a teacher training course at London University Institute of Education. Taught at Regent Street Polytechnic, 1938–40 and 1946–63, with a break for Army and camouflage service in Middle East and North Africa. From 1963–79 was senior lecturer at Chelsea School of Art, from 1975 onwards teaching at Royal Academy Schools. Was elected RA, 1975, having been elected ROI in 1952 and Hon. ROI in 1974. Also showed with RHA, RBA, NEAC and elsewhere. Among his awards were Roy Miles Award at RA Summer Exhibition, 1978; and Charles Wollaston Award at same venue, 1984. Commissions included 1956 mural for Anglican Church of St Luke, Leagrave. Blamey was a consummate draughtsman whose work had three main themes: family, ecclesiastical pictures and commissioned portraits. He aspired to "stillness and permanence" in his work. Touring retrospective show was based on Norwich Gallery, 1992–3. Tate Gallery holds Blamey's work.

Edmund BLAMPIED 1886–1966 Landscape and figure painter in oil, watercolour and wash; etcher and lithographer. Born in Jersey, he studied art under Philip Connard and at the London County Council Bolt Court Art School, 1905–13. Exhibited at RA, Fine Art Society, RBA, RE, RSW, RHA, Paris Salon and at other venues. Won a gold medal for lithography at the Paris International Exhibition in 1925. Blampied was a noted etcher, with a fine, swirling line. He designed Jersey occupation stamps and a Jersey liberation stamp in connection with World War II. His work is in a number of British and foreign collections. Lived at Beaumont, Jersey.

Emily Beatrice BLAND 1864–1951 Painter, especially of flowers in oil, studied at Lincoln School of Art, then at the Slade School of Fine Art under Henry Tonks and Fred Brown, 1892–4. Exhibited RA, NEAC, Fine Art Society, Goupil Gallery, Ridley Art Club, SWA and elsewhere. Chantrey Bequest bought her Striped Camellias and Yachts at Lymington, both now in the Tate Gallery. Other British and some overseas galleries hold her work. A prolific painter, she had her first one-man show at the Leicester Galleries in 1922. Lived in London.

Sydney Frances Josephine BLAND 1883– Painter in tempera and watercolour, born in York, she studied art at Heatherley's School of Fine Art, 1920–2, under Henry Massey, at Goldsmiths' College School of Art, 1922–3, with Harold Speed, and privately, including time with Bernard Adams. Exhibited SWA, RP, RI and had one-man exhibitions. Produced a number of posters for industry. Lived in Newlyn, Cornwall, and was a member of both the Newlyn and St Ives Societies of Artists.

Frances BLANE 1954– Painter and draughtsman, born and lived in London, who studied at the Byam Shaw School of Painting and Drawing, 1988–91, and Slade School of Fine Art, 1991–3. She won the Graham Hamilton Drawing Prize in 1991. Exhibitions included Ben Uri Gallery from 1991; Into the Nineties, Mall Galleries, 1993; Café Gallery, 1994; and In the Looking Glass, Usher Gallery, Lincoln, and tour, from 1996. This included Blane's Expressionistic Self-Portrait, of 1993. Mouths and heads were key features of her work, as "I am a very oral person." Had a solo show at Curwen Gallery, 1995, others in 1997 at 231 St John Street and Shillam and Smith.

Jeremy Nicholas BLANK 1957– Painter, artist in multi-media, performance, film and video, and teacher, born in Hampton Court, Middlesex. He studied at Colchester School of Art for foundation studies, 1976–8, gaining Prix de Rome/Munnings Award; obtained an honours degree in fine art painting from Chelsea School of Art, 1978–81, teachers including Ken Kiff, Stephen Buckley and Anne Rees-Mogg; and attended Colchester Filmmakers Workshop between 1983–5, teaching life drawing at The Minories, Colchester, 1984–6. Blank was a member of the National Society for Education in Art & Design. He held a number of residencies, including the Eastern Arts Art in School Scheme, 1988. Among Blank's prizes was a first national prize for painting at New Contemporaries, ICA, 1981, and he was a John Moores Liverpool Exhibition prizewinner in 1987. Blank began making experimental work with electronic media in the early 1980s and showed in international film festivals. In Freezeframe at Lamont Gallery, 1996, Blank showed Flare, a collage of film in which he focused on its ephemeral nature by burning and melting it down. Other mixed performances, events and exhibitions included Turin International Film Festival, 1984; Video Danse Internationale, Paris, 1992; and Ritzy Cinema, 1996, paintings and drawings. Had a solo show at Minories, 1983, and at Ganz Gallery, 1991. Blank said that his main works were his neo-classical ones, 1979–84; the Head painting series, 1986–91; and video works, 1991–6. Colchester Institute, Essex University, University of Texas, Waltham Cross Museum, International Video Dance in Austria and Danse Video, Paris, hold his works. Lived in London.

Slavomir Stanislas BLATTON 1943– Artist and teacher, born in Limanowa, Poland. He was initially educated in Warsaw where he attended the Academy of Fine Arts, 1962–9. Gained a Ministry of Culture Scholarship. In 1970 settled in London, where he taught etching at the Working Men's College. Exhibited in London and the provinces and was included in Berry Street Open Studios Exhibition, 1984.

Susannah BLAXILL 1954– Botanical watercolourist and draughtsman, born in New South Wales, Australia, who began painting full-time in 1985 after five years' study at University of East Anglia, Norwich. Her draughtsmanship was meticulous, and she used a fine brush and many layers of watercolour to achieve an intense, brilliant image. Exhibition at Royal Horticultural Society, Chelsea Flower Show and Society of Botanical Artists, of which she became a member in 1989. Showed solo at Spink & Son, 1994.

Susanna BLECH 1959– Artist and teacher, born in London, who studied at Wimbledon School of Art and at Brighton Polytechnic, gaining an honours degree in painting in 1982. Taught at Blackheath School of Art and Merton Adult College, with a private teaching practice in Wimbledon. Worked both figuratively and abstract, with a special interest in Greek mythology and horses. Showed at Camden Arts Centre and Kingston Hill Art Gallery and was included in People and Places at Gagliardi Gallery, 1993.

Christopher BLEDOV 1957– Painter and teacher, born in Staffordshire, who lived in Nigeria, 1961–3. After attending Hereford College of Art, 1976, taught part-time there, then attended Slade School of Fine Art, 1977–82, with film studies at University College, 1980–1. He won the Sir William Coldstream Prize in 1978, in 1982 gaining the Robert Ross Prize and a Boise Travelling Scholarship. The Slade holds his work. Group exhibitions included Northburgh Gallery, 1981; LG, 1982; Sandford Gallery, 1983; and Berry Street Open Studios, 1984. Elisabeth Gallery gave him a solo show in 1983.

Edith BLENKIRON 1904–1992 Painter, notable as a floral illustrator, born in Northumberland. She studied at Goldsmiths' College School of Art and married the artist Rowland Hilder in 1929. Showed at RA and assisted Hilder with *Wildflowers of the Countryside*, a popular series completed for Shell in the mid-1950s. Their son was the artist Anthony Flemming. Lived in Greenwich, southeast London.

Ernst M BLENSDORF 1896–1976 Sculptor in wood, clay and cement, born in Denmark and studied widely in Europe. Exhibited UA, RBA, RSA, RCamA, Leicester Galleries and Wadham College, Oxford, plus one-man shows at the Cambridge Building Centre and in London. The French publication *La Revue Moderne* featured his work on several occasions. Lived in Bruton, Somerset.

Witold John BLESKY 1934– Sculptor and painter, born in Poland, of American nationality, who was educated in Poland, England and America at San Francisco State College. He showed at Marjorie Parr Gallery, with Free Painters and Sculptors of which he was a member at Loggia Gallery, Round House Gallery, Paris Salon and elsewhere. Private collections in Britain and America held his works. Lived in Walderslade, Kent.

Maurice BLIK 1939– Sculptor and teacher, born in Netherlands. As a Jew he spent three years in Belsen concentration camp, in Germany, in World War II. Moved to Britain with his mother and attended Hornsey College of Art, 1956–60. From 1967–8 was at University of London Institute of Education, gaining a teaching certificate with distinction. Participated in many group exhibitions, including Four Sculptors at Heal's Art Gallery, 1978; Wapping Artists, 1984; RA Summer Exhibition from 1986; Stamford Sculpture Park, Stamford, Connecticut, 1988; RBS at RWA Gallery, Bristol, 1989; and The Sculpture Project, Ardingly, Sussex, 1990. Took part in Sculpture at Canterbury, 1991. Solo exhibitions included Ben Uri Gallery, 1980; Alwin Gallery, 1985; sponsored exhibition with support from Arts Council and Whitechapel Art Gallery, 1989. Blik produced much commissioned work, including sculptures for East India Dock and London Docklands Development Corporation, 1991. He was principal lecturer in fine art at Middlesex Polytechnic. Lived in London.

Douglas Percy BLISS 1900–1984 Painter, wood engraver, writer and teacher, born in Karachi, who attended Edinburgh University, graduating with a master's degree in 1922. Then studied painting at Royal College of Art under William Rothenstein and wood engraving with Sir Frank Short as a postgraduate during 1922–4. The several strands of Bliss's versatile career then began to unwind. In 1927 he shared a show at the St George's Gallery with Edward Bawden and Eric Ravilious, artists with whom he had a strong affinity. Also showed at RA, SWE and NEAC and had one-man exhibitions with Reid and Lefevre. In the 1930s Bliss taught at Hornsey and Blackheath Schools of Art, just after World War II – during which he served in the Royal Air Force – at Harrow School of Art, then from 1946–64 was the influential director of Glasgow School of Art. In the 1920s Bliss had laid the foundations of his reputation as a writer by acting as London art critic of *The Scotsman* newspaper and publishing, in 1928, his *A History of Wood Engraving*; this was followed over the years by many learned essays and in 1979 his monograph *Edward Bawden*. Bliss, who illustrated many books, was a fine wood engraver; his black-and-white work has tended to overshadow his achievement as a painter. He was married to the portrait painter Phyllis Dodd and lived mainly in Glasgow.

Gunther BLOCH 1916– Sculptor in various materials and teacher, born in Germany. He studied art there as well as at Leeds College of Art and Regent Street Polytechnic School of Art. His work appeared in the Britain Can Make It exhibition as well as at Cooling, Ben Uri and Berkeley Galleries and in the provinces. Lived in London, where he taught in several schools.

Martin BLOCH 1883–1954 Painter and draughtsman in many media, born in Neisse, Silesia. Initially studied music and architecture. Then opted for art, studying in Munich and Berlin, notably with Lovis Corinth. First one-man show at Paul Cassirer Gallery, Berlin, 1911. Bloch then continued his art education mainly solo for some years in France, Spain and Italy. By 1920 he was able to have a retrospective at the Cassirer Gallery. Until 1933, when he left Germany for England, spending a year on the way in Denmark, Bloch associated with the Expressionists, for 10 years running an art school. Expressionism left an indelible mark on his style and palette even after he settled in Britain, whose citizenship he took in 1947. In Britain Bloch painted mainly in London, Dorset and Wales, although after World War II he was to travel widely in America and Canada, teaching for a time in Minneapolis. For three years before World War II he had run an art school in Britain with Roy de Maistre. Bloch exhibited widely internationally and in Britain, including LG, AIA, Ben Uri Gallery, Leicester Galleries and RA. Memorial exhibitions at Beaux Arts Gallery, 1955, Arts Council, London, and touring, 1957, Kaplan Gallery, 1959, and Ben Uri Gallery, 1963. Work in many galleries, including Tate Gallery. Lived in London.

Gwilym John BLOCKLEY 1921– Painter, teacher and writer, born in Knighton, Radnorshire. Showed with PS and RI, of both of which he was a member, RA and in the provinces. Pitman published his watercolour painting course as well as his book *The Challenge of Watercolour*, and he ran private classes. The John Blockley Gallery was at Stow-on-the-Wold, Gloucestershire.

Freda BLOIS 1880–1962 Painter. Lady Blois studied art in Florence. She went on to exhibit with the RA, RBA, NEAC, SWA and the Reading Guild of Artists.

Giles BLOMFIELD 1925– Architect and sculptor, born in Penzance, Cornwall, who settled in Truro. His paternal grandfather was the architect Sir Reginald Blomfield. Studied at Bartlett School of Architecture with Albert Richardson and Hector Corfiato, and at École des Beaux-Arts, Paris, with Eugene Beaudouin. He won the Donaldson Medal, 1954, and RIBA Bronze Medal, 1965. After being attached to a series of architectural practices from 1954, from 1974–87 ran his own, Blomfield Cartlidge, Bayly, in Truro. Blomfield's striking sculpture The Altar of the Sword's Point is in Canterbury Cathedral.

Leslie BLOMFIELD 1920– Painter and architect, born in London, from a long line of architects including Sir Reginald Blomfield. Leslie Blomfield worked as an architect for about 30 years, mostly abroad. He settled in the York area in 1984 and practised as a self-taught watercolourist, establishing his reputation by painting a series of cathedrals and churches. His pictures were reproduced as prints by the National Trust and York Civic Trust and in 1990 the Yorkshire Wildlife Trust commissioned him to paint four nature reserves it administered. Blomfield's work was included in Images of the Yorkshire Landscape, organised by Sheeran Lock at Leeds Civic Hall, 1991.

Maxwell BLOND 1943– Painter and printmaker, born in St Annes, Lancashire. He studied at Bath Academy of Art, Corsham, under Howard Hodgkin, and Slade School of Fine Art with Patrick George, leaving in 1965. Blond used a strident, colourful palette, producing pictures with rich imagery. Showed in many mixed exhibitions, including LG, and had solo exhibitions at his brother Jonathan's Allerton Gallery, Liverpool, and in London at Blond Fine Art. Lived in Hoylake, Cheshire.

Paul BLOOMER 1966– Painter and printmaker, born in Dudley, Worcestershire, whose work could have a strong imaginative quality, using an unusual, rich palette, as in his oil Voices, at Royal Over-Seas League Open, 1994. He studied at Stourbridge College of Art, Nottingham Polytechnic and the Royal Academy Schools. Among prizes won were the Arthur Hacker Prize and Hennington Award, both 1992; Dudley Art Gallery Purchase Prize, 1993 (it and Walsall Art Gallery hold Bloomer's work); and the John Purcell Print Prize and Joseph Webb ARE Commemorative Fund Award, both 1994. Had a solo show at The Weathered Wall Gallery, Seattle, America, 1993.

Sandra BLOW 1925– Abstract painter who also used materials such as polyethylene and willow cane to construct pictures. She was born in London, where she continued to live, also having a studio in St Ives, Cornwall. She studied at St Martin's School of Art, 1941–6, under Ruskin Spear, at the Royal Academy Schools, 1946–7, and at the Academy of Fine Arts in Rome, 1947–8. In the late 1940s she travelled in Spain and France. Had first one-man show at Gimpel Fils in 1951, worked in Cornwall, 1957–8, then from 1960 taught at Royal College of Art. Participated in many group exhibitions in Britain and abroad, including John Moores Liverpool Exhibition, 1961, where she won a second prize for painting, as she did in 1965; Camden Arts Centre, 1969, English Landscape in the 20th Century; in 1977 British Painting 1952–1957, at RA, to which she was elected in 1978; and in 1994 RA gave her a retrospective. Blow has been said to be concerned pre-eminently with the problems of pure painting: balance and proportion, tension and scale. Tate Gallery holds her work.

William James BLOYE 1890–1975 Sculptor and teacher, born in Cornwall, but moved to Birmingham in mid-1890s. Bloye studied at Birmingham School of Art, 1904–9, gaining the William Kenrick Scholarship for 1905–6; from 1910 until World War I began Bloye studied sculpture at Royal Academy Schools. After a couple of years teaching modelling part-time in Birmingham art schools, in 1919 Bloye joined Birmingham School of Art, where he became head of sculpture until his retirement in 1956. Early in 1920s Bloye studied for short periods with Eric Gill, which had a lasting impression on his work. By the mid-1920s Bloye had a busy studio of his own in Birmingham, employing assistants trained by him at the School of Art. He carried out a large amount of civic sculpture in Birmingham and carved the Dudley, Worcestershire, war memorial and reliefs on its town hall buildings. After retirement in Solihull Bloye continued to handle his own commissions. Elected fellow of RBS in 1938. Died in Arezzo, Italy.

Judith BLUCK 1936– Artist, born in London, who progressed through various media to sculpture and who worked on a large scale in a number of materials. She revived the use of pressed brick, her most important work being The Legend of the Iron Gates, an 80-foot relief commissioned by Sainsbury's for a supermarket in Wilmslow. This won the Otto Beit Medal of the RBS, of which she was a fellow. Was also a brother of Art Workers' Guild. Bluck also held bronze and silver medals from the Société des Artistes Français. Among other works by Bluck are a fountain group of Otters, for Carlisle City Council, at The Lanes, where her Jimmy Dyer mural is sited; a 28-foot Crucible Fountain at Moorfoot, Sheffield; and five new designs of Royal Insignia for Crown Court and prison sites. Bluck's Sheep, in bronze, were sited in Fenny Stratford, funded by the Milton Keynes Foundation. Morris Singer Foundry cast her work. Lived in Yorkshire.

Alfred Richard BLUNDELL 1883–1968 Painter, printmaker and glass engraver, born in Bury St Edmunds, Suffolk. After education there he attended the Slade School of Fine Art, 1913, following a period as a railway clerk. Blundell painted a large number of architectural subjects in Britain and on the continent, showing at RA, NEAC, Alpine Club Gallery and extensively in the provinces. Fitzwilliam Museum in Cambridge, other provincial museums and the Luxembourg, Paris, hold his work. Lived in Icklingham, Suffolk, and for many years at Cavenham Mill, Bury St Edmunds.

Margaret Leah BLUNDELL 1907– Mural painter, commercial artist and printmaker, born at Wallasey, Cheshire. After attending Cheltenham Ladies' College she studied at Liverpool School of Art with Frederick Carter and George Marples, 1925. Exhibited Walker Art Gallery, Liverpool, SWE and RBA. She carried out a number of murals in London and Blackpool in hotels and shops and drew for women's magazines and *Radio Times*. Lived at Rhydwyn, near Holyhead, Anglesey.

Martyn BLUNDELL 1955– Artist and teacher who attended Southport College of Art, 1977–8, and Loughborough College of Art and Design, 1978–81. Taught part-time at Bootle Technical College. Showed in northwest of England, notably in Merseyside Artists 3, Walker Art Gallery and tour, 1986–7.

Peter Alfred BLUNSDEN 1949– Abstract sculptor in steel, born in Norwich, Norfolk, who studied at the School of Art there, 1984–8, graduating with honours in fine art sculpture. His mixed exhibitions included Whitworth Young Contemporaries, Whitworth Art Gallery, Manchester, 1987; L'École Regional des Beaux-Arts, Rouen, 1988; Wingfield College Outdoor Exhibition, Suffolk, and Open Studio Exhibition, Hardingham, Norfolk, both 1992. His workshop involvements included Hardingham Sculpture Workshop, 1990, and Triangle Workshop, New York State, 1992. Philip and Muriel Berman Collection, America, holds his work. Had a studio at Hardingham and lived in Reepham, Norfolk.

Ferdinand Victor BLUNDSTONE 1882–1951 Sculptor, born in Switzerland, who studied at the South London Technical Art School and then the Royal Academy Schools, winning a gold medal and travelling studentship and Landseer Scholarship, also studying in Egypt, Greece, Italy and France. In 1925 gained a Silver Medal, Paris Exhibition. Showed extensively at RA, also RSA and Royal Glasgow Institute of the Fine Arts. Among his works is the Plimsoll Memorial on London's Victoria Embankment. He was a fellow of RBS and his works The Elf and Atalanta are illustrated in the volume *RBS: Modern British Sculpture*, published 1939. Lived in London and West Drayton, Middlesex.

Wilfrid BLUNT 1901–1987 Artist, teacher, writer and curator, born in Ham, Surrey. His brother was the art historian and spy Anthony Blunt. Began to paint in childhood. Left Oxford University after two terms and studied in Paris at the Atelier Moderne under Othon Friesz and at the Académie de la Grande Chaumière, Paris, where he had his first one-man show. Entered Royal Academy engraving school in 1922, where his teachers included Frank Short, and worked under Leon Underwood in his studio. Taught at Haileybury for 15 years, interrupted by a period studying singing in Germany and Italy; he sang professionally for a while. Became art master at Eton College, 1938–59, then curator of the Watts Gallery, Compton, Surrey. Showed in England and at Paris Salon. Wrote about two dozen books, including a witty, entertaining autobiography *Married to a Single Life*, 1983, and *Slow on the Feather*, 1986.

Robert Henderson BLYTH 1919–1970 Landscape and figure painter in oil, gouache and watercolour. Born in Glasgow, Blyth studied art under Forrester Wilson at Glasgow School of Art, 1934–9, and under James Cowie at Patrick Allan-Fraser School of Art, Hospitalfield, Arbroath, 1938. He became head of drawing and painting at Gray's School of Art, Aberdeen. Showed widely, including Royal Glasgow Institute of the Fine Arts, RSA, RSW and SSA. The Ministry of Works, Dundee City Art Gallery and Dunbartonshire County Council bought his work, which often has a strongly romantic flavour. Memorial exhibition was held at Aberdeen Art Gallery, 1972. Lived in Aberdeen.

Robert Cresswell BOAK 1875–1949 Painter, printmaker and teacher who was married to the artist Margaret Cooper. Born in Letterkenny, Donegal, he was educated in the north of Ireland and Scotland, then attended Londonderry School of Art, Glasgow School of Art, the Royal College of Art as well as studying in France and Italy. During the period 1900–17 he taught at several art schools in England and Wales. Exhibited RA, RCamA, RHA and provinces, and had several one man shows. Lived in London.

Andrzej BOBROWSKI 1925– Sculptor and medallist, notable as one of the Polish paper sculptors who flourished in England in post-war years. He studied during World War II at Warsaw Academy of Art, participated in the Warsaw Uprising in 1944 and was a prisoner of war in Germany. After hostilities he studied art in Rome, then at Slade School of Fine Art under A H Gerrard, F E McWilliam and Henry Moore. Became a freelance artist and designer for advertising and display, his figures often witty and satirical and capable of movement for animated films. The coronation of Queen Elizabeth II, the London Hilton, Hoover and the electrical firm Philips all absorbed his talents. Worked for both the Diana and De Mayo Studios. Bobrowski created bronze and steel welded sculptures and commemorative medals. Exhibited widely on the continent, in South Africa and in Britain, where he was included in Polish Paper Sculpture at Polish Cultural Institute, 1995. At the Olympiada d'Arte e Cultura, Albano, Italy, he won a gold medal for sculpture. Lived in London.

George Alfred BODEN 1888–1956 Painter, printmaker and black-and-white artist. Born in Lincoln, he studied at the School of Art there, Atelier Colarossi, Paris, Académie des Beaux-Arts, Antwerp, at Camberwell School of Arts and Crafts and at John Hassall's poster school, in London. Exhibited RA, RBA, RI, in the provinces and at the Paris Salon. Glasgow Museum and Art Galleries hold his work. Lived in Lincoln.

Leonard BODEN 1911– Portrait painter, born in Greenock, Renfrewshire, married to the artist Margaret Boden. After Sedbergh School Boden studied at Glasgow School Art and Heatherley's School of Fine Art. As well as showing at RP of which he was a member, exhibited at RSA and completed portraits of dignitaries including the royal family and His Holiness Pope Pius XII. Chelsea Arts Club member who lived in London.

Margaret BODEN fl. from 1940s– Portrait painter like her husband Leonard Boden, she was born in Ecclesmachen, West Lothian. She studied at Glasgow School of Art and Heatherley's School of Fine Art. Exhibited with UA, SWA and PS all of which she was a member, and RP, ROI and the Royal Glasgow Institute of the Fine Arts. Lived in London.

Neville BODEN 1929–1996 Abstract sculptor in metal, draughtsman and teacher, born in Albert Town, South Africa, who learned many skills as a boilermaker. From 1958 studied under George Fullard at Chelsea School of Art and was later a Gregory Fellow at Leeds. Taught at London College of Printing, Chelsea, Camden School of Art, Central St Martin's and Kingston. Had a solo show at Whitechapel Art Gallery, 1973, and was president of LG, 1973–8. In later life lived in La Indiana, Andalusia, Spain, but died in London. Arts Council holds his sculpture Red Cross and Tate Gallery Blow in Her Ear.

Miles BODIMEADE 1959– Sculptor in stone and wood, and draughtsman, born in Arundel, Sussex. He attended West Sussex College of Art and Design, 1979–80, then Liverpool Polytechnic Department of Sculpture, 1980–3. Among group exhibitions in which he participated were Southern Counties Drawing Competition, 1986; On The Wall Gallery, New York, 1989; and Arundel Gallery Trail, 1989–90. His one-man shows were at Arun Art Centre, 1985; Duff Gallery in Arundel and On The Wall Gallery, 1987; and he shared a show at England & Co, 1991. Bodimeade said that he used the figure "as a springboard for ideas, and abstract it to a greater or lesser degree depending on the theme". NBC Television, New York, holds his work.

Josselin BODLEY 1893–1974 Painter of architectural and landscape subjects, son of the historian J E C Bodley. He studied in Paris, where he died, and was wounded during World War I service in Belgium. Showed at Leicester and Beaux Arts Galleries, at Manchester City Art Gallery and in Paris. Manchester holds his Landscape, oil on canvas, of 1941.

Francesca BOEHM 1910– Painter in watercolour, born in Germany, who after settling in Britain lived in Cardiff, South Wales. She showed extensively with WAC, WSW of which she was for some time secretary, RWS, SWA and elsewhere and shared two-man shows at Llantarnam Grange, Cwmbran. Oxford Education Authority holds her work.

BOHDAN: *see* **Bohdan PARASZCZUK**

Marian BOHUSZ-SZYSZKO 1901–1995 Painter and teacher, born in Trokienniki, Poland. He studied at Department of Fine Art at Wilno University, 1921–3, then at the Academies of Fine Arts in Cracow and Warsaw, 1923–7. Bohusz-Szyszko was imprisoned as a Polish soldier by the Germans in World War II, then on liberation became teacher of a group of Polish art students in Rome before settling in Britain in 1946, when he founded the Polish School of Art. His own work drew on religious subject matter and was Expressionist in the Colourist tradition. He showed extensively in Britain and continental Europe, solo exhibitions including a retrospective at Drian Galleries in 1963. In 1981 there was a show at National Museum, Gdansk, and in 1993 he was included in the City Art Centre, Edinburgh, show Polish Roots – British Soil. The Bishop's Palace and Chapel, Winchester, and National Museums of Gdansk, Warsaw and Wroclaw hold his work. More than 60 of his pictures are on permanent display at the St Christopher's Hospice, Sydenham, where he died. He had become artist-in-residence there in 1977 and in 1980 took as his second wife Dame Cicely Saunders, founder of the modern hospice movement. Bohusz-Szyszko was termed "a great artist" by *Guardian* critic Eric Newton on the occasion of the painter's first London show in 1959, at Grabowski Gallery.

Cyril Thompson BOLAM 1908– Painter, self-taught, who was born in Newcastle upon Tyne, Northumberland, where he continued to live. He exhibited at the Laing Art Gallery and Museum, Newcastle, and the Shipley Art Gallery, Gateshead. He held official positions in both the West End Art Club, Newcastle, and Federation of Northern Art Societies.

John BOLAM 1922– Painter, designer and teacher, born in Amersham, Buckinghamshire. The landscape of the Chilterns, English Romantic painters and poets and modern French artists such as Braque and Degas all influenced Bolam's work. He studied furniture design at High Wycombe School of Art and painting at Hornsey School of Art. Went on to become head of the School of Art in Cambridge, 1970–83. Showed at AIA Gallery, Leicester Galleries and one-man exhibitions included New Art Centre. Fry Art Gallery in Saffron Walden holds his work.

Sean BOLAN 1948– Artist specialising in transport and architecture, using ink and watercolour, born in Rowlands Castle, Hampshire. He was educated in Havant, then studied nearby at Portsmouth College of Art, 1965–8. Showed in mixed exhibitions, work being held by several local authority collections. Was a member of the Great Western Society and lived for some time at Moreton-in-Marsh, Gloucestershire.

John BOLD 1895–1979 Painter and draughtsman, born in Manchester, where he continued to live. Attended Manchester School of Art and showed regularly at MAFA, serving on the selection committee for its centenary exhibition; also exhibited at Walker Art Gallery, Liverpool, the Mid-Day Studios in Manchester and other northern shows. Manchester City Art Gallery holds his An Aran Village; An Aran Landscape; The Church, Inishmaan; Portrait of a Cat; and A Suburban Landscape, all in Bold's typically precise style.

William BOLGER 1941– Painter in oil on canvas, mainly landscapes of St Ives, Cornwall, where he settled, and symbolic pictures based on Aztec imagery. Bolger was born in Liverpool, where he studied at the College of Art, 1962–5, gaining his master's degree at the Royal College of Art, 1965–7, under Merlyn Evans and Carel Weight. Group exhibitions included Salt House Gallery, St Ives, 1995, with a solo show at St Ives Public Library, 1994. Casablanca Club, Liverpool, and private collections hold his work.

Elaine BOLTON: *see* **Elaine GILMOUR**

Richard BOLTON 1950– Watercolourist and writer who studied at Shrewsbury College of Art, where he developed acute observation and attention to detail. The British landscape, including such features as old farm implements and abandoned cars, was a favourite subject. Wrote a number of books on aspects of watercolour painting. Exhibitions included The Linda Blackstone Gallery, Pinner, and widely abroad.

Tim Scott BOLTON 1947– Landscape painter and teacher who trained as a land agent, then turned to art as a career. Visited the Middle East and India, taught watercolour painting twice a year and took groups of artists abroad. Had his own gallery in Wiltshire. He also showed with the Malcolm Innes Gallery in London and Edinburgh, Tryon & Moorland Gallery in London and Nairobi, Bruton Gallery at Bruton, Somerset, and with Oliver Swann and Mathaf Galleries.

Michael BOLUS 1934– Sculptor and teacher, born in Cape Town, South Africa. Bolus moved to England in 1957 and studied at St Martin's School of Art, 1958–62. For a time he was an assistant to Anthony Caro, who taught there. In 1963–4 Bolus went back to Cape Town on a visit, having a solo show there in the latter year. In 1965 he had a one-man exhibition at Waddington Galleries, the first of a series, then had a solo show at Kornblee Gallery, New York, in 1966. About this time Bolus was teaching at St Martin's, also at Central School of Art and Design. Bolus' work underwent a number of transformations. He was originally a modeller, then a carver rather in the manner of Brancusi, then produced floor-based metal sculptures, abstract and coloured, latterly making grid-style and lattice-form pieces such as he showed in The Condition of Sculpture exhibition at Hayward Gallery in 1975. Bolus' work formed part of The Alistair McAlpine Gift, shown at Tate Gallery in 1971, and the Arts Council also has his work. Among his open-air commissions is Untitled, 1981, in aluminium and steel, at Sutton Manor Arts Centre, Sutton Scotney.

David BOMBERG 1890–1957 Painter and influential teacher, born in Birmingham of Polish Jewish refugee stock. In London from 1905 Bomberg studied with Walter Bayes at City and Guilds evening classes and, having become acquainted with artists such as John Singer Sargent, Ossip Zadkine and Solomon J Solomon, in 1908 broke his indentures while an apprentice to a chromolithographer to study art. For several years studied with W R Lethaby at the Central School of Arts and Crafts and with Walter Sickert at Westminster School, then 1911–13 attended the Slade School of Fine Art full-time, where he won several awards. Prior to World War I designed for Roger Fry's Omega Workshops; travelled to Paris where he met Picasso, Derain and Modigliani; and received acclaim from Wyndham Lewis, being invited to show with the Vorticist Exhibition, in 1915. Exhibited with the Friday Club, NEAC and was a founder-member of the LG. First one-man show at Chenil Galleries, 1914. Travelled extensively in the 1920s and 1930s, notably to Spain and Palestine, which inspired some strongly Expressionist landscape paintings. Began teaching during World War II, forming with his students the Borough Group in 1946. This was followed by the Borough Bottega seven years later with which a retrospective was held in 1954. Bomberg's wife Lilian, whom he often painted, and other members of his family were associated with the Borough Group. Several memorial exhibitions held and a major retrospective at the Tate Gallery, which holds his work, 1988. Died in London.

Lilian BOMBERG: *see* **Lilian HOLT**

Arnold BOND 1905– Painter, artist in scraperboard and line, and teacher, born in Bexleyheath, Kent. Studied at Goldsmiths' College School of Art and Bath Academy of Art, Corsham.

Showed with RA, Corsham Group and Eastbourne Society of Artists, of which he was a member. Taught art at Eastbourne Technical Institute and lived in St Leonards-on-Sea, Sussex.

Arthur J F BOND 1888–1958 Painter, printmaker and draughtsman, born in Devonport, who after education in Tavistock attended Heatherley's School of Fine Art, Goldsmiths' College School of Art and the Central School of Arts and Crafts. Most of his life was lived in the Thames River area, and he was a member of the Wapping Group of Artists and RSMA. Also exhibited RA, RI and Paris Salon. Lived at Holmbury St Mary, Surrey.

Henry BOND 1966– Artist, born in London, who attended West Surrey College of Art, Farnham, 1984–5, graduating with honours from Goldsmiths' College, 1985–8. His group exhibition appearances included East Country Yard Show, Surrey Docks, and The Mulitiple Projects Room, Air de Paris, Nice, both 1990; and Spy-Stories, Sergio Casolini, Milan, Il Compo, Rome, 1991. Solo shows included Documents, with Liam Gillick, at Karsten Schubert Ltd; James Hockey Gallery, Farnham; and Documents, with Liam Gillick, Centre d'Art Contemporain, APAC Nevers, all 1991.

John BOND 1945– Painter of landscapes in oil on card using a rich palette, who was obsessed by painting from childhood in Cromer, Norfolk, where he was born and attended school. After studying at Norwich and Central Schools of Art Bond in 1965 became a designer for a book publisher in Guildford, where The Chaucer Studio Gallery gave him a first solo show. A second successful exhibition, at Majorie Parr's gallery in Chelsea, saw Bond established as an independent artist, other exhibitions following at Ralph Lewis Gallery, Brighton; The Upstairs Gallery at RA; and The Westcliffe Gallery, Sheringham. His main outlet was Century Galleries, Henley-on-Thames, where he had an exhibition in 1995.

Marj BOND fl. from mid-1950s– Artist, born in Scotland, who studied at Glasgow School of Art, 1955–60, taught by Alex Dick, David Donaldson, Mary Armour and Benno Schotz. She was a figurative painter, in the Scottish Colourist tradition, with strong poetic and symbolic elements. In 1988 Bond made a trip to India which opened up new visual channels and gave her the opportunity to work on handmade paper. In 1992 she took part in a summer sculpture workshop in Tuscany; 1993 brought journeys to Yucatan, Mexico, and Urbino in Italy; and in 1994 she had a painting residency at Annaghmakerrig, the Tyrone Guthrie Centre, in Ireland. Among her awards was the Anne Redpath Award, 1984; Crawford Arts Centre Special Award, St Andrews, 1987; and an English Speaking Union scholarship, 1994. Was elected a professional member of SSWA in 1975, later a council member; a member of the Dundee Printmakers' Workshop, 1987; and in 1989 member of both RSW and SSA. Showed at RSA regularly from 1983. Showed solo with Open Eye Gallery, Edinburgh, from 1984, Thackeray Gallery from 1992. Edinburgh University, Perth Art Gallery and Art in Hospitals hold examples.

Charles BONE 1926– Painter, muralist and ceramist, born in Farnham, Surrey, married to the sculptor Sheila Mitchell. He studied at Farnham School of Art and Royal College of Art. Bone was president of RI for 10 years, a director of the RI Galleries and later the Mall Galleries. Also showed with RA, RBA, NEAC and Federation of Canadian Artists, of which he was an honorary member. He had many solo exhibitions, including Medici Gallery; Gainsborough's House at Sudbury; Canaletto Gallery, Tom Morgan Gallery, Pasadena; New Ashgate Gallery in Farnham; Surrey University; Upper Grosvenor Gallery, and elsewhere. He was an honorary member of the Medical Art Society and of the Society of Botanical Artists. Private collections around the world held his work and he completed murals in Spain, Italy and Malta. In 1989 he gained the Hunting Group Prize for watercolour and in 1991 his book *Charles Bone's Waverley* was published, with a foreword by HRH The Prince of Wales. Lived in Puttenham, Surrey.

Helen BONE fl. from late 1980s– Painter who said that although there was "an obvious gulf between my apparently abstract work and perceptual reality, I am a realist at heart". From 1985–7 studied for a painting diploma at Mid-Warwickshire College; attended Coventry University, 1987–90; from 1990–2 working for a master's degree in fine art at University of Central England, Birmingham. Early exhibitions included Florida and Buenos Aires, then Herbert Art Gallery in Coventry, Bonhams, and Pacesetters at Peterborough Museum and Art Gallery, 1995. Lived in Dunchurch, near Rugby, Warwickshire.

Muirhead BONE 1876–1953 Painter, but mainly printmaker and draughtsman, born in Glasgow, the Bone family producing a number of artists, writers and critics, including Stephen and James Bone. Bone initially trained as an architect, 1890–4, simultaneously attending art classes at Glasgow School of Art under Archibald Kay. Moved to London in 1901 and soon began exhibiting at the RA and NEAC. Had his first one-man show at the Carfax Gallery in 1903, a year later becoming a founder-member of the Society of Twelve. Became the first official war artist in 1916, again serving as a war artist to the Admiralty in World War II. His first book was *Glasgow* in 1901, but he went on to illustrate many more by members his family. He was a trustee of the National Gallery, Tate Gallery and Imperial War Museum. Knighted 1937. The Tate Gallery holds his work, which has a strong, linear quality, much of it based on travels on the continent. Died in Oxford, is commemorated with a tablet in the crypt of St Paul's Cathedral, London. Memorial exhibitions in Manchester and at the Arts Council, 1955.

Phyllis Mary BONE 1896–1972 Sculptor of animals in bronze. Born at Hornby, Lancashire, she studied at Edinburgh College of Art and on the continent. She exhibited at the RA, RSA, Royal Glasgow Institute of the Fine Arts, the provinces and abroad. Aberdeen Art Gallery and Dumfries Art Gallery hold her work, which is in the realist tradition. Illustrated in Eric Newton's *British Sculpture 1944–1946*. Lived in Kirkcudbright, Scotland.

Stephen BONE 1904–1958 Painter, wood engraver, illustrator, critic, broadcaster and writer. Born in Chiswick into a family of writers and artists. Stephen's father was the painter Sir Muirhead Bone and Stephen married the artist Mary Adshead. After Bedales School he studied at the Slade School of Fine Art, 1922–4. From 1920 began showing with NEAC; won a gold medal for wood engraving at the 1925 Paris International Exhibition; in 1926 shared a show with Robin Guthrie and Rodney Burn at the Goupil Gallery; and two years later painted a decoration for Piccadilly Circus underground station (eventually replaced by advertisements). Travelled extensively with his wife in the British Isles and on the continent and exhibited widely in the 1930s, including Fine Art Society, Lefevre Gallery and Redfern Gallery. In the late 1930s was active in the AIA, helping German refugees to settle in England and find work. During World War II became an officer in camouflage operations in Leamington Spa, from 1943–5 serving as an official war artist attached to the Royal Navy. Bone's speciality was the small oil panel "snapshot". They brilliantly evoke the scenes of his wide travels and illustrate his book *Albion: An Artist's Britain*, published in 1939. After the war his pictures fell out of favour and he concentrated on his ability to communicate with words. Bone could be a spellbinder, with a prodigious memory for facts. He served as art critic for the *Manchester Guardian* in 1948; wrote articles for the *Yorkshire Post* and *Glasgow Herald*; broadcast on radio and television, in such programmes as *The Critics* and *The Brains Trust*; and wrote children's books, sometimes working with his wife. In 1957 was appointed director of Hornsey College of Art. The Tate Gallery holds his work. Retrospective Sally Hunter Fine Art, 1986. Lived in London.

Hein BONGER 1952– Self-taught sculptor, born in Arnhem, Netherlands. Exhibitions included RA Summer Exhibition, 1993; Chappel Galleries, Chappel, from 1994 (in 1996 with Tessa Newcomb); and Ernst & Young, Cambridge, 1995. Bonger was based in Suffolk.

Eliza BONHAM CARTER 1961– Abstract painter who studied at Ravensbourne College of Art, 1982–5, then Royal College of Art, 1986–8, being awarded Abbey Major Scholarship to British School, Rome in the latter year. Group shows included Todd Gallery, 1991, and Aiding and Abetting, at The Gallery at John Jones, 1994. Solo shows included The Berkeley Square Gallery, 1989, and Galleria Sprovieri, Rome, 1992.

George BONNER 1924– Painter, born in Toronto, Canada. Educated at the South-West Essex Technical College, he exhibited at the RA, New Vision Gallery, Towner Art Gallery, Eastbourne – which holds his work – and abroad. Bonner painted in oil and acrylic, his pictures being noted for their texture, as well as in collage. Lived at Bexhill, Sussex.

Lesley BONNER 1954– Artist working in such materials as wood and concrete who studied at Harrow School of Art and Bristol Polytechnic. She was employed as community artist in Milton Keynes, Buckinghamshire, from 1977–83 and settled there. The city's Development Corporation commissioned a range of work from her including Totem Pole, Griffin and Lodge Gates Carving.

Mary BONNING: *see* **Mary JOHNSTONE**

Susan BONVIN 1948– Artist and teacher whose work included abstract sculptures and constructions, with pigment. Was born in London of Anglo-Swiss nationality. Studied at Wimbledon School of Art, 1964–6, then gained an honours degree in fine art painting at Falmouth School of Art, 1966–9, in the latter year winning the Sir Edward Nichol Painting Prize. Was joint editor of the arts anthology *Wallpaper*, also participating in *Wallpaper on Cassette*, Audio Arts. Had an artists in schools residency, Eastern Arts Board, 1989. Between 1970–94 did part-time teaching in schools, further and higher education, from 1994 teaching at Tresham Institute, Kettering. Group shows included On Site, Arnolfini Gallery, Bristol, 1979; *The Economist* Gallery, 1991; and The Table Studio Group, The Living Room, 1996. Had a solo show at Ascham Street Studio, 1986, later ones including Gallery 4, Shad Thames, 1993. Arts Council holds her work. Lived in Southwick, Peterborough, Cambridgeshire.

James William BOOTH 1867–1953 Painter in oil and watercolour keen on country subjects, born in Manchester. born in Manchester. Showed extensively at RCamA of which he was a member, RA, Walker Art Gallery in Liverpool and elsewhere. Lived in Scalby, Scarborough, Yorkshire. Manchester City Art Gallery holds examples.

Peter BOOTH 1940– Painter, born in Sheffield, Yorkshire. He attended the College of Art there in 1956–7, emigrated to Australia in 1958, then from 1962–5 studied at National Gallery School in Melbourne, where he continued to live. In the early 1970s worked in framing department of the National Gallery of Victoria, coming into contact with the work of William Blake, which had a profound effect. Booth produced figurative, gestural and semi-abstract works. They were lit by a light that was rarely daylight and while drawing on his experience of the Australian landscape were inspired by dreams and the subconscious. One of the leading Australian painters of his generation, Booth showed widely in mixed exhibitions in that continent. He had his first one-man show at Strines Gallery, Melbourne, in 1967, after that showing often in Melbourne and Sydney; with CDS Gallery, New York, in 1985–7; and had his first European show at Albemarle Gallery in 1988. National Gallery of Victoria and Metropolitan Museum, New York, hold his work.

Roberta BOOTH 1947– Painter and printmaker who studied at Luton School of Art, 1964–6; fine art at Coventry College of Art, 1966–9, gaining her diploma; then obtained her master's degree in printmaking at Royal College of Art, 1969–72. In 1982 obtained an Eastern Arts Association grant. Mixed shows included Hachette Gallery, and British Council Exhibition in Linz, Austria, both 1971; Cracow Print Biennial, Poland, 1972; Five Realists, Minories, Colchester, and Summer Show I, Serpentine Gallery, both 1976; Cambridgeshire Artists, Kettle's Yard, Cambridge, 1983; and Society of Botanical Artists, 1995. Had a solo exhibition at Duncan Campbell Contemporary Art, 1996, of paintings completed 1974–89, in which Booth transformed everyday objects as analogues for humanity, giving them a Surrealistic hint of menace. Victoria & Albert Museum and University of Waikato, New Zealand, hold examples.

Daphne BOOTHBY fl. from late 1950s– Sculptor, painter and draughtsman who studied at West of England College of Art, Bristol, gaining a diploma with first-class honours, and an art teacher's diploma. She travelled in Italy, studying painting and sculpture at Academy of Fine Arts Pietro Vannucci, Perugia. In 1981 was elected a brother of the Art Workers' Guild. Boothby worked in fine hardwoods, direction of the grain relating to carefully developed abstracted forms. Italian historic urban architecture was a constant influence on her paintings and drawings, which were also abstracted. Group shows included Loggia Gallery from 1981. From 1965 held regular open studio exhibitions in west London. Others included William Penn House, 1968; University of Surrey, 1970; Ice House Gallery, 1982; Palazzo del Priori, Perugia, 1989; and Quaker Gallery, 1994. BBC, London College of Furniture and Church of St John the Baptist, Neath Abbey, hold examples.

Karolina BORCHARDT 1913– Painter, born in Minsk and educated in Krakow, Poland, who later adopted British citizenship. Studied art at University of Stefan Batory in London and in Italy. Was a member of Free Painters and Sculptors, showing at Loggia Gallery, also in mixed exhibitions at Barbican Art Gallery, Centaur Gallery and abroad. Solo shows were held at Richmond and Barrett Galleries and in America. Lived in London.

Dorothy BORDASS 1905–1992 Painter, artist in collage and printmaker, born in London. She studied with several teachers throughout the 1920s, including R T Mumford, at Académie Julian in Paris, and at Heatherley's School of Fine Art under Iain Macnab. Took part in many group shows, including Redfern and Mercury Galleries and extensively abroad; had solo shows at New Vision Centre Gallery, Woodstock Gallery, in the provinces and overseas. South London Art Gallery, other British and Commonwealth galleries hold her work. This sometimes has both a seemingly naive and jokey quality. A show of her output over the period 1954–90 was held at Chappel Galleries, Chappel, Essex, in 1992. Lived for some years in Cambridge.

Wendela BOREEL 1895–1985 Painter and printmaker, born in Pau, France, she studied at the Slade School of Fine Art, the Westminster Technical Institute under Walter Sickert and the Central School of Arts and Crafts. Boreel became closely associated with the Sickert circle and it was because of her brilliant studies in gouache that he became interested in the medium. She was an especially accomplished printmaker and her subjects, such as the actress Gwen Frangcon-Davies, the Café Royal and London street scenes, owe much to his influence. She exhibited RE, NS, NEAC, Redfern and Walker's Galleries and had a number of one-man shows in London and abroad. Victoria & Albert Museum holds her work. Finally lived in Mougins, France.

Wyn BORGER 1933– Painter and teacher, born in Withington, Manchester, her father a senior London Midland and Scottish Railway freight official. After education at Whalley Range High School for Girls, spent two years at Manchester School of Art, then three at Bath Academy of Art, Corsham, teachers including Colin Thompson, Reg Butler, Peter Potworoski, William Scott,Peter Lanyon, Litz Pisk, Brian Wynter, James Tower and Lyn Chadwick. From 1959–83 was head of art department and exhibitions organiser at Brunel University. In 1957 married the behavioural psychologist Robert Borger (previously exhibited under her maiden name Winifred Frost). Exhibitions included Bath Library, LG, Bedford Park Festival and elsewhere. Lived in London.

Christine BORLAND 1965– Artist using such media as photography and installations, born in Darvel, Ayrshire. She gained an honours degree at Glasgow School of Art, 1983–7, then her master's at University of Ulster, Belfast, 1987–8. Group shows included Speed at Transmission Gallery, Glasgow, 1991; Aperto, Venice Biennale, 1993; Institute of Cultural Anxiety, ICA, 1994; and British Art Show, with tour, 1995–6. Solo shows included From Life at Tramway, Glasgow, 1994, and Kunstwerke, Berlin, and the British Council Gallery, Prague, both 1995.

Deirdre BORLASE 1925– Painter, printmaker, collagist and teacher, born in London, who from childhood wanted to paint, but received little early encouragement. She studied at Bromley School of Art, 1940–4, then at the Royal College of Art, 1944–6, where teachers included Ruskin Spear and Carel Weight and where she met her future husband Frederick Brill (she was included with him and their children in Relative Values at The Smith Art Gallery & Museum, Stirling, 1993). Lectured at Harrow School of Art, 1946–8, and Kingston School of Art, 1948–50. Bringing up a family curtailed her artistic activity for some years, although she continued to fill sketchbooks. After the Brills bought a cottage in Carperby, North Yorkshire, in 1967 she began to paint the landscape, Venice being another favourite subject of her pictures, which often took a witty turn. During 1977 Borlase attended a course in printmaking at Morley College, in 1992 began to decorate furniture and also began experimenting with a computer paintbox. Showed extensively at RA Summer Exhibition from 1946 and elsewhere in mixed shows. Had a solo show at David Thompson Gallery, 1979, later ones including Broughton House Gallery, Cambridge, from 1989. Commissions included six paintings for St Luke's Hospital, Bradford. Graves Art Gallery, Sheffield, holds her work.

Daisy Theresa BORNE 1906– Sculptor in a variety of materials, and teacher, born in London. An interest in religious themes was a feature of her output, which was elegant and conservative while being tinged with modernism. Borne travelled widely with her family, being educated partly in America, then returned to London where she studied sculpture at Regent Street Polytechnic School of Art with Harold Brownsword. Also studied singing, but declined to take up the stage professionally. Learned to carve with Joyce Bidder, with whom she shared a studio in southwest London for many years. Some work was signed TB, joined. Showed at RA, RBS of which she was an associate, and was vice-president of RMS. Her work was included in a two-artist show with Joyce Bidder at Fine Art Society, 1987.

Jacob BORNFRIEND 1904–1976 Painter in oil and tempera, mainly of landscape and still life. Born in Zborov, Czechoslovakia (as Bauernfreund, later Anglicised), he was educated at the Academy of Fine Arts, Prague, 1930–5, under Willi Nowak. All early work lost when he moved to England in 1939. First one-man show at Roland, Browse and Delbanco, London, in 1950. Painted a large mural for the Jews' College, London, in 1957, having done mural work in Czechoslovakia. The Tate Gallery, Southampton City Art Gallery, several colleges at Oxford and many galleries abroad hold his work. Lived in London.

Eleanora Anderson BORRIE: *see* **Eleanora HOPE HENDERSON**

Charles Gordon BORROWMAN 1892–1956 Watercolour, pastel and pencil artist, born in Edinburgh. Having attended Edinburgh University, he studied at the College of Art there on occasions between 1912–20 with David Alison and William Walls. After being commissioned in the Indian Army just before World War I, Borrowman served for over 30 years with the 4th Gurkha Rifles, whose history he wrote. Exhibited RSA, RSW, Royal Glasgow Institute of the Fine Arts and RSMA. The Indian Army Museum, Sandhurst, and the Russell-Cotes Art Gallery and Museum, Bournemouth, hold his work. Lived at Dunkeld, Perthshire.

Jiri BORSKY 1945– Painter and teacher, born in Dobrany, Czechoslovakia. He drew from an early age, then while attending Building College in Prague in 1960 began painting. From 1964 attended Prague University to study architecture, at instigation of father and to avoid military service, and began to exhibit pictures. After first visit to England in 1967 and another in 1968, in 1969 moved permanently, settling in Potteries, working as draughtsman for Wedgwood's, then as architectural assistant with borough of Newcastle-under-Lyme. Became British citizen in 1975, in 1976 enrolled at North Staffordshire Polytechnic to study painting and graduated in fine art in 1979. Took part in mixed shows in Midlands and elsewhere. After a one-man show at Brampton Museum, Newcastle, in 1971, others included Keele University on several occasions from 1977, and City Museum & Art Gallery, Hanley, Stoke-on-Trent, 1980. Taught at Keele, which holds his work, as do several provincial galleries including Stoke. Borsky's work was figurative, often autobiographical, influences being Klee, Miró, Chagall, Dubuffet and Dix.

Alfred Edward BORTHWICK 1871–1955 Painter, stained glass artist and printmaker, born in Scarborough, Yorkshire. Studied at Edinburgh College of Art, in Antwerp and at Académie Julian, Paris, under Adolphe Bouguereau. Served in Army in both Boer War and World War I. Prolific exhibitor, especially at RSW and RSA, also at RA, RE, RP and Royal Glasgow Institute of the Fine Arts. Elected RSA, 1938. Lived in Edinburgh.

Derek BOSHIER 1937– Artist who painted, sculpted and became involved in printmaking, photography and films, writing and books; teacher. He was married to the artist Patricia Gonzalez. Boshier was born in Portsmouth, Hampshire, and attended Yeovil School of Art, 1953–7, and Royal College of Art, 1959–62. After showing with Young Contemporaries in 1959 Boshier was included in several hundred mixed exhibitions internationally. He had a first solo exhibition, Image in Revolt, at Grabowski Gallery, 1962, several dozen following after that, later ones including Texas Gallery, Houston, and Mandeville Gallery, University of California, both 1991, Galerie de Centre, Paris, 1993, and Connaught Brown, 1996. From 1963–73 Boshier was an instructor at Hornsey College of Art, from 1963–79 at Central School and from 1973–9 at Royal College of Art. Many further appointments followed in Britain and abroad, then in 1980 Boshier joined University of Houston, Texas, eventually becoming professor. In the early 1990s he returned to live in England, settling in Kingsbury Episcopi, Somerset. Boshier's art went through various phases, touching on Pop Art, hard-edge Op Abstraction and politically radical conceptual art. Tate Gallery, British Museum, Victoria & Albert Museum and several dozen other notable international collections hold Boshier's work.

Marcus Arthur BOSS 1891– Painter in oil and watercolour, mainly of portraits, Boss was born in London and studied at Birkbeck School of Art, Heatherley's School of Fine Art, 1908–11, and the Royal Academy Schools, 1911–16. Exhibited widely, including the RA, ROI, RP, International Portrait Society and in the provinces. Lived in London and was a member of the Chelsea Arts Club and London Sketch club, where he was a noted character.

Ervin BOSSANYI 1891–1975 Figure painter in oil and tempera, stained glass artist and ceramics maker. Born in Hungary where he initially studied art, then at Académie Julian, in Paris, and Camden School of Art, London. Exhibited RA and Beaux Arts Gallery. One-man shows in London, Edinburgh and Germany. As well as extensive official purchases abroad, Bossanyi's work is held by the Tate Gallery and Victoria & Albert Museum. He lived at Eastcote, Pinner, Middlesex.

James BOSTOCK 1917– Printmaker, painter and illustrator, born in Hanley, Staffordshire. He studied at Medway School of Art, Rochester, 1933–6, and Royal College of Art, 1936–9. Was on staff of Bristol Polytechnic. His book *Roman Lettering for Students* was published in 1959, his wood engravings for *Poems* *of Edward Thomas* appearing in 1988. Showed at RA, NEAC, Crafts Centre of Great Britain and RBA. Victoria & Albert Museum and British Museum hold his work. Was a member of SWE and East Kent Art Society. Lived in Broadstairs, Kent.

Allan BOSTON 1951– Painter, born in Hastings, Sussex. He studied at University of Newcastle, 1973–6, then Chelsea School of Art, 1975–6. Exhibited in groups in Britain and America, and was included in John Moores Liverpool Exhibition from 1976, his oil Car and Hand winning a prize in 1985. Had a solo exhibition at Serpentine Gallery in 1975. Arts Council holds his work. Lived for a time in London.

James BOSWELL 1906–1971 Painter, illustrator, political cartoonist and printmaker. Born at Westport, New Zealand, Boswell began studying at the Elam School of Art, Auckland, in 1924; after coming to London in 1925 studied at the Royal College of Art, 1925–9. Began showing paintings from 1927 with the London Group and lithographs with the Senefelder Club. Became interested in politics in the late 1920s, in 1932 giving up painting. Joined the Communist Party and took to illustration and graphic design. In 1933 was a founder-member of the AIA, with which he illustrated, at the same time drawing for *Left Review* and contributing anti-Fascist cartoons to the *Daily Worker* under the name Buchan. Boswell combined his position as art director of the publicity department of Asiatic – later Shell – Petroleum with his radical activities. Travelled widely during World War II in the Army, after which he rejoined Shell for two years before joining the staff of *Lilliput* magazine until 1950. Began to exhibit widely, including the RA, Drian Gallery and Paris Salon. Boswell was a persuasive writer, publishing *The Artist's Dilemma* in 1947. While working as editor of the house journal of J Sainsbury Ltd, the retail firm, he wrote its centenary history. The bitingly satirical cartoonist and printmaker, whose work has been compared to that of the German George Grosz, diversified in the 1950s and 1960s. In 1951 he finished a large mural for the Sea and Ships pavilion for the Festival of Britain; he designed the poster Let's Go With Labour and the party's entire publicity campaign for the 1964 general election; film posters included *It Always Rains on Sunday* and *The Blue Lamp*, for Ealing Studios. Having established himself as a fine Colourist, Boswell later worked as an abstract painter. His work is held by many galleries in Britain and New Zealand, including the Tate Gallery. Lived in London.

William Aubrey BOSWELL 1926– Painter in watercolour and oil and teacher, born in Nottingham. He studied at Nottingham College of Arts and Crafts, 1941–3; was a lithographer in the Royal Engineers, 1944–9; meanwhile attending Kingston School of Art part-time, 1945; Geniefa College, Suez, part-time, 1946; and Royal Air Force School of Art and Architecture, Heliopolis, part-time, 1947. Held a number of teaching posts, eventually becoming principal design officer for county planning for Clwyd, in which he settled at Wrexham. Wrote and illustrated guides to parts of Wales, such as Llangollen, Wrexham, Denbigh and Corwen. He was a member of RCamA and a founder and chairman, 1960–70, of Wrexham Art Group. Also exhibited at Williamson Art Gallery, Birkenhead; Royal Welsh Show; and Manchester City Art Gallery.

Winifred Doris BOSWORTH 1900–1957 Watercolour painter, etcher and embroiderer, born in Bideford, Devon, who signed her work with her maiden name, D Goaman. Studied at Bideford School of Art, 1916–21 under Hugh Heard, and at Bristol College of Art, 1921–3, with Reginald Bush. She held a series of teaching posts, notably at Bideford School of Art and the West of England College of Art in the 1920s and 1930s. Exhibited RWA and elsewhere, Bristol City Art Gallery holding her work. Lived in Carlisle.

Paul BOTHWELL KINCAID 1946– Sculptor and graphic artist, born in Birmingham, Warwickshire, who studied at Stourbridge College of Art and Design, and Dyfed College of Art, 1980–3. Became a member of SGA in 1979, showing with it and around Wales. Bishop Vaughan School in Swansea holds his work. Lived for a time in Newcastle Emlyn, Dyfed.

Dennis Roxby BOTT 1948– Watercolourist, born in London. He studied at Colchester School of Art, 1967–9, then Norwich School of Art, 1969–72, his teachers including Edward Middleditch. He worked full-time as an artist after 1975, claiming "wide-ranging subject matter, including architecture or other man-made influences in landscape". Was elected RWS in 1983, also participating in group shows at Agnew. Had solo exhibitions at Gallery 33 in Billingshurst from 1977; Ogle Gallery, Eastbourne, 1978; and Bourne Gallery, Reigate, from 1986. Towner Art Gallery in Eastbourne and public galleries in Brighton and Hove hold his work. Lived in Milford, Surrey.

BOTTERILL: *see* **ANTON**

Albert Ernest BOTTOMLEY 1873–1950 Painter born in Leeds who studied art with the landscape artist William Edwin Tindall. Exhibited prolifically at RA, RBA, RCamA as well as at many other venues, public galleries in Leeds and Worthing buying his work. Lived at Reigate, Surrey.

Fred BOTTOMLEY 1883–1960 Landscape painter in oil and watercolour. Studied at the Slade School of Fine Art. Exhibited RA, RBA, ROI and with the St Ives Art Club. Lived at Stratford-upon-Avon, Warwickshire.

Peter BOTTOMLEY 1927– Artist in watercolour, gouache and graphic techniques, Bottomley was born at Goole, Yorkshire. He studied at Doncaster School of Art under Thomas Alexander Anderson and at the Royal College of Art under Robert Austin. After studies lasting 1942–52 Bottomley began to exhibit in Britain and America, including the RA and RE. He became principal of Southport College of Art. Lived at Southport, Merseyside.

Pauline BOTY 1938–1966 Painter, who created some of the most memorable images of the 1960s, and actress, born Carshalton, Surrey. She attended Wallington County Girls' School, winning a scholarship to study stained glass at Wimbledon School of Art. From 1959–61 she attended the Royal College of Art. She showed at AIA Gallery in 1961 with notable 1960s artists such as Peter Blake; in 1962 was included in New Approaches to the Figure at Arthur Jeffress Gallery; in 1963 taking part in Pop Art at Midland Group Gallery, Nottingham. In that year she held her first solo exhibition at Grabowski Gallery. As an actress Boty appeared in Frank Hilton's *Day of the Prince* at Royal Court Theatre in 1962, in the same year being featured in Ken Russell's film *Pop Goes the Easel* with Blake, Derek Boshier and Peter Phillips. Boty was married to Clive Goodwin, who was involved in the film business and who died in tragic circumstances in California. Boty died in London after the birth of their daughter. She was featured in The Sixties Art Scene in London, at Barbican Art Gallery, and had a small commemorative show at Mayor Gallery, both in 1993.

Allan BOULTER 1940– Painter, draughtsman and lino-cut artist, born in Reading, Berkshire. He attended Willesden Art School, 1953–6, Harrow Art School and gained his Royal Academy Schools certificate, 1961–3, notable teachers including Charles Mahoney. He won three David Murray Scholarships: London, Cornwall and Aix-en-Provence University, France. In 1973 Boulter won the Laing Calendar Prize Competition. Group shows included Penzance Library Art Centre Gallery, 1980–7, and Hampstead Town Hall, 1985–6. Showed solo at Deal Library from 1979, Deal Serendipity Gallery from 1981 and Royal Cinque Ports Yacht Club from 1984. Wandsworth Borough Council holds his work. Lived in Deal, Kent.

Dick BOULTON 1939– Self-taught artist known mostly for his pastels, although also worked for long periods in watercolour. Produced highly stylised landscapes which later tended towards abstraction. Showed with PS, RI, Patricia Wells Gallery in Thornbury and elsewhere and had over a dozen shows in Somerset and Bristol. There was a retrospective at The Strata Gallery, Upper Norwood, 1997. Boulton lived near there, also at Ashcott, near Bridgwater, Somerset.

Doris BOULTON: *see* **Doris BOULTON-MAUDE**

Janet BOULTON 1936– Artist in watercolour, paper relief and pencil, born in Wiltshire, who studied at Swindon School of Art & Design, 1953–5, then Camberwell School of Art, 1955–8, in the latter year winning the David Murray Landscape Painting Scholarship. Began part-time teaching in a Swindon grammar school, 1959, other appointments including Swindon School of Art, 1960–2 and from 1972; Chelsea Westminster Evening Institute, 1962; Hreod Burna School, Swindon, 1970; Pangbourne College, with residency, 1981; residency at Radcliffe Infirmary, 1986; and art teaching at Abingdon School, 1988. Events in Boulton's career were development of an interest in botanical studies, gardens and garden history from 1981, which led to widespread painting of gardens in England, Italy and Scotland; attendance at a papermaking workshop at Oxford Polytechnic, 1987; and the editing of Paul Nash's letters to Mercia Oakley, 1989. Boulton was a member of the Royal Horticultural, Garden History and British Ivy Societies. She admired the work of Juan Gris, Morandi and Lucy Rie. Her still lifes of bottles and jars were notable, and they enabled her "to confront the duality between the vertical and horizontal planes and to exploit their rhythmic potential". Her many mixed shows included Reading Museum & Art Gallery, RA Summer Exhibition, Browse & Darby, LG, Scunthorpe Art Gallery, RWS Open and Flying Colours Gallery in Edinburgh. Solo exhibitions included a series at Mercury Gallery from 1988. Southern Arts, Oxford and Isle of Wight Health Authorities and National Gallery of Canada in Ottawa hold examples. Lived in Abingdon, Oxfordshire.

Doris BOULTON-MAUDE 1892–1961 Printmaker (born Doris Boulton, her original exhibiting name) who studied at Burslem School of Art, Stoke-on-Trent, then at Royal College of Art, 1916–21. She showed at RA and was an associate of RE, 1918–21. Went to Egypt, reportedly teaching art in Cairo, and making prints of views there. Back in London in 1930 she attended Slade School of Fine Art for a term and began exhibiting again. Came into contact with modern art movements, was influenced by Franz Marc and the Blaue Reiter style and changed to relief printing methods. Married Lionel Maude, whom she had met at a Fabian summer school (his parents Aylmer and Louise Maude, members of a strongly Socialist family, were Tolstoy's authorised English translators and biographers; they had been part of a late-1890s Tolstoyan community at Purleigh, Essex), and began to exhibit as Doris Boulton-Maude. Showed at NEAC, Redfern Gallery, Walker Art Gallery in Liverpool, SWA and RBA. Lived at Great Baddow, Essex. In 1995–6 a Chelmsford Museums Service show toured the county. Chelmsford and Essex Museum holds her work.

Diana BOURDON SMITH 1933– Painter in oil and watercolour and book illustrator, born in Wallington, Surrey. She studied at Kingston School of Art, 1950–4, under Robin Child and James Anthony Betts. Showed at NEAC, RA, RWA of which she was made an associate in 1984, and elsewhere in south and west of England. RWA holds her work. Lived in Bath, Avon.

Doris BOURGUIGNON fl. from 1940s– Artist whose work fell into two distinct periods, and who worked in a range of media. She studied at Belfast College of Art, then Royal College of Art, initially producing academic work. During World War II she painted American and British personnel and their activities in Northern Ireland and blitzed areas of Belfast. Had two solo exhibitions in Belfast, one in 1948 at the Museum and Art Gallery, which holds her early work (painted under her unmarried name of Doris V Blair) and later contemporary output.

Bourguignon studied for that under Wallace Harrison in New York and in Paris with Fernand Léger and André Lhote. In 1975 Bourguignon, living in Belgium, had a solo exhibition at Galerie L'Angle Aigu in Brussels. In mid-1990s settled in London where Bourguignon was painting acrylic works of "Figurative Abstraction". In 1945 she had illustrated *Various Verses* by John O' the North.

Bob BOURNE 1931– Painter, born in Exmouth, Devon. Although mainly self-taught, in the 1950s he attended St Martin's School of Art and West of England Academy in Bristol part-time. Painted abstract and figurative works. Showed with Arthur Tooth, 1973; was included in the Arts Council tour Fragments Against Ruin, 1981–2; and the RWA exhibition Artists from Cornwall, 1992. Arts Council holds his pictures Lover's Leap, 1972, and Self Portrait, 1977. Bourne lived a simple life in a fisherman's cottage at Newlyn, Cornwall.

Christopher BOURNE 1930– Artist and teacher, born in Wolverhampton. After education there and in Newcastle he held a series of teaching posts, including Bath Academy of Art and Chelsea School of Art. A versatile artist, he participated in many group shows, including John Moores Exhibition in Liverpool, SEA, Whitechapel Art Gallery, Piccadilly and Rowan Galleries and New Art Centre.He also did graphic work for Editions Alecto; was commissioned by the BBC to design *Façade*, which was performed at the Barber Institute, Birmingham, and in Cheltenham at the Music Festival; and his sculpture Nativity was completed for Bangor Cathedral. One-man shows included University College of North Wales, Bangor. WAC holds his work.

John Frye BOURNE 1912–1991 Painter in oil and watercolour, who became a popular portraitist. Born in London, he was educated at Bishop's Stortford College, then studied at the Royal Academy Schools, where his teachers included Walter Westley Russell. Bourne claimed to be the youngest student at the Schools since J M W Turner, and was there 1929–34. He showed at RA, RCamA, RP, RWS and elsewhere, his work being published in *Royal Academy Illustrated.* Chelsea Arts Club member who lived in Sidbury, Devon.

Peter BOURNE 1931– Painter in oil and watercolour, and teacher, born in Madras, India, who studied at Glasgow School of Art, 1949–54, with David Donaldson. Went on to combine teaching and painting, being a member of RSW and SSWA. "The Fauves, British colourists and Pop" were among influences on his work, which appeared in group shows in Glasgow and Edinburgh, where he also exhibited solo, also in groups in Kendal, Perth and Newcastle upon Tyne. Paintings in Hospitals, Abbot Hall Art Gallery in Kendal, Edinburgh's city art collection and Mobil Oil have examples. Lived in Aberfeldy, Perthshire.

Regis de BOUVIER DE CACHARD 1929– Artist in oil, gouache and bronze and printmaker, born in Paris, France, who studied at the École Boule there, then was at the Machasson Textile Studio for Haute Couture, designing for Paris fashion houses. His work comprised stylised landscapes, figure and still life works, using a distinctive palette, with a Surrealist tinge. Group exhibitions included Salon des Indépendants, Paris, 1955; O'Hana Gallery, 1958; and The Guildhall, 1972. Had a series of international solo exhibitions, latterly including Kandinsky Gallery, Madrid, 1976; Sala Giannini, Madrid, 1976; Mall Galleries, 1981; with a retrospective at Tadema Gallery, 1987. Courtauld Institute holds a catalogue raisonné. Public collections include Tate Gallery, Museum of Modern Art in Paris; private collections Duke of Bedford, Alan Ladd, Dean Martin, Frank Sinatra and David Wolfson. Count de Bouvier de Cachard lived latterly at Lyme Regis, Dorset.

Howard BOWCOTT 1956– Sculptor and artist in other media, born in Manchester. He studied fine art at Newcastle University, 1975–9, from the early 1970s having long stays in area of Blaenau Ffestiniog, Merionethshire, to draw, paint and photograph. Moved to Blaenau Ffestiniog, working as a stonewaller and civil engineer on the railway there, with subsequent years spent working in the landscape. In 1985 Bowcott was assistant to David Nash at Kroller Muller Museum, Arnhem, Netherlands. In 1987 went on cultural exchange visit, part-funded by British Council, to Zimbabwe, with a return visit in 1988. In that year he was also artist-in-residence, National Museum of Wales, Llanberis, and assistant to David Nash at Tournus, France. Took part in extensive group shows, notably in Wales. His solo exhibitions included Bulawayo City Art Gallery and British Council, Harare, Zimbabwe, in 1987, later ones including Glynn Vivian Art Gallery, Swansea, 1993. Bowcott's work is in the collections of Gwynedd County Council and Swansea City Council.

Cliff BOWEN 1942– Sculptor, draughtsman and teacher, born in Ogmore Vale, Glamorgan. He studied at Newport College of Art, then went on to teach at Swansea, Sheffield and Derby Colleges of Art, 1966–72, when he joined Glasgow School of Art's sculpture department. Four years later he was made head of the department. Bowen drew on the countryside and nature for his work, but changed the scale of things to match his own remembered scale of importance. Showed WAC, Axiom Gallery in Exeter and Glasgow School of Art staff show. Had one-man exhibition at Compass Gallery, Glasgow in 1983.

Denis BOWEN 1921– Painter and gallery owner, born in Kimberley, South Africa, but took United Kingdom citizenship in 1962. He was married for a time to the artist Judy Stapleton. Bowen received early education in north of England, and attended Huddersfield Art School on a County Award. He was accepted at Royal College of Art in 1940, but Royal Navy service, which involved extensive travel, put back his studies there to 1946–50, his teachers including Rodrigo Moynihan, John Minton and Carel Weight. Bowen soon began to make a name as a leading experimental painter; he taught at various provincial art colleges as well as Royal College and Central School of Arts and Crafts; in 1952 along with other members of the ICA he founded the Free Painters' Group; and from 1956–66 he founded and directed the New Vision Centre, with Frank Avray Wilson and Halima Nalecz, which became a focal point for the work of advanced artists from Europe and elsewhere. Bowen was appointed associate professor at Victoria University, British Columbia, 1969–72. Contributed to art publications in Britain and abroad and showed extensively internationally. Bowen had a first retrospective show at Bede Gallery, Jarrow, in 1973, and a second at Huddersfield Art Gallery in 1989. In 1984 Bowen co-founded Celtic Vision, a group representing contemporary art from Europe's main Celtic regions. Bowen's work is in dozens of international public galleries, including Victoria & Albert Museum and British Museum. Lived in London.

John BOWEN 1914– Painter, born in Lanelli, Carmarthenshire. After attending Llanelli and Swansea Schools of Art he taught at Llanelli School of Art, 1939–60, also at the Boys' Grammar School there apart from wartime service in the Royal Air Force. He was an artist member of SWG and also showed WAC and at the Royal National Eisteddfod. In 1968 he had a retrospective at Parc Howard Mansion, Llanelli. Painter of landscapes in Britain and abroad and still life, in oil and watercolour whose work is in many public collections, including WAC and Newport Art Gallery and Museum.

Keith BOWEN 1950– Artist who was born in Wrexham, Denbighshire, and trained at Manchester Polytechnic. He was a frequent exhibitor at the Royal National Eisteddfod, gaining first prize in 1983. In 1988 he designed a postage stamp to celebrate publication of William Morgan's *Welsh Bible*, 1588. National Library of Wales in Aberystwyth holds his work.

Owen BOWEN 1873–1967 Painter, born in Leeds, who attended the High School there. He acquired his artistic training studying with Gilbert Foster and also studied printmaking and pottery design. Although Bowen painted on the continent, he was particularly known for his views of Yorkshire, for he settled in Leeds and established his own school of painting there. Also illustrated books. After World War II he was president of RCamA for a number of years, exhibiting with it prolifically, also with Walker Art Gallery, Liverpool, and RA and ROI. Several northern public galleries, including Leeds, Rotherham and Rochdale, hold his work.

Thomas BOWEN 1909– Specialist in lithography and fore-edge painting; designer, born in London. Studied at his local School of Art in Clapham, at London School of Printing and at Bolt Court School. Was by profession an industrial and engineering draughtsman. Showed RWS and in the provinces, Warsaw Museum in Poland holding his work.

Bernard BOWERMAN 1911– Painter, technical illustrator and designer, born in London, who attended Leyton School of Art, West Ham School of Art, classes in Walthamstow and privately studied with various artists. Member of the Wapping Group of Artists and showed at RA, RI, RBA and elsewhere, signing his pictures Bernard-Bowerman. Lived at Buckhurst Hill, Essex.

Kelvin BOWERS 1946– Painter, collagist, writer and poet and athlete, born in Stoke-on-Trent, Staffordshire. He was British Junior Indoor mile record holder in 1964, and in 1974–5 travelled to Australia on foot, the longest distance run ever, recorded in his book *Closing the Distance*, published in 1980. Bowers began writing poetry and making collages while training in Australia in 1966–7. In 1983 he enrolled at Staffordshire Polytechnic where he met the artist Jo Baker, with whom he lived in a converted cowshed in the Staffordshire countryside and collaborated on many projects. Bowers graduated with an honours fine art degree in 1986, the year that he published *Fantaisie Valse*, a limited-edition book of collages, with Baker; in that year they shared a show at New Victoria Theatre, Newcastle-under-Lyme. Other shared ventures included two-man exhibitions at Galerie Sud, Galerie Forum and Galeries Kooring-Verwindt, Amsterdam, 1987; in 1989 a photo-montage mural commission for St Edwards Mental Hospital, Cheddleton, and visits to New York and Mexico; and in 1990 a first joint London show at England & Co. They parted in 1991 and from 1992 Bowers lived with the artist Dooze Storey, latterly in London. In 1995 had solo shows at Salt House Gallery, St Ives, and England & Co; and State Gallery of Art, Sopot, Poland, 1996. Bowers was winner of a purchase prize at the Fifth Open Exhibition, Stoke-on-Trent City Museum and Art Gallery, 1991. His work was also owned by the artists Peter Blake, Gordon House and Denis Bowen and is in the permanent exhibition of contemporary British painting assembled in New York by Robert and Susan Summer. Bowers' work mixed Expressionist colour, Primitivism, fantasy and Surrealism.

John BOWES 1899–1974 Painter, pen and ink draughtsman and singer, born in Oldham, Lancashire. He was educated at Manchester Grammar School and attended the Royal Military Academy, Sandhurst, in World War I. Was professional singer, while also painting, for 20 years until 1943, then when became deaf took up full-time painting. Was made member of RCamA in 1965, also joining Manchester and Liverpool Academies, Manchester Society of Modern Painters and Lancashire Group of Artists. Had solo shows starting with 1946 at Salford Art Gallery, including retrospective at Atkinson Art Gallery, Southport, 1971. Public galleries in Derby, Liverpool, Salford, Southport and Newcastle upon Tyne hold his work. Lived in Southport, Lancashire.

Druie BOWETT 1924– Painter, writer and poet, born in Ripon, Yorkshire. She studied at Harrogate School of Art and later with Jean-Georges Simon, a pupil of Bourdelle. She wrote a memoir of him and her illustrated book of poems *Painter's Poetry* was published in 1986. Parisian influences were apparent in Bowett's pictures, which while showing a strong command of natural form had a notable pattern element. Was a member of Midland Group,

Industrial Painters' Group, WIAC and other international bodies, also showing at RA, Paris Salon, LG, RP and RSA. Had many solo exhibitions from 1957 at Midland Group Gallery, Nottingham, later ones including The Pierrepont Gallery, Newark, 1991, and Cartwright Hall, Bradford, 1995. HRH The Duke of Edinburgh holds her work. Lived in Blyth, Nottinghamshire.

Olwyn BOWEY 1936– Painter and draughtsman, born Stockton-on-Tees, County Durham. Attended West Hartlepool School of Art and the Royal College of Art and was awarded a travelling scholarship. For a time she taught at Waltham Forest School of Art. Showed at New Grafton Gallery and elsewhere, and became RA in 1974, also being a member of RBA. Work held by Tate Gallery, Arts Council, RA, Ministry of Public Building and Works and provincial galleries. Lived in Heyshott, Midhurst, Sussex.

David BOWIE 1947– Musician, actor, painter and sculptor, born in London as David Jones. His first hit single record, in 1969, was *Space Oddity*, after which many followed, including *The Rise and Fall of Ziggy Stardust and the Spiders from Mars*, 1972, *Scary Monsters and Super Creeps* in 1980 and *Never Let me Down*, 1987. In 1989 Bowie was executive producer and wrote the score for *The Delinquents*. Among his films were *The Man Who Fell to Earth*, 1976, and *Absolute Beginners*, 1986, and he appeared in stage and television plays. Before committing himself to performing Bowie had studied art, which he collected, notably works by modern British painters. In 1997, Bowie and others launched the 21 partnership, which sought to open up art writing to a younger audience by publishing more approachable titles. Bowie's own artworks appeared in Bosnia War Child at Flowers East, and in Minotaur Myths & Legends at Berkeley Square Gallery, both in 1994, and in Minky, Manky at Arnolfini Gallery, Bristol, 1995. His solo exhibition New Afro Pagan and Work 1975–95 was held at The Gallery in Cork Street, 1995. In 1995 he was also commissioned to prepare the Montreux Jazz Festival poster. Whitworth Art Gallery in Manchester, the Jacksonville Museum of Modern Art in Florida and Saatchi Collection hold examples of Bowie's work, which can be highly colourful.

Jonathan BOWKER 1963– Painter of Expressionistic figure groups, born in Huddersfield, Yorkshire. He graduated from Lanchester Polytechnic, Coventry, in 1987 with an honours degree in fine art. He took a studio in the Coventry Canal Basin, was a member of Coventry Artists' Group and showed in the city, in Liverpool and in the Pacesetters 8 exhibition in Peterborough, 1988. Had a solo show at Cotton Art Gallery, Midlands Arts Centre, Birmingham, in 1989, and in 1990 shared a three-man show at Woodlands Art Gallery.

Frank BOWLING 1936– Painter, born in Bartica, Guyana, who completed his schooling in England from the age of 14. Originally intended to be a writer, but after travelling on the continent and seeing the work of certain European masters he returned to England, began work as an artists' model and decided to become a painter. Attended City and Guilds School, joined the Royal College of Art in 1959 and after a short time at the Slade School of Fine Art returned to the Royal College to complete his master of arts degree in 1962. Bowling had already made his mark with work showing the influence of Francis Bacon, his picture Mirror being made Painting of the Year at 1966 RA Summer Exhibition. Disenchanted with the art scene in London Bowling moved to New York in 1966, receiving Guggenheim Memorial Foundation Fellowships in 1967 and 1973. Returned to London in 1976, but continued to show widely internationally, with several one-man shows at Tibor de Nagy, New York; Serpentine Gallery, 1986; RWA, Bristol, 1989; and City Gallery, Leicester, 1996, entitled Bowling on Through the Century. Tate Gallery, Arts Council and several major American galleries hold his work. Participated in The Other Story at Hayward Gallery, and tour, 1989–90.

Betty BOWMAN 1923– Painter, etcher and teacher, born in Ealing, west London. Her father was head of a glass and pottery firm, Edward Bowman & Son, and for many years Betty Bowman worked in it as a designer, being the first artist since Ravenhead to produce freehand decoration which could be fired into opalescent ware and glass. Studied at Central School of Arts and Crafts, 1944; privately with Mabel B Messer; Regent Street Polytechnic School of Art from 1953, where her teachers included Norman Blamey; and City and Guilds of London Art School, 1967–70, where she studied under Rodney Burn and Robin Guthrie. Moved to Cotswolds where she converted an old mill and ran her own school. As well as many group show participations had regular solo exhibitions, starting with Woodstock Gallery, 1963, others including John Whibley Gallery, Drian Gallery and Mall Galleries. Noted for her portraits and atmospheric landscapes in pastel, many of which were featured on the sets of television programmes. Davy International Corporation holds her work. Lived in Stourton, Warwickshire.

Pat BOWRING fl. from 1970s– Painter, draughtsman and printmaker whose work contained an element of fantasy. She studied painting with Morris Weidman in Tunbridge Wells in 1970–7, then moved to Greenwich and worked with the painter George Gault and sculptor Gerda Rubinstein. She was a member of NS, chairman of the Blackheath Art Society, 1981–4, a member of Greenwich Arts Council and Woodlands Art Gallery advisory group. Showed with RBA, UA, South London Artists and elsewhere. Shared a show at Tudor Barn Art Gallery in Eltham in 1983, was one of four artists who exhibited at Woodlands in 1988 and also showed solo.

John BOWSTEAD 1940– Artist, born in Northampton, who obtained a national diploma in design, painting, at Coventry College of Art, 1958–62. At Coventry a fellow-student was Roger Jeffs, and together they had a show, A New Kind of Brightness, at the Umbrella Club, Coventry, in 1961. In that year Bowstead took part in Eclectics at Nottingham Art Gallery and exhibited in

Midland Young Contemporaries, also in Nottingham. In 1962 Bowstead shared a show at ICA with Maurice Agis, David Hockney and Peter Phillips and was included in an Arts Council tour selected from Young Contemporaries. Arts Council acquired Bowstead's oil on board The Language of Love, of that year. Bowstead attended the Slade School of Fine Art, 1963–4. In the latter year he, Jeffs and two other Slade students, Terry Atkinson and Bernard Jennings, formed Fine Artz, which produced the work Action Chair. They also presented a project and sound show called Miss Misty and the Tri-Cool Data at Birmingham Polytechnic in 1966. After Fine Artz Bowstead continued working with Jeffs until 1968–9 in Light-Sound Workshop, a research unit at Hornsey College of Art. Bowstead settled in east London.

David T BOWYER 1950– Printmaker, born in Coventry, Warwickshire. Attended Bournville School of Arts and Crafts, Birmingham; Ravensbourne College of Art and Design, Bromley; then did postgraduate work at Manchester Polytechnic. Bowyer was trained as an abstract painter, but matured as an etcher with an interest in landscape, wildlife and architecture. In 1980 he was engaged to work on the *Banks Florilegium* project for Editions Alecto and British Museum, in 1982 moving to Clarendon Graphics to work with contemporary artists under Anthony Benjamin. From 1987 worked in own studio at Blackheath, southeast London. Showed with Greenwich Printmakers and was a member of it and Printmakers' Council. Many mixed shows included RA Summer Exhibition and Whitechapel Open, at Whitechapel Art Gallery. Solo shows included Axis Gallery, Brighton, 1977, and later Woodlands Art Gallery, 1992.

Jason Richard BOWYER 1957– Painter and teacher, born London, son of the artist William Bowyer. Jason Bowyer attended Camberwell School of Arts and Crafts, 1975–9, and Royal Academy Schools, 1979–82. Among his many awards were the British Institution Award in 1982; Elizabeth Greenshields Award in 1983; and British Council Visit Award to Bulgaria in 1990. Bowyer was artist to Fulham Football Club, 1985–6. His mixed shows included RA, NEAC and Christie's Post-Graduate Exhibition, 1982. Had a solo show at Lyric Theatre, Hammersmith, with a series at New Grafton Gallery from 1991. He was a part-time lecturer at Sir John Cass College, ran the NEAC school of drawing and offered short courses from his studio, in the Kew Bridge Steam Museum. His work was held by Arts Club, S G Warburg, the Museum of Modern Art at Smolyen, Bulgaria and Museo Taurino, Pamplona, Spain. Lived in Brentford, Middlesex.

William BOWYER 1926– Painter and teacher, father of the artists Jason and Francis Bowyer. He was educated at Burslem School of Art and Royal College of Art. Bowyer won the City of London Art Award in 1963. Went on to become head of fine art at Maidstone College of Art, 1971–82. As well as painting landscapes Bowyer was a noted portrait painter, his portraits of Arthur Scargill, the miners' leader, and Viv Richards, the cricketer, being bought by National Portrait Gallery in 1988. He was commissioned by Marylebone Cricket Club to paint the Bicentenary Game at Lord's in 1988. Bowyer was a member of RWS, RP and RBA and was honorary secretary of NEAC, also showing at RA, to which he was was elected in 1981, New Grafton Gallery and elsewhere. RA, Chantrey Bequest, Arts Council and other public collections hold his work. Lived in London.

E BOX 1919–1988 Painter in a poetic, naive style reminiscent of the work of the Douanier Rousseau, her real name was Eden Fleming. She adopted E Box when she began exhibiting in the late 1940s, having trained for two years at Regent Street Polytechnic School of Art, then being prevented from painting by the war years. Was married to Marston Fleming, senior research fellow at Imperial College, and with him travelled widely in continental Europe, North America, Russia, Africa and Asia, what she saw contributing to her pictures. An admirer of these was the artist Howard Hodgkin, who wrote an appreciation for the catalogue of her retrospective at David Carritt Ltd, 1981. Other retrospectives were held at St George's Hall, King's Lynn, 1956, and Fermoy Art Gallery there, 1979. Tate Gallery, Arts Council, Southampton City Art Gallery and Dunedin Art Gallery in New Zealand hold examples.

Richard BOX 1943– Painter, draughtsman, fabric collagist and teacher who studied fine art at Hastings School of Art, 1960–2, then Goldsmiths' College School of Art, 1962–5. Taught at Eltham Green Comprehensive School for three years, then at Avery Hill College. His exhibitions included a one-man at Woodlands Art Gallery, 1980, where flowers were the main theme.

Sonia BOYCE 1962– Painter, artist in collage and mixed media, born in London of parents from Barbados and Guyana. Studied at Stourbridge College of Art and Technology, 1980–3. Attended first National Conference of Black Artists in Wolverhampton in 1982. Artist-in-residence, Skinners Company's Girls' School, 1985. Using a combination of figurative and decorative images, Boyce was concerned to regenerate her cultural identity in what she considered a racist society. Solo shows included Black-Art Gallery, 1986, and Whitechapel Art Gallery, 1988. In 1998, Boyce had a show at Cornerhouse, Manchester, following a residency at Manchester University, based in the department of art history. A publication documented her time there. Boyce participated in The Other Story, Hayward Gallery and tour, 1989–90. Arts Council and Tate Gallery hold her work.

Hugh BOYCOTT BROWN 1909–1990 Painter and teacher, born in Bushey, Hertfordshire, where his father Allan Robert Brown was art master at the Royal Masonic School. Several other members of the family were artists (including Hugh's brother Michael, whose surname used a hyphen). Boycott Brown learned from his father and studied at the Margaret Frobisher School, Bushey. In 1929 he began teaching at Royal Masonic Junior

School, but he continued his studies in the evenings at Watford School of Art; during holidays studied at Heatherley's School under Frederic Whiting and Bernard Adams; and during the 1930s was much encouraged by Sir John Arnesby Brown. By then Boycott Brown had begun his association with the East Anglian coast, a major theme in his work, although he also painted a lot abroad. Catching fleeting effects of light and colour, especially sky effects, were the artist's strong point, using small panels and oils. In 1947 Boycott Brown bought a cottage in Blakeney, Norfolk, where he lived permanently after retiring in 1970. Later exhibitions included Southwell Brown Gallery, Richmond, 1985; Belgrave Gallery, 1986; and in 1991 there was a memorial show at Abbott and Holder. Signed work HBB and must not be confused with Hercules Brabazon Brabazon, the much-faked artist who did the same.

Michael BOYCOTT-BROWN 1910– Abstract artist, using collage, watercolour and oil, and teacher, brother of the painter Hugh Boycott Brown (who chose not to hyphenate the surname). He was born in Bushey, Hertfordshire, and studied at British Colombia College of Art in Vancouver; at Datillo Rubbo's School of Art, Sydney; at Académie Julian, Paris; and at Westminster School of Art under Mark Gertler and Blair Hughes-Stanton. Worked as an assistant at Zwemmer Gallery, 1938–9, and taught at Paston Grammar School, North Walsham, and at Norwich School of Art. He was an honorary member of Hampstead Artists' Council and a member of National Collage Society. Took part in numerous mixed exhibitions from 1958, with the Cambridge Society of Painters and Sculptors, at Arts Council Gallery, Cambridge, later ones including Eastern Open/93 and 95 Exhibitions at Fermoy Gallery, King's Lynn; Heffer Gallery, Cambridge, Laing Art Competition, 1995; Business Arts Fair, Islington, 1995; and English Artists at the Académie Julian, at Michael Parkin Gallery, 1996. By 1996 Boycott-Brown, who named Kurt Schwitters and Nicolas de Staël among key influences, had had two dozen solo shows, mainly in Cambridge, Heffer Gallery, Clare Hall and Gallery Soleil among the venues. In 1996 Boycott-Brown shared a show at Cambridge Arts, Ely, with his wife Eira John. They lived in Cambridge.

Arthur BOYD 1920– Painter and artist in variety of media such as tapestry, ceramics and sculpture, born in Melbourne, Australia, brother of the artist David Boyd. Boyd's grandfather Arthur Merric Boyd gave him lessons in painting and he had his first show in Melbourne aged 19. He attended evening classes at National Gallery of Victoria School of Art, then after war service founded a pottery with his brother-in-law John Perceval. That lasted until 1958, the following year settled in England, and then he divided his time between the two countries. Boyd was a powerful and mystical landscape and figure painter who drew on his own folklore associated with Aboriginal life. Among other activities he illustrated Pushkin's fairy tales; designed the décor for the ballet *Renard* for the 1961 Edinburgh Festival; and was commissioned to complete a big series of ceramic panels for the 400th Shakespeare Anniversary, also for Edinburgh. Participated in many group shows and had series of solo exhibitions at Fischer Fine Art, which represented him. Among retrospectives of his work were Whitechapel Gallery, 1962, and Richard Demarco, Edinburgh, 1969. Arts Council, National Gallery of South Australia in Adelaide and many other public galleries hold his work.

Cherith BOYD: *see* **Cherith McKINSTRY**

David BOYD 1924– Ceramic sculptor, painter and potter, grandson of the artist Arthur Merric Boyd and brother of the painter Arthur Boyd. His studies took place within the family and at Melbourne National Gallery School. In the 1950s Boyd became noted for his ceramics. He later became a painter to produce a series of large panels inspired by Arthur's work and influenced by his brother-in-law, John Perceval. Boyd lived in England, France and Spain, 1950–5; was president of the Contemporary Art Society in Melbourne, 1960–1; but resigned to accept an Italian Government Travelling Art Scholarship, which took him to Rome, after which he worked in England. Boyd's painting style was original and figurative with an almost sculptural depth. He showed in the Antipodean exhibition in Melbourne in 1959 and at Whitechapel Art Gallery in 1960. Examples of his pottery are in the National Museum of Modern Art, Tokyo, and other work is in Australian state galleries.

Graham BOYD 1928– Abstract painter and teacher, born in Bristol, who attended Watford School of Art, gaining his diploma in 1951, with a year at Institute of Education at London University until 1952. Was resident in Southern Rhodesia, 1953–5. Boyd was visiting artist at Reading University, 1975–83, having had a similar post at Plymouth State College, in America, 1972–3. Among other positions held was head of painting, Hertfordshire College of Art & Design. Boyd was influenced by American abstract painters, learning there the technique of working with large canvases on the floor, freeing him to apply paint in broad, sweeping bands of colour. Landscape was an inspiration. Mixed shows were participated in at Waddington Galleries from 1957; he also took part in John Moores Liverpool Exhibitions, LG and RA. Had a solo show at AIA in 1962, later ones including Spacex Gallery, Exeter, 1983. In 1994 he shared an exhibition with Katherine Gili at The Charterhouse Gallery. Walker Art Gallery in Liverpool holds his work. Lived in Chipperfield, Hertfordshire.

Jamie BOYD 1948– Painter, printmaker and draughtsman, born in Melbourne, Australia, son of the painter Arthur Boyd. Moved to London with his family in 1959, starting to paint full-time in 1965. In 1968 went to the Michael Karolyi Foundation in south of France on a painting award. Boyd was given technical instruction by his father and attended Central School for two weeks in 1969 on a diploma course, but was essentially self-taught. Turner, the Impressionists and Bonnard were influences. Although he went with his wife and children to live in New South Wales in 1978

Boyd remained based in London, returning to Australia every few years to paint the landscape. He had many solo exhibitions commencing with Bonython Galleries, Adelaide, 1966, later shows including Palazzo Strozzi, Florence, 1989, and Boundary Gallery, 1990. Universities of South Australia and Western Australia are among public collections with his works.

James BOYD 1943– Artist, notable as a printmaker, born in Dundee. He studied at Duncan of Jordanstone College of Art there and at Patrick Allan-Fraser School of Art, Hospitalfield, Arbroath. In 1982 was elected RE. Showed at RSA, International Print Biennales in Korea and Republic of China, at Mercury Gallery, International Art Fair in Basle, 1985, and in The Compass Contribution at Compass Gallery, Glasgow, 1990. Had a solo show at that gallery in 1976.

James Davidson BOYD 1917– Artist in oil, watercolour and enamel, and gallery curator, born in Glasgow. He was married to the artist Elizabeth A Ogilvie. Studied at Falkirk High and Technical Schools, then Glasgow School of Art, 1936–40. Was director of Dundee Art Galleries and Museums, 1949–82. Lived in Dundee, Angus.

Jane BOYD 1953– Painter, draughtsman and teacher, born and worked in London. She studied at Camberwell School of Arts and Crafts, 1971–5, and went on to teach at several art colleges. Her work was concerned with people and their surroundings, paintings being evolved over a long period. Group shows included McMurray Gallery, 1975, and Summer Show I at Serpentine Gallery, 1981.

John BOYD 1957– Painter, who studied at Slade School of Fine Art, 1976–8, after a foundation year at Newcastle College of Arts, then at Newcastle University, 1978–80. Boyd's group appearances included Northern Young Contemporaries, Manchester, in 1980; the Open Eye Gallery, Edinburgh, in 1987–8; and Christopher Hull Gallery, 1988. Boyd had a solo show at Below Stairs Gallery, Newcastle, in 1981, with others following in Newcastle, Antibes and Rotterdam until in 1989 Christopher Hull gave him a first one-man show in London.

John G BOYD 1940– Painter in oil and teacher, born in Stonehaven, Kincardineshire. He studied at Gray's School of Art, Aberdeen, 1958–62, and Patrick Allan-Fraser School of Art, Hospitalfield, Arbroath, 1961, teachers including Robert Henderson Blyth and David Michie. He moved to Glasgow in 1962 and became a part-time lecturer at the School of Art, 1967–88, later in further education. Boyd's main works were portraits, still life and composition. He was a member of RP and Royal Glasgow Institute of the Fine Arts, also showing at RA, RSA, Fine Art Society and Cormund Gallery in Glasgow, Open Eye Gallery and Bourne Fine Art in Edinburgh and Portland Gallery. Lillie Art Gallery, Milngavie; Paisley Museum & Art Gallery; and People's Palace in Glasgow hold his work. William Hardie Gallery, Glasgow, held a retrospective in 1994.

Margaret BOYD 1920– Painter and artist in ceramics, born in Bristol. She studied at West of England Art College there and went on to exhibit extensively, including LG, SEA, WIAC, RWA, Redfern and Leicester Galleries. Coventry Training College holds her work. Lived in Bristol.

Muriel BOYD: *see* **Muriel Boyd SANDEMAN**

Patrick BOYD 1960– Artist in a variety of media who studied at London College of Printing, West Surrey College of Art in Farnham and then holography at Royal College of Art. He went on to make a special study of holography. As well as gaining a Fulbright Arts Fellowship in Light Transmission and a fellowship at the Academy of Media Arts in Cologne, he was artist-in-residence at the Museum of Holography in New York, 1989–90. He took part in many solo and group exhibitions, contributing boxed constructions to Art in Boxes at England & Co, 1992.

BOYD and EVANS 1968– This is the year the partnership began of Fionnuala Boyd (born Welwyn Garden City, Hertfordshire, 1944) and Leslie Evans (born St Albans, Hertfordshire, 1945). Boyd studied at Leeds University, 1963–7, Evans at Leeds College of Art, 1967–8. Boyd and Evans used photography and painting to create their representational yet allegorical art, several examples of which are held by Arts Council. Their first solo show was held at Angela Flowers Gallery in 1971, after which many such exhibitions were held there. Boyd and Evans were twice prizewinners in the Bradford Biennale in the 1970s, also participating in Tokyo Biennale and John Moores Exhibition, Liverpool, both in 1974. In 1977–8 they travelled in America as Bicentennial Fellows, did work in that country and showed at Fendrick Gallery, Washington, in 1978. A Decade of Paintings toured from Milton Keynes Exhibition Gallery, 1982–3. In 1991 Boyd and Evans were invited by the Royal Geographical Society to join the Brunei Rainforest Project as artists-in-residence, and resulting paintings toured in England and abroad from Flowers East in 1993. Tate Gallery, Arts Council, British Council and many British provincial and foreign collections hold examples.

Glynn BOYD HARTE 1948– Painter in watercolour, draughtsman in coloured pencil and lithographer, and teacher, born in Rochdale, Lancashire, married to the artist Caroline Bullock. He studied at Royal College of Art, 1970–3, teachers including Brian Robb, Edward Bawden and Peter Blake. Taught part-time at Cambridge School of Art, 1973–83. Boyd Harte became a brother of the Art Workers' Guild. He illustrated the literary page of *The Times*, 1986–90, the *Sunday Telegraph* from 1990. Decorated the Dolphin Brasserie, 1986; started the Dolphin studio, for fabrics and wallpapers, 1989; and did murals for Crabtree & Evelyn in Rockefeller Center in New York, 1991. He produced *Venice*, 1988, and *Mr Harte's Holiday*, 1990, as well as publishing several limited edition books of lithographs, including *Metro-land*, with verse by Sir John Betjeman. Boyd Harte said that he intended to "carry on the English tradition of Bawden and Ravilious, topographical views and applied decorative art". He took part in innumerable group shows, his solo shows including a series at Francis Kyle Gallery from 1978, also at Albermarle Gallery from 1988 and Portland Gallery from 1992. Victoria & Albert Museum holds his work. Lived in Veules-les-Roses, northern France.

Bertha Stanfield BOYDELL 1899–1978 Sculptor and potter, born in Cobridge, Staffordshire. She attended Hanley School of Art under Ernest W Light, 1916–20, and Goldsmiths' College School of Art, 1920–2, under Frederick Marriott, thereafter for a short period assisting the potter Charles Vyse. She was married to the artist Phillip Boydell and signed her work B S B. Exhibited RA and RMS. Lived in London.

Phillip BOYDELL 1896–1984 As well as being an artist in oil and watercolour, Boydell was a notable designer and typographer whose career included positions as art master at Croydon and Blackheath Schools of art and at the Royal College of Art 1923–6. Born at Tyldesley, Lancashire, he studied art at Manchester School of Art and then at the Royal College of Art under Sir William Rothenstein and Robert Anning Bell. For 35 years from 1926 he was with the London Press Exchange, holding posts as art director and creative director. He designed the typeface known as Festival for the Festival of Britain in 1951. Because of his work on many national press and poster campaigns he was well qualified to write *The Artist in Advertising*. He was also a book illustrator. The Imperial War Museum and Trinity College, Oxford, own examples of his work. Married to the sculptor Bertha Stanfield Boydell. Lived in London.

Alma BOYES fl. from late 1970s– Sculptor, ceramist, designer and teacher who had a special interest in wildlife sculptures, notably of endangered species, developed during a long association with wildlife sculptor William Timym. Graduated as a ceramist from Bath Academy of Art in 1978, in 1980 gaining a British Council Scholarship to work in Mexico. From 1982 she attended North Staffordshire Polytechnic, concentrating on industrial production techniques, gaining her master's degree in 1984. Lectured at several universities and colleges and was included in 1st RWA Open Sculpture Exhibition, 1993. Lived in London.

Alicia BOYLE 1908–1997 Painter, quill pen draughtsman, muralist, printmaker, theatre designer and teacher. A rather solitary figure, her work was influenced by Surrealism and the light, colour and landscapes of Greece, Ireland and Spain. She was born in Bangkok, Thailand, and spent her early years in Limavady, County Londonderry, then London, where she studied at Clapham School of Art for four years, which she regarded as a waste of time. Won a scholarship to Byam Shaw School of Drawing and Painting, under Ernest Jackson. As a student had first picture accepted at RA in 1932; in 1934 gained a commission for a mural of St James' Park for the nurses' home of Great Ormond Street Hospital. After staying in the School for Artists in Mykonos, Greece, in World War II taught in Northampton. Showed with Leicester and Leger Galleries, where her use of light and colour, swirling imagery and allegory were praised. Boyle began to show in Ireland, at CEMA in Belfast and Waddington Gallery, Dublin. In 1971 settled at Reenacapull, County Cork, later living in Dublin. The Sweeny Series of paintings, from 1978, based on the mad, seventh-century northern king, was important. Had many solo shows, from Peter Jones Gallery, 1945, including Crawford Municipal Art Gallery, Cork, 1988, with a catalogue of work, 1932–88. That gallery, Bank of Ireland and Irish Arts Council hold her work.

Mark BOYLE 1934– (and family) Artist, born in Glasgow, who worked as one of a team, other members of which were Joan Hills, born in Edinburgh in 1936; and the Boyle children: Sebastian, born 1962, and Georgina, born 1964. Mark Boyle after Army service studied law at Glasgow University, 1955–6, then did a variety of jobs such as clerk and waiter. In addition, he put on exhibitions and took part in performance art. In 1964 he and Hills made a replica of a piece of ground, the beginning of a project called The Journey to the Surface of the Earth. The aim of this was to duplicate meticulously 1,000 portions of land, normally about six feet square, chosen by throwing darts at a map. A cast of the section was exactly painted to reproduce it. Boyle aimed at complete objectivity. He also produced a series of constructions using modern consumer waste. Exhibitions included ICA, 1969; Hayward Gallery, 1986–7; and abroad. Arts Council holds Boyle family work.

Judy BOYT fl. from 1980s– Sculptor and ceramist who trained at Wolverhampton and graduated with a master's degree in industrial ceramics from Stoke-on-Trent. She worked in the design industry for several years, producing figurative work for bone china and porcelain production. Her first freelance commission was a high-bas relief of polo playing for Garrard, the Crown Jewellers. Then in 1991 she won the British Sporting Art Trust Award. As an experienced rider Boyt was well equipped to create the statue of Grand National and Cheltenham Gold Cup winner Golden Miller; she also consulted trainers, jockeys and contemporary newsreels to finish the bronze, at Cheltenham race-course. Boyt handled royal commissions. She showed on the continent, in America and with the Tryon Gallery. The Morris Singer Foundry handled her work.

Rosemary BRABANT 1915– Painter, whose work had both Impressionistic and abstract influences, born in Cottesloe, Western Australia. She studied at Melbourne National Gallery Art School, at Hammersmith College of Art and in Italy. In 1970 was elected to Free Painters and Sculptors, and also exhibited at New Vision Centre, Woodstock Gallery, Cockpit Theatre, AIA and abroad in mixed and solo shows. Lived in London.

Dorothea BRABY 1909–1987 Illustrator, printmaker, commercial artist and painter, born and lived in London. After attending St Felix School in Southwold, between 1926–30 she studied at Central School of Arts and Crafts under John Farleigh, in Italy, at Heatherley's School of Fine Art, and in France. For 30 years she freelanced, Imperial Chemical Industries, *Radio Times* and *The Studio* using her work. Showed with SWA, Hampstead Artists' Council, Arts Council and abroad. Her instructional book *The Way of Wood Engraving* was published in 1953. Among books illustrated by her were John Keats' *Poems*, 1950, and Oscar Wilde's *Lord Arthur Savile's Crime*, 1954.

Arthur BRADBURY 1892–1977 Painter, etcher and teacher who before taking up painting was a merchant marine cadet; the sea and ships were fond subjects of his. Studied art at St John's Wood School of Art and Royal Academy Schools. Exhibited RA, RWA, RI, extensively at Walker's Galleries, and elsewhere. Imperial War Museum and Russell-Cotes Art Gallery and Museum, Bournemouth, hold his work. Lived at Sandbanks, Poole, Dorset.

George Eric BRADBURY 1881–1954 Sculptor and designer, born in London, son of the sculptor Frederick Bradbury. Studied at Lambeth School of Art, where he won several medals, after this studying stained glass design. Exhibited RA, Walker Art Gallery, Liverpool, in France and America. He specialised in memorial plaques and tablets. Lived at Ringmer, Sussex.

Susan BRADBURY 1949– Stained glass artist and teacher, born in Stoke-on-Trent, Staffordshire, who studied at Swansea College of Art, 1977–80, with Tim Lewis and Majory Walters. She was a fellow of both the British Society of Master Glass Painters and Royal Society of Arts and a member of the Scottish Glass Society. Among teaching posts were lecturing part-time at Sunderland Polytechnic, 1984–6, and in 1982 at the Architects' Institute, Leningrad, and Artists' Union, Moscow, and in 1990–1 to Indonesian art colleges. In 1981 Bradbury with Paul Lucky formed the Stained Glass Design Partnership and in 1981–3 she was town artist for Irvine New Town, completing nine commissions there. Bradbury's work was architectural, and included stained glass windows and screens at Newcastle School of Art; a window at Cockermouth School, Cumbria; and two windows for Laigh Kirk, Kilmarnock. Solo shows included Harbour Arts Centre, Irvine, 1984, and Northern Centre for Contemporary Arts, Sunderland, 1986. Worked at Kilmaurs, Kilmarnock.

Dorothy BRADFORD 1918– Painter and printmaker, born in Cockermouth, Cumberland. She studied at Liverpool College of Art, Leeds College of Art, Central School of Arts and Crafts and St Martin's School of Art, her teachers including Ruskin Spear and Maurice de Sausmarez. Showed at Bluecoat Gallery in Liverpool, Woodstock Gallery, at Royal Festival Hall and American Embassy in London, as well as abroad. She held a number of versatile roles during her career, such as art adviser to Ilkley Council, in Yorkshire, and official artist to the New Philharmonia Orchestra during its 1971 American tour. Continued to live and work mainly in the Liverpool area.

Geoffrey BRADFORD 1947– Maker of box sculptures from odds and ends of material found on various coasts. He was born in Leytonstone, southeast Essex. Exhibitions included Contemporary Art Fair in Islington, Beside the Seaside at Worcester City Art Gallery and Y Tabernacl International Open (where he was a prize winner), Machynlleth, all 1994; The Boat Show, Kilvert Gallery, Clyro, 1995; and Gordon Hepworth Fine Art at 23 Smith Street, 1997. Two-man exhibitions included Kilvert Gallery, 1994, and Cleveland Craft Centre, Middlesbrough, 1995.

Robert BRADFORD 1945– Painter in acrylic, film-maker and teacher, born in London. He studied at Beckenham School of Art, 1961–3, Ravensbourne College of Art, 1964–7, and Royal College of Art, 1967–70, his teachers including Brian Fielding and Alan Green. Taught part-time at Maidstone College of Art, but his exhibiting career was established in the west of England, where he showed with Arnolfini Gallery, in Bristol where he lived, Bath Festival Gallery and elsewhere; also showed at ICA. Sometimes signed work R B.

Eric BRADFORTH 1920– Artist born in Sheffield, Yorkshire, where he studied at the College of Art, later at Royal College of Art. Although destined for teaching, instead Bradforth took up an invitation to establish a graphic arts department for the Royal Artillery at Manorbier, Pembrokeshire, described to him as "Paradise". He built up a team of artists, photographers and model-makers which created resources used globally by the Royal Artillery. When the school closed he and his team moved to Larkhill, Wiltshire, but on retirement Bradforth returned to Pembrokeshire, settling in Tenby. Included in his War Office work was the building of a realistic Malaysian jungle; the drawing of a life-sized Russian bomber for a firing range; design of a battle scene in a display window at the main recruiting centre in the Strand so effective that it disrupted traffic; and creation of exhibitions and displays for the Royal Tournament and the Aldershot Tattoo. After retirement Bradforth painted a seagull's eye-view of sixteenth-century Tenby for the town's Museum – which gave him a solo show in 1995–6 – and a large mural depicting Tenby history in its market hall.

Florence BRADLEY 1902– Painter and artist in black-and-white, born at Gledhow, Yorkshire. After education at Leeds Girls' High School and privately in London, she studied art with Albert Ludovici, 1916–32, having settled in Hampstead. Elected UA, 1944, and was a founder member of the Milldon Art Society. Exhibited SWA, RBA and widely in the provinces.

Frank BRADLEY 1903– Painter, theatrical designer and chartered architect, born in Manchester, where he attended the College of Technology and School of Art, then the Newlyn School of Painting under Stanhope Forbes. He was a member of RCamA, also showing with UA, at Victoria & Albert Museum, at Manchester City Art Gallery, with the Lancashire and Cheshire Artists and abroad. Had a solo show at Salford Art Gallery in 1958. Lived in Chinley, Derbyshire.

Helen BRADLEY 1900–1979 Artist in oil and watercolour, born in Oldham, Lancashire, who attended the local Art School for two terms only in 1914, but did not start painting seriously until 1960. Her pictures reflected her childhood world in a naive style and were compared with those of L S Lowry, although she insisted they had nothing in common. Her work became very popular in reproduction through her books such as *And Miss Carter Wore Pink*, *The Queen Who Came To Tea* and *Miss Carter Came With Us*. Died in Wilmslow, Cheshire.

James Tomlinson BRADLEY 1919– Sculptor, painter and teacher, born in Droylsden, near Manchester. Although he was mainly self-taught, Bradley attended some life classes at Leeds College of Art He went on to teach maladjusted children for a time and also lectured part-time at Somerset College of Art, in Taunton. Bradley showed widely in the north of England, including Manchester Arts Club, MAFA, RWA and elsewhere, and had a one-man show at the New Vision Centre of his sculpture in 1958. Signed his work J B. Finally lived in Winscombe, Somerset, where he taught in a local school.

Martin BRADLEY 1931– Painter, draughtsman, muralist and sculptor, born London. He was an illegitimate orphan initially living in deprived circumstances, but eventually enabled through a wealthy father to attend St Paul's School. Ran away to sea at 14 and for several years served as a cabin boy on the Central and South American run, during which he began serious painting, mostly academic portraits of shipmates. Was a dishwasher or waiter in London restaurants and became well known to artistic circles as The Rimbaud of Soho because of his drinking, drug-taking and promiscuous life. A number of prestigious galleries, such as Gallery One, Gimpel Fils and the Redfern Gallery began to show his work. Went to Paris where he was taken up by Rudolphe Augustinci, director of the Rive Gauche Gallery, showing artists such as Max Ernst, Yves Tanguy and René Magritte. Notable British collectors such as Sir Roland Penrose, Sir Herbert Read and Dame Barbara Hepworth acquired Bradley's work. In 1962 Bradley decided to rethink his career, left Paris and travelled for many years in the Far East. Served for a period in the Spanish Foreign Legion, seeing action. This period cultivated Bradley's ability as a linguist; he was able to speak about ten languages, including Chinese, Japanese, Tibetan and Hindi. Became converted to Nichiren Shoshu Buddhism "which changed the whole foundation of my thinking". Bradley's work, largely abstract, is difficult to pigeonhole, having strong calligraphic, symbolic influences. It is in many international collections, including the Museum of Modern Art, New York. England & Co showed Paintings: 1950–1970, in 1988.

Sarah BRADPIECE 1954– Artist who studied at Hornsey College of Art, 1976–7, then Chelsea School of Art, 1978–9. Was included in 1981–2 Woodlands Art Gallery touring show of Greater London Arts Association award winners. Also showed in 1980 at ICA, Arnolfini Gallery in Bristol and Third Eye Centre, Glasgow, and in 1981 in Summer Show 3 at Serpentine Gallery. She worked as an animatronics designer for the *The Muppets* show on television. Lived in London.

Brian BRADSHAW 1923– Printmaker, painter and teacher, born in Bolton. Studied at Bolton and Manchester Schools of Art, at the Royal College of Art through a scholarship, 1948–51, then at the British School in Rome for two years. In the 1950s Bradshaw was appointed to teach etching at the Heginbottom Art School in Ashton-under-Lyne, where his northern directness was said to be appreciated by students, and in 1960 he took up the post of professor of fine art at Rhodes University, Grahamstown, South Africa. Bradshaw exhibited at RA, RE, with Liverpool Academy of Fine Arts and frequently at the Manchester Academy, as well as Crane Gallery, Manchester, and elsewhere. He was one of the painters contributing to a new post-war Lancashire realist school. Lived in Bolton and Fachwen, Caernarvonshire.

Constance BRADSHAW fl. from c.1898–1961 Painter in oil. Studied Spenlove School of Art. Exhibited RA, RBA, ROI, NEAC, Goupil Gallery, SWA – of which she was acting president for several years prior to World War II – Paris Salon, in the provinces and in New Zealand and Canada. Several of her landscapes, mainly in Wales, were reproduced. Lived at Bickley, Kent.

Dorothy BRADSHAW 1897– Oil and watercolour painter, born in Calcutta, India. She studied art under Jack Merriott in Polperro, Cornwall, and went on to exhibit at the Chelsea Art Society, Leighton House in Kensington, the RI and SWA. Lived at Budleigh Salterton, Devon.

George Fagan BRADSHAW 1887–1960 Marine painter who had a career as a Naval officer. Born in Belfast, he was educated at HMS Britannia, Dartmouth, gaining his artistic education in St Ives and Malta. Exhibited with RSMA, of which he was a founder-member, St Ives Art Society, RA and RSA. Sunderland Art Gallery holds his work. He lived at Ship Studio, St Ives, Cornwall, and was the husband of painter Kathleen Bradshaw.

Kathleen BRADSHAW 1904– Painter who was married to the artist George Fagan Bradshaw. She was closely associated with the artistic life of St Ives, Cornwall, where she studied, exhibited and was a member of the Society of Artists. Also showed at RA, ROI and Paris Salon.

Laurence BRADSHAW 1899–1978 Sculptor, painter and printmaker, born in Cheshire. After attending Liverpool University went to the School of Art there, 1916–7, under William Penn. Also worked in Frank Brangwyn's studio in the 1920s and studied sculpture in London and Paris. Exhibited at the RA, RWS, St George's Gallery, in Budapest, Prague and Moscow; one-man exhibitions at Architectural Association Gallery. His work is held by the Victoria & Albert Museum,

Brompton Oratory, Worthing Town Hall and the Marx-Engels Museum, Moscow. He made a number of portrait busts, including the journalist Hannen Swaffer for the London Press Club, Karl Marx, Lenin and the British Communist leader Harry Pollitt, some of these pieces being in the Soviet Union. In 1958 he was master of the Art Workers' Guild. Lived in London.

Peter BRADSHAW 1931– Painter, mostly in oil, born in London, who studied at Northampton School of Art, 1945–7. After leaving school he found no artistic employment, doing other jobs for 30 years, taking up painting as a hobby in 1961, then "found that my work was saleable, which eventually enabled me to turn professional". His pictures were "mainly railway subjects, landscapes and old-time gaslit scenes." Showed with UA, ROI and in the area of Northampton, where he lived, and had work published on greetings cards. Private collectors throughout the world held his pictures, which "featured trademarks of a cat and a robin".

Raymond Henry BRADSHAW 1918– Painter, draughtsman and teacher who studied at Bancroft's School, where he eventually taught art. Attended West Ham School of Art, 1935–6, then Westminster School of Art, 1936–8, where his teachers included Bernard Meninsky and Mark Gertler. Showed RA, RBA, RP and elsewhere. Lived in Loughton, Essex.

Kenneth Russell BRADY 1884–1953 Businessman, architect, artist, cartoonist and writer, born in Northern Ireland of a Donegal family. Settled in England in 1900, trained as an architect in Newcastle, moved to Manchester in 1909 and in 1910 joined the *Manchester Guardian* as a cartoonist and illustrator. After Army service as an officer in France in World War I, Brady returned to become business editor of the *Manchester Guardian Commercial.* In 1924 he became first director of the Liverpool Organisation, being responsible for the first Liverpool Week. In 1926 Brady joined Manchester Ship Canal Company, retiring in 1949 having held senior positions, remaining an architectural consultant. He had during these years written articles on industrial design, decorative art and architecture and showed at MAFA. Brady was responsible for persuading the editor of the *Manchester Guardian,* C P Scott, to sit for T C Dugdale, and he presented the portrait to Manchester Press Club in 1928. Brady's own portrait, by Ronald Allan, is held by Manchester City Art Gallery.

Philip BRAHAM 1959– Painter, born in Glasgow. He studied at Duncan of Jordanstone College of Art, Dundee, 1976–80, then was visiting artist at University of California, Los Angeles, 1981–2. Notable for his Scottish landscapes. Braham took part in Scottish Art Today – Artists At Work, a 1986 Edinburgh Festival exhibition, and the following year in The Vigorous Imagination at Scottish National Gallery of Modern Art, Edinburgh. Solo exhibitions include Glasgow Arts Centre, 1987; Scottish Gallery, Edinburgh, 1988; and Raab Gallery, 1989. Lived in Edinburgh.

Kate BRAINE 1964– Figurative sculptor, who learned marble carving at Carrara, Italy, and attended Heatherley's School of Fine Art followed by City & Guilds of London Art School. Commissions included Ian Board, Saffron Aldridge and David Tang. Braine also took body casts. Showed widely in London, including Birch & Conran and Berkeley Square Gallery, and was included in Sixteen Sculptors at Sladmore Contemporary, 1997.

Percy BRAISBY 1910– Sculptor, potter and teacher who studied at Gloucester and Cheltenham Colleges of Art. He became head of painting at the Gloucestershire College of Art in Cheltenham, where he lived, in 1964 converting Barratts Mill into a studio, helped by his assistant Miss D G Sutton. Braisby showed at Royal Society of Arts, RWA, the 1951 Festival of Britain, was a prizewinner at the International Eisteddfod in Wales in 1952 and in 1962 was included in 19 Young Sculptors at Hillfield Gardens, Gloucester. Cheltenham Art Gallery & Museums holds Braisby's clay figure of a potter, of about 1950.

Barbara BRAITHWAITE 1930– Artist in variety of media, latterly with an interest in stained glass, born in Sheffield, Yorkshire. She studied with Eric Jones at the College of Art there and at Slade School of Fine Art under William Coldstream, Lucien Freud, Thomas Monnington and Graham Sutherland. Between about 1960 and 1988 Braithwaite stopped painting while raising a family, resuming after her husband's death. Showed at ICA, Beaux Arts Gallery, Zilla Bell in Thirsk and Brantwood Gallery, Coniston, having solo exhibitions at Old School Workshops, Middleham, and at Swaledale Festival, North Yorkshire. Arts Council holds her work. Lived in Horsehouse, Leyburn, North Yorkshire.

Christopher BRAMHAM 1952– Painter and teacher, born in Bradford, Yorkshire. Although his father was a newsagent and his mother a school dinner lady, who split up when Bramham was young, he was enabled to spend some time at a preparatory school, but failed Common Entrance. An old part-work magazine inspired Bramham to be an artist. He attended Bradford College of Art, 1970; his desire for a more traditional teaching and to work from nature took him to Kingston School of Art, 1971–3, after which he was a part-time teacher in schools, 1974–86, by now with a family and hard up. A meeting with Lucien Freud in 1982 led to Bramham showing with Agnew, although he was several times rejected by the RA, so he became disillusioned with the selection procedure. Had a show with Fine Art Society in 1988, then from 1992 had a series of highly successful exhibitions with Marlborough Fine Art, craftsmanlike and intense landscapes, still lifes and interiors. Bramham admired Freud (who owned his work and painted him and his family), Bacon, Andrews, Auerbach and, among foreign artists, Giacometti, Picasso and Matisse. Lived in Richmond, Surrey.

Leonard Griffiths BRAMMER 1906–1994 Painter and printmaker, born in Burslem, Stoke-on-Trent; he eventually became supervisor of art for the local Education Authority, 1951–69. Studied at Burslem School of Art, 1923–6, under Gordon Forsyth, then Royal College of Art, 1926–30, where his teachers included

William Rothenstein, Malcolm Osborne and Robert Austin. Was elected RE in 1956, also showing RA. Victoria & Albert Museum, Tate Gallery and Ashmolean Museum, Oxford, hold his work. Brammer was noted for his depictions of the industrial landscape of the Potteries, its ovens, kilns, workshops and canals. Lived finally in Porthmadog, Gwynedd.

Walter BRAND 1872–1959 Artist in pencil and wash; architect, born in Ipswich, Suffolk. Studied at Ipswich School of Art and Heatherley's School of Fine Art. Exhibited RBSA, RIBA, Leicester Society of Artists and extensively in the Midlands. Lived in Leicester.

Margaret Elizabeth BRANDEBOURG 1926– Sculptor, born in Surbiton, Surrey. She studied at Kingston School of Art and at the Royal Academy Schools under Denis Dunlop. Lived in Kingston upon Thames, Surrey.

Stephen BRANDES 1966– Artist working in mixed media, sometimes on a huge scale, born in Wolverhampton, Staffordshire. He studied at Bournville College of Art and Design, 1984–5, and at Bath Academy and Bath College of Higher Education in 1985–8. Exhibited widely in West Country and gained RWA award in 1988–9. In 1989–90 his picture (The Return of) The Prodigal Farmer appeared in John Moores Liverpool Exhibition. One of Brandes' more remarkable achievements was his Hill Figure for Bath, a 70-foot drawing in 12 tons of Bath stone. Lived in Bath, Avon.

Marion BRANDIS 1956– Mural and mosaic artist and teacher, born in Hamburg, West Germany, who had a studio in Brighton, Sussex, from 1985. She gained an honours degree at Edinburgh College of Art, 1977–81, with a postgraduate diploma in 1982, then was junior fellow in ceramics at South Glamorgan Institute of Higher Education, Cardiff, 1983–4. Teaching included Loughborough College of Art and Central St Martins School of Art, and she was an external course adviser at Edinburgh College of Art. Among Brandis' awards was a South East Arts Travelling Grant to visit Hispano-Mooresque architecture in Spain, 1993. Exhibitions included Design for Living, Gardner Arts Centre, Brighton, 1987; garden show at Oxford Gallery, 1989; and a similar exhibition at Barbican Centre, 1991. Commissions included mosaic mural for Ashford Library, Kent, with Nicholas Martin, 1990; tiled mural for Northampton Guildhall extension, 1993; and large glass tile mosaics for Govan Housing Association, 1994.

Rolf BRANDT 1906– Painter, designer, illustrator and teacher. Although born in Hamburg, Brandt was British. Lived permanently in England from early 1930s and as well as studying art in Paris attended Amédée Ozenfant's London school. Showed at LG, Arts Council, AIA and had several one-man shows in England and Italy, one at Paris Gallery, London. Did some mural work; had illustrations in publications such as *The Listener* and *Radio Times*; and illustrated a number of books, including works by Balzac and Rabelais, his pictures often having a droll but eerie quality. Taught for some years at London College of Printing and Byam Shaw School of Drawing and Painting. Lived in London.

Frank BRANGWYN 1867–1956 Decorative painter often on a large scale, creator of murals and printmaker. Born in Bruges, Belgium, where a museum to commemorate him was opened in 1936, Brangwyn had tuition from his architect father, but was mainly self-taught. After working in William Morris' business, 1882–4, Brangwyn went to sea and he retained a love of the sea and travel. As a young man lived in Kent, selling drawings, then from the mid-1880s started to exhibit at the RA and to establish his reputation which soon became international. Won a gold medal at Chicago Exhibition for his picture The Convict Ship. Elected RA in 1919. By then he had painted mural decorations for Skinners' Hall, 1904–9. Other notable such large-scale works were murals commissioned for the House of Lords in 1926, rejected and acquired by Swansea City Centre seven years later; and murals for the Rockefeller Center, New York, 1932, where Brangwyn's collaborators were José Maria Sert and Diego Rivera. A 1924 retrospective in London was extremely successful, being opened by the new Labour prime minister Ramsay MacDonald. Brangwyn exhibited prolifically, notably at Fine Art Society and RA. Received many academic honours. Further retrospectives followed in Worthing, 1951, RA, 1952, and a memorial show was held at the Fine Art Society, 1958. Brangwyn, who died at his Ditchling, Sussex, home, remains famous for his grandiose and colourful pictures of exotic and historical scenes. Tate Gallery holds his work. In *Brangwyn Talks* his friend William de Belleroche records the artist's opinions.

Leslie Maurice Leopold BRANGWYN 1896– Wood engraver and etcher, born in London. He studied at Goldsmiths' College School of Art with Stanley Anderson and James Bateman. Became a member of the Art Workers' Guild in 1949, retiring in 1966. Exhibited RA, NS, RCamA, RSA and Paris Salon. Lived in Orpington, Kent.

Alison BRANIGAN 1969– Sculptor, medallist, jeweller, photographer and performance artist, sometimes working in mixed media, who was educated in Scarborough, Yorkshire. She completed a foundation year, diploma credit, at Harrogate College of Art and Technology, 1988–9; gained a fine arts honours degree at Birmingham Institute of Art and Design, 1989–92; then from 1995 was on the master's degree applied art and visual culture course at Sir John Cass, London Guildhall University. Her work experience included art classes at Salvation Army hostel, Digbeth; assisting the sculptors Malcolm Poynter and Bo Carter; and working on the restoration of St Paul's statue in St Paul's Cathedral. Awards included Jerwood Allied Craft Award, first prize, 1996, and joint first prize at the Birmingham Assay Office Silver Design Awards, 1997. In 1996 was elected an associate member of the Society of Numismatic Artists and Designers. Took part in many mixed shows, one-mans including Sad Tidings at Simmons Gallery, 1997. Lived in London.

Edward Eaton BRANNAN 1886–1957 Painter, printmaker and potter, studied under Herbert Rollett at Grimsby School of Art. His sons were the artists Noel Brannan and Peter Brannan. Exhibited RA, Walker Art Gallery, Liverpool, RWS, RCamA, UA and Paris Salon. One-man show at Usher Gallery, Lincoln, which holds his work. He was a member of the AIA and Lincolnshire Artists' Society. Lived in Lincoln.

Noel BRANNAN 1921– Artist and teacher, born in Tynemouth, Northumberland, who worked in oil, watercolour and felt pen and wash. He studied at Lincoln School of Art, 1947–51, then Leicester College of Art, 1951–2, although he had begun painting in 1940. Taught art for 28 years, taking up full-time art in 1980. Was one of the painters chosen for Jack Beddington's 1957 book *Young Artists of Promise*. Became member of AIA, also showing with RA, RBA, LG and elsewhere including Lincolnshire and South Humberside Artists' Society. Brannan liked to work on the spot, with an inclination for industrial subjects. Had a solo show at Willoughby Memorial Trust Art Gallery, 1985, in Corby Glen. Usher Gallery, Lincoln, and Nuneaton Art Gallery hold his work. Lived in Burbage, Leicestershire.

Peter BRANNAN 1926– Painter, draughtsman, printmaker and teacher, born in Cleethorpes, Lincolnshire. He studied at Grimsby School of Art, then Leicester College of Art. He taught mainly in Newark, Nottinghamshire. Brannan was elected RBA in 1960 and was president of Lincolnshire and South Humberside Artists. He showed in mixed exhibitions at RA, NEAC, LG and elsewhere, having a series of solo shows with Trafford Gallery, one at Usher Gallery, Lincoln, 1978, and a retrospective at Goldmark Gallery, Uppingham, in 1995. Usher Gallery, Grundy House Museum in Blackpool and Lincolnshire Education Committee hold his work. Brannan admired the work of French Post-Impressionists, also Cotman and Chardin. Lived in Welbourn, Lincoln.

Allan BRANSBURY 1942– Sculptor and teacher, born in Jersey, Channel Islands. He studied at Bristol's West of England College of Art, then University of London Institute of Education. He next studied in North America for a while. Was especially interested in large-scale sculptures sited in natural settings. After serving as artist-in-residence at the University of Sussex, Brighton, in 1976, Bransbury was from 1977–80 principal of Bromley Centre for Arts and Crafts, then was attached to the Highlands and Islands Development Board, in Scotland, living for some years at North Kessock, Inverness.

Rosa BRANSON 1933– Painter, artist in embroidery and fabric collage, daughter of the artist Clive Branson, she married and divorced the painter Alan Hopkins, who was diagnosed a schizophrenic. She had four years at Camberwell School of Arts and Crafts and one at the Slade School of Fine Art, but regarded herself "as a classical painter". Dissatisfied with her art school training Branson came to spend six years in the National Gallery, copying and learning the techniques of the Renaissance. Her early work stemmed from painstaking sketches of London scenes, such as cafés; there was a period of embroidery pictures and fabric collages; many years painting still life, portraits and landscapes; then after the death of her second husband Branson, although an athiest, painted a long series of heavenly scenes and Red Cross panoramas in which friends and neighbours were used as models. These, like her many still lifes of fruit, were on a large scale. By the mid-1990s she had completed almost 500 pictures. Mixed exhibitions included RA, ROI, LG, Young Contemporaries, Royal Festival Hall and Mermaid Theatre. Had a solo show at Woodstock Gallery in 1962, later ones including Lyric Theatre, 1987, Highgate Cemetery Chapel, 1992, and Brontë Restaurant, Oulton Hall, 1993. Branson won the Morrison International Decanter Design Competition and was guest at the 1993 Woman of the Year lunch at Savoy Hotel. De Vere Hotel Group, Marquess of Sligo, Lambeth Palace and the Nuffield Foundation hold examples. Lived in London.

John BRASON 1924– Painter, draughtsman and teacher, who was born in South Shields, County Durham. Attended the School of Art there, 1940–4, then the Royal College of Art, 1944–7, under Gilbert Spencer, Percy Horton and Eric Gill. For a time taught at St Martin's School of Art and Camberwell School of Arts and Crafts. Brason also had musical and theatrical interests. Exhibited RA, Arts Council and elsewhere. Lived in London.

David BRASSINGTON 1947– Collagist, painter in oil and screenprinter, born in Coventry, Warwickshire. He studied art in Leamington Spa with Trevor Halliday, also the history of art at Ealing Polytechnic and at Camden Institute. Had solo shows at Square Gallery, 1990, and with David Birkett, 1991. Kurt Schwitters, Robert Rauschenberg, John Walker and Juan Gris were influences. Lived in London.

Jean BRATBY: *see* **Jean COOKE**

John BRATBY 1928–1992 Painter, novelist and teacher, born in London. He studied at Kingston School of Art, 1948–9, then Royal College of Art, 1951–4. Married the painter Jean Cooke, 1953, marriage dissolved in 1977. Through the 1950s Bratby regularly showed at Beaux Arts Gallery in solo exhibitions, the first being in 1954. He won Abbey Minor, Italian Government and Royal College of Art Minor Travelling Scholarships in 1954, the year following receiving a prize in the *Daily Express* Young Artists Competition. Bratby taught at Carlisle College of Art, 1956, then at Royal College of Art, 1957–8. He represented Britain at Venice Biennale in 1956 and gained the Guggenheim Award, and in 1958. In that year he was commissioned to paint the pictures for the film of Joyce Cary's novel *The Horse's Mouth*. He wrote his own first novel, *Breakdown*, 1960. Bratby was a prolific exhibitor, having painted over 1,500 portraits alone by 1991, when a retrospective was held by National Portrait Gallery, which holds his work. In the same year there was a solo show at Albemarle Gallery and the Mayor Gallery included him in The Kitchen Sink Artists Revived, which drew attention to his

1950s pictures. There was another solo show at Sue Rankin Gallery, with a retrospective at The Catto Gallery in 1997. Bold images, thick paint and primary colours were Bratby's trademarks. He was elected RA in 1971. Lived in Hastings, Sussex.

Allin BRAUND 1915– Painter, printmaker and teacher, born in Northam, Devon. Studied at Bideford School of Art, 1932–6, then Hornsey School of Art, 1936–9. He went on to teach at Hornsey College of Art and was ultimately a lecturer at Middlesex Polytechnic. Showed widely, including RE, Redfern Gallery, St George's Gallery, Zwemmer Gallery, RA and abroad. Arts Council, British Council, Victoria & Albert Museum and a number of provincial and foreign galleries bought his work. Lived for many years in London, where his panels, representing abstract motion, on the Harrow Road elevation of Paddington Green police station were a notable feature.

Phyllis BRAY 1911–1991 Painter, illustrator, muralist and collector, born in Norwood, London. She was married for several years to the painter John Cooper, until the marriage was dissolved, their daughter being the artist Philippa Cooper, then married Eric Phillips. Her father was William de Bray, who had been attaché to Maria Fyodorovna, mother of the murdered Tsar Nicholas II. As a child she wanted to be an artist and claimed to be the youngest scholarship student at the Slade School of Fine Art when she joined it, was a favourite of Henry Tonks and won a Slade Drawing Prize. In the mid-1920s Cooper spearheaded formation of the East London Group of painters with which Phyllis Bray was closely involved. Her connection with the East End was strengthened when she completed three large murals for the People's Palace in the Mile End Road. For over 40 years helped the mural painter Hans Feibusch, working in many churches around Britain. Bray joined LG in 1934, showing with it regularly, also at Leicester Galleries, Wildenstein, Drian Gallery and Mignon Gallery, Bath. She also did a large volume of publicity, including work for Shell, the John Lewis Partnership and London Transport; her book illustrations included Alison Uttley's *A Traveller in Time*. In the 1950s and 1960s Bray collected medieval and Renaissance jewellery for modest sums; the Phyllis Phillips collection was sold at Christie's in 1989 for £576,000. Parkinson's Disease latterly prevented her from painting, and she died in Hampstead, north London. Memorial show at Collyer-Bristow, 1998.

Richard BRAY 1951– Sculptor in wood and photographer, born in London. He studied photography at the Polytechnic of Central London before turning full-time to sculpture and carving wood. Bray created abstract works which explored and exploited the nature of each piece of timber. He was included in the three-man exhibition Sculpting at Fine Art Society, 1996. Bray lived and worked near Cambridge.

Antanas BRAZDYS 1939– Sculptor in stainless steel, and teacher, born in Lithuania. He studied at Art Institute of Chicago, 1962–4, then Royal College of Art. Went on to become senior sculpture lecturer at Cheltenham College of Art for a time. Brazdys participated in a number of influential group exhibitions, including Towards Art II, Arts Council, 1965; Open-air Sculpture Exhibition, Battersea Park, 1966; and the RA's British Sculptors '72. Solo shows included Hamilton Galleries, 1965; Arnolfini Gallery, Bristol, 1966; and Annely Juda Fine Art, 1971. A tie-up with a New York dealer meant that he did not have solo shows for some time in Britain, although he did show at RA and did commissioned work for Harlow New Town, some on a very large scale. Arts Council and British Steel Corporation hold his work. Lived in Tewkesbury, Gloucestershire, and had a studio in London.

Alfred Keeley BRAZIER 1894–1979 Painter and craftsman who originally began as an apprentice ceramic artist at Coalport China Works, in Ironbridge. Then studied art under William Hentry Gates at Coalbrookdale School of Art, 1911–15, later at Birkenhead and Hammersmith Schools of Art. Early on he favoured still life in oil, but later turned to landscape watercolours. He was a skilled carver. Member of BWS, also showing with UA, RWA, RBSA, RCamA and NWG and was a founder and chairman of Merioneth Artists' Society. Lived in Barmouth, Merionethshire.

Charles BREAKER 1906–1985 Painter and teacher, born in Bowness-on-Windermere, Westmorland. He worked with his father as a boatbuilder, then during the 1930s travelled widely in Europe with his lifelong friend, the painter and illustrator Eric Hiller, who was to show extensively at Goupil Gallery. When World War II broke out Breaker returned to England and worked for Vickers Armstrong in the drawing office. In 1947 he and Hiller moved to Cornwall, settling in Newlyn where they founded the Newlyn Holiday Sketching Club, This they ran for 15 years, and when Hiller died Breaker moved to Penzance. Showed widely in Britain and on the continent, in later years his work being exhibited by Nina Zborowska Fine Paintings, Painswick.

Ian BREAKWELL 1943– Artist using a variety of media; teacher; administrator. Born in Derby, Breakwell studied at the local College of Art, 1961–5. In 1967 he staged his performance Restaurant Operations at Exeter Festival and Bristol Arts Centre. In 1969 Unword 1 was staged at Compendium Bookshop, Unword 2 following at ICA. By then Breakwell had established his preoccupation with the relationship between word and image, which was to appear in many forms in ensuing years. After being visual arts director at Bristol Arts Centre, 1967–8, Breakwell taught at Somerset College of Art, 1969–73. Other examples of the artist's output were: one-man shows at Angela Flowers Gallery, Arnolfini Gallery and Scottish Arts Council Gallery, Edinburgh; the making of the films *Repertory* and *The Journey* in the 1970s; and his publication of *Diary Extracts*, *Continuous Diary* and *Fiction Texts*. Arts Council holds his work.

William Ramsden BREALEY 1889–1949 Portrait painter in oil, born in Sheffield where he studied at the School of Art, then

Royal College of Art. Exhibited RA, RBA especially, ROI, RSA and Paris Salon, where he gained an Honourable Mention in 1925. The Ministry of Information bought his picture The Gas Mask during World War II. Lived in London.

Antony BREAM 1943– Extensively internationally travelled landscape painter and etcher, born London. He studied with Peter Greenham at Royal Academy Schools, 1964–7. Among Bream's shows were Fine Art Society, 1979; Jonathan Poole Gallery, New York, 1983; Richmond Gallery, 1988; and a solo exhibition at Cadogan Contemporary, 1992. Bream did a lot of commissioned work. In 1981 he travelled to North Yemen on an expedition, preparing work for a book and two exhibitions; in 1985 he painted in Colorado for *Forbes Magazine*; and in 1989–90 he engaged in industrial commissions to paint gold mining in Spain and cable-laying in Bermuda.

Evelyn BREARLEY 1906–1985 Painter and teacher, born in Douglas, Isle of Man. After education in England and Wales she attended Manchester College of Art, teaching part-time while still a student. A number of further school appointments followed in the north of England and finally Wales, where she was also a part-time teacher for the Workers' Educational Association and Gwent County Council. Showed in groups at Bradford City Art Gallery, Paris Salon, SEA, SWG, NEAC and widely in the provinces; one-man shows included Newport Museum and Art Gallery, Exeter University and University College, Cardiff. CASW holds her work. This was representational and abstract, strong in colour and line. Lived in Griffithstown, Pontypool, Gwent.

Alan BREESE 1922– Sculptor. Breese for a while attended the London County Council School of Building in Brixton. His art studies were pursued at Richmond School of Art under the sculptor James Wedgwood; City and Guilds School, Kennington; London School of Art with the sculptor Edgar Allan Howes; and drawing with Ralph Middleton Todd and with Vivian Pitchforth at Camberwell School of Arts and Crafts. For some time Breese was involved with work on St Paul's Cathedral. Exhibited RA, LG, RBA and elsewhere. Breese's plaster Head of a Painter is illustrated in Eric Newton's monograph *British Sculpture 1944–1946*. Lived in London.

Jane BRENNAN 1966– Producer of site-specific paintings, recalling Renaissance frescoes, as included in New Contemporaries, 1996, at Tate Gallery, Liverpool, and Camden Arts Centre. She was born in Edinburgh, and gained a fine art degree at Central St Martin's School of Art and Design, 1989–92, then a postgraduate higher diploma in sculpture from Slade School of Fine Art, 1993–5. She was included in a number of 1995 exhibitions: Gasworks Group Show at Gasworks Gallery, Cardoso Art 95 in Cardoso, Italy, and White Trash at Lost-in-Space.

Robert BRENNAN 1925– Painter, printmaker and illustrator, born in London, who had no formal art training. Brennan began painting seriously in 1950, after wartime Army service in Italy and work as a medical laboratory technician at Hammersmith Hospital. After travelling, including living on a boat, in the early 1950s, moved to Cornwall, settling in Penzance, showing with the Penwith Society in 1953. Was elected a member in 1957. Brennan began making monotypes in 1958, "after watching the poet W S Graham make some during all-night sessions"; in 1962 did illustrations for *Jazz Monthly* and *Audio and Record Review*; and in 1970 spent three months in Amsterdam. Had a first solo show at Objet d'Art in Action, with a catalogue introduction by David Lewis, 1956. Later solo shows included Orion Gallery, Penzance, 1973, and Mill House Gallery, Penzance, 1990.

Sara BRENNAN 1963– Artist who produced woven tapestries, using differently coloured square and rectangular shapes, as in New Art in Scotland, Centre for Contemporary Arts, Glasgow, 1994. She was born and lived in Edinburgh, where she attended the College of Art, 1982–6, after National Arts School, Papua New Guinea, 1981–2. Exhibitions included Artist in Industry, tour including Aberdeen Art Gallery, 1989; Interwoven, Abbot Hall, Kendal, 1990; Fine Art Consultancy, Shad Thames Gallery, 1992; and Artist of the Week, Collective Gallery, Edinburgh, 1994.

Catherine BRENNAND 1961– Painter and graphic artist who studied at Bishop Otter College, Chichester. Work in the construction industry as a technical and graphic artist promoted Brennand's interest in architecture. She employed watercolour with wax resist to create a rich pattern of textures and travelled widely in Britain, on the continent and in America for inspiration. John Piper, Graham Sutherland and Winslow Homer were influences. Won a Winsor & Newton Young Artist's Award at RI in 1991, then a Frank Herring & Sons award for the Best Painting of an Architectural Subject in 1992, after which she was elected RI. Also exhibited at The Linda Blackstone Gallery, Pinner.

Michael BRENNAND-WOOD 1952– Artist, designer and lecturer, born in Bury, Lancashire, who attended Bolton College of Art, 1969–72; gained an honours degree in textiles at Manchester Polytechnic, 1972–5; and his master's degree in textiles at Birmingham Polytechnic, 1975–6. In 1977 he established a studio in Bedfordshire, where he settled at Sandy, and was largely concerned with the construction of individual textiles/mixed-media works. Brennand-Wood was from 1977 associated with Goldsmiths' College as a part-time lecturer, being senior lecturer, 1983–9. Other teaching posts included University of Ulster, Royal College of Art, Glasgow School of Art, Middlesex and Trent Polytechnics and elsewhere, and he lectured extensively overseas. He was on many committees, notably for the Crafts Council and Eastern Arts Board, and held extensive British and overseas residencies. Among awards received were medallist, Munich Exempla Exhibition, 1980; British Council Award and Travel Grant and a Major Award, Visual Arts/Crafts Board of the Australia Council, all 1988; and Distinguished Visiting Fellow, British Council, Kyoto City University, Japan, 1990–1. He was curator for the Japanese Fibre Exhibition Restless Shadows, which toured the United

Kingdom, 1991–2. Commissions included Law Courts, Ilkeston Council, 1975–6; Cheshire County Council, 1980–2; LRC International, 1987; and in 1989 Automobile Association, Basingstoke, and Robin Gibson/St Stephen's Cathedral, Brisbane, Australia. Brennand-Wood took part in numerous group shows, solo exhibitions latterly including Galerie RA Amsterdam, Netherlands, and Gallery/Gallery, Kyoto, Japan, both 1990, and Canberra Institute of Arts, Australia, 1991. Victoria & Albert Museum, Crafts Council, National Museum of Modern Art, Kyoto, and many other local authority, overseas public gallery and corporate collections hold examples, including Conoco in Warwick; its work, Overlays, was made of recycled books and tea tins.

Angus BRENT 1903– Painter of landscapes and seascapes, whose full name was Ralph Richard Angus Brent. He studied at St Martin's School of Art with Bertram Nicholls. Exhibited widely in New Zealand and in Britain, including RA, RBA, Fine Art Society and in the provinces. Much of his work was done in Hampshire, where he showed in Southampton and Bournemouth and lived at Fordingbridge.

Gillian BRENT 1959– Abstract sculptor, born in Bedfordshire. She attended Wimbledon School of Art, 1978–81, then St Martin's School of Art, 1981–3, for postgraduate studies. In 1984–5 her work appeared in Have You Seen Sculpture From The Body?, Tate Gallery and tour. She shared a four-man show at Woodlands Art Gallery, 1990. Had a solo show at Worcester City Art Gallery, 1988. Worked in Sheffield, Yorkshire.

Dorothy BRETT 1883–1977 Painter of figure subjects and latterly of Indian life, born in London, daughter of Reginald Brett, 2nd Viscount Esher. She studied at Slade School of Fine Art, 1910–16. Showed in England at NEAC and elsewhere and in America, having a retrospective at America British Gallery, New York, 1950. She had gone to live in New Mexico in 1924 with the writer D H Lawrence and his wife. She remained there, dying in Taos. In 1933 she published the book *Lawrence and Brett: a Friendship*. Tate Gallery holds her work. Although formally known as The Honourable Dorothy Brett she came to be known to friends just by her surname.

William BRETT 1932– Painter, notably a watercolourist, born in London. Showed throughout his working life, varying from a commercial art studio to Dover Harbour Board. Showed with South London Artists' Group from 1965 and was an active member of the Arts Group in Sandwich, Kent, where he lived, Canterbury Society of Art and East Kent Art Society. Had a solo show at Deal Library Gallery in 1995.

Walter BRETTINGHAM 1924– Painter in oil and teacher, born in London. He studied at Sir John Cass College, 1948–51, when Bainbridge Copnall was principal; St Martin's School of Art, 1951–3, with Frederick Gore as head of painting; and Bournemouth College of Art, 1953–4. Taught at several schools from 1954, finally art and art history at Spelthorne College, Ashford, Middlesex, 1959–81. Was a life member of National Society for Education in Art & Design. Brettingham's mixed shows included Plymouth Artists, 1957; Swindon Artists, 1958; ROI from 1963 – winning a prize in 1987, but being disqualified for being over age; Furneaux Gallery, Wimbledon, 1970; Staines Artists, 1973; and Holkham Gallery, 1982. After a solo show at Berystede Hotel, Ascot, in 1972, later exhibitions included Bloomsbury Gallery, London University, 1984. Lived in Virginia Water, Surrey.

David BREUER-WEIL 1965– Artist who was born and lived in London, who completed a foundation course at St Martin's School of Art, but opted to read English at Cambridge University. Although working in a responsible job, he was prolific as an artist, as shown in his solo exhibition at Boundary Gallery, 1997. Breuer-Weil produced autobiographical paintings and drawings; landscapes, often tiny, with an abstract, dreamlike quality; and sculptures, based mainly on the male figure, made from smashed rocks which were reassembled.

Henry Charles BREWER 1866–1949 Painter, especially in watercolour, son of the artist Henry William Brewer. Studied at Westminster School of Art with Fred Brown. Exhibited extensively at Fine Art Society and RA, RI of which he was a member, extensively in provinces and abroad. Lived in London, views of which he painted.

Paul BREWER 1946– Photographer and draughtsman whose methods included photo-mechanical printmaking. He was born and based in Cardiff, from 1972 having a studio there. Studied at Newport College of Art, 1965–9; from 1972–3 was at University of Wales Institute of Science and Technology; from 1973–4 at Cardiff College of Art's art education department. Brewer won a series of WAC Awards and was in its collection, also in National Museum of Wales, Cardiff, and Newport Museum and Art Gallery. Exhibited widely in Wales, including WAC tour of Recent Purchases by CASW in 1979, and had a series of solo shows, including Oriel, Cardiff, 1981.

Martyn BREWSTER 1952– Painter, printmaker and teacher, born in Oxford. He studied, 1970–1, at Hertfordshire College of Art and Design, then from 1971–5 at Brighton Polytechnic. In 1977 he gained Eastern Arts Awards. Brewster went on to teach for a time at East Herts College, being a visiting lecturer at Winchester School of Art. As well as participating in many group shows, Brewster showed solo frequently. These included Harlow Playhouse Gallery, Essex, 1982; Bury St Edmunds Art Gallery, 1984; Warwick Arts Trust, 1986; and The Winchester Gallery, Winchester, and tour, 1986; and Jill George Gallery, 1994. Using a mainly bright palette, Brewster's work hovered on the edge of figuration and abstraction. Brighton Polytechnic, The Open University and Winchester School of Art own his work. There were retrospectives at Russell-Cotes Art Gallery & Museum Bournemouth and at Coram Gallery, in 1997.

Sydney BRIAULT 1887–1955 Painter and illustrator, born in London. Initially studied art at evening classes at the Regent Street Polytechnic School of Art, and at St Martin's School of Art. He did a large amount of commercial work: book jackets and illustrations and drawings for *Strand* and *Windsor* magazines. During World War II he was for several years studio manager with a leading London advertising agency. A member of Croydon Art Society, he lived at Shirley, Surrey.

Michael BRICK 1946– Painter and teacher who studied fine art at Newcastle University where he eventually taught, also being a visiting lecturer elsewhere. Won a Granada Fellowship in Painting at York University. His group exhibitions included John Moores Exhibition, Liverpool, 1978, where he was a prizewinner; Surfaces at Postgraduate Gallery, Hull, 1979; Centrum Beeldende Kunst, Groningen, Netherlands, 1988; and the Newcastle Group show The Northern Lights, DLI Museum & Arts Centre, Durham, and tour, 1990. Solo exhibitions included a series at Anne Berthoud Gallery from 1981. Arts Council, British Council and Contemporary Art Society hold his work. Lived in Newcastle.

Elizabeth BRIDGE 1912–1996 Painter in oil and watercolour of still life, figures and landscapes, sometimes with a pattern element, who aged 17 gained a scholarship to Hornsey School of Art. She began by carrying out small commissions and illustrations for newspapers. Was a member of RI and ROI, also exhibiting at RA, SWA, RSA and with the Industrial Painters Group, and gained an Hon. Mention at the Paris Salon. Many of her flower paintings and some of her portraits were reproduced. In 1997, Christie's South Kensington included a group of Bridge's pictures in a Modern British sale.

Millie BRIDGE 1934– Artist in various media, including collage, and teacher, born in Rome, Italy. She studied at St Martin's School of Art, teachers including Ruskin Spear, John Minton and Frederick Gore. Bridge began as a graphic designer in advertising agencies, then taught in Hampshire and Sussex, latterly art at Chichester College of Further Education. She preferred abstract work, with rocks, cliffs and mountains key later themes. Group shows included Redfern Gallery, Mall Galleries, Westminster Gallery and Bishop's Palace, Chichester. Her work is held in many collections in Britain and abroad. Lived in Chichester, Sussex.

John BRIDGEMAN 1916– Sculptor and teacher, working in bronze and ciment fondu. He was born in Felixstowe, Suffolk, studied at Colchester School of Art with Barry Hart and Edward J Morss, later at Royal College of Art, 1947–9, with Frank Dobson. He became head of Birmingham Polytechnic school of sculpture, 1955–81. Bridgeman was made a fellow of RBS in 1960 and was a member of RBSA. His commissions included Madonna Dolorosa, for Coventry Cathedral; a Group of Warriors, for St Catherine's College, Cambridge; sculptural decorations for the 1951 Festival of Britain Dome of Discovery; and Cosmic Energy, an abstract panel for Aston University, Birmingham. He showed with RA; Roland, Browse & Delbanco; public galleries in Birmingham and Liverpool; and at Anthony Hepworth Fine Art, Bath. Lived in Leamington, Warwickshire.

Peter BRIDGENS 1947– Sculptor and teacher who studied at Bath Academy of Art, Corsham. Teaching experience included ceramics at Bristol Polytechnic and head of the School of Art and Design in Queen's Road, Clifton. Landscape, architecture and stone structures in the Cotswolds, Pembrokeshire and Umbria were influences on Bridgens' abstract work. He was included in the 2nd Open Sculpture Exhibition at RWA, 1996. Lived in Marshfield, Chippenham, Wiltshire.

Alan BRIDGWATER 1903–1962 Sculptor, painter, printmaker and teacher. Studied at Birmingham College of Art, 1923–33, the staff of which he later joined. Exhibited RA, NEAC, RBA, RSA and RBSA. Birmingham City Museum and Art Gallery holds his work and he also completed a war memorial for Kings Norton Grammar School. Bridgwater also had strong links with Dudley, teaching at its School of Art, 1948–54. With Charles Upton he formed the sculpture partnership Bridgwater and Upton, and their work included novel sculptural decoration for Dudley police headquarters. Lived in Edgbaston.

Barbara Helen BRIDGWATER 1919– Painter, textile artist, photographer and teacher who was married to the sculptor Alan Bridgwater. She studied at the College of Arts and Crafts in Birmingham, 1936–41. Started teaching at Malvern College of Art in 1941, later appointments including senior lectureship at City of Birmingham College of Education, 1956–75, and Birmingham Polytechnic Centre for Education, 1975–7. Showed at RA, RBA, NEAC and elsewhere. Lived latterly at Hawkhurst, Kent.

Emmy BRIDGWATER 1906– Surrealist painter, draughtsman and, from the 1970s, collagist, born in Birmingham. She studied art there, in Oxford and London. When in 1936 she saw the International Surrealist Exhibition in London this shaped the future course of her work, and soon after this she joined the Birmingham Group of Surrealists and the Surrealist group in England in 1940. During the 1940s she contributed to several international Surrealist publications, then in 1947 was invited by André Breton to the Galerie Maeght international Surrealist show in Paris where she signed the English group's *Declaration.* After some years of neglect, when she was unable to paint because of family responsibilities, interest was revived in Bridgwater's work when she was included in the Hamet Gallery's Surrealist show in 1971, as she was in several further reviews in the 1980s. Blond Fine Art gave her a solo show in 1990. Lived just outside Birmingham.

Edith Elizabeth BRIER: *see* **Elizabeth SCOTT-MOORE**

Argent BRIERLEY 1893–1960 Landscape painter and teacher who after attending George Heriot's School in Edinburgh gained his diploma at the College of Art. After World War I service with the Royal Scots Regiment he taught at Manchester School of Art, L S Lowry being a pupil. Later appointed art master at William Hulme's Grammar School, taking a similar post in 1945 at Lawrence Sheriff School, Rugby, eventually settling in Salisbury, Wiltshire. He died on a business trip to Manchester, where the City Art Gallery holds many examples. Showed at MAFA, RSA, with Wessex Artists and with Civil Defence Artists, having been a warden in World War II.

E Irlam BRIGGS fl. c.early 1890s–1950 Modeller, painter and artist in fresco who studied at Wimbledon College of Art after private education. Also attended St John's Wood School of Art, Royal Academy Schools and Académie Julian, Paris. Miss Briggs was brought up in a religious environment and did work for a number of churches in England and America. Exhibited RA, Walker Art Gallery, Liverpool and elsewhere in the provinces. She was closely associated with the East Dorset Art Society, living at Parkstone.

William BRIGGS 1888–1978 Painter, engraver and photographer, born in London, where he had a studio at 22 Chenies Street. He was educated at the Borough Polytechnic and Bolt Court art school. Was elected a member of The Royal Photographic Society in 1933, being admitted as a full fellow in 1936. Showed at Ridley Art Club, ROI and extensively along the south coast, where he settled at Steyning, Sussex.

Isobel BRIGHAM 1963– Painter, born in Fareham, Hampshire, who studied at Chelsea College of Art, 1988–92, teachers including Helen Chadwick, and Slade School of Fine Art, 1992–4, where "I was unhappy". Her figurative, painterly pictures were usually made over sustained periods, "change the whole time and I do a lot of scraping off". She admired Rembrandt, Van Gogh, Ingres and Goya. Exhibitions included The Discerning Eye, Mall Galleries, 1991; BP Portrait Award at National Portrait Gallery and Royal Over-Seas League Open, both 1992; Fresh Art, Business Design Centre, 1994; and In the Looking Glass, Usher Gallery, Lincoln, and tour, 1996–7. Lived in London.

Kate BRIGHT 1964– Painter, born in Suffolk, who attended Ipswich School of Art, 1983–4, then Camberwell School of Arts and Crafts, 1985–8. The structure of natural and man-made features in landscape was of key interest to Bright, who took part in group shows at London Institute Gallery, 1987; Homerton College, Cambridge, 1989; and South Bank Centre's touring exhibition The British Art Show 1990. Had a strong connection with Yugoslavia, having a solo show at Galerija Arts, Llubljana, 1989. Lived in London.

Ken BRIGHT 1939– Sculptor and draughtsman, notable for bird and animal subjects; teacher. He was born on the Isle of Wight and studied at Portsmouth College of Art and Goldsmiths' College School of Art. Became head of ceramics at Goldsmiths' and a member of the Crafts Centre of Great Britain. Had work shown in England abroad and in private collections worldwide. Had solo exhibition at Woodlands Art Gallery, 1978, work being made from studies at Falconry Centre, Gloucestershire, and Police Stables, Dulwich.

Charlotte BRILL 1950– Artist, born in London, daughter of the painters Frederick Brill and Deirdre Borlase, whose activities included set and costume design, performance art and stand-up comedy, storytelling, site-specific sculpture, works on and with paper and arts administration. She was strongly committed to feminism, radicalism and direct verbal address rather than creating the permanent art object. Studied at Wimbledon School of Art and Central School of Art & Design, 1968–72, then worked as a theatre designer, 1972–80; as a performer, 1979–83; then from 1984 as an administrator. She was included in Relative Values, the Brill family exhibition, at The Smith Art Gallery & Museum, Stirling, 1993.

Frederick BRILL 1920–1984 Teacher, painter and writer, born in London. He studied at Hammersmith School of Art, 1934–9, Slade School of Fine Art, 1940–1, and Royal College of Art, 1941–5, where he won a medal for distinction in painting. After six years of part-time teaching Brill in 1951 became a lecturer at Chelsea School of Art, rising to become principal, 1965–79. He wrote a monograph on *Matisse*, 1967, and another short publication on *Turner's Burial at Sea*, 1969, which contained prose compared with John Ruskin's. Showed with LG, RBA, RA and NEAC and had several solo shows. In 1985 Chelsea School of Art staged a memorial exhibition. Lived finally at Carperby, Yorkshire, an area much painted by him. Was survived by his wife, painter Deirdre Borlase, and was included with her in Relative Values, The Smith Art Gallery & Museum, Stirling, 1993.

Patrick BRILL 1963– Performance artist, born in London, married to Jessica Voorsanger, also known as Jessica Voorsanger-Brill. He was the son of the artists Frederick Brill and Deirdre Borlase and was included in the Brill family exhibition Relative Values, The Smith Art Gallery & Museum, Stirling, 1993. He studied at the University of Reading, 1981–5, winning a Rome Prize in the latter year. Gained a Harkness Fellowship with the Cooper Union School of Arts and Sciences, New York, America, 1988–90. After Brill's solo exhibition I want children's TV: I want children's TV banned, at Sue Williams Gallery in 1991, Brill turned from the painted image to satirical performance. He invented Bob Smith and simulated game shows in which members of the audience participated using his Home Sculpture System. An example was Dont Hate Sculpt, at Arnolfini Gallery, Bristol, 1997–8, in which both Bob and Roberta Smith rather than Patrick Brill were billed.

Reginald BRILL 1902–1974 Artist in oil and watercolour and fine draughtsman of landscapes, figure studies and portraits. Born in London, Brill studied under Henry Tonks at the Slade School

1921–4 after a period at the St Martin's School of Art. Won the Prix de Rome for painting and was at the British School in Rome 1927–9. Worked in Cairo, 1930. Exhibited at the RA, Leicester Galleries and in East Anglia, where he lived, at Lavenham. Was principal of Kingston School of Art. Wrote *Modern Painting* and *Art as a Career*.

Victoria BRILL 1958– Artist, designer and teacher using a wide range of media, born in London daughter of the painters Frederick Brill and Deirdre Borlase and married to the artist Stephen Gavin. Allegory, moral issues, everyday objects and routines and art history references were all found in her work. She studied at Camberwell School of Arts and Crafts, 1976–7, then Kingston Polytechnic, 1979–82, winning a Stanley Picker Travelling Scholarship to Venice, 1981, and the *Guardian* Purchase Prize, New Contemporaries, 1983. Designed *Faust* set and costumes for Mantis Dance Theatres, 1985, designing and painting model theatres for Channel 4 Television's *A Map of Dreams*, 1986. From 1989 taught for North Yorkshire County Council. Was Artist of the Day, Angela Flowers Gallery, 1985; Showed at Linton Court Gallery, Settle, 1987–90; and at Stonegate Gallery, York, 1987–91. In 1993 she was included in the Brill family show Relative Values at The Smith Art Gallery & Museum, Stirling.

Fredda BRILLIANT 1908– Sculptor, born in Lodz, Poland, married to the film producer Herbert Marshall. She established an international career. In England she showed at RA, RWS, Leicester Galleries, Whitechapel Art Gallery and elsewhere. Among her public works are the Mahatma Gandhi memorial in Tavistock Square and the portrait of Sir Isaac Hayward for the Royal Festival Hall, while her head of the statesman Krishna Menon is in the National Art Gallery in New Delhi and Southern Illinois University and National Art Gallery in Sydney, New South Wales, also hold her work. Lived for a time in Sussex, also in Carbondale, Illinois, in America. In the 1980s a number of books by her were published in India, including the short story collection *Truth in Fiction*; *Women in Power*; and *The Black Virgin*.

Max BRIMMELL 1917–1993 Artist, notably of watercolour landscapes, actor and bookseller, born in London. His real name was Ronald Arthur Brimmell, Max stemming from a part played on the stage. During World War II Brimmell was in the Royal Navy, rising from the rank of ordinary seaman to the command of several ships. After the war he studied at Putney School of Art under John Bowyer and Francis Edwin Hodge. Showed at RI, UA, PS, RBA and at the Stables Theatre and Museum in Hastings, where he settled from 1963, being a founder-member of Old Hastings' Town Week, president of its Preservation Society and a founder- and playing member of its Cricket Club. As an actor Brimmell appeared in a film with Boris Karloff, on the West End stage, for 18 years in the radio serial *The Archers* as the vicar and on television as the sidekick of chief superintendent *Fabian of the Yard*. Realising he could make more money from antiquarian bookselling than acting, Brimmell turned to this, becoming an authority on children's literature and publishing two books. Continued to paint at weekends, when he reckoned to complete two pictures. Finally lived at Bexhill-on-Sea, Sussex.

Sharon BRINDLE 1958– Draughtsman and painter working in pastel/conté and oil on canvas, born in Staffordshire. She studied at Camberwell School of Art, 1979–82. Took part in a number of mixed shows, including Art '92 and Art '93, Islington; and at Camden Galleries. Had a solo show at Boundary Gallery in 1992, another at Portland Gallery, 1993. Brindle was notable as a draughtsman of the female nude, believing that "all the universe and its forces are concentrated in the unclothed human body". Her work was included in Ron Bowen's 1992 book *Drawing Masterclass*. Lived in London.

Donald BRINDLEY 1928– Sculptor of horses in various materials, born at Penkull, Stoke-on-Trent, Staffordshire. He studied at Burslem College of Art, then at Royal College of Art until 1951, teachers including John Skeaping and Frank Dobson. He was a consultant to several British and foreign porcelain makers, including Royal Worcester Porcelain and Josiah Wedgwood & Sons. Was elected a fellow of RBS in 1973. HM The Queen holds his work. Lived in Stoke-on-Trent.

John BRINE 1920– Painter and teacher, born in Sydenham, southeast London. He attended Clapham School of Art, 1935–9, teachers including Roland Pitchforth, then Royal College of Art, 1946–9, under Ruskin Spear and Rodrigo Moynihan. Went on to become head of fine art school at Ravensbourne College of Art & Design. Was a member of RBA and showed at RA, LG and SEA. Hertfordshire Education Committee bought his work. Lived in Bromley, Kent.

Mike BRISCOE 1960– Painter and advertising illustrator, born and lived in Colwyn Bay, Clwyd. He studied at Wrexham College of Art under David Cooper, 1978–9, then Sheffield City Polytechnic, 1979–82, where teachers included Terry Lee. Showed at RA Summer Exhibition from 1983, at Piccadilly Gallery from 1984 and in same year at Palais des Nations, Paris. Was a Stowells Trophy prizewinner.

Stuart BRISLEY 1933– Painter, producer of structures in various materials, performance artist and teacher, born in Haslemere, Surrey. He attended Guildford School of Art, 1949–54; Royal College of Art, 1956–9, with an Abbey Minor Scholarship in the latter year; in 1959–60 won Bavarian State Scholarship and studied at Akademie der Bildenden Künste, Munich; then studied at Florida State University, Tallahassee, 1960–2. Brisley gained a Fulbright Travel Award for 1960–4 and the Hille Fellowship, 1970–1. In 1973–4 Brisley won DAAD Berlin Artists' Programme Award. He was town artist at Peterlee, County Durham, 1976–7. Brisley became reader in charge of media-fine art at Slade School of Fine Art in 1985. He followed a period producing fairly formalist structures with the utilisation of movement and light and work as a performance artist. This comprised various rituals which carried social and political messages. He had retrospectives at ICA in in 1981 and Serpentine Gallery in 1986, with a show at South London Gallery, 1996. Arts Council holds his work. Lived in London.

Nan BROACKES 1908– Painter and draughtsman who studied at Leeds College of Art under Arthur Pope. Showed her work at RA, SSA and Royal Glasgow Institute of the Fine Arts. Lived for a time at Currie, Midlothian.

Clio BROAD 1934– Artist in watercolour, gouache and pastel, and teacher, born in Aberystwyth, Cardiganshire. She attended Lancaster and Morecambe College of Art, 1951–3, and Swansea College of Art, 1953–5, taught by Howard Martin and William Price. From 1955–6 Broad worked as a stained glass painter for Bell's, of Bristol, then taught art in Maesydderwen Comprehensive School, Ystradgynlais. Mixed show appearances included Attic, Mumbles and Ceri Richards Galleries, Swansea; National Museum of Wales, Oriel Albany and Manor House Fine Arts, in Cardiff; Mold National Eisteddfod; Llewellyn Alexander Gallery; and Coal Industry National Art Competition & Exhibition, Blackpool. Had solo shows at Ystradgynlais Library and Gorseinon Institute. Lived in Ystradgynlais, Swansea.

Arthur BROADBENT 1909–1994 Painter, ceramist and teacher, born in Belfast, Northern Ireland. Studied at Royal College of Art design school, teachers including Henry Moore. Taught at Lincoln College of Art; was a camouflage officer in Royal Air Force, 1939–45; then taught at Shrewsbury School, 1945–70. His main works included murals in St Tim's and St Ambrose, Everton, demolished 1970. Broadbent, who adored the work of Bonnard, showed with Shropshire Art Society, elsewhere in the country and had a solo exhibition at Shrewsbury School in 1980.

Robina Margaret BROADFIELD 1906– Painter, born in Hebburn, Country Durham, married to the art teacher Aubrey Broadfield. Apart from six weeks of evening classes at Leicester College of Art she was self-taught. She was a leading member of Leicester Society of Artists and showed at public galleries in Leicester and Nottingham, in Germany and Italy. Her work was "from memory, or imagination" and was signed with initials. Lived in Glenfield, Leicester.

Barry BROADIE 1940– Painter and teacher, born in Manchester. He was educated at George Heriot's School in Edinburgh, where he settled. Taught art at Basil Paterson Tutorial College. Broadie showed widely in Scotland, including RSW, RSA and Scottish Gallery group shows and had a number of solo exhibitions in the city. Royal Edinburgh Hospital owns his work.

John Christopher BROBBEL 1950– Painter, teacher and writer, born in Hartlepool, County Durham, where he settled. He studied at the local College of Art, 1969–71, at Byam Shaw School of Drawing and Painting, 1971–4, then at Royal Academy Schools, 1974–7, where his teachers included Peter Greenham and Norman Blamey. Showed RA, NEAC and RBA and had several solo exhibitions. Sometimes signed work only with initials. Wrote *Pencil Drawing* and *Drawing with Ink* and taught for a time at Hartlepool College of Further Education and Cleveland College of Art.

Henry Matthew BROCK 1875–1960 Illustrator, designer and watercolourist, born and lived in Cambridge, younger brother of the illustrator Charles Edmund Brock. Studied at local School of Art, worked alongside his brother and by the mid-1990s was a busy illustrator of periodicals. His work appeared in *Boy's Own Paper*, *The Graphic*, *Pearson's Magazine* and *The Strand Magazine*, plus many others, and he illustrated many books. He was elected RI in 1906, also showing at RA, RSA and Walker Art Gallery in Liverpool, producing attractive landscapes.

Albert Ernest BROCKBANK 1862–1958 Painter who was born and lived in Liverpool, studying at the School of Art there, in London and at Académie Julian in Paris. He was president of both the Liverpool Academy and Liverpool Sketching Club and showed extensively at Walker Art Gallery which holds his work, as does Harris Museum and Art Gallery, Preston. Also showed at RCamA, RBA, RA and RI.

Russell BROCKBANK 1913– Humorous illustrator, born in Niagara Falls, Ontario, Canada. Brockbank was educated at Ridley College, Ontario, studying art at Buffalo New York School of Art in America, then with Harold Sandys Williamson at Chelsea School of Art, 1931–2. Showed at SGA, but was most known for his illustrations in a variety of magazines, notably *Punch*, of which he was art editor for just over a decade from 1949. Also illustrated a number of books, including *The Brockbank Omnibus*. Lived in Thursley, Surrey.

Gerald Leslie BROCKHURST 1890–1978 Painter, etcher, draughtsman and teacher, born in Edgbaston, Birmingham. So gifted was Brockhurst as a draughtsman that he was admitted to Birmingham School of Art aged 12. He entered the Royal Academy Schools in 1907, in 1913 winning a gold medal and a travelling scholarship. In 1913–14 he visited Paris and in Italy studied the Quattrocento painters, whose style influenced his own portraits. Had a one-man show at Chenil Gallery in 1919, in 1920 deciding to concentrate on etching, which he did lucratively for the next decade. Brockhurst's election to RE in 1921 and RP in 1923 was followed in 1928 by his winning associate status at RA and being elected a visitor to the Royal Academy Schools. He was elected RA in 1937. Two years later Brockhurst left for New York with his model Kathleen – known as Dorette – Woodward, whom he was to marry after divorce from his wife Anaïs, also a notable model for his work. By this time Brockhurst was established as a sought-after portrait painter, able to ask 1,000 guineas a canvas. His models were to include The Duchess of Windsor, Marlene Dietrich and J Paul Getty. For his remaining years

Brockhurst undertook many lucrative portrait commissions, exhibiting with Knoedler and Portraits Incorporated, dying at Franklin Lakes, New Jersey, with a reputation which had largely faded in Britain, although collectors remembered him as a masterly etcher. His reputation was revivified by the 1986–7 exhibition of his work which toured from Graves Art Gallery, Sheffield. Public galleries there, in Oxford, Preston, Hull, Glasgow and elsewhere hold his work.

Keith BROCKIE 1955– Wildlife illustrator and artist, born in Haddington, East Lothian, he moved to Strathmiglo, Fife, aged 13, from there going to Bell Baxter High School, which had a good art department. After school spent four years at Duncan of Jordanstone College of Art, Dundee, gaining a diploma in illustration and printmaking. Worked for some months as illustrator for Dundee Museum, but disliked working in an office so went freelance. He believed in constant field work, and was a bird ringer. Showed Brotherton Gallery and elsewhere and had a Scottish Arts Council show in 1981. Lived at Carse of Gowrie, Scotland.

Michael BROCKWAY 1919– Painter, son of the musician Sir William Harris, who studied at Stowe School and Cambridge University. Attended Farnham School of Art, 1946–50, Cheltenham School of Art, 1950, and Ruskin School of Drawing in Oxford, 1951–4. He was a member of NEAC, also showing with RA, RBA and RI. His study of the watercolourist Charles Knight was published in 1952. Lived in Burford, Oxfordshire.

Laurence BRODERICK 1935– Sculptor in various materials of animals, birds and human figures; teacher. After six years in Regent Street Polytechnic School of Art and Hammersmith School of Art until 1961, with a large family to support Broderick for the next 20 years was an historical and educational illustrator and painter and teacher. Began sculpting full-time in 1981. Showed at RWA, RBA and RA. Had one-man show at Belgrave Gallery, 1979; Otter Trust, Bungay, 1982; Manor Gallery, Royston, 1986; Warrington Museum and Art Gallery, 1992; and in the same year at Gallery An Talla Dearg, Isle of Skye, the island which was the source of much of his inspiration. Commissioned work included Madonna and Child, All Saints, Weston-super-Mare; The Swimming Otter, The Otter Trust, Earsham; and Teko – The Swimming Otter, Clan Donald Centre, Armadale. Worked at Waresley, Bedfordshire.

Muriel Alice BRODERICK 1910–1954 Designer, illustrator and teacher, born at Torquay, Devon. Studied at the Southern College of Art, Bournemouth, 1928–34, under Leslie Ward and Harold Williamson, where she later taught. Exhibited RA and elsewhere, sometimes as M A B. Completed a lot of commercial work, illustrated books published in Britain and America, drew for the *Illustrated London News* and *Sketch* and widely for women's magazines, including *Woman's Own* and *Woman's Journal*. Lived in Bournemouth, Hampshire.

Sally BRODHOLT fl. from 1970s– Printmaker, born in West Indies. She studied at Centre for Arts and Crafts, Bromley. Showed at RA, Mall Galleries and was included in Group '77 Printmakers at Woodlands Art Gallery in 1981. Lived in London.

Carol R BRODY 1943– Sculptor in a variety of materials who was born in New York. She studied at the Art Students' League of New York and at the New York School of Design, then in London, 1973–7, at Camden Arts Centre, Hampstead. Showed with NS of which she was a member, SWA, NEAC and elsewhere. The Israeli Embassy, London, holds her depiction of the Israeli politician Golda Meir. Lived for a time in Gerrards Cross, Buckinghamshire.

Frederick J BRODY 1914– Designer, craftsman, painter in tempera and teacher, born and lived in Sheffield. He studied at the local College of Art, 1929–34, then at Royal College of Art, 1934–7, his teachers including Eric Ravilious, Ernest Tristram, Edward Bawden and Barnett Freedman. Showed at Paris International Exhibition in 1937, Festival of Britain in 1951 and in America.

Horace BRODZKY 1885–1969 Artist, writer, critic and teacher, born in Melbourne, Australia, of Jewish parents. In 1901 he enrolled for drawing tuition at National Gallery of Victoria School of Art, then in 1904 moved to America, where in 1906 he joined the National Academy of Design, in 1908 moving to London. There he enrolled at City and Guilds Art School and had a first solo show. He became friendly with such artists as Henri Gaudier-Brzeska, Jacob Epstein, David Bomberg and Mark Gertler; his biography of Gaudier appeared in 1933. Brodzky's theatrical design work was included in a show which toured the continent. In 1914 he joined the LG and began to be included in modern art shows, in New York, 1915–23, editing several magazines. Taught at London County Council evening classes from 1924–34. Brodzky was included in the first show of British lino-cuts organised by Claude Flight at the Redfern Gallery in 1929. Six years later James Laver's *Forty Drawings by Horace Brodzky* revealed the artist's stature as a fine draughtsman. Among Brodzky's later publications were a biography of Pascin and one of Gaudier-Brzeska's drawings, both in 1946. Eightieth birthday shows took place at the Ben Uri Gallery and Oxford Union Cellars in 1965. Other retrospectives were at the Jewish Museum of Australia, Melbourne, 1988, and Boundary Gallery, 1989.

Michael BROIDO 1927– Artist and teacher, born in London, who lived in South Africa, 1929–49. He was a self-taught artist who worked in the clothing industry for many years and lived in Cornwall, 1956–80. He was a part-time gardener for the artist Patrick Heron, having an attic studio in his Eagles Nest home, 1956–8; moved to St Ives and was a studio assistant to Barbara Hepworth, 1959–62, teaching at Truro Art School, 1960–80. Showed regularly with Penwith Society and then Fore Street Gallery and was included in Belgrave Gallery 1992 show British abstract art of the 50s and 60s. After producing little work for about 20 years from 1965, Broido resumed painting. Pier Gallery Arts Centre, Stromness, holds his work.

William David BROKMAN DAVIS 1892-pre-April 1993 Painter and printmaker, born in Birmingham, who studied at the School of Art there. Exhibited RA, RSA, RCamA and elsewhere and was an associate of RE; its records show that Brokman Davis became an honorary retired associate in 1967 and died "pre-April 1 1993". He was also a member of Chelsea Arts Club. Work is held by British Museum, National Museum of Wales in Cardiff, British Council, British provincial museums and galleries overseas. He lived for a time in Leek, Staffordshire, latterly at West Parley, Dorset.

Tom BROMLY 1930– Painter, draughtsman, photographer and teacher, born in Los Mochis, Mexico. He studied at Canterbury College of Art, 1946–50, then Leeds College of Art, 1953–4. Began teaching painting, 1955–61, at Newcastle College of Art & Design, eventually becoming dean of the faculty of arts and design at Newcastle Polytechnic, 1987–92. Bromly was closely connected with the development of art and design education throughout Britain. In 1992 he was co-author of *Capability Through Art & Design*. Bromly was a founding member of the Newcastle Group in the 1960s, creating large hard-edge pictures, but the constraints on his time determined a change in scale and subjects over the years. As well as mixed shows in the northeast and elsewhere Bromly had a series of solo exhibitions, with a retrospective at University Gallery, University of Northumbria, 1993–4. Newcastle Polytechnic portrait collection includes his work.

Birgitte BRONDUM-NIELSEN: *see* **Bitte B-N**

Licia BRONZIN 1960– Artist in various media, born in Adelaide, Australia. She studied painting at the Academy of Fine Arts, Venice, 1980–4, then film and video at London College of Printing, 1987–90. Portraits and film work combining animation and live action were special interests. She showed at New Era Gallery, Adelaide, in 1985, her first main exhibition in Britain being John Moores Exhibition, Liverpool, in 1991–2, with Woman with Colours. Lived in London.

George BROOK 1898– c.1955 Painter, designer and black-and-white artist, born in Leicester. Studied at the College of Art there. Showed at Leicester Museum and Art Gallery and was a member of Leicester Sketch Club. Illustrated children's and educational books and magazines. Lived in Leicester.

Ian BROOK 1934– Watercolourist, born in Sheffield, Yorkshire. He began painting in France aged 15. As a businessman from 1957–90 he painted all over the world, exhibiting in Britain and France, then became a professional from 1990. Brook said that he was a "strong believer in painting from nature in the open air". He was taught by Agnete Varming, in Copenhagen, 1964–5, and Josh Partridge in London, 1978–84. Had a solo show of landscapes of Provence at Eygalières, 1990, then one of Thailand landscapes at Joy Thornton, 1992. Logica Ltd holds his work. Lived in London and in Khon Sawan, Chayaphum Province, Thailand.

James BROOK 1959– Painter, born in Huddersfield, Yorkshire. He studied at Exeter College of Art, 1981–4, then Chelsea School of Art, 1989–90. He held a solo show at Red Herring Gallery, Brighton, in 1986. Exhibited with LG, 1989; Riverside One, 1990, winning a prize; New Contemporaries, 1990–1, at Arnolfini Gallery, Bristol, and tour; and in 1991–2 he won a prize at John Moores Exhibition, Liverpool, with his picture Water. For this he used television and magazine photographs as source material. His 1995–6 entry was the ingenious Road (with Raindrops, Eye). Lived in London.

Peter BROOK 1927– Painter, born in Holmfirth, Yorkshire. After Barnsley Grammar School he attended Huddersfield School of Art and Goldsmiths' College School of Art. He was one of Jack Beddington's chosen *Young Artists of Promise*, in the 1957 book of that title. Initially Brook painted industrial scenes, then from the 1960s Pennine rural landscapes, especially winter scenes, from 1980 Scottish and Lancashire landscapes. From 1979–83 completed 52 Hannah Hauxwell pictures. Was elected RBA in 1962. In 1960 had a solo show at Wakefield City Art Gallery; from 1968–72 was contracted to Agnew, with seven solo shows, two in Palm Springs and two in Adelaide; in 1990 had retrospective at Brighouse Art Gallery. Many notable actors owned Brook's pictures, including James Mason, 30 examples; Tommy Steele; Alan Ladd; and Keith Barron. Lived in Brighouse, West Yorkshire.

Anne BROOKE 1916– Painter and teacher, born at South Crosland, Yorkshire, who worked in oil, the Bible being a key theme of her work. She attended Chelsea School of Art, 1937–9; Huddersfield School of Art, 1939–41; and London University Institute of Education, 1941–2. Was a member of Leeds Fine Art Club. Showed with RA, RSA, RCamA, WIAC, NEAC, RBA, ROI and Paris Salon. Had a solo show at Swarthmore Centre, Leeds, 1962, and Renoir Gallery, Harrogate, 1977. Her work was held by public galleries in Harrogate, Keighley, Wakefield and Southend, and by local education committees in Hertfordshire, Lincolnshire, Northumberland and Bristol. Lived in Harrogate, North Yorkshire.

Eleanor Christina BROOKE fl. c.1955– Painter who studied at Académie Julian, Slade School of Fine Art and Heatherley's School of Fine Art. Showed in London and provinces, sometimes signing work E C B. Lived for a while at Eastcombe, Gloucestershire.

Geoffrey Arthur George BROOKE 1920– Painter in oil, born in Bath, Somerset. He came from a Naval family and served in the Navy after attending Royal Naval College in Dartmouth. In 1949–50 he studied art with the painter Sonia Mervyn and went on to show with the Army Art Society. Lived in Sussex, at Ringmer, then in Balcombe.

Horace BROOKE 1897– Watercolourist and printmaker, mainly doing commercial work. Brought up in Yorkshire, he attended Ossett Municipal Technical School and Royal College of Art, Leeds College of Art and Royal College of Art. Showed RA and elsewhere and lived in St Albans, Hertfordshire.

Iris BROOKE 1908– Portrait painter and draughtsman, book illustrator and writer. Studied at Croydon School of Art, 1923–6, and Royal College of Art, 1926–9. Although Brooke sometimes ventured into humorous books, her reputation is based on volumes concerned with historical costume, launched by the title *English Children's Costume*, 1930. Lived for some time at Widworthy Barton, near Honiton, Devon.

James Leslie BROOKE 1903–1973 Decorative artist in a variety of media, born and lived in Huddersfield, Yorkshire, who studied at the College of Art there with John Gauld. Also studied in Italy, France and North America. Exhibited at RA, RBA and in Yorkshire.

William BROOKER 1918–1983 Painter in oil, especially of interiors and still life. Born in Croydon, Surrey, Brooker studied at Croydon School of Art 1936–9, Chelsea School of Art 1947–9 and Goldsmiths' College School of Art 1948–9. From 1949–53 he taught at Bath Academy of Art, living for a time with Brian Wynter, then Terry Frost. Howard Hodgkin, a pupil, called him "a great teacher". In 1953 Brooker became head of painting at Willesden School of Art, 1958, senior lecturer in painting at Harrow School of Art and was at Ealing School of Art from 1960. In 1965 became senior lecturer at the Central School, then was principal of Wimbledon School of Art 1969–81. Exhibited from early 1950s with LG, also with Arthur Tooth and Son and Agnew. A retrospective was held at Newcastle Polytechnic in 1987, toured to Agnew. Brooker's work can be reminiscent of pictures by Walter Sickert, palette and subjects being similar, although Brooker remained his own man. His work is held in a large number of public collections in Britain and abroad, including the Tate Gallery, Arts Council, Aberdeen Art Gallery and galleries in Canada, Australia, New Zealand and Brazil. Lived at Carshalton, Surrey.

Daysi May BROOKES 1886–1981 Painter, especially of portraits and miniatures, born in Norwich, Norfolk. After initial education there she studied art with J S Watkins in Sydney, Australia, and at the Julian Ashton school there. Exhibited widely in Australia; was a member of the council of the Australian Art Society for several years after World War II; and had a miniature accepted by the National Gallery of New South Wales, Sydney. In Britain she exhibited RMS, SM, Paris Salon and with the Norfolk and Norwich Art Circle. Lived latterly in Norwich.

Kenneth BROOKES 1897–c.1978 Watercolourist and commercial artist, born in Manchester. Studied at Watford and Harrow Schools of Art, 1913–16. Member of London Sketch Club, of which he was president in the early 1950s, also showing at RA, RBA and RI. Lived in Harrow, Middlesex.

Lionel BROOKES 1915– Painter and teacher, a native of Staffordshire who studied at Royal College of Art under Gilbert Spencer, 1937–40. For a time he was on the staff of Northampton School of Art and had work in the Central Museum and Art Gallery there. Showed at RA and RBA. Lived in Loughborough, Leicestershire.

Malcolm John BROOKES 1943– Artist in oil, gouache and pastel, and teacher, born in Birmingham. He attended the College of Arts and Crafts there, 1959–64, when Gilbert Mason was head of the painting school. Started teaching at local grammar school, then at Droitwich High School, from 1984 being head of design and technology at Stourport-on-Severn High School. In his own work Brookes favoured "a regular change of emphasis which keeps me alert and avoids predictability. I most admire the understatement and contemplative quality of such artists as Morandi and Gwen John." Was a member of RBSA and an associate of RCamA, other group appearances including Ikon Gallery in Birmingham, RWA, Mall Galleries and Dudley Art Gallery. Had a series of solo shows in Midlands, including Worcester Art Gallery; Bulls Eye Gallery, Lichfield; Compendium Gallery and Midlands Art Centre, both in Birmingham. That Centre, RBSA and Worcester College of Higher Education hold examples. Lived in Bromsgrove, Worcestershire.

Alan BROOKS 1965– Artist and teacher, born in Southend, Essex, who studied at Jacob Kramer School of Art, Leeds, Reading University and Slade School of Fine Art. From 1993 he was a visiting lecturer at Reading. He gained an Owen Ridley Drawing Prize, 1990; a Royal Academy Grant, 1991; a Slade Project Grant for study in Berlin, 1992; and a London Arts Board Award, 1996. Group exhibitions included New Art in Yorkshire, University Art Gallery and St Paul's Gallery, Leeds, 1987; Into the Nineties IV, Mall Galleries, 1992; Los Angeles Art Fair, 1993; and in 1996 Whitechapel Open at Whitechapel Art Gallery and Royal Over-Seas League Open, where Brooks won first prize. Had a solo show at Wet Paint Gallery, 1994. Reading University holds his work. Lived in London.

Ern BROOKS 1911–1993 Painter and illustrator, born in Manchester into a large working-class family. Was an apprenticed lithographer with George Faulkner, studying painting and drawing at Manchester School of Art. Worked as a commercial artist, which sapped his strength for other painting, while keeping abreast of European trends in art, being a keen disciple of Picasso. In 1951 Brooks created the mural Public Health for a floating exhibition on HMS *Campania*, part of the Festival of Britain; and in that year his lino-cut Men of Tolpuddle sold to raise funds for the *Daily Worker* newpaper. His lifelong companion, the painter Barbara Niven, also a Communist Party member who died in 1971, ran the *Worker's* Fighting Fund for over 20 years. In the

1930s they had helped found the Manchester Theatre Union, in which the director Joan Littlewood and folk singer Ewan McColl were involved. Brooks showed at AIA, of which he was a member, Gimpel Fils and Arts Council shows of realist work at Whitechapel Art Gallery. A major theme in his later work was the field gate, symbol of an uncertain future.

Jason BROOKS 1969– Figurative painter whose work has been compared in style with that of Hans Bellmer and Francis Bacon. Born in Yorkshire, he studied at Rotheram College of Arts & Technology, 1986–7; Goldsmiths' College, 1987–8; Cheltenham and Gloucester College of Art, 1988–91, with a Rome Travel Bursary, British School at Rome, 1990; and Chelsea College of Art and Design, 1991. Group exhibitions included Remakes, Young Unknowns Gallery, 1990; Gerald Davies Gallery, Dublin, 1992; British Telecom New Contemporaries, Manchester and tour, 1993; and Art94, with Paton Gallery, Business Design Centre, Islington, 1994. In 1996 Brooks shared a show at Paton with Clive Head. Won a purchase prize and portrait commission from Cheltenham & Gloucester Building Society, 1991, another prize at John Moores Liverpool Exhibition, 1997–8. Showed solo at Entwistle, 1997–8. Llved in London.

John Charles Vine BROOKS 1901–1991 Painter of landscapes, mainly in oil in the Post-Impressionist manner, born in Tonbridge, Kent, where he lived, dying nearby in Tunbridge Wells. He was married to the artist Mary Brooks from 1933. Owing to disability, Jack Brooks had no formal schooling, apart from individual music tuition (he composed for the piano) and painting lessons in the 1940s from Hesketh Hubbard. For about 20 years until 1936, Brooks was an employee and director of Chas Baker & Company, the family car distribution firm. During World War II, he was an observer in the Royal Observer Corps, later devoting time to his property interests. From 1930 for about 40 years, Brooks originated and developed a system of Colour Harmony, despite being dyslexic, leaving raw material later put into final form by his son Dominic. Elliott Seabrooke was one artist impressed by the idea. Brooks also designed his own rotating perspective ruler. The innovations were employed in Brooks' own work, hung between 1937–45 at LG, NEAC, RBA, RA, RWS and elsewhere.

Louie BROOKS 1900– Part-time painter, born in Manchester, who studied at the College of Art there, teachers including Albert Dodd. She was a member of MAFA from 1943, showing elsewhere in the Lancashire area, with RBA and RP. Lived latterly in Colwyn Bay, Clwyd.

Marjorie BROOKS 1904–1980 Painter and decorative artist, born and lived in London, married to the architect Lord William Holford, who died in 1975; she was sometimes known as Marjorie Holford. Studied at Central School of Arts and Crafts and Royal Academy Schools, winning its Gold Medal and Edward Stott Travelling Studentship, 1927, and bronze medals for design, decoration and figure painting. Showed at RA, Walker Art Gallery in Liverpool (where she designed costumes for the Liverpool Playhouse) and elsewhere. Worked for the British Council. She bequeathed her picture Tea On the Lawn to Brighton Museum and Art Gallery in 1980.

Mary BROOKS 1897–1991 Artist in oil, watercolour and pastel of landscape and still life, originally known as Edith Mary Brown (a limited amount of work was completed using the name Mary Brown), born in Barnsley, Yorkshire. She studied at Leeds School of Art, 1915–20, teachers including Haywood Rider and Walter Pearson, and Royal College of Art, 1920–4, with William Rothenstein and Gerald Moira. Her contemporaries there included Henry Moore, Barbara Hepworth, Eric Ravilious, Douglas Percy Bliss and Phyllis Dodd (Bliss' wife, who painted a portrait of Mary in 1930). Mary was married to the Royal College-trained artist George Konow Branson until 1933, when after divorce she married the painter J C V Brooks. His Colour Harmony theory was to influence her pictures. She was art mistress at Cambridge County School, 1924–8, and showed at RA, WIAC of which she was a member, RBA and elsewhere. Lived for many years at Tonbridge, Kent, dying near Bath, Somerset.

Mary BROOKS 1906– Self-taught painter who was born and lived in London. She was a member of Free Painters and Sculptors and was closely involved in running the Loggia Gallery. Showed in London, the provinces, America and France.

Drake BROOKSHAW 1907–1993 Painter in oil, artist in line and wash and lithographer, born in London. He studied at Central School of Arts and Crafts with John Farleigh, Bernard Meninsky and F C Herrick. Brookshaw's career was as an illustrator, designer, painter and teacher of lithography at Goldsmiths' College School of Art. He worked for International Wool Secretariat; *The Times*; London Transport; Shell-Mex and B P; J Arthur Rank; *Radio Times*; British Rail; and completed drawings and book covers for numerous publishers. His work is in the Royal Air Force Museum, Hendon, and in the Fleet Air Arm Museum. From 1964 he lived part-time in Spain, painting portraits and landscapes, and in 1991 Homenaje to Drake Brookshaw was held by Ayuntamiento de Mijas (Town Hall). From 1959 he showed regularly in Cornwall, where he lived finally in a nursing home in Wadebridge. Was a member of the Senefelder Club and Art Workers' Guild.

Marion BROOM fl.c.1920–1960 Painter in oil and watercolour. Born in Norfolk, she studied at the Royal College of Music and sang in opera for a time. Exhibited RA, RI, RWA and RCamA. Leamington Spa Art Gallery and several overseas galleries hold her work. Lived at High Wycombe, Buckinghamshire.

Mollie BROOME 1910–1994 Painter and photographer, notable for portraits, born in the Southsea area, Hampshire, her father a bank cashier. During World War II she served in the Auxiliary Territorial Service, commissioned acting junior commander, involved partly in photography at an anti-aircraft battery. After the war she studied art, industrial design and drawing. Worked at a studio in Ilford for two years, then opened her own photographic studio in Fareham, Hampshire. After marrying Wing-Commander George Potter in 1959 she resigned as a technical illustrator for the civil service and moved to Bushey, Hertfordshire, where she set up studio at home and concentrated on portraits. Bushey Museum Trust holds Broome's work.

Frances BROOMFIELD 1951– Painter in oil and tempera on wood panels with gesso ground, usually on a small scale; also an illustrator. C G Jung's ideas of the collective unconscious were an influence, painting being Broomfield's "way of exploring the world of the imagination". Born in Warrington, Lancashire, she attended the local College of Art and Newport Art School, in 1990 joining Cecil's Collins' life classes at the Central School of Art. Published work included book jackets for Cape, Bodley Head, Century Hutchinson, Little, Brown & Company and others; the 1995 calendar for Colin Dann's *Farthing Wood* series; and greetings cards for Royle, Santoro Graphics, Pharaoh Fine Arts and others. She was a member of the Women's Art Library and was featured in the International Women Artists' Diary in 1988 and 1996. Awards included North West Arts, 1989; Pollock Krasner Foundation, 1991; Oppenheim-John Downes Trust, 1993; and London Arts Board, 1995. From 1977, Broomfield showed almost exclusively with Portal Gallery. Other shows included Sue Williams Gallery and Art Works for London Lighthouse, both 1988; Birmingham City Art Gallery, 1991; and she shared an exhibition at Bremen Art Gallery, Germany, 1992.

James BROTCHIE 1909–1956 Painter in oil and watercolour and museum curator. Born in Glasgow, Brotchie studied art at the School of Art there, 1928–32, then in several centres on the continent. He was the son of Theodore Brotchie, an artist who was primarily an art administrator, and James spent most of his life on similar work, eventually becoming keeper of prints and drawings at the National Gallery of Scotland, Edinburgh. He also published articles in a number of Scottish publications, including *The Scotsman*, *Scottish Art Review* and *Glasgow Herald*. Exhibited RSA, SSA and the Royal Glasgow Institute of the Fine Arts. Lived in Edinburgh.

William BROTHERSTON 1943– Sculptor and teacher, born in Edinburgh. He studied at Cambrige University, 1962–5, and from 1965–71 at Edinburgh College of Art, where he then began teaching. He exhibited regularly at RSA, Federation of Scottish Sculptors of which he was a member, as he was of SSA. As well as taking part in a number of group shows of Scottish sculpture, Brotherston showed solo at Pier Arts Centre, Stromness, and elsewhere. Scottish Arts Council holds his work.

Alan BROUGH 1890–1986 Sculptor, born at Morley, near Wilmslow, Cheshire. He studied at Manchester School of Art and was a member of MAFA, where he exhibited. Moved to Prestbury, Cheshire, in 1930, where he established a small shop to exhibit his carvings and to deal in antiques. Brough had a studio in Wilmslow, adjacent to the railway station. He retired in the 1960s, and from then on did little work. As well as doing some traditional carvings of figures including members of his family, Brough did more advanced sculpture in stone and wood. Manchester City Art Gallery holds his sculpture Primavera, of 1927. Although he continued to live in Prestbury, Brough died at his daughter's house in Marchamley, near Shrewsbury.

Robert BROUGH 1916–1984 Painter and draughtsman, born in Cambuslang, Glasgow, who was by profession an electrical engineer. After education at Rutherglen Academy he studied art in Glasgow and London. Exhibited extensively throughout Britain and Ireland in group shows, including PS, UA, Ridley Art Society of which he was vice-chairman, Ealing Arts Society and Bladon Arts Society and had solo shows in London and the southern counties. Barclays Bank Ltd bought his work. Brough was especially known for his marine pictures and landscape and portrait pastels. Lived in Brentford, Middlesex.

Aya BROUGHTON 1912– Painter, muralist and lecturer, born in Kyoto, Japan. After education in Japan she studied at Newton Abbot School of Art and Dartington Adult Centre. She was a member of NS, Free Painters and Sculptors, WIAC, SWA and was an Associate of Société des Artistes Français. Also showed at RA, RI, RBA and elsewhere and in 1972 gained silver medal at Paris Salon. Private collections worldwide hold her work. Also used painting name Aya. Lived in Torquay, Devon.

BROUN-MORISON of Finderlie fl. c.1950–1970 Henry de Annand, nineteenth Laird of Finderlie, painted flowers in oil on wooden panels. Exhibited London and the provinces. Signed work with letter F.

Allan Robert BROWN c.1889–1947 Landscape watercolourist and teacher, father of the painter Hugh Boycott Brown. He was senior art master at the Royal Masonic Senior School in Bushey for many years, and gave lessons to his son. Was a member of Watford and Bushey Art Society. In 1994 Bushey Museum Trust held a joint exhibition of both artists' pictures.

Arnesby BROWN 1866–1955 Painter of landscapes, especially with cows. Born in Nottingham, John Arnesby Brown studied art there, with Andrew McCallum and then with Sir Hubert von Herkomer at his Bushey School of Art, 1889–92. Brown's wife Mia was also a painter. Brown's reputation became international, but he concentrated his work on St Ives, in Cornwall, and Norfolk, although for about the last 20 years of his life, after his wife's death, he lived in London for much of the time. Exhibited RA, Leicester Galleries, Goupil Gallery, RSA and at many other venues. In 1934 Brown was represented at the Venice Biennale, having a retrospective at Norwich Castle Museum the following year. Tate Gallery holds three typical scenes: Morning, Silver Morning and The Line of the Plough. Brown was elected RA in 1915 and was knighted in 1938. Died at Haddiscoe, Norfolk, in 1955, with a memorial exhibition in Norwich, 1959.

Atri BROWN 1906– Sculptor, married to the painter Veronica Picris. He studied at Wolverhampton School of Art under Robert Emerson and at the Royal College of Art under Ernest Cole. Brown was a Prix de Rome winner in 1928. Exhibited RA, NS and in America and the British Council bought his work, 1939. Taught at Chelsea Polytechnic School of Art, 1934–9. Sometimes signed work Atri. Lived in London.

Bonnie BROWN 1952– Artist in oil, gouache and mixed media and teacher, born Dorking, Surrey, married for a time to the painter Padraig Macmiadhachain. She attended Winchester School of Art, graduating with honours in 1981, in 1982 gaining a postgraduate diploma in printmaking. Obtained a travel award to Holland. Began teaching in 1982, appointments including Southampton Institute of Higher Education, Chelsea and Winchester Schools of Art and Maidenhead College of Art and Design. Exhibitions included Picture Post Gallery, 1981; Salisbury Playhouse, Salisbury, 1984; Stephen Bartley Gallery from 1988; RWA from 1990; The Discerning Eye, 1992, where she won a prize; and Laing Competition, Winchester, 1993. Lived at White Yard Studio, Swanage, Dorset. The Purbeck landscape and seascapes were cited as her "biggest influence".

Cecil BROWN 1902– Painter and architect who was educated at St Paul's School and studied art privately. Showed RA, Guildhall Library and Art Gallery, New Zealand House and Grundy House Museum in Blackpool. He illustrated a number of books to do with ecclesiastical architecture. Lived in London.

Charles William BROWN 1882–1961 Primitive artist, born at Robin Hill, north Staffordshire, son of a miner; he had a hard, poverty-stricken childhood. Left school at 12 and worked on farms and in pits. Eventually became manager at Newbury Collieries, Coleford, in 1923, but this job turned sour and he was employed elsewhere in mining until retirement in 1948. Then concentrated on his painting, showing with Society of Staffordshire Artists. Lived for much of his life in Etruria, Staffordshire, and bequeathed a collection of pictures and autobiographical writings to City Museum and Art Gallery, Stoke-on-Trent. It held a retrospective exhibition in 1993.

Christopher BROWN 1953– Printmaker and illustrator, born in London. He left Royal College of Art in 1980, then went on to work as an illustrator for *Radio Times*, *The Observer* and on book covers for Penguin Books and Faber & Faber. Illustrated Somerset Maugham's *Short Stories* for The Folio Society, had his colour linocut *The Sculler*, 1984, issued by Merivale Editions and showed his work at Michael Parkin Gallery.

Colin BROWN 1962– Painter, artist in construction and collage, born in Dundee, Angus, raised in Kingussie, Inverness-shire, who attended Duncan of Jordanstone College of Art, Dundee, 1982–7. After periods in Glasgow and Düsseldorf, Germany, from 1995 settled in Stonehaven, Aberdeenshire. Brown gained a RSA John Kinross Scholarship, 1987, and a Pollock-Krasner Award, 1996. He took part in numerous group exhibitions, including Diadem Centenary, Perth (second prize), 1984; RSA and Compass Gallery, Glasgow, from 1986; Fine Art Society, Glasgow, from 1991; Open Eye Gallery, Edinburgh, 1995; and Roger Billcliffe Gallery, Glasgow, 1997. Had a solo show at Barbizon Gallery, Glasgow, 1989, later ones including Peacock Gallery, Aberdeen, 1997, with frequent solo exhibitions in Germany. Highland Regional Council and Norddeutsche Landesbank, Hanover, hold examples.

Deborah BROWN 1927– Sculptor in glass fibre, papier mâché and bronze, born in Belfast, where she settled. Brown developed from being a painter. Her work was figurative and abstract, noted for its delicate colour, serenity and calm. She studied painting at Belfast College of Art, 1946, then National College of Art in Dublin, 1947–50, subsequently in Paris. Her teachers included Maurice McGonigal and Sean Keating. She took part in many mixed exhibitions, including RHA, RUA, WIAC. Had a solo show at CEMA Gallery, Belfast, in 1951, others including New Vision Centre, 1959–64; Arts Council Gallery, Belfast, 1962; David Hendriks Gallery, Dublin, 1966–84; and a mid-career retrospective at Ulster Museum, Belfast, and tour, 1982. In that year she became a member of the Sculpture Society of Ireland. Among her commissions was a Drover and Seven Sheep for Arts Council of Northern Ireland Sculpture Park, installed 1992. The Council, Municipal Gallery of Modern Art in Dublin, Arts Council of Southern Ireland and other collections hold her work.

Denise BROWN fl. from mid-1930s– Printmaker and painter, born in London, daughter of artist Frederick Peter Brown. After education in Germany she studied at Royal College of Art, having gained a British Institution Scholarship; her teachers were Malcolm Osborne and Robert Austin; after gaining her diploma, in 1935, in 1936 she won a Rome Scholarship in Engraving and a Travelling Scholarship. Brown was elected RE in 1959. Was a regular exhibitor at RA and RWA and abroad, as well as illustrating children's and gardening books. Victoria & Albert Museum and Ashmolean Museum in Oxford hold her work. Lived in Church Westcote, Oxfordshire.

Dexter BROWN 1942– Artist in nearly all media, born in Hayes, Middlesex, settling nearby at Pinner. He attended Harrow School of Art, 1956–9. In 1960 Brown, who also worked under the name De Bruyne, became a freelance illustrator, in 1965 taking up automobile art, for which he became noted, having great ability to depict authentic cars at speed. Between 1969–79 Brown had a period of portraiture including pop stars. His work appeared in periodicals such as *Car Collector* and *Ferrari World*. Solo shows included Monte Carlo Galleries, Alexandria, Virginia. Also showed at Auto Art in Connecticut, and Abarth Galleries and Porsche Museum in Tokyo. Was commissioned by Pininfarina in Turin, Italy.

Diana Elizabeth BROWN 1929– Painter and illustrator who sometimes worked on china, born in Cambridge. She specialised in wildlife subjects and was a member of SWLA. Studied at Tunbridge Wells School of Art, 1947–51. Showed with SWLA and in Scotland and illustrated for periodicals as well as a number of books. Lived in Aboyne, Aberdeenshire.

Elaine BROWN 1961– Painter, born and lived in London, who graduated with honours in fine art, 1980–4, at University of Reading, then gained a postgraduate diploma from Cyprus College of Art, 1985–6. Her pictures, serene and considered, placed objects in a format where they interacted, suggesting metaphysical aspects. Group shows included New Contemporaries 1984 at ICA; Three Women Painters, Rochester Art Centre, 1987; and Espace Vega, Paris, 1994. Among her solo exhibitions was Harriet Green Gallery, 1995.

Frank Percival BROWN 1877–1958 Designer of mosaics and other works. Born in Staffordshire, studied art at the Royal College of Art, 1902–7 under Gerald Moira, W R Lethaby and others. Held a number of teaching positions in London, including visiting art master at Merchant Taylors' School. Was for a time chairman of the South Kensington Sketching Club and began the old students' association at the Royal College of Art just before World War I. Did design work for Josiah Wedgwood and Sons. Lived at Rottingdean, Sussex.

Glenn BROWN 1966– Painter, born in Hexham, Northumberland, who did a foundation course at Norwich School of Art, 1984–5, gained an honours degree in fine art at Bath Academy of Art, 1985–8, then a master's at Goldsmiths' College, 1990–2. Brown was included in Young British Artists V, at Saatchi Gallery, 1995, where he showed a range of paintings which took the works of artists such as Dali, Auerbach and Appel as their starting point, displaying great technical skill. Lived in London.

Hannah BROWN 1886– Painter and draughtsman, born in London. She studied singing privately and painting with the watercolourist Myles Birket Foster. However, she was mostly self-taught, studying intensively while living in Italy for about 10 years from the late 1920s. Brought up at the Foundling Hospital in London, she recalled her experiences in *The Child She Lay Bare*, published in 1919 under the pen-name A Foundling. Exhibited RA and in Sussex, where she lived latterly at Rottingdean.

Hilary BROWN 1963– Sculptor and teacher working in a variety of materials. Born in Portsmouth, she studied at Ruskin School of Art, Oxford, 1981–4, then Birmingham Polytechnic, 1985–6. She had a sculpture fellowship at Cheltenham College of Art, 1986–7. Went on to become a visiting lecturer at various art schools and colleges, including Birmingham, Cheltenham and Ruskin. Her sculpture The Weak Spot was included in East & South Norwich Gallery/Kent Institute of Art and Design exhibition in 1992. Lived in London.

John BROWN 1887–c.1961 Painter who was educated at Cambridge University, then studied at Westminster School of Art, 1926–9, with Walter Bayes. Showed at RBA, RCamA, Paris Salon and Lincolnshire Artists' Society, sometimes just signing work J B. Lincoln's Usher Gallery holds his works: A Break in the Clouds, November Sky and Humberstone Foreshore, all presented by Sir Hickman Bacon in the 1930s. Lived at Grimsby, Lincolnshire.

John BROWN 1931– Sculptor producing stone carvings and bronzes, mainly based on the human form, realistic, simplified or abstracted. He studied at Hornsey School of Art and at Hampstead Garden Suburb Institute with Howard Bate. Was an associate member of RBS. In 1989, he was the first prize winner of a Business Arts Award, and in 1995 Brown's Love of the Family was placed in the children's wing of King's College Hospital. He carried out a number of church commissions. Linda Blackstone Gallery, Pinner, and The John Russell Gallery, Ipswich, were among galleries showing Brown's work.

John Caldwell BROWN 1945– Artist and teacher, born in Scotland, who graduated from Glasgow School of Art, 1963–8, teachers including David Donaldson and Duncan Shanks. Brown won many awards, including latterly Arts Club Award, SSWA, and Scottish Provident Award there, both 1993; and Heinzel Gallery Award, 1994. He taught from 1968, later positions including head of art at The Edinburgh Academy, Edinburgh from 1988; visiting lecturer, Leith School of Art, Edinburgh, 1991–4; and from 1994 visiting lecturer at Edinburgh College of Art and board director at Leith School of Art. Brown regularly exhibited with RSW, RSA, Royal Glasgow Institute of the Fine Arts and SSWA, taking part in many other group exhibitions, especially in Scotland. Had a solo show in 1970 at both Glasgow School of Art and Ayr Gallery, Ayr, later ones including The Open Eye Gallery, Edinburgh, and Duncan R Miller Fine Arts, both 1996. Commissions included Portrait of Hugh McDiarmid, 1968; Portraits of Two Royal Archers, 1970; and Portrait of Viscount Arbuthnot, 1972. Brown constantly experimented with form, expression, colour and texture, employing a rich palette in oils, collage and mixed media, figurative and abstract elements. Lived in Edinburgh.

John Ernest BROWN 1915– Sculptor, painter and teacher, born in Shawforth, Lancashire. Studied at Manchester's Municipal School of Art and after World War II taught at Monmouthshire Training College. He became closely involved with the development of art studies in Wales and was a member of SEA and National Union of Teachers. During World War II War Artists' Advisory Committee had bought his work, as had the War Office; he also showed at public galleries in Southport, Manchester and Belfast and at the National Museum of Wales, Cardiff. Based at the Monmouthshire Training College, Caerleon.

Keith BROWN 1947– Sculptor and teacher, born in Hexham, Northumberland. He won a scholarship to Michigan University, in America, 1969, studying at Royal College of Art, 1972–5. Taught in early 1980s at Manchester Polytechnic. Solo shows included Serpentine Gallery, 1977, Leeds Polytechnic, 1979. Brown's multi-piece Untitled, 1981, in wood, is held by South Hill Park Arts Centre, Berkshire.

Mary BROWN: *see* **Mary BROOKS**

May Marshall BROWN 1887–1968 Painter and teacher, born in Edinburgh, was married to the artist William Marshall Brown. She studied at Edinburgh College of Art, in Ireland and on the continent. Taught at St Margaret's School, Edinburgh, for many years. She contributed to the Pilgrim Trust *Recording Britain* project and exhibited RSA and RSW extensively, also Royal Glasgow Institute of the Fine Arts and in the English provinces. The art gallery in Auckland, New Zealand, holds her work. Member of SSA. A May Marshall Brown Award is made at the RSW's annual exhibition. Lived in Edinburgh.

Mimi BROWN 1920–1996 Painter of still life and landscape with a careful regard for tonal values, born in Belgium. She married two British bankers, taking her name from the first. Travelled widely abroad. Lived finally in Eastbourne, Sussex, where she died in a nursing home in The Meads. Sometimes signed work M B. Premier Gallery, Eastbourne, showed work after her death.

Mortimer BROWN 1874–1966 Sculptor of religious and classical subjects, born in Stoke-on-Trent, Staffordshire. He studied at Hanley School of Art around 1890, then for several years in the early 1890s at Royal College of Art and at Royal Academy Schools, 1896–1901; his teachers included Richard Ledward, Alfred Gilbert and Éduardo Lantéri and he won a number of medals and awards. Further study followed in Italy and Greece. For some years Brown worked with the sculptor William Hamo Thornycroft. Showed RA, ROI and RI and was made a fellow of RBS. Tate Gallery holds his bronze Shepherd Boy. Lived in Twickenham, Middlesex.

Neil Dallas BROWN 1938– Painter and teacher, born in Elgin, Moray. He studied at Dundee College of Art, and Patrick Allan-Fraser School of Art, Hospitalfield, Arbroath, as well as Royal Academy Schools. Won a travelling scholarship to the continent and a number of notable awards and prizes. In 1967 visited New York with a Scottish Arts Council Award; in 1970 took part in the Arts Council of Northern Ireland Open, winning a major prize; and in 1981 won a bursary to the Scottish Arts Council studio in Amsterdam. From 1968–78 was visiting lecturer at Duncan of Jordanstone College of Art in Dundee, then joining the staff of Glasgow School of Art. Dallas Brown participated in dozens of group shows in Britain and abroad and his one-man schedule was equally hectic. He had a one-man show at Duncan Institute, Cupar in 1959; others followed at Compass Gallery, Glasgow; there was a series at Piccadilly Gallery; a retrospective toured from Stirling University in 1975; and Perth Art Gallery followed in 1987 and Thackeray Gallery in 1989. Birds and humans featured in Dallas Brown's pictures which are tinged with mystery, menace and Surrealism. Walker Art Gallery in Liverpool, Arts Council of Northern Ireland and many Scottish galleries hold his work. Lived in Newport-on-Tay, Fife.

Nellie BROWN fl. c.1930–1970 Artist in oil, watercolour and black-and-white. Born in Wolverhampton, she studied at the School of Art there. Exhibited RA and RBSA, principally rural views. She signed her work NB with the date. Lived in Wolverhampton, Staffordshire.

Percy BROWN 1911–1996 Sculptor and potter. Studied at the Royal College of Art. Then taught sculpture at Leicester College of Art, was head of the school of sculpture and pottery at Leeds College of Art, later head of the department of art and architecture at Hammersmith College of Art. Exhibited RA, Leicester Galleries, Gimpel Fils and at other London galleries. Leicester Museum and Art Gallery and several other public collections hold his work. Brown's work was in two phases as shown in his retrospective at The Canon Gallery, Chichester, in 1991: from 1937–55 he did portraits and sculptures related to buildings, including ceramics and nude studies; from 1963 he started abstract compositions in bronze and wood. Lived at St Margaret's on Thames, Middlesex.

Philip BROWN 1925– Painter and stained glass artist, born in London, who did a lot of work for religious buildings. Was educated at St Paul's School, then Oxford University. Studied art at Slade School of Fine Art, 1945–7, at L'Académie de la Grande Chaumière, 1948, and also in Paris at L'Ateliers d'Art Sacré, 1949–50. There followed a stream of work for churches in Britain and overseas, notably in Liverpool, Scunthorpe, Pershore and Eastbourne. Brown also exhibited in mixed exhibitions and had solo shows at the Galerie St Placide, Paris, and Ashley Gallery in London in the early 1950s. Lived in St Leonards-on-Sea in Sussex, later in Madrid, Spain.

Philip BROWN 1958– Versatile artist, born in Leeds, Yorkshire, where he did a foundation course at Jacob Kramer School of Art, 1977–8; gained an honours degree in fine art at Manchester Polytechnic, 1978–81; and a higher diploma at Slade School of Fine Art, 1981–3. In 1983–4 Brown used a Boise Travelling Scholarship to study Islamic architecture in Morocco and its influence in Spain; in 1984–5 he held a residency at Lady Lodge Arts Centre, Peterborough, working with local industries, and in 1986 a brief residency at Bretton Woods School there, helping with the organisation of three murals. Shows included MAFA from 1979; Beaumanor Hall, Leicestershire, 1983; Werner-Jaeger Halle, Viersen, West Germany, 1986; and Art '87, at Peterborough's Lady Lodge Arts Centre, 1987. Solo shows included one there, 1984–5.

Ralph BROWN 1928– Sculptor and teacher, born in Leeds, where he studied at the College of Art, 1948–51, following encouragement at Leeds Grammar School and Royal Air Force Service from 1946. Early inspirations were Henry Moore and Jacob Epstein. Was then at Hammersmith School of Art, 1951–2, taught drawing by Leon Underwood, followed by tuition from Frank Dobson and John Skeaping at Royal College of Art, 1952–6. Also studied under Zadkine, but was less influenced by him at this time than by the sculpture of Germaine Richier and that of Rodin. Brown was to live in France 1973–76. Held a number of teaching posts in England, including Royal College of Art, 1958–72, being elected RA in latter year. Showed Leicester Galleries and Taranman Gallery and completed many public commissions, including Swimmers for Hatfield New Town and Meat Porters for Harlow New Town. Brown's bronzes were often of figures in motion, and if they sometimes appear awkward they are always infused with a strong sense of passion and humanity. The retrospective at Henry Moore Centre for the Study of Sculpture, Leeds, in 1988, indicated Brown's abilities as a draughtsman. Tate Gallery and Arts Council hold his work. Lived in Amberley, Gloucestershire.

Reginald Victor BROWN 1897– Painter, designer and teacher, born in Brighton, Sussex. He was brought up in Hull where he attended the School of Art, then going to Manchester School of Art and Milan. During World War II he was an official war artist attached to Ford Motor Company, in Trafford Park, Manchester. He earned his living thereafter as a commercial artist. He was a life member of the Manchester Athenaeum Graphic Club and helped to organise exhibitions at the City Art Gallery on Rowley Smart, the Annual Athenaeum Graphic Exhibitions and the Five Manchester Art Clubs Exhibition of 1929 and the Six Manchester Art Clubs Exhibition of 1930, for which he designed the catalogues. Also showed at Walker Art Gallery in Liverpool, RA, RCamA and elsewhere in the north of England, Manchester City Art Gallery buying his picture The Wye River. Lived for 50 years in Manchester, then at Harwood, Bolton, Lancashire.

Richard BROWN 1965– Self-taught sculptor working mainly in sandstone and slate, born in Lanarkshire. He was winner of the 1995 Royal Glasgow Institute of the Fine Arts N S Macfarlane Charitable Trust Award, shared with William Selby. Ewan Mundy Fine Art in Glasgow, where Brown lived, included him in the 1996 exhibition Spring '96. Brown's figurative reliefs, in the manner of Eric Gill whom he much admired, often used the pale red sandstone retrieved from demolished Glasgow buildings.

Robin BROWN 1950– Sculptor, painter and teacher. He attended Bromley College of Technology, 1967–8 and University of York, 1969–72. From 1973 at various times he studied part-time at Instituto de Espana, City Literary Institute and painting with Roy Oxlade. Brown was sculptor-in-residence at Kent Institute of Art & Design, 1989–91. His group exhibitions included Galeria Nueva, Banco Central, Bogota, in 1983; Hall Palace, Bexley, 1985–7; and Sculpture at Canterbury from 1990. In 1991 he had a commission from St Paul's Church, Canterbury. Brown was noted for sculpting with a variety of woods.

Rodger BROWN 1961– Sculptor in mixed media and teacher, who gained an honours degree in fine art at Sheffield Polytechnic, 1983–6, then his master's degree at Nottingham Polytechnic, 1988–90. Went on to work in the school of art and design at University of Derby. His sculptures appeared in many mixed shows including Mappin Art Gallery, Sheffield; Whitworth Art Gallery, Manchester; Castle Museum, Nottingham; Bread Street Gallery, Penzance; Smith's Gallery; and in East, in 1991, at Norwich School of Art Gallery. His 1990 work Bookshelf there was made up of shelf brackets, books and nests. Lived in Wirksworth, Derbyshire.

Samuel John Milton BROWN 1873–1963 Watercolourist and draughtsman of marine views. Born at Wavertree, Liverpool. Studied at the Liverpool School of Art, 1888–1900, under John Finnie. Exhibited RI, Walker Art Gallery, Liverpool and RCamA. Liverpool Corporation bought his picture Ploughing Her Way. Published several books on Liverpool, illustrated by him. Was at various times president of the Liver Sketching Club, Liverpool Academy of Arts and Flintshire Art Society. Lived at Upton, Chester.

Simon BROWN 1968– Painter of colourful small pictures, full of whimsical figures, in unusual frames. Born in Kent, Brown did a foundation course at Maidstone College of Art, 1988–9, then studied at Leeds Polytechnic, 1989–92. In 1989 he was runner-up in the Light in Art competition in Leeds. His 1992 appearances included Northern Graduates Exhibition and in 1993 he shared a show at New Academy Gallery and Business Art Galleries.

Tina BROWN fl. from early 1980s– Artist in various media who studied at Cyprus College of Art, 1978, then Royal College of Art, 1979–82. She exhibited in Stowells Trophy, 1978; British Council in Nicosia, 1979; Kyklos Gallery, Nicosia, 1981; Hayward Annual, 1982; and in British Artists at Cyprus College of Art at Woodlands Art Gallery, 1983.

Varuni BROWN: *see* **VARUNI**

William BROWN 1953– Painter and printmaker, born in Toronto, Ontario, Canada, of Scottish parents. He trained as a sculptor and went on to travel and read widely, reflected in his work. This used stylized imagery and appeared naive, his landscapes having an emphasis on the solid structure of objects, rhythm and design being other key features. Brown gained several awards, including a South West Arts Travel Award (Tunisia and Algeria), 1986, and a WAC Award (Orkney), 1992. He was the organiser of several projects including Contemporary Printmaking in Wales, 1993–6, which toured Britain and the continent, and 6 x 6, which toured, 1994. Had a major exhibition at Glynn Vivian Art Gallery, Swansea, 1996. Plymouth City Museum, National Maritime Museum and Peel Heritage Museum in the Isle of Man hold examples. Lived in Bridgend, Mid Glamorgan.

Alan Charlson BROWNE 1903–1970 Painter and photographer who studied at Liverpool School of Art, in Hope Street, and at Christchurch School of Art, in New Zealand. While in New Zealand Browne exhibited widely and was a member of

Canterbury Society of Arts, appearing in its *Jubilee Catalogue 1881–1930*. Browne also showed at RCamA, Walker Art Gallery in Liverpool, Royal Geographical Society (of which he was made a fellow in 1933) and at a number of public galleries in the north of England. During World War II he was attached to the Air Ministry as a camouflage officer. Lived near Wigan, Lancashire.

Charles Egerton BROWNE 1910–1996 Artist noted for his animal sculptures, and engineer, whose early education was blighted by dyslexia, so that he resorted to night school and self-education. Trained as a toolmaker, he became a chartered engineer. Was the founder and chairman for over 40 years of the Egerton Group of Companies, which from the early 1940s was involved in the aerospace industry, based in Burnt Oak, Middlesex. Browne studied sculpture in the studios of L Cubitt Bevis and Ernest Shone-Jones; pastels and oil with Helen Wilson at Heatherley's School of Fine Art (he helped save it when it hit hard times in the late 1960s); animal painting with Marguerite Frobisher in Bushey; and bronze casting with Michael Gillespie at Hertfordshire College of Art and Design, St Albans. Browne mainly worked in bronze, also using marble, stone, terracotta, cement and plaster, and engraved glass with an abrasive wheel. Exhibited in many London exhibitions, especially at SWLA, RBA, NEAC and Hesketh Hubbard Society, and had solo shows at Watford and Bushey Museums. He was made an associate member of the Société des Artistes Français in 1984, winning the Salon Gold Medal that year, and in 1995 was made an associate of RBS. Two years before, he had been elected a fellow of the Zoological Society of London, having researched animal subjects extensively at London and Whipsnade Zoos. The French animalier tradition, Édouard Lantéri, Sir Alfred Gilbert, Lucy Kemp-Welch, Sir Alfred Munnings and Frank Calderon were key inspirations. He was a keen medal-winning shot and fisherman. Browne created public works for Whitbread's stable block and the Farmers' Club, both in London; the Shire Horse Society headquarters in Peterborough; and the memorial to Bushey artists in St James' Church there. Bushey Museum, which gave him a memorial exhibition in 1996, holds his work.

Clive Richard BROWNE 1901–1991 Painter, mainly of landscapes in oil, and teacher of art, born in Keelby, Lincolnshire, who attended St John's College, York. He studied at Grimsby Art School and under Herbert Rollett. Was a member of North Lincolnshire Art Society and of Lincolnshire Artists' Society, also exhibiting at RA, RCamA RBA, RHA, RBSA, NS, Walker Art Gallery in Liverpool and at Paris Salon. His main works included On the Cornish Coast, Still Grinding and Near Lizard Point. Usher Gallery, Lincoln, holds his work. For many years lived at Waltham, Lincolnshire, latterly at Horsforth, Yorkshire.

Gilbert BROWNE 1954– Artist, notably a printmaker, born in Girvan, Ayrshire. He studied at Leeds Polytechnic, 1973–6, under Norman Webster, then Chelsea School of Art, 1976–7, with Dick Hart. Went on to establish own studio in London, showing at RA Summer Exhibition, Christie's Contemporary Art, Graffiti Gallery and abroad.

Kathleen BROWNE 1905– Painter, printmaker, teacher and art historian, born in Christchurch, New Zealand. Studied and taught at Canterbury College School of Art, Christchurch, 1920–4, from 1925–31 teaching at various schools. Browne attended Chelsea School of Art, 1932–3, as well as evening classes at Central School, in 1934 Royal College of Art. In 1935 was proposed as a candidate for Prix de Rome, but was too old. Taught at various venues until in 1949 founded own school. In running this she was helped by Marian Kratochwil, whom she married in 1961. Retired in 1979 to concentrate on her own work, notably portraits, which included the pianist Krystian Zimerman, and moved to Hampstead. Browne won a bronze medal at Paris Salon, 1947. She was a member of the Senefelder Club and Graphic Arts Society and showed at RA, RSA, Leicester Galleries and in 1950 shared a three-man exhibition at Prince Galitzine Gallery. Painted on the continent, notably in Portugal. National Portrait Gallery, British Museum and Cambridgeshire Education Authority hold her work. At one time she was art education policy adviser to the colour-makers George Rowney and Company. A perceptive monograph was published privately on her work by her husband, with whom she shared a retrospective at Polish Cultural Institute, 1994.

Matthew BROWNE 1959– Painter, draughtsman and teacher whose output included abstract works such as Home, oil on canvas, shown at Royal Over-Seas League open, 1995. He studied at Camberwell School of Arts and Crafts, then began a series of teaching appointments, including drawing tutor with Hackney Adult Education, 1988; visiting tutor at Chelsea College of Art & Design, 1989–90; visiting tutor at Outreach Community Art Centre, Auckland, 1992; plus several other New Zealand posts. Group shows included Iraqi Prize Exhibition, South London Art Gallery, 1982; RP, Mall Galleries, 1986; The Family in Art, New Zealand Academy of Fine Arts, Wellington, and Wallace Awards, Customs House, Auckland, both 1994. Had a solo show at Sue Rankin Gallery, 1986, later ones including Souvenir, Ferner Gallery, Auckland, 1995.

Richard BROWNE 1921–1990 Sculptor in various materials, born in London. He studied at Wimbledon School of Art, 1948–52, then Slade School of Fine Art, 1953. Browne was made a fellow of RBS and became president of SPS, being noted for his portraits. These included the ballerina Dame Alicia Markova, in 1992 taken into National Portrait Gallery collection. Work by Browne is in Guildford Cathedral, City of London University and Crawley New Town. Lived in Old Heathfield, Sussex.

Rory J BROWNE 1966– Painter, draughtsman and teacher, born in Alton, Hampshire, who graduated from Chelsea School of Art in 1988. He became head of art at St George's, a Hertfordshire comprehensive school, and settled in St Albans.

Exhibited in many mixed shows, including regularly in RA Summer Exhibition. Browne was a finalist in several national art competitions and won an Elizabeth Greenshields Award. He sometimes employed collage to give depth to the urban landscapes for which he was noted, being interested in natural and man-made structures such as girders and gasometers. Had a solo show at Edith Grove Gallery, 1997. London Borough of Barnet, British Gas and Mowlem, the building firm, owned examples.

Amy Katherine BROWNING 1882–1978 Painter in oil and teacher, follower of the Impressionists, subjects including flowers, children and landscape. She was born at Bramingham Hall, Bedfordshire, one of eight children, was brought up in the country and was encouraged by her parents to paint. After schooling in Ripon and Luton she went, aged 18, to Royal College of Art under Gerald Moira, gaining a scholarship to continue without paying, then studied in Paris, where she worked much in the open air, concentrating on problems of painting sunlight. In 1916 married the painter T C Dugdale. Taught at Camberwell School of Arts and Crafts, then replaced Percy Hague Jowett at Bromley and Beckenham School of Art until end of World War II. During war ran a Red Cross point and took in evacuees. In Paris she had exhibited at the Salon, where she won gold and silver medals; the French government bought two pictures for the Luxembourg collection, including The Red Shawl. Exhibited flower paintings at Fine Art Society in 1925, and also showed RA, NEAC, NS, ROI and extensively abroad. Her work is in many British provincial collections, including Manchester, Southampton and Glasgow, and those abroad. Brownie, as she was known to artist friends, latterly lived in Chelsea, where she had a studio, and Saxmundham, Suffolk, where she painted flowers from her own garden, insisting that "bought flowers have no character". The artist's great-niece, the actress Joanna Dunham, organised a large show of Browning's work at Christchurch Mansion, Ipswich, 1995.

Stephen James BROWNING 1953– Painter who went on to manage Greenwich Theatre and oversee its Art Gallery and who was born and lived in London. He graduated from Oxford University in 1974 with a degree in modern history, after attending Marlborough College. In 1971 he studied at Putney and Byam Shaw Schools of Art. Showed with Free Painters and Sculptors, at Mall Galleries and in the provinces.

Harold BROWNSWORD 1885–1961 Sculptor in bronze, wood and marble. Born in the potteries area of the West Midlands, son of a book-keeper at Wedgwood's, Brownsword studied at Hanley School of Art, then at the Royal College of Art, 1908–13. While at Hanley he won a gold medal for the design of a sundial, at the Royal College winning a travelling scholarship to Rome. He then taught sculpture, 1914–38, and was headmaster of Regent Street Polytechnic, 1938–50, where he executed a bronze relief of Major Robert Mitchell. Brownsword exhibited in London and the provinces and designed and executed war memorials at several locations, including Hanley and Northallerton, Yorkshire. He was a sculptor in the classical tradition, capable of images of great tenderness, as in his The Little Flower, illustrated in *RBS: Modern British Sculpture*, published in 1939. Brownsword was a fellow of the RBS. Lived in London.

Neil BROWNSWORD 1970– Ceramic artist, modeller and teacher, born in Stoke-on-Trent, Staffordshire, who studied at Newcastle-under-Lyme College; Cardiff Institute of Higher Education; and Royal College of Art. Brownsword was winner of the 1995 Royal Over-Seas League Award at the Royal College, providing two trophies for the League's Open in that year. Browne held a number of modelling and designing posts in the period 1990–94, including work for Josiah Wedgwood and *Spitting Image* Workshops, the firm that provided satirical puppets for television; then was assistant to Martin Smith at the Royal College and resident artist at Charleston Farmhouse, both 1994; and in 1995 taught at Bath College and Cardiff Institute of Higher Education and was modeller and assistant to Sir Eduardo Paolozzi. Awards included Potclays Award for Ceramics, 1990 and 1994; Cardiff Institute Award, 1992; Examiner's Award at Royal College, and Fletcher Challenge Ceramics Award, Auckland, both 1995. Group shows included Annual Open Art Exhibition, Stoke-on-Trent Museum & Art Gallery, from 1990; Workshop Gallery, Chepstow, 1993; and Museum of Mankind Student Showcase, 1995.

Anne BRUCE 1927– Painter and designer, born in Stoke Poges, Buckinghamshire. She studied theatre design and painting and drawing at Slade School of Fine Art, 1945–53, her teachers including Vladimir Polunin, then went on to Edinburgh College of Art. Was a prizewinner at John Moore's Exhibition, Liverpool, 1962. Showed widely, including New Art Centre, RA, Richard Demarco Gallery in Edinburgh and Galerie Creuze, in Paris. One-man exhibitions included Camden Arts Centre, 1978, and she had a shared exhibition at Austin/Desmond Fine Art, Sunninghill. Bruce was pioneer and director of Burleighfield Art, 1970–6, and was chairman of WIAC, 1973–9. From 1981 she lived in Somerset. She worked in watercolour on a large scale, producing landscapes of England and abroad, describing her pictures as "the summing up of my experience of living".

George J D BRUCE 1930– Painter in oil, born and lived in London, who attended Westminster School, then Byam Shaw School of Drawing and Painting, his teachers including Peter Greenham and Patrick Phillips. The Hon. George Bruce was elected RP in 1959 and occupied senior positions, being vice-president from 1984.

Marion BRUCE 1946– Artist in various media who was for some years with Ballet Rambert as a dancer from early 1960s. Began art studies in 1967, later concentrating on printmaking at Wimbledon School of Art. From 1980 she took part in many group exhibitions, including Camden Arts Centre, Arnolfini Gallery in Bristol and England & Co's 1992 Art in Boxes. She designed for Houston Ballet and showed in Houston, Texas.

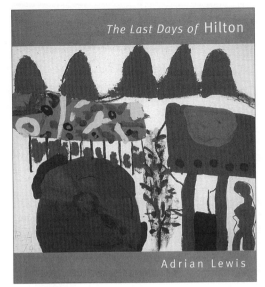

SCOTTISH ARTISTS' BENEVOLENT ASSOCIATION

Patron:	HRH Princess Alexandria	Honorary President: Angus Macdougall	
COUNCIL 1998			
President:	Jack B Firth RSW		
Vice-Presidents:	James D Robertson RSA RSW RGI	Miss Anne Donald DA AMA	
	Alistair Sharp	Bill Wright RSW RGI PAI	
Honorary Secretaries:	Dr Michael C G Rennie MC ChB	Barclay Lennie	
Honorary Treasurer:	John G Barclay CA HRSW		
Council:	Mrs Brenda Lenaghan RSW	Norman Kirkham RGI	Archibald D McIntosh RSW RGI
	Norman Edgar RGI	Mrs Morag Sharp	Charles T K MacQueen RSW RGI
	Jack Knox RSA RSW RGI	Albert L Robson	Gordon K Mitchell ARSA RSW

Secretary and Treasurer: R C Liddle CA, 5 Oswald Street, Glasgow G1 4QR Telephone: 0141-248-7411

OBJECT – to afford relief to distressed deserving Artists – whether subscribers to the Fund of the Association or not – their Widows, Orphans or Dependants.

The President and the Council appeal to Artists and those interested in Art to become Members, Subscriptions and donations will be received by any Members of the Council, or by the Secretary and Treasurer. Applications for assistance should be sent to the Secretary.

A donation of not less than £25 constitutes Life Membership. The Association was founded in 1889. The Council acknowledges with thanks support received from art societies and commercial companies.

Public Art Development Trust

PUBLIC ART DEVELOPMENT TRUST is an organisation engaged in an exciting and innovative dialogue which takes art and artists out of traditional contexts and into the wider world.

PADT commissions artists to create new work within the cultural landscape of public places and engages the public in the aesthetic, social and environmental issues of our times through the work of living artists. Over the years, London has been the location from which PADT's projects move outward, nationally and internationally.

PADT's projects manifest themselves in different forms, whether that be the temporary event, permanent or more long term installations. Recent projects have taken place along the River Thames, at King's Cross, at Heathrow Airport, and London Hospitals and for artranspennine98 and include:

Grenville Davey's **One and Four Thirds** at London's Docklands
Henry Bond's book and video work **Deep, dark water**
Angela Bulloch's **From the chink to Panorama Island**
Vong Phaophanit's **Ash and Silk Wall** at the Thames Barrier
Catherine Yass's **Corridors** at Springfield Hospital
Magdalena Jetelova's **Crossing King's Cross**
Julian Opie's **Imagine You're Moving** at BAA's Heathrow Airport
Joseph Bartscherer's **Canal** for artranspennine98

These projects have taken place through arts, business and public alliances which are sufficiently adventurous to enable the commissioning of innovative new works of art for unexpected places. PADT produces publications under its Documentary Notes series and holds periodic seminars and lectures.

PADT's work engages with a wide spectrum of participant audiences and dispels the notion that the best of contemporary art in Britain takes place only in the museums and galleries.

PADT was set up as a charitable trust in 1983 and currently receives financial support from the London Arts Board.

Kirkman House, 12-14 Whitfield Street, London W1P 5RD
Tel: +44 171 580 9977 Fax: +44 171 580 8540
e-mail: padt@padt.demon.co.uk

LONDON ARTS BOARD

Matt BRUCE 1915– Artist in various media and teacher, born in Shanghai, China. He studied at Edinburgh College of Art, 1932–9, teachers including John Maxwell and William Gillies. Went on to teach in several schools, including Varndean School for Boys in Brighton, where he settled, and part-time at College of Art there. Showed at RI of which he was a member, RA and RBA.

John Harold BRUCE-LOCKHART 1889–1956 Watercolour painter, born at Beith, Ayrshire. Was educated at Sedbergh School, of which he was later headmaster, Cambridge and on the continent. Exhibited RA, RI, RSW and with the Lake Artists' Society. Lived at Sedbergh, Yorkshire.

Mabel BRUCE LOW 1883–1972 Watercolourist and printmaker, born in Edinburgh, educated at Dulwich High School and in Germany. Studied art under Walter Sickert at Westminster School of Art and with Robert Burns at Edinburgh College of Art and Richard Jack at London School of Art. Exhibited RA, RSA, IS, NEAC, SWA and especially at RBA. British Museum and several provincial galleries hold her work, which often features flower paintings. Lived in Bournemouth, Hampshire.

BRÜER fl. from late 1950s– Artist and teacher, full name Brüer Tidman, who was especially interested in the human figure. Born in Norfolk, he trained at Great Yarmouth College of Art, 1957–61, and at Royal College of Art, 1961–4. Taught at Chesterfield College of Art and then at Lowestoft College School of Art and Design, 1976–84. Group shows included Athena International Awards at Mall Galleries, 1985, where he was a prizewinner; 1986, Fermoy Gallery, King's Lynn, East Anglian Artists Open Exhibition, first prizewinner; RA Summer Exhibition, 1989; British Artists of the 90s, RBSA, 1991; and Gallery K, 1992. Solo exhibitions included Lowestoft Art Centre, 1984; Fermoy Gallery, 1991; and Chappel Galleries, Chappel, 1993. Castle Museum in Norwich holds Portrait of the Artist's Mother, a drawing of 1992. Lived in Lowestoft, Suffolk.

Tony BRUMMELL SMITH 1949– Artist working in various media including pastel, born in Berkshire. He worked in commercial art and music before settling to painting seriously and professionally in 1970, working from a studio near Harrogate, north Yorkshire. The countryside and gardens featured strongly in his work. Group showings included RWS, PS and Bankside Gallery; in 1989 he was a Royal Horticultural Society Silver Medal Winner, and in the 18th Laing Art Competition, 1990, he was a regional first prize winner. Brummell Smith had a solo show at Century Gallery in Henley-on-Thames in 1975, later ones including Duncalfe Galleries, Harrogate, 1989–90, and Bourne Gallery, Reigate, 1993.

Reginald BRUNDRIT 1883–1960 Landscape and figure painter in oil and watercolour. Born in Liverpool, he studied at Bradford School of Art, the Slade School of Fine Art and under the animal painter and sculptor John M Swan. Exhibited RA, ROI, NEAC, RSA, Walker Art Gallery, Liverpool, Paris Salon and elsewhere abroad. Yorkshire was a favourite subject of Brundrit's, and the Tate Gallery holds several examples. Other English provincial and Australian galleries hold his work. Elected RA 1938. Lived at Masham, Yorkshire.

John BRUNSDON 1933– Printmaker, painter and teacher, born in Cheltenham, Gloucestershire, where in 1949–53 he attended the College of Art. Moved to Royal College of Art, 1955–8, under Julian Trevelyan. He became head of printmaking at St Albans School of Art and wrote a standard textbook: *The Technique of Etching and Engraving*, 1965. Among his commissions was one for Houlder Bros, for their Mahe Beach Hotel, Seychelles. Showed widely in mixed exhibitions in Britain and abroad. Solo shows were held in Lund, Sweden, 1965, and Curwen Gallery, 1967, later ones including Alice Simsar Gallery, Ann Arbor, Michigan, John Owen Gallery in Cardiff and Chapman Gallery, Canberra, all in 1984; his Celebration of the Shakespearian Properties, at Shakespeare Centre, Stratford-upon-Avon, 1990; CCA Galleries, 1996; with a retrospective at Bankside Gallery (he was an associate of RE) in 1998. Although Brunsdon's early work was influenced by the American Abstract Expressionists, his mature pictures were representational. He was a full-time artist from 1977, with a studio in Stradbroke, Suffolk. Arts Council, British Council, Tate Gallery Museums of Modern Art in Edinburgh and New York and other public collections hold examples.

Ann BRUNSKILL 1923– Printmaker, draughtsman and painter, born in London. She studied at Central School of Arts and Crafts and Chelsea College of Art, gaining her diploma in 1962. Crafts Advisory Committee Index of Craftsmen awarded her a bursary which enabled her to study art and design in India. Her ideas were mainly about people and their relationships. Showed with RE of which she was for a time a member, RA and Victoria & Albert Museum. Solo shows included Easton Rooms, Rye, from 1983; Drew Gallery, Canterbury, 1991; and Duncan Campbell Contemporary Art, 1994. Victoria & Albert, Library of Congress in Washington, National Library of Australia in Canberra and other notable international collections hold her work. Lived latterly in Egerton, Kent.

Elizabeth York BRUNTON fl. c.1905–1960 Painter and wood engraver in colour who studied at Edinburgh College of Art, then in Paris. She exhibited RSA, RSW, Paris Salon, Royal Glasgow Institute of the Fine Arts and extensively abroad. British Museum holds her work. Lived in Edinburgh.

Violet BRUNTON 1878–1951 Miniature painter and woodcarver, born at Brighouse, Yorkshire, daughter of the artists Arthur and Annie Brunton. She was educated at Southport and Liverpool Schools of Art and the Royal College of Art. Won several medals there and the County Palatine Scholarship in Liverpool. Exhibited RA, RMS, RBA, Walker Art Gallery, Liverpool, and had several one-man shows. Victoria & Albert Museum holds her work. Lived in London.

Winifred Mabel BRUNTON 1880–1959 Watercolourist specialising in miniatures. After early art education in South Africa, studied at the Slade School of Fine Art. Married the Egyptologist Guy Brunton and wrote several books on ancient Egypt. Showed in Egypt and South Africa, where galleries hold her work and in England at the RA, RBA and RMS. Many one-man shows at the Arlington Gallery. Signed work with initials W M N B. Lived at White River, Eastern Transvaal, South Africa.

John BRYAN: *see* **Bryan de GRINEAU**

Mary BRYAN 1918– Embroiderer and textile designer, painter and teacher, born in London. Attended Putney High School, then studied at Bromley College of Art, 1936–41, and Royal College of Art. In 1949 she joined Brighton College of Art specialising in dress, following several years at Worthing School of Art, staying at Brighton for many years. She exhibited extensively, including Heal's Mansard Gallery, Crafts Centre of Great Britain, Red Rose Guild, UA, RBA and in industrial design touring shows. Her work was illustrated widely in crafts and design magazines and was bought by Victoria & Albert Museum and London County Council. Lived in Worthing and later in Lower Beeding, Sussex.

Dena BRYANT 1930– Artist, gallery owner and restorer, born in Gloucester, who studied at Royal West of England Academy, Bristol. Went on to run her own gallery for 26 years. Showed at St Albans Museum, 1970; St Albans Gallery, which holds her work, from 1975; at Salon des Nations in Paris, 1983; Royal Horticultural Society International Exhibition, at Mall Galleries, 1984; Galerie Salammbo, Paris, 1988; and had solo show of flower watercolours in St Albans Abbey, 1991. Sometimes signed work Dena, with initials or snail. Lived in St Albans, Hertfordshire, and at East Hyde, Luton, Bedfordshire.

Emma BRYANT fl. from early 1980s– Painter, muralist and teacher who trained from 1978–84 at Camberwell School of Arts and Crafts, Brighton Polytechnic and Central School of Art & Design. She showed regularly from 1982 and was included in a four-man exhibition at Woodlands Art Gallery, 1988. There she showed work which built up a picture of southeast London's river front. Bryant worked on several mural projects at school and hospital locations and taught at Morley College and Goldsmiths' College School of Art.

Gordon BRYCE 1943– Painter and teacher, born in Edinburgh. He studied drawing and painting at Edinburgh College of Art, 1960–5, in 1965 winning an Andrew Grant Travelling Scholarship to Spain. From 1968 he was a lecturer in printmaking at Gray's School of Art, Aberdeen. A painter of still life and landscape, Bryce employed a rich, warm and luscious palette in the Scottish tradition. Elected RSW, 1976. He won many awards, including a Sir William Gillies Travelling Scholarship; Scottish Arts Council Award; and an RSW May Marshall Brown Award. Was elected RSA and showed often at RA and SSA. Had two solo shows at New 57 Gallery, Edinburgh in 1966 and 1968. Later showed at Scottish Gallery, Edinburgh; Yperifanos Gallery, New York; and Sue Rankin Gallery. Numerous public collections hold Bryce's work, including Scottish National Gallery of Modern Art, Scottish Arts Council and National Trust for Scotland. Lived in Aberdeenshire.

Ken BRYCE 1956– Painter, draughtsman, printmaker and lecturer, born in Mancot, Flintshire, who after foundation and degree studies in Wales went to Royal College Art, gaining his master's in printmaking, 1988. Won WAC awards and commissions in 1979 and 1981. Was a visiting lecturer at Chelsea and Falmouth Schools of Art, Manchester and Seychelles Polytechnics and Chesterfield College of Art & Design. Took part in mixed and two-man shows in London, the provinces and Wales and had a solo show at Lamont Gallery before, in 1990–2, living in the Seychelles archipelago. The outcome was a solo exhibition, Reflections from a Small Island, at Oriel Contemporary Art, 1996. Rank Xerox, Penguin Books, Lowick House Print Trust, WAC and Royal College of Art hold Bryce's work. Lived in Hampshire.

Una BRYCE 1964– Painter and teacher, born in Londonderry, Northern Ireland, who did a foundation course in Liverpool, graduated from Coventry Polytechnic, then gained her master's degree in fine art painting, 1988, from Birmingham Polytechnic. She held a fellowship at Limerick College of Art and Design, where she was artist-in-residence, 1991–2, and was a visiting lecturer at Cork and Limerick Colleges of Art. Showed in England, Greece and extensively in Northern Ireland, being based in Queen Street Studios, Belfast.

Dilys BRYON 1930– Painter, printmaker, ceramist and teacher, using a rich palette, who was a purely figurative artist until the early 1970s; then a painting Trapped Bird, using bright colour constrained by a black grid, led her to move towards abstract, stained glass-like works. She studied at Wimbledon School of Art, obtaining a national diploma in design (painting), gaining her art teachers' diploma at London University. In 1974 began to study etching and mezzotint with Mark Balakjian at Morley College, in 1991 studying the etching techniques of S W Hayter at Atelier Contrepoint, Paris. Taught as head of department in private and state schools at secondary level, in adult education and higher education colleges. Was vice-chairman and chairman of the Printmakers' Council, also a member of NS, and exhibited with North and South Printmakers and Wandsworth Printmakers. Open exhibitions included RE; Curwen Gallery; Barbican Centre; and National Open Print Exhibition, Mall Galleries. Had a solo show at Gallery 20, Brighton, 1978, later ones including Pump House Gallery, 1995. Scarborough Art Gallery, Brunel University and several foreign collections hold examples. Lived in Fetcham, Surrey.

Mary BRYSON 1905–1994 Painter, printmaker and draughtsman of cool, restrained portraits and landscapes, born in Douglastown, growing up in Forfar, the countryside and people of Angus featuring in her early work. From 1921, studied at

Edinburgh College of Art with David Foggie, Henry Lintott and D M Sutherland, but when her family moved to London in 1923 she transferred to the Central School of Arts and Crafts, later to Chelsea College of Art where Terence Cuneo was a friend. She was employed at the School of Tropical Medicine and at the Cancer Hospital (later the Royal Marsden) as a medical draughtsman. There she met Charles Bryson, married him just before the outbreak of World War II, changing her name from May Johnston Riach to Mary Bryson, and when he was appointed a consultant pathologist at the Whittington Hospital in north London they settled nearby in Highgate. In the 1950s she attended a portrait class run by Jesse Dale Cast at Hornsey School of Art. After her husband's death, in 1972, she painted little, concentrating on her garden. Early in her career she had shown at the RSA, Senefelder Club and SWA. In 1997 there was a memorial show at The Highgate Gallery.

BUCHAN: *see* **James BOSWELL**

Dennis BUCHAN 1937– Painter and teacher, born in Arbroath, Angus. Buchan studied at Duncan of Jordanstone College of Art in Dundee and continued with postgraduate studies at Patrick Allan-Fraser School of Art, Hospitalfield, Arbroath, 1954–9. He taught part-time at Dundee in 1962–5, then joined the full-time staff. Buchan participated extensively in group shows in Scotland. He won a number of awards, gaining the Keith Prize and Latimer Prize at RSA in the early 1960s, in 1973 winning a Scottish Arts Council Major Award. In 1988 he gained the William J Macaulay Award for the most distinguished work in the RSA, to which he was elected. Buchan's first one-man was at Malcolm's Furnishing Store, Dundee, in 1959. Others included Compass Gallery, Glasgow, in 1994. Scottish Arts Council holds his work.

Anne BUCHANAN 1929– Painter, born in London where she continued to live; she was also known as Anne Buchanan-Crosby, having been the first wife of the sculptor Theo Crosby. Studied at Worthing School of Art and in 1948 at Camberwell School of Arts and Crafts with John Dodgson. She was a member of LG and was included in the Arts Council's British Painting '74, in 1974, where two Scenes from the Myths of Antiquity were shown, accompanied by a lengthy artist's statement. Had solo shows at AIA, 1971, and Meridian House International, Washington, 1979.

Elspeth BUCHANAN 1915– Painter in watercolour and oil, and teacher, born in Bridge of Weir, Renfrewshire. Studied at Edinburgh College of Art, 1933–8, on an Andrew Grant Open Scholarship, her teachers including Hubert Wellington and Robert H Westwater; then gained a Travelling Scholarship, 1938–9. During World War II worked in Naval Intelligence in Oxford, where in 1943 she studied art with Bernard Meninsky. Buchanan was noted for her small watercolour landscapes of Edinburgh, in a representational style. She showed with RSA, RA, NEAC and LG while teaching, 1947–72. Was a member of SSWA and SSA. Had her first solo show at Great King Street Gallery, Edinburgh, 1972, and lived in the city.

Hugh BUCHANAN 1958– Landscape and still life painter, born in Edinburgh, who studied for a degree in drawing and painting at College of Art there, 1976–80. In the latter year an Andrew Grant Travelling Scholarship took him to the Middle East. After undertaking a postgraduate course back at Edinburgh College with distinction, 1980–1, Buchanan in 1981 gained a Helen Rose Bequest to Northern Italy and Yugoslavia, also undertaking commissions for the National Trust. He went on to travel extensively in Britain and the continent, architecture featuring strongly in the resulting work. In addition to group showings, including Fine Art Society and Francis Kyle Gallery, Buchanan had solo exhibitions which included Scottish Gallery, Edinburgh, and Francis Kyle. HRH The Prince of Wales and the National Trust hold his work.

June BUCHANAN 1920– Artist mainly in pastel, full name Elizabeth June Buchanan, born in Ashwell, Hertfordshire, into an artistic family (the metalworker Edward Spencer was an uncle, the painter Ethel Spencer, a pupil of Gauguin, an aunt). In 1932 she gained a full certificate from the Royal Drawing Society, under her maiden name June Spencer. Work and bringing up a family prevented her from pursuing art until later in life. During World War II Buchanan was an ambulance driver. Studied at Marlborough Institute, Sloane Avenue, with I Bassingthwaighte. Mainly showed at Hurlingham Club exhibitions. The work of Paul Maze, colour and light inspired her. Lived in London.

Mary BUCHANAN 1876–1958 Sculptor and watercolourist who studied at Paisley School of Design and Glasgow School of Art under the sculptor Johan Keller. She lived for a long time in Paris, working in the studios of Bourdelle and Zadkine, showing at the Salon. Also exhibited at RA, Royal Glasgow Institute of the Fine Arts and at Sculpture in the Open Air, Glasgow, 1949. Notable for figures and heads in wood and marble; she presented her Female Portrait, in oolitic limestone, to Glasgow's Art Gallery and Museum, Kelvingrove, in 1945. Late in life she became an enthusiastic watercolourist.

Oughtred BUCHANAN 1883–1979 Painter, whose full name was Evelyne Oughtred Buchanan, born at Stockton-on-Tees, County Durham. After attending the High School there she studied for a few months with Stanhope Forbes, but mainly taught herself. Showed at RA, RSA, SSA, Royal Glasgow Institute of the Fine Arts, SSWA with which she was closely associated, and extensively in the English provinces. Glasgow Museums and Art Galleries hold her work. Lived in Edinburgh.

Ian BUCHANAN-DUNLOP 1908– Painter and draughtsman in ink, full name Archibald Ian Buchanan-Dunlop, he was born in Whitefield, Lancashire, and became a professional soldier, attaining the rank of brigadier. Was educated at Sandhurst's Royal Military Academy. Showed at RWS of which he was a member, and in military art shows. Until 1975 after retirement from the Army he was principal of the Scottish Office. Mainly known as a watercolourist. Lived in Colinton, Edinburgh.

John Sandford BUCK 1896–1988 Painter, draughtsman and printmaker, born in Minehead, Somerset, but his family soon moved to Monmouth where he attended Monmouth School. In 1914 he joined the Army but contracted rheumatic fever on Salisbury Plain and was ill for three years, being discharged as "unemployable". He went to live with his parents at Brains Green, Blakeney, in Gloucestershire, where he eventually settled. After trying to train for office work at Clark's College in Bristol and having studied etching with Reginald Bush at the Municipal School, Buck decided to make his living as a painter. His pictures were mainly local or holiday scenes, worked up from pastel sketches on the spot. Showed with BWS of which he was a member, RWA, RBSA and RI. Newport New Museum and Art Gallery holds his work. Member of Wye Valley Art Society and Gloucestershire Society of Artists. Retrospective show at Dean Heritage Centre, Soudley, Gloucestershire, in 1988.

Jon BUCK 1951– Figurative sculptor and teacher, born in Bristol. He attended Cardiff College of Art, 1975–6, Trent Polytechnic, where he obtained a bachelor's degree in fine art, 1976–9, and Manchester Polytechnic, 1979–80, for his master's degree. Buck was appointed fellow in sculpture at Cheltenham College of Art, 1980–1, was sculptor-in-residence for Borough of Thamesdown, 1985, and from 1987 lectured at Southampton Institute. His highly stylised work was shown at RWA annual exhibition from 1987; Sculpture in the Garden, Abergavenny, 1990; Gallery Pangolin, Stroud, from 1991; and Bath Art Fair, 1992. Buck's public commissions included Clifton Zoological Society, Bristol, 1986–7, and Old Cattle Market Site, Swindon, 1989–90. His work is in many private collections worldwide. Lived in Bath, Avon.

Michael BUCK 1954– Painter and teacher who studied at High Wycombe College of Art and Further Education, at Ruskin School of Drawing in Oxford and at Bretton Hall College of Further Education, Yorkshire. Buck was a fine, atmospheric landscape painter who reckoned that his knowledge of the countryside was deepened by an interest in hang-gliding and in garden design. He lectured at the Inchbald School of Garden Design, Banbury College of Art and several schools. Showed in group exhibitions at RA, Dwarves Gallery in Oxford and Sue Rankin Gallery, his solo shows including Sue Rankin, 1987. Lived in Oxford.

Allan BUCKETT 1953– Sculptor and teacher, born and lived in London, who studied at St Martin's School of Art, 1971–5. Worked at Meridian Bronze Foundry, 1976–9, then became a visiting lecturer at Edinburgh College of Art. Group shows included New Contemporaries at Camden Arts Centre, 1975, St Martin's Sculpture at South Bank in 1977 and Summer Show 3 at Serpentine Gallery, 1980. There he showed smallish mild steel works which "would generate some fresh ideas. Using colour was important. I wanted to discover, for myself, if colour could be useful in sculpture."

John BUCKLAND WRIGHT 1897–1954 Painter, draughtsman, but primarily an etcher and engraver who was self-taught. Born in Dunedin, New Zealand, Buckland Wright studied history at Oxford and then architecture in London. He soon realised that he wanted to be an artist more than an architect and by 1921 he was living in Belgium and was elected a member of the Gravure Originale Belge in 1925. Was also a member of Xylographes Belges, SWE and LG. During the 1930s Buckland Wright lived and worked in Paris and frequently visited S W Hayter's Atelier 17. He had one-man shows in London and throughout the continent, sometimes signing his work J B W. Work held by Victoria & Albert Museum, British Museum and many galleries and museums in Europe and America. A master printmaker with an assured, swirling line, Buckland Wright passed on his skills after World War II when he taught at Camberwell School of Arts and Crafts, from 1948, and the Slade School of Fine Art, from 1953, the year that his book *Etching and Engraving: Techniques and the Modern Trend* was published. He illustrated over 50 books. Retrospective Blond Fine Art, 1981. Lived in London.

Claude BUCKLE 1905– Painter, especially in watercolour, born in London, educated at Wolverhampton Grammar School. He trained as an architect, but gave this up in the late 1920s to become a full-time painter, exhibiting widely in England and America. He was a member of both RSMA and RI. Lived for many years in Andover, Hampshire.

Sydney H BUCKLE 1912– Painter, printmaker, designer and teacher, born in Stockton-on-Tees, County Durham. Attended Darlington School of Art, Northern Polytechnic and Garnet College. He held a number of teaching posts in the Stockton and Darlington areas and was a member of Darlington Society of Artists. Lived in Stockton.

Guy BUCKLES 1964– Artist born in Iowa, America, who studied at Hong Kong University; Hastings College of Art; and the Slade School of Fine Art. Showed at Victory Gallery, Hastings from 1989; Rye Society Summer Show from 1992; and from 1992 at Royal Over-Seas League Open, having a solo exhibition there in 1994.

Howard BUCKLEY 1909– Watercolourist, printmaker and teacher, born in Croydon, Surrey. Studied at Croydon School of Art and Royal College of Art. Buckley went on to teach, eventually becoming principal at Derby School of Art. Exhibited RA, RWA, in the provinces and in Chicago. He completed mural paintings in Worthing pier pavilion, Sussex, and other work held by Southampton and Brighton Art Galleries. Lived in Wheatley, Oxfordshire.

Jim BUCKLEY 1957– Highly versatile artist, born in Cork, Ireland, who attended Crawford School of Art there, 1975–80.

Buckley was involved in a series of imaginative creations, ranging across boxes with interiors, video and ambitious installations such as Flood, at Meiho, Japan, 1993, involving concrete tanks, water, paint and lights. Group exhibitions included World in a Box, City Art Centre, Edinburgh, and tour, 1994, preceded by Human Properties, Ikon Gallery, Birmingham, 1992, and Speed at Transmission Gallery, Glasgow, 1991. Solo shows included Illuminations at The Collective Gallery, Edinburgh, 1991; Access, at University of Strathclyde, 1992–3; and Kyoni Gallery, Tokyo, 1994. Lived in Dennistoun, Glasgow.

Stephen BUCKLEY 1944– Artist and teacher working in an often unconventional range of materials. He was influenced by Pop Art and Dada and while his work appears abstract it hints at everyday objects and appearances. Born in Leicester, Buckley studied at University of Newcastle upon Tyne, 1962–7, then Reading University, 1967–9. He taught at Canterbury and Leeds Colleges of Art and Chelsea School of Art, 1969–71; was artist-in-residence at King's College, Cambridge, 1972–4; and was visiting tutor at Royal College of Art, 1976 and 1986. After showing in Six at the Hayward, Hayward Gallery in 1969, Buckley had a one-man show at Nigel Greenwood in 1970. He was a John Moores Exhibition, Liverpool, prizewinner in 1974 and 1979. Buckley soon built up an impressive list of British and foreign showings and had a retrospective at Museum of Modern Art, Oxford, 1989, with an exhibition at University Gallery, University of Northumbria, 1994. Arts Council holds his work. Lived in London.

Sydney BUCKLEY 1899–1982 Painter and printmaker with a strong interest in Lake District and architectural subjects. He was born in Oldham, studied at the School of Art there and between 1927–32 was on its staff. He was an architect by training and during World War II was engaged in war claims work. After the war he went to live in Cartmel, Cumbria, with a sister, unmarried like himself, who was a craftsman and weaver. For some time they had a studio in the Cartmel Priory gatehouse. He showed in his studio and RI, RSA, RSW, Lake Artists' Society and MAFA. Helped to illustrate a Forestry Commission handbook. Oldham Art Gallery holds two pictures by him of local scenes. His sister died a month before him early in 1982.

Martin Arnold BUCKMASTER 1862–1960 Painter, teacher and writer, born in London, where he finally lived. Studied at Royal College of Art, where he specialised in architecture, a subject on which he wrote several books and published many articles. Exhibited RA, RI and RBA. Taught art at Tonbridge School. Member of the Arts Club.

George BUDAY 1907–1990 Printmaker, teacher and writer, born in Hungary, where he was educated at Kolozsvar and Szeged University, gaining his doctorate in 1934, also studying art in Italy. He lectured on graphic arts at Franz Joseph University, 1934–41. In England he became a book illustrator, published his own *Little Books* for a number of years and in 1954 *The History of Christmas Cards*. Buday was elected RE in 1953 and a fellow of SWE in 1954. Also showed at RA and elsewhere. Arts Council bought his work. Lived latterly in Coulsdon, Surrey.

Herbert Ashwin BUDD 1881–1950 Painter and teacher, born at Ford Green, Staffordshire. After private education he attended Hanley School of Art, then the Royal College of Art, 1903–8, under Gerald Moira. Taught at St Martin's School of Art, 1929–49, and Hornsey School of Art, 1930–49. Married to the artist Helen Mackenzie. Exhibited RA, NEAC, RP, ROI and Royal Glasgow Institute of the Fine Arts. Imperial War Museum and galleries in Bradford and Oldham possess his work. Lived in London.

Kenneth George BUDD 1925–1995 Designer of murals, mosaics and windows, born in London, who studied at Beckenham School of Art, 1941–4, then Royal College of Art, 1947–50, his teachers including John Cole, Kenneth Rowntree and Charles Mahoney. He exhibited at RA, Young Contemporaries, AIA and in the Power and Production Pavilion at London's South Bank Festival Site. Budd also did a substantial amount of advertising designing, but was better known for public building designs, including windows in the Church of the Good Shepherd, Brighton; a coat-of-arms in the foyer of Guy's Hospital; and work in the Medical Centre at Westerham, Kent, where he lived. Budd was a member of the Art Workers' Guild.

Rachel BUDD 1960– Painter, born in Norfolk, who graduated from Newcastle University, 1978–82, gained her master's degree at Royal College of Art, 1983–6, then obtained a fellowship at Kingston Polytechnic, 1986–7. Among her awards were the LG Henry Moore Prize, 1987, Mark Rothko Memorial Trust Fund travel grant to America in 1988 and British Council Botswana workshop grant, 1991. Took part in the Three Ways Arts Council/Royal College of Art European tour, 1990–3. Later solo shows included Purdy Hicks Gallery, 1993, and University of Northumbria 1994. Government Art Collection and Contemporary Art Society hold examples.

Graham BUDGETT 1954– Artist and teacher using photography, who graduated in fine art from Trent Polytechnic, 1973–7; did an advanced diploma in sculpture at St Martin's School of Art, 1977–8; and a master's in fine art at Stamford University, California, based in sculpture, 1979–82. From 1977–8 Budgett co-ordinated seminars for advanced students at St Martin's, from 1979–82 taught at Stamford University and from 1982–5 lectured at University of California, Santa Barbara. Exhibited widely, later shows including collaboration with Jane Mulfinger on the work A Grey Area, for the touring exhibition Boxer, 1995, Walsall Museum & Art Gallery. This installation in Plasticine and Astroturf recorded the names of boxing champions. Victoria & Albert Museum holds Budgett's work in its photographic collection.

Friedel BUECKING 1946– Sculptor who used a variety of materials, such as railway sleepers, carpet, stone and wood. Took up carving and sculpture full-time in 1979, then between 1985–90 took a part-time honours degree in fine art/sculpture in Hertfordshire. Work in public spaces and exhibitions included a nativity set for St Albans Cathedral, comprising chainsaw carvings, 1984; Wharf – carving and construction on Gasriec's Wharf, South Bank, 1989–90; Hull Dock Museum, the installation of wood and stone Atlantis, 1991; and Sculpture at Canterbury, 1992. One-man works included an installation at Tobacco Dock, 1992. Worked in London.

Michael BUHLER 1940– Painter in oil, creator of painted wood boxworks and teacher, born and lived in London, son of the artist Robert Buhler. He studied at Royal College of Art, 1960–3, teachers Carel Weight, Ceri Richards, Ruskin Spear and Colin Hayes. Buhler taught part-time in many art schools, university art departments and at Imperial College. He was a prolific exhibitor, including RA, John Moores Exhibition in Liverpool, Camden Arts Centre, Arts Council of Northern Ireland and elsewhere. Had solo shows at New Arts Centre, 1966–71, Architectural Association, 1968, and Maclean Gallery, 1981–92. Arts Council, British Museum, Eastern Arts Association and Liverpool University hold his work.

Robert BUHLER 1916–1989 Painter and teacher, born in London of Swiss parentage, he was early encouraged to paint. In the early 1930s he studied painting initially in Zürich and Basle, and attended Bolt Court, St Martin's School of Art and the Royal College of Art. He left the Royal College after a few months and with the help of a little money left to him took a studio and began to paint professionally, encouraged by the patron Edward Marsh. His mother had a café in Charlotte Street, so he became familiar with Fitzrovia and was friendly with the Euston Road School painters, whose style left an imprint on his work. Around the late 1930s Buhler did work for Shell-Mex and BP; was associated with the AIA; began a notable series of portraits with Dickie Green and Stephen Spender, bought by the Contemporary Art Society in 1938; and contributed to exhibitions at the Leicester Galleries. He exhibited with the NEAC from 1945, showed at the RA from1946, becoming RA in1956. Taught at Chelsea School of Art, Central School of Arts and Crafts and from 1948–75 was a tutor at the Royal College of Art. Three of his pictures were bought under the terms of the Chantrey Bequest and there are quite a lot in collections in the provinces and abroad. Buhler preferred to choose the subjects of his portraits, who included the critic John Davenport, the actor Sir Donald Wolfit and the poet Laurie Lee. In later life he concentrated more on landscape. Buhler, whose son was the painter Michael Buhler, lived in London.

Simon BULL 1958– Etcher, teacher and illustrator, born in Bedfordshire. He travelled the world with his parents before settling in Yorkshire in 1977, where he studied fine art at Leeds Polytechnic. He taught etching part-time at Leeds University and Bretton Hall College and illustrated several books. Bull liked to work on location, especially in the Lake District and Yorkshire dales. Mixed exhibitions included RA Summer Exhibition, Leeds Art Fair and 8th British International Print Biennial, Bradford. Had a solo show at Hong Kong Hotel, Hong Kong, 1976, a series at Fairfield Halls, Croydon, from 1978, also Bretton Hall College, 1984. Had studio at Clayton, Bradford, Yorkshire.

Paul BULLARD 1918–1996 Painter mainly in oil, born in London. Studied at Clapham School of Art, 1934–8, then Royal College of Art, 1938–40 – war service in the Royal Artillery intervened – and 1946–7, notable teachers being R V Pitchforth and Charles Mahoney. Bullard taught at various London art schools during 1947–58, from 1958–78 being head of the department of foundation studies at Camberwell School of Arts and Crafts. His exhibitions included Phoenix Gallery, 1947, RA from 1948 onwards, LG, NEAC, the Football Centenary Exhibition in 1953 and Belgrave Gallery, 1988. Collections holding his work include Imperial War Museum, Football Association and Shropshire Education Committee. Lived at Stanstead, Suffolk. Died in St Helena Hospice, Colchester.

Anne BULLEN 1914– Painter, draughtsman and illustrator, born in Norwich, Norfolk. She specialised in animal subjects, especially horses, and came from a military family, a connection strengthened by marriage. After education privately and in Paris, she studied art at Académie Julian there, in 1930, followed by Chelsea School of Art. Showed at UA and in Devon; lived for a time at Charmouth, Dorset. She illustrated a number a books with horse and pony themes, fiction and non-fiction.

Maud BULLEN 1906– Watercolourist, born and lived in Dorking, Surrey. A physically handicapped, naive artist, she studied with Ursula Hulme at Rentwood Occupational Therapy Centre at Fetcham. Took part in mixed exhibitions at Mall Galleries, New Metropole Arts Centre in Folkestone and in Best of British Naive Artists at Lyric Theatre. Had a solo show at Loggia Gallery, being a member of Free Painters and Sculptors.

Molly BULLICK fl. from late 1970s– Artist who gained a diploma in architecture, 1964, then began printmaking in 1978–9. She was awarded a Barcham Green Printmaking Competition Student Prize, 1980; gained two Scottish Arts Council bursaries, 1979 and 1981; and was elected to SSA in 1982. Took part in Scottish Print Open Three, 1983, organised by the Dundee Printmakers' Workshop, also showing with RSA and SSWA.

Angela BULLOCH 1966– Versatile conceptual artist in a variety of media, born in Ontario, Canada. She gained an honours degree in fine art at Goldsmiths' College of Art, 1985–8, won a Whitechapel Artists' Award, 1989, and had a two-month residency, Arcus-project, Moriya, Japan, 1994. Bulloch said that she was "interested in how things evolve, or shift their meaning when you move them into various different contexts ... I like the apparent contradictions of defining something which is always subject to change." She first showed her work in the 1988 exhibition Freeze in the PLA Building, thereafter participating in numerous group exhibitions internationally and getting wide press coverage.

In the mid-1990s she was working on a number of public projects, including Belisha Beacon Indicator System, 1996, a permanent work at the Leipziger Messe, Leipzig, and Panorama Island, a project for a disused jetty on the Thames, in front of Bankside Power Station. She was keen on the idea of sculptures as places of social interaction. Video compilations included 240 minuten, 1992, and Unplugged: the Demo Video Tape, 1993. Bulloch's first solo exhibition was at Interim Art, 1990. Many others followed in Europe and America, later ones including, in 1996, Galerie Walcheturm, Zürich, and Robert Prime. Lived in London.

Caroline BULLOCK 1947– Naive painter, born in Cornwall, working in oil and gouache. She was married to the artist Glynn Boyd Harte. Attended Bedales School, taught by Christopher Cash. Mixed appearances included Penwith Society, in St Ives, and she had solo exhibitions at Sheviock Gallery in Cornwall and Michael Parkin Gallery. Lived in Veules-les-Roses, Seine-Maritime, France.

Hazel BULLOCK fl. from 1960s– Painter who studied at Sir John Cass School of Art, teachers including David Graham and Roland Pitchforth. In 1970 she was elected to Free Painters and Sculptors, also showing at RBA and Browse & Darby. Had solo show at Loggia Gallery in 1973, later ones including Phoenix Gallery in Lavenham and Highgate, both 1989. Lived in London.

Jean BULLOCK 1923– Sculptor in a variety of materials, designer and printmaker, born in Bristol, married to the artist John Bullock. She studied at Watford School of Art and Camberwell School of Arts and Crafts, her teachers including Karel Vogel. She was elected to SPS in 1964, also showing with RA, in the provinces and abroad. South Norwood School and Ministry of Defence hold her work, and she designed a stained glass window for St Giles, Lockton, not far from her home near Pickering, North Yorkshire.

Stephen BULLOCK 1889 c.1972/3 Painter in oil and watercolour, born in Salisbury, Wiltshire. He studied under Austin Garland at Lincoln School of Art. Showed at Foyles Gallery and in the provinces. From 1927–70 he showed with the Lincolnshire Artists' Society at the Usher Gallery, Lincoln, being the Society's chairman and deputy chairman at times in the late 1940s/early 1950s. Usher Gallery holds two watercolours by him: Romance; and Farmstead, Donington on Bain. He lived in Lincoln.

Clifford Derek BULLOUGH 1917– Painter and teacher, born in Barrow-in-Furness, Lancashire. He studied at Bolton School of Art, 1935–9, and Manchester School of Art, 1939–40. Exhibited PS; Manchester City Art Gallery holds his work. Lived in Isleworth, Middlesex.

Lionel BULMER 1919–1992 Painter and teacher, born in London. Was married to the artist Margaret Green. Bulmer studied at Royal College of Art just after World War II and taught for many years at Kingston College of Art. His special subject was the Suffolk landscape, often small pictures painted with a quiet, sensitive precision and using such colours as lemon, emerald and lilac. As well as showing at Leicester Galleries, RA, NEAC and RWS (of both of which he was a member), Bulmer had solo exhibitions at New Art Centre. Lived at Onehouse, near Stowmarket, Suffolk.

William Harold S BUNCE 1921– Painter and teacher, who gained art and teaching diplomas at Manchester School of Art, becoming art master at Stretford Grammar School. Stationed in Germany in World War II he attended a painting course at Gottingen University. Showed with MAFA; his Peak Farm, of 1958, bought from its Centenary Exhibition, 1959, was painted in Derbyshire, a favourite subject. Lived in Hale Barns, Cheshire.

John BUNTING 1927– Sculptor in wood, stone and bronze, born in London. He attended Ampleforth College, 1941–4, and Oriel College, Oxford, 1945, serving in Royal Marines, 1945–7. After Robert Thompson, Kilburn, in 1948, Bunting studied under Walter Marsden at St Martin's School of Art, 1949–51, then with John Skeaping and Leon Underwood at Royal College of Art, 1951–4. He showed with RA, York Festival, and elsewhere in mixed exhibitions. Had a solo show with Fischbacher, Paris, in 1965, and a retrospective at Billingham Forum in 1972. Bunting did much public work for schools, churches, hospitals, community centres and memorials, the War Memorial Chapel at Hambleton, Yorkshire, being a key work. He was a fellow of RBS, 1972. Lived in Nunnington, York.

Peter BUNTING 1947– Painter whose work included Surrealist-type images, born in Switzerland. He was educated at Cambridge University and Byam Shaw School of Painting. Group exhibitions included Moira Kelly Gallery, 1982; New Grafton Gallery, 1985; Contrariwise (Surrealism and Britain 1930–86), touring show, 1986; Richard Pomeroy Gallery, 1987; and Sandra Higgins Fine Arts, 1990. Solo shows included Pomeroy Purdy Gallery 1989. Churchill College in Cambridge and Sheffield City Art Galleries hold examples.

Biddy BUNZL 1952– Painter and sculptor who studied at Vienna Kunst Akademie, 1969–70, then obtained degree in sculpture at Camberwell School of Arts and Crafts. She spent a year at Rietveld Akademie in Amsterdam on a British Council scholarship and undertook postgraduate studies at Reading University. Bunzl turned to painting in 1980 and showed widely, in group shows – including RA Upstairs Gallery, Hayward Annual and Riverside Gallery – and solo at Odette Gilbert Gallery. Bunzl initially made purely abstract, formal colour paintings, then moved on to more figurative work, which employed a rich palette.

James BURBIDGE 1959– Sculptor and creator of mixed-media constructions who studied at West Surrey College of Art and Design, Farnham. Mixed show appearances included LG,

Smith's Gallery and England & Co, 1991, in Art in Boxes. Had a solo show called Made for Other Reasons in 1989 at Michaelson and Orient, another at England & Co in 1992. There Burbidge showed small lead foil-covered boxes containing strange and haunting worlds created from materials such as papier mâché, wood and polished brass.

Claire BURBRIDGE 1971– Multi-media artist and teacher whose special interest was the human figure in motion, influenced by her association with dancers of the Royal Ballet and Rambert School. Burbridge gained an honours degree in fine art at Oxford University, then her master's in printmaking at Camberwell College of Arts. In 1991–2 she curated the Magdalen College art collection; in 1992 edited *Isis* magazine and undertook an exchange scholarship at Karl Marx University, Budapest; and in 1993 gained the Vivien Leigh Prize, having work bought by the Ashmolean Museum, Oxford. Exhibited in 2nd Open Sculpture Exhibition at RWA, 1996. Lived in London.

Lawson BURCH 1937– Artist, teacher and writer who worked in various media, notably acrylic, born in Belfast, Northern Ireland. He studied at Stranmillis College with Cyril Mount, and with Belfast College of Art with John Luke. Between 1959–78 taught in various secondary and grammar schools, then became a full-time artist. Burch was an academician of RUA and chairman of Ulster Arts Club, 1986–8. In 1980 he won the George Campbell Award, which enabled him, like Campbell, to live and work in Spain, and to exhibit there. Burch had stories broadcast on BBC radio and presented arts programmes on television. The poet Gerard Manley Hopkins was an inspiration, as was the wild beauty of the Donegal landscape, where he settled in Glenties. Group exhibitions included RHA; Independent Artists, Solomon Gallery and The James Gallery, all in Dublin; and Irish Contemporary Art, Boston. Solo shows included Arts Council and The Bell Galleries and Queen's University, all in Belfast; Image Gallery, Dublin; and The Willow Island Gallery, Enniskillen. Arts Council, Queen's University, Northern Ireland Tourist Board and Department of the Environment and the national self-portrait collection at Limerick University all hold Burch's work.

Gina BURDASS 1953– Painter of abstracts, such as Soliton 3, acrylic with marble dust on canvas, in 1997–8 John Moores Liverpool Exhibition. Born in Shrewsbury, Shropshire, Burdass studied at Hammersmith College of Art, 1972; Central School of Art, 1973–6; and Wimbledon School of Art, 1982–5. From 1986–91 she was a part-time assistant to the the artist Bridget Riley. Showed widely internationally in group exhibitions, which included Space Open Studios from 1993 and Salon des Graphiques, Curwen Gallery, from 1995. Lived in London.

Alan BURDEN 1938– Artist and teacher, born in Stanmore, Middlesex, originally studied and worked as a metallurgist. At Harrow School of Art, 1962–6, gained a diploma in painting and lithography, a diploma in education at University of Newcastle upon Tyne, 1966–7. Taught at a Newcastle comprehensive, 1967–72, then was head of art departments in Wigan and Essex. Took part in North West One, Chenil Gallery, 1976; Five Painters, at Salford City Art Gallery, 1979; and MAFA, 1980. Shared an exhibition at Scene Gallery, Newcastle, 1969, having a solo exhibition at Colin Jellicoe Gallery, Manchester, 1981. Burden said that his paintings "strive for autonomy, but the emotional drive behind them is, more often than not, some well-loved place, some memory or feeling about that place that I wish to encapsulate within an essentially two-dimensional surface."

Daniel BURDEN 1928– Painter, artist in collage and print-maker, born in Paris. After education at Kilburn Grammar School in northwest London, Burden attended Willesden Art School, 1949–52, where his teachers included James Neal, and the Royal College of Art, 1952–5, where teachers included Ruskin Spear, John Minton and Rodrigo Moynihan. He exhibited with RWA of which he was a member, RA, AIA, LG, elsewhere in England and also in France, where he settled for some years at Miramont de Guyenne in the Lot-et-Garonne region in the southwest. University of Leicester and RWA hold his work.

Angela BURFOOT fl. from 1960s– Painter and draughtsman who studied at Slade School of Fine Art with William Coldstream, while there gaining the Philip Wilson Steer Prize for Still Life and Landscape and a Henry Tonks Drawing Prize. She was the wife of the artist Ian Armour-Chelu and mother of the painter Louise Armour-Chelu. Commissioned portraits were a feature of her work. She showed at RA Summer Exhibition, had solo shows in London and abroad and in 1990 took part in a family exhibition at Markswood Gallery, Great Bardfield. Lived in Wissett, near Halesworth, Suffolk.

Arthur James Wetherall BURGESS 1879–1957 Marine artist and editor, born in Bombala, New South Wales, Australia. He studied art in Sydney and St Ives, Cornwall. As well as being art editor of *Brassey's Naval and Shipping Annual*, Burgess was Australia's official naval artist in 1918. Showed at RI and ROI both of which he was a member, RA, RHA, RBA and elsewhere. National Art Gallery of New South Wales in Sydney and several British public collections, including Lincoln and Nuneaton, hold examples. Settled in London, where he was a member of Langham Sketch Club. Malcolm Innes Gallery held a show of Burgess' marine, fishing and ski-ing oils and watercolours in 1996.

Cefyn BURGESS 1961– Artist, notable as a textile designer, born at Bethesda, Caernarvonshire, settling nearby at Penmaenmawr, Gwynedd. He did an arts foundation course at Birmingham Polytechnic, 1979–80; gained an honours degree from the fashion/textiles department of Manchester Polytechnic, 1980–3; and obtained a master's degree at Royal College of Art, 1983–5. Was a member of the Craft Council of Wales Committee, National Eisteddfod Craft Committee and North Wales Art Association Committee and showed in the principality.

Christine BURGESS 1937– Sculptor in weatherproof and low-fired ceramic and other materials, painter and draughtsman in various media, and teacher, born in Manchester, where she attended the Regional College of Art, 1954–9, with a Lady Whitworth Scholarship. Teachers included William Tocher, William Bailey and Harry Sutcliffe. In 1959, she married Peter Burgess, lecturer in ceramics, and from then taught full- or part-time in schools and colleges of art. After raising a family, in the early 1970s resumed personal work mainly in ceramics, in 1984 settling in Oxford and concentrating on sculpture. After remarriage in 1989, in early 1990s diversified materials and started experimenting with surfaces. Became chairman of Oxford Art Society and co-ordinator of the Oxford Confederation of Artists and Makers, a group pressing for a city gallery. Burgess' sculpture stemmed from the human form, although she avoided working direct from the model "because this is found to be inhibiting and sometimes inappropriate to the medium". Institution of Mechanical Engineers gave her a Queen's Silver Jubilee Award design commission. Group exhibitions included Museum & Art Gallery, Swindon; County Museum, Woodstock; Pittville Gallery, Cheltenham; Museum of Modern Art, Oxford; RBSA; RWA and elsewhere. Later solo shows included Bentlies Gallery, Woodstock, 1993. Wiltshire Country Council and Thamesdown Councils hold examples.

Eliza Mary BURGESS 1878– Watercolourist, especially of portraits, born in Walthamstow, where she studied, also at the Royal Female School of Art with the aid of a scholarship. Gained several medals. Exhibited RA, RSA, Cooling Galleries, Walker Art Gallery, Liverpool, Paris Salon and elsewhere abroad. Walker Art Gallery, Liverpool, and Graves Art Gallery, Sheffield, hold her work. Lived in London.

Paul BURGESS 1961– Printmaker, designer, illustrator, artist in mixed media and teacher, he studied printmaking at Camberwell School of Arts and Crafts and textiles at Royal College of Art. He then freelanced in a number of fields. Showed at Whitechapel Open; New British Design, in Tokyo; Royal Festival Hall in South Bank Picture Show, where he was a prize-winner; England & Co Art in Boxes, 1992, and elsewhere.

Peter BURGESS 1952– Painter, born in St Albans, Hertfordshire. He attended Watford School of Art, 1970–1, Wolverhampton Polytechnic, 1971–2, Wimbledon School of Art, 1972–4, and Royal Academy Schools, 1974–7. He won the David Murray Award in 1975–6–7 and the British Institution Award, 1976. Burgess was notable for his depictions of beaches and the seaside in vibrant colours. Showed at RA, Nottingham Castle Museum and Derby City Art Gallery in mixed shows, winning several prizes. Had a solo show at Nottingham Castle Museum in 1982; Blackfriars Arts Centre, Boston, Lincolnshire, 1986; and from that year showed at Thackeray Gallery. Contemporary Art Society, Nottingham City Council and several local authorities hold his work. Lived in Nottingham.

Victor BURGIN 1941– Artist and teacher, born in Sheffield, Yorkshire. Burgin used text, photographs and prints to create his pedagogically oriented art in which issues such as power in society and sex were examined. Burgin studied at Royal College of Art, 1962–5, then Yale University, 1965–7. He took part in When Attitude Becomes Form at ICA in 1969, then from 1970 soon built up an impressive range of one-man shows, venues including Daniel Templon Gallery, Paris; Protech-Rivkin Gallery, Washington; Lisson Gallery and Nigel Greenwood; and Museum of Modern Art, Oxford, where he had a retrospective in 1978. Later shows included ICA and Kettle's Yard, Cambridge, both 1986; Family Romance at Karl Bornstein Gallery, Los Angeles, and John Weber Gallery, New York, both 1990; and and in 1991–2 Passages, at Musée d'Art Moderne, Villeneuve d'Ascq/Ville de Blois. From 1973 Burgin taught at Central London Polytechnic; from 1976 at Yale, Princeton and elsewhere; he held a DAAD German Government Fellowship in 1978–9; and in 1980 became Picker Professor at Colgate University, New York. Arts Council and Royal College of Art hold examples.

Greig BURGOYNE 1968– Figurative artist, born in Glasgow, who studied at Cumbria College of Art & Design, Carlisle, 1987–9, West Surrey College of Art & Design in Farnham, 1989–92, and Royal College of Art, 1992–4. Public commissions included murals for stairwells at West Surrey College, 1991, and in 1992 extensive murals for Old Arcade Shopping Centre in Aldershot. Exhibitions included Ditchling Gallery, Ditchling, 1990–1, LG at Morley Gallery in 1993 and in 1994 Five RCA Painters at Paton Gallery. TI Group Art Collection holds his work.

Robert BURKALL MARSH: *see* **Robert MARSH**

Ian BURKE 1955– Painter, draughtsman and teacher. He studied at Newcastle University and Goldsmiths' College ATC Department. Went on to teach at Wandsworth Comprehensive School. Burke's exhibitions included Northern Contemporaries, 1976; Mid-Wales Open and Moira Kelly Summer Show, both 1981; and Goldsmiths' exhibition at Woodlands Art Gallery, 1983.

Patrick BURKE 1932– Painter, printmaker and teacher, born in Shoreham, Sussex. He studied at Brighton College of Art and Royal College of Art and was a Rome Scholar, 1957–9, specialising in etching. Burke taught at Brighton College of Art and became head of painting at Brighton Polytechnic, retiring in 1989. Some of his work was Pop-influenced, as in The Sussex Scene, Towner Art Gallery, Eastbourne, 1993.

Peter BURKE 1944– Artist and lecturer, born in London, who after City of Bath Technical School studied art at Bristol Polytechnic, 1973. Had a solo show with Gilbert Parr Gallery in 1978, later venues including Victoria Art Gallery, Bath, 1986. Was elected to RWA in 1985, which holds his work. Lived at Bradford-on-Avon, Wiltshire.

Thomas BURKE 1906–1945 Painter and designer, born and died in Liverpool, who studied at College of Art there and Royal College of Art. He travelled extensively, was a radio officer in the Merchant Navy and during World War II was a prisoner of war during which he designed posters. Showed at RA, RP, RHA and Walker Art Gallery in Liverpool, which holds his canvas The Student.

Averil BURLEIGH 1883–1949 Painter whose husband was the painter C H H Burleigh, her daughter the artist Veronica Burleigh. A versatile painter, she showed at the RA, RI, SWA, Sussex Women's Art Club and RCamA and was elected an associate of the RWS shortly before she died. Brighton Art Gallery held a memorial show in the year of her death. Lived in Hove, Sussex.

C H H BURLEIGH 1869–1956 Painter of landscapes, townscapes, still life and interiors. These sometimes featured his family, his wife being the artist Averil Burleigh, his daughter the painter Veronica Burleigh. He studied at Brighton School of Art and in Paris, where his teachers included Jacques-Emile Blanche. Showed at RA, Fine Art Society, ROI of which he was a member, and RI. Lived in Hove, Sussex.

Veronica BURLEIGH 1909– Painter in oil and watercolour, daughter of the artist C H H Burleigh, born in Hove, Sussex. Studied at Slade School of Fine Art, 1927–30, under Henry Tonks. Exhibited at RA, SWA, Sussex Women's Art Club and with the Sussex Painters, at Worthing, where the public gallery holds her work. Her main works included Little Ballet Dancers, Scene Painters and Calliope. During World War II served in the Women's Auxiliary Air Force. Burleigh's work was mainly portraits until 1970, when she moved into the country, living at Henfield, Sussex. For 20 years she commuted yearly to Rhodesia, where she held 23 one-man shows.

David William BURLEY 1901–1990 Watercolourist, commercial artist, printmaker and teacher, born in Greenwich, southeast London. He studied at Goldsmiths' College School of Art and showed at RA, RBA, RI and in the provinces. Was an adult tutor, conducting painting holidays. Lived in Birchington, Kent.

Barry BURMAN 1943– Mixed-media artist, born in Bedford, and teacher. He studied at Coventry College of Art under Michael Sandle, then Royal College of Art with Harry Weinberger. He was a part-time lecturer in painting at Mid-Warwickshire College of Art, 1974–92, then became a full-time artist, being represented by the Goldmark Gallery, Uppingham. Burman was a prizewinner in Mercia Art at Herbert Museum and Art Gallery, Coventry, which holds his work, 1985, and he gained first prize in the 1991 Hunting/*Observer* Awards. His mixed exhibition appearances began with Through Drawing at ICA, 1966; was also in Modern Drawings at Angela Flowers Gallery and in British Figurative Art in Copenhagen, both 1972; also Mayor Gallery, 1988. Had a solo show at Coventry College of Art, 1969, later ones including Nicholas Treadwell Gallery, 1982, and Goldmark Gallery, 1992. His work was included in several books on erotic and Superhumanist art. Lived in Leamington Spa, Warwickshire.

Chila Kumari BURMAN 1957– Artist and teacher, born in Liverpool, who attended Southport College of Art, 1975–6; Leeds Polytechnic, winning a first-class honours degree, 1976–9; and Slade School of Fine Art, 1980–2. Burman worked in a wide range of media, including etchings, cibachrome prints, photo-based works and three-screen video installation with sound track. When her retrospective was held at Bluecoat Gallery, Liverpool, in 1995 she was said to stand "at the vanguard of politically radical art, occupying a position within discourses around black art and issues of cultural identity, representation and gender". From 1984 Burman taught widely on a visiting or part-time basis, including Brighton Polytechnic, Central School of Art, Birmingham Polytechnic, Chelsea School of Art and Middlesex University. She conducted a range of workshops and presentations, holding many residencies. Commissions included the mural Southall Black Resistance, with Keith Piper, for Great London Council, 1985; mural for London Borough of Haringey, 1987; and work Body Weapons for Walsall Art Gallery, 1992. Mixed shows included New Contemporaries, ICA, 1981; Artists Against Apartheid, Royal Festival Hall, 1985; and Contemporary Black Art, Stoke-on-Trent Garden Festival, 1986.

Gerald Maurice BURN 1859–1945 Painter and printmaker concerned with marine and architectural subjects. He was born in London, son of the architect and painter George Adam Burn. Studied at South Kensington, later studies taking place in Germany, Belgium and France. Often working on a large scale, Burn showed at RA, RBA, Walker Art Gallery in Liverpool and with Portsmouth and Hampshire Art Society. Travelled widely, eventually settling in 1907 in Amberley, Sussex, to use the studio of the watercolourist Rose Barton. National Maritime Museum, Science Museum and other public venues in Britain and abroad hold his work.

Hilary BURN 1946– Bird artist and illustrator, born in Macclesfield, Cheshire, who graduated in 1967 in zoology from Leeds University. She showed with Wildfowl Trust and Royal Society for the Protection of Birds, illustrating its *Book of British Birds*, 1982. Was a member of SWLA from 1983 and lived at Huish Champflower, Somerset.

Rodney Joseph BURN 1899–1984 Figure and landscape painter, mainly in oil. Born in London into a wealthy family, Burn went to Harrow School, then after a period in the Army during World War I he attended the Slade School under Henry Tonks, Walter Russell and Philip Wilson Steer. At the Slade he had a brilliant career, winning six major prizes between 1918–22, and he merited an article on him while still a student in the *Burlington Magazine*. Married the sculptor Margaret Sharwood-Smith. Held several teaching posts, at the Royal College of Art before and after World War II, at the City and Guilds School and at

Camberwell School of Art. From 1931–4 he and the painter Robin Guthric were appointed joint directors of painting and drawing at the Boston Museum School of Fine Arts, in America. The Chantrey Bequest and Contemporary Art Society bought his work, which is in the Tate Gallery, British Museum print room and in galleries in Bristol and Brighton. Independent means enabled Burn to spend his later years sailing, in European travel, staying on the south coast of England near Chichester and working in his final studio, on the banks of the Thames at Chiswick. Retrospective Austin/Desmond Fine Art, 1989.

Geoffrey BURNAND 1912– Painter, theatrical designer and mural artist. After education at Imperial Service College, Windsor, Burnand studied art at Farnham School of Art, with Otway McCannell, 1929–31, and at the Royal Academy Schools, 1931–2, under Thomas Monnington. He was a Prix de Rome winner and attended the British School in Rome, 1933–5. Exhibited RA, RBA, NEAC and throughout the West Country. Signed work with initials plus date. Completed a number of church commissions in the south of England and East Anglia. Lived at Bordon, Hampshire.

Robert BURNAND 1929– Watercolourist, printmaker, glass engraver and teacher, born in Malacca, Malaya. He studied at High Wycombe, Harrow and Brighton Colleges of Art, his teachers including the painter and illustrator Morgan Rendle. Became an associate of RE in 1968 and was a member of Somerset Society of Artists, living at North Petherton. Among books illustrated was Rider Haggard's novel *She*.

James Walton BURNETT 1874– Watercolourist, especially of architectural and marine subjects; he retired as a marine architect shortly before World War II, and worked for some time for the shipbuilders Cammell Laird at Birkenhead, Cheshire. Studied at Birkenhead School of Art, 1889–92, then at Liverpool School of Art in 1900 and again in 1907–8. Liver Sketching Club member. He showed at at the public galleries in Liverpool, Manchester and Southport, RCamA and had a one-man show at Williamson Art Gallery and Museum, Birkenhead, which holds his work. Lived in Bebington, Cheshire.

Christopher Anthony BURNHAM 1956– Painter and printmaker, born in London. After East Ham Grammar School he studied at Cardiff College of Art with Ian Grainger. Showed Chapter Arts Centre in Cardiff, where he lived at Roath, and elsewhere.

David BURNHAM 1940– Artist, craftsman and teacher working in a variety of media. Initially Burnham trained as a bookbinder, then studied design under Edgar Mansfield at London School of Printing and Graphic Art. In 1960 he began painting and experimenting with sculpture, in 1968 moving on to pottery and ceramic sculpture. Taught pottery for some time at Eltham Adult Education Institute. His exhibitions included Ewan Phillips Gallery, 1965–7; Tudor Barn Gallery, Eltham, 1974; Blackheath Gallery from 1975; and Woodlands Art Gallery, 1977. In 1964 British Drug Houses commissioned a bronze from Burnham. Lived in London.

Alexander Sillars BURNS 1911–1987 Painter and draughtsman, born in Newmilns, Ayrshire. He did diploma and post-diploma studies at Gray's School of Art, Aberdeen, followed by a travelling scholarship. Additional studies included a short time at Slade School of Fine Art, for drawing, and in France. He won the Keith Prize in the RSA competition in 1934. Showed in a variety of exhibitions and was a member of SSA. Aberdeen Art Gallery and Newport Art Gallery hold his work. Lived in Aberdeen.

Brendan Stuart BURNS 1963– Abstract painter and teacher, born in Nakuru, Kenya. He did a foundation course in Cardiff, 1981–2, then gained his honours degree in fine art there, 1982–5, from 1985–7 doing postgraduate painting at Slade School of Fine Art. In 1989 he won a WAC Travel Grant, to study in Florence; in 1991 was artist-in residence at Llanfrechfa Grange Mental Health Unit, Cwmbran; then in 1993 won Gold Medal in Fine Art, National Eisteddfod of Wales. Had widespread teaching experience from 1991, including Pontypridd College of Art & Design. Was an extensive mixed show exhibitor from 1983, including Young Masters, *You* Magazine Exhibition, Solomon Gallery, 1987; inaugural Welsh Contemporaries Annual, Red Square Gallery, 1991; and 56 Group Wales, National Museum of Wales, Cardiff, where he lived, 1996. Had a first solo London show at Oriel Contemporary Art, 1996. County of South Glamorgan, City and County of Cardiff and Leicestershire Education Authority hold examples.

Kitty BURNS 1925– Painter, notably of frescoes and murals, born in Edinburgh, whose full name was Katherine Burns McKeon. She studied at Edinburgh College of Art, 1946–50, where her teachers included William Gillies and Leonard Rosoman. She won a number of painting prizes, including a first prize at RSA, also showing in Scotland with SSA and Arts Council. In addition she showed widely internationally, including completing murals for the Hong Kong and Shanghai Bank in Paris and the Queen Elizabeth Stadium in Hong Kong. Lived for some years at Flayosc in the Var region of southern France.

Pamela BURNS 1938– Artist working in a range of media including oil, gouache and charcoal and photography, and teacher, born in London, although she moved to Worcestershire in 1945. Studied painting at Leicestershire College of Art, 1957–60; won a college bursary award and visited Italy, 1960; studied painting at Royal Academy Schools, and visited France, 1960–3. Further European travels were to include the Netherlands. Futher teaching included Ravensbourne College of Art and Design, Southend College of Art, London College of Furniture and St Martin's Schoolof Art. Wasa member of AIA. Sheshowed there from 1965; at theDowns Gallery, Manchester,1967; at Parkway Focus Gallery, 1975; and was in the Hayward Annual, at Hayward Gallery, 1978.

William BURNS 1921–1972 Painter, especially of landscapes, born in Newton Mearns, Renfrewshire. He studied at Glasgow School of Art, 1944–8, his teachers including Ian Fleming and David Donaldson. Showed widely in Scotland, was a member of RSW and had several solo exhibitions with Aitken Dott, Edinburgh. Is in RSA collection and in public collections in Paisley, Dundee and Glasgow. Lectured in art at Aberdeen College of Education and lived in Balmedie, Aberdeenshire. Sea Crane, held by Glasgow's Kelvingrove Art Gallery, is typical of Burns' almost childlike landscape- or seascape-cum-abstracts which have a strong-image quality.

William BURNS 1923– Painter and architect, full name Cecil William Burns, born in Sheffield, Yorkshire. He briefly attended Sheffield College of Art; qualified as an architect in 1956; then from 1962–88 ran his own practice alongside a burgeoning career as a painter. Burns appeared in mixed shows at RA, ROI and at Mall Galleries. He had solo shows at Mayfield Gallery, Sheffield, 1985–6, then began to show solo in London, later exhibitions including Medici Gallery, 1991–2. Burns was a fellow of RIBA and of Society of Architectural Illustrators. Lived in Sheffield.

Vivien BURNSIDE 1958– Artist in a wide range of media, teacher and administrator who after graduating in fine art at University of Ulster in Belfast, where she was based at the Queen Street Studios, returned for her master's degree, 1993–5. In between studies Burnside was an arts administrator and part-time tutor in Belfast; in 1992, with an Arts Council Bursary and Travel Award, studying Renaissance drawing in Florence. She was later artist-in-residence at Crescent Arts Centre, Belfast. Group shows included Irish Women Artists, Douglas Hyde Gallery, Dublin, 1987, and Relocating History, Fenderesky Gallery, Belfast, and tour, 1993. Solo exhibitions included Bluecoat Gallery, Liverpool, 1985.

James BURR 1926– Relief printer, teacher, writer and critic, born in Bedfordshire, who studied at Bromley School of Art, Slade School of Fine Art, and in Paris at Académie de la Grande Chaumière, Atelier 17 and L'École des Beaux-Arts. He won a Wilson Steer Medal for Painting in 1951 and a State French Scholarship, 1952. Was a founder-member of the Printmakers' Council of Great Britain and a member of the International Association of Art Critics. Became head of the art department at the City Literary Institute, 1961–88, was art critic for *Apollo Magazine*, 1961–91, and also wrote for *Printmaking Today*. Exhibitions included Roland, Browse & Delbanco, 1959; Zwemmer Gallery, 1965; Consort Gallery at Imperial College, 1970; Curwen Gallery, 1976; St John's Smith Square, 1987; and Burgh House, Hampstead, 1991. His work was in many public and corporate collections in Britain and abroad, including Leeds University; Walker Art Gallery in Liverpool; New York Public Library; University College; Cincinnati Museum of Fine Art; and London Business School. Lived in London.

Joan BURR fl. from 1960s– Sculptor and painter who studied sculpture at Chelmsford School of Art and Camberwell School of Arts and Crafts. She produced little work while bringing up her children during the following six years, but started making constructions in 1968 and began to paint in 1970. Among her exhibitions was Space from the Quadrangle at Woodlands Art Gallery, 1973.

Victor BURR 1908– Painter, born in London, who attended West Sussex School of Painting and Drawing under R O Dunlop. Showed at RA, NEAC, RP and in Sussex, where he lived for many years at Crawley.

Edward BURRA 1905–1976 Watercolourist, draughtsman and printmaker, born into prosperous circumstances in London. While still at school he developed anaemia and rheumatic fever which terminated early his formal education, but from 14 he was able to devote his energies to drawing. Studied at Chelsea School of Art, 1921–3, and Royal College of Art, 1923–4. Had his first solo show at Leicester Galleries, 1929. He was a member of Unit One in 1933 and showed with the English Surrealists later in the 1930s. Despite his poor health Burra travelled widely. Influences on his work, usually watercolour on a large scale in strong colour, were many: the negro dives of Harlem; the Spanish Civil War; English horror novels and books by older French and Spanish writers; and the work of artists such as Picasso, Wyndham Lewis and Dali. They prompted an art concerned with the sinister, bizarre and picaresque. Also designed for the stage, including the Camargo Society's ballet *Rio Grande* and Sadler's Wells' *Miracle in the Gorbals*. Tate Gallery, which holds his work, gave him a retrospective in 1973. Lived near Rye, Sussex.

Lorraine BURRELL 1963– Artist in a wide range of media who graduated from Liverpool Polytechnic in 1989. Her work gained considerable media attention and was included in many group exhibitions, including Old Museum, Belfast, 1991, and One Oxford Street and Flax Studios there, 1992, as well as Head Gallery in Dublin, 1994. Had solo exhibitions in Belfast, where she was based at the Queen Street Studios, at Crescent Arts Centre in 1992 and The Plaza, 1993.

Louie BURRELL 1873–1971 Miniaturist, portrait and landscape painter, born into a family of artists, father William Luker, mother Ada Margetts. They did not wish her to study painting and took her away from the South Kensington Art School, sending her to teach art in a local high school. By 1900 she had earned enough money to attend Herkomer's School, Bushey, where she was a star pupil, showing annually at the RA. Leaving Bushey in 1904 she moved to Cape Town, married Philip Burrell, but returned to England in 1907 for the birth of her daughter Philippa. Her husband having died Burrell resumed her career, becoming a leading miniaturist, painting members of the royal family, showing at Fine Art Society, Walker and other galleries. In 1912 she moved to Ottawa to restore her health from overwork, and embarked on a life of extensive travel, including visits to America, India and Canada again, eventually returning to England again, where she died in Barnet, Hertfordshire. Bushey Museum

Trust held a major show in 1989 and acquired a selection of Burrell's work, as did the Victoria & Albert Museum and National Gallery of Canada, Ottawa. Her life is included in her daughter's autobiographical books *The Golden Thread*, *The Horses & the Charioteer* and *The Dance of the Opposites*.

Frederick BURRIDGE 1869–1945 Printmaker and teacher, born in London, studying under Frank Short at Royal College of Art. He was finally, from 1912–30, principal of the Central School of Arts and Crafts. He was elected RE in 1898 and was also a member of Art Workers' Guild, showing at RA, Walker Art Gallery in Liverpool and Royal Glasgow Institute of the Fine Arts. Before Burridge settled in London he taught for 15 years in Liverpool.

Peter BURRIDGE 1960– Jewellery designer, printmaker and teacher, born in Taunton, Somerset. He studied at Solihull College of Art, 1977–9, and Birmingham Polytechnic. Showed at RA Summer Exhibition, Zebra One Gallery, Barbican Centre and abroad. Lived in Solihull, West Midlands.

Helen BURROUGH: *see* **HELEN**

Thomas Hedley Bruce BURROUGH 1910– Watercolourist, draughtsman and architect, who wrote and lectured on architecture at Bristol University. He was born in Newport, Monmouthshire, studied at Clifton College and then Royal West of England Academy school of architecture, 1928–32. Was married to the artist Helen Burrough. He became a member of RWA, which holds his work. Burrough's writings included *An Approach to Planning* and *Bristol Buildings*. Lived for many years at Frenchay, near Bristol.

Dorothy BURROUGHES fl. from c.1920–1963 Poster artist, printmaker and illustrator, born and lived in London. She studied at Slade School of Fine Art, Heatherley's School and in Germany, produced animal posters for London Underground, illustrated for magazines such as *Bystander* and *Illustrated London News* and for a string of her own children's books with animal themes. Was for a time a member of RBA, also showing with Fine Art Society and SWA. Victoria & Albert Museum holds her work.

James BURROUGHS 1961– Sculptor, born and worked in London, who lived in Bedford, 1963–81. Did a foundation course at Mander College there, 1981, then a bachelor's degree in fine art at Wimbledon School of Art, 1982–5, after which he set up a studio in Peckham. Exhibitions included Cannizaro Park, Wimbledon, from 1982; Spirit in the Mass, Wells Arts Centre, Norfolk, 1986; Leighton Buzzard Arts Centre, 1987; and Carving in Christchurch at Christchurch Park, Ipswich, 1988. In that year he had a solo show at 47 Gallery, Great Russell Street. Bedford County Council holds Burroughs' work.

Victor Hugh Seamark BURROUGHS 1900– Painter in oil and watercolour, born in London. Studied art at Camberwell School of Arts and Crafts, Southampton Row School of Design, Goldsmiths' College School of Art and at Reading University. Exhibited RA, RMS, RCamA and Paris Salon, where he won a silver medal in 1973. Lived near Reading, Berkshire.

Geoffrey BURROWS 1934– Figurative painter in oil and watercolour, born in St Faiths, Norfolk, the county where he settled at Spixworth. Burrows was self-taught and began serious painting in the late-1960s. He was a member of Norfolk and Norwich Art Circle and showed at RA Summer Exhibitions from 1980, also ROI, RBA, RSMA, RI, NEAC and Paris Salon. Atkinson Art Gallery in Southport and Norfolk County Council hold his work.

Kevin BURROWS 1954– Painter who studied at Southend School of Art, 1973–6, and Winchester School of Art, 1976–9. In 1981 gained financial support from Eastern Arts for the making of large works and was on Eastern Artists' Register, in 1983 being on Epping Forest District Museum Artists' Register. Mixed shows included Stowells Trophy at RA, 1979; Trends 80, Mall Galleries, 1980; Artists in Essex, Loughton School of Art, 1984; and in 1985 shared four-man exhibition at Woodlands Art Gallery. Had solo show at Towngate Theatre Gallery, Basildon, 1983.

Roy BURROWS 1922– Painter of landscapes and teacher, born in Crewe, Cheshire. He attended Nottingham University and studied art at St Peter's College, Peterborough, 1947–8, and at Nottingham College of Arts and Crafts, 1948–50. He taught at Cartref Melys School, in Conway, also teaching art summer schools at Coleg Harlech. Showed with RCamA and elsewhere in Wales and the provinces and one-man shows included Peterloo Gallery, Manchester. Stoke-on-Trent City Museum and Art Gallery holds his work. Lived in Colwyn Bay, Clwyd.

Donald BURT 1923– Artist in watercolour, gouache and clay, teacher and poet, born in Southampton, Hampshire. He studied at Exeter College of Art, 1940–2 and 1945–7, with William Ruscoe for ceramics, and at London University, 1947–8. Became ceramics senior lecturer at Stourbridge College of Art. "Form and texture in ceramics, composition and vigour in paintings and rhythm and humour in poetry" were criteria. Burt's work was featured in *Ceramic Review* and his poems were published by Arrival Press of Peterborough and the International Society of Poets. Group shows included London Artists at Shrewsbury School, 1968; Nesscliffe Gallery; Sidmouth Visual Arts; and Queen Elizabeth Hospital and the Design Centre in Birmingham. Had one-man shows at Butlin Gallery, Dillington House, Somerset; and Theatre on the Steps, Bridgnorth. Signed work with a D B monogram in a square. Lived at Sidmouth, Devon.

Lawrence BURT 1925– Sculptor and teacher, born in Leeds, Yorkshire. Between 1939–49 Burt worked as an industrial metal worker, apart from service in the Army in World War II, although he did sculpt in his spare time. From 1948–55 he studied part-time at Leeds College of Art, making assemblages, sculptures and reliefs, then he taught at Leeds, 1956–60. This was the first of a series of teaching posts throughout England, including art colleges in Leicester, Cardiff, Wolverhampton and Falmouth. He had his first one-man show at Drian Gallery in 1961, others following at Exe Gallery, Exeter, and Angela Flowers. Oriel Gallery, Cardiff, gave him a retrospective in 1980. Burt had a close connection with Cyprus, living and working there for a time, with two others opening the Pisces Art Gallery in Famagusta in 1972 and teaching at summer school there. Work held by Arts Council, WAC, Tate Gallery, Cyprus Cultural Office and Public Collection and other public galleries.

George Ray BURTENSHAW 1888– Painter who studied at Reigate Commercial School and Redhill Technical School, Surrey, some time with William Tatton Winter. Exhibited in Birmingham, widely in Surrey and lived in Reigate. Sometimes signed work Geo. Ray.

Alice Mary BURTON 1893– Painter and draughtsman, born in Nogent-sur-Oise, France, but was educated in England. She studied at the Byam Shaw and Vicat Cole School of Art and at the Regent Street Polytechnic School of Art, winning a series of medals. She was noted for her charcoal drawings and pictures of people and flowers and showed frequently at RA, 1929–68, also at RP and Paris Salon, where she gained an Honourable Mention. With the artists Elsie Gledstanes and Agnes Tatham she ran the Unique Studio for Children art school in London for some years. Regent Street Polytechnic bought decorative panels by her. Lived in London and latterly in Silverstone, Towcester, Northamptonshire.

Andrew BURTON 1961– Sculptor and draughtsman, born in Kent. He took a first-class honours degree in fine art at Newcastle University in 1983, gaining his master's degree there in 1986, when a British Academy Travelling Scholarship took him to India. Burton won a prize for sculpture in 1983 at the Tyne Tees Northern Open, in 1991 taking the McGrigor Donald Sculpture Prize. In 1990 he won commissions for three bronzes for Newcastle Business Park and Gateshead Garden Festival, then in 1991 commissions for Stevenage Museum. From the outset he was a busy exhibitor, including RA, the 1988 Manchester City Art Gallery Summer Exhibition and Pelter/Sands, Bristol, which gave him a solo show in 1991. Towers, ziggurats and elephants featured in the Bristol show, which revealed Burton's gift of mischievous wit. Lived in Newcastle upon Tyne, Tyne and Wear.

Charles BURTON 1929– Painter and teacher, born in Treherbert, Mid Glamorgan, Wales. He studied at Cardiff College of Art and the Royal College of Art. Went on to hold a number of teaching posts, including head of the department of art at Liverpool College of Art and head of the department of art and design at Glamorgan College of Education, in Barry. Had one-man shows there and at the Prospect Gallery, in London, group shows including SEA, SWG and WAC. He gained a gold medal at the 1954 Royal National Eisteddfod. Work is held by Cambridge University, WAC and Department of the Environment. Lived for a time at Southport, Lancashire, then retired to south Wales.

Philip BURTON 1936– Bird artist, born in London, who graduated from University College, London, as a zoologist in 1958, gaining his doctorate 11 years later. Went on to work in natural history department of British Museum. A keen ornithologist, he showed with SWLA of which he was a member, and his illustrations appeared in a number of bird books. Ulster Museum, Belfast, holds his work. Lived in Berkhamsted, Hertfordshire.

Phyllis Marie BURTON 1913– Painter who studied at Cheltenham School of Art, under Seaton White, 1932–3, then at Reading University, under Anthony Betts, 1933–6. Exhibited SWA, RBA and Association of Sussex Artists. Lived at Hoddesdon, Hertfordshire.

Ralph Molyneux BURTON 1922– Sculptor in a variety of materials and teacher, brought up in Cheshire and educated at King's School, Macclesfield. Studied at Royal College of Art, 1947–50, where his tutors included John Skeaping and Frank Dobson. Taught for some years at the Adult Education Centre in Tunbridge Wells, Kent, and completed public commissioned work, mainly in the south of England. Lived in Ticehurst, Sussex.

Rosemary BURTON 1951– Painter and draughtsman who studied at Slade School of Fine Art, 1972–8. Mixed exhibitions included Barry Barker Gallery and her Drawing of a Man, of 1976, was included in Arts Council tour Fragments Against Ruin, 1981–2, having been taken into their collection. Lived in London.

William Francis BURTON 1907–1995 Painter in oil, born in North Walsham, Norfolk, whose first wife was the artist Elizabeth Crampton-Gore, their daughter being the painter Georgina Saunders. Burton was mainly self-taught, although he had some lessons in the mid-1940s from his father-in-law William Gore. Travelled extensively through India, Singapore and Australia, where he exhibited as Angelo Perini. Turner, Seago, Montague Dawson and William Russell Flint influenced Burton's style. He was noted for his marine paintings and for views of East Anglia, where he lived much of his life, dying at Ramsey, Essex. Showed with RSMA, at Guildhall and elsewhere and had many paintings reproduced as prints; *Evening Gold* and *Eventide*, scenes at West Mersea, were among the most popular prints of the late 1960s.

Keith BURTONSHAW 1930– Painter of "traditional landscape and marine subjects, especially the Lake District", born and lived in Beckenham, Kent, who was self-taught and retired early after part-time painting to be a full-time artist. His full name was John William Keith Burtonshaw. He was a member of BWS, UA, NS and London Sketch Club and he showed at RSMA and RI, having solo exhibitions in Croydon.

Ernst BURWELL 1911– Painter and stage designer, full name William Ernst Burwell, born in Kingston-upon-Hull, Yorkshire. Studied at Hull and Brighton, Sussex, Colleges of Art. Showed at NEAC, RI, RA, in the northern provinces, including Hull's Ferens Art Gallery, and in Australia. Imperial War Museum holds his work. Lived at Hillingdon, Middlesex, and Eton in Buckinghamshire.

Adrian BURY 1891–1991 Artist and writer, born in London, his father being a sculptor and bronze-caster, his uncle the sculptor Alfred Gilbert. Bury's first job was as an office boy in a tobacco-pipe factory. Learned shorthand in the evenings and joined the Graphic Photo Union, then the *Bystander* where he became familiar with many artists and writers. Attended evening art school, then in 1914 began studies at the Académie Julian, Paris, and Atelier Colarossi. Rejected for Army service, in London began work as freelance writer and cartoonist, then joined the *Sunday Pictorial*. In early 1920s studied art at English School in Rome. Continued to travel widely throughout his life. Chelsea Arts Club stalwart. In 1947 Bury changed his name from Buhrer to Bury, under which he had written for many years. Published his autobiography, *Just a Moment, Time*, in 1967. Other books include volumes on Francis Towne, Reginald Eves and Alfred Gilbert. Exhibited RA, Leger Gallery and RWS, whose Club's annual volume he edited for a time. Lived in London.

Morley BURY 1919– Painter in oil and teacher, born Bournemouth, Hampshire, and christened John Morley Bury. Grew up in Holdenhurst and "made up my mind to be an artist while I was still at the village school." After Bournemouth School he attended Bournemouth Municipal College Art, 1937–9, where his teacher Johnny Walker was a strong influence, then Reading University, 1939–40. Then spent six years in the Army, with a tank regiment in the Western Desert, then as a prisoner of war in Italy and Germany, being freed by Russian troops and repatriated. After the war Bury returned to Reading University, where he met his wife, art historian Shirley Bury, also attending Regent Street Polytechnic and Goldsmiths' College. He also attended evening classes in textiles at Central School of Arts and Crafts and a course of lectures at the Courtauld Institute. He taught part-time at Emanuel School, Wandsworth, from 1948–58, then part-time at Hornsey College of Art until retirement in 1984. Mixed shows included NEAC, 1950; LG and *Daily Express* Young Artists, both 1954; Vision and Reality, Wakefield City Art Gallery, 1957; 3 Artists, South London Art Gallery, 1961; Centaur Gallery, 1970; and The Forgotten Fifties, Graves Art Gallery, Sheffield, and tour, 1984. Bury also showed with AIA, Hampstead Artists' Council, Heal's Mansard Gallery and Everyman Foyer, Hampstead, where he had a series of solo exhibitions from 1960. Public collections include Victoria & Albert Museum, Salford Art Gallery, Nuffield Foundation and various education committees, plus Cambridge University and corporate collections including Staveley Industries, Lintas and Rank Xerox. Tate Gallery archive holds Bury's self-portrait. Bury's interest in figure subjects in the 1950s changed to landscape in the 1960s, landscapes "not real but a collection of seen ideas. Gradually texture of the paint became more important." He wrote that "studies in the organisation of colour relationships and the optical qualities which create a sense of space" were important to him. Lived in London.

George BUSBY 1926– Painter and draughtsman, born in Birmingham, full name Cecil George Busby. He attended evening classes at Birmingham College of Art, teachers including Bernard Fleetwood-Walker and William Eggison. Busby worked as a designer/illustrator in the display business for many years, taking up watercolour in 1969 and becoming a freelance artist in 1978. He was a member of the Chartered Society of Designers, RBSA and Guild of Railway Artists. Busby was especially interested in buildings, canals, railways and industrial archaeology in his work, which was shown at Mall Galleries, Ombersley Galleries and Westcliffe Gallery, Norfolk. He shared a show at Edwin Pollard Gallery, Wimbledon, having solo exhibitions at Tegfryn Gallery, Menai; Heathrow Airport; and Solihull Library. National Library of Wales, Aberystwyth, holds his work. Lived in Solihull, West Midlands.

John BUSBY 1928– Painter, sculptor, designer and teacher, born in Bradford. He studied at Leeds and Edinburgh Colleges of Art, being awarded a postgraduate period of study and a Major Travelling Scholarship. From 1956 he was on the staff of Edinburgh College of Art. In 1978 he was artist-in-residence in Orkney. For almost 20 years from 1958 Busby was actively involved in the 57 Gallery in Edinburgh. Busby was a founder-member of the SWLA with a special interest in birds. Ornithology took him on trips to Jordan and the Indian Ocean and he visited Shetland to illustrate Hugh Miles' book *Track of the Wild Otter*. He was the author of *The Living Birds of Eric Ennion* and *Birds in Mallorca*. Busby designed a big tapestry for Edinburgh Tapestry Company and made carvings for St Martin's Church, Bradford. He was president of SSA, 1973–6, and was elected RSW in 1982. Exhibited at Pier Arts Centre, Stromness; Darlington Arts Centre; Peter Potter Gallery, Haddington; Compass Gallery, Glasgow, and abroad. Scottish Arts Council, Oxford University and many provincial galleries hold his work. Lived at Ormiston, East Lothian, Scotland.

G Felicity BUSH 1913– Painter and modeller, born in St Helens, Lancashire. She studied at Liverpool School of Art under Will Penn, 1929–34, then at Royal College of Art, 1934–8, with Gilbert Spencer. Exhibited at RA and in the provinces. Lived in London.

Harry BUSH 1883–1957 Painter of landscapes, figures and townscapes, born in Brighton, Sussex, married to the artist Noel Laura Nisbet. He studied at Regent Street Polytechnic School of Art and elsewhere in London, where he lived. Sometimes signing his work H B, he showed with ROI of which he was a member, RA, RWA, RSA and Paris Salon. Work is held by British and Australian galleries. In 1985 Oscar and Peter Johnson had an exhibition.

Reginald Edgar James BUSH 1869–1956 Painter, draughtsman, printmaker and teacher, born in Cardiff, Wales. He was married to the watercolourist Flora Bush, his father James Bush having been head of Cardiff School of Science and Art. Reginald studied there and at Royal College of Art. He went on to teach, being principal of Bristol Municipal School of Art for about 40 years from 1895. Exhibited RA, RWA, RE extensively, Walker Art Gallery, Liverpool, Paris Salon and elsewhere overseas. Bristol and Cardiff bought prints by him. Lived for many years in Bristol, and in London.

Fred BUSHE 1931– Sculptor and teacher, born in Coatbridge, Lanarkshire. He studied at Glasgow School of Art, 1949–53, and University of Birmingham's School of Art Education, 1966–7. Fred Bushe lectured in sculpture at Liverpool College of Education, 1962–9, and Aberdeen College of Education, 1969–79, when he became a full-time artist. He played a big part in widening interest in sculpture in Scotland, establishing the Scottish Sculpture Workshop in 1979 and the Scottish Sculpture Biennale Exhibition from the early 1980s, besides promoting several other such gatherings. As well as taking part in important mixed shows in Britain and abroad, Bushe had solo exhibitions: at 57 Gallery, Edinburgh, in 1962; Bluecoat Gallery, Liverpool, 1966; and more recently Talbot Rice Art Centre, Edinburgh, 1982. Elected RSA in 1986. Scottish Arts Council and Aberdeen Art Gallery are among public collections with his work. Lived in Lumsden, Aberdeenshire.

Robbie BUSHE 1964– Artist in mixed media and teacher whose work was tinged with a unique wit. Born in Aberdeen, where he became a lecturer at Gray's School of Art, Bushe completed his degree and postgraduate diploma in painting at Edinburgh College of Art, graduating in 1990. Quickly had a series of solo exhibitions, won two awards in RSA shows and was included in 1993 Thompson's Gallery exhibition Contemporary Art From Scotland. Edinburgh College of Art, Edinburgh City Council and RSA hold examples.

Lynn BUSHELL 1946– Artist whose work included stylised landscapes in a rich palette, born in Kent. Studied at Edinburgh University and Edinburgh College of Art. Mixed exhibitions included Roland, Browse & Delbanco; Scottish Gallery and Richard Demarco Gallery, Edinburgh; and a four-man show at Thackeray Gallery, 1977.

Simon BUSSY 1870–1954 Painter and draughtsman, notably in pastel, who used a bright palette, had a strong decorative sense and completed many small pictures of animals and birds from observation in London Zoo. Bussy was born in Dôle, France, into a peasant family. A scholarship took him to Paris where in 1886 he entered École des Arts Décoratifs. Four years later moved to École des Beaux-Arts where he studied under Delaunay and Moreau. Whistler and Japanese prints were key influences. Had his first solo show at Galerie Durand-Ruel, Paris, in 1897, then went on to show widely in England and France. He married Dorothea Strachey in 1903 and settled in Roquebrune, in the south of France, spending frequent summers in Britain. Among his portraits were Lady Ottoline Morrell, in Tate Gallery collection. Died in London. In 1964 Sotheby's held two important sales of Bussy's pictures from the John Strachey collection.

Alice Caroline BUTLER 1909– Watercolour miniaturist, born in Kent, who studied at St Albans School of Art. Before she was married, in 1938, ran a studio-shop in Malmesbury, Wiltshire. She illustrated her husband Maurice H Bizley's book *Friendly Retreat*. Was a member of RMS and St Ives Society of Artists, specialising in wild flowers and cats. Lived in Perranporth, Cornwall.

Anthony BUTLER 1927– Painter and teacher, born in Liverpool, who studied at the local School of Art, 1944–5 and 1948–50, interrupted by Royal Air Force service. His teachers included Martin Bell, Alfred Wiffen and Allan Tankard. He taught at St Helens Art School, then, until retirement, as head of art at Birkenhead School. Showed at RA, Crane Gallery in Manchester and at the City Art Gallery there, at Agnew and in Northern Young Contemporaries. Butler's output was not large but of high quality, with a leaning towards nostalgic subjects and abstraction. Walker Art Gallery in Liverpool and several other leading northern galleries hold his work. Was elected RCamA in 1960. Lived at West Kirby, Wirral, Merseyside.

Arthur Stanley George BUTLER 1888–1965 Architect, painter and writer who, after attending St Andrews University, studied at the Architectural Association. Keen European traveller, whose books included *The Substance of Architecture* and *Plain Impressions*. Was a member of Chelsea Arts Club. Exhibited RA and RI and lived in London. Manchester City Art Gallery holds his work.

Auriol BUTLER fl. from 1930s– Artist in oil, watercolour and pastel, notably of landscapes and portraits. These included HRH The Princess Royal. Butler started at Exeter School of Art as a child, then was at Byam Shaw School with Ernest Jackson, at Slade School of Fine Art with Randolph Schwabe and in Paris at Académie Julian, L'Académie de la Grande Chaumière and elsewhere. Was a member of Tavistock Group of Artists and Devon Art Society, also showing with LG, RBA and elsewhere. Lived in Cornwood, Devon.

G A BUTLER 1927– Painter who studied at Liverpool College of Art during late 1940s. In 1959 he was appointed head of art at Birkenhead School. From the early 1950s showed RA and with Crane Kalman Gallery in London, but was mainly represented in the north of England, showing at Liverpool Academy and with local societies. Was also a member of RCamA. Birkenhead, Liverpool and Manchester Corporations hold his work. Butler's tiled mosaic for the Churchill shopping precinct at Dudley, Worcestershire, was of a striking Cubist design.

George BUTLER 1904– Watercolourist, born in Sheffield, Yorkshire, who attended the College of Art there, 1922–3, then Central School of Arts and Crafts, 1923–6. Joined the advertising agency J Walter Thompson, 1925–60, and in 1960–80 lived partly in Provence, France. Butler became a member of NEAC, RBA and RWS. The Graves and Mappin Art Galleries in Sheffield hold examples. Lived in Bakewell, Derbyshire.

James BUTLER 1931– Sculptor and teacher, born in London, who studied at Maidstone School of Art, 1948–50, then St Martin's School of Art, 1950–2, followed by National Service, 1953–5, in Royal Corps of Signals. Taught for many years at City & Guilds of London Art School after working as a stone carver for 10 years. Butler's work was figurative, especially the female figure. As a contrast, his first major commission was a twice-life-size portrait statue of President Jomo Kenyatta of Kenya, for Nairobi. Other commissions included more African statues; one from the Richard III Society for a memorial statue of the king at Castle Gardens, Leicester; portrait statue of Sir John Moore, at the barracks of that name, Winchester; John Wilkes, the political figure, in New Fetter Lane; and Skipping Girl, Harrow. Was elected RA in 1972, RWA in 1980 and a fellow of RBS in 1981. Lived at Radway, Warwickshire.

Jonathan BUTLER 1960– Stained glass artist, born in Surrey, who attended Reigate School of Art and Design for four years studying architectural decoration. After graduating in 1981 he worked independently as a designer/maker, believing that contemporary designs could be used in any context depending on the sensitivity of the designer. He was awarded the Worshipful Company of Glaziers Stevens Competition first prize in 1980, third prize in 1981 and the Sir Arthur Evans Travelling Scholarship in 1981. His commissions for stained glass include Our Lady's Church, Battersea, 1985; six windows for a Saudi Arabian palace, 1986; Fulham United Reformed Church, 1987; Lambeth Community Care Centre, 1988, and many other works in private homes and commercial properties. Worked in London.

Liz BUTLER 1948– Watercolourist, illustrator and teacher, born in Brampton, Cumberland, who attended Liverpool College of Art, 1966–70, gaining her master's degree from Royal College of Art, 1970–3. She later studied the history of garden design at Birkbeck College, and took part in The Art of the Garden exhibitions at venues throughout England. Teaching included Colchester School of Art, 1973–82, Camberwell College of Arts and Crafts, 1982–92, and elsewhere. In 1996, Butler was made an associate of RWS. From 1979 showed solo with Francis Kyle Gallery. Her clients included British Gas, *Times* Newspapers, Usborne Publishing, Penguin Books and The National Trust; The Earl of Harewood commissioned a series of paintings; and in 1983 the General Post Office sought designs for stamps commemorating British gardens. Butler's publications included *The Herb and Spice Book*, 1979, and *The Seasons*, an exploration of twelve country walks, 1982. Government Art Collection and Abbot Hall Art Gallery, Kendal, hold examples. Lived in London.

Margaret BUTLER 1932– Painter and printmaker, born in Cleckheaton, Yorkshire. Studied at Dewsbury and Batley Technical and Art School and at Royal College of Art, where her teachers included Edward Ardizzone and Edwin La Dell. Showed Victoria & Albert Museum, Batley Art Gallery, elsewhere in north of England and at Yale University in America. Lived in Cleckheaton.

Paul BUTLER 1947– Painter, muralist and draughtsman, and teacher, born in Bristol. Butler studied there at the West of England College of Art, 1965–6, and at Kingston upon Thames College of Art, 1966–9. In the 1980s he worked on a number of London murals, including the Shepherds Bush Peace Mural, near where he lived, and the Labour History Mural at the Trades Union Congress National Education Centre. Mixed exhibitions included Hunting/*Observer* Awards, 1992, and John Moores Liverpool Exhibition, 1995–6. Had a first solo show at Air Gallery, 1980, one at Montpelier Sandelson in 1996 indicating Butler's affinity with Frank Auerbach, Leon Kossoff and Jack Yeats in his handling of paint. The anonymous dramas of city life were featured. Arts Council, Harris Museum and Art Gallery in Preston, Rochdale Art Gallery, Museum of London, National Museum of Mineworkers and Edinburgh City Council hold examples. From 1988 Butler was head of painting at Surrey Institute of Art & Design, Farnham.

Reg BUTLER 1913–1981 Sculptor and teacher who trained as an architect. Born at Buntingford, Hertfordshire, Butler became an Associate of the Royal Institute of British Architects in 1937, practising between 1936–50 as Cottrell Butler. Lectured for a time at the Architectural Association School, then worked as technical editor of *The Architect's Journal* in the late 1940s. In 1941–5 Butler had worked as a blacksmith in Sussex. He started to become a sculptor in 1947, in that year joining Henry Moore as an assistant. His first one-man show was at the Hanover Gallery, London, two years later. The early 1950s were years of sharp advance in Butler's career. In 1950 he began teaching at the Slade School and became Gregory Fellow at Leeds University, two years later being represented at the Venice Biennale. He became famous in 1953 when he won the grand prize in The Unknown Political Prisoner sculpture competition. Finished teaching at Slade 1980. Towards the end of his life he produced a series of drawings and sculptures concentrating on nude female figures, featured in his Tate Gallery retrospective 1983–4. Lived in Berkhamsted, Hertfordshire.

Richard BUTLER 1921– Painter and designer, born in Essex, who studied at Salisbury School of Art. Showed RA, Arts Council, Walker's Galleries and elsewhere and lived for many years in Horsham, Sussex.

Stephen BUTLER 1954– Painter and collagist, born and lived in Nottingham, who gave up working as a computer programmer in 1978 to attend West Surrey College of Art and Design, Farnham, graduating with honours in fine art, 1979–82. He wrote that his paintings were "heavily influenced by Surrealism, while my collages bring together found objects both natural and man-made in a variety of configurations". Butler was a founder-member of Can Studios in Nottingham, 1988. Group shows included 12 Notts Artists, Palace of Culture, Poznan, Poland, 1992; Innovart, Leicester Museum and Gallery, 1993; and Fragments, Ikon Gallery, Birmingham, and tour, 1994. Had a solo show at Castle Museum and Gallery, 1991, and Yard Gallery, Wollaton Park, 1998, both in Nottingham. Butler's main works were the Earth Table series of collages, 1992; Lost Haven, painting, 1995; and Talisman, collage, 1997. His work appeared in A Pearce's *The Art and Craft of Collage*, 1997, and Nottingham Trent University and the Boots company hold examples.

Vincent BUTLER 1933– Sculptor of figurative-naturalistic work, mainly in bronze, and teacher, born in Manchester. He studied at the Accademia di Belle Arti, Milan, with Marino Marini, and went on to be head of the sculpture school at University of Northern Nigeria, 1960–3, then lectured at Edinburgh College of Art, 1963–90. Was a member of RSA and Royal Glasgow Institute of the Fine Arts. Had solo shows at New Grafton Gallery; Birley Gallery in Manchester; Goosewell Gallery, Menston; the City Art Centre, Open Eye Gallery and Kingfisher Gallery, all in Edinburgh; plus Finkbeiner Galerie, Wolfsburg. Also participated in numerous group exhibitions. Scottish National Portrait Gallery, Edinburgh, holds his work. Lived in Edinburgh.

Hamad BUTT 1962–1990 Installations artist, born in Lahore, Pakistan, who graduated from Goldsmiths' College in 1990. He made three installations: Transmission, at Milch Gallery, 1990; Familiars, at John Hansard Gallery, Southampton, 1992, which was remade two years later at Milch; and he exhibited in 1995 at Tate Gallery as part of the show Rites of Passage. Before he died he began to plan a publication about his work, which formed part of a posthumous book, with contributions by others, issued in 1996 – as *Familiars – Hamad Butt* – by the Institute of International Visual Arts with John Hansard Gallery.

Victorine BUTTBERG 1904– Painter, teacher and designer, born in Edinburgh, where she continued to live and show oils and watercolours. Aquatic scenes and harbours and flowers were favourite themes. For a number of years after leaving school Miss Buttberg drew for fashion advertising in the studio of the Edinburgh department store Jenner's, prompted by economic need. She then obtained a diploma in drawing and painting from Edinburgh College of Art and from 1934, having gained her art teacher's certificate at Moray House College of Education, Edinburgh, taught art in several schools until retirement. Was a member of SSA, with which she showed regularly, also with RSA.

Francis BUTTERFIELD 1905–1968 Mainly abstract painter and draughtsman, born in Bradford, Yorkshire, who attended evening classes with Henry Butler at the local School of Art while working in woolstapling. From 1929 he rebelled against this and began painting in earnest under considerable difficulty, but encouraged by collectors such as Sir Michael Sadler. Butterfield became a member of the Seven and Five Society and had solo shows with Zwemmer Gallery in 1934 and Leicester Galleries in 1937. He settled in London about 1937, spending some time in a studio on the Left Bank in Paris, then his career faded, and he was latterly art editor and wrote for a glossy magazine. Having suffered from heart trouble and cancer he died in Greenwich Hospital. Some of Butterfield's work had landscape allusions; sometimes he painted in hot glue, sprinkling this with sand or brickdust; cement and a flashlamp were also used. Public galleries in Leeds, Sheffield and Wakefield acquired Butterfield's pictures, as did the museum of the Raja of Aundh, India.

Ron BUTTERFIELD 1920– Sculptor and designer in various materials, born and lived in Sheffield, who studied at the local College of Art full- or part-time, 1934–40. He was a member of Guild of Yorkshire Craftsmen and Society of Church Craftsmen and completed much ecclesiastic work. This included pieces in churches in Sheffield, Nuneaton, Melksham, Bradwell and abroad.

Sarah BUTTERFIELD 1953– Artist in oil and watercolour, born and lived in London. The Hon. Sarah Willetts studied painting at Ruskin School, Oxford, 1975–8, where her teachers included Jane Dowling. Also studied architecture at Edinburgh and Bristol Universities, qualified as an architect and practised until the mid-1980s, then chose to paint full-time. Beach, garden and sporting pictures were a strong feature of her work, often rich in sunlight. She was a member of NS and showed in groups at Agnew, Mall Galleries and Richmond Gallery. Solo shows included Judd Street Gallery, 1987, and Cadogan Contemporary, 1991.

Elizabeth BUTTERWORTH 1949– Painter, draughtsman and printmaker, with a strong interest in natural history subjects depicted with delicacy and precision, born in Rochdale, Lancashire, and attended the School of Art there, 1966–8; Maidstone College of Art, 1968–71; and Royal College of Art, 1971–4. Group shows included British Drawing 1952–1972, Angela Flowers Gallery, 1973; English Realists – The Figurative Approach, Fischer Fine Art, 1976–83; 8 British Realists, Louis K Meisel, New York, 1981; and The Rainforest Art Exhibition, Natural History Museum, 1990. Had a solo show at Angela Flowers Gallery, 1975, later ones including Redfern Gallery, 1997. Butterworth's work is held in many international collections, including British Government Art Collection, Museum of Modern Art in New York and Victoria & Albert Museum.

John Malcolm BUTTERWORTH 1945– Painter, printmaker and teacher, born in Lancashire, who studied at Rochdale College of Art, 1961–3, Newport College of Art, 1965–6, then Cardiff College of Art, 1965–6, gaining a Royal Academy David Murray Scholarship in 1965. Went on to teach art at

Southampton Institute of Higher Education. Showed at National Museum of Wales in Cardiff, Cleveland Drawing Biennale and abroad in mixed exhibitions; solo shows included University of Surrey and Southampton City Art Gallery. Surrey University and several education authorities hold his work. Lived in Winchester, Hampshire.

Jon BUTTERWORTH 1968– Painter whose work "reaches out to the ambitions of the later Abstract Expressionists", born in Oldham, Lancashire. He studied at Loughborough College of Art and Design in Leicestershire, where he lived, 1987–90. Contributed to East at Norwich Gallery, 1991.

Alfred BUXTON 1883–1963 Sculptor, born in London. Studied at City and Guilds of London Art School, Finsbury School of Art and Royal Academy Schools, under Hamo Thornycroft and Thomas Brock. Buxton won a gold medal and Travelling Scholarship for sculpture, which enabled him to study widely on the continent. Exhibited RA, Paris Salon, where he gained an Honourable Mention in 1924 for his statue Isabella, based on Keats' poem, and other venues. He completed a large volume of church and memorial carving. Lived in London.

Jennifer BUXTON 1937– Artist in various media, notably a miniaturist, born in London. She studied at Frobisher School of Animal Painting, 1948–53, then Byam Shaw School of Drawing and Painting, 1954–7, her teachers including Lucy Marguerite Frobisher and Bernard Dunstan. Was made a member of RMS in 1970, also showing widely in provinces and at Paris Salon. Lived in Ulverston, Cumbria.

Judy BUXTON 1961– Painter, draughtsman and teacher, born in Sydney, New South Wales, Australia, who moved to England in the early 1980s, where she eventually settled on the Lizard peninsula, Cornwall. "To create grandeur and evocation of space rather than figurative representation" was a key aim. Studied at Falmouth College of Art and Royal Academy Schools, later teaching at Falmouth. Awards included the Richard Jack Interior and Portrait Awards and Henfield Drawing Award, all 1992; in 1993 the Creswick Landscape Prize, David Murray Travel Scholarship, RWS Award and the Painter-Stainers' postgraduate Cyril Sweet Award; winning the Painter-Stainers' 1st Prize, 1996. Group exhibitions included New Generation at Newlyn Orion, Cornwall, 1990; Salt House Gallery, St Ives, 1994; and Royal Over-Seas League Open, 1996. Solo shows included The Oxford Gallery, Oxford, 1996. Cornwall County Council and several corporate collections hold examples.

Donald BUYERS 1930– Painter and teacher who was born and lived in Aberdeen. He studied at Gray's School of Art there, 1948–51. Was a member of RSW, mixed exhibition appearances including Young Scottish Contemporaries, Arts Council, 1963–4; Glasgow Group Exhibition, 1975–80; BWS, 1987; and Open Eye Gallery, Edinburgh, Six East Coast Artists, 1990. Had a solo show at Gaumont Gallery, Aberdeen, 1954, later ones including University of Aberdeen, from 1970, and Torrance Gallery, Edinburgh, 1991. HRH The Duke of Edinburgh, Scottish Arts Council and many other Scottish public and private collections hold his work.

Edwin BYATT 1888–1948 Landscape and flower painter, especially in watercolour. His early career was spent working as a lithographer, then as a commercial artist with a printing company. Medici Society reproduced his work, and he exhibited RA, RI, ROI, Walker Art Gallery, Liverpool, and Paris Salon. Russell-Cotes Art Gallery and Museum in Bournemouth holds his work. Lived in Ewell, Surrey.

Gordon BYATT 1907– Painter and decorative artist, born in Cleethorpes, Lincolnshire. Exhibited at Foyles Gallery, Usher Art Gallery in Lincoln and elsewhere in provinces. Lived in Cleethorpes.

Leonard BYNG 1920–1974 Sculptor, born in London. After attending Harrow School and Oxford University Byng studied at the Ruskin School of Drawing and Fine Art, Oxford, 1939, under Albert Rutherston, and in 1944 at the Slade School of Fine Art with Randolph Schwabe. His sculpture has a classical simplicity, as shown in Eric Newton's monograph *British Sculpture 1944–1946*. Exhibited RA and was an associate RBS. Lived at various times in Sandwich, Kent, Paris and London.

Charles BYRD 1916– Painter, sculptor and kinetic artist working in a variety of materials, born in Pontypridd, Glamorgan. After an elementary education Byrd did a variety of jobs, ranging from photographer to aircraft fitter, becoming a full-time artist in 1950. From the early 1950s he participated in a wide range of group shows, including WAC, Compendium Gallery in Birmingham and Howard Roberts and Arlington Galleries, Cardiff. In the early 1970s he participated in Kinetic Art, in Glynn Vivian Art Gallery in Swansea, and in Edinburgh; and Wales and the Modern Movements, at University College of Wales, Aberystwyth. One-man shows included Chapter Arts Centre, Cardiff. Glamorgan, Merthyr and Gwent Education Authorities hold his work.

John BYRNE 1940– Painter, designer and writer, born in Glasgow. He attended the School of Art there, 1958–61; Edinburgh College of Art, 1961–2; Glasgow School of Art, 1962–3; then a travelling scholarship took him to Italy in 1963–4. Among his many pursuits Byrne worked as a graphic artist for Scottish Television; did carpet design; and designed record sleeves and book jackets. He had his first one-man show at Glasgow's Third Eye Centre in 1975, having become a full-time painter in 1968, signing his work Patrick. This early work was frequently of a whimsical Scottish nature, work under his own name being more mainstream. Byrne was strongly associated with Portal Gallery. Developed another career as a scriptwriter and playwright, writing the successful television series *Tutti Frutti* and *The Slab Boys Trilogy*.

Alfons BYTAUTUS 1955– Artist and teacher, who gained his diploma at Edinburgh College of Art (drawing and painting), 1972–7, lecturing in printmaking there, 1978. From 1979 he was employed as a printmaking technician in the Edinburgh Printmakers' Workshop, studying at Atelier 17, Paris, 1983. He showed at Printmakers' Workshop Gallery, Edinburgh, 1981; Peacock Printmakers' Gallery and Forebank Gallery, in Dundee, both 1982; and was included in Scottish Print Open Three, 1983, organised by Dundee Printmakers' Workshop. Was made an associate of RSA and lived in Edinburgh.

Marjorie BYWATER 1905– Painter and teacher, born in Ealing, where she studied at the local School of Art, at the Royal College of Art, 1927–30, under Ernest Tristram and Reco Capey, then from 1935–6 at the Slade School of Fine Art with Vladimir Polunin. Exhibited RA, RWS, WIAC and Paris Salon. Active member of Questors Theatre Club, Ealing. Lived in London.

C

C: *see* **Christopher Herbert Henry CATLIN**

Anthea C: *see* **Anthea CHAPMAN**

Leonard CACKETT 1896–1963 Painter of landscapes and seascapes, in London. Studied Bolt Court School of Art and Hackney Institute. Exhibited RA, RWA, RSMA, PS, RWS and widely in the provinces. Was a member of St Ives Society of Artists, the Society of Sussex Painters and the West Sussex Arts Club. Folkestone Museum and Art Gallery holds his work. Lived at Ferring, Sussex.

Panayotis CACOYANNIS 1955– Artist whose work included mixed media constructions. Studied at Oxford University, Central School of Art and Design, Middlesex Polytechnic and Royal College of Art. Showed in mixed exhibitions at LG, Royal Over-Seas League and in 1991 Art in Boxes, at England & Co. In 1993 was a finalist in Bank of Cyprus Art Award, work shown at Gallery K. Had solo shows at Angela Flowers, Todd Gallery and Alexander Roussos Gallery.

Kathleen CADDICK 1937– Painter, designer and printmaker who studied at High Wycombe College of Art. She worked for several years as a graphic designer before starting to paint full-time in 1968. Began etching in 1976, combining a strong line with delicate colouring. Weathered buildings, bleached grasses, winter trees and snow were recurrent themes. Caddick showed extensively in the Britain, where Belgravia Contemporary Arts sold her work, in the Middle East and gained a large following in Germany. In 1977 a major show of her pictures toured Europe.

Florence St John CADELL fl. from c.1900–1960 Landscape and figure painter who spent much time in Scotland, sister of the artist Agnes Morison Cadell. She travelled widely and showed at Alpine Club Gallery, RSA, Royal Glasgow Institute of the Fine Arts and elsewhere.

William CADENHEAD 1934– Painter, draughtsman and teacher, born in Aberdeen. He studied at Duncan of Jordanstone College of Art, Dundee, under Alberto Morrocco, 1951–5, later teaching there; in Italy and France, 1956; at Patrick Allan-Fraser School of Art, Hospitalfield, Arbroath; and under Peter Greenham at Royal Academy Schools, 1957–61, gaining the David Murray Scholarship in 1957. In 1969 was elected a professional member of SSA, also showing at RSA, RSW and Compass Gallery, Glasgow. Showed solo at Scottish Gallery, Edinburgh, from 1981, and Woodstock Gallery. Scottish Arts Council and members of the royal family owned his work. Lived at Muir of Lownie, Forfar, Angus.

Michael CADMAN 1920– Painter and teacher, born in Epsom, Surrey. Studied at Wimbledon School of Art, 1937 and 1940–1, under Gerald Cooper and Robert Buhler, then Royal College of Art, 1941–4, with Gilbert Spencer, Percy Horton and Robert Austin. He taught at Epsom School of Art from 1947–68/9. Cadman said that design, colour and atmosphere were most important in his work, notable features being architectural and hedgerow themes, water reflections and cattle compositions. Was a member of RI, 1970, also St Ives Society of Artists and some minor societies. Showed at ROI, RWS, RA, RBA and in many other group shows. His solo exhibitions included Canaletto Gallery, 1963–4, Whitehall Galleries, Cheam, 1967, and Southampton, 1982. Work also appeared in Royle's *Artists' Britain* calendars. Lived in Sherborne, Dorset.

John CAHILL 1954– Painter and gallery owner, born in Golborn, Lancashire. He studied at Wigan Technical College for foundation work, 1971–3, gained his honours degree in fine art at Portsmouth Polytechnic, 1973–6, then his master's degree in painting, 1977–80, at Royal College of Art. Among his awards were Jeffrey Archer Prize for best painting by an artist under 30, 1980; two Elizabeth Greenshields Foundation Sponsorships, 1980–2; and first prize at Royal Bath & West Show, 1987. In 1988 he opened The Harbour Gallery, Tenby, Dyfed. Mixed exhibitions included RA Summer Exhibition from 1982 and Wales Art Fair, Cardiff, 1993. Had a one-man show at Harris Museum & Art Gallery, Preston, 1978, and at Wyeside Arts Centre, Builth Wells, 1986. Cahill painted minutely detailed landscapes.

CAI XIAOLI 1956– Painter and teacher, born in Xian, central China, married to the artist Wang Jianan. She graduated in 1982 from the Chinese Painting Department of the Central Academy of Fine Art of China and went on to teach in the Academy. Became director of the Contemporary Fine Brush Painting Association. The artists worked individually and jointly and won prizes in the 6th National Art Exhibition of China and the Beijing Artists' Association in 1986. In 1988 they moved to Britain. They evolved a unique technique of watercolour painting based on traditional methods from the Shong dynasty for painting on silk. The two artists outside China showed widely, including Eastern Art Gallery, 1988; OneOneNine Gallery, 1989; RA and Royal Festival Hall on several occasions; in Hamburg, Tokyo and Hong Kong; and in 1992 they shared an exhibition at Gruzelier

Modern and Contemporary Art. Collections include Central Academy of Fine Art, China; British Museum; and Victoria and Albert Museum.

CAI YUAN 1956– Painter, born in China, who took images from printed sources "to express my mixed feelings towards the contemporary art scene". After Nanjing Academy of Arts studied at Chelsea College of Art and Royal College of Art. Group shows including his work were: 2nd Biennale of European Art Schools, Antwerp, 1989; LG, Royal College of Art, 1990; Beardsmore Gallery, 1993; and Journeys West, University of Essex touring exhibition, 1995. Awards included J Andrew Lloyd Scholarship, 1991.

Judith CAIN 1944– Painter and teacher, born in York, who earned her national diploma in painting at Leeds College of Art, 1960–4, teachers including Harry Thubron and Tommy Watt, then gained her teacher's certificate at Goldsmiths' College of Art, 1965. For some years after leaving college Cain taught textile design and printmaking, lecturing part-time at many colleges including Canterbury, Colchester Technical, Jacob Kramer in Leeds and at the Polytechnic there. From 1985 was full-time painting co-ordinator at Leeds Metropolitan University's department of fine art. In 1995 she was Laing Regional Exhibition 1st Prize Winner; its National Exhibition major prizewinner; and was a prizewinner, Harewood Award, at Harewood Landscape Open. Later solo exhibitions included Thackeray Gallery and Dean Clough Galleries, Halifax, both 1996. Leeds University and Leeds Metropolitan University both hold examples. Cain only rarely used brushes, her fluid, translucent pictures resulting from the use of devices such as rags and sponges. Images which nourished her work included early Roman glass, Middle Eastern carpets, Indian miniatures and flower and tree forms in early Italian pictures.

Osmund CAINE 1914– Artist in oil, watercolour and stained glass and teacher, born Manchester. Studied at Birmingham College of Art, 1930–7, and in Italy, 1938. Gained an honours degree in medieval and modern history and studied singing at Guildhall School. He taught, 1945–7, including principal lectureship in graphic design at Twickenham College of Technology. Took part in numerous mixed exhibitions, including NEAC, RBSA and RA, and had 14 solo shows in Britain and France, later ones including Duncan Campbell Fine Art, 1986, and Galerie Salammbo, Paris, 1987. English hill figures, British castles, monumental effigies, Kew Gardens and France were notable themes in his work. Caine completed 15 stained glass windows in Britain and abroad, including St Gabriel's Church, Cricklewood, and St Cuthbert's Church, Copnor. Ministry of Transport and London University, City of Birmingham Art Gallery and Victoria & Albert Museum hold his work. Lived in Kingston upon Thames, Surrey.

Florence Blanche CAINS 1905– Painter and artist in patchwork and knitwear; teacher. She was born and lived in Bristol, studying at the School of Art there, 1922–7. For her art teacher's diploma she specialised in calligraphy and embroidery. Became head of art department at St George Grammar School, Bristol. Was a member of SWA and showed at RA, RI and RWA. From around 1960 her works "assumed abstract forms, influenced by wood grains and bones".

Gerald Albert CAINS 1932– Painter and teacher, born in Stubbington, Hampshire. He attended Southern College of Art, Portsmouth, 1949–53. After National Service in Egypt, gained art teacher's diploma, at Bournemouth, then an advanced diploma in art education at Cardiff, 1977. Notable among his teachers was John Elwyn. Taught art, 1957–85, mainly in Bristol, then painted full-time. Cains was early influenced by the social realism of Camden Town and LG painters, and was notable for subdued-colour townscapes. He was elected RWA in 1978, also being a member of Bath Society of Artists. His work was included in Football and the Fine Arts, Football Association show in 1953; also RA from 1964; ROI from 1983; and Brewhouse Open Art, Taunton, 1986. Had a solo show at Patricia Wells Gallery, Thornbury, 1976, also Harlequin Gallery, Bath, 1982. RWA holds his work; Walsall Education Authority holds Towards Temple Meads; and Longleat House's Wessex Collection The Miner in his Garden. Lived in Clandown, near Bath, Avon.

Joyce W CAIRNS 1947– Painter and teacher, born at Haddington, East Lothian. She graduated at Gray's School of Art, Aberdeen, followed by a postgraduate year. Further studies at Royal College of Art earned her a master's degree and a fellowship course at Gloucester College of Art and Design, Cheltenham, followed. Joyce Cairns won a large number of prizes and awards, including the Hospitalfield Prize, 1969; RSA Student Prize, 1970; Carnegie Travelling Scholarship to America, 1971, and the English Speaking Union Scholarship there in 1972; and the RSA's Latimer Award in 1978 and the first prize in its Morrison Portrait Competition in 1989. She was elected RSW in 1979. From 1977 Cairns was a lecturer at Gray's School of Art while also teaching at Dundee and Glasgow Art Schools. In 1985 she was the first woman president of Aberdeen Artists. She took part in many group exhibitions, including RA and SSA, and after a solo show at Compass Gallery in 1980 others were at Perth Museum and Art Gallery in 1986, the 369 Gallery in Edinburgh in the same year and the Third Eye Centre, Glasgow, 1987. Her pictures drew on partly fictional and partly biographical material to create densely packed and compelling images.

CALBEAM: *see* **Frederick Harold BEAMISS**

Alexandra CALINESCU 1967– Artist whose work included abstract paintings such as At the Still Point of the Turning World, in Royal Over-Seas League Open, 1994. She was born in Cambridge, studying there at the Cambridgeshire College of Arts & Technology; City and Guilds of London Art School; and Royal Academy Schools. Won a series of awards, including Philip Connard Travel Award, 1988; Richard Ford Award for Travel, 1989; Landseer Scholarship, 1991; David Murray Travel

Scholarship, 1991–2. Took part in many group shows, including Janus Avivson Gallery, 1990; Bankside Gallery Open, 1991; LG Open, Barbican, 1993; and ASC Studios, 1994.

Edward CALLAM 1904–1980 Painter in oil and watercolour of landscapes and architecture, black-and-white artist, designer and typographer. Born at Great Kimble, Buckinghamshire, he studied art under F F May. Exhibitions included the RA, Société des Artistes Français, RBA, ROI, the Russell-Cotes Art Gallery and Museum, Bournemouth, Foyles Gallery and the Brighton and Worthing Art Galleries, in Sussex. Was a member of the Society of Sussex Painters. Official purchases include Maidstone Corporation, Luton Art Gallery and Luton Corporation. *Sphere*, *Tatler*, *The Christian Science Monitor* and Penguin Books used his work. Lived at Bexhill, Sussex.

Ruth CALLAND 1963– Artist and teacher, born in Scunthorpe, Lincolnshire, who attended Lincolnshire College of Art, 1981–2; gained a first-class degree in fine art from Coventry (Lanchester) Polytechnic, Coventry, 1982–5; then her master's in painting, Chelsea School of Art, 1986–7, with a Boise Travelling Scholarship in 1987. From 1987–8 was fellow in painting at Gloucestershire College of Art & Technology (Gloscat), Cheltenham, founding the Gloscat Women's Group, 1987. Held a number of visiting lectureships, including Wimbledon School of Art, Croydon and Barnet Colleges and Nene College in Northampton. Other features of her career included membership of Coventry Artists Group, 1985–6; freelance art consultancy, 1989–90; being a counsellor for Relate from 1992; and between 1994–6 being a member of the Stoke Newington Arts Project and the Newham Counselling Forum. Mixed shows included New Contemporaries, ICA and tour, 1986; Three Figurative Painters, Paton Gallery, 1987; New Art, Atrium Gallery, 1991; An English April, Lamont Gallery, 1992; and Unquiet Voices, which she also curated, at Doncaster Museum & Art Gallery, 1997. She had a solo exhibition there, 1998, having had one at Atlantis European, called Mother's Suite, 1995–6. Leicestershire Collection, Coventry (Lanchester) Polytechnic, British Gas and Slade School of Fine Art hold examples. Lived in London.

Elaine CALLEN fl. from early 1980s– Artist notable for depictions of natural forms in pastel, who lived and worked in Belfast, Northern Ireland, and was a founder-member of Queen Street Studios there. She graduated from the University of Ulster in 1981 and took part in many group shows in England, Scotland and Ireland including Works on Paper at Queen Street Studios, 1994. Her many solo shows included Lyric Theatre, 1989, and Harmony Hill Arts Centre, 1990, both Belfast.

Robert CALLENDER 1932– Artist working in a variety of materials to make realistic objects; painter and curator. He was born in Mottingham, Kent. Studied at South Shields Art School, 1948–9. After attending Edinburgh University, 1951–4, and the College of Art, 1954–9, he gained an Andrew Grant Scholarship which took him to the British School in Rome. First solo show at 57 Gallery, in Edinburgh, in 1963, becoming its director, 1966–9. By this time Callender was well established as a constructor of objects. They could be boats or part of boats, made from paper, card or balsa-wood and realistically painted. Callender had a number of solo shows: Talbot Rice Art Centre, Edinburgh, 1985; Third Eye Centre, Glasgow, 1986; and Mayor Gallery, 1986. He was president of SSA, 1969–73. Scottish National Gallery of Modern Art holds his work.

Simon CALLERY 1960– Painter, born and lived in London, who studied at Berkshire College of Art and Design, 1979–80, and South Glamorgan Institute of Higher Education, 1980–3. He won Arts Council Young Artists Awards in 1983 and 1986, gained a Gold Medal at Welsh National Eisteddfod, 1986, and won a prize at John Moores Liverpool Exhibition, 1993–4. Solo exhibitions include Anderson O'Day, 1993. Saatchi Collection holds his work.

Roy CALNE 1930– Painter in all media whose works depicted transplant surgery, patients, nurses and medical colleagues "from the human point of view". Calne was born in Richmond, Surrey, was a medical graduate of Guy's Hospital, 1952; served as medical officer to a Gurkha Regiment in Hong Kong and Malaya, 1954–6; taught anatomy at Oxford University, 1957–8; trained in surgery at the Royal Free Hospital and started research on organ transplantation in 1959; lectured in surgery at St Mary's and Westminster Hospitals, 1961–5; in 1965 taking up the appointment as professor of surgery at Cambridge University. He became one of the most distinguished surgeons in the transplant field and was knighted in 1986. Calne was a Sunday painter, encouraged in art at school, whose later teachers included Francis Russell Flint and Ron Ranson. A decisive turn came with the arrival of the painter John Bellany at Addenbrooke's Hospital in 1988; this third teacher of Calne's convinced the surgeon of the therapeutic effect of art. Calne's exhibition The Gift of Life toured from the Barbican Centre in 1991, sales of pictures and catalogues supporting The University of Cambridge Children's Liver Fund. Calne also showed in Germany, Singapore and in Japan's Kyoto Museum in group exhibitions. Other solo shows included Richmond Gallery and Science Museum which holds his work, as do Wellcome Museum and Royal College of Surgeons. Lived in Cambridge.

Gwendoline May CALVERT 1908– Sculptor in terracotta and painter, born in Swansea, who was a nurse by profession. She studied art at the Bolt Court School, Fleet Street, and showed at Guildhall in London and widely in the provinces, from 1978–88 being a member of Hesketh Hubbard Art Society. Burnley Hospital holds her work. Lived for some years at Brierfield, Lancashire.

David Young CAMERON 1865–1945 Painter, notably of rather dour Scottish mountain subjects, and printmaker, born in Glasgow. Studied at evening classes in the early 1880s at Glasgow School of Art, in 1885 joining Royal Institution, Edinburgh, as a full-time student. Cameron soon built up an

impressive exhibiting record. He was made a member of RWS in 1906, RSA in 1918 and RA in 1920. In 1924 he was knighted and was made King's Painter and Limner in Scotland, 1933. During World War I the Canadian government commissioned him to paint war pictures in France. Cameron was a trustee of the Scottish National Galleries and of the Tate Gallery, which holds his work, 1921–7. He was a noted etcher, examples being featured in a number of books, including Sir Herbert Maxwell's *Story of the Tweed*, 1905. From 1898 Cameron lived in Kippen, Stirlingshire, whose church includes his work and that of other notable Scottish artists. His sister was the artist Katherine Cameron. He died in Perth.

Emma CAMERON 1964– Painter and printmaker, born in Ross Shire, who attended Fortrose Academy, 1975–81. Did a foundation course in art and design at Camberwell School of Arts and Crafts, 1981–2; an honours degree in fine art (painting), at Central School of Art and Design, 1982–5; and a diploma in advanced printmaking at the Central, 1985–7; with a postgraduate certificate in education, University of East Anglia, 1990–1. Mixed shows included RA; RSA; Artefact, Bankside, Stephen Bartley, Boundary and October Galleries; Alba Fine Art; and Phoenix Gallery, Lavenham. In 1996 had a solo show at Chappel Galleries, Chappel.

Gordon Stewart CAMERON 1916–1994 Painter and teacher, born in Aberdeen. He was married to the painter Ellen Malcolm. After education at Robert Gordon's College in Aberdeen Cameron attended Gray's School of Art there, 1935–40, his teachers including D M Sutherland. He went on to teach at Duncan of Jordanstone College of Art, in Dundee. His work, which shows a fine knowledge of anatomy, is in several Scottish collections, including Aberdeen Art Gallery. Lived in Invergowrie, Perthshire.

Katherine CAMERON 1874–1965 Painter, printmaker and book illustrator. Born in Glasgow, sister of the artist D Y Cameron. Studied at Glasgow School of Art, 1898, under Fra Newbery, then at Atelier Colarossi, Paris. Exhibited flower paintings and landscapes prolifically in Britain and abroad, including RA, Royal Glasgow Institute of the Fine Arts, RSW, Walker's Galleries. The Tate Gallery, Victoria & Albert Museum, British Museum and Library of Congress, Washington, in America, hold her work. Contributed to *The Yellow Book* and illustrated a number of other titles, including James Aitken's *In a City Garden*, 1913, and Iolo Williams' *Where the Bee Sucks*, 1929; her husband, Arthur Kay, was more enthusiastic about this work than she was, for she preferred painting. Had a one-man show at the Annan Gallery, Glasgow, 1959. Lived in Edinburgh.

Moira CAMERON 1962– Artist born and lived in London who spent some time working in New York. She attended Ravensbourne College of Art, 1980–4, gaining a first-class honours degree, then won her master's degree at Chelsea College of Art, 1984–5. Group shows included Mall Galleries, 1984; Lisson Gallery, 1985; Patricia Knight Gallery, from 1987; LG from 1989; and Twining Gallery, New York, 1992. Solo exhibitions included Twining Gallery, 1991. Curwen Gallery also stocked her work.

Shirley CAMERON 1944– Sculptor and events artist, born in Oxford. She studied at Sutton School of Art, 1959–62, then in the sculpture department of St Martin's School of Art, 1960–6. Had a period as a youth leader in the late 1960s. Lectured 1969–72 at Dyfed College of Art, then received an Arts Council grant for work with Roland Miller. In the early 1970s she took part in a variety of events in Britain and on the continent, including Railway Images, at Leicester Arts Festival; Swansea Valley (Land Art); Coventry Arts Festival; and Fanfare for Europe, Hull and Cardiff. One-man shows included University College, Swansea.

Zoe CAMERON 1959– Painter, draughtsman and teacher who studied at Maidenhead College of Art & Design, 1975–7, then Gloucestershire College of Art & Design, Cheltenham, 1977–80, where she graduated with honours. From 1990 lectured part-time at Falmouth School of Art. From 1980 showed with Cheltenham Group at Cheltenham Art Gallery & Museum; Rooksmoor Gallery from 1981; Delahaye Gallery, Cirencester, 1985; and Stephen Bartley Gallery, 1991. Solo show at Rooksmoor Gallery, 1984, later one-man exhibitions including Salt House Gallery, St Ives, Cornwall, 1990. In 1993 shared a show at Cadogan Contemporary. Her pictures attempted "to express a recognition of the human condition in all its extremes". Lived in Cornwall.

Florence CAMM 1874–1960 Stained glass artist who studied at Birmingham School of Art. She was in business under her father's name, Thomas William Camm, with her brothers Robert and Walter Herbert Camm. Exhibited extensively RA, Walker Art Gallery, Liverpool, RSA and abroad. Lived at Smethwick, Birmingham, and continued to work into her eighties, being referred to by her brother Walter as "our best man".

Robert CAMM 1878–1954 Stained glass artist who studied at Birmingham School of Art. He was in business under his father's name, Thomas William Camm, with his brother Walter Herbert and sister Florence. Exhibited RA and in Turin, Italy, where at the International Exhibition he won the only prize for stained glass. Lived at Smethwick, Birmingham.

Walter Herbert CAMM 1881–1967 Stained glass artist who studied at Birmingham and West Bromwich Schools of Art. His father had founded the family stained glass business about 1850, selling it later and starting afresh in 1885 not far away in Smethwick, Birmingham, where it remained. When Thomas William Camm died the business was taken over by Walter Herbert Camm, his brother Robert and sister Florence, who all worked in it to an advanced age. Camm exhibited extensively at RA, RSA, Walker Art Gallery in Liverpool and elsewhere. In 1911 the Camms won a medal in Turin for a window called Dante and Beatrice and their last big window was a Warwickshire Regiment memorial in Warwick Parish Church. Other work was done for

Christchurch in New Zealand, for the collector J Pierpont Morgan in America, for a children's hospital in Kimberley, South Africa, as well as extensive windows in England. A room devoted to the family's works was created in the Staffordshire industrial museum at Shugborough Hall. Camm lived at Warley Woods, Oldbury.

Donald CAMMELL 1934–1996 Film director, screenwriter and portrait painter, son of the writer and poet Charles Richard Cammell. He began to paint when aged three, being judged a prodigy. Left Westminster School at 16, attended Byam Shaw School of Art, gained a scholarship to the Royal Academy Schools, then studied in Florence with Pietro Annigoni (his father's *Memoirs of Annigoni* appeared in 1956). Became a full-time portrait painter in the early 1950s, with a studio in Chelsea. Although he had success, including a society portrait of the year (the subject was Sheridan, Marquis of Dufferin and Ava, a page boy at the coronation of Queen Elizabeth II), Cammell decided to change course, in 1961 moving to Paris, but he failed to find a satisfactory new style. Exhibitions included a solo show at Gallery One, with another at Bertha Schaefer Gallery, New York, 1961. In Chelsea Cammell had met the Greek film actress Maria Andipa, whom he married, and in the 1960s films displaced art as his main preoccupation. His first screenplay, *Duffy*, was produced in England in 1968. In 1970, *Performance*, which Cammell wrote and co-directed with Nicholas Roeg, caused a stir, with its atmosphere of surreal decadence, the cast including James Fox and Mick Jagger. Cammell's first Hollywood film was *The Demon Seed*, 1977, starring Julie Christie. *The White of the Eye*, 1988, and *The Wild Side*, 1995, were also directed by Cammell, who was latterly based in Los Angeles. His second wife, China Kong, who worked with Cammell on many of his screenplays, was introduced to the former painter by his friend Marlon Brando. Cammell killed himself with a shot in the head.

Jane CAMP 1932– Self-taught painter in oil and gouache, born in Clapham, south London. She began painting in 1981 and took her subjects from her immediate environment, people in their daily occupations, her garden, animals and children; she also enjoyed creating dramatic sporting pictures. Lived near Dorking, Surrey, being a member of its Group of Artists, other mixed shows including RI and SWA, and Medici Society published cards of her pictures. Had a series of solo shows at The Westcott Gallery, Westcott.

Jeffery CAMP 1923– Artist and teacher, born in Oulton Broad, Suffolk. He studied first at Lowestoft and then at Ipswich School of Art, then from 1941–4 was at Edinburgh College of Art under William Gillies and John Maxwell. He returned to Suffolk at the end of 1944 and won an Andrew Grant Travelling Scholarship in 1945 and a David Murray Bursary for landscape painting in 1946. His first solo show was with Beaux Arts Gallery in 1959. He was married to the painter Laetitia Yhap for a while from 1964, living in Hastings, although he later moved to London. Camp taught at Slade School Fine Art, 1963–88, and was elected RA in 1984. In addition to several shows at Beaux Arts he had major solo exhibitions at New Art Centre, 1968; a retrospective at South London Art Gallery in 1973; Serpentine Gallery, 1978; several at Nigel Greenwood Gallery from 1986; and RA, 1988. Camp's pictures were included in several major international touring exhibitions in the 1980s. In 1981 published the book *Draw*, which was frequently reprinted. Art Council holds several examples of Camp's work, which was full of movement and colour and often featured south of England coastal scenes, as well as landscapes with figures.

Alex CAMPBELL 1932– Artist in acrylic and gouache, and teacher, born in Edinburgh, where he lived. He studied at Edinburgh College of Art, where he was on the staff from 1960, studying under William Gillies and Robin Philipson, and obtaining his master's degree with honours, 1951–8; gained an Andrew Grant Travelling Scholarship to France, did a post-graduate scholarship and then obtained an Andrew Grant Travelling Scholarship to Spain, Morocco and Italy. Among a series of awards was the RSA Guthrie Award, 1963; May Marshall Brown Awards, 1979 and 1986; Grampian Region Award, 1980; and Alexander Graham Munro Award, 1991. Campbell became a member of SSA, 1966; SWLA, 1967; RSW, 1976; and RSA, 1981, being its librarian in 1982. Campbell took part in many group shows, especially in Scotland, from 1962. Had a string of one-man exhibitions, later ones including Kingfisher Gallery, Edinburgh, 1990; Lamp of Lothian Collegiate Trust, Haddington, 1991; and Loomshop Gallery, Lower Largo, 1993. Among many public collections holding examples were Edinburgh City Art Centre, Government Art Collection, Keighley Art Gallery, RSA and Scottish Arts Council.

Catriona CAMPBELL 1940– Painter, mainly in oil of figurative work, born in Dollar, Clackmannan, whose sister was the illustrator Jennifer Campbell and whose daughter was the artist Gwen Jones. Campbell was early taught by her portrait painter father Ian Campbell, then she attended Glasgow School of Art, 1957–61, under David Donaldson and Mary Armour. After marriage and a family and some teaching, she from 1981 painted full-time, "for my enjoyment and that of the viewer. Arrangement of shapes in a space and the play of light upon them seems enough to strive for". Velasquez, Van Dyck, Uccello, Degas and Picasso were mentioned as influences. Campbell was a member of SSWA, also exhibiting in open exhibitions with RSA, RP, SSA, Royal Glasgow Institute of the Fine Arts, and in group exhibitions at Stirling Gallery, Stirling, 1981; Peter Potter Gallery, Haddington, 1982; Gatehouse Gallery, Glasgow, from 1992; Gallery 41 and Firth Gallery, both Edinburgh in 1994; and Catto Gallery, 1996. Later solo shows included Dundee Repertory Theatre, 1985, and Gallery Quinn, St Andrews, 1986. BBC Scotland held her work. Lived in Letham, Cupar, Fife.

Christopher CAMPBELL 1956– Sculptor, born in Blackpool, Lancashire, who studied at the local College of Technology and Trent Polytechnic in Nottingham, where he settled. His large wooden sculpture Camel was sited in 1984 at Milton Keynes

General Hospital, commissioned by the Development Corporation. Leicestershire Education Authority and Sheffield City Art Galleries also hold examples.

Felicity CAMPBELL 1909– Painter, illustrator and commercial artist, brought up in Sussex. Studied art widely on the continent and in London with the illustrator Edmund J Sullivan. Exhibited Walker's Galleries, IS and elsewhere. She illustrated a number of books, including *The Pond*, by Marjorie Bowen. Lived for some time at Guestling, Sussex.

George E CAMPBELL 1899–1976 Portrait, figure and religious sculptor, born in Liverpool, who worked mainly in bronze, wood and terracotta, some stone. After Royal Navy service, 1916–18, Campbell studied for five years at Royal College of Art, winning the Whitechapel 1st Prize, then continued his studies in France, Italy, Switzerland and America. Lived in several places in France, 1930–9, followed by World War II service with Royal Air Force and Royal Navy, then reopened his studio in London. Was elected a fellow of RBS in 1951. Showed at RA, RSA and Royal Glasgow Institute of the Fine Arts. Glasgow's Art Gallery and Museum, Kelvingrove, has Campbell's Torso, in wood, of 1944.

Ian CAMPBELL 1902–1984 Painter, notably of portraits, also landscapes, and teacher, father of the artist Catriona and the illustrator Jennifer Campbell. He was born in Oban, Argyll, and studied at Glasgow School of Art, 1921–6, under Maurice Greiffenhagen, who remained an influence. Campbell taught art for 40 years, at first in Glasgow schools, from 1937 until he retired in 1968 as head of department at Dollar Academy, Clackmannanshire, where he died. Continued to paint until the day of his death. Showed widely, including RSA (won the Guthrie Award, 1931), Royal Glasgow Institute of the Fine Arts, RI, RA, RWS, SSA and elsewhere. His drawing of Cosmo Lang, Archbishop of Canterbury, completed in 1936, is held by National Portrait Gallery.

Irene CAMPBELL 1914– Painter in oil, gouache and acrylic, and teacher, born London. Studied in 1930–5 at Chelsea and Hornsey Schools of Art, teachers including Henry Moore and Graham Sutherland. She taught in London and worked at Harefield Hospital, 1940–6, then married and raised a family in Newlyn, Cornwall, where she settled. After these responsibilities returned to painting pictures that were "exciting with colour and composition that warrant further study". Her abstracts were based on windows and doors in her house and abroad, as well as old family photographs, work with a strong sense of pattern with a felicitous line. Showed at Chenil Gallery in the 1970s and Newlyn Orion Gallery in 1980s and in 1985 had a solo show at Penzance Arts Centre.

Joan Betty CAMPBELL 1923– Watercolourist, miniaturist and teacher, born in London. Apart from some lessons at evening school in Ilford, was mainly self-taught. Became a member of SWA in 1975, RMS in 1980. Sometimes signed her work with initials only. Showed at Bankside and Mall Galleries, at Paris Salon and in America. Lived in Ickenham, Middlesex.

Scott CAMPBELL 1924– Painter, maker of reliefs and teacher, born in Buxton, Derbyshire. After attending Bradford Grammar School he studied art at King's College, Newcastle upon Tyne, 1948–53. He worked for the North East Regional Office of the Arts Council, 1953–5, and taught art at King's College. Had several solo shows, including Drian Gallery, 1960–3, and Hatton Gallery, Newcastle, 1962. Was included in the Arts Council show Construction England in 1963 and in Belgrave Gallery's 1992 exhibition British abstract art of the 50s and 60s. Lived in Newcastle.

Steven CAMPBELL 1953– Painter, born in Glasgow where he spent seven years in a steelworks as an engineer after leaving school. Studied at Glasgow School of Art, 1978–82, winning the J D Kelly Award, Bram Stoker Gold Medal and a Fulbright Scholarship which took him to New York. There he held two one-man shows in 1983, at Barbara Toll Fine Arts and at the John Weber Gallery, and other exhibitions in America, Germany and London soon followed. In 1987 he had a major show at Marlborough Fine Art and another three years later at Third Eye Centre, Glasgow. Also took part in extensive group shows in Britain and abroad. Campbell's pictures, often with complex titles, owe much to Dada and Surrealism in the way that they question traditional logic and ways of looking at things in a satirical way. Scottish National Gallery of Modern Art holds his work.

J CAMPBELL-BRADY 1943– Artist, born in Glasgow, who said that "the potent exile of the mind, which is well known to many Scots, is vital for my work". He studied at Camberwell School of Arts and Crafts and in 1980 had a first solo show at Bristol Arts Centre. Also had a shared exhibition with Richard Kennedy at Neville Gallery, Bath; showed at first International Arts Fair at Barbican, London, where work was bought by the committee; and showed with the Open Circle, Glasgow, at the Growth Festival. William Hardie Ltd, of Glasgow, represented Campbell-Brady at the London Contemporary Art Fair, Art 92.

Eleanor CAMPBELL-ORDE 1908–1996 Painter, charity worker and lifelong Christian Scientist, born Eleanor Watts in Cheadle Hulme, Cheshire, her father's warehouse business in Manchester funding a private education. Studied history at Lady Margaret Hall, Oxford, where her friends included John Betjeman, Osbert Lancaster and Stephen Spender, but left the University early to join the Central School of Arts and Crafts. A long engagement to the actor Valentine Dyall (later famous as the radio storyteller The Man in Black) ended when she left to study in Florence. During the 1930s she was a pupil of the Georgian artist Prince Aleksandr Konstantinovich Schervashidze and the Russian painter Mikhail Larionov, helping them to produce backcloths for the Ballets Russes in Britain and Spain. In 1938 she married Sir

Simon Campbell-Orde, banker and Scottish landowner. After World War II the Campbell-Ordes set up a market garden at Bishop's Stortford. They continued to support educational and artistic projects: the Arts Educational Schools, Tring; Yehudi Menuhin's music school; and the Harlequin Ballet Trust, for which she designed and painted more attractive sets. She was a considerable world traveller who eventually settled in Dedham, Essex, where she showed her work locally and died. Her husband had predeceased her in 1969.

Oliver CAMPION 1928– Painter and teacher. Campion painted still life and landscape. His scenes in the south of France and still life studies were in colour and construction in the Cézanne tradition. He studied at Central School of Arts and Crafts and Slade School of Fine Art. Campion taught at Oxford School of Art, Morley College and at Camberwell. After solo shows at Mayor Gallery in 1968 and 1971 he had a succession of exhibitions from 1975 at New Grafton Gallery. The Arts Club, *Financial Times* and Magdalen College, Oxford, are among the owners of his work.

Sue CAMPION 1944– Colourist with strong sense of design, who trained and worked as a display artist, 1960–9, studying at Nottingham Polytechnic, 1986–90. Mixed exhibitions included Barnes Gallery from 1991; Wykeham Galleries, Stockbridge, from 1992; and Alresford Gallery, Alresford, 1997. She was a Patchings Award prize winner, Patchings Gallery, Nottingham, 1991. Had solo exhibitions with Artz Gallery Bors, Belgium, and Rowleys House Museum, Shrewsbury, both 1984, later ones including New Grafton Gallery, 1997. Rowleys House and Swedish Airlines Arts Club, Stockholm, hold examples.

Leslie CANDAPPA 1927– Painter and sculptor, brought up in Ceylon. He showed paintings, gouaches and collages at New Vision Centre Gallery in 1958. Lived for a time in London.

Eric CANEY 1908–1979 Illustrator in watercolour, ink and pencil. Born in London Caney, an architect, showed at the RA, RI, RBA and NS as well as locally in Chelsea. Lived in Guildford, Surrey.

Ashton CANNELL 1927– Mainly a watercolourist, teacher, born Edward Ashton Cannell in the Isle of Man. He attended the School of Art there, then Liverpool College of Art. He taught at Isle of Man School of Art and became head of art for various London schools as well a senior assessor for examinations. Became a full-time painter in 1973. Carried out commissions for British Petroleum, Bass International. Foyles and Cassells. Was a member of RSMA, London Sketch Club, BWS and Wapping Group, also exhibiting at RA, Linda Blackstone Gallery in Pinner, Archer Gallery and Paris Salon, where he won a silver medal in 1973, a gold in 1975. Department of the Environment holds his work. Lived in London.

Michael CANNEY 1923– Painter, relief maker, writer, broadcaster and teacher, born in Falmouth, where he was early on taken to art shows. His teacher at school in Taunton, W Lyons-Wilson, encouraged Canney, who at start of 1940s joined full-time classes at Redruth and Penzance Schools of Art and St Ives School of Painting, under Leonard Fuller. After Army service, 1942–7, which included travel to Italy, where he continued to draw, Canney studied at Goldsmiths' College School of Art, 1947–51, and after a bout of pulmonary tuberculosis spent six months in postgraduate study at Patrick Allan-Fraser School of Art, Hospitalfield, Arbroath. Around the time that he was teaching in London, 1952–7, Canney started making reliefs and pursued neo-Cubist work. In 1956 he was appointed curator of Newlyn Art Gallery, supplementing a meagre stipend with freelance broadcasting, contributing about 200 documentary programmes to radio and television. In 1964–5 Canney taught part-time at Plymouth College of Art; was in 1965–6 appointed visiting gallery director and lecturer at University of California, Santa Barbara; then joined the staff of West of England College of Art (subsequently Bristol Polytechnic), 1966–83. In 1984 Canney chose to live in Italy, in a village between San Gimignano and Siena, continuing to paint, but in 1985 scripted a documentary film for television on painting in Newlyn which won an award in New York. Canney exhibited regularly at group exhibitions in Britain and abroad. His later one-man shows included Newlyn Art Gallery, 1983; Prescote Art and Design, Edinburgh, 1984; and Belgrave Gallery from 1990. Plymouth City Art Gallery and several other public collections hold his work. Lived in Devizes, Wiltshire.

Neil CANNING 1960– Painter and illustrator, born in Enstone, Oxfordshire. Rather than attend an art school he chose to study in the studio of a professional artist. Canning had his first solo show at Bodkin Gallery, Chipping Norton, 1979, and he soon exhibited at RA and RI. Further solo shows followed at Swan Gallery, Burford; Linacre College, Oxford; West Wharf Gallery, Cardiff; and Century Galleries, Henley-on-Thames. In 1982 Canning's work was bought for the Nuffield Fund Paintings in Hospitals scheme. He illustrated Graeme Garden's *The Skylighters*, published in 1988.

James CANT 1911–1982 Versatile artist, born in Melbourne, Victoria, Australia, married from 1945 to the artist Dora Chapman. He studied in Sydney with Dattilo Rubbo and Julian Ashton, at the East Sydney Technical College and at the Central School of Arts and Crafts in London, having moved there in the early 1930s. Cant experimented with several styles, became associated with the Surrealists and showed with the new modern generation of British painters such as Victor Pasmore, John Piper, Graham Sutherland and Francis Bacon. Cant returned to Melbourne in 1939, by which time he had embraced Social Realism, evidenced in a number of powerful anti-war pictures such as The Merchants of Death and The Bomb, in the collection of the Art Gallery of South Australia, Adelaide. He enlisted in World War II and after it helped to found SORA (Studio of Realist Art). For about five years to 1955 Cant lived in England, where he was included in the first exhibition of the Australian Artists' Association, at the RWS' Conduit Street gallery, 1953.

He exhibited widely internationally. Settled in Adelaide, where his wife came from, Cant became famous for hyper-realistic studies of nature which had an abstract, patterned quality. During his final years multiple sclerosis confined Cant to a wheelchair and prevented him painting pictures, but he was able to decorate pots produced by his wife. There were retrospectives at the South Australian Art Gallery, 1984, and Niagara Galleries, Melbourne, 1993.

Jean CANTER 1943– Artist in various media and teacher, born and lived in Epsom, Surrey. She studied at the local School of Art, 1956–61, then Wimbledon School of Art, 1961–3. Taught part-time for Mid-Surrey Adult Institute. Canter became a member of SGA in 1977, later vice-president and in 1984 was its Rexel Prizewinner. Also showed with RI and RWS. Ewell Museum holds her work.

Davide CANTONI 1965– Artist born in Milan, Italy, who studied at Kingston Polytechnic, 1983; Slade School of Fine Art, 1985–9, with a period at the Hochschule der Kunst, Berlin, 1988; and in 1991–3 at Royal College of Art. His exhibitions included an installation for Negative Image in Art of Photography at Royal College in 1989. His work Bend in the Nile was included in East & South at Norwich Art Gallery/Kent Institute of Art and Design, 1992, and in 1993–4 two panels, computer spray on canvas, entitled Sat F, were included in John Moores Liverpool Exhibition. Lived in London.

Estella CANZIANI 1887–1964 Painter, decorator and artist in black-and-white, writer and muralist. Born in London, the daughter of the painter Louisa Starr, Canziani studied at Arthur Cope and Erskine Nicol's School, in London, and the Royal Academy Schools early in the century. Exhibited prolifically and widely, including RA, Walker's Galleries especially, SWA, RMS, RI, RBA and on the continent; held a number of one-man shows. A multi-talented woman, she did medical illustration during World War I; collected peasant dress and handicrafts and wrote about them in such books as *Costumes, Traditions and Songs of Savoy*, 1911, and *Through the Appenines and the Lands of the Abruzzi*, 1928; was a member of the National Art Collections Fund and a fellow of the Royal Geographical Society; and wrote about the house where she was born and continued to live in *Round about Three Palace Green*, 1939.

Nuria CAPDEVILA 1963– Painter, printmaker and teacher, born in Barcelona, Spain, to which she returned to live after three years in Britain from late 1980s. She gained a degree in fine arts at University of Barcelona, 1981–6, followed by a postgraduate printmaking year, 1987, also studying at Academia Ramon Sanvicens Barcelona, 1982–4. In 1992 she participated in the international symposium Behind the 7 Seas at Stadt Wernigerode, Germany. Capdevila's awards included an East Midlands Arts Starter Grant, 1990, and Project Grant, 1991. Among her prizes were first prizes at Banco de Vizcaya and first prize Club Turo Blanc, both Barcelona, 1987, and a third prize, Silver Palette, Derby Museum, 1990. Capdevila undertook extensive teaching plus artist-in-residencies, including Highland Printmakers, Inverness, Leicester Print Workshop and Nottingham Castle Museum. Group shows included Open Exhibition, Castle Museum, Nottingham, and Prisoners Abroad, Blackbull Gallery, both 1990; and The Discerning Eye, Mall Galleries, 1992. Solo shows included Vases in the Sky, Castle Museum, Nottingham, 1991.

Reco CAPEY 1895–1961 Designer for industry in many materials, but also showed paintings and sculpture. Born at Burslem, Staffordshire, he studied art at the Royal College of Art, 1919–22, and widely on the continent. He held several positions at the Royal College for 30 years from 1924 and was chief examiner in industrial design for the Board of Education, 1937–40. Exhibited RA and widely overseas. Lived at Alfriston, Sussex.

John CAPLE 1966– Self-taught painter, and illustrator, who began painting in the mid-1980s, attracted by the independent style of primitive painters like Alfred Wallis and the folk art of the West Country. For generations Caple's family had been farmers and land workers in the Mendips, and much of his art was concerned with the light, scenery, inhabitants and mythology of that part of Somerset. Caple's illustrations appeared on many of Penguin Books' covers, notably an edition of Roald Dahl's novels. Showed paintings with John Martin of London.

John CAPSTACK 1957– Painter, born in Halifax, West Yorkshire. He studied at Percival Whitley College, Halifax, 1975–7, and at Manchester Polytechnic, 1977–80. He was a figurative painter concerned with man, his environment and symbols, as shown in his entry for East, Norwich Gallery, 1991; also in East & South, at same gallery and tour, 1992; and in his prizewinning Expulsion No II at John Moores Exhibition, 1991–2. Lived in Leeds, Yorkshire.

Malcolm CARDER 1936– Artist and teacher who studied architecture, sculpture and painting at Kingston College of Art, 1955–9, then worked as a freelance graphic designer, 1959–61. From 1961–4 lectured at Plymouth College of Art; from 1964–6 taught constructional sculpture at Farnham School of Art; then in 1967 took up a research fellowship in visual communications (media) at Portsmouth School of Architecture. Carder received a commission for the British Pavilion, Expo '67, in Montreal. Between 1969–71 Carder worked on exhibitions with Nigel Greenwood, London; Hans Meyer, Krefeld; Hayward Gallery; and Wilfried Reckermann, Koln. Carder then worked for Theo Crosby at Pentagram on the Arts Council exhibition and book *The Environment Game*, where his assistant again was the artist Judy Clark. Carder's own mixed shows included Constructions at Axiom Gallery, 1966; Unit-Series-Progression, Arts Council, Cambridge, 1967; L'Art Vivant, Fondation Maeght, France, and Prospect '68, Düsseldorf, both 1968; and Plans & Projects as Art, Kunsthalle, Berne and Munich, 1969. There was a solo exhibition at Axiom, 1968. In 1974 Carder went with Judy Clark to India and he became involved with the teacher Baghwan Shree Rajneesh and lived at the ashram at Poona, Maharashtra, until about 1981. When the ashram moved to Oregon in that year Carder, then called Swami Anand Yatri, went briefly to London before going on to Oregon. He was involved in the production of books documenting lectures by Rajneesh published by Osho International (Rajneesh was latterly known as Osho by his followers), which had offices in London. In 1996 Yatri declared that "Malcolm Carder no longer exists. He is no longer a sculptor." Carder's work, latterly sold by Nigel Greenwood, is held by Arts Council, Tate Gallery, Contemporary Art Society, Kelvingrove Art Gallery in Glasgow, Middlesbrough's public gallery and several American collections.

Margaret CARDEW 1899–1961 Painter, born in Wolverhampton, Staffordshire, as Margaret Stokes, being related to an eminent local family. She studied at Slade School of Fine Art and Académie Julian, in Paris. She showed at Paris Salon and elsewhere, living in Paris and London. Her small, subtle oil Normandy Village is in the Garman-Ryan Collection at Walsall Museum & Art Gallery.

Seth CARDEW 1934– Artist in ceramics, sculptor and teacher, son of the potter Michael Cardew, born in Winchcombe, Gloucestershire. He studied under Karel Vogel at Camberwell School of Arts and Crafts, 1955–9. Sculpted and taught at Twickenham College of Technology for 10 years, in 1975 starting to work at Wenford Bridge Pottery, St Breward, Bodmin, Cornwall. He was a member of the Craftsmen Potters' Association and Cornwall Craft Association. In 1968 was included in From Life at Camden Arts Centre. His solo shows included Craftsmen Potters' Gallery, 1984. Cardew's main works were large dishes with characteristic painting. He said that Vogel was "a strong influence on the visual side. Later an ethic of tactile quality became added". Victoria & Albert Museum holds his work, which he expounded at workshops abroad.

Conrad H R CARELLI 1869– Watercolourist who, after private education in England, attended Académie Julian, Paris. Son of the artist Gabriel Carelli. Exhibited RA, RI, Walker Art Gallery, Liverpool, and had one-man show at Walker's Galleries. Queen Mary bought his work. Was a member of Langham Sketch Club and lived in London.

Margaret CAREY 1961– Artist in various media who gained an honours degree in fine art at Liverpool Polytechnic, 1981–4. She completed 16 glass panels for International Garden Festival in Liverpool, 1984; was included in Artists under 30 at Royal Liverpool Hospital, 1985; and was in Walker Art Gallery, Liverpool, touring Merseyside Artists 3, 1986–7. Had a solo show at Bridewell Gallery in the city, 1986.

Penny CAREY 1939– Landscape painter, designer, teacher and illustrator, born in east Yorkshire. She trained at Académie Julian, Paris, Kingston School of Art and Brighton College of Art. She taught in Battersea, then worked as a freelance illustrator and book jacket designer, later returning to teaching in Plumstead, southeast London. Among her exhibitions was a four-man show at Woodlands Art Gallery in 1981.

Peter Leonard CAREY 1931– Painter, sculptor and administrator, born in Manchester, who sometimes signed his work P L C. Studied at Oldham School of Art, 1946–51, then trained as a teacher at Manchester College of Art, 1951–2. Exhibited Northern Young Artists of which he was a member, Archer Gallery, Crane Gallery in Manchester and in public galleries in Oldham, Salford and Wakefield. He completed a mural for Park Mill Spinning Company, in Dukinfield, Cheshire. Lived in Oldham, later in London.

Anne CARLINE 1862–1945 Naive painter, wife of the artist George Carline, and mother of the painters Richard, Sydney and Hilda. She started painting in watercolour, in the hope that she could illustrate stories she wrote for children, in 1928. She had an exhibition at French Gallery in 1934, around then beginning to paint in oil. In 1939, on the initiative of the artist André Lhote, she held an exhibition at Galerie Pittoresque, in Paris, where Soutine was among her admirers. Also exhibited at LG and AIA and was included in the 1971 Leicester Galleries show The Carline Family.

Hilda CARLINE 1889–1950 Painter, born in London, whose family were artists, notably her brothers Richard and Sydney. She studied at Percyval Tudor-Hart's Académie de Peinture in Hampstead in 1913, then during World War I worked in the Women's Land Army in Suffolk. Studied at Slade School of Fine Art from 1918, taking several prizes, and through Gilbert Spencer got to know his brother Stanley, the painter, whom she married in 1925, eventually settling in Cookham. There were two daughters, Shirin, and Unity who also studied at the Slade. She showed at RA, Goupil Gallery and NEAC, but the breakup of her marriage was followed by a decline in health in 1942. Although she resumed painting, another breakdown followed. Was included in The Carline Family exhibition at Leicester Galleries, 1971. Harris Museum and Art Gallery, Preston, holds her work.

Nancy CARLINE 1909– Artist notable for landscapes and townscapes and deft portraits, born and lived in London. Married the artist Richard Carline. She studied at Slade School of Fine Art under Henry Tonks and Allan Gwynne-Jones, 1928–31. From 1933–5 worked at Sadler's Wells Ballet, in 1933–4 attending Vladimir Polunin's class for stage design at Slade, then late in 1930s Euston Road School. Was for many years an art examiner for Cambridge Local Examinations Syndicate. Joined Hampstead Artists' Council, also showing with AIA, LG, NEAC and RA. Was represented in The Carline Family, Leicester Galleries, 1971, and Spencers and Carlines, Morley Gallery, 1980, and tour. Had a retrospective at Camden Arts Centre, 1985. Latterly lived in Oxford.

Richard CARLINE 1896–1980 Painter, writer and administrator, born in Oxford. His father, George Carline, his mother Anne and brother Sydney, his sister Hilda (Mrs Stanley Spencer) and his wife Nancy were all painters. Carline in 1913–15 attended Percyval Tudor-Hart's Académie de Peinture, in Paris, then London. After a short period teaching Carline served in World War I in the Army, in the Royal Flying Corps, then as a war artist. With his brother he became noted for war pictures from the air. Elected LG in 1920 and at this time the Carlines' Downshire Hill house became a centre for artists such as Henry Lamb, John Nash and Mark Gertler. Between 1924–9 Carline taught at Ruskin School of Drawing, Oxford, in 1928 making an extensive lecture tour of North America. He had his first solo show at Goupil Gallery, 1931. The mid-1930s saw Carline involved in negro art, organising a show at Adams Gallery in 1935, and contributing the main text to *Arts of West Africa*, edited by Michael Sadler. During World War II Carline supervised camouflage of factories and airfields. He was involved in AIA, helping to found the Hampstead Artists' Council in 1944; in 1946–7 was first art counsellor of Unesco; and from 1955–74 was chief examiner in art for the Cambridge Local Examinations Syndicate. His books included *Pictures in the Post, the story of the Picture Postcard*, 1959: *Draw They Must*, 1968; and *Stanley Spencer at War*, 1978. Carline died in Hampstead and in 1983 Camden Arts Centre there organised a memorial show, and tour. Imperial War Museum holds his work.

Anne CARLISLE 1901– Painter, born in London into a military family. After private education she attended Byam Shaw School of Art, also studying in Romania and France. She showed at Redfern, Mayor and Lefevre Galleries, also showing in Paris and New York; her first one-man show was in the late 1920s at Marcel Bernheim's Paris gallery. She wrote a book on *English Drawings of the 19th Century*. She held a number of art administrative posts, including two regional directorships, of CEMA and then the Arts Council; and partly concurrently, in the 1940s and 1950s, the post of art adviser to the United States Information Service, in London. Lived latterly for some years at Chateauneuf-de-Grasse, in France.

Fiona CARLISLE 1954– Painter, born in Wick, Caithness. After studying at Edinburgh College of Art, 1972–6, she was granted an Andrew Grant Postgraduate Scholarship, 1976–7. From 1978 she had a series of solo shows at 369 Gallery, Edinburgh, and she showed in many exhibitions of mixed work in Scotland and London. In the 1980s she tended to abandon her earlier style employing flat areas of colour and black lines for more vigorous brushwork, her palette gaining strength. In 1984 she went to live on Crete.

Michael CARLO 1945– Versatile artist using all print processes, draughtsman, watercolourist and teacher, born in Glemsford, Suffolk, later settling in Boxford. He attended Colchester School of Art, 1961–4, notable teachers including Edward Bawden, Peter Coker, John Nash and Edward Middleditch. Then was at Royal College of Art, 1964–7. He taught part-time in art schools, then set up own studio. Landscape was the theme of Carlo's work, documenting a small area around his studio, a mile from his birthplace. The Set Aside farm scheme was a feature of his exhibition Changing Suffolk at Christchurch Mansion, Ipswich, in 1992. Carlo was a member of RE, also showing at RA Summer Exhibition, Serpentine Gallery and elsewhere. Solo exhibitions included Bolton Museum, Usher Gallery in Lincoln, Southampton City Art Gallery and John Russell Gallery in Ipswich from 1985. Tate Gallery, Laing Art Gallery in Newcastle and London Transport hold his work, which is also in American collections.

Ron CARLSON 1936– Sculptor, ceramics artist and teacher, born in Newport, Monmouthshire. He studied at Newport College of Art, 1952–6, and the Royal College of Art, 1956–9, then aided by two government scholarships worked in Belgium and Sweden. Went on to become senior lecturer at Newport College. Participated in group shows at Piccadilly Gallery, Demarco Gallery in Edinburgh and widely in Wales, including Royal National Eisteddfod, Howard Roberts Gallery in Cardiff, and WAC, which holds his work. One-man shows included Howard Roberts and Keele University, Staffordshire. Included in WAC touring exhibition of drawings The Probity of Art in 1980.

John CARLYON 1917–1982 Sculptor in stone, born in Cornwall. Exhibitions included RSMA, SWLA and Mall Galleries. Had a one-man show at the Moorland Gallery, which specialised in the wildlife subjects Carlyon favoured. His work is in the RSMA's Diploma Collection. Lived at the Lizard, Cornwall.

Andrew CARMICHAEL fl. from 1970s– Conceptual sculptor and installations artist, born in Hull, Yorkshire, who trained at Goldsmiths' College, Royal College of Art and the British School at Rome. Mixed shows included Woodlands Art Gallery, 1985, and Made in Greenwich, at The Living Room, 1994. Had solo shows at Mario Flecha Gallery. In 1993 he completed an artist placement for the Greenwich Waterfront Development Partnership. Was based in London.

Rodick CARMICHAEL 1931– Painter, born in Edinburgh. He studied at the College of Art there, 1948–53, then at British School in Rome, 1957. Among group exhibitions participated in were Young British Artists, Museum of Modern Art, New York, 1953; the Arts Council 4 Scottish Painters, 1959–60, Edinburgh and tour; Unesco's 25 Years of British Painting, 1972; and University of New South Wales Invitation, 1984–6. Among prizes won were the Georges Invitation Prize in 1976; the Capital Permanent Prize in 1978–80; and the Gold Coast Prize, 1983. After a solo show at the 57 Gallery, Edinburgh, in 1959, others were held at the Scottish Gallery there; Gallery West, Los Angeles, 1969; Bartoni Gallery, Melbourne, 1975; Melbourne University Art Gallery in 1983; a Perth Festival retrospective at University of Western Australia in 1984; and in 1989 Scottish

Gallery in London held An Antipodean Decade 1979–1989, to coincide with a major show at Macquarie Galleries, Sydney. Among Carmichael's publications was *The Iconic Language of Painting*, in 1981, and *Artisan and High Technology*, 1985.

Andrew CARNIE 1957– Painter, born in London, where he continued to live. He studied at Goldsmiths' College School of Art, 1979–82, and at Royal College of Art, 1983–6. Took part in group exhibitions at Bluecoat Gallery, Liverpool, 1984, Whitechapel Open from 1987 and in 1989–90 John Moores Liverpool Exhibition showed the canvas Swing. Exhibited solo with Angela Flowers in 1987 and Giray Gallery, 1988.

Anthony CARO 1924– Sculptor and teacher, born in London. After studying engineering at Cambridge University, 1942–5, Caro studied sculpture at Regent Street Polytechnic, 1946, then at the Royal Academy Schools, 1947–52. He worked as a part-time assistant to Henry Moore, 1951–3. From 1952–79 Caro taught at St Martin's School of Art, a dynamic period in which it was said that his students learned "not a style, not a dogma, but a discipline of doubt and enquiry". Also taught at Bennington College, Vermont, in mid-1960s. Caro's first one-man show was at Galleria del Naviglio in Milan in 1956. Then showed at Venice and Paris Biennales and elsewhere worldwide. A retrospective was held at Museum of Modern Art, New York in 1975 with tour; there was a large Tate Gallery exhibition in 1991–2 which showed that although Caro had become famous for bolted and welded steel and aluminium sculptures which were light and graceful he was later capable of monumental works such as After Olympia; in 1994 a seventieth birthday retrospective was held at Annely Juda Fine Art; in 1995 a major show being held at Tokyo's new Museum of Contemporary Art. Caro's initial work was figurative in lead and bronze, but 1959 saw a change to non-figurative pieces. He was knighted in 1987. In 1996 Caro was part of a team, that included the architects Sir Norman Foster and Partners and the engineers Ove Arup and Partners, which won an international design competition for a new pedestrian bridge to link St Paul's Cathedral to the new Tate Gallery of Modern Art at Bankside and the Globe Theatre. The Tate, the Arts Council and other major collections hold Caro's work.

Paul CARO 1958– Versatile artist, fond of bright colours, born and based in London, who attended Oxford University to study zoology and the Slade School of Fine Art. While in Oxford he organised a Kenneth Noland retrospective show, then in 1987 he worked at the André Emmerich Gallery in New York. Caro attended Emma Lake and Triangle Artists Workshops; took part in group exhibitions, including Whitechapel Open from 1988, and Made in Greenwich at The Living Room, 1994; and had solo shows, including The Pike Gallery.

David Lawrence CARPANINI 1946– Painter, draughtsman, printmaker and teacher, born in Abergwynfi, West Glamorgan, married to the artist Jane Carpanini. He studied at Gloucestershire College of Art, 1964–8, Royal College of Art, 1968–71, and University of Reading, 1971–2. Taught at Oundle School, later becoming head of art and design in faculty of education at Wolverhampton Polytechnic. Carpanini was a member of RBA, 1976, being awarded its de Laszlo Medal in 1980; fellow of RE, 1981; and in 1983 a member of RWA and NEAC. Also showed at Piccadilly Gallery, New Art Centre, Agnew and Business Art Galleries. Carpanini's work was largely devoted to the industrial scene in South Wales. National Museum of Wales in Cardiff, National Library of Wales in Aberystwyth, Contemporary Art Society for Wales and other public collections hold examples. Lived in Leamington Spa, Warwickshire.

Jane CARPANINI 1949– Watercolourist, born in Bedfordshire, married to the artist David Carpanini. She was a regular tutor on weekend courses and contributed to the instructional magazines *The Artist* and *Leisure Painter*. Studied at Luton College of Technology, 1967–8, Brighton College of Art, 1968–71, and Reading University, 1971–2. She was elected to RWA in 1977, and in 1978 to RBA and RWS, eventually serving as its honorary treasurer. Much of Carpanini's work was inspired by Snowdonia; she lived at Caernarfon, Gwynedd. Her pictures were tinged with an intense, almost severe realism. She showed at many private galleries, including Patricia Wells Gallery, Thornbury; Fosse Gallery in Stow-on-the-Wold; and Albany Gallery, and her pictures were reproduced in limited edition prints, as postcards and Christmas cards. Solo shows were organised by WAC and National Museum of Wales, Cardiff. The Museum and National Library of Wales, Aberystwyth, hold her work.

Sue CARPENTER 1957– Performance artist who made sculptures to wear, working with children and women, and on large-scale public art events; teacher. She studied fine art at Newcastle University, 1975–81, starting her teaching and performing in 1979. Her appearances included Pompidou Centre, Paris, and with New Moon Group, including its show at Woodlands Art Gallery, 1987.

Allan CARR 1914– Painter, draughtsman and teacher, born in London. Studied at Thanet School of Art, 1933–5, then at the Slade School of Fine Art, 1935–8, with Randolph Schwabe. Taught for a while at Edinburgh College of Art. Exhibited NEAC, SSA and RSA. Lived in Edinburgh.

Barbara CARR: *see* **Barbara GILLIGAN**

David CARR 1915–1968 Painter and collector, born in London into wealthy family. Attended Uppingham School and left to join the family biscuit-making business, but left because he hated it and went to read history at Oxford University. On holiday in Italy he determined to become an artist against his father's wishes, studied briefly at Byam Shaw School in the late 1930s, then for several years at Cedric Morris's East Anglian School of Painting and Drawing where his future wife, Barbara Gilligan was also a student. Bought Starston Hall, Harleston,

Norfolk, and began to paint there and in London, where he became a discerning collector and the friend of painters such as the Roberts Colquhoun and MacBryde and other Soho-based artists. Although Carr was prominent in the Norfolk Contemporary Art Society and was included by Bryan Robertson in a survey of British painting at Whitechapel Art Gallery in 1953 and in a show at Southampton City Art Gallery a few years later, it was not until the Mayor Gallery show of 1987 that his true stature was appreciated in London (he had died just before a show at the Bertha Schaefer Gallery in New York). Carr completed a remarkable series of oils in a post-Cubist style on the theme of man and the machine and a series of inventive late watercolours described by Robertson as "of special importance in British art of this period". In 1997, his work was shown alongside that of his friend Prunella Clough at Austin/Desmond Fine Art.

David CARR 1944– Painter, draughtsman and teacher, born in Middlesbrough, Yorkshire. He studied at Slade School of Fine Art, 1962–6, where he won the Tonks Drawing Prize, prizes for landscape drawing and first prize in the Summer Composition. On leaving, a David Murray Landscape Scholarship awarded by RA and a Boise Travelling Scholarship from University College permitted Carr to spend time at British School in Rome. In 1965 he was president of Young Contemporaries. Carr was head of pre-foundation studies at Camden Arts Centre, 1969–82, eventually returning there as tutor. Other teaching was done at Goldsmiths' College School of Art, Birmingham School of Art's postgraduate department and Kingston School of Art. Carr showed with RA and LG, being elected to LG in 1987. His prizes included the Cleveland Drawing Biennale and South Bank Picture Show. Carr had solo shows at Camden Arts Centre in 1987, Cadogan Contemporary in 1989 and The Walk, 1997, in which his interest in landscape in Britain and abroad were exemplified. Inner London Education Authority and University College London held his work.

Edith CARR 1875–1949 Portrait and miniature painter, born in Croydon, Surrey. After private education she studed at Croydon School of Art and in Paris. Member SWA. Exhibited RA, RMS, SWA and Paris Salon. Lived in South Croydon.

Eric CARR 1916–1991 Painter and sculptor, born in Liverpool, where he died. After attending primary school in Everton Carr left aged 14 to work as a signwriter, then in the 1930s joined the Bertram Mills Circus, for which he was a scene designer. After World War II Royal Air Force service he returned to Merseyside and with his brother Leslie set up signwriting in Birkdale. From then he became a prolific sculptor and painter. He was noted for his ecclesiastical work, including carved Stations of the Cross for the Roman Catholic Cathedral in Salford and a large statue of Christ for the Liverpool International Garden Festival, in 1984. He also did work for public houses and restaurants and was a member of Liverpool Academy. A large exhibition of his work was held by Liverpool's Central Library in 1991.

Francis CARR 1919– Artist in many media, teacher, administrator and writer who moved to England from Hungary in 1938, settling in London. Carr, who was originally Francis Peters, was called "a maverick, a citizen of the world" and "a socially motivated artist". He studied at Central School of Arts and Crafts, 1938–41, then after five years' war service, from 1948 for many years held a series of teaching appointments including London College of Printing, Croydon College of Art and Open University. He was a pioneer in exploiting the creative potential of silkscreen printing. From 1965–8 Carr was design consultant to the Greater London Council Housing Division, in 1967 devising the Artists & Architecture show at The Building Centre, which gave him a retrospective in 1993. From 1968–74 Carr was chairman of The New Organisation, concerned with the visual quality of the urban environment. In 1972 Carr organised the Urban Cinema Festival at the National Film Theatre. As well as participating in many group shows in Britain and abroad, Carr had solo exhibitions, his Woodstock Gallery show in 1959 marking a turning point towards a monumental, three-dimensional approach and polychrome sculpture. Carried out many commissions, including a mixed-media relief mosaic at Holman Hunt Infant School, 1961; commemorative area and sundial, Port Talbot Tidal Harbour, 1970; and in 1990 his The Tree of Life stone maze, in Kazakhstan. Arts Council and British Museum hold his work.

Henry CARR 1894–1970 Landscape and portrait painter in oil and watercolour. Born in Leeds, Carr studied at Leeds College of Art and the Royal College of Art. He exhibited at the RA – he was elected RA eventually – as well as the NEAC, RBA, RP, provincial galleries and the Paris Salon, where he won a gold medal in 1956. His work was widely reproduced, in *The Artist*, *The Studio*, *Time* and *Life* and in the book *War Pictures by British Artists: Air Raids*. Carr was an official war artist with the First Army in North Africa and Italy for some years in World War II. The Imperial War Museum holds his work. Carr wrote the book *Portrait Painting* and lived in London.

Tom CARR 1909– Painter, born in Belfast. From Oundle School he went to Slade School of Fine Art, 1927–9, studying under Henry Tonks. He then spent a year at Settignano, near Florence. In the 1930s he was associated with the Objective Abstractionists and the Euston Road group of painters, but his naturally lyrical manner, best shown in his landscape pictures, did not make him a satisfactory theory painter. Returned to Ireland in 1939, having established himself in mixed shows such as LG and NEAC, and he had shown with Victor Pasmore and Ceri Richards at Zwemmer Gallery, 1933. First solo show was at Wildenstein, in 1940. Although in the next decade he had shows with Redfern Gallery, Leicester Galleries, Wildenstein again and Agnew, apart from a retrospective at Ulster Office in 1980 Carr showed mainly in Ireland. He had a big retrospective in Belfast and Dublin in 1985 and in 1989 three eightieth birthday shows were held: at Eakin Brothers, Belfast; Tom Caldwell Gallery, Belfast; and National Gallery of Ireland, Dublin. Tate Gallery, Ulster Museum in Belfast and other public collections hold Carr's work.

Tom Dickens CARR 1912–1977 Sporting painter, illustrator and printmaker with a special interest in hunting. Carr began as a colliery blacksmith, working for the Royal Navy in World War I. Industrial injury money enabled him to attend King's College at Newcastle upon Tyne and to study under George Vernon Stokes. The Midlands and north of England became his favourite painting spots.

Alexander CARRICK 1882–1966 Sculptor and notable teacher, born in Musselburgh, Midlothian. Carrick originally trained as a stone carver in the studio of Birnie Rhind, Edinburgh, then studied sculpture at the College of Art there and Royal College of Art. He joined the staff of Edinburgh College of Art in 1914, and apart from a break for military service, 1916–18, he was to continue his teaching career at the College until around 1942, for the last 14 years being head of sculpture. Carrick showed at RSA, RA and Royal Glasgow Institute of the Fine Arts, but he is especially remembered for his sculptures related to architecture. Between the wars he carried out many commissions on a large scale, including the Animal Wall extensions at Cardiff Castle, 1923; the exterior figures of Justice and Courage and the interior bronze reliefs for the Scottish War Memorial, 1924–7; and the carving of William Reid Dick's designs for St Andrew's House, Edinburgh, 1936. RSA holds his figure Felicity.

Edward CARRICK 1905–1998 Printmaker, painter, film art director and designer, and writer, born in London. His real name was Edward Anthony Craig, he was the son of the artist Edward Gordon Craig and grandson of the actress Ellen Terry. For many of his early years he lived with his father and studied in Italy, returning to England soon after the mid-1920s. Exhibited at St George's and Redfern Galleries, at Art Institute of Chicago and with the Grubb Group, of which he was founder and president; his illustrations appeared in such publications as *Artwork*, *Architect's Review* and *Bookman's Journal* as well as in several books, including Edmund Blunden's *In Summer* and Edith Sitwell's *In Spring*, both 1931; and he painted murals in a number of theatres, including Cambridge Theatre, the Victoria News Theatre and at Easton Manor, near Dunmow, Essex. He was art director for Ealing Studios, 1936–8, then the Crown Film Unit and Army Film Unit, 1939–47. He founded the first school in England specialising in the study of cinema, in 1937. Carrick was the author of *Designing for Moving Pictures*, *Art & Design in the British Film* and *Designing for Films*. His many film credits included *Western Approaches*, 1944; *Tiger Bay*, 1959; *Macbeth*, 1960; and *Nanny*, 1965. In 1968, Carrick published *Gordon Craig: the story of his life*, and he was responsible for establishing collections about his father throughout the world (there is a notable archive at Eton College). British Museum, Victoria & Albert Museum and Metropolitan Museum of Art in New York hold examples of Carrick's work. Died at Thame, Oxfordshire.

Elsie CARRICK 1894– Painter and draughtsman, mainly working in watercolour with some oil, born in Middlesbrough, Yorkshire. Miss Carrick attended Sunderland High School, then the Slade School of Fine Art, 1915–17, gaining first-class certificates in drawing, painting, design and perspective and a first prize in artistic anatomy. She went on to teach and joined the Norfolk and Norwich Art Circle in 1946 after she had moved to Norwich to teach at the Blyth School, serving on the Circle's council and as its secretary. After over 30 years she left Norwich and the Circle.

Ian CARRICK 1939– Sculptor and teacher, born in Rugby, Warwickshire, who gained his National Diploma in sculpture, 1962, and Slade Diploma in 1964. He lectured at Wrexham School of Art, 1964–6, was head of fine art at University of Nigeria, 1966–8, was senior lecturer in sculpture at at Liverpool Polytechnic, 1968–76, then was head of sculpture and of fine art and vice-principal at Falmouth School of Art and Design, 1976–91, continuing to live in the Cornish town. Showed at Herbert Art Gallery in Coventry, Penwith Gallery in St Ives, Bluecoat Gallery in Liverpool and elsewhere, and was in Falmouth Connections at Falmouth Art Gallery in 1994. Australian and New Zealand High Commissions and Ford Motor Company commissioned him.

Donald P CARRINGTON 1907– Painter and teacher, born at Outwood, near Wakefield, Yorkshire, where he attended the Grammar School, the School of Art, 1924–6, then the Royal College of Art, 1926–30. He taught at the Huddersfield, Sheffield and Leicester Schools/Colleges of Art. Exhibited RA and extensively in northern municipal galleries including Graves Art Gallery, Sheffield, which holds his work. Lived in Leicester.

Joanna CARRINGTON 1931– Painter and teacher, daughter of the publisher Noel Carrington and niece of the artist Dora Carrington. She studied with Cedric Morris at the East Anglian School of Painting and Drawing, in Suffolk, with Fernand Léger in Paris and at Central School of Arts and Crafts. She went on to teach at Hornsey College of Art, Regent Street Polytechnic School of Art and at Byam Shaw School of Art. Her book *Landscape Painting for Beginners* was published in 1979. Among her many solo shows was one at New Grafton Gallery in 1982, where in 1991 she shared one with her husband Christopher Mason, later ones including Thackeray Gallery, 1997. Lived mostly in France, in the early 1990s settling in St Savin, Vienne. Gauguin, the Nabis, Bonnard and Matisse were important influences, as was a film made by her husband about Alfred Wallis in 1973. She painted landscape, still life and kitchen interiors in oil, using a rich palette.

Leonora CARRINGTON 1917– Surrealist artist and writer, born at Crookhey Hall, Cockerham, Lancashire, daughter of a cotton magnate. She began writing and illustrating stories as a small child, her birthplace being frequently featured in her art. After a convent education Carrington went to Miss Penrose's finishing school in Florence and was presented at court. In 1936 joined Amédée Ozenfant's private art school in north London, met the Surrealist Max Ernst and returned with him to France to live together, settling in the south in 1937. But it was a difficult relationship, as Ernst was married, and in 1940 Carrington had a breakdown, described in her autobiographical writing *Down Below*. By this time she was a member of the Surrealist circle, having shown her work for the first time in Paris in 1937. By the time of her breakdown Carrington was living in Spain, where in Picasso's studio she met a diplomat, Renato Leduc, whom she married and accompanied to New York. In 1942 they went to live in Mexico, where she remained until her move back to New York in 1985. She eventually settled near Chicago, still working. Carrington wrote in French and English, her stories including *The House of Fear*, 1938, her first book, as well as *The Oval Lady*, 1939, and *Little Francis*, 1986. A retrospective of her paintings, drawings and sculpture was held at Serpentine Gallery, 1991–2.

Derek CARRUTHERS 1935– Artist in various media and teacher, born in Penrith, Cumberland. Studied art at King's College, Newcastle University, 1953–7, teachers including Victor Pasmore and Lawrence Gowing. Taught at Sunderland College of Art, 1957–64, and eventually retired as professor of fine art at Trent Polytechnic, Nottingham. Carruthers was early influenced by Pasmore, but eventually went through what he called a "post-Modernist rethink" and produced metaphysical landscapes. He had solo shows at Univision Gallery, Newcastle, in 1957 and at Drian Galleries, 1963–5. Was included in the Arts Council show Construction England, 1963, and in Belgrave Gallery's 1992 exhibition British abstract art of the 50s and 60s. Leicester University and public galleries in Bradford and Kendal hold his work. Lived in Nottingham.

Mary CARRUTHERS 1878–1962 Painter and modeller, born in London, sixth daughter of the 1st Baron Trevor. The Honourable Mrs Carruthers' second husband was Douglas Carruthers, the explorer. She studied at Norwich School of Art, 1928–30, then at the Grosvenor School of Modern Art, 1929–30, with Iain Macnab. For a time she was chairman of the Norfolk and Norwich Art Circle. Exhibited with RBSA, RSA, SWA, RI, Paris Salon and prolifically with the Art Circle, especially portraits and flower pictures. Late in life, when settled in Burnham Market, she again studied at Norwich School of Art.

Rose CARRUTHERS: *see* **Rose ELLENBY**

Fiona CARSON 1947– Sculptor, draughtsman and teacher, born in Edinburgh. She gained an honours degree in art history at Courtauld Institute, London University, 1965–8, then travelled in India, drawing, 1969–71. After lecturing in art history at West Surrey College of Art, Farnham, 1972–5, Carson completed a degree in fine art (sculpture) at St Martin's School of Art, 1976–80, after a period of "dawning feminism". From 1976 she also taught part-time at various centres including Goldsmiths' College. Her abstract sculptures featured found objects. Showed in groups at Clare College, Cambridge, 1967; Lauderdale House, 1978; LG, 1982; and Woodlands Art Gallery, 1983.

John Paddy CARSTAIRS 1916–1970 Painter in oil, gouache and watercolour, writer and film-maker. Studied art at the Slade School of Fine Art, exhibited at Leicester Galleries, RBA, RA and Paris Salon. Extensive one-man shows, including Redfern Gallery, Leger Galleries and Walker's Galleries. Wrote a book: *Watercolour is Fun*. Is in the collections of Trinity College, Oxford, City Art Gallery, Manchester, and Kircaldy Museum and Art Gallery, Fifeshire. Carstairs began his film career as a camera assistant and went on to direct 45 feature films. The first was *Holiday's End*, 1937, and among his versatile output was a series with the comedian Norman Wisdom, starting with *Trouble in Store*, 1953. He wrote over 30 books. Lived at Kingston Hill, Surrey.

Thelma CARSTENSEN 1906–1992 Artist, mainly watercolour and etching, born in London. She studied at Hornsey School of Art, 1924–7, then Slade School of Fine Art, 1927–30, her teachers including Allan Gwynne-Jones, Randolph Schwabe and Norman Janes. Was a member of WIAC, also showing at Goupil Gallery, Walker's Galleries, RA, NEAC and in the provinces. Lived in Moulsford, Oxfordshire.

Robert CARSWELL 1969– Abstract artist whose work employed grids. He was born in Edinburgh, where he attended the College of Art, 1986–91, then Chelsea College of Art & Design, 1991–2. In 1992 Carswell gained a Repton College painting residency. Group shows included Bruntsfield Gallery, Edinburgh, 1989; Malvern Open Drawing Competition in Great Malvern, 1992; LG at Morley Gallery, 1993; and Aspects of Abstraction at Paton Gallery, 1995.

Albert Clarence CARTER 1894–1958 Sculptor and goldsmith, born in London, who was a goldsmith's apprentice and studied art at Lambeth and Central Schools. Carter was made a fellow of RBS, showing at RA. His marble figure Primavera is illustrated in Eric Newton's 1947 monograph *British Sculpture 1944–1946*. In later years he was based in Reading, Berkshire.

Albert Henry CARTER 1928– Painter and teacher who graduated with honours from St Paul's College, Cheltenham, 1973–7. Taught art at Oundle School. He showed at RBA, of which he became a member in 1983, then honorary treasurer, also at RWA and in the provinces. American Embassy holds his work. Lived in Oundle, Northamptonshire.

Bernard CARTER 1920– Painter and curator, born in London where he continued to live, married to the artist Eugenie Alexander. Carter was educated at Haberdashers' Aske's School, then Goldsmiths' College School of Art. He went on to be keeper in charge of pictures and conservation at National Maritime Museum, Greenwich, retiring in 1977. With his wife he published *Art for Young People*. Had a solo show with Arthur Jeffress in 1955, then a long series with Portal Gallery. Also appeared at RA, British Council, Arts Council and abroad. Carter's Abstract Composition, completed in the mid-1950s, was included in Paule Vézelay's Groupe Espace exhibition at Royal Festival Hall in 1955.

Bernard Arthur Ruston (Sam) CARTER 1909– Painter in oil, teacher and writer, born in Kenilworth, Warwickshire. He was married to the artist Jane Tresidder. Sam Carter gained his master's degree in the modern languages tripos at Cambridge, 1930–2. He also attended Grenoble and Innsbruck Universities, and the Central School of Arts and Crafts part-time, his teachers including John Cooper, John Farleigh, Fred Porter and Bernard Meninsky, as well as the Euston Road School. He was on the staff of Camberwell School of Art, 1945–9, and of the Slade School of Fine Art, 1949–78, becoming professor of perspective at Royal Academy Schools, 1975–83. Contributed to a number of learned journals on perspective, as well as *Oxford Companion to Art*, 1970. Showed with East London Group, LG, Arts Council Euston Road touring exhibition, 1948–9, and RA Summer Exhibitions. Arts Council, London Museum, Contemporary Art Society and other collections hold his work. Lived in London.

Frederick CARTER 1885–1967 Painter, printmaker and writer, born in Bradford, he studied art in France, Belgium and London. Exhibited extensively at RE and Baillie Gallery, also RA, NEAC and ROI. Among his books were *The Dragon of the Alchemists* and *Florentine Nights*. Chelsea Arts Club member. Lived in London.

Jack CARTER –1992 Painter in watercolour, who died in about his eightieth year. Was a greengrocer and self-taught flower painter of professional standard who showed locally in the Horsham, Sussex, area where he lived, his work always being in demand. He was said to have declined a contract with the dealer Frost & Reed, which could have given him a national name.

John CARTER 1908–1983 Painter and designer, born in London where he lived for many years, eventually settling in Hastings, Sussex. He studied at Regent Street Polytechnic School of Art, Central School of Arts and Crafts and St Martin's School of Art, 1925–30. Worked for Heal's in London from 1963–74, and managed their design studio. Showed with RI and RBA, both of which he was a member. Carter won the Philip de Laszlo Medal and was a runner-up for the Hunting Group's watercolour of the year award.

John CARTER 1942– Painter and teacher, born Middlesex. Was at Twickenham School of Art, 1958–9, and Kingston College of Art, 1959–63. In 1963–4 he won a Leverhulme Travelling Scholarship, enabling him to work on the continent including a period at British School in Rome. In 1966 he was assistant to Bryan Kneale and began teaching at London College of Printing. After travelling to America on a Peter Stuyvesant Foundation Travel Bursary, 1966–7, Carter taught widely, including Royal College of Art and University of Reading. From 1968 had a series of solo shows at Redfern Gallery, later showing with Nicola Jacobs Gallery. Was a Tolly Cobbold Exhibition prizewinner in 1981. Carter's work was enigmatic, abstract, graceful and still, with a painter's interest in colour and space. Arts Council holds examples.

Kenneth CARTER 1928– Yorkshire-born sculptor in stone and metal and teacher for a time at Exeter College of Art. He won the Leeds Gold Medal for sculpture in 1973 and was a fellow of RBS. Exhibited in RA Summer Exhibition. Public work includes carvings on Exeter Cathedral and stone reliefs at Queen's Gardens in Kingston-upon-Hull. Lived for a time in Lympstone, Devon.

Mary CARTER 1909– Painter in oil who was educated at Bury Grammar School and Queen Elizabeth College in London. Mrs Carter studied at Heatherley's School of Fine Art and Sir John Cass School of Arts and Crafts. Showed and lived in London. Member of Free Painters and Sculptors and ICA.

Mary Elizabeth CARTER 1947– Painter, born in London, was married to the artist J B Hiscock. She studied at Kingston School of Art, then Royal College of Art. There her teachers included Carel Weight and Roger de Grey. She won the Princess of Wales Scholarship and British Institution Award and in 1985 was winner of the Three Friends Prize at RA, at which she showed from 1968. Showed at New Grafton Gallery, RMS, RWA and elsewhere and in 1991 shared an exhibition at Llewellyn Alexander. Mary Carter's work was on a small scale and dealt with daily life in the home and country and portraits. RA holds her work. Lived in Hemyock, Devon.

Simon CARTER 1961– Painter, brought up in East Anglia, whose work stemmed from its landscape although veering towards abstraction. He completed a foundation course at Colchester Institute, 1980–1, then in 1981–4 an honours degree at North-East London Polytechnic. Appeared in many group shows, especially in East Anglia, including Colchester Arts Centre, 1981–4; the 1987 East Anglian Artists' Open, in King's Lynn, where he was specially commended; The Glory of the Garden at Brett Gallery, Hadleigh, 1991; and St John's Gallery, Bury St Edmunds. Had a one-man show at Stamford Arts Centre, 1988, and another at Chappel Galleries, in Essex, 1992. Suffolk County Libraries loan collections hold his work.

Tony CARTER 1943– Sculptor who used mainly found objects which acquired a new meaning when assembled by him. He studied at University of Newcastle upon Tyne, graduating in fine art, 1962–6, obtaining his master's degree at University of Reading, 1966–8. He was Henry Moore Foundation artists fellow at Christ's College and Kettle's Yard, Cambridge, 1990. Among Carter's awards were Peter Stuyvesant Foundation Prize, Young Contemporaries, 1967, with a similar prize at Northern Young Contemporaries, 1968. He also gained an Arts Council Major Award, 1975–80. Carter was a prizewinner at Tolly Cobbold Open Exhibitions in 1977–85, and in 1988 gained Unilever Award in Whitechapel Open Exhibition. Carter took part in numerous group exhibitions from Young Contemporaries, 1967, in Britain and abroad. He had a solo show at Garage Ltd in 1975, later ones including Imperial War Museum, 1992, the year he also showed at Anthony Reynolds Gallery. Arts Council and Contemporary Art Society hold his work.

Walter Dyke CARTER 1894–1966 Painter and etcher. Studied at Royal College of Art and Manchester University and Bolton Schools of Art. After World War II he was art master at Prince Henry's Grammar School, Otley, in Yorkshire, becoming a member of both the Otley Arts Club and Bolton Art Circle. Exhibited RA, RCA and in public galleries in Liverpool, Manchester, Preston and Bradford. Died in the Walsall area of Staffordshire.

Edward CARTER PRESTON 1885–1965 Sculptor, designer, painter and printmaker, father of the artist Julia Carter Preston, born in Walton, Lancashire. He received his early training at the University Art Sheds, Liverpool, one of the tutors being Augustus John. Although early in his career Carter Preston worked in many two-dimensional media, later he developed an interest in three-dimensional ones, producing sculptures in stone and wood. He became proficient in designing and producing medals, largely encouraged by his success in winning the open competition for the next of kin plaque at the end of World War I – under assumed names he won first and second prizes, the same design being used for World War II. Commissions for many medals followed, including the Distinguished Flying Cross, Coronation Medal and Queen's Seal for the County Palatine of Lancashire. In 1930 a major commission came in the form of sculpture for the Anglican cathedral, Liverpool, work that continued for almost 35 years; it was to involve aspects such as processional silver, robes and service sheets. Other ecclesiastical commissions followed, notably for buildings by Giles Gilbert Scott. Carter Preston was a founder member of the Bluecoat Society of Arts and a member of the Sandon Club. Showed with Fine Art Society, RMS of which he became a member in 1929, Walker Art Gallery in Liverpool which holds his work and elsewhere. Died in Liverpool.

Julia CARTER PRESTON fl. from 1960s– Ceramist and teacher, for long based in Liverpool, daughter of the sculptor Edward Carter Preston. She studied at the local College of Art, combined studio work with teaching in Lancashire art colleges, ran the ceramics section of Liverpool Polytechnic, then worked full-time at a studio in Bluecoat Chambers. Her work unusually combined earthenware with sgraffito decoration. Had major shows at Bluecoat Display Centre from 1966, exhibited in Merseyside Artists' exhibitions from 1983, also at Walker Art Gallery, Liverpool; Williamson Art Gallery in Birkenhead; Atkinson Art Gallery, Southport, and elsewhere. Liverpool's Anglican Cathedral, Town Hall and University hold examples. Carter Preston produced many commemorative and presentation items and ecclesiastical ceramics, usually font bowls, including St Nicholas and Our Lady, Liverpool; St Columba's Church, Anfield; and The Church of the Holy Family, Southport. In 1988 was artist-in-residence at Walker Art Gallery.

Doris H de CARTERET 1897–1956 Landscape painter in oil. Studed at Byam Shaw and Vicat Cole School of Art, 1915–19. Exhibited RA, RBA, ROI, RSA, Ridley Art Club and widely in the provinces. Lived in Arundel, Sussex.

William CARTLEDGE 1891–1976 Painter and teacher, born in Manchester where he studied at the School of Art, then Slade School of Fine Art where his teachers included Henry Tonks, Fred Brown and Tancred Borenius. He held a number of teaching positions in Liverpool, Shipley and Pudsey, finally – from 1932–51 – being principal of Staffordshire County School of Art and Crafts as well as art adviser to the county. Exhibited RA, Alpine Club Gallery, RCamA, extensively at Arlington Gallery, and RBA. Manchester City Art Gallery and several other northern galleries hold his work. Finally lived at Birdham, Sussex.

Hilary CARTMEL 1958– Sculptor, notably in wood, born in Wendover, Buckinghamshire, who studied at Exeter College of Art, 1976–7, then Trent Polytechnic, 1977–80. Held a number of residencies, including Carlton Hayes Hospital, Leicestershire, 1982–3. Solo exhibitions included Centre Gallery in Cheltenham, 1982, and Loughborough Art Centre, 1983. Arts Council holds Sprawling Red Woman, 1984, in stained wood, bought from Bluecoat Gallery, Liverpool, and Rufford Country Park, Ollerton, has several examples.

John CARTMEL-CROSSLEY 1933– Painter and teacher, born Southport, Lancashire, who studied at local Art College and Liverpool College of Art, 1949–54. For 15 years from 1954 worked as a non-figurative painter in and around Merseyside, then taught in London, 1969–72, and Norfolk, 1972–4. Then moved to Orkney Isles to work as a full-time artist, concentrating on water-colours. After 10 years moved to Northumberland to set up Rock South Studio and Gallery. Showed at Patricia Wells Gallery, Thornbury, and held many solo exhibitions from 1955. Work held in public and private collections throughout the world. Lived at Alnwick, Northumberland.

Peter CARTWRIGHT 1939– Abstract painter and teacher, born in Derby, attending its College of Art, 1956–8, then Royal College of Art, 1958–61. Then lived in Nottingham and taught at its College of Art. Showed with Young Contemporaries, AIA Gallery and was included in 1965 John Moores Liverpool Exhibition. In 1967 Cartwright's oil on canvas Three was included in Survey '67 Abstract Painters at Camden Arts Centre and it was taken into Arts Council collection.

Reg CARTWRIGHT 1938– Artist and illustrator, born in Leicester, who settled in Leicestershire at Kibworth Beauchamp, 1970. Cartwright did his National Service as a musician in the Leicester Regiment, 1957–60, then worked in studios as a commercial artist and art director for 13 years, becoming a full-time painter and illustrator in 1974. Mixed shows included Portal Gallery, 1972; Piccadilly Gallery, 1979; 16th Exhibition of Original Pictures of International Children's Books, Japan, 1981;

and Royal Festival Hall Books of the Year Exhibition, 1986. Solo shows included Portal from 1974; Leicester Museum and Art Gallery, which holds his work, 1980–1; Woods Gallery, Leicester, 1990; and Goldmark Gallery, Uppingham, 1995.

Richard CARTWRIGHT 1951– Painter of imaginative, dreamlike landscapes, he studied at Goldsmiths' College School of Art and drew inspiration from sources as diverse as the early Sienese School, Alfred Wallis, Samuel Palmer, Morandi and Corot. In 1990 he was elected a member of RWA. Group shows included Campbell and Franks, 1976–7; Jablonski Gallery, 1987; and Waterman Fine Art, 1990. Cartwright had a solo show at Marches Gallery, Hereford, 1977, later ones including Rooksmoor Gallery, Bath, from 1987, and Adam Gallery there, 1993.

Simon CARTWRIGHT fl. from mid-1980s– Painter who studied at University College of Wales, 1980–4; University of California, San Diego, Santa Cruz, 1982–3; and London University, 1988–9. Group shows included Fosse Gallery, Stow-on-the-Wold, and Selective Eye Gallery, Jersey, both 1991. Had a solo exhibition at Frost & Reed, 1990. This featured a number of themes common to Cartwright's work: still life, effect on landscape of the post-war agricultural revolution, architecture and political assassinations.

Caroline CARY 1940– Painter in acrylic and watercolour. She studied at Camberwell and Chelsea Schools of Art in the late 1950s, her teachers including Lawrence Gowing. She ceased painting professionally while bringing up her family, but then resumed, much of her work stemming from travels in Africa, India and the Far East. Although tending towards the abstract, she said that her works revealed "a strong physical presence". Mixed shows included Mall Galleries, Guildford University, Clarges and Jonathan Poole Galleries. From the mid-1970s was a frequent solo exhibitor, notably at Loggia and Langton Galleries, later shows taking place at Leighton House, 1983, and Sue Rankin Gallery, 1990. Worked in London and Devon.

Ateo J CASADIO 1905–1987 Painter of Italian descent, who spent most of his life in England, noted for still life. In 1969 showed Adam and Eve in RA Summer Exhibition and work also handled by Phipps & Company. Lived in Nazeing, Essex.

Wyn CASBOLT 1914– Painter, draughtsman and printmaker, she was born in London. Studied at Slade School of Fine Art with Norman Janes and Randolph Schwabe. Exhibited WIAC, Redfern Gallery, with Newbury Art Society and abroad. For much of her life Casbolt suffered poor health, but this did not prevent her producing fine landscapes and abstracts in the late 1950s and early 1960s. Lived in Newbury, Berkshire, later in southwest London.

Tony CASEMENT 1949– Abstract artist, noted for paintings on canvas and paper with an emphasis on the use of colour, direct mark and surface, and teacher, born in St Eval, Cornwall. He studied at the fine art department at the University of Newcastle upon Tyne, 1967–71, then was one of a specialist printmaking group at Brighton Polytechnic, 1971–2, returning to Newcastle as research assistant fine art, printmaking, media, 1972–4. His teachers included Ian Stephenson. After being a part-time lecturer at Hertfordshire College of Art, St Albans, 1976–8, from 1978 Casement was a visiting lecturer at venues including Hull and Canterbury Colleges of Art; Portsmouth Polytechnic; Sir John Cass; Southend and Suffolk Colleges; and Norwich School of Art. Between 1990–4, he was a founder-member and co-ordinator for Open Studios and Workshops in northeast Suffolk, where lived at Yoxford; joined Health Images, 1991; spent some time in Dhaka, Bangladesh, and was a member of Halesworth Gallery committee, both 1992; and joined Bearing 090° (European artists exchange), 1993. Mixed shows included Young Generation, Norrköping Museum, Sweden, and International Drawing Biennale, Teesside, from 1973; Eastern Open, Fermoy Centre, King's Lynn, from 1987, being a prizewinner in 1992; and Kettle's Yard Gallery Open, Cambridge, 1995. Had a solo show at Calouste Gulbenkian Gallery, Newcastle Polytechnic, 1973, later ones including Martha Stevns Gallery, Fressingfield, 1995.

Francis Milton CASHMORE 1892–1971 Architect and painter whose buildings and watercolours were marked by an urbane style. He was born in London and attended University College School, where he developed as a fine pianist, noted mathematician and perspective draughtsman. Studied architecture at Regent Street Polytechnic and at Royal Academy Schools, where Edwin Lutyens was his mentor. After World War I service with the Aircraft Manufacturing Company as a design engineer, in 1920 Cashmore qualified at RIBA, of which he was made a fellow in 1932. In 1921 joined Dunbar Smith and Cecil Brewer, who were involved with National Museum of Wales in Cardiff and Heal's department store, London. Aged 35 Cashmore joined Messrs Joseph as design architect, becoming a partner in 1932; in 1960 he became senior partner and the firm was renamed Messrs Joseph, F Milton Cashmore and Partners. Among notable buildings he worked on were Shell-Mex House, on the Embankment; Melbury Court, Kensington High Street; Springbok House, Leatherhead Court, Surrey; and Britannic House, Moorfields. Many watercolours of buildings made by Cashmore in the post-war period have become valuable records. A successful show was held at Comedy Gallery, 1963, with another at The Medici Gallery, 1992, to celebrate his centenary.

Ann CASIMIR 1935– Sculptor and printmaker, born in Montreal, Canada, where she studied at McGill University. Studied art at Montreal Museum of Fine Arts, in Italy and at Sir John Cass School of Art. Showed at Free Painters and Sculptors, of which she was a fellow, and elsewhere in London, where she had several solo exhibitions and lived.

Nigel CASSELDINE 1947– Painter, notable for richly coloured, painterly landscapes of Ireland and East Anglia, as in his solo show at The Medici Galleries, 1996. He initially worked as a studio assistant to F V Magrath, studying part-time at the Sir

John Cass and Camberwell Schools of Art, 1967–72. After this, he formed the Romney Studio Workshop. Casseldine won The Brandler Painting Prize in 1988 and in 1991 was elected a full academician at RWA, having been an associate from 1985. Also exhibited at Nina Zborowska Fine Paintings in Painswick, RA, Rooksmoor and Adam Galleries in Bath, Wykeham Gallery and Penwith, St Ives. Lived in Chalford, Stroud, Gloucestershire.

Julia CASSELS fl. from 1980s– Painter who after a couple of years in advertising and design went to live in Africa for a time in the Rift Valley, Kenya. On her return to England, not wishing a routine job she pursued her enthusiasm for painting by producing watercolours for exhibition and commission. Travelled in Italy and Britain. Exhibitions included Guildhall Gallery, Winchester; Mall Galleries, Art for Youth Exhibition, 1990; Hurlingham Gallery; Percy Bass Ltd; and in 1991 she had a solo show at Charlotte Lampard Gallery.

Hugh CASSON 1910– Architect, watercolourist and illustrator and author, born and lived in London. He studied architecture at Cambridge University; Craven Scholar, British School at Athens, 1933; and at Bartlett School, University of London. He was in private practice as an architect from 1937. During World War II was camouflage officer with the Air Ministry. From 1948–51 was director of architecture for the Festival of Britain. He held many official appointments. Casson was knighted in 1950; was elected RA in 1970; was president of the RA, 1976–84; and was made a Companion of Honour, 1985. His publications included *New Sights of London*, 1937; *Bombed Churches*, 1946; *Diary*, 1981; *Hugh Casson's Oxford*, 1988; and *Hugh Casson's Cambridge*, 1992.

Lucy CASSON 1960– Creator of small sculptures, born in Prestwood, Buckinghamshire, who graduated from Camberwell School of Arts and Crafts in 1981. Went on to show her witty, colourful works in Britain and abroad, in 1996 being given a small show at Hove Museum & Art Gallery in its First Sight showcase. Casson said that her work was "made of recycled tin, wire, twigs, cloth, rubber, gloves and found objects, soldered, rivetted or stuck together. I gather my inspiration from observation of people and animals, instances, stories, moments and moods."

Simon John CASSON 1965– Artist and teacher, born in York, who lived in Zambia, until 1982. Gained a first-class honours degree in fine art painting at Exeter College of Art and Design, 1985–8, in 1987 studying in Rotterdam; attended Central St Martins College of Art and Design, part-time, for a post-graduate diploma in printmaking, 1988–90; then gained his master's degree at the Royal Academy Schools, 1991–4. Among many awards and prizes won were the Cecil Collins Memorial Prize for Fine Art, 1990; David Murray Studentships, Travel Scholarships to Spain and Italy, 1993 and 1994; and in 1994 the Royal Academy Gold Medal for Painting. Teaching included Bournemouth and Poole College of Art and Design. Mixed exhibitions included RA Summer Exhibition and RE, both from 1989 (he was made an associate of RE in 1992); National Printmaking Exhibition, Mall Galleries, 1994; and Ainscough Contemporary Art, 1996. In 1996 had a solo show at Long & Ryle.

Jesse Dale CAST 1900–1976 Painter, draughtsman and teacher, born in London. From 1914–17 Cast studied at School of Building, Brixton, intending to become an interior decorator, then for three years was employed successively in design studios of Maples, Harrods and H & C Davis (Radiation Ltd). He attended life classes at St Martin's School of Art in the afternoons, and in the evenings at Camberwell School of Arts and Crafts. In 1919 a large watercolour was hung in the architectural room of the RA. Awarded a scholarship by London County Council, Cast studied at Camberwell 1920–2, under Albert Rutherston, then from 1922–6 under Henry Tonks at Slade School of Fine Art, winning first prize in painting from life and first prize in decorative design, 1924–5; first prize in drawing heads from life, 1925–6; and, on leaving, the Robert Ross Scholarship in Fine Art. Cast showed at NEAC for first time in 1926 at the start of a period when he lived abroad, in Bruges, Belgium; then Soller, Majorca. From 1930–9 Cast showed at RP, to which he was elected in 1957, and annually at RA from 1934, but he later declined offers of nomination for election. During the war Cast worked in the Ministry of Aircraft production, then afterwards taught at Harrow School of Art, Central School of Art and Design and Hornsey College of Art, where he accepted a permanent appointment. Because he was so self-critical and because a large number of paintings was destroyed during the war, Cast's extant output is small. He was highly regarded by his peers as a meticulous draughtsman and craftsman. A memorial show was held at South London Art Gallery, 1980, another at University College, 1994. Tate Gallery and British Museum hold examples. Lived in Tunbridge Wells, Kent.

Eva CASTLE 1922– Sculptor, potter and designer, born in Aarhus, Denmark. She studied at Royal Academy in Copenhagen, 1944–7, then at Slade School of Fine Art, 1948–50, with A H Gerrard and F E McWilliam. Produced textile designs and ceramics in Britain and on the continent. Was a founder-member of SPS in 1953 and was a fellow of RBS. Her sculpture Clearance was in the Football Association's show Football and the Fine Arts, 1953, and in 1956–7 she was guest artist at Chelsea Pottery. Showed at RA from 1951 as well as in leading London and provincial galleries. Her Madonna is in St John's Church, Newbury. Castle was married to the actor Tony Britton and lived in London.

Florence E CASTLE 1867– Painter and illustrator, brought up in Croydon, Surrey. Studied at Lambeth School of Art with Sir William Llewellyn, then in Paris. Showed RA, ROI, SWA and NEAC. Lived in London.

Patricia CASTLE fl. from 1940s– Artist, born and eventually returned to London, who studied for a short time at Camberwell School of Arts and Crafts, also in evenings at St Martin's School of Art. In early 1970s she moved to Ramsgate, became involved in town conservation and converted a disused hardware shop into a gallery. Castle later showed and travelled in America. Mixed exhibitions included Datchet Gallery in Datchet, 1978; Flint House Gallery, Broadstairs, 1982; Plaza Gallery, Houston, 1985; New Academy Gallery, 1987; The Heifer Gallery, from 1990; and Platform Gallery, Folkestone, 1991. Had a first solo show in early 1960s, later ones including Canterbury Festival, 1988, and Burgh House, Hampstead, 1990–1.

Shelley CASTLE 1967– Artist working in mixed media, born and lived in London, who obtained a first-class honours degree from Central St Martin's College of Art & Design, 1989–92. Showed at Cromwell and Ward and Fresh Art, 1992 and in Biennale in Naples, Madrid and Brussels, 1993, sharing an exhibition at Morley College in the same year. Chelsea Arts Club holds work.

Edmund CASWELL 1938–1996 Artist, notably a muralist, born in Bangalore, India, remaining there seven years before his family returned to England, where Edmund grew up in Coventry. Although at 13 he won a scholarship to the local School of Art, a love of horses prompted him to study at agricultural college in Oxford, after which his varied career including being a coal miner, soldier, decorator and stage designer. Aged 38, Caswell decided to be a full-time artist, attending life classes at Heatherley and St Martin's Schools of Art and a part-time foundation course at Sir John Cass. At 40, Caswell was accepted for the fine arts degree course at Middlesex Polytechnic, and in his first year completed a mural in the geriatric ward of Colindale Hospital. In his final year, 1980, Caswell began his huge mural based on J M Barrie's *Peter Pan* at the Hospital for Sick Children, Great Ormond Street, a vivid depiction of 450 figures drawing on his Indian memories. It was finished in 1988, and thereafter Caswell was involved with a number of *Peter Pan* ventures for Barrie's birthplace at Kirriemuir. Further projects included 10 large paintings linked to Mussorgsky's *Pictures from an Exhibition* music; it developed into a live multi-media production which had a Scottish première at Dundee University and an exhibition there, both in 1993. Caswell also produced a painting for Dundee developer Michael Johnston's new headquarters in 1994, and soon after he painted Robert Burns' *Tam O'Shanter* for the same building. Caswell did illustrations for Jane Austen's *Pride and Prejudice*, for Black Swan Press, 1985–6, and in 1994–5 painted portraits for Dundee University, including one of Barrie. Caswell's last painting was for St Mary Magdelene Church in Dundee, where his funeral service was held after his death from cancer. Ninewells Hospital in the city, where he had lived from 1990, held a memorial exhibition, 1996–7.

Heather O CATCHPOLE 1942– Miniaturist, notable for her portraits, born in Winnipeg, Canada. She studied at Natal School of Arts and Craft, South Africa. Became a member of RMS, also exhibiting at RA, Hilliard Society and elsewhere. Lived at Fitzhead, Somerset.

John Denis Harwood CATLEUGH 1920– Painter, designer, architect, theatre designer and collagist, born in King's Lynn, Norfolk. He was also a noted collector of British ceramics, especially William De Morgan. Catleugh attended Oundle School and London University, qualifying as an architect in 1949 after World War II service. Apart from this, Catleugh did not have a formal art training and his career was multi-faceted. Early on he made a series of Perspex and wood reliefs and did furniture designs, as well as creating collages and relief paintings in plaster. In 1953 he was a prizewinner in the Furniture Makers' Guild Coronation Design Competition. In 1951 Catleugh designed sets for Picasso's play *Desire Caught by the Tail*, at the Watergate Theatre. A significant development was seeing in 1949 a Jackson Pollock exhibition in Venice, which launched the artist on an exploration of the drip-and-pour technique; it led to a series of space-time pictures. Among the important group shows in which he participated were British Abstract Art at Gimpel Fils, in 1951 and This is Tomorrow, at the Whitechapel Art Gallery, 1956. AIA and Redfern Gallery also exhibited the work of Catleugh and England & Co gave him a shared show with John Milnes-Smith in 1988. Lived in London.

Christopher CATLIN 1902–1977 Self-taught artist, born and lived in London, who commonly signed his work C. After attending elementary school he eventually became a taxi-cab driver. Painted from early in life, favouring pastel and tempera, his subjects market scenes and people, with a special interest in people and their faces. His work brought him a circle of friends including notabilities such as Sir Charles Tennyson and C V Wedgwood, and artists Polly Hill Clark and Helen Stuart Weir. Catlin's wife cleaned for the artist Orovida Pissarro and, in gratitude for the Catlins' help and friendship, Orovida bought them a house in Fulham after selling one of her father, Camille's, pictures. Catlin was a member of RBA, showed at RA and in local independent exhibitions and had a solo show in Kensington Church Street shortly before he died.

Brian CATLING 1948– Artist working in a wide variety of media, including abstract sculpture in steel, born in London. He studied at North-East London Polytechnic and Royal College of Art and in 1982–5 was the first Henry Moore Fellow at Norwich. Exhibited at Air Gallery, 1977, Camden Arts Centre, 1979, Arnolfini Gallery, Bristol, in 1980, and Ikon Gallery, Birmingham, 1981. In 1983 was included in British Artists at Cyprus College of Art at Woodlands Art Gallery. Arts Council holds several examples.

Lance CATTERMOLE 1898–1992 Painter who studied at Central School of Arts and Crafts, 1922–3, teachers including Bernard Meninsky and James Grant, then Slade School of Fine Art, 1923–6, under Henry Tonks and Philip Wilson Steer. Showed with RA, ROI of which he was made a member in 1938, RBA and widely in the provinces. National Army Museum holds his work. Lived for many years at High Salvington, Sussex. Cattermole came from a line of artists: his father was Sydney, a painter who followed on from George, illustrator of Charles Dickens' *The Old Curiosity Shop* and other works.

Fred CATTON 1889– Self-taught watercolourist, brought up in London. Exhibited RWS, RBA, UA and with Civil Defence Artists. Lived in London and later at Welling, Kent.

Louise CATTRELL 1957– Painter, notably of landscape, born in Glasgow. She studied at Duncan of Jordanstone College of Art, Dundee, 1975–80, then at Royal College of Art, 1980–3. Among her awards were the Duncan of Drumfork Travelling Scholarship, in 1978; an Adam Bruce Thomson Award from RSA and a Scottish Education Travelling Scholarship, in 1979; the Farquhar Reid Award, in 1980; and the John Minton Award, in 1983. Cattrell took part in a number of group shows, including SSA, RA and the Whitechapel Open, and in 1992 had solo exhibition at Beaux Arts, Bath.

Patrick CAULFIELD 1936– Painter, printmaker and teacher, born in London, where he continued to live. He studied at Chelsea School of Art, 1956–9, and Royal College of Art, 1960–3. In the latter year he taught at Chelsea School of Art. By then Caulfield had shown several times with Young Contemporaries and in 1964 was in The New Generation at Whitechapel Art Gallery. Caulfield's first one-man show was at Robert Fraser Gallery in 1965, and he soon made an impression in mixed and solo international shows. A print retrospective toured California in 1977; in 1981 there was a retrospective at Walker Art Gallery, Liverpool, and Tate Gallery; then Serpentine Gallery in 1992–3. The artist's early mature works were black-and-white, depicting familiar objects, and he was seen as one of the later generation of Pop painters. When he worked in colour this was black-outlined and without modulation, although later works depended more on painterly illusion, such as in the 1984 acrylic on canvas Fish and Sandwich, in the Saatchi Collection. Arts Council and many other public collections hold his work. Elected RA, 1993.

Ian CAUNCE 1947– Sculptor who studied at Liverpool Polytechnic, 1982–5. His exhibitions included Riverside, Widnes, 1981; Beaumanor Hall, Leicestershire, 1985–6; and the Walker Art Gallery touring Merseyside Artists 3, 1986–7.

William Sidney CAUSER 1876–1958 Painter in various media, born in Wolverhampton, Staffordshire. Studied at Wolverhampton School of Art, in London and in several countries on the continent. Exhibited RA, NEAC, Leicester Galleries, RI and Royal Glasgow Institute of the Fine Arts; one-man shows Fine Art Society and Leger Gallery. Work held widely in provincial collections. His books include *An Artist in Spain*. Lived in London.

Peter CAVACIUTI 1952– Painter whose work reflected an interest in classical Chinese art and Japanese poetics. He used handmade paper from China, Korea, Japan and Nepal; Chinese ink and traditional pigments; and developed methods of mixing colours from seventeenth-century Chinese recipes. Cavaciuti spent seven years studying with the foremost Chinese artist Fei Cheng Wu; continued with Professor Bao, the noted flower and bird painter; and attended the Central School of Art, Beijing. Exhibitions included RA Summer Exhibition, RWS, Sebastian Pearson Gallery, Broughton House Gallery in Cambridge, Benjamin Hargreaves and Belgium and Japan.

John CAVANAGH 1931–c.1995 Artist, born in Manchester, who studied there at the College of art and Design. Had a solo exhibition at City Art Gallery, Salford, 1961, then a series in the north of England, also at Drian Galleries from 1974, including figurative-towards-abstract pictures, and Compendium Galleries, Birmingham, 1975.

Sue CAVE 1949– Painter and muralist, born in Grimsby, Lincolnshire. She studied at the local School of Art, 1965–8, then Kingston College of Art from 1968, in 1971 gaining a scholarship to study in Egypt. Was commissioned to paint a mural for Grimsby Parish Church and painted harpsichords created by the musical instrument maker Robert Goble. These were exhibited at music festivals in Britain and on the continent. Had a first solo exhibition at Oxfordshire County Museum in 1981 and in 1985–6 was included in the Piccadilly Gallery's show The Brotherhood of Ruralists and Friends.

Herbert Harry CAWOOD 1890–1957 Sculptor, notably of portraits, and founder, born in Sheffield. He studied at the Technical School of Art there, winning several medals subsequently at the Royal Academy Schools. He exhibited at RA and in the provinces. Cawood was a fellow of the RBS, becoming honorary treasurer for a time just after World War II. Lived in London.

Alfred CAWS 1912– Painter, draughtsman, designer and teacher, born in Bembridge, Isle of Wight. He studied at Heatherley's School of Fine Art under Patrick Larking and Frederic Whiting and went on to teach in further education classes. Caws said that his main objectives were "relationship of shapes and unity of colour". He was a member of NS, also showing with ROI, Artists of Chelsea, AEB, Wessex Artists and elsewhere. His work was reproduced in commercial publications. Lived in Shanklin, Isle of Wight.

Hermon CAWTHRA 1886–1971 Monumental sculptor, draughtsman and teacher, born Joseph Hermon Cawthra in Baildon, Yorkshire. From the ages of 14–21 he was apprenticed to a monumental mason, but studied in the evenings from 1904 at Saltaire Art School and in 1907–9 at Leeds School of Art. Then studied full-time at Royal College of Art, 1909–11, and Royal Academy Schools, 1912–16, when he was found unfit for Army service so carved propellors for the Royal Flying Corps. Worked for a short time for the sculptor Paul Montford after the war, then was on his own until 1939, when World War II forced him to close his studio. He had been elected a fellow of the RBS in 1937.

When war broke out Cawthra joined Brighton College of Art, in 1941 going to Hull as head of sculpture, where he stayed until war's end. After reopening his London studio Cawthra taught part-time, until he had to retire, at 70, at Bournemouth Municipal College of Art. Cawthra, who intensely disliked the modern movement in sculpture, had made his name with the Bootle War Memorial in 1922. Other notable works included the Burns statue in Dumfries; The Orator, drawn from life at Hyde Park Corner; Britannia and the Lion, on the County Fire Office, in Piccadilly; and the memorial to the Earl of Meath at Lancaster Gate. Cawthra worked for the leading architects of his day and much of his sculpture went overseas, having a strong Empire theme. After Sir William Reid Dick he was one of the leading classical sculptors of his time. He showed at RA extensively as well as in Bradford, Liverpool and Glasgow. Cawthra was a brilliant portrait draughtsman and a sculptor of great range, examples being included in the volume *R B S: Modern British Sculpture*, published in 1939; and in Eric Newton's monograph *British Sculpture 1944–1946*. Latterly lived in Sheen in southwest London, but died on a visit to Cottingley, Yorkshire.

Mark CAZALET 1964– Painter, notable for fantastic landscapes, born in London. He studied at Chelsea and Falmouth Schools of Art, 1982–6. Won many awards, including a French Consul National Studentship at L'École Nationale Supérieure des Beaux-Arts, in Paris; a residency at the Cité-Internationale des Arts, also in Paris; and a Commonwealth University Scholarship to Baroda University, India. As well as being included in many group shows, Cazalet showed solo at Arts Centre Group, Waterloo, and at Gallery 7 in Bombay, but his first major exhibition in London was at Christopher Hull Gallery, 1992.

CAZIEL 1906–1988 Painter whose work was strongly influenced by Cézanne and Cubism, born in Sosnowiec, Poland. His real name was Kazimierz Zielenkiewicz, with which he signed his work until in 1940s the name Caziel was adopted as more easily memorable. He studied at Warsaw Academy of Fine Arts, 1931–6, showed in Poland and then gained a state scholarship to Italy and Paris, 1937. In 1939 he volunteered for the Polish Army in France, settled in the country in 1946 in Aix-en-Provence, then in Paris, and designed Poland's pavilion for the Unesco International Exhibition of Modern Art. In 1947 had a solo show at Galerie Allard, Paris, shortly after which he began a long friendship with Picasso. In 1951 the Musée National d'Art Moderne bought a big canvas by Caziel, and two years later the Vatican commissioned four large pictures for its Museum of Religious Art. In 1957 Caziel married the Scottish painter Catherine Sinclair. He had the first of several one-man shows at Grabowski Gallery in 1966, three years before setting in Somerset, where he died. He bequeathed 10 paintings to the National Museum of Modern Art in Warsaw. In 1990 the Polish Cultural Institute in London held a memorial exhibition, another show being organised by Whitford Fine Art in 1995. Tollemache House at Thurso, Caithness, contains a fresco designed by Caziel in 1963.

Janina CEBERTOWICZ 1953– Painter, draughtsman and teacher, born in Manchester, with a special interest in art and musical education. She studied at Bath Academy of Art, 1972–5, and Manchester Polytechnic, 1977–8, gaining an honours degree in fine art, her teachers including Donald McKinlay, Peter Kinley, Michael Kidner, William Scott, David Pearson and Adrian Heath. Held a number of teaching posts in Lancashire, where she lived at Cloughfold, Rossendale, from 1989 being head of art at Bury Grammar School for Girls. Residencies included Royal Northern College of Music from 1991. Cebertowicz was elected to MAFA from 1984 and was active in its running. Group shows included Portraits North at Salford Art Gallery, 1988; Bede Gallery, Jarrow, Van Gogh Centenary Exhibition, 1990. Had a solo show at Bluecoat Gallery in Liverpool, 1981, later ones including Tib Lane Gallery, Manchester, from 1989 and Royal Northern College of Music there from 1992.

Karol CEBULA 1946– Painter and artist in mixed media who also employed means such as tape recordings; teacher. He was born in Pittenweem, Fife. Studied at Edinburgh College of Art, 1964–9, gaining the Andrew Grant Travelling Scholarship, 1969–70. He attended Moray House College of Further Education in 1972. Two years later Cebula won a Scottish Arts Council Award. He was for a time an art teacher in Dunfermline. Cebula participated in group shows held by Young Scottish Contemporaries in the late 1960s, was included in Seven Scottish Artists at ICA in 1969, the Arts Council Travelling Exhibition Art Spectrum Scotland in 1971 and in A Choice Selection at Fruit Market Gallery, Edinburgh, 1975. In 1974 he had a solo show at Kynd Kyttock's Gallery, Falkland. Fife Education Committee and Scottish Arts Council hold his work.

Roger CECIL 1942– Painter, draughtsman and teacher who lived in the house in Abertillery, Monmouthshire, where he was born and brought up. He produced work rich in imagery, poetry and colour which drew on his environment, the industrial valley towns and mountains. Prolific and obsessive, he was a solitary artist, with affiliations to no group. Cecil joined Newport College of Art in 1959, teachers including John Wright and Thomas Rathmell; in 1963 he gained the highest award that year in the national diploma in design. Won the David Murray Landscape Award from the RA. Cecil was offered a place at Royal College of Art, but after a few weeks was unsatisfied and took up manual work in opencast mines and on building sites. The BBC made a television documentary on Cecil's work called *The Gentle Rebel*. Taught in Ebbw Vale. In 1995–7 he gained his master's with distinction in communication design from Central St Martins College of Art & Design. For a long time Cecil did not exhibit, through choice, and it was friends who helped to promote him. Had a series of exhibitions at Business Art Galleries from 1987 and in 1995 the Hill Court Gallery, Abergavenny, held a retrospective of work special to the artist. In 1998 Gordon Hepworth and Y Tabernacl both showed Cecil's pictures.

Rose CECIL 1956– Painter and draughtsman who studied at Byam Shaw School of Art and City and Guilds of London Art

School. Had a show of docklands pictures at Michael Parkin Gallery, 1988; travelled in Tibet, China, Nepal, Guatemala and Belize; and had a show in 1996 at Parkin of Galapagos Islands paintings.

Ashton CHADWICK 1944– Artist and teacher, born in Cornwall. Studied at Falmouth School of Art, 1961–5, Brighton College of Art, 1965–6, and Royal Academy Schools, 1966–9. Teaching appointments included Basingstoke Technical College and widely in adult education, being an exhibitor at Artists in Adult Education at Woodlands Art Gallery, 1982. Other exhibitions included Oxford Press Gallery, 1969, Heal's Mansard Gallery, 1969–71, and Camden Arts Centre, 1981, where Chadwick was senior lecturer and Centre head.

Enid Mary CHADWICK 1902–1987 Church decorator, book illustrator and calligrapher, born in Basingstoke, Hampshire. Studied art with W B Morrell in Exeter and in Brighton at the College of Art with Lawrence Preston and with Louis Ginnett. Reflecting her religious upbringing Chadwick concentrated on children's book illustration with a Christian theme and she decorated a number of churches mainly in Britain but also in America and South Africa. The Shrine of Our Lady of Walsingham contains her work. She was artist at the Shrine, near where she lived, from 1934–87. Signed work E M C.

Ernest Albert CHADWICK 1876–1956 Watercolourist, wood engraver and draughtsman, son of the artist John Chadwick, born in Marston Green, Warwickshire. He was one of the most prolific exhibitors at RBSA, of which he became a member in 1912. Was also a member of New Society of Artists, 1924, RCamA, 1929, and RI, 1939. Chadwick was noted for his pictures of English rural life, especially Cornish fishing villages, and used a bicycle to carry his painting equipment. Birmingham City Museum and Art Gallery holds his work. Lived in Henley-in-Arden, Warwickshire.

Helen CHADWICK 1953–1996 Artist in various media, born in Croydon, Surrey. She studied at Brighton Polytechnic, 1973–6, gaining an honours degree, obtaining her master's at Chelsea School of Art, 1976–7. Twice nominated for the Turner Prize, Chadwick unsettled many with her concentration on subjects such as defecation and delay. Piss Flowers, 1994, was a series of 12 bronzes cast from holes in the snow where she and her partner had urinated. She was in the group shows Long Live the New Flesh, Kettle's Yard, Cambridge, and Postmodern Prints, at Victoria & Albert Museum, both 1991; and in Twelve Stars, Belfast Arts Council Gallery and tour, 1992–3, which showed her Self Portrait, 1991, in ciba transparency, aluminium on glass, electrics, acquired for the European Parliament Collection. Tate Gallery and British Council also hold examples. Began showing solo soon after graduation, including Aspex Gallery, Portsmouth; Museum of Modern Art, Oxford; Museum of Modern Art in New York; and in 1996 the exhibition she was working on at the time of her death was held at Portfolio Gallery as part of the Edinburgh International Festival.

Lynn CHADWICK 1914– Sculptor in metal, born in London. He is noted for his mobiles and for abstract shapes, dancing children and waiting and watching figures. After education at Merchant Taylors' School, although Chadwick wanted to become a sculptor, his family persuaded him to enter an architect's office, and he stayed an architectural draughtsman until World War II, when he became a Fleet Air Arm pilot. Working with the architect Rodney Thomas after the war Chadwick began experimenting with mobiles, partly inspired by the work of Alexander Calder. First showed at LG in 1950, in that year having initial one-man show at Gimpel Fils. Gained a national prize in The Unknown Political Prisoner competition in 1953; won International Sculpture Prize at Venice Biennale, 1956; and first prize at Concorso Internazionale del Bronzetto, in Padua, 1959. Showed regularly with Marlborough Gallery since 1961. Exhibited extensively around the world, being represented in many major collections, including Tate Gallery and Museum of Modern Art, New York. Retrospective at Yorkshire Sculpture Park, 1991–2. Lived at Stroud, Gloucestershire.

Paxton CHADWICK 1903–1961 Illustrator and designer with a strong interest in natural history. Born in Fallowfield, Lancashire, he attended Manchester School of Art. Exhibited in London, Manchester, in France and North America. He illustrated a large number of books on plants, birds and animals for leading publishers, such as the Educational Supply Association and Penguin Books Ltd. Lived at Leiston, Suffolk.

Sam CHADWICK 1902–1992 Watercolourist and printmaker, notable for his pictures of the Yorkshire dales. He was born in Leeds and, with the exception of 18 months spent in York in the early days of his training and two years in a London studio, lived and worked there. Upon retirement after 50 years as a commercial artist he devoted the last 15 years to landscape painting, employing a soft and fluid palette with refined tonal qualities. Chadwick was also an accomplished photographer.

Douglas H CHAFFEY 1924– Artist born and lived in Poole, Dorset, who ran the Trinity Art Gallery in Wareham. He was self-taught and had exhibitions widely in the provinces.

Hayman CHAFFEY: *see* **HAYMAN**

Marc Camille CHAIMOWICZ 1946– Artist, born in Paris. He studied at Camberwell School of Arts and Crafts, 1964–8, then Slade School of Fine Art, 1968–70. In 1971 had a solo show at Sigi Krauss Gallery, others following in 1972 at Gallery House and Serpentine Gallery. Chaimowicz went on to exhibit internationally, taking part in a number of performances. In 1977 Doubts, a sketch for video camera and audience, was presented at several venues on the continent and in London; in the same year he published *Dream*, an anecdote, through his dealer Nigel Greenwood. Arts Council holds several examples of his work, using objects such as adapted photographs, glass, gloss paint and wood, as in (For Mantelpiece) Interval No. 3, 1979.

Martyn CHALK 1945– Creator of reliefs and floor sculptures and draughtsman who lived and worked in Hull from 1967. He reconstructed reliefs by the Russian artist Tatlin which were widely shown in museum exhibitions and were held by many public and private collections. Exhibited his own work widely, including Ferens Art Gallery, Hull, having a solo show in 1992. Of those works he said: "Apparent references to objects or to direct visual experience have no more (and no less) significance in the final form of each construction than geometric and non-objective shape, or than details produced by structural necessity." Also showed solo at Juda Rowan Gallery on a number of occasions and abroad. Contemporary Art Society, Ferens Art Gallery and University of Hull hold his work.

Michael CHALK 1933– Painter who studied at Royal College of Art, winning an Abbey Major Scholarship in 1958. Showed at Gimpel Fils and in the provinces and lived in South Croydon, Surrey. Was included in The 1960's at England & Co, 1993.

Jack CHALKER fl. from late 1930s– Artist, illustrator and teacher who studied graphics and painting at London University, 1936–9, served in the Royal Artillery during World War II, was captured by Japanese at the fall of Singapore, in 1945 being attached to Australian Army Headquarters as a war artist and illustrator. Studied at Royal College of Art, 1946–9, having in 1939 had to decline a scholarship due to the war. In 1950 moved to Falmouth as principal of Falmouth School of Art, which he helped establish, also being county art adviser for Cornwall. From 1958–84 was principal of West of England College of Art in Bristol with a concurrent lectureship at local University. Exhibited widely throughout world, including Falmouth Connections at Falmouth Art Gallery, 1994, shortly after he had published a book of his Japanese prisoner of war drawings. He also illustrated children's books and medical and surgical books and in 1991 was elected fellow of the Medical Artists' Association. Solo shows were held at RWA, Cheltenham Art Gallery, Cardiff and Bridgwater Arts Centre. Lived near Wells, Somerset.

Brian CHALKLEY 1948– Painter and teacher, who studied at Chelsea School of Art, 1970–3, and Slade School of Fine Art, 1973–5. He taught at Norwich School of Art, 1975–84, in 1983–4 holding a six-month placement with British Steel Corporation as Artist in Industry on Teesside. Went on to be a part-time teacher at Chelsea School of Art, in 1989 gaining a six-month Rome Award in Painting spent at British School in Rome. Chalkley made frequent appearances at John Moores Liverpool Exhibition from 1980 and was included in Artists in Industry at Hatton Gallery, Newcastle, with tour, in 1984. Had several solo shows in northeast of England, others including Howard Gardens Gallery, Cardiff, 1985, and Lanchester Gallery, Coventry Polytechnic, 1988. Arts Council holds his work. Lived in London.

Rosemary Ann CHALKLEY 1931– Painter and designer for television, born in Hull, Yorkshire. Studied at Central School of Arts and Crafts, 1950–51, her teachers including Keith Vaughan and Victor Pasmore; Byam Shaw School of Art with Peter Greenham and Patrick Phillips, 1952–3; in 1952 with Ernest Jackson; and in 1953 with David Murray. Showed at RA and NEAC and lived in Richmond, Surrey.

Mike CHALLENGER 1942– Painter, sculptor and printmaker who studied at Goldsmiths' College School of Art and Slade School of Fine Art in the early 1960s. His highly coloured, hard-edged and forceful screenprint Red Snort, of 1971, was included in Mods and Shockers at Cheltenham Museum & Art Gallery, 1996. Lived in London.

Sarah CHALMERS 1957– Painter in oil and watercolour of landscape in Britain and abroad. She did a foundation course at Chelsea School of Art, then gained her bachelor's degree in fine art at Hornsey College of Art. Six months were spent at L'École des Beaux-Arts, Aix-en-Provence, in France. Showed at King Street Gallery, Bristol, Maas and Cadogan Galleries. After organising several one-man shows in and around London, Chalmers had a solo exhibition in 1992 at New Grafton Gallery, others including Art First, 1998.

Michael CHALWIN 1943– Artist in a variety of materials and teacher, brought up in Oxfordshire, who attended Oxford School of Art, 1959–63. After a period teaching, two years on the Isle of Skye, an education course in Oxford and more teaching, Chalwin settled in Newlyn, Cornwall, in 1978. He became a member of the Society of Artists there. His work was included in the 1989 Newlyn Orion Galleries exhibition A Century of Art in Cornwall 1889–1989. Images, icons and the topography of Cornwall were important features.

Brenda CHAMBERLAIN 1912–1971 Painter and poet, born in Bangor, where she died. First wife of the artist John Petts, with whom she founded the Caseg Press. After a visit to Copenhagen in 1930, where she was much impressed by Gauguin's early work, Chamberlain in 1931–6 studied at Royal Academy Schools, Ernest Jackson and Walter Westley Russell being among her teachers. She also studied at University College of North Wales, Bangor. Chamberlain participated in many group shows, including Heal's Mansard Gallery, 1948; The Influence of Wales in Painting, Brighton, 1957; and Eisteddfod Gold Medallists, WAC, 1967. One-man shows included Gimpel Fils on several occasions in the 1950s; Zwemmer Gallery, 1962; and a memorial exhibition at National Museum of Wales, Cardiff, 1973. Her books included *The Green Heart*, 1958; *The Water Castle*, 1963; and *The Protagonist*, a play performed in Bangor in 1970. Her work is widely held in Welsh collections, including National Museum of Wales.

Christopher CHAMBERLAIN 1918–1984 Painter, draughtsman and teacher, born in Worthing, Sussex, as George Christopher Chamberlain. He was married to the artist Heather Copley. After private education Chamberlain studied at Clapham School of Art, 1934–8, in 1935 being awarded a London County

Council three-year intermediate scholarship. In 1938 he accepted a Royal Exhibition and studied at Royal College of Art, 1938–9 and 1946–8, interrupted by war service, his final year being for postgraduate studies. Chamberlain taught at Camberwell School of Arts and Crafts and Bromley College of Art, ending as principal lecturer at Camberwell, his visiting lectureships including Sheffield, Colchester, Bournemouth and Ravensbourne. In 1984 he was selected to get a Civil List Pension. Chamberlain carried out a substantial volume of graphic work for such clients as Phoenix House, The Bodley Head, National Savings and Jonathan Cape. Commissioned works included British Rail and British Electricity Authority. He contributed to the Football Association show Football and the Fine Arts, 1953, was a regular exhibitor at RA Summer Exhibitions and had a solo show at Trafford Gallery, 1953. Asa landscape painter Chamberlain believed in knowing his location meticulously, as shown in The Dangerous Corner, owned by Tate Gallery and painted near where he lived in Chelsea.

Edmund CHAMBERLAIN 1968– Artist, born in Beverley, Yorkshire, who studied at Newcastle University, 1986–90 and in 1994 won an Elizabeth Greenshields Foundation Award. Shared a show with his brother Lewis Chamberlain at The Guillaume Gallozi Gallery, New York, in 1993, when he made his first appearance in BP Portrait Award at National Portrait Gallery. In 1996 was included in a three-man exhibition, Drawing, at Fine Art Society.

Lewis CHAMBERLAIN 1966– Artist born in Hull, Yorkshire, who studied at Slade School of Fine Art, 1984–8. In 1994 he won the Pollock-Krasner Foundation Award. Shared a show with his brother Edmund Chamberlain at The Guillaume Gallozi Gallery, New York, in 1993, having had a solo exhibition there is 1991. In 1994 took part in BP Portrait Award, National Portrait Gallery, in 1996 taking part in three-man show, Drawing, at Fine Art Society.

Trevor CHAMBERLAIN 1933– Painter, born in Hertford, who was self-taught. Apart from National Service in the Army, 1953–5, until 1964 Chamberlain worked as an architectural assistant, then painted full-time. He liked to paint his pictures of the sea, townscapes and landscapes in one session on the spot, which gave them great spontaneity. Chamberlain was elected a member of NS in 1968, RSMA in 1970 and ROI in 1972, also being a member of Chelsea Art Society and Wapping Group of Artists. Among awards won were Lord Mayor of London's Art Award, 1976; James Bourlet Prize at ROI, 1980; Chris Beetles Watercolour Award at RWS Open, 1987; and Llewellyn Alexander Award at ROI, 1991. Solo shows included Ash Barn Gallery, Petersfield, 1971–83, and Oliver Swann Galleries, 1989. Guildhall Art Gallery and National Maritime Museum, Greenwich, hold his work. Lived in Hertford, Hertfordshire.

Eddie CHAMBERS 1960– Artist in collage, born in Wolverhampton, who attended Lanchester Polytechnic, Coventry, 1980, and Sunderland Polytechnic, 1983. While still doing his foundation course he became noted for his work Destruction of the National Front. With other artists, notably Keith Piper, he established The Pan-Afrikan Connection. A show was held at Wolverhampton Art Gallery in 1981, Chambers claiming that the black artist's work should be "a tool to assist us in our struggle for liberation." Exhibited widely in London and the provinces and participated in The Other Story, Hayward Gallery and touring, 1989–90. Arts Council and Sheffield City Art Galleries hold his work. He was based in Bristol, Avon.

Stephen CHAMBERS 1960– Painter and printmaker, born in Montevideo, Uruguay, who studied at Winchester School of Art, 1978–9; St Martin's School of Art, 1979–82; and gained his master's degree at Chelsea School of Art, 1982–3. Gained a Rome Scholarship, 1983–4; in 1985 was artist-in-residence at Portsmouth Polytechnic; was painting fellow at Winchester School of Art, 1986–7; in 1987 won Greater London Arts Association and Oppenheim-John Downes Trust Award; with a Mark Rothko Memorial Trust Travelling Award in 1989; and an Elephant Trust Award, 1995. Books included *Long Pig* and *Four Heads*, both published by Imprints. Chambers took part in numerous group shows, including Warwick Arts Trust, 1983; Nigel Greenwood Gallery, 1988; Artists' Books at Eagle Gallery, 1993; and The Hare, City Gallery, Leicester, 1996. Had a solo show, Strange Smoke, Winchester Gallery, 1987, then a series at Flowers East from 1989. Arts Council, Manchester University, Victoria & Albert Museum and Metropolitan Museum of Art, New York, hold examples.

Barbara CHAMIER 1885– Miniaturist and painter in oil, born in Faizabad, Uttar Pradesh, India. She studied at King's College Art School; in London her teachers included Rex Vicat Cole and Byam Shaw. Exhibited RMS, of which she was an associate, RA, SWA, Royal Glasgow Institute of the Fine Arts and in Paris. Lived latterly at Warsash, near Southampton.

Catherine CHAMNEY 1894– Watercolourist whose early life was spent in India and South Africa, her father being a civil servant. Studied art with L Burleigh Bruhl. Showed at RI, RCamA, Walker Art Gallery, Liverpool, SWA and elsewhere. She was a noted painter of the British landscape and is represented in Northampton Central Museum and Art Gallery. Lived in Bushey, Hertfordshire.

Walpole CHAMPNEYS 1879–1961 Painter, designer and teacher, born in Woking, Surrey. After part-education in France, he attended Teddington School of Art, and, after marriage in 1907, continued studies at South Kensington School of Design, winning first-class honours in design. In 1910–11 Champneys studied anatomy at King's College Hospital and attended life classes at Bolt Court. During World War I Champneys' career as a designer gained momentum, with jobs as varied as book covers for the *Tarzan* series, posters for London Underground and war posters. His circle of friends included the artists Robert Bevan, Walter Bayes and Walter Sickert. Although Champneys was appointed to the demanding post of master of the decoration course at the Architectural Association, 1923–7, he undertook many major public commissions during the 1920s and 1930s, including murals for the British pavilion at the big international decorative arts exhibition in Paris in 1925; designs for the Savile Theatre and Savoy Hotel; a mural for the Wembley Exhibition; and he was appointed colour consultant for the Shakespeare Memorial Theatre, Stratford-upon-Avon. Champneys retired in 1939 and died in Brightlingsea in Essex. A major retrospective was held at The Minories, Colchester, 1977. In addition to his public work Champneys made tiny pictures for his own pleasure, landscapes and visionary studies which owe much to William Blake, Paul Nash and the marshland of East Anglia. Gothick Dream Fine Art promoted their cause. Victoria & Albert Museum holds Champneys' work.

John CHANCELLOR 1925–1984 Painter of sailing ships over the period 1780–1970 in oil and watercolour, marine draughtsman and writer, who was obsessed by drawing and the sea as a small boy in Portugal. After his family had returned to England, aged 11 Chancellor was granted a reprieve from school to attend Vita Art Studio, Bexhill, winning Royal Drawing Society medals. Boarded at Wycliffe College until in 1942 he signed as an apprentice officer in the merchant marine. During World War II was sunk twice by enemy action. Bought and renovated his own sailing barge; did illustrating work for nautical journals such as *Yachting Monthly*; drew a strip-cartoon, Captain Crest, for the comic *Eagle*; and illustrated Fred Cooper's *Sailing Barge Handbook*. Chancellor worked for Lapthorns, a barge and tug operator, in 1963 settling in Brixham, Devon, where he fished and then did hydrographic surveys with his own vessel, *Exact*. By the early 1970s Chancellor was turning more to painting, in 1973 having a sell-out exhibition – one of several – organised by Triton Gallery, Torquay. Chancellor's pictures could take up to six months to paint and are notable for their exact detail combined with superb sea and atmospheric effects. A few of Chancellor's pictures appeared as signed limited editions. A selection of his work, *The Maritime Paintings of John Chancellor*, was published in 1984, including accompanying text by the artist; in 1989 *John Chancellor's Classic Maritime Paintings* appeared, introduced by his widow, Rita.

Alec CHANDA 1962– Painter and teacher who studied at Camberwell School of Arts and Crafts, 1979–83. For two years he then travelled through Indonesia, Australia and India, returning in 1985 to paint in London, teaching art part-time in Richmond. He showed at the Whitechapel Open in 1985; the John Player Portrait Award at the National Portrait Gallery, 1988; at Cadogan Contemporary, with Simon Barry, in 1989; and in 1990 he won second prize, Hunting Group Art Prizes, at Mall Galleries. In 1991 he shared a show with two painters at Cadogan Contemporary.

Cynthia CHANDLER 1937– Painter and illustrator, born in Isleworth, Middlesex. She studied at Twickenham School of Art. Showed at PS, UA and in the Midlands, being a member of Rugby and District Art Society and Coventry and Warwickshire Society of Artists. Lived in Rugby, Warwickshire.

Eileen CHANDLER 1904–1993 Painter and draughtsman, born in London where she died, was married to the illustrator Roland Chandler from 1930 until he died in World War II. Studied at Hornsey School of Art, gaining a scholarship to Royal Academy Schools. She was a noted portrayer of children, and an article in *Illustrated London News* launched her on a successful career making watercolour portraits of film stars in Hollywood. Liza Minnelli the singer and actress, Sheridan Morley the writer and Bamber Gascoigne, the television personality and author, were among her subjects. Chandler became better known in America and Sweden than in Britain, her many Swedish commissions including the royal family. On her wide travels she completed effective watercolour landscapes.

Robert CHANDLER 1952– Artist, art dealer (he ran the Mowbray Gallery, Hampstead, where he settled) and picture framer, born in London. He was self-taught, having studied with Anthony Green at Highgate School, and later was notable for abstract works. Mixed shows included Andrew Usiskin Contemporary Art and 33 Mossop Street both from 1993; RA Summer Exhibition, 1993; Llewellyn Alexander Gallery and Beatrice Royal Gallery, Eastleigh, both 1994; and Contemporary Art Society, from 1995. Solo shows included Andrew Usiskin, 1992, and Courcoux & Courcoux, Salisbury, 1993.

Avinash CHANDRA 1931–1991 Painter, born in Simla, India, who studied at Delhi Polytechnic, 1947–52, and won first prize at the First National Exhibition of Art in New Delhi in 1954. Had several one-man shows there in the early 1950s before moving to London in 1956, the following year having his first British solo show at Commonwealth Institute. Won a gold medal at the Prix Européene in Ostend in 1962, three years later moving to New York. Won several fellowships in America before returning to live in London in 1971. Showed extensively in Britain, on the continent and in America, notably at Bear Lane Gallery in Oxford, 1961; Patricia Judith Gallery, Miami, 1984 and 1985; and Horizon Gallery, London, 1987. Participated in The Other Story, Hayward Gallery and touring, 1989–90. His work, influenced by that of Van Gogh and Soutine, was noted for its strongly erotic element, although the later paintings were more poetic, turning less to the human figure, rather to birds and flowers. Tate Gallery, Victoria & Albert Museum and Arts Council hold his work.

Chien-Ying CHANG 1915– Watercolourist, born in Kiangsu, China, married to the artist Cheng-Wu Fei. She graduated from National Central University, Nanking, 1931–5, then studied at Slade School of Fine Art, 1947–50, under Randolph Schwabe and William Coldstream. Was a member of RI, RWA and SWA, also showing at RA and RBA. Had a series of solo exhibitions at Leicester Galleries from 1951. Graves Art Gallery, Sheffield, and

St John's College, Oxford, hold her work, which was signed in Chinese characters. Lived for many years in north London.

Leslie Thomas CHANNING 1916– Landscape watercolourist who was by profession an architect, born in Weymouth, Dorset. He studied at Regent Street Polytechnic School of Architecture, 1934–9. During World War II he was involved in Royal Air Force camouflage, then worked as an architectural assistant to London County Council and Middlesex County Council, finally with the Church Commissioners, 1956–78. Became a member of UA, 1973, also being vice-president of Thames Valley Arts Club, a member of Richmond Art Society and associate member of NS. Showed at RI and had solo exhibitions at Fairfield Halls, Croydon, and St George's Church, Hanworth. Lived at Hampton Wick, Middlesex.

Marie F CHANT 1917– Painter in oil, gouache and watercolour, lithographer and textile designer. Born in Rugby, Warwickshire, she studied at Rugby School of Art, the Slade School of Fine Art and the Central School of Arts and Crafts. Work reproduced in a number of magazines, including *Vogue*, *House and Garden* and *Homes and Gardens*. Exhibited RBA, Walker's Galleries and the provinces. Lived at Tilehurst, Reading, Berkshire.

Bob CHAPLIN 1947– Printmaker, artist in film and photography and teacher, born in Hastings, Sussex. He studied at Ravensbourne and Brighton Colleges of Art, 1965–73. Mixed shows included Tate Gallery and Victoria & Albert Museum, which hold his work, and International Print Biennales in Cracow, Llubljana, Biella, Florence, Wakayama, Kanagawa and Fredrikstad, where he was a prizewinner. Chaplin also won prizes at 5th, 6th and 9th British Print Biennales. His solo shows included Riverside Studios, Arnolfini Gallery in Bristol and Gardner Arts Centre, Brighton, as well as abroad. Chaplin's work is represented in over 90 collections in Europe. His teaching experience included West Sussex College of Design in Horsham as well as visiting lectureships at Chelsea, Brighton, Ravensbourne and Maidstone Colleges of Art. Lived latterly in New York.

Michael CHAPLIN 1943– Printmaker and teacher, born in St Neots, Huntingdonshire, who went on to study at Watford College of Art, 1961–4, and Brighton College of Art, 1967–8, for postgraduate work. Taught at Maidstone School of Art and Kingston Polytechnic. Showed at RA Summer Exhibition and elsewhere. Lived in Maidstone, Kent.

Anthea CHAPMAN 1933– Painter and teacher, brought up in Sussex, living for a time at Herstmonceux. She was married to the painter David Chapman. Educated in Hove, she studied art at Brighton College of Art and Crafts, 1949–55, with Raymond Cowern and Charles Knight. Taught at Eastbourne School of Art, was a member of the Eastbourne Group. Her work, signed Anthea C, is in the collections of the Tel-Aviv Museum, Israel, and Stoke-on-Trent City Museum and Art Gallery.

David CHAPMAN 1933– Painter, draughtsman and teacher who was educated at Brighton Grammar School and the local College of Art, 1949–54. After teaching in a number of schools for 12 years, Chapman worked with dancers in a specialist college of physical education. He joined the faculty of art and design at Brighton Polytechnic in 1972, teaching drawing, and also worked as an external examiner, eventually becoming head of foundation at Brighton. In 1986 he had a six-month sabbatical to develop his own work which culminated with a show at Wren Gallery, Piccadilly. In addition to mixed shows in London and the provinces Chapman shared an exhibition at Brighton Polytechnic Gallery in 1988. Latterly lived in Brighton and in France.

Della CHAPMAN 1931– Etcher, christened Adella, born in Bolton, Lancashire, and married to the artist Martin Chapman. She did not study etching at Goldsmiths' College School of Art, which she attended 1949–53, as it was "very rarely done by anyone at that time"; instead, her teachers were Adrian Ryan and Kenneth Martin, painters, and the sculptor Robert Jones. Settled at Hitcham, Suffolk, where close-up study of nature was of key importance. Group shows included Greenwich Printmakers, RA Summer Exhibition, Gainsborough's House Print Workshop in Sudbury and Suffolk Craft Society. Solo exhibitions included Luton Museum, Gainsborough's House and elsewhere in East Anglia.

Dinos and Jake CHAPMAN Creators of sculptures and dioramas, the brothers worked jointly. Dinos was born in 1962 and gained his bachelor's degree at Ravensbourne College of Art, 1979–81, his master's at Royal College of Art, 1988–90. His brother gained his master's there at the same time, having obtained an honours degree at North-East London Polytechnic, 1985–8. Examples of the brothers' work were their life-size version of the castration of Spanish prisoners, using shop dummies, based on Goya's Disasters of War series of etchings, smaller versions of the etchings being made painstakingly from tiny model soldiers. Group shows included Matter & Fact, Katherine Hamnett Building, 1993; Liar, Hoxton Square, 1994; and General Release: Young British Artists, Venice Biennale, Scuola di San Pasquale, 1995. We Are Artists was a solo installation at Hales Gallery, 1992, others including Great Deeds Against the Dead, Victoria Miro Gallery, 1994, and Bring me the head of Franco Toselli!, Ridinghouse Editions, 1995. Saatchi Collection holds their work.

George CHAPMAN 1908–1993 Painter and printmaker, born London. Studied at Gravesend School of Art, Royal College of Art and Slade School of Fine Art, having worked in advertising to save money to study. Earliest influences were Walter Sickert and the Euston Road School painters. Early in World War II he visited the Rhondda Valley, Wales, which gave his work new direction, leading to a prolific period. In 1957 won the National Eisteddfod gold medal for painting. Lived in Great Bardfield, Essex, 1948–60, then moved to Aberaeron, Wales, in 1960. He was the subject of a BBC *Monitor* television programme in

1961, the Chapman script appearing in Sir Huw Wheldon's book *Monitor* in 1962. Chapman took part in many mixed shows, one-man exhibitions including Piccadilly Gallery, Zwemmer Gallery and Howard Roberts Gallery, Cardiff. His work is in a number of public collections, including Victoria & Albert Museum, Whitworth Art Gallery, Manchester, and Glynn Vivian Art Gallery, Swansea. Chapman withdrew from exhibiting for much of the 1970s, but this period of reinterpretation led to a new spate of work in the 1980s. Retrospective Aberystwyth Arts Centre 1989 and touring, another at Goldmark Gallery, Uppingham, 1992. Chapman, who in 1957 won the Gold Medal for Fine Art at Royal National Eisteddfod, described his association with the mining communities of south Wales as "a love affair". He died at Aberaeron.

Jake CHAPMAN: *see* **Dinos and Jake CHAPMAN**

John Lewis CHAPMAN 1946– Painter noted for meticulous pictures of transport and machinery subjects, sometimes in rural and period settings. He was born in Blackburn, Lancashire, and left school in 1961 to work as a layout artist for the local evening newspaper. Studied at Blackburn Art College, 1963–4, then in 1965–8 worked as a technical illustrator for a local engineering company. Chapman was a member of Blackburn Artists' Society and showed at the local public gallery as well as RA Summer Exhibition, W H Patterson, Warrington Art Gallery and elsewhere. A number of signed limited edition prints were produced of his scenes. Blackburn Art Gallery holds his work. Lived in Bolton, Lancashire.

June CHAPMAN 1939– Painter in oil, born in Ruislip, Middlesex. She studied at Camberwell School of Arts and Crafts, 1955–6, and went on to paint professionally, specialising in interiors, domestic scenes and still life. Showed at RA, ROI, RBA, UA, Edwin Pollard Gallery and Blackheath Gallery. In 1982 she was awarded the Diploma of Merit at University of Arts, Parma, Italy.

Martin CHAPMAN 1930– Artist and teacher, married to the etcher Della Chapman, who studied at Goldsmiths' College School of Art, 1946–9, then Royal College of Art, 1951–4. Chapman, who painted in oil and had an extensive knowledge of the history of art, lectured part-time at Morley College from 1969. Had work in a number of private collections including that of Gustav Delbanco, one of the partners in Roland, Browse & Delbanco. Worked in Suffolk, where he lived at Hitcham, and in Cornwall and Dorset.

Max CHAPMAN 1911– Versatile artist, critic, illustrator and poet, born and lived in London. Chapman's mother, Bertha Cregeen, and her two sisters were artists. He attended Dulwich College and Byam Shaw School, 1927–30, where he was taught and befriended by the artist Charles Ricketts, who funded a scholarship to Italy, 1934, and "the European Grand Tour". This disturbed Chapman, who felt that instead he must adjust his art to modern trends. Although Chapman was a figurative artist who later returned to figuration, much of his work was abstract. Zdzislaw Ruszkowski, John Coplans and Jackson Pollock were influences. Collage noyé was one of Chaman's innovations while experimenting with new media. He showed at RA, LG, RBA and elsewhere and had solo exhibitions at Storran, Leger, Molton and Leicester Galleries, Camden Arts Centre, New Vision Centre Gallery and in Paris and Zurich. In 1981 there was a selective retrospective at Middlesbrough Art Gallery when Oswell Blakeston also showed. They were companions for decades and collaborated on projects. Chapman was art critic for *What's On in London* for about 25 years.

Robin CHAPMAN 1944– Printmaker and photographer, born in Essex. Studied, 1961–4, at London College of Printing where he gained a first-class diploma. In the mid-1960s emigrated to America and joined big photographic studio in New York, returning to England soon after to avoid the Vietnam draft. In London opened a freelance studio specialising in still life and worked for most of top advertising agencies. Tired of commercial photography he moved to Spain and for a decade worked in film production of television commercials. Again in London, Chapman divided his time between painting and managing an art gallery. His screenprints were sold by Belgravia Contemporary Arts.

Dick CHAPPELL 1954– Painter and teacher, born in Chesterfield, Derbyshire, who studied at local College of Art, 1972, then at Goldsmiths' College School of Art, 1973–6. After working at British Museum, 1977–85, taught art at Lincoln, Portsmouth and Hereford. Regularly showed at RA Summer Exhibition from 1980s; with Islington Group, 1983–4; Hill Court Gallery, Abergavenny, 1992; Keith Chapman Gallery, 1993; and shared a show with Dewi Tudur at Martin Tinney Gallery, Cardiff, 1994.

Agnes CHARLES fl. from early 1930s– Designer and maker of stained glass windows and painter in oil. She studied at Royal Academy Schools, 1930, and Central London Polytechnic, 1952. Her business St Crispin's Glass was based at her home in Codicote, Hertfordshire. Her work can be seen in churches in Codicote, Knebworth and Houghton Regis and in Brentwood Cathedral. She exhibited at RA, Leicester, Leger and Alpine Galleries and elsewhere in London.

Eleanor CHARLESWORTH 1891– Painter, notably of flowers, who studied at the Slade School of Fine Art. Exhibited widely, especially at ROI and SWA, also at RA, RI, NEAC, RSA and Paris Salon. Lived in London.

Kristin CHARLESWORTH 1955– Painter who studied at Camberwell School of Arts and Crafts, 1973–4; Bath Academy of Art, 1974–6; and Hornsey College of Art, 1976–8. Among the mixed exhibitions she took part in were Haringey Arts Centre, 1979, gaining the award for the best overall exhibit; Foyles Gallery, 1979; RA and NEAC. In 1990 had a solo show at New Grafton Gallery.

Nicole CHARLETT 1957– Artist who studied fine art at Portsmouth Polytechnic, where she began a systematic and constructive approach to her work. From 1978, she inquired into quantitative and qualitative colour relations in paintings, drawings and prints. Charlett's work was included in The House Construction Show, 1981; in Colour Presentations, Gardner Centre Gallery, Sussex University, and tour, 1986; and Complexions, at Galerie L'Idee, Zoetermeer, Netherlands, and Dean Clough, Halifax, 1989. Arts Council holds her work. From 1979 she lived in London.

Alan CHARLTON 1948– Painter, born in Sheffield. He attended Camberwell School of Art and the Royal Academy Schools. In reaction against the traditional figurative and landscape work being taught Charlton began to create simple, grey abstracts based on rectangular shapes. Usually they have a planned location, where they take on the light and space of the space occupied, and they call for a measured response by the viewer. After 1972 Charlton showed frequently, especially on the continent. He was in The New Spirit in Painting in 1981 and Documenta 7, Kassel, 1982, and was included in the South Bank Centre's touring exhibition of 1988–9, The Presence of Painting. After 1979 he had frequent solo shows, including Amsterdam, Eindhoven, Brussels, Edinburgh and London, where Annely Juda exhibited 10 paintings in 1996. Arts Council holds his work.

Alan Bengall CHARLTON 1913– Watercolourist and draughtsman, born in North Shields, Northumberland. Studied art at the King Edward VII School of Art, Durham University, and under Percy Bradshaw at the Press Art School. Exhibited RI, Manchester City Art Gallery and at Laing Art Gallery, Newcastle. Lived at Corbridge, Northumberland.

Evan CHARLTON 1904–1984 Painter, teacher and administrator, born in London, husband of the artist Felicity Charlton and brother of George. He studied at London University, 1923–7, then at the Slade School of Fine Art, 1930–3. Began teaching in Bristol in 1935 and became head of Cardiff School of Art, 1938–45, being a war artist during World War II. From 1945–66 he was an Her Majesty's Inspector for art in Wales. Charlton took part in a number of group exhibitions, mainly in Wales, including SWG, Royal National Eisteddfod, WAC and National Library of Wales, Aberystwyth. He had a series of solo shows, including Welsh Gallery, Abergavenny, 1973. Charlton's work can have a slightly Surrealist quality, as in Promenade Restaurant, held by Glynn Vivian Art Gallery, Swansea. National Museum of Wales, Cardiff, which gave him a memorial show in 1985, also holds his work. Died at Porthkerry, South Glamorgan.

Felicity CHARLTON 1913– Painter in oil and watercolour, born in Clifton, Bristol. She studied 1932–7 West of England College of Art, Bristol, where her teachers included the painter Evan Charlton, whom she married. Her work consisted of "scenes of interiors and gardens, with imaginary figures and other details", and was widely exhibited in group shows including RWA, WAC, Royal National Eisteddfod and Howard Roberts Gallery, in Cardiff. WAC, Newport and Swansea art galleries hold her work. Had a number of shows with husband including a major retrospective at Newport Museum and Art Gallery in 1981. The gallery gave her another retrospective in 1993. Other solo shows included Andrew Knight Gallery in Cardiff, 1985; Underground Gallery, Bath, 1989; and Rooksmoor Gallery, Bath, 1991. Lived at Porthkerry, near Barry, South Glamorgan.

George CHARLTON 1899–1979 Painter and teacher, born in London. He studied at the Slade School of Fine Art from 1914, joining the staff in 1919. Taught at Willesden School of Art, 1949–59, and was an examiner in art for the University of London school examinations for many years. Was a governor of several schools of art. Showed widely in London, having first one-man show at Redfern Gallery in 1924, also showing solo at Beaux Arts Gallery. Tate Gallery has his picture Elephants and the Arts Council his watercolour of Brighton. His wife, Daphne Charlton, who survived him until 1991, was for many years a close associate of the painter Stanley Spencer. Charlton's house in Hampstead, north London, was described as "an Aladdin's cave of pictures". The artist Evan Charlton was George's brother.

Mervyn CHARLTON 1945– Painter, born in Woodford, Essex. He attended Nottingham Art College, 1974–7. Was artist-in-residence at Guildford House, Guildford, in 1983, the year he won Gulbenkian Printmaker Award. Charlton participated in many group exhibitions, including Whitechapel Art Gallery, RA, Bath Festival Show and Thumb Gallery. He had two solo exhibitions at Moira Kelly Fine Art in the early 1980s and later two with Sally Hunter Fine Art, 1985–9. Charlton used a sophisticated technique to create a fantasy world in which archetypal and everyday images coalesced. British Petroleum Ltd, Achim Moeller Ltd and Unilever Ltd own his work.

Clifford CHARMAN 1910–1993 Painter who was born and worked in Bexleyheath, Kent. He studied at Regent Street Polytechnic School of Art, 1936–9 and 1948–50. Showed at RA, NS, RBA, Chelsea Art Society, Bristol City Art Gallery, New Metropole Arts Centre in Folkestone and abroad. He was elected ROI in 1954 and won the James Bourlet Prize at the 1982 centenary exhibition. Charman was also a prizewinner in the 1977 Greater London Council Spirit of London show. City of London Guildhall holds his work.

Siegfried CHAROUX 1896–1967 Sculptor of figures and draughtsman, born in Vienna where he studied at the School of Arts and Crafts, then at the Vienna Academy of Fine Arts. Was a political cartoonist until 1933, when he began a series of monuments in Vienna. Moved to England in 1935 and was naturalised 11 years later. Charoux was interested in sculptural techniques employed in classical times, as evident in his terracotta Youth, in the Tate Gallery. Exhibited RA, LG, Royal Glasgow Institute of the Fine Arts, Piccadilly Gallery and widely in America. Elected RA in 1956. Among his public works are a memorial to the flyer

Amy Johnson in Hull and his huge group The Islanders for the South Bank Exhibition, 1951, as well as carvings for the School of Anatomy and the Engineering Laboratory at Cambridge. His figure Motor Cyclist stands outside Shell Centre, on London's South Bank. There was a retrospective at Ashgate Gallery, Farnham, 1975. Lived in London.

Lord CHARTERIS OF AMISFIELD 1913– Sculptor, educated at Eton College and Sandhurst, who served in the Army in World War II in Palestine, attaining the rank of lieutenant-colonel. Then became private secretary to HM The Queen, 1952–72; was keeper of HM Archives, 1972–7; and was a permanent Lord in Waiting from 1978. He was provost of Eton, 1978–91, was a trustee of the British Museum and chairman of the trustees of the National Heritage Memorial Fund. Was created Baron (life peer, United Kingdom), 1977. Lord Charteris' sculpture was inspired by the work of Oscar Nemon, with whom he studied and shared a studio in St James' Palace for many years. In addition to many private commissions, including a fountain in the shape of a lion's mask for the Marquess of Anglesey at Plas Newydd, north Wales, his work was included in Sixteen Sculptors at Sladmore Contemporary, 1997. Lived at Wood Stanway, Cheltenham, Gloucestershire.

Michael CHASE 1915– Painter in watercolour and designer, gallery director and lecturer, born in London. He was the son of the painter William Chase and his second wife was the artist Valerie Thornton, with whom he often showed. They formed a distinguished art collection, part of which was shown at The Minories, Colchester, in 1994. Chase attended evening classes at Hornsey, Central and Chelsea Schools of Art. After war service he became a trainee in a firm of interior decorators, then ran the Kensington Art Gallery; Zwemmer Gallery, 1954–65; and The Minories, 1966–74. His technical mentors were John Nash and Edward Bawden, and Paul Nash, Arthur Boyd and Paul Klee were a constant source of inspiration. He was "not concerned with actual places as with the visual ingredients they portray". Took part in many mixed shows, including RA Summer Exhibitions and Colchester Art Society, and won the Barcham Green Company award at open exhibition at Bankside Gallery in 1986. Solo exhibitions included a tour based on The Minories, 1981, later shows including Clare Hall, Cambridge, 1992; Printworks, Colchester, and John Russell Gallery, Ipswich, both 1994; and Chappel Galleries, Chappel, 1996. Department of the Environment, International Chemical Industries and public galleries in Bolton, Leicester and Sheffield hold his work. Lived at Woolpit Green, Bury St Edmunds, Suffolk, then near Ipswich.

Peter CHASE 1921– Printmaker, photographer and teacher who took an honours degree in fine art at school of fine art, Newcastle upon Tyne University. Later spent four years as a studio assistant at Slade School of Fine Art, then taught printmaking at Burslem School of Fine Art and Bournemouth College of Art. Pathé made a film of Chase's work, *Lithography on Stone*, 1966. He became a member of Printmakers' Council. The big city, with its heavy industry, dockland, slums and bars was Chase's subject. Exhibited widely including RA Summer Exhibition, 1984, AIA, Senefelder Club, Hiscock Gallery in Portsmouth, Lamont Gallery, Zella Nine and elsewhere. Solo exhibitions included Chiltern and Woodstock Galleries, Univision Gallery in Newcastle upon Tyne and Southampton Art Gallery. Lived in Shirley, Southampton, Hampshire.

Daniel CHASIN 1967– Painter and photographer, born in New York. He studied at King's Lynn College of Arts and Technology. His work was included in Young Painters Exhibition at Blenheim Gallery in 1989; showed photographs at East West Gallery; and had exhibits in England & Co's 1990 show Art in Boxes. Victoria & Albert Museum holds his work.

Philip CHATFIELD 1958– Sculptor in stone, born in Southsea, Hampshire. After education at Monmouth School Chatfield declined a sponsored commission in the Royal Artillery in favour of a place at Newcastle University fine art department, where learned stonemasonry and lettering under Roy Kitchin and Jonah Jones. After this Chatfield was a stonemason in Somerset and Dorset; becoming self-employed, he interspersed masonry and lettering with making sculpture in his Taunton studio. After a solo show at Swansea Arts Workshop in 1983 he became employed by Swansea City Council on its maritime development scheme. Was included in Seven Sculptors Working in Wales at Glynn Vivian Art Gallery & Museum, Swansea, in 1986.

William Henry CHATTAWAY 1927– Sculptor and draughtsman, born in Coventry, Warwickshire. After King Henry VIII School went to Art School in Coventry, 1943–5, then Slade School of Fine Art, 1945–8. Two years later he settled in Paris. He showed in inaugural ICA show in 1950 and John Moores Exhibition, Liverpool, 1956. On the occasion of the dedication of Coventry Cathedral in 1961 he took part in exhibition at Herbert Art Gallery, which holds examples of his sculptures and drawings. Chattaway also showed at Hanover and Leicester Galleries, having a solo show at that gallery in 1969. Also exhibited extensively in Paris, New York and Belgrade. Commissions executed included ones for Sir Basil Spence, the architect, Hutchinson Press and Midland Bank, overseas branch, London.

Shiavax CHAVDA 1914– Artist, born in India, who studied at Slade School of Fine Art and in Paris. He showed paintings and drawings of India at AIA Gallery in 1955. Tate Gallery archive holds his Self-Portrait, scraperboard and Indian ink.

Daniel CHATTO 1957– Painter and draughtsman who was educated at Westminster School. He started painting in his early thirties after an acting career, working on a modest scale. He did a foundation course at City and Guilds of London Art School, and he also attended New College, Oxford. Chatto travelled widely in Britain, northern Spain and the Western Himalayas. He had a show at Cadogan Contemporary in 1992.

Enid CHAUVIN 1910– Artist and teacher, born in Blackheath, southeast London, where she attended the School of Art under John Platt, also going to Goldsmiths' College School of Art. Prior to World War II she taught in Hong Kong, then held a series of appointments in the southeast of England. Exhibited RA, AIA, ROI, UA, SWA, NS, Redfern Gallery and elsewhere. Lived in Weybridge, Surrey, later in Corsica.

Malvina CHEEK 1916– Painter, studied at Wimbledon School of Art and Royal College of Art. She took part in the Pilgrim Trust *Recording Britain* project and exhibited with war artists at the National Gallery. Exhibited at RA, RBA, NEAC and elsewhere. Victoria & Albert Museum holds her work. Lived in London.

Bernard CHEESE 1925– Printmaker, watercolourist and teacher, born in Sydenham, southeast London. He was the husband of the artist Sheila Robinson, their daughter being the artist Chloë Cheese. Studied at Royal College of Art, 1947–50, where Edwin La Dell persuaded Cheese to make lithographs. Taught printmaking at St Martin's School of Art, Goldsmiths' College and Central School of Art and Design. Was elected RE in 1988. Exhibitions included Senefelder Club, Beaux Arts and St George's Galleries, Heffer Gallery in Cambridge, John Russell Gallery in Ipswich and RA. HM The Queen, Arts Council, Victoria & Albert Museum, Fry Art Gallery in Saffron Walden and several major American collections hold examples. Cheese went to live in Thaxted, Essex, in the 1950s and remained for many years in the county.

Chloë CHEESE 1952– Illustrator and printmaker, born and lived in London, daughter of artists Bernard Cheese and Sheila Robinson. She attended Cambridge School of Art, 1970–3, Royal College of Art, 1973–6, winning a drawing prize in 1972, then worked in Paris in 1974. Began drawing for *Sunday Times Colour Magazine* and also worked for *The Observer*. Her prints were sold through Curwen Gallery and Christie's Contemporary Art. Cheese's first solo exhibition was at Curwen Gallery in 1979, others taking place at Thumb Gallery; in Japan, with which she had a strong working connection; and at Coram put on a retrospective to 1973 in 1996. In 1985 a British Council touring exhibition was entitled British Illustration from Caxton to Chloë, acknowledging her contribution. Work is held by Fry Gallery, Saffron Walden, and Arts Council.

Doreen CHEESMAN 1915– Artist in oil, watercolour and chalk, wife of the painter Harold Cheesman. She studied at Plymouth School of Art and the Royal College of Art and went on to teach at Parsloe's School in Dagenham and Onslow School, Guildford, later teaching adults and children in Farnham, Surrey, where she settled. Marriage interrupted her painting, but she showed at Rye Art Gallery and with Farnham Art Society.

Harold CHEESMAN 1915–1982 Painter, mainly of landscapes, in oil, watercolour and gouache, born in Rye, Sussex. He married the artist Doreen Cheesman. After study at Hastings School of Art he attended the Royal College of Art, left in 1938. Showed at RA, NEAC, RWS, and in the provinces, having a series of exhibitions at the Ashgate Gallery, Farnham, between 1963–80. The Imperial War Museum, Towner Art Gallery in Eastbourne Melbourne City Art Gallery and other provincial galleries hold his work. Lived in Farnham, Surrey.

Henry CHEETHAM 1877– Watercolourist who was a professional commissioned soldier in the Indian Army, born in London. He studied part-time by post with Sam Spencer. Showed at Fine Art Society, at the public gallery and Little Gallery in Worthing, and with the West Sussex Art Club and Lancing Art Club, in Sussex, which he founded in 1953. Lived in Worthing, Sussex.

Edward CHELL 1958– Painter and teacher, born in Huddersfield, Yorkshire, who studied at University of Newcastle upon Tyne, 1977–81, and at Royal College of Art, 1987–9. Took part in Hunting Group Awards, 1988, winning first prize; Snapshots, Eagle Gallery, 1993; and John Moores Liverpool Exhibition, from 1995–6. Had a solo show at Dove Arts Centre, Stockton, 1985, later ones including Anthony Wilkinson Fine Art, 1995. Arts Council holds his work. Lectured at Canterbury College of Art. Lived in London.

Gang CHEN 1961– Painter, born in Nanjing, China. He attended the Art Academy there, 1983–4, after Jiangxi Art College, 1972–81. Studied at Chelsea College of Art, 1990–1. Awards included Delfina Studios Trust and BT New Contemporaries, both 1992; and Arthur Andersen Prize, 1993. Group exhibitions included Bernard Jacobson Gallery, 1992; and John Moores Liverpool Exhibition and Paton Gallery, both 1993. In that year had a solo show at 63 Union Street Gallery in London, where he lived, with another at Aspex Gallery, Portsmouth, 1994. In 1995 gained an Abbey Award in Painting at the British School at Rome.

Jonathan CHEQUERS 1954– Sculptor in stone, wood and plaster, born in Croydon, Surrey. His work was mainly abstract, related to organic forms. He studied with Open College of the Arts, on short courses and privately and showed with Sussex Sculptors and at Star Gallery, Lewes. Lived in West Hoathly, Sussex.

Peggy CHERNIAVSKY 1923– Modeller, strongly influenced by the idea of the clown and the Italian comedy tradition, born in Bristol. Studied at Camberwell School of Arts and Crafts, 1951–2, then concentrated on sculpture at Chelsea School of Art, 1957–60, with Willi Soukop and Bernard Meadows, and was at Royal College of Art, 1960. Showed RA, RMS, Whitechapel Art Gallery and elsewhere. Sometimes signed work PCC. Imperial Arts League member who lived in London.

Arthur William CHESHER 1895–1972 Primitive painter born in Bedfordshire. He remained a countryman, having worked originally on his father's farm and become enthusiastic about traction engines and steam lorries as a young man. Accidents forced him to retire in his mid-40s, so he turned to painting, rural life and old farm machinery forming the core of his subject-matter in brightly-coloured pictures. In a quarter of a century he produced about 300 of these. Showed at Arthur Jeffress Gallery, then when that closed at the Portal Gallery. Was the subject of a Ken Russell *Monitor* BBC television documentary in the mid-1960s.

Sheila CHESSER 1915– Painter, born in Cheshire, married to Dr Eustace Chesser, the noted medical practitioner and writer. A self-taught artist, she belonged to WIAC and Free Painters and Sculptors, and showed at Redfern and Leicester Galleries, Whitechapel Art Gallery, Bradford City Art Gallery and in Ireland in mixed exhibitions. Solo shows included Midland Group Gallery in Nottingham and Greenwich Theatre Gallery. Leicester University holds her work. Lived in London.

Charles Sidney CHESTON 1882–1960 Painter and etcher. Born in London, he studied at the Slade School of Fine Art, 1899–1902. Exhibited widely, including RA, RHA, Goupil Gallery, RWS, Fine Art Society and NEAC. First one-man show at Colnaghi's in 1929, the year his artist wife Evelyn Cheston died. He published a monograph *Evelyn Cheston: Member of the New English Art Club 1908–1929*, in 1931. Lived at Polstead, near Colchester, Essex.

Manuel CHETCUTI 1939– Sculptor and teacher, born in Cardiff, where he attended the College of Art, 1959–63. After a period lecturing at Newport College of Art and Chelsea College of Art he joined the staff of the department of art at Sheffield Polytechnic in 1974. Welsh Theatre Company and Llandaff Cathedral commissioned work by him, which was also shown in group shows at Camden Arts Centre, Demarco Gallery in Edinburgh and by WAC, which holds his work.

Annette CHEVALLIER 1944– Artist in mixed media and teacher, born in West Sussex. She attended West Sussex College of Art, 1961–3, and Chelsea College of Art, 1963–6. After working in London, 1966–78, she moved to the northeast of England and settled in Tynemouth, teaching part-time at Cleveland College of Art. She gained Northern Arts Awards in 1980–1, a Charlotte Press Printmaking Bursary in 1981 and a Northern Arts Purchase Award, 1982. Chevallier's work was abstract, sometimes using repeated notations. She took part in many group shows: RA and LG from 1966; Whitechapel Art Gallery from 1968; Art and the Sea, at Ceolfrith Gallery, Sunderland, 1981; Engelsk Grafikk Gallery F15, Moss, Norway, 1982; and Six Artists from the Coast, Laing Art Gallery in Newcastle and Scandinavian tour, 1983. After 1971 solo show at Richmond College, later one-man exhibitions included Camden Arts Centre, 1980, and Hatton Gallery, Newcastle, 1982. Sussex University and Northern Arts hold her work.

Charlotte CHEVERTON 1960–1991 Artist and teacher, born Charlotte Ramsden and known as Lottie. She was born in Sleningford, Yorkshire, and attended the Slade School of Fine Art, 1978–81. She married the artist Mark Cheverton and after teaching at Fettes College she in 1988 with her husband founded the Leith School of Art in Edinburgh in a building which had housed the Mission for Norwegian Seamen. Like Mark she was a committed Christian, which expressed itself in her painting. With him she was killed in a road accident at Wooler, Northumberland. Memorial show at Leith School of Art, 1992.

Mark CHEVERTON 1952–1991 Artist and teacher, born in London. He became art teacher at Marlborough College, 1974–80, then travelling secretary in art for the University and Colleges Christian Fellowship, 1980–2, then in 1982–88 was head of art at Edinburgh Academy. In 1988 with his wife, Charlotte, he founded the Leith School of Art. As a painter and printmaker Cheverton expressed his deep religious faith. He was killed with his wife in a car accident at Wooler, Northumberland. Memorial show at Leith School Art, 1992.

Hugh CHEVINS 1931– Painter, mural artist, designer and illustrator, born in Retford, Nottinghamshire. Studied at Twickenham School of Art, in Paris and at the Royal Academy Schools, winning a bronze medal in 1953. Showed UA, Piccadilly Gallery, in the provinces and at Paris Salon, where he won two silver medals in the 1950s. Did a variety of work for firms such as Imperial Chemical Industries and Shell Petroleum. Science Museum holds his work. Lived in Shepperton, Middlesex.

Maria CHEVSKA fl. from mid-1970s– Painter, draughtsman, printmaker and teacher, based in London, who attended Byam Shaw School of Art, 1970–4, including postgraduate studies. Awards included Arts Council, 1977; Greater London Arts Association, 1979–84; Gulbenkian Foundation Printmakers Award, 1982; and Austin Abbey Award, British School at Rome, 1994. Chevska became head of painting at Ruskin School of Drawing and Fine Art, Oxford. She was a prolific exhibitor, who was included in Sister Wendy Beckett's 1988 survey *Contemporary women artists*. Group shows included Art and Sea, John Hansard Gallery, Southampton, and ICA, both 1981; Whitechapel Open, from 1983; Crossover, Anderson O'Day Gallery, 1991; and White Out, Curwen Gallery, 1995. Had a solo show at Air Gallery, 1982, later ones including Weight, Andrew Mummery, 1996; and Spoken Image, Kunstmuseum Heldenheim and Museum Goch, Germany, and BWA Gallery, Wroclaw, Poland, all 1997. Arts Council, Gulbenkian Foundation, Bolton City and Oldham Art Galleries and corporate collections hold examples. Lived in London.

Albert Ranney CHEWETT 1877–1965 Artist and photographer, born in Toronto, Canada, who travelled to England with his family in the late 1890s, attending Herkomer's School at Bushey, Hertfordshire, for several years before studying at Académie Julian, Paris. After time in Canada, where hedecorated the Rotunda of the Prince George Hotel, Toronto, with scenes of pioneering life and showed at the Ontario Society of

Artists show in 1905, Chewett had a studio in Florence, Italy, then returned to Bushey, where he settled. Latterly became more interested in photography and radio than art. Showed at RA and Walker Art Gallery in Liverpool and was included in A R Chewett and Friends, mounted by Bushey Museum Trust, 1986.

Anna CHEYNE fl. from mid-1970s– Sculptor and Batik artist. She attended Kingston School of Art, then Slade School of Fine Art, studying painting and sculpture. In 1982 gave up a job as a supplier of pottery materials to concentrate on own sculpture. Showed extensively in Ireland and England from mid-1970s, including Lisnagarvey Art Society annual shows, RUA, Oireachtas in Dublin and Cork and Guinness Hop Store, Dublin. Had a solo show at Peacock Gallery, Craigavon, 1984, later exhibitions including Rooksmoor Gallery, Bath, 1988, and Cavehill Gallery, Belfast, 1991. Took part in a number of workshops, including a ceramic workshop with Eduardo Paolozzi, Dublin, 1988. Commissions included ornamental plasterwork for ceiling of Old Town Hall, Belfast, 1982, and a coat of arms for the headquarters of the Northern Ireland Fire Authority, Lisburn, 1987. She was a member of the Society of Sculptors, Ireland, and Association of Artists of Ireland. Lived in Lisburn, County Down.

Ian CHEYNE 1895–1955 Colour woodcut artist and painter, born in Broughty Ferry, Angus. After education at Glasgow Academy, Cheyne studied at Glasgow School of Art under Maurice Greiffenhagen. Originally Cheyne concentrated on painting, but increasingly his time was devoted to colour woodcuts, notably Scottish and continental landscapes. He showed at SSA, RSA, Redfern and Cooling Galleries and was treasurer for the Society of Artist-Printmakers. His work had a marked Art Deco quality. Scottish National Gallery of Modern Art holds. Lived in Bearsden, Glasgow.

Heather CHILD 1911–1997 Painter, calligrapher and writer, born in Winchester. She studied at Chelsea School of Art and gained an exhibition to Royal College of Art where the noted calligrapher Edward Johnstone taught. Among Child's books were a number dealing with Johnstone's methods; a collection of these books and manuscripts is held by Victoria & Albert Museum. Other books included *Decorative Maps*, 1956; *Heraldic Designs: A Handbook for Students*, 1965; and *The Calligrapher's Handbook*, 1985. Child showed with RMS, was a member of Art Workers' Guild and several other crafts-oriented societies. Lived in Petersfield, Hampshire, for many years with the portrait painter Dorothy Colles, who survived her.

St John CHILD fl. from 1960s– Artist in various media who studied at Hornsey College of Art and Royal College of Art, specialising in fine art. Showed at Redfern, Brook Street, Molton and Woodstock Galleries, New Art Centre, Sussex University, Brighton College and in 1993 had solo show at Hove Museum & Art Gallery. That was Windmill Paintings, completed by the artist during cycle rides through Suffolk and Sussex.

Elizabeth CHILTON 1945– Artist in oil, watercolour and bronze, born in Darlington, County Durham. She studied at Ruskin School of Drawing in Oxford where her teachers included Richard Naish and Geoffrey Rhoades. Showed at RA, NEAC, ROI and Paris Salon, work including landscapes, portraits and abstractions. Some Oxford University colleges hold her work. Lived in Toot Baldon, Oxfordshire.

Michael CHILTON 1934– Painter, draughtsman, creator of constructions in a variety of materials, and teacher, born in Leeds, Yorkshire. Chilton's output embraced a wide span in the belief that "a person has many facets, and you would be extremely dull if you only ever saw the world in one way". However, a selection of elements from nature was a key feature of his output, drawing on the landscape. He studied at Leeds College of Art, 1952–6, under Harry Thubron, gained a travel scholarship to Spain in 1956, from 1956–9 studied painting and lithography at Slade School of Fine Art, in 1959 gaining an Abbey Minor Travel Scholarship. Chilton joined Leicester College of Art, 1960–4, being a visiting lecturer at Nottingham and Coventry Colleges of Art in 1963–4, then was a senior lecturer at Hull College of Art, 1965–73. During the 1960s he showed at Grabowski Gallery and in other mixed exhibitions. Had a solo show at Ferens Art Gallery, Hull, and at Suzanne Fischer Gallery, Baden-Baden, 1975. Later solo exhibitions included a major retrospective at Usher Gallery, Lincoln, 1991, and work from 1960–92 at Ferens in 1992. Lived in Hull.

Vasant Narayan CHINCHWADKAR: *see* **VASANT**

James CHINNECK 1973– Artist whose work included his four glass and metal Suitcases, 1996, shown in New Contemporaries that year at Tate Gallery, Liverpool, and Camden Arts Centre. Chinneck was born in Hertford, Hertfordshire, and gained a fine art degree at Leeds Metropolitan University, 1993–6. Other exhibitions included the MISC Group Show at the University's gallery, 1995, and before that Diverse 13, Granary Wharf, Leeds, 1994.

James CHISHOLM 1917– Painter who was born in Edinburgh, where he continued to live. Studied at Edinburgh College of Art under Francis M'Cracken and at Edinburgh and Glasgow Universities. Showed at RSA and other Scottish galleries. The Reverend Chisholm was for a time director of arts and crafts for the Church of Scotland, later lecturing at Edinburgh University.

Derek CHITTOCK 1922–1986 Painter, notably of portraits, whose work contained a strong element of Socialist Realism, art critic and historian, who studied at the Slade School of Fine Art, 1942–7, under Randolph Schwabe, and at the Royal Academy Schools under Philip Connard. Exhibited at RA, RP, RBA and NEAC. At the end of World War II Chittock did portrait work for the War Artists' Advisory Committee. In the early 1950s he was one of the artists recruited from the AIA to form a selection committee for the Artists for Peace Exhibitions. Chittock was a paid-up member of the British Communist Party until the Hungarian uprising in 1956 prompted his resignation, and he also was art critic of the *Daily Worker*. He completed covers for the magazine *John Bull*, ranging from the Test Match to London buses, and sometimes used the name James Dudley. His daughter was the actress Emily Morgan, his brother the film critic John Chittock. Lived in Hertford, London and the Sevenoaks area of Kent.

Tim CHITTY 1956– Artist who studied at Burslem School of Art. He drew on Victorian and Edwardian images to inspire boxes, collages and mechanical creations. Among his appearances was Art in Boxes at England & Co, 1991, where his Untitled mixed media assemblage was shown.

Herbert William CHOAT 1912– Painter and commercial artist, born in Southsea, Hampshire. After initial education in Portsmouth he studied at the School of Art there, 1928–33. Showed at RA, elsewhere in London and in the provinces. Lived for many years at South Ruislip, Middlesex.

Adam CHODZKO 1965– Artist using various materials, born and lived in London. He gained his bachelor's degree at University of Manchester, 1985–8, and master's at Goldsmiths' College, 1992–4. Group exhibitions included Malania Basarab Gallery, 1992; Making People Disappear, Cubitt Street Gallery, and Mandy Loves Declan 100%, at Mark Boote Gallery, New York, both 1993; Galleri Nicolai Wallner, Copenhagen, 1994; and Brilliant! New Art from London at Walker Arts Center, Minneapolis, and tour, and Venice Biennale, both 1995. Had a solo show at Bipasha Ghosh, 1992. Arts Council holds his work.

Henri CHOPIN 1922– Poet, painter, graphic artist and designer, typographer, publisher film-maker, broadcaster and advocate of the international avant-grade, born in Paris, France. Chopin was subjected to forced labour in Germany during World War II from 1943, serving in the French Army in Vietnam, 1948–9. From 1955, Chopin was acquainted with the poet and champion of Surrealism André Breton, writer on art Michel Seuphor and the Lettristes. During the late 1950s and 1960s his activities included radio work in France, Sweden and Czechoslovakia; shows with Jiri Kolar, John Furnival and others; and his classic audio-visual magazines *Cinquième Saison* and *Ou*, each issue containing recordings and texts. Chopin continued publishing *Ou*, his activities as a concrete and sound poet, international performances and recordings while exiled in England, at Ingatestone, Essex, from 1968 into the 1980s. Returned to Paris, 1985. Exhibitions of his work included Queensland College of Art Gallery, Australia, 1992, and Norwich Gallery, Norwich School of Art and Design, 1998.

Adrian CHORLEY 1906– Painter, draughtsman and printmaker, especially of landscapes, born in East Bergholt in Suffolk, Constable country. After attending St Paul's School Chorley went to Byam Shaw School of Drawing and Painting, 1924–7, and Royal College of Art. Showed RA, ROI, RBA, NEAC and elsewhere. Lived in Edenbridge, Kent.

Graham CHORLTON 1953– Painter and teacher, born in Leicester. After studying at University of Leeds, 1972–6, he was at Birmingham Polytechnic, 1977–8. He taught there and elsewhere in the West Midlands and was commissioned by Birmingham City Council. Chorlton's group shows included Facade: The City's Face, at Ikon Gallery, Birmingham, with tour, 1987–8; Unfinished Business, Lanchester Gallery, Coventry Polytechnic, 1990; and the 1991–2 John Moores Exhibition, Liverpool. The urban landscape and experience were features of his work, as in the John Moores picture Apartment. Showed solo at Wolverhampton Art Gallery, 1983, and Midlands Arts Centre, 1989. Lived in Stirchley, Birmingham.

Eleanor CHRISTIE 1929– Sculptor, especially in ciment fondu, and teacher, wife of the artist Fyffe Christie, with whom she showed at Woodlands Art Gallery, 1979. She studied at Glasgow School of Art and Camberwell School of Arts and Crafts. Taught sculpture at Marylebone Institute. Full-length figurative works were a strong feature of Christie's output. Lived in London.

Fyffe CHRISTIE 1918–1979 Painter, draughtsman, muralist and teacher, born in Bushey, Hertfordshire, son of a commercial artist and illustrator, George Christie. From the age of 12 Christie lived in Glasgow, from 1934 working in a solicitor's office, then became an apprentice lithographic draughtsman and during World War II served in the Scottish Rifles, resulting work finding its way into the Imperial War Museum. Christie studied at Glasgow School of Art, 1946–50, mural painting under Walter Pritchard. He gained the Newbery Medal in 1950 and a post-diploma year's study. After a period teaching and a six-month travelling scholarship taken on the continent Christie resumed teaching and completed many murals, including Glasgow University and the Iona Community House. With his wife Eleanor, a sculptor, he moved to London in 1957 and again taught, while completing murals and much other work. Christie and his wife held a show at Woodlands Gallery in 1979, shortly before he died. This showed him to be a painter with a rich palette, notable for his female nude studies, as well as a consummate draughtsman. Cyril Gerber Fine Art, Glasgow, held a show in 1988.

Stella CHRISTIE fl. from early 1990s– Artist and teacher who gained a first-class honours degree in textiles at Glasgow School of Art, 1983–7, then in 1988–9 was a master of fine art candidate on a Fulbright Scholarship at Tyler School of Art, Philadelphia, America, 1988–9. While in America she taught at Tyler; under the Hope Scott Trust Fund had a studio in New York; and travelled from there to Los Angeles. Further experience included teaching at Elmvale Centre and Easterhouse School, Glasgow, 1990; being a design consultant for the plays *Mourning*

Becomes Electra and *Man and Superman* at Citizen's Theatre, Glasgow, 1991; having a studio at British School, Rome, 1992; another six months painting in New York, 1994–5; and voluntary work in the Victoria & Albert Museum prints and drawings department, 1996. Group shows included RSA, 1992; Laing Exhibition at Mall Galleries and Atholl Gallery, Dunkeld, both 1993; and Long & Ryle Art International, 1994. Had a solo shows at Whitechapel Open Studios and Tricycle Gallery, both 1994, and in 1996 shared a three-artist exhibition at Harriet Green Gallery.

Talbot Patterson CHRISTIE 1946– Painter and draughtsman, born in Montreal, Canada. He studied at Byam Shaw School of Art, 1966–70, teachers including Maurice de Sausmarez, then Royal Academy Schools, 1970–3. Exhibitions included Heim Gallery, National Museum of Wales in Cardiff, the provinces and Paris. Lived for a time in Oxford.

John CHRISTOFOROU 1921– Powerfully gestural abstract and figurative artist using a brilliant palette, born in London to parents of Greek origin. Christoforou's mother died when he was a baby, his father in 1932, two years after he and John had moved to Athens. Before returning to England in 1938 Christoforou studied at L'École des Beaux-Arts in Athens, where Byzantine art impressed him. After serving in the Royal Air Force, 1941–6, Christoforou studied modern art by visiting the National and Tate Galleries, in 1949 having a first solo show at 20 Brook Street Gallery. During a stay in Paris, 1951–2, where he continued to visit major galleries, Christoforou destroyed all his prentice works. Returned to London, 1953, Christoforou showed with Gimpel Fils and at Victor Musgrave's gallery and made the acquaintance of writers including Maurice Collis, Colin Maclnnes and Denis Silk. He married in 1956 and decided to settle in Paris. In 1965 Christoforou received the prize of the International Association of Art Critics in London. Went on to exhibit extensively, retrospectives including Randers Kunstmuseum, Denmark, 1974; L'École Regionale des Beaux-Arts d'Angers, and tour, 1985; and Fondation d'Art Moderne en Picardie, Amiens, 1988. He took French nationality in 1990. Tate Gallery archive holds Christoforou's self-portrait.

Ann CHRISTOPHER 1947– Non-figurative sculptor in bronze, born Watford, Hertfordshire. Inspiration ranged from the cycladic pieces of ancient Greece to modern buildings such as skyscrapers, lending them a contemplative presence. She studied at Harrow School of Art, 1965–6, then West of England College of Art, Bristol, 1966–9, her teachers being Ralph Brown and Robert Clatworthy. After graduating she worked as a freelance sculptor. Among her main works was a bronze in Tower Bridge Road, London, completed in 1990, and another, Lines from Within, for Castle Park, Bristol, 1993. She was elected RWA, 1983, RA in 1989. Among Christopher's awards were first prize in the Harrison-Cowley Sculpture Competion, 1968; the Peter Stuyvesant Award, 1971; Birds Charity Award, 1973; and South-West Arts Award in 1976. Began showing in mixed exhibitions at Mignon Gallery, Bath, and RWA, 1969; RA Summer Exhibition from 1971; Marjorie Parr Gallery; LG and JPL Fine Arts, 1975; New Art Centre, 1987; and Lynne Stern Associates, 1988. Showed solo at City of Bristol Museum & Art Gallery and Mignon Gallery, 1972, later shows including New Ashgate Gallery in Farnham, 1987, and Dorset County Museum & Art Gallery, Dorchester, 1989. Bristol University, RWA, Contemporary Art Society and Glynn Vivian Art Gallery, Swansea, hold her work. Lived in Marshfield, near Chippenham, Wiltshire.

Anne CHRISTOPHERSON 1921– Painter in oil and teacher, born in Simla, India, married to artist John Christopherson. Although between 1958–67 she moved from the figurative to the abstract, her work was mainly figurative, notably maritime industrial scenes based on the Thames. Christopherson studied at Bournemouth College of Art, 1946–8, Goldsmiths' College School of Art, 1948–50, and Hornsey School of Art, 1950–1, her teachers including Leslie Ward and Kenneth Martin. From 1951–62 she taught art at Blackheath High School. Was a member of Blackheath Art Society, Hampstead Artists' Council, WIAC and Greenwich Open Studios, and in addition had a series of solo shows, starting with Siri Colvin Gallery, 1967. Later ones included Higherwater Gallery, 1990. National Maritime Museum, Greenwich, holds her work. Lived in London.

John CHRISTOPHERSON 1921–1996 Painter and artist in collage, born in Blackheath, southeast London, where he mostly lived. After a series of administrative jobs in 1959 resigned from the Civil Service to paint full-time, although he had only studied for a short period in the evenings from 1955 at Chelsea School of Art. Christopherson became attracted to the art world at the time of the 1951 Festival of Britain, when he began collecting modern paintings and sculpture. His influences were many: pictorial, literary and musical, especially the music of Debussy and Ravel. Encouraged by Jean Dubuffet, Victor Pasmore and Anthony Caro he began showing at mixed exhibitions at the Leicester, Redfern and Mercury galleries. He had a one-man exhibition at the Hyde Park Gallery in 1961, followed a string of solo shows at such galleries as ICA, Marjorie Parr and England & Co, which gave him a memorial exhibition in 1997. There were retrospectives at Woodlands Art Gallery, 1972 and 1995. Arts Council holds Christopherson's work, which range from a private-image world of abstraction to haunting, unpeopled townscapes of deceptive simplicity. Was married to the painter Anne Christopherson.

José CHRISTOPHERSON 1914– Painter and artist in mixed media, born in Manchester, who was married to the artist Richard Weisbrod. She studied in London for five years, notably with Iain Macnab at Grosvenor School of Modern Art. She exhibited in London and Manchester, then her career was interrupted by World War II forces service. Appeared in group exhibitions put on by Lucy Wertheim and was influenced by the work of Chagall and Christopher Wood; showed at Mid-Day Studios and with Manchester Group and at Great House Gallery near Bolton. Had solo shows in London, Manchester and Winnipeg in Canada. The circus and landscape were leading features of her pictures, which are held by Blackburn and Salford Art Galleries. Lived latterly in Vaud, Switzerland.

Frank Harcourt CHUBB 1894– Painter and teacher who specialised in watercolours, born in Plymouth, Devon. He was largely self-taught. Showed at RI, RBA and at Paignton Art and Crafts Society, of which he was a prominent member. Lived in Paignton, Devon.

Ralph Nicholas CHUBB 1892–1960 Imaginative watercolourist, illustrator and teacher. Born in Harpenden, Hertfordshire, he was educated at Cambridge University and the Slade School of Fine Art, where he gained the life painting prize. Went on to become art master at Bradfield College and tutor of life drawing at St Martin's School of Art. Exhibited RA, Goupil Gallery, NEAC, Alpine Gallery and in the provinces. Notable titles were The Sacrifice and The Torture of Creation. Manchester City Art Gallery holds his oil on canvas Berkshire Farm, 1926. He lived in the county near Newbury.

Brian CHUGG 1926– Artist, author and lecturer, born and lived in Braunton, Devon. He studied at Bideford School of Art, 1946–9, then Camberwell School of Arts and Crafts, 1949–50. After architectural experience, 1944–6, Chugg lectured in art at North Devon College, 1953–79. From 1980 he was a freelance author and artist. Group show appearances included RBA, Woodstock and Piccadilly Galleries. He had a retrospective in Barnstaple in 1953, showing rock paintings in 1958. Between 1964–87 Chugg was a contributor to Country Diary in *The Guardian*. His publications include *Victorian & Edwardian Devon*, 1975, and *Devon: A Thematic Study*, 1980.

Jagjit CHUHAN 1955– Painter, draughtsman and teacher, born in India, who studied at Slade School of Fine Art, 1973–7, where her teachers included William Coldstream, Lawrence Gowing and Jeffery Camp. On leaving the Slade Chuhan's work was Expressionistic; then experimented with various ways of working, including semi-abstracts based on nature, which later incorporated figures from Indian classical dance; and in mid-1990s was painting series of self-portraits. In 1992, Chuhan was granted a Fellowship in Sculpture, funded by The Henry Moore Foundation, established at Liverpool John Moores University, where she was a part-time lecturer, visiting lectureships including Royal College of Art. Mixed exhibitions included In the Looking Glass, Usher Gallery, Lincoln, and tour, from 1996. Had a solo show at Oldham Art Gallery, Oldham, 1984, later ones including Drumcroon Arts Centre, Wigan, 1992. Arts Council holds her work. Lived in Chorlton, Manchester.

Katherine CHURCH 1910– Painter, born in London, married for a time to the writer Anthony West. She attended Brighton Art School, 1928–30; Royal Academy Schools, 1930–3; then the Slade School of Fine Art, 1933–4. Took part in mixed shows including RA, NEAC, AIA, National Museum of Wales in Cardiff and Tate Gallery. Had a show at Wertheim Gallery in 1933, others including Sally Hunter & Patrick Seale Fine Art, 1984. Contemporary Art Society and National Museum of Wales, Cardiff, hold her work. Lived in Wimborne, Dorset.

John Spencer CHURCHILL 1909–1992 Painter, especially of murals, sculptor, writer and flamboyant character, the nephew of Sir Winston Churchill. He was the son of Major John Churchill, grandson of Lord Randolph Churchill. He was educated at Harrow School and Oxford University where he was a distinguished gymnast. After briefly working on the Stock Exchange he studied at Royal College of Art, Central School of Arts and Crafts, Westminster School of Art and Ruskin School of Drawing. He also receive private tuition from several artists including Bernard Meninsky and William Nicholson. His first commission was a mural for Lady Islington, followed by one to decorate the Renaissance palace in India of the Maharanee of Cooch Behar. Many others followed, for or featuring Spencer Churchill's society friends. Spencer Churchill also successfully sculpted a figure of his uncle. After a period in Spain at the time of the civil war, he opened a shop in front of his studio in Chelsea, then during World War II worked in camouflage and was claimed to have been the only artist present to make sketches of the Dunkirk evacuation. A prodigious drinker, Spencer Churchill was arrested with his wife in 1955 for being drunk and disorderly. He was accused of howling like a dog, but claimed to have been singing opera. Published his autobiography, *Crowded Canvas*, in 1961.

Martin CHURCHILL 1954– Painter, born in Glasgow. He lived in Edinburgh and studied at the College of Art, 1972–76, being awarded a postgraduate year in 1976–7 and the Adam Bruce Thomson Prize. In 1980 he won a Latimer Award and in 1981 a Guthrie Award. Churchill appeared in group exhibitions at the Stirling Gallery, the 369 Gallery in Edinburgh, and the Roseangle Art Centre in Dundee; in 1981 he participated in Scottish Gallery, Edinburgh, show Contemporary Art from Scotland. Churchill had solo exhibitions at 369 Gallery and Chenil Gallery. Hove Museum and Art Gallery holds his work.

Vernita CHURCHILL 1882– Painter, born in London. She studied art privately and at Heatherley's School of Fine Art. Showed at ROI, RI and NEAC. Lived in London.

Winston Spencer CHURCHILL 1874–1965 Statesman, politician, soldier, writer and artist. Born at Blenheim Palace, elder son of the Right Hon. Lord Randolph Churchill, he was educated at Sandhurst, thereafter serving abroad as a soldier and war correspondent. Entered parliament as a Conservative in 1900, later being successively a Liberal and a Conservative. Became a minister in 1905, over the next 35 years at various times being given a series of senior positions such as First Lord of the Admiralty and Chancellor of the Exchequer under various governments. Prime minister 1940–5 and 1951–5. Awarded Nobel Prize for Literature, 1953. Among his books are

Marlborough, *World Crisis* and *History of World War II*. Made Companion of Honour, 1922, awarded Order of Merit, 1946, and knighted, 1953. Although Churchill only painted part-time, he produced over 500 pictures. He describes in his book *Painting as a Pastime*, 1948, how he began. Exhibited at the RA from 1947 and was elected Hon. RA in 1948. The Tate Gallery and RA Diploma Gallery hold his work. Churchill had a retrospective exhibition at the RA, 1959, with an American and Commonwealth tour, and there was an exhibition at Sotheby's in 1998. Although he attempted portraits and interiors, Churchill is best known for his landscapes, of Kent where he lived and abroad. Died in London.

Colin CINA 1943– Painter and teacher, born in Glasgow. He attended the School of Art there, 1961–3, then moved to London to take up a postgraduate course at Central School of Art, 1963–6. He went on to become head of fine art at Chelsea School of Art. A Peter Stuyvesant Foundation Bursary awarded in 1966 enabled Cina to travel in America for several months, where the work of artists such as Barnett Newman and Frank Stella made a major impression. Over the following years his work was to pass through a series of phases, with influences from Surrealism and Pop Art. A notable series was the MH paintings of the 1970s where a unified surface is crossed by thin vertical and angled lines. The careful arrangement of colours and forms in a Cina picture can give it a lively surface, similar to the work of the Russian artists Kandinsky and Malevich. Cina had many one-man shows, including Serpentine Gallery, 1970 and 1980. Scottish National Gallery of Modern Art holds his work.

Ricardo CINALLI 1948– Figurative artist who employed gouache, and pastel on tissue paper layers, to create works with mythological themes, sometimes with a teasing quality. He was born in Argentina, where he obtained a degree in psychology/philosophy at the University of Rosario, 1966–72. Moved to England in 1973, studied at Harrow School of Art, 1977, and Hornsey College of Art, 1978–80. Among his public commissions were King's Observatory, Kew Gardens, 1984; Londesborough Room, Alexandra Palace, and Embassy of Argentina, both 1987; British Petroleum, Hemel Hempstead, 1989; and a frontdrop design for NationalTheatre's production of Jean Cocteau's *Les Parents Terribles*, 1994. Group exhibitions included Five Drawings, Classon House, 1981; Homage to the Square, Flaxman Gallery, 1989; and Galleria Futura, Stockholm, 1994. Had many solo shows, including Galerie de l'Université, Montreal, 1979; Museum of Modern Art, Rio de Janeiro, 1984; Jill George Gallery, 1988; James Hockey Gallery, Farnham, 1992; and Beaux Arts, 1994–5. Lived in London.

Doug CIPRIANI 1928– Artist and designer, full name Douglas Cipriani-Bond, born in London. He studied at Twickenham College of Art, 1942–6, and privately. He was a member of Free Painters and Sculptors, also showing at Victoria Art Gallery in Bath, Towner Art Gallery in Eastbourne and elsewhere. Solo exhibitions included Worthing Museum and Art Gallery and Sussex University. Lived in Hove, Sussex.

Ferdinand CIREL 1884–1968 Cirel was by profession a transport driver for Cardiff Corporation, self-taught as an artist. Around 1920 he began showing his work locally, then showed with SWG, Royal National Eisteddfod, SEA, in the English provinces and RA. WAC gave him a retrospective in 1953. It holds his work, as does the Glynn Vivian Art Gallery, in Swansea, and the National Museum of Wales, Cardiff. Cirel died in Cardiff.

CJA-STONES: *see* **Christopher John ASSHETON-STONES**

George CLAESSEN 1909– Self-taught artist, born in Colombo, Ceylon. He moved into pure abstraction about 1947. Claessen was a founder-member of the '43 Group in Ceylon, also belonging to Victorian Artists' Society in Melbourne and in London Free Painters and Sculptors, Hampstead Artists' Council and Islington Art Circle. Showed at Venice Biennale in 1956 and at its equivalent in São Paulo, Brazil, in 1959, where he won an award. Solo shows included Velasquez Gallery, Melbourne, 1947; Archer Gallery, 1949; and New Vision Centre, 1962. In 1945 War Artists' Advisory Committee bought a work by Claessen, who sometimes signed with initials only. Lived in London.

CLAIRE 1907– Painter, born in Glasgow, full name Claire Ritson. She studied at Edinburgh College of Art, at Frobisher School of Painting, with Hayward Veal and Arthur Segal. Member of WIAC; also showed RBA and ROI and with Hampstead Artists. Lived in London.

Christopher CLAIRMONTE 1932– Painter, draughtsman and teacher, producer of decorative views notable for a felicitous line, who studied at Wimbledon School of Art and the Royal College of Art, teachers including John Minton. Became a full-time lecturer at Epsom School of Art. Lived in Hove, Sussex, where the Museum and Art Gallery holds his ink and gouache The Natural History Museum, London. Had a solo exhibition with Patrick Seale Gallery, 1981, sharing one with Roy Spencer at Sally Hunter Fine Art in 1987. Terrace Gallery in Worthing and Cowfold Gallery, Cowfold, also showed Clairmonte, who later lived in Cyprus.

Helen CLAPCOTT 1952– Painter, notably of landscape, and teacher, born in Blackpool, Lancashire, who gained an honours degree in fine art from Liverpool School of Art, then did postgraduate studies at Royal Academy Schools. In Liverpool she won the David Murray Travelling Scholarship, painting in Morocco, and in 1975 had a solo show at the Liverpool Academy, which invited her to join. She won the David Murray prize three years in succession at the Academy Schools, and in her final year show the RA bought her picture Life Room. On leaving the Academy she won the Elizabeth Greenshields Foundation scholarship which enabled her to paint for a year, when she began to paint pictures of her home town, Stockport. Teaching included Northwich School of Art and Southampton College. Clapcott soon gained a flurry of solo exhibitions, in 1984 alone showing at Salford City Art Gallery, Stockport War Memorial Gallery and The Ginnel Gallery, Manchester. Mixed shows included long associations with RA Summer Exhibition and New Ashgate Gallery, Farnham.

Molly CLAPHAM: *see* **Molly FIELD**

Peter CLAPHAM 1924– Creator of constructions in various materials, space light structures, painter and draughtsman, born in London, who studied at the Architectural Association, 1947–52. Group exhibitions included AIA from 1962; Richard Demarco Gallery, Edinburgh, from 1966; Marlborough New London Gallery, Marlborough-Gerson Gallery in New York and Marlborough Graphics, all from 1967; The Jewish Museum, New York, 1969; and Galerie Contemporaine, Geneva, 1971; and Hampstead Artists' Council, 1974. Solo shows included Battelle Gallery in Geneva and Kenwood, both 1971. Arts Council holds his work.

Thomas John CLAPPERTON 1879–1962 Figure and memorial sculptor, born in Galashiels, Selkirkshire, who studied at Glasgow School of Art and Royal Academy Schools, winning a Gold Medal and travelling scholarship. He was elected a fellow of RBS and his figure of King Robert the Bruce, at gateway of Edinburgh Castle, and his Galashiels war memorial, Border Chivalry, are illustrated in *R B S: Modern British Sculpture*, published in 1939. Showed at RA, RSA and Royal Glasgow Institute of the Fine Arts. Lived in London.

John CLARE 1911–1983 Painter, draughtsman and teacher, born in Manchester. Apart from five years' World War II service in the Middle East, he lived and worked there all his life. He began painting in middle age and attended part-time classes at Manchester Regional College, Withington College of Further Education and Manchester Polytechnic. For the last seven years of his life he conducted weekend courses in life drawing and painting at North Hulme Centre, Manchester. For a time Clare was chairman of Salford Art Club, which inaugurated a John Clare Award annually when he died. A memorial show was held at City of Salford Art Gallery, 1984.

Peter CLARE 1935– Painter of pictures with Christian themes, born in London. Raised as a Quaker, he converted to Catholicism in 1958. Clare was brought up and educated in Sheffield and at Southampton University, graduating in mathematics in 1963, for many years teaching this subject in secondary schools and colleges. Clare exhibited widely from 1959, with over 20 solo shows, many in central galleries in London, Birmingham, Manchester, Portsmouth and abroad. His main cycle of pictures was The Journey, worked on from 1979, first shown at St George's Church, Bloomsbury, during Lent, 1993, then toured. It provided a platform to raise funds for projects including street children in Latin America. Clare's other themes included The Earth Mother, The Cana Cycle and The Little Flowers of St Francis. Lived in Cleobury Mortimer, Shropshire.

Stephen CLARE 1958– Painter with a special interest in the British tradition of landscape painting from Constable through to Bomberg. He was born in Walsall, Staffordshire, and studied at the School of Art there, 1975–6, then Sir John Cass College of Art, 1977–80. His exhibitions included Poole Fine Art, London and New York, 1983 (a two-man show with Michael Ayrton); 20th Century Gallery, 1984; Adam Gallery, 1985; Jablonski Gallery, 1986; and John Moores Liverpool Exhibition, 1987, where he showed Beachy Head after a Storm, one of a series, and a departure from earlier imagined landscapes. Lived in London.

Alan CLARK 1926– Watercolourist, born at Campsall, near Doncaster, Yorkshire, son of the artist Edwin Clark. He studied design at Leeds School of Art, from the early 1950s worked in the printing industry and was a founder-member of Scolar Press, which specialised in the production of facsimile publications of rare books from the Bodleian Library, in Oxford, and the British Museum. Clark began painting in 1980, as a landscape watercolourist becoming noted for his Dales pictures, reproductions of which he supervised. Showed with British Society of Painters in Ilkley and was included in Images of the Yorkshire Landscape, organised by Sheeran Lock at Leeds Civic Hall, 1991. Lived at Askwith, Wharfedale, Yorkshire.

Alan Nicholas CLARK 1939– Painter and teacher, born in Leeds where he also lived. After Worksop College Clark studied at Ruskin School of Drawing, Oxford, his teachers including Geoffrey Rhoades and Percy Horton. Among Clark's exhibiting venues was 65 Group, of which he was secretary, a public schools masters' group. He was married to the artist Sherras Clark.

Anthony CLARK 1942– Painter and teacher who studied at Sunderland College of Art, then from 1963–6 at Royal College of Art, his teachers being Carel Weight, Peter Blake and Roger de Grey. Became head of fine art at Monkwearmouth College, Sunderland. Showed in RA Summer Exhibitions, at Hyde Park and Edith Grove Galleries and in 1993 was included in People and Places at Gagliardi Gallery. Clark had over a dozen solo exhibitions and has work in collections of Universities of Durham and Surrey.

Bruce CLARK 1937– Artist in oil and multi-media and teacher, born in Bedfont, Middlesex. He studied at Bath Academy of Art, Corsham, 1958–60, teachers including Howard Hodgkin, Gwyther Irwin and William Crozier. Clark held a number of posts teaching full- and part-time in Surrey, Worcestershire and Kent, latterly part-time lecturing in adult education. He obtained his master's degree in art and design education in 1985 and was a member of the National Society for Education in Art & Design. Clark's own work was "mainly abstract, with strong landscape influence". His numerous group show appearances included France and North America. Had solo shows at Chiltern Gallery, 1961–2; Worcester City Art Gallery, 1968; University of Kent, 1985; and One Off Gallery, Dover, 1990. Surrey County Council holds his work. Lived in Bossingham, Canterbury, Kent.

Caroline McAdam CLARK: *see* **McADAM CLARK**

Cosmo CLARK 1897–1967 Painter, born in London. His father was the artist James Clark, his wife the painter Jean Clark. Studied at Goldsmiths' College School of Art, 1912–14 and 1918, Académie Julian, Paris, 1918–19, and Royal Academy Schools, 1919–21, there winning a gold medal and Travelling Scholarship. At one time directed the Rural Industries Bureau and was a trustee of the Imperial War Museum. Was elected RA, 1958. Clark, whose work is sometimes similar to that of Edward Wadsworth, exhibited at the RA, NEAC, Leicester Galleries, RI and ROI as well as on the continent and in North America. Huddersfield Art Gallery and the Graves Art Gallery, Sheffield, hold his work. Lived in London.

Edwin CLARK 1897– Landscape painter using a variety of media, born in Adwick-le-Street, near Doncaster, Yorkshire, where he eventually settled in Harrogate. He was a self-taught painter, father of the artist Alan Clark, who oversaw the printing of reproductions of Edwin's work. For many years Edwin Clark was a technical adviser to the National Coal Board. He began painting in middle age, took it up seriously on retirement in the early 1960s and continued into his nineties. His Dales water-colours were based on sketches and memory and were shown at local arts club shows, notably Otley, of which he was long a member. His work was included in Images of the Yorkshire Landscape, organised by Sheeran Lock at Leeds Civic Hall, 1991.

Jake CLARK 1966– Painter, born and lived in London, who studied at Falmouth School of Art, 1985–6, Derbyshire College, 1986–8, Brighton Polytechnic, 1989–91, and Royal College of Art, 1991–3. His awards included Mario Dubsky Travel Award and Christie's Fine Art Prize, both 1992, and Atlantis European Studio Prize, 1993. Christie's Corporate Collection holds Clark's work. Mixed exhibitions included Maze Gallery, Brighton, 1989, Royal Over-Seas League Annual Open, 1992, and John Moores Liverpool Exhibition, 1993–4. In 1994 shared a three-man exhibition at Paton Gallery, sun-filled pool scenes incorporating collage elements.

Jean CLARK 1902– Painter, born in Sidcup, Kent, who was married to the artist Cosmo Clark. She studied at Sidcup School of Art and the Royal Academy Schools. Was made a member of RWS in 1972, and she had a retrospective at Bankside Gallery in 1983; also an honorary member of NEAC, 1981. Additionally exhibited at RBA and NEAC. Completed murals for Corpus Christi Church in Weston-super-Mare and ceiling painting for Woodford Green United Free Church. Lived in London, later in Shottisham, Suffolk.

John CLARK 1943–1989 Painter and teacher, born in Yorkshire. After studying at Hull College of Art, 1961–5, gained a Fulbright Scholarship to study at Indiana University, in America. He lectured in colleges in Britain, America and Canada and from 1978–83 lived and worked in Canada, where he was co-ordinator of painting and drawing at Nova Scotia College of Art and Design. He returned to Britain in 1983, becoming head of painting at Hull College of Further Education. Clark's paintings were seen in many group shows, and he had solo shows at Ian Birksted Gallery; 49th Parallel Gallery, New York; and Wynick/Tuck Gallery, Toronto; and shared a show with David Sweet at Castlefield Gallery, Manchester. Arts Council of Northern Ireland and several important foreign collections hold his work. Died in Alberta, Canada.

John M'Kenzie CLARK 1928– Painter and draughtsman, born in Dundee, Angus, where he continued to live. He studied at the local College of Art, 1945–50, and Norwich College of Art, 1950–1, as well as Patrick Allan-Fraser School of Art, Hospitalfield, Arbroath, 1953, and St Martin's School of Art, 1955–6. Was a member of Royal Glasgow Institute of the Fine Arts and showed at RA, RSW, SSA and RSA. Dundee City holds his work.

Judy CLARK 1949– Artist in a range of media, designer, teacher and administrator, born in Portsmouth, Hampshire. She did a foundation course at Portsmouth Polytechnic fine art department, 1967–8, then gained her diploma with grade one honours (painting/sculpture), 1968–71, teachers including Jeffrey Steele, David Saunders and Noel Forster. Clark obtained her higher diploma in fine art (painting/experimental) from Slade School of Fine Art, 1971–3, taught by William Townsend and Bernard Cohen. Between 1969–71 she was assistant to Malcolm Carder during work for major galleries in Britain and abroad, and she also helped him when he worked for Theo Crosby at Pentagram on the Arts Council exhibition and book *The Environment Game*, 1972–3. Between 1973–4 Clark was a visiting and part-time lecturer at Bath Academy of Art, Hornsey, Winchester, Wolverhampton, the London College of Furniture and elsewhere, in 1974 gaining a Boise Travel Scholarship. Between 1974–80 Clark undertook a period of travel and personal study, including a trip to India with Carder. On returning, Clark resumed teaching and in 1981–2, during Pentagram's refurbishment of Unilever House, she was responsible for design of carpets and other decorative architectural details. After working 1985–9 as a freelance designer for the fashion textile industry – Clear Cut Design, Today Interiors and Sanderson were among her clients – Clark helped run the Sandra Higgins Fine Arts and Nigel Greenwood Galleries, 1989–91. She moved to West Dean College in 1991 as assistant short-course organiser, becoming head of department in 1994. Clark had had a solo show, Issues, at Garage Art, 1973. Later exhibitions included Badge Art, Angela Flowers Gallery, 1982; Whitechapel Open, Whitechapel Art Gallery, 1984; and Open Studios, Carpenters Road, 1989–90. Her initial interest was in mixed-media "issue-based" art, involving "an investigation into the nature of taboo, particularly in relation to women". Later work was "based around ideas concerning consumption". Mary Douglas' book *Purity and Danger* was important. Arts Council and Tate Gallery hold examples.

Kenneth CLARK 1922– Ceramist who studied at Slade School of Fine Art, 1945–8, then Central School of Arts and Crafts, 1949. With his wife Ann Clark he ran Kenneth Clark Pottery based at Lewes, near his home in Ringmer, Sussex. Exhibited in many group shows and had solo exhibitions at Piccadilly and Zwemmer Galleries.

Laurie CLARK 1949– Artist notable for work in pen and ink, influenced by artists such as F L Griggs and T J Cooper, and interested in dark, shadowy aspects of nature. She was educated in Cheltenham, settled in Nailsworth, Gloucestershire, and ran a contemporary art gallery. Her picture Swan Bank, Nailsworth, of 1994, was included in Mods and Shockers, at Cheltenham Art Gallery & Museum, 1996.

Michael CLARK 1918–1991 Sculptor, son of the sculptor Philip Lindsey Clark, born in Cheltenham, Gloucestershire. Studied at Chelsea School of Art, 1935–7, then at City and Guilds of London Art School, Kennington, 1947–50. Showed at RA and carried out a great deal of commissioned work, notably at Carmelite Friary at Aylesford, Kent. He gained the Otto Beit Medal for Sculpture for his statue of the Virgin of the Glorious Assumption there, illustrated in the Friars' publication *Image of Carmel*, 1974. Was president of RBS, 1971–6. Had a studio at Churt, Surrey.

Michael CLARK 1954– Artist in oil on canvas, pencil on paper and mixed media, born in Manchester. Intensive study of paintings by such artists as Rembrandt, Titian, Holbein and Chardin in the National Gallery was important to his work. Clark was noted for his realistic portraits, including the artist Francis Bacon, Sickert's model Marguerite Kelsey and Muriel Belcher, proprietor of Soho's Colony Room drinking club. This was commended in the BP Portrait Award 1992 at National Portrait Gallery and Clark contributed to the tribute to Belcher at Michael Parkin Fine Art, 1982. Mixed shows also included 75 Years of the London Group, Royal College of Art, 1988; Acquisitions 1986–1990, British Museum, 1990; and The Portrait Now, National Portrait Gallery, 1993–4. Had a solo exhibition at Birch & Conran Fine Art, 1988; Graves Art Gallery, Sheffield, 1989; City Art Gallery, York, 1990; Pallant House, Chichester, 1993; and Wounds – New Work, at Rebecca Hossack at St James', 1994. This was an intensive study of the human condition through a series of small paintings of wounded flesh. British Museum, Pallant House and Chichester Cathedral hold examples of Clark's work.

Michael CLARK 1959– Painter and designer notable for pleasing, summery watercolours, born in Ayr. After two years as a golf professional Clark went to Edinburgh College of Art where he was taught by Elizabeth Blackadder, John Houston and Robin Philipson, and specialized in illustration, graphics and photography. Worked with the BBC, 1983–9, concentrating on design and animation, then moved to London, freelancing as a visualizer for a golf magazine. Had a first solo show at Sally Hunter Fine Art in 1996, of watercolours which formed the basis of a range of greetings cards published by Woodmansterne.

Norman CLARK 1913–1992 Painter and teacher, born in Ilford, Essex. He studied at Central School of Arts and Crafts, 1929–30, with John Farleigh and Bernard Meninsky, then was at the Royal Academy Schools, 1930–5, under Tom Monnington, Ernest Jackson and Walter Russell. Among a number of awards was the gold medal for historical painting. Clark taught at Brighton College of Art and Brighton Polytechnic, 1947–77. Was elected RWS in 1960. Clark showed at RA between 1933–74, also exhibiting at Brighton Art Gallery, Sussex Watercolour Society, Worthing Art Gallery and elsewhere. Imperial War Museum and Harris Museum and Art Gallery in Preston hold watercolours by Clark, who lived in Hurstpierpoint, Sussex, and drew on idiosyncratic local characters for the subjects of many watercolours. Clark's daughter was the artist Penny Hopkins.

Peter Christian CLARK 1950– Painter and printmaker, born in Bingley, Yorkshire, son of the artist and teacher the Clark. He attended Ruskin School of Drawing in Oxford under Richard Naish. Exhibited in London, where he lived, and elsewhere.

Philip Lindsey CLARK 1889–1977 Sculptor in various materials, born in London, son of the sculptor Robert Lindsey Clark. Educated in Cheltenham, where he initially studied sculpture from 1905–10, his father being a major influence. Then studied at City and Guilds Art School, 1910–14, and Royal Academy Schools, 1919–21. Won the Distinguished Service Order during World War I. Exhibited RA, RBA, RSA and Royal Glasgow Institute of the Fine Arts. Clark completed a number of war memorials, notably the Belgian soldiers' memorial at Kensal Green, London; he was a fellow of the RBS, and his relief of St Thomas More is illustrated in the volume *RBS: Modern British Sculpture*, published in 1939. Signed work P L C. Like his son Michael he contributed to the restoration of the Carmelite Friary at Aylesford, Kent, being a Carmelite tertiary, featured in the Priory's publication *Image of Carmel*, 1974. Lived in London, finally in the West Country.

Rachel CLARK fl. from mid-1970s– Painter who gained a first-class degree in fine art at West Surrey College of Art and Design, Farnham, 1976, in that year showing in New Contemporaries at RA and with LG at Camden Arts Centre. Other shows included John Moores Liverpool Exhibition, 1978; 4 Elements at Towner Art Gallery, Eastbourne, 1991; BP Portrait Awards, National Portrait Gallery, 1993; RP, Mall Galleries, 1994; and Pacesetters at Peterborough Museum and Art Gallery, 1995. Mrs Clark lived in London.

Robert D CLARK 1951– Painter, teacher and writer, born in Blackburn, Lancashire. He studied at Leeds Polytechnic, graduating with honours in fine art. Went on to teach at Chesterfield College of Art and to write often for *The Guardian*. Solo shows included Leeds Polytechnic Gallery, 1975; Bede Gallery, Jarrow, 1982; Mappin Art Gallery, Sheffield, 1987; and Chesterfield Arts Centre, 1990. Clark's abstract work was shown in mixed exhibitions in Spain, Poland and Britain, and in 1991 he shared a three-man show at Woodlands Art Gallery. Lived in Sheffield, Yorkshire.

Sherras CLARK 1936– Painter and teacher, full name Elisabeth Sherras Clark, married to the artist Alan Nicholas Clark. She was born in Surbiton, Surrey, and after the Arts Educational Trust studied at Ruskin School of Drawing, Oxford, teachers including Richard Naish and Percy Horton, from 1961–4. As well as exhibiting did illustrative work for British Museum fossil catalogue. Lived for a time in Leeds, Yorkshire.

Thomas Humphrey CLARK 1921– Watercolourist, black-and-white artist and teacher, born in Manchester, father of the artist Peter Christian Clark. He studied at Bradford Regional College of Art, teachers including Fred Cecil Jones. Taught at St Aldate's College, Oxford, and was a member of National Society for Art Education. Exhibited in the provinces, living in Oxford, later in Beemire, Cumbria.

Anne CLARKE 1944– Artist and teacher, born in Londonderry, Northern Ireland. She graduated from the University of Ulster in Belfast, 1985. Held residency at the Tyrone Guthrie Arts Centre, Annamakerrig, 1993, having held one at Sculpture Symposium, Waterford, 1990. Lectured at the University of Ulster, at College of Technology in Londonderry and elsewhere. She was a leading member of Queen Street Studios, Belfast, and took part in Works on Paper there, 1994. Solo exhibitions included Temple Court, Belfast, 1993.

Audrey M CLARKE 1926– Artist and designer in various media, born and lived in Huncote, Leicestershire. She studied at Leicester College of Art, 1943–8, and showed at City Art Gallery and elsewhere in the provinces.

Bethia CLARKE fl. from c.1890–1958 Interior and landscape painter in various media. Born in Blackheath, she studied art in London and Paris. Exhibited widely, including RA, RBA, ROI, SWA and Ridley Art Club. Lived in London.

Brian CLARKE 1953– Prolific stained glass and set designer, using a rich palette to produce abstract and figurative works, born in Oldham, Lancashire. His childhood, the son of a miner and mill worker, was hard. From 1965 began full-time art education at Oldham School of Arts and Crafts under a junior scholarship, involved in such aspects as heraldry, gilding and pigment-making. An interest in art and architecture was inspired by trips to York Minster, Lancashire Priory and Fountains Abbey and by the mid-1960s film of Michelangelo's life *The Agony and the Ecstasy*, starring Charlton Heston. Attended Burnley School of Art, 1968; won a first-class distinction in his diploma at North Devon College of Art & Design, attended from 1970; gaining the Winston Churchill Memorial Travelling Fellowship to study art and architecture in Rome, Paris and Germany, 1974, with a second part in 1975 which covered contemporary painting in New York and Los Angeles. In 1975 Mid-Pennine Arts Association put on an exhibition of Clarke's glass works, the first of many in British and foreign galleries, later ones including Oldham and Mayor Galleries, 1993. Clarke's glass commissions were also international, including King Khaled International Airport, Riyadh, 1982; Government Building, Doha, Qatar, 1984; Cavendish Arcade, Derbyshire, 1987; Stansted Airport, 1991; EAM Building, Kassel, 1993. Was awarded honorary fellowship of RIBA, 1993. Devised sets for several Paul McCartney World Tours and for a ballet by Wayne Eagling in tribute to Rudolph Nureyev, The National Ballet, 1993. Clarke lived in London (the spectacular studio of the artist William Russell Flint) and Hastings, Sussex.

Derek CLARKE 1912– Painter and teacher. Clarke studied at Slade School of Fine Art, then from 1947–79 lectured at Edinburgh College of Art. Shortly after World War II he and his wife visited Connemara, where he completed a remarkable series of pictures featuring local people in their houses. After retirement Clarke painted portraits and landscapes and did work for churches, including a set of windows in engraved glass. He was a member of RSW and RP and had solo shows with Scottish Gallery, Edinburgh, where he lived. Scottish Arts Council, University of Edinburgh and Dunfermline Art Gallery hold his work.

Dora CLARKE fl. from c.1915– Sculptor in various materials, but notably a direct carver, born in Harrow, Middlesex. Gained a scholarship to Slade School of Fine Art, where she studied under Henry Tonks and J Havard Thomas. She was made a member of RBA, also showing at RA, NEAC, Royal Glasgow Institute of the Fine Arts and elsewhere. Was a fine figure sculptor and draughtsman with work held by Ministry of Information and Ashmolean Museum, Oxford. Lived in London for many years.

Edward CLARKE 1962– Painter who studied at Hartlepool College of Art, 1981–2, Sheffield Polytechnic, 1982–5, and Royal Academy Schools, 1985–8. He showed at RA Summer Exhibition from 1986, in the John Player Portrait Exhibition at the National Portrait Gallery in 1988, at WB Gallery in Sheffield in 1989 and in The Broad Horizon, Agnew, 1990.

Eularia CLARKE 1914–1970 Artist in oil, watercolour and pastel, born in London, mother of the artist Rachael Sherlaw-Johnson. She produced mainly landscapes and portraits until 1960, then a series of religious paintings until her death. She studied at the Ruskin School of Drawing, Oxford, under Gilbert Spencer. Group shows including Wessex Artists, Southampton Art Gallery, 1968. Participated in The Church & the Artist (the Methodist Church's collection) at venues including Walker Art Gallery in Liverpool and Manchester City Art Gallery, 1963–5.

Had numerous solo shows, later ones including Imperial College, 1968, Winchester Cathedral and Lymington Community Centre, both 1969, and Yoxford Gallery in Yoxford, 1970. As well as the Methodist Church's collection of twentieth-century Christian Art, Clarke is represented in the National Museum of Wales in Cardiff, with slides and archives in the Women's Art Library. Died in Southampton.

Geoffrey CLARKE 1924– Sculptor and artist in stained glass and mosaic, and teacher. He was born in Darley Dale, Derbyshire. Studied at Preston and Manchester Schools of Art, then served in Royal Air Force, 1943–7. Studied Royal College of Art, 1948–52. Went on to teach in Colchester and became head of the department of light transmission and projection at Royal College of Art, 1968–73. Had first solo show at Gimpel Fils, 1952, but worked substantially on commissions. Coventry, Chichester and Lincoln cathedrals all have work by Clarke, who also worked on *Time-Life* Building, 1952, and Thorn Electric Building, St Martin's Lane, 1958. Clarke completed forged and welded sculptures, acquiring knowledge on a course at British Oxygen Company. There was a touring retrospective of sculpture and graphic works organised by Ipwich Museums and Galleries, 1994–5. Tate Gallery, Arts Council and Victoria & Albert Museum hold Clarke's work. His son was the sculptor Jonathan Clarke. Lived in Hartest, Suffolk, where he cast works in his own studio. He was elected RA in 1976.

Graham CLARKE 1941– Printmaker, author and humorist who was educated at Beckenham School of Art and Royal College of Art under Edward Bawden. He went on to become one of Britain's most popular image-makers, creating hundreds of pictures of English rural life and history and of the Englishman's view of Europe. He considered himself a Man of Kent, living in the village of Boughton Monchelsea, with a strong sense of tradition and of religious, social and historical continuities. His incident-packed prints were sold in numerous galleries. Clarke's books included *Balyn and Balan* and *Vision of Wat Tyler*, which was praised by Kenneth Clark. Wildenstein held a series of exhibitions of his watercolours, starting in 1990. Examples of Clarke's output are held in royal and public collections, including Victoria & Albert Museum, Tate Gallery, New York Public Library and Hiroshima Peace Museum.

Helen CLARKE 1966– Sculptor who studied at Suffolk College and Canterbury College of Art. Her work was included in a three-man show of sculptures and drawings at High Street Exhibition Galley, Ipswich, 1992, in which an interest in the living image was the common factor. She set up a studio at Polstead, Suffolk.

Hilda Margery CLARKE 1926– Artist in oil and other media, born in Monton, Eccles, Manchester. She studied privately with L S Lowry; in Hamburg, 1946; at Southampton College of Art, 1960–8; Ruskin School, Oxford, print workshop, 1975; gaining her bachelor's degree, Southampton, 1982. The University there holds her work. Mixed exhibitions included Southampton City Art Gallery, 1963–76; Free Painters and Sculptors, 1974–6; Tib Lane Gallery, Manchester, 1978; and Chalk Farm Gallery, 1981–2. Had a solo show at Hamwic Gallery, Southampton, 1970, later ones including Hiscock Gallery, Southsea, 1977, and The First Gallery, Bitterne, which she ran, 1989. Lived in Bitterne, Southampton.

Jonathan CLARKE 1961– Sculptor, son of the sculptor Geoffrey Clarke, under whom he served an apprenticeship from 16. He went on to work mainly in sandcast aluminium from his own studio and foundry in Hartest, Suffolk. Shows included Phoenix Gallery in Lavenham; Moya Bucknall, Solihull; Galerie Am Plats Eglisau, Zürich; Coach House Gallery, Guernsey; and RA Summer Exhibition from 1989. In 1993 had a shared show at Chappel Galleries, Chappel, with a solo exhibition there, 1996.

Joseph William CLARKE 1898– Watercolour painter, industrial designer and teacher. Studied at Chester School of Art under Walter Schroder, 1915–17, then went on to teach art in Chester, where he lived and exhibited. Also exhibited RCamA and with Flintshire Artists.

Pat CLARKE fl. from late 1960s– Painter, draughtsman, printmaker and teacher who studied at Reigate Art School, 1966–9. She taught part-time in adult education and various community-based projects. Clarke moved to Cwm Prysor, North Wales, in 1981, in 1984 opening Oriel y Ddraig art gallery with her husband in Blaenau Ffestiniog, Gwynedd, where they then lived. The Welsh landscape became an important feature in Clarke's work. She was a member of NS, Free Painters and Sculptors, Printmakers' Council and Association of Artists and Designers in Wales. Took part in many group and joint shows. Had a solo show at Fairfield Halls, Croydon, in 1978, later ones among several dozen that followed including Hereford City Art Gallery, 1992. The City Museum there holds her work.

Paul Montem CLARKE 1915– Painter, lithographer and teacher, born in Nova Scotia, Canada, who studied art at Croydon School of Art under Ruskin Spear, 1935–9, then with Spear, Robert Buhler and Rodrigo Moynihan, 1946–9, at Royal College of Art where he gained a silver medal for painting. Exhibited UA, NEAC and elsewhere. Lived in East Croydon, Surrey.

Peter John CLARKE 1927– Watercolourist and printmaker who studied at Northampton School of Art, his teachers including Henry Bird. He showed at RI, UA and elsewhere and lived in Moulton, Northamptonshire.

Richard CLARKE 1955– Painter born in Newcastle upon Tyne who studied at Slade School of Fine Art, 1973–7, a Robert Ross Travelling Scholarship taking him to Rome, 1977–9. In 1989 gained a New York Foundation for the Arts Fellowship. Early in the 1980s he showed with Brooklyn Waterfront Artists in New York, later with The Rotunda Gallery and at the Metropolitan Museum of Art there. The Museum holds his work, which was notable for being oil and tempera on linen. As well as landscapes and portraits Clarke made subject pictures such as New World Order and his Fledgling Democracy, shown in his solo exhibition at Browse & Darby in 1992, which make points about the modern world. Earlier, Clarke had had one-man shows with Drian Gallery, 1980, and John Figura Gallery, Washington.

Richard Cambridge CLARKE 1909– Watercolourist, printmaker and teacher, born in Ilford, Essex, who attended Regent Street Polytechnic School of Art, 1937–8, having attended Bishop's Stortford College, 1921–6, later training as an engineering draughtsman. Between 1957–79 was self-employed as an illustrator and Workers' Educational Association lecturer. In 1981 gained an honours degree through the Open University. Took part in mixed exhibitions at RI, Piccadilly Gallery, elsewhere in London and the provinces, and had solo shows in Bishop's Stortford area every two years from late-1960s. Letchworth Museum and Art Gallery holds his work. Lived in Saffron Walden, Essex.

Robert CLARKE 1947– Abstract painter, born and lived in London, who attended Ravensbourne College of Art, 1969–73, then Chelsea School of Art, 1973–5. In 1977 he was elected a member of LG, with which he had shown from 1974. Other mixed exhibitions included RA Summer Exhibition and Wapping Artists Open Studios, both from 1979; John Moores Exhibition in Liverpool, 1980; and 16 Artists at Battersea Arts Centre, 1982. Unilever and several other corporate collections hold Clarke's work.

Roger CLARKE 1966– Artist whose work included floor-based abstract works in steel, born in Buckinghamshire. He studied sculpture at Slade School of Fine Art, 1985–9, and was Henry Moore Sculpture Fellow at Winchester School of Art, 1991, The Winchester Gallery giving him a solo exhibition in 1992. In 1987 he had had a solo exhibition of monoprints at Café Casbar. Also exhibited at Whitechapel Open; was involved in the site-specific exhibition Windfall in Hyde Park, 1988; and showed in Bremen, 1989.

Terence CLARKE 1953– Representational artist, born in Manchester, who said that he "endeavoured to make simple pictures with uncomplicated intentions". He gained his bachelor's degree in fine art at Lanchester Polytechnic's department of art and design, 1972–5; in 1975 won a David Murray Landscape Scholarship; in 1976–9 attending Royal College of Art, while there editing and producing the College magazine *1132*. Took part in Stowells Trophy, 1973; showed drawings at 5 Dryden Street, 1978; and had a series of solo exhibitions at Edward Totah Gallery.

Thomas Flowerday CLARKE fl. c.1930–1960 Painter who studied at Heatherley's School of Fine Art and Central School of Arts and Crafts. Exhibited RA, ROI, Cooling Galleries and in the provinces. Bank of England bought his work. Member Langham Sketch Club and Wapping Group of Artists. Lived at South Croydon, Surrey.

Tim CLARKE fl. from 1970s– Painter and draughtsman who studied at Stourbridge and Cheltenham Colleges of Art, then at Trent Polytechnic. He began exhibiting in 1979, taking part in many group exhibitions in the Midlands and north of England. He also had a number of solo shows, including Sue Rankin Gallery, 1990. Clarke's childhood attachment to Yorkshire led to his frequently painting in that county and the north.

Edna CLARKE HALL 1879–1979 Draughtsman, watercolourist and printmaker, born in Shipbourne, Kent. Her maiden name was Edna Waugh, under which she originally worked. She married William Clarke Hall in 1899, a barrister who was in 1932 knighted for his penal reform work. He encouraged her parents to let her study at Slade School of Fine Art, which she entered in 1894. She was a star pupil of Henry Tonks, winning a Slade Scholarship in 1897. She showed at NEAC, Friday Club and AAA, and had a solo show at Chenil Gallery in 1914. A much larger show followed at Redfern Gallery in 1924, after which she often showed there. Clarke Hall was noted for her lively draughtsmanship, notably in a series of illustrations which she did for Emily Brontë's novel *Wuthering Heights*, but they were not completed or published. She also wrote poetry. Although she was plagued by ill-health, when her husband died in 1932 she took up farming to overcome financial difficulties. There was a retrospective at Manchester City Art Gallery in 1939; New Grafton Gallery held a small hundredth birthday show in 1979, and another in 1982; and Graves Art Gallery, Sheffield, held a major show in 1985. Tate Gallery, British Museum and Victoria & Albert Museum hold her work. Lived in Upminster Common, Essex, for many years.

Jack CLARKSON 1906–1986 Sculptor in various materials, but wood carving was his favourite method of work. Also painted in oils. Born in Silsden, Yorkshire and studied at Keighley School of Art and Royal College of Art, among his teachers being Henry Moore. He was the head of the sculpture department at Sheffield College of Art, 1930–44, then was for over 20 years principal of the Newcastle, Staffordshire, School of Art. Exhibited RA, in Glasgow and Sheffield and has work in Hanley and Newcastle Art Galleries. In his retirement he devoted his time to wood carvings of birds in foliage and of the human form. Lived in Newcastle.

Pamela CLARKSON 1946– Printmaker, painter and teacher, born in Lancashire, who studied at Manchester College of Art, 1963–4; Central School of Art and Design, 1964–7; Royal College of Art, 1967–70; University of Chile, Santiago, 1973; and the Catholic University there, 1974. Awards included David Murray Landscape Scholarship, 1967; John Minton Travelling Scholarship, 1970; and President of Chile Scholarship, 1973. While in Chile, Clarkson was artist-in-residence and English teacher at the Grange School, Santiago. Teaching in England included printmaking appointments at Winchester School of Art, Ulster Polytechnic in Belfast, Loughborough College of Art and Design and Wolverhampton Polytechnic. Took part in many group shows including John Moores Liverpool Exhibition, 1976. Solo exhibitions included Penwith Galleries, St Ives, 1978, and Harris Museum and Art Gallery, Preston, 1982. Clarkson admired the work of Peter Lanyon and Roger Hilton and her output included strongly abstracted landscapes.

Shaun K CLARKSON 1961– Sculptor and creator of mixed-media assemblages who studied at West Sussex College of Art and Design and Kingston Polytechnic. His work, which had an ornate quality, was shown at Black Bull Gallery, Crucial Gallery and England & Co, where his two 1991 creations Knife and Fork were shown in Art in Boxes, 1991.

Robert CLATWORTHY 1928– Sculptor, draughtsman and teacher who also designed for theatre, born in Bridgwater, Somerset. He studied at West of England College of Art, 1944–6, Chelsea School of Art, 1949–51 and Slade School of Fine Art, 1951–4. Went on to teach at Royal College of Art and West of England College of Art. He was also governor of St Martin's School of Art and head of department at Central School of Art and Design. Had first exhibition at Hanover Gallery in 1955 with Rosemary Young, and also showed at Basil Jacobs Gallery, RA and Austin/Desmond Fine Art. Major works in London are in Finsbury Avenue and in Alton Housing Estate, Roehampton. Clatworthy's early work involved Expressionistic portrayal of bulls and horses; later he moved further towards abstraction in his human heads, which can be uncompromisingly, almost brutally powerful. Tate Gallery and Victoria & Albert Museum hold his work. Elected RA, 1973. Lived in London for many years.

Richard CLAUGHTON 1917– Sculptor in a variety of materials, and teacher, born in London. He studied at Slade School of Fine Art, 1946–9, with Randolph Schwabe, later becoming senior lecturer in sculpture there. Exhibited NEAC, RBA, LG, in the provinces and the Netherlands. His work is to be found decorating a number of British buildings as well as in Lagos Cathedral, Nigeria. He was a fellow of the RBS and lived in London.

William Lionel CLAUSE 1887–1946 Painter in oil and watercolour, born in Middleton, Lancashire, who studied at Slade School of Fine Art. He was a notable painter of rural figure subjects and landscapes whose work became freer in style later in his career. Began showing with NEAC in 1914, later becoming honorary secretary and treasurer. Also exhibited at RA, Cooling and Goupil Galleries, Fine Art Society and elsewhere and, after his death, his work was revived by Gallery Edward Harvane. Bradford's Cartwright Hall Art Gallery holds his picture Marguerite, lent to the 1986 Christie's NEAC centenary show. Lived in London.

Rupert CLAUSEN 1960– Painter, born in Copenhagen, Denmark. He studied at South Glamorgan Institute of Higher Education, 1978–9, then Birmingham Polytechnic, 1979–82. He showed in John Moores Exhibition, Liverpool, in 1989–90 and in 1991–2, his pictures depicting biomorphic forms. Clausen also showed in The Discerning Eye, at Mall Galleries, 1991. Lived in London.

A Bourne CLAVERDON: *see* **Alice Buxton WINNICOTT**

Beryl CLAY 1889– Painter, draughtsman, printmaker and teacher, born in London. Educated at Clifton High School, Bristol, where she eventually taught art. Then studied at the Grosvenor School of Modern Art, 1929–31, under Iain Macnab, and in 1936 at the Central School of Arts and Crafts. London Passenger Transport Board reproduced her work. Exhibited LG, Senefelder Club, NEAC and WIAC. Lived in London.

Monica Mary CLAY 1912– Painter, designer and teacher, born in Halifax, where she studied initially at the School of Art, 1929–35. Then studied at Leeds College of Art, her teachers including John Frederic Greenwood, and Bradford Regional College of Art under Reginald Aird, where she specialised in textile design, 1938–41. She held a number of teaching positions including Tiverton School of Art and Poole College for Further Education. Exhibited at public galleries in Leeds, Manchester, Wakefield and elsewhere. Lived in Halifax and latterly in Parkstone, Dorset.

Phillippa CLAYDEN 1955– Artist in oil, collage, inks and pastel, and teacher, born and worked in London. She created a haunting, dreamlike world in her pictures, which were populated by bizarre, memorable figures. After initial ceramic work in Italy in 1972, Clayden was at Central School of Art and Design, 1973–7, graduating with honours. Was a freelance painter and teacher, commencing several years' study of drawing with Cecil Collins, an important influence. Studied stained glass at Central School, 1979–81, doing a postgraduate diploma course at Royal Academy Schools, 1979–82, followed by more teaching. She participated in many mixed exhibitions, starting with New Contemporaries and Whitechapel Open in 1977. Had a solo show at Camden Arts Centre in 1978, with others at Boundary Gallery latterly, starting in 1991. In 1991 was nominated as one of four most promising young artists of that year.

Harold CLAYTON 1896–1979 Painter of flower pictures in the style of the Dutch Old Masters, such as The White Fluted Vase, Morning Glory, Birth of Spring and Floral Palette, and published by Venture Prints. Although Clayton's pictures commonly fetched good sums in the auctions rooms and were handled by Richard Green, W H Patterson and Frost & Reed Ltd, the artist remained a shadowy figure. Born in the city of London, Clayton studied at Hackney, Harrow, Hornsey and St Martin's Schools of Art, notably under Norman Janes the printmaker. Early in the 1930s Clayton lived in Harrow, showing several times at

RA, including a wood engraving. Also worked in Hampstead in north London and in Suffolk, then in a remote old farmhouse in Devon.

Inge CLAYTON fl. from 1970s– Artist working in oil, watercolour, collage and as a printmaker, brought up in Salzburg, Austria. Her work, centred on the human figure, was termed "sensuous, sometimes erotic", owing something to the Vienna Secessionists and Jugendstijl. Clayton came to England in the 1960s, initially working as an interior architect and jewellery designer. From 1976–84 she studied collage with Jack Yates and life drawing with John Nicholl at Camden Arts Centre, also printmaking at St Albans School of Art with Peter Jacques. As well as showing in group exhibitions at RA, in America and widely in Europe, Clayton had a number of solo shows, including Margaret Fisher Gallery, 1979; Chalk Farm Gallery, 1985; Boundary Gallery, 1988; and St Jude's, 1990. Lived in London.

Peter CLAYTON 1959– Artist and teacher, born in Wigan, Lancashire, who did a foundation course at Preston Polytechnic, 1977–8; gained an honours degree in fine art there, 1978–81, tutors Bill Sharp and Alan Powell; and in 1983–4 completed a postgraduate certificate in education at Leicester Polytechnic, and settled there. Clayton had periods as a community arts worker in Lancashire and Leicester; he co-ordinated public art events; was art tutor at Fosse Arts Centre, Sir Jonathan North Community College and Fullhurst Community College in Leicester; and carried out numerous mural commissions for restaurants, leisure centres and schools. He was artist-in-residence, Grizedale Forest, Cumbria, in 1995. Clayton said that his paintings were "concerned with conveying a sense of place and are based on sketches, photographs and memories of my local environment and places I visit... By integrating bold brushwork, rough textures, random scratches and subtle glazes, I want to create images of the landscape that combine strength and beauty with a feeling of being eroded and weather-beaten." Exhibitions included Leicester City Art Gallery Open Exhibition from 1986 (Prizewinner, 1989 and 1991); Present Prints, Royal Festival Hall, 1989; Art for Conservation, Chelsea College of Art, 1991; Wild West, Woods Gallery, Leicester, 1994. He had a solo show at Abbot Hall Art Gallery, Kendal, 1997. The Grizedale Society and Peterborough Arts Council hold examples.

John CLEAL 1929– Artist, craftsman and teacher, born in South Africa. He trained four years as a signwriter, then worked as a layout artist and illustrator. In London in the 1950s he was an illustrator for a newspaper with his own weekly column as well as being cartoonist for a Norwegian sports paper. Returning to South Africa, Cleal established a design studio for 10 years, then returned to England in 1960 where he became a partner in Henrion Design Associates. In 1962 Cleal moved to Fishguard, Wales, farmed for eight years and then set up the craft complex Workshop Wales, also an art gallery. Clwyd Exhibition Services toured a show of Cleal's work in 1985 called Leather, Wood and Stone.

James CLEAVER 1911– Painter, illustrator, printmaker and writer, educated in London. He studied at Camberwell School of Art, 1930–4, then Royal College of Art, 1934–8. His books included *The Theatre Through the Ages*, 1946; *The Theatre at Work*, 1947; and *A History of Graphic Art*, 1963. He was a member of the Authors' Club and of the Society of Industrial Artists. Showed at RA, other London galleries and in the provinces. Later solo shows included one of landscape and theatrical subjects at Arts Club, 1982, and a retrospective at Southend Central Library, 1988. In his eighties he was working on theatrical subjects, portrait heads of literary figures and writing his memoirs. Lived latterly at Westcliff-on-Sea, Essex.

Richard CLEGG 1966– Artist who employed techniques such as hologram, paint and neon and strikingly shaped canvas on panels. He was born in Blackpool, Lancashire, studying at Blackpool and Fylde College, 1985–6, Canterbury College of Art, 1986–9, and Royal College of Art, 1990–3. Group shows included On Sight at Tower Bridge Piazza, 1991, Cooling Gallery in 1992 and Robert & Susan Summer Residency Exhibition, Connecticut, America, 1994. In that year he shared a three-man show at Paton Gallery. Awards included Pemberton Travel Award and John Minton Travel Award to Barcelona, both 1991; Henry Moore Foundation Scholarship, 1992; and Susan Kasen Summer Study Award to Cologne and Summer Fellowship to America, both 1993. British Rail holds his work.

Benjamin CLEMENS fl. from c.1905–1957 Sculptor. Studied at Royal College of Art and afterwards worked as assistant to Édouard Lantéri. Exhibited RA especially, 1906–44, also RSA and Royal Glasgow Institute of the Fine Arts. Among Clemens' public sculpture was work on Africa House in London's Kingsway and a concrete lion for the government building at the 1924 Wembley British Empire Exhibition, illustrated in the volume *RBS: Modern British Sculpture*, published in 1929. Clemens was elected a fellow of the RBS. Lived in London.

Winifred CLEMENT SMITH 1904– Painter and embroiderer, born, educated and lived in Tunbridge Wells. Studied at its School of Art, also at Regent Street Polytechnic School of Art. Showed at ROI PS, RI, SWA, elsewhere in London and in the provinces. Mrs Clement Smith was a member of Tunbridge Wells Art Club.

Joy CLEMENTS 1921– Artist in wide range of media, notably pastel, born in Burwell, Suffolk, whose paternal grandmother, Alice Munnings, was a cousin of Sir Alfred Munnings. Serious application to painting began in the 1970s, and she was taught at Ulster Polytechnic by John Turner. Dreams were an important influence on "a personal kind of Expressionism ... using rich colours, particularly blues". Main works were figure paintings, still life and portraits, including two of the Duchess of Abercorn. Clements was made an associate of RUA in 1983, was president of the Ulster Society of Women Artists and vice-president and chairman of the Ulster Watercolour Society. Group shows included Eakin Gallery, Belfast, and Jonathan Swift Gallery,

Kilroot, and in 1979 she had a solo exhibition with Malone Gallery, Belfast. Ulster Television holds her work. Lived in Newtownabbey, County Antrim, Northern Ireland.

Keith CLEMENTS 1931– Painter, draughtsman, teacher and writer, born in Brighton, Sussex. He attended the local College of Art, 1947–53. After National Service he was a visiting teacher of art in Orkney, 1955–8. Following several years teaching in Sussex he did an advanced diploma in art education at Birmingham University and College of Art, 1964–5, becoming senior lecturer in art at Eastbourne College of Education, 1965–76, principal lecturer in art at East Sussex College of Higher Education, 1976–8, then senior lecturer in art history at Brighton Polytechnic, 1978–88. He wrote for *The Artist* magazine and published *Henry Lamb: the Artist and His Friends*, 1985, having completed his doctoral thesis on Lamb. Among Clements' solo shows were Orkney County Library, 1956–8, National Film Theatre, 1972, Castle Rushen in the Isle of Man, 1978, in 1988 he shared a show with David Chapman at Brighton Polytechnic Gallery, further solo exhibitions including Bloomsbury Revisited at the Bloomsbury Workshop in 1992, and New Vistas: Sussex from the Bypass, Pallant House, Chichester, 1996. Lived in Newhaven, Sussex.

Raymon CLEMENTS 1927– Painter, sculptor and teacher, born in Dudley, Worcester. Studied at Birmingham School of Arts and Crafts, teachers including Bernard Fleetwood-Walker. Taught for many years at Rowley Regis Grammar School and Rowley Regis College, also lecturing at Leamington School of Art and Birmingham College of Technology. Showed widely in the provinces, continental Europe and South America. Lived at Penn, Wolverhampton, Staffordshire.

William Charles CLEMENTS 1903–1983 Painter and tutor to adult classes, born in London. He studied under Norman Janes at Hackney Technical College, at South-West Essex Technical College, then with Andrew Gordon at Walthamstow. Showed UA, RBA and East End Academy in Whitechapel. Was president of London Sketch Club and chairman of Essex Art Club. Lived in Chingford, Essex, for many years but moved to Northampton in 1981.

Katie CLEMSON 1951– Printmaker, teacher and writer, born in Temora, New South Wales, Australia. She studied at Croydon College of Art and Central School of Art and Design. Clemson lectured extensively on printmaking, also writing several books on the subject. Was a prizewinner for relief prints at International Print Biennal at Bradford, exhibiting widely elsewhere in England, including RA, RE, Redfern Gallery, where she had a solo show in 1997, and abroad. Was based at White Gum Press, Minstead, Hampshire.

Nola CLENDINNING 1943– Painter who was educated in South Africa and moved to England in 1965. She started painting soon after, self-taught, using watercolour and gouache. Figures, animals and landscapes were copied freely from medieval drawings, bestiaries, church carvings and sketchbooks. Exhibitions included a solo show at University of Southampton Gallery.

Ian CLENTON 1969– Artist, born in Woking, Surrey, who attended Northwich College of Art and Design, 1988–90, then graduated from Goldsmiths' College in fine art and art history, 1990–3. Clenton's early works were made of found objects, to which colour was applied. Later works were on deep, square canvases, with monochrome but textured grounds, as in his solo show at The Blue Gallery, 1996.

Henry CLIFFE 1919–1983 Painter, printmaker and teacher, born in Scarborough, Yorkshire. When he was in Army in World War II met the painter William Scott in Wales, then in 1946 enrolled as student at Bath Academy of Art. He was invited to join the staff and became an influential teacher. Married colleague, Valerie May. The work of Cliffe and his students was shown in a number of international exhibitions, such as Cincinnati International Lithography Exhibitions, 1954 and 1960, and at two Venice Biennales. Cliffe had first solo show of paintings at Redfern Gallery in 1956, and three years later his first one-man print show at St George's Gallery. In 1960 Cliffe won first purchase prize at Philadelphia Print Club and in the following year gained a Ford Foundation Scholarship, Pratt Institute of Art, New York. In 1965 his book *Lithography: A Studio Handbook* appeared. Cliffe had a retrospective show of prints, 1970, at Arnolfini Gallery, Bristol, and in 1977 and 1980 one-man shows of paintings and drawings at Festival Gallery, Bath. In 1996 Phillips auctioned Works from the Studio of Henry Cliffe, revealing four decades of constant inventiveness and experiment, from figurative to abstract and finally back to figurative.

James CLIFFE 1906–1994 Painter and draughtsman, notably of accomplished portraits, born in Liverpool, where he lived at Wavertree. Cliffe was a mainly self-educated artist who attended evening classes for life drawing. He began painting scenery for theatres; did publicity for local picture houses; and worked in the display studio of a city centre store before becoming a self-employed book illustrator, then a portrait painter. For many years Cliffe was a familiar sight at Bluecoat Chambers, in his small black beret, smock and corduroy trousers, having a studio there for over 25 years. His speciality was Liverpool characters such as the sculptor Arthur Dooley; also lord mayors and mayoresses and Queen Elizabeth II. Cliffe's portrait of barrow girl Lizzie Christian is in the Maritime Museum, Liverpool. Showed at RCamA and the Liverpool Academy, where he also exhibited solo. He retired in 1986, the year after he was mugged, and gave a portrait to the Victims of Violence Group to auction for its funds.

Clare M CLIFFORD 1894–1975 Miniaturist and watercolour painter, born in Hythe, Kent. She studied under the miniaturist S Arthur Lindsay. Went on to show with RMS and Exeter Art

Society. Her early work carried the signature Clare M Ogilvie (the surname of her first husband; later she was Clare Lady Clifford of Chudleigh). Lived at Newnham, Hampshire.

John Grant CLIFFORD 1944– Painter and teacher, born in Perth, Scotland. He attended Duncan of Jordanstone College of Art in Dundee, 1962–7, then Royal College of Art, 1966–7. He gained a British Institute Award in 1973 and a Latimer Award. For a time he lectured at Duncan of Jordanstone. Among group exhibitions in which he was included were RSA Summer Exhibitions from the early 1970s, Six Dundee Painters at the local art gallery in 1974 and A Choice Selection at Fruitmarket Gallery, Edinburgh, 1975. Scottish Arts Council and Scottish Television hold his work, which included figurative, highly decorative canvases.

Robin CLIFFORD 1907– Painter, born in Gillingham, Kent. Clifford gained a master's degree at Cambridge University. He studied at Maidstone and St Martin's Schools of Art. Exhibited RA, ROI, NEAC. Clifford was a connoisseur, with a collection of pictures featuring leading modern British artists. Lived at Rochester, Kent.

John CLINCH 1934– Sculptor of large works in metal of a populist nature born in Folkestone, Kent. He studied at Kingston School of Art and at Royal College of Art sculpture school. Clinch showed widely in the UK, including RA Summer Exhibition. Merseyside Development Corporation, Thamesdown Borough Council for Swindon city centre, Milton Keynes Development Corporation and Cardiff Bay Development Area commissioned works. Arts Council holds Clinch's Mr "Fats" Waller, the jazz musician, of 1981, in fibreglass. Lived in Tregaron, Dyfed.

Gordon CLOSE 1958– Artist in various media and lecturer, trained as a sculptor, and born in Sunderland, County Durham. He attended the local College of Art, 1979–82, at that time producing often large sculptures with a heavy use of classical imagery. He had early success, pursuing public and private commissions and exhibiting at such venues as Aspex Gallery in Portsmouth, Yorkshire Sculpture Park and Wordsworth Museum in Grasmere. From the early 1990s Close concentrated on two-dimensional works (by this time his sculpture was more limited and on a smaller scale), with classical, mythological and domestic themes, their much-refined surfaces having a glowing, luminous quality, as in a shared show at Sally Hunter Fine Art, 1997. He was then a visiting lecturer in sculpture and drawing at Sunderland University, living in Northumberland.

Peter CLOSE 1959– Sculptor, born in Somerset where he settled near Long Sutton. Ernst Blensdorf, Umberto Boccioni, Bob Scrivens and Alberto Giacometti influenced Close, who was included in 1st RWA Open Sculpture Exhibition, 1993. Close's early work specialised in whale sculpture carved in local limestone, which brought commissions from Greenpeace and The Whale and Dolphin Conservation Society, which sold his work worldwide. Music and sculpture was a later preoccupation.

Val CLOSE 1949– Abstract painter and teacher, born in Sunderland. She studied at Sunderland Polytechnic and Syracuse University in America. Her awards included the Backhouse Drawing Prize, Syracuse University Scholarship and a Northern Arts Major Bursary and a Travel Award. Close was artist-in-residence with Northumbria Police, 1984–5. She taught in Britain and America, including Newcastle and Sunderland Polytechnics. Group appearances included New Contemporaries, at ICA, 1980; Spacex Gallery, Exeter, 1983; and the Newcastle Group show The Northern Lights, at DLI Museum & Arts Centre and tour, 1990. Later solo exhibitions included Laing Art Gallery, Newcastle, 1988. Contemporary Art Society holds her work. Lived in Newcastle.

Peter CLOSSICK 1948– Painter and art lecturer in adult education, born in London, where he settled. He studied at Leicester Polytechnic, 1966–9, Camberwell School of Art, 1974–8, and Goldsmiths' College School of Art, 1978–9. His group show exhibitions included LG, ROI, Whitechapel Open, RA Summer Exhibition and John Moores Exhibition, Liverpool, 1991–2. Had solo exhibitions at Sweet Waters Gallery, 1989, as well as Phoenix Gallery, 1991, and in the provinces.

Anne CLOUDSLEY 1915– Artist in a wide range of media, teacher and writer, born in Reigate, Surrey, who studied at the City Literary Institute, 1971; Byam Shaw School, 1972–6; and Goldsmiths' College, 1976–7. Teachers included John Flavin, Bill Jacklin, Euan Uglow, Bernard Dunstan, Diana Armfield and Peter Gerrard. From 1978–81, Cloudsley was founder and honorary gallery manager at the Africa Centre, from 1982–5 chairman of Westminster City Council's visual arts committee. She was a visiting lecturer at the fine art department at University of Nigeria, Nsukka, 1981, and lecturer in lithography for the Working Men's College, 1982–90. Cloudsley wrote and broadcast on remote peoples and their environments, publications including *Women of Omdurman: life, love and the cult of virginity*, 1983. The culture and life of the Sudanese and other Arab societies as well as abstract works were among her output. Group shows included Air Gallery, 1976; Berry Street Annual Open Studios, 1979–90; RA Summer Exhibition, from 1992; New Burlington Gallery, 1994; and Atrium Gallery, 1997. She completed a design for the Biological Council Medal and had work in the collection of Statoil (UK). Lived in London.

Colin CLOUGH 1903–c.1980 Painter whose correct name was Thomas Collingwood Clough. Born in Glen Conway, Denbighshire, Wales, he was the son of the painter Tom Clough. He studied at the Slade School of Fine Art under Henry Tonks in 1925–7, then at the Royal College of Art from 1928–30 under William Rothenstein. He exhibited at RA, LG and elsewhere. Went on to work widely in Wales, France and Canada. During World War II was a camouflage officer in the

Middle East. Lectured at Sir John Cass School of Art and lived in London.

Pauline Susan CLOUGH 1943– She studied at Bournville School of Art, Birmingham, and later became an heraldic embroidery designer before taking up art full-time. Favoured watercolour and pastel, although she was fond of experiment, "so variable, and for me so exciting". Showed at PS of which she was made a member in 1982, RA, RBSA and elsewhere in the provinces and abroad. She won the Daler-Rowney Award, PS, 1982 and 1985; Everyman Award, RBSA, 1986; Daler-Rowney Major Pastel Award, PS, 1987. Lived in Newick, Sussex.

Prunella CLOUGH 1919– Painter and printmaker, born in London, where she continued to work with forays into the provinces. Studied at Chelsea School of Art, 1938–9, then during World War II did various jobs, including a stint as a draughtsman. Had a first solo show at Leger Gallery, 1947, later exhibitions following at Roland, Browse and Delbanco; Leicester and Grosvenor Galleries; New Art Centre, and elsewhere. She had a retrospective at Whitechapel Art Gallery in 1960; another at Graves Art Gallery in Sheffield a dozen years later; Warwick Arts Trust, 1982; Annely Juda Fine Art, 1989; and in 1996 there was a toured show of work from 1970 which included Oriel 31, Newtown, and Camden Arts Centre. Clough's early work was concerned with industrial subjects which leaned towards abstraction, which later became the dominant mode, with a surprising range of colours and motifs. Tate Gallery and Arts Council hold examples.

Chris CLOVER 1948– Self-taught artist, born in Manchester, who left school at 15. Manchester City Art Gallery holds Clover's Your Memory is Your Bible, Your Imagination Your Future, acrylic on hardboard. Clover claimed to have developed his own form of art, Symbolic Perspective, explained in the artist's privately produced publication *Before the Parable: A Fordigraph Sketch (with poems)*, a copy of which is held by the Gallery's archive.

Harry CLOW 1940– Painter, born in London, who entered world of commercial art aged 16 and two years later become a freelance artist. He specialised in military history, sea battles from Roman times through to Vietnam and other marine work. Many of his pictures were commissioned for the walls of major shipping firms. Clow's range was wide, from yachts to commercial vessels to warships, and he also completed some aviation paintings. With the publisher and former captain Colin Squire, Clow teamed up in the early 1990s to work on what they called the Ultimate Collection, paintings of some of the world's most beautiful yachts and power boats, limited edition prints being produced. The Collection was launched at Superyacht '91 held at the Barbican, London, in 1991. Strict accuracy was a criterion.

Shelagh CLUETT 1947– Sculptor and teacher, born in Dorset. She studied at St Martin's School of Art, 1966–7, Hammersmith College of Art, 1967–8, Hornsey College of Art, 1968–71, and Chelsea School of Art, 1971–2, where she later taught. Gained the Sainsbury Award in 1972 and Greater London Arts Association Major Award in 1979. Went on to show on many group exhibitions from 1972 at Museum of Modern Art, Oxford, including New Sculpture at Ikon Gallery, Birmingham, 1979; Acme Gallery, 1980; Paris Biennale, 1982; and Kruithuis, S'-Hertogenbosch, Netherlands, 1983. Was included in 9 Artists from Wapping British tour, based at DLI Museum & Arts Centre, Durham, 1983. Showed solo at Nicola Jacobs Gallery from 1982. An abstract sculptor who was based in London.

Jan CLUTTERBUCK 1919– Artist in watercolour and pastel and teacher, born in Newton, Massachusetts, America. She studied printmaking with Michael Carlo at Harrow School of Art and with Michael Rothenstein, but was largely self-taught. Among her teaching experiences were work at Cassio College, Watford, and summer courses for Cambridge Drawing Society, as well as watercolour workshops in Sarratt, Hertfordshire, where she lived. She was chairman of WIAC, 1965–75. Also exhibited at RA Summer Exhibitions, American Embassy, Hurlingham Gallery and elsewhere. Had a solo show at Forge House Gallery, 1973. Coventry and Gloucester Education Committees hold her work. She said that her pictures were "tranquil studies of isolated places in which there is a quality of timelessness … I like wide, open spaces with solitary buildings, sheep or cows."

Alan CLUTTON-BROCK 1904–1976 Painter who was better known as art critic of *The Times* and writer of books on painting. He was educated at Eton College and Cambridge University, also studying at Westminster School of Art. Showed at RA, LG and elsewhere. His books include *Italian Painting* and *An Introduction to French Painting*. Sometimes signed work only with initials. Was for a time after World War II a National Gallery trustee and from 1955–8 Slade professor of fine art at Cambridge. Lived in Hadleigh, Suffolk, and finally at Moreton-in-Marsh, Gloucestershire.

Maggi CLYDE 1952– Painter and printmaker, born in Glasgow. She studied at Edinburgh College of Art, 1970–5, and Royal College of Art until 1979. Showed in Norway and elsewhere and had a group of etchings included in Arts Council tour Fragments Against Ruin, 1981–2. Scottish Arts Council also holds her work. Lived for a time in London.

Henry Horne CLYNE 1930– Sculptor in various materials and teacher, born in Wick, Caithness. He produced individually handmade ceramic sheep, dated, stamped and signed by the artist, under the name Sheepshapes. Studied at Edinburgh College of Art, 1948–54, then at Moray House Teachers' Training College, 1954–5. Gained a Harkness Fellowship in America in 1959–61, attending a ceramics course in Tokoname, Japan, 1986. From 1962–73 taught at art schools in Norwich and Cheltenham, being principal lecturer in sculpture at Winchester, 1973–86.

Took part in many group shows, from Sculpture Centre, New York, 1961, having solo exhibitions at Arlington Mill, Gloucestershire, 1967, and Eastleigh Museum, Hampshire, 1992. Among larger works completed was painted wooden structure titled Opening Bend, bought by Scottish Arts Council, 1966, in collection of Stirling University. Lived in King's Somborne, Hampshire.

Thora CLYNE 1937– Artist and teacher, born in Wick, Caithness. She gained her master's degree with honours in fine art at Edinburgh University and College of Art in 1960, teachers including William Gillies and Derek Clarke, then was awarded a year's postgraduate scholarship and travelling fellowship, Andrew Grant Bequest. Was principal assistant at Aberdeen Art Gallery, 1960–1, in 1963 studying printmaking at University of Colorado in America. From 1963 lectured part-time at Edinburgh College of Art. Prizes included the Anne Redpath Award, 1979, and special prize, 1984, both SSWA of which she was a member. Was also a member of SSWA and regularly exhibited at RSA, RSW and at RA. Also exhibited in group shows in France and America. Had a solo show at Torrance Gallery, Edinburgh, 1991. Parisian street scenes, wild gardens, cats and unspoilt agrarian landscapes were among key themes. Gillies Bequest at RSA holds her work. Lived at Milnathort, Kinross-shire.

William Daniel CLYNE 1922– Painter, draughtsman, illustrator and teacher, born at Stirkoke Mains, Caithness, in which county he eventually settled at Lybster. Studied at Edinburgh College of Art from 1940–2 and 1946–8, his teachers including John Maxwell and William Gillies; also at the School of Art in Hospitalfield, Arbroath, under Ian Fleming, 1949. Showed at SSA, Society of Caithness Artists, RSA, RSW and in Canada. Edinburgh College of Art holds his work.

Peter COATE 1926– Painter in oil and watercolour and teacher, born in Nailsea, Somerset. He studied at Chelsea School of Art under Ceri Richards and Robert Medley until 1950. Went on to teach in various colleges and schools; from 1972–87 ran The Mendip Painting Centre. Coate painted in Somerset, Suffolk and Wales, churches and country houses and landscape, "the wilder and rockier the better". Was a member of R WA, also showing at RA and ROI. Solo shows included MignonGallery in Bath and Mall Gallery, Clifton. Lived in Stone Allerton, Somerset.

Andrew COATES 1939– Artist working in construction, printmaking and drawing media, and teacher, born in Leeds, Yorkshire. He studied at Batley School of Art, 1959–64, under Robert Lee, and at Birmingham Polytechnic, 1975–6. His work was "based on collections of natural and man-made objects which have achieved a richness of colour and texture through exposure to the elements". After lecturing at Shenstone College, Bromsgrove, 1964–8, Coates became senior lecturer at Westhill College, Birmingham, 1969–89, from then being principal lecturer at Newman and Westhill Colleges. He was a member of the National Society for Education in Art and Design. Group appearances included Cleveland International Drawing Biennale, 1979; Midland View IV, at Herbert Art Gallery, Coventry, 1987; The Experience of Touch, at Walsall Art Gallery, 1989; and Ikon Gallery tours, 1989–90 and 1992. Had a solo show at Midlands Arts Centre, 1984, later ones including Bretton Hall, 1991. Lived in Birmingham.

Joe COATES 1948– Artist in mixed media and teacher, born in Liverpool. He attended the College of Art there, St Martin's School of Art and Reading University between 1967–75. From 1979 taught at the School of Art, Falmouth. He was a member of Newlyn Society of Artists and his work was included in the 1989 Newlyn Orion Galleries exhibition A Century of Art in Cornwall 1889–1989. Coates lived with the artist Mary Mabbutt.

Tom COATES 1941– Artist in oil, watercolour and pastel in the spontaneous, English tradition. He studied at Bournville College of Art, 1956–9, Birmingham College of Art, 1959–61, and Royal Academy Schools, 1961–4, his teachers including Peter Greenham. Won several prizes and scholarships during his studies and many after. As well as showing widely in mixed shows in London and the provinces, Coates was for a time president of the RBA and a member of RWS, RP, NEAC and PS, of which he was president. His one-man shows included a number at New Grafton Gallery. Coates carried out a series of prestigious commissions, including one for the RWS in 1990 to paint the ceremonial procession celebrating HRH The Queen Mother's ninetieth birthday. Wrote *Creating a Self-Portrait*, 1990.

Maureen Margaret COATMAN 1919– Sculptor in various materials, born in Woking, Surrey. She attended Sherborne School for Girls and gained her art tuition privately, watercolour painting with William T Wood and sculpture with Enid Fenton Smith. Went on to complete a number of publicly sited works: in churches and schools in the Home Counties. Examples are to be found in churches at Monks Risborough, Buckinghamshire, and Sonning Common, Berkshire. Sometimes signed work M M C. Lived at Askett, Buckinghamshire.

Helen COATON fl. from late 1930s– Sculptor who after Bristol University studied art at Leicester College of Art with Percy Brown, 1937–42. Exhibited Leicester Museum and Art Gallery and with Leicester Society of Artists, of which she was a member. Also a member of AIA. Lived at Chelmsford, Essex.

Alice Margaret COATS 1905–1978 Wood engraver and painter, born in Birmingham. She studied at the School of Art there, 1922–8, specialising in illustration and lettering and was attracted to the Japanese method of colour printing. Pattern-making is a strong element in her work. She also studied at Slade School of Fine Art, took lessons from the wood engraver Clifford Webb and in Paris in 1930s attended André Lhote's school. Coats showed at WIAC, Redfern Gallery, Ruskin Galleries, Central Club of Colour Woodblock Engravers of which she was a founder-member in 1927, RBSA and with Birmingham Group, of which she was honorary secretary in 1938. Her books on botanical illustration were notable: *Flowers and their Histories*, 1956; *The Quest for Plants*, 1969; and *The Book of Flowers*, 1973. Birmingham City Museum and Art Gallery holds her work. Lived in Birmingham.

David COBB 1921– Painter and draughtsman of marine scenes, born in Bromley, Kent, married to the painter Jean Main. After education at the Nautical College, Pangbourne, he studied with the Cornwall-based painter Borlase Smart. Exhibited RBA, SMA and ROI. Charles David Cobb lived in Brockenhurst, Hampshire.

John COBB 1946– Sculptor in wood, and draughtsman, born in Suffolk. He studied for a short time at Great Yarmouth College of Art, at Coventry College of Art and then the Royal College of Art. His sculptures are beautifully constructed and take several forms: some have head themes, as in the Arts Council's Head Case IV, of 1978; the chair was another theme. Among Cobb's showings was the 8th Paris Biennale, of 1973; the 1977 Silver Jubilee Exhibition in Battersea Park; in 1979–80 in Wood at the Yorkshire Sculpture Park; and he participated in the Welsh Sculpture Trust's 1983 Margam exhibition Sculpture in a Country Park. Cobb won the Walter Neurath Award for Sculpture in 1971 and the Sainsbury Award in 1974. In 1980–1 he was the resident fellow-in-sculpture at Yorkshire Sculpture Park and in 1985–8 held a Henry Moore Fellowship in Sculpture at Norwich School of Art. Later group exhibitions included 1st RWA Sculpture Exhibition, 1993, and later solo shows Anne Berthoud Gallery, 1991. Lived in Woodbridge, Suffolk.

Hilary COBBETT 1885– Painter and teacher, born in Richmond, Surrey, daughter of the artist William Cobbett. She studied at Richmond School of Art 1903–5, then again 1924–7. Exhibited RA, SWA, SMA and elsewhere. Lived in Richmond.

Anne COBHAM: *see* **Anne SAÏD**

Jason COBURN 1969– Artist, born in Manchester, whose contribution to New Contemporaries in 1996, at Tate Gallery, Liverpool, and Camden Arts Centre, included the New Contemporaries compliments slip signed with his first name. Coburn gained a degree in fine art at Middlesex University, 1991–4, then a master's in curating and commissioning contemporary art at Royal College of Art, 1994–6. Other exhibitions included Quirk, at The Chocolate Factory, 1994; Deep End, at The Tannery, 1995; and Annexed, 1 Hoxton Street, 1996.

Elizabeth COCHRANE 1966– Artist in watercolour and charcoal, and teacher, born in Manchester. She studied at the Polytechnic there, 1984–5, under Norman Adams, then in 1985–9 at Newcastle upon Tyne where she gained the John Christie Prize for Painting and Oliver Hicks Memorial Prize. Went on to run painting courses in Cortona, Tuscany, and in England. Her main works were landscape watercolours, using a rich palette. Group exhibitions included RSW Open Exhibition and Beatrice Royal Art Gallery, Eastleigh. Had a solo show at Galleria d'Arte G Severini, Cortona. Lived in Hale, Cheshire.

Helen Lavinia COCHRANE 1868–1946 Painter, born in Bath, Somerset, who studied at Liverpool School of Art, in Munich and London. From 1915–18 she directed military hospitals in France and Italy, where she painted extensively. She was a member of RI and SWA and showed at RA, Walker Art Gallery in Liverpool and RBA. Had solo exhibitions at Fine Art Society. Lived in Italy and then in London.

Rosemarie COCKAYNE fl. from 1960s– Painter and draughtsman whose work had an Expressionist colour and strength. She was born in Montreal, Canada, moving to England when young. She trained at Royal Ballet School under such dancers as Tamara Karsavina and appeared at Covent Garden, dancing leading roles in London and on the continent and became prima ballerina at Basle State Ballet. Her study of painting began at Irene Ironside's school in Kensington under her nephew Christopher Ironside; went on to study art at Kunstmuseum in Basle, influenced by the work of Emil Nolde and Edvard Munch; she later studied at St Martin's School of Art. Cockayne did stage designs for *Nutcracker*, *Coppelia* and *Jazz Ballet*, Dublin. Exhibitions included a series of solo shows at Clarges Gallery and a shared one at Primrose Hill Gallery in 1990. University College Hospital, Clydesdale Bank and Christ's Hospital Art Centre own examples. Lived in London.

Gordon COCKBURN 1944– Painter and draughtsman, born in Maybole, Ayrshire, educated at Carrick Academy. Had a first solo show at Maclauren Art Gallery in Ayr in 1977, then went on to exhibit at John Moores Exhibition in Liverpool and at Walker Art Gallery there. This was followed by a Scottish Arts Council touring exhibition. Cockburn also showed at New Solen Gallery and Shore Gallery in Edinburgh, the Dick Institute in Kilmarnock, Rozelle House in Ayr and the Royal Glasgow Institute of the Fine Arts and had a solo show of drawings made as a tribute to the French mime artist Marcel Marceau at Graeme Mundy Gallery, Glasgow.

James Mitchell COCKELL 1893– Watercolourist and photographer, born in Swindon, Wiltshire, where he continued to live. Studied by post with Percy Bradshaw's Press Art School. Showed at RI, elsewhere in London and extensively in Swindon area.

Douglas COCKER 1945– Sculptor and teacher, born in Alyth, Perthshire. He studied at Duncan of Jordanstone College of Art, Dundee, 1963–8, and won many awards, which enabled him to travel, including extensive trips through Greece, study in Italy and America. From 1972–81 he lived in Northampton, returning to Scotland to Gray's School of Art, Aberdeen, where he became a senior sculpture lecturer. Cocker was a frequent exhibitor, including Glasgow Garden Festival, New Sculpture in Scotland at Crammond Sculpture Centre and abroad. Had many solo shows, including a key one at Third Eye Centre, Glasgow, 1985. Arts Council, Scottish Arts Council and several education authorities and universities hold his work. Until the early 1970s this was mainly metal-based, but Cocker then moved towards box constructions including wood and collage elements; from 1985 larger works employing rough logs were assembled, similar to classical architecture. Comments on the current social scene were a feature of the later work. Lived in Aboyne, Aberdeenshire.

Christabel Annie COCKERELL 1863–1951 Painter of children and landscapes. She was a first cousin of Sir Sydney Cockerell, who was director of the Fizwilliam Museum, Cambridge, 1908–37; the wife of the sculptor Sir George Frampton, who like her enrolled at the Royal Academy Schools in 1882; and the mother of the painter Meredith Frampton, who painted a fine portrait of her. She exhibited at RA, New Gallery, ROI, RBA and elsewhere and lived for many years in London.

George COCKRAM 1861–1950 Landscape painter in watercolour, born at Birkenhead, Cheshire. Studied at Liverpool of Art, 1884, then in Paris, 1889. Exhibited RCamA, of which he was a member, especially; also prolifically at RI and Walker Art Gallery, Liverpool, and at RBA and RA. His work is held by public galleries in Oldham, Hull and Birkenhead and the Tate Gallery's example, Solitude – a wide stretch of sand washed by the tide under a grey sky – is typical of this single-minded watercolourist. Lived at Anglesey, North Wales.

Maurice COCKRILL 1936– Painter and teacher, born in Hartlepool, County Durham. He had a peripatetic childhood and after leaving school did a variety of jobs. In the late 1950s he studied painting at evening classes, then in 1960 was accepted by Denbigh Technical College to study painting full-time, attending University of Reading, 1963–4. Taught, including Liverpool College of Art and Liverpool Polytechnic. Took part in group shows including Neptune and Everyman Theatres in Liverpool, Bluecoat Gallery there, Liverpool Academy, Portal Gallery and RCamA. Also showed one-man in Liverpool and in the early 1980s moved to the metropolis, showing at Bernard Jacobson Gallery. Cockrill's Liverpool work was in line with that of such artists as Sam Walsh and Adrian Henri, employing Pop and Photo-Realist styles. Later, he moved towards Romantic Expressionism, as shown in his retrospective at Walker Art Gallery, Liverpool, 1995. Cockrill also published poetry in magazines such as *Ambit* and *Poetry Review*.

Bertram H COCKS 1883– Painter, draughtsman and miniaturist on ivory, born in Goring-on-Thames, Oxfordshire. He lived in Reading, Berkshire, and studied at Reading University, 1905–10, with W G Collingwood. Showed at Foyles Gallery, RMS, Mid-Day Studios in Manchester, in the Reading area and in Christchurch, New Zealand.

John Whitlock CODNER 1913– Painter and teacher, born in Beaconsfield, Buckinghamshire, son of the artist Maurice Codner, father of the painter Stephen Codner. He studied at Regent Street Polytechnic School of Art under Harry Watson, 1930–2. Taught at Sir John Cass School of Art, 1947–51. Codner showed at RWA of which he was a member from 1947, also at RA and RP. Had solo shows in London and the west of England, RWA holding his work. Until the death of his father in 1958 Codner signed pictures John Whitlock, thereafter John Codner. Lived in Stokenham, Devon.

Maurice CODNER 1888–1958 Portrait painter, educated at Stationers' Company School. He showed RP, of which he was for a time a member and honorary secretary, RA, RI, NEAC and Paris Salon, where he gained an Honourable Mention in 1938. Imperial War Museum holds his work. Arts Club member who lived in London and was the father of the painter John Codner.

Stephen Milton CODNER 1952– Painter and printmaker, born in Clevedon, Somerset, son of the artist John Codner. He studied at Camberwell School of Arts and Crafts and the City and Guilds of London Art School and showed at RA, RWA and elsewhere. Lived in London.

John CODRINGTON 1898–1991 Watercolourist who was a professional soldier, being a lieutenant-colonel in the Coldstream Guards. The watercolours he did reflected his extensive, compulsive travels as well as battle scenes ranging from the Somme, in 1916, to the Falklands War, in 1981. The enormous output of Coddy, as he was known to fellow-members of the Beefsteak Club, also embraced his love of gardens and garden design. Although he had no solo exhibition when alive, Michael Parkin Gallery staged a memorial show of watercolours 1916–90 in 1992. Lived in London.

John COFFEY 1965– Artist who employed video, born in Belfast, Northern Ireland, who obtained a degree in fine art at Wimbledon School of Art, 1993–6. Exhibitions included Bandits-Mages, Video Festival, Bourges, 1995, and New Contemporaries, at Tate Gallery in Liverpool and Camden Arts Centre, 1996.

Henry COGLE 1875– Painter, printmaker and teacher, born in Plymouth, Devon. His initial education was at the Devonport Dockyard School, after which he attended Plymouth School of Art. He went on to hold several teaching appointments, being an assistant at Belfast School of Art, then headmaster of Battersea Polytechnic. School of Art until 1936. Showed at RA, LG, Leicester and Redfern Galleries, RHA and elsewhere; had a one-man show at Plymouth Museum and Art Gallery in 1948. That gallery and British Museum hold his work. Lived in Torquay, Devon.

Alfred COHEN 1920– Painter, born in America, who studied at the Art Institute of Chicago. In 1929 was awarded a foreign travel scholarship which took him to Europe. He continued studying in Paris at L'Académie de la Grande Chaumière, showing his work in France and Germany. In 1960 Cohen settled in England and had a long series of shows with Roland, Browse & Delbanco. His interiors, still lifes and seascapes had a chunky, richly coloured style. Cohen's work is in many public collections including Contemporary Art Society, Nuffield Foundation, Pembroke College in Oxford and galleries in Rye and Hull, as well as widely abroad.

Bernard COHEN 1933– Painter of abstracts and influential teacher, born in London, where he eventually settled. Brother of the painter Harold Cohen. Studied at South-West Essex Technical College and School of Art, 1949–50, St Martin's School of Art, 1950–1, and Slade School of Fine Art, 1951–4. Awarded a French government scholarship in 1954 and a Boise Travelling Scholarship in 1956 and worked in France, Spain and Italy. Had first solo show at Midland Group Gallery, Nottingham, in 1958, in the same year showing one-man at Gimpel Fils. From the 1960s Cohen began to build up an impressive list of British and foreign exhibition appearances, showing at the Venice Biennale in 1966; having a retrospective at Hayward Gallery in 1972; followed by key appearances in Milan and Paris in the 1970s. In London he showed with Waddington Galleries. Cohen taught for periods at Ealing School of Art, Chelsea and Wimbledon and was Slade professor and chair of fine art, London University, from 1988. The Tate Gallery and other public collections hold his work which was early on influenced by Abstract Expressionism and later was very colourful and detailed, full of imagery and a variety of texture, as shown in the special 1995 Tate display.

Dave COHEN 1932– Sculptor, ceramics artist and teacher, born in Milwaukee, Wisconsin. He became head of ceramics at Glasgow School of Art after holding a similar position at Edinburgh College of Art. Was active in promoting the Scottish Craft Centre. As early as 1963 Cohen showed at Sacramento Museum Craft Exhibition in America. Arrived in Scotland he showed at 57 Gallery, Edinburgh, British Craft Centre and Carnegie Trust Sculpture Exhibition. Also showed, solo or in groups, at Compass Gallery, Glasgow; Boundary Gallery; and widely overseas.

Harold COHEN 1928– Abstract painter and designer of textiles and furniture, born in London, elder brother of the painter Bernard Cohen. He studied at Slade School of Fine Art, 1948–52, in the latter year winning an Abbey Travelling Scholarship which took him to Italy. He had his first solo show at Ashmolean Museum in Oxford in 1951, followed by a series at Gimpel Fils, the first in 1954. While in America on a Harkness Commonwealth Fellowship, 1959–61, he had a show at Allan Stone Gallery in New York, about the time he was contributing to the Situation exhibitions. Taught at Slade School of Fine Art. Arts Council and Tate Gallery hold his work.

Isaac Michael COHEN 1884–1951 Portrait painter, born in Ballarat, Victoria, Australia. Studied in Melbourne at National Gallery of Victoria, in 1905 winning a travelling scholarship that took him to further studies in Paris. Exhibited RP, RA, ROI and Walker Art Gallery, Liverpool, exentensively and in Paris at the Salon, where he won gold and silver medals. Williamson Art Gallery and Museum, Birkenhead, and galleries in South Africa and Victoria hold his work. Lived latterly in London.

Mary COHEN 1910– Painter and draughtsman who was born and lived in London. She attended St Felix School, Southwold, and studied in Italy, then went to Slade School of Fine Art, 1928–31, under Henry Tonks and Randolph Schwabe, and several years later the Euston Road School under the direction of Claude Rogers, Victor Pasmore and William Coldstream. Showed at RA, LG, New Grafton Gallery and elsewhere. Whitworth Art Gallery, Manchester, holds her work.

Ola COHN 1892–1964 Sculptor, teacher and writer, born Carola Cohn in Bendigo, Victoria, Australia. Studied at Bendigo School of Mines, 1909–19, Swinburne Technical College, 1920–5, and in London at the Royal College of Art, 1926–30, where she received much tuition from Henry Moore. Also studied bronze-casting and wood-carving and travelled extensively in Europe. In 1931 she returned to Australia to spread the word about modern sculpture such as that of Moore and Jacob Epstein, but her own work is said to have later become sentimental and folksy. She taught, including the Kindergarten Training College, Melbourne, and her books included *Fairies Tree* and *More about Fairies Tree*. She was in Europe again, 1949–51. In London exhibited RBA, SWA, Leicester Galleries, Redfern Gallery and LG, as well as at Paris Salon and widely in Australia. She won a number of prizes for her work, which is held by public galleries including the National Gallery of South Australia, Adelaide, and the National Gallery of Victoria, Melbourne. Was president of the Melbourne Society of Women Painters and Sculptors, 1948–64, to which she left her Melbourne home as a memorial centre.

Dorothy COKE 1897–1979 Painter and teacher, born at Southend, who was noted especially for her watercolours. Studied at Slade School of Fine Art under Fred Brown and Henry Tonks, 1914–18. She painted troop scenes during World War I and during World War II was an official war artist. Began to teach at Brighton College of Art and settled nearby at Rottingdean, retiring in 1963. Exhibited RA, RWS, NEAC, SWA and elsewhere. Imperial War Museum holds her work which in watercolour has a free, washy, open-air quality.

Peter COKER 1926– Painter, draughtsman, writer and teacher, born in London. He studied at St Martin's School of Art, 1947–50, then Royal College of Art, 1950–4, winning a Royal Scholarship in 1951. A British Institution Scholarship followed three years later. From 1954–73 Coker taught at St Martin's School of Art. When he left college Coker became associated with the Kitchen Sink realist painters and had the first of a string of shows at Zwemmer Gallery in 1956. In 1962 he participated in the Arts Council touring exhibition British Painting 1950–7, in 1966 in another Arts Council show, Painters in East Anglia. By then his attention had been diverted from the early butcher's shop subject, which shocked many people, to landscape, which remained his preoccupation. Structure, texture and movement were key features of Coker's analysis of the world around him. He showed regularly with Thackeray Gallery for many years. In 1972 he was elected RA, the year of his retrospective at The Minories, Colchester; a further followed at Chelmsford and Essex Museum in 1978; in 1979 the butcher's shop series was featured in a retrospective in Liverpool plus tour; and in 1992 a retrospective of landscapes toured from Abbot Hall, Kendal. In 1976 Coker published *Etching Techniques*. Sheffield City Art Galleries is one of several provincial galleries holding his work. Lived in Mistley, Essex.

Colin COLAHAN 1897–1987 Painter, noted for his portraits, latterly also a sculptor, born into well-to-do family in Woodend, Victoria, Australia. He studied medicine at the University in Melbourne, 1915–16, then art at Max Meldrum School there, 1916–19 (in 1917 publishing *Max Meldrum, His Art and Views*), also in London and Paris. Colahan was a founder-member of the Australian Academy of Art. Moved to London between the wars and was an official war artist with the Australian forces from 1942. As well as exhibiting at the RA, ROI, elsewhere in England and at the Paris Salon, Colahan also showed with the Australian Artists' Association, of which he was president, formed in London in 1951. He lived in Whistler's house in Tite Street, where the Association met. By this time the monocled Colahan was well established in England, but in the mid-1960s with his wife Ursula Marks (of the Marks & Spencer chain store family), he moved to the Riviera and died in Menton. He is well represented in Australian public collections.

Anthony COLBERT 1934– Versatile artist, illustrator and teacher, working in oil, acrylic and watercolour, born in Newport, Isle of Wight. Attended West Sussex College of Arts and Crafts, Worthing, 1949; while doing National Service in the Army studied at Farnham Art School. After three years' agency and studio work Colbert was staff artist on *The Observer* for eight years. In 1967 he went to South Vietnam for the Save the Children Fund, resulting works being shown at AIA Gallery that year. In 1968 Colbert became a freelance illustrator. Work included illustrations for the national press, advertising, magazines and billboard hoardings, clients including Penguin Books, *The Times Educational Supplement*, *Nova*, BBC and The Folio Society. He wrote and illustrated two children's books: *Amanda Has a Surprise*, 1971, and *Amanda Goes Dancing*, 1972. For 20 years Colbert lectured part-time at Camberwell, Brighton, Exeter and other art colleges/polytechnics, and was an external assessor at Goldsmiths' for three years. Was a member of the Association of Illustrators. Took up landscape painting in 1986 and held solo shows annually at The Little Gallery, Arundel; the Old Chapel Gallery, Pembridge; and Penrhos Court, Kington. From 1988 lived at Staunton-on-Arrow, Herefordshire.

William COLDSTREAM 1908–1987 Painter of portraits, landscape and still life and influential teacher. He was born at Belford, Northumberland, then studied at the Slade School 1926–9, being awarded Slade Scholarship in 1927. In the 1920s and 1930s he became friendly with the poet W H Auden and the painters Victor Pasmore, Claude Rogers and Walter Sickert. He worked on documentary films with the GPO Film Unit 1934–7, collaborating on one with Auden. In 1938 he participated briefly with the painter Graham Bell in Mass Observation. Was a founder with Rogers and Pasmore of the Euston Road School of Drawing and Painting, later becoming an official war artist in the Middle East and Italy. From 1945–9 he was a visiting teacher at Camberwell School of Art, becoming Slade Professor of Fine Art 1949–75. *The Coldstream Report*, which stemmed from his chairmanship of the National Advisory Council on Art Education 1959–60, was of key importance. Among his official positions were those of trustee of both the Tate and National Galleries. Work in many public collections, including the Tate Gallery which gave him a retrospective show in 1990–1. Coldstream's work was based on a system of painstaking measurement, which meant that a portrait could take 60 sittings, with small, red registration marks often left visible on the finished picture. Was knighted in 1956. Lived in London. Coldstream's first wife was the painter Nancy Sharp.

Elsie Vera COLE 1885–1968 Painter, printmaker and teacher, born in Braintree, Essex. Educated in Gravesend, Kent, she studied art at Norwich School of Art, 1908–10, then at Chelmsford School of Art, 1911–19, under Charles Baskett. For roughly 20 years she taught at Norwich School of Art, starting just after World War I. Showed at RI, SWA and with the Norfolk and Norwich Art Circle, to which she belonged, being noted for her drawings of Norwich, where she lived.

Ernest COLE 1890–1980 Sculptor, draughtsman and teacher. Born at Greenwich, Cole studied at Goldsmiths' College School of Art and went on to become professor of sculpture at Royal College of Art in 1924–6. He was discovered at the age of sixteen and a half by Charles Ricketts and Selwyn Image when examining at Royal College of Art. He had a prodigious talent, being compared to Alfred Stevens. Ricketts bought drawings which later went to Fitzwilliam Museum, Cambridge. Cole was commissioned to sculpt two large groups for the London County Council building; many other drawings were bought by collectors for high prices. Commissioned during World War I in the Army, Cole was sent on a mission to America where he met his artist wife, Laurie, who predeceased him by about 10 years. His career did not live up to its early promise. When after the war he was converted, as Ricketts said, to "modern art nonsense" Cole lost contact with the collector, who had hoped he would acquire an international reputation as an apostle of classical art. Lived at Kingston, near Canterbury, Kent.

John COLE 1903–1975 Painter in oil and stained glass artist. Born in London, Cole was the son of the artist Rex Vicat Cole. John Cole is most noted for his unsentimental depictions of London shop fronts, often quaint and old-fashioned. He exhibited widely, including the RA, NEAC, RBA, in the provinces and at the Paris Salon, where he won a silver medal in 1952 and a gold medal two years later. His work was widely reproduced, by the Medici Society and others. He held official positions with a number of artistic bodies, such as the Campden Hill Club and the St James' Art Society, of both of which he was chairman. Pictures in public galleries in Britain and abroad, including Hastings Public Museum and Art Gallery, Sussex. Lived in London.

Jonathan COLE 1962– Painter whose output included abstracts such as Untitled, in Royal Over-Seas League Open, 1994. Born in Fareham, Hampshire, he studied at Bristol Polytechnic; École des Beaux-Arts, Marseilles; and Royal Academy Schools. Group shows included Ten Young Artists, Mall Galleries, 1988, and Camden Film Co-operative, 1993. Had a solo exhibition at Earl's Court Gallery, 1991, and Riviera Art Gallery, Hastings, 1994.

Laurie COLE 1890–c.1970 Sculptor, painter, printmaker and artist in black-and-white. Born in New York, she had a distinguished academic career before settling in England, having studied at Columbia University and become a doctor of jurisprudence. Studied art in France and Germany, then with her husband, the sculptor Ernest Cole, with whom she settled near Canterbury, Kent. Exhibited RA, Royal Glasgow Institute of the Fine Arts, Paris Salon and at Columbia University in 1947.

Leslie COLE 1910–1976 Painter and teacher, studied at Swindon School of Art with Harold Dearden, 1927–32; at Birmingham College of Art, 1932–3, with Harold Holden; then Royal College of Art, 1934–7, with Malcolm Osborne and Ernest Tristram. Exhibited RA, RP and widely abroad. Cole was a notable war artist, working for the Ministry of Information in Malta, then for the Admiralty and War Office. For some time he taught at the Central School of Arts and Crafts. Imperial War Museum and Ferens Art Gallery, Hull, hold his work, which is reproduced widely in anthologies of pictures by war artists. In 1985–6 the War Museum staged an exhibition of Cole's World War II pictures called To the Front Line. Lived in London.

Philip William COLE 1884–1964 Painter, stained glass artist and metalworker, born at St Leonards-on-Sea, Sussex. After attending King's College, London, Cole went to Hastings School of Art and the Royal College of Art, 1909–13. He exhibited RA, RBA, Paris Salon and provincial galleries. Was a member of the Art Workers' Guild. Viscount Montgomery and Sir Winston Churchill were among recipients of silver presentation caskets made by Cole, who also completed a number of memorials and stained glass windows in East Sussex churches, notably at East Dean and Bexhill. Lived at Fairlight, Sussex.

Richard COLE 1952– Sculptor and teacher whose work was inspired by the English northern landscape. He was born in Kent and studied at Newcastle University. He was a visiting lecturer at various places including Royal College of Art, eventually lecturing in sculpture at Humberside College of Higher Education. Participated in many group shows, including Northern Young Contemporaries at Whitworth Art Gallery Manchester, 1975–7; Moira Kelly Gallery, 1982; Open Air Sculpture Exhibition, Hull and Lincoln Castle, 1986; and the Newcastle Group show The Northern Lights at DLI Museum & Arts Centre, Durham, and tour, 1990. Later solo shows included Bondgate Gallery, Alnwick, 1986. Completed big outdoor sculpture commissions including Windy Nook, Gateshead, Wakefield District Council, 1989, and National Garden Festival, Gateshead, 1990. Lived in Gateshead, Tyne and Wear.

Robert COLE 1964– Sculptor who studied at Thurrock Technical College, 1981–3, then Wimbledon School of Art, 1983–6. From 1986 participated in various group exhibitions. In 1992 took part in British Contemporary Drawing & Print at Isis Gallery, Leigh-on-Sea, and in 1993 in Drawing Towards Sculpture at same venue.

Deanne COLEBORN 1931– Painter and etcher, born in Stourbridge, where she attended the School of Art, later the Royal College of Art. She was the second wife of the painter Keith Coleborn. Originally a glass designer, she then moved to etching and painting, showing at RA, RWA and RE in group exhibitions, one-man shows including Greenwich and Lyric Theatre Galleries and Woodlands Gallery. Member of the Greenwich Printmakers, RE and Printmakers' Guild. Lived at Downe, Kent.

Freda M COLEBORN 1911–1965 Painter, designer, embroiderer and teacher. Born in India, she was married to the artist Keith Coleborn. Studied at Royal College of Art. Signing her work F M C, she exhibited at the RA and in many international shows, being noted for her glass designs. Lived at Downe, Kent.

Keith COLEBORN 1909– Painter, printmaker, stained and engraved glass-maker and teacher, born in Portsmouth, Hampshire. Was married to two artists: Freda Coleborn, then Deanne Coleborn. Studied at Royal College of Art, his teachers including Edward Bawden, Eric Ravilious and Reco Capey. Held a number of teaching posts from 1935 at Stourbridge and Wallasey, finally being principal of Bromley/Ravensbourne College of Art, 1946–75. Was involved in work for university-level recognition of art training. Showed widely, including RA, and internationally. Lived in Downe, Kent.

Alan COLEMAN 1920–1998 Sculptor and teacher, born in Croydon, Surrey, who studied at Goldsmiths' College School of Art and Royal College of Art, where he passed first-class in 1951. In 1952 he was elected to RBA, in 1961 a fellow of RBS. Died after a brief illness. Lived for many years at Wonersh, Surrey.

Trevor COLEMAN 1936– Artist in a wide range of styles and media, photographer, potter, teacher and editor, born in Johannesburg, South Africa. His early studies included chemistry and geology. Attended Witwatersrand Technical College, 1958–60. Decided to concentrate on art as a career and when in London, 1961–5, attended Central School of Arts and Crafts part-time. On returning to Johannesburg taught at the Visual Arts Research Centre, 1966, and privately. He also ran the Trevor Coleman Gallery, 1977–85, and edited *Gallery* magazine, 1981–3. Was a leading member of the South African Association of Arts. Coleman was keenly interested in archaeology, geology, anthropology and African art. He travelled extensively in Africa and abroad, reflected in colourful, hard-edge pictures. Showed widely in group and solo exhibitions in South Africa. In England Coleman was a member of Hampstead Artists' Council, showed in mixed exhibitions at Grosvenor and Whitechapel Arts Galleries, 1964, and with Nicholas Treadwell Gallery, 1965. Had a series of solo shows, including Everyman Theatre Gallery, 1963, and ICA, 1964. Victoria & Albert Museum print room, Johannesburg Art Gallery, University of the Witwatersrand and other South African collections hold examples. Lived in Johannesburg.

Nathan COLEY 1967– Artist using photography and wall pieces, as in New Art in Scotland, at Centre for Contemporary Arts, Glasgow, 1994. For these, he said that "the reality of images, their authenticity and the cultural trust we place in them, is a point of entry". Coley was born and lived in Glasgow, where he gained a fine art honours degree, 1985–9. Other mixed shows included Festival of Plagiarism, Transmission Gallery, Glasgow, 1989; Love at First Sight, The Showroom, 1992; Swarm, Scottish Arts Council Travelling Gallery, 1995; A Scottish Collection, Berwick Gymnasium Gallery, Berwick, 1997; and Correspondences, Scottish National Gallery of Modern Art, Edinburgh, 1997–8. Coley was commissioned to work on the refurbishment of Stills Gallery's Edinburgh premises, 1996–7, from which stemmed *Urban Sanctuary*, a book and solo exhibition at IPA, Edinburgh.

Grace Marion COLLCUTT 1875–1954 Landscape painter, daughter of the architect Thomas Edward Collcutt, among whose buildings were London's Savoy Hotel and the Imperial Institute. She studied at Richmond School of Art and the Slade School of Fine Art, and exhibited at the RA, Abbey, Baillie and Goupil Galleries, Walker Art Gallery in Liverpool, SWA and elsewhere. Settled in Brighton, Sussex, where the Museum and Art Gallery holds local views in watercolour by her.

Henry COLLER 1886–1958 Magazine illustrator in line and wash. Born in Wood Green, London, he studied art at Manchester School of Art. Went on to work prolifically for many publications, including *Wide World*, *John Bull* and *My Home*, as well as drawing for advertisements. Lived in London.

Dorothy COLLES 1917– Artist in oil, pastel and pencil, notable for portraits, mainly of children. She was born in Cairo, Egypt, and studied at the Westminster School of Art before World War II with John Farleigh, Bernard Meninsky and Mark Gertler. Between 1940–5 served in the Women's Auxiliary Air Force in the United Kingdom and the Middle East. After hostilities, she worked in Egypt for the Egyptian Exploration Society and for the Jordanian government before returning to London, after which she freelanced. She said that pastelists such as Chardin, Degas, La Tour and Angelica Kaufmann and the draughtsmen Augustus John, Rubens and Ingres were influences. Colles was a member of PS, also exhibiting at RP and RA. In 1962 she had a solo show at Leighton House. She wrote *Portraying Children*, 1953, and in 1970 published *Christian Symbols Ancient & Modern* with Heather Child, the artist and calligrapher, who was a lifelong companion. They lived at Petersfield, Hampshire.

Ruth COLLET 1909– Painter, printmaker and illustrator, born in Barley, Hertfordshire. After Bedales School she studied at Slade School of Fine Art, where her teachers included Philip Wilson Steer, Henry Tonks and Franklin White. She showed extensively at Goupil Gallery, RA, WIAC, NEAC, LG, Leicester Galleries and Gainsborough's House, Sudbury, and was a member of Hesketh Hubbard Art Society. Did a number of book jacket illustrations and hundreds of lino-cuts for Westminster Synagogue. Israeli Embassy and Ben Uri Art Society hold her work, "which was influenced by Dürer, Van Gogh and Rembrandt." Later solo exhibitions included Sue Rankin Gallery, Sternberg Centre for Judaism and Moss Galleries, 1991. Lived for many years at Northwood, Middlesex.

William Frederick COLLEY 1907–1957 Birmingham-based painter, printmaker and teacher who taught art and design at the city's College of Art. He came into prominence in the 1930s and 1940s, undertaking murals (including a commission for the Federation of British Industrialists in Birmingham) and exhibiting his watercolours and lithographs at the RBSA of which he was a member, RA, NEAC and Redfern Gallery. The discovery of a body of Colley's work prompted an exhibition of his lithographs at the 20th Century Gallery, 1997. The prints, often large, occasionally in colour, indicated his strong interest in the decorative and bizarre and the industrial and leisure activities of Midlands people.

Brian COLLIER 1945– Painter and draughtsman, born in Bolton, Lancashire. He studied at the College of Art and Design there, 1960–5, teachers including Tony Bates; at Brighton College of Art, 1965–6, with Jennifer Dickson; Atelier 17 in Paris, 1967, with Stanley William Hayter; then as a Rome Scholar at British School in Rome, 1966–8. Showed at RA, Hayward Gallery, Air Gallery, Serpentine Gallery and elsewhere. Victoria & Albert Museum holds his work. Lived for some time in Hove, Sussex.

Graham COLLIER 1923– Painter, full name Alan Graham Collier, and teacher; born in Manchester. Initially educated in Lancashire and Yorkshire, he studied art at Lincoln School of Art, 1940–2, Newark School of Art, 1942–4, and the Slade School of Fine Art, 1944, with Randolph Schwabe. He went on to hold a number of teaching posts in Yorkshire, then in 1954 became art director at Lancing College, Sussex. Showed LG, at the Leeds and Bradford public galleries and elsewhere. In the late 1940s he was art correspondent for the *Yorkshire Evening Press*. Painted a number of musicians' portraits, including the official Hallé portrait of Sir John Barbirolli, the orchestra's conductor. Chelsea Arts Club member.

June COLLIER 1943– Painter and teacher who studied at the Slade School of Fine Art, 1961–5, gaining a French government scholarship in painting in the latter year. From 1965–79 taught at Byam Shaw, Camberwell, Canterbury, Falmouth, Gloucestershire, Liverpool, St Martin's and Wimbledon Schools of Art. In 1979–80 she spent nine months at the Shree Rajneesh Ashram, India. Was included in Contemporary Artists in Camden at Camden Arts Centre, 1981.

Stephen COLLINGBOURNE 1943– Sculptor and teacher, born in Dartington, Devon, where he attended Dartington Hall School, 1948–60, and Dartington College of Art, 1960–1. Was at Bath Academy of Art, Corsham, 1961–4. After teaching at a comprehensive school in Oxford, lectured from 1965–70 at Dartington College of Art. Then did a foundry course at Royal College of Art, 1970; worked at the Serpentine Gallery, 1971; was assistant to the sculptor Robert Adams, 1972; lived and worked in Malaysia, 1972–3; was fellow in sculpture at University College of Wales, 1974; then was appointed lecturer in sculpture at Edinburgh College of Art, 1976. As well as extensive mixed show appearances, Collingbourne had a series of solo shows, starting with Dartington Hall, 1968, later ones including MacRobert Arts Centre, Stirling University, 1979. Commissions included Leicester University Library, 1974, and Royal Mile, Edinburgh, 1983. Scottish and Welsh Arts Councils hold his work. Although early on a painter, Collingbourne said that from 1988 "I have spent most of my time working in two dimensions on paper." He was "not interested in instant impact, but in making sculpture which is capable of changing visual experience and has a timeless quality." Lived in West Linton, Peebleshire.

Anthony COLLINGE 1934– Painter of abstracts and lecturer, born in Cheshire, who studied at Liverpool College of Art under Arthur Ballard and George Mayer-Marton, and at the Slade School of Fine Art under Claude Rogers, Anthony Gross, Ceri Richards and Robert Medley. While at Liverpool was awarded the Blond Travelling Scholarship, visiting Italy, staying at the British School at Rome. Taught at Canterbury College of Art and London College of Printing, then from 1963–96 at Goldsmiths' College School of Art, being head of art education, 1976–85, colleagues including Anton Ehrenzweig and Harry and Elma Thubron. Tony Collinge's exhibitions included LG 75th Anniversary, RCA, 1988; joint show with Elma Thubron, Storey Institute Gallery, Lancaster, 1994; solo exhibition at Woodlands Art Gallery, 1995; and Museum of Installation, 1997. That museum, Arts Council and Goldsmiths' hold examples. Lived in London and Benhall, Saxmundham, Suffolk.

Albert Henry COLLINGS fl. from c.1895–1947 Prolific and versatile painter, born and lived in London, where he studied. He was a member of RI and RBA, also exhibiting at RA, Fine Art Society and ROI. Won a Gold Medal at Paris Salon, 1907. He did commissioned work for Portsmouth Town Hall and completed portraits of HRH The Prince of Wales.

David COLLINGS 1949– Painter and teacher who studied at Redruth School of Art, 1965–9, then Berkshire College of Education, 1969–72. He lived in Newlyn, Cornwall, and showed with Newlyn Society of Artists of which he was a member, in southwest of England and abroad. Contemporary Art Society holds his work.

Anthony COLLINS 1944– Painter, born in Dublin, Ireland, where he eventually returned to work. Participated in many group shows and early had two solo exhibitions. From 1980–90 he helped establish Austin/Desmond Fine Art. In 1991 studied at Cyprus College of Art in Paphos, showing resulting work at Jonathan Cooper, 1993. Collins said of his method: "I like to use photographs instead of preliminary drawings ... The scene shot in an instant faster than the eye can recall."

Cecil COLLINS 1908–1989 Figure, landscape but essentially visionary painter in oil, pastel, watercolour and gouache, printmaker and draughtsman, Collins is one of the notable individual figures not uncommon in British art. Born in Plymouth, Devon, Collins won a scholarship while at the Plymouth School of Art which took him to the Royal College of Art in 1927–31. Shortly after leaving the College Collins married Elisabeth Ramsden, also an artist, an important influence on his work. She appeared in his pictures throughout his career. Collins had his first one-man show at the Bloomsbury Gallery in 1935 and in the following year took part in the International Surrealist Exhibition. At Dartington Hall he met the American artist Mark Tobey who fostered his interest in Far Eastern art and philosophy. From 1951 taught at the Central School of Arts and Crafts for many years, where his influence was outstanding. In 1947 Collins published *The Vision of the Fool*, the Fool being a recurrent image in his pictures. Designed tapestries and the Icon of Divine Light, for Chichester Cathedral. Many one-man exhibitions, including a major retrospective at the Tate Gallery in 1989 and a commemorative exhibition in 1995. Tate and other important collections hold examples. Lived in London.

Elisabeth COLLINS 1904– Painter and sculptor, brought up in Yorkshire. Her family owned the *Halifax Courier and Guardian* of which her father was editor. She studied sculpture at Leeds School of Art, then with Henry Moore at Royal College of Art. There she met her husband the artist Cecil Collins, and they were married shortly after leaving, in 1931. She originally exhibited at SWA under her maiden name of Ramsden. After marriage the opportunity to pursue her own work was curtailed, as she helped foster her husband's gift. Her work was not unlike his, with its fokloric, fantastic elements, and it was one of her early drawings, The First Fool, that released in him the inspiration for his long series of works on the theme of the Fool. Her most prolific period was when they were living at Dartington Hall from 1937 until the end of World War II. A retrospective was held at Albemarle Gallery in 1989, another at England & Co, 1996. Lived in London.

George Edward COLLINS 1880–1968 Painter, printmaker and teacher with a strong interest in natural history subjects, son of the artist Charles Collins, who studied at Epsom and Lambeth Schools of Art. His appointments included art master at Guildford Royal Grammar School. Collins' pictures illustrated a number of books, such as Gilbert White's *The Natural History and Antiquities of Selborne*. Showed extensively at RCamA, RBA, Brook Street Art Gallery, RA and elsewhere. Lived in Gomshall, Surrey.

Hannah COLLINS 1956– Artist in various media, born in London. She studied at Slade School of Fine Art, 1974–8, then gained a Fulbright Scholarship to America, 1978–9. Her group shows included Antidotes to Madness, Riverside Studios, 1986; L'Invention d'un Art, Pompidou Centre, Paris, 1989; and The Last Days, Arenal Gallery, Seville, 1992. Solo shows included Film Stills at Matt's Gallery, 1986, later ones including Museum of Modern Art, San Francisco, 1992. Her Nomad II, of 1991, was included in Twelve Stars, Belfast Arts Council Gallery and tour, 1992–3, which was acquired for European Parliament Collection. Arts Council and British Council also hold her work.

Helen COLLINS 1921–1990 Artist and teacher, born in Dorking, Surrey, daughter of the watercolourist George Edward Collins and flower painter Clare Perrin and grand-daughter of Charles Collins. She studied at Guildford School of Art and Royal College of Art after World War II. Among her output were drawings of heavy horses in the *Surrey Advertiser*. She taught at Englefield Green School. Guildford Borough collection includes her view of North Street, Guildford.

Henry COLLINS 1910–1994 Painter, designer and teacher, born in Colchester, Essex, who continued to work in that area. He was married to the artist Joyce Pallot. Collins studied at Colchester School of Art and the Central School of Arts and Crafts. After World War II service with the Army he worked as a freelance designer, establishing himself through commissions for Central Office of Information at the 1951 Festival of Britain. He taught for many years in the graphic design department of St Martin's School of Art, at Colchester School of Art and in adult education classes. With his wife he worked on many exhibition designs and murals, including Shell Centre, General Post Office Tower and Grosvenor House; Essex County Council; and Jamestown Festival in America. The two artists shared a retrospective show at The Minories, Colchester, 1984 and 1995, and in 1995–6 Essex County Libraries toured a Collins memorial show.

Jamie COLLINS 1959– Artist, designer and teacher, born in London, who graduated from Falmouth School of Art in 1982. In 1984 he joined Sculptors in Greater Manchester Association, having his studio there for some years. Collins subsequently turned to painting and poetry as a means of expression. An exhibition at Manto's, Manchester, in the mid-1990s won critical acclaim. Collins designed sets and costumers for Duchy Opera's production of Mozart's *The Magic Flute* and carried out a number of large-scale commissions in Manchester. He held the post of lecturer in sculpture at Bolton Institute of Higher Education, 1987–93. In 1996 Collins was included in North by North West, at Bolton Museum and Art Gallery, paintings which flowed "from an eight-and-a-half years' relationship lived under the shadow of Aids".

Marjorie COLLINS 1941– Painter in acrylic and watercolour, born in Chicago, Illinois, America, who graduated in fine art, University of Michigan, Ann Arbor, 1958–62, also studying part-time at school of the Art Institute of Chicago, moving to England in 1975, where she settled in Oxford. Initially, Collins' work was people and places, mainly buildings, but from 1990 she focused on still lifes and floral pictures. Although her work was representational, "the actual subject I choose to paint ... is less important than the resulting abstract patterns of light, shape and colour that they create." Joined Oxford Art Society, 1983, SWA, 1994. Group shows included RA Summer Exhibition, Hunting/*Observer* Art Prize, ROI, RWS and Museum of Modern Art in Oxford. Solo shows included Green College in Oxford, Joy Horwich Gallery in Chicago, Barbican Centre, Shire Hall Gallery in Stafford, and Stables and Sunshine Galleries. Oxford City Council, Cole Taylor Bank in Chicago, Cabinet Office and Daler-Rowney hold examples.

Michael COLLINS 1936– Artist in graphic media and teacher, born in New Malden, Surrey. After five years in the management of Clan Line Steamers, Collins studied at Wimbledon School of Art, 1962–5, then Swansea College of Art, 1965–6, his teachers including Lionel Ellis and E M Scales. He eventually became head of the art department at Emanuel School, London. Collins was a topographical draughtsman who showed with SGA and Society of Architectural and Industrial Illustrators, of both of which he was a member. Sometimes signed work with initials only. Lived in Petersham, Surrey.

Peter COLLINS 1935– Painter and teacher, born in Inverness, whose work could have a Surrealistic quality. He studied at Edinburgh College of Art, 1952–6, and gained a Post-Diploma Scholarship and an Andrew Grant Major Travelling Scholarship in 1957, studying in Italy, 1957–8. Lectured at Duncan of Jordanstone College of Art, Dundee. He was a professional member of SSA. Group shows included Arts Council of Northern Ireland, New Charing Cross Gallery in Glasgow and in 1970 he was included in Scottish Arts Council show Seven Painters in Dundee, where he lived. Had a solo show at Scottish Gallery, Edinburgh, 1968. Aberdeen Art Gallery, Scottish Arts Council and Edinburgh Education Authority hold examples.

Peter Gerald COLLINS 1923– Painter and draughtsman, born and lived in London, who studied for several years at Royal College of Art from 1946, teachers including Rodrigo Moynihan, Ruskin Spear, John Minton and Robert Buhler. He worked in advertising, ran an antique shop and gallery in Sussex and completed posters for organisations such as British Rail, British European Airways and J Lyons & Company. Showed at RA, Balcombe Galleries, in open studio and at Zella Nine Gallery. Leicester Education Authority holds his work. Chelsea Arts Club member.

Roland COLLINS 1918– Painter, designer, photographer, printmaker and writer, born in London, who studied at St Martin's School of Art, teachers including Leon Underwood and Vivian Pitchforth. Collins early began recording the London scene, showing at RA, while working for London Press Exchange advertising agency. After World War II, during which he did agricultural work as a conscientious objector, Collins studied in 1947 in Morris Kestelman's life class at Central School and exhibited at most of London's societies, including LG, PS, RBA, ROI, RSMA, RWS, and in the provinces. In 1945 Collins designed the sleeve for Britain's first long-playing record, issued by Decca; in 1951 wrote a children's book, *The Flying Poodle*; in 1952 edited and illustrated *The Young Ballet Dancer* magazine; and in 1954 illustrated with colour lithographs Noel Carrington's *Colour and Pattern in the Home*. Had a first solo show in 1966 at Fitzroy Tavern, being long active in the association to preserve the Fitzrovia area; had another show at Illustrators' Gallery, 1987; and one at Michael Parkin Gallery, 1994. London Borough of Camden owns his oil of Bankside. Settled in Padstow, Cornwall.

William Wiehe COLLINS 1862–1951 Watercolour painter, born in London, who studied at Lambeth School of Art, 1884–5, and Académie Julian, Paris, 1886–7. Exhibited prolifically, notably at Walker's Galleries, RI, ROI and at Fine Art Society, as well as abroad. He painted widely in England and on the continent, publishing several books on the cathedral cities of England, Italy and Spain. Manchester City Art Gallery holds his work. Lived at Bridgwater, Somerset.

Hugh COLLINSON 1909– Painter and illustrator, especially of townscapes, and teacher, born in Ipswich, Suffolk. Studied at the School of Art there, 1926–9, under Leonard Squirrell, then at Royal College of Art, 1929–32. Showed RA and extensively in the provinces, Ipswich Art Gallery holding his work. Lived in Leicester, where he taught for a time at the College of Art.

Maurice COLLIS 1889–1973 Writer and critic, administrator and painter, born in Ireland, who after a career as an Indian Civil Servant in Burma, 1912–34, returned to London to pursue a literary life. His daughter was the art critic and writer Louise Collis. He published 35 books, including a biography of Stanley Spencer; was art critic for *The Observer* and *Time & Tide*; and numbered among his many artist friends Henry Moore, L S Lowry, Cecil Collins and Barbara Hepworth. Collis began painting in 1956 and intuitively and spontaneously created his own brightly coloured, phantasmagorically figured and almost surreal world. Although his first solo show, when he was 71, achieved some favourable critical reaction, it was left to England & Co to revive interest in the work with an exhibition in 1998.

Peter COLLIS 1929– Painter, notably of landscapes in a rather sombre palette. He was born in London and studied at Epsom College of Art. Settled in Ireland, where he concentrated on depicting the County Wicklow region near his home. Awards included Royal Trust Company Ltd Award, 1975; Olreachtas Maurice MacGonigal Landscape Prize, 1981; Claremarris Open Exhibition Prizes, 1982, 1990 and 1992; and Oireachtas Irish Pensions Landscape Prize, 1983. Collis was a member of RHA. Showed extensively in group exhibitions, including RA, RP, UA, Austin/Desmond Fine Art and elsewhere. Showed solo at Emmet Gallery, Dublin, 1975–7, later one-mans including John Martin of London, from 1996. Limerick University, National Self Portrait Collection in Ireland and many corporate collections hold examples.

Mat COLLISHAW 1966– Artist who was born in Nottingham. Studied at Trent Polytechnic, 1985–6, then graduated with honours from Goldsmiths' College, 1986–9. Group exhibitions included Ghost Photography, The Illusion of the Visible, Italian tour, 1989, and Modern Medicine, Building One, and A Group Show, Karsten Schubert Ltd, both 1990. Solo shows included Riverside Studios in 1990 and Karsten Schubert, 1991, with a shared exhibition following a residency at Camden Arts Centre, 1995–6.

Alfred James COLLISTER 1869–1964 Painter, mainly of watercolours, brought up in Isle of Man. Studied at Royal College of Art and showed extensively at RBA of which he was a member, RI, Walker Art Gallery in Liverpool and elsewhere. Lived in London for a time but settled finally at Clymping, Sussex.

Nina COLMORE 1889–1973 Painter of equestrian subjects, specialising in Lipizzaner stallions and Egyptian racing ponies. Also painted inn signs. Born in Hounslow, Middlesex, her father was Colonel Gostling Murray, her mother an amateur artist. Colmore studied at Heatherley's School of Fine Art with Henry Massey, in Paris at the Académie Julian and in several studios. She showed at the NEAC and at the Paris Salon, where she won a diploma. Among her patrons were HRH The Maharajah of Jaipur, HRH The Prince Ali Khan and the Duchess of Westminster. During World War I Colmore, who enjoyed travel, drove a mobile canteen in the Middle East. Late in life she drove a car across Africa. Lived near Andover, Hampshire.

Russell COLOMBO 1947– Artist, born in London, who studied drawing and painting at Edinburgh College of Art, 1969–73, completing postgraduate studies in art therapy at Hertfordshire College of Art, St Albans, 1980–1. Then worked as a freelance art therapist. Was included in Scottish Print Open Three, 1983, organised by Dundee Printmakers' Workshop.

Marzia COLONNA 1951– Sculptor and painter, born in Pisa, Italy, who settled in Evershot, Dorset. Studied in Pisa at the Instituto Statale d'Arte, 1963–8, then in Florence at the

Accademia, 1968–70. Mixed exhibitions included Upper Grosvenor Galleries, 1972; Christopher Hull Gallery, 1984; Warwick Arts Trust, 1988; Hannah Peschar Sculpture Garden, 1993; and Glydebourne Festival Gallery, 1994. Solo shows included Campbell & Franks from 1979, and Gillian Jason Gallery from 1987. Commissioned work included portraits of Princess Helietta Caracciolo and a small memorial sculpture of the two Vasconsuellos brothers who died in the *Marchioness* boat disaster on the Thames. The writer David Garnett, who owned her small bronze head Emmanuel, said that it was "a precious possession with which I have lived for some years. It is a creation; not a portrait but an imaginary head full of individuality."

Ithell COLQUHOUN 1906–1988 Painter, draughtsman, poet and lecturer, born in Shillong, Assam, India. Studied at Slade School of Fine Art, 1927–31, where her teachers included Henry Tonks and Vladimir Polunin, then privately in Paris and Athens. Showed extensively, including LG, Contemporary Art Society, Tate Gallery and abroad, and had solo shows at Fine Art Society, Mayor Gallery and elsewhere. Bradford and Cheltenham public galleries hold her work, which is often of an exotic nature, revealing fine draughtsmanship. She was interested in such things as natural health cures, psychodynamics and Celtic prehistory. Lived for many years in Paul, Cornwall.

Robert COLQUHOUN 1914–1962 Painter, printmaker and theatre designer, born in Kilmarnock, Ayrshire. He won a scholarship to Glasgow School of Art in 1933 where he met the painter Robert MacBryde. "The Roberts" remained together for life, which was often temperamentally turbulent. Gauguin and Percy Wyndham Lewis were early influences on Colquhoun, who in 1937–9 was enabled to travel in France and Italy with MacBryde. After a brief period in the Army he was invalided out and lived in London with MacBryde and John Minton and associated with other Neo-Romantic artists and Jankel Adler, who encouraged Colquhoun to concentrate on lone figure studies rather than landscapes. Hieratic individuals and abstract forms now became a hallmark of Colquhoun's art. In 1946 the artist visited Ireland, from which monotypes of Irish women emerged; in 1947–8 he worked for the Miller's Press in Lewes; further visits to the continent followed. Colquhoun with MacBryde designed for the ballet *Donald of the Burthens* at Covent Garden in 1951 and for *King Lear* at Stratford two years later. In 1958 a retrospective show was held at Whitechapel Art Gallery. Arts Council, Tate Gallery and Scottish National Portrait Gallery hold his work. Died in London.

Peter COLQUITT 1936– Artist and teacher who studied at Nuneaton School of Art and Birmingham College of Art. Went on to teach at Bishop Milner School, Dudley, Worcestershire, where he lived. He exhibited at the RBSA Open, Midland Art Medical Society, Wolverhampton Art Gallery and with the General Post Office, Dudley. Solo exhibitions included Cannon Hill and Compendium Galleries, Birmingham, and at Midland Arts Centre, 1970. Vaughan College holds his work.

Richard COLSON 1955– Painter and draughtsman, born in Edinburgh, who attended Goldsmiths' College, 1973–7, and Garnett College, 1984–6. He was notable for his impastoed landscapes, figure paintings and interiors. Group shows included Art and Computers, Cleveland Gallery, 1988; New Grafton Gallery, 1989; Francis Kyle Gallery, 1990; and Jonathan Clark Fine Art, 1993. In 1996 he had a solo exhibition at Theo Waddington Fine Art. Pearson Holdings and Thomas Agnew and Sons hold examples.

Brendan COLVERT 1961– Painter, born in Dorset, who studied at Bristol Polytechnic, 1984–7. He showed in a range of mixed exhibitions, including Northlands, Cheltenham, 1987; the Bristol/Hannover Exhibition, Bristol, in the same year; in collaborations at The Cottages and at the St John's Road Site, Bristol, both 1989; and in 1991–2 John Moores Exhibition, Liverpool, where his picture Untitled was a powerful image subtitled The Problem of Pain. Lived in Kingsdown, Wiltshire.

Henry (or Harry) Morton COLVILE 1905– Painter of portraits and landscapes who in 1925 studied in Paris with André Lhote. In 1932 he settled in Aix-en-Provence, three years later exhibiting in Paris at Galerie Zak. Exhibited at RA Summer Exhibition in 1944, when he was living in London, in 1945 sharing an exhibition at Berkeley Galleries with Henry Moore and Matthew Smith, with whose work Colvile's had much in common. Exhibited at Salon d'Automne, Paris, in 1953, three years later being included in Wildenstein's Some Contemporary British Painters show. Colvile's paintings were acquired for Renand Collection, Paris, and for other collections in England, France and America.

Calum COLVIN 1961– Painter, sculptor and photographer, born in Glasgow. He studied at Duncan of Jordanstone College of Art, Dundee, 1979–83, at first concentrating on painting, then sculpture, then photography. His photographic studies were continued at Royal College of Art, 1983–5. Colvin began constructing installations made from found junk objects; onto these he would paint the outlines of figures which would be coloured in sophisticated and complex ways; photographs were then taken and the installation destroyed. The Constructed Narratives focused on hero-worship, fantasies and desires. The Photographer's Gallery held a show in 1986, and Scottish National Gallery of Modern Art holds Colvin's work, which was featured in the Scottish Art since 1900 show, 1989–1990, at the Gallery and touring.

Melanie COMBER 1970– Abstract artist, who did a foundation course at Kent Institute of Art & Design/Maidstone College of Art, 1989–90; gained an honours degree in fine art painting from Wimbledon School of Art, 1990–3; and her master's in the same subject at Chelsea College of Art, 1993–4. She was a nominee for the David Murray Scholarship, RA, 1992–3; a finalist in the New Art Award, Cubitt Street, 1993; and a finalist in the Swiss Bank Corporation European Art Competition, 1994. Group shows included Cooltan Arts and Galerie Dagmar, both 1993; No

Turkeys at Raw Gallery, 1994; and Jinan Gallery, 1995. Solo shows at The Blue Gallery began with Elemental, 1995. Comber's work included evocations of natural organic structures, as in her Blue Gallery show of 1996, where she built up ribbed, even scarred surfaces with lavish quantities of chalk, sand, oil paint and natural pigments, so that the pictures teetered on the brink between two and three dimensions.

William Edmund Hunt CONDON 1886– Watercolour painter and illustrator. Born in Cawnpore, India, Condon pursued a military career, attaining the rank of brigadier. Condon studied art under George W C Hutchinson, in Clifton, Bristol, then in Montreux, Switzerland. Prior to World War II his work appeared for several years in the *Illustrated London News* and elsewhere. While in India he exhibited widely. In 1952 he was made life president of the Exeter Art Society. Lived at Newton Abbot, Devon.

Roy CONN 1931– Painter, born in London. Trained as a structural engineer, he was mainly self-taught as an artist. In 1958 he moved to St Ives, Cornwall, and became a member of the Penwith Society. He had solo shows at Rowan Gallery, 1966, and Arnolfini Gallery, Bristol, 1969, and in 1992 was included in Belgrave Gallery's British abstract art of the 50s and 60s. Victoria & Albert Museum, Contemporary Art Society and Arts Council of Northern Ireland hold his work.

Philip CONNARD 1875–1958 Painter and teacher, born in Southport, Lancashire. At first he worked as a house painter and studied art part-time until he won a scholarship to the Royal College of Art and in 1898 a British Institution Prize which took him to Paris. Returning to London he illustrated and taught at Lambeth School of Art. Showed widely, including RA, Leicester Galleries, RWS and NEAC as a member of both, Fine Art Society and elsewhere. Also showed solo at Leicester Galleries, and at Barbizon House. In World War I was an official war artist; painted murals for Queen Mary's Dolls' House, Windsor; also did decorations for the liner *Queen Mary*. Was elected RA in 1925 and Keeper, 1945–9. Connard was a painter of many facets, as his holding in the Tate Gallery shows. Died at Twickenham, Middlesex.

Wendy CONNELLY 1969– Painter and teacher who was born in Liverpool. After summer school art courses at the Menia and Nelson Centre, North Wales, 1986–8, did a foundation course at Cheshire College of Further Education, 1987–8; an art history course in northern Italy, 1987, with further tuition there in 1988; and gained an honours degree in painting at Central St Martins School of Art and Design, 1988–91. In 1989 she taught at Menia and Nelson Centre summer school. Among her awards was the Boise Scholarship for travelling in Spain in 1992. Group exhibitions included Winsford Lodge, Cheshire, 1987; RCamA Summer Exhibition from 1990; Mostyn Art Gallery, Llandudno, 1991; and Bath and Islington Art Fairs, 1992. Her first solo show, at Bernard Jacobson Gallery in 1993, sold out. TSB Group holds her work. Lived in Cheshire.

Angela CONNER fl. from 1960s– Sculptor and painter, self-taught, although she was an apprentice with Barbara Hepworth and gained a painting scholarship to Rhodes. She showed with Gimpel Fils, RA Summer Exhibition and Tryon Gallery and had solo exhibitions at Browse & Darby and Lincoln Center, New York, 1971. Was a member of New Grafton Gallery's Portrait Centre. Her subjects included Duke of Devonshire, the artist Lucien Freud, the poet Sir John Betjeman and Lord Goodman. Arts Council holds her work. Lived in London.

Joan CONNEW fl. from 1940s– Painter, calligrapher and illuminator, born in Sydenham, Kent. She studied at Brighton School of Art, Beckenham School of Art and Central School of Arts and Crafts, her teachers including the painter Henry Carr. Showed with RA, SWA, RSMA, RBA and Arts and Crafts Exhibition Society. Ministry of Information bought her work. Lived for many years at Shortlands, Kent.

Brian CONNOLLY 1961– Multi-media artist, teacher and events organiser who graduated from the University of Ulster in Belfast, 1984, gaining his master's degree in 1985. He instigated a number of significant arts events including Available Resources, Londonderry, 1991, and was on the editorial board of *Circa*. Won many Arts Council awards. Taught at Nova Scotia College of Art, Sheffield Polytechnic, University of Ulster, Queen's University and Colleges of Art in Cork and Limerick. His commissioned sculpture Turning Point was sited in St Anne's Square, Belfast, where he was a member of Queen Street Studios. Showed there in Works on Paper, 1994, also internationally.

William John CONNON 1929– Painter, draughtsman and teacher, born in Turriff, Aberdeenshire. He studied at Gray's school of Art in Aberdeen, his teachers including Ian Fleming and Robert Henderson Blyth. He later taught at that school and lived in Aberdeen. Was a member of SSA, also showing with Aberdeen Art Society and RSA. Scottish Arts Council holds his work.

Liam CONOR: *see* **William CONOR**

William CONOR 1881–1968 Painter and illustrator, born in Belfast, where he was especially known for his pictures of the city's shipyards and working-class street life. Was born William Connor and sometimes signed work Liam, Liam Conor or Liam O'Conocohair. Began studies at Belfast Government School of Art in 1894. Became an assistant teacher in antique at the Municipal Technical Institute in 1903, leaving the following year to join the lithographic firm David Allen and Sons. Left there after about 10 years to become a full-time painter. Was an official war artist in both World Wars. Works first hung at Belfast Art Society in 1910, and from then on showed extensively in the city, at RHA, Royal Glasgow Institute of the Fine Arts, RA and elsewhere. Founder-member of NS and member ROI. Elected RHA in 1946. Illustrated a number of books, including his friend Lynn Doyle's *Ballygullion* and *The Ballygunnion Bus*. Retrospective held by Arts Council of Northern Ireland at Ulster Museum, 1968.

Arts Council of Northern Ireland, Ulster Folk Museum and Manchester City Art Gallery hold his work.

Alfred Charles CONRADE 1863–1955 Painter and modeller who studied art in Germany, France and Spain. Exhibited RA, RIBA and Paris Salon. He was principal artist at the White City, 1911–14, and his work had a strong architectural bias. Lived at Kingston upon Thames, Surrey.

Stephen CONROY 1964– Painter, born in Helensburgh, Dunbartonshire. He studied painting at Glasgow School of Art, 1982–7. In 1986, just before he began his postgraduate year, Conroy won first prize for painting at the RA's British Institute Fund Awards, the year that he also had a solo commissioned exhibition at Dumbarton District Council. Group shows included Royal Glasgow Institute of the Fine Arts, 1986; The New British Painting, Cincinnati Contemporary Arts Center and tour, 1988; and Scottish Art since 1900, 1989–90, at Scottish National Gallery of Modern Art, and touring. Conroy had a one-man show at Marlborough Fine Art, 1989. The artist was an admirer of the Scottish painter James Cowie, and in the older artist's manner Conroy's work is exact, tighter and more studied in its brushwork than much modern Glasgow painting. Conroy's reality is mysterious, with a tinge of Surrealism. Scottish National Gallery of Modern Art holds his work. He lived and worked near Glasgow.

Blanche CONSTABLE 1882–1956 Watercolour painter and designer, born in Malton, Yorkshire. Studied at Bradford School of Art under Charles Stephenson, then held a series of teaching posts, notably at Varndean Grammar School, Brighton. Exhibited IS and in the provinces. Member of the Sussex Women's Art Club. Lived in Brighton.

Martin CONSTABLE 1961– Painter and teacher, born in Toronto, Canada. He studied at Richmond-upon-Thames Polytechnic, 1978–9; St Martin's School of Art, 1979–80; Coleg Elidyr, Camphill, in south Wales, 1980–1; then graduated with first-class degree from Camberwell School of Art, 1983–6; gaining his master's at Goldsmiths' College School of Art, 1988–90. He was a part-time tutor at Central St Martins School from 1994, becoming co-ordinator and drawing course tutor from 1995. Among mixed exhibitions were South London Art Gallery, Thames & Hudson Prize Show, 1986; RA Summer Exhibition and John Moores Liverpool Exhibition, from 1987; The Discerning Eye, Mall Galleries and tour, 1991, where Constable was a first prize winner; Eagle Gallery, 1993; and Royal Over-Seas League Open, 1995. Had solo shows at Long & Ryle Art International, 1992–4. Arts Council, The London Institute and several corporate collections hold examples. Lived in London.

Richard CONSTABLE 1932– Artist in gouache and teacher, born in Lewes, Sussex. He gained an art scholarship to Marlborough College, 1945–50, later attending Trent Park Training College and becoming an art teacher in various schools, 1959–67. Participated in group exhibitions with Bath Society of Artists of which he was a member, Ipswich Art Club and SGA. From 1967 had over 40 solo exhibitions, including Heal's Gallery, Cooling Galleries, Radlett Gallery, Mignon Gallery in Bath and extensively abroad. Constable produced "Surrealist landscapes influenced by oriental art". Lived in Norton sub Hamdon, Stoke sub Hamdon, Somerset.

Lyn CONSTABLE MAXWELL 1944– Figurative sculptor, born in London, who was educated at St Mary's, Wantage. She studied fine art at Byam Shaw School and sculpture at Heatherley's School of Fine Art with Cubitt Bevis. An overland trip to India in 1970 led to a first bronze Nepalese Mother and Child. In 1977 Constable Maxwell won a diploma at the Venice Concourso Internationale di Pittura. Became artist-in-residence at Winchester Cathedral in 1991. Among her commissions was the Fourteen Stations of the Cross for St Gregory's Church, Alresford, known as the Patrick O'Donovan Memorial. Had solo shows at Bury Street Gallery in 1981–5, another in 1988 sponsored by Martini Rossi at The Newbury Festival. Work was cast by The Morris Singer Foundry.

Diana CONSTANCE fl. from 1950s– Artist, born in New York City, America, where she gained a scholarship to the Arts Students' League. She was assistant art director for Reporter Publications; did graduate work at the University of New Mexico; then during a five-year residence in Rome developed an interest in photography. Exhibitions included Albuquerque, New Mexico, 1960; at Camden Arts Centre: in 1970, Life Photographs, and in 1973, shared show with the sculptor John Farnham; Space Open Studios, from 1974; LG at Royal College of Art, 1978; and Contemporary Artists in Camden, Camden Arts Centre, 1981. Camden Borough Council, Leicester Education Authority and Mobil Oil Group hold her work. In 1988 her solo exhibition Aids (and nobody wants to know) was held at the Peoples Gallery. Lived in north London.

Hervé CONSTANT 1951– Painter, inspired by the poet Arthur Rimbaud, who explored the visual connection between what people see and say and employed a number of treasured forms: the triangle the symbol of the soul, windows of perception and the Christian cross. He was born in Casablanca of a Moroccan Jewish mother and French father and suffered a dislocated childhood. Initially determined to be an actor, but turned to painting. Studied at Conservatoire National de Musique de Toulon, 1967–70; École Nationale Superieure des Arts et Techniques du Theatre, Paris, 1971–3; and Beaux-Arts de Toulon, for printmaking, 1980–3. Group shows included Fischer Fine Art, 1978; Stamford Arts Centre, 1985; Air Gallery, 1989; and Tricycle Gallery, 1993. Also had many mixed exhibitions in France and solo shows from late 1960s; British one-mans included in 1995 Ben Uri Art Gallery, Tricycle Gallery and The Living Room. Commissions/collections included St Martin's Church, Gospel Oak, 1987; Arthur Andersen, 1991; Lynam Richard Partnership, 1994; and Earl Estates Ltd, 1995. Lived in London.

Frank CONSTANTINE 1919– Painter, restorer and curator, born Harry Frank Constantine in Sheffield, where he settled. Studied at Sheffield and Southampton Colleges of Art and at the Courtauld Institute. While in the Army in 1939 began work for Sheffield City Art Galleries, becoming director in 1964 and retiring in 1982. Showed RA, with Sheffield Society of Artists of which he was president, at Graves Art Gallery in Sheffield and elsewhere in the provinces. The Sheffield collection holds a number of landscapes by him.

Ellen CONTI 1884– Painter and draughtsman, born in London, of English origin but who married the actor, singer and artist Guiseppe Conti, of Italian background. Educated in south London and in Surrey, she studied art at West Croydon Art School, where she excelled as a pencil draughtsman, later attending Chelsea Art School under Ernest Borough Johnson, Clapham Art School, Heatherley's School of Fine Art and St Martin's School of Art, where her teachers included Conrad Lomax. Showed principally in the Ipswich and Norwich areas and lived at Cavendish, Suffolk.

Dorab Dadiba CONTRACTOR 1929– Artist, notably a sculptor, born in Bombay, India, who became a naturalised British citizen. He studied at Sir J J School of Art, Bombay, qualifying in 1929. Showed in mixed exhibitions with NS of which he was a member, Romford Central Library and Mall Galleries. Had a solo show at India House, 1972, and Woodstock Gallery, 1975, later ones including Kenneth More Theatre, Ilford, 1988. HM The Queen and other members of the royal family hold his work, sometimes signed Dorab. Lived in Gidea Park, Essex.

Francis CONVERY 1956– Painter, draughtsman and teacher, born in Paisley, Renfrewshire. After working as a mechanical engineer, 1972–6, and travel to Europe, 1978, Convery attended Edinburgh College of Art, 1979–83, during which he travelled to Turkey, in 1984 gaining his diploma in postgraduate studies. After part-time lecturing at the College, 1984–6, during which time he visited New York, Convery was appointed lecturer in drawing and painting at Gray's School of Art, Aberdeen, in 1987. His awards included first prize in the Rowney Competition for painting, 1982; Carnegie and John Kinross travelling scholarships in 1983; and a series of RSA awards, including the Latimer in 1984, Scottish Post Office Board, 1992, and Highland Society of London, 1994; and the Shell Expro Award, 1995. Convery was elected an associate of RSA in 1994. Took part in many mixed shows including Scottish Gallery in Edinburgh; Fosse Gallery, Stow-on-the-Wold; and Mercury Gallery. Solo exhibitions included Scottish Gallery from 1991. Edinburgh's University, College of Art, Council and City Arts Centre hold his work.

Dianne CONWAY fl. from late 1960s– Painter and teacher who started on her art training at Aberdeen College of Education, 1968–71, where she worked under James Hardie. After bringing up her family, in 1985 she began a course in fine art at Plymouth, then moved to Exeter for another three years to obtain a degree and professional teaching qualification. Went on to teach in a comprehensive school. Style of painting changed radically over the years, from vigorous representational pictures to more contemplative abstracts. Had a first comprehensive show at Cleveland Bridge Gallery, Bath, in 1991, with a second there in 1992 based on a journey the year before across China.

Edward CONWAY 1872– Flower painter in oil and watercolour, who studied under Henry Tonks at the Slade School of Fine Art, then at Académie Julian, Paris. Exhibited RA, RWA and elsewhere. Lived at Burford, Oxfordshire.

Jennifer CONWAY 1935– Miniaturist and painter in various media, born in Brecon, Wales, who attended Bedford College of Physical Education, 1954–7. She became a member of RMS in 1979 and SM in 1981, also exhibiting at RA, SWA and in America. Brecknock Museum holds her work. Lived in Maescelyn, Powys.

Ben COODE-ADAMS 1964– Sculptor noted for wrought-iron work. He took a first-class honours degree in sculpture at Camberwell School of Arts & Crafts, 1982–6, doing a postgraduate certificate of education at Middlesex Polytechnic, 1986–7. Then did a postgraduate course in bronze casting at Royal College of Art, 1987–8, and his master's degree in sculpture there, 1989–92. He received a number of awards, scholarships, sponsorships and residencies. Exhibited at South London Art Gallery in the Sogat 82 Sculpture Show from 1985; Hannah Peschar Gallery from 1986; Arts Club, Bryan Kneale's Choice, 1990; Geffrye Museum, 1992; and in Drawing Towards Sculpture, 1993, at Isis Gallery, Leigh-on-Sea, in which he showed witty, slightly Surrealist drawings.

Alice May COOK 1876–1960 Book illustrator, especially children's books, sometimes under her maiden name of May Barnett; miniature painter. Studied at St John's Wood School of Art and the Royal Academy Schools. Exhibited RA, RMS, SWA, RSA and RHA, in Canada and South Africa. Lived at Spixworth, Norwich, Norfolk.

Barrie COOK 1929– Abstract painter and teacher, born in Birmingham, where he studied at the College of Arts and Crafts under Bernard Fleetwood-Walker, 1949–54. Taught in secondary schools, then taught at Coventry College of Art, 1961–9; was head of the fine art department at Stourbridge College of Art, 1969–74; senior fellow in fine art, painting, at Cardiff College of Art, 1974–7; Gregynog Fellow, University of Wales, 1977–8; then head of fine art at Birmingham Polytechnic, 1979–83. Was artist-in-residence, Fishguard Arts Festival, 1984, then at the National Museum & Art Gallery, Cardiff, 1987–8, having a studio base in the city until 1992, when he moved to Helston, Cornwall. Cook took part in numerous mixed shows, including Marjorie Parr Gallery, 1963; John Moores Liverpool Exhibition, from 1967; the Arts Council's British Painting '74, 1974; The Presence of Painting, the South Bank Centre's 1988–9 tour; and Cross Currents, Reed's Wharf Gallery at the Barbican Centre, 1996. His work could be both monumental, as at Camden Arts Centre in 1971, and delicate and discreet. Had a long series of solo shows, starting with Herbert Art Gallery, Coventry, 1966, later ones including Spray Paintings, Barbican Centre, 1995. Arts Council, Tate Gallery, WAC and many other public collections hold examples.

Ben COOK 1967– Artist, born in Thornbury, Gloucestershire, who studied at Sunderland Polytechnic, 1986–9. In 1991 he took part in Granada Celebration, Albert Dock, Liverpool, and in 6 Manchester Artists at Castlefield Gallery, Manchester, in 1993–4 being included in John Moores Liverpool Exhibition. Had a first solo show at Chapman Gallery, Salford, in 1993. Lived in Manchester.

Beryl COOK 1926– Popular painter in oil of daily life with a ribald tinge, born in Egham, Surrey. Left Kendrick School at 14 to work in an insurance office. In 1943 began short career as a show-girl, became a model and worked for several dress firms. In 1946 with her mother bought a riverside tea-garden at Hampton and married Merchant Navy officer John Cook. After running a public house in Essex they moved to Southern Rhodesia where Beryl did several jobs and began painting. After a period in Zambia settled in Cornwall, where she started painting on her favourite support, wood. Beryl ran a boarding-house at Plymouth Hoe, Devon, where she settled, and which was the inspiration for many pictues. In the mid-1970s Plymouth Arts Centre put on a show, after which her fame grew fast, with exhibitions at Whitechapel and Portal Galleries. Her first book of paintings, *The Works*, was published in 1978, a second, *Private View*, in 1980. *Beryl Cook's London* followed in 1988. Had a retrospective in that year at Plymouth City Museum, with tour, with another in 1995. In 1998 she moved to Bristol.

Brian COOK 1910–1991 Painter, designer, writer, publisher and politician, educated at Repton School. In 1928 he joined the family publishing firm B T Batsford in the production department, but attended part-time classes at Central School of Arts and Crafts. His bright, wrap-around cover for *The Villages of England* led to his being used as sole illustrator for the British Heritage series and over 100 distinctive covers in an Art Deco style. He also designed railway, holiday and travel agency posters and showed in Paris. After World War II service in the Royal Air Force he rejoined the firm and took the surname Batsford (his mother's maiden name); his painting career dwindled as he moved to become chairman. He became a Conservative member of parliament in 1958 and held a number of important government and party positions. Sir Brian, knighted in 1974, was chairman of the Royal Society of Arts, 1973–5. The Hayward Gallery show Landscape in Britain in 1983 led to a revival of interest in his work; in 1987 he published *The Britain of Brian Cook* and had a retrospective at the Parkin Gallery. Died in Winchelsea, Sussex.

Christopher COOK 1959– Painter, poet and teacher, born in North Yorkshire. He attended Exeter College of Art & Design, 1978–81, gaining the Gladys Hunkin Poetry Prize, then obtained master's degree in painting, Royal College of Art, 1983–6. Also studied at Rietveld Akademie, Amsterdam, 1985; gained an Italian Scholarship, 1986; and in 1987–8 attended Accademia di Belle Arti, Bologna. Won a number of prizes, including first prize at Camden Annual, 1984. Cook was fellow in painting at Exeter College of Art, 1989; guest artist, Stadelschule Frankfurt-am-Main, Germany, 1991, the year he was head of painting, Exeter Faculty of Art, University of Plymouth, 1991; visiting artist, Akademie van beeldende Kunsten, Rotterdam, Holland, 1992; and visiting fellow at Oxford University, 1993. In addition to many mixed shows in Britain and abroad, had solo show at Camden Arts Centre, 1985, later ones including a series at Benjamin Rhodes Gallery from 1987–8. British Museum and other public collections hold his work.

David COOK 1940– Wildlife artist notable for his birds, photographer, paper sculptor and lecturer, born in Rochester, Kent. He attended Medway College of Art, 1956–9, under Stanley Hayes, then Regent Street Polytechnic School of Art, 1962. Cook was a photographer with *Country Life* magazine, then a research photographer with Bowater, followed by a career in law, becoming a freelance wildlife artist and paper sculptor. He formed the Cookco Press "to promote not only my own work but that of artists I admire". He gave workshops around the world and demonstrated, mainly for Rexel Ltd with Derwent pencils. Showed with UA, RA, SWA and RSMA and had solo exhibitions widely in Britain. His work is held by a number of civil, corporate, educational and private collections. Lived in Carlisle, Cumbria.

David COOK 1944– Painter and printmaker, whose work included landscapes and Surreal compositions. He was born in Bingley, Yorkshire, in the mid-1970s settling in Malham. Studied at Bradford College of Art and Royal College of Art. Exhibited widely abroad and was included in Images of the Yorkshire Landscape, organised by Sheeran Lock at Leeds Civic Hall in 1991. Majestic landscapes of Malham and Gordale Scar were an important feature of Cook's output.

David COOK 1957– Artist, born in Dunfermline, Fife. He studied at Duncan of Jordanstone College of Art, Dundee, 1979–84, and won a travel fellowship that took him to Paris, Amsterdam, Belgium and Cyprus. Cook garnered a number of awards, including first prize at the RSA annual student show, 1983; RSA Guthrie Award, 1985; Scottish Arts Council Awards, 1985–8–9; and McGregor Donald Sculpture Award second prize, 1990. Cook had extensive group showings, including RSA, Mercury Gallery in Edinburgh, Warwick Arts Trust, and Scottish Gallery in Edinburgh and London. A solo show at Traverse Theatre in Edinburgh in 1982 was followed by a series which included 369 Gallery, Edinburgh, 1987–9, and Gruzelier Modern and Contemporary Art, 1991.

Francis Ferdinand Maurice COOK 1907–1978 Painter, born in London, son of Sir Herbert Frederick Cook, Bart. Sir Francis studied art under Harold Speed, John Arnesby Brown and S J

Lamorna Birch over a decade from 1926. He then exhibited widely, including RA, RBA, LG and Walker Art Gallery, Liverpool, one of several provincial collection holding his work, which is sometimes of an allegorical-cum-religious nature. Sometimes signed work with initials F M C plus date. Had a special interest in the techniques of the Old Masters and connections with St Ives and Jersey artists' colonies and lived in St Aubin, Jersey.

Frederick T W COOK 1907–1982 Painter in oil and gouache of landscapes, marine scenes and flowers. Born in London, Cook studied at the Hampstead School of Art and during World War II was an official fireman-artist. He exhibited widely, at the RA, RSA, RWA and the Leicester, Redfern and Trafford Galleries. The Imperial War Museum and Plymouth City Museum and Art Gallery, Devon, hold his work. *Studio*, *Sphere* and *Tatler* used his pictures. Lived in Polperro, Cornwall.

G Lewis COOK 1913– Painter and designer who was self-taught, born in London where he continued to live. Showed at UA, RBA and RI.

Hubert COOK 1901– Painter, printmaker and teacher, born in Wroughton, Wiltshire. He studied with Harold Dearden at Swindon School of Art, 1926–34, then at the Central School of Arts and Crafts, 1935–38, with Noel Rooke and Percy Hague Jowett. Taught at Portsmouth Technical College. Exhibited RA, UA, RWA, Senefelder Club, Leicester Galleries and overseas. Swindon Museum and Art Gallery is among several holding his work. Lived in Swindon.

Ian David COOK 1950– Artist and teacher, born and lived in Paisley, Renfrewshire. He studied at Glasgow School of Art, 1969–72, teachers including David Donaldson, with a post-graduate diploma, 1972–3. Gained the Hutcheson Drawing Prize, 1972; Cargill Travelling Scholarship to Spain and North Africa, 1974; and a Scottish Arts Council Travelling Bursary to Central Africa, 1984. He was a member of RI and RSW, 1978, also exhibiting with Royal Glasgow Institute of the Fine Arts and extensively elsewhere. Showed solo with Kelly Gallery, Glasgow, from 1979, later exhibitions including Flying Colours Gallery in Edinburgh, 1989, and African Images at Scottish Gallery there, 1990. BBC and Trustee Savings Bank hold examples.

Jenny COOK 1942– Artist born in Preston, Lancashire, who studied at Harris College locally, 1960–5, then Leicester College of Art, 1965–6. She showed in mixed exhibitions at RA from 1975 and Medici Society reproduced her work. Showed solo at Mercury Gallery from 1976 and Leicester Museum and Art Gallery, 1982. Lived in Leicester.

John Kingsley COOK 1911–1994 Painter, muralist, wood engraver and teacher, born in Winchcombe, Gloucestershire. He studied at Royal Academy Schools under Thomas Monnington and Walter Westley Russell, gaining the Gold Medal and Travelling Scholarship; then at Central School of Arts and Crafts, for wood engraving under Noel Rooke. Cook served as a Merchant Navy radio officer in World War II, making an extensive record of his experiences at sea and in an Algerian prison camp. Imperial War Museum as well as London's Guildhall Library, the Library of Congress in Washington and Bristol Museum and Art Gallery hold his work. Cook went on to become head of the design school at Edinburgh College of Art. He also produced a book of poems and wood engravings called *Aftermath* and toured a moving image show called *Microcosm*. Was a member of SWE and SSA, also showing in mixed exhibitions at RA Summer Exhibitions, RSA and elsewhere. Solo exhibitions included Demarco Gallery and Open Eye Gallery, both in Edinburgh; and at the Gallery Upstairs, at RA. In 1995 there was a memorial show at Edinburgh College of Art. John Sell Cotman and Samuel Palmer were influences cited by Cook, who also had an abstract phase and produced large pictures on ecological themes. Lived finally in London.

Olive COOK 1916– Writer and painter, born in Cambridge, who was married to the artist Edwin Smith. After reading modern languages at Cambridge University, Cook worked as a typographer for the publisher Chatto and Windus, then joined the staff of the National Gallery. Although not professionally trained as a painter, she gained help from her husband and Thomas Hennell, and spent a short time at Cedric Morris' East Anglian School of Painting and Drawing. Early watercolour landscapes were acquired for the Pilgrim Trust's *Recording Britain* project. In 1954 Cook was second prizewinner in an Italian government painting competition, she showed at Leicester Galleries, LG and WIAC and she had solo exhibitions at Arcade Gallery and at the Old Fire Engine House, Ely, 1979–84. Ferens Art Gallery, Hull, and Nuffield Foundation hold her work. Lived for many years in Saffron Walden. She wrote the guide to the Fry Art Gallery's collection there, and is represented in it. Contributed to *The Saturday Book.*

Richard COOK 1947– Painter, draughtsman and teacher, born in Cheltenham, Gloucestershire. Having begun to paint in his early teens Cook left boarding school as soon as he could and went to St Martin's School of Art, 1966–70, where he became impressed by the work of David Bomberg and Leon Kossoff, influences seen in his own figure paintings and landscapes. After Royal College of Art he eventually moved from London to Cornwall in 1985, settling in Newlyn, from 1990 teaching part-time at Falmouth School of Art and Design. Among the group exhibitions he appeared in were The Human Clay, an Arts Council show at Hayward Gallery, 1976; British Art 1940–1980, in 1980, with a similar sponsor and venue; Serpentine Gallery Summer Show in 1982; A Century of Art in Cornwall, at County Hall, Truro, in 1989; and Stephen Bartley Gallery, 1991. After a solo show at House Gallery in 1981 he had another with Odette Gilbert Gallery, 1989, and Newlyn Art Gallery, 1992. Arts Council and British Museum hold his work.

Richard COOK 1949– Painter of portraits and landscapes, born in Grimsby, Lincolnshire. He studied at the College of Art there,

Maidstone College of Art, 1968–71, and Royal Academy Schools, 1972–5. While there he won the E T Greenshields Award for Study Abroad and the David Murray Landscape Award. In 1980 he held a one-man show at Royal Academy Schools' Gallery and gained a Richard Ford Travelling Scholarship to Spain to study at the Prado. Ford showed often at RA, was a member of RBA and also took part in mixed exhibitions at NEAC, RP, RI and widely in the provinces. Lived in Brighton, Sussex.

T R COOK 1964– Painter, creator of collage boxes and painter who studied at Harlow Technical College and Birmingham Polytechnic. Cook's work had a witty quality, as seen in several examples at England & Co in the 1991 show Art in Boxes. Had one-man exhibitions at Swiss Cottage Library and Playhouse Gallery, Harlow, and at England & Co in 1994.

Anthony R COOKE 1933– Artist and teacher, born in London. He studied at Worthing School of Arts and Crafts, then at Royal Academy Schools, his teachers including Peter Greenham, Carel Weight and Ruskin Spear. Exhibited widely, and was chosen by Jack Beddington for his 1957 volume *Young Artists of Promise*. Public galleries in Batley, Leicester, Nottingham, Preston and Worthing hold his work. Taught at West Sussex College of Art and Design. Signed work with initials. Lived at Shoreham-by-Sea, Sussex.

Beth COOKE 1920– Landscape and plant painter and draughtsman, born in East Dulwich, southeast London, full name Elizabeth Hannah, her father the ecclesiastical and heraldic designer Percy John Hill. Graduated in horticulture at Studley hoping to make a career in plant-hunting, but war diverted her into agricultural research at Rothamsted, where she met her husband-to-be, the notable soil scientist George William Cooke, whom she married in 1944. Having illustrated a Pitman manual *Botany for Gardeners*, Cooke began studying with Gerhart Frankl from 1950–1, but the use of colour and the inspiration of Emil Nolde and German Expressionism turned her towards painting. Had work accepted for Redfern Gallery Summer Exhibition in 1951; by Derbyshire Education Department, 1953; WIAC and LG in 1955; then concentrated on her family until after her husband's death in 1992. Later solo shows included Royal Agricultural Show, Stoneleigh, from 1993; CRA Gallery, St Albans, 1994; and Atrium, from 1995. Cooke's landscapes, real and imaginary, had as their main literary influence writings by the Westmorland novelist Constance Holme. The artist lived in Harpenden, Hertfordshire.

E F COOKE 1905–1963 Painter in oil, born at Stone, Staffordshire. After education at Stafford Girls' High School, Mrs Cooke studied art at the Kitchener Institute, in Stone, then at Carlisle School of Art. She continued to live in Stone, exhibited widely in the north of England and was associated with the Whitehaven Art Club.

Ida COOKE fl. from late 1930s– Artist in various media, born in New Plymouth, New Zealand. She studied at Slade School of Fine Art where she won a prize for life painting; also attended Oscar Kokoschka's School, Salzburg, Austria. Exhibited extensively in mixed exhibitions, including RA, RP, John Whibley Gallery and elsewhere. Gained gold medal, Accademia Italia. Had solo shows at Woodstock Gallery, 1966, and Clarges Gallery, 1973, later ones including Centaur Gallery, 1980. Lived in Windsor, Berkshire.

Jean COOKE 1927– Artist in oil, watercolour, pastel and clay, and teacher, born and lived in London, married to the painter John Bratby. Some of her work, such as the Tate Gallery's Self-Portrait, of 1959, was inscribed Jean Bratby. She painted Bratby and appeared in many of his works. She studied at Central School of Arts and Crafts, 1943–5; Camberwell School of Arts and Crafts and Goldsmiths' College School of Art, 1945–9, and at City and Guilds School of Art; and at Royal College of Art, 1953–5, under Carel Weight and Ruskin Spear, having run a pottery workshop in Sussex, 1950–3. Was a lecturer at Royal College, 1965–74. In 1972 was elected RA, was also a member of RBA. In addition to mixed show appearances had many solo exhibitions, early ones including Establishment Club, 1963, and Leicester Galleries, 1964, later ones including Agnew and Ansdell Galleries, 1974. Cooke was noted as a realistic painter of everyday life, citing "figures in light and space" as an important theme.

Randal COOKE 1946– Painter, printmaker and teacher, born in southeast London. He studied painting at Camberwell School of Arts and Crafts and Chelsea School of Art. Went on to become a tutor in lithography at Camberwell and Cambridgeshire College of Art and Technology. Among his many exhibitions was a four-man show at Woodlands Art Gallery, 1988. Had a solo show at Kent Institute of Art & Design, Maidstone, 1993. Lived in east London.

Stanley COOKE 1913– Painter in oil and watercolour and free-lance commercial artist, He was born in Mansfield, Nottinghamshire, between 1924–32 studying at the local School of Art, then illustration through Percy Bradshaw's correspondence Press Art School. Cooke's work was reproduced on greetings cards and he showed in mixed exhibitions at RA, ROI and UA. Drian and Mansfield Art Galleries gave him solo shows. Lived for many years in Guildford, Surrey.

William Cubitt COOKE 1866–1951 Watercolourist, draughtsman, printmaker and teacher, born and lived in London. He was apprenticed to a chromo-lithographer and did a lot of commercial work, studying at Heatherley's and Westminster Schools of Art, also at Cook's, but was mainly self-taught. He was a member of Langham Sketch Club and walked constantly with a sketchbook. His work appeared in magazines such as *Illustrated London News* and *Harmsworth's* and in books published by Blackie, Dent, Methuen and others. Showed at RA, RI and RBA.

Julian COOKSEY 1960– Figurative and non-figurative sculptor, and teacher, employing a range of natural and man-made materials. He gained a degree in English literature from Magdelen

College, Oxford, 1979–82; was a management trainee with Trafalgar House, 1982–5; regional administrator, Association for Business Sponsorship of the Arts, 1985–8; did a foundation course at Chelsea School of Art, 1988–9; then graduated in sculpture from Central St Martins College of Art & Design, 1989–92. During that time he was a part-time foundry worker at Arch Bronze, Putney, from 1993–5 undertaking technician work and part-time teaching at Brunel University Arts Centre and Kingston University, from 1994 also teaching sculpture part-time at Kensington & Chelsea College. Exhibitions included 1st RWA Open Sculpture Exhibition, 1993, and a shared show with Barbara Delaney at Brunel University, 1997. Had a London studio.

Charles John Franklin COOMBS 1907–1989 Painter, illustrator, naturalist and medical practitioner, born in Bristol. He was self-taught as an artist, although he was much-influenced and helped by the artist Robert Gillmor. Coombs studied at Clifton College and Cambridge University and was a Bachelor of Civil Law. While in general practice in the area of Truro, Cornwall, for 40 years Coombs was heavily involved in ornithological research, belonging to a number of related organisations. Was a member of SWLA, showing elsewhere in Britain and abroad. Among books illustrated were his own *The Crows*, 1978. Ulster Museum in Belfast holds his work.

Daniel COOMBS 1971– Artist who was born and lived in London. He gained an honours degree at Ruskin School of Art, Oxford, 1989–92; obtained his master's degree in painting from Royal College of Art, 1992–4; then won a Scholarship to the British School at Rome, 1994–5. Exhibitions included Young British Artists VI, Saatchi Gallery, 1996. Coombs said that his work was "about the blandness that comes from not having a voice beyond the common, anonymous popular one".

Caroline COON fl. from 1960s– Figurative painter who as a child boarded at Legat Russian Ballet School, later at Royal Ballet School, appearing at Covent Garden. Attended Central School of Art and in 1965, while working as a model, appeared in Ken Russell's television film *Rossetti*. In 1967 she co-founded the drugs advisory group Release, in the 1980s managed the Punk group The Clash, in 1988 publishing *The Punk Rock Explosion*. Coon was included in The Sixties Art Scene in London, at Barbican Art Gallery, 1993, in the same year in People and Places at Gagliardi Gallery. The poet Christopher Logue, the actress Julie Christie and other notable collectors acquired Coon's work.

Hubert COOP 1872–1953 Painter notable for his landscapes and seascapes of England, which he travelled widely. He was born in Olney, Buckinghamshire, and worked as a draughtsman in industry, being elected to RBA aged 22. Ebb Tide, Whitby and Chalk Cliffs at Dover are among his main works. Showed at Walker Art Gallery in Liverpool, RA, RCamA and RI and had work bought by Oldham Corporation. Lived latterly in Northam, Devon.

Alfred Egerton COOPER 1883–1974 Portrait and landscape painter, born in Tettenhall, Staffordshire, who studied at Bilston School of Art and Royal College of Art, graduating in 1911. Served in Artists' Rifles in World War I. He was elected RBA in 1914. In 1921 Cooper's picture London from an Airship was a notable feature of the RA Summer Exhibition and three years later he won an Honourable Mention at Paris Salon. Also showed Walker Art Gallery in Liverpool, ROI, RI and Goupil Gallery. King George VI and Sir Winston Churchill were among Cooper's portrait subjects. Lived in London and was a member of Chelsea Arts Club.

Austin COOPER 1890–1964 Maker of abstract collages, watercolourist, poster designer and teacher, born in Souris, Manitoba, Canada. The family moved to Cardiff, Wales, when Cooper was six years old. He studied at the School of Art there, winning a scholarship to the Patrick Allan-Fraser School of Art, Arbroath, where he studied 1905–9. In London, in 1910, he attended evening classes under Innes Fripp at the City and Guilds School. After a period in Canada as a commercial artist and interior designer Fripp served in the Army during World War I, had another spell in Canada, returning to England in the early 1920s where he designed posters and began to paint seriously in the early 1940s. First one-man show at London Gallery in 1948; showed at Gimpel Fils from 1955; also exhibited at Galerie Craven, Paris. Tate Gallery holds several examples. Lived in London.

Constance COOPER 1905– Painter, born in Shoreham, Kent, who studied at Croydon College of Art. She was a member of SWA and showed in London, the provinces and abroad. Lived in Croydon, Surrey.

David COOPER 1952– Painter and draughtsman, born in London. Cooper was a mature student at Goldsmiths' College School of Art under Leonard McComb, having worked for a decade from 1968 as a mason pavior for the London Borough of Southwark. After four years at Goldsmiths', from 1978, Cooper began to show in mixed exhibitions, notably New Contemporaries. In 1985 he shared a show at Goldsmiths', exhibiting large figurative paintings. The following year he participated in Cityscape: The changing face of London, an Arthur Andersen and Company exhibition, then in 1986–7 he was included in A Reputation Amongst Artists, a Norwich School of Art Gallery touring exhibition. Cooper was a meticulous artist who drew on his experiences in London's East End and its street life, notably the theme of children playing. Arthur Andersen and Leicestershire Education Authority hold his work.

Eileen COOPER 1953– Painter, draughtsman, printmaker and teacher, born in Glossop, Derbyshire. Aged 17 she did a foundation course in Ashton-under-Lyne, then was at Goldsmiths' College School of Art, 1971–4, then Royal College of Art, 1974–7. Later she was a visiting lecturer at Central St Martins. Cooper was noted for her studies of the human figure, often large and of a Chagall-like intensity. From the mid-1980s she participated in numerous mixed exhibitions in Britain. After a solo exhibition at Air Gallery in 1979 others included House Gallery in 1981; Blond Fine Art, 1982–3–5; Artsite Gallery, Bath, 1987; then a series at Benjamin Rhodes Gallery from 1988. Among her commissioned work was a Staircase Project at ICA, 1982, and a series of book covers and frontispieces. Arts Council, British Council and Victoria & Albert Museum hold her work.

Francis Glanville COOPER 1918– Watercolourist, potter and teacher, born in Portsmouth, Hampshire. Studied at Kingston School of Art with Henry Hammond, 1945, then the Burslem School of Art in 1947 and Woolwich Polytechnic. Younger brother of the potter Ronald Glanville Cooper. Like his brother he went on to teach, for periods at Sheffield and Maidstone Colleges of Art and Southend School of Art. Cooper showed at Design Centre, Red Rose Guild of Craftsmen and elsewhere. Wakefield City Art Gallery holds his work. Signed his work in monogram form. Lived in Sheffield for some years.

George Ralph COOPER 1909– Painter and businessman, born in Aylmerton, Norfolk. Initially educated in Norwich, he later attended the University of Wales and obtained a doctorate of philosophy. He studied art in the 1920s and 1930s in Wales, America and Scotland. Showed at RA, ROI, AIA and with Hertford Art Society, which he founded in 1953. Official collections in Bedford and Letchworth hold his work. Lived in St Albans, Hertfordshire.

Gerald COOPER 1898–1975 Painter, sculptor and teacher whose works included children's portraits, landscapes and horses, but who was noted for his meticulous flowers in the manner of the Dutch Old Masters. Cooper studied at Royal College of Art, where in 1925 he shared the Drawing Prize of the school of painting with Phyllis Dodd. Cooper became principal of Wimbledon School of Art and was keenly interested in art education. He was a member of the Bray and National Committees on Art Education and was an examiner for the Ministry of Education. Was also a member of NS, and showed at NEAC, E Stacy-Marks in Eastbourne, RA extensively until the year of his death and elsewhere in Britain. Lived in London.

Isolde Frances COOPER 1903–1953 Painter in oil, born in London, she was the daughter of Lord Borthwick and married Sir George Cooper. Lady Cooper studied at Heatherley's School of Fine Art under Iain Macnab. Exhibited RBA and ROI. Lived at Hursley, Winchester, Hampshire.

Ivor COOPER 1899–1987 Advertising executive and part-time artist who studied architecture in England and America. He took a first job in advertising with Wilson's agency in 1919, then eventually joined Lever House Advertising House Advertising Service aged 26. After the formation of the Lintas agency in 1928 his charismatic personality helped give it an international thrust. He retired from Unilever in 1964 to give himself time for interests including painting and his work was included in the Lintas Beyond the Horizon show at Agnew in 1988.

John F COOPER 1929– Artist, teacher and educationist, born in Merthyr Tydfil, Glamorgan. He studied painting and stained glass from 1949–56 at Swansea College of Art and was technical assistant at Glynn Vivian Art Gallery for two years. Held a number of teaching posts in the Midlands and South Wales, then did a diploma in art education at Cardiff College of Education in the late 1960s. Took part in a number of group shows including Young Contemporaries at Chenil Galleries, 1953, then in Wales at Royal National Eisteddfod, SWG, WAC and elsewhere.

John Hubert COOPER 1912– Artist and teacher, born in Pemberton, Lancashire. Cooper studied at Wigan School of Art, 1930–5; at Liverpool University Department of Education; taught at Gosport Country Grammer School and Bay House School, Gosport, 1936–75, also being an adult education tutor; in the 1970s graduating through the Open University. Was a member of BWS and Royal Drawing Society, also showing in Hampshire and Wessex Artists Exhibitions and at Paris Salon. Designed and etched windows for Gosport Town Hall. Lived latterly in Banstead, Surrey.

Josephine Mary COOPER 1932– Miniaturist, painter and printmaker, born in Brighton, Sussex. She studied at St Albans School of Art, Mid-Hertfordshire College of Further Education and privately. Had a number of solo shows; was a member of SM from 1974; UA from 1975; RMS from 1983; and SWA from 1988, also exhibiting at RSMA and at Paris Salon, where she gained a Silver Medal, 1974. Lived in Welwyn Garden City, Hertfordshire.

Julian COOPER 1947– Painter and teacher, born in Grasmere, Westmorland, who lived for a time at Ambleside, Cumbria. He studied at Lancaster School of Art, 1964–5, and Goldsmiths' College of Art, 1965–9, winning a Boise Travelling Scholarship, 1969–70. He held a Karolyi Foundation in France in 1976, followed by a fellowship at VCCA in Virginia, 1981, won a Northern Art Bursary in 1982 and was visiting lecturer at Sunderland Polytechnic the same year. Cooper's series of pictures Under the Volcano, based on the novel by Malcolm Lowry, was important and was featured in Summer Show 2 at Serpentine Gallery, 1983. Other group exhibitions included RA Summer Exhibition, 1972; Deck of Cards, JPL Fine Art, 1976; and Northern Open at Ceolfrith Gallery, Sunderland, 1982. Cooper was a frequent exhibitor with LG annual shows from 1967. Solo shows included Laing Art Gallery, Newcastle, 1974, and JPL Fine Art, 1978. Arts Council, University College in London and galleries in Bolton, Lancaster and Newcastle hold examples.

Margaret COOPER 1893– Painter and writer who was married to the artist Robert Cresswell Boak. After studying at Queen's University, Belfast, she attended the Slade School of Fine Art, then studied in Paris. Lived in London.

Mary COOPER 1911– Collagist and artist in various materials who studied at Central School of Arts and Crafts with Bernard Adeney. She showed at RA, Leighton House and was a member of Free Painters and Sculptors. Signed work with initials. Lived for a time at Richmond, Surrey.

Michael COOPER 1943– Painter in oil, born in Birmingham, self-taught and by profession a picture restorer. Music "played an important part" in creating his small, subtle, understated pictures which were exhibited at RA Summer Exhibition, Bruton Street Gallery, Phoenix Gallery at Lavenham and Towner Art Gallery, Eastbourne. Showed solo with Star Gallery, Lewes. Cooper sometimes signed pictures with initials only.

Michael COOPER 1944– Sculptor, often on a monumental scale in stone and marble, born in Dublin, Ireland. He studied in England under Anthony Gray, showing widely in England, Ireland and America. As well as a nine-foot Sailfish sited in Florida, and a Troubador figure in the Mandarin Hotel, Hong Kong, Gray completed large pieces for public and private sites in England. Was included in Sixteen Sculptors at Sladmore Contemporary, 1997.

Paul COOPER 1923– Sculptor in many materials, born and lived in Wool, Dorset, married to the artist Audrey Carnaby. He studied at Poole College of Art, 1939–41, at Goldsmiths' College School of Art, 1948–51, then at Lincoln College in 1958. Showed at RA, with RBS of which he was a fellow and elsewhere in London and the provinces. Did widespread church work in Britain and abroad. Oxford and Lincoln Education Authorities hold examples.

Paul COOPER 1949– Sculptor and teacher, born in Manchester. He studied sculpture at Newcastle University and went on to lecture at University of Lancaster. In 1981 he was in Baltimore as a visiting artist at the Maryland Institute of Art. Cooper worked at various times in wood, mild steel and hollow cast concrete, in the last case usually in limited editions which could be placed at various locations. He was interested in patterns to be found in both man-made and natural forms and pursued a special study of mathematical systems and series. Showed in the Welsh Sculpture Trust Margam Park Sculpture in a Country Park exhibition in 1983; solo exhibitions included Leeds Polytechnic, 1980; and commissioned works included Quincunx, 1983, five concrete spheres, at Rufford Country Park, Ollerton.

Philippa COOPER 1934– Representational painter in watercolour and pen and ink, printmaker and teacher, born and lived in London, daughter of the artists John Cooper and Phyllis Bray. She admired the work of William and Ben Nicholson, John Sell Cotman, Eric Ravilious and Edward Bawden. After South Hampstead High School, she was granted a major scholarship to Slade School of Fine Art, 1950, gained her diploma in 1954, and was awarded postgraduate study year, 1954–5. Teachers included William Coldstream, Lucien Freud, B A R Carter, John Piper, Edward Ardizzone, Robert Medley and John Buckland Wright. She had a strong interest in architecture, her first husband being Geoffry Powell, winner of the Golden Lane Housing scheme and founder of Chamberlin, Powell & Bon, architects of the Barbican scheme for the City of London. She was for 26 years planning adviser to the Borough of Ealing for the conservation of Bedford Park. Teaching included London County Council and Inner London Education Authority schools, Wormwood Scrubs Prison and Chiswick Polytechnic. Mixed shows included Young Contemporaries; A Family of Painters – 3 Generations, Queen Mary College, 1978 (which she organised); and Sally Hunter Fine Art and Collyer-Bristow Gallery, both 1997. Had solo exhibitions at Judd Street Gallery, 1987 and 1990.

Phyllis COOPER 1895– Miniaturist and heraldic artist, born in London. She studied at Frank Calderon's School of Animal Painting, with the miniaturist Norah Bourne and elsewhere in London. Showed at RA, RMS, SWA, RI and Walker Art Gallery in Liverpool. Much of her work was done for Debrett's Peerage Ltd. Member of SM, and lived in Worthing, Sussex.

Rosamund COOPER fl. from early 1930s– Painter, commercial artist and teacher, educated in Hampstead, north London. Studied at Heatherley's School of Fine Art, her teachers including R O Dunlop, Frederic Whiting and Bernard Adams. She was there 1938–40 and again in 1947, early in World War II having a spell in an advertising agency. Later taught art in Norfolk, settling there at Sheringham. Exhibited at Heal's Mansard Gallery, RBA, ROI, Cooling Galleries and in Norwich.

Simon COOPER 1960– Artist, born in Newcastle upon Tyne, who graduated from Duncan of Jordanstone College of Art, Dundee, 1979–83, with an honours degree in illustration and printmaking. In 1983 was included in Scottish Print Open Three, organised by Dundee Printmakers' Workshop.

Stephen COOPER 1951– Painter and creator of wall-mounted, abstract, totem-like objects from such objects as cistern ballcocks, paint and refuse bags. He was born and based in London and attended St Martin's School of Art, 1971–5, then Royal College of Art, 1976–9. Awards included Pratt Award at St Martin's, 1974; John Minton Travel Award, 1976; Anstruther Drawing Prize, 1977; Berger Award (major), Royal College, 1979; and a painting fellowship at Ulster University, Belfast, 1980. Took part in many group shows including Young Contemporaries at ICA, 1975; John Moores Liverpool Exhibition, 1976; Winchester Gallery, Winchester, 1984; On a Plate, Serpentine Gallery, 1987; and Made in Greenwich, The Living Room, 1994. Had a solo show at Hull School of Art, 1979, from 1989 having a series at Smith Jariwala/Kapil Jariwala Galleries.

Thomas Joshua COOPER 1946– Artist using framed photographs and brief texts who, according to the catalogue of New North (Tate Gallery Liverpool, 1990), was "not concerned to document facts. Instead he employs the camera in search of a greater sense of meaning … The significance of the work resides in our own imaginative response to all that the artist has embraced in his involvement with the places he depicts." Born in San Francisco, California, America, Cooper became founding head of the Glasgow School of Art's fine art school, in 1982. After leaving America, Cooper lived in Derbyshire, then the west of Scotland. Later solo shows included Where the Rivers Flow, Fruitmarket Gallery, Edinburgh, 1997–8. Arts Council holds examples.

William COOPER 1923– Self-taught artist who was born in Merthyr Tydfil, Glamorgan. He attended Westminster School and Cambridge University. Cooper was for many years on the staff of Sherborne School, also lecturing independently and for Bristol University extra-mural department. Cooper began specialising in collage and mixed media in 1963, later adding oil, acrylic and watercolour. He was elected RWA in 1973, joining its council in 1991. His many mixed exhibition appearances included RA, NEAC, Swansea University and Newlyn Orion Gallery. Solo shows included Drian Gallery, 1971, and Albany Gallery in Cardiff, 1972, later ones Rona Gallery, 1988. Cooper was winner of a first prize at International Exhibition of Artists, 1964; prize-winner Westward Television Open, 1973; also at Wessex Artist, 1977; and South West Open, Plymouth, 1992. Welsh Development Corporation, Staffordshire Education Authority, Bryanston and Sherborne Schools hold his work. Lived in Sherborne, Dorset.

William Heaton COOPER 1903–1995 Landscape painter, writer and lecturer, born in Coniston, Lancashire. Studied partly with his father, Alfred Heaton Cooper, and at Royal Academy Schools, 1922–5. His many depictions of the Lake District were based on years of experience as a fell walker and climber. Cooper was an honorary life-member of the Lake Artists' Society. His book *Illustrated Hills of Lakeland* appeared in 1938, later ones including *Lakeland Portraits*, 1954, and *Mountain Painter*, 1984. Alpine Club and Abbot Hall Art Gallery, Kendal, hold his work. He was elected RI in 1953, also showing at RA and RBA and having several solo exhibitions. Was married to the sculptor Ophelia Gordon-Bell. Lived in Grasmere, Cumbria.

Mira COOPMAN 1924– Painter and draughtsman in pen and ink, born in Lodz, Poland. She was educated in Poland, Israel and Beirut and studied art in Jerusalem in the mid–1940s, then attended Slade School of Fine Art, 1946–8. Exhibited in Middle East, with British Council and in London with Ben Uri Art Gallery. Lived in London.

Mark COOTE 1932– Painter, draughtsman and teacher, born in London. Coote was given a mural commission for Festival of Britain in 1951, then attended Royal College of Art, 1954–7. He soon established a following, appearing through the 1950s in Young Contemporaries, in a 1955 Arts Council travelling show and at Leicester and Redfern Galleries. In 1957 he was one of six young painters chosen for a Critics' Choice exhibition at Gimpel Fils. But Coote wanted to avoid being manipulated and sought time to work out his own ideas. Eventually moved north and became senior lecturer in art at Warrington College of Education, giving up teaching in 1983 for a period of self-imposed isolation and intense work. By this time his pictures had attracted the attention of Kenneth Clark and Graham Sutherland, who noted Coote's special abilities as a landscape painter. From the early 1970s Coote had a series of one-man exhibitions, notably at Didsbury, 1972; Portland Gallery, Manchester, 1974; then a series with Tom Caldwell Galleries in Belfast, Dublin and London, having an Irish retrospective in 1988. Manchester City Art Gallery, Bolton Museum and Art Gallery and North West Arts Collection hold his work.

Barry Gordon COPE: *see* **ABBOTT**

Elizabeth COPE 1952– Painter of bold, colourful still lifes and landscapes, born in County Kildare, Ireland, setting in County Kilkenny. She attended the National College of Art and Design, Dublin, 1970; Sir John Cass School of Art, 1972–4; and Chelsea School of Art, studying fine art, 1974–7. Among many awards were a Spanish Government Grant to Segovia and Madrid, 1974; a French Government Grant to Aix-en-Provence, 1982; a Travel Award to Zurich, 1992–3; and an Arts Council Travel Bursary to Somalia, 1994. Group shows included Odette Gilbert Gallery, 1987; Claremorris Open from 1989; Brontë Contemporary Art, Boston and Florida, 1993; and John Martin of London, 1995. Had a solo exhibition at Peacock Theatre, Dublin, 1979, then showed frequently, later ones including Solomon Gallery, Dublin, and Park Walk Gallery, both 1995.

Jill COPE 1944– Painter, draughtsman, printmaker and teacher, born in Shrewsbury, Shropshire, where she attended the College of Art and Leeds College of Art in the 1960s. Taught in Manchester, in 1974 moving to Dorset where she was head of art at Gillingham Comprehensive School. Left full-time teaching in 1988, moved back to Shropshire, settling at Woolston, Craven Arms, in a converted cowshed with a garden studio, and began painting seriously in 1990. Mixed exhibitions included Hereford Museum and Art Gallery and Millfield Open Art Exhibition, both from 1991; West Midlands Open, Dudley, and Davies Memorial Gallery, Newtown, both 1992, and in both a prizewinner; and Millfield Open, Machynlleth Tabernacle Open and Newtown Open in Powys, all three in 1993, a prizewinner in each case. Had a solo show at Museum of Modern Art, Machynlleth, 1994. It, Millfield School and Dudley Museum and Art Gallery hold examples. Cope wrote that she loved "making marks, laying on paint or scratching a line … I suppose I should be an Abstract Expressionist" but "the figure, whether human or animal has been the primary basis for representational art and I find myself bound to that tradition."

Constance Gertrude COPEMAN 1864–1953 Painter, printmaker, poster designer and teacher. Was born in Liverpool, where she studied under John Finnie at the School of Art, 1891–1900, then in St Ives, Cornwall, with Julius Olsson. Sometimes signed work C G C. Exhibited extensively at RCamA, RE and especially Walker Art Gallery Liverpool, which holds her work; also at RA and Royal Glasgow Institute of the Fine Arts. Lived in Liverpool where records show her to have died "very poor".

John COPLANS 1920– Painter, educated in Johannesburg, South Africa, self-taught as an artist. Showed at RBA, AIA, LG and Redfern Gallery as well as extensively overseas; one-man shows included paintings and drawings at New Vision Centre Gallery, in 1957. Represented in Plymouth and Hull public galleries and in Museum of Modern Art, New York. Lived for some years in London.

Heather COPLEY 1918– Painter, graphic artist and teacher, full name Diana Heather Pickering Copley, born in Brewood, Staffordshire. She was married to the artist Christopher Chamberlain. Studied at Clapham School of Art, 1933–9, and Royal College of Art, 1940; after part-time teaching she returned to Royal College, 1945–7, in 1948 having a postgraduate year. Among her notable teachers were Vivian Pitchforth, W A Wildman and Carel Weight. From 1948–83 taught mainly part-time at St Martin's School of Art, drawing and painting. Between 1955–68 did graphic work for various outlets including Phoenix House, Bodley Head, Law Society and John Lehmann. Showed at RA Summer Exhibitions from 1950; Arts Council travelling exhibitions from 1960; Seven Dials Gallery, 1982; and Richard Allan Gallery, 1988. RA holds her work Lake Trasimeno, bought in 1978. Lived in London.

John COPLEY 1875–1950 Painter and printmaker, born in Manchester. Studied at the University there, then at the School of Art; at the Cope and Nicol School of Art; then at the RA Schools. Married to the artist Ethel Gabain. Travelled extensively in Italy. Exhibited extensively at Cooling Galleries, Goupil Gallery and RBA, also with NS, NEAC and abroad. Became honorary secretary of the Senefelder Club, 1910–16, only three years after taking up lithography, for which he won principal awards at an international exhibition at Chicago Art Institute in 1930. Was an honorary foreign member of Pulchri Studio, in The Hague. British Museum, Victoria & Albert Museum, provincial and foreign galleries hold his work. In 1985 Garton & Cooke put on a show of prints by Copley and his wife; in 1990 the Yale Center for British Art, in America, and Agnew both staged exhibitions by Copley. Semi-reclusive and a semi-invalid, Copley lived in London.

Edward Bainbridge COPNALL 1903–1973 Sculptor and painter. Born in Cape Town, South Africa, Copnall – father of the painter John Copnall – studied at Goldsmiths' College School of Art and at the Royal Academy Schools. He turned to sculpture in the late 1920s. He exhibited widely, including RA, LG, NEAC, RP, RSA, NS, ROI and at the Paris Salon. His commissions included figures on the RIBA building, Portland Place; St Columba's, in Pont Street; and several dozen carvings for the liners *Queen Mary* and *Queen Elizabeth*. Copnall was head of Sir John Cass College, 1945–53, and president of the RBS, 1961–6. His work is in a number of British and foreign collections. Lived at Littlebourne, Canterbury, Kent.

Frank Thomas COPNALL 1870–1949 Portrait painter, born in Ryde, Isle of Wight, married to the artist Teresa Copnall. He studied at Finsbury College and began a business career in Liverpool, painting in his spare time, then a commission enabled him to become a professional portrait painter from 1897. He was a member of NPS, Liverpool Academy and Liver Sketching Club, also showing at Liverpool Autumn Exhibition, RA, RP, RSA and abroad. Williamson Art Gallery & Museum, Birkenhead, has several portraits of local dignitaries by Copnall.

John COPNALL 1928– Painter and teacher, born in Slinfold, Sussex, son of the sculptor Bainbridge Copnall. He studied at the Architectural Association, 1945–6; did his National Service in the Army; from 1949–50 studied with his father at Sir John Cass College; then under Henry Rushbury at the Royal Academy Schools until 1954, the year he won the Turner Gold Medal for landscape painting. Went to Spain to live until 1958, initially being a figurative painter, but by the time he returned he was committed to abstraction. Gesture and colour are distinguishing features of Copnall's work, themes derived form sources such as jazz, window-bars in a studio or landscape. Copnall taught for many years from 1973 at Central School and was a visiting teacher at Canterbury College of Art for a time. He won an E A Abbey Scholarship in 1970; Arts Council Awards, 1972–3; a British Council Award, 1979; and in 1989 was elected a LG member. Group shows included Wildenstein, 1958; Annely Juda Fine Art, from 1969; John Moores Liverpool Exhibition, from 1972; RA Summer Exhibition, from 1980; British and Irish Modernist Art, Christie's, 1986–9; and Cross Currents, Reed's Wharf Gallery at Barbican Centre, 1996. Had a solo exhibition at Piccadilly Gallery, 1955, later ones including Reed's Wharf and De La Warr Pavilion, Bexhill-on-Sea, both 1996. Arts Council, Aberdeen and Bristol public galleries and other notable collections hold examples. Lived in London.

Teresa COPNALL 1882–1972 Painter, notably of flowers, born at Haughton-le-Skern, near Darlington, County Durham, married to the artist Frank Thomas Copnall. She studied in Brussels, then at Slade School of Fine Art under Frederick Brown and Henry Tonks and at the Herkomer School in Bushey. Showed at RA, ROI, RCamA, RSA, SWA, at Paris Salon, in Canada and at UA and Deeside Art Group of which she was a member. Work was reproduced by Medici Society Ltd and Raphael Tuck. Walker Art Gallery in Liverpool holds her work. Lived in Hoylake, Cheshire.

Sioban COPPINGER 1955– Sculptor and teacher, whose childhood was spent abroad. She gained an honours degree at Bath Academy of Art, 1974–7. Taught at Downe House School, Hermitage, Berkshire, 1991–2. Coppinger worked extensively in the field of public sculpture. In 1982 won competition and was commissioned by Nottinghamshire County Council to create sculpture for Rufford Country Park; in 1991 completed work for Donnington Valley Hotel; in 1992 Elephant Waterworks for Basingstoke District Hospital. She was made an associate of RBS in 1991, later being elected to council. In 1993 was included in 1st RWA Open Sculpture Exhibition and showed at Chelsea Harbour Yacht Club Gallery. A sense of fun was a strong feature of Coppinger's work. Lived in Newbury, Berkshire.

Helen Dorothy COPSEY 1888– Painter, notably in tempera, and teacher. She was born in London, her father being an art dealer. Attended Regent Street Polytechnic School of Art, 1905–10, then Royal College of Art, 1910–12. She exhibited NEAC, RA, RBA, WIAC of which she was a member, and SWA. Her work is illustrated in George Orwell's monograph on *The English People* and she has pictures in the collections of Derby Museum and Art Gallery and Russell-Cotes Art Gallery and Museum in Bournemouth. Lived in London.

Horace COPSON 1903– Watercolourist and designer, born in Bedford. He studied at Northampton Art and Technical School, then privately. Exhibited with ROI, RBSA and with NS, of which he became a full member in 1968, showing annually until 1979, also at Paris Salon. Later solo shows included Alfred East Gallery, in Kettering, 1974, and Woburn Abbey, 1975. Lived in Northampton.

Lydia CORBETT 1934– Watercolourist, born in Paris into an artistic environment, her father being a dealer, her mother a painter. Corbett was self-taught, her pictures having a springy line and gay washes, featuring still lifes and figure studies with witty additions. During the 1950s Corbett met Picasso at Vallauris on the French Riviera. She became the model for a sustained cycle of works, known as the Sylvette paintings. Moved to England in 1968, settling in Devon. She was represented by Francis Kyle Gallery from 1989, when she appeared in the theme show Blue and White. From 1989 held solo shows with the gallery.

Thomas James CORBIN 1906– Painter, printmaker and teacher, born in London. Studied at Croydon School of Art, 1922–7, with Oswald Crompton, then at Royal College of Art, 1927–30, with Reco Capey. Corbin held several teaching appointments for almost 20 years from 1930, including Edinburgh and Leicester Colleges of Art, eventually becoming a schools inspector specialising in art. He showed at RA, in the provinces and in Sweden and wrote several books on fabric printing and design. Lived in Elsworth, near Cambridge.

Roger CORCORAN 1943– Artist whose work included collage, born in Liverpool. He attended the College of Art there and Royal College of Art. Group exhibitions included Liverpool Academy; London Artists at Shrewsbury School, 1968; BBC Television and elsewhere. Lived for a time in Streatham, south London.

Philip CORE 1951–1989 Figure painter and draughtsman, also well known as a broadcaster on arts and as a photographic critic in British national press. He was born in Dallas, Texas, spent the first few years of his life in India, then returned to New Orleans. Aged six he entered military academy, and aged seven won first prize in the Vieux Carré Artists Open Competition. While at Middlesex School at Concord, Core won every possible prize for art and literature during the period 1963–9, when he entered Harvard on a scholarship. After a short period he obtained leave to go to Paris, where he helped research a book on the Symbolists, returning to graduate in 1973. Later that year he attended Ruskin School of Drawing, Oxford, then in 1974 Accademia di Belle Arti, Florence, moving permanently to London in 1975. Core's work appeared in *Vogue*, *Vanity Fair*, *New Society*, *Illustrated London News* and elsewhere. Core carried out a number of commissions, including a mural for the Ritz Hotel in 1980; Cyclorama, commissioned by BBC Television in 1984; and Joy, a sculpture for The London Lighthouse Project, in 1987. His publications included *Camp: the Lie that Tells the Truth*, 1984. Took part in mixed shows in London and abroad and was given a memorial exhibition at St Jude's, 1990. Arts Council holds his work.

Alfred James CORFIELD 1904– Painter, designer and teacher, born in Portsmouth, Hampshire. Although mainly self-taught, he studied for short periods in the 1920s and 1930s with private teachers. He lived in Newton Heath, Manchester, and exhibited widely in that area, including Stockport and Oldham art galleries, Stockport Art Guild and Oldham Society of Artists.

Colin CORFIELD 1910–1991 Painter of portraits, full name Thomas Charles Collingwood Corfield, who specialised in boardroom commissions. He studied at Leeds College of Art, Royal College of Art, gained a travelling scholarship in 1934, and attended Académie des Beaux-Arts in Paris. A Chelsea Arts Club member, he showed at RP and elsewhere. Lived in Chelsea, later in Selling, Kent.

Michael CORKREY 1962– Painter who was educated at Bedford College of Higher Education, 1981–2. Then studied at Leeds Polytechnic, 1982–5, and Royal Academy Schools, 1986–9. In 1987 Corkrey won the Henfield Award, followed by Worshipful Company of Painter-Stainers' Prize in 1988 and the De Segonzac Travelling Scholarship in 1989. Among mixed exhibitions Corkrey in the second half of the 1980s appeared at John Player Portrait Award Exhibition at National Portrait Gallery; he was a Winsor & Newton Finalist, ROI, at the Mall Galleries; and was in the Cadogan Contemporary Christmas Show, 1989. In 1990 he shared a show with two other painters at New Grafton Gallery.

John Elmer CORLEY 1950– Painter, printmaker and stained glass artist, born in Peterborough, Huntingdonshire. He studied at Northampton School of Art, 1968–70, teachers including Henry Bird, then at Canterbury College of Art, under Geoffrey Rigden and Stass Paraskos. Showed at New Metropole Arts Centre, Folkestone, 1973, Northampton Art Gallery, 1974, and elsewhere. Lived in Tilmanstone, Kent.

David CORNELL 1935– Sculptor and painter, born in London. From 1952–62 he attended the Central School of Arts and Crafts and Harrow School of Art, teachers including Roger Hilton and Philip Turner; was then at Academy of Fine Art, University of Pennsylvania, in America, studying anatomy under Robert Beverley Hale, 1968–70; and worked in collaboration with Marc Chagall in France. Gained five Arts Council Awards. In 1965 Cornell won a Royal Mint national selection and was appointed coin and medal engraver/sculptor, a position held until 1969. He was elected a fellow of RBS in 1971, becoming vice-president of SPS in 1977. In 1982 Cornell was awarded the Diploma di Merito Universita delle Arti, in Italy. Cornell took part in many exhibitions in Britain and abroad, including RA, 1967;14th International Medaille, Koln, 1971; Plazzotta Studio, 1984; Cadogan Gallery, and Armstrong-Davis Gallery, Arundel, both 1985; and Henry-Brett Galleries, Stow-on-the-Wold, 1991. Among Cornell's commissions was one by jockey Lester Piggott to sculpt his retirement bronze riding Nijinsky; also completed a life-size unicorn in bronze for The Welcome Foundation building in Euston Road, London. Lived in Tunbridge Wells, Kent.

Christopher CORNFORD 1917–1993 Artist, cartoonist, writer and teacher who was born and died in Cambridge. His great-grandfather was Charles Darwin and his mother Frances and brother John were both poets. After education at Stowe School and Leys School, Cambridge, attended Chelsea and Slade Schools of Art. Cornford was in the 1930s politically active as a member of the Communist Party and remained a rebel in spirit. His first important post was in 1947 at Newcastle and finally he was head of humanities at Royal College of Art, 1962–79. From 1984 taught in Cambridge for University of the Third Age. Cornford's book of cartoons *Drawn to Protest* was published by Cambridge Campaign for Nuclear Disarmament shortly before his death.

Marcus CORNISH 1964– Sculptor and teacher who studied at Camberwell School of Arts and Crafts, 1982–6; Middlesex Polytechnic, to gain a Certificate in Education, 1986–7; Royal College of Art, 1987–8, for postgraduate studies in bronze casting; then obtained his master's degree there, 1989–92. From 1985 he exhibited widely, initially in the South London Art Gallery Sogat 82 Sculpture Show; Hannah Peschar Gallery from 1986; Arts Club, Bryan Kneale's Choice, 1990; The Discerning Eye, Mall Galleries, 1992; and in 1993 at Isis Gallery, Leigh-on-Sea, in Drawing Towards Sculpture. Cornish gained a large number of residencies and awards, notably Henry Moore Foundation Scholarship, 1989–91, and Elizabeth Greenshields Foundation Award, 1992. Solo shows included Artist of the Day at Angela Flowers, 1994. Held a number of residencies, including Ravensbourne School, 1990, and Ibstock, West Hoathly, 1993, the year he was elected an associate of RBS. Commissions included Reading Town Council, Reading Civic Society sculpture of Francis Kendrick, 1991, and Head of Alberti, sponsored by Olivetti, 1992. Later teaching posts included De Montfort University, 1994, and Royal Academy Schools postgraduate school, 1995. Cornish's father was the artist and teacher Peter Cornish and his wife Mary Anne Aytoun-Ellis. He lived in Lewes, Sussex.

Norman CORNISH 1906– Sculptor and modeller in various materials, son of the architect Stephen Cornish. Educated at the Grammar School in Eastbourne, Sussex, he attended the School of Art there, 1922–9, studying under Arthur Reeve-Fowkes and Oliver Senior. Later was employed by the British film production company Gainsborough Pictures in their studios. Exhibited at RA and lived in London.

Norman CORNISH 1919– Painter, draughtsman and teacher whose work concentrated on the mining world of the northeast of England. Born in Spennymoor, County Durham, aged 14 he became a miner, like his father, retiring from the National Coal Board after 30 years. Then taught at Sunderland Art College. Showed at Northern Academy and with the Stone Gallery, Newcastle upon Tyne, later exhibitions including Nicholas Bowlby, Tunbridge Wells, 1995. In 1962 Cornish was commissioned by Durham County Council to paint a big canvas for the new County Hall. He appeared in a number of television films, including the BBC's *Two Border Painters* (the other was Sheila Fell) in 1963 and Tyne Tees Television's *Shapes of Cornish*, 1976. The library of the University of Northumbria, in Newcastle upon Tyne, has a unique collection of pictures by Cornish on permanent display, including the major paintings Pit Road near a Colliery, Winter, and Pit Road with Telegraph Pole and Lights.

Stroud CORNOCK 1938– Artist in sculpture and print, interactive systems. draughtsman and curator, born John Stroud Cornock in Epsom, Surrey. He attended Kingston and Royal Colleges of Art, teachers including Hubert Dalwood and Peter Atkinson. In the late 1950s Cornock was engaged in sculpture restoration; in Minimal sculpture to 1968, his main work being Labyrinth; then was involved in interactive art systems, 1968–72. Eventually became curator of the collection of the Council for National and Academic Awards, preparing its catalogue in 1992, when it was shown at John Jones Gallery. Cornock's own exhibition appearances were Sculpture Annual, AIA Gallery, from 1962; Young Contemporaries, FBA Galleries, from 1963; Survey '68: Abstract Sculpture, Camden Arts Centre, 1968, and elsewhere. He was involved in the organisation of a number of exhibition and inter-disciplinary group projects and participated in many conferences, regularly at conferences of the Society for General Systems Research, Design Research Society and Brain Research Association, 1970–82. He was co-author of *A Sculptor's Manual*, 1968, and contributed frequently to scholarly publications. Lived in London.

Arthur CORNWELL 1920– Artist, notably an illustrator interested in marine subjects, born in Vancouver, British

Columbia, Canada. His education included Page Military Academy, California. Attended Art Centre School in Los Angeles; Regent Street Polytechnic School of Art; Heatherley's School of Fine Art; and Académie Julian, Paris. Showed at RA, which holds his work, also SGA, RSMA, and in the provinces. Lived in Ruislip, Middlesex.

Ken CORNWELL 1955– Artist and teacher who studied at Liverpool Polytechnic, 1972–7, gaining an art honours degree, also a teacher's diploma. Went on to lecture at Mabel Fletcher College in Liverpool. He showed at Sculpture in the Garden at Bluecoat Gallery, Liverpool, 1984, and from 1985 was included in Walker Art Gallery's touring Merseyside Artists shows. In 1986–7 he showed the collage Tua Poh, produced in response to a trip to Southeast Asia in 1985.

Elizabeth CORSELLIS 1907– Painter and etcher who studied art under Graham Sutherland at Chelsea School of Art. Exhibited RA and NEAC. She was the aunt by marriage of the painter Jane Corsellis. Lived at Ham, Marlborough, Wiltshire.

Jane CORSELLIS 1940– Painter, draughtsman and printmaker, born in Oxford. She termed herself a "member of the modern figurative movement, continuing a great tradition that began with Sickert and his early followers". She studied at Byam Shaw School of Art, 1960–4, gaining the Leverhulme Scholarship and final year painting prize. While still a student showed with Young Contemporaries and at RA Summer Exhibition. After college she painted in Spain before teaching for two years. From early 1970s she travelled extensively, including Canada, Malaysia, India, Thailand, Indonesia and Australia. As well as showing abroad she continued to exhibit with NEAC and RBA, both of which she was a member. From 1985 had series of solo shows at New Academy Gallery. Her book *Painting Figures in Light* was published in 1982. Lived in London.

James COSGROVE 1939– Printmaker, painter, sculptor, artist in ceramics and teacher, born in Glasgow. After joining the Army in 1955 as a cartographic draughtsman, Cosgrove was a telecommunications officer for a decade, then studied in prints and textile department of Glasgow School of Art, 1967–71. He concentrated on screenprints. After graduation Cosgrove worked in the department, becoming its head a few years later. In 1982 he took over as head of first-year studies. Cosgrove was mainly a painter, although in 1980 he had an exhibition of drawings at Glasgow Print Studio, followed six years later by a paintings show at Corners Gallery, Glasgow. In 1989 Cosgrove took part in the show Crossing Boundaries at Compass Gallery, Glasgow.

Milein COSMAN 1922– Draughtsman, printmaker and painter in oil, born in Gotha, Germany. She was married to the musician and broadcaster Hans Keller and was noted for her portraits of musicians, dancers and figures in movement. After education in Germany and Switzerland she studied at Slade School of Fine Art, 1939–42, notable teachers including Harold Jones for lithography. Her work appeared in a number of musical books, and in periodicals such as *Radio Times*, *Ballet* and *Opera*. In 1958 she prepared a schools drawing course for Independent Television. Mixed shows included RA, Mercury and Roland, Browse & Delbanco Galleries, RE and abroad. Had many solo exhibitions including Berkeley Galleries, 1949; Camden Arts Centre, 1969; British Council, Paris, 1970; Ryder Gallery, Los Angeles, 1974; Menuhin School and Dartington Hall, both 1982; Clare Hall, Cambridge, 1990; and Belgrave Gallery, 1996. Victoria & Albert Museum, *Financial Times*, University College in Cardiff, National Portrait Gallery and several overseas collections hold her work. Lived in London.

Mary COSSEY fl. from 1970s– Painter, printmaker and draughtsman who studied fine art at Bromley College of Art. In 1970 she gave up work in advertising to paint full-time, in 1979 returning to part-time work. Showed at RA Summer Exhibitions; Spirit of London at Royal Festival Hall; ROI; NEAC; South London Art Gallery and elsewhere. Had solo show at Woodlands Art Gallery, 1983. The artist favoured still lifes of plants.

Brian S COSTALL 1943– Painter, printmaker and teacher, born in London. He attended Harrow School of Art, 1959–64, then Royal College of Art, 1964–7, where his teachers included Carel Weight and Peter Blake. Showed at Trafford Gallery and elsewhere.

Jensine COSTELLO 1886– Painter born in Norway, where she was brought up, also in America. Then studied at Heatherley's School of Fine Art under Bernard Adams and Frederic Whiting. Exhibited ROI, SWA, NS, RP and Paris Salon. Lived in Exmouth, Devon.

Simon COSTIN 1962– Artist in various materials who studied biology and taxidermy at Natural History Museum and theatre design at Wimbledon School of Art. Among his exhibitions were Aspects Gallery; Bergdorf Goodman, in New York; Rebbeca Hossack Gallery; and in 1990 he was included in England & Co's Art in Boxes. Costin made jewellery for Derek Jarman's film *Caravaggio*.

Mabel Winifred COTTEE 1905–1991 Watercolourist who was by profession a civil servant. She attended Nottingham College of Art part-time, 1924–34, belonged to Nottingham Society of Artists and exhibited at the Nottingham Castle Art Gallery, as well as elsewhere in the provinces. Lived in Nottingham.

Fran COTTELL 1954– Abstract sculptor and teacher, born in Bexley, Kent. She studied at Reading University department of fine art, 1973–7, then worked for her master's degree in fine art at Goldsmiths' College School of Art, 1979–81. Taught part-time in adult education while maintaining a studio in London. Exhibitions included John Moores Liverpool Exhibition, 1978, Waterloo Gallery from 1980 and in 1982 shared an exhibition at Woodlands Art Gallery.

Arthur COTTERELL 1917– Artist in oil and watercolour, noted for his landscapes, born in London. He attended Regent Street Polytechnic School of Art, 1937–9, notable teachers including Norman Blamey, then during World War II studied at Leicester, Hereford and Hamburg Art Schools. After 20 years of self-employment and a period on the staff of London University, Cotterell retired early to paint full-time. He was a member of UA from 1979, and was president of Cantium Group, also belonging to South-East London Art Group and London Sketch Club. Showed at ROI, Guildhall and Mall and Westminster Galleries in mixed exhibitions. Solo shows included Fairfield Halls in Croydon and Woodlands Art Gallery, 1980. Whitbread held his work. Lived in Orpington, Kent.

Allan COTTERILL 1913– Painter, sculptor and teacher, born in Southport, Lancashire. Attended the School of Art there, Liverpool School of Art and Central School of Arts and Crafts. He held a series of teaching posts, including Carmarthen School of Art and Cardiff College of Art. Showed in public galleries in Preston, Southport and Liverpool. Lived in Winchester, Hampshire.

Alan COTTON fl. from 1960s– Painter, teacher and writer, born in Redditch, Worcestershire. Studied at Ruskin Hall, Bournville School of Art, Birmingham College of Art and, after three years in the painting school there, completed his training at Birmingham University. In late-1970s he became a research fellow at University of Exeter, and for some years was senior lecturer in charge of painting and art history at Rolle College, Exmouth, resigning in 1982 to paint full-time. Did work for Open University, wrote articles for art magazines and was co-author of a book on child art: *Learning and Teaching through Art and Crafts*. Showed with RBA, RWA, at Stroud and Sidmouth Festivals and had several dozen exhibitions, including City of Plymouth Art Gallery, City of Exeter Art Gallery and elsewhere throughout the west of England. In 1990 David Messum showed French and Italian pictures by him in which thick impasto and a rich palette were features. Had a studio at Colaton Raleigh, Devon.

Christopher COUCH 1946– Realistic painter, born in Hemel Hempstead, Hertfordshire, who studied at the Art School at Leamington Spa, Warwickshire, 1963, where he eventually settled, attending Slade School of Fine Art for a term in 1964. He then worked on his own, exploring various styles including abstraction, but on seeing a Rembrandt exhibition in the Netherlands in 1968 decided to abandon painting, entering an Anglican order as a novice, remaining for five years. In 1978 Couch, supported by a small legacy, took a house in Brighton and set himself to work out a style under the influence of Pablo Picasso and Francis Bacon. Regulation of the quality of light was of key importance in Couch's pictures: still lifes, figure studies and self-portraits. He believed that "painting should look ordinary, part of everyday experience," defining a good work of art as a "perfect balance of intellect, spirit, emotion and body." In 1982 Couch was artist-in-residence at Birmingham Museums and Art Gallery, which acquired Afternoon, 1982, for the permanent collection. From 1986 had a series of solo shows at Marlborough Fine Art.

Francis COUDRILL 1914–1989 Enterprising painter, puppeteer, ventriloquist, designer and inventor, born in Warwick, father of the artist and musician Jonathon Coudrille. Coudrill was originally a science teacher, then a self-taught artist, holding a successful first solo show at Warwick Galleries, Birmingham. In the 1930s Coudrill did extensive publicity work for British film companies, including a life-size model of the actress Anna Neagle for Herbert Wilcox and Seven Dwarfs masks for the film *Snow White*. Painted inn signs for Ind Coope. Coudrill had taught himself ventriloquism, making his own puppet, William Casanova, including hair from his mother's head. To support his art, Coudrill toured the variety halls, signing for his first professional engagement in 1947; he entertained troops in the Middle East; then appeared on television with Hank the Cowboy, who became a star on BBC Television's *Whirligig*. When commercial television came, Coudrill wrote, animated and filmed Hank cartoons, creating his own superbly crafted alternative animation machine. Through the 1950s fan mail arrived by the sackful, and no home was complete without Hank glove puppets, guns, jigsaws and tea towels. Determined to be a serious painter, Coudrill settled in Cornwall and opened the Mermaid Art Centre in St Ives, later moving to Studio Golva, Cadgwith. Showed in St Ives and Newlyn. In 1991 David Lay's Penzance auction house sold Coudrill's studio contents, including figurative and abstract art.

Jonathon COUDRILLE 1945– Surrealist painter, writer, composer and guitar virtuoso, born in Warwickshire, son of the artist and performer Francis Coudrill and married to the South African poet M J (Gretl) van der Merwe. He was taught silversmithing by Art Nouveau jeweller Poppy Quelch; studied at High Wycombe School of Art; sculpture under Denis Mitchell at Redruth Art School; then painting with John Tunnard. Parallel with art, Coudrille was a musician. He was musical director on his father's *Hank Rides Again* cowboy cartoon series; had his own programme, *Young Tomorrow*, on Westward Television; in the late 1960s performed with experimental and fringe bands; was topical singer-songwriter on the radio programme *Day By Day*; and toured with the World Famous Kazatka Cossacks. His children's books included *Farmer Fisher*, the first picture book on the British market to incorporate a record. Mixed shows included Penwith Society and The Cadgwith Society of Painters, of which he was a member. Solo exhibitions included The Picture House Gallery, St Ives, 1995. Produced a series of pictures: Laying the Ghost of my Father's muse. Bank of Nova Scotia, Canada, holds his work. Lived at Studio Golva, Cadgwith, Cornwall.

Mary Louise COULOURIS 1939– Painter and printmaker, born in New York, daughter of the actor George Coulouris. Educated in London, she studied at Slade School of Fine Art,

1958–62, where her teachers included Anthony Gross; the École des Beaux-Arts, in Paris, 1963–4, in the former year gaining a French government scholarship; and for the same period at Stanley William Hayter's Atelier 17. Became a noted professional printmaker and member of the Printmakers' Council, showing extensively at RA and having one-man shows in London, the provinces and abroad. New York Public Library and Bibliothèque Nationale, Paris, hold her work. Lived for periods in London and in Linlithgow, West Lothian.

Melanie COUNSELL 1964– Artist involved in site-specific installations, born in Cardiff. She studied at South Glamorgan Institute, 1982–6, gaining a bachelor's degree in fine art, and was at Slade School of Fine Art, 1986–8. Gained a Boise Travel Scholarship in 1988 and a Whitechapel Artists' Award in 1989. Her group shows included Anthony Reynolds Gallery, 1988, and she was in South Bank Centre's touring exhibition The British Art Show 1990. Had a solo show at Matt's Gallery, 1989. Lived in London.

Graham COUPE 1950– Painter and teacher born in Accrington, Lancashire. He studied at Rochdale College of Art, 1969–70, Ravensbourne College of Art, 1970–3, then Goldsmiths' College School of Art, 1974–5. Went on to teach part-time in east London. His work was included in a Goldsmiths' show at Woodlands Art Gallery, 1983.

Glenys COUR 1924– Painter, artist in collage and teacher, born in Fishguard, Pembrokeshire. Studied at Cardiff College of Art, then went on to lecture in painting at Swansea College of Art. Took part in a number of group shows, including stained glass at Victoria & Albert Museum in 1957, SWG of which a member, and CASW; had shared shows with her husband Ronald Cour, Victor Neep and Ray Howard-Jones in Wales. Completed commissions for murals for Trustee Savings Bank in Swansea area. Was a member of WAC art committee for a time. Had a solo show at Swansea University in 1974, others including Universities of Exeter and Swansea in 1982 and Glynn Vivian Art Gallery, Swansea, 1986. That gallery, WAC and CASW hold her work.

Ronald COUR 1914–1978 Sculptor and teacher, born in Swansea, South Wales, where he attended the College of Art and then Royal College of Art. In 1947 joined the staff of Swansea College, to which he was attached for many years. He completed a number of commissions, including a head of the Member of Parliament Percy Morris for Swansea Guildhall and work for the Foreign Office. Participated in many group shows including SWG of which he was for a time chairman, Glynn Vivian Art Gallery in Swansea and New Vision Centre. Also had one-man exhibition at University College, Swansea. In 1936 Cour won the Royal National Eisteddfod Sculpture Prize. WAC and many other institutions hold his work.

Tim COURAGE 1967– Abstract artist, born and lived in Poole, Dorset. He studied at Wimbledon School of Art, 1987–90, and exhibited at East & South, Norwich Gallery/Kent Institute of Art and Design, 1992. His work Untitled was one of a series which he said were "parodies of formalist abstraction".

Emily COURT fl. from 1905–1957 Painter in oil, especially of flowers, born in Newport, Essex. She studied at the Slade School of Fine Art under Henry Tonks and Walter Westley Russell. Court exhibited RA, NEAC, ROI and SWA extensively, and abroad. Lived in London.

Ethol COURT 1898– Portrait miniaturist in oil and watercolour. Born in Preston, Lancashire, she studied with Harold Charles Bartlett and Margaret Oldbridge. Exhibited at RA, RMS, Paris Salon and in Brussels. She was a member of Ealing Art Club and lived at Southall, Middlesex, where she taught miniature painting.

Jeffery COURTNEY 1947– Painter, notably of portraits. These included Lord Amory, four portraits of former Lord Mayors of London and Masters for the Worshipful Company of Haberdashers, the Earl of Cranbrook and Viscount Runciman. He studied at Hornsey College of Art and Royal Academy Schools until 1972, in that year winning the Elizabeth T Greenshields Scholarship. Showed at RA, RP, New Grafton Gallery and elsewhere and had several solo exhibitions. Had a studio in London.

Ruth Margaret COUSENS 1930– Watercolourist and teacher, born in London. She studied at Rolle College, Exeter, 1948–50, then went on to teach, including Maidstone Technical High School and Sittingbourne Girls' Grammar School. Showed at RA, RI and Paris Salon, gaining a gold medal there in 1973. Solo shows included Townley House, Ramsgate, 1973, and Royal Museum, Canterbury, 1978. Thanet Council holds her work. She was founder and project director of the Castle Trust Arts Centre in Ramsgate, Kent, where she lived.

Timothy COUSINS 1952– Gestural, Expressionistic artist and teacher, especially in acrylic and gouache, whose work was "rooted in an attempt to assert an identity on a surface". Cousins was born in Weston-super-Mare, Somerset, and studied at Exeter College of Art and Design, 1976–7; Ravensbourne College of Art and Design, 1977–81; and Roehampton Institute, 1982–3, Brian Fielding being an important teacher. Taught in London, where he was based at The Art in Perpetuity Trust Studios. Exhibitions included Citizens' Gallery in Woolwich and Harlech Biennale, both 1996, and Clevedon: Sharing a View, APT Gallery and tour, 1997–8, with a solo show at Colston Hall, Bristol, 1977.

Graça COUTINHO 1949– Painter, born in Lisbon, Portugal, where she studied at School of Fine Art, 1969–71, then St Martin's School of Art, 1974–7. Group appearances included John Moores Liverpool Exhibition from 1987, other provincial shows in England and Wales, on the continent and in South America. Showed solo in Portugal from mid-1970s including

Calouste Gulbenkian Foundation, Lisbon, 1989, as well as Todd Gallery. Lived in London.

Kenneth COUTTS-SMITH 1929– Painter and art critic. Studied at Heatherley's School of Fine Art. Among his books was *The Dream of Icarus*. Took part in group exhibitions in Britain, on the continent and in North America and had a string of one-man shows, including New Vision Centre Gallery, 1963. Towner Art Gallery, Eastbourne, is one of several British collections holding his work, which is also in galleries in Yugoslavia and America. Lived in London.

Jack COUTU 1924– Printmaker, watercolourist, sculptor and teacher, full name Raymond John Coutu, born and lived in Farnham, Surrey, area. He studied at local School of Art, 1947–51, sculpture; Royal College of Art, 1951–4, stained glass; and Central School of Art, 1951–5, where Merlyn Evans was a notable influence on Coutu's printmaking. Coutu taught printmaking at Central School, 1957–65, then at Farnham, West Surrey College of Art & Design, 1965–85. His career as a notable carver of netsuke began in 1968, and he became a member of the America-based Netsuke Kenkyukai Society. Was also a member of RE and Printmakers' Council. The Japanese influence on Coutu's work was "due to a stay during my Army career with the occupation forces". Showed in groups at RA, at Bradford Print Biennale and elsewhere in the provinces; in leading netsuke conventions; had a two-man show with Michael Rothenstein at Alecto Gallery, 1965; and a solo exhibition at Graphic Arts Gallery, 1968. Arts Council and Victoria & Albert Museum hold his work.

Lucie-Renée COUVE DE MURVILLE 1920–1995 Painter in oil, ink wash using Chinese brushes and pastel, born in Majunga, Madagascar, of Anglo-French nationality. She spent all her early life in France, was in Mauritius, 1935–9, returning to Paris just before the war. Studied by correspondence with ABC School of Art, 1937–9, then under Emma Ruff in Paris for five years while her father, who was British, hid in the family flat. She moved to England in 1945 and contributed to mixed shows in London, Wakefield, Bradford and Bristol. In 1975 had a solo show at RWA covering her career to date. In 1957 she was chosen by Jack Beddington for inclusion in his book *Young Artists of Promise*. She was made Chevalier de l'Ordre des Palmes Académiques in 1967 and in 1982 Chevalier de l'Ordre National du Mérite. Couve de Murville specialised in portraits, flower studies, landscapes and seascapes, signing her work C de M. Young Women's Christian Association holds an example. Lived for many years in Clifton, Bristol.

Ethel Louise COVE 1916–1978 Artist, calligrapher, designer and teacher, born in Sidmouth, Devon, married to the artist and teacher Harold Cove. She attended Leeds School of Art, 1935–7, then the design school of Royal College of Art, 1937–40, teachers including Ernest Tristram and Edward Johnston. Among her commissions was *Book of the Dead and the Living*, Earls Barton, 1946, her last being *The Family Tree of Sir John Barton Townley, Bilsborough Hall, Lancaster*, 1978. Was a member of the Scribes Society. In 1964 she showed an abstract fabric collage in The Teaching Image, work by staff of Leeds College of Art at the City Art Gallery. Died at Horsforth, near Leeds, Yorkshire.

Frederick Halford COVENTRY 1905– Artist in various media, born in New Zealand. Studied at Elam School of Art in Auckland, Julian Ashton Art School in Sydney and in London at Grosvenor School of Modern Art. Was made a member of the Society of Industrial Artists in 1946, next year joining the Society of Mural Painters. Showed widely, including RA, Council of Industrial Design, Imperial Institute as well as in Australia and New Zealand. British Museum, Imperial War Museum and overseas collections hold his work. Lived in London for many years.

Keith COVENTRY 1958– Painter and sculptor, born in Burnley, Lancashire, who graduated from Brighton Polytechnic, 1978–81, gaining his master's degree at Chelsea School of Art, 1981–2. Coventry was included in Young British Artists V, at Saatchi Gallery, 1995, where he exhibited apparently white abstracts which had an underlying reference to the royal family and establishment, the privileged and ceremonial. Was also included in Sensation, at RA, 1997, the year of his solo exhibition at The Showroom. Coventry has works in the collections of the Arts Council; British Council; Contemporary Art Society; and in America at the Museum of Modern Art, New York; Walker Art Center, Minneapolis; and Museum of Modern Art, San Diego. Lived in London.

Victor COVERLEY-PRICE 1901–1988 Painter and writer who was for about 20 years from 1925 a professional diplomat. Was born in Winchester, Hampshire, and obtained his Master of Arts degree from Oxford University. He published *An Artist Among Mountains*, illustrated books for children and showed widely abroad as well as at RA, RI, UA and in the provinces. Lived in Cirencester, Gloucestershire.

Peter COVIELLO 1930– Painter, potter and teacher, born in Harrow, Middlesex. He studied at Willesden and Guildford Schools of Art, gaining his diploma in painting in 1951, and went on to teach at Maidstone College of Art and Central School of Arts and Crafts, 1957–68. His first solo show was in 1957 and he represented Britain in abstract painting exhibitions in Scandinavia and Australia, 1960–1. Coviello moved to Canada in 1968 and became co-ordinator of creative art, Sheridan College, Oakville. From 1969 he was involved with pottery after meeting Glasgow-born Liz Brown, whom he married. In both pottery and painting Coviello worked on a big scale. Arts Council holds Coviello's abstract Hanuman, of the mid–1960s. Lived for some years at Plainfield, Ontario, often showing with his wife. Later returned to London and was a resident artist at Florence Studios, showing with England & Co in 1993.

James COWAN 1948– Painter and draughtsman, born in Glasgow in 1948. His awards included Morland Lewis Travelling

Scholarship, 1981, and Tower Hamlets Arts Award, 1984. Among his many exhibition appearances were New Contemporaries at ICA, 1979; Stowells Trophy at RA and LG at Morley Gallery, 1981; Cockpit Theatre Gallery and City University, 1983; Aspex Gallery, Portsmouth, 1984; and in 1985 participated in four-man exhibition at Woodlands Art Gallery. Peterborough City Art Gallery holds his work.

Jean Hunter COWAN fl. c.1935–1965 Sculptor and painter, educated at St Leonard's School, St Andrews, Fife. She showed at RSW, RSA, SSA, Royal Glasgow Institute of the Fine Arts and SSWA, of which she was president for most of the 1950s. She had a number of other careers, winning international golf and tennis titles; performing as a notable amateur violinist; travelling extensively, especially in Africa; and being claimed as the first woman to fly, in 1911 (a record disputed by the Royal Aeronautical Society). Lived in Edinburgh.

Judith COWAN 1954– Artist in various media, and teacher, born in London. She did a foundation course at Bristol College of Art, 1973–4, followed by Sheffield College of Art, 1974–7, then Chelsea School of Art, 1977–8. She was a Gulbenkian Rome Scholar, attending British School there in 1978–9. From 1979 taught at various art schools and was a sessional lecturer at Reading University. Her exhibitions included Northern Young Contemporaries, at Whitworth Art Gallery, Manchester, from 1975, being a prizewinner in 1977; Rassegna Internazionale di Scultura Contemporanea, San Marino, Italy, 1979, where she was a prizewinner; and Woodlands Art Gallery touring show, 1981–2, of Greater London Arts Association award winners. Had a solo show at Kettle's Yard, Cambridge, 1996, of sculpture and photo-sculpture. Arts Council holds her work.

Noël COWARD 1899–1973 The author of over 50 plays; 25 films as writer, director or star; hundreds of songs; a ballet and two autobiographies, he began sketching during his childhood in south London. He resumed watercolour painting in the early 1930s, usually at home in Kent. He was encouraged by Sir Winston Churchill to take up oils, which Coward employed to create colourful, stylish, a little naive and sometimes theatrical views around his English, Swiss and above all Jamaican homes. Artists such as Derek Hill, who painted his portrait, also advised him. Coward had an allergy to turpentine, so he wore gloves when painting and used casein as a medium. Although Coward, knighted in 1969, did not design for his own shows, he completed a poster for his musical *Sail Away*. He gave a few pictures away, but they did not reach public notice until an auction of 34 at Christie's in 1988 fetched £786,000. In that year Sheridan Morley's *Out in the Midday Sun: The Paintings of Noël Coward* told their story. Died in Jamaica.

Kate COWDEROY 1875–1972 Painter and miniaturist who studied at Herkomer Art School at Bushey, Hertfordshire, from 1899. The Cowderoy family eventually settled there, and Kate became one of a circle of artists celebrated with an exhibition by the Bushey Museum Trust in 1988. From 1904 for a time Cowderoy lived in Karlsruhe, Germany, looking after two girls, through a Herkomer family connection. In the summer of 1914 Cowderoy visited Paris for a few months, later showing at the Salon, and she painted landscapes in northern France and Belgium. As well as landscapes, portraits and genre pictures, she gained many commissions for miniatures, latterly favouring flowers, gardens and cats as subjects. Exhibitions also included RA and Walker Art Gallery, Liverpool.

Ian COWELL 1964– Painter who studied at Manchester Polytechnic, 1983–4, and Leicester Polytechnic, 1984–7. Showed widely, including Smith's Galleries; Cleveland College of Art and Design; MAFA; RP from 1989; and at Agnew in The Broad Horizon, 1990.

Raymond Teague COWERN 1913–1986 Although he was a versatile painter and illustrator, Cowern is noted especially for his fine work as an etcher. Educated in Birmingham, he went on to study at the Central School of Art there and at the Royal College of Art and just before World War II at the British School, Rome. The British Museum as well as galleries in Glasgow, Birmingham, Liverpool, Oxford and abroad own his work. He exhibited at the RA – of which he became an associate in 1957 and a full academician in 1968 – as well as the RWS, RE and other leading London and provincial galleries. There was a large show at Stables Gallery, Oxford, in 1996. Lived in Whitehaven, Cumbria.

Hilda COWHAM 1873–1964 Illustrator of children's books and painter, born in London, who married the artist Edgar Lander. Studied at Wimbledon and Lambeth Schools of Art and Royal College of Art. After winning a prize in a competition run by the magazine *Studio* she quickly built a reputation as a magazine illustrator, noted for her facility in drawing with the brush in the Chinese and Japanese manner. One of the earliest women illustrators to work for *Punch*, she also drew for *The Graphic*, *Little Folks*, *Pearson's Magazine*, *The Sketch*, *The Sphere* and many others and illustrated a number of books. James Thorpe cites her "fantastic impressions of children" in the magazine *Moonshine*. Exhibited RA, RWS, in the provinces, Paris Salon and in North America. Wrote a number of children's stories and like her husband did some etched work. Lived in Guildford, Surrey.

Bel COWIE 1943–1983 Printmaker, watercolourist, teacher and theatre designer, born in Dundee. She studied at Gray's School of Art, Aberdeen, 1960–64, and in Berne, Switzerland. She taught at Gray's School of Art and at Aberdeen College of Education; was involved in theatre design; and between 1975–8 was director of Aberdeen's Peacock Print Workshop. Took part in many Scottish group shows including SSA of which she was a member, RSA, RSW and Compass Gallery, Glasgow. Public collections include Scottish Arts Council. Lived in Aberdeen.

James COWIE 1886–1956 Painter, draughtsman and teacher, born in Cuminestown, Aberdeenshire. In 1906 he started studying for an English degree at Aberdeen University, but association with the art teacher James Hector deflected Cowie's enthusiasm to art, and he eventually passed teacher-training examinations in drawing. From 1909 Cowie was art master at Fraserburgh Academy, then from 1912–14 he studied at Glasgow School of Art and was appointed art master at Bellshill Academy, in the Glasgow area. War cut this appointment short, but Cowie was able to resume at Bellshill, 1918–35, after a time in the Pioneer Corps as a conscientious objector. The pupils at Bellshill inspired his own painting which was meticulous in its draughtsmanship and preparation and which from the 1940s took on a Surrealist tinge. Cowie was one of the great individualists of modern Scottish painting. In 1935 he was appointed head of painting at Gray's School of Art, Aberdeen, two years later becoming warden of the Patrick Allan-Fraser School of Art, Hospitalfield, Arbroath. In 1943 he was elected RSA. Scottish Arts Council, Aberdeen Art Gallery and Museum and other Scottish galleries hold his work, of which there was a memorial show organised by Scottish Arts Council in 1957. Died in Edinburgh.

Barbara COWLES 1898– Oil painter, born in Melksham, Wiltshire. After education at Trinity Hall, Southport, she exhibited at RA. Lived in London.

Allan Rees COWNIE 1927– Artist in oil and watercolour, pastel and black-and-white, born in Cardiff, south Wales. From 1970 he was a freelance portrait painter. Cownie studied at Kingston School of Art and Manchester Regional College of Art. His group shows included Alderley Gallery; Royal Exchange and Colin Jellicoe Galleries, Manchester; and Weaver Gallery, Weaverham. His series of solo exhibitions included Salford Art Gallery; Pitcairn Gallery, Knutsford; Howarth Gallery, Accrington; and University of Manchester. His portraits included the singer Sir Geraint Evans and the astronomer Sir Bernard Lovell. Reynards Ltd and Barr's Soft Drinks Ltd hold his work. Lived in Pwllheli, Gwynedd.

Frank Cadogan COWPER 1877–1958 Painter of historical subjects in the manner of the Pre-Raphaelites; portrait painter. Born at Wickham, Northamptonshire, he studied art at the St John's Wood School of Art, 1896, at the Royal Academy Schools, 1897–1902, and with the American-born historical painter E A Abbey, followed by studies in Italy. Exhibited prolifically at the RA; also showed at ROI, Fine Art Society, Walker Art Gallery, Liverpool, RP and elsewhere. Elected RA in 1934. He completed mural paintings in the Houses of Parliament, London, and the Tate Gallery and Leeds City Art Gallery hold his work. Lived in Cirencester, Gloucestershire.

Geoffrey COWTON fl. from 1950s– Watercolourist, printmaker, teacher and gallery proprietor, born and educated in Bradford, Yorkshire. Trained as a teacher of art at St John's College, York, later studying printmaking at Leeds College of Art. For some years he was head of art and design in a Halifax school, later working as a freelance artist and proprietor of Glendale Studio in Halifax, West Yorkshire. Cowton was a noted Dales landscape painter, his love of the area beginning with a school geography excursion to Grassington and Malham. His son Martin was an artist.

David COX 1914– Painter in oil, and teacher, born in Falmouth, Cornwall, who studied art in London, France and Italy. He was closely associated with the St Ives Society of Artists and the Penwith Society of Arts in Cornwall, being honorary secretary of both. He showed at many venues, including RA, ROI, NEAC, RWA, NS, Leicester Galleries, Leger Gallery, Marlborough Gallery and widely overseas. Had one-man shows in London. Living at Stoke-by-Nayland, near Colchester, he ran his own art school for several decades.

David COX 1947– Artist in various media who began to create sculpture, toys and furniture in early 1970s, within a few years being granted a bursary by Southern Arts to work full-time. It eventually organised a touring show of Cox's creations. He also showed solo at Bath Festival, Winchester Gallery and Victoria Art Gallery in Bath and in 1992 his mixed-media constructions were included in Art in Boxes at England & Co. Cox held a series of artist-in-residencies.

Dorothy COX 1882–1947 Landscape artist and portrait miniaturist whose early years were spent in London and its southern suburbs. In 1901 she was elected RMS, also showing widely at Walker Art Gallery in Liverpool, RA, RHA, RI, Fine Art Society and elsewhere. In 1925 she settled in Shoreham-on-Sea, Sussex, where the Brighton Art Gallery holds her watercolour The Abandoned Quarry.

Elijah Albert COX 1876–1955 Painter, poster and mural artist and book illustrator, born in London. He studied at the People's Palace Technical School, Whitechapel, then at Bolt Court School. Worked as a designer in industry, which later proved useful in his public poster and mural work. Also assisted Frank Brangwyn. Exhibited RA, RI, SGA, Whitechapel Art Gallery and elsewhere. Illustrated several books. Public galleries, including Preston, Bristol and Canterbury, hold his work. Lived at Woolage Green, near Canterbury, Kent.

Ernest Moses COX 1885– Painter, born in Kettering, Northamptonshire. Studied at Bradford College of Art and exhibited extensively in Yorkshire. He was a leading member of Bradford Arts Club, with which he exhibited at Cartwright Hall for the last time in 1958. Lived in Shipley, Yorkshire.

Gertrude Florence Mary COX fl.c.1930–1980 Painter in oil and watercolour and etcher. Studied art under R Kirkland Jamieson, she went on to exhibit widely, including ROI, RBA, Paris Salon, RWA and RI. The Royal Albert Memorial Museum and Art Gallery, Exeter, holds her work. Lived in Exeter.

Ian COX 1951– Representational painter and teacher, with a crisp, fresh style, who attended Southend College of Art, 1970–2, received the Lord Leverhulme Scholarship to attend the Byam Shaw School of Drawing and Painting and in 1975 won the David Murray Landscape Prize. Taught at Southend College of Art. From the mid-1990s showed in the Essex Open Exhibition at Beecroft Art Gallery, Westcliff-on-Sea, Essex, where he lived. In 1997 was included in Four British Artists at Grosvenor Gallery.

John COX fl. from late 1980s– Wildlife painter and illustrator with a special interest in birds who in 1989 won the Bird Illustrator of the Year award presented by *British Birds* magazine, when living in Romford, Essex, and working in a London office. The year before, he had won its Richard Richardson Award for Bird Artists under 21. His painting career was launched when Chevron UK Ltd, the oil company, asked Cox to illustrate its 1990 calendar. Many commissions for books and magazines followed, Cox began to exhibit and was elected a member of SWLA, joining its council and showing with it at the Mall Galleries. In 1997 he exhibited in Chevron's calendar artists show at the ICA.

Philip COX 1945– Self-taught artist using cardboard and salvaged paper papier mâché, born and lived in the Nottingham area. Until 1986 Cox worked in industry and local government, after which he was a full-time artist, working to commission, creating exhibitions and undertaking residencies. He made life-size figures, wryly observed, in everyday situations. Cox participated in the Open Show at Nottingham Castle Museum and Art Gallery from 1982, other mixed show appearances including The Crescent Gallery, Scarborough, 1987, and Whitworth Art Gallery, Manchester, 1989. His solo exhibition Scrap People toured from Midland Group Arts Centre, Nottingham, 1986; later tours included People in Place, nationally, based on The Turnpike Gallery, 1990–3. Cox created 60 figures for the permanent exhibition The Tales of Robin Hood. Bedfordshire and Somerset County Councils and Epping Forest District Museum hold Cox's work.

Sally COX 1955– Sculptor, born in London, who worked as a gardener and dress designer before moving to Yorkshire in 1990 "to enable me to concentrate on art". An exhibition of Zimbabwean sculpture at the Yorkshire Sculpture Park persuaded Cox to focus on local stone. After gaining an honours degree in history at University of York, 1974–7, she trained as a teacher at the Froebel Institute, 1977–8. Took part in sculpture and life drawing classes at Camden and Islington Adult Education, 1988–90, at periods between 1989–92 continuing her studies at Open College of the Arts and Rochdale College. Her work was included in Islington Arts Group at Hardware Gallery, 1989; Turret Studio Group, The Turret, Hebden Bridge, 1992; Yorkshire Women Artists, Elizabethan Gallery, Wakefield, 1993; and it was also shown by The Gallery, Manchester.

Stephen COX 1946– Sculptor, born in Bristol. He studied there, at Loughborough and at Central School of Art, 1964–8. He first showed in London in 1976, after which he exhibited widely elsewhere in Britain and on the continent, notably at the Lisson Gallery. In 1985 had a major exhibition at Arnolfini Gallery, Bristol, which reviewed his work from 1977–85. He usually worked in stone, but also employed materials such as sand and lime on plasterboard and wood. Cox was preoccupied with architectural shapes and the Italian Renaissance tradition of stone carving and chose to spend much of his time in Italy. The marble Tondo 1981 in Tate Gallery collection employed red marble from Verona, carved under his supervision by local craftsmen. In 1995 Cox had a show at The Henry Moore Institute, Leeds, called Surfaces and Stones of Egypt. Arts Council holds several of his works.

Sue COX 1933– Artist in ceramics and porcelain, born in Singapore, who studied with Lucie Rie and Hans Coper at Camberwell School of Arts and Crafts, 1960. Her early work was architectural ceramics and studio pottery, sculptural work starting in 1990, "influenced by colour and simple form and calligraphy". Was a member of the Society of Sussex Sculptors, Society of Scribes and Illuminators and North Downs Calligraphers. Showed at Brighton Pavilion, Worthing Art Gallery and Museum and at East Grinstead Autumn Art Show. Allied Dunbar and CP Carpets hold her work. Lived in Oxted, Surrey.

Bernadette COXON 1958– Painter and draughtsman who studied at Newport School of Art, 1977–80, teachers including David Dobson, then Royal Academy Schools under Peter Greenham. She graduated with honours in 1980, four years later gaining a Sir James Knott Scholarship. Showed at RA, National Portrait Gallery and in the provinces, signing work with initials. Lived for a time in London.

Raymond COXON 1896–1997 Painter, mural artist, printmaker and teacher, born in Hanley, Stoke-on-Trent, Staffordshire. After serving in Cavalry in Palestine in World War I he studied at Leeds College of Art, 1919–21, and Royal College of Art, 1925. At Leeds he knew Henry Moore, of whom he painted a notable portrait, as he did of the sculptor Jacob Epstein. With Moore, Leon Underwood and others he formed the British Independent Society in 1927. Taught at Richmond School of Art. Was associated with the Chiswick Group and also showed with LG of which he was a member, and the Redfern, Leicester and Cooling Galleries. Had first solo show with London Artists' Association at Cooling in 1928. Official war artist in World War II. Married the artist Edna Ginesi, with whom he had a joint show at Parkin Gallery in 1985. There was a retrospective at Stoke-on-Trent City Museum and Art Gallery in 1987. Tate Gallery and Manchester City Art Gallery hold examples. Lived in London.

Damien COYLE 1957– Artist, born in Dungannon, County Tyrone, Northern Ireland, who gained his bachelor's degree in fine art from University of Ulster, 1981, his master's in 1982. He was a founder-member of Queen Street Studios, Belfast, and in 1993 was invited to join the editorial board of *Circa*, to which he regularly contributed. Exhibited in Independent

Artists at Douglas Hyde Gallery, Dublin, in 1984; in a three-man show at Arts Council Gallery, Belfast, 1993; in two shows associated with the Queen Street Studios in 1994, Works on Paper and Beyond the Partitions; and in the Netherlands and America.

Moya COZENS 1920–1990 Painter, printmaker and teacher, born in Forest Hill, London, who spent some of her early life in Australia. She studied at Slade School of Fine Art, 1938–41, winning prizes. Exhibited RA, Ashgate Gallery in Farnham, Herbert Art Gallery in Coventry, Heal's Mansard Gallery, Zwemmer's Gallery and in America and South America.

Richard CRABBE 1927– Artist in oil, acrylic, watercolour, chalk and collage, and teacher, born in Horley, Surrey. He was at Croydon School of Art, 1941–5; did National Service in coal mines, 1945–8; then was at Royal College of Art, 1948–51, under Ruskin Spear, John Minton and Carel Weight. Taught full-time at Derby and Manchester Colleges of Art and Portsmouth Polytechnic, 1951–87. Was exchange professor, Eastern Illinois University, 1975; gained an Arts Council bursary, 1976; founder-member and director of Art Space, Portsmouth, from 1980; and for two months in 1984 was resident artist for city of Düsseldorf. Was a member of International Association of Artists. Crabbe's work "passed through three main periods, in all of which colour played a major role: 1943–65 figuration; 1965–87 Geometric Abstraction; from 1987 returned to figuration." Took part in four-man show at Galleri 17, Stockholm, 1984. Had a solo exhibition at Peterloo Gallery, Manchester, 1976, later ones including Havant Arts Centre, 1990. Portsmouth City Museum, Wigan Education Committee and overseas collections hold Crabbe's work. Lived in Southsea, Hampshire.

Jack CRABTREE 1938– Painter and teacher, born in Rochdale, Lancashire. He attended the local College of Art, 1955–7, St Martin's School of Art, 1957–9, and Royal Academy Schools, 1959–61. Teaching positions included Colleges of Art in Salford, at Royal College, Newport and Belfast. Crabtree participated in many group shows, including membership of 56 Group, SWG and Royal National Eisteddfod. In the 1970s Crabtree was known as a Social Realist, being commissioned by National Coal Board to paint the working lives of miners in south Wales. Other commissions included British Petroleum, Rochdale Education Authority and a mural for the Diocese of Monmouth. Solo shows included the Howard Roberts Gallery in Cardiff, Trafford Gallery and Kerlin Gallery, Dublin, 1990, where he showed several dozen studies of the Irish writer Francis Stuart, some paying homage to the painter Francis Bacon, whose work Crabtree revered. National Museum of Wales in Cardiff and many provincial collections hold Crabtree's work. The Glynn Vivian Art Gallery, Swansea, has Save This Pit, a fine example of his hard-hitting style.

Peter CRABTREE 1930– Painter and teacher, born in Morecambe, Lancashire, but brought up in industrial West Riding of Yorkshire. At Leeds College of Art, 1947–51, Crabtree was impressed by the teaching of Tom Watt. He then studied at Royal College of Art, where the teachers included John Minton, Ruskin Spear and Carel Weight, 1953–6, in the latter year winning an Abbey Minor Scholarship, enabling him to study in Italy. Crabtree taught at Yeovil School of Art, 1957–8, Batley College of Art, 1958–62, then for many years at Liverpool College of Art. Crabtree was notable as a landscape painter whose big canvases were brought to fruition over a long period and which had a singular quality of light and atmosphere. Among group shows he participated in was Norwich School of Art Gallery's 1986–7 touring exhibition A Reputation Among Artists. Early in 1960s showed solo with Crane Gallery in Manchester and at Crane Kalman Gallery, later exhibitions including Bluecoat Gallery in Liverpool in 1975 and the city's Royal Hospital, 1986. Lived in Southport, Lancashire.

Trevor CRABTREE 1945– Sculptor and teacher, born in Bradford, Yorkshire, who studied at the local College of Art, then Hornsey and Royal Colleges of Art, in 1970–2 being a Rome Scholar. Held a number of teaching posts, from 1975 being senior lecturer at Manchester Polytechnic/Manchester Metropolitan University. Exhibited widely from 1965, when appeared in Young Contemporaries, later appearances including RA Summer Exhibitions from 1987; Grundy Art Gallery, Blackpool, 1989; Storey Institute, Lancaster, 1992; and 1st RWA Open Sculpture Exhibition, 1993. Lived in Rusholme, Manchester.

Adrienne CRADDOCK 1964– Artist and teacher, a printmaker creating hand-coloured drypoints and collographs, born at Lower Eaton, Herefordshire. Her father was Kenneth Craddock, principal of Herefordshire College of Art. Adrienne grew up in a farming area on the Welsh border, and her interest in rural life and the relationship of man and animals was reflected in her bold, imaginative work. She did a foundation course at Hereford College of Art, 1982–3; gained a first-class honours degree, specialising in printmaking, from North Staffordshire Polytechnic, 1983–6; then studied fine art printmaking at Manchester Polytechnic for her master's degree, 1987–9. From 1989 lectured in printmaking at the Polytechnic and taught in art centres, schools and colleges around Britain. In 1989 was included in Whitworth Young Contemporaries at Whitworth Art Gallery, Manchester; in 1990 in Open British Printmaking at Bankside Gallery; in 1993 was elected a member of MAFA; participated in 1994 in BBC Television's *The Art* educational series, and was shown at Benjamin Rhodes Gallery, also being included in Short Stories – Tall Tales, a tour organised by City Art Gallery, Leicester. In 1995–8 Chanticleer: Prints and Sculpture by Adrienne Craddock and Marjan Wouda toured the United Kingdom, organised by Sheeran Lock. Craddock lived in Brockhall Village, near Whalley, Lancashire.

Vivian Claud CRADDOCK WILLIAMS 1936– Artist in oil, pen and wash and ceramics, born in London, who signed his work V C C W. He was educated at Repton School under Arthur Norris and Denis Hawkins, then at Ruskin School of Drawing in Oxford under Percy Horton. Craddock Williams worked in London at studios in the World's End and Parsons Green and with the Chelsea Pottery. From 1971 he worked in Africa. He was a member of Wye Valley Art Society, Art Centre Foundation of Zambia and National Arts and Crafts Committee, Uganda. Showed with the Wye Valley Art Society, 1950–60, and with Chelsea & Kensington Art Society Exhibition, 1960–70. Kensington Borough Council and Zambia National Gallery, Lusaka, hold examples. Craddock Williams cited the sculptor Jacob Epstein and his son the painter Theo Garman as influences. Lived in Kampala, Uganda.

Tony CRAGG 1949– Sculptor and teacher, born in Liverpool. he studied at Gloucester, Wimbledon and the Royal College of Art, 1969–77. In that year he moved to Wuppertal, Germany, teaching at Düsseldorf Kunstakademie. Within a decade he had several dozen solo shows, including London, Berlin, Hamburg, Paris, Naples, Genoa, Tokyo, New York, Toronto and Middleburg. In the late-1980s Cragg represented Britain at the Venice Biennale and won the Turner Prize. From the outset Cragg used found objects to create his sculptures, as diverse as seashore objects or plastic debris. Cragg was also interested in the creation of monolothic forms, from metal, stone and glass, as in Subcommittee, shown in his 1991 Lisson Gallery exhibition. Much of Cragg's work with everyday objects started with the idea that it was the artist's duty to discover the poetry, pathos and hidden values in them to transform our way of looking at them. Retrospectives in 1992 at Tramway and Centre for Contemporary Art, Glasgow, with one at Whitechapel Art Gallery, 1996. Cragg was elected RA in 1994. Arts Council and Tate Gallery hold his work.

Barry CRAIG 1902–1951 Landscape and portrait painter, full name Frank Barrington Craig. After studying at Slade School of Fine Art, spent several years teaching in South Africa, returning in mid-1930s. Was elected NEAC in 1946, RP in 1949, also showing at RA, Goupil and Cooling Galleries, RI and elsewhere. Bradford's Cartwright Hall Art Gallery holds his Concarneau Harbour, a bold design in the Fauve style, lent to Christie's NEAC centenary show in 1986. Lived in London.

Edward Gordon CRAIG 1872–1966 Theatrical designer, printmaker, actor and writer. Craig was the son of the architect E W Godwin and the great actress Ellen Terry, and the father of Edward Anthony Craig (who worked as Edward Carrick), artist, theatre and film designer. A flamboyant polemicist, Craig told of his early life in *Index to the Story of my Days*, 1957. He was for a time an actor, but gradually turned to the theory and practice of scene design and direction, his extremely simple sets having a big influence on the theatre in America and in continental Europe, rather less in England. Early on he became interested in wood engraving, in which he was substantially self-taught and prolific, although he learned simplification of design from William Nicholson and James Pryde, working as the Beggarstaff Brothers. Was an original member of the SWE. Among books illustrated by him are his own *Book of Penny Toys* and *The Art of the Theatre*, 1905, and W B Yeats' *Plays for an Irish Theatre*, 1913. He also contributed to periodicals such as *The Dome* and *The Mask*, which he founded while living in Italy.

Michael CRAIG-MARTIN 1941– Sculptor and teacher, born in Dublin. He made works which brought together a number of materials and objects – such as milk bottles, metal brackets and water – his earlier productions employing texts, his later ones large wall projections. Craig-Martin went to America in 1946 and studied at Yale University, 1961–3, and Yale School of Arts and Architecture, 1964–6. From 1966 he was resident in Britain, his teaching appointments including Bath Academy of Art and Canterbury College of Art, then Goldsmiths' College School of Art, 1973–88, where he nurtured talents at the forefront of British art in the 1990s. Craig-Martin's belief that "a thing was not a work of art because it was made of bronze or paint, but defined by something else," giving the artist "the opportunity to use all the materials in the world" led to attacks by more conservative critics. After a first solo show at Rowan Gallery in 1966 he exhibited there frequently, also taking part in important international mixed shows. He had a retrospective at Whitechapel Art Gallery in 1989 and an exhibition at Waddington Gallery in 1993. He was a trustee of the Tate Gallery. Arts Council holds his work.

Heather CRAIGMILE 1925– Painter and draughtsman, born in Birkenhead, Cheshire. She was educated at Downe House, Newbury. Studied at Chester School of Art and privately with Harold Workman and Arnold Mason. Was a member of UA and Chelsea Art Society, also exhibiting with RCamA and RBA. Had solo exhibitions in Wales, where she lived at Conway, Gwynedd.

Anthea CRAIGMYLE 1933– Painter, brought up by the River Thames on Chiswick Mall, where she later had a studio. She studied at Chelsea School of Art, 1950–2. Took part in mixed shows at RA, Toswitta Haftmann Gallery, Zürich, and New Grafton Gallery. It gave her one-man exhibitions in 1984–8–92, previous solo shows having taken place at Clytie Jessop Gallery, 1970, and Yehudi Menuhin School, 1973. Lady Craigmyle lived in London.

Elizabeth CRAMP 1929– Painter, born near Rye, Sussex, wife of the artist Jonathan Cramp. She studied at Hastings School of Art and Royal Academy Schools until 1953, in 1954 settling in Wales. Was a member of WSW and RWS and showed with NEAC, at RA and elsewhere, including own home in Fishguard, Pembrokeshire. HRH The Prince of Wales and WAC hold her work.

Jonathan CRAMP 1930– Painter and teacher, born in Ninfield, Sussex, married to the artist Elizabeth Cramp. He studied at Hastings School of Art and Bournemouth College of Art into early 1950s, his teachers including Vincent Lines. He was a teacher and head of art at Fishguard County Secondary School,

1954–81. Showed with NEAC and RWS of which he was a member, LG, New Art Centre, RWA and elsewhere, as well as at home in Fishguard, Pembrokeshire. WAC and National Museum of Wales, Cardiff, hold his work.

Leigh CRAMPTON 1937– Artist working in a variety of media, born in Surrey, who studied at Finnish Academy of Fine Art, 1962–4, then Camberwell School of Arts and Crafts, 1966–70. Went on to teach part-time in London, where he lived. Showed at Air Gallery, 1975, and in Summer Show 2, at Serpentine Gallery, 1980. Solo exhibitions included Gardner Centre for the Arts, University of Sussex, and University of Essex, 1977.

Seán CRAMPTON 1918– Sculptor and printmaker, born in Manchester, who also created some silverwork and mosaics; full name was Arthur Edward Seán Crampton. Son of the architect Joshua Crampton. Studied at Vittoria School of Art, Birmingham, 1930–3, then Central School of Art there, and in Paris. Showed RA, Leicester Gallery, RSA and Alwin Gallery. Taught sculpture for several years in late 1940s at Anglo-French Art Centre, London. Sometimes signed work with his initial only, encircled. Had many solo shows in London and was included in 1st RWA Open Sculpture Exhibition, 1993. Figure groups, nude male and female figures, birds and animals were favourite subjects. Lived in Calne, Wiltshire.

Elizabeth CRAMPTON-GORE 1925– Painter in various media, born in London, but brought up in France among professional artists. She was taught from early childhood by her artist father William Gore, also attending Folkestone Art School for seven years part-time. She taught art, music and languages. Showed with Folkestone Art Society, of which for a time she was a member, and elsewhere. Her work included flower studies, sea and landscapes, religious, Symbolist and abstract pictures. Crampton-Gore (later Mrs Elizabeth Parry-Crooke) was the first wife of the artist William Francis Burton, their daughter Georgina Saunders also being a painter. Crampton-Gore lived in Folkestone, Kent.

William CRAMPTON GORE: *see* **William GORE**

Doris CRANE 1911– Sculptor, born in London, studied with William Everatt Gray, who like her worked in wood and ivory. Showed with RMS of which she became a member in 1958, RA, RSA and Paris Salon. Was a member of Deben Art Club. Lived for many years at Old Felixstowe, Suffolk.

Andrew CRANSTON 1969– Painter, born in Hawick, Roxburghshire, who studied at Manchester Polytechnic, Gray's School of Art in Aberdeen and Royal College of Art. He gained the NatWest Prize for Art and John Kinross Travelling Scholarship, both in 1993, and Alistair Gilchrist Fisher Memorial Awards, 1996. Group shows included Project Perec at French Institute, Edinburgh, 1993; Aberdeen Artists' Society, Aberdeen Art Gallery, 1994; and Royal Over-Seas League Open, 1996.

Alistair CRAWFORD 1945– Painter, printmaker, photographer, art historian and teacher, born in Fraserburgh, Aberdeenshire. He attended Glasgow School of Art, 1962–6, under Robert Stewart, and began teaching in 1966. His appointments included professor of art at University College of Wales, Aberystwyth, the first in its history, from 1990. Crawford travelled in Norway, Italy, Holland, France, Greece and America. Among his many activities he gained a commission for the mural The Palio at Siena, University of Leeds, 1971; in 1978 he made Vedute di Roma prints at the British School at Rome; gained a British Council Artists Award, 1981; won the Gold Medal in Fine Art at Royal National Eisteddfod of Wales, 1985; and in 1988 founded Aberystwyth Printmakers with Robert Meyrick. Crawford took part in over 100 exhibitions in Britain and abroad, having over two dozen solo shows. His work was held by many collections, including WAC, Hunterian Museum and Art Gallery in Glasgow, British Council and Imperial College. He was co-author of *John Thomas 1838–1905: Photographer*, 1977, and author of *Mario Giacomelli*, 1983, and several other books. He was the younger brother of the artist John Crawford and lived in Comins Coch, near Aberystwyth, Dyfed.

Heather CRAWFORD 1926– Painter, notably of posters, artist in various materials and teacher, born in East Boldon, County Durham. Studied art at Lincoln Training College, 1944–6, College of Arts and Crafts in Hull, 1951–2, Sunderland College of Art and in Glasgow. Exhibited with Federation of Northern Art Societies and at Shipley Art Gallery, Gateshead. Also showed with Sunderland Art Club of which she was a member, living at Roker, Sunderland.

Hugh Adam CRAWFORD 1898–1982 Painter, mural artist, designer and teacher, born in Busby, Lanarkshire. Was married to the artist Kathleen Mann. Crawford studied at Glasgow School of Art under Maurice Greiffenhagen, 1919–23; at Central School of Arts and Crafts, 1924–5; and at St Martin's School of Art. He joined the staff of Glasgow School of Art in 1925, where he was an influential teacher, and was head of painting until 1948 when he became head of Gray's School of Art, Aberdeen. He was there until 1954, then was principal of Duncan of Jordanstone College of Art, Dundee, 1954–64. Crawford painted a strong series of portraits in the 1930s. Among his murals were some for the Roman Catholic chapel at Bellahouston and others for John Brown's shipyard and Scottish Brewers, Glasgow. Glasgow Art Club gave him a retrospective in 1971, the Third Eye Centre in Glasgow showing selected works from 1928–78 in 1978. His work is in Scottish collections.

John Gardiner CRAWFORD 1941– Painter and teacher, born in Broadsea by Fraserburgh, Aberdeenshire, older brother of the artist Alistair Crawford. After Fraserburgh Academy he studied at Gray's School of Art, 1959–64, including a postgraduate year, and at Patrick Allan-Fraser School of Art, Hospitalfield, Arbroath. He was made a member of RSW in 1974, RBA in 1983 and RI in 1984. Among his awards was first prize for painting at Gray's in 1962; first prize in Scottish Arts Council Open Exhibition in 1969; and Hunting Award, first prize for watercolour, 1982. Having come from a long line of fishermen, Crawford painted boats and the sea in great detail. His teaching appointments included Dundee College of Education until 1980, when he left to concentrate on painting, although he was artist-tutor at Newbattle Abbey College, Midlothian, 1980–85. His solo exhibitions included William Hardie Ltd, Glasgow, 1993. Robert Fleming Holdings holds his work. Lived in Arbroath, Angus.

Thomas Hamilton CRAWFORD fl. from c.1890–1948 Artist in watercolour and mezzotint, son of the sculptor John Crawford. He studied in Glasgow and Edinburgh and showed at RA, RSW, RSA, Fine Art Society and Paris Salon. He was a Savage Club member who lived at Berkhamsted, Hertfordshire.

Eileen CRAWFURD 1916– Painter born in Haywards Heath, Sussex, who attended Roedean School, then studied at Slade School of Fine Art with Randolph Schwabe, 1934–5, as well as the Sir John Cass School of Arts and Crafts. She showed at SWA of which she was a member, RWA, RI, in the provinces and on the continent. Lived in Salcombe, Devon.

Alwyn CRAWSHAW 1934– Popular painter, lecturer and demonstrator, born in Mirfield, Yorkshire, who studied under Vincent Lines at Hastings School of Art, 1949–51. From 1957–80 directed Russell Artists Merchandising in Kingston upon Thames, and also demonstrated for Daler-Rowney & Company. Crawshaw was a member of SEA and BWS, also president of the National Acrylic Painters' Association. His solo exhibitions included Harrods, Barclay Art Gallery in Chester and Guildford Galleries in Surrey. As well as radio and television appearances Crawshaw was author of many instructional books, such as *Learn to Paint Boats and Harbours* and *Sketching with Alwyn Crawshaw. The Artist at Work* was tutorial with an autobiographical strand. Felix Rosenstiel's produced his first print. Lived in Dawlish, Devon.

E Burnett CRAWSHAW fl. c.1930–1950 Painter who was by profession a barrister and medical practitioner. Exhibited RA, RMS and Paris Salon. Lived in Epsom, Surrey.

Frances CRAWSHAW 1876– Painter who was married to the artist Lionel Crawshaw. She attended Scarborough and Westminster Schools of Art, as well as studying in Italy. Exhibited RA, WIAC, RSA, NEAC and elsewhere. Lived in Droitwich, Worcestershire.

Lionel CRAWSHAW 1864–1949 Painter and printmaker who was born near Doncaster, Yorkshire, and married the artist Frances Crawshaw. He attended Cambridge University, qualified as a solicitor, then studied art in Germany and Paris. Early in the century he worked in Yorkshire, based at Whitby. Exhibited RA, Walker's Galleries, RSW, ROI and at many other galleries. Signed work L C in the form of of a monogram. Towards the end of his life lived at Newton Abbot, Devon.

John CRAXTON 1922– Painter and designer, born in London, son of the pianist Harold Craxton. When only 10, he had paintings exhibited in schools group at Bloomsbury Gallery. In 1939 studied life drawing at L'Académie de la Grande Chaumière, Paris, returning to study in 1940 at Westminster School of Art and Central School of Art with P F Millard and Eric Schilsky. The following year he studied drawing at Goldsmiths' College School of Art with Clive Gardiner. About this time Craxton was friendly with Graham Sutherland and Lucian Freud and became recognised as a member of the Neo-Romantic group of painters. He had his first solo show at Leicester Galleries, 1944. In 1946 Craxton visited Greece for first time, whose landscape was eventually to leave its mark on his work. After a joint show with Freud at London Gallery in 1947, with whom he had worked in Greece, in 1948 Craxton visited Crete for the first time; in 1960 he rented a house in Hania there which subsequently became his home, although Craxton was an indefatigable traveller in several continents. In 1951 Craxton designed sets and costumes for *Daphnis and Chloe* at Covent Garden; in 1966 he helped restage it for Athens Festival and completed designs for the ballet *Apollo* at Covent Garden. Between 1971–4 worked on Landscape with the Elements as the Cottrell Memorial Tapestry for the McRobert Centre, Stirling University. Craxton had a retrospective show at Whitechapel Art Gallery in 1967 and in 1985 a show of paintings and drawings appeared at the Chrysostomos Gallery, Hania; British Council, Athens; and Christopher Hull Gallery. Tate Gallery and other major collections hold his work. Elected RA, 1993.

Fred CRAYK 1952– Painter who said that his work exploited "the tension between abstraction and representation". The decaying mining landscapes and communities of West Lothian were one of his subjects. Born in Portsmouth, Hampshire, Crayk studied in Paris, 1971–2, Duncan of Jordanstone College of Art, Dundee, 1972–6, then Edinburgh College of Art, 1976–7. He was awarded a Scottish Education Department Minor Travelling Scholarship to France; won the Greenshields Foundation Scholarship (Canada) in 1978; in 1980 won Scottish Arts Council Amsterdam Studio Bursary. As well as participating in many group shows, Crayk had one-man exhibitions at Torrance Gallery in Edinburgh and Compass Gallery, Glasgow, and at Lamont Gallery, 1997. Scottish Arts Council and City Art Centre, Edinburgh, hold his work.

John CREALOCK 1871–1959 Painter in oil of portraits and landscapes. Born in Manchester, after education at Sandhurst Royal Military Academy and service in the Boer War, Crealock studied art at the Académie Julian, Paris, 1901–4. Exhibited RA, RP, Goupil Gallery, NEAC and elsewhere. Williamson Art Gallery & Museum, Birkenhead, and several other galleries in England and France hold his work. Lived in Hove, Sussex.

Anne-Marie CREAMER 1966– Artist, born and lived in London, whose work drew on photographic and cinematic sources, as in her canvas Chimera (Dynamite Lady), shown in 1992 at East & South, Norwich Gallery/Kent Institute of Art and Design. She studied at Middlesex Polytechnic, 1986–8, then Royal College of Art, 1988–90.

Alexander CREE 1929– Artist in pastel, oil watercolour and teacher, born in Dunfermline, Fife. Cree studied at Edinburgh College of Art, 1946–52, his teachers including William Gillies, Robin Philipson, William MacTaggart and Leonard Rosoman. He won an Andrew Grant Postgraduate Scholarship, 1950–1, and Travel Scholarship, 1951–2. Taught in state schools, from 1963–87 being principal teacher of art at Dunbar Grammar School. Showed with RSA, SSA, RSW and Royal Glasgow Institute of the Fine Arts. His solo shows included Lyceum Gallery, Edinburgh, 1957, Demarco Gallery, Edinburgh, 1968; and Macaulay Gallery, East Lothian, 1990. Cree said of his subjects that these were "mainly the landscape of lowland Scotland, but I am also interested in the people". Scottish Arts Council, Nuffield Foundation and British Transport Hotels hold his work. Lived in East Linton, East Lothian.

Janet CREE 1910–1992 Painter, notably of portraits in tempera with an early-Italian feel, born in London. She was married to the barrister John Platts-Mills and was the mother of the film-maker Barney Platts-Mills, notable for the 1970 film *Bronco Bullfrog*. She studied with Ernest Jackson at Byam Shaw School of Drawing and Painting. Showed at RA, Phoenix Gallery in Lavenham and elsewhere. Tate Gallery holds her early Oriental Portrait. Lived in London and near Uckfield, Sussex. Died in London.

Dennis CREFFIELD 1931– Painter and draughtsman, born in London. From 1948–51 he studied with David Bomberg at Borough Polytechnic and from 1957–61 at Slade School of Fine Art. Creffield became Gregory Fellow in Painting at University of Leeds, 1964–7. By then he had taken part in many mixed exhibitions, including John Moores Exhibition, Liverpool, 1961, where he was a prizewinner, and with LG, of which he was elected a member in 1962. He had a solo show at Leeds City Art Gallery in 1966, others including Queen's Square Gallery, Leeds; Brighton Polytechnic Gallery; and Serpentine Gallery, 1980. He won a Major Arts Council Award in 1977. Creffield had an ambition to draw every cathedral and abbey church in England, and from this stemmed the South Bank touring exhibition of 1988–90 and *English Cathedrals*, with a text by Creffield, published in 1987. His first one-man show at a private venue in London was at Albemarle Gallery in 1991. Paintings and Drawings of London, 1960–90, was held at Barbican Gallery in 1992 and his Paintings of Petworth toured from Gillian Jason Gallery, 1993–5. Creffield was a powerful artist in the Bomberg Expressionist tradition. His work is held by Arts Council, Tate Gallery and many other public gallery and university collections. Lived in Brighton, Sussex.

Benjamin CREME 1922– Painter, designer and illustrator, born in Glasgow. He began painting aged 14, left school at 16 to paint but was too young to enter local School of Art, although he attended life classes there. Feeling he had become a modern painter and that the School of Art was too academic Creme declined to pursue studies. In 1940 held a joint show with Douglas Campbell at a trade union club, where Josef Herman and Jankel Adler gave encouragement. Studied for several years with Adler. In 1942 Creme and Robert Frame illustrated W S Graham's poems *Cage Without Grievance*. Moved to London in 1946 when Creme met up with John Minton, Prunella Clough and Keith Vaughan and his pictures had a marked Neo-Romantic tinge. In the mid-1940s Tyrone Guthrie commissioned Creme to do sets for his production of *Carmen* and Creme began to show widely, at AIA, LG, Gimpel Fils, Redfern and Leger Galleries. A visit to south of France in 1950 prompted Creme to adopt a lighter palette and to move towards abstraction. Had one-man show at Gallery Apollinaire in 1952 and exhibited in America, other solo shows including St George's Gallery, 1955; Bryant M Hale Gallery, Los Angeles, 1964; and Dartington New Gallery, 1977. After Jane England organised a retrospective at Themes and Variations Gallery in 1985 England & Co gave Creme several partial retrospectives. Victoria & Albert Museum and British Museum hold his work. In addition to his painting Creme was frequent lecturer, advocating the mission of Maitreya the Christ.

Alexander CRESSWELL 1957– Watercolourist and teacher, who studied history of art at Winchester College. Then went on to West Surrey College of Art and Design and Byam Shaw School of Drawing and Painting. Cresswell began painting professionally in 1981 and participated in many group shows as well as holding numerous solo exhibitions in Britain and abroad. Later ones included Spink & Son, The Atlantic Hotel, in Jersey, and Save Britain's Heritage, at Mappin & Webb site, all in 1991, then Cadogan Gallery in 1992. Cresswell's fine technique as a watercolourist was employed for the Spink show, called The Silent Houses of Britain, in which over five years he recorded 45 grand country houses, since abandoned. This coincided with the publication of his book of the same title. Cresswell was a tutor at The Prince of Wales' Summer School in Civil Architecture, in Rome, in 1991. Cresswell's commissioned work included Wiggins Teape plc, Burmah Castrol plc and the Parliamentary Art Collection in the Palace of Westminster.

Emily Grace CRESWELL 1889– Miniaturist and portrait painter, born in Ravenstone, Leicestershire. She studied art, after attending University College, Reading, at Leicester School of Art. This was followed by periods at Harrogate and Leamington Schools of Art plus some time with the miniaturist S. Arthur Lindsay in Chelsea. She sometimes signed her work E G C or G C and exhibited RMS, RI, SWA and elsewhere. Lived in Harrogate, Yorkshire.

Joseph CRIBB 1892–1967 Sculptor, draughtsman and letter-cutter, son of Herbert William Cribb and brother of Lawrence

Cribb, both artists. From 1906–13 was apprenticed to Eric Gill, settling in Ditchling, Sussex. After World War I service became almost a founder member of the Guild of St Joseph and St Dominic and for many years was in charge of the stonemason's shop. Cribb did a lot of work for the Brighton architectural practice of John Denman and worked on the tabernacle of the London church of St Simon Stock. Cheltenham and Hove Museums and Art Galleries hold his work.

Kevin CRIBB 1928– Sculptor and letter-cutter, son of Lawrence Cribb and nephew of Joseph Cribb, both artists. He was born in Abergavenny, Monmouthshire. He was apprenticed to his father and David Kindersley in the Eric Gill workshop and worked for many years with Kindersley before going independent. Cribb exhibited in Bath, many times in Cambridge and in Bruges, Belgium. He worked in wood and stone, completed a headstone commemorating the inventor Barnes Wallis and has works in Winchester Cathedral and Wye College, Kent. Lived in Haslingfield, Cambridgeshire.

Lawrence Walter CRIBB 1898–1979 Sculptor, born in Twickenham, Middlesex, father of Kevin Cribb, son of Herbert William Cribb and younger brother of Joseph Cribb, all artists. He studied under his brother and Eric Gill, working with Gill from 1921. After the death of Gill in 1940 Cribb carried on in the workshop with Denis Tegetmeier, moving to north Wales late in the 1950s. From 1925 Cribb had many exhibitions. He worked with Gill on the League of Nations mural and St James' Park Underground Station as well as other commissions. Died in Barrington, Cambridgeshire.

Frances CRICHTON STUART 1951– Artist in oil, tapestry and pencil, muralist and illustrator, born in Dublin, Ireland, adopted and brought up in Scotland, educated at a Catholic convent. In 1972 enrolled at St Martin's School of Art, taught by Gillian Ayres, John Hoyland, Frederick Gore and Jennifer Durrant. Crichton Stuart was early influenced by Seurat, the Symbolists and Jung; also interested in travelling, "the different values of Man and Man's search for enlightenment" and the Painting and Prayer Movement, serving it as a tutor. Activities included murals at St Bartholomew's Hospital radiotherapy unit and Laycock School, Islington, 1973; in 1976–7, after leaving St Martin's, a mural at Charing Cross Hospital, aided by an Arts Council grant; in 1977–8 was assistant to artist Gary Stephan, in New York; lived in Greece, 1981; helped organise Matthew Smith show at Barbican Gallery, 1983; travelled in Australia, Colombia, Yugoslavia and Italy, 1986–7; began designing and making tapestries, 1988; and illustrated *Alex*, by Peter Ryde, 1994. Later exhibitions included solo at Stephen Bartley Gallery, 1989; and mixed shows at Mossop Street Gallery and Kirkcaldy Museum and Art Gallery, both 1993. Lived in London.

Stephen CRIPPS 1952–1982 Pyrotechnic sculptor and performance artist, who was early encouraged at Cranleigh School by his art master Howard Pickersgill. Attended Bath Academy of Art, Corsham, 1970–4, where he reconstituted salvage and explored the possibilities of automatism. Then took a studio in east London, 1975–9. Economic pressures made Cripps take on a series of temporary jobs, such as scene shifting at Raymond's Revue Bar and photographing for a detective agency, then in 1979 he joined the London Fire Brigade, where as a nonconformist in a regulated atmosphere he found life tough going on occasions. Striving to break free of alcohol and heroin dependency Cripps misjudged a dose of methadone and died the following morning. Cripps had three shows at Acme Gallery, between 1978–81. Among the many multi-media performances he took part in were those with Paul Burwell and Anne Bean, whose Bow Gamelan Orchestra worked with the sculptor Richard Wilson. Bean and Burwell helped form The Stephen Cripps Trust, to prevent dispersal of his work. An installation and a performance to mark the tenth anniversary of Cripps' death took place at Serpentine Gallery in 1992, along with publication of an extensive monograph, supported by Acme Housing Association.

CRISPIN: *see* **Geoffrey WHEELER**

Keith CRITCHLOW 1933– Figurative and abstract artist, architect, teacher and writer. He studied at St Martin's School of Art and Royal College of Art, 1954–7, teaching at the Royal College from 1973. He was an early disciple of the American architect Richard Buckminster Fuller, whose first London exhibition he organised, and he ran his own architectural consultancy, Keith Critchlow Associates. Critchlow was interested in a variety of subjects related to art and architecture: geometry, mathematics, pattern and order in space. He was an expert on sacred architecture. Was represented in the 1988 Royal College of Art show Exhibition Road. Lived in London.

Michael Bernard CRITCHLOW 1904– Painter and illustrator, brought up in Wolverhampton, where he attended the School of Art under Robert Emerson. Did a considerable amount of illustrative work for magazines such as *Strand Magazine*, *Britannia and Eve* and *Nash's Magazine*. Exhibited RA, NEAC, ROI and elsewhere. Chelsea Arts Club member who lived in London.

Ariel CRITTALL 1914– Painter and draughtsman, born in Essex where she settled at Great Bardfield. Studied in Munich, Germany, 1934, then courses in life drawing and sculpture at St Martin's School of Art, 1935, and Slade School of Fine Art, 1935–6, her teachers including Vivian Pitchforth and A H Gerrard. Crittall's painting and drawing was confined to her spare time until 1980, when her husband died, then she concentrated on it seriously. Mixed shows included Bury St Edmunds Art Gallery, 1983; work accepted for RA Summer Exhibition, 1985; and in 1994 both Braintree Town Hall and Fry Art Gallery, Saffron Walden. Had a solo show at Quay Gallery, Sudbury, 1986, later ones including University of Essex, 1992; Braintree Town Hall, 1994; and Guild Hall, Thaxted, 1996. Crittall was a member of

Colchester Art Society and was included in its Fiftieth Anniversary Exhibition at Chappel Galleries, Chappel, 1996. Gwen John, Winifred Nicholson and Matisse were cited as influences and Crittall aimed at "a palimpsest: richness and depth of tone, one thing half seen through another". Essex University Library, Braintree Library and Sir Stephen and Lady Tumim held examples.

Andrew CROCKER 1962– Artist, born in North Yorkshire, who studied at Cleveland College of Art, 1981–2, then graduated from Goldsmiths' College with a degree in fine art, 1982–5, with postgraduate studies there, 1987–9. Exhibitions included Cleveland International Drawing Biennale 1989; Cricket Hill Gallery, New York, USA, 1993; Lamont Gallery, 1995; and Paul Smith, New York, 1996. Commissions and collections include London Underground, Ladbroke Group and Ernst & Young.

Barbara CROCKER 1910– Painter of pictures and murals, printmaker and illustrator and art lecturer, born in London, married to the writer Eric Whelpton. She studied at Slade School of Fine Art, 1927–30, under Henry Tonks, Philip Wilson Steer and Tancred Borenius, continuing her studies in France and Italy. Worked as a professional painter backed up by lecturing, notably to troops in World War II. Travelled throughout Europe, the Middle East and Russia. Showed with LG, RSW, Alpine Gallery and WIAC. From 1960 held studio shows about once a year. Completed murals in offices and restaurants in London, also in Natural History Museum. Art gallery in Rye, Canada House in London and New York Museum hold her work. Among her publications was *Art Appreciation Made Simple*. Lived in Rye, Sussex.

Jeremy CROCKER fl. from early 1980s– Painter, printmaker, muralist and teacher, who did a foundation course at Somerset College of Arts and Technology, 1977–8; gained a first-class honours degree in painting from Wolverhampton Polytechnic, 1978–81 (including a term at Orleans, France); then did post-graduate studies in printmaking at Central School of Art and Design, 1983–5. Crocker gained a Tim Turner Travelling Scholarship, 1981; Prix de Rome (Printmaking), British School at Rome, 1986–7; and an Italian Government Bursary to study in Rome, 1990. Crocker's work included figure groups, including nude and clothed figures, giving them a slightly stagey quality, as in A Clear Picture at Collyer-Bristow Gallery, 1997. Other mixed shows included Stowells Trophy from 1980; The Brewhouse Open, Taunton, from 1981; Open Print Exhibition, Bankside Gallery, from 1988; and LG, from 1992. Later solo shows included 30 Brook Street, 1994. Crocker held a teaching fellowship at Christ's Hospital, Horsham, 1985–6; was a visiting lecturer at the Central School (The London Institute), 1987; he taught at St Paul's School from 1988; and also gave adult classes. Commissions included four mural paintings at the Royal Surrey Hospital, Redhill, commissioned by the Public Art Development Trust, 1985.

John CROFT 1923– Artist in oil and collage, born in London. He was by profession a civil servant who after Westminster School studied at Oxford University, London University's Institute of Education and the London School of Economics, obtaining his master's degree. Had no formal art training and produced "non-figurative, Minimalist, work derived from landscape". Participated in group shows at Piccadilly and John Whibley Galleries, at Camden Arts Centre in its survey of abstract artists in 1967, Bear Lane Gallery in Oxford in 1968 and in Arts in Mann, 1992. Had a solo exhibition at University of Sussex's Gardner Centre in 1970, a year later at Warwick University. London Borough of Camden and London School of Economics hold his work. Lived in London, latterly at Peel, Isle of Man.

Marjorie CROFT 1889– Painter and printmaker. She showed NEAC, SWA, RA, RBA and elsewhere and lived in London for many years after an early period in Penshurst, Kent.

Richard John CROFT 1935– Artist in a wide range of media, and teacher, born in London, who studied at Bromley College of Art, 1951–5, then Brighton College of Art, 1957–8. Between 1958–86 he taught, for a time being head of the art department at Annadale Grammar School, Belfast; in 1984 he moved from Belfast to Dundrum, County Down; and in 1986 began to paint full-time. Croft began as a realistic painter but quickly became influenced by Geometric Formalisation and later by Geometric Abstraction, leading to constructions in wood and Perspex. In the 1960s he produced several kinetic works; in the 1970s slowly returned to realism, but still with a bias towards Geometric Cubism and a simplification of statement, using very thin paint and pale colour; with the move to Dundrum the move to realism continued, but his palette brightened. From 1962 Croft regularly showed work at the Irish Exhibition of Living Art in Dublin and Belfast, RHA and RUA; he became an Ulster Academician in 1967, and won the Conor Prize in 1970. In 1963 Croft was a founder-member of Group '63 and in 1973 with his artist wife Helen Kerr he helped found the Octagon Gallery. After a solo show at Piccolo Gallery, Belfast, in 1960 Croft regularly had one-man exhibitions, a retrospective at Flowerfield Arts Centre, Portstewart, going to several venues in 1993–4. Ulster Museum, Oxford and London Universities, Northern Ireland Arts Council and many other public and corporate collections hold examples.

Stuart CROFT 1970– Artist who painted and used adhesive tape, who said that his work had "always formed an exploration into the possibilities and history of abstractions". Studied in 1989 at Harrogate College of Arts and Technology, in 1990–2 at Newcastle upon Tyne Polytechnic, in the latter year having an Erasmus EC placement at the National College of Art and Design, Dublin. From 1992–3 lived in Berlin, in 1993–4 attending Wimbledon School of Art. Exhibitions included Squires Gallery, Newcastle, 1991; Zwemmer Gallery, Courtauld Institute, 1993; three-man show at University of Surrey, Guildford, 1994;

and Pacesetters, Peterborough Museum and Art Gallery, 1995. Lived in London.

Michael John CROFTON 1961– Sculptor, restorer and teacher who obtained first-class diploma in sculpture from City and Guilds of London Art School, 1980–4. Crofton engaged in a wide variety of work, including wax and rubber moulding, freelance casting for sculptors and part-time teaching at Fulham and Chelsea Adult Education Institute, 1987–9. Showed at RSA and RA from 1988; Keith Chapman Gallery, 1989; West Wales Art Centre, Fishguard, 1992; and 1st RWA Open Sculpture Exhibition, 1993. Lived in Hebron Whitland, Dyfed.

Stella Rebecca CROFTS 1898–1964 Painter, sculptor and potter of portraits and animals, born in Nottingham. Studied at Central Schoolof Arts and Crafts, 1916–22, and Royal College of Art, 1922–3. Exhibited RA, RMS, SWA, Crafts Centre of Great Britain and widely abroad. Nottingham Castle Museum, Hanley Museum in Stoke-on-Trent and Manchester City Art Gallery hold her work, as does Victoria & Albert Museum. Lived at Billericay, Essex.

Gertrude CROMPTON 1874– Watercolour and oil painter and teacher, born in West Tanfield, Yorkshire. After initial education in London she studied at the Westminster School of Art under William Mouat Loudan, then in Paris. She exhibited SWA, Goupil Gallery, with the St Ives Society of Artists and at the Paris Salon. While living in Cornwall was a justice of the peace, retiring just after World War II. Then lived at Nailsworth, near Stroud, in Gloucestershire.

David CRONE 1937– Painter and teacher, born in Belfast, Northern Ireland, who attended Belfast College of Art from 1956, then taught art at Larkfield Secondary School in the city, 1961–3, next at his old grammar school, Annadale, 1963–75, then went on to teach at Ulster College. He gained a number of awards, including an Arts Council of Northern Ireland travel scholarship to the continent, 1964, commissions including a mural for Ulster '71. As well as painting portraits Crone was a significant landscape artist whose pictures variously showed Expressionist and Cubist influences. Exhibitions included CEMA, Magee Gallery in Belfast, Arts Council of Northern Ireland which holds his work and Tom Caldwell Gallery, Belfast.

Hugh CRONYN 1905–1996 Painter in oil, watercolour and mixed media, and teacher, born in Vancouver, British Columbia, Canada. He was educated at Ridley College and after a brief period in business studied with the landscape painter Frank Johnston, one of the Group of Seven, then at the Art Students' League of New York, 1929; in 1930 at the American School of Fine Arts, Fontainebleau; then for several years in Paris including time with André Lhote, 1932. After settling in London, with the outbreak of World War II Cronyn was commissioned in the Royal Naval Volunteer Reserve, 1940, serving in several ships, his final posting being to Saigon. Early in the war Cronyn had volunteered for bomb disposal; he was awarded the George Medal for defusing a bomb in the volatile tanker *Chesapeake.* After demobilisation, Cronyn became director of art at the Architectural Association's school of architecture, 1946–9, then taught painting at Colchester School of Art, 1949–69. He showed at The Minories, Colchester; Canada House; Nancy Poole's Studio, Toronto; Phoenix Gallery in London and Lavenham (with a retrospective there in 1990); RA; and LG. In 1989, by which time Cronyn's eyesight was failing, he published a memoir, *Steady As You Go; A Canadian At Sea.* Finally lived in London, spending part of the year at a house in the southwest of France.

Gordon CROOK 1921– Painter, tapestry designer and teacher, born in Richmond, Surrey. After initial education in Chichester, Sussex, Crook attended St Martin's School of Art and the Central School of Art & Design. He showed at Redfern and O'Hana Galleries, at the Bear Lane Gallery in Oxford, in Scotland and in America. Lived in Great Yeldham, Essex.

P J CROOK 1945– Pam Crook was born in Cheltenham, and was married to another painter, Richard Parker. She studied at the Gloucestershire College of Art, 1960–5. Showed at RA Summer Exhibition from 1978, RWA and John Player Portrait Award Exhibition at National Portrait Gallery, 1986. Had a series of solo shows at Portal Gallery from 1980, in 1986 and 1995 at Cheltenham Art Gallery & Museum, which holds her work, and from where a retrospective toured in 1996. Westminster Cathedral, Tewkesbury Abbey and the parish church in Bishop's Cleeve, Gloucestershire, where she lived, also hold examples. Crook's figurative works had a slightly Surrealist, haunting quality and were unusual in that the image spilled from the canvas on to the wooden frame.

Thomas Mewburn CROOK 1869–1949 Sculptor and teacher, born at Tonge Moor, Bolton, Lancashire. After a religious schooling he attended Manchester Technical School and then the Royal College of Art, gaining three silver and five bronze medals and his diploma in 1902, followed by extensive studies on the continent. He was elected RBA in 1910 and a fellow of RBS in 1923. Crook's Mysteries and his Pieta, erected in St Katherine's, Rotherhithe, are illustrated in *RBS: Modern British Sculpture*, published in 1939. Showed at RA, Royal Glasgow Institute of the Fine Arts, RBA, ROI and RI. Between 1894–5 Crook taught modelling at the Royal College, then from 1896–1905 modelling and anatomy at Manchester School of Art. He was an Arts and Savage Club member who lived in London.

Irene M CROOKENDEN 1880–1957 Flower painter in oil, pastel and watercolour. Born in Camberley, Surrey, into a military family, she studied art at the Slade School of Fine Art and the British School at Rome, where she won the Calderon Prize for portraiture. Exhibited RA, Goupil Gallery, SWA, RBA and widely in the provinces. Lived in London.

Barbara CROOKS 1904– Painter in oil, born in London. She was educated at Southend High School, The Froebel Institute at Roehampton and London Academy of Music & Dramatic Art, becoming a kindergarten teacher. From the 1960s "to prove that I can paint and as a prophylactic against family tragedy" Crooks took up painting in oil, attending evening classes at Southend-on-Sea Art School and adult leisure classes, mainly producing landscapes. Was a member of NS and Southend Art Club and also showed at ROI, NEAC, Paris Salon and elsewhere. Sometimes signed work B G A, her full name being Barbara Gwendolen Anne Crooks. Lived in Thorpe Bay, Essex.

John CROPTON: *see* **David STAINER**

William CROSBIE 1915– Painter, draughtsman and mural artist, born in Hankow, China, of Scottish parents. The family stayed in China until 1926; Crosbie had a Chinese tutor, and Oriental philosophy remained a potent force in his life and work. After toying with the idea of a commercial career back in Glasgow, Crosbie decided instead to be a painter and studied at the School of Art, 1932–5. A Haldane Travelling Scholarship took him to Paris, where he studied history of art at the Sorbonne and worked under Fernand Léger and Aristide Maillol. He then joined an archaeological expedition to Egypt, where he copied friezes on temple walls, but was back in Britain to serve in the Merchant Navy and Civil Defence during World War II. Crosbie now made a name as a mural painter through his association with architects such as Basil Spence; the Victoria & Albert Museum's Britain Can Make It show in 1946 and the Festival of Britain, in 1951, were examples. He did some book illustration, designed the sets of Eric Chisholm's ballet *The Earth Shapers* and produced wood and stone carvings for churches. Crosbie showed regularly in mixed Scottish exhibitions, having many solo shows. There were retrospectives at Scottish Gallery, Edinburgh, in 1980, and at Ewan Mundy & Celia Philo, Glasgow and London, 1990, and Ewan Mundy put on an eightieth birthday exhibition in Glasgow in 1995. Crosbie was made an associate of RSA in 1953, a full RSA 20 years later. His work is hard to classify, as he was extremely versatile, a fine draughtsman and brilliant Colourist. Scottish Arts Council and Scottish National Gallery of Modern Art hold his work. Latterly Crosbie worked mainly at Petersfield, Hampshire.

Clem CROSBY 1958– Painter, born in Aldershot, Hampshire, who studied at Trent Polytechnic, Nottingham, 1979–82. Group exhibitions included Wonderful Life, 1994, and in 1995 Six Painters, both Lisson Gallery; and in 1995 Real Art at Southampton City Art Gallery. Lived in London.

Theo CROSBY 1925–1994 Architect, sculptor and writer, born in Mafeking, South Africa. He studied at University of Witwatersrand, Johannesburg, moved to London in 1947 and that year studied part-time at Sir John Cass School of Art, then Central School of Arts and Crafts, 1950–4, and St Martin's School of Art, 1956–8. Crosby was a fellow of RIBA and of the Chartered Society of Designers and was made RA in 1990. He became a partner in Pentagram Design Partnership. As a sculptor he made large terracottas and stone carvings, in later years moving towards a more classical imagery and technique. He was commissioned to make a drinking fountain in Hyde Park for the Great Children's Party, 1979, also working on the Shakespeare Globe Centre and National Police Memorial in The Mall. His publications included *Le Corbusier*, 1959, and *Let's Build a Monument*, 1987. Crosby was professor of architecture and design at Royal College of Art, 1990–3. His first wife was the artist Anne Buchanan, his second Polly Hope. Lived in London.

Dorothy CROSS 1956– Artist, designer and teacher, born in Cork, Ireland, who employed unorthodox materials such as cows' udders and snakes in silver cases. She gained a bachelor's degree at Leicester Polytechnic and her master's degree in fine art from San Francisco Art Institute, California. Teaching and lecturing experience included Crawford School of Art, Cork; National College of Art and Design, Dublin; Waterford and Belfast Colleges of Art; Williams College, Massachusetts; Oberlin College, Ohio; and School of the Museum of Fine Arts, Boston. In 1992 and 1994 handled set and costume designs for Opera Theatre Company for various Irish venues. From 1985–8 Cross was a committee member for the Irish Exhibition of Living Art, from 1992 a member of Aosdana. Group shows included Strongholds, Tate Gallery in Liverpool and Hilden Museum, Tampere, Finland, 1991; Welcome Europe, Holsterbro Kunstmuseum, Jutland, Denmark, 1992; and Fetishism, South Bank Centre tour, 1995. Later solo shows included Frith Street Gallery, 1994; Kerlin Gallery, Dublin, 1995; and Arnolfini Gallery, Bristol, 1996. Irish Museum of Modern Art, Dublin; Arts Councils of Ireland and Northern Ireland; and Tate Gallery hold examples.

Gwen CROSS 1900–1966 Painter, printmaker, jeweller, cutler, sculptor, illustrator and teacher, born in Bristol, married to the artist Fred Whicker. Despite family opposition she studied at Bristol Municipal School of Art under Reginald Bush, returning to teach there until towards the end of World War II. In 1934 she was a founding member of New Bristol Arts Club, serving as its first president, its aim being to enliven the city's art scene. Cross made etchings of Bristol, in its City Art Gallery collection. Soon after the war the Whickers moved to Falmouth and became members of the St Ives Society of Artists. Gwen became a noted flower painter, a leading figure at Falmouth School of Art as a teacher and governor. She showed at RA, SWA, RWA, ROI and extensively overseas. The Whickers' lives in Cornwall, as representational artists overtaken by the modern movement, were lived in straitened circumstances. There was a joint retrospective at Falmouth Art Gallery and RWA in 1994.

Nicolette CROSS 1930– Painter in variety of media, born in London, who studied at Byam Shaw School of Drawing and Painting, 1947–52, with Peter Greenham and Patrick Phillips. She eventually moved to Canada, settling latterly in Bowen Island, British Columbia, after some years in Vancouver. She was a member of UA and Federation of Canadian Artists, also exhibiting with NS, NEAC, RWA and elsewhere.

Roy CROSS 1924– Painter of historical ships and aircraft, born in London. His work was widely available in limited-edition prints. Became a member of Society of Aviation Artists in 1952 and 25 years later the RSMA. Showed at Börjessons Gallery, Gothenburg, Sweden, from 1975 and Marine Arts Gallery, Salem, Massachusetts, from 1976. Lived in Langton Green, Tunbridge Wells, Kent.

Tom CROSS 1931– Painter, printmaker, constructions maker, teacher and writer, born in Manchester. He attended the College of Art there and Slade School of Fine Art. In 1956–8 travelled and painted in Italy and France on Rome and French Government Scholarships. From 1959–63 was assistant director of the WAC. He then held several teaching posts in Britain and abroad, being from 1976–87 principal of Falmouth School of Art. He was a member of LG and chairman of Penwith Society of Arts, 1982–4. In the latter year he published *Painting the Warmth of the Sun, St Ives Artists, 1935–75*. Wrote *Artists and Bohemians: 100 years with the Chelsea Arts Club*, 1992. Cross was a prolific exhibitor, group exhibitions including John Moores Exhibition in Liverpool, Reading Museum, SWG, SEA and elsewhere. His one-man show Drawings of Wales and Italy was held at Everyman Theatre, Hampstead, 1963; others included Penwith Galleries, Montpelier Studio, and Austin/Desmond Fine Art, 1989. Lived in Constantine, Cornwall.

Will CROSS 1888–1971 Painter in oil of portraits and landscapes, born in London. After education at King's College, he studied with W R Lethaby at the Central School of Arts and Crafts, at the Slade School of Fine Art under Randolph Schwabe and with Albert Rutherston in Oxford at the Ruskin School of Drawing. Exhibited at UA, RBA, RI, with Artists of Chelsea and the Chelsea Art Society, in the provinces and America. Lived in Sutton Courtenay, Berkshire.

Bob CROSSLEY 1912– Painter and printmaker, born in Northwich, Cheshire, who attended Heybrook School, Rochdale. Crossley was always an experimental artist, who had a deep interest in form and colour tensions and whose pictures attained almost pure abstraction. His early career was in the north of England. After military service in the Royal Air Force, 1941–5, Crossley showed in various exhibitions such as RA, SGA, Paris Salon and Manchester Academy, being elected a member in 1950. In 1959 he moved to St Ives, Cornwall, and London, showing with Penwith Society of Arts, Newlyn Society of Artists, AIA, Piccadilly and Redfern Galleries and elsewhere. Had a solo show at Crane Kalman Gallery, Manchester, 1959, later ones including Bristol Art Centre in 1980 and a retrospective at Penwith Galleries, St Ives, 1992. Contemporary Art Society, Winnipeg Art Gallery in Canada and Museum and Art Gallery in Durban, South Africa, hold Crossley's work. Lived in Porthgwidden, Cornwall.

Clare CROSSLEY fl. from 1920s– Painter and draughtsman, notable for small, delicate landscapes of scenery around her home Combermere Abbey, Shropshire. Her father was Brigadier Alan Thomson, her sister Baroness Tweedsmuir, her husband the politician Anthony Crossley and her daughter Taisa Camu, an artist. She had early encouragement in sketching from Robert Morley, then from Augustus John, a neighbour in Chelsea in the 1920s. She attended Académie Julian, Paris, in 1925; Slade School of Fine Art under Henry Tonks; in the 1930s was with Vladimir Polunin as a private pupil and at the Slade again, in 1936; also making abstract colour prints at S W Hayter's Atelier 17, in Paris. Showed at NEAC, LG, Leicester Galleries and Trafford Gallery. Had a solo show at Storran Gallery in 1931, another at Chenil Galleries, 1969, and in 1975 was one of Three Women Painters at Michael Parkin Fine Art.

Cuthbert CROSSLEY 1883–1960 Painter, printmaker and designer, notable for landscapes and architectural subjects, sometimes employing unusual means. He was born in Halifax, Yorkshire, where he early showed artistic gifts. Studied advanced applied design at the local School of Art, winning a King's Prize. Crossley was a member of the School of Art Sketching Society and a founder-member, around 1907, of Halifax Arts and Crafts Society. Soon after World War I Crossley became a designer for John Crossley & Sons, carpet makers, at the Dean Clough works, but by the early 1920s had become a full-time artist. He drew for the *Halifax Courier*; in 1928 completed etchings of old Halifax, including the three gates of the Piece Hall; and in 1933 illustrated T W Hanson's *Old Inns of Halifax*. Showed in Yorkshire and at RA, RI, RSA, RBA, Walker Art Gallery in Liverpool and at the Paris Salon. Bankfield Museum in Halifax and public galleries in Leeds and Newcastle upon Tyne hold Crossley's work, which could sometimes show a Cubist influence. Moved from Halifax soon after World War II to St Ives, Cornwall, where his wife shortly, and he later, died. In 1962 there was a Crossley Memorial Exhibition at Bankfield, with a further show there in 1973.

Gordon CROSSLEY 1929– Painter and teacher, born in Surrey, who studied at Wimbledon School of Art. He became senior lecturer in art and design at Barking College of Technology. Showed with NS of which he became a member in 1983, RA and NEAC, and had a series of solo exhibitions in East Anglia. Lived at Sheering, Hertfordshire.

Harold CROSSLEY 1900– Sculptor, painter and printmaker, born in Thornton, Yorkshire, attending the nearby Bradford Art School, 1915–19. He showed at public art galleries in Bradford, Liverpool, Preston and Manchester but latterly did not contribute to exhibitions. Was for some years a member of Bradford Art Club. Lived in Knott End-on-Sea, Blackpool, Lancashire.

Patrick CROUCH 1954– Sculptor and teacher who was an assistant to Edward Bainbridge Copnall, 1970–3, studying sculpture and anatomy with Tony Gray, 1970–2, and attending Sir John Cass School of Art, 1970–3. Between 1973–5 Crouch studied construction with Vincent Arnall and church organ restoration with Tom Robbins. From 1974–5 he was again at Sir John Cass, in 1976–9 graduating with an honours degree in sculpture from St Martin's College of Art. Crouch had substantial teaching experience in the mid-1980s in adult education in the southeast of England, and at Canterbury College, the John Makepeace School of Craftsmen in Wood, Central St Martins College of Art and Kent Institute of Art & Design, Canterbury, where in 1992 he took part in Sculpture at Canterbury. His residencies included Tunbridge Wells, Sevenoaks Festival and Harlow Carr Gardens in Harrogate, 1983–6. Crouch showed in numerous mixed exhibitions, including RA, New Metropole in Folkestone, Christopher Hull Gallery, Roy Miles Gallery and LG 92 at Morley Gallery.

Barbara CROW 1942– Printmaker, illustrator and teacher, born in Liverpool. She studied at Slade School of Fine Art, 1959–62, under William Coldstream, then did a postgraduate course in printmaking at Bristol Polytechnic, 1982–4. Was a member of RCamA, Association of Illustrators and the Association of Artists/Designers in Wales. Also exhibited at Arnolfini Gallery and RWA, both in Bristol. Lived in Llangattock-vibon-Avel, Gwent.

Derek Walter CROW 1928– Painter, draughtsman, printmaker and potter, born in Strood, Kent. He was brought up in Rochester, then studied at Medway School of Art, 1945–7, and at Royal College of Art, 1949–52, where his teachers included Rodrigo Moynihan, John Minton and Robert Buhler. Went on to teach in Jersey, Channel Islands, where he settled in St Helier. Showed Young Contemporaries, RI, RBA, SGA, in the provinces and elsewhere. National Film Theatre, London, holds his work.

Kathleen Mary CROW 1920– Painter in mixed media, mainly oil and watercolour, born and lived in Oxton, Nottinghamshire. Studied at Nottingham Polytechnic, 1964–76, with Ronald Thursby, then at Leicester, 1976–82, with Leslie Goodwin, both part-time. Became member of NS in 1983 and ROI in 1988, also showing with RA Summer Exhibition, RI, Nottingham Society of Artists and Rufford Craft Centre. She had a joint exhibition with Leslie Goodwin at RWA. Crow was a landscape painter who signed work with a monogram of her three initials.

Ron CROWCROFT 1953– Painter and writer, born in Hastings, Sussex. He was educated partly in Cyprus, partly in Chichester, Sussex. Attended West Sussex College of Design, Worthing, and Leeds Polytechnic in the early 1970s, his teachers including Jeff Nuttall and Glynn Williams. Showed at Sheffield College of Art and Leeds University Gallery, Leeds City Art Gallery holding his work in its collection. Lived for a time in Leeds, Yorkshire.

Barbara CROWE fl. from 1950s– Painter in oil and watercolour of English landscape and flowers. She taught painting widely in England and Wales and wrote and illustrated verses and stories for children. Born in the northwest of England, Crowe studied at Croydon and Bolt Court Schools of Art. She was a member of RI, SWA and Society of Botanical Artists, also exhibiting with Westminster and Chenil Galleries. Had a series of solo shows in Surrey, where she lived in Hammerfield, Abinger Hammer.

Maida CROWE: *see* **MAIDA**

Victoria CROWE 1945– Painter and teacher, born in Kingston upon Thames, Surrey. She studied at Kingston School of Art, 1961–5, and Royal College of Art, 1965–8. From 1968 she became a part-time lecturer at Edinburgh College of Art. Crowe won the David Murray Landscape Scholarship in 1968, the Anne Redpath Award in 1973, Scottish Arts Council Bursaries in 1969 and 1975 and the *Glasgow Herald* Art Exhibition Award in 1981. The following year she was elected RSW, since when she won a number of awards and prizes. Crowe showed extensively in mixed shows in Scotland and England. She had solo exhibitions at Waterhouse Gallery in 1969 and 1971, a series at Scottish Gallery, Edinburgh, in the 1970s, then at Thackeray Gallery, Mercury Gallery in Edinburgh, Fine Art Society in Edinburgh and Glasgow and Bruton Gallery, Somerset, in 1989. Scottish Arts Council, Scottish National Gallery of Modern Art and many other public collections hold her work. Lived at Carlops, By Penicuik, Midlothian.

Graham CROWLEY 1950– Artist and teacher whose work could include bizarre and fantastic elements. He was born in Romford, Essex, and studied at St Martin's School of Art, 1968–72, and Royal College of Art, 1972–5. Gained Arts Council awards in 1976–8. Crowley was artist-in-residence at St Edmund Hall, Oxford, 1982–3; was senior fellow in painting, South Glamorgan Institute of Higher Education, 1986–9; and in 1991–2 held the Riverscape International Drawing Residency, Cleveland. Group shows included RA; John Moores Liverpool Exhibition on several occasions including 1987 when he was joint second prizewinner; Peter Moores Liverpool Project 7 As of Now, 1983–4; and Twinings Gallery, New York, 1985. His one-man show Home Comforts toured in 1983 and other major solo exhibitions included Totah Gallery New York, 1986, and London from 1984, including Lamont Gallery, 1995 and 1997. Arts Council holds his work and he lived in London.

Hugh Melvill CROWTHER 1914– Artist in oil and pastel, born at Newby, near Scarborough, Yorkshire. He studied at Newport College of Art, becoming a freelance painter and teacher at further education classes in Chepstow for 21 years. Crowther was a member of West Gloucestershire Art Society, Wye Valley Art Society and Gloucestershire Society of Artists. His portraits and landscapes were also shown at Royal Glasgow Institute of the Fine Arts, elsewhere in the provinces and in London. Newport Museum holds his work. Lived in Tidenham, Gwent.

Michael CROWTHER 1946– Painter and teacher, born in County Durham. He studied at Leeds College of Art, 1964–8, and from 1970 taught at South Glamorgan Institute of Higher Education. He was included in WAC show The Probity of Art and the Paris Biennale in 1980, and was included in John Moores Liverpool Exhibitions starting in 1982. Had solo shows in London, Aberdeen, Exeter and Newcastle. Arts Council holds his acrylic on cotton duck Salvo II, of 1981. Lived in Cardiff.

Stephen CROWTHER 1922– Artist in oil, pastel, charcoal and conté, and teacher, full name Deryck Stephen Crowther. He was born in Sheffield, Yorkshire. Studied at the College of Art there, winning a Royal College of Art scholarship, 1941. After war service, 1941–6, was at Royal College, 1946–9, teachers including Gilbert Spencer, Rodrigo Moynihan, Carel Weight and Ruskin Spear. From 1950–87 was a lecturer in drawing and painting at Cleveland College of Art & Design, Hartlepool. Crowther was included in Jack Beddington's 1957 volume *Young Artists of Promise*. He was made a member of RBA in 1958 and became president of Hartlepool Art Club. Crowther said that he owed a debt to the Old Masters and tried "to apply the lessons learnt to my own work, which reflects my life and environment". In 1989 Crowther won a Higgs & Hill Bursary, being commissioned to paint Port Solent Marina, Portsmouth, for the company. In 1992 two oils were commissioned by Sultan of Oman. Showed at RA, RP, Leicester Galleries and elsewhere in mixed exhibitions. Showed solo at Gray Art Gallery & Museum, Hartlepool, from 1967; Billingham Art Gallery, 1970, later shows including Middlesbrough Art Gallery, 1984. Lived in Seaton Carew, Hartlepool, Cleveland.

Kathleen CROZIER fl. from 1970s– Artist in various media, and teacher. She studied at Fishponds College of Education, Hastings; Birmingham Central and Goldsmiths' College Schools of Art; and at Morley College. Taught art, notably ceramics, in schools and at adult institute level. Upon retirement concentrated on printmaking, mainly etching, and was a founder member of Greenwich Printmakers' Association. Was elected to NS in 1976. Showed widely in group exhibitions in London and Sussex and took part in four-man show at Woodlands Art Gallery, 1988. Solo shows included Stables Gallery, Hastings, from 1976; Conway Hall, 1983; and Tudor Barn Art Gallery, Eltham, 1985.

Philip CROZIER 1947– Painter and teacher, born and lived in London. He trained at Bath Academy of Art, Corsham, and Goldsmiths' College. Had solo shows at Caius College, Cambridge; Gardner Centre for the Arts, Brighton; and in 1979 at Woodlands Art Gallery. Work there had a strong pattern element, containing "many direct and indirect borrowings from forms and processes of painting outside the Fine Art sphere, as well as non-Western art," the artist wrote. Crozier taught at Woolwich College.

William CROZIER 1930– Painter and teacher, born at Yoker, Glasgow, who studied at the School of Art there, 1949–53. Having worked for two years as a theatre decorator, Crozier from the mid-1950s travelled widely in Europe. He then taught at Bath Academy of Art, the Central School of Arts and Crafts and Winchester School of Art. He retired as head of fine art there in 1987 to devote all his time to painting. From 1957 Crozier had a series of solo exhibitions at Drian Galleries, abstracts with landscape references. He was influenced at this time by American Abstract Expressionism. His later work employed more obvious landscape references, but vibrant colour and vitality continued to be key elements. Crozier exhibited at Arthur Tooth and Sons, Compass Gallery in Glasgow, Serpentine Gallery, Scottish Gallery and abroad. Scottish National Gallery of Modern Art gave him an important show in 1995. Collections in Glasgow, Aberdeen, Birmingham and overseas hold examples.

Audrey CRUDDAS 1912–1979 Stage designer and painter, born in Johannesburg, South Africa. She was educated in England and attended St John's Wood School of Art, Royal Academy Schools and Byam Shaw School of Drawing and Painting. After painting for a year in Europe and North Africa, during World War II Cruddas was in the Women's Land Army, strenuous work which made her ill, and during convalescence she began stage design. This led to Robert Helpmann asking her to create the costumes for his production of *The White Devil*, by John Webster. Cruddas became a noted stage designer, working for Covent Garden, The Old Vic, the York Mystery Plays and the Edinburgh Festival, producing both costume and set designs. She retired to Great Bardfield, Essex, in the late 1950s to concentrate on watercolour painting and showed locally, with Augustin Gallery and with Leigh Underhill Gallery. Victoria & Albert Museum, British Museum and Fry Art Gallery, Saffron Walden, hold her work.

Colin CRUMPLIN 1946– Painter and teacher, born in Hertfordshire. He attended Leicester School of Art, 1964–5, then Chelsea School of Art, 1965–8, and Slade School of Fine Art, 1968–70, having from 1967 begun showing at LG and at Young Contemporaries. Group show appearances included John Moores Liverpool Exhibition from 1987 and Corsham A Celebration, Victoria Art Gallery, Bath, 1988–9, and tour. His solo exhibitions included Garage Art Ltd in 1975; 1985 Salisbury Festival; 1986 Axiom Gallery, Cheltenham; and in 1997 both Todd Gallery and John Hansard Gallery at University of Southampton. Taught at various art colleges, eventually becoming head of fine art at Bath College of Higher Education. Arts Council holds his work. Lived in Bath, Somerset.

R H CRUTCHLEY 1943– Sculptor and teacher who studied at Birmingham College of Art, then became senior lecturer at Bournville College of Art. Exhibitions included Portfolio, RBSA, 1988; Ikon Gallery, Birmingham, 1991; and 1st RWA Open Sculpture Exhibition, 1993. In 1990 he created statue of St Michael for St Michael's Church, Manor Park. Lived in Hockley, Birmingham.

Michael CRYER 1940– Printmaker, painter and teacher, born in Blackburn, Lancashire, son of the painter and engraver Wilfred

Fairclough, husband of the artist Mary Malenoir. He studied at Kingston College of Art, 1957–61, was a Rome Scholar in Engraving, 1964–6, attending the British School in Rome, 1964–7, and Stanley Hayter's Atelier 17 in Paris, 1967. Taught for a time at Farnham School of Art. Lived in Kingston upon Thames, Surrey.

Michael CUBEY 1964– Painter whose output included abstract pictures, born in Wellington, New Zealand, where he studied at Elam School of Fine Arts and Auckland University. Group shows included Bowen Galleries, Wellington, from 1985; South Bank Picture Show, Royal Festival Hall, 1991; Beardsmore Gallery, from 1992; Cable Street Open Studios and Wellington City Art Gallery, Wellington, both 1994; and Royal Over-Seas League Open, 1995. Had solo shows at Bowen Galleries from 1986, later ones including Islington Arts Factory, 1993, and Beatty Gallery, Sydney, Australia, 1994–5. University of Wellington holds his work.

Mikey CUDDIHY 1952– Abstract artist and teacher, born in New York, America, who studied at Edinburgh College of Art, 1969–71, Central School of Art and Design, 1971–4, then Chelsea School of Art, 1974–5. As well as doing a range of jobs, from working in an art gallery to time as a waitress, she taught part-time, including Newcastle Polytechnic and St Martin's School of Art. Showed with LG, Angela Flowers and Air Galleries and in Summer Show 2 at Serpentine Gallery, 1981. Solo shows included The Gallery, Acre Lane, 1980, later ones Aimee in Galashiels and other paintings, Flowers East, 1995.

Nick CUDWORTH 1947– Draughtsman, illustrator and teacher with a special interest in anatomical art, born in Derby. He attended the College of Art there, 1964–6, then did graphic design at Chelsea School of Art, 1966–9, his teachers including Brian Mills and Edward Wright. During the ensuing years Cudworth, as well as being a freelance artist, did a variety of jobs, ranging from recording musician, ward orderly in a geriatric hospital and postman to lecturer in graphic design at Trent Polytechnic, Nottingham, and lecturer in drawing at Winchester School of Art. He took part in numerous group exhibitions, including Mall Galleries, Arnolfini Gallery in Bristol, La Scala opera house in Milan and the New York Art Fair. He had a solo show at Newcastle University in 1969, others including Thumb Gallery, ICA, Battersea Arts Centre and Nicholas Treadwell Gallery, with which he was long associated. Arnolfini and Nicholas Treadwell Galleries hold his work. Lived in Stroud, Gloucestershire.

Bill CULBERT 1935– Painter and artist using a range of freestanding objects and light installations. He attended Canterbury University School of Art, in New Zealand, 1953–6. Won a travelling scholarship in 1957, and attended Royal College of Art, 1957–60, where he gained a silver medal for painting. He won first prize in the Open Painting Competition, Arts Council of Northern Ireland, in 1964, four years later gaining another prize. Was artist-in-residence at Museum of Holography, New York, in 1985. The year after, Culbert had a retrospective at ICA. In 1997, there was an exhibition at Serpentine Gallery Lawn. His dealer in London, where he lived, was Victoria Miro. Culbert's work took a profound shift in the mid-1960s, when he changed from painting to using such items as a light bulb-holder, a light bulb and a jug to create his work. Royal College of Art and Arts Council hold examples.

Gordon CULLEN 1914–1994 Architect, artist and writer, full name Thomas Gordon Cullen, he was educated at Prince Henry's Grammar School in Otley and then trained as an architect at Regent Street Polytechnic. Cullen was assistant to the Russian architect Berthold Lubetkin and worked on major buildings such as the Finsbury Health Centre, for which he supplied an entrance mural, and Highpoint apartment block, Highgate. For most of World War II Cullen was in Barbados with the Colonial Office planning team, in 1946 becoming deputy editor of the *Architectural Review*, which developed his interest in urban renewal. His ignored proposals for the redevelopment of Westminster, *Westminster Regained*, were regarded by many as visionary. He became a cult figure, and his style of drawing was much-copied. Cullen's book *Townscape* appeared in 1964 and there were exhibitions of his work all round Europe. By then he had become townscape consultant to the Ford Foundation in New Delhi and Calcutta, other consultancies following for Liverpool, Llantrisant, Tenterden, Peterborough, Ware, London Docklands and Glasgow. With David Price he founded his own architectural practice. Cullen won the American Institute of Architects Gold Medal in 1976 plus many honorary doctorates.

Patrick CULLEN 1949– Painter who studied at St Martin's and Camberwell Schools of Art from 1972–6. He won a number of prizes, including Spirit of London Competition, Royal Festival Hall, 1984–5; Watercolour Prize, RA, 1989; Daler-Rowney Prize, PS Annual Exhibition, 1990 and 1995; and Abbott and Holder Travel Award, RWS Open Exhibition, 1991. In 1991 Cullen was elected PS. Notable for his landscapes of Italy. Cullen's solo shows included Ogle Gallery, Eastbourne, 1978; several at the Amalgam Art Ltd; and Thackeray Gallery, from 1992. RA, Sheffield City Art Galleries and Paintings in Hospitals hold examples. Lived in London.

Matthew CULLERNE-BOWN 1956– Artist in mixed media, born and lived in London. Attended Camberwell School of Art, 1975–9, Slade School of Fine Art, 1979–81, Stroganov Institute in Moscow, and the Moscow University. Showed with Northern Young Contemporaries, Whitworth Museum and Art Gallery, Manchester, 1979; New Contemporaries, ICA, 1980–1; Whitechapel Open, 1983; Warwick Arts Trust and Air Gallery, 1984; and in 1986 The Wissarth Gallery, Berlin, and The Minories, Colchester, where he was one of 4 London Artists. Also showed in four-man exhibition at Woodlands Art Gallery, 1989.

Derek CULLEY 1952– Self-taught artist, born and educated in Dublin, Ireland, with an Irish father and English mother. Culley did his master's degree in marketing at Brunel University, 1992–4, his dissertation subject being "Marketing of the visual artist in Britain – are there lessons to be learned from Europe?" Culley was a founder and chairman of Celtic Vision with the painters John Bellany and Denis Bowen, and participated in the group's exhibition tour in 1986–7. He took part in many other group shows, including LG tour, 1987; Knapp Gallery, from 1988; 2000 Years Celebration, Customs House, Dublin, 1991; Modern Irish Painting, Dillon Gallery, 1995; and Skopje Museum of Contemporary Art, Republic of Macedonia, 1996. Solo shows included Five Years of Culley, Royal Hospital Kilmainham, Ireland, 1989, and The Irish Club, 1996. Strong chiaroscuro, heavy impasto, vigorous brushwork and direct, expressive handling were characteristics of Culley's work, in which Celtic imagery and associations were important. Lived in Windsor, Berkshire.

Michael CULLIMORE 1936– Painter and teacher, born in Bradford-on-Avon, Wiltshire, who studied at Swindon College of Art and Goldsmiths' College School of Art. Early in the 1960s he moved to north Wales and taught and from the early 1970s was curator of the University College of North Wales, Bangor, Art Gallery. Retired in 1983 because of ill-health and returned to Wiltshire to live in Hindon. Participated in a number of touring exhibitions and had one-man shows including Bangor Art Gallery and Austin/Desmond Fine Art. WAC, National Museum of Wales in Cardiff and Swansea's Glynn Vivian Art Gallery hold Cullimore's work, which is in the English romantic landscape tradition.

Charlotte CULLINAN 1959– Painter who studied at Canterbury, Ravensbourne and Royal Colleges of Art, also with George Baselitz. Showed at RA, Smith's and New Academy Galleries, at Sainsbury Centre in Norwich and Camden Arts Centre. Was included in Six Young British Painters, toured Spain, 1991–2.

Frederick George Rees CUMING 1930– Painter, born in London, of English, Scottish and Irish descent. A subtle colourist who specialised in landscapes in Britain and on the continent. He trained at Sidcup School of Art, 1945–9, and after National Service attended Royal College of Art, 1951–5, winning an Abbey Minor Travelling Scholarship which took him to Italy. Was elected RA in 1974. He took part in many mixed shows and had a string of one-man exhibitions, including New Metropole Gallery, Folkestone; Leonie Jonleigh, Guildford; Little Studio, New York; and from the early 1980s a number at New Grafton Gallery. He was joint winner of the Grand Prix Contemporary Art Award, Monte Carlo, 1977; and the Sir Brinsley Ford Award, NEAC, 1986. His work is in a number of British public galleries, including National Museum of Wales, Cardiff; Towner Art Gallery, Eastbourne; and Monte Carlo Museum. Lived for some years at Ashford, Kent.

Belle Skeoch CUMMING 1884–1964 Watercolourist, studied at Liverpool School of Art, Byam Shaw School of Art and Edinburgh College of Art. Was married to the artist William Skeoch Cumming. Exhibited RSA, RSW, SSWA, Royal Glasgow Institute of the Fine Arts and Paris Salon. Was a member of Glasgow Lady Artists' Club. Lived in Edinburgh.

Diana CUMMING 1929– Painter, draughtsman and printmaker, born in Hereford. Cumming said: "I draw when I paint," drawing being "not easy, but essential." Her pictures could be witty or apparently naive with elements of fantasy, and sometimes employed a Pointillist style. She studied at Slade School of Fine Art, 1950–4, teachers including William Coldstream, B A R Carter and F E McWilliam. Won several awards, including Rome Scholarship, 1954–6. Took part in many group exhibitions, including Young Contemporaries, 1952; Walker Art Gallery, Liverpool, 1957–63; LG, 1958–9; and RA Slade centenary exhibition, 1971. Had a solo show at Beaux Arts Gallery, 1964, later ones including Cooling Gallery and Hereford Museum and Art Gallery, both 1990. Arts Council, Contemporary Art Society and Ministry of Works hold examples. Lived in London.

James CUMMING 1922–1991 Painter and teacher, born in Dunfermline, Fife. He studied at Edinburgh College of Art, 1939–41, then after five years with the Royal Air Force Volunteer Reserve returned to the College, 1946–50, for postgraduate work and travelling scholarships. He was in many mixed exhibitions in Britain and abroad. In 1955 he had a solo show at Gallery One in London, others following steadily, especially at the Loomshop Gallery in Lower Largo, Fife, and there was a series of retrospectives, including Lothian Region Gallery, Edinburgh, in 1981. Collections include HRH The Duke of Edinburgh, Arts Council and Scottish National Gallery of Modern Art. Cumming was a member of SSA, being its president for a time, and was treasurer and secretary of the RSA and a member of RSW. From 1950 for many years he taught at Edinburgh College of Art. Cumming's work for long drew its inspiration from life on the Isle of Lewis, but in the early 1960s it changed course and examined abstract themes, such as cellular structure, while retaining his unique colouring. Scottish Gallery in Edinburgh, where Cumming lived, held a memorial show in 1995.

Peter CUMMING 1916– Painter and teacher, born in London, who was educated at St Paul's School. Studied art at Royal Academy Schools, 1936–40, under Sir Walter Westley Russell after a period at Hammersmith Art School. Exhibited RA and RBA, of which he was a member. Lived Lancing, Sussex, where he joined Brighton Arts Club, later living in Old Woodstock, Oxfordshire.

Albert Runciman CUMMINGS: see Albert RUNCIMAN-CUMMINGS

Jane CUMMINGS 1917– Painter, printmaker, illustrator and teacher, born in Richmond, Surrey. Studied at Harrow School of Art, Chelsea School of Art under Graham Sutherland and Harold Williamson and Central School of Arts and Crafts with Clarke

Hutton. She exhibited in south of England and had work purchased by the London County Council and Hertfordshire Education Committees. Published a title in the Penguin Books Limited Puffin series: *Theatre You Can Make*. Lived in Northwood, Middlesex.

Gus CUMMINS 1943– Painter and teacher who studied at Sutton and Wimbledon Schools of Art and Royal College of Art. He taught at Hammersmith, Sutton and Croydon Schools of Art and part-time posts included Ravensbourne, Chelsea, Hastings, City & Guilds of London and Royal Academy Schools. Cummins was noted for his industrial scenes. Among awards won were Henry Moore Prize (LG), 1982; First Prize, Hunting Group, 1990; and Blackstone Award, 1992. Showed annually at RA Summer Exhibition from 1982, in 1992 being elected RA; Rye Society of Artists, Rye, from 1983; and New Grafton Gallery from 1991, having a solo show there in 1993. Lived in Hastings, Sussex.

Charles CUNDALL 1890–1971 Painter, pottery and stained glass artist, born in Stratford, Lancashire. After working as a designer for Pilkington's Pottery Company under Gordon Forsyth, Cundall studied at Manchester School of Art, obtaining a scholarship to Royal College of Art, 1912. After World War I Army service he returned to Royal College in 1918, then was at Slade School of Fine Art, 1919–20, and in Paris. Cundall travelled widely in several continents and became noted for his panoramic pictures, such as Bank Holiday, Brighton, in Tate Gallery's collection. He was a member of NEAC, RP, RWS and other bodies and was a prolific RA exhibitor. Had first solo show at Colnaghi, 1927. Official war artist in World War II, during which he was elected RA, 1944. His wife was the painter Jacqueline Pietersen. Lived in London.

Nora Lucy Mowbray CUNDELL 1889–1948 Painter and writer, born in London, grand-daughter of the artist Henry Cundell. She studied art at Blackheath School of Art, Westminster Technical Institute with Walter Sickert and part-time, 1911–14 and 1919, at the Slade School of Fine Art. Cundell was noted for her figure compositions, having won the Melvill Nettleship Prize for Figure Composition in 1914. Cundell exhibited at RA, NEAC, Goupil Gallery, SWA, NS and elsewhere, and her picture Smiling Woman is in the Tate Gallery. She was one of the founder-members of the NS in 1930, five years after her first one-man show, at Redfern Gallery. Travelled widely in America. Wrote and illustrated *Unsentimental Journey*, 1940. Lived at Dorney, near Windsor, died in London, and had a memorial show at RBA.

Clifford Benjamin CUNDY 1925–1992 Sculptor and painter, born in Wallasey, Cheshire. Awarded a scholarship to Oxford University to study engineering in 1944, Cundy was rusticated two years later for being unable to pay his wine bill. By then he had attended part-time classes under Albert Rutherston in drawing at Ruskin School of Drawing and life classes with Peter Greenham. Did several jobs to earn a living; was in Iran for a period; and returned in 1948 with the object of becoming a monk; but marriage to his muse Hazel Hazlewood determined Cundy to become a full-time painter, which he did in 1964. His portraits and still lifes in oil owed much to the inspiration of Van Gogh. From early 1970s Cundy mastered sculptural techniques, creating free-standing figures and bas-reliefs; he used the lost-wax method and eventually built his own foundry in his Richmond, Surrey, garden. A prolific worker, he showed at NS of which he was a member, as he was of the Sketch Club, also exhibiting at RP, RA, Alwin Gallery and Upper Street Gallery in Islington.

Nell Tenison CUNEO 1867–1953 Illustrator and painter, especially of portraits, born in London. Her original name was Nell Marion Tenison. After working as an illustrator, she met her future husband, the American-born artist Cyrus Cuneo, at the Atelier Colarossi, Paris, having previously studied in London at Cope and Nicol's School of Art. Her son was the artist Terence Cuneo. She exhibited RA, SWA, Goupil Gallery and elsewhere and illustrated especially girls' and women's magazines and a number of girls' books, such as Angela Brazil's *A Terrible Tomboy*, 1915. When her husband died in 1916 she travelled widely in England, latterly living at Shamley Green, Surrey.

Terence CUNEO 1907–1996 Painter in oil, noted for his realistic, atmospheric pictures of railway engines. He was born in London, son of the artist Nell Tenison Cuneo. He studied at Chelsea School of Art and Slade School of Fine Art. Became a member of War Artists' Advisory Committee, a member of Royal Glasgow Institute of the Fine Arts, vice-president of the Guild of Aviation Artists and president of the Society of Equestrian Artists. Showed at RA, ROI and RP. Exhibited one-man at RWS Galleries from 1941, Sladmore Gallery from 1971 and in 1988 had major exhibition at Mall Galleries. Cuneo painted a number of portraits of HM The Queen, notably on the occasion of her coronation, as well as portraits of Field-Marshal Bernard Montgomery and the one-time prime minister Sir Edward Heath. Cuneo's pictorial trademark was a tiny mouse, and in 1977 he published his autobiography *The Mouse and His Master*. Lived in East Molesey, Surrey.

Vera CUNINGHAM 1897–1955 Painter, draughtsman and theatre designer. After brief study at the Central School of Arts and Crafts, she began exhibiting with the LG in 1922. In the same year she became friendly with Matthew Smith, who frequently painted her, and with him exhibited in Paris, at the Amis de Montparnasse and the Salon des Indépendants. She had her first one-man show at the Bloomsbury Gallery in 1929. Towards the end of the 1930s did a series of theatre designs, but although the stage world appealed to her extravert, bohemian personality, she opted to return to easel painting to avoid having her independence threatened. Helped to organise the Civil Defence Artists shows at Cooling Galleries during World War II; also exhibited with the Storran Gallery and Redfern Gallery. Support for her work after World War II came mainly from the Paris dealer Raymond Creuze, who put on three shows, in 1948, 1951 and 1954, and who assembled an important collection of her pictures, publishing a lavish monograph on her in 1984. Although Vera Cuningham's figure paintings of the 1920s and 1930s are of their period, in her later work she developed a singular style, using a curving line and sombre palette: an English original, as she was as a character. Lived in London. A retrospective show was held at the Barbican Art Gallery in 1985.

Mitzi Solomon CUNLIFFE 1918– Sculptor in many materials, and designer, born in New York. She was educated in America, Sweden and France, her art tuition including Art Students' League of New York, 1930–3, and Columbia University, 1935–40. Exhibited widely in several continents, especially in North America, including Festival of Britain in 1951. Solo exhibitions included Exeter University, 1969. Work widely reproduced, especially in architectural journals, and is held by Leeds and Liverpool Universities. Lived for periods in Manchester, Brighton and London.

John CUNNINGHAM 1926– Painter, born in Lanarkshire. He studied at Glasgow School of Art, then lectured there until becoming a full-time painter in 1986. Cunningham was elected to Royal Glasgow Institute of the Fine Arts in 1980 and won the Torrance Award as well as the MacFarlane, Cargill and Scottish Amicable Awards. He showed in group exhibitions at RSA, Glasgow Art Club and Portland Gallery. Glasgow's Kelvingrove Art Gallery, Hunterian Gallery and University of Glasgow hold his work, which was in the Scottish Colourist tradition.

Keith CUNNINGHAM 1929– Painter who studied at Central School of Arts and Crafts, 1949–52, then the Royal College of Art, 1952–5. In the 1950s he showed at RA, Beaux Arts Gallery, with LG and elsewhere in London, where he lived.

Owen CUNNINGHAM 1954– Sculptor and teacher, born in Birmingham, who studied at Manchester Polytechnic, 1975–8. After St Martin's School of Art, 1978–80, Cunningham was assistant to Anthony Smart, 1980–1. Then went on to teach at St Martin's and in north of England. Gained The Sykes Prize (1st) in 1980. Showed with Northern Young Contemporaries and MAFA in 1977; Liverpool University Senate House Gallery, 1978; and in Have You Seen Sculpture from the Body? at Woodlands Art Gallery, 1983. Tyne and Wear Museums Service holds his work.

Elizabeth B CUNNINGTON 1914– Sculptor and watercolourist who was born in London and studied at Oxford University. Studied at Slade School of Fine Art under Randolph Schwabe and George Meldrum, 1936–9. Showed at NS, RWS, RA and elsewhere and lived near Oxford.

Peter CURL 1921–1959 Painter, printmaker and designer. Born at Southsea, Hampshire, Curl studied at the Southern College of Art in Portsmouth and at Brighton College of Art. Taught at Mansfield School of Art in the late 1940s, then from 1950 at Tunbridge Wells School of Art. He did a wide range of commercial design work, clients including the Council of Industrial Design, book publishers and BBC. Lived in Cranbrook, Kent.

Peter CURLING 1955– Painter whose speciality was the racehorse in action and the atmosphere of the racecourse. He was born in Waterford, Ireland, studying in England at Stonyhurst College and then Millfield, where he won an art scholarship. From 1971–3 he studied under Signorina Simi in Florence, in 1974 briefly with John Skeaping. His first solo show was with Tryon Gallery in 1976, which continued to exhibit his work. Curling was closely involved in racing: he rode on the Berkshire Downs and at Newmarket; rode his own horse Caddy, trained by Edward O'Grady, to victory in a bumper race in Ireland; and he hunted regularly with the Tipperary, where he settled. Curling completed many commissioned pictures of well-known horses; he also painted landscapes; and his largest assignment was a huge mural for John Mangier at Coolmore.

Muriel CURR fl. from 1940s–1993 Painter and teacher, daughter of the artist Tom Curr, she was born in Edinburgh, which she continued to use as her base although she held a number of posts in England. Studied at Edinburgh College of Art, 1938–43. She taught in Hertfordshire and in London and was attached to Pinewood Studios, the film studio, for a time. Showed with SSA and SSWA, both of which she was a member, as well as RA and elsewhere.

Tom CURR 1887–1958 Artist and cartoonist, born in Edinburgh, where he continued to live. He was educated at Daniel Stewart's College, the old Life School at the Mound and at Edinburgh University. From the life class he went to Edinburgh College of Art when it opened in 1909, where he met his wife, who taught drawing. After commissioned Army service in World War I Curr returned to the printing firm McLagan and Cumming, which he had entered as an apprentice artist, eventually becoming managing director. Much of his early work was black-and-white, but later he showed annually in RSA and other exhibitions, finding many subjects in the countryside. Work bought by Scottish Office, London. Curr was a staunch Baptist, active in the life of Edinburgh, of which he was a bailie.

Alan CURRALL 1964– Artist using video, born in Stoke-on-Trent, Staffordshire, who gained a degree in fine art at the county University, 1989–92, with a master's at Glasgow School of Art, 1993–5. Exhibitions included Videos aus Glasgow Un-Fair, Cologne, and Five British Artists at Kunstalle, Mannheim, both 1995; and Pandaemonium, ICA, and New Contemporaries, at Tate Gallery, Liverpool, and Camden Arts Centre, all 1996, the year that Curral was artist-in-residence, Fringe Gallery, Glasgow. In 1997, Currall participated in Video Positive 97: Escaping Gravity, organised by Fact, Bluecoat Arts Centre, Liverpool.

Peter CURRAN 1949– Artist and teacher, born and lived in Bristol who began painting at 17 inspired by the English landscape school, especially Turner, Palmer and Constable, and who favoured on-site drawing. Studied graphics at West of England Academy, 1965–7; did a foundation course at Filton Technical College, 1969–70; studied fine at and printmaking at Central School of Art and Design, 1970–3, under Cecil Collins, Adrian Berg and Paul Huxley; then did a postgraduate certificate in education at Bristol University, 1974–5. From 1989 attended a life drawing class, with a renewed interest in the human figure. Early work was signed Peter Curran Murphy (Murphy was his stepfather's name). Curran wrote that he was "much disappointed with modern art since 1945, and find much abstraction decorative." Over the 30 years from the mid-1960s Curran found inspiration in many sources, including Poussin, Piero della Francesca and de Chirico; the Italian Futurists; Sickert, Auerbach and Bacon; cricket; the Severn Estuary; and the decommissioning of Berkeley nuclear power station. Group shows included Arnolfini Gallery, Bristol, 1979; RA Summer Exhibition, 1983; Summer Show at England & Co., 1989; and The Horse in the Environment, 1993. Later solo exhibitions included First Barcelona Works, Eye Gallery, Bristol, 1989. Nuffield Foundation, Imperial Chemical Industries and British Institute in Florence, Italy, hold examples.

Esmé CURREY fl. from c.1905–1973 Artist in tempera and pencil; printmaker. Born in London, Miss Currey studied at the Slade School of Fine Art, in Melbourne, Australia, under Max Meldrum, and at Goldsmiths' College School of Art under the engraver Stanley Anderson. She is noted for her precision of line, like Anderson. She exhibited at many venues, including RA, RBA, RE, UA and Paris Salon. Lived in London.

Ken CURRIE 1960– Painter, printmaker, mural artist and filmmaker, born in North Shields to Scottish parents who moved with him to Glasgow when he was a baby. Currie studied social science at Paisley College of Technology, 1977–8, then attended Glasgow School of Art, 1978–83, his teachers including Alexander Moffat. He won several awards. Currie's intention was to pursue film production as a career, and from 1983–5 he directed and produced films at Cranhill Community Arts Project. But in 1985 the problems and expense involved in film-making turned Currie back to painting. A committed Socialist, he projected a series of pictures devoted to labour history in Scotland. A key work was the Glasgow Triptych, of 1986, now in Scottish National Gallery of Modern Art. Murals for The People's Palace followed. By 1988 Currie had a solo show at the Third Eye Centre, Glasgow, and the Raab Gallery, Berlin.

Denis CURRY 1918– Sculptor, painter, draughtsman and teacher who combined a profound knowledge of nature's engineering structure with a poetic vision. He was born in Newcastle upon Tyne and drawing was central to his life from the age of about three, "even on my mother's black skirt with white chalk". After studying architecture at Durham Curry graduated in painting and sculpture from the Slade School of Fine Art, 1945–6 and 1949–50, where he won numerous prizes. Slade teachers included William Coldstream, A H Gerrard, Henry Moore, Stanley Spencer and Reg Butler. Gerrard, who called Curry "one of the most outstanding thinkers since Leonardo", used him as his assistant on large commissions including Hemel Hempstead town centre. Curry's first full-time teaching post was as head of sculpture at Exeter College of Art. Moved to Bristol in 1961 and was head of the department of foundation studies at a critical time in its history, 1962–76, when Curry left to pursue his own work on a remote hill farm at Llanycefn, Clynderwen, Dyfed. In 1976 Pelter/Sands Gallery, Bristol, held a comprehensive show of Curry's work called Shapes of Flight. Curry had long been interested in animal flight. In 1967 he was granted the first patent for a variable-geometry ornithopter (in 1978 being invited by the Historic Aircraft Museum to place it there). A paper was published by the Royal Aeronautical Society in 1975. The wild life of Pembrokeshire inspired much of Curry's later work, and in the mid-1990s he worked on a series of earth paintings involving tractor wheel patterns. Elected RCamA 1992; also showed at RA, LG, RWA, WSW, West Wales Arts Centre in Fishguard and National Eisteddfod of Wales. National Museum of Wales in Cardiff, Pembrokeshire Museum and Bristol Schools Art Service hold examples.

Stanley CURSITER 1887–1976 Painter, printmaker, writer and curator, born in Kirkwall, Orkney. Cursiter originally served apprenticeship as a chromolithographic designer before studying at Edinburgh College of Art. He was a keen follower of Post-Impressionism and of the Futurists, which he saw in London and Scotland just before World War I. His seven Futurist works, all painted in 1913, are superbly composed and very elegant. He also painted fine interiors, landscapes and portraits in a more conventional manner. Exhibited RA, RSA, Royal Glasgow Institute of the Fine Arts and elsewhere. His work is in a number of Scottish and English galleries. For a time Cursiter was keeper of the Scottish National Portrait Gallery, was responsible for pioneering work in art education and picture restoration while director of the National Gallery of Scotland, 1930–48, and in 1948 he was appointed King's Painter and Limner in Scotland, after which he retired to Orkney. Among his books are one on the artist S J Peploe, 1947, also *Looking Back: A Book of Reminiscences*, 1974. Centenary exhibition held at Pier Arts Centre, Stromness, 1987.

Anthony CURTIS 1928– Painter, and in 1960s–70s ceramist, born in Wakefield, Yorkshire. He studied at Loughborough College, 1948–50, at Bath Academy of Art, Corsham, 1950–1, and did postgraduate diploma at London University, 1974–6, his teachers including William Scott, Peter Potworowski, Bryan Wynter, Peter Lanyon and Kenneth Armitage. In 1957 he was included in Jack Beddington's book *Young Artists of Promise*. Was a member of Free Painters and Sculptors, also showing at RWA, LG, RSW, Redfern and Zwemmer Galleries. In 1960–1 was included in Arts Council tour Modern Stained Glass. Solo shows began with Bear Lane Gallery, Oxford, 1959, later ones including Management College, Henley, 1991, and Woburn

Festival, 1992. RWA and Bristol Education Committee hold his work. Lived at Flackwell Heath, High Wycombe, Buckinghamshire.

David Jan CURTIS 1948– Self-taught artist, designer and teacher, born and in lived in Doncaster, Yorkshire. He served an apprenticeship in industry, then headed an engineering design team with Hawker Siddeley, commencing full-time painting in 1988. Curtis painted in many parts of Britain. He was a commission painter for Federation of British Artists, lectured to art groups and taught part-time at Doncaster Faculty of Art and Design. He was elected a member of RSMA in 1983 and of ROI in 1988. Took part in many mixed exhibitions, including RA Summer Exhibition, RWS Open and elsewhere. He was a Stanley Grimm Memorial Prizewinner at ROI in 1991. Had series of solo shows with Richard Hagen Ltd, Broadway, from 1990. The Sultanate of Oman, HM Crown Commissioners and British Gas hold his work.

Gertrude M CURTIS: *see* **Gertrude M KNOPP**

Mark CURTIS 1964– Painter who studied at City & Guilds School of Art, 1988–92. He won the Chadwick Healey Painting Prize in 1991 and 1992 and the Villiers David Travel Prize in 1992. Exhibitions included Fresh Art at Business Design Centre and Art Parcels at Frost & Reed, both 1992; Arcana Open Studios, 1993; and Tradition and Consequence at Hyde Park Gallery, 1994. Curtis had a solo exhibition at The Blue Gallery, 1995, when his work was described as "figurative, abstract, Constructivist and conceptual all at the same time".

Noel William CUSA 1909–1990 Wildlife artist in watercolour and pen and ink, born in Hull, Yorkshire, who was self-taught. He graduated with a Bachelor of Science degree from University College, Nottingham, 1930, obtaining his doctorate, 1933. He was a patents and research chemist with Imperial Chemical Industries until 1966, then a full-time artist. Was a member of SWLA from 1965, becoming its chairman, also a member of MAFA, showing regularly at both venues, in the provinces and abroad. British Museum and Natural History Museum hold his work, which also appeared in a number of books on birds. Lived in Topsham, Devon.

Eugene CUSACK 1940– Painter, draughtsman and printmaker, noted for his portrait studies and Rembrandt-like etchings, born in New York, America. From 1963–5 he attended the Art Students' League of New York as a Ford Foundation Scholar; studied in Mexico, 1965–8; and won a series of John and Anna Lee Stacy Scholarship Fund Awards between 1968–72. Cusack won the Jane Peterson Prize for Oils, 1968, and the Salmagundi Club Prize for Oils, 1971, both at the Allied Artists Exhibition. He also showed at the Audubon Exhibition in 1971 and at the Nineteenth Annual Print Exhibition at Brooklyn Museum, 1974. His solo exhibitions in America included a series from 1969 at the Harbor Gallery, New York; one at Court Galleries, Cincinnati, Ohio, 1971, and Capricorn Gallery, Bathesda, Maryland, 1973. In 1971, Cusack moved to Clifton, Bristol, in England, and in 1972 had a solo exhibition at David Cross Fine Art. Eventually returned to New York. Smithsonian Institution, Washington, bought Cusack's etching Father.

Alan CUTHBERT 1931–1995 Painter in oil and teacher, born in Southend-on-Sea, Essex. After studying geology, working for a surveying firm, serving in Royal Air Force signals and working for John Taylor & Sons, mining engineers throughout the period 1948–57, Cuthbert in 1957–61 studied at Goldsmiths' College School of Art, 1957–61, under Sam Rabin and Kenneth and Mary Martin. After teaching part-time at Wimbledon School of Art, 1961–3, between 1963–79 Cuthbert was head of foundation and vice-principal at Wimbledon, from 1979 until retirement in 1991 being vice-principal. Cuthbert was a member of the Colour Group of Great Britain, long interested in colour research and its application. In this connection he was in 1969 involved in colour related to the Calder motorway bridge; in 1979 designed the ballet *Counterpoint*, to music by Benjamin Britten, at Adeline Genée Theatre, East Grinstead; in 1981, devised an interior for Holy Trinity Church, Forest Row, Sussex; and in 1990 was consultant for the BBC television series *The Colour Eye*. Mixed shows included Structural Growth in Natural Form, Whitechapel Art Gallery, 1967; The Painting School at Montmiral, Camden Arts Centre, 1989; and Diagonale des Arts, Cahors, France, 1995. In 1991 there was a selective retrospective at Wimbledon Library Gallery and the artist's studio. Graves Art Gallery in Sheffield; Towner Art Gallery in Eastbourne; Bedales School; New Metropole Arts Centre, Folkestone; and Universities of Surrey, Kent and Sussex hold examples. Retired to Puylaroque, France, 1992, where he died.

Alfred CUTHBERT 1898–1966 Watercolourist, born in South Shields, County Durham, who went into business as a broker. Studied at South Shields School of Art and continued to live in the area, being a member of the Art Club there. Exhibited RI and elsewhere. Sunderland Art Gallery holds his work.

David CUTHBERT 1951– Versatile artist and teacher, born in Norwich, Norfolk, married to the artist Ros Cuthbert. He attended Somerset College of Art, Taunton, 1969–70; gained his painting diploma at Central School of Art & Design, 1970–3; then was at Institute of Education, London University, 1973–4. Taught at Working Men's College, 1973–6; then did extensive teaching, part-time and summer courses in France and Italy, with periods at Wimbledon College, Loughton College of Further Education and St Martin's School of Art. Was a member of Artists 303. In 1983 gained an artist's placement from South West Arts at Kings of Wessex School, Cheddar. From 1984–90 edited *The Looker*, an art and ideas magazine. Mixed shows included Swiss Cottage Library and Burgh House Contemporary Artists in Camden, both 1981; Off Centre Gallery, Bristol, 1990; and Brought to Book, Flowers East, 1994. Solo exhibitions included Parkway Focus, 1976–84; Consort Gallery, Imperial

College, 1981; and his Winscombe Farm Studio, Avon, 1995. Kings of Wessex School and Electrografia Museo International, Cuenca, Spain, hold examples.

Ros CUTHBERT 1951– Painter, draughtsman, printmaker and teacher, full name Rosalind Cuthbert, born in Somerset, settling in Winscombe, Avon. She was married to the artist David Cuthbert. She studied at Somerset College of Art, Taunton, 1969–71; Central School of Art & Design, 1971–4, teachers including Blair Hughes-Stanton and Cecil Collins; gaining her master's degree in painting at Royal College of Art, 1974–7, under Keith Critchlow and Peter de Francia. Among awards were RWA first prize, 1982. Was tutor in charge of relief printing at Central School, 1978–92, and directed and taught Mendip Painting Centre from 1985. Group exhibitions included Arnolfini Gallery, Bristol, Avon Open Exhibition, 1983; Portrait 1980s, Fermoy Centre, King's Lynn, and tour, 1985–7; and Self-Portraits, Plymouth City Art Gallery, 1992. Solo shows included Camden Galleries, 1989, and Anthony Hepworth Fine Art, Bath, 1995. Published a number of instructional books, and illustrated with wood engravings Yellow Fox Press publications. Contemporary Art Society, National Portrait Gallery, Sheffield City Art Gallery and Eton College hold examples. Was a member of Artists 303.

E CUTNER: *see* **Effie SPRING-SMITH**

Herbert CUTNER 1881–1969 Graphic artist and printmaker. Born in Hull, Cutner studied at the London County Council-run Bolt Court School of Art and at the Central School of Arts and Crafts, his teachers including Walter Bayes and Frank Emanuel. Married the artist Effie Spring-Smith. Cutner, who sometimes signed his work H C, mainly showed at the SGA. He was a journalist who wrote on diverse subjects, from articles in the rationalist publication *The Freethinker* to *Teach Yourself Commercial Art* and *Teach Yourself Etching*. Lived in London.

Christiana CUTTER 1893–1969 Painter and draughtsman, born in Wisbech, Cambridgeshire. In 1910 moved to London and attended Slade School of Fine Art prior to World War I under Henry Tonks. There she met the artist Marjorie Lilly, whose brother George she married in 1919. Showed at LG, NEAC and Walker's Galleries and in 1974 was included in Parkin Gallery exhibition The Sickert Women and The Sickert Girls. Died in Chichester, Sussex.

George CUTTS 1938– Sculptor in stone and steel, maker of mobiles and teacher, born in Rugby, Warwickshire. While working at Goole Shipyard he obtained a place at Doncaster School of Art, 1956–8, then the Royal College of Art, 1958–60, teachers including John Skeaping. He later taught there, at Royal Academy Schools, Chelsea School of Art and elsewhere. Exhibited widely in Britain, on the continent and in America, as well as carrying out public commissions. Landscape and the sea were key inspirations. His The Kiss, of 1991, and Sea Change, 1996, were moving sculptures included in the Sculpture at Goodwood displays.

Michael CUTTS 1937– Painter and teacher, born in London, who in 1953 had a trial for Chelsea Football Club, then attended Regent Street Polytechnic School of Art, 1954–8, and London University Institute of Education, 1958–9. For some years worked as a full-time teacher in the Forest of Dean, Newcastle upon Tyne and London, teaching part-time at Camden Institute. In 1967 a series of abstract paintings by Cutts was included in Camden Arts Centre's Survey '67 Abstract Painters. By that time he had had two solo shows: in 1963 at People's Theatre, Newcastle, and in 1966 at Gordon Gallery, Wimbledon. Also exhibited with Young Contemporaries and at Grabowski Gallery. Cubism and the ideas of Marshall McLuhan, on whom Cutts lectured, were important to the artist, who reckoned that he "could make a reality quite apart from the seen world if one regarded paints and brushes as the first stage in a making process, rather than the last act of expressing oneself."

Tadeusz CZERWINKE 1936– Sculptor in various materials, potter and teacher, born in Poland, noted for extensive work in churches in Britain and on the continent. He studied at Winchester School of Art, 1957, teachers including Norman Pierce, and went on to teach at Shoeburyness Comprehensive School. From 1976 was a member of SPS, also showing with Association of Polish Artists and abroad. St Peter's, Hinckley; St Sebastian and St John the Baptist, Preston; and General Sikorski Museum in Prince's Gate, London, hold his work. Lived in London.

Andrzej CZYŻOWSKI 1919– Artist, designer and editor, one of the Polish paper sculptors who flourished in England after World War II. Fought in the Polish Campaign and in France, was interned Switzerland studying at Fribourg University, then served in the Polish Army press unit in Italy. After arriving in Britain in 1946, Czyżowski worked until 1964 as a freelance designer, producing paper and metal sculptures for a range of clients including Diana Studio. Humour and satire marked his output. For almost 20 years from 1966 worked for Radio Free Europe in Munich. Returned to London and held a post in the Polish Government in Exile and then, until 1991, was editor-in-chief of *The Polish Daily*. His work was included in Polish Paper Sculpture at the Polish Cultural Institute, 1995.

D

Richard D: *see* **Richard DENT**

Charles DABORN 1920–1968 Painter in oil, born at Woking, Surrey, who attended Kingston School of Art, 1936–9, under Reginald Brill and the Royal College of Art, 1939–40 and then 1946–8, under Percy Jowett. Taught at Winchester School of Art. Completed a mural in the town's council offices. Exhibited RA, at the Bladon Gallery at Hurstbourne Tarrant and at the public galleries in Mansfield and Birkenhead. Lived at Winchester, Hampshire, where colleagues knew him as Stuart, his middle name. His daughter was the painter Erica Daborn.

Erica DABORN 1951– Painter, draughtsman and teacher, born in Winchester, Hampshire, daughter of the artist Charles Stuart Daborn. From 1976–85 she was married to the printmaker Anthony Davies, from 1985 to the American film maker Dennis Lanson. She studied at Winchester School of Art, 1968–72, with John Bellany and William Crozier, and at the Royal College of Art, 1973–4, and 1975–7, with Peter Blake, David Tindle and Leonard Rosoman. Daborn took up a teaching fellowship at Cardiff College of Art, 1977, having a studio at Chapter Art Centre until 1983. Had a residency at the MacDowell Colony, New Hampshire, 1984, moving to America to live in 1985, in California until 1996, then taking a teaching post at Boston Museum of Fine Arts. Daborn created her own world of bizarre people and animals. From 1985–9 her work was "based on social critique. From 1989 to the present the dominant theme is motherhood, images evolving through a painting process that accesses the unconscious." Was a member of 56 Group Wales, 1980–6. Group exhibitions included many in Britain and America; solo exhibitions began with Air Gallery, 1981, later ones including Sherry Frumkin Gallery, Santa Monica, 1993, and Phyllis Kind Gallery, Chicago, 1995. Awards included a number from WAC. It, Contemporary Art Society for Wales, Welsh Development Agency, Newport Museum and Art Gallery and other British and American collections hold examples. Lived in Winchester, Massachusetts.

Hugo (Puck) DACHINGER 1908–1995 Painter, designer and draughtsman, born in Gmunden, Austria, who from 1943 was married to the artist Meta Dachinger Gutman. Dachinger studied art in Leipzig, 1929–32, then from the latter year worked in Vienna as a freelance artist and designer. He invented and patented a lettering method that was used principally in window displays. In 1938 when German troops entered Austria Dachinger decided to leave Leipzig, making his way to Denmark, then England. In 1940 he was interned at Huyton, then in the Isle of Man for several months, but on release settled in London to work as an artist. Dachinger was notable for his witty studies of figures and groups of people, which were tinged with a strong humanity. He had an appearance in the Leipzig Kunstalle in a mixed show in 1932; held exhibitions in the Ramsey, Isle of Man, camp in 1940; then soon began to appear at Redfern and Leger Galleries. In the 1950s he also showed with Ben Uri Gallery and Jack Bilbo's Modern Art Gallery. Dachinger showed with his wife in Gmunden in 1980, then six years later appeared in the Art in Exile show; Berlin, Oberhausen, Camden Arts Centre and John Denham Gallery. That gallery gave him a solo show in 1989, a memorial in 1997. His wife Meta (1916–1983) was also an artist.

Tom DACK 1933– Painter and artist in pen and ink, born in Newcastle upon Tyne, where he attended the College of Art & Design. Most of his working life was spent in advertising agencies and commercial art studios as an illustrator and designer. His own work was concerned with marine, aircraft and landscape subjects. Showed at Darlington Art Gallery; Bede Museum in Jarrow; Sally Port Gallery, Berwick-upon-Tweed; Patricia Wells Gallery, Thornbury, and elsewhere. Lived in Whitley Bay, Tyne and Wear.

Winifred DACRE: *see* **Winifred NICHOLSON**

William St Alban Rae DADY 1938– Painter, sculptor and teacher, born in Delhi, India. He studied at Goldsmiths' College School of Art, 1956–61, teachers including Sam Rabin, Kenneth Martin and Ivor Roberts-Jones, and became head of art at Stowe School. Joined SPS in 1979, also showing with Federation of British Artists and RA. Lived in Buckingham, Buckinghamshire.

Arnold DAGHANI 1909–1985 Versatile artist, notable as a draughtsman, and writer, who produced over 4,000 works. He was born in Suceava, then in the Austro-Hungarian Empire, now part of Romania, and showed artistic promise at school. Although he attended art school in Munich, Daghani obtained no formal qualification. Aged 23 he was conscripted into the Army, then after early discharge in the early 1930s he worked for a publisher, doing clerical work, in Bucharest. With his wife Daghani was placed in a forced labour camp by the Nazis, but they escaped and were repatriated. After World War II Daghani lived as an English translator and tutor while practising his art, but, at odds with the regime, in 1959 he took an exit visa to Israel – forfeiting over 900 works on leaving Romania, then settled in Vence, France, 1961–70, and Iona, Switzerland, 1970–7. Among his French achievements was decorating the Anglican chapel of St Hugh, Vence, using an original means of painting on glass. His final move, in 1977, was to Hove, Sussex, where he died. Wartime privations and an unsettled existence had for years undermined his health, and he felt an isolated figure artistically. Arnold Daghani, A relentless spirit in art, was held at Brighton Polytechnic, 1984, and in 1992 Barbican Centre and Ben Uri Art Society, which holds his work, put on shows.

Eric DAGLISH 1894–1966 Wood engraver, watercolour painter and illustrator who was notably an artist depicting birds and country life. Born in London, Daglish attended university there and in Bonn, Germany. Although he exhibited at Redfern Gallery, SWE of which he was a member, and NEAC, Dr Daglish was most known for his illustrative work in which attention to detail was paramount. Paul Nash taught him engraving just after World War I and was friendly with him and Alice Daglish when living at Dymchurch, Kent. Among books illustrated by this naturalist artist were *Woodcuts of British Birds*, 1925; Henry David Thoreau's *Walden*, 1927; and Gilbert White's *The Natural History of Selborne*, 1929. Lived at Speen, near Aylesbury, Buckinghamshire.

Peter DAGLISH 1930– Printmaker, painter and teacher who studied at École des Beaux-Arts in Montreal, Canada, 1956–60, then did postgraduate studies at Slade School of Fine Art, 1963–5. From 1973 taught printmaking on the master of arts course at Chelsea School of Art and painting and printmaking at the Slade, postgraduate students. Daglish's pictures, featuring real and unreal women, had a Pop Art-like directness, and were both jazzily coloured and monochrome. He was a member of RE and showed widely nationally and abroad. Tate Gallery, Victoria & Albert Museum, major Canadian collections and public galleries in Bradford and Hull hold examples. Lived in London.

Michael D'AGUILAR 1924– Painter in oil and printmaker, born and lived in London, brother of the artist Paul D'Aguilar, educated privately in France, Italy and Spain. D'Aguilar studied at Royal Academy Schools, 1948–53, teachers including Bernard Fleetwood-Walker and William Dring. There he won the Armitage and silver medal, 1949, as well as several Royal Drawing Society medals. He showed in mixed exhibitions at RA, NEAC, Young Contemporaries and Leicester Galleries, work distinguished by a rich palette, also having solo exhibitions at New Grafton Gallery, Gimpel Fils and elsewhere.

Paul D'AGUILAR 1927– Painter and draughtsman, born and lived in London, brother of the artist Michael D'Aguilar. He was privately educated in France, Italy and Spain and studied at Royal Academy Schools, 1948–53, under Henry Rushbury. In 1949 D'Aguilar gained first prize for drawing at RA, also winning several Royal Drawing Society medals. Also studied in Italy. Showed in mixed exhibitions at RA, RBA, NEAC and the New Grafton, Leicester and Redfern Galleries, as well as abroad.

Deirdre DAINES 1950– Painter and teacher who studied at Walthamstow School of Art and Royal Academy Schools. She won the Eric Kennington Prize for Drawing, David Murray Prize for Landscape as well as silver and bronze medals. Showed in mixed exhibitions at RA, Langton Gallery, Agnew and New Grafton Gallery. Her solo shows included RA Common Room, 1981, and Cale Art Gallery, 1982. Daines was a sensitive portrait painter. She taught at Harrow and Croydon Colleges of Art as well as adult education classes for the Inner London Education Authority. Lived in London.

Adrian DAINTREY 1902–1988 Painter, illustrator and writer, born in London and educated at Charterhouse, where he early showed a talent for drawing. Studied at Slade School of Fine Art, 1920–4, but found its regime unsympathetic. Instead preferred the company of Augustus John and his circle, sometimes assisting in John's studio. A congenial man, Daintrey gathered a wide circle of friends, who included the artists Nina Hamnett and Rex Whistler, Matthew Smith and Alvaro Guevara and the writer Anthony Powell. After the Slade he continued his studies in the Louvre and L'Académie de la Grande Chaumière, Paris, then became art master at Dean Close School, Cheltenham. First exhibition shared with Paul Nash at Dorothy Warren's gallery in 1928, and as a result Daintrey gained aristocratic patrons who helped ease his money worries. During World War II served widely abroad and was involved in camouflage work. Finding himself unfashionable as an artist after the war he held shows in his studio. He also served as the magazine *Punch*'s art critic, 1953–61; published a pleasant volume of reminiscences, *I Must Say*, in 1963; and from the late 1960s taught part-time at the City and Guilds Art School, eventually becoming its librarian. Latterly Daintrey had successful exhibitions of his witty and attractive paintings and drawings, often featuring the area around his studio in Little Venice, London, at South London Art Gallery, Michael Parkin Fine Art and Sally Hunter Fine Art. British Museum and Imperial War Museum hold his work.

Gabriel DAKEYNE 1916– Artist in collage, watercolour and acrylic, born in Marske-by-the-Sea, Yorkshire. She studied at Swindon School of Art, 1934, under Harold Dearden; in the Netherlands; and in 1953 through Percy Bradshaw's Press Art School. Exhibited at RA, SWA, RWA and at Paris Salon. Had a solo show at St Aldate's in Oxford, 1978. Lived in Winnersh, Berkshire.

Arthur D'ALBERTSON –1964 Painter, black-and-white and commercial artist. Studied at Putney School of Art under R O Dunlop and John Bowyer. Later worked for Henry Squire & Company, advertising agents, and was director and associate editor of *Art Quarterly*. Was chief cartoonist for *Seven Seas Magazine* for several years in the 1930s and also drew for *Punch*. Exhibited RA, ROI, RWA and Paris Salon and had one-man shows in London and the provinces. Lived at Binstead, Sussex.

Arthur DALBY 1900–1961 Printmaker, studied at Liverpool School of Art and the Royal College of Art. By profession he was a government-appointed inspector of art schools. He exhibited RA and Walker Art Gallery, Liverpool. Lived in Camberley, Surrey.

Claire DALBY 1944– Artist in watercolour, gouache and wood engraving, daughter of the watercolourist Charles Longbotham, born in St Andrews, Fife. She studied at City and Guilds of London Art School, 1964–7. Dalby said that in her landscapes and still lifes she was "interested in light falling on objects and in the relationships of objects in the space they occupy". In botanical illustration she strove "to convey the structure of plants as well as appearance". Became a member of RWS in 1973, RE in 1978 and was also a member of SWE. She was elected a vice-president of RWS in 1991. Also exhibited with Clarges Gallery from 1968 and at Halifax House, Oxford, 1987. Had a solo exhibition in Camberley, Surrey, where she lived, in 1975, later ones including Imperial College from 1981 and Shetland Museum, Lerwick, from 1988. Natural History Museum published two wall charts by her on lichens and in 1989 *Claire Dalby's Picture Book* appeared. Science Museum, Natural History Museum, Victoria & Albert Museum and Ashmolean Museum, Oxford, hold her work.

Tom DALE 1935– Artist in various media and teacher, born in Greenock, Renfrewshire. He attended the local High School, then Glasgow School of Art, 1953–7. Went on to become art master of Selwood School, Frome, Somerset, not far from his home at West Horrington. Showed at Burwood Gallery, Wells, and elsewhere in West Country and became a member of RMS in 1982.

Anthony DALEY 1960– Painter, born in Jamaica. He studied at Leeds College of Art, 1978–9, graduating at Wimbledon College of Art, 1979–82, gaining his master's degree at Chelsea School of Art, 1982–3. Among his group shows were Christie's Inaugural, 1983; Turnpike Gallery, Leigh, Greater Manchester, 1987; Basel and London Art Fairs, 1986; and Smith's Gallery, 1988. Showed solo with Angela Flowers Gallery from 1986, with a one-man at Woodlands Art Gallery, 1990. Worked in Greenwich Artists' Studios. Daley worked on a large scale, figurative pictures tending towards abstraction.

Angela DALLAS 1946– Painter, printmaker and designer, born in Bradford, Yorkshire. Attended Harrogate School of Art, 1963–4, then Cardiff College of Art, 1964–7. In 1965–6 she attended a fine art summer course at the Academy of Fine Art in Perugia, Italy, and a summer course in photography at Barry Summer School. During 1967 she participated in WAC's poster project, in which a screen print was chosen for enlargement to poster size for use in public throughout Wales. Dallas in 1969 set up as a freelance designer with a special interest in fashion in London, but in 1971 moved to Cyprus. There she continued to paint, with a particular interest in murals. Exhibited widely in Cyprus and in Britain in group shows in Whitechapel Art Gallery; Albany Gallery, in Cardiff; and with WAC, which holds her work.

John E S DALLAS 1883– Watercolour painter of landscapes and townscapes. After education at Alleyn's School, Dulwich, Dallas was at St Martin's School of Art. Showed at RCamA. Lived in Leatherhead, Surrey.

Terence Henry DALLEY 1935– Artist and illustrator, born in Kusumu, Kenya, who worked mainly in watercolour or drawings in pencil or charcoal pencil. He attended St Martin's School of Art, 1954–7, and Royal College of Art, 1957–60, then was at Hochschule für Gestaltung, Ulm, West Germany, 1960–1. Taught at Wimbledon School of Art from 1967. Showed with RWS at Bankside Gallery and in several shows at Mall Galleries. Had a solo exhibition at Upper Grosvenor Galleries, 1971, and elsewhere. Worked as a freelance illustrator for a number of firms and publishers, views of London a common feature, as shown in Peter Marcan's book *Artists and the East End*, 1986. Museum of London and The Fishmongers' Company hold Dalley's work. Lived in London.

Derek DALTON 1929– Painter and teacher, born in Lancashire. He studied at Blackpool and Hornsey Colleges of Art and was for some years head of painting at Newcastle Polytechnic. Dalton was a painter of the northern landscape. Although he did some abstract work, his later pictures were distinguished by a vertical grid-type motif, tending to divide the scene into strips. He showed extensively in group exhibitions, including John Moores Exhibition, Liverpool, 1972; Tom Caldwell Gallery, Belfast, 1978; Ukrainian Institute of Modern Art, Chicago, 1986; Washington Arts Centre, 1989; and the Newcastle Group's The Northern Lights show at DLI Museum & Arts Centre, Durham, 1990, and tour. Awards included a purchase prize at Northern Art Exhibition, 1978, and first prize at Tyne Tees Northern Open, 1985. Later solo shows included Sunderland Arts Centre, 1983, and Grey's Gallery, Newcastle, 1985–6. Lived in Corbridge, Northumberland.

Lisa DALTON 1954– Painter and teacher, born in London. She studied at Chelsea School of Art, 1974–7, gaining a first-class honours degree in fine art, then her master's degree after study there, 1977–8. From 1980 was for some years a visiting lecturer at University of Reading fine art department. Completed a number of commissioned works, notably portraits. In 1978 her paintings were used in Arnold Wesker's *Love Letters on Blue Paper*, at National Theatre, and in 1988 a painting appeared in John Schlesinger's film *Madame Sousatzka*. Dalton appeared in many group shows from late 1970s, including Whitworth Art Gallery, Manchester, Young Contemporaries, 1977; Washington, Chicago and Basle Arts Fairs, 1980; Jonathan Poole Gallery, New York, 1983; and Bury St Edmunds Art Gallery, 1988. After a solo show at Robin Gibson Gallery, Sydney, 1979, others included Thackeray Gallery, 1989.

Dexter DALWOOD 1960– Figurative painter and teacher, born in Bristol, who studied at St Martin's School of Art, 1980–5, and Royal College of Art, 1988–90. Went on to be associate lecturer at University of Northumbria, in Newcastle upon Tyne. Mixed shows included Whitechapel Open from 1992; Base/Salama–Caro Gallery, 1994; and John Moores Liverpool Exhibition, 1995–6. Solo shows included Paton Gallery, 1987; Smith Jariwala Gallery, 1992; and Galerie Unwahr, Berlin, 1995. Arts Council holds his oil The Room, 1984–5. Based in London.

Hubert DALWOOD 1924–1976 Sculptor and influential teacher, born in Bristol. He worked in a variety of materials, sometimes moulding and sometimes casting his forms, which were abstract and resembled primitive art. For much of World War II Dalwood was apprenticed to the British Aeroplane Company, then after a period in the Royal Navy he attended Bath Academy of Art, Corsham, 1946–9. He held a number of teaching posts at schools of art in England, latterly head of the sculpture department at Hornsey College of Art, 1963–73, holding the same position at the Central School of Arts and Crafts from 1974–6. He showed for many years at Gimpel Fils; won first prize for sculpture at the Venice Biennale in 1962; and was given a retrospective memorial show at the Hayward Gallery in 1979; another at Hebden Bridge Arts Festival, 1996. Lived in London.

Jehan DALY 1918– Painter and draughtsman, notably in pastel, born in Llanelli, Carmarthenshire. His father was the painter William Daly, principal of Kidderminster School of Art, which Jehan attended. Then studied at Royal College of Art under Gilbert Spencer. Did some magazine illustration, including *House and Garden*, early in career and exhibited RA, NEAC, Agnew and in Canterbury area, where he latterly lived a simple, reclusive life. Was reluctant to exhibit, although his drawings were prized by other artists. Daly was of French and Irish extraction the name Jehan – pronounced John – being of medieval French origin.

William Edward DALY 1879–1962 Painter and artist in glass, born in Manchester. He attended the School of Art there, Royal College of Art and studied in Paris. He was principal of Kidderminster School of Art after Llanelli School of Art, Carmarthenshire. Completed windows in several churches. Showed RA, Manchester City Art Gallery and elsewhere in the provinces. After his retirement from the Kidderminster School about the end of World War II Daly took up portraiture, examples of which were shown at the local Art Gallery in 1950 in a one-man exhibition. It holds two landscapes by him: The Pool, Boncourt; and The Valley of the Loire. Lived in Kidderminster, Worcestershire, and died in Worcester. The artist Jehan Daly was his son.

Matthew DALZIEL 1957– Artist using sculpture, photography and installations, born in Irvine, Ayrshire, who as well as showing individually worked jointly with Louise Scullion as Dalziel & Scullion. He gained an honours degree in fine art (sculpture) from Duncan of Jordanstone College of Art, Dundee, 1981–5, winning the Dalgetty Dunn Scholarship. Won a higher national diploma in documentary photography from Gwent College of Higher Education, 1985–7, then was awarded a postgraduate diploma in sculpture and fine art photography from Glasgow School of Art, 1987–8. He was artist-in-residence for Shell UK Exploration and Production at the St Fergus gas plant, 1988–9; won a Scottish Arts Council Major Bursary, moving to St Combs, 1990–1; gained a short artist's residency at Addenbrooke's Hospital in Cambridge, 1992; then in 1994–5 was artist-in-residence for Banff & Buchan District. Exhibitions and commissions included Forces, Gwent College of Art, 1987; Artists in Industry, Aberdeen Art Gallery, 1990; and Satellites & Monuments, a large light work, commissioned by Lux Europae, Edinburgh, 1992.

DALZIEL & SCULLION– The name under which Matthew Dalziel and Louise Scullion collaborated from early 1990s, working in a range of media. Commissions included 4 Minutes, Science Museum, 1994; and in 1995 The Most Beautiful Thing, for the Scottish Arts Council, and The Gifted Child, outdoor installation for Eastwood Arts Festival, Glasgow. Dalziel & Scullion were artists-in-residence for Banff & Buchan District, 1994–5. They had an exhibition at Arnolfini Gallery, Bristol, 1996. This included impressions of the flat, minimal landscape of northeast Scotland where they lived, unsettling video images of 80,000 battery hens and large photographs accompanied by a scented text. In 1997 Scottish National Gallery of Modern Art, Edinburgh, exhibited their video Endlessly. Arts Council, Science Museum and Victoria & Albert Museum hold their work.

Nikki DANBY 1957– Painter and draughtsman, born in Victoria, British Columbia, who began drawing and painting from an early age. From 1980–3 she studied at Byam Shaw School of Art. Then went on to contribute pictures to mixed shows, including Charlotte Lampard Gallery, Cadogan Contemporary and Zella Nine. In 1992 had first solo show at Cadogan Gallery, of works done between 1987–91, during which time she had received several portrait commissions in Europe and Australia. Her images were described as "sensual and rich in colour and tonal variety".

John Alexander DANFORD 1913–1970 Sculptor, mural painter and watercolourist. Born in Dublin, he studied at Wimbledon School of Art, 1929–34, under S Nicholson Babb, and at the Royal Academy Schools, 1934–9, where he won a gold medal in 1935. He was granted the Landseer Scholarship in 1934 and a British Institution Scholarship three years later. Exhibited RA, RHA and in Nigeria. Danford was British Council representative for a time in Sierra Leone and his work is in permanent collections in West Africa and Ireland. Finally was known as a colourful character in Kinsale, County Cork, Ireland, walking around the town with a male companion both dressed in African finery. He also completed African murals in Ballinacurra House, where he lived.

Alice Laura DANIEL 1892– Painter and draughtsman. She studied art privately with the watercolourist J Paul Brinson. Exhibited BWS. Lived near Stockport, Cheshire.

Alfred DANIELS 1924– Painter, teacher and writer of books on art, born in London, where he continued to live. Daniels studied at Woolwich Polytechnic, 1943–4, then service in the Royal Air Force, resuming his studies at Royal College of Art, 1947–50, undertaking postgraduate studies in mural design, 1950–2. Daniels was to hold a number of teaching posts: from 1951–76 at Hornsey College of Art; from 1964–9 part-time at Royal College of Art; from 1973–88 part-time at Sir John Cass, City of London Polytechnic; 1976–80 part-time at Middlesex Polytechnic; then again at the Royal College, 1984–7. Daniels showed widely in mixed shows from the early 1950s. He was one of Jack Beddington's *Young Artists of Promise*, in the 1957 book of that title, and his stylised depiction of people and places remained remarkably consistent. He handled a number of commissions, including murals for Hammersmith Town Hall. His books included *Painting and Drawing*, 1961; *Drawing Made Simple*, 1962; and *Landscape Painting in Watercolour and Oil*, 1980. His many solo shows included Zwemmer Gallery from mid-1950s, later ones including Belgrave Gallery, 1989: Alfred Daniels in Israel. Daniels was a member of RWS and RBA. Leeds University and Greater London Council held his work.

Harvey DANIELS 1936– Printmaker, painter and teacher, born in London, was married to the artist Judy Stapleton. He studied at Willesden College of Art, 1951–6, Slade School of Fine Art with Lynton Lamb and Ceri Richards, 1956–8, and at Brighton College of Art, 1958–9. Was a member of the Printmakers' Council of Great Britain, taught at Brighton College and at London University. Victoria & Albert Museum, Towner Art Gallery in Eastbourne and several American museums hold his work. Solo shows included Pallant House, Chichester, 1995. Lived in Brighton, Sussex.

Leonard DANIELS 1909–1998 Influential administrator, teacher and painter, with a special interest in portraiture, born in London, who studied at Regent Street Polytechnic and Royal College of Art, 1929–32, gaining the portrait prize in his final year. He early on showed sporting prowess, notably as a runner and long-distance cyclist. Exhibited at Goupil and Redfern Galleries in the 1930s. After teaching in several schools, including Taunton's in Southampton, Daniels was on the staff of Southampton and Portsmouth Schools of Art; during World War II, as well as being head of painting at Leeds College of Art, he did commissioned work for the War Artists' Advisory Committee; then in 1947 was appointed principal of Camberwell School of Art retiring in 1974. His predecessor William Johnstone had laid the foundations of an impressive staff, to which Daniels added, teachers during his time there, as its longest serving principal, including Edward Ardizzone, Martin Bloch, William Coldstream, Richard Eurich, Robert Medley, Victor Pasmore, Claude Rogers, Michael Rothenstein and Karel Vogel. Under Daniels' civilised, calm direction, Camberwell was steered through major changes. He was elected president of the National Society for Art Education in 1965. After retirement, Daniels taught adult education classes in Kingston, before moving to Midhurst, Sussex. Died in Winchester, Hampshire, where there was an exhibition of work by him and his wife soon after in the cathedral. Imperial War Museum and Southampton City Art Gallery hold examples.

Peter DANIELS 1937– Landscape painter using a rich palette, born in Salford, Lancashire. He trained at Manchester College of Art, worked in London in advertising and marketing, then in 1975 began painting full-time. In 1984 he moved to Pembrokeshire, in 1987 opening the Pink House Gallery, Nine Wells, Solva, Haverfordwest. Exhibitions included Adams Fine Art, Albany Gallery in Cardiff and Dessin Gallery, in Los Angeles, all 1991; and Cleveland Bridge Gallery, Bath, and International Art Expo, New York, both 1992.

Stephen DANIELS 1955– Sculptor who did a part-time course at Bath Academy of Art, 1973–80. Took part in group exhibition at Mignon Gallery, Bath, 1977, from same year showing at RWA Autumn Open; with Bath Society of Artists from 1978; and in 1st RWA Open Sculpture Exhibition, 1993. Had solo show at Alwin Gallery, 1984, which continuously exhibited his work. Horse and Rider, Dark Crusaders and Seafarers were leading themes of his sculptures. Lived in Colerne, Wiltshire.

George DANNATT 1915– Artist in all media, photographer and writer on music who from 1940–70, apart from Army service, 1941–4, was a chartered surveyor in the family business, qualifying in 1940. He was born in Blackheath, London, and attended Colfe's Grammar School and the College of Estate Management. From 1944–56 was a regular *News Chronicle* music critic, being an authority on Sir Arthur Bliss. In 1948 Dannatt began his association with the Dorset area, photographing it and taking up part-time residence in 1958, two years after reviving his interest in painting. In this he was self-taught. From 1963 Dannatt began an association with the Cornish painters. He was influenced by Penwith artists and especially John Wells through Ben Nicholson. Became an associate of Penwith Society of Art and a member of Newlyn Society of Artists. Dannatt had a three-man show with Wells and Alexander Mackenzie at Orion Gallery, Penzance, in 1975, having a solo show at Newlyn Art Gallery, 1976. Other solo exhibitions included Galerie Schreiner, Basel, Switzerland, in 1980–1; Galerie Artica, Cuxhaven, Germany, from 1984; New Ashgate Gallery, Farnham, 1992; Dorset County Museum, Dorchester, 1993; Book Gallery, St Ives, 1995 and 1997. There was a retrospective at Newlyn Art Gallery in 1981. Royal Air Force Museum, Hendon, holds his work, which employed geometric forms with lyricism and which used a warm and economic palette. Lived in Tisbury, Wiltshire.

Peter DARACH 1940– Artist working in a range of media, born in Spondon, Derbyshire. He studied at Royal College of Art, 1962–5, and was an "? [sic] outsider painter since 1968, living in Scotland, Italy and France", later in London. His large oil on board … Rolled into One won a prize in the 1995–6 John Moores

Liverpool Exhibition. Arts Council acquired a series of pencil drawings, Sue in Love, from the artist in 1985.

Stephen John DARBISHIRE 1940– Painter, musician and teacher, born in Greenodd, Lancashire. He won a scholarship to Byam Shaw School of Drawing and Painting, 1957–9, teachers including Peter Greenham, Peter Garrard and Bernard Dunstan. In 1960–1 Darbishire was a lay missionary to West Africa with the Irish Missionary Fathers, teaching art and English, then between 1962–7 was a musician and singer with a band. He then studied at Charlotte Mason, Ambleside, teachers' training college, spending a year at St Martin's in Lancaster, obtaining an honours degree, followed by teaching, 1972–83, then full-time painting. Darbishire was made a member of RBA in 1983, also belonging to Lake Artists' Society, and he showed at RA, RP and NEAC. From 1989 he had annual shows at Richard Hagen Gallery, Broadway. Henry Ling & Sons published greetings cards of Darbishire's work.

Phil DARBY 1938– Self-taught artist in oil and oil pastel, born in Birmingham. Left school at 15 and worked in the printing trade. After finishing his National Service in 1960 Darby began seriously to study painting, taking many jobs to finance it. In 1979 moved to Sennen, Cornwall, where he built his own studio and painted full-time. Became a member of Newlyn Society of Artists in 1974. Showed with RWA, Newlyn Orion Galleries in Penzance, Wills Lane Gallery in St Ives and elsewhere. Had solo shows in 1987 at Galerie Artica, Cuxhaven, Germany, at Queen's Elm Gallery and at Brown's Gallery, Penzance. Open University holds his work. Darby's pictures were mostly small, "both abstract and what I call my Voyages of the Red Ship (a series of highly stylised seascapes suggesting dreamlike voyages)."

Andrew DARKE 1948– Creator of constructions from wood, born in Preston, Lancashire, who began sculpting in mid-1960s. Although he obtained some support from Yorkshire Arts, Darke did a number of part-time jobs. Showed at Huddersfield Piazza, Yorkshire Sculpture Park, and Kenwood House in Hampstead, 1983. Among Darke's publicly sited sculptures are Oak Log Fall, 1981, at Oakwell Country Park, near Leeds, and Sliced Log 4, 1983, overlooking Chesil Beach, Dorset. Darke was a self-taught artist who lived in Holmfirth, West Yorkshire.

Michael DARLING 1923– Painter, born in London, who studied at Harrow School of Art and at the Royal Academy Schools with Henry Rushbury. Showed at NEAC, RA and RBA and London County Council bought his work, which he signed M D. Lived in London.

John Leonard DARLISON 1931– Artist in watercolour, pastel and oil, and teacher, born in Leyton, Essex. He was mainly self-taught, but did have lessons from Angus Rand, John Blockley and Edward Wesson, 1980–3. Darlison became a full-time artist in 1982, ran courses in France until 1986, then from his home address in Glasbury, Herefordshire. Using an Impressionistic technique Darlison aimed "to produce a sense of place and atmosphere in landscape painting". Group exhibitions included Albany Gallery in Cardiff, New Gallery in Swansea and David Curzon Gallery. Had a series of solo exhibitions, including Arts Club, Fairfield Halls in Croydon, St David's Hall in Cardiff, Riverside Gallery in Crickhowell and Island Gallery in Victoria, British Columbia. Government Art Collection (Queen's Jubilee Purchase) holds Darlison's work, as do many private collections in Britain and abroad.

Robin DARWIN 1910–1974 Painter and principal of the Royal College of Art. Born in London, Darwin after Eton College and Cambridge University attended the Slade School of Fine Art. He exhibited at the RA and other main London galleries. After World War II service in the Ministry of Home Security, Darwin was in 1945–6 at the Council of Industrial Design. While there he wrote a report titled *The Training of the Industrial Designer*, which led to his appointment as head of the Royal College, where he stayed from 1948–71. Darwin's reforms were considerable. Although he advocated initially that the training of the industrial designer – seen to be essential by the Ministry of Education – meant that easel painting was not a priority, in practice he became an adept promoter of the College's special contribution to the fine arts. The College assumed independent university status under his direction. Darwin's administrative abilities – he was knighted in 1964 – overshadowed his very real talent as a painter. Landscape was his main interest, although he was a good portrait painter, and he produced highly professional and atmospheric examples in oil and watercolour in Britain and abroad. Lived near Marlborough, Wiltshire.

Geoffrey DASHWOOD 1947– Sculptor and draughtsman, most noted for his sculptures of wildlife; a keen naturalist from his early years. For some years Dashwood worked for the Forestry Commission, then for about a decade sold drawings to local collectors, illustrating official wildlife literature. In the early 1960s spent a few weeks at Southampton College of Art, but the environment did not suit him. In 1986–7 Dashwood won Best Sculpture Award for exhibits at SWLA. Showed at Sladmore Gallery; Courcoux and Courcoux, Salisbury; Wildfowl and Wetlands Trust, Slimbridge; and John Davies Contemporary, Stow-on-the-Wold.

May Lilian DAUBAN 1907–1989 Watercolourist, born in Worthing, Sussex, daughter of Sir Claude Ricketts. She was educated at St Michael's, Guildford, also studying art in Paris. Her husband was in the Army and she exhibited widely in India and Pakistan before World War II, winning a gold medal in Calcutta. In Britain was a member of RWS and showed at RBA Galleries and in the provinces, although she withdrew from exhibiting in later years. Lived in Selsdon, Surrey.

Pamela DAUKES 1930– Painter in oil who studied at Bromley College of Art, latterly with Tom Coates and Roy Freer. Was a member of the Reigate Society of Artists; won a drawing award with UA, 1995; other group shows including Cider House Gallery, Bletchingley, Bank Street Gallery in Sevenoaks and Century Gallery, Datchet. Had a solo exhibition at Talent Store. Lived in Oxted, Surrey.

Frank DAVENPORT 1905–1973 Painter, born in Harrow, Middlesex, who studied at Harrow Technical School, then Royal College of Art, gaining his painting diploma in 1927. Showed at RA, LG and at *Daily Express* Young British Artists. Among his main works were Pinner View Lane and Crown Street, Harrow on the Hill. Lived at Hillingdon Heath, near where he was born, for many years, later in Norwich, Norfolk.

Ian DAVENPORT 1966– Abstract painter, born in Sidcup, Kent. He studied at Northwich College of Art and Design, 1984–5, and Goldsmiths' College School of Art, 1985–8. His group exhibitions included Young Contemporaries, at Whitworth Art Gallery, Manchester, 1985; Karsten Schubert Gallery, 1988; and the South Bank Centre's touring exhibition The British Art Show 1990. Davenport's method of working, as exemplified by his Waddington Galleries show in 1993, was to pour paint from a small scaffold using a vessel with an adjustable head to regulate the breadth of each pour. Was nominated for the Turner Prize in 1991. Lived in London.

Edith DAVEY fl. c.1915–1950 Portrait painter, black-and-white artist and miniaturist, brought up in Lincolnshire, who studied at Lincoln School of Art, then Royal College of Art, where she won a silver medal. Exhibited RA, RI, RMS, WIAC, SWA, Walker Art Gallery, Liverpool, and Paris Salon. Davey did a number of book illustrations and had work purchased by Huddersfield Art Gallery. Lived in London.

Grenville DAVEY 1961– Abstract sculptor, born in Launceston, Cornwall. He studied 1981–5 at Exeter College of Art and Design and Goldsmiths' College School of Art, gaining a bachelor's degree in fine art. Took part in many mixed shows internationally and in Britain, including Venice Biennale, 1988; National Museum of Modern Art, Tokyo, 1989; in 1990 Newport Harbor Museum in California and South Bank Centre's touring exhibition The British Art Show 1990. From 1987 had solo shows at Lisson Gallery, others including Primo Piano, Rome, 1989; Stichting De Appel Foundation, Amsterdam, 1990; Galerie Crousel-Robelin Bama, Paris, and Kunsthalle, Berne, 1991; and Kunstverein für die Rheinlande und Westfalen, Düsseldorf, Galleria Franz Paludetto, Turin, and Chisenhale Gallery, all in 1992. In that year won Turner Prize Award, at Tate Gallery. Lived in London.

Leonard John DAVEY 1913– Ceramic sculptor and potter, born in Nottingham. He studied at Leicester College of Art, 1926–8, and Edinburgh College of Art, 1945–9. Ran the Davey Pottery at Bridge of Dee, Kirkcudbrightshire, and showed in crafts exhibitions throughout Scotland. Leicester Museum and Shipley Art Gallery in Gateshead hold examples.

Peter DAVEY 1946– Painter in oil, tempera and watercolour, performance artist and teacher, born in Teignmouth, Devon. He studied at Reading University under Claude Rogers and Terry Frost, 1967–8; at Chelsea School of Art under Myles Murphy and Brian Young, 1968–71; and there again with Ian Stephenson, 1975–6. Between 1972–5 Davey was a member of Bernsteins, founders of Obstacle Art; he did occasional performances with The Kipper Kids, and solo; and was a furniture painter, teacher and painter and decorator. Lived in Munich, Germany, 1977–9, and 1992–3. Group shows included Garage, 1975; ICA, Northern Young Contemporaries and Stowells Trophy, all 1976; Hayward Annual at Hayward Gallery and Galerie Defet, Nuremberg, both 1979; and in the 1990s especially in Nuremberg, including Art 5, 1990, and in America. Solo shows included Garage, 1975; Felicity Samuels, 1977; and in 1988 at Kunstfocus, Munich. Davey's main works comprised trompe l'oeil wood and marble grain, 1973–6; large figurative works, 1988–92; large abstract works, 1992–3; and from 1994 watercolours, on-the-spot landscapes. Soutine, John Marin and William Gillies' watercolours were admired by him. Lived in Ashurst Wood, Sussex.

Illtyd DAVID 1906–1992 Self-taught painter and sculptor, born at Abertridwr, near Caerphilly, South Wales. He was brought up on a farm, left school at 13 to work on a farm and became a ploughing and hedging champion. After five years in Canada, 1927–32, was an agricultural engineer, 1933–57, then a colliery engineer. Began painting in 1964, inspired by the biography of Sir John Millais by his son. David was a member of RCamA, also showing with NEAC, RA, SEA, at Royal National Eisteddfod and at Paris Salon, where he won gold and silver medals in the mid–1970s. WAC and National Museum of Wales hold his work. Lived at Deri, Mid-Glamorgan.

Michele DAVID 1968– Painter who gained an honours degree in fine art, painting, at Glasgow School of Art, 1986–90, where she won the John and Mabel Craig Bequest in the latter year. Among other awards were a Scottish Arts Council Grant in 1993 and the Villiers David Travel Prize, 1996. She was a member of the Glasgow Society of Women Artists. She was artist-in-residence, Shetland Isles, appointed by the Scottish Arts Council and Shetland Arts Trust, in 1992, in 1994–5 holding a residency at Drumcroon Education Centre, Wigan. In 1995 The Archer Group Commissioned her, and in 1996 both Victoria Hospice, Kirkcaldy, and Shetland Isles Calendar (for 1997). Group shows included Berkeley Square Gallery, 1990; Ben Uri Gallery, 1991; Worcester Art Gallery & Museum, Worcester, 1994; and Christopher Hull Gallery, 1996. In 1997 she shared a show at Cadogan Contemporary, later solo shows including Shetland Museum (which holds her work), 1996.

Nathan DAVID 1930– Figurative sculptor and teacher, born and lived in London, who was in advertising until 1960, teaching graphic design part-time at Watford College of Art. Studied sculpture at City & Guilds of London Art School, teaching it part-time at Sir John Cass College. Showed at RA Summer

Exhibition. Commissions included Ondine, Dame Margot Fonteyn, 1975, near Reigate railway station, and fountains, 1982, at Sutton Court, Surrey, all works in bronze.

Ian Stuart DAVIDSON 1936– Sculptor and teacher, son of an artist, born in Sheffield, Yorkshire. He was educated in South Africa, studying art at Camberwell School, 1960–1, Chelsea College of Art, 1962–3, and did a postgraduate certificate under Bernard Meadows at Royal College of Art. Lectured at Rochdale College of Art and at other schools in the provinces, showing in London and elsewhere. Manchester Loan Collection holds his work. Lived for a time in Brixham, Devon.

Lindsay DAVIDSON 1948–1986 Artist, born in Yorkshire, who studied at Exeter Art School, 1966–9. She was a founder-member of the Black Box Theatre, an experimental visual theatre company formed by John Epstein in 1969, which until 1972 gave performances throughout the country. These included Museum of Modern Art, Oxford, and the Round House. Davidson's group shows included LG, Whitechapel Art Gallery, 1972; The Nude, Morley Gallery, 1976; and Award Winners, Thorndike Gallery, Leatherhead, 1979. In 1982 she shared a show, Figurative Art Today, with John Epstein and Dennis Creffield, at 7 Dials Gallery. Later solo shows included Morley Gallery and Southover Gallery, Lewes, both 1979, the year Davidson won a major award from South East Arts Association.

Majel DAVIDSON 1885–1969 Artist, born in Aberdeen where she was educated at the High School, then graduated in 1907 from Gray's School of Art, having specialised in painting and pottery. In 1908 Davidson moved to Paris, studying with Charles Guérin and starting a life's friendship with the artist Edward Overton-Jones who was through his family strongly connected with the pottery industry. Although Davidson exhibited at the Salon d'Automne in 1912, World War I interrupted; she earned the Military Medal as a volunteer ambulance driver. Prompted by the Canadian artist Katrina Buell, Davidson moved to Toronto in the mid-1920s where she associated with Group of Seven artists. Back in Europe, she concentrated on pottery and her work for the International Council of Women, only returning seriously to painting in her mid-sixties while living near Stirling. Her work shared a show with that of Alexander Graham Munro which was put on in 1989 at Portland Gallery, in association with William Hardie.

Aubrey Claud DAVIDSON-HOUSTON 1906–1995 Painter and draughtsman, born in Dublin, Ireland, into a military family. He attended Royal Military College, Sandhurst, and was a regular soldier for 23 years, always interested in art. While a prisoner of war in Germany for five years made drawings of 600 fellow-prisoners. Upon retirement in 1949 Davidson-Houston studied at Slade School of Fine Art with William Coldstream for three years. Attended St Martin's School of Art part-time and worked for a time with Sir Gerald Kelly. Davidson-Houston was noted as a portrait painter, exhibiting at RP, NS, RCamA, RSA and at Paris Salon. Had a solo show at Walker's Galleries. HRH The Duke of Edinburgh was among his subjects and his works are held by several members of the royal family. Lived in Esher, Surrey, with a studio in London. Died at Allington Court, St Albans, Hertfordshire.

Alan DAVIE 1920– Painter, born in Grangemouth, Stirlingshire, whose father was a painter and printmaker. Studied at Edinburgh College of Art, 1937–40, where he was influenced by John Maxwell. Won several scholarships. After serving in Army in World War II Davie worked for a time as a professional jazz musician. He was also interested in writing poetry, designed textiles and pottery and worked as a jeweller. By the time of his first solo show, at Grant's Bookshop, Edinburgh, in 1946, Davie's interest in the work of Paul Klee and primitive artists was evident. Over the years there were a number of such influences on his work: the American Abstract Expressionists such as Pollock and Gorky, Oriental mysticism including Zen Buddhism, gliding and swimming and Indian mythology. Davie viewed art as a way of gaining spiritual enlightenment. His later work was less expressionistic, more full of symbolism. In 1947 Davie married the artist and potter Janet Gaul, travelled in Europe and met Peggy Guggenheim, the collector, which expanded his horizons. From 1950 he was having solo shows with Gimpel Fils and had his first New York exhibition at the Catherine Viviano Gallery in New York in 1956. Was Gregory Fellow at Leeds University, 1957–9. In 1962 Davie had retrospective at Stedelijk Museum, Amsterdam, which toured, and from then he consolidated his international reputation with a number of overseas retrospectives. Fifty-year retrospective at McLellan Galleries, Glasgow, 1992, another at Barbican Art Gallery, 1993. Tate Gallery holds his work. Lived in Hertfordshire, St Lucia and Cornwall.

Joseph DAVIE 1965– Artist, notable as a printmaker, who was born in Glasgow and studied at its School of Art, 1983–7. He won the Guthrie Award at RSA in 1990. His exhibition A Journal of the Blackout was shown at Glasgow Print Studio in 1991, the year when he participated in Danger Artists at Work, a City Art Centre, Edinburgh, touring show. The city's collection holds his work.

Alexander William DAVIES: *see* **J A D**

Anthony DAVIES 1947– Printmaker, born in Andover, Hampshire. He studied at Manchester School of Art and Royal College of Art, winning the Prix de Rome, British School in Rome. In 1985 Davies established his own printmaking workshop in Belfast, the year following gaining a printmaking fellowship at the Royal College of Art. Participated in many group shows in Britain and abroad and had many solo exhibitions, including Birmingham Polytechnic; Compass Gallery in Glasgow; Bluecoat Gallery, Liverpool; Hendricks Gallery, Dublin; and Limerick Gallery. In 1988 and 1989 he was resident artist in Northern Ireland and in 1990 in Hungary. Several dozen public collections in Britain, on the continent and elsewhere abroad hold work by

Davies, which is infused with a strong sense of social conscience. Was married for a time to the artist Erica Daborn. Eventually moved to Grey Lynn, Auckland, New Zealand.

Arthur Edward DAVIES 1893– Painter and draughtsman born in Pontrhydygroes Ystrad Meurig, Cardiganshire. He studied at Metropolitan School of Art in Dublin. Showed RA for many years, RWA, in the provinces and abroad. National Library of Wales in Aberystwyth holds his work. Lived in Norwich, Norfolk.

Austin DAVIES 1926– Painter and teacher, born in Liverpool, which was the focus of his career. Studied at Liverpool School of Art, 1946–51, with Arthur Ballard and Martin Bell. Davies was a prominent exhibitor in the Liverpool Academy in the 1950s, often showing taut, gritty pictures of the city. He painted a notable portrait of the local Member of Parliament Mrs Bessie Braddock, and Davies' portrait of his wife, the novelist Beryl Bainbridge, is in the collection of Manchester City Art Gallery. Davies also showed Arts Council, AIA, public galleries in Salford and Newcastle upon Tyne and had several one-man shows including Piccadilly Gallery, and Coombs Contemporary, 1997.

Benedict DAVIES fl. from c.1935– Painter and teacher who sometimes worked under name Turkletob and whose real name was Beatrice Rozenberg (Davies being her maiden name). She was born and educated in London and studied at Royal Academy Schools, 1934–9, under Sir Walter Russell. During World War II taught for a short time at Bideford School of Art. Showed at RA and had one-man exhibitions, in 1962 and 1976, at Ben Uri Art Society. As well as still-lifes, portraits and genre scenes, in latter years she painted a major series of compositions on Jewish holocaust, having researched vanished Jewish communities in Eastern Europe. John Lewis Partnership holds her work. Son Asher was also a painter. Lived in Bushey Heath, Hertfordshire.

Charles Richard Anthony DAVIES 1930– Painter, potter and teacher, born in Broadstairs, Kent. Studied at Southport School of Art, 1945–53, and Manchester Regional College of Art. He held a number of teaching appointments, including his old college in Manchester and Durham Technical College. Showed RCamA, at public galleries in Salford, Southport and Preston and in Belgium. Lived for some time in Durham.

Douglas DAVIES 1946– Painter, potter and teacher, educated in Edinburgh, where he studied ceramics and glass design, 1966–70, at the College of Art, with a postgraduate scholarship in ceramics and a travelling scholarship to Italy, 1970–71. Davies taught part-time at Moray House College of Education, 1971–2 and lectured in ceramics at Glasgow School of Art, 1973–86, then becoming a full-time potter and painter. His pots, stoneware and porcelain, were functional, decorative and exuberant in style; his gouache and acrylic paintings used the shape, pattern and colour of landscape almost to abstraction. Davies was a regular solo exhibitor, later shows including Macaulay Gallery in Stenton and Castlegate House, Cockermouth, both 1994, and The Scottish Gallery, Edinburgh, 1996. He had a studio gallery at Skirling, Biggar, Lanarkshire.

Emrys DAVIES fl. from 1920s– Self-taught artist, born in Pont-rhyd-y-groes, Cardiganshire. He was by profession a retail chemist. He was made a member of PS in 1928, also exhibiting at NS and in France. Lived for many years in Maidenhead, Berkshire.

Geoff DAVIES 1944– Printmaker, painter and teacher, born in St Albans, Hertfordshire. He attended Goldsmiths' College School of Art, 1960–3 and the Royal College of Art, 1963–6. Then went to Cardiff College of Art to lecture. Took part in a number of group shows in Wales, including WAC and 56 Group, of which he was a member; as well as group exhibitions in London, including RWS show Graven Image, in 1963. Designed several theatrical sets for the Welsh Theatre Company. National Museum of Wales, Cardiff, holds his work.

Gerald DAVIES 1957– Artist and teacher born in South Wales who gained an honours degree in fine art at Wolverhampton Polytechnic, 1977–80, and his master's degree at Royal College of Art in painting, 1981–4. His teaching experience included both Wolverhampton and the Royal College as well as Bournemouth and Poole College of Art, Sunderland Polytechnic and Lancaster University, where he taught drawing full-time. He was also a visiting professor at Purdue University in America, to which he gained a Fulbright Scholarship, 1990–1. Davies was the winner of a scholarship at Cité Internationale des Arts, Paris, 1983; was artist-in-residence at Durham Cathedral, 1988–9; was commissioned by the Fawe Street Press to produce work for a limited edition book *More songs from the recent wars* in 1989; and in 1993 was visiting artist in Norfolk schools. Group shows included Printmakers' Council, 1986; Artists who studied with Peter de Francia, Camden Arts Centre, 1987; and Cheltenham National Drawing Competition, 1994. He shared a show with Paul Gladwyn at East West, 1995. Later solo shows included Recent Drawings at Contact Gallery, Norwich, 1993.

Gordon DAVIES 1926– Painter, muralist, worker in many other media, designer and teacher, born in London. After Army sevice in World War II Davies studied at Camberwell School of Arts and Crafts, 1948, and Royal College of Art, 1950–3. Taught drawing part-time at Canterbury College of Art. In 1962 assisted his friend John Ward with murals at Challock Church, Kent, and went on to complete others for Braxted Park, Essex, the Chateau Segonne in Bordeaux, the Chandos Memorial Chapel, Whitchurch, and elsewhere. Work regularly appeared at RA Summer Exhibition from early 1950s. Had solo shows at Wye College, 1967, Waterhouse Gallery, 1973, from 1977 at King Street Gallery and in 1993 at Sally Hunter Fine Art. Had a retrospective at Royal Museum and Art Gallery, Canterbury, in 1990. Extensive work for *House & Garden*, wallpaper designs for Shand-Kydd and Sanderson, shell-work panels and carpet designs were other aspects of Davies' output.

Hanlyn DAVIES 1942– Painter, printmaker and teacher, born in Dunvant, Swansea. From 1960–3 was at Swansea College of Art and from 1963–4 there and at University College, Swansea. From 1964 Davies' career was America-oriented. After two years as an assistant at Yale School of Art and Architecture and assisting Joseph Albers, held posts at Universities of Vermont and Massachusetts. Having exhibited in Britain at WAC, Royal National Eisteddfod and Glynn Vivian Art Gallery in Swansea, Davies had many solo shows in America, winning a large number of prizes. WAC and a series of American public collections hold work.

Hugh DAVIES 1949– Painter and teacher, born in Germany. He studied at Brighton College of Art, 1964–8, then Chelsea School of Art, 1968–9, eventually becoming senior lecturer at Chelsea. He exhibited at John Moores Liverpool Exhibition, 1987, having solo shows at Redfern Gallery from 1984 and at Cartwright Hall, Bradford, 1986. Artificial light and space and theatricality were features of Davies' work, which was "more concerned with the metaphor than the simile". Lived in London.

Ivor DAVIES 1935– Painter, printmaker, performance artist, writer and teacher, born in Treharris, Glamorgan, where he settled at Penarth. From 1952–6 Davies studied at Cardiff College of Art; 1956–7 at Swansea College of Art; then was at University of Lausanne, 1959–61, as an assistant teacher of English. A series of university teaching posts followed; Davies was from 1971–8 curator of Talbot Rice Art Centre, University of Edinburgh; and from 1978–88 was principal lecturer in history of art and head of the school of cultural studies, Gwent College of Higher Education, Newport. Exhibited widely in mixed shows, including Royal National Eisteddfod, SWG and SEA and was a member of RCamA, The Welsh Group, WSW and Beca, as well as the Association of Art Historians and International Association of Art Critics. Had a solo show at Traverse Theatre, Edinburgh, 1968, later ones including touring exhibition from Wrexham Arts Centre, 1992–3; Bruton Gallery, Bath, 1993; Martin Tinney, Cardiff, 1994; and Brecknock Museum, Brecon, 1995. WAC, Edinburgh and Stirling Universities hold examples. Among Davies' interests were the organisation of multi-media and experimental theatrical performances, participation in seminars on such topics as Kinetic Art and Space Art, and languages: he was fluent in, or had a working knowledge of, Welsh, English, French, Spanish, Italian, German and Russian.

John DAVIES 1946– Sculptor, painter and teacher, born in Cheshire. He studied painting at Hull and Manchester Colleges of Art, then after two years at Slade School of Fine Art he won a sculpture fellowship at Gloucester College of Art. Arts Council and Tate Gallery hold Davies' work, the Tate's Young Man, of 1969–70, stemming from the period when Davies was teaching at Cheltenham Art College. His first sculptures were shown at Whitechapel Art Gallery in 1972 and prompted attention because of their disturbing realism. Davies' young men had parts, such as heads and hands, cast from life, lifelike wigs and items of clothing worn by the artist or bought at jumble sales. During the 1970s Davies produced groups of figures. Later he made small, acrobatic figures and a series of huge heads. From the end of the 1970s Davies took part in many group shows in Europe, South America and Australia and held one-man shows at Marlborough Fine Art.

John A DAVIES 1901– Painter in oil and watercolour with a strong interest in maritime subjects, born in Ware, Hertfordshire, not far from where be finally settled at Therfield. After education at Clifton College and the Royal Military Academy at Woolwich, he studied painting at Heatherley's School of Fine Art, with additional tuition from Jack Merriott and other painters. Was a keen member of the Wapping Group, for a time being its chairman. Showed there, RWS and RSMA and also as a member and elsewhere. National Maritime Museum, Greenwich, holds his work.

John Elwyn DAVIES: *see* **John ELWYN**

John R DAVIES 1899–1985 Painter and draughtsman, born in Wolverhampton, Staffordshire, who on leaving school at 14 attended evening classes at Manchester School of Art. After serving in Lancashire Fusiliers from 1917, Davies studied full-time at the School under Adolphe Valette with whom, after he joined the family business, Davies continued to study as well as at the studio of MAFA, of which he became a member. He was also a member of Stockport Art Guild, becoming its president in 1959, was elected RI and on retiring became a member of Haslemere Art Society and was a founder-member of the Art Society in Midhurst, Sussex, where he lived. Showed at RA and had several solo shows in Buxton and Manchester, where Tib Lane Gallery exhibited a selection of his work in 1994. Oldham, Buxton and Stockport public galleries hold examples.

Michael DAVIES 1947– Painter and teacher who was born in Tonbridge, Kent. He studied at Hastings College of Art and Technology, 1976–81, gained an honours degree in fine art at Canterbury College of Art, 1981–4, then his master's degree at Manchester Polytechnic, 1984–5. Among his teachers were Dennis Creffield, Fabian Peake and Stass Paraskos. Davies was a part-time lecturer at Hastings College of Art, 1986–9, also teaching at Cyprus College of Art, Paphos, 1987–91. Group shows included Olympia Contemporary Art Fair, 1986, and The Big Fight, Vanessa Devereux Gallery, 1987. He had solo exhibitions at Wedges Bistro, Hastings, 1988, and Music Room Concerts, St Leonards-on-Sea, 1993. Towner Art Gallery, Eastbourne, holds his work. Was a member of the Society of Sussex Downsmen. Lived in Bexhill-on-Sea, Sussex.

Ogwyn DAVIES 1925– Painter, ceramist and teacher, born in Trebanos, near Swansea. After Royal Air Force service, 1943–7, Davies attended Swansea College of Art, 1947–52, then taught in several schools in England and Wales, at Tregaron Secondary School, 1955–85. Group exhibitions included Leicester Galleries, CASW, Royal National Eisteddfod, SWG and Howard Roberts

Gallery, Cardiff. Showed solo at University College, Wales, Aberystwyth, where the National Library holds several pictures, with religious themes. WAC also holds Davies' work. Lived at Tregaron, Dyfed.

Paul DAVIES 1947–1993 Sculptor, performance artist, art historian and teacher, born in Mumbles, Swansea, went to school in Wales, West Germany and Devon. He was at Northampton School of Art, 1965–6, studied sculpture at St Martin's, 1966–9, sociology at University of Essex, 1969–72, and did postgraduate design at University of Liverpool. After temporary posts he became head of art at Plymouth and Mannamead College, 1973–4; lecturer at Cheshire School of Art and Design, 1974–80, and held various visiting lectureships; then was lecturer in art and design at Coleg Gwynedd, Bangor. He was involved in many Welsh groups, including 56 Group, and showed widely in Wales. Inspired by the Rebecca Riots of 1843, he and his brother Peter launched the Beca Group in 1983. By then Davies was known as a radical figure, having as a student burned oil-painted surfaces to blistering finishes; been involved in the International Destruction in Art Symposium in Better Books' basement, 1966–7; also the occupation of Hornsey College of Art, 1968. The National Eisteddfod was a notable venue where in 1974 Davies dressed as a type of red dragon with a concealed flame-thrower. He helped establish art classes for the unemployed and a community arts centre. Died of a heart attack in Bangor during the organisation of the show Official Status – Beca at the Gate, Colwyn Bay Library, 1993–4, plus tour.

Peter DAVIES 1937– Artist in a variety of media, born in Liverpool, who studied at Swindon School of Art until 1961. He was dissatisfied with "the then accepted concept of painting", and with the encouragement of the sculptor John Hoskin and the painter Patrick Caulfield set out to develop his "own completely personal means of expression", living in London. In 1965 Davies returned to Swindon and set up a workshop with other artists, helping to promote local craftsmen. By 1966 it had begun to claim too much of his time, so he moved to Oxford. After a year of painting had a show at Mansfield College there in 1968.

Peter DAVIES 1953– Writer on art and painter, born in Pontypool, Monmouthshire, whose pictures were mainly plein-air landscapes, especially of Cornwall and France. Davies studied art history at the University of East Anglia, 1972–6, then life drawing under Joe McGill at Chelsea School of Art evening classes, 1985–90. Davies wrote a string of books on modern British art, including the pioneering *A Northern School*, 1989, and *Liverpool Seen*, 1992, also *St Ives Revisited*, 1994. Group shows included A Northern School, Grundy Art Gallery, Blackpool, 1990; Domino Gallery, Liverpool, 1992; Harlech Biennale and Graham Gallery, Tunbridge Wells, both 1996; and Clevedon: Sharing a View, APT Gallery and tour, 1997–8. Had solo exhibitions at Bridewell Studios, Liverpool, 1992; Porthmeor Gallery, St Ives, 1994; and in 1995 shared an exhibition at The Living Room with Charmian Leonard. Private collections holding his work include Jilly and Leo Cooper, George Melly, Bob Simm, Michael Kenny and Denis Bowen. Lived in Bristol.

Peter DAVIES 1970– Painter, born in Edinburgh, who graduated from Goldsmiths' College in 1996. His work appeared in Die Yuppie Scum, at Karsten Schubert, 1996; in 1997 in Artists and their Spread, 53 Exmouth Market, and in the Saatchi Collection-related show Sensation, at the RA. There he was described as making "obsessional paintings about the medium of painting itself ... The work is at once fastidious and awkward, painted in a faux-naïf style". In 1997, Davies was commissioned by Habitat to create a work entitled Small Circle Painting.

Philip DAVIES 1953– Painter and teacher, born in Pudsey, Yorkshire. He attended Loughborough College of Art, 1972–5, then Royal College of Art, 1978–81. He went on to teach at Brighton Polytechnic and Ulster University. From the mid-1970s Davies was a prolific exhibitor, making several appearances at John Moores Exhibition in Liverpool, at LG, Christopher Hull and Cooling Galleries and Royal Over-Seas League. In 1986 he was winner of the League's first prize. Had a solo show at Polytechnic Gallery, Stoke, in 1987, others including Christopher Hull Gallery 1988–90–92. Lived in London.

Raymond Edgar Monson DAVIES 1924–1995 Artist in watercolour and mixed media whose chief interests were landscape and the buildings in it. By profession he was a pharmaceutical journalist, being a Master of Pharmacy of the University of Wales. He was largely self-taught, but did a correspondence course tutored by G John Blockley. Davies began painting in 1974. He belonged to NS, 1983, also showing with RI, RBA and RMS and in Surrey, where he lived at Woodham.

Roger DAVIES 1938– Painter, born in Neath, Glamorgan. After attending Lancing College, Sussex, 1951–6, Davies went to Swansea College of Art, 1956–7, and then Chelsea College of Art, 1957–61, Bernard Meadows and Prunella Clough being among his teachers. For a time he then worked in the family steel company while continuing to paint. In 1963 he won a WAC Prize at SWG exhibition, and he also showed at SEA and with Howard Roberts Gallery, Cardiff. WAC holds his work.

Roland DAVIES 1904–1993 Cartoonist, commercial artist and painter, born in Stourport, Worcestershire. Aged 13 he attended evening classes at Ipswich School of Art for two years, then full-time for two more. Left home and became apprenticed to a litho-printing firm in West Drayton, designing cinema and other posters. Began to offer cartoons as a freelance to *Motor Cycle News* and *Autocar* magazines. Davies created his genial, plodding carthorse cartoon strip Come On, Steve!, which appeared in the *Sunday Express* from 1932–9, then in the *Sunday Dispatch*. The character also featured in animated films, and Davies developed a career drawing for other papers and children's comics. In World War II Davies worked for the Ministry of Information. By 1972, under the guidance of art dealer Alan Class, Davies had turned to painting in oils, creating nostalgic London street scenes, marine and cowboy pictures. Showed at RBA, RSMA and elsewhere.

Rosemary DAVIES fl. from 1970s– Painter and muralist who trained at Harrow School of Art and Mid Warwickshire College of Art. Showed in many mixed exhibitions, including four-man show at Woodlands Art Gallery, 1988. Painted two murals for East Birmingham Hospital, 1985, and Warwick Central Hospital, 1987, pictures by her being bought by the Paintings in Hospital committee. From 1979 had a series of solo shows.

Ruth Llynfi DAVIES fl. c.1940– Miniaturist and portrait painter, often working on ivory, born in Llansamlet, near Swansea, South Wales. Studied mainly at Swansea School of Art and showed at RA, in Wales and Scotland. Lived at Mumbles, Glamorgan.

Siobhan DAVIES 1966– Artist who through the medium of installations worked "to capture things intangible and transitory." An example was her neon lights piece Window (proposition for gaining time) in the show East, Norwich Gallery, 1991. Davies studied at Newcastle Polytechnic, 1986–9, then Birmingham Institute of Art and Design, 1990–1. Showed in BT New Contemporaries, ICA, 1993. Lived in Moseley, Birmingham.

Stephanie DAVIES 1910–1990 Artist, designer and costume historian, born in Bristol where she attended the West of England College of Art, also the University, 1927–32. At various times she was head of painting at the Ladies' College, Cheltenham; director of the Channel Islands School of Painting; and taught at Schools in Chester and Malvern. As well as showing extensively on the continent Davies exhibited at RBA, SWA, UA, NS and in the provinces. Solo shows included Bristol Old Vic and University College, Exeter. Lived in Malvern Link, Worcestershire, then Upper Breinton, Herefordshire.

Thomas DAVIES 1899– Painter in oil and watercolour. Born at Colwyn Bay, Denbighshire, North Wales, Davies studied art privately under Robert Evans Hughes. He went on to exhibit with the Flintshire Art Society, North Wales Group and Denbighshire Art Society; had a one-man show at Gwrych Castle. Lived at Abergele, Clwyd, Wales.

Tim DAVIES 1960– Artist and teacher, born in Haverfordwest, Pembrokeshire, who, after several years engaged in music, did a foundation course at Ravensbourne College of Art & Design, 1986–7; gained an honours degree in fine art at Norwich School of Art, 1987–90; then his master's, on issues of art and architecture, at Kent Institute of Art & Design, Canterbury, 1991–2. After an unsatisfactory experiment with painting, Davies made the site-specific installation Flags over Solva, 1992, which pointed the way to the creation of others as well as performance works which explored dispossession and disempowerment. These were painstakingly crafted using a multiplicity of materials, and included Paran Chapel, 1993; Solfach, Burnt Wall, 1993–4; Alphabeca, 1995; and Tatters, 1996. Davies' work experience included a residency at Bedford Modern School, 1990–1, and part-time teaching at Carmarthen College of Technology & Art and at HM Prison, Swansea, 1995. Davies was a member of the Beca Group and of Artists' Project. Showed widely in Britain and abroad, with solo exhibitions at Spacex Gallery, Exeter, and at Glynn Vivian Art Gallery, Swansea, where he lived, in 1997.

William DAVIES 1928– Painter in oil, born in South Wales, who served in the Royal Navy until 1962. He was noted for his fluent, on-the-spot pictures of Venice and London, where he also painted from the life over several years at the Royal Academy of Music. Was a member of the Wapping Group, also showing at ROI and RSMA. Lloyd's of London used one of Davies' Thames scenes on its calendar. Solo shows included Omell Galleries, Windsor, 1990. Lived in West Hyde, Rickmansworth, Hertfordshire.

W Mitford DAVIES 1895– Illustrator and painter who studied at Liverpool School of Art, 1920–4. Exhibited RCamA. He was principally known as an illustrator of books in Welsh who was closely associated with the Welsh League of Youth. Lived at Gaerwen, Anglesey.

Arna DAVIS fl. from c.1990– Sculptor and Jungian analyst, born in Finland, who settled in Britain as a young adult, eventually at Watford, Hertfordshire. In 1973, she qualified as a social worker while training to become a psychotherapist, becoming a member of the British Association of Psychotherapists and a member of the International Association for Analytical Psychology. Long interested in art, Davis started art training at St Albans School of Art and Design, 1989, obtaining her honours degree in fine art from University of Hertfordshire in 1995. Group shows included Hertfordshire Visual Arts Forum, CRA Gallery, St Albans, 1992; Take 16, Margaret Harvey Gallery, St Albans, 1993; Sculpture Exhibition, Watford Area Arts Forum, Royal Caledonian Schools, Bushey, 1996; and Unquiet Voices, Doncaster Museum & Art Gallery, 1997. Had a solo show, Screen 24 x 24 = 576, sculpture, University of Hertfordshire, 1995–6.

Arthur Joseph DAVIS 1878–1951 Watercolourist who was an architect by profession. Studied at L'École des Beaux-Arts, Paris, 1896–1900. Exhibited RA. Was an Officer of the Legion of Honour. Lived in London.

Bernard J DAVIS 1932– Artist, notably a sculptor and mosaicist, born in the Farnham area of Surrey, married to the painter Diana Hammond. He studied at Winchester School of Art, 1949–53, and Royal Academy Schools, 1953–5, Maurice Lambert among his teachers. At RA Summer Exhibition in 1955 showed two heads, one of an Eastern girl, also exhibiting at Herbert Art Gallery, Coventry, and Towner Art Gallery, Eastbourne, which holds a bronze cast, Pandora. Davis' body of ecclesiastical and school commissions included work for St Philip's Cathedral in Birmingham, Holy Family Church in Dagenham, the Augustinian

Priory, Hammersmith, and Imberhorne School, East Grinstead. Was based for periods at Debenham, Suffolk, and Haywards Heath, Sussex.

Derek DAVIS 1926– Ceramist, born in London, who studied painting at Central School of Arts and Crafts with Robert Buhler and Keith Vaughan, 1946–50. He gained a fellowship as artist-in-residence, University of Sussex, 1967, and a Southern Arts Association Bursary, 1978. He was a member of Contemporary Applied Arts and of International Academy of Ceramics and a fellow of the Craft Potters' Association. His exhibitions included Primavera, Cambridge, 1965; University of Sheffield, 1971; Blond Fine Art, 1985; and Sheila Harrison from 1986; also showed extensively abroad. Davis was "influenced by painters, Picasso among others", in his work, which was held by Victoria & Albert Museum, Southampton City Art Gallery, Westerwald Keramic Museum, Germany, and elsewhere. Lived in Arundel, Sussex.

Elizabeth DAVIS 1921– Painter, constructions artist and restorer, born in Johannesburg, South Africa, where she was educated. In the late 1960s-early 1970s she showed extensively in Italy, winning the Viscontea Prize, Milan, in 1970. Solo shows included Galleria Pater, Milan, 1969, and Woodside Gallery, 1972. She directed that gallery for some years in Epsom Downs, Surrey, where she lived.

Heather St Clair DAVIS 1937– Equestrian artist, born in Cheltenham, who grew up on a farm in the Cotswolds hunting country. Studied at Cheltenham College of Art & Design and Birmingham College of Art, graduating in life drawing, sculpture and three-dimensional design. After hair-raising trip across Altantic in a converted cutter, eventually settled with young family in Vermont, America, in the early 1960s, where she farmed, bred and trained event horses, was an International Dressage judge, painted and taught art in local schools. Encouraged by art dealers Frost & Reed, she returned to Gloucestershire to paint seriously in 1988, thereafter showing with that gallery. Continued to live in Vermont, and was a member of the American Academy of Equine Art.

George Horace DAVIS 1881–1963 Artist, born in London, who studied at Ealing School of Art. He was for a time staff artist on the publications *Graphic* and *Sphere* and in 1923 became chief staff artist on the *Illustrated London News*. During World War I he was head of aerial diagrams for the Royal Flying Corps and an official war artist. Davis wrote many articles connected with marine illustration and was very prolific as an illustrator, famous for his diagrammatic drawings and cross-sections of ships. He was a member of RSMA and a founder-member of the Society of Aviation Artists. Showed at RA, Imperial War Museum which holds his work and elsewhere. Lived in Ewell, Surrey, then latterly in Brighton, Sussex.

Hilda DAVIS fl. c.1935–1960 Painter who was married to the artist Cyril Davis. She studied at the Grosvenor School of Modern Art, with Iain Macnab, 1935–9. Exhibited NEAC, RBA, ROI, AEB and widely in the provinces. NS member. Lived in London.

James DAVIS 1926– Sculptor and restorer in stone, born in London, who studied at Sir John Cass School of Art, 1949–53, under Edward Bainbridge Copnall. He became a freeman of the Worshipful Company of Painter-Stainers in 1972. Showed at Guildhall, Leighton House and Mall Galleries. Chelsea and Kensington Town Hall and St Nicholas' Church in Elm Park, Essex, hold examples. Had a studio and lived in Shoeburyness, Essex.

James Spence DAVIS 1944– Painter of landscape, born in Glasgow, where he studied at the School of Art with William Armour and David Donaldson, graduating in 1967. He was a member of The Scottish Ruralists who worked on-the-spot regardless of climate. Was an exhibiting member of Glasgow Art Club, Royal Glasgow Institute of the Fine Arts and Paisley Institute of Fine Arts, also showing regularly with RSA and RSW. In 1993 was included in Contemporary Art From Scotland at Thompson's Gallery. HRH The Duke of Edinburgh holds his work.

John Warren DAVIS: *see* **WARREN DAVIS**

Judith DAVIS 1933– Artist in oil, acrylic, watercolour, pastel and Batik, born in Dewsbury, Yorkshire. She studied at Wimbledon School of Art, 1951–4, then Royal College of Art, 1954–5, notable teachers including Gerald Cooper. Married straight from College and after her children were in their teens began teaching: Bury's Court Preparatory School and adult education classes. Joined the Reigate Society of Artists in 1973, becoming honorary secretary. Group shows also included *Daily Express* Young Artists Exhibition at New Burlington Galleries, 1955; RA, 1980; SWA, 1982 and 1989 at Mall and Westminster Galleries; Fairfield Halls, Croydon, 1987 and 1995; and Guildford Gallery, 1991. Lived in South Nutfield, Surrey. Early work was signed with her maiden name, Judith Fitton.

Kate DAVIS 1960– Mixed-media and performance artist who studied at Hertfordshire College of Art and Design, 1978–9, then Falmouth School of Art, 1979–82. Group shows included Ox-Skull/Pterodactyl, an installation with Graham Hubbard at Falmouth School Gallery, 1981; New Contemporaries at ICA, 1982; and Wapping Artists Open Studios, from 1983. In that year took part in Fairies and Water Maidens are the only other Alternatives (The myth of Housework being a Creative Activity), Loughborough Polytechnic and Central Art School. Lived in London.

Marie Thérèse DAVIS 1964– Artist employing strong figurative images, and teacher. She graduated from Queen's University, Belfast, in social anthropology in 1986, then, having completed her postgraduate certificate in education there in 1987, Davis gained a certificate in art and design from Oxford Polytechnic, 1990. In that year she worked as a visiting artist in a young offenders institution in Oxfordshire, and was a visiting lecturer in Oxford Polytechnic's printmaking department, also teaching music. She was associated with Queen Street Studios in Belfast, taking part in the 1994 shows Works on Paper and Beyond the Partitions. In the same year she had a solo exhibition at Harmony Hill Arts Centre.

Mike DAVIS 1946– Stained glass artist and conservator, and teacher, born in London, who did a foundation course at St Martin's School of Art, 1965–6, then his diploma at Hornsey College of Art, 1967–70, tutor Jack Smith. A course at Patrick Reyntiens' studio in 1968 prompted an interest in architectural glass. He held a fellowship in stained glass at Digswell Arts Trust, Welwyn Garden City, 1970–4, and worked there until 1981, when he set up a studio in Durham. Became senior lecturer in architectural glass at University of Sunderland from 1994, having taught part-time at Sunderland Polytechnic from 1982. Davis was an associate of The British Society of Master Glass Painters and of Art and Architecture. Exhibitions included RIBA Gallery, The Design Centre, Southwark Cathedral and Victoria & Albert Museum, which holds his work. Davis carried out many commissions, churches including St John's Church, Digswell; St Nicholas' Hospital Chapel, Gosforth; and St Elizabeth of Hungary, Aycliffe. Secular commissions included Monkseaton Metro Station, Tyne and Wear; Guildhall, Durham; and entrance screen for Greatham Hospital. His main concern was "to render the image by the texture of light". Lived in Brandon, County Durham.

Myra DAVIS 1915–1994 Artist using charcoal, oil, pencil and collage, born in London, who attended Heatherley's School of Fine Art in the mid-1930s (Michael Ayrton was a contemporary), with Paul Drury as one teacher, also studying with André Lhote in Paris prior to World War II. Although her work attained a high standard, Davis was shy of exhibiting. Her first public show was in John Minton and Friends, at Michael Parkin Gallery, 1997. Minton was a friend, and they produced portraits of each other. Died in Sussex.

Noel Denholm DAVIS 1876–1950 Primarily a portrait painter, Davis was born in Nottingham, where he studied at the School of Art for five years in the 1890s and was then at the Royal Academy Schools. Worked for a decade in London as a portrait painter, but continued to show in Nottingham. Among his portraits were General William Booth of the Salvation Army and the Victoria Cross-holder Captain Albert Ball. He eventually returned to live in Nottingham and in 1929 his frescoes in the Council House Arcade were unveiled, showing scenes from city history. Died on a visit at Goring-on-Thames, Oxfordshire.

Pamela DAVIS fl. from 1970s– Painter of botanical subjects in a realistic style who studied at Twickenham College of Art. She was a founder-member of the Society of Botanical Artists, a vice-president of SWA, a member of RMS and Hilliard Society. In 1987 she won the Suzanne Lucas Award, in 1991 winning RMS Gold Memorial Bowl. Mixed exhibitions included Medici Gallery and Linda Blackstone Gallery, Pinner.

Percy Charles Clement DAVIS 1867– Watercolourist who served lifelong with the Great Western Railway. Exhibited BWS, of which he was a member, and widely in the Midlands and south Wales. Lived in Cambridge.

Peter DAVIS 1926– Painter, draughtsman and teacher, born in Brentford, Middlesex. He attended Ealing School of Art, 1941–5; Central School of Art (John Cass Institute), 1946–8, under Nicholas Egan and Stanley Spencer; then as a Royal Scholar was at Royal College of Art, 1948–51, teachers including John Nash, Ruskin Spear and John Minton. He lectured at Hammersmith School of Art, 1955–75, then at Chelsea School of Art, 1975–80, retiring to paint full-time. Davis' main works were Eros and Agape, Don Quixote and Gethsemane. Exhibitions included Piccadilly Gallery and Miami Beach, Florida. Solo shows included Felix Gallery, 1957; Pantiles, Tunbridge Wells, 1962; Framlingham Castle Gallery, 1965; and Aldeburgh, Suffolk, 1970. Lived in Metfield, Harleston, Norfolk.

Peter DAVIS 1972– Painter, born in Sutton, Surrey, who studied at Goldsmiths' College, 1990–3. Group exhibitions included Six Painters at Karsten Schubert, 1994, and Real Art at City Art Gallery in Southampton, 1995. Had a solo show at Karsten Schubert in 1994.

Philomena DAVIS 1949– Sculptor of works of a populist nature, born in London, who trained at City and Guilds of London Art School and Royal Academy Schools, winning the Gold Medal in 1973. She lived in Japan for over two years, studying Japanese art and architecture. Moved to Milton Keynes, Buckinghamshire, in 1980, opening a bronze foundry in New Bradwell. Milton Keynes Development Corporation commissioned her bronzes Dream Flight, Flying Carpet and High Flyer, sited in 1989 in the Shopping Building, Queens Court. In 1990 Davis was elected president of RBS.

Robin DAVIS 1925– Self-taught artist who was educated at Bournemouth Grammar School and St Catherine's College, Oxford, who began painting in 1956. Had solo exhibitions at Woodstock Gallery, 1960, St Martin's Gallery, 1962, New Vision Centre, 1964, and Aston University, Birmingham, 1965, showing Abstract Expressionist work. From 1966–79 Davis did little painting, training as a psychologist, psychotherapist and group analyst, restarting with wood collages and then paintings again, in an abstract style. His work was "full of skeletal forms, fractured images and eroded earth qualities which lead to an impression of continued disintegration and re-integration", as shown at Belgrave Gallery, 1995, to mark Davis' 70th birthday. Cornwall was for many years an important influence on Davis' output, "its rocky coastline, and the way in which the light plays on the sea", and he finally settled there, in Penzance.

Roger C DAVIS 1942– Sculptor, draughtsman, jeweller and teacher, born in Weymouth, Dorset. Became seriously interested in art aged 16, then from 1961–2 studied with the artist Sven Berlin at his New Forest studio. Spent three years on Isle of Portland familiarising himself with stone, then a decade involved in jewellery, abandoning this in 1979 to teach art at Weymouth Grammar School. Wales, Celtic cultures, mythology and poetry influenced his work. Exhibitions included solo show, Drunk on the Moon, Dorset County Museum, Dorchester, 1988.

Rosemary DAVIS fl. from late 1940s– Painter, draughtsman, illustrator and teacher, she won scholarships to Wallasey and Chelsea Schools of Art, 1945–7. As a freelance she concentrated on fashion illustration for magazines and newspapers and taught art to children before turning to fine art in 1981. Showed at Knapp and Heifer Galleries, with British Council in Cyprus and elsewhere.

Francis DAVISON 1919–1984 Painter and collagist, born in London. He was married to the artist Margaret Mellis. Davison was brought up by adoptive parents in France and England. After reading English and anthropology at Cambridge University he wrote poetry, then began to draw in 1946. Two years after he married Margaret Mellis, in 1948, they moved to Suffolk, running a smallholding at Syleham for much of the time, in 1976 settling in Southwold, where Davison died. By the early 1950s his paintings became simplified shapes, then in 1952 he became a collagist. Over the next 20 years reference to landscape disappeared and the colour range was extended. Davison said that he was the only true collagist, as he relied entirely on found, used and not painted papers, which were cut and fitted with great exactness. When he was half-paralysed Mellis would hold the papers while he tore them. Davison was included in the South Bank Centre touring show The Experience of Painting, in 1989. He had solo shows at Graves Art Gallery, Sheffield, 1981; Museum of Modern Art, Oxford, 1982; and Hayward Gallery, 1983. Redfern Gallery has mounted several posthumous exhibitions. Arts Council holds his work.

George Mark Oswald DAVY 1898–1983 Painter and sculptor, born in Doncaster, Yorkshire, who was by profession a soldier, his military training including Royal Military Academy. He had private teaching as an artist, 1904–15, attending Byam Shaw School, 1959–62, under Peter Garrard. Exhibitions included RBA, NS, RWS, RSA and Paris Salon, and he was vice-president of Chelsea Art Society. Imperial War Museum holds four works by Brigadier Davy, including a painting of the sinking of HMS *Eclipse* and two sculptures of Admiral of the Fleet Sir Algernon Willis, a former chairman of the museum's trustees. Davy lived latterly at Alyth, Perthshire.

Cedric DAWE 1906– Artist in conté crayon, born in London, who studied at Royal College of Art and elsewhere in London. He was by profession a film art director. Belonged to UA, also showing with RA, RI, ROI and RWS. Lived in Chartridge, Buckinghamshire.

Sidney DAWLSON 1917–1990 Artist in various media, born and lived in London, who worked for the daily parliamentary record *Hansard*. He studied at Central School of Arts and Crafts, 1937–8. Was a member of Free Painters and Sculptors, also exhibiting with RSMA, ROI, RBA and in the provinces. Solo shows included Loggia Gallery, 1975.

Denys DAWNAY 1921–1983 Versatile artist, educated at Westminster School, who attended the Euston Road School and who showed in its exhibitions and at RA. Developing diabetes as a child and tuberculosis as a young man hindered his pursuing a full artistic career. Dawnay was a close friend of King George VI and other members of the royal family. He suggested to the Duke of Edinburgh that he take up painting shortly after his marriage in 1947, giving him his first paintbox and easel, long in use; he subsequently helped Princess Margaret design a tea service, made by Spode in 1956, later in regular use at Kensington Palace; and he also gave painting instruction to the Prince of Wales. The Queen asked Dawnay to paint a game book, which was not finished, and he produced a book of dog caricatures for Lord Lambton, the dogs dressed as famous artists. Later in life, living in Scotland, Dawnay became an accomplished photographer and created a sensational garden. Dawnay's work was in the collections of Humphrey Brooke and Sir Houston Shaw-Stewart, Dawnay's step-brother and first cousin, Lord Salisbury, Lady Harrod, Lady Mersey and the royal family. He died in hospital at Greenock, Renfrewshire. He is sometimes referred to as Denis or Dennis Dawnay.

Alva DAWSON 1915– Artist and teacher, born in Leicester, who studied at Nottingham School of Art and part-time at Goldsmiths' College School of Art, 1933–8. She was head of art at Rock Hills Girls' School, Bromley, to 1975 and from 1947 was an art tutor in adult education in Nottingham, Bromley and Sevenoaks. Buildings, demolition, docks with shipping and roof tops were her principal subjects. She was president of Bromley Art Society and a member of Sevenoaks Art Club. Also exhibited at Keele University in Staffordshire, Sevenoaks Library and The Old Bakehouse Gallery, Sevenoaks. Lived in Sevenoaks, then in Chipstead, Kent.

Byron DAWSON 1896–1968 Artist, illustrator and teacher, born in Banbury, Oxfordshire, with a special interest in architectural subjects. As an engineering apprentice in Newcastle upon Tyne, where he settled, he was encouraged to study art at Armstrong College, teaching there until 1927. Success at the RA in 1928 launched his professional painting career, which soon was concentrated in the northeast of England, although Dawson did show briefly at RSA. Drew for the *Newcastle Journal*. Dawson contributed nine Lancashire scenes to the Pilgrim Trust *Recording Britain* project and was included in the 1990 show at the Victoria & Albert Museum, which holds his work, as do Laing Art Gallery in Newcastle and Shipley Art Gallery, Gateshead. His latter years until a final illness were marked by financial hardship.

Chris DAWSON 1942– Abstract sculptor in various materials and teacher, born in Liverpool. He studied at the School of Art there and Royal College of Art. Making forms that allowed people to become part of them, Dawson showed at AIA Gallery and Camden Arts Centre. He was eventually appointed to the staff of the University of East London.

David DAWSON 1960– Painter of abstracts on a large scale, born in north Wales. He did a foundation course at Cardiff College of Art, 1980–1, then an honours degree in fine art, painting, at Chelsea School of Art, 1984–7, completing his master's degree in painting at Royal College of Art, 1987–9. Dawson won a David Murray Studentship in 1988. He exhibited in group shows from the mid-1980s, including Young Masters at Solomon Gallery, 1987; The Abstract Connection at Flowers East, 1989; and at Cooling Gallery, 1991. In 1989 he was given an Artist of the Day solo show at Flowers East, chosen by Joe Tilson.

Edward DAWSON 1941– Painter who was born in Northumberland, where he was educated at Alnwick. He graduated from King's College, Durham University, 1960–4, teachers including Victor Pasmore. Was a member of NEAC, solo shows including a series at Edwin Pollard Art Gallery from 1985. Lived in Buckhorn Weston, Dorset.

Eric DAWSON 1918– Watercolourist and commercial artist, born in east London, who began drawing when very young. He was encouraged at his secondary school by his art master Rupert Shephard and gained a scholarship to West Ham Art School. During war service in North Africa and the Middle East Dawson drew for forces' publications, worked in camouflage and taught drawing in the Army School of Education at Beirut University. On demobilisation he chose commercial art as a career, for many years working as a freelance art director. After a first one-man show at Sally Hunter Fine Art in 1987 Dawson gave up all commercial work to concentrate on exhibiting. His series of solo shows included a second with Sally Hunter in 1991. Dawson's watercolours take a wry look at everyday life, contemporary and of his childhood.

Gladys DAWSON 1909– Artist in watercolour, line and wash, born in Rochdale, Lancashire, who sometimes exhibited under her married name Gladys Woodruff. She studied at Heatherley's School of Fine Art, 1936–9, teachers including R O Dunlop, Paul Drury and Frederic Whiting. She was successful in a number of commercial fields, such as textile designs for Liberty and Courtauld, greeting cards for Raphael Tuck and Valentine and book jackets. She was a member of RCamA from 1946, SWA from 1953, becoming its vice-president and president. Also exhibited with RI, RWA, Walker Art Gallery in Liverpool and elsewhere. She had a number of solo shows including several in Colwyn Bay, 1947–54; Trinidad, 1954; Kenya, 1963; and Bourne Hall, Epsom, 1974. Williamson Art Gallery in Birkenhead holds her work. She specialised in making watercolour records of windmills, castles and old buildings plus birds and the small animals of Britain. Lived in Banstead, Surrey.

Mabel DAWSON 1887–1965 Painter, decorator and embroiderer, born in Edinburgh, where she studied at the College of Art under William Walls and Frank Calderon. Exhibited her work, which regularly featured animals and birds, at RA, RSW and RSA especially, Royal Glasgow Institute of the Fine Arts and abroad. She did work for the Scottish Society for the Protection of Wild Birds in the 1930s. Newport Museum and Art Gallery holds her work. Lived in Edinburgh.

Montague DAWSON 1895–1973 Painter of ships and the sea in oil and watercolour. Born in London, Dawson studied under the noted marine painter Charles Napier Hemy. Contributing to Dawson's background were the fact that his grandfather had been the painter Henry Dawson, his father was a sea captain and Dawson himself served at sea during World War I and afterwards. After Royal Navy service he began painting full-time, contributing pictures to the RA, leading London and provincial galleries as well as showing overseas. His work is owned by the National Maritime Museum, provincial and foreign galleries. Dawson's clipper ships are distinctive, and he retains his position as a premier marine painter in the realist tradition regardless of changes in artistic fashion. Lived at Milford-on-Sea, Hampshire.

Patricia Vaughan DAWSON 1925– Printmaker, watercolourist and artist in papier mâché, and teacher, born in Liverpool. Until marriage in 1948 she showed under the name Patricia Wright. She studied at Croydon School of Art, 1941–5, under Reginald Marlow and Ruskin Spear. Some of her work was inspired by the writings of the novelist John Cowper Powys and was illustrated in *The Powys Review*. From 1945–6 Dawson worked in the studio of Raoh Schorr, a Swiss sculptor based in Chelsea; from 1946–8 taught art at Ashfold, a preparatory school; then in 1963–6 she lectured at the Tate Gallery. She produced a series of slide strips and booklets introducing art to children. Showed with LG, Bear Lane Gallery in Oxford, London Building Centre and elsewhere. Had a solo show at St John's, Smith Square. British Museum, Victoria Art Gallery in Bath and other provincial collections hold her work. Lived in Ludlow, Shropshire.

Peter DAWSON 1947– Artist in oil, watercolour and mixed media and teacher, born in Leeds, Yorkshire. He studied at Bingley College of Education, 1967–71, teachers including Robert Lee. Until 1979 Dawson painted almost entirely in oils, mainly the human figure; there followed several years' experiment with watercolours; some years of exploration, involving buildings and things seen during extensive travels; then work affirming past interests and using objects such as Egyptian wall paintings, icons and Islamic miniatures. Was elected RI in 1982. Solo shows began with Anthony Parton Gallery, Bradford, 1972, later ones including Luton Art Gallery, 1982. In 1989 Dawson was co-author and co-illustrator with his wife Andrea of *Albania – a Guide and Illustrated Journal*. Many of Dawson's pictures were in public and private collections, some being published as limited editions, posters and reproduction prints. Lived in Little Hadham, Hertfordshire.

Phyllis DAWSON 1903– Illustrator and wood engraver, born in London. She studied at Clapham School of Art with William Washington, then at Canterbury School of Art under John Austen. Drew for magazines and showed at RBA and in the Kent area. Work in Canterbury Royal Museum. Lived in Canterbury.

P Norman DAWSON 1902– Painter and teacher, born in Chadderton, Lancashire. He had a widespread education, including Glasgow University, universities in Canada, Royal College of Art, 1921–7, where his teachers included Frank Short, the British School in Rome and elsewhere abroad. He held a number of teaching appointments, including Camberwell and Winchester Schools of Arts and Crafts and the principalship of the Southern College of Art. Exhibited LG, Leicester Galleries, Cooling Galleries, London Gallery and at the Museum of Modern Art, New York, which holds his work. Lived in Winchester, Hampshire.

Rhoda DAWSON 1897–1992 Artist and craftsman, born in London where she died, daughter of the artists Nelson and Edith Dawson. She married the sculptor John Bickerdike. After St Paul's School Dawson attended Hammersmith School of Art and then the Royal Academy Schools, where her teachers included Walter Sickert. She then worked for Heal's Art Gallery until 1930, when she went for some years to Newfoundland and Labrador to join the Grenfell Medical Mission. There she taught crafts and rug design, examples including her own work being shown at Canada House in 1991. After returning to England Dawson studied anthropology briefly at London School of Economics, aided Bickerdike with models for the Museum of Ghana and worked in Gunnersbury Museum. She had a show of her Canadian watercolours at Fine Art Society in 1989, and a large group was bought by the Memorial University Art Gallery in St John's.

Robert DAWSON fl. from c.1900–1948 Decorative designer, painter, craftsman and teacher, born in Bingley, Yorkshire, where he eventually returned. After studying at Royal College of Art Dawson was assistant master there for two years, was headmaster of Belfast Municipal School of Art for 18 years, then became principal of Manchester's equivalent School, 1919–39, where he greatly expanded its role in the region. He showed at RHA, RA and Walker Art Gallery in Liverpool.

Harold Armstrong Edward DAY 1924– Painter of landscape in a rather naive style, born in Crewe, Cheshire, who obtained a Ford Scholarship and qualified as a mechanical engineer. Went on to deal in pictures in Eastbourne, Sussex, as Eastbourne Fine Art, his son John taking over the business in the early 1970s. Wrote a number of books on Constable, Stannard and the East Anglian painters. *Day's Diary* described a year's dealing and *I Harold* was his diary as an artist after moving to Nedlands, Perth, Australia. Day built up a collection of Australian artists.

Pamela DAY 1953– Painter and teacher, born in Halifax, Yorkshire. She studied at Percival Whitley College of Further Education there, 1971–2, then Byam Shaw School of Art, 1972–5. After Royal Academy Schools, 1975–8, Day was at University of London Goldsmiths' College ATC Department, 1979–80. Taught in London for a year, then from 1982 at Stourbridge College of Technology and Art. Among Day's Awards were Eric Kennington Prize, Armitage Prize and Landseer Prize at Royal Academy Schools. Shows included RA Summer Exhibition from 1977; Pictures for Schools at National Museum of Wales, Cardiff, 1978; Two Young Painters at Chalmers Art Gallery, 1980; and Woodlands Art Gallery Goldsmiths' show, 1983.

Paul DAY 1967– Sculptor of reliefs, notably in terracotta, and draughtsman, who did a foundation course at Colchester Institute, 1987–8; attended Dartington College of Arts, 1988–9; and gained an honours degree in fine art at Cheltenham School of Art, 1989–91. Although featuring modern people and settings, Day's reliefs had a magical, poetic quality and included recurring images such as sleepers and staircases. Awards included The Sir Alfred Munnings Prize, 1988; Prince's Trust Award, 1991; and The Taylor Foundation Prize, Salon des Artistes Français, 1993. Among commissions was the Conversation Triptych, for Hilton International's headquarters at Watford, 1996. Group shows included Fresh Art, Business Design Centre, Islington, 1991, and Unicorn Pictures Ltd, Palace of Westminster, 1997. Had a solo show at Cheltenham Museum and Art Gallery, 1992; a series in France; then Duncan Campbell Contemporary Art, 1997. Houses of Parliament and Lord Archer hold examples.

Michael DAYKIN 1947– Artist, teacher, exhibition organiser, studio manager and editor, who studied at Watford School of Art, 1970–1, St Martin's School of Art, 1971–4, and Royal College of Art, 1974–7, there gaining his master's degree. He won the Oppenheim-John Downes Memorial Award. After teaching at Havering Technical College, 1978–84, Daykin taught extensively in England and America, latterly at Barnfield College, Luton, and Middlesex Polytechnic from 1991. Organised extensive exhibitions, notably at Black Bull and St James' Galleries, 1989–92. Between 1980–93 was founder and partner, Metropolitan Wharf and Cable Street Studios. For periods in the 1980s he was listings editor for *London Art & Artists Guide* and *Art Line Magazine*. Mixed exhibitions included Stowells Invitation, Mall Galleries, 1972; San Mateo University, California, 1976; Air Gallery, 1984; XO Gallery, 1992; and Gallery K, 1995. Later solo and two-man exhibitions included Studio Gallery, 1984, and XO, 1991. Benchmark Holdings; Musée d'Art Contemporaire, in Skopje; Northern Arts; and Quaglino's hold examples. Lived in London.

Charles Ernest DEACON fl. c.1934–1965 Watercolourist who studied at Richmond School of Art. Exhibited RA, RBA, RI,

RWS, of which he was an honorary member, RCamA, SMA, Paris Salon and widely in the provinces. Lived at High Wycombe, Buckinghamshire.

Richard DEACON 1949– Sculptor and teacher, born in Bangor, Caernarvonshire. He studied at Somerset College of Art, St Martin's School of Art and Royal College of Art, 1968–77. Went on to teach at Central School of Art and Bath Academy of Art. The artist became caught up in the movement to redefine the ways of making sculpture and its purpose. He worked in a variety of materials, ranging from metal and wood to linoleum, and was especially interested in day-to-day objects such as pots and chairs. The German poet Rainer Maria Rilke and the philosopher Martin Heidegger aided Deacon's studies of language and meaning. As well as taking part in key group shows Deacon had many one-man exhibitions, including Sheffield Polytechnic Gallery, Riverside Studios, Lisson Gallery and Serpentine Gallery, 1997. He was included in the Arts Council's 1993–4 tour Recent British Sculpture. Public commissions include University of Warwick and Bank Centre in Auckland, both in 1991, and Musée d'Art Moderne, Villeneuve d'Ascq, France, 1992. Arts Council and Saatchi Collection hold his work. Elected RA, 1998.

Liz DEAKIN 1929– Artist in various media and teacher. She studied at Poole School of Art, 1948. Showed with SWA of which she was a member and elsewhere. Lived in Butts Knapp, Shaftesbury, Dorset.

Cyril DEAKINS 1916– Painter, draughtsman, printmaker and teacher, born in Bearwood, near Birmingham. He studied at Hornsey College of Art, 1934–40 and 1946–7, teachers including J C Moody, Norman Janes and Douglas Percy Bliss, his studies interrupted by Army service. He taught at Edmonton County School, 1947–8; lectured in illustration at Willesden School of Art, 1949–52; was art editor for Iliffe & Sons, 1953–7; was a free-lance illustrator, 1957–71; then from 1971–81 was head of art at St John Payne School, Chelmsford. Deakins showed with RA, NEAC, RBA, RI and RE. His solo shows included Reade Gallery, Aldeburgh, 1973, and a retrospective at Thaxted Guildhall, 1986. Victoria & Albert Museum and South London Art Gallery hold his work. Lived in Great Dunmow, Essex. The artist Tom Deakins was his son.

George DEAKINS 1911–c.1982 Painter in oil, self-taught, born in Gosport of a naval family. Deakins served with the Royal Navy for 22 years from 1927. During this time he exhibited throughout the world, with over 60 one-man shows. When he retired he opened a studio at Dunster, Somerset, where he lived.

Tom DEAKINS 1957– Painter, especially of the East Anglian landscape, and teacher, born in Essex, son of the artist Cyril Deakins, growing up at Duton Hill, near Dunmow. Gained a fine art honours degree at Newcastle Polytechnic, 1980, then an art teacher's certificate, Leeds Polytechnic, 1982. Taught full-time from 1982–4, then part-time 1984–91, at Felstead, Essex. Mixed exhibitions included RA Summer Exhibitions from 1983; from 1984 at ROI, where he was several times a finalist in the Winsor and Newton Young Artists Award; 1988 onwards at Fry Gallery in Saffron Walden; and in 1992 at Khoetsu Fine Art, Tokyo. Had a solo exhibition at Medici Gallery, 1989; William Hardie, Glasgow, 1991; and Chappel Galleries, Chappel, 1995. Year before was elected chairman of Dunmow Art Group. Newcastle University, Beecroft Art Gallery in Southend and Epping Forest District Museum hold examples.

Joxé de ALBERDI 1922– Sculptor and teacher, born in Azcoitia, Spain, where he was initially educated. Studied art in San Sebastian and London. For a time he lectured at St Martin's School of Art and at Sir John Cass School of Arts and Crafts. Showed RA, LG, NS and in the provinces. Lived in London but returned to Spain in the early 1970s, where he also exhibited. His aluminium Abstract Form, 1972, was sited in Stevenage New Town.

Catherine DEAN 1905–1983 Painter and teacher, married to the artist Albert Houthuesen. She was born in Liverpool where she attended the School of Art, then Royal College of Art. She lectured in art at St Gabriel's Training College in London, where she lived. Late in life she showed with Mercury Gallery. Tate Gallery holds her picture Sheep's Skull and Ferns.

Frank DEAN 1865–1947 Painter, born in Headingley, Leeds, Yorkshire, who studied at Slade School of Fine Art and in Paris. He travelled widely in North Africa, the Middle East and India and lived in various parts of England. Was a prolific exhibitor, showing Fine Art Society, RSA, ROI, Walker Art Gallery in Liverpool, NEAC and elsewhere. For a time Dean was a member of RBA.

Graham DEAN 1951– Watercolourist who worked on a large scale, concerned with the human figure and using a bright palette. Dean was born at Birkenhead, Merseyside. He attended Laird School of Art there, 1968–70, was at Bristol Polytechnic faculty of art and design for three years, was a full-time painter from 1974, then in 1991 was awarded a Senior Abbey Award in Painting at British School in Rome for 1992. Dean was also involved in a number of films and collaborated with Darshan Singh Bhuller of London Contemporary Dance on several productions. Dean participated in many mixed shows after appearing with British Realists at Ikon Gallery, Birmingham, in 1976, both in Britain and abroad. He had a solo show at Bristol Arts Centre in 1973, others including several exhibitions with Nicholas Treadwell Gallery from 1974, Roundhouse in 1982, Austin/Desmond Fine Art from 1988 and Nerlino Gallery in New York from 1989. Arts Council, Contemporary Art Society and Victoria & Albert Museum plus several foreign collections hold his work.

John DEAN 1930– Self-taught artist, born and lived in Grassington, North Yorkshire. He was a notable painter of his home area, producing large oils as well as piano key ivory miniatures. He trained as a master butcher, worked in farming and the building trade and was an experienced dry stone waller. Took up painting after leaving the Army in 1950. Dean was a fellow of the British Society of Painters and a member of RMS and SM. Shell Oil and John Ward Textiles hold his work.

Margaret DEAN fl. from 1960s– Painter, muralist and teacher, born in Lancashire, married to the sculptor Roger Dean. She trained at Liverpool College of Art and obtained a European travelling scholarship in 1963. From then she taught in a number of art colleges in Britain; at the Red Deer College of Arts in Alberta, Canada; and from 1990 at Exeter Community Centre, for Devon County Council. Showed widely in mixed exhibitions in London, the provinces and North America, solo exhibitions including Kayler and Spacex Galleries in Exeter, Bluecoat Gallery in Liverpool, Compendium Gallery in Birmingham and Bowes Museum, County Durham. She completed site-specific works for Oxford Architects' Partnership, 1983–6, and a large mural for Exeter City Swimming Pool, 1984. City councils in Exeter, Liverpool, Manchester and Plymouth hold examples. Lived at Pennsylvania, Exeter, Devon.

Roger DEAN 1937– Sculptor and teacher, born in Warrington, Lancashire, who modelled in clay, cast into a variety of materials. He studied at Liverpool College of Art, 1953–9, under Philip Hartas and George Yoonson, then spent several months at Brera Academy in Milan under Marino Marini. Teaching experience included Bradford and Liverpool Colleges of Art, Red Deer College in Canada and eventually Exeter College of Art, where Dean was head of sculpture. He was also external examiner to many colleges. Dean said that the main influences at the start of his career were Rodin and Germaine Richier, "work concerned with the structure and mechanics of organic forms within a literal framework, dealing with the cycle from birth to death and the regeneration thereafter". Main works were Armillary Sphere, Customs House, Exeter, 1991; Market Arch Relief Sculptures, Ilfracombe, 1992; and Memorial Fountain, fiftieth anniversary of the Exeter Blitz, 1993. Mixed shows included John Moores Liverpool Exhibition, where he was a prize winner, 1964; Millfield Open Exhibition, and Peri-Renneth Gallery, New York. Had a series of solo shows including Bluecoat Gallery in Liverpool; Compendium Gallery, Birmingham; Lane Gallery, Bradford; Exe Gallery, Exeter; and the University there and at Keele. Walker Art Gallery, Liverpool; Atkinson Art Gallery, Southport; Keele University, Crewe & Alsager College in Staffordshire and Gulbenkian Foundation hold examples. Lived in Pennsylvania, Exeter, Devon. His wife Margaret was also an artist.

Ronald DEAN 1929– Self-taught artist who was by profession an insurance broker. Born in Farnborough, Hampshire, he attended the local Grammar School. Became a member of RSMA in 1970, also showing at RBA, National Maritime Museum in Greenwich, with Tonbridge Art Group of which he was a member, and abroad. Lived in Bidborough, Kent.

Tacita DEAN 1965– Artist who employed film and installation, studied at Slade School of Fine Art, 1990–2. Among her awards were BT New Contemporaries Award Winner, 1992; Arts Council of Great Britain Film and Video Award and Barclays Young Artist Award, runner-up, both 1993; London Arts Board, 1994; and FRAC Award in Bourges, France, 1995. Group shows included Six Slade Students, Rijksakademie, Amsterdam, 1992; Peripheral States at Benjamin Rhodes Gallery, 1993; Dew of Gold, Frith Street Gallery, 1995; and British Art Show 4, with tour, 1995–6. Her Foley Artists solo show was at the Tate Gallery, 1996.

Angela DEANE: *see* **Angela THORNE**

Frederick DEANE 1924– Portrait painter, born in Manchester, where he studied at the Junior School of Art, Manchester College of Art, 1940–2, then the Royal Academy Schools, 1946–51, taught by Philip Connard. Had several one-man shows. He did a number of portraits in a formal style of notable people and dignitaries, including the writer Lord David Cecil. Manchester City Art Gallery holds his portrait of Edward John Stanley, Earl of Derby. Chelsea Arts Club member who lived at Donnington, Berkshire.

Chris DEARDEN 1941– Painter in watercolour and oil and teacher, born in Halifax, Yorkshire, who studied at Huddersfield School of Art. He was a textile designer in Bradford and Belfast for 18 years, from 1982 teaching landscape painting. Settled in Ireland from 1973, living at Greenisland, County Antrim. Dearden was an associate of RUA and a member of Ulster Watercolour Society. Also showed with RHA; Narrow Water Gallery, Warrenpoint; Kelly Hotel, Wexford, annual show from 1988; and at Dublin Castle, 1995. Among awards was the Queen's Award for Export, 1978. Had many solo shows, including a series at Queen's University, Belfast, also Ulster Arts Club, Newry Art Centre, Seymour Gallery in Lisburn, Trooperslane Gallery, Carrick, and Cavehill Gallery, Belfast. HRH The Prince of Wales, BBC, Albert Reynolds the former Irish prime minister and many private collections in Britain and abroad hold examples.

Harold DEARDEN 1888–1962 Painter in oil and watercolour, draughtsman in ink and wash. Dearden studied at Rochdale School of Art under H Barrett Carpenter, 1905–10, then at the Royal College of Art for five years under Gerald Moira. Dearden, a strong draughtsman, went on to become head of Swindon Art School for 30 years from 1920 and was president for a time of Swindon Artists' Society. He exhibited in London and provincial galleries and Swindon Museum and Art Gallery holds his work. Lived in Swindon.

Alison DEBENHAM 1903–1967 Painter, whose work was closely concerned with her family, London house and the south of France. Family money – her father, Sir Ernest Debenham, ran the store business – enabled her to choose her life. After a finishing school in Paris she entered Slade School of Fine Art for several years in 1921, in 1928 moving to Paris, in 1929 to south of France where she studied with Simon Bussy and met painters and writers such as Matisse and André Gide. Married the artist René Leplat in 1930. They showed at Galerie Vignon, Paris, Alison in 1932. In 1935 had a show at Zwemmer Gallery, London, and was associated with the Euston Road painters. There was a memorial show at Richmond Hill Gallery, 1968, another show at Belgrave Gallery in 1976.

De BRUYNE: *see* **Dexter BROWN**

Coralie de BURGH: *see* **Coralie KINAHAN**

Lydia de BURGH 1923– Painter in oil and watercolour, notable for her portraits, born in London. As a child she was taught by Ruth Stalder, of Switzerland. Later in London she studied privately with Sonia Mervyn the portrait painter, 1948–51, more teaching coming from Byam Shaw School of Art, 1952, and Edward Wesson. She was elected RUA, 1984, being a member of Chelsea Art Society, SWLA, Ulster Watercolour Society and the Ulster Society of Women Artists. Also exhibited at RP, RBA and Royal Glasgow Institute of the Fine Arts. Solo shows included Ulster Office, London, 1956. Most of de Burgh's work was commissioned. She had a contract with Rowland Ward Gallery in London and Nairobi from 1960–9 to paint African wildlife. Painted HM The Queen and other members of the royal family from personal sittings. Her autobiography, *Lydia's Story*, was published in 1991. Lived in Clough, County Down, Northern Ireland. Her sister was the artist Coralie Kinahan.

John DEE 1938– Sculptor, born in Northampton, who studied at Reading University and Slade School of Fine Art. He was included in the Arts Council's touring Contemporary British Sculpture of 1966, by which time his work was "a synthesis of the forms of art known as 'painting' and 'sculpture', 'costructivism and 'surrealism'", he said. The Arts Council acquired Dee's 1966 abstract work Revelation, in fibreglass and plywood. Also took part in mixed shows at AIA Gallery and Leeds (Merrion Centre) National Sculpture Competition, in which he won a prize. Solo shows included Hull University, 1966.

Geoffrey DEELEY 1911– Sculptor and teacher, born in Netherton, Worcestershire. He studied sculpture at Wolverhampton School of Art and Royal College of Art, winning Prix de Rome which enabled him to study in Rome in 1935. The relief with which he won the prize was bought by Dudley Art Gallery and is called The Conquest of Air by Man. Deeley went on to become head of sculpture at Goldsmiths' College School of Art, retiring in 1975. Deeley's Staindrop Sandstone sculpture Christ and Mary Magdalene, in Gornal Wood Crematorium Garden of Remembrance in Dudley, completed in 1962, has slightly Primitivist tendencies, in the manner of Epstein.

Polly de FALBE 1961– Painter, notable for still life, who studied at Slade School of Fine Art, gaining a bachelor's degree, 1979–83. Mixed shows included Christie's Pick of Graduate Art, Wigmore Hall Foyer, 1983; Kingsgate Workshop Gallery, from 1985; and Blenheim Gallery, 1988. Shared a show with David Drey at Bartley Drey Gallery, 1995.

Georges F M de FOSSARD 1898– Painter, miniaturist, illustrator and mural artist. He studied under the portrait painter Robin Watt, 1924–6, then at St Martin's School of Art, 1927–8. Exhibited SGA, PS, RMS, NS and elsewhere. Lived for a time in London.

Robert de FRESNES 1908– Painter in oil and watercolour, subjects including portraits, thoroughbred racehorses, still life and flowers. He was a member of the Interior Decorators and Designers' Association and acted as a consultant designer. Born in Glasgow, de Fresnes' original name was Conroy-Robertson; he assumed the title of Baron de Fresnes by deed poll in 1944. He studied art in France, Italy and America from 1934–9, having been at Glasgow School of Art, 1930, under W O Hutchison. His work was held by many private collections in Britain and abroad. Lived in Galston, near Kilmarnock, Ayrshire.

Paul DEGGAN 1932– Painter who attended Chichester High School in Sussex. Studied at Kingston School of Art, 1945, under Reginald Brill, then at Chichester School of Art, 1952–3. Showed at RA, LG, Young Contemporaries, Piccadilly Gallery and David Paul Gallery, Chichester.

Wilfred Gabriel de GLEHN 1870–1951 Painter, born in London, studied at the South Kensington Schools and École des Beaux-Arts, Paris. Married to the painter Jane de Glehn. Early on in his career de Glehn began exhibiting at the Paris Salon, RA and NEAC, as well as Fine Art Society, Leicester Galleries RP, RA, RHA and at many other venues. First one-man show at Carfax Gallery, 1908. De Glehn travelled widely, which provided many of his subjects and additional exhibition venues. He was a painter of beautiful people and places, rather in the manner of John Singer Sargent. Elected RA, 1932. David Messum held an exhibition in 1989. Lived at Stratford Tony, near Salisbury, Wiltshire.

Jules de GOEDE 1937– Abstract painter and sculptor and teacher, born in Rotterdam, Netherlands. He studied at Academie voor Beeldende Kunsten en Kunstnieverheid, Arnhem, 1953–5; Eindhoven School of Art, 1955–61; Orban School of Art, Sydney, Australia, 1957–9, then Canberra School of Art, 1959–61. He went on to be associate senior lecturer at Middlesex Polytechnic, visiting other colleges. De Goede showed with Young Contemporaries in Sydney, 1966, followed by extensive mixed exhibitions in Britain and abroad, including Five Dutch Artists, Serpentine Gallery, 1974; Arts Council Collection, Design Centre, 1989; and Unilever Collection, International Art Fair, Olympia, 1991. Showed at Studio Nundah, Canberra, solo from 1963, with a series at Grabowski Gallery from 1967, and House Gallery from 1979, later one-mans including XO Gallery, 1992. Arts Council,

Contemporary Art Society and provincial galleries in Newcastle and Bristol hold his work. Lived in London.

Roger de GREY 1918–1995 Landscape painter and teacher, born in Penn, Buckinghamshire, nephew of the painter Spencer Gore and married to artist Flavia Irwin. Was at Chelsea School of Art, 1936–9 and again 1946–7, his teachers including Ceri Richards, Robert Medley and Raymond Coxon. His time at Chelsea was divided with Army service in World War II. Taught at King's College, Newcastle upon Tyne, 1947–54, then until 1973 at Royal College of Art, when he became principal of City and Guilds of London Art School. From 1984–93 he was president of the RA, having been elected in 1969 and treasurer for a time. He showed at RA and New Art Centre, having had his first one-man exhibition at Agnew, 1954. De Grey's landscapes, near his studio in Kent or house in the Charente Maritime, France, were quiet in colour and orderly in construction and were given a memorial show at RA in 1996. Tate Gallery and Arts Council hold de Grey's work. He was knighted in 1991.

Bryan de GRINEAU 1883–1957 Draughtsman, illustrator, painter and printmaker, born and lived in London. He was christened Charles William de Grineau and published early work as John Bryan. His father was the artist Alfred Bryan and the son drew from an early age in his studio. During World War I de Grineau served as captain and adjutant in the 41st Brigade, Royal Field Artillery, and sent home vivid sketches from the front for *Illustrated London News* and *Illustrated War News*. For some years after 1919 he lived abroad because of shell-shock, studying with Maurice Denis in Paris and Joseph Pennell in New York. In 1939 de Grineau had a solo show of Caribbean drawings at Walker's Galleries. He became noted for his motor racing pictures, early achievements in aviation and architecture, having a special ability to depict cars at speed. Fine examples were included in the Royal Automobile Club's Diamond Jubilee Exhibition which toured Britain in 1957. The artist also drew for the *Sporting and Dramatic News*, covered events such as the Queen's wedding and coronation and was *Illustrated London News* special correspondent in World War II. Some 237 drawings by him from the magazine's archive are held by the Imperial War Museum at Duxford Airfield.

Anthony DEIGAN 1945– Painter, printmaker, collagist, draughtsman and teacher, born in Ireland. Moved to Essex as a boy and studied at Walthamstow, then at Maidstone College of Art, 1964–7. In 1968 won an Anglo-French Scholarship to study printmaking in Paris. From that year he taught at St Martin's School of Art. Deigan travelled widely in Australia and Indonesia, where he also taught. Had a first solo show at Editions Alecto in 1969, otherwise appearing at Bradford International Print Biennale, RA, Kettle's Yard in Cambridge and abroad. Deigan painted several murals in Saffron Walden, Essex, where the Fry Art Gallery holds his work. It is also in the collections of Fitzwilliam Museum in Cambridge, British Council and Sheffield University. Lived in Saffron Walden for some years.

Brian DEIGHTON 1950– Painter and teacher, born in Harrogate, Yorkshire. He attended Byam Shaw School of Art as a mature student as well as Goldsmiths' College School of Art, his teachers including Robin Klassnik and Wynn Jones. The work of Joel Fisher and Tony Bevan were influences. After gaining his master's degree Deighton went on to teach part-time. He was a founder-member of the Riverside Artists Group, 1986, showing in Soviet Union in 1988–9. Public art projects participated in were Shepherd's Bush and Shaftesbury Mosaics, 1989–91. His work was included in East & South Norwich Gallery/Kent Institute of Art and Design show, 1992. Lived in London.

Dorrit DEKK 1917– Painter, printmaker and designer, born in Brno, Czechoslovakia. She studied at Kunstgewerbe Schule, Vienna, 1936–8, then Reimann School, London, 1938–9. After working as a radio intelligence officer in the Women's Royal Naval Service in World War II Dekk began a career in graphic design. She worked for Central Office of Information, 1946–8; was a stage designer and illustrator in Cape Town, 1949; then between 1950–79 was in private practice in London, where she continued to live, clients including Air France, British Rail and London Transport. She illustrated several books. Was elected a fellow of the Society of Industrial Artists in 1956. Dekk returned to painting after a design career, having a fascination with back streets and their inhabitants, markets and ruins in Britain and abroad. Mixed shows included Barbican Centre, The Best of British Naive Artists, 1984; Sue Rankin Gallery, 1987; and Edith Grove Gallery, 1988. Solo shows included Clarendon Gallery, 1984–86 and Maltings Gallery, Farnham, 1985.

Lucette de la FOUGÈRE fl. from 1950s– Painter and ceramist, born in London where she continued to live. She was educated there and in France, studying art with Léopold Pascal, her husband. She was a member at various times of Free Painters and Sculptors, ROI, RBA and NS, also exhibiting at RA Summer Exhibitions. Had a solo show at Mall Galleries. National Museum of Wales, Cardiff, holds her work.

Muriel de la HAYE 1937– Painter in oil and teacher, born in Oldham, Lancashire, who studied in the early 1950s at Manchester Regional College of Art under L S Lowry. She taught art for five years, spent eight years with Jersey Potteries in the Channel Islands, then lived and worked in Wales at Borth, Dyfed. Her work was "mainly figurative, colour and composition almost as important as Expressionistic approach to figures in landscape". From 1970 took part in many exhibitions in Wales and in 1994 won first prize in an open competition, The Sea, The Sea, at Y Tabernacl, Museum of Modern Art, Machynlleth. She showed solo there, also at Oldham Library Art Gallery and in Aberystwyth at the Museum and the Arts Centre. Y Tabernacl holds her work.

Louise de la HEY 1959– Painter, born in London where she continued to work. She attended Byam Shaw School of Drawing and Painting, 1977–81, then in 1982 worked in Italy. She was a resonant Colourist, fond of still life and interiors. Her work appeared in RBA, RA, Newburgh Street Gallery, Charlotte Lampard Gallery and other mixed shows. In 1990 she shared an exhibition at Cadogan Contemporary.

Barbara DELANEY 1941– Painter, draughtsman and teacher, born in Osnabrueck, Germany, who was married to Patrick Delaney, a student of Peter Lanyon. She studied at Central School of Art and Design, 1968. Gained an Arts Council Award, 1972; a Greater London Arts Award, 1976; and was a finalist for a Gregory Fellowship, Leeds University, 1978. From 1979–85 was a part-time lecturer in fine art (painting) at de Montfort University, Leicester; Kingston University; and Camberwell College of Art. Group shows included Kansas City Art Institute, America, 1975; Anne Berthoud and Redfern Galleries, both 1980; New York Contemporary Art Fair, 1992; Hong Kong Contemporary Art Fair, 1995; and Art96, 1996. Solo exhibitions included Air Gallery/Surrey University, Guildford, 1978; Atkinson Art Gallery and Museum, Southport, 1979; Sally East Gallery, 1981; and Bassetlaw Museum, Retford, 1996. Of her abstract works Delaney said: "After-images interest me, also double images: a thing being more than itself – reflections in water, on glass", or "music like Satie's piano works, or jazz". Public collections holding examples include Government Art Collection; Contemporary Art Society; Brunel, Open, Southampton and Surrey Universities; and Nuffield Foundation. Lived in London.

Elise D'ELBOUX 1870– Painter, draughtsman and teacher, born in Southampton, daughter of the artist Walter D'Elboux. She studied at Hartley Institute School of Art, Royal College of Art, Académie Julian in Paris, Camden School of Art and Chelsea School of Art with Ernest Borough Johnson. Signing her work E D' E, she exhibited at RA, Walker Art Gallery in Liverpool, RSA and elsewhere. She held a number of teaching positions, including Royal College of Art, 1897–1901. Lived in London.

Lillian DELEVORYAS 1932– Artist and designer, born in Chicopee Falls, Massachusetts, America. She studied at Pratt Institute in Brooklyn, graduating from Cooper Union for the Advancement of Science and Art. She exhibited in mixed and solo shows in Britain, America and Germany, one-mans including Medici Galleries. Temple Newsam, Leeds, holds her work. Lived in Stroud, Gloucestershire.

Denys DELHANTY 1925– Painter and teacher, born in Cardiff, where Delhanty attended the College of Art, 1942–4 and 1947–50. From 1951–64 was then head of art department at Cheltenham Ladies' College, other posts including senior lectureship at Gloucestershire College of Education. Took part in many group shows, including RWA, Cheltenham Group of Artists, Royal National Eisteddfod, SWG and SEA. National Museum of Wales in Cardiff, RWA and WAC hold work.

DELLA: *see* **Della HOLLOW**

Ron DELLAR 1930– Self-taught artist in watercolour and oil, born in London. He worked "in solitude and without any external connections". Dellar showed at RP, New Art Centre, Leicester Galleries, *Daily Express* Young Contemporaries and elsewhere in mixed exhibitions. Showed solo at Archer Gallery and several times in Germany. He did a quantity of magazine and other commercial work. The Rother levels in Romney Marsh were a feature of his later pictures. Lived in Rye, Sussex.

Jeff DELLOW 1949– Painter and teacher, born in Newcastle upon Tyne. He studied at St Martin's School of Art, 1968–9, Maidstone College of Art, 1969–71 and Slade School of Fine Art, 1972–4, followed by a Cheltenham Fellowship, 1974–5. He then went on to appear nationally in group shows, including John Moores Exhibition, Liverpool, in 1976, 1989 and 1991–2, when he was a prizewinner. He had solo shows at Castlefield Gallery, Manchester, 1988, and Todd Gallery, 1989. Dellow was also an Athena Awards prizewinner in 1988. Was head of painting at Kingston Polytechnic. Lived in London.

Koert DELMONTE 1913– Painter and black-and-white artist, born in Amsterdam, Netherlands. Studied there and in Brussels. As well as showing on the continent, in England he exhibited with Wildenstein, Redfern Gallery and RA. British Transport used his posters. Lived in Purley, Surrey.

George Frederick DEMAINE 1892–1966 Architectural sculptor and landscape painter, notably in watercolour, born in Keighley, Yorkshire. Studied at the local School of Art, then gained a West Riding County School Scholarship to Royal College of Art, winning his diploma in 1921, and an exhibition. Showed at RA, RWA, Alpine Club Gallery and Cartwright Hall, Bradford, main works including Westminster Embankment, Hampstead Heath and Poole Harbour. Joined Art Workers' Guild in 1950. Lived in London and in Bushey Heath, Hertfordshire.

Richard DEMARCO 1930– Artist, illustrator, gallery director and teacher, born in Edinburgh, where he continued to live. He studied at the College of Art there, 1949–53, then after Army service in 1954–6 was art master at Duns Scotus Academy, 1956–7. In 1963 Demarco was a founder-member of Traverse Theatre. The 1960s also saw him launch the Richard Demarco Gallery and become elected to SSA and RSW. The gallery became a focal point for innovative art and theatre, and in 1975 Demarco gained a Scottish Arts Council Award for services to the contemporary Scottish art world. Demarco was closely involved in promoting eastern European events in Britain, in 1976 gaining the Gold Award of the Polish People's Republic. He directed the Edinburgh Arts Summer School, was closely involved in the Edinburgh Festival and was a visiting lecturer at over 50 educational institutions in Europe and North America. Red tape and reliable funding were problems Demarco enterprises commonly encountered. Demarco's publications included *The Artist as Explorer*, 1978, and *The Road to Meikle Seggie*, 1979. He published a number of suites of prints, including *The*

Malta Suite for Editions Alecto, 1970. Victoria & Albert Museum, Scottish Arts Council and Philadelphia Museum of Art hold his work.

Adrien de MENASCE: *see* **MENASCE**

Rosalie de MERIC 1916– Painter in oil and acrylic, draughtsman and teacher, born in Weymouth, Dorset. Her earliest training was with the Vorticist artist Claude Flight in France and Dorset. Then studied with Mark Gertler and Bernard Meninsky at Westminster School of Art, 1936–9; at St Martin's and Central Schools, 1939–45; at Medway School of Art, Rochester, 1945–8; then obtained an honours degree in fine art from Norwich School of Art, 1984–7. Her early work was landscape, followed by a series of imaginative allegorical pictures, a period of Abstract Expressionism, hard-edge geometric acrylic pictures, then a return to landscape from 1983. De Meric, who was married to the poet Thomas Blackburn, was a fellow of Free Painters and Sculptors. She showed at Leeds, Bradford and Wakefield public galleries, Grabowski and Drian Galleries as well as abroad. Later solo exhibitions included Halesworth Gallery, Halesworth, 1989. Between 1963–77 de Meric was a lecturer at Sir John Cass School of Art, London College of Printing and Croydon College of Art. Lived for many years at Westleton, Suffolk.

Cathy de MONCHAUX 1962– Sculptor of enigmatically titled, often richly ornamented works, created from a variety of materials who was born and continued to live in London. She studied at Camberwell School of Arts and Crafts, 1980–3, and Goldsmiths' College School of Art, 1985–7. She gained a Steinberger Group Award in 1988, in 1989 the Greater London Arts Individual Artist's Award. From 1986 showed at Whitechapel Open; had a two-man show at Goldsmiths' Gallery in 1989, the year she was in Barcelona Biennial, in Spain; and then was in The British Art Show 1990, toured by South Bank Centre. Had solo shows at Winchester Gallery in 1985; Mario Flecha Gallery, 1988, the year when she was an Artist of the Day at Angela Flowers Gallery; Laure Genillard Gallery, 1990; and Whitechapel Art Gallery, 1997. Arts Council holds her work. Her father was the sculptor Paul de Monchaux.

Paul de MONCHAUX 1934– Sculptor in stone and metal, draughtsman and teacher, born in Montreal, Canada, father of the artist Cathy de Monchaux. He studied at the Art Students' League of New York, 1952–4, and the Slade School of Fine Art, 1955–8, teachers including Reg Butler, F E McWilliam and A H Gerrard. After teaching at the Nigerian College of Technology, 1958–60 and Goldsmiths' College, 1960–5, de Monchaux was at Camberwell School of Arts and Crafts as head of sculpture, 1965–83, then head of fine art, 1984–6, after which he mainly concentrated on commissioned sculpture. He gained an Arts Council Major Award, 1980, and a Northern Electric Environment Award, 1990. Was a member of LG, mixed show appearances including John Moores Liverpool Exhibition, 1961; Notices, Camden Arts Centre, 1979; the Serpentine Gallery/South Bank Centre's Sculpture Show, 1983, for which he was a selector; and Whitechapel Open, 1994. Had a solo exhibition (artist-in-residence), Chesil Gallery, Portland, 1991. Commissioned work included Bench Sculptures for British Rail, 1990; Basilica for Coventry Crown Court, 1991; and Wilfred Owen Memorial, Shrewsbury Abbey, 1993. Contemporary Art Society and Colchester District Health Authority also hold examples. Lived in London.

Lisa de MONTFORT 1906–1990 Portrait painter and miniaturist, born in Pietermaritzburg, Natal, South Africa. She was educated in South Africa and England, then studied art with Henry Tonks and Philip Wilson Steer at the Slade School of Fine Art, finally in Italy. Exhibited RMS, of which she was a member, RA, NEAC, LG, RP and elsewhere. She was a member of the group of artists in the 1950s living around Charlotte Street, London (including Harry Jonas, who drew her), written about in Clifford Bax's book *Rosemary for Remembrance.*

Miles Fletcher de MONTMORENCY 1893–1963 Painter, baronet, son of Hervey Lodge de Montmorency and husband of the artist Rachel de Montmorency. He studied at Dover School of Art, the Byam Shaw and Vicat Cole School of Art and Royal Academy Schools. Exhibited RA, RBA, Walker's and Cooling Galleries, ROI and at the National Gallery, London, with war artists. Elected RBA, 1935, of which he was in the mid-1940s honorary librarian. Wrote *A Short History of Painting in England.* Lived in London.

DENA: *see* **Dena BRYANT**

John DENAHY 1922– Painter and draughtsman, born in London, who studied art at Eltham Art Centre. He was elected to NEAC in 1980, also showing with RA, RWE and with Eltham Group. Won Daler-Rowney first prize at RBA in 1987. Had solo shows with Anna-Mei Chadwick gallery from 1989. Bank of England holds his work. Lived in Sidcup, Kent.

David DENBY 1946– Artist, notable for his sensitive portrait drawings and imaginative still lifes, who attended St Albans Art School, 1965–6, Walthamstow Art School, 1966–8, then Royal Academy Schools, 1968–71. Among his awards were the David Murray Landscape Scholarship and Leverhulme Scholarship, 1968–9, and Royal Academy Schools Portrait Silver Medal, 1969–70. His work was included in exhibitions at RA from 1969; at Mall Galleries, 1988; in Continuing the Tradition, Chappel Galleries, Chappel, 1993; and he also exhibited regularly in Sweden and Denmark. Solo show at Chappel Galleries, 1994.

Henry DENHAM 1893–1961 Painter, draughtsman, commercial artist and teacher. Born in Bristol, he studied at Bristol School of Art, 1906–13, under Reginald Bush and John Fisher, after which he was painting and life master there for a decade. Member of Langham Sketch Club and of the Wapping

Group. Exhibited at RA, Cooling Galleries, RI, RWA, RSMA and many public galleries in the provinces. Lived at West Wickham, Kent.

DENIS 1913–1997 Painter, printmaker, draughtsman and critic, full name Denis Mathews. He was born in London, son of the Canadian artist Richard George Mathews. Attended Highgate School and was at the Slade School of Fine Art, 1930–3 and 1935–6. Worked as a medical artist and during World War II showed in war artist exhibitions organised by Vera Cuningham. From 1945–56 Mathews was secretary of the Contemporary Art Society. He also appeared on the BBC's radio programme *The Critics*. His work reflected wide travels in several continents. Mathews was a francophile, who illustrated Pierre Poupon's and Pierre Forgeot's *A Book of Burgundy*, published in 1958. Showed with LG, Agnew, Redfern Gallery and had a first solo exhibition at Leicester Galleries, 1947. There was a retrospective of work done 1940–75 at Bartley Drey Gallery in 1994, another at Y Tabernacl, Machynlleth, 1997. Lived for many years at Felin Fach, Brecon.

Dominic DENIS 1963– Artist, born in London, studied at Chelsea School of Art, 1984–6, graduating with honours from Goldsmiths College, 1986–9. Group shows included Freeze, PLA Building, 1988; and Modern Medicine, Building One, and British Art, Basel, both 1990. Had a solo show with Harry Zellweger, Lugano, 1990.

David DENISON 1939– Surrealist artist and teacher, born in Wakefield, Yorkshire, who studied at Doncaster College of Art, 1972. Showed with Camden Arts Centre and widely in north of England in mixed exhibitions. Had solo exhibitions at Manor House Museum and Art Gallery, Ilkley, from 1970, later ones including Cartwright Hall, Bradford, 1980. Brighton Museum and Art Gallery holds his work. Lived in Burley-in-Wharfedale, Yorkshire.

Stephen DENISON 1909– Landscape painter in oil, born in Leeds, he was self-taught. Was educated at Oundle School and Oxford University. A member of the Arts Club, he contributed to *Isis* magazine while at Oxford, 1929–31, and later exhibited at the RA. Lived at Ramsgill, near Harrogate, Yorkshire.

Gladys DENMAN 1900– Painter and miniaturist, born in London as Gladys Denman-Jones, a name that sometimes appeared on her earlier work. Studied with Henry Tonks and Walter Westley Russell at the Slade School of Fine Art, 1919–23, exhibiting at RMS, of which she became a member in 1960, RP, ROI and elsewhere. Lived in Chagford, Devon, later in London.

Gladys DENMAN–JONES: *see* **Gladys DENMAN**

Noel DENNES 1908–1988 Painter, notably in tempera, and printmaker, born in Lowestoft, Suffolk. He studied at Norwich School of Art under Ernest Whydale. From 1961–2 was chairman of Norfolk and Norwich Art Circle and showed at NS, RE and RA. His solo shows included Assembly House, Norwich. Lived at Costessey and died at St David's Nursing Home, Sheringham, Norfolk.

Trevor DENNING 1923– Artist, teacher and writer, born in Moseley, Birmingham, studying painting and graphics at the College of Art there and continuing to live in the city. Denning became senior lecturer in the faculty of art and design at Birmingham Polytechnic (now University of Central England) school of foundation studies/art education until 1985. He was co-organiser of the Birmingham Artists' Committee, 1948–52; in the 1950s was hon. secretary of the RBSA; became a member of the Society of Industrial Artists and Designers, 1956 (worked in book design and film); and in 1965 was a founder-member of the Ikon Gallery, Birmingham. Denning completed several mural decorations, including mosaic, and had a solo show at Ikon, 1966. He was in 1972 a founder-member of the International Playing-Card Society and become a world authority on Spanish playing-cards. In 1989 Denning was made the first Member of Honour of the Asociación Española de Coleccionismo e Investigación del Naipe, Madrid, and in 1993 won the (International) Modiano Prize for the best work of research into the history of playing-cards. Publications included *The Playing-Cards of Spain*, 1997.

F Madeline DENNIS fl.from c.1925– Miniaturist and landscape painter who studied at the Slade School of Fine Art with Henry Tonks and Walter Westley Russell, then in Italy. Sometimes signed work F M D. Exhibited RA, RI, SWA and SM, of which she was a member. Lived in London, then at Angmering-on-Sea, Sussex.

Jeffrey DENNIS 1958– Painter and teacher, born in Colchester, Essex, who said that he wanted "to make a new kind of Pre-Raphaelite painting; but not in a revivalist or nostalgic sense". Studied at Slade School of Fine Art, 1976–80. From the late 1970s Dennis took part in many group exhibitions, including Whitechapel Open, 1980; Castello Colonna, Genazzano, Italy, 1985; Comic Iconoclasm, at ICA, 1987; South Bank Centre tour The British Art Show, 1990; and John Moores Liverpool Exhibition, 1997–8. One-man shows began with 5 Dryden Street Gallery and University of Essex, both 1979; a series with Salvatore Ala Gallery, New York, Milan and London, from 1985; and Anderson O'Day Gallery, 1994. He was tutor in fine art at Ruskin School of Drawing, Oxford, from 1991. Arts Council holds his work. Lived in London.

Michael DENNIS 1941– Sculptor in wood, iron and stone, born in Los Angeles, California, America, who studied at Reed College, Portland, Oregon, 1963, and Stanford University, Stanford, California, 1967, where he gained his doctorate. Was involved in teaching and research in neurobiology at Harvard Medical School, Boston, 1967–70; at University College London, 1970–2; and at University California Medical Centre, San Francisco, from 1972, becoming professor, 1978–80. Decided to abandon this career, moving to Denman Island, British Columbia, where he had bought land in the late 1960s and where until 1984 he was self-employed in residential design and construction. During a period at University of Nicaragua in 1984 Dennis took up sculpting, and on return to Denman concentrated on this. He won the Design Vancouver Sculpture Competition, 1992, and in 1993 the Sculpture Margam International Competition with a year's residency at Margam Park, Port Talbot, Wales. On Denman Island, Dennis followed loggers, "retrieving large hunks of cedar trees and sculpting from them archetypal forms which allude to the human figure," sometimes draping "these minimal forms with rent auto body metal." Later, he "became interested in creating outsized archetypal tools ... monuments to the first utensils of our forebears." Exhibitions included Emily Carr College, Vancouver, 1986; Surrey Art Gallery, Surrey, British Columbia, 1989; Diane Farris Gallery, Vancouver, 1993; American Visionary Art Museum, Baltimore, Inaugural Show, 1995; and Outsider Art Fair, New York, 1996. A number of public collections in British Columbia and Washington state; University of California, San Francisco; and Volary, Czech Republic, hold examples. Two sculptures completed for Margam were sold at Phillips, London, 1997.

Lynn DENNISON 1958– Artist, born in Penrith, Cumberland, who studied at Norwich School of Art, 1981–2, then Slade School of Fine Art, 1987. She was included in the Arts Council touring show The Tree of Life, 1989–90, Reclaiming the Madonna at Usher Gallery, 1993–4, and was an Artist of the Day at Angela Flowers Gallery, 1994, chosen by Tai-Shan Schierenberg. Solo and group exhibitions were held at Diorama Gallery from 1987.

Robyn DENNY 1930– Painter and teacher, born in Abinger, Surrey. He studied at St Martin's School of Art, 1951–4, then Royal College of Art, 1954–7, and was exhibiting with Young Contemporaries in 1953. In 1958 he had his first solo show at Gallery One. Denny was influenced by American colour-field painters and produced rectilinear abstracts. He wrote on art for *Das Kunstwerk* and *Art International*. Teaching posts included Bath Academy of Art, Slade School of Fine Art and visiting professorship at Minneapolis School of Art. Denny participated in many international group shows and had solo exhibitions widely abroad. He represented Britain at Venice Biennale in 1966 and seven years later had a retrospective at Tate Gallery. Showed with Waddington Galleries and Bernard Jacobson in New York. Arts Council holds his work.

Joyce DENNYS 1893–1991 Illustrator, painter and writer, born in Simla, East Punjab State, India. Soon after studying at art school in London she completed World War I propaganda posters. She also made her name as a writer of the *Doctor Dose* books in the 1930s and in World War II wrote humorous articles for *The Sketch* magazine, reprinted in book form in the 1980s as *Henrietta's War* and *Henrietta Sees it Through*, followed by plays and a West End musical, *Kookaburra*. She took up oil painting at 70, initially flowers and later pictures of Budleigh Salterton, Devon. Imperial War Museum holds her work. Lived in London.

Ann Langford DENT 1924– Painter and teacher, born in London. Because of her Quaker origins Ann Dent did not attend any school. She studied at Coventry School of Art, 1940–2; St Martin's School of Art, 1942–3; Central School of Arts and Crafts, 1946–7; and École des Beaux-Arts, 1948–9, in Paris, her teachers in London including Rodrigo Moynihan, Ruskin Spear and Robert Buhler. From 1943–6 during World War II she worked in the government codes and ciphers section at Bletchley. She went on to teach at Colet Court Boys' School and Kensington High School for Girls. Exhibited RA, LG and Chelsea Art Society, of which she was a member; shared a show with Trevor Chamberlain at Newbury Festival in 1982. Her work, which often features scenes of London, is owned by Hinckley Borough Council in Leicestershire and several notable private collectors. Lived in London.

Richard DENT 1902–1981 Self-taught artist who also did repoussé work in copper and enamel. Born in Hereford he exhibited with the Loggia Gallery, Free Painters and Sculptors and elsewhere. Sometimes signed work Richard D. Lived in London.

Robert Stanley Gorrell DENT 1909–1991 Watercolourist, etcher and teacher, born in Newport, Monmouthshire. In late 1920s he entered an engineering course at Newport Technical College, but later moved to Art School. From there he gained a place at Royal College of Art in the engraving school, 1931. In 1933 he gained his diploma and the British Institution Scholarship and was runner-up in Prix de Rome Scholarship, 1935, when he joined staff of Cheltenham School of Art. Served in Army, 1942–4, and resumed teaching at Cheltenham when invalided out, becoming principal in 1950 until 1974. Was appointed RE, RWS and RWA, also showing at RA, RSA, NEAC, RBA, Art Institute of Chicago and elsewhere. A memorial exhibition of his etchings was held at Cheltenham Art Gallery in 1991. It, Newport Art Gallery and Museum, RWS, RWA and National Library Wales, Aberystwyth, hold his work. Lived in Charlton Kings, Cheltenham, Gloucestershire.

Kenneth DENTON 1932– Painter in oil of traditional landscape and marine pictures, and teacher, born Chatham, Kent. He won a scholarship to Rochester School of Art in 1944, in 1946 becoming an apprentice to decorative artist Arthus Charles Gull. Also studied at night classes and was encouraged by the painter and musician David Mead. After National Service in the Army, in 1954 Denton set up as a freelance decorative artist while gaining fellowship of the British Institute of Interior Designers and The Chartered Society of Designers. Had several teaching posts, including Maidstone College of Art and Royal School of Military Engineering. Became a member of RSMA and International Society of Marine Painters. In 1983 Denton won the Hunting Group Art Award. He held several dozen solo shows in Britain and abroad. National Maritime Museum, Greenwich, holds his work. Lived in Sporle, King's Lynn, Norfolk.

Jenifer de PASS fl. from early 1970s– Painter, designer and printmaker, forbidden at the age of 17 by her parents to attend art school. While bringing up a family, she attended the City Literary Institute one day a week, studying the designing and screen-printing of fabric. Moved to Suffolk in 1973, taking over the house and studio of Josef Herman, and began self-taught painting, initially of landscape, later concentrating on still life, deriving "my inspiration from the intrinsic quality and beauty of individual objects grouped together". Shortly after starting to paint had a solo show at Minories, Colchester, later ones including Chestenet European Arts Centre, 1980, Digby Gallery in Colchester, 1987, and Chappel Galleries, Chappel, 1997.

Robert de QUIN 1927– Sculptural artist in a variety of materials; teacher. He was born in Namur, Belgium, and studied at Hornsey College of Art, 1945–50. Member of NS and Free Painters and Sculptors, of which for a time he was vice-chairman. Took part in many group exhibitions in Britain and abroad and had solo shows at Mall Galleries and elsewhere. Lived for some time in London.

Susan DERGES 1955– Artist and lecturer working in a variety of media, including etching, photography, acrylic, card on wood and enamel on Perspex. Born in London, she studied at Winchester School of Art, 1972–3; gained a first-class honours degree in painting at Chelsea School of Art, 1973–6, while there helping in the workshop of John Ernest with experiments in sound vibration; then in 1977–9 made postgraduate studies at the Slade School of Fine Art in painting and computer graphics, with DAAD and Boise travelling scholarships to Germany and Japan, the former involving metamorphosis and periodic transformation of visual elements. Derges continued to have close connections with Japan: in 1981–2 she won a Rotary Foundation Scholarship there, in 1982–3 doing research into audio-visual media at Tsukuba University, later organising workshops in Tokyo. From 1978 held a series of visiting lectureships in London and the provinces, and became department of media lecturer at University of Plymouth, Exeter, in 1994. Group exhibitions included Hayward Annual, at Hayward Gallery, 1978; Presence 2, Gallery On, Poznan, 1988; New Acquisitions, Arts Council Collection, South Bank, 1993; and Cameraless Photography, Yokohama Museum of Art, Japan, 1994. Showed solo with Gallerie im Zentrum, West Berlin, from 1978, later exhibitions including James Danziger Gallery, New York, and Arnolfini Gallery, Bristol, both 1995. Victoria & Albert Museum, Metropolitan Museum of Modern Art in New York and several Japanese public gallery and corporate collections, hold examples. Lived in Okehampton, Devon.

Brigid DERHAM 1943–1980 Artist and teacher, born and died in London. Derham was a prolific painter of large, colourful and vibrant pictures, such as circus scenes, figurative but tending towards abstraction. She studied at Slade School of Fine Art, 1961–6, gained her diploma with distinction in painting in 1965, then a postgraduate diploma in 1966. Her teacher Frank Auerbach remembered her as a "rather beautiful and brilliant" student, and Michael Andrews and Bert Irvin also admired her work. Derham won the Walter Neurath Prize for Drawing and Painting, 1962; an Italian Government Scholarship for study in Italy and an Ian Stevenson Travelling Scholarship, both 1965; Boise Travelling Scholarship, 1966; and an Arts Council Grant, 1972. She taught part-time at Byam Shaw School of Art and occasionally at the Slade. Group exhibitions included New Art Centre, where she had a solo show in 1974, and RA Summer Exhibition; she was included in British Painting '74 by the Arts Council in 1974.

Jupp DERNBACH: *see* **Jupp DERNBACH-MAYEN**

Jupp DERNBACH-MAYEN 1908–1990 Versatile artist in many media, although he was mainly interested in painting in oil and watercolour and printmaking. He was born Appollonia Herman Joseph Dernbach in Mayen, Germany (he later added Mayen to his surname and styled himself Jupp Dernbach-Mayen; there was a monogram of the three initials in a box, which was sometimes used). Jupp, whose father was a stonemason, was when aged 12 apprenticed to a house painter, acquiring skills later useful in supplementing income from such jobs as scene painting at the Berlin State Theatre. His employer paid for him to attend Cologne Art School in the mid-1920s, from which he won a scholarship to study under Max Kaus and Hans Orlowski at the Berlin Academy. In the early 1930s Jupp met his wife-to-be, Miette. Although a Roman Catholic he helped Jewish friends flee Nazi Germany, but found it prudent to move abroad; after living in Ibiza and France he closed his Berlin studio in 1938 and settled in England. After internment at Huyton, service in the Pioneer Corps and a nervous breakdown, Jupp shortly after World War II became assistant to the potter Lucie Rie for about four years. Began working on his own account, an early commission being a big mosaic for the 1951 Festival of Britain Dome of Discovery. Other commissions included mosaics and fountains for Sanderson's, 1960; a welded sculpture for the Westminster Bank, New Oxford Street, 1962; a fountain for Centrepoint, St Giles Circus, and a font and cross for the Church Missionary Society, Waterloo Road, both 1966. Mixed shows included Society of Mural Painters, first exhibition, 1950, and Smithsonian Institution, Washington, and tour, 1962. There was a memorial show at Belgrave Gallery, 1996. Victoria & Albert Museum holds ceramic work by Dernbach-Mayen, who lived in London.

Sophie de ROMER 1890– Painter and printmaker, born in Dorpat, Poland. She studied art in Munich and in Paris, including some time with Jacques-Emile Blanche. She had strong connections with Vilno where she was educated, exhibited and whose local museum bought her work. Also showed extensively at Beaux Arts Gallery and widely abroad, including Latvia, Egypt and America. Was a member of the RBA and lived in London.

Gerard de ROSE 1918–1987 Portrait painter and teacher, born in Accrington, Lancashire, his father a surgeon and professor of music of Russian descent. Attended Accrington School of Art, then won a Royal Exhibition in textile design to Royal College of Art. He studied there in 1939 and returned to the painting school, 1946–50; during World War II served in the Royal Engineers, taking part in the Dunkirk evacuation. From 1950–8 de Rose taught at various art colleges, including London College of Printing, then was head of the faculty of fine art, Maidstone College of Art, 1958–67. He was elected RBA in 1961, also showing at RA, RP, Zaydler Gallery, Bradford and Manchester Art Galleries, Paris Salon and other venues. Solo shows included Trafford, Alwin and William Ware Galleries, Haworth Art Gallery in Accrington which holds his work and widely in America. In the 1960s de Rose developed a reputation as a painter of the famous, subjects including the Duke of Bedford, Julie Christie, Vita Sackville-West, Rod Steiger, Sammy Davis Junior, Claire Bloom and Vladimir Nabokov, this portrait appearing on the cover of *Time* magazine. The portraits are notable for their astute placing of the subject against a plain background. By his peers de Rose was remembered as a flamboyant character. A small man with red hair and a stutter, he was a convivial member of the Chelsea Arts Club, a skilled amateur magician and in his youth a formidable boxer. Died in Hammersmith Hospital.

Freda DERRICK 1892–1969 Artist in pen and ink and watercolour, and writer, born in Cheltenham, Gloucestershire, where she eventually settled, although from youth until 1950, her most prolific period, she worked occasionally from a hut at East Brent, Somerset. She was the daughter of the Reverend J G Derrick, chaplain to the Cheltenham Workhouse and a keen amateur photographer, and was educated at Pate's Grammar School for Girls, Cheltenham School of Art and at London art schools. From 1920 travelled extensively by bicycle, mainly in Gloucestershire and Somerset, putting up at farms where they would take her in. She made meticulous drawings of churches, farm buildings, village scenes, country crafts and working life, inspired by William Morris and the Arts and Crafts Movement. Most were for magazine articles or her own books; she also produced animal books and alphabets for children. Her first publication was *The Ark Book*, 1921. Others included *Gothic Wanderings in Somerset*, 1930; *Tales Told in Church Stones*, 1935; *A Traveller Among The Farms*, 1936; *Country Craftsmen*, 1945; *Cotswold Stone*, 1948; and *A Trinity of Craftsmen*, 1950. In 1995 Cheltenham Art Gallery and Museums, which holds her work, put on an exhibition.

Thomas DERRICK 1885–1954 Painter of pictures and murals; book illustrator. Born in Bristol, studied at the Royal College of Art, where he later taught decorative painting. Sometimes signing his work T D, he exhibited at the RA, NEAC, Fine Art Society, IS and overseas. Derrick was employed by Hilary Pepler as an illustrator for St Dominic's Press, based at Ditchling, Sussex. Lived in Newbury, Berkshire, later in Canada.

Kenneth DERRINGER 1925– Painter and teacher, born and lived in Liverpool. He studied at Liverpool University School of Architecture and Liverpool College of Art and eventually became principal of Warrington School of Art. Derringer was a Sandon Studios, Liverpool Academy and Wirral Art Society member who also showed with RCamA, and public galleries in Birkenhead, Preston, Manchester and Liverpool, where the Walker Art Gallery holds his gouache April Showers, bought from the artist in 1951.

Pamela DERRY 1932– Artist in oil, born in Welwyn Garden City, Hertfordshire. A painter of atmospheric landscapes, she was self-taught. She was a member of NS and showed at ROI, SWA, RBA, NEAC, Century Galleries in Henley-on-Thames and widely in south of England and at Paris Salon. Russell-Cotes Art Gallery and Museum, Bournemouth, holds her work. Lived in Holt, Wimborne, Dorset.

Maurice de SAUSMAREZ 1915–1969 Painter, teacher and writer on art education who after Christ's Hospital studied at Royal College of Art. Among his teaching positions were the principalship of Byam Shaw School of Drawing and Painting and a period as head of the department of fine art at Leeds University. He participated in the Pilgrim Trust *Recording Britain* project. Among his writings was the book *Basic Design*, which had a revolutionary effect on art education in many parts of the world. Showed at RA, LG, NEAC and Leicester Galleries. In 1971 Homage to Maurice de Sausmarez at Upper Grosvenor Galleries included work by him and his friends. Works are held by Victoria & Albert Museum and several northern galleries. He was a Chelsea Arts Club member who lived finally in London.

Alice Des CLAYES 1891– Painter and illustrator, born in Aberdeen, Scotland, sister of Berthe Des Clayes and Gertrude Des Clayes, both painters. Studied at Bushey School of Art with Lucy Kemp-Welch and Rowland Wheelwright, at the Newlyn School of Art, then with Dudley Hardy at Ambleteuse, in France. Like her sisters, Alice Des Clayes spent some time in Canada and like them exhibited there, but whereas Alice and Gertrude ultimately settled in Britain, Berthe opted for Lunenburg, Nova Scotia, and died in 1968. Alice, like her sisters, painted pastoral scenes, all having a fondness for horses. She exhibited in England at RA, in the provinces and at Paris Salon and has work in the collection of the National Gallery of Canada, Ottawa. Finally lived in Newton Abbot, Devon.

Gertrude Des CLAYES 1879–1949 Painter, born in Aberdeen, Scotland, sister of the artists Alice Des Clayes and Berthe Des Clayes. She studied with Bertha Herkomer at Bushey School of Art, then with Tony Robert-Fleury and Jules Lefebvre at Académie Julian, Paris, but was substantially self-taught. She painted a large number of portraits and genre scenes, such as The Pearly King, exhibited in 1934 in Winnipeg. Spent many years in Canada, like her sisters, but returned to London where she died. She exhibited RA, Paris Salon and widely in Canada, and

National Gallery of Canada, in Ottawa, holds her picture Young Canadian Girl, of about 1920.

Steven des LANDES 1962– Painter, graphic artist and teacher, born in Preston, Lancashire, where he gained his honours degree in fine art, 1980–3. He then worked as a full-time painter and community artist, teaching painting in workshops and being closely associated with Liverpool Education Authority. He was also a part-time lecturer at Southport College of Art and Arts Centre, 1989. Mixed shows included Acorn Gallery in Liverpool from 1987 and Broekman Gallery in Chester from 1992. Had a solo exhibition at Bridewell Gallery, Liverpool, where he lived, 1987. Others included Skillion Business Centre Liverpool Visionfest, 1992.

Anne DESMET 1964– Painter, printmaker and teacher, born in Liverpool. Graduated from the Ruskin School, Oxford, 1986, with a master's degree in 1991, gaining a postgraduate diploma in printmaking at Central School in 1988. Went on to lecture at Royal Academy Schools, Ruskin School, Middlesex University and Leeds Polytechnic. She was elected a fellow of the RE in 1991, being its honorary curator of prints. As well as regularly showing with the RE, in 1991 Desmet was elected a member and exhibited with SWE, and she showed with Printmakers' Council and at RA Summer Exhibitions. Awards and prizes included Elizabeth Greenshields Foundation Award, 1989; British School at Rome Scholarship in Printmaking, 1989–90; and artist-in-residence, Oriel 31, Newtown, 1990. Completed commissions for Oxford University Press and *The Times*. She showed solo with Ruskin School in 1990, with Duncan Campbell Gallery from 1991 and Royal Over-Seas League, 1992. Ashmolean Museum holds her work. Lived in London.

Pascoal de SOUZA 1928– Painter in oil, born in Goa, Portuguese India, who studied at Sir John Cass and St Martin's Schools of Art, gaining the de Laszlo Award in 1959. Was a member of RBA and ROI, showing at RA and Paris Salon, and having a series of solo exhibitions at Trafford and Alwin Galleries. Lived for many years at St Margaret's, Twickenham, Middlesex.

Paul DESSAU 1909– Painter in oil who studied at Hornsey School of Art, then St Martin's School of Art. Exhibited RA, RP, Cooling Galleries, in the provinces and in North America. Work purchased by the Government Art Collection and is in several public galleries in the Midlands, including Worcester Art Gallery. Lived in London and then in London Colney, Hertfordshire.

Gerard de THAME 1958– Painter and sculptor, born and lived in London. He studied at Brighton Polytechnic, 1978–81, Chelsea School of Art, 1981–2, in 1982 won a one-year Rome Scholarship in sculpture and in 1984 a Mark Rothko Travel Award to America. Arts Council holds his acrylic on paper Tall and Old, bought from Air Gallery, 1983. Also in 1983 de Thame showed at Hayward Gallery; in 1984 at Riverside Studios; and in 1985 at Nicola Jacobs Gallery and John Moores Liverpool Exhibition, where he was a prizewinner.

Edward Julius DETMOLD 1883–1957 Watercolourist, illustrator and printmaker specialising in natural history subjects and the creation of his own fantastic worlds. Like his twin brother Charles Maurice he was educated privately and studied creatures in the zoo, and he worked with him until Charles Maurice's death in 1908. Edward Julius settled in Montgomeryshire, by which time he had established a reputation as a book illustrator, working with great exactitude. *The Fables of Aesop*, 1909, and Maurice Maeterlinck's *The Life of the Bee*, 1911, were notable examples. For a few months in 1905 the brothers were associates of RE, but resigned. Edward Julius was a prolific exhibitor at Fine Art Society, Brook Street Art Gallery, Arlington and Baillie Galleries, NEAC, RA, RI and elsewhere. Committed suicide.

Anthony DEVAS 1911–1958 Painter, principally of portraits. Born in Bromley, Kent, he studied at the Slade School of Fine Art, 1927–30, where he was friendly with William Townsend, Geoffrey Tibble and others associated with the Euston Road School in the late 1930s. Married Nicolette Macnamara, the writer and painter. In the 1930s began to establish a reputation as a portrait painter, painting HM The Queen in 1957. First exhibited at Cooling Galleries in 1936, from 1940 at the RA. Also showed at Agnew, NEAC, RP and the Leicester Galleries. Devas' work is in several public collections, including the Tate Gallery, which has his portrait of the poet Dylan Thomas' wife Caitlin, sister of Nicolette Macnamara. Devas' portraits of women and children can be very sensitive as his memorial show at Agnew in 1959 showed. Exhibitions at Graves Art Gallery, Sheffield, in 1991, and Tenby Museum and Picture Gallery, 1992, concentrated on the Devas family circle pictures. Lived in London.

Nicolette DEVAS 1911–1987 Painter and writer, daughter of the Irish wit and landowner Francis Macnamara, of Ennistymon, County Clare. Her sister Caitlin married the poet Dylan Thomas. The story of her unusual bohemian childhood is told in her book *Two Flamboyant Fathers*, 1966, in which Augustus John's family features strongly. Aged 16 she entered the Slade School of Fine Art, studying under Henry Tonks. There she met the painter Anthony Devas, whom she married in 1931. Seven years after he died, in 1958, she married the artist Rupert Shephard. Birds were a favourite theme in Devas's paintings. She showed at NEAC, RA and LG and had a solo show at Storran Gallery, her painting name sometimes being Macnamara. Bringing up a family restricted her painting and she developed her writing, in 1958 publishing her first novel *Bonfire*; several other books followed. In 1987 her work was included in a show of Slade Contemporaries at Sally Hunter Fine Art.

Bob DEVEREUX 1940– Painter, performance poet, librettist, gallery proprietor and festival organiser, born in Dorking, Surrey, who trained as a graphic artist at Kingston School of Art,

1957–61, moving to Cornwall in 1965, based in St Ives. Founded the Salt House Gallery in 1979, having previously run Sloop Gallery, to show his own pictures, 1973. Devereux exhibited widely, including Newlyn Orion Gallery in Penzance on various occasions; Manchester City Art Gallery, 1983; Black Horse, Frome, 1991; in 1992 was included in Artists from Cornwall, RWA; and Showcase, Truro Museum, 1994–5. Later solo shows included Salt House Gallery, 1996. Devereux began work as a performance poet with the group Mask, 1970; among his many other activities in subsequent years were the pamphlet *Be Green's* publication in 1973; first performance with Clive Palmer, founder-member of The Incredible String Band, 1974; a first collaboration with the composer Christopher Brown, on *Seascapes*, 1979; libretto for the children's opera *The Ram King*, with Brown, 1982; in 1985–6 librettos for Rudi Van Dijk for the opera *Kalma Loka* and Jonathan Lloyd for the chamber opera *The Uncertainty Factor*; in 1988 presentation of a programme about St Ives artists for BBC World Service; publication of six poems in Martin Leman's *Just Bears*, 1992; and the cantata *Fluid Form*, with composer Stephen McNeff, 1994. Devereux was closely associated with the St Ives Festival from 1970. His work was widely distributed throughout Europe.

Richard DEVEREUX 1956– Sculptor, born in Lincolnshire, who studied at Portsmouth College of Art, where he won a scholarship. He had a first solo show in 1979 at Axis Gallery, Brighton, after which he was involved in many mixed exhibitions, showing regularly at the New Art Centre and Sculpture Garden, Roche Court, Wiltshire. In Stillness and in Silence, "a collection of works reflecting on the sacredness of the earth", toured from Usher Gallery, Lincoln, in 1994. Tate Gallery, Bodleian Library in Oxford and several other libraries hold his work, which ranged over a wide variety of media.

Phyllis DEVEY 1907– Portrait painter in oil and teacher, born in Birmingham. She studied at the College of Arts and Crafts there, her teachers including Bernard Fleetwood-Walker. Went on to hold a number of teaching posts in the Midlands, notably at Windylow School in Solihull and at the Bournville School of Art. She showed at NS, SWA, ROI, Paris Salon and extensively in the provinces. Lived Wootton Wawen, Warwickshire.

Pamela de VILLE 1923– Sculptor in bronze and ciment fondu, born in Saxilby, Lincolnshire. She studied and worked under T B Huxley-Jones, Anthony Gray and Nathan David. Lady de Ville was a member of RMS. She showed with SPS, MAFA, Lake Artists' Society, SWA, Phoenix Gallery at Lavenham and Pitcairn Gallery, Knutsford, and cast bronzes in her own foundry. Private collections in Britain and abroad hold her work. Lived in Sonning, Berkshire.

George DEVLIN 1937– Painter, printmaker, artist in ceramics and teacher, born in Glasgow. He attended Glasgow School of Art, 1955–60. Was awarded several prizes, including the Robert Harr, Chalmers, Haldane and Carnegie Travelling Scholarships. In 1968 he was awarded a Major Arts Council Award, in 1971 the Cargill Award and seven years later the Exhibit of the Year Award at Royal Glasgow Institute of the Fine Arts. He was elected RSW in 1964, chairman of the Glasgow League of Artists in 1977 and a member of the Royal Glasgow Institute in 1989. In the late 1960s he set up his own painting school in France, re-establishing it in 1989. For some years he taught in design department of Glasgow College of Building and Printing. Travelled extensively in Europe and Africa. Devlin designed and illustrated books and in 1973 designed the set and costumes for Scottish Ballet. Had one-man shows at Scottish Gallery and Demarco Gallery in Edinburgh, Leicester University and Kelly Gallery, Glasgow, in 1989. Scottish National Gallery of Modern Art holds his work. Lived in Glasgow.

Gerry DEVLIN fl. from mid-1970s– Painter and teacher who won his bachelor's degree and an advanced diploma in painting from University of Ulster, Belfast, 1977–8, then gained a Ford Foundation Grant to study at Syracuse University, New York, where he won his master's degree in 1981. As well as being artist-in-residence for the Artists in Prison Scheme, Dublin, Devlin taught widely in Ireland, including Dublin, Cork, Waterford and Belfast Colleges of Art and the Workers' Educational Association. He was invited to contribute to the *Great Book of Ireland*, shown at Ulster Museum, Belfast, 1991. He was a prizewinner in 1987 and 1994 at the Claremorris Open Exhibition, also at Works on Paper at the Fenderesky Gallery, Belfast, 1988. In 1994 he was included in Beyond the Partitions, put on by Queen Street Studios, Belfast, with which he was associated. Solo shows included Crawford Municipal Art Gallery, Cork, 1990.

Andy DEWAR 1944– Artist and teacher, born in Dundee, Angus, who studied graphics and silversmithing at Gray's School of Art, Aberdeen, 1962–6, lecturing for a period at Aberdeen College of Commerce from 1969. He was a member of the management committee of Peacock Printmakers, Aberdeen, where he exhibited, other group shows including RSA, Aberdeen Artists' Society, Aberdeen Arts Centre and Scottish Print Open, at Artspace in Aberdeen and tour. Had solo shows at Peacock Gallery and elsewhere. Public, private and local authority collections hold Dewar's work.

Hugh de WET 1931–1998 Painter of landscape and still life in oil, born in South Africa, who was a reporter there and then on *The Times* in London. Trained as an artist at City and Guilds of London Art School. Showed at RA Summer Exhibition, NEAC, various commercial galleries and had a solo show at 20 Fournier Street, Spitalfields, in 1996.

Louis de WET 1930– Painter using an Old Master mixed technique, egg emulsion and oil glazes combined, born in Durban, Natal, South Africa, which he left permanently at the end of 1952. Studied in Paris at L'Académie de la Grande Chaumière, 1953–6, and in the meisterklasse, Academy of Art in Vienna, 1969–71, under Rudolf Hausner. Had a studio in London, then in 1983 bought Wenlock Abbey, Much Wenlock, Shropshire, which he and his actress wife restored. Was a member of the Historic Houses Association. De Wet was "much influenced by continental Old Masters, but [I] paint as a twentieth century painter." He believed that originality was not merely innovation, but that it and real value were "new links in a very old chain. I see my roots as Flemish, English, French and German." In later years sold only to private clients direct from his studio, although he had solo shows in Paris, Milan, Brussels and Venice in 1994.

Paul Edward DEWS 1961– Artist and musician, born in Hitchin, Hertfordshire, working in a range of media. After leaving school Dews became a landscape gardener, a silkscreen printer for eight years, then studied Art and Social Context at Dartington College of Art, graduating with an honours degree in 1989. From then he worked in Huddersfield, Yorkshire. His work was strongly figurative, often incorporating a narrative text. Mixed exhibitions included The Northern Art Show, Mall Galleries, 1994. Had a series of solo shows including Fairbairn House, Leeds; Bradford Community Arts Centre; Walton Gallery, Guisborough; Marsden Mechanics, Huddersfield; and Gallery on the Street, Cambridge.

Sheila DEWSBURY 1939– Painter in oil and teacher who studied at Sedgley Park College. She taught in comprehensive and further education painting semi-professionally until 1989, then painted full-time. Her main theme was "elemental aspects of nature, spending most time painting the wilder parts of Britain and the west of Ireland". Dewsbury was a member of MAFA. She exhibited with ROI, RCamA, and at the Edinburgh Festival and Bath Contemporary Arts Festival. Showed solo at Saddleworth Festival regularly from 1984. Lived in Greenfield, Oldham, Lancashire.

James DEXTER 1912– Artist and designer who studied at Leicester College of Art. He lived in Leicester for many years and the local corporation owned his work. Showed at RA, LG, NEAC and in the provinces.

Walter DEXTER 1876–1958 Painter in oil and watercolour and illustrator. Born in Wellingborough, Northamptonshire, he studied at Birmingham School of Art, 1892–1900, at the Birmingham Royal Society of Artists and on the continent. Exhibited RA, RBSA, RI, ROI, RBA and elsewhere. Castle Museum, Norwich, holds his work. Dexter was a prolific writer on art and illustrated a number of books, including E V Lucas' *A Wanderer in Paris*. Lived at King's Lynn, Norfolk.

Henry Cotterill DEYKIN 1905–1989 Painter in oil, sculptor, furniture maker and teacher, born in Edgbaston, Birmingham. He studied at the College of Arts and Crafts there and at Slade School of Fine Art. Deykin taught at Warwick School, 1936–65, except for a period in camouflage work in World War II. In 1950–1 Deykin was commissioned by Geoffrey Pugh, head of Atco Ltd, the lawnmower company, to complete 23 paintings showing the progress of grass sports in the twentieth century. They were given a countrywide tour. The collection was sold at Sotheby's in 1982. Some are illustrated in M A Wingfield's *Sport and the Artist*, volume one on ball games, published in 1988. Showed RA, Whitechapel Art Gallery and elsewhere in mixed shows. Sponsored solo shows included Eton, Harrow and Cambridge and Norwich Art Schools. Latterly Deykin concentrated on furniture, until arthritis made it difficult for him to stand. Lived at Leamington Spa, Warwickshire.

Avtarjeet DHANJAL 1939– Sculptor, born in Dalla, Punjab, into a crafts-oriented peasant family. After working as a carpenter and at other jobs, he studied at Government College of Arts, Chandigarh, 1965–70, then went to East Africa, where he taught sculpture at Kenyatta University College, in Nairobi, Kenya, for two years. After arriving in Britain in 1974 he did the advanced sculpture course at St Martin's School of Art, but left after a short time. As artist-in-residence at Alcan Aluminium at Tipton, in the Midlands, he was sponsored to complete a number of sculptures, having a show at Dudley Castle in 1975. Travelled widely, including a return to Punjab, to take part in sculpture seminars. Much of Dhanjal's work was for public commissions, using man-made and natural features, abstract and often untitled. Had a solo show at Horizon Gallery, 1987; participated in The Other Story, Hayward Gallery and tour, 1989–90; and was given a major exhibition at Pitshanger Manor and Gallery, Ealing, 1997, in which Dhanjal's concern to explore and resolve opposing elements and polarities, his striving for formal simplicity and clarity of purpose and his range of work from kinetic aluminium sculptures to slate pieces were explored.

Pierre DIAMANTOPOULO 1952– Self-taught figurative sculptor, born in Cairo, Egypt, of a Greek father and French mother, moving to England during the Suez Crisis of 1956. He obtained an honours degree in literature from University of Essex, 1973, and was an advertising copywriter for the agency Foote, Cone & Belding, 1974–89. In the latter year he took his first studio as a professional sculptor in Brighton, Sussex, where he continued to live. Exhibitions included Tryon Gallery from 1990; Garrard, 1991; Harrods, 1991–2; South Bank Centre National Touring Exhibition, 1995; and in 1996 Beaux Arts in Bath and 2nd RWA Open Sculpture Exhibition.

Colin DICK 1929– Painter. Studied painting for four years full time at St Martin's School of Art under Frederick Gore, R V Pitchforth and James Stroudley. He was closely associated with the Thames, living for six years in the Thames Valley as a child, at Henley and later on at Chiswick Mall. Showed at RA from early 1960s. Herbert Art Gallery and Museum, Coventry, has many paintings of local interest in its collection.

William DICK 1950– Versatile artist who gained his diploma in art, drawing and painting at Dundee College of Art, 1972–7, with a postgraduate course at St Martin's School of Art, 1977–8. Exhibitions included Paperworks at Aspex Gallery in Portsmouth and LG, Camden Arts Centre and tour, both 1982; and Scottish Print Open Three, 1983, organised by Dundee Printmakers' Workshop.

William Reid DICK 1879–1961 Sculptor in the classical tradition of portraits, figure studies and public monuments. Born in Glasgow, he studied at the School of Art there until 1907, then at the City and Guilds School, Kennington. Showed at the RA from 1912, and was elected RA, 1928. He was president of the RBS, 1915. Knighted in 1935. Was King's Sculptor in Ordinary for Scotland, 1938–52, and Queen's Sculptor from 1952. Also exhibited Royal Glasgow Institute of the Fine Arts, IS, RSA, RSW, RI and Paris Salon. Reid Dick was an astute businessman who fulfilled many public commissions, whose work can achieve technical excellence with dignity and sensitivity. Among his notable works are heads of Sir Winston Churchill and King George VI; Dawn, in the Tate Gallery; the equestrian group Controlled Energy on Unilever House, London; Godiva, for the City of Coventry; the Kitchener Memorial Chapel, in St Paul's Cathedral; and the statue of David Livingstone at Victoria Falls, in Africa. Lived in London. Reid Dick's daughter Mary Hart was an artist.

Sophie DICKENS 1966– Sculptor in a variety of materials interested in the dynamism and rhythm of the human form, for which she made special anatomical studies at London University, 1991. She was educated at Charterhouse, Godalming, 1982–4; gained an honours degree in art history at the Courtauld Institute, 1984–7; trained at Sir John Cass School of Art, 1988–92, in the latter year winning the sculpture prize; in 1991 also studying ceramic shell bronze casting at Central St Martins School of Art. Exhibitions included Fresh Art, Business Design Centre, 1992; Albion Fine Art, 1994; and Usiskin Gallery and The McHardy Sculpture Company, both from 1995. Had a solo exhibition at Andy Elton Studios, 1994.

Charles George Hamilton DICKER 1896–1977 Painter and Church of England priest, born in Ouse, Tasmania, his father also an ordained minister. After his mother's early death, was taken to England by his father and was brought up by two maiden aunts. Studied at Oxford University and in late 1920s at Slade School of Fine Art, where William Coldstream was a close friend. Supported by a small private income, Dicker continued to paint until World War II, showing at East London Group Lefevre exhibitions, NEAC and elsewhere. Had long been interested in religion and in 1942 was ordained in Leicester. Eventually became vicar of South Stoke, near Bath, in 1948, where he remained for 18 years, then retiring to Wells. Is buried at South Stoke, Somerset.

John DICKERSON 1939– Ceramist, draughtsman, mixed media sculptor and teacher, born in Swaffham, Norfolk. He studied at Goldsmiths' College School of Art, Art Students' League of New York and Pratt Institute there, gaining his master's degree in 1968, then doctorate from Royal College of Art, 1971–4. He wrote extensively on raku ware. His own work was shown and held widely in Britain and abroad. Lived in London where he was in the fine arts division of Richmond College, The American International College.

Robert DICKERSON 1924– Australian painter and draughtsman and printmaker, born in Sydney. He was self-taught from an early age, left school at 14, became a professional boxer two years later and at 18 joined the Royal Australian Air Force, serving in Borneo in World War II. After the war Dickerson worked for a decade as a labourer, continuing to paint, selling a picture to the National Gallery of Victoria in 1956 and three years later becoming a full-time painter. In 1959 he was the only Sydney representative in the Antipodeans, a group set up in support of figurative art. Recent Australian Paintings, at the Whitechapel Art Gallery, in 1961, and the 1963 show Australian Painting at the Tate Gallery were dominated by the Antipodean style. Dickerson made the loneliness of city life his special theme. He went on to show widely in Australia, and is represented in all state and provincial galleries. In 1989 he travelled in Britain, Germany and Netherlands and in 1991 England & Co gave him a solo show.

Edward Montgomery O'Rorke DICKEY 1894–1977 Painter, printmaker, teacher, administrator and curator, born in Belfast. He obtained his master's degree from Cambridge University and studied painting under Harold Gilman at the Westminster School of Art. From 1926–31 Dickey was professor of fine art and director of King Edward VII School of Art, Armstrong College, Newcastle upon Tyne. He was then staff inspector of art, Ministry of Education, 1931–57, but from 1939–42 was secretary of the War Artists' Advisory Committee, in 1942, on the recommendation of Kenneth Clark, joining the committee, while returning to the Ministry, until the war's end. Eventually Dickey became first curator of The Minories, Colchester. The Imperial War Museum holds extensive wartime correspondence involving Dickey and a copy of a television documentary on war art in which he appeared. The Minories' collection of Dickey's work includes a self-portrait. Dickey painted extensively on the continent, public galleries in Manchester, Belfast and Cork holding examples. He showed at RA, NEAC and LG. An upright, gentlemanly figure, Dickey was notable for always carrying a sketchbook in his pocket. Lived latterly at Turvey, Bedfordshire.

Mary DICKINSON fl. from c. 1935– Painter and draughtsman in black-and-white, born in Liverpool. She was initially educated in England, France and Germany, then studied at Liverpool School of Art and in London at Frank Spenlove-Spenlove's Yellow Door School of Art. Exhibited widely, including ROI, RA, PS and SWA both of which she was a member, NEAC, NS and Paris Salon, where she gained an Honourable Mention. RSA, where she also exhibited, bought her work. Lived in London.

Adam DICKS 1967– Freelance illustrator and painter, born in London, who chose to create "paintings about people, their characters and how they behave (to each other) or react to their environments". He studied at Richmond-upon-Thames College and Middlesex Polytechnic. Commissions included cover illustrations for publishers including Macmillan Publishers and HarperCollins. Group shows included Chartwell House, 1992; Summer Show at Burlington New Gallery, 1994; and Royal Over-Seas League Open, 1996.

Evangeline Mary Lambart DICKSON 1922– Artist mainly in watercolour, mixed media and pastel, born in Sheffield, Yorkshire, studied under Violet Garrod and Anna Airy. The British landscape and its history were key themes in her work, as in her show Ancient Places, at Salisbury & South Wiltshire Museum in 1992. Commissioned work included illustrations for *In Search of Heathland*, by Lee Chadwick, 1982. She was a member of BWS and exhibited in many shows in London and East Anglia, notably RI, RWS, and at Paris Salon. Solo shows include Clarges Gallery and Christchurch Mansion, Ipswich. Graves Art Gallery, Sheffield, and Ipswich hold her work. Lived in Westerfield, Ipswich, Suffolk.

James Marshall DICKSON 1942– Painter and draughtsman, born in Kirkcaldy, Fife, where he settled at Lochgelly. Studied at Edinburgh College of Art, 1960–4, teachers including Stuart Barrie. Was made a member of RSW in 1972, also showing with public galleries in Kirkcaldy and Perth and at Royal Glasgow Institute of the Fine Arts. Angus and Banff County collections hold his work. Dickson was in charge of art at Lochgelly Centre.

Jennifer DICKSON 1936– Painter, printmaker and teacher, born in Piet Retief, South Africa. She studied at Goldsmiths' College School of Art, 1954–9, then at S W Hayter's Atelier 17 in Paris, and is mainly noted for her prints. She exhibited internationally and work is held by the British Museum, Victoria & Albert Museum, Metropolitan Museum in New York and other collections. RE member, elected RA, 1976. Was in charge of printmaking at Brighton College of Art, then taught at the Faculty of Fine Arts at Concordia University, Montreal, Canada. Latterly lived in Ottawa, Ontario. The City Gallery showed new works in 1997.

Joan DICKSON 1913– Painter and teacher, born in Southampton, where she studied at the School of Art, 1929–35, and Royal College of Art, 1935–8. She later taught for some years at the Southampton School. Showed at RA, LG and NEAC. Married to the artist Michael Platt and lived for a time at Brockenhurst, Hampshire.

Nell Gwenllian DICKSON 1891–1967 Watercolour landscape painter, born in Reading, Berkshire. She studied art prior to World War I under W G Collingwood, at Reading University with Alan Seaby, then at Heatherley's School of Fine Art with Herbert Maryon; from 1935–38 she studied with Leonard Richmond, later working under Hervey Adams and David Cox. Exhibited RA, SWA, RBA, RSA and with the Norwich Art Circle. Had several one-man shows in Norwich, where she lived, in the 1950s and 1960s. Was chairman of the Norfolk and Norwich Art Circle in 1951.

Rodney DICKSON 1956– Painter, sculptor in wax and teacher, born in Bangor, County Down. Studied at Liverpool College of Art, 1979–83, graduating with grade 1 honours. From 1983–4 lived in Amsterdam with his partner the designer Judith Hone, then returned to live in Devon for five years, followed by Liverpool. Dickson went to New York in 1992 under an Ireland/America Arts Exchange. Among his other awards were a David Murray Travelling Scholarship, 1983. He was a John Moores Liverpool Exhibition prizewinner, 1987, and won several South West Arts and Northern Ireland Arts Council Awards. Dickson taught part-time at Southport and Liverpool Art Colleges, and was artist-in-residence at Walker Art Gallery, Liverpool, 1990. Had a solo show there, 1990, others including Cartwright Hall, Bradford, 1992–3. Dickson painted on a large scale in oil, the paint often thick and dark, the images sometimes disturbing. Walker Art Gallery, University of Liverpool and Arts Council of Northern Ireland hold his work.

Thomas Elder DICKSON 1899–1978 Painter, teacher and writer, born in Barrhead, Renfrewshire. He studied at Glasgow School of Art, 1920–4, under Maurice Greiffenhagen, then went on to hold a number of teaching posts, latterly as vice-principal of Edinburgh College of Art, where he lectured on the history of art. He wrote several books on painting and design and wrote for art magazines. Exhibited SSA, of which for a time he was president after World War II, RSA, RSW and Royal Glasgow Institute of the Fine Arts. Dr Dickson lived in Edinburgh.

Wesley DICKSON 1925– Painter and draughtsman, by profession a civil servant, born in Belfast where he continued to live. Studied art at Belfast Academy with John Turner and exhibited RUA.

Xenia K DIEROFF 1965– Artist using video, born in Hamburg, West Germany, who gained a degree in fine art at University of Brighton, 1990–3, and her master's at Goldsmiths' College, 1994–6. Exhibitions included BT New Contemporaries 92, tour, 1992; Nobby Stiles, Vandy Street, 1995; and New Contemporaries, Tate Gallery in Liverpool and Camden Arts Centre, 1996.

Grace DIGBY 1895– Landscape painter, jewellery designer and musician, born in Scarborough, Yorkshire. Studied art in Brussels. Exhibited RA, Walker Art Gallery, Liverpool, RCamA, on the continent, in Australia and America. Lived at Edgbaston, Birmingham.

Violet M DIGBY fl. from 1930s–1960 Artist in oil and pastel who was born in Plymouth, Devon. Studied at Hastings School of Art under Philip Cole and Leslie Badham, at the Slade School of Fine Art, 1938, and the following year in Paris. She exhibited ROI, RCamA, UA, at the Paris Salon and in India.

Lived at St Ives, Cornwall, where she was a member of the St Ives Society of Artists.

Jane Chadderton DIGGLE 1882– Painter and poster artist, born in London, who after education there and in Paris studied at Heatherley's School of Fine Art, the Central School of Arts and Crafts and privately. Exhibited RA, RI, WIAC, NS and elsewhere. Lived in Tenterden, Kent.

Stanley Victor DIGGLE 1919– Painter, draughtsman and teacher, born in Leicester, where he settled. His father's job as a landscape gardener probably contributed to his interest in depicting the countryside, which features in much of his work. Studied at Leicester College of Art, 1947–9, then in 1949–51 at Camberwell School of Arts and Crafts, where his teachers included Claude Rogers and Richard Eurich. Showed Young Contemporaries, AIA, NEAC and South London Art Gallery. Held several art teaching posts, latterly in Coventry.

Megan Ann di GIROLAMO 1942– Ceramist, teacher and illustrator, born in New Delhi, India, married to the artist Romeo di Girolamo. She studied at High Wycombe College of Further Education, Hornsey School of Art and South Glamorgan Institute of Higher Education, gaining her master's degree in ceramics in 1987. She illustrated several books, including *The Crab and its Relatives*. Exhibited in London and Ireland. Lived in Wendover, Buckinghamshire.

Romeo di GIROLAMO 1939– Painter and teacher, born in Civitella, Italy. He was educated in England and studied art at High Wycombe School of Art, 1954–9, on a county scholarship. He won the Granada Theatres National Painting Prize in 1957, the RA's David Murray Travelling Scholarship in 1959. Eventually became head of painting at Amersham College of Further Education. Was a member of RBA, also exhibiting at RA and elsewhere in mixed shows as well as solo shows. Lived in Wendover, Buckinghamshire, married to the ceramist Megan Ann di Girolamo.

Paul DIGNAN 1962– Abstract painter employing bright, narrow bands of vertical and horizontal colour. He was born in Dundee, Angus, and attended Gray's School of Art, Aberdeen, 1981–5, and Slade School of Fine Art, 1985–7. In 1993 Dignan was awarded a residency by the Reykjavik Municipal Art Museum in Iceland, in 1995 gaining a Rome Scholarship, British School at Rome. Group exhibitions included RSA Student Exhibition, Edinburgh, 1985; Vik Gallery, Edmonton, Alberta, 1988; Abstract Art – The Next Generation, Mall Galleries, 1994; and Aspects of Abstraction at Paton Gallery, 1995.

Beatrice DILLISTONE 1899– Painter, illuminator, black-and-white artist and teacher, born in Brighton, Sussex, where she continued to live. Attended Brighton School of Art, 1917–21, then the Royal College of Art, 1921–3. Taught art at Wakefield School of Art and Crafts and Thornes House School, 1923–59. Among illuminated work commissioned was a roll for York Minster.

Angela DILLON 1955– Abstract artist whose works reflected her Spanish/Mexican antecedents and who was born in Campeche, Mexico. She was educated at Robert Gordon University and Gray's School of Art, Aberdeen, 1992, then Royal College of Art. In 1992 gained the RSA's Thompson Award. Exhibitions included Aberdeen Artists' Exhibition and RSA, 1991–2, Atlantis Galleries, 1993, and in 1994 Battam Studio in Connecticut, America, and Five RCA Painters, at Paton Gallery.

Norman DILWORTH 1931– Sculptor, draughtsman, painter and teacher, born in Wigan, Lancashire, attending its School of Art, 1949–52. Then studied at Slade School of Fine Art, under William Coldstream, 1952–6, winning the Tonks Prize, and the *Sunday Times* Drawing Prize, 1956. Gained a French Government Scholarship to study in Paris, 1956–7. Dilworth participated in many group shows from Young Contemporaries in 1953, John Moores Liverpool Exhibition, 1959, LG for some years, and progressively abroad. After a solo show at Redmark Gallery, 1968, in 1970 he began to show on the continent, especially in the Netherlands. Later shows included Galerie Elke Dröscher, Hamburg, and Art Affairs, Amsterdam, both 1993. From the mid-1970s Dilworth had a base in Amsterdam, settling there in 1982. His major commissions included a fountain for the Crown Offices, Cardiff, first prizewinner in Arts Council competition; relief for Stadsdeel Zeeburg, Amsterdam, 1990; and tower for Rijkerswoerd, Arnhem, 1991. Arts Council, Tate Gallery, British Council and many continental collections hold Dilworth's work. He became progressively a sculptor, completing wooden abstract floor and wall pieces, saying of his work: "It is the parallel to nature which fascinates me … I am not attempting to make an illusion of something else."

Steve DILWORTH 1949– Sculptor using a wide range of found and other objects, and teacher, born in Kingston-upon-Hull, Yorkshire. He studied at Maidstone College of Art, 1967–71, and won a series of awards from Arts Council, Scottish Arts Council and Henry Moore Foundation. Was a visiting lecturer at Winchester, Cheltenham, Wolverhampton, Dundee and Glasgow Colleges of Art; Royal Academy Schools; and Ruskin School of Drawing, Oxford. Exhibitions included Upper Street Gallery, 1975–6; Ikon Gallery, Birmingham, 1980; Goldmark Gallery, Uppingham, 1991; Paper Works IV, Dundee, where he was first prize winner, 1993; and The Gallery in Cork Street, 1994.

Phyllis DIMOND 1911– Watercolourist, born and lived in London, whose work was "mostly topographical, mainly local, commissioned and sold privately". She attended Hammersmith School of Arts and Crafts, 1926–9, and Royal College of Art design school, 1931–4, for her diploma, tutors Edward Bawden and Eric Ravilious. From 1934–9 she gave part-time tuition at Bolt Court School of Photo-Engraving and Lithography; was also a freelance designer; and did some animated cartoon drawing. Her career "took off after 1942". She contributed 12 London pictures to the *Recording Britain* project, and was included in the associated National Gallery show, 1942–3, and Victoria & Albert Museum's 1990 exhibition. Also showed at RA, 1958; Lord Mayor's Award Shows, 1963–5–6; and Westminster Artists, 1966. Latterly contributed watercolour still lifes to St John's Wood Church Christian Aid Exhibitions. Victoria & Albert Museum and St Marylebone Library local history collection hold examples of Dimond's work, which also appears in the volume *Londoner's England*, 1947.

Maria DINELEY 1971– Painter of landscape with a bravura style in oil and colourful palette, born in Dorset, where she established a strong local following for her views around Berwick St John. In the early 1990s attended the Charles Cecil Studios in Florence. Had a solo show at Christopher Wood Contemporary Art, 1995.

Naomi DINES 1968– Sculptor and artist in various media, born in Fareham, Hampshire. She gained a first-class honours degree in fine art, sculpture, at Chelsea School of Art, 1988–91, then her master's degree at Royal College of Art, 1991–3. Dines won an Alfred Munnings Award in 1988, Paul Dowson Memorial Trophy, 1989, and in 1992 was a prizewinner at East & South, at Norwich Gallery/Kent Institute of Art and Design. Other exhibitions included Osborne Gallery, 1989; in 1990 Art '90, at Business Design Centre; and Under Sail at 1991 Chichester Festival. Lived in Maldon, Essex.

Jan DINGLE fl. from 1970s– Printmaker and designer who originally studied graphic design at Hornsey College of Art, taking up etching some years later. Subsequently worked in studios and ateliers developing the varied techniques used in her coloured etchings. The Norfolk Broads, where she cruised for much of the year, featured strongly in her pictures. Showed at RA Summer Exhibition, with other major societies and had a series of solo shows. These included Trumpington Gallery, Cambridge, 1984; Medici Gallery and Casson Gallery, Eastbourne, both 1986; and Stevenage Leisure Centre, 1990. Lived in Waltham Abbey, Essex.

Kenneth DINGWALL 1938– Painter, constructions artist and teacher, born at Devonside, Clackmannanshire. Dingwall studied at Edinburgh College of Art, 1955–9. After being an Andrew Grant Postgraduate Scholar, 1959–60 and living in Greece, 1961–2, Dingwall began teaching at Edinburgh College of Art in 1963. From 1973–4 he was visiting professor at Minneapolis College of Art and Design in America. In 1988 he was appointed professor at the Cleveland Institute of Art, Ohio. It was from around 1973 that Dingwall developed his abstract paintings and constructions, influenced through work seen in America by Mark Rothko and Robert Ryman. Dingwall's method of painting was laborious and careful, usually in sombre colours, his aim being to reveal shifts between what we feel and what we reveal. Dingwall had solo shows at Scottish Gallery, Graeme Murray and Scottish Arts Council Galleries, all in Edinburgh, in the 1960s and 1970s. A more recent solo show was at the Peter Noser Galerie, Zurich, 1987. Scottish National Gallery of Modern Art holds his work.

Ernest Michael DINKEL 1894–1983 Painter of landscapes, Biblical subjects, flowers and portraits who practised in oil, tempera, watercolour and pencil, and who also worked in stained glass, engraved glass and made sculpture. Born in Huddersfield, of German descent, Dinkel was a man in the arts and crafts tradition. He studied at Huddersfield School of Art and at the Royal College of Art 1921–5. Dinkel won the Owen Jones Travelling Scholarship to study art and architecture in France and Italy. Married the artist Emmy Dinkel–Keet. Assistant to Ernest William Tristram at the Royal College 1925–40, was principal of the School of Art, Stourbridge in 1940–47, from 1947–61 being head of the school of design at Edinburgh College of Art. Designed inn signs and posters, for London Transport. Exhibitions include RA, NEAC and RWS, with a major exhibition at the Art Gallery, Cheltenham, 1980. Official purchases include the Tate Gallery. Lived at Bussage, near Stroud, Gloucestershire.

Emmy Gerarda Mary DINKEL-KEET 1908– Painter noted for exquisite fine brush drawings and watercolours, and teacher, married to the artist Michael Dinkel. During World War I Dinkel Keet left her native Holland to join her father in England. She won the Essex County Art Scholarship in 1927 to attend Southend College of Art, 1927–30, then was at Royal College of Art, 1930–3, teachers including William Rothenstein, Ernest Tristram, Malcolm Osborne, Edward Johnstone, Edward Bawden and Eric Ravilious. Studied peasant embroidery and design in Hungary, teaching these subjects at London Country Council Institutes and arts and crafts at Sherborne School for Girls. After freelancing, 1937–9, she taught at Malvern College of Art, married, then taught part-time in Scottish schools. She was made RWA in 1987, also showing at RSA and RA and sharing a show with her husband at Stroud Festival, 1984. Lived at Bussage and then Cirencester, Gloucestershire.

Mary DINSDALE fl. from 1960s– Painter and illustrator who trained at Guildford and Harrow Schools of Art. She began painting in 1980, having previously worked as a freelance illustrator, including a long spell with *Radio Times*, latterly illustrating for *Punch*. Worked in a variety of media, notably gouache. Drawing was a strong element in her work, which had a Neo-Romantic flavour. Dinsdale showed widely in the south of England. She was a member of Rye Society of Artists and Hastings Arts, showing regularly at Easton Rooms, Rye. Work also appeared at Hastings Museum and Art Gallery, Wedges Gallery in Hastings and Dandelion Gallery, Tunbridge Wells. Work held in public collections.

Eve DISHER 1894–1991 Painter, born in London, who studied at Hornsey School of Art. During World War I she worked for the

London Fire Service. After leaving home to marry the theatre critic Willson Disher she became friendly with members of the Bloomsbury Group. When her marriage broke up in the late 1920s she began a relationship with a member of John Grierson's General Post Office film unit and became involved in its work. After the war she travelled widely, living in South Africa and Jamaica, paying her way by painting portraits. For many years shared a studio with Vera Cuningham, whose work influenced her style. Disliking the smell of oil paint Eve Disher opted for gouache, and as well as portraits – which included Professor J B S Haldane, now in the National Portrait Gallery – she sometimes painted flower pictures and urban scenes. Showed with London Artists' Association, SWA, WIAC and Mattheisen Gallery. Died in London.

Arturo Di STEFANO 1955– Artist working in various media who was born in Liverpool, where he completed a foundation year at the Polytechnic, 1973–4. He then studied at Goldsmiths' College School of Art, 1974–7, and Royal College of Art, 1978–81. His first solo show in 1985 was followed by a year at Accademia Albertina, Turin, backed by an Italian Government Scholarship. He was a prizewinner at John Moores Exhibition, Liverpool, 1991–2. His solo show appearances included Pomeroy Purdy Gallery, 1989–91, several abroad and Walker Art Gallery, Liverpool, 1993.

Alan DIXON 1936– Artist, poet and teacher who began making sculpture from scrap metal during National Service in the Royal Air Force, 1954–6, work that has not survived. Studied at Goldsmiths' College, 1956–63, where he was unsympathetic to the "subdued, laborious naturalism of a Euston Road kind" then prevailing "and was fascinated by Dada, particularly the earliest brief outbreak in Zürich," had "Robert Motherwell's pioneering book on more-or-less permanent loan from the library" and "found out about Schwitters' works at Lords Gallery." Dixon went on to teach art in schools in London and Peterborough, 1959–87. He published several collections of poems, some decorated with his own woodcuts; some were produced by Poet & Printer, a press which used Dixon's woodcuts in other publications. His poems were also published in *The Listener*, *The Observer*, *London Review of Books*, *The Times Literary Supplement* and elsewhere. Dixon published translations of Hungarian poems and poems by Max Jacob. In the early 1960s Dixon showed woodcuts, paintings and drawings at the AIA Gallery. In 1990 an exhibition of his drawings and watercolours of cats was held at David Holmes Contemporary Art, Peterborough, and constructions from scrap materials in 1995–6. He also made stone carvings.

Anna DIXON fl. from c.1915–1959 Painter who was born in Edinburgh. Studied at the Royal Scottish Academy Schools under Charles Mackie and E A Walton. Exhibited RA, Royal Glasgow Institute of the Fine Arts, RSA, RSW and in the Scottish and English provinces. President of the SSWA, 1930–42. Lived in Edinburgh.

Jane DIXON 1963– Painter, printmaker, draughtsman and teacher, born in Bolton, Lancashire, who studied at the College of Higher Education there. Also attended West Surrey College of Art & Design, Farnham; and Royal College of Art. She was course tutor at Goldsmiths' College, 1991–3; and in 1994 visiting tutor at the Royal College of Art and Gray's School of Art, Aberdeen, also working on Macmillan's *Dictionary of Art*. Dixon gained a Rome Scholarship in printmaking, 1989; a British Council Travel Grant for Czechoslovakia, 1992; a Purchase Prize, Oriel Mostyn Open, Llandudno, 1993; and was artist-in-residence, Lowick House, Cumbria, 1994. Took part in numerous group shows, including Fresh Art, Barbican Centre, 1986; Work in Progress, Anderson O'Day, 1988; Editions 1/90, International Art Fair, Basel, 1990; and Royal Over-Seas League Open, 1994. In 1992 had solo exhibitions at Café Gallery and Co-existence Art. Oriel Mostyn, Sussex County Council and Leeds Borough Council hold examples.

Jo DIXON 1950– Figurative artist, born in Willingham, Lincolnshire, who believed strongly in good drawing. She studied at Hammersmith College of Art, 1969–72, later at Whitelands College, then taught art in several London schools. After bringing up her children she returned to exhibiting after a dealer had noticed her work, initially in Devon where she lived with her general practitioner husband. Countryside Gallery, Tiverton, gave her a show, and she sold regularly from Drewe Arms, Broad Hembury. In 1996 had a successful exhibition at St John's Smith Square.

Joe DIXON 1915– Painter and teacher who studied at Royal College of Art, being awarded a postgraduate year and a Travelling Scholarship. He went on to teach at Camberwell School of Arts and Crafts and was senior fellow at British School in Rome, 1980. He showed at Opix Gallery, Woodlands Art Gallery, in other mixed exhibitions and in Italy in Rome and Assisi. A figurative artist, notable for his landscapes.

Rex DIXON 1939– Artist, born in London, and teacher. He studied at Newton Abbot School of Art, 1966–8, then Stourbridge College of Art, 1968–71, where he later taught part-time. Was also visual arts officer for Midlands Arts Centre. He showed solo there from 1973, also exhibiting at Ikon Gallery, Birmingham, 1971, and Dudley Art Gallery, 1976. Lived for a time at Stourbridge, Worcester.

DIZ: *see* **Edward ARDIZZONE**

Zoran DJORDJEVIC 1952– Painter of abstract work, and teacher, who studied at Hornsey College of Art, 1972, Chelsea School of Art in 1973 and gained a French government scholarship in 1976, the following year setting up a studio in Rotherhithe. In 1979 he taught at Barnfield College school of art and design and was manager of Round House Gallery. Exhibitions included Westminster Artists at Alpine Gallery, 1978; 5 Dryden Street and Moira Kelly Fine Art, both 1980; and LG at

Morley Gallery and Contemporary Artists in Camden, at Camden Arts Centre, both 1981.

M Wilson DOAR 1898– Painter, draughtsman and wood carver specialising in depictions of dogs. Miss Doar studied at Heatherley's School of Fine Art, 1936, with Frederic Whiting and Bernard Adams, then went on to show with RSA, RCamA, RBA and elsewhere. Lived in London.

Stanley DOBBIN 1929– Printmaker, draughtsman and mixed media artist, and teacher, born in Birmingham. He studied at the College of Art there, 1947–52. Taught at Newton Abbot Grammar School, 1954–9, then Manchester College of Art/Polytechnic, 1959–84. German Expressionism, the British Neo-Romantics and Edward Wadsworth were influences. Was a member of MAFA. Also showed at Bluecoat Gallery, Liverpool, in mixed exhibitions in 1970s; 1983 in Woodworks at Plymouth Art Centre; 1987–93 at Acorn Gallery, Liverpool; in 1990 in Vincent at Bede Gallery, Jarrow, and elsewhere. Had solo shows in 1970s at Bluecoat and in 1980s at Acorn. Figure and landscape woodcuts done in Scotland, Cornwall and North Devon were cited by Dobbin as his main works. Provided illustrations for Jack Clemo's *Clay Cuts* poems, 1991, and Fiona Pitt-Kethley's poems *A School for Life*, 1993. Lived in Cheadle Hulme, Cheshire.

Honor DOBBS 1902–1987 Printmaker and painter who studied Beckenham School of Art. She took part in mixed shows at RA from 1964, others being at Free Painters and Sculptors of which she was a member, Bankside Gallery, Fairfield Halls in Croydon and Ripley Arts Centre. In 1985 she shared a four-man exhibition at Woodlands Art Gallery. Solo exhibitions included Woodlands and the Churchill Library, Bromley. Lived in Chislehurst, Kent, and Cushendall, County Antrim.

Frank Sellar DOBLE 1898– Painter who was by profession a photographer. He was brought up in the Liverpool area and went to the School of Art there and continued to live at Crosby. Doble was a member of the Liverpool Academy of Arts and Liver Sketching Club and exhibited there and at the Walker Art Gallery. Was president of Liver Sketching Club in 1934.

Antoni DOBROWOLSKI 1919–1987 Painter, designer and sculptor, one of the Polish paper sculptors who flourished in Britain after World War II. He was born in Pinsk, was commissioned in the Polish Army and granted leave to study art at the Academy in Rome, where his strongly individual style developed. Intricate detail, charm and accuracy and imaginative use of materials characterised his output. Moved to England in 1947 where he enrolled at the Sir John Cass School of Arts and Crafts. Worked for Diana Studio. During the coronation of Queen Elizabeth II, despite being confined to bed with illness, Dobrowolski was heavily involved in decorative work for the celebrations in Regent and Oxford Streets. Industrial clients included Vat 69 Whisky, British Railways and KLM, work being done for the Brussels World Exhibition. Decorations for the grand ballroom of the Dorchester Hotel, Hoover and the White Eagle, Knightsbridge, were notable successes. His work was included in Polish Paper Sculpture at the Polish Cultural Institute, 1995.

Cowan DOBSON 1893–1980 Portrait painter, born in Bradford, Yorkshire, son of the artist Henry John Dobson. He was educated at George Watson's College, Edinburgh, studying art in the Scottish capital, London and Paris. Showed at RA from 1913–59, including portraits of notable sitters including Admiral of the Fleet the Earl Beatty, 1934, and The Earl Attlee, 1956. Was elected RBA in 1922, also exhibiting at Fine Art Society, Royal Glasgow Institute of the Fine Arts, RSA, Walker Art Gallery in Liverpool and elsewhere. Glasgow Corporation bought his work. Lived finally in London and was an Arts Club member.

Eric DOBSON 1923–1992 Artist and influential teacher, born in County Durham, who gained a scholarship to Dame Allen's School, Newcastle, 1934–41, then received a first-class honours degree at King's College 1942–3 and 1946–50, studies interrupted by Royal Navy service. Dobson stayed on to work as a tutorial student under Lawrence Gowing, Roger de Grey and Christopher Cornford, later becoming a full-time member of staff at Newcastle University. An accidental head injury led to his retirement in 1989. Dobson was a representational and abstract painter, the Euston Road School and especially Victor Pasmore being influences. He showed in London and Paris and had a memorial exhibition at University of Northumbria, Newcastle, in 1994.

Frank DOBSON 1886–1963 Sculptor, draughtsman and painter in oil and watercolour. Born in London, the son of an artist with whom he initially studied, Dobson first attended Leyton School of Art, 1900–2, was an apprentice studio boy with the sculptor Sir William Reynolds-Stephens, 1902–4. After a time in Cornwall was, 1906–10, at Hospitalfield Art Institute, Arbroath, finally attending the City and Guilds School, Kennington, 1910–12. Although he made his first wood carving just before World War I, Dobson's first one-man show, at the Chenil Galleries, 1914, was of paintings and drawings. During World War I enlisted in Artists' Rifles and continued working, Imperial War Museum acquiring his large oil The Balloon Apron. After the war Dobson met Wyndham Lewis and exhibited with Group X in 1920; had first one-man show as a sculptor at Leicester Galleries, 1921. First sculptures were very stylised, but later work influenced by the work of Aristide Maillol. During the inter-war years Dobson consolidated his reputation – with Epstein he was called "a keeper of tradition", bridging classical and modern sculpture – by making the backdrop for the first performance of William Walton's *Façade*; showing internationally; designing glazed pottery reliefs for Hay's Wharf, London; completing his large carving Pax and notable portraits. Official war artist in World War II. Professor of sculpture at the Royal College of Art, 1946–53. Elected RA, 1953. Dobson is represented in many public galleries, including the Tate Gallery. Arts Council memorial exhibition 1966, and touring; retrospective Kettle's Yard,

Cambridge, 1981–2, toured; major reappraisal at Henry Moore Institute, Leeds, 1994. Died in London.

Martin John DOBSON 1947– Artist in oil, chalk pastel and photography, born in Manchester. He was self-taught and began painting seriously and exhibiting in the early 1970s while employed in commercial photography, later dividing interest between the two. Dobson's main theme was steam railways in landscape. He chiefly worked "in monochrome or muted colour to evoke the atmosphere of the steam railway in its declining years". Was a member of Guild of Railway Artists. Showed extensively in group and open exhibitions, including Colin Jellicoe Gallery, Manchester; Manchester Academy; Astley Cheetham Gallery, Stalybridge; Bath and Edinburgh Festivals; Torr Top Gallery, New Mills; and Lyric Theatre. Solo shows included Past Trains, Manchester and Salford University Library, 1979; and Fire and Water, Colin Jellicoe, and Charlotte Mason College, Ambleside, both 1988. Greater London Council bought two works. Lived in Hyde, Cheshire.

Mary E DOBSON 1912– Painter, draughtsman, mural artist and illustrator, born in London. Studied at Bournemouth Municipal School of Art, 1930–4, Chelsea Polytechnic, 1936–7, then in 1938 at Central School of Arts and Crafts. During World War II she served in the Women's Royal Naval Service. She drew for a wide range of publications, including *Strand Magazine*, the *Daily Mail* and *Daily Herald* and *Nursery World*. Exhibited RA, SWA and NEAC. Lived in London and in Shipbourne, Kent.

Scott DOBSON 1918– Painter, designer, art critic and teacher whose full name was Edward Scott Dobson and who was born in Blyth, Northumberland. Studied art at King Edward VII College, Newcastle; at Freckleton, in Lancashire; and Leeds College of Art. Sometimes signing work only S D, showed New Vision Centre, Redfern Gallery, RSA and in his home area of Newcastle upon Tyne. For a time he was art critic of the *Evening Chronicle* newspaper there and he also taught art for several years at Manchester Grammar School, as well as running the Westgate Gallery in Newcastle. Shipley Art Gallery in Gateshead and Laing Art Gallery and Museum in Newcastle hold his work.

Michael DOCHERTY 1947– Painter and creator of artworks using found objects, born in Alloa, Clackmannanshire. He studied at Edinburgh College of Art, 1964–8, an Andrew Grant Scholarship permitting him to travel in France and Spain. Docherty gathers found objects, which he paints and which together chronicle his travels. Scottish National Gallery of Modern Art holds an example: An Object Fixed in Time, constructed in 1977. He was in the Gallery's exhibition Scottish Art since 1900, 1989–90, which toured; Docherty's first solo show was in 1970 at Richard Demarco Gallery, Edinburgh.

Alan DODD 1942– Painter, muralist and designer, born in Kennington, Ashford, Kent. He studied at Maidstone College of Art, 1958–63, teachers including Christopher Ironside, Robin Ironside, Gerard de Rose, Margery Gill and David Hockney; then at Royal Academy Schools, 1963–6, under Peter Greenham, Charles Mahoney, Fred Dubery, Graham Arnold, Edward Bawden, Richard Eurich and Gertrude Hermes. Until 1975 Dodd concentrated on easel pictures, then he added mural works, small architectural details and became an advisor on historic colour detail. Dodd was a member of the Art Workers' Guild from 1982. He took part in the RA Bicentary Exhibition, 1967–8, and had a series of solo shows at New Grafton Gallery, 1969–72. He completed five capriccio panels for the Painted Room, Victoria & Albert Museum, 1986; work in the Painted Hall, Great Fosters, Egham, 1989; and in New Picture Room, Sir John Soane's Museum, 1992. Lived in London.

Francis DODD 1874–1949 Draughtsman, painter and printmaker, especially of portraits, born at Holyhead, Anglesey. Studied at Glasgow School of Art under Fra Newbery and Archibald Kay, winning the Haldane Scholarship in 1893, travelling to France, Italy and later to Spain. For about 10 years from 1895 lived in Manchester, then settled in Blackheath in southeast London, which he often painted and drew. Dodd was an official war artist during World War I and was a trustee of the Tate Gallery, 1928–35, being elected RA in 1935. Dodd exhibited extensively at NEAC, RA and RWS and at many other venues and his work is in a number of British public collections, including Tate Gallery, in South Africa and Australia. His work is comparable to that of his brother-in-law, Muirhead Bone, although Dodd can be a lively and perceptive portrait painter: witness his portraits of the critic Edward Garnett in the Tate Gallery and the painter Henry Lamb in Manchester's City Art Gallery. A retrospective of Dodd's work was held at Cheltenham in 1944. Memorial shows took place at Bluecoat School, Liverpool, 1949, and South London Art Gallery, 1950.

Phyllis DODD 1899–1995 Painter, notably of portraits, born in Chester. Her parents encouraged her early interest in art. She won a Royal Drawing Society prize in 1909 and her mother took in paying guests to send her to Liverpool School of Art, 1917–21, where Will Penn taught her the use of a limited palette; by the 1950s she developed an interest in more positive colour. In 1921 won a Royal Exhibition, one of many awards, to Royal College of Art, 1921–5. While teaching at Walthamstow Technical College, 1925–30, obtained portrait commissions through William Rothenstein, in 1928 marrying the artist Douglas Percy Bliss. She being a perfectionist in all things, domestic life eroded Dodd's time for painting. Although when a student she had painted so concentratedly that she forgot to eat and became ill, as a housewife she said that "when there is dust on the stairs, I cannot settle down to painting." Showed at RA, with a notable success in 1939; had a joint exhibition with her husband at Derby Museum & Art Gallery, 1947; another joint show at St Michael's Gallery, Derby, 1983; a ninetieth birthday show at Hatton Gallery, Newcastle, 1989; and a retrospective at the public gallery, Derby, again in 1995. Glaucoma was diagnosed in 1976; she suffered a major stroke which badly damaged her sight in 1986, a year after she painted her last major portrait; and in 1992 she became totally blind. Lived for many years in Glasgow.

William DODD 1908– Watercolourist who studied at Kendal School of Art, 1926–33. He was a member of Lancaster Art Group and the Lake Artists' Society. Showed NEAC, RWA, RCamA and elsewhere. Lived at Arnside, Westmorland.

Andrew DODDS 1927– Watercolourist, illustrator and teacher, born in Gullane, East Lothian. He studied at Colchester School of Art, 1942–5, then Central School of Arts and Crafts, 1947–50, teachers including John Minton, Keith Vaughan, Bernard Meninsky, Ruskin Spear, R S Badmin and John Farleigh. He was a part-time tutor at St Martin's School of Art, 1952–75, then principal lecturer in the art and design department of Suffolk College, Ipswich, 1975–89. Dodds illustrated several dozen books, including *East Anglia Drawn*, 1987. He was a member of Colchester Art Society, which held his work, and exhibited at RA. Had a solo exhibition at Studio Club, 1961, others including Minories, Colchester, from 1970; Mermaid Theatre, 1975; and Digby Gallery, Colchester, 1991. Lived in Lower Raydon, Ipswich, Suffolk.

James DODDS 1957– Artist born in Brightlingsea, Essex, who was an apprentice shipwright, 1972–6, then attended Colchester School of Art, 1976–7, Chelsea School of Art, 1977–80, and Royal College of Art, 1981–4. From 1980 was a prolific exhibitor, including The Minories, Colchester, 1983, Hatton Gallery at Newcastle upon Tyne, 1985, Camden Arts Centre, 1987, Gallery 44 at Aldeburgh Festival, 1990, and Sue Rankin Gallery, 1992. Solo exhibition of recent paintings was held at Chappel Galleries, Chappel, 1994. Ipswich and Horniman Museums and the Britten-Pears Library hold examples. Commissions included two big paintings for Clacton and Rochford Hospitals, The National Trust and Kent Opera and Tollesbury stained glass window working with Stourside Glassworks.

Joan Kathleen DODDS 1918– Artist and illuminator, born and lived in York and studied at the School of Art there. She was by profession a bank clerk but also did part-time art teaching. Dodds joined the PS in 1967, belonged to York Art Society and showed with RI and Paris Salon. York Minster holds illuminated work by her. Latterly she retired from exhibiting.

Eveline DODGSON 1901–1995 Artist who was born at Long Marston, Yorkshire, first cousin of the artist John Dodgson. After her parents died when she was young she was brought up by her uncle Campbell Dodgson, keeper of prints and drawings at the British Museum. She studied at Edinburgh College of Art and Slade School of Fine Art, in Paris and Italy. She was married to James Byam Shaw, second son of the artist Byam Shaw, then to William Winkworth, an authority on Oriental ceramics. Exhibited NEAC and elsewhere and decorated All Hallows Church, Poplar, in 1924. After her husband's death Eveline converted to Roman Catholicism and liked to be called Margaret. Lived latterly in the Isle of Wight.

John DODGSON 1890–1969 Painter, printmaker, teacher and collector, born in Murree, Punjab, India. His mother was a keen amateur painter, his uncle Campbell Dodgson, of the British Museum, and early on he gained a love of Renaissance Italy. After attending Oxford University, 1909–13, Dodgson studied at Slade School of Fine Art, 1913–15, with Henry Tonks. Served with Army during World War I, carried out a commission for Imperial War Museum and in 1919 was for a short time assistant director at National Gallery under Sir Charles Holmes. Showed with NEAC, LG of which he was president in 1950–2 and with London Artists' Association, of which he was also a member. After World War II Army Service Dodgson taught at Camberwell School of Arts and Crafts, 1946–50, then at Chelsea School of Art, 1950–8. His first one-man show was at Claridge Gallery, 1928; he had another, in 1959, at Beaux Arts Gallery. Dodgson's work owes something to the Camden Town and Euston Road traditions, but there is a strong Symbolist strain, as in the Tate Gallery's Giant Snail. Dodgson was a keen collector, having private means, and owned pictures by Bonnard, Pasmore, Steer, Claude Rogers and Duncan Grant, as well as by his students. His own studio was burned to the ground in 1964, so remaining work is limited. Memorial show at South London Art Gallery, 1971. Major show at Fine Art Society and tour, 1995. Lived at Chelsworth, Suffolk.

Tom DODSON 1910–1991 Self-taught painter, born in and lived in the Salford area of Lancashire, the eldest of a poor family of five children. Although keen on art as a child – top of the class for drawing, he chalked the local pavements with his depictions of local characters – he had to leave council school at 14 and join the grocery trade, during his life doing a number of jobs in industry to support his family. Shortly before retiring as a caretaker he took up art again, painting scenes of his youth with sincerity and warmth, having a first solo show at Bell Galleries, Sale, in 1974. This sold out, and soon over 30,000 prints from 36 of his original paintings were sold (usually the signed, limited editions were 850). By 1985, some paintings were selling at almost £2,000. Tom and his wife Lily toured Lancashire in their Reliant Robin three-wheeler to find new subjects. In 1998, Salford Quays Heritage Centre, helped by Studio Arts, Lancaster, put on a commemorative exhibition.

Samuel DODWELL 1909–1990 Painter, draughtsman and broadcaster, born in London, who attended Regent Street Polytechnic School of Art and began painting seriously after World War II. Impressionism, sound draughtsmanship and a tendency towards abstraction all played a part in his diverse output, which included portraiture. Dodwell was elected RI in 1965, also taking part in mixed shows such as RA Summer Exhibition, RP and RBA. Held solo exhibitions in London, the provinces and abroad, including Athens and Amsterdam. Among Dodwell's commissions was a large mural of sunflowers for the Imperial Hotel, Torquay, one for the American Chamber of Commerce, London, and portraits in Beirut, Lebanon, where he appeared on television. He also featured in *Portrait in Oils*, a Westward Television programme. The Nuffield Foundation bought three works. Lived in Reigate, Surrey, later in Lostwithiel, Cornwall.

Ruth DOGGETT 1881–1974 Painter, printmaker and teacher in the Camden Town Group tradition, second eldest of 10 children, born in Cambridge, of George Doggett. He was a director of Robert Sayle, a local general store, and a strong non-conformist. Miss Doggett studied for several years at Westminster School of Art, teachers including Walter Sickert, gaining a medal in 1913. Because she became a teacher Doggett's own painting was restricted to holidays, so her output was small. East Anglia, the West Country and Cornwall were favourite painting spots. Doggett lived in London until 1939, when she returned to Cambridge, and about this time seems to have stopped painting. She was a member of the LG, showed at ROI and at Walker Art Gallery in Liverpool and had a solo show at Fine Art Society in 1934, where a few pictures sold. Although Doggett's work is not often shown Sickert, Harold Gilman – who painted a notable portrait of her – and the critic Frank Rutter all thought highly of her abilities. In 1946 she settled in St Leonards-on-Sea, Sussex, with several sisters, devoting much time to botany and gardening.

Mary Jo DOHERTY 1971– Ceramic artist, born in Londonderry, Northern Ireland, who studied at University of Ulster and Royal College of Art. She gained a Northern Ireland Education Board Scholarship, 1994–6, and a Wedgwood Scholar Prize, Royal College of Art, 1996. Won the Royal Over-Seas League Trophy Commission in 1996, the resulting work being inspired by seventeenth-century Meissen figurines.

Moira DOHERTY fl. from mid-1980s– Figurative artist, muralist and teacher who graduated from the University of Ulster, Belfast, with a fine art degree in 1985. She was involved in the education of the young disabled and the supervision of drama workshops and murals. The resulting work won many awards, including the first prize, Barclays Young Artist Award, and was performed and shown throughout Northern Ireland. Showed with the Claremorris Open Exhibition, in the annual Independent Artists Exhibition at Arts Council in Belfast and in Beyond the Partitions, put on by Queen Street Studios, Belfast, with which Doherty was associated.

Willie DOHERTY 1959– Artist employing photographs and text, born in Londonderry, where he continued to live. Studied at Ulster Polytechnic, Belfast, 1977–81. From early-1980s took part in many mixed shows, including Performance, Live Work, at Crescent Arts Centre, Belfast, 1982; Oliver Dowling Gallery, Dublin, 1987; Three Artists, Battersea Arts Centre, 1988; and South Bank Centre's The British Art Show 1990. Had solo shows at Orchard Gallery, Londonderry, from 1980, and elsewhere. Was included in Twelve Stars, Belfast Arts Council Gallery and tour, 1992–3, showing work chosen for the European Parliament Collection.

Maxwell DOIG 1966– Painter, draughtsman and printmaker who abandoned a graphics course in the early 1980s because it restricted his vivid imagination. Encouraged by the artist David Blackburn he was accepted for Manchester School of Art in 1985. The following year he had a two-man show at Manchester University, had work accepted for Manchester Academy Summer Exhibition and won a prize for the best print shown. By the time Doig graduated in 1988 he had shown at Whitworth Art Gallery, Manchester, in the Young Contemporaries exhibition and at Bankside Gallery, in 1990 winning the Joseph Webb Scholarship for the best draughtsman under 35. Doig took up a postgraduate scholarship to Slade School of Fine Art 1988–90, where he won a Laura Ashley Scholarship. His first show after finishing at the Slade was at Hart Gallery, Linby, Nottingham, in 1990, which continued to show him. Universities of Manchester and London hold examples.

Peter DOIG 1959– Painter, born in Edinburgh, who attended Wimbledon School of Art, 1979–80, St Martin's School of Art, graduating 1980–3, then gained his master's degree at Chelsea School of Art, 1989–90. Mixed exhibitions included New Contemporaries at ICA, 1983, and Barclays Young Artist Award, Serpentine Gallery, 1991. Showed solo at Articule, Montreal, Canada, 1990, and Whitechapel Artist Award, Whitechapel Art Gallery, 1991,with another exhibition in 1998. Doig's land-scape Stealth House, 1992, was included in Twelve Stars, Belfast Arts Council Gallery and tour, 1992–3, being acquired for European Parliament Collection. Doig won first prize in John Moores Liverpool Exhibition, 1993–4, and in 1994 won the Eliette von Karajan prize in Salzburg, Austria, and had a solo exhibition at Victoria Miro Gallery. Tate Gallery, Contemporary Art Society, Arts Council and European Parliament hold examples. Lived in London.

Miriam DOKOTLIVER 1954– Painter using mixed media, born in Ukraine, who studied for an honours degree in fine art at Glasgow School of Art, 1987–91, gaining her master's in fine art and design, Gray's Art School/Robert Gordon University, Aberdeen, where she lived, 1993–4. Mixed shows included Ben Uri Gallery, 1990; RSA from 1991; Roger Billcliffe, Compass Gallery and Royal Glasgow Institute of the Fine Arts, all Glasgow in 1994; and Rendezvous, Candlewick and the City Art Gallery, all in Aberdeen in 1996. Later solo exhibition included The Lemon Tree, Aberdeen, 1995, and The Gallery at Heatherslaw Mill, Northumberland, 1996.

Germaine DOLAN 1945– Artist and teacher in acrylic and watercolour, born in Cambridge of Irish parents. She travelled extensively with her Royal Air Force family and subsequently. Studied at Ealing School of Art, 1969–70, and Canterbury College of Art, 1970–3, notable teachers including Geoffrey

Rigden and Mali Morris, with Matisse a key influence. Dolan said that "I draw fast – gathering information – and paint slow, synthesising and considering. Attention must be rigorously drilled by hand and eye to be limber. New signs must be found, the briefest possible indication." Took part in many mixed shows in Canterbury and in Clevedon: Sharing a View, APT Gallery and tour, 1997–8. Solo exhibitions included The Grange Museum, Neasden, 1985; Darwen College, University of Kent, 1992; and in 1996 at The Friars Gallery, Canterbury, where she lived. The Sinai Desert was her second home, where she ran occasional art courses.

Patrick DOLAN 1926–1980 Painter of abstracts in oil, and teacher, born in Ireland. He studied at Architectural Association in 1950s, was an associate of Francis Bacon and, largely due to Adrian Heath, in 1960s moved to St Ives, Cornwall, in 1965 becoming a member of Penwith Society of Arts. From 1969 until his death he was a senior lecturer at Cardiff School of Art. In 1962 Dolan shared a show with Anthony Shiels and Alan Wood at Gallery 60 in Chichester, organised by Rawlinsky Gallery; in 1965 he shared an exhibition with Wood at Queen Square Gallery in Leeds, also showing with Midland Group in Nottingham; and in 1995 a group of Dolan's works was shown by Belgrave Gallery. He remains a rather mysterious figure, who died of cancer.

James DOLBY 1909–1975 Painter, printmaker and draughtsman, born at Oxenhope, near Haworth, Yorkshire. Studied at Keighley School of Art and at the Royal College of Art under Robert Austin and Malcolm Osborne. Exhibited RA, SWE, RBA, in the provinces and widely abroad. The Victoria & Albert Museum and Whitworth Art Gallery, Manchester, among a number of provincial galleries, hold his work. Dolby was on the staff of Bournemouth College of Art in the 1930s, then was head of Blackburn School of Art, 1947–69. He served in the Royal Navy during World War II and wrote a book called *The Steel Navy*. His work ranged over a variety of subjects, including industrial scenes, interiors and abstract paintings of the sea. Lived at Southampton.

M F DOMMEN: *see* **Marguerite France DOUGLAS**

Jacqueline DONACHIE 1969– Artist using sound installations and photographs, born and lived in Glasgow, who studied at the School of Art there, 1986–91. In 1995–6 she gained a Fulbright Fellowship to New York. Group exhibitions included Information, Paisley Museum and Art Galleries, 1989; New Art in Scotland, Centre for Contemporary Arts, Glasgow, 1994; Make Believe, Royal College of Art, 1995; and Correspondences, Scottish National Gallery of Modern Art, 1997–8. Had a solo show, Part Edit, at Tramway, Glasgow, 1994, later ones including Home Taping, Marian Goodman Gallery, New York, 1996.

Rita DONAGH 1939– Draughtsman, painter, collagist and teacher, born in Wednesbury, Staffordshire. After studying at University of Durham, 1956–62, she taught at Reading University's School of Fine Art, 1964–72. Further teaching followed at Slade School of Fine Art and Goldsmiths' College School of Art. Donagh participated in a number of influential group shows and had a first solo exhibition at Nigel Greenwood in 1972, showing thereafter. In 1977 had retrospective at Whitworth Art Gallery, Manchester, and tour. Arts Council holds her work, which was often of a highly experimental nature, drawing on inspirations as diverse as police photographs of nightlife in New York; an Irishman killed in Dublin by a car bomb; and the American writer of *Walden*, H D Thoreau. Her working method was painstaking, with precise draughtsmanship.

Anne DONALD 1941– Painter, printmaker and museum keeper, born and lived in Glasgow, who studied at the School of Art there, 1959–63, under David Donaldson, William Armour and W Drummond Bone. She worked at Glasgow Art Gallery and Museum, 1959–63, latterly as keeper of fine art; was a part-time artist until 1993, then full-time. Was a member of Royal Glasgow Institute of the Fine Arts, Glasgow Society of Women Artists and SSWA, also showing at RSA and RSW and with several Glasgow dealers in mixed exhibitions. Had a two-man show at Lillie Art Gallery, Milngavie, 1977; a four-man there in 1994; with a solo exhibition at Greenock Arts Guild, 1978. Glasgow Art Gallery and Museum, Strathclyde University, Lillie Art Gallery and Tayside Regional Council hold Donald's work, which was still life and landscape "influenced by Scottish art from the Glasgow Boys and Scottish Colourists onwards".

George DONALD 1943– Painter and teacher, born in Ootacamund, southern India. He was awarded an Andrew Grant Scholarship in the mid-1960s, attending Edinburgh College of Art, 1966, winning a postgraduate scholarship in 1967 and a Helen A Rose Travelling Scholarship, 1967–8. Donald was a visiting scholar at Benares University in 1967, then was at Hornsey College of Art, 1969. In the 1970s he won a series of awards and bursaries followed by more in the 1980s, including the RSA Gillies Prize and RSW May Marshall Brown Award. Donald was a member of RSA, RSW and SSA. He worked as a visiting artist in China and Thailand, lectured at Edinburgh College of Art and was director of Edinburgh Festival Summer School in the Visual Arts. Donald showed widely in Britain and abroad in mixed exhibitions. Main solo exhibitions ranged from 57 Gallery, Edinburgh, in 1971, through Scottish Gallery and Open Eye Gallery there to Christopher Hull Gallery in 1992. Donald did commissioned portraits for Scottish Arts Council and Glasgow University and a window design for the Scottish National Library. Victoria & Albert Museum, Scottish Arts Council and Glasgow University hold his work.

Antony DONALDSON 1939– Painter and teacher, born in Godalming, Surrey. His work often reflected ephemeral events and personalities and the media. Studied at Regent Street Polytechnic School of Art, 1957–8, and Slade School of Fine Art, 1958–62, obtaining a London University postgraduateship of fine art in 1962–3. He showed with Young Contemporaries and LG and had first one-man show at Rowan Gallery in 1963. Joined teaching staff of Chelsea School of Art in 1962, the year before he won a second prize in John Moores Liverpool Exhibition. Later showed at Felicity Samuel's gallery. Tate Gallery and Arts Council hold his work.

David DONALDSON 1916–1996 Painter and teacher, born in Chryston, Lanarkshire. He was married to the artist Marysia Donaldson. He studied at Glasgow School of Art, 1932–7. In 1936 Donaldson won the Directors Prize and a year later the Haldane Travelling Scholarship, visiting Italy and France. After additional tuition at Glasgow School of Art he took up part-time teaching there, becoming a full-time teacher and eventually head of the department of drawing and painting. Was elected RSA and won its Guthrie Award. In 1977 he was appointed Painter and Limner to HM The Queen in Scotland. Although versatile, Donaldson became known as one of Scotland's leading portrait painters. He participated in many group shows in Britain and abroad. Had a one-man exhibition at Henry Hillier's Studio, Glasgow, in 1961, others including the French Institute, Glasgow, and Mall Galleries, 1980. Donaldson's work is held by HM The Queen, Scottish Arts Council and many Scottish galleries. Lived in Glasgow, but had a house in France.

Kim DONALDSON 1952– Painter and sculptor, born in Rhodesia. He grew up on his grandfather's ranch, where he began to sketch while still at school. After experimenting in various styles and media, in 1972 he became a full-time artist, wildlife his subject. Donaldson developed an encyclopaedic knowledge of the flora and fauna of southern Africa and was noted for his subjects' anatomical accuracy, based on living rough close to them in the wilderness. Donaldson's work, which was included in several books on wildlife art and was reproduced in limited edition plates, had many solo showings. His exhibition Safari was held by The Halcyon Gallery, Birmingham, 1994. Donaldson latterly settled in Florida, America.

Marysia DONALDSON fl. from 1950s– Painter, sculptor and designer, born in Warsaw, Poland. She moved to Scotland at an early age, where she was educated. Studied at Glasgow School of Art under her husband-to-be, the painter David Donaldson, and afterwards with Hugh Adam Crawford. On leaving art school she took up sculpture and fashion design, later returning to painting, in which she was a rich Colourist. Showed at RSA, RA, Royal Glasgow Institute of the Fine Arts and Fosse Gallery, Stow-on-the-Wold, in mixed exhibitions. She had solo shows at Macauley Gallery, Stenton, in 1985; at Washington Gallery, Glasgow, 1986; and in 1987 at Ancrum Gallery, Roxborough. Her work is in collection of HRH The Duke of Edinburgh and in many private holdings throughout the world. Had a studio in London.

Rory DONALDSON 1965– Artist in mixed media, notable for photomontage work, born in Aberdeen, Scotland. Studied at Gray's School of Art, Aberdeen, and after graduating with honours studied at University of Ulster to gain master's degree, over period 1982–7. In 1986 gained Shell UK Prize, also Rank Xerox, Marlow, award. Group exhibitions included Time at Museum of Modern Art in Oxford, 1988; the Fruitmarket Open, at Fruitmarket Gallery, Edinburgh, 1990; and Gruzelier Modern Art, 1992. Solo exhibitions included Physical Manners at Project Gallery, Dublin, and Interference, Art Advice, Belfast, both 1989. In 1992–3 Donaldson was included in the Arts Council Gallery, Belfast, show Twelve Stars, the work State 13, of 1991, being acquired for European Parliament Collection.

Thea DONIACH 1907–1986 Artist in oil, watercolour and ink, she was born into an artistic family at Chevreuse, France, her father being the Polish Jewish painter Leopold Pilichowski. In 1932 she married the distinguished scholar of Judaic and Semitic languages, lexicographer, linguist and civil servant Nakdimon Doniach, who died in 1994. After education at the Lycée Français de Londres Doniach in the early 1950s studied art in London, first under Frederick Gore at St Martin's School of Art, then at Goldsmiths' College. She acted as a part-time tutor in Oxford, where she lived. Work is in the collections of RWA and City of Oxford Education Committee and the junior common rooms of Corpus Christi and University Colleges, Oxford.

Mary DONINGTON 1909– Sculptor and musician, born in London, who studied at Royal Academy of Music. She was mainly self-taught in art, but had a year under the sculptor Frank Dobson, 1945–6. Showed at RA, WIAC, NS and elsewhere. Lived for many years at Headley Down, Hampshire.

Godfried DONKOR 1964– Artist, curator and teacher, who graduated in fine art painting at Central St Martins College of Art, 1984–9; studied painting under a Unesco grant in Barcelona, Spain, 1991–2; then gained his master's degree studying African art history at the School of Oriental and African Studies, 1994–5 (he had a solo show there, 1995). In 1995, he lectured on African art at the Royal Academy. Donkor worked as a curator at 198 Gallery, 1995–8, where he also exhibited. He gained a *Daily Mail* Best Newcomer Exhibition award at Olympia, 1991. Group shows included Thapong International Artist Exhibition, Botswana, 1994, and Transforming the Crown, American tour, 1997. Installations included The Seven Lives of Picasso, 1994, and Glamour, 1995, both Harvey Nichols. Smithsonian Institution, Washington, America; Paintings for Hospitals; University of Helsinki, Finland; and Unilever collections hold examples. Lived in London.

Leonard David DONNE 1926– Painter, printmaker and teacher, born in Leicester. He studied at the College of Art there under the portrait painter Donald Carrington, eventually becoming head of art at Cheshunt School. Donne, who signed his work D D, was a member of Free Painters and Sculptors, having a series of solo shows at Loggia Gallery from 1973. Others included Hitchin Museum, 1977. Lived for many years at Ware, Hertfordshire, latterly at Leintwardine, Herefordshire.

Frances DONNELLY 1970– Painter, born in Lurgan, Northern Ireland, who studied at Kingston University, 1988–9; University of Ulster, 1991–3 (which owns her work); and Royal College of Art, 1993–5. In 1992, she gained a placement at Bazalel Academy of Art and Design, Jerusalem, in 1994 a travel award to Asilah Studio, Morocco. After leaving the Royal College, Donnelly began establishing a name as an abstract painter, but by the time of her solo exhibition at Paton Gallery, 1997, her work was figurative, with a forceful style, a tendency to pattern making and elements of Symbolism. She was "interested in the collective memory of enchanted places". Group shows included Belfast Young Contemporaries, Oxford Street Gallery, Belfast, 1992, and Stratocruising at Raw Gallery, 1996.

Micky DONNELLY 1952– Artist, teacher and writer in whose work enigmatic images and symbols were featured. Was born in Belfast, where he gained his bachelor's degree at University of Ulster in 1979, his master's two years later, then in 1985 won the Arts Council of Northern Ireland Scholarship at the British School at Rome. He wrote and lectured extensively on art, and was for a time on the editorial board of *Circa*. He was chosen for many key Irish art exhibitions which toured abroad, including On the Balcony of the Nation, America, 1990–2, and The Fifth Province, Canada, 1991–3. In 1994 he was included in the shows Works on Paper and Beyond the Partitions, put on by Queen Street Studios, Belfast, with which Donnelly was associated. Had numerous solo shows in Ireland and abroad, including Taylor Galleries, Dublin, 1988 and 1992, and Anderson O'Day, 1991. Ulster Museum in Belfast; Arts Councils of Great Britain, Northern Ireland and the Republic of Ireland; British Council; and the European Parliament hold his works.

Arthur DOOLEY 1929–1994 Self-taught sculptor in metal who scorned art schools, born and worked in Liverpool. Big Arthur, as he was known, was a Liverpudlian character who applied to be town planner because he was against a tower block city, helped reform the Liverpool Academy, being its chairman, and campaigned to revive the South Docks. After leaving school at 14 Dooley served on Mersey tugboats and was also to work on the *Ark Royal* in Cammell Laird's shipyard, important to his development as a sculptor. He joined the Irish Guards playing as a bagpiper; went absent without leave and served as a colonel with the Palestine Liberation Organization; and was jailed for his absence, in prison experimenting with sculpture. Back in London he joined a drawing class at Whitechapel Art Gallery, worked as a janitor and part-time model at St Martin's School of Art and eventually returned to Liverpool where a time working for Dunlop's at Speke helped him refine his sculptural technique. An important breakthrough was getting a commission to work on the Stations of the Cross for St Mary's Church at Leyland, near Preston. Other work included The Risen Christ for Our Lady of the Wayside in Solihull and the statue of St Mary in the Mariners' Chapel of the Quay in the Liverpool parish church of St Nicholas. Dooley, a Communist and a Catholic, spurned London art galleries, although his shows included the dungeons of Windsor Castle in 1990. Latterly his son Paul, a trained stonemason, helped him. Walker Art Gallery, Liverpool, holds The Soldier.

DORAB: *see* **Dorab Dadiba CONTRACTOR**

Barbara DORF 1933– Artist in oil, watercolour and charcoal pencil, and art history teacher, born and lived in London. Dorf favoured architectural subjects in a distinctive style characterised by delicate tonal watercolour washes against clear, simple forms. She attended Central School of Arts and Crafts, teachers including Keith Vaughan, and Slade School of Fine Art, leaving in 1962, under Tom Monnington, E H Gombrich and Francis Haskell. Dorf's teaching appointments included Ruskin School of Drawing, Oxford, and Brookes University there. Among her mixed shows were RA Summer Exhibition and NEAC. Solo shows included Michael Parkin Gallery from 1978, Montpelier Sandelson, 1981, and Maas Gallery from 1986. In 1993 she was in a three-artist exhibition at Jerram Gallery, Salisbury. British Museum; Lady Margaret Hall and St Edmund Hall, Oxford; Sir Ernst Gombrich; the actress Dame Judi Dench; and actor Alec McCowen held examples.

Simon DORRELL 1961– Painter and illustrator, born in Worcestershire. After an arts foundation course in Hereford, in 1984 Dorrell gained an honours degree from Maidstone College of Art. Then moved to Camberley, Surrey, to pursue career as a freelance illustrator. After a period in Herefordshire from the mid-1980s, where he returned to an earlier interest in landscape painting, in 1989 set up a studio in Elan Valley, mid-Wales, where he restored and developed an Edwardian garden as well as painting. Showed widely, including Five Dials Gallery, 1984; Silk Top Hat Gallery, Ludlow, 1988; Upton Lodge Galleries, Tetbury, 1991; and Sue Rankin Gallery, 1992, where he also in same year shared a show.

Bartolomeu Dos SANTOS 1931– Printmaker and teacher, born in Lisbon, Portugal. He studied at Escola Superior de Belas Artes in 1950–6, then studied at Slade School of Fine Art until 1958. Returned to Portugal while retaining connections with London. After Anthony Gross's retirement, in 1961 took over as professor of printmaking at Slade. Showed in Britain, Portugal and elsewhere, his prints sometimes incorporating photographic imagery. Retrospective was held at Centro de Arte Moderna of the Gulbenkian Foundation in Lisbon in 1989; in 1990–1 was included in British Museum show Avant-Garde British Printmaking 1914–1960; and in 1996 his exhibition Reminiscences on Fernando Pessoa was held at Strang Print Room, University College, following his retirement from the Slade. Lived in London.

John DOUBLEDAY 1947– Sculptor, born in Maldon, Essex, where he continued to live. Doubleday studied in Paris and at Goldsmiths' College School of Art, 1965–8. Had a solo show at Waterhouse Gallery, 1968, followed by several dozen others, latterly Beecroft Art Gallery, Southend-on-Sea, 1985; Boundary Gallery, 1989; and Oriel Gallery, 1990. Among his many public works were Dr Michael Ramsay, Archbishop of Canterbury, Lambeth Palace, 1974; Earl Mountbatten of Burma, Broadlands, 1976; Charlie Chaplin, Leicester Square, 1981; The Beatles, Liverpool, 1984; and The Cricketer, County Square, Chelmsford, 1992. Ashmolean Museum in Oxford, Tate Gallery, Victoria & Albert Museum and National Museum of Wales, Cardiff, hold his work.

Eric John DOUDNEY 1905–1986 Industrial designer, sculptor in many materials and teacher, born in Watford, Hertfordshire, as Henry Eric John Doudney; he signed work E J D. After Acton and Chiswick Polytechnic Doudney studied at Richmond School of Art, then Royal Academy Schools sculpture department and Kennington School of Art, his teachers including Charles Wheeler, William McMillan and E S Frith. Taught before World War II at Twickenham Technical College, then designed for Hawker Aircraft and Halex Ltd before joining the staff of the University of Canterbury in Christchurch, New Zealand, in 1950. Showed in England at RA, RBA and elsewhere, his work being sited on various public buildings in London and the north of England. Was elected a fellow of the RBS, his Slate Carving, in the manner of Eric Gill, being illustrated in the book *R B S: Modern British Sculpture*, published in 1939.

John DOUGILL 1934– Painter, artist in variety of graphic and photographic media, and teacher. He attended West Sussex College of Art, 1950–5, then Royal College of Art, 1957–60, becoming a tutor at Royal College in 1977. In the early 1970s Dougill, a committed teacher, gravitated to the organisation of students in photographic, film and poster work, becoming interested in community and environmental affairs. Participated in RA exhibition Thirty London Painters in 1985 and was included in Royal College of Art's show Exhibition Road in 1988. Lived in London.

Anne DOUGLAS 1948– Sculptor, draughtsman and teacher. After studying anthropology at Durham University Douglas studied sculpture at Camberwell School of Arts and Crafts. She was Rome Scholar in Sculpture, 1976–8, and artist-in-residence at the British School in 1984. In 1987 she gained a travel grant to New York. Douglas' teaching venues included Slade School of Fine Art and Royal College of Art. She took part in many group shows including British School, 1977–8; Newcastle Polytechnic Gallery, 1978–9; Artsite Gallery, Bath, 1986; and the Newcastle Group's 1990 show The Northern Lights at DLI Museum & Arts Centre, Durham, and tour. Her later solo shows included Bondgate Gallery, Northumberland, 1986, and St Martin's Gallery, 1989. Arts Council holds examples. Douglas said that she was "concerned with constructing a plastic equivalent for experience," not just imitating reality. Lived in Gateshead, Tyne and Wear.

David DOUGLAS 1965– Artist in various media, born in Daventry, Northamptonshire. He studied art at foundation school, Nene College, Northampton, 1981–3, and Maidstone College of Art, 1983–5. Showed at RA and elsewhere. Paintings in Hospitals bought his work. Lived in Weedon, Northamptonshire.

Emma Cathleen DOUGLAS fl. from 1970s– Printmaker who did a foundation course at Central School, 1975–6, graduating in fine art from Middlesex Polytechnic, 1976–9. Was affiliated to the École des Arts Decoratifs, Paris, 1979–80, gaining a master's degree in printmaking at Royal College of Art, 1980–3. Shows included Stowells Trophy at RA from 1979; Hayward Annual, 1982; Battersea Arts Centre, 1985; Angela Flowers Gallery, 1986; and Royal Over-Seas League, 1988. She was Lowick House artist-in-residence, 1984, and a junior fellow in the Royal College of Art's department of printmaking, 1988. Lived in London.

Jane DOUGLAS 1918– Painter, stage designer and teacher. She studied at the Slade School of Fine Art, at St Martin's School of Art and at Goldsmiths' College School of Art. Showed RA, LG, SWA and in the provinces. Lived in London.

Marguerite France DOUGLAS 1918– Painter and printmaker and farmer, born in Derbyshire of Swiss parents. She sometimes signed work M F Dommen, her unmarried name, also M F D. Studied with Ernest Townsend in Derby, followed by a year in 1935 at Lausanne École des Beaux-Arts, then painting, 1936–9, at Royal Academy Schools with Walter Westley Russell, Tom Monnington and Ernest Jackson. Between 1939–45 Douglas was in the Women's Land Army, mostly as a timber measurer in the New Forest which inspired an interest in trees. Showed landscape and portraits with SSA and with SWA. In 1959 Douglas became a corresponding member of the International Institute of Arts and Letters and in 1968 showed in Ancona, being awarded a Diploma of Merit. William Johnstone much influenced her work in the 1970s. Lived in Earlston, Berwickshire.

Phoebe Sholto DOUGLAS 1906– Portrait miniaturist, painter, enameller and teacher, born in London. She studied at Eastbourne College of Art under Arthur Reeve-Fowkes and Oliver Senior. Was a member of RMS from 1972, exhibiting at RI, RA and in the Kent area, where she lived at Goudhurst, teaching art at Bethany School. Sunderland Museum & Art Gallery holds her portrait of the artist Lawson Wood.

Sokari DOUGLAS CAMP 1958– Sculptor in welded steel, often of everyday people and events. She graduated from Central School of Art and Design, 1983, gaining her master's degree at Royal College of Art. Among awards was the Saatchi and Saatchi Award in 1982 and the Prince of Wales Scholarship and Henry Moore Bursary, both in 1983. Took part in many group shows from New Contemporaries, 1983; From Two Worlds, Whitechapel Art Gallery and tour, 1986–7; and Africa Explores, at New Museum for Contemporary Art, New York, and tour, 1991–3. Had solo show at Bluecoat Gallery, with tour, 1988, later ones including Redfern Gallery, 1993. Arts Council holds her work. Lived in London.

Pat DOUTHWAITE 1939– Painter, born in Glasgow. As a small girl she studied movement and mime with Margaret Morris, wife of the painter J D Fergusson; he encouraged her to paint, but otherwise she was self-taught. In 1958 she lived in Suffolk with a group of artists, including Robert Colquhoun, Robert MacBryde and William Crozier. From 1959 for some years she travelled worldwide, then settling to work in Britain. Had first solo show at 57 Gallery, Edinburgh, 1958. Participated in many group shows in Britain and abroad and had regular one-man exhibitions, including a retrospective at Third Eye Centre, Glasgow, in 1988–9, and tour; and several with William Jackson Gallery. Douthwaite's pictures, often tinged with sadness or anguish, pursued a variety of themes, such as the Manson Trial, American Women Bandits and Amy Johnson, Aviator. Aberdeen Art Gallery, Ferens Art Gallery in Hull and Scottish Arts Council hold her work.

Stephen DOVE 1949– Prolific artist and teacher, born in Leicester, a notable Colourist as a painter. Dove said that his paintings "lie in that area that exists between abstraction and figuration … The human form and the landscape are frequent sources that are referred to directly or else merely hinted at." He gained his art and design diploma, attending Lanchester Polytechnic in Coventry and Hull College of Art, obtaining his art teacher's diploma at Birmingham Polytechnic. In 1976 Dove moved to Zennor, Cornwall, from 1980 settling in St Ives. He gained South West Arts Minor Awards, 1980 and 1981. Taught part-time at Falmouth School of Art, Falmouth School and Richard Lander School in Truro. Dove was a member of the Penwith Society and Porthmeor Printmakers, both in St Ives, and Newlyn Society of Artists. He had many mixed exhibition appearances, including Cannon Hill Arts Centre, Birmingham, 1974; Salt House Gallery, St Ives, from 1980; New Street Gallery, Plymouth, 1987; Demarco's Choice, Newlyn Gallery, 1993; and Eight Painters, Rainy Day Gallery, Penzance, 1994. Had a solo show at Plymouth Arts Centre, 1980; at Salt House, from 1981; and Beaux Arts, Bath, 1984. St Thomas' Hospital, Royal Cornwall Museum in Truro and Cornwall School Collection hold examples.

Peter DOVER fl. from 1980s– Abstract relief printmaker and teacher, born in Merseyside, who gained a first-class honours degree at Leeds Polytechnic, 1981–4, and his master's in fine art, with Alistair Grant, at Royal College of Art, 1986–8. Won many awards, including *Galleries Magazine* award (Open to Print), 1988; London Contemporary Arts and Friends of Bradford Art Galleries awards, 11th British International Print Biennale, 1990; *Printmaking Today* award, Federation of British Artists Print Exhibition, 1994; and Stinger Purchase Prize and Estonia National Art Museum Purchase Prize, Tallinn International Print Triennale, 1995. Held many residencies and lectureships, later visiting posts including Leeds Metropolitan University and Kent Institute of Art and Design. Among Dover's commissions was a silkscreen mural project for Great Ormond Street Hospital, 1990–1. He was made an associate of RE in 1995 and took part in many group exhibitions, including Marlborough Graphics, 1991; British Art Fair, Royal College of Art, 1993; Salon des Graphiques at Curwen Gallery, 1995; and Bracknell Gallery, South Hill Park, 1996. Showed solo with New Academy Gallery from 1991. Tate Gallery, Ashmolean Museum in Oxford, Estonia National Art Museum and public galleries in Dudley and Plymouth hold examples. Lived in London.

Alexander Warren DOW 1873–1948 Painter, printmaker and writer, born in London. Studied at Cambridge University in the 1890s, then studied art with Norman Garstin in Penzance, with Frank Brangwyn in London, at Heatherley's School of Fine Art and in Paris. Exhibited RBA extensively, also at RI, ROI, Walker Art Gallery, Liverpool and Paris Salon. Wrote on painting for such publications as *John O'London's Weekly, Daily News, The Tablet* and *Colour*, to whose staff he was attached. Lived in London.

James H DOWD 1884–1956 Painter, draughtsman and printmaker who spent part of his early life in Sheffield but later settled in London. He contributed to publications including *Punch* and produced a popular book, *Important People*. Exhibited RA, RP, Cooling Galleries and elsewhere in London.

Natalie DOWER 1931– Painter and sculptor in various media, born in London, where she eventually settled to work part of the year, also in Portugal. She was also a teacher, including St Albans, Camberwell and Byam Shaw Schools of Art; Bath Academy of Art in Corsham; and at the American School of Tangier, Morocco, where she lived from 1966, moving to Portugal in 1973, returning to Britain in 1982. Dower said that her style moved from that of the Euston Road School to Constructivism. She attended St Martin's School of Art, 1948–9; Camberwell School of Art, 1949–52; and Slade School of Fine Art, 1952–4. Group shows included Fox Fine Art, 1977; Hayward Annual, 1982; Systematic Constructive Drawings at Wentworth Gallery, University of York, 1986; Chicago International Art Exposition from 1988; and First International Female Artists' Art Biennial, Stockholm, 1995. Had a solo show at Polytechnic of Central London, 1979, later ones including Out of the Arc, Curwen Gallery, 1995, and Mathematics – The Visual Arts, Rowley House, Oxford, 1996. Arts Council, Government Art Collection and Arthur Andersen & Company hold her works.

Sean DOWER 1965– Artist educated at Camberwell School of Art and Rijksakademie van Beeldende Kunsten, Amsterdam, Netherlands. He was included in prominent group exhibitions: Lost Property, W139, Amsterdam, and Great Western Studios, 1995; and Against, Anthony d'Offay Gallery, Pandemonium at ICA and Rational Behaviour, The Tannery, all 1996. In 1997, Dower completed his first major commission for a public gallery, No Room in Hell (Absent Qualia), for Matt's Gallery, a three-dimensional video installation mixing the visual conventions of low-budget 1970s horror films with contemporary street culture and the mythology of the undead found in voodoo.

Ann DOWKER fl. from 1970s– Painter, draughtsman, printmaker and teacher, born in Sheffield, Yorkshire. After studying at Bath Academy of Art, Corsham, she taught in East End of London, attending evening classes in life drawing at St Martin's School of Art. In 1978 she began etching one day a week at Camden Institute, in 1981 taking part-time course in lithography at Central School of Art. She taught part-time at adult education classes and at Byam Shaw School of Art. Dowker was a prolific artist, interested in the human figure, who viewed her work "as a form of research, a process of discovery, invention and constant optimism". Showed in group exhibitions at House Gallery, 1981, and Moira Kelly Gallery, 1982, and was included in the Norwich School of Art Gallery 1986–7 touring show A Reputation Amongst Artists. Had a solo exhibition at Christchurch Mansion, Ipswich, 1994, another at Theo Waddington Fine Art, 1997. Government Art Collection holds her work.

Jane DOWLING 1925– Painter and teacher who was married to the artist Peter Greenham. She took a degree at Oxford University, 1943–6. Studied at Slade School of Fine Art and Ruskin School of Drawing, Oxford, Byam Shaw School of Art and Central School of Art, concluding her studies in the early 1960s. She went on to teach at Byam Shaw, Maidstone College of Art and Royal Academy Schools. Showed at RA from 1961. She had a series of solo shows at New Grafton Gallery from 1974. Had a joint Arts Council and Norwich School of Art touring show in 1984–5 with her husband. Her work was bought by Farringdon Trust, more being in John Radcliffe Hospital, Oxford. Had a 20-year retrospective at Mompesson House, Salisbury, 1992. Lived at Otmoor, Oxfordshire.

Avril DOWN 1900– Painter and teacher, born in Penang Island, Malaya. Educated in England, she attended Slade School of Fine Art, where her teachers included Henry Tonks and Walter Russell. She went on to teach in the Bishop's Stortford area, where she belonged to the local Art Society, living at Elsenham, Hertfordshire. She showed with UA, RI, in the Bishop's Stortford and Sutton Coldfield areas and in India. Completed a number of murals in public buildings in England and India. Sometimes signed work with initials only.

Vera DOWN 1888– Painter and printmaker, born in London. She studied at Walter Donne's Grosvenor Life School, the Central School of Arts and Crafts and in Paris. Taught for a time. Showed at RA, Walker's Galleries, Ridley Art Club, SWA and elsewhere. Lived in Woldingham, Surrey.

Kate DOWNIE 1958– Artist employing a variety of media, including film and performance, who was born in America. Studied at Gray's School of Art in Aberdeen, 1975–80. Downie made a number of residencies, including Scottish Arts Council residency in Amsterdam and at Total's North Alwyn oilfield in the North Sea. Solo shows included Amsterdam and Denmark and one at Collins Gallery, Glasgow, in 1990 after a year's residency in Paris. She showed frenetic images evoking the speed and bustle of the city. Downie's work was in Through Women's Eyes, at City Art Centre, Edinburgh, 1992–3. Is represented in collections throughout Europe and America.

Linda DOWNIE 1964– Artist born in Dunfermline, Fife, who gained a fine art honours degree at Duncan of Jordanstone College of Art, Dundee, 1982–6, with postgraduate studies at Nova Scotia College of Art, Halifax, Canada, 1984; then attended Royal College of Art, 1987–9, for her master's in fine art, with an exchange scholarship in Vienna, 1988. Among awards were an Elizabeth Greenshields Memorial Award, 1987, and a London Institute Purchase Award, 1996. Participated in group exhibitions in Britain and Switzerland, solo shows including Category & Allegory, Lamont Gallery, 1998, where fantastic images mingled human, animal, bird and vegetable elements and drew on ancient myth. Publications included *Le Bain* and *The Bad Book Suit*.

Nigel DOWNING 1964– Painter, draughtsman and teacher, born Middlesbrough, Yorkshire. He did a foundation course at Cleveland College of Art and Design, 1984–5, an honours degree in fine art at Canterbury College of Art, 1985–8, and his master's degree in fine art (painting) at University of Newcastle, 1988–90. In 1988 won a Chatham College of Further Education mural award. Held a residency at Sir William Turner 6th Form College, Redcar, in 1991, the year he was also artist-in-residence at Pilkington Glass International Ladies' Tennis Championships at Eastbourne. Downing taught part-time at University of Newcastle. In 1990 he had a solo show at Picture Gallery, Newcastle, the year after at Cleveland College of Art. In 1992 Downing was artist-in-residence at Towner Art Gallery, Eastbourne, which gave him a one-man show of his Pilkington tennis pictures. These showed Downing's fluid use of paint, bright palette and studies of figures in action to good effect.

Peter DOWNING fl. from 1950s– Artist and teacher who lived near the edge of Morecambe Bay, Lancashire. His work celebrated its peculiar qualities and light as well as being, in his words, "landscapes of an interior space that mirrors and reflects the external flow and change". Downing studied at Leeds and Royal Colleges of Art. Was a teacher of fine art, 1954–84, when he took early retirement from his post of principal lecturer at Preston (later Lancashire) Polytechnic. Then painted full-time. From 1952 Downing's work was seen throughout the country in many solo and mixed exhibitions. These included an Arts Council tour, Bradford Print Biennale, the International Drawing Biennale in Cleveland and Lancashire South of the Sands, which toured from the County and Regimental Museum, Preston, 1988.

Edgar DOWNS 1876–1963 Painter, especially of animals, born at Claughton, Birkenhead, Cheshire. After education in Birkenhead he studied at Munich Academy of Arts, winning a silver medal. Exhibited extensively at ROI, also at RCamA, RA and Walker Art Gallery, Liverpool. Latterly lived at Mudeford, Hampshire.

John DOWNTON 1906–1991 Painter and draughtsman, born in Erith, Kent. He read art history at Cambridge, 1925, gaining a first-class honours degree. Then entered Slade School of Fine Art, 1928, under Henry Tonks and Philip Wilson Steer. A private income enabled Downton to travel widely in Western Europe in the period before World War II. What he saw in museums, his reading and understanding of the Italian Quattrocento encouraged him to develop a style of portraiture, mainly in tempera, of meticulous heightened realism. The artist was a keen Morrisian Socialist and pacifist and a conscientious objector. His pictures were shown to acclaim at RA Summer Exhibitions in late 1930s and his portrait of Joan Harris was included in Prominent Living Artists at Russell-Cotes Art Gallery, Bournemouth, in 1937. Otherwise his work remained unseen until a retrospective at Fine Art Society in 1993; followed by a major tour from Graves Art Gallery, Sheffield, during 1996. Downton lived variously in Cambridge, London and Florence, settling finally at the family home near Sevenoaks, Kent.

Katharine DOWSON 1962– Sculptor, born in London, daughter of the president of the RA, Sir Philip Dowson. She studied at Heatherley School of Art, 1984–5; gained her degree at Camberwell School of Arts and Crafts, 1985–8; then studied for her master's degree in sculpture at Royal College of Art, 1989–92. Among awards were the Princess of Wales Scholarship, 1989–92, and 1st Prize for Egg Loo at Royal College, 1991, the year she won a Granada Foundation Prize. Took part in many group shows, including On Site, Tower Bridge Piazza, 1991; BT New Contemporaries tour, 1992–3; Art in Boxes, England & Co, 1993; and Growth, Norfolk & Norwich Hospital, Norwich, 1994. Had a solo show at 181 Gallery, 1993, in 1995 Mayor Gallery staging her exhibition Growth, in which such topics as "the physical interiors of man and nature" and "human mortality in relation to the universal" were explored. The Saatchi Collection held her work. Lived in London and Norfolk.

James DOXFORD 1899–1978 Painter and teacher, born in North Shields, Northumberland. After education locally he studied at department of fine art, Durham University, under E M O'Rorke Dickey and Richard Hatton, 1922–6. He was principal of Bridgwater Art and Technical School, 1932–8, its equivalent at Barnstaple, 1938–44, then for many years from 1945 was head of the art department at Gateshead Grammar School. Showed with RWA, of which he was a member, RA and elsewhere in the provinces. RWA, Laing Art Gallery in Newcastle and Shipley Art Gallery, Gateshead, hold his work. Lived in Gateshead for many years, latterly in Canterbury, Kent.

Rem DOXFORD: *see* **Anthony HILL**

John DOYLE 1928– Artist in watercolour, pastel and oil, born in London. He began an iron foundry and then put in a manger so that he could attend evening classes at Maidstone School of Art under John Ward. He believed painting could not be taught formally, learning most "just from being with other painters and observing". In 1994 Doyle won a runner-up prize in the Singer & Friedlander/*Sunday Times* Watercolour Competition with a picture which was one of 400 made during a staged walk to Rome. They were to celebrate the foundation of Canterbury Cathedral by St Augustine, held in 1997. The Vatican holds Doyle's work. Was a member of RWS who also exhibited at RA and with the East Kent School in Canterbury Museum. Solo shows included Spink & Son and Canterbury Cathedral. Lived at Warehorne, Ashford, Kent.

Elizabeth DRAKE 1866–1954 Painter, printmaker, miniaturist and teacher, born at Chatham, Kent. After studying at Rochester and Westminster Schools of Art she lived in Paris, working at Atelier Colarossi. Exhibited RA, RWS, RI and elsewhere. Painted widely throughout England, France and South Africa, where her work is in public collections. Lived at Wokingham, Berkshire.

Chris DRAPER 1965– Artist in various media who studied at St Martin's School of Art and Royal College of Art. He was notable for his mixed-media boxes, displayed at England & Co's Art in Boxes in 1992 and incorporated in moving form in a video made for the band Miro. Other group appearances took place in England, France, Japan and Netherlands and in 1990 he had a solo show at Wave Gallery, Tokyo.

Kenneth DRAPER 1944– Sculptor, draughtsman and painter, and teacher, born in Sheffield, Yorkshire. He studied at Chesterfield College of Art, 1959–62, at Kingston School of Art, 1962–5, then Royal College of Art, 1965–8. Draper won the sculpture prize at Young Contemporaries in 1965, then four years later had a one-man show at Redfern Gallery The 1970s saw him taking part in important foreign shows and in British Sculptors '72 at RA, the year he gained a commission for John Dalton Building, Manchester Polytechnic. An important commission, in 1977–8, was his Oriental Gateway for Bradford University. In 1977 Draper took part in the Silver Jubilee Contemporary British Sculpture Exhibition in Battersea Park, the year he won a Major Arts Council Award. Arts Council holds several examples of his work, which was abstract. From mid-1970s taught at Goldsmiths' College School of Art and Camberwell School of Arts and Crafts. Had retrospective at Warwick Arts Trust, 1981. Later solo shows included Austin/Desmond Fine Art and Glen Green Gallery, Santa Fe, 1991, the year Draper was elected RA, and Hart Gallery, 1996. Draper latterly lived on the island of Menorca.

Jasmina DRAŠKOVIĆ-JOHNSON 1943– Icon painter and restorer, born in Kruševac, Yugoslavia, brought up and educated in Belgrade. Studied prehistoric and classical archaeology and art history at Universities of Belgrade and Michigan, in America, gaining a master's degree. Went on to work as an archaeologist, conservator and illustrator, participating in field expeditions and museum work in Europe, Africa, the Middle East and North America. Worked on restoring the monastery church of St Peter in Ras, Yugoslavia; excavating a medieval church near Siena, Italy; on classical Greek vase painting in the British Museum;

and as an artist-conservator at American Museum of Natural History, New York. Icons mainly in the Serbian Byzantine style were shown at four-man exhibition in Woodlands Art Gallery in 1981.

Shmuel DRESNER 1928– Artist in a range of media, including printmaking and collage, born in Warsaw, Poland. With the help of the Central British Fund charity organisation Dresner arrived in England in 1945, starting to paint during a four-year stay in sanatoriums. He then studied at Heatherley School of Fine Art, 1949, and at Central School of Arts and Crafts, 1953. St Martin's Gallery gave him shows in 1962 and 1966; Ben Uri Art Society, which holds a range of examples, in 1975; Galerie Roche, Henstedt, 1980; and Galerie Slavia, Bremen, 1981. Lived latterly in Middlesex.

George Cuthbert DRESSER 1872–1951 Landscape watercolourist, younger brother of the artist Alfred Dresser, who was born and lived in Darlington, County Durham. By profession he was a draughtsman, showing for many years with Darlington Society of Arts of which was a member and RI. The local art gallery holds his work.

Jacob DREW 1909– Painter, decorative artist and teacher, born in Stoke-on-Trent, Staffordshire, where he attended the School of Art, 1926–9, then the Royal College of Art under Ernest Tristram and William Rothenstein, 1929–33. After World War II Drew was head of painting for several years at Camberwell School of Arts and Crafts, then became principal of Willesden and Ealing Schools of Art. He was honorary secretary of the Arts and Crafts Exhibition Society and a council member of the Craft Centre of Great Britain. Showed at RA, and Victoria & Albert Museum holds decorated glass by him. Lived for many years in London, in 1993 moving to France. He was married to the artist Jean Drew.

Jean DREW 1904–1994 Painter, weaver and teacher who studied textiles and weaving at the Royal College of Art and had a studio in Chelsea. She taught in London art schools and ran the textile department at Guildford College of Art. Her rugs were sold under the name Jean Finn at Heal's store and she received many commissions, including the Festival of Britain, 1951. Victoria & Albert Museum hold examples. An exhibition emphasising Drew's flower painting, which flourished with the making of two gardens following her move to Llangorse, 1964, and then Brecon, Powys, in 1988, was held at Brecknock Museum, Brecon, in 1995. Strong design and a feeling for colour were enhanced by her world travels in later years. Her husband was the artist Jacob Drew.

Pamela DREW 1910–1989 Artist in various media, born in Burnley, Lancashire, who studied with Dorothy Baker, with Iain Macnab at the Grosvenor School of Modern Art and in Paris. For five years during the 1950s Drew was an Air Ministry accredited war artist, during which time she handled the Royal Air Force Coronation Review. Had many solo shows in Britain and overseas, work being held by Imperial War Museum, Port of London Authority and Royal Air Force Museum, Hendon. Lived in Milnthorpe, Cumbria.

Knowles DREWE 1878– Painter and teacher who was born Reginald Frank Knowles Drewe. He studied art with Audley Mackworth and showed at RA and Paris Salon. Medici Society reproduced his work. Lived at Berkhamsted, Hertfordshire.

Eva DREWETT 1957– Sculptor in metal and ceramic, born in Warsaw, Poland, who moved to England in the late 1970s, studying at Chelsea School of Art, 1982–3; Central School of Art and Design, 1983–7; and Royal College of Art, 1987–9. She drew on the human form to produce powerful, abstracted works, often on a big scale, as in The Human Side of Being II, of 1991, displayed in Sculpture at Goodwood, 1996–7. Royal Hong Kong Jockey Club, at Kowloon Sculpture Park, holds Drewett's sculpture.

Geoffrey Crellin DREWITT 1921– Painter, muralist and teacher, born in Little Gaddesden, Hertfordshire, whose school has murals by him. After Berkhamsted School he studied at Westminster School of Art and Central School of Arts and Crafts, 1938–40, then in 1946–7 at University of London Institute of Education. Began teaching at Pinner County School, 1947, and after appointments in Norwich and Liverpool was art advisor to Northumberland from 1967, living in Newcastle upon Tyne. Showed at RA, NS, RBA and ROI.

Yvonne DREWRY 1918– Painter, printmaker, typographer and teacher, born in Chiswick, west London, who studied at Liverpool College of Art, 1934–6, then at Edinburgh College of Art, with a Senior Andrew Grant Scholarship, where teachers included William Gillies, Joan Hassall and John Maxwell. She lived in Suffolk for 50 years, finally based at Hollesley, Woodbridge, teaching "students from 8–80 years to see and to paint, print, engrave" (including Maggi Hambling, at Amberfield School, Nacton). Drewry ran a private press, Centaury Press, producing small books, and claimed to be "a lone worker". Was a member of Ipswich Art Society, mixed shows including Laing Art Competition at Mall Galleries, 1991, highly commended 1994; Drawings for All, Gainsborough's House, Sudbury; and Ipswich Open at Wolsey Art Gallery, Ipswich, 1995. Had solo exhibitions at Ipswich, Woodbridge, Colchester, Aldeburgh and Sudbury. Work in many private collections in Europe and Australia.

Agnes DREY c.1890–1957 Painter in oil, born in Withington, Manchester, sister of the art and theatre critic Oscar Raymond Drey who was husband of the artist Anne Estelle Rice. She studied with Frances Hodgkins, who painted her portrait, in the Drey family collection. In the early 1930s Drey moved to St Ives, Cornwall, where she died. She exhibited with WIAC, the Newlyn and St Ives Societies, Lanham's Gallery and Castle Inn in St Ives and was a founder-member of the Penwith Society, which holds her work and gave her a memorial show. Designs by Drey and others were screenprinted onto table mats by the local firm Porthia Prints.

David DREY 1962– Painter who gained a diploma in acting at Drama Centre, Chalk Farm, 1981–4. He then attended John Cass, 1986–7, winning his diploma from Byam Shaw School of Art, 1987–90. Took part in Summer Show, Chenil Galleries, 1990; Florence Trust Open Studio, 1993; and Digswell Trust Group Exhibition at Whiteley's, 1994. In 1995 shared a show with Polly de Falbe at Bartley Drey Gallery. David Drey came from an artistic background. His father was the antique dealer David Drey, his mother the dealer Gill Drey, his grandfather the art critic O Raymond Drey, whose wife was the painter Anne Estelle Rice.

James DRING 1905–1985 Painter in oil and watercolour. Born in London he studied at Clapham School of Art from 1920–7, then at the RCA under Sir William Rothenstein. Exhibited at the RA, RBA, ROI, Wertheim Gallery, in provincial galleries as well as abroad in Paris, Brussels, Sweden and the USA. The Contemporary Art Society purchased his work and the Medici Society, London, reproduced it. The Victoria and Albert Museum, Southampton Art Gallery and Brussels and Mons Museums hold examples. Between 1943–72 he taught at the St Martin's School of Art. Younger brother of the painter William Dring. Lived in London.

Melissa DRING 1944– Artist in pastel and oil, born in Hampshire, daughter of the artist William Dring. She studied at Winchester School of Art and Royal Academy Schools and worked as a portrait painter, police forensic and television courtroom artist. Showed at RA, RP, RBA and PS of which she was a member. Lived in Northampton, where the Central Museum & Art Gallery holds her work, as do Trades Union Congress headquarters and Wellington Park Hotel, Belfast.

William DRING 1904–1990 Painter, draughtsman and teacher, born Dennis William Dring in London, known colloquially as John; brother of the artist James Dring; married the painter Grace Elizabeth Rothwell; his daughter Melissa Dring was also an artist. Studied under Henry Tonks at Slade School of Fine Art, 1922–5, and emerged as a fine draughtsman, a sympathetic portrait painter, fond of using his family as subjects, and deft watercolourist. Won several prizes and scholarships at the Slade. Taught until 1940 at Southampton School of Art, then became an official war artist, whose work is well represented in the Imperial War Museum. After the war he became a noted RA exhibitor, being elected RA in 1955, producing a stream of boardroom and official portraits and depicting a number of royal occasions. Lived at Compton, near Winchester, Hampshire.

Zorica DRLJACHA 1942– Sculptor and draughtsman, brought up initially in Yugoslavia. Was educated partly there, partly at Luton College of Technology before studying at Goldsmiths' College School of Art, then Royal Academy Schools. Her teachers included Charles Mahoney and Sir Henry Rushbury. Won several prizes and Landseer Scholarship. Showed RA, RBS and elsewhere and did commissioned work for Expo '67, held in Montreal, Canada. Lived for some years in London.

George DROUGHT 1940– Artist and teacher who studied at St Helens School of Art, Liverpool College of Art and Central School of Arts and Crafts. Drought won a John Moores Scholarship, taught etching at Bluecoat Chambers in Liverpool and showed widely in mixed exhibitions in the northwest as well as having many solo shows. Two drawings by him were included in the Walker Art Gallery, Liverpool, 1986–7 touring Merseyside Artists 3.

Elsie DRUCE fl. from c.1905–1965 Painter and printmaker, born at Weybridge, Surrey. After education at Roedean School, studied art under William Rothenstein. Exhibited RA, SWA, Goupil Gallery, RP and at many other venues. Member of East Kent Art Society and lived at Rye, Sussex.

Amy Julia DRUCKER 1873–1951 Painter, miniaturist, printmaker and teacher. After initial education in London she studied at St John's Wood and Lambeth Schools of Art and Atelier Colarossi, Paris. She was a versatile, prolific and much-travelled artist who as well as exhibiting at London venues such as RA, RMS, Goupil Gallery, RI and ROI showed abroad, where her work is widely distributed. Was commissioned to paint a portrait of the Emperor of Abyssinia, Haile Selassie. Ben Uri Art Society holds examples. Lived in London.

Michael DRUKS 1940– Artist who used "a variety of techniques ... My work is mainly concerned with group and individual behaviour in the environment. I focus on the conflict between the individual and the crowd." Born in Jerusalem, Druks from 1966–7 studied at the Bat-Yam Institute of Art and the Art High School in Tel-Aviv. He began showing in the early 1960s, participating in the 10+ group. Having in 1970 gained the Working Award for the Creative Artist from the American-Israeli Cultural Foundation, he spent three months in America. In 1971 he taught at Jerusalem's Bezalel Academy of Art, also organising his first street event, the peeling of a public notice-board, aided by the Tel-Aviv city authorities and the Israeli Broadcasting Association. After visiting Amsterdam in 1972 Druks moved to London, where he settled, helping to found the Art Meeting Place in Covent Garden in 1974. Photography, video tapes and sound were features of his work, which was shown in Contemporary Art in Camden, in 1981, at Camden Arts Centre. Solo exhibitions included Whitechapel Art Gallery, 1976, and Beardsmore Gallery, 1997. In 1973 Druks received the W Sandberg Prize from the Israeli Museum, which holds his work, as do the Tel-Aviv Museum, Museum of Modern Art in Haifa and Jan van Eyck Academie, Maastricht.

Blaise DRUMMOND 1967– Painter, born in Liverpool, who contributed "an epic painting, at least for me", entitled Little Western World, oil on canvas on board, to the 1997–8 John

Moores Liverpool Exhibition. Drummond studied at Edinburgh University, 1985–9, then at the National College of Art and Design, Dublin, 1990–4, and for his master's degree at Chelsea College of Art, 1997–8. Later solo exhibitions included The Natural Order of Things, Rubicon Gallery, Dublin, 1997.

Gordon DRUMMOND 1921– Watercolourist, scale modeller and miniaturist, born in Sale, Cheshire. Immediately prior to World War II, during which he served in the Royal Engineers, L T Gordon Drummond was apprenticed as an architect in Manchester. After Army service he was a freelance artist for a while, his art training being undertaken at Manchester College of Art. Showed there, also RWS, but was mainly known as a commercial artist employed by fine art publishers such as Kardonia Ltd, of which he was for a time senior artist. Lived in Potters Bar, Middlesex.

Violet Hilda DRUMMOND 1911– Illustrator and writer of children's books, watercolourist and printmaker, born and lived in London. She studied at St Martin's School of Art. Her book *Mrs Easter and the Storks*, 1957, won her the Kate Greenaway Award. The *Little Laura* series of books by her resulted in cartoon films which she produced for BBC Television. Showed at Oliver Swann Galleries.

Chris DRURY 1948– Sculptor, born in Colombo, Ceylon, who gained his sculpture diploma at Camberwell School of Art, 1966–70. He won a South East Arts Award, 1976, and a British Council Northern Norway Exchange, 1988. Group shows included The Unpainted Landscape, a Scottish Arts Council tour, 1987; Woodlands, Angel Row Gallery, Nottingham, 1990; and Art in Nature, Arte Sella, Sella Valley, Italy, 1994. Had a solo show, Medicine Wheel, Coracle, 1983, later ones including Rebecca Hossack Gallery, 1993, and Vessel, Towner Art Gallery, Eastbourne, and tour, 1995. Later public commissions included Covered Cairn, Tickon Sculpture Park, Langeland, Denmark, 1993, and Vortex, Lewes Castle, Sussex, 1994. Drury travelled extensively and used various, including found, materials to create baskets, cairns and shelter forms. Arts Council, Contemporary Art Society, Royal Botanic Garden in Edinburgh and galleries in Leeds and Cheltenham hold examples.

Henry Myles Reilly DRURY 1904– Watercolourist, printmaker and architect, born in Marlborough, Wiltshire. A qualified architect and fellow of the RIBA, Drury was by profession surveyor to the Dean and Chapter of Exeter Cathedral, having studied at the Architectural Association, 1922–7. He exhibited in the Exeter area, mainly with Exeter Art Society, and lived at Ebford, Devon.

Paul DRURY 1903–1987 Printmaker, painter and teacher, born in London, son of the sculptor Alfred Drury, his mother was also an artist. Studied at Goldsmiths' College School of Art under Edmund Sullivan, Malcolm Osborne, Clive Gardiner and Stanley Anderson, becoming one of the finest exponents of the Goldsmiths' school of printmaking, his work being influenced by the pastoral tradition of Samuel Palmer. Drury went on to teach at Goldsmiths', also at Sir John Cass School of Art. Although he left Goldsmiths' for a time in the late 1930s he returned after World War II part-time and retired in 1969, having been principal of the School of Art for two years. During the war Drury worked in the plaster department at Queen Mary's Hospital, Roehampton, putting to use skills learned working in his father's studio. He also did work for the War Artists' Advisory Committee. Exhibited widely in Britain, continental Europe, in North and South America. British Museum, provincial and foreign galleries holding his work. Retrospective at Goldsmiths' College Gallery, 1984. Lived at Nutley, Sussex.

Alexandra DRYSDALE 1962– Abstract artist, born in London, who studied fine art at Chelsea School of Art, 1980–4. She exhibited in London, Stockholm and Amsterdam and in 1996 had a solo show at Gainsborough's House, Sudbury, having moved to East Anglia two years before. Drysdale's works were grids of repeated relief forms combining delicate pencil draughtsmanship with paper cubes, sewing thread, feathers and other materials. Intricately made and largely monochromatic, they were intended "to emphasise the impermanence of physical forms by drawing attention to shadows and using simple materials and motifs".

Russell DRYSDALE 1912–1981 Painter of landscapes and figures, mainly of Australian subjects, whose full name was George Russell Drysdale. Born in Bognor Regis, Sussex, he went as a child to Australia where his family had interests in farming. Drysdale first visited Europe early in the 1930s, one of a series of visits, after which he decided to relinquish farming and to study art with George Bell in Melbourne for three years from 1935. He was again to study with Bell in 1939–40, but meanwhile he studied in Paris at L'Académie de la Grande Chaumière and Atelier Colarossi, then in London with Iain Macnab at the Grosvenor School of Modern Art. Back in Australia his reputation steadily grew after his first one-man show at the Macquarie Galleries, Sydney, 1942. Had first London one-man show at Leicester Galleries in 1950, other following in 1958, 1965 and 1972. Represented in many Australian Galleries and in Tate Gallery. Retrospective at National Gallery of Victoria, Melbourne, in 1960. Died at Hardy's Bay, New South Wales.

Jaroslav DUB 1878– Painter, born in Veltrusy, Bohemia, who attended Prague School of Art. Initially exhibited in that city, then after settling in Rhyl, Flintshire, about start of World War II began exhibiting RCamA.

Fred DUBERY 1926– Painter and teacher, a native of Suffolk, where much of his work – intimate, in the manner of Bonnard and Vuillard – was painted. He studied at Croydon School of Art, 1949–50 and at Royal College of Art, 1950–3. From 1964 he taught for many years at Royal Academy Schools, being appointed professor of perspective in 1984. From 1950 was a regular RA exhibitor, also showing at NEAC, Leicester Galleries and Roland, Browse & Delbanco. He had solo shows at Trafford Gallery, 1957 and 1963, and New Grafton Gallery, 1974 and 1989. Wrote several books on drawing and perspective. The Arts Club and public galleries in Brighton and Huddersfield hold his work. Lived at Great Finborough, Suffolk.

Du BROUILLARD: *see* **Neil FOGGIE**

Mario DUBSKY 1939–1985 Painter and teacher, born in London. He studied at Slade School of Fine Art, 1956–61, the final year doing postgraduate work. Between 1962–3 Dubsky undertook part-time painting, including Morley College. An Abbey Major Scholarship took him to the British School in Rome, 1963–5. During rest of the 1960s and early 1970s Dubsky taught at various art schools and colleges, including Camberwell, Wimbledon, Brighton, and Central, while a Harkness Fellowship was granted him in 1969–71 for travel to America. Dubsky lived in New York, 1973–4, and he was artist-in-residence at British School, Rome, 1982. He was a tutor at Royal College of Art, 1981–5, having a retrospective at South London Art Gallery in 1984, 15 years after his first one-man, at Grosvenor Gallery. Took part in mixed shows in Britain and abroad. Dubsky was a powerful painter, whose work featured harrowing subjects such as the Holocaust. Arts Council holds. Lived in London.

Ernest John DUCKETT 1916– Painter, notably of portraits, born at Much Wenlock, Shropshire. He studied at art schools in Shrewsbury and Stoke-on-Trent. Was elected PS in 1951 and showed at RA, NS, in the provinces and at Paris Salon. Lived for many years in Kent, at Sevenoaks and later at Southborough.

Aidron DUCKWORTH 1920– Sculptor, painter and teacher, born in Lincoln. He was married to the sculptor and potter Ruth Duckworth. After initial education in Spalding, Duckworth in 1949 studied with Seán Crampton at the Anglo-French Art Centre; also at Chelsea School of Art, 1949–51, where his teachers included the sculptor Willi Soukop, and at the Royal College of Art, 1951–4. Showed widely in England and America, including Woodstock Gallery, New Art Centre and Arnolfini Gallery, Bristol. Was for some time professor of sculpture at Syracuse University, New York, and lived for a while in Kew, Surrey.

Barbara DUCKWORTH 1913– Artist in various media, professionally engaged in medical work, born in Wallasey, Cheshire, settling eventually nearby in Heswall, Wirral. She was a State Registered Nurse and studied at Liverpool College of Art, 1934–8. As well as illustrations for medical books and periodicals, showed with Liver Sketching Club and Walker Art Gallery, Liverpool. She was a fellow of the Medical Artists' Association.

Ruth DUCKWORTH 1919– Sculptor and potter, born in Hamburg, Germany. Studied art in Liverpool, 1936–40 and Kennington School of Art, 1942–3; studied pottery at Hammersmith School of Art and Central School of Arts and Crafts. Showed at RA, elsewhere in London and in North America, including several solo shows. Worked for some time in Chicago, notably on the design for a huge mural on University of Chicago's geophysical building. Lived for some years in Kew, Surrey, and was married to the sculptor Aidron Duckworth.

Wilfred DUDENEY 1911– Sculptor and teacher, born in Leicester. He was educated at St Paul's School, then Central School of Arts and Crafts, 1928–33, with Alfred Turner. Held a number of teaching posts, latterly at Isleworth Polytechnic, Middlesex. Showed, sometimes only signing with initials, at RA, NEAC, RHA and elsewhere. Dudeney's carved elm Falcon is illustrated in Eric Newton's monograph *British Sculpture 1944–1946*. Elected a fellow of RBS in 1952. Lived in London.

Gerry DUDGEON 1952– Artist and teacher, born in Darjeeling, India. He gained an honours degree in modern languages at Cambridge University, 1970–4, studying German art history at Freiburg University, Germany, 1972–3, then worked for Museum of London on excavations, 1974–5. Gained an honours degree in fine art, 1975–9, then his master's degree at Reading University, 1979–81. Won a Boise Travelling Scholarship to New York, 1981, then was a visiting lecturer at art colleges and polytechnics in England from that year. Showed with New Contemporaries from 1977; RA Summer Exhibition from 1983; Riverside Open in 1986; and Change of Seen Gallery, Dorchester, 1988. Solo exhibitions included Derby Hall, Bury, 1982, and Vortex Gallery from 1986. Lived in Beaminster, Dorset.

Anna DUDLEY: *see* **Anna Dudley NEILL**

Colin DUDLEY 1923– Painter, sculptor and teacher, born in Greenwich, southeast London. After initial education at Eltham College he studied art at Sidcup School of Art and Goldsmiths' College School of Art. He held a number of teaching positions in schools and training colleges, including Christ Church College, Canterbury, Kent. Showed at RA, NEAC, SEA, LG and elsewhere, London County Council and Derbyshire Education Committee buying his work.

Geoffrey DUDLEY 1918–1986 Sculptor and teacher, born in Wednesfield, Staffordshire, who studied at Wolverhampton School of Art, 1936–9, and Royal College of Art, 1939 and 1945–6, being a Travelling Scholar in 1946. Dudley had worked as an engineer, 1940–5, and his sculpture, in metal, blending realism and abstraction, was preoccupied with themes such as trains and railways. He lectured in sculpture at Newcastle upon Tyne University, 1946–63, being an extra-mural lecturer at Durham University, 1949–58. Between 1963–84 he held several posts at Chelsea School of Art, being head of the department of sculpture from 1974. Did extensive commissioned work. Showed at AIA Galleries, RA, RSA, Stone Gallery in Newcastle and elsewhere and had memorial exhibitions at Chelsea School of Art, 1986, and Hatton Gallery, Newcastle, 1987. The lost wax method of casting was used by Dudley, who had work acquired by West Midlands Arts, RA (Chantrey Bequest) and Inner London Education Authority.

James DUDLEY: *see* **Derek CHITTOCK**

John DUDLEY 1915– Painter and miniaturist, born in Eton, Buckinghamshire, taught art at home by his mother, the artist Ada Dudley. He retired from the Army and began painting seriously in 1967. Joined PS, 1972, RMS, 1984, and SM in 1985. Dudley painted over 400 portraits and was accredited portraitist to the Army Air Corps and Parachute Regiment. Lord Aberdare, the Bishop of Credition, Admiral of the Fleet Sir Henry Leach and General Sir Frank King were among his subjects. He also painted landscapes, horses and dogs. In 1984 he won the Bill Mundy Gold Sovereign Award. Lived at Chilmark, Salisbury, Wiltshire.

Debbie DUFFIN 1953– Versatile artist and teacher who studied at Coventry University, taking part in degree show at Herbert Art Gallery there, 1976, in the same year being a prizewinner at Winsor & Newton Exhibition at Mall Galleries. Other mixed show appearances included Masks, Café Gallery, 1984; London Pride at Lamont Gallery, 1986; A Drawing Show, Waterman's Art Centre, 1990; and John Jones Open, The Gallery at John Jones, 1994. Awards included Oppenheim-John Downes Memorial Award to Artists, 1985; Publication Grants from Arts Council, 1987 and 1992; and London Arts Board Award, Research and Development, 1994. Had a solo show at The University, Keele, 1975, later ones including Trespass, at Adam Gallery, 1991, and Barbican Centre, 1996. In that, Duffin showed fragile and elegant linear constructions which stemmed from intensive drawing. In 1995 Duffin was commissioned by British Telecom to create a sculpture out of the relics of old telephone exchange equipment. Duffin had extensive teaching experience, including workshops on professional practice. Latterly this included course co-ordinator and tutor for Open College of the Arts, 1990–2; from 1994 co-ordinator, professional practice, Wimbledon School of Art; and from 1995 visiting lecturer at Central St Martin's School of Art. Coventry University and Women's Art at New Hall College, Cambridge, hold examples.

John DUFFIN 1965– Painter, draughtsman and printmaker, born in Barrow-in-Furness, Lancashire, where took an apprenticeship at Vickers Shipbuilding & Engineering and qualified as a draughtsman, 1981–5. Attended Goldsmiths' College, 1985–8, graduating in fine art, completing a postgraduate diploma in advanced printmaking at Central St Martins College of Art, 1988–90. Based in London, between 1989–91 Duffin worked with Tom Phillips, including all the etchings in Dante's *Inferno*; also with Norman Ackroyd on a mural for Lloyds Bank, 10 feet by 150 feet, in etched stainless steel. Mixed shows included Lake Artists' Exhibition, Grasmere, 1986; Whitechapel Open, at Whitechapel Art Gallery, 1988; RA Summer Exhibition, from 1990; Bankside Gallery, Members' Show, 1992; and Kerb Scrawlers, The Living Room, Greenwich, 1994. Solo exhibitions included Coachhouse Gallery, Grasmere, 1992.

Daniel J DUFFY 1878-c.1955 Painter in oil, born at Coatbridge, Lanarkshire. Studied at Glasgow School of Art under Fra Newbery and widely on the continent. Exhibited RA, RSA, ROI, RHA, Royal Glasgow Institute of the Fine Arts and Paris Salon, where he gained Honourable Mentions in 1936 and 1938. Member of Glasgow Art Club. Lived in Coatbridge.

Emlyn DUFFY 1916– Artist in coloured inks with a science fiction bias. Born in Croydon, Surrey, Duffy, who signed his work Dy, held a number of one-man shows in the 1970s at galleries including the Loggia, Woodstock Gallery and the Paris Salon. Regency Press published two volumes of poetry written and illustrated by Duffy. He also had work reproduced by *Science Fiction Monthly* as well as German and Dutch periodicals. By profession a biologist, he worked in London's Natural History Museum.

Manny DUFFY 1954– Artist and illustrator who attended Harrow College of Art from 1971, then Norwich School of Fine Art from 1973. During the 1970s she worked as an artist for a publishing house, was a natural history illustrator for an educational design group and began working as a freelance artist in advertising and publishing. Belgravia Contemporary Arts showed her work.

Terry DUFFY 1948– Painter, born in Liverpool, who studied at College of Art there, 1973–6. He was Liverpool chairman of the British Art and Design Association. Duffy's mixed show appearances included Contemporary Art Society art market; the Francis Graham-Dixon and Benjamin Rhodes Galleries; and in 1991–2 John Moores Exhibition, Liverpool, where he showed the abstract: The Miraculous Draught of Fishes. He showed solo at Air Gallery, 1981, Harris Museum and Art Gallery, Preston, where he had a North West Arts Major Fellowship, 1984; Laing Art Gallery in Newcastle upon Tyne, 1989; and The New Millennium Gallery, St Ives, 1997. Lived in the Wirral Peninsula, also having a studio in east London.

Thomas Cantrell DUGDALE 1880–1952 Painter mainly of portraits in oil; textile designer. Born in Blackburn, Lancashire, T C Dugdale studied at Manchester School of Art, Royal College of Art, the City and Guilds School in Kennington, then at the Académie Julian and Atelier Colarossi, Paris. From early in the century he showed with the NEAC and RA, being elected RA in 1943. Having served in the Army during World War I, he held an exhibition in 1919 at the Leicester Galleries of pictures of the Middle East. Married to the painter Amy Katherine Browning. During the inter-war period Dugdale consolidated his position as a leading portrait painter and was for 20 years from 1919 art adviser to Tootal Broadhurst Lee, the textile company. Exhibited widely in Britain and overseas, the Tate Gallery and many provincial galleries acquiring his work. Lived in London.

Arthur Radclyffe DUGMORE 1870–1955 Painter and printmaker of landscapes, animals and birds. Born in Betws-y-coed, Wales, after an international schooling Dugmore studied art in

Italy and America. He went on to travel widely to study wild life in Europe, America, Africa and Asia, sometimes lecturing. He also wrote magazine articles and published many books, including *Nature and the Camera* and *African Jungle Life*. Lived in Christchurch, Hampshire, and was president of the Southbourne Art Society, 1947–50.

John DUGUID 1906–1961 Painter, teacher and traveller, associated with the Downshire Hill group of artists in London's Hampstead. His brother was the writer Julian Duguid, author of *Green Hell*. After Harrow School and New College, Oxford, Duguid (pronounced Doogid) studied there with Sydney Carline at Ruskin School of Drawing in the late 1920s, then at Bauhaus in Germany with Josef Albers and Wassily Kandinsky, 1931–2. Duguid's letters to the painter Richard Carline graphically illustrate the tense atmosphere at the Bauhaus between Nazis and Communists. In 1930 Duguid had sailed with Carline to Venezuela on one of the last square-rigged ships, *Grace Harwar*. Duguid worked and taught in Chile from 1936–48. He showed at Goupil Gallery, RA, LG and contributed to an exhibition of Negro Art at Adams Gallery in 1935. Had a solo show at Grabowski Gallery, 1960. Died in Aberystwyth General Hospital. A memorial show was organised by Anglo-Chilean Society at Canning House, Belgrave Square, in 1962. The catalogue is an excellent review of his life and work. Abbot Hall Art Gallery, Kendal, holds Duguid's pictures.

Ken DUKES 1943– Artist in mixed media, acrylic and wood, stage designer and teacher, brother of the artist Ashley Dukes. He studied at Swansea College of Art, Brighton Polytechnic, then taught in schools with all age groups, eventually in a sixth-form college. Work in the theatre included repertory and small touring opera companies. Exhibited with SWG of which he was a member, having solo shows at Blue Room in Weymouth, and in Worcester at the City Art Gallery, Arts Workshop and Swan Theatre. Influences cited were Josef Albers, William Coldstream, Euan Uglow, Carl André and Henri Edmond Cross. Lived in Worcester.

Edmund DULAC 1882–1953 Leading book illustrator, decorative artist and painter. Born in Toulouse, France, he initially studied law at Toulouse University, then attended the Art School for three years, followed by brief studies at Académie Julian, Paris. Although he had shown portraits at the Paris Salon early in the century, Dulac was especially attracted by British book illustration, so he moved to England to work on periodicals such as *The Pall Mall Magazine* and in 1912 took British naturalisation. Dulac proved a versatile artist, designing theatrical costumes and scenery, producing designs for medals, banknotes and stamps, as well as designing furniture. He was a fastidious draughtsman, whose most notable achievement was his illustrations for fine books, including Edgar Allan Poe's *The Bells and Other Poems*, 1912, Robert Louis Stevenson's *Treasure Island*, 1927, and Alexander Pushkin's *The Golden Cockerel*, 1950. Represented in a number of public collections. A centenary exhibition toured from Mappin Art Gallery, Sheffield, 1982–3. Dulac's death was probably brought about by a heart attack, prompted by his late enthusiasm for flamenco dancing. Lived in London.

David DULY 1946– Artist, designer and teacher, born in Hastings, Sussex. He studied physiology and pathology in Oxford, and art at the Ruskin School there, at the Brassey Institute and at Brighton College of Art. Work experience included theatre design and direction and teaching anatomy and drawing, including classes in Winchester. Duly's group shows included St Edmunds Gallery, Salisbury, 1977, and in 1979 Centra, Reading, and Hayward Annual. Solo exhibitions/ performances included Boldrewood Gallery, Southampton, 1975.

Elizabeth Althea du MANOIR 1910– Portrait artist, born in Bushey, Hertfordshire, daughter of the Royal Academician figure and portrait painter George Harcourt. She studied at Slade School of Fine Art, was a member of SWA and showed in England, America and South Africa, signing work with initials. Settled finally in Charmouth, Dorset.

Royston du MAURIER-LEBEK: *see* **ROYSTON**

Ted DUMMETT 1906–1989 Self-taught painter in oil, acrylic and watercolour, sometimes known by his full name, Edwin James Dummett. He was born at Castle Cary, Somerset. Worked in the building trade until 1939, was then in HM Forces until 1945, was a civil engineer, 1945–71, retiring to Trefriw, Gwynedd. He was elected RCamA in 1977, in 1978 to its governing council. Dummett won a number of Italian awards, including Accademico d'Italia con Medaglia d'Oro, Salsomaggiore; Premio Il Centauro d'Oro, Accademia Italia, Salsomaggiore, 1982; Diploma di Maestro di Pittura Honoris Causa, Seminario Internazionale d'Arte Moderna e Contemporanea, Salsomaggiore, 1983. His work appeared in 1972 show An Alternative Tradition, WAC and Scottish Arts Council tours. Also showed at Williamson Art Gallery, Birkenhead; Victoria Art Gallery, Conway; Mostyn Art Gallery, Llandudno; and Salon des Nations, Paris.

Elizabeth DUN 1923–1995 Artist in various media, excluding oil, using figurative and abstract modes. She was born in Rawalpindi, India, where her father was British Army medical officer. Began school in Heliopolis, Egypt, being sent aged eight to board at Wycombe Abbey preparatory school, then went to Sherborne and read social studies at Edinburgh University. Studied art in Italy in the studio of Renato Guttuso and first exhibited. Then worked part-time in London hospitals to enable her to study at Central School of Arts and Crafts. Went to Hong Kong where she was director of the Save the Children Fund, creating day and residential centres for poor street children. Studied art with Lui Shou Kwan, her paintings then reflecting a mix of Chinese and Western styles. Returned to England, she spent 17 years at Westminster Hospital, caring for neurological patients and their families. Created paintings, embroideries and stained glass in studios in Islington and Spitalfields. Travelled repeatedly to Italy, perfecting her Italian. Became the first woman to qualify as a London Guide, guiding on the continent, too, in Italian. Exhibitions included Comedy Gallery, 1961; Ashmolean Museum, Oxford, 1969; Warwick Gallery, Warwick, 1972; Pinacoteca Civica, Macerata, Italy, 1981; and Sackhouse Gallery, Wells-next-the-Sea, 1985.

Emma DUNBAR fl. from mid-1980s– Artist using variety of techniques, with a strong sense of colour and decoration, whose prolific output reflected her fondness for travel. She gained an honours degree in fine art, printmaking, from West Surrey College of Art and Design, Farnham, 1981–4, and then exhibited widely. Group exhibitions included Sue Williams Gallery, 1988; CCA Galleries, Farnham, from 1990; Turtle Fine Art, Cheltenham, 1992; and Ansty House, Alton, 1996. Had a solo show at Wandle Gallery, Sutton, 1985, later ones including New Ashgate Gallery, Farnham, 1998.

Evelyn DUNBAR 1906–1960 Painter, mural artist, illustrator and teacher, born in Reading, Berkshire. She studied at Rochester and Chelsea Schools of Art and Royal College of Art, 1929–33. A member of the Society of Mural Painters, she painted murals at Brockley County School, Kent, 1933–6, and at the Training College, Bletchley, in Buckinghamshire, 1958–60. During World War II she was an official war artist, being especially known for her paintings of the Women's Land Army. Was a visiting teacher at Ruskin School of Drawing, Oxford, from 1950. Latterly she concentrated on portraits. There was a strong pastoral theme in Dunbar's work, and she was an apt choice, with Cyril Mahoney, to illustrate *Gardener's Choice*, in 1937. Showed with NEAC and Goupil Gallery. Imperial War Museum, Tate Gallery and Manchester City Art Gallery hold her work. Died near Ashford, Kent.

Lennox DUNBAR 1952– Painter, printmaker and teacher, born in Aberdeen, where he attended Gray's School of Art, 1969–74, eventually returning there as printmaking subject leader. After studying at Gray's, Dunbar was etching technician at Peacock Printmakers, 1978–86; visiting artist-tutor at Louisiana State University, America, 1986; also a visiting lecturer at various art schools. Awards included a series of travel awards across Europe and to America; the RSA's Meyer Oppenheim Award, 1976 (he was made an RSA associate in 1990); its Latimer Award in 1978, the year he set up the Amsterdam Studio for the Scottish Arts Council; the RSA Guthrie Award, 1984; and Shell Expro and the RSA Highland Society of London Awards in the early 1990s. In 1987 Dunbar won 1st Prize in the Paisley Art Institute Drawing Competion, two years after winning the 2nd Prize. He was a Major Prizewinner, Cleveland Drawing Biennale, 1989. Selected exhibitions included Double Elephant, British Prints, Barbican Centre, 1985; Printmakers' Drawings, Mercury Gallery, Edinburgh, 1987; and Paperworks IV, Seagate Gallery, Dundee, 1993. There was an important solo show at Hatton Gallery, Newcastle, and Peacock Printmakers, Aberdeen, 1995. The strongly patterned pictures in this exhibition drew on implements and materials used to shape the traditional landscape around Dunbar's studio at Auchnagatt, as well as new images such as kit house building and plantation trees. Collections holding his work include Scottish Arts Council, RSA, and Aberdeen, Paisley and Middlesbrough public galleries.

Peter DUNBAR 1929–1983 Painter, illustrator, graphic designer and art editor, working in oil and pen and ink, born and died in London. He attended Woolwich Polytechnic art school, 1944–46; Camberwell School of Art, 1946–7, where John Minton and Lawrence Gowing were influences; and the Anglo-French Art Centre, 1948–9. Dunbar was an illustrator on the *Financial Times*; art director of *The Economist*, 1959–68, then a consultant; director of PD Associates; Matthews, Miller, Dunbar; and art director, Ballantine Books. Group shows included St George's Gallery, 1953; 4 Young Painters, Blackheath, 1955 (the others were Robert Hunt, Gordon Richards and Owen Wood); and Camberwell School of Art, 1964–5.

Clare DUNCAN 1956– Artist in various and mixed media, including performance work, and poet, born Anne Clare Cardew Duncan, who also worked under her married name Clare Turner. She was born in Arusha, Tanganyika, and was educated in Edinburgh, attending Telford College, 1975–6, and from 1979–81 Portsmouth and Canterbury Colleges of Art, then Lanchester Polytechnic. Was elected UA in 1979, also exhibiting at SWA and RSA, having a solo show at Hiscock Gallery, Portsmouth. Lived for a time in Cranfield, Bedfordshire.

Clive DUNCAN 1944– Sculptor and teacher, born in London, married to the painter Janet McQueen. Studied at High Wycombe College of Art, 1961–4; Camberwell School of Arts and Crafts, 1964–6, under Sydney Sheppard and Giacomo Baragli; and City and Guilds of London Art School, 1966–8, under James Butler and David McFall. Taught sculpture at Heatherley School of Art (head of School); was principal lecturer in charge of sculpture at Sir John Cass School of Art, London Guildhall University (head of School, 1972–1993), and was a visiting teacher at Slade Summer School and City and Guilds Sculpture School. Was elected a fellow of RBS in 1983, a member of RBA in 1984 and was president of the Thomas Heatherley Trust, 1973–94. Apart from portrait sculptures, Duncan's work, in a variety of materials, was dominated by serious political, social and sexual themes. He developed ideas in the early 1970s for sculpture, dance and music. Among his portraits is Myfanwy Piper, wife of John Piper. His nine-foot-high Rose Images are also notable. Exhibited frequently at RA fom 1968, also RP, Royal Glasgow Institute of the Fine Arts, Portland Sculpture Park, Nicholas Treadwell Gallery and elsewhere. He was an exhibition consultant for Sotheby's and produced a booklet for Victoria & Albert Museum: *From Lost Wax to Found Bronze*. Solo shows included London Guildhall and Playhouse Gallery, Harlow. Lived in Shiplake, Oxfordshire.

Colin DUNCAN 1966– Painter and designer, born in Floriana, Malta, who studied at Cumbria and Canterbury Colleges of Art & Design. He was stage set designer for Blur, world tour, 1993, and construction assistant for the Agongo Exhibition, Edinburgh International Festival, 1994. Group shows included Herbert Read Gallery, Canterbury, from 1986; CD Show, Collective Gallery, Edinburgh, 1992; Demarco European Art Foundation, Edinburgh, 1994; and Royal Over-Seas League Open, 1995. Had a solo show at Fruitmarket Gallery, Edinburgh, 1991, later ones including Chessel's Gallery, Edinburgh, 1994.

James DUNCAN 1946– Painter who specialised in stylised landscapes and figurative work influenced by the Scottish landscape where he lived in Aberdeenshire. For some years he restored a castle there, making a gallery to show work by himself and other artists with local connections. Duncan studied at Edinburgh College of Art. Awards included the Andrew Carnegie Award and a bronze medal, Salon des Nations. Shows included RSA Summer Exhibition, 1983; Greenwich Gallery and Museum Gallery in Elgin, both 1986; Talent Store, 1987; and in 1997 he shared an exhibition, Land & Sea, with Christopher Stiling at Gallery Forty Seven.

Janet McQueen DUNCAN 1944– Painter, designer and teacher, born in Marlow, Buckinghamshire, wife of the sculptor Clive Duncan. She worked in watercolour, drawing media and oil, landscape and studies of light on water being notable themes. Studied at High Wycombe School of Art. She was a theatre set designer, was involved in theatre wardrobe, and taught art to advanced level and privately. Showed with RBA, at Castle Hill Gallery in High Wycombe and at Henley's Arts and Music Festival. Had many solo exhibitions including Century Galleries in Henley and Hartley Wintney and in Windsor, and also worked to commission. Lived in Shiplake, Oxfordshire.

Jean DUNCAN 1933– Painter, printmaker and video artist, originally known as Jean Fraser, whose son Alastair Duncan was a tapestry artist. She was born in Edinburgh, where she obtained her diploma at the College of Art, 1951–5, under William Gillies, Robin Philipson and Leonard Rosoman, gaining a postgraduate diploma in printmaking, 1980–1, under David Barker at University of Ulster. Became co-director of Seacourt Print Workshop at Bangor, County Down, Northern Ireland, having settled in Belfast. She was an academician of RUA and a member of the Artists' Association of Ireland. Interested "in the power of repetitive shapes and rhythms in visual art", in 1993 Duncan began a series of etchings prompted by composer John Tavener's *The Protecting Veil*, shown at Royal Northern College of Music, Manchester, in 1994. Later solo shows included One Oxford Street, Belfast, 1995. Awards included Mini Print International, Cadaqués, Spain, 1988, and Arts Council of Northern Ireland, 1990. It holds her work, as do University College in Dublin, Dundee City Art Gallery and other public collections. Duncan held a residency at Tyrone Guthrie Centre, Annaghmakerrig.

John DUNCAN 1866–1945 Painter, illustrator, mural artist, stained glass designer and teacher, born in Dundee, Angus. As a schoolboy he began evening classes at the local School of Art and for some years became a newspaper illustrator in Dundee and London. Further studies followed in Antwerp and Düsseldorf, in Dundee with George Dutch Davidson and in Rome, where the early Italian artists made a lasting impression. In Edinburgh Duncan became involved with the Celtic Revival leader Patrick Geddes, for whose home he painted murals. After a visit to America with Geddes in 1899, Duncan taught at Chicago University, 1902–4, before settling back in Edinburgh. He was made RSA in 1923 and RSW in 1930. Scottish National Gallery of Modern Art holds his work.

McG DUNCAN: *see* **T G McGILL DUNCAN**

Marjorie DUNCAN 1905– Painter, born in London, who studied at Froebel Educational Institute and art with Bernard Adams. She was a member of The Eastbourne Group and exhibited with NS, RP, Royal Glasgow Institute of the Fine Arts and elsewhere. Lived for many years in Alfriston, Sussex.

Mary DUNCAN 1885–1964 Painter and etcher, born in Bromley, Kent, where she attended the School of Art. Later went to the Slade School of Fine Art and studied in Paris. Exhibited extensively at RHA, RA, NEAC, RSA, ROI and Goupil Gallery. Leamington Art Gallery and Plymouth City Museum and Art Gallery among others hold her work. Lived at Mousehole, Cornwall.

Stephen DUNCAN 1952– Sculptor, born and worked in London, who did a foundation course in art and design at Watford School of Art, 1970–1; graduated with a first-class honours degree in sculpture and printmaking from Wimbledon School of Art, 1971–4; gained a postgraduate certificate in sculpture and printmaking, with a Silver Medal, Royal Academy of Art, 1974–7; with further postgraduate studies, under a British School Scholarship, at Accademia di Belle Arti, Rome, 1978–9; and was at British School at Rome, Rome Award in Sculpture, 1992–3. Teachers included Peter Startup at Wimbledon and Willi Soukop at Royal Academy Schools. Worked in Britain, widely on the continent and in America, and obtained a South East Arts Travel Award, from 1973. As well as sculpting, Duncan practised as a poet, lectured in fine art in universities and colleges and wrote for journals including *Artscribe*. The use of mythology, metaphor and narrative were important. He was an associate of RBS and took part in group shows including Artspace, Oxford, and Philippe Daverio Gallery, both 1994, and Ben Uri Gallery from 1994. Had a solo exhibition at St Albans Cathedral in 1979, later ones including Lanchester Gallery, Coventry University, 1995, and Woodlands Art Gallery, 1997. Commissions included River God relief at Elm Quay, Nine Elms Lane, 1988, and Lotus, bronze sculpture at Nottingham Trent University, 1994. Wandsworth Council and National Hospitals Collection also hold works.

Terence Edward DUNCAN: *see* **TERRY**

Brian Redvers DUNCE 1937– Artist in all two-dimensional media, born in Surrey, where he had a studio at Wonersh. In the late 1950s he studied at Guildford and Salisbury Schools of Art and at Reading University, teachers including Jack Rodway and Peter Startup. From 1960 Dunce worked in art and design practice and was involved in the curating and design of Arts Council exhibitions. British romantic art, mythology, folk culture, Celtic imagery and the work of Paul Nash and Ivon Hitchens were influences on Dunce's work, which included autobiographical, moon and ambiguous landscape series as well as a modern crucifixion, sponsored by Winsor & Newton. Dunce was a member of PS and took part in numerous mixed shows, including Bankside Gallery, RI, NEAC, London Contemporary Art Fair, Kettle's Yard in Cambridge and Mall Galleries. By the mid-1990s he had had 14 solo shows including Chelsea School of Art, University of Surrey, Yehudi Menuhin School, Cobham, and St Martin's Gallery. Price Waterhouse & Company and English Trust Company hold examples.

Peter DUNHAM 1911– Painter in oil and watercolour and architect, born in Luton, Bedfordshire. He studied at the Bartlett School of Architecture and part-time at Slade School of Fine Art. Dunham was a fellow of RIBA and was a practising architect from 1933, when he was a Donaldson medallist. He always painted, mostly landscapes in East Anglia, Italy and Austria, and was influenced by his uncle and aunt, the painters T C Dugdale and A K Browning. Was a member of Architect Artists of RIBA and showed at RA Summer Exhibitions, in East Anglia and in Austria. Lived at Sternfield, Saxmundham, Suffolk.

Keith DUNKLEY 1942– Painter and teacher, born in Corbridge, Northumberland. He studied at Kingston School of Art, 1960–4, then Royal Academy Schools, 1964–7. Dunkley taught at Sheridan College, Toronto, in Canada, 1969–73. He showed with RWS, of which he was a member, RA and elsewhere, and from 1978 had a series of one-man exhibitions with John Davies in Stow-on-the-Wold. Dunkley painted in the Scottish borders country, in France and elsewhere on the continent and lived near Edinburgh.

Sue DUNKLEY 1942– Painter, printmaker, teacher and writer. She studied at Bath Academy in Corsham, 1959–61, Chelsea School of Art, 1961–3, and Slade School of Fine Art, 1963–5. Among her awards were a Morland Lewis Travelling Scholarship to Australia, 1963, and a Boise Travelling Scholarship to Italy, 1965. In 1967 she was art correspondent for the magazine *Nova*. From about this time she began a series of teaching appointments, which included Chelsea School of Art, St Martin's School of Art, Goldsmiths' College and Slade School of Fine Art. Undertook a number of grant-sponsored work trips and was artist and technical advisor on location for filming in Donegal in 1991. Unpeopled landscapes and small-scale, intimate studies of women were aspects of Dunkley's art, shown in mixed exhibitions at LG, Nicholas Treadwell Gallery and abroad; and in solo shows at Bolsover Street Gallery, 1973, Thumb Gallery from 1979 and Curwen Gallery, 1986. Borough of Camden and Unilever hold her work.

Hazel Bruce DUNLOP 1911– Painter, mainly of portraits, born into a military family in British North Borneo and studied at Slade School of Fine Art with Henry Tonks, Philip Wilson Steer and Randolph Schwabe. She was married to the artist Francis Edwin Hodge. Member of the UA, with which she showed, also with SWA, ROI, RA and Paris Salon. Lived in London.

Ronald Ossory DUNLOP 1894–1973 Painter in oil of landscapes, seascapes, figure studies, portraits and still life. Born in Dublin, Dunlop studied at Manchester School of Art, then Wimbledon School of Art and in Paris. Had spent some time working in an advertising agency. He became a prolific exhibitor, venues including the RA, NEAC, Leicester and Redfern Galleries, RSA, RHA and the Royal Glasgow Institute of the Fine Arts. His first one-man show was at the Redfern Gallery, 1928. In 1923 Dunlop founded the Emotionist Group of writers and artists, and his own work is characterised by a painterly exuberance. Dunlop's work is in a number of public galleries, including the Tate. He wrote *Understanding Pictures* and his autobiography, *Struggling with Paint*, 1956. Lived at Barnham, Sussex.

Albert DUNN 1908– Landscape painter, born in Farnborough, Hampshire. He was educated in Newcastle upon Tyne, studying art there, 1925–30, with William Fenton. He settled in Powick, Worcestershire, belonged to Worcester Art Society and Malvern Art Club, showed in RA Summer Exhibitions and had several solo exhibitions at Malvern Art Gallery.

Alfred DUNN 1937– Artist and teacher, born in Wombwell, Yorkshire. He studied at Royal College of Art, 1959–61, eventually becoming senior tutor there. Showed at Redfern Gallery from 1965 and extensively in Germany and Italy. Arts Council holds his work. Lived at Trawden, Lancashire. Sometimes signed work E(rnest) A(lfred) Dunn.

Anne DUNN 1929– Painter, born in London. She was married first to the artist Michael Wishart, in whose autobiography *High Diver* she appears, then Rodrigo Moynihan. She attended Chelsea School of Art, 1947–50, the Anglo-French Art Centre, 1951, then in 1952 Académie Julian, Paris. From the mid-1950s she was a regular exhibitor for many years at Leicester Galleries, also participating in mixed shows at NEAC, RA and abroad. From 1964–8 was editor of *Art and Literature*. Had many solo exhibitions, starting with a series from 1957 at Leicester Galleries, then an extended series from 1967 at Fischbach Gallery, New York, later shows including Maison des Jeunes et de la Culture, Paris, in 1988, and Christopher Hull Gallery in 1990. Arts Council, CAS and other public collections hold her work. Lived in Lambesc, France.

Ernest Alfred DUNN: *see* **Alfred DUNN**

George DUNN 1914– Sculptor who was educated at Bemrose School, Derby, 1926–32, where he proved a distinguished academic and sports all-rounder. Gained a scholarship to Derby School of Arts and Crafts, 1932–7, where he won a string of first prizes for landscape and still life, designed and painted scenery for Derby's Centenary of Local Government Exhibition in 1935, exhibited at Winsor & Newton's Exhibition of Contemporary Art in Birmingham in 1936 and was secretary of Derby Graphic Club, 1935–7. Studied at Slade School of Fine Art, 1937–40, on a number of Derby Borough Major Scholarships, winning a series of prizes, with a refresher course in sculpture and drawing, 1946–7. Eventually joined staff of Leeds College of Art, in charge of photographic records, and was included in The Teaching Image, College staff show in 1964 at Leeds City Art Gallery. Showed elsewhere in Yorkshire.

Reginald George DUNN 1907– Painter, born in Windsor, Berkshire. The Reverend Dunn studied at the All Nations Missionary College, in London, privately in Greece during World War II and then at Torquay School of Art, 1949–50. Showed RCamA and elsewhere and lived in Paignton, Devon, for some years.

Chris DUNSEATH 1949– Sculpture and lecturer, who gained an honours degree at Gloucestershire College of Art and Design, Cheltenham, 1968–71; did postgraduate diploma studies at Slade School of Fine Art, 1971–3; and held a sculpture fellowship at Cardiff College of Art and Design, 1973–4. From 1986 Dunseath was associate senior lecturer head of sculpture, at Coventry School of Art and Design, Coventry University, his visiting lectureships including Cheltenham, Birmingham, Manchester, Falmouth and Portsmouth Colleges of Art, the John Makepeace School for Craftsmen, Royal Academy Sculpture School, University of Wales Institute in Cardiff and the Universities of Warwick and the West of England. His many group shows included New Sculpture, Ikon Gallery, Birmingham, 1978; Yorkshire Sculpture Park, 1980; Alwin Gallery, 1988; Portrait: An Exploration, The Coventry Gallery, 1994; and 2nd RWA Open Sculpture Exhibition, 1996. Had a solo show at Oriel Gallery, Cardiff, 1974, later ones including Department of National Heritage and Civic Trust, 1994. Dunseath won a major commission for West Bromwich High Street, Sandwell, 1989; another for The Waterfront, Dudley, for Richardson Developments, 1992. Arts Council, WAC, South West Arts, Henry Moore Institute in Leeds and other collections hold examples. Lived in Hinton St George, Somerset.

Bernard DUNSTAN 1920– Painter, draughtsman and teacher, born in Teddington, Middlesex. He was married to the painter Diana Armfield. Dunstan was a painter on a small scale brought up in the Sickert-Degas-Vuillard tradition, who developed a keen following for his intimate interiors with nude and semi-draped figures and views of Venice. He studied at Byam Shaw School of Art, 1939, then Slade School of Fine Art, 1939–41. From 1946–9 taught at West of England School of Art in Bristol, Camberwell School of Art, 1950–64, Byam Shaw 1953–74, Ravensbourne Art College, 1959–64, and City and Guilds of London Art School, 1964–9. His reputation was established with a series of solo shows at Roland, Browse and Delbanco, then Agnew. He was a member of NEAC, RWA (being its president in 1979) and was elected RA in 1968. Among his several books were *Learning to Paint*, 1970, and *Painting Methods of the Impressionists*, 1976. Arts Council holds his work. Lived in Kew, Surrey.

Thea DUPAYS fl. from early 1950s– Painter, draughtsman and teacher who studied painting at Goldsmiths' College School of Art for four years in early 1950s. She then went to West Africa where she held her first solo show and illustrated books for Oxford University Press and Longmans. On returning to England in 1960 she settled in Bath and continued to illustrate, teach and paint, but family concerns reduced her painting time until in 1984 she returned seriously to work. Showed RWA, RP and Bath Art Society and in 1992 had solo show at Hill Gallery, Bradford-on-Avon. Dupays was notable as a landscape painter, with an ability to match her style to the place depicted.

H Enslin du PLESSIS 1894–1978 Painter and journalist, born in Standerton, Transvaal, South Africa. Was educated in Cape Town, but had no formal art training. During World War I saw service in wide area of Middle East and acted as a correspondent for newspapers in South Africa. Took up painting seriously in his thirties and showed in England from the late 1920s. Exhibited extensively with Goupil and Arlington Galleries; also Leicester Galleries; Roland, Browse and Delbanco; LG and elsewhere. Contemporary Art Society and Arts Council bought his work, which is in a number of South African galleries. Manchester City Art Gallery's Boats, La Rochelle, is typical of the artist's delicate, Impressionist manner. Press Club member who lived in London.

Charles DURANTY 1918– Watercolourist, born in Romford, Essex, who was self-taught. He worked in journalism, agriculture and for most of his life in book publishing, finally with Gerald Duckworth & Company. He published a small collection of his verse, *Audition*. Duranty said that his pictures were "a personal interpretation of rural life in Essex and Suffolk in the past half century". He took part in many group shows, including Thackeray, New Grafton and Leicester Galleries; Roland, Browse & Delbanco; Mercury and Zwemmer Galleries and abroad. Solo exhibitions included Thackeray and New Grafton Galleries. Paintings in Hospitals, the Wentworth Hotel in Aldeburgh and private collections hold Duranty's works. Lived in Merrow, Guildford, Surrey.

Sarah DURCAN 1969– Painter, born in London, who studied at National College of Art & Design, Dublin, and Winchester School of Art. She won an Arts Council materials grant, 1991; Arts Flight, 1994; and EVA Open Award, 1995. Group shows included Triskel Arts Centre, Cork, 1988; Iontas, Sligo Art Gallery, Sligo, 1993–4; Delfina Studios Gallery, Byam Shaw

School and Royal Over-Seas League Open, all 1995. Had a solo show at Arts Council, Dublin, 1992.

James DURDEN 1878–1964 Painter born in Manchester, where he studied at the School of Art, then Royal College of Art. Exhibited RA, ROI, RP, Royal Glasgow Institute of the Fine Arts and Paris Salon, where he gained a silver medal in 1927. Also showed in the provinces, South Africa, New Zealand and Australia. Manchester City Art Gallery and several foreign galleries hold his work, which was reproduced by the Medici Society. Lived near Keswick, Cumberland.

Nommie DURELL 1905–1989 Painter and teacher, born and died in London, christened Mary Louise Lasenby. She was related to the Liberty family and was brought up in the libertarian arts and crafts tradition. After Roedean School she attended Slade School of Fine Art, married Harry Durell the architect and pioneered art teaching methods which gained the approval of Herbert Read and other educational progressives. Her exhibition of child art at Zwemmer Gallery in 1938 gained much attention. During World War II she and her husband, as conscientious objectors, moved to Dartington Hall and worked on the land. She resumed her teaching, including a spell at Bedales, then when divorced after the war set up a boarding-house in Hampstead. Journeyed annually to a cottage at Menton, on the French Riviera, to paint, later working each year in Greece. She had shown in mixed exhibitions such as NEAC before World War II, but much of her output remained unshown until Sally Hunter Fine Art exhibited some in 1992.

Terry DURHAM 1936– Versatile artist, born in East Ardsley, Yorkshire, father a steel worker, his mother employed in a mill. Worked as a painter and decorator, attending Batley College of Art part-time, then studied for a year at Leeds College of Art, working mornings in a Wakefield mill to pay for the course. After National Service washed dishes and painted in the Isles of Scilly for two years, then spent about 10 years in London, returning to Yorkshire in the early 1970s. Mixed shows in London included Nicholas Treadwell Gallery, and had a series of solo exhibitions including New Vision Centre Gallery, 1963, and Queen Square Gallery, Leeds, 1965. Durham's other works included a huge abstract mural for Morley Corporation swimming baths, early 1970s; publication of the book *Angus Pangus* and the *One Jump Giant*, 1973; from the late 1970s creation of pictures based on real-life Yorkshire characters; and in 1992 production of forest folk sculptures at his studio in the Walkley Clogs complex, Mytholmroyd. Muriel Spark and Olivia Manning, the novelists, Pop music star Bill Wyman and scientist Dr Jacob Bronowski all owned Durham's pictures.

Alan DURMAN 1905–1963 Verstile artist and photographer, born in Weymouth, Dorset, who trained there with a photographer, then moved to London, where he made window displays. He next worked as an artist and photographer with Imperial Tobacco Company, then with the printer Mardon, Son and Hall, and in World War II was commissioned in the Royal Army Service Corps. Durman moved to Bristol about 1950. He was elected an artist member of Bristol Savages in 1946, was made its president in 1952 and exhibited prolifically, 1946–63, portraits and landscapes, and with RWA occasionally, 1934–49. The Savages held work by, and a caricature of, Durman, who was remembered as "small in stature with a twinkle in his eye … When he joined the club he was clean shaven, but in the late 1950s he grew a moustache and beard." Durman also produced posters and murals, venues including the Berkeley Café, Saltford Community Hall and the Cabot Grill. A copy of Ernest Board's famous picture of Cabot leaving Bristol was another of Durman's notable pictures.

Jennifer DURRANT 1942– Painter and teacher, born in Brighton, Sussex, where she studied at College of Art, 1959–63, then Slade School of Fine Art, 1963–6. In 1964 she received an Abbey Minor Scholarship and two years later was a Young Contemporaries prizewinner. After participating in several important group exhibitions, such as John Moores in Liverpool in 1970, Durrant had a one-man show at Serpentine Gallery in 1974. Others included Arnolfini Gallery in Bristol, 1979; retrospective at Serpentine Gallery, 1987; and Barbican Concourse Gallery, 1992. Taught at various colleges including Royal College of Art and Chelsea School of Art. She was an Arts Council award winner in 1976, and has work in its collection, and won the Athena Prize, 1988. Durrant painted abstract pictures on a large scale which can be complex, ambiguous and lyrical. Lived in London.

Roy Turner DURRANT 1925–1998 Painter and poet, born in Lavenham, Suffolk. After a childhood addiction to drawing aeroplanes, he did war service in the Army, then attended Camberwell School of Arts and Crafts, 1948–52, being influenced by Keith Vaughan and John Minton. In 1950s developed from figuration to abstraction. He said that any titles on his pictures were "meant to be interpreted as poetry, to engender a state of mind rather than describe exactly what the particular picture is". Was influenced by European abstractionists and by English poetry, such as that of Gerard Manley Hopkins and Thomas Hardy, also by the work of James Joyce, Samuel Beckett and Dylan Thomas. As well as painting, Durrant was employed in administrative work at Vickers from 1956–63 and was a director of the Heffer Gallery, Cambridge, 1963–76. Showed with Free Painters and Sculptors, of which he was a fellow, and with NEAC, of which he was a member, and quite often with RA from 1950. In 1960 his poetry *A Rag Book of Love* was published. After a solo show at Guildhall, Lavenham, in 1948, he showed regularly, later exhibitions including Loggia Gallery, Gallery of Britsh Art in Lausanne and Belgrave Gallery, 1991. Several dozen public collections hold his work, including Imperial War Museum, Bradford City Art Gallery and Balliol College, Oxford. Lived in Cambridge.

Alan Lydiat DURST 1883–1970 Sculptor in wood, stone and ivory of figures, religious subjects and animals. Born at

Alverstoke, Hampshire, Durst studied at the Central School of Arts and Crafts under Richard Garbe before and after World War I, during which he served with the Royal Marines (he had been in the Marines for some years prior to his Central School entry in 1913). Durst also studied in Chartres, France. After several years working as a sculptor, he taught wood carving at the Royal College of Art 1925–48, with the exception of the war years, when he again served in the Marines and was at the Admiralty. Durst had his first one-man show at the Leicester Galleries in 1930 and was a member of the LG for about 25 years from the late 1920s. Wrote *Wood Carving* in 1938. Durst carved figures for the Royal Academy of Dramatic Art in 1931, did a quantity of ecclesiastical carving, including the west front of Peterborough Cathedral, and a memorial to the artist Randolph Schwabe in Hampstead Parish Church graveyard. The Tate Gallery holds his work, which is also illustrated in Arthur T Broadbent's monograph *Sculpture Today in Great Britain 1940–1943*. Durst, who sometimes signed his work A L D plus the date, lived in London.

Graham DURWARD 1956– Painter, born in Aberdeen, who studied at Edinburgh College of Art, 1973–7, with a postgraduate year in 1977–8. In 1982 he won a Scottish Arts Council Young Artists Bursary. Among group shows Durward participated in the Scottish Arts Council's Scottish Art Now show in 1982, and his one-man exhibitions included 369 Gallery, Edinburgh, 1979 and 1981. He also did some film work. Durward's work pursued an Expressionistic form, at the same time adopting a strong vein of Post-Cubism. Lived in Edinburgh.

Philip G DUTHIE 1957– Painter and draughtsman, born in Aberdeen, where he studied at Gray's School of Art, 1957–9. He then painted full-time, based in Belmont and Wasps Studios in Aberdeen, eventually settling in Edinburgh, where he exhibited at RSA from 1981. Also showed in Members' Drawings, at Peacock Printmakers, and Inaugural Exhibition, Artspace Galleries, both Aberdeen in 1980; and Cleveland 5th International Drawing Biennale, 1981. Gray's and private collections in Britain and America hold Duthie's works.

Harold John DUTTON 1889–1971 Painter, draughtsman, scraperboard artist and teacher. born in Birmingham. Studied at the School of Arts and Crafts there with Arthur J Gaskin. He was a leading figure in the Nottingham Society of Artists and showed extensively in Nottingham, Birmingham and other Midlands and northern towns. Nottingham Castle Art Gallery and Museum holds his work. Dutton moved to Nottingham aged 20 and taught at Claremont Secondary School. He was noted for landscape pencil drawing of great charm and delicacy and encouraged many pupils to take up art as a career. Lived in Sherwood, Nottingham.

Orlando DUTTON 1894–1962 Sculptor and portrait painter whose career was mainly in Australia. Born in Walsall, Staffordshire, Dutton initially studied art locally, then in 1909 was apprenticed to the Lichfield-based sculptor Robert Bridgeman. From the 1920s he built a reputation for himself in Australia, where he exhibited widely and worked extensively on public buildings. The National Gallery of South Australia, Adelaide, holds his work, as do Melbourne University, Anzac House, St John's Church and St Patrick's Cathedral, all in Melbourne. Lived at Wayville, near Melbourne.

Ron DUTTON 1935– Medallist, sculptor and teacher, born in Nantwich, Cheshire. He studied in the department of fine art at the University of Newcastle upon Tyne and was for some years head of sculpture at Wolverhampton College of Art from 1964. Showed at RA; in London Artists at Shrewbury School, 1968; Crane Kalman, 1977; The Medal, Mirror of History, at British Museum, 1979; and at Ina Broerse Gallery, Amsterdam, 1982. Had a solo show at Laing Art Gallery, Newcastle, 1964, later exhibitions including Tettenhall Gallery, Wolverhampton, where he lived, 1982 and 1984. Gained a number of awards and has work in public and private collections in Britain and abroad. Carried out many medal commissions, including Victorian Society, 25th anniversary, 1983; and in 1984 Fabian Society and Wolverhampton Art Gallery centenaries.

Dorothy Zinaida DUVAL 1917– Painter in oil and teacher, born in Ipplepen, Devon. She studied under Anthony Devas and attended Slade School of Fine Art, 1949–55. As an artist Duval had an aptitude and liking for capturing subjects on the spot, and admired Manet and Corot. She taught at Felixstowe College, girls' public schools and at adult classes. Showed at UA of which she was a member; was also a fellow of British Academy and a lay member exhibitor at RSMA shows. Also exhibited at RBA, ROI, RP and Ashmolean Museum in Oxford. Gained silver medal at Paris Salon in 1959, an Accademia Italia gold medal in 1980. Solo shows included Saffron Gallery, Saffron Walden, 1973; Broadstairs Library Gallery, 1978; and Margate Library, 1989. Grenadier Guards holds her portrait of the Victoria Cross winner Harry Nicholls. Lived in Kingsgate, Broadstairs, Kent.

Leslie DUXBURY 1921– Painter who in the 1950s produced pictures of the type popularly known as Kitchen Sink School. He was born in Accrington, Lancashire, attending the local Art School, then was briefly at Royal College of Art in 1941, returning to it, after Army service, in 1944–6. Settled in London and showed with LG; Roland, Browse & Delbanco; and AEB, from which his oil on canvas Tenement Dwellers was acquired in 1956 by Arts Council. In 1984 he was included in the Graves Art Gallery, Sheffield, touring show The Forgotten Fifties.

DY: *see* **Emlyn DUFFY**

David DYE 1945– Sculptor, photographer and teacher, born in the Isle of Wight. He studied sculpture at St Martin's School of Art, 1967–71, and showed with Young Contemporaries in 1970 and in the following year in English avant-garde at New York Cultural Centre and Art Systems at Museum of Modern Art, Buenos Aires. In 1972 Dye had first one-man show at ICA, also teaching 1972–6 at Brighton Polytechnic, moving to Newcastle Polytechnic in 1979. Won an Eastern Arts Grant in 1978. Further one-man shows followed at Lisson Gallery and Robert Self Gallery, London and Newcastle. Arts Council holds his work. Lived for a time in Saffron Walden, Essex.

Alan DYER 1944– Painter, born in Nelson, Lancashire. He took a business training for six years before attending art school in Bristol and studying for a Master of Philosophy degree at Reading University. Showed in RA Summer Exhibition and had solo show at Sandford Gallery, 1981. His multi-image Desert Painting No 3, of 1979, was included in Arts Council tour Fragments Against Ruin, 1981–2, and is now in the collection. Lived for a time in Coventry, Warwickshire, and was also known for a series of family portraits.

Dorothy DYMOCK 1881–1984 Painter in oil, aunt of the artist Rachel Windham, born in Bedford. Dymock was a hospital cook with the Red Cross during World War I. Then received a grant from WTE – Central Committee on Women's Training to study full-time at the Slade School of Fine Art, 1921–2, under Henry Tonks, on whom she made a good impression. Dymock considered continuing for the 1922–3 session, then cancelled. She also attended Westminster School of Art. Showed at RA, SWA, Ridley Art Club, ROI and elsewhere. Miss Dymock produced her strong, Colourist work until she was 91 and even during her later blindness maintained a keen interest in painting.

Lucy DYNEVOR 1934– Painter, printmaker and restorer, born Sheffield, daughter of art expert Sir John Rothenstein and niece of the artist Michael Rothenstein. She studied painting under Percy Horton at Ruskin School of Drawing, Oxford, and restoration with Helmuth Ruhemann. For some years she combined painting with freelance restoration. She was noted for her paintings of trees. Was a member of Oxford Printmakers' Co-operative. Had first solo show in London at New Grafton Gallery in 1991. Lived at Shotover, Oxford.

Noel DYRENFORTH 1936– Batik artist, born in London and continued to live there. After education at St Clement Danes, London, went on study and travel tours throughout Asia, Far East and America. Extensive international exhibitions, including many one-man shows which included Heal's Mansard Gallery, Oxford Gallery, Lincoln Craft Centre. Wrote several books on the technique of Batik. Work held by Victoria & Albert Museum.

Douglas DYSON 1918– Artist in oil, pastel, pen and pencil and teacher, born in Halifax, Yorkshire, married to the painter Sylvia Dyson. He studied at Huddersfield School of Art, 1935–9, then Royal College of Art, 1946–9, teachers including Gilbert Spencer, Rodrigo Moynihan, John Minton, Ruskin Spear and Carel Weight. He joined the Manchester Muncipal School of Art staff in 1949, which became the faculty of art and design, Manchester Polytechnic, retiring in 1981. Dyson said that "my first priority has always been as a teacher." He was a member of MAFA. Also showed at RA, Manchester City Art Gallery which holds his work, Manchester Polytechnic and Atkinson Art Gallery, Southport. Baptism of Christ, an oil in St John's Church, Newton Heath, Manchester, was a principal work. Lived in Hale, Altrincham, Cheshire.

Julian DYSON 1936– Draughtsman and painter who qualified as a dental surgeon in 1959, but 10 years later reduced his surgery hours to concentrate on painting. Took part in numerous mixed exhibitions, including Ashbarn Gallery, Petersfield; Aberystwyth University; Cleveland Bridge Gallery, Bath; Newlyn Orion Gallery, Newlyn; and Gordon Hepworth Gallery, Newton St Cyres. When The Group of Twelve was formed in 1992, Dyson was elected president. Solo exhibitions included Rainy Day Gallery, Penzance, 1992. In 1996 the book *36 Drawings by Julian Dyson* was published. Although he worked in many parts of the country Dyson, a self-taught artist born in Cornwall, returned there in the early 1980s, its landscape being a key element in his work. Lived at St Mawes.

Sylvia DYSON 1917–1987 Watercolourist and illustrator who was brought up in Lancashire. She attended Huddersfield School of Art, 1935–40, then Royal College of Art, 1940–3, under Ernest Tristram. Married the artist Douglas Dyson and lived at Hale, Cheshire. She illustrated for Penguin Books and showed with LG, NEAC and elsewhere.

André DZIERZYNSKI 1936– Painter and critic, born in Warsaw, Poland, as Andrzej-Leszek Dzierzynski, who was brought up in the country near the Kazimierz-on-Vistula art colony. He studied history of art at Warsaw University, 1953–7, then moved to London, where he was encouraged by the sculptor Irena Kunicka to take up painting in 1958. Travelled widely on the continent. Mixed shows included Upper Grosvenor Gallery, The Sail Loft Gallery in St Ives and Crane Kalman Gallery. In 1963 he shared a show at the Centre Charles Peguy with Elena Gaputyte and had over a dozen solo exhibitions, including Upper Grosvenor and Hamet Galleries and abroad. Dzierzynski said that he worked "outside main streams and fashions" and "as a policy does not want to be included in any public collection". He was noted for egg or beeswax tempera landscapes on wood panels and mixed-technique pictures. Between 1960–75 they stemmed from extensive travels in the Middle East Asia and North and Latin America, although latterly Umbria and Tuscany, where he was based in a remote hermitage near San Gimignano, were inspirations. He was a member of several associations of art critics and contributed to the BBC's Polish language service.

Krystyna Shackleton DZIESZKO fl. from 1970s– Versatile artist and teacher, born in London of Anglo-Polish origin, who explored ideas about crossing boundaries, location and dislocation, cultural identity and diversity. Completed a foundation course at St Martin's School of Art, 1965–7; gained an art and design diploma at Manchester School of Art, 1967–70; then a postgraduate certificate in education at Manchester Polytechnic, 1970–1. Taught art at Marylebone Paddington Institute, 1973–6, other appointments including Camden Arts Centre, 1978–92. Commissions included panels for Churchill Hotel, 1968, and constructions for Holloway Community Centre, 1973. Group exhibitions included BP Arts Festival, Barbican, 1985; Hampstead Artists, Camden Arts Centre, 1986; On Uncommon Ground, Arts Council exhibition at Cartwright Hall, Bradford, 1991; and Instituto Nacional de Bellas Artes, Mexico City, 1994. Held a number of solo shows at Posk Gallery and East End Open Studios in Milborne Street, both from 1989. In 1990, Stanislaw Pater made a film, *The Evolving Image*, about her for Polish National Television.

Kazimierz Tadeusz DŹWIG 1923–1994 Artist, born in Craców, Poland, in 1923, who after the outbreak of World War II was sent by the Germans to a labour camp from which he escaped to Italy in 1943, joining the Italian partisans and Polish Second Corps. Studied painting at Academy of Fine Arts in Rome until the end of 1946 when he moved to England and soon joined the Sir John Cass School. Also took lessons with Henryk Gotlib in 1948–9 and with Camberwell School of Arts and Crafts. In 1952 he began work in Thomas De La Rue's banknote design department, retiring from it in 1988. Continued to paint in his spare time and showed widely in Britain, Poland and elsewhere. In 1995 the Polish Cultural Institute held a retrospective show. National Museums in Warsaw and Gdańsk hold examples.

E

Paul EACHUS 1944– Artist in various media, born in Liverpool, where he attended the College of Art, 1961–6, then Royal College of Art, 1967–70. Exhibitions included Liverpool University, Reeves Bi-centenary Pictures for Schools, London Artists at Shrewsbury School, 1968, and later exhibitions East at Norwich Gallery, Norfolk Institute of Art & Design, 1991. Nuffield Foundation and Gloucester Education Committee hold examples. Lived in London.

Russell EADE 1969– Versatile painter, born in Epsom, Surrey, who studied at Camberwell School of Art. He was resident artist, Paynes Poppets Chocolate Factory, 1987; Heathrow Airport, 1989–90; and London Transport, 1993–4. Was a foundryman at Meridian Fine Art Bronze Foundry, 1995, the year his oil on cotton duck Immortally Yours was shown at Royal Over-Seas League Open. Other group shows included Young Unknowns Gallery, from 1988; Limboland, Imperial College, 1989; The Discerning Eye, Mall Galleries, 1992; and Pulse, at Minet Road Gallery, 1993.

Robert EADIE 1877–1954 Painter, printmaker and poster designer who was educated in Glasgow, studied at School of Art there and in Munich and Paris. In World War I served in the Royal Engineers. He was a member of Glasgow Art Club, living in Cambuslang, and the city's Art Gallery holds his watercolour Stirling Bridge. Other main examples of Eadie's work include St Monans; Snow on the Roofs; Old Bridge, Stratheven; and Dinan Market. He was elected RSW in 1916, also showing at RSA, Royal Glasgow Institute of the Fine Arts, RA and Walker Art Gallery in Liverpool.

Aileen EAGLETON 1902–1984 Wood engraver, painter in oil and watercolour. Born in Bexley, Kent, studied art under Louis (Louisa) Thomson. A member of the SGA, she exhibited with the RA, SWA, RI and ROI, Walker Art Gallery, Liverpool, and Paris Salon. Lived at East Molesey, Surrey.

Godfrey EAGLETON 1935– Painter, draughtsman and teacher, full name Godfrey Paul Eagleton (sometimes painted as Paul). Studied for national diploma in painting and textiles at Camberwell School of Arts and Crafts, 1955, teachers including Gilbert Spencer and Martin Bloch; did National Service in Army as a photoprinter artist, 1955–7; obtained diploma in painting and etching, with first-class honours in art history, at Slade School of Fine Art, 1957–9, teachers including Claude Rogers; and gained art teacher's certificate at University College, 1959–60. Extensive teaching included Camberwell School of Art and Putney Art Centre, both 1962–7; Regent Street Polytechnic, 1963; London College of Fashion, 1967; Henry Thornton Youth Centre, 1972–6; Lewisham Inner London Education Authority Art Centre, 1976–87; and Summer Craft Centres in Westminster and Lambeth, 1989–90. Was a member of South London and South-East London Groups. Had a series of solo exhibitions including Battersea Art Centre and Opus Gallery, showing figurative and non-figurative work. Lived in London.

Paul EAGLETON: *see* **Godfrey EAGLETON**

Angela EAMES 1951– Abstract artist in various media, born in Malmesbury, Wiltshire, who taught part-time and lived in London. She studied at Bath Academy of Art and Slade School of Fine Art. Among her exhibitions was Five at Woodlands Art Gallery, 1982.

Enid EARDLEY fl. from 1940s– Painter, notable for portraits, who studied at Central School of Arts and Crafts in 1939, then in mid-1960s with Stanley Grimm and Steven Spurrier. She was a member of SWA and had a series of solo exhibitions including Alpine Gallery, 1981. Lived in Old Amersham, Buckinghamshire.

Joan EARDLEY 1921–1963 Painter and draughtsman, born in Warnham, Sussex. In 1938 she enrolled at Goldsmiths' College School of Art, staying for several months, then was at Glasgow School of Art, 1940–3, under Hugh Adam Crawford, graduating with several prizes. After a brief period at Jordanhill College of Education and a period as a joiner's labourer, in 1947 Eardley spent six months under James Cowie at the Patrick Allen-Fraser School of Art, Hospitalfield, before in 1948 taking up her post-diploma scholarship at Glasgow School of Art. A travelling scholarship took her to France and Italy in 1948–9, the resulting work being shown at her first solo exhibition at Glasgow Art School in 1949. Eardley now embarked on her two main themes as a painter: Glasgow tenement life, with its studies of children; and from 1951 pictures of the sea and coast at Catterline, on the northeast coast, where she latterly spent much time, these works having an Abstract Expressionist force. In 1960 she was a guest teacher at Hospitalfield. Eardley was elected SSA in 1948 and RSA in 1963 not long before dying of cancer in hospital near Glasgow. Scottish National Gallery of Modern Art has an extensive collection of her work. In 1988 a major retrospective was held at Talbot Rice Centre and RSA, Edinburgh.

Paul EAREE 1888–1968 Artist who was professionally trained as an ecclesiastical architect, art teacher and illustrator, but poured his spare-time creative energies into paintings, etchings and drawings with a strong regional content. Although he showed locally, Earee was rarely persuaded to part with his work for money, and only gave it away if he was sure the recipient's feelings for it matched his own. As an architect Earee designed council houses and the pulpit of St Gregory's Church, Sudbury, Suffolk, where he was a notable personality. Earee was a friend of the artists Rowland Suddaby and John Rimmer, their ideas strongly interacting. In 1920 Earee was a founder of the Sudbury Dramatic Society. He collaborated with his architectural business partner H A F Haslewood to paint scenery for the original, locally famous production of *Brer Rabbit and Mr Fox* at the Victoria Hall in 1921 and for *La Poupée* in 1923. There was a retrospective show, Landscapes and Dreams, at The Quay Theatre in 1983 and in 1996 Chappel Galleries, Chappel, included Earee in its Colchester Art Society Fifty Years Anniversary Exhibition.

Honor EARL 1901–1996 Portrait painter and draughtsman, whose natural talent for art (what she called her ability "to do certain tricks") helped her overcome the demoralizing effects of dyslexia and to support charities. Edith Honor Betty Earl was the second daughter of the 1st Viscount Maugham, Chancellor of the Exchequer under Neville Chamberlain and brother of writer W Somerset Maugham. Although the Hon. Honor Earl's subjects were often drawn from the top rank of society, including four generations of the British royal family and stars of stage and screen, she chose to mix with the under-privileged. In 1937 Earl became a prison visitor; during World War II she worked to employ refugee talent; she raised funds for the All-Nations Voluntary Service League; and donated the proceeds of exhibitions to such causes as the National Council for the Unmarried Mother and Child, the Actors' Orphanage and The National Society for Prevention of Cruelty to Children. She founded, and acted as chairman of, the Young Musicians' Fund. Earl was especially good at portraying children, holding their attention while sketching with one hand and operating a glove puppet with the other, or playing tunes with a comb and paper. Lived in London and at Martyr Worthy, Hampshire.

Donald Maurice EARLE 1928– Artist in various media and teacher, born in Melksham, Wiltshire. He attended West of England College of Art, Bristol, 1944–7, and 1949–51. Dr Earle was head of art department in various schools in Britain, latterly Great Baddow School in Chelmsford, Essex, where he lived. He showed with RWS, NEAC, RWA, RBSA and Colchester Art Society. Solo exhibitions included Mercury Theatre, Colchester, 1983; Barbican Centre, 1986; and Norwich, 1988.

Tom EARLY 1914–1967 Painter with a naturally primitive style and rich palette, by profession a doctor, whose talent was spotted by Ben Nicholson when Early was convalescing in Carbis Bay, Cornwall, 1946. He was befriended by the sculptor Denis Mitchell, with whom he had three shows in St Ives: two at Castle Inn, 1947–8, and one at Downing's Bookshop, 1949. Returned to medicine in 1952 after marrying Eunice Campbell, who published a memoir of him (*The Magic Shuttle – The Story of Tom Early: St Ives and After*), 1994, which coincided with a memorial show at Belgrave Gallery and later at The Book Gallery, St Ives. Early became registrar at the county mental hospital, Derby, and was a founder member of the Derby Group, which held its first show at Derby Art Gallery, 1961. His last solo show was at Midland Group Gallery 1965.

Anthony EARNSHAW 1924– Painter, creator of cartoon strips, prints, boxed assemblages and "books of a sort" who was born in Ilkley, Yorkshire. He was an autodidact who "through an enthusiasm for poetry discovered Surrealism in the mid-40s 'which changed my life'". This started him on making his various artefacts and "all in all making a general nuisance of myself". His assemblages sometimes used found objects and were noted for their biting wit and singular vision. Tony Earnshaw was the subject of several television films. His exhibitions included a retrospective at Leeds Institute, 1966; Angela Flowers, 1972; Dean Clough Contemporary Art Gallery, Halifax, 1986–8–92; retrospective at Leeds City Art Gallery, 1987; Graves Art Gallery, Sheffield, 1988; and Flowers East, 1989. Arts Council and Leeds City Art Gallery hold his work. Lived at Saltburn-by-the-Sea, Cleveland.

Thomas EASLEY 1949– Portrait painter and miniaturist working on various supports, self-taught, born in Oroville, California. Showed in America, in Venice and in London with RMS of which he was a member, Medici Society Ltd, ROI and elsewhere. London Sketch Club member. Work in many private collections including that of TRH The Prince and Princess of Wales. Lived for some years in Venice, Italy.

Max EASTLEY 1944– Artist, musician and teacher, born in Torquay, Devon. He studied sculpture at Middlesex Polytechnic (Hornsey College of Art), 1969–72. Eastley was fellow/lecturer in audio/visual art at Exeter College of Art, 1972–3, and in sculpture at North-East London Polytechnic, 1974–5, also being a visiting lecturer at Slade School of Fine Art and Falmouth School of Art. He taught musical instrument construction at Morley College and at Science Technology & Craft Centre, 1974–8. Eastley won an Arts Council Bursary, 1977. Group exhibitions included 6 Times, Serpentine Gallery, 1976; he shared a show with David Toop at Chapter, Cardiff, 1978; and had solo shows at Exe Gallery in Exeter, 1973, and Spectro Gallery, Newcastle upon Tyne, 1977. As a sculpture student Eastley began to investigate the relationship of chance to music, using shadow projections, graphic scores and kinetic sound machines. As an instrument builder he worked in performances ranging from his own installations and machines to musical compositions, recording and improvisation. In 1990 the range of Eastley's work in sound and vision was documented in a television film, *The Clocks Of The Midnight Hours*, shown on Channel 4. Later examples of his works included a Concert tour of Japan with Toop, 1993; *Buried Dreams*, with Toop, Beyond Records, 1994; Installation and concert, Purcell Room, South

Bank, 1995; and another at Cannon Hill Park, Birmingham, 1996. Lived in London.

Arthur EASTON 1939– Painter, printmaker and teacher, born in Salfords, Surrey. He attended Reigate School of Art, 1963–6. Went on to teach part-time at Reigate and Bletchingley Adult Education Centres and ran his own art classes, having previously taught at Reigate School of Art. Also worked as an art therapist in psychiatric hospitals. Easton gained a diploma of merit, University of Arts, Italy, in 1982 and the Stanley Grimm Prize at ROI annual show in 1991. He was a member of ROI and NS. Easton was a still life painter of meticulous exactness, in the northern European tradition. One-man shows were frequent, including Phoenix Gallery in Lavenham, 1991, and he shared an exhibition with three painters at Mistral Gallery, 1992. HRH The Princess Michael of Kent and the Museum of British Labour hold his work. Lived in Reigate, Surrey.

Hugh EASTON 1906–1965 Artist in stained glass, born in London, who studied art in France and Italy. Completed many windows, including examples at St Andrew and St Patrick, Elveden, Suffolk; and Brechin, Durham and Winchester Cathedrals. Lived in London.

Isabella EASTON 1971– Painter, printmaker and collagist, born in Epsom, Surrey, daughter of the artist Timothy Easton and restorer Christine Easton. Studied at Suffolk College of Further and Higher Education for a national diploma in art and design, 1988–90, then gained an honours degree in fine art, painting at Winchester School of Art, under Vanessa Jackson, 1990–3. Undertook a number of study visits in France, Germany, Spain and Italy; in 1992 went on a three-month exchange to Hochschule der Kunst, Berlin; and in 1997 began three-year postgraduate course at Royal Academy Schools. She said that, "using architecture as the main reference, my geometric compositions are constructed by superimposing one image over the other by the multi-layering of glazes in the watercolours and oil paintings. The etchings consist of two and three plates separating the various colours which, when overlaid, are intended to give the illusion of the interaction of space and solid." Awards included R K Burt Award for imaginative use of paper, 1993, and Eaton Fund for Artists, 1995. In 1995 Easton was elected a member of United Abstract Artists. Exhibitions included County Architect's Office, Winchester, 1992; Winchester Gallery, Winchester, and Slaughterhouse Gallery, both 1993; Tabernacle and Ben Uri Galleries, both 1995; and Battersea Arts Fair, 1996. Lived in London.

Timothy EASTON 1943– Painter and sculptor, born in Tadworth, Surrey. From 1960–4 Easton attended Kingston College of Art and Heatherley's School of Fine Art, studying painting. He began making his living as a mural and portrait painter and soon had offers to exhibit in Chicago and Kansas, where his work proved a success. In 1966–7 he travelled in Italy and northern Europe on scholarship. In 1969 he had a solo show at Woodside Gallery, Ewell, with many exhibitions – mixed and group – following in Britain and abroad. Easton's sculptures dated from about 1970. They were strongly influenced by classical themes, were produced in the lost wax way and were in bronze overlaid in silver and gold. Many of Easton's paintings were associated with the restoration of his fifteenth-century house near Woodbridge, Suffolk, on which he wrote for learned journals. Easton was also a student of the idea of The Fool, which has appeared for centuries in art and literature. In 1989 Easton painted Restoration to commemorate 50 years of the unit at the Queen Victoria Hospital, East Grinstead, set up to deal with treatment and rehabilitation of injured airmen by the plastic surgeon Sir Archibald McIndoe and the oral surgeon Sir William Kelsey-Fry. A 1996 Winston Churchill Travelling Fellowship enabled Easton to work in Italy and Spain. Later solo exhibitions included Chris Beetles Ltd, 1990; Cadogan Gallery from 1991 (part of his Henley series in 1996); and Bourne Gallery, Reigate, 1997 (coinciding with the publication of his book *Oil Painting Techniques*). One daughter, Isabella, was a painter, his daughter Lucy a jeweller.

William George EASTON 1879– Scraperboard artist, draughtsman and watercolour painter, born in London, who studied at Bolt Court School with Cecil Rea, then at Lambeth School of Art with Innes Fripp. Signed work W G E. Illustrated for national press and did book illustration. Exhibited RA and lived in London.

Nicholas EASTWOOD 1942– Artist and lecturer, who said that his paintings were "like visual records of an idea". Born in Winchester, Hampshire, Eastwood studied at Exeter College of Art, 1959–62, and from 1972 was on the staff of University of Exeter New Library, where he was deputy head and co-founder of the audio-visual section. Eastwood was a busy lecturer in Britain and abroad, modern and contemporary art being key subjects. Mixed shows included Harry J Lunn Gallery, New York, 1960; Whitechapel Art Gallery, 1976; Spacex Gallery, Exeter, from 1982; and Gordon Hepworth Gallery, Newton St Cyres, 1991, in Devon Artists. Had a solo exhibition at Galerie Jean Camion, Paris, 1960, later ones including Falmouth Art Gallery, 1997. Lived at Pinhoe, Exeter, Devon.

Roger EASTWOOD 1942– Artist mainly in oil and pastel, born in Ashton-under-Lyne, Lancashire. He was mainly self-taught, subjects being the street scenes of Oldham, Rochdale and Manchester and female nude studies. Eastwood was elected to MAFA in 1979, also showing with Oldham Society of Artists, Oldham Group of Artists and Colin Jellicoe Gallery, Manchester. Lived in Delph, Oldham, Lancashire.

Edwin EASYDORCHIK 1949– Artist producing abstract work in mixed media and teacher, born in Northumberland, who settled to work in Tynemouth, Tyne and Wear. He studied at Central School of Art 1968–71, in 1971 travelling to Italy with a Sir James Knott Travelling Scholarship. In 1973–5 he was a postgraduate painter at Newcastle University. From 1974 held several part-time lectureships, from 1982 lecturing in painting at Newcastle University. In 1979 gained an Arts Council Purchase Award, and won several Northern Arts Grants. Took part in many group shows, from Young Contemporaries, 1970, others including Sunderland Arts Centre and tour, 1975; XI Paris Biennale, 1980; and Six Artists from the Coast, Laing Art Gallery in Newcastle and Scandinavian tour, 1983. One-man exhibitions began with Sunderland Arts Centre, 1975, later ones including the same venue, 1983, and Atlantis Gallery, also 1983. Arts Council holds several drawings.

David EATWELL 1960– Self-taught artist, born in Oxford, who left school at 16 and began painting aged 25. His early work was concerned with the effects of nature on man-made and natural surfaces; later pictures were abstract: referential, geometric and organic. Eatwell showed in small-scale exhibitions in London and the provinces, later at The Lower Nupend Gallery, Cradley.

John EATWELL 1923– Painter and creator of mixed-media constructions. Studied painting at Chelsea School of Art. He showed widely in Britain, Germany and America, mixed exhibition appearances including LG, Warwick Arts Trust, Portsmouth City Art Gallery and England & Co. Had a solo show at The Minories, Colchester, 1989. Surface tones and textures were key features of his abstract studies.

John EAVES 1929– Painter, ceramist and teacher, born in Bristol. He studied at Bath Academy of Art in 1949–52, then began teaching pottery there, remaining on staff until 1979. In 1963 he had a solo ceramics exhibition at Forum Galleries in Bristol, the year later at New Vision Centre Gallery. In 1966 Eaves had a solo show of paintings at Arnolfini Gallery in Bristol, and he won a Winston Churchill Memorial Trust Fellowship to work as a painter in New Mexico. In 1986–7 he gained a Leverhulme Emeritus Fellowship to study Emile Nolde and paint in Germany. Eaves continued to exhibit widely, having a retrospective at Victoria Art Gallery, Bath, in 1987. Arts Council holds his work. Lived in Bath.

ECCLES 1920– Painter, designer and illustrator, full name Ferelith Eccles Williams, born in Oxford. She was initially educated in Wantage, then studied at Oxford Technical School, 1937–9, the Slade School of Fine Art, 1939–40, and Central School of Arts and Crafts, 1945–6. Her work was widely illustrated on the printed page, including *London Opinion*, *Sunday Times*, *Designers in Britain* and *Lilliput*. Showed at Heal's Mansard Gallery, LG, AIA and elsewhere. Lived for many years in London.

Harry Norman ECCLESTON 1923– Painter in watercolour, printmaker and teacher, born in Bilston, Staffordshire. He studied at the College of Art in Birmingham under Richard Stubbington, 1939–42, then at Royal College of Art under Robert Austin, 1947–51. From 1952–8, lectured in printmaking and illustration at South-East Essex Technical College. From 1958–83 he was artist designer at Bank of England Printing Works, where he was designer of the Series D notes: £1, Newton; £5, Wellington; £10, Nightingale; £20, Shakespeare; and £50, Wren. He was elected RE in 1961, being its president in 1975, the year he was elected a fellow of RWS. Was also a member of RWA and honorary member of RBSA, also a member of Art Workers' Guild. Eccleston's watercolours were much concerned with subjects on the water's edge and his prints, mainly of industrial subjects, included a water-edge suite, 1987. Also showed at RA from 1949, at NEAC and at Art Fairs in London and Bath. Bank of England Museum, British Museum and Ashmolean Museum in Oxford hold his work. Lived in Harold Hill, Romford, Essex.

Tom ECKERSLEY 1914–1997 Designer, muralist, illustrator and teacher, born in Newton-le-Willows, Lancashire. He studied at Salford College of Art, 1930–4, under Martin Tyas. Moved to London in 1934, where with a fellow-student, Eric Lombers, he established Eckersley Lombers, with a reputation for fine poster design. Eventually Eckersley counted among his clients London Transport, Shell-Mex, the Post Office, Gillette and the Royal Society for the Prevention of Accidents. His posters got their message over simply in two-dimensional form, with a strong idea, taste and good humour, with words well matched to the graphics. Eckersley Lombers was forced to close during World War II. Eckersley served as a cartographer in the Royal Air Force, eventually moving to the Air Ministry's publicity office. After the war Eckersley Lombers was briefly revived, then Eckersley built up a successful freelance practice. Before the war Eckersley had taught at the Westminster School of Art and Borough Polytechnic. For 20 years from 1957 he was head of graphic design at the London College of Printing, which gave him a retrospective in 1975. He published *Poster Design* in 1954. Among several books illustrated was his first wife, Daphne's, *Cat o'Nine Lives*, in 1947 (his second wife was the artist Mary Kessell). Among Eckersley's murals is that at Heathrow Airport underground station. Eckersley's work was shown at many international exhibitions and is included in the collections of the Victoria & Albert Museum, Imperial War Museum, London Transport Museum and in overseas holdings. Among honours received was his appointment as a Royal Designer of Industry, 1963, and Chartered Society of Designers' medal, 1990. Lived in London.

Maurice EDELMAN 1911–1975 Politician, writer and recreational painter who was educated at Cardiff High School, was an exhibitioner in modern languages at Trinity College, Cambridge, 1929, graduated in 1932 and gained his master's in 1941. From 1932–41 was involved in the application of plastics to aircraft building, then was a journalist and war correspondent in North Africa and France. After World War II held various appointments in international bodies, notably with a French connection, and was vice-chairman of the British Council, 1951–67. He was Labour Member of Parliament for Coventry constituencies between 1945–74. Books included *The Birth of the Fourth Republic*, 1945;

political novels, including *Who Goes Home*, 1953; and television plays. There was a memorial show at Herbert Art Gallery, Coventry, 1977.

Andrew EDEN 1946– Artist and teacher whose work included abstract sculptures in various materials, including pigment. He attended Byam Shaw School of Art, 1963–4, then gained a first-class honours degree in fine art painting at Wimbledon School of Art, 1964–9. He was joint editor/contributor, *Wallpaper* arts magazine, also participating in *Wallpaper on Cassette*, Audio Arts, Whitechapel Art Gallery, Gallery. From 1983 was associate lecturer in painting and history of art, Tresham Institute of Further and Higher Education, Kettering. Group shows included Young Contempories, 1968; On Site, Arnolfini Gallery, Bristol, 1979; Six Attitudes, Peterborough Museum and Art Gallery, 1983; and The Table Studio Group, The Living Room, 1996. Had a solo show at Daniel Shackleton Gallery, Edinburgh, 1971, later ones including Tower Bridge Piazza Gallery from 1991, and Streitenfeld Gallery, Oberursel, Frankfurt, 1995.

Denis EDEN 1878–1949 Painter, son of the watercolourist William Eden, born in Liverpool. He was educated at University College School, studying under F G Stephens; at the St John's Wood School of Art; and at Royal Academy Schools. Historical subjects were a feature of his work, which was shown at RA, Royal Glasgow Institute of the Fine Arts, Fine Art Society and RSA. Lived at Woodstock, Oxfordshire.

Max EDEN 1923– Artist in various media, teacher, born in St Helens, Lancashire. He attended Liverpool College of Art, 1948–51, at École des Beaux-Arts in Paris, 1951–2, and at Royal Academy in Copenhagen, 1954. A landscape painter in a rich palette, Eden claimed as his chief influences Cézanne and the School of Paris; Spain, the Lake District and Scotland were favoured subjects. Eden showed in France and Denmark in the 1950s. In Britain showed at Redfern Gallery and in many group shows in the northwest. Had a solo show at Acorn Gallery in Liverpool, 1985; Atkinson Art Gallery, Southport, 1988; and with his son John Eden at Orsini Gallery, 1991. Atkinson Art Gallery holds his work. Eden lived in Southport, Merseyside, and was a lecturer at College of Art there, 1960–85.

Norman EDGAR 1943– Painter in the Scottish Colourist tradition of landscape and still life, and teacher, born in Paisley, Renfrewshire. He studied painting at Glasgow School of Art, 1966–70, then taught until 1990, when he resigned to paint full-time. In 1991 Edgar was elected a member of the Royal Glasgow Institute of the Fine Arts, also showing at RP, RSA, Fosse Gallery in Stow-on-the-Wold, Richard Hagen Gallery in Broadway and elsewhere. Edgar received many portrait commissions, from bodies such as the University of Glasgow, The Archdiocese of Glasgow and the Royal College of Obstetricians. Had a solo show at Glasgow Art Club in 1977, later ones including Roger Billcliffe Fine Art, Glasgow, in 1996. Paisley Art Gallery and HRH The Duke of Edinburgh hold Edgar's work. In 1993 he was made president of Glasgow Art Club. Lived in Gourock, Renfrewshire.

Ursula EDGCUMBE 1900–1985 Sculptor in bronze, stone and wood, and painter, of figure groups and birds. Born at Sandy, Bedfordshire, Edgcumbe worked in the studio of the sculptor Havard Thomas, then studied under him at the Slade School where she won the scholarship for sculpture in 1918. When she left in 1921 she turned from modelling to direct carving for architectural projects, especially for George Kennedy. Lack of commissions and of sympathy with current trends prompted Edgcumbe in 1940 to turn from sculpture to painting. She had had a one-man sculpture show at the Leger Galleries in 1935; several painting shows followed after World War II. Commissioned work includes the large granite war memorial at Zennor, Cornwall. Work reproduced in William Aumonier's *Modern Architectural Sculpture*, Kineton Parkes' *The Art of Carved Sculpture* and the Fine Art Society catalogue *Sculpture in Britain Between the Wars*, 1986. Signed work with her initials. Lived at Ballingham; Hereford.

Reginald Edward EDGECOMBE 1885–1966 Painter, draughtsman, printmaker and designer-craftsman in glass and metal, born in Birmingham, where he finally lived. Studied at Birmingham School of Art, where he won the Messenger Prize for metalwork. Around this time he was a keen athlete, competing as a gymnast with the British team at the Antwerp Olympic Games in 1920. Member of Birmingham Art Circle. Exhibited RBSA on many occasions, also in Royal Society of Arts competitions.

Henry EDION 1905–1987 Artist on paper, born Heinrich Edelstein in Vienna, Austria. While in a Nazi concentration camp was encouraged to paint by the German Expressionist Gert Wollheim, also a prisoner, then after World War II attended L'Académie de la Grande Chaumière, in Paris. Lived and worked in Indo-China, Australia, Italy, France, Canada and America, eventually moving to England for his wife to be treated for cancer. The threat of nuclear war and rockets were a recurrent theme in Edion's work, which employed humour, strong colours and thick black lines, as in his exhibits in Fragments Against Ruin, the Arts Council touring show of 1981–2. Edion also exhibited in North America, with Crane Kalman Gallery in 1962, and after his death was shown at that gallery in 1993 and at Ben Uri Art Society, 1994, which holds examples. Lived finally in west London.

John EDKINS 1931–1966 Figurative and hard-edge abstract painter, photographer, draughtsman and teacher, born in Bromley, Kent. Attended Ealing Junior School of Art, 1942–5, then the senior school, 1945–8. Between 1945–8 Edkins painted, gardened and taught part-time, then entered the school of painting at Royal College of Art, 1954–7. After a travelling scholarship to Greece, from 1958–61 taught at Bideford School of Art, lecturing in painting at Liverpool College of Art, 1961–6. Exhibited at

Liverpool Academy and was a prizewinner at John Moores Liverpool Exhibition in 1965. Although Edkins was absorbed in his work, three major heart operations undermined his strength. He was a dedicated teacher, a man with wide, lively and quirky enthusiasms, ranging from music, personal products of the industrial age and motor racing to the making and launching of fire balloons. Had a solo show, organised by the Liverpool Academy, at Bluecoat Chambers, 1966, shortly after he married and went to live in the Formby, Lancashire, area. Died in Guy's Hospital. Walker Art Gallery, Liverpool, which owns his work, organised a retrospective in 1967, toured to the Royal College of Art.

Edith EDMONDS fl. c.1920–1955 Watercolourist who studied at Liverpool School of Art, 1921–2 and in Paris at Atelier Delbos, 1923–4. Showed at RA, SWA, RCamA, in the provinces and at Paris Salon. Lived in Conway, Carnarvonshire.

Michael EDMONDS 1926– Sculptor, watercolourist and draughtsman. After education in the south of England he served in south Wales coal mines, 1944–7, then qualified as an architect in 1953. First one-man show at Cooling Galleries, 1943. Was a founder-member of the 56 Group and joined the Society of Christian Artists. Had further one-man shows in London and in Wales and has taken part in group shows including RCamA, WAC, SWG and *Daily Express* Young Artists Exhibition in 1955. Commissioned work included National Union of Mine Workers and Medical Research Council, for which he completed a tile mural. Contemporary Art Society and Pembroke College, Oxford, bought his work.

Simon EDMONDSON 1955– Artist who was born and lived in London. He studied at City & Guilds School of Art, 1973–4; Kingston Polytechnic, 1974–7; and at Syracuse University, New York, 1978–80. He held a first solo exhibition at Syracuse in 1979, after which he had one-man shows in Berlin, Zürich, New York and London, where Nicola Jacobs Gallery exhibited him for a time. Later solo shows included Jason & Rhodes Gallery, 1995. In 1987 Edmondson was included in The Self Portrait: A Modern View tour, originating at Artsite Gallery, Bath.

Nellie Mary Hepburn EDMUNDS fl. from 1895–1953 Miniature and portrait painter who studied at Slade School of Fine Art under Fred Brown and at Westminster School of Art. She was a prolific exhibitor at RMS, in which she held a number of senior positions. Also showed at RA, SWA and RI. Lived in Bexhill, Sussex.

May de Montravel EDWARDES 1887– Painter and miniaturist who studied at the Cope and Nicol School, in South Kensington, then at the Royal Academy Schools, 1907–12, where she was a bronze and silver medallist. Exhibited RA, RI, SM, of which she was a member, Brook Street Gallery and Paris Salon. She was fond of historical subjects and her picture of General Wolfe on the Heights of Abraham before the Battle of Quebec was one notable example. Lived in London.

Alan EDWARDS 1947– Artist and teacher who gained an honours degree at Liverpool Polytechnic, 1979–82, and who taught at Plessington High School. He showed at Five Artists, Liverpool's Unity Theatre, 1980; Stowells Trophy at RA, 1982; and was included in Walker Art Gallery, Liverpool, touring exhibition Merseyside Artists 3, 1986–7, showing the wood/collage Door II.

Arthur Sherwood EDWARDS 1887–1960 Architect and sculptor who spent much of his spare time painting. He was born in Leicester and studied in Grimsby and Newcastle, where he gained a bronze medal. Notable among his public works are his mosaic of the Battle of Waterloo for Manchester's Free Trade Hall; Sculptures at the back of that building; and his prizewinning war memorial at Sale, Cheshire, to the 10th Battalion Lincolns, a marble statue of St George. Few of his paintings were commissioned and most remained unframed until the death of his wife, after which there was a studio sale at the Manchester Auction Mart in 1980. Manchester City Art Gallery holds his work, which was also exhibited at RA, RI, RCamA, Walker Art Gallery in Liverpool and at Royal Glasgow Institute of the Fine Arts. Lived for some years in Ashton-on-Mersey, Cheshire.

Benjamin Ralph EDWARDS 1950– Painter, printmaker, draughtsman and teacher, born in London, where he lived. He studied art privately, at City and Guilds of London Art School, 1968–72, then with S W Hayter at Atelier 17 in Paris, 1972–3, and Roderic Barrett at Royal Academy Schools, 1973–7. Taught part-time at City and Guilds. Showed from 1977 at RA Summer Exhibitions, RE and abroad and illustrated several books. Victoria & Albert Museum holds his work.

Cyril Walduck EDWARDS 1902– Painter in oil and watercolour, mainly of landscapes. Studies pursued at Regent Street Polytechnic School of Art. Exhibited at RA, RBA, RI, ROI and Paris Salon, Laing Art Gallery in Newcastle buying his work. Lived at Upper Wyche, near Malvern, Worcestershire.

Griff EDWARDS 1920– Painter and teacher, born in Port Talbot, Glamorgan. After attending Swansea College of Art Edwards did military service 1940–7, but managed to study part-time at Bournemouth College of Art, completing his formal studies at Paignton School of Art, 1947–9. From 1949 was on staff of Swansea College Art, latterly as the head of technical graphics department. Showed RCamA, SEA, Royal National Eisteddfod and elsewhere in Wales, where his drawings of chapels were a notable feature done in connection with WAC.

Helen EDWARDS 1882– Landscape painter and writer on art who also worked under her maiden name Helen Sutton. She studied at Algernon Talmage's school in St Ives, Cornwall, and with A Moulton Foweraker, 1906–8, and H Dawson Barkas in Reading, 1909. Showed at SWA, PS, UA and in the provinces, notably with art societies in Hampshire and Dorset, where she lived at Parkstone. Medici Society reproduced several pastels, including *After the Shower* and *Untrodden Snow*.

John EDWARDS 1938– Painter and teacher, born in London, where he continued to live. Edwards studied at Hornsey College of Art, 1953–60, with a spell in Royal Air Force, 1956–8. In the early 1960s Edwards taught at Brighton College of Art and Leeds University Institute. After a British Council Scholarship took him to Belgium in 1963–4, Edwards embarked on a busy teaching career which included periods at Chelsea and Brighton and St Martin's School of Art, where he was senior lecturer in painting. In the mid-1970s he taught at a number of American colleges and universities and was artist-in-residence at Syracuse University, New York. Edwards took part in many group exhibitions and from 1967 had extensive solo shows at Rowan Gallery. In 1979 a Newcastle upon Tyne Polytechnic Art Gallery show toured England. Edwards' abstract pictures had many influences over the years, including Rothko, Noland, David Smith and Anthony Caro. The surfaces could be highly charged and sometimes he used basic configurations in series, such as X's, T's, crosses and arcs. Arts Council holds his work.

John EDWARDS 1940– Portrait, wildlife and sporting artist who aimed to "continue the traditional methods of naturalistic painting, drawing and sculpture" in his work. He was born in Kidderminster, Worcestershire. Was at Stourbridge Art School, 1953–5, then was a carpet designer, 1955–62. From 1962–3 studied art with Pietro Annigoni in Florence, then was at Royal Academy Schools. Gained four silver and bronze medals and the Elizabeth Greenshields Memorial Foundation Award, 1965–6 and 1968–9. Edwards was made a member of RP in 1970. In 1986 won the World Wildlife Fund Art Award. Among Edwards' subjects were the politician Margaret Thatcher and the actress Helen Mirren. He showed with Moorland and Malcolm Innes Galleries; Solent Gallery, Lymington; Chesterville Gallery, Kidderminster; RA Summer Exhibitions; SWA; Ashmolean Museum in Oxford, and elsewhere. Gordonstoun School, The Kennel Club and Oxford and Cambridge University colleges hold his work. Lived in Kidderminster.

John D EDWARDS 1952– Painter, sculptor and teacher, born in London. He studied, 1971–4, at Harrow School of Art and Central School of Art and Design, his teachers including Adrian Berg, John Hoyland and Paul Huxley. In 1973 Edwards was the first president of New Contemporaries, was an assistant to both Hoyland and Berg and began a working relationship with Waddington Galleries interspersed with teaching. In late-1970s travelled extensively through Europe and America. The early-1980s saw Edwards working as the sculptor Barry Flanagan's assistant, also with Allen Jones and Ivor Abrahams. Edwards had his first solo show with Odette Gilbert Gallery in 1985, several more following.

Kevin EDWARDS 1962– Artist who after a foundation year at Bangor, 1981–2, studied at Liverpool Polytechnic, 1982–5. Showed with Liverpool Four at Theatre Gwynedd, 1984; Bluecoat Gallery BA Graduates, 1985; and with Walker Art Gallery, Liverpool, 1986–7 touring exhibition Merseyside Artists 3. In 1986 shared a show at Theatre Gwynedd.

Laurence EDWARDS 1967– Sculptor, draughtsman and teacher, born in Suffolk, where he set up a foundry at Laxfield and ran classes. He studied at Canterbury College of Art and in 1988 went to study bronze casting and sculpture at Royal College of Art. There he was awarded a Henry Moore Bursary, the Angelani Prize for Bronze Casting and an Intach Travelling Scholarship, enabling him to study in India traditional casting methods. Had a solo show at High Street Exhibition Gallery, Ipswich, in 1994.

Lionel EDWARDS 1878–1966 Painter and draughtsman, magazine and book illustrator and writer, famous for his sporting, particularly fox- and stag-hunting, and military subjects. Edwards studied with the painter Arthur Cope and at Frank Calderon's School of Animal Painting. Edwards reported in Spain for *The Graphic* in 1910, then served with the Army Remount Service during World War I. Thereafter he became a favourite contributor to sporting and other magazines, such as *Punch*, and began to be known for his illustrations to several dozen books with horsing and country themes. He was the author, mostly on hunting subjects, of more than a dozen books. His *Reminiscences of a Sporting Artist* appeared in 1948. For a time he was a member of the London Sketch Club. Edwards knew his subjects at first hand, as he hunted with 91 packs of foxhounds and at the age of 80 was still jumping gates. A quiet, gentle man who looked like an old soldier, he earned a reputation as a first-class sporting artist, exemplary at representing the English landscape during the seasons. Exhibited RCamA and RI especially, also RA and Walker Art Gallery, Liverpool. British Sporting Art Trust held his work. Lived at Buckholt, Wiltshire.

Mary Stella EDWARDS 1898–1989 Mystic poet, painter and model-maker, born in London. Studied at Battersea and Regent Street Polytechnic Schools of Art. There she met Judith Ackland, with whom she spent the rest of her life, painting around Britain and exhibiting together and jointly making models and dioramas, Edwards painting the settings. Windsor Guildhall holds examples. She illustrated for publishers such as Chapman and Hall; showed at SWA, RBA and elsewhere; and published several volumes of poetry. The first book, *Time and Chance*, was published by Leonard and Virginia Woolf at Hogarth Press, 1926. London Museum holds her work. Lived in Staines, Middlesex.

Peter EDWARDS 1955– Figurative painter in oil, born in Chirk, Denbighshire, who studied at Shrewsbury, 1974–5, and Cheltenham, 1975–8, after which he was based in Shropshire, settling in Oswestry. Showed at RA Summer Exhibition and regularly in portrait exhibitions at National Portrait Gallery, which toured his Contemporary Poets show, 1990–3. The Liverpool poets, Seamus Heaney, John Heath-Stubbs, Michael Longley, Douglas Dunn and Bobby Charlton were among Edwards' main works. National Portrait Gallery, Ulster Museum in Belfast, Ferens Art Gallery in Hull, National Library of Wales in Aberystwyth, Williamson Art Gallery in Birkenhead and a number of university colleges hold examples. Chelsea Arts Club member.

EFF: *see* **Roy FERGUSON**

Felim EGAN 1952– Painter and sculptor, born in Strabane, County Tyrone. Studied at Northern Ireland Polytechnic, then 1975–7 did Slade School of Fine Art postgraduate study. Mixed shows included Third Eye Centre, Glasgow; Graeme Murray Gallery, Edinburgh; Art Cologne '88 and '89; and Fruitmarket Gallery, Edinburgh. From 1979 had a series of solo shows at Oliver Dowling Gallery, Dublin. Others included Arts Council Gallery, Belfast; Douglas Hyde Gallery, Dublin; Madeleine Carter Fine Art, Boston, America; and Scottish Gallery, 1990. Two major commissions carried out by Egan were a neon construction for Ardhowen Theatre, Northern Ireland, 1986, and a wall construction for the conference hall in Dublin Castle, 1989. Ulster Museum, Belfast; Arts Council of Northern Ireland; and Contemporary Irish Arts Society hold Egan's work, which included Minimalist paintings and bronzes, abstract with landscape references. Worked in Dublin and Edinburgh.

Shan EGERTON 1948– Landscape artist in pastel and oil, born in London but brought up on the Welsh border, her mother a painter from an artistic family. From 1966–70, Shan studied at Byam Shaw School of Art, teachers including Bernard Dunstan and Diana Armfield. After art school she divided her time between her home near Hay-on-Wye and London, which she eventually gave up. Travelled in India, China, Nepal, Mongolia and Tibet, making sketches later worked up in the studio. Mixed appearances included RA Summer Exhibitions, PS, NEAC and Kilvert Gallery in Clyro. Had several solo exhibitions at Oliver Swann Galleries from 1980, later ones including Sally Hunter Fine Art, 1997.

Frank EGGINTON 1908–1990 Watercolour painter of landscapes, born in Wallasey, Cheshire, son of the artist Wycliffe Egginton and brother of Lucy Egginton. Studied with his father, at Newton Abbot and Exeter Schools of Art. Showed extensively at Fine Art Society, RCamA of which he was a member, RHA, Annan and Sons in Glasgow and elsewhere. Lived in Donegal, in the west of Ireland, for some years.

Wycliffe EGGINTON 1875–1951 Landscape painter, born in Birmingham. Educated there and at Liscard Art School, Wallasey. Exhibited prolifically at Fine Art Society and Walker's Galleries, at both having one-man shows, also at RA, RCamA, RI and RHA. Father of the artists Frank and Lucy Egginton. Victoria & Albert Museum, Walker Art Gallery, Liverpool, several other English provincial galleries and the public gallery in Auckland, New Zealand, hold his work. Lived in Teignmouth, Devon.

William Stanley EGGISON fl. from c.1910–1956 Portrait painter and teacher who studied at Birmingham Municipal School of Art and won a scholarship which he chose to take in Paris at Académie Julian just before World War I. Although Eggison had been the most brilliant student of his period in Birmingham, problems in leaving France and the loss of all his work done there exacerbated health problems and and his promise faded. He painted and showed little on return to England, but was elected a member of RBSA in 1930 and was recognised as a fine teacher in the life class at Birmingham School of Arts and Crafts.

Philip EGLIN 1959– Ceramic figure sculptor, born in Gibraltar, who studied at Harlow Technical College, 1977–9; Staffordshire Polytechnic, 1979–83; and Royal College of Art, 1983–6. He showed with Contemporary Applied Arts from 1986; Garden Show, Gainsborough's House, Sudbury, 1989; The Decade Ahead, Scottish Gallery, Edinburgh, 1990; Colours of the Earth, British Council show touring India, 1991; and The Raw and the Cooked, Barbican Art Gallery and tour, 1993–4. Victoria & Albert Museum, Fitzwilliam Museum in Cambridge, Contemporary Art Society and public galleries in Brighton and Hove, Gateshead and Portsmouth hold examples. Eglin won the Jerwood Prize for ceramics in 1996.

Uzo EGONU 1931– Painter, designer and typographer, born in Onitsha, Nigeria. In his early teens he won a national school art competition in Nigeria, then came to England, finishing his initial education in Norfolk. Studied at Camberwell School of Arts and Crafts, 1949–52, having been encouraged to seek London art education in Nigeria by the sculptor Ben Enwonwu. Egonu travelled widely in Europe, supporting himself by lecturing and selling his work. Back in London in 1954 he was lucky to find a private patron for several years. Egonu began as a naturalistic painter, but his painted world became more stylized as he parted company with straight realism "to explore all the possibilities to use form". Took part widely in group shows in Europe. One-man exhibitions included Commonwealth Institute, 1973 and 1982; Black-Art Gallery and Royal Festival Hall, 1986. Participated in The Other Story, Hayward Gallery and tour, 1989–90, and the Institute of International Visual Arts toured a solo show by him in 1997, venues including Oldham Art Gallery. Victoria & Albert Museum, provincial and overseas galleries hold his work.

Georg EHRLICH 1897–1966 Sculptor of animals, draughtsman and etcher. He was educated and studied art in Vienna at the Kunstgewerbeschule, 1912–15, and began to exhibit widely on the continent. Settled in England and showed at the RA, RSA, with the Arts Council of Great Britain and elsewhere, as well as continuing to show widely on the continent and in North America. He completed public sculpture in Britain and abroad. Extensive one-man shows, including Venice Biennale, 1958, a series in London from 1938–60, and in Columbus, Ohio,

1948. His work was widely reproduced and is in many public collections, including Tate Gallery, British Museum and Victoria & Albert Museum. Lived in London.

Cae EINION: *see* **Raymond George PERRY**

Ernst EISENMAYER 1920– Sculptor in various materials and painter, born in Vienna, Austria. After secondary education there he moved to London in 1939 and studied at Camberwell School of Arts and Crafts, 1947, teachers including Victor Pasmore. Showed at Leicester Galleries and Marjorie Parr Gallery and had a series of solo shows at Mercury Gallery between 1964–72. Among his international commissions was metal sculpture for British pavilion at Expo '70, in Japan. His Family Group, stylised figures in bronze presented in 1970, stands at Carlton Forum Estate in Nottingham. Eisenmayer later moved to Italy.

George EISLER 1928–1998 Expressionist painter, draughtsman, printmaker, illustrator and teacher, born in Vienna, Austria, son of the composer Hanns Eisler, his mother the singer Charlotte Eisler. From 1936 Eisler spent 20 months with his mother in Moscow, but during the return to Vienna they learned that Hitler had arrived there, so they stayed in Prague, having to move to England in 1939. Settled in Manchester, Eisler attended the Central High School for Boys and was encouraged in his painting by art historian Margaret H Bulley, who acted as a patron. Eisler attended the Stockport, Manchester and Salford Schools of Art, in 1944 showing at Foyles Gallery in an exhibition of Austrian artists in England including Oskar Kokoschka, who taught him. Eisler had his first solo show in Manchester in 1946, the year he returned to Vienna, where he studied life drawing in the evenings at the Academy. From the late 1940s Eisler travelled and showed extensively across Europe. Notable events included Otto Klemperer's request for set and costume designs for Mozart's *The Magic Flute* at Covent Garden's Royal Opera House, 1962; award of the Austrian Staatspreis for painting and major shows at the Vienna Secession and at Weinmüller's, Munich, 1965; election as president of the Secession in 1968 (until 1972); publication in 1970 of a monograph by Otto Breicha on Eisler's works, with a solo show at the Secession; award of the Prize of the City of Vienna, 1971; of the Cross of Honour for Science and Art, 1974; and the Klimt Award of the Vienna Secession in 1976; followed by a retrospective in Graz in 1977. In 1979 Edition Tusch published a portfolio of Eisler's etchings, entitled *Imaginary Portraits – 14 Poets*, the year he illustrated Dashiell Hammett's detective stories. Eisler participated in the Venice Biennale in 1982. Eisler's teaching included International Summer Academy in Salzburg, 1981–2–4, and the University of New Mexico, 1983–5. His later exhibitions included Landscape of Exile, 1988, at Manchester City Art Gallery, evocative views of the city.

Andrew EKINS 1961– Artist and lecturer, born in Preston, Lancashire, who studied at Medway, Canterbury and Camberwell Colleges of Art. He was artist-in-residence at the Chisenhale Gallery, 1995, having lectured part-time at Kensington & Chelsea College from 1991 and Epping Forest College from 1992. Won a City of Westminster/Arts Council Award, 1992, and a South East Arts Travel Award, 1995–6. In 1986 gained work commission for Collins/Granada Publishers. Group shows included Barbican Centre, 1985; A Simple Twist of Fate, Riverside Studios, 1992; and Royal Over-Seas League Open, 1996. Had a series of solo shows, including South Hill Park Arts Centre, Bracknell, 1995. Riverside Health Authority held Ekins' work which was non-descriptive but made "oblique references to elements from my experience and habitat".

John ELDERFIELD 1943– Curator, historian, teacher, writer and painter, born in Yorkshire. He studied at University of Manchester school of architecture, 1961–2; University of Leeds department of fine art, 1962–6; taught at Winchester School of Art, 1966–70; was awarded a Harkness Fellowship, research in history of art, at Yale University, 1970–1; researched at Museum of Modern Art, New York, 1971–2; and from 1972 studied at Courtauld Institute, gaining his doctorate. Taught art at University of Leeds, 1973–5. From 1975 was on the staff of the Museum of Modern Art in New York. Among his published works was *Henri Matisse: A Retrospective*, to coincide with the exhibition at the Museum in 1992. Producing abstract works, Elderfield took part in a number of mixed shows, including Cunningham Ward Gallery, New York, and British Painting '74, organised by the Arts Council, both 1974. Solo shows included University of Guelph, Canada, 1971, and Park Square Gallery, Leeds, 1974. Was a contributing editor to *Artforum*, 1972–4, and *Studio International*, 1973–5. Lived in New York.

Harold ELDRIDGE 1923– Painter, muralist and teacher, born in London. He attended Camberwell School of Arts and Crafts, Royal College of Art and went on to teach at art school in Coventry, Warwickshire, where he settled. Showed at RA, LG and elsewhere. One of his murals is in Mortlake Primary School, Surrey. His portrait of John Minton was included in John Minton and Friends, Michael Parkin Gallery, 1997.

Mildred E ELDRIDGE 1909–1991 Painter, muralist and book illustrator, born in Wimbledon, Surrey. She studied at the School of Art there, Royal College of Art and at British School in Rome. She was involved in *Recording Wales* for the Pilgrim Trust, 1944–6. Completed a 120-foot mural for the nurses' home at Robert Jones and Agnes Hunt Orthopaedic Hospital, Oswestry. Showed with SEA, WAC, RCamA, RSA, RWS and elsewhere. She had a show at National Library of Wales, Aberystwyth, in 1959, and at Powys Fine Art Room, Welshpool, in 1961. In 1993 there was a tribute show at Abbott and Holder. Victoria & Albert Museum; National Museum of Wales in Cardiff; and Oldham and Sheffield Councils hold her work. Lived at Rhiw, Pwllheli, Gwynedd.

Gertrude ELIAS 1913– Artist producing cartoons, graphic art and posters, by profession an illustrator, born in Vienna, Austria, studying at the State School of Applied Art. She won the Werkbund Prize for a poster, aged 19. She did extensive commissioned work Bodley Head, Constable, Collins, Frederick Muller, Duckworth and Contemporary Films. Exhibitions included Women's Images of Men, ICA, 1980; Art & Society, Whitechapel Gallery, and Contemporary Artists in Camden, Burgh House, both 1981; and Midland Group, Nottingham, and Intergrafik, Berlin, both 1984. Had a retrospective at Margaret Fisher, 1984. In 1993–4 her autobiography appeared: *The Suspect Generation*, extensively illustrated mainly with political cartoons from British and foreign journals for which she had written articles. Victoria & Albert Museum and The Museum of Labour History, Manchester, hold examples. Lived in London.

Ken ELIAS 1944– Painter and teacher who originally studied medical laboratory technology at Neath General Hospital/Neath Technical College, 1961–5, before taking a foundation course at Cardiff College of Art, 1965–6. Gained an honours degree from Newport College of Art and Design, 1966–9, did a postgraduate teaching certificate at University College Cardiff, 1969–70, gaining his master's in fine art at South Glamorgan Institute of Higher Education, 1985–7. After a series of teaching posts from 1970, from 1980 Elias was head of the art department at Aberdare Girls' Comprehensive, being a visiting lecturer at South Glamorgan Institute, 1988. He won several WAC awards and is represented in its collection as well as those of West Wales Arts Association and Bangor Normal College. Exhibitions included Neath and District National Eisteddfod of Wales, 1994. Lived in Neath, West Glamorgan.

Benno ELKAN 1877–1960 Sculptor, printmaker and draughtsman, born in Dortmund, Germany. Studied painting in Germany, Switzerland and then took up sculpture privately in Paris. Exhibited widely on continent and in London and the provinces, having settled in England in the early 1930s. Elkan's work was purchased widely for European collections and is in the House of Lords, bust of Marquess of Salibury and King's College, Cambridge, Lord Keynes. Sometimes signed work B E. Among his books was *Spain Seen by an Artist*, which he illustrated. Lived in London.

Rose ELLENBY fl. from 1940s– Painter and illustrator, born and lived in London. Sometimes she exhibited under her married name Rose Carruthers. She studied at Central School of Arts and Crafts, 1939–43, with Bernard Meninsky and Noel Rooke. Among her book illustrations were two King Penguins: *Edible Fungi* and *Poisonous Fungi*. Showed at New Burlington Galleries and Victoria & Albert Museum, which owns her work.

Ashley ELLIOTT 1974– Painter of abstracts, born in Bristol, who gained a fine art degree at Slade School of Fine Art, 1992–6. Exhibitions included Detour, Disused Bus Depot, King's Cross, 1994, and in 1996 New Contemporaries at Tate Gallery, Liverpool, and Camden Arts Centre.

David Raymond ELLIOTT 1942– Watercolourist, born and lived in Stockport, Cheshire. He was mainly self-taught apart from studies with Francis Pratt at Montmiral, France. Elliott left the printing trade in 1988 to become a freelance artist. Limited-edition prints from watercolours of the Lake District were sold in the northwest of England. Elliott's interest was mainly landscape, influences being the work of William Russell Flint and John McCombs. He was a member of Stockport Art Guild and showed with BWS and Ginnel and Colin Jellicoe Galleries in Manchester.

Geoffrey ELLIOTT 1935– Painter, muralist, draughtsman, printmaker and teacher, born in Tideswell, Derbyshire. He studied at Derby and Brighton Colleges of Art, 1952–7. After lecturing at Brighton and Wolverhampton Colleges of Art and winning an Italian Government Travelling Scholarship, 1969, in 1983 Elliott emigrated to Australia, establishing a studio in Brisbane. Travelled and worked in Australia, Britain, America, Bali, on the continent and in Cyprus. Exhibited widely in solo and group shows in England and Australia. There his main works included pictures for Jupiter's Casino, Ramada, and Sea World, Nara, on the Gold Coast; Daydream Island Hotel in the Whitsundays and Kooralbyn Valley Heart Resort in the Gold Coast hinterland. Completed large murals for Dockside Restaurant, Kangaroo Point, Brisbane, and Kooralbyn Valley Conference Centre, a triptych for Albert Park Motor Inn, four big still lifes for the Brisbane Hilton, two large landscapes for Brisbane City Travelodge and large works for the members' stand at Rosehill Racecourse, Sydney. Tate Gallery, British Council, Australian and many corporate collections hold examples. Lived in Indooroopilly, Queensland.

Marguerite ELLIOTT 1943– Artist and teacher who studied at Brighton College of Arts & Crafts, 1959–63, Royal Academy Schools, 1964–7, then British School in Rome, 1967–8. She went on to become a part-time teacher at Chester College of Further Education. Took part in mixed shows at Mercury and Odette Gilbert Galleries, RA Summer Exhibition from 1985 and at Ash Barn Gallery in Petersfield. In 1986–7 she had a number of still lifes, a key interest, in Merseyside Artists 3, toured by Walker Art Gallery in Liverpool. Had a solo show at Duncan Campbell Contemporary Art, 1997. Hove Museum and Art Gallery, BBC and Lever Bros hold her work.

Marion ELLIOT 1964– Artist with a special interest in ceramic figures. She studied for a bachelor's degree in fine art at Liverpool Polytechnic, 1982–5, then worked for a diploma in ceramics at Sir John Cass, City of London Polytechnic. She was included in Artists under 30, Royal Liverpool Hospital, and Graduates '85, at Liverpool's Bluecoat Gallery, both 1985. In same year began showing with Walker Art Gallery's touring shows Merseyside Artists.

Richard ELLIOT 1960– Painter, born in London. He attended Ravensbourne College of Art, 1982–3, then did an honours degree in painting at Duncan of Jordanstone College of Art, Dundee.

Showed at RSA, the 1988 South Bank Show, Art Miami '92 at the Miami Beach Convention Centre and at Art92, Islington Business Design Centre, represented by Contemporary Artists' Forum. In 1990 had a solo show at Boland's Gallery. Of his large, colourful townscapes in thick impasto Elliot commented that his ambition was "to produce paintings with figurative and abstract elements supported by a loose, almost coincidental, narrative". Lived in London.

Richard ELLIOT 1964– Atmospheric landscape painter in oil and watercolour who studied at Chester School of Art, 1983–4, Manchester Polytechnic, 1984–7, then did postgraduate painting at Royal Academy Schools, 1987–90. Among his awards were 1987 David Murray Landscape Studentship; 1988 Singer & Friedlander/*Sunday Times* Watercolour Competition Student Prize; and 1990 *Antique Dealers' and Collectors' Guide* Prize. Elliott was commissioned to produce pictures for the oil company Chevron's 1991 calendar. Shows included Manchester Polytechnic, 1986; Mall Galleries and Lynne Stern Associates, both 1988; and solo exhibitions Gallery North, Cumbria, and Art Directions, both 1989.

Walter Albert ELLIOT 1936– Artist in various media, born in Wembley, Middlesex. He studied at de Havilland Aero College, became a design and development engineer with de Havilland Engine Company and was elected a fellow of the British Interplanetary Society for his contribution to rocket design. Studied art at Harrow College of Art and Hammersmith Polytechnic. Was a member of PS and UA and of the Torbay Guild of Artists and was president of Ilfracombe Art Society. Also showed with RI and in Paris and in 1981 won gold medal and membership of Accademia Italia. Lived in Ilfracombe, Devon.

Belinda ELLIS 1949– Abstract painter, born and lived in London, who studied at Sir John Cass School of Art, 1967–9, and North-East London Polytechnic, 1969–72. Mixed shows included Space Open Studios, 1975; 55 Wapping Artists, 1979; and from 1980 Wapping Artists Open Studios.

Bill ELLIS 1944– Painter in oil and watercolour, born in Rhyl, Flintshire, where he continued to live. He was "self-taught, but had good advice from Welsh artist Robert Evans Hughes, who lived in Rhyl". Ellis was an insurance agent before taking up art full-time. He painted many portraits, including the acting partnership Richard Burton and Elizabeth Taylor; landscapes; and abstracts, where the "main influence was Salvador Dali". Ellis was a member of the Prestatyn 57 Group, Clwydian Art Society and Flint and Deeside Art Society and exhibited in many libraries, including Rhyl, and in Rhyl Town Hall. He had a great interest in music hall and published *Seaside Entertainment: 100 Years of Nostalgia*, and *Rhyl in Old Photos*.

Brendan ELLIS 1951– Versatile artist and teacher, based in Belfast, Northern Ireland, who studied at Ulster College Northern Ireland Polytechnic for diploma (first-class honours) and post-diploma work until 1974, having left St Mary's Grammar School in 1969; in 1977 he gained his master's degree at Royal College of Art, also winning the John Minton Drawing Prize. Between 1974–9, Ellis held a number of positions, including teacher, mural painter for Belfast City Council and clerical officer with the Water Service, from 1979 being a medical artist at Royal Victoria Hospital in Belfast. From 1987 he was shop steward for the Confederation of Health Service Employees at the Hospital. His output was varied, including Stations of the Cross for St Columba's Roman Catholic Church, Annan, Dumfriesshire, 1984; commissions for churches in England, from 1990; and a commissioned self-portrait for the National Collection, Limerick, 1992. Solo shows included Kerlin Gallery, Belfast, 1990. Arts Council of Northern Ireland holds Ellis' work.

Clifford ELLIS 1907–1985 Printmaker, designer, painter and teacher, married to the artist Rosemary Ellis. He was born in Bognor Regis, Sussex. He spent a year at St Martin's School of Art before studying illustration at Regent Street Polytechnic School of Art, 1924–7; Ellis then did a year's postgraduate teacher-training course and in 1929 gained a diploma in art history at London University. It was while teaching at Regent Street Poly from 1928–36 that Ellis married his wife, with whom he was to collaborate on so much work. During the early 1930s they did many notable book jacket, mosaic and poster designs, patrons including London Transport and the Post Office. In 1936 Clifford Ellis joined the staff of Bath Technical College, in 1938 was appointed head of the School of Art, eventually Bath Academy of Art, where he devised a pioneering syllabus and assembled a notable staff. Although Ellis was always busy with his own work, designing book jackets for the Collins *New Naturalist* series, working for the Pilgrim Trust *Recording Britain* project and being active in Bath Art Club, the Academy was his main achievement, as the exhibition at Michael Parkin Gallery in 1989 and its catalogue showed.

Edwina ELLIS (E N ELLIS) 1946– Engraver and printmaker, born in Sydney, Australia. She studied painting at National Art School there and at John Ogburn Studio, 1963–9. Moved to London, 1972, studying metal engraving at Sir John Cass College, then wood engraving with Simon Brett Summer School, 1981 and 1983. Ellis was elected to SWE membership in 1984 and fellowship of RE in 1987. Showed with RA Summer Exhibition from 1984, at Lumley Cazalet group shows and at Bradford Print Biennale in 1990. Had a solo exhibition at Oxford Gallery, Oxford, 1984, later ones including Godfrey and Twatt, Harrogate, 1991. Her main works included The Maxims of the Duc de la Rochefoucauld, 1986; Seven Products of Virtue as Garden Prigs, 1987; and Three Locks, 1990. Victoria & Albert Museum, Ashmolean Museum in Oxford and Fitzwilliam Museum Cambridge as well as American and Australian collections hold her work. Ellis moved to Wales in 1991, living at Tyn-y-Graig, Ystrad Meurig, Dyfed, although travel in Africa, Arabia and Australia remained an inspiration to her work, which showed a preoccupation with warm light and colour engraving.

Harold ELLIS 1917– Painter, draughtsman and commercial artist, born and lived in Baildon, Yorkshire. He attended Bradford Grammar School, then entered the commercial art studio of Field, Sons & Company, Bradford, 1933–9. Was a Bradford Arts Club member who also exhibited at Cartwright Hall in the city.

Lionel ELLIS 1903– Painter, wood engraver, modeller and teacher, specialising in portraits, flowers and horses. Born in Plymouth, Devon, Ellis studied at Plymouth School of Art, 1918–22, Royal College of Art, 1922–4, where he obtained a Travelling Scholarship, Atelier Colarossi in Paris, and in Italy. Ellis' liking for the Old Masters of painting influenced his illustrations, in the 1920s, of Robert Herrick, Theocritus and Catullus for the Fanfrolico Press. He exhibited at RA, NS, of which he was a member, NEAC and extensively at Redfern Gallery. Victoria & Albert Museum, British Museum and several provincial galleries, including Plymouth, hold his work. Lectured on painting at Wimbledon School of Art, 1937–68, although in his later years led a reclusive, back-to-the-land type of existence at Headley, Surrey.

Noel ELLIS 1917– Painter and printmaker, born in Plymouth, Devon. He studied at the School of Art there and then at Royal College of Art until 1948. Showed at RA, LG, NEAC, ROI and in the provinces. Lived in London for many years.

Norman ELLIS 1913–1971 Painter who was by profession a builder, born and lived in Leicester. He studied at the College of Art there and Lincoln College of Art and was a member of Leicester Society of Artists and Leicester Sketch Club. He also showed with ROI, RBA and widely in the Midlands. Leicester Museum and Art Gallery holds his work.

Peter ELLIS 1955– Painter, born in Manchester. He attended Camberwell School of Arts and Crafts, 1979–83, then Royal College of Art, 1984–7. Ellis often painted in acrylic, abstracts employing circles and elliptical themes. Won the Mario Dubsky Travel Award in 1987 and gained a Rothko Fellowship in 1990. Appeared in group exhibitions at Pomeroy Purdy Gallery, Camden Arts Centre, Nigel Greenwood Gallery, Fischer Fine Art and Cooling Gallery. In 1989 he was an Artist of the Day at Flowers East; he was in American Passion: The Collection of Susan Kasen Summers and Robert Summers, McLellan Galleries in Glasgow and Royal College of Art, both 1995; and in the 1997–8 John Moores Liverpool Exhibition. Exhibited solo with Anthony Wilkinson Fine Art.

Ray ELLIS 1921– Painter who was born in America into an artistic family. He studied from 1939–41 at Philadelphia Museum School of Art and graduated from Pennsylvania Academy of Fine Arts. After four years in the Navy he resumed painting, had a successful solo show at Pennsylvania Academy of Arts, but on marrying he moved professionally into advertising until 1969, when he set up a studio at Chatham and became involved in New York's art scene. He had been made a member of New Jersey Watercolour Society in 1960, in 1964 became a member of Salmagundi Club and in 1967 had work accepted by the American Watercolour Society, also becoming a member. His book of watercolours *South by South-East*, text by Walter Cronkite, recording a voyage from Chesapeake Bay to Key West, was published in 1983; it sold over 150,000 copies and led to more such volumes. Chris Beetles Ltd gave solo shows to Ellis in 1987 and 1989, the latter comprising pictures of a journey along the Thames. Lived latterly in Savannah, Georgia.

Richard H ELLIS 1905– Sculptor and painter. He exhibited at Lucy Wertheim's Gallery in 1931 and at the Storran Gallery and lived in London.

Robert ELLIS 1928– Painter, illustrator, designer and teacher, born in Northampton. Studied at the School of Art there, 1942–7, where his teachers included Frederick Courtney, and then at Royal College of Art, 1949–52, under Rodrigo Moynihan, Ruskin Spear, John Minton and others. He exhibited RA, RWS, AIA, SEA, in New Zealand and America. Had a series of one-man shows in Auckland. Derbyshire Education Committee and galleries in Invercargill and Hamilton, New Zealand, hold his work. For four years from 1953 Ellis taught at Yeovil School of Art, then took a post in 1957 lecturing at Auckland University, where he eventually held a senior post in the fine arts department.

Rosemary ELLIS 1910–1998 Artist and teacher, born in London, wife of the artist Clifford Ellis, with whom she closely collaborated. She studied at Regent Street Polytechnic School of Art, from about 1927–31, marrying her husband while there, and with him worked in the early 1930s on many poster designs, mosaics and book jackets, clients including London Transport, Jonathan Cape and Shell-Mex and BP. Living in Bath, in 1938 Rosemary Ellis began to teach art at the Royal School for Daughters of the British Army and became closely associated with local art life. With her husband she designed many book jackets for Collins from 1945 and in 1946 a mural for the Britain Can Make It exhibition at Victoria & Albert Museum.At Bath Academy of Art with her husband Rosemary Ellis taught many subjects as the need arose, creating one of Britain's key art learning centres after World War II. Latterly lived in Devizes, Wiltshire.

George Montague ELLWOOD 1875–1955 Decorator and designer, born in London. Studied art at Camden School of Art, Royal College of Art, where he won medals, and on the continent. Exhibited RA, RI, Paris Salon, where he won a silver medal in 1900, in the provinces and elsewhere in Europe. Signed work G M E. Was married to the painter Ida Ellwood. Ellwood completed a large volume of commercial work, such as theatre and railway posters; painted some murals; and wrote books on architecture, furniture and anatomy, notably *Studies of the Human Figure* and *Human Sculpture*. During World War II he was for a time design master at Camden School of Art. Lived at Boscombe, Hampshire.

Sheila ELMHIRST 1920– Painter and illustrator, born in Eastbourne, Sussex. Studied at the Slade School of Fine Art, 1936–9, under Randolph Schwabe and at the London Polytechnic. Exhibited RA, SWA and ROI. Was a keen collector of early English portraits. Lived in London, later in Ipswich, Suffolk.

Pat ELMORE 1937– Sculptor, notably of portraits, born in Rugby, Warwickshire. She attended Wellingborough High School and Dame Alice Harpur School. Showed at RBA, RWA and elsewhere in west of England in group exhibitions. Solo shows included Bedford Library, Wantage Museum and Central Library in Oxford. Thamesdown Arts holds her stone sculpture Heidi and the Duck. Lived in Faringdon, Oxfordshire.

Essil R ELMSLIE 1880–1952 Figure and portrait painter, wife of Charles Rutherston, brother of the artists William Rothenstein and Albert Rutherston. Charles Rutherston was a noted collector, who made a bequest of works to Manchester City Art Gallery in 1925; it holds Elmslie's oil on canvas Emma, Covent Garden, of 1909. She exhibited at NEAC, London Salon, Goupil Gallery and Walker Art Gallery, Liverpool.

William Graham ELPHINSTON fl. from 1930s–1952 Watercolour painter, born in Winchester, who served in the Indian Army, 1905–38. Studied at Regent Street Polytechnic School of Art under Giffard Lenfestey, then at the Slade School of Fine Art, 1938–9, under Randolph Schwabe, also privately with William Wood. Exhibited RA, RI, NS and RBA. Lived in London.

Joseph ELSE 1874–1955 Sculptor and teacher, born in Nottingham, who studied at Royal College of Art, taught at Belfast School of Art and then became principal of the School of Art in Nottingham. Later lived in Newnham-on-Severn, Gloucestershire. Showed at RA and at public gallery in Nottingham. He was a fellow of RBS and his Bronze Mask and powerful Zeus, The Philanderer are illustrated in the 1939 volume *RBS: Modern British Sculpture*.

Cecile ELSTEIN 1938– Artist and teacher who was born in Cape Town, South Africa. She worked as a laboratory technician, studying sculpture at Michaelis School of Art and with Nel Kaye. Always an extensive traveller, Elstein settled in England in 1960. She studied ceramics with Catherine Yarrow, 1965–9, setting up a studio in Southampton, 1969–70, where she extended the range of her work. After studying sculpture and printmaking at West Surrey College of Art and Design, Farnham, 1975–7, in 1978 set up Spath Road Workshop where she lived in Didsbury, Manchester, teaching "awareness through art". Showed in many group exhibitions including MAFA, Hampstead Artists' Council, with Chilford Hall Press and abroad. In 1983 she gained a North West Bursary Award concerned with designs for inflatable spaces, 1986 bringing a colour prize at British International Print Biennale, Bradford. Had a series of solo shows including Boldrewood Gallery, Southampton, 1974, later ones featuring Clare Hall, Cambridge, and Casabella Gallery, Manchester, both 1988.

Ray ELTON 1914– Self-taught painter in oil, born in Cardiff, south Wales, father of the sculptor Andrew Elton. Elton lived in London for many years and was a member of Hampstead Artists' Council, exhibiting in mixed shows around Britain. Landscapes and abstracts featured in his output, sometimes geometrical and brightly coloured. Elton had a solo exhibition at Wilson Gallery in 1945. Others included Nicholas Treadwell Gallery, 1970; Camden Arts Centre, 1987; and Camden Art Gallery, 1990. Works were signed with a monogram.

Brian ELWELL 1938– Painter, printmaker, mural designer and lecturer, born in St Helier, Jersey. He studied at Chelsea School of Art, Birmingham Polytechnic and Wimbledon School of Art. He was a Leverhulme Scholar and gained the Falkiner Award. Elwell was senior lecturer in fine art at Southampton Institute of Higher Education and was a visiting lecturer at Tower Hamlets College. He was interested "in light, movement and change in nature, subjects mainly landscape and water reflections". Major exhibitions were at the Ikon Gallery in Birmingham; John Hansard Gallery, Southampton; Southampton City Art Gallery; and Morley College. Also sold work through Berkeley Square Gallery. Southern Arts Association, Southampton University, Salisbury General Hospital and Falkiner Fine Papers hold examples. Lived in New Forest at Nomansland, near Salisbury, Wiltshire.

Frederick William ELWELL 1870–1958 Versatile painter, notably of genre scenes, born in Beverley, Yorkshire, son of the wood carver James Elwell. Studied at Lincoln School of Art, winning the Gibney Scholarship in 1887. Next studied at Academy Schools, Antwerp, worked for a while in London and Beverley, then continued his education at Académie Julian, Paris. From mid-1890s exhibited at RA and Paris Salon, also showing at ROI, RSA, Walker Art Gallery, Liverpool, and in Scotland. Elwell's career became based in Beverley from the early years of the century. His picture of the Beverley Arms kitchen is held by the Tate Gallery and the town's gallery has a collection of pictures by Elwell and his wife Mary Dawson Elwell (Holmes). He was elected RA in 1938. A large retrospective was held at Laing Art Gallery, Newcastle upon Tyne, 1993–4.

Mary Dawson ELWELL 1874–1952 Painter, notably of interiors, also landscapes, born in Liverpool, daughter of a shipping merchant. She married Hull oil broker George Holmes who died in 1913, then the painter Fred Elwell, with whom she studied, in 1914. His portrait of his wife is held by the Borough Council in Beverley, Yorkshire, where they settled. Her money enabled the Elwells to travel extensively on the continent. She exhibited often at RA, also at SWA, RSA, Walker Art Gallery in Liverpool and elsewhere, although a stroke in 1945 incapacited her. There was a retrospective of the work of the two Elwells in 1953 at Beverley Art Gallery and Ferens Art Gallery, Hull.

Cecilia ELWES 1874–1952 Flower painter. Studied in Cornwall with Stanhope Forbes and S J Lamorna Birch, then in

Switzerland. Exhibited ROI, SWA, RI, SWA, in the provinces and Montreux. Wrote *Flower Painting in Water-colour*, 1932. Lived in Oxford.

Helen ELWES 1958– Painter, born in London. She attended Ruskin School of Art, 1979–82, after West Surrey College of Art and Design, 1976–7. Then was taught by Peter Greenham at Royal Academy Schools, 1983–6. Among awards won were Worcester College Travel Award, 1981, Landseer Scholarship and Arthur Hacker Portrait Prize in 1984, Fred Elwell Prize and Humphrey Brooke Award, 1985, and Richard Ford Award, 1986. In 1987 gained a setting-up grant from WAC. Showed at RA Summer Exhibitions from 1984, New Grafton Gallery, RP, NEAC and elsewhere and in 1982 had solo exhibition Oxford Arts Centre. Her portrait of Frank O'Donnell, head boatman of St Michael's Mount, Cornwall, was commissioned by the National Trust. Lived in Mells, Somerset.

Luke ELWES 1961– Painter who studied at Bristol University and RWA, 1980–3, then at Camberwell School of Art, 1983–4. From mid-1980s quickly had several solo exhibitions, including Rebecca Hossack Gallery, 1990. Among mixed exhibitions he took part in The Broad Horizon, Agnew, 1990.

Simon ELWES 1902–1975 Portrait painter in oil, born at Theddingworth, near Rugby. He studied at the Slade School of Fine Art under Henry Tonks, 1918–21, and in Paris, some time with André Lhote. Exhibited at RA from 1927 and was elected RA 40 years later. Also showed Arts Council, RP of which for a time he was a council member, Royal Glasgow Institute of the Fine Arts, Walker Art Gallery, Liverpool, and Paris Salon, where he gained a silver medal in 1948. During World War II he was an official war artist in India and Southeast Asia and painted leading military figures, such as Field-Marshal Sir William Slim and Field-Marshal Jan Smuts. Imperial War Museum holds his work. Lived for a time in London and died in Amberley, Sussex. His son Dominic was also an artist, his father the singer Gervase Elwes.

John ELWYN 1916–1997 Painter, printmaker, book illustrator and teacher, born in Newcastle Emlyn, South Cardiganshire, his real name being William John Elwyn Davies (early work could be signed J E D). He studied at Carmarthen Art School, 1933–7, Bristol College of Art, 1937–8, Royal College of Art, 1938–9 and 1946–7. Elwyn taught at Portsmouth College of Art, 1948–53, then for many years at Winchester College of Art. Elwyn was closely identified with the landscape of Cardiganshire and its people, notably groups emerging from chapel on a Sunday morning in Sunday-best and dark suits and bowler hats. He wrote that he "continued using figures until about 1962, then for about 10 years worked in a semi-abstract manner with subjects taken from my garden. Eventually I returned to the landscapes of West Wales, without figures." Elwyn took part in numerous mixed shows in Britain and abroad from 1942. One-man exhibitions included Leicester Galleries, Howard Roberts Gallery in Cardiff, National Library of Wales, Tegfryn Gallery in Anglesey and in 1988 he shared a show with Thomas Rathmell at Ceri Richards Gallery, Swansea. National Library of Wales, Aberystwyth, put on an eightieth birthday retrospective in 1996. Commissioned work was done for Barclays Bank, Shell, *Radio Times*, Harlech Television and the General Post Office. Originally a Welsh speaker, Elwyn was made an honorary member of the Gorsedd of Bards and of RCamA. In 1956 he won the Royal National Eisteddfod gold medal. Elwyn's work is held by many public collections, including National Library of Wales, Aberystwyth; National Museum of Wales, Cardiff; Welsh Arts Council; and Leeds University. Lived in Winchester, Hampshire.

Charles Herbert Lewis EMANUEL 1868–1962 Painter and craftsman in various materials, such as silver and ivory. He was educated at Harrow School and Oxford University, graduating with a master's degree, and became a solicitor by profession. A keen photographer, he exhibited with the London Salon of Photography, also SGA, with the Goldsmiths' Company and in Italy. Was a member of Art Workers' Guild from 1933, its honorary librarian, 1938–62. Lived in London.

Frank Lewis EMANUEL 1865–1948 Painter, printmaker, draughtsman and writer, born in London. After the Slade School of Fine Art under Alphonse Legros, Emanuel worked under W A Bouguereau at the Académie Julian, Paris. From the late 1880s he began to show at the RA and Paris Salon, also exhibiting NEAC, ROI, RI and many other galleries. Emanuel had a varied career, travelling widely in Europe, Africa and Ceylon; being chief examiner for the Royal Drawing Society; publishing art criticism and topographical drawings in the *Manchester Guardian* and *Architectural Review*; and teaching etching at the Central School of Arts and Crafts, 1918–30. Was a keen collector of water-colours. Wrote a number of books, including *Etching and Etchings*, 1930. In his writings Emanuel opposed new trends in art. The Tate Gallery holds his picture Kensington Interior. Lived in London.

John EMANUEL 1930– Painter in oils and mixed media, born in Bury, Lancashire. Emanuel served an apprenticeship in decorating, signwriting and graining and did his National Service with the Army in Hong Kong. Did not begin painting until in his thirties and then did not show any work for a decade. Lived in St Ives, Cornwall, from the mid-1960s where, although he had no formal art training, he was helped by Denis Mitchell, John Wells and Alexander Mackenzie. Emanuel was noted for nude studies which he said were "also about Penwith, its standing stones, cliff faces and countryside, about living here". He was a member of Penwith Society of Arts and of Newlyn Society of Artists, of which he was chairman, 1977–8. Took part in numerous mixed shows in Britain and abroad. Had two solo shows at Wills Lane Gallery, St Ives, 1975–6, others including Montpelier Studio from 1979 and Beaux Arts Gallery, Bath, from 1988. Cornwall County Council Schools Library Service and Parnham House, Beaminster, hold his work.

Ronald EMBLETON 1930– Painter and illustrator, born in London. Studied art with David Bomberg at South-East Essex Technical College and showed in London, the English provinces and in America. Some of his work was of an experimental nature. Wrote and illustrated for children. London Sketch Club member who lived for some years in Bournemouth, Hampshire.

Arthur EMERY 1896–1980 Painter and draughtsman, born in Penmaen, Glamorganshire, he spent much of his life as a merchant navy officer. Studied at the Slade School of Fine Art, in Oxford then in London, for two periods: 1939–40, then 1946–8, his teachers including Randolph Schwabe and Allan Gwynne-Jones. He did a variety of ephemeral illustrative work, but also showed at RA and RCamA. A slow worker, Emery painted mainly landscapes in watercolour, with a few portraits. Lived in Bodfean, Caernarvonshire.

Rowland EMETT 1906–1990 Humorous illustrator and inventor of eccentric machines, born in London, son of a journalist and amateur inventor. Emett studied at Birmingham School of Arts and Crafts, then worked in a commercial studio in that city. After war work as a draughtsman concerned with jet engine design Emett's reputation as a cartoonist and illustrator gained momementum. His second contribution to *Punch* about the time World War II was getting under way began a strong association with the magazine, where his endearing steam engines and the Far Twittering and Oyster Creek Railway attracted a keen following. The Railway was given tangible life during the 1951 Festival of Britain, which led to a new career as a creator of comical working machines. They were commissioned by industry and others and have been shown in places such as Ontario's Science Museum and Washington's National Museum of Air and Space. He worked on the 1968 film *Chitty Chitty Bang Bang* and in 1974 unveiled his large Rhythmical Time Fountain in the Victoria Centre, Nottingham. Emett was also a noted book illustrator, particularly for Walter de la Mare. In 1988 he had a show at Chris Beetles Ltd, which travelled to America. Lived in Ditchling, Sussex, and died nearby at Hassocks.

Tracey EMIN 1963– Artist using a variety of materials, born and worked in London, who gained a bachelor's degree in fine art from Maidstone College of Art, 1986. Mixed shows included Hotel Carlton Palace Chambre 763, at Hotel Carlton Palace in Paris, 1993; Karaoke & Football, Portikus, Frankfurt, 1994; Brilliant! New Art from London, Walker Art Center, Minneapolis, 1995 (in which Emin exhibited a tent inside which she had sewn the names of everyone she had slept with); and A Grapefruit in the World of Park, Transmission Gallery, Glasgow, and Sad, at Gasworks, both 1996. In 1993 Emin with the artist Sarah Lucas for several months ran The Shop, at 103 Bethnal Green Road. In 1994 Emin conducted Exploration of the Soul – Journey across America, in which readings were staged at venues including the Museum of Contemporary Art in San Diego, and My Major Retrospective was held by Jay Jopling at White Cube. Other solo shows included Exorcism of the Last Painting I ever Made, Galleri Andreas Brändström, Stockholm, 1995, and in 1996 Full House at Wolfsburg Museum, Wolfsburg. In 1995 the artist set up the Tracey Emin Museum at 221 Waterloo Road. British Museum and South London Gallery, where in 1997 Emin appeared in I Need Art Like I Need God, hold the artist's works, as do several American collections.

Lohan EMMANUEL 1971– Painter, born in Sri Lanka, who spent most of his life in England and who graduated from St Martin's School of Art, 1994. From 1995 had a series of solo shows with Cassian de Vere Cole Fine Art. Emmanuel's canvases were in the style of the Old Masters, with figures whose heads faded into the landscape, giving them a slightly Surrealist quality.

John Victor EMMS 1912– Painter and teacher, born in Bordon, Hampshire. He studied at Woolwich Polytechnic Art School, 1930–4, where his teachers included Louis Prince; Hornsey School of Art, 1946–8, with Frederick Mitchell and Arthur Mills; then Goldsmiths' College School of Art, 1948–9. Emms held several teaching posts, including latterly Woolwich Polytechnic Secondary Art School. He exhibited with RA, East End Academy, Liberty the London store and in provincial galleries. Lived in Leatherhead, Surrey.

Kenneth EMSLEY 1921– Watercolourist, pen and ink draughtsman and teacher, born and lived in Shipley, Yorkshire. He was educated at Loughborough College and Cambridge University, obtaining his master's degree. His studies at various art schools included tuition by Arnold Dransfield and Edward Wesson. Emsley was a member of Leeds Fine Art Club, chairman of Bradford Arts Club and president of both SM and BWS. He showed at Mall and Bankside Galleries, in the provinces and in America.

Paul EMSLEY 1947– Draughtsman, painter, designer and teacher, born in Scotland. His family went to South Africa in 1949 and he obtained his national diploma in graphic design at Cape Technical College, 1969. Worked in advertising, 1970–6, latterly beginning to draw and paint, being self-taught as a painter. From 1976–7 Emsley lived in England, and on returning to South Africa taught design and drawing, from 1983 at Department of Creative Arts, University of Stellenbosch. Emsley said that constant drawing had taught him "the deep significance of even the most ordinary forms … I try to draw not only what I see, but also what I wish I had seen." He took part in South African Art, 1978–9, touring America, which went to São Paulo, Brazil; and in Cape Town Biennial and Triennials from 1979. Later solo shows included Redfern Gallery, 1994. Johannesburg Art Gallery and other notable collections hold his work.

Rosalie EMSLIE 1891–1977 Painter, draughtsman and artist in black-and-white, born in London. She was the daughter of the artist Alfred Edward Emslie and daughter of the miniaturist Rosalie M Emslie. After private education she attended the Royal Academy Schools, 1913–18, then studied in France, Italy and

Spain. Exhibited extensively at RBA, also at RA, Goupil Gallery, SWA, NEAC, in Italy and America. Canadian government bought her work. Lived in Petersfield, Hampshire, and in Reigate, Surrey, with the painter Florence May Asher.

Ruth END 1959– Versatile artist and teacher, born in London, who worked especially in acrylic and oil on canvas. Her paintings depicted "single figures or groups and their relationships with each other, or with themselves. I choose the setting and objects to enhance or question the nature of these." End studied from 1977–8 at Jacob Kramer, College, Leeds, graduating in fine art from South Glamorgan Institute of Higher Education, 1978–81. In 1980 held a solo show of sculpture, prints and performance at Kingsgate Gallery, exhibiting in Stowells Trophy at RA in 1981. In 1982 End moved to Cheltenham, Gloucestershire. There she held workshops for children at Bournside School, 1988–90. In 1992 was commissioned to design and make a donation box for Pittville Pump Room Museum and held a show at Turtle Gallery of bowls, boxes and wall reliefs. Held a workshop for mentally ill adults in 1993, in 1994 being commissioned to design and make a donation box for Holst Birthplace Museum Trust, Cheltenham. In 1995 held a solo exhibition at Veale Wasbrough, solicitors, Bristol, in which three-dimensional wooden cartoons, made to commission, were featured.

Eden ENDFIELD 1960– Painter, notably of portraits, born in London, who studied at Camberwell, Chelsea and Slade Schools of Art. Won a Wyndham Lewis Scholarship and an Elizabeth Greenshields Foundation Award. Group shows included A New Perspective, Leighton House Gallery, 1990; BP Portrait Award, National Portrait Gallery, 1994; and Royal Over-Seas League Open, 1995. National Westminster Bank and Lord Irvine of Lairg hold examples.

Florence ENGELBACH 1872–1951 Painter, principally of flowers, born in Jerez de la Frontera, Spain, of English parents. Studied at Westminster School of Art, at the Slade School of Fine Art, in the mid-1890s, with Fred Brown, then in Paris. Began exhibiting under her unmarried name of Neumegen, but after marriage early in the century ceased painting, resuming about 1930. Exhibited RA, ROI, NS, Lefevre and Goupil Galleries and elsewhere. First one-man show at Beaux Arts Gallery, 1931, and memorial show at Leicester Galleries, 1951. Tate Gallery holds her work. Engelbach's interest in flower painting was inspired by her Warwickshire garden after she had returned to the easel having brought up her family. She also painted good landscapes and delicate, atmospheric nudes. Lived latterly in London.

Frederick ENGLAND 1939– Artist, designer, teacher and gallery proprietor, born in London. He studied at Brighton College of Art, 1956, teachers including Raymond Cowern, Charles Knight and Ernest Sallis Benney, in Norway, 1960, and in 1961 at London University with Ronald Horton. Went on to teach at Leek School of Art. England was president of the Society of Staffordshire Artists and a member of the Free Painters and Sculptors. Showed at RI, RBA, widely in the provinces and at Paris Salon, where he won silver and gold medals. Solo shows included Octagon Gallery in Bolton, University of Keele and abroad. Stoke-on-Trent City Museum and Art Gallery holds England's work. Lived in Leek, Staffordshire, where he ran his own gallery.

Nora ENGLAND 1890– Painter and versatile designer for interiors and the performing arts, born in London, daughter of the artist Edwin Ward. She studied art at Royal College of Art and Westminster School of Art and with the figure and portrait painter Sir James Shannon. She exhibited RA, SWA, RI, IS, RP and elsewhere. Lived in London.

Robert ENGLAND 1949– Artist whose work employed everyday objects in unfamiliar settings. He studied at Thurrock Technical College, 1973–5, Maidstone College of Art, 1975–8, and was included in 1983 in a second year master's show, Goldsmiths' College School of Art, at Woodlands Art Gallery. Other exhibitions included Rye Art Gallery, 1979, and The Hall, Stanford, Essex, 1980.

Grace ENGLISH 1891–1956 Painter and etcher, born in London. Studied at the Slade School of Fine Art, 1912–14, where she won a painting prize, then learned etching under Sir Frank Short at the Royal College Art, 1921. Exhibited RA, RP, NEAC, RBA and in the provinces. Leeds City Art Gallery holds her work. Lived in London.

James ENGLISH 1916–1988 Painter, collagist and teacher, born and lived in Bristol. He studied at West of England College of Art there, his teachers including Evan Charlton, Reginald Bush and Donald Milner. English held several teaching appointments in Bristol, including latterly Clifton High School, and until 1952 assisted at evening classes at West of England College of Art. Was from 1949–53 a member of SGA and was for many years an associate of RWA, which holds his work. Also exhibited at Arts and Crafts Exhibition Society.

Michael ENGLISH 1941– Multi-faceted artist, born in Bicester, Oxfordshire, who attended Ealing School of Art, studying under a number of avant-garde teachers and participating in The Ground Course, "a revolutionary method of art teaching" which "released a great wealth of creative talent". In 1967 English became involved in the hippie movement in England and America, producing large volumes of psychedelic posters and painting fashionable shopfronts. Was involved in forming the rock group Hapshash & the Coloured Coat in 1968, named after the design partnership that he formed with Nigel Waymouth. An album was released on the Liberty label. With the decline in hippiedom English in 1969 – the year of his first solo show, at Motif Gallery – shifted towards a personal style of Super-Realism, which manifested itself in limited-edition prints entitled *Food Synaesthetics and Rubbish*, as the result of which his work gained global exposure. In 1973 began to paint canvases, abandoning the more Pop-oriented work of the prints, man-made objects taking the role of pollutants, as in his painting No Deposit No Return. From 1975 there was a shift in content, monumental works of great detail featuring transport machinery. From 1986 English became dissatisfied with Hyper-Realism, seeking a new personal style. English's books include *3-D Eye*, 1979, and *The Anatomy of an Illusion*, 1989. He showed at galleries in London, New York, Tokyo, Paris and the south of France and was featured in the Barbican's The Sixties Art Scene in London, 1993. Museum of Modern Art in New York, Arts Council and British Council and Victoria & Albert Museum hold examples. Much of English's later work was sold direct to the buyer instead of through galleries plus some advertising commissions "which I enjoy". Lived in London.

Simon ENGLISH 1959– Figurative painter on a grand scale but with a restricted palette, English was concerned with the contemporary world while harking back to the Old Masters and traditional icons, as in his works at The Saatchi Gallery Young British Artists III show, 1994. He was born in Berlin, Germany, and did a foundation course at Bournemouth College of Art, 1977–8, then an honours degree in fine art painting at Central School of Art & Design, 1978–81. Solo exhibitions included Laurent Delaye, 1992. Saatchi Collection holds his work.

Stanley Sydney ENGLISH 1908– Sculptor and artist in ceramics, born in Romford, Essex. Studied at City and Guilds of London Art School under a scholarship, then at Royal Academy Schools with William McMillan. He went on to spend much of his career in the Liverpool area, where he lectured at the College of Art from 1946. Member of Sandon Studios Society Club. Showed at RA and elsewhere. Work also done for Bank of England, South Africa House and a number of churches in the Liverpool locality, where he lived, having a studio in Bluecoat Chambers. Married to the artist Rachel Russell.

Augustus William ENNESS 1876–1948 Landscape painter, born in Bocking, Essex. Studied at Slade School of Fine Art and at Académie Julian in Paris, and was elected RBA in 1925. He was a prolific exhibitor there and at ROI and Fine Art Society, also showing at RA, Ridley Art Club, RSA and Walker Art Gallery in Liverpool. Lived in London.

Eric Arnold Robert ENNION 1900–1981 Bird artist, naturalist and teacher, born in Kettering, Northamptonshire. He was educated at Epsom, Cambridge University, St Mary's Hospital and worked as a general practitioner, 1926–46. Dr Ennion was next to be warden of Flatford Mill Field Centre, Suffolk, 1946–51; ran Monks House Bird Observatory and Field Research Centre, Northumberland, 1951–61; then retired to Shalbourne, Marlborough, Wiltshire, but remained active painting and conducting courses. Ennion was a self-taught artist, his son being the wild life painter Hugh Ennion. Dr Ennion was founder-chairman of SWLA. He carried out many commissions, notable illustrations appearing in the *Shell Bird Book*, 1966. Among other volumes including his work was the posthumous *The Living Birds of Eric Ennion*. He had four solo shows at Ackerman's, 1937–9, then every year he participated in many solo and shared exhibitions, including Sladmore Gallery, Henley Galleries and William Marler Gallery.

Hugh ENNION 1932– Watercolurist and teacher, born in Burwell, Cambridgeshire, son of the bird painter E A R Ennion. Hugh Ennion was "self-taught under the wing of my father, starting in 1966". Ennion used broad, graduated and superimposed washes to convey atmosphere and place, later defining small areas of detail. Edward Seago and Edward Wesson were influences. Latterly he began drawing and painting birds, having established a reputation as a landscape and estuarial artist. Ennion was an Army officer from 1952–63; was a watercress farmer from 1963–72; then taught from 1973, latterly part-time. He shared shows at Croft Gallery, Bristol; Bernard Rose Gallery, Newbury; RI; and Manor House Gallery, Chipping Norton. Solo exhibitions included Patricia Wells Gallery, Thornbury. HRH The Duke of Gloucester bought his work. Lived in Shalbourne, Wiltshire.

Brian ENO 1948– Rock musician, artist and teacher, born in Woodbridge, Suffolk, who from the mid- to late-1960s attended Ipswich and Winchester Schools of Art. He was a founder-member of Roxy Music, then left it in 1973 and began his solo career with the album *Here Come the Warm Jets* and released a number of critically acclaimed records. He also collaborated with such artists as John Cale, Nico, Robert Fripp and the band James. As a record producer, Eno was noted for his ability to steer artists into radical new areas; he was a pioneer in tape-looping and other versions of sound manipulation. Eno continued to work in the visual medium, his video installations being shown around the world, including the Stedelijk Museum in Amsterdam; at the Venice Biennale; the Pompidou Centre in Paris; as well as a permanent exhibition opened in 1995 at Austria's Swarovski Museum. As a visiting professor at the Royal College of Art, in 1995 Eno collaborated with Laurie Anderson and some of his students on the Self-Storage installation in Wembley. In 1996 Eno's work was included in Freezeframe at Lamont Gallery. His ambitious installation Lightness – described by him as "something between cinema, firework display, environmental music and installation" – was staged at the Russian Museum's Marble Palace, in St Petersburg in 1997.

Kathryn ENSALL fl. from mid-1980s– Artist, notably in pastel, and teacher. She studied from 1975–86 at University of Lancaster, Leeds Polytechnic and Newcastle Polytechnic. Went on to teach at Huddersfield Polytechnic and at Huddersfield College. Held a number of residencies and awards, including artist-in-residence, Yorkshire and Humberside Museums Council. Worked for a time in the artists' workshops at Tate Gallery, Liverpool. Among her frequent exhibitions was a three-man shared show at Woodlands Art Gallery, 1991, where her work explored "the themes of image-making between the sexes". Lived near Huddersfield, Yorkshire.

John ENSOR 1905– Industrial designer and painter, born in Cardiff. Studied art in Italy and at Royal College of Art. Worked for Imperial Chemical Industries as a designer in 1930s and in World War II was a war artist. Showed RA, NEAC, Leicester Galleries and widely in North America, Imperial War Museum holding his work. For many years Arthur John Ensor worked in Canada, establishing Ensor Industrial Design Associates in Toronto, where he also lived.

Ben ENWONWU 1921–1994 Painter, sculptor and teacher, born in Onitsha, Nigeria, where he died in Lagos. His gifts were noted when he was at primary school and flourished at Government College, Umuahia, between 1934–9. Taught from 1940–4, then a Shell Mexico scholarship took him to Britain after an early work, Making Man, in woodbrush and leaves, gained attention. Enwonwu studied at Goldsmiths' College School of Art, 1944; Ruskin School of Drawing, Oxford, 1944–6; then achieved a first-class honours degree at Slade School of Fine Art, 1946–8. HM The Queen sat for him for a statue which was placed at entrance of Parliament Buildings, Lagos. In 1959 Enwonwu rejoined Nigerian public service as art supervisor, giving up this job nine years later to concentrate on his own work, holding exhibitions in Europe, North America and elsewhere. In 1971 went as visiting professor in African studies to Howard University, Washington, in America, in the same year being appointed professor of fine arts at University of Ife, Illife, Nigeria, retiring in 1975. Died at his home in Ikoyi, Lagos.

Jacob EPSTEIN 1880–1959 Sculptor of monumental works and portraits, watercolourist and draughtsman. Born in New York of Polish Jewish parents, he was interested in art from childhood. Aged about 16 attended classes at the Art Students' League and at night school. Money earned by illustration paid for him to travel to Paris, where he studied the work of Rodin and other sculptors, also attending the École des Beaux-Arts and Académie Julian. Moved to London in 1905, becoming a British citizen two years later. He became a controversial figure as the result of several commissions: figures on the British Medical Association building in the Strand, London, 1907–8; the Oscar Wilde Memorial, Paris, 1910–11; and the W H Hudson Rima memorial in Hyde Park, 1925. After meeting advanced artists such as Picasso and Brancusi in France just before World War I Epstein became associated with the Vorticist movement in England, producing his Rock Drill construction in 1913–14. Successful both as a modeller and a carver, Epstein continued for several decades to produce busts of notable people, such as Joseph Conrad, Albert Einstein and Somerset Maugham; to create religious and other public sculptures; and to produce controversial images such as Genesis and Adam. Founder-member of the LG, exhibited many times at the Leicester Galleries and had first one-man show at the Twenty-One Gallery, in 1913. Published his autobiography *Let There Be Sculpture*, 1940. Knighted 1954. Many galleries, including the Tate, which held a retrospective in 1980, have his work. Lived in London. His son was the painter Theo Garman.

John EPSTEIN 1937– Artist and teacher, born in Sutton, Surrey, who studied painting at Central School of Arts and Crafts, 1957–61. Epstein was a member of Situation, taking part in the RBA Gallery show in 1960 and Situation's Arts Council tour, 1962–3; also showed with LG, 1977–8. His solo exhibitions included University of Essex, 1979. Theatre productions were an important part of Epstein's career. In 1969 he founded the Black Box Theatre, an experimental visual theatre company, which until 1972 performed throughout Britain, including Museum of Modern Art, Oxford, 1970, and Round House, 1970–1. Had extensive teaching experience, including Exeter College of Art, Bristol and Belfast Polytechnics as well as Morley College and Sir John Cass School of Art part-time. Latterly Epstein suffered from Alzheimer's Disease and lived in London.

John ERNEST 1922–1994 Sculptor and maker of reliefs, born in Philadelphia, America. He studied at its Settlement School of Music and Art with Antonio Cortizas, 1939–41. Lived and worked in Sweden, 1946–9, and in Paris, 1949–51, settling in London in 1951. Studied sculpture at St Martin's School of Art, 1952–6. During the latter part of the 1950s Ernest began making geometric constructions and scientific models. He taught at Bath Academy of Art, Corsham, Regent Street Polytechnic School of Art and Chelsea School of Art. Showed in Britain and abroad. Commissions included a relief mural and tower, International Union of Architects Congress, 1961. Arts Council holds his work, which was produced slowly and little of which survives. Died in Exeter, Devon.

Ilene ERSKINE 1933– Printmaker, notable for etchings in colour using a rich and distinctive palette and strong images, and teacher, born in Stirlingshire. She said that "like Matisse, I want my work to be colourful and cheerful." Graduated with a master's honours degree from University of Edinburgh, 1955, gaining her master's in education, 1964, adding an honours degree in sculpture, 1991, from Edinburgh College of Art. For most of her life she worked as a teacher and psychologist, then as a printmaker, taking part in many group exhibitions. Was a professional member of SSWA. Lived in Edinburgh.

Ken ERSSER 1940– Painter who studied at Camberwell School of Arts and Crafts and Royal Academy Schools. In 1965 he won the David Murray Scholarship, in 1966 the Leverhulme Award. Mixed shows included Young Contemporaries, Ikon Gallery in Birmingham, Opix Gallery and Figurative Painters at Woodlands Art Gallery, 1980. Had a solo show at Arnheim Centre in 1969; later ones including British Council in Athens, where he completed a mural, 1971; and Petit Gallery, Chicago, 1978.

Edward Frederick ERTZ 1862–1954 Painter and printmaker, born in Chicago, where he began as an illustrator and engraver, becoming involved in artists' organisations in the city. After working on a publication *The Century* in New York in the mid-1880s, Ertz travelled to Paris to continue his artistic education, where he taught for most of the 1890s. Eventually he settled in England, exhibiting at RBA extensively, as well as RA, ROI, Royal Glasgow Institute of the Fine Arts and Paris Salon. Was married to the miniature painter Ethel Horsfall Ertz. His work is in a number of public collections. Lived at Pulborough, Sussex.

Amy ESHOO 1961– Artist and lecturer, born in America, who studied at Wellesley College, 1979–83; Art Institute of Chicago School, 1986–7; then Goldsmiths' College School of Art, 1988–90. Lectured at National and Hayward Galleries. Her An Open Book was included in East & South at Norwich Gallery/Kent Institute of Art and Design, 1992. Lived in London.

Tom ESPLEY 1931– Artist in oil, tempera and watercolour and teacher, born in Aberdeen. He studied at Camberwell School of Arts and Crafts, then Slade School of Fine Art. His teachers included William Coldstream, Claude Rogers, B A R Carter, Robert Medley, Patrick George, Andrew Forge and Victor Pasmore. After National Service in the Royal Air Force as a photographer Espley worked in special effects with the film company Metro-Goldwyn-Mayer at Borehamwood, 1957–63, then taught part-time painting, drawing and photography at Camberwell, Hornsey and Central Schools of Art. Espley painted still life, nudes, landscapes and portraits, appearing regularly at RA Summer Exhibitions; Browse & Darby; Camden Arts Centre; South London Art Gallery and elsewhere. Solo shows included Green and Abbott, Belgrave and Amwell Galleries, Menuhin School and Alliance Building Society. British Rail, Chase Manhattan Bank and several other firms hold Espley's work. Lived in London.

EST: *see* **Elizabeth SCOTT-TAGGART**

Jack ESTERHUISEN 1949– Artist and teacher who studied at Canterbury College of Art, 1969–70, Brighton Polytechnic, 1970–3, and Royal Academy of Arts and Liu Academy of Taoist and Ch'an Buddhist Arts, 1974–7. From 1978 Esterhuisen held a number of part-time teaching posts, including Winchester and Canterbury Colleges of Art, North-East London Polytechnic and Cyprus College of Art. In 1983 he was included in British Artists at Cyprus College, at Woodlands Art Gallery. From 1982 he taught full-time at Newcastle Polytechnic.

Frederick ETCHELLS 1886–1973 Painter, draughtsman, architect and translator, born in Newcastle upon Tyne. Etchells studied for several years at Royal College of Art and for an equal period in Paris up to World War I, where he became interested in Fauve and Cubist painting. He showed with Roger Fry's Post-Impressionist exhibitions in London in 1912–13, by which time he was practising as an architect; became involved in the Omega Workshops; then accompanied Wyndham Lewis when he left to found the Rebel Art Centre. Participated in the Vorticist movement and contributed drawings to *Blast*. Also showed with Group X and LG, of which he was a founder-member. As a war artist he was notable for his painting of Armistice Day for the Canadian War Memorial. He then abandoned painting for architecture, becoming a fellow of RIBA in 1931. Among his notable buildings are the new library at Godolphin and Latymer School, Hammersmith, and the Crawford Building, Holborn. Did much church work and wrote on architecture and Anglican worship. Also translated Le Corbusier's *Towards a New Architecture*. Tate Gallery holds his work. Died in Folkestone, Kent.

Ken ETHERIDGE 1911– Writer, painter and teacher, born in Ammanford, Carmarthenshire. He attended Swansea School of Art and studied English at University College, Cardiff, for three years from 1933. After various teaching jobs he was from 1947–71 head of the art department at Queen Elizabeth Boys' Grammar School, Carmarthen. Showed Paris Salon, Piccadilly Gallery, Woodstock Gallery and for many years at Royal National Eisteddfod where he won a number of awards. Had several solo shows, including Woodstock Gallery. Among his writings were books on scenic design and stage costume; a number of radio plays in English and Welsh; and *Collecting Drawings*. WAC holds his work.

Margaret EULER fl. from c.1925– Painter and teacher, born in London. Studied at Goldsmiths' College School of Art and at the Royal Academy Schools under various teachers, including Sir George Clausen and Sir Walter Westley Russell. Showed at RA, AIA of which she was a member, at Paris Salon and in the provinces. Lived in Bromley, Kent.

Richard EURICH 1903–1992 Painter and draughtsman, born in Bradford, Yorkshire, who settled for many years at Dibden Purlieu, near Southampton, and who had as a principal theme the sea, ships, ports and beach life. Father of the photographer Crispin Eurich. Richard Eurich's interest in painting was encouraged at Bradford Grammar School, then he went on to study at Bradford School of Art, 1920–4, and at the Slade School of Fine Art, 1924–6. There he concentrated on drawing, having his first one-man show of drawings, at the Goupil Gallery, in 1929, work of impressive quality. First one-man show of paintings at the Redfern Gallery four years later. He was aptly made an official war artist attached to the Admiralty during World War II, during which he completed his notable picture Survivors from a Torpedoed Ship, in the collection of the Tate Gallery. Imperial War Museum, National Maritime Museum at Greenwich and many provincial galleries hold his work. From 1949 taught for a period at Camberwell School of Arts and Crafts. Elected RA in 1953. Retrospective exhibition Bradford Art Galleries and Museums, 1979–80, and tour, and there was a memorial touring show based on Southampton City Art Gallery, 1994. Eurich's work depicted everyday events but sometimes had an English element of oddness, as in his picture The Mummers, in Hove Museum of Art. Other national and regional collections hold examples.

Barry EVANS 1923– Mural painter and illustrator, born in London, married to the artist Mary Evans. Studied at Kingston

School of Art, then at Royal College of Art, 1941–3, under Ernest Tristram. Exhibited Festival of Britain and Central Office of Information, also illustrating publications and magazines such as *Lilliput* and *Picture Post*. Lived in Braughing, Hertfordshire.

Bernard EVANS 1929– Painter, draughtsman and teacher, born in Liverpool where he studied at the College of Art. Also studied at Camberwell School of Arts and Crafts, teachers including Richard Eurich and Martin Bloch. He went on to direct the Mounts Bay Art Centre in Newlyn, Cornwall, where he settled, being chairman of the Society of Artists there. Exhibited widely throughout England, sometimes signing work only with initials.

Bob EVANS 1947– Painter, artist in ceramics and lecturer, born in Cardiff where he attended the College of Art, 1964–8. Was next at Chelsea College of Art, 1968–9, and Hornsey College of Art, 1970–1. Did a variety of jobs then, while continuing to paint. Showed Young Contemporaries, 5 Artists at University College in Cardiff, Royal National Eisteddfod, SEA and SWG and had a one-man exhibition at Serpentine Gallery, 1972. WAC holds his work and he was included in its 1980 touring show of drawings The Probity of Art. Lived in London for a time.

Cerith Wyn EVANS 1959– Tape, slide, video and film artist, born in Llanelli, Carmarthenshire. Did a foundation course at Dyfed College of Art, 1976–7; obtained a first-class honours degree in fine art at St Martin's School of Art, 1977–80; and a master's honours degree in film and television, Royal College of Art, 1981–4. Awards included The Worldwide Video Festival, The Hague, first prize, with a similar prize at 3e Semaine Internationale de Video, Geneva, both 1989. Participated in extensive exhibitions and screenings, including solo show at London Film-makers' Co-op, 1981; another at B2 Gallery, 1982; The New Art, Tate Gallery, 1983; Cinema as Art, National Film Theatre, 1986; Retrospective screenings at London Film-makers' Co-op and masterclass lecture at Riverside Studios, both 1988; and Signs of the Times, Museum of Modern Art, Oxford, and Video sculpture, installation commissioned by Kijkhuis in Den Haag, part of a retrospective, both 1990. Was included in Sensation, at RA, 1997.

David EVANS 1929–1988 Painter of landscape, still life, fantasies and murals, born in London. Studied at Central School of Arts and Crafts with Keith Vaughan. Early in his career he showed photomontages at Gallery One and gained several commissions; these included a design for the Hollywood Room in the *Observer* Film Exhibition, 1956, and a mural for the Soup Kitchen, Knightsbridge. He began painting watercolours and gouaches in 1967, two years before he settled in Suffolk. They were not shown until 1973, when his work was included in a mixed show at Deben Gallery, Woodbridge. In 1975 his work was included in summer show at Redfern Gallery, where he held solo exhibitions from 1979, after showing one-man at McMurray Gallery for three years, 1976–7–8. After his death in a road accident, Redfern gave him a small memorial show in 1988.

David EVANS 1942– Painter and teacher, born in Abercarn, Monmouthshire. He studied at Newport College of Art, 1959–62, then at Royal College of Art, 1962–5; in 1965 he won the College's Silver Medal for Painting. Travelled in Spain and Morocco before becoming a lecturer at Edinburgh College of Art, being based in the city. Evans was Granada Arts Fellow at University of York, 1968–9, and travelled through America in 1975–6. He was a member of RSW and was elected RSA in 1989. Evans was noted for his Hyper-Realist interiors which often have a tinge of suspense or mystery about them. He had a one-man show at New 57 Gallery in Edinburgh in 1966, others following at Marjorie Parr and Gilbert Parr in London. Lived in Edinburgh.

David EVANS 1950– Artist, especially in pastel, who did much landscape work in Kent and Surrey. He studied at Croydon College of Art, 1973–7. After that he had many exhibitions including Green Party Fayre, 1988; Holland Gallery, 1989; Laing Collection Art Show, 1990; London Ecology Centre, 1990; and in 1992 he shared a show with three other artists at Anna-Mei Chadwick.

David Lloyd EVANS 1916– Painter and teacher who married the book illustrator Grace Gabler. He studied at Wimbledon School School of Art with Gerald Cooper, 1935–8 and at the Royal College of Art with Gilbert Spencer, 1938–40. For two years from 1943 was art master at Sedbergh School, Yorkshire, then instructed at Stoke-on-Trent Art Schools. Exhibited RA. Lived near Stone, Staffordshire.

Evelyn EVANS 1915– Painter, designer, printmaker and teacher who was born in Burford, Oxfordshire. She studied at Cheltenham School of Art, 1932–5, with Gerald Gardiner, then at the Royal College of Art, 1935–9, with John and Paul Nash and Edward Bawden. Exhibited RA, RBA, and NEAC. Victoria & Albert Museum holds her work. She taught at Blackpool School of Art, then Epsom and Ewell School of Art. Lived in Puttenham, Surrey, for some time.

Garth EVANS 1934– Sculptor, draughtsman and teacher, born in Cheadle, Cheshire. From 1955–7 studied at Manchester School of Art, then at Slade School of Fine Art, 1957–60. Evans showed at John Moores Exhibition, Liverpool, in the 1960s, and had his first solo exhibition at Rowan Gallery in 1962, the first of many there. In 1964 he gained a Gulbenkian Purchase Award, in 1966 an Arts Council Sabbatical Award. In 1966 Evans began teaching at St Martin's School of Art, gained a British Steel Corporation Fellowship in 1969 and the year following became a visiting lecturer at Slade School of Fine Art. Other teaching posts were at Royal College of Art, Camberwell School of Arts and Crafts and Minneapolis College of Art and Design. Evans took part in many influential mixed shows in Britain and abroad. Commissions included Ebbw Vale Urban District Council and Peter Stuyvesant Sculpture Project, Cardiff, 1972. Tate Gallery, Museum of Modern Art in New York and Victoria & Albert Museum hold his work, the Arts Council holding his abstract works Relief in White

No. 7 and Blue No. 30, of 1962 and 1964. Later shows included Mayor Gallery, 1991. From late 1970s lived in New York.

Geraint EVANS 1968– Painter and draughtsman, born in Swansea, south Wales, where he studied at the Institute of Higher Education, 1986–7, then at Manchester Polytechnic, 1987–90, and Royal Academy Schools, 1990–3. Exhibitions included Into the Nineties, Mall Galleries, 1993; Whitechapel Open and Mostyn Open, Llandudno, both 1994; and John Moores Liverpool Exhibition, 1995–6. Had a solo exhibition at Gallery 1010, University of Tennessee, America, 1994. Lived in London.

Gwyn EVANS 1931– Painter, born Tonypandy, Glamorgan, who attended Cardiff College of Art, 1948–54. After a period teaching in Coventry in the late 1950s he returned to Tonypandy to teach at the Grammar School. Showed with Young Contemporaries in London in 1950, then with Royal National Eisteddfod, SEA and SWG.

Handel EVANS 1932– Painter, draughtsman and printmaker, born in Pontypridd, Glamorgan. He studied at Cardiff College of Art, 1949–54, teachers including David Tinker and Eric Malthouse. From 1947–58 Evans made studies in the Alexander Technique and music, attending the Clifford H Lewis School of Music, receiving the Licentiate of the Royal Academy of Music diploma in 1958. After painting in the Caribbean (where he taught briefly), Germany and Italy, 1959–62, in 1962–3 Evans was at the British School at Rome. In 1975–6 he studied with Stanley William Hayter at Atelier 17, Paris, other teachers including the etcher Anthony Gross. Otherwise, Evans lived by painting in the Caribbean, notably the Bahamas, the Americas and many European countries. Music remained a key influence on pictures which had man and technology as a theme and which indicated an acquaintance with Futurism, Surrealism and Cubism, using a distinctive palette. Had extensive exhibitions in Germany, including Deutscher Beamtenbund Berlin, 1992, and Preussen Elektra, Kassel, 1995. British shows included Mario Flecha Gallery, 1982, and Clare Hall, Cambridge, 1987. Ashmolean Museum in Oxford, Clare Hall and National Gallery of Jamaica hold examples.

Hugh EVANS 1946– Printmaker and designer, born in Cardiff. After studying at Newport College of Art, where in the early 1970s he worked for a few years as a technician, Evans studied textile design in Denmark and Finland. From 1973 he worked as a printmaker in his own studio. Showed at Glynn Vivian Art Gallery in a show called Welsh Artists One and at Royal National Eisteddfod. Did some work on sets for the television station HTV.

James EVANS 1964– Sculptor, born in Romford, Essex. He studied at Central School of Art and Design, 1984–7, then University of Colorado, 1987–90. He went on to teach part-time at several colleges of art. A leading interest of Evans' work was opulent domestic interiors, especially of the Victorian era, as in his clay Thigh Grasp Comforter, shown in the 1992 East & South Norwich Gallery/Kent Institute of Art and Design show. Lived in London.

Margaret Fleming EVANS 1952– Painter and teacher, born in Glasgow where she studied at the School of Art, 1970–4, teachers including David Donaldson, Leon Morrocco and James Robertson. She taught in adult education, was a member of UA and showed in London and the provinces. Lived in High Halden, Kent.

Merlyn EVANS 1910–1973 Painter, printmaker, sculptor and teacher, born in Cardiff, noted for his Surrealist and abstract works which often have an overtone of menace. He studied at Glasgow School of Art, 1927–30, a travelling scholarship enabling him to work extensively on the continent until he resumed studies at the Royal College of Art, 1931–3. Further studied under Stanley William Hayter in Paris, 1934–6. Was influenced by Surrealism and the Vorticists, exhibiting at the International Surrealist Exhibition in London in 1936. Began teaching in London, then lived and taught in South Africa, 1938–42, having his first one-man show at Durban's City Art Gallery in 1939. After widespread World War II Army service Evans settled in London, where he became a member of LG. With his ex-Army grant took a refresher course at Central School of Arts and Crafts. From 1965–73 taught at Royal College of Art. Tate Gallery and other major galleries hold his work. Retrospective at Whitechapel Art Gallery, 1956, and memorial show at National Museum of Wales, Cardiff, 1974. Evans was married to the pianist Margerie Few, sister of Elsie Few, Claude Rogers' wife. Lived in London.

Nick EVANS 1907– Painter, sculptor and teacher, born and lived in Aberdare, Mid Glamorgan. Evans was self-taught as an artist and began painting at the age of 70, using his fingers and rags. His father was a miner and mining was a leading feature of his work, along with the Jewish Holocaust, of which he produced a record. Evans' grim, large monochrome pictures of mining life in the 1920s and 1930s were featured in a solo show at St David's Hall, Cardiff, in 1993. He was elected RCamA in 1981, also showing with RA, Turner Gallery in Penarth, Browse & Darby, RWA, Swansea University and abroad, winning many prizes. Tate Gallery, National Museum of Wales in Cardiff, Arts Council and WAC hold his work. Evans published a book on his work, *Symphonies in Black*, in 1987.

Peter EVANS 1943– Painter, designer and businessman, born in Handsworth, Birmingham. From 1960 attended Birmingham College of Arts and Crafts to study exhibition design. While employed as a designer produced in his own time abstract constructions and paintings which were included in shows at Compendium Galleries, Birmingham; Pentagon Gallery, Stoke-on-Trent; Bear Lane Gallery, Oxford; and Compendium II, London. From 1966–84 took over Warwick Fine Arts, dealer and picture framer, in Edgbaston. In 1978 Evans abandoned abstraction and became interested in what was termed Romantic Realism. By 1984 and retirement to paint full-time, Evans was established as an exhibitor at RA. He went on to have solo shows at Seen Gallery, 1986; and from 1987 several with John Davies Contemporary Painters, Stow-on-the-Wold. Davies was noted for his pictures of town and countryside in France. Lived in Solihull, Warwickshire.

Powys EVANS 1899–1981 Caricaturist and painter, also known as Quiz, born in London, son of a county court judge, William Evans, and brother of the artist Gwen Evans. He studied with Spencer Gore and Robert Bevan, the Camden Town Group painters; under Henry Tonks at Slade School of Fine Art, 1915–17; and with Walter Sickert and Sylvia Gosse with a period at Westminster School of Art. Served with Welsh Guards on the Western Front in France, 1918. Visited Sickert in Dieppe, 1920. Evans' early aspirations as a painter of London scenes were cut short when he began drawing for publications which included *The London Mercury* and *The Saturday Review*. His caricatures could be cruelly grotesque, as work in his two Leicester Galleries exhibitions in the mid-1920s and one at Colnaghi, in 1932, the latter two sell-outs, showed. He drew five prime ministers, four chancellors of the exchequer and 30 judges. His books included *The Beggars' Opera*, 1922; *Eighty-Eight Cartoons*, 1926; and *Fifty Heads drawn by Powys Evans*, 1928. An enigmatic figure, he retired when still at the height of his powers to Dolgellau, Merioneth, where he lived as a semi-recluse. In 1975 there was a retrospective at Langton Gallery, which gave him and Edmond Xavier Kapp a show in 1985. National Portrait Gallery holds many sketchbooks and studies by Evans, including Sir Arnold Bax the composer, Sir Jacob Epstein the sculptor and writers A A Milne and J B Priestley.

Ray EVANS 1920– Painter, illustrator, writer and teacher, born in Hale, Cheshire. He studied at Instituto di Belle Arti, Florence, 1945–6; Manchester College of Art, 1946–8; and Heatherley's School of Fine Art, 1948–50, under Iain Macnab, termed "a great influence". Evans worked for six months with the advertising agents Colman, Prentis & Varley, 1950–1, then as a freelance. Among various teaching appointments was Southampton College of Art, 1956–66. Did commissioned work for major companies such as British Petroleum, Eagle Star, banks and government. Many solo exhibitions included Thackeray, Furneaux and Canaletto Galleries; Winchester city art gallery; and Ashbarn Gallery in Petersfield. RA and RI, of which he was a member, RBA and RWA were among group show appearances. Among Evans' books were *Travelling with a Sketchbook*, 1980, and *How to be a Successful Illustrator*, 1993. National Library of Wales in Aberystwyth, Southampton Education Authority and Winchester gallery hold his work. Lived in Salisbury, Wiltshire.

Sybil EVANS fl. from 1950s– Painter who studied at The College in Pontypool, Monmouthshire; in the same county at Newport College of Art; and at Hornsey College of Art. Showed at RA, NEAC and elsewhere. Lived for some time in Torquay, Devon.

Vincent EVANS 1896– Painter, printmaker and teacher, born in Ystalyfera, Glamorgan, south Wales. Studied at Swansea School of Art and at Royal College of Art under William Rothenstein and Frank Short. He went on to become art master at Slough Grammar School, 1940–61, after a period in New Zealand, then taught at Slough College until 1968. Exhibited RA, NEAC, RWS, Leicester Galleries and Paris Salon. National Museum of Wales, Cardiff, and Glynn Vivian Art Gallery, Swansea, bought his work. Lived in Slough, Buckinghamshire.

Will EVANS 1888–1957 Painter, designer and printmaker, born and died in Swansea, south Wales. After leaving school at 14 Evans became an apprentice tinplate printer at South Wales Canister's works, eventually becoming their chief designer after attending lessons part-time from 1910 at Swansea School of Art. Showed RCamA, SWG, SWAS and elsewhere and was given a memorial show at Glynn Vivian Art Gallery, Swansea in 1958, a dozen years after his one-man exhibition there. That gallery and National Museum of Wales, Cardiff, hold his work which was frequently landscapes of the Swansea area in watercolour.

William EVANS 1911– Painter, born in London, studied at Hammersmith School of Art and Royal Academy Schools. Showed at RA, LG, RBA and RP, his work being held by public collections in Oxford, Cambridge and Reading. Lived at Abinger Hammer, Surrey.

Esmé EVE 1920– Painter in gouache, teacher, book illustrator and designer, born in London. She studied at Croydon School of Art and Royal College of Art. Miss Eve taught graphics at various art colleges and embroidery design at Royal School of Needlework. Book illustrations were completed for Blackie, Odhams, Longman's, Macdonald's, Hamlyn and other publishers, and she contributed designs for charity greetings cards, as well as Medici. She wrote and illustrated *The Christmas Book* under the name Eve, which she sometimes used for pictures. Lived in Seaford, Sussex.

Roberta G EVERETT 1906– Sculptor and teacher, born in Surrey, who attended Goldsmiths' College School of Art and City and Guilds of London Art School. She taught at Brentwood College of Education, Essex. Exhibited RA, Royal Glasgow Institute of the Fine Arts and at Paris Salon. Lancashire Education Committee holds her work. Lived in Hornchurch, Essex, then Harrow, Middlesex.

Graham EVERNDEN 1947– Printmaker and designer, married to the painter Sue Evernden. He was born in Kent and studied at Maidstone College of Art, graduating with a first-class honours degree in 1970. Worked in London as a graphic designer and illustrator for four years, going freelance in 1974. In 1975 was elected to Printmakers' Council. Set up own printmaking studio in

Sussex, running a separate studio for editioning etchings for other artists. Dorset and Sussex were key elements in his work, which was shown at RA Summer Exhibition from 1977, Mall Galleries from 1978 and widely abroad. Gillridge Gallery, Crowborough, gave him a solo show.

Leonard Charles EVETTS 1909–1997 Stained glass artist, teacher, watercolourist and, like his father, a skilled letterer. He was born in Newport, Monmouthshire. Aged 18, he won a short scholarship to the Royal College of Art, with a three-year one covering the years 1930–3. His teachers included Edward Johnston for calligraphy, for whom he served as a demonstrator, and Martin Travers for stained glass. Evetts taught at Edinburgh College of Art from 1933–7, in 1938 publishing his book *Roman Lettering*, which establish him as an authority on ancient calligraphy. From 1937 Evetts taught for about 40 years in the department of fine art at King's College, Newcastle, eventually becoming department head. During World War II he was engaged by the government for camouflage work. Newcastle's Cathedral Church of St Nicholas has a fine east window, of 1962, by Evetts, one of over 300 completed in Britain and abroad. He favoured traditional architecture as a setting. In 1995, the Church of England acknowledged Evetts' achievement with a Lambeth doctorate. Showed at RA. Laing Art Gallery, Newcastle, holds his watercolour Bamburgh Castle. Died at Woolsington, Tyne and Wear.

David EVISON 1944– Abstract sculptor in metal and wood, sometimes painted, and teacher, born in China. He studied at Leeds College of Art, 1963–7, then St Martin's School of Art, 1967–8, where he taught part-time. Group shows included Stockwell Depot I and Prospect '69, Düsseldorf, Germany, both 1969; Sculpture in Holland Park, 1972; and The Condition of Sculpture, Hayward Gallery, 1975. Had solo shows at Kasmin Gallery, 1971–2, and at Museum of Modern Art in Oxford, 1976. His Untitled sculpture, of 1979, was sited in Grizedale Forest Sculpture Park. Arts Council and Whitworth Art Gallery in Manchester hold examples. Lived in southeast London.

David Shanks EWART 1901–1965 Painter, born in Glasgow, who spent most of his life there. After a short period in business after leaving school, Ewart attended Glasgow School of Art, his teachers including Maurice Greiffenhagen and Fra Newbery. On graduating in 1924, he used a scholarship to take him to Italy and France. On his return, in 1926 his picture The Emigrants was a great success at Royal Glasgow Institute of the Fine Arts show, a companion picture, The Return (now in the collection of Scottish National Gallery of Modern Art), appearing the following year. Ewart showed also at RA and RSA, where he won the Guthrie Award in 1926 and the Lauder Award in 1927. His work is notable for its hard-edged, ultra-realistic quality, very suited to the pictures of American tycoons and their wives which he painted during prolonged visits from the mid-1940s.

Michael EXALL 1950– Painter, printmaker, draughtsman and teacher, born in Norwich, Norfolk. Attended Hornsey College of Art, 1968–72, under Norman Stevens, and Royal Academy Schools for postgraduate studies, 1972–5. Anthony Gross and Giorgio Morandi were influences. From 1976 Exall taught part-time at Manchester Polytechnic and University, providing him time and money for his own work. Group exhibitions included Bradford International Print Biennale from 1976, the year he showed in British Realists at Ikon Gallery, Birmingham; Hull Print Exhibitions from 1984; and RA Summer Exhibitions. Had a solo show at Trinity College, Oxford, 1974; Angela Flowers Gallery and City Art Gallery in Barnsley, both 1986; Dean Clough, Halifax, 1990; and Salford Art Gallery, 1991. Public galleries in Leeds, Norwich, Sheffield and Wakefield hold examples, as does Skopje Museum in former Yugoslavia. Lived in Todmorden, Lancashire.

James Robert Granville EXLEY 1878–1967 Painter, printmaker and teacher, born at Great Horton, Bradford, Yorkshire. He studied at Skipton Art School and Royal College of Art, graduating in 1907. Among his appointments was headmaster of Hull Municipal Art School, 1912–19. Natural history and the countryside were key subjects. Exley was elected RE in 1923, also showing at RA, Redfern Gallery and Royal Glasgow Institute of the Fine Arts. British Museum, Victoria & Albert Museum and Fitzwilliam Museum in Cambridge hold examples. Lived in London, then at Grassington, Yorkshire.

Ray EXWORTH 1930– Sculptor, draughtsman and teacher, born in Ipswich, Suffolk. He attended the local School of Art, 1951–5, then Royal College of Art, 1955–9. He had a solo show at Whitechapel Art Gallery, 1975, Felixstowe Remembered, 1970–4, as well as other sculptures and drawings; was also shown at Chappel Galleries, 1992, and in same year was included in Artists from Cornwall at RWA. Awards included Arts Council, 1975–7–84, and a South West Arts Fellowship, 1985. Taught at Falmouth School of Art and lived in Praze, Camborne, Cornwall. Arts Council holds several examples.

Frank EYRE 1953– Painter and draughtsman who graduated from University of Belfast, 1989, later studying there for his master's degree. Showed in mixed exhibitions throughout Ireland, including Works on Paper and Beyond the Partitions, put on in 1994 by Queen Street Studios, Belfast, with which Eyre was associated. His work sometimes used unconventional media, such as charcoal and car spray. Solo exhibitions included Rubicon Gallery in Dublin, 1990, and One Oxford Street, Belfast, 1992.

Anthony EYTON 1923– Painter and teacher, born in London, where he continued to live. He was educated at Canford School, Dorset, then studied fine art for a term at Reading University in 1941, serving in the Army, 1942–7, painting occasionally. From 1947–50 studied at Camberwell School of Arts and Crafts, in 1951–2 gaining an Abbey Major Scholarship to work in Italy. Began to show with LG and RA and in 1955 had first one-man exhibition at St George's Gallery. From 1957 Eyton taught at

Camberwell School of Art, other teaching following at Royal Academy Schools from 1965 and in 1969 at St Lawrence College, Kingston, Ontario. Among other notable events in Eyton's career were winning a prize at John Moores Exhibition, Liverpool, in 1972; travels in Italy and India in the 1970s; membership of LG, RWA, RWS and NEAC and election to RA in 1987. Eyton showed with Browse & Darby and had a retrospective South London Art Gallery and tour in 1980. He was a landscape and still life painter in the tradition of Euston Road School and Camberwell School of Art who believed that art stemmed from a regard for nature, balancing fact and abstract. Arts Council, Tate Gallery and Imperial War Museum hold his work.

F

F: *see* **BROUN-MORISON of Finderlie**

Miche FABRE-LEWIN 1956– Artist and art therapist, born in what is now Zimbabwe, who moved to England in 1980, settling in Oxford. She gained an honours degree in comparative literature/art history at East Anglia University, Norwich, 1975–80; studied stained glass at École des Beaux-Arts, Aix-en-Provence, 1978–9; and was apprenticed to the Patrick Reyntiens Stained Glass Studio, Beaconsfield, 1980-1; gained an art therapy diploma, Hertfordshire College of Art and Design, St Albans, 1988–9; then obtained her master's in art therapy at Hertfordshire University's school of art, 1992–4. Group shows included Three Women, at The Studio, Oxford, 1986; Diorama Arts Centre, 1990; Wolfson and Stables Galleries in Oxford, both 1992; Ben Uri Gallery, Annual Open, 1995; and Unquiet Voices, Doncaster Museum & Art Gallery, 1997.

William Bateman FAGAN 1860–1948 Sculptor, born and lived in London, educated at Dulwich College and married to the painter Betty Fagan. He was elected a fellow of RBS in 1938 and showed at RA, Royal Glasgow Institute of the Fine Arts, Walker Art Gallery in Liverpool, ROI and elsewhere. Was a Chelsea Arts Club member.

Mateusz FAHRENHOLZ 1963– Creator of boxed constructions, printmaker, born in St Andrews, Fife, his parents Polish exiles. He explored suffering and exile in his work, which used photographs of unknown people and places and a range of domestic items which he specially aged. In 1984–5 did summer studies at Academy of Fine Arts in Craców, Poland, then in 1984–8 gained an honours degree in fine art, printmaking, from Gray's School of Art in Aberdeen, doing his postgraduate diploma there, 1988–9. Gained a Go and See grant from the Prince's Trust, 1990, and a Go Ahead grant to work with the Polish sculptor Piotr Bies in 1992. In 1991 was artist-in-residence at Aberdeen Art Gallery. Group shows included Polonia Society, Craców, 1984; Open Prints Exhibition, Bankside Gallery and New Generation Artists at Compass Gallery, Glasgow, both 1988; and CD3, Collective Gallery, Edinburgh, 1994. Had a solo show at Aberdeen Art Gallery in 1991, later ones including England & Co, 1995. Aberdeen Art Gallery, National Library of Scotland and the libraries at St Andrews and Dundee Universities hold his work.

Jonathan FAIRBAIRN 1961– Ceramist and teacher who studied at Laird School of Art, 1977–8, next Wallasey School of Art, 1978–81, then becoming a ceramics technician and lecturer at Wirral Metropolitan College. Fairbairn said that his work was designed "with the mystical lost rituals and ceremonies of ancient cultures in mind", such as Ceremonial Jug, shown in the 1986–7 Walker Art Gallery, Liverpool, Merseyside Artists 3 touring exhibition. Also exhibited at Wirral Spring Exhibition, Williamson Art Gallery, Birkenhead, 1986, and in same year Fourplay at Acorn Gallery, Liverpool.

Bernard FAIRCLOUGH 1915– Painter and teacher, born in Glossop, Derbyshire. He studied at Manchester School of Art, teachers including Leslie Baxter, going on to teach for many years until 1975 at Darlington School of Art, of which he became head. Showed with RSA, Arts Council, Whitechapel Art Gallery and widely in the provinces. Manchester Education Committee holds his work. Lived in Newbiggin, Barnard Castle, County Durham.

Mary FAIRCLOUGH 1913– Painter, printmaker, illustrator, potter and writer, born in Keynsham, near Bristol, Somerset, where she continued to live, was a councillor and was active in Keynsham Local History Society (later Keynsham Civic Society). She studied at home with Kit Gunton, 1926–30, then part-time at West of England Art College, Bristol, until 1939. Served in Women's Voluntary Service in World War II, but her mother's illness and failing sight and her own asthma restricted her activities. Through Gunton Miss Fairclough showed with Clifton Arts Club and had her work seen by Claude Flight, participating in his lino-cut exhibitions ("as a group we exhibited at the Ward Gallery, London and Brighton"); also showed with RWA; and locally in Keynsham. Fairclough illustrated, mostly books and magazines for children, for publishers including Macmillan, Evans Brothers, George Newnes and Pearson's. She published *Miskoo The Lucky, a tale for children with illustrations*, 1947; *Little Dog and The Rainmakers*, 1949; *The Blue Tree*, 1960; and *John Barleycorn*, 1962. Her ballad opera *John Barleycorn*, for which she wrote the libretto and designed the costumes, was performed at Wellsway School, Keynsham, in 1968, music by Bruce Montgomery and published by Novello. Fairclough's smaller art works and crafts were signed M F in monogram form, with the date.

Michael FAIRCLOUGH 1940– Printmaker, painter, muralist and teacher, born in Blackburn, Lancashire, son of the artist Wilfred Fairclough, married to the painter Mary Malenoir. He studied at Kingston School of Art, 1957–61; was a Rome Scholar in Engraving, 1964–6, at British School in Rome, 1964–7; then was at S W Hayter's Atelier 17, Paris, 1967. After teaching at Belfast College of Art, 1962–4, was at West Surrey College of

Art, Farnham, 1967–79. He completed the National Trust commemorative stamps for the Post Office in 1981. Among his solo exhibitions was Bohun Gallery, Henley-on-Thames, 1981. Ashmolean Museum in Oxford and Victoria & Albert Museum hold his work. Was made a fellow of RE, 1973, and a member of Printmakers' Council, 1981. Lived in Farnham, Surrey.

Wilfred FAIRCLOUGH 1907–1996 Etcher, watercolourist and teacher, born in Blackburn, Lancashire, husband of the painter Joan Vernon-Cryer and father of the artist Michael Fairclough. Left school at 14 to work in a mill, then trained as an audit clerk while attending evening classes at Blackburn School of Arts and Crafts, passing the Board of Education's drawing examination in 1930, the year he was appointed a part-time teacher at Blackburn. Determination gained him entry to the Royal College of Art's engraving school, where he excelled, 1931–4, under teachers Malcolm Osborne and Robert Austin. He was a Rome Scholar in Engraving, 1934, attending the British School in Rome, 1934–7. Rome was a favourite subject, later replaced by Venice. Lived in Kingston upon Thames, Surrey, and was principal of the School of Art there, 1962–70, assistant director of Kingston Polytechnic, 1970–2. Fairclough had joined the staff at Kingston in 1938, then spent his wartime service in the Royal Air Force; he worked on models employed in planning the bouncing bomb attack on the Mohne dam; and was latterly in India. Fairclough was elected RE, 1946, and RWS, 1968, also showing at RA, RSA, Royal Glasgow Institute of the Fine Arts and at the Redfern Gallery, as well as widely overseas. Contemporary Art Society bought his work, also held by Ashmolean Museum in Oxford and Victoria & Albert Museum, which has the almost 60 watercolours which Fairclough completed during World War II for the Pilgrim Trust's *Recording Britain* project.

Frederick Park FAIRER 1910– Portrait painter, born in Hull, Yorkshire. He studied art at the Borough Polytechnic with David Bomberg in 1948, City and Guilds of London Art School in Kennington in 1950 and the Central School of Arts and Crafts in 1951–3. Showed at RA, NEAC and RP. Lived in London.

Michael FAIRFAX 1953– Sculpture and lecturer, born in Windsor, Berkshire. He attended Portsmouth College of Art for foundation studies, 1976–7, then graduated with honours from Gwent College of Higher Education, 1977–80. Gained several Southern Arts and WAC grants and was an Eisteddfod prize-winner, 1992. Did an extensive amount of educational and lecturing work in Britain and abroad; residencies included Margam Sculpture Park, 1991, and Forestry Commission, Garw Valley, 1992. Between 1986–91 travelled in Italy, Egypt, Spain and America. His work in public places included Margam Sculpture Park and Ebbw Vale, for Garden Festival. Had a solo show at Newbury Spring Festival, 1983, another at St David's Hall, Cardiff, 1991. Lived in Canton, Cardiff, south Wales.

Edmund FAIRFAX-LUCY 1945– Painter who studied at City and Guilds of London Art School, 1963–6, then Royal Academy Schools under Peter Greenham, 1967–70. He won the David Murray Travelling Scholarship, 1966, 1967 and 1969. From 1967 he was a regular exhibitor at RA, and was also a member of NEAC. Showed in group exhibitions at New Grafton Gallery, which gave him a first solo show in 1971. Fairfax-Lucy was noted for his sensitive landscapes and interiors in which the play of light was a special feature. Lived at Charlecote Park, Warwick.

James FAIRGRIEVE 1944– Painter and teacher, born in Prestonpans, East Lothian. He studied at Edinburgh College of Art, 1962–8, and was awarded an Andrew Grant Scholarship and one-year postgraduate study, David Murray Landscape Award and Travelling Scholarship to Italy. He went on to teach painting and drawing at Edinburgh College of Art. Fairgrieve was a member of RSW and was president of SSA in 1978. Birds, animals and the natural world featured strongly in his pictures, which were shown widely in Scottish group exhibitions. One-man shows included New 57 Gallery and Scottish Gallery, in Edinburgh, and Mercury Gallery in London and Edinburgh. Scottish Arts Council and many other Scottish collections hold his work. Lived in Gordon, Berwickshire.

Angus FAIRHURST 1962– Artist in mixed media, born in Kent, where he studied at Canterbury College of Art, 1985–6, completing an honours degree at Goldsmiths' College School of Art, 1986–9. Among his group shows was Modern Medicine, Building One, 1990, and Summer Group Show, Karsten Schubert Ltd, 1992. The year before had a solo show at Karsten Schubert. Fairhurst's Scuba Blue Attachment, of 1992, was acquired for the European Parliament Collection and was shown in the Arts Council, Belfast, touring show Twelve Stars, 1992–3. In 1998 he shared an exhibition, Odd-Bod Photography, with Sarah Lucas at Sadie Coles HQ.

Enoch FAIRHURST 1874–1945 Painter, miniaturist, designer and illustrator, born and lived in Bolton, Lancashire, father of artist Jack Fairhurst. He was elected a member of Manchester Academy, 1932, and of RMS in 1943, having earlier been an associate for a time. Showed also at Walker Art Gallery in Liverpool, RA, RSA and RCamA.

Jack FAIRHURST 1905–1989 Painter, draughtsman and teacher, son of the miniaturist Enoch Fairhurst, born in London. He studied at Camberwell School of Art, 1919–23, under Albert Rutherston, then Royal College of Art, 1923–7, with William Rothenstein and Randolph Schwabe. Held several teaching appointments in the London area, between 1941–57 acting as head of Richmond School of Art. Was a member of Ridley Art Club, South London Group, Richmond Art Group and the Society of Fulham Artists, also showing RA, RP and in the provinces, having several solo shows in and out of London. Lived latterly in Dallinghoo, Suffolk.

Miles Christopher FAIRHURST 1955– Painter, born in Norwich, son of the landscape artist Joseph Fairhurst. He studied art with his father and at University of Aix-en-Provence, France. Showed his work in his own gallery in New King's Road, London, and in various mixed exhibitions, having a first substantial showing at Park Grosvenor Galleries in 1992. In late-1980s returned to East Anglia to breed waterfowl and paint landscape, which he did rather in the manner of Edward Seago.

Dorothy M FAIRLEY 1894– Etcher, wood engraver, painter and stone carver. Studied at Richmond Art School and Regent Street Polytechnic. One-man show in 1946 at Walker Galleries, also showed in mixed exhibitions at many venues, including RA, NEAC, SWA, Paris Salon and Chicago Institute of Fine Art. Lived at Robertsbridge, Sussex.

George FAIRLEY 1920– Painter, sculptor and teacher, born in Dunfermline, Fife. After studying at Edinburgh College of Art Fairley was for 15 years from 1947 lecturer in fine art at Swansea College of Art, then moving to head the foundation studies department at Croydon College of Art. Showed with 56 Group of which he was a member, Leicester Galleries, SEA, WAC and in other group shows, having several solo exhibitions with Gimpel Fils, at Bear Lane Gallery in Oxford and at the Universities of Southampton and Surrey. Among his commissions were stainless steel murals for National Westminster Bank in the Home Counties area. WAC and Worcester College, Oxford, hold his work. Lived in Horsham, Sussex.

Churton FAIRMAN 1924–1997 Sculptor in wood and stone, broadcaster, actor, photographer and musician, born in London, full name Austin Churton Fairman, son of the actress Hilda Moore, leading lady for Gerald du Maurier. Attended Aldenham School and Oxford University, but left early to joint the Ballet Rambert. After World War II service in the Ulster Rifles, Fairman became a ballet photographer. His first wife was Spanish; with her he returned to Spain and wrote *Another Spain*, 1952, about its countryside. Through the director Peter Brook, he became involved in the theatre; then Independent Television religious programmes; and, as Mike Raven, as a disc jockey for pirate radio and BBC Radio 1, eventually with the *Mike Raven Blues Show*. Appeared as Mike Raven in several horror films, including *Crucible of Terror*, 1971. Early in the 1970s Fairman and his second wife, Mandy, moved to Cornwall to live in a converted pigsty, from 1980 running a dilapidated farm near Blisland, by which time Fairman had been carving about six years. A first show in Cornwall ran into difficulties because of the controversial nature of Fairman's work, but he was to have two exhibitions at St George's Church, Bloomsbury, in 1990 and 1992, and in 1993 his The Deposition from the Cross was exhibited in the Images of Christ touring show in Northampton and at St Paul's Cathedral.

Sheila FAIRMAN 1924– Artist in oil and miniaturist, born in South Benfleet, Essex. She attended Southend College of Art, 1938–40. Fairman's main works were still life, her Shells and Feathers series being shown at various venues. In 1967 with a revived interest in painting she returned to Southend College of Art to study portrait and life drawing at evening classes and she began painting miniatures in 1979. She was a member of RMS from 1981; was a member of Hilliard Society of Miniaturists; in 1985 was elected to SWA; and in 1986 was a founder-member of Society of Botanical Artists. Also exhibited at RSMA, ROI, RI and in the provinces. She gained several placings in the Hunting Group Art Prizes and won the RSM Gold Bowl in 1989. Beecroft Art Gallery, Southend, holds her work. Lived in Leigh-on-Sea, Essex.

Tom FAIRS 1925– Artist in mixed media, stained glass designer and teacher, born and lived in London. He studied at Hornsey College of Art, 1948–50, and Royal College of Art, 1950–4. Became senior lecturer in theatre design at Central School of Art & Design. Fairs after a period of abstract work painted landscape, interiors and still life. He showed at RA Summer Exhibitions, Rooksmoor, Covent Garden and Thackeray Galleries. Was a member of the Society of Landscape Painters and the Society of Small Paintings. Stained glass was prepared for baptistry and day chapel lights for Our Lady of the Wayside, Shirley, Birmingham; Holborn College of Law, Languages and Commerce; and Officers' Club, Bahrain.

Dorothy FAIRWEATHER 1915– Artist in various media, born in Folkestone, Kent. She attended the local School of Art, Liverpool University and Richmond Art School. At times was engaged in photography and running an art gallery. Exhibited solo at Turnpike Gallery at Leigh; Stables Gallery in Hastings; The Old Bakehouse, Sevenoaks; Woodlands Art Gallery; and Mount Street Post Office. Mixed exhibitions included RA, the provinces and abroad. Lived in Sevenoaks, Kent.

Ian FAIRWEATHER 1891–1974 Painter, born at Bridge of Allan, Stirlingshire. He is believed to have studied forestry and botany as a young man before serving in World War I, during which he was a prisoner of war in Germany. Then studied art in Netherlands and was at Slade, 1920–3. Although he had shows at Redfern Gallery in 1930s, Fairweather's life for much of the inter-war years was that of a traveller, especially in the Far East and Australia, which became his home. During World War II he served in British Army. In 1952 he tried to sail to Timor on a home-made raft, was reported missing but turned up shortly after in Timor, was sent to Britain and then back to Australia, where he lived at Bribie Island, Queensland. His work is original, brilliant and sensuous and often employs unconventional materials. It is in Tate Gallery and all Australian state galleries. Died in Brisbane.

FAISAL 1969– Artist, notably a printmaker, and teacher, full name Faisal Abdu'allah, who did a foundation course at Harrow School of Art, 1987-8; gained a first-class honours degree in fine art printmaking at Central St Martins School of Art, 1989–91, in 1989 attending the Massachusetts College of Art in Boston, in America; then gained his master's degree in fine art printmaking at the Royal College of Art, 1991–3. He had a residency at Furness School, 1993, and gained the Art in the City Award,

1995–6. Teaching included Falmouth School of Art, Middlesex and East London Universities, Royal College of Art and Wolverhampton University. Faisal's work appeared in many magazines and newspapers. Exhibitions included Brent Arts Festival, 1987; Photographers' Gallery, from 1993; and University of East London, 1996. Had a solo show at 198 Gallery, 1993. Victoria & Albert Museum holds his work. Lived in London.

Leila FAITHFULL 1896–1994 Artist in a variety of media, born in Walton, Lancashire, daughter of Sir James Reynolds, Bart, but brought up in Liverpool. She married George Faithfull in 1917 and after he died in early 1940s took as her second husband in 1943 the writer and critic Cuthbert Worsley. After the war while they were on a trip through France he left her, in Marseilles, and she stayed on to work. She frequently painted alone abroad. Faithfull studied at Slade School of Fine Art, 1923–4, later at L'Académie de la Grande Chaumière, Paris. For a time Faithfull was surgical artist to Sir Archibald McIndoe, the pioneer plastic surgeon, at Queen Victoria Hospital in East Grinstead. Leila (pronounced Lyla) Faithfull was noted for her portraits, shown extensively at Leicester Galleries, NEAC, RBA, RA, ROI and elsewhere. She was in the private collections of Lord Clark and Sir Edward Marsh and had works accepted by War Artists' Advisory Committee and Contemporary Art Society and public galleries in Aberdeen, Birmingham and Manchester. In later years she created heads, figures on horses and the occasional dancer in metal: cut-outs from sheets or as wire shapes and outlines, but these were not commercially successful. Died in St Angela's Convent, Bristol, where she had lived for several years.

Bushra FAKHOURY 1942– Sculptor, born in Beirut, Lebanon. Dr Fakhoury attended St Paul's, Wimbledon School of Art, Beirut University College, American University of Beirut and London University. Exhibitions included Bloomsbury and Mall Galleries, 1986; Jablonski Gallery, 1987; Kufa Gallery, 1989; and 2nd Open Sculpture Exhibition at RWA, 1996. Her themes and subjects included human and animal, some merging into surreal figures of myth and fantasy. Lived in London.

Roland FALCON 1914– Sculptor in various materials and photographer, educated in Copenhagen, Berlin and London. He was official sculpture photographer for the Tate Gallery and exhibited his photographs in London. Also showed RMS, RSA, Russell-Cotes Art Gallery and Museum in Bournemouth and Foyles Gallery. Lived in Edgware, Middlesex.

Brian FALCONBRIDGE 1950– Sculptor, draughtsman and teacher, born in Norfolk. He studied at Canterbury College of Art, 1968–9, Goldsmiths' College School of Art, 1970–3, and Slade School of Fine Art, 1973–5. Gained the Walter Neurath Art History Award in 1972, Arts Council Minor Award, 1976, the Eastern Arts Association Award in 1977, and four years later the Tolly Cobbold/Eastern Arts Regional Prize. In 1991 Falconbridge won the Blackstone Prize at RA. Went on to teach at Goldsmiths' and the Slade. Falconbridge took part in Goldsmiths at South London Art Gallery in 1972; showed with LG and New Contemporaries; RA; and in 1983 was Artist of the Day at Angela Flowers Gallery. In 1984 The Minories put on a show of his work which toured England. Falconbridge's coloured, abstract sculptures were on a small scale, in wood and other materials, and employed geometrical shapes. Arts Council, Contemporary Art Society and University of East Anglia hold his work. Lived in London.

Conor FALLON 1939– Self-taught sculptor, born in Dublin, Ireland, where he latterly settled in Kinsale, County Cork, with his painter wife Nancy Wynne-Jones. Between 1966–72 Fallon lived in Cornwall. Group shows included Newlyn Orion Gallery from 1966; RHA from 1977; and Contemporary Artists from Ireland, Austin/Desmond Fine Art, 1990. Had a solo show at Newlyn Orion, 1972, later ones including Arts Council tour, 1983.

Keith FALLSHAW 1946– Commercial artist, painter and sculptor, born in London. He studied typographical design at London College of Printing; was also a pupil of the portrait painters Leonard and Margaret Boden. Showed at NS, UA, elsewhere in London and at Deben Gallery, Woodbridge. Lived in Bishop's Stortford, Hertfordshire.

Joe FAN 1962– Painter, draughtsman and designer, born in Hong Kong. He studied graphic design at Aberdeen College of Commerce, then at Gray's Art School, Aberdeen, under Alexander Fraser and Gordon Bryce. Fan obtained a first-class honours degree in drawing and painting. His pictures mixed Eastern figures, over-ripe fruit, pigs and carved grotesques and were painterly with a pleasingly muted palette. In the mid-1980s Fan acquired a batch of awards, including first prize in the Commonwealth Section of the 1985 Rank Xerox Selected National Competition 86; a first prize in the 1987 Wood Group Young Artists' Award; and in 1988 a Carnegie Travelling Scholarship, RSA. Group shows included RSW. Solo exhibitions at Compass Gallery, Glasgow, and Sue Rankin Gallery, both 1991. Scottish Arts Council, Gray's School of Art and Aberdeen Royal Infirmary hold his work.

Barry FANTONI 1940– Cartoonist, designer, writer and broadcaster who studied at Camberwell School of Arts and Crafts as a Wedgwood Scholar. He was a member of the satirical magazine *Private Eye*'s staff from 1963; was cartoonist for *The Listener*, 1968–88; wrote art criticism for *The Times*, 1973–7; and was its diary cartoonist from 1983. Fantoni also designed film and television posters and painted a mural at the Queen Elizabeth Conference Centre, 1985. Among his books was *The Best of Barry Fantoni Cartoons*, 1990. Was chairman of Chelsea Arts Club, 1978–80. His solo shows included Woodstock Gallery, 1963; Brunel University, 1974; and he had a retrospective at Cadogan Contemporary, 1991.

Cyril Arthur FAREY 1888–1954 Architect and watercolourist, born and lived in London, father of the architect and painter

Michael A J Farey. He was educated at Tonbridge School, won a Gold Medal at Royal Academy Schools and a Sloane Medallion from RIBA. Exhibited extensively at RA, also at RSA and Royal Glasgow Institute of the Fine Arts. In 1996 Gallery Lingard held a show of Farey's architectural sketches and watercolours, Thumbnotes & Masterpieces.

Tim FARGHER 1952– Painter, born in Lincolnshire, who graduated from St Martin's School of Art, 1979. His exhibitions included Camden Arts Festival, 1978; RP; Fraser Gallery, Woodbridge; Long & Ryle Art International; and Portland Gallery, 1992. He was guest artist at Glyndebourne Festival Opera in 1991. Fargher's commissions included 14 big oils on a theme of mythological and extinct creatures for Tim Walker, late chairman of the World Wildlife Fund, in 1985; and 85 paintings for HM The Sultan of Oman, 1985–8. Portrait commissions included Sir Peter Pears, 1980; Sir Kenneth Berrill, 1988; and The Reverend Dr Edward Carpenter, 1989.

Elsie FARLEIGH: *see* **Anne NEVILLE**

John FARLEIGH 1900–1965 Oil and watercolour painter, wood engraver and printmaker. Studied at the Central School of Arts and Crafts, 1917–21, under James Grant, Bernard Meninsky and Noel Rooke. Married to the artist Elsie Farleigh. Exhibited LG, Leicester and Redfern Galleries, RE, RSA and in the provinces. He taught at Rugby School, 1922–4, then joining the Central School staff as head of the book production department. Published several books, including his autobiography *Graven Image*, 1940. 20th Century Gallery showed Farleigh's wood engravings in 1997. Lived in London.

Charles William FARLEY 1893–1982 Portrait and genre painter in oil and watercolour who served in the Queen's Westminsters in World War I and was a captain/adjutant in the Army in World War II, having seen service in India and the North-West Frontier. Prior to the second war Farley was living at Richmond, Surrey, showing at RA Summer Exhibition and elsewhere, later at East Molesey. After demobilisation in 1945 he moved to Cheltenham, Gloucestershire, where he was a member of the Cotswold Art Club and a founder-member of Cheltenham Art Club. He also exhibited with RI, 1940, RWA from 1956, and RP from 1957. Cheltenham Art Gallery holds his picture The Woodyard.

Francis FARMAR 1948– Painter, draughtsman and art consultant, educated at Eton College. He spent every spare moment in the drawing schools there before continuing his studies in Italy, St Martin's School of Art and West of England College of Art, Bristol. He joined the auctioneers Christie's in 1971, remaining to 1986 by when he had become director of their modern British picture department. Farmar then took the radical step of moving to the Morayshire coastal village of Findhorn to concentrate on his own painting while continuing as a consultant for Christie's and for private clients. He was responsible for the Painters of Camden Town exhibition and catalogue at Christie's in 1988. Farmar's work, influenced by the St Ives and Neo-Romantic painters, included landscapes around his Scottish home and in the south of France. William Hardie Gallery gave him a solo show in Glasgow in 1991. Lived latterly in Sedgehill, Dorset, and London.

Bernard FARMER 1919– Painter and maker of abstract constructions, born and lived in London. He studied at Chelsea Polytechnic School of Art and showed with LG, New Vision Centre, St Martin's Gallery and AIA. Solo exhibitions included Heal's Art Gallery, 1964, and Angela Flowers Gallery, 1982. Farmer said that "the more simple I can make an image the better I like it … The less can always expand in the mind, whereas more either constricts or becomes too much." Farmer was co-organiser with Malcolm Hughes of Directions-Connections at AIA Gallery, 1961, and had work reproduced in Frank Avray Wilson's *Art as Understanding*, 1963. The painter Adrian Heath was a strong advocate of his work. Arts Council and Contemporary Art Society hold examples.

John FARNHAM 1942– Sculptor and draughtsman, born in Perry Green, Hertfordshire. In 1958 he joined his father's building business, in 1965 becoming a full-time assistant to Henry Moore, having previously worked part-time. At first Farnham's sculptures were fairly conventional, but in the mid-1970s they began to get more personal and complex, with a greater exploration of the abstract. In 1969 Farnham showed at Pace Gallery, then after further showings had a solo exhibition in 1973 at Old Bakehouse Gallery, Sevenoaks, the year he carried out his first major commission: Winged Figure, commissioned by Department of the Environment for Royal Air Force, Naphill. In 1973 also gained an Arts Council grant. Further commissions included Life Form, of 1980, commissioned by Institute of Biology. Other exhibitions included a one-man show at New Art Centre, 1976, and a shared exhibition at Leeds City Art Gallery, 1984, and tour.

Emma FARQUHARSON: *see* **Roy HOBDELL**

Giles FARQUHARSON: *see* **Roy HOBDELL**

Linda M FARQUHARSON 1963– Printmaker, illustrator and lecturer, born in Aberdeen, who gained an honours degree, specialising in illustration and printmaking, from Duncan of Jordanstone College of Art, Dundee, in 1985, winning the Sekalski Prize for printmaking. Stayed on for a year under a postgraduate scholarship in design specialising in printmaking, from 1993 lecturing there part-time. In 1990 Farquharson bought and restored a Columbian printing press. Showed at Compass Gallery, Glasgow, 1986; Printmakers' Workshop, Edinburgh, 1990; Barbican Centre and SSA, both 1993; RSA, 1995; and Roger Billcliffe Fine Art, Glasgow, 1996. Bank of Scotland, The Royal Bank of Scotland, The Scottish Office and other collections hold her work.

Mo FARQUHARSON 1953– Sculptor and draughtsman, born in Aberdeenshire, to which she frequently returned from London. She trained as a sculptor in Edinburgh under Edward Gage; for three years at the Ruskin School of Drawing, Oxford, where Chris Dorset was influential; and for a year at Massachusetts College of Art, Boston, in America. Became a member of RBS. Exhibited widely in Britain, including a solo show at The Gallery in Cork Street, 1997. This included expressive sculptures and drawings of animals, birds, fish and people, including figures exploring urban relationships. These were inspired by her London Bridge sculpture, acquired by Paribas Ltd. Other commissions included Edinburgh Zoo, bust of its president, Viscount Arbuthnott; two life-size coal miners for Hamilton, Lanarkshire, for Akeler (Scotland) Ltd; and a figure of John Lennon, commissioned by record company HMV for charity auction at the Silver Clef Awards. HRH The Duke of Edinburgh holds Farquharson's work.

Heather FARR 1912– Painter, especially of landscapes, born in Nottingham, initially educated in Scarborough, Yorkshire. She studied art at Nottingham School of Art and the Slade School of Fine Art, exhibiting at NEAC, WIAC and Nottingham Museum and Art Gallery. For a time she taught art at Geffrye Museum and lived in London.

Anthony FARRELL 1945– Painter, draughtsman and teacher, born in Epsom, Surrey. He studied at Southend School of Art, 1961–3, Camberwell School of Arts and Crafts, 1963–5, and Royal Academy Schools, 1965–8. From 1976 he taught part-time at various art schools and centres, in 1981–2 winning an Eastern Arts Association Fellowship and the Association's Exhibition Award. Farrell took part in many group exhibitions, notably RA, Serpentine Gallery mixed shows and the Norwich School of Art Gallery's 1986–7 touring exhibition A Reputation Among Artists. His first solo show was at Brunel University in 1972, later ones including Riverside Studios in 1982 and Art Space Gallery, 1992. Farrell lived at Leigh-on-Sea, Essex, and was notable for his lively, figure-packed seaside scenes. Arts Council, Minories and Epping Forest Museum hold his work.

Christopher FARRELL fl. from 1990s– Painter who graduated with first-class honours in visual arts, painting, from De Montfort University, Leicester, going on to study for a postgraduate diploma in painting at the Royal Academy Schools. He twice won the RA's David Murray Scholarship for Landscape Painting. Exhibited at the Summer Exhibition from 1996, the year he won the British Institution Award for painting. Farrell's Seascape I was chosen for the 1997 Chevron UK Ltd calendar, he appeared in the oil company's ICA show that year and took part in group exhibitions at the Jelly Leg'd Chicken Gallery, Reading.

Julia FARRER 1950– Artist whose work included geometrical abstractions, and teacher, born and lived in London. She studied at Slade School of Fine Art, 1968–72, then taught there for two years. A Harkness Scholarship took her to America, 1974–6, and she worked in Paris, 1978–9. Also taught at Wimbledon and Byam Shaw Schools of Art. Group exhibitions included First Nuremberg Drawing Biennial, 1979; British Artists' Books, Atlantis Gallery, 1984; Harkness Artists 58–85 at Air Gallery, 1985; and in 1988 Composition/Structure at Galerie Lüpke, Frankfurt. Had a solo show at JPL Gallery, 1980; Air and Huddersfield City Art Galleries, both 1983; Curwen Art Gallery and Imprints, both 1986; and Francis Graham-Dixon Gallery, 1995. Ashmolean Museum in Oxford, University of Austin in Texas and University College, London, hold examples.

John FARRINGTON fl. from 1950s– Painter and teacher whose work has a gritty realism. He attended School of Art in Dudley, Worcestershire, influenced by the principal, Joe Jago, and Ivo Shaw, who encouraged Farrington to study illustration and printmaking. In 1957 did teacher training year at Leicester College of Art. Christopher Wood, Edward Bawden, John Minton, Jack Smith, Edward Middleditch, Alan Reynolds and Oskar Kokoschka were influences. Farrington painted the Black Country and also worked in series, such as bird men, flying men, Icarus, fairgrounds and circuses. He depicted the grimmer aspects of farming, having worked as a cowman. In 1984 Farrington produced the paintings for Granada Television's *The Ebony Tower*, based on John Fowles' novel. Solo shows included Goldmark Gallery, Uppingham, 1993.

Anne C FARROW 1928– Painter and draughtsman, born in Great Yarmouth, Norfolk. She was initially convent-educated in Reading, attended the University there, joined the town's Guild of Artists and showed elsewhere in the area, where she settled.

Stephen FARTHING 1950– Painter, printmaker and teacher, born in London. He attended St Martin's School of Art, 1968–73; Royal College of Art, 1973–6; was an Abbey Major Scholar at British School, Rome, 1976–7; lectured in painting at Canterbury College of Art, 1977–9; taught painting at the Royal College, 1980–5; was head of department of fine art, West Surrey College of Art & Design, Farnham, 1985–89; was artist-in-residence at the Hayward Gallery, 1989; then in 1990 was elected Ruskin Master at Ruskin School of Fine Art & Drawing and professorial fellow of St Edmund's Hall, Oxford. Farthing's early work showed some reference to Pop Art, drawing on diverse images. He was a figurative painter who responded in different ways to the environment in which he was placed, his work sometimes having a sinister edge. Took part in numerous group shows, including New Contemporaries, 1975; John Moores Liverpool Exhibition from 1976 at Walker Art Gallery, Liverpool, being several times a prize winner; New Art Centre, 1979; Edward Totah Gallery, from 1985; Heritage Exhibition at Cornerhouse Gallery, and tour, 1990; 20th Century Drawings, Ashmolean Museum, Oxford, 1994; and Collecting the Contemporary, University of Essex, 1995. Had a solo show at Royal College of Art, 1977, later ones including Tales of Topophilia, at Coram Gallery, 1994, resulting from a series of visits overseas as guest of the British Council; The Knowledge:

SE1/South, at The Cut Gallery, 1995 (the previous year it had held SE1/North); and Absolute Monarchy, Anne Berthoud, 1996. Ashmolean Museum, Arts Council, British Council, National Museum of Wales in Cardiff and many other public collections hold examples. Elected RA, 1998. Lived in Oxford.

Suzy FASHT 1964– Painter, born and lived in London, who began her studies with a foundation course at Sir John Cass School of Art, 1991–2; gained a fine art honours degree, painting, at Wimbledon School of Art, 1992–5; then did a postgraduate fine art diploma at the Royal Academy Schools, 1995–8. In 1997 she won the M&G RA Summer Exhibition prize for an artist under 35, the Creswick Prize for landscape and the RA Silver Medal. She was commissioned by Chevron UK Ltd to provide watercolours of Lewis and Harris, Outer Hebrides, for its 1998 calendar, and was featured in the oil company's show in 1997 at the ICA. Mixed shows included Cut Gallery, 1994; Wimbledon Library Gallery, 1995; Attendi and Ben Uri Galleries, both 1996; and Beatrice Royal Gallery, Eastleigh, 1997. Had a solo show in that year at The Cromwell Hospital.

Kaffe FASSETT 1937– Self-educated textile and knitwear designer, painter and writer, brought up in California, America, where his parents ran a restaurant. There he met people from Britain, became interested in its culture and moved there in the mid-1960s. After a time in Bath, he settled in London to paint seriously and became inspired by the street markets and the Victoria & Albert Museum (it was to give him the first major exhibition for a contemporary textile artist in 1988). Friendship with the designer Bill Gibb and a trip to Scotland inspired Kaffe (pronounced Kayf) to start serious knitting. He held successful exhibitions around the world and produced books such as *Glorious Knitting*, 1985; *Family Album*, 1989; and *Glorious Interiors*, 1995. In 1997 there was a sixtieth birthday show at The Catto Gallery of his colourful still life paintings.

George R FATHERS 1898–1968 Painter and teacher, born in Derby, son of sculptor Caleb Fathers. Studied at Ipswich School of Art, 1918–22, under George Rushton, then at the Royal College of Art, 1922–6, under William Rothenstein. Fathers made a career on the art side of publishing and in process engraving. He exhibited RA, NEAC and in the provinces and was notable for his landscapes. Fathers was a member of both Bradford and Ipswich Art Clubs. At various times he was a visiting teacher at Borough Polytechnic, Leeds and Hull Colleges of Art. Lived in Bradford.

James Alexander FAULDS 1949– Painter and teacher, born and lived in Glasgow. He attended Duncan of Jordanstone College of Art, Dundee, 1968–72. Exhibited at RSA, SSA, Group 81 in Glasgow of which he was a founder-member, RSW and in Germany. Was a Glasgow Art Club member.

Amanda FAULKNER 1953– Painter, draughtsman and printmaker. She studied printmaking at Ravensbourne College of Art, then worked for her master's degree at Chelsea School of Art, 1982–3. She spent two years in South America, part of a two-man team making anthropological films of the Canai Indians of Ecuador, and also worked there as an illustrator of short books on the mythology of an Amazonian group. Among Faulkner's group appearances were Young Contemporaries, ICA, 1981. In 1983 she had a solo show at Woodlands Art Gallery. Her work there and works held by Arts Council, bought from Angela Flowers, 1983, were much concerned with women. Plymouth Arts Centre included Faulkner in a three-artist exhibition in 1996. For a time she lived in Chatham, Kent.

Howard FAULKNER 1894–1979 Watercolourist, designer and teacher, born in Birmingham, where he was at school. Attended Dudley School of Art. 1910–14, then Royal College of Art, 1919–22, where his teachers included Ernest Tristram. He went on to hold a number of art teaching posts, in Cornwall, Wiltshire and finally in Eastbourne, Sussex, where he settled and where he was a member of the Society of Artists. Showed PS, NEAC and elsewhere. Victoria & Albert Museum and Towner Art Gallery, Eastbourne, hold his work.

Richard FAULKNER 1917–1988 Painter, born in Belfast, where he studied at the College of Art. Showed at RHA, RUA of which he was a member, and Belfast Museum and Art Gallery. Lived for many years in Ballycastle, County Antrim.

Trevor FAULKNER 1929– Sculptor and teacher, born Robert Trevor Faulkner in Sheffield, Yorkshire. He worked in most three-dimensional media, with a special interest in metal. Faulkner claimed to "have developed hand-wrought and welded sculpture to a uniquely high level, with a technique impossible to duplicate." He studied at Sheffield School of Art, 1946–50, and with Frank Dobson and John Skeaping at Royal College of Art, 1952–5, after holding a commission in the Army, 1950–2. In 1955 he was a vehicle designer, then went into teaching, becoming principal lecturer at Sheffield City Polytechnic. From 1988 sculpted and worked as a consultant full-time, being a fellow of RBS. He showed with Young Contemporaries, RA and Moorland Gallery. Had solo shows with John Hutton Gallery, Peterborough, 1968; Alwin Gallery, 1980; then became gallery artist with John Noott, Broadway. He carried out work for a number of firms, including British Steel, Expamet and BOC. Cartier, Bond Street, holds his work. In 1978 Faulkner published *Direct Metal Sculpture*. Lived in Bradway, Sheffield.

Emma FAULL 1956– Painter, draughtsman and writer, notable for her studies of birds. She was described by the naturalist and bird painter Sir Peter Scott as "an artist of great distinction. Her bird paintings are large, scientifically accurate and enormously decorative." Born in England, she graduated in geography from Oxford University, then in 1979 travelled to Athens as a draughtsman with the British School of Archaeology. In 1980 she gained a scholarship from the Greek government to write *The Imagery of the Bird in Ancient Greece*. Her book *Endangered Birds* was published in 1992. Among Faull's exhibiting venues were

Cadogan Gallery, Addison Ross Gallery, Spink & Son, National Museum of Greece, Wildlife Art Gallery in Lavenham and elsewhere. HM The Queen and HRH The Duke of Edinburgh hold her work. Lived in Jersey.

James FAURE WALKER 1948– Painter, born and based in London, who studied at St Martin's School of Art, 1966–70, and at Royal College of Art, 1970–2. Was editor of *Artscribe* magazine and occasionally taught. Group exhibitions included Stowells Trophy Exhibition, Chenil Gallery, 1969, in which he won a prize; Space Open Studios, 10 Martello Street, from 1973; Style in the Seventies, at Arnolfini Gallery, Bristol, and tour, 1979; John Moores Liverpool Exhibition, 1982; and Summer Show 2, Serpentine Gallery, 1983. Leicester Education Authority holds his work.

Shelley FAUSSET 1920– Sculptor in various materials, especially stone, and teacher, born in Newbury, Berkshire. In 1930s studied under Eric Gill. Fausset later started his own press, Linden Press, which published fine illustrated broadsheets on handmade paper. Fausset had attended Friends' School in Saffron Walden and during World War II did farm work and was with a Friends' Ambulance Unit in northern Europe. From 1946–8 was assistant to Henry Moore, then was at Chelsea School of Art, 1948–52, and Slade School of Fine Art, 1952–4. Was a part-time teacher in Cambridge area, 1948–54; was full-time, 1958–81, being head of foundation studies at Central School of Art & Design from 1963; then taught part-time, 1981–7, at Central School and Architectural Association. Fausset took part in many mixed shows from 1955, including Leicester, Obelisk and Brook Street Galleries, RA, LG and New Art Centre. From 1960–70 did not show, working to establish a basis in elemental forms. Had a solo show at Mercury Gallery in 1973. In 1979 organised the Amnesty sculpture exhibition in St Paul's Cathedral; in 1983 was commissioned by Harlow Art Trust; at LG Royal College of Art show in 1984 was nominated for Henry Moore prize; gained Nina Hosali Award for Sculpture, 1989; in same year was commissioned as sculptor for Magna Park development, Leicestershire, completing the 36-piece task in 1991. Elected member of RBS in 1979. WAC holds his work. Lived at Pirton, Hertfordshire.

Pat FAUST fl. from 1950s– Painter, theatrical designer and muralist, born in Lancashire, who studied at Manchester Regional College of Art and Birmingham's Crescent Theatre. Miss Faust was a member of Leeds Fine Art Club and the Arts Society in Scarborough, Yorkshire, not far from where she lived for many years at Filey. Showed with MAFA, RA, RCamA, Royal Glasgow Institute of the Fine Arts and at Paris Salon. Solo shows included University of Hull. Scarborough Corporation owns her work.

Randa FAWZI fl. from 1970s– Painter of strong, colourful images in acrylic which used the triangle as a building block, born in New York, America, educated in England and Switzerland. Seeking her cultural roots she studied at the College of Fine Art, Cairo; did a postgraduate course at Goldsmiths' College; then trained in tempera techniques with Theodor Zeller in Germany. Exhibitions included John Sears Gallery, 1976; Regent Gallery, 1982; Jablonski Gallery, 1987; and Duncan Campbell Contemporary Art, 1997, as well as widely abroad. The Campbell show was based on work done during a decade-long stay in Scotland; latterly, Fawzi lived in England and Germany.

Alan Hardy FAYERS 1926– Painter and teacher, born in Accrington, Lancashire. He studied at Accrington Regional College of Art from 1943–4, then after a wartime break from 1947–51, completing his studies during 1951–2 at Bretton Hall, Wakefield. Held a number of teaching positions, including Malton Grammar School. Exhibited widely in Lancashire, notably with the Lancashire Artists and West Riding Artists. Lived in Ilkley, Yorkshire.

Gordon FAZAKERLEY 1937– Gestural abstract painter, born in Widnes, near Liverpool, his family including a line of grocers. He studied at Liverpool College of Art from 1952, teachers including George Mayer-Marton and Arthur Ballard, then Central School of Arts and Crafts, 1956–7, where he studied painting and stained glass, teachers including William Turnbull. While doing his National Service in the Army Lawrence Alloway showed Fazakerley's work to Herbert Read, which led to a first solo exhibition at ICA, 1959. After the Army Fazakerley did a number of jobs. Having won a small sum of money he went over to Hardy Strid, in Sweden, later to Jørgen Nash and took part in building up the Bauhaus Situationist at Drakabygget, although he later rejected Situationist ideas. In 1962 he met his Danish wife-to-be and settled in Denmark. Exhibited widely in Europe.

Moira FEARBY 1969– Artist whose work included abstract pictures, born in Sydney, New South Wales, Australia, and studied at Curtin University of Technology, Western Australia. Group exhibitions included An Aspect, Art Rage Festival, Fremantle, 1991; Young Emerging Artists Exhibition, Crafts Council, Perth, 1992; Moira Fearby & Helore Roberts, Alternative Arts, 1994; and Royal Over-Seas League Open, 1995. The Bar Chambers Collection, Perth; Highlands Sculpture Gallery, California; and 4011/2 Workshop Collection hold examples.

Ian FEARN 1934– Artist and teacher, born in Newport-on-Tay, Fife. He studied at Duncan of Jordanstone College of Art in Dundee, 1950–6. A Travelling Scholarship took him to the continent and Cyprus in 1956–7. He taught art in Fife for three years from 1959 and in 1962 began to lecture at Duncan of Jordanstone. Among group shows in which Fearn participated were Dundee City Art Gallery; Scottish Arts Council; Compass Gallery; and Dundee Print Workshop. SAC holds his work. Lived in Dundee.

Charmian FEARNLEY 1932– Sculptor in all three-dimensional materials who studied at Gloucestershire College of

Art, 1955–7, and Royal College of Art, where she won the Feodora Gleichen Award. Showed at RA, AIA, RWA and Royal Glasgow Institute of the Fine Arts and in 1962 was included in 19 Young Sculptors at Hillfield Gardens, Gloucester, when she was living at Rodborough Manor, Stroud. Fearnley was commissioned to complete a number of portraits and sculpture for BBC Television and the *Daily Mirror* (design for 26 trophies).

Edmund Owen FEARNLEY-WHITTINGSTALL 1901–1972 Painter, draughtsman and teacher, born in Marlow, Buckinghamshire. He was educated at Haileybury College and studied art at Regent Street Polytechnic School of Art, 1922–5, his teachers including Harry Watson, and the Royal Academy Schools, 1925–8, under Charles Sims and George Clausen. For five years shortly after World War II he taught painting and drawing at Sir John Cass School of Arts and Crafts. Showed at RA, RP, NS and elsewhere. He shared his time between London and Ickford, Buckinghamshire.

James FEARON fl. from mid-1980s– Figurative artist who graduated in fine art from University of Ulster, Belfast, 1984. In 1989 he was invited to take up a residency at Banff Arts Centre in Canada and in 1992 he took part in a Belfast/Berlin Exchange, funded by Aer Lingus and Arts Council of Northern Ireland. Showed at Mall Galleries and in 1994 was included in Works on Paper and Beyond the Partitions, put on by Queen Street Studios, Belfast, with which Fearon was associated. Solo shows in Belfast included Kerlin Gallery, 1988, and Orpheus Building, 1990.

Judith FEASEY 1945– Painter, etcher and teacher, born and lived in London. She studied at Guildford School of Art, 1965–9; Royal Academy Schools, 1973–6; and Goldsmiths' College, 1976–7, for a teacher's certificate. While studying she gained the David Murray Landscape Scholarship, 1975–6, the Turner Gold Medal for landscape painting, 1976, and in the same year the Arthur Hacker Silver Medal for portrait painting, among other awards. Many exhibitions included RP, RA Summer Exhibitions, Greater London Council Spirit of London Competitions, Greenwich Printmakers, RWS and Bermondsey Artists' Group Exhibitions. Feasey taught at Brixton College.

Yan Kel FEATHER 1920– Painter of strong figurative pictures, born in Liverpool, son of the Austrian artist Wilhelm Feder. He began painting in 1939 and had a first solo show at Gibbs Gallery, Manchester in 1940. During World War II Feather studied alone at the National and Tate Galleries. He cited Velasquez, Fuseli, Ivon Hitchens, Roger Hilton, Francis Bacon and L S Lowry as influences. After a visit to Cornwall in 1947 Feather returned to Liverpool, for some years running a night club and an antique shop, eventually returning to settle in St Ives in 1977 to paint full-time. Meanwhile, he had continued to paint, solo shows including Archer Gallery, 1950, and Hanover Gallery, 1951; he won The Wolfson Memorial Prize in 1957; was a member of Liverpool Academy, 1960–70; having a solo show at Bluecoat Society, 1972. Became a member of Newlyn Society of Artists, 1980–90, and showed widely in the West Country/Cornwall. Had a retrospective at The New Millennium Gallery, St Ives, 1996.

William FEATHERSTON 1927– Sculptor and teacher, born in Toronto, Canada, who lived and worked in Britain 1957–71. The latter 10 years of this time was spent teaching at Cardiff College of Art, after which Featherston taught in California and worked as a freelance artist in Vancouver. Featherston showed internationally and while in Britain exhibited with the 56 Group and SEA, having solo exhibitions at Woodstock, New Vision and Grabowski Galleries in London. WAC, Glasgow University and many overseas public collections hold his work.

William FEAVER 1942– Writer on art, broadcaster, teacher and painter. He read history at Oxford as an Open Scholar, 1961–4; taught at Royal Grammar School, Newcastle upon Tyne, 1965–71; then was a James Knott Research Fellow at Newcastle University, 1971–3. Contributed to many national publications on art; was art critic of *Vogue* and *Artnews New York* from 1973; art critic of *Financial Times*, 1973–5; art adviser to *Sunday Times Magazine*, 1973–5; and art critic of *The Observer* from 1975. Was a member of Arts Council's art panel, 1974–9; chairman of Serpentine Gallery, 1975–6; and member of art advisory committee for National Museum of Wales from 1991. He taught at many art schools; was an external assessor at Royal College of Art and University of Ulster; and organised a number of exhibitions. Among his books were *Pitmen Painters*, 1988, and *Van Gogh*, 1990. Northumberland was a favourite painting subject. Among exhibitions shown in were A Personal View at Nigel Greenwood Gallery, 1988, and a three-critic show at Cadogan Contemporary, 1992. Lived in London.

Hermann FECHENBACH 1897–1986 Printmaker and painter, born in Wurttemberg, Germany, into a Jewish family. From an early age drawing became a passion and refuge for his shy nature, but his parents wanted a commercial career for him, so he became a window dresser in Dortmund. Conscripted in 1916, in 1917 Fechenbach was badly injured, having a leg amputated. In 1918 he began training at a Stuttgart handicraft school for invalids, graduating to studies of painting and restoration at the Stuttgart and Munich Academies, 1919–22, Max Liebermann being an influence. A year studying classical artists in Florence from 1923 was followed by travels through Pisa, Venice, Vienna and Amsterdam. Returned to Stuttgart in 1924, Fechenbach worked and showed in the contemporary style. In 1930 he married the photographer Greta Batze and they taught students in their studio until Nazi pressure led them to England in 1939. Fechenbach was interned in the Isle of Man, where he produced a powerful series of anti-Nazi lino-cuts. Settled in Oxford in 1941 Fechenbach began to exhibit to critical acclaim, then he had a first London show at the Anglo-Palestinian Club in 1944, the year he moved to the capital. In the mid-1940s he showed at Ben Uri Gallery, which holds examples in its collection. Although Movietone produced a news feature on Fechenbach about 1951, the artist increasingly retired from exposure, settling in Denham, Buckinghamshire, from 1962. In 1969 he published *Genesis*, illustrated with enlarged prints from many small wood engravings, and in 1972 the partly autobiographical *The Last Jews of Mergentheim*, appeared. A show at Blond Fine Art in 1985 revived interest in Fechenbach.

Daphne FEDARB 1912–1992 Painter, born in London, who married the artist Ernest Fedarb, and whose daughter Paulette was also a painter. She studied at Beckenham School of Art, 1928–30, Slade School of Fine Art, 1931–4, then at Westminster School of Art, 1936–9, where Mark Gertler taught her painting and Bernard Meninsky drawing. She married Ernest Fedarb in 1932 and in 1935 they had a joint show at Fine Art Society. Daphne Fedarb became a member of NS, 1940–55, of the RBA in 1948 and WIAC, 1955–68. Between 1961–73 she showed work at RA, NEAC and LG, in America and on the continent. Had a solo exhibition at Gallery 34, Shaftesbury, in 1968, another at Chilham Gallery, Kent, 1972, and shared a second show with Ernest at Sally Hunter & Patrick Seale Fine Art, 1986. Daphne Fedarb won first prize in the Laing Landscape Competition, 1981, and a second prize in 1983, and gained the RBA De Laszlo Medal in 1982. Lived in Nackington, Kent.

Ernest FEDARB 1905– Watercolourist and teacher, born in Canterbury, Kent, married to the artist Daphne Fedarb, their daughter Paulette also being a painter. In 1918 Fedarb attended first art classes at Sidney Cooper School of Art (later Canterbury School of Art), then was at Beckenham School of Art, where his teachers included Percy Jowett, Vivian Pitchforth and Henry Carr. In 1924 he became art master at Kent College, Canterbury, a year later at King's School Canterbury, in 1935 joining the staff of Westminster School of Art, then in 1939 becoming art master at Merchant Taylors' School. In 1940 his Hampstead home was destroyed by a bomb, which cost all his painting equipment and much of his early work. When the Hammersmith School of Art returned from evacuation in 1944 Fedarb joined its staff, then from 1947–65 was a Ministry of Education inspector for art. Fedarb had first showed with RBA in 1926. From the mid-1930s he showed regularly in London and provincial galleries and for many years from 1960 was honorary secretary to the United Kingdom Committee of the International Association of Art, delegate to International Art Congresses in New York, Amsterdam and London. In 1985 he was made president of NS. He had a joint show with his wife at Fine Art Society in 1932 and a second at Sally Hunter & Patrick Seale Fine Art in 1986. The Fedarbs were regular painters in France, Ernest's speciality being delicately coloured still lifes of flowers. Lived in Nackington, Kent.

Paulette FEDARB 1934– Artist in oil, watercolour, pen and ink and teacher, born in Canterbury, Kent, daughter of the artists Ernest and Daphne Fedarb. She studied at Chelsea School of Art, 1951–5, Bromley College of Art, 1955–6, then Hornsey College of Art, 1956–7, after which she taught full-time and continued to paint. Family commitments gave little time for painting after marriage in 1964, but from 1968–87 she taught part-time in adult evening classes, including Workers' Educational Association courses for Nottingham University, 1977–9. In 1981 returned to painting, in 1987 giving up all teaching to paint full-time. Her book *Pen and Ink Techniques* was published in 1992. Fedarb said that "my work is figurative, mainly of landscape and plant-derived forms. Textures of surface and pattern are important." Mixed shows included WIAC, NS and Midland Group. Had a solo show at Basement Gallery, Midland Group, 1964, also The Garden, Loughborough, Leicestershire, where she lived, 1985.

Bryant FEDDEN 1930– Glass engraver, letter-cutter and sculptor, born in Esher, Surrey, who was educated at Bryanston School and Cambridge University, where he read history and English, 1950–3. He taught in Britain and Pakistan, 1953–60, turning to letter-cutting and sculpture as a livelihood in 1960. Exhibited in London and the provinces, being included in 19 Young Sculptors at Hillfield Gardens, Gloucester, 1962. Victoria & Albert Museum, Cheltenham Art Gallery & Museums and several cathedrals hold examples. Was a member of the Gloucestershire Guild of Craftsmen and lived in the county at Littledean.

Mary FEDDEN 1915– Painter, notably of murals, and teacher, born in Bristol, married to the artist Julian Trevelyan. She studied at Slade School of Fine Art, as a scholar, 1932–6. She taught painting – the first woman tutor – at Royal College of Art, 1958–64, from 1965–70 at Yehudi Menuhin School. Was a member of LG, 1962-4, and participated in many other mixed shows. Solo shows included Redfern Gallery from 1953, Hamet Gallery from 1970, Heal's Mansard Gallery, Arnolfini Gallery in Bristol and elsewhere in the provinces. Major exhibition at RWA in 1988, by which time she had been its president for several years. Mural commissions included Festival of Britain in 1951, the P & O liner *Canberra* in 1961, one with Julian Trevelyan at Charing Cross Hospital in 1980, and one for Colindale Hospital, 1985. Fedden was noted for her domestic, modest-sized still lifes, rich in colour and with an immaculate pattern element. HM The Queen, Chantrey Bequest for Tate Gallery and Contemporary Art Society bought her work. Lived in London. Was elected RA, 1992.

Cheng-Wu FEI 1914– Painter and teacher, married to the artist Chien-Ying Chang. Studied at China's National Central University, 1930–4, teaching at the Fine Art College there, 1941–6, further studying at Slade School of Fine Art, 1947–50. Published *Brush Drawing in the Chinese Manner*. Showed at RA, NEAC, RWS and elsewhere, having solo exhibitions at Leicester Galleries. Public galleries in Derby and Sheffield hold his work and Tate Gallery archive holds his Self-Portrait, 1953. Lived for many years in north London.

Hans FEIBUSCH 1898–1998 Mural painter, draughtsman and printmaker, born in Frankfurt-am-Main, Germany. After education in Frankfurt, he studied art in Germany, France and Italy for six years from 1919, exhibiting widely on the continent. In England Feibusch showed at Lefevre Gallery extensively from the late 1930s, also RA, RHA, Cooling Galleries, Leicester and Redfern Galleries, but he was mainly known as a mural painter, a strong draughtsman and colourist with an interest in religious themes. Victoria & Albert Museum and Leeds City Art Gallery hold his work, but it is predominantly in churches and on public buildings, examples being Chichester Cathedral, which has his Baptism of Christ; a number of parish churches in London and the provinces; Dudley Town Hall, in Worcestershire; and the Civil Centre in Newport, Monmouthshire. Was author of the book *Mural Painting*, 1946. Feibusch continued working to an advanced age and lived in London, to which he had moved in the 1930s when the Nazis condemned and destroyed his work in Germany. Retrospective at Pallant House Gallery, Chichester, and tour, 1995–6.

Frederick FEIGL 1884–1965 Painter, born in Prague in what is now the Czech Republic, who was originally known as Friedrich Feigl. He studied at Prague's Academy of Arts, then at Antwerp Academy in 1904–5, and in Paris. Settled in Germany, where he had a show in Berlin at J B Neumann Graphisches Kabinett in 1912, returned to Czechoslovakia, after a year in Palestine, in 1933, but six years later left for England, where he died in London. In 1940 he had a show with Lucy Wertheim's Gallery, others including one at Ben Uri Art Society, which holds several examples, in 1964.

Maurice FEILD 1905–1988 Painter, printmaker, and teacher. He studied at Slade School of Fine Art in 1920s, then after three years went to teach art at The Downs, a Quaker preparatory school at Colwall, near Great Malvern, where he remained until after World War II. He inspired several dozen notable painters by his direct, open-air teaching methods, including Kenneth Rowntree, Lawrence Gowing, Patrick George and Francis Hoyland. After World War II Feild taught for a time at Camberwell School of Arts and Crafts and he was invited by William Coldstream to teach at the Slade. Feild was a keen painter of landscape who showed at Cooling's and Walker's Galleries and latterly at Austin/Desmond Fine Art. In 1970 Coldstream organised a Grosvenor Gallery retrospective. Lived in London.

June FEILER: *see* **June MILES**

Paul FEILER 1918– Painter, originally of representational, but later of abstract work; teacher. He was born in Frankfurt-am-Main, Germany, arriving in England in 1933. Feiler attended Slade School of Fine Art, 1936–39, then during World War II was interned and sent to Canada. Returning to England, he taught at combined colleges of Radley and Eastbourne until the end of the war, then at West of England College of Art from 1946, being head of painting, 1963–75. His first wife was the painter June Miles. He later married the artist Catharine Armitage. Feiler became associated with the St Ives painters after his first visit in 1949, the year before his work moved towards abstraction, and in 1953 he settled in Stanhope Forbes' old studio at Kerris, near Newlyn. Had first solo show at Redfern Gallery in that year, followed by several others. Additional individual exhibitions included Crawford Arts Centre, St Andrews, 1981, which toured; Austin/Desmond Fine Art, 1990; and retrospective Tate Gallery, St Ives, 1996. Carried out several architectural commissions for Yorke, Rosenberg & Mardell. Work held by Aberdeen Art Gallery and Museums, Arts Council, many British provincial and overseas galleries.

Florence Isabel FEIST 1878– Watercolourist and miniaturist, born in London. Studied at Crystal Palace School of Art under Matthew Webb and Herbert Bone. Exhibited RMS and in the provinces. Lived at Henfield, Sussex.

Trevor FELCEY 1945– Painter of figures and landscape and teacher, born in Ferring, Sussex. He studied at Camberwell School of Art, 1963–6, then Royal College of Art, 1966–9. He won Andrew Lloyd and David Murray Scholarships. Went on to teach part-time at Wimbledon and Byam Shaw Schools of Art. Felcey's work appeared in RA, at British Drawing at Hayward Gallery in 1982 and in the Norwich School of Art Gallery touring show A Reputation Among Artists, in 1986–7. Had solo shows at Brunel University in 1976 and Ian Birksted Gallery, 1982. Lived in London.

Carl FELKEL 1896–1980 Landscape, figure and portrait painter, studied in Vienna and Munich. In addition to exhibiting widely on the continent, Felkel showed in Britain at the Goupil Gallery and the RA. He travelled extensively in Europe and America. The Vienna Albertina as well as public galleries in Manchester and Derby hold his work. Lived in London.

Brian FELL 1952– Sculptor, born in Liverpool. He studied at Manchester Polytechnic, 1975–9, then spent a year as Fellow in Sculpture at Cheltenham College of Art. He went on to lecture part-time at Blackpool and Rochdale Colleges of Art. Fell was awarded a Major Award by North West Arts and in 1981 the Yorkshire Arts Association Artists in Industry Fellowship. He used pre-formed steel for his sculpture, and this was an opportunity for him to work in a steelworks, surrounded by his material at all its stages of formation. Although Fell's sculptures were abstract, they made allusions to human or machine counterparts, dynamic while being quite compact. Fell took part in a number of group shows, including New Contemporaries at ICA in 1978, the Manchester Academy exhibitions and he was included in the Welsh Sculpture Trust's 1983 Margam event, Sculpture in a Country Park.

Eleanor FELL fl. from c.1900–1946 Painter and printmaker, born in Thetford, Norfolk, and educated in Tewkesbury. She studied at Westminster School of Art, where she won several prizes, and in Paris. Her practice of landscape painting was facilitated by a keen interest in caravanning. She was elected an associated of RE in 1908, also exhibiting at RA, NEAC, SWA, Royal Glasgow Institute of the Fine Arts and at Walker Art Gallery in Liverpool. Lived in Worthing, Sussex.

Michael FELL 1939– Artist and teacher, notable as a printmaker, born in London. After a foundation course at St Martin's School of Art he attended the City & Guilds School of Art, also studying painting and printmaking under a travelling scholarship on the continent. Fell taught at City & Guilds School. He was a fellow of the Society of Designer Craftsmen and organised the show Vision and Innovation in St Paul's Cathedral, part of the Society's centenary celebrations. Group shows included Galleria Renata, Chicago, 1988; Allan Art Galleries, Singapore; Belanthi Gallery, New York; and in 1993 the Chappel Galleries, Chappel, show Continuing the Tradition. British Museum, Arts Council and Royal Academy hold his work. Had a solo exhibition at Grosvenor Gallery, 1996, richly coloured landscapes of the Armagnac region.

Phyllis FELL 1901– Painter and miniaturist, born in Plymouth, Devon. She was of a military family, was educated in Bexhill, Sussex, and studied at Blackheath School of Art, but returned to Plymouth to live. Signing her work P F, she showed at RA, RMS of which she was a member, and elsewhere.

Sheila FELL 1931–1979 Painter, draughtsman and teacher, born in Aspatria, Cumberland, her father a miner. Attended Carlisle School of Art, 1947–9, encouraged to take up textile design; then St Martin's School of Art, 1949–51, with R V Pitchforth and John Napper. Although she left Cumbria at 18 and thereafter only returned on visits, its landscape predominated in her work, her depictions of it being painterly but generally dour. Had a daughter by the Greek sculptor Takis Vassilakis in 1957, the year following winning a Boise Scholarship to Greece. First solo show at Beaux Arts Gallery in 1955, one of a series in the 1950s and 1960s. Joined teaching staff of Chelsea School of Art in 1958, the year after she won a prize in John Moores Liverpool Exhibition. Exhibited also at RA, being elected RA in 1974; Ashgate Gallery, Farnham; and New Grafton Gallery. There was a small memorial show at Abbot Hall Art Gallery, Kendal, in 1981, and a larger one at Salford Art Gallery, and touring, 1990–1. Tate Gallery and Arts Council hold her work. Lived in London.

Michael FELMINGHAM 1935– Painter, muralist, printmaker, watercolourist and teacher, born in Worcestershire. His first artistic work was published in 1956, and from then on he exhibited in leading galleries in Britain, accepting commissions from major companies including Allied Lyons and Texaco. Between 1968–89 he was lecturer in design history at Coventry College of Art (later Lanchester Polytechnic). He made prints for Royal Academy Graphics Collection at Curwen Studio, was a Saunders Waterford prizewinner in 1981, winning an award in the Laing Competition in 1992. In 1977 he had a retrospective at Herbert Art Gallery and Museum, Coventry. Later solo shows included Midlands Contemporary Art in 1990 and in 1992 Venice Observed at Waterman Fine Art Ltd. A series of watercolours of local views were commissioned by Herbert Art Gallery and are in its permanent collection. Felmingham's *The Illustrated Gift Book 1880–1930* was published in 1990.

Shirley FELTS fl. from 1950s– Artist in various media who was born in West Virginia, America. She graduated from University of Texas with fine art degree in 1958, then did post-graduate work in graphics at San Francisco Institute of Art. After working in the city as a graphic artist she travelled through Asia and the Far East, 1962–4, eventually settling in southeast London. Showed in mixed exhibitions in America and Europe and had two solo shows in Corpus Christi, Texas, in 1959. Others included The Old Fire Engine House, Ely, from 1970, Gallery 27 in Tonbridge from 1975, Washington Arts Centre in Cumbria, 1983, and Woodlands Art Gallery, 1984. In that show Felts showed landscapes bordering on abstraction. In 1979 Felts was profiled on BBC Anglia Television. Clare College in Cambridge and King's School in Ely hold her work.

Rachel FENNER 1939– Sculptor, painter and teacher, born in Scarborough, Yorkshire. She studied at Wimbledon School of Art, 1958–62, then sculpture at Royal College of Art, 1962–6. Won a Sainsbury Award Grant in 1966. From 1966 taught sculpture at Winchester and West Surrey Colleges of Art and Wimbledon School of Art and was a visitor to Royal Academy Schools, 1974–6. Arts Council Major Award in 1976 was among several won. Solo shows included House, 1976; Taranman and DLI Museum and Arts Centre, Durham, both 1978; Aspex Gallery, Portsmouth, and Abbot Hall Art Gallery, Kendal, both 1981; and Duncan Campbell Contemporary Art, 1993. Among many commissions were Saxon Column for Hamwick, Southampton, 1989–90, and Earthworks for Castle Park, Bristol, 1991. Arts Council holds her work.

Greta FENTON 1932– Landscape and figure painter, teacher, born London, who studied at Wimbledon College of Arts and Crafts and Central St Martin's College of Art & Design. She worked in the art department of Condé Nast Publications on *Vogue* and *House and Garden* and was an art director for two London advertising agencies. Taught art at Brighton College of Technology. She was an award winner of the International Federation of Art Societies at City of London Guildhall. Showed at Brighton Festival, Guild of Sussex Artists, Hove Museum & Art Gallery and The Grange, Rottingdean. Shared an exhibition at Duncan Campbell Contemporary Art, 1995. Lived in Hove, Sussex.

Max FENTON 1956– Oil on canvas and installations artist; exhibitions organiser, born in Dundee, Angus. He attended Duncan of Jordanstone College of Art there, 1975–9. Among shows participated in were Interference, Riverside Studios, 1986;

Riverside Open, 1987; Anomie, Patent House, and Brick Lane Open, both 1992; and Itself, Transmission Gallery, Glasgow, 1993. Lived in London.

Samuel FENTON 1923– Painter and draughtsman who was by profession a commercial traveller, born in London. He studied art at Regent Street Polytechnic School of Art under Harold Brownsword and at Harrow Technical School. Showed RA, NS, RBA and Sussex County Arts Club. Lived in Brighton, Sussex.

Simon FENTON 1970– Artist in various media, born in Hertfordshire. He studied at Harlow College, 1987–9, obtained an honours degree at Norfolk School of Art & Design, 1989–92, then attended Brighton University for his master's degree, 1992–4. Group exhibitions included Harlow Playhouse, 1989; Black Sheep Gallery, Brighton, 1992; then he in 1993 took part in In Piper's Footsteps at New Academy Gallery. Among Fenton's commissioned work was a mural for Harlow College Sports Hall; another for the College Library; and a set and costume design for *Mask of the Red Death* at Harlow Playhouse.

Cathy FENWICK 1955– Painter and draughtsman who graduated with first-class honours in sculpture from Gloucestershire College of Art & Design, 1977–80, gaining her master's degree from Royal Academy School, 1982–5. She won a Henry Moore Fellowship in 1982 and the Landseer Prize, 1983. Fenwick's work included an unpredictable sense of colour and uncompromising images. Group exhibitions included Ikon Gallery, Birmingham, 1980; Arts Council touring show of drawings, 1980–1; Birch and Conran from 1987; and BP Portrait Award at National Portrait Gallery, 1994. In 1980 had solo show at Jordan Gallery, with a sculpture show at Ikon. From 1992 showed solo at East West. Arts Council holds her work.

Cyril Lawrence FEREDAY: *see* **Joseph FEREDAY**

Joseph FEREDAY 1917– Artist in oil and acrylic, beyond 1976 mainly an etcher and engraver, teacher, born in Dudley, Worcestershire. He studied at Wolverhampton and Birmingham Colleges of Art and the Slade School of Fine Art, 1946–8. Was elected a fellow of RE in 1986. In 1976–8 Fereday conducted two summer schools in printmaking at Hope College, Holland, Michigan. He took part in several shows in Michigan, at Hope College and at Pravna Gallery, Saugatuck; also at RA; Redfern, Piccadilly and Leicester Galleries; and at galleries in the English provinces. Solo shows included Dudley Art Gallery, Wolverhampton Art Gallery, Boldrewood Gallery at Southampton University, Woodstock Gallery and abroad. Plymouth, Bilston and Portsmouth public galleries hold his work. His full name was Cyril Lawrence Joseph Fereday and until election to the RE he was known as Cyril Lawrence Fereday. Lived in Brading, Isle of Wight.

FERELYTH 1916– Sculptor in wood, stone, plastics, bronze and resin bronze, and lecturer, born in London, full name Ferelyth Alison Wills. Studied with John Skeaping at Central School of Arts and Crafts, 1935–9, then did war service, 1941–5. Was a member of Society of Designer-Craftsmen and Petersfield Arts and Crafts Society. She gave illustrated talks and demonstrations on sculpture, animal movement in art and choice of materials. With Bill Wills she wrote *Sculpture in Wood*, 1975. Retired in 1990. Showed at RA, Crafts Centre of Great Britain of which she was a member until 1970, Wildlife Society exhibitions and elsewhere. Lived in Emsworth, Hampshire. Pallant House, Chichester, holds Ferelyth's sculpture Fox.

Dan FERGUSON 1910– Painter and printmaker, brother of the artist Roy Ferguson, born and lived in Motherwell, Lanarkshire. He studied at Glasgow School of Art after Motherwell's Dalziel High School. Became ROI in 1958. Ferguson also showed at RSW, Royal Glasgow Institute of the Fine Arts, gained a silver medal at Paris Salon in 1961 and a gold medal at Italian Academy in 1980. Public galleries in Glasgow and Paisley hold his work.

John David FERGUSON 1932– Painter in all media, born in Buxton, Derbyshire, who studied at the West of England College of Art, Bristol, and at the Slade School of Fine Art under William Coldstream and William Townsend. Exhibited with LG; *Sunday Times* Exhibition, first prize, 1957; Leicester Galleries; Singer & Friedlander/*Sunday Times* Watercolour Competition, 1994; and in South Africa. Arts Council (he took part in its travelling exhibitions), Derbyshire Education Committee, University College London, University College of St Mark and St John in Plymouth, and Bristol City Art Gallery hold examples. Lived at Pendeen, Penzance, Cornwall.

Malcolm Alastair Percy FERGUSON 1913– Painter, born in Blackwater, Hampshire. He attended Portsmouth and Croydon Schools of Art, 1935–8, and Slade School of Fine Art, 1939 and 1948–51. Was a member of RWA, also exhibiting at RA, RP, Paris Salon and in the provinces and having solo shows in Britain and abroad. Completed a number of paintings in churches in South Africa and Zimbabwe. Plymouth City Museum and Art Gallery holds his work. Lived in North Petherton, Somerset.

Nancy FERGUSON fl. c.1950–1970 Painter and silversmith, born in Belfast, where she continued to live. Studied at Belfast College of Art and showed at RHA and RUA.

Neil FERGUSON 1955– Painter born in Dunfermline, Fife, who studied at Edinburgh College of Art, 1973–7, then Goldsmiths' College School of Art, 1978–9. His many group shows included Seven Young Artists at Talbot Rice Art Centre, Edinburgh, 1977; LG from 1980; Whitechapel Open, 1985; Celtic Vision, 1986–7, Madrid and European tour, where Ferguson shared the Scottish representation; and Tom Allen Centre retrospective and New Moon Group Show, Woodlands Art Gallery, both 1987. Had a solo show at Sir John Cass School of Art, 1985, others including Windsor and Jersey Arts Centres, 1987.

Roy FERGUSON 1907–1981 Watercolourist, caricaturist, teacher and writer, born in Motherwell, Lanarkshire, where he settled. He was the brother of the painter Dan Ferguson. Studied at Glasgow School of Art and taught at Dalziel High School for over 25 years. Showed at RA, NEAC, RBA, RSW of which he was a member, RSA, on the continent – including Paris Salon, where he gained a silver medal – and in Canada. Glasgow Museums and Art Galleries and the corporation in Newport, Wales, hold his work. Ferguson was a caricaturist for the *Scottish Sunday Express*, contributed nature notes to *The Scotsman* and wrote poetry, a collection being published by *The Motherwell Times* in 1972. His caricatures were signed eff.

John Duncan FERGUSSON 1874–1961 Painter, draughtsman, sculptor and writer, born in Leith, Midlothian. Although he matriculated in medicine at Edinburgh University, Fergusson opted to become an artist, inspired by Glasgow painters. From the mid-1890s Fergusson began to travel on the continent, studying at Atelier Colarossi, in Paris. From 1907 until World War II Fergusson settled in the French capital, began to paint in the Fauve manner, was befriended by the painter Dunoyer de Segonzac and began to sculpt in a Cubist style. In 1911 he was appointed visual arts editor of *Rhythm* magazine, a time when his own work was inspired by vital contemporary dance music. He had had a first one-man show at the Baillie Gallery in London in 1905, and as well as showing in France he had four works in the Post-Impressionist and Futurist Exhibition at the Doré Galleries in London in 1913. In that year he met his wife, the dancer Margaret Morris, who was in 1974 to publish *The Art of J D Fergusson*. After they settled in Scotland in 1939 Fergusson was a founder-member of the New Art Club a year later. From this emerged the New Scottish Group in 1942 and a revitalisation of the Scottish art scene. He was art editor of *Scottish Art and Letters* and author of *Modern Scottish Painting* in 1943, his first retrospective show opening in Glasgow in 1948. Fergusson died in Glasgow. Shortly after, a memorial exhibition was held, Arts Council, RSA and touring. Fergusson will always be remembered as a vibrant Colourist and incisive draughtsman whose luscious depiction of French countryside, life and character and whose sensuous nudes are unmistakable.

Maria-Theresa FERNANDES fl. from 1970s– Artist in various media, noted for textural reliefs, and teacher, born in Nairobi, Kenya. She studied at Sir John Cass College, 1967–8, then Manchester College of Art and Design, 1968–71 and 1975–6. Gained a number of awards, including British Council, 1981, and Embroiderers' Association of Canada, Toronto, 1982. Held many teaching posts, including Ulster Polytechnic; HM Styal Prison, Cheshire; School for the Mentally Handicapped, Northwich; Manchester Polytechnic; and Belfast School of Fashion and Textiles. Took part in many group shows in Britain and America, including Commonwealth Institute, 1972; RA, 1978; MAFA 1981; and Tennessee State Museum, 1982. Had a solo show at Covent Garden Gallery, 1973, others including Bretton Hall, Yorkshire, 1978, and Woodlands Art Gallery, 1983. Lived in America.

Roberto Gonzalez FERNANDEZ 1948– Artist, born in Monforte de Lemos, Spain, who studied fine arts at Escuela Superior de Bellas Artes de San Fernando, Madrid, 1969–74, living in Edinburgh from 1977. In 1983 he was included in Scottish Print Open Three, organised by Dundee Printmakers' Workshop.

Martin FERRABEE 1957– Sculptor, born in Nottinghamshire, who attended Jacob Kramer College of Art, Leeds, in 1980–1, then St Martin's School of Art, 1981–3. Took part in Kornarija Symposium of Sculpture, Yugoslavia, 1982, and in Have You Seen Sculpture from the Body? at Woodlands Art Gallery, 1983.

Brian FERRAN 1940– Painter, administrator and teacher, born in Londonderry, Northern Ireland. He studied at St Joseph's College of Education, 1959–62, then St Mary's College of Education, 1962–3, both in Belfast, then taught art, 1963–6. Obtained an honours degree in art history from Courtauld Institute and a postgraduate diploma in business administration from Queen's University, Belfast. In 1970–1 Ferran spent a year at Brera Academy of Fine Art, Milan, Italy. From 1966 he was on the staff of the Arts Council of Northern Ireland, becoming director. He served on many committees and boards and was a member of RUA. Posters, murals and films were among his special interests. The *Irish Times* critic Brian Fallon described his work as "often poetically suggestive rather than explicit". Took part in many group shows in Ireland and abroad, solo exhibitions including David Hendriks Gallery, Dublin; New and Tom Caldwell Galleries, Belfast; Queen's University, Belfast; University of Durham; and a series in America, including University of Wisconsin, Milwaukee, 1992. In 1989 Ferran completed three large stained glass windows for a church at St Patrick's College, Maghera, and in 1990 a mural at the entrance of St Columb's College, Londonderry. Arts Council of Northern Ireland, Ulster Museum, Gordon Lambert Collection, Queen's University and many other Irish collections hold examples. Lived in Belfast.

Moira FERRIER 1939– Watercolourist who was born in Glen Lethnot, Angus, into a farming family. After Brechin High School she attended Gray's School of Art, Aberdeen, her teachers including David Michie, Ian Fleming and Robert Henderson Blyth, gaining her diploma in 1961. Ferrier was a regular exhibitor at RSW, of which she became a member in 1979, and she had a series of solo exhibitions, including Ancrum Gallery, Ancrum, 1991. Lived for a time at Strathdon, Aberdeenshire.

David Dawson FERRY 1957– Painter, printmaker, artist in mixed media and teacher, born in Blackpool, Lancashire. Ferry did foundation studies in fine art at Blackpool College of Higher and Further Education, 1974–6; he gained a first-class honours degree at Camberwell School of Arts and Crafts, 1976–9, with a commendation in printmaking, Agathe Sorel being a notable teacher; then did postgraduate studies in printmaking at Slade School of Fine Art, 1979–81, notably under Mario Dubsky. In 1981–2 did extended studies certificate in printmaking at

Camberwell. Ferry held a number of teaching posts. In 1991 he was appointed senior lecturer in fine art at Kent Institute of Art & Design, Canterbury, also visiting lecturer at Fachhochschule Design, Düsseldorf. His *Painting Without A Brush* was published in 1991, the year he was commissioned by British Nuclear Electric to produce a picture of Sizewell B Power Station. Group exhibitions included 2nd National Exhibition of Modern British Prints, Grundy Art Gallery, Blackpool, 1981; RA Summer Exhibitions, from 1985; Five Contemporary Printmakers, National Museum of Wales, Cardiff, and tour, 1987; and Volcanic Landscapes, Boundary Gallery, 1991. Later solo shows included Drew Gallery, Canterbury, 1992. Public galleries in Blackpool and Maidstone hold his work. Lived in Canterbury, Kent.

Edori FERTIG 1957– Painter, printmaker and teacher, born in New York City. Studied at Massachusetts College of Art, Boston, 1980–2, after a design course at Rhode Island School of Design, Providence, 1975–9. Showed widely in group shows on America's east coast, then in London at Diorama Arts Centre, 1986, and Morley Printmakers at Morley Gallery, 1989. In 1990 she shared a three-man exhibition at Woodlands Art Gallery. Taught at American Community School in Surrey.

Elsie FEW 1909–1980 Painter in oil, artist in collage and teacher, brought up in Jamaica. She studied at the Slade School of Fine Art, in Paris and at the Bartlett School of Architecture. Married the artist Claude Rogers in 1937 and became associated with the Euston Road School, participating in the Euston Road exhibition at Wakefield City Art Gallery in 1948. She exhibited in London, having her last exhibition in 1980, which included sensitive landscapes from the Euston Road period and abstract collages, which she had begun to create in 1968 shortly before a stroke and partial paralysis. For a time she was a member of LG and RWA and was senior lecturer and head of the art department at Gipsy Hill Training College. Victoria & Albert Museum and Arts Council bought her work. Lived for some years at Somerton, Suffolk.

Michael FFOLKES 1925–1988 Cartoonist, illustrator and writer, born and lived in London, his real name was Brian Davis and he was the son of commercial artist Walter Davis. He chose his pseudonym out of *Burke's Peerage*, and it suited his quirky, flamboyant, irreverent personality. ffolkes was educated at Leigh Hall College, Essex, then St Martin's School of Art, 1943, under John Farleigh. After Royal Naval service he was at Chelsea School of Art, 1946–9, with Ceri Richards and Robert Medley. After graduation for seven years ffolkes freelanced; his work was to appear in *Punch, Playboy, Reader's Digest, Private Eye* and the *New Yorker*. He created characters in the *Daily Telegraph's* Peter Simple satirical column and illustrated over 50 books, including Claud Cockburn's *Aspects of English History* and the Folio Society edition of Anita Loos' *Gentlemen Prefer Blondes*. His own publications included *How to Draw Cartoons*, 1963; *ffolkes' Companion to the Pop Scene*, 1977; and his picture autobiography *ffundamental ffolkes*, 1985. Balliol College, Oxford, contains a set of commissioned caricatures of eminent dons by him.

Charles FFOULKES 1868–1947 Museum curator, writer and painter, born in London, who studied at Oxford University, and in Paris including lessons from Carolus Duran. He became an expert on armoury, for many years curator of armouries at the Tower of London, from 1917–33 curator at Imperial War Museum. He lectured at Oxford University and wrote a series of books, including *The Armourer and his Craft*. Showed at RA, RBA, Walker Art Gallery in Liverpool and at Paris Salon. Lived finally in Oxford.

Elizabeth FIDDAMAN 1911– Painter, mural artist, printmaker and teacher; her father was an architect, William Fiddaman. She was educated in Coulsdon, Surrey, and continued to live in that locality, latterly at Sanderstead. She studied at Croydon Art School, her teachers including Kenneth Holmes and Maurice Wheatley, 1930–4, then at the Royal College of Art, 1934–7. During the war she was engaged in camouflage work for Ministry of Home Security for five years, then taught part-time at Croydon and Sutton Schools of Art. Exhibited RA.

Nic FIDDIAN-GREEN 1963– Sculptor and draughtsman, notable for his studies of horses' heads, heads of Christ and romantic landscapes in charcoal. Fiddian-Green gained a foundation diploma at Chelsea College of Art; an honours degree in sculpture at Wimbledon College of Art; then a diploma in lost-wax bronze casting at Central St Martins College of Art. He was married to the potter Henrietta Hutley. For the first two years they lived on the island of Gozo, where he established the first foundry, and from the early 1990s he worked on commissions for the cathedral and Capuchin monastery there. Fiddian-Green showed widely in Malta and London, where in 1997 he participated in a mixed show at the Sladmore Gallery and had a solo exhibition at Air Gallery. Walton Contemporary Art, Melitensia Gallery near Valletta, Glyndebourne Opera House and the Hannah Peschar Gallery & Sculpture Garden at Ockley had work on permanent exhibition. Fiddian-Green cast pieces at his foundry in a barn adjoining his cottage at Bramley, Surrey; he worked mainly in bronze, also in lead, marble, copper and clay.

Constance Louise FIDLER 1904– Portrait painter and teacher. She was educated at Wigan Girls' High School, then attended Liverpool City School of Art, under George Marples, and Royal College of Art under William Rothenstein. After studying to teach she held a series of art teaching posts, latterly in the Southport and Liverpool area, where she was associated with the Boys' Clubs movement. Exhibited NEAC, RBA and had one-man shows in Birmingham and Liverpool, where the City Libraries bought her work. Member of Sandon Studios Society and Liverpool Academy. Lived at Freshfield, near Liverpool.

Dick FIELD 1912– Painter, draughtsman and teacher, born in Winson, Gloucestershire, who was married to the artist Molly

Field. Studied at Cheltenham School of Art under Gerald Gardiner and the Royal College of Art with Gilbert Spencer. Taught at Dewsbury School of Art, Yorkshire. He exhibited RA and widely in the provinces. Lived in Wakefield, Yorkshire.

Dorothie FIELD 1915–1994 Painter, draughtsman, art promoter and teacher, born in London, who sometimes signed work Dorothie Langridge. She studied at Highbury Hill School (with Nan Youngman), 1927–31; Chelsea School of Art (teachers including Henry Moore), 1931–2; Nottingham School of Art, 1933–6; and Birmingham University, for a social services diploma, 1941–2. Despite two marriages and having children, she continued to paint, in a variety of styles. Field was a full-time artists' consultant and freelance exhibitions organiser from 1964, founding the Gallery 359 and Field Galleries. Coal mining, war and peace, the origins of life and death and environmental problems were key themes, pursued over long periods. She was represented in group shows organised by the Arts Council, SEA, AIA and Pictures for Schools. Had numerous solo shows, starting with Wertheim Gallery, 1937, with a retrospective at Nottingham University, 1990; and exhibitions at Manor House, Ilkley, 1992; Usher Gallery, Lincoln, 1994; and Rufford Craft Centre, 1995. Bradford University and other public collections hold examples.

Molly FIELD 1912– Painter, born in Keighley, Yorkshire, who originally worked under the name of Molly Clapham. Married the artist and teacher Dick Field. After Keighley Girls' Grammar School attended Leeds College of Art, 1932–3, then Royal College of Art, 1934–8, with Ernest Tristram. Showed at RA, WIAC and the Art Gallery, Wakefield, the Yorkshire town where she lived.

Natalie FIELD 1898–1977 Painter and miniaturist, born in London, but resident in South Africa from the year of her birth. She studied at Slade School of Fine Art, 1916–22, where her teachers included Henry Tonks, Frederick Brown and Philip Wilson Steer, and at the Westminster School of Art under Walter Sickert. Returning to South Africa, she lived at Umkomaas, Natal, and took part in group exhibitions and had many solo shows. She was a member of the South African Society of Artists and just before World War II helped found the Transvaal Art Society, of which early on she was president. South African National Gallery, Cape Town, holds her work.

Patricia FIELD 1926– Mural painter and illustrator, born in Hull, Yorkshire. Attended Malvern College for Girls, then Manchester School of Art, 1945–8, under Ian Grant. Exhibited Festival of Britain and in Yorkshire, where she lived at Hessle.

Peter L FIELD 1920– Painter, modeller, printmaker and teacher, born in Winson, Gloucestershire. He studied at Cheltenham School of Art, 1937–9, with A Seaton-White, then at Goldsmiths' College School of Art, 1946–9, under Clive Gardiner. After teaching in Paignton and Swindon he went to Birmingham, retiring in 1982 as head of the art and design faculty at City of Birmingham Polytechnic. Showed at RA and in the provinces and Swindon Museum & Art Gallery holds his work. Lived in Bournville, Birmingham.

Stanley FIELD 1908– Watercolourist and teacher, born in London. He studied at St Martin's School of Art and at the Royal College of Art, his teachers including Gilbert Spencer and William Rothenstein. Taught for London County Council from 1934, until World War II followed by periods at Reimann and Bath Schools of Art. After wartime service lecturing on art to servicemen and as an official war artist Field taught at Gravesend School of Art and Borough Polytechnic before moving to South Africa until 1958 where he lectured at Witwatersrand Technical College and was from 1954–8 a senior lecturer and then head of the Port Elizabeth Technical College. While there he had several solo shows. In 1958 Field emigrated to Australia.

Steve FIELD 1954– Artist in acrylic, true fresco, mixed media and sculpture, including bronze, steel and concrete. He was born in Saltash, Cornwall, graduating from Sheffield University and gaining his master's degree in fine art from Wolverhampton Polytechnic, 1981–4, teachers including Malcolm Hughes, Knighton Hosking and Graham Cooper. Field was a joint research fellow at Wolverhampton Polytechnic, 1981–4; was a member of the West Midlands Public Art Collective, 1985–8; from 1989 being artist-in-residence for Dudley. In 1992 he won a Royal Society of Arts Art for Architecture Award. Was a member of LG, Midlands Group, Art and Architecture and the Birmingham Art Trust. Field's murals were influenced by the artists Edward Wadsworth and Percy Wyndham Lewis, his sculptural works by organic, especially spiral forms, as in his Thomas Attwood memorial at Halesowen. He shared a show at Wolverhampton Polytechnic, 1984, also being featured at Ikon Gallery, Birmingham. Lived in Leamington Spa, Warwickshire.

Brian FIELDING 1933–1987 Painter and teacher, born in Sheffield, Yorkshire, where he attended the local College of Art, 1950–4, then Royal College of Art, 1954–7. He gained an Abbey Minor Travelling Scholarship in 1958. Although he had a one-man show at Rowan Gallery in 1962 and again in 1964, Fielding's work was rather neglected by the dealers. His works, influenced by Zen Buddhism, were highly regarded by his peers. Fielding was an influential teacher at Ravensbourne College of Art and Design from 1962. He was included in the Survey of Abstract Painters at Camden Arts Centre in 1967 and had several more solo exhibitions before gaining a retrospective at Mappin Art Gallery, Sheffield, and tour, 1986. In 1995 David Holmes Contemporary Art, Peterborough, reviewed Fielding's output. Arts Council and Royal College of Art hold examples. Lived in London.

Jim FIELDING 1962– Painter, illustrator and maker of mixed-media constructions. He studied at Camberwell School of Arts and Crafts and Royal College of Art. Showed at Royal College as well as Cartoonists Gallery, Coliseum Theatre, Royal Festival Hall, Gardner Arts Centre in Brighton and England & Co, where his Locomotive was included in the 1991 show Art in Boxes.

Duggie FIELDS 1945– Painter in acrylic on canvas, born in Salisbury, Wiltshire, brought up in Tidworth, who attended Chelsea School of Art, 1964–8, after briefly studying architecture at Regent Street Polytechnic. Teachers included John Hoyland, Ian Stephenson, Lawrence Gowing, Allen Jones, Patrick Caulfield and Bernard Cohen. As a student his work moved from Minimal, Conceptual and Constructivist phases to a more hard-edge, post-Pop figuration. After he had visited America for the first time in 1968, Fields said that "my perspective on life was never the same." By the mid-1970s his work included many elements that were later defined as Post-Modernism. In 1983 in Tokyo, sponsored by the Shiseido Corporation, a gallery was created especially for his show, and the artist and his work were simultaneously featured in a television, billboard and subway advertising campaign throughout the country. In London Fields lived in a flat that reflected the 1950s–1960s, wore makeup and a Teddy-boy haircut. Mixed shows included Fashion and Surrealism, Victoria & Albert Museum, 1988. Had a solo show at Hamet Gallery, 1971, later ones including Albermarle Gallery, 1987, and Rempire Gallery, New York, 1990. Arts Council holds his work, which had wide international press and television documentary coverage.

Ray FIELDS 1930– Graphic designer and film-maker who from 1960 was employed as a full-time teacher of graphic design after studying in various schools. He went on to become senior lecturer in the faculty of art and design at Liverpool Polytechnic. Fields' films were shown at ICA in London and widely in the north of England. Showed from 1954 with Liverpool Academy, with RCamA of which he was president and elsewhere. Solo exhibitions included Rushworth Gallery, Liverpool.

Jini FIENNES 1938–1993 Writer and painter, born in Chichester, Sussex (her unmarried name was Jennifer Lash, which she used for some of her books), her father Brigadier Hal Lash, of the Indian Army. She married farmer-turned-photographer Mark Fiennes, with whom she led a nomadic life in England and Ireland, renovating many properties. They raised seven children, including a foster-child, among them the actors Ralph and Joseph Fiennes. An unhappy childhood spurred Jini to give out to people, her intense spirituality evident in her books and pictures. After an unhappy convent schooling she left home, worked as under-matron in a preparatory school and at 23 published her first novel, *The Burial*, to critical acclaim. Her last novel, *Blood Ties*, published posthumously in 1997, was featured in a BBC2 Television programme, in *The Works* series, that year. Jini, who worked in gouache, charcoal and oil, attended Farnham Art School, 1954, and Byam Shaw School of Art, 1982. Took part in a group show at Penwith Gallery, St Ives, in 1985; also had solo exhibitions in Suffolk at Halesworth and Westleton Chapel Galleries, both 1987, and in London's Holland Gallery, 1988. In 1986, she developed cancer and embarked on a tour, on foot and with a backpack, of the holy sites of France and Spain, the book *On Pilgrimage* appearing in 1991. Died in Odstock, Wiltshire.

Susannah FIENNES 1961– Painter and teacher who was born and continued to work in London. She attended Slade School of Fine Art, 1979–83, obtaining a first-class honours degree. In 1983 she won a Boise Travel Scholarship to Italy, the year following gaining an RA British Institution Fund Award. Taught art and history of art at Dulwich College part-time, 1985–7, then conducted a private drawing class. Fiennes showed in Christie's Pick of Graduate Art in 1983, two years later appearing in a watercolour show at Alpine Gallery. Other mixed exhibitions included Agnew Young Contemporaries in 1988 and John Player Portrait Award in 1989. In 1990 Fiennes shared a show at Cadogan Contemporary, having a solo exhibition there in 1992.

FIENNES-FOSTER 1918– Painter whose married name was Barbara Otley. She studied painting in early 1960s with Kristin Berge, a student of Oskar Kokoschka. Became a member of Free Painters and Sculptors in 1964, also belonging to Chichester and Downland Art Societies and other Sussex groups. Showed also at Chenil and Mall Galleries. Lived in Rustington, Sussex.

Denis FILDES 1889–1974 Painter, born in London, son of the Victorian narrative artist Sir Luke Fildes. He was educated at Stone House, Broadstairs, and at HMS *Britannia* and became a professional sailor, attaining the rank of commander. He was badly injured and burned when the HMS *Natal* was blown up at Cromarty in 1915. Invalided out, he turned to painting for a living. Early on he produced flower pictures and seascapes but, failing to find a market, concentrated on portraits. Fildes considered his finest examples were HM Queen Elizabeth II at the Royal Air Force Club; Field Marshal Lord Montgomery, at St Paul's School, Barnes; and Sir Edmund Hilary, conqueror of Everest. The large double portrait of The Queen and Duke of Edinburgh at the Royal Naval College, Greenwich, is stiffer and less successful; Fildes was an uneven painter. He was a member of the United Services Club and exhibited at Walker's Galleries, RA, Walker Art Gallery in Liverpool and elsewhere. For many years he was curator of the Antrobus family museum at Amesbury, Wiltshire, but health in 1973 forced him to give up residency there, and he had a bungalow built nearby. The Imperial War Museum has Fildes' archive.

Michael FINCH 1957– Artist and teacher, born in London, who graduated in fine art from Ravensbourne College of Art, 1976–80, obtaining his master's at Royal College of Art, 1982–6. Won the Wiggins Teape Award, 1976; Milner Kite Award, 1982; Burston and Unilever Awards and Unilever Purchase Prize, all 1985. As well as a number of visiting lectureships, including Ravensbourne, Wimbledon and St Albans Schools of Art and Kent Institute of Art & Design, Finch taught at Richmond College, London, 1988–91, and from 1994 at Parsons School of Art, in Paris. Showed at Northern Young Contemporaries,

Manchester, 1978; Peter de Francia and Artists Who Studied Under Him, Camden Arts Centre, 1987; *Economist* Building Gallery, 1993; Credo, 1994, at Purdy Hicks (he had been co-ordinator and curator for its predecessor, Pomeroy Purdy Gallery, 1989–92); and Towards An Abstraction, David Holmes Contemporary Art, Peterborough, 1995–6. Had a solo show at City Museum, Peterborough, 1983, later ones including Purdy Hicks, 1994, and David Holmes, 1995. Lived in Senlis, France.

Patricia FINCH 1921– Sculptor of figurative works in clay, teacher, born and lived in London. She was the daughter of a doctor and studied medicine, including two years' anatomy at King's College and West London Hospital, her ambition "to be a plastic surgeon or a sculptor". Studied art at the Hampstead Institute, 1953–7, and taught dancing part-time. Finch received her first portrait commission in 1958. Was elected to SWA and Contemporary Portrait Society and became a fellow of RBS in 1990. She was a demonstrator to the Tate Gallery Summer Course in Sculpture, 1983, and tutor to the Hulton Studio for the Visually Handicapped, 1986–90. Showed at RA and had exhibitions in London and widely abroad. Royal Academy of Dancing holds her commemorative medal of Dame Margot Fonteyn, and Bank of England Museum, Royal Academy of Music and Poetry Society also hold her work.

Richard Henry Carew FINCH 1908–1985 Landscape painter in oil. Born in London, Finch studied at the Bartlett School of Architecture, 1928–33, and for a time practised as an architect. He then studied art at the Grosvenor School of Modern Art. Exhibited at the RHA and elsewhere in Dublin, where he lived, signing his work C F or Carew Finch. Finch wrote a number of pamphlets on aspects of architecture and is remembered as "a quiet, unassuming gentleman of a very charitable disposition".

William Robert FINCH 1905– Self-taught artist in various media, journalist and teacher, born in Lowestoft, Suffolk. He trained to teach at College of St Mark and St John. Showed at RA, East End Academy and widely in the provinces. He was head of the art department at Beal Grammar School, Ilford, and Chigwell School. Lived at Weybread, Diss, Norfolk.

Peter Gillanders FINDLAY 1917– Painter and teacher, born in Madras, India. He was educated in Suva, Fiji, then in Yorkshire. He studied art at Leeds College of Art, 1935–9, under Douglas Sharpus Andrews, then at the Slade School of Fine Art, with Randolph Schwabe, from 1939–40, then after a war interval from 1944–5. Taught for a period at Accrington School of Art, Lancashire. He did some technical book illustration and showed widely in Yorkshire. Lived in Accrington.

Sheila FINDLAY fl. from early 1950s– Painter, designer and illustrator, born in Auchlishie, Kirriemuir, Angus. She was noted for her richly coloured, decorative domestic scenes and still lifes. Studied at Edinburgh College of Art, specialising in stained glass and mural painting and working in the department of design, 1945–51, her teachers included John Maxwell and Leonard Rosoman. In 1949 gained a postgraduate studentship, followed by a year's senior travelling scholarship, spent in France, Italy and Sweden. In 1950s worked in London as a freelance designer and illustrator, working for major publishing houses while showing at RA, LG and elsewhere, being elected RWS in 1968. Had solo show at Catto Gallery, 1990. Was married to the artist Alfred Hackney and lived in Cobham, Kent, with another studio in Edinburgh.

FINE ARTZ 1964– A group formed in this year by Slade School of Fine Art students Terry Atkinson, John Bowstead, Roger Jeffs and Bernard Jennings which collaborated on a work called Action Chair. In 1966 Fine Artz presented a projection and sound show entitled *Miss Misty and the Tri-Cool Data* at Birmingham Polytechnic. Jeffs later wrote that although Fine Artz was shortlived it "served its purpose (thorn in the side of the Slade and we had fun!). Apart from the Chair, etc, we wrote essays which appeared in *Ark*, journal of the Royal College of Art, circa 1964–5, the nearest we got to a Fine Artz manifesto."

Stephen FINER 1949– Painter, mainly of the human head on a small scale, born in London. Mixed shows included Small Work, Nicola Jacobs Gallery, 1981–2; Berkeley Square Gallery, from 1988; and Basle Art Fair, 1991. Had a series of solo exhibitions at Four Vine Lane from 1981, later ones including Bernard Jacobson Gallery from 1992. Arts Council, British Council and Contemporary Art Society hold examples.

Peter FINK 1948– Sculptor and teacher, born in London, graduated as an engineer from University of Prague, Czechoslovakia, 1969; studied sculpture at St Martin's, 1969–72; taught there for three years; then graduated in philosophy at University College, 1978. He was sculpture consultant to Newport, Gwent, where he was based, 1988, gaining a research fellowship at Cardiff Art School, 1989. Fink said that he was "interested in working with architects and others who are committed to the built environment," which stemmed from "my belief that artists should work openly in the public domain." Commissions included Shiva, Punjabi University, India, 1980; Castle Cross, Banbury, Oxfordshire, 1981; Ark, Jerusalem, Israel, 1986; and Riverfront Promenade, Newport, 1989. Fink latterly worked extensively with the performance artist Anne Bean. In 1992 they realised Light Year, then the largest temporary public art project in the United Kingdom, which took Canary Wharf as a canvas for a huge light sculpture, seen over 40 kilometres by millions of Londoners.

Ian Hamilton FINLAY 1925– Writer and artist in many media, born in Nassau, Bahamas, of Scottish parents; brought to Scotland as a child. After a short period at Glasgow School of Art Finlay saw military service in Germany, then did a variety of agricultural jobs including shepherding in the Orkneys. Began to write fiction, drama and poetry, some single-word poems presaging concrete poetry. In 1961 Finlay with Jessie McGuffie started the Wild

Hawthorn Press to publish contemporary work, for most of the 1960s publishing the magazine *Poor. Old. Tired. Horse.* In 1966 Finlay and his wife Sue moved to an isolated farmhouse near Dunsyre, Lanarkshire, transformed the garden into a sculpture park as an antidote to the modern movement and sought to promote an art which pays homage to a lean, classical tradition. Aptly he changed the name of his home to Little Sparta. Finlay had many solo shows, including Scottish National Gallery of Modern Art in 1972 and Serpentine Gallery, 1977. He was shortlisted for the Turner Prize in 1985. The Scottish National Gallery of Modern Art holds a body of work by him.

Donald FINLEY 1902–1981 Artist and writer, born in Australia at Victoria, studying art in Melbourne at its National Gallery. He moved to England and became films and exhibitions officer at Australia House, 1945–67. An industrious man, Finley helped found the Australian Artists' Association in London. He had an interest in amateur theatricals, and in the Association's first exhibition at the RWS Conduit Street gallery in 1953 showed two stage designs. In 1963 his book *Modern Australian Painting* was published, an excellent, well-illustrated account. The National Library of Australia, Canberra, holds Finley's archive, and typescript of *John Peter Russell: the lost impressionist 1858–1930*, compiled between 1963 and 1981.

Jean FINN: *see* **Jean DREW**

Michael FINN 1921– Painter, administrator and teacher, who grew up near Brooklands, Surrey. His father was an architect. After serving in World War II in the Royal Air Force, training as a pilot in Canada, Finn taught in Somerset, then became head of Falmouth School of Art, 1958–72, and Bath Academy of Art, Corsham, 1972–82, starting to paint full time in the latter year. Earthy, luminous colours were a characteristic of his work, which was shown in Artists from Cornwall, RWA, 1992. He also took part in mixed shows at Newlyn Orion Gallery, Penzance, at the Wolf at the Door gallery there and at Penwith Society of Arts. Solo shows were held at Festival Gallery, Bath, 1978; Newlyn Orion, 1989; and Wolf at the Door, 1990. Lived in St Just, Cornwall.

Paul FINNEGAN fl. from early 1980s– Figurative artist whose work had a strong decorative element, he graduated from University of Ulster in Belfast, Northern Ireland, 1981, where he remained. Showed widely through Ireland and had work chosen for shows in England, France and Scotland. Took part in RUA Exhibition, Ulster Museum, and in Oireachtas, both 1986; in 1994 participated in Works on Paper and Beyond the Partitions, put on by Queen Street Studios, Belfast, with which he was associated. Solo shows included several in Belfast: Crescent Arts Centre, 1983, Fenderesky Gallery, 1984, and Art Advice Gallery, 1989, and his Head to Head was shown at Zakks Barbers Shop, 1990.

Rose FINN-KELCEY 1945– Sculptor, performance and installations artist, teacher, born Northampton. She studied at the School of Art there, at Ravensbourne College of Art and Chelsea School of Art for postgraduate work. Finn-Kelcey usually created for a particular space, such as Steam Installation, 1992, for Chisenhale Gallery, likened to a huge steam press. Group exhibitions included the Arts Council's The British Art Show, 1984; Shocks to the System, Royal Festival Hall and tour, 1991; and Young British Artists II, Saatchi Gallery, 1993, which, like Arts Council, holds her work. Solo shows included Bureau de Change at Matt's Gallery, 1988, and Camden Arts Centre, 1997. Teaching included Byam Shaw School of Art. Lived in London.

Richard FINNY 1909–1987 Painter, draughtsman and teacher, born in London. After Dulwich College Finny attended Byam Shaw School of Drawing and Painting. He won the Rome Scholarship for mural painting in 1929, the youngest winner at the time and the first from Byam Shaw. His two years in Rome, however, were overcast by the depression which was to plague the rest of his life. In 1934 he began teaching art in schools, including Oundle. During World War II he was in Royal Engineers' camouflage section, seeing service in India and Burma. Unable to paint on demobilisation, he joined the Old Bleach Linen Company in Northern Ireland as assistant to director of design and publicity, but after two years returned to London to paint, then teaching, which he did until 1966. Alcoholics Anonymous helped him overcome a drink problem, but depression continued. Retrospective at Byam Shaw in 1988, proceeds to Medical Research Council. Finny's output was small, as he was so self-critical, but he did show at RA and Nineteen Thirties Society. Lived in Camberley, Surrey.

Joy FINZI 1907–1991 Portrait draughtsman of great sensitivity, musician and writer, born as Joyce Black in London where she studied at Central School of Arts and Crafts with John Skeaping. She married the composer Gerald Finzi in 1933 and they built their home at Ashmansworth, near Newbury in Berkshire, just before World War II, where she died. When early in the war Finzi founded the Newbury String Players she was administrator and played in the violins. She was careful in nurturing Finzi's work even after his terminal illness was diagnosed in 1951 and after his death founded the Finzi Trust. Many of her drawings were of musicians and writers, including Ralph Vaughan Williams, Howard Ferguson, Helen Thomas and David Jones. Her *Portrait Drawings* were published in 1987 and several volumes of poetry. Work held by National Portrait Gallery.

Sylvia FINZI 1948– Painter, draughtsman, printmaker and teacher who studied at Slade School of Fine Art. In 1983 she was visiting artist at Westfield College and she taught as visiting lecturer at Heatherley's School of Fine Art and at Munich's Volkshochschule. She was commissioned to make a mural for a new wing of Lewisham Hospital in the late 1980s. Finzi took part in many group exhibitions, including 1982 Hayward Annual and Woodlands Art Gallery in 1988. Also had a series of shows in England and abroad. Victoria & Albert Museum and Bibliothèque Nationale, Paris, hold examples. Lived in London.

Margaret FIRTH 1898–1991 Painter, especially of still life which latterly moved towards abstraction, born in Saltaire, Yorkshire. She rarely left the West Riding. Firth was born into prosperous circumstances, her father a Bradford textile manufacturer, surrounded by paintings and art books. Studied at Bradford School of Art from 1914–21, although her mother's health prevented regular attendance. Teachers were Fred Stead and Harry Butler. Eventually set up her own studio and additionally studied with Bertram Priestman and Arthur Reginald Smith, although for 20 years Firth found little time to paint, showing occasionally at RA, LG and in Yorkshire. After the death of her parents and brother, in 1948 Firth settled in Ilkley and began painting seriously again, attending Maurice de Sausmarez's art history lectures, travelling extensively in Italy and establishing a keen local following for her work. This included textile collage flowerpieces and Tulips, sold to Wakefield Art Gallery in 1950. Had three solo shows at Hawksworth Gallery, Ilkley, between 1984–7, then in 1988 Bradford Art Galleries and Museums, which holds her work, organised a touring exhibition.

FISH fl. from c.1913–1964 Painter, illustrator and textile designer, born in Bristol, Anne Harriet Fish in 1918 married Walter Sefton. She studied under Charles Orchardson, John Hassall, at the London School of Art and in Paris. She exhibited at RA and Fine Art Society, which gave her a solo show. Did extensive work for *Punch, Tatler, Vanity Fair, Vogue* and *Cosmopolitan* and illustrated a number of books including her own *Awful Weekends and Guests*, 1938. Her work was stylish and Beardsleyesque with a satirical tinge. Tall and and rather grand in manner, she lived in St Ives, Cornwall, where she collected some good local paintings and was a member of the Penwith Society of Arts and St Ives Society of Artists.

Alfred Hugh FISHER 1867–1945 Painter, printmaker and writer, born in London. After working in a city office he gained a scholarship to Royal College of Art, then studied in Paris. For three years he travelled the British Empire as artist attached to the Visual Instruction Committee of the Colonial Office, writing books including *Through India and Burmah with Pen and Brush.* He was a prolific exhibitor at RE of which he was an associate, RA, NEAC and elsewhere. Lived in Princes Risborough, Buckinghamshire.

Chris FISHER 1950– Artist and teacher, born in London. He studied at Winchester School of Art, 1967; St Martin's School of Art, 1967–70; and Royal College of Art, 1970–3. He won an Abbey Major Travelling Scholarship, the John Minton Award and the Anstruther Award, 1973. From 1974–94 Fisher taught at Royal College of Art, from 1993 being fine art course director at Goldsmiths' College. Fisher was keen that an artist should not repeat himself, his own work employing mixed media and an interest in unconventional tapestry. Royal College holds his Mixed Media Composition, 1974, the Arts Council his tapestry Blindfolded, 1977. From 1989 Fisher translated and illustrated a series of European poets for Cahill Press. Fisher showed regularly in London. He was a prizewinner in the 1976 John Moores Liverpool Exhibition, also showing in the 1995–6 show. Lived at Weston, Newark, Nottinghamshire.

Don Mulready FISHER 1923– Painter and designer for films and the theatre, born in London. Studied art in Hampstead, 1940–1, then at St Martin's School of Art with Ruskin Spear, 1943–6. Was a member of the Society of Industrial Artists and Free Painters and Sculptors, also exhibiting at NS, ROI, LG and Piccadilly Gallery. Solo exhibitions included Loggia Gallery, Barbican Centre and Salon des Nations in Paris. Lived in Paris, France.

Gareth FISHER 1951– Versatile sculptor and teacher, born in Keswick, Cumberland, who from early on was influenced by the American sculptor Donald Judd. Fisher's mature work reflected contemporary issues, was built in plaster and used found material and could take some time to complete. He attended Edinburgh College of Art, 1969–76. Went on to live in Dundee, Angus, where he lectured in sculpture at Duncan of Jordanstone College of Art. From 1978 Fisher showed at New 57 Gallery, of which he was chairman, 1979–80, and Talbot Rice Gallery, both in Edinburgh; Artists' Space Gallery in New York; Art Gallery of Nova Scotia, Halifax; Hatton Gallery in Newcastle upon Tyne; Camden Arts Centre; and Third Eye Centre, Glasgow. His 1984 solo show at Mercer Union, Toronto, included Sprouting Head, featured in the Arts Council's tour The British Art Show, 1984. A 1986 solo exhibition at The Fruitmarket Gallery, Edinburgh, toured Scotland. From 1984–6, Fisher was chairman of the Blackness Public Arts Programme, Dundee, where the Museum and Art Gallery holds his work.

Joel FISHER 1947– Sculptor, draughtsman and teacher, born in Salem, Ohio, America, who lived in Britain periodically from 1970, mainly between 1976–83. He graduated from Ken on College, 1969, Magna Cum Laude, Phi Beta Kappa. Gained a number of awards, prizes and fellowships, including Thomas J Watson Traveling Fellowship, 1969; Gast der Berliner Kunstlerprogram des DAAD, 1973–4, 1994; Pollock-Krasner Foundation, 1993; and John Simon Guggenheim Fellowship, 1993–4. Had extensive teaching experience, including Goldsmiths' College, 1978–9, and Bath Academy of Art, 1980–2, mainly in America. Fisher said that his lineage was "directly from the teaching of Josef Albers"; he later spent some time with Albers and at Goldsmiths' "once taught a variation on Albers' excellent colour course". Participated in numerous group shows internationally, British ones including the Arts Council's British Art Show with tour, 1984; Vessel, at Serpentine Gallery, 1987; and Todd Gallery, from 1994. Showed solo extensively with Nigel Greenwood Gallery until 1989; later solo shows included Lawrence Markey Gallery, New York, 1994, and Galerie Rochefort, Montreal, 1995. Fisher's work was included in several dozen international public collections, Arts Council, Leeds City Art Gallery and Victoria & Albert Museum having examples.

Myrta FISHER 1917– Painter, initially in oil, later in acrylic, and teacher, born in Wimbledon, Surrey. She attended Huddersfield Art School, 1935–7, then Slade School of Fine Art, 1937–40, being a Henriques Scholar. She had periods of full-time and part-time teaching after World War II and had a year in Greece, 1954–5, a student of the British School at Athens. Showed with AIA and Eastbourne Group, of which she was a member, for many years, solo exhibitions including AIA, Ansdell Gallery, The Grange in Rottingdean, and two private shows in Newhaven. Harold Mockford, Braque and other early twentieth-century painters were influences. Towner Art Gallery, Eastbourne, holds her work. Lived in Newhaven, Sussex.

Norman FISHER 1958– Painter of landscapes, usually small and in oil on board, which had a luminous quality. He was born in Darlington, County Durham, and studied at Humberside College of Higher Education. Concentrated on painting the Humberside estuary and Wolds region. Fisher set up and administered the Unit 50 Studios on the River Hull in 1983 and was a leading member of Hull Artists' Group. There was a major show of his landscapes at Scarborough Art Gallery in 1990 and in 1991 he was included in Images of the Yorkshire Landscape, organised by Sheeran Lock at Leeds Civic Hall.

Roger FISHER 1919–1993 Marine painter, born in Dover, Kent. After Clifton College he was 37 years in the Royal Navy, which gave his pictures great authenticity. Was elected to RSMA in 1983, also showing with Wapping Group of Artists and Armed Forces' Art Society. Royal Naval Lifeboat Institution and Yarrow Shipbuilders hold examples. Lived in Snape, Suffolk.

Sandra FISHER 1947–1994 Figurative painter and printmaker, born in New York, her mother an artist. In 1968 graduated from California Institute of the Arts. After working for a year at Gemini print studio in Los Angeles moved to London, becoming studio assistant to R B Kitaj, whom she married in 1983. Her fluent, colourful work became popular through the 1989 picture Boating at Regent's Park, commissioned by London Underground and used for the poster *Days on the water*. Had solo show at Lefevre Gallery, 1993. Fisher's pictures were commonly modest in scale. She admired the work of Delacroix, Monet and Matisse, from the Israeli painter Avigdor Arikha absorbed the rule that a picture should be finished in one session and chose to paint in front of the subject. The male nude was a favourite. She collaborated several times with the poet Thomas Meyer on fine, limited edition books. Died in London where British Museum holds her work.

Stefani Melton FISHER 1894–1963 Painter, notably of portraits, printmaker and teacher, son of the artist Melton Fisher, born and lived in London. He was educated at Westminster School, studying then at Byam Shaw and Vicat Cole School of Art and Royal Academy Schools. Became art master at Dulwich College. Was a member of ROI and PS, also showing at RA, RI and elsewhere.

Tyson FISHER fl. from c.1920–1962 Painter of murals and stage sets as well as pictures, born in Waterloo, Lancashire. Studied art in the south of France. Lectured on art and was a member of the Liver Sketching Club. Exhibited RCamA, Walker Art Gallery, Liverpool and RWS. Lived at Crosby, Lancashire.

Gerald FISHON fl. from mid-1950s– Painter whose work showed the influence of such artists as Beckmann, Nolde and Soutine, born in London. In 1955 he studied at St Martin's School of Art with James Dring. Subsequently he attended City & Guilds of London Art School, Sir John Cass College and Morley College, teachers including Maggi Hambling, John Bowles and David Graham. Fishon worked as a commercial artist, helping to prepare major exhibitions on the history of the Crusades and French Revolution. In 1976 he showed a self-portrait in the Whitechapel Art Gallery exhibition of East End artists. Fishon also participated in two two-man shows at Primrose Hill Gallery, 1989–93.

Clifford FISHWICK 1923–1997 Painter and teacher, born near Accrington, Lancashire, married to the painter Patricia Fishwick. He attended Liverpool School of Art, 1940–2, then after Naval service returned to complete his studies, 1946–7, including art teacher's diploma. Fishwick combined a busy painting career with teaching at Exeter College of Art, becoming principal, 1958–84. He was a member of the Newlyn Society from 1952–83 and exhibited at the Penwith Society in 1950s–1960s and had a solo show in 1983. Fishwick showed solo at St George's Gallery, in 1957, others including Dartington Hall, 1959; Exeter University, 1961; Plymouth City Art Gallery, 1966; Essex University, 1976; Spacex Gallery, Exeter, 1982; and works of the 1950s at Austin/Desmond Fine Art, 1989, with other works, 1990. Also showed with Bruton Street Gallery. Over the years Fishwick's style changed as certain influences took effect, the Neo-Romantics, the Cornish painters and the second School of Paris painters such as Nicolas de Staël. His later work was darker, more loosely put together and more abstract. Public galleries in Exeter, Plymouth and Bradford hold examples. Lived in Topsham, Devon.

Patricia FISHWICK 1929– Artist in oil, pen and watercolour and teacher, born in Liverpool, where she attended the College of Art, 1947–9, then Exeter College of Art, 1949–52, where she was taught by Clifford Fishwick, whom she married. She taught history of art at Exeter College, 1972–84. Patricia Fishwick was a member of Newlyn Society of Artists, 1952–83. also a member of the Kenn Group of Artists and Exeter Society of Artists. She took part in RWA shows, John Moores Liverpool Exhibition and Westward Television Open Art. Solo shows included Exeter University. Plymouth City Art Gallery holds her work. Lived in Topsham, Devon.

James FITTON 1899–1982 Painter, advertising and poster designer, draughtsman and printmaker, born in Oldham,

Lancashire, where he was educated at a board school. Was apprenticed as a calico designer in Manchester where for some years he attended the School of Art part-time, getting to know the painter L S Lowry. In London attended evening classes under A S Hartrick at Central School of Arts and Crafts from 1925, in 1928 marrying the artist Margaret Cook and settling in Dulwich, where he continued to live. The 1930s were very active for Fitton, who exhibited at such venues as RA and NEAC; was appointed art director for the C Vernon and Sons advertising agency; had his first one-man show, in 1933, at Arthur Tooth and Sons; and began to teach in that year at Central School. Fitton's father had been a trade union leader, active in the Labour movement, attitudes which left their mark on Fitton. He became active in AIA, drew cartoons for the *Daily Worker* and *Left Review* and became known for his brilliantly witty and adroit caricatures of political leaders such as Mosley, Churchill and Mussolini. Other work over the years included posters for London Transport; illustrations for *Lilliput* and other magazines; wartime work for the Ministry of Food, Ministry of Information and Ministry of Education; and a number of notable film posters. Elected RA in 1954. In his pictures Fitton was a shrewd and perceptive observer of London low life, of its cafés, markets and characters.

Judith FITTON: *see* **Judith DAVIS**

Margaret FITTON 1902–1988 Painter, illustrator and sculptor, born in London, married to the artist James Fitton. Her mother had studied at Royal Academy Schools and her uncle had founded the Cook School of Art. She studied at Central School of Arts and Crafts under Bernard Meninsky and met her husband in a lithography class there in the 1920s. Renoiresque in appearance, she modelled for a number of artists including Barnett Freedman. First job was illustrating books for Warne & Company and also illustrated for *Lilliput* and *The Listener*. Sculpted a head of her husband, who frequently used her as a model. Exhibited RA, AIA, LG, Arts Council and Storran Gallery. In 1937 the critic Anthony Blunt wrote that Margaret Fitton's Ironing and Airing was the one submission worth noting in an RA spring exhibition. She was an AIA and Arts Club member and lived in London.

Peggy FITZGERALD 1923– Painter and draughtsman, born in Hastings, Sussex, where she attended the High School, then the School of Art, 1944–6. Free Painters and Sculptors member who also showed with UA, at Loggia Gallery and widely in the provinces, especially Home Counties. Farnham Art Society member who lived in Aldershot, Hampshire.

Pete FITZGERALD fl. from late 1960s– Painter, sculptor, draughtsman, printmaker and teacher, born in Woolwich, southeast London. He studied at Central and Camberwell Schools of Art. Went on to teach in London social priority schools, in 1978–9 painting on secondment at Goldsmiths' College School of Art. Had a solo show at Woodlands Art Gallery, 1981. The works on show, heads and figures, were, according to Fitzgerald, "not arrived at by abstracting down from a human starting point, but rather in a building up of shapes until a human presence is suggested".

Elizabeth FITZHERBERT: *see* **Elizabeth MACFADGEN**

David FITZJOHN 1963– Painter, born in Wembley, Middlesex. He studied at High Wycombe College of Higher Education, 1981–2, then Canterbury College of Art, 1983–6. Took part in group exhibitions in Aylesbury and Canterbury in mid-1980s and participated in John Moores Liverpool Exhibition, 1987. Lived in Aylesbury, Buckinghamshire.

Joyce FITZWILLIAMS 1912–1969 Prolific artist whose life in parts remains a mystery. Her father was in the Army, so her childhood was unsettled, and she was educated by a governess. She attended Royal Academy Schools, 1933–8, winning the Landseer Prize and a Silver Medal for a painting of two figures from life. After teaching art for a time Fitzwilliams went into a convent, but near to taking her final vows she became ill and left. She then taught at Llandysul County School, for girls, near Newcastle Emlyn, Cardiganshire, location of her family home Cilgwyn. Joyce was to live in its dower house for a time with her mother. Eventually she went to America and taught art at the Annie Wright Seminary, Tacoma, Washington state, run by a cousin. She was there, 1960–8, was known as Miss Joyce and in 1967 gained her master's degree from the University of Puget Sound. Fitzwilliams' output moved from straight figuration towards Surrealism, and in America she took up screenprinting. Learning that she had cancer, Fitzwilliams went to the Philippines hoping for a faith healing cure. This did not happen and she died in Honolulu, Hawaii. An endowment fund was donated to the Seminary (now the Annie Wright School) in her memory. National Library of Wales, Aberystwyth, holds her picture Hafod.

Barry FLANAGAN 1941– Sculptor in a variety of materials, draughtsman, film and furniture maker and teacher, born in Prestatyn, Flintshire. He studied at St Martin's School of Art, 1964–6, receiving the ICA Dover Street Materials Award in 1965. In 1972 he won the Gulbenkian Foundation Grant to work with the dance company Strider, three years later gaining an Arts Council Award, which allowed him to undertake kiln work. Flanagan's teaching included St Martin's School of Art, 1967–71, with further sessions at Newport School of Art and Omaha Municipal University, Nebraska. After a first solo show at Rowan Gallery in 1966, Flanagan showed there many times, and also exhibited solo at Hester van Royen Gallery and Waddington Galleries as well as widely overseas. In 1978 had one-man show at Serpentine Gallery. Among his commissions were Peter Stuyvesant Sculpture Project, Cambridge, 1972, and City Square, Ghent, 1980. Exhibition at Yorkshire Sculpture Park, 1992. Arts Council holds a wide selection of Flanagan's work. He was elected RA in 1991.

Terence P FLANAGAN 1929– Painter, draughtsman and teacher, born in Enniskillen, County Fermanagh, Northern

Ireland. He studied at Belfast College of Art, 1949–53, in 1954 starting to teach at St Mary's College of Education. Flanagan was a notable landscape watercolourist. He participated in many mixed exhibitions, including Four Ulster Painters, at Arnolfini Gallery, Bristol, 1965; Two Irish Painters, with Colin Middleton, Herbert Art Gallery and Museum, Coventry, 1968; The Gordon Lambert Collection, at Hugh Lane Municipal Gallery of Modern Art, Dublin, 1972; Armstrong Gallery, New York, and Smithsonian Institution, Washington, and tour, 1986; and Contemporary Artists from Ireland, Austin/Desmond Fine Art, 1990. Flanagan had a solo show at CEMA, Belfast, 1961, later exhibitions including an Arts Council of Northern Ireland 1967–77 retrospective in 1977 and Places, 1960–85, Fermanagh County Museum, 1986. Lived in Belfast.

Dennis FLANDERS 1915–1994 Artist in watercolour, carbon pencil and black and brown ink, born in Walthamstow, Essex. He attended Merchant Taylors' School, worked for periods in chartered accountancy, interior decorating, then printing, then became a freelance artist. "The beauty of Britain and its architecture and landscape" were leading themes in Flanders' work; as well as the early English watercolourists he cited Piranesi, Meryon, Muirhead Bone, F L Griggs and Henry Rushbury as influences. Flanders' art education was evening classes at Regent Street Polytechnic School of Art. By the early 1990s he had completed over 3,000 drawings, mainly of Britain, also of Venice and Rome. Flanders was a member of RWS and RBA and an honorary freeman of the Painter-Stainers' Company. Flanders' books, such as *Dennis Flanders' Britannia*, 1984, and *Dennis Flanders' London*, 1986, were celebrated with shows at Fine Art Society and Guildhall Library. The Library and Guildhall Art Gallery hold an extensive collection of his work. Lived in London.

Moyna FLANNIGAN 1963– Painter, born in Scotland, who gained an honours degree at Edinburgh College of Art, 1985, then her master's degree from Yale University School of Art in America, 1987. She had obtained a Yale University Scholarship in 1985, other awards including Scottish Arts Council Artists Award in 1994. Flannigan was artist-in-residence at Aberdeen Art Gallery, 1990. Showed widely in Scotland and had a solo exhibition at 369 Gallery Edinburgh, 1990, later ones including William Jackson Gallery, 1994. Aberdeen Art Gallery, City Art Centre in Edinburgh and Scottish Arts Council hold examples.

Joseph Otto FLATTER 1894–1988 Versatile artist, born in Vienna, Austria, where he enrolled at the Academy of Fine Arts in 1914. Had to serve as an infantry officer for over three years before he could resume his Academy studies, supported by work as an itinerant portrait painter. In 1934 Flatter married the concert pianist Hilda Loewe, settling with her in England in 1935. Shortly before World War II Flatter produced a series of cartoons warning of the Nazi threat. Nevertheless, when war began he was interned on the Isle of Man, although he was soon released to do extensive propaganda work for the Ministry of Information and the exiled Belgian government. Flatter was commissioned as an Army captain and made an official war artist at the Nuremberg Trials. After the war Flatter found it hard to resume his career as a portrait painter, in which Rembrandt was always his main inspiration. Instead he bought and restored Old Masters. His own final series of pictures was in tempera, many influenced by the death of his wife in 1976; much of the work was satirical, drawing on literature and personal experience, and it also emphasised essential human values. Imperial War Museum holds a large collection of Flatter's war illustrations. Some were included in Art in Exile in Great Britain 1933–45, Camden Arts Centre, 1986. Lived and worked in London.

Zena FLAX 1930– Artist and designer, born and lived in London. She attended Chelsea School of Art, 1949–53, focusing on illustration, then became interested in etching, which she pursued at Central School of Arts and Crafts, 1953–5. Worked as a graphic designer. Showed etchings at Whitechapel Art Gallery, RA Diploma Gallery, elsewhere in London and in the provinces. Was a member of Printers Inc. Workshop. Exhibited with it at Ben Uri Art Society, which holds her work, in 1990, and in 1991 had a solo exhibition at Sternberg Centre for Judaism.

Bernard FLEETWOOD-WALKER 1893–1965 Painter and draughtsman mainly of figures and portraits. Born in Birmingham, where he lived most of his life. Initially was a modeller and metalworker, then studied painting at Birmingham School of Arts and Crafts, followed by London and Paris. Wounded and gassed during World War I service in Artists' Rifles, but continued to paint and draw. After war taught for about 10 years at King Edward's Grammar School, Aston, in 1929 leaving to teach at Birmingham School of Arts and Crafts. Exhibited extensively at RA from 1925 – he was elected RA 1956 – and otherwise showed mainly at RWS, NEAC, RBSA and RP. Also had a one-man show at Ruskin Gallery, Birmingham, 1925, and won a silver medal at Paris Salon. Moved to London after retirement from teaching in Birmingham in 1951 to give more time to students at Royal Academy Schools, where he had been appointed assistant keeper. RA, Leeds City Art Gallery, other provincial and foreign galleries hold his work. Memorial exhibition in Birmingham, 1965; retrospective John Lindsay Fine Art, Solihull/Belgrave Gallery, 1981.

Arthur FLEISCHMANN 1896–1990 Sculptor in various materials, notably a pioneer in the use of carved Perspex and water, and teacher, born in Bratislava, Slovakia, then part of Hungary. He studied medicine and art at the Prague Academy, winning a scholarship to the Master School of Sculpture in Vienna, also studying in France and Italy. Fleischmann taught art in Vienna, 1935–7, and also held classes for the Czech Army. After periods in South Africa, Bali and Australia, where he lived from 1939, he settled in London from 1948, there exhibiting at RA, NS and RBA. Public galleries in Bratislava, Sydney and Blackburn, Lancashire, hold his work, which is contained in buildings and churches in Britain and abroad. Fleischmann was a devoted Roman Catholic. He was the only artist to sculpt four Popes from life. Among his many other portrait sitters were the industrialist Lord Robens, the singer Kathleen Ferrier and the actor Trevor Howard. Fleischmann's work was originally figurative, becoming more abstract from the 1960s. He was a fellow of the RBS. Died in Tenerife, Spain.

George FLEMING 1941– Painter and lecturer, his figurative work related to public concerns and social issues. After some years in the Royal Navy and British Merchant Navy, Fleming graduated from University of Ulster, Belfast, 1987–91, completing a postgraduate diploma in applied arts in 1992. Ran workshops at Ulster Folk and Transport Museum, Harmony Hill Arts Centre and the Slane Arts and Crafts Gallery. Also lectured to such bodies as the Northern Ireland Patchwork Guild and Quilt Art Workshops as well as his old university. Took part in many group shows in Belfast, including Arts Council Gallery, 1988, and in 1994 Works on Paper and Beyond the Partitions, organised by Queen Street Studios, Belfast, with which he was associated. His solo show Echoes toured Northern Ireland, 1993–4.

Ian FLEMING 1906–1994 Painter, printmaker and teacher, born in Glasgow where he attended the School of Art, 1924–9. Chika Macnab and Charles Murray were his initial printmaking teachers, then he worked with Robert Sargent Austin and Malcolm Osborne for several months of a travelling scholarship at Royal College of Art, additional studies being made in France and Spain. Fleming taught at Glasgow School of Art, 1931–48, at Hospitalfield from 1948–54, then he was principal of Gray's School of Art, Aberdeen, 1954–72, where he developed printmaking. Fleming was elected RSA in 1956. Having been a permanent member of the council of the Society of Artist Printmakers, he was in 1974 appointed chairman of Peacock Printmakers. Fleming scored an early success in 1931 when he engraved Gethsemane, bought by the French government and also in the collection of Scottish National Gallery of Modern Art. His later work was notable for experiment both in printmaking and in watercolour. Glasgow School of Art holds Fleming's fine picture The Painters Robert Colquhoun and Robert MacBryde, who were his pupils. Died in Aberdeen.

Jean FLEMING 1937– Painter and draughtsman, born in Glasgow. She studied at the School of Art there, 1953–8, and at Patrick Allan-Fraser School of Art, Hospitalfield, Arbroath. Showed Royal Glasgow Institute of the Fine Arts, RSW of which she was a member and elsewhere. Paisley Art Gallery and the Nuffield Foundation hold her work. Lived in Crail, Fife.

John B FLEMING 1912–1991 Watercolourist, draughtsman and academic registrar at Glasgow School of Art. He was born in Dumbarton, Dunbartonshire, and studied at the Academy there. Went to Glasgow School of Art, 1930–5, his teachers including W O Hutchison, then in 1943 to Art Students' League of New York. Fleming was made a member of Society of Industrial Artists and Designers, 1956, RSW, 1960, and an honorary member of Royal Glasgow Institute of the Fine Arts, 1985. Also showed at RSA and in private galleries. Public galleries in Glasgow and Paisley hold examples. Lived finally in Crail, Fife.

Ken FLEMING 1944– Printmaker, designer and illustrator who showed in range of exhibitions. He was born in Middlesbrough, Yorkshire, and grew up in London. Leaving school in 1963 he rejected formal art training, instead working in an advertising agency. While serving in several agencies he began to make prints, initially lithographs, in 1968 moving back to Yorkshire where he ran his own design business from 1972–6. After a return to London and becoming a freelance illustrator Fleming gradually concentrated on print making. Meticulously detailed areas of printing in otherwise simple images often produced an ethereal, dreamlike result.

John FLEMONS 1934– Abstract painter and teacher who studied at Chelsea School of Art, 1951–3, then 1955–8. Then went on to University of London Institute of Education, 1958–9, and Birmingham School of Art Education, 1970–1. Flemons won the Morland Lewis Travelling Scholarship (second prize), 1956, (first prize), 1958. He taught at Morley College as head of art and design. Was included in Woodlands Art Gallery 1982 show Artists in Adult Education. Other exhibitions included John Moores Liverpool Exhibition, 1961, Gallery 273 at Queen Mary College, 1975, and Brunel University, 1977. Had a solo exhibition at Morley Gallery in 1993. Lived in London.

Alan FLETCHER 1936–1958 Painter, draughtsman and printmaker, born in Glasgow. He studied at the School of Art there, 1952–5, and was awarded a travelling scholarship to Italy in 1957, where he died in an accident the following year. Consequently Fletcher's exhibiting career was short, although his work was shown in London and New York in the late-1950s and he was included in Painters in Parallel at Edinburgh College of Art in 1978. Scottish Arts Council, Dundee and Aberdeen Art Galleries and Glasgow University hold his work.

Doreen FLETCHER 1952– Painter and draughtsman, notable for scenes of London's East End, where she settled. She studied at Newcastle School of Art and Croydon College of Art. Tower Hamlets Central Library held an exhibition of her work in 1985.

Eileen FLETCHER 1948– Self-taught painter who began painting in 1970, influenced by medieval, Oriental and primitive art and who admired artists such as Rousseau, Chagall and Richard Dadd, whose apparently naive images found a reflection in her own acrylics and gouaches on board. Born in Liverpool, after a period in London she moved to the Isle of Man in the mid-1970s, settling in Laxey and bringing up a family. Group shows included RA Summer Exhibition from 1972; 7 Dials Gallery, 1981; and Summer Show 2 at Serpentine Gallery, 1983.

Frank Morley FLETCHER 1866–1949 Noted colour woodblock printer, painter and teacher, born in Whiston, Lancashire. He studied at Atelier Cormon, in Paris. Fletcher was head of the art department at University College, Reading, 1898–1906, from 1908 being director of Edinburgh College of Art. In 1923 he left Edinburgh for California, three years later being naturalised an American citizen. Fletcher showed paintings and prints at RA, ROI, RSA, Paris Salon and especially at IS, of whose council he was a member, 1903–9. He was responsible for promoting the colour woodcut in the Japanese style and in 1916 published *Wood-block Printing*. Scottish National Gallery of Modern Art holds his colour woodcut Girl Reading.

Geoffrey Scowcroft FLETCHER 1923– Painter and draughtsman, born in Bolton, Lancashire, where he attended the School of Art, later the Slade School of Fine Art under Randolph Schwabe. Exhibited RA, RBA, NEAC and in the north of England. Drew for newspapers and books for children. Lived at Ashtead, Surrey.

Hanslip FLETCHER 1874–1955 Watercolour painter and printmaker with a special interest in London's architecture. Born in London, he was educated at Merchant Taylors' School. Became a member of the Art Workers' Guild. Fletcher's work featured regularly in London's serious daily and Sunday newspapers, and he exhibited RA, Goupil Gallery, NEAC, RI and in other London galleries. The Guildhall Library and Southampton Art Gallery hold his pictures. Lived in London.

Henry FLETCHER 1901– Painter and teacher, born in Bradford, Yorkshire, where he studied and taught at College of Art. His teachers there, 1915–18, included Fred Stead. Was then at St Martin's School of Art under John Allen, 1921–2, after spending 1920 in Paris at Atelier Colarossi. Showed at RA, Goupil Salon RBA and widely in the provinces. Lived for some years in Earley, Berkshire.

Michael FLETCHER 1944– Painter and teacher, born in Gloucestershire, who studied at Chelsea School of Art, 1962–6. He went on to teach at Putney School of Art and was included in 1982 Woodlands Art Gallery show Artists in Adult Education. Other exhibitions included Young Contemporaries and Arts Council's Young Contemporaries Travelling Exhibition, 1965, LG from 1973 and South London Art Gallery, 1980.

Rosamund M B FLETCHER 1914–1993 Sculptor and letterer, daughter of the artist William Blandford Fletcher, born in Dorking, Surrey. She studied at Ruskin School of Drawing in Oxford and Slade School of Fine Art. Was a member of the Guild of Lettering Craftsmen and a fellow of RBS. Fletcher's work was heavily biased towards religious subjects. She showed at RA and RBA, but much of her output is in churches, schools and religious houses in Britain and abroad, as in St Mary's Convent, Ascot; St Mary's Roman Catholic Primary School in Wimbledon; and Richmond Roman Catholic Secondary School. In 1948 Fletcher gained both the RBS's Feodora Gleichen Memorial Fund award and Olympic Bronze Medal. She lived in Oxford, later at St Francis Convent, Braintree, Essex.

James FLETCHER-WATSON 1913– Watercolourist, mainly of landscape, and teacher, born in Coulsdon, Surrey. He was a student at Royal Academy School of Architecture, gaining a silver medal for design, 1936, but as a watercolourist was essentially self-taught, between 1930–4, concentrating on Cotman and the Norwich School. During World War II he was in the Army as a major, working in camouflage and runway construction in India and Burma. He taught at summer schools and wrote several instructional books. Fletcher-Watson was elected RI in 1952, RBA in 1957. He showed at RA and at Paris Salon in mixed exhibitions and had solo shows in own gallery at Windrush, Oxfordshire, where he lived, in Australia and America and at Chris Beetles Ltd, 1989. Fletcher-Watson said that he was "a *strong* believer that we should maintain the traditional thread from the early watercolourists right through to the future and let the modern ideas come and go as they please on the way."

Alex FLETT 1914– Painter, born in Findochty, Banffshire. Studied at Gray's School of Art, Aberdeen, under D M Sutherland. Showed RA, RSA, SSA, Leicester and Redfern Galleries and NEAC. Lived for many years in London.

Charles W FLIESS 1899–1956 Painter and draughtsman, born in Germany, who moved to England in 1939. In 1954–5 he was included in an exhibition called Four Palettes at Derby Museum and Art Gallery. The year after he died Derby was given three pictures by Fliess' brother, Dr Robert Fleiss of New York, through the artist Clifford Hall. Ben Uri Art Society also holds examples.

Claude FLIGHT 1881–1955 Painter, printmaker, interior designer and sculptor. Born in London, Flight trained as an engineer, then became a librarian, in 1906 beginning seven years of beekeeping and farming in Sussex. Began to study at Heatherley's School of Fine Art, resuming his studies in 1918 after Army service, with a special interest in lino-cutting, of which he was to become a master. In the 1920s began to exhibit on the continent, in 1925 having lino-cuts bought by the Contemporary Art Society and the British Museum. Two years later formed interior decorating business with the artist Edith Lawrence, experimenting with lino-cutting, textiles, picture panels and wall hangings. In 1931 had one-man show at Redfern Gallery, in 1935 a joint exhibition with Edith Lawrence at the French Gallery. They were responsible for the First Exhibition of British Lino-Cuts at the Redfern in 1929, an annual event until 1937. During World War II many of Flight's paintings and colour blocks were destroyed by enemy action. For a time Flight was editor of *Arts and Crafts Quarterly*, and he also published a number of books, including *Lino-Cuts*. S C Kaines-Smith called Flight "the only true futurist that this country has produced". His vital, dynamic prints were early recognised as masterpieces in a neglected medium. In later life lived with Edith Lawrence at Donhead St Andrew, Wiltshire. Memorial show at Parkin Gallery, 1973.

E M FLINT 1883–1968 Painter and teacher, born in Loughborough, Leicestershire. She attended Birmingham School of Art. From 1914 she was principal of Lichfield School of Art and from 1915–49 art director of Queen Mary's Grammar School for Boys, Walsall, where she originally went temporarily and made a lasting impression. Known as Emma, she was acknowledged to be a strict disciplinarian who did not suffer fools gladly; she was also a character, who prior to World War I was riding a motorcycle with her mother in the sidecar. Shortly before her death she was made mayor and when she successfully fought to get an art gallery in Walsall it was named after her. Miss Flint set up Queen Mary Grammar School's art sixth form and in the year after her death 32 old boys were attending Birmingham School of Art. Showed at RA, RBSA and RWA and lived in Walsall, Staffordshire.

Francis Russell FLINT 1915–1977 Oil and watercolour painter. Studied at the Grosvenor School of Modern Art, Royal Academy Schools and in Paris. Son of Sir William Russell Flint, RA, Francis was an official Admiralty artist who exhibited at the RA, RSA, elsewhere in Britain, Africa, Canada and the USA. His pictures were mainly of marine subjects and they were reproduced in many publications, including *Royal Academy Illustrated, Illustrated London News, Sketch* and *Tatler*. He wrote for *The Artist* and *The Studio* and several books on watercolour painting. Lived at Burgess Hill, Sussex.

Geoffrey FLINT 1919– Painter and teacher, born in Woking, Surrey. Studied at Kingston School of Art and Royal College of Art and eventually became principal of Eastbourne School of Art, latterly the College of Art and Design. The local Towner Art Gallery holds his work. Lived in Eastbourne, Sussex.

Purves FLINT 1883–1947 Landscape artist and printmaker, born in Edinburgh, son of the artist Francis Wighton Flint and younger brother of the painter William Russell Flint. His full name was Robert Purves Flint. He was educated at Daniel Stewart's College in Edinburgh and served in the Army in France in World War I. He was a member of RSW and an associate of RWS and was a prolific exhibitor, also showing at Leicester Galleries, Fine Art Society, Royal Glasgow Institute of the Fine Arts and elsewhere. Lived for many years in Whitstable, Kent.

Robert FLINT 1880– Sculptor in wood and stone, born at Shoreham-on-Sea, Sussex. Studied at Putney School of Art under Charles Doman, 1929–39, then City and Guilds, London, 1939–41. He exhibited at the RA and in the provinces and his work is held by Russell-Cotes Art Gallery and Museum, Bournemouth. Was elected RMS in 1948. Lived at Southwick, Sussex, and was a member of the Society of Sussex Artists.

William Russell FLINT 1880–1969 Watercolourist, printmaker and illustrator, born in Edinburgh. He was the son of the artist Francis Wighton Flint, elder brother of the landscape painter Purves Flint and father of the artist Francis Russell Flint. Apprenticed when he left school to a firm of lithographers, Flint attended art classes, and after moving to London at the turn of the century worked as a medical illustrator before joining *The Illustrated London News'* staff. In his spare time he studied at Heatherley's School of Fine Art. His first book illustration success was H Rider Haggard's *King Solomon's Mines*, 1905, to be followed by many titles including *The Song of Songs*, 1909, Charles Kingsley's *The Heroes*, 1912, and Homer's *The Odyssey*, 1924. Took up etching, which he studied at Hammersmith School of Art, 1914. After service in the Royal Naval Volunteer Reserve and Royal Air Force in World War I Flint continued to establish his reputation as a technically superb watercolourist and skilled etcher. His books, such as *Models of Propriety*, 1951, and *Minxes Admonished or Beauty Reproved*, 1955, gained him great popularity, along with prints produced for wide distribution, but his concentration on semi-draped pin-ups in continental settings took him out of critical favour. He was a prolific exhibitor, especially at Fine Art Society, RWS, RSW and RWA, and his work is in many public collections around the world. Elected RA, 1933, and knighted, 1947. Lived in London.

Helen FLOCKHART 1963– Painter, born in Hamilton, Lanarkshire. She studied at Glasgow School of Art, 1980–5, then in following year at State Higher School of Fine Art in Poznan, Poland. Flockhart's work was reminiscent of primitive paintings and was influenced by naive, folk art pictures and icons. Woman's role as Maiden, Madonna and Mother were features of her meticulously painted canvases. She showed solo in Poznan in 1986 and at Fruitmarket Gallery, Edinburgh, 1990. In 1992–3 she appeared in Through Women's Eyes at Edinburgh City Art Centre. Scottish Arts Council holds her work.

Alan FLOOD 1951– Painter and etcher, born in Lancashire, who attended Blackburn School of Art and Leeds School of Fine Art. He began his career as a freelance illustrator, but after six years resumed painting. Flood's subjects included portraits, cityscapes, interiors and still life. Exhibitions included Blackburn and Manchester City Art Galleries, National Portrait Gallery, Leeds University Gallery and Opera North Grand Theatre, Leeds, 1996. In 1993 Flood completed a series of etchings of the playwright Samuel Beckett, *A Beckett Metamorphosis*, and *The Leeds Centenary Print Edition*, both published by Sheeran Lock Fine Art. Two years later, Flood finished a residency with Opera North; in 1996 was commissioned by the Christian charity Caring for Life to produce drypoint etchings; and in 1996–7 Opera North commissioned Flood for portrait work. Commissioned portraits included Geoffrey Lehmann, R A Clegg, Charles and Elizabeth Noble and the Solabarrieta family. National Library of Ireland, West Yorkshire Playhouse, Leeds City Art Gallery and Leeds General Infirmary and Thomas Danby College hold examples. Flood was based in Leeds.

Mary Sargant FLORENCE 1857–1954 Painter of pictures and murals working in tempera and watercolour. Born in London, sister of the sculptor Francis W Sargant, she studied at the Slade School of Fine Art under Alphonse Legros and in Paris, partly at Atelier Colarossi. Exhibited RA, NEAC, SWA and elsewhere. She was interested in the theory of colour, on which she wrote. The Tate Gallery owns her work. She designed her own house at Marlow, Buckinghamshire, but died at Twickenham, Middlesex.

Cedric FLOWER 1920– Painter, draughtsman, stage designer, illustrator and writer, born in Sydney, New South Wales, Australia, eventually settling in the state at Werri Beach. Flower left school to work as a commercial artist, attending evening classes at the Dattilo Rubbo Studio. From 1950–5 he was overseas, in Britain "making a living in the more mundane branches of advertising" and taking part in the first Australian Artists' Association exhibition at the RWS Conduit Street gallery, 1953. Back in Australia, he had many solo shows in Sydney, Melbourne and Adelaide, becoming known for pictures with a strong decorative quality. His books include *Duck and Cabbage Tree*, 1968; *The Antipodes Observed*, 1974; and *Illustrated History of New South Wales*, 1981. National Gallery of Australia, Canberra, and other Australian public collections hold examples.

Nigel A FLOWER 1931– Painter, designer and teacher, born in Ashbourne, Derbyshire. Flower attended Cardiff College of Art, 1947–53, then held a number of teaching posts, returning to Cardiff College, 1964, to study graphics and photography. He then joined Rhondda Borough Council, in Wales, as a graphic designer and photographer. Showed Royal National Eisteddfod, SWG and WAC, which holds his work.

Peter FLOWERS 1916–1950 Landscape painter. Initially educated in Switzerland, he studied art under Bertram Nicholls, then went on to show at the RA, RBA and ROI, also becoming a member of the Society of Sussex Painters. His work was reproduced by the art dealer Frost and Reed and the greetings card firm Raphael Tuck. Lived at Steyning, Sussex.

Christina FLOYD 1949– Artist and teacher, born in London, who studied at Central School of Art, 1968–9, Hornsey College of Art, 1969–72, then Royal College of Art, 1972–5. She taught at University of Pittsburgh, in America, 1975–8, later teaching part-time at Stourbridge College of Art and Hull College of Higher Education. Group shows included Northern Young Contemporaries, at Whitworth Art Gallery in Manchester, 1974; Museum of Art, Carnegie Institute, Pittsburgh, 1976; and Summer Show 3 at Serpentine Gallery, 1980. There she exhibited work in a variety of media. Solo exhibitions included, 1977, University of Pittsburgh, which holds her work, as does Leicester Education Authority. Lived in Ilford, Essex.

Donald Henry FLOYD 1892–1965 Painter of the Monmouthshire landscape, born in Plymouth, Devon, where he studied at Plymouth College, 1908–12, with the Cornish artist John Barlow. During World War I served with the Devon Regiment in India and Egypt, painting while off-duty. In 1920 married a Newport, Monmouthshire, teacher Annie Rogers, moving to Chepstow to live. Became a regular exhibitor at RA, 1920–1950. In 1948, was commissioned by Ceylon government to produce a suite of 68 pictures to celebrate independence. Many public and private collections hold Floyd's work, shown in A Feeling for Landscape by Newport Museum and Art Gallery in 1998.

Ceal FLOYER 1968– Artist employing slide projection and such objects as bulb and flex, and film, who was born in Karachi, Pakistan. Obtained a degree in theatre studies at Dartington College of Arts, 1989–90; did an art and design foundation course at Sir John Cass School of Art and Design, 1990–1; obtaining a degree in fine art at Goldsmiths' College, 1991–4. Group shows included Hit & Run, Tufton Street, 1992; Fast Surface, Chisenhale Gallery, 1993; General Release, Scuola di San Pasquale, Venice, 1995; and British Art Show 4, with tour, 1995–6.

Herbert FLUGELMAN 1923– Sculptor, painter, printmaker and teacher, Bert Flugelman was born in Vienna, Austria, settling in Australia in 1938. He attended the National Art School and East Sydney Technical College, both in Sydney, 1947–50, then travelled and worked in Britain, continental Europe and America, 1951–6. Support from the RA enabled Flugelman to work on the island of Ibiza, 1951. In 1953 he took part in the first Australian Artists' Association exhibition at the RWS Conduit Street gallery and had a solo show of paintings at the Piccadilly Gallery. Flugelman held a number of teaching posts in Australia, notably at the University of Wollongong, where he was made a professional fellow from 1991. After early developing as a painter, despite the crippling limitations of polio he became noted as a sculptor, winning many awards and competitions, his metal sculptures being well suited to public places. Commissions included University of New South Wales, 1964; Festival Hall, Adelaide, 1973; and Lawrence Hargrave Memorial, Wollongong, 1988. Later solo exhibitions included Irving Sculpture Gallery, Sydney, 1988. National Gallery of Australia, Canberra, Wollongong University and other Australian public galleries hold examples.

Michael FLYNN 1947– Painter, sculptor in ceramic and metal, printmaker and teacher, born in Ireland. Over many years of exhibiting in mixed and solo shows Flynn built a name primarily as a sculptor whose work had a notable animal energy, its own symbolism, humour and a special concern with organs of touch. His reputation was especially strong on the continent, where he worked and taught, as he did in colleges of art in Britain. Group shows included International Print Biennale, Epinal, France, 1977; Fire and Smoke, Midland Group, Nottingham, and touring, 1983–4; Sculpture from Wales, Oxford Gallery, 1987; and Gainsborough's House, Sudbury, 1991. Selected one-man exhibitions included painting, Ikon Gallery, Birmingham, 1975; Sculpture in Ceramic and Bronze, 3D Gallery, Bristol, 1986; Goya Gallery, Antwerp, 1991; and Martin Tinney Gallery, Cardiff, 1993. Crawford Municipal Art Gallery, Cork; Crafts Council; and Victoria & Albert Museum hold his work. Lived in Cardiff.

Florian FOERSTER 1968– Printmaker and teacher, born in Oldenburg, West Germany, who moved to England in 1989. He did a foundation course at Manchester Polytechnic, 1989–90, from 1990–3 obtaining a fine art degree, art and design, at Liverpool and Manchester Polytechnics, specialising in printmaking (in 1991 spending several months travelling in Brazil, studying printmaking at the Museu Lasar Segall, São Paulo). From 1993–4, taught printmaking part-time at Salford University College. Between 1994–7, Foerster obtained a structural engineering degree at Manchester Victoria University. Group exhibitions included Skelmersdale Arts Centre, 1993; MAFA Open, 1994 (awarded a print prize, another in 1996); Tib Lane Gallery, Manchester, from 1994. Had a solo exhibition at Liverpool University School of Architecture, 1995, with two others in 1996 at Royal Northern College of Music, Manchester, and Galerie Zunge, Berlin, Germany.

Mary FOGG 1918– Painter, ceramic sculptor and teacher, born in Poulton-le-Fylde, Lancashire. From 1942–4 she studied at Preston and Liverpool Arts Schools part-time, then worked widely in England and Wales as a radiographer during the rest of the war. In 1945 settled in North Wales and studied etching and sculpture, in 1964–7 studying painting and ceramics at Bath Academy of Art, Corsham. Did a variety of teaching in the Oswestry, Shropshire, area where she lived. Fogg was a member of WIAC, The Welsh Group and Free Painters and Sculptors. Showed at Royal National Eisteddfod, RCamA, WAC and elsewhere and had a series of solo shows. Among her commissions was a Mother and Child for St John's Church, Stoke-on-Trent. University College of Wales, Aberystwyth, holds her work.

David FOGGIE 1878–1948 Painter, draughtsman and teacher, born in Dundee, where he studied at the High School. Encouraged by the local Art Society and with £30, Foggie went to Antwerp to study art, remaining ten months on that sum. After further studies there Foggie established himself as an artist in Dundee. In 1919 he moved to Edinburgh, where he obtained a part-time teaching post at the College of Art, held until 1939. Foggie was elected RSA in 1930, six years after being made RSW, then in 1932 he was made secretary of the Academy, a post he held until his unexpected death during an attack of asthma, which had plagued him since his early thirties. Foggie's abilities as a fine painter and superlative draughtsman have been for many years underrated. He was a master of the human figure, but he never became a society portraitist and lack of commissions forced him to select models from manual workers, professional models, members of his own family or friends – especially people of character. He painted at every opportunity. Examples of his work are in galleries in Dundee, Paisley, Edinburgh, Aberdeen, Glasgow and elsewhere. The National Portrait Gallery has a series of Edinburgh portraits. Centenary show 1978 at Dundee Museums and Art Galleries. His son was the painter Neil Foggie. Lived in Edinburgh.

Neil FOGGIE 1912–1995 Artist and teacher, born in Balmullow, Fife, son of the artist David Foggie and married to the painter Margaret Hendry. Foggie was predominantly a landscape painter, mostly in oil, who drew cartoons as Du Brouillard. He attended Edinburgh College of Art, 1930–4. Was art master at Dollar Academy, 1934–48 (interrupted by war service with the Argyll & Sutherland Highlanders, where he rose to major), then was principal art teacher at Galashiels Academy, 1948–72. In 1955–6 Foggie made a teaching exchange to Toronto, Canada, where modern Canadian painting, especially the work of the Group of Seven, impressed him, and where he showed and sold well. Years later, Canadians would seek out Foggie's Scottish works. Showed at Royal Glasgow Institute of the Fine Arts, RSA, SSA, Aberdeen Artists' Society, RSW and elsewhere. Solo shows included Old Gala House, Galashiels, 1952, and Galashiels Public Library, 1972. Lived partly in Edinburgh, partly in Mull, where he died.

Brian FOJCIK 1960– Figurative painter and draughtsman, born in Kirkcaldy, Fife, who studied at Duncan of Jordanstone College of Art, Dundee, 1979–83, with a postgraduate year, 1983–4. Prizes included John Milne Prize in Painting; George Duncan of Drumfork Travelling Scholarship, both at Duncan of Jordanstone; Elizabeth Greenshields Award, 1988; and Maude Gemmell Hutchison Prize, RSA Summer Exhibition. Fojcik was elected to SSA in 1992 and to SSWA in 1993. Group shows included Gallery 22 and Compass Gallery, both in Glasgow, and RSA, all 1988; RA Summer Exhibition, 1989; and Roots, Kirkcaldy Museum and Art Gallery, 1993. Had a solo show at Gallery 22, Cupar, 1984, later ones including The Scottish Gallery in Edinburgh, from 1993, and Thackeray Gallery, 1996.

Peter FOLDES 1924–1977 Artist and film director, animator and scriptwriter, born in Budapest, Hungary. He studied at Courtauld Institute from 1946, also at Slade School of Fine Art and had an exhibition at Hanover Gallery, 1953. Returned to Hungary to make films, but had his greatest success in France from the mid-1960s. Among his titles was *Bilitis*, 1968, and a Canadian film, *La Faim*, about world famine, 1973. In the year of his death a documentary about Foldes, *Image de Peter Foldes*, drew attention to his contribution as an early computer-animation man. Tate Gallery archive has his striking Self-Portrait, 1953.

Charles FOLKARD 1878–1963 Illustrator and painter, born in London, father of the sculptor Edward Folkard. He attended Goldsmiths' College School of Art, Blackheath, Sidcup and St John's Wood Schools of Art and is most famous for creating the comic strip for children *Teddy Tail* in the *Daily Mail* in 1915, which lasted for 45 years. Also drew for other newspapers, for magazines and illustrated several dozen books. These include

Aesop's Fables, 1912; *Mother Goose's Nursery Rhymes*, 1919; and George Macdonald's *The Princess and the Goblin*, 1949. Lived in London for some years, finally in Heathfield, Sussex.

Edward FOLKARD 1911– Sculptor, son of the illustrator Charles Folkard, born in London. He studied at Goldsmiths' College School of Art and the Royal Academy Schools and was elected a fellow of the RBS in 1955. Showed at RA, RBA, LG and Royal Glasgow Institute of the Fine Arts and was a member of Chelsea Arts Club. Sometimes signed work E F. Lived in London.

Peter FOLKES 1923– Painter in oil, watercolour and acrylic, and teacher, born in Beaminster, Dorset. Studied at West of England College of Art, Bristol, 1941–50, his studies being interrupted by Army service, 1942–7, abroad. He went on to become head of the department of fine art, Southampton Institute of Higher Education, retiring in 1989. Became a tutor for Artscape Painting Holidays and a consultant and demonstrator for Winsor & Newton. In 1963 Folkes won a Goldsmiths' Travelling Scholarship which enabled him to travel widely in America. In 1959 he was elected RWA, in 1969 RI, holding senior positions with both bodies. Had a series of solo shows, beginning with Rumbold Gallery, Midhurst, 1962, later ones including RWA, 1986, and St Paul's School Gallery, 1992. Arts Council and RWA hold his work. Lived in Swaythling, Southampton.

Ron FOLLAND 1932– Largely self-taught artist in oil, acrylic and watercolour, who studied for a time in Paris having been born in Portsmouth, Hampshire. He was noted for his landscapes, especially of English villages. Folland twice achieved the number one position in the Fine Art Trade Guild nationwide poll and was for many years from 1965 rated in the Top Ten Artists Poll more times than any artist. His solo shows included Frost & Reed, Bristol, from 1976; *To-Day*, Southern Television, from same year; Frost & Reed, Worthing, 1978; and St Helier, Jersey, 1980. His limited-edition prints sold widely and included *Spires of Paris, Springtime in London* and *Dimanche*. Collectors around the world hold examples. Lived in Ickenham, Middlesex.

Ursula FOOKES 1906–1991 Lino-cutter and painter in oil and watercolour, whose early life is a mystery. She studied at the Grosvenor School of Modern Art, 1929–30. Her highly stylized work showed the influence of one of its founders, Claude Flight, who included it in exhibitions at the Ward Gallery in the 1930s, a period when Fookes travelled and painted abroad with her artist friend Pauline Logan, with whom she shared a studio in Pimlico, and produced more conventional Post-Impressionist works. These were exhibited at NEAC, and she also showed at Redfern Gallery and SWA. In 1939 Fookes, her mother and an aunt moved to Lymington, Hampshire, where she did war work, then she travelled to the continent in 1945, running a mobile canteen for the troops. Later settled in Norfolk and bird watching became a keen interest, while the art work had diminished. It was only after her death that a body of pictures was found, reviving interest in her earlier output, and dealers began to show them. Fookes' diary of her time in Germany, 1945–6, was edited for private circulation by Alan Guest, a copy being placed in the Imperial War Museum.

Susan FOORD 1945– Painter, born in London, who studied at Jacob Kramer College and at Leeds Polytechnic faculty of art and design. She created small, delicate pictures which tended "to be evocative of landscape or seascape and sometimes still life". Showed at RA, RWA, Waterman Fine Art, in Hong Kong at Gallery 7 and in Eight by Eight at Pallant House, Chichester, in 1997, the year she had a solo exhibition with Offer Waterman & Co Fine Art. Provident Financial Art Collection holds her work. Lived in Bristol.

Victorine FOOT 1920– Artist in oil, watercolour and pastel and teacher, born in Pembury, Kent, from 1946 married to the sculptor Eric Schilsky. She studied at Central School of Arts and Crafts, Chelsea School of Art and Edinburgh College of Art, teachers including Morris Kestelman, Ceri Richards, Leonard Rosoman and William Gillies. After settling in Edinburgh she taught at the College. Foot was one of Jack Beddington's *Young Artists of Promise* in the 1957 book of that title. Painting "moments that surprise me", she exhibited at LG, NEAC, RA, RSA and SSA in mixed shows, having several solo exhibitions at Scottish Gallery, Edinburgh, from 1969. Scottish Arts Council and War Artists' Advisory Committee acquired her work, Foot having worked under the Directorate of Camouflage during World War II.

Winslow FOOT 1939– Sculptor, painter and teacher who studied at Philadelphia Museum College of Art in America. He taught at Leeds College of Art and was included in its staff exhibition The Teaching Image at Leeds City Art Gallery, 1964. Was later on the staff of Wolverhampton Polytechic in the product design department, then lived in London.

Arthur FORBES: *see* **Arthur FORBES-DALRYMPLE**

Donald FORBES 1952– Painter in oil, by profession a restorer with National Gallery in Edinburgh, where he lived. He was born in Glasgow, studying at its School of Art, 1970–4, teachers including David Donaldson. Showed with RSA and Royal Glasgow Institute of the Fine Arts, solo exhibitions including Lillie Art Gallery, Milngavie.

Michael FORBES 1968– Artist, born in Dingwall, Ross and Cromarty, where he attended the Academy, 1979–85, starting to paint full-time in 1989. In 1997, Forbes was a finalist in the J D Fergusson Arts Award for the most promising young Scottish artist. Group exhibitions included Myth and Symbol, Inverness Art Gallery, 1993; Compass Gallery, Glasgow, 1995; and RSA, 1996. Solo exhibitions included Eden Court Theatre, Inverness, 1989; Flying Colours Gallery, Edinburgh, 1991; and Chalk Farm Galleries, from 1996. United Distillers holds his work.

Richard FORBES 1953– Painter, born and based in London, who trained in art schools there, 1972–9. He went on to work in the technical services department of the Tate Gallery. Forbes produced paintings concerned with theories of colour and language in the manner of the Systems Group: groups of multi-coloured squares and rectangles. His work was included in A Disquieting Suggestion, John Hansard Gallery at the University of Southampton, 1988. Arts Council and Conoco Centre, Warwick, hold examples.

Ronald FORBES 1947– Painter and teacher, born Braco, Perthshire. He studied at Edinburgh College of Art, 1964–9, with Robin Philipson, and at Jordanhill College of Education in Glasgow. Forbes taught at Bell College, Hamilton, then was appointed Leverhulme Senior Art Fellow at Strathclyde University, Glasgow. He next moved to Cork where he was head of painting at Crawford School of Art, returning to Scotland in 1978 to be artist-in-residence Livingstone, West Lothian. He then lectured at Glasgow School of Art for four years, from 1983 being on the staff of Dundee College of Art. In the early 1970s Forbes was founder-chairman of the Glasgow League of Artists and when in Livingstone was chairman of the Art Foundation there. He won a number of awards for films. Forbes had solo shows at Compass Gallery in Glasgow, Drian Galleries, Third Eye Centre in Glasgow and at Seagate Gallery, Dundee, 1990. Arts Council of Northern Ireland, Cork Art Gallery and SAC hold his work. Lived in Livingston, West Lothian.

Stanhope Alexander FORBES 1857–1947 Painter and teacher, born in Dublin, who was married to the artist Elizabeth Armstrong. Forbes studied at Lambeth School of Art, Royal Academy Schools, 1874–8, then for two years in Paris. He was influenced by Jules Bastien-Lepage. Settled in Cornwall in 1884, became a leading member of thc Newlyn School of open air painters specialising in local landscapes and the lives of fishermen and their families. The Tate Gallery's picture The Health of the Bride is a good example. Forbes was a founder-member of NEAC in 1886 and two years later began showing with RA, being elected RA in 1910. Also travelled extensively on the continent. With his wife he founded the Newlyn School of Art in 1899, and he remained an influential teacher for many years. Died in Newlyn.

Arthur FORBES-DALRYMPLE 1912– Painter in oil, gouache, pastel and watercolour. Born in Edinburgh, he studied under Henry Massey at Heatherley's School of Fine Art, 1930–2, and at Goldsmiths' College School of Art under Clive Gardiner, 1932–4. Exhibited RA, NS, ROI, NEAC, RBA and extensively in Paris, including the Salon. Sometimes signed work Forbes. Lived in London.

George Henry FORD 1912–1977 Sculptor, studied at Hornsey School of Art under Harold Youngman. Exhibited RA, Royal Glasgow Institute of the Fine Arts, Walker Art Gallery, Liverpool, and elsewhere in the provinces. His teak figure Eve is in the collection of Bradford City Art Gallery. Work also featured in Arthur T Broadbent's monograph *Sculpture Today in Great Britain 1940–1943*. He was a fellow of the RBS and lived in London.

Jane FORD: *see* **Jane TRESIDDER**

Jenifer FORD 1934– Painter, born in Cape Town, South Africa. She studied at Michaelis School of Fine Art, University of Cape Town, 1951–3, then 10 years later with Bernard Adams in London. Showed NS of which she was a member, ROI, RP and elsewhere and had a number of solo shows including British Council, Munich, West Germany, where she lived for some years.

Laura FORD 1961– Artist in various media who studied at Bath Academy of Art, 1978–82, with an exchange term at Cooper Union, New York, then Chelsea School of Art, 1985. Her group shows included Whitworth Art Gallery, Manchester, 1982; Serpentine Gallery, 1983; Sculpture in the City, Bath, 1986; Mappin Art Gallery, Sheffield, 1988; and Six of the Best at Christopher Hull Gallery, 1989. Had a solo show at Nicola Jacobs Gallery, 1987; Benjamin Rhodes, Gallery, 1991; and Spacex Gallery, Exeter, 1996. Arts Council, Contemporary Art Society and Unilever plc hold examples.

Leslie FORD 1885–1959 Pastel and watercolour artist, born in Bow, London. Studied at West Ham School of Art under Mervyn Lawrence and Arthur Legge. Exhibited PS, RI and elsewhere in London. Was an active member of the Wapping Group of artists, of which he was secretary for a time after World War II, and the Langham Sketch Club. Sunder and Museum and Art Gallery holds his work. Lived at Gidea Park, Essex.

Malcolm Stephen FORD 1914– Painter, printmaker and teacher, born in Newport, Monmouthshire. He studied at Newport School of Art and Royal College of Art. Did work as a book illustrator and jacket designer and held a number of teaching posts, being vice-principal of Birmingham College of Art for some years, then dean of art and design at Birmingham Polytechnic. Lived at Sutton Coldfield, Warwickshire.

Mary FORD 1944– Painter of figurative pictures, of restricted palette and simplified form to emphasize their abstract qualities, born in London. She was brought up in Cornwall from the age of six, having "an idyllic childhood" on the family ketch moored at St Mawes. From 1970–6 attended Byam Shaw and Royal Academy Schools, where William Scott taught her. The work of the St Ives painters Alfred Wallis ("painted purely from the heart") and Ben Nicholson ("I admire the sophistication") was a strong influence. Group exhibitions included New Contemporaries, 1972; Wills Lane Gallery, St Ives, from 1975; Eastgate Gallery, Chichester, 1987; and Roy Miles Gallery, 1994. Had solo exhibitions at Sadler's Wells Theatre, 1975, and Eastgate Gallery, 1986.

Michael FORD 1920– Painter and black-and-white draughtsman who handled a wide variety of subjects, including portrait commissions. He studied at Goldsmiths' College School of Art, 1937–40, teachers including Clive Gardiner. Went on to do war artist work, several pictures being held by Imperial War Museum. Ford's War Weapons Week in a Country Town is illustrated in Eric Newton's 1945 book *War Through Artists' Eyes*. Ford showed RA, RBA, NEAC, Towner Art Gallery in Eastbourne and at Paris Salon and continued painting at an advanced age despite being profoundly deaf. Lived in Winsor, Southampton.

Peter FORD 1937– Artist and printmaker, born in Hereford, where he attended the College of Art, 1955–6. Was then at St Mary's College for teacher training, at Strawberry Hill in Twickenham, 1957–60; Brighton College of Art, 1960–1; and London University Institute of Education to gain diploma in education of maladjusted children. Among Ford's awards were a bursary from Scottish Arts Council, 1976, and a South West Arts Minor Award, 1980, the year he took part in its touring show Seven Print Makers. In 1977 Ford was elected a member of the Printmakers' Council, in 1979 a participating member of World Print Council. Mixed shows included RA Summer Exhibition from 1975. Solo show included The Whole Spectrum, Margate, 1977, and Shady Characters, Leicester, 1979. Lived in Bedminster, Bristol.

Reginald William FORD 1909–c.1973 Designer, calligrapher, illustrator and artist, born in Reading, Berkshire, where he settled at Earley. Studied part-time at the local university. Worked for Oxford University Press, Macmillan and others. His book *Record of a Pilgrimage* was published in 1936. Showed with Reading Guild of Artists and had work bought by the Corporation and Art Gallery.

Chris FORDHAM 1949– Abstracted landscape painter working in mixed media, born in London. Fordham studied for an interior design diploma in London, 1967–71, obtained a diploma in art, Alexander Mackie, Sydney, Australia, 1976–9, postgraduate work at Alexander Mackie, 1981. In 1984 gained a Bachelor of Arts degree at City Art Institute, Sydney. Lived in Sydney, 1974–87, showing regularly in mixed exhibitions and competitions in New South Wales from 1976. Had solo exhibition at Arcana Gallery, Kelso, 1977, and Montmartre Gallery, Canberra, 1982. In 1982 gained Warringah Contemporary Art Prize, in 1983 Blackheath Art Prize. After returning to Britain Fordham showed in mixed exhibitions in south of England and had a one-man show at Albion Gallery, Lewes, 1990. Several public collections in Australia and Bank of Ireland hold work.

Mollie FORESTIER-WALKER 1912–1990 Painter and draughtsman. Brought up in Devon, she studied at the West of England School of Art, in Bristol, and privately with T P Anderson. During World War II the War Artists' Advisory Committee bought her portrait of Wing-Commander Guy Gibson for the Imperial War Museum. Exhibited RP, NS, PS and Paris Salon, where she gained an Hon. Mention in 1949. Lived in London and at St Mawes, Cornwall.

Andrew FORGE 1923– Art critic and writer, teacher and painter, born in Hastingleigh, Kent. He studied at Camberwell School of Arts and Crafts, 1947–9, under William Coldstream and Victor Pasmore. Was senior lecturer at the Slade School of Fine Art, 1950–64; head of the department of fine art at Goldsmiths' College, 1964–70; and from 1975–83 was professor at the School of Art, Yale University, and dean. He held a number of official appointments, including trustee of the Tate Gallery, 1964–71 and 1972–4 and of the National Gallery, 1966–72. Was president of LG, 1964–71. Wrote books on a series of artists, including Klee, Vermeer, Soutine and Manet. Tate Gallery holds his work. Lived at Elmsted, Kent.

Charlotte FORMAN fl. from 1950s– Painter, illustrator and teacher who trained at the Central School of Arts and Crafts, 1940–3 and 1946–8, then Bath Academy of Art, Corsham, 1957–9. She taught at Southwark College, in London schools and adult education. Did book illustrations and jacket designs for such publishers as Michael Joseph, Victor Gollancz and Bodley Head. Her pictures, in a detailed style, were shown at LG, Pictures for Schools, AIA, Hampstead Artists' Council, South London Artists and in a four-man show at Woodlands Art Gallery, 1981.

Robert FORMAN 1912– Interior decorator and artist in wash and pen and ink, born in Berwick-upon-Tweed, Northumberland. He was self-taught. Wrote a number of books, including *The Art of Scraperboard* and *Design for Commercial Artists*. Lived in Redland, Bristol.

Archie FORREST 1950– Artist and teacher, born in Glasgow where he studied at the School of Art, 1969–73. He was then a teacher at Dunbartonshire schools, 1974–85, and a tutor at Glasgow School of Art, 1978–85, in the latter year becoming a full-time artist. Forrest was a prolific exhibitor in group shows, including Kelly Gallery in Glasgow, Lillie Gallery in Milngavie, Fine Art Society in Glasgow and Royal Glasgow Institute of the Fine Arts, to which he was elected in 1988. He was a winner of its Torrance Award and of the Benno Schotz Sculpture Award, Scottish Amicable Painting Prize and Arthur Andersen Award. Forrest painted a lot in France and Italy, his one-man shows including a series of own-studio exhibitions and Portland Gallery, 1990. The Duchess of York, Scottish National Portrait Gallery and Glasgow Art Club hold his work.

Edwin FORREST 1918– Painter in oil, born in Birkenhead, Cheshire, self-taught apart from criticism from his friend and noted local teacher Will Penn. Became a freelance decorative artist and signwriter and was curator of the Williamson Art Gallery and Museum. Two key influences on Forrest's pictures were "the story of landscape and transient effects of sunlight and shadow across sea and land". Forrest was a member of RCamA. Exhibited in groups including Festival of Britain and Merseyside Artists, both at Walker Art Gallery, Liverpool; Atkinson Art Gallery, Southport; Grosvenor Museum, Chester; MAFA; and Williamson Art Gallery. Had solo shows with RCamA, Conway; Rushworth's Gallery, Liverpool; and Lady Lever Art Gallery, Port Sunlight. Lived in Trefriw, Gwynedd.

Norman John FORREST 1898–1972 Sculptor in wood. He studied under Thomas Good at Edinburgh College of Art. Went on to exhibit at RSA, SSA, Royal Glasgow Institute of Fine Arts as well as in London and the provinces. Forrest did a lot of ecclesiastical work as well as sculptures for the liners *Queen Mary* and *Queen Elizabeth.* His work often has a strong, elemental, primitive quality in the manner of Epstein. Illustrated in Eric Newton's monograph *British Sculpture 1944–1946*. Lived in Edinburgh.

Denzil FORRESTER 1956– Painter, brought up in Grenada until in the late-1960s he moved to London. He attended Central School of Art and Design, 1975–9, and Royal College of Art, 1980–3, a Rome Scholarship in the latter year taking him to the British School in Rome, 1983–5. A Harkness Fellowship took him to live in New York, 1986–8. Forrester's pictures were commonly on a large scale, mixing West Indian and European culture, Rastafarianism and traits to be found in German Expressionism and Italian Futurism, with bold, radiating lines of brilliant colour. He had his first solo show at Riverside Studios in 1983; another at Commonwealth Institute in 1986; was included in Exhibition Road show in 1988 at Royal College of Art which, like the Arts Council, holds his work; and had a further solo exhibition at 198 Gallery in 1995.

John FORRESTER 1922– Painter, born in New Zealand. After war service he lived in St Ives, Cornwall, 1953–8, then from 1960 in Paris. Among his solo shows in England were Gimpel Fils, 1955, and McRoberts and Tunnard, 1962, and he also exhibited in France and New Zealand. He was included in Belgrave Gallery's 1992 shows British abstract art of the 50s and 60s. Arts Council holds his canvas Two of a Kind, 1962. Julian Hartnoll and Paisnel Gallery also handled Forrester's work.

Anthony Gordon FORSEY 1926– Painter and printmaker, born in Birmingham, where he studied at the College of Arts and Crafts. He also studied etching and engraving with Robert Austin at the Royal College of Art. Exhibited RA. Lived for some time in London.

Catherine FORSHALL 1958– Painter and draughtsman with a special interest in the landscape of the Lot region, France, where she settled in 1985. She was born in Scotland, studied art in Florence, moved to London to begin a career in ceramic restoration, then returned to Scotland to paint. Had a first solo show in 1988 in Cahors, began to exhibit regularly at Salon d'Automne, Paris, other shows taking place elsewhere in France and New York. Had a first solo show in London in 1996 at Portland Gallery.

Juliana FORSTER 1943– Sculptor, born in Dorchester, Dorset, who studied with Willi Soukop and Elizabeth Frink at Chelsea School of Art, 1962. She became an associate of RBS in 1970. Exhibitions included Ewan Phillips Gallery and David Paul Gallery, Chichester. Lived in West Lavington, Sussex.

Noel FORSTER 1932– Abstract painter and teacher, born in Seaton Delaval, Northumberland. He studied at University of Newcastle upon Tyne from 1950–3 and 1955–7. During the 1960s had solo shows at Ikon Gallery, Birmingham, and University of Sussex, while taking part in group exhibitions, including John Moores Exhibition, Liverpool; there he gained a third prize in 1972 and a first prize in 1978. From 1970–1 Forster taught at Minneapolis College of Art and Design, teaching at Slade School of Fine Art from 1971. In 1975–6 Forster won an Arts Council Major Bursary, became artist-in-residence at Balliol College, Oxford, and showed at Museum of Modern Art there. In the mid-1970s he won the Gulbenkian Award. In the mid-1980s he began teaching at Camberwell School of Arts and Crafts. Arts Council holds his picture Two Units, One in Grey, of 1975, acrylic on linen, a favourite support used by Forster. From 1987 Forster showed solo regularly with Anne Berthoud Gallery. Lived in London.

Gordon Mitchell FORSYTH 1879–1952 Painter, stained glass artist and potter, born at Fraserburgh, Aberdeenshire. He studied at Gray's School of Art, Aberdeen, and at the Royal College of Art, completing his studies in 1903. He worked as a designer at Pilkington Tile and Pottery Company as well as serving as art director at Stoke-on-Trent School of Art. Signing his work G M F, he exhibited mainly landscapes and townscapes at RA, RI, Fine Art Society and the Royal Glasgow Institute of the Fine Arts. Eton College as well as galleries in Leeds, Stoke-on-Trent and Newcastle upon Tyne hold his work. He wrote several books on the art and craft of pottery. Lived at Woore, near Crewe, Cheshire.

James FORSYTH 1910– Painter in oil who studied at Cambridge University. Studied art at the Slade School of Fine Art, 1932–3, with Randolph Schwabe, then two years later in Florence. Showed RA, Leicester Galleries, NEAC and in the provinces. Lived in London.

Moira FORSYTH 1905–1991 Stained glass and pottery designer and watercolourist, born in Cresswell, Staffordshire, daughter of the ceramic designer Gordon Forsyth. She was encouraged to work in clay from an early age and trained in ceramics at Burslem School of Art. Lack of work prompted her to enter the Royal College of Art with a national scholarship to study pottery, but having seen the glass in Chartres Cathedral she instead studied glass design with Martin Travers. Exhibited at RA and at public galleries in Bristol and Stoke-on-Trent. During

World War II attached to the research department of the Ministry of Town and Country Planning she worked on two major surveys, on Oxford and Canterbury, then returned to glass work. An ardent Catholic, she especially liked making windows for Catholic churches, and among her major commissions are a transept window at the Benedictine Abbey in Fort Augustus. Her most significant works are in two cathedrals, Guildford and Norwich, and in St Columba's Church in Pont Street, London, where she lived.

Philip FORTIN 1901–1985 Painter, printmaker, sculptor, draughtsman and teacher, born in London. He was a talented violinist who early had to choose between a career in music and art. Attended St Martin's School of Art, 1917–20, under the sculptor Harry Parr, then the Royal College of Art, 1920–3, teachers including Gerald Moira and William Rothenstein. Showed at Zwemmer Gallery, New Burlington Galleries and elsewhere. Did some advertising work, occasionally condensing his name as a signature to Pif, by which he was generally known to his students and family. Fortin held several teaching posts, including Ipswich School of Art. On retirement in 1962 he moved from the Suffolk town to Cassis, in the south of France. Exhibited abstract paintings and drawings there and in Marseilles, jointly with his wife Yetta. After her death Fortin became reclusive, describing himself as an "aggressive eccentric", but he remained a great communicator on art, history and music and an enthusiastic advocate of the twentieth century. He returned to live with his daughter in St Osyth, Essex, where he died.

Peggy FORTNUM 1919– Artist in various media, designer, book illustrator and teacher, born in Harrow on the Hill, Middlesex. She was married to the artist Ralph Nuttall-Smith. She studied at Tunbridge Wells School of Art with E Owen Jennings and then at Central School of Arts and Crafts with John Farleigh and Bernard Meninsky. She was an arts and crafts teacher, 1940–1; an Auxiliary Territorial Service signals operator, 1942–3, being discharged with a pension and war grant after injury; an illustrator of children's books, 1944–89; and a textile designer, 1947–50. Fortnum was noted for her sprightly line as a book illustrator, notably accompanying Michael Bond's many Paddington Bear books; in 1975 her own *Running Wild* appeared. Fortnum also did work for Imperial Chemical Industries and for BBC Television programmes, *Playschool* and *Jackanory*. Exhibited at The Minories, Colchester, British Museum, Victoria & Albert Museum and in regional books shows, as well as abroad. Lived in West Mersea, Essex.

Rebecca FORTNUM 1963– Painter who was born and continued to work in London. She attended Oxford University to read English, 1983–6, before gaining a Master of Fine Arts degree from Newcastle University, 1986–8. Travelled to New York on a Northern Arts Travel Award in 1989, then held the 1989–90 fellowship in painting at Exeter College of Art. She exhibited widely, including solo shows at the Collective Gallery in Edinburgh and Southwark College Gallery and group exhibitions at Spacex Gallery, Sheffield, Pomeroy Purdy and Herbert Art Gallery, Coventry. In 1991 she took up a fellowship at Skowhegan School of Painting and Sculpture in America, then in 1992–3 was the visiting fellow in painting at Winchester School of Art.

Hubert FORWARD 1927– Painter, ceramist, printmaker and calligrapher and teacher, born in north London. He studied at Hornsey School of Art, 1945–52, teachers including Russell Reeve, Allin Braund and Henry Holzer. Held several teaching posts, eventually becoming head of ceramics at Norwich School of Art, 1953–82. Was a member of Federation of British Artists, Norwich Twenty Group and SGA and showed with RI and East Anglian Artists. University of East Anglia holds his work. In 1957 Forward was chosen for inclusion in Jack Beddington's *Young Artists of Promise*, his picture Hayfever, 1954, being illustrated. Signed some work with initials only. Lived in Norwich, Norfolk.

Anthony FOSTER 1909–1957 Sculptor in stone and wood and teacher, born in India, father of the sculptors Peter and Stephen Foster. He was a pupil of Eric Gill, 1930–8. Worked as a sculptor, 1939–57, farming as a conscientious objector from 1941–5. Taught at Camberwell School of Arts and Crafts, 1953–7. Foster's work was figurative with a strong Christian content. He showed at RA and Ashley Gallery. Died in London.

Bell FOSTER 1900– Painter, designer and illustrator, his full name was Arthur Bell Foster. Brought up in Northallerton, Yorkshire, he attended Sheffield School of Art, 1924–9. Exhibited RA, RSA, RI, RCamA, RBSA, NEAC, Royal Glasgow Institute of the Fine Arts, Paris Salon and widely in the provinces. Darlington Art Gallery holds his work. Lived in Moseley, Birmingham.

Deryck FOSTER 1924– Marine artist with a strong interest in sailing, born in Bournemouth, Hampshire. After King's School, Canterbury, he studied at Southern School of Art, 1939–42, teachers including Leslie Ward and Geoffrey Baker, then Central School of Arts and Crafts, 1946, where John Farleigh, Laurence Scarfe and Jesse Collins were on the staff. In 1957 Foster was included in Jack Beddington's book *Young Artists of Promise*, his Lady Francesca Entering St Vaast illustrated. Was a member of RSMA and has work in National Maritime Museum, Greenwich. Lived in Yarmouth, Isle of Wight, later in Bailey's Bay, Bermuda.

Graham FOSTER 1950– Painter and sculptor, born in Halifax, Yorkshire, who settled nearby at Skipton. He studied at Bradford College of Art, 1968–70, Leeds Polytechnic, 1970–3 and Royal College of Art, 1973–6. His work could be fetishistic, with overt sexual imagery, sculptures using a range of materials. Showed in north of England, solo exhibitions including Cartwright Hall, Bradford, 1978. His large Untitled, of 1976–9, in oil, acrylic and industrial paint, was included in Arts Council's 1981–2 tour Fragments Against Ruin, being taken into the collection.

John FOSTER 1951– Sculptor, born in London. He studied at Epsom School of Art with Peter Hide, 1969–73. Hide was then at Stockwell Depot, 1973–5; Triangle Workshops, New York State, with Anthony Caro, 1982 and 1985; and in 1986–8–90 organised Hardingham Sculpture Workshops. His Lazy E, made in steel painted and waxed, an abstract piece, was shown in the show East at Norwich Gallery, 1991. Foster's publicly sited sculpture includes Untitled, 1980, in metal, commissioned by Peterborough Development Corporation for Herlington Township Centre. Lived in Hardingham, Norfolk.

Lilian Lee FOSTER 1897– Painter, born in Boston, Lincolnshire. She was educated in Boston, then studied at Leeds College of Art, 1928, with the watercolourist and etcher Harold Holden. She showed widely at public galleries in Leeds, Bradford, Hull and Lincoln and at RWA. Was a member of Lincolnshire Artists' Society.

Marcia Lane FOSTER 1897–1983 Her favourite medium was wood engraving, and she also painted portraits in oil and watercolour, did pen and ink book illustration, silkscreen printing and extensive publicity work for firms such as Kodak, Cadbury and Nestlé. Born in Seaton, Devon, Foster – who married the artist and writer Dudley Jarrett – began studies at St John's Wood School of Art during World War I, where she was influenced by the teaching of Leonard Walker. Was then at Royal Academy Schools and Central School of Arts and Crafts, where she learned wood engraving under Noel Rooke. She illustrated several dozen books, notably titles by Viola Bayley and Pamela Brown. Never had a solo show, but was a prolific exhibitor with RA, RE, SWE, NEAC, at the Paris Salon and the Art Institute of Chicago. Her sketches of children, called *Let's Do It*, was published in 1938. Died in Wincanton, Somerset.

Peter FOSTER 1943– Sculptor in stone and wood and letter-cutter, son of the sculptor Anthony Foster and older brother of the sculptor Stephen. He attended High Wycombe College of Art under Darsie Rawlins, then City and Guilds of London School of Art, 1964. Worked as a sculptor and letter-cutter, 1965–72, emigrated to Australia, 1972–6, then from 1976 worked in Britain. Church work was especially important in Foster's output and he acknowledged his father, Eric Gill and David Jones as "exerting a strong influence". His Saint Martin and Beggar is in St Martin's Church precinct, Basildon, Essex. Lived for a time at Frieth, Henley-on-Thames, Oxfordshire.

Richard FOSTER 1945– Artist in oil, watercolour and gouache, born and lived in London. He grew up in Norfolk and was educated at Harrow School and Oxford University. Studied art at Studio Simi, Florence, 1963–6, then City and Guilds of London Art School, 1967–70. Foster was made a member of RP in 1976, becoming vice-president in 1991, also belonging to Art Workers' Guild. He showed regularly at RA and in 1972 won a Lord Mayor's Award. Had a solo show with Jocelyn Feilding, 1974, with Spink & Son from 1978. Many public and private collections hold examples.

Tony FOSTER 1946– Artist, administrator and teacher, born Lincolnshire, who studied at Birmingham College of Arts and Crafts, 1972–4, and at Cardiff School of Art, 1976–8, with an interval teaching in the Cayman Islands. Began work as an arts organiser, notably with South West Arts, Exeter. Then in 1986 he returned to painting full-time, having established a studio at Tywardreath, near Par, Cornwall. He became a renowned traveller who walked hundreds of miles in wild places to paint "a celebration of the wilderness and the idea of a journey or series of journeys". His Thoreau's Country was featured at Yale Center for British Art, New Haven, Connecticut, 1985; John Muir's High Sierra at Smithsonian Institution, Washington, 1989; and Rainforest Diaries at Royal Albert Memorial Museum and Art Gallery in 1993. Foster's work was included in the Newlyn Orion Galleries 1989 exhibition A Century of Art in Cornwall 1889–1989. In 1988 Foster was awarded the Yosemite Renaissance Prize and his work is in the collection of Yosemite National Park.

Simon FOSTER-OGG 1960– Sculptor and teacher. He studied at Maidstone College of Art, 1982–3, and Goldsmiths' College School of Art, 1983–6. For three years, 1978–81, he had been a stonemason working on Canterbury Cathedral. He went on to teach at Kent Institute of Art & Design, South Kent College and Portland Sculpture Park, where he had a residency, from the early 1990s. Public commissions were carried out for Whitstable Sea Front in 1990 and Portland Sculpture Park in 1991. Among Foster-Ogg's group appearances were Light Waves Dark Tidings at Herbert Read Gallery, Canterbury, in 1991; in the following year he was in Sculpture at Canterbury.

Lesley FOTHERBY 1946– Painter and teacher, born in London. Studied at Bath Academy of Art, Ravensbourne College of Art and Leicester Polytechnic. She left teaching in 1984 to become a professional watercolourist. Exhibited regularly at Royal Horticultural Society, winning two of its silver medals. She had a first solo show at Chris Beetles Ltd in 1985, others following in 1987–9. Lived in Yorkshire.

Clare FOTHERINGHAM 1890– Painter in oil and watercolour. Born at Ovenden, Halifax, she studied at Goldsmiths' College School of Art, 1909–14, under Frederick Marriott and Percy Buckman. She went on to teach art and exhibited widely, including RA, RI, SWA, RSA and RBA. Lived at Hollingbourne, Kent.

James FOTHERINGHAME 1970– Painter interested in depicting wildlife who studied at Mid-Warwickshire College, 1989–90; Nottingham Trent University, 1990–3; and Royal Academy Schools, 1993–6. Group exhibitions included RA Summer Exhibition from 1994, the year he was awarded the British Institution Fund, W H Patterson Prize and gained third prize, Singer & Friedlander/*Sunday Times* Watercolour Competition. Had a solo show at Cadogan Contemporary, 1995, another at New Grafton Gallery, 1997.

FOUGASSE 1887–1965 Cartoonist, illustrator and designer, real name Cyril Kenneth Bird. After Cheltenham College, Bird studied engineering at King's College, London, but also attended classes at Regent Street Polytechnic School of Art and Bolt Court, Fleet Street. World War I injuries prevented his practising as an engineer, so took course with Percy V Bradshaw's Press Art School, and his work soon appeared in *Punch*. He became art editor of the magazine in 1937, then was editor four years from 1949. Bird's sparse, graphic style became famous during World War II when he designed posters for the government, notably *Careless Talk Costs Lives*. He also exhibited extensively at the Fine Art Society and at RSA. Illustrated a number of books, including *A Gallery of Games*, 1921, *The Changing Face of Britain*, 1940, and A P Herbert's *A School of Purposes*, 1946. Was master of the Art Workers' Guild for a time and on the council of both the Imperial Arts League and the SGA. Married to the artist Mary Holden Bird. Lived at Laughton, Sussex.

Helen FOULDS 1902– Painter and teacher, born in Romiley, Cheshire. She obtained a Froebel diploma, studying art at Camden Art Centre, Hampstead, where she also exhibited. Showed at SWA, RWS and had solo exhibitions in post offices in London, where she lived.

Cherryl FOUNTAIN 1950– Painter and teacher. She studied at Reading University, 1968–72, and Royal Academy Schools, 1974–7. From 1973 she taught in Kent schools and education centres. Fountain won a number of prizes and awards, which included a bursary from the Worshipful Company of Painter-Stainers, in 1975, also the David Murray Studentship for Landscape Painting. She won the Studentship again in 1976, the year she won the Richard Jack Award for Portraiture. In 1977 she gained the British Institution's First Prize for Drawing and a first prize in the *Observer* Jubilee Print Competition. The Italian Government bursary for landcape painting and study of art history, which took her to Perugia, was won in 1978, three years before winning the Richard Ford Award to study in the Prado Museum, Madrid. As well as exhibiting at RA from 1975 and in other mixed shows including Maas Gallery and Piccadilly Gallery, Fountain had a solo show at Royal Museum, Canterbury, in 1983, shared a show at New Grafton Gallery in 1981 and had a solo exhibition there in 1986. Fountain's pictures frequently featured gardens and plants, painted with great intensity.

Marian FOUNTAIN 1960– Sculptor and medallist, born in New Zealand, who lived and worked in Auckland, London, Rome and Paris. She graduated in sculpture and design at Elam School of Fine Arts, University of Auckland, 1979–82, studying at Scuola della Medaglia, Rome Mint, Italy, 1985–6. Awards and residencies included Queen Elizabeth II Arts Council Major Travel Grant, 1984; residency at National Gallery of Modern Art, Edinburgh, and Prix de Sculpture, first prize, French Mint, both 1990; and Lipworth Foundation Sculpture Prize, 1993. She won a number of commissions from the British Art Medal Society, 1985–90. Group shows included National Exhibition, Crafts Council, Wellington, 1981; MAFA Open, 1988; and Press Museum, Istanbul, 1996. Was a frequent solo exhibitor from 1983, later shows including Simmons Gallery, 1997.

Christian FOURNIER 1962– Abstract painter, born in Livry-Gargan, near Paris, France, mainly working in oil but also mixed media. From 1979–82 studied graphic design at Lycée Corvisart in Paris, then attended L'École des Beaux-Arts there, 1982–5, gaining a part-time diploma at City of London Polytechnic, 1987–91. To support his studies and painting Fournier did a number of jobs: in Paris, 1984–5, working as a layout artist, other positions including sales assistant in a London card shop. Exhibitions included Southwark Open, 1995, and 1995–6 his Untitled canvas appeared in John Moores Liverpool Exhibition.

Nancy FOUTS fl. from late 1960s– Artist and gallery owner, born in America, who studied at Chelsea School of Art, 1964–8, then Royal College of Art, 1968. She established the Shirt Sleeve Studio, then in 1987 the Fouts and Fowler Gallery. She had a first solo show at Angela Flowers Gallery in 1974 and in 1994 was an Artist of the Day there, chosen by Les Coleman.

David FOWKES 1919– Painter in oil and teacher, born in Eastbourne, Sussex, son of the artist Arthur Reeve-Fowkes. He studied at Reading University, 1938–40 and 1946–8, under Anthony Betts. Fowkes first taught at Winchester School of Art, then for 30 years at Gray's Art School in Aberdeen, resigning as senior lecturer in the painting school in 1980, moving to live in York. He was a figurative artist, working from drawings made in and about York and in and around Italy, which he visited annually. Piero della Francesca, Seurat and Balthus were influences. Group exhibitions included NEAC, Michael Parkin Gallery and Scottish Arts Council tours. Had a solo show at Douglas and Foulis, Edinburgh, 1970, later ones including Abbot Hall, Kendal, and Charlotte Lampard, both 1989. Scottish Arts Council, Aberdeen Art Gallery and HM The Queen and HRH The Duke of Edinburgh hold examples.

Bertha FOWLE 1894–1964 Painter of miniatures, flowers and landscapes, born at Gravesend, Kent. Studied and taught at the School of Art there. Exhibited RA, RMS and RI especially, SWA and Walker Art Gallery, Liverpool. HM Queen Mary bought her work. Lived at Gravesend.

LeClerc FOWLE fl. from 1950s–1992 Painter and draughtsman, born in Haslar, Hampshire. She studied privately and at Slade School of Fine Art. Was a member of RWA and ROI. Exhibited in mixed shows at RA, NEAC, RSA and in the provinces, won first prize in Laing Competition in 1979 and gained gold and silver medals at Paris Salon. Had a series of solo shows. Lived in London.

Richard FOWLER 1921– Sculptor in all three-dimensional materials and teacher who studied at West of England College of Art in Bristol and at the Royal College of Art. He was a member of Cheltenham Art Group and showed at RA and RWA and in 19 Young Sculptors at Hillfield Gardens, Gloucester, 1962. Fowler became head of sculpture at Gloucestershire College of Art and Design, Cheltenham. After retirement, Dick Fowler lived in France.

Ron FOWLER 1916– Versatile printmaker, born in London. He studied at Glasgow School of Art, 1941, Warrington School of Art, 1955, and Chester College of Adult Education, 1979–80. Began printmaking in 1978 after retiring from a career in chemical engineering, having attended Birkbeck College at London University. Fowler joined SGA in 1982, becoming a member of its council in 1985. Showed with Society of Botanical Artists, NS and Mall Prints. Buxton Museum and Art Gallery holds his work. Lived in Lower Whitley, Cheshire.

FOWOKAN 1943– Sculptor, full name Kenness George Kelly, born in Kingston, Jamaica, mainly self-taught and practising from 1980. Fowokan was involved in promoting African history and art to schools and other educational institutions around Britain. Commissions included three pieces for Greater London Council South Bank Spring Festival, 1983; two for Borough of Hammersmith and Fulham Marcus Garvey centenary, 1987; and one for African Peoples' Historical Foundation building, Brixton, 1988. Exhibitions included Brixton Art Gallery opening show, 1983; 198 Gallery, from 1988; RA Summer Exhibition, 1991; and Transforming the Crown, Harlem Studio Museum, New York, America, 1997.

Christine FOX 1922– Sculptor and teacher, born in Bridlington, Yorkshire, who specialised in sculpture at Bath Academy of Art in Corsham, 1956–9. She was a part-time lecturer in sculpture at Cambridgeshire College of Arts & Technology, 1964–88. Took part in many sculpture park shows, including Sculpture in a Garden, Tatton Park, Cheshire, 1982; Yorkshire Sculpture Park, Bretton Hall College, Wakefield, 1986; and Art of Sculpture, Broxbourne Civil Hall, Hertfordshire, 1993. Showed annually with Cambridge Society of Painters & Sculptors from 1970 and in the Studios & Sculpture Gardens Open, triennially during the Cambridge Festival, from 1975. Solo exhibitions included Richard Bradley Atelier, Norfolk, 1972; Marjorie Parr Gallery from 1976; Gilbert Parr Gallery, 1980; and latterly Sculpture into Landscape at Peterborough Arts Centre, 1990, and Landscape of Trees, Broughton House Gallery, Cambridge, 1995. Sculpture bought for public places included Axe Carrier, Clare Hall Garden Court, Cambridge University, 1975; Batrachian Cascade, Stony Stratford, Milton Keynes, 1981; Gathering of Owls, Darwin's Aviary, New Hall, Cambridge University, 1992; and Sentinel, Girton College, Cambridge, 1993. Worked in Coton, Cambridge.

Kathleen FOX 1948– Artist employing oil on board, oil on gesso and collage and three-dimensional work in bone and wax, born in Durban, South Africa, her son being the painter Nicholas Fox. She studied in Durban, 1966–70, and in Cape Town with Michael Pettit, 1980–1. She was a member of the Women's Art Library, South East Arts and Hourglass. Fox defined her artistic interests as "mystery, ambiguity, dreams and childhood memories, subconcious levels of thought, mythology, forces that move beneath the observable surface of reality". Group exhibitions included Forum Gallery, Cape Town, 1981; UVA, Paris, 1991; England & Co, 1992; Rye Art Gallery, Rye, 1994; and Mall Galleries, 1995. Had a solo exhibition with South African Association of Arts, Cape Town, 1986, later ones including Trinity Arts Centre, Tunbridge Wells, and St Martin-in-the-Fields, both 1990; and Trinity Arts Centre, 1996. Ernst & Young and PPP Ltd hold examples. Lived in Cranbrook, Kent.

Mary FOX 1922– Painter and printmaker, born in Atherstone, Warwickshire, who studied at Leicester School of Art, 1939, then lithography at the Central School of Arts and Crafts. She was very influenced by the work of Polish and German painters, including several who moved to England, particularly Zdzislaw Ruszkowski, Walter Nessler and Jan Wieliczko. Group shows included RA, NEAC, WIAC, Christopher Hull Gallery and the Camden Annual. Had a series of shows at John Whibley Gallery from 1960, later ones including Sue Rankin Gallery, 1986, and Stables, Birmingham, from 1993. Her work was included in Ian Simpson's 1990 book *The Challenge of Landscape Painting*. Arts Council; Victoria & Albert Museum; Nuneaton, Beecroft in Southend and Portsmouth Art Galleries; and many education committees held Fox's work. Lived in London.

Peter FOX 1952– Artist notable for mixed-media assemblages. He studied at Kettering Technical College and Falmouth School of Art. Fox envisaged Art as having power to counter potentially technologically harmful forces. He showed in groups at Newlyn Orion Gallery, Penwith Gallery and in Art in Boxes, England & Co, 1991. His solo exhibitions included Falmouth School of Art, Yeovil Museum and Salthouse Gallery, St Ives, Cornwall.

Lesley FOXCROFT 1949– Abstract sculptor, born in Sheffield, Yorkshire. She studied at Camberwell School of Arts and Crafts, 1970–4. Her group shows included Fruitmarket Gallery, Edinburgh, 1981, Victoria Miro, 1991, and in 1993–4 she was in the Arts Council's touring Recent British Sculpture. Her solo shows included Konrad Fischer Gallery, Düsseldorf, 1974, Museum of Modern Art, Oxford, 1975, Laure Genillard Gallery, 1988, and Cairn Gallery, Nailsworth, 1993. Lived in London.

Maurice FOXELL 1888–1981 Watercolour painter, artist in pastel, lino-cutter and wood engraver. From an ecclesiastical family, Maurice Foxell, who took holy orders, was educated at

Christ's Hospital and Queen's College Oxford. Exhibited at the Abbey Gallery and Walker's Galleries in the inter-war years. Was a Knight Commander of the Royal Victorian Order and lived in retirement in Lingfield, Surrey.

Nigel FOXELL 1931– Draughtsman and watercolourist, born in London where he continued to live. He studied at various evening classes in London, notably at Central School of Arts and Crafts under Merlyn Evans. Had an especial interest in depicting aspects of London before demolition and lectured on architecture for Workers' Educational Association. Ran the private Earl's Court Gallery at his home in Earl's Court. Showed at RBA, East Kent Art Society and elsewhere.

Meredith FRAMPTON 1894–1984 Painter and etcher, born in London, full name George Vernon Meredith Frampton. He was the son of Sir George Frampton, sculptor of Peter Pan, his mother being the artist Christabel Cockerell. Meredith Frampton attended Westminster School, had additional art tuition, then after some months in Geneva learning French enrolled at St John's Wood Art School. From 1912–15 and in later years during some evenings he studied at Royal Academy Schools, winning a first prize and a silver medal. After World War I Army service Frampton began his professional career. He was already a member of the Art Workers' Guild. From 1920–1945 he showed at RA, being elected RA in 1942 but retiring in 1953. By the end of World War II he had found that his eyesight was insufficient for the type of detailed work he did. Frampton was a slow worker, producing meticulous portraits of singular realism which nevertheless often give a sense of unease, of the slightly sinister. After years of obscurity a retrospective at the Tate Gallery in 1982 revived his reputation. His subjects included King George VI, Sir Johnston Forbes-Robertson the actor and the architect Sir Edwin Lutyens. Tate Gallery and Imperial War Museum hold his work. Died in Wiltshire.

Peter de FRANCIA 1921– Painter, draughtsman, teacher and writer, born in Beaulieu, France. He studied at Academy of Brussels and Slade School of Fine Art, 1938–40. In the late-1940s and early-1950s de Francia worked in Canada, was at the American Museum in New York and for several years was in British television, responsible for arts programmes. From 1954–61 he taught at Morley College and St Martin's School of Art; was at Royal College of Art from 1961–9; then after a few years at Goldsmiths' College School of Art in 1972 de Francia joined Royal College of Art as professor of painting, a position he held until 1986. He was held in high regard as a teacher. He was an acknowledged and published expert on Fernand Léger, his important study appearing under the Yale University Press imprint in 1983. De Francia was a fine draughtsman who worked in series, his figurative pictures often having a political or social message. Retrospectives at Camden Arts Centre, 1977 and 1987. Arts Council holds his work. Lived in London.

Brian Jabez FRANCIS 1927– Glass engraver, born in Dersingham, Norfolk. Attended London and Nottingham Universities and studied art at Canterbury and Exeter Colleges of Art. Showed RMS and SGA, of which he was a member, and overseas. Paris Salon medallist. Lived in Thorney, Cambridgeshire.

Eric Carwardine FRANCIS 1887– Architect, born at St Tewdric, near Chepstow, Monmouthshire. Francis studied with the Royal Academician and architect Sir Edward Guy Dawber. Francis' work was shown at the RA and RWA, which holds it in the permanent collection. *The Architectural Review* and *Country Life* printed examples. Lived at West Monkton, Taunton, Somerset.

Iris FRANCIS 1925– Painter and printmaker, born in Dereham, Norfolk. Studied at Slade School of Fine Art, 1942–3 and 1945–6, with the intervening two years at Norwich School of Art; then at Manchester School of Art, 1947–8, with Harold Williamson, Swindon School of Art, 1948–50 with Harold Dearden, and the East Anglian School of Painting and Drawing with Cedric Morris. Exhibited SWA and widely in East Anglia including Norfolk and Norwich Art Circle, of which she was a member and which holds her work. Lived in Norwich.

Mark FRANCIS 1962– Abstract artist, born in Newtownards, County Down, Northern Ireland. He studied at St Martin's School of Art, 1981–5, then Chelsea School of Art, 1985–6. Was included in New Contemporaries at ICA, 1983; Whitechapel Open, 1990; Twelve Stars, Arts Council Gallery, Belfast, and tour, 1992–3 (Francis' work Union 2, of 1992, was shown there, being acquired for European Parliament Collection); in 1993 won the Grand Prize at Tokyo International Print Exhibition; and was in the 1995–6 and 1997–8 John Moores Liverpool Exhibitions. Later solo shows included Harewood House, Leeds, 1996, and Mary Boone Gallery, New York, 1997.

Mike FRANCIS 1938– He was born in Tooting, south London, lived for a while in Sidcup and settled in Eltham. While training to become an illustrator, Francis studied at St Martin's and Central School of Art. Joined the Furneaux Gallery in 1960, where he had his first solo show; in 1972 won the National Gallery's 150th anniversary poster award; also exhibited with Nicholas Treadwell in Britain and widely abroad. Had a solo show at Whitford Fine Art, 1998, which comprised Super-Realist pictures strong in sexual allusion and innuendo. Jamaican Embassy and a number of corporate collections, including Pears and Shell UK, hold examples.

FRANCYN fl. c.1940–1970 Painter, born in Portsmouth, Hampshire, whose real name was Cynthia Dehn Fuller. She showed with WIAC and NS both of which she was a member, Hampstead Artists' Council and Free Painters and Sculptors and abroad and had several one-man shows. Lived in London.

Eva FRANKFURTHER 1930–1959 Artist, born in Berlin, Germany, who was brought to England by her family in 1939, settling in London's East End. Attended St Martin's School of

Art, 1947–52, but taught social work at the London School of Economics. Her book *People* had an introduction by the artist and critic Mervyn Levy. Ben Uri Art Society, which has her Portrait of a Woman, gave her a show in 1962, three years after she committed suicide.

Gerhart FRANKL 1901–1965 Artist in various media who developed his own techniques and who late in life pursued religious themes. He was born in Vienna, Austria, the only son of cultured parents, and briefly studied chemistry before concentrating on art. Although he studied for several months in 1920–1 with Anton Kolig in Noetsch, Frankl was mostly self-taught, not wishing to join any art movement. From 1922 he travelled in North Africa and widely in Europe and held several exhibitions; in 1930 the Munich Pinakothek bought a landscape and the art historian Hans Tietz wrote a monograph cataloguing Frankl's etchings. Emigrated to England in 1938. Participated in the Venice and São Paulo Biennales and the Pittsburgh Triennale and in 1961 the president of Austria, which he occasionally visited, bestowed the title professor on Frankl. After his death in Vienna there was a memorial show at Hayward Gallery in 1970 organised by the Arts Council which, like Pallant House Gallery Trust in Chichester, holds Frankl's work, with another exhibition at Fitzwilliam Museum, Cambridge, in 1997. There is a Gerhart Frankl Memorial Trust, based in London.

John FRANKLAND 1961– Artist working in a wide range of materials, born in Rochdale, Lancashire. He did a foundation course at the College of Art there, 1979–80, then an honours degree in fine art at Goldsmiths' College, 1980–3. After leaving college Frankland supported himself as a carpenter and decorator, refurbishing old houses. Was included in Young British Artists IV at Saatchi Gallery, 1995. The work Ohne Titel employed part of a tree trunk and paint; Untitled was a garden shed in reflective silver polythene over wood. Was also included in British Art Show 4, and tour, 1995–6. Had solo exhibitions with Hales Gallery fom 1993 and one at Matt's Gallery, 1996: What you lookin' at? Lived in London.

Alan FRANKLIN 1954– Sculptor in a variety of materials, born in Oxford. He studied at Banbury School of Art, 1972–3, St Martin's School of Art, 1973–4, worked as a landscape gardener in southern Spain, then studied at West Surrey College of Art & Design, Farnham, 1975–7. His exhibitions included South Hill Park Arts Centre, Bracknell, from 1979; Johnson Wax Kiln Gallery, Farnham, 1981; Aspex Gallery, Portsmouth, and Reading Museum and Art Gallery, 1982; and in 1983 a Goldsmiths' show at Woodlands Art Gallery.

Ben FRANKLIN 1918–1986 Sculptor and teacher, born in Petworth, Sussex. From 1933–9 he worked as a lithographic artist, for the last three years studying part-time at Croydon School of Art. He resumed his studies there after Army service in World War II, resolving to be a sculptor. From 1947–50 studied at Goldsmiths' College School of Art under H Wilson Parker, in 1950 being assistant to Frank Dobson for Festival of Britain work. Started showing at RA. From 1949 Franklin began a series of teaching posts, culminating in his appointment as head of sculpture at the West Surrey College of Art and Design, in Farnham, Surrey, 1969–81. Showed widely in Britain and abroad and carried out many private and public commissions, figurative and abstract. Franklin's involvement in Buddhism, Indian and Chinese art and philosophy gave his work qualities of tranquillity and harmony. Retrospective at West Surrey College of Art and Design, 1988, and touring. Lived in Farnham, Surrey.

Jenny FRANKLIN 1949– Painter and teacher, born in Durban, South Africa. She studied at University of Natal, 1967–72, gaining a postgraduate honours degree; gained an education diploma at University of Cape Town, 1975; settled in London in 1979, obtaining a postgraduate diploma in art and design from Goldsmiths' College, 1979–80; her master's degree in painting, Royal College of Art, 1986–8; then was at British School at Rome, 1988–9. For many years she undertook part-time teaching and she travelled widely. Took part in many group shows, solo exhibitions including Artist of the Day, selected by Jennifer Durrant, Flowers East, 1989; and Crane Kalman Gallery from 1991. Graves Art Gallery in Sheffield holds her work which used a rich and vibrant palette and imagery derived from such subjects as graffiti, textile decorations, mythical birds or fish.

Kim Hunsdon Eastwood FRANKLIN 1955– Painter, notably in tempera, born in Natal, South Africa. He studied at Michaelis School of Fine Art, Cape Town, graduating in 1977. Was a member of SWLA, showing elsewhere in Britain and abroad. National Gallery of Botswana holds his work. Lived in Teddington, Middlesex.

L Michèle FRANKLIN 1958– Painter, printmaker, sculptor and teacher, born in Vermont State in America, of American/British nationality. Attended Camberwell School of Arts and Crafts, gaining an honours degree in fine art with a commendation for sculpture. In 1984 studied etching there, also at International School of Graphics, Venice. In 1981 did part-time teaching including art therapy, women's art classes, in 1988 taking up post of associate lecturer at Camden Adult Education Institute. Mixed exhibitions included RA, 1982; Wapping Wall Studios, 1984; Ben Uri Art Society, 1987; and Whitechapel Open Studios – At Home, 1992. Shared a show at Sue Rankin Gallery, 1992. Ben Uri holds her work. Lived in London.

Alexander FRASER 1940– Painter and teacher, born in Aberdeen. He studied at Gray's School of Art there, 1958–62, completing a postgraduate year. A Travelling Scholarship took him to France and Italy. Fraser won a number of awards including the RSA Guthrie Award, the Sir William Gillies Bequest allowing him to travel in Egypt. Fraser joined the staff of Gray's School and became senior lecturer in charge of painting. From the mid-1960s he had a steady stream of solo exhibitions, figurative and abstract work, including 57 Gallery, Edinburgh; Sheffield University; Compass Gallery, Glasgow; Aberdeen Art Gallery; Talbot Rice Art Centre, Glasgow, 1987; and Cyril Gerber Fine Art, Glasgow, 1995. In that exhibition Fraser showed small paintings and drawings intended to engage the viewer's imagination and which were "open to interpretation", tinged with a Surrealist oddness. Among Fraser's administrative roles were serving on Grampian Hospitals and Health Care Art Project Committee, and on the councils of the SSA, Aberdeen Arts Society, RSA and RSW.

Colin FRASER 1956– Teacher and painter of still life and interiors whose work included a strong autobiographical symbolism, born in Glasgow. He gained an honours degree at Brighton and had a first solo show there in 1978. Many others followed, including Catto Gallery in 1994. Also exhibited in RA Summer Exhibitions and with NEAC and RWS. Spent many years perfecting the egg tempera process. Moved to Sweden in 1985, where he lived in Lund and taught at its School of Art.

Donald Hamilton FRASER 1929– Painter, printmaker, writer and teacher, born in London. He studied at St Martin's School of Art, 1949–52, having his first solo show at Gimpel Fils in 1953. Showed frequently there and at Paul Rosenberg & Co in New York and elsewhere abroad in mixed exhibitions. The ballet and landscape were common themes in his work, which was largely figurative and influenced by the School of Paris, where he studied under a French Government Scholarship, 1953–4. Taught at Royal College of Art, 1957–83. Was elected RA in 1985 and was a member of Royal Fine Art Commission in 1986. Arts Council holds his work. Lived in London.

Elizabeth FRASER 1914– Sculptor in various materials and painter, born in Teddington, Middlesex. She studied at Birmingham, Central and Westminster Schools of Art and at Edinburgh College of Art under the sculptor Eric Schilsky. Showed with SPS of which she was a member, RA and in the provinces, having a series of solo exhibitions. Lived in London.

Eric FRASER 1902–1984 Painter in oil and watercolour, stained glass designer but especially an outstanding pen and ink draughtsman. Fraser studied at Goldsmiths' College School of Art under Frederick Marriott, Edmund J Sullivan and Clive Gardiner, all strong black-and-white men. He exhibited at the RA and SSA, but it is on the printed page that he established his reputation. He worked for the Folio Society, Golden Cockerel Press, *Radio Times, The Studio* and *Punch*, among many others. Murals were done for the navigators memorial in Westminster Abbey and Babcock House, and a huge one in connection with the Festival of Britain in 1951. Latterly Fraser said that he preferred commissions which meant he could use his imagination and did not have to represent reality. A wide-ranging exhibition of Fraser's work was held at the Royal College of Art in 1991, sponsored by British Gas, Fraser having invented Mr Therm, the gas symbol. The firm was one of Fraser's many industrial clients. Lived at Hampton, Middlesex.

Ian FRASER 1933–1987 Painter, printmaker and teacher, born in Newcastle upon Tyne, Northumberland. Fraser studied at Leeds College of Art, 1949–53, then at Royal College of Art, 1955–8. He taught at Hornsey College of Art and was head of the BA Hons Fine Art course at Middlesex Polytechnic. Lived in Shepperton, Middlesex.

Jean FRASER: see Jean DUNCAN

Neil FRASER 1955– Versatile artist, maker of boxed sculptures which he called 3D collages, inspired by a single object for which he created a life history. Born in Ealing, Middlesex, Fraser early wanted to be an artist, from 12 inspired by Surrealism, notably Magritte, Ernst and de Chirico and the wonders of the Science Museum. He graduated from the Central School of Art and Design, 1973–7, where he was interested in performance art, particularly lighting and building, while carrying on his own sculpture. Fraser used objects from the Greenwich foreshore near his home, or, in the case of his show Gas Pie, at The Mayor Gallery, 1998, ideas gleaned on a trip to eastern Europe. Work themes included "disasters, airships, evolution".

Norman FRASER 1943– Artist, notably a draughtsman, and teacher, whose work was influenced by Op Art, Celtic designs and the computer at various stages. He was born in Belfast, Northern Ireland, and studied at the College of Art there, 1960–5, and Hornsey College of Art, 1965–8. Returned to Belfast to teach, appointments including a lectureship at Ulster College. In 1974 he gained a travel bursary from Arts Council of Northern Ireland, which holds his work, to research computer art in North America. Exhibitions included the Arts Council of Northern Ireland's Gallery in Belfast, Octagon Gallery in the city and Third Eye Centre, Glasgow.

William Miller FRAZER 1864–1961 Landscape painter, born at Scone, Perthshire, who attended Perth Academy, then studied at Royal Scottish Academy Schools, winning the Keith Prize, then in Paris. Elected RSA in 1924. Exhibited there and prolifically at Royal Glasgow Institute of the Fine Arts, and at RA, RBA, RHA and ROI. Closely involved with Scottish Arts Club, of which he was for a time president. Lived in Edinburgh.

Nigel FREAKE 1959– Painter, born in London, who studied at Exeter University/College of Art & Design, 1978–81, then Goldsmiths' College, 1991–3. He was finalist, New Art Award for Postgraduates, in the latter year. Group exhibitions included Library Gallery, Exeter University, 1982; Spacex Gallery, Exeter, 1983; Cable Street Studios Open Studios, 1990; Into the Nineties 5, Mall Galleries, 1993; and Cable and Wireless, 1995. In Blush, shared with Julie Major at Paton

Gallery, 1996, Freake showed work indicating Carl André's Minimalist influence. Painted in acrylic and synthetic resin on linen, the paintings had as their origin dresses, patterned fabrics on a moving female body. The Courtauld Institute East Wing Collection holds Freake's work.

Harry FRECKLETON 1890–1979 Painter in oil, born in Nottingham, where he continued to live. He was the husband of the artist Vera Freckleton. He attended Nottingham School of Art, 1904–12, his teachers including Wilson Foster, and was influenced by the local painter Arthur Spooner. Freckleton worked as a lithographic artist, served in the Army during World War I, worked as an artist for New Zealand Ciné Studios and then ran his own photographic business, 1924–65. He showed at RA, RP, RBA and with the Nottingham Society of Artists of which he was a member. Represented in public collections in Nottingham, Blackpool, Huddersfield and elsewhere.

Vera FRECKLETON 1899–1989 Painter and miniaturist, noted for her work on ivory, born in Nottingham, where she continued to live. She was the wife of the painter Harry Freckleton, and her uncle Arthur Redgate and grandfather Sylvanus Redgate were both Nottingham artists. Studied at local College of Art, 1917–20. She showed her work at RMS, 1955–74, of which she became a full member in 1971. Also exhibited at Paris Salon where she gained an Hon. Mention in 1955, a silver medal in 1965 and a gold medal in 1972.

Waveney FREDRICK 1921– Artist in various media, notably pastel and charcoal, born in Luton, Bedfordshire. She studied at King Edward VI School, Birmingham, where she lived, and art at East Anglian School of Painting with Cedric Morris. Became a member of RBSA in 1978 and PS in 1983. She won the Feeney Award, Birmingham, 1977, PS' Herring Award, 1983, and Pastel Society of Canada Award, 1989. Took part in Five Artists at RBSA Galleries, Birmingham, 1990. Solo shows included Birmingham University; Oxford University; Keele University; Walsall Art Gallery; Royal Shakespeare Theatre, Stratford-upon-Avon; and in America.

Katerina FREDYNA 1906– Painter and draughtsman, notably in gouache, born in Kharkov, Russia. After education there she studied at St Martin's School of Art from the mid-1950s under Muriel Pemberton. Was a member of WIAC, Free Painters and Sculptors and Campden Hill Club, also exhibiting at Whitechapel Art Gallery, Camden Arts Centre and at Paris Salon. Bibliothèque Nationale, Paris, holds her work. Lived in London.

Susan FREEBOROUGH 1941– Figurative sculptor who gained a first-class honours degree at Chichester College of Higher Education, 1986, then an honours degree in fine art at Cheltenham College of Art, 1991. Between 1991–2 she was employed by Pangolin Editions sculpture foundry at Chalford, Gloucestershire. Showed in degree exhibition at Cheltenham College and in Fresh Art at Business Design Centre, Islington, both 1991, and in 1st RWA Open Sculpture Exhibition, 1993. Lived in Sheepscombe, Stroud, Gloucestershire.

Colin FREEBURY 1946– Painter producing large gestural abstracts in which pastel colours were predominant, born in London. Studied for his art and design diploma at Falmouth School of Art, gaining a teaching qualification from Cardiff University. In 1979 became a member of Penwith Society of Arts and worked in a studio in Penwith Gallery, St Ives, Cornwall. Exhibitions included Rainy Day Gallery, Penzance, 1994, and The Edge of Beyond, Belgrave Gallery, 1995.

Barnett FREEDMAN 1901–1958 Painter, printmaker, draughtsman and teacher, born in east London to a poor Jewish family recently arrived from Russia. He was bedridden for several years as a child and largely taught himself basic education, music and to draw. By 1916 he was able to earn his living as a draughtsman to a monumental mason. For five years he studied part-time at St Martin's School of Art. The personal influence of William Rothenstein enabled him to study full-time at the Royal College of Art, 1922–5. Then he went through a lean period as a freelance. After two years he was commissioned to illustrate Laurence Binyon's poem *The Wonder Night*, he began to exhibit at the NEAC and became a pioneer in reviving colour lithography. At various times taught at the Working Men's College, Crowndale Road, Ruskin School of Art, Oxford, and the Royal College of Art. Official war artist in World War II. By his death Freedman had established an enviable reputation as an illustrator and designer of posters, stamps, books and book-jackets. He believed there was no such thing as commercial art, "only good art and bad art". First exhibition at the Literary Bookshop, Bloomsbury, 1929; memorial exhibition Arts Council, 1958, and tour; Manchester Polytechnic, which holds the Freedman archive, held a major show in 1990. Freedman lived in London, married to the artist Beatrice Claudia Freedman. Tate Gallery holds his work.

Beatrice Claudia FREEDMAN 1904–1981 Artist, illustrator and teacher, born in Formby, Lancashire, of Sicilian ancestry. She worked as Beatrice Claudia Guercio, her maiden name; Claudia Freedman; or just C F. Was married to the artist Barnett Freedman. She studied at Liverpool School of Art under Frederick Carter, then at the Royal College of Art with Malcolm Osborne. Exhibited at RA and Walker Art Gallery, Liverpool. In addition she did a wide variety of graphic work, designing an alphabet for the Baynard Press; producing designs for advertising; as well as drawings for the General Post Office, Fortnum and Mason, Medici Society and Curwen Press. Among books illustrated were her own *My Toy Cupboard*; the *Little Book of Parables*, 1944, perhaps her most important work in this field, for which her husband did the page layouts; and Eleanor Graham's editing of *The Puffin Book of Verse*, 1953. Victoria & Albert Museum holds her work. Lived in London for many years, but died in Sussex.

Claudia FREEDMAN: see Beatrice Claudia FREEDMAN

Constance FREEDMAN 1927–1982 Sculptor in a variety of materials and painter, wife of a furniture manufacturer, Joseph Freedman. She studied at Sir John Cass School of Art, 1963–8. In 1979 she was awarded a Church Fellowship for environmental and functional sculpture. For most of her life Freedman lived in Hackney, east London. The Chalmers Art Gallery there holds her portrait bust of Big Dave, a market character, and in 1980 Prince Philip unveiled her powerful Javelin Thrower, in welded copper, which stands outside the Britannia Leisure Centre, Shoreditch. Generals Eisenhower and Montgomery were portrayed by her and her head of the ballet dancer Anton Dolin is on permanent view at Sadler's Wells Theatre. Showed at RA, Whitechapel and Ben Uri Galleries, Paris Salon and elsewhere abroad and had a series of solo exhibitions, including Chalmers, 1969–72, and Brunswick Gallery, 1977. She was a member of SPS and was made a fellow of RBS in 1978. Freedman died in the Royal Marsden Hospital, Fulham.

Barbara FREEMAN 1937– Painter, printmaker, sculptor and installations artist, and teacher, born in London. She studied at St Martin's, Camberwell and Hammersmith Colleges of Art, gaining her diploma in 1962, doing a postgraduate diploma at University of Leeds, 1972. Taught part-time in several colleges. Freeman made sculpture until 1982, when she changed to painting and printmaking, including mixed media pieces. She travelled widely, which was reflected in the subjects of her work, both figurative and abstract, often using a rich palette. She was a member of the Association of Irish Artists. Group exhibitions included Magnetic North, Orchard Gallery, Londonderry, 1987; Art London 89, Art Fair, 1989; and Abstract Representation, Triskel Arts Centre, Cork, 1991. Was later represented by Hart Gallery, Nottingham. West Yorkshire County Council, Leeds City Council and University of Bradford are among British and foreign collections holding examples. Lived in Belfast, Northern Ireland.

Barry FREEMAN 1947– Self-taught painter, notably in oil and pastel, of landscapes, coastal and figure pictures. His shows included Fairfield Halls, Croydon, 1985–9; Edwin Pollard Gallery, 1987; Bourne Gallery, Reigate, 1990–1; Beaton Brown Fine Paintings, 1990; PS, 1990–1; RBA, 1990; and in 1992 he shared a show with three artists at Anna-Mei Chadwick.

Esther J FREEMAN 1939– Sculptor who worked in a variety of traditional and modern materials. She studied at West of England College of Art in Bristol and at the Slade School of Fine Art. Her plaster Sculpture of Haptikos, of 1962, was included in that year in 19 Young Sculptors at Hillfield Gardens, Gloucester, at which time she was living in London.

John Tatchell FREEMAN 1958– Artist, notably a printmaker, born in London, who studied at Chelsea School of Art, 1977–80, after Bath Academy of Art, 1976–7. Held a number of Arts Council residencies, including Folly Hill School, Farnham, and Winston Churchill School, Woking, both 1991. Books illustrated included *The Graphic Guide to Thatcher*, by Ed Harriman, 1986, and *Jazz in the Synagogue*, by Lawrence James, 1994. Group shows included John Player Portrait Exhibition at National Portrait Gallery, 1984 and 1989; Gardner Arts Centre, University of Sussex, 1991; Collins Gallery, University of Strathclyde, Glasgow, and Kerb Scrawlers, The Living Room, Greenwich, both 1994. Later solo shows included Balliol College, Oxford, and South Hill Arts Centre, Bracknell (which, with Ashmolean Museum, Oxford, holds his work), both 1994.

Lily FREEMAN 1920– Painter and lecturer, born in Vienna, Austria. She studied art there and with Arthur Segal in London. Exhibitions included Loggia Gallery, Cockpit Theatre, Ben Uri Gallery, Hampstead Town Hall and Royal Over-Seas League. Lived in London.

Mary FREEMAN 1888–1974 Watercolourist, born on St Patrick's Day and known as Pat. She trained at Kingston School of Art, having been born in Surbiton, Surrey, then lived for 40 years in Shere, only moving to an old people's home in Woking in her seventies when she became ill. She was then still painting and was known for her watercolours of local woods and the market and cafés of Guildford. A group of her paintings was donated to Guildford House Gallery, and there are works by her in other galleries in the southeast of England.

Ralph FREEMAN 1945– Painter of abstract pictures in oil and watercolour, designer and teacher, born in London. He studied at St Martin's and Harrow Schools of Art, 1961–5, then worked as a jazz pianist, artist and designer in London, Hamburg and Frankfurt. Commissions included murals and social, film and exhibition posters, 1965–74. He also lectured at Bournemouth College of Art. Later commissions included the stage set for *Nevermore* at Half Moon Theatre, 1985, and a series of works on Man, Spirit and Energy, 1990. Freeman was a member of Newlyn Society of Artists and Penwith Society of Arts. Mixed show appearances included Boundary and Ben Uri Galleries, Camden Arts Centre and Anderson O'Day. He had a solo show at Camden Arts Centre in 1983, later ones including several in Milan and Hamburg and Royal Cornwall Museum Galleries, Truro, 1992. Lived in St Ives, Cornwall.

Allen FREER 1926– Painter, miniaturist and illustrator, he was a frequent solo exhibitor at Tib Lane Gallery, Manchester, from 1970. Later solo shows included Linton Court Gallery, Settle; Oriel 31, Welshpool; and Austin/Desmond Fine Art. Freer also appeared in mixed shows at Agnew, Hamet Gallery and New Grafton Gallery. He illustrated books for Cambridge University Press and T R Henn's autobiography *Five Arches*. Freer was noted for his landscapes, notably those of the English countryside, which had a fine sense of atmosphere.

Mavis FREER 1927– Landscape painter and teacher who was born in Chesterfield, Derbyshire. From 1943–9 she studied at the

School of Art there and Goldsmiths' College School of Art. Taught part-time at Grinling Gibbons School, Deptford. Showed frequently in mixed shows and had a solo exhibition in Canterbury in 1976, another at Woodlands Art Gallery in 1977.

Roy FREER 1938– Painter using a rich palette, and teacher, born in Birmingham. He trained at Bournville School of Art and Birmingham College of Arts and Crafts between 1956–8. He was a member of ROI, PS and RI whose later work became looser and broader, more about the substance of colour, brushmark and paint. Freer took part in many mixed shows, including RA Summer Exhibition, NEAC, Linda Blackstone Gallery in Pinner and Adam Gallery in Bath. A large number of solo exhibitions included Anna-Mei Chadwick, 1993. Among his awards were the RI bronze medal in 1986; ROI Cornelissen Prize same year; PSCD Soar Prize, 1990; and ROI Catto Gallery Prize, 1992. Open University holds his work. Lived in London.

Hubert Andrew FREETH 1912–1986 Etcher and painter, especially of portraits and figure subjects. Born in Birmingham, he attended the School of Art there, then won an engraving Rome Scholarship in 1936, subsequently spending three years at the British School in Rome. During World War II he was an official war artist in the Middle East, his drawings and prints being bought by the War Artists' Advisory Committee. Work also owned by British Museum and many other public collections. Freeth contributed to the Pilgrim Trust *Recording Britain* project and was widely anthologised in collections of war artists' work. Exhibited RA, and was elected RA 1965, also RE, RWS, RP and elsewhere. Freeth was noted for his superbly accomplished etchings. Taught at St Martin's School of Art and Central School of Arts and Crafts. Lived at Northwood, Middlesex.

Peter FREETH 1938– Printmaker and teacher, born in Birmingham, who studied at Slade School of Fine Art, 1956–60, gaining the Prix de Rome for engraving, 1960. He taught at Royal Academy Schools and Camden Institute. From 1973 showed at RA, elsewhere in mixed shows in London, as well as extensively abroad. In 1986 he was joint winner of the best print prize at RA Summer Exhibition. In the following year was elected associate of RE and was also RA Elect. From 1987 had solo shows at Christopher Mendez. British Museum, Victoria & Albert Museum, Arts Council and Metropolitan Museum hold his work. Lived in London.

Thomas FREETH 1912– Painter, draughtsman and teacher who worked for a time as a designer/painter on porcelain, studied at Royal College of Art for four years, then travelled in France and Spain. He joined the Army in April 1941, from September that year serving as a sapper with Headquarters, 9th Armoured Division. War Artists' Advisory Committee bought several works by Freeth, in collections of Imperial War Museum and Royal Pavilion Art Gallery and Museums, Brighton. At that time he was based in Halifax, Yorkshire, but by late-1940s, when he showed at RA Summer Exhibitions, Freeth was living in Bromley, then Beckenham, Kent, where he taught at the Art School. He was remembered by a former colleague as "a sound man, rather retiring, a loner".

Annie FRENCH 1872–1965 Watercolourist, illustrator, designer and teacher, born in Glasgow and married to the artist George Wooliscroft Rhead, who predeceased her by 45 years. French studied at Glasgow School of Art under Fra Newbery and taught in the department of design there from 1909, but after marrying Rhead she settled in London in 1915. She was a prolific exhibitor at RSA and Royal Glasgow Institute of the Fine Arts, also showing at RHA, RA and elsewhere. Her work was highly detailed, mixing Art Nouveau, the style of Jessie M King and a touch of Aubrey Beardsley. Scottish National Gallery of Modern Art holds several works by her.

Dick FRENCH 1946– Painter, born in South Shields, County Durham. He studied at Sheffield College of Art, 1962–7, his teachers including Robin Plummer and Kevin Farrell, then at Royal College of Art, 1967–70, under Carel Weight and Peter Blake. For a time he was resident artist at Lanchester Polytechnic, Coventry. He won the Harmstone Bequest, 1967, and Burston Award in 1970. Among mixed exhibitions were John Moores Liverpool Exhibitions, 1976 and '87, in both of which he won prizes, as well as City Artists, 1985–6. Had solo shows at South Hill Park in 1985 and City Artists Gallery, 1986. Public galleries in Wolverhampton and Sheffield hold his work. Lived in London.

Stanislaw FRENKIEL 1918– Painter, writer and teacher, born in Cracow, Poland, where he attended the Academy of Fine Arts, 1937–9. During the Nazi occupation he escaped to Lvov, was arrested by the Russians and deported, in 1942 joined the Polish Army in Russia and travelled to the Middle East, moving to London in 1947. His *Beirut Drawings 1944–7* was published in 1986. Frenkiel was eventually emeritus reader at London University and head of the Institute of Education, 1973–83. He was a member of LG and the Association of Polish Artists in Great Britain and RWA. His colourful figurative paintings were shown in Britain and continental Europe, and he was included in City Art Centre, Edinburgh, 1993 show Polish Roots – British Soil. His solo exhibitions included Grabowski Gallery from 1960; Tamara Pfeiffer Gallery, Brussels, from 1973; Newman Galleries, Philadelphia, from 1976; a Polish retrospective tour, 1981–3; and retrospectives at Bloomsbury Gallery, London University, 1983–7. That university, the University of Pennsylvania and several Polish museums hold his work. Lived in London.

M Hanbury FRERE 1866–1956 Watercolour and pastel artist, born at Horham, Suffolk. Studied at Wimbledon with Leonard Pocock and Alfred Drury, then exhibited in London and in East Anglia. HM Queen Mary bought her work. Lived in Norwich.

Lucian FREUD 1922– Painter and teacher, born in Berlin, son of Ernst Freud, architect, and grandson of the analyst Sigmund

Freud. Arrived in England in 1932 and became British subject seven years later. During the next few years studied at Central School of Art, East Anglian School of Painting and Drawing and Goldsmiths' College School of Art, having first one-man show in 1944 at Lefevre Gallery. In 1946–8 visited France and Greece and in 1951 won Arts Council Prize at Festival of Britain Exhibition. Three years later a group of his works was shown at British Pavilion at Venice Biennale. Taught at Norwich School of Art and Slade School of Fine Art. A series of solo shows in 1970s at Anthony d'Offay Gallery and a one-man exhibition at Davis & Long Company, in New York, consolidated Freud's position as a leading British realist painter, notable for his almost clinically raw portraits and nude studies. There was a retrospective at Hayward Gallery in 1988 and in 1993 a major show at Whitechapel Art Gallery was toured to Metropolitan Museum, New York, and Reina Sofia, Madrid. Several critics termed Freud Britain's greatest living painter. Tate Gallery, Arts Council and other major collections hold his work. Freud was granted the Order of Merit in 1993.

Jacqueline FREWING 1937– Sculptor in a variety of materials, painter in oil mainly of portraits and teacher, born in West Wickham, Kent. She studied at St Martin's School of Art, 1955–8, with Vivian Pitchforth, Frederick Gore, Anthony Caro and Elisabeth Frink. After a short period as a freelance illustrator, Frewing was involved in advertising, 1960–5, then had family commitments for almost 20 years; from 1985 returned to Brighton University to retrain, diversifying into oil painting, sculpture and teaching, teachers including Helen Collis and Robert Ellis. As a sculptor Frewing said that her "working approach is to build with clay, rather than to scrape away, which accounts for the textured surface typical of my work". Was a member of the Society of Sussex Sculptors and Three Counties Sculpture Society. Showed widely in Sussex and at Westminster Gallery, SWA. Had a solo show at Kilvert Gallery, East Grinstead. Lived in Copthorne, West Sussex.

David FRIED 1958– Artist who worked in a wide range of media, including three-dimensional, born and based in London. He did a foundation course at East Ham Technical College, 1975–6; gained an honours degree in fine art at Middlesex Polytechnic, 1976–9; obtained a master's in painting, Royal College of Art, 1980–3; then studied for a postgraduate diploma in art therapy at Hertfordshire College of Art, 1990–1. Notable teachers included the sculptor Paul Neagu and the painter John Loker. From 1992 was a member of the British Association of Art Therapists, from 1993 the Japanese Vintage Motorcycle Club. Illustrated many German publications, notably books by Erich Fried and Geoffrey Trease, and was included in Peter Marcan's 1992 publications *An East London Album* and *A Bermondsey and Rotherhithe Album*. Fried tended to show at publicly funded venues and public spaces temporarily converted for exhibitions rather than commercial galleries, and had no dealer.

Klaus FRIEDEBERGER 1922– Artist mainly in oil paint, born in Berlin, Germany. He arrived in England in 1939, Australia in 1940, and studied painting as an ex-service student at East Sydney Technical College, 1947–50, returning to London in 1950, settling in Blackheath. Friedeberger won the Mosman Art Prize, 1949, the Europe Prize, Ostende, 1964 gold medal. An important series of Friedeberger's pictures was about children. From the 1970s his paintings were not about something outside themselves. "I want them to have a presence with a convincing reality of their own." As well as many group shows in Europe and Australia from 1944 Friedeberger had solo exhibitions at Hamilton Galleries and New Gallery, Belfast, 1963; Warwick Arts Trust, 1986; Eva Jekel Gallery 202, 1990; and a retrospective at Woodlands Art Gallery, 1992.

Arthur FRIEDENSON 1872–1955 Painter of landscapes and coastal scenes, born in Leeds, Yorkshire. After apprenticeship to a sign painter, from late-1880s he studied at Académie Julian, Paris, and at Académie Royale des Beaux-Arts, in Antwerp. Worked in Netherlands, where he was influenced by local landscape painters. From about 1910 he worked at various locations in Dorset, dying at Parkstone after prolonged ill-health. Friedenson showed prolifically at RA, Fine Art Society, Goupil Gallery and elsewhere, and Tate Gallery holds his work.

Ian FRIEND 1951– Sculptor, born in Eastbourne, Sussex. He studied at Exeter College of Art, 1969–70, Birmingham College of Art, 1970–3, and Slade School of Fine Art, 1973–5. In latter year gained Boise Travelling Fellowship. Group exhibitions included Third British International Drawing Biennale, Dorman Museum, Cleveland, 1977; House Gallery, 1979; and Serpentine Summer Show 1, 1980. Also had a solo exhibition at House Gallery, 1978. Lived in London.

Ian FRIERS 1910–1975 Sculptor who was by profession a civil servant, brother of the artist Rowel Friers. After initial education at the Model School and College of Technology in Belfast, where he was born, Friers was a self-taught artist who held senior positions in the RUA. He exhibited there, RHA and in Bradford, CEMA in Northern Ireland buying his work. Lived in Dundonald, County Down.

Rowel FRIERS 1920– Painter, cartoonist, book illustrator, stage designer and muralist, born in Belfast, Northern Ireland, brother of the artist Ian Friers. He attended Belfast College of Art on a scholarship, having trained in lithography with S C Allen, Belfast. Most Irish newspapers went on to use Friers' work, plus periodicals such as *Radio Times* and *Dublin Opinion*. He was noted for his amusing caricatures of notabilities, such as the politicians Enoch Powell and Ian Paisley, in the National Portrait Gallery. Ulster Museum and Art Gallery and Arts Council of Northern Ireland also hold his work. He was a member of RUA and Ulster Watercolour Society. Friers was granted an honorary master's degree by the Open University for contributions to art. He showed with CEMA, RHA, Arts Council of Northern Ireland and in the American tour of Contemporary Ulster Artists. His books included *Wholly Friers* and *The Revolting Irish*. Lived in Holywood, County Down.

Elisabeth FRINK 1930–1993 Sculptor, draughtsman and teacher, born Thurlow, Suffolk. Studied at Guildford School of Art, 1947–9, and Chelsea School of Art, 1949–53, under Willi Soukop and Bernard Meadows. She taught at Chelsea School of Art, 1951–61, St Martin's School of Art, 1954–62, and at Royal College of Art, 1965–7. After early exhibiting with LG, Frink had a one-man show at St George's Gallery in 1955 and four years later at Bertha Schaefer Gallery, New York. Over the years she established herself as a sculptor concerned with themes, such as goggle men, running men and horses with and without riders. She worked on many major public commissions, such as Wild Boar for Harlow New Town; Blind Beggar and Dog, at Bethnal Green; and a noble horse and rider, Piccadilly, London. The predatory and the vulnerable are both important aspects of Frink's work. She was elected RA in 1977 and five years later became Dame Elisabeth Frink. Made a Companion of Honour, 1992. Exhibited extensively internationally, with work in major collections including Tate Gallery and Arts Council. While fighting cancer Frink struggled to complete her last commission, a monumental but unusual figure of Christ for the front of the Anglican cathedral in Liverpool, unveiled a week before her death in Woolland, Dorset. There was a memorial show at Yorkshire Sculpture Park, Bretton Hall, 1994. Frink's son was the painter Lin Jammet.

Paul FRIPP 1890–1945 Painter, draughtsman, photographer and teacher, born in Mansfield, Nottinghamshire, into a family which on both sides included artists. He attended Bristol and Leicester Schools of Art, then in 1909 won the Bennet Scholarship and a free studentship to the Royal College of Art; returned to Leicester for two years to train for his painting diploma; and postponed return to the Royal College when World War I began. He was commissioned in the Army and served in Gallipoli, Egypt and Palestine, was mentioned in despatches and was twice wounded. With a miniature camera in his tobacco pouch he took hundreds of films (in 1931 Fripp was elected a fellow of the Royal Photographic Society and he won several medals). Returned to Royal College in 1919, graduating in 1921. Taught at Cheltenham Ladies' College, becoming a member of Cheltenham Camera Club and then its president and showing with Cheltenham Group of Artists, 1921–32. Also showed at RA and NEAC. After heading the Art Schools at Bideford and Bath Fripp was appointed principal at Carmarthen, where he died. He was a big, humorous, enthusiastic man, always preoccupied by some invention or idea. Fripp was celebrated with a show at Cheltenham Museum and Art Gallery, 1986. Carmarthen Museum holds examples.

Clifford FRITH 1924– Painter, draughtsman and teacher, born in London. He studied at Camberwell School of Arts and Crafts, where he later taught, and at St Martin's School of Art. His teachers included Victor Pasmore and R V Pitchforth. Frith also taught at Goldsmiths' College School of Art. Exhibited RA, Wildenstein and Redfern Galleries and elsewhere. Did lithographic work for the catering firm J Lyons & Co and had work bought by Contemporary Art Society. Lived in London.

Edgar Silver FRITH 1890–1974 Sculptor and teacher, born and lived in London, son of the sculptor William Silver Frith. Studied at Kennington and Lambeth Schools of Art and Royal Academy Schools and went on to become head of the sculpture section at City and Guilds of London Institute, Kennington and Lambeth Art School. Joined Art Workers' Guild in 1923 and was made an associate of RBS in 1932. Showed at RA, Walker Art Gallery in Liverpool and elsewhere.

Michael FRITH 1951– Painter and illustrator, born in Kingston upon Thames, Surrey, who studied graphic arts at Canterbury College of Art. Among his many illustrative jobs was sketching the trial of the politician Jeremy Thorpe at the Old Bailey and, for Independent Television News, that of the Yorkshire Ripper murderer, Peter Sutcliffe. He also painted the portrait of the publisher Robert Maxwell for the National Portrait Gallery. Exhibited at Smith's Gallery, the Illustrators' Gallery and National Portrait Gallery and in 1993 had a solo show at John Adams Fine Art Ltd with Canon Gallery of restaurant watercolours done while illustrating the Craig Brown Table Talk column in the *Sunday Times*.

Marguerite FROBISHER 1891–1974 Painter and teacher, born Lucy Marguerite Frobisher in Leeds, Yorkshire. She studied at the Kemp-Welch School of Painting from about 1911, and like her teacher specialised in animal subjects. Between 1916–21 Frobisher returned to Leeds, then went back to Bushey, lived with Kemp-Welch and became secretary of her school. Two years after it was closed, in 1928 Frobisher opened her own, as The Frobisher School of Art. Although she continued to teach until her death, from the early 1940s until Kemp-Welch died in 1958 Frobisher again lived with her as friend and companion. Kemp-Welch left Frobisher her property and pictures and for some years from 1967 a Lucy Kemp-Welch Memorial Art Gallery existed, until the pictures had to be put into store. Frobisher exhibited widely, including RCamA and SWA both of which she was a member, also RBSA, Paris Salon, RSA and other venues. Bushey Museum has shown her work.

Fanchon FRÖHLICH fl. from 1960s– Printmaker, philosopher and painter, born in Iowa, America, as Fanchon Angst. She studied philosophy at University of Chicago, continuing her studies with Rudolph Carnap and doing postgraduate work in Oxford with Sir Peter Strawson. A section of her thesis on The Logical Qualities of Material Objects was published in *Mind*. Married the theoretical physicist Herbert Fröhlich. Began painting under her married name, studying at Liverpool College of Art under a postgraduate scholarship; with Peter Lanyon in Cornwall; Japanese ink painting with Goto San in Kyoto; and etching with S W Hayter, of Atelier 17, in Paris. Hayter's ideas were important to Fröhlich, who wrote papers for conferences and contributed to books on such subjects as aesthetics and the relation of physics to biology. Formed a group of artists known as Collective Phenomena in Liverpool, where she lived, in 1990. In the group, "two or more painters intertwine their strokes and areas of colour on the same canvas according to visual counterpoint." Exhibited at Picton Library, Liverpool, in 1992, and in Paris in 1994 "where several people painted before the audience accompanied by music by a composer improvising according to our movements" and had work exhibited. Exhibited her own work in Atelier 17 shows internationally, also in Japan and at Liverpool Academy. Walker Art Gallery, Liverpool, and Bowes Museum, Newcastle, hold Fröhlich's work.

Hester FROOD 1882–1971 Painter, draughtsman and printmaker, notably of architectural subjects, born in New Zealand. She was educated at Exeter High School and studied art in the city and at Atelier Colarossi, Paris, for six months. In 1906 on a visit to Scotland she met the artist David Young Cameron who said that he would teach her to etch. She early on showed at RA and RSA with success and had a first solo show at Colnaghi's in 1925, followed by another at Dunthorne's in 1927. Towards the end of World War II Frood had the first of two shows in Glasgow, and in 1946–9 final exhibitions with Colnaghi's. By then she was long settled in Topsham, Devon. Fry Gallery put on a show of her work in 1990. British Museum, Victoria & Albert Museum and Scottish National Gallery of Modern Art hold examples.

Millie FROOD 1900–1988 Painter, draughtsman and teacher, born in Motherwell, Lanarkshire. She studied at Glasgow School of Art and taught at Bellshill Academy. Early on she showed with RSA and RSW and with the arrival of the painter J D Fergusson and his dancer wife Margaret Morris from France in 1939, and the influx of foreign painters such as Josef Herman and Jankel Adler, Frood became part of a movement which revitalised the arts in the city after World War II. She showed with the New Scottish Group and designed the costumes and set for the ballet *The Harvesters*, put on in 1961, dance in Scotland having been given new life with Margaret Morris' Celtic Ballet Club, the Celtic Ballet of Scotland and the resulting Scottish National Ballet. Frood had a number of solo shows in Lanarkshire and Glasgow, latterly her work was exhibited in America and Japan and in 1989 Cyril Gerber Fine Art, Glasgow, held a show linking her with the New Scottish Group.

Andy FROST 1957– Sculptor and draughtsman, born in Bedford. Andrew Frost studied at Lanchester Polytechnic, Coventry and Reading University. In 1979–80 Frost was in Rotterdam on a Royal Netherlands Scholarship, then in 1982 visited America on a Boise Travel Scholarship. He then became Henry Moore Foundation Fellow in Sculpture at Camberwell School of Arts and Crafts. His sculptures utilised a range of materials, from wood and steel to plastic and fibreglass. Although they had titles such as Batmobile (1983, Arts Council collection) and E1 Cid Chancing his Arm and could be entertaining and amusing, Frost's creations were often quite frightening and dynamic depictions of energy and power. He showed in a number of British galleries, was included in New Contemporaries at ICA, was in the 1983 Whitechapel Open Exhibition and in the Welsh Sculpture Trust's Margam event Sculpture in a Country Park in the same year.

Anthony FROST 1951– Painter in acrylic and teacher, born in St Ives, Cornwall. His family moved to Banbury when he was young and he went to the Art School there, 1967–70, then Cardiff College of Art, 1970–3. Returned to live in Cornwall in 1974, at Morvah, with a studio in Penzance. He commonly worked to a background of rock music and designed an album cover and backdrop in 1990 for the world tour of a favourite group, The Fall. Frost was much in demand as a teacher of colour to children. He said he wanted his own pictures "not to be influenced. I want them to be colour and shape. I don't want people to see things in them … It's like creating your own language." Took part in many mixed exhibitions, solo shows including Newlyn Art Gallery, 1979, later ones Gordon Hepworth Gallery, Newton St Cyres, and Royal Cornwall Museum Galleries, Truro, both 1991. Contemporary Art Society, Nuffield Trust and John Moores hold examples. His father was the artist Terry Frost.

C J Fenton FROST: *see* **Cyril James FROST**

Cyril James FROST 1885– Portrait painter and printmaker, born in Croydon, Surrey, who studied at the School of Art there under Francis Jackson. Exhibited RA, RP, UA and RBA, sometimes signing his work C J Fenton Frost. Lived at Banbury, Oxfordshire.

Dennis FROST 1925– Portrait painter in oil and pastel. Born in London, Frost studied art at St Martin's School of Art and Putney School of Art. Exhibited RP. He illustrated Ernest Savage's book *Painting in Pastel* and Joe Singer's *Figures in Pastel* and it is in this medium that many think Frost's best work was done. Lived at Eastergate, near Chichester, Sussex.

Shirley Jane FROST 1935– Painter, craftsman, jeweller and teacher, born in London. She was educated partly in England at Roedean School, partly in South Africa and attended Worthing and Wimbledon Schools of Art and the Royal College of Art, 1957–60. Went on to teach at Birmingham Polytechnic. Showed at London Design Centre, elsewhere in Britain and on the continent and in America.

Stuart FROST 1960– Sculptor, born in Bath, Somerset, using a variety of materials, whose output was characterised by an interest in natural objects, their place within an environment and their relationship to culture, myth and history. Frost drew inspiration from wide travels, including the Central Americas and Scandinavia, where he was based in Bergen, Norway. Frost attended Bristol Polytechnic, 1979–80; gained a fine art honours degree from Wolverhampton Polytechnic, 1980–3; and obtained his master's in sculpture from the Royal College of Art, 1983–6. From 1984 held many residencies, later ones including Dumfries and Galloway, 1997. Group shows included Mikkeli Taide

Museo, Finland, 1988; Nordnorsk Samtidskunst, Norway, 1991–6; and Høstutstillingen, Oslo, 1994–6. Had a solo exhibition at Oulu Taide Museo, Finland, 1988, later ones including Victoria Art Gallery, Bath, 1997. Several Norwegian collections, including its Arts Council, hold examples.

Terry FROST 1915– Painter, printmaker and teacher, born in Leamington Spa, Warwickshire. Did a variety of jobs after leaving school, then served in the Army and was held as a prisoner of war. Imprisoned in Bavaria he met the painter Adrian Heath who encouraged Frost to paint in oil. After the war Frost studied in the evenings at Birmingham College of Art, then at St Ives School of Painting and at Camberwell School of Art in the late 1940s. Frost later went on to teach at a number of art schools, including periods at Reading and Newcastle Universities and at Banff Summer School, Canada. Frost began abstract painting in 1949, shortly before returning to St Ives where he worked, 1950–2, as assistant to the sculptor Barbara Hepworth. Frost is notable for his use of primary colours and of shapes reflecting Cornish marine life, its bobbing boats and heaving water. Completed much work in paint and collage, which has a spare, taut quality. He exhibited widely internationally and in England, notably at Redfern Gallery, New Art Centre and Austin/Desmond Fine Art. Frost, whose son was the artist Anthony Frost, was elected RA in 1992 and was knighted in 1998. Tate Gallery holds his work. Had a studio at Newlyn, Cornwall.

Winifred FROST: *see* **Wyn BORGER**

Jonathan FROUD 1958– Sculptor, whose output included installations and performance pieces, and teacher, born in Hengistbury Head, Dorset. Direct contact with the public was important to Froud when creating works, which included materials such as plastic waste pipes and computer printouts. Froud studied at Bournemouth and Poole College of Art, 1975–6; Brighton Polytechnic, 1976–9; and Royal College of Art, 1979–82 (he later taught there part-time). In 1982–3 he worked and travelled in South America. Awards included Cox Award; Royal College Award to work in Carrara, Italy; British Council Royal Wedding Award; Royal College Major Travelling Scholarship; a Henry Moore Foundation Award; Greater London Arts Association Award; and Chelsea Arts Club/Guinness Award for Most Promising Young Sculptor. In 1984–5, Froud was Fourth Merseyside Artist in Residence at the Bridewell Studios and Walker Art Gallery, having a solo show at the Walker in 1985. Other exhibitions included New Contemporaries, ICA, 1979 (where he was a prize winner); Quarries, Camden Arts Centre, 1983; and Drawings, Chelsea School of Art, 1985.

Martin FROY 1926– Painter, mural artist and teacher, born in London. After studying history at Cambridge University and service in the Royal Air Force, Froy was at Slade School of Fine Art, 1949–51, being Gregory Fellow in Painting at University of Leeds, 1951–4. From 1953–8 Froy was artist-consultant to Coventry's city architect. He also designed murals for the Belgrade Theatre there. From 1953–5 Froy taught engraving at Slade School of Fine Art; taught at Bath Academy of Art, 1954–65; was head of painting at Chelsea School of Art, 1966–72; from then being professor of fine art at University of Reading. Froy had a solo show at Leicester Galleries in 1961, others following at University of Sussex, Arnolfini Gallery in Bristol, Park Square Gallery in Leeds, and Reading University in 1979. Arts Council holds several examples of his work.

Anthony FRY 1927– Painter and teacher, born in Theydon Bois, Essex. Studied under Maurice Feild at the Downs School, Colwall, and attended Bryanston, where he continued to paint. Was at Edinburgh College of Art, 1946–7, then Camberwell School of Art, 1948–50, and was Rome Prize winner 1950. Having been taught by Victor Pasmore and Claude Rogers at Camberwell, Fry was a natural participant in the 1948 Wakefield City Art Gallery Euston Road Group show. He became member of teaching staff at Bath Academy of Art in 1954, joining Camberwell two years later. Had first one-man show at St George's Gallery in 1954 and in New York at Durlacher Bros in 1961. Also showed at LG of which he was a member, ICA, RWA and elsewhere. Arts Council and Tate Gallery bought his work. Lived in Box, Wiltshire.

Gladys Windsor FRY 1890– Artist in various media and teacher, married to the painter Windsor Fry. She met him in 1906 when he was teaching and she was a student at Hammersmith School of Art, marrying him 16 years later. She also studied with the Horsham-based artist Florence Davey and with G H Catt, in Chichester. Fry was a King's Prize winner for design and gained City and Guilds embroidery honours. Her publications included *Working Drawings for Embroidery* and *Embroidery and Needlework*. Showed at RBA, Walker Art Gallery in Liverpool, at the Festival of Britain in 1951 and in the provinces. Lived for many years at Hove, Sussex, later in Brighton.

James FRY 1910– Artist in watercolour, pastel and oil. Fry was born in London and studied at Watford School of Art under Arthur Scott, well known as a painter and etcher. Fry lived at Corfe Castle, in Dorset.

Malcolm FRY 1909– Artist in various media, full name Arthur Malcolm Fry, who studied at Bournemouth School of Art, his teachers including Leslie Ward. He was at various times director of RWS of which he was a member, RE and SPS. Showed in main London galleries, in the provinces and abroad and had a series of one-man exhibitions. Bournemouth Corporation holds his work. Lived in Orpington, Kent.

Maxwell FRY 1899–1987 Architect, teacher, painter and collector, born in Wallasey, Cheshire, full name Edwin Maxwell Fry, educated at the Liverpool Institute and Liverpool University School of Architecture, graduating in 1923. With several other forward-looking architects in 1931 he established the Modern Architectural Research (MARS) group, which was influential in

Britain and abroad. In 1943 with his second wife Jane Drew he was appointed town planning adviser in West Africa and in 1951 he went to India as senior architect with Le Corbusier for Chandigarh, the new capital city of Punjab. Fry's books included *Autobiographical Sketches* and *Art in the Machine Age*. In his later years he became the RA's professor of architecture and turned to painting. He had been elected a fellow of RIBA in 1930, winning its Gold Medal in 1964. Fry was elected RA in 1972 and showed with Drian and Fieldborne Galleries. He was a noted patron of young artists. Lived finally at Cotherstone, County Durham.

Windsor FRY 1862–1947 Painter and teacher, full name Harry Windsor Fry, born in Torquay, Devon, married to the artist Gladys Windsor Fry, whom he met while he was teaching at Hammersmith School of Art. He was educated privately in Torquay, studying at St John's Wood School of Art and Royal Academy Schools, where he was a medal winner. During World War I he served with the Royal Fusiliers, 1914–19, and was renowned for his physical fitness and brilliance as a swordfighter. Fry was a prolific exhibitor, showing many times with RBA of which he was a member, RA, RHA, RI, ROI and elsewhere. Liverpool Corporation bought his picture Youth and Age. Lived in London.

Katherine Mary FRYER 1910– Painter, wood engraver and teacher, born in Leeds, Yorkshire, where she studied at the College of Art, 1926–31. Went on to teach at Bath School of Art for a period, living in Bath, Somerset. She exhibited Redfern Gallery and in north of England galleries, Wakefield and Harrogate Art Galleries buying her work. Later lived at Harborne, Birmingham.

Stan FRYER 1906– Painter and draughtsman, born and lived in Manchester, who studied at the local School of Art, in Italy and Africa. He did a considerable amount of illustrative work for national and provincial press. Showed at RI, RCamA, with Army Art Society, UA and widely in the provinces.

Wilfred Moody FRYER 1891–1967 Painter, commercial draughtsman and teacher, born in London. Studied at Bradford School of Art. Exhibited RA, RBA, RI and widely in the provinces. Was a member of Croydon Art Society; Langham Sketch Club, of which for a time he was chairman; and the Wapping Group of Artists, of which he was president. Lived at Addiscombe, Surrey.

Akiko FUJIKAWA 1948– Printmaker, born in Kyoto, Japan, married to the artist Geoffrey Earle Wickham. She gained her bachelor's degree at Kohka College, Kyoto, 1970, then studied traditional Japanese woodblock printing, moku hanga, at Asahi School of Art, 1977–81, with Takeji Asano. From 1980 showed with Shinanokai Group in Kyoto, in 1985 taking further courses with Japanese masters. In 1986 set up Chapel Studio, Burnham-on-Crouch, Essex, with Wickham. Took part in open exhibitions at Beecroft Gallery, Southend-on-Sea, from 1990. Solo shows included Mildmay House, Burnham, 1993. British Museum holds her work.

Raf FULCHER 1948– Sculptor and teacher, born in Essex, who studied at University of Newcastle upon Tyne, 1966–72. Went on to teach at Sunderland Polytechnic, settling at Ramshaw, Bishop Auckland, County Durham. Fulcher worked in a variety of materials and was included in the Serpentine Gallery/South Bank Centre's The Sculpture Show, 1983, at that time contending that British art was "characterised by a peculiar reserve or reticence when dealing with the intensely subjective". His Garden Front, of 1981, was sited at Jesmond Metro Station, Newcastle.

George FULLARD 1923–1973 Sculptor in metals, wood, rubbish and objects from toy shops. Was also an outstanding draughtsman and teacher. Born in Sheffield, Yorkshire, the son of a miner, he studied art at the College of Art there, 1938–42. After war service in the Army, during which he was badly injured at the battle for Cassino, Fullard studied at Royal College of Art, 1945–7 under the sculptors Frank Dobson and Richard Garbe, then lived in Paris. From 1963 he was in charge of the sculpture department at Chelsea School of Art. Militarism and ships and the sea were leading themes in Fullard's work, which was always an exploration into unknown possibilities. He said that "the artist works towards the miracle of making visible that which apparently did not exist." He showed in John Moores Liverpool Exhibitions from 1957; Contemporary British Sculpture, the Arts Council touring show, from 1958; Gimpel-Hanover Gallery, Zürich, 1963; British Sculpture at Redfern Gallery in 1972, and elsewhere. Had a solo show at Woodstock Gallery in 1958; Gallery One, 1961; Marlborough New London Gallery, 1964; Park Square Gallery, Leeds, 1972; there was a major retrospective at Serpentine Gallery, 1974; a selective one at Yorkshire Sculpture Park, 1997; another key show at Mappin Art Gallery, Sheffield, 1998. Arts Council, West Riding Education Authority, Ferens Art Gallery in Hull and Australian and American collections hold examples. Lived in London.

James FULLARTON 1946– Painter and lecturer, born in Glasgow, where he studied at the School of Art under David Donaldson, gaining his diploma in 1969. From that time he painted full-time while lecturing for Scottish Arts Council. He won the David Cargill Award, 1976, the Britoil Award, 1986. Fullarton used a broad palette, with colour the dominant feature, for portraits, landscape and still life in oil and acrylic. Showed with RSA and Royal Glasgow Institute of the Fine Arts. Solo exhibitions included Lillie Art Gallery, Milngavie; John D Kelly Gallery and Ewan Mundy Fine Art, both Glasgow; and Macaulay Gallery, Stenton. Lillie Art Gallery, Robert Fleming Holdings and Royal College of Physicians and Surgeons, Glasgow, hold examples. Lived in Straiton, Ayrshire.

Cynthia Dehn FULLER: *see* **FRANCYN**

Dorothy FULLER 1904– Painter and teacher who was born and lived in Brighton, Sussex, for many years. Her earlier work was signed with her unmarried name Dorothy Sawyers. She studied at Brighton College of Art, 1919–26, with Louis Ginnett; gained the Turner Gold Medal and British Institutional Scholarship in 1927, then the Edward Stott Travelling Scholarship and Gold Medal in 1929, while studying at Royal Academy Schools under Walter Westley Russell; then travelled abroad, 1929–30. Taught at Worthing College of Art, 1931–42. She was a member of Sussex Women's Art Club and Reynolds Club and showed at RA and public galleries in Brighton and Hove.

Leonard John FULLER 1891–1973 Portrait, figure, still life and landscape painter in oil. Fuller studied art at Clapham School of Art and the Royal Academy Schools, then began his notable career as a teacher of painting and drawing at St John's Wood Art Schools 1922–32. From 1927–37 was assistant art master at Dulwich College, where he had been educated. In 1938 Fuller moved to St Ives, Cornwall, where he founded the St Ives School of Painting, which he ran until he died. Although Fuller was a painter of a traditional kind, he was open to new ideas, advocating a more tolerant approach to modern art in 1953 in St Ives, four years after the founding of the Penwith Society of Arts, of which he was elected chairman. Advanced artists such as Terry Frost and Bob Law were to study with Fuller. Fuller exhibited widely, including RA, RSA, RP and Paris Salon, where in 1927 he gained a silver medal. Newport City Museum and Art Gallery and Plymouth City Museum and Art Gallery hold his work. Lived in St Ives.

Martin FULLER 1943– Painter and draughtsman, born in Leamington Spa, Warwickshire. He attended Mid-Warwickshire College of Art, 1960–2, then Hornsey College of Art, 1962–4, in the latter year being awarded a Guggenheim-Mckinley Scholarship, American Workshop, Italy. Fuller's work was abstract with references to landscape and figurative allusions and was described as having "painterly elegance and wit". Among Fuller's group appearances were Richard Demarco Gallery, Edinburgh Festival; Arnolfini Gallery in Bristol; Angela Flowers and Redfern Galleries and Barbican Centre. After a solo show at Arnolfini in 1968 others followed there, also Bear Lane Gallery in Oxford, Grabowski Gallery, Thumb Gallery, Austin/Desmond Fine Art in 1990, KDK in 1998. Bristol City Art Gallery holds his work. Lived in London, but for a time was artist-in-residence in Santa Fe, America.

Overton FULLER fl. c.1940–1960 Painter whose full name was Violet Overton Fuller. After education in Belgium and Wales she attended Beckenham School of Art, under Percy Hague Jowett, the Central School of Arts and Crafts with Robert Kirkland Jamieson and St Martin's School of Art. She was especially fond of painting flowers. Her husband was an Indian Army officer, so that she exhibited partly in India, but also widely at RWS, UA, BWS, SWA, PS, WIAC.

Ron FULLER 1936– Maker of witty animated models and toys, printmaker and teacher, born in Cornwall. He studied fine art at Plymouth, Falmouth and the Royal College of Art, then taught printmaking in Bristol and in London colleges. In 1972, Fuller moved to Laxfield, Sussex and reduced his teaching commitments to concentrate on toys and models, gaining international recognition. He used largely traditional techniques in painted wood and sheet metal and was influenced by folk art. His masterwork was his contribution to The Ride of Life, an extraordinary fairground-style ride made in sections by over 20 artists, commissioned for a shopping centre in Sheffield, but not installed. It was resurrected for Fuller's solo show at Gainsborough's House, Sudbury, 1996.

Violet FULLER 1920– Artist in watercolour and oil, born in north London, who studied at Hornsey School of Art, 1937–40, with Russell Reeve, then at Stroud School of Art, 1942–4. She "concentrated mainly landscape, the elements and the quality of light" in her work. Fuller, who did graphic work, was a prolific exhibitor. She was a fellow and founder-member of the Free Painters and Sculptors, having solo shows including the Loggia Gallery, Woodstock Gallery and Old Bakehouse Gallery, Sevenoaks. Mixed shows included RA, RBA, RI, and NEAC. London Boroughs of Enfield and Haringey hold her pictures. Lived in Woodingdean, Sussex.

Hamish FULTON 1946– Artist, born in London, who created "art resulting from the experience of individual walks". Between 1964–9 Fulton studied at Hammersmith College of Art, St Martin's School of Art and the Royal College of Art. From 1969 he made walks through several continents, adhering to strict, self-imposed programmes, such as "a continuous 106-mile walk without sleep", featured in Into the Night at Annely Juda Fine Art, 1993. Showed frequently and widely in Britain and abroad, and numerous public collections, including Tate Gallery; Bibliothèque Nationale in Paris; Metropolitan Museum, Tokyo; and The Brooklyn Museum, New York, hold examples.

William FURLONG 1944– Artist and teacher, born in Surrey, who attended Guildford School of Arts and Crafts, 1960–5, then the Royal Academy Schools, 1965–8. Went on to be head of the foundation department at Wimbledon School of Art. With Michael Archer he ran Audio Arts (see separate entries). Lived in London.

Stephen FURLONGER 1939– Sculptor in all media and teacher, born in Hindhead, Surrey. He studied at Christchurch University, New Zealand, and Royal College of Art under Bernard Meadows. Furlonger was a Gulbenkian Rome Scholar who did part-time teaching at various colleges. Then taught full-time at Lanchester Polytechnic and became head of sculpture at Central School of Art & Design and Central St Martins College of Art & Design. Furlonger wrote that most of his work "has involved the use of water as a medium." Collective exhibitions included Towards Art II; Survey '68: Abstract Sculpture, at

Camden Arts Centre, 1968; Jubilee Show of British Sculpture, Battersea; and Hayward Annual, 1978. Solo exhibitions included Galerie Swart, Amsterdam, and a number of studio shows. Arts Council and public galleries in Auckland and Wellington, New Zealand, hold examples.

James FURNEAUX 1935– Watercolourist, printmaker and teacher who gained his diploma from Gray's School of Art in Aberdeen, where he continued to live, in 1958, the year he won the RSA Chalmers-Jervis Prize. Exhibited for many years with RSA, SSA and Peacock Printmakers in Aberdeen. Was included in Six Members of Staff, Aberdeen College of Commerce, at Artspace, 1981; 10 North-East Artists, Artspace Aberdeen Edinburgh Festival show and tour, 1981–2; and Scottish Print Open Three, organised by Dundee Printmakers' Workshop, 1983. Solo shows included Aberdeen Arts Centre, 1978, and restaurant at Aberdeen Art Gallery, 1997.

Paul FURNEAUX 1962– Painter, born in Aberdeen. He studied at Edinburgh College of Art and won a postgraduate diploma with distinction. Furneaux's pictures are singular, being inhabited by mystical figures. The painter won many awards. These included the RSA's Keith Award for Best Student in 1986; Young Scottish Artist of the Year, sponsored by Miller Homes, which provided him with a studio in Paris for a year; and the *Sunday Times Scotland* Mayfest Award in 1989. After working in Paris he had a solo show at Todd Gallery and at Compass Gallery, Glasgow. Aberdeen Art Gallery is among several public collections holding his work.

Jane FURNESS 1931– Painter, artist in collage and mixed media, draughtsman and teacher, full name Valerie Jane Furness, who was born in South Molton, Devon. She studied at Wimbledon School of Art with John Ward and Gerald Cooper, also at University of London Institute of Education. Landscape, the human figure and a series based on families in part of Bristol were among her subjects. From 1957–63 worked in Cornwall, showing regularly at Newlyn Gallery and Penwith Society of Arts, joining it in early 1960s. She later lived and taught in London, Bristol and Cornwall and was head of art at Red Maids' School, Bristol, 1979–86, and taught in illustration department of Falmouth School of Art, 1986–94. In 1962 had first show at Oxford Gallery, later ones including Porthmeor Gallery in St Ives, 1991, and Beatrice Royal Gallery, Eastleigh, 1994. Queen's Hotel in Penzance and Nina Zborowska hold examples. Lived finally in Clifton, Bristol.

John FURNIVAL 1933– Artist in pen and ink, mixed media, printmaker and teacher, born in London. He attended Wimbledon College of Art, 1951–5 and Royal College of Art, 1957–60. In 1960 he moved to Gloucestershire, settling in Woodchester. He taught at Stroud and Cheltenham Art Colleges until 1966, when he taught initially at Bath Academy of Art and then at Bath College of Higher Education. With Dom Sylvester Houédard set up Openings Press in 1964 and with him staged many shows of concrete poetry stemming from schemes worked on at Bath Academy with students. Took part in international shows and had retrospective at Laing Art Gallery in Newcastle upon Tyne in 1971. The following year he won Arts Council Prize at International Print Biennale, Bradford. Arts Council holds his work.

Roger FURSE 1903–1972 Artist in various media, film and stage designer. Born at Ightham, Kent, he studied under Henry Tonks at the Slade School of Fine Art, 1920–4, after education at Eton College. Exhibited at the Leicester and Berkeley Galleries and the Salon d'Automne, Paris. The Imperial War Museum holds his work. Furse was principally known as a theatrical designer, of settings and costumes. He had to his credit dozens of productions at major London theatres, such as the Old Vic, Lyric and Haymarket, plus provincial and foreign venues. He also designed costumes and armour for Laurence Olivier's film *Henry V*, in 1944, plus other notable films such as *Odd Man Out, Spartacus* and *The Roman Spring of Mrs Stone*. Lived in London.

Hideo FURUTA 1949– Artist and teacher, notable as a sculptor, born in Hiroshima, Japan. From 1969–71, Furuta attended Tokyo Visual Art College, Tokyo, for foundation and sculpture; for five years, after involvement in the student movement, studied art, mathematics and physics; concentrated on etching and engraving at Hijiyama Art College, Hiroshima, 1977–8; then comparative philosophy and aesthetics at Hiroshima University, 1978–80. He worked as a quarry man at Ishizaki Quarry, Kurahashi Island, 1982–3. After a period teaching in Chile in 1984, Furuta in 1985 began teaching and sculpting in Wales, and went on to hold a large number of posts and residencies in Britain; was a visiting lecturer at Trondheim Art College, Norway, in 1991; and was Henry Moore Fellow in Sculpture at Northumbria University, Newcastle, 1992–4. His sound works and public performances included an African Drum Performance there, 1993. Furuta took part in many group shows in Britain and abroad. He had a solo exhibition of silkscreen prints at Saeki Gallery, Hiroshima, 1977, later ones including sculptures, drawings, photos and video works at University Gallery of Newcastle, 1997. This featured granite and basalt spheres and cones, carved at a quarry on the Solway Firth, when Furuta was described as "an artist who powerfully embodied a synthesis of conceptual and physical concerns". By that time, Furuta's public commissions numbered almost a score, later ones including a monumental outdoor sculpture for Gateshead Sculpture Park, Gateshead: Axiom, in white granite and black basalt, 1993–6. Collections holding his work included Margam Sculpture Park, Port Talbot; Edinburgh Printmakers' Workshop, Edinburgh; Gallery Oriel 31, Newtown; and Glynn Vivian Art Gallery and Museum, Swansea.

Irena FUSEK-FOROSIEWICZ fl. from 1950s– Painter, born in Oharewicze, Poland, who settled in Britain in the early 1950s and studied with Marian Bohusz-Szyszko in London. Working in the Post-Impressionist tradition of colour and light, she made the landscapes of the Sussex Downs, Italy and Spain her main themes. Was active in the Association of Polish Artists in Britain and had a solo show at Polish Cultural Institute in 1996.

Michael FUSSELL 1927–1974 Painter, collagist and teacher who did figurative and abstract work, with a special interest in weather and the sea. He was born in Southampton and educated in Bournemouth, Hampshire. Studied at City & Guilds Art School, St Martin's School of Art, 1946–9, and Royal College of Art, 1949–52, under Rodrigo Moynihan. Taught at St Martin's and from 1964 was head of fine art at Wimbledon School of Art. Showed at RA, Young Contemporaries and in the provinces and had a first solo exhibition at Beaux Arts Gallery in 1956. Tate Gallery and Arts Council, which in 1976 staged a retrospective, hold examples. Lived for many years in London and was married to the artist Evelyn Williams.

G

Christa GAA 1937–1992 Watercolourist, born in Hamburg, Germany. She was married to the painter Ken Howard. The artist studied German philology and art history in Cologne, Bonn and Florence, 1957–60, then painting at Fachhochschule für Kunst und Design in Cologne, 1975–80. Gaa moved to England in 1980. She showed in mixed exhibitions at New Grafton Gallery, New Ashgate Gallery in Farnham, in RA Summer Exhibition and elsewhere. She shared an exhibition at New Grafton in 1984, had a solo show there in 1990 and it held her memorial exhibition in 1992. A typical Gaa watercolour celebrates an informal domestic still life, although she did some landscapes in Britain and abroad. Her technique showed a quiet restraint. Died in Cologne.

Ethel GABAIN 1883–1950 Printmaker and painter, born in Le Havre, of mixed French and Scottish descent. She married the artist John Copley in 1913, their son being the actor Peter Copley. After spending her first 14 years in France Gabain attended an English boarding school, then studied at the Slade School of Fine Art, Collin's studio in Paris and lithography at Central School of Arts and Crafts. With Copley she was a founder-member of the Senefelder Club in 1910. Despite continuing poor health she travelled on the continent and was a prolific printmaker; turned to painting in Italy in 1924, making her first appearance with an oil painting, Zinnias, at RA in 1927. Also exhibited at Goupil, Redfern and Chenil Galleries; with Colnaghi; RSA; Walker Art Gallery in Liverpool; and was a member of RBA (which gave her a memorial exhibition in 1950), ROI and SWA (becoming its vice-president). Gabain's favourite themes were adolescent girlhood and a figure against a window, one model – Carmen – being painted over 50 times. In World War II Gabain was an official war artist. Imperial War Museum holds her work, which is in other collections including Manchester City Art Gallery. In the 1930s Gabain, with scripts supplied by her husband, became a popular lecturer on art history to schools, to boost family funds. In 1985 Garton & Cooke held an exhibition of both artists' prints. Lived in London.

Neville GABIE 1959– Abstract sculptor and teacher, born in Johannesburg, South Africa. After studying at Hull College of Art, 1980–3, and Royal College of Art, 1986–8, Gabie went on to teach at Cheltenham and Gloucester College of Higher Education. He was included in the River exhibition at Goldsmiths' Gallery in 1990 and in the 1993–4 Arts Council touring show Recent British Sculpture. Solo shows included Camden Arts Centre, 1987, and Spacex Gallery, Exeter, 1991. Gabie lived near Stroud, Gloucestershire.

Naum GABO 1890–1977 Constructions artist in a variety of materials, designer, writer and teacher, born in Bryansk, Russia, as Naum Pevsner, brother of the painter Antoine Pevsner. As a young man he changed his name to Naum Gabo so as not to be confused with his brother. Gabo entered Munich University in 1910 to study medicine, then natural sciences, but also attended art history lectures. In 1912 transferred to an engineering school in Munich, in 1913–14 joining his brother in Paris. When World War I broke out he moved to Copenhagen, then Oslo, in 1915 beginning to make constructions. Although sometimes figurative, these were generally abstract, simple and beautiful using a variety of materials, notably later Perspex when he came to England. From 1917–22 Gabo was in Moscow, where he knew advanced artists such as Tatlin and Kandinsky. In 1920 with Pevsner he produced a *Realistic Manifesto* outlining the tenets of pure Constructivism. From 1922 for a decade he was in Berlin in contact with the artists of the de Stijl and Bauhaus movements; with Pevsner he designed for Diaghilev's ballet *La Chatte* in 1926; then from 1932–6 lived in Paris, and was a member of the Abstraction-Création group. After arriving in England in 1936 he helped edit the manifesto volume *Circle*. By now he was married to the painter Miriam Israels, and with her he settled in St Ives, Cornwall, where he was an influential figure. Soon after World War II Gabo moved to America, where he became an American citizen in 1952, carried out important commissions and became professor of the Graduate School of Architecture, Harvard University. He had a retrospective show at Tate Gallery in 1966; again in 1976, after which he gave the gallery a group of works; and there was a retrospective at the Tate in 1987. Gabo died in Wateringbury, Connecticut.

Caroline Sylvia GABRIEL 1912– Early a painter in oil, she later carved in wood and stone. She taught at Avery Hill College of Education and at evening classes and published educational textbooks. Gabriel studied under Randolph Schwabe and George Charlton at Slade School of Fine Art after attending North London Collegiate School. Showed at RA, RBA, SPS, RSA and elsewhere. Lived in Ashington, Sussex.

Edith Mabel GABRIEL 1882–1972 Sculptor, born in Richmond, Surrey. She studied at Heatherley's School of Fine Art and in Paris. Her sculpture was classical with a modern tinge, as in her Mother and Child, illustrated in the volume *RBS: Modern British Sculpture*, published in 1939. Eventually elected a fellow of RBS. Showed RA, RSA, Walker Art Gallery in Liverpool and elsewhere. From 1915 rented 1 Mall Studios, Hampstead, where she remained until her death.

Michael GABRIEL 1931– Sculptor in metals, wood and stone, who studied at Coventry and Cheltenham Colleges of Art. Was a member of Cotswold Art Club and Cheltenham Group of Artists, exhibited at RWA and was included in 19 Young Sculptors at Hillfield Gardens, Gloucester, in 1962, when he was living in Cheltenham. In 1976 Gabriel had a solo show at Trinity College, Oxford.

Andrew GADD 1968– Figurative painter in oil who produced dramatic studies strong in chiaroscuro, he studied at Falmouth School of Art and Royal Academy Schools. Showed at RA Summer Exhibition, Paton Gallery and had a solo show at Agnew, 1995. Metropolitan Museum, New York, holds his work. Lived in Richmond, Surrey.

Anthea Dominique Juliet GAGE 1956– Painter and teacher, born in Edinburgh where she continued to live, daughter of the painter Edward Gage. She studied at Edinburgh College of Art, 1974–9, her teachers including George Donald and David Michie. Went on to teach at Royal High School, Edinburgh. Was a regular exhibitor with SSA and RSW, of both of which she was a member.

Edward GAGE 1925– Painter, illustrator, stage designer, writer and teacher, born in Gullane, East Lothian. He studied at Edinburgh College of Art, 1941–2 and 1947–52, his teachers including William Gillies. Served in Army during World War II in India and Malaya. A postgraduate scholarship and travelling scholarship took him to Majorca. Gage taught at Fettes College until 1968, when he joined the staff of Napier College of Science and Technology, for 20 years from 1958 being a part-time lecturer at Edinburgh College of Art. He was a member of RSW and was president of SSA in 1960–4. Gage also worked as a freelance set designer for Gateway and Citizen's Theatres in the early 1950s; illustrated for a number of publishers, including *Radio Times*; was art critic for *The Scotsman*; and wrote *The Eye in the Wind: Contemporary Scottish Painting since 1945*, published 1977. Gage had a series of solo shows at Scottish Gallery, Edinburgh. Scottish Arts Council, Aberdeen and Edinburgh Universities hold his work. He was the father of the artist Anthea Gage and lived in Edinburgh.

Sylvia Petula GAINSFORD 1942– Artist and illustrator working in acrylic, watercolour and line and as a printmaker, teacher, and gallery owner with her husband Leon Olin. She was born in Tonbridge, Kent, and attended Tunbridge Wells School of Art, studying wood engraving with E Owen Jennings, painting with J Weidman. Gainsford taught and travelled extensively abroad, then from 1974 toured Britain in a mobile studio with her husband; settled in Kent; then went to work at Rhosycaerau, Goodwick, Dyfed, helping to run Gallery One at Fishguard. She worked for publishers including Bishopsgate Press and Bell and Hyman and was commissioned by A G Müller, of Switzerland, to illustrate and design *The Tarot of the Old Path*, 1990. Group shows included Frances Iles Gallery, Rochester, and Nuffield Art Centre, Southampton. She showed solo there with Hamwic Gallery. Gainsford's main interest was wildlife, her aim being "to capture the living spirit and character of the animal". Kallis Foundation in Beverly Hills, California, holds Gainsford's work.

Paul GAISFORD 1941– Landscape and figure painter in oil and watercolour, born in Dorking, Surrey. He studied at Camberwell School of Art, 1956–61; Slade School of Fine Art, 1961–4; and Berlin Academy, 1964; teachers included Sir William Coldstream, Claude Rogers and Frank Auerbach. Solo shows included Ibis, Langton, Piers Feetham and Meldrum Walker Galleries. University College and Berlin Academy of Fine Arts hold examples. For many years Gaisford kept handsome, Moroccan leather-bound diaries which chronicled his life and pre-occupations such as his horse Rosie and gypsy caravan. Lived at Great Rissington, Cheltenham, Gloucestershire.

Richard GALE 1946– Painter, born in Portishead, near Bristol. After attending local art college in Taunton he studied at Kingston School of Art, 1965–8, and Royal College of Art, 1970–3. Work was shown at Basel Art Fair in 1975, Düsseldorf Art Fair in 1976, RA from 1981 and it was selected at National Portrait Gallery for Imperial Tobacco Portrait Award, 1982–3. Had his first solo show at Parkin Gallery, 1977. Gale was a slow worker, finishing only a handful of paintings annually, and they sometimes took several years to germinate. Was noted for his portraits and figure studies employing a realistic technique. Lived in Clevedon, North Somerset.

Neil GALL 1967– Painter, born in Scotland, who studied at Gray's School of Art, Aberdeen, 1987–91, and Slade School of Fine Art, 1991–3. In 1993 he gained an Abbey Major Award to study at the British School at Rome, showing there in 1994, in 1995 taking part in the two-man exhibition Rome Scholars at Gray's School gallery. Gall's oil on canvas Flower Painting No. 7 was included in the 1997–8 John Moores Liverpool Exhibition. Following a year's residency at Durham Cathedral, his exhibition Durham Paintings toured from the Reg Vardy Gallery, Sunderland, 1997–8. Lived in London.

Anya GALLACCIO 1963– Artist, born in Glasgow, who studied at Kingston Polytechnic, 1984–5, and then graduated from Goldsmiths' College with honours, 1985–8. Group exhibitions included Poetic Figuration in the Eighties, Lauderdale House, 1988; The Return of Ulysses, English National Opera, 1989; and Next Phase, Wapping Pumping Station, 1990. Her work was included in the exhibition of sculpture and installations Sweet Home, originated by Mostyn Art Gallery, Llandudno, and tour, 1994. In 1996 she filled the Wapping Pumping Station with an installation of ice, salt, steam and light, in 1997 creating an installation for the lawn of the Serpentine Gallery.

Brian GALLAGHER 1935– Painter and draughtsman who studied with Herbert Green. He showed with London Sketch Club of which he was a member, PS in which he held several key positions, SWLA and in the provinces. Lived in Ashford, Middlesex.

Mary GALLAGHER 1953– Painter, born in Glasgow, where she continued to lived. She attended the School of Art there, 1974–8, having a postgraduate year in 1979. After a period of consolidation, during which the work she produced was well-received, Gallagher decided to paint full-time. She showed at Royal Glasgow Institute of the Fine Arts, Lillie Art Gallery in Milngavie, Perth Museum and Art Gallery and Barclay Lennie Fine Art in Glasgow, having a first solo exhibition in London in 1989 at Portland Gallery. Gallagher was not a prolific artist, her striking still lifes having the studied appearance and rich colour of S J Peploe's.

Arthur GALLINER 1878–1961 Painter, art historian and lecturer, born in Zinten, Germany. Studied art in Berlin, Munich and widely in Italy. Exhibited at a number of galleries in Germany and in England at RI, RBA and elsewhere in London. Royal Library, in Copenhagen, Denmark, holds his work. Wrote a book on the German Impressionist painter Max Liebermann and held several teaching posts, including Hammersmith School of Art, 1947–50, and Borough Polytechnic, 1950–2. Lived in London. He was distantly related to the artist Edith Galliner.

Edith Marguerite GALLINER 1914– Painter in acrylic, potter, etcher and teacher, born and lived in London, distantly related to the artist Arthur Galliner. Her German-Jewish family returned to Germany in the year she was born, she was educated in Berlin, then moved to England again to escape arrest in 1933. As well as studying in Paris, attended Camberwell School of Arts and Crafts and Central School of Art and Design. Taught in Cork, Ireland, and in London. In the early-to-mid-1960s returned to Berlin to paint. Galliner was influenced in Germany by the Bauhaus and Brücke movements, in England by advanced artists such as Ben Nicholson and Victor Pasmore. Group exhibitions included Hamilton Galleries, from 1966; Hampstead Artists' Council, from 1967; Camden Arts Centre, 1970; Annely Juda, from 1970; RE, 1973; German Embassy, 1978; and Art in Exile in Great Britain 1933–45, Camden Arts Centre, 1986. Had a solo show at Hamilton Galleries, 1967, later ones including Galerie Wolfgang Gurlitt, München, 1973. National Gallery in Berlin holds her work.

Vincent GALLOWAY 1894–1977 Painter, mainly of portraits, born in Hull and educated at Ushaw College. Studied at Hull College of Art, in London and the Netherlands. During World War I Galloway served in the East Yorkshires, being wounded at the battle of Oppy Wood, in France, and he also served in the Middle East. He took over as curator at the Ferens Art Gallery, Hull, in 1928, serving until 1960, and he began the collection of local marine artists. Was vice-president of Hull Art Club. Exhibited RA, with RP, of which he was a member, in Nottingham and at RBA. Galloway painted about 250 portraits, a third of which were shown in a retrospective at the Ferens Art Gallery in 1972. The gallery holds several pictures by Galloway, also a portrait of him by G K Beulah. Died in Reading, Berkshire.

Kay GALLWEY 1936– Painter and illustrator who also hand-painted her own frames and created screens in the Oriental style. She began studying at City and Guilds School of Art aged 15, then attended Goldsmiths' College School of Art, in 1953 obtaining a scholarship to Royal Academy Schools, where she remained only six months. Became an illustrator with Artists Partners for *Harper's & Queen* magazine and others while developing as a costume designer and portrait painter. In addition, Gallwey had pastels used by Royle's for their colour 1992 calendar; had paintings accepted by London Underground Posters; and produced books based on her pets. Showed in Britain and America and solo several times with Catto Gallery.

Martina GALVIN 1964– Mainly a painter, but also did some installation work, born in Dublin, Ireland. She studied at the National College of Art & Design, there, and after graduating did her master's degree at South Glamorgan Institute of Higher Education, Cardiff. She took part in many group exhibitions in Ireland and Britain, and had solo shows in Skibbereen, County Cork, and in Cardiff, with one at Mulligan's, Cork Street, in 1994. The paintings there were part of a new series, "where the colour and light of particular landscapes plays a dominant role … These paintings are imaginings of a mythical place, informed by real landscapes."

Abram GAMES 1914–1996 Graphic designer and teacher, born and lived in London, who was self-taught apart from two terms at St Martin's School of Art, 1930, and evening life classes. In 1936, the year he won first prize in a poster competition to publicize London County Council evening classes, Games was dismissed from the commercial art studio Askew-Young for horseplay, and decided to concentrate on his freelance career. He was not by nature an organisation man, although big organisations such as London Transport, Shell and the General Post Office were quick to employ his talents. During World War II Games designed posters for the War Office, 1941–6, some of his Socialistically inclined productions proving controversial. He was also responsible for British and Israeli postage stamps; the 1951 Festival of Britain, Queen's Award to Industry and BBC Television emblems; and gained first prizes in poster competitions in Finland, Portugal, America, Sweden and Spain. Taught at the Royal College of Art, 1946–53, his 1960 book *Over My Shoulder* explaining his methods of work. Games was made a Royal Designer of Industry in 1959 and in 1991 gained the Designers and Art Directors' Association President's Award. Had a series of solo shows overseas and in Britain, including a 60-year retrospective at Camden Arts Centre in 1991 and a show of war posters at the Imperial War Museum in 1994.

Mary GAMLEN 1913– Sculptor, painter and teacher, born in London. She studied at Hornsey School of Art and was on its staff, 1937–45. Became an honorary member of UA, also

exhibiting with RA, NEAC and in the provinces. Settled in Southrepps, Norfolk, and completed a number of village signs in the county as well as church work. Royal Marines Museum holds her Lying-in-State of Sir Winston Churchill.

Nick GAMMON 1958– Abstract painter who studied at Chelsea School of Art, 1976–7, then Bath Academy of Art, Corsham, 1977–80. He was assistant to Howard Hodgkin, 1981–90. Gammon produced dazzling, hard-edged abstracts composed of small rectangles, as shown in Cross Currents, Reed's Wharf Gallery at Barbican Centre, 1996. Had shows at Heritage Centre, 1992; Berning & Daw, 1993; and Blue Gallery, 1995. Lived in Dingle, County Kerry, Ireland.

Reg GAMMON 1894–1997 Painter, draughtsman and writer, born in Petersfield, Hampshire. He was educated at Churcher's College and studied privately with an uncle, Frank Patterson, prior to World War I. In 1918 Muirhead Bone offered to get Gammon into the Slade School of Fine Art, but being married he declined, taking up a career as an illustrator and writer. He drew for *Punch*, cycling and motoring magazines and in the 1930s wrote and illustrated a country feature for the *News Chronicle*. Made extensive walking and cycling trips in Britain, Ireland and Brittany, painting watercolours. After World War II was a hill farmer in the Black Mountains until 1953, then took up oil painting seriously, settling in Cannington, Somerset. He was influenced by Gauguin, using a rich palette to depict simple rural life. Was a member of ROI and RWA, which gave him a retrospective in 1985. Also held a number of exhibitions with New Grafton Gallery. In 1990 Gammon published his autobiography *One Man's Furrow – 90 Years of Country Living*, which sold out on publication. RWA, WAC and several provincial galleries hold his work. Died in a nursing home at Bridgwater.

Valerie GANZ 1936– Artist and teacher, born at Mumbles, near Swansea, who studied painting, sculpture and stained glass at the College of Art there, remaining as a tutor, 1957–73, when she returned to full-time painting. Her teachers included Alfred Janes, William Price and George Fairley. Ganz became preoccupied by the landscape of south Wales, concentrating on industrial, especially mining, areas. In 1985 Ganz took a house and studio at Six Bells, Abertillery, for nearly a year depicting the lives of the miners at its colliery, underground and on the surface, with their families at choir practice, in the snooker halls and at chapel. The work was widely exhibited, notably at the mining show at Glynn Vivian Art Gallery, Swansea, in 1986. In 1990 Ganz was commissioned by British Coal Opencast to study three sites in south Wales and she later worked at Tower Colliery. Other subjects covered by Ganz included jazz musicians, in New Orleans and at the Brecon Jazz Festival; the Chinese landscape; master classes at Dartington Music School; and the urban landscape of New York. Exhibitions included National Museum of Wales in Cardiff, National Library of Wales, Aberystwyth, National Industrial and Maritime Museum, Cardiff, and Royal National Eisteddfod. CASW holds her work. Lived in Llandeilo, Dyfed.

Robert Lambert GAPPER 1897–1984 Sculptor in a variety of materials, letterer and teacher, born in Llanaelhaearn, Carnarvonshire. After a period at Goldsmiths' College in London and a year teaching art and woodwork in Pwllheli School, in Wales, Gapper served in the Army during World War I, after which he obtained a Bachelor of Science degree in electrical engineering at University College of North Wales and worked as an engineer in Rugby. Having attended Rugby School of Art and being asked to teach there, from 1923–7 he attended the Royal College of Art while, as at Rugby, attending evening classes at Chelsea School of Art and Central School of Art. After a travelling scholarship which took him widely across the continent, Gapper in 1928 began working in North Wales granite quarries and won his first commissions for sculpture. From 1934–62 was a lecturer in art at the University College of Wales, Aberystwyth. In 1973 he gained an honorary Master of Arts degree from the University of Wales. Carried out many commissions, mainly in Wales, including the Thetis memorial, at Holyhead, Gwynedd, and the portrait bust of Alun Lewis in Aberdare. Lived in Aberystwyth.

Elena GAPUTYTE 1927–1991 Sculptor, draughtsman, installations artist, gallery proprietor and teacher, born in Shiaulai, Lithuania. Her parents were farmers, and she retained a love of the land and a kinship with country people. With three brothers and a sister Gaputyte (pronounced Gaputeeta) escaped from the Communist incursion by fleeing to Germany in 1944. She left a displaced persons camp to study history of art at Ludwigs University, Frieburg, and drawing and weaving at L'École des Arts et Métiers there. After two years, in 1948 she left for Canada, settling in Montreal and studying at L'École des Beaux-Arts. In 1951 she moved to Toronto and after working for a year as a bank clerk enrolled in the sculpture class at Ontario College of Art. Became a Canadian citizen and moved to Paris in 1953, studying at L'École des Beaux-Arts under the sculptor Marcel-Antoine Gimond. Moved to St Ives in Cornwall in 1956, becoming a member of the Penwith Society of Arts, and in 1960 opened The Sail Loft Gallery, the year she obtained a French government scholarship, studying again briefly with Gimond. In 1963 at the Sail Loft, she held a Peter Lanyon retrospective. After moving to London Gaputyte studied bronze casting at Hammersmith College of Art. She was in charge of the sculpture department at Digby Stuart College, 1964–77, was an examiner for London University's Institute of Education, 1969, and was recognised as a London University teacher in 1976. In 1975 Gaputyte was winner of the Arts Council and Eastern Arts Association Open Air Sculpture Competition, Key Theatre, Peterborough. In the late-1970s she progressed to installations, mainly concerned with the memory of the war dead. Took part in many exhibitions internationally from 1953 and from 1961, when she had a show at The Gallery, Penzance, had around two dozen solo exhibitions. Later ones included Richard Demarco Gallery, Edinburgh, and

Transmission Gallery, Glasgow, both installations and in 1989. Work is held by public and private collections in many countries.

Richard GARBE 1876–1957 Sculptor in various materials of figures and animals. Born in London, the son of a maker of ivory and tortoiseshell objects, to whom he was apprenticed. Then studied at Central School of Arts and Crafts and the Royal Academy Schools. Became an instructor in sculpture at the Central School, 1901–29, then professor of sculpture at the Royal College of Art, 1929–46. Garbe was a fellow of the RBS, began exhibiting at the RA from 1908 and was elected RA in 1936. Also exhibited RMS, Walker Art Gallery, Liverpool, and Royal Glasgow Institute of the Fine Arts. Monumental work includes some on the National Museum of Wales, Cardiff. Tate Gallery and many provincial galleries hold his work. Lived at Westcott, Surrey.

Meta GARBETT 1881– Painter, notably in pastel, born at Heene, Sussex. She was educated privately, and also art privately with the miniaturist Edwin Morgan. Was a member of St Ives Society of Artists and PS, at both of which she showed, also RI, UA and at Paris Salon. Finally lived in Paignton, Devon.

Anna GARDINER 1966– Painter and draughtsman, born and lived in London, who passed out with a distinction in her diploma at Chelsea School of Art, 1986–8; graduated at Brighton Polytechnic, 1988–91; then did a Royal Academy Schools diploma, 1991–4. Won a British Institute Fund Prize for Painting, 1993; and in 1994 a George Isted Prize and NatWest 90s Prize for Art first prize. Mixed shows included Art for Youth, Mall Galleries, and RA Summer Exhibition, 1992–3; New Discoveries, Boundary Gallery, 1994; and No Turkeys – Part II, Raw Gallery, 1995. Had a solo exhibition at Art First, 1996, remarkable for a series of paintings of small girls, Velasquez's pictures of children in the Prado, Madrid, having been an inspiration. NatWest Group, Arthur Andersen & Company, Capital Group Studios and De Vigier Foundation in Switzerland hold Gardiner's work.

Clive GARDINER 1891–1960 Designer, illustrator, printmaker, painter and teacher, born in Blackburn, Lancashire. His father was the editor of the *Daily News*, A G Gardiner, his wife the painter Lilian Lancaster. Gardiner was educated at University College School, toyed with journalism, then studied at Slade School of Fine Art, 1909–12, Royal Academy Schools, 1913–14. After World War I duties at the Ministry of Munitions Gardiner took an art teaching course, then taught at Brighton School of Art. Under the influence of Puvis de Chavannes he had shown for several years at RA and NEAC. In 1918 Gardiner became a part-time teacher at Bolt Court School of Art and Goldsmiths' College School of Art. Gardiner began to extend his range, illustrating his father's books, painting portraits and completing posters. These included notable work for London Underground, Empire Marketing Board and Shell. On the strength of that he was appointed headmaster/later principal of Goldsmiths', 1929–57, where he had considerable influence in advancing the modern movement, his own style being successively impressed by Cézanne, Derain, Picasso and Braque. In 1936 he had his only one-man show, of paintings, at French Gallery. Gardiner carried out substantial work as a decorator, including murals for Sir John Benn's Hostel, Stepney; Toynbee Hall; and the Students' Union of London University. During World War II he advised on the design and decoration of British Restaurants. In his final years Gardiner produced small oils and watercolours in his original more reflective vein, regularly visiting the Scilly Isles. Arts Council put on a memorial show in 1963, South London Art Gallery, 1967.

Dan GARDINER 1966– Painter and mixed media artist. His abstract pictures drew imagery from industrial backgrounds and had an underlying social concern, as in his prizewinning canvas Boom? at John Moores Liverpool Exhibition 1989–90. Gardiner was born in Hitchin, Hertfordshire, studying at Hertfordshire College of Art and Design, St Albans, 1984–5, and Liverpool Polytechnic, 1986–9. Was included in Girobank National exhibition at Mercury Court, Liverpool, 1988, and in 1989–90 showed works at Liverpool Airport in conjunction with Merseyside Boroughs. Lived in Hitchin for some time.

Gerald GARDINER 1902–1959 Landscape painter in oil, and teacher. Born in London, he studied at Beckenham School of Art, under Percy Jowett, 1919–23, then at the Royal College of Art, 1923–7. Exhibited RA, NEAC, RSA and Cooling Galleries. During World War II he completed wall decorations for the Cheltenham Services Club, a year later illustrating Fred Kitchen's book *Jesse and His Friends*. Work in several public collections. Gardiner's landscapes are notable for their translucent colour. Lived in Stroud, Gloucestershire.

Mary GARDINER 1931– Artist in pencil, pastel, watercolour and textiles, and teacher, sometimes known as Meg Gardiner, who was born and lived in Barry, Glamorgan. Her husband was the sculptor Robert Thomas, her son the painter Ceri Thomas. She studied at Cardiff College of Art, 1947–50, and Royal College of Art, 1950–3, under Margaret Leischner, gaining a Cotton Board Scholarship, 1951–2. She married Robert Thomas in 1952 and taught textiles at Ealing School of Art, 1954–69, returning to Wales in 1971, where she taught until retirement in 1991. Close contact with the designer Ernest Race and his wife Sally was cited as a key influence on Gardiner's development. Fidelis Furnishing Fabrics, Moygashel/Stevenson & Sons, Otterburn Tweeds, Lurex Dobeckmen & Company and Tootal used Gardiner's talents. She showed at Albany Art Gallery, Cardiff, in 1989.

Meg GARDINER: *see* **Mary GARDINER**

Stanley Horace GARDINER 1887–1952 Painter, notably of landscape, and teacher, born in Reading, Berkshire, winning a scholarship to its University, also studying at Patrick Allan-Fraser School of Art, Hospitalfield, Arbroath, having on leaving school been apprenticed to a decorator. Gardiner taught for a time at University College in Reading and also worked and taught in

America, returning to England in World War I to enrol. In the mid-1920s he moved to Lamorna, near Penzance, Cornwall, where initially he endured poverty, although eventually he began to exhibit widely and ran his own small painting school from home. He was elected an associate of RWS and a member of the New Society of Artists, also showing at Fine Art Society, RWA, Irish Salon, RA, Walker Art Gallery in Liverpool and Berkshire Art Society.

Vanessa GARDINER 1960– Painter and collagist. She was a student at Oxford Polytechnic for its arts foundation course, 1978–9, then graduated from Central School of Art and Design with an honours degree in fine art, 1979–82. Her work was specifically based on the coastal and inland landscapes of West Dorset, but instead of being representational it abstracted the forms of sea and land. Gardiner appeared in mixed exhibitions at Allsop Gallery, Bridport, 1991–2; at Athelhampton House, Dorset, in 1992; and from 1991 showed solo at Duncan Campbell Gallery.

Alexandra GARDNER 1945– Painter and draughtsman and teacher, born in Bellshill, Lanarkshire. She studied at Glasgow School of Art, 1963–8, with David Donaldson and William Drummond Bone, then lectured there, 1968–88. Ill health prompted early retirement, but after a successful second kidney transplant in 1990 Gardner "continued to paint, but more prolific and yet more disciplined." Uccello, Vermeer and Morandi were influences on Gardner's work, but her themed pictures remained distinctively her own. These included still life, nude, bar interior, American diner and barbershop series. Gardner was a member of the Royal Glasgow Institute of the Fine Arts. She won a series of awards, including Glasgow Society of Women Artists, Scottish Arts Council Lady Artists' Fund and Cleveland 5th International Drawing Biennale. Was a prolific exhibitor in mixed exhibitions, including RSA, 1969; RSW, 1976; Fine Art Society, 1981; Lillie Gallery, Milngavie, 1986; and Art Expo, New York, 1993, with Duncan Miller Fine Art. Had a solo show at Royal Scottish Academy of Music & Drama, Glasgow, 1968, later ones including Mayfest, Gatehouse Gallery, Glasgow, 1993. Kelvingrove Art Gallery in Glasgow and Glasgow Corporation hold her work.

Ann GARDNER 1964– Painter who studied at Slade School of Fine Art. She obtained an honours degree in 1986, The Slade Higher Diploma in Painting three years later. Among her group appearances was The Slade in the North, Halifax, and Four Counties Show, 1987; Whitechapel Open, 1989; The Prose of Painting, at Austin/Desmond Fine Art, 1991; and A Second Perspective, at Leighton House, 1991. She won 10 awards and prizes between 1982–92, including The Pearson Prize for Drawing and Painting; The Henry Tonks Prize; The Monnington Prize; First Prize for Painting, British Institution Fund of the RA; and a Boise Scholarship to travel and paint, which took her to New York. Had a solo show at Bedford Library in 1991 and shared an exhibition at Cadogan Contemporary in 1992. She was a fluid painter, interested in fleeting effects of light and atmosphere. Lived in London, but worked some of the time in France.

Annette GARDNER 1920– Painter in oil and teacher, born in London. She studied at Twickenham Art School, 1952–4, after always drawing and painting as a child. Then attended Hampstead Garden Suburb Institute, 1954–6, and St Martin's School of Art, 1960–3, under David Tindle. Gardner, who sometimes painted as Annette Gardner-Wood, was particularly interested in Abstract Expressionism and cited Walter Nessler as her main teacher and influence. When her husband died in 1972 she took over the principalship of Wood Tutorial College, teaching art and other subjects until 1988. She was a member of the Ben Uri Art Society, Free Painters and Sculptors and Hampstead Artists' Council and participated in many group and travelling shows. Lived in Edgware, Middlesex.

Derek George Montague GARDNER 1914– Marine artist in oil and watercolour, born in Gerrards Cross, Buckinghamshire, entirely self-taught. He served in the Royal Naval Volunteer Reserve, 1934–47, retiring as a commander, and was mentioned in dispatches, HMS *Broke*, 1942. From 1947–63 Gardner worked as a chartered civil engineer for the Ministry of Works in Kenya. Was elected to RSMA in 1966, in 1988 being made honorary vice-president for life. Gardner's work was featured in many marine painting reference books. He took part in group shows of the Kenya Art Society, 1950–63; UA and RSMA from 1958; and from 1982 at Mystic Maritime Gallery in America, and elsewhere. Had a series of solo shows at Polak Gallery from 1972. National Maritime Museum at Greenwich, Britannia Royal Naval College in Dartmouth and the Bermuda Maritime Museum hold examples. Lived at Corfe Mullen, Wimborne, Dorset.

Ian GARDNER 1944– Painter and teacher, notable as a landscape watercolourist. He studied at Lancaster School of Art and Nottingham College of Art. He pursued a full-time lecturing career until 1979, after which he taught part-time at several Colleges of Art, most notably as professor in art and design at University of Illinois, 1986–7. Between 1981–6 he was co-editor, with Patrick Eyres, of *New Arcadian Press*, a quarterly journal dealing with landscape issued in text and image. Began working in watercolour in 1969, eventually concentrating on the Morecambe Bay area of Lancashire with its dramatic coastline, and his own allotment, as seen in North by North West, Bolton Museum and Art Gallery, 1996. Work in many public and private collections.

Pam GARDNER 1920– Painter, draughtsman and jewellery designer, born in Bray, Berkshire. She studied art at London Polytechnic and jewellery with Goldsmiths' and Silversmiths' Company. Showed mainly in west of England, notably at Days Mill Gallery in Nailsworth and Cygnet Gallery in Stroud, near where she lived in Amberley, Gloucestershire.

Peter GARDNER 1921– Painter in oil and teacher, born in London. He studied at Hammersmith School of Art, 1935–8 and

1946–50, teachers including Herbert Holt and Harold Workman, then London University Institute of Education, 1950–1. Taught for a time at Plaistow Grammar School and was honorary secretary of the Society of Fulham Artists. Was elected ROI in 1977, also showing with Trafford Gallery, RA and NEAC. Hammersmith Borough Council and Nuffield Foundation, York University, hold his work. Lived latterly at Shaftesbury, Dorset.

Stephen Reginald GARDNER 1948– Painter, born in Prestwich, Lancashire, who studied art locally and showed in Manchester at Colin Jellicoe Gallery and in Lincolnshire, notably at Portfolio Gallery, Scunthorpe. Lived in Manchester.

Annette GARDNER-WOOD: *see* **Annette GARDNER**

William GARFIT 1944– Painter and draughtsman with an interest in country subjects, born in Cambridge, near where he settled at Harlton. He attended Cambridge School of Art, 1963; Byam Shaw School of Drawing and Painting, 1964–7, under Maurice de Sausmarez; and at Royal Academy Schools, 1967–70, with Peter Greenham. He illustrated a number of countryside books. Exhibited with Cambridge Drawing Society and RBA both of which he was a member, and had solo exhibitions at Tryon and Moorland Gallery and elsewhere.

Margaret Lester GARLAND 1893–1976 Artist, born in Oxford, who attended Royal College of Art design school, 1925–7, where she met Helen Binyon, who became a lifelong friend. During 1930s showed with NEAC and painted a mural for Holy Trinity Church, Bath, destroyed during World War II. After war taught briefly at Bath Art School, then at Bath Academy of Art, 1946–58. By then she had settled in Bath, showing with Bath Society of Artists. Showed at Arcade Gallery; Barber Institute in Birmingham; Leva Gallery; and at David Paul Gallery, Chichester, in 1978.

Mollie GARLAND 1920– Painter and teacher, educated in Liverpool, who studied at the City School of Art there, 1938–41, under Will Penn, then at the Slade School of Fine Art, 1941–2. Was a member of the Sandon Studios Society and Liverpool Academy and joined the staff of Liverpool City School of Art. Exhibited RA, RBA, Manchester Academy and widely in the Liverpool area, where she lived. Liverpool's Walker Art Gallery holds her work.

Daphne GARMAN 1913– Sculptor, born in Beaconsfield, Buckinghamshire, as Evelyn Daphne Garman. Trained as a sculptor in 1933–8 with Anne Acheson and showed with SWA as a student. Her nursing career in the war and family commitments interrupted her sculpting until the early 1970s, when she studied recent developments in casting and resumed working in clay or wax for finishing in bronze, resin bronze plaster or terracotta. Was elected to NS in 1980 and SWA in 1985, also exhibiting with SPS and in the provinces and having several shows with her husband, R C Garman. She specialised in portraits human and animal, especially of horses and dogs. An interest in sight-hounds led to a commission from Asprey for a galloping saluki. Winsor & Newton ordered portrait bronzes of their founders, on display in the firm's museum, and Garman also made religious works and imaginative pieces in limited editions. Lived latterly in Cheltenham, Gloucestershire.

Theo GARMAN 1924–1954 Painter and draughtsman, son of the artist Jacob Epstein and his most famous model, Kathleen Garman. A gifted child, he aspired to an academic career after Oxford University. In preparation for this he did a correspondence course after leaving school while, as a conscientious objector in World War II, working as a cowhand in Sussex, and intensively painting, the result being a severe breakdown. Continued to paint, living in London, and had two exhibitions, at Redfern Gallery, in 1950–2. His work was much admired by Wyndham Lewis, Kenneth Clark and Matthew Smith, who called Garman a "genius". An unworldly man, Garman was familiar with the art treasures of Europe and was, like his father, a fervent collector, concentrating on medieval religious pieces. His own pictures were intense and richly coloured, not unlike those of Van Gogh. Garman-Ryan Collection at Walsall Art Gallery holds his work. A small selection was shown in a retrospective at Fine Art Society in 1989.

Edith Mary GARNER 1881– Painter, born at Wasperton, Warwickshire. She was married to the artist William Lee-Hankey and modelled for some of his pictures. After education at the North London Collegiate School, she studied at the Slade School of Fine Art and on the continent. Had an interest in the theatre. Showed RA, NS, ROI and Paris Salon. Her work is held by Leamington Art Gallery. Lived in London.

Angelica GARNETT 1918– Artist, daughter of the painter Vanessa Bell, born at Charleston Farmhouse, Firle, Sussex. In 1936 she attended the London Theatre Studio drama school, in 1938 the Euston Road School to study art, which she then taught at Langford Grove School, 1940. In 1941 she worked on the Berwick Church murals with her mother, Duncan Grant and Quentin Bell, the next year marrying the writer David Garnett, by whom she had four daughters. Continued to paint, organise art courses and run exhibitions while living in Huntingdonshire. Garnett worked with George Bergen in New York, 1967–8, lived in Sussex from 1977, in 1984 settling in France at Forcalquier. Solo shows included Grafton, Upper Street and Marjorie Parr Galleries and Southover Gallery, Lewes. Later exhibitions included The Crescent Gallery, Cedar Springs, Dallas, Texas, 1986, and Deborah Gage (Works of Art), where her 1993 exhibition Transformations comprised objects made from plastic bags, bottles, cans, corks and feathers. Garnett also gained a reputation as a designer of textiles, book jackets, pottery decoration and mosaics.

Eve GARNETT 1900–1991 Landscape painter, muralist, book illustrator and writer, born in Worcestershire. She studied at Chelsea Polytechnic School of Art, at Royal Academy Schools, where she won the Creswick Prize and Silver Medal, and with Alexander Jamieson. Travelled extensively. Exhibited at Tate Gallery, ROI, SWA and NEAC. Was most noted for her children's books and *The Family from One End Street*, 1937, which won the Carnegie Gold Medal, and its sequels. In 1948 she illustrated Robert Louis Stevenson's *A Child's Garden of Verses*. The volume *First Affections* told of her early childhood. Lived in Lewes, Sussex.

Geoffrey Sneyd GARNIER 1889–1970 Printmaker, born in Wigan, Lancashire, he was married to the painter Jill Garnier. Left Charterhouse in 1907, obtained a City and Guilds certificate in engineering and while working in Toronto decided on art as a career. Returned to England in 1910, studied for two years at the School of Painting, Bushey, then in 1912 joined Stanhope Forbes' school in Newlyn, Cornwall, where he continued to live. Garnier's early work was often religious. Meticulously researched the lost art of the aquatint, but later concentrated on engraving. Showed at RA, RSA, RWA, SGA and in the north of England, where his work is held by Oldham Art Gallery and Museum and other galleries.

Jill GARNIER 1890–1966 Painter, especially of portraits, and fine draughtsman, born in Quidenham, Norfolk as Jessie Caroline Dunbar Blyth. Studied at Cheltenham Ladies' College, then from 1915 at Stanhope Forbes' school in Newlyn, Cornwall, where she met her husband the printmaker Geoffrey Sneyd Garnier. Exhibited at RA, RWA and was a member of both the Newlyn and St Ives Societies of Artists. A talented embroiderer, she reproduced some of her own pictures. Lived in Newlyn.

Charles GARRAD 1952– Artist, designer and teacher notable for his creation of atmospheric, unpeopled rooms. Born in Somerset, he studied at Stourbridge College of Art, 1969–70; Cardiff College of Art, 1970–3; and Chelsea School of Art, 1973–4. Went on to teach, including Chelsea. After being artist-in-residence at the Institute of Modern Art in Brisbane, 1979, in 1980 he lectured throughout Australia, in 1982 working in television design. He gained a Greater London Arts Association Major Award in 1981. Group shows included New Contemporaries '74 at ICA, 1974; Out of the Blue, Acme Gallery, 1978; mural work for Greater London Arts Association in Covent Garden, 1980; and Summer Show 1 at Serpentine Gallery, 1983. Had a solo show at Chapter Arts Centre, Cardiff, 1973, later ones including Institute of Modern Art, Brisbane, 1979. Lived for a time in London.

Peter John GARRARD 1929– Painter who studied at Byam Shaw School of Drawing and Painting. He was a member of RBA, of which he was president for a time, RWA, NEAC and RP, also exhibiting in RA Summer Exhibition. Lived in London.

Rose GARRARD 1946– Versatile artist, designer, sculptor and teacher, born in Bewdley, Worcestershire. She did a foundation course at Stourbridge College of Art & Design, 1965–6; gained a first-class honours degree in sculpture from Birmingham College of Art, 1966–9; did a postgraduate master's degree (higher diploma in sculpture) at Chelsea School of Art, 1969–70; then gained a British Council/French government scholarship to École des Beaux-Arts, Paris, 1970–1. Garrard won a number of international awards and residencies, including The South London Gallery, 1994, where for her show Arenas for Conversation she based works of art on chats with people who visited her. Garrard had numerous mixed and solo shows, the latter including Talisman, Louise Hallett Gallery, 1988; Calgary Conversation, New Art Gallery, Calgary, 1991; and Disclosing Dialogues, Vancouver Art Gallery, Canada, 1992. She lectured widely, including Reading University, Trent and Sheffield Polytechnics, Croydon College of Art and Dartington College of Arts. Was also a freelance designer, notably for BBC and to architects, including The Spirit of the City, a 30-foot bronze wall sculpture near Old Street tube station. Arts Council, Henry Moore Sculpture Trust and Victoria & Albert Museum hold examples.

John Geoffrey GARRATT 1914–1986 Artist in oil, watercolour, pen and ink. Born in Wallasey, Merseyside, Garratt studied at Brighton College of Art and made his career as a bookseller. He became known as an expert on model soldiers and wargaming, publishing a series of books on the subject, including the *World Encyclopedia of Model Soldiers*. He also wrote a book on drawing landscape in pen and ink and *Westcountryman's England*. He exhibited widely, including the RA, Imperial Institute and galleries in Brighton, Bolton, Eastbourne, Cheltenham and Blackpool. Several museums and galleries hold his work, including his home town of Farnham, Surrey.

Sam GARRATT 1865–1947 Painter of landscapes and historical scenes and etcher, born in Barwell, Leicestershire. His father was a farm labourer, Sam became a bootmaker and studied for 15 years in the evenings at the local School of Art. He settled in Brecon and showed at the Eisteddfod, his picture King Charles Leaving the Priory, Brecon, winning a prize. Also showed at RCamA, RHA, Walker Art Gallery in Liverpool, RA and elsewhere. He was a member of Brecon Conservative Club.

Albert Charles GARRETT 1915–1983 Painter in oil, and wood engraver. Born at Kingsclere, Hampshire, he studied painting under Sir William Coldstream and engraving with John Buckland-Wright, attending successively Camberwell School of Art in 1947–9, the Anglo-French Art Centre in 1949–50 and the Slade School of Fine Art 1950–1. Among Garrett's appointments was senior art lecturer at the Polytechnic of North London, chairmanship of Mall Prints and presidency of the SWE. Among his many books and papers, some of which were learned analyses of light and colour in particular environments, were volumes on the *Wood Engravings and Drawings of Iain Macnab* and *British Wood Engraving of the 20th Century*. Garrett participated in numerous international exhibitions, where he won several medals. One-man shows included the Woodstock Gallery in 1961, Mall

Galleries in 1972 and the University of Windsor, Ontario, in 1979. Derby Art Gallery, the Ferens Art Gallery, in Hull, and several other British and foreign galleries hold his work. Lived in Ruislip, Middlesex.

Violet Nellie GARROD 1898–1981 Painter, draughtsman, miniaturist and teacher, born in north London, who studied at Hampstead Garden Suburb Central Institute and St John's Wood School of Art, with Leonard Walker. Showed at RMS, SM of which she was a member, PS and elsewhere, winning gold medals for her miniatures at RA and Salon d'Été, Paris. During World War II Miss Garrod moved with her parents to Southbourne, founding the Art Group there; when she went to New Milton after the war she started a second group; following her parents' death, she and her sister moved to a flat overlooking the Royal Lymington Yacht Club, and the Palette Club began in 1954; on moving to Milford she taught in a hut in her garden, from which developed the Milford Art Group, in 1958. Among her portraits were large ones of Bishop Kenneth Lamplugh, Reverend Darrell Bunt, chaplain of the fleet, and of Olive Troke, first woman mayor of Lymington. Russell-Cotes Art Gallery and Museum, Bournemouth, holds her work. For her last decade lived in Swanage, Dorset, finally suffering a stroke.

Alethea GARSTIN 1894–1978 Painter, born in Penzance, daughter of the artist Norman Garstin. Began sketching with her father in France as a child, starting to paint seriously at 16, so that at 18 her first work was accepted by RA. Had no formal training apart from a brief period at Heatherley's School of Fine Art life drawing. For a time she drew for publications such as *Punch*, *The Tatler* and *The Sketch*. From 1912–77 she showed regularly in England and France, in all at nearly 60 galleries. Travelled extensively in Europe, Africa, Australia and the Caribbean. Some early work was in the Fauve manner, and her friends Edward Wolfe and Morland Lewis were also influences. The catalogue of the major exhibition of her father's and her work at the Penwith Gallery in 1978, which toured, records that she "had no theories" and "lived in the present"; and her pictures of places and people have a French spontaneity. Bristol City Art Gallery, National Trust and others hold her work. RWA member. She lived most of her life in Penzance, then when her studio was destroyed because of redevelopment she moved to Zennor, where she died.

Ray GARVEY 1943– Painter, graphic artist and teacher who studied at St Martin's School of Art, Kingston College of Art and London University, 1963–8. His teaching experience included Croydon College of Design and Technology and Putney School of Art and in 1982 he was included in Artists in Adult Education at Woodlands Art Gallery. Other shows included Cockpit Theatre, 1970, Serpentine Gallery, 1974, and Towner Art Gallery, Eastbourne, 1981.

Tirzah GARWOOD 1908–1951 Wood engraver, painter and modelmaker, born in Gillingham, Kent, but grew up in Eastbourne, Sussex, where aged 17 she entered Eastbourne School of Art. There she met her future husband, the artist Eric Ravilious. Next went to Central School of Arts and Crafts and began to exhibit her prints. Showed at SWE in 1927 and received commissions from BBC, Kynoch Press and Golden Cockerel Press. After Garwood married Ravilious in 1930 her output was restricted by domestic chores, but she collaborated with him on mural work. In the mid-1940s Garwood began painting, and creating her paper models of houses and chapels, with their singular, childlike charm. She continued this work after marrying Henry Swanzy in 1946, living for some time in Hampstead, London, but dying at Copford, near Colchester, in Essex. Towner Art Gallery, Eastbourne, held a memorial show in 1952 and a further comprehensive exhibition in 1987. Fry Art Gallery, Saffron Walden, holds her work.

Rosemary GASCOYNE fl. from early 1980s– Artist in oil on canvas or board, born in Norwich, Norfolk, who gained a diploma from Amersham College of Art, then an honours degree from Brighton University, 1981, where teachers included Chris Le Brun and Jack Smith. Took part in many group shows, including Centaur Gallery, 1985; Towner Art Gallery, Eastbourne, 1986; Brighton University, 1987–90; and Gracefield Art Centre, Dumfries, 1997. Had a solo exhibition at Trinity Arts Centre, Tunbridge Wells, 1986, later ones including Chambers Gallery, Moffat, and Gracefield Art Centre, both 1996. In 1993, Gascoyne moved to Dumfries and Galloway, establishing The Cree Gallery, Gatehouse of Fleet, where she exhibited.

Michael GASKELL 1963– Artist born at Billinge, Wigan, Lancashire, who studied at St Helens College of Art & Design, Coventry Polytechnic and Bretton Hall College. Went on to conduct many workshops for galleries, museums and art departments. Group shows included Mercia Artist Open, Herbert Art Gallery, Coventry, 1986; MAFA at Manchester City Art Gallery, from 1987; Make it Paper, Gateshead public gallery, 1995; and Royal Over-Seas League Open, 1996. Had a solo show at The Old Town Hall, Halton, 1990.

Nora GASTON fl. from mid-1960s– Artist and teacher whose work employed rich colours and a strong decorative element. She obtained a national diploma in design, painting and printing from Belfast College of Art, 1964, in 1979 graduating with a bachelor's degree in education from University of New Brunswick, Canada. She was arts adviser for the New Brunswick School Board before taking up the post of head of printmaking and surface design at New Brunswick Craft School, Fredericton, 1982. After a period as a member of Gallery Connection Studios there, Gaston moved to Saudi Arabia, working as an arts consultant and as adviser to Falcon Fine Art Gallery, Riyadh. In 1990 Gaston was appointed to the visual arts committee of the Northern Ireland Arts Council. Gaston was commissioned to make stained glass windows for a church in New Maryland, 1982, and for a hospital in Fredericton, 1984, and to complete a mural for Musgrave Park Hospital, 1992. Took part in many group shows, notably at Arts Council Gallery, Belfast, from 1989, and was included in the 1994 exhibitions

Works on Paper and Beyond the Partitions, organised by Queen Street Studios, Belfast, with which she was associated. Had a series of solo shows in America, Canada and Saudi Arabia. Lived in Belfast, Northern Ireland.

Rosalind GATEHOUSE fl. c.1915–1950 Watercolourist educated in England and in Dresden, Germany. She exhibited RA, RCamA, Walker Art Gallery in Liverpool and RBSA, signing work with R G monogram. Lived in Witham, Essex.

Rupert GATFIELD 1959– Painter, draughtsman and printmaker, born in Kuala Lumpur, Malaya, who studied at Pangbourne College, where for his advanced-level course he was taught by artist Richard Shirley Smith who "greatly inspired" him. Did a foundation course in Worthing but considered himself "to be a self-taught Surrealist", painting full-time from 1983. The 1990s saw him concentrating on the theme of A Garden, square pictures in which Gatfield created his own world. Group exhibitions included Park Walk and Images Galleries, both 1984; RA Summer Exhibition from 1987; RWS and Royal Over-Seas League Exhibitions, both 1989; and Bordeaux Salon d'Hiver, 1993 (first prize). Had a solo show at Danziger Metcalfe, 1986; Konicus, Bristol, 1995; and Beaux Arts, Bath, 1996. Lloyd's of London and North Devon Academy of Art hold his work. Lived in Bristol.

Stuart Luke GATHERER 1971– Painter in oil of figurative works with an enigmatic story element, tense situations and artificial light predominating. Seventeenth-century Dutch painting, especially that of Vermeer, was a strong influence. He was brought up in the eastern highlands of Scotland, and graduated with his master's degree in fine art from Edinburgh College of Art, in 1995. Showed in Scotland and the north of England and was exhibited at Art97, Contemporary Art Fair, in 1997 by Portland Gallery, which that year gave him a first London solo show.

Jason GATHORNE-HARDY 1968– Painter, born in Malaya, who was brought up near the Suffolk coast. After studying zoology at Oxford University and researching conservation biology at the University of Kent, he took up drawing and painting full-time in 1993. His aim was "to translate the energy of the land into paintings for other people to see", and this he did by creating abstract, calligraphic shapes out of mud which he smeared and shaped. They had titles such as Orwell Estuary or Elmstead Market, as in his contribution to Cross Currents at Reed's Wharf Gallery at the Barbican Centre, 1996. In 1995 Reed's Wharf and Aldeburgh Cinema, Suffolk, gave him solo shows, as did Snape Maltings, nearby, in 1996.

John Richardson GAULD fl. from 1911–1962 Painter, muralist and lithographer, born at Gateshead, County Durham. Studied at King Edward VII School of Art, Durham University, Royal College of Art and lithography at London County Council School. Became chief assistant at Huddersfield School of Art, eventually principal of Bolton School of Art, 1930–51. Was president of MAFA and of Bolton Art Circle. Exhibited RA, Goupil Gallery and Royal Glasgow Institute of the Fine Arts. Victoria & Albert Museum, British Museum and provincial galleries hold his work. Lived at Bolton, Lancashire.

Annabel GAULT 1952– Painter and draughtsman, born in West Sussex, who was notable for remote, bleak and eerie landscapes, She studied at West Surrey College of Art, 1973–7, then Royal Academy Schools, 1977–80. Mixed exhibitions included Oxford Gallery from 1979; Thackeray Gallery, 1989; Pallant House, Chichester, 1993; and City Gallery, Leicester, 1994, the year when her work was shown in Redpath Gallery, Vancouver, in Three British Artists, with Brendan Neiland and Patrick Procktor. From 1994 showed solo with Redfern Gallery. Hampshire County Council commissioned work, which was also owned by Arts Council.

George GAULT 1916– Painter and teacher, born in Belfast. Gault joined the British Army aged 18 and served until 1946. He then studied at Camberwell School of Arts and Crafts, 1948–51, his teachers including William Coldstream, Kenneth Martin, Victor Pasmore and William Townsend. Gault went on to teach painting at the Greenwich Adult Education Institute for 20 years. In 1957 Gault was one of Jack Beddington's *Young Artists of Promise*, in the book of that title. He showed at RA, LG, NEAC, RBA, RP, Fine Art Society and Austin/Desmond Fine Art. Won a silver medal at 1954 Paris Salon. Solo show at Sweet Waters Gallery, 1989; retrospective at Woodlands Art Gallery, 1995. Lived in London.

Kate GAULT 1954– Painter, draughtsman and dancer. She studied drawing and painting at The Academy, Florence, and the Byam Shaw School, then dance, music and choreography at the London School of Contemporary Dance. For several years she worked with dance companies in New York, London and Amsterdam, painting in her spare time. In Ethiopia she was commissioned by the Ministry of Culture to form a dance company trained in both Western and traditional styles. In 1984 Gault moved to Italy to become a full-time painter, then to the Pyrenees and finally Mallorca. Gault's work was simple and colourful, reflecting the environments where she had lived. As well as exhibiting in mixed shows at Piccadilly Gallery she had a solo show at Christopher Hull Gallery, another at Sue Rankin Gallery in 1991. She was sister of the artist Annabel Gault, and latterly exhibited as Katherine Hamilton.

Elena GAUSSEN MARKS 1938– Portrait and landscape painter and draughtsman, and teacher, born in Kent. She studied at Southern College of Art, Portsmouth; Royal Academy Schools; and Camberwell School of Arts and Crafts. Her notable teachers included Claude Rogers, Peter Greenham, Henry Rushbury and Robert Buhler; until his death she shared a studio with Buhler, saying: "My aim is to justify his faith in my work." Gaussen Marks aspired "to combine the figurative and the abstract in painting by colour relationships, form/shape, subject matter subservient to the whole." From 1973–9 she was head of the art department at Queen's College. Among her main works were portraits of Lord Tonypandy, former speaker of the House of Commons, Leo Marks and Helene Hanff, the author. Mixed shows included RA Summer Exhibitions from 1983, RP, NEAC, Bath Festival and Society of Landscape Painters, of which she was a member. Alpine Club Gallery, Spink and Stephen Bartley Gallery held solo exhibitions of Gaussen Marks' pictures, which are in Chelsea Arts Club and Southampton University collections. Lived in London.

William GAUNT 1900–1980 Painter of landscapes, urban scenes and witty draughtsman, art critic and writer. Born in Hull, son of the artist William Gaunt, went on to study at Westminster School of Art in 1924–5 under Walter Bayes and Bernard Meninsky. Exhibited at RA, Redfern Gallery and Lefevre Gallery and had a number of one-man shows. Gaunt was a lively and illuminating writer on aspects of British art, notably *The Pre-Raphaelite Tragedy*, *The Aesthetic Adventure* and *The March of the Moderns*. Lived in London.

William Norman GAUNT 1918– Painter and teacher, who was born in Leeds but educated in Morecambe, Lancashire. He studied at Lancaster School of Art, 1946–9, with Walter Bayes. Showed RWS, RI, with Lancaster Art Group, of which he was a member, and elsewhere in the provinces. Lived in Morecambe and then in Giggleswick, Yorkshire.

James GAVIN 1928– Painter and teacher, born in Duns, Berwickshire. He studied drawing and painting at Edinburgh College of Art, 1955–9, followed by private study in 1960 in Paris, then went on to teach at Cumbria College of Art and Design. He showed in group exhibitions in England, Scotland and Ireland. After a one-man show at 57 Gallery, Edinburgh, in 1961 others followed in the city at Scottish, Richard Demarco and Alexander Galleries.

Stephen GAVIN 1953– Painter, photographer, draughtsman, collagist and teacher, born in Dover, Kent, married to the artist Victoria Brill (with whom he was included in the Brill family show Relative Values, The Smith Art Gallery & Museum, Stirling, 1993). Gavin produced both abstract and figurative works, was interested in objects connected with ritual and cult practices and employed animated sequences created on a computer paintbox in his later creations. Gained a first-class degree in painting and photography at Kingston Polytechnic, 1972–5, then his master's at the Royal College of Art, 1976–9. Between 1978–85, Gavin won the College's Travelling Scholarship to Amsterdam and Basle, a John Minton Travelling Scholarship to Rome and an Italian State Scholarship and Beryl Ash Award. He was Stanley Picker Fellow in Painting, Kingston Polytechnic, 1979–80. Gavin taught at Goldsmiths' College, 1983–4; Clapham and Battersea Institute, 1985–8; and from then on design and technology at Queen Margaret's School, York.

Barbara GAY 1921– Painter and potter, born and lived in Bristol, where she studied at West of England College of Art, 1936–46, teachers including Roy Smith. In 1949 worked at Monkton Combe Pottery, near Bath, with Rachel Warner. Showed at RWA, of which she was an associate, and carried out commissioned work. St George's, Brandon Hill, Bristol, contained several pieces by her.

Bernard GAY 1921– Painter, writer and lecturer, by profession an inspector of schools, born in Exmouth, Devon. Attended Willesden School of Art, 1947–51, where his teachers included Maurice de Sausmarez. Gay was a versatile man, who wrote on diverse aspects of painting including his book *The Art of Sandro Botticelli*; he was also prominent in arts administration in the London suburb of Hampstead, where he co-founded the Camden Arts Centre, being at one time chairman of its Trust. Showed widely, including solo exhibitions at ICA, Camden Arts Centre, Piccadilly Gallery, Wildenstein and other leading London galleries. Sometimes signed work with initials only. Oxford University and a number of county council collections, including Hertfordshire and Essex, bought his work. He was one of Jack Beddington's *Young Artists of Promise*, in the 1957 book of that title. Gay said that he was "passionately interested in the organisation, planning and design of didactic design exhibitions". Examples were his Classics of Modern Design, Maker Designers Today and De Stijl shows. He lived latterly in Mansel Lacy, Herefordshire.

Francisco GAZITUA fl. from late 1960s– After studying philosophy at Catholic University of Chile, 1963–7, Gazitua pursued sculpture at University of Chile, 1967–9. Over the next eight years he taught and founded a handicrafts centre and was assistant to the sculptor Samuel Roman. Under a British Council Scholarship he attended St Martin's School of Art, 1977–9, then teaching there. From 1980 for several years organised and taught at summer school at Kornarija, Yugoslavia. As well as exhibiting extensively and carrying out commissions in Chile, Gazitua showed at British Council in London, 1978; St Martin's at the Polytechnic of North London, 1979; and in 1983 at Woodlands Art Gallery in Have You Seen Sculpture from the Body? Banco Real de Brasil, in São Paolo, holds his work.

Frances GEAKE 1903–1955 Painter and musician who taught music, born in Torquay, Devon. Studied at Newton Abbot Art School and also privately with the watercolourist Gladys Best. She exhibited RWA, NS, RI and with the Exeter Art Society, of which she was a member. Victoria & Albert Museum holds her work. Lived in Exeter.

William GEAR 1915–1997 Painter and administrator, born in Methil, Fife. He studied painting at Edinburgh College of Art, 1932–7, and the Edinburgh University Fine Art Class, 1936–7, his teachers including William Gillies and John Maxwell. After study in Paris with Fernand Léger in 1937 he travelled in Italy and the Balkans area on the strength of a scholarship. After World War II service in the Army and a period in the Control Commission in Germany, Gear lived in France until 1950, when he returned to Britain and in 1951 won a Festival of Britain Purchase Prize. In 1958 was made curator of Towner Art Gallery in Eastbourne. He was appointed head of the faculty of fine art in Birmingham College of Art in 1964; guest lecturer at National Gallery of Victoria, Melbourne, and University of Western Australia, Perth, in 1966; and in 1975 won the Lorne Fellowship and retired as head of the department of fine art at Birmingham Polytechnic. By then Gear had built up an impressive international exhibiting record, a painter of abstract compositions, often dancingly powerful in colour, who made a significant contribution to European painting through his association with the COBRA group in the immediate post-war years. Fifty-year retrospective at Redfern Gallery, 1997. William Gear and COBRA toured from Aberdeen Art Gallery, 1997–8. Tate Gallery and many provincial and foreign collections hold Gear's work. Elected Senior RA, 1995. Lived in Birmingham.

Robert GEARY 1931– Artist in inks and watercolour and illustrator, born in Battersea, south London. He attended Hammersmith School of Building and Arts & Crafts, 1945–8, teachers including Ernest Fedarb, William Washington and Dalgleish Playfair. He was made a member of SGA in 1969, a fellow of Chartered Society of Designers in 1980 and of Royal Society of Arts in 1981, also showing with RBA. Ronald Searle and Charles Keeping were cited as influences on Geary's work, which was used in periodicals such as *Radio Times* and *Punch*. Illustrated a number of books, including Chris Powling's *Dracula in Sunlight*, 1989. Geological Society and London Hospital hold his work. Lived in Sidcup, Kent.

Steve GEARY 1962– Painter and commercial artist, born and lived in London, who studied for a graphics degree at Goldsmiths' College in the early 1980s under Derek Cooper. As well as carrying out postcard and advertising commissions, Geary became one of the chief illustrators for the satirical television series *Spitting Image* and the only British artist providing covers for *MAD* magazine. In 1998 Geary showed Varying Shades of Pink at Air Gallery, touring to America, each painting inspired by a Pink Floyd rock group album, with limited-edition prints available. To complete the series, which had Surrealist overtones, Geary chose to work through the night to the music's blaring accompaniment, having been a fan of the Floyd since he was 14.

Charles W GEBHARD 1923– Painter, draughtsman and potter, born in London, married to the sculptor Jennifer Gebhard. He studied at Bromley College of Art with Keith Coleborn, 1947–50, then with Henry Rushbury at the Royal Academy Schools in 1950. Exhibited RA, LG, RBA, in the provinces and in Kenya. Lived for some years in London.

Margaret GEDDES 1914– Painter and draughtsman, born in Cheam, Surrey, educated in Eastbourne, who studied at Westminster School of Art, 1932–7, teachers including Walter Bayes, Bernard Meninsky and Mark Gertler. Geddes became a member of NS, AIA and WIAC, also showing at RA, LG, NEAC and Redfern Gallery. Solo exhibitions started at AIA, 1950, later ones including Halesworth Gallery, Suffolk, and a studio retrospective in Teddington, Middlesex, both 1973. Geddes' work moved from figuration to abstraction. She was an adventurous, inquiring artist, well aware of developments on the continent and in America, as demonstrated in the monograph on her, by Denys J Wilcox, which accompanied her retrospective at Woodlands Art Gallery, 1998. Leicestershire Education Authority holds her work. In 1996 Geddes, who suffered from Alzheimer's Disease, moved to a nursing home in Taunton, Somerset.

Stewart GEDDES 1961– Painter and teacher. He did a foundation course at Canterbury College of Art, 1979–80, then completed an honours degree in fine art at Bristol Polytechnic, 1980–3. Geddes, a painterly painter, took his landscape subjects from a wide range, from flour mills and gasometers to scenes in the Mediterranean area. From 1985 he taught foundation courses, in Weston-super-Mare and at Bristol Polytechnic. Exhibited in a wide range of mixed exhibitions, including Stowells Trophy Exhibition at RA in 1983; regularly from 1984 at RWA Open; from 1985 at Gloucester City Museum; and from 1986 at RA. After sharing a show at Rooksmoor Gallery, Bath, in 1987, he had solo shows there, 1989–91. Also in 1991 had solo exhibition at Cadogan Contemporary.

Wilhelmina GEDDES 1887–1955 Stained glass designer, printmaker and painter, born in Ireland where she studied in Dublin and Belfast. She showed at RHA, in London and Edinburgh, on the continent and in North America and was especially noted for her window designs, which included Belfast's Assembly Hall, the city's Museum and Art Gallery holding her window Children of Lir. Lived for a time in London.

Arthur GEE 1934– Wildlife, landscape and seascape artist, mainly in watercolour, but also pastel and oils and prints. He was born in and lived in Warrington area of Cheshire. After several years in industry and Royal Air Force, from 1955–83 was an engineering draughtsman, then becoming a self-employed artist. Gee was mainly self-taught, but had one year full-time in fine art, 1983–4, at St Helens College of Art and Design. Peter Scott, the Impressionists and early English watercolourists were among influences. He was a "romantic painter, looking for atmospheric conditions, also strong lighting and chiaroscuro". Gee was elected to SWLA in 1969 and became an associate of BWS in 1988. Group shows included Mall Galleries, East African Wildlife Society, Mini-Print International at Barcelona, in Spain, where he was a purchase prize winner, and the provinces. Solo shows included Great House Gallery, Rivington, Bolton; Warrington Art Gallery; and Brentwood Arts, Warrington.

Frank GEERE 1931–1991 Painter of atmospheric equestrian pictures and portraits, born in southwest London, self-taught apart from occasional night school classes. His first attempt at an equestrian picture was in 1961, when he saw a print of a horse and foal on his aunt's wall and copied it. Geere spent some years in Australia and worked for a lithographic publisher in the West End of London before being made redundant, when he concentrated on painting. He painted from photographs and from racecourse visits, where he obtained commissions for pictures. Included in his output were portraits of the ballet dancer Rudolf Nureyev and the jockey Lester Piggott and a number of studies of the racehorse Desert Orchid. Sold regularly from a pitch in the Bayswater Road until illness intervened. In 1985 Geere joined The Society of Equestrian Artists as a friend and showed with it on several occasions at the Mall and Westminster Galleries. In 1988 the *Daily Mail* offered the owner of the winner of its Leisure Stakes, at Lingfield, a commissioned portrait of his horse by Geere in addition to the £20,000 prize money. Geere died in Burgess Hill, Sussex.

William GELDART 1936– Painter and illustrator, born in Marple, Cheshire. He studied at Manchester Regional College, 1956–7. Showed at RA, in the Manchester area and at Geldart Gallery, Henbury, Macclesfield, Cheshire. He wrote and illustrated *Geldart's Cheshire* and illustrated many other titles. Manchester Grammar School holds his work.

William GELLER 1930– Artist in pen and ink, pencil and gouache, born in Essex. He was a City of London apprentice in commercial art, studying at South-West Essex Technical College and Central School of Arts and Crafts. After becoming an advertising agency art director Geller was a freelance artist and designer. For a time was a member and president of SGA. Geller was noted for marine pictures with technical authority but careful composition. He lived in Maldon, Essex, where he was a member of the Art Society and Stone Sailing Club. Group exhibition appearances included RSMA, Wapping Group and touring shows of Federation of British Artists. Port of London Authority holds his work.

Margaret GENEVER fl. from 1940s– Painter and printmaker, born in London, daughter of the architect Charles Genever. She studied from mid-1940s for many years at St Martin's School of Art, teachers including Herbert Holt and Otway McCannell; Hammersmith School of Art under Carel Weight and Ruskin Spear; and Central School of Art. Showed at RA, Free Painters and Sculptors and in provinces and solo at the Loggia Gallery. Lived for many years in Guildford, Surrey.

Caroline GENTILLI 1959– Artist in etching and mixed media, born in London, who attended Epsom School of Art, 1977–8, and Bristol Polytechnic, 1978–81. From 1982–6 Gentilli did non-arts-related jobs, then went back to full-time printmaking, from 1991 being "a part-time artist and full-time mother". Gentilli was a member of the Printmakers' Council and Bath Society of Artists. She said that "the use of colour and textures are very important to me as a means of expression. My two main influences are forms taken from the plant and rock world and the primitive art of Latin America." Group show appearances included RWA, 1986; RE Open, 1987; Royal Festival Hall, 1989; RA Summer Exhibition, 1990; and overseas shows in Canada, Spain, America, South Korea and Malta. Lived in Bishopston, Bristol.

Jeremy GENTILLI 1926– Painter, printmaker, draughtsman, tapestry designer and artist in collage. Born in London of English parents, Gentilli was of Italian origin through his grandfather; his mother was the painter Madge Gentilli. He studied at Oxford University, 1946–8. Also attended Heatherley's School of Fine Art and Camberwell School of Arts and Crafts under Claude Rogers. Gentilli moved to Paris in 1951 and settled in France at Croissy sur Seine, Yvelines. In 1950s he studied in the atelier of Fernand Léger, S W Hayter's Atelier 17 and for tapestry worked with Pierre Daquin at Atelier de Saint Cyr latterly in 1971. Gentilli showed internationally, group exhibitions including the 1961 Biennale in Ljubljana, Yugoslavia; the 1962–3–5 Salons du Trait in Paris; and the 1964 Roter Reiter–Künstler Gruppe, Munich, West Germany. One-man exhibitions included Galerie Giraudoux, Paris, 1960; Eric Locke Gallery, San Francisco, 1963; Gallery A at South Yarra, Australia, 1964; and Galerie Vasse in Lillie, 1973. In the 1970s and 1980s he showed several times at Galerie Antares, in Paris. Gentilli's work was acquired by the Bibliothèque Nationale, Paris; Bibliothèque Royale, Brussels; Arts Council and Victoria & Albert Museum, London; and Museum of Modern Art, New York.

Madge Hope GENTILLI 1897–1963 Painter in oil, born in London, mother of the artist Jeremy Gentilli and sister of the playwright, man of letters and Labour Member of Parliament Benn W Levy. She studied at Heatherley's School of Fine Art under Bernard Adams and exhibited at ROI, RBA and RP, also in Chelsea where she lived. Died in Menton, France.

Bernard GENTLE 1913– Painter and lithographer, born in Watford, Hertfordshire. Studied with Francis Hodge at St Martin's School of Art. Exhibited with RA, Norwich Art Society and Leger Galleries. Lived at Blofield, Norfolk.

Iqbal GEOFFREY 1939– Painter, born in Chiniot in what is now Pakistan. A precocious, multi-talented man, Geoffrey was editor of the *Pakistan Post* and *Law School Journal* in the 1950s, being called to the Bar in Pakistan in 1959, with distinction. By this time he had travelled through Pakistan and India to study ancient monuments, decided to take up painting full-time although mainly self-taught, and travelled to England in 1960, having his first one-man show at the Galerie de Seine, London, in 1961. He was awarded a Huntingdon Hartford Foundation Fellowship in 1962 and worked in America. Geoffrey claimed to have pioneered abstract painting in Pakistan, his work being partly inspired by Hindu mythology and Eastern calligraphy. While in America Geoffrey was graduate editor of the *Harvard Art Review*, 1965–6, and was visiting professor of fine arts at St Mary's College, Indiana, 1967–8, studying art criticism at the Fogg Art Museum. His work is in a number of notable collections of modern painting, including the Tate Gallery, Arts Council and Boston Museum of Fine Arts. Returned to live and work in Pakistan.

Grace Courtenay GEORGE 1909– Painter, printmaker and teacher, born in Bristol. She studied at West of England College of Art there, teachers including Reginald Bush, and for most of her teaching career, 1939–69, taught art at grammar school, Chipping Sodbury, showing locally. Lived latterly in West Harnham, Salisbury, Wiltshire.

Helen GEORGE fl. from early 1920s– Sculptor and painter who after initial education at Talbot Heath School, in Bournemouth, studied sculpture with Antoine Bourdelle in Paris. She exhibited RA, Goupil Gallery, SWA, Leicester Galleries, Paris Salon and widely in America. Her work was bought by Victoria & Albert Museum, Salford Museums and Art Galleries and Manchester City Art Gallery. Lived at Blandford Forum, Dorset.

Janie GEORGE 1962– Painter, printmaker, muralist and teacher, born in East Pakistan, who studied at Somerset College of Art; West Surrey College of Art, Farnham; and Slade School of Fine Art. Held a number of teaching posts, including Slade School, 1990–2, and Bath College of Higher Education, 1993–4, then became a freelance muralist. Mixed shows included Printmakers at Farnham, Maltings, 1984; Macau University Print Exhibition, Macau, 1989; RA Summer Exhibition, 1992; and Royal Over-Seas League Open, 1994. Had a solo show at Horniman Museum, 1993.

Jon GEORGE 1944– Painter, printmaker and teacher, born in Ulverston, Lancashire, notable for use of egg tempera and the invention in 1989 of Castprinting. This inexpensive technique employed wet clay to make a painting in relief. George trained at Falmouth School of Art, 1965–8, eventually becoming a self-employed artist and teacher. As well as organising projects with children, pensioners and artists, he also taught Castprinting in Wormwood Scrubs prison and elsewhere. George cited Indian painting and Persian miniatures as influences. "To describe a landscape in time and space, to tell a story and concern with gesture" were important in his work. Between January and May 1991 George travelled by bicycle through nine West African countries, resulting work being shown at Bancroft Road Library, near his Chisenhale Studio, in 1992. Solo shows included Furness Museum, Lancashire, 1986, and Tyn-y-coed Gallery, Barmouth, 1989.

Patrick GEORGE 1923– Painter and teacher, born in Manchester. He studied at Edinburgh College of Art as an Andrew Grant Scholar, 1941–2; was in the Royal Naval Volunteer Reserve, 1942–6; then studied at Camberwell School of Arts and Crafts under William Coldstream, 1946–9. Was on the staff of Slade School of Fine Art from 1949, going as head of department to Nigerian College of Art & Technology, Zaria, 1959. From 1960 George was a member of the art panel to implement the *Coldstream Report*, of the Arts Council and of Eastern Arts. Obtained a personal chair at Slade, 1983, being Slade Professor, 1985–8. A self-effacing artist, George was a distinguished figurative painter in the Euston Road School tradition, a seeker for the essential structure and feel of the scene surveyed. Group exhibitions included Eight Figurative Painters, Mellon Center for British Art, Yale, and elsewhere in America, 1981; Hard Won Image, Tate Gallery, 1983; A Singular Vision, Royal Albert Memorial Museum, Exeter, 1984; and Five Protagonists, Browse & Darby, 1994, a gallery which gave him a series of solo shows from 1984. Previously he had shown at Gainsborough's House, Sudbury, 1975, and there was an Arts Council Retrospective at Serpentine Gallery, 1980. Arts Council, Government Art Collection, Tate Gallery and other public collections hold examples. Lived in London and Great Saxham, Suffolk.

Will G GEORGE 1851–1945 Primitive painter, born in Mousehole, Cornwall. He was the grandfather of the artist Jack Pender. Between the ages of 10 and 75 George was a fisherman, who retailed his exploits to Pender, who found them an inspiration. On retirement he took up painting, working on scraps of card and paper, producing many meticulous watercolours of Mousehole. George was promoted by the painter Alethea Garstin, who introduced him to the Passmore Edwards Art Gallery, Newlyn, and to other artists. His work was included in Artists from Cornwall, at RWA in 1992.

Nicholas GEORGIADIS 1925– Stage designer, artist in acrylic and oil on board and gouache on paper, born in Athens, Greece. He studied at Slade School of Fine Art, 1953–5, with Robert Medley. Worked substantially for leading ballet, opera and theatre companies as a set and costume designer. The Theatre Museum holds his work. Showed at Documenta, Kassel; Venice Biennale; and Carnegie Exhibition, Pittsburgh. He had solo exhibitions at Redfern and Hamilton Galleries and elsewhere in London, where he lived, and in Milan and Athens.

Elpida GEORGIOU 1958– Painter who was born in London. She studied at St Martin's School of Art, 1983–6, then at Royal Academy Schools, 1987–90. Georgiou gained the Winsor & Newton Painting Award in 1988, the Guinness Award for a first-time exhibitor at RA Summer Exhibition in 1991 and Elizabeth Greenshields Award in 1992. Took part in a variety of mixed shows from mid-1980s, including ROI in 1990, where she was a prizewinner, and Whitechapel Open in 1992. Had first London solo show at Christopher Hull Gallery in 1992. Her work is in the collections of Unilever and Guinness. Lived in London.

Charles March GERE 1869–1957 Painter, illustrator, designer of wall decorations and stained glass and teacher. Born in Gloucester, Gere won scholarships to Birmingham School of Art, where he studied under Edward Taylor and later taught. Gere's early work was much influenced by the Pre-Raphaelite-favoured Italian painters and for a time he studied tempera painting in Italy. Worked with William Morris at the Kelmscott Press and later at the Ashendene Press and did much to make the Birmingham

School a centre of excellence for book design, contending that illustrations and type should be complementary. Was interested in the revival of wood engraving. Gere was a member of the Birmingham Group of Painters and Craftsmen, which was strongly arts and crafts-oriented. Brother of the artist Margaret Gere. He exhibited prolifically, especially at RWS and NEAC, also Fine Art Society, Carfax Gallery, RA and Goupil Gallery. Elected RA, 1939. Tate Gallery holds his work. Gere's landscapes are notable for their careful design and serene atmosphere. Lived at Painswick, Gloucestershire, and died in Gloucester.

Margaret GERE 1878–1965 Painter, notably in tempera, born in Leamington Spa, Warwickshire. She was the sister of the artist Charles March Gere, studied under him from 1897 at Birmingham School of Art and like him was an original member of the Birmingham Group of Painters and Craftsmen. The copying of Piero della Francesca in tempera in Florence in 1901 had a marked effect on her work, and she further studied at Slade School of Fine Art, 1905. Showed with and was a member of NEAC and RBSA and had first exhibition with her brother at Carfax Gallery, 1912. Represented in The Earthly Paradise exhibition at Fine Art Society, 1969. Cheltenham Art Gallery devoted a show to her in 1984. Tate Gallery holds her picture Noah's Ark. She and her sister Edith, who married the artist Henry Payne, were known as "the masterful Miss Geres".

Bruce GERNAND 1949– American-born sculptor and draughtsman, producing enigmatic, abstract sculptures in a wide range of materials. He studied at Pennsylvania State University, 1966–8; graduated in philosophy at San Francisco State College, 1968–70; attended City and Guilds of London Art School, 1971–2; Central School of Art and Design, 1972–4; and Royal College of Art, 1975–6. Among awards received were those from the Arts Council, 1977; Eastern Arts Association, 1987; and he was Henry Moore Fellow in Sculpture at Central St Martins College, 1992–4, working in its foundry. Gernand showed in Britain from the early 1980s; had an exhibition in Coopers & Lybrand's Atrium Gallery, 1994; was included in the Osaka Triennale of Sculpture, 1995, in Japan; and in 1996–7 had work in the Sculpture at Goodwood display.

Alfred Horace GERRARD 1899–1998 Sculptor, ceramist and teacher. His first wife was the artist Kaff Gerrard, with whom he had a show at Colnaghi's, 1931. Gerrard studied at Manchester School of Art, then Slade School of Fine Art. He served in the Army and Royal Flying Corps in World War I, in the Army in World War II and was a war artist, 1944–5. He joined the Slade's staff in 1925, was its temporary head in 1948–9, and was professor of sculpture there, 1948–68, thereafter professor emeritus. Won the RBS Silver Medal in 1960. Gerrard's stone relief The North Wind is on London Transport headquarters. His work was included in The Slade 1871–1971 exhibition at RA in 1971. Lived at Leyswood, Tunbridge Wells, Kent. Gerrard, known as Gerry, was a revered teacher of students as diverse as Karin Jonzen, Eduardo Paolozzi and F E McWilliam, who wrote a catalogue tribute for the Gerrard retrospective at South London Art gallery in 1978.

Charles GERRARD 1892–1964 Painter in oil, born in Antwerp. Studied at Lancaster School of Art, 1907–14, and at the Royal College of Art, 1917–22, under Robert Anning Bell and Gerald Moira. Exhibited RA, NEAC, Redfern Gallery and elsewhere, the City of Birmingham Museum and Art Gallery holding his work. Gerrard also showed in North America, Italy and India, where he taught for a time and was an official art adviser in Bombay. He was an expert on Indian art and iconography. Work appeared in *The Studio* and *Colour* magazines. Lived at Denham, Buckinghamshire.

Kaff GERRARD 1894–1970 Painter and potter, born Katherine Leigh-Pemberton, who was married to A H Gerrard, for many years professor of sculpture at Slade School of Fine Art. She attended the Slade, 1922–4, under Henry Tonks and Philip Wilson Steer, and was a star pupil. She won first prize for painting from the cast in 1922, second prize for life painting and first prize for portrait painting in 1923. She was a visionary, almost pantheistic artist who drew inspiration from Paul Nash and the landscape of Sussex and the South Downs. During World War II she painted some topical scenes of rural devastation. Also completed highly coloured abstracts, often with a strong symbolical component. Although she was out on the South Downs almost every day painting Gerrard only had one public show, in 1931 at Colnaghi's; this was of sculpture and pots by Kaff Gerrard and her husband, including some joint efforts. Her paintings were not shown until the exhibition in 1991 at Royal Museum and Art Gallery, Canterbury, when several public galleries acquired examples, including Imperial War Museum.

Thomas A GERRARD 1923– Painter, by profession a chartered surveyor, born in Gaerwen, Anglesey. He showed with Royal National Eisteddfod, SWG, WAC, Howard Roberts Gallery in Cardiff, and shared a two-man show at Tegfryn Art Gallery, Menai Bridge. Gwent and Merthyr Tydfil Education Authorities hold his work.

Arnold GERSTL 1888–1957 Painter, restorer and gallery curator. Born in Prague, studied art there and in France, Austria and Spain. Exhibited RA and widely on the continent, including one-man shows. Prior to World War I he was a film studio artist for a short time. After World War II took over as curator at the Burton Art Gallery in Bideford, Devon, where he lived.

E A GEYDUSHEK-GEYDON 1893–c.1970 Painter in oil, she was educated in Vienna, where she studied at the Academy of Arts. In London studied at Regent Street Polytechnic School of Art. Exhibited RA, LG, with Ealing Arts Club and overseas. Lived in Ealing, west London.

Karl GHATTAS 1958– Self-taught painter who graduated in medicine from London University, 1982, gaining his Master of

Science philosophy degree from the London School of Economics in 1989. Ghattas' career as an artist was successful after he gave up a lucrative position as an ear, nose and throat surgeon and lecturing in philosophy at the London School of Economics. Between 1994–6, he was a visiting lecturer at Winchester School of Art, and was an assessor for Westminster Arts. Group exhibitions included The Laing Open, Mall Galleries, 1991; Affordable Art Company, Connaught Brown, from 1993; and Courtauld Institute of Art's Biennial, 1996. Had a solo show at Z Gallery, New York, 1992, later ones including Images of God, Hirschl Contemporary Art at the Gallery in Cork Street, 1996. This drew inspiration from world religions. Metropolitan Museum in New York and Ferens Art Gallery, Hull, hold examples.

Nikos GHIKA 1906–1994 Artist and designer in a range of media, and teacher, born in Athens, Greece. He later lived there, in London and Paris. Was educated at the Lycée in Paris and after studying art in Athens attended Académie Ranson, Paris. After living for about a dozen years in Paris, where he had his first solo show in 1927 at Galerie Percier, in 1934 returned to Greece. There he designed for the theatre; with friends published a monthly review called *The Third Eye*; and from 1941–59 taught at National Technical University in Athens, later becoming professor emeritus. He also illustrated a number of books, including Kazantzakis' *The Odyssey*, and Cavafy's *Poems*. His many solo shows included Leicester Galleries, 1955, from which Tate Gallery's Petite Composition en Gris was bought. Musée National d'Art Moderne, in Paris, and Metropolitan Museum, New York, hold examples. Byzantine art and Cubism were marked influences on Nikos Ghika's pictures. His first retrospective was held at the British Council in Athens in 1946, there was a major retrospective at Whitechapel Art Gallery in 1968 and he was elected an Hon. RA in 1986. Died in Athens.

David GHILCHIK 1892–1974 Painter and draughtsman, born in Romania. He studied at Manchester School of Art, 1907–15, where his wife Josephine was a fellow-student of Adolphe Valette, then he attended the Slade School of Fine Art under Henry Tonks and Ambrose McEvoy. He exhibited widely, including RA, ROI, NEAC, RP and Walker Art Gallery, Liverpool. Was a member of London Sketch Club and contributed to *Punch* between the wars and *Daily Sketch*. Ghilchik's oil paintings can be similar in style to those of Christopher Wood, landscapes having a breezy freshness. He was featured in Manchester City Art Gallery's 1976 exhibition of Valette. Lived in London.

Arthur GIARDELLI 1911– Artist in watercolour and relief construction, born in London, whose name came "from my grandfather who, under Garibaldi, fought for the liberation of Italy". Studied at Alleyn's School and Oxford University, 1930–4, gaining a master's degree. Studied art at Ruskin School of Drawing, Oxford, 1930, and with Cedric Morris, 1943–6. Went on to teach at University College of Wales, Aberystwyth, 1958–78, winning a British Council Award, 1979. In his studio in Warren, Pembroke, Dyfed, Giardelli made his elegant, technically skilful constructions from mostly local materials, "paper from old books, disused sacks, scrap metal, watch and clock parts, jetsam and sea shells". He was a member of the Association of Artists and Designers of Wales, International Artists' Association and was chairman of 56 Group Wales. Group shows also included Tate Gallery, Bear Lane Gallery in Oxford, Whitworth Art Gallery in Manchester and abroad. Solo exhibitions included WAC, National Library of Wales in Aberystwyth and Manchester College of Art. Tate Gallery, National Museum of Wales in Cardiff and Arts Council hold his work.

Phelan GIBB 1870–1948 Painter and potter, born in Alnwick, Northumberland, his full name was Harry Phelan Gibb. He was the son of the artist T H Gibb. Phelan (pronounced Faylan) Gibb studied in Newcastle, Edinburgh, Paris, Antwerp and Munich. For a quarter of a century he worked in Paris and was influenced by the work of Cézanne. He exhibited in group exhibitions at Salon d'Automne, the AAA as well as Wertheim, Alpine and Redfern Galleries, RHA, RSA and in New York. Had first solo show at Baillie Gallery, 1911. Gibb's rather earthy and apparently naive work was highly thought of by Roger Fry, Gertrude Stein and the dealer Lucy Wertheim. She supported him and his wife in their declining years with money, assistance to travel to France and even clothes but Gibb, an uneven painter, was unable to match his finest work of the period 1910–20. Tate Gallery holds.

Stanley Watson GIBB 1898–1973 Landscape watercolourist and designer. Born in Lythe, North Yorkshire, Gibb initially studied art at Scarborough School of Art under Albert G Strange, then at Goldsmiths' College School of Art under Frederick Marriott. He exhibited at the RA, RI and the Lake Artists' Society, living at Keswick, Cumberland.

Elizabeth GIBBARD 1913– Sculptor, painter and wood engraver, she studied art at Banbury School of Art and Bath School of Art. As well as exhibiting in mixed shows at the RA and UA, Gibbard had one-man exhibitions in Oxford. Hertfordshire County Council Education Department bought her work. Lived at Cricklade, Wiltshire.

Joan Lever GIBBINGS: *see* **Joan LEVER**

Robert GIBBINGS 1889–1958 Wood engraver, sculptor, writer and teacher. Born in Cork, Ireland, he was educated at the university there, then at the Slade School of Fine Art and at the Central School of Arts and Crafts where he joined Noel Rooke's design class. Commissioned in Munster Fusiliers in World War I, but was wounded by a bullet through the neck while serving in the Dardanelles and was invalided out. While abroad developed engraving style based on strong light and shade found in buildings in snow or bright sunlight, pattern counting more than the subject. Also worked in more naturalistic style. After the war founded SWE. When the Golden Cockerel Press, for which he was working, was threatened with closure, he took it over. During 1924–33 Gibbings' press published 72 books. In 1936 appointed lecturer in book design at Reading University. Travelled widely abroad, including Tahiti. Showed at Redfern Gallery, IS, SWE and RHA. Work held by British Museum, Victoria & Albert Museum and many other galleries in Britain and abroad. *Sweet Thames Run Softly* is his most famous book, published in 1940. It was followed in 1942 by *Coming Down the Wye* and in 1945 by his first Irish volume, *Lovely is the Lee*, chosen by the Book of the Month Club in America. In 1955, Gibbings bought a cottage in Berkshire, near the Thames, and there wrote and illustrated his last book, *Till I End My Song*. In 1972 there was an exhibition of Gibbings' work at the Dorchester Abbey Festival.

Benjamin GIBBON 1914– Painter and mural artist who studied at Ruskin School of Art, Oxford, then the Slade School of Fine Art. Exhibited RA, Goupil Gallery, NEAC, Cooling Galleries and RBSA. Lived at Pershore, Worcestershire.

Faith GIBBON: *see* **Faith O'REILLY**

Sidney GIBBON 1895–1988 Painter, draughtsman and teacher, born in Leamington Spa, Warwickshire. He attended Leicester and Brighton Colleges of Art. Went on to teach, from 1930–57 being head of Newark-on-Trent School of Art. He had an interest in architecture and in puppetry. Showed in the Midlands and has work in Newark Municipal Museum. Lived finally at Acomb, York.

Carole GIBBONS 1935– Painter, born in Glasgow, where she continued to live. She studied at the School of Art there, 1957–61, first showing with Allan Fletcher and Douglas Abercrombie in Glasgow in 1958. From 1965–7 she worked in Spain, then returned to Glasgow. She had her first solo show as a studio exhibition in 1965, having her second at Traverse Gallery, Edinburgh, 1968, then another in 1969 at Compass Gallery, Glasgow. A retrospective followed at the North Briton Gallery, Gartocharn, in 1973. A large-scale show of her work was held at Third Eye Centre, Glasgow, in 1975. She continued busily exhibiting in mixed and group shows, having another retrospective at McLellan Galleries, Glasgow, in 1986. Her work is held by Scottish National Gallery of Modern Art and by Scottish Arts Council, whose award she won in 1970.

Jeff GIBBONS 1962– Painter, born and lived in London, who studied at Ravensbourne College of Art, 1980–1; Middlesex Polytechnic, 1981–4; and London University, 1989–91. He was included in Pick of the New Graduate Art at Christie's in 1984 and won a prize in John Moores Liverpool Exhibition, 1995–6. Shared a show at Morley Gallery, 1994, and solo exhibitions included Somerville College, Oxford, 1991.

John GIBBONS 1949– Sculptor, born in Ireland, who attended Limerick School of Art, 1969–70, then St Martin's School of Art, 1972–6. He gained a number of awards, including a Macaulay Fellowship in Sculpture, 1975; two GLAA Awards, 1978–85; and an Arts Council Award, 1979. He was several times a visiting artist, including Sculpture Space, Utica, New York, 1980; Clayworks Studio Workshop and Syracuse University, both New York in 1983; and School of the Museum of Fine Arts, Boston, 1984. Took part in many group shows, solo exhibitions starting with International Arts Centre, 1975; others including Serpentine Gallery, 1986; Madeline Carter Fine Art in Boston, America, 1988; Angela Flowers/Flowers East from 1992; and Whitworth Art Gallery, Manchester, 1997. Arts Council, Tate Gallery, Gulbenkian Foundation and several foreign public collections hold examples. Gibbons' abstract steel sculpture, sometimes painted, related to seen objects, notably the American architectural landscape.

Evelyn GIBBS 1905–1991 Printmaker, draughtsman, painter and teacher, born in Liverpool, where she studied at the School of Art, 1922–6; at Royal College of Art, 1926–9; then at British School in Rome, 1929–31. Taught at Goldsmiths' College School of Art and was married to Sir Hugh Willatt. Showed at RA, NEAC, RE and other major galleries and there was a posthumous exhibition at Morley Gallery in 1994. Gibbs was a fine draughtsman in the classical tradition and her work is held by Arts Council, Ashmolean Museum in Oxford and other public collections. Lived in London.

Leonie GIBBS fl. from early 1980s– Figurative sculptor who trained at Edinburgh and Wimbledon Art Colleges in the early 1980s. In 1989 she was elected an associate of RBS. The ancient civilisations of Greece, Egypt and the Picts were inspirations for her expressive bronzes. Completed many commissions, including portrait heads, and showed frequently in London and Scotland, where she exhibited at RSA and lived in Invernesshire. Had a solo show in 1997 at The Bruton Street Gallery.

Patrick GIBBS 1959– Landscape painter and teacher. He studied fine art at Magdalen College, Oxford, graduating in 1981. Gibbs was at one time a teacher, working in several schools, one of them King's College School, Wimbledon, where he had been a pupil. After graduation he decided to concentrate on landscape painting, working in oil, acrylic and watercolour on a large and small scale. Worked for extended periods in southern Europe, notably Tuscany, but also in Scotland, Turkey and the London area. For a time he favoured a horizontal format, stemming from experiments with panoramic views based on photographs. Mixed shows included New Grafton and Moss Galleries, one-man exhibitions taking place at Fine Art Trade Guild, 1987–8, and Hurlingham Gallery, 1990. Lived in London.

Snow GIBBS 1882–c.1970 Painter who studied at Central School of Arts and Crafts, in New York and at L'École des Beaux-Arts, Paris, 1907–14. Exhibited RCamA, Walker Art Gallery, Liverpool, BWS, of which for a time he was secretary, RWA and Paris Salon. Lived in Leigh-on-Sea, Essex.

Thomas Binney GIBBS 1870–1947 Painter of landscape and portraits and teacher, born in Darlington, Yorkshire. Binney Gibbs was educated at Liverpool North-West School of Art and Liverpool University before studying briefly in London. Although he was early on quite successful as a painter living in Manchester and then at Chapel-en-le-Frith in Derbyshire, for a time he was art master at New Mills. In 1910 he moved to Whistler's old studio in Chelsea and began to concentrate on portraits, having shown several family portraits at RA. Also showed at IS and Paris Salon. In 1939 he settled in Stunts Green, Sussex, where he continued to paint local people and landscapes. Jeremy Wood Fine Art, Cranleigh, had a show of his work in 1975.

Tim GIBBS 1923– Painter, muralist and teacher, working with a bright palette and a bold, firm style. He studied history at Oxford University, 1946–8, and art at Ruskin School of Drawing in Oxford, 1946–9. Between 1956–84 did a large volume of part-time teaching, including Ruskin School, Bath Academy and Morley College. He was deputy Ruskin Master and head of fine art at Oxford University, 1974–80, being acting Ruskin Master in 1976, devising the degree course in fine art. Also did summer school work in Britain and abroad. Completed murals for The Blue Lion in Fen Ditton, 1958, and for Barclays Bank in Guildford, 1968. Took part in mixed shows at RA, LG, John Moores Liverpool Exhibition and elsewhere. Had a solo show at Piccadilly Gallery, 1955, later ones including Nelson Rockefeller Collection, New York, 1986, Clarendon Gallery, 1987–90, and Cadogan Contemporary, 1993. Royal College of Music and several education authorities hold his work.

Jason GIBILARO 1962– Painter, born in London. He studied at St Martin's School of Art and Brighton Polytechnic. Appeared in many mixed exhibitions, including Stowells Trophy, Whitechapel Open, Royal Over-Seas League (BA Travel Prize to India), Angela Flowers Gallery, Brighton Festival and elsewhere. His first substantial show was at Christopher Hull Gallery, 1990, called Berlin – Before and After the Wall, to which Gibilaro's punchy, colourful style was well suited. Lived in London.

Charlotte Ellen GIBSON 1902– Sculptor and teacher, born in Launceston, Cornwall. She studied at Regent Street Polytechnic School of Art under Harold Brownsword, 1925–31, then at the British School in Rome, 1931–2. Married the artist J T A Osborne. She went on to teach sculpture at Regent Street Polytechnic 1933–63 and was elected fellow of the RBS in 1951. Exhibited RA, RSA, Royal Glasgow Institute of the Fine Arts and in the provinces. Two examples of her portrait work are illustrated in Arthur T Broadbent's *Sculpture Today in Great Britain 1940–1943*. Lived in Orsett, Essex.

James GIBSON 1948– Painter and teacher, born in Glasgow. He studied art history at Edinburgh University, then taught English for some years while teaching himself the practical side of painting in his spare time. After an initial solo show at Compass Gallery, Glasgow, in 1985 Gibson showed at a number of venues in mixed exhibitions in Scotland and London. He had a solo show at Artspace Aberdeen in 1989 along with a second one-man at Compass. Gibson's pictures, slightly naive in appearance and carefully structured, deal with the sadness, loneliness and vulnerability of people.

James Brown GIBSON 1880– Painter, printmaker, designer and modeller, born in Glasgow where he studied at the School of Art, his teachers including Maurice Greiffenhagen. Glasgow Art Club member. Showed there, also RSA, RSW, Walker Art Gallery, Liverpool, and Royal Glasgow Institute of the Fine Arts. Lived in Killin, Perthshire.

Jean GIBSON 1927–1991 Sculptor and maker of reliefs, born in Stockport, Cheshire, studied at Royal College of Art, 1951–5, graduating with first-class honours and winning a travelling scholarship. Took part in many group exhibitions, including RA Summer Exhibitions, 1978–91, and LG, of which she became a member 1987. Solo exhibitions included Leicester Galleries from 1968; Nicola Jacobs Gallery, 1981; Oriel Gallery, Cardiff, 1985; Lynne Stern Associates, 1991; and The Redfern Gallery, 1995. Commissions included Commonwealth Institute, 1967; P&O Lines, for the *Oriana*, 1969; Record Industry Awards, 1975–8; Tel-Aviv Museum, Israel, 1976; and Cecil Denny Highton Group of Architects, 1982. When shown at the Redfern, Gibson's reliefs were said to "deal with the manic struggle between feeling and those things that impose constraints on its free expression. They are lyrical and romantic yet disconcerting in the profound sensitivity that they betray." Lived in London, married to the painter Anthony Whishaw.

Lloyd GIBSON 1945– Artist and teacher in many media who studied at Newcastle University from 1963, taught at the local Polytechnic and lived in Newcastle. He was included in The British Art Show touring exhibition, chosen by critic William Packer and put on in 1980 by Arts Council, which holds Gibson's work. Solo exhibitions included Gulbenkian Gallery, Newcastle, 1969; Richard Demarco Gallery, Edinburgh, 1977; and Mappin Art Gallery, Sheffield, 1978.

Tom GIDLEY 1968– Artist using various materials, such as mixed media with motor in his 1995 Venice Biennale submission Always on my Mind. He was born in Birmingham and gained his bachelor's degree from Central St Martins School of Art, 1987–90, his master's there, 1990–1. Group shows included How Noisy Everything Grows, Royal College of Art, 1992; The Daily Planet, Transmission Gallery, Glasgow, 1993; Beyond Belief, Lisson Gallery, 1994; and in 1995 In Search of the Miraculous at Starkmann Ltd. Had a solo exhibition at British Council Window Gallery, Prague, 1993. Lived in London.

Colin GIFFARD 1915– Painter, architect and teacher, born in London. He gained his master's degree from Cambridge University, studying architecture at University College, London. Giffard gained the RIBA Schools Drawing Prize, 1932, and was a

Rome Finalist, architecture, 1939. Studied at Bath Academy of Art, 1948–51, teachers including William Scott and Peter Potworowski, teaching at the Academy, 1951–68. Giffard was a member of RWA, also showing with RA, LG and abroad. Solo exhibitions included several in Bath and at Woodstock Gallery between 1958–69. RWA holds his work and he completed murals for educational authorities in Lancashire and Hertfordshire. Lived in Freshford, Bath.

Andrew GIFFORD 1970– Painter whose work was mainly concerned with the transient effect of weather on landscape. Gifford studied fine art at University of Newcastle and by the time he had graduated with first-class honours had held a solo show at Middlesbrough Art Gallery. He was included in a three-man exhibition at John Martin of London, 1996, and in group shows at SSA and Fruitmarket Gallery, Edinburgh.

Helen GILBART 1955– Painter, draughtsman and printmaker influenced by David Bomberg. She studied at Lancaster University, 1975–6, then undertook a postgraduate painting course at Cyprus College of Art, under a Peter Minet Trust Award, 1983–4. Completed an advanced diploma in printmaking at Central School of Art and Design, 1985–7. An Oppenheim-John Downes Trust Travel Award enabled her to paint in Spain for a year in 1989. Solo shows include Bedarte Gallery, Almeria, Spain; and South Hill Park Arts Centre. In 1991 took part in Towner Art Gallery, Eastbourne, David Bomberg and his followers exhibition, and in 1997 twenty-fifth anniversary exhibition at Bury St Edmunds Art Gallery. Lived in Middleton, near Saxmundham, Suffolk.

GILBERT and GEORGE Performance artists, creators of photo-montage, publishers and film-makers. Gilbert (Proesch) was born in the Dolomites, Italy, in 1943. Studied at Wolkenstein School of Art, Hallein School of Art and Munich Academy of Art. George (Passmore) was born in Plymouth, Devon, in 1942. He studied at Dartington Adult Education Centre, at Dartington Hall College of Art and Oxford School of Art. They met when studying at St Martin's School of Art in 1967. From 1968 they showed work and were living sculptures, their first appearance being at Frank's Sandwich Bar, London, in that year. Many other appearances included Robert Fraser Gallery, Nigel Greenwood Inc and at Robert Self and Anthony d'Offay Galleries. They also appeared several times at Whitechapel Art Gallery and at Hayward Gallery, 1987, as well as widely abroad. In addition to featuring in films and videos, Gilbert and George produced works in edition and books such as *Gilbert and George The Complete Pictures 1971–1985*, in which their art philosophy was expounded, seeking "to speak across the barriers of knowledge directly to People about their Life and not about their knowledge of art". A typical Gilbert and George performance was miming to an old record of *Underneath the Arches* while wearing their formal suits and ties, their faces and hands bronzed. Arts Council and other major collections around the world hold their work. There was a 30-year retrospective at the Musée d'Art Moderne, Paris, in 1997. Lived in London.

Anthony GILBERT 1916–1995 Designer, illustrator and painter who studied at Goldsmiths' College School of Art. From 1943–69 he worked for the advertising agency J Walter Thompson and produced famous anonymous designs such as the After Eight chocolate mint box. Gilbert, a member of the Society of Industrial Artists, completed murals for the Festival of Britain in 1951 and designed stained glass. Was a prolific illustrator for publications such as *Radio Times*, *Vogue*, *House and Garden* and *Lilliput*. In his final years he worked from a studio in Charlbury, Oxfordshire, producing a series of exquisite still lifes, portraits and other pictures redolent of Art Nouveau and Henri Matisse. There was a memorial show at David Messum Fine Art, 1996.

Dennis GILBERT 1922– Artist in oil, watercolour and pastel, born and lived in London. For many years he was married to the artist Joan Gilbert, also known as Joan Musker. Gilbert studied at St Martin's School of Art, 1946–50, teachers including Roland Pitchforth. He became a visiting teacher at four London art schools and was eventually a senior lecturer at Chelsea School of Art. In 1957 Gilbert was chosen as one of Jack Beddington's *Young Artists of Promise*, in the book of that title. He was a member of NS, NEAC, Society of Landscape Painters, Contemporary Portrait Society and Chelsea Art Society. His main works were portraits and landscapes. Also showed at RA, RP, RBA, Stephen Bartley Gallery, Langton Gallery and Paris Salon.

Donald GILBERT 1900–1961 Sculptor in a variety of materials. Born at Burcot, Worcestershire, son of the sculptor Walter Gilbert, he studied with him, with Sir Alfred Gilbert, at Birmingham Central School of Art, at the Royal College of Art under Derwent Wood and at the Royal Academy Schools under William Reid Dick and Henry Poole. At the Schools he won silver and bronze medals. Also studied for a time in Italy. Exhibited RA, RSA, SWEA and RHA. Gilbert completed a wide range of work, including busts of the composer Sir Edward Elgar and the conductor Sir Henry Wood, military badges and memorials, ecclesiastical sculpture and Inspiration to Flight, on the British Overseas Airways Corporation building at Brentford. Gilbert's work is illustrated in the volume *RBS: Modern British Sculpture*, published in 1939, and in Arthur T Broadbent's *Sculpture Today in Great Britain 1940–1943*. Lived near Billingshurst, Sussex.

Ellen GILBERT fl. from 1950s– Painter and printmaker who graduated from Cornell University in America before attending the School of Visual Arts, where she studied with Jack Potter, Chaim Koppelman and others, as well as the High School of Music and Art, The Art Students' League of New York and the workshop in lithography at London College of Printing. She moved to United Kingdom in 1969 from New York and began experimental etching with Islington Studio, learning transparent printing techniques developed at S W Hayter's Atelier 17, in Paris. Trips to Scotland, Wales and Ireland revived Gilbert's interest in watercolour. She was a member of Greenwich

Printmakers' Association, Printmakers' Council, Hampstead Artists' Council and Islington Art Circle. Mixed shows included RA, Square and Heifer Galleries. Solo exhibitions included Burgh House and Everyman Cinema both in Hampstead, Woodstock Gallery and Radlett Gallery in Radlett.

George GILBERT 1939– Artist using pen and wash, watercolour and acrylic, and teacher, whose subjects were mainly the coast of Fife, where he lived at Crail, and still life. Gilbert was born in Glasgow, graduated from the School of Art there, 1957–61 (was awarded the Guthrie Book Prize for Portraiture), with postgraduate studies (highly commended), 1961–2. Was elected a member of RSW in 1973 (joining its council in 1994), SSWA in 1991 and Paisley Art Institute, 1992. Gilbert taught in Scottish schools from 1963–89, then painted full-time. Group shows included Commonwealth Arts Festival, Glasgow, 1965; Shed 50 Gallery, St Monans, from 1974; Contemporary Scottish Painting, Middlesbrough Art Gallery, 1988; series of Fife Connection exhibitions including the first at Kirkcaldy Art Gallery, 1990; and Scottish Fine Art, Catto Gallery, 1996. He won the Paisley Art Institute's Artstore Award, 1992; RSW's Sir William Gillies Award, 1993; and gained 1st Prize, Marine Life, Portsoy Festival, 1994. Had a solo exhibition at Blythswood Gallery, Glasgow, 1967, later ones including The Open Eye Gallery, Edinburgh, 1994. Public collections holding examples include Nuffield Foundation; Paintings in Hospitals, Scotland; and Fife Regional Council.

Jim GILBERT 1933–1995 Artist who grew up in the East End of London and who was dishonourably discharged from National Service aged 21, turning to a life of crime. Gilbert was a huge, powerful man who spent much of his life in jail for crimes ranging from drug smuggling to robbery. Confined in the 1960s he began painting as a form of mental release, often without a model and with only poor materials. Although he later painted gentle watercolours of Morocco, much of Gilbert's output, in a sombre palette, reflected his earlier harsh experiences. He had his first show in Bath in 1972, almost two dozen following. He was the first recipient of the Arthur Koestler Award for prisoners' art in 1973 and was chosen by the Dylan Thomas Society to paint the picture of the poet presented to President Jimmy Carter in 1978. When he married his wife Lynne in 1990 Gilbert changed his surname to Barrington, his middle name, to start a new life. Died in southern Spain, where he was temporarily staying alone to paint. Nicholas Bowlby, Tunbridge Wells, had a memorial show in 1995 which transferred to Royal College of Art.

Joan GILBERT 1928– Painter, printmaker, illustrator and tapestry designer, born in India but educated at Badminton School. She married the artist Dennis Gilbert. Studied at St Martin's School of Art, 1945–50 and went on to show with Zwemmer Gallery, SEA, AIA, RA and Arts Council; had one-man shows at Travers Gallery. Work bought by Inner London Education Authority and West Riding Education Authority. Lived in London for many years and was also known as Joan Musker.

Richard GILBERT 1957– Painter, born in Plymouth, Devon. He studied at Falmouth, Wimbledon and Chelsea Schools of Art. In 1984 he gained a one-year Abbey Major Rome Scholarship and received the Barclays Bank Young Painter of the Year Award, his work was shown in Wet Paint at Bath Festival Gallery and at Warwick Arts Trust. In 1985 Gilbert's picture Reverie was included in John Moores Liverpool Exhibition. Lived for a time at Sevenoaks, Kent.

Stephen GILBERT 1910– Painter, sculptor and architectural designer, born in Fife, grandson of the sculptor Sir Alfred Gilbert. He studied at Slade School of Fine Art, initially architecture, but Henry Tonks advised him to take up painting, and he won the Slade Scholarship in 1930. After showing with LG and RA, Gilbert had his first solo show with Wertheim Gallery in 1938, three years after marrying the Canadian sculptor Jocelyn Chewett. Gilbert then had several years in Paris and Dublin, returning to Paris after World War II. In 1948 Gilbert's painting became abstract, he became a member of the COBRA group and exhibited with the Salon des Réalités Nouvelles and Salon des Surindépendants. In the mid-1950s Gilbert became involved in three-dimension constructions and his interest in architecture was reawakened as he worked alongside the experimental architect Peter Stead in Huddersfield. Projects involving colour in architecture and metal buildings eventually led to structures in aluminium utilising curvilinear planes. Although he continued to be based in Paris, Gilbert's work was shown in Britain at Drian Gallery, Austin/Desmond Fine Art and other venues. Arts Council and Tate Gallery hold examples.

Terence J GILBERT 1946– Painter, designer and illustrator, largely self-taught, who studied and copied Old Master techniques in the National Gallery. He worked in advertising studios until 1965, then for a decade was a freelance illustrator in England, on the continent and in America for advertising, film and publishing firms. After travelling in the Middle East and America, in 1976 he decided to devote all his time to painting scenes in those countries, animal studies and portraits. Showed widely at Mathaf Gallery, for which he worked under contract. Completed some historical reproduction pictures.

Vic GILBERT 1938– Painter and draughtsman, born and lived in London. He was a member of the Free Painters and Sculptors from 1977, also showing at Hampstead Artists' Council, ROI and elsewhere.

Wally GILBERT 1946– Sculptor, jeweller, metalworker and teacher, born in Sussex, who aimed "to create an organic and expressive whole based upon a strong formal structure". He attended West Sussex School of Art and Design, 1964–6, then Chelsea School of Art, gaining his diploma in sculpture, 1966–8. From 1975–87 he was an associate lecturer in art and design and jewellery; worked for Louis Osman, architect and goldsmith, 1982–8; from 1989 being associate lecturer in general art and design and media at the Royal National College for the Blind,

Hereford. In 1994 Gilbert was granted freedom of the Worshipful Company of Goldsmiths. Group shows included Plastic Precisely, Arnolfini Gallery, Bristol, 1980; WAC tour, 1985; 20 Artists at Artwear, New York, 1992; and Made in the Middle, West Midlands tour, 1995–6. Had a solo show at Roger Billcliffe Fine Art, Glasgow, 1996. Contemporary Art Society, Victoria & Albert Museum and Birmingham and Worcester Museums and Art Galleries hold examples.

Walter GILBERT 1871–1946 Sculptor, metalworker, designer, teacher and writer, born in Rugby, Warwickshire. He was educated at the Municipal School of Art, in Birmingham; at South Kensington; and in France, Belgium and Germany. Travelled widely in America and India. Taught at Rugby School and Harrow School. Gilbert, who wrote on industrial art, became art adviser to several major firms in this field and was a founder-member, and chief designer for, the Bromsgrove Guild. Ornamental metalwork for the council buildings in Dudley, Worcestershire, is by Gilbert, who was also engaged on aspects of the great gates at Buckingham Palace, Liverpool Cathedral and on war memorials in Liverpool, Burnley, Crewe, Troon, and elsewhere. Lived in Birmingham and London.

Michael GILBERY 1913– Portrait painter and teacher, born and lived in London, who studied at St Martin's School of Art, 1928–32, then until 1935 at Royal College of Art, teachers including Gilbert Spencer and Vivian Pitchforth. Taught for many years at St Martin's School of Art. Showed at RA, NS, NEAC, RP and elsewhere. Tel-Aviv Museum in Israel holds his work.

Garry GILCHRIST 1952– Painter, brought up in the Gorbals area of Glasgow, where he was born and studied at the School of Art, 1969–71. Using a rich and unusual palette, Gilchrist was notable for his series of heads, sometimes distorted into shapes such as triangles. Bank robbers was another theme. Exhibitions included St Martin's Gallery, Leicester, 1976; Sundance Studios and Press Club, both 1982; Stephen Bartley Gallery, 1984; Windsor Arts Festival from 1987; West Wharf Gallery, Cardiff, 1990; Bohemian Café, Blackheath, 1993; and City Art Gallery, 1994. In 1997 had a solo exhibition at Air Gallery. Lived in London.

Philip Thomson GILCHRIST 1865–1956 Painter, especially of marine subjects, born at Stanwix, near Carlisle. Studied in Hampshire and under the painter Tom Mostyn, after a period in business. Exhibited RA, RSA, especially at RBA, also Walker Art Gallery, Liverpool, RHA and Royal Glasgow Institute of the Fine Arts. He was a member of both the Liverpool and Manchester Academies, public art galleries in those cities buying his work. Lived at Sunderland Point, near Lancaster.

Paul GILDEA 1956– Figurative painter, born and lived in London, who studied at Camberwell School of Arts and Crafts, 1975–6, then Middlesex Polytechnic, 1976–9. Mixed exhibitions included Serpentine Gallery Summer Show 1 of 1982; Greater London Council's Spirit of London, 1982, as second prize winner; RA Summer Exhibition from 1987; and John Moores Liverpool Exhibition, 1995–6. Had a solo show at Galerie Quincampoix, Paris, 1989.

Theresa GILDER fl. from 1960s– Artist and designer, notable for her stone carvings. Born in Manchester, she studied at the School of Art there, then became a textile designer. She settled in Cornwall and was influenced by the work of Barbara Hepworth in St Ives. Was taught by John Tunnard, E Bouverie Hoyton and Barbara Tribe at Penzance School of Art. As well as portraits, Gilder made a reputation for her carved intertwining figures, as shown in Artists from Cornwall at RWA, 1992. She also showed at Newlyn Orion Gallery, Penzance; Truro City Museum; and Artful Eye, New Jersey, in America. Truro City Gallery and the Child Development Centre, Plymouth, hold her work. Lived in Penzance, Cornwall.

Frank Lynton GILES 1910– Artist in many media, full name Albert Frank Lynton Giles, born in London. He studied at Goldsmiths' College School of Art and St Martin's School of Art, teachers including Clive Gardiner, James Bateman, Stanley Anderson and Vivian Pitchforth. Was elected RWA in 1978. He showed at RA, RP, RBA, RI, RWS, extensively in the provinces and at Paris Salon, where he won a silver medal in 1948. Principal works included The Milliner, Cornish Fisherman and My Son Geoffrey. Public collections in Sheffield, Worthing and Bristol and RWA hold examples. Lived in Worthing, Sussex.

Graham GILES 1942– Landscape painter and teacher, who made his first paintings as a schoolboy on the tow-path of the Grand Union Canal at Berkhamsted, Hertfordshire. Studied at Regent Street Polytechnic School of Art, 1960–3, then Chelsea School of Art, 1963–4. Awards included RA David Murray Scholarship, 1962; Swedish Government Scholarship to study at the Royal Academy of Fine Arts, Stockholm, with Evert Lundquist, 1964; and a French Government Scholarship to study at L'École Nationale Supérieure des Beaux-Arts, Paris, 1965. Taught extensively from mid-1960s, latterly being a visitor at both Hull and Grimsby Colleges of Art and senior lecturer in theoretical studies, Norfolk Institute of Art & Design. Mixed exhibitions included LG, Thackeray and South London Art Galleries and Phoenix Gallery, Lavenham. Solo shows included Cadogan Contemporary, from 1988. Shared an exhibition with his wife Julie at The John Russell Gallery, Ipswich, 1997. Lived in Suffolk.

Julie GILES 1946– Painter, draughtsman and teacher, born in Bedford, who obtained her diploma from Camberwell School of Arts and Crafts, 1965–9. She taught at Centro d'Arte in Verrocchio, Italy, and at Norwich School of Art. Mixed exhibitions included Gainsborough's House, Sudbury, Drawings for All, 1984; Wykeham Galleries, Hampshire, from 1988; and Home and Abroad, The John Russell Gallery, Ipswich, 1997, the year she shared an exhibition there with her husband, Graham Giles. Had a series of solo exhibitions, starting with Bury Art Gallery, 1972, later ones including Cadogan Contemporary, 1988, and John Russell, 1989. British Rail holds her work. Lived in Suffolk.

Lesley GILES 1953– Artist in oil, pastel and watercolour, born in Bristol, who supported herself working part-time for local government social services. She studied at Goldsmiths' College School of Art, 1972–6, with Peter Cresswell, Albert Irvin and John Bellany, then at Royal College of Art with Ken Kiff, Andrew Brighton and Peter Allen. Giles' work was featured in a number of books on landscape painting. Her work was notable for its careful organisation and an absence of people, sometimes creating a slightly Surrealist atmosphere. Group shows included Subjective City, Cleveland Gallery, Middlesbrough, and tour, 1990. She was in Two London Painters, at Swiss Cottage Library, 1983. Solo shows included Dungeness Paintings, Rye Art Gallery, 1992, and Deserted Landscape, at Barbican Centre, 1994. London Boroughs of Camden and Hounslow hold her work. Lived in London.

Peter GILES 1939– Artist in various media, singer and teacher, born in Perivale, Middlesex. He attended Ealing School of Art, 1954–9, and Hornsey College of Art, 1959–60, making a special study of illustration. Taught part-time at several schools in Kent, lectured in North America and showed in the provinces. Lichfield Art Gallery holds his work. Lived at Bridge, Canterbury, Kent.

Tam GILES 1930– Sculptor and teacher, born in Britain, who from age of 10 lived mostly abroad. First art studies were with Joaquin Torres Garcia and the George Washington University and Corcoran School of Art in Washington, America. Her nomadic existence ended with settling in London in 1971. From then she taught first part-time at Byam Shaw School of Art, in 1979 full-time, resigning in 1986 to devote all her energies to environmental projects. Associated with other British Constructivist artists, she showed at Sally East Gallery and in group shows in Britain and on the continent. Carried out commissioned work, believing that new materials and construction methods should be employed by artists "to humanise them and bring them into our world of images".

Tony GILES 1925– Painter, born in Taunton, Somerset. He worked as a draughtsman with the Admiralty, 1941–59, teaching himself to paint. Began to make a reputation after settling in Cornwall in 1961, railways and landscape being a favourite theme in his work. He won the English China Clay competition Art in Industry in 1971. Mixed exhibition appearances included RA Summer Exhibition, and he was a participant in Artists from Cornwall at RWA, 1992. Solo shows included Salthouse Gallery, St Ives, 1984; Park Gallery, Cheltenham, 1988; and Penwith 65th Birthday Retrospective, 1990. Kettle's Yard Gallery, Cambridge, and public galleries in Stoke-on-Trent and Birmingham hold examples.

Tom GILHESPY 1944– Sculptor, artist in mixed media and teacher, born in Ferryhill, County Durham. He attended Leicester College of Art, 1962–6, and the Accademia di Belle Arti, Florence, on an Italian Government Scholarship, in 1966–7. Went on to become a part-time lecturer for a time at Newport College of Art. A member of the 56 Group, Gilhespy showed with it as well as SWG, at Royal National Eisteddfod and WAC, which holds his work. Included in WAC The Probity of Art touring show of drawings, 1980.

Katherine GILI 1948– Sculptor and teacher, born in Oxford. Studied at Bath Academy of Art, 1966–70, then St Martin's School of Art, 1971–3. In 1972 she began teaching at Norwich School of Art, at St Martin's in 1975, later joining the City Lit. Gili began to exhibit in mixed shows in the early 1970s, at Museum of Modern Art in Oxford; Chelsea Gallery; Norwich Cathedral; Stockwell Depot; and in Silver Jubilee Contemporary British Sculpture Exhibition, Battersea Park, 1977. Later appearances included Yorkshire Sculpture Park at Bretton Hall in 1983, when she also took part in Have You Seen Sculpture from the Body? at Woodlands Art Gallery. Had a solo show at Salander/O'Reilly Gallery, New York, 1981, and shared an exhibition with Graham Boyd at The Charterhouse Gallery, 1994. Gili was a creator of abstract sculptures analagous to human figures, in steel but with sensuous, dance-like connotations. Arts Council holds her work. Her father was the noted bookseller, publisher, Spanish scholar and translator J L Gili, who died in 1998.

GILL 1930– Watercolourist, born in London, married to the artist David Green. Gill Green studied at Hornsey College of Art under Jesse Cast and Norman Janes. Exhibited widely with her husband, including Heffer's in Cambridge, Century Gallery in Henley-on-Thames, Rye Art Gallery, 44 Gallery in Aldeburgh and Wigmore Hall. Cards and prints of her work were published. Lived in Woodbridge, Suffolk.

Alison GILL 1966– Sculptor, born in London. She attended Kingston Polytechnic, 1984–5, Brighton Polytechnic, 1985–8, and Royal College of Art, 1990–2. She worked in a variety of media, as in her exhibit Untitled – paper, nail varnish, tar and paint – in East & South, Norwich Gallery/Kent Institute of Art and Design, 1992. In 1993 she took part in the Brick Lane Open 3, Spitalfields Heritage Centre, and in Drawing Towards Sculpture, Isis Gallery, Leigh-on-Sea. Lived for a time in East Molesey, Surrey.

Angela GILL 1964– Painter, born in Middlesex, who studied at Harrow School of Art, 1983–4, Portsmouth Polytechnic, 1984–7, and Royal College of Art, 1991–3. Her exhibitions included A Place For Art at Brighton Polytechnic, 1989; BT New Contemporaries, 1992; Paton Gallery, 1993; and in 1993–4 her powerful Heavy and Clenched was included in John Moores Liverpool Exhibition. Lived in Hayes, Middlesex.

Cecil GILL 1897–1981 Painter, brother of the artists Eric and MacDonald Gill, born Brighton, Sussex. Was by profession a doctor who studied medicine at Edinburgh University. After service as a pilot in World War I he was for eight years from 1925 a medical missionary in India and the Far East, after which he was a general practitioner in England and Wales until 1968. For some time he was a member of SWG, and he also showed with SEA, Royal National Eisteddfod, Newport Art and Craft Society and WAC, which also holds his work. Did some painting in Corsica.

Eric Peter GILL 1914– Artist in watercolour and associated media and teacher, born in Birkenhead, Cheshire. He studied at Liverpool School of Art with Will C Penn. He taught there, 1937–40 and 1946–50, during World War II serving in the Royal Air Force as a cartographic draughtsman. Was principal of St Helens School of Art, 1950–74. Group shows included Wirral Society of Arts of which he was a member, Walker Art Gallery in Liverpool, Liverpool Academy of Art shows and at Rob Piercey Gallery, Portmadog. Had solo shows at St Helens Museum and Art Gallery and Williamson Art Gallery in Birkenhead. The Walker and Williamson hold his work. His later work included "studies of Welsh landscape, the rugged terrain of remote valleys, southern Snowdonia mostly". Lived in Bromborough, Wirral.

Lilly Kathe Elizabeth GILL 1922– Animal sculptor and artist, born in Germany, who trained as an art teacher, later in life attending adult education classes in pottery and ceramics. Took part in group exhibitions with SWA, SWLA, Radlett Art Society shows and elsewhere. Had solo shows at Boreham Wood Civic Centre, Hertsmere Council Offices, Watford and Stanmore Libraries, Watford and Bushey Museums and Holkham Hall, Norfolk. Belonged to Watford & Bushey and Radlett Art Societies. Bushey Museum Trust holds her work. Italian sculptors in the Victoria & Albert Museum and Sir Edwin Landseer were cited as key influences. Lived in Bushey, Hertfordshire.

MacDonald GILL 1884–1947 Architect, mural painter, calligrapher, designer and teacher, full name Leslie MacDonald Gill and known as Max. He was the brother of the artists Eric and Cecil Gill and was born in Brighton, Sussex. He studied at Royal Naval Academy and art at Chichester School of Art and Central School of Arts and Crafts. Early in the century was articled as an architect, was eventually elected fellow of RIBA and worked at such buildings as Lincoln Cathedral and the House of Commons, being noted for his murals. Was also an Imperial War Graves Commission designer and for a time a lecturer on architecture and completed posters for the Empire Marketing Board and London's Underground Railway. Tate Gallery holds. Died in London.

Madge GILL 1884 (some sources say 1882)–1961 Prolific figurative artist (original name Maude Eades) who drew, painted, embroidered and knitted her works in a unique naive style, born illegitimately in London, where she spent most of her life. During her early years she was brought up by her mother and an aunt and spent some time in orphanages in London and Canada, returning to England in 1903. Living with another aunt, she was introduced to Spiritualism. Madge married her cousin Thomas Gill in 1907; of four children born, only two sons survived, Laurie during his life doing much to promote his mother's work. Madge lost the sight of an eye, later replaced by a glass one, but despite this around 1919–20 began to create her strange objects and drawings – singular for their delicate patterning and cross-hatching and the inclusion of an oval-faced female figure – in bed by oil lamp light. She was guided by a spirit called Myninerest, and in 1920 became a medium. Although she exhibited at the East End Academy from the 1930s and gained much press interest, she shunned publicity and sales, saying her works belonged to her spirit guide. Through the 1950s Madge worked hard, often through the night, standing in front of a roll of calico which unwound from a frame fixed up by Laurie, with whom she finally lived in a gloomy house in East Ham. Exhibitions which did much to promote her name after her death included one by Newham Arts Council at Newham Town Hall, 1969, with another at Leeds Playhouse Gallery in 1976. She was later included in mixed shows such as Outsiders & Co, at England & Co, 1996. Gill's work is in many public collections, including the Outsider Collection and Archive.

Ruth GILL 1915– Artist, mainly doing commercial work, born in London. Studied at Chelsea School of Art, then for a time was art director of the advertising agency John Tait and Partners, in London. Exhibited LG. Work widely reproduced in women's magazines. Lived in London.

Sheila GILL 1925– Painter, potter, designer, calligrapher and teacher, born in Leeds, Yorkshire. Studied at Leeds College of Art, her teachers including Douglas Bisset and John Frederic Greenwood. Showed in the area of Leeds, near where she lived at Shadwell, teaching at Roundhay School for Boys.

Stanley Herbert GILL 1912– Painter, printmaker and teacher, born in Leeds, Yorkshire, his father Fred being a lithographer. Studied at the local College of Art, 1928–31, then at Royal College of Art, 1931–5, teachers including Gilbert Spencer. From 1936 began teaching at art schools in Yorkshire, being on the staff of Salisbury College of Art, 1947–72. Showed with RA, Bethnal Green Museum of Childhood and widely in the provinces. Lived in Salisbury, Wiltshire.

Ernest GILLAM 1897– Painter, notably in watercolour, born in Brighton, Sussex. He was self-taught as a painter. Showed at RA and in the provinces. His work appeared in *The Artist* magazine and the publishers awarded Gillam a gold medal for watercolour in 1932. Lived in north London, then at Woodingdean, near Brighton.

Régie GILLARD 1919– Artist in watercolour, born in Brentry, near Bristol, married name Régine Virgon. She studied with Donald Milner at the West of England College of Art, Bristol, then became involved in designing greetings cards for Medici, Dixon's and Gordon Fraser, for whom she worked exclusively on cards and other material for over 30 years. Her work was shown all over the world, exhibitions including

RWA and Clifton Arts Club. Lived latterly at Vellow, Williton, Somerset.

Edwin GILLBE 1917–1974 Painter in oil, gouache and watercolour; typographer and designer. Gillbe studied art at St Martin's School of Art under Herbert Ashwin Budd and Stafford Leake, at the City and Guilds of London Art School under James Grant, then at the Camberwell School of Art under Victor Pasmore. As well as having his design work featured in national newspapers and advertisements, Gillbe exhibited at the ROI, RBA and RWS. Lived in London.

Joan GILLCHREST 1918– Artist, born in London, who trained under Iain Macnab at Grosvenor School of Modern Art and in Paris. During World War II she drove an ambulance in London. In 1958 she moved to Cornwall. From before the war she had begun to exhibit in mixed company, over the years showing with RA, LG, NEAC and Whitechapel Art Gallery. Also showed in Cornwall at Newlyn Orion Gallery, Penzance, and Wills Lane Gallery, St Ives, and she was included in Artists from Cornwall at RWA, 1992. Had solo shows at Plymouth City Art Gallery, 1969, Newlyn Orion in 1973–6, Bodmin Fine Arts, 1974–8, and Windsor Fine Arts, 1978.

Joan GILLESPIE fl. from 1970s– Painter of highly coloured still lifes and landscapes, who studied at Duncan of Jordanstone College of Art, Dundee, 1972–5, gaining a diploma in drawing and painting from Edinburgh College of Art, 1975–6. After being a designer with the Royal Museums of Scotland in Edinburgh, 1979–86, began to paint full-time. Was a finalist in Morrison Portrait Competition, RSA, 1991, and Laing Landscape Competition, Mall Galleries, 1992, also showing at Royal Glasgow Institute of the Fine Arts, RWS and SSWA, as well as many private galleries. Shared a show with Geri Morgan at Duncan Campbell Contemporary Art, 1998. City of Edinburgh, corporate and private collections hold examples.

Michael GILLESPIE fl. from 1950s– Sculptor and teacher who studied at Hammersmith College of Art, learned bronze casting and cast for Jacob Epstein, who was a major influence. Took part in a lot of mixed shows, including 1st RWA Open Sculpture Exhibition, Bristol, 1993, and had many solo shows. Much of his work was abstract, although Gillespie disliked the distinction between it and figurative sculpture. In 1969 with John W Mills he published a standard manual, *Studio Bronze Casting*, and he taught latterly at Hertfordshire University. Lived in Histon, Cambridgeshire.

Raymond GILLESPIE 1955– Painter, designer and teacher, born in Dungannon, County Tyrone. He attended Ulster College of Art and Design, where he graduated after four years in 1978, the year he won the Philip Smiles Award – Gold Medal. Was with Ulster Museum, 1978–85. His teaching included Rupert Stanley College, Belfast, and the University of Ulster. From 1985–91 Gillespie was a partner in design and advertising practices, leaving to become a full-time painter. Among group shows in which Gillespie showed were Heritage Centre, Bangor, 1988; 4 Ulster Painters, Heritage Centre, Bangor, 1991; and Tom Caldwell Summer Shows in Belfast and Dublin, 1991. Atmospheric landscapes on a small scale were a feature of Gillespie's work.

Stirling GILLESPIE 1908–1993 Self-taught painter, teacher, traveller and film-maker, born in Stirling, Stirlingshire, as James Stirling Gillespie. From boyhood his aim was "to portray in watercolour (and some oil) the beauty of the Scottish scene". Although an outstanding schoolboy athlete, Gillespie's interest remained art, but his father's business failure in 1928 prevented his taking up a place at Glasgow School of Art. Became a journalist, in 1936 joining Dalrymple Educational Film Productions; in 1938 travelled through Africa to make educational films; and in 1939 published his experiences in the book *Celluloid Safari*. Gillespie also sailed yachts across the North Sea, Baltic Sea and Bay of Biscay. Eventually concentrated on landscape painting, in 1958 settling in Rothesay, Isle of Bute, after three years in Ballarat, Australia, and one in the Yoruba region of Nigeria, where he taught art. Joined Glasgow Art Club, becoming vice-president, and showed at Royal Glasgow Institute of the Fine Arts, being exhibitor of the year by popular acclaim in 1979–80–81. Solo shows included Kelly Gallery in Glasgow and Pitlochry Theatre. In 1985 illness prevented use of his right hand and arm, so he ceased to paint. By then he had sold well over 1,500 pictures.

Leonard Christopher GILLEY 1915– Versatile artist and teacher, born in Camberwell, southeast London, where he attended the School of Arts and Crafts, among his notable teachers being Edward McKnight Kauffer. During World War II Gilley was a cartographer in the Royal Air Force. Industrial commissions were undertaken for Shell, Castrol, Ministries of Transport and Agriculture, Dunhill and Hoover, and he illustrated for Odhams Press, Constable and other publishers. Gilley was noted for his marine paintings, "influenced by the work of William van de Velde", and portraits. Showed at Fishmongers' Hall and galleries in Bath, Bristol, Monmouth and Tetbury. Lived latterly at Trelleck, Monmouth, Gwent.

Ken GILLHAM 1934– Sculptor, modeller and teacher, born and lived in London. He studied at Medway College of Art, 1950–4, and Royal Academy Schools, 1956–8, teachers including Peter Greenham and Maurice Lambert. In his final year gained the Silver Medal and Landseer Scholarship. Gillham's work, in a variety of media, was used in many trade fairs and exhibitions, including Royal Society of Scientific Instrument Makers, British Museum and Walt Disney Productions, in America. He was an associate of the RBS.

Ernest GILLICK 1874–1951 Sculptor, born in Bradford, who studied at the Royal College of Art, where he won a Travelling Scholarship. Married to the sculptor Mary Gillick. Exhibited RA, RSA and Walker Art Gallery, Liverpool. Gillick was awarded the

RBS medal in 1935, three years later becoming a fellow. Was master of the Art Workers' Guild in 1935, served on the faculty of sculpture of the British School in Rome and on the Imperial Arts League's council. Gillick completed a large volume of public sculpture, including the Frampton memorial in St Paul's Cathedral, London; medals for the Royal Mint, RA and Inner Temple; London's Lord Mayor's seal; plus a variety of work for Commonwealth countries. Lived in London.

Liam GILLICK 1964– Artist and critic who was born in Aylesbury, Buckinghamshire. Studied at Hertfordshire College of Art, 1983–4, then Goldsmiths' College, graduating with honours, 1984–7. Group exhibitions included The Multiple Projects Room, Air de Paris, Nice, 1990. Solo shows included 84 Diagrams, at Karsten Schubert Ltd, 1989; and Documents, with Henry Bond, Karsten Schubert, 1991. With Andrew Renton co-edited *Technique Anglaise: Current Trends in British Art*, 1991.

Mary GILLICK fl. from 1911–1965 Sculptor and medallist, married to the sculptor Ernest Gillick. She studied at Royal College of Art and exhibited at RA and elsewhere. She carried out commissioned work for the Wellcome Foundation, London; Bishop Bell, for Chichester Cathedral; and medals for the Royal Society, London. Lived in London.

William George GILLIES 1898–1973 Painter and teacher, born at Haddington, East Lothian. After World War I service he attended Edinburgh College of Art, 1919–22, and was a founder-member of 1922 Group. A travelling scholarship took him to the continent, where he studied with André Lhote in Paris. On his return he taught for a year at Inverness Academy, then joined Edinburgh College of Art where he remained for 40 years, becoming principal in 1960 and retiring six years later. Through his quiet life Gillies was influenced by a number of painters, including Munch, Matisse and Bonnard, but he remained essentially a Scottish painter of still life and landscape whose work is strong in pattern and colour. The area around his home in Temple, Midlothian, featured strongly in his work. He was elected RSA in 1947 and in 1963 was made president of RSW. In 1970 elected RA, was knighted and Scottish Arts Council arranged a major touring retrospective, 22 years after Gillies had had his first one-man show in Edinburgh at the French Institute. Tate Gallery, Edinburgh's Scottish National Gallery of Modern Art (which held a big exhibition of Gillies' watercolours in 1995) and other Scottish galleries hold examples.

Barbara GILLIGAN 1913–1995 Painter, born in London, married to the artist David Carr. Like him she studied at Cedric Morris's East Anglian School of Painting and Drawing and at Slade School of Fine Art with Vladimir Polunin for stage design, 1934–5. With her husband she was the subject of one of Morris's finest portraits. Showed at Cooling Galleries, in Sladey Ladies at Parkin Gallery in 1986, at Galerie Salamanda, Paris, 1987, and elsewhere abroad. Had a solo show at Leicester Galleries in 1948. Lived at Starston Hall, Harleston, Norfolk.

Margaret GILLISON 1916– Artist in watercolour, oil and graphic media, born in Warwick. She was on the staff of the Grosvenor Museum, Chester, 1966–77. Was a member of Clwydian Art Society, also exhibiting with North Wales Federation of Art Societies and its south Wales equivalent and National Eisteddfod. She was a Royal Horticultural Society Silver Gilt and Silver Medallist and an Alpine Garden Society Gold Medallist. Sometimes exhibited under her married name of Margaret Gillison Todd. Lived in Mold, Clwyd.

Tricia GILLMAN 1951– Painter, born in Johannesburg, South Africa, who produced colourful, abstract works. She studied at Universities of Leeds, 1970–4, and Newcastle upon Tyne, 1975–7. Her group show appearances included several at John Moores Exhibition, Liverpool, from 1982; Forces of Nature, at Manchester City Art Gallery, 1990; and Three Ways, a British Council touring show to eastern Europe, in the same year. Her first solo show was at Parkinson Gallery, Leeds, in 1978. Later exhibitions included several at Benjamin Rhodes Gallery, from 1985, and Laing Art Gallery, Newcastle upon Tyne, and tour, 1989–90. Taught at St Martin's School of Art and Royal College of Art. Lived in London.

Robert GILLMOR 1936– Artist in watercolour, acrylic, pen and ink and scraperboard, and teacher, noted for his natural history pictures. He was born and lived in Reading, Berkshire, studying in fine art department of Reading University, 1954–9, with J A Betts and William McCance. He taught art and craft at Leighton Park School, Reading, 1959–65, then went freelance. Gillmor was a prolific book illustrator, around 90 titles containing his work; he was art editor of *Birds of the Western Palearctic* from 1966; was a founder-member of SWLA from 1964, being its president from 1984; and was president of Reading Guild of Artists, 1969–85. Showed solo at Reading Museum & Art Gallery, which holds his work, 1970; Washburn Gallery, Boston, America, 1971; Tryon Gallery, Nairobi, Kenya, 1973; and had a touring exhibition in France, 1983–4. Ulster Museum & Art Gallery, Belfast, also holds his work.

William GILLON 1942– Painter and teacher brought up in Leith, Edinburgh, settling in the city. As a youth he taught himself to draw, then studied at the College of Art, 1960–6, gaining top marks in his post-diploma final year. He was then granted a travelling scholarship to France and Spain in 1965. Teaching included Scotus Academy. When Gillen's work was included in the Scottish Realism show, by Scottish Arts Council, which holds his work, in 1971, he was described as “a violently energetic visionary”. He found drawing “hard work” and painted “to make a discovery, to investigate my feelings in paint.” Had a first solo show at Edinburgh International Festival in 1965, others including Scottish Gallery, Edinburgh, 1970.

Maeve GILMORE 1917–1983 Painter in oil and writer, born in London, where she died. She was married to the artist Mervyn Peake and mother of the painter Fabian Peake. Studied at the

Westminster School of Art, originally sculpture, then switched to painting on meeting Peake, whom she married in 1937. Maeve put Mervyn's work first, sacrificing her own talent. She had a number of shows in London, including Woodstock Gallery, sharing some with Mervyn, her pictures including portraits, still lifes and imaginary landscapes. When Peake became too ill to work, for many years she promoted his stature. She wrote *A World Away*, the story of their lives, 1970, as well as several other books. Was president of the Mervyn Peake Society, 1975–83.

Sidney GILMORE 1923– Sculptor in various materials, born in London, who attended Willesden College of Technology. Was a member of Free Painters and Sculptors, also exhibiting at RA, in the provinces and abroad. Lived in Wembley, Middlesex.

Albert GILMOUR 1923– Artist and draughtsman, noted for his railway pictures, born in West Hartlepool, County Durham, married to the artist Elaine Gilmour. Gilmour's intimate knowledge of the railway stemmed from his career as a fireman and then as a driver with British Rail. His studies included Gateshead Technical College; Bewick Studio; King's College, Newcastle; Ormsby Hall, Yorkshire; and Slade School of Fine Art. Was a member of West End Group in Newcastle and Gateshead Art Club and exhibited elsewhere in north of England. Lived at North Gosforth, Newcastle upon Tyne.

Elaine GILMOUR 1931–1990 Artist in oil and collage, and teacher, born in Hetton-le-Hole, County Durham, who originally showed under her maiden name of Elaine Bolton. She was married to the painter Albert Gilmour. Gained a University of Durham teachers' certificate with art distinction, also studying art at Neville's Cross College, Durham, and Sunderland College of Art. Was a member of West End Art Club in Newcastle upon Tyne, where she lived, also showing with Sunderland, Gateshead and Newcastle public galleries.

George Fisher GILMOUR fl. from 1940s– Painter in oil, born and lived in Kingston upon Thames, Surrey, where he studied at the School of Art under James Anthony Betts. Gilmour went on to exhibit widely, at venues including RA, Paris Salon, NEAC, RBA, NS, UA, Cooling Galleries and out of London at Blackpool, Darlington, Bootle, Merthyr Tydfil, Edinburgh and Aberdeen. Work was reproduced in *The Studio* and *The Listener*.

Hugh GILMOUR 1965– Painter, born in Kilwinning, Ayrshire. He gained a first-class honours degree in painting at Gray's School of Art, Aberdeen, 1983–7, then his master's degree at Royal College of Art, 1987–9. Among his awards were a Hospitalfield Scholarship, 1986, and a Rome Scholarship, British School at Rome, 1989–90. Gilmour used disembodied, broken forms to depict humiliation, anger, illness and breakdown of communication, as in his solo show at William Jackson Gallery, 1994. His first one-man exhibition was in 1989 at Irvine Arts Centre, Irvine, 1989, and he participated in many group shows, including RSA Student Exhibition, 1986–7; Rome Scholars, 1980–1990, Royal College of Art, 1990; and Greenwich Festival Open Studios, 1992.

John GILROY 1898–1985 Painter and teacher, born in Newcastle upon Tyne. He was for some years on the staff of Camberwell School of Arts and Crafts. Gilroy studied in Newcastle, then at the Royal College of Art and on the continent. Showed extensively at Fine Art Society, also RA, ROI, RP and Manchester City Art Gallery. Public galleries in Belfast, Hull and the Laing Art Gallery, Newcastle, hold his work. In 1998 a centenary exhibition which toured from the Laing, organised by the History of Advertising Trust, showed Gilroy's many Guinness stout posters, featuring toucans, a sea lion, an ostrich and other animals; his World War II posters for the Ministry of Information, such as *Careless Talk Costs Lives* and *Dig for Victory*; and portraits of the royal family, Winston Churchill and John Gielgud. Gilroy was a Chelsea Arts Club member who lived in London, but died in Guildford, Surrey.

Natalie GILTSOFF 1941– Painter of exuberantly rich flower pictures and interiors, and teacher, born in Richmond, Surrey. She studied from 1955–62, originally for three years in the junior department, at Camberwell School of Arts and Crafts, specialising in textile design. Teachers included Anthony Eyton, Dick Lee, Euan Uglow, Patrick Symons and Philip Matthews, with whom she lived in his last years. She then concentrated on embroidery at Goldsmiths' College, 1966–7. From 1967–9 was a part-time lecturer in colleges of art in London, Hertfordshire, Avon and Wiltshire. Mixed exhibition appearances included The Flower Gallery, where she also showed solo; John Noott, Broadway; Anna-Mei Chadwick; RWA and elsewhere. Later solo exhibitions included Beatrice Royal Art Gallery, Eastleigh, 1994. Lived in Devizes, Wiltshire.

Christopher GILVAN-CARTWRIGHT 1966– Artist, illustrator and teacher, born in Dorking, Surrey, who studied at Weston School of Art, Central St Martin's School of Art & Design and Cracow Academy of Fine Art, Poland. Lectured at Weston School part-time, 1988–96, and from 1996 at West Herts College in Watford. In 1996 curated the No Visa Required III show at Polish Cultural Institute. Gilvan-Cartwright won a Thames Television Travel Bursary, 1987–8, and a British Council/Polish Government Travel Scholarship, 1990–2. Heinemann, Penguin, Quartet Publishing and national newspapers commissioned his work. Group shows included Art for Aids, Royal Festival Hall, 1987; Artforum, 1995; and Royal Over-Seas League Open, 1996. Later solo shows included The Sun Calls me Home, Sydney House, 1996. Gilvan-Cartwright's paintings were "landscape themes in which something magical is about to, or has, happened".

Edna GINESI 1902– Painter, stage designer and decorator, born in Leeds, married to the artist Raymond Coxon. She studied at Leeds College of Art and Royal College of Art, 1920–4. In the latter year a West Riding Travelling Scholarship took her to several countries on the continent. Showed in group exhibitions at LG of which she was a member, Cooling and Leicester Galleries, had her first solo show at Zwemmer Gallery in 1932 and in the early 1930s did décor for Camargo Ballet. Was an ambulance driver in World War II. Retrospective show at Bradford in 1956 and shared an exhibition with her husband at Parkin Gallery, 1985. Represented in Tate Gallery and lived in London.

John GINGELL 1935– Painter, performance and structures artist, and teacher, born in London. He studied at Goldsmiths' College School of Art and went on to lecture at Cardiff College of Art. Was a founder-member of the ZOO Group and a contributor to its statements as sponsored by WAC; also to Everyday Something Changes, ZOO Group exhibition at Chapter Arts Centre, Cardiff, in 1972; and to Tate Gallery's Tate Kidsplay environmental installations in early 1970s. Took part in a number of performances, including Rover and Bonzo in Wonderland at Studio Theatre at University College, Cardiff. In Gingell's installation exhibition Soft City, held in Vancouver in 1982, he brought together a variety of objects and materials found in the city in an attempt to describe his experience as a visitor there.

Phyllis GINGER 1907– Watercolourist and illustrator, born in London. She attended Richmond School of Art, 1932–5, then Central School of Arts and Crafts, 1937–9, her teachers including William Palmer Robins, John Farleigh and Clarke Hutton. She took part in the Pilgrim Trust's *Recording Britain* project and illustrated several books. Became a member of RWS in 1958 and in 1990 was featured artist in its 1990 Spring Exhibition, with 13 works shown. Victoria & Albert Museum and Museum of London hold her pictures. Lived in Kew, Richmond, Surrey.

Graham GINGLES 1943– Artist, born in Larne, Northern Ireland, who settled there in Ballygalley, County Antrim. He studied at Belfast College of Art, 1962–6, then Hornsey College of Art, 1966–7, attending the British School at Rome, 1970–1, under an Arts Council of Northern Ireland Rome Scholarship. Took part in many group shows, including Learning Design, WAC tour, 1968; 8 Northern Ireland Artists, Third Eye Centre in Glasgow, 1977; Photo Realism, Orchard Gallery in Londonderry, 1979; Boxed Show, Artsite Gallery, Bath, 1986; and RHA, October Exhibition, invited artist, 1991. Had a solo show with Arts Council Gallery in Belfast, 1961, later ones including Project Arts Centre, Dublin, 1992.

Charles GINNER 1878–1952 Painter in oil and watercolour and occasional printmaker, born in Cannes, France. From 1899 in Paris he studied architecture, then turned to painting. Was from 1904–8 at the Académie Vitti, under the Spaniard Anglada y Camarosa, then at the École des Beaux-Arts. Ginner's sister was the dance teacher Ruby Ginner Dyer. Ginner made a journey to Buenos Aires, Argentina, in 1909, where he held his first one-man show. His oil paintings showed the influence of Vincent Van Gogh, the paint thick, making them difficult to handle. Having shown with the AAA in 1908, Ginner after the Buenos Aires trip settled in London, where he became a key member of the Fitzroy Street, Camden Town and Cumberland Market groups. He was especially friendly with Harold Gilman and in 1914 in the *New Age* spelt out their painting creed known as New Realism. In that year he showed jointly with Gilman at the Goupil Gallery. During World War I Ginner painted for the Canadian War Records, and he was an official war artist during World War II. Ginner's watercolours are unmistakeable, with meticulous detailing of trees and buildings. The Tate Gallery and many other galleries hold his work, the National Portrait Gallery a typically precise self-portrait. Arts Council memorial show and touring, 1953–4.

Louis GINNETT 1875–1946 Painter of portraits, interiors and murals, stained glass designer and teacher. He was educated at Brighton Grammer School and studied in London and then at Académie Julian in Paris. Taught at Brighton School of Art. He showed at RA, ROI, RWA and elsewhere. Brighton Royal Pavilion Art Gallery and Museums holds Ginnett's The Coat of Many Colours and his Design for Stained Glass Windows for the Chapel of the Royal Masonic Institute for Girls. Lived at Ditchling, Sussex.

Michael GINSBORG 1943– Abstract artist and teacher, born in Ealing, west London. He studied at Central School of Art & Design and Chelsea School of Art, 1964–9. Among his teaching posts was head of fine art at Wimbledon School of Art from 1991. Ginsborg was included in the critic William Packer's British Art Show touring exhibition, organised Arts Council, 1980, and his canvas The Gate was in 1993–4 John Moores Liverpool Exhibition. Solo exhibitions included Lisson Gallery, 1969; Serpentine Gallery, 1973; and Benjamin Rhodes Gallery from 1989.

Ann GINSBURY: *see* **PELOUSE**

Joseph GINSBURY 1892– Charcoal portrait specialist who after private art studies attended Birkbeck School of Art. Drew for such papers as *Sporting Life*, *Time and Tide* and *Financial Times*. Lived in London.

Sheila GIRLING fl. from 1970s– Painter, notably in watercolour, and collagist, born in Birmingham. She studied at the School of Art there and at Royal Academy Schools. Girling's work had a strong sense of place. She began to experiment with collage during a visit to Barcelona in 1983; her pictures were composed from previously painted fragments of canvas, secured in place and then repainted and glazed to create a variety of rich textures. The landscapes of Canada and Dorset were favourite subjects. Showed in London, including Francis Graham-Dixon Gallery, New York, Hamburg and Canada, having a solo show in Edmonton and Calgary in 1978. Lived in London.

Geraldine GIRVAN 1947– Painter of rich still lifes and interiors, in the tradition of the Scottish Colourists. Born in Derby she studied at Edinburgh University and Edinburgh College of

Art. Working mostly in gouache and oil, she contributed regularly to open shows at RSA, RSW and RWS. Her first solo show with Chris Beetles Ltd in 1989 was a marked critical and commercial success.

Joy GIRVIN 1961– Painter and teacher who studied at Newcastle upon Tyne Polytechnic, 1981–4, then Royal Academy Schools, 1984–7. Among her awards were an Italian Government Scholarship to Rome, 1989–90. From 1983 she took part in many mixed exhibitions including Stowells Trophy, Tyne Tees Northern Open, Whitworth Young Contemporaries, Camden Annual Exhibition, RA Summer Exhibition and The Broad Horizon, at Agnew, 1990. She had a solo show at Newcastle upon Tyne Polytechnic Gallery, 1989; Blason Gallery, 1991; and Cadogan Contemporary, 1993. Between 1990–2 she was a visiting tutor at Hertfordshire College of Art and Design. Lived in London.

Christine GIST fl. from 1970s– Sculptor and designer who was inspired by architecture and who worked for some years with an architect. She used a variety of materials for abstract works. Gist attended Chesterfield College of Art and Design, studying textile design, 1963–5. Then obtained a bachelor's degree in fine art – sculpture from University of Washington, Seattle, 1978–81, gaining a master's degree in sculpture at Yale University School of Art, 1981–3. Among her awards were a Fashion Group Inc. Scholarship, 1978; a Ford Foundation Sculpture Grant, 1979; a Pacific Northwest Sculpture Award, 1981; and a Connecticut Commission for the Arts Independent Project Grant, 1989. Gist participated in many shows in Britain and America, later ones including City Gallery, Leicester, 1990, and Sculpture at Canterbury, 1991.

Rodney GLADWELL 1928–1979 Painter, born in Didcot, Berkshire. He studied in Paris at Atelier Colarossi, 1949–50. Went on to show with Archer Gallery, O'Hana Gallery, Piccadilly Gallery, in Paris and the English provinces, Molton Gallery, with the dealer Lucy Wertheim who owned his work, and at Sussex University, which gave him a retrospective in 1962–3. The University commissioned him to execute large painting for its main hall in 1962. He also carried out work in 1959 for Georgian Club, in London, and in the same year designed an exhibition combining modern fabrics and paintings for Cotton Board of Great Britain, in Manchester, which was shown in Australia and New Zealand. Johannesburg University and Arts Council hold his work, which included heavily stylised female nudes. After a disappointing show at J-P Lehmans' Gallery in 1974 Gladwell disappeared in the mid-1970s from the English exhibiting scene, having married in 1972 and spent some time touring Canada. Lived in London for some years and was latterly represented by the Swiss dealer Walter Feilchenfeldt, in Zürich.

Paul GLADWYN 1956– Painter, draughtsman and collagist, born in Anglesey, Wales. Among his works were colourful landscapes which included abstracted shapes. He gained a first-class honours degree at Trent Polytechnic, 1980–3, and completed postgraduate studies at Slade School of Fine Art, 1993–5. Mixed exhibitions included Stowells Trophy, RA and Riverside Studios, all 1983; 4th Highland Open Exhibition (prizewinner) and Gulacsy Gallery, Budapest, both 1990; and Winter Paintings, The Ceilidh Place, Ullapool, 1994. In 1994 the Highland Regional Council and Scottish Arts Council toured Gladwyn's solo show Out of The Darkness, the year that he began showing solo with East West and with The Ceilidh Place. Scottish Arts Council, Highland Regional Council, the Socomer Group in Belgium and Robert Fleming & Company hold examples. Gladwyn was based in northwest Scotland.

Christopher GLANVILLE 1948– Painter and marine illustrator, born in London, son of the artist Roy Glanville. He attended Heatherley and Byam Shaw Schools of Art and Royal Academy Schools, his teachers including Peter Greenham and Bernard Dunstan. Glanville was elected a member of RWA, showing with it annually from 1980. Exhibited in RA Summer Exhibition from 1972. Exhibited extensively elsewhere, including NEAC, RBA, National Museum of Wales in Cardiff, Woburn Abbey, Ashgate Gallery in Farnham and Sinfield Gallery, Burford. RWA and Richmond Museum hold his work. Lived in Kingston upon Thames, Surrey.

Roy GLANVILLE 1911–1965 Marine artist, born and died in London, father of the painter Christopher Glanville. He studied at Hammersmith School of Art. Glanville was elected to RSMA in 1950 and to RBA in 1954, and was a member of Wapping Group of Artists. Also showed at RA and was a De Laszlo Medal winner. Walker Art Gallery, Liverpool, holds his work.

Sidney Herbert GLANVILLE 1884–1953 Painter, educated at Woodford, Essex, who exhibited RA, UA and RBA. Lived at Fittleworth, Sussex.

Jane GLASFURD 1909– Painter, full name Margaret Jane Glasfurd, born in Chelwood Gate, Sussex. Studied at Regent Street Polytechnic School of Art, 1930–33, then from 1933–4 at Kunstgewerbeschule in Munich, Germany. She showed at WIAC and Cookham Art Club, to both of which she belonged, and in Sussex, where she lived at Southease.

Edwin GLASGOW 1874–1955 Painter in oil and watercolour. Born in Liverpool, attended university there and in Oxford, several books of sketches of which he published. Was keeper of the National Gallery for several years in the 1930s. Exhibited RA, RI, provincial galleries and Paris Salon. Laing Art Gallery and Museum, Newcastle upon Tyne, holds his work. Lived at Charlbury, Oxfordshire.

Leslie GLASGOW 1955– Sculptor, born in Scotland. He attended Wimbledon School of Art, 1984–5, Central School of

Art and Design, 1985–8, and Royal College of Art, 1988–90. His work appeared in The Leicester Collection, 1988, at Art Directions, 1989, and RA Summer Exhibition, 1990, and in 1991 several works based on the theme Ship of Fools were included in Sculpture & Sculptors' Drawings at William Jackson Gallery. Lived in London.

Margaret GLASS 1950– Artist, notably in pastel, born in Chesham, Buckinghamshire. She was a member of PS and of Société des Pastellites de France. Lived in Debach, Suffolk.

Pauline GLASS 1908– Painter mainly in oil, she studied in Brussels, Belgium, then with Bernard Fleetwood-Walker at Birmingham College of Art. Showed at RA, RP, ROI and RBSA and lived at Harborne, Birmingham.

Peter GLASS 1917– Painter in the Impressionist manner, notable for urban scenes, born in Melbourne, Victoria, Australia. He was a pupil of Max Meldrum at the Swinburne Technical College, Melbourne, and furthered his studies with stays in London and Paris, 1951–5. In 1953 he exhibited both in the Paris Salon and in the first Australian Artists' Association show at RWS Conduit Street gallery. Glass won a number of awards in Australia and showed especially in Melbourne galleries. National Gallery of Australia in Canberra, University of Melbourne, corporate and many private collections hold examples.

William Mervyn GLASS 1885–1965 Painter of the Scottish highlands and islands who studied at Aberdeen School of Art and Royal Scottish Academy Life School. As well as being a member of RSA and president from 1930–3 of SSA, showed at RA, Royal Glasgow Institute of the Fine Arts and Walker Art Gallery, Liverpool. Was a member of the Edinburgh Group and lived in the city for many years.

Lancelot GLASSON 1894–1959 Painter who was born in Twickenham, Middlesex. After attending Marlborough College he studied at the Royal Academy Schools. During World War II he was engaged in camouflage work for the Air Ministry and Ministry of Home Security. He exhibited RA, RSA, Royal Glasgow Institute of the Fine Arts and Walker Art Gallery, Liverpool. Brighton and Rochdale galleries hold his work. Was a member of the Arts Club and of Art Workers' Guild from 1933. Lived in London.

Gerry GLEASON 1946– Painter, sculptural installation and mixed-media artist, born and worked in Belfast, Northern Ireland, who was interested in social, political and historical conflict, as in The Ulster Saga, at Newlyn and Middlesbrough Art Galleries, 1994–5. His images and palette could be rich, primitive, powerful. In 1989 Gleason designed colour illustrations for Brian McAvera's book *Art and Politics in Ireland*; in 1990 his Monumental Head image made a poster for Yeats Theatre Festival at Abbey Theatre, Dublin. Also in 1990 he gained Arts Council of Northern Ireland and Department of Foreign Affairs, Dublin, awards. In addition to many group shows in Ireland and abroad, later solo exhibitions included Orchard Gallery in Londonderry and tour, 1989, and QQ Gallery, Cracow, Poland, 1990. Londonderry City Council holds his work.

John GLEDHILL 1950– Painter in oil and draughtsman, full-time professional artist from 1971. He was born in Manchester and obtained his master's degree after three years at Royal Academy Schools, teachers including Peter Greenham and John Lessore. Showed with Calder Rural Artists Group of which he was a member, RA Summer Exhibition from 1985, Lancashire Contemporaries, Leeds City Art Gallery and elsewhere, his main works being urban landscapes, ship paintings and figure compositions. Had a solo show in 1990 at Castlefield Gallery, Manchester. In Cardiff, National Museum of Wales holds his work. Lived and worked in Hebden Bridge, Yorkshire.

Elsie GLEDSTANES 1891–1982 Painter in oil, pastel, watercolour and tempera of figure groups, portraits and landscapes. Born at Ealing, Middlesex, Gledstanes studied in Paris, and for periods at the Slade School of Fine Art, Byam Shaw School of Art and Vicat Cole School. She went on to become a prolific exhibitor, with work characteristic of artists who were at the Slade in the early part of the century; an especially accomplished watercolourist. Exhibiting venues included RA, RBA, SWA, Walker's Gallery, Ridley Art Club, plus other provincial and Scottish galleries. Had studios at Prenteg, Portmadoc, in North Wales, and in London.

Tom GLEGHORN 1925– Painter, administrator and teacher, born in Thornley, County Durham. He moved to Australia as a child. Had no formal art training but was assisted by the painter William Dobell and undertook travel studies to England and the continent early in the 1960s and in 1970 and showed widely in England, where his work is held by Manchester City Art Gallery and by other public galleries in Middlesbrough, Swansea and Newcastle upon Tyne, where the Stone Gallery represented him. All Australian state galleries also hold his pictures. Taught widely in Australia, notably at Bedford Park Teachers' College, Adelaide, from 1973. For about a dozen years from 1958 he directed the Blayland Galleries, in Sydney, where early on he had worked as a designer. Gleghorn was a painter of eclectic style.

Lady Helena GLEICHEN 1873–1947 Painter of landscapes and animals, born in London where she continued to live. She was the daughter of His Serene Highness Prince Victor of Hohenlohe, a British Navy admiral and also a sculptor. Her sister was the artist Lady Feodora Gleichen. Helena Gleichen was educated privately, then studied art in Rollshoven and in London, notably at Frank Calderon's School of Animal Painting. She showed at RA, City of Birmingham Museum and Art Gallery, New Gallery and in France and Italy. Several Italian public galleries bought her work. Pictures of the Italian war front and subscription hunt paintings were notable features of the work of Gleichen, who was keen on shooting and lived part of the year at Much Marcle, Herefordshire.

Ena GLEN: *see* **Ena RUSSELL**

Katie GLIDDON 1883– Painter, draughtsman and teacher, born in Twickenham, Middlesex. She studied at Slade School of Fine Art with Henry Tonks and Fred Brown, 1900–4, and developed a special talent for watercolours of flowers. Exhibited RA, NEAC, SWA, with the Arts Council and elsewhere. Lived for a time in Sanderstead, Surrey.

John Ainsworth GLOVER 1949– Painter, printmaker and teacher, born in Maryland, America, although he was educated at King's School, Harrow, and at Chiswick Polytechnic. Studied at Ealing Art School, 1968–9, with Derek Hirst, then at Slade School of Fine Art, 1969–72, under Keith Critchlow. Took part in a number of mixed exhibitions in London, including American Embassy, 1971, two years later having a one-man show at Amwell Gallery near where he lived in Islington, north London.

Louis GLOVER 1912–1982 Oil painter specialising in pictures of dogs, and potter. Born in Coventry, Glover studied art at the Royal College of Art under the painter Ernest Tristram and the potter William Staite Murray in the early 1930s. Glover became principal of the School of Art in Barnsley, Yorkshire, was art adviser to the county borough and was honorary director of the Cooper Art Gallery. Exhibited with the Yorkshire Society of Artists and elsewhere in the provinces. Wrote the *Batsford Book of Poodles* and the *Batsford Book of Dogs*, plus illustrations of dogs in *Dog World*. Lived in Stourbridge, Worcestershire.

Norah GLOVER 1923– She combined private practice as an architect with architectural perspectives and painting, gradually turning almost wholly to painting. After education at Malvern Girls' College, Glover studied architecture at Regent Street Polytechnic and, after qualifying in 1946, joined Sir Patrick Abercrombie's office. She was awarded the Andrew Prentice Bursary in 1948, Owen Jones Studentship in 1949 and was elected a fellow of RIBA in 1969. Showed at RA, Society of Architect Artists, Stock Exchange, Gilbert Parr Gallery and The Patricia Wells Gallery, Thornbury, which also gave her a solo exhibition in 1979. Prior to that she had had eight one-man shows at John Whibley Gallery, 1962–75. Painted acrylic and watercolour landscapes in England and on the continent and flower studies, pictures noted for their light, depth and delicacy of handling.

GLUCK 1895–1978 Painter, born in London into the family which founded the J Lyons & Co catering empire. Although she drew an allowance from her family, she rejected her name Hannah Gluckstein, calling herself Gluck (say it like duck). She early established herself as an eccentric, dressing in men's clothes. Attended St Paul's Girls' School, Hammersmith, her work winning a Royal Drawing Society silver star in 1913. Student at St John's Wood School of Art, then during World War I began to work with Newlyn School artists at Lamorna Cove, Cornwall. Established a distinctive style as an exquisite painter of portraits, flowers and landscapes, her work having a crisp 1920s look. Gluck held five exhibitions, in 1924, 1926, 1932, 1937 and 1973, being closely associated with the Fine Art Society, which held a memorial show in 1980–1. A special Gluck Room was created in the gallery in 1932 and the Gluck Frame – three symmetrically stepped panels – was patented by her. Litigious and obsessive by nature, for many years Gluck battled to raise the quality of artists' materials, especially paints, on which she became an expert. Lived latterly in Sussex, where she died at Steyning.

Felix GLUCK 1923–1981 Printmaker notable for lino-cuts in the German Expressionist tradition, painter of the English landscape, teacher and editor, born in Fürth, Bavaria. Fled with family from the Nazis in 1936; studied at the Free Academy of Art, Budapest, 1941–4, under Aurel Bernath and Robert Bereny; was imprisoned in Mauthausen concentration camp, 1944–5, where he contracted tuberculosis, which had to be treated at a sanatorium in Davos, 1946–8. An aunt in Newcastle enabled him to visit England from 1948, where he was able to study at King's College, Durham University, under Christopher Cornford and Lawrence Gowing. Before returning to Hungary in 1950 Gluck began to exhibit, gaining first prize in the Giles Bequest Relief Print Competition, organised by the Victoria & Albert Museum. Gluck worked as art editor for Hungary's state publishing house, 1953–6, but with the uprising he fled to England, settling in Twickenham, Middlesex. Gluck was made art editor at Rathbone (later Aldus) Books, 1957–66; lectured in graphic design at Hornsey College of Art, 1966–9, Chelsea College of Art, 1969–71, and Twickenham College, 1973–7; edited *Modern Publicity*, 1967–81, and founded the Felix Gluck Press in 1971, which lasted until just after his death. Gluck had solo shows at Woodstock Gallery, 1962, and Keele University, 1974. He died at Royal Marsden Hospital, 1981, and there was a retrospective at Orleans House Gallery, Twickenham, 1986, with another show at Durham Art Gallery and DLI Museum, 1995.

Paulien GLUCKMAN 1951– Sculptor in stone of figurative work, born in The Hague, Netherlands. She studied with Michael Marriott at Sir John Cass College, from 1993 being an apprentice with the sculptor John Skelton. She was a teacher of young children. Medardo Rosso and Brancusi were influences on the work of Gluckman, who was a member of Sussex Sculptors and Sussex County Art Club. She showed at Brighton, Hove and Worthing Museums and Art Galleries, at the Brighton Festival and at Charleston Farmhouse, Firle. Lived in Brighton, Sussex.

Daphne GOAD 1925– Painter and lecturer on art, born in Wallington, Hertfordshire. She studied at Central School of Arts and Crafts, 1943–7, Chelsea School of Art, 1943–7, L'École des Beaux-Arts, 1947–8, and Le Centre des Spectacles, 1947–8. Showed with RI, NEAC, SEA and elsewhere, Kent Education Committee buying her work. Lived in Hertford.

D GOAMAN: *see* **Winifred Doris BOSWORTH**

Victoria GOAMAN 1951– Botanical artist, born in London. She trained and worked as a freelance botanical illustrator with Dr Edmund Launert at the Natural History Museum, continuing this work for Royal Botanic Gardens, Kew. From 1974 she began to use watercolour for botanical flower paintings for publication and private collections. Where possible she preferred to work from live specimens rather than photographs. Among the books she illustrated were *Culinary Herbs*, produced by the Royal Horticultural Society in 1974; *Understanding Wild Flowers*, by Ros Evans, 1982; and *Garden Flowers*, by C Grey-Wilson and the artist, where the illustrations took over three years as she was restricted by seasonal work. Also did illustrations for *Illustrated London News, Natural World* and *Midland Bank Calendar*. Won several Royal Horticultural Society awards, including a gold medal for watercolour painting in 1978. Exhibited with Austin/Desmond Fine Art, Sunninghill, 1990.

Tony GOBLE 1943– Painter and gallery director, who studied at Wrexham School of Art. He went on to be director of the gallery at Llanover Hall Arts Centre in Cardiff, where he lived. He was a member of the Welsh Group, Association of Artists/Designers in Wales and RCamA. Also showed with RA, LG and abroad in Europe. Goble's work, which could be stridently coloured with a generous use of red and a rich personal imagery, was given a big exhibition, Dream Seeds, at Glynn Vivian Art Gallery, Swansea, in 1995. WAC holds Goble's work.

Francis Ambrose GODDARD 1868–1962 Self-taught painter, who developed his interest in art after retiring as a career soldier with the rank of lieutenant-colonel, signing work F A G. Exhibited RA, ROI and RBA. At various times he was chairman of the Army Art Society and president of the RMS. Lived in London.

John GODDARD 1924– Painter and teacher, born in Cardiff, where he attended the College of Art in 1941–3 and 1947–51, interrupted by the war, his teachers including James Tarr, Ceri Richards and Evan Charlton. He went on to teach at the College for a time as well as at a number of Welsh schools including Lewis School in Caerphilly, where he lived. Showed LG, SEA, SWG, WAC and elsewhere.

Judith GODDARD 1956– Artist who employed video, born in Crosshouses, Shropshire. She studied at Berkshire College of Art, 1973–5; gained an honours degree in fine art at Reading University, 1975–9; and a master's degree in environmental media, 1981–3. Awards included one from the Arts Council, 1983; installation for Sound/Vision, Plymouth and Exeter, 1985; and video for Video Positive, Tate Gallery, Liverpool, 1988–9. Took part in Signs of the Times at Museum of Modern Art, Oxford, 1990, and in 1995 contributed to Open House: two exhibitions for Jim Ede's centenary at Kettle's Yard, Cambridge, in which her contribution focused on Ede's wife, Helen.

Preston GODDARD 1928– Painter and designer, born in Liverpool. Studied at Croydon School of Arts and Crafts under Robert Arthur Wilson, 1945–6 and 1948–50. Goddard exhibited widely in mixed shows in London and the provinces. A one-man show at the Beaux Arts Gallery in 1955 was followed by others at Leicester Galleries, Somerville College in Oxford and the Fairfield Halls, Croydon. Leicestershire and Surrey Education Committees hold his work. Lived for many years in Croydon, Surrey, and sometimes signed pictures Preston.

Charles Edward Victor GODDEN 1901–1976 Draughtsman of figures in pencil and chalk; printmaker. Studied at Portsmouth School of Art, 1922–4, then from 1934–9 with James Bateman and Stanley Anderson at Goldsmiths' College School of Art. He exhibited at the RA, other leading galleries, Bath Society of Artists and RWA, being a trustee of it for 20 years from 1952. Lived at Corsham, Wiltshire.

Nicola Jane Averill GODDEN 1959– Sculptor, born in Germany but educated in Somerset. She graduated from West Surrey College of Art and Design, in Farnham, and went on to show with David Messum, Mall Galleries and at Eton College. Was a director of Linden Contemporary Sculpture. Lived for a time in London.

Angela GODFREY 1939– Artist, notably a sculptor, and teacher, born in London, who did a large amount of commissioned work for churches. Gained a fine art degree, Newcastle University, 1957–61, then taught at Mid-Warwickshire School of Art, 1962–4. Exhibitions included Letchworth Art Gallery, 1975, and Kodak House in Hemel Hempstead, 1977. Among her public works are Entrance Door, 1974, for St Bernardine Friary Church in Buckingham, and an impressive, stylised Christ on the Cross, 1976, at Weston Favel Roman Catholic Church, Northamptonshire.

Ian GODFREY 1942–1992 Ceramic sculptor and potter whose creations were spiced with wit and playfulness, featuring small creatures and drawing on ideas from a range of cultures. Born in Ely and educated in London, Godfrey attended Camberwell School of Arts and Crafts from 1957, initially to study painting, although turned to pottery in the department run by Dick Kendall. His teachers included Hans Coper and Lucie Rie. In 1962 he started a workshop in Islington; in 1967–8 gained a pottery fellowship at Royal College of Art; in 1975 moved to Denmark, setting up a domestic pottery workshop in Jutland; then returned to Highgate in 1980. Showed widely in Britain and overseas from 1962, including Osaka, Expo '70; Faenza, Concorso Internazionale Ceramica d'Arte, in 1974, where he gained a gold medal; and Heltborg Museum, Denmark, 1992. In 1993 Godfrey was given a memorial show by Galerie Besson. Public galleries in Glasgow, Aberdeen and Paisley hold his work, as does the Victoria & Albert Museum and several overseas galleries.

Jim GODFREY 1945– Painter and draughtsman, born in Kingston upon Thames, Surrey. He studied at Camberwell School of Arts and Crafts, 1964–8. Showed at Greenwich Theatre Gallery, 1967; Bakehouse Gallery, 1982; and had a solo show at Woodlands Art Gallery, 1983.

Laura GODFREY–ISAACS 1964– Painter and teacher, born in London, where she settled to work. She studied at Kingston Polytechnic, 1982, Brighton Polytechnic, 1983–6, and Slade School of Fine Art, 1986–8. In the latter year she won a Boise award and a Fulbright Fellowship, so becoming artist-in-residence at Pratt Institute, New York. In 1990 she took up a similar position at Tate Gallery, Liverpool, having a solo show there called Pink. Other solo exhibitions included Sue Williams Gallery and John Milton Gallery, both 1991. In 1991–2 her picture Body with Little White Holes was included in John Moores Exhibition, Liverpool, the holes "shifting uneasily between provocative physicality and sensual allure". Worked on public arts projects in Central America, Romania, New York and in Britain, including Whitechapel Gallery. Became a senior lecturer at Winchester School of Art.

Ada Charlotte GODSON fl. c.1920–1960 Painter and miniaturist, born at Tenbury, Worcestershire. She studied at Cheltenham Ladies' College, then at Sir Arthur Cope's School of Art, in France, Germany and Italy. Exhibited RI, SM, RBSA, UA and Paris Salon, her work being widely reproduced in France. Lived in London.

Keith GODWIN 1916–1991 Sculptor, draughtsman, collagist and teacher, born in Warsop, Nottinghamshire. He studied at Nottingham College of Art, 1934–6, Leicester College of Art, 1936–9, and sculpture at Royal College of Art, 1939–40 and 1946–8, World War II being spent in Royal Air Force Intelligence. He won the Royal College's Silver Medal in 1947, the Travelling Scholarship in 1949. Godwin became head of sculpture at Hammersmith College of Art, 1957–67, then at Manchester Polytechnic, 1967–82, becoming head of fine arts there, 1979–81. He showed at RA, RBA of which he was a member and Manchester Academy. Carried out many commissions, abstract and figurative; notable works were his sculpture for the centenary of the *Manchester Evening News*, 1971, work for the Reed Paper Group, British Rail and Commonwealth Institute. Memorial show at Woodlands Art Gallery, 1992. Lived in Sudbury, Suffolk.

Mary GODWIN 1887–1960 Painter, born at Stoke Bishop, near Bristol. Studied art in the women's department of King's College under Byam Shaw, also with Walter Sickert and Harold Gilman and at Westminister Polytechnic. Her work retained a Camden Town Group flavour. Exhibited at RA, AAA, Goupil Gallery, Cooling Galleries, NEAC, LG and had one-man show at Leger Gallery. Paintings were reproduced in *The Studio* and *Colour*. Lived in London.

Walter GOETZ 1911–1995 Painter and illustrator for newspapers and magazines, born in Cologne, Germany. He attended school in England from 1922, Bedales from 1923. When his parents were ruined in the Depression, Goetz in 1929 declined to read history and English at Cambridge University and returned to Berlin to study painting. The political climate made him move to England again in 1931 (he was naturalised three years later), where he became a notable illustrator and cartoonist for the *Daily Express* (as Walter) and magazines as varied as *Lilliput*, *Strand* and *Vogue*. In World War II Goetz worked in the Foreign Office intelligence department and closely with the BBC, broadcasting black propaganda to Germany. From 1951–72 Goetz lived in Paris, illustrating Pierre Daninos' *Major Thompson* books and from 1959 dealing in high-value pictures. Exhibited his own work in Paris and in London at Lefevre, Wertheim and Bloomsbury Galleries and had one-man shows at St George's Gallery and Leicester Galleries. Goetz was first married to the designer artist Jill Greenwood. He settled permanently in London from 1980.

Nicholette GOFF fl. from 1980s– Artist who gained an honours degree in fine art at Maidstone College of Art, 1981–4; was at Birkbeck College, University of London, 1989–91, for diploma studies; then obtained her master's in art criticism and theory at Kent Institute of Art & Design, Canterbury, 1994–6. Exhibitions included Common Ground, Milton Chantry, Gravesend, 1985; West End Studios Group, Medway Arts Centre, Chatham, 1989; Visions of Life, Gagliardi Gallery, 1993; and Fantasy, a United Arab Emirates tour of work by 15 British women artists, 1995. Solo shows included Post Nostalgia Gallery, Teddington, 1995. Goff's work in the Kent Institute of Art & Design show Diverse, 1996, was based mostly on found objects revolving around a notion of trace: "a suggestion of possible meaning invoked by the objects and the situation in which they are placed".

Harry GOFFEY 1871–1951 Miniatures painter and printmaker, born in Liverpool. He studied at Liverpool School of Art, under Sir Hubert von Herkomer at his School of Art at Bushey, Hertfordshire, 1892–4, then at Chelsea Polytechnic. Exhibited RA and Walker Art Gallery, Liverpool. British Museum holds his work. Lived at Berkhamsted, Hertfordshire.

Grace GOLDEN 1904–1993 Painter, printmaker, illustrator and teacher, born and lived in London. She studied at Chelsea School of Art, 1920–3, with John Revel; at Royal College of Art, teachers including William Rothenstein, 1923–6, teaching there, 1926–7; and at Regent Street Polytechnic School of Art. Golden worked for magazines and produced book illustrations, often having to work to tight deadlines and research historical detail meticulously. Her own book *Old Bankside*, 1951, was so detailed that she was invited by Sam Wanamaker, planning to rebuild Shakespeare's Globe Playhouse, to be official archivist to the project. Golden also did posters for the General Post Office; worked for the Ministry of Information; and drew historic buildings for the Pilgrim Trust. During World War II she placed work with the War Artists' Advisory Committee. Showed at RA, Fine Art Society and Leicester Galleries and had a retrospective at

South London Art Gallery, 1979. Tate Gallery and Museum of London hold much of her work.

John GOLDING 1929– Teacher, writer, painter and exhibition organiser, born in England but educated in Mexico and Canada, at the University of Toronto. From 1951–7 Golding did postgraduate work at Courtauld Institute, his doctoral thesis being published in 1959 as *Cubism 1907–14*. In 1959 he began teaching at Courtauld, then was a tutor at Royal College of Art, 1971–86, being senior tutor, 1981–6. In 1978 Golding was Slade Professor of Fine Art at Cambridge University. Golding's pictures were abstract, reflecting and contemplative. He had his first solo show at Gallery One in 1962, others including Rowan Gallery, Hayward Gallery and Kettle's Yard, Cambridge. In 1994 Golding had a show of work at Mayor Gallery coinciding with the Tate Gallery's big sculpture and painting exhibition which he co-curated. Arts Council holds work by Golding, who lived in London.

Hilde GOLDSCHMIDT 1897–1980 Painter and printmaker, born in Leipzig, Germany, where she began her studies in 1914. Between 1920–3 she was a master pupil of Oskar Kokoschka at Dresden Academy. From 1923–32 she travelled to New York, Paris, the south of France, Italy and then returned to Germany where she had a first solo exhibition at Gallery Caspari, Munich, in 1932. Settled in Kitzbuehel in 1933, the Tyrolean scenery being an inspiration. Fearing a Nazi threat, in 1939 she moved with her mother to London, settling at Langdale, Westmorland, in 1942. She lived by making fur and leather goods, continued to paint and befriended the artist Kurt Schwitters. During her time there her lyrical Expressionist style became more structured. Always figurative, her pictures were richly coloured, sometimes symbolic and very moving. Had a show in Manchester in 1949, the year before her return to Kitzbuehel. Later shows included a number in Austria; Annely Juda Fine Art, 1969; and Abbot Hall Art Gallery, Kendal, and tour, 1973. Abbot Hall, Tate Gallery and several Austrian collections hold her work.

Shelly GOLDSMITH 1962– Versatile artist and teacher whose work could have a strong abstract pattern quality, as in Untitled, Royal Over-Seas League Open, 1994. Was born in Corringham, Essex, studying at West Surrey College of Art & Design, Farnham; Royal College of Art; and Winchester School of Art. Held a number of lectureships, including Manchester Polytechnic, 1992, then tapestry at West Dean College, Sussex. Commissions included Collins Book Publishers, 1987; Victoria & Albert Museum Contemporary Collection and Lewis Moberly Design Group, both 1989. Mixed shows included Contemporary Textile Gallery from 1987; Rebecca Hossack Gallery from 1990; and Gift for Life, Imagination Gallery, 1993. Had a solo show, Vital Spark, Gainsborough's House, Sudbury, 1992.

Andy GOLDSWORTHY 1956– Sculptor and draughtsman, born in Cheshire. He attended Bradford Art College in 1975, then Preston Polytechnic, 1975–8. During 1989 he worked at Ellesmere Island, Canada, and at North Pole. Travelling widely to make sculptures in a particular environment was a feature of Goldsworthy's work. Goldsworthy had a series of one-man shows at Fabian Carlsson Gallery from 1987, later ones including Leeds City Art Gallery, a touring exhibition, Hand to Earth, in 1990; Aline Vidal Gallery, Paris, 1990; and Arts Club of Chicago, 1991. In that year his work was included in Sculpture & Sculptors' Drawings at William Jackson Gallery. Lived in Dumfriesshire, Scotland.

Mark GOLDWORTHY 1962– Painter and printmaker, born in London as Alan Mark Goldsworthy. He attended Great Yarmouth College of Art & Design, Medlock Fine Art Centre and Manchester Polytechnic, 1983–6. After a three-month tour of European countries and their galleries Goldsworthy set up studio in St Mary's Works, Norwich, which remained his home, and helped organise several shows for Contact Gallery, an artists' co-operative. He was also an itinerant artist in South Africa, 1989–90, in 1991 visited America and was artist-in-residence for Circus Project at King's Lynn Arts Centre. An interest in dreams gave Goldsworthy's pictures a surreal quality. Mixed exhibitions included Gainsborough's House, Sudbury; Knapp Gallery; Mall and Bankside Galleries; and several French galleries. Among his solo exhibitions was Chappel Galleries, Chappel, 1990.

Oliver GOLLANCZ 1914– Painter, printmaker and teacher, born and lived in London, son of Sir Israel Gollancz and cousin of the publisher Victor Gollancz. He became senior lecturer in the history and theory of art at Sir John Cass School of Art, taught for the Open University, University of London Extra-Mural Department and for Syracuse University London Centre. As a part-time mature student Gollancz studied with Cecil Collins and Hans Tisdall at Central School of Art & Design. He described himself as "committed to working in oil on canvas … to revitalise painting as a significant form of contemporary art". His Colourist work was "increasingly non-figurative in interpretation of visual and emotional experience". Gollancz took part in group shows at Camden Arts Centre and in France, where he had a second home in the Cevennes. Gollancz's series of solo shows included Square Gallery, 1992, and in 1994 Ben Uri Art Society, following a residency at Mizpe Ramon in the Israeli Desert.

Chris GOLLON 1953– Self-taught figurative painter, originally of portraits, then in an allegorical style. Gollon dealt with the tragedy and misfortune of the human condition, his subjects including tramps, grotesques and misfits, sometimes with a manic quality. He was a finalist in Hunting Group Prizes, Mall Galleries, 1989, also showing at ROI from 1990. Solo exhibitions included Ferens Art Gallery, Hull, 1993, televised and so popular it was extended two weeks; Lawrence Batley Centre, West Bretton, 1994; The Pump House Gallery, 1995; and The Road to Narragonia, Lamont Gallery, 1996; and Galerie Simoncini, Luxembourg, 1997, the year that Independent Art Promotions successfully exhibited Gollon's work in Bahrain. University of Hull and a number of corporate collections hold examples.

Hazel GOMES 1952– Versatile and colourful artist and designer, born in Goa, who early started painting, in which she was largely self-taught. Until 1971 attended the Sir J J School of Applied Arts in Bombay; then, after a visit to America, from 1973 studied fashion at St Martin's School of Art. She established a studio in Paris, designed for Yves St Laurent, worked for continental journals and had designs for Dutch firm Peek and Clopenburg shown at Stedelijk Museum, Amsterdam. Returned to London after eight years and continued to exhibit widely, including People and Places at Gagliardi Gallery, 1993.

David GOMMON 1913–1987 Painter in gouache and watercolour, muralist and teacher, born in London. He early wanted to be a painter and from 16 enrolled in art school at Battersea Polytechnic. Aged 19 he was given a solo show by Wertheim Gallery, then for several years Lucy Wertheim took most of his work and paid him £2 a week. Gommon came into contact with the theatre and continued his programme of self-education in the arts, which remained a passion. Living in Dorset his attachment with the romantic English landscape – a strong element in his work – was begun. Disillusioned with art on his return to London and aware of social unrest and deprivation, Gommon largely gave up painting. After a period in London Fire Service in World War II Gommon taught at a progressive school in Kent, then from 1946–77 taught art at Northampton Grammar School. Gaining a teaching qualification took time, because of the unacademic nature of his work. In 1959 Gommon held his second solo show, at Northampton Art Gallery, then had occasional exhibitions. His work found its way to Canberra Grammar School, Australia; he completed a huge mural for St Crispin Hospital, near Northampton; and public collections bought his work or were given it by Lucy Wertheim. Angel Row Gallery, Nottingham, held an exhibition 1991–2, which toured. Gommon lived in Hardingstone, near Northampton.

Patricia GONZALEZ 1958– Painter, draughtsman, printmaker and teacher, born in Cartagena, Colombia, a naturalised American citizen, wife of the artist Derek Boshier. She did a foundation course at Central School of Art & Design, 1976–7, graduated in painting and printmaking from Wimbledon School of Art, 1977–80, then did advanced printmaking at Glassell School of Art, Houston, 1982–3. After teaching art at George Washington School, Cartagena, 1980–1, Gonzalez held a number of appointments in Colombia and America, being visiting assistant professor at University of Houston, 1990–2. Mixed shows included Young Contemporaries at ICA, 1979; Colombian Artists, Canning House, 1983; Contemporary Arts Center, New Orleans, 1988; and Angela Flowers Gallery, 1993. Had a solo show at Graham Gallery, Houston, 1984, later ones including Art Museum of Southeast Texas, Beaumont, 1990, and Graham Gallery, 1991. Lived latterly at Kingsbury Episcopi, Somerset.

Amabel GOOCH 1899–1954 Painter, born at Weston, Hertfordshire. Self-taught artist who exhibited mainly in Norfolk, notably with the Norwich Art Circle. Lived near Diss, Norfolk.

Charles Stephen GOOD 1905– Painter, calligrapher, black-and-white artist and teacher. Studied at Harrogate School of Art with Richard Parker, then at Royal College of Art with Reco Capey, Edward Johnston and Ernest Tristram. From the late 1920s he held a series of positions at schools of art in the Midlands, north of England and London until World War II, which saw him working for such bodies as the Air Ministry. After the war taught at Hull College of Art. Exhibited RA, RP, RBA and widely in the north of England. Member of the Yorkshire Group of Artists and lived in Hull.

John Strickland GOODALL 1908–1996 Watercolourist and black-and-white illustrator, born in Heacham, Norfolk, into a family with a long medical tradition. He was educated at Harrow School, where he showed a talent for art, caricaturing the masters. His father, a Harley Street physician, reluctantly let Goodall be "trained to be a mid-Victorian art student" under Arthur Cope and John Watson Nicol, later with the noted draughtsman Harold Speed and at the Royal Academy Schools, 1925–9. There he met his future wife, Margaret Nicol. Began as a fortnightly contributor to *Radio Times* and went on to illustrate for periodicals such as *Bystander*, titles by E Nesbit and Miss Read and a series of his own books with Victorian and Edwardian settings. Because these contained no words beyond the title-page, children could make up their own story, and they were readily marketable overseas. Group shows included RA as well as RBA and RI, of both of which he was a member. During World War II Goodall, already a member of the Territorial Army, was posted to India where he worked in camouflage and had his first solo exhibition, of local landscapes, at the Government School of Art, Calcutta, in 1943. After the war Goodall settled at Tisbury, Wiltshire, in a cottage which featured in his books. He continued to paint landscapes, in Britain and abroad, and portraits, subjects including the Duchess of Kent and the actor Michael Redgrave. From 1984 showed regularly with the Christopher Wood Gallery, in 1993 also at The Jerram Gallery, Salisbury. Died in Shaftesbury, Dorset.

Francis Philip GOODCHILD 1904– Artist and teacher, born in London. He studied at High Wycombe School of Art, 1919–23, then as a Royal Exhibitioner at Royal College of Art, 1923–6, teachers including Ernest Tristram and William Rothenstein. Was principal of Newton Abbot College of Art, 1947–64. Showed at RWA and elsewhere in west of England. Lived for many years in Brixham, Devon.

Mervyn GOODE 1948– Painter in oil, born in Cambridgeshire. He studied landscape architecture at Gloucestershire College of Art, but decided in 1969 to pursue his vocation as a landscape artist. His first solo show was a marked success, at Highton Gallery, 1970, and within 20 years Goode had had 30 one-man exhibitions. Later ones included Medici Galleries, 1990, and Reid Gallery in Milford, Surrey, 1991. Had many mixed show appearances and his work was reproduced by Medici Society, Bucentaur Gallery and Kingsmead Publications. Goode said that his "inspiration is the English landscape in all its moods and seasons.

I am a keen naturalist and conservationist". Lived in Hawkley Hurst, Hampshire.

Stephen Frederick GOODEN 1892–1955 Printmaker and illustrator, born in Rugby, who studied at Rugby School. Gooden then studied at the Slade School of Fine Art, 1909–13, and after World War I service and some years' experience with lithography, wood engraving and etching, he turned to copper engraving in the early 1920s. During the late 1920s he concentrated on this medium, reintroducing it to book illustration while working with the Nonesuch Press. Gooden exhibited RE, RMS, RA and NEAC, but his main outlet was the printed page. Among books he illustrated were Abraham Cowley's translation of *Anacreon*, 1923, Edward Marsh's translation *The Fables of Jean de la Fontaine*, 1931, and the American author O Henry's *The Gift of the Magi*, 1939. Whitworth Art Gallery, Manchester, holds his work. Lived at Chesham Bois, Buckinghamshire.

Walter GOODIN 1907–1992 Originally a railway porter, this landscape painter's talent was nurtured from 1926 in Beverley, Yorkshire, by the artist Fred Elwell. Goodin attended the Royal Academy Schools, where he won the Gold Medal, the Elwells helping to fund his studies. After World War II, during which he served overseas, Goodin settled in Bridlington, Yorkshire, and married. Ferens Art Gallery, Hull, holds Goodin's The Old Custom House, and he was also exhibited at RA and at the Carnegie Institute, Pittsburgh, America. Elwell's portrait of Goodin, painted shortly after his Royal Academy studies in 1937, is owned by Sewerby Hall, Yorkshire.

Catherine GOODMAN 1961– Painter, draughtsman and teacher, born in London. She attended Camberwell School of Arts and Crafts, 1979–84, for a foundation degree, completing a postgraduate diploma at Royal Academy Schools, 1984–7. From 1990 she taught at Camberwell. While studying she had won the Tom Phillips Drawing Prize, in 1984, the David Murray Travelling Scholarship, 1984–5, the Royal Academy Gold Medal in 1987 and the Richard Ford Award in 1988. Exhibited in RA Summer Exhibitions, at the RA's Art Al Fresco in 1988 and in 1991 had a solo show at Cadogan Contemporary.

David GOODMAN 1918– Painter, designer and teacher who studied at St Martin's School of Art and showed first at RA while still a student. With his friend Peter Lanyon he taught art to the armed forces in Naples in 1945, then after World War II at Chichester School of Art. He was art director for several national magazines; a director of the David Paul Gallery in Chichester, and was chairman of Chichester Design Associates; was art adviser to the Festival Theatre there; and designed sets and costumes for Glyndebourne opera house and the ostrich symbol for Pallant House, Chichester, which holds his work as part of the Kearley Bequest. Goodman's wife Pearl was a singer, who was a leading member of Joan Littlewood's Theatre Workshop. Goodman won two Italian gold medals for painting and a Design Council Award. Although principally a landscape painter in the English romantic tradition, he also made portraits, which included the playwright Christopher Fry and actress Kate O'Mara. In 1993 had a retrospective show at Vicars Hall, Chichester. Lived near the Sussex town at Halnaker.

Sheila GOODMAN fl. from 1965– Artist, notably in pastel, who worked in England and travelled extensively in Europe and Canada to complete landscapes and coastal scenes. Born in Lancashire, she studied graphic design at High Wycombe College of Art, 1966–9. Went on to show in group exhibitions at Daler Gallery, Wykeham Gallery, Century Gallery, PS, SWA, Society of Botanical Artists and RA. Had solo shows at Bettles Gallery in 1989–90–91 and shared an exhibition with three artists at Anna-Mei Chadwick, 1992.

Jane GOODWIN 1944– Artist who was educated in Australia and London, where she eventually took a studio, living in Puttenham, Surrey. Did a foundation course at Brisbane School of Art, Queensland, 1962. Her work experience included retailing in Australia, America and Nigeria; acting as advertisement manager for Thomson Publications' *Ambassador Magazine*; and being advertisement traffic manager in the production department for the agency J Walter Thompson. Between 1992–5, Goodwin gained an honours degree in fine art from West Surrey College of Art and Design, Farnham, then her master's degree in sculpture from Brighton University, 1995–7. Exhibitions included Reflections of Life and Festival of Women's Art, both at Coventry Gallery, 1994; DNA at Whiteleys' Gallery, 1995; Private View, Cable Street Gallery, 1996; and Unquiet Voices, Doncaster Museum & Art Gallery, 1997.

Leslie GOODWIN 1929– Painter and illustrator, born and lived in Leicester, attending the College of Art there, 1949–55. Showed with RWA of which he was a member, RA and PS and had a series of solo exhibitions. Bristol Old Vic owns his work.

Sarah GOODWIN 1937– Painter of landscapes in England and on the continent, still lifes and interiors in the tradition of the NEAC with which she exhibited, also with RA Summer Exhibition, RWA, RBA and the Small Paintings Society, of which she was a member. Studied at Byam Shaw School of Drawing and Painting, 1955–9, teachers including Peter Greenham, Bernard Dunstan, Charles Mahoney and Allan Gwynne-Jones. Had a solo exhibition at The Jerram Gallery, Salisbury, 1995. Lived in Fordingbridge, Hampshire.

Bruce GOOLD 1948– Artist in various materials, but notably a printmaker, born in Newcastle, New South Wales, Australia. Aged 10, Goold attended Saturday morning art classes, then in 1964 began to study painting at Newcastle Technical College, in 1967 joining National Art School, Sydney. For some years Goold was involved in various artistic enterprises, designing sets and costumes and creating environments for exhibitions and cabarets.

After travels through Asia with his wife in 1974 Goold settled in Palm Beach, near Sydney, and began lino-cutting. Had his first show of cuts at Queen Street Gallery, Sydney, 1979, and a one-man show at Paul Craft Gallery, Melbourne, 1980. Further solo shows followed, along with a commission for 25 designs for a limited edition book; fabric designing and mural painting; and a poster for Australian Museum. In 1987 he designed the official poster for Bi-Centennial Festival of Sydney. Goold's work had strong ties with German Expressionism, as shown in his solo exhibition at England & Co, 1988, the year he travelled to Europe for the first time, living and working in Ireland.

Paul GOPAL-CHOWDHURY 1949– Painter and teacher, born in Calcutta, India. He attended Camberwell School of Art, 1967–8, Slade School of Fine Art, 1968–73. Gopal-Chowdhury began lecturing at Chelsea School of Art and obtained a Boise Travelling Scholarship and French Government Scholarship, 1973–4; between 1975–7 lectured at Leeds University, where he was awarded a Gregory Fellowship, and Byam Shaw School of Art; and in 1983–4 was artist-in-residence at Gonville and Caius College and Kettle's Yard Gallery, Cambridge. Took part in many group exhibitions, including British Painting '74, Hayward Gallery, 1974; Hayward Annual and Summer Show 3, Serpentine Gallery, both 1979; A Taste of British Art Today, Brussels, 1981; and RA Summer Exhibition, 1988, invited artist. Solo shows included Newcastle upon Tyne Polytechnic Art Gallery, 1980; Ian Birksted Gallery, from 1981; Kettle's Yard Gallery, 1984–5, and tour; and Benjamin Rhodes Gallery, from 1986. Contemporary Art Society; Chase Manhattan Bank, New York; and public collections in Bolton and Doncaster hold examples. Lived in London.

Dora GORDINE 1906–1991 Sculptor, especially modelled heads in bronze, often of Oriental subjects. She was born in St Petersburg, Russia, and studied music in Paris until 1922. Then the sculptor Maillol gave her encouragement and she began showing at Salon des Tuileries and RA from late 1920s. First solo show held at Leicester Galleries in 1928. She then lived for about five years in China, settling in England in mid-1930s and marrying the diplomat the Honourable Richard Hare, who became professor of Russian literature at London University. She designed their house and studio in Richmond. In 1949 elected a fellow of RBS, about the time she began making trips to America to teach and work. Commissions included bronzes for Singapore Town Hall and work for Esso Refinery, Milford Haven, in Wales. After her husband's death in 1966 Gordine lived a reclusive life surrounded by their collection of Russian art objects, sold at auction by Phillips in 1994. Proceeds went to Kingston University to finance a Russian art centre at Doritch House where the rest of the Gordine collection was put on display. Tate Gallery holds several examples of her work.

Alan GORDON 1924– Painter, teacher and commercial artist, born in Salford, Lancashire. After Manchester Grammar School he attended Salford School of Art, 1941–2, then Manchester Municipal School of Art, 1942–7. He held a series of government and industrial jobs. Showed at Mid-Day Studios in Manchester and elsewhere in the northern provinces. Lived in Eccles, Lancashire.

Anne GORDON 1941– Painter, draughtsman and teacher, born in Glasgow. She studied at the School of Art there, then taught art in schools. This was followed by peripatetic teaching in west Stirlingshire, where she settled. Much of her work was inspired by the local landscape, the Western Isles, Greece, Turkey, Tuscany and Andalucia, exploration of colour, tone and mood being important. Was elected an artist member of Glasgow Art Club in 1991. Also exhibited in San Francisco, and annually with RSA, Royal Glasgow Institute of the Fine Arts, Glasgow Society of Women Artists and SSWA. Gordon won Lauder Awards in 1986–7. In 1995 shared a show at Duncan R Miller Contemporary.

Cora Josephine GORDON fl. from c.1908–1950 Painter, printmaker, illustrator and writer, born in Buxton, Derbyshire, who studied at Slade School of Fine Art. She showed extensively in Paris and at Lefevre and Cooling Galleries, SWA, ROI, RBA, Walker Art Gallery in Liverpool and elsewhere. With her artist and writer husband Jan Gordon, who predeceased her by six years, she travelled widely, producing popular books such as *Two Vagabonds in the Balkans*, 1925, *Two Vagabonds in Albania*, 1927, and *London Roundabout*, 1933. Otherwise lived in London.

Douglas GORDON 1966– Video installation artist, born in Glasgow, who graduated from the School of Art there, 1984–8, gaining his master's, 1988–90. Drew on a variety of sources, such as film noir and home videos found in Glasgow's back-street markets. His many group exhibitions included Barclays Young Artist Award, Serpentine Gallery, 1991; Speaker Project, ICA, 1992; Chambre 763, Hotel Carlton Palace, Paris, 1993; Watt at Witte de Witte Centre for Contemporary Art-Kunsthal, Rotterdam, 1994; and British Art Show 4, and tour, 1995–6. Had a solo showing at Glasgow Tramway and Kunst-Werke, Berlin, of 24-Hour Psycho, 1993, others including Lisson Gallery, 1994, and The End at Jack Tilton Gallery, New York, 1995. British Council and Contemporary Art Society hold Gordon's work. Gordon won the Turner Prize in 1996.

Esmé GORDON 1910–1993 Artist, normally in watercolour, architect and writer, born and lived in Edinburgh. From boyhood Alexander Esmé Gordon "put pencil, paint and paper as all-important, believing that happy people are those who use their hands." After Edinburgh Academy Gordon studied architecture at Edinburgh College of Art, 1928–34, winning the Owen Jones Scholarship in his final year. From 1937 until shortly before he died he maintained a small private practice which did mainly church work, including restoration in St Giles' Cathedral and Canongate Kirk. Early in World War II he designed troop canteens, then served in the Royal Engineers until 1945. Gordon was made a fellow of the Royal Incorporation of Architects in Scotland, 1953, a fellow of RIBA, 1956, was an honorary life member of SSA and was elected to RSA in 1967. From 1973–8 he was its honorary secretary, making significant archive finds. Among Gordon's books were *The Royal Scottish Academy 1826–1976*, 1976. Piranesi and William Walcot were cited by him as influences on his own work. Gordon was a scholar of Oriental art, and a keen collector of Japanese woodblock prints and Chinese jade. Travelled widely in Italy, India and the Far East, recording the trips in watercolours and drawings. Had a solo show at Scottish Gallery, Edinburgh, 1988.

György GORDON 1924– Painter in the European Expressionist tradition, born in Hungary. He gained his diploma in painting at the Academy of Fine Art, Budapest, in 1953, but during the Hungarian uprising against the Communists three years later fled to England. Despite lack of good English he found work and in 1964 moved to Wakefield, Yorkshire, to take up post at College of Art. Eventually took early retirement to paint. Noted for sombre figure paintings in which the images are isolated and distorted. Showed widely, including National Portrait Gallery. Work in public and private collections in Britain, on the continent, in America and Australia. National Portrait Gallery and Hart Gallery held retrospectives in 1995.

Hilda May GORDON 1874–1972 World-travelling artist, born of Scottish parents who had lived in South Africa but had settled in the Isle of Wight. Studied at Bushey School of Art, afterwards making sketching trips to continent. By 1907 was holding a show in Bond Street, then while working in Europe and Middle East as a volunteer nurse in World War I continued to paint. Set off from Britain for Dalmatian Coast in 1922 "for no particular reason", as she noted in her extensive journals, not returning to London until 1928. By then she had taken in countries such as Greece, India, Burma, China, Korea, Japan and America. On her return had show at Fine Art Society. Continued to travel through her sixties, until World War II brought her to rest in London. Martyn Gregory Gallery held a retrospective in 1987.

Ian Charles GORDON 1925– Painter, draughtsman and architect, born in Sevenoaks, Kent, working in oil, watercolour and charcoal. While a student at the Bartlett School of Architecture, Gordon studied with David Bomberg at the Borough Polytechnic, and continued to follow Bomberg's principles as a spare-time painter while working as an architect in Edinburgh, 1951–1980, and after retirement. Was a fellow of RIBA and a founder-member of the Borough Bottega, 1953, with which he showed, also exhibiting at RSA, Society of Scottish Architect Artists and Dumfries & Galloway Art Society. Lived in Thornhill, Dumfriesshire.

Susan GORDON 1942– Sculptor in various materials and part-time teacher, born in Wembley, Middlesex. She studied at Hammersmith School of Art, 1964–5, Wimbledon School of Art, 1965–6, and the City and Guilds of London School, 1966–9. Showed at RA, Nicholas Treadwell Gallery and elsewhere. RBS Feodora Gleichen Memorial Fund Award-winner. Signed work with initials. Lived in London.

Tania GORDON 1901–1994 Painter, notable for her use of the palette knife, born in Vilna, Russia, full name Tamara Tania Gordon. She married Sholom Gordon, from another prominent Vilna family, and they emigrated first to South Africa in the late 1920s and then to London, where her husband was an industrialist. Her son Max became a leading designer of art galleries. She took up painting in her fifties and showed at the Arthur Jeffress and Whibley Galleries and abroad, including Paris Salon.

Virginia GORDON 1937– Sculptor who studied at Royal Academy Dramatic Art, 1953–7, Morley College, 1976–8, then took advanced course at St Martin's School of Art, 1978–80. Mixed exhibitions included Morley College Group Exhibition and Art into Landscape at Serpentine Gallery, 1976–7; Wapping Artists 1981; and 10 London Artists, Taidemuseo in Helsinki and Finnish tour, 1983. In that year was included in 9 Artists from Wapping British Tour, based at DLI Museum & Arts Centre, Durham. Capital Radio holds her work, which could be abstract in various materials. Lived in London.

W R GORDON 1872–1955 Painter and teacher, born at Moira, County Down, Northern Ireland. He studied in his spare time at Birkenhead's Laird School of Art while working in the Port Sunlight soap factory and in Belfast attended the School of Design. From 1901 through World War II Gordon taught art at Royal Belfast Academical Institution, also teaching evening classes. He was a founder-member of Ulster Arts Club and showed at RHA in Dublin. Arts Council of Northern Ireland holds his work.

Ophelia GORDON-BELL (sometimes not hyphenated) 1915–1975 Sculptor in various materials and watercolourist. Born in London she came of an artistic family, her father being the etcher F Lawrence Bell, her mother the animal painter Winifred Gordon Bell. Joan Ophelia Gordon Cooper, her correct name, was married to the Lake District painter William Heaton Cooper. She studied art privately and at Regent Street Polytechnic School of Art, 1932–6. Showed at RA, RSA, Royal Glasgow Institute of the Fine Arts and Lake Artists' Society. Among several official commissions was a portrait bust of the Everest climber Sir Edmund Hillary, acquired by New Zealand National Gallery, Wellington. Lived in Grasmere, Westmorland.

Michael GORDON-LEE 1943– Painter and sculptor who was by profession a landscape architect for Cheshire County Council. He was born in Harrow, Middlesex, and attended Hammersmith College of Art. He showed with PS from 1983, in 1984 being elected a member shortly after winning its Award for Best Picture by a Non-Member; MAFA from 1984; and RWA from 1985. In 1986–7 Gordon-Lee was included in the Walker

Art Gallery, Liverpool, touring Merseyside Artists 3. Lived in Tarporley, Cheshire.

Frederick GORE 1913– Painter, teacher and writer, born in Richmond, Surrey, son of the artist Spencer Gore. He studied at Trinity College and Ruskin School of Drawing, Oxford, 1932–4, finally at Westminster School of Art and Slade School of Fine Art, 1934–7. In the latter year he had his first one-man show at Redfern Gallery, followed by a series there after World War II. In 1938 he travelled in Greece, showing the resulting work in Paris. Greece, Majorca and France were favourite landscape subjects for Gore, whose rich palette had more in common with the French than the English tradition. Gore taught at Westminster, Epsom and Chelsea Schools of Art and was head of the painting department at St Martin's School of Art, 1951–79. He was elected RA in 1973 and was chairman of its exhibition committee, 1976–87. His publications included *Abstract Art*, 1956; *Painting: Some Basic Principles*, 1965; and *Piero della Francesca's The Baptism*, 1969; plus many RA catalogue introductions. In 1979 he had retrospectives at Gainsborough's House in Sudbury and Bury St Edmunds Art Gallery, with an important one at RA in 1989. Southampton, Plymouth and Reading public galleries hold his work. Lived in London.

William GORE 1871–1946 Versatile painter, doctor of medicine, musician and composer and linguist, full name William Crawford Crampton Gore, born in Enniskillen, Fermanagh (his daughter Elizabeth Parry-Crooke, also a painter, changed her name to Crampton-Gore using a hyphen, which was how she signed her work; the hyphen has sometimes been used in her father's name). Gore studied medicine at Trinity College, Dublin, qualifying in 1897; practised; then from 1901 concentrated on art, studying for several years at Slade School of Fine Art under Henry Tonks and Philip Wilson Steer, also in Paris. In his diaries Gore said that his greatest debt was to the Norwegian painter Fritz Thaulow. Gore worked as a ship's surgeon before and during World War I and travelled extensively. Spoke six languages, including Russian. He continued to practise medicine later in life; from 1932 lived in Colchester, Essex, where he died and where he was a civilian doctor at the Military Hospital. Simultaneously with painting, Gore studied music, receiving help from Charles Wood, and was a prolific composer, notably of lyrics, his compositions being publicly performed and broadcast. Much of Gore's life was spent in France. Married a French wife in 1923 in Montreuil-sur-Mer, where he had rented a studio. They bought a house there and lived a bohemian life until returning to England, visitors including Dermod O'Brien, Philip Connard and Augustus John. Was elected RHA in 1919, also exhibiting at RA, Paris Salon where he gained several Hon. Mentions, NEAC, ROI and Fine Art Society, and had solo shows. Was a Chelsea Arts Club member. A memorial exhibition was held at Victor Waddington Galleries, Dublin, in 1946.

Charles Harris GORHAM 1916– Painter, graphic designer and teacher, born in Bexley, Kent. Studied at Royal College of Art with William Rothenstein and Ernest Tristram. Victoria & Albert Museum holds his work and he exhibited in London, the provinces, Germany and Denmark. Lectured at Maidstone College of Art. Lived in Borough Green, Kent, for many years.

Maro GORKY 1943– Painter, notably of richly coloured, patterned landscapes, daughter of the American artist Arshile Gorky. Although he died when she was young, he greatly influenced Maro's work. She studied at the Slade School of Fine Art before marrying the artist and writer Matthew Spender and moving to a remote farmhouse in Tuscany, Italy. Bernardo Bertolucci's film *Stealing Beauty*, released in 1996, celebrated the marriage of Gorky and Spender. She had a series of solo shows with Long & Ryle Art International.

Des GORMAN 1960– Painter of still life, portraits and interiors, born in Glasgow, who graduated from Gray's Art School, Aberdeen, in 1988 with an honours degree in fine art. Won a number of awards, including first prize, David Gordon Memorial Trust, RSA, and the Elizabeth Greenshields Foundation Award, both 1988; Armour Award, Royal Glasgow Institute of the Fine Arts, 1989; and Contemporary Fine Art Gallery Award, 1993. Mixed shows included Open Eye Gallery, Edinburgh, 1991; Kelly Gallery, Glasgow, 1993; and Ten Young Painters, Thompson's Gallery, 1994. Had a solo show at Paisley Art Centre, 1989, later ones including John Martin of London in 1995. Strathclyde Police and corporate and private collections hold Gorman's work.

Ernest Hamilton GORMAN 1869– Painter and black-and-white artist, whose varied art education included periods in Portsmouth, with Alfred Emslie and at Goldsmiths' Institute with Amor Fenn. For many years he was honorary secretary of the Liver Sketching Club, where he exhibited, as well as Walker Art Gallery, Liverpool. Lived at Lower Bebington, Cheshire.

James GORMAN 1931– Painter in oil, acrylic and watercolour, and teacher, born in Gourock, Renfrewshire. He studied at Glasgow School of Art, 1949–53, a notable teacher being Walter Pritchard for mural painting, in which Gorman gained his diploma, also winning a travelling scholarship. His own murals include Trinity College, Glasgow, 1953–4; a mural design for Eastwood Senior High School, 1966; and for Moorfoot Primary School, Gourock, 1970. His National Service included various art work and a mural, now in the War Office. He went on to be principal teacher of art and design at John Neilson Institute, Paisley, and at Port Glasgow High School. Gorman's work ranged from delicate landscape watercolours to strong figurative pictures. He claimed a "Celtic influence in my use of nets to generate images". Was a member of the Royal Glasgow Institute of the Fine Arts and as well as mixed exhibitions had many solo and joint shows, venues including Paton Gallery, Edinburgh, 1976; Greenock Arts Guild, 1984; and Graeme Mundy Gallery, Glasgow, 1988. Lived latterly at Corriegills, Isle of Arran.

Antony GORMLEY 1950– Sculptor and draughtsman who was born and lived in London. He was educated at Cambridge University, 1967–70, Central School of Art, 1973–4, Goldsmiths' College School of Art, 1975–7, then Slade School of Fine Art, 1977–9. In the latter year he won a Boise Travelling Scholarship to America. In 1980 gained Greater London Arts Association Award, in 1981 first prize in the Kent County Council/Arts Council Singleton Sculpture Competition, in 1994 the Turner Prize. Gormley was concerned with the relationship between culture and nature, life and death, the profane and the sacred. Sometimes his methods were unconventional: in 1981 he made a sculpture by eating the double negative form of his own body out of layers of sliced white bread. In that year he gained a solo show at Whitechapel Art Gallery, the year following participating in British Sculpture in the Twentieth Century (part II) at Whitechapel as well as the 1982 Venice Biennale. Gormley took part in Objects & Figures at Fruitmarket Gallery, Edinburgh, and tour, 1982–3; showed at Coracle Press Gallery in 1984; and in 1992 was included in Contemporary Art Society purchase show at Camden Arts Centre. Gormley's most noted achievement was the completion, in 1998, of the Angel of the North, the tallest sculpture in Britain, made in three parts from weathering steel; the huge winged figure project overcame initial opposition to be sited at the head of the Team Valley, near Gateshead, next to the A1(M) road. Arts Council, Contemporary Art Society and other collections hold the work of Gormley, who was married to the painter Vicken Parsons.

Mary GORRARA 1923– Sculptor in various materials and teacher, born and lived in London. She studied at Camberwell School of Arts and Crafts; City and Guilds of London Art School, where her teachers included A R Middleton Todd; and Sir John Cass School of Art. Went on to teach at Camden Arts Centre, Hampstead. She was made a fellow of RBS in 1975, also belonging to Free Painters and Sculptors. Mixed shows included RA, Kenwood House and Lincoln Cathedral. Her solo exhibitions included Camden Arts Centre, 1972, and Jonathan Poole Gallery, 1983. Camden Borough Council holds her work.

Hester GORST 1887– Painter and modeller, born in Liverpool, she married the Queen's Counsel Elliot Gorst. Studied at Slade School of Fine Art, 1904–6, with Henry Tonks, and in Brussels. She showed at Royal Drawing Society where she won silver and gold medals, Goupil Gallery, NEAC, in the Netherlands and America and at the Paris Salon into the late 1960s, gaining an Hon. Mention for figurines. Early work signed Hester Holland, her maiden name. Lived in London. Was active into her nineties, having a show and appearing on television, until loss of sight incapacitated her.

Alexander GORTON 1916–1969 Draughtsman in pen and ink, poster designer and printmaker, employed by London Transport. He died in service as a divisional superintendent. Studied art with the Press Art School and in Southwark. London Transport art exhibitions and its publications were his main outlet, although he also drew for other transport magazines. London Transport Museum lists a number of works by Alec Gorton, including 67 Safety on the Track designs. Lived at Woodford Green, Essex.

Annabel GOSLING 1942– Painter, born in Overbury, Gloucestershire, brought up in Suffolk. She attended Ipswich School of Art, 1958, Angers Beaux-Arts in France in 1959, then Byam Shaw School of Drawing and Painting, 1960–4; was awarded Leverhulme and Byam Shaw Scholarships, 1960. Gosling's work was impressed by an intense interest in light and colour, the work of Matisse and Cézanne and extensive travels in Europe and India. Showed at RA, RBA, NEAC and Archer Gallery in mixed exhibitions. Had solo show at Ansdell Gallery, 1971; Royal Festival Hall, 1980; Mall Galleries, 1991; and Mistral Galleries, 1992. Work held by the royal family of Abu Dhabi, Scottish Educational Development Authority, Savoy and Berkeley Hotels.

Mary Rose GOSLING 1926– Painter and draughtsman, also known as Mary Rose Hardy, born in Birmingham as Gosling. She studied at Birmingham College of Art with Bernard Fleetwood-Walker, 1943–7, then in Paris, 1950, at L'Académie de la Grande Chaumière. Showed SWA, RBA, RI, WIAC and elsewhere. Lived for a time at Forest Row, Sussex.

Sylvia GOSSE 1881–1968 Painter in oil and watercolour and etcher of landscape, still life, figure studies and interiors. Born in London, the daughter of writer and critic Sir Edmund Gosse, she studied at the St John's Wood School of Art, Royal Academy Schools and the Westminister School of Art under Walter Sickert. From 1909–14 she taught at Sickert's Rowlandson House, London, school. His influence is evident in much of her work. She exhibited at the AAA, RA, LG, RBA and RE and had her first one-man show at the Carfax Gallery in 1913. Like Sickert, she painted a lot in London and in Dieppe. Her work was reproduced in magazines such as *The Studio, Apollo* and *Print Collectors' Quarterly* and is in many British and foreign collections, including the British Museum, Tate Gallery and Ashmolean Museum. Lived at Ore, Hastings, Sussex.

Imre GOTH 1893–1982 Painter, notably of portraits, and inventor, born in Szeged, Hungary, who studied at Budapest Academy of Fine Arts, then in the 1920s in Berlin. He became noted for fashionable portraits of film stars and among his patrons was Field Marshal Hermann Goering, the Nazi air chief. After a successful exhibition in Birmingham at the New Galleries, in 1935, Goth moved to England where through friendship with the Hungarian film director Alexander Korda he came to paint portraits used in productions starring Ralph Richardson, Michael Wilding, Ann Todd and Margaret Leighton. When later in life Goth's eyesight failed he returned to inventing. In Berlin he had designed parachutes and headlights for cars. In London he formed a company to market his inventions, which included the non-drip device in bottles. His exhibitions included Ferens Art Gallery,

Hull, and Russell-Cotes Art Gallery, Bournemouth, both from 1939; RP, 1948; and Grundy Art Gallery, Blackpool, 1949.

Henryk GOTLIB 1890–1966 Painter, printmaker, sculptor and writer, born in Cracow, Poland. Studied at the Academy of Fine Art, Cracow, later in Munich, Amsterdam and Paris. Had first one-man show in Warsaw in 1918, a year later returning to Cracow, where he became leader of advanced Formist movement. Early in the 1920s Gotlib had shows in Berlin and Amsterdam, then during the rest of the decade he lived mainly in France. Early in the 1930s he travelled extensively in Europe but exhibited in Poland and took part in Polish shows overseas. In 1934 returned to Cracow where he continued to write, then to broadcast on art. Having travelled to Cornwall just before World War II, he decided to remain in England where he began to exhibit, notably one-man shows with Roland, Browse and Delbanco in the 1940s. Later solo shows were held with O'Hana and Crane Kalman. The Arts Council acquired The Boat in 1961, the Gulbenkian Foundation two pictures in 1962. Gotlib's book, in English, *Polish Painting* appeared in 1942, and *The Travels of a Painter*, earlier commissioned by a Polish publisher, in 1947. Gotlib's early work was much influenced by Bonnard, tinged with Kandinsky's mysticism. His later pictures were less picturesque, less seductive. An exhibition was held at the Scottish National Gallery of Modern Art, 1970, with tour; another at Morley Gallery, 1971; Boundary Gallery, 1988; and Connaught Brown, 1996. Lived in South Godstone, Surrey.

John GOTO 1949– Artist, born in Stockport, Cheshire, who studied at Berkshire College of Art, 1965–7, and St Martin's School of Art, 1967–70. He gained British Council Scholarships to Paris, 1977, and Prague, 1978, and in 1988–9 was artist-in-residence at Kettle's Yard, Cambridge. In 1990 his The Atomic Yard toured from Kettle's Yard, part of his major project Seven Tales from the Twentieth Century, to be completed by the year 2000. Goto won a prize with his Nastagio in Bosnia acrylic on canvas included in John Moores Liverpool Exhibition, 1993–4. Later solo exhibitions include Andrew Mummery and Portfolio Gallery, Edinburgh, both 1997, and Museum of Modern Art, Oxford, 1998. Arts Council and other public collections in Britain and abroad hold Goto's work.

Basil GOTTO 1866–1954 Sculptor, born in London, educated at Harrow School. He studied in Paris with Adolphe Bouguereau and in the late 1880s at the Royal Academy Schools, where he won the Landseer award in 1890. In 1899 he was Boer War correspondent in South Africa for the *Daily Express*. Exhibited RA extensively, also RI, ROI, Royal Glasgow Institute of the Fine Arts and Paris Salon. Southampton Art Gallery holds his work. Lived at Twyford, Hampshire.

Ernst GOTTSCHALK 1926– Sculptor and painter, interior and exhibition designer, born in Hamburg, Germany. He studied at Edinburgh College of Art, the Anglo-French Art Centre and Chelsea School of Art. Until 1990 Gottschalk worked mainly in Britain, then settled in France at Bandol, where as well as exhibiting and working to commission he kept a studio open to the public. He was a member of ICA and the Society of Industrial Artists and Designers and his work was featured in *Architectural Review, Design, Ideal Home, The Listener* and *House and Garden*. Exhibited widely throughout Europe, including Air, Alwin, Ben Uri, Gimpel Fils, Grabowski, Portal and Treadwell Galleries; Centre 't Hoogt, Utrecht; Galerie Robert Boeuf, Toulon; Sculpture Actuelle, Toulouse, where Gottschalk gained a first prize; and Van Gogh Museum, Amsterdam. Works were held by many collections around the world.

Alexander GOUDIE 1933– Painter, notably of portraits, born in Paisley, Renfrewshire. He studied at Glasgow School of Art, 1950–5, under William Armour, Benno Schotz and David Donaldson. He was awarded the Somerville Shanks Prize for Composition, Newbery Medal, postgraduate scholarship, Keith Award (RSA), and in 1953 a travelling scholarship enabled him to visit Paris. From the late-1950s Goudie, who married a French wife, frequently visited France, including annual painting trips to Loctudy, Brittany. His first major exhibition of Breton pictures was at The Scottish Gallery, Edinburgh, in 1966. There was a retrospective at The Fine Art Society, Glasgow, 1983, and a solo show at Roger Billcliffe Fine Art, Glasgow, 1992. In 1987–9 Goudie carried out décor for the Brittany Ferries flagship *Bretagne*. Goudie's stylish portraits included HM The Queen, Billy Connolly the comedian and Lord Mackay when Lord Chancellor. Robert Fleming Holdings Ltd has his work. Goudie was a member of Glasgow Art Club, RP and Royal Glasgow Institute of the Fine Arts.

Alan GOUK 1939– Painter, teacher and writer, born Belfast, moved to Glasgow when still small. He studied architecture at the School of Art, 1957–9, part-time while working for an architect; he adopted a similar procedure at Regent Street Polytechnic, 1959–60, when working for London County Council. Upon moving to Edinburgh, 1961–4, to study philosophy and psychology at the University, Gouk began to paint in an Abstract Expressionist style. From 1964–7 he worked for the British Council. From 1967, when he began to lecture at St Martin's School of Art, where he eventually became head of advanced painting and sculpture, Gouk could concentrate fully on his painting. Moving away from acrylics to oils from the mid-1970s, Gouk was concerned to avoid flatness in painting, exploring pictorial space created by colour in wide canvases and using a heavy impasto. His work was featured in the Four Abstract Artists show at the Fruitmarket Gallery, Edinburgh, 1977; in the Scottish Painting since 1900 exhibition at Scottish National Gallery of Modern Art, 1989–90, and tour; he had a solo show at Smith's Galleries in 1986; another at Flowers East, 1997. Gouk was also a jazz composer. Lived in London.

Alec Carruthers GOULD 1870–1948 Landscape painter and illustrator, born in Woodford, Essex, full name Alexander Carruthers Gould. He was the son of the caricaturist Francis

Carruthers Gould, settled in Porlock, Somerset, and illustrated E W Hendy's *Wild Exmoor Through the Year*, 1930. He was a member of RBA where he was a prolific exhibitor, also being a member of RWA and showing at RA, ROI, NEAC and other galleries.

Charles GOULD 1925–1987 Watercolourist, born in Ealing, west London. Studied at the local School of Art, 1948–51, and continued to work in Ealing. Showed RI, NS and abroad, notably Paris Salon. Philadelphia Art Gallery, in America, holds his work.

David GOULD 1947– Painter and teacher, notable for watercolours, many of Italy where his wife originally lived. He was born in London and studied at Gloucester College of Art in Cheltenham, 1965–9, and Royal College of Art, 1969–72. He won an Abbey Major Scholarship to Rome, 1972–3, and a painting fellowship at Cardiff College of Art, 1974–5. After five years teaching at Byam Shaw School, he returned to teach at Cardiff. Mixed exhibitions included Oriel (WAC), Cardiff, 1975; Air travelling exhibition, 1977; Spirit of London at Royal Festival Hall, 1980; and Summer Show 1 at Serpentine Gallery, 1982. Solo shows included Chapter Arts Centre, Cardiff, 1985; St David's Hall, Cardiff, 1989 and 1993; and Oriel Contemporary Art, 1996.

Thomas GOURDIE 1913– Painter, calligrapher and teacher, born in Cowdenbeath, Fife. He studied at Edinburgh College of Art, 1932–7, under Herbert Hendrie. He took part in war artists' exhibitions in London in World War II, from which official purchases of watercolours were made. Also showed RSA, SSA, RSW and in Arts Council exhibitions. For some time taught at the High School in Kirkcaldy, Fife, where he lived.

Alan Stenhouse GOURLEY 1909–1991 Painter, stained glass artist, theatre designer and teacher, born in Ayr, Scotland. Studied at Glasgow School of Art, 1928, and Edinburgh College of Art, 1929–31, where his teachers included William Gillies. Moved to South Africa where from 1932–7 taught at Johannesburg Technical College and created window designs for cathedrals in Pretoria and Johannesburg. Studied at École des Beaux-Arts, 1938–40, in Paris; during World War II was an instructor in camouflage; studying at Slade School of Fine Art in 1945, his teachers including Randolph Schwabe. Travelled throughout the world, but found time to design for the theatre; exhibiting, mainly at Mall Galleries; and was for some years president of ROI. South Africa House in London has carpet designed by him and his work is in the collection of HM Queen Elizabeth The Queen Mother. Lived in Bromley, Kent.

James GOVIER 1910–1974 Painter, printmaker and teacher, born in Oakley, Buckinghamshire. Studied 1930–5 at Swansea School of Art, where his teachers included William Grant Murray, and 1935–40 at Royal College of Art, under Malcolm Osborne and Robert Austin. Sickert, Constable, Rembrandt, Degas and Chardin were some influences on Govier, a traditionalist who disliked commercialism and modern influences. Augustus John and Dylan Thomas were friends of Govier in Wales and London. During World War II Govier served in the Royal Air Force, making models of the D-Day landings and Dambusters raids, meeting Barnes Wallis, inventor of the bouncing bomb. Showed with RA, Ipswich Art Club and elsewhere. An important exhibition of his work was held in 1993 at Christchurch Mansion, Ipswich. National Museum of Wales, Cardiff, and Glynn Vivian Art Gallery, Swansea, hold pictures by Govier, who lived finally at Hoxne, Diss, Norfolk.

Dorothy Willett GOW fl. from c.1925– Modeller and potter whose correct name was Dorothy Ermyntrude Gow, Willett having been her maiden name. Studied at Central School of Arts and Crafts after initial education in England and France. Showed at RBA, SWA of which she was an associate, and in the provinces. Lived in London.

Lucienne GOW fl. from early 1930s– Painter and printmaker, she studied at Heatherley's School of Fine Art and in Paris, after initial education at Roedean School. Exhibited RA, SWA, RBA and completed some posters, sometimes signing work lugow. Lived in London.

Francis GOWER 1905–1995 Painter, notably of portraits, teacher and illustrator. He studied from early 1920s at St Martin's School of Art with Stafford Leake; won a scholarship to Royal College of Art, 1929–32, where his teachers included Randolph Schwabe, Gilbert Spencer and Barnett Freedman; studied at evening classes for a diploma in the history of art at London University; and continued with evening classes at St Martin's. His 1930s work included a period with the Lintas advertising agency. During World War II Gower worked in psychiatric hospitals, making studies later worked up into oil paintings. Went on to show at RA, RP and was included in the Lintas Beyond the Horizon show at Agnew, 1988. Gower also designed the jackets for children's books and taught at the Working Men's College as well as lecturing in history of art at Harrow and Willesden Schools of Art and at Hampstead Garden Suburb Institute. In 1986 a show of his work was held at Watford Museum, in 1996 a memorial exhibition at Bushey Museum.

Lawrence GOWING 1918–1991 Painter, teacher, writer and administrator, born in London, where he died. His first art teacher was Maurice Feild, at The Downs preparatory school, Colwall. Then studied under William Coldstream at the Euston Road School. Conscientious objector during World War II. First one-man show at Leicester Galleries in 1948. Professor of Fine Art at Durham University and principal of King Edward VII School of Art, Newcastle upon Tyne, 1948–58; principal of Chelsea School of Art, 1958–65; keeper of the British collection and deputy director of the Tate Gallery, 1965–7; professor of fine art at Leeds University, 1967–75; and Slade Professor of Fine Art at University College, London, 1975–85. Knighted in 1982 and made RA in 1989. Wrote books and catalogues on wide range of artists, from Hogarth to Lucien Freud and made a number of lucid television programmes on aspects of painting. As an inquiring teacher he enthused students and fellow members of staff. Gowing was a sensitive painter of still life, portraits and landscape, Sickert and Cézanne being notable influences. Tate Gallery is among a number of public collections holding his work. Arts Council retrospective 1983.

Alice Kirkby GOYDER 1875–1964 Painter, wood carver and printmaker, born in Bradford, Yorkshire. She studied at Bradford School of Art and with Louise Jopling. Was very interested in depicting animals and won a silver medal at Women's Exhibition in 1897. She showed with RA, SWA, Walker Art Gallery in Liverpool and elsewhere. Belonged to Bradford Arts Club, East Kent Art Society and Ipswich Art Club. British Museum holds her work. Her death was registered in Bromley, Kent, although she lived for some years in Orford, Suffolk.

Dennis GRAFTON 1922– Painter in oil, born at Penn, near Wolverhampton. Brought up in the West Country, he returned to study at Wolverhampton School of Art part-time, 1937–44, his teachers including Robert Emerson and John Holden. Exhibited RA and RBA. Lived in Wolverhampton, Staffordshire.

Brian GRAHAM 1945– Painter, mainly in acrylic, also in mixed media, born in Poole, Dorset, settling at Swanage. He was "briefly at Bournemouth College of Art, but consider myself self-taught." Graham spent many years in design/advertising, but reckoned "that my *obsession* with painting started in 1975." Graham's work tended towards the abstract, but drew its inspiration from "the hills, the soil and the sea. Wild places, gentle places, sacred places". He hoped "to make the indefinable attainable". Graham participated in many mixed shows, in 1992 winning first prize in the RWA autumn exhibition donated by Brandler Galleries. After a solo show at Poole Arts Centre, 1986, later ones included On Line Gallery, Southampton, and Alpha Gallery, Swanage, both 1993. Upton House Heritage Centre; Scaplans Court Museum, Poole; and Bank of Industry, San Francisco, hold examples.

Carol GRAHAM 1951– Artist, notable as a portrait painter, born in Belfast, Northern Ireland, who gained a diploma in fine art at the local Art and Design Centre, 1970–4, married Michael Ballard in the latter year and did a post-diploma course in 1975. She won an Arts Council of Northern Ireland Bursary in 1976 and its Major Award, 1980. She was elected RUA in 1985, the year she won its Gold Medal (Portrait). Was accepted by the National Portrait Collection in 1987. Group shows included Tom Caldwell, 1975; RHA from 1978; and Bath Art Fair, 1983. Tom Caldwell gave her a solo show in 1982. Major portrait commissions included James Galway, flautist, 1987; Sir Derek Birley, vice-chancellor of the University of Ulster, 1990; Joan Trimble, pianist, 1992; and Dr Mary Robinson, president of Ireland, 1993. In 1982 she did the cover of Bernard McLaverty's book *Secrets*. Lived in Lisburn, County Antrim.

David GRAHAM 1926– Painter and teacher, born and lived in London. He studied at Hammersmith and St Martin's Schools of Art and Royal College of Art and in 1957 was included in Jack Beddington's book *Young Artists of Promise*. Went on to become senior lecturer at Sir John Cass School of Art. Showed at RP of which he was a member, RA, Leicester Galleries, with Roland, Browse & Delbanco and abroad. In 1987 he had a retrospective at Herbert Art Gallery and Museum in Coventry. Contemporary Art Society and Guildhall Art Gallery hold his work.

George GRAHAM 1882–1949 Painter and printmaker, born in Leeds, Yorkshire, where he studied and in London under various teachers. He was a member of ROI, RI and RSW, and a leading figure in the Yorkshire Artists and Society of Sussex Painters. Was a prolific exhibitor, showing at Fine Art Society, RA and elsewhere. Public galleries in Bradford, Leeds and Worthing hold examples. Lived latterly in Winchelsea, Sussex.

Peter GRAHAM 1959– Painter, born in Glasgow, where he attended the School of Art, studying mural design and optical art. His studies of the human brain's appreciation of colour and his mixing of colours not normally associated with each other contributed to the vibrant appearance of Graham's canvases, as did the often exotic locations. Upon graduation Graham became a film editor with BBC for four years, although on returning to painting he continued to do freelance film work. After a holiday in Sardinia Graham held a solo show at Tricycle Gallery, 1986. As well as showing in many mixed exhibitions in Scotland and London Graham continued to hold regular solo shows, including Nanyang Academy of Fine Arts, Singapore, 1990, where he was artist-in-residence under a British Council sponsorship; in 1991 at Flying Colours Gallery in Edinburgh and 90s Gallery, Glasgow; and Bourne Gallery, Reigate, 1992. Graham was a member of New Glasgow Colourists. British Council, Singapore; the Nanyang Academy of Fine Arts; and Western Baths Club, Glasgow, hold his work.

Rigby GRAHAM 1931– Painter, printmaker, muralist, illustrator, writer and teacher, born in Stretford, Lancashire. In 1943 his family moved to Leicester, where he settled. Studied mural painting at Leicester College of Art, teachers including D P Carrington and Cyril Satorsky. From 1954 taught for two years in local schools before returning to the College, initially in the book-binding department, which stimulated his interest in the art of the book. Graham went on to illustrate over 300 books and was strongly associated with the private press movement, including the Brewhouse, Cog, New Broom, Pandora and Saint Bernard's Presses. His most opulent book was *Graham's Leicestershire*, 1980. It shows Graham's interest in urban blight and industry. He was strongly influenced by the Neo-Romantics, although his colour owed much to German Expressionism. Travelled widely in Europe. Murals for local schools included Woodstock Junior, New Parks House Junior and Eyres Monsell Junior, and Leicester Royal Infirmary. Graham had over 40 solo shows. These included retrospectives at Hemel Hempstead Arts Trust, 1977, and

Goldmark Gallery, Uppingham, 1991. University of Wales, Aberystwyth, holds examples.

Roberta M GRAHAM 1954– Artist notable for light-box sculptures, born in Londonderry, Northern Ireland, who studied at West Surrey College of Art, 1971–3, and North-East London Polytechnic, 1974–7. Aspects of beauty, violence and death were key themes in Graham's work. Group exhibitions included Whitechapel Open at Whitechapel Art Gallery, 1977; Hayward Annual, at Hayward Gallery, 1979; and Summer Show 1 at Serpentine Gallery, 1983. Solo shows included Spectro Gallery in Newcastle upon Tyne; Arnolfini Gallery, Bristol; and Orchard Gallery in Londonderry, all 1983. Arts Council holds her work. Lived for a time in London.

Bernard Montague GRAINGER 1907– Painter, draughtsman and designer in a variety of materials such as ivory and metal; teacher. Grainger was born in Paddock Wood, Kent, and after attending Ardingly College studied at Maidstone School of Art, Royal College of Art and the Central School of Arts and Crafts. He went on to hold a number of teaching posts, at Sheffield College of Art and in Sheffield University's architecture department. Member of Sheffield Society of Artists and keen caving enthusiast in Pennine area. Lived for some time at Bradwell, Derbyshire.

Esther GRAINGER 1912–1990 Painter, teacher and artist in embroidery collage and calligrapher, born and mostly based in Cardiff, south Wales, where she studied with William Pickles at the School of Art, 1928–34. Other influences included Constance Howard, Heinz Koppel and George Mayer-Marton. In the 1930s Grainger taught crafts to the wives of unemployed miners, later organising painting classes and exhibitions at the Pontypridd Settlement. There she met Cedric Morris, who taught her at his Benton End East Anglian School. In 1950 with David Bell of the Arts Council Grainger organised the first open exhibition of paintings at the National Eisteddfod and was secretary for the Welsh Pictures for Schools shows. Among her exhibitions was a retrospective at the Minories, Colchester, 1973, with watercolours at Manor Gallery, Pontcanna, Cardiff, 1990. A member of SWG and WSW, Grainger also exhibited with WAC, which holds her work, as well as SEA. A number of education authorities also hold examples.

Ian GRAINGER 1942– Printmaker, draughtsman, designer and teacher who created highly original images, drawing on many literary and natural sources, tinged with wryness and self-criticism. He studied at Sunderland College of Art, 1965–8, then Birmingham College, 1968–9; was awarded a fellowship in painting at Chicago Art Institute in America, 1969–70, then Prix de Rome, engraving, 1971–3. Was made an associate of RE in 1974. Taught part-time and in 1980 was Gregynog Fellow under the auspices of WAC and University of Wales. Was included in Text and Image, Curwen Gallery, 1978, and Serpentine Summer Show 1, 1980. His solo exhibitions included Arnolfini Gallery, Bristol, 1980. WAC and Northern Arts hold examples.

Christian GRANDJEAN 1945– Printmaker and photographer, born in Paris, where he studied photography in various studios, 1961–4. He worked as a freelance photographer, 1965–74, eventually becoming a London-based printmaker. Mixed-show appearances included in 1969 Point 50, Paris, where he also had solo exhibitions in 1970–1; Wapping Artists 1981; Bradford Print Biennale, 1982; and Whitechapel Open in 1983, when he participated in 9 Artists from Wapping British Tour, based at DLI Museum & Arts Centre, Durham. London Borough of Tower Hamlets and University of Calgary, Alberta, hold his work.

Lee GRANDJEAN 1949– Sculptor, draughtsman and teacher, born in London, although he lived for part of his youth in Romania. Studied at North-East London Polytechnic, 1967–8, then Winchester School of Art, 1968–71. Grandjean had a studio in London, 1971–80, then moved to Reepham, Norfolk. From 1980–1 he was research fellow in sculpture at Winchester School of Art, having lectured at Wimbledon School of Art since 1976. In 1991 became sculpture tutor at Royal College of Art. Grandjean worked in various materials and was interested in "the transformation of material" and with non-European and ancient civilisations shared a desire to "render raw materials into another expressive substance". Included in his output were reclining nudes, parents and children, and head sculptures, sometimes on a large scale, such as his Head of Glynn Williams, of 1982. He showed in outdoor exhibitions, such as Yorkshire Sculpture Park, Cannizaro Park in Wimbledon and he participated in the 1983 Welsh Sculpture Trust Margam show, Sculpture in a Country Park. Arts Council holds examples.

Edith GRANGER: *see* **Edith GRANGER-TAYLOR**

Simon GRANGER 1955– Artist born in London who studied at Slade School of Fine Art, 1973–9, including postgraduate work, in 1984–5 gaining a residency at Aycliffe, County Durham. He appeared in Whitechapel Open Exhibition from 1983; Wild Creatures, an Arts Council touring exhibition, 1988; was an Artist of the Day at Angela Flowers Gallery, 1994, chosen by Andrew Stahl; and was included in 1997–8 John Moores Liverpool Exhibition. Arts Council and Northern Arts hold examples. Lived in London.

Edith GRANGER-TAYLOR 1888–1958 Painter, born Edith Granger in Grassington, Yorkshire, the family moving to Little Milton, Oxfordshire, in 1894. In 1915 she married Godfrey Taylor, consulting engineer and captain in the Royal Engineers, after which she used Granger-Taylor professionally. Her son Jerry Granger-Taylor and grandson Nicholas Granger-Taylor were both painters. She studied for a term at Royal Academy Schools in 1910; at St John's Wood Art School before 1914; had lessons in portraiture from Philip de Laszlo; did a term at Slade School of Fine Art, 1919; returning there in 1933 for Vladimir Polunin's stage painting classes. During the 1920s and 1930s showed extensively with RBA, RWS and NEAC all as a member;

also with PS, NS and in 1921 won *The Times'* women's supplement's April cover competition. Solo exhibitions were at Grosvenor Galleries, 1922; Blomqvist Gallery, Oslo, 1930; Beaux Arts Gallery, 1932; Walker's Galleries, 1958; and Gillian Jason Gallery, 1989.

Nicholas GRANGER-TAYLOR 1963– Painter, notably of portraits, born in London. He was educated at Latymer Upper School, then completed foundation studies at Kingston Polytechnic, 1981–2. After obtaining his degree in fine art from Bristol Polytechnic, 1982–5, Granger-Taylor did a postgraduate diploma in painting at Royal Academy Schools, 1987–90. He obtained a special commendation in John Player Portrait Award in 1987, gaining second prize that year in the British Institution Fund Painting Award. Several other awards followed, including in 1990 the Elizabeth Greenshields Foundation Award and the Richard Ford Award, which enabled him to study at Prado, Madrid. Granger-Taylor fast established a reputation in mixed shows including RA, the Festival Hall's South Bank Picture Show and Cadogan Contemporary Summer Exhibitions. That gallery gave him a solo show in 1988, another following at Waterman Fine Art in 1991. His father and grandmother, Jerry and Edith Granger-Taylor, were also artists.

Alistair GRANT 1925–1997 Painter, printmaker, artist in collage and teacher born in London, where he settled. He attended Birmingham School of Art, 1941–3, was four years in the Royal Air Force, then was at Royal College of Art, 1947–50, with a continuation scholarship, 1950–1. From 1955 for many years Grant taught printmaking at Royal College of Art, where he became head of the department in 1970, taking the chair of printmaking in 1984, retiring in 1990. Grant had a keen, painterly sense of colour in pictures that were at first figurative, later abstract. His dexterity as a draughtsman was exhibited in John Huston's film *Moulin Rouge*, based on the life of Toulouse-Lautrec, made in 1953, where Grant drew on camera. Grant showed RA, AIA, NEAC, at Redfern, Piccadilly and Zwemmer Galleries and was a prizewinner at the Cracow Print Biennale in 1972. After the death of his second wife Joan Strickland (who had worked with him at the Royal College), in 1995, Grant lived partly in France, partly in England, showing in both. His mother came from Etaples, in northern France, where he went to school, and he retained the family home there. Grant's work is held by the Victoria & Albert Museum, British provincial and many overseas galleries. There was a memorial show at Art First, 1997.

D Marion GRANT 1912– Artist in stained glass, born in Bromley, Kent. She was educated at Central School of Arts and Crafts, 1931–5, then embarked on a career which encompassed a large amount of ecclesiastical work. Exeter Cathedral, Glasgow Cathedral and a number of English churches contain windows by her. Lived in London.

Duncan GRANT 1885–1978 Painter and decorative artist, designer for the theatre and of pottery and textiles. He was born at Rothiemurchus, Inverness-shire, but spent his early years in India. After studying at Westminster School of Art in 1902 Grant spent a time in Italy, studied under Jacques-Emile Blanche in 1906, then for a short period at the Slade School of Fine Art. During the period 1907–9 Grant lived in Paris, where he met Matisse, whose talent for felicitous decoration is often found in Grant's own work over the years. Grant then travelled widely in Europe and Tunisia; was influenced by French Post-Impressionists during Roger Fry's first show of them in London in 1910–11, Grant contributing to the second show in 1912; and became a member of the Camden Town Group and later LG. Grant's association with the Bloomsbury Group around this time and his work with Roger Fry's Omega Workshops was of lasting importance to his career, his association with Vanessa Bell being a notable aspect of this. While living at Charleston, Firle, Sussex, which remained his home, they and Quentin Bell decorated the church at Berwick, near Firle, in 1943. Grant had his first one-man show at the Carfax Gallery in 1920. He was in many group shows, including the Leicester, Redfern, Lefevre and Leger Galleries, also having one-man shows at Agnew. Represented in many public collections, including Tate Gallery, which staged a retrospective exhibition in 1959, with Arts Council tour.

Ian GRANT 1904–1993 Painter, art historian and teacher, born in Scotland. He studied at Glasgow School of Art, 1922–6, under Maurice Greiffenhagen, then in 1927 at Atelier Colarossi, Paris, and Royal College of Art, 1927–30. Grant became senior lecturer at Manchester Regional College of Art, staying there, 1937–69; his wife Margaret Gumuchian, whom he married in 1953, was a student in his class. Other appointments included part-time work at Mauldeth Road College of Further Education, 1959–79, and lecturing in art history at Manchester University extra-mural department. Grant was for a time vice-president of MAFA, where he won a major prize in 1986. In 1989 he was included in The Last Romantics at Barbican Art Gallery. Manchester City Art Gallery holds his work, which was exhibited at solo shows at Salford Art Gallery and elsewhere in the north. Lived in Stockport, Cheshire.

James Ardern GRANT 1887–1973 Printmaker, painter and teacher, born in Liverpool. He studied at the School of Art there, where he later taught, at Académie Julian in Paris and in London at Central Technical School. Eventually became vice-principal of Central School of Arts and Crafts. Before World War I in Liverpool Grant was a member of Sandon Studios Society, in 1932 becoming a fellow of RE, also a member of NS and PS of which he was president. Showed extensively, including RA, Chenil Gallery, NEAC, RSA, Walker Art Gallery and elsewhere. Walker Art Gallery holds his portrait of the theatrical designer George Harries, Whitworth Art Gallery, Manchester, his striking pastel Woman in a Grey Hat. Latterly lived in London.

Keith Frederick GRANT 1930– Artist in all painting media, teacher, born Liverpool. Attended Willesden School of Art,

1952–5, then Royal College of Art, 1955–8, where he gained a silver medal for mural painting. In 1958 he won a travelling scholarship to France, in 1960 a Norwegian Government Scholarship, in 1962 and Icelandic Government Scholarship, in 1973 a Gulbenkian Award and in 1976 a grant from the Norwegian government to visit Norway. He was head of painting at Maidstone College of Art, 1969–71, later becoming head of the department of art at Roehampton Institute of Higher Education. Grant showed at Roland, Browse & Delbanco; Crane Kalman Gallery; Gillian Jason Gallery and elsewhere and was a member of the Society of Landscape Painters. He was the subject of a *Look, Stranger* programme for BBC Television, which featured his 1971 open-air sculpture at Shaw Theatre based on *Joan of Arc*. He also completed murals for Rhodesia House in 1959, Middlesex Hospital in 1972 and Gateshead Metro Station, 1981–3. Dramatic, simple landscapes of the Norwegian fjords, moving towards abstraction, were a feature of Grant's work, and he was also interested in the world seen from space. Arts Council, Contemporary Art Society and Fitzwilliam Museum in Cambridge hold examples.

Leslie GRANT 1923– Painter, notably of landscapes and townscapes, draughtsman and teacher. After serving in Royal Air Force air crew in World War II Grant studied at Bromley and Brighton Colleges of Art. He taught at Mansfield School of Art; in Germany; at several London schools; and became head of art at Plumstead Manor School. Grant showed at South London Art Gallery; in the provinces, notably with Midland Group of Artists; in Germany; and in 1979 at Woodlands Art Gallery.

Marianne GRANT 1931– Painter in oil, born in St Gallen, Switzerland. She studied in Zürich and Geneva, eventually returning to live in Zürich after a period in Romford Essex. As well as showing in Switzerland she exhibited with NS of which she was a member and had a number of English solo shows including BH Corner Gallery, Century Galleries in Henley-on-Thames and Royal Northern College of Music. Standard Telephone and Cables bought her work and some of her work was produced in print form. Essex Art Club member.

Edgar GRANTHAM 1926– Painter, calligrapher and teacher, born in York. He was initially educated in Bradford, then studied art between 1947–52 in Liverpool, Bradford and Leeds. After World War II he taught for a couple of years in the Army, eventually joining the staff of Sheffield Central Technical School, where he remained for some years. Showed mainly in Yorkshire, where he lived in Sheffield.

Alastair GRANVILLE-JACKSON fl. from 1950s– Sculptor, printmaker and teacher, born in Woodstock, South Africa. He studied art history at University of Cape Town, where he obtained his bachelor of arts degree in 1954, obtaining a master of arts degree from Columbia University in 1982. In 1957 he studied in Florence and in the same year at Slade School of Fine Art with Reg Butler, the sculptor. Further studies included periods in the early 1960s at Central School of Arts and Crafts and St Martin's School of Art, with Anthony Caro, then Cranbrook Academy of Art, 1965–7, Birmingham, Michigan, in America. As well as exhibiting in South Africa and in America, Granville-Jackson showed at AIA, LG, RBSA as well as Heal's Mansard Art Gallery. Lived for some time in New York.

William GRAVENEY 1904–1984 Sculptor in bronze, stone, terracotta and wood. Born in London, Graveney studied at the school of wood carving at the Royal College of Art, then later at City and Guilds School, Kennington, under Charles Leonard Hartwell, RA. He won several silver medals. Became a tutor in wood carving at Morley College, in South London. Exhibited at the RA from 1926. The Tate Gallery holds his oak carving Cormorants. Wrote several books on carving. Lived in Chiswick, London.

Lorna GRAVES 1947– Sculptor in raku-fired ceramic and painter, born in Kendal and settled at Hunsonby, Penrith, Cumbria. She gained a Bachelor of Science degree at London University, 1969–72; was librarian at Oxford University, 1972–4; attending Cambridge College of Art, 1974–6. In 1981–4 obtained Cumbria College of Art & Design diploma in fine art. Won an Arts Council Award in 1978; a series of regional arts awards, 1984–8; and the David Canter Memorial Award, 1991. The Eden Valley and Cumbrian landscape, the nearby stone circle Long Meg and her Daughters were key influences. The poet Kathleen Raine saw in Graves' work "a kind of grave simplicity, something tender and enduring". Mixed exhibitions included Temenos, Dartington Hall, 1988; Aberdeen Art Gallery, 1990; Pyramid Gallery, York, 1994; and Bleddfa Gallery, Powys, 1995. Later solo exhibitions included Roger Billcliffe Fine Art, Glasgow, and Montage, Castleton, both 1995. Tate Gallery, Metropolitan Art Gallery in New York, Victoria & Albert Museum and public galleries in Aberdeen, Kendal, Carlisle and elsewhere hold examples.

Guy GRAVETT 1919–1996 Photographer and painter, born in Kent, who studied at Lewes Grammar School and, determined to be an artist, attended Brighton College of Art under Walter Hayes. To make a living he joined HM Customs and during World War II was commissed in the Royal Engineers, ending as the Naples port commandant. He was a lifelong keen sailor. Demobilised and unable to make a living as a painter Gravett taught himself photography and set up a studio in Lewes, not far from the opera house at Glyndebourne. Eventually he was to become the photographer for the Festival Opera there, meticulously covering each production and the building of the new opera house in 1993–4. Major commissions also came from *Picture Post, The Sunday Times*, British Petroleum and wine merchant Peter Dominic. Wine was another of Gravett's passions, and he provided illustrations for the early editions of Hugh Johnson's *World Atlas of Wine*. Gravett returned to painting in the 1970s, France – its vineyards and the Normandy countryside, in particular – being a favourite subject. His watercolours and oils of Dieppe were made into a show at the port in 1993.

Anthony GRAY 1915–1972 Sculptor in stone, bronze, wood, resins and other materials. Gray studied art in several countries on the continent in the late 1930s. After World War II he studied at Camberwell School of Art, 1946–9, then at St Martin's School of Art, 1949–50. He taught for a while and undertook architectural and portrait commissions, being for a time vice-president of the SPS. Exhibited SPS and RA. Among his many portraits of famous people were Earl Attlee, Sir John Barbirolli, Sir David Low and Nubar Gulbenkian. Lived in London.

Dorothy GRAY 1901–1962 Painter of miniatures of flowers on ivory, born in London. Exhibited RMS, RA, SWA and Foyles Gallery. Lived at Bexhill-on-Sea, Sussex.

Douglas Stannus GRAY 1890–1959 Bravura painter in oil of figures, portraits, landscapes, still life and his own family. Born in London, in 1900 he attended art school in Clapham, in 1904 becoming a full-time pupil at Croydon School of Art. In 1908 accepted at Royal Academy Schools, where his teachers included Ernest Jackson and Charles Sims, but the strongest, lasting influence remained Schools visitor John Singer Sargent. Won Landseer Scholarship in 1912, British Institution Scholarship in 1914, suspended during military service. Because of injuries, was retired with a life pension. Travelled in France and in the 1920s began to have success with pictures at the Royal Academy, where his portrait of his sister Rosalind was bought by the Chantrey Bequest. Also showed at ROI and RP. In 1947 taught portrait class at Brighton Art College. Gray's career went through lean periods, but his reputation received a boost in the 1980s with exhibitions at Spink & Son. The Tate Gallery holds his work. Gray's daughter was the artist Virginia Susanne Douglas Robinson. He lived at Southwick, Sussex.

Elizabeth GRAY 1928– Musician and self-taught painter, born in Scarborough, Yorkshire, whose speciality was sporting and wildlife pictures. Had solo shows at Tryon Gallery, in the provinces and in America at Sportsman's Edge Gallery, New York. Bank of England holds her work. Lived at Awre, Newnham-on-Severn, Gloucestershire.

Ethel GRAY 1879–1957 Painter, printmaker, stained glass designer, potter and embroiderer. Born in Newcastle upon Tyne, she studied at Leeds College of Art, York School of Art and Royal College of Art. Taught for many years, including Leeds Training College for over 30 years to 1944. Exhibited RA, SWA, RWS, Paris Salon, extensively in the provinces and in South Africa, where she finally lived in Johannesburg.

Frederick GRAY 1911–1960 Painter and designer, of jewellery and for television and films. Born at Colchester, Essex, he studied at the Royal College of Art. Exhibited in London, where he lived. Took part in the Pilgrim Trust *Recording Britain* project.

Jane GRAY 1931– Stained glass artist, born in Lincoln. She studied at Kingston School of Art, 1948–52, under Reginald Brill, then at Royal College of Art, 1952–5, with Lawrence Lee. For the next three years she assisted Lee with his windows in Coventry Cathedral. Elected a liveryman of the Worshipful Company of Glaziers in 1983. Examples of her work are to be founded in Hillingdon Hospital Chapel, Oxford County Hall and Glaziers Hall, London. Lived in Uxbridge, Middlesex, then in Shrawardine, Shrewsbury.

Jane GRAY fl. from 1960s– Printmaker and teacher who studied at London University and Camberwell School of Arts and Crafts, where she was awarded a postgraduate scholarship in graphics. She taught at various schools in the southeast of England. Made a BBC Television series with John Berger on animal prints. Lino-prints of animals were featured when her work was shown in Group '77 Printmakers at Woodlands Art Gallery, 1981. Gray's prints were exhibited widely and illustrated in the national press.

Janice GRAY 1966– Watercolourist who studied at Glasgow School of Art, 1984–8. Awards included Elizabeth Greenshields Scholarship and W O Hutchison Prize for Drawing, both 1988; and Alexander Graham Munro Travel Award and Maude Gemmell Hutchison Award, both 1996. Gray was elected to RSW in 1995. Exhibitions included RSA, 1987; Atholl Gallery, Dunkeld, 1990; Scottish Gallery, Edinburgh International Festival Exhibition, 1996; and Ainscough Contemporary Art, 1997, amusing watercolours of acrobatic animals. Aberdeen Art Gallery and BBC Scotland, Glasgow, hold examples.

Joseph GRAY 1890–1962 Painter, printmaker and illustrator, born in South Shields, County Durham, attending the School of Art there. He travelled extensively through Europe and Russia, served in the Black Watch in World War I, eventually becoming war artist for *The Graphic*. The Imperial War Museum acquired his painting titled A Ration Party, and the British Museum and Victoria & Albert Museum holds examples. Showed with Aitken Dott in Edinburgh, also Fine Art Society and RSA. Lived in Broughty Ferry, Angus.

Milner GRAY 1899–1997 Graphic designer, draughtsman and teacher with a respect for craftsmanship and materials, creator of such well-known symbols as the Jaeger stores lettering, born in Blackheath, southeast London. He was educated locally at Colfe's Grammar School and Goldsmiths' College School of Art (where he was later a tutor, also teaching at Royal College of Art and Central School, as well as being principal of Sir John Cass School of Arts and Crafts). During World War I Gray served in Army camouflage. In the early 1920s he formed half of the pioneering consultancy Bassett-Gray (later the Industrial Design Partnership) and shared digs with Graham Sutherland, who did work for it. Sutherland painted his final portrait of Gray for the Society of Industrial Artists and Designers, which Gray had helped form in 1930, of which he was twice president and from which he received its first Design Medal for outstanding achievement. Invited by Frank Pick of London Transport to join the Ministry of

Information exhibition team in World War II, Gray was involved in such famous campaigns as Dig for Victory. He was persuaded to form the Design Research Unit with Kenneth Bayes and Misha Black. Over several decades jobs included the Britain Can Make It exhibition, the Festival of Britain and commissions for Imperial Chemical Industries, British Rail, and the Post Office. Gray was made Royal Designer of Industry, and was a member of the Council of Industrial Design and of the Royal Mint design committee. He was a convivial member of the Arts Club.

Ronald GRAY 1868–1951 Painter, born in London, who after working for a time in the family heating engineering business around the mid-1980s studied with Percy Jacomb-Hood in his studio, at the Westminster School of Art under Fred Brown and at the Académie Julian, Paris. In the first decade of this century visited America several times. Had one-man show at Goupil Gallery, 1923, and also exhibited RA, NEAC, RWS, Fine Art Society and at the Paris Salon, where he won a silver medal. Was a friend of Philip Wilson Steer, Gray's watercolours being especially similar in style to his friend's. Lived in London.

Stuart GRAY 1925– Lithographer in watercolour, born in Streatham, south London, where he attended the Grammar School. Was a member of NS and UA, RI and RSMA, being notable for his marine paintings. Lived in East Cowes, Isle of Wight.

William Everatt GRAY 1892–1957 Sculptor, studied art at Regent Street Polytechnic School of Art under Charlotte Osborne and Harold Brownsword. Exhibited RA, RSA, RHA, RMS, NS and Paris Salon. Was especially fond of working in wood, and wrote articles on the technique. The General Post Office, Ministry of Agriculture and Russell-Cotes Art Gallery and Museum, Bournemouth, hold his work. Lived near Chessington, Surrey.

Ashley GREAVES 1961– Painter, born in Croydon, Surrey, who studied at Ravensbourne College of Art; Portsmouth Polytechnic; and Cyprus College of Art. Was leader of the art group for Urban Spaces Scheme, Polytechnic of North London, 1985–7. Group shows included Mountbatten Gallery, Portsmouth, 1983; Kyklos Gallery, Paphos, 1985; Leeds Polytechnic Gallery, Leeds, 1987; Open Exhibition, Johnson Wax Kiln Gallery, Farnham, from 1989; and Royal Over-Seas League Open, 1995, showing the acrylic on paper Girl Showing Parents Her Strawberry Tattoo.

Christopher GREAVES 1913– Designer, painter and teacher, born in Gidea Park, Essex, the son of an architect. He studied at Chelsea School of Art and Central School of Arts and Crafts. Shortly after World War II he taught for a while at London School of Printing, then was art editor of several magazines, as well as being art director of the advertising agency S T Garland. Showed at UA and elsewhere. Lived in Ascot, Berkshire.

Derrick GREAVES 1927– Painter, artist in collage and teacher, born in Sheffield. From 1943–8 he was an apprentice signwriter, which he said taught him more than subsequent teaching. After attending evening classes he won a scholarship to the Royal College of Art, 1948–52, then with an Abbey Major Scholarship worked in Italy, 1952–3, where he was influenced by the Italian Realists, notably Renato Guttuso. Sheffield and Italy featured in his first one-man show at the Beaux Arts Gallery in 1953, and it was in the 1950s that he became a notable member of the Kitchen Sink School. With other Kitchen Sink painters he exhibited at the Venice Biennale in 1956, in the following year appearing in the Looking at People show at South London Art Gallery and Pushkin Museum, Moscow. In the same year he was awarded a gold medal for painting at the Moscow Youth Festival and he was also a John Moores Liverpool Exhibition prizewinner. Taught for several years at St Martin's School of Art. From the 1960s Greaves' work lost its Kitchen Sink grittiness, becoming more poetic, linear and allusive. Graves Art Gallery in Sheffield held a retrospective in 1980. Tate Gallery holds his work. Lived in London.

Jack GREAVES 1928– Sculptor, artist in oil, pastel and watercolour and teacher, born in Leeds, Yorkshire, who studied at the College of Art there, 1948–51; Royal College of Art, 1951–4; and British School in Rome, 1960–1. After teaching in Stroud, he was appointed head of the department of sculpture at Cheltenham College of Art. He had a studio in the Cotswolds, 1955–64; was at Ohio State University, 1964–8; worked in America and the Cotswolds, 1968–88; then had a studio in Yorkshire, living in Snainton, Scarborough. Greaves was a member of RWA. Group exhibitions included Three Humanist Sculptors, Zwemmer Gallery, 1960; 19 Young Sculptors, Hillfield Gardens, Gloucester, 1962; Bruton Gallery, from 1970; and widely in America from 1977. Solo shows included Ohio State University, 1966; Stroud Festival, 1969; Search Gallery, 1973; Vorpal Gallery, New York, 1978; and Gallery 200, Columbus, from 1985. Main works included Christ Teaching, Columbus, 1978; The Guardian, Toledo, Ohio, 1981; The Naiad Fountain, Columbus, 1984. RWA, public galleries in Bristol and Coventry and Columbus Museum of Art hold examples.

Leonard GREAVES 1918–1949 Painter, teacher and writer who after attending London University studied at Chelsea School of Art, 1934–8. Prior to World War II he was for two years assistant lecturer at the National Gallery, from 1945 becoming a visiting instructor at St Martin's School of Art. He exhibited RA, NEAC, LG, UA and AIA and had several one-man shows in the 1940s, including Redfern Gallery. Also exhibited abroad. The Contemporary Art Society bought his work, which is held by Bristol and Wakefield public galleries. This was sometimes signed L G. *The Artist*, *The Saturday Book* and *The Listener* published his pictures and he wrote widely, mainly for art and architectural periodicals. Lived in London.

Anne GREBBY 1944– Painter and teacher, born in Lincoln. After graduating at Birmingham College of Art Grebby did post-graduate studies at Hornsey College of Art and the British School in Rome. She taught at Sheffield College of Art; was visiting lecturer at art colleges in Manchester, Birmingham, Liverpool, Cheltenham, Newcastle and at the Central School of Art; then in 1988 she was appointed head of painting at Sheffield Polytechnic. As a painter she was concerned with themes including women's issues and wildlife survival. She showed widely in France and in group shows at Whitworth Art Gallery, Manchester, and in John Moores Liverpool Exhibitions. In 1980 she shared a show at Compass Gallery, Glasgow, with Paul Hodges, in the following two years having solo exhibitions at Paton Gallery.

Alan GREEN 1932– Painter, printmaker and teacher, born in London, married to the artist June Green. He attended Beckenham School of Art, 1949–53, and after National Service in the Far East was at Royal College of Art 1955–8, winning a Major Travelling Scholarship which took him to France and Italy in 1958–9. Won many awards and prizes in Britain and especially abroad. Among his teaching posts were Hornsey and Leeds Colleges of Art and Ravensbourne College of Art and Design. While at Leeds he took part in The Teaching Image, a Leeds College staff show at the City Art Gallery. He also showed extensively in mixed exhibitions overseas. Showed also particularly with Annely Juda Fine Art. Arts Council, British Council and Guggenheim Museum, New York, hold his work, which was abstract, as seen in The British Art Show, chosen by the critic William Packer, which was toured by Arts Council in 1980.

Anthony GREEN 1939– Painter and teacher, born in London. Green exhibited in Young Contemporaries in 1956, the year he went to Slade School of Fine Art, where he was until 1960, when a French Government Scholarship took him to Paris. Two years after that he had a first one-man show at Rowan Gallery, with which he showed for many years. In addition he showed with LG, being elected a member in 1964, and RA, to which he was elected in 1977. Green won a Gulbenkian Purchase Award in 1963 and gained a prize at John Moores, Liverpool, show in 1974. In 1967 he won a Harkness Fellowship to America, where he lived until 1969, by which time he had begun to establish an impressive international exhibiting career. In 1964 he taught at the Slade, shortly after beginning a long period of teaching at Royal College of Art. He had a retrospective at RA in 1978, a year in which his work was shown extensively in the provinces, and in Japan in 1987–8, and A Green Perspective was held at Pallant House, Chichester, in 1994. Green's work was produced slowly and featured his family and their surroundings, until the late 1980s the flat where he had been brought up and continued to live, then he moved to Little Eversden in Cambridgeshire and his pictures reflected the landscape. Green created his own perspective, a little like what is seen through a fish-eye lens, favoured oddly shaped supports and latterly pictures on free-standing structures. Arts Council holds his work. His daughter Katie was a painter.

Daphne GREEN 1926– Painter, born in London, who studied at the Oxford School of Art, her teachers including Peter Greenham, Evelyn Dunbar and Bernard Meninsky. Did some poster work and exhibited Ashmolean Museum, Oxford, and with the local Art Society. Signed work D G. Lived for a time in Oxford.

David GREEN 1929– Watercolourist, teacher, writer and illustrator, born in Southport, Lancashire, married to the artist Gill Green. Began his art training at Exeter in 1946 and moved to Royal College of Art school of design (ceramics) after National Service with the Royal Artillery. Changed direction to study at Hornsey College of Art, 1949–53, painting with Jesse Cast, etching with Norman Janes and lithography with Henry Holzer. Between 1953–7 taught part-time at Harrow, Willesden and Medway Colleges of Art and showed at RA, Leicester Galleries and RE. For next 24 years taught full-time in ceramic department at Carlisle College of Art and the school of three-dimensional design at Bath Academy of Art, taking early retirement in 1981. In 1983 an exhibition of Green's work was held at King's Circus Gallery, Bath, then from 1985 shared regular shows of watercolours with his wife, including Heffer's in Cambridge, Century Gallery in Henley-on-Thames, Linfield Gallery in Wells and elsewhere. Green was a landscapist and many thousands of cards and limited edition prints were sold. Among books illustrated were *Good Food from Farthinghoe*, by Nicola Cox, 1981, and *English Stone Building*, by Alec Clifton-Taylor, 1983. Green's own books, mainly on pottery, included *Understanding Pottery Glazes*, 1963, and *Experimenting with Pottery*, 1971. His father was William Green, artist and principal of Exeter School of Art. Lived in Woodbridge, Suffolk.

David GREEN 1935– Painter in oil and watercolour, born in London. He became a full-time painter in 1968. Was a member of ROI and NS. Showed at Mall Galleries, Luton Museum, Heffer Gallery in Cambridge, Stamford Arts Centre and in Bedford, near where he lived. Mayor's Parlour in Bedford, Texas Instruments and English Gallery, Boston, in America, hold his work.

Elizabeth Helen GREEN: *see* **Helen BEALE**

Gill GREEN: *see* **GILL**

June GREEN 1935– Sculptor and teacher who studied at Sunderland College of Art and Royal College of Art. While on the staff of Leeds College of Art, in 1964 with her husband Alan Green took part in The Teaching Image exhibition at Leeds City Art Gallery. Later lived in Llangattock Vibon-Avel, Monmouth, Gwent.

Madeline GREEN 1884–1947 Painter in oil on canvas, born in London, who studied at Royal Academy Schools. Won a Silver Medal at Paris Salon in 1923 and also exhibited prolifically at Agnew in Manchester, RWA, RA, SWA, Royal Glasgow Institute of the Fine Arts and elsewhere. Spink & Son included two impressive figure pieces in their Twentieth Century British show in 1984. She lived for a time in Ealing, Middlesex.

Margaret GREEN fl. from c.1950– Painter, notably of small landscapes in a reticent style, born in West Hartlepool, County Durham, married to the artist Lionel Bulmer. She studied at the local School of Art and Royal College of Art, 1944–7, winning Henriques and Travelling Scholarships, a Silver Medal and Painting Prize. Showed with RA, LG, NEAC, Leicester Galleries, William Ware Gallery and in several provincial galleries and touring exhibitions in Britain and abroad. Had a solo exhibition at New Grafton Gallery in 1972. Chantrey Bequest, *Financial Times*, Ministries of Information and Public Works and public galleries in Carlisle, Coventry, Leeds and Nottingham hold examples. Lived at Onehouse, near Stowmarket, Suffolk.

Paul GREEN 1951– Painter, born in Pontypridd, Glamorgan. He studied at Maidstone College of Art, 1969–70; Cardiff College of Art, 1970–4; and Slade School of Fine Art, 1974–6. Showed in the Whitechapel Open, at the Air Gallery and was a prizewinner in the 1995–6 John Moores Liverpool Exhibition. After a first solo exhibition at Oriel Gallery in Cardiff in 1974 had a series in London, where he lived. His 1983 oil on canvas Graig Yr Hesg is held by the Arts Council.

Roland GREEN 1896–1972 Painter of birds in oil and watercolour. Born at Rainham, Kent, Green studied at the Art School in Rochester and then at Regent Street Polytechnic. He had many one-man shows at Arthur Ackermann and Son and in East Anglia. A reclusive man, Green had a studio at Hickling Broad, Norfolk, where he studied meticulously birds and their habits. He illustrated a number of books by himself – *How I Draw Birds*, and *Wing Tips* – and others, including work on Australian birds.

Ron GREEN 1923– Painter, born in Lincolnshire. He was a chartered engineer until 1979, although he was always interested in watercolour painting. Studied under R A Tucker at Gloucester College of Art and held a show there, also exhibiting locally. Upon retirement Green began painting full-time in the Lake District. He showed with Broughton Gallery, Peebles, Thornethwaite Gallery, Keswick, Lake Artists' Society in Grasmere and elsewhere, such as Patricia Wells Gallery, Thornbury. Green was especially keen on northern British landscapes. Lived in Lorton, near Cockermouth, Cumbria.

Stephen GREEN 1918– Painter, printmaker, graphic artist and designer, born in Cobham, Surrey. He was the son of the watercolourist R H Green. Studied at Reading University, 1935–7, and at Royal College of Art, 1937–9 and again in 1942. Exhibited RA, NEAC, Leicester Galleries, AIA and in Denmark. He completed a volume of commercial work for *The Times*, London Transport and so on. Lived in London.

William GREEN 1894–1972 Painter, potter and teacher, born in Hanley, Staffordshire. He attended Hanley School of Art and then the Royal College of Art, 1920–2, under William Rothenstein and Ernest Tristram. Until about the mid-1920s he held appointments as a pottery designer, including a period with Crescent Pottery in Stoke-on-Trent, after which he was on the staff of several art schools, becoming principal of Exeter School of Art from early in World War II, retiring in 1958. He was a noted collector of English watercolours, showing his own work at RA, RWA and elsewhere. His son was the artist David Green. Lived in Exeter.

William GREEN 1934– Painter and teacher, born in Greenwich, southeast London, strongly influenced by German Expressionist art and orchestral music. After several jobs including working in an architect's office, Green from 1952–4 attended the School of Art in Sidcup, Kent, where he eventually settled, influenced by Edward Eade. Having been accepted by the Royal College of Art in 1954 he was not able to start until 1955 as his pacifist leanings put him in prison for three months as a conscientious objector. Influenced by American Abstract Expressionism Green turned to making black abstracts, creating them by pouring and hurling bitumen paint on hardboard and treating the surface brutally, dragging a bicycle on it and setting it on fire. In 1957 Green was included in New Trends in British Art, Rome-New York Art Foundation, Rome; and Dimensions, British Abstract Art, 1948–57, O'Hana Gallery; and he was in Ken Russell's film *Making an Action Painting*, which led to international coverage. In 1958 Green had a first solo show at New Vision Centre Gallery and left the Royal College with a first-class honours degree. Showed in first Situation exhibition at RBA Gallery, 1960, and was lampooned in Tony Hancock's film *The Rebel* in 1961, about the time Green was experimenting in an American Pop Art style. Teaching included a working men's college; Harrow, Walthamstow and other Schools of Art; and Goldsmiths' and Havering Technical College, from which he retired in 1981. Green withdrew from exhibiting from mid-1960s until a solo show at England & Co, 1993, when he was included in The Sixties Art Scene in London, Barbican Art Gallery.

David GREENALL 1947– Creator of semi-abstract works who left school at 15 and worked in the fishing and building industries, starting to paint in 1975. Did a foundation course at Norwich School of Art, 1982, gaining an honours degree in fine art from Winchester School of Art, 1983–6. Settled in the Outer Hebrides where the singular landscape of Lewis and the image of the Butt of Lewis lighthouse featured strongly in his pictures. Mixing his own colours from raw pigment and blending mediums such as wax, resin, oil and tempera he produced works of great vigour. Exhibitions included Flying Colours Gallery, Edinburgh, 1993, and Coombs Contemporary, 1994.

Judith GREENBURY 1924– Painter and writer, born in Bristol. She studied at West of England College of Art, 1943–6, with George Sweet, then under Randolph Schwabe at Slade School of Fine Art, 1946–7. She painted portraits, landscapes and figures in landscape. Was elected to RWA in 1979, also exhibiting at NEAC and RA. Her solo shows included Forest Row and Alpine Galleries. RWA holds her work. After her husband's death in 1989 and a serious accident in 1995, during recovery

Greenbury wrote *Spey Portrait*, an illustrated memoir of their fishing the Scottish river, published 1997. The following year published her memoir of George Sweet. Lived in Henley-on-Thames, Oxfordshire.

William GREENGRASS 1895–1970 Printmaker who was a pupil at Grosvenor School of Modern Art and was a keeper at Victoria & Albert Museum. Fond of the lino-cut, he produced images that owe much to Vorticism. Redfern Gallery showed his work.

Robert GREENHALF 1950– Artist whose main subjects were landscape and wildlife. He was born at Haywards Heath, Sussex, studied at Eastbourne and Maidstone Colleges of Art and graduated in 1971. Greenhalf chose to sketch in the field and usually used only one etching plate, printing in up to eight colours. His work was shown in many mixed and solo exhibitions, in London, including RA Summer Exhibition, the provinces and abroad. In 1979 it was featured in the Royal Society for the Protection of Birds magazine *Birds*. In that year he was elected a member of the Printmakers' Council, in 1981 the SWLA and in 1982 RBA. Lived near Rye, Sussex.

Jane GREENHAM: *see* **Jane DOWLING**

Peter GREENHAM 1909–1992 Painter and teacher, brother of the artist Robert Duckworth Greenham, married to the painter Jane Dowling. He was educated at Dulwich College and won a scholarship to read history at Oxford, although he read English. Studied at Byam Shaw School of Drawing and Painting under Ernest Jackson, 1935–9. He then became a schoolmaster in Oxford but continued to paint. Was elected RA in 1960. Greenham succeeded Sir Henry Rushbury as keeper of the Royal Academy Schools in 1964, retiring in 1985. Showed widely in mixed exhibitions and from 1972 had many solo exhibitions at New Grafton Gallery. He was a member of its portrait centre, and among his subjects were Sir Isaiah Berlin, Dr F R Leavis and Lord Hailsham. Tate Gallery holds his work. In 1984–5 the Arts Council and Norwich School of Art put on a touring show of work by Greenham and his wife. They lived at Otmoor, Oxfordshire.

Robert Duckworth GREENHAM 1906–1976 Painter, printmaker, mural artist and draughtsman. Born at Streatham, Surrey, brother of Peter Greenham. Studied at Byam Shaw School of Art and at the Royal Academy Schools, where he won several scholarships and medals. Exhibited RA, RP, NEAC, LG, RSA, ROI, in the provinces and abroad. Principal works include Bathing Beach, purchased by the Australian government, Near Cromer and Snow in Dulwich. Greenham was especially fond of painting beach scenes, his slightly stylised draughtsmanship and unique palette being instantly recognisable. Lived at Gillingham, Dorset.

Martin GREENLAND 1962– Painter, born in Marsden, West Yorkshire, whose work was rich in symbol and imagery. He studied at Nelson and Colne College of Art, 1979–81, and Exeter College of Art, 1981–5. Showed at Whitworth Young Contemporaries, 1985; Gallery North, Kirkby Lonsdale, 1987–8; and several times at John Moores Liverpool Exhibition, including 1991–2 and 1995–6. Held regular solo shows from 1987 in Cumbria, where he lived at Sedbergh, including Lyth Gallery, Kendal, 1995. For some time his work was permanently on show at New Year Gallery in the town.

Edwin GREENMAN 1909– Painter, printmaker and teacher, born in Beckenham, Kent, where he studied at the School of Art, 1926–9, under Henry Carr; was then at Royal College of Art, 1929–33, teachers including Gilbert Spencer and Ernest Tristram. Elected RP in 1968, also exhibiting at RA, in Czechoslovakia and America. His teaching positions included head of Sir John Cass School of Art. Victoria & Albert Museum holds his work. Lived latterly in Donnington, Chichester, Sussex.

John GREENSMITH 1932– Watercolourist and teacher, born and lived in Sheffield, Yorkshire. He studied at the College of Art there and taught art locally at All Saints School. Was elected to NEAC in 1978 and five years later to RWS, also showing with RA and RCamA.

Joseph GREENUP fl. from c.1915–1946 Portrait and figure painter who won scholarship to Royal College of Art around 1913–16, after a period at Birmingham Municipal School of Art. Greenup became a member of RI in 1936 and RBSA in 1945 and showed at RA, including posthumously in 1947. Lived in London.

Eileen Constance GREENWOOD 1915– Painter, craftworker and teacher, born in London. Was married to the artist Ernest Greenwood. She studied at the London County Council School of Arts and Crafts and then at Royal College of Art, 1934–7, with Ernest Tristram. She went on to hold a number of teaching posts, including principal of Sittingbourne College of Education. Showed RA, RI, SWA, LG and Kensington Salon, having joint shows with her husband at Kensington Gallery in 1951 and 1953. She was an enthusiastic member of SEA and several education committees including Middlesex bought her work. Lived at Broad Street, near Hollingbourne, Kent.

Elizabeth GREENWOOD 1942– Painter, draughtsman and teacher whose work sometimes had a jokey, popular culture-related quality. She was born in Cheshire and trained at Coventry College of Art, St Martin's School of Art and Goldsmiths' College School of Art. Taught in London schools, in adult education and youth centres and Avery Hill College of Education. Her work appeared in many mixed shows and she had solo exhibitions at Proscenium Gallery, Greenwich Theatre Gallery and, in 1978, at Woodlands Art Gallery.

Ernest GREENWOOD 1913– Artist and teacher, born in Welling, Kent, husband of the painter Eileen Greenwood. He studied at Gravesend Grammar School, painting at the Royal

College of Art under William Rothenstein and, after a travelling scholarship enabled him to work at the British School in Rome, he entered the etching and engraving school of the Royal College under Malcolm Osborne and Robert Austin. Greenwood's World War II Army service, 1941–6, included a time on the staff of the School of Military Engineering as an architectural draughtsman. Retired in 1961, having been a teacher then an inspector of art education with Inner London Education Authority and Kent Education Committee. Had a first solo show in 1947 at Kensington Art Gallery, about a dozen following by retirement. During this he travelled extensively, for a decade as a specialist art lecturer with Swan's Hellenic Voyages. Showed with RA and RI and was elected a member of RWS in 1973, being president for eight years from 1976 during which time the Society re-established itself at Bankside. Had a retrospective at New Metropole Arts Centre, Folkestone, 1972, another at County Hall, Maidstone, 1997. Tate Gallery and several provincial galleries hold his work. Lived in Broad Street, Kent.

Frank GREENWOOD c.1883–1954 Etcher who studied under Frank Short at South Kensington and in Paris under Maxime Lalanne. He was mainly known for his views of Manchester which record vanished buildings. Showed at Walker Art Gallery in Liverpool and at Manchester's City Art Gallery where in 1976 he was included as an associate of the local artist Adolphe Valette in his centenary show.

Jill GREENWOOD 1910–1995 Artist and designer, born and lived in London, originally Gillian Crawshay-Williams, her mother the miniaturist Joyce Kilburn, her grandfather the painter John Collier, for whom she sat. Studied at Central School of Arts and Crafts, 1927–30, a great friend of the illustrator Lynton Lamb, then learned etching in Florence. In 1931 she joined the clothes firm Jaeger, where she was known as Crawshay, staying with them about 30 years and revitalising their displays. The first Regent Street decorations were hers, for the Festival of Britain, in 1951; in 1954 she designed the Street's Christmas lights; and in 1959 she decorated Oxford Street's lamp-posts. During World War II, at the Ministry of Works, she wrote and illustrated a best-selling booklet *Make Do and Mend*. From 1938 was married briefly to the artist Walter Goetz, in 1940 marrying Tony Greenwood, the Labour Member of Parliament who in 1970 became Baron Greenwood of Rossendale. Lady Greenwood remained a staunch Socialist, a leading worker for the Campaign for Nuclear Disarmament who also set up the Hampstead Community Centre and the Tony Greenwood Charitable Trust. In later years she taught art to pensioners at Age Concern in Hampstead. She was a skilled sketcher of political personalities, contributing to the *Daily Mail*. Had two solo shows of her own pictures, which frequently featured cats, at Barron Gallery, with a notable exhibition at Camden Arts Centre in 1978.

John GREENWOOD 1959– Painter, born in Leeds, Yorkshire, who studied at York College of Arts and Technology, at Cheltenham and Royal College of Art. He constructed meticulous, pictorially mischievous and witty pictures in which sexuality was a recurrent theme. They owed much to artists he admired: Yves Tanguy, Max Ernst and Salvador Dali and had a Surrealistic quality. In 1990 Greenwood won the Midland Bank Purchase Award and the Burston Award and spent three months in residence at Cité Internationale des Arts, Paris. Works were exhibited in group shows in Switzerland and London and in 1992 were featured in Young British Artists at The Saatchi Collection, which holds Greenwood's work.

John Frederic GREENWOOD 1885–1954 Printmaker and watercolour painter, born at Rochdale, Lancashire. Studied at Shipley School of Art, 1904–7, Bradford School of Art, 1907–8, and the Royal College of Art, 1908–11, under W R Lethaby. He became head of the school of design at Leeds College of Art until 1948. Exhibited RA, RBA, RE and widely throughout several continents. The British Museum and Victoria & Albert Museum hold his work. Lived at Ilkley, Yorkshire.

Julia GREENWOOD 1951– Watercolourist and draughtsman in pen and ink. She studied at Camberwell School of Arts and Crafts. Was given many commissions, ranging from a drawing of the boat used by the Transglobe Expedition to a copy of an Elizabethan map for the Aldeburgh Society. Settled in Suffolk, had two shared shows in Aldeburgh and a solo show at Sue Rankin Gallery, 1990.

Orlando GREENWOOD 1892–1989 Painter, designer and draughtsman, born in Nelson, Lancashire. From the age of 13 he worked in his uncle's cotton mill. After studying at Goldsmiths' College School of Art and Army service in World War I, in the 1920s Greenwood became notable as the mill worker-turned-artist, famous for his still lifes and classical set-pieces. Greenwood painted still life and many self-portraits because he said that he was too poor to afford models, although his exhibition with Spink in 1925 was termed "a triumph" by the *Daily Mail*, and 28 works out of 30 were sold for £2,500. Greenwood showed widely with RBA of which he was a member, RA, Colnaghi's, Beaux Arts Gallery and abroad. After Greenwood's house was bombed in World War II he moved with his wife to the north, settling in 1967 in Ulpha, Cumberland, the year he gave up painting. Greenwood had a baffling range of styles. As well as poster designs for London Underground and Great Western Railway and shop advertisements for Liberty's and Whiteleys, his own painting ranged from nineteenth-century academic to pictures in an almost gaudy palette influenced by Cubism. Studio sale at Christie's South Kensington, 1990. A small centenary show was held at The Bloomsbury Workshop, 1992.

Philip GREENWOOD 1943– Printmaker and painter, born in Dolgellau, Merionethshire. He studied at Harrow College of Art, 1961–5, teachers including Christopher Sanders and T W Ward, then at Hornsey Teachers' Training College, 1965–6, with Peter Green. Was elected to RE in 1982, also showing at RA, Tate

Gallery and several overseas printmakers' shows. Arts Council, Tate Gallery and galleries in Derby, Lincoln, Oldham and Sheffield hold examples. Lived in Cobham, Surrey.

Robin GREENWOOD 1950– Sculptor and teacher, born in Manchester, who studied at Wimbledon School of Art, 1968–71, then St Martin's School of Art, 1971–2. He later taught at both, living in London. In 1978 Greenwood gained an Arts Council Major Award. Group exhibitions included Northern Young Contemporaries, 1967; New Sculpture at Norwich Cathedral, 1974; Arts Council Exhibition at Serpentine Gallery, 1979; and Woodlands Art Gallery, 1983, in Have You Seen Sculpture from the Body?

Sydney GREENWOOD 1913– Painter, printmaker and teacher, born in Stalybridge, Cheshire. He studied at Goldsmiths' College of Art, Croydon School of Art, Westminster and privately in Paris in the early 1930s and again in 1946. Obtained a London University diploma in art teaching. Lectured at Manchester College of Art, becoming vice-principal of Southampton College of Art in 1950–73. Was a member of RWA, also showing with Arts Council, RA, Upton Lodge Gallery in Tetbury and elsewhere. Represented in private and public galleries in Britain and North America. Did mural work for Barclays Bank and illustrations for Longman, Oxford University Press and other publishers. Greenwood was "particularly interested in landscape with an abstract element rather than a descriptive treatment". Lived in Sway, Hampshire.

Timothy GREENWOOD 1947– Painter and etcher of wildlife (the Royal Academician Frank Short bequeathed him his etching equipment), born in Chatham, Kent. Aged 10, Greenwood won his first prize as a schoolboy in a Fry's Chocolate-sponsored national competition for a painting of The Creation. Six years later, he used as his first model a rat found by his mother in her deep-freeze. Attended Ravensbourne and Camberwell College of Art, aged 20 became the youngest member of SWLA, and appeared in national newspapers and was filmed by the BBC Television programme *Animal Magic*. Greenwood was employed by the Royal Society for the Protection of Birds as a warden, also working as a keeper on Forestry Commission land. He was commissioned to illustrate the bird section of the 1971 *Shell Nature Guide*, in that year being funded by the company to travel through Spain and Morocco to gather material for a book on European and North African birds of prey, part of his extensive research travels abroad. The first volume of *The Atlas of Rare Pheasants*, a collector's item, illustrated by Greenwood for Palawan Press, appeared in 1997. Greenwood also showed at RA, Arthur Tooth and Sons and Gallery 77 and had solo exhibitions at Furneaux Gallery from 1971. Lived at Loch Tummel, near Pitlochry, Perthshire.

Thomas Affleck GREEVES 1917–1997 Draughtsman, architect and writer who began making fantastical drawings while at Radley College. Spent a year at Slade School of Fine Art, then studied architecture at Cambridge and at Architectural Association, interrupted by World War II service, and practised as an architect for many years. Showed at RA Summer Exhibitions and had solo exhibitions at Robin Garton Gallery, 1978, and Garton & Cooke, 1987. The heart of Greeves' work was a series of views of cities in varying stages of ruin and decay using a technique inspired by Piranesi. RIBA drawing collection holds several examples. Greeves' work was published in *The Saturday Book, Country Life* and *The Architects' Journal*. He published an illustrated monograph on Bedford Park, where he lived, 1975, and in 1994 his *Ruined Cities of the Imagination* and other drawings appeared in a limited edition.

Barbara GREG 1900–1983 Wood and lino engraver and watercolourist. Born in Styal, Cheshire, Barbara Greg studied at the Slade School under Henry Tonks and the Central School of Arts and Crafts under William Palmer Robins. Married the artist Norman Janes. Greg exhibited widely, including the RA, NEAC, RE, RHA, RWS and SWE. The Contemporary Art Society bought her work. She illustrated a number of books with natural history themes, such as *Pastures New*, by Ian Niall, and *Enigmas of Natural History*, by E L Grant Watson. Lived in London and died in hospital in Enfield.

Annabelle GREGORY 1941– Artist in collage, antique textile dealer and teacher, born in Richmond, Surrey. She studied at St Martin's School of Art, 1958–9, and Camden Arts Centre, 1973–4, teachers including Elisabeth Frink and Joe Tilson. Was a member of the Oxford and Banbury Art Societies, also exhibiting with SWA and at Artweeks, Oxfordshire, and Museum of Modern Art, Oxford. Had a solo show at Deddington Art Gallery in Oxfordshire, where she lived at Adderbury. Specialised in portraits, flowers and figure work.

Bessie Denton GREGORY 1894–1970 Watercolourist who was brought up in Cheshire. She studied at Wallasey School of Art, showing at RCamA, BWS and elsewhere. Exhibited at RCamA, of which she was honorary secretary for a time, from 1945 until just before her death, in Wallasey, Merseyside. Mainly lived and painted in the Carnarvonshire area of north Wales.

Christine GREGORY fl. c.1905–1960 Sculptor, potter and teacher, born in London. Exhibited frequently at RA, also at RMS, Walker Art Gallery, Liverpool, SWA, Walker's Galleries, extensively in provinces, in Paris and Toronto, Canada. She was elected a fellow of RBS and her figure Rhythm is illustrated in its volume *RBS: Modern British Sculpture*, published in 1939. City Museum and Gallery in Stoke-on-Trent and Ulster Museum, Belfast, hold her work. Between 1918–37 Gregory was modelling instructor at Hammersmith School of Arts and Crafts. Lived in London.

Dorothy Craven GREGORY 1927– Painter and teacher, born in London. Her studies included a period, 1944–8, at Chelsea

School of Art with Ceri Richards and Raymond Coxon. Exhibited RA. NEAC, SWA, LG and elsewhere. Lived in London.

Malcolm GREGORY: *see* **MacGREGORY**

Margaret GREGORY 1927– Painter in oil and acrylic of richly coloured abstract/figurative works, born in Belfast, Northern Ireland. Graduated from the Guildhall School of Music, 1945, in 1955 attending evening classes in art under Kulwant Aurora. Music, Samuel Palmer, Odilon Redon and Buddhism were cited as influences. Between 1956–75 Gregory was in the Royal Opera House chorus, taught drama and was a member of Edward Lucie-Smith's poetry group, in 1975 moving to Bristol to paint. Exhibited at RWA, Cleveland Bridge Gallery in Bath, Plumbline Gallery in St Ives and Beatrice Royal, Eastleigh. Fuji Art Museum holds her work.

Nuala GREGORY 1965– Artist and lecturer who gained a first-class degree in fine art from University of Ulster, Belfast, 1988. She lectured there and ran many workshops. Showed in the Claremorris Open Exhibition, 1990; with Belfast Young Contemporaries, One Gallery, 1992; and in 1994 in Beyond the Partitions, organised by Queen Street Studios, Belfast, with which she was associated. Solo shows included Works on Paper, 1990, at Peacock Gallery, Craigavon. She was later commissioned by the Arts Council of Northern to make a big screen for their offices in Belfast.

Stephen GREGORY fl. from 1970s– Artist and teacher who trained at Newcastle University and Manchester Polytechnic and showed in group and solo exhibitions in north of England and in London. He was artist-in-residence in Milton Keynes, 1977–9, and in the next two years was a part-time lecturer at Sheffield Polytechnic. From 1982 he held a series of positions as a community art worker, including Northampton, Cheshire and Nottingham. Department of the Environment, Manchester Polytechnic, Open University and Milton Keynes Development Corporation hold his works.

Steven GREGORY 1952– Sculptor, stonemason and teacher, born in South Africa. He gained an honours degree in fine art at St Martin's College of Art and held a City and Guilds craft and advanced craft qualification in stonemasonry. Gregory was an indentured apprentice for five years at Westminster Abbey and Hampton Court and did three years as foreman mason on Richmond Terrace restoration, Whitehall. He periodically worked in the construction industry as a project and construction manager; lectured at art colleges and polytechnics on titanium and metal processes, also teaching sculpture to adults and art classes for children; spent three years on the design and mass production of titanium jewellery; and was invited to collaborate with the ion implantation group at the Department of Nuclear Physics, Harwell, on a since-patented product. Exhibited Sculpture at Goodwood from 1995, and his work The Sentinel was part of the 1997 Lewes Sculpture Trail. RTZ Corporation and Cass Electronics commissioned his work, also held by Leicestershire Education Authority. Lived in London.

Donald GREIG 1916– Painter and printmaker with a strong interest in marine subjects, married to the artist Rita Greig. He was born in London, son of the watercolourist James Greig, and studied at Southend College of Art with the watercolourist Charles Taylor. Was elected a member of RSMA in 1967, the year he won a Gold Medal at Paris Salon, also showing at RA, RI and NEAC. National Maritime Museum, Greenwich, holds Greig's work. Lived in Woodleigh, Devon.

Rita GREIG fl. from 1960s– Painter and printmaker, born in Norwich, Norfolk, married to the artist Donald Greig. After grammar school studied art privately. She was elected to both NEAC and ROI in 1974, the year she won a Silver Medal at Paris Salon, becoming a member of RWA in 1983. Chase Manhattan Bank holds her work. She was based in Woodleigh, Devon.

Hugo GRENVILLE fl. from 1970s– Painter and teacher who, using a rich palette, specialised in painting aspects of the theatre and performers, and theatrical moments in daily life. Attended life classes at Chelsea School of Art, 1978, while serving in the Coldstream Guards, 1977–83. After working for the advertising agency J Walter Thompson, 1983–4, ran a company dealing in contemporary art, 1984–9, then became a full-time painter, having attended Heatherley's School of Art open studio in 1988. Mixed shows included Chelsea Art Society from 1975; Armed Forces Art Society from 1980; Young British Artists, Alpine Gallery, 1986–7; ROI from 1991; and Brian Sinfield Gallery, Burford, 1994. Solo shows included Tryon & Swann Gallery, 1995. Commissions included studies and a large painting of the tercentenary masque at Chatsworth House, 1994; among portraits were General Sir Michael Gow and the former Archbishop of Canterbury Lord Runcie.

Harold GRESLEY 1892–1967 Landscape and figure painter in oil and watercolour. Born in Derby, he was the son of the painter Frank Gresley. Studied at Derby School of Art, 1912, then with Arthur Spooner, 1919, at Nottingham School of Art, and at the Royal College of Art. Exhibited RA, Cooling Galleries, RWS, UA and elsewhere. Derby Museum and Art Gallery and Nottingham Art Gallery hold his work. Gresley, who was assistant art master at Repton School, lived at Chellaston, Derbyshire, and was a member of Derby Sketching Club.

Nicola GRESSWELL 1954– Artist and teacher, born in Oxford, who attended the Polytechnic there where she did a foundation course, 1972–3, followed by Camberwell School of Arts and Crafts, 1973–6, studying painting and textile printing. In 1976–7 took a course at London University's Institute of Education. After three years' part-time teaching at a London comprehensive school and Amersham College of Further Education, set up own silkscreen print studio near Oxford while continuing to live and paint in London. Showed at RA

Summer Exhibition from 1983, also exhibiting at Casa Pupo Gallery, Cale Art and Thumb Gallery. Had a solo print show at Barbican Centre Foyer, 1984, a solo show of watercolours at Minsky's Gallery, 1985.

Hugh GRESTY 1899–1958 Architectural and landscape painter. Born at Nelson, Lancashire, he studied at the Lancashire School of Art and at Goldsmiths' College School of Art under Edmund Sullivan. Exhibited RA, RBA, RI, RSA and Walker Art Gallery, Liverpool. Lived at St Ives, Cornwall. Manchester City Art Gallery holds his work.

Kenneth H GRESTY 1928– Painter and teacher, born in Manchester, where he studied under Harold Williamson at Regional College of Art from 1944–51, with a two-year break from 1946. Held several teaching appointments in the area, finally at Bolton Sixth Form College. Was elected to MAFA in 1954, also showing with RA and elsewhere. Lived in Sale, Cheshire, later at Borth-y-Gest, Gwynedd. Manchester City Art Gallery holds his work.

Frederic Millward GREY 1899–1957 Painter, draughtsman and printmaker, born in London. Studied art at Central School of Arts and Crafts under F E Jackson, Bernard Meninsky, A S Hartrick and Richard Garbe. He was a lecturer at the National Gallery and Tate Gallery early in the 1920s, went to the National Gallery of South Australia, Adelaide, and then set up the North Adelaide School of Fine Arts, which he ran until 1942. Extensive work in Australian public collections. He was eventually president of the Royal South Australian Society of Arts and principal of the state's School of Arts and Crafts. Lived at Toorak Gardens, South Australia.

Nina GREY 1907– Sculptor, born in Eastern Galicia in what was then Austria, moving to Vienna as a child. Having studied at a Jewish teachers' college she taught from late 1920s to 1939, when with her husband she settled in London. Studied at Hornsey and St Martin's Schools of Art. Exhibitions included Ben Uri Art Society, 1962, which holds her work.

Florence GREY-EDWARDS 1892– Painter, chiefly in oil, born in Brookline, Massachusetts, America, her father being the artist George Lee. She was educated in Boston and in Paris, studying with William James at Boston's Museum of Art, then in England at the Slade School of Fine Art, 1925–7, with Henry Tonks and Philip Wilson Steer. Signing her work F G E, she showed at RA and NEAC. Lived in London.

Michael GREY-JONES 1950– Painter using a variety of media, notably watercolour, and teacher, born in Carmarthen, who lived for many years in Kent, settling at Rainham. He studied at Maidstone College of Art and the Royal Academy Schools. Went on to teach watercolour part-time at Eton College. In 1994 his meticulous depiction of terrace houses, Chatham, won the £15,000 first prize in The Singer & Friedlander/*Sunday Times* Watercolour Competition. Grey-Jones had gained an award in 1992 but, realising the rules excluded paintings previously shown in London as ineligible, he withdrew and the prize went to another painter.

Ralph Glanville GREYSMITH 1874–1953 Painter and designer, born in Manchester of an artistic family. Studied at Brighton School of Art and Académie Julian, Paris. He was eventually responsible for art teacher training at Brighton School of Art. Exhibited RA, RBA, RI, NEAC and in the provinces. Brighton Museum and Art Gallery holds his work. Finally lived in London.

Launce Benedict GRIBBIN 1927– Painter, printmaker, sculptor, photographer and teacher, born in Gateshead, County Durham. He studied at Sidcup School of Art, 1944–6, then Goldsmiths' College School of Art, 1948–9, his teachers including Ruskin Spear and Drake Brookshaw. Studied art history at Courtauld Institute, 1950–3, gaining an Italian government scholarship for postgraduate studies in Venice, 1953–4. Gribbin was in the education department of the Victoria & Albert Museum, 1972–7, was head of the history of art and design at London College of Printing, 1977–8, then lectured for Sotheby's Educational Studies, 1989–91. Gribbin first showed at NEAC in 1946, later at LG, RA, Paris Salon and elsewhere. He had two London solo shows in 1952–3. Although he enjoyed "a 'success of esteem', this was never an economic proposition, and since 1963 I have been instead a photographer who lectures to his own slides on art history." He had "no interest in non-figurative painting". Lived in St Albans, Hertfordshire.

Bernard Finegan GRIBBLE 1873–1962 Painter, especially of architectural and marine subjects, born in London, son of the architect Herbert Gribble. Bernard was married to the artist Eleanor Mabel Gribble. His first art tuition was with his father, then he studied at the South Kensington Schools and with Albert Toft. Exhibited RA extensively, also ROI, Royal Glasgow Institute of the Fine Arts and elsewhere. His work is in public galleries in Bournemouth, Preston and overseas. He was marine painter to the Worshipful Company of Shipwrights. Member of the Savage Club. Lived at Parkstone, Dorset.

Eleanor Mary GRIBBLE 1883–1960 Painter, designer, book illustrator and teacher, born in London, who studied at Ipswich School of Art, Royal College of Art and at British Museum. She taught at Ipswich School of Art, designed for Tibbenhams in Ipswich and ran her own private studio school. She was a keen student of ecclesiastical decoration and Queen Mary bought her work. Showed at RA, SWA and abroad. Lived in Ipswich, Suffolk.

Kenneth GRIBBLE 1925– Draughtsman, painter and teacher, born in Sparkbrook, Birmingham. He studied at Harrow School of Art, 1943, with Ernest Heber Thompson; Camberwell School of Art, 1946–7, teachers including William Coldstream, Claude

Rogers, Laurence Gowing and Victor Pasmore; and Slade School of Fine Art, 1947–50. Gribble then began a series of teaching posts, latterly being art advisor to Somerset Council Council Education Department, 1972–80, then principal of Maidstone College of Art, 1980–4. Showed at MAFA from 1956, with Lincolnshire Artists at Usher Gallery in Lincoln from 1961, RWA from 1970 and elsewhere. Had a solo show at Phillips Gallery, Middlesbrough, 1955, later ones including Taunton Brewhouse Theatre, 1977. Manchester City Art Gallery, Usher Gallery and galleries in Middlesbrough, Salford and Ilminster hold examples. Gribble said that the Slade tradition, Sickert and the later Euston Road School were important influences. Lived in Sidmouth, Devon.

Mary GRIERSON fl. from 1950s– Botanical watercolourist born in Bangor, North Wales. From her childhood she was drawing and painting plants. During World War II she joined the Women's Auxiliary Air Force, working as an interpreter for the photographic reconnaissance unit, then joined an aerial survey firm. Studied with the painter and plantsman John Nash, and with his encouragement applied for the post of botanical illustrator at Royal Botanical Gardens, Kew, which she held until retirement. She then freelanced, jobs including painting endangered species in Israel for the Nature Reserve Authority; and from 1974 she regularly went to Hawaii at the invitation of the National Tropical Botanic Garden, to add to its archives. Chose to work from the living plant in pure transparent watercolour, which meant her output was governed by the seasons. Work appeared in many scientific journals, including *Curtis's Botanical Magazine*, and books illustrated included *Mountain Flowers* by Anthony Huxley, 1967, and C Grey-Wilson's *The Genus Cyclamen*, 1988. Was awarded five gold medals by the Royal Horticultural Society. Held a series of solo exhibitions, including Spink & Son, 1990.

Peter GRIERSON 1963– Artist who studied at St Martin's School of Art and in Northampton, gaining an honours degree in fine art. Group shows included the 1982 John Player Portrait Award at National Portrait Gallery; Laing National Art Competition at Mall Galleries in 1991; *The Guardian* Art for Sale exibitions at Whiteleys from 1992; and in 1994 he was a finalist in The Alasdair Gilchrist Fisher Memorial Award at Cadogan Contemporary, with Abstract Expressionist work. Had a series of solo shows at Alba Fine Art from 1986, in 1987 showing at Barke Gallery, New York.

Ronald GRIERSON 1901– Multi-faceted artist and designer who studied at Grosvenor School of Modern Art, 1926–9, with Iain Macnab. From 1946–9 he was a visiting teacher at Camberwell School of Arts and Crafts. In 1930 Grierson married fellow-art student Enid Martin; inspired by Edward McKnight Kauffer they taught themselves to weave. Ronald Grierson's designs caught the spirit of each decade of his career and show a continued interest in painting, Braque and Rothko being notable influences. Among his activities are working as a consultant designer for S J Stockwell (Carpets) Ltd; designing for Liberty's and Heal's; a rug for Guildford Cathedral; lino-cuts; and the book *Woven Rugs*, 1979. Showed at Victoria & Albert Museum, which holds a considerable archive, Leicester and Redfern Galleries. Lived in London.

Peter GRIEVE 1936– Abstract sculptor and teacher, born and lived in London. He studied at Bromley College of Art, 1954–7, and Royal Academy Schools, 1957–61, taught in Greece, 1961–4, then became senior lecturer in sculpture at Birmingham Polytechnic. His exhibitions included Young Contemporaries, 1960; RA Summer Exhibition from 1973; and Serpentine Summer Show 1, 1980. In that year he shared a show at Air Gallery. Solo exhibitions included Ikon Gallery, Birmingham, 1975.

Robert GRIEVE 1924– Painter, printmaker, collagist and teacher, mainly of abstract work containing an allusive interplay of colour and images. He said: "I don't think you should get everything out of a painting at one glance. You should be able to come back to it and see other connections." Chinese album paintings were an influence. Bob Grieve studied lithography with Henry Trivick at Regent Street Polytechnic School of Art, 1953–5, and at Swinburne Technical College, Melbourne, 1956–8. He made several study trips to Japan in the 1960s and to the Soviet Union and Cuba in the 1980s. He won a series of awards over 25 years from 1959 and taught graphic art widely in Victoria, being president of the Print Council of Australia, 1973–8. While in England, Grieve took part in the first Australian Artists' Association exhibition at the RWS gallery in Conduit Street in 1953. Other notable group shows included Tokyo Print Biennial from 1960; Contemporary Australian Printmakers, Tokyo and New York, 1984; and Australian Artists at Landell Galleries, California, 1987. Later solo shows included a series at Holdsworth Galleries, Sydney, from 1985, and David Ellis, Melbourne, from 1987. Australian National Gallery in Canberra and many other Australian public collections hold examples.

Chris GRIFFIN 1945– Figurative and abstract artist in various media, born in Maes-y-cwmmer, Mid-Glamorgan, who studied fine art at Gloucestershire College of Art in Cheltenham and at Royal College of Art. He was a freelance artist then from 1977, showing at RA Summer Exhibition, Riverside Gallery in Crickhowell and at 1993 Wales Art Fair, Cardiff. Rural and industrial scenes of south Wales were a speciality.

Ella GRIFFIN 1898–1953 Painter and teacher. Studied at Chelsea School of Art, 1915–20, where she later taught. Exhibited extensively, including RA, SWA, ROI, NEAC and elsewhere. Lived in London.

Frederick GRIFFIN 1906– Artist and designer, born in Nottingham, who studied at the local School of Art with the sculptor Joseph Else. Griffin did a wide range of commercial work, including British Railways, British Overseas Airways Corporation and shipping firms. He was a member of SGA, ROI and NS from 1970–6. Showed RA, RSA, LG, RSMA and elsewhere. Lived in London.

Peter GRIFFIN 1947– Painter and teacher, born in Wakefield, Yorkshire. He went to an elementary school and then worked as guillotine operator for a printer's. He had always wanted to be a painter, and when he saw a newspaper item that it was possible to study art without formal qualifications he applied and did foundation studies at Wakefield School of Art, 1970–1. Was then at Loughborough College of Art, 1971–4, and Royal College of Art, 1974–7. Gained Rome Scholarship in Painting to British School in Rome, 1977–9. Rome became a major influence on his work. From 1979–83 was lecturer at Canterbury College of Art, then during 1980s taught at many art schools as a visiting tutor. After being artist-in-residence at Patrick Allan-Fraser School of Art, Hospitalfield, Arbroath, in 1987 and similarly at Cyprus College of Art, Paphos, 1989–90, Griffin taught at West Surrey College of Art part-time. From 1974, when he showed with West Riding Artists, Griffin was in many group shows, being a prizewinner in the 1982 Spirit of London Exhibition at Festival Hall. Had a solo show in Wakefield in 1974; later solo shows included Angela Flowers Gallery, 1986; Gallery Gloria, Nicosia, 1991; and Austin/Desmond Fine Art, 1991. Griffin's work, which had a jokey, Surrealistic element, was based on personal themes, such as the Icarus, Man and Dog and Ram Series. He believed in "pushing paint to the point of destruction, and then starting all over again".

Edward Hales GRIFFITH 1909–1982 Painter and teacher, born in Birkenhead, Cheshire, who attended Birkenhead School, Liverpool College of Art, 1926–9, then the Royal College of Art, 1930–3. He did part-time teaching at Laird School of Art and St Anselm's Secondary School, Birkenhead, 1934–9; Alsop Grammar School, Liverpool, 1940–1; was in the Army as a gunner-signaller, 1941–7; then taught at Liverpool College of Art from 1947 for over 20 years. In the late 1970s, after retirement, he returned to the College to paint in the life room. Griffith was a member of the Liverpool Academy of Arts. He also exhibited in Watercolours, Gouaches and Drawings by Liverpool Artists, at Bluecoat Chambers, 1950. Finally moved with his daughter to live in the Sudbury area of Suffolk. Walker Art Gallery, Liverpool, and the Museum of Liverpool Life have works by him.

Hanmer GRIFFITH 1880–1969 Painter of landscapes, born Monmouth. Retired there having been an estate agent in Ystradgynlais, Breconshire. He showed with SWG and Wye Valley Art Society and had several solo exhibitions in Ross-on-Wye. His illustrations for W J Smart's *Where Wye and Severn Flow*, of 1949, typify his interest in the landscape of this border area, where he died at Skenfrith.

Lillian E A GRIFFITH 1877– Sculptor, painter, miniaturist and teacher, born at Abersychan, Monmouthshire. She studied at Wimbledon School of Art, the Slade School of Fine Art and Westminster School of Art, her teachers including Alfred Drury. Exhibited for many years at RA, Walker Art Gallery in Liverpool and at Paris Salon. National Museum of Wales, Cardiff, holds marble and bronze panels by her, notably Bindie, the head of a boy, to which she was much attached. For several years she held art classes for Glamorgan County Council and taught miniature painting at Swansea School of Art. Lived at Hengoed, Glamorgan.

Andrew GRIFFITHS 1956– Sculptor – notably a stone carver – and teacher, who did a foundation course at Wrexham College of Art, 1974–5, then gained an honours degree in fine art sculpture at Central School of Art & Design, 1983–6. He studied bronze casting with Ab Abercrombie and did two years' life drawing with Cecil Collins. Griffiths' work experience included assisting the sculptors Barry Flanagan, Bill Woodrow and Liliane Lijn and the printmaker Norman Ackroyd; working in the A&A Sculpture-Casting Foundry; and teaching at Slade School of Fine Art. From 1994 Griffiths was lecturer in sculpture at Carmarthen College of Art & Technology. Commissions included bronze figures for a Tokyo theatre park, 1992. Took part in many mixed shows, with a solo exhibition at Swansea Botanical Gardens, 1995. Had a studio at Llangennech, Dyfed.

Anthony GRIFFITHS 1960– Artist, born in Oxford, who studied at Bournville School of Art and Craft, 1978–80, and at Bath Academy of Art in Corsham. Among his mixed shows was The Self Portrait: a Modern View, which toured from Artsite Gallery, Bath, 1987, in which Griffiths showed work in limewood. He had had a first solo show in the city the year before.

Barbara GRIFFITHS fl. from mid-1970s– Painter and teacher, notably a landscape watercolourist, who graduated with honours at Maidstone College of Art, 1973–6. She taught watercolour painting at adult education centres in Kent. Among her exhibitions were RE, 1976; Drew Gallery, Canterbury, 1982; Newbury Spring Festival, 1985; and three-man show at Woodlands Art Gallery, 1989.

David GRIFFITHS 1939– Painter, teacher and gallery owner, born in Liverpool. After attending Pwllheli Grammar School he went to the Slade School of Fine Art, 1957–61, then taught art in Birmingham for several years in the 1960s. In the latter part of the 1960s he opened the David Griffiths Gallery in Cardiff, later the Albany, and organised Pwllheli Art Gallery during the summer. Did some television work. He was well-known as a portrait artist, completing a lot of public commissions, including Bertrand Russell for University College, Swansea, and Lord Hailsham for the House of Lords. Liverpool University and Eton College also hold his work.

Glyn GRIFFITHS 1926– Painter, graphic designer and teacher, born in Treorchy, Glamorgan, but brought up in Cardiff, where he attended the School of Art, 1942–5. After Naval service he returned to Cardiff College of Art, 1948–50, then began a series of teaching appointments. From 1958–66 he lectured in graphic design at Birmingham College of Art, although he later farmed in west Wales and lived in Huntingdon, teaching part time while painting. Participated in many group shows, including SEA, SWG, University of Birmingham and WAC. CASW bought his picture Landscape of an Industrial Town.

Hugh GRIFFITHS 1916– Painter who was born in Karachi. Was educated at Canford School and the Dragon School, Oxford. Showed at RA, RBA and NEAC. Lived at Winchelsea and later St Leonards-on-Sea, Sussex.

Mary GRIFFITHS 1956– Painter and draughtsman who studied at Dyfed College of Art, 1974–5, then Croydon College of Art, 1975–8, her teachers including John Bellany, Bruce McLean and Gus Cummins. She was artist-in-residence at Oast Room Gallery, The Malting House, Cambridge, 1992. Prizes included Lady Evershed Drawing Prize – Eastern Open, 1988, and was highly commended – Britain's Painters, 1991. Mixed show appearances included Eastern Open from 1987; New Gallery, Swansea, 1990; Three Painters at Bow House Gallery, Barnet, 1991; and BP Portrait Award, at National Portrait Gallery, 1992. After a solo show at ADC Theatre, Cambridge, 1987, later ones included St John's Gallery in Bury St Edmunds, 1991, and Chappel Galleries, Chappel, 1993. Strong figurative work was a notable feature of Griffiths' output.

Michael GRIFFITHS 1951– Printmaker, draughtsman, painter and teacher, born in London. He studied fine art for his degree at Brighton Polytechnic, doing a postgraduate course in printmaking there. Went on to teach at Winchester School of Art and Southampton Institute of Higher Education. From 1976 Griffiths was represented in many group shows in Europe and America, including the Varna Print Biennale in Bulgaria, the First International Miniature Print Biennale in Britain and the Cleveland International Drawing Biennale. In 1990 he shared a three-man show at Woodlands Art Gallery. Had over a dozen solo shows in Britain. From 1981 was a member of the Printmakers' Council. His work was in many public and private collections throughout the world. Lived in Hampshire, where he had his own printmaking studio.

Tom GRIFFITHS fl. from 1930s– Painter, draughtsman, illuminator and teacher, educated in Norwich, where he continued to live. He attended the School of Art there, where he lectured, 1942–9, also studying at Heatherley's School of Fine Art, Grosvenor School of Modern Art and privately with Bernard Adams. Griffiths was chairman of Norfolk and Norwich Art Circle on several occasions, also president from 1983. *The County War Memorial Book of Remembrance*, in Norwich Cathedral, was among his many illuminated vellums. He showed at RA, NS and elsewhere.

Ronald Edwin GRIGG 1917– Painter and commercial artist involved in the advertising industry, born in Wells, Somerset. Studied at Leicester College of Art, 1934–7. Exhibited at the public gallery in Leicester and the Sketch Club and Society of Artists there, to both of which he belonged. The local corporation bought his work. Lived in Leicester.

John GRIGSBY 1940– Printmaker and painter, born in Staffordshire, who studied at Stoke-on-Trent and Leicester Colleges of Art. Showed with RE of which he became a member in 1978, RA, RWS, RWA, LG, in the provinces and abroad. National Museum of Wales in Cardiff, Graves Art Gallery in Sheffield and other public collections hold examples. Lived in Beckenham, Kent.

Winsor GRIMES 1928–1996 Artist, designer, draughtsman and teacher, born in Pontypool, Monmouthshire, who described himself as "A child of the 30s Depression – although showing talent as an artist, I started work on the coalface at the age of 14. Later I went to work in a Nylon spinning factory, where I started on the shop floor, but became works artist." Grimes' pictures reflected working people's hard lives. He gained his adult teacher's certificate at Newport College of Technology, but continued in industry in south Wales. His first show of paintings was in Risca in 1972; during following years he exhibited widely in Wales, London and abroad; then shared a show with Helen Lush at the Old Library Gallery, Cardiff, in 1995. An enthusiastic, infectious teacher, he taught in England and Wales, and was finally based in Abergavenny, Monmouthshire.

Stanley GRIMM 1891–1966 Painter, born in London, but studied in Riga, Russia, and in Munich just prior to World War I. After being a prisoner of war in Germany came to live in England, settling in London. As well as showing widely abroad, Grimm exhibited extensively in England, including RA, Redfern Gallery, ROI, Goupil Gallery, Leicester Galleries and Gallery Edward Harvane. Member of Chelsea Arts Club where Adrian Bury remembered him as a giant of aristocratic appearance, "hospitable in the extreme". Served in Royal Navy in World War II, using his expert knowledge of Russian.

William GRIMMOND 1884–1952 Painter, designer and illustrator, born in Manchester. He attended the School of Art there. Exhibited widely, including RA, NEAC, Fine Art Society, RI and RBA. Manchester City Art Gallery holds his work. Was a member of the Art Workers' Guild. Lived at Rowledge, near Farnham, Surrey. While in Manchester Grimmond was a member of the Unnamed Society, director Frank Sladen Smith, other artist members being Lilian Reburn and Eric Newton.

Tom GRIMSEY 1960– Sculptor who was born in London. He studied at Wimbledon School of Art, 1979–82, then St Martin's School of Art, 1982–3. Exhibitions included Spacex Gallery Exeter, from 1979; Contemporary Sculpture at Hounslow Sculpture Park from 1980; Woodlands Art Gallery in Have You Seen Sculpture from the Body?, in 1983; and Bath Contemporary Art Fair in 1992. Grimsey worked in steel, modern and Indian dance movements sometimes being used as the basis for abstract pieces. Lived in London, then West Didsbury, Manchester.

Reginald GRIMSHAW 1910– Painter and teacher, born in Farsley, Yorkshire, married to the potter Gladys Grimshaw. Studied at Pudsey School of Art, 1927–30, Leeds College of Art, 1930–1, then Royal College of Art, where his teachers included Ernest Tristram. He taught at schools of art in Maidstone and Cheltenham from mid-1930s, for many years being head of Oxford School of Art. Showed at RA, RBA and elsewhere. Lived in Noke, Oxfordshire.

Trevor GRIMSHAW 1947– Painter and draughtsman who was notable for depicting industrial Lancashire, born in Hyde, Cheshire. He studied at Stockport College of Art. Showed at RA, RSA, RCamA, MAFA and in 1973 in Saddleworth Art Group exhibition at Woodlands Art Gallery. His solo shows included Colin Jellicoe Gallery, Manchester.

Alan GRIMWOOD 1949– Sculptor in various materials and teacher who attended Kingston School of Art, 1969–71. He held a number of part-time teaching posts, including Harrow School of Art, Essex and Brunel Universities. Had a solo show at Sunderland Arts Centre in 1982. Arts Council holds a selection of stylised figurative works by Grimwood, who has Large Rabbit and Figure in a Pond, both 1980, in the Grizedale Forest collection, Cumbria.

Antony Gibbons GRINLING 1896–1982 Sculptor and businessman, educated at Harrow School, 1910–14, where he showed an aptitude for art under W Egerton Hine. He was the son of Gibbons Grinling, a director of the wine merchants Gilbey. Served with the Hertfordshire Regiment in World War I, in which he was commissioned, wounded and won the Military Cross; in World War II he rose to lieutenant-colonel with the same regiment. Grinling convalesced in Taormina, Sicily, 1919–20, where he studied sculpture, then made his career, 1921–61, with Gilbey's, becoming a managing director. As a sculptor he often worked with Serge Chermayeff. Commissions included garden statues for Queen Mary's Dolls' House at Windsor, a relief for the Cambridge Theatre and a room of sculpture and furniture for Whiteley's store. Had a solo show at Tooth's in 1934, also exhibiting at RA, Upper Grosvenor, Leicester and Worthing Art Galleries, signing work with initials. Grinling's figurative sculptures could be both tender and exuberant, as in the Fine Art Society's 1986 exhibition Sculpture In Britain Between the Wars. Grinling was also a perceptive collector. A small bronze figure group by Henry Moore bought in the early 1950s for £50 sold at Phillips in 1995 for £124,700. Lived at Dyrham, near Chippenham, Wiltshire.

John GRINSTEAD 1920–1987 Painter, designer, calligrapher and teacher, born in Leeds, Yorkshire, full name Edgar John Grinstead. After attending Wakefield Cathedral School he was at Wakefield College of Art, Central School of Arts and Crafts, 1946, then Royal College of Art, 1950. Became senior lecturer at Kingston upon Thames Polytechnic. Showed RA, RUA and in the provinces and had a number of presentations made to members of the royal family. Lived in East Molesey, Surrey.

Michael GROARKE 1943– Designer and painter, born in Manchester. He attended Calico Printers' Association Design School, Manchester Polytechnic and Rochdale College of Art and showed with RA, RCamA, RWS and elsewhere. Lived in Marple, Cheshire.

Michael GROGAN 1947– Painter, printmaker and illustrator, born in Lyndhurst, Hampshire. After basic navigational training he attended Winchester College of Art, 1967–8; Liverpool College of Art, 1968–71; and Royal College of Art, 1971–4, also studying for a short time in Paris. Did some illustrative work for Sutton Hoo treasure catalogue in British Museum. Had one-man show at Gallery 273 at Queen Mary College and at Jordan Gallery. Lived in London and Totton, Hampshire.

Jon GROOM 1953– Painter with an interest in sculpture, and teacher, born in Powys. Studied at Cardiff College of Art, 1971–2 and 1974–6, Sheffield Polytechnic, 1972–3, and Chelsea School of Art, 1976–7. Groom's abstract pictures carefully balanced the volumes of each unit in a work. He was meticulous about surface. He was included in John Moores Liverpool Exhibition, 1987, and in the South Bank Centre's 1988–9 survey The Presence of Painting. His first solo show was at Riverside Studios, 1978. Other exhibitions included Rochdale Art Gallery, 1983, Ruth Siegel Gallery in New York, 1985, and Nicola Jacobs Gallery, 1986. For some years he was fellow in painting at Gloucester College of Art and Design, Cheltenham. Arts Council holds his work.

Jean GROSE 1926– Painter, born in Cambridge, who studied at Royal College of Art and in Italy. Showed SEA, WIAC and NEAC. Taught bookbinding at Hammersmith School of Art and lived in London.

Anthony GROSS 1905–1984 Painter, illustrator, creator of animated cartoons, watercolourist and outstanding etcher. Born in London, Gross studied at the Slade School of Fine Art, at the Académie Julien, Paris, under Pierre Laurens, at the École des Beaux-Arts and in Madrid. Had his first one-man show at the Leicester Galleries in 1934, after which he had several dozen one-man shows in Britain and abroad. The Victoria and Albert Museum gave him a major retrospective in 1968. He also took part in many mixed exhibitions, including the RA, being elected a Royal Academician in 1980. Galleries holding his work include the Tate, British Museum, Victoria & Albert Museum and the Imperial War Museum. Was an official war artist in World War II in the Middle East, India and Europe. By then he had married his French artist wife Marcelle (Daisy) Florenty, had travelled extensively in North Africa and Europe and had worked on animated cartoons, such as *La Joie de Vivre*, *The Fox Hunt*, for

Alexander Korda, and *Round the World in Eighty Days*. Book illustrations included *The Forsyte Saga* and *Six Idylls of Theocritus*. Taught at the Central School of Arts and Crafts and at the Slade. Worked extensively in France, having bought a house at Le Boulvé in 1955. Wrote an authoritative book on *Etching, Engraving and Intaglio Printing*. Lived in London.

Richard Oliver GROSS 1882–1964 Sculptor in marble and bronze, born at Barrow-in-Furness, Lancashire. Studied at Camberwell School of Arts and Crafts under Albert Toft. Exhibited RA. Went to live in Auckland, New Zealand, where he carried out a large volume of public sculpture. Was elected a fellow of the RBS, 1948.

Athalie GROSVENOR fl. from late 1930s– Sculptor and painter, born in Beaconsfield, Buckinghamshire, as Stella Athalie Henderson. She was educated in Hampstead, north London, where she settled, studying at Slade School of Fine Art with Randolph Schwabe and A H Gerrard. Became a member of RBS and Hampstead Artists' Council, also exhibiting at RA. Had a solo show at Foyles Gallery in 1968.

Martin GROVER 1962– Painter, born in Carshalton Beeches, Surrey. He studied at Croydon School of Art, 1980–1, Trent Polytechnic, Nottingham, 1981–4, and Royal Academy Schools, 1984–7. Grover's detailed, stylized figurative paintings can have a strong atmosphere of surreality and tension. His picture The Wait, the first in a series based on observations made while working in a hospital, was included in John Moores Liverpool Exhibition, 1989–90, his acrylic on canvas Two Slightly Anxious Sisters winning a prize there, 1993–4. Showed solo with Merz Contemporary Art and lived in London.

John Michael GROVES 1932– Painter and draughtsman, born and lived in London. He attended Camberwell School of Arts and Crafts, 1953–7. Became a member of RSMA in 1977, also showing elsewhere in London.

Lavender GROVES 1932– Artist in oil, pen and ink and ceramics, born in Manchester. She attended Chelsea School of Art, gaining her diploma in 1954, teachers including Harold Sandys Williamson, Raymond Coxon and Frederick Brill. Groves worked the Upton Pottery with her husband Mark Beard. Animals, notably horses, as well as heraldry were among her subjects and she claimed to be "the only potter to do calligraphy on earthenware using my technique". Became a member of ROI in 1960, also exhibiting with RA and RBA. National Museum of Wales in Cardiff and City of Birmingham Museum & Art Gallery hold examples. Lived in Upton-on-Severn, Worcestershire.

Gerald GRUBB 1912–1994 Artist in oil, pastel and acrylic whose work covered a range of subjects. Born in Dublin, Ireland, he was educated at St Stephen's Green School, studying art at the Metropolitan College and RHA life class; Académie des Beaux-Arts in Brussels; and in London at Central School of Arts and Crafts and Anglo-French Art Centre. Became a member of Free Painters and Sculptors in 1986, its Loggia Gallery giving Grubb a memorial show in 1995. A self-effacing, prolific artist, Grubb showed widely elsewhere, including RA and Hampstead Artists' Council. Lived in London.

Pegi GRUFFYDD 1960– Painter and printmaker, born in Pwllheli, Caernarvonshire. She studied at Manchester Polytechnic, 1978–9, Wolverhampton Polytechnic, 1979–82, and Royal Academy Schools, 1983–6. She showed at RA Summer Exhibition, Royal National Eisteddfod, North Wales Open and elsewhere, having a solo exhibition at Theatre Gwynedd. Bangor. Lived at Chwilog, Gwynedd.

Cuthbert GRUNDY 1846–1946 Painter of landscapes and figure studies, Sir Cuthbert Grundy was educated at Victoria University, New South Wales, Australia. He is most remembered with his brother J R G Grundy as the donor of the Grundy Art Gallery, Blackpool. Cuthbert Grundy, author of works on chemistry and plant life, showed at leading London galleries. He was from 1913–33 president of RCamA and held senior positions in RWA, RBC and SWAS. He was represented in the centenary show of RCamA in 1982. Was knighted in 1919 and died in Blackpool.

Jim GRUNDY 1956– Painter, born in Leicester. He studied at the Polytechnic there, 1974–5, then Maidstone College of Art, 1975–8. Group exhibitions featuring his work included Artists from Space Studios at Norfolk House, 1982; Open Studios at Norfolk House, 1983–4; Ten Artists at South London Art Gallery, 1983; and he was in a show of four artists at Woodlands Art Gallery, 1984. Grundy had solo shows at Greenwich Theatre Gallery, 1981, and Maidstone College of Art, 1984. Photographs of figures from theatrical scenes formed the starting point for most of Grundy's pictures at Woodlands, an abstract composition developing from the original image. Kent County Council and Nuffield Foundation hold his work.

Mavis Wilson GRÜNEWALD 1931– Painter, draughtsman, printmaker and teacher, full name Eleanor Mavis Grünewald (Wilson was her maiden name), born in Stockton-on-Tees, County Durham. She studied at Middlesbrough School of Art, then Leeds College of Art; in the late 1950s she taught at Heginbottom Art School in Ashton-under-Lyne, Lancashire. Showed at Middlesbrough Art Gallery, Macclesfield Art Gallery and in Germany, where she settled in Frankfurt. Middlesbrough Town Council bought her work, which is also in German public collections.

Helen GRUNWALD 1925–1988 Painter, draughtsman, designer, artist employing glass and mirrors and teacher, born in Vienna, Austria. Educated in Vienna, she studied art at Beckenham School of Art, 1941–4, with Henry Carr, then with Carel Weight at Royal College of Art, 1949–52. Showed widely including AIA, the

Leger, Leicester and Berkeley Galleries, New Art Centre and in the provinces. Completed a mural at St Thomas's Canterbury. Music and architecture were leading themes in her work. Sometimes signed work hel or Helen. Lived in London.

Vaughan GRYLLS 1943– Creator of photo-collages and pun-sculptures, and teacher, born in Newark Nottinghamshire. The targets of his work included linguistic philosophy, the press, contemporary art, current events and international relations. He studied at Wolverhampton College of Art, 1964–7, under Roy Kitchin; Goldsmiths' College of Art, 1967–8; and Slade School of Fine Art, 1968–70, with Reg Butler, Phillip King and Richard Wollheim. Briefly from 1973 Nicholas Wegner and Grylls operated The Gallery in a Paddington back street, an offbeat alternative to the conventional commercial gallery system. Mixed exhibitions included Northern Young Contemporaries, Whitworth Art Gallery, Manchester, 1967; Whitechapel Open, 1978; and Photographers' Gallery from 1983. Had a first solo show at Wolverhampton Polytechnic, 1970. Grylls taught for several years in America and in 1989 was appointed the first professor and head of the school of art and design at Wolverhampton Polytechnic. An inaugural exhibition commemorating the appointment was held at Wolverhampton Art Gallery in 1989 (selected works 1964–89, catalogue containing complete works). His later solo shows included Herbert Read Gallery at Kent Institute of Art & Design, Canterbury, 1998, Grylls having been appointed the Institute's second director in 1996. University College London, WAC, Contemporary Art Society and other collections in Britain and abroad hold examples. Lived in London and at Westmarsh, Kent.

Beatrice Claudia GUERCIO: *see* **Beatrice Claudia FREEMAN**

Alan Douglas GUEST 1931– Artist, born and lived in Nottingham, who attended Mundella Grammar School, 1942–9, and was a chartered librarian, 1952–89, retiring early, having from 1974 been senior librarian, bibliographical services section, Nottinghamshire Public Libraries. Guest was taught art by his uncle, the painter Joseph Arthur Jackson, having begun painting as a schoolboy. During National Service in the Royal Air Force, 1949–51, drew and painted influenced by Aubrey Beardsley, Jean Cocteau and Paul Klee. Other influences on his strongly linear work were botany and Byzantine art. Guest also produced Surrealist collages, with his own texts, with Max Ernst an influence. For many years he studied printmaking, lecturing to library assistants on book production and illustration. In 1992 he wrote sections on colour woodcuts and lino-cuts and contributed to the biographical dictionary in *British Printmakers 1855–1955*, edited by Robin Garton. Was a member in 1960s and 1970s of Midland Group of Artists, also of SWE. Group shows included England & Co from 1989; Leicester Collection for Schools and Colleges, annual exhibition, from 1990; Nottingham Castle Museum, Box Art, 1993; Woods Art Gallery, Leicester, 1994; and in 1997 Body Parts at David Holmes Contemporary Art Peterborough, and Derby City Open Art Competition.

Alvaro GUEVARA 1894–1951 Painter, born in Valparaiso, Chile. Although he began painting when small, it was only when he spent two years in Bradford, having travelled to England in 1908 to join the cloth trade, that he began studying art at the College of Art. Then studied at Slade School of Fine Art, 1912–16, winning a scholarship in 1914. Became associated with Roger Fry and the Omega Workshops and began to show with NEAC of which he was a member, and elsewhere. In the mid-1920s he spent several years back in Chile, painting and boxing at championship level, then had a show of his Chilean pictures at Leicester Galleries in 1926. Married the painter Meraud Guinness in 1929 and went to live in France, concentrating on imaginary portraits and landscapes. His portrait of Edith Sitwell, in Tate Gallery collection, is one of his finest works. Showed in Paris at Galerie Mouradian in 1938. Died in Aix-en-Provence.

Meraud GUEVARA 1904–1993 Painter, often of bizarre, Surrealist pictures, born in London as Meraud Michael (a name used to sign pictures) Guinness into a wealthy family. She was a 1920s bright young thing who married the Chilean artist Alvaro Guevara in 1929, having a long and stormy relationship with him. She studied at Slade School of Fine Art under Henry Tonks intermittently, 1923–7. Had a solo show in Paris in 1928, her teacher there being Francis Picabia. She was a member of a set including Christopher Wood, whom she almost married, Gertrude Stein, Nancy Cunard and Lord Berners. In 1940 she had a show at Valentine Gallery in New York. Winston Churchill owned Alvaro's portrait of Meraud. After Alvaro died in 1951 Meraud supervised his estate and arranged for his writings to be published and memorial shows to be held. She resumed painting with enthusiasm. Died in Paris.

Derrick GUILD 1963– Artist born in Perth who studied at Duncan of Jordanstone College of Art in Dundee, 1982–7, and at Art Institute of Chicago, 1984. He was in The New Generation at Compass Gallery, Glasgow, 1986, in Figuration to a Degree at Paton Gallery, 1993, and in Paton Gallery at *The Economist*, 1994. Paton gave Guild a solo show later that year/early 1995, work which "though its expression is streaked with Christian symbolism" was "a vision of a pre-Fall world whose creatures of land, sea and air are undiminished by guilt". Among Guild's other solo shows was Choice Bread at Paton Gallery in 1997, stemming from the artist's winning The Villiers David Award in 1995 which "enabled me to experience Spanish painting and culture at first hand during a critical stage in the development of my work." Dundee City Art Gallery, Scottish Arts Council and several corporate collections hold examples.

Harriet GUINNESS 1970– Painter, born and lived in London, who studied at Chelsea College of Art, 1989–92, and Royal Academy Schools, 1992–5. Showed with LG, 1993, and in RA

Summer Exhibition from that year and had an oil on canvas titled Block in 1995–6 John Moores Liverpool Exhibition.

Lindy GUINNESS 1941– Painter who took up painting in 1961 after meeting Duncan Grant, who became a close friend. She studied at Chelsea School of Art and with Oskar Kokoschka in Salzburg. In 1964 married Lord Dufferin. Worked for *Harper's and Queen* as a journalist and photographer, then at ICA before becoming a full-time artist in 1969, with added studies at Slade School of Fine Art. She travelled in India, Italy and Greece and showed in London and Ireland. Solo exhibitions included Gallery Edward Harvane, 1975; Eyre and Hobhouse Ltd, 1979; The Maclean Gallery, 1981; and The Solomon Gallery, Dublin, 1983. Lived in London and Clandeboye, County Down, Northern Ireland.

Thomas Gladstone Middleton GUISE 1916–1984 Painter in various media, born in Davidston, Ross and Cromarty. He was by profession a process engraver and printer. Studied at Edinburgh College of Art, 1947–9, with Adam Bruce Thomson. Over 35 years Guise worked in many styles, completing landscapes, figure studies and abstracts which have a strong poetic quality. He favoured watercolour and Pointillism. Showed in many group exhibitions including RSA, RSW, RBA, NEAC, SSA and with Free Painters and Sculptors. Solo shows from 1966 included Randolph Gallery, Edinburgh Festival; Stanford University, California, and also in America at Los Robles Gallery, Palo Alto; the Ian Clarkson and the Abacus Gallery, Edinburgh; and Sally Port Gallery, Berwick-upon-Tweed. Work widely held internationally in private collections. Lived in Edinburgh.

GUITTI: *see* **Guitti BARRATT-DENYER**

Alan GUMMERSON 1928– Artist and teacher who attended Bradford and Leeds Colleges of Art. While teaching at Leeds College, in 1964 took part in The Teaching Image staff exhibition at Leeds City Art Gallery, showing oils and constructions. Solo exhibitions included Wakefield, Lane Gallery Bradford and New Vision Centre. Latterly lived at Blackshaw Head, Hebden Bridge, Yorkshire.

Margaret GUMUCHIAN 1927– Painter, printmaker and teacher, born in Manchester of Armenian parents. While studying at Manchester Regional College of Art met her future husband, the artist Ian Grant, who was teaching there. She went on to teach art at grammar schools in Manchester and Stockport, Cheshire, where she settled. Gumuchian was a member of MAFA, also showing at RBA, with Northern Young Artists and widely in the north of England. In 1988 she was the outright winner in the northwest Laing Competition. Salford Art Gallery holds her work.

Gordon GUNN 1916– Artist in watercolour, ink and charcoal. Born in Glasgow, Gunn studied art at Glasgow School of Art for five years in the late 1930s under Ian Fleming and Sir William O Hutchison. Gunn went on to exhibit widely in Britain and abroad, venues including RA, RSMA, RI, RBA, the Glasgow Institute of the Fine Arts as well as galleries in Bermuda and Germany. Aberdeen Art Gallery, the Corporation Art Gallery in Harrogate and Leamington Spa Art Gallery hold his work, among others. In 1978 Gunn had a retrospective at Woodlands Art Gallery which in addition to his wide-ranging landscapes included a series of cosmic pictures executed between 1953–74 "concerned with the Universe as a background to our activities". Latterly he had studios in Blackheath, London, and Arisaig, Scotland.

James GUNN 1893–1964 Painter of portraits and landscapes. Herbert James Gunn was born in Glasgow, studied at the School of Art there, then at Edinburgh College of Art and Académie Julian, Paris. Exhibited RA, RSA, Fine Art Society, RP, Cooling Galleries and Goupil Gallery. Awarded gold medal at Paris Salon, 1939; elected president of RP, 1953; elected RA, 1961; knighted, 1963. Although known as a portrait painter, having painted a state portrait of HM The Queen in 1953–4, Gunn was also a brilliant painter of figures and scenes in sunlight and action, in the manner of Lavery, Peploe and the French Impressionists. The National Portrait Gallery holds his work. Lived in London, where he was a member of many notable clubs, such as the Athenaeum, Chelsea Arts and Garrick. Scottish National Portrait Gallery held a retrospective, 1994–5.

James Thomson GUNN 1932– Painter and designer, born in Gorebridge, Midlothian, settling nearby at Dalkeith, where he attended the High School. Gunn studied at Edinburgh College of Art, 1950–6, teachers including William Gillies and Robin Philipson. He obtained a travelling scholarship, 1954–6, which took him extensively through Europe. A versatile artist, Gunn showed at RSA, RSW of which he was a member, SSA, RI and elsewhere, having several solo exhibitions. In 1985 he gained the Highland Society of London Award, RSA. Argyll Education Committee holds his work.

William Archibald GUNN 1877– Painter in watercolour and pastel of landscapes and townscapes. After initial education in Hereford he attended Glasgow School of Art, 1897–1901. Exhibited Walker Art Gallery, Liverpool, and in other northern provincial cities. Graves Art Gallery, Sheffield, holds a view of the city by him. Lived in St Ives, Cornwall.

James GUNNELL 1947– Watercolourist, notable for his flower pictures, born in Surrey. He attended West Surrey College of Art and Design, 1969–73, and Royal Academy Schools, 1973–6, winning the David Murray Prize for Landscape Painting, 1972–4. In 1974 he showed with Young Contemporaries; was a frequent exhibitor with RA; showed at Beaux Arts Gallery, Bath; Towner Art Gallery, Eastbourne; and Gardner Arts Centre, Brighton. From 1986 had regular solo shows at Thackeray Gallery. In 1992 he was commissioned to provide the illustrations for British Gas (Southern)'s corporate calendar.

Beatrice GUNTHORP fl. c.1925–1965 Portrait painter, born in Rhyl, Flintshire, who studied at Royal Academy Schools. She married the artist Cecil Gunthorp. Exhibited at RA Summer Exhibition from 1926–65 and lived in London.

Cecil GUNTHORP fl. from mid-1920s–1983 Sculptor, married to the portrait painter Beatrice Gunthorp. He was born in London, having a studio in the south at Balham. Studied at City and Guilds of London Institute and at Royal College of Art. Was a member of Art Workers' Guild from 1930 and showed at RA.

Kit GUNTON 1900–1980 Artist in oil, watercolour, lino-cut, scraperboard and other media who spent most of her life in Bristol. After attending Culverhay School, Keynsham, she studied at Bristol School of Design, under John Fisher, 1916–18, then Bristol College of Art, 1918–21, with R E J Bush. From 1920–79 she was a prolific exhibitor at RWA, being made an associate in 1972. Also showed at SWA. In 1938 *Birdsworth*, with a text by the Bristol writer and artist Donald Hughes, was published, including several dozen lino-cuts of birds by Gunton, who operated from the Pelican Studio in Whiteladies Road. Bristol City Art Gallery, Bristol Corporation Schools Loan Collection and RWA hold examples of Miss Gunton's work. By 1976 she had moved to Bournemouth, where she died.

George GURR 1911–1978 Landscape and coastal painter mainly in watercolour. Studied at Leicester College of Art, 1932–7, under Ralph Middleton Todd. Showed with NEAC and for many years with Leicester Society of Artists, of which he was a member. He was the son of another local painter, Albert Gurr, who worked in watercolour until he died aged 101.

Herbert GURSCHNER 1901–1975 Painter, printmaker and theatrical designer, born in Innsbruck, Austria. He studied there, in Vienna and for several years with Franz von Stuck at Munich Academy, also having private tuition with Egger Lienz. Gurschner showed extensively between the wars at Cooling Gallery, had his first solo show at Fine Art Society in 1929, also exhibiting widely on the continent and in America. He lived in England from 1932, serving in the British Army in World War II, becoming a British subject in 1946. Designed for a number of stage plays. Tate Gallery holds his work.

Graham GUSSIN 1960– Artist born and living in London, who gained his master's degree at Chelsea School of Art, 1989–90. Group exhibitions included New British Sculpture, Chisenhale Gallery, 1987; Installation Work, Chrome Factory, 1988; New Identities, Camden Arts Centre, 1989; Five British Artists, Thomas Backhaus Gallery, Düsseldorf, Germany, 1991; Angles Gallery, Los Angeles, America, 1992; Landscape Paintings, Transmission Gallery, Glasgow, 1993; and Video Positive 97, Fall (100–1), Cornerhouse, Manchester, 1997. Solo shows included Primo Piano, Rome, and Chisenhale Gallery, both 1993, and in 1998 an installation at the Tate Gallery, in which Gussin's preoccupation with the nature of space was evident.

Derek GUTHRIE 1936– Painter, born in Liverpool, who studied at the West of England Art College, Bristol, 1953–6, and L'Académie de Feu, Paris. Simplified pictures of ships and the sea were a feature of his work, which was shown in a series of solo exhibitions at Portal Gallery. Guthrie lived in Brittany, Spain and Cornwall, where he settled at Newlyn, near Penzance. He said that: "A painter has a relationship with the place where he has chosen to live, and this should be a vital part of his painting."

James GUTHRIE 1874–1952 Painter, illustrator, designer, printer and writer, born in Glasgow, father of the artist Robin Guthrie. While working in the family metal business studied part-time at Heatherley's School of Fine art and at the British Museum. In 1895 founded *The Elf* magazine and four years later the Pear Tree Press. He published his own books, being responsible for all the processes. His own graphic work is sometimes experimental, often intense in feeling. Exhibited IS, Baillie Gallery, RA, RSA and at the Barcelona International Exhibition, winning a gold medal. His own books include *An Album of Drawings* and *The Proportional System of Typographical Composition*. Lived at Flansham, Sussex.

Jane Gordon GUTHRIE 1927– Painter, born in Farningham, Kent. She studied at Sidcup Art School, 1944–6; Goldsmiths' College School of Art, 1946–7; the Royal College of Art, 1947–50, teachers including Leonard Appelbee, Ruskin Spear and Carel Weight; then in 1959 with Oskar Kokoschka. Showed at RA, RP and NEAC and had several solo exhibitions. Lived in Boxley, Kent.

Kathleen GUTHRIE 1905–1981 Painter in oil and opaque watercolour, silkscreen printer, textile designer and mural painter. Writer of children's books. Born in Feltham, Middlesex. Studied at the Slade School under Henry Tonks and at the Royal Academy Schools. Married the artist Robin Guthrie in 1927 and after divorce the constructivist painter Cecil Stephenson in 1941. Early work is signed K Maltby, her maiden name. At the Slade was influenced by Stanley Spencer's The Nativity, then in the late 1920s by the French Impressionists and her husband's more conventional, Augustus John-like style. With Robin Guthrie went to Boston in 1931 for two years, where he was invited with Rodney Burn to become a co-director of the School of Fine Art. One-man show by Kathleen Guthrie, of figure paintings and landscapes, at Boston's Stace Horne Gallery, in 1932. Her style was further modified when she married Stephenson and associated with the avant-garde of Hampstead. Completed a mural for a local welfare centre. In 1948 had one-man show at Wolf Mankowitz's Little Gallery, in 1951 at the Crane Gallery in Manchester. Began to move from pictures with a whimsical, poetic feeling towards pure abstracts. Retrospective at Drian Gallery in 1966. She illustrated successful children's books, *The Magic Button* and *Magic Button to the Moon*, which contain short poems by her. Lived in London.

Robin GUTHRIE 1902–1971 Painter, draughtsman, illustrator and teacher, born in Harting, Sussex. He was the son of the artist and printer James Guthrie and the husband of the artist Kathleen Guthrie, after divorce from her marrying Deborah Dering. Studied at Slade School of Fine Art, 1918–22, with Philip Wilson Steer and Henry Tonks; Guthrie was like Tonks a fine, sensitive draughtsman, especially of portraits. In the early 1930s he was with Rodney Burn joint director of painting and drawing at the School of the Museum of Fine Arts in Boston, in America; with Burn and Stephen Bone he had his first show at the Goupil Gallery in 1926. Also exhibited at NEAC of which he was a member, Leicester Galleries, Arthur Tooth and Sons, Tate Gallery and many other venues. The Tate, British Museum, Victoria & Albert Museum, National Portrait Gallery and other public institutions hold his work. Guthrie also taught at St Martin's School of Art, City and Guilds School and Royal College of Art, 1950–2. His book illustrations include Eleanor Farjeon's *All the Way to Alfriston*, 1919, and his father's *A Wild Garden*, 1924. Lived in London.

GUY 1956– Self-taught artist in acrylic notable for exuberantly coloured flower still lifes, born and worked in London, full name Guy Stocker. His work was widely reproduced in greetings cards, calendars and posters. Group shows included Contemporary Fine Art Gallery, Eton; Liberty; Images, Zebra 1; and St Albans and York Arts Fairs. Had a series of solo exhibitions at Charlotte Lampard Gallery from 1988 and at Greencroft Gallery from 1989.

Alexander GUY 1962– Painter and teacher, born in St Andrews, Fife. He studied at Duncan of Jordanstone College of Art in Dundee, 1980–4, then Royal College of Art, 1985–7. From 1987 he taught part-time at Glasgow School of Art. Guy won many awards, including first prizes at Diadem Centenary, Scotland, and Scottish Young Contemporaries, both 1984; an Elizabeth Greenshields Foundation Award, 1985, with a second Award in 1987; and a prize in the 1993–4 John Moores Liverpool Exhibition for his spiked bed canvas, "one of a series I have done about pain and punishment, worry and guilt." Showed solo at Paton Gallery from 1989 and lived in London. Unilever, Robert Fleming & Company and Scottish Arts Council hold examples.

Edna GUY 1897– Watercolour painter, born in Sutton, Surrey. She studied art in South Africa with John Amschewitz in 1920, then at Académie Julian, Paris, 1921–2, at the Spenlove School with Reginald Eves, 1934–5, and at the Slade School of Fine Art, 1936, under Randolph Schwabe. Exhibited RA, SWA, RI, Paris Salon and widely abroad. Member of RWS. Lived in London.

Louella GWILLIM 1950– Painter and teacher, who studied at City and Guilds of London Art School, 1975–8. Went on to teach for Ravensbourne and Hammersmith and North Kensington Adult Education Institutes. Appeared at RA Summer Exhibition, Whitechapel Open, Camden Open, Royal Over-Seas League and in 1985 was included in Figurative Painters at Woodlands Art Gallery. Lived in London.

Elis GWYN: *see* **Elis Gwyn JONES**

Allan GWYNNE-JONES 1892–1982 Painter in oil and watercolour, etcher, illuminator and decorator whose landscapes, still lifes and portraits gain their effect with a quiet, understated charm. Born in Richmond, Surrey, Gwynne-Jones went to Bedales, then was articled to study law. In 1913 exhibited a picture on silk at the NEAC, with which he continued to show for many years. Served with distinction in World War I, then attended the Slade School 1919–22, his studies having been interrupted in 1914. Won several first prizes. Became professor of painting at the Royal College of Art in 1923, about the time he began to hold one-man shows. Resigned to join the Slade staff in 1930, staying there until 1959. During World War II he also taught part-time at the fine art department, University of Reading. Was married to the artist Rosemary Allan, their daughter being the painter Emily Gwynne-Jones. Exhibited regularly at the RA from 1950, elected RA in 1965. Wrote several books, including *Portrait Painters* and *Introduction to Still-Life*. Gwynne-Jones' work is in many public collections in Britain, including the Tate Gallery and Ashmolean Museum, as well as abroad. Memorial exhibition in 1982 at National Museum of Wales, Cardiff. Lived at Eastleach Turville, Gloucestershire.

Emily GWYNNE-JONES 1948– Painter, daughter of the artists Allan Gwynne-Jones and Rosemary Allan and married to the painter Frank Beanland. Between 1965–6 she studied at the Royal Academy Schools, with travel on the continent, then at the Royal College of Art, under Carel Weight, 1967–70, working in Paris in 1968. She won a British Council Travelling Scholarship to Budapest, Hungary, in 1971; worked on costumes for English National Opera, 1973–5; then studied at North-East London Polytechnic and etching with Norman Ackroyd and textiles at Central School of Arts and Crafts, 1977–8. Showed from mid-1960s at RA Summer Exhibitions, also at NEAC and New Grafton Gallery and was a member of the Contemporary Portrait Society. Had solo shows with Michael Parkin Gallery in 1977, King Street Gallery in 1983 and Heveningham Hall, 1993. RA, Eton College and Paintings in Hospitals hold examples. Lived in Fressingfield, Suffolk.

Pauline GYLES 1931– Watercolourist with no formal art school training who specialised in miniature portraits, still lifes and flowers. She was born in Dorset, where she settled in Poole. After leaving school she hand-coloured photographic portraits to a high standard, then began miniatures around 1970. She was a founder-member of the Society of Botanical Artists, also belonging to RMS and the Hilliard Society. Also exhibited with Medici and Llewellyn Alexander Galleries and with Linda

Blackstone Gallery in Pinner. Russell-Cotes Art Gallery and Museum in Bournemouth and the Society of Apothecaries hold examples. Her work appeared in the RMS' *100 Years of Miniatures*, by Suzanne Lucas; *How to Paint Miniatures*, by Robert Hughes; and *The Techniques of Painting Miniatures*, by Sue Burton.

H

H: *see* **Kathleen Finlay HORSMAN**

Liam H: *see* **Liam HANLEY**

Norman Douglas H: *see* **Norman Douglas HUTCHINSON**

Vivien H: *see* **Vivien HISLOP**

Alfred HACKNEY 1926– Printmaker, painter and teacher, born in Stainforth, Yorkshire, brother of the artist Arthur Hackney. He studied at Burslem School of Art in Stoke-on-Trent, then Edinburgh College, with a travelling scholarship to France and Italy. He was a visiting teacher at Willesden School of Art, then senior lecturer at Medway College of Art in Rochester. Was a member of RWS and an associate of RE, also showing with RA, SEA, LG and SSA. RA holds his work. Lived in Cobham, Kent.

Arthur HACKNEY 1925– Painter, etcher and teacher, older brother of the artist Alfred Hackney, born in Stainforth, Yorkshire. He was an apprentice engraver in the Potteries, studying with Reginald Haggar at Burslem School of Art, Stoke-on-Trent, then Royal College of Art with Robert Austin, winning a travelling scholarship. Went on to be head of department at West Surrey College of Art and Design, Farnham, 1950–86. He was a member of RWS, being vice-president, 1973–6, and of RE, also showing at RA and widely elsewhere in Britain and abroad. Victoria & Albert Museum, Ashmolean Museum in Oxford and many other collections hold examples. Lived in Tongham, Farnham, Surrey.

Charles HADCOCK 1965– Sculptor, born in Derby, who trained at Gloucestershire College of Arts and Technology, 1984–7, then the Royal College of Art, 1987–9. Residencies included Hurricane Sculpture, London Borough of Ealing, 1987–8, and Millfield School, Street, 1997. Group shows included Uley Arts Centre, Gloucestershire, 1987; New Art Centre Sculpture Garden, Roche Court, Salisbury, 1989; and Lewes Sculpture Trail, Lewes, 1997. Later solo exhibitions included Reed's Wharf Gallery, 1996, and University of Essex, 1997. Hadcock made two types of sculpture: casts of polystyrene packaging, and large metal constructions (such as his 10-ton, cast-iron Caesura IV, in 16 sections, installed at Goodwood Sculpture Park, in 1995, rather like a yet-to-be-finished piece of architecture on which the viewer could speculate). Public and corporate commissions included Brighton and Hove Council, Imperial Chemical Industries, British Airports Authority Gatwick Airport and Allied Domecq. Lived and worked in London.

Vincent HADDELSEY fl. from 1960s– Self-taught horse painter, brought up in a small village south of Lincoln where learned to ride and hunt. Haddelsey left England aged 18 for British Columbia, and extensive travels through the continent, Mexico, Asia and Inner Mongolia followed. He broadened his equestrian knowledge and began to paint what he saw. In 1995 Rona Gallery gave him his first solo show in England for over a decade. Collingbourne Fine Arts issued signed, limited-edition prints, some in a period setting. HM The Queen, the Mellon Collection of Sporting Art in America and a number of English museums hold examples. Haddelsey latterly spent much time in France.

Aldridge HADDOCK 1931–1996 Self-taught artist in mixed media, full name Edwin Aldridge Haddock, known as Fin and born in Durham. He attended the University there graduating as a bachelor of medicine and of surgery in 1953, gaining a diploma in obstetrics from the Royal College of Obstetricians and Gynaecologists in 1955. He was house surgeon and house physician at a number of hospitals in Newcastle and Middlesbrough. Haddock was a member of Lincolnshire Artists' Society and Free Painters and Sculptors. He had several dozen solo shows, including Ferens Art Gallery, Hull; Graves Art Gallery, Sheffield; Woodstock Gallery; Drian Galleries; and Century Galleries in Henley-on-Thames. Public galleries in Hull, Doncaster and Newcastle hold examples. Lived in Grimsby, Lincolnshire.

John HADDOCK 1934– Professionally an interior designer who painted. Studied furniture design at Birmingham College of Art, in 1963 being elected a member of the Society of Industrial Artists and Designers, later The Chartered Society of Designers. Began painting in 1972 at Eltham Institute Art Centre. Showed at RA Summer Exhibitions, Tudor Barn Art Gallery in Eltham and had two four-man exhibitions: at Greenwich Theatre Gallery and in 1985 at Woodlands Art Gallery. Painted still life and landscapes widely in England and France. Lived in London.

John Marshall HADDOCK 1914–1963 Painter, illustrator and commercial artist, son of the painter J M Haddock. Studied at Regent Street Polytechnic School of Art, where he concentrated on architectural work, also at Putney School of Art, 1933–8, with Adrian Hill and Francis Hodge. Showed at RA and RBA and did magazine illustration. Sometimes signed work J M H. Lived in London.

Susan HADLEY 1940– Sculptor, painter, draughtsman and teacher, born in Redhill, Surrey, great grand-daughter of the

Danish painter Vilhelm Marstrand. From 1959–60 she studied at Lycée Français de Londres, a bilingual secretarial course in French and German, then in 1982–6 at West Sussex Institute, where she gained a first-class honours degree in art and design. Hadley spent half the year teaching (which included West Dean College, 1991–4), half on her own work. This reflected "all aspects of life, and the Christian content comes naturally from my human experience." Recurrent themes included vulnerability, arms and relationships. In 1993, the BBC Television programme *Glimpses of God* centred on her sculpture. Hadley was included in John Plowman's 1995 book *The Encyclopedia of Sculpting Techniques*. She was a member of the Art Centre Group. Lived in Chichester, Sussex, where she opened her house and garden during its annual Festivities. Mixed shows included Regnum Club, Chichester, and Terrace Gallery, Worthing, both 1988; Goodwood House, Goodwood, 1990; Eastgate Gallery, Chichester, from 1991; Mark Jerram Gallery, Salisbury, 1995; and Thompson's Gallery, from 1996. Had solo exhibitions at Pallant House, Chichester, 1987–8.

Karl HAGEDORN 1889–1969 Painter, commercial artist, designer of fabrics and teacher, born in Berlin. After initial education in Germany Hagedorn settled in England in 1905, training in textile production. He attended Manchester School of Technology and the city's School of Art, Slade School of Fine Art and in Paris, 1912–3, where he was in the school run by Maurice Denis. The Cubist and Futurist influences acquired in Paris profoundly affected Hagedorn's work as shown in the Society of Modern Painters, Manchester, 1913–6; the impact of his pictures in a provincial city, before his work became more conventional, was covered in Manchester's First Modernist Karl Hagedorn 1889–1969 at Whitworth Art Gallery, Manchester, 1994, and Chris Beetles Ltd, 1995. Hagedorn became naturalised at the outbreak of World War I, during which he served in the Army, producing war pictures. He showed widely in Paris and was a member of Salon d'Automne, was honorary treasurer of the RBA and showed at Fine Art Society, AAA, NEAC, RI and elsewhere. Did commercial work for Empire Marketing Board, Shell and *Radio Times*. Taught part-time at Epsom School of Art. British Museum, Victoria & Albert Museum and Manchester City Art Gallery hold examples. Lived at Lower Feltham in Middlesex and in London. A Hagedorn Trust exists to enhance his reputation.

Arthur T HAGG 1895– Painter and designer. Studied at Norwich School of Art, 1912, then at the Westminster School of Art under Walter Bayes and Bernard Meninsky. Taught for some years in Sussex. Exhibited RA, RI, NEAC and RBA. Lived in London.

Reginald George HAGGAR 1905–1988 Painter, pottery designer and writer, illustrator and teacher, born in Ipswich, Suffolk. Aged 12 he became a delivery boy for a florist's, then was at local Art School, 1922–6, followed by Royal College of Art, to which he won a Royal Exhibition and where he was taught by Reco Capey. Joined Mintons Ltd in 1929 and soon became art director, but left in 1935, miffed at resistance to his efforts to improve designs. He became head of Stoke School of Art until 1941, holding a similar position at Burslem School of Art until 1945, when he became a freelance painter, writer on pottery and porcelain and lecturer. His books on *Lane Delph*, *Staffordshire Chimney Ornaments*, *English Country Pottery* and his two *Encyclopaedias of English and Continental Pottery and Porcelain* were scholarly and readable. Showed RA, RWA, RSA and elsewhere and was from the mid-1940s for over 30 years president of the Society of Staffordshire Artists. He lived in Stoke-on-Trent where the City Museum and Art Gallery, in common with galleries in Ipswich and Dudley, holds his work.

Brian HAGGER 1935– Painter in oil and watercolour, draughtsman in pencil and teacher, born in Bury St Edmunds, Suffolk. He studied at Ipswich School of Art, 1952–6, then Royal College of Art, 1958–61, teachers including Colin Moss, Pif Fortin, Carel Weight, Ruskin Spear and Ceri Richards. Numerous mixed shows included RA Summer Exhibition, Phoenix Gallery in Lavenham and Highgate and with Norwich Twenty Group. Had a series of solo shows at Bramante Gallery, 1968–71; Thackeray Gallery, 1972–5; and Langton Gallery, 1976. Between leaving College and 1976 Hagger produced around 350 marvellously evocative paintings of London, mainly of Fulham and the unfashionable end of King's Road, Chelsea. He also painted Brighton, Norwich and the East Coast. In the mid-1990s, seeking a new theme, Hagger was concentrating mainly on drawing. Did occasional teaching, including Salisbury College of Art, and Great Yarmouth College of Art and Design, including adult education. Bolton Art Gallery holds his work. Lived latterly in Norwich, Norfolk.

John HAGGIS 1897–1968 Portrait, landscape and figure painter in oil and watercolour, black-and-white artist and etcher. Born in London, Haggis studied art in Australia and at Royal College of Art under Malcolm Osborne. Showed widely, including Walker's Galleries, RA, RP, NEAC, RCamA, RWA and Paris Salon. His work is in Australian and British provincial museums. He was official portrait painter to the British studio Gainsborough Pictures, travelling as far afield as Barbados to complete portraits. These included Fredric March, Mai Zetterling and Claire Bloom. Painted many landscapes in Britain, especially in Yorkshire and Hertfordshire, where he lived at Welwyn. In 1921 he founded the Welwyn Garden City Art Club.

Philip HAGREEN 1890–1988 Wood engraver, painter, ivory carver, letter-cutter and cartoonist born into a family of artists. He studied as a painter in Cornwall with Norman Garstin, Harold and Laura Knight, then at New Cross Art School, joining the Army in World War I. After the war Hagreen assembled artists who formed SWE in 1920. In early 1920s settled in Ditchling, Sussex, and joined the Guild of St Joseph and St Dominic, with Eric Gill learning letter-cutting and helping complete the Stations of the Cross for St Cuthbert's in Bradford. For 15 years from 1934 contributed amusing cartoons for *The Cross and The Plough*, the magazine of the Catholic Land Federation. Retired from Guild in 1957, in later years being bedridden.

Jonathan HAGUE 1938– Artist and teacher, born in Llandudno, Caernarvonshire. He attended Liverpool College of Art, 1957–63, then Royal Academy of Fine Art, The Hague, 1964–6. He was a part-time lecturer at Coventry College of Art, then a lecturer at Birmingham College of Art. Showed at RA, Redfern Gallery and widely in the Netherlands, which had granted him a State Scholarship. Had a solo show at Orez International Gallery, The Hague, in 1964, others including Royal Institute Gallery, 1967. Lived in Leamington Spa, Warwickshire.

Sheila HAGUE 1920– Painter, illustrator and cartoonist who was brought up in Sussex. She attended Wimbledon School of Art under Gerald Cooper and Robert Barnes, then the Royal College of Art with Gilbert Spencer and Percy Horton. Exhibited RA and AIA. Lived in London.

Ghulam HAIDER: *see* **YUNUS**

George Douglas, The Earl HAIG 1918– Painter, born in London, son of Field-Marshal Earl Haig whom he succeeded in 1928. After education at Stowe School and Oxford University, Earl Haig served in the Army in World War II, being a prisoner of war in Italy and Germany. In 1945–7 he attended Camberwell School of Arts and Crafts, his teachers including William Johnstone and Claude Rogers; during the holidays he studied with Paul Maze. From 1945 Lord Haig had a series of one-man shows over several decades at the Scottish Gallery, Edinburgh, as well as showing widely elsewhere in Britain and on the continent, latterly including Clarges Gallery and Gallery 10, London. Scottish Gallery gave him a seventieth birthday show in 1988. His work is in the collections of HM The Queen and other members of the royal family, Scottish National Gallery of Modern Art and further public collections. Lord Haig was a member of the Scottish Arts Council and of the Royal Fine Art Commission for Scotland and a trustee of the National Galleries of Scotland. As a landscape painter he was fond of simple, almost naive images infused with a rich palette. Lived in Bemersyde, Melrose, Scotland.

Alfred Grenfell HAIGH 1870–1963 Painter in oil and watercolour, born in Parkgate, Cheshire. He studied art in Paris, then started to paint professionally at the age of 30. Haigh was a keen horseman and favoured hunting and racing subjects. He did not exhibit but had a number of patrons, including HRH The Aga Khan, the Duke of Portland and Lord Rosebery. Made several painting trips to America. The Duke of Northumberland has Haigh's portrait of the ninth Duke, painted in 1933. Was included in The British Sporting Art Trust's 1983 show at Alpine Gallery.

Peter HAIGH 1914–1994 Painter in oil and draughtsman, born near Huddersfield, Yorkshire, and brought up on his uncle's farm. He sold his first painting aged 15; trained as a textile sample dyer, which gave him an early understanding of colour, tone and shape; then travelled the country, sketching and painting. After seven years in the Army in World War II, mostly in the Far East, Haigh – who always insisted that he was self-taught – between 1946–9 attended Heatherley's School of Art under Iain Macnab and Goldsmiths' School of Art, where John Mansbridge and Bernard Hailstone taught and where Haigh met his future wife, Patricia, who became a commercial artist. At the start of the 1950s, following his work being shown at Wildenstein, Haigh was financed to work in France for six months by a Shell oil executive and collector. Between 1949–55 Haigh's pictures were included in mixed exhibitions at RBA, NS, UA, at Roland, Browse and Delbanco and at the Beaux Arts, Zwemmer, Leicester and Redfern Galleries, but then he withdrew from showing, keen to develop in his own way. His early pictures were in the spirit of Walter Sickert, whose work with that of Augustus John he much admired, but gradually he moved towards geometrical abstraction, commonly in a muted palette. Haigh was a meticulous craftsman, noting when he last worked on a picture and could safely return to it, and utilising all available time from morning light until four in the afternoon. To survive he did a variety of clerical jobs, worked as a barman and learned framing and gilding with the firm of Savage before setting up on his own for several years until pressure on painting time made the business impracticable. In 1988 The Pride Gallery put on a retrospective, another show being held at Ambiente Gero, Galeria de Arte, in Valencia, 1991. Lived in London and died in Chelsea and Westminster Hospital.

Richard Neville HAILE 1895– Portrait painter and photographer, born in London. Educated at St Mark's College, Chelsea; Chelsea Polytechnic; and Regent Street Polytechnic School of Art. Exhibited RA, London Salon, PS and in a number of photographic shows. On several occasions he was president of the Institute of British Photographers. Lived in Bognor Regis, Sussex.

Sam HAILE 1909–1948 Artist, potter and teacher. Went to evening classes at Clapham School of Art, winning a scholarship to Royal College of Art, 1931–5, initially concentrating on painting, then on pottery under the potter William Staite Murray. During the late 1930s Haile showed with Surrealist Group and AIA. From 1939–44 he lived in New York, but served with British Army towards end of World War II. In 1946 he joined the Rural Industries Bureau as its pottery consultant, but was killed in a motoring accident two years later. Haile's pictures mixed strong themes, including concern at the threat of Fascism, sexuality and violence. Review exhibitions of his work were held at Crafts Centre in 1951, Birch and Conran, 1987, and Holburne Museum, Bath, 1993.

Bernard HAILSTONE 1910–1987 Portrait painter, brother of the artist Harold Hailstone. After education at the Judd School, Tonbridge, Hailstone attended Goldsmiths' College School of Art, under Clive Gardiner, then the Royal Academy Schools, with James Bateman and Walter Westley Russell. At the outbreak of World War II Hailstone joined the Auxiliary Fire Service, drew his comrades and Blitz scenes and held an exhibition at the RA. In

1941 he was asked to become an official war artist, initially attached to the Ministry of Transport. Later he painted convoys in the Atlantic and Mediterranean, then in 1944 joined South-East Asia Command, painting Lord Louis Mountbatten and key members of his staff, pictures now in Imperial War Museum. A gregarious, outgoing man, Hailstone went on to paint Sir Winston Churchill, Lord Olivier, Paul Mellon – he worked a lot in America – and members of the royal family, but he as happily painted ordinary members of the public. Also exhibited LG, RBA and NEAC. Lived at Hadlow, near Tonbridge, Kent.

Harold HAILSTONE 1897–1982 Illustrator and cartoonist in watercolour, black-and-white and oil. Born in London, studied at Goldsmiths' College School of Art. During World War II served in the Royal Air Force as an official artist and exhibited with the War Artists. The Imperial War Museum holds his work. Illustrated widely for magazines such as *Punch*, *Illustrated London News*, *Passing Show* and *Tatler*. Brother of the artist Bernard Hailstone. Lived at Hadlow, near Tonbridge, Kent.

June HAINAULT fl. from 1950s– Painter and printmaker who studied at Regent Street Polytechnic School of Art and at Heatherley's School of Fine Art, teachers including Iain Macnab and Frederic Whiting. Was a member of Free Painters and Sculptors, also of Eastbourne Group, and had a number of solo exhibitions, including Il Traghetto Gallery in Venice, 1966; New Town Gallery, Uckfield, from 1969; Upper Street Gallery, from 1972; and Hanover Galleries, Liverpool, 1986. Lived in Five Ashes, Sussex.

Lett HAINES 1894–1978 Artist in various media and teacher, correct name Arthur Lett-Haines. Was educated at St Paul's School and served in the Army in World War I. He was early a member of an artistic set including E McKnight Kauffer, John Middleton Murry and D H Lawrence. Lett Haines was always an experimental artist whose work had a strong linear element and who admitted a big debt to Picasso. In 1918 he met the painter Cedric Morris and they lived together for 60 years as lovers, although it was sometimes a stormy partnership. A less consistent painter than Morris, Haines chose to take over the running of the East Anglian School of Painting and Drawing household. As a teacher Haines believed in giving students freedom to develop along independent lines. There was a retrospective at Redfern Gallery, 1984.

Tony HAINES 1959– Painter, born in Harborough Magna, Leicestershire. He attended Loughborough College of Art and Design, 1977–8, then Ravensbourne College of Art and Design, 1979–82. Among his exhibitions were Stowells Trophy, RA, 1982; Deptford Artists Group Show, 1984; New Moon Group Show, Woodlands Art Gallery, from 1986; and Showroom Gallery. A gestural abstract painter.

George HAINSWORTH 1937– Painter in a rich palette, sculptor and teacher, born in Leeds, Yorkshire. He attended Leeds College of Art, 1955–60, then Slade School of Fine Art, 1960–2, under William Coldstream. In the following year he gained a Gulbenkian Scholarship in Sculpture at British School, Rome, 1962–3. Hainsworth taught fine art at Leeds College of Art, 1963–70, joining the staff of Leeds Polytechnic in 1970, eventually becoming senior lecturer in the centre for art and contemporary studies at Leeds Metropolitan University. Hainsworth took part in numerous mixed exhibitions. Had a solo show at Sue Rankin Gallery, 1991. Worked non-figuratively for many years, then resumed representational subjects, flowers, mythology and politics being recurrent themes. He was a member of MM Arts Group and the Yorkshire Sculptors' Group. Baring Capital Investors and Provident Financial Group owned examples. Hainsworth's wife Lucy was also an artist and they lived at Hunsingore, near Wetherby, Yorkshire.

Lucy Mary HAINSWORTH 1935– Sculptor, draughtsman and printmaker; teacher, born in Johannesburg, South Africa. She studied at Bromley College of Art, 1955–9, and Slade School of Fine Art, 1959–62, teachers including Frank Auerbach. In 1971 she gained her graduate certificate of education. Was a visiting tutor at Leeds Metropolitan University and other colleges. The figure in movement, the northern industrial landscape and political issues, such as Apartheid, were featured in her work. She was a member of Yorkshire Sculptors' Group and St Paul's Printmakers, Mirfield. In 1990 Hainsworth had a residency at Cartwright Hall, Bradford. Took part in many mixed shows, sharing some with her husband George, including Doncaster City Art Gallery, 1995. Solo shows included Cookridge Street Gallery, Leeds, 1989, and Imperial Chemical Industries Works, Huddersfield, 1992. Provident Financial Group and Eastthorpe Gallery, Mirfield, hold examples. Lived at Hunsingore, near Wetherby, Yorkshire.

Guy Donne Gordon HAKE 1887–1964 Architect and architectural painter and draughtsman. Studied at L'École des Beaux-Arts, Geneva, and at the Architectural Association School, London. Exhibited RA, RWA and Bristol City Art Gallery, which bought drawings by him of wartime bomb damage. Wrote on architectural draughtsmanship. He became principal of RWA School of Architecture for 30 years from 1922. Lived at Honiton, Devon.

Leslie HAKIM DOWEK 1960– Artist born in Beirut, Lebanon, who moved to Britain in 1976. She studied at Camden Arts Centre, Central School of Art, Camberwell School of Arts and Crafts, Slade School of Fine Art and Norwich School of Art. She showed in groups at RA, Edward Totah Gallery, Whitechapel Open, Royal Over-Seas League Annual Exhibition, where she won a joint first prize, and at England & Co's Art in Boxes, 1991. The vulnerability of Nature and its decline were a feature of her assemblages. She showed solo at Spacex Gallery, Exeter, in 1989, and Manchester City Art Gallery, 1991 Lived in London.

Elsie HALE 1913– Artist in oil and watercolour, a member of the Hilliard Society of Miniaturists. She was born in Worcester and studied at the College of Art there, 1929–33. At Paris Salon she gained a gold medal in 1978, also showing at RA and elsewhere in London and the provinces. Lived in Salisbury, Wiltshire.

Helen HALE 1936– Painter and sculptor, born in Harpenden, Hertfordshire. She studied at St Martin's and Sir John Cass Schools of Art. Was a member of Hampstead Artists' Council, Free Painters and Sculptors, NS, WIAC, ROI and SWA, also exhibiting in Scotland and France. Lived in Hampstead, north London, later in Rudgwick, Sussex.

Irina HALE 1932– Artist and teacher, half Russian, half Irish, who had an English childhood. Left school aged 11 and lived for six years with her mother in France, portrait painting for a living. Between 1951–4 studied at Bath Academy of Art, Corsham, and travelled on scholarships. Spent the next two years teaching art to children. From 1957–61 she lived in a mountain village near Rome and travelled. After painting for three summers under Kokoschka in Salzburg Hale gained the City of Salzburg Prize, moved to Paris, then back to Italy. Took part in mixed shows at Leicester and Mercury Galleries; Richard Demarco Gallery in Edinburgh; and with WIAC. Solo shows included Crane Kalman Gallery, 1966, and Hambledon Gallery, Blandford, 1968.

John Howard HALE 1863–1955 Painter of portraits and landscapes, born at Farnham, Surrey. Studied at Farnham School of Art, South Kensington Schools and Westminster School of Art under Fred Brown. Studies continued in Holland, where he concentrated on nineteenth-century Dutch art, and he also studied landscape painting with George Boyle. He was for many years head of Blackheath School of Art. Exhibited RA, RBA especially, ROI, Paris Salon, provincial galleries and in Canada. Lived at Farnham, Surrey.

Kathleen HALE 1898– Painter, printmaker, writer and illustrator, born at Broughton, Peeblesshire. Studied at Manchester School of Art, Reading University with Allen Seaby, 1915–17, the Central School of Arts and Crafts, 1928–30, with Bernard Meninsky, and the East Anglian School of Painting and Drawing, 1938, with Cedric Morris. Although she exhibited NEAC, LG, RBA, Leicester and Lefevre Galleries and elsewhere, Hale is most noted for her work for the printed page. After a variety of jobs she gained a reputation as a poster and book artist, then for her series of around 20 books featuring Orlando, the Marmalade Cat, the first appearing just before World War II. Widely travelled in several continents. Retrospective at The Gekoski Gallery, 1995.

Sydney HALE 1907– Portrait painter in oil, pastel and pen and ink. Studied under Bernard Fleetwood-Walker at Birmingham College of Arts and Crafts, then went on to teach life and portrait drawing and painting at Birmingham College of Art and Coventry School of Art. Had one-man shows in the West Midlands area, as well as exhibiting in mixed shows at the RA, LG, RBA and RBSA. Lived at West Bromwich, West Midlands.

Gordon HALES 1916– Artist in oil, watercolour and pastel, born in Matlock, Derbyshire. He studied at Leicester College of Art and Northampton School of Art. Hales' favourite subjects were "ships and the sea, the Thames, men at work, the streets of London, the half light". He was a member of RSMA, an associate of RBA, a member of the Langham Sketch Club, Wapping Group of Artists and the Artists' Society and a founder-member of the London Muster of Artists. Also showed at PS and elsewhere. Lived in Watford, Hertfordshire.

Adrian HALL 1943– Sculptor and teacher, born in Cornwall, whose uncompromising and witty output made use of materials as diverse as badges, light bulbs, vacuum cleaners and symbols such as the swastika. Hall attended Plymouth College of Art, 1959–63, and Royal College of Art, 1964–7. He gained several scholarships and was at Yale University in America, 1967–9, then held a series of teaching appointments in Los Angeles in California, Auckland in New Zealand and Ulster College, Belfast, where he became principal lecturer in sculpture in 1973. Two years later Arts Council of Northern Ireland granted him a commission for a land sculpture, Northern Ireland Housing Executive, Kilcooley Estate, Bangor. His many shows included Arnolfini Gallery in Bristol, Young Contemporaries at Tate Gallery, Project Gallery in Dublin and Pinacotheca, Melbourne, in Australia.

Arthur Henderson HALL 1906– Painter in oil and watercolour, printmaker and illustrator. Born at Sedgefield, County Durham, Hall studied art at Accrington and Coventry Schools of Art, the Royal College of Art and at the British School in Rome. Obtained Prix de Rome for engraving in 1931. Exhibitions included RA, Leicester Galleries, RWS, LG and RE. Hall went on to become head of the school of graphic design at Kingston School of Art. He illustrated several books on gardening and children's educational books. Work bought by the British Museum and Cambridge University. Lived at East Molesey, Surrey.

A H Morgan HALL 1900–1984 Painter, born in Cardiff. After attending grammar school he worked for most of the 1920s and 1930s in his father's gallery while studying painting, in the late 1930s working in an architect's office. For 25 years from 1939 he worked for the Ministry of Works, on retirement in 1965 painting full-time. He was a leading figure in SWG and WSW, showing at RA, NEAC, RBA, WAC and elsewhere in group exhibitions. In 1971 shared a show with William Selwyn at Albany Gallery, Cardiff. WAC and University College of Wales, Aberystwyth, hold his work.

Christopher HALL 1930– Painter in oil, born in Slaugham, Sussex. He was noted for his precise, colourful depictions of the town of Recanati, in the Marche region of Italy, which he visited regularly. Hall attended Slade School of Fine Art, gaining his diploma in 1954. In 1957 a picture of his was the frontispiece of Jack Beddington's book *Young Artists of Promise*. Hall was made a member of RBA in 1988, also exhibiting at National Library of

Wales, Aberystwyth, the Stafford and Reading Art Galleries and at Jackson Gallery, Delaware. Arthur Jeffress, Portal and New Grafton Galleries gave Hall solo shows, and he had one of Italian pictures in 1992 at Waterman Fine Art. Arts Council, Museum of London and National Library of Wales hold examples. Lived in Newbury, Berkshire.

Clifford HALL 1904–1973 Painter in oil and watercolour, draughtsman and etcher. Born in London, Hall early in the 1920s began to study at Richmond Art School, then Putney Art School. At the Royal Academy Schools, in 1926–7, was influenced especially by Walter Sickert, and much of Hall's work bears the stamp of Sickert's palette and subject-matter: landscapes, genre scenes and London low life. In the late-1920s he lived in Paris, studying with André Lhote. Had a one-man show at the Beaux Arts Gallery in the mid-1930s, then served with a stretcher party during much of World War II. In 1946 he had the first of a number of one-man exhibitions at Roland, Browse and Delbanco, and his monograph on *Constantin Guys* was published. Making a living in bohemian Chelsea was often a struggle for Hall, who recorded his experiences in an unpublished journal covering 50 years from the 1920s. In the late 1960s he began a new series of pictures: women wrapped in towels, mysterious with unseen faces. His work is in many public collections in Britain, including the Imperial War Museum, Victoria & Albert Museum, and Arts Council, and abroad. Memorial exhibition at Belgrave Gallery in 1977, studio sale at Christie's, London, 1982. Hall latterly married one of his students at Regent Street Polytechnic School of Art, Ann Hewson, and they lived in London.

David HALL 1937– Sculptor and teacher, born in Leicester. Hall attended Leicester College of Art, 1954–60, then Royal College of Art, 1960–4, studying with Bernard Meadows. In 1964 he won the Young Contemporaries Kasmin Prize, in 1965 the Prix des Jeunes Artistes and Prix de la Ville de Paris, IV Biennale de Paris. He gained a number of awards and grants from the Arts Council, British Council and British Film Institute. In 1972 Hall became head of mixed-media activities at Maidstone College of Art's department of fine art. Hall was an extensive exhibitor, showing in Young Contemporaries in 1961 and 1964; at Richard Feigen Gallery, New York, in 1966, and Sculpture in the Open Air, Battersea Park, the same year; at ICA in 1972; and in the Royal College of Art's 1980 exhibition Bernard Meadows at the Royal College of Art 1960–1980. Arts Council holds examples of Hall's abstract works in welded steel, polyurethane and laminboard.

Edward HALL 1922–1991 Painter, especially of official portraits in oil, born in Barwell, Leicestershire. Studied at Wimbledon School of Art and Slade School Fine Art. He went on to become honorary secretary of RP and became noted for portraits of Prince Rainier of Monaco, the Prince of Wales, the Duke of Gloucester and other military, clerical and civic dignitaries. Showed at RA, Agnew, NEAC and elsewhere. Lived in London.

Grahame HALL: *see* **Claude MUNCASTER**

Joseph HALL 1890– Painter and draughtsman, born in Thornaby-on-Tees, Yorkshire. Studied at Goldsmiths' College School of Art with Edmund Sullivan and Clive Gardiner. Showed at RA, RBA, RI and in the provinces, HRH The Duke of Edinburgh buying his work. Lived in Bromley, Kent.

Kenneth HALL 1913–1946 Painter, draughtsman and designer, born in Surrey, educated at Lancing College. For a time Hall studied agriculture, then began designing furniture with an interior design firm in London. In 1934 he showed a portfolio of his pictures to Lucy Wertheim, and although he had not exhibited before she soon gave him a show at Wertheim Gallery, where several important collectors acquired Hall's work. Became involved with Basil Rákóczí and his Society for Creative Psychology, where Hall met Juan Stoll and had the few lessons in art he ever had. In 1935 decided to paint full time and during the next few years travelled in Europe with Rákóczí and became aware of modern movements such as Surrealism. With advent of war, they settled in west of Ireland, then in 1940 moved to Dublin, reviving the Society and the White Stag Group, which they had begun in London, holding group and mixed shows with prominent Irish painters. Initially Hall was a landscape painter, but birds and fishes feature strongly in his later work. In 1945 Hall returned to London, showing with Redfern Gallery, but in a depressed state he committed suicide. Hall appears in Lucy Wertheim's book *Adventure in Art*, 1947, where his strongly outlined work is illustrated. European Modern Art had a retrospective show in 1991 in Dublin.

Nigel HALL 1943– Sculptor, draughtsman and teacher, born in Bristol, where he studied at West of England College of Art. In 1964–7 he attended Royal College of Art, having a first solo show at Galerie Givaudon, Paris, in the latter year. In 1967–9 a Harkness Fellowship enabled Hall to travel and work in America, Canada and Mexico. Hall's international exhibiting career now began to grow, and he settled to showing in England with Annely Juda Fine Art. From 1972–4 Hall taught at Royal College of Art, then became principal lecturer at Chelsea School of Art. Commissions included Peter Stuyvesant Sculpture Project, Sheffield, 1972. Hall was much concerned with spatial relationships and the interplay between exterior and interior forms in his work, as shown in the several examples held by Arts Council and in his retrospectives at Sunderland Art Centre and Warwick Arts Trust in 1980. Lived in London.

Oliver HALL 1869–1957 Painter and etcher, mainly of landscapes. Born in London, studied at Royal College of Art, 1887–90, also at Westminster and Lambeth Schools of Art in the evenings and privately with Daniel Williamson and W L Windus. Father of the painter Claude Muncaster. Hall travelled widely on the continent. Began exhibiting at RA in 1890, being elected RA in 1927 and Senior Academician in 1945. Also showed extensively at RWS, Fine Art Society, RE, Leicester Galleries and many other London venues, having his first one-man show at Dowdeswell Gallery, 1898. Represented in many public collections, including Tate Gallery, which holds his Avignon, Shap Moors and Vale of Festiniog. Hall's method of painting in oil was to complete a picture in the studio from watercolour studies done on the spot. Lived at Ulverston, Lancashire.

Patrick HALL 1906–1992 Watercolourist who early on made drypoints and etchings, born in York and educated at Sedbergh School. He attended York and Northampton Art Schools and while a teenager helped with the conservation of York Minster's windows. Worked in the family tanning business at New Earswick as a young man and when it broke up after World War II moved to London and took a studio full-time. Showed at RA, RSA, NEAC and Paris Salon. His many solo exhibitions included Waddington Galleries, Gilbert Parr Gallery, Marjorie Parr Gallery, Austen Hayes Gallery in York, Montpelier Studio and Thames Gallery, Windsor. Hall sketched the landscape of Europe, especially scenes with rivers, canals and buildings, returning to his home in Sellindge, Kent, to complete the final pictures. He said that he tried "to take watercolour to greater tonal values and richness". Imperial War Museum, Guildhall Art Gallery and many public galleries in the provinces and the National Galleries of Australia and New Zealand hold examples.

Pauline Sophie HALL 1918– Versatile printmaker, born in Birmingham. She studied at the University there and Oxford University, gaining a science degree including biology in 1938. Attended Michaelis School of Art in Cape Town, South Africa, 1955–60. Showed with RE and SWLA and in local exhibitions in aid of conservation such as The Dorset Naturalists' Trust, Dorset County Museum, 1982–3. Solo shows included Shakespeare Centre, Stratford-upon-Avon, 1984. Lived in Snitterfield, Warwickshire.

Sean HALL 1961– Abstract painter who gained an honours degree in fine art at Ravensbourne College of Art and Design, 1981–4. Appeared in mixed shows at RA Summer Exhibition from 1983; Whitechapel Open, at Whitechapel Art Gallery, from 1984; and Greenwich Theatre Gallery, 1987. Shared a four-man show at Woodlands Art Gallery, 1988. Lived in southeast London.

Sharon HALL 1954– Painter, born in Darlington, County Durham. She studied at Coventry Polytechnic and Slade School of Fine Art. In 1981 she gained a French Government Scholarship and worked in Paris for six months. Showed widely and was included in four-artist show at Woodlands Art Gallery, 1989. Lived in London.

Marilyn HALLAM 1947– Artist and teacher, born in Yorkshire. She studied painting, 1965–9, at University of Reading fine art department, gaining her master's degree there, 1970–2. In 1969 Hallam won a Boise Travelling Scholarship. Went on to lecture part-time at colleges including Reading University and Hull College of Higher Education. Exhibitions included Platform '72, in 1972, at Museum of Modern Art, Oxford; Spirit of London, at Royal Festival Hall, 1979–80; Hull Print Competition, at Ferens Art Gallery, Hull, 1980–1; and Painters + Sculptors from the Greenwich Studios, at Woodlands Art Gallery, 1981.

William HALLÉ 1912– Painter, notably of landscape in oil, born in Richmond, Surrey. His father was related to the Hallé who founded the orchestra, and his mother was a direct descendant of Sir Peter Lely, court painter to Charles II. Hallé decided to become a painter after looking at a book of reproductions in his public library, having gone to live in the East End of London aged 20, and attended evening classes at Bethnal Green Men's Institute. During war service in the Army he joined local art schools where he was stationed, after demobilisation continuing at Battersea Men's Institute and working at night as a telephonist. A visit to France during the war and later trips to South Africa, where he showed solo at Alder Gallery, Johannesburg, were important. Jack Beddington included Hallé in his 1957 book *Young Artists of Promise*. Hallé took part in mixed shows, showed one-man at Wildenstein several times and had a string of solo exhibitions at O'Hana Gallery, where he painted a patio mural. When it closed on the death of its owner Hallé "could not get another gallery to take me on"; he filled sketch-books, but did little painting for about 20 years. Revived interest in the mid-1990s prompted him to paint again, and he showed at Bartley Drey Gallery. Latterly lived in sheltered accommodation in southwest London. Public galleries in Hull and Bury hold examples.

Ellen Kathleen HALLETT 1899–1988 Painter, embroiderer, artist in various materials and teacher, born in Bristol, where she continued to work. She studied art at West of England College of Art in Bristol under Reginald Bush and went on to teach at Fairfield Grammar School. In 1921 she gained a Board of Education drawing certificate and in 1937 passed first-class in the City and Guilds of London Institute examination. Was a member of the Embroiderers' Guild and at the age of 75 spent over six months completing a fabric collage of Athelhampton House, at Dorchester. Showed at RA, RE, RCamA, SWA and extensively elsewhere. Cheshire County Training College bought her pencil drawing Moondaisies and Sorrel and Derbyshire Education Committee Museums Service her fabric collage Frozen Garden. Wrote *Blue Print and Dye Line* for schools.

Phyllis HALLETT 1926–1990 Artist and teacher, born in South Norwood, south London. She studied at Goldsmiths' College School of Art in the 1950s, influenced by Clive Gardiner and, especially, Betty Swanwick. Began teaching in Croydon, then in 1974 was appointed by the National Maritime Museum, in Greenwich where she finally lived, to run a children's centre, which became the Half-Deck Club; when she retired she was head of education at the Museum. While there she published and illustrated three books, *The White Galloper*, *Olly's Round* and

Jumping Cats. After retirement she resumed painting, in vivid and delicate colours, varied subjects such as gardens, cats and unusual objects which fascinated her.

Roger HALLETT 1929– Painter in oil and tempera, born in Bristol, who painted in different styles under his own name and as Gidleigh Prowz. He studied at the Slade School of Fine Art, 1954–7, his teachers including Tom Monnington, William Coldstream and Lucien Freud. From 1957–60 Hallett was a television designer in Australia, where he began to have one-man exhibitions, including Macquarie Gallery, Sydney; Gallery A and Farmer's Blaxland Gallery, in Melbourne; and at Broken Hill City Art Gallery. Also showed one-man in Paris and Bristol and in London at the AIA and Temple Galleries. London Sketch Club member. Hallett spent four years painting Hallett's Panorama, at the Thames Barrier Visitor Centre, which depicts Georgian Bath as seen from a hot air balloon. Lived in Twerton, Bath, and in Saliès de Bearn, Pyrenées Atlantiques, France.

Alan HALLIDAY 1952– Figurative and abstract artist and draughtsman. He was trained at the Courtauld Institute of Art, where he graduated, obtaining an Oxford University doctorate on English artists in Paris during the Napoleonic period. Halliday was notable for his spare drawings of the human figure; at the same time his paintings were eloquent and colourful. Halliday had a special affinity with the ballet and in a long association with the Royal Ballet had a number of shows at Royal Opera House, Covent Garden. Was a frequent exhibitor in mixed shows including CCA Galleries in London and Tokyo, Ebury Gallery, Clarendon Gallery, Music Theatre Gallery and Westbourne Gallery. Painted throughout the world. In 1987 formed and led the European Artists' Group at Frankfurt Festival, subsequently transferring to Los Angeles. Later one-man shows included Bruton Street Gallery, 1992.

Charlotte Mary Irvine HALLIDAY 1935– Topographical painter and illustrator, daughter of the artist Edward Halliday, born and lived in London. She studied at Royal Academy Schools, 1953–8. Her work was reproduced in books published by Hutchinson & Company and Ginn & Company. She was made a member of RBA in 1960, NEAC in 1961 and RWS in 1976, also showing with RSMA and elsewhere. A solo show at Sally Hunter Fine Art in 1998 celebrated Halliday's love of architecture.

Edward Irvine HALLIDAY 1902–1984 Painter in oil and watercolour mainly of portraits. Born in Liverpool, Halliday studied at the City School of Art there, in Paris at the Atelier Colarossi and at the Royal College of Art. He was awarded the Prix de Rome and worked at the British School there. Exhibited at RA, RBA, Paris Salon and RP, of which for a time he was president. His work is in the collections of HM The Queen, Walker Art Gallery, Liverpool, the Athenaeum Club, Wolverhampton Royal Hospital and Bootle Dyeworks. His work was reproduced in *The Studio*, *Illustrated London News* and *The Times* and he was interviewed by Stanley Casson for his book *Artists at Work*, published in 1933. In 1997, the University of Liverpool held an exhibition which concentrated on Halliday's efforts to popularise art between the wars. Halliday's daughter Charlotte was also an artist. He lived in London.

Irene HALLIDAY 1931– Painter and teacher, born in Kingsmuir, Angus. After Arbroath High School she attended Duncan of Jordanstone College of Art, Dundee, 1948–53, teachers including Alberto Morrocco. Went on to lecture at Didsbury College of Education in Manchester. Was elected to RSW in 1955, also showing at RA and Royal Glasgow Institute of the Fine Arts. Had several dozen solo exhibitions in north of England, Scotland and America. Public galleries in Bolton, Dundee, Salford and elsewhere hold examples. Lived in Arbroath, Angus.

John Alexander HALLIDAY 1933– Painter, notably of murals and in tempera, born in Kirkcudbright, Kirkcudbrightshire, where he studied at the local Academy. Halliday was at Glasgow School of Art, 1949–53, gaining a RSA Travelling Scholarship. He carried out many murals for private clients and businesses and had solo shows in Britain and on the continent. Lived for a time in Edinburgh and in Dunsyre, Lanarkshire.

Thomas Symington HALLIDAY 1902– Sculptor, stained glass designer, painter – especially of shipbuilding on the Clyde – and teacher at Dundee High School, born in Thornhill, Dumfriesshire. Studied at Ayr Academy, in Glasgow to be a marine engineer, then at Glasgow School of Art under Robert Anning Bell and Maurice Greiffenhagen. Halliday was elected SSA in 1943 and was a founder-member of the Guild of Aviation Artists in 1963. J D Fergusson included him in his New Scottish Group. In 1947, with the poet George Bruce, Halliday edited *Scottish Sculpture*. He showed at RA, RSMA, RSA, Royal Glasgow Institute of the Fine Arts, Paris Salon and elsewhere abroad. Halliday carved the war memorial in the parish church of Wormit, Newport-on-Tay, Fife, where he lived for over 50 years; also the coat of arms for Newport Town Council; designed several stained glass windows, including Ayr and Dundee Parish Churches; and painted a large mural of the Battle of Narvik for the Royal Naval Dockyard, Rosyth. HM The Queen, HRH The Duke of Edinburgh and galleries in Derby, Glasgow, Dundee and the Imperial War Museum hold examples. A ninetieth birthday show was held at Wormit Arts and Crafts in 1992.

Trevor HALLIDAY 1939– Painter and teacher, born in Birmingham, where he studied at the College of Arts and Crafts, 1954–60, then Royal Academy Schools, 1960–3. He held a number of fine art teaching posts and until 1989 was head of the fine art school at Birmingham Polytechnic. Among his group show appearances were Objects and Documents, Arts Council, 1971–2; Recent British Painting, at Hayward Gallery, 1974; Twenty One for Twenty One, at Ikon Gallery in Birmingham and tour, 1985; and John Moores Exhibition, Liverpool, 1991–2. He had a solo retrospective at Ikon Gallery, 1975. Lived in Grimsby, South Humberside.

Lesley HALLIWELL 1965– Painter and teacher, born in Gainsborough, Lincolnshire, who studied at Lancashire Polytechnic, Dartington College of Arts, Nottingham Polytechnic and Goldsmiths' College. She held a residency in Patagonia, Chile, in 1991, and from 1993 was a part-time lecturer at Cambridge Regional College. Group shows included Northern Graduates at New Academy Gallery, 1989; NEAC, Mall Galleries, 1990; Eastern Open, at King's Lynn Art Centre, from 1993; and Royal Over-Seas League Open, 1996. Solo shows included In Patagonia, Burgh House, 1994.

Susan HALLS 1966– Ceramic artist and teacher, born in Gillingham, Kent, who gained her diploma in ceramics with distinction at Medway College of Art & Design, 1984–6; her higher national diploma there, with distinction, 1986–8; and her master's degree in ceramics, with distinction, 1988–90. In 1990–1, Halls gained a six-month residency at Banff Center for the Arts in Alberta, Canada. Teaching included Royal College of Art, the Museum of Modern Art in Oxford, and Staffordshire, Manchester Metropolitan and Wolverhampton Universities. Among Halls' awards and commissions were one from Kent County Council for a ceramic mural for the County Hall at Maidstone, 1988–9; first prize winner, Campbell's Soup Tureen Design Project (the Toad tureen is in Campbell's Museum Collection, in America), 1989; and a commission for a life-size figure for Christie Cancer Hospital, Manchester, 1994–5. Showed annually with SWLA at Mall Galleries from 1989; The Decorative Beast, Crafts Council, 1990; Colours of the Earth, British Council tour of India, 1992; Ceramic Contemporaries, Victoria & Albert Museum, 1993; and Lynne Strover Gallery, Fen Ditton, 1997. Had a first solo exhibition at Andrew Usiskin Contemporary Art, 1992. Victoria & Albert Museum, Contemporary Art Society and The Sackler Foundation hold examples.

Reginald HALLWARD 1858–1948 Painter and stained glass designer. Studied at Slade School of Fine Art and Royal College of Art. Exhibited extensively, especially at Dowdeswell Galleries, RA and NEAC. Christopher Wood Gallery held a show in 1984. Lived in Arthog, Merionethshire.

Frederick James HALNON 1881–1958 Sculptor and teacher, born and lived in London. He studied at Goldsmiths' Institute from the age of 11, won two national gold medals in 1902–3, and was a pupil of the sculptor Alfred Drury. Went on to become modelling master at Goldsmiths' College. Showed at RA, RI, Royal Glasgow Institute of the Fine Arts and elsewhere and was a fellow of RBS. Williamson Art Gallery in Birkenhead acquired his work and he completed a war memorial panel for Ashford, Kent. A sensitive sculptor in the classical tradition.

Julian HALSBY 1948– Figurative and representational painter in oil, writer and teacher, born and lived in London, married to the printmaker Miranda Halsby. He studied under Kyffin Williams at Highgate School, gained his master's degree in history and history of art at Cambridge University, 1967–71, and was senior lecturer at Croydon College of Art, 1971–80, then freelanced. Halsby was elected a member of RBA in 1994 and of the International Association of Art Critics, 1995. From 1990, he wrote the In Conversation series for *The Artist* magazine. His books included *Scottish Watercolours 1740–1940*, 1989; *Venice: The Artist's Vision* and *Dictionary of Scottish Painters 1600–1960*, both 1990; *The Art of Diana Armfield*, 1995; and *The Art of Lincoln Taber*, 1998. Group shows included NEAC, from 1987; RA Summer Exhibition, from 1989; New Academy Gallery Cancer Relief Exhibition, 1993, and widely elsewhere. Was in a four-man show at Jerram Gallery, Salisbury, 1996; two-man at Pembroke Gallery, Windsor, 1997; and solo at Abbott and Holder, 1998.

Miranda HALSBY 1948– Artist, notably a printmaker, born and lived in London, married to the painter and writer Julian Halsby. After the North London Collegiate School, she studied at Kingston College of Art, 1966–7; Hornsey College of Art, 1967–8; part-time at Chelsea College of Art and Camden School of Art, 1990–1; and etching at Hampstead School of Art, 1994–7. In 1997 attended the Artichoke Printing Workshop. Halsby took part in mixed exhibitions from 1988, being a member of the Small Paintings Group from its inception in 1991. Exhibiting venues included Highgate, King Street, Bartley Drey, Piers Feetham and Thompson's Galleries, Sarah Samuels in Chester and Woodhay Picture Gallery, Newbury.

Helene HALSTUCH 1954– Painter and muralist, born in New York City. Studied at Pratt Institute there, 1972–4, Central School of Art, 1974–7, then London University Institute of Education, 1977–8. Went on to work for the London Borough of Southwark and Lambeth Youth Service, and completed a mural for Southwark. Her exhibitions included Ben Uri Summer Show, 1979; a shared exhibition at Ben Uri in 1980; RA Summer Exhibition, 1981; a shared show at Ice House, 1989; and also in that year she took part in a four-man exhibition at Woodlands Art Gallery. Was married to the painter Peter Morrell. Lived in London.

Paul HAMANN 1891–1973 Artist and teacher, born in Hamburg, married to the painter Hilde Guttmann. He studied at the local Arts and Crafts School and with Rodin in Paris. Served in World War I, then returned to be prominent in artists' colonies and Hamburg artistic social life. With the emergence of Nazism in 1933 moved to Paris, three years later settling in London. From 1938 he had a studio in Hampstead, with his wife established a private art school and eventually became a member of the Hampstead Artists' Council. Was a founder-member before World War II of the Free German League of Culture (FDKB), in which Oskar Kokoschka and Fred Uhlman were involved; helped to organise and took part in shows of German, Austrian and Czech artists' work at New Burlington and Lucy Wertheim Galleries. Was interned in the Isle of Man in 1940, but about a dozen years later adopted British citizenship. Hamann was in

1986 included in Art in Exile in Great Britain 1933–45, at Camden Arts Centre.

Alan HAMBLETON 1954–1998 Artist, born in Leek, Staffordshire, who trained at West Surrey College of Art & Design, Farnham, 1975–8, then Manchester Polytechnic, 1979–80. Hambleton worked for Dundee Printmakers' Workshop from 1980. In 1983 he was included in Scottish Print Open Three, which the Workshop organised; he was a Yorkshire Arts Artist in Industry; and was studying at Tamarind Institute, University of New Mexico, in America.

Harry HAMBLING 1902–1998 Self-taught painter, by profession a banker, living in Hadleigh, Suffolk, father of the artist Maggi Hambling. It was at her insistence that he began to experiment with oils at the age of 65. Although he had painted some watercolours when young and occasionally visited exhibitions, he then took up painting seriously. Work was notable for its strong design, visionary intensity and powerful colour, and it frequently featured the Suffolk countryside. His solo show at Brett Gallery, Hadleigh, in 1991 was a great success, and he had several others.

Maggi HAMBLING 1945– Artist, born in Suffolk, the daughter of the artist Harry Hambling, whom she encouraged to paint. She studied with Arthur Lett-Haines and Cedric Morris, 1960, who ran the East Anglian School of Painting and Drawing; at Ipswich School of Art, 1962–4; Camberwell School of Arts and Crafts, 1964–7; and Slade School of Fine Art, 1967–9, in the latter year gaining a Boise Travel Award which took her to New York. Hambling began to appear in group shows, such as A Space of 5 Times at Grabowski Gallery, the John Player Biennale in Nottingham and on several occasions at John Moores Exhibition, Liverpool. In 1967 the artist had her first solo exhibition at Hadleigh Gallery; she showed solo again at Morley Gallery in 1973 and in 1977 at Warehouse Gallery, when she also appeared at RA and won an Arts Council Award. Hambling, whose work is held by Arts Council, was an Expressionistic painter with vigorous brushwork, noted for her portrait and figure studies, including Max Wall the comedian and A J P Taylor, the historian. In 1980–1 Hambling was the first artist-in-residence at the National Gallery. She had solo shows at Serpentine Gallery, 1987; Bernard Jacobson in 1990, which included mature landscapes; and a first exhibition of sculptures at Marlborough Fine Art, 1996. Lived in London.

Arthur Creed HAMBLY 1900–1975 Landscape watercolourist, black-and-white artist, illuminator and etcher. Studied art at Newton Abbot School of Art with Wycliffe Egginton and Conway Blatchford, then at Bristol School of Art under Reginald Bush. Hambly went on to be a prolific exhibitor, venues including the RA, NEAC, SGA, Walker Art Gallery, Liverpool, and in America. His work is in public collections in Australia and New Zealand. He taught at Salisbury School of Art and Camborne and Redruth School of Art in Cornwall. Lived at Chilcompton, Bath, Somerset.

Cheryl HAMER 1952– Painter and mosaicist, born in Penang, Malaya. She studied at Maidstone College of Art, Reading University and Newcastle University. She was a mosaic artist at Newcastle Art Centre, 1985, then two years later artist-in-residence at Fleming Hospital in Newcastle, where she lived. Group exhibitions included New Contemporaries, 1976; Sheffield Open at Mappin Art Gallery, 1983; Richard Demarco Gallery, Edinburgh, 1988; and the Newcastle Group's The Northern Lights show in 1990 at DLI Museum & Arts Centre and tour. She had a solo show at that venue in 1986, later ones including Bondgate Gallery, Alnwick, 1988. Northern Arts and Kent Education Authority hold her work.

Dan HAMER 1923–1990 Artist who was born and educated in Bolton, Lancashire. He was a lifelong rock climber and mountaineer, which was reflected in his pictures. When World War II began he was still at school, enlisting in the Royal Air Force in 1941. He spent the remainder of the war around the Mediterranean, sketch pads charting his movements: sea front at Alexandria, burnt-out buildings at Tobruk, and pictures of Malta, Sicily and Italy, especially Mount Etna and Vesuvius. After the war he entered the Civil Service and began an outdoor career as a surveyor with the Ordnance Survey, always with a sketch pad. In 1949 he settled in Mossley, near Saddleworth, continuing mountaineering in the Lake District, Scotland and the Alps. Became a member of Saddleworth Art Group in 1950 and showed oils and watercolours at Saddleworth, Accrington, Haslingden, Bradford, regularly at Tib Lane Gallery in Manchester, and in 1973 in The Northern Scene at Woodlands Art Gallery.

Frank HAMER 1929– Painter, potter and teacher, born in Accrington, Lancashire. He studied at the School of Art there, 1944–7 and 1949–50, Burnley School of Art, 1950–1, with Harold Thornton, and at Leeds College of Art, 1951–2. Went on to exhibit in the Accrington area and taught for a time at both his old Art School in that town and at Wolverhampton College of Art. Lived for a time in Wolverhampton.

Margarete HAMERSCHLAG 1902–1958 Painter, illustrator, printmaker, writer and teacher, born in Vienna, Austria. She worked variously as M H, Hamerschlag, later Berger-Hamerschlag or Margarete Berger-Hamerschlag, Margarete (or Margareta) Berger, Margareta Livia Berger or just Berger. From 1908–17 studied at the children's art class run by Franz Cizek, a profound influence, then in 1917–22 at Kunstgewerbeschule. In 1922 married the architect and artist Joseph Berger. For the next dozen years she exhibited in Austria and abroad, wrote and illustrated several books, including Edgar Allan Poe's *The Mask of the Red Death*. After living in Palestine, 1934–6, settled in England, and showed at Wertheim and Arcade Galleries and elsewhere, after World War II with Hampstead Artists' Council and Heal's Art Gallery. Taught at Monkey Club, Knightsbridge, then at youth clubs in Paddington, her experiences there, published in 1955 as *Journey into a Fog*, selling 25,000 copies. Died in London. There was a show of her watercolours at Würthle, Vienna, in 1987, and in 1993 Österreischische Galerie there acquired two of her oil paintings. Victoria & Albert Museum holds woodcuts by her.

Constance HAMERSLEY fl. c.1905–1960 Painter, born in Timaru, New Zealand. After private education in Canada, Italy and England she studied art at the Slade School of Fine Art with Henry Tonks and Philip Wilson Steer, 1906–7, in Munich, in 1933, and four years later with André Lhote, in Paris. Exhibited RA, SWA and WIAC. Finally lived at Long Crendon, near Aylesbury, Buckinghamshire.

Cuthbert HAMILTON 1884–1959 Artist, muralist and potter, born in India. He studied at the Slade School of Fine Art on a scholarship, 1899–1903, teaching art at Clifton College, 1907–10. In 1912–13 while working on murals and screens for Madame Strindberg's Cabaret Theatre Club resumed friendship with Wyndham Lewis. He was invited by Roger Fry to exhibit with Grafton Group in 1913 and joined Omega Workshops, although with Lewis and others he left after a row with Fry. Hamilton joined Lewis' Rebel Art Centre and was a signatory to the Vorticist manifesto in *Blast*, helping to illustrate the first issue. After World War I he took part in the Group X exhibition, showing abstract-oriented work and pottery from the studio he had founded, Yeoman Potteries. Died in Cookham, Berkshire. His reputation was revived by Vorticism and its Allies, Hayward Gallery, 1974; The Omega Workshops, Anthony d'Offay Gallery, 1984; and The Avant-Garde in Britain 1910–1960, at Fine Art Associates.

Ian HAMILTON fl. from late-1980s– Painter and draughtsman who graduated with a degree in fine art from Manchester College of Art, 1987. Hamilton took part in mixed shows at Belltable, Limerick, 1990; One Oxford Street Gallery, Belfast, 1992–3; and in 1994 Beyond the Partitions and Works on Paper, both organised by Queen Street Studios, Belfast, with which he was associated for a time. Hamilton's work was chosen for BP Young European Artists, Brussels, 1991, and Belfast Young Contemporaries, Belfast and London, 1992. Solo shows included Project Art Centre, Dublin; Navan Arts Festival; and Kerlin Gallery, Belfast, all 1990. Lived and worked in Galway, Irish Republic, and County Down, Northern Ireland.

John HAMILTON 1919–1993 Painter in oil of major sea battles of the twentieth century and historical sailing ships, notable for accurate detail. After Bradfield College he served in the Army in the Far East, winning the Military Cross. After the war he worked in a Suffolk Borstal; went to the Gold Coast to start the approved school system there; after eight years returning to England to work in industry. Holidaying in Tresco, in the Scilly Isles where he later settled, he decided to become a painter, in which he was self-taught. His first big collection covered the war in the Atlantic, over 70 pictures now in the Imperial War Museum's HMS *Belfast*. The war in the Pacific was depicted in about 100 pictures, now in the Pentagon, in America; there was also a series on the Falklands campaign; and Hamilton then started on a run of 200 Antarctic paintings, setting up a branch of the Antarctic Heritage Trust in 1992. He showed with RSMA and had solo shows in Hamburg, 1979, and London, 1980.

John HAMILTON fl. from mid-1980s– After working in the civil service, Hamilton graduated in fine art from University of Ulster, Belfast, in 1984. In 1985 he participated in an Alternative Lifestyles bookshop exhibition, *Belfast*; in 1986 and 1989 he exhibited with Harmony Hill Arts Centre, in the city; and in 1994 Hamilton took part in the shows Works on Paper and Beyond the Partitions, sponsored by the Queen Street Studios, with which he was associated. In 1985 shared a show at Otter Gallery, Belfast. Hamilton's drawings and paintings had strong elements of Symbolism and the surreal.

Katherine HAMILTON: *see* **Kate GAULT**

Maggie HAMILTON 1867–1952 Painter and embroiderer, daughter of a bobbin manufacturer, James Hamilton of Glasgow, who settled the family in Helensburgh, Dunbartonshire. Her elder brother was the Glasgow School artist James Whitelaw Hamilton, she married the painter Alexander Nisbet Paterson in 1897 and their daughter was the artist Viola Paterson. She was an embroiderer of painstaking determination, one of her works in The Paterson Family show at Belgrave Gallery, in 1977, having taken five years to finish. Showed widely at RSA and Royal Glasgow Institute of the Fine Arts as well as RA and Walker Art Gallery in Liverpool.

Richard HAMILTON 1922– Painter, teacher, exhibition organiser and artist employing a variety of means such as holographs, cibachrome and the Quantel paintbox computer. He was born in London where in 1936 he studied at Westminster Technical College and St Martin's School of Art in the evenings. After a short period working in the Reimann Studios Hamilton studied at Royal Academy Schools in 1938, and in 1946, during the intervening period studying to be an engineering draughtsman, skills which he employed with the firm EMI. While he was at Slade School of Fine Art, 1948–51, Hamilton in 1950 had first solo show at Gimpel Fils Gallery. This was the start of an impressive exhibiting career which saw Hamilton's work shown at such locations as Robert Fraser Gallery; Studio Marconi, Milan; Stedelijk Museum, Amsterdam; and Vancouver Art Gallery. Hamilton was a prizewinner at John Moores Exhibition, Liverpool, in 1969, the year before his retrospective at Tate Gallery. He had a show at Serpentine Gallery in 1975, then it was 1991 before he had a major exhibition in London, this time at Anthony d'Offay. Hamilton taught at Central School of Art in 1952–3; was at King's College, University of Durham, 1953–66; and in 1957–61 taught at Royal College of Art. Hamilton was a disciple of Marcel Duchamp; he reconstructed Duchamp's Large Glass in the mid-1960s and shortly after organised the exhibition The Almost Complete Works of Marcel Duchamp at Tate Gallery. The Tate, which gave

Hamilton a major retrospective in 1992, holds his work, as does Arts Council.

Susie HAMILTON 1950– Painter, born and lived in London, whose work used violent contrasts in tone and hard, bright colours and was "to do with ideas of the desert or wasteland". She studied at St Martin's School of Art, 1969–72, gaining her diploma, notable teachers including Henry Mundy, Gillian Ayres and Albert Herbert. During the mid-1970s she was a cartoonist for magazines such as *Spare Rib* and *Time Out* and worked in publishing as an editor/designer. Hamilton from 1977–81 read English at London University, gaining an honours degree and her doctorate in 1989, combining later studies with lecturing in English at Middlesex Polytechnic and West London Institute of Higher Education. She attended Byam Shaw School of Art 1989–92, for a fine art diploma, teachers Wynn Jones and Julia Farrer. Showed at Capsule Gallery, 1992; in 1993 The Gallery at John Jones, Battersea Contemporary Art Fair and The Coventry Gallery; in 1994 sharing a show at Coram Gallery. *The Economist* holds her work.

John HAMILTON–HOLDEN: *see* **John Hamilton HOLDEN**

HAMILTON MACK 1903– Painter, printmaker and teacher, born in London as Mary Hamilton Mack. After initial education in east London she studied at the Slade School of Fine Art, her teachers including Henry Tonks and Walter Westley Russell, where she was a Slade Scholarship and Melville Nettleship award-winner. In the 1920s she worked in Australia, partly in Sydney, and exhibited. Also showed RA, Goupil Gallery, NEAC, RBA and was an ICA member. Taught art at Fulham County Secondary School for a time, living in London.

Paul HAMLYN 1953– Artist in various media, born in Stockport, Cheshire. He studied at Goldsmiths' College School of Art, 1979–80; St Martin's School of Art, 1980–3; then returned to Goldsmiths' in 1986–8. In 1991 he created the site-specific installation PITCH and showed at Alternative Arts. His picture Lucifer was chosen for John Moores Exhibition, Liverpool, in 1991–2. Lived in London.

Medina HAMMAD 1963– Painter, draughtsman and teacher, born in Middlesex. She studied at Chelsea School of Art, 1981–2, and Newport College of Art, Gwent, 1982–5. She went on to teach at Lincolnshire College of Art and Design. Much of Hammad's work explored her Sudanese/English background with freshness, vitality and a bold use of colour. She exhibited at Usher Gallery, Lincoln, in 1988, and was included in the Norwich Gallery travelling show History and Identity, 1991–2. Lived in Lincoln.

Alice Berger HAMMERSCHLAG 1917–1969 Painter and administrator, born in Vienna, who moved to Northern Ireland in 1938, dying in Belfast. As well as designing for publishers she created stage sets throughout Ireland, was closely involved in running the New Gallery and was a versatile painter in whose work Expressionism and grand themes were significant. She studied, 1929–38, under the pioneer child art teacher Franz Cizek, at the Kunstgewerbeschule and Vienna Academy of Arts. Exhibitions included Queen's University in Belfast, Avgarde Gallery in Manchester, Dawson Gallery in Dublin, Ulster Office, RSA and SSWA. Ulster Museum, Ulster Television and Arts Council of Northern Ireland hold examples. Her husband Heinz Hammerschlag set up the Alice Berger Hammerschlag Award to help artists after her death.

Tom HAMMICK 1963– Artist and teacher who gained a first-class honours degree at Camberwell School of Art with print-making commendation, followed by master's degree studies. In 1992 he was appointed head of painting and drawing at Eton College. Hammick won the *Spectator* Award in 1988, in 1994 being a finalist in The Gilchrist Fisher Memorial Fund competition at Cadogan Contemporary with work which was close to abstraction. Took part in group shows at Redfern Gallery, with a solo exhibition there in 1996, three years after one at Star Gallery, Lewes. Arts Council holds his work.

Beryl HAMMILL 1942– Textile artist, born in Harrogate, Yorkshire, who studied at Batley and Leeds Colleges of Art. In the 1970s Hammill mostly produced experimental textiles, in 1979 concentrating on tapestry weaving. Using wools that she often hand-dyed, Hammill worked from her favourite landscapes of Ilkley Moor, Yorkshire, on the edge of which she lived, and the west coast of Scotland. Her tapestries were exhibited in Denmark, Australia and in Britain, including Images of the Yorkshire Landscape, organised by Sheeran Lock at Leeds Civic Hall in 1991.

Hermione HAMMOND 1910– Artist in a wide range of media, except acrylic, born in Hexham, Northumberland. She studied at Chelsea Polytechnic with Henry Moore and Graham Sutherland and at Royal Academy Schools with Walter Russell and Tom Monnington. She also studied etching at night classes. After winning the competition to decorate the ceiling of the new Senate House of London University in 1937 Hammond won the Rome Scholarship in painting in 1938, her time there being cut short by the start of World War II. After war service she seized the opportunity after the Blitz to capture many views of the city of London never before visible, soon to be hidden again. Miss Hammond continued to live by her brush, painting in Canada, America, Europe and the Near East. She had many commissions to paint portraits, including Professor Francis Wormald for the Society of Antiquaries and Dr Kate Bertram for Lucy Cavendish College in Cambridge. The Fitzwilliam Museum there and Museum of London hold her work. Her solo shows included Bishopsgate Institute, 1956; Hartnoll & Eyre, 1978; and Michael Parkin Gallery, 1993. Lived in London.

Joel HAMMOND 1963– Self-taught painter who was born in Littletown, County Durham. His first major showing was at

John Moores Exhibition, Liverpool, 1991–2, a highly-charged, colourful, autobiographical picture called Three. Lived in London.

Mark HAMMOND 1967– Painter of gestural, lyrical abstracts, born in Harpenden, Hertfordshire, who gained a degree in fine art at Kingston Polytechnic, 1988–91, then a postgraduate higher diploma at Slade School of Fine Art, 1993–5. He was awarded a two-year scholarship by the Worshipful Company of Painter-Stainers. Exhibitions included Elemental at The Blue Gallery, 1995, which gave him his first solo show in 1996: The Deluge Paintings. In 1996 Hammond was included in New Contemporaries at Tate Gallery, Liverpool, and Camden Arts Centre.

Paul HAMMOND 1947– Artist employing acrylic on hardboard, assemblage and collage, born in Derby, who attended the College of Art there, 1965–6, under Brian Mills; Leeds College of Art, 1966–9, studying with Patrick Hughes and Glyn Williams; and Slade School of Fine Art, 1969–71, under Robyn Denny. Hammond considered that he worked "with a guarded fealty, in the orbit of Surrealism", and his output was widely illustrated in publications covering that field, such as J H Matthews' *The Imagery of Surrealism*, 1977, as well as *Surrealism*, *Melmoth*, *SUBobJECTIVITÉS*, *The Hourglass Review*, *Dies und Das* and *The Day Book*. Group show appearances included The World Surrealist Exhibition, Gallery Black Swan, Chicago, 1976; Surrealism Unlimited, Camden Arts Centre, 1978; In the Spirit of Surrealism, Bradbury & Birch Fine Art, 1984; Le Mouvement PHASES 1952–1988: l'expérience continue, Musée des Beaux-Arts André Malraux, Le Havre, and Surrealism Is Dead, Long Live Surrealism!, The Crawshaw Gallery, both 1988; Quadrinom: Hammond-Pusey-Welson-West Galerie 13, Hanover, 1991; and 87 images, 71 artistes, 23 pays de la planisphere PHASES, Galeries d'art à vocation pédagogique des collèges publiques de Plemet, Plouec-Lié y Quintin, Bretaña, 1994. Settled in Barcelona, Spain.

Roy HAMMOND 1934– Topographical watercolourist who was an engineering designer for Ford Motors. He was able to paint full-time on retirement and to travel. He had a number of sell-out shows with Chris Beetles Ltd, including Roy Hammond in Egypt, 1987; In Istanbul, 1988; and Roy Hammond's London, 1990.

Nina HAMNETT 1890–1956 Painter, draughtsman and writer. Born in Tenby, Wales, she studied art at the Pelham School of Art, South Kensington, under Arthur Cope, then at the London School of Art under John Swan, William Nicholson, Frank Brangwyn and George Lambert. She soon became acquainted with Walter Sickert, of whom she painted an excellent portrait, and Henri Gaudier-Brzeska, who sculpted her. Began to exhibit, in the Albert Hall, at the NEAC and LG. Went to Paris, quickly becoming a member of the bohemian set, meeting artists such as Modigliani and Brancusi and working at Marie Wassilieff's Academy, where Fernand Léger taught. She went on to exhibit at the RA, Leicester Galleries, Redfern Gallery, Arthur Tooth and Son and the Salon d'Automne, Paris. Her life was recounted in *Laughing Torso*, 1932, and *Is She a Lady?*, 1955, discursive but amusing books. She also illustrated the *People's Album of London Statues*, by Osbert Sitwell. After World War II Hamnett, a good painter and fine draughtsman whose achievement could have been much greater, became known as a hard-drinking member of the group of artists and writers who haunted Fitzrovia, in London, where she died, a noted character. Tenby Museum held a centenary show in 1990.

Nichollas HAMPER 1956– Painter, employing unconventional media such as car spray and Hammerite; teacher, born in Chatham, Kent. He studied at Slade School of Fine Art, 1975–9, and Royal College of Art, 1980–2. Went on to teach at Oxford Polytechnic, 1988–91, and was also visiting lecturer at Ruskin School of Drawing. Group show appearances included Tolly Cobbold, 1985; Smith's Gallery, 1985–8; and Raab Gallery, 1988. In 1991–2 he was a prizewinner at John Moores Exhibition, Liverpool, with a dynamic, large canvas: The Intervention of the Doner Kebab. He had solo shows at Fischer Fine Art in 1985; at Oxford Polytechnic and Ruskin School 1990; as well as abroad. Lived in Oxford.

John HAMPSON 1898– Painter and architect, born in Tyldesley, Lancashire. He studied at Manchester University, studying painting privately with several teachers. Exhibited at Mansfield Museum and Art Gallery which holds his work, with Denbighshire Art Society of which he was a member and elsewhere in north Wales. Lived for many years in Rhyl, Flintshire.

Roger HAMPSON 1925–1996 Painter, printmaker and teacher, born in Tyldesley, Lancashire. Hampson was noted for his straightforward depictions of southeast Lancashire, mines and miners. He studied at Manchester College of Art, 1946–51, with Paul Keen and Norman Jaques. Hampson began teaching at Bolton Secondary Technical School, 1951–3; lectured at Hereford School of Art, 1953–4; was a graphic designer, 1954–61; was at Bolton College of Art & Design, eventually as principal, 1961–7; then was principal of Loughborough College of Art & Design, 1978–86. He was a member of MAFA, being its president, 1969–76, and was a fellow of the Chartered Society of Designers. Took part in over 100 group shows and had some 30 solo exhibitions, including Tib Lane Gallery, Manchester, from 1963. Lived finally in Hereford. Lancashire Mining Museum, Salford, held a memorial show and The Gallery, Manchester's Art House, a retrospective, both in 1996.

Michael HAMPTON 1937– Painter of birds and other natural history subjects, full name F Michael Hampton, born in Croydon, Surrey, attending the School of Art there. He was a member of SWLA, also exhibiting with Royal Society for the Protection of Birds, Blackheath Gallery and in the provinces. A number of SWLA calendars reproduced his work. Lived in Shirley, Surrey.

Hugh HAMSHAW-THOMAS 1959– Installations artist who attended Central School of Arts and Crafts, 1978–9, then Bath Academy of Art in Corsham, 1979–82. His brand of conceptual art consisted of collecting, categorising and assembling found objects, treating twigs, leaves or artificial flowers as if they were scientific specimens and thereby exploring human perceptions of reality. Exhibitions included East 94 at Norwich Gallery, 1994; and in 1995 Collective Evidence at Northbank Gallery and Bruce Castle Museum. Lived in London.

David HAMSHERE 1902– Artist in oil, pastel, charcoal and pencil, born at Freretown, Mombasa. Hamshere studied art with Stanhope Forbes, the Newlyn School painter, in the late 1920s, followed by a period in Florence, at the Byam Shaw School under Francis Jackson, and at the Slade School in the early 1930s under Allan Gwynne-Jones. He exhibited widely, including the RA, Hesketh Hubbard Art Society and NEAC, one-man shows including the Canaletto Gallery in London and galleries in Cyprus, Florence and Turkey. Lived in London.

Dennis John HANCERI 1928– Artist and designer with a strong interest in marine subjects, born and lived in London. He studied at St Martin's School of Art. Was a member of RSMA from 1970, also the Wapping Group of Artists and showed widely in America.

Kenneth W HANCOCK 1911– Painter, notably of portraits and flowers, born in Mumbles, Swansea. He studied at the Swansea School of Art and Royal College of Art and went on to teach, notably as principal of Swansea College of Art. Showed with RCamA, SWG, Royal National Eisteddfod and elsewhere. WAC, National Museum of Wales in Cardiff and Glynn Vivian Art Gallery, Swansea, hold his work.

Frederick HAND 1880– Painter who studied at the Brook Green School, which the artist Leon Underwood opened in 1921, where life drawing was the mainstay of instruction. Hand exhibited RA, ROI, Walker's Galleries, Lefevre Gallery, Fine Art Society and in the provinces. Lived in London.

Martin HANDFORD 1956– Artist in pen and ink and pencil, born in London. He was best known for the *Where's Wally?* cartoon books, incorporating many tiny characters, one of the most successful children's ideas of all time. Over 25 million copies had been sold by the early 1990s in over 20 countries in 19 languages. Made into a television series for British television in 1993 and one book was the first children's book ever advertised on the moving lights billboard in Times Square, New York. Cinema epics and playing with toy soldiers were early influences on Handford, who attempted to recapture the excitement by drawing crowds of stick figures. He worked for three years in an insurance office to finance his degree at art college. Each Wally picture took eight weeks to draw. Handford also showed in the RA Summer Exhibition, at Leonie Jonleigh Studio, Wonersh, Guildford, and was included in the Arts Council's tour Fragments Against Ruin, 1981–2, with The Battle of Chacabuco. Lived for a time at Cobham, Surrey, and at Axminster, Devon.

Fred HANDO 1888–1970 Illustrator, writer, local historian of the Monmouthshire area and teacher. After service in World War I Hando was appointed headmaster of Hatherleigh School, Newport. He wrote and illustrated, in pen and ink, seven books which stemmed from his extensive travels around the nooks and corners of Gwent, recording many houses and places now disappeared. To some extent the books were based on the almost 800 articles he wrote for the *South Wales Argus*, called "Monmouthshire Sketchbook", starting in the 1950s and ending just before his death. The writer Arthur Machen, associated with the same area, wrote a foreword to Hando's book *The Pleasant Land of Gwent*, published in 1944.

Christopher HANKEY 1911– Untaught painter, born in Oxted, Surrey, who graduated in modern history from Oxford University in 1932. He became a trainee with a civil engineering firm, obtaining a degree in that subject from University College in 1939, then served a year as private secretary to his father, Lord Hankey, a member of the War Cabinet. Served in the Royal Engineers/Royal Marines, 1940–6, widely overseas, then became a civil servant, initially with the Ministry of Labour, then with the Ministry of Overseas Development until 1972 and official retirement. For six years he did similar work with a quango. Although on walking holidays in Europe Hankey sketched constantly, his later work concentrated on the architecture and countryside around his home near Westerham, Kent, as shown in his first solo exhibition, at Mistral Galleries, Westerham, in 1992. Hankey's landscapes and seascapes were mostly small, "the main characteristic of which is clear, clean colours with a sense of space". He was a member of the Armed Forces' Art Society, also showing with RA, NS, ROI and RBA.

Roderick HANLAN 1928– Sculptor and teacher, born in Penygraig, Glamorgan. After National Service, 1946–8, Hanlan lectured in three-dimensional design in Kingston. He lived in Germany for several years in the 1960s. Group shows included Archer Gallery, New Art Centre, Arnolfini Gallery in Bristol, SEA, SWG and WAC. One-man exhibitions included several in Germany and Drian Gallery, constructions. Commissions included WAC award-winning sculpture Look Up, sited in Newtown.

Cliff HANLEY 1948– Artist and musician, born Glasgow, using as media acrylic, oil, lithography and wood engraving. Cliff Hanley, writer, was his father, and David Hanley, cameraman, his uncle. Hanley attended Glasgow School of Art, 1967–72, teachers including William Bone and Geoff Squires. Hanley said that by the time he finished there he was "utterly sick of art." He started his first band half way through the art school, and after leaving "spent about 15 years concentrating on rock, but most of the money came from design, letterheads to interiors. Those discos and pubs we designed were like nothing else … A little bit of journalism, a sci-fi strip, but it was my rock band that got me to London." In 1984 Hanley suffered a brain haemorrhage, which affected his left hand, and after recuperating in 1986 he was urged to paint again. Hanley became most famous for his many paintings and lithographs of fleeting glimpses of people in cars, prompted by an experience in Toronto in 1986; for him they were "protagonists in modern-day icons". Hanley was a member of National Artists' Association. Mixed shows included Royal Glasgow Institute of the Fine Arts, 1988; South Bank Picture Show, 1991; Workers Against Racism, The Edge Gallery, 1993; ArtExpo, Jacob Javits Center, New York, 1995; and New Year Show at St Thomas' Hospital, which holds his work, 1996. Later solo exhibitions included The Gallery, Gabriel's Wharf, and Whiteleys' Atrium, both 1996. Lived in London.

Liam HANLEY 1933– Artist in oil on cotton on paper and watercolour, born and lived in London. Hanley was a part-time student at Central School of Art briefly, but was mainly self-taught. His painting life began in the mid-1950s. He was a journalist at night, painting during the day, and did not become a full-time artist until he was 55, in 1987. There were many changes in Hanley's work, the most lasting influences being Ben Nicholson and Morandi. "I do not paint *of* things," he wrote, but "*about* things and feelings." Among Hanley's many mixed show appearances were AIA Gallery, St Pancras and Camden Festivals, Tib Lane Gallery in Manchester, RA Summer Exhibitions, Phoenix Gallery in Lavenham and Thackeray Gallery. He had a solo show at Royal Society of Arts in 1962, later ones including, in 1991, Broughton House Gallery in Cambridge, Phoenix Gallery and Bronwen White Gallery, New Orleans. In 1964 Hanley made illustrations for a limited edition of *Face of Winter*, by James Hanley, his father. Graves Art Gallery in Sheffield, Abbot Hall Art Gallery in Kendal and a number of local authorities hold examples. He sometimes painted as Liam H.

Charles Arthur HANNAFORD 1887–1972 Landscape painter in watercolour. Studied at Plymouth Art School. The son of the painter Charles E Hannaford, he opted to sign his pictures Hannaford Junior. Wrote *The Charm of the Norfolk Broads* and exhibited principally at the RBA, as well as the RA and Royal Glasgow Institute of the Fine Arts. Lived at Wroxham, Norfolk.

Charles E HANNAFORD 1863–1955 Watercolourist of landscapes, who studied under Stanhope Forbes and in Paris. Father of the artist Charles Arthur Hannaford. Exhibited RA, RI, RBA, RCamA and had several one-man shows before World War I at Walker's Galleries. Lived at Stalham, Norfolk.

Andrew HANNAH 1907– Painter and museum curator, born in Glasgow, where he remained, the son of a local authority art supervisor. Hannah graduated from Glasgow University with a Master of Arts degree and studied at the city's School of Art, 1932–5, where his teachers included Hugh Adam Crawford and J D Revel. As well as being deputy director for art for Glasgow Museums and Art Galleries Hannah was for some years in charge of the Burrell Collection. He also edited the publication *Architectural Prospect*. Glasgow Art Club member.

Clifford HANNEY 1890–1990 Painter of marine, landscape and figure subjects and teacher, married to the artist Eirene Hutton-Seed. He was born at Publow, Pensford, near Bristol and studied at the University there and art at West Marlands School of Art, Southampton, and Bristol Municipal School of Art under R E J Bush. He was art master at Kimbolton Grammar School, 1923, then after a number of appointments was principal of Crewe School of Art, 1943–50. Was elected an associate of RWA, 1923, was one of the founders of the New Bristol Art Club in 1933 and was elected to Bristol Savages in 1951, becoming its president in 1963. Showed at ROI, Walker Art Gallery in Liverpool, Manchester City Art Gallery and Oldham Art Gallery. Among his main works were Twilight, Sea Hawks and The Schooner. Lived in Bristol but was buried at Publow churchyard.

Brian HANSCOMB 1944– Printmaker, born near Watford, Hertfordshire, who aged 16 was apprenticed as a copperplate letterpress engraver, qualifying aged 24. In 1975–7 attended Hertfordshire College of of Art and Design, moving to Frome in 1978 to work as a gravure engraver. In 1979 left industry to work as a full-time artist/engraver from his home. Was a member of Bristol Printmakers' Co-operative, 1978–80, being elected to Printmakers' Council of Great Britain in 1981. Mixed shows included RA Summer Exhibition from 1976, NEAC from 1977 and RWA from 1979. Solo shows included one in Berlin, 1977, another in Bath, 1981. Department of the Environment holds his work. Lived at St Breward, Bodmin, Cornwall.

Marcelle HANSELAAR 1945– Painter, draughtsman, illustrator and teacher, born in Rotterdam, Netherlands, who studied at Royal Academy of Visual Arts, The Hague, 1962–4, and Rijks Academie, Amsterdam, 1977–8. She painted and travelled extensively in Europe, Central Asia and the Far East. Teaching included Central and St Martin's Schools of Art, 1987–8; lectures at Sotheby's Institute from 1989; and in China from 1993 at several colleges. Hanselaar had a great interest in the European Expressionist tradition, reflected in her own figurative work and unusual palette. German painters such as Beckmann, Heckel, Hacker, Lüpertz and Fetting influenced work which from 1991 was "involved with themes of the human condition such as ageing, fear, a search for identity in our make-believe world and my anger and rebellion against soulless social behaviour … I portray this with with a sense of compassion and humour". Illustrations included *Buddhism Now* from 1989; Ajahn Sumedho's *Teaching of a Buddhist monk*, 1990; *Elements of Zen*, by David Scott, 1992; and work for *Risk* magazine. Group shows included Morley Gallery, 1983; Links of Affinity, Knapp Gallery and Glasgow Art Club, 1989; and Identity, Towner Art Gallery, Eastbourne, 1995. Had a solo show at De Kosmos, Amsterdam, 1976, with a string of exhibitions in Netherlands and Britain after that, later ones including Royal Netherlands Embassy, 1993, and Galerie Reisel, Rotterdam, 1994. In 1996

Hanselaar shared a show with Peggy Postma at Collyer-Bristow Gallery. Lived in London.

Lys HANSEN 1936– Painter, born in Falkirk, Stirlingshire. She gained her diploma at Edinburgh College of Art, 1955–9; Edinburgh College of Speech & Drama, where she graduated, 1955–8; completed postgraduate studies at the College of Art, 1960; did a year's fine art studies at Edinburgh University, 1961; and attended Moray House College of Education for teacher training in 1963. Hansen gained a number of travelling scholarships which allowed her to work in France, Italy, the Netherlands and Germany, having a studio in Berlin, 1985–6. She gained a number of awards and was artist-in-residence, École de Peinture, Castelnau de Montmiral, Tarn, France, in 1988. Hansen was an energetic exhibitor in group and solo shows, where her strongly gestural figurative paintings were immediately recognisable. Among the solo shows were Camden Arts Centre, 1986; City Art Centre, Edinburgh, 1988; McLaurin Gallery, Ayr, 1990; and Richard Demarco Gallery, Edinburgh, 1991. Scottish Arts Council, University of Stirling and City Art Centre, Edinburgh, hold her work.

Markus HANSEN 1963– Artist using photographic images, born in Heidelberg, West Germany. He graduated with honours from University of Reading, 1981–5. Group exhibitions included South Hill Park Performance Festival, Bracknell, 1984; Internationale Photozene, Museum Ludwig, Cologne, 1988; and Interim Art, 1990. Solo shows began with Keeping the Peace, Wunschik Peterson Gallery, Düsseldorf, 1988, later ones including James Hockey Gallery, Farnham, 1991.

Joseph Mellor HANSON 1900–1963 Painter, especially of Cubist-influenced works, and teacher, born in Wheatley, near Halifax, Yorkshire, son of a farmer. He studied at Halifax Technical College and School of Art, 1917–24, on a private scholarship, was briefly art master at Rishworth School, then in 1925 moved to Paris, France, for a decade, studying under Friesz, Léger, Lhote, Le Corbusier and Ozenfant, whose assistant he became. Exhibited solo and at Salons in Paris, at the International Exhibitions in Zürich, Berlin and Stockholm and in England at Yorkshire Artists Exhibitions in Leeds and Wakefield. Having in 1932–3 lived "absolutely from hand to mouth", he returned to England to become art master at Newport Grammar School, Shropshire, two years later showing solo with Lucy Wertheim. Bankfield Museum, Halifax, gave him a retrospective in 1938, the year he moved to New York with his South African-born wife. In 1945 he joined the staff of Cornell University, becoming professor of painting in the School of Architecture there. Hanson died during conversion of a former school at Bodle Street Green, Hailsham, Sussex, for retirement, which was due in 1964. Museum of Modern Art in New York and several other American and Welsh collections hold examples.

Siobhán HAPASKA 1963– Sculptor, born in Belfast, Northern Ireland, of Irish/Parsee parentage, who studied for a degree at Middlesex Polytechnic, 1985–8, gaining her master's from Goldsmiths' College, 1990–2. In 1993 she won a Barclays Young Artist Award. Mixed exhibitions included Guinness Peat Aviation Awards for Emerging Artists, Gallagher Gallery, Dublin, 1990; Making People Disappear, Cubitt Street Gallery, and Wonderful Life, Lisson Gallery, both 1993; and Entwistle, 1996. She had her first solo show at ICA, 1995–6, large structures with opalescent finishes. Hapaska's favoured medium was fibreglass, flawless surfaces sprayed and polished to perfection. Speed, fantasy and the future were elements in her work.

Anne HARCOURT 1917–1985 Painter in oil, watercolour, pen and wash, born in Arbroath, Scotland. She was the daughter of the RA George Harcourt. Studied at the Slade School of Fine Art and privately with Bernard Adams. Exhibited at RA, RP and RWA and had solo shows at the Mayfair Art Gallery in 1954 and in America. Lived at Boxford, Newbury, Berkshire.

George HARCOURT 1868–1947 Painter, born in Dunbartonshire, husband of the artist Mary Lascelles Harcourt, their daughters being the painters Anne, Aletha and Mary Edeva Harcourt. He studied for three years with Hubert von Herkomer at Bushey School of Art and was from 1901–9 governor of the Patrick Allan-Fraser School of Art, Hospitalfield, Arbroath. He was elected RBA in 1897, RP in 1912 and RA in 1926 and was also a member of the Arts and Chelsea Arts Clubs. A prolific exhibitor, Harcourt showed also at Fine Art Society, Walker Art Gallery in Liverpool, RSA and Royal Glasgow Institute of the Fine Arts. National Gallery of South Australia in Adelaide, Bank of England and Winchester College acquired his works. Lived latterly at Bushey, Hertfordshire.

James HARDAKER 1901– Painter, born in Bradford and a member of the Arts Club there. He studied at Bradford School of Art, 1915–17, his teachers including Fred Stead. Exhibited widely in Yorkshire, including Leeds, Bradford and Wakefield, and did some magazine illustrating. Lived for many years at Bingley, Yorkshire.

Gerald A C HARDEN 1909– Painter, printmaker, calligrapher and teacher, born in Charlton Kings, Gloucestershire. He attended the School of Arts and Crafts in Cheltenham and Royal College of Art. From 1932–71 he taught, latterly at Cambridgeshire High School, Cambridge, where he lived. Exhibited at RA, Tate Gallery and widely in the south of England.

Alexander Merrie HARDIE 1910–1989 Artist in watercolour, pastel, oil and gouache, born in Aberdeen. Hardie was a self-taught artist with a fine sense of colour in the Scottish tradition, who painted mainly landscapes, latterly still life and portraits. He obtained his master's degree from Aberdeen University in 1931, became a Bachelor of Science in 1934 and obtained his doctorate in 1959. After time as a research engineer with Metropolitan Vickers, then commissioned service in the Royal Air Force, 1939–46, Hardie lectured in electronics at Aberdeen University and was professor of physics at the University of Bath. He was elected RWA in 1970 and was a member of the Bristol Savages. He showed with Aberdeen Artists' Society, RSA and had several solo exhibitions, including Rooksmoor Gallery and Holburne Museum, both in Bath, at RWA and at Logie Gallery, Tain, in Ross-shire, where he settled at Cromarty. RWA, Gloucester Education Authority and University of Bath hold his work.

Gwen HARDIE 1962– Painter, teacher and artist in cement, plaster and mixed media, born in Newport, Fife. She studied at Edinburgh College of Art, 1979–84, winning the RA's Richard Ford Award in 1983. In 1984 went on a scholarship to Berlin, where she remained until 1990, then settling in London. Hardie was a versatile painter. Some of her work depicted the female figure with the woman as hero rather than as a male-observed object. For this she used herself as a model. The resulting pictures were large, while depicting only a fist or a navel. Her prizewinning entry in the 1997–8 John Moores Liverpool Exhibition, the oil Cleave (I), was a Minimalist image. Took part in many mixed shows, including The New British Painting, 1988–90, with extensive American tour; and Cabinet Paintings, Gillian Jason Gallery, 1991. Had a solo show at Studio Gallery, Glasgow, 1984; a major exhibition at Fruitmarket Gallery, Edinburgh, with tour, 1987; Scottish National Gallery of Modern Art, Edinburgh, 1990; and Annely Juda Fine Art, 1994. Taught exensively, including Oxford Brookes University. Scottish National Gallery of Modern Art, British Council and several foreign collections hold examples.

James HARDIE 1938– Painter and teacher, born in Motherwell, Lanarkshire. He was educated at Larkhill Academy, then studied at Glasgow School of Art, 1955–9, where his teachers included David Donaldson. He gained the Keith Award and the Chalmers Bursary, enabling him to travel in Holland and France. He lectured at Aberdeen College of Education for a dozen years, then from 1980 taught at Glasgow School of Art, in 1989 being exchange tutor with the Chicago Art Institute. From the end of the 1960s Hardie began flying, gaining his pilot's licence. His work was influenced by his love of flying and home area on the edge of the Firth of Clyde, verging on the abstract. Showed widely in Scotland, including one-man shows at Blythswood and Compass Galleries, Glasgow, and Scottish Gallery, Edinburgh. Scottish Arts Council and Aberdeen Art Gallery hold his work.

Martin HARDIE 1875–1952 Watercolour painter, printmaker, writer and museum curator, born in London. After studying at Cambridge University Hardie studied art at the Royal College of Art under Frank Short. Hardie went on to become keeper of the departments of painting and engraving, illustration and design at the Victoria & Albert Museum, from which he retired in 1935. He exhibited watercolours in a traditional style at RA, RSW, RWS, RSMA, NEAC and elsewhere, along with fine etchings at RE. The Victoria & Albert Museum plus many provincial galleries hold his work. He was a distinguished writer on art, notably of the standard three-volume work *Water-colour Painting in Britain.* Lived at Tonbridge, Kent.

Nell HARDIE 1912– Watercolour painter and writer, born Helen Wightman Robertson, in Dumbarton. In 1925 she won a silver medal in the Glasgow Corporation Drawing Competition. She was married in 1939 and on her husband's return from active service in 1945 they resumed their life together, a cottage in Roxburghshire becoming their second home. Over the next 10 years she recorded in watercolour many wild flowers in the area. Her *Wild Flowers and Memories of the Scottish Borders* was published in 1992 by William Hardie Gallery, Glasgow.

Alfred Frank HARDIMAN 1891–1949 Sculptor, born in London, who initially studied at the Royal College of Art under Édouard Lantéri, 1912–16, then at the Royal Academy Schools and finally the British School in Rome, 1924. Won the RBS medal in 1939, being elected RA five years later. Among his works are the memorial to Earl Haig in Whitehall, London, and sculpture for St John's College, Cambridge, and Kippen Church, Stirling. *RBS: Modern British Sculpture*, published in 1939, illustrates his bust of Cecil Rhodes, for Rhodes House, Oxford, and bronze of St George, both in a muscular classical tradition. Was a fellow of the RBS and lived in London.

Melville HARDIMENT 1915– Painter and teacher, born in Wisbech, Cambridgeshire, who was for a time head of the art department at Bromsgrove Art and Technical School, Worcestershire. Hardiment studied art at Peterborough Training College, at the Camberwell School of Arts and Crafts under Claude Rogers and Victor Pasmore, as well as in Birmingham and St Ives. Showed LG, AIA, of which he was a member, and in the Midlands, where he had a series of one-man shows.

Alexis HARDING 1973– Artist, born and lived in London, who gained an honours degree in fine art at Goldsmiths' College, 1992–5. Exhibitions included Stephen Friedman Gallery and Multiple Orgasm, Lost-in-Space, both 1995; and Nine Lives at 26 Chiltern Street and New Contemporaries at Tate Gallery, Liverpool, and at Camden Arts Centre, all 1996. Harding's contribution to New Contemporaries included Hung I, 1995–6, an abstract in oil and gloss paint on canvas. He was included in the 1997–8 John Moores Liverpool Exhibition. Solo exhibitions included Andrew Mummery, 1998. Arts Council holds Harding's work.

David HARDING 1944– Painter and teacher, born in Bath, Somerset. He studied at High Wycombe School of Art, 1961–5, and the Slade School of Fine Art, 1965–7. Went on to teach at Bath College of Higher Education from 1972. He participated in Sainsbury's touring show Images for Today, 1982–3; RA Summer Exhibitions from 1985 and group shows at Museum of Fine Art in Alexandria, Egypt, and at Victoria Art Gallery, Bath, the same year. In 1987 his picture Old Earth was included in John

Moores Liverpool Exhibition. Arts Council holds his work. Lived in Bradford-on-Avon, Wiltshire.

Jennifer HARDING 1956– Artist in acrylic, watercolour and gouache, born in Fordingbridge, Hampshire. She did a foundation course at Salisbury College of Art, 1974, an honours degree in fine art at Canterbury College of Art, 1975–8, a postgraduate course at Cyprus College of Art in Paphos, 1979, then attended Athens School of Fine Arts, 1983–4, under a Greek Ministry of Education Scholarship. Among her awards was an Oppenheim-John Downes Memorial Award in 1987. She was several times a visiting artist at Cyprus College of Art from 1986 and in 1987 was an archaeological illustrator with the British Institute of Archaeology in Ankara, Turkey. Harding's group shows included Stowells Trophy at RA, 1978; John Moores Liverpool Exhibition, 1983; Whitechapel Open, 1985; and Omphalos Open Exhibition, Sandwich, 1993. She had a solo show at British Council Gallery in Athens, 1984, another at Finnegan Fine Art, 1990. Lived in London.

Morris HARDING 1874–1964 Sculptor, painter and teacher, born in Stevenage, Hertfordshire, who studied in the studio of his uncle Harry Bates, also with John M Swan. Taught at London County Council's Technical Institute. In 1925 Harding moved to Northern Ireland, where he settled at Holywood, County Down, and worked for many years on Belfast Cathedral. He was a member of RBS, RHA, RUA of which he was president and of the Society of Animal Painters. Harding also showed at RA, Walker Art Gallery in Liverpool, Royal Glasgow Institute of the Fine Arts and elsewhere. Ulster Museum, Belfast, holds his work.

Robert HARDING 1954– Sculptor and teacher, born in Lancashire. He employed a variety of materials, although he most favoured steel, and was interested in the public siting of sculpture. Harding studied at Exeter College of Art, followed by post-graduate research at University of Lancaster into contemporary sculpture in urban areas. In 1985 he co-produced a Welsh Sculpture Trust show, Sculpture & Architecture: Restoring the Partnership, which toured widely. He showed in open-air exhibitions at Tatton Park, Cheshire, St Donats Arts Centre and elsewhere, including the 1986 Glynn Vivian Art Gallery & Museum, Swansea, Seven Sculptors Working in Wales. The gallery holds his work. Lived in Uplands, Swansea, and taught part-time at Dyfed College of Art, Carmarthen. Had solo shows at Swansea Arts Workshop.

Robert HARDING 1957– Painter and sculptor of abstract work, born and lived in London. He studied at Salisbury School of Art, 1973–6, and Camberwell School of Arts and Crafts, 1976–9. Showed at John Moores Liverpool Exhibition from 1982; RA Summer Exhibition, 1984; Open Studios, Greenwich, 1986; and The Table Studio Group, The Living Room, 1996. Later solo shows were at Smith Jariwala Gallery from 1990.

Winifred HARDMAN fl. c.1915–1975 Painter in oil and tempera of figure subjects, mural painter and signboard creator. Born at Rawtenstall, Lancashire, Hardman studied at the St John's Wood School of Art, then at the Royal Academy Schools, where she won bronze and silver medals. Exhibited at the RA, RSA, NEAC, Tate Gallery, Redfern Gallery and elsewhere. Her work was widely reproduced, examples being *The Studio*, *Yorkshire Post*, *The Listener* and *The Sphere*. Among her murals was one for St Peter's Church, Hammersmith. She was a member of the Society of Sussex Painters. Lived in London.

Beatrice M HARDY 1897– Painter, born in London, daughter of the landscape painter and miniaturist Dorofield Hardy. She studied at the Royal Academy Schools under Charles Sims and exhibited SWA and RP. Lived in Cranbrook, Kent.

Irma HARDY 1912– Painter and draughtsman, notable for portraits and scenes from the ballet, born in Budapest, Hungary, where she attended the Royal Academy of Arts, 1931–6. Showed in Hungary to mid-1940s, then in England with SWA of which she was a member, RP, PS and had several solo shows, including Cooling Galleries. HM The Queen holds her work. Lived in London.

Jim HARDY 1930–1992 Painter in oil and acrylic whose lack of self-promotion denied him the solo shows he deserved. Studied at Hornsey College of Art, worked for some years as a scene-painter at Sadler's Wells Theatre, in Islington where he lived, finally being a media resources officer with an east London college. Was a member of Islington Art Circle.

Mary Rose HARDY: *see* **Mary Rose GOSLING**

Robert HARDY 1952– Painter who worked on a small scale, who studied at Stoke-on-Trent and Chelsea School of Art and, after travelling in India for several years, attended life classes run by Cecil Collins. He was in the British visionary tradition, influences including religious folk art, votive painting, Indian and child art. Hardy aimed "to depict those presences and places that lie between the real world and the world of the spirit, between earth and heaven." Began exhibiting in 1982, solo exhibitions including England & Co, 1996.

Daphne HARDY HENRION 1917– Sculptor in clay, plaster, terracotta and bronze, notable for portrait heads and figure groups, these tinged with suffering and heroism. She was born in Amersham, Buckinghamshire, as Daphne Hardy, under which name she at first worked, marrying the designer F H K Henrion in 1947. Hardy Henrion left school at 14 and studied privately in the Netherlands for a year with Marian Gobius and Albert Termote in 1931, having been educated in The Hague since 1923. Attended Royal Academy Schools, 1934–7. Aged 20 she won the Gold Medal and Travelling Scholarship which took her to France and Italy for two years. When the Munich Crisis occurred she escaped from France by ship. She was a member of the Cambridge Society of Painters & Sculptors, 1980–95, also RBS. Also exhibited with Hampstead Artists' Council, WIAC, RBA, Pictures for Schools and Contemporary Portrait Society. Early solo exhibitions were at Beaux Arts Gallery, 1946, and AIA Gallery, 1956, later ones at Ditton Hall Barn, Fen Ditton, 1984, and Clare Hall, Cambridge, 1987. Hardy Henrion said that her approach to work was "entirely traditional and not at all intellectual, being a direct expression of my perception of people and situations". In 1951 Hardy Henrion produced a large cement figure for exhibition at the South Bank for the Festival of Britain. Her bronze relief Family Group is at Addenbrooke's Hospital, Cambridge, having originally been commissioned by Misha Black for the Alliance Building Society. In the mid-1980s she made a head of the writer Arthur Koestler (whose *Darkness at Noon* she had translated in 1940), casts held by National Portrait Gallery, Edinburgh University and the Koestler Foundation. Lived in Cambridge.

Joe HARGAN 1952– Painter and teacher, born in Glasgow, where he attended the School of Art, 1970–4, teachers including David Donaldson and Danny Ferguson. He showed at Glasgow Art Club of which he was a member, SSA, BWS and Royal Glasgow Institute of the Fine Arts. Hargan won a number of awards, including David Cargill Award at Royal Glasgow Institute, 1982, and the James Torrance Memorial Award there, 1984; the Meyer Oppenheim Prize, RSA, 1986; and Paisley Art Institute Award, 1993. BBC, Strathclyde Education Department and South of Scotland Electricity Board hold examples. In 1996, The Contemporary Fine Art Gallery, Eton, gave Hargan a solo show, which included his colourful landscapes and singular figure studies. He lived at Paisley, near Glasgow.

T HARGRAVE-SMITH 1909– Watercolourist, born in Newport, Monmouthshire, where he attended the Art School in 1925–7. In the late 1930s he studied watercolour painting with the landscape artist Wycliffe Egginton. Was a professional soldier for some years, so showed with Army Art Society and has work in Imperial War Museum; also showed RA, RWS, of which he was a member, and abroad. Lived in London.

Sally HARGREAVES 1946– Painter and draughtsman, born in Blackburn, Lancashire. She studied at Harris College of Art, Preston, 1963–5; Chelsea School of Art, 1965–8; and Camberwell School of Art, 1968–9. Gained an Italian Government Bursary, Perugia, 1969, and an Italian Government Scholarship, Florence, 1971. Hargreaves said that she was "drawn to flat, formal shapes; horizontal and vertical lines; wide open spaces; dark skies and brilliant light; the simplicity of a striped Indian Navajo blanket … the Fen landscape fascinates me." Group exhibitions included John Moores Liverpool Exhibition, 1972; British Drawing, Hayward Annual, and Three Painters, Norwich Castle Museum, both 1982; and Peterborough Art '87, Lady Lodge Arts Centre, 1987. She had a solo show there in 1985.

Ethel HARKER fl. from 1915– A versatile painter in oil and watercolour who studied at Chester School of Art and privately. Was a member of Liver Sketching Club. Exhibited RCamA and Walker Art Gallery, Liverpool. Lived at Heswall, Cheshire.

Beth HARLAND 1964– Artist in mixed media who attended Salisbury College of Art, 1983–4, then studied at Ruskin School of Art in Oxford, 1984–7, gaining scholarship status and a travelling bursary to study in Germany. She completed her master's degree at Royal College of Art, 1987–9, spending a term at Cité Internationale des Arts in Paris. Harland showed at Sandra Higgins Fine Art and Contemporary Art Society Market. She was involved in collaborative work with the i/x group, including in 1991 a show at Quicksilver Gallery, Middlesex Polytechnic, then participated in (dis) parities at Mappin Art Gallery, Sheffield, in 1992, and at Herbert Art Gallery, Coventry, 1993.

Dennis HARLAND 1924– Sculptor and teacher who studied at King's College, Newcastle upon Tyne. Joined the staff of Leeds College of Art, where he was involved in three-dimensional studies. Was included in the College staff show The Teaching Image, 1964, at Leeds City Art Gallery, showing three plaster reliefs. Lived at Austwick, Clapham, Yorkshire.

Dennis F HARLE 1920– Painter with a strong interest in wildlife subjects, born and lived in Sandwich, Kent, by profession a nature reserve warden. He studied at evening classes, Ramsgate and Canterbury Schools of Art, and was a founder-member of SWLA. Had several solo shows in Kent.

Primrose HARLEY 1908– Painter of pictures and murals and printmaker, born in London. She studied at Chelsea Polytechnic under Graham Sutherland and Percy Hague Jowett, then at the East Anglian School of Painting and Drawing under Cedric Morris and Arthur Lett-Haines. Showed RA, NEAC, SWA, LG and elsewhere. Completed murals for British European Airways, Dorland Hall, in London's Regent Street, and lived in London.

Kevin HARLOW 1952– Sculptor and teacher who used "humour as a way of addressing serious issues without becoming bogged down in rhetoric", materials including "fibreglass, angle grinders and acrylics … Influences vary – anything from television and magazines to High Art, Folk Art, Pop Art and real people." Born in Peterborough, Huntingdonshire, Harlow studied at Birmingham College of Art, 1970–1; Leeds Polytechnic, 1972–5; and Birmingham Polytechnic, 1977–8. Taught art in Bradford, 1978–87, then was an artist and sculptor full-time. Exhibitions included Norwich and Poole Arts Centres, both 1978; Bradford Open Artists Exhibition, 1981–5; Leeds Arts Space, 1985; and with Nicholas Treadwell Galleries and widely in international art fairs from 1990. Had a solo exhibition at Leeds Playhouse, 1984.

Rod HARMAN 1942– Artist and teacher who studied at Brighton College of Art and Royal College of Art. Taught for a time at the College of Further Education in Hastings, Sussex, where he eventually settled. Had a solo show of watercolour drawings and patterns at Woodlands Art Gallery, 1979–80.

Desmond HARMSWORTH 1903–1990 Publisher and painter, whose daughter Margaret was also an artist. After education at

Eton College and Oxford University, where he obtained his master's degree, Harmsworth worked for several years in the family newspaper and publishing business Associated Newspapers. Then studied drawing at Académie Julian in Paris and had his first show at the Galerie des Quatre-Chemins in 1933, his first London show with Wildenstein five years later. Worked with British Information Services in New York, 1940–6, during which he continued to show, his first post-war exhibition in London being at Roland, Browse and Delbanco in 1954. He did not have a solo show again until one in 1988 at Berkeley Square Gallery, critically well received. Among his portraits were James Joyce, Osbert Sitwell and Havelock Ellis. Finally lived in Egham, Surrey, having become 2nd Baron Harmsworth on his father's death in 1948.

Frederick Bertrand HARNACK 1897–1983 Oil, watercolour and woodcut artist specialising in marine subjects. Born in London, studied with Arthur Briscoe, then exhibited at RA and other galleries in London, the provinces and on the continent. Sometimes signs his pictures Fid Harnack. Wrote *Sailing Ships through the Ages* and was illustrated in the yachting press. Lived at West Mersea, Essex.

Arto der HAROUTUNIAN: *see* **ARTO**

Edward Steel HARPER 1878–1951 Painter of landscape in oil, born in Birmingham, son of the artist Edward Steel Harper. After education at King Edward VI High School, Birmingham, where his father taught at the School of Art, the son went on to teach at Wolverhampton Grammar School, retiring in 1942. Exhibited RA, ROI and RBSA. City of Birmingham Museum and Art Gallery holds several of his landscapes. Signed work with monogram incorporating a harp. Lived at Harborne, Birmingham.

Eric HARPER 1918– Painter and draughtsman, full name Stanley Eric Harper, born in West Kirby, Cheshire. Studied at Malvern School of Art under Victor Moody, 1937–9; Wolverhampton School of Art, 1937, with Robert Emerson; at the Royal Academy Schools, where his teachers included William Dring and Ralph Middleton Todd and where he won a gold medal and Travelling Scholarship, in 1948; then finally at the British School in Rome. Showed at RA, RBA, SGA and NEAC. Lived in west London.

Geoffrey Felix HARPER 1913– Painter and designer of stained glass and murals, born in Wolverhampton, Staffordshire. Studied at Wolverhampton, Birmingham and Blackheath Schools of Art, Goldsmiths' College School of Art and Central School of Arts and Crafts. Exhibited RA and elsewhere, but was mainly noted for stained glass in many churches in London and the Home Counties. Lived in Harpenden, Hertfordshire.

Stephen HARPER 1954– Painter, born in Northern Ireland, who studied at Ulster College of Art & Design, 1971–3; Bath Academy of Art, Corsham, 1972–5; Ulster College again, 1975–6; Liverpool Polytechnic 1977–8; and at Goldsmiths' College, 1979–81, to gain his master's degree. Harper was noted for his intense, meticulous still life drawings and paintings, in which the placing of objects was of key importance. Group exhibitions included Four by Four at Project Gallery, Dublin, 1976; Works on Paper at Edward Totah Gallery, 1979; and Summer Show 2 at Serpentine Gallery, 1983. In 1992 had a solo show at England & Co. Arts Council of Northern Ireland holds his work. Lived in London.

Hildred HARPIN 1907– Painter, notably of murals, and teacher, born in Marsden, Yorkshire, son of the artist E Harpin. Studied at Huddersfield School of Art, Royal College of Art and in Italy. Taught art at Keighley School of Art, Yorkshire, near where he lived at Silsden. Exhibited in London and widely in the north of England. Much of Harpin's work is in churches throughout England in the form of murals and panels, including Ludlow, Keighley, Silsden, Cricklade and at the Passionist Monastery, Ilkley.

Sydney HARPLEY 1927–1992 Sculptor and teacher, born in London. He left school at 14 to work as an electrician. During National Service in the Army in Egypt, 1945–8, saw a head of Ramases II which inspired him to be a sculptor. After work in the artificial limb factory at Roehampton and evening art classes, in 1950 he enrolled as full-time student of sculpture at Hammersmith School of Art. Was most helped by John Skeaping at Royal College of Art, 1953–6, and in 1954 made first appearance in RA Summer Exhibition with Seated Girl. Harpley was to become known for his sculptures of attractive girls, using props such as swings, bicycles and hammocks. He was elected a fellow of RBS in 1963, RA in 1981. From 1972 he taught for a time at Leicester Polytechnic. Harpley carried out a number of ambitious figure groups in bronze, such as Dockworker for London County Council for the Lansbury Estate in Poplar. An over-life-size portrait memorial to Jan Christian Smuts led to solo shows in Cape Town and Johannesburg, South Africa. His busts included Edward Heath, Lee Kuan Yew and Prince Albert of Monaco. He had two successful shows at Chris Beetles Ltd in 1987 and 1990. In final years lived in Somerset and then Kilkenny and died in Dublin, Ireland.

Hywel HARRIES 1921– Painter, designer, illustrator and teacher, born in Tumble, Carmarthenshire. Attended Llanelli School of Art and Cardiff College of Art, then went on to hold a number of teaching posts. A member of RCamA, he also showed with Royal National Eisteddfod, NWG and Cardiganshire Art Society. For many years he was a cartoonist for *Cambrian News*; did book illustration and jacket design for Welsh printing presses; and illustrated the HM Stationery Office publication *Cambrian Forests*, 1958. One-man shows included National Library of Wales, Aberystwyth, 1970. CASW bought his oil Buarth Road, Snow.

Claire HARRIGAN 1964– Painter and teacher, born in Kilmarnock, Ayrshire, later settling to work nearby at Girvan, although she travelled widely overseas. Studied at Glasgow

School of Art, 1982–6, winning the Mary Armour Award. In 1990 she added the Lily McDougall Award. Was artist-in-residence at London Hall, Ayr, 1986, and in 1989 became a visiting tutor at Glasgow School of Art. Harrigan exhibited in many national open shows, including RSA, SSWA, Royal Glasgow Institute of the Fine Arts, Mercury Gallery in London and Edinburgh, Open Eye Gallery in Edinburgh and elsewhere. Had a series of solo exhibitions at Macaulay Gallery, Stenton, and Christopher Hull Gallery from 1988. In both landscape and still life Harrigan was a rich, intense colourist, as seen in the show she shared with her parents, James and Elspeth Harrigan, at Vicarage Cottage Gallery, North Shields, 1995. She was elected a member of RSW.

Elspeth HARRIGAN fl. from mid-1950s– Watercolourist who confined her work to the flora of Scotland and those countries travelled in with her painter husband James. She studied at Glasgow School of Art, 1956–60. Won the Royal Horticultural Society Silver Medal, 1985 and 1986; the LAS Group Award for watercolour at SSWA, 1986; Lily McDougall Prize from same group, 1987; and showed at Flying Colours Gallery, Edinburgh, and Barclay Lennie Fine Art, Glasgow. Her plates illustrated J H Dickson's *The Wild Flowers of Glasgow*, 1991. In 1995 she and her husband shared an exhibition with their daughter Claire at Vicarage Cottage Gallery, North Shields.

James HARRIGAN 1937– Painter and teacher, married to the artist Elspeth Harrigan, their daughter Claire also being a painter. He studied at Glasgow School of Art, 1956–61, gaining his diploma in drawing and painting 1960, postgraduate diploma in printmaking, 1961. Won the Laing Landscape Competition, 1980, the *Scotsman* Art Competition in 1985. Regular showed in mixed exhibitions in Scotland; shared a show with his wife and daughter at Vicarage Cottage Gallery in North Shields, 1995; solo exhibitions included Flying Colours Gallery in Edinburgh.

Alfred HARRIS 1930– Painter and printmaker, born and lived in London, who in mid-1950s attended Willesden School of Art and Royal College of Art. For a time he was involved in the running of the art and design department of London University's Institute of Education. Participated in mixed shows at Tate Gallery. New Vision Centre and Whitechapel Art Gallery and had solo exhibitions at Ben Uri and Drian Galleries and in Sweden. Ben Uri Art Society holds his work. Lived in London.

Annie HARRIS fl. from late 1970s– Painter who attended Camberwell School of Arts and Crafts, 1979–83. She went on to teach there, 1983–5. An admirer of Velasquez and Vuillard, she painted in Tuscany and Scotland, sometimes working on a large scale. As well as taking part in group shows she shared a show at Cadogan Contemporary in 1991 and she had a solo show there in 1993. The National Trust commissioned her to paint The Bookroom, Sissinghurst.

Charles HARRIS fl. from 1970s– Painter and draughtsman who did a foundation course at Epsom College of Art and Design, 1970–1, then a vocational course at Hammersmith College of Art and Building, 1971–4. He won a scholarship to Royal Academy Schools, 1977–80, then a scholarship to the postgraduate course, 1980–30. He won a number of prizes there, including the David Murray Scholarship in Landscape Painting for 1979–80 and 1981. Showed at RA Summer Exhibition from 1979, Mall Galleries from same year and won membership of Free Painters and Sculptors, 1981. Had solo show at Woodlands Art Gallery, 1982.

Derrick HARRIS 1919–1960 Printmaker, painter, illustrator and designer. Born at Chislehurst, Kent, he studied art at the Central School of Arts and Crafts under Noel Rooke and John Farleigh. Exhibited SWE. He taught wood engraving and illustrating at Kingston and Reigate Schools of Art, in Surrey. Did commissioned work for the Festival of Britain, in 1951, illustrated several books for the Folio Society and has work in the collection of the Victoria & Albert Museum. Sometimes signed work D H. Lived in London.

Edwin HARRIS 1891–1961 Landscape painter in watercolour and tempera, especially of Sussex scenes. Educated in Littlehampton, Harris went on to exhibit at RA, Cooling Galleries, RBA and elsewhere, public galleries in Eastbourne, Hove and Accrington buying his work. His picture Moonrise was reproduced by the Medici Society. Was a member of the Association of Sussex Art Clubs and Brighton Art Club. Lived in Washington, Sussex.

Geoffrey HARRIS 1928– Sculptor, printer and teacher, born in Nottingham. He attended Leeds College of Art, 1948–51, then Royal College of Art, 1951–4. From 1953–4 he was a visiting lecturer at Dockland Settlements, then assisted the sculptor Leon Underwood and David John in 1954 and William Bloye in 1955–7. He held visiting lectureships meanwhile at Birmingham College of Art and Stourbridge School of Art. Harris assisted the sculptor Henry Moore, 1957–60, was visiting lecturer at Bromley College of Art, 1960–4, lectured at Ravensbourne College, 1964–70, then was senior lecturer there, 1970–86. Harris' commissions included Baildon Primary School, Yorkshire, 1951, the year he was awarded a Travelling Scholarship to Italy by Leeds College of Art; London County Council Maitland Park Housing Estate, St Pancras, 1964; and Smead Dean Centre, Sittingbourne, 1984. Mixed shows included Obelisk Gallery from 1957; Leicester Galleries from 1959; LG from 1965; and Goldsmiths' Hall, 1975. He had solo shows in 1964 at Leicester Galleries and Queen's Square Gallery, Leeds. From the late- 1980s Harris concentrated on painting as well as sculpture. Lived in Faversham, Kent.

Jane HARRIS 1956– Painter, born in Dorset. She studied at Bournemouth College of Art, 1975–6, Camberwell School of Arts and Crafts, 1976–7, Brighton Polytechnic, 1977–9, Slade School of Fine Art, 1979–81, and Goldsmiths' College School of Art, 1989–91, where she completed her master's degree. Harris gained a number of awards: the Boise Travelling Scholarship, to Japan, 1981; a French Government Scholarship at Paris, 1985–6;

Erasmus Exchange, Grenoble, 1990; and to Amsterdam in 1991. Participated in various group shows including Stowells Trophy, RA, 1979; New Contemporaries, ICA, 1981; and shared exhibitions in 1984 at Woodlands Art Gallery and in 1988 at Alpha Gallery, Swanage, and Holland Gallery. Had a solo show at University College London, 1981, and then at Anderson O'Day, 1992. Harris was a painter who reduced to a minimum the elements in her work, working on a large and small scale. At Anderson O'Day she restricted her format to that of an ellipse with fluctuating edges placed within a space of a different colour.

Jeffrey HARRIS 1932– Abstract painter and teacher, born in Leeds, Yorkshire, studying at the College of Art there. Awarded a travelling scholarship to Paris in 1953. From 1956–64 Harris worked and lived in St Ives, Cornwall, then taught painting at Harris College, Preston. Returned to St Ives in 1965. Exhibitions included Passmore Edwards Gallery in Newlyn, Penwith and Fore Street Galleries in St Ives, Plymouth City Art Gallery and New Art Centre. In 1963 he shared an exhibition with Jane Beeson at Rowan Gallery, in 1965 having a solo exhibition at Mowan Gallery, Manchester. The City Art Gallery there holds works by him, and Arts Council has his oil on board Black, Grey and White, of 1959. In the 1970s Harris moved to Australia with his second wife, the Australian artist Gwen Leitch, where he taught and painted. The new landscape gave a different direction to his pictures.

Josephine HARRIS fl. from 1950s– Painter, printmaker and glass engraver, who studied with William Mann at Plymouth College of Art, 1948–52. For a time she was secretary to the Royal Academy Schools. She was a member of RWA, NEAC and RBA, also showing at RA Summer Exhibition. Public galleries in Plymouth and Sheffield hold examples. Lived in London.

Lyndon Goodwin HARRIS 1928– Painter and etcher, born in Halesowen, Worcestershire. He studied at Birmingham College of Art; Slade School of Fine Art, teachers including Randolph Schwabe and William Coldstream; and Central School of Arts and Crafts under Andrew Freeth. Among Harris' awards were Slade Scholar. In 1957 he was chosen for inclusion in Jack Beddington's book *Young Artists of Promise*. Harris was a member of RI, RSW and RWA, also showing with RA from age of 13, RBA, NEAC and Royal Glasgow Institute of the Fine Arts. At the Paris Salon he gained a Gold Medal, painting, and an Hon. Mention, etching. The Government Art Collection and University College hold his work.

Phyl HARRIS 1925– Artist in pen, watercolour and pencil, and teacher, born and lived in London, full name Phyllis Harris. She studied at Reading University School of Art, Brighton College of Arts and Crafts and Camberwell School of Art, and at evening classes, her teachers including Anthony Betts and John Minton. She was made a member of SWA in 1975, SGA in 1991 and was also a member of Art Societies in Wembley and Harrow. Also showed at Knapp Gallery and Westminster Central Gallery. Harris' work was semi-abstract; she was "interested in the design and pattern of landscape and still life".

Richard HARRIS 1954– Sculptor and teacher, born in Newton Abbot, Devon, who graduated in fine art from Gloucester College of Art, 1973–5. Taught in Australia, 1979–81, exhibiting at First Australian Triennial in Melbourne, 1980–1. Harris was closely associated with Grizedale Forest, Cumbria, initially holding a fellowship there, 1977–8. His large Quarry Structure, 1978, in slate and wood, is sited at Grizedale. Was included in Arts Council's The Sculpture Show, 1983, living in Newcastle upon Tyne, completing a commission in Gateshead for Arts Council and Northern Arts.

Tim HARRIS fl. from mid-1980s– Painter who studied initially in Taunton, 1978–9. He gained an honours degree at Winchester School of Art, 1979–82, then his master's degree from Chelsea School of Art, 1982–3. His mixed show appearances included Tony Carter Studio, Brixton Artists' Co-op, Winchester Gallery and Hardware Gallery, and in 1991 he was a prizewinner in The Discerning Eye at Mall Galleries, and tour. One-man shows included 1988 Mermaid Theatre and Hardware Gallery. Winchester School of Art library holds his work.

Tomás HARRIS 1908–1964 Artist in many media, picture dealer and collector, born in London. His father Lionel Harris founded the Spanish Art Gallery which Tomás later helped to run, having dealt on his own. Studied at Slade School of Fine Art, 1923–6, having won the Trevelyan-Goodall Scholarship, under Henry Tonks; then for a year at British Academy in Rome; etching at the Slade after World War II; and wood engraving in the early 1950s with John Buckland-Wright. During the war Harris' knowledge of Spain was invaluable to the Security Service. He was a principal organiser of Operation Garbo, which misled the Germans on Allied plans for the invasion of France. After the war Harris gave up dealing to devote himself to collecting and painting. In 1943 he showed solo with Lefevre Gallery. He also exhibited with Knoedler in New York and widely in Spain, where he was the first independent artist since Goya to have his cartoons woven at the Royal Tapestry Factory in Madrid. With Juliet Wilson, in 1964 he produced a scholarly two-volume book on the etchings of Goya, his fine collection being shown at the British Museum in 1963–4. Public galleries in Toledo, America and in Sâo Paulo, Brazil, hold Harris' work. Finally settled for many years in Camp de Mar, Majorca, Spain, drawing on the landscape to produce pictures reminiscent of Van Gogh. He died in a motor accident and his friend Anthony Blunt organised a memorial show at Courtauld Institute Galleries in 1975.

Vera Furneaux HARRIS 1904– Painter, miniaturist, illustrator and teacher who sometimes worked on ivory, born in Ross, Herefordshire. She was educated at the Grammar School in Maidstone, then at the School of Art there, at the Slade School of Fine Art and in Paris. Exhibited RA, RMS of which she was a member, Paris Salon and elsewhere and did work for the religious publisher A R Mowbray and Company. Lived in Loose, Kent.

Claude HARRISON 1922– Artist, notably in tempera, born in Leyland, Lancashire. He was married to the artist Audrey Johnson in 1947, their son being the potter Tobias Harrison. He was educated at Preston College of Art, 1939–41, Liverpool College of Art, 1941–2, then after Royal Air Force service in India, Burma and China, at Royal College of Art, 1947–50. Harrison was a painter of murals, portraits, conversation pieces and imaginative figure compositions including harlequin-type and masked figures and using a delicate palette. He showed with RP of which he was an honorary member, RA, RBA and elsewhere in mixed exhibitions and had numerous solo shows including Contemporary Fine Art Gallery, Eton, 1992. In 1991 he shared a show with his wife at Phoenix Gallery, Highgate. Harrison published *The Portrait Painters' Handbook*, 1968, and *The Book of Tobit*, 1969. Harris Art Gallery in Preston and galleries in Kendal and Lancaster hold his work. Lived in Cartmel Fell, Cumbria.

Coela Pryce HARRISON fl. c.1920–1960 Watercolourist, born at Thorpe near Norwich, Norfolk, into a military family. She attended St Felix's School, Southwold, and studied art in St Ives with Leonard Fuller, at Heatherley's School of Fine Art with Iain Macnab and elsewhere. Showed at RWS, SWA, RI, in India and Malta. Lived for a time at Dedham, Essex, completing small pictures of the local countryside.

Colin HARRISON 1939– Painter, draughtsman and teacher, born in Boston, Lincolnshire. His specialities were nudes and portraits, and he was noted for subjects from the entertainment world such as the singer Ruby Murray and the dancers Fred Astaire and Ginger Rogers. Harrison attended Leicester College of Art, 1957–61, then Royal Academy Schools, 1961–4, obtaining a David Murray Scholarship in his first year and a Silver Medal in his last. Lectured at Ulster College of Art and Design, 1964–73, and was a visiting lecturer at Wolverhampton Polytechnic. In 1970 Arts Council of Northern Ireland, which along with Ulster Museum holds his work, gave him a project award for film-making with William Bogle. Exhibitions included New 57 Gallery, Edinburgh; Brown Thomas Gallery in Dublin; Richard Demarco Gallery in Edinburgh; and Tom Caldwell Gallery, Belfast.

Edward Stroud HARRISON 1879– Painter, born in Edinburgh, where he studied at Heriot-Watt College and the University. Exhibited RSA extensively, SSA of which he was a member, Walker Art Gallery, Liverpool, and Royal Glasgow Institute of the Fine Arts. Lived for many years in Elgin, Moray.

Ian HARRISON 1935– Painter, miniaturist and teacher, born in Staines, Surrey, educated partly in England, partly in Nairobi, Kenya, where his art education was obtained. Went on to teach history of art and design at Halton College of Further Education, Widnes. Showed with RMS, Hesketh Hubbard Society and elsewhere and had several one-man shows at Woburn Abbey, Bedfordshire. Lived in Northwich, Cheshire.

John Cyril HARRISON 1898–1985 Artist who specialised in natural history, born in Tidworth, Wiltshire. He began drawing as a small boy, his family living in British Columbia from 1912–15, learning anatomy from taxidermy and concentrating on birds of prey. After service in World War I Jack Harrison studied at Slade School of Fine Art, then moved to Norfolk, settling in a studio in Haynford. He illustrated books on birds, notably his friend Seton Gordon's *Days with the Golden Eagle*, of 1927; in 1949 wrote and illustrated *Bird Portraits*; and in 1968 completed all illustrations for Brown and Amadon's *The Birds of Prey of the World*. Harrison's travels included Scotland, Iceland and latterly Africa. The Tryon Gallery regularly held his shows and published prints of his game bird subjects, which had popular appeal, as did his watercolours. Harrison, who listed his recreations as shooting and fishing, died after finishing all the pictures for his spring 1985 exhibition. His prints continued to be sold by the Tryon and Moorland Gallery.

John Francis HARRISON 1904– Versatile and colourful artist, one of the Pitmen Painters, Jack Harrison was the son of a miner, born at Waterhouses, County Durham, moving to Ashington, Northumberland, in 1909. When 13 he started at Ellington Colliery, went to Bothal Pit at Ashington Colliery at 15 and worked until he was made redundant at 63. Harrison endured long and unsociable shifts, working hard coal in cramped conditions for meagre pay, rising to be a deputy overman. In the 1950s he joined the Ashington Art Group, consistently experimental and individual in his approach, "although it was often difficult to buy paints and materials and framing my work has been very costly". The Group's paintings went to Germany and China, the first post-Communist Western art show there. Harrison worked widely in Northumberland, "particularly liked the coastal areas from Berwick to North Shields". The mining community "was a rich source of inspiration". He had a retrospective at Woodhorn Church Museum in 1994 and the Colliery Museum there holds his work, which was signed with a JFH monogram.

Laura HARRISON fl. from late 1960s– Painter and draughtsman, notable for portraits in a rich palette, born and lived in Glasgow, where, under David Donaldson, she graduated in drawing and painting from the School of Art, 1967. Among privately commissioned portraits were the naturalist David Bellamy; her work was also in many corporate and private collections. Exhibitions included RP from 1990; Glasgow Society of Women Artists, Royal Glasgow Institute of the Fine Arts and Bruton Street Gallery, all from 1993–4; and William Hardie, Glasgow, 1995. Also exhibited with Flying Colours Gallery. In 1996 had a solo show at Gatehouse Gallery, Glasgow.

Margaret HARRISON 1940– Artist in mixed media, sometimes on a large scale, as in Rape, of 1978, owned by Arts Council; teacher. She studied at Carlisle College of Art and Royal

Academy Schools. Among her awards was a Royal Academy Schools Bronze Medal, a British Council Scholarship to Italy and Northern Arts and Arts Council grants. Went on to teach widely, including Royal College of Art, Slade School of Fine Art and Goldsmiths' College. Mixed exhibitions included Art for Society, Whitechapel Art Gallery and tour, 1978; Some British Art from the Left, Artists' Space, New York, 1979; and Woodlands Art Gallery and tour, 1981–2, in Greater London Arts Association award show. Solo shows included Carlisle City Art Gallery and tour, 1980–1.

Margot HARRISON 1915– Painter, born Margaret Amy Harrison in Madras, southern India. She studied privately with Edwin Pascoe Holman, later with Kingsley Sutton and was for four years a part-time student at Farnham Art School with John Wilkinson. For a time she was a member of SWA and RWS Art Club. Harrison exhibited at Paris Salon, ROI, RBA and in provincial galleries and had several solo shows in London. British Petroleum commissioned her to paint views of the rivers Tamar and Test and the National Trust Clumber Park. Lived in Odiham, Hampshire.

Marguerite HARRISON 1927– Painter, draughtsman and teacher, born in Llandudno, Caernarvonshire, Wales. She was educated at the Royal Masonic School at Rickmansworth and was mainly self-taught as a painter although she studied for a while with Kenneth Jameson. Exhibited RA, RCamA and with Wirral Society of Arts. She was a Froebel-trained teacher who taught in the Birkenhead area of Cheshire and privately, living in Birkenhead. For some years Harrison painted under her unmarried name Marguerite Hazel Roberts.

Mary Kent HARRISON: *see* **Mary KENT**

Stephanie HARRISON 1939– Artist using watercolour, gouache, pen and pencil, born in King's Lynn, Norfolk. She attended Medway College of Art, Rochester, 1955–60, teachers including John Ward and Fred Cuming. After working as an illustrator and graphic designer in industry Harrison worked for the Science Museum and British Museum, becoming a freelance artist in 1979. She illustrated several books, including *Reader's Digest Wild Flowers of Great Britain*, and designed greetings cards for Henry Ling and Company. She was a member of RMS and the Society of Botanical Artists, showing also with RI and Francis Iles Gallery, Rochester. Harrison was a gallery artist at Linda Blackstone Gallery, Pinner, and had a number of solo exhibitions in London and Kent. As well as botanical, house and garden studies she painted landscape, still life and meticulous studies of aircraft and motor transport. Lived at Stick Hill, Edenbridge, Kent.

Thomas Michael HARRISON 1969– Painter and teacher, born in Wigan, Lancashire. He gained an honours degree at University College of Wales, Aberystwyth, in 1990, winning several prizes. Went on to complete his master's degree and in 1991–2 taught at the College. His work was shown at exhibitions at University College of Wales, Coach House Gallery in Wigan and Mall Galleries and in 1993 was included in Aberystwyth Artists at The Deffett Francis Gallery, Swansea Institute of Higher Education.

Robert Edward HARRISSON 1922– Painter and teacher, born in London, educated in Edmonton where he continued to live. Studied at Hornsey School of Art, 1938–42, then after war service in the Royal Navy at Royal College of Art, 1946–9, where his teachers included Rodrigo Moynihan and Ruskin Spear. Showed with Enfield Art Circle and elsewhere, Royal Dental Hospital holding his work. This he signed R E H.

Tim HARRISSON 1952– Sculptor, draughtsman, painter and teacher, who attended Hammersmith College of Art, 1969–70, Norwich College of Art, 1970–3, and Byam Shaw School of Fine Art, 1975. After working as a woodman and welder, 1976–80, in 1980–3 Harrisson was lecturer in painting and drawing, adult education, for Wiltshire and Dorset Council. In 1988 he was sculptor-in-residence, Red House Museum, Christchurch, organised by the Hampshire Sculpture Trust. Spatial relationships were of key importance to Harrisson's abstract sculptures. Millfield School, Somerset, gave him a commission in 1989, in collaboration with Artsite Gallery, Bath. Mixed exhibitions included Salisbury Library, 1981; Harris Museum, Preston, 1985; in 1987 he was a winner in international competition organised by Metro Art, New York; 1991, *The Economist* Plaza, St James'; and 1994, New Art Centre Sculpture Garden at Roche Court, Salisbury. Had a solo show at New Art Centre, Sloane Street, 1993.

Frederick Samuel HARROP 1887–1969 Painter, potter, printmaker, designer and teacher, born in Batsford, Stoke-on-Trent. Harrop was a student at Hanley Municipal School of Art, 1906–9, where he won a number of prizes and medals, then at Royal College of Art, 1909–13. In 1913 Harrop went to Siam, holding a series of art teaching positions, finally being organising art master to the Ministry of Public Instruction, Bangkok. He also designed Siamese currency notes. Won Order of the Crown of Siam, third class, in 1920, two years after gaining the Order of the White Elephant, fourth class. From 1930 he was back in England holding teaching positions at Willesden Polytechnic, Paddington Technical Institute and Hammersmith School of Building and Arts and Crafts. As well as showing in Siam, Harrop exhibited at RBA, Crafts Centre of Great Britain and had a memorial show at Camden Arts Centre in 1970. Lived in London.

Frank HART 1878–1959 Graphic artist and painter. Born in Brighton, Sussex, he studied at Heatherley's School of Fine Art. Exhibited RA, RI, RWS and abroad. Among his books are *Dolly's Society Book* and *Master Toby's Hunt*, and he also had work in *Punch* and *Men Only*. Lived at Cooden, Sussex.

John HART 1921– Painter, engraver and teacher, born in Manchester and educated at Merchant Taylors' School, Crosby.

Studied at Liverpool College of Art and in Paris, then ran teacher training at Liverpool College and at Goldsmiths' College. While in Liverpool Hart appeared in John Willetts' *Art in a City*, 1967, as "a slight, bespectacled figure of buzzing energy" who not only ran "an outstanding department at the College but produces a steady output of non-figurative paintings". Exhibition venues included John Moores Liverpool Exhibitions; Bear Lane Gallery in Oxford; LG, Annely Juda, Marjorie Parr, Beaux Arts and Redfern Galleries, and abroad. Completed a mural at Daresbury Nuclear Physics Laboratory. Walker Art Gallery in Liverpool, Dudley Art Gallery, the Universities of Liverpool, Manchester and York and several education authorities hold examples. In retirement lived in Montbrun-les-Bains, France.

Jonathan HART 1949– Abstract artist whose work often derived from landscape and observation of nature, born in Ripon, Yorkshire. Studied at Scarborough School of Art, 1968–9, then Canterbury College of Art, 1969–72. Did a variety of jobs to support his painting. His mixed show appearances included Stowells exhibition at Mall Galleries, 1972; Some Canterbury Painters, at Canterbury Library, 1974; and Summer Show 2 at Serpentine Gallery, 1982. Had a series of open studio solo exhibitions, living for some time in London.

Philip HARTAS 1930– Sculptor and teacher who studied at Leeds College and Slade School of Fine Art under Henry Moore and Reg Butler. He held teaching posts at Derby, during which time he was chosen by Jack Beddington as one of his *Young Artists of Promise*, in the 1957 book of that title; Liverpool College of Art; Bournemouth and Leicester; then finally at Brighton Polytechnic/Brighton University. Exhibited at Liverpool Academy and elsewhere. Hartas completed a number of commissions when resident in Liverpool, including a relief in Lewis' department store.

Christine HART-DAVIES 1947– Watercolourist, born in Shrewsbury, Shropshire. She read fine art and typography at Reading University, 1966–70, teachers including Rita Donagh and Michael Twyman, where she graduated with honours. She worked for several years with a London design group, mainly on educational books, then in 1975, after sailing and travelling in Europe and North Africa, settled in Poole, Dorset, becoming known for precise botanical watercolours. Hart-Davies became a member of RMS in 1975 and a founder-member of the Society of Botanical Artists in 1985. She was especially interested in mosses and lichens, and her work on these was four times awarded the Gold Medal of the Royal Horticultural Society. Her exhibitions included Contemporary British Watercolours, RI and Hilliard Society of Miniaturists from 1983; and Paris Salon and Flowers and Gardens from 1984. Her solo exhibitions included Spring Hill Gallery, Brisbane, from 1984, and Young Masters Gallery, Brisbane, from 1987. The book *A Year in a Victorian Garden*, 1990, includes her work, which is held by the Hunt Institute of Botanical Documentation, Carnegie-Mellon University, Pittsburgh.

Jack HARTERT 1922–1975 Versatile painter and draughtsman, producing figurative work with an emphasis on line, whose father owned a gallery on Madison Avenue, New York. Jack drew from an early age, contributing to school magazines, and studied art at university and the National Academy of Design. After Army service in World War II Hartert joined the family business, based in Paris where he purchased European paintings which were shipped back to America, at the same time continuing with his own work. Although Hartert was lukewarm about much of what he bought, notably the Impressionists and especially Monet, he seems to have had a high regard for Degas, as he did for the Dutch Old Masters and advanced artists like Magritte. Still lifes in the Dutch manner and pastels of nudes were special features of Hartert's output; one later theme was the slightly Surrealist Tower of Babel series of oils. After a few years in America Hartert in 1961 moved to England, settling in Clifton where his brother William, who had married a Bristol girl, lived. Jack married in 1970, but did not want children, having seen many injured and orphaned ones in the Pacific during the war, two of whom he and friends unofficially adopted during hostilities. Hartert refused any medals. Later, the Arab-Israeli conflict prompted several powerful anti-war drawings. Hartert was a serious, unassuming artist whose friends often knew nothing of his work. He had no compulsion to sell, and showed infrequently in New York, London, Paris and the Netherlands. In 1975, after his death from cancer, there was a memorial show at David Durant's gallery in Clifton, where examples of Hartert's trompe l'oeil painted furniture were included. Hartert was remembered locally as a larger-than-life character, often seen in the city's better restaurants, a generous, cigar-smoking host and companion, noted for his amusing anecdotes.

Alex HARTLEY 1963– Artist using a variety of media, born in West Byfleet, Surrey, who did a foundation course, 1983–4, then an honours degree, 1984–90, at Camberwell School of Arts and Crafts, gaining his master's at Royal College of Art, 1988–90. Group exhibitions included International Departures, Kavalere Kazerne, Amsterdam, 1990; Crossover, Anderson O'Day Gallery, 1991; Young British Artists from the Saatchi Collection, Art Cologne, Cologne, 1993; Fall Out, Walker Fabrik, Darmstadt, 1996; and Sensation. Young British Artists from the Saatchi Collection, RA, 1997. Later solo shows included Victoria Miro Gallery, 1997, where Hartley's work Viewer was composed of a vast, fully functioning slide viewer and oversized 35-millimetre slides. Arts Council, Contemporary Art Society, De Beers and Caldic Collections hold examples.

Kathleen HARTNELL 1886-c.1965 Painter and printmaker, born in Bristol. She was also known as Katherine Hartnell, and was the sister of the artist Hilda E Jefferies, also known as Hilda E Bonsey. Paintings were signed in her married name, Kathleen Hartnell, etchings with her maiden name, Kathleen G(rant) Jefferies. She studied at Slade School of Fine Art under Henry Tonks, Philip Wilson Steer and Walter Westley Russell, winning several prizes. Exhibited extensively at

Beaux Arts Gallery, RA, NEAC, LG, Leicester Galleries and RSA. Aberdeen and Bristol public galleries hold her work. She was also a musician, trained at the Royal Academy of Music. Lived in London.

Archibald Standish HARTRICK 1864–1950 Illustrator, printmaker, painter and teacher, born in Bangalore, Madras, India. Hartrick studied at Edinburgh University, the Slade School of Fine Art and in Paris, notably at Académie Julian, where he met such luminaries as Toulouse-Lautrec and Van Gogh. In 1887 showed first picture at Paris Salon. Returned to Scotland, then from 1889 worked in London as a black-and-white illustrator for *The Pall Magazine*, *The Graphic* and *The Daily Graphic*. Hartrick was notable for his drawings of country life, of which the British Museum has fine examples. Although he later lived in London a period with his wife, the artist Lily Blatherwick, in Gloucestershire inspired Hartrick with rural subjects. Taught at Camberwell and Central Schools of Arts and Crafts. Hartrick showed prolifically at RWS and NEAC of both of which he was a member, as he was of Senefelder Club; had a show with his wife at Continental Gallery, 1901; and had a retrospective at Fulham Public Library in 1936; and a memorial show at Arts Council, 1951. *A Painter's Pilgrimage through Fifty Years*, which he published in 1939, reflects his chequered life.

Charles Leonard HARTWELL 1873–1951 Sculptor in marble and bronze, born in Blackheath, London. Studied at City and Guilds School, Kennington, privately with Onslow Ford and Hamo Thornycroft and at the Royal Academy Schools. Exhibited extensively at RA, as well as RI, ROI, RSA and RP. Chantrey Bequest bought A Foul in the Giants' Race as well as Dawn, both now in Tate Gallery collection. Elected RA in 1924 and was awarded the RBS silver medal for The Goatherd's Daughter five years later. Member of the Arts Club. Hartwell's usual method of working was to make an accurate plaster model of a work which assistants would then principally carve, Hartwell adding the final touches. Died at Aldwick, Sussex.

William John HARTWELL 1922– Painter, born in Amington, Staffordshire. He studied at Goldsmiths' College School of Art with Kathleen Allen, 1940–2 and 1948–9. Exhibited AIA, Whitechapel and Leicester Galleries and RBA, sometimes signing his work only with initials. West Riding Education Committee, in Yorkshire, bought his work. Lived for some time in Norwich.

Charles W HARVEY 1895–1970 Painter and teacher, born in London, whose family moved to Belfast, Northern Ireland, in 1906, where he remained based. He trained as a damask designer and studied at Belfast School of Art and for a short time at Dublin's Metropolitan School of Art. From 1932–60 Harvey taught at St Mary's Training College, initially part-time, becoming head of department. He exhibited principally at Ulster Arts Club and Arts Council of Northern Ireland put on a retrospective in 1976.

Daniel HARVEY 1959– Sculptor, born in Dorking, Surrey. He did a fine art sculpture course at Cardiff College of Art, 1977–8, then was at Royal College of Art, 1983–6. Mixed shows participated in included LG at RCA Galleries, 1984; Outside Sculpture Show, Camden Lock, 1985; Vanessa Devereux Gallery, 1986; and Kettle's Yard, Cambridge, 1988. Had solo shows at Birch & Conran from 1987. Harvey worked with the Laboritorio Aperto of Bussana Vecchia in Italy in 1985. In 1988 his environmental sculpture was included in Peter Greenaway's film *Drowning by Numbers*; in 1989 living sculpture by him was featured in Derek Jarman's film *War Requiem*.

Denis HARVEY 1925–1992 Sculptor, writer, photographer and teacher, born in Chelmsfield, Kent. He was educated at Bryanston School, worked in forestry for four years, completed an apprenticeship in stone masonry, studied sculpture at Wimbledon School of Art and later taught the subject at Reigate and West Surrey Colleges of Art. He showed his sculptures and photographs in London, Paris and Italy and completed stone monoliths for National Westminster Bank in Kingston upon Thames, heraldic and figure sculpture restoration work for London County Council and many portraits and sculptures in stone, marble, wood and bronze. When he was 17 Harvey became fascinated by the gypsy way of life, learned to speak the Romany language, to live like the travelling people and wrote about them. He was co-author of *The English Caravan*, 1972; *The Gypsies: waggon-time and after*, 1979; and just before he died, in Crawley, Sussex, finished *Plaiting the Magic.*

Gail HARVEY 1954– Painter, whose landscapes had a strong Expressionist content, born in Glasgow. She studied at the School of Art there, 1972–7, including post-diploma, with time at Hospitalfield Summer School, Arbroath, 1975. Harvey won a Scottish Education Department Travelling Scholarship in 1977, and a John Murray Thomson Award at RSA, 1985. Showed regularly at RSA, also RSW and Royal Glasgow Institute of the Fine Arts. Had a solo exhibition at Macaulay Gallery, Stenton, 1991, later ones including Roger Billcliffe Fine Art, Glasgow, 1997. Shetland Arts Trust and Highlands and Islands Enterprise hold examples. Harvey moved to Shetland in 1988, which was a strong theme in her output.

Gertrude HARVEY 1889–1966 Flower and landscape painter, self-taught, married to the artist Harold Harvey. A keen gardener, she settled in a cottage in Newlyn, Penzance, Cornwall, and showed at RA, SWA, Walker Art Gallery in Liverpool, Fine Art Society and Goupil Gallery. Had a solo show at Leicester Galleries, having received encouragement from the writer George Bernard Shaw. He wrote the catalogue introduction for the sell-out show where all exhibits cost five guineas. Gert Harvey was a witty, forthright character who died in a nursing home in St Just.

Hilda HARVEY 1890–1982 Painter, notably of portraits, printmaker and miniaturist on ivory. She was daughter of the artist

John Rabone Harvey, her older brother being Herbert Johnson Harvey. Attended Birmingham School of Art for about six years from age of 15, then worked for firm of Birmingham silversmiths, closed down by World War I, the owners being German. She joined London couture house Mechinka, studying part-time, then full-time at Slade School of Fine Art under Henry Tonks. In London was courted by the artist Gilbert Spencer. After going with another artist to Paris in early 1920s and catching paratyphoid fever she was advised not to winter in England so lived in south of France for two years. After her return she married Charles Meeke of Birmingham and had one son, Harvey, before divorcing him. After periods in Cornwall and Llangollen during World War II she returned to St Ives where she continued to paint until 1950. Showed at NEAC, RA, Paris Salon and RBSA, being elected an associate in 1933.

Jake HARVEY 1948– Sculptor, born in Kelso, Roxburghshire. He studied sculpture at Edinburgh College of Art, 1966–72, during 1971 under a travelling scholarship visiting Greece and the Greek islands. He further travelled to India in 1989. Harvey was a trustee of the Scottish Sculpture Trust, 1984–7. His sculptures, such as Poacher's Tree and Poacher's Vane, both shown at Scottish Art in the 20th Century, at RWA, 1991, are full of mysterious signs and symbols, the sculptor favouring forged and welded steel. Had a one-man show at Third Eye Centre, Glasgow, 1985, Scottish Gallery in Edinburgh, 1993. Scottish Arts Council and Contemporary Art Society hold his work. Major commissions included Hugh MacDiarmid Memorial, Langholm, 1985; and Symbol Stone for Compaq Computers, Glasgow, 1988. Harvey was elected RSA in 1989. Lived at Maxton, St Boswells, Roxburghshire.

John HARVEY 1935– Painter and teacher, born in Plymouth, Devon. After a career in printing and commercial art Harvey graduated with honours in fine art painting, 1975–8, from Camberwell School of Arts and Crafts, then obtained his art teacher's certificate from Brighton Polytechnic, 1978–9. He taught at a Cornish school before retiring early to paint in Penzance. Harvey mostly completed work on the spot, notably colourful coastal and beach scenes. Mixed exhibitions included Parkway Gallery; Phoenix Gallery, Lavenham; Whitechapel Art Gallery; and Salthouse and Porthmeor Galleries, St Ives. In 1993–4 he had a solo exhibition at Gordon Hepworth Gallery, Newton St Cyres.

John HARVEY 1959– Artist whose work included constructed paintings, teacher and writer, born in Nantyglo, Monmouthshire. He gained a fine art honours degree at Gwent College of Higher Education, 1977–81, then a master's degree in visual art at University College of Wales in Aberystwyth, 1982–4, getting his doctorate, 1986–90. He was appointed its lecturer in fine art in 1992. The visual culture of Welsh nonconformity was a special interest. Showed in group exhibitions in southwest England and in Wales, including Aberystwyth Artists at The Deffett Francis Gallery, Swansea Institute of Higher Education, 1993.

John Wynn HARVEY 1923–1989 Sculptor, painter, draughtsman and writer, born in London, son of the diplomat Oliver Harvey, Lord Harvey of Tasburgh, whose diaries he was to edit. Educated at Eton, Westminster and Cambridge University, he was at the Central School of Art, 1947–9. In the 1950s Harvey enjoyed considerable success as a sculptor, by the 1960s turning to drawing and painting as his main means of expression, chief subjects being wildly coloured sculptural figures and Welsh landscapes. In 1960 Harvey published his first novel, *Within and Without*, a bestseller made into a film; his second, *Beside the Sea*, 1967, enjoyed critical success. Much of Harvey's later life was spent at the maternal family home at Meifod, Powys, where he farmed, although he died in Rome. Harvey was deeply influenced by his friend, Henry Moore. He argued that the vitality of abstract art, and in particular its heightened sense of form and colour, must be channelled to constructive effect. He believed in a marriage between the creativeness of abstraction and the disciplines of figurative art. Group show appearances included Leicester Galleries, SPS and RP. Solo exhibitions included Galerie La Licorne, Paris, 1951, Glebe Gallery, 1985, and Bernheimer Fine Arts, 1988. There was a retrospective at Cadogan Contemporary, 1991. Musée d'Art Moderne, Paris, and Pembroke College, Oxford, hold examples.

Marcus HARVEY 1963– Painter using richly coloured impasto, strongly gestural marks and an overlying black linear image. He was born in Leeds, Yorkshire and studied at Goldsmiths' College School of Art, 1982–6, gaining an honours degree in fine art. Teachers included Harry Thubron, Albert Irvin, Basil Beattie and Michael Craig-Martin. Was included in Young British Artist IV at Saatchi Gallery, 1995, where such pictures as Half Way Up, Julie From Hull, Reader's Wife 1 and My Arse Is Yours contained frequent references to the female nude, knickers and bottoms. In 1997, Harvey's portrait of the Moors child murderer Myra Hindley, made using casts of a child's hand prints, prompted outrage when exhibited at the RA in Sensation: British Artists from the Saatchi Collection, being kicked and splattered with eggs and ink. Harvey lived in London.

Mark HARVEY 1921– Sculptor and teacher, creating figurative and abstract works in metal and stone, born in Birmingham. He studied at Chelsea School of Art, 1944–6, and teaching posts included Regent Street Polytechnic and Goldsmiths' College Schools of Art and Morley College. Did commissioned work for churches and public sculptures including the Portland stone Polar Bear, 1964, in Glebe Shopping Centre at Stevenage New Town.

Michael Anthony HARVEY 1921– Artist in oil, watercolour and crayon and art critic, born in Kew, Surrey, who studied at Bryanston School, then Epsom School of Art, 1948–50, and Wimbledon School of Art, 1955–7, teachers including R O Dunlop and David Birch. He was art critic for the *Surrey Mirror* Series of Newspapers and art correspondent for the *Croydon Advertiser* Series, as well as contributing to many other periodicals and books. Harvey was a member of SGA, also of Art

Societies in Chichester, Reigate and Bognor Regis. He showed at John Whibley Gallery, Rutland Gallery, Qantas Gallery and widely abroad, having many solo and dual shows. Royal Borough of Camden and East Sussex County Council hold examples: the oil Limehouse Reach, held by Johns Hopkins University, Baltimore, is one of his principal works. Lived in Bognor Regis, Sussex.

William HARVEY 1957– Painter, born in Hampshire, who studied at Gwent College of Higher Education, 1980–3, then Birmingham Polytechnic, 1983–4. His mixed shows included Cleveland International Drawing Biennale, 1985, and John Moores Liverpool Exhibition, 1987, where he was a prizewinner with Liners. His solo shows included Worcester City Art Gallery, Winchester Gallery and Spitalfields Workspace, 1986. In 1986–7 he was fellow in painting at South Glamorgan Institute of Higher Education, Cardiff. Arts Council holds his work. Lived in London.

John Hammond HARWOOD 1904–1980 Painter, especially of landscape in watercolour, and illustrator. Born in Darwen, Lancashire, he was educated in Ripon, Yorkshire, then attended Harrogate School of Art, 1921–4, also Royal College of Art, 1924–8, under William Rothenstein. He became principal of Gloucester School of Art, 1939–45, then Sheffield College of Art, 1945–64. Was a member of Sheffield Society of Artists, where he taught and exhibited for many years. Also exhibited RA, NEAC and LG. He illustrated a number of books in the Puffin series. Sheffield Arts Department bought his work, which often featured the Dorset coast; he died in Dorset, but lived for many years in Sheffield.

Lucy HARWOOD 1893–1972 Painter and draughtsman, born at Belstead Park, near Ipswich, although soon after her birth the family moved to East Bergholt. She wanted to be a pianist, but an operation went wrong, leaving her right side partly paralysed, so she turned to painting, attending the Slade School of Fine Art prior to World War I. When Cedric Morris opened the East Anglian School of Painting and Drawing in Dedham, in 1937, Harwood, still unmarried and living at home, became a student, which she remained, moving to be near the School when it relocated at Benton End, Hadleigh, in 1940. She was a key figure in its social life. Her pictures, painted with her left hand, were spontaneous, innocent and colourful, still life and landscapes of Suffolk around her home at Upper Layham. She sold them locally and the first show of her work was at The Minories, Colchester, 1975. Further shows included several at Sally Hunter Fine Art. Ipswich Museum and Colchester Art Society hold Harwood's work.

Jun HASEGAWA 1969– Painter and draughtsman, born in Japan, who gained a bachelor's degree in fine art at Goldsmiths' College, 1992–5. Exhibitions included White Trash and Multiple Orgasm, both at Lost-in-Space, 1995; and New Contemporaries at Tate Gallery, Liverpool, and Camden Arts Centre, 1996.

Ron HASELDEN 1944– Sculptor who worked in a variety of media, born in Gravesend, Kent. He studied sculpture at Gravesend School of Art, 1961–3, then Edinburgh College of Art, 1963–6. Involved in multiples, film and performance for several years from 1973, then concentrated on installation. His group appearances included New Light on Sculpture at Tate Gallery, Liverpool, 1990, and Arts Council touring show Recent British Sculpture, 1993–4. His solo shows included Seaward at Serpentine Gallery, 1977. Whitechapel Art Gallery, 1988, and Golden Crescent at South London Art Gallery, 1993. Lived in London.

Ray HASLAM 1942– Painter and teacher, born in Bolton, Lancashire. He studied at the local College of Art, 1957–62, continuing his training at Sheffield College of Art. He later became a teacher in secondary education and from 1972 worked in the department of art at St Martin's College of Higher Education, Lancaster. Haslam's Hyper-Realist pictures examined aspects of urban decay, as in his Crashed Cortina, Wellington Road Garage, Lancaster, 1983, included in Lancashire South of the Sands, which toured from County and Regimental Museum, Preston, 1988.

Ernest William HASLEHURST 1866–1949 Watercolourist, principally of landscapes, born in Walthamstow. Studied at the Slade School of Fine Art under Alphonse Legros. Exhibited RA, RBA, RI, RWA and Ridley Art Club; had several one-man shows in London. Haslehurst's work was extensively reproduced, notably in Blackie's *Beautiful Britain* series. His work is in the collections of a number of British provincial galleries – notably Bristol, Sheffield, Oldham and Newport – as well as galleries in Canada, New Zealand and Sri Lanka. For some time he was president of the Midland Sketch Club. Lived in London.

Joan HASSALL 1906–1988 Wood engraver, painter, typographer and teacher, born in London, daughter of the artist John Hassall and sister of the writer, poet and librettist Christopher Hassall. After attending a Froebel Training College for teachers Joan Hassall was at the London School of Art, 1925–7, Royal Academy Schools, 1928–33, and at Bolt Court, 1931–4. She taught book production at Edinburgh College of Art, 1940–6. Showed at SWE and RE, of both of which she was a member, RA, SWA, RHA and elsewhere. Illustrated many books, including Jane Austen, Robert Louis Stevenson, Mary Webb and many of *The Saltire Chapbooks*. For almost 15 years before her death poor sight prevented her cutting her delicately detailed blocks. Work held by British Museum. Lived in Malham, Yorkshire.

John HASSALL 1868–1948 Cartoonist, illustrator, designer, painter and teacher, born in Walmer, Kent. He was father to the artist Joan Hassall and the writer Christopher Hassall. After education in England and Germany Hassall farmed in Canada, began contributing sketches to *The Graphic*, then early in 1890s spent several years studying art in Antwerp and at Académie Julian,

Paris. In England Hassall became a popular cartoonist and designed posters such as *Skegness is* So *bracing*. Hassall illustrated numerous books and periodicals such as *The Idler*, *London Opinion*, *Pearson's Magazine* and *The Tatler*. For many years he ran his own school of art. He was a member of RI, RWA and Arts, London Sketch and Savage Clubs. Lived in London.

David HASTE 1938– Artist and teacher who studied at St Martin's School of Art and Royal College of Art. He began teaching in 1970 and became head of the fine art course at Canterbury School of Art. Among his mixed shows was Volcanic Landscapes at Boundary Gallery, 1991. After a summer climbing around Mount Etna in Italy Haste showed canvases at the Geological Museum in 1986 under sponsorship of the British Museum, one of several solo exhibitions. Victoria & Albert Museum holds his work.

Francis John HASTINGS 1901–1990 Mural painter, teacher, politician and writer who became the 15th Earl of Huntingdon. He was educated at Eton College and Oxford University and as a young man while travelling became enthused by the mural paintings of the Mexican left-wing artist Diego Rivera. He worked with Rivera extensively in America as well as completing his own work. On returning to England he taught at Camberwell School of Arts and Crafts and Central School of Arts and Crafts. During the 1940s he became involved with local politics in Andover, Hampshire, near where he lived, then in national government, being parliamentary secretary to the Ministry of Agriculture and Fisheries, 1945–50, in the Attlee Labour administration. Among his books is *Commonsense about India.* Showed at Wertheim Gallery, Lefevre Gallery and overseas and was chairman of the committee of the Society of Mural Painters, 1951–8. The Marx Memorial Library, London, has a remarkable mural by him. Was a member of Art Workers' Guild, AIA and was president of the Society of Mural Painters. Was married to the writer Margaret Lane. New Grafton Gallery held an eightieth birthday retrospective in 1981. Lived in Beaulieu, Hampshire, and in London.

Erica HASTINGS-GRAY 1890– Watercolour painter and calligrapher, born in London. She studied at London School of Art, 1914–16, with John Hassall and Ernest Borough Johnson, with Frank Spenlove-Spenlove and with Hesketh Hubbard. Exhibited UA, WIAC and East Sussex Art Club, of which she was a member. Lived in Battle, Sussex.

Ethel C HATCH 1870–1975 Painter, especially of figures and flowers, mainly in watercolour. Born in Oxford into a religious and scholastic family, she attended the High School there, then the Slade School of Fine Art under Henry Tonks, Fred Brown and Philip Wilson Steer. Exhibited RA, Goupil and Chenil Galleries, NEAC, SWA and Paris Salon, having a one-man show at Walker's Galleries in mid-1920s. Lived for a time in Italy, and in London.

Lionel HATCH 1949– Typographer, printmaker and artist in pastel, born in Bolton, Lancashire; he settled nearby at Atherton. Studied at Bolton College of Art, 1966–9, where his teachers included Roger Hampson. Showed in the area.

Mona HATOUM 1952– Artist, born in Beirut, Lebanon, who took part in many exhibitions, screenings and performances. She studied at Byam Shaw School of Art, 1977–79, then Slade School of Fine Art, 1979–81. Among her awards were Greater London Arts, 1982, and Arts Council Video Bursary, 1985. She was artist-in-residence at Western Front Art Centre in Vancouver, Canada, 1984; other residencies occurring at 911 Contemporary Art Centre, Seattle, America, in 1986, Chisenhale Dance Space, 1986–7, and Western Front Art Centre again, 1988. From 1989–92 was senior research fellow in fine art at South Glamorgan Institute of Higher Education, Cardiff. From 1981 group appearances included New Contemporaries, at ICA; Festival of Video Art, SAW Gallery, Ottawa, 1985; Essential Black Art, Chisenhale Gallery and tour, 1988; South Bank Centre's The British Art Show and tour, in 1990; and The Quality of Light, The Tate at St Ives, 1997. Retrospective at Museum of Modern Art, Oxford, 1998. Lived in London.

Doris HATT 1890–1969 Painter, designer and printmaker, born in Bath, Somerset. She studied at the School of Art there, after initial education in England and Germany, then at Royal College of Art and in Vienna. She eventually returned to live in the West Country, finally settling at Clevedon, Somerset, in a house and studio built to her own design. Showed mainly in that area. Exhibitions included RA, Leicester and Redfern Galleries, Jack Bilbo's Modern Art Gallery, and Foyles Gallery; in the 1950s and 1960s she had a series of one-man shows, including Minerva Gallery, Bath, and Osiris Gallery, Oxford, with a retrospective at RWA, Bristol, 1960.

Paul HATTON 1951– Artist in mixed media and teacher, born in Luton, Bedfordshire. He trained at Nelson and Colne College and the University of Lancaster. Taught part-time at St Martin's College in Lancaster, Edge Hill College in Ormskirk, Lancashire Polytechnic and Tuson College in Preston, also being fellow in 3D at the University of Lancaster. From 1983 he showed widely in Lancashire galleries and was included in the 1988 exhibition Lancashire South of the Sands, which toured from County and Regimental Museum, Preston. Hatton was a founder-member of Luneside Studios, Lancaster, and was interested in small incidents such as the lines of floating foam and grass; relevant materials were employed in the final images, although these were not direct representations.

Peter HATTON 1956– Artist, born in Rossendale, Lancashire, who was a member of TEA (see separate entry). Studied at Rochdale College of Art, 1974–5, then Liverpool Polytechnic, 1975–8. Hatton worked on a number of commissions with Janet Hodgson.These included Liquid Matter at Serpentine Gallery and Watershed, Queen Elizabeth Hall, both 1993. Lived in London.

Anthony HATWELL 1931– Sculptor and teacher, born in London, married to the artist Elizabeth Hatwell. He studied from 1947–9 and 1951–3 at Bromley College of Art; from 1952–3 at Borough Polytechnic with David Bomberg; from 1953–7 at Slade School of Fine Art; then gained a Boise Travelling Scholarship, 1957–8. Was assistant to Henry Moore, 1958. From 1969–90 was head of the school of sculpture at Edinburgh College of Art. Between 1959–69 Hatwell was a member of LG, its vice-president in 1961–3. Group exhibitions comprised Borough Bottega with Bomberg, 1953–5, in London, Oxford and Cambridge; Open Air Exhibition, Middelheim Park, Antwerp, 1959; Contemporary British Sculpture, Arts Council, 1960–4; Battersea Park Open Air Exhibition, 1963; LG Jubilee Exhibition, Tate Gallery, 1964; British Sculpture in the Twentieth Century, Whitechapel Art Gallery, 1981–2; Built in Scotland, Third Eye Centre, Glasgow, and tour, 1983; and Bomberg And His Students, South Bank University, 1992. Hatwell's work is held by Scottish National Gallery of Modern Art, Edinburgh, and Arts Council. Lived in Belhaven, Dunbar, East Lothian.

Elizabeth HATWELL 1937– Painter who also sculpted, and teacher, married to the sculptor Anthony Hatwell. She was born in Brighton, Sussex, graduated with honours in fine art from Chelsea School of Art, 1962–6, then taught at Edinburgh College of Art, 1969–79, and was a visiting lecturer at Duncan of Jordanstone College of Art, Dundee, 1976–7. In 1988 she published *The Artist's Daybook*. Group shows included LG from 1965; Roland, Browse & Delbanco and Marjorie Parr Gallery, both 1975; Scottish Arts Council, Small Sculpture, 1978; and Richard Demarco Gallery, Edinburgh, and tour, from 1988. Had a solo exhibition at Stirling Gallery, 1976, and Scottish Gallery and Royal Edinburgh Hospital, Edinburgh University, both 1979. Scottish Arts Council and Argyll Education Department hold examples. Lived in Belhaven, Dunbar, East Lothian.

David HAUGHTON 1924–1991 Painter, printmaker and teacher, born in London where he eventually settled, although he spent his early life in India. Haughton studied at Slade School of Fine Art and in 1947 moved to Nancledra, near St Ives, Cornwall. He was for short periods a member of the St Ives Society of Artists and of the Penwith Society. In 1951 left Cornwall and took up teaching appointment at Central School of Arts and Crafts until 1984. As well as showing in Cornwall in group exhibitions, Haughton was featured in the Arts Council touring show Contemporary Cornish Painting in 1949, the ICA's Contemporary English Landscape in 1957 and Cornwall 1945–55 at New Art Centre in 1977. An exhibition of his etchings originating at the St George's Gallery toured several continents, 1960–3, a Newlyn Art Gallery show of 1979 touring England. In 1992 Gordon Hepworth, Exeter, showed a retrospective of Haughton's St Just paintings, 1948–79. He was both a representational and abstract artist. Died in London.

Derrick HAUGHTON 1955– Painter whose picture in acrylic and household paint on canvas From the Day You Were Born was included in the 1997–8 John Moores Liverpool Exhibition. Born in Kingston, Jamaica, Haughton studied at Cardiff College of Art, 1974–5; Trent Polytechnic, Nottingham, 1975–8; Slade School of Fine Art, 1978–80; and Goldsmiths' College, 1992–4. From the mid-1980s he took part in group shows including Into the Nineties, Mall Galleries, 1994, and Foil, 202 Great Sufffolk Street, 1996. Lived in London.

Patrick HAUGHTON 1942– Painter, construction and assemblage artist, and teacher, using cool colours and clean lines, in whose work a sense of place, particularly the coastal landscape of Cornwall, was important. Haughton was born in Devonport and grew up in Barnstaple, north Devon, moving to Exeter to study architecture in 1960. The artist Nicholas Eastwood encouraged him to paint, and this he studied at Exeter College of Art, 1962–3, transferring to West of England College of Art, Bristol, 1963–6. Paul Feiler was head of painting, visitors including Peter Lanyon, William Scott and Karl Weschke. Qualified as a teacher and worked in primary schools in Kent, and Cornwall for 26 years, taking early retirement in 1995 to be a full-time artist. Haughton was a member of Newlyn, Penwith and Penzance Art Societies. Group exhibitions included Broad Street Gallery, Penryn, 1989–90; and Royal Cornwall Polytechnic Open, Falmouth, 1997. Solo shows included Falmouth Art Gallery, 1997 and Michael Wright Fine Art, Bristol, 1998. Lived in Penryn, Cornwall.

Wilfred HAUGHTON 1921– Artist in watercolour, oil and pastel, and writer, born in Hillmount, County Antrim, Northern Ireland. He became a member of RUA in 1956 and was for a time its president, was president and founder of Ulster Watercolour Society in 1977 and was a member of the Watercolour Society of Ireland. He also showed with RHA, RI and elsewhere and had a series of solo exhibitions in London, Belfast, Dublin and Limerick. After a business career he became a full-time artist from 1968. Haughton was virtually self-taught, although he attended courses by Jack Merriott and Edward Wesson. He aimed "to preserve the pure watercolour technique in the face of many additives that take away from the clarity and sparkle of this medium." Wrote the books *Brush Aside* and *Purely Watercolour*. Belfast's Museum and Art Gallery hold his work. Lived in Cullybackey, Ballymena, County Antrim.

Gerwyn HAVARD 1962– Painter born in Crickhowell, Breconshire, who studied at Central London Institute and Central St Martins College of Art & Design. From 1985–7 assisted at Nicola Jacobs Gallery. Group exhibitions included Annexe Gallery, 1990; Department of Education, 1992; Seven Sisters Gallery and Alexandra Palace Open, both 1994; and Saddleworth Open in Lancashire, Llangibby Open in Brecon and Royal Over-Seas League Open, all 1995. At the last show Havard's depiction of trees in an almost abstract pattern, Petrified Forest, oil on canvas, was exhibited.

Mandy HAVERS 1953– Artist and teacher who worked in mixed media, born in Portsmouth, Hampshire. She studied at its

College of Art and Design, 1971–2; at Coventry Polytechnic, 1972–5; then at Slade School of Fine Art, 1976–8. From 1980 she was a visiting lecturer at the Slade, Coventry Polytechnic and Trent Polytechnic in Nottingham. Among mixed shows was The Self Portrait: a Modern View, which toured from Artsite Gallery, Bath, 1987. Held a solo show at Arnolfini Gallery in Bristol which toured England and Ireland, also having one-man exhibitions in London, Brussels and Birmingham and with Nicholas Treadwell in Bradford.

Ashley HAVINDEN: *see* **ASHLEY**

Paul Douglas HAWDON 1953– Painter and printmaker, born in Manchester, who graduated with honours from St Martin's School of Art, 1978–82, was at Royal Academy Schools, 1982–5, attending British School in Rome as a Rome Scholar, 1988–9. Showed at RA, LG, RE and elsewhere. Lived in London, then in Birmingham.

Meredith William HAWES 1905– Artist in oil, watercolour, gouache and pastel, and teacher, born in Thornton Heath, Surrey. He attended Croydon School of Art, 1924–5, then Royal College of Art, 1926–30, teachers including William Rothenstein, Randolph Schwabe and Henry Rushbury. He held a number of teaching posts including being principal successively of Bournville, Portsmouth and Birmingham Colleges of Art. Completed murals in Manchester, Bournemouth and Birmingham and did book illustrating for leading publishers including John Murray and Oxford University Press. Hawes was a member of RWS, NEAC and SGA. Also showed at RA, leading London galleries, in France and America. RWS holds his work in the diploma collection. Lived latterly at Millbrook, Torpoint, Cornwall.

Peter HAWES 1940– Artist employing a range of approaches, including photographs, collages, paintings and assemblages, and teacher, who studied at Great Yarmouth and Norwich Schools of Art; Tilburg Academy, Netherlands; and Hornsey College of Art. Went on to become a principal lecturer at Brighton Polytechnic. Took part in several dozen shows, solo exhibitions including Landforms, The Gallery, Brighton Polytechnic, 1980; and Gardner Centre, University of Sussex, 1985–6. Works held by private and public collections in Britain and America.

Marjorie HAWKE 1894–1979 Draughtsman and painter in oil, born in London. She studied at Heatherley's, the Central School of Arts and Crafts and the Westminster School of Art, under Bernard Meninsky. Her work found its way into many private collections in Britain and abroad from mixed exhibitions at LG, Leicester Galleries, O'Hana and galleries in Greece, France and Italy. One-man shows included Bear Lane Gallery, Oxford, and the Rotunda Gallery. Lived in London.

Anthony HAWKEN 1948– Sculptor, jeweller and artist in various other media, born in Erith, Kent. He studied at Medway College of Art, Rochester, 1965–8, then with Willi Soukop at Royal Academy Schools, 1968–71, winning the Landseer Scholarship and Bronze Medal. He was assistant to Leon Underwood, 1972. Hawken was elected to RBS. His commissions included a medal for Motorola, Maidenhead; sculptured taps for the Prince of Dubai; and collections of jewellery for Roland Klein and Alistair Blair. Mixed shows included RA, Mario Flecha Gallery and Greenwich Theatre Gallery. Had solo shows at Blackheath Gallery; Minories, Colchester; and Woodlands Art Gallery, 1987. Citibank, Strand, holds his work. Lived in London.

Derrick HAWKER 1936– Painter and mixed media artist and teacher, experimental in approach, in whose work a dot technique, jigsaw shapes and the reduction of what was seen to its essence all played a part. The Irish landscape was a favourite subject. Hawker was born in Seaton, Devon, between 1953–9 attending South Devon College of Art and Cardiff College of Art. He held a number of teaching posts including Ulster College of Art and Design, 1965–73, after which he became principal of Teesside College of Art, Middlesbrough. Exhibitions included Woodstock Gallery, Arts Council of Northern Ireland Gallery in Belfast – it holds his work – and Barrenhill Gallery, Dublin.

Susan HAWKER 1949– Painter in oil and watercolour, born in Surrey. She attended Sutton School of Art, 1965–6, Epsom School of Art, 1968–71, and Royal College of Art, 1971–4, being awarded a John Minton Scholarship. Among various awards won was first prize in the Laing Painting Competition, 1981. Was elected RWS in 1975 and also showed in mixed exhibitions at RA, Leonie Jonleigh Studio in Guildford, Camden Arts Centre and elsewhere. From 1976 had a series of solo shows at Thackeray Gallery. Carlisle City Art Gallery, Chantrey Bequest and National Westminster Bank hold her work. Hawker was a landscape painter whose work was on more than one occasion compared to that of Cézanne.

Yvonne HAWKER 1956– Painter and printmaker, born in Madeira. She studied at Goldsmiths' College School of Art and Ravensbourne College. Showed extensively in Britain and Sweden, including RWS, RBA, RA, International Art Fair in Stockholm in 1983 and Smith's Gallery. In 1987–8 had solo show called Five Rooms in two parts: at Richard Demarco Gallery, Edinburgh, and at Bruton Gallery, Bruton, Somerset. This was based on rooms in Black Clauchrie, the artist's former Victorian shooting lodge home set in remote moorland at Barrhill by Girvan, Ayrshire. Hawker's pictures were about the dignity and beauty of inanimate, man-made objects transformed by time.

Julian HAWKES 1944– Sculptor, notable for abstract works in various materials, born in Gloucester. He studied at Slade School of Fine Art, 1967–9, gaining a Sainsbury Award in 1966. Was assistant to Phillip King, 1969–75, in the latter year winning a Gulbenkian Award and having a solo show at Woburn Arts Centre. Showed solo with Rowan Gallery from 1978, Arts

Council from the first exhibition acquiring Untitled, in canvas and wood, of 1976–7. Hawkes' Untitled, 1979, in oak and York stone, was commissioned by Peterborough City Council.

Justin HAWKES 1955– Painter and conservator, whose own works were richly coloured abstracts with landscape allusions. Hawkes studied at Cambridge Anglia Polytechnic, 1974–6, and in 1976–80 at Byam Shaw Art School, teachers including Frank Bowling and Simon Willis. In his second year he gained the Graham Hamilton Drawing Award. Undertook five-year apprenticeship as a painting conservator at School of Helmut Ruhemann and became a visiting teacher to art schools. Was a member of the International Institution for Conservation and the Association of British Restorers. Hawkes' main works were T Junction, 1979; Victorian, 1988; and Arbudus Point, 1993. Exhibitions included Mario Flecha Gallery, 1987; Edogawa Culture Centre, Tokyo, 1990; Collective Gallery, Edinburgh, 1994; and a shared exhibition with John Maltby, Andrew Vass and Richard Day, Amalgam 1995. Had a solo exhibition at Ginza, Tokyo, 1990, and shared one with Mark Reddy at Lynne Strover Gallery, Fen Ditton, 1997. Hawkes said that he was "influenced by British colour-field painters such as Robyn Denny, Richard Smith and Bridget Riley". Lived in Cambridge.

John HAWKESWORTH 1920– Painter, designer, writer and producer. He attended Rugby School and Oxford University and in between spent five months in Paris at Académie Julian. During Army service in World War II continued to paint. After demobilisation in 1946 pictures by Hawkesworth in Redfern Gallery were seen by the film director Alexander Korda's designer brother Vincent, who invited Hawkesworth to join the art department of London Films. Hawkesworth was art director for such films as *The Third Man*. In 1955 he gained the chance of learning the role of producer with the Rank Organisation and later moved into television as creator, writer and producer. Among the many films and television plays and series Hawkesworth was responsible for were *Tiger Bay*; *Upstairs, Downstairs*; *The Duchess of Duke Street*; *The Tale of Beatrix Potter*; and *Sherlock Holmes*. In 1991 an exhibition of his film design work of the 1950s was shown at Austin/Desmond Fine Art. Lived near Oakham, Rutland; and in London.

Dennis HAWKINS 1925– Painter, sculptor, printmaker and teacher who studied at Ruskin School of Drawing, Oxford, 1947–9, then Slade School of Fine Art, 1949–52, teachers including William Coldstream and Graham Sutherland. He was a member of the Printmakers' Council and Midland Group of Artists. Showed at Gimpel Fils, AIA, LG, Redfern Gallery and New Vision Centre and International Print Biennales in Tokyo and Florence. Commissions included murals and bas-reliefs at New Hospital, Netheredge, Sheffield, and a series of panels for Royal Children's Hospital in Liverpool. Arts Council, Victoria & Albert Museum, provincial art galleries, education authorities and overseas galleries hold Hawkins' work. He became director of art at Repton School, living at Repton, Derbyshire.

Peter HAWKINS 1934–c.1980s Sculptor and teacher, born in London, who studied at Kingston and Chelsea Schools of Art and Royal College of Art. Showed with Young Contemporaries, 1958; Cultura Ingles, Porto Alegre, Brazil, 1959; Wakefield and Bradford City Art Galleries, both 1962; and LG and Redfern Galleries, Arts Council Exhibition of Sculpture in Reading and A Painter's Collection at RA (Edward Le Bas' collection; he held several of Hawkins' works), all 1963. Hawkins lectured at the School of Furniture and Design, High Wycombe, into the 1960s, living in a converted barn in Abingdon, Berkshire. Went to India and America and was interested in yoga, mysticism and aestheticism, his later work becoming more conceptual, influenced by Minimalism.

Phillip Dennis HAWKINS 1947– Painter in oil, draughtsman, illustrator and photographer, born and lived in Birmingham, who studied at the College of Art there, 1964–8. He was a technical illustrator in the railway industry and press photographer who became noted for his depiction of current and historical railway subjects worldwide, "concentrating on the unique atmosphere of the steam railway in all its forms". Was in 1979 a founder-member of the Guild of Railway Artists, becoming its president in 1988, exhibiting extensively with the Guild. Also had solo shows in Birmingham, Solihull and York. Hawkins' articles appeared regularly in the railway press, from 1986 appeared in the *Footplate Calendar* and had fine art prints produced by Quicksilver Publishing. Completed works for railway companies, such as European Passenger Services' Eurostar trains, 1995. Other works held by Freightliner, BBC, *Birmingham Post and Mail*, Bristol United Press and Brown & Root-Booz Allen Ltd.

Anthony HAWKSLEY 1921– Sculptor, designer and artist in precious metals, born in Coventry, Warwickshire. He studied at Regent Street Polytechnic, Maidstone College of Art and the Royal College of Art. Showed at Ewan Phillips Gallery, Oxford Gallery and widely overseas. His work is held by Magdelene and Keble Colleges at Oxford University. Lived at Deddington, Oxford.

Dorothy Webster HAWKSLEY 1884–1970 Painter in watercolour and tempera of figures and portraits; black-and-white artist. Studied at St John's Wood School of Art, where she won a silver medal, and at the Royal Academy Schools, under George Clausen, where she won a silver medal and the Landseer Scholarship. Exhibited at many venues, including the RA, Fine Art Society, RI, SWA, Walker Art Gallery, Liverpool, and the Paris Salon, where she won a silver medal. Represented in several British provincial public collections, and in galleries in North America. Hawksley was capable of painting impressive, slightly stagey pictures in the manner of Charles Ricketts. Lived in London.

Rozanne HAWKSLEY 1931– Artist and teacher, born in Portsmouth, Hampshire, who attended the Southern College of Art there, then Royal College of Art, with postgraduate studies at

Goldsmiths' College School of Art. Hawksley worked originally as a freelance illustrator and designer/maker, including textile art, while teaching part-time in schools of art, including two years in America. Later part-time and visiting teaching posts included Goldsmiths', Royal College and Slade School of Fine Art. Hawksley's sculptures comprised clay, wax, wood, bone and jewels; the resulting images could be disturbing, not finding a ready outlet in commercial galleries. In the mid-1990s her work was "influenced by an Arts Council study tour to Andalucia and Spanish art of Catholique Morticole, together with the effects of war, sickness, death and poverty on the individual and the loneliness of the suffering individual." Exhibitions included the Museum of Modern Art, Kyoto, Japan; Crafts Council; Plymouth City Art Gallery; Cornerhouse, Manchester; Camden Arts Centre; RSA; and Kettle's Yard, Cambridge. Hawksley's work was held by Imperial War Museum, Kennedy Center in America and the Museum of Textiles in Poland. She was first married to the illustrator Åsgeir Scott, secondly to the actor Brian Hawksley. Lived at Newport, Dyfed.

Jann HAWORTH 1942– Artist and teacher, born in Hollywood, California, who was for a time married to the artist Peter Blake. She was one of the seven founders of The Brotherhood of Ruralists in 1975 which had its first show at RA in 1976. Haworth studied at University of California, Los Angeles, 1959–61, and at Slade School of Fine Art, 1962–3. In the 1970s founded The Looking Glass School in Wellow, Avon, for children, with a group of similarly minded parents to share teaching. As well as painting she created masks and figures in terracotta and other materials. Contributed to group shows, including Four Young Artists, 1963, and The Obsessive Image, 1968, at ICA; RA; and Ruralist exhibitions. Solo shows were held at Robert Fraser Gallery, 1964–9; Arnolfini Gallery, Bristol, and Leslie Waddington, both 1974, and elsewhere. Was included in the survey exhibition The 1960's at England & Co, 1993, and in the same year had her first solo show for 20 years at Gimpel Fils. With the writer Richard Severy she created a series of illustrated children's books.

Lilian HAWTHORN 1909–1996 Painter, born and lived in London, who was married to the artist Elwin Hawthorne. Originally exhibited under her maiden name Lily Leahy. While working in the city, in her teens she attended various drawing classes at Regent Street Polytechnic, then joined John Cooper's classes at the Bow and Bromley Evening Institute, which she stayed with during the 1930s. Showed with the East London Group at Lefevre Gallery. Did various jobs, including decorating china and window dressing, continuing to paint and exhibit and do imaginative tapestry work until an advanced age. Also showed in East Ham area and with Whitechapel Art Gallery.

Raymond Humphrey Millis HAWTHORN 1917– Wood engraver and teacher, born in Poole, Dorset. He studied at Coventry School of Art, 1935–9, and gained his teaching diploma from Hornsey School of Arts and Crafts, 1939–40, teachers including Norman Janes and Douglas Percy Bliss. Hawthorn had several teaching appointments, starting with Coventry School of Art, 1946, latterly lecturing full-time at Wirral College of Art and Design and Adult Studies, 1976–8, part-time 1978–80. He was elected a fellow of RE in 1975, being invited to join SWE, 1985. Also showed in mixed exhibitions at Wirral Society of Arts and Atkinson Art Gallery in Southport. One-man shows included Folio Gallery, 1959, and Williamson Art Gallery, Birkenhead, 1980. Atkinson and Williamson Galleries hold examples. Hawthorn's leading themes in book illustration were mainly classical and medieval history, in prints mainly landscapes and in paperback cover illustration *The New Testament*. Lived in Bebington, Wirral, Merseyside.

Wilfred Charles HAWTHORN 1877–1955 Painter, draughtsman and teacher. Born at Kettering, Northamptonshire, he studied at Wyggeston Art School, Leicester, 1890–2, in the studio of Walter Gash, Kettering 1895–1902, Wimbledon School of Art, Académie Julian, in Paris, 1901, then in the studio of Sir Alfred East for many years. He exhibited at the RA and extensively in the provinces. He published books on art education and practice. Work held by Herbert Art Gallery and Museum, Coventry, and the Alfred East Gallery, Kettering. For some time Hawthorn was president of the Coventry Art Guild. Was for a period chief assistant art master at Loughborough College of Art. Lived in Coventry.

Elwin HAWTHORNE 1905–1954 Painter, printmaker and teacher, born and lived in London, his wife the painter Lilian Hawthorn, his uncle the part-time artist Henry Silk. Like them he showed with the East London Group at Lefevre Gallery, having studied from 1927 with John Cooper at the Bow and Bromley Evening Institute. Through the Group Hawthorne (his full name was Elwin Henry Hawthorn; the added e was a mistake in a review which Lefevre chose to retain; some very early work is signed Elwin H Hawthorn or E H H) met Walter Sickert, whose studio assistant he was for three years. He was eventually under contract to Reid & Lefevre and had two solo exhibitions with them, 1934 and 1938. In World War II Hawthorne served with ARP (Air-raid Precautions) and St John's Ambulance Brigade, witnessing harrowing scenes which affected this sensitive man deeply. Then served in the Army, after which he worked for Plessey's, handling wages. Died on his way to one of several evening classes he taught. Pictures by Hawthorne of pre-World War II London are of deceptively simple design, in which he captures the atmosphere of almost-deserted streets with a near-surreal style. Among collectors were the Duke of Rutland, Earl of Sandwich, Sir Edward Marsh, Charles Laughton and J B Priestley. Manchester City Art Gallery holds Hawthorne's Church near Blackheath, presented by Contemporary Art Society.

Ian HAY 1940– Artist in pastel and watercolour, and teacher, born in Harwich, Essex. He studied at Colchester School of Art, 1955–60, then Royal College of Art, 1960–3, teachers including John Nash, Ruskin Spear and Roger de Grey. He taught at St

Martin's and Norwich Schools of Art and was senior lecturer in drawing at the school of art at Colchester Institute. Hay was noted for his pastels of the Thames, its changing moods in different climates. He was a member of Colchester Art Society, also showing with Phoenix Gallery in London and Lavenham; Minories, Colchester; RA Summer Exhibitions and elsewhere. Public galleries in Sheffield and Doncaster hold examples. Lived in Colchester, Essex.

John Arthur Machray HAY 1887–1960 Portrait painter, born in Aberdeen, who studied under George Harcourt at Patrick Allan-Fraser School of Art, Hospitalfield, Arbroath. He was a member of RP and London Portrait Society and showed also at RA, Royal Glasgow Institute of the Fine Arts and Walker Art Gallery, Liverpool. He lived in London and painted portraits of the nobility.

Peter Alexander HAY 1866–1952 Versatile painter, born in Edinburgh, who studied at Royal Scottish Academy Schools, at Académie Julian in Paris and in Antwerp. He was elected RSW in 1891, RI in 1917. A prolific exhibitor, he also showed at RA, RSA, Royal Glasgow Institute of the Fine Arts and many other galleries. Lived in London.

Rudolf HAYBROOK 1898–1965 Portrait and figure painter and theatre designer, born in London where he was based, son of the landscape painter Rudolf Heubach. Educated at Brighton College, he served in France during World War I, being demobilised after suffering shell shock. Began his largely self-taught career as an artist in the 1920s, spending some time at Chelsea Polytechnic School of Art with J D Revel, and working in association with Stanley Lupino. After living in South Africa he returned to England just before World War II and enlisted in the Auxiliary Fire Service. In his spare time he painted pictures of the Blitz, reputedly based on sketches on active service. War Artists' Advisory Committee declined to give Haybrook a commission, but they bought works by him, one of which is in the Imperial War Museum, which has since acquired others. Showed RA and had one-man shows at Brook Street Gallery in 1930s and at Leicester Galleries, which showed a big collection of his war pictures in 1940. Haybrook lectured on fire-fighting techniques in North America. After the war he developed a lung complaint brought on by his fire service work, and giving up painting spent some years as a courier, being a fluent French and German speaker.

Reg HAYDEN 1917– Painter, draughtsman and teacher, born in Brighton, Sussex, where he attended the College of Art, 1933–8, under Walter Bayes and Lawrence Preston; then studied at Slade School of Fine Art with Randolph Schwabe, 1939–40. He held a series of teaching posts, including Portsmouth College of Art and Bradford College of Art, eventually becoming head of fine art at Liverpool Polytechnic. Exhibited RA, LG, Leicester Galleries, Sussex University and elsewhere. Lived in Liverpool.

Colin HAYES 1919– Artist in oil and watercolour, writer and teacher, born and lived in London. Hayes gained his master's degree from Oxford University and studied at Ruskin School of Drawing in Oxford. He "greatly valued Peter Greenham's drawing lessons at the City School, Oxford." Between 1940–5 Hayes was commissioned in the Royal Engineers. He was on the staff of the Royal College of Art, eventually as reader, 1949–84. Hayes was president of RBA and was elected RA in 1970. He wrote a series of books on painting and painters, including *Renoir* and *Rembrandt*, *Stanley Spencer* and *Ruskin Spear* as well as *A Grammar of Drawing*. Showed in RA Summer Exhibitions, at Agnew, New Grafton and Fieldborne Galleries and in the provinces. In later years Hayes' palette lightened, he was fond of painting in Greece and there was a strong pattern element in his richly coloured landscapes. Arts Council, British Council and many other public collections in Britain and abroad hold examples. New Grafton Gallery held a retrospective in 1996.

Edward HAYES 1932– Painter and draughtsman, born in Dublin, Ireland, living in London from 1957, whose output included stylised figurative pictures. From 1958, when he had a one-man exhibition, Walls, at Hammersmith Art Gallery, Hayes had others every few years, with a series at Drian Gallery from 1964, including Lines for Beckett, 1970; Chamber Music, 1973; and (Study) Oliver Plunkett's Head, 1981. He also showed works at Redfern Gallery, New Vision and New Art Centres; in America at the Heritage Gallery and Barnsdale Museum, both in Los Angeles, and Long Beach Museum, California; and in Poland at the National Museum, in Warsaw.

Georgia HAYES 1946– Painter and draughtsman, born in Aberdeen, who studied with Roy Oxlade, 1977–82. She participated in a number of group exhibitions including RA; Oxford County Museum, Woodstock; Victoria Art Gallery, Bath; and Usher Gallery, Lincoln. Included in the 1991 David Bomberg and his followers exhibition at Towner Art Gallery, Eastbourne. Her picture Embalmed With A Cat was selected for the 1992 East & South Norwich Gallery/Kent Institute of Art and Design show. Hayes was a part-time art teacher at Tunbridge Wells Adult Education Centre, 1986–90. Lived at Bells Yew Green, Sussex.

Jonathan HAYES 1969– Artist using such media as etching, photograph and crayon, and teacher, born in the Isle of Sheppey, Kent. Studied at University College of Wales, Aberystwyth, gaining a first-class honours degree, 1991, winning several prizes. Then worked for his master's degree, and taught as a part-time lecturer and studio assistant. He took part in exhibitions at the College's Art Centre and was in 1993 Aberystwyth Artists exhibition at The Deffett Francis Gallery, Swansea Institute of Higher Education.

Margaret C HAYES: *see* **Margaret Clarisse TOULMIN**

Peter HAYES 1946– Sculptor and ceramist who studied at Birmingham College of Art. He then travelled extensively and worked in Lesotho, Swaziland, Botswana, India, Nepal, Japan, South Korea and in continental Europe, all of which contributed to his unique style. Among his shows were Sotheby's and Christie's; Scottish Gallery, Edinburgh; Graham Gallery, New York; Martha Sneider, Chicago; and Running Ridge Gallery, Santa Fe. He had a solo show at Anthony Hepworth Fine Art, Bath, 1992. For a time Hayes had a studio in Cornwall.

Malcolm HAYLETT 1923– Painter, illustrator, photographer and writer, born in Montreal, Canada, who studied at Southend College of Art. His work appeared in a wide number of newspapers and periodicals, such as the *Daily Mail*, *Illustrated London News* and *Britannia and Eve*. He was for a time president of the Arts Club in St Ives, Cornwall, where he lived, also showing with St Ives Society of Artists.

Patrick HAYMAN 1915–1988 Painter, often on driftwood, poet and publisher, born in London where he finally lived. Was educated at Malvern College, but lived in New Zealand in 1936–47, starting to paint in Dunedin, in 1938. Returned to England in 1947, eventually settling in Cornwall. Although he finally moved from Cornwall permanently he often returned there and it remained an inspiration for his painting. He much admired the work of the primitive artist Alfred Wallis; his own pictures also drew on images of the sea and have an apparently childlike quality, vigorous, vivid and direct. From 1958–63 founded and edited the magazine *The Painter and Sculptor*, influential in its advocacy of figurative art. In 1988 the Louise Hallett Gallery published *Painted Poems* by Hayman. Showed widely in group shows and had solo exhibitions in Cornwall, London and abroad. A large retrospective show was at Camden Arts Centre and then toured in 1990. Tate Gallery and Arts Council hold his work.

HAYMAN CHAFFEY 1920– Painter and designer, born in Hastings, Sussex, full name Frederick William Hayman Chaffey. He studied at Hastings School of Art, Hornsey School of Art and privately. Exhibited RA, RBA, NS, Leicester and Heal's Galleries and at Paris Salon. Lived for a time at Charing, Kent, and in Barcelona, Spain.

Dan HAYS 1966– Painter, born and lived in London, who graduated in fine art from Goldsmiths' College, 1987–90. He was first prize winner at the 1997–8 John Moores Liverpool Exhibition with his oil on canvas Harmony in Green, his depiction of a green hamster cage, exactly the artist's height, with "a very slight perspective. My early obsessions with Escher and Op Art resurface." Group shows included Thirty Seven Seconds, The Slaughterhouse, 1989; Moving Pictures, Clove Gallery, 1993; 22Ovolt Message, Hooghuis, Arnhem, Netherlands, 1995; and the Arts Council new purchases tour Ace!, 1996–7. Solo shows included Laure Genillard Gallery, 1996.

Christopher HAYSOM 1939–1989 Sculptor, painter and teacher, son of a mason "and a three-hundred-year-old tradition". Left school aged 16, first studied sculpture under Ralph Brown and then under Paul Fletcher at Bournemouth College of Art, later with Bernard Meadows at the Royal College of Art. Taught sculpture at Central School of Art and Design from 1973. In 1988, Haysom began preparing stone blocks for a studio, built in Acton, near Worth Matravers, Dorset. When cancer stopped him carving, he turned to painting. A memorial show was held at Central and St Martins School of Art, a few weeks after his death, in May 1989.

Stanley William HAYTER 1901–1988 Engraver, painter, teacher and writer, born in London, son of the painter W H Hayter. After taking a degree in chemistry at King's College, London University, in 1921, Hayter worked for Anglo-Iranian Oil Company in Abadan in the early-1920s. He had begun to experiment with printmaking and in 1926 left the oil company, moved to Paris and enrolled at Académie Julian, where his fellow-students included Balthus, Calder and Anthony Gross. In 1927 he founded Atelier 17 to research the technique of engraving and thereafter was greatly influential as a teacher. Was married three times, his second wife being the American sculptor Helen Phillips. Hayter was an early member of the Surrealist movement; he exhibited widely in Europe and America; wrote books on *Jankel Adler*, 1948, and *New Ways of Gravure*, 1949, plus numerous articles. Received the Légion d'Honneur in 1951. He took part in numberless exhibitions throughout the world, including a retrospective exhibition at Whitechapel Art Gallery in 1957 with an Arts Council tour in 1958, transferred that year to the Venice Biennale; print retrospective at Victoria & Albert Museum, 1969. Although Hayter had spent the period 1940–50 in New York, where he ran Atelier 17, he took it back to Paris in 1950, closing the New York branch in 1955, and it was in Paris that he died. A man of great enthusiasm and energy, Hayter continued painting to the end of his life, during which period his pictures took on a new, glowing colour.

Margaret HAYTHORNE 1893– Painter, printmaker and designer, born in Liverpool, where she attended the City School of Art under William Penn, then the Central School of Arts and Crafts under Francis Jackson and Noel Rooke. Was sister of the artist Edmund Haythorne and was a member of the Sandon Studios Society. She exhibited RA, RCamA, Redfern Gallery and SWE. Whitworth Art Gallery in Manchester holds her work. Lived in Liverpool.

Alfred HAYWARD 1875–1971 Painter and mural artist strongly influenced by the Impressionists. Born in London, he was within a few months taken to live in Hooe, Sussex, at Quiddleswell Mount, which he sold only in 1948 when his finances were low and he was in receipt of a Civil List Pension. From 1891–4 attended South Kensington Schools, then was at Slade School of Fine Art, 1895–7. During the period up to World War I Hayward travelled to West Indies, Central America and Italy, which he always loved. After serving in Artists' Rifles Hayward was appointed an official war artist, 1918–9, his resulting work being held by Imperial War Museum. By the end of the 1920s Hayward was faring well as a painter, but his income dipped sharply in the 1930s. Exhibited RA, NEAC, of which he was a member, Leicester Galleries, Wildenstein, RP, RWS and Gallery Edward Harvane, 1970. Work held by Tate Gallery, provincial galleries and galleries overseas. Centenary exhibition Belgrave Gallery, 1975. Hayward was a keen member of Chelsea Arts Club, a dapper, immaculate man of old-fashioned manners. Finally lived in London.

John HAYWARD 1929– Stained glass artist who studied as a painter at St Martin's School of Art, 1946–9. He learned stained glass with a firm in Westminster, then went freelance in 1961 with a large commission for east and west windows at St Mary Le Bow. After this Hayward "was continuously busy mostly with glass, but some furniture and metalwork, all commissioned work in churches and other public places." He was a fellow of the British Society of Master Glass Painters. His work included east windows, St Michael, Paternoster Royal (Dick Whittington's church); east window in St Peter's, Oxford; nave windows, Grantham Parish Church; and nearly all windows in Dunstable Priory (a booklet on the glass there features Hayward's work); and the east window in Walsingham Church. Hayward said that he was "influenced by icons, Braque, Sutherland and Seurat. My design tends to be figures in landscapes." Ely Cathedral Stained Glass Museum holds Hayward's work. Lived in Corscombe, Dorchester, Dorset.

Pete HAYWARD fl. from 1960s– Painter and teacher who studied at Eastbourne School of Art, 1963–5, and West Sussex College of Higher Education, 1965–8. Until 1972 taught in Essex and at an approved school in County Durham, then became head of art and arts co-ordinator for Walton Comprehensive School, Peterborough. Exhibitions included Wisbech Museum, Usher Gallery in Lincoln, Yarrow Gallery in Oundle and in 1987 he was included in Peterborough's Art '87, at Lady Lodge Arts Centre.

Tony HAYWARD 1954– Sculptor and teacher who studied sculpture at St Martin's School of Art in the early 1970s, then ceramics at the Royal College of Art, 1983–5. He taught part-time in art colleges, also running educational workshops in schools and museums for primary-age children. His work included assemblages of wall-mounted objects and constructions using found objects. Exhibited in many group shows in Britain, continental Europe and America. Solo appearances included Orchard Gallery, Londonderry, 1986; Artsite, Bath, 1990; and Winchester Gallery, Winchester, 1993. In 1997 an exhibition of Hayward's collection of utilitarian objects and toys bought during six trips to India, from 1988, was shown at Hove Museum & Art Gallery.

Eric HAYWARD-YOUNG 1908– Painter of pictures and murals and miniaturist, born in Sheffield, son of the artist Walter Hayward-Young. Studied art privately and showed at RA. Lived in London.

Carol HAYWOOD 1941– Sculptor, ceramist and teacher, born in Clifton Hampden, Oxfordshire, who as well as drawing worked in porcelain and bronze. She studied fine art at St Martin's School of Art, 1958–62, teachers including Peter Blake, Derrick Greaves, Elisabeth Frink, Peter de Francia, Frederick Gore, Joe Tilson and John Farleigh; then gained her master's in ceramics at Cardiff, 1992–4, under Mick Casson, Geoffrey Swindell and Peter Starkey. Working from the figure arose from a lifelong interest in dancing and yoga. Haywood taught yoga for over 20 years and art to children and adults, and from 1994 drawing at degree level in the ceramics department at Cardiff (she had her own studio in the city). Group shows included Meridian, Hay-on-Wye; Candover Gallery, Alresford; and RWA 2nd Open Sculpture Exhibition, all 1996. She was a member of the Crafts Council Register.

John HAYWOOD 1936–1991 Painter and falconer, based in Coventry, Warwickshire, where he attended the College of Art. Then spent a year on the continent where he "sketched, played piano in bars and learned to play the Flamenco guitar." Back in England working for his father Haywood's teenage interest in flying birds of prey was rekindled, and at his suggestion he flew falcons for display at Twycross Zoo Park. After three years there Haywood helped a wealthy client to train birds of prey, also working with falcons and eagles for films and television. Working with Countess Marie de Beningsen, co-founder of the Quill and Palette Partnership, which sold pictures to banks and business premises, Haywood combined his bird and artistic talents and sold his own paintings "from Aldwych to Hong Kong". Eventually Haywood flew around 200 birds of prey. Haywood sold well through the Mathaf Gallery to Middle Eastern clients and himself flew falcons in North Africa. When King Fahd of Saudi Arabia visited London in 1987 Mathaf held a special exhibition featuring Haywood's pictures and Genesis Publications produced a 500-copy, signed book.

Mark HAYWOOD 1952– Printer, draughtsman, photographer and teacher, born in Oldham, Lancashire. He studied at Jacob Kramer College of Art in Leeds, 1971–2, then at the Medlock Fine Art Centre in Manchester, 1972–5, where his teachers included the sculptor Keith Godwin. Went on to teach at Salford College of Art. Exhibited at Chenil Galleries, also widely in Lancashire, including Oldham Art Gallery and Portland Gallery. Manchester Polytechnic holds his work. Lived at Whalley Range, Manchester.

David HAZELWOOD 1932–1994 Self-taught artist, born and lived in Ipswich, Suffolk. He used collage, acrylic and mixed media. Hazelwood's work could be meticulous and subtly coloured, sometimes employing tiny pieces of sheet music. He was a member of Free Painters and Sculptors for a time, was a photo-lithographic artist, 1948–85, from then on a professional artist. Hazelwood took part in many group exhibitions including RA Summer Exhibition from 1977; Bath Festival from 1983; International Art Fairs from 1985, including Basle, Chicago, Cologne, Frankfurt and Madrid; Anthony Dawson Museums

Tour, 1987; and Continuing the Tradition, Chappel Galleries, Chappel, 1993. Had a one-man show at Bedford College, 1970, later ones including Frankfurt Art Fair, 1991, and Galerie Peerlings, Krefeld, and Galerie Krakeslatt, Brömolla, both 1993. Victoria & Albert Museum, Department of the Environment, Camden Arts Centre and many provincial galleries hold his work. Hazelwood's idol was Nicolas de Stäel, other influences being Ben Nicholson, Mark Tobey, Kurt Schwitters, Antonio Tapiés and Roger Bissière. In 1995 a tribute show was held at Christchurch Mansion, Ipswich.

Robin HAZLEWOOD 1944– Painter and teacher, born in Warwickshire, where he studied at Coventry College of Art, 1961–5, then attended Liverpool College of Art, 1965–6. Taught widely in adult education in London, including Putney and Wandsworth and Camden and Stanhope Adult Education Institutes. In 1982 was included in Artists in Adult Education at Woodlands Art Gallery. Other shows included Coventry Museum and Art Gallery, 1965; Nuffield Gallery, Southampton, 1974; Scribes Gallery from 1979; and South London Art Gallery, 1980.

Charles Walker HAZZARD 1964– Figurative sculptor, born in Birmingham, who did a foundation course at Bournville Art School there, 1983–4; gained an honours degree at Gloucestershire College of Arts and Technology, 1984–7; did postgraduate study at Sir Henry Doulton School, 1988–90; then obtained a postgraduate higher diploma in sculpture at City & Guilds of London Art School, 1990–1. Hazzard was elected an associate of RBS in 1992, becoming a member of its council and several of its committees. In 1996–8 he was appointed to a Henry Moore Fellowship in Sculpture at Loughborough College of Art and Design. Commissions in 1990–1 included portraits of the art critic Peter Fuller; Lord Jack Ashley; Leon Krier, architect to the Duchy of Cornwall; and Professor Roger Scruton. In 1993 Hazzard completed a lantern for St James the Less, Pimlico. Exhibitions included MAFA and LG, both 1992; RA Summer Exhibition, 1993; Cheltenham Society of Artists and Whitechapel Open, both 1994; and RWA 2nd Open Sculpture Exhibition, 1996. Had a first solo show at The Hyde Park Gallery, 1993, with one at Exchange Square, The Broadgate Centre, 1996. Lived in London.

Clive HEAD 1965– Painter, born in Maidstone, Kent. He studied visual art at University College of Wales, Aberystwyth, and University of Lancaster. Head produced meticulous paintings of places, using a camera "to isolate and record" the image. He showed widely from 1985 and in 1991 shared a three-man exhibition at Woodlands Art Gallery. Lived in South Yorkshire.

Richard HEAD 1951– Artist in pen and ink, gouache, oil and drypoint, born in London, who attended Eton College, 1964–8, under Peter Sumsion and Oliver Thomas; in 1969 did a pre-university course in Italy; was taught at West Surrey College of Art & Design by John Morris, 1970; then did a fine art degree at Bristol Polytechnic, 1971–4, in 1972 being a David Murray student, teachers including David Ferguson and Michael Canney. Became a full-time gardener at The Royal Horticultural Society, Wisley, from 1979. John Piper, Keith Grant, Christopher Wood, Walter Sickert and Monet were influences, subjects of work including landscapes, seascapes and views of old buildings. Head was a member of Guildford Art Society. Took part in mixed shows including RA Summer Exhibition from 1979, Michael Parkin Fine Art from 1984 and Sally Hunter Fine Art from 1986. Solo shows included Dillington House, Ilminster, 1980, and The First Gallery, Bitterne, 1995. Lived in Woking, Surrey.

Tim HEAD 1946– Artist, born in London where he continued to live, and teacher. He studied at Newcastle upon Tyne department of fine art, 1965–9. In the summer of 1968 he was assistant to Claes Oldenburg in New York. Head was then at St Martin's School of Art, 1969–70. After being assistant to the artist for the Robert Morris show at Tate Gallery in 1971, Head taught at Goldsmiths' College School of Art and Slade School of Fine Art. During 1977–8 he was artist-in-residence at Clare Hall and Kettle's Yard, Cambridge. Painting, slide projections and mirrors were used by Head for environmental pieces created for specific sites in which he questioned the nature of reality and illusion. As well as showing widely internationally he showed at such venues as Museum of Modern Art in Oxford, Rowan Gallery and Arnolfini Gallery, Bristol, with a retrospective of work since 1984 at Whitechapel Art Gallery, 1992–3, and tour. Arts Council holds examples.

Douglas A HEALD 1943– Artist in various media who was born in York, where he eventually settled, setting up a studio and gallery. He early developed an artistic talent, with a special interest in natural history and architecture. Studied for three years at York School of Art, then spent a period in studios in north of England. Next travelled extensively in North America, Europe and North Africa, continuing to travel to fulfill commissions. Among those presented with his work were members of the royal family and Cardinal Basil Hume, Archbishop of Westminster.

George HEALER 1936– Sculptor in various materials and teacher. He went to school in Chester-le-Street, County Durham, where he settled and attended Sunderland College of Art, 1952–6, teachers including Harry Thubron and Bob Jewell. After National Service in the Army, 1956–8, Healer did a variety of jobs, being employed in the family fruit business; working as a commercial designer and church furniture designer; as a ceramics restorer at Beamish Open Air Museum; and as a commercial sculptor for Swanbridge Art Company, Sunderland. He also taught sculpture and casting design, including adult education classes and at Sunderland College of Art, 1968–74, and with Peterlee & Aycliffe Development Corporation, 1982–4. Was an associate of RBS, gaining its Diploma for Distinction in 1974. Showed at Westgate Road Galleries, Newcastle, 1960; Durham University, 1963; Royal Edinburgh Academy, 1965; RA, 1967; Royal Institute of Fine Art, 1978, and elsewhere. Bowes Museum, Barnard Castle, County Durham, holds his work.

Christine HEALEY fl. from c.1980– Painter, printmaker and teacher active in northwest England who worked in adult education as a tutor/therapist from 1982 while showing extensively. She was part-time curator and organiser of the Chapman Gallery, University of Salford, where she also held the post of artist-in-residence. In addition to her work in Britain she tackled international topics. Her exhibition Impressions of Brunei: A British Eye was shown at Malay Museum, Brunei, 1988, shortly after Aspects of Sri Lanka appeared at the British Council Hall, Colombo. In 1992 had a solo show at Chapman Gallery, The Ultimate Experience, and in 1994 No Pelicans in Pembrokeshire at Portico Library Gallery, Manchester.

Eithne HEALY 1964– Sculptor who studied at Wimbledon School of Art, 1988–91, graduating with honours in sculpture. Showed in annual outdoor exhibit of sculpture in Cannizaro Park, Wimbledon, from 1989; Gagliardi Contemporary Art and Design, 1992–3; and in 1993 at Isis Gallery, Leigh-on-Sea, in Drawing Towards Sculpture. In 1992–3 had sculpture placed at Tamworth High School, Mitcham.

Timothy HEALY 1901– Watercolour painter and black-and-white artist who did commercial work as well as exhibiting. Born in Manchester, son of the artist Timothy Healy, William Timothy Joseph Healy – his full name – studied at Bolt Court, Fleet Street, under Geoffrey Pocock and Sylvan Boxius. Exhibited RI. Work was reproduced by magazines such as *Mother and Home* and *Woman and Home*. Lived at Southborough, Kent.

Andrew HEARD 1958–1993 Painter and printmaker, born in Hertford, Hertfordshire. He attended Chelsea School of Art, 1979–80, having in late–1970s worked as a waiter at Blitz night-club while studying history and history of art at London University, 1976–9. After graduation he lived for a year in West Berlin. For some time Heard's work was best known on the continent. Two of his most successful shows were at Friedman-Guinness Gallery in Germany, at Heidelberg in 1987 and Frankfurt in 1989. He also had one-man shows in 1980s in Athens, Amsterdam, Paris and Zürich. In England Heard was chosen in 1986–7 for Whitechapel Open exhibitions, in 1988 he had a show at Salama-Caro Gallery and in 1992 Connaught Brown held his exhibition Strange Fruit. Heard's work, which had a strain of uneasiness, celebrated popular figures such as the actor Terry-Thomas, the actress Barbara Windsor and comedian Max Miller. He wanted it to be like "a slap in the face". The later large circular canvases of Strange Fruit were brighter, more playful, with less of an uncomfortable message. Dressed like a skinhead, Heard was an advocate of his friend artist and writer David Robilliard's work, admired the plays of Joe Orton and sought to interpret the culture of the 1950s and 1960s. Died of Aids in London. There was a memorial show at Salama-Caro in 1994.

Michael HEARD 1931–1994 Artist born in Romford, Essex, settling in East Anglia in 1964 and living finally at Wivenhoe. He studied at Central School of Arts and Crafts, 1952–4, then at RWA, 1955, followed by time in London, 1956–9, then St Ives, Cornwall, 1959–63. Group shows included Penwith Society in St Ives, Plymouth City Art Gallery, Portal and Mall Galleries, Agnew, John Moores Liverpool Exhibition at Walker Art Gallery, and Aldeburgh Festival Gallery. In 1996 he was included in Colchester Art Society Fifty Years Anniversary Exhibition at Chappel Galleries, Chappel. Solo shows included Newlyn Art Gallery in Newlyn, Mercury Gallery, Gainsborough's House in Sudbury and several at Essex University Gallery and Wivenhoe Arts Club.

Nancy Hastings HEARSEY fl. c.1940–1960 Painter born in Ontario, Canada. She studied at Heatherley's School of Fine Art and in Paris. Showed at RA, NS and Paris Salon. Lived for a time in London.

John HEARTFIELD 1891–1968 Versatile politically committed artist of the left, born Helmut Herzfeld in Berlin Schmargendorf, Germany; he adopted the name John Heartfield in 1916 because of the German political slogan "May God Punish England", regarding it as war-mongering. His parents, both politically active, abandoned Heartfield, his brother and sisters, in 1899. In 1905, after elementary school, Heartfield began an apprenticeship in Wiesbaden; studied at the Royal Bavarian Arts and Crafts School, Munich, 1908; in 1912 worked as a commercial artist for a printing firm in Mannheim; in 1913 studied at the Arts and Crafts School in Berlin under Ernst Neumann; then during world War I spent a short period in the Army until a feigned nervous breakdown prompted his release and he was able to run a publishing company with his brother Wieland. In 1918 Heartfield, by then director of the Military Educational Film Service (later UFA), became a member of the Berlin Club Dada and joined the Communist Party with Wieland and George Grosz. The 1920s and early-1930s saw Heartfield hectically active, responsible for book jackets, typography and layout, articles, set designs, posters and photomontages, associated with radical leftwing groups, spending some time in the Soviet Union. With the Nazi takeover in 1933 Heartfield fled to Prague, then to England in 1938, where in 1939 he became involved with the AIA and Free German League of Culture, which honoured his fiftieth birthday in 1941, the year after he was interned as an enemy alien and became severely ill. Worked as a designer for publishers such as Penguin Books, and as a freelance cartoonist. In 1950 Heartfield returned to Leipzig to continue his work, and a first comprehensive exhibition of this in the German Democratic Republic was held in 1957, when Heartfield moved to Berlin. After growing recognition – there were exhibitions around Europe in 1964–5 – he died there. In 1992 there was an exhibition at the Barbican Art Gallery.

Adrian HEATH 1920–1992 Painter and teacher, born in Maymyo, Burma, he arrived in England as a small boy, studied at Bryanston School and was taught in Newlyn by Stanhope Forbes, 1938, and the Slade School of Fine Art, 1939, then evacuated to Oxford. Was in Royal Air Force, and was a prisoner of war in

Germany, returning to study at Slade, 1945–7. Although at first his work was representational, in the late-1940s it became abstract, his initial abstracts being shown at LG. By then he had spent a year in the south of France at Carcassonne, where he had a solo show at Musée de Carcassonne in 1948. First one-man exhibition in Britain was at Redfern Gallery, 1953. Had numerous group show appearances in Britain and abroad and regular solo exhibitions, including many at Redfern Gallery and two retrospectives, at City Art Gallery in Bristol in 1971 and at Graves Art Gallery, Sheffield, in 1972. An articulate painter who nevertheless cautioned that "artists should be wary of the written statement," Heath in 1953 published the important monograph: *Abstract Art, its Origin and Meaning*. He continued to expound his beliefs as a teacher at Bath Academy of Art, 1955–76, the University of Reading, 1981, and elsewhere. Work held by many international public collections, including Arts Council, Tate Gallery, Victoria & Albert Museum and Whitworth Art Gallery, Manchester. Lived in London, but died in France at Montmirail, while teaching at a summer school. In 1953 Heath married the stage designer Corinne Lloyd.

Claude HEATH 1964– Artist in mixed media, born and lived in London. He gained a degree in philosophy from King's College, 1983–6. Heath's exhibitions included Young British Artists VI at Saatchi Gallery, 1996, which included work centered around a cast of his brother's face. By the time of the exhibition this intricate pursuit had produced 198 drawings, with more of the series to come. He was a prizewinner at John Moores Liverpool Exhibition, 1997–8.

Irene HEATH 1906– Painter, illustrator and writer of books for children, born in Bedford. Studied at St John's Wood School of Art, Heatherley's School of Fine Art and at Regent Street Polytechnic School of Art. Exhibited RA, NS and ROI. Her books included *A Birthday Book for Children*, *Capricorn Colony* and *Heard by a Mouse*. Lived in London.

Isobel HEATH 1908–1989 Painter and poet who was associated with St Ives, Cornwall, for some 50 years. She studied at Atelier Colarossi, Paris, and with Leonard Fuller in St Ives. During World War II she worked as an artist with the Ministry of Information. She exhibited with RSA, RCamA, ROI, RI and was a member of the St Ives Society of Artists. In 1949 she was a founder-member of the breakaway Penwith Society of Arts. Heath had a romantic obsession with the Cornish landscape and would drive onto the moors, where she would work and sleep for days at a time, painting at night with the aid of a tin miner's hat and lamp. Expressionist abstraction was a strong feature of Heath's pictures, featured in a show at Tadema Gallery, 1990, and she was also noted for her portraits. Her books included *Passing Thoughts*, 1971; *Love*, 1973; and *Reflections*, 1978.

Lewis Edward HEATH 1911– Artist in gouache, watercolour and pen and ink, he was born in Hastings, Sussex, and studied art at the School of Art there under Philip William Cole. Then attended the Royal College of Art under Ernest Tristram and the calligrapher Edward Johnston. Heath – who sometimes signed his work Leharca – held a series of teaching posts in England, finishing as head of the art department at Burton upon Trent grammar school, where he lived. He published a book on outdoor sketching, was interested in marionette-making and was a member of the British Puppet & Model Theatre Guild.

Marjorie HEATHER fl. from late 1940s–1989 Painter of semi-caricature figure groups in oil and watercolour, born and lived in Newbury, Berkshire. She believed in the importance of line drawing, constantly carried a sketch-book, saying that it was "essential to sketch as fast as you write", working up paintings in her studio which retained a strong outline. As a mature student Heather attended Ruskin School of Drawing, Oxford, 1945–8, under Albert Rutherston, winning prizes for figure composition and still life painting; then was at Byam Shaw School of Drawing and Painting, 1948–50. For 30 years her work was selected regularly for RA, RWS, RP and other galleries in the provinces and abroad. She was a founder-member in 1947 of Newbury Art Group and helped set up the Bussock Mayne Group. A memorial show was held at Newbury District Museum in 1991.

Cecil HEATHFIELD 1893–1969 Artist, commercial designer, teacher and administrator, born in Croydon, Surrey, who studied at the School of Art there and at the London County Council Bolt Court School, under Walter Bayes. When his first wife, Dorrie, was appointed head of a school in Polegate, Heathfield moved to Sussex, travelling to London daily to work as a commercial artist. Early in the war, when work diminished, he gave up the London studio and stayed in Sussex. Settled in Lewes, Heathfield aimed to bring art to a wider public, teaching in the prison, running a social club for teenage evacuees and holding classes in villages. He became art adviser to East Sussex Education Committee, was a governor of Brighton College of Art and chairman of Lewes Theatre Club. After Dorrie died in 1941, Heathfield married the Lewes-born artist Evelyn Fawsset and converted derelict stables into Paddock Studios, where classes were held and they showed work jointly. Among Heathfield's solo exhibitions was one at County Town Gallery, Lewes, in 1961, which showed him turning towards abstraction, Surrealism and collage. He was noted as a fine draughtsman. Heathfield was a prominent member of Brighton and Lewes Art Clubs, Eastbourne Society of Artists and Battle Arts Group. When Evelyn died in 1980, aged 87, she gave Paddock Studios to East Sussex County Council under the auspices of the Charity Commission, and in various guises they continued to be used for teaching and exhibitions.

Bobby HEAVEN 1922– Artist in oil, oil pastel, acrylic and stained glass, born in Rochdale, Lancashire, correct name Elizabeth Anne Heaven. Attended Bristol Polytechnic/Filton College for many years from 1975, one tutor being Anthony Rossiter. Heaven painted landscapes and made sketches in Provence, Ireland and the Somerset area where she lived at Clevedon, using a distinctive and colourful palette. Showed with

RA, RWA, Clifton and Clevedon Art Clubs, Bath Society of Artists, ROI and Lynda Cotton Gallery at Watchet. Had a solo show at Pier Gallery, Clevedon, 1991, and The Court Gallery, Nether Stowey, 1994. She appeared in Chris Chapman's Channel 4 television series *Secrets of the Moor*, shown in 1996.

Eric HEBBORN 1934–1996 Draughtsman, sculptor, painter, teacher, writer and faker of Old Master and some modern drawings, born in London the son of a grocer's assistant. As a boy he was sent to Borstal but became interested in art and attended Chelmsford Art School, 1949–51, under Charles Archer, then Walthamstow Art School under Stuart Ray and Kurt Roland. While studying at Royal Academy Schools, 1955–8, he won a number of scholarships and prizes, including the Silver Medal and Hacker Portrait Prize. Spent two years in Italy having won the Rome Scholarship in Engraving for 1959. He taught at Walthamstow and Reigate and Redhill School of Art. Having worked for a time as a restorer and being interested in the techniques of the Old Masters, he set up Pannini Galleries Ltd in London, eventually moving to Italy, where he settled in Anticoli. Many drawings in the styles of the Old Masters fooled the experts, exchanged hands for large sums and entered notable collections, as told in Hebborn's entertaining book *Drawn To Trouble, The Forging Of An Artist*, 1991. Hebborn showed his own work, too, having a successful show of sculptures at Alwin Gallery, 1978, and large retrospective at the British School, Rome, where he had studied. In 1994 Julian Hartnoll and Archeus Fine Art organised further extensive shows. Died in Rome in mysterious circumstances, a magistrate suggesting homicide as the cause.

Godfrey HECHT 1902–1980 Painter in oil, gouache and other media of an experimental bent. Born in London, where he continued to live, Hecht was educated at Downside School. Exhibited in mixed shows with the Free Painters and Sculptors, ROI, NS and SGA. One-man show at the Woodstock Gallery. Hecht was a member of the Reform Club.

Peter HEDEGAARD 1929– Architect and artist whose works included rectangular abstracts, born in Copenhagen, Denmark. He studied at Oxford University and Bartlett School of Architecture. Solo shows included Architectural Association, 1967; Curwen Gallery, 1969; Consort Gallery at Imperial College, 1974; and Peterloo Gallery in Manchester and Oxford Gallery, Oxford, both 1976. In 1981 he was included in Contemporary Artists in Camden at Burgh House, Hampstead, near where he lived. Victoria & Albert Museum; Sussex and Salford Universities; and public galleries in Belfast, Bolton, Hull and Sheffield hold examples.

Ray HEDGER 1944– Painter, printmaker, artist in film and performance, and teacher, born in Wiltshire. He studied at Gloucestershire College of Art, in Cheltenham, and at Central School of Art. Hedger tried to create an image embracing "that single moment when one sees something that no camera is capable of capturing because it contains so many elements beyond the 'real' and the present." He was a member of SWE, illustrated two poetry anthologies and made a film based on the book *Crow* by Ted Hughes. Was also involved in creating a dance piece with the dancer Alex Howard, music by the Czech composer Pavel Novak. Mixed shows included Fitzwilliam Museum and Kettle's Yard, Cambridge; Oxfam tour Art for a Fairer World; Birmingham City Museum & Art Gallery; and Contemporary Art Holdings, Cheltenham. Solo shows included The Nude and Landscape, Cheltenham Art Gallery & Museum, 1994. Lived in Fairford, Gloucestershire.

Russell HEDGES 1945– Painter whose work inclined towards abstraction, generally on a large scale. Brought up in Buckinghamshire, Hedges as a young man was a musician in Cornwall, then attended Norwich School of Art, 1978–82, and Chelsea School of Art, 1982–3. He returned to Cornwall, living in Penzance, and showed with Newlyn Society of Artists and elsewhere. His picture Moon Anchor was included in the 1989 Newlyn Orion Galleries exhibition A Century of Art in Cornwall 1889–1989.

Dora HEDGES 1881–c.1955 Painter and potter, born in Sheffield, Yorkshire. After education at Derby High School she studied at Chiswick School of Art and the Royal College of Art. Although she was an exhibitor at SWA and RWS she was better known as a potter, writing the book *Pottery in the Making* and having her work accepted by the Victoria & Albert Museum. She was married to the artist Richard Lunn and sometimes exhibited under the name Dora Lunn, notably at Walker Art Gallery, Liverpool, before World War II.

Crispin HEESOM 1950– Artist notable for landscapes "not concerned with topographical detail, but with light, mood, dreams and memories inspired by the places". He was born in Oundle, Northamptonshire, and settled nearby at King's Cliffe. Studied at Norwich School of Art, 1970, then Byam Shaw School of Painting and Drawing, 1971–3. Exhibitions included The Museum, Ashton, 1979; The Annexe Gallery, Wimbledon (Group Show), 1980; Peterborough Museum & Art Gallery, 1984; Stamford Arts Centre, 1985; Art '87, at Peterborough's Lady Lodge Arts Centre (Group Show), 1987; and Green Man Exhibition, Yarrow Gallery, Oundle (Group Show), 1995. In 1982 Heesom carried out a mural commission in Girdlers Road, Hammersmith.

Bé van der HEIDE 1938– Painter, muralist, printmaker and teacher, born in the Netherlands, who studied painting at the Academy for Fine Arts in Enschede, 1956–60, also in Montreal, Canada, having emigrated in 1960. Travelled extensively in Middle East and Africa, returning to Canada in 1964, and in 1967 was commissioned to produce a large mural, in nails on board, for the Dutch pavilion at Expo '76, Montreal. After three years in Istanbul, Turkey, in the late 1960s, returned to Montreal in 1970, moving to London in 1982. She took part in the Triangle workshop in New York in 1984 and in 1992 was guest artist of the Outer Mongolian Artist Union. Participated in numerous group show around the world, including Links of Affinity, Knapp Gallery, 1989, and had many solo exhibitions, starting with

Rijksmuseum Twenthe, Enschede, 1963, later ones including Bruton Street Gallery, 1992; Powell Moya Partnership, 1993; and Chancery Gallery, Royal Netherlands Embassy, 1994. City of Enschede; Bibliothèque Nationale de Quebec; National Film Board of Canada; Quebec Government; and several corporate collections own examples.

Michael HEINDORFF 1949– Painter, highly versatile printmaker and teacher, Heindorff attended art college and University of Braunschweig, in Germany, 1970–4. He gained a German National Scholarship, 1972–6, and a DAAD Scholarship for London, 1976–7, attending Royal College of Art, 1975–7. Heindorff was at home in various media and styles, although over the years he edged away from figuration to abstraction. He won an award at John Moores Exhibition in Liverpool in 1976, a few years later gaining the Schmidt-Rottluff Prize and the Villa Massimo Prize, in Rome. A retrospective of his work covering the decade from 1977 was held at Northern Centre for Contemporary Arts in 1987. For many years his pictures were handled by Bernard Jacobson in London and New York. Arts Council holds. Heindorff taught at Royal College of Art from 1980 and was included in its Exhibition Road show in 1988. Lived in London.

HEL: *see* **Helen GRUNWALD**

Julie HELD 1958– Painter and teacher, born in London where she continued to work. Studied for bachelor's degree in fine art-painting at Camberwell School of Art, 1977–81, then did post-graduate diploma at Royal Academy Schools, 1982–5. Taught widely from 1981 including Kingston Polytechnic and University of Wolverhampton. Held won a Stanley Picker Fellowship at Kingston, 1981–2; first prize in Royal Over-Seas League Annual Exhibition, 1984; and Lucy Morrison Prize at same exhibition, 1986. Mixed shows included Whitechapel Art Gallery, 1977; Boundary Gallery from 1988; and RA Summer Exhibition, 1992. Had solo shows at Kingston Polytechnic, 1982; Wilson Hale Gallery, 1990; and Piccadilly Gallery, 1993. Keele University and Nuffield College at Oxford University hold her work.

HELEN 1917– Painter and draughtsman, full name Helen Burrough, who was born in Ceylon. She was married to the artist Thomas Hedley Bruce Burrough. Studied from 1937–9 in London and Stockholm and showed in mixed exhibitions including RWA, of which she was a member. Lived for many years at Frenchay, near Bristol.

HELEN: *see* **Helen GRUNWALD**

Jack HELLEWELL 1920– Painter and designer, working mostly in acrylic; his imaginary landscapes were created with patches of colour, and he also painted still life. Hellewell was born in Bradford, Yorkshire, where he attended the College of Art, then worked as a graphic designer until the mid-1970s, when he started to paint full-time. He worked on the edge of Ilkley Moor, Yorkshire, which provided inspiration, as did trips on the continent, North Africa and Australia. Showed at RWS and Business Art Galleries; in 1990 had a solo at Manor House Ilkley; and was included in Images of the Yorkshire Landscape, organised by Sheeran Lock at Leeds Civic Hall in 1991.

Glenn HELLMAN 1938– Sculptor and teacher, born in Walthamstow, north London. Studied at the local art school, 1959–61, then at Hornsey College of Art under Robert Adams, 1961–4. In 1964 Hellman came into prominence as the winner of a nationwide sculpture competition. He was Robert Adams' assistant, 1964–6, and had several one-man shows at Leicester Galleries in subsequent years. Taught at Morley College and Goldsmiths' College School of Art. His Twosome, in bronzed steel, of 1970, was shown with The Roland Collection at Camden Arts Centre, 1976. Hellman's Eagle, 1982, in aluminium, stands on a huge slate megalith in Cardiff. Lived in Headcorn, Kent.

Jeff HELLYER 1947– Artist and teacher, born Oxford, who studied part-time at Ruskin School of Drawing, 1964–7, then did a foundation course at Oxford Polytechnic, 1967–8; studied painting at Chelsea School of Art, 1968–71, then painting and mixed media at Slade School of Fine Art, 1971–3. In 1973 won a Boise scholarship to study in France and Italy and until 1981 taught part-time at many colleges including Cheltenham, Chelsea, Ravensbourne, Bath, Portsmouth and Reading. From 1981 taught at Falmouth School of Art. In 1990 Hellyer was artist-in-residence at the School of Painting, Montmirral, Tarn, France. Showed widely from 1977 on the continent, also at Annely Juda Fine Art, Newlyn Orion Gallery and Penwith Gallery in Cornwall, where he lived in Falmouth. In 1994 Hellyer was included in Falmouth Connections at the town's Art Gallery.

Francis HELPS 1890–1972 Painter, draughtsman and teacher, born in Dulwich, southeast London. At Dulwich College, 1903–7, Helps was the only boy to take art lessons and had a private tutor. In 1908 went to Slade School of Fine Art, where taught by Henry Tonks and Fred Brown. In 1915 Helps volunteered for service with Artists' Rifles, serving in France. In 1924 he joined the 1922–4 Everest Expedition as official artist, completing 80 paintings and drawings, most now in America. Between 1931–4 Helps taught at Royal College of Art, then volunteered to be evacuated with it to Ambleside, in the Lake District, 1940–4. From 1953 until his retirement Helps was head of the school of painting in Leeds, where he settled, returning in his last year to Bromley, Kent. Helps showed with RBA, of which he was elected a member in 1933, and in 1924 had a show at Alpine Club Gallery of his Himalayan work. Further shows were at City Art Gallery, Leeds, 1959; Manor House Museum and Art Gallery, Ilkley, 1971; and South London Art Gallery, 1979.

Alison HELYER 1965– Painter, born in Cleveland, where she attended Cleveland College of Art, 1983–4, De Montfort University, Leicester, 1984–7, then Chelsea College of Art, 1991–2. Awards included Prince's Trust Bursary and Exhibition

Award Northern Arts, both 1992. Mixed shows included Fab Four at Loseby Lane Gallery, Leicester, 1989, Whitechapel Open at Atlantis Gallery, 1994, and in that year she shared a three-man exhibition at Paton Gallery, showing huge toy dogs blown up on a white ground.

Nicholas HELY HUTCHINSON 1955– Painter, influenced initially by Dufy and Matisse, also drawing on the English Neo-Romantic tradition. He settled near Blandford, Dorset, and the countryside of that county and Wiltshire, horse racing, interiors and still life were among his subjects. Studied at St Martin's School of Art and Bristol Polytechnic. Showed solo with Montpelier Studio from 1984, later exhibitions including Wattis Fine Art, Hong Kong, from 1992, and The Jerram Gallery, Salisbury, 1995. Government Art Collection, Barbican Centre and Unilever hold examples. Hely Hutchinson was the third son of the 8th Earl of Donoughmore, an old Irish family.

Andrew HEMINGWAY 1955– Painter, born in Yorkshire, who studied at Barnsley School of Art, 1973–4, then Camberwell School of Art, 1974–7. With the aid of a bursary he travelled to Italy and Norway, 1977–8, being sent under private sponsorship to Japan to paint landscapes. He showed at RA from 1980, the year he began exhibiting in mixed shows at Piccadilly Gallery. In the 1980s he appeared in Basle, Düsseldorf and Cologne International Art Fairs. After a solo show at Johnston Gallery, Edmonton, Alberta, in 1978, others included a series at Piccadilly Gallery from 1981 and a major show at Brian Sinfield, Burford, 1992. Hemingway was a slow worker, notably in egg tempera, producing only about 30 pictures a year.

Harold HEMINGWAY 1908–1976 Painter, draughtsman and designer, born and based in Rochdale, Lancashire, best known for his depictions of the town between 1930–70. In the 1950s Hemingway and L S Lowry would walk around Rochdale, selecting planned-for-demolition buildings which should be recorded using Hemingway's distinctive colour and light. The son of a painter and decorator, Hemingway left school at 13 and worked at John Bright's Mill, eventually as a carpet designer. While working he trained at the local Art School, winning many awards for the design of fabrics, carpets and posters. Hemingway was a member of Rochdale Art Society and the Lancashire Group of Artists and undertook several commissions for Rochdale Corporation. His set designs for Rochdale Curtain Theatre formed the basis of his first exhibition in 1938, and subsequent shows, as well as London and Cambridge, were held widely in Lancashire. Rochdale Art Gallery has eight of his works, which in all are reckoned to number over 1,000.

Gordon HEMM fl. from 1920–1956 Architectural artist who was also an architect and fellow of RIBA. Studied at Liverpool School of Art. Exhibited Walker Art Gallery, Liverpool, and RA. Lived in Manchester.

Charles HEMMING: *see* **Laurence Charles HEMMING**

Laurence Charles HEMMING 1950– Artist in oil, acrylic, watercolour and pen and ink, born in Mynythislwyn, near Pontllanfraith, Monmouthshire. He studied at Goldsmiths' College, London University, 1973–7, notable teachers including Ivor Roberts-Jones, Carl Plackman, Michael Kenny and Peter Creswell. Hemming, who sometimes signed his work Charles Hemming, sometimes L C H, was originally concerned with conceptual sculpture, poetry related to 3D objects, which developed into an interest in illusion in objects and surfaces and in writing and illustration. Andrew Wyeth, Edward Hopper, Magritte, Arthur Rackham, Aubrey Beardsley, Rex Whistler and Osbert Lancaster were special influences. Decorative work for the Travellers' Club and Institute of Directors, the College of Arms and Sheikh of Dubai were among principal works. In 1990 Hemming was reserve decorative artist for the National Trust. From 1992 he did extensive book illustration and cartoon work for Ravette Books. His own books included *Paint Finishes*, 1985, and *British Painters of the Coast and Sea* and *British Landscape Painters*, 1988–9, the latter winning the *Yorkshire Post* Book Prize, 1989. He showed at Radlett Gallery, Radlett, 1978; Francis Kyle Gallery, 1981–2; and Portal Gallery, 1979–83. Lived in London.

Rachel HEMMING BRAY 1947– Born in London, painter and draughtsman working in oil, watercolour, pastel and drawings in all media, and teacher. Studied at Central School of Art, London, 1965, and College of St Mathias, Bristol 1966–9. Showed in mixed exhibitions at RA and RWA, and many one-man shows, including George's Gallery, Bristol 1981–82, Rooksmoor Gallery, Bath, 1985, Pelter/Sands, Bristol 1988, National Theatre, South Bank, London, 1991 and Bristol City Art Gallery, 1994. Worked regularly on individual and small group portraits, and in 1990s developed something of a niche in corporate commissions of people in their working environments. These latter she likened to "the manner of a war artist, with the subjects not 'sitting' for their portraits, and my having to cope with a great deal of movement". Such commissions included Bristol Old Vic, Theatre Royal; BBC Natural History Dept; Bristol City Museums and Art Gallery, and musicians at the Pump Room, Bath. Also painted landscapes, interiors and works of memory and imagination. Corporations holding her work include Bristol City Museums and Art Gallery, BBC Art Collection, University of Bristol Theatre Collection and Nat West Life Collection. Lived in Bristol.

Paul HEMPTON 1946– Painter, printmaker and teacher, born in Wakefield, Yorkshire. He studied at Goldsmiths' College School of Art, 1964–8, teachers including Andrew Forge, and at Royal College of Art, 1968–71, with Carel Weight, and obtained his master's degree. He taught at Wolverhampton Polytechnic, Nottingham University and Reading University's department of fine art. Arts Council holds his oil on canvas Marker V – Hill, Rod and Stone, of 1976–7, bought from Ikon Gallery, Birmingham, and several provincial collections have examples, including Wakefield Art Gallery. In 1980, Hempton represented Great Britain at the 11th Biennale de Paris. Lived in Minchinhampton, Gloucestershire.

Antony HEMSLEY 1965– Painter, born in Manchester. He studied painting at Trent Polytechnic, Nottingham, where he settled to work in Oldknows Studios. His first show in a public gallery was A Long Snake Summer at Mappin Art Gallery, Sheffield, 1989–90, which showed him to be an energetic, vibrant Colourist.

Philip HEMSLEY 1933– Painter, draughtsman and teacher, born in Stocksbridge, Yorkshire, full name George Philip Hemsley. He studied at Kingston School of Art and Royal Academy Schools with Henry Rushbury and Peter Greenham, gaining his certificate in 1958, the year he won a British Institution Award. Also gained Royal Academy Silver Medal, Landseer and Leverhulme Scholarships. Hemsley was a part-time adult education tutor. In his work he favoured "an imaginative, representational approach based on drawing". Showed at RA, RBA, RP, NEAC and Redfern Gallery. City of London Guildhall, Leicestershire Education Authority, Ashford Hospital and several other public collections hold examples. Was a Ridley Art Society member who lived in Woking, Surrey.

Gerard HEMSWORTH 1945– Sculptor who was born and lived in London. He attended St Martin's School of Art, 1963–7. Among his many mixed show appearances were Survey '68: Abstract Sculpture, at Camden Arts Centre, 1968; British Sculpture out of the Sixties, ICA, 1970; Carlisle Museum and Art Gallery, 1976; Tony Shafrazi Gallery, New York, 1988; and Galeria Comicos/Luis Serpa, Lisbon, 1991. Among dozens of solo shows were Nigel Greenwood Gallery, 1970; Museum of Modern Art, Oxford, 1972; Matt's Gallery, 1983; ICA, 1986; Anthony Reynolds Gallery, from 1987; and in 1991 Steendrukkerij BV, Amsterdam, and Galerie Cintrik, Antwerp. Arts Council holds several examples of his work.

Arthur Edward HENDERSON 1870–1956 Architectural artist and draughtsman, born in Aberdeen, where he attended the School of Art. Also became an architect, studying at the Architectural Association and City and Guilds School, in both places winning medals. Obtained the Owen Jones Travelling Scholarship of RIBA, in 1896, and was engaged in excavations at the Temple of Diana, Ephesus, in Greece. Exhibited RA, UA and RBA. Lived at Crawley Down, Sussex.

Belinda HENDERSON 1908–1988 Painter, designer, illustrator and teacher, daughter of civil servant Sir Horace Hamilton, she attended King Alfred's School, Hampstead. Just before World War II she studied at Chelsea School of Art, Henry Moore, Ceri Richards and Graham Sutherland being notable teachers. She also attended Cedric Morris' East Anglian School of Painting and Drawing. During the war she served as a guide lecturer and draughtsman for the Ministry of War. She also created painted fabrics, illustrated books and designed jackets for publishers such as Hamish Hamilton. In the late-1940s she began teaching drawing and painting, and in 1948 married the writer Philip Henderson. Showed in Hampstead galleries, WIAC, RA Summer Exhibitions and elsewhere, and there was a memorial show at 20th Century Gallery.

Elsie HENDERSON 1880–1967 Draughtsman, printmaker, painter and sculptor, she was principally a delineator of wild animals, although she also did landscapes and figure studies. Born in Eastbourne, Sussex, she was encouraged by her amateur painter mother. Studied at Slade School of Fine Art, 1903–5, then widely in Paris, in 1908–9, including periods at Académie Moderne, Atelier Colarossi, La Palette and Cercle Russe. In 1912 studied with Othon Friesz, the following year working in Italy. On the outbreak of war she returned to Guernsey, where she had spent much of her childhood, but in 1916 she enrolled at Chelsea Polytechnic to study lithography with Ernest Jackson. She began to draw at Regent's Park Zoo and won critical acclaim in 1917 with a zoo poster for London Underground. Started her own press and became a member of Senefelder Club, WIAC, Monarro Group and other exhibiting bodies. Her first solo show was at Leicester Galleries, 1924. In 1928 married the French consul in Guernsey, Baron Henri de Coudenhove, and lived on the island until 1946, when after the privations of the occupation and her husband's death she settled at Hadlow Down, Sussex. An exhibition reviving her memory, which also showed work by her friend Orovida Pissarro, was held at Parkin Gallery, 1985. Work in many public collections, including Tate Gallery, British Museum and Fitzwilliam Museum, Cambridge.

Ewen HENDERSON 1934– Experimental, Expressionist ceramic sculptor, draughtsman, printmaker and teacher, born in Staffordshire, both parents from Scottish medical families, his father the doctor in a lunatic asylum. After failing to obtain a short-service commission, Henderson did his National Service in the Royal Air Force Regiment in Germany, on release working for a chemical company. Based in Cardiff, Henderson visited museums and attended evening art classes; joined the Barry Summer School, meeting Harry Thubron, Terry Frost and Kenneth Martin; then studied at Goldsmiths' College, 1964–5, and Camberwell School of Arts and Crafts, 1965–8, tutors including Hans Coper and Lucie Rie. Henderson rebelled against symmetrical conformity and the art/craft gap; he built vessels instead of using a wheel, and eventually employed a mix of clays and paper pulp. Music was an inspiration, megaliths latterly a key theme. Henderson taught part-time and participated in numerous mixed exhibitions in Britain and abroad. Later solo shows included Hart Gallery and Galerie Besson, both 1994, and a Midlands Art Centre touring show, 1996. In 1990 Henderson completed a Triparteid Bird Form for the Saatchi Building, Berkeley Square. Among several dozen public collections holding examples are British Council; National Museum of Wales, Cardiff; Stedelijk Museum, Amsterdam; Ulster Museum in Belfast; and Victoria & Albert Museum. Henderson was based in London.

Keith HENDERSON 1883–1982 Painter, muralist and illustrator of great individuality, educated at Marlborough College.

Studied art at Slade School of Fine Art, then in Paris. Initially he was principally a portrait painter. After Army cavalry service in World War I Henderson travelled widely, including Africa and South America, the local plants and wildlife finding their way into his often colourful work. Official war artist attached to Royal Air Force in World War II. Among books that Henderson illustrated are W H Hudson's *Green Mansions*, 1926, and *The Purple Land*, 1929, and he published several titles himself, including *Palm Groves and Humming Birds*, 1924. Exhibited RA, Fine Art Society and RWS extensively, as well as ROI and RSW. Pelter/Sands, Bristol gave him a solo show in 1980. Galleries in Glasgow, Manchester, Preston, Worthing and elsewhere hold his work. Lived at Spean Bridge, Inverness-shire.

Kevin HENDERSON 1963– Sculptor who said his works were "organisations of images". He was born in Singapore and studied at Gray's School of Art in Aberdeen, 1981–6, also Oregon State University, America, 1982–3. His group exhibitions included New Scottish Art at Third Eye Centre, Glasgow, 1989, and South Bank Centre's tour The British Art Show 1990. In 1987 had solo show at Eden Court Theatre, Inverness. Lived in Edinburgh.

Nigel HENDERSON 1917–1985 Artist and teacher working in a wide range of media, born in London, who attended Stowe School, 1931–3, then through his mother became connected with the Bloomsbury Group. In 1935–6 studied biology at Chelsea Polytechnic, and was active in the Group Theatre with Rupert Doone and Robert Medley. While assisting Helmut Ruhemann the picture restorer Henderson, with the encouragement of Peggy Guggenheim, developed as a Surrealist painter and collagist, showing at Guggenheim Jeune. After serving as a pilot in Coastal Command in World War II Henderson suffered a nervous breakdown, but recovered to study at Slade School of Fine Art and experimented with photograms using bomb site debris. In the early 1950s Henderson combined teaching creative photography at Central School of Arts and Crafts with photojournalism for *Flair*, *Architectural Review* and *Melody Maker* and did posters for jazz musician Ronnie Scott. In 1952 with his friend Eduardo Paolozzi was involved in founding the Independent Group, and together they set up Hammer Prints Ltd, 1955–61. From 1957–60 Henderson taught part-time at Colchester School of Art, in 1965–8 taking over the photography department at Norwich School of Art, with which he was long connected. In 1976 Henderson completed a mural for University of East Anglia, Norwich. Henderson had a retrospective at Kettle's Yard, Cambridge, 1977. A major show toured from Norwich School of Art Gallery, 1982–3. Tate Gallery holds his work. Lived for many years at Landermere Quay, Essex.

Sheila Scott HENDERSON 1910– Landscape and portrait painter in oil, Henderson was at the Yellow Door School of Art under Frank Spenlove-Spenlove, which he had founded in 1896, and under the portrait painter Reginald G Eves. Henderson then went on to exhibit widely and prolifically, at the RA, NEAC, Brook Street Art Gallery, ROI, RSA, RP, the Paris Salon and others. Lived in Reigate, Surrey.

William HENDERSON 1903–1993 Painter of conversation pieces and draughtsman, born into privileged circumstances near Frome, Somerset, which obviated the need to earn a living. He attended Eton College, was at Cambridge University for a year with another in Paris taking drawing lessons. Was also advised privately by Judith Lear and the Polish journalist and artist Rom Landau, who persuaded Henderson to attend Westminster School of Art under Mark Gertler and Eliot Hodgkin. During World War II was a captain in the Royal Marines in India, including a period as aide-de-camp to General Archibald Wavell. In 1950s had two notable shows at Redfern Gallery. Travelled extensively and died at Tisbury, Wiltshire.

William HENDERSON 1941– Painter, designer and teacher, born in Ringmer, Sussex. He studied at Brighton College of Art, 1959–63, and Slade School of Fine Art, 1963–5. Made stage designs for Royal Opera House, Covent Garden. Showed at John Moores Liverpool Exhibition from 1969, RA Summer Exhibition from 1986 and Athena Awards, 1987. Solo shows included Arnolfini Gallery, Bristol, 1983, and Newcastle Polytechnic Gallery, 1984. Taught at Central St Martins School of Art from 1981. Rhythm and pattern were strong elements in Henderson's work, as in Arts Council's example Gjalla, of 1979, and Juggler's Mirror, in John Moores 1989–90 show. Lived in London.

Birgitte HENDIL 1944– Miniaturist, born in Copenhagen, Denmark, who studied at Edinburgh College of Art, 1964–9, teachers including Harry More Gordon. Showed at RSA, Scottish Arts Council and Stirling Gallery, in Stirling.

Kevin HENDLEY 1961– Painter and etcher working on a small scale and using rich colours. His inspiration came "from the atmosphere of pubs, cafés, bars, concerts and street scenes. These provide me with bizarre and humorous characters which are wonderful subjects." Hendley, a miner's son, grew up in Cresswell, Derbyshire, at 15 taking an apprenticeship which led to his becoming a master butcher after eight years. In 1985 he moved to London, attended life classes and took a foundation course at the City Lit. In the summer of 1993 he obtained his bachelor's degree in fine art painting at Central St Martins College, his degree show being a sell-out. Went on to become artist-in-residence at Royal Opera House. Showed at Sue Williams Gallery and elsewhere.

Robert Leslie HENDRA 1912– Stained glass and watercolour artist, born in London. Attended Camberwell School of Arts and Crafts and Central School of Arts and Crafts and worked in the studio of Martin Travers. Was a leading member of the British Society of Master Glass Painters. His work is to be found in Westminster Cathedral and a number of English provincial cathedrals. Lived in Harpenden, Hertforshire.

Herbert HENDRIE 1887–1946 Stained glass artist, painter and teacher, born in Manchester, who studied at Royal College of Art and Slade School of Fine Art. He became head of the design school at Edinburgh College of Art. Welbeck, Buckfast, Ampleforth and Paisley Abbeys contain windows by him and Kippen Parish Church, Stirling, has the outstanding Cameron Window, in memory of the artist D Y Cameron's wife; Hendrie strove for the effect of "crushed jewels and mother of pearl". Showed at RA, RSW, RSA, NEAC and elsewhere. Lived in Edinburgh and was a member of Chelsea Arts Club.

Archibald Hunter HENDRY 1890– Oil and watercolour painter, born at North Leith, Midlothian, Scotland. He studied art at the Royal High School, Edinburgh, and at the College of Art there, where his teachers included a number of notable Scottish painters, D M Sutherland and David Foggie. Exhibitions included RSW, SSA, RSW and the Edinburgh and Stirling Triennial. Was a member of the Royal Scots Club who lived at Middleton, Midlothian.

Heinz HENGHES: *see* **Henry HENGHES**

Henry HENGHES 1906–1975 Sculptor and teacher, born in Hamburg, Germany, as Heinz Henghes, by which name he is sometimes known. He was educated in Germany and America but was a self-taught sculptor who became head of fine art at Winchester College of Art. Produced the sculpture Orpheus for the 1951 Festival of Britain; it was eventually sited at Camden School for Girls. Birmingham City Art Gallery and the Museum of Modern Art in New York also hold his work. Lived latterly in Winchester, Hampshire, and in Tursac, Dordogne, France. Remembered by a colleague "as a brusque man. He was a devil – but I liked him!"

Joseph HENNAH 1897–1967 Painter in oil and watercolour who was born and lived mostly in Newport, Monmouthshire, later in Weymouth, Dorset. Showed at RA and RWA. Hennah had a love of the countryside and liked making studies of less obviously picturesque aspects, such as farmyard corners, hedges and gravel pits. He painted a large number of gouaches of South Africa and was particularly attached to the Cornish fishing villages of Polperro and St Ives.

Thomas HENNELL 1903–1945 Watercolour painter, draughtsman, writer and poet. Born at Ridley, Kent, studied at Regent Street Polytechnic for several years in the early 1920s, then qualified as a teacher with Marion Richardson. Taught art for several years. Began to research his first book, *Change in the Farm*, in Britain, and Ireland, mainly by bicycle. Was a meticulous recorder, in words and pictures, of vanishing country crafts and ways. In 1931 became friendly with Edward Bawden, Eric Ravilious and other artists based in Great Bardfield, Essex. From 1932–5 was treated for psychiatric illness, which he wrote about in *The Witnesses*. During World War II Hennell was an official war artist in Europe and the Far East, dying in mysterious circumstances in Java. The Imperial War Museum holds a large collection of his pictures, which are in many other public galleries. Hennell was a keen student of English watercolour painting and wrote well on it. Although not a great natural draughtsman, he improved his technique to become a fine atmospheric and distinctive watercolourist. Victoria Art Gallery, Bath, held a survey show in 1995.

Hubert HENNES 1907– Painter, draughtsman and teacher, born in London. Married to the artist Hilary Miller. Hennes studied at the Working Men's College, Crowndale Road, London, where he won the Lowes Dickinson Scholarship, which permitted a short period of travel to continental art centres; also St Martin's School of Art, 1928–30, and Royal College of Art, 1930–4. After seven years' teaching at Leicester College of Arts and Crafts, 1934–41, Hennes at the end of World War II took up a post at Oxford School of Art. Exhibited RA and RBA. Lived in Oxford.

Adrian HENRI 1932– Painter, poet, performance artist and writer, born in Birkenhead, Cheshire, where he remained based. He was closely identified with the 1960s Liverpool Pop scene and sought to produce popularly understandable art, as with Kop football series from the 1970s. He studied at King's College, Newcastle upon Tyne, and Durham University, 1951–5, graduating with a fine art degree. First exhibited in 1958 at Liverpool Academy, becoming its president, 1972–81. Showed frequently at John Moores Liverpool Exhibition from 1961 and gained second prize in 1972 with Painting One. Other series of paintings by Henri encompassed food, debris and magic places, as in Dream Palace (Homage to Ferdinand Cheval), shown at John Moores, 1989–90. Took part in poetry readings and performed at Isle of Wight rock festival in late 1960s with his Liverpool Scene band. Among his publications was *The Postman's Palace*, a book for children, 1990. Henri had a series of solo shows, including a retrospective, The Art of Adrian Henri, held in 1986 at South Hill Park, Bracknell, and tour, and in 1997 an exhibition of his 1960s work at Whitford Fine Art. Walker Art Gallery in Liverpool and Arts Council hold his work.

Frank Watson HENRICKSEN 1915–1955 Artist in gouache and line, born and lived at Wallsend, near Newcastle. He was mainly self-taught and exhibited with Newcastle Society of Artists, Shipley Art Gallery in Gateshead, and at Laing Art Gallery, Newcastle, which holds his work.

Daphne Hardy HENRION: *see* **HARDY**

Ben HENRIQUES 1967– Painter, born in Cheshire, who went to live in Scotland aged nine, being educated in Perthshire. He attended the fine art department at University of Newcastle, 1986–90. The island of Tiree off Scotland's west coast was a favourite subject, as shown in shared exhibition he had at William Hardie Gallery, Glasgow, in 1992. Worked in Scotland and London.

Rose HENRIQUES 1889–1972 Social worker, artist and musician, born and lived in London, daughter of James Loewe, communal worker and scholar. She studied the piano in Breslau,

Germany, then in 1914 was persuaded by Basil Henriques, whom she married, to enter social work. Basil was knighted for his work in London's East End in 1955. He and Rose were wardens of the Bernhard Baron St George's Jewish Settlement from 1914–48, and continued to live there even after officially retiring. Rose was known to the boys and girls as "the Missus". In addition, she was a nurse at Liverpool Street Station in World War I; was an air-raid warden and organised an emergency feeding scheme in World War II; in 1945 went to Bergen-Belsen to tackle welfare problems after the closing of the notorious camp; was chairman of the British Ose Society for promoting physical and mental health; and in 1954 founded the Workrooms for the Elderly in east London. Henriques fostered local interest in ballet, music and drama and as an artist painted east London's streets and docks. In 1947 the Whitechapel Art Gallery held a show Stepney in War and Peace; in 1961 Vanishing Stepney at the Gallery included several hundred paintings and drawings by her. *Fifty Years in Stepney*, by Rose Henriques, was published by the Settlement in 1966, based on broadcast talks. Tower Hamlets Public Libraries holds a large collection of her pictures.

Bruce HENRY 1918– Wildlife and landscape artist, born in Kandy, Ceylon, working in watercolour, pastel and oil, who travelled widely. His father George Morrison Reid Henry and brother David M Reid-Henry [sic] were also wildlife artists with an international reputation. Bruce Henry was educated in Britain and after graduating from London University entered the church, serving with his wife in India for many years. He later became head of religious studies at Worthing Sixth Form College for a decade, in 1980 retiring to paint full-time. Was a member of SWLA, showed widely in England and had several solo exhibitions. His illustrated book *Highlight the Wild – The Art of the Reid Henrys* was published in 1986. The collection Nature in Art, Gloucester, holds his work. Lived in Worthing, Sussex.

George Morrison Reid HENRY 1891–1983 Wildlife artist, notable for his bird paintings, born in Ceylon on a tea estate where his father was manager. As one of 11 children he had little formal education, but extensive reading and observation helped him by 15 to begin establishing a reputation as a naturalist and artist. Was appointed assistant in systematic entomology at Colombo Museum, where he worked until retirement. In 1927 the government published the first of a series of 64 paintings of birds, entitled *Coloured Plates of the Birds of Ceylon*, with his illustrations and text by W E Wait. Later illustrated several bird books, including *Indian Hill Birds*, by Salim Ali, and in 1955 Oxford University Press also published his key work, *A Guide to the Birds of Ceylon*, written and illustrated by him and still a standard work. Travelled widely abroad, including a visit to Australia when he was 88, continuing to sketch from life in small, lined notebooks. His work was exhibited in London, Zimbabwe and elsewhere. His sons Bruce Henry and David M Reid-Henry were also bird artists.

Olive HENRY 1902–1989 Stained glass designer and painter, born and lived in Belfast, Northern Ireland. During evening classes at Belfast School of Art she became interested in stained glass, took an apprenticeship with W F Clokey & Company and stayed with them. She was elected RUA, was a founder-member of Ulster Society of Women Artists, also showing with Watercolour Society of Ireland and RHA. Ulster Museum holds her work.

Susan HENSEL 1944– Artist working with oil, tempera, painted wood and collage, and teacher, born in Amersham, Buckinghamshire, married to the sculptor and jeweller David Hensel. Hensel did a foundation course at Wimbledon School of Art, 1965–6, gained an honours degree in fine art at Brighton College of Art, 1966–9, with a further year at Reading University, 1969–70. She taught art in local schools and at adult education classes. Her own work showed a surreal influence and she exhibited widely in England and abroad, including Wraxall Gallery, 1981; Doktor Glas, Stockholm, 1982; Ankrum Gallery, Los Angeles, 1984; Gallery Reich, Cologne, and Milligan Gallery, Storrington, both 1991. Lived in East Grinstead, Sussex.

John HENSHALL 1913– Painter, calligrapher and teacher, born in Stockport, Cheshire, where he lived. He studied art at Stockport College and showed with RI, Society of Church Craftsmen, Red Rose Guild and elsewhere, having a series of solo exhibitions in the north of England and north Wales. Art galleries in Stockport and Wigan hold examples.

Yvonne HENTHORNE 1942– Painter and teacher, born in Wetherby, Yorkshire, who studied at Goldsmiths' College School of Art, 1961–6, teachers including Andrew Forge and Patrick Millard. Between 1969–75 she received a series of Italian, Brazilian and West German grants and scholarships. Taught at Havering Technical College. Was elected to RBA in 1978, also showing with SWA, at Young Contemporaries and Midland Group Gallery, solo exhibitions including Ikon Gallery, Birmingham. Lived in London.

Deirdre HENTY-CREER fl. from late 1930s– Painter, and creator of small ceramic flower studies, born in Sydney, Australia, in art self-taught after private education. She was accredited to the Ministry of Information, 1940–5; was at various times on the council of UA and Chelsea Art Society and on the committee of the Armed Forces' Art Society; and represented Great Britain in Sport in Art in the VII Olympiad at the Victoria & Albert Museum. Showed at RA, RBA, NEAC and elsewhere. Had a solo exhibition at Fine Art Society, 1941, later ones including Qantas Gallery from 1970, with a retrospective of 60 years at Bartley Drey Gallery, 1997. Medici Society, Warren of Ware, Chryson's of California and Gruhen of Innsbruck reproduced artworks by Henty-Creer, which included portraits of HRH Prince Michael of Kent and Sir John Kerr, Governor-General of Australia. HRH The Prince of Wales holds her work, also in museums in Cape Town and Oxford. Her sister was the painter Pam Mellor. Lived in London.

Tony HEPBURN 1942– Sculptor and teacher using a variety of materials, born in Manchester, who studied at Camberwell School of Arts and Crafts, 1959–63, and London University, 1963–5. Went on to lecture at the faculty of art and design at Lanchester Polytechnic in Coventry; also being a visiting professor at Carnegie-Mellon University in Pittsburgh, Pennsylvania; then at Alfred University, Alfred, New York, as head of the division of art and design. Exhibitions included Primavera Gallery, 1967; Victoria & Albert Museum, 1968; Bradford City Art Gallery, 1971; and Clay Sculpture, Yorkshire Sculpture Park, 1980. In 1982 took part in the three-man Convergent Territories, The Banff Centre School of Fine Arts, Alberta. Solo shows included Covent Garden Gallery, 1969. Victoria & Albert Museum, Inner London Education Authority, Stoke-on-Trent Museum and several overseas collections hold examples.

David HEPHER 1935– Painter, collagist and teacher, born in Surrey. He studied at Camberwell School of Arts and Crafts and Slade School of Fine Art, 1955–61. In the 1960s he participated in group shows at Young Contemporaries, LG and Piccadilly Gallery, then had first solo show at Serpentine Gallery in 1971. In 1972 showed solo with Angela Flowers Gallery, at which he was to continue exhibiting. Hepher also taught part-time in London. In the 1970s Hepher participated in Germany and France in several shows devoted to realist or Hyper-Realist painting, and became noted for his minute depictions of suburban domestic house fronts, with their bow-windows, stained glass fanlights and privet hedges. In 1974 Hepher had retrospective exhibitions at Mappin Art Gallery, Sheffield, and Whitechapel Art Gallery, with one at the Museum of London, 1996, entitled Streets in the Sky, featuring graffiti-marked south London council tower blocks. Hepher lived nearby in Camberwell. Sheffield City Art Galleries, British Council and Boysmans Museum in Rotterdam are among public collections holding his work.

Ruth HEPPEL 1926– Painter and draughtsman, born in London, who studied at Regent Street Polytechnic School of Art, teachers including Norman Blamey and Arnold Auerbach. She showed at RA, RP, RHA and in Germany, and had several solo exhibitions. Lived at Nether Winchendon, Buckinghamshire.

Norman HEPPLE 1908–1994 Painter, born in London, where he lived, full name Robert Norman Hepple. The family came from the village of Hepple, Northumberland. He was the son of the painter Robert Hepple and the nephew of Wilson Hepple, the Northumberland animal painter. Studied at Goldsmiths' College School of Art and Royal Academy Schools, under Sir Walter Russell. During World War II Hepple joined the London Fire Service and became an official war artist to the National Fire Service, the Imperial War Museum holding resultant work. Hepple was elected RP in 1948, being its president, 1979–83; was elected NEAC in 1950; and in 1961 was made RA. Hepple's many portraits included HM The Queen, HRH The Duke of Edinburgh and other members of the royal family. He also painted landscapes, horses and flowers for relaxation, as shown in his show at Spink & Son, 1987.

Arthur Jackson HEPWORTH: *see* **Arthur JACKSON**

Barbara HEPWORTH 1903–1975 Sculptor of formal and abstract figures in bronze, stone and wood. Born in Wakefield, Yorkshire, Hepworth studied at Leeds School of Art, then from 1921 at the Royal College of Art, from 1924–5 living in Italy as the result of a West Riding Travelling Scholarship. Married the sculptor John Skeaping in 1924, marriage dissolved 1933, and exhibited with him. In Rome had learned the technique of carving. In the early 1930s her interest in abstract sculpture developed, encouraged by several developments. She had met the painter Ben Nicholson in 1931 – marrying him shortly afterwards, marriage dissolved 1951 – and with him visited the studios of Arp, Brancusi, Braque, Picasso and Gabo. Hepworth in the 1930s became a member of several forward-looking groups, such as the 7 & 5 Society, Unit One and Abstraction-Creation. In 1939 Hepworth moved to St Ives, Cornwall, where she became an influential member of the artistic community, being a founder-member of the Penwith Society in 1949. In 1947–8 she had made her notable series of drawings of operating theatres, and in 1949 a first one-man show of drawings at Durlacher Bros, in New York, extended her growing reputation. Two works were commissioned for the Festival of Britain in 1951 and she won second prize in The Unknown Political Prisoner competition two years later. Although in the 1950s she was to design décor for productions at the Old Vic theatre and for Covent Garden opera house, she was to concentrate on consolidating her position as Britain's premier female sculptor, being given several retrospective exhibitions and having work purchased by major international galleries. She became Dame Barbara Hepworth in 1965. Died in a fire in her studio in St Ives, where a Barbara Hepworth Museum was opened in 1976.

Dorothy HEPWORTH 1898–1978 Painter, the lifelong friend and companion of the painter Patricia Preece, whom she met at the Slade School of Fine Art. While studying there she first showed at RA and in 1918–19 graduated with first-class honours. With Preece she set up a studio in London, then spent four years with her in Paris, where Hepworth studied at Atelier Colarossi. After returning to England in 1925 they rented cottages in the west of England, in 1927 settling in Cookham, Berkshire, where she lived with Patricia Preece until she died, even during Preece's bizarre marriage to the painter Stanley Spencer, which she sought to discourage. Much of Patricia Preece's output is known to be by Dorothy Hepworth, especially the later work, but how much is unclear. A studio sale at Christie's in 1984 encompassed 500 paintings and over 1,500 drawings from Dorothy Hepworth's studio; these included studies of girls, still lifes and landscapes, especially of the Cookham area. A small woman of masculine dress, Dorothy Hepworth latterly led a reclusive life with Patricia Preece, who predeceased her in 1971. Hepworth left two sixteenth-century statues to the Victoria & Albert Museum in her will.

Stephen HEPWORTH 1963– Non-traditional sculptor, born and lived in London, who gained his honours degree in fine art at

Brighton Polytechnic, 1984–7, his master's degree at Goldsmiths' College, 1988–90. In 1991–3 he won a number of British Council Awards. Hepworth "rendered language solid, creating a short circuit between the encoding of language and desire through his adoption of the role of a translator." Group exhibitions included Barclays Young Artist Award, Serpentine Gallery, 1991; and in 1992 Joy and Pain at Institute of Contemporary Art, Amsterdam, and Génériques: Le Visuel et L'Écrit, Hôtel des Arts, Paris. Solo exhibitions included 121 Art Gallery, Antwerp, 1991, and in 1992 Galerie Gutharc Ballin, Paris, and ArsFutura Galerie, Zürich.

Albert HERBERT 1925– Painter, printmaker and teacher, born in London. Left school early and briefly worked in newspapers, attending life drawing classes part-time at St Martin's School of Art with R V Pitchforth. After Army service, on which he 40 years later made a television film, attended Wimbledon School of Art, 1947, then Royal College of Art, 1949. Began exhibiting at RA in 1951, the year when he married Jacqueline Henly, a sculpture student. A Royal College of Art Travelling Scholarship in 1952–3 enabled him to travel on the continent and an Abbey Major Scholarship in 1953–4 took him to Rome, where he encountered the Italian Realists. Worked for a time in the Kitchen Sink style and was one of Jack Beddington's selections for the book *Young Artists of Promise.* Between 1955–6 lectured at Dudley School of Art, in 1956–64 at Birmingham College of Art, joining St Martin's School of Art in 1964, where he became principal lecturer. A flirtation with abstract painting then in vogue left him dissatisfied and Herbert returned to figurative painting through etching. A British Council-financed trip to the Far East directed Herbert's mind to Biblical subjects – he was a Catholic convert, long interested in Buddhism – which led to a series of small but powerful pictures in a quasi-primitive style. Had a number of one-man shows including England & Co, 1989. Lived at Cliftonville, Dorking, Surrey. His daughter Madeline was an artist.

Barry HERBERT 1937– Printmaker, painter and teacher, born in York. He studied at Archbishop Holgate's School there and at James Graham College and went on to head the fine art department at Leeds University. As well as mixed exhibitions Herbert had several dozen solo shows, including Serpentine Gallery, 1971; Galerie Brechbühl, Switzerland, from 1972; and Gilbert Parr Gallery, 1982. Editions of his prints were published in Britain and on the continent. Lived in Leeds, Yorkshire.

Jacqueline Anne HERBERT 1928– Sculptor, printmaker, draughtsman and illustrator, brought up in Kent, wife of the painter Albert Herbert. She studied at Beckenham School of Art, 1946, with Carel Weight, at Goldsmith's College School of Art, 1947–9, Royal College of Art, 1949–52, with the sculptor John Skeaping, and in Spain and Italy. Showed AIA, Leicester Galleries, ICA, British School in Rome and elsewhere. Shell, the oil company, bought her work.

Kathy HERBERT 1955– Artist and teacher working in a wide range of materials who graduated from University of Ulster in fine art in 1990, having transferred from the National College of Art and Design, Dublin, where she spent three years. Herbert was artist-in-residence at St Patrick's College, Dublin, in 1992 and worked for some years as a teacher for the adult life drawing class at Crescent Arts Centre and Royal Ulster Academy Association, Belfast. Her sculpture was chosen for a number of significant events, including The Boglands Symposium, County Wicklow, 1990, and The Snow Sculpture Symposium, Luleå, Sweden, 1992. She was a prizewinner at the Íontas Small Works Competition, Sligo, 1991. Also took part in The Oireachtas Exhibition, RHA Gallery, Dublin, 1993, and in 1994 Beyond the Partitions, put on by Queen Street Studios, Belfast, with which she was associated.

Madeline HERBERT 1957– Artist, designer and teacher, daughter of the artist Albert Herbert. She studied at Camberwell School of Arts and Crafts and Goldsmiths' College School of Art. Designed for stage, puppet theatre and films and taught costume drawing. Was included in England & Co's Art in Boxes, 1991.

Ian HERDMAN 1957– Sculptor, painter, draughtsman and teacher, born Newcastle upon Tyne. After attending the Royal Grammar School there he was at University of Reading, 1976–80, gaining a fine arts degree. From 1980 Herdman appeared regularly in group shows, including New Contemporaries at ICA, 1980; Serpentine Gallery Summer Show, 1982; Cheltenham Sculpture Biennale, 1985; Sue Williams Gallery, 1988; staff exhibition at Croydon College, 1990; and Sculpture at Canterbury, 1991. Solo exhibitions included Air Gallery, 1984, and Jablonski Gallery, 1986. Hunterian Gallery, Glasgow, and University of Reading hold his work.

Gordon HERICKX 1900–1953 Sculptor and teacher, born in Birmingham, where he died. Herickx won a scholarship to Birmingham College of Art in 1914, to which he returned after World War I, winning the Rylands Scholarship. His teaching included Walsall School of Art, but his career was mainly based in Birmingham, working in stone and bronze. Herickx had a special interest in fine lettering, but his main achievement was a small body of effigies of corn, cyclamen and chestnut bud which can be sensual, with the subtle simplifications of Brancusi. Among Herickx's better-known commissions were the interior decoration of the Cunard Steamship Company's offices and work at Cecil Sharp House, in London. The Barber Institute in Birmingham and the city's Museum and Art Gallery hold his work, as do a number of other provincial collections. There was a memorial show in Birmingham Museum and Art Gallery in 1953, shortly after an exhibition at Kensington Art Gallery. Herickx was a friend of the poet Louis MacNeice, appearing in his autobiographical narrative poem *Autumn Sequel* as Wimbush, and in Jon Stallworthy's biography of MacNeice.

John HERITAGE 1931–1994 Painter, sculptor and teacher, born in Liverpool, where he studied sculpture with Charles Gardiner at the School of Art, after National Service attending

Slade School of Fine Art in 1955 under Reg Butler. After teaching in Liverpool, Heritage studied at British School, Rome, 1961, where he concentrated on drawing and painting. Returned to Liverpool, Heritage taught and became secretary of the Liverpool Academy. From 1972–9 he was head of Wallasey School of Art and then vice-principal of Wirral College of Art, then from 1980–92 was dean of Clwyd College of Art, Wrexham. Heritage retained his connection with the northwest, maintaining a home in Wallasey, Cheshire. Much of Heritage's work had a satirical and social comment side. He had a photographic memory and would on occasion work intensively at night for long stretches. Heritage took part in mixed and solo shows in London, America and South Africa. What proved to be a memorial exhibition toured from Theatre Clwyd Gallery, 1994–5. Liverpool's Walker Art Gallery holds examples.

Bridget HERIZ 1949– Sculptor and teacher, born a British citizen in Hamburg, West Germany, daughter of the glass engraver Patrick Heriz-Smith and the painter Audrey Pilkington. She studied at Goldsmiths' College, 1973, with Carl Plackman, and at Ravensbourne College of Art & Design, 1974–7, with Eric Peskett and Brian Fielding. From 1978–86 Heriz taught at the Clock House Art Centre, Suffolk, from then on working full-time as a self-employed sculptor. Of her work Heriz said that it was "based on human experience, and therefore strongly uses the human figure, but entwined with images of biological and geological metamorphoses, the theme being one of growth". Mixed exhibitions included Sculpture in Anglia, Corn Exchange, Ipswich, from 1979; prizewinner, SGA, 1985; and 20th Century British Artists, Oriel Gallery, Cambridge, 1991. Bromley Parish Church commissioned her work. Lived in Badingham, Suffolk.

Patrick Ambrose Lewis HERIZ-SMITH 1920– Glass engraver, artist in pastel and teacher, husband of the artist Audrey Pilkington and father of the sculptor Bridget Heriz. He was born in Bournemouth, Hampshire, attending Reimann School of Art, 1937–9, teachers including Leonard Rosoman, then Slade School of Fine Art, 1939–41, under Allan Gwynne-Jones. Heriz-Smith taught in schools, 1941–64, including Gordonstoun; from 1964–78 he ran an independent adult residential school in Suffolk; from 1978–88 running a similar but non-residential school at Exeter. Heriz-Smith was a member of Suffolk Craft Society, Devon Guild and a fellow of the Society of Designer-Craftsmen. The composer Benjamin Britten and the singer Peter Pears owned his work. Lived in Exeter, Devon.

Stella HERKLOTS 1938– Sculptor, born in Hong Kong, her father a scientist and botanical artist. She was interned during World War II in the Philippines, then travelled extensively throughout the world. After gaining an economics degree, 1957–60, began sculpting in 1967, in London studying briefly with the Czech sculptor Irena Sedlecká. She worked for some years in interior design and landscape garden design, then gained a fine arts degree in sculpture at Leicester Polytechnic from 1986–9. Herklots worked mainly to private commission, notably portrait busts. Exhibitions included a relief at the headquarters of the Committee of Directors of Polytechnics, 1989, and 1st RWA Open Sculpture Exhibition, 1993. Lived in Melton Mowbray, Leicestershire.

Andrew HERMAN 1961– Artist who employed miscellaneous media such as wood, synthetic rubber, canvas and copper tacks. He was born and continued to work in London. Studied at Bath Academy of Art, 1980–3, then Goldsmiths' College School of Art, 1988–90. Gained a British Council Award 1991–2. He created a series of paintings, such as his entry for East & South, Norwich Gallery/Kent Institute of Art and Design, 1992, in which a work was dismantled and reconstructed. The idea was that "a painting can be conceptually divided into parts, and that each constituent part plays an independent role."

Josef HERMAN 1911– Painter, draughtsman and writer, born in Warsaw, Poland, son of a Jewish cobbler. In 1929–31 studied at School of Art and Decoration, Warsaw, then worked as a graphic artist and designer in the Polish capital, beginning to exhibit his pictures, which had Expressionist tendencies. In 1938 left Poland for Brussels, where he was influenced by Permeke. Moved to Britain in 1940; lived in Glasgow for a time where he met Jankel Adler and began to paint nostalgic pictures of childhood; then moved to London where he had a show at Lefevre Galleries. A period of great importance began when Herman settled for about a decade from the mid-1940s in the Welsh mining village of Ystradgynlais and began his series of sombre-hued paintings and ink drawings of miners and their environment. In 1946 had first of a long series of exhibitions at Roland, Browse and Delbanco, and began to show internationally. Contributed pictures to Festival of Britain in 1951, and in 1956 had first of several retrospectives at Whitechapel Art Gallery, others including Swansea and Glasgow public galleries in 1963 and 1975 respectively. Although he lived in London from 1953, Herman travelled widely. In addition to the mining series he also drew land workers and peasants. In 1975 published his autobiography, *Related Twilights*. Work in many public galleries, including Tate. Was made RA in 1990.

Gertrude HERMES 1901–1983 Sculptor, wood engraver, linocutter, illustrator and designer of great versatility. Born at Bromley, Kent, Gerts, as she was known to her friends, first wanted to be a farmer and worked for a year on the land in Essex. Then she had a year at Beckenham School of Art and a year in Germany to learn the language, followed by four years at Leon Underwood's School of Painting and Sculpture at Hammersmith, 1922–6. In 1926 married the artist Blair Hughes-Stanton, divorced 1933. Was influenced by the work of Henri Gaudier-Brzeska and Brancusi and tribal sculpture in the 1920s and '30s. First commission for a portrait bust was of the writer A P Herbert, in 1931, and she became noted for her busts of writers, such as Kathleen Raine (Tate Gallery) and David Gascoyne, and heads of children. Worked for the Cresset Press, Gregynog Press and Golden Cockerel Press. During World War II went with her children to Canada and America, where precision drawing in shipyards and factories in black and white led to her turning to colour on return to England in 1945. She had taught at St Martin's before the war, and after it taught at that school as well as Camberwell, the Central School and Royal Academy Schools. Elected RA in 1971. In 1981 the Academy gave her an eightieth birthday show. Hermes' work has warmth, elegance and vitality, tinged with a functional spareness. Lived in London.

Patrick HERON 1920– Painter, designer, writer and teacher, born in Leeds, son of T M Heron the founder of Cresta Silks; as a child Heron lived for some time in Cornwall, where he eventually settled at Zennor, St Ives. Studied at Slade School of Fine Art, 1937–9. As a conscientious objector during World War II he worked on the land, also having a short time at Leach Pottery, St Ives. In London in 1945 he resumed painting and had first solo show at Redfern Gallery, 1947. Wrote on art for *New English Weekly*, also for *New Statesman and Nation* and for *Arts*, the New York-based publication, his views gaining a wide readership. Painted frequently in Cornwall during visits, buying his permanent home, Eagles Nest, in 1955. Taught at Central School of Arts and Crafts, 1953–6. In mid-1950s Heron began to paint abstract works, and he was Britain's strongest link with the New York Abstract Expressionists, discussing the first exhibition of their works in Europe in 1956. The group show that he advised on – Metavisual, Tachiste, Abstract Painting in England Today – at Redfern Gallery in 1957 was a landmark. His soft-edged lozenges of vibrant colour became unmistakeable, and were shown in a number of solo exhibitions at Bertha Schaefer Gallery, New York, from 1960 and elsewhere widely abroad. Camden Arts Centre showed big new abstracts in 1994. Susanna Heron was his daughter. Tate Gallery, which with other major public collections holds his work, gave Heron an important exhibition in 1998.

Susanna HERON 1949– Artist in a variety of media and writer, born in Cornwall, where she grew up. She was the daughter of the painter and writer Patrick Heron. Attended Falmouth School of Art, 1967–8, then Central School of Art & Design, 1969–71. In 1978–9 she was in America under a United Kingdom/United States Bicentennial Arts Fellowship. She also won a British Council/National Endowment for the Arts. In 1989 Heron gained a Thornton Bequest for Bronze Casting from the Arts Council and won a sculpture prize in the Tree of Life Exhibition, South Bank Centre, and tour. Her solo exhibitions dated from 1985 at Whitechapel Art Gallery, later ones including Newlyn Art Gallery and tour, 1992. Camden Arts Centre, where she had shown in 1989, had an exhibition in connection with her book *Shima: Island and Garden*, based on the family home Eagles Nest, in Cornwall, published 1992. Cibachrome prints and slate carvings were features of Heron's work. This was held by Victoria & Albert Museum, National Museum of Wales in Cardiff, Contemporary Art Society and overseas. Lived in London.

George HERRAGHTY 1949– Painter, often of miniatures, draughtsman and artist in collage, born in Letterfourie, Banffshire. He studied at Duncan of Jordanstone College of Art, Dundee, 1967–71, where his teachers included Alberto Morrocco and David McClure. He went on to do post-diploma work and in 1972 a Major Travelling Scholarship took Herraghty extensively around Europe. Showed RSA, SSA, elsewhere in Scotland, and in Germany. Lived in Dundee, Angus.

Eugen HERSCH 1887–1967 Painter, mural artist, printmaker and teacher, born in Berlin, where he was trained in the old master tradition at the Koniglichen Kunstakademie. After graduating he won the Rome Prize and spent 1910–12 in Italy. Returning to Berlin he established a fine career as a portrait painter, broken by a period during World War I as a war artist. As life became hard for Jews in Nazi Germany, Hersch with his wife left for England in 1939 where, after a period of internment in the Liverpool area, he began to reshape his career. Showed at RA, PS, RP, Whitechapel Art Gallery and elsewhere and completed a large mural Triptych in Blue for Wandsworth Town Hall. His final work, which took five years, is a huge mural of twelve paintings: A Requiem to Comfort the Bereaved. His work is in several public collections in Germany and was commemorated with a show at John Denham Gallery in 1990. Lived in London.

Samuel Irvine HERTFORD fl. c.1890–1960 Landscape painter, born in Liverpool but educated in America, including time in Detroit, Michigan, and Jersey City, New Jersey. Studied at Liverpool School of Art. He was a member of the Liverpool Academy and was in the mid-1920s president of the Liver Sketching Club. Exhibited RA, RCamA, Walker Art Gallery, Liverpool, widely in the north of England and in America. The critic George Whitfield described Hertford's Sound of Iona, in a 1930s Liverpool Academy show, as being a "masterpiece of its kind", in the manner of the Scottish Colourists. Stretford Art Gallery, Manchester, bought Hertford's work. Lived in Wallasey, Cheshire.

Ivie HERTSLET 1883–1977 Painter, draughtsman and writer, born in Fawkham, Kent, into a family of Swiss ancestry with a long tradition of service to Court of St James. By 1895 showed artistic talent and was sent to Westminster and then Lambeth Schools of Art, being taught at Lambeth by Philip Connard. In 1906–7 she showed four pictures at Walker Art Gallery, Liverpool, but then turned her attention to writing stories and poems in magazines and newspapers, including *Home Notes*, *The Idler*, *T P's Weekly*, *The Times*, *Country Life* and *Little Folks*. In 1917 married John Craik-Henderson, a lawyer and politician, eventually becoming Lady Craik-Henderson. Visits to France in the 1940s revived her interest in art and she became prolific, especially landscapes of France, Scotland and Sussex, where she settled at Brewhurst. Showed latterly at RA and Royal Glasgow Institute of the Fine Arts. She was painted by Glyn Philpot, Eric Kennington and Archibald McGlashan, these portraits being included in a retrospective of her work at Alpine Gallery, 1979.

Pascal HERVEY 1969– Artist who used a mix of coloured gloss paints sprayed with a mastic gun into bubblewrap in horizontal and vertical bands to create Untitled, in the 1997–8 John Moores Liverpool Exhibition. Hervey was born in Swindon, Wiltshire, and settled in London. After studying at the Slade School of Fine Art, 1989–93, he attended Chelsea College of Art, 1993–4. In 1996 he showed at Bund and Lotta Hammer Galleries, in 1998 having a first solo exhibition at Deutsch-Britische Freundschaft.

Sophie HERXHEIMER 1963– Painter and lecturer, born in London, who studied at Camberwell School of Arts & Crafts, Chelsea School of Art and École des Beaux-Arts in Montpellier, France. Herxheimer was a visiting lecturer at Winchester School of Art and Central St Martin's College of Art & Design. Showed at Whitworth Young Contemporaries at Whitworth Art Gallery, Manchester, 1985; Riverside Open at Riverside Studios, 1986; South Bank Picture Show, Royal Festival Hall, from 1989; BP Portrait Award at National Portrait Gallery, 1993; and Royal Over-Seas League Open, 1995. Had a solo exhibition at Bloomsbury Theatre, 1988, later ones including Atlantis, 1994. Publications including Herxheimer's work included *Wonder Tales*, edited by Marina Warner, 1994, and Pomme Clayton's retelling of *Tales of Amazing Maidens*, 1995. London Lighthouse holds Herxheimer's work.

Walter HERZ 1909–1965 Commercial artist, illustrator, painter and bibliophile, born in Naetirisch Ostrak, Austria (later Czechoslovakia) into a middle-class but uncultured family. His small stature made him a bookworm, and through a strong character and intelligence he developed knowledge of book collecting and talents for painting and drawing while studying law. When Hitler invaded Czechoslovakia Herz fled without his family to Poland, then England, arriving in 1939. Became a freelance commercial artist, a job he always disliked, although he went on to illustrate many books on Jewish subjects and books for children. From 1947 he joined his lifelong friend V V Rosenfeld in a commercial art business. The work eliminated time for his own painting. In 1945 Herz tried to commit suicide through a drugs overdose, having heard his mother had been murdered by the Nazis. He was resuscitated, but the experience clouded the rest of his life. Became an obsessive and knowledgeable book collector who specialised in sixteenth-century volumes, old and first editions of the Greek and Roman classics, English literature of the eighteenth century and art. Died of heart failure. Through Rosenfeld his library was donated to The Jewish National & University Library, Jerusalem. Ben Uri Art Society holds work by Herz, who designed the Holocaust memorial for Leicester Synagogue.

Raya HERZIG fl. from early 1970s– Painter, born at Kartuzy, near Gdańsk, Poland. As a small child of a cultured family she had to endure the terror of the ghetto and the concentration camp, only her sister surviving, experiences which left a mark on her work. For years she carried her ideas inside her until one day she started to paint, after which she worked in a number of styles, including Surrealism and fantasy. One series included nudes with faces replaced by motionless masks; then there were the Transformer and Monuments series. After World War II Herzig lived in Sweden, Switzerland and Italy, taking up Swiss citizenship and working as a professional painter from 1971. She became a member of the Union of Swiss Painters, Sculptors and Architects (GSMBA) in 1973. In 1990 she moved to Britain and eventually to Dartmouth, Devon. From 1971 she showed with the annual exhibition of Basle artists, Kunsthalle Basle, elsewhere in Switzerland and abroad in mixed shows, including Swiss Painters in Britain at October Gallery, 1991. Showed in solo exhibitions from 1972, at Galerie Niggli, St Gallen and Galerie Mascotte, Basle; at Stara Kordegarda, Warsaw, 1980; and in 1992 at Polish Cultural Institute.

Barbara HESELTINE 1906–1996 Theatre designer, costume specialist and painter, known as Billy Heseltine and married to Chartres Molony. After school she studied at Central School of Arts and Crafts and trained as a teacher, but, not wanting to teach indefinitely beyond a short time at the Central, she went to the Old Vic to learn theatre work. After several years there, in the second half of the 1930s Heseltine freelanced, clients including the Shakespeare Theatre at Stratford, Sadler's Wells and Regent's Park Open Air Theatre. The war years were spent at Birmingham Repertory, after which Heseltine returned to Sadler's Wells for a few years, then retired. The war had proved a strain, so she began painting again for her own pleasure. Her work included individualistic landscapes completed during a number of holidays in Ireland, and portraits. Heseltine also took up the circus as a subject, having a backstage pass to Bertram Mills at Olympia where she made numerous sketches, some of which she worked up into finished watercolours and oils. Little of Heseltine's work was sold in her lifetime. She lived latterly in London, although her funeral was at Stourbridge Crematorium in Worcestershire.

John HESELTINE fl. from 1940s– Painter, illustrator and teacher, husband of the artist Pam Masco, noted for his English and continental scenes, figure studies and portraits. London-born Heseltine studied at South-East Essex College of Art, obtaining a teaching diploma and scholarship to the Royal College of Art, 1942. In 1941 he gained the Farquharson Memorial Prize. After Royal Naval service for four years he worked as art editor for Norman Kark Publications, then in 1949 began a freelance career as an illustrator. In 1969 Heseltine was commissioned by International Publishing Corporation to paint the investiture of the Prince of Wales. He lectured at Wellington College and adjudicated for South-East Essex College of Art through the 1970s. RP, Bourne Gallery in Reigate and David Messum Gallery showed Heseltine's pictures, which included large, textured, quasi-abstract works. He produced a number of marine subjects among which are two paintings of H M S *Hermes* in the South Atlantic, which hang in the officers' mess at Yeovilton and in the Dartmouth Naval Museum. Lived in Petworth, Sussex.

Florence HESS 1891–1974 Landscape painter, born in Leeds. She studied at Leeds School of Art and from 1905 with the

Yorkshire painter Mark Senior, whose friend and assistant she became, accompanying him on his visits to Bruges and Holland. She painted along the coast of Yorkshire and Norfolk, her earlier work showing Senior's influence especially. Exhibited RA, NEAC, WIAC and widely in the provinces. Was a keen member of Fylingdales Group. Lived in London for some time and at Alwoodley, near Leeds.

I J Berthe HESS 1925– Painter and teacher whose work as well as being signed was authenticated by a thumb-print on the back. She was born in Paris, her father being a Sunday painter, and she studied at Académie des Beaux-Arts, free classes during World War II, but was largely self-taught. Moved to London in 1967 with her technocrat and sculptor husband Adolph, having travelled widely, and opened the BH Corner Gallery near St Paul's Cathedral, where her work was shown. Above it Hess ran an academy where she taught Bertisme, a technique by which a painting was sculpted by brush out of enormous quantities of paint; finished surfaces could be several inches thick and take two years to dry. Museums in Britain, France and Germany showed Hess's pictures. In 1972 part of BH Corner Gallery was turned into a permanent display of the work, while others' pictures were also on view, and in 1973 another permanent exhibition was set up in the Rue Faubourg Poissonièrre, Paris.

Rene HETHERINGTON 1921– Sculptor in a variety of materials, and teacher, born in Yorkshire. She attended Leeds College of Art and the Royal College of Art. Her work is held in a number of private collections in Britain and abroad and was bought by Leeds Education Authority. RBA member. Lived in Carlisle, Cumbria.

Charles HETT 1939– Painter, conservator and teacher, born in Freshford, Somerset, grandson of the artist Ambrose McEvoy. He studied at Byam Shaw School, 1958–60, then at Royal Academy Schools, 1961–5, winning the Armitage Prize. From 1965–7 Hett taught part-time and painted mostly landcape in the Fens and Cornwall. After studying artifact conservation, 1968–9, he worked mostly in that field, in Mexico, 1969–72, subsequently in Ottawa, Canada, where he lived. While in England, 1965–8, Hett worked on stage with The Alberts group. He showed at NEAC, RBA and at Leicester Galleries, having a one-man show in 1967, from which Lord Goodman bought work. Garman-Ryan Collection at Walsall Museum & Art Gallery also holds.

Lucette HEUSEUX 1913– Painter, brought up in Brussels, Belgium, where she attended the university. As well as exhibiting in Belgium she showed at RA, RP, RWS, widely in the provinces and in North America. She lived there in New York and in London.

Harold Cornelius HEWARD 1881–1973 Landscape, marine and figure painter in various media; black-and-white illustrator Born in Southsea, Hampshire, Heward studied at Lambeth School of Art and privately. Exhibited at RA, RI, RSW, ROI, in the provinces and at the Paris Salon. Lived in Surbiton, Surrey.

Joseph HEWES 1954– Painter who studied for two terms at Taunton College of Art, 1970, having attended secondary modern school. He was included in the Piccadilly Gallery's 1985–6 show The Brotherhood of Ruralists and Friends. Lived at Warleggan, Cornwall.

William HEWISON 1925– Painter and illustrator, born in South Shields, County Durham. He studied at the Art School there, 1941–3, Regent Street Polytechnic School of Art, 1947–9, and London University. Became art editor of the magazine *Punch*, 1960–84. As well as humorous work for the press Hewison took part in Young Contemporaries, Whitechapel Art Gallery and Arts Council exhibitions. Lived in London.

Forrest HEWIT 1870–1956 Painter, born in Salford, Lancashire, who studied with Walter Sickert and T C Dugdale and who was closely associated with the MAFA. Hewit was a good figure painter whose works have much in common with Sickert's in approach. He painted many landscapes in England, on the continent, in China and elsewhere. Hewit was a director and vice-chairman of the Manchester-based Calico Printers' Association. This enabled him to help more needy painters, notably Frances Hodgkins, who acted for a time as designer. Hewit exhibited widely, including RA, NEAC, Cooling Galleries and RBA. Work held by several public collections. Lived in Wilmslow, Cheshire.

Geoffrey HEWITT 1930– Painter, illustrator and teacher, born in Horden, County Durham. Studied at Royal College of Art and went on to lecture at Birmingham College of Art. Exhibited widely in group shows, including RA, RBSA, LG and overseas, and had a series of one-man exhibitions including Shipley Gallery, Univision Gallery and Arden Gallery. Illustrated books and magazines. City Art Gallery, Birmingham, holds his work.

May R HEWITT fl. c.1940–1960 Painter in oil, born in Newcastle upon Tyne where she studied art part-time at King's College. She showed locally, at the Laing Art Gallery in Newcastle and Shipley Art Gallery in Gateshead, where she lived, and belonged to the local Art Club. In the 1950s she was for much of the decade secretary of the Federation of Northern Art Societies.

Pauline HEWITT 1907– Landscape and portrait painter in oil who went on to teach after studying at the Slade School of Fine Art and in Paris. Exhibited RA, SWA and RI. Lived in St Ives, Cornwall.

Elsie HEWLAND 1901– Painter of figure and genre subjects, educated in the north of England, who attended Sheffield College of Art, 1921–4, then the Royal Academy Schools, 1926–30, under Walter Westley Russell. Exhibited RA, RWS and in the provinces, but is especially known for her World War II pictures, which depict life on the home front. Imperial War Museum holds her work, which was much-anthologised in war-related books, such as Eric Newton's *War Through Artists' Eyes*. Lived at

Chalfont St Giles, Buckinghamshire, for a time, also near Ventnor, Isle of Wight.

Francis HEWLETT 1930– Painter, ceramic sculptor and teacher, born in Bristol. He studied painting and etching at West of England College of Art there, 1948–52; was at École des Beaux-Arts, Paris, 1953; studied at Slade School of Fine Art, 1953–5, and worked for a time with William Coldstream and Claude Rogers. He was head of painting at Falmouth School of Art, 1960–81, settling in the Cornish town after moving to the county in 1957. In 1977 Hewlett was Gregynog Arts Fellow, University of Wales, in Newtown. Hewlett worked in ceramics, mainly large-scale sculpture, 1968–75, then from 1981 concentrated on pictures of the Bristol Empire theatre, based on much earlier drawings. The colourful, evocative pictures were shown at Browse & Darby in 1993. Hewlett showed at RA, RWA of which he was a member and at Newlyn Orion Gallery and in 1992 was included in Artists from Cornwall at RWA. Ulster Museum in Belfast; National Library of Wales in Aberystwyth; and public galleries in Leicester, Plymouth, Portsmouth and Southampton hold examples. Lived in Falmouth, Cornwall.

Charles HEWLINGS 1948– Abstract sculptor, and teacher, producing large works in such materials as concrete, steel, wood, pigment and fired clay. He gained an honours degree in fine art at University of Newcastle upon Tyne, 1967–71, then did an advanced sculpture course at St Martin's School of Art, 1971–3. Interspersed with periods as a part-time lecturer, Hewlings held a Wilhelm Lehmbruck Scholarship in Duisburg, West Germany, 1982–4; took part in the Triangle Artists' Workshop, Pine Plains, New York, 1984; was visiting sculptor at School of the Museum of Fine Arts, Boston, America, 1986, in the same year participating in the Hardingham Sculpture Workshop in Norfolk; and in 1991 held the Picker Lectureship, Kingston Polytechnic. Took part in numerous mixed shows, including Platform '73, Museum of Modern Art, Oxford, 1973; Arts Council Purchases and Awards, Serpentine Gallery, 1979, the year of his Arts Council Major Award; Sculpture at Cannizaro Park, 1985; and Galerie Dagmar, 1993. Had a solo show at Acme Gallery, 1976, later ones including a series at Smith Jariwala/Kapil Jariwala Galleries from 1990. London Borough of Hounslow; Wilhelm Lehmbruck Museum, Duisburg; and St Matthew's Church, Brixton, also hold examples.

Ann HEWSON 1933– Painter, draughtsman and clay sculptor, born and lived in London. Studied at South-West Essex Technical College after leaving school; lived in the country without much painting; then returned to London, attending evening classes at Regent Street Polytechnic School of Art. Married one of her teachers, Clifford Hall. Showed in various London galleries, including a shared exhibition with Nigel Lambourne at Belgrave Gallery, 1976, and a solo show at John Denham Gallery, 1985.

Cicely HEY 1896–1980 Painter and modeller of miniature period figures, born at Faringdon, Oxfordshire. She studied at the Brussels School of Art, Central School of Arts and Crafts and Slade School of Fine Art. She was married to the art critic and editor of the *Burlington Magazine*, R R Tatlock. Her friendship with the painter Walter Sickert is well recorded in books on him. He met her at a Roger Fry lecture in 1922 after which he drew and painted her many times in the 1920s, much attracted by her boyish humorous expression. Hey began to exhibit in group shows about this time. She showed with the LG and Denbighshire Art Society for long periods, as well as with the NS, WIAC and SGA. Her first one-man show was of portrait drawings at Reid and Lefevre in 1933. In 1941 she moved to Wales, after which she concentrated on her period figures, which were shown widely. Hey's work is in the collections of Glynn Vivian Art Gallery, Swansea, British Museum and Reading University's Rural Life Museum. Lived at Llysfaen, Clwyd.

Anthony HEYWOOD 1957– Sculptor and teacher who worked in mixed media. He studied at Newcastle Polytechnic, 1971–4, obtaining an honours degree in sculpture, then was at Christ Church College, Canterbury, 1975–6. Heywood had enormously varied teaching experience. Apart from teaching at Kent Institute of Art & Design, Canterbury, he was a part-time social worker, ran children's classes, classes for the mentally and physically handicapped and taught at South Kent College, Cyprus School of Art, Royal College of Art and elsewhere. Among his awards were a Harkness Fellowhip, British Council Award and a South East Arts Artists' Award. He was well written up in the national press and appeared on television programmes such as *Wogan* and *Blue Peter*. Also showed in numerous group exhibitions including RA Summer Exhibition, Minories Gallery and Sculpture at Canterbury, 1992. His solo shows included Christa Nagel Gallery, Koln, Germany.

Sally HEYWOOD 1964– Painter, born in Liverpool, who studied at Oxford University, 1982–3, then Royal Academy Schools, 1984–7. Among awards won in 1987 were the Creswick Landscape Prize, David Murray Landscape Award and the Dunoyer de Segonzac Travelling Scholarship. In 1987–8 Heywood won a fellowship in painting at Gloucestershire College of Art, a British Council Scholarship to the German Democratic Republic following in 1990–1, and from 1990 she lived and worked in Berlin. Heywood's abstract work was gestural with very thick impasto and a rich palette, as seen in a three-artist show at Paton Gallery in 1994. Group exhibitions included Red Herring Art Gallery, Brighton, 1989, other appearances at Paton Gallery and elsewhere on the continent, especially in Germany. Solo exhibitions included Midland Bank Headquarters, 1986; Paton Gallery, 1990; Sperl Gallery, Potsdam, 1991; and Ministry of Culture, Land Brandenburg, 1992. Metropolitan Museum of Art, New York; Stroud District Council; and Art in Hospitals hold examples.

Alfred HEYWORTH 1926–1976 Painter, draughtsman and teacher, born in Birmingham. He attended Moseley Junior Art School, 1939–42, Birmingham College of Art, 1942–6, Royal

College of Art, 1946–50, and Académie de la Grande Chaumière, in Paris, 1950–1. He gained a French Government Scholarship. Went on to be a visiting teacher at Kingston College of Art and Epsom School of Art. Heyworth was a member of RWS, RBA and NEAC. Public galleries in Birmingham, Bradford, Preston and Sheffield hold examples. He was a Chelsea Arts Club member who lived in Chiswick, west London, and died in Charing Cross Hospital.

David HIBBERT 1946–1991 Painter and draughtsman, born in Berkshire, who left school in 1959 to concentrate on painting. Produced haunting figure and landscape paintings in soft, earthy colours. He studied sculpture with Shelley Fausset for two years in 1960s, then attended Croydon College of Art, 1966–7, where he claimed he learned little. Went through rigorous study of such artists as Leonardo, Breughel and Dürer and became interested in surface and texture. Patrick Hayman, Bernard Leach and Peter Lanyon were key influences as were the Malvern Hills, where he lived much of his life, moving to Hastings, Sussex, in 1982. Its Museum and Art Gallery gave him a memorial show, 1992–3. Hibbert's solo shows were at Search Gallery, 1973, and Hereford City Museum, 1985. Mixed exhibitions included RA Summer Exhibition from 1987; LG 75th Anniversary Exhibition, at Royal College of Art, 1988; and in same year Louise Hallett Gallery.

Phyllis I HIBBERT 1903– Flower painter and teacher. She studied at Preston and Liverpool Schools of Art and went on to teach at a College of Further Education in the Lytham St Annes area of Lancashire where she lived. Showed at RA, SWA, RCamA, Manchester Academy and Walker Art Gallery in Liverpool. Harris Museum and Art Gallery in Preston holds her watercolour Nasturtiums. Hibbert was a regular exhibitor in Lancashire for some 45 years from 1927 at the Lancashire Art Exhibition, her watercolours of flowers often incorporating pottery or statuettes.

Allanson HICK 1898–1975 Architect and painter in oil and watercolour, born in Hull, Yorkshire. He attended the Grammar School there and College of Art. Exhibited widely. From 1935–55 his works were accepted annually at RA and he was a founder-member of RSMA. Ferens Art Gallery, Hull, holds a batch of work by him and he is also represented in Mansfield Art Gallery. Member of Art Workers' Guild and Chelsea Arts Club. Lived in Hornsea, Yorkshire.

Norman HICKIN 1910–1990 Artist in scraperboard, born in Birmingham. He was self-taught but was influenced by Bernard Fleetwood-Walker while at Aston Grammar School. Hickin trained as an entomologist, graduating in 1936 and obtaining his doctorate in 1940. For a time he was a rubber technologist at Dunlop, then became scientific director of Rentokil, the pest control firm. He was primarily a naturalist who loved drawing. Among his books, which he illustrated, were *African Notebook*, 1969, and *Beachcombing for Beginners*, 1975. Also showed with SWLA, of which he was a member. Died at Bewdley, Worcestershire.

Jason HICKLIN 1966– Painter and printmaker who attended Stafford College of Art, with distinction, 1984–5, and Central St Martins, 1985–93, graduating in painting with a diploma in advanced printmaking. Group shows included Bankside Open, Bankside Gallery, 1992; RE and RA, both from 1994; and NEAC, 1996. Showed solo with Attendi from 1996.

Edward Albert HICKLING 1913– Painter and technical illustrator, born in Nottingham where he attended the College of Art, 1927–39, under Arthur Spooner. Showed at RA, ROI, RSMA, RP and elsewhere. Member of the Sketching Club in Derby. Lived in Breaston, Derbyshire.

Arthur Ernest HICKMAN-SMITH 1876–1956 Landscape painter, singer and teacher, born in Birmingham, father of the artist Eileen Hickman-Smith. He studied at Birmingham School of Art under Edward Taylor and James Valentine Jelley. Hicky, as he was known, served as a captain in World War I, was for a time a regimental bandmaster and ran seaside concert parties, being an accomplished baritone. He was a poet, wrote books of stories and and was a fellow of the Royal Society of Arts. Exhibited at RA, RBA, PS and widely in the provinces. Was co-founder and secretary of Islington Art Circle, living in Highbury, north London, for many years. He died in Winchmore Hill Hospital.

Eileen HICKMAN-SMITH fl. c.1940–1970 Sculptor, painter in oil and journalist, born in London, daughter of the painter Arthur Ernest Hickman-Smith. Miss Smith studied art at Regent Street Polytechnic School of Art under Harold Brownsword and Geoffrey Deeley. She attended Highbury Hill School, living her life in the north London suburb. Exhibited at RA, RI, NS, WIAC, RBA and Islington Art Circle. The local town hall has a panel by her. At the time of her father's death, in 1956, she was already under medical care.

Amy Elizabeth Blanche HICKS 1876– Watercolourist and teacher, born in Devoran, Cornwall. She studied at Truro, Falmouth and Redruth Schools of Art and in Newlyn in Norman Garstin's studio. Showed at RI, in Cornwall and at Paris Salon, in 1951. Lived in Newquay, Cornwall.

Anne HICKS 1928– Artist in oil and gouache and teacher, born in London, married to the artist Jerry Hicks. She studied at Slade School of Fine Art with Randolph Schwabe, George Charlton and William Coldstream, then was a freelance artist in Bristol from 1952. Was visiting lecturer to Bristol University School of Architecture, taught in adult education and elsewhere. Bristol University has a swimming pool mural by her; she did other murals and stage designs with her husband. Mediterranean landscapes, portraits and wild animals in natural habitats, mainly large cats, were among Hicks' favourite subjects. She was a member of RWA, which holds her work. Exhibited in British Women Painters at Museum of Modern Art in Paris, in the English provinces and held joint shows with her husband. Lived in Bristol.

Jerry HICKS 1927– Artist in oil and pastel and teacher, born in London, full name Gerald Anthony William Hicks, married to the artist Anne Hicks. He studied at Slade School of Fine Art, 1944–5 and 1948–50, notable teachers including Randolph Schwabe, William Coldstream, Lucien Freud and William Townsend; and with Walter Bayes in Lancaster and London. Went on to teach at Cotham Grammar School, settling in Bristol, becoming a freelance artist in 1980. Hicks was a Judo 6th Dan which he said "influenced dynamic work". He did stage designs and murals with his wife, working in the European realist tradition, and they were extensively committed to environmental work. He was chairman of the Bristol City Docks Group, was a member and chairman of the Bristol Civic Society and was vice-chairman of the South-West Council for Sport. Hicks was a member of RWA which holds his work, exhibited at RA, RBA, at Arnolfini Gallery in Bristol and elsewhere in the provinces. He had several solo shows in London and Bristol and shared some with his wife. Hicks was winner of the Bristol 600 Competition in 1973, won the Queen's Silver Jubilee Award with a picture of Roger Bannister's sub-four minute mile and in 1984 gained an Olympic painting prize. Portraits included Lord Methuen, the Member of Parliament Marcus Lipton and the actor John Woodvine. In 1997 completed a mural commission of I K Brunel for the SS *Great Britain.* His *Judo through the Looking Glass,* with illustrations, was published in 1994, in which year he was made a Member of the Order of the British Empire "for services to sport and the community in the south west". Bristol, Brunel and Liverpool Universities and Bristol Merchant Venturers hold examples.

Lesley HICKS 1964– Artist often working in mixed media on paper. She studied at the fine art department at the University of Newcastle upon Tyne, then graduated from Royal Academy Schools in 1989. Her awards included the Richard Ford Award to study in Spain, 1989. From the early 1980s she participated in many mixed shows in the provinces and London, notably The Broad Horizon, at Agnew, 1990. Work was commonly signed L F Hicks.

L F HICKS: *see* **Lesley HICKS**

Nicola HICKS 1960– Sculptor and draughtsman, born and lived in London, noted for her fine depictions of animals. She attended Chelsea School of Art, 1978–82, Royal College of Art, 1982–5. Took part in many mixed shows including Christie's Inaugural Graduate Exhibition, 1982; Artist of the Day, Angela Flowers Gallery, 1984; Basel Art Fair in Switzerland and '85 Show, Serpentine Gallery, both 1985; Yorkshire Sculpture Park, 1986; Bryan Kneale's Choice, at Arts Club, 1990; and Drawing Towards Sculpture, Isis Gallery, Leigh-on-Sea, 1993. Began showing with Angela Flowers in solo exhibitions in mid-1980s in London and Ireland, later shows including Peter Scott Gallery, Lancaster, and Castlefield Gallery, Manchester, both 1993. Contemporary Art Society holds her work. Commissions included a monument in Battersea Park.

Philip HICKS 1928– Painter, married to the sculptor Jill Tweed. He attended Winchester College, then Chelsea School of Art and Royal Academy Schools. Hicks exhibited at Marjorie Parr and Robert Self Galleries, New Art Centre and widely abroad. Tate Gallery and Imperial War Museum hold examples. Lived in London.

Clive HICKS-JENKINS 1951– Artist in mixed media, choreographer, stage designer and director, born in Newport, Monmouthshire, who was educated in theatre studies at Italia Conti School and Ballet Rambert. He began his career as a dancer, and eventually created productions for leading companies worldwide, as well as working in television and film. In the late 1980s Hicks-Jenkins "cut down on theatre and design work to explore other areas of creative activity. I began to make and exhibit masks." In the early-1990s he met his partner Peter Wakelin, "my teacher and mentor, who gradually encouraged me to develop my painting, which is now my life." Hicks-Jenkins' masks shows included The Old Library, Cardiff, 1992–4; Oriel Myrrddin, Carmarthen, and tour, 1994–5; and Pennine Arts, Burnley, 1995. Solo exhibitions included New Theatre, Cardiff, 1984; Theatre Clwyd, Mold, 1986; and Newport Museum and Art Gallery, 1986 and 1992. Mixed shows of pictures included Attic Gallery, Swansea, and Gordon Hepworth Gallery, Newton St Cyres, and Hicks-Jenkins shared an exhibition with Charles Shearer at Kilvert Gallery, Clyro, 1996. Commissions included frieze murals for natural history department at Newport Museum and Art Gallery and posters for Cardiff New Theatre and Theatre Clwyd. Theatre Museum, Covent Garden, holds his work. Lived in Pontcanna, Cardiff, where Hicks-Jenkins sought "to find a truly Welsh art, which explores the special and the profound in Welsh landscape and culture."

Charles Christopher HICKSON 1957– Painter in oil and watercolour and lecturer, born in Hull, Yorkshire. Gained an honours degree in fine art, having studied at Medlock Fine Art Centre, Manchester Polytechnic, 1976–9. He combined painting with part-time lecturing in colleges in northwest of England. Group shows included Urban Landscape at Stockport Art Gallery, and Lancashire South of the Sands, which toured from the County and Regimental Museum, Preston, both 1988; and Attitudes to the Contemporary Nude, at the latter venue, 1989. Solo shows included Lewis Textile Hall, Blackburn, 1987; Warrington Museum and Art Gallery, 1988; and Towneley Hall, Burnley, 1990. Eastern Arts Association and Towneley Hall own examples. Lived in Sale, Cheshire.

Peter HIDE 1944– Sculptor in steel and teacher, born in Carshalton, Surrey. He studied at Croydon College of Art, 1961–4, then St Martin's School of Art, 1964–7. There he was one of the first of the younger British sculptors to adopt Anthony Caro's methods, although in Hide's work structure rather than spatial arrangement was the key principle. Later Hide said that he wanted to regain "a sense of steel parts and relations between them". Taught at Norwich School of Art, 1968–74; St Martin's, 1971–8; and was professor of sculpture at the University of

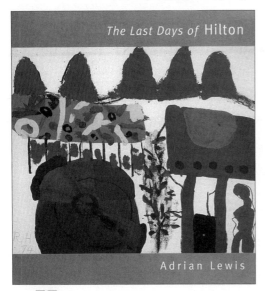

Alberta, in Canada, from 1977. From the late-1970s Hide took part in many workshops in North America and Europe and he visited England each year to work for several weeks in Norfolk. Hide had early exhibitions at Stockwell Depot from 1968, at Serpentine Gallery, 1976, and Arnolfini Gallery, Bristol, 1979. There was a show at Alberta House, 1984; a 10-year retrospective at Edmonton Art Gallery in 1986, the year when a series of exhibitions started at Kathleen Laverty Gallery there; and a show at André Emmerich Gallery, New York, 1990. Tate Gallery, Arts Council, City of Barcelona Museum of Modern Art and a series of North American collections hold examples.

Charles HIGGINS 1893– Oil and watercolour painter, and writer. Born at Belgrano, Buenos Aires, Higgins studied art in London, France and Italy. Often signing his pictures Pic (in his books used the pen-name Ian Dall), Higgins exhibited at galleries in London, in the USA, Rome and Paris. The Contemporary Art Society bought his work. Was married to the painter Kate Olver. Lived in London.

Dorothy Mary HIGGINS fl. from 1940s– Painter and teacher, born in Seikyi, Burma, but educated in Yorkshire. She attended Leeds College of Art, 1940–5. Showed at RSA, RP, WIAC, ROI and elsewhere. Lived at Sleights, Yorkshire.

Lawrence HIGGINS 1964–1988 Painter and printmaker, born in Bury, Lancashire, of British and Afro-Caribbean parents. After attending Cardinal Langley Grammar School, Middleton, Higgins went to Rochdale College of Art for an arts foundation course; in 1983 he won the Student of the Year Foundation Prize. Higgins attended Goldsmiths' College School of Art in that year, graduating in 1986. Shortly after graduation a set of prints by him was bought for the Arts Council collection. The subject of Higgins' prints was daily life in Peckham, where he lived. He also painted exuberant oils of figures on beaches. Higgins committed suicide and was commemorated in 1992 with a South Bank Centre exhibition.

Lloyd George HIGGINS 1912– Painter of contemporary Lancashire scene, born in Mossley, Lancashire. He studied at Royal College of Art, Salford. Gained Diploma in Industrial Design (1st Prize) of Royal Society of Arts. Was a founder-member of Saddleworth Art Group and appeared in a show of its work at Woodlands Art Gallery, 1973. Also showed at Manchester Academy, Tib Lane Gallery and elsewhere in northwest.

Wilfred HIGGINS 1893–1978 Portrait painter, full name Francis Wilfred Higgins, who was born and finally lived in Chester and who attended the School of Art there. Also studied in London and Italy. Showed RA, RHA, widely in Canada as well as in Australia and on the continent, notably at the Paris Salon. Joined the Art Workers' Guild in 1936.

Derek HIGGINSON 1930– Painter born in Oakhill, Stoke-on-Trent, Staffordshire, where he attended the College of Art, 1944–50, his teachers including Frith Milward. Showed with Free Painters and Sculptors of which he was a member, Staffordshire Artists' Club of which he was a founder-member, with the Unit Ten Group of former Stoke students and elsewhere widely in the Staffordshire area.

Jo HIGSON: *see* **Jo SCANNELL**

Rowland HILDER 1905–1993 Landscape and marine painter, mainly in watercolour, printmaker and illustrator. Born at Greatneck, Long Island, America, with British parents, Hilder was initially educated in Morristown, New Jersey. After settling in England, he studied illustration and printmaking at Goldsmiths' College School of Art under Edmund Sullivan for three years in the 1920s. He was later to lecture at that College between the wars, also at the Central School of Arts and Crafts, Royal College of Art and Farnham School of Art. During World War II Hilder served in the Army, concerned with camouflage. He was involved in several fine art publication companies, was a pioneer silkscreen printmaker in Britain, did extensive advertising work, notably for Shell-Mex and BP and illustrated many books. He was assisted in his Shell work by his wife Edith, originally Edith Blenkiron. Hilder's book illustration commissions included Herman Melville's *Moby Dick* and Robert Louis Stevenson's *Treasure Island*. His own books *Starting with Watercolour* and *Painting Landscapes in Watercolour* and the two volumes *Rowland Hilder's England* and *Rowland Hilder Country* presented his own pictures. Hilder achieved great popular success with his portrayal of the English countryside, notably Kent, with the characteristically delineated trees and oast-houses. He showed at RA, RI of which he was president 1964–74, RHA and NEAC. He had his first solo show at Fine Art Society in 1939, and there was a retrospective at Woodlands Art Gallery, 1985. Hilder early on was a keen sailor, marine artist and illustrator of boys' sea adventure stories. Although he lived in London he kept a coast-guard's cottage at Shell Ness, as a base for marine painting. His son also painted, under the name Anthony Flemming.

Muriel B G HILEY 1906– Sculptor and designer of medals, born in Cardiff. After private education she studied at Goldsmiths' College School of Art, 1926–9, then sculpture at Royal Academy Schools, 1929–34. From 1929 she showed at RA, also with RCamA and with Lewisham Society of Arts. From the late-1920s she obtained a large number of commissions including medals of David Lloyd George, Neville Chamberlain and Jan Christian Smuts; a commemorative plaque for Brooklands motor racing track jubilee in 1957; and in 1966 a large copy of the World Cup for Wembley Stadium. Imperial War Museum, Glynn Vivian Art Gallery in Swansea and National Museum of Wales, Cardiff, hold her work.

Richard HILEY 1921– Painter, illustrator and teacher, born in Halifax, Yorkshire, where he continued to live. Studied at Halifax School of Art, 1936–40, then after World War II at Royal College of Art, 1946–9, his teachers including Kenneth Rowntree and Rodney Burn. Taught at Huddersfield School of Art.

A Stuart HILL: *see* **A STUART-HILL**

Adrian HILL 1895–1977 Painter, mainly of landscapes in watercolour, and illustrator. Born at Charlton, Kent, studied at St John's Wood School of Art, 1912–14, then at the Royal College of Art, 1919–20. During World War I Hill was an official war artist, producing outstanding pictures from the front line, now in the Imperial War Museum. Exhibited at the RA, RBA, NEAC, RHA, ROI, in the provinces and overseas, including Paris Salon. His work is in many public collections, including the Victoria & Albert Museum. Hill was an exemplary, enthusiastic teacher. For a time he taught at Hornsey School of Art and on screen in the early days of television after World War II. He wrote many books on painting techniques, such as *On Drawing and Painting Trees*, 1936, and *The Pleasures of Painting*, 1952. Lived at Midhurst, Sussex.

Andrea HILL 1954– Artist noted for her box and collage creations. She studied at Bournemouth and Poole College of Art and Design and Goldsmiths' College School of Art. Showed at Slaughterhouse Gallery, Shipley's Bookshop and England & Co, in Art in Boxes, 1991.

Anthony HILL 1930– Constructivist artist working in a variety of materials, painter and teacher. Born in London where he continued to live. He studied at St Martin's School of Art and Central School of Art and Design, 1947–51, in 1951–2 visiting Paris. He had painted in Dadaist and Surrealist styles in 1950, but after meeting Picabia, Kupka and Vantongerloo his painting became more disciplined, he made his first relief in 1954 and two years later abandoned painting. His first solo show of reliefs was at ICA in 1958. Two years later he was an organiser of Construction: England: 1950–60, at Drian Gallery. Went on to show widely internationally in exhibitions of abstract and constructivist art. Taught for a time at Polytechnic of Central London, Chelsea School of Art, gained a Leverhulme Fellowship at mathematics department of University College in London, 1971–3, and eventually became visiting research associate there. From mid-1970s Hill signed some works Redo, others Rem Doxford. Commissions included large screen for headquarters of the International Union of Architects' Congress, 1961. Hill had a retrospective at Hayward Gallery in 1983. Tate Gallery, Victoria & Albert Museum, Arts Council and other public collections in Britain and abroad hold examples.

Barrie HILL 1936– Artist and musician, born in Sheffield, Yorkshire, who took up drawing and painting at Camden Adult Education Institute in 1970. After opting for early retirement from the National Economic Development Office in 1988, he devoted much time to painting and playing the cello, taken up in 1985, with the East London Late Starters Orchestra. With his cello teacher Pat Legg Hill produced *The Better Late ... Cello Book*. Chamber music was the main inspiration for Hill's pictures. In 1992, his large oil painting of the Lindsay String Quartet was exhibited at the Conway Hall and at the Quartet's twenty-fifth anniversary concerts at the Wigmore Hall and Crucible Theatre, Sheffield. Showed at Sheffield Chamber Music Festival from 1988 and from 1995 his pictures of chamber musicians in concert were permanently exhibited at Conway Hall. Later lived in Fougères, France.

Caroline HILL 1935–1983 Painter, draughtsman, etcher and fabric designer, who studied at the Slade School of Fine Art, 1952–6, in 1955 being awarded the Catherine Maude Pearce Scholarship permitting a year of postgraduate study. Exhibited with Young Contemporaries, 1955–6, in 1956 with Leicester Galleries, in 1957 marrying Nicolas Hill. In 1975, she had a solo show at William Darby. Hill painted mostly on a small scale, delicate and charming works which harked back to Bloomsbury and the Euston Road School. In 1976 she completed a watercolour portrait of the writer Graham Greene at his Antibes home. In 1985, a complete catalogue of her work was privately published, with introductions by Richard Morphet and William Packer. Lived in London.

Derek HILL 1916– Painter notable for perceptive portraits and subtle landscapes, stage designer, exhibition organiser and writer. He was born Arthur Derek Hill in Bassett, Hampshire. Was educated at Marlborough College, then studied stage design in Munich, Paris and Vienna, 1933–5, and began life drawing. Although he designed sets and costumes for the ballet *The Lord of Burleigh* at Sadler's Wells in 1937, in Paris a year later he chose to paint rather than pursue designing. During World War II he worked on a farm in England, painting spare-time. Contributed articles to *Penguin New Writing*, *New Statesman* and other magazines. The 1940s and 1950s were busy years for Hill, for he had a first solo show at Nicholson Gallery, 1943; designed for *Il Trovatore* at Covent Garden, 1947; painted in Ireland and Italy, where he was encouraged by the critic Bernard Berenson; organised the Degas exhibition at Edinburgh Festival, 1952; had a series of shows at Leicester Galleries; and was art director of the British School in Rome, 1953–4, and 1957–8. Had retrospectives at Whitechapel Art Gallery, 1961, and Colnaghi's, 1994, with a solo show at King's Lynn Festival, 1986. Created a gallery showing his own fine collection of pictures at his home in Donegal, Ireland. He painted part of the year on Tory Island, where he discovered and promoted a group of fishermen-painters, who went on to exhibit widely. Collaborated on several books on Islamic architecture. Hill's work is in collections of Tate Gallery; Arts Council; Fogg Museum, Harvard; National Gallery of Ireland, and elsewhere.

E D HILL 1900– Painter, born in Caernarvon. She lived there as a housewife and did not start painting until 1964. Mrs Hill then showed in the WAC exhibition Alternative Tradition and with the Caernarvon and Nantile Valley Art Groups. The Caernarvon Institute Building gave her a solo show in 1972, for which she obtained much local press coverage.

Edith HILL fl. from late 1960s– Printmaker, painter and draughtsman who studied at Beckenham Centre for Arts and Crafts. She showed at RA Summer Exhibitions, in Kent and was included in Group '77 Printmakers at Woodlands Art Gallery, 1981. Lived in Beckenham, Kent.

Harriet Mena HILL fl. from late 1980s– Artist who did a foundation course at Camberwell School of Arts and Crafts, 1985, obtaining her honours degree there, 1986–9. She appeared in mixed shows at Intaglio Printmakers, 1989; New Scottish Painters, at Fine Art Society, Glasgow, 1991; and in the same year she was a prizewinner at the Mall Galleries, and tour, in The Discerning Eye. She shared a show at Eagle Gallery, An Open Reality, in 1991, the previous year having had a solo exhibition at Duncan Campbell Fine Art. Government Art Collection and St John's College, Oxford, hold her work.

John HILL 1905– Painter and decorative artist who was born in Bassett, Hampshire, and educated at Marlborough College. In 1945–6 studied at Camberwell School of Arts and Crafts under Lawrence Gowing and Victor Pasmore. Signing his work J H, he showed at LG, Redfern Gallery and RA. Lived in London.

Mary F HILL 1926– Painter and teacher, born in Frampton Cotterell, Gloucestershire. She was initially educated in Bristol, attending the West of England Art College there under Donald Milner, 1943–7. Lived in Chippenham, Wiltshire, where she taught art at the Grammar School.

Oliver HILL 1887–1968 Architect and painter, born in London. Educated at Uppingham School, then was self-taught as an artist. Exhibited RA, Royal Glasgow Institute of the Fine Arts and had two one-man shows at Leicester Galleries. Lived at Sapperton, Gloucestershire.

Philip Maurice HILL 1892–1952 Landscape and marine painter, born in Southampton, who married the artist Megan Rhys. After attending Oxford University, Hill studied art in London and St Ives, with which his work was strongly associated. Exhibited RA, NEAC, RBA, Goupil Gallery, UA, SMA and with the St Ives Society of Artists, of which he was a member. He held several senior positions in the RSMA. Hill's picture of Polperro was used as a poster by the Great Western Railway. Alongside his career as an artist Hill worked for the Chamber of Shipping, of which for a time he was general manager. Lived variously in London, Wadhurst in Sussex and St Ives, Cornwall.

Raymond Arthur HILL 1916– Watercolour painter, engraver and designer. Born in Leicester, Hill studied art at Tunbridge Wells School of Art, 1933–6, under its principal E Owen Jennings, then during 1936–40 at the Royal College of Art under Ernest Tristram. Hill went on to show silverwork designs at a number of venues, including the Goldsmiths' Hall. He was successively head of Worcester School of Art, 1947–50, Swindon School of Art, 1950–3, then head of industrial design at Liverpool College of Art, 1953–64. Lived in Liverpool.

Robert HILL 1932–1990 Painter, draughtsman and teacher, born in Watford, Hertfordshire, where he lived. Hill studied at Watford School of Art and Royal Academy Schools in 1950s, where he several times won the David Murray Scholarship in landscape, plus other awards, teachers including Henry Rushbury, Peter Greenham and Bernard Fleetwood-Walker. Went on to teach at Matthew Arnold School in Staines. He was a member of ROI, UA, NS and NEAC and showed at RA, Woodstock and Beaux Arts Galleries. Nottingham Museum and Art Gallery and several other provincial galleries hold Hill's work.

Ronn HILL 1933– Artist in oil, watercolour, pen and ink and mixed media, and teacher, born in London. He studied at Willesden Technical College and Heatherley's School of Fine Art, 1958–65, teachers including Jack Merriott, Harry Riley and Patrick Larking. Taught in adult education in Borough of Ealing, then took on private freelance teaching in 1972 in southern English counties, later giving private tuition at Orpheus Studio, Kingston Lisle, Wantage, in Oxfordshire. Hill was a believer in fine draughtsmanship. He belonged to UA and SGA and exhibited with RBA and at Paris Salon. Had a series of solo shows.

Rowland HILL 1919–1979 Painter and draughtsman, born in Belfast. Went to work at 14, but wishing to become an artist Hill studied in the evenings at Belfast Technical College and at Belfast College of Art, where his teachers included Fred Allen. At the age of 16 he had three oils hung at the annual exhibition of the Ulster Academy of Arts. He later showed at RHA, in London and widely overseas and held many one-man exhibitions in Belfast. Lived in Jordanstown, County Antrim.

Rowland Henry HILL 1873–1952 Painter, black-and-white artist, born in Halifax, Yorkshire. Studied at Halifax and Bradford Schools of Art, also at the Herkomer School at Bushey and extensively abroad, mainly on the continent. Exhibited RA, Walker Art Gallery, Liverpool, and elsewhere in the provinces. Imperial War Museum and many northern public galleries hold his pictures. Hill was a member of the Staithes Group of painters, who worked in the Staithes and Runswick Bay area of Yorkshire, featured in a series of exhibitions at Phillips & Sons, Marlow. Lived at Hinderwell, Yorkshire.

Vernon HILL 1886–1972 Carver, draughtsman and print-maker, born in Halifax, Yorkshire. After Board School, at 13 was apprenticed to lithography at a printing works. Left at 18 hoping to become a teacher at technical school. Won a poster competition prize and worked with John Hassall; then for the publisher John Lane; served in Army for three years; and had two exhibitions at Leicester Galleries, 1924–7. Made carvings for St Joan of Arc, Farnham, 1930. From 1932–56 worked with Sir Edward Maufe on Guildford Cathedral. Other commissions included Runnymede Memorial, 1952; Church of St Columba, Pont Street, 1954; and Middle Temple, 1955. Was included in Sculpture in Britain Between The Wars, Fine Art Society, 1986. A large collection of

Hill's visionary Art Deco drawings is held by Southampton City Art Gallery.

Jan Stanley HILLER 1918– Painter, printmaker and teacher, born in London. Studied at Hornsey School of Art with John Moody and Herbert Budd, 1935–9, then after World War II in 1946–7. He taught at Prince Henry's Grammar School, Evesham, Worcestershire, where he lived, showing RI, SGA of which he was a member and at Worcester Corporation Art Gallery.

Susan HILLER 1942– Artist in mixed media, teacher, born in America. She studied at Smith College, Northampton, Massachusetts, 1957–61, then at Tulane University, Louisiana, 1961–5, concentrating on anthropology. She then did field work in South America, but became disillusioned with this and began painting again, earlier an optional study. Moved to Europe and settled in London in 1967 and soon had a solo touring show organised by United States Information Service. In 1968 she gained the Karolyi Foundation Award. Four years later her exhibition Photography into Art took place at Camden Arts Centre, and touring. Hiller was artist-in-residence at Sussex University in 1975, followed in 1976 by solo shows at Serpentine Gallery and Gardner Arts Centre at University of Sussex. In that year, too, Hiller won the Gulbenkian Foundation Visual Artists' Award, also in 1977. Many more solo shows followed, including Hester van Royen Gallery; Museum of Modern Art, Oxford; and Tate Gallery, Liverpool, retrospective, 1996. For some of her early working years as an artist Hiller concentrated on a type of performance art, then she also mixed drawing, photography, video, texts, sculpture and painting, sometimes in large installations. The artist said that "as well as potsherds, postcards and dreams are some of the materials used as the starting point for works that look at the repressed or unacknowledged content of our society's artefacts." Arts Council, Tate Gallery, Imperial War Museum and many other galleries in Britain and abroad hold her work. Lived in London.

David HILLHOUSE 1945– Artist, teacher and curator, born in Wirral, Cheshire, who worked in watercolour and egg tempera. In the 1960s–1970s he studied at Laird School of Art and Liverpool College of Art. He graduated in 1969 and was elected a member of RCamA in 1979, becoming its vice-president. Hillhouse was a teacher, curator of the Williamson Art Gallery in Birkenhead and principal museums officer for Wirral. He showed with Wirral Society of Arts and Deeside Art Group, both of which he was a member, on Merseyside and elsewhere. Lived at Greasby, Wirral.

John HILLIARD 1945– Artist who sculpted, used photographs and text. He was born in Lancaster and studied at St Martin's School of Art, 1964–7, a travel scholarship taking him to America in 1965. Hilliard had his first one-man show at Lisson Gallery in 1971, then often exhibited there. He also appeared in notable overseas group shows and one-man, venues including Galerie Hetzler & Keller, Stuttgart; John Gibson Gallery, New York; and Musée d'Art Moderne, in Paris. Arts Council holds a selection of his work. His publications include *Analytical Photography*, 1977, and *From the Northern Counties*, 1978.

Victoria HILLIARD 1960– Creator of three-dimensional works in mixed media who studied at Exeter College of Art; she gained a diploma in typographic design for print, with a distinction. Hilliard began to develop her own work while acting as manager of the graphic studio of a busy London newspaper and began showing at Liberty's. She also worked in Cornwall and in the Scilly Isles as a gardener and florist. Her work had a strong fantasy element and used a rich palette. She designed tapestries, garden rooms and a travelling circus bus. Exhibitions included Bient and Bient, 1988; The Hat Shop, Powys, 1991; and she shared a show at John Davies, Stow-on-the-Wold, 1993. Lived in Cornwall.

Tristram HILLIER 1905–1983 Painter of landscapes and still life and some religious subjects, his pictures have a hard-edged clarity and surreal quality while appearing overtly realistic. Born in Peking, China, Hillier studied art at the Slade School in 1926 under Henry Tonks, then in Paris under André Lhote and at the Atelier Colarossi. In the 1930s he was one of the group of artists who formed Unit One. After he finished his studies until 1940 he travelled widely on the continent, often living alone for several months in Spain, France and Portugal, his scenes of sparsely populated villages or townships under a bleaching sun being developed during the winter months in Somerset. He met Braque and was impressed by the use of black in his pictures and those of Velasquez and some of the Flemish painters; black is a feature of some of Hillier's still lifes such as Harness (Tate Gallery). His work shares characteristics with that of his friend Edward Wadsworth, with whom he painted abroad. After his first one-man show at the Lefevre Gallery in 1931 Hillier's work was popular with the picture-buying public and he went on to show widely in Britain and abroad. Elected RA 1967. His autobiography *Leda and the Goose* was published in 1954. Retrospective show at Worthing Art Gallery in 1960 plus a touring retrospective which included the RA in the year he died. Lived at East Pennard, Shepton Mallet, Somerset.

Peter HILLS 1925– Sculptor in a variety of materials and teacher, born in Bearsted, Kent. He studied at Bromley College of Art, 1948–50, Royal Academy Schools, 1950–5, then for several years was assistant to the sculptor Maurice Lambert. In 1972 he was Churchill Fellow in Sculpture. He taught art at Tonbridge School, where he had studied, during 1960s–1970s. Hills was a fellow of RBS and a member of the public schools art masters' 65 Group. Lived in Tonbridge, Kent.

Arthur Cyril HILTON 1897–1960 Self-taught painter and sculptor, whose work embraced abstract and Surrealist styles, born in Manchester. He served overseas in World War I and was wounded on the Somme, 1916. Worked for Manchester Education Committee as a school registrar and as a librarian at the Committee's offices. Showed at Walker Art Gallery in Liverpool,

Manchester City Art Gallery which holds his work, with Manchester Athenaeum Graphic Club, Southport Spring Exhibition and as a member of Manchester's Society of Modern Painters from the 1930s, being elected chairman in mid-1950s. Had a solo show at Salford Art Gallery and a first one-man exhibition in London at Crane Kalman Gallery, 1959. Lived in Chorlton-cum-Hardy, Manchester.

Bo HILTON 1961– Artist who gained his master's degree in fine art printmaking at Brighton, 1985–8, then lived and worked in London and Cornwall, where he was a member of the Newlyn Society of Artists. Showed from 1993 at Newlyn Orion Gallery, RA and NEAC and from 1994 at New Grafton Gallery. Frequently exhibited at major London art fairs. In 1995 had a first solo show at Cassian de Vere Cole Twentieth Century British Art. His father was the painter Roger Hilton.

Matthew HILTON 1948– Artist, notably a printmaker, born in London, son of the painter Roger Hilton. He spent three years studying photography and film at Bournemouth College of Art, then in 1972 travelled to north of England to live and work with Welfare State Theatre Company. From 1974–85 was a member of the Fire Service, but continued with his own work. He had a show of photographs at Holdsworth Gallery, Hebden Bridge, in West Yorkshire, 1981, another of lino-prints at same gallery in 1982. In 1983 gained a North West Arts printmaking bursary at the Manchester Print Workshop. During the 1980s Hilton continued to show his lino-prints in solo and mixed exhibitions and was artist-in residence, Fieldhead Hospital, Wakefield, in 1987. After a solo show at Austin/Desmond Fine Art in 1988 Hilton had another in 1990, the year after he had travelled around the Baltic by ship. Latterly set up studio in Norfolk.

Roger HILTON 1911–1975 Figurative and abstract painter and draughtsman, teacher, a key member of the St Ives art colony in Cornwall and the last major painter to settle there. He was born in Northwood, Middlesex, the family name being Hildesheim, changed during World War I because of anti-German feeling. Studied at Slade School of Fine Art, 1929–31, under Henry Tonks; although he won a Slade Scholarship in 1931 he did not take it up, but during the 1930s studied for periods in Paris, part of the time with Roger Bissière at Académie Ranson. First one-man show was at Bloomsbury Gallery in 1936. During World War II he served in the Army, part of the time as a commando, for about three years being a prisoner of war after the Dieppe raid of 1942. Was a schoolteacher for a time after the war, also teaching at Central School of Arts and Crafts, 1954–6. His first abstract paintings date from 1950. During the 1950s and 1960s Hilton began to spend more time in west Cornwall, and the landscape there influenced his pictures, which were never to be as entirely abstract again as those of the early 1950s. Hilton took part in numerous group shows in Britain and abroad, winning first prize at John Moores Liverpool Exhibition in 1963. Retrospective exhibition at ICA in 1958, and similarly important shows included Serpentine Gallery in 1974; Graves Art Gallery, and touring, in Sheffield 1980; Leicester Polytechnic Gallery and tour, 1984–5; Hayward Gallery, 1993–4; and Tate Gallery St Ives, 1997–8. Alcoholism hindered Hilton's output; he was confined to bed by illness (he suffered peripheral neuritis) from 1972. Arts Council holds his work. Died at Bottallack, Cornwall.

Rose HILTON 1931– Painter, born in Kent. After initial training at Beckenham School of Art she went on to study at Royal College of Art, 1954–7. From there travelled to Rome for a year on an Abbey Minor Scholarship. Back in England she met and married the painter Roger Hilton and they moved to Botallack, Cornwall. She then brought up her children and looked after her husband during his long illness, but painted little herself. After Roger's death she resumed painting and took drawing lessons in the mid-1980s from Cecil Collins. Her exhibitions included Newlyn Orion Gallery, 1977 and 1987; Michael Parkin Gallery, 1988; Oxford Gallery, 1989; and David Messum, 1991. She was a richly colourful painter of people and interiors.

George HIM 1900–1982 Designer, illustrator, watercolourist and teacher, born in Lodz, Poland; his working name was an abbreviation of Himmelfarb. For about a decade from 1917 he was variously at university in Moscow, Berlin and Bonn and studying graphic art in Leipzig, then returned to Poland. For just over 20 years from the early 1930s he collaborated with Jan Le Witt as a design partnership, moving the business to London in 1937. Lewitt-Him created notable wartime posters and the Festival of Britain clock in 1951. From 1954 Him worked independently, illustrating many children's books, working on animated films, designing toys and painting landscape watercolours, such as Shikun Petach Tiqvah, in Ben Uri Art Society collection. For eight years from 1969 taught at Leicester Polytechnic. Showed at London College of Printing in 1976 and Ben Uri in 1978. Died in London.

Lubaina HIMID 1954– Painter, designer, mixed media artist, administrator and teacher, born in Zanzibar, Tanzania, but arrived in England in the year of her birth. Studied theatre design at Wimbledon School of Art, 1973–6, working in theatre and interior design after that. In the early 1980s she was both a part-time teacher and youth worker, obtaining her Master of Arts degree in cultural history at the Royal College of Art, 1982–4. Organised exhibition at Africa Centre in 1983, which included her own work and that by other women of Afro-Caribbean or African descent, in which "their anger shines through", she said. Himid's work had a multi-pronged polemical content, satirising white society, poking fun at society's heroes and celebrating black creativity. Showed widely in mixed exhibitions, including The Other Story, Hayward Gallery, 1989–90, and tour; and Picturing Blackness, at Tate Gallery, which holds her work, 1995–6. Arts Council and Rochdale Art Gallery also have examples. In 1986 Himid opened her own gallery, The Elbow Room.

Frederick HINCHLIFF 1894–1962 Painter and teacher, born in Queensland, Australia, as George Frederick Hinchliff. After studying at Huddersfield Technical College he attended the School of Art there and Royal College of Art. He held a series of art teaching posts in Leicester, Sheffield, Batley and Guildford, from 1936–60 being principal of Croydon School of Art. Exhibited at RA, NEAC and widely in the provinces. Hinchliff was involved in the restoration of St Stephen's Chapel in the Palace of Westminster, was noted for his murals and was active in art circles in Croydon, Surrey, where he lived.

Arthur Mayger HIND 1880–1957 Art historian, curator and watercolour painter. Born at Burton upon Trent, Staffordshire, he studied at Cambridge University. Entered British Museum in 1903, being keeper of prints and drawings 1933–45. He was Slade Professor of Fine Art at Oxford, 1921–7. Published a number of scholarly works on prints. Exhibited RA, Agnew, Goupil Gallery, NEAC and Colnaghi's. Work held by Ashmolean Museum, Oxford, Graves Art Gallery, Sheffield, and galleries abroad. Lived in Henley-on-Thames, Oxfordshire.

Albert HINDLE 1888– Painter and draughtsman, born in Accrington, Lancashire. He studied at the School of Art there, Royal College of Art, 1910–12 and Académie Julian, Paris, 1912–13. Showed at RA, ROI, UA, NS, NEAC and elsewhere. Lived in Kingston upon Thames, Surrey.

Yvonne HINDLE 1963– Painter and teacher who studied at Newcastle upon Tyne Polytechnic, 1981–4, and Royal College of Art, 1985–7. She gained the Audun Gallery Prize and Painters and Stainers' Cyril Sweet Award, both 1987, and obtained a fellowship in painting at Cheltenham School of Art, Cheltenham, Cheltenham & Gloucester College of Higher Education. In 1993 became acting head of painting at University of Northumbria, Newcastle. Mixed shows included Whitechapel Open Part I, Spitalfields Gallery, 1992, and Aiding and Abetting, The Gallery at John Jones, 1994.

Kay HINWOOD 1920– Painter who was born and lived in Bromley, Kent. She studied with Sonia Mervyn as a private student; at City and Guilds of London Art School; then at Kathleen Browne Painting School with Browne and her husband Marian Kratochwil. She was a member of UA and PS, also exhibiting at SWA, RP and ROI.

Roland HIPKINS 1895–1951 Painter, notably of landscapes, born in Bilston, Staffordshire, where he attended the School of Art, then the Royal College of Art, 1919–22. Hipkins went on to make his career in New Zealand, where he taught at the Teachers' College, Wellington, 1931–49. He was prominent in the art world there, being a member of the council of the New Zealand Academy of Fine Arts. Exhibited RBSA and extensively in New Zealand, where his work is in several collections, including Auckland Art Gallery. Lived in Wellington.

Chris HIPKISS 1964– Draughtsman, notable for large, monochrome, fantastic cityscapes, as shown in Outsiders & Co at England and Co, 1996. Hipkiss left school at 16 to be apprenticed to his father's joinery business and began to draw seriously, creating his own Utopia on paper. Eventually gave up joinery and moved to a Kent village where he continued with his drawing, began an environment group and planted trees. Working on a large roll of cartridge paper he sometimes needed to use the village hall as a studio and drew inspiration from his travels, television and "stray thoughts". Showed in London and New York.

Percy HIPKISS 1912– Painter and designer, born in Blackheath, Birmingham, educated locally. He was a member of RBSA, Birmingham Watercolour Society and Dudley Society of Artists. Warwick Central Museum and Art Gallery, Dudley, holds his work, which included jewellery design. Lived in Warley, West Midlands.

John S HIRD 1885– Painter, born in Ambleside, Westmorland. Studied at Oxford and Bordeaux Universities, an educationist, in art largely self-taught, he also painted for periods under several teachers including Ian Grant and Brian Bradshaw. Showed mainly in the Lakes and Yorkshire areas, where he was a member of Kendal Art Society and Bradford Arts Club. Sometimes signed work Stalker Hird. Settled in Ambleside.

Stalker HIRD: *see* **John S HIRD**

Barry HIRST 1934– Painter, illustrator, designer and teacher, born in Padstow, Cornwall. He attended Alleyn's School, Dulwich, then was at Camberwell School of Arts and Crafts 1950–2, studying and teaching there, 1954–6. After a period of two years at Slade School of Fine Art, from 1958–9 Hirst was a freelance designer with Le Comet and Berthon Muchler, Animated Films, Paris, and Silver Pine Potteries in London. After teaching at Watford, Croydon, Heatherley's and Chelsea Schools of Art, 1959–71, Hirst became head of the School of Art and Design, Sunderland Polytechnic. Hirst participated in many group shows from the late-1950s in Britain and abroad, having two solo exhibitions in 1965 at Hanover Gallery and Stone Gallery, Newcastle upon Tyne. Later shows included several with Mercury Gallery, in London and Edinburgh, from mid-1980s. Hirst also illustrated for private press books, including the work of C Day Lewis, Roy Fuller and R S Thomas. British Council, Contemporary Art Society and provincial British and foreign galleries hold his work.

Damien HIRST 1965– Artist, born in Yorkshire, who attended Jacob Kramer College of Art, Leeds, 1983–4, then Goldsmiths' College, 1986–9. His group show appearances included Whitworth Young Contemporaries, Manchester, 1987; Freeze, at PLA Building, 1988; New Contemporaries, at ICA, 1989; and Modern Medicine and Gambler, both at Building One, 1990. In 1994 Hirst curated Some Went Mad, Some Ran Away at the Serpentine Gallery, by which time he had become famous, in the words of critic Andrew Graham-Dixon, as the "virtuoso of dead animals and flies, the man who sold Charles Saatchi a tiger shark suspended in formaldehyde", for the Saatchi Collection. Hirst's winning entry for the Turner Prize, 1995, Mother and Child Divided, showed a cow and calf bisected longitudinally and presented in a glass case. It was said to explore the themes of mortality and isolation. Hirst also exhibited two of his spot paintings, white canvases covered with a slightly irregular grid of coloured circles. In 1996 BBC 2 Television showed *Hanging Around*, a dark comedy written and directed by Hirst.

Derek HIRST 1930– Painter and teacher, born in Doncaster, Yorkshire, where he attended the local School of Art, 1946–8. He then studied at Royal College of Art, 1948–51, after that for 25 years teaching widely in London. In the early-1970s Hirst also taught at Philadelphia College of Art and York University, Toronto, from 1976–87 being principal lecturer in painting at Kingston Polytechnic. Hirst was artist-in-residence at Sussex University in 1966, five years after his first one-man show, at Drian Galleries. Other solo shows included Sussex University, the Towner Art Gallery in Eastbourne and a retrospective at Angela Flowers Gallery in 1979. Hirst's work remained basically figurative with fundamental preoccupations, although its outward appearance seemed periodically to change quite radically. A visit to Japan in 1985 was a key influence. Arts Council holds examples. Lived in Chichester, Sussex.

Norman HIRST 1862–1956 Printmaker and painter, born in Liverpool, who in 1885 took up a two-year scholarship at Herkomer's School in Bushey, where he remained until 1895. Later lived on the south coast, notably at Seaford, Sussex. While in Bushey Hirst learned his engraving and mezzotint skills at the fine art printing studios of H T Cox, and after he moved he continued to use the studios for mezzotinting, at which he was an expert. His reputation was mainly as a mezzotint engraver of works by Gainsborough, Lawrence, Watteau and Romney, and in 1917 he was called as an expert witness in a notable court case in which an attribution was disputed. (Hirst's opinion that the work was not by Romney was eventually borne out.) Hirst was made an associate of the RE in 1931. Frost & Reed published his works *Sea Melodies* and *Capture* and Agnew *The Mall* and *Gamme d'Amour*. Showed extensively at RA, also at Fine Art Society, Abbey Gallery and RI, but a lack of interest in original mezzotints after World War II prompted Hirst's executors to burn most of his studio collection. Some of what remained was exhibited in Three Bushey Artists by the Bushey Museum Trust in 1991.

Jeannette HISCOCK 1895–c.1977 Watercolourist, born and lived in Oxford, where she was educated. Studied at the Ruskin School of Art there and with Sydney Carline. Exhibited RI, SWA and Oxford Art Society, of which she was a member, 1935–77.

Simon HISCOCK 1960– Painter of enigmatic abstracts, and teacher, born in London, who studied at Byam Shaw School of Art, lecturing at Lewisham College, 1990–2. Group shows included Brixton Art Gallery, 1985; East End Open Studios from 1987; Triangle Artists' Workshop in New York and St James' Gallery, both 1990; and Royal Over-Seas League Open from 1994.

Andrew Healey HISLOP 1887–1954 Painter, printmaker and artist in black-and-white. Born in Edinburgh, he studied at the College of Art there, 1908–13, in his final year going on to the British School in Rome. For many years taught at his old College and became president of the SSA. Married to the artist Margaret Hislop; the artist Vivien Hislop was their daughter. Exhibited RSA, SSA and Royal Glasgow Institute of the Fine Arts. Lived in Edinburgh where he was a member of the Arts Club.

Margaret HISLOP 1894–1972 Painter in oil who was married to the artist Andrew Healey Hislop. Studied at Edinburgh College of Art and exhibited at RSA, RA, RSW and Royal Glasgow Institute of the Fine Arts. Glasgow Museum and Art Galleries bought her work. Lived in Edinburgh.

Vivien HISLOP 1926– Landscape artist in pen and wash, fashion artist, illustrator and journalist. Daughter of the artists Andrew Healey Hislop and Margaret Hislop, she was born in Edinburgh. Studied at the University there and the College of Art, 1944–8, under her father, William Gillies and Joan Hassall. Did a great deal of journalistic work, including periods on the *London Evening News* and the *Daily Mail*. Showed at SSA and RSA. Sometimes signed work Vivien H or just with initials. Lived in Sutton, Surrey.

Frederick Brook HITCH 1877–1957 Sculptor, notably of memorials. Born in London, the son of the sculptor Nathaniel Hitch, he studied at the Royal Academy Schools. Notable among his works are the statue of Captain Matthew Flinders and the Sir Ross Smith memorial, both erected in Adelaide, South Australia (and illustrated in the volume *RBS: Modern British Sculpture*, published in 1939), a statue of Charles Wesley in Bristol and one of Admiral Horatio Nelson, in Portsmouth. Was a fellow of the RBS. Lived in Hertford, Hertfordshire.

Harold HITCHCOCK 1914– Painter in watercolour and gouache, born in London as Raymond Hitchcock, whose pictures are of a visionary nature and have been called "the visual embodiment of Jung's philosophy". Financial problems prompted Hitchcock's parents to send the children to live with the maternal grandparents in Thundersley, Essex, where in a cultured environment he began to paint at the age of nine. At Thundersley he had a vision "of harmony and well-being and peace" which influenced his subsequent development, his painting being an attempt to recapture this. Back in London aged 13 he began painting imaginary natural landscapes. His work was seen by the painter Laura Knight and he was called a child prodigy, but he entered a long period doing commercial artwork – broken by service during World War II as a non-combatant, volunteering for bomb disposal – which often left him depressed. For years was plagued by trigeminal neuralgia until surgery in 1958 cured this.

In 1947 had first public showing of his work at the International Art Centre; by 1964 was able to give up commercial work; in 1965 had an exhibition at Woburn Abbey, his picture The Mill being purchased for the Lidice Memorial Museum, Czechoslovakia; and in 1967 had first major retrospective at RI galleries. Had a successful tour of America in 1969. Hitchcock's pictures owe much to those of Claude Lorrain and J M W Turner, being idealised, light-drenched landscapes peopled with mysterious figures. Essentially self-taught, he employed a form of automatism as advocated by André Breton. Hitchcock's joining the Subud Brotherhood, a religious-type group, in 1960 was a profound influence. Lived in Ugborough, Devon.

Malcolm John HITCHCOCK 1929– Artist in oil, oil over egg tempera, gouache and pen and wash, born in Salisbury, Wiltshire. He studied at Andover School of Art, then did "a variety of work to keep the wolf from the door," becoming a full-time artist in mid-1980s. His main works were Pointillist railway paintings in oil and semi-abstract, mixed media nudes. Hitchcock was a member of RWA. He also exhibited at RA and Paris Salon and in the provinces; his solo shows included Bramante Gallery, Ashgate Gallery in Farnham and Hiscock Gallery in Southsea. Reading Museum and Art Gallery holds his work. Lived in Padworth Common, Reading, Berkshire.

Raymond HITCHCOCK 1922–1992 Artist and writer, born in Calcutta, India, son of a professional soldier. Was educated partly at Denston College, Staffordshire, then in 1939 went to Cambridge University. Army service interrupted his education, but he returned to Cambridge to gain a degree in mechanical sciences, then joined Cable and Wireless. From the mid-1950s Hitchcock began to paint in oils, at first Surrealistic Biblical and autobiographical works, by the 1960s abstracts. Through that decade he showed often in London and Oxford. As a writer he made his name with the 1969 novel *Percy*, a satire on transplant surgery, which was successfully filmed two years later. Nine more published novels and some television and radio plays followed. Hitchcock's paintings of the 1970s and 1980s returned to narrative themes. He drew for *Tatler* and *Punch.* A retrospective exhibition of Hitchcock's work was held at Guildhall Gallery, Winchester, where he lived, in 1992.

Theodore HITCHCOCK 1892– Painter and teacher who studied at Hornsey School of Art, after attending London University, his teachers being Adrian Hill and John Charles Moody. Exhibited ROI, RBA, NEAC and RA. Lived in Enfield, Middlesex. Hitchcock was involved in the design of his house including a series of stained glass windows, some abstract, which remained intact after his death.

Ivon HITCHENS 1893–1979 Painter in oil of landscapes, flowers, decorative pictures and figures. Born in London, the son of the painter Alfred Hitchens; Ivon Hitchens was father of the painter John Hitchens. After education at Bedales, Ivon Hitchens studied art at St John's Wood and the Royal Academy Schools, where he was influenced by John Singer Sargent and William Orpen, although this is not readily apparent in his mature work. Later notable influences were the French Post-Impressionists Cézanne, Braque and Matisse. Hitchens had his first one-man show at the Mayor Gallery in 1925, later showing at Tooth's, the Lefevre and Leicester Galleries. He was a member of a number of forward-looking groups before World War II, including the 7 & 5 Society, London Artists' Association and LG. He moved to Sussex from London in 1940 and gradually became famous for his long, rural scenes which used bold, sweeping brushstrokes, increasingly bright colours and edged gradually towards abstraction. Waterfall, Terwick Mill, of 1945, and Winter Walk, No. 4, of 1948, are typical of his landscapes at their best. Hitchens completed a number of notable murals, at Cecil Sharp House, London, and for several universities. He is widely represented in public galleries around the world, including the Tate Gallery. There were several retrospective exhibitions during his lifetime and one at the Serpentine Gallery, 1989. Lived at Petworth, Sussex.

John HITCHENS 1940– Painter in oil, son of the artist Ivon Hitchens and grandson of the painter Alfred Hitchens. John Hitchens' landscapes and flower paintings were similar to his father's, with their broad strokes of paint and rich colours. After Bedales School Hitchens attended Bath Academy of Art. He showed from the 1960s, having a solo show at Marjorie Parr Gallery, 1964. Exhibited there until 1976, showing from 1967–71 with Ditchling Gallery; 1967–82 with David Paul Gallery, Chichester; and 1977–9 with Gilbert Parr Gallery. Later solo shows included a series with Montpelier Studio from 1983 and one at Davies Memorial Gallery, Newtown, 1987. In 1979 West Sussex Education Committee commissioned a huge mural, A Landscape Symphony, from Hitchens, who was born in the county, settling at Byworth, Petworth. His work is held by many other collections, including public galleries in Brighton, Bradford and Hull.

Simon HITCHENS 1967– Sculptor producing abstract forms from stone and other media, son of the painter John Hitchens and grandson of Ivon Hitchens. Simon studied at West Surrey College of Art & Design, 1985–6, then gained an honours degree at Bristol Polytechnic's faculty of art and design, 1987–90. He was assistant to the sculptors Peter Randall-Page, 1990, and Anish Kapoor, 1993–6. Group exhibitions included LG Open from 1992; Galerie de L'Avancon, Bex, Switzerland, 1993; Hannah Peschar, Surrey, and Contemporary Art Society, both from 1994; and Eight by Eight at Pallant House, Chichester, 1997. He was selected by the British Council for sculpture symposiums in Slovakia, 1994, and Colombia, 1996, and was made an associate of RBS, 1997. Lived and worked in London.

Stephen HITCHIN 1953– Sculptor in stone, draughtsman and teacher who studied at Liverpool Polytechnic, 1972–6, gaining his master's degree at Manchester Polytechnic, 1976–7. He went on to become head of art and design at Glenburn School,

Skelmersdale. Hitchin said that his sculpture was "initially evolved from the human form, being derived from a variety of experiences, observations and sources", as in Girl's Head, included in Walker Art Gallery, Liverpool, 1986–7 touring show Merseyside Artists 3. Hitchin showed with Liverpool Academy as a member in 1980, MAFA in 1982 and RA. Had a solo show at Atkinson Art Gallery in Southport, 1981, and shared one at Liverpool University Senate House, 1986. In 1978 he gained a Merseyside Arts Association Award. Lived in Higher Bebington, Wirral, Merseyside.

Ting-Fay HO fl. from early 1980s– Abstract artist whose greatest sources of inspiration were Western classical music and Eastern calligraphy. She was born in Hong Kong and studied at Chelsea and Central St Martins Colleges of Art and Design. Group exhibitions included Drian Galleries, 1983; Warwick Arts Trust, from 1986; The East-West Connection, Oval House Gallery, 1988; Galeria Lieco Recreo, Orense, Spain, 1993; and Journeys West, University of Essex touring show, 1995. Had a solo exhibition at Fulham Library, 1982, others including Centre 181 Gallery, 1986.

Harold Frank HOAR: *see* **ACANTHUS**

Michael HOARE 1928– Painter, muralist, illustrator and teacher. He qualified in fine arts at Croydon College of Art in 1950 and then went to study theatre design at Old Vic Theatre School. He worked in the theatre in England and Australia, taught widely, illustrated books and record sleeves and painted a number of murals, notably at All Saints, Cleadon, County Durham. In 1969 he settled in France, in a remote village in the southwest. As well as showing in France, Hoare had several shows with Sue Rankin Gallery from 1990. National Gallery of New South Wales, Sydney, holds his work. Degas, Corot, Millet and Rembrandt were admired painters.

Marjorie HOARE fl. from late 1920s–1953 Watercolour painter and draughtsman. After private education she studied at the Slade School of Fine Art under Henry Tonks, 1927, then in Sussex with Franklin White. Exhibited RA, NEAC, RHA, Goupil Gallery and in the provinces. Lived at Barcombe, Sussex.

John HOBART 1922– Self-taught artist working in various media, born in London. He was "a Sunday painter from the 1950s, full-time since 1982". Hobart graduated in natural science at University College. He was visiting professor of forest entomology at University of British Columbia, Vancouver, 1972–3, then head of the school of animal biology and dean of the science faculty at University College of North Wales, Bangor, of which he was a fellow. It holds his work. Peter Lanyon, Roger Hilton, William Scott and Kurt Schwitters were influences. Hobart was a vice-president of RCamA. He showed with NWG, Newlyn Orion Gallery, Penwith Society of Arts of which he was an associate and elsewhere. He had a solo show at Bangor Gallery. Lived at Ludgvan, Penzance, Cornwall.

Charles HOBBIS 1880–1977 Silversmith, metalworker, all-round craftsman, teacher and watercolourist. He was born in Sheffield, studying at the School of Art there 1893–1902; he won a Queen's Prize, four King's Prizes, a bronze medal and in 1902 a gold medal for which he was awarded a Royal Exhibition to study design at the Royal College of Art. Was at the Royal College, 1902–7, under W R Lethaby and made a special study of silversmithing and metalwork with Henry Wilson, called "the most outstanding metalworker of his time". Hobbis also trained in heraldry and lettering under Edward Johnston. In 1919 appointed headmaster of Norwich School of Art, where he remained until 1946. His tenure was celebrated by a special exhibition in 1974. Hobbis was remembered as a perfectionist, although he did not encourage study of the modern movement in art. Showed at RA and in Norfolk, the Norwich Castle Museum and Art Gallery holding his work. Lived in Norwich.

James HOBBS 1960– Draughtsman who graduated from Winchester School of Art, 1988. The previous year Hobbs had found a copy of H V Morton's 1927 book *In Search of England* in a car boot sale. He set out to recreate Morton's journey, keeping a journal and making 400 drawings of places and buildings Morton had seen. The drawings showed the influence of Hobbs' teacher Dennis Creffield and through him the approach of Creffield's own teacher David Bomberg. A group of the drawings was shown at Wolseley Fine Arts, 1996.

Peter HOBBS 1930–1994 Artist, musician and teacher, born and lived in London. After working as a jazz pianist from 1953–5, studied at Central School of Art, taught there for a year at the start of the 1960s, then began teaching soon after that at Camberwell School of Arts and Crafts, where he remained over many years. Hobbs was an abstract Constructivist whose mixed exhibitions included Situation at RBA Galleries, 1960; an Arts Council touring exhibition, 1962–3; and later he was featured in The Sixties Art Scene in London, Barbican Art Gallery, 1993. Had a series of solo shows, the first at ICA, 1960. Alcohol was Hobbs' problem, prompting erratic behaviour such as turning up at Camberwell to teach on the wrong day of the week, but he was remembered with affection by an ex-staffer as a highly amusing colleague. Worked finally in a studio in Hampstead.

Roy HOBDELL 1911–1961 Painter, muralist and designer who grew up in south London and by age 14 had begun classes at Camberwell School of Arts and Crafts under Stanley Thorogood. Leaving Camberwell in 1927 he worked in an art studio, then in 1932 joined the Lintas advertising agency, where he spent almost the rest of his life. Attended life classes at St Martin's School of Art. A friend of the photographer Angus McBean, Hobdell worked on some of his backdrops; the stage remained a main interest, and he designed sets for Ballets Nègres. As a muralist Hobdell completed trompe l'oeil commissions for Lord Faringdon, at Buscot Park, Barnsley Park and Brompton Square. Also did illustrative work for *The Leader*; made flower paintings on glass for the Festival of Britain in 1951; and large doorways for *Observer* Film Festival in 1956. In 1950s began to show work with Redfern and Arthur Jeffress Galleries and sold pictures through Peter Jones' store in Sloane Square, signed with the names of his cats, Giles and Emma Farquharson. Hobdell was included in the Lintas Beyond the Horizon exhibition at Agnew, 1988.

Nicky HOBERMAN 1967– Painter who was born in Cape Town, South Africa, and who gained a degree in modern history at Oxford University, 1986–9; then a fine art degree at Parsons School of Design, Paris, 1989–93; and a master's at Chelsea College of Art, 1994–5. Showed during Battell Stoeckel Fellowship, Yale Summer School of Art, 1992, and was included in New Contemporaries at Tate Gallery, Liverpool, and Camden Arts Centre, 1996.

Ronald HOBLING fl. from 1930s– Painter and draughtsman, notable for portraits, born and lived in London. He studied at Hornsey School of Art, teachers including Russell Reeve and J C Moody, also portraiture with Frank Emanuel. Showed at RI, Whitechapel Art Gallery, Artists of Chelsea and in the provinces.

Alice HOBSON 1860–1954 Watercolourist, born in Leicester, who studied with James Orrock, John Fulleylove and Wilmot Pilsbury. She was elected RI, also showing occasionally at RA and Walker Art Gallery, Liverpool. Travelled extensively on the European continent and in Africa and settled eventually at Praa Sands, Cornwall.

Marion Grace HOCKEN 1922–1987 Painter, born in Zennor, Cornwall, who showed early talent which led her to study with Arthur Hambly at Redruth School of Art in her teens. After World War II showed at Downing's Bookshop in St Ives with Peter Lanyon, Brian Wynter, Isobel Heath and other luminaries. She was a founder-member of Penwith Society of Arts in 1949. As well as showing at RA and ROI, of which she was a member, Hocken was a botanist inspired by nineteenth-century natural history painters and Fantin-Latour. Her flower studies were acclaimed at Paris Salon. Hocken's fame mainly rests on a large 1955 canvas The Hollow Men, based on the T S Eliot poem, which when showed in 1957 caused a row, because of its deeply satirical comments on modern St Ives life. For the next 30 years Hocken led a reclusive life in Carbis Bay following the reception of The Hollow Men. She was physically handicapped and the condition worsened, although she did marry in later years. With her husband she shared a keen interest in unidentified flying objects. After her death Whitford and Hughes handled the sale of The Hollow Men.

James HOCKEY 1904–1990 Painter, printmaker and teacher, born in London. After education at Alleyn's School, in Dulwich, Hockey attended Goldsmiths' College School of Art, 1922–7, then went on to teach, being principal of Farnham School of Art, 1945–69, then joint principal of West Surrey College of Art and Design, 1969–71. He was a key figure in art education development and was for a time president of Farnham Art Society. Showed at RA, RBA, NEAC and elsewhere, and was noted for his flower paintings, Contemporary Art Society buying his work. Lived in Farnham, Surrey.

Susan-Jayne HOCKING 1962– Painter in oil and watercolour and oil, often on a small scale, who graduated from Bristol Polytechnic and Royal Academy Schools. Mixed exhibitions included Ten Young Artists, Mall Galleries, 1988; RA Summer Exhibitions, from 1989; and Cadogan Contemporary, 1991. She was a seasoned traveller, and her solo exhibition at New Grafton Gallery, 1996, included impressions of India, Myanmar, Vietnam, Thailand and China. Lived in London.

David HOCKNEY 1937– Painter, graphic artist, photographer, theatre designer, teacher and writer, born in Bradford, Yorkshire. Hockney was a brilliant draughtsman, the best-known British painter of his generation, who gained international success from his mid-twenties. His work had a homo-erotic strain, but became widely popular through its satirical imagery and its attractive images of swimming pools, showers and Californian life. Hockney attended Bradford School of Art, 1953–7, and Royal College of Art, 1959–62; there he won a Gold Medal and the Guinness Award for Etching. His studies had been interrupted for a two-year period of hospital work as a conscientious objector. Hockney worked at various times in London, Paris and California, but from 1977 was based in Los Angeles, where the light had a marked influence on his work. In 1962 he was an instructor at Maidstone College of Art, then through the 1960s held various teaching appointments at the Universities of Iowa, Colorado and California, and was Slade Professor of Fine Art, Cambridge University, 1990. Hockney won painting prizes at the John Moores Liverpool Exhibition, 1961 and 1967, to which he added major awards in Paris, Craców, Stuttgart and New York, for graphics and photography. Hockney had first one-man show at Kasmin Gallery, 1963, the Alan Gallery in New York, 1964, then had a continuous stream of international one-man shows. Notable in later years were appearances at Los Angeles County Museum of Art (travelling to Metropolitan Museum of Art, New York), and retrospectives at Tate Gallery, 1988, and Manchester City Art Gallery, 1996. Hockney's work is held by the Tate Gallery, Victoria & Albert Museum, Arts Council, Art Institute of Chicago, Los Angeles County Museum of Art and elsewhere. Notable works for the printed page are his etched illustrations for Cavafy's *Poems*, 1967, and *Six Fairy Tales of the Brothers Grimm*, 1969. For the stage he designed set and costumes for Stravinsky's *The Rake's Progress* and Mozart's *The Magic Flute*. His book *David Hockney by David Hockney* appeared in 1976, and *That's The Way I See It*, in 1993. He was elected RA in 1991 and was made Companion of Honour in 1997.

Joan HODES 1925– Figure and landscape painter and draughtsman, born and lived in London. She studied under Franklin White at Slade School of Fine Art, 1945–8, then was a pupil of Oskar Kokoschka, 1947–53, "a revelatory experience" (in

1948–9 Hodes visited Paris for a year, with studies at Académie Julian and Académie de la Grande Chaumière). Completed landscapes over a wide area of Britain, Ireland and continental Europe. Group shows included Contemporary Portrait Society, Leicester and Mercury Galleries and RA Summer Exhibition. Had solo exhibitions at Foyer Gallery, 1962 and 1971, later ones including Boundary Gallery, 1994. Victoria & Albert Museum holds her work.

Francis Edwin HODGE 1883–1949 Artist who was born in Devon, educated privately and then studied at Westminster School of Art and Slade School of Fine Art, his teachers including Augustus John, William Orpen and Frank Brangwyn, with further studies in Paris. In World War I he was commissioned in the Army, and Imperial War Museum, Victoria & Albert Museum and Plymouth City Art Gallery hold examples. He was a member of RBA from 1915, ROI 1927, RP 1929 and RI in 1931. For a time he was assistant to Gerald Moira at Royal College of Art. Also showed at NEAC, RA, Goupil Gallery, RSA and elsewhere. Was a member of Authors' and Chelsea Arts Clubs and lived in London.

Jessie Mary Margaret HODGE 1901–1964 Painter, muralist, illuminator and illustrator, born and lived in London. She was educated at Norland Place School and in art at Lime Grove and the Royal Academy Schools, gaining a bronze medal for life painting and a Landseer Scholarship. By the mid-1930s Hodge had become artist to St Mary's Hospital, had exhibited at RA, RSA, RMS, Royal Glasgow Institute of the Fine Arts, Walker Art Gallery, Liverpool, and Paris Salon, and had achieved notable commissions. These included lettering around the Kitchener Memorial in St Paul's Cathedral; decorations in Vigo House, featured in *The Builder* magazine; tablets lettered for The Second Church of Christ Scientist; fresco panels for the hall of the Eastman Dental Clinic; an illumination to commemorate Sir Ernest Shackleton; and medical and surgical illustrations for Sir Duke Elder, Glasgow University and elsewhere. At this time Jessie retained her interest in fishing, golf and tennis, but a neighbour, who knew her as Peggy, remembers her by the early-1960s as sociable but solitary, "a bit careworn", and asthmatic, "probably brought on by nerves". Jessie's father, the sculptor Albert Hemstock Hodge, had died in 1918, and Jessie, her mother and brother Norman settled in Hampstead Garden Suburb. Frustrated, Jessie appears to have resented her mother's devotion to Norman, who suffered from bad skin trouble and "looked like an ogre", so that he and his mother never went out. When mother died in 1963, Jessie and Norman planned to move permanently to a country cottage near Campbeltown which they owned and used for several weeks each summer, but Jessie died as they prepared to leave. Norman remained in Hampstead, then moved to the cottage helped by a neighbour, but soon died. Jessie was buried at Acton Cemetery.

Rodney Hellyer HODGE 1906–1963 Painter, born in Plymouth, Devon, son of David Hodge, principal of the School of Art there. Rodney Hodge began his studies there, then was at Royal College of Art, 1928–31. Having served as art master at the County High School, Redditch, Worcestershire, 1932–51, Hodge then moved to head the School of Art. Sometimes signing his work R H H, Hodge exhibited at public galleries in Plymouth, Birmingham and Liverpool. Also designed for stained glass, pottery and carved wood. Lived in Redditch.

Simon HODGE 1903–1973 Painter and draughtsman born in Glasgow, where he studied at the School of Art, 1920–4. He lived in London and Johannesburg from 1923 and from 1963 in Ibiza, Spain, dying in Edinburgh. While in South Africa Hodge was well known as a landscape and wildlife painter. He was president of the Johannesburg Art Club from 1931–2 and showed widely, including a series of exhibitions in the 1950s at the Pieter Wenning Gallery, Johannesburg. In the late 1950s Hodge and his wife did a year-long motoring and painting tour of the African continent. In Britain he showed at RA, RI and the Society of Artist Printers in Glasgow, having a solo show at the Royal Glasgow Institute of the Fine Arts. Rio Tinto Zinc in London and the Kruger National Park and Standard Bank in South Africa hold his work.

Wendy HODGE 1953– Painter, designer and illustrator, born in Canada. She attended Algonquin College in Canada to study advertising art, 1970–2, then did an illustration course in New York in 1979. Gained an Ottawa University Scholarship in 1982–3, then studied at Byam Shaw School of Art, 1983–5, and Royal College of Art, 1985–7. In addition to a Byam Shaw Scholarship she gained a British Commonwealth Scholarship. Hodge was a prizewinner at Royal Over-Seas League in 1985. Her other exhibitions included a solo show at Flaxman Gallery, 1987; London Picture Show, 1989, where she was a prizewinner; then in 1990 she was one of Flowers East's Artist of the Day, chosen by Lucy Jones.

Joanne HODGEN 1964– Painter, born in Glasgow, who studied at Bath Academy of Art in Corsham, then at Reading University. Mixed shows included 1st Portobello Open, Tabernacle Centre, 1989; A Woman's Point of View, Warehouse Gallery, Kendal, 1992; and Whitechapel Open and Royal Over-Seas League Open, both 1994.

Cyril Walter HODGES 1909– Artist in pen and ink, watercolour and oil, and writer, born in London. He studied at Goldsmiths' College School of Art, 1923–6, under Edmund J Sullivan. Hodges was noted for his book illustrations, stage designs, historical writings for children and adult works on the Elizabethan theatre, as well as architectural reconstructions of theatres. *Columbus Sails*, 1939; *The Marsh King*, 1967; and *Plain Lane Christmas*, 1978, were among his titles. His detailed work, *Shakespeare's Theatre*, 1964, was awarded the Kate Greenaway Medal for its illustrations. He also drew for *Radio Times*. He was included in the Box of Delights travelling exhibition of children's book illustrations, 1991–2. Had a solo show at Shakespeare

Institute, Stratford-upon-Avon, 1982, another at Folger Shakespeare Library, Washington, America, in 1988; it holds his work. Lived in Lewes, Sussex.

Merrett HODGES fl. from c.1895–1961 Painter, printmaker and photographer, full name William Merrett Hodges, who was also an art dealer for a time. He was elected an associate of RBSA in 1917 and exhibited extensively there, also at Walker Art Gallery in Liverpool, RCamA, RA and elsewhere in northern public art galleries. He lived in Birmingham and was a member of the Midlands Arts Club.

Paul HODGES 1950– Painter, from Cardiff, who did the foundation course at Bath Academy of Art, graduating with an honours degree at Sheffield College of Art. For many years he was a part-time and visiting lecturer at art colleges and polytechnics in Liverpool, Birmingham, Cheltenham, Sheffield and Stoke in north Staffordshire. In 1990 he was artist-in-residence at Harewood House, Leeds, working on an education and conservation programme, ending with a solo show at Terrace Gallery there. Hodges won the Stowells Trophy at Mall Galleries in 1975 and in 1976 at the same venue the Winsor and Newton Award. He exhibited in France, the Natural History Museum in London, Tolly Cobbold Exhibition Tour and Paton Gallery. He shared a show at Compass Gallery, Glasgow, in 1980 with Anne Grebby. The previous year Hodges had had a solo show at University Gallery, Sheffield.

Roberta HODGES 1903– Painter, draughtsman and teacher, born in Harlesden, northwest London. Studied at Goldsmiths' College School of Art with Frederick Marriott, then Slade School of Fine Art with Henry Tonks and Philip Wilson Steer. She married the artist Jozef Sekalski. Exhibited RA, RHA, NEAC, SSA, Paris Salon and elsewhere. Lived in St Andrews, Fife.

Eliot HODGKIN 1905–1987 Painter, notably in tempera, of small, highly detailed pictures of flowers and fruit; mural painter; writer. Born at Purley, near Reading, Berkshire, Hodgkin after Harrow School studied at Byam Shaw School of Art and at the Royal Academy Schools under Ernest Jackson. First one-man show at Picture Hire Gallery, 1936. Later showed at RA, Wildenstein, Leicester Galleries, NEAC, RBA and in New York. Among his books are *She Closed the Door*, 1931, and *Views of London*, 1948. Tate Gallery holds his work. Hodgkin sought to show things "exactly as they are, yet with some of their mystery and poetry, and as though seen for the first time". Hodgkin, a religious man, was a notable collector. A selection from his collection was shown in a memorial exhibition at Hazlitt, Gooden and Fox in 1990, and it included Sir Thomas Lawrence, Corot, Rubens, Graham Sutherland, Degas and Japanese prints. Lived in London.

Howard HODGKIN 1932– Painter, printmaker and teacher, born in London, where he eventually settled. Hodgkin was evacuated as a child to America, but was educated at Eton College, where the art master Wilfrid Blunt was influential. Studied at Camberwell School of Art, 1949–50, then at Bath Academy of Art, 1950–4, under Clifford Ellis, whom he considered "a teacher of genius". From 1954–6 was part-time assistant art master at Charterhouse School before teaching at Bath Academy of Art, 1956–66. Hodgkin then taught for six years at Chelsea School of Art, in 1976–7 being fellow in creative art at Brasenose College, Oxford. He had his first solo show at Arthur Tooth and Sons in 1962, after which he participated in notable international group shows. His further one-man exhibitions included Galerie Muller, Cologne, in 1971; Museum of Modern Art, Oxford, 1976, and tour; Hayward Gallery and tour, 1983; an appearance at Venice Biennale, 1984; a retrospective at Whitechapel Art Gallery in 1985, the year he won the Turner Prize; with another retrospective at Hayward Gallery, 1996. Latterly showed with Anthony d'Offay. From 1972–6 Hodgkin was a Tate Gallery trustee and he was knighted in 1992. Indian Mughal miniatures, which he collected for a time, were important to Hodgkin. Although originally a figurative artist, his mature, richly coloured pictures hovered on the edge of abstraction, although he insisted that "I can't paint without a subject." He said that "memory is the principal subject of all my pictures. I'm painting a feeling." Arts Council holds several examples. While at Bath Hodgkin married the artist Julia Lane, but they separated in the mid-1970s.

Jonathan Edward HODGKIN 1875–1953 Self-taught watercolourist who was by profession an electrical engineer, born and lived in Darlington, County Durham. He was chairman and director of many companies, chairman of Darlington Society of Arts and a trustee of the Bowes Museum and Art Gallery, Barnard Castle. His *Little Guide to County Durham* was popular. He was a member of RBA from 1928, showing there extensively, also at Walker's Galleries, Laing Art Gallery in Newcastle and Leeds City Art Gallery.

Frances HODGKINS 1869–1947 Painter, teacher and illustrator of landscape and still life, born in Dunedin, New Zealand, where her barrister father, an amateur painter, taught her watercolour. She showed with Otago Art Society locally and attended Dunedin Art School, 1895–8. After teaching and working as an illustrator she travelled to Europe in 1901 and had a solo show at W B Paterson's Gallery six years later. Having settled in Paris in 1908 she taught at Atelier Colarossi and in her own school. Had now established a reputation as an open-air watercolourist. She continued to travel and show in Australia, New Zealand and elsewhere, taking up oil painting in 1915. In the mid-1920s she worked for two years as a designer for Calico Printers' Association, in Manchester, living with Hannah Ritchie and D Jane Saunders. Seeing the work of Matisse several years before had given her work a modern impetus, indicated at her solo show at Claridge Gallery in 1928. Was taken up by the St George's Gallery, which was interested in younger, more advanced artists, as told in its owner Arthur Howell's book: *Frances Hodgkins, Four Vital Years*, 1951. Working in France and Spain she now showed with the 7 & 5 Society and produced work of great transculency and vigour. Died in Dorchester, Dorset. Tate Gallery and other major galleries hold her work. Several memorial shows held including Tate Gallery and Arts Council provincial tour, 1952, The Minories in Colchester showing late work in 1991.

Cecil HODGKINSON 1896-c.1961 Watercolourist, farmer and land agent whose work reflected his country background. Born in Billingborough, Lincolnshire, he showed in the Lincoln area and was chairman of the Lincolnshire Artists' Society in the mid-1950s. Lived at Greatford, near Stamford, in that county.

Wilfred HODGKINSON 1912– Artist, teacher and writer who was educated in Kidderminster where he attended the School of Art, then Birmingham College of Art. From 1939–46 was principal of Bilston School of Art and curator of the local art gallery. Later freelanced. Lived for a time at Shrawley, Worcestershire.

Carole HODGSON 1940– Sculptor and draughtsman, born in London. She studied at Wimbledon School of Art, 1957–62, then Slade School of Fine Art, 1962–4. Hodgson's work cleverly mixed abstraction, landscape and the human figure. She held solo exhibitions with Angela Flowers Gallery from 1973, later Flowers East. Other shows along the way were with WAC, Cardiff, 1976; Fine Arts Galleries, University of Wisconsin, 1980; Llanelli Festival, 1984; and New Ashgate Gallery, Farnham, 1991. Arts Council, WAC, British Council and other public collections in Britain and abroad hold her work.

David HODGSON 1959– Gestural abstract artist, born in Cheshire. He attended North Staffordshire Polytechnic, 1980–1, then Croydon College of Art, 1981–4. Hodgson's exhibitions included Waterloo Live, at Waterloo Gallery, 1981, and New Acquaintances, at Fabian Carlsson Gallery, 1987. In 1988 he was in Time Out Live, at Olympia, and was a nominee for Young Artist of the Year at Whitechapel Art Gallery. In 1990 Hodgson was the Boyle Family's choice as Artist of the Day at Flowers East.

Janet HODGSON 1960– Artist, born in Bolton, Lancashire, who studied at Lincoln College of Art, 1978–9, then theatre design at Wimbledon School of Art, 1979–82. Carried out a series of commissions, including The Boat, Birkenhead Park, Merseyside, 1990; Arrivals, Settle Market Place, with Peter Hatton, one of a series of collaborations with him, 1992; and Piltdown Bungalow, Uppermill, 1993. Group exhibitions included A Pool of Signs II, Bluecoat Gallery, in Liverpool where she was based, 1992; Manchester Airport Terminal Two, 1993; and in 1995 Making it at Tate Gallery, Liverpool, where her White Cube, Black Square was made of granulated sugar, royal icing, steel, molasses and pump.

Louisa HODGSON 1905–1980 Painter and teacher, daughter of London and North Eastern Railway official Edward Hodgson, amateur artist and member of Berwick Art Club. She was educated at Whitley Bay and Monkseaton High School, then studied under Richard Hatton at Armstrong College, Newcastle. Won an Abbey Scholarship in mural decoration in 1928, spending three years at the Royal College of Art, where she specialised in mural decoration, joining the staff of Armstrong College's art school part-time in 1931. In 1931–2 Hodgson completed a lunette for the Laing Art Gallery, Newcastle, which illustrated the local Shipwrights' Guild passing along the quayside around 1450. The Laing also has her striking picture The Collingwood Monument, Trafalgar Night. Hodgson was a frequent exhibitor 1934–52 at RA Summer Exhibition, notable for unusual subjects such her 1936 entry In Search of Peace, in egg tempera, acquired by Manchester City Art Gallery. Ferens Art Gallery, Hull, has her 1938 exhibit The Birth of Venus. Hodgson ground her own pigments and while at Armstrong College worked with scientists there to reproduce colours used by the Italian Old Masters. Lived in Tynemouth, finally at Alnmouth, Northumberland, as a virtual recluse, her final years cloaked in mystery.

John HODSON 1945– Artist in oil and marble, born in Oxford. He studied at Courtauld Institute, 1970. Hodson began painting landscapes in 1970 "using a colourful, Impressionist technique", then sculpted from 1975. He took part in group exhibitions in France and Italy and had a solo show at Woodstock Gallery, 1972. Lived in London.

Ron HODSON 1916– Painter, decorative artist and lecturer, born in Bolton, Lancashire. He studied at the School of Art there, his teachers including John Gauld, then at Manchester School of Art under Robert Dawson. Exhibited widely in north of England, including Manchester, Liverpool, Southport and Preston, and at Lefevre Gallery, London. Salford Museums and Art Galleries hold his work. He lectured to the Workers' Educational Association and lived in Burnley, Lancashire.

Franz Peter HOFFER 1924– Painter, stage designer, illustrator and writer, born in Berlin, Germany. He was educated in Kent at a boarding school, then attended St Martin's School of Art, 1939–41, under Sydney Litten. Hoffer had a multi-faceted career. Among his many activities he did stage design at the Glasgow Citizens' Theatre, for the theatre in London and at Stratford-upon-Avon; he designed for *Reader's Digest* Association Ltd; worked for the Central Office of Information; and wrote for magazines such as *Lilliput* and *Saturday Book*. Showed with Leicester Galleries, Arts Council, RBA and overseas. Lived in London and in Milan, Italy.

Erik HOFFMANN 1952– Painter and teacher, born in Leoben, Austria. He attended Kassel School of Art, 1975–80, having moved to Germany in 1960; from 1981–2 was a teacher of painting at Kassel, then attended Glasgow School of Art, 1982–3. Although Hoffmann continued to live in Kassel he spent part of the year on the island of Barra, in the Outer Hebrides. Working in tempera and acrylic Hoffmann completed portraits of great exactness and figure studies in landscapes with an intense atmosphere. From 1977 he won a number of awards in Germany and Scotland, including a grant from the German Academic Exchange Service for Glasgow in 1982 and in 1989 the Morrison Scottish Portrait Award, RSA. Showed at APEX-Gallery, Göttingen, in 1980, and at Savignyplatz Gallery, Berlin, in 1981–2. In 1988–9 had a first Scottish touring show, Portraits from the Western Edge, with Ulrike Kanne, An Lanntair, Stornaway, also showing with St Andrews Arts Centre, Aberdeen Art Gallery and Richard Demarco Gallery, Edinburgh. Later shows included Bruton Gallery for the Bath Festival, 1992.

Gerard HOFFNUNG 1925–1959 Humorous illustrator, writer and broadcaster with a special interest in music. Born in Berlin, was educated at Highgate School and at Harrow School of Art under John Platt. Hoffnung then began to mix careers as an illustrator and as a teacher. He was art master at Stamford School, 1945–6; staff artist on the *Evening News*, 1946; worked for Contact Publications, 1947–8; joined the staff of Harrow School, 1948; and was staff cartoonist for Cowles Magazines, New York, 1950–51. He freelanced widely, for publications including *Punch*, *Lilliput*, *Graphis*, *Daily Express* and *Saturday Evening Post*. Intermingled were forays into broadcasting for BBC, where his fruity, wheezy voice soon became instantly recognisable; playing the tuba; and organising his music festivals, at the Royal Festival Hall, in the 1950s, where unlikely instruments were played. He exhibited at the Little Gallery, Piccadily, 1949, and at the Festival Hall in 1951 and 1956. Books included *The Maestro*, *The Hoffnung Symphony Orchestra* and *Ho Ho Hoffnung*. Lived in London.

Eileen HOGAN 1946– Painter, designer, printmaker, illustrator and teacher who studied graphic design and then painting, under Carel Weight, at Royal College of Art, 1971–4, following a period at Camberwell School of Arts and Crafts, 1963–7, and British School of Archaeology, Athens, 1970–1. Showed solo on many occasions, including British Council, Athens, 1971; Royal College of Art in 1977; a series at Fine Art Society, London and Glasgow, from 1980; Imperial War Museum, 1984; and Graduate School of Library Services University of Alabama, 1988. She illustrated a number of books, including *Fragments from Sappho*, 1973; *The Dream of Gerontius*, 1976; and *A Selection of Poems by C P Cavafy*, 1985. The British School in Athens commissioned a mural in 1971, and other commissions included Imperial War Museum, 1983–4, Women at Work in the Royal Navy; *Illustration: A Working Art*, commissioned by Batsford, 1989; and Royal Mail stamps, 1990–1. Public collections holding Hogan's work include Victoria & Albert Museum plus many overseas collections. She was a member of RWS. In 1992 The London Institute awarded her a professorship.

Lizzie HOGARTH 1879–c.1953 Painter and draughtsman, born in Aberdeen. She studied art there with James Hector and at St Martin's School of Art. Exhibited at RSA, extensively at RBA and SWA of both of which she was a member, and in the provinces. Still life and landscape were the mainstays of her contributions to SWA, where she was a prolific exhibitor, 1919–52. Lived latterly in Petworth, Sussex.

Paul HOGARTH 1917– Painter, illustrator, printmaker and teacher, born in Kendal, Westmorland, full name Arthur Paul Hogarth. Sometimes signed work P H. Studied at Manchester School of Art, St Martin's School of Art and obtained doctorate at Royal College of Art. He was senior tutor in the faculty of graphic art there, 1964–71. In 1981 was commissioned by Imperial War Museum to depict the Berlin Wall. His work is also in Fitzwilliam Museum in Cambridge, Victoria & Albert Museum and many other public galleries in Britain and abroad. Hogarth was a Royal Designer of Industry, and was elected ROI, 1979, RA in 1984 and RE in 1988. Retrospective at Abbot Hall Art Gallery, Kendal, 1985. In 1990 his exhibition Cold War Reports 1947–67 was at Norfolk Institute of Art, with a tour. Much of Hogarth's early work was of a left-wing committed nature, and he was associated with AIA, desiring to be "a communicator rather than a painter". He was in the English tradition of the artist-traveller and among his books were *Looking at China*, 1955; *Majorca Observed* (with Robert Graves), 1965; *Drawing Architecture*, 1973; *The Mediterranean Shore* (with Lawrence Durrell), 1988; and *Drawing a Life: the autobiography of Paul Hogarth*, 1997. Among his awards was the *Yorkshire Post* Award for the Best Art Book, 1986. Settled finally at Hidcote Manor, Gloucestershire.

Philip HOGBEN 1945– Landscape and figure painter who studied at Derby and Winchester Schools of Art, 1961–6. In 1969 settled in Cornwall to teach at Falmouth School of Art. Showed in west of England and abroad and in 1992 was included in Artists from Cornwall at RWA. Two years before, he gained *Western Morning News* prize at Newlyn Contemporaries show. Hogben was a member of Newlyn Society of Artists and lived in Helston.

William HOGGATT 1880–1961 Painter, mainly of landscapes of the Isle of Man. He was born in Lancaster, of a Cumbrian father and Scottish mother, won a scholarship to the Royal College of Art which he did not take up, but became apprenticed to a local stained glass makers, continuing his studies at the school of art in Lancaster's Storey Institute. Aided by one of the Storeys, Hoggatt studied at the Académie Julian in Paris, 1901–5. While working on a commission at the Tate Gallery he came to know his future wife, Dazine, sister of Leonard Archer who managed the pianist Paderewski, then travelled to Isle of Man to inspect his future home. Hoggatt liked the light and landscape and decided to stay, living at Port St Mary until 1925, then at The Darragh, Port Erin, which became one of the island's intellectual centres. Hoggatt was a prolific and widespread exhibitor, especially at the RA Summer Exhibition, also RSA and RSW. He was a member of a number of exhibiting societies, including RI, RBC and RCamA, and was president of the Manx Artists. In 1934 he won a competition to design a stained glass window commemorating the work of T E Brown, the island's national poet. Foxdale Valley, in the collection of Pallant House,

Chichester, is a typical solidly drawn pastel. Other works by Hoggatt are in the Manx Museum Art Gallery and in the collections of public galleries in Liverpool, Manchester, Oldham and Preston, as well as several Australian galleries.

Chris HOGGETT 1927– Painter, sculptor, ceramist, stage designer, teacher, illustrator and writer, born and lived in Cheltenham, Gloucestershire. He studied at Royal College of Art, 1950–3, where Rodney Burn and Carel Weight were influential teachers, others including John Minton, Rodrigo Moynihan, Charles Mahoney and Robert Buhler. Hoggett went on to teach and work in a wide range of media and illustrate many books. His own books included *Stage Crafts*, published in Britain and America. In later years Hoggett returned to his main interest, paintings landscapes, especially in the wilder areas of Scotland and New Zealand. During this time "a more abstract approach developed as the result of combining figurative elements with landscape". Showed mainly in West Country, including RWA and with Cheltenham Group of Artists.

Pete HOIDA fl. from 1960s– Painter, poet and teacher, born and brought up in Birkenhead, Cheshire. After working as a landscape architect for London County Council in the early 1960s he studied painting at Hammersmith College of Art and Building and Goldsmiths' College. During the 1960s and 1970s volumes of his poems were published and readings given at many colleges and universities, the Traverse Theatre in Edinburgh and ICA. Taught at Chelsea School of Art, 1978. From 1974 he lived and painted at the same location outside Stroud, Gloucestershire. Hoida's seemingly abstract paintings, in acrylic on elongated, horizontal canvases, were much-inspired by the Toadsmoor Valley. Rothko, Pollock, Matisse, Braque and Picasso were cited as influences, "mediated by Hilton, Heron and others". Group exhibitions included New Young Contemporaries, Camden Arts Centre, 1973–4; Six Gloucestershire Painters, Spacex, Exeter, 1980; Kilvert Gallery, Clyro, 1992–3; and Oriel Senig, Harlech, 1994. Had a solo show at International Arts Centre, 1975, later ones including Museum and Art Gallery, Cheltenham, 1995.

Ashley HOLD 1964– Artist who studied painting at Falmouth School of Art and Design. He exhibited with Penwerris Community Arts Group in Falmouth, Cornwall, and at Newlyn Orion Gallery as a member of Newlyn Society of Artists. Also showed with Independent Schools Exhibition, Dulwich Art Gallery and Oxford in 1986, and in Painting Today auction at Bonhams, 1991–2, was included in Falmouth Connections at Falmouth Art Gallery in 1994 and in same year had a portrait at BP National Portrait Award at National Portrait Gallery. Hold undertook several group murals and workshops in the local community, including a mural for Truro School.

Cliff HOLDEN 1919– Painter, designer, draughtsman, printmaker and teacher, born in Manchester. He initially studied agriculture and veterinary science, then philosophy at the City Literary Institute from 1944 where he met David Bomberg, Edna Mann and Dorothy Mead (with whom Holden was closely associated for 11 years). In 1945 these artists followed Bomberg to the Borough Polytechnic and joined his group from the Bartlett School of Architecture in drawing at various venues. In 1944–5 Holden and Bomberg conceived the Borough Group, established 1946, the first of seven shows taking place in 1947. Holden was its president, 1946–8, but resigned over policy issues. Bomberg reorganised the group, which disbanded in 1951. Holden met the Swedish artist Torsten Renquist and in 1952 showed in Four Englishmen in Gummesson's Gallery, Stockholm; in 1956 he was invited to show more in Sweden and set up a design studio in Gothenburg with Lisa Grönwall and Maj Nilsson; in 1959 Holden and the studio moved to Marstrand, the trio becoming known internationally as Marstrand Designers. Holden also taught in Sweden and abroad, including Goldsmiths' College. Participated in many group shows and solo exhibitions were held in Sweden, later ones including Möbelcentrum, Stockholm, from 1977, and Marstrand Designers (with his son Thomas Holden, the painter), 1979. Holden was a member of LG, was a fellow of the Free Painters and Sculptors and Chartered Society of Designers, a design associate of the American Institute of Interior Designers, as well as several Swedish artists' organisations. Extensive public commissions included hotels, ships, offices, embassies and consulates. Tate Gallery, Arts Council, Victoria & Albert Museum, Scottish National Gallery of Modern Art in Edinburgh, Manchester City Art Gallery and a series of Swedish collections hold examples. Holden promoted Swedish artists in Britain and British artists in Sweden, such as the sculptors Armitage, Chadwick and Butler.

Douglas Hamilton HOLDEN 1919–1972 Painter, printmaker, creator of found-object assemblages and teacher, son of Harold Henry Holden and brother of John Hamilton Holden, both artists. Douglas studied at Birmingham School of Arts and Crafts with Beatrice Johnson (as his wife known as Trixie Holden) before World War II. During the war Douglas served in the Royal Navy, then in 1946–7 he and Trixie studied at the Royal College of Art. Douglas taught at St Martin's School of Art and showed at the RA Summer Exibition in the 1950s while living in London; was elected an RWS associate in 1953 and RWS in 1961; and exhibited at The New Art Centre, 1965. In April 1988 Douglas' work was included in a studio sale of several Holdens' works at Burstow & Hewitt, Battle.

Harold Henry HOLDEN 1885–1977 Watercolour painter, etcher and teacher, born in Settle, Yorkshire, father of three artists: Geoffrey H Holden, John Hamilton Holden and Douglas Hamilton Holden. He studied at Skipton School of Art, Leeds College of Art and the Royal College of Art after initial lessons near his home in Settle. He exhibited at RA, RBSA, RWS and abroad, Leeds City Art Gallery, among others, holding his work. He became art department head at Leeds Modern School in 1910; principal of Cheltenham School of Arts and Crafts, 1914; principal of Leeds College of Art, 1922; director of art education and principal of the College of Arts and Crafts, Birmingham, 1928–46. Holden's work could be sombre, and he favoured strongly organised pictures. Lived finally in Westbury-on-Trym, Bristol, with his fourth son, Rupert, a civil engineer.

John Hamilton HOLDEN 1913–1980 Artist and administrator who worked as John Holden. Born in Leeds, he went on to study at Birmingham College of Art, of which his father, Harold Holden, was for a time principal. Then he studied at Royal College of Art. Holden became progressively principal of Wolverhampton College of Art, Manchester College of Art and Design and then deputy director of Manchester Polytechnic, from which he retired in 1978. Holden's considerable contribution to building up the Manchester College is chronicled by David Jeremiah in *A Hundred Years and More*, published by Manchester Polytechnic in 1980. Among official positions held by Holden were the presidency of both the National Society for Art Education and the Association of Art Institutions. Holden wrote on art and education and showed at RA and provincial galleries. Lived in Wilmslow, Cheshire. Sometimes he is incorrectly listed as John Hamilton-Holden.

John HOLDEN 1942– Painter and teacher, born in Gillingham, Kent, who studied at Medway College of Art and Design, 1959–63, and Royal Academy Schools, 1963–6. From 1986 he was principal lecturer in fine art at Liverpool John Moores University. Showed regularly at RA from 1968; in Parallel Lines, at Cardiff Institute of Higher Education, 1993; and in the 1995–6 John Moores Liverpool Exhibition, with You are the One, a geometrical abstract. Had a solo exhibition at RA in 1974. Lived in Long Buckby, Northampton.

John Vivian HOLDEN 1931– Painter, printmaker, muralist and teacher who studied at various London art colleges and in Paris studios in 1940s and 1950s. He went on to teach painting, etching and the history of art for about 35 years, travelling frequently in Europe. Holden had shows at National Theatre in London, Orleans House in Richmond and at Cleveland Bridge Gallery, Bath. He did a number of murals for companies, including Dunlop Rubber Company. Holden was described as an "intense admirer of the irrational and neurotic in art". He had a fine understanding of the human figure, on which his work was based, forms materialising on the canvas in deft strokes of colour, giving an impression of restless energy.

Thomas HOLDEN 1957– Painter, muralist, designer and printmaker, son of the artists Cliff Holden and Lisa Grönwall, he was born in Gothenberg, Sweden. From 1972 pursued his own work and from 1975 exhibited with his parents under the name Marstrand Designers. Collaborated on numerous projects and public commissions, being represented in Swedish embassies and consulates, hotels, hospitals, factories, banks, ferries and cruise ships. Strindberg Museum in Stockholm has Holden's large silkscreen portrait of the writer. Group exhibitions included David Bomberg-linked show at Towner Art Gallery in Eastbourne, 1991. Had many solo exhibitions in Sweden from 1977, later ones including Gallery St Nikolaus, Stockholm, 1985.

Edgar Thomas HOLDING 1870–1952 Landscape painter, born in Horncastle, Lincolnshire, who became full-time painter in maturity. Was at various times president of the RWS Art Club, secretary of the Society of Sussex Painters and a member of the Art Workers' Guild. Regular exhibitor at RWS, also showed at RA, Fine Art Society, Goupil Gallery, Walker Art Gallery, Liverpool, and many other venues. He was extensively illustrated in books, such as the *Old Water-colour Society's Annual*, and by firms such as Vickers Brothers. Public galleries in Brighton, Bristol, Southport, Leeds and Worthing hold his work. Lived for many years in Sutton, Sussex.

Marjorie HOLFORD: *see* **Marjorie BROOKS**

Florence Mabel HOLLAMS 1877–1963 Painter of horses, dogs, flower studies and the countryside. She studied at the Calderon School of Animal Painting and at Académie Julian, Paris, and was a keen horse and dog woman. In the 1920s and 1930s Hollams produced many equine portraits, using samples of the horses' coats and manes for reference, finishing her work with great speed. Exhibited RA and Ackermann.

Claerwen HOLLAND 1952– Painter, draughtsman, printmaker and teacher, born in Radnorshire, where she continued to live. Her subjects were rooted in the countryside and domestic still life. She studied at Byam Shaw School of Drawing and Painting under Maurice de Sausmarez, who awarded her the principal's prize for landscape in oils. Won a David Murray Studentship in landscape painting given by RA. Exhibited in many mixed shows, including RA and NEAC. Had solo exhibitions at Sue Rankin and Thackeray Galleries. Holland was a member of the Artists and Designers of Wales, and for them she demonstrated etching at Royal Welsh Showground at Builth Wells, where she also showed Beulah Speckled Faced Sheep, which featured in much of her work.

Dudley HOLLAND 1915–1956 Painter, muralist, designer, printmaker and teacher whose work had a Neo-Romantic tinge and a strong sense of design. Holland was educated at Kingston Grammar School, Chelsea and Willesden Schools of Art. He was awarded a Royal Exhibition to the Royal College of Art, 1936, which he refused, preferring to paint on his own. Taught design, painting and drawing at Willesden, Harrow and Goldsmiths' College Schools of Art, then was appointed principal of York School of Art, 1949, of Guildford School of Arts and Crafts, 1951. He completed mural decorations for Cunard Line, schools and libraries. Exhibited at RA from 1937, also with NEAC, LG, with Redfern Gallery and in touring shows. In 1950 he shared an exhibition with Austin Wright at York City Art Gallery which holds his work, as does the Arts Council. Holland was killed when his motorcycle hit a lorry; he was rushed to Kingston Hospital but was dead on arrival. One version says that Holland would not have used the motorcycle again, as he was on the way to collect a new car. Another that he was furious at a wrongly detrimental inspector's report and by mistake tipped the lorry. Lived at Hale, near Farnham, Surrey.

George Herbert Buckingham HOLLAND 1901–1987 Painter, educated at the Grammar School in Northampton, where he was born and made his career. He worked as a commercial artist before studying at Leicester School of Art and Chelsea Polytechnic. Was a founder-member of Northampton Town and County Art Society and its president in 1949–50. He was noted for his portraits and showed at RP, Alpine Club Gallery, ROI and elsewhere. National Portrait Gallery, Royal Academy of Music and National Library of Wales hold his work.

Harry HOLLAND 1941– Painter, draughtsman, printmaker and teacher, born in Glasgow. After an attempt to study at Wimbledon College of Art which fell through because of lack of funds, Holland attended a commercial college, then was at St Martin's School of Art, 1965–9. Taught at Chelsea Community Centre, Coventry College of Art until 1972, at a series of art schools in the Midlands, then at Cardiff College of Art, 1974–8, when he left to paint full-time. While at Coventry several pictures were bought by the collector Charles Saatchi. Holland began to show with Nicholas Treadwell Gallery, then Ian Birksted Gallery in 1983 and Thumb Gallery, 1986 (later the Jill George Gallery). Holland's mixed shows included Aspects of Realism, 1976–8, which toured Canada; The Probity of Art, a WAC touring show, 1980; in the same year the British Art Show, an Arts Council exhibition which toured; and People in Great Britain, 1989, a British Council touring show. Had a solo show at Roundhouse Gallery, 1979; the following year WAC toured his one-man exhibition; then he showed regularly, with a Jill George UK travelling retrospective in 1991. Holland's work – impeccably crafted – went through several phases, including realism with a hinted-at – even sinister – narrative element; still life; and still life with a Surrealistic atmosphere which explored aspects of reality. Tate Gallery, WAC and Metropolitan Museum of Art in New York hold his work. Based in Cardiff.

Hester HOLLAND: *see* **Hester GORST**

James HOLLAND 1905–1996 Designer, painter, teacher and writer, born in Gillingham, Kent, son of a naval blacksmith, who early on won the president's prize of the Royal Drawing Society and a scholarship to Rochester School of Art with his ship drawings. From 1924 attended Royal College of Art painting school, where James Boswell became a close friend. In 1933 they helped to found the AIA. Holland held the first of many exhibitions while still at the Royal College, where he was active in the sketch club. On graduating Holland joined the advertising agency Foote, Cone & Belding, and was commissioned, with John Betjeman, to write copy for Shell by Jack Beddington; was active in LG and NEAC; helped decorate the Peace Pavilion at the 1937 Paris World Fair; and was a freelance illustrator. During World War II Holland worked in the Ministry of Information's exhibition design department, invaluable experience when he was asked to oversee the Sea and Ships section of the Festival of Britain in 1951 and to be chief designer of the *Campania* floating exhibition hall which toured 10 ports. From 1952–63 Holland was group art director for Erwin, Wasey and Company, the advertising agency, from 1963–71 head of the faculty of visual communication design at Birmingham Polytechnic. Holland was closely involved in the work of the Society of Industrial Artists and Designers, being its president, 1960–1, in 1980 publishing its history, *Minerva at Fifty*. Died in Pembury, Kent. Retrospective at Art Connoisseur in 1997.

Vera HOLLAND fl. c.1950–1975 Oil painter, tapestry designer and embroiderer. Born and lived at Sileby, Leicestershire, studying with Edgar Lander, then at Loughborough School of Art. Exhibited widely throughout Britain, including RI, SGA, SWA and locally in Leicester. Her work was reproduced in a number of publications, including *The Listener*, *Country Fair*, *The Countryman* and *The Lady*.

Laura HOLLIDAY 1958– Creator of wall-based sculptures – often humorous, sinister, or jokey portraits – made from found objects, papier mâché and paint, which could evolve over a period. She was born in Sydney, Australia, where she spent nine years before her family moved back to its roots in Penarth, near Cardiff, where she settled eventually at Roath. Gained an honours degree in fine art from South Glamorgan Institute of Higher Education, Cardiff, 1976–80, and her master's degree from Royal College of Art, 1982–5. In 1983 she won a Young Artists Grant from WAC, in 1986 a Pirelli Commission. Mixed shows included Stowells Trophy, RA, 1980; Invited Artists, WAC Gallery, Cardiff, 1986–7; Women Artists Open Exhibition, Cardiff Central Library, 1990; and The All-Women Cardiff Artists Show, Oriel Contemporary Art, 1996. Had a solo exhibition, Gossiping Teapots, The Old Hall, Cowbridge, 1982, later ones including Sculpture at St David's Hall, Cardiff, 1988, and Face to Face, Old Hall, Cowbridge, 1993.

Sarah HOLLIDAY 1960– Self-taught watercolourist whose London Unveiled show at New Academy Gallery, 1998, focused on the capital's changing scene. Holliday was elected a full member of RWS in 1996. In 1991 she had won the Saunders Waterford Award there, in 1989 the Arrobus Award for Watercolour at Camden Arts Centre. She was artist-in-residence, Commonwork Land Trust, Kent, 1990, and expedition artist to Borneo for Raleigh International, 1994. Mixed shows included David Curzon Gallery, 1992; SWA, 1993; and RSW, 1998.

Stephen HOLLINGSWORTH 1967– Artist using a variety of materials to create installations, as at New Art in Scotland, Centre for Contemporary Arts, Glasgow, 1994. Hollingsworth was born in Leeds, attended Gwent College of Higher Education, 1988–91, and the School of Art, Glasgow, 1992–4. He said that his work was "concerned with how as human beings we experience the world through our senses and the passage of time." Mixed shows included Leeds Open Artists Exhibition, from 1991, and Danger, School of Art Institute, Chicago, 1993, the year he had a solo show at the White Room, Glasgow School of Art.

Gerald HOLLIS 1908– Painter, educated privately. Exhibited RA, Leicester Galleries, RBA and in provinces. Had a number of one-man shows at Brook Street Art Gallery. Lived in Fulwood, Lancashire.

Richard HOLLIS 1934– Painter in oil lacquer, graphic designer and teacher, born in London, where he settled. He studied at Chelsea School of Art, 1954–5, Wimbledon School of Art, 1955–7, and Central School of Arts and Crafts, 1958–9, under William Turnbull. Between 1960–80 taught in various art schools, practised graphic design and in 1994 published *Graphic Design: A Concise History*. Hollis' own work was influenced by Venezuelan painting of the 1950s and Swiss Concrete Art. He showed at New Vision Centre Gallery and in 1993 was included in The Sixties Art Scene in London at Barbican Art Gallery. Richard Hollis: Graphics for the Whitechapel was held at Whitechapel Art Gallery, 1984.

Della HOLLOW 1922–1980 Artist in collage and watercolour who also practised interior decoration. Born at South Molton, Devon, Della Hollow – who sometimes signed her work only with her first name – studied art at Exeter School of Art, 1938–41, under Ruth Wood and Leighton Woollatt; she also had private lessons with Patrick Larking. Exhibited SWLA, RI and NS. Lived at Colyton, Devon.

Geoffrey HOLLOW 1944–1998 Self-taught painter of abstracts, born and based in London, who began painting in 1972. He had awards from the Arts Council, Elephant Trust and British and American Arts Foundation and held visiting lectureships in Britain and overseas. Took part in extensive group shows, including Made in Greenwich, The Living Room, 1994. Solo shows included Air Gallery, 1981; Greenwich Theatre Gallery, 1989; and Kepler Gallery, 1992. In 1993 he held a residency at City Museum & Art Gallery, Hanley, Stoke-on-Trent, with an accompanying exhibition. Several corporate collections hold examples.

Douglas Raymond HOLLOWAY 1923– Watercolourist and architect, born in London, who attended Royal West of England Academy School of Architecture, also studying watercolour with James Michie. He was in private practice in Bristol, then in the County Architect's Department for Kent, then Lancashire, 1959–84. He was a member of RWA. For many years Holloway concentrated mainly on the Lancashire scene, but also north Wales and Andalucia, where he spent part of each year. He used "a limited palette and avoided unnecessary detail which results in an apparent simplicity or Impressionist style. Most of my work is done in the studio, although I prefer to paint on the spot." Mixed shows included RCamA, Gloucester City Art Gallery and the Society of Architect Artists. In 1981 he had a solo show at Dallas Inman Gallery and in 1989 another at Vernon Gallery, both in Preston, Lancashire, where he lived at Longton. RWA holds his work.

Edgar HOLLOWAY 1914– Printmaker, watercolourist, calligrapher and teacher, born in Doncaster, Yorkshire, where his father was a frame maker. Aged 14 he began to attend classes at local School of Art and in 1931 had first solo show in London. While earning his living from etchings and portrait commissions Holloway studied under Randolph Schwabe at Slade School of Fine Art, where he proved an outstanding draughtsman. During World War II taught for a while, but illness prevented him continuing. Holloway became a Catholic and married a disciple of Eric Gill. He settled in Ditchling, Sussex, in 1949 and became a member of the Guild of St Joseph and St Dominic in which Gill was involved. By now Holloway had taken up lettering, signwriting, calligraphy and wood engraving, and he designed and worked as a cartographer for major publishing houses. In 1969 he returned to watercolour and, after his retirement, line engraving. Holloway showed at RBA and the Society of Artist Printmakers, both of which he was a member, as well as RA, RI and NEAC. He gave a large collection of his prints to Ashmolean Museum in Oxford, which held a show of them in 1991. Holloway was the father of Tim Holloway the artist. Edgar Holloway at 80 was at Kendal's Abbot Hall Art Gallery and Museum as part of a tour in 1994.

Edgar HOLLOWAY: *see* **James NOBLE**

Robert Charles HOLLOWAY 1914–1986 Painter in gouache and pastel, and teacher, born in Chelsea. He studied at Clapham School of Art and Royal College of Art under Sir William Rothenstein and Percy Hague Jowett. Holloway became art master at King's College School, where he established a small press producing art books. He showed at RA, RBA and NEAC and lived in Epsom, Surrey.

Ted HOLLOWAY 1926–1987 Painter, draughtsman and teacher, born in Upham, Hampshire, who left school at 15 and became a forestry worker for three years. At 18 he became a Bevin Boy in the Durham Coalfield, by which time he was drawing and painting. At 28 he attended classes at Durham University Extra-Mural Department, in 1958 won a bursary to study full-time at Sunderland College of Art, then gained an art teacher's diploma, with distinction, at London University. Holloway became head of art at Jarrow Springfield Comprehensive School, then gave up teaching to paint full-time in 1981. Moved to Charlton Kings, Gloucestershire, where he became fascinated by early Celtic art and mythology, but is best known for his long series of drawings based on his mining career. These were featured in a touring show, after his death on a painting trip to Scotland, originating in Stoke-on-Trent Art Gallery, in 1993. Accompanying it, Holloway's artist wife Gill produced a book of his drawings: *A Bevin Boy Remembers*.

Alexander HOLLWEG 1936– Painter, draughtsman, coloured wood relief maker and teacher, born in London, the grandson of the artist Edward Wadsworth. He said that his subject "has always been the same, people and their houses – where they work and where they play." After reading French and German at Oxford he studied at Camberwell School of Arts and Crafts from 1960–3. By

David Holmes in St Ives

DAVID HOLMES CHYWIDDEN, 6 CARNCROWS STREET, ST IVES, CORNWALL, TR26 1PJ • TEL: 01736 797068

1973 he was head of department at Maidstone College of Art, later teaching part-time at Bristol Polytechnic. After a solo show at Whitechapel Art Gallery in 1971, followed by shows at Felicity Samuel Gallery, 1972–7, there were several abroad. Was included in 5 Modern British Artists, Mark Glazebrook, 1983. Lived in Nettlecombe, Avon.

Agnes Gladys HOLMAN 1885–c.1967 Commercial artist and illustrator, specialising in animals, sculptor and miniaturist. Born at Charlton Kings, Gloucestershire, she studied at St John's Wood School of Art, then made a personal study of animals. Served in Women's Land Army during World War I. For some years was a member of council of the Royal Drawing Society, for which she was an examiner. Did an extensive amount of illustrative work for Oxford University Press, educational publications, *Western Daily Mail* and for book jackets. Exhibited SWA, RWA, RI, PS, in the provinces and abroad. Lived in Bath, Somerset.

George Alfred HOLMAN 1911– Sculptor and medallist, his talent was early spotted at school. Studied art at Hornsey School of Art under the sculptor Harold Youngman, 1927–34, after Hackney School of Art, 1925–27. Exhibited at RA and other London provincial galleries. Holman's sculpture has a feeling of mass and solidity, as in his Boy and Duck, illustrated in Eric Newton's monograph *British Sculpture 1944–1946*. Southgate Borough Council commissioned a bas-relief in stone for Broomfield Park. Lived at Leigh-on-Sea, Essex.

Jamie HOLMAN 1973– Artist using video and film, born in Inverness, who gained a fine art degree at Chelsea College of Art, 1994–7. Was included in Titanic Numbers at Blackburn College, 1994; Student Film Festival, Cornerhouse, Manchester, 1995; and New Contemporaries at Tate Gallery, Liverpool, and Camden Arts Centre, 1996.

Clyde HOLMES 1940– Landscape painter and poet, born in London, who trained at Hornsey College of Art, 1961–4, then St Martin's School of Art, 1964–5. Holmes moved with his family to a remote shepherd's cottage in Snowdonia National Park in 1970 – Capel Celyn, Frongoch, near Bala, Gwynedd – to live "in what most people would consider abject poverty". Initially, there was no telephone or electricity, no running water or gas, and the cottage was two miles from the nearest road. The wild, wet landscape became Holmes' subject. He published several volumes of verse, poems appearing in the *Anglo-Welsh Review, Poetry Wales, Poetry Review, London Magazine, Outposts* and elsewhere. Holmes gained a WAC Award for Painting, in 1978, also a commendation in WAC Award for Literature (Poetry) and a New Poetry Prize. Group shows included Canaletto Gallery, 1974; Our Native Land, Mostyn Gallery, Llandudno, 1979; Royal National Eisteddfod of Wales, from 1989; and Artists in National Parks, Victoria & Albert Museum, 1992. Had a solo show at Treadwell Gallery, 1973, later ones including Welsh Gallery, 1994. Hagen Museum, Germany, holds his work. In 1997, Holmes was featured in the documentary series *Visions of Snowdonia* on BBC2 Television.

David HOLMES 1939– Artist, teacher and gallery owner, born in Great Yarmouth, Norfolk. He studied at Leicester College of Art and Leicester University, 1957–62, then worked in Turkey in 1963. From 1963–78 Holmes taught at several London colleges, including a lecture tour of Europe, 1977. He settled in Peterborough, Cambridgeshire, in 1978, establishing the David Holmes Art Gallery in 1987. Holmes' own exhibitions included Foyles Art Gallery, 1961; Young Contemporaries, 1962; Ulster Museum, Belfast, 1964; AIA Gallery from 1966 (he was AIA news correspondent until it closed in the 1970s); and LG, 1976. In 1984 Holmes had a solo show, The Naked and the Nude, at City Museum & Art Gallery, Peterborough, influences being "a long-standing admiration for the Spanish poet Federico Garcia Lorca and a deepening sense of outrage at the political and social blunders of our time". From 1998 lived in St Ives, Cornwall, where he showed at Plumbline Gallery, having had a solo show there in 1996 at Salt House Gallery.

Frank HOLMES 1960– Painter and teacher who graduated in fine art from University of Ulster, Belfast, 1990. Went on to teach at St Mary's Training College, 1991, and Dunmurry High School, 1991–2. Took part in many group shows in the Belfast area, including Works on Paper and Beyond the Partitions, both in 1994 and put on by the Queen Street Studios, Belfast, with which Holmes was associated. Holmes participated in workshops, including The East Belfast Festival, 1991, and The Adventure Playground, Berlin, 1992, taking part in both the Belfast/Berlin Exchange and the Belfast/Bristol Exchange in that year.

Gilbert HOLMES 1952– Sculptor of steel abstracts, born in Otley, Yorkshire. He studied at Hull College of Art and St Martin's School of Art. Was included in Garden Exhibition 2, Camden Arts Centre, 1978. Lived for a time in London.

John HOLMES 1893–1980 Painter, teacher, administrator and writer, born in Derby, son of the watercolourist George Holmes, married the painter Vera Cathleen Taylor. Studied at Slade School of Fine Art, 1918–20, under Henry Tonks and Philip Wilson Steer, Royal College of Art, 1920–1, in Sweden and Germany. He went on to teach, including periods at Harrow School and as principal of the Regional College of Art, Manchester, also lecturing in education at Manchester University. Showed at Manchester City Art Gallery, Derby Art Gallery and elsewhere. Wrote several books, including *Applied Perspective* and *The Art of Interior Decoration.* While he was at the Manchester College Holmes, who was familiar with developments at the Bauhaus and in Scandinavia, introduced what was probably the first basic design course in an English art school, although he regarded the period prior to World War II, teaching colour theory at the Architectural Association, as his most important such achievement. Lived in Naphill, Buckinghamshire.

John HOLMES 1935– Artist working in oil, acrylic and Caran d'Ache who studied with Tom Eckersley at London College of Printing. He was an art director in advertising and was involved in that field and illustrated publishing throughout the world for 20 years. He had group appearances throughout Europe and solo shows with Nicholas Treadwell Gallery; Galerie L'Oeil Écoute, in Lyon; and Galerie "W", Annemass. Female Eunuch was a notable work of a painter interested in Surrealism. Museum of Modern Art in New York holds his work. Lived at Gooderstone, King's Lynn, Norfolk.

Katharine HOLMES 1962– Landscape painter, born in Malhamdale, Yorkshire, with a studio in Malham, whose subject was the local limestone terrain which she began painting in 1990. Studied fine art at Newcastle University and exhibited regularly, including 1996 Leeds Art Fair, and kept an open studio. Her landscapes were "not so much portraits of the landscape but evocations of the atmosphere of a place".

Keith HOLMES 1944– Artist in oil, pastel and charcoal, conservator and teacher, born in Richmond, Yorkshire. He gained a fine art degree at West Surrey College of Art and Design, Farnham, 1969–73 (teachers including Robin Ball and Harold Cheeseman), then a diploma in paper conservation at Camberwell School of Arts and Crafts, 1973–5. He was a fellow of the International Institute of Conservation. In 1977, Holmes was visiting professor teaching conservation at postgraduate level at New York University. During the 1970s and 1980s, he ran his own private press, producing limited editions which he printed, illustrated and bound by hand. His work can be found in the British Library, Victoria & Albert Museum and Trinity College in Dublin. British war artists influenced Holmes' work, in which sound draughtsmanship, detached analysis of spatial depth, a strong sense of colour and the fall of light were features. Holmes was artist-in-residence at the Science Museum, 1994–6, and painted a portrait of its director, Sir Neil Cossons. In 1990, work was commissioned by the officers' mess of the Royal Marines to commemorate the close of the School of Music, Deal. Holmes' many mixed shows included RSMA, PS, NEAC, ROI and Guild of Aviation Artists. Had a solo show at Greenwich Theatre Art Gallery, 1985, later ones including Royal Albert Hall, Army Flying Museum and Imperial College, all 1997, and The Royal College of Pathologists, 1998. Lived in London.

Kenneth HOLMES 1902– Painter, printmaker, writer, designer and teacher. Born in Skipton, Yorkshire, Holmes attended the School of Art there, 1919–21, Leeds College of Art, 1921–3, with periods at Central School of Arts and Crafts and Chelsea School of Art, Royal College of Art, 1923–7, then 1927–8 in Italy. Held a number of design consultancy posts and teaching positions, finally as principal of Leicester College of Art, 1934–56. Exhibited RA, NEAC, Fine Art Society, RHA, in the provinces and abroad and showed with war artists at National Gallery, London, during World War II. Victoria & Albert Museum and a number of provincial galleries hold his work. Wrote and broadcast on art. Holmes was especially noted as a fine architectural draughtsman. Lived for much of his life in Leicester, but retired near Boscastle, Cornwall.

Lesley HOLMES 1958– Untrained watercolourist, born in Lusaka in what became Zambia, West Africa. She spent her early life there before returning to England where she settled in Chipping Norton, Oxfordshire, setting up a studio open to the public part-time. Holmes was noted for her delicate watercolour views of the Cotswolds and for pictures of cats, reproduced as prints, cards and calendars by a number of commercial companies.

Marcus HOLMES 1875–1951 Painter, printmaker and teacher, born in Ipswich, Suffolk. Studied at Aberdeen School of Art, 1896–9, three years as a scholar at Herkomer School at Bushey, also in Paris and Florence. Holmes was a keen athlete, playing soccer for Dorset, cricket for Aberdeenshire, hockey for Hertfordshire and was a good middle- and long-distance runner. Was art master and a housemaster at Monmouth School, 1906–46, and was an Oxford University extension lecturer on art history, an occasional pungent remark showing that he was not in sympathy with every modern development. In 1930 with his wife, also an artist, Holmes formed the Wye Valley Arts Club (later Society). Exhibited RA, RCamA, RWA as an associate, Walker Art Gallery in Liverpool and Paris Salon. National Museum of Wales in Cardiff and Newport Museum and Art Gallery hold examples. Lived in Monmouth.

Mary Dawson HOLMES: *see* **Mary Dawson ELWELL**

Paul ROBERTS-HOLMES 1964– Sculptor and teacher who did a foundation course at Roehampton Institute, 1983–4, then a diploma in fine art at RA Schools, 1984–7. He became curator of Roche Court Sculpture Park and was an outreach tutor for RA. He showed at RA Summer Exhibitions from 1987, also at New Art Centre Sculpture Park from 1988, Crypt Gallery, 1990, and 1st RWA Open Sculpture Exhibition, 1993. Leicester County Council holds his work. Lived in East Winterslow, Wiltshire.

Philip HOLMES 1931– Painter and teacher whose father, John Holmes, was a wood carver. He studied at St Martin's School of Art, 1948–53, then in 1953 Hammersmith College of Art, also attending Borough Polytechnic classes under David Bomberg, whose teaching had a lasting effect on his work. In 1954 Holmes attended L'Académie de la Grande Chaumière, Paris, and in that summer Borough Bottega, Ronda, where he completed notable canvases. Holmes went on to teach at Havering Technical College. Painted widely abroad, including Israel, France, Greece, Italy and America. Showed solo at RBA Galleries, ICA, Studio Gallery and Beaux Arts Gallery. Was included in Borough Group show at Fine Art Associates, 1989.

Ronald HOLMES 1924–1970s Printmaker and teacher who studied at Sheffield and Royal Colleges of Art. He taught at Willesden School of Art, next at the College of Art in Leeds, where he lived, where he was head of printmaking, then of graphic design. Lino-cuts were a notable feature of his output. Was included in The Teaching Image, a Leeds College of Art staff show at Leeds City Art Gallery in 1964. Also took part in Arts Council travelling exhibitions. British Museum holds the work of Holmes, who was remembered as having "a good teaching ethic" by his Leeds student Derek Hyatt, who found a dead crow on Holmes' instruction for his outstanding print of that title. Holmes and his wife were killed in a car crash in the 1970s. British Museum holds colour woodcuts by him.

Lawrence HOLOFCENER 1926– Sculptor, playwright, lyricist, actor and director, born in Baltimore, Maryland, America. Holofcener modelled in clay and cast in bronze, and claimed Michelangelo, Rodin and Epstein as influences. He studied for a year at the Maryland Institute and at the New School in New York "at a class given by Chaim Gross. I lasted an hour." Holofcener took part in group exhibitions in Bucks County, Pennsylvania; Princeton, New Jersey; and in London. Had a first solo show at Gibbes Museum, Charleston, South Carolina, 1977, and latterly at Bruton Street Gallery, 1996, and The Catto Gallery, 1997. Catto commissioned Holofcener to produce a limited-edition maquette of his life-size sculpture Allies (Churchill and Roosevelt), unveiled in Bond Street in 1995. Other works by him included Faces of Olivier (28 in bas-relief), unveiled by Lord Olivier in 1985 at Chichester Theatre, Sussex; and Thomas Paine, unveiled in 1997 at Bordentown, New Jersey. For the stage, Holofcener wrote *Mr Wonderful*, starring Sammy Davis, Jr, on Broadway. His plays included *Before You Go*, Broadway and West End, and *The Bench*, off-Broadway. He acted on Broadway in *Stop The World* and *Hello, Dolly*. After he had settled in Ventnor, Isle of Wight, Holofcener began singing there in cabaret. Applied for British citizenship. Mrs Sammy Davis, Jr; Mayor Joseph Riley and the Unitarian Church, both in Charleston; AT&T, New Jersey; Actor's Equity in New York and British Equity; and the Screen Actor's Guild, New York, hold Holofcener's work.

Charlie HOLT 1947– Printmaker, painter, computer artist and teacher, born in Hitchin, Hertfordshire. He studied at Rochdale College of Art, 1964–6, with a travelling scholarship to Italy; then gained first-class diploma at Loughborough College of Art, 1966–9; obtained art teacher's certificate from Brighton Polytechnic, 1969–70; then his master's degree at Manchester Polytechnic, 1984–5. Holt went on to teach in schools and colleges, latterly at Liverpool Institute of Higher Education. Influences on his work cited were Hitchens, Dufy, Gauguin, Morandi and Magritte. Holt's pictures had "their roots in the Garden of Eden, in a cycle of life". Exhibitions included Manchester Academy, from 1977; Liverpool Academy, 1980; RA Summer Exhibitions, from 1982; Hanover Gallery, Liverpool, 1986; Royal Festival Hall, 1990; and Colin Jellicoe Gallery, Manchester, 1992. Lived at Croston, Lancashire.

Eric Stace HOLT 1944–1997 Painter, especially in tempera, and draughtsman, brought up in Surrey where he initially worked as a painter in Purley, later living near Sandringham, Norfolk. Attended Epsom and Ewell School of Art, 1959–62, where his teachers included Eric Rodway and Leslie Worth; then Wimbledon School of Art, but left after a short time to paint on his own. Economic demands caused him to take up a number of dead-end jobs, then he freelanced as a glass painter and antiques restorer, which revived his interest in painting. Showed in mixed exhibitions at RBA and RA, where his pictures prompted an overwhelming response from public and dealers. Had several one-man shows in 1970s with Maltzahn Gallery, later showing with Piccadilly Gallery. Holt's work falls into two broad categories: Biblical incidents in modern dress and scenes from country and suburban life. The design element is strong, the artist distorting figures if he felt it necessary. Holt was a slow, meticulous and self-critical artist, with a strong interest in the countryside, its crafts and pursuits. He continued to work, even after contracting the brain cancer that killed him.

Gwynneth HOLT 1909– Sculptor in a variety of materials, born in Wednesbury, Staffordshire, married to the sculptor T B Huxley-Jones. After a convent education in Birmingham Holt studied at Wolverhampton School of Art, 1925–30, under the sculptor Robert Emerson. Holt's work could be graceful and stylised, as shown in the three examples in Arthur T Broadbent's 1949 monograph *Sculpture Today in Great Britain 1940–1943*. She was a fellow of RBS and was for a time an associate of RBSA. Also showed at RA, in the provinces and with Royal Glasgow Institute of the Fine Arts. St Felix' School in Southwold; St Margaret Church, Downham; and the Church of the Immaculate Conception, Chelmsford, hold examples, as do Aberdeen, Leamington and Wolverhampton public galleries. Lived in Eynsham, Oxfordshire.

Herbert HOLT 1891–1978 Portrait painter in oil, son of stained glass artist Henry Holt. Attended St Helens School of Art, Liverpool School of Art and Slade School of Art. Exhibited RA, RCamA, Paris and Walker Art Gallery, Liverpool, which holds his work. In 1958 he published *Portrait Painting in Oils*. Member of Chelsea Arts Club and lived latterly in London.

Lilian HOLT 1898–1983 Painter, born in London. She attended Putney School of Art, but economic necessity forced her to work for Prudential Assurance Company from 1915–22, when she studied at Regent Street Polytechnic School of Art. Married to the art and antiques dealer Jacob Mendelson, 1923–8, then married the painter David Bomberg. Painted with Bomberg widely overseas and became a founder-member of Borough Group, showing Archer Gallery, Arcade Gallery and elsewhere. Had a retrospective at Ben Uri Gallery in 1980, from which Tate Gallery bought a landscape, like much of her work strongly influenced by Bomberg, called Tajo Ronda. After Bomberg's death Lilian, supported by her daughter Dinora Mendelson, also a member of the Borough Group, devoted years to promoting David Bomberg's work.

Roy HOLT 1942– Painter and teacher, born in Sutton, Surrey. He studied at Epsom and Ewell School of Art, 1959–62, Royal

Academy Schools, 1962–6, and Goldsmiths' College School of Art, 1985–7. Became a senior lecturer at Liverpool Polytechnic. Holt participated in many group shows, notably in London, and his related abstract canvases Bands Eroded were included in John Moores Liverpool Exhibition, 1989–90. Had a solo exhibition Contexts and Thresholds at Flaxman Gallery, 1989, another at Dean Clough Contemporary Art Gallery, Halifax, 1990. Lived in London.

Brenda HOLTAM 1960– Painter and teacher, born in Whiteway, Gloucestershire, who studied at Gloucestershire College of Art and Design, 1979; with Francis Hewlett at Falmouth School of Art, 1980–3, gaining a first-class honours degree; then did a postgraduate diploma in painting, 1983–6, under Peter Greenham. Taught adult education classes from 1988. Was elected RWS in 1992. Mixed exhibitions included Newlyn Orion Gallery in Penzance, 1982, RA Summer Exhibitions from 1985, NEAC from 1987, and Wherry Quay Gallery, Ipswich, from 1991. Shared a show with Victoria Rees at Cadogan Contemporary, 1994. Lived in London.

Robin HOLTOM 1944– Artist and teacher who worked in oil, charcoal, ciment fondu and screenprinting. He studied at Chelsea School of Art, 1963–6, then Royal College of Art, 1967–70, teachers including Patrick Caulfield and Ken Kiff. Holtom worked as an art therapist, 1970–80; from 1984–94 ran residential courses in Wales, where he settled at Llechryd, Cardigan; then was a full-time artist. His main works included paintings of oak trees, hill landscapes and dancers. Group shows included Fountain Gallery, Llandeilo; Dyfed Open; PS Annual; and Y Tabernacl, Museum of Modern Art, Wales, in Machynlleth, which holds his work. Solo shows included Battersea Arts Centre; Chapter Arts, Cardiff; CCA Gallery, Bath; Oriel Contemporary Art, 1995; and Ozten Zeki Gallery, 1996, where his exhibition The Road to Mensano indicated Holtom's liking for powerful colours and a simplification of shape in landscape.

Dora HOLZHANDLER 1928– Painter in the naive style, born in France. She became a student at Anglo-French Art Centre in London in 1946 where she met her future husband, George Swinford, and settled in Hampstead. She exhibited at Young Contemporaries in 1949 and at Beaux Arts Gallery in 1954 in mixed exhibitions, and many such appearances followed in Britain and abroad. Had a solo exhibition at Chenil Gallery in 1960, others including a series at Langton Gallery in the 1970s, Concourse Gallery, 1984–5, Crane Kalman, 1985, Graham Modern Gallery in New York in 1986, Bowmoore Gallery, 1989–91, and Beaux Arts, Bath, 1996. Eric Newton, the *Manchester Guardian* critic, called Holzhandler's work that of "a temperamental primitive ... colourful as a Persian illumination, always brilliant, but never harsh." Nuffield Foundation and a number of notable private collectors hold examples.

Gordon HOME 1878–1969 Painter, draughtsman and writer with a special interest in topography and history, British and foreign. Born in London, he was a self-taught painter who showed at RA and Royal Glasgow Institute of the Fine Arts. Member of Art Workers' Guild. He had work illustrated in magazines such as *The Studio*, *Connoisseur* and *Illustrated London News*, his books including *Yorkshire Coast and Moorland Scenes*, 1904, and *History and Antiquities of Cyprus*, 1958. Lived in St Boswells, Roxburghshire, and in London.

Grace HOMER 1907– Painter, teacher, born in Liverpool. She attended Liverpool College of Art in 1940s, her teachers including Will Penn. She went on to teach locally, notably at the Mabel Fletcher Technical College, following a period at Liverpool School for the Blind, where she taught art. Took up embroidery and won a prize in the International Poliomyelitis Embroidery Competition in 1958. Also showed pictures at RA, SWA, RBA and elsewhere. Lived in Liverpool where she was a member of the Sandon Studios Society Club.

Arthur HOMESHAW 1933– Artist in various media and teacher who attended West of England College of Art, Bristol, 1951–4, then 1956–7. He went on to teach at Queen Elizabeth's School in Crediton, Devon, where he lived. Homeshaw completed a mural for Temple Meads Station, Bristol. He was a member of RWA, which holds his work, and showed at RA, RE and elsewhere. Had a one-man show with Patricia Wells Gallery in Thornbury in 1981.

Evie HONE 1894–1955 Painter and artist in stained glass, born in Dublin. She was descended from Joseph Hone, brother of the Royal Academician Nathaniel Hone, and she was partly crippled by infantile paralysis. After studying with Walter Sickert at Westminster School of Art Hone attended Byam Shaw School of Drawing and Painting and was with Bernard Meninsky at Central School of Arts and Crafts. The 1920s were spent largely in Paris, where she studied briefly with André Lhote, then for a much longer period with the pioneer Cubist painter and theoretician Albert Gleizes. In 1924 Hone and her friend Mainie Jellett shared a show at Dublin Painters' Gallery. She also showed with the 7 & 5 Society for some years and exhibited widely in Paris, being a founder-member of Abstraction-Création in 1932. Under the influence of Rouault, Hone turned to stained glassmaking, and her burgeoning reputation led to some impressive commissions. Eton College Chapel and St Michael's in Highgate are two examples, and the Tate Gallery has The Crucifixion by her. Arts Council held memorial show in 1959.

Michael HONNOR 1944– Painter and printmaker who between 1962–8 studied at Oxford University, Hornsey College of Art and Byam Shaw School of Drawing and Painting. From 1969 he lived in Devon as an artist whose work was especially concerned with weather and water: the Atlantic coast of Cornwall, Dartmoor rivers and the Yorkshire Dales. He was director of the print workshop at Dartington Hall Craft Education Centre and Wilkey's Moor Print Workshop. One-man shows included St Catherine's College, Oxford, 1964; Greenwich Theatre Gallery,

1970; Exeter Arts Centre from 1984; Sue Rankin Gallery from 1988; and Thackeray Gallery, 1996. Collections included many British High Commissions and Embassies; Worcester College, Oxford; London Institute of Education; and corporate collections including Barclays Bank, Citibank and Trust House Forte. Honnor's pictures caught the essence of a place, sparkling and atmospheric, using a rich palette.

Ernest HOOD 1932–1988 Painter, born in Edinburgh, son of a lithographer. Studied at Glasgow School of Art, 1952–6. He became a member of the Royal Glasgow Institute of the Fine Arts, also showing with RSW, RSA, RWS and elsewhere. The Kelvingrove Art Gallery in Glasgow, where Hood lived, holds his work.

Harvey HOOD 1946– Sculptor and teacher, born in Staffordshire. He studied at Birmingham College of Art, 1965–9, and Royal College of Art, 1969–72. Lectured part-time at Leicester Polytechnic, 1972–3, then became senior lecturer at Cardiff College of Art and visiting lecturer at various colleges. Hood's awards included a prize for young contemporaries from Arts Council, 1971; Sainsbury Award, 1973; Arts Council Major Purchase Award, 1981; and artist-in-residence, Bishop's Palace, St Davids, 1986. In 1990 he gained a WAC Special Project Grant for researching the way architects and artists were educated, travelling to many countries. In 1981 Hood created Archform at Newport Station, commissioned by British Rail. Participated in many exhibitions including The Young Contemporaries, Arts Council tour, 1968; Ikon Gallery, Birmingham, 1969; Mostyn Art Gallery, Llandudno, 56 Group Show, 1981; Six Sculptors from Wales, touring Finland, 1987; and Sculpture at Canterbury, 1991. Solo shows included Oriel, WAC, Cardiff, 1979. Lived near Raglan, Gwent.

Harry HOODLESS 1913– Artist in oil and tempera and teacher, born in Leeds, where he studied at the College of Art, 1929–33, then at Royal College of Art, 1933–6, teachers including Edward Bawden and Eric Ravilious. Hoodless taught at Norwich School of Art, 1936–9, then at Laird School of Art in Birkenhead, 1939–76, from 1946 being principal. Hoodless was noted for his landscapes featuring dockyard debris and decay, and he cited Seurat, Edward Wadsworth, Tristram Hillier and Graham Sutherland as influences. Hoodless was a member of Liverpool Academy and Wirral Society of Arts. His exhibitions included RA, Leeds City Art Gallery, Bluecoat Gallery in Liverpool and Atkinson Art Gallery, Southport. He also showed at two galleries which hold his work: Walker Art Gallery in Liverpool and Williamson Art Gallery in Birkenhead. Lived in West Kirby, Wirral.

Charlie HOOKER 1953– Born and based in London, Hooker was interested in exploring and fusing aspects of music, dance and the visual arts. His systems-based works were focused on specific spaces and were not repeated elsewhere. Hooker studied at Croydon College of Art and Brighton Polytechnic. He produced a series of audio and video tapes. Performances included Six Sound Pieces, Robert Self Gallery, 1975; Percussion Walk 23 (one of a series), Chelsea School of Art, 1978; Tate Gallery, 1981; James Hockey Gallery, Farnham, 1990; and Camden Arts Centre, 1991. Arts Council holds examples.

Dora HOOPER fl. c.1920–1960 Painter in oil and watercolour. Studied at St John's Wood Art School, 1913–14, under Leonard Walker, then at the Westminster Technical Institute. Exhibited UA, RI, SWA, RWS, RCamA and Paris Salon. Lived near Penzance, Cornwall.

George HOOPER 1910–1994 Painter in oil and watercolour, and teacher, born in Gorakhpur, India. In 1912 he moved to England to live with his grandfather and to be schooled. After two years with the Westminster Bank Hooper studied in 1930–1 at Slade School of Fine Art, moving to Royal Academy Schools under Tom Monnington in 1931–5. There he won two gold medals, a travelling scholarship and the Rome Scholarship in Painting, which gave him two years in Rome after a few months in Madrid, 1935–8. During World War II Hooper served in Air Raid Precautions and was invited to join the Pilgrim Trust's *Recording Britain* project. In the 1950s Hooper designed posters for General Post Office, Esso, Shell and other companies. By then he had begun to teach: from 1943–5 at Watford Grammar School; 1945–77 at Brighton Polytechnic department of fine art; and from 1948–77 he lectured for Workers' Educational Association, affiliated to London University. A visit in 1958 to Italy appears to have released Hooper's rich palette, perhaps nurtured in India. In mid-1940s began exhibiting at Leicester Galleries, also appearing in mixed shows with LG and RBA. Later solo shows included Odette Gilbert Gallery, 1984–6, and Sally Hunter Fine Art, 1988, with a memorial show at Michael Parkin Gallery, 1995. Victoria & Albert Museum and British Museum hold examples. Wrote articles for *The Artist* magazine. Lived in Redhill, Surrey.

John HOOPER 1939– Painter of geometrical abstracts, and teacher, born in Morocco, who studied at Camberwell School of Art, 1958–62; Royal College of Art, 1962–5; in latter year won the J Andrew Lloyd Royal College Scholarship for Landscape, which took him to Greece, and an Italian Government Scholarship, to Perugia. A French Government Scholarship enabled Hooper to work in Paris in 1965–6, a Canada Council Grant facilitating travel in Canada and to New York in 1969. He also taught in Canada on several occasions. Mixed shows included Young Contemporaries at RBA Galleries from 1960; LG at same Galleries from 1961; John Moores Liverpool Exhibition, 1963; RA Summer Exhibition, 1965; and Wapping Artists Open Studios from 1980. Solo shows included University of Surrey, Guildford, 1976. Lived in London.

Miriam Mabel HOOPER 1872–1953 Landscape watercolourist, born and lived in Redhill, Surrey, also home of her nephew the painter George Hooper. She studied at Croydon School of Art under Walter Wallis and James Shannon whose work she much admired, and she also went on sketching parties with William Tatton Winter, to whom she was related through her brother's marriage. She sketched extensively in England and on the continent. Exhibited at RA, RI, Walker Art Gallery in Liverpool and RWA and was a member of RSW Art Club. There was an exhibition at Bourne Gallery, Reigate, in 1994.

Polly HOPE 1934– Artist who trained as a ballet dancer and subsequently at the Slade School School of Fine Art. Hope worked extensively throughout Europe. Although she studied initially as a painter and sculptor, she made her reputation with large quilted fabric works, mostly on an architectural scale. Commissions included Cwmbran New Town, St Peter's Church in Whitstable, the headquarters of NMB Bank, Amsterdam, and the Victoria & Albert Museum. She had many solo shows in Europe and America and was the second wife of the sculptor Theo Crosby.

Rosa HOPE 1902–1972 Painter, etcher and teacher, born in Manchester, twin sister of the portrait painter Muriel Hollinger and daughter of an art teacher. In 1919 attended Slade School of Fine Art under Henry Tonks and Philip Wilson Steer; was later at Central School of Arts and Crafts. In 1926 her etching Adoration of the Shepherds won Prix de Rome. In 1935–8 taught etching and drawing at the Michaelis School of Fine Art in South Africa, from 1938–57 being a senior lecturer at University of Natal. Exhibited extensively in Britain and South Africa, including RA, NEAC, RE, Natal Society of Artists, South African Academy and on the continent. Frequently painted the Drakensberg Mountains and the Transkei. Hope's work showed technical mastery of her medium, but was doggedly conservative in style. Represented in many South African galleries as well as British Museum and Victoria & Albert Museum. Died at Kokstad, Cape Province.

Eleanora HOPE HENDERSON 1917– Painter in oil and watercolour, born in Edinburgh as Eleanora Anderson Spence. She painted until 1966 as Eleanora Anderson Borrie; "I just used the name Borrie." She was a student at Edinburgh College of Art, 1935–40, under William Gillies, John Maxwell and Robert Westwater. She "won the highest award for my year and a Travelling Scholarship". Hope Henderson was elected SSA and won the Guthrie Award. She also showed at RA, RSA, RP, with Dumfries Art Society and elsewhere in Scotland and England. Solo exhibitions included Woodstock Gallery. Lived in Achie, New Galloway, Kirkcudbrightshire.

Don HOPES 1935– Artist, born in Bristol, originally trained as an engineer, who studied painting at Slade School of Fine Art. For a time he worked with the sculptor Kenneth Martin. An example of Hopes' cleverly engineered kinetic sculpture is the aluminium Untitled, 1983, in Portsmouth City Museum and Art Gallery's garden. Exhibitions included that gallery, 1980 and 1983, with a show of drawings at the local Aspex Gallery in 1995 which had been prepared originally for a room at Glynn Vivian Art Gallery, Swansea.

Alan John HOPKINS 1930–1974 Painter in oil, born in Harrow, Middlesex, who studied at the local School of Art with John Gerald Platt and Christopher Sanders, at Slade School of Fine Art under Claude Rogers and at Royal Academy Schools. Although a brilliant student Hopkins suffered from schizophrenia, which prevented him reaching his full potential. His first wife was the artist Rosa Branson, with whom he shared a show at Woodstock Gallery in 1962. Also exhibited in Four Young Painters at Parsons Gallery, 1955, RA Summer Exhibition RBA, LG and Young Contemporaries. Died from cancer at Royal Marsden Hospital, Sutton, Surrey.

Clyde HOPKINS 1946– Painter and teacher, born Bexhill, Sussex. Graduated from Reading University, 1969, and went on to paint and teach part-time, eventually becoming head of painting at Winchester School of Art. Hopkins' abstract works evoked huge space and cloud-like forms, his later work having a darker surface with light sources behind. He was represented in a number of survey shows, including the South Bank Centre's 1988–9 touring exhibition The Presence of Painting. In 1985–6 a one-man show toured Britain including Ikon Gallery, Birmingham, and had solo exhibition at Francis Graham-Dixon Gallery, 1992. Had a studio in Hastings, Sussex.

Louise HOPKINS 1965– Painter, born in Hertfordshire, who gained a bachelor's degree in fine art at Newcastle Polytechnic, 1985–8, and her master's at Glasgow School of Art, 1992–4. Was included in New Art in Scotland, at CCA, Glasgow, 1994; Swarm, a Scottish Arts Council touring show, 1995; and New Contemporaries at Tate Gallery, Liverpool, and Camden Arts Centre, 1996. Solo shows included Tramway, Glasgow, and Andrew Mummery, both 1996; artconnexion, Nice, and Galerie Isabella Kacprzak, Berlin, both 1997; and Galleria Raffaella, Cortese, Milan, 1998. Arts Council, Aberdeen Art Gallery in Aberdeen, British Council and Saatchi Collection hold examples.

Penny HOPKINS 1943– Painter mainly in watercolour with some oils, and teacher, born in Haywards Heath, Sussex, daughter of the artist Norman Clark. She studied at Brighton Art College, 1961–5, teachers including Charles Knight, her father, George Hooper, Raymond Briggs, Justin Todd, John Lord, John Lawrence, Jennifer Dickson and John R Biggs. Hopkins was a part-time teacher with private pupils and did some commission work in early years. After divorce in 1988 she became assistant art teacher at Burgess Hill School and began painting again. Was a member of Sussex Watercolour Society, taking part in group shows at RWS, Southover Gallery in Lewes and at Hove Museum and Art Gallery. Had solo exhibitions at Burstow Gallery in Brighton, Rottingdean Gallery and Terrace Gallery, Worthing. Lived in Cowfold, Sussex.

John HOPKINSON 1941– Figurative artist who studied at Grimsby School of Art. Among his shows were Drawings of Importance at Roland, Browse & Delbanco, 1978; Wingfield

Gallery, 1988; Camden Arts Centre, 1990; and in 1993 he was in Two Plus Two at 33 Mossop Street.

Gill HOPLEY 1947– Artist who did a foundation course at Liverpool Polytechnic, 1980–1, then an honours degree there, 1981–4, winning a Sir John Moores Scholarship in final year. She was featured in Stowells Trophy Exhibition at RA, 1984; Sir John Moores Scholarship Retrospective, 1985; and showed with Walker Art Gallery, Liverpool, Merseyside Artists tours from 1985. In 1985 she obtained a Belle Vale Murals Commission.

Ruth HOPWELL 1923– Painter and teacher, initially educated in Northampton. Attended Northampton School of Art, 1939–42, then Royal College of Art, 1942–5, under Francis Helps, Gilbert Spencer and Percy Horton. Exhibited RA and Bradford City Art Gallery, Hertfordshire Education Committee buying her work. From 1945 taught at Howell's School, Denbigh, north Wales, where she lived.

Richard HORE 1935– Painter, muralist and teacher, born in Clacton-on-Sea, Essex, who attended Colchester School of Art, 1951–5, teachers including John O'Connor, then Royal College of Art, 1956–60, with Leonard Rosoman, Carel Weight and Ruskin Spear, winning a silver medal for mural painting in the latter year. Went on to teach at Wrexham College of Art. Showed at RA, WAC, Mostyn Art Gallery in Llandudno, and elsewhere. National Maritime Museum in Greenwich holds his work. Lived in Chester, Cheshire.

Ronald T HORLEY 1904– Painter and draughtsman of architectural subjects, born in Pinner, Middlesex. Attended Radley College, Berkshire, then studied art at Heatherley's School of Fine Art, 1921–4, St John's Wood School of Art and Central School of Arts and Crafts. Showed at RA and RI. Lived in London.

David HORN 1937– Sculptor, draughtsman and teacher, born in London, but moved shortly after to Pembroke Dock, Wales, where he attended the Grammar School. Attended Chelsea School of Art, 1956–60, then Royal College of Art, 1960–4, winning the drawing prize in 1964. Left to teach at St Martin's School of Art, followed by other teaching posts in London, Leicester, Watford and Nottingham. Showed in many group exhibitions, including AIA Gallery, Young Contemporaries at RBA Galleries, Sculpture 60–66 Arts Council touring exhibition, Time Space at Bristol University, Royal National Eisteddfod and WAC. In 1965 completed sculpture for Cwmbran New Town. Arts Council owns his bronze Asleep in the Sofa, of 1963–64, and WAC also has work.

Eric HORN 1910–1953 Primarily a commercial artist, Wilfrid Eric Horn was born at West Bergholt, Essex. Studied at Colchester School of Art, Camberwell School of Art under Eric Fraser, St Martin's School of Art and Sutton School of Art. He was art director for several advertising agencies. Lived in West Wickham, Kent.

Winifred HORNBLOWER 1879– Bank clerk who painted part-time until she retired. She studied at the Laird School of Art and at RMS with Alyn Williams. Hornblower exhibited extensively at Walker Art Gallery in Liverpool, RA, RCamA, Royal Glasgow Institute of the Fine Arts and at Paris Salon. Was a member of Liver Sketching Club and lived in Birkenhead, Cheshire.

Anna HORNBY 1914– Painter and calligrapher who was educated at Westonbirt School, Gloucestershire, eventually settling in the county at Upper Slaughter. After a brief period of study in Italy with landscape and flower painter Aubrey Waterfield Hornby attended Byam Shaw School of Drawing and Painting, 1934–40, teachers including Francis Ernest Jackson. She was a member of the Art Workers' Guild and NEAC, also showing with RA, RWA and RBA.

Jocelyn HORNER 1902–1973 Sculptor and teacher, born in Halifax, where she continued to live. She entered Leeds School of Art in 1920 to train as a sculptor, with Henry Moore and Barbara Hepworth as fellow students. During the 1920s Miss Horner began a series of children portraits and animal studies and during World War II became a home teacher for the blind. After 1945 she returned to Leeds as a student and in the early-1950s became a part-time teacher of modelling and woodcarving at the Percival Whitley College, Halifax, also teaching at Halifax Art College. Her later work came increasingly under the influence of Jacob Epstein, and the 1960s saw her sculptures exhibited locally and nationally. Horner won the Leeds Gold Medal under the annual award for work by artists born of Yorkshire parents. Her head of a blind man is in the London headquarters of the Royal National Institute for the Blind; she did a group of the Brontë sisters for the Parsonage Museum, Haworth; and her bust and hands of Sir John Barbirolli are held by the Hallé Concert Society in Manchester. A memorial show was held at Stable Court Galleries, Temple Newsam, Leeds.

Elizabeth HOROSZY-RIDLEY 1948– Artist in paint, ceramics and mixed media born in Warsaw, Poland, where she studied history of art at Warsaw University. Settled in England from 1968, with extended periods in Greece and France. Graduated in fine art with honours at London Guildhall University (formerly Sir John Cass School). She worked voluntarily with those suffering from chronic mental health illnesses and gave workshops, some for children with learning disabilities. Group shows included Heifer Gallery from 1993; Hop Exchange, part of Southwark Festival, from 1994; and Etcetera Gallery, 1996. Solo exhibitions included Ashford Library and in the National Museum, Nieborow Palace, Poland, both 1997. Lived in London.

Michael HOROVITZ 1935– Experimental artist, performance poet, jazz musician, song writer and singer, editor and writer, born in Frankfurt, Germany, but moved to London aged two years. Graduated in English at Oxford University, 1954–9. In the late-1950s was associated with jazz music scene in London and Pop generation. In 1959 helped to start New Departures publications. Improvised first jazzpoems with Dudley Moore, Joe Harriott, Ronnie Scott and others and was on the road in extensive jazz gigs. Conducted Live New Departures art circuses. In 1963 published monograph on artist Alan Davie, by whose work he was influenced. During 1960s showed at AIA, RBA, Ben Uri and ICA. In the 1970s published *Love Poems*, then *The Wolverhampton Wanderer*. Horovitz gained the Arts Council Writers' Award in 1978 and the Translators' Award for the book *Egghead Republic* by Arno Schmidt in 1979. Later activities included compiling and presenting *Poetry Now* programmes for BBC Radio 3; publishing *Growing Up: Selected Poems & Pictures 1951–79*, in 1979; and launching Poetry Olympics in 1980. In 1986 his *Midsummer Morning Jog Log* appeared with drawings by Peter Blake, in memoriam Frances Horovitz. From the mid-1980s returned to substantial art work. Had solo show at Combined Harvest Gallery, 1987; Bop Paintings, Collages, Picture-Poems, 1962–1971, was held at England & Co, 1989; and there was a 50-year retrospective at Amberden Estates in 1997.

Artur HOROWICZ 1898–1962 Commercial artist in tempera and line. Born in Warsaw, he studied art there and in Berlin in the early-1920s. Exhibited in London and on the continent and in Britain illustrated books and drew for such publications as *The Illustrated London News* and *The Sketch*. In Poland he had served as artist to the War Ministry, 1927–39, to the Polish Air Force, 1940, and to its Air Ministry, 1943–6. Lived in Surbiton, Surrey.

Nancy HORROCKS 1900–1989 Abstract artist with a fine feeling for texture, born in Compton, Hampshire, daughter of the architect Brook T Kitchin. She attended Winchester High School, also studying at Slade School of Fine Art, 1918–20, and Chelsea School of Art. Was married to Lieutenant-General Sir Brian Horrocks, notable World War II soldier (their only daughter drowned while swimming in the Thames in 1979), who latterly became a popular television broadcaster on military matters. Horrocks was included in WIAC and travelling exhibitions, 1958–65; New Vision Centre Gallery and Knott Gallery, Dallas, both 1961; Grabowski Gallery, 1962; Heal's Mansard Gallery, 1964; and in 1965, Bradford and Northampton City Art Galleries and Grosvenor Gallery. Solo exhibitions included AIA Gallery, 1960, and New Gallery, Belfast, 1965. The abstract artist Adrian Heath thought highly of her pictures, writing that "The quality … in all her works is directness." Lived at Singleton, Sussex; latterly at Knowle Park Nursing Home, Cranleigh; with a funeral at Putney Crematorium.

William Eric HORSBRUGH-PORTER 1905–1985 Painter and writer, born in Dalkey, near Dublin, Ireland, commonly known as Eric. He went to Bedales School, then attended Slade School of Fine Art, 1924–8, under Henry Tonks; he gained Slade and Robert Ross Scholarships and was a prizeman. Horsbrugh-Porter's friends included such fellow-students as William Coldstream and William Townsend, in whose journals he appears. He was a keen tennis player of high standard. Helped Stephen Bone on his Piccadilly Underground station murals. During World War II Horsbrugh-Porter served in the Royal Navy as a first lieutenant on aircraft carriers, including *Indomitable*. In 1929 Horsbrugh-Porter had married Monica Maude, daughter of Captain Anthony Maude and Eva Beresford, of Belgard Castle, Dublin. After the war he joined his father's stockbroking firm there, Porter, Millard and Irvine. In 1947 Horsbrugh-Porter, as Eric Porter, published *Saturn's Child*, a fairly racy novel based on the life of the Spanish painter Goya, which was translated into several languages. He showed at RHA, 1926–52, also at Cooling Galleries, RA, NEAC, ROI and elsewhere. His most successful works, sometimes commissioned and known in the family as his "grassy pictures", gave a worm's eye view of meadows of vetch, ladybirds, and so on. Latterly he used coloured glass in large landscapes and seascapes, one being bought by Shelbourne Hotel, Dublin. Sometimes signed his pictures with the initials H P.

Hannah HORSFALL 1963– Artist, born in London. She studied at Central School of Art and Design, 1982–3. Moved to the Isle of Skye, in 1985 she began drawing with Malcolm Bell, their drawings being joint efforts; each had the right to make and obliterate marks. An example of their abstract work was Twentysixth Drawing, in 1992 East & South Norwich Gallery/Kent Institute of Art and Design show. Eventually worked in London.

Nicholas HORSFIELD 1917– Artist in graphic media and oils and teacher, born in New Malden, Surrey. He studied at Royal College of Art, 1935–8, under Sir William Rothenstein, Percy Jowett and Gilbert Spencer, then after war service, 1939–46, became Arts Council regional officer for visual arts for the north-west region in Manchester, 1948–56. From 1956–77 Horsfield lectured at Liverpool College of Art/Liverpool Polytechnic, then became part-time faculty tutor in life drawing, 1977–82. Horsfield was a member of Liverpool Academy of Art from 1954, being president, 1960–5, and was also a member of Merseyside Contemporary Artists. Solo shows included Bluecoat Chambers, Liverpool, from 1963; University of Shefield, 1974; University of Durham, 1975; and Chateau Musée in Dieppe and Camden Arts Centre, 1984. Sickert and de Staël were both influences on Horsfield's work and Normandy was a recurring subject from the early 1950s as the landscape of the Crosby area of Liverpool, where he settled, was to become. Arts Council, Liverpool University, Atkinson Art Gallery in Southport, Manchester City Art Galleries, Chateau Musée and Walker Art Gallery in Liverpool (which gave Horsfield a retrospective in 1997) hold examples.

Susan HORSFIELD 1928– Artist in wide variety of media and teacher, born in Poona, India. She graduated in fine art from Regent Street Polytechnic School of Art in 1952, teachers having included Patrick Millard, Norman Blamey, David Smith and Ian Mackay. She did varied freelance work alongside teaching, including James Gardner Associates. From 1969–86 she was head of art department at Farrington's School, Chislehurst, also lecturing in further education and at field study centres. Lived at Bessels Green, Sevenoaks, Kent, drawing on the Shoreham Valley landscape for her work. Horsfield was a member of WIAC. She showed with RBA, RWS and LG. Had a solo show at Walker's Galleries, others including Bear Lane Gallery, Oxford, 1962; Heal's Mansard Gallery, 1968; Sheffield University, 1980; Digby Gallery, Colchester, from 1984; and St John's, Smith Square, 1987.

Malcolm HORSLEY 1925–1991 Painter and yachtsman, born in Sydney, Australia. After active Army service in Far East Horsley studied painting with Desidirius Orban and at Sydney College of Art, graduating in 1950. He moved to London and managed the Savage Gallery. Although he painted in Spain and Corsica, producing figurative, lyrical work, and having shows in London, Barcelona and Paris, Horsley's interest in art had by the early 1960s begun to give way to his early passion for sailing, dating back to the building of his own dinghy in Sydney in the early 1940s. From the 1960s he raced, chartered and refitted seagoing yachts; at Porto Cervo in Sardinia running the port, the charter boat company, berth sales and acting as a consultant; established himself as an independent marine surveyor and worked for three years with Northrop and Johnson of Cannes; and formed Malcolm J Horsley International. Lived in his own-build house in Corsica for a time, where he also farmed. Died in Singapore.

Kathleen Finlay HORSMAN 1911– Artist in gouache and potter, born in London. Studied at Hornsey School of Art, 1929–33, with John Moody, then at the Royal College of Art, 1933–7, with William Staite Murray, the potter. She held a number of teaching positions, notably at Edinburgh College of Art. Exhibited RSA, SSA and elsewhere in Scotland, signing her work H. RSA holds her work. Lived in Edinburgh.

Walter HORSNELL 1911– Painter and designer, born in Ware, Hertfordshire. He studied at Bolt Court School of Art and St Martin's School of Art. Between 1929–39 Horsnell was a graphic artist for various London art studios, then was art designer for motion picture presentation, 1936–9. Was in photographic reconnaissance in Royal Air Force, 1941, then was an official technical illustrator with Ministry of Aircraft Production, 1942–7. Horsnell was noted for his landscapes and townscapes in Britain and abroad. Showed in RA, RBA and elsewhere, solo exhibitions including Harrogate Festival, 1970. Grundy Art Gallery in Blackpool and Lambeth Palace hold examples. Lived in Harrogate, Yorkshire.

Francis Cecil HORSTMANN 1906–1968 Painter, calligrapher, decorator and teacher, born at Weston-super-Mare, Somerset, where he studied at the School of Art, followed by Royal College of Art. He held a series of art teaching posts in Northampton, London, Glasgow and Bristol, where he was vice-principal and head of the design school at the West of England College of Art. He wrote a number of books on painting, drawing and building. Lived at Weston-super-Mare.

Brian HORTON fl. from c.1970s– Artist, notably in gouache. Studied at Cheltenham College of Art, worked in the City of London and was a picture restorer before deciding to paint full-time. Horton painted the English countryside and coastal areas, his pictures having an ethereal, visionary quality. Had several exhibitions with David Messum, in Beaconsfield and London. Lived in an old rectory in Taplow, Buckinghamshire, which he and his artist wife Sheila covered with paintings, including painted car hub caps, inside and out. Three daughters were artists.

George HORTON 1859–1950 Painter, notably in watercolour, printmaker and teacher, born in North Shields, Northumberland. He had an unhappy childhood, working as a delivery boy in his father's butcher's shop, in the evenings copying reproductions of old masters in the Free Library. Encouraged by local art enthusiasts, Horton began to support himself as a professional artist after leaving home. He took a studio and advertised lessons in art. In about 1918 Horton settled permanently in London, by which time was establishing a wide reputation, and in 1922 had his first one-man show in Britain at Greatorex Gallery. He also showed at Laing Art Gallery in Newcastle, at RA, RSA and to much acclaim in Netherlands and Paris. The artist continued to make regular visits to northeast England and, after his London studio was bombed in 1940, lived in Spital Tongues, Newcastle, until 1945, but died in London. Mills, canals and coastal scenes in Holland and the northeast were his speciality. Memorial and centenary shows were held at South Shields Public Library and Museum in 1951 and 1959.

Julie HORTON 1965– Painter, designer and illustrator who studied at Solihull College of Technology and Kingston Polytechnic. She was featured in The Discerning Eye exhibition at Mall Galleries, 1990, and in 1991 at England & Co in Art in Boxes.

Percy HORTON 1897–1970 Painter and draughtsman, born in Brighton, Sussex. Studied at Brighton School of Art, 1918–20, where he had a scholarship. Horton was a man of strong radical convictions, and because he was an absolute conscientious objector he had to endure two years' hard labour in Carlton Prison, Edinburgh, 1916–18, during World War I. From 1916–18 was at Central School of Arts and Crafts under A S Hartrick and Ernest Jackson, then with a Royal Exhibition attended Royal College of Art, under Randolph Schwabe and Allan Gwynne-Jones, 1922–5. Horton went on to teach at the Royal College, 1930–49, where he was a highly respected figure, becoming Ruskin Master of Drawing at Oxford University, 1949. Taught voluntarily at the Working Men's College, London, for a time. Horton's social commitment is evident also in his early membership of the AIA, writings in the *New Left Review* and subject matter, such as his picture Unemployed Man, held by Sheffield City Art Galleries, which held a major show of his work in 1982. Tate Gallery also holds his picture The Invalid, of his mother. Horton was a realistic painter, influenced by Cézanne, who showed from 1926 with

NEAC, also RA and Goupil Gallery. His younger brother was the artist Ronald Horton. Lived in Lewes, Sussex.

Ronald HORTON 1902–1981 Painter, draughtsman, printmaker, photographer, teacher and bibliophile with strong left-wing convictions, born and died in Brighton, Sussex, brother of the artist Percy Horton. He studied at Brighton School of Art, 1919–23, in 1924 moving to London to work for the sculptor William Aumonier. From 1920 until his death Horton was a member of the Communist Party, and from 1924–6 he was politically very active, working part-time for the book dealer Birrell & Garnett (his collection of Russian children's books went to the Victoria & Albert Museum, his games, puzzles and toys to the University of Wales, Aberystwyth) and studied in the evenings at St Martin's School of Art. Horton gained a scholarship to the Royal College of Art under William Rothenstein, 1926–9, and visited Paris. Between 1930–40 Horton's many activities included helping Rex Whistler with murals and stage sets; researching for Stanley Morison's *The English Newspaper*; extensive teaching (from 1932–55 part-time with Parmiter's School, Bethnal Green), including lectures to teachers on child art; showing at RA, NEAC, Bloomsbury and Zwemmer Galleries; and contributing to *Athene*, *Art & Craft* and *Education*. In 1944 Horton returned to Brighton as head of art teacher training at the School of Art, retiring officially in 1966, but not from work. In the 1950s and 1960s Horton travelled extensively abroad. He was an active member of SEA, Art Workers' Guild, AIA and Artists for Peace, organising key exhibitions, including the Lenin Centenary and the Centenary of the Paris Commune. Retrospective at Brighton Polytechnic, 1982.

John HORWILL 1927– Painter and teacher who served in the Merchant and Royal Navy for four years, then attended Carlisle College of Art from 1949, gaining a scholarship to Royal College of Art, 1953, becoming an associate in 1956. Taught for 26 years, for 17 being principal lecturer in art at St Mary's College, Strawberry Hill, Twickenham, also doing extensive examining for London and Middlesex Regional Examining Boards. Showed widely, including John Cleal's gallery in Fishguard. Walker Art Gallery, Liverpool; Middlesbrough and Hereford City Art Galleries; Inner London Education Authority; and Leeds Training College hold examples. Lived in Llanrwst, Gwynedd.

Angela HORWITZ 1934– Sculptor and painter, born and lived in London, who studied art at Marylebone Institute and Sir John Cass College. She was a member of NS and Ridley Art Club, also exhibiting at Alpine and Smith's Galleries.

Nina HOSALI 1898–1987 Painter, writer and teacher, born in London of Indian-Celtic parentage. She studied art privately and trained in Margaret Morris movement at the London School founded by the painter J D Fergusson's wife; the Fergussons were great friends of the Hosalis. Nina Hosali obtained a Master of Science degree at London University and wanted to research in seismology but abandoned this when with her mother she went to North Africa to help neglected and suffering animals. She was founder of the Nature Cure Clinic in London and was involved in founding the Free Painters and Sculptors. Also showed with WIAC, RBA, ROI and had many solo shows in Britain and overseas. Published *A North African Diary* and a book of poems entitled *Children of Allah*. Her pictures showed individual imagination and used exotic colours. Lived in Biggin Hill, Kent.

David HOSIE 1962– Painter, draughtsman and printmaker, born in Glasgow, Scotland, whose figure paintings sometimes had an unsettling element. Hosie graduated in drawing and painting from Edinburgh College of Art, 1980–5, gaining a postgraduate diploma in printmaking, 1986. His awards included Richard Ford Travelling Scholarship, RA, 1985; a George Jackson Hutchison Award and an Andrew Grant Major Award and Travelling Scholarship, all 1986; and a Royal Glasgow Institute Award, 1992. Group exhibitions included New Generation Show, Compass Gallery, Glasgow, 1986; Germinations, Centre de la Vieille Charité, Marseilles, and tour, 1987–8; opening exhibition of Raab Gallery, Millbank, 1989; and Art94 (Jill George Gallery), 1994. Had a solo show at Raab Gallery, 1987, later ones including Jill George Gallery from 1992. Scottish Arts Council and RSA hold examples.

John HOSKIN 1921–1990 Sculptor in metal of figurative and abstract work, and teacher, born in Cheltenham, Gloucestershire. Left school aged 14 and worked for an architect until World War II Army service, then returned to drawing office. In 1950 began painting and working on reliefs and constructions until by 1953 he was seriously engaged in sculpture, showing at LG from 1954. Assisted the sculptor Lynn Chadwick until an opportunity to lecture part-time at Bath Academy of Art arose in 1957, and he was there until 1968, finally as principal lecturer in sculpture. After being sculptor in residence at Lancaster University, 1968–71, Hoskin was professor of fine art at Leicester Polytechnic, 1978–86. First one-man show was at Lords Gallery in 1957. Others occurred at Matthiesen Gallery and Arnolfini Gallery, Bristol. One of Hoskin's most notable pieces is the Exalted Christ for St Stephen's Church, in Bristol. Tate Gallery and Arts Council hold examples. Died in London, was buried in Herefordshire and in 1994 there was a memorial show at Storey Gallery, Lancaster.

Hugh Richard HOSKING 1904–1991 Painter, designer, mural artist, stage designer and teacher, born in Twickenham, Middlesex. Dick Hosking was married to the sculptor Alma Ramsey. He was a student of Bournemouth College of Art, 1922–5, and Royal College of Art, 1925–9. Held several teaching posts, latterly being principal of Ryland Memorial School of Art in West Bromwich, 1943–7, then principal of College of Art in Coventry, 1947–64. Prominent in bodies concerned with art education. Showed at AIA, Leicester Society of Artists and elsewhere. Best-known public commissions were the design for the Martyrs of Coventry mosaic in Broadgate House, Coventry, 1951, and a memorial stained glass window in St Nicholas Church, Warwick, 1964. A founder-member of the Warwick Society, in retirement he worked for many years in the Warwickshire county archives restoring documents and maps and was involved in church restoration. Lived in Warwick.

Knighton HOSKING 1944– Painter and teacher, born in Sidmouth, Devon. He attended Exeter College of Art, 1959–63, then Central School of Art and Design, 1963–6. In 1966 he won a Peter Stuyvesant Foundation Bursary to travel in America. By then Hosking had begun to show in mixed exhibitions, such as Young Britons at Altman Gallery, in New York. He went on to show at John Moores Liverpool Exhibitions in 1978–82–85. In 1968 Hosking began teaching at Wolverhampton Polytechnic and in 1970 had his first solo show there. Another followed in 1974, the year he had a one-man at Serpentine Gallery. Later solo shows included Wolverhampton Art Gallery in 1985. In the mid-1970s Hosking went to live in the country again, and the landscape became a key feature of his work; he turned away from working only in the studio and began to use on-location drawings and photographs. Arts Council holds his acrylic on canvas Earth Band, of 1974–5. Settled in Penn Common, Wolverhampton, Staffordshire.

Ned HOSKINS 1939– Painter, etcher, teacher and exhibitions organiser, born in Croydon, Surrey, although he moved to Yorkshire in 1944. Studied art at Harrogate Technical School, 1953–5; Harrogate School of Art, 1955–60; and Royal College of Art, 1961–4. There he "mixed with the Pop Artists and worked with David Hockney on his early etchings." Although Hoskins moved to Sussex in 1964, working as a designer and part-time lecturer at West Sussex College of Art, in 1968 he moved to Buckinghamshire, lecturing at High Wycombe College of Technology and Art. A 1973 fine art fellowship at University of Southampton was followed by lecturing at Buckinghamshire College of Art and Design, lecturing in California, 1976–7, and the founding in 1987 of the Fiveways Artists' Group in Brighton. In 1992 Hoskins retired from full-time lecturing to paint. He became art exhibition co-ordinator for Komedia Theatre Gallery, Brighton, where he had settled, in 1995. Took part in numerous group shows, his many solo exhibitions including London and Southampton Universities; Gardner Art Centre, Brighton; Richmond Art Centre, Richmond, California; Brighton Museum and Art Gallery; and Rottingdean Grange Gallery, Sussex. Hoskins said that he worked "from aspects of landscape, based on the theme of the juxtaposition of unusual and familiar forms and objects found on my rambles".

Dom Sylvester HOUÉDARD 1924–1992 Concrete poet, typographical artist, teacher and writer, born in Guernsey, Channel Islands, as Pierre Sylvester Houédard. He was evacuated to England in 1940 and gained his master's degree in history at Oxford University, 1942–9, interrupted by Army Intelligence service, 1944–7. Entered the Benedictine Abbey of Prinknash, at Cranham, Gloucestershire, in 1949, where he died, having been 41 years a monk, 32 years a priest. He studied philosophy at the Benedictine University of Sant' Anselmo, Rome, 1951–5. Apart from his own contribution to concrete poetry, published and exhibited, he played a key role in the international dissemination of the movement from 1962. He gave the first lectures, at Royal College of Art and ICA, and his work was shown in dozens of exhibitions in Britain and overseas, such as the 1971 Victoria & Albert Museum touring show d s h, dom sylvester houédard, visual poetries.

Liz HOUGH 1966– Painter who studied at Mid-Cheshire College of Art and Design, 1984–5. Then graduated from Manchester Polytechnic, 1985–8, and did postgraduate painting at Royal Academy Schools, 1988–91. Hough won the Creswick Prize and Landseer Scholarship in 1990, the year she obtained the Daler-Rowney Award for an artist under 30 years of age and was a finalist in the Young Painters' Award Scheme. In 1991 she gained the Vincent Harris Prize. Her work was described as "a sort of gentle Expressionism", with James Ensor, the Belgian painter, among its influences. She began showing in mixed exhibitions in 1989 at Pyramid Arts, and also exhibited at RA, ROI, Piccadilly Gallery, Albany Gallery and elsewhere. In 1992 shared a show at Cadogan Contemporary.

Barrie HOUGHTON 1941– Painter and actor, born in Shorne, Kent, who left a business career to study painting at St Martin's School of Art and on scholarship in Paris. After travelling through eastern Europe, he had several solo shows in London and Edinburgh, mainly exhibiting big abstracts. During further travels through southern Europe and in north Africa Houghton encountered travelling theatre groups; on returning to England he became a theatre designer in Canterbury, went to drama school and acted, notably with advanced companies. Film roles included the Biblical character Judas, the painter Vincent Van Gogh and Adolf Eichmann, tried for war crimes against the Jews. Early in the 1990s Houghton resumed full-time painting, inspired by East Anglia's landscape, and moved to Woodbridge, Suffolk. The Simon Carter Gallery there gave him a solo show in 1995.

Eve HOUGHTON 1908– Painter, wood engraver and teacher, born in Sagaing, Burma. She studied at Ruskin School of Drawing, Oxford, under Sydney Carline and the Royal Academy Schools with Sir Walter Westley Russell and Thomas Monnington. Held a number of teaching posts, including Mount School, York. Exhibited RA, in provinces and at National Gallery of Canada, Ottawa, and latterly extensively with East Kent Art Society of which she was a member. Lived in Teynham, Kent.

Gill HOUGHTON 1962– Artist in mixed media who attended Sheffield Polytechnic, 1984–5, before studying at North-East London Polytechnic, 1985–8. From 1989–91 she attended Royal College of Art, during that time spending a term at Cité Internationale des Arts in Paris. Her work was exhibited in many group shows in Britain and on the continent, including New Ways in Painting, Institute Mathilderhöhe in Germany and at Galerie zur Altendeutschen Schule in Switzerland. Her work also appeared at Art'91, International Contemporary Art Fair, Olympia, and in (dis)parities, Mappin Art Gallery, Sheffield,

1992, and at Herbert Art Gallery, Coventry, 1993. At that time she was Picker Fellow at Kingston Polytechnic. It was said of Houghton's work that it was "predicated on an open-endedness, the paces and gaps between the pieces are as rich and thoughtful as the pieces themselves."

Geoffrey HOUGHTON BROWN 1903–1993 Artist and aesthete, born in London, of private means. He was educated at Rugby School, studying art with Maurice Denis in Paris and at Slade School of Fine Art. In the 1920s–40s Houghton Brown carried out wall paintings and decorative schemes in restaurants and private houses, including Blue Train Restaurant, the Five Hundred Club, for Syrie Maugham, Nigel Playfair and Edward James; he renovated large houses, such as Oving Hall and Winslow Hall, filling them with rare objects, of which he was a connoisseur; and was a partner in Cotter's Market, which sold painted furniture. His own pictures were religious, in a Byzantine-Cubist style, and these he showed in mixed exhibitions at Leicester, Leger and Mayor Galleries, also having solo shows at St Michael's Workshop, Oxford, in 1942, and at Ebury Street Gallery, 1946. Was a devout Roman Catholic from 1924, a member of the Guild of Catholic Artists and Craftsmen; he helped set up the Church Decorators' Society and was a strong supporter and a chairman of the Latin Mass Society. A panel in tempera on the life of Saint Neot is in the Catholic church in St Neot's, Cambridgeshire. Died in a nursing home in Kingston upon Thames, Surrey.

Francis William HOUNSELL 1885–1956 Painter and teacher, born in London, specialising in watercolours. Studied at Brighton School of Art, then Royal College of Art. His teaching career was interrupted by World War I, in which he served in the Army in France and the Middle East. Latterly lived in Derby, where he was principal of the School of Arts and Crafts. Exhibited with Derby Sketching Club, the Society of Present-Day Artists, Midlands Artists and elsewhere in the provinces.

Shelagh HOURAHANE 1941– Painter, printmaker and teacher, born in Cardiff where she studied history at University College, 1959–62. After a year in youth work she became a tutor at Great Yarmouth College of Art, followed by a similar position at Stourbridge College of Art before doing a postgraduate diploma in fine art at University of Edinburgh, 1965–6. Went on to lecture in art history at University College of Wales in Aberystwyth. Took part in mixed shows in Wales, WAC possessing her work.

Miranda HOUSDEN 1965– Sculptor employing exotic materials, found objects and video, born in Lusaka, Zambia. She studied at Falmouth School of Art, 1984–7, and Chelsea School of Art, 1988–9, in 1990 being Rome Scholar at British School in Rome. Housden hoped to "disturb or unsettle the viewer" with her creations such as Breathless, a video and fur object featured in 1992 East & South Norwich Gallery/Kent Institute of Art and Design show. She was included in its forerunner, East, at Norwich Gallery, 1991. Lived in London.

Gordon HOUSE 1932– Printmaker, painter, designer, typographer and teacher, born in Pontardawe, Glamorgan. He studied at Luton and St Albans Schools of Art, 1947–50. From 1950–2 House worked in an advertising agency and was assistant to an ecclesiastical sculptor; he was a designer for Imperial Chemical Industries, 1952–9; then was a graphic designer for Kynoch Press, 1959–61. From then on he pursued his own artistic work, while teaching part-time at Central School of Art, St Albans and Hornsey Schools of Art and Luton College of Technology, 1961–4. House took part in the Situation British Painting show at RBA Galleries, 1960, and New London Situation at Marlborough New London Galleries, 1961, and was included in The Sixties Art Scene in London, Barbican Art Gallery, 1993. His solo shows began with New Vision Centre Gallery, 1959, among the later ones being After Powhatan, Ashmolean Museum, Oxford, 1993–4, abstract works based on its collection of curiosities. Arts Council, British Council, Victoria & Albert Museum and many other public collections hold examples. Lived in London.

William S HOUSE 1909– Painter, born in London. Studied at Central School of Arts and Crafts, 1925–6, under Gerald Spencer Pryse, then at Bolt Court School of Art, 1926–30, with Sylvan Boxsius. Exhibited extensively in north London area and settled finally in France at St Cyprien, near the Spanish border.

Edith Giffard HOUSEMAN 1875– Painter, printmaker and draughtsman in pencil. Born at Bredwardine, Herefordshire, she was educated at Bedford High School, then studied art under Claude Hayes, Frank Calderon and Walter Donne. She went on to teach art at Northend House School, at Petworth, Sussex. Exhibited widely, including RA, SWA, Cooling Galleries, SSWA and SGA. The Towner Art Gallery, Eastbourne, holds her work. Lived at Petworth.

Shirazeh HOUSHIARY 1955– Sculptor, draughtsman and teacher, born in Iran, where early on she studied calligraphy and the theatre. Left Iran at 18 and studied at Hornsey College of Art, Middlesex Polytechnic, 1975–6; then Chelsea School of Art, 1976–9; becoming a junior fellow in fine art at Cardiff College of Art, 1979–80. Went on to be a visiting lecturer at several art colleges. Early work was described as "rough, grotesque, almost monstrous", clay and straw over a wooden maquette which was "allowed to grow mould". Later she immersed herself in Sufism, turned to painting and in her sculpture addressed the questions Who am I? Where do I come from? And where do I go? Based on precise drawings, Houshiary's sculptures were constructed by Andy Everett, who had also trained as a sculptor. Was included in the 1982–3 Fruitmarket Gallery, Edinburgh, touring exhibition Objects and Figures and in Arts Council's 1993–4 tour Recent British Sculpture. Solo shows included Chapter Arts Centre, Cardiff, 1980, and Kettle's Yard Gallery Cambridge, 1982, with later continental touring exhibitions. Had a studio in south London.

Paul HOUSLEY 1964– Abstract painter, born in Stalybridge, Cheshire. He studied at Tameside College of Technology,

1981–2, and Sheffield Polytechnic, 1983–6. He showed at Smith's Gallery, Islington Arts Factory and Graves and Mappin Art Galleries in Sheffield. In 1991–2 his picture The Electrician was chosen for John Moores Exhibition, in Liverpool.

Laurence HOUSMAN 1865–1959 Dramatist, novelist and artist, born in Bromsgrove, Worcestershire, younger brother of the classical scholar and poet A E Housman. He studied art at Lambeth School of Art and South Kensington from early 1890s. Eventually he concentrated on writing, although some of his publications were brought out with his own illustrations, as he had worked for a time as an illustrator. His first book of verse, *Green Arras*, appeared in 1895. He was notable for *Victoria Regina*, produced in 1937, and *Happy and Glorious*, 1945. His autobiography, *The Unexpected Years*, appeared in 1936. Whitworth Art Gallery, Manchester, holds his work. Lived in Street, Somerset, dying in Glastonbury.

George HOUSTON 1869–1947 Painter and printmaker, born in Dalry, Ayrshire, where he continued to live, also in Glasgow. He was elected RSW, RI and RSA, also showing at Royal Glasgow Institute of the Fine Arts, Walker Art Gallery in Liverpool, Fine Art Society and elsewhere. Much of his work was done in Ayrshire and Argyllshire. He was a member of Edinburgh Arts and Glasgow Art Clubs. Several public galleries hold examples of work by an artist who painted in the Impressionist manner.

Ian HOUSTON 1934– Artist in oil, watercolour and coloured pencil, born in Gravesend, Kent. He studied at Royal College of Music, briefly with St Martin's School of Art, then moved to Norfolk in 1964 where, under the guidance of Edward Seago, he became committed to a career as a painter. Houston became president of the East Anglian Group of Marine Artists. He had a first solo show at Usher Gallery, Lincoln, in 1964, then showed at Mandell's Gallery, Norwich, each year until 1986. Other shows included Monazo Fine Arts, Monte Carlo, from 1981; Falmouth Art Gallery, from 1984; Beehive Corner Gallery, Adelaide, 1986; and Mongerson Wunderlich Galleries, Chicago, 1990. His work was also shown with RI and Paris Salon, where he won a silver medal for watercolour. Houston was awarded a gold medal with rosette by the National Society for French Culture. Polak Gallery was his London agent.

John HOUSTON 1930– Painter and teacher, born in Buckhaven, Fife, married to the artist Elizabeth Blackadder. Houston studied at Edinburgh College of Art, 1948–54, his final year being spent in Italy on a travelling scholarship. He returned to Edinburgh to teach at the College. In 1957 Houston helped start the 57 Gallery in Edinburgh, having his first solo show there in 1958. Other one-man shows were held at Scottish Gallery, Edinburgh, and Mercury Gallery for many years. A keen traveller, Houston exhibited widely abroad. He was a member of SSA and RSW and was elected RSA in 1972. Houston tended towards Expressionism in his landscapes, Munch being a key influence, employing bold colours. Scottish National Gallery of Modern Art holds his work.

Albert HOUTHUESEN 1903–1979 Painter of religious and visionary works, teacher, born Amsterdam, son of artist and musician Jean Charles Pierre Houthuesen (pronounced Howthozen, stress on second syllable). When her husband encouraged Albert to paint, his mother struck Jean Charles on the head, and he died from the blow not long after. This tragedy, poor health and poverty pursued Albert Houthuesen for years, long after the family had moved to London in 1912. Albert was naturalised 10 years later. After leaving elementary school aged 14 he did a number of pointless jobs, studying at St Martin's School of Art evening classes, 1917–23. Won scholarship to Royal College of Art, 1923, studying there until 1927. Four years later married painter Catherine Dean. Taught at the Working Men's College, 1928–36, then after the war, when he was a draughtsman in locomotive works in Doncaster, at St Gabriel's College. Although he showed at NEAC did not have first solo show until 1961, at Reid Gallery. In 1977 had three London shows and appeared with success on television. Tate Gallery holds his work. Lived in London.

Charles HOWARD 1899–1978 Abstract and Surrealist painter, born in New Jersey, America. Studied at University of California, travelled on the continent, lived for a time in Paris where he was influenced by Jean Hélion, then settled in London, 1939–40. Initially Howard painted murals, and was employed to paint Edward Wadsworth's nautical designs on the wall of the de la Warr Pavilion in Bexhill, 1936, the year he exhibited with the British Surrealist Group in the first London Surrealist Exhibition. Howard had a show of abstract pictures at Guggenheim Jeune Gallery in 1939. After an absence he returned to Britain in 1946, was given a retrospective at Whitechapel Art Gallery in 1956 and became a British citizen in 1963. He was included in The Surrealist Spirit in Britain, Whitford and Hughes, 1988.

Constance Mildred HOWARD 1910– Printmaker, teacher and embroiderer, born in Northampton, she was married to the sculptor Harold Wilson Parker. She studied at Northampton School of Art, 1925–31, with Lewis Duckett, 1929–31, and at the Royal College of Art, 1931–5, where her teachers included Eric Ravilious and Edward Bawden. Held a number of teaching posts, including Kingston School of Art, 1939–46. Showed at SWE, Arts Council, Arts and Crafts Society and elsewhere. Arts Council bought her work which was used widely in magazines such as *Illustrated London News* and *The Listener*. Lived for many years in London.

Diana HOWARD 1947– Painter, born in Surrey, married to the artist John Morley. She studied at Sutton and Epsom Colleges of Art and, as a postgraduate student, at Royal Academy Schools under Peter Greenham until 1971. Gained David Murray Studentships in Landscape, 1967–9, and Landseer Prize and Royal Academy Schools Bronze Medal for Painting, 1970. She was an associate of The Brotherhood of Ruralists and was

included in their shows, her work having a sense of mystery. An early interest in the poems of Dante and later in Celtic mythology and the subject of the Holy Grail led on to an involvement with Eastern mysticism. Took part in many group exhibitions, including Piccadilly Gallery, New Grafton Gallery and Arnolfini Gallery, Bristol. Her solo shows included Festival Gallery, Bath, 1982; Somerset Rural Life Museum Gallery, 1988; and Chappel Galleries, Chappel, 1991. Lived in Stoven North Green, Suffolk.

Francis HOWARD 1874–1954 Painter, critic and administrator. Brought up as a Roman Catholic, Howard was educated widely on the continent and in England, his art studies including Herkomer School at Bushey. Was a founder-member of NPS and IS, where he exhibited. Also showed at Walker Art Gallery, Liverpool, which bought his work, and overseas. Signed pictures F H. Wrote criticism and did research for a number of publications. Member of Chelsea Arts Club and lived in London.

Ghislaine HOWARD 1953– Painter noted for Expressionist landscapes, born in Manchester, who studied fine art at the University of Newcastle upon Tyne. She worked in London and Paris, in 1980 returning to the northwest of England, settling in Glossop, Derbyshire. Wrote for *The Artist* magazine on her work and methods. Showed widely in England, including Images of the Yorkshire Landscape, organised by Sheeran Lock at Leeds Civic Hall, 1991. Manchester's City and Whitworth Art Galleries and Graves Art Gallery, Sheffield, acquired her work.

Ian HOWARD 1952– Painter, draughtsman and teacher, born in Aberdeen. He studied at Edinburgh University and College of Art. He won a Travelling Scholarship to Italy, later winning the RSA Guthrie Award in 1978; first prize in the Scottish Open Drawing Competition in 1985; and was a Tolly Cobbold Eastern Arts National Competition prizewinner. Howard taught at Gray's Art School in Aberdeen, then from 1986 was head of painting at Duncan of Jordanstone College of Art, Dundee. Howard's works were described as "usually an intriguing, carefully balanced blend of fine draughtsmanship, fantasy and classical references". He exhibited them in many mixed shows in Britain and abroad and had solo exhibitions at Compass Gallery, Glasgow. Contemporary Art Society, City Art Centre in Edinburgh and many Scottish galleries hold his work. Lived in Aberdeen.

James Campbell HOWARD 1906– Painter and graphic artist, born in London, who was self-taught. He showed at RA and RI and was a Langham Sketch Club and SGA member. Lived finally in Ditchling, Sussex.

John HOWARD 1958– Mainly a printmaker, Howard was noted for his meticulous but atmospheric depictions of industrial and grand architecture in the Midlands and Black Country, documenting the past. He studied at Birmingham Polytechnic, 1986–9, with Jean Vaudeau and Kim Kempshall. Prior to this he worked for a decade in industry, "five of which I spent in foundries and related industries, as well as factories, warehouses, and so on". His main influences were Piranesi, Brangwyn and Joseph Wright of Derby. Howard was a member of the Birmingham Artists' Group and Birmingham Arts Trust and an associate of RBSA and RE. Showed at RA Summer Exhibitions, Bankside Gallery, Mall Galleries, MAFA Open and elsewhere and in 1991 had a one-man exhibition at Midlands Contemporary Art, Birmingham. Victoria & Albert Museum, Birmingham University, Surikov Academy of Arts in Moscow and other public collections hold examples. Lived in Warley, West Midlands.

Ken HOWARD 1932– Painter, born in London, where he continued to live, married to the artist Christa Gaa. He studied at Hornsey College of Art, 1949–53, Royal College of Art, 1955–8, and won a British Council Scholarship to Florence, 1958–9. Was elected NEAC, 1962; ROI, 1966; RWA, 1981; RWS, 1983; and RA, 1991. His many awards were the First Prize in the Lord Mayor's Art Award, 1966; First Prize Arundel Art Centre, 1969; he was a prizewinner at John Moores Exhibition, Liverpool, 1978; and at John Laing Exhibition, 1979. Won First Prize, Hunting Group Award, 1982; was a prizewinner at RWA in 1983; and at NEAC Centenary Exhibition, 1986. Howard was appointed official artist in Northern Ireland by Imperial War Museum in 1973–8. Between 1973–80 worked with Army in Germany, Cyprus, Oman, Hong Kong, Nepal, Norway, Canada, Belize and Brunei. Howard did much commissioned work, including The Drapers' Company, The Haberdashers' Company, United Nations and elsewhere. Appeared in numerous mixed shows. One-man exhibitions included Plymouth Art Centre, 1955; John Whibley Gallery, 1966–8; and from 1971 a series with New Grafton Gallery. Howard was a painter noted for his handling of light and for his depictions of nudes in interiors. Imperial War Museum, Plymouth City Art Gallery, National Army Museum and other provincial British galleries hold his work.

Margaret Maitland HOWARD 1898– Painter and draughtsman, notably in black-and-white, born in London. She studied at the Byam Shaw and Vicat Cole School of Art and Royal Academy Schools, where she was a multiple silver medal-winner plus other awards. Exhibited RA, NEAC, SWA, RP and ROI. Just after World War II she was appointed draughtsman to the Institute of Archaelogy at London University. Ridley Art Club member, daughter of the artist Henry James Howard. She lived in Sutton, Surrey.

Norman HOWARD 1899–1955 Painter and illustrator. Studied at Camberwell School of Arts and Crafts, 1918–20, then at Westminster School of Art for four years under Walter Bayes. Exhibited RSMA, RA, IS, Goupil Gallery and NEAC. The Admiralty bought his work in 1945, and eight years later he did decorations for the P&O liner *Arcadia*. Lived in Richmond, Surrey, where in 1951 he was president of the Art Group.

Ray HOWARD-JONES 1903–1996 Painter, especially in gouache, draughtsman, mosaicist and muralist, writer and poet, born in Lambourn, Berkshire, as Rosemary Howard-Jones. She was educated at St Hilda's School, Penarth, and the London Garden School, then the Slade School of Fine Art from the age of 17 for four years. From the late-1930s through World War II she led a varied life, working as an archaeological draughtsman at National Museum of Wales, Cardiff; helped the unemployed and deprived children in the city; with the composer Gomer Llewellyn ran the East Moors Theatre; with Coastal Defence recorded fortified islands in the Bristol Channel; and was a Royal Navy war artist recording loadings for D-Day. After the war moved to London and worked as a medical draughtsman. In 1946 attended Patrick Allan-Fraser School of Art, Hospitalfield, Arbroath, under James Cowie. Although based in London, Howard-Jones in later years travelled as far as Spain, Cyprus and America and was especially associated with west Wales and the islands offshore. From 1949–58 she spent long periods on the tiny island of Skomer. Nature and a deep inner spiritual life and Celtic mystery and legends were sources of inspiration. Her mosaics include one for Thomson House, Cardiff, 1958; another for Grange Church, Edinburgh, 1964–5. Published *Poems and Stories*, 1968. Howard-Jones had a first solo exhibition at Bloomsbury Gallery, 1935. Regular shows followed, including Leicester Galleries, 1964, where she was a frequent exhibitor; there was a WA retrospective and tour, 1974; a West Wales Arts retrospective, 1983; one put on by West Wales Arts Centre, Fishguard, 1992; and another by Rocket Press in 1993. Imperial War MuseumWAC and National Museum of Wales hold examples, commonly signed Ray.

Charles Wilfred HOWARTH 1893– Painter in oil, watercolour and line artist, Howarth established a reputation as an illustrator of newspapers, periodicals and books. After studying at Sheffield School of Art under A C C Jahn and Oliver Senior in 1910–12, Howarth spent two years at Birmingham School of Art. He exhibited with the Sheffield Society of Artists, at the RSA, in Birmingham and in Wales. Lived at Conway, North Wales.

Constance HOWARTH 1927– Watercolourist and textile designer, born in Rochdale, Lancashire. She gained her design diploma in 1947, having studied at Manchester Regional College of Art. Her work was exhibited in a number of notable exhibitions in the textile design field and is held by Victoria & Albert Museum. Lived in London for many years.

Maggy HOWARTH 1944– Artist in pebble mosaic, born in Warrington, Lancashire, who attended Reading University's school of fine art, 1962–6. For 20 years she worked with outdoor theatre companies, from 1983 undertaking pebble mosaic pavement commissions. "I think I am the only pebble mosaic practitioner in the United Kingdom." Her book *The Art of Pebble Mosaic* was published in 1994. She was a member of Art and Architecture and Artists Working to Commission and her work was to be found in Rose Street, Edinburgh; Discovery Point in Dundee; in Stockton High Street; and East Cleveland Hospital. Showed at Stoke Garden Festival, 1986. Lived at Wennington, Lancaster.

Russel HOWARTH 1927– Artist and teacher, born and lived in Oldham, Lancashire. He was educated locally, starting an engineering apprenticeship in 1941 while drawing in his spare time. Howarth began painting in 1950 after completing his technical studies. He taught pottery at part-time evening classes from 1962, giving up engineering in 1981 and teaching in 1992. Joined the Saddleworth Art Group in 1951 and took part in mixed shows at Museum Gallery, Brown Hill Centre and Mill Yard Gallery, all in Uppermill; Oldham Art Gallery; RBA and elsewhere. His solo shows included Royal Northern College of Music and Tib Lane Gallery, Manchester.

Winifred HOWE 1880–c.1948 Painter in oil and watercolour, born in West Horsley, Surrey. She was daughter of the painter A D Peppercorn and changed her name from Peg Peppercorn to avoid confusion with her father. After study at home she attended Slade School of Fine Art, where she gained her certificate and studied under Henry Tonks. Howe showed from 1907 including RA, NEAC, ROI, Goupil Salon and by invitation at the *Daily Express* Women's Exhibition in 1922. Her sister, Gertrude Peppercorn, a concert pianist, was married to the writer Stacy Aumonier, another sister being married to the writer and typographer Francis Meynell. Manchester City Art Gallery holds her work. Lived for many years at Ashtead, Surrey, but developed cancer and finally lived in a nursing home.

Cheryl HOWELD 1944– Artist in oil and watercolour, born in St Albans, Hertfordshire. She studied at Hornsey College of Art, 1962–3, with John Hoyland, John Simpson and Fred Cuming. Howeld's work concentrated on the figure and landscape, which took her on trips around England, notably Norfolk and Sussex, the south of France, Italy, Scotland and Russia, in which she had a special interest. Took part in many mixed shows, including Hampton Hill Galleries, Twickenham, from 1980; Original Picture Shop, 1985; Walton Gallery, 1988; PS, 1989; NEAC from 1990; and Richmond Gallery, 1992. Had a solo show at Maddermarket, Norwich, 1984, later ones including Churzee Studio Gallery, which she opened in 1988. Lived in London.

David HOWELL 1965– Painter, born in Ross-on-Wye, Herefordshire, who studied from 1984–8 at the Coventry Polytechnic, settling nearby at Stoke. As well as showing in the Coventry Open in 1992 and winning a prize at John Moores Liverpool Exhibition, 1993–4, Howell shared several exhibitions, including Omphalos Gallery, Sandwich, 1992.

Neale HOWELLS 1965– Artist in oil, acrylic, pastel, pencil and wood, in which irregular shapes, pastel colours – notably blue – and graffiti were important elements. He was born and worked in Neath, Glamorgan, and studied at Neath Tertiary College (it holds his work), under Ian Wagstaff, 1985–7; gained an honours degreee at Bath College of Higher Education, 1987–90; and obtained WAC travel grants to Berlin, 1996, and New York, 1998. Mixed shows included National Eisteddfod, Conway, 1995; National Eisteddfod, Bala, 1997; and 9th Mostyn Open, Oriel

Mostyn, Llandudno, 1997. Solo exhibitions included Berlin Works 96 at Swansea Arts Workshop, 1997.

Allan HOWES 1888–1969 Sculptor, notably of figures, born Edgar Allan Howes in East Dereham, Norfolk, Howes studied at the Royal Academy Schools, where he won the Landseer prize plus several other prizes and a silver medal, also studying at the Slade School of Fine Art. Exhibited extensively at RA, RMS, RSA and Royal Glasgow Institute of the Fine Arts, and was elected a fellow of RBS. Howes' Madonna and Child as well as his Torso, typical works, are illustrated in the volume *RBS: Modern British Sculpture*, published in 1939, and his bronze Dawn, of 1942, is shown in Arthur T Broadbent's *Sculpture Today in Great Britain 1940–1943*. Howes' work is in several public collections. Lived in London, afterwards in Saffron Walden, Essex.

Anne HOWESON 1952– Artist in gouache, conté and oil, born in Kent. She attended Central School of Art, 1970–1, for a foundation course; graduated from St Martin's School of Art, 1971–4; then gained her master's degree at Royal College of Art, 1975–8. Howeson did a large amount of illustrative work, including *Independent Review*, *Saturday Times Review*, *German Playboy* and *The Spectator*. In 1990 she was a judge for the *Reader's Digest* Illustration Competition, she took part in a number of workshops and seminars and devised a summer course for Massachusetts College of Art, Boston, in 1992. Exhibitions included Galerie Mokum, Amsterdam, 1980; Association of Illustrators shows from 1981; Talbot Rice Centre, Edinburgh, 1985; and South Bank Picture Show from 1990. Lived in London.

James HOWIE 1931– Artist and teacher, born in Dundee. He studied at Duncan of Jordanstone College of Art there, 1949–54, then after National Service studied ceramics at Liverpool College of Art, 1956–7. In the next five years he lived in London and on the continent for a while, returning to teach at his old College of Art in Dundee, 1962–7. After some time away, partly in the south of England, Howie returned to Dundee as artist-in-residence at Dudhope Art Centre. He took part in many group shows. Had a solo exhibition at New Art Centre in 1960, his later appearances including Edinburgh College of Art, Richard Demarco Gallery in Edinburgh and Compass Gallery, Glasgow. Was included in Painters in Parallel at Edinburgh College of Art, 1978. Scottish Arts Council, Glasgow University and Dundee City Art Gallery hold his work.

B HOWITT-LODGE 1883–1948 Painter and architect, who studied in London. He did much illustrative work for publications such as *Our Dogs*, *Dog World* and the *Encyclopaedia Britannica*. Exhibited RMS, RA, ROI and elsewhere and was a member of the London Sketch Club. Worked for Air-raid Precautions (ARP) during early part of War II, when he painted the Blitz. His pictures Business as Usual and London Carries On were official purchases. Lived in London.

Sally HOWKINS 1961– Painter and printmaker, born in Nottingham. She studied at Mansfield College of Art, 1977–9, then Newcastle upon Tyne Polytechnic, 1979–82. Group shows included Northern Contemporaries, 1981; Gallery 7, Newcastle upon Tyne from 1983; Warwick Arts Trust, which holds her work, from 1987; and Oxford Visual Art Week, from 1991. Had a solo show at Cadogan Contemporary, 1993, atmospheric landscapes moving towards abstraction.

Alan James HOWLETT 1940– Painter, printmaker, collagist, creator of wood reliefs and teacher, born in London. He attended Ealing School of Art, 1958–60, then Royal College of Art, 1960–3, his teachers including Frank Auerbach and Bernard Cohen. From the early-1960s through the 1970s Howlett did part-time teaching, including around 10 years at Norwich; he was a freelance broadcaster for BBC music programmes; and undertook photography for record companies, including Harmonia Mundi in France and Vanguard in America. Howlett also taught music, on which much of his painting was based; he had a special interest in music of the Trecento and Quattrocento in Italy and France. From 1980 Howlett painted and taught in Italy. Although he took part in many group shows in his student days he then rejected the commercial gallery system, selling largely privately, especially to musicians.

Nancy HOWORTH 1912– Landscape painter, educated in Eastbourne, Sussex, where she attended the School of Art, 1930–2, later studying privately. Showed with SWA, Free Painters and Sculptors and with Association of Sussex Artists of which she was a member. Had several solo exhibitions, including Ditchling Gallery. Lived in North Chailey, Sussex.

Ray HOWORTH 1914– Painter, designer and teacher, born in Wealdstone, Middlesex. He studied at Harrow Technical and Art School under John Gerald Platt. After Army service in World War II held a number of teaching posts, following a period as a freelance, becoming head of the design department at Manchester College of Art and Design. As well as having work reproduced in many publications Howorth showed at RA, ROI and widely in the provinces. Lived in Knutsford, Cheshire.

Diana HOWSE 1956– Artist, arts administrator and editor, born in Oxfordshire, who gained fine art honours degree at Exeter College of Art and Design, 1975–8. Howse was at this time involved in Spacex, an artists' studio complex, where she ran a gallery until 1981, when she left to concentrate on her own work. During the 1980s Howse was editor of the *South West Arts Newsletter to Artists*; was education officer for Spacex until 1984; became involved in film and video; in the mid-1980s moved to Bristol to work at Watershed, Britain's first media centre; met David Lascelles (whom she married in 1990); and began her ongoing involvement with Harewood House, Yorkshire, creating the Terrace Gallery there, which opened in 1989. She had had a solo installation, Ghost Town, in 1985, and on moving to London in 1987 Howse began seriously painting again, participating in

Cross Currents at Reed's Wharf Gallery at the Barbican Centre, 1996, showing lush, Expressionist abstracts, with landscape references.

Melanie HOWSE 1968– Glass artist, who attended Portsmouth Art College, with a distinction in three-dimensional design foundation studies, 1987–8, achieving further merits and distinctions during an architectural stained glass course at Swansea Institute of Higher Education, 1989–92. Among awards were the British Society of Master Glass Painters Stevens Competition first prize, 1991, and the Howard Martin Award, for outstanding merit, 1992. Howse completed eight square metres of glass for the Swansea Institute library, during a residency, 1992, and lancet windows and a roundel, St Illtyd's Church, Port Tennant, Swansea, 1993. In 1997 moved to Emsworth, Hampshire, and set up her own business. In that year showed figurative works on glass with background illumination at Eight by Eight, Pallant House, Chichester.

Rose Chicheliana HOWSE 1892–1981 Miniaturist and painter in watercolour, born in Waterford, Ireland, whose full name was Henrietta Rose Chicheliana Howse. She studied art in Brussels, then miniature painting in London with the miniaturist S Arthur Lindsey. He confided in her his medium for painting on ivory, a secret which remained after she died with her family. Howse painted in watercolour, but not to sell, the subjects being Scottish and Swiss scenes, figures, dogs, cats and flower arrangements. Became an associate of RMS. Her husband was in the Navy and travelled a lot, but eventually they settled in Scotland at Kilmacolm, Renfrewshire.

Cherry HOWSON 1912– Watercolour artist who was born at Tipton, Staffordshire. Studied art at the School of Art in Lancaster under the painter and etcher Charles Ripper, then with the Kendal artist George Mortram Moorhouse. She exhibited quite widely in the north of England, at venues including Walker Art Gallery, Liverpool, Atkinson Art Gallery, Southport, the Lake Artists' Society and with the RS. Lived at Evesham, Worcestershire.

Peter HOWSON 1958– Painter and mural artist, born in London, moving to Glasgow as a small boy. He attended Glasgow School of Art 1975–77, then took two years off to do a number of jobs, was in the Army for a time and travelled in Europe. He resumed his studies and graduated in 1981. His time off mid-studies provided Howson with useful material for his painting which is characterised by its powerful draughtsmanship, simple imagery and theatrical lighting to depict a masculine world, tough and gritty. Howson soon built up a reputation on leaving college. From 1982–3 he painted murals at the Feltham Community Association, then in 1985 he was artist-in-residence at the University of St Andrews. He won the Arthur Andersen Purchase Award at Compass Gallery, Glasgow, Barras show for the 1986 Mayfest. Howson showed widely abroad and his British solo exhibitions included a retrospective at McLellan Galleries, Glasgow, 1993. A turning-point in Howson's life and career was being chosen as official war artist for Britain in Bosnia, sponsored jointly by *The Times* newspaper and the Imperial War Museum. It and Howson's dealer Flowers East put on critically acclaimed shows of the resulting work in 1994. Scottish Arts Council, Scottish National Gallery of Modern Art, Tate Gallery, Victoria & Albert Museum and many provincial galleries hold Howson's work. Lived in London.

Henry HOYLAND 1894–1948 Painter who studied in Sheffield, London and Paris. He exhibited RA, NEAC, RBA, in the provinces and at the Paris Salon and had one-man shows in London and in the provinces. Was a member of Chelsea Arts Club and the Arts Club. From 1921–9 Hoyland was on the staff of Sheffield College of Art and for five years during World War II he was deputy chief camouflage officer for the Ministry of Home Security. Work by Hoyland, a subtle Colourist, was bought by the RA out of the Edward Stott Fund and provincial galleries hold his work. Lived at Leamington Spa, Warwickshire.

John HOYLAND 1934– Painter, printmaker, designer and teacher, born in Sheffield, Yorkshire. He enrolled in junior art department at Sheffield College of Art in 1946 instead of attending grammar school, then from 1956–60 was at Royal Academy Schools, where in 1959 his entire diploma show of abstracts was taken down by order of the RA's president Sir Charles Wheeler. Hoyland was elected RA in 1991. He became an influential teacher, at Hornsey College of Art, Croydon School of Art, Chelsea College of Art (where he was principal lecturer from 1965), St Martin's School of Art, Royal Academy Schools and Slade School of Fine Art, from which he resigned in 1989. Hoyland won a number of prizes, including Calouste Gulbenkian Purchase Award, 1963; first prize at John Moores Exhibition Liverpool in 1982; joint first prize in Korn Ferry International Award Exhibition in 1986; and in the following year first prize in the Athena Art Awards Exhibition. Hoyland developed a strong attachment to America, from the late 1960s making visits to New York and setting up a studio there and in 1972 becoming Charles A Dana professor of fine arts, Colgate University, Hamilton. He was in close touch with such abstract painters as Noland and Motherwell and in 1988 travelled in America selecting and curating the Hans Hofmann show for the Tate Gallery. In 1986 he designed sets for Sadler's Wells ballet *Zansa*. Hoyland exhibited widely internationally, including Whitechapel Art Gallery, Waddington Galleries, Serpentine Gallery with tour, 1979–80, Compass Gallery in Glasgow and Flowers East. Tate Gallery, British Council and other major collections hold his work. Lived in London.

Denise HOYLE 1935– Painter and potter. She was born in Paris and studied there at L'Académie de la Grande Chaumière. Married to the artist Walter Hoyle. She was especially interested in natural history, early botanical drawings and the ballet. Designed posters for the Post Office. Showed at Old Fire Engine House, Ely, and in Saffron Walden at Church Street Gallery. The Fry Art Gallery in Saffron Walden holds her work. Lived in Hastings, Sussex.

Jonathan HOYLE 1957– Painter and draughtsman, he studied at Rochdale College of Art, Gloucestershire College of Art and the Royal Academy Schools, 1979–82. He gained the Elizabeth Greenshields Scholarship in 1981; a prize for drawing at the Royal Academy Schools in 1982; an Italian Government Scholarship for 1982–3; and the Oppenheim-John Downes Memorial Award in 1989. Hoyle's figurative pictures were notable for their strong abstract design. He showed in mixed exhibitions including Pick of Graduate Art, at Christie's, in 1982; RA 1985 Summer Exhibition; in 1986 at New Grafton Gallery; and in the Laing Collection, Mall Galleries, 1990. He had a solo show at Wellington Crescent, Winnipeg, in 1985; at Judd Street Gallery, in 1990; and in that year shared a show at Thackeray Gallery. HRH The Prince of Wales bought his work.

Walter HOYLE 1922– Watercolourist, printmaker, designer and teacher, born in Rishton, Lancashire, married to the artist Denise Hoyle. He studied at Beckenham School of Art and at Royal College of Art, 1940–2 and 1947–8, under Edward Bawden. From 1948–9 he was artist attached to the Byzantine Institute in Istanbul. Work that he saw there influenced Hoyle, who also claimed to be "an English romantic with a love of France". Hoyle taught at St Martin's School of Art, 1951–60; Central School of Arts and Crafts, 1960–4; and Cambridge School of Art, 1964–85. While in Cambridge he launched Cambridge Print Editions, which produced limited editions of artists' prints. Editions of his own prints were commissioned by Editions Alecto, Christie's Contemporary Art and Folio Society. He designed wallpapers and painted murals for the Natural History Museum and for the Sealink ship *St David*. Showed at RA, Leicester Galleries, Zwemmer Gallery, Kettle's Yard in Cambridge, the Great Bardfield Exhibitions in mid-1950s and elsewhere. Other commissioned work was done for Shell, BBC and Post Office. Tate Gallery, British Museum and Victoria & Albert Museum hold his work. Lived in Hastings, Sussex.

Louis HOYLES 1914– Although primarily an industrial designer, Hoyles was also a sculptor and draughtsman. Born in London, he studied art with Harold Youngman and Russell Reeve. Exhibited in Britain and abroad, mainly in design-oriented shows. Lived in Stanmore, Middlesex.

Edward Bouverie HOYTON 1900–1988 Printmaker, watercolourist and teacher, born in London. He studied at Goldsmiths' College School of Art, 1918–26, then at British School in Rome, 1926–8. He went on to become principal of Penzance School of Art, 1941–66. With his wife Inez Hoyton, the artist, he was a notable figure in Newlyn art circles and showed widely locally as well as at RA, RBA, and elsewhere in the provinces. Hoyton's work covered a wide range, from early prints in the manner of Samuel Palmer and F L Maur Griggs – as illustrated in *The Studio* volume *Artists' Country*, by C Geoffrey Holme and G S Sandilands – to abstract etchings of Tresco, in the Isles of Scilly, of the late-1940s. He was also a notable portraitist. In all his work there is strong emphasis on sound draughtsmanship. He had a final show of The Lifetime's Work at St Ives Society of Artists in 1987.

Inez HOYTON 1903–1983 Painter in oil and watercolour, designer, weaver and embroiderer, Hoyton studied at Leeds College of Art. It was there that she trained to teach, eventually becoming art teacher, during World War II, at Benenden School, in Kent. When her husband, the artist Edward Bouverie Hoyton, became principal of Penzance School of Art, Inez taught there, from 1946–68. Although her second name was Estella, she sometimes signed her work Inez B Hoyton. She and her husband became strongly associated with Cornish artistic life; Inez was a member of the Newlyn Society of Artists, the St Ives Society of Artists and the Penwith Society, in St Ives. She travelled widely, notably in Greece, Italy and Spain. Inez exhibited at the RA, the Orion Gallery in Penzance and widely in Britain. Lived at Newlyn.

Waclaw HRYNIEWICZ 1909–1987 Architect and sculptor, one of the group of Polish paper sculptors who made such an impact in Britain after World War II. After graduating from Warsaw Institute of Technology's department of architecture he spent two years in the studio of Le Corbusier, returned to Warsaw to work on the modernisation of Polish Railways, then in 1938 with Osiecki and Skolimowski gained first prize for the design of the Polish pavilion at the New York World Fair. After deportation to Siberia by the Soviet Union, in 1941 he was released to join the Polish Army and served in North Africa and Italy, later designing and overseeing the erection of the Polish War Cemetery at Monte Cassino. In 1947 with Osiecki and Skolimowski set up Studio 2, offering architects' and designers' services, clients served by Hryniewicz including Creda and Swan Mill and many international fairs and exhibitions. Eventually he reverted to architecture. Was included in Polish Paper Sculpture at Polish Cultural Institute, 1995.

Xiao Peng HUANG 1960– Artist, born in China, who attempted "to return to the traditional spirit of Oriental art from Minimalism". He studied at Guangzhou Academy of Arts in China, then at Slade School of Fine Art. Group exhibitions included Guangzhou Academy from 1983; Six Slade Students, Rijksakademie, Amsterdam, 1992; Artists' Open Studios, Tudorleaf Centre, 1993; and Journeys West, University of Essex touring show, 1995.

Deirdre HUBBARD 1935– Sculptor, born in New York City, America, who graduated Summa cum Laude at Harvard University in 1957. Studied with Andreas Feininger, in the studio of Elisabeth Frink and at Chelsea College of Art. Showed at RA, Royal Glasgow Institute of the Fine Arts, National Museum of Wales in Cardiff, Usher Gallery in Lincoln, Camden Arts Centre and at RWA, where in 1996 she was included in the 2nd Open Sculpture Exhibition with the near-abstract Wingless Bird. Many private collections in Britain and abroad hold her work. Lived in London.

Hesketh HUBBARD 1892–1957 Painter, printmaker, furniture designer, printer, writer and lecturer. Born in London, he studied at Heatherley's School of Fine Art, Croydon School of Art and Chelsea Polytechnic. Hubbard was founder and director of the Forest Press; for a time master of the Art Workers' Guild; and the author of over a dozen books, including *A Hundred Years of British Painting 1851–1951*. He was a member of many societies connected with painting and printmaking in Britain and overseas. Exhibited widely, including ROI, RSA, RA, RBA and Ridley Art Club. Many galleries in Britain and abroad hold his work. Lived in London.

John HUBBARD 1931– Painter, designer and printmaker, born at Ridgefield, Connecticut, America. He studied at Harvard University, 1950–3, completed three years' military service including time in Japan, then in 1956–8 studied at Art Students' League of New York and with Hans Hofmann. From 1958–60 Hubbard lived in Rome and travelled through Europe, then moved to Dorset in 1961, settling in Chilcombe. Among a wide variety of activities Hubbard in 1968 designed décor and costumes for Dutch National Ballet's *Le Baiser de la Fée*; in 1983 designed décor for the Royal Ballet's production *Midsummer*; in 1985 painted the backcloth for *Sylvia pas de Deux* for the same company; was in 1988 invited resident artist at Poet's House, New Harmony, Indiana; then in 1990 was guest in Malaysia of the National Gallery of Malaysia. Group exhibitions included The Sea at Laing Art Gallery, Newcastle upon Tyne, 1986; Forces of Nature at Manchester City Art Gallery and tour, 1990–1; and John Moores Liverpool Exhibition, 1991–2. Hubbard's first solo show after moving to England was at New Art Centre in 1961, after which he added many international one-man exhibitions. He had a series of shows with Fischer Fine Art from 1984, after a retrospective at Warwick Arts Trust, 1981, another following at Yale Center for British Art, New Haven, Connecticut, 1986. Tate Gallery, Scottish National Gallery of Modern Art, British Council and other public collections hold his work. Hubbard won the Jerwood Prize in 1996.

Edgar HUBERT 1906–1985 Abstract painter, born Norman Edgar Hubert in Billingshurst, Sussex, and one of the mysterious curiosities of modern British painting. He was at school at Sherborne, and after studying art at University of Reading was at the Slade School of Fine Art, 1926–9 (gaining a certificate for drawing, 1926–7). Henry Tonks was among his teachers and he shared rooms with William Townsend, in whose journals he appears. Although he socialized with such painters as Geoffrey Tibble, William Coldstream and Rodrigo Moynihan and was involved in the Objective Abstractions group in the mid-1930s, Hubert was a shy man who became a recluse, exhibited little and whose work is generally unknown. He exhibited with the AIA, 1939; in La Jeune Peinture en Grande Bretagne, at La Galerie René Drouin in Paris, 1948, exhibiting four gouache compositions, one lent by the British Council, which organised the show; in the same year having solo show at the Mayor Gallery, where he had begun exhibiting in 1946, offering 20 Compositions, I–XX, "prices on application". After living with his family in Beaconsfield after World War II Hubert settled in Seaford, Sussex, where he continued to paint for himself, working in a variety of styles including a geometrical phase and abstracting out of his head rather than from nature. Hubert kept abreast of art developments, but was reluctant to talk about his own work. He painted at least one portrait, of his mother, held by the family. Finally his health was not good and he died of broncho-pneumonia and chronic broncho/asthma in a nursing home.

Andrew HUDSON 1935– Artist, born in Birmingham, who studied at Oxford University, graduating in English literature and language, 1957. Attended Slade School of Fine Art, 1957–9, and the University of Saskatchewan, Canada, 1961–2. From 1965 he lived in Washington, America. Group exhibitions included Corcoran Gallery of Art, Washington, from 1979; Basel Art Fair, with Bernard Jacobson, 1980. Showed widely in America, Germany and Canada, solo exhibitions including Klonardis, Inc, Toronto, from 1981; Brody's Gallery, Washington, from 1985; and Gallery 163, Seattle, 1989. Public collections holding examples include National Gallery of Canada, Ottawa; Corcoran Gallery of Art and George Washington University, both in Washington; and Pallant House Gallery Trust, Chichester, presented by Hudson by way of a memorial to Charles Kearley, a major Pallant House benefactor, the two being cousins.

Anna Hope HUDSON 1869–1957 Painter, also known as Nan Hudson, who was born in New York but brought up in Washington. She produced landscape, figure and architectural pictures in the manner of Walter Sickert, who admired her work. Went to Paris to study art in early 1890s, meeting her lifelong friend the painter Ethel Sands; spent five years in Eugène Carrière's atelier from 1896, also studying with Henri Evenepoel. As well as showing in Paris, she shared a show with Sands at Carfax Gallery, 1912, was a founder-member of LG in 1913, a member of WIAC and also showed at London Salon, NEAC, Baillie Gallery as well as Cooling, Goupil and Leicester Galleries. Pictures by her were included in Camden Town Recalled at Fine Art Society, 1976, and The Painters of Camden Town, at Christie's, 1988.

Erlund HUDSON 1912– Painter and designer, born in south Devon as Eleanor Erlund Hudson. She studied at Royal College of Art, teachers including Robert Austin and Malcolm Osborne, becoming an associate in 1937. Her studies were extended for two years with Continuation and Travelling Scholarships. War Artists' Advisory Committee bought her work, which is in the Imperial War Museum. Hudson was made a member of RE in 1946 and RWS in 1949, also showing at RA and abroad. She was a costume designer and was artistic adviser to the Brooking Ballet School. Lived in London for many years.

Nan HUDSON: *see* **Anna Hope HUDSON**

Tom HUDSON 1922–1997 Teacher and artist, born in Horden, County Durham, into a working-class, mining environment with little exposure to art. Association with such key figures as Harry Thubron and Herbert Read honed Hudson's natural ability to inspire and motivate others. Hudson studied at Sunderland College of Art, at King's College at the University of Durham, then did a postgraduate course in art history at Courtauld Institute, 1950–1. Began teaching at Lowestoft School of Art, other appointments following in Leeds, Leicester, Cardiff College of Art where he was director of studies and in Vancouver, Canada. He held a number of consultancies in Britain and abroad, and was interested in a range of subjects including education, colour and the history of art. Group shows included Drian Galleries, Grabowski Gallery where he also had a solo show in 1973, and abroad. In 1972 he completed a mural for University Hospital Wales in Cardiff. Hudson was a member of the 56 Group, also exhibiting with SEA, at Royal National Eisteddfod and elsewhere. Died in Bristol.

Yvonne HUDSON 1924–1985 Sculptor, artist in various fields including watercolours and embroidery, puppet-maker and teacher, born in Wanstead, Essex. She studied at the Slade School of Fine Art in 1943–8, winning the sculpture prize in the latter year. For a time she was arts adviser to the Scottish Association of Girls' Clubs, then after marriage she lived at Earnley, Sussex. Taught at Portsmouth School of Art and later at Horsham Art School. She was a keen Anglican, and much of her work had religious themes and was done for Chichester Cathedral and Sussex churches; it is also held by Worthing Art Gallery. She was a fellow of the RBS and showed at RA, RBA and elsewhere and had several solo shows in Chichester, Earnley and Winchester. Retrospective at Chichester Centre of Arts in 1987.

Henry Percy HUGGILL 1886–1957 Paintmaker, printer, teacher and curator, born in London. Studied at the Royal College of Art, 1908–14, under W R Lethaby, Gerald Moira and Sir Frank Short. Exhibited RA, RE, provincial and overseas exhibitions. Huggill's work is held by a number of northern art galleries, including Atkinson Art Gallery, Southport. He was principal of Southport School of Art, 1921–30, and curator of the local art gallery for that period. From 1930 he was principal of Liverpool College of Art for 21 years. Lived at Dyserth, Flintshire.

John HUGGINS 1938– Sculptor and teacher, born in Wiltshire. He studied sculpture at West of England Art College, Bristol, 1956–61, gaining among awards the prize for sculpture in both 1959–60. He became a part-time lecturer at Bristol Polytechnic and Bath Academy of Art until 1977, then decided to sculpt full-time. Huggins' affinities were with artists such as Brancusi and Duchamp-Villon, being concerned with forms and their interaction and impeccable craftsmanship. Mounting on black bases was a feature of his sculptures. Initially he showed in the Bath and Bristol area, then signed with Alwin Gallery, later Art Scene, to handle his output exclusively, having a series of solo exhibitions, although he had a one-man at Anthony Hepworth Fine Art, Bath, in 1993. Was a member of RWA and associate of RBS. Arts Council and Bristol City Art Gallery hold his work. Lived in Woodford, Berkeley, Gloucestershire.

Angela HUGHES 1964– Painter and draughtsman who studied at Darlington Sixth Form College, 1984–5, Newcastle University, 1985–9, and Royal Academy Schools, 1989–91. From 1985 she gained a string of awards, including the John Christie Memorial Prize twice at Newcastle University, 1986–7; Eric Kennington Drawing Prize, 1990–1; and the David Murray Landscape Scholarship at RA, 1991. In that year, too, she gained a Northern Arts Artists' Bursary. Again in 1991 Hughes was granted a National Trust for Art Commission and a Procter & Gamble Ltd Commission. Her work was described as being about "the power and atmosphere of places", tough and uncompromising. She began to show in mixed exhibitions in 1987 at Hatton Gallery, Newcastle University; other venues included RA, Mall Galleries and The Artists' View, Docklands, 1991. In 1992 she shared a show at Cadogan Contemporary and in 1994 won The Alasdair Gilchrist Fisher Memorial Award there. Lived in Darlington, County Durham.

Christopher HUGHES 1881–1961 Painter, printmaker, illustrator and teacher, born in St Albans, Hertfordshire, he studied privately and acquired his artistic training from his father, Wyndham Hughes, who was a specialist in ecclesiastical decoration and stained glass. Christopher Hughes served at Marlborough College, 1920–46, as art master. Exhibited RA, Foyles Gallery, Walker's Galleries and in the west of England. Lived at Marlborough, Wiltshire.

Donald HUGHES 1881–1970 Artist, principally in watercolour and crayon, born in Clifton, Bristol, who continued to live in the city. He was a student at Heatherley's School of Fine Art under Iain Macnab and Henry Massey. Went on to become auctioneer and estate agent, but retired early to paint. Showed in London and the provinces and had first one-man show at Clifton Arts Club in 1924; for a time he was chairman of the Club. Was also a member of the Bristol Savages, being originally elected as a literary member, for he wrote several volumes of verse. In 1938 he wrote the text for the artist Kit Gunton's book *Birdsworth.* Bristol City Art Gallery holds Hughes' work. He bought Blaise Hamlet, and when his offer of it was refused by Bristol Corporation presented it to the National Trust.

Edith HUGHES fl. c.1910–1960 Painter, printmaker and designer who after initial education, partly in France, in 1913 attended Heatherley's School of Fine Art; also studied painting with Harold Gilman and Walter Sickert and printmaking with Ernest Jackson. Exhibited RA, RCamA, NPS, ROI, Goupil Gallery and Paris Salon. Lived in London.

Eleanor HUGHES 1882–1959 Watercolourist, born in Christchurch, New Zealand. After initial education in New Zealand, she studied in Newlyn, Cornwall, with Stanhope Forbes and Elizabeth Forbes. Continued to live in Cornwall, at St

Buryan, and was married to the artist Robert Morson Hughes. She exhibited RA, Goupil Gallery, NEAC, RI, SWA, Walker Art Gallery, Liverpool, and elsewhere. Oldham Art Gallery & Museum, Lancashire, holds her work.

Frank HUGHES 1905–1987 Painter, draughtsman and teacher, a Londoner born in St Pancras who settled in Muswell Hill. Although trained at St Martin's School of Art, Hughes worked for the capital's water board in an administrative capacity, a chore which enabled him to live and pay for his painting materials. A longstanding friendship with the painter Edward Bishop was important. With his companion Kathleen, Hughes travelled in France and Italy, producing drawings and watercolours of landscapes and café scenes which he would work up later into oil paintings. These, like his sensitive portraits, can be small and quite dark. Hughes, an exhibiting member of the NEAC, was very left-wing, a hater of the Establishment, who did, however, exhibit three landscapes at RA Summer Exhibitions between 1954–61. His diffidence prevented his showing widely. He was heavy smoker, starting with a cigarette, changing next to a cigar, then a pipe, and as a result suffered from emphysema.

Frederick George HUGHES 1924– Sculptor in plastic, born in Gibraltar. He was a member of Royal Glasgow Institute of the Fine Arts, also exhibiting in group shows including RA Summer Exhibitions, 1966–72, and Majorie Parr Gallery. Lillie Art Gallery, Milngavie, holds two works in the manner of Naum Gabo, bought in 1973, Cyclops and Germination, Perspex and string abstracts. Lived in Henley-on-Thames, Oxfordshire.

Frieda HUGHES fl. from 1980s– Painter of strong figurative works, daughter of the poet laureate Ted Hughes and the poet Sylvia Plath, brought up in Devon. She attended Bedales, then studied at St Martin's School of Art after an early marriage, selling greetings cards and three years in the Civil Service in Exeter. Travelled to Australia in 1988, where she bought a farm to which she returned periodically, also having a studio in south London. Showed with Anna-Mei Chadwick.

Ian HUGHES 1958– Painter, art therapist, photographer and installations artist, born in Glasgow. Hughes studied at Duncan of Jordanstone College of Art, Dundee, 1976–80. For much of the 1980s he worked with the mentally sick, in the art therapy department at Stobhill Hospital, Glasgow, then at Royal Edinburgh Psychiatric Hospital. He had his first one-man show at 369 Gallery, Edinburgh, in 1985. In 1988–9 he worked as artist-in-residence at Scottish National Gallery of Modern Art, Edinburgh; had a solo show there in 1989 and in that year showed widely on the continent. Several large museums, as well as the Scottish National Gallery of Modern Art, hold his work which was deeply influenced by his time with the mentally deranged and which can be sad and disturbing but powerful.

Jim HUGHES 1934– Designer and teacher, born in Glasgow where he attended the School of Art, 1950–4, then Jordanhill College, obtaining his teaching certificate. Went on to lecture at Glasgow University's extra-mural department. Was elected to SGA in 1972. Showed in the Glasgow area, having work in the local public gallery. Lived in Ayr.

Ken HUGHES 1927– Sculptor and teacher, born in Liverpool. He attended Slade School of Fine Art, 1951–5, under A H Gerrard, Reg Butler and F E McWilliam. Hughes went on to teach at Birmingham College of Art and Bath Academy of Art, where he was head of sculpture, 1965–85. Hughes' main works were a Holy Family group in Southwark Cathedral and portraiture. His painted sculpture in relief and in the round was "influenced by German painting of the Weimar Republic" on which he lectured. Hughes took part in various group shows, including RA Summer Exhibition, and had solo shows at Ikon Gallery, Birmingham, and at Festival Gallery, Bath. Birmingham and Bristol City Art Galleries hold examples. Lived in Bristol.

Malcolm HUGHES 1920–1997 Systematic Constructivist artist, draughtsman, painter and teacher, born in Manchester. From 1938–9 he attended the College of Art there, then Royal College of Art in 1946–50. He taught part-time initially at Bath Academy of Art, where he remained 1960–70. From 1966–70 taught at Chelsea College of Art, from 1968–82 at Slade School of Fine Art, becoming emeritus reader in fine art at University of London. In 1969 Hughes was co-founder of the Systems Group. Hughes had his first one-man show at ICA in 1965. Among the group shows he contributed to were Four Artists: Reliefs, Constructions and Drawings, at Victoria & Albert Museum in 1971; Basically White at ICA in 1974; and British Art in the 60s, Tate Gallery in 1977; he also appeared in many overseas group shows; and in The Non-Objective World Revisited at Annely Juda Fine Art in 1988. Hughes' work is held by British Council and Manchester City Art Galleries. The artist Jean Spencer was Hughes' companion for over 25 years, becoming his second wife in 1997. They lived in London.

Nigel HUGHES 1940– Painter, sculptor and printmaker, born in Camberley, Surrey, who became a full-time artist from 1977 when he attended the Royal Academy Schools under Peter Greenham and Norman Blamey. To produce his landscapes and wildlife studies in the romantic, figurative tradition Hughes travelled extensively, including the continent, Arabia, Africa, New Zealand, the South Pacific, South and Central America. Mexico was a special favourite. His solo exhibitions were held in Britain and widely abroad. He had a show in London at the Mexican Embassy when its president visited in 1985; at Guy Morrison in 1987; plus a series at Oliver Swann Galleries. Hughes' work featured in David Hicks' book *Living with Design*, 1979, and in several archaeological works on ancient American civilizations. Hughes guided a tour to Yucatan in 1987. Commissions included HRH The Prince of Wales, the Grenadier Guards, National Trust and Tower of London. Limited edition prints were produced of his works. Lived in County Down, Northern Ireland.

Patrick HUGHES 1939– Painter, designer, teacher and writer, born in Birmingham. He studied at James Graham Teachers' Training College, Leeds, 1959–61, in the latter year having his first solo show at Portal Gallery. In 1961 also he showed in John Moores, Liverpool, Exhibition, the first of several appearances. For three years in the early 1960s Hughes taught in Leeds schools before becoming senior lecturer in painting and drawing at Leeds College of Art, 1964–9. After a year studying art education at London University Hughes taught for four years at Chelsea and Wolverhampton Schools of Art from 1970. In that year he had a one-man show at Angela Flowers Gallery, the first of many there. Hughes was included in a show of Surrealist pictures at Crawshaw Gallery in 1988. His pictures had a strong jokey element, featuring odd perspectives, rainbows and visual paradoxes. These were themes taken up in books such as *Upon the Pun, Dual Meaning in Words and Pictures*, produced with Paul Hammond, in 1978, and *Moron Oxymoron*, of 1983. Hughes' work is held by Arts Council, Tate Gallery and British Council. He was the second husband of the writer and artist Molly Parkin. Lived in London.

Robert Alwyn HUGHES 1935– Painter, graphic artist, film maker and teacher, born in Dowlais, Glamorgan. He attended Newport College of Art, 1953–7, Leicester College of Art, 1957–8, and Royal College of Art, 1958–61. From the early 1970s, he was in charge of Taliesin Films, becoming known for experimental films and photographic projects. Showed at Howard Roberts Gallery in Cardiff, McRoberts and Tunnard in London, SWG, Royal National Eisteddfod and abroad. Among his films was a semi-documentary on the poet Idris Davies. CASW bought his oil painting Send Back Your Homing Pigeons, Dai.

Robert Evans HUGHES 1896–1970 Painter and draughtsman, born in Llanwrst, Denbighshire. Having lived in Australia with his family he volunteered for service with the Australian Army and during action in France was blown up and almost paralysed. In Australia he began painting under the tuition of Maud Russell. Later had tuition at the Royal Society, studied in Rome and at Central School of Arts and Crafts under Bernard Meninsky and F J Porter. Settled in North Wales, finally at Rhyl, where he was a founder-member of the Colour Society and Prestatyn 57 Group; was also a member of the UA and was president of the Denbighshire Art Society, Colwyn Bay. Showed UA, ROI, NS, RCamA and elsewhere. Flintshire Education Committee owns his work. Retrospective exhibition at Rhyl Library Museum and Arts Centre in 1988. Hughes was notable for his Welsh landscapes and for the fact that he overcame colour blindness to paint.

Robert Morson HUGHES 1873–1953 Primarily a landscape painter, in oil, Hughes married the painter Eleanor Waymouth (Hughes). He attended Lambeth School of Art and the South London Technical Art School. Exhibited RA, IS, ROI, Goupil Gallery and NEAC. Leeds City Art Gallery holds his work. Lived finally at St Buryan, Cornwall.

Ronnie HUGHES 1965– Painter who gained a first-class degree in 1988 from University of Ulster in Belfast where he was born, then his master's degree in fine art, 1989. Architectural images and words were notable features of his canvases. His work won first prize at the Taylor Awards in 1989; it was chosen for the Claremorris Open Exhibition in 1989 and 1992; and it appeared in the 1994 shows Works on Paper and Beyond the Partitions, put on by Queen Street Studios, Belfast, with which he was associated. His later solo exhibitions included City Reformed, at Rubicon Gallery, Dublin, and Limerick City Gallery of Art, both 1993. Hughes' work received wide media coverage and is held by Arts Council of Northern Ireland, Irish Contemporary Arts Society and Monaghan County Museum.

Stephen HUGHES 1952– Artist and teacher working in a variety of materials, primarily known as a sculptor, who was born in Salisbury, Southern Rhodesia. Before attending Goldsmiths' College School of Art, 1984–7, where he gained an honours degree in fine art, Hughes worked in factories, including ceramics and brass. After Goldsmiths', he was Picker Fellow at Kingston upon Thames Polytechnic. He lectured at Goldsmiths', 1992–3, from then on at Kingston University. His many group appearances included Adam Gallery, 1986; Mandy Loves Declan 100%, Mark Boote Gallery, New York, 1993; Arts Council's tour Recent British Sculpture, 1993–4; Computer World, The Tannery, 1996; and John Moores Liverpool Exhibition, Walker Art Gallery, 1997–8, where he was a prize winner. Had solo exhibition at The Showroom, 1987, and Galerie Philippe Casini, Paris, 1992. Arts Council holds examples. Lived in London.

Thomas Gwynfryn HUGHES 1923– Printmaker and teacher, born in Ynyshir, Glamorgan. He attended Cardiff College of Art, in the late-1940s starting a teaching career that included the senior lectureship in illustration and printmaking at Newport College of Art. In 1974 was involved in An Iconograph of the Mabinogion, concerned with the Medieval collection of Welsh folk stories, in connection with the Royal National Eisteddfod and WAC; he also showed with SWG and Northampton Arts Society. WAC holds his work.

Blair HUGHES-STANTON 1902–1981 Wood engraver, painter, draughtsman and teacher, born in London, son of the artist Sir Herbert Hughes-Stanton, his first wife was the printmaker Gertrude Hermes. He was educated at Colet Court and HMS *Conway*, then studied art at Byam Shaw School, 1919–22, Royal Academy Schools, 1922–3, and at Leon Underwood's School, 1923–5. While married to Gert Hermes he collaborated with her to illustrate John Bunyan's *The Pilgrim's Progress*, 1928. He succeeded John Maynard as head of the Gregynog Press, 1931, and with his second wife, Ida Graves, established the Gemini Press, illustrating her *Epithalamion* in 1934. In 1938 he won an International Prize for Engraving at Venice Biennale. Hughes-Stanton taught at Westminster School of Art, 1934–9; Colchester School of Art, 1945–7, after war service; St Martin's School of Art, 1947–8; and Central School of Arts and Crafts,

1948–80. He was a member of LG, SWE and a founder-member of the International Society of Wood Engravers. Showed with Redfern, Leicester and Cooling Galleries. Royal Glasgow Institute of the Fine Arts and RHA. Contemporary Art Society, Whitworth Art Gallery in Manchester and other public collections hold examples. Lived latterly in Manningtree, Essex.

Julian HUGHES-WATTS 1969– Painter, born in Cardiff, whose work included geometrical abstracts in bright colours, such as his acrylic on canvas Delodur, Royal Over-Seas League Open, 1995. Hughes-Watts studied at Birmingham College of Fine Art and Royal Academy Schools. He gained a Leverhulme Scholarship, 1991–4, and the Worshipful Company of Painter-Stainers Award, RA, 1994. Group exhibitions included 22 Cork Street, 1993, and in 1994 Premiums Exhibition, Sotheby; New Burlington Gallery; and Fresh Art, Business Design Centre, Islington.

James HUGONIN 1950– Painter and teacher, born in Barnard Castle, County Durham. He studied at Winchester School of Art, West Surrey College of Art and Design in Farnham and at Chelsea School of Art. Went on to teach at Chelsea and at colleges in the northeast of England. He was a member of the Newcastle Group of artists and was included in South Bank Centre's touring show of 1988–9, The Presence of Painting. One-man shows included Galerie Brigitte Hilger, Aachen, 1983; Graeme Murray Gallery, Edinburgh, and Bede Gallery, Jarrow, 1985; and Galerie Hoffman, Friedberg, 1987. Reacting against free, gestural painting surrounding him at art school in the 1970s Hugonin sought a style by which he could create work balanced "between extreme complexity of means on the one hand and the apparent simplicity of the overall image on the other". Tiny fragments of colour created a texture with sweeps and rhythm. Arts Council holds his work. Lived in remote Cheviot Hills, at Wooler, Northumberland.

Thelma HULBERT 1913–1995 Painter and teacher, born in Bath, Somerset, where she studied at the School of Art. During the 1930s Hulbert was close to the group of artists which included William Coldstream, Victor Pasmore, Claude Rogers and Graham Bell which eventually became the Euston Road School. After the interruption of the war years she travelled in America, Africa and on the continent, while continuing to paint in her London studio. From 1962–72 she taught at Central School of Art and Design. Hulbert took part in numerous exhibitions, including solo shows at Leicester, Redfern and Marjorie Parr Galleries and a retrospective at Whitechapel Art Gallery in 1962. Arts Council, Contemporary Art Society, provincial and foreign galleries hold her work. Died at home in Honiton, Devon.

Frederick W HULL 1867–1953 Belfast, Northern Ireland, businessman, born in Drogheda, County Wexford, who took up painting in his thirties. Studied part-time at Government School of Design and privately with the landscape and flower artist David Gould. Harvey was a member and president of Ulster Arts Club and a member of Belfast Art Society, also showing at Walker Art Gallery in Liverpool and RHA. Ulster Museum holds his work.

James HULL 1921–1990 Painter and interior designer, born in London, where he died. From a working-class background, Hull studied architectural design before World War II, during which he served in the Army, 1939–46, eventually becoming a toymaker and scenery designer. His first paintings were Surrealistic, but this changed to a Constructionist style using pure colour and basic geometrical shapes. With the help of Herbert Read Hull had his first exhibition in the Brook Street Gallery in 1949, then his reputation as a member of the avant-garde grew as he showed at Gimpel Fils and painted his mural The Story of Coal for the Festival of Britain's Dome of Discovery in 1951. Began to show in Paris and New York, but economic pressures spurred him to enter and win a competition to design the interior of the *Daily Mirror* building, and he worked for the IPC publishing conglomerate until 1970. After an idyllic sojourn in Ibiza he did a variety of designing jobs in several continents, returning to London in straitened circumstances in 1980. During the period before his death his reputation as a pioneer abstractionist was re-established with shows at the Camden Galleries and Whitford and Hughes.

Norman Thomas Stephen HULL 1901-c.1978 Painter and ceramic artist. Born at Church Gresley, Staffordshire, he studied art at Nottingham College of Art, Derby College of Art and Stoke-on-Trent College of Art. Exhibited RI, in the provinces and America, and at the Paris Salon, where he won a bronze medal in 1957. He was managing director of Honiton Art Potteries and the Norman Hull Pottery, Devon, and his work is in various royal collections. Was a fellow of the Royal Society of Arts until he died, and lived at Worthing, Sussex.

Michael HULLIS 1955– Sculptor and teacher who studied at Ipswich School of Art, 1974–5, Bristol Polytechnic, 1975–8, then became a technician at Sir John Cass School of Art, 1979–82. From 1982 was a part-time lecturer there and at Sidcup Arts Centre. Hullis' mixed show appearances included a Goldsmiths' exhibition at Woodlands Art Gallery, 1983.

Ursula HULME 1917– Artist in various media, textile designer and art therapist, born in Cottbus, Germany. She lived in Berlin and studied at the Reimann School there under Maria May, moving to England in 1938 where she worked as a freelance fabric designer. From 1961 Hulme worked as a voluntary art therapist for several medical centres. In 1978 she founded and became president of the registered charity Conquest, The Society for Art for Physically Handicapped People. Hulme was a member of Free Painters and Sculptors and of Richmond Art Group. She had several solo shows at Woodstock Gallery, 1960–70, and at Talent Store, 1990. Lived in East Ewell, Epsom, Surrey.

Gary HUME 1962– Painter whose output ranged from early rigorous geometrical abstracts and a series of door-based images to later exuberantly colourful figurative pictures. Hume was born in Kent, and studied at Liverpool Polytechnic, 1985–6, and Goldsmiths' College School of Art, 1986–8. Group shows included Lorence Monk Gallery, New York, and Esther Schipper, Cologne, both 1989, and South Bank Centre's touring The British Art Show, 1990. Had solo exhibitions at Karsten Schubert Ltd from 1989; one of strange, pathetic and unsettling new works at ICA in 1995; and in 1997 a range of his pictures was shown, in a shared exhibition with Fiona Rae, at Saatchi Gallery. In 1996 he was included in the Turner Prize exhibition at the Tate Gallery and in 1997 won the Jerwood Prize. Lived in London.

Effie HUMMERSTON 1891– Watercolourist, born in Leeds where she studied at the School of Art and continued to live. Exhibited RI, RWS, in Leeds and at Walker Art Gallery, Liverpool.

Campbell HUMPHREYS 1910–1948 Artist in black-and-white and wash and typographer. Studied at Glasgow School of Art, 1927–38, under Hugh Adam Crawford and Henry Alison. Then worked mainly in the advertising industry. Lived at Falkirk, Stirlingshire.

David HUMPHREYS 1937– Artist in acrylic, watercolour and etching, and teacher, born in London but with strong Welsh connections. He studied at Durham University, 1958–62, with Victor Pasmore as tutor, and gained the Thomas Penman Scholarship and a State Scholarship. After graduation Humphreys taught at Ravensbourne College of Art & Design, 1963–9, then painted and travelled full-time. While most of his landscapes were set in Wales, Humphreys spent part of each year in the Hebrides, also visiting countries such as Czechoslovakia, Mexico, Peru and Chile. The relationship of figures to landscape and elements of Symbolism were aspects of Humphreys' work. Took part in many group shows including Arts Council Young Contemporaries, 1960; John Moores Liverpool Exhibition from 1967; Royal National Eisteddfod of Wales from 1968; RCamA, 1989; and The Discerning Eye, Mall Galleries from 1991. He had a series of solo shows at Galerie Basilisk, Morgue, Switzerland from 1972, later shows including Dieter Matschke, Leipzig, Germany, 1991, and Gottesman, Jones & Partners, 1992. Arts Council, several education authorities and provincial universities hold Humphreys' work. Lived in St Davids, Pembrokeshire.

Henry Norman HUMPHREYS 1905–1955 Painter, designer and teacher, born in Liverpool. Studied at the School of Art there, 1925–31, under William Penn and George Marples, then from 1931–3 at the Royal College of Art under Sir William Rothenstein and Barnett Freedman. Held a number of teaching posts, including Leamington Spa, Hastings and Wrexham Schools of Art. Exhibited RA, Walker Art Gallery, Liverpool, and other provincial galleries. Illustrated a Welsh translation of *Aesop's Fables*. Bootle Museum and Art Gallery holds his work. Lived at Lower Foxdale, Isle of Man.

Johanne HUMPHREYS 1968– Sculptor and teacher making abstracted works in a variety of materials, who "dealt with the influence modern farming methods have on landscape, surrounding my area of Suffolk." She was born there in Lowestoft. Gained a first-class honours degree at Manchester Polytechnic, 1989–92, experience then included organising exhibitions for Clock House Artists Association; being a foundry mould-maker; backdrop painting for photographers; and visiting lecturing at Lowestoft College of Further Education. In 1998 participated in return project in Minnesota, America. Exhibitions included Yew Tree Open, 1st Open Studio Exhibition, Laxfield, 1992; two-man show at Peter Pears Gallery, Aldeburgh, 1994; On the Border, Christchurch Mansion, Ipswich, 1997; and a shared show at Chappel Galleries, Chappel, 1998. Had a solo exhibition at Neal Street, Covent Garden, 1993. Humphreys' husband was the artist Laurence Edwards.

John HUMPHREYS 1929– Painter in oil, born in Bethlehem, in South Africa's Orange Free State. After education in Johannesburg he attended Heatherley's School of Fine Art under Iain Macnab, then with Stanley Grimm in the mid-1950s. He joined ROI in 1977 and won the Stanley Grimm Prize four years later. Also showed with RA, RI, RSMA and at Paris Salon. Lived in Greenford, Middlesex.

Winifred O HUMPHREYS 1895–1975 Versatile artist and teacher working in many media, born in Liverpool, where she attended the School of Art, then Slade School of Fine Art. In the inter-war years she worked mainly in the city, being a student tenant at the Bluecoat School and a member of the Sandon Studios Society. Humphreys completed portraits, murals, woodcuts, modelling and decorative panels for ships, stores, clubs, churches; stage and costume design for David Lewis, Sandon and Playhouse theatres; design of floats and costumes for Liverpool Centenary Railway Exhibition and the Lancashire Cotton Pageant at Belle Vue, Manchester, in the 1930s. In the 1940s she began the Quiet Club at the Royal Institution for services personnel. Taught in schools and technical colleges in Liverpool and north Wales, in 1946 moving to Naid-y-March, Holywell, Flintshire, where she died. Humphreys latterly developed a technique for mosaic plaques and panels using broken china and tiles. Showed at IS, Walker Art Gallery in Liverpool and Manchester City Art Gallery. A privately printed monograph on Humphreys was published in 1980, three years after a memorial show in Mold.

Mark HUMPHRYS 1925– Painter, mural artist, carver in wood and stone and teacher, born in Monaco. He studied at Winchester School of Art, where his teachers included Leonard Daniels; Southampton and Bournemouth Colleges of Art. Went on to lecture at St Hild's College, Durham. Showed with LG, Wessex Artists and Hampshire Artists. Lived in Durham.

Cecil Arthur HUNT 1873–1965 Landscape painter, born in Torquay, Devon. Studied at Cambridge University, practised as a barrister, then during World War I took up painting full-time. Was by that time known for his writings on the law. Hunt was especially fond of his watercolour portraits of mountains, dramatic and with an assured handling of broad planes. His work were reproduced in the *Alpine Journal* and *Alpine Calendar*, by the Medici Society and in many publications. Exhibited prolifically at RWS, of which for several years in the early 1930s he was vice-president, Fine Art Society, RBA, Ridley Art Club, Walker's Galleries and elsewhere. British Museum, Victoria & Albert Museum, Fitzwilliam Museum in Cambridge and many provincial galleries hold his work. In 1996 Chris Beetles Ltd held an exhibition of Hunt's pictures with a catalogue comprehensively covering his life, travels and output. Lived in London and at Manaton, Devon.

Georgina HUNT 1922– Painter, born in Reading, Berkshire, who worked in many media, mainly in acrylic and oil. Her abstract, spray-painted paintings had a feeling of calmness and mystery. Hunt worked to liberate colour from the restraints of imagery, feeling that all shapes or lines had associational connotations. She studied with William Coldstream at Slade School of Fine Art, 1945–50. In 1976 she won a Greater London Arts Association major award, in 1993 gaining the Osaka 21st Century Association Prize, Osaka International Triennale. Group exhibitions included Blackheath Art Society, 1966; Hunter College, New York, 1972; LG, Barbican Centre, and Chelsea Arts Club (of which she was a member), both 1992; and United Abstract Artists, Mall Galleries, 1994. Had a solo show at Drian Gallery, 1967, with series at Space Studios from 1974 and Camden Studios from 1984. Hunter College; London Borough Hounslow Picture Loan Scheme; and Contemporary Arts and Culture Centre, Osaka, hold examples. Lived in London.

Gerry HUNT 1927– Abstract painter and draughtsman, born in London. He studied at Camberwell School of Art, 1953–5, and Slade School of Fine Art, 1955–7, then went on to teach at Camberwell for many years. Showed widely in London and at John Moores Liverpool Exhibition, 1963, 1965 and 1989–90. Coracle Press published his *Some Principles and Practice of Twelve Modern Art Styles* in 1980, and he showed with Coracle. Had exhibitions of drawings at Camberwell School in 1986–8. Lived in London.

Kay HUNT fl. from 1960s– Painter and teacher who was born in London. She studied at Camberwell School of Art and went on to teach at West Surrey College of Art and Design, Farnham. She showed at AIA Gallery, LG, South London Art Gallery, Camden Arts Centre and in a long series of Space Exhibitions, including Space from the Quadrangle at Woodlands Art Gallery, 1973. Had a solo show at Courtauld Institute.

Sue HUNT fl. from 1980s– Painter, printmaker and teacher who did a foundation course at High Wycombe College of Art, 1977–8; gained an honours degree in fine art, Canterbury College of Art, 1978–81; then her master's in fine art, Cardiff College of Art, 1985–7. Teaching experience included senior lecturer in printmaking at Norwich School of Art from 1991. In 1986 Hunt gained a WAC award to study in America and Mexico City researching murals; in 1988 under a Wales/Philadelphia Exchange, Brandywine Printworkshop, she was involved in producing a suite of lithographs and organising a student coalition to design and make a large mural in downtown Philadelphia; and in 1992 gained a WAC travel grant to research paper-making and wood block printing in Rajasthan, India. Hunt became a member of Association of Designers and Artists of Wales and of Pioneers Arts Group/Art Wales, both 1981; and of 56 Group Wales, 1994. Exhibitions included Wish you were here, Chapter Art Centre, Cardiff, 1986; Welsh Printmakers' Council touring show, 1989; Hyde Park Gallery, 1992; and Castle Museum, Norwich, 1994. Solo exhibitions included University Hospital Wales, 1991. Lived in Adamstown, Cardiff.

Tom HUNT 1920– Artist, born in Swinton, Lancashire, working mainly in oil and alkyd. Won a scholarship to Regional College of Art, Manchester, 1934–6, studied figure drawing at evening classes, 1943–7, then taught himself to paint after seeing the Gauguin Centenary Exhibition in Paris in 1949. First showed at Mid-Day Studios, Manchester, 1948–51, then from 1950s held solo shows at his studio in Victoria Park, at galleries across the northwest and participated in group exhibitions in England and Wales. In 1962 he showed a series of paintings interpreting music at Bridge House Galleries which received an enthusiastic response from the conductor of the Hallé Orchestra, Sir John Barbirolli. Hunt wrote that he "liked new challenges", and other subjects included landscape, people, still life, car crashes and football. There was a retrospective at The Portico Gallery, Manchester, 1995. He lived nearby at Ashton-under-Lyne.

Alec Butler HUNTER 1899–1958 Textile designer, born in London, who studied at Byam Shaw School of Art under Ernest Jackson. He was a director of Warner and Sons Ltd. Lived at Thaxted, Essex.

Alexis HUNTER 1948– Artist who employed photography, born in Auckland, New Zealand. She studied at Elam School of Art, 1966–9, and took a teaching diploma in art and art history in 1971. Became a member of the Association of Cinematographers and Television Technicians. Showed at Hayward Annual, 1978; Palais des Beaux-Arts, Brussels, 1979; Summer Show 2 at Serpentine Gallery, 1981; and Woodlands Art Gallery, 1981–2, touring exhibition of Greater London Arts Association award winners. Solo shows included ICA, 1978, and New 57 Gallery, Edinburgh, 1980. Arts Council, Scottish National Gallery of Modern Art and Otago University in New Zealand hold examples. Lived in London.

Elizabeth HUNTER 1935– Painter in oil, printmaker, curator and teacher, born and lived in Bristol, who studied at Slade School of Fine Art under Claude Rogers, Anthony Gross and Lucien Freud, gaining her diploma with special commendation, 1958. From 1964–6 she was curator of the Passmore Edwards Art

Gallery in Newlyn, later becoming teacher of life drawing at the School of Art & Design, Bristol. Group shows included Young Contemporaries; Kunstverein in Hanover, Germany; Penwith and Newlyn Societies; RA Summer Exhibitions, and elsewhere. Solo shows included Arnolfini Gallery, Bristol, 1964, and Bath College of Higher Education, 1994, where Hunter's key Inanna Series was shown, "potent and glowing images of birds, beasts and mythologies". Was a member of the Newlyn Society.

Ian HUNTER 1947– Environmental sculptor and teacher, born in Londonderry, Northern Ireland. He gained his diploma in sculpture from Ulster College of Art and Design, Belfast, 1965–9; did his teacher training at Leeds Polytechnic, 1969–70; gained his master's degree at University of Case Western Reserve, Cleveland, Ohio, in America, 1975–7; and obtained his doctorate from Manchester Polytechnic, 1987–92, on The Relevance of Environmental Sculpture Practices to Landscape Architecture. Hunter was education officer at the National Art Gallery, Wellington, New Zealand, 1971–5; was curator of painting and sculpture there, 1978–80; its acting director, 1978–9; in 1981 was a visiting lecturer at University of Canterbury, Christchurch, New Zealand; worked freelance in New Zealand and London, 1982–6; was artist-in-residence for the Rossendale Groundwork Trust/ North West Arts, Rossendale, 1986–7 (during which time he worked on projects with the local farmer and stone carver Stan Yates); was a consultant on environmental education and the arts to the Forestry Authority from 1992 onwards. In 1989 Hunter founded Projects Environment, a charitable trust. Examples of work done by Hunter were included in Lancashire South of the Sands, 1988, toured from the County and Regimental Museum, Preston. Took part in other group shows and had a series of solo exhibitions, including sculpture installations at Rossendale, 1987–9. Main works included Willow Dome and Snake Maze for Garden Festival Wales, Ebbw Vale, 1992. Lived at Turn Village, near Ramsbottom, Lancashire.

John Frederick HUNTER 1893–1951 Multi-talented artist, whose work included prints, enamels, stained glass and metalwork, and administrator, brother of the artist Mercy Hunter. He was born in Manchuria at Chin-Chow, his father being an Irish Presbyterian Church missionary. He studied at Trinity College in Dublin, at that city's Metropolitan School of Art and at Royal College of Art, graduating in 1922. In 1923 became art inspector for Ministry of Education, Northern Ireland, and was closely associated with CEMA, which organised his memorial show in 1952 in Belfast. Hunter was elected to RUA, becoming its president, also showing at RHA. Ulster Museum and Arts Council of Northern Ireland hold examples. Died at Whitehouse, Antrim.

John Young HUNTER 1874–1955 Painter, son of the painter Colin Hunter and husband of the artist Mary Young Hunter, his first wife. He was born Glasgow and studied at the Royal Academy Schools, his teachers including John Singer Sargent and Lawrence Alma-Tadema. Travelled extensively with his wife on the continent. He was at first influenced by the Pre-Raphaelites and was later mainly a portrait painter, his pictures sometimes being rather glamorous with a high finish. He lived in Suffolk for some time, but the latter part of his life was spent in America and died in Taos, New Mexico. Exhibited widely, including RA, Fine Art Society and elsewhere. Tate Gallery holds his Chantrey Bequest picture My Lady's Garden. Later work was signed John Young-Hunter.

Kenneth HUNTER 1916– Printmaker, illustrator, painter and teacher, born in Leeds, Yorkshire, where he was initially educated. A self-taught artist, he became vice-principal of the Press Art School, 1946–54, the correspondence course founded by Percy V Bradshaw. As well as exhibiting in London and the provinces, Hunter illustrated a number of books and drew for *Radio Times*, *Lilliput*, *Picture Post* and other periodicals. Lived finally in Leyburn, Yorkshire.

Kenny HUNTER 1962– Versatile sculptor, born in Edinburgh, who gained an honours degree at Glasgow School of Art, 1983–7. Among his awards were a John Kinross Scholarship to Florence, 1987; Benno Schotz Award, 1991; East prizewinner, Norwich Gallery, Norfolk Institute of Art and Design, 1993; and Friends of the RSA Artist's Award, 1995. Among Hunter's professional experience was construction worker and hospital porter, 1980–2; technical assistant, Glasgow School of Art, 1988–90; visiting artist in schools and set design for Theatre Romania's production of *The Last Night of Socrates* at Tramway, Glasgow, all 1993; and in 1995 installation of outdoor sculpture as part of the Stevenson Trail, for Sunderland City Council, 1995. Mixed shows included Compass Gallery, Glasgow, New Generation, 1987; Cyril Gerber Fine Art, Glasgow, 1990; Fuse, at Collins Gallery, Strathclyde University, 1993; and Swarm, Scottish Arts Council tour, 1995. Had a solo exhibition at Compass Gallery, 1992, later ones including The Spell of Plato, Glasgow School of Art, 1993, and Norwich Gallery, 1996. British School at Athens and Scottish Arts Council hold examples.

Margaret HUNTER 1948– Painter and ceramic sculptor, born in Irvine, Ayrshire. She studied at Glasgow School of Art, 1981–5, then awards enabled her to study under Georg Baselitz at the Hochschule der Künste in Berlin, 1985–6. After this she shared her time in Berlin and Fairlie, on Scotland's west coast. Hunter's theme was the female form, mother-and-child relationships and more latterly the female related to other individuals. Her brushwork was free and gestural. To lessen her dependence on the Western figurative tradition she turned for inspiration to primitive forms. Hunter had early solo shows, in 1986, in Berlin and Ayr. Also exhibited at Vanessa Devereux Gallery and at Art First, 1997. Scottish National Gallery of Modern Art, Edinburgh, holds her work.

Mary Sutherland HUNTER 1899– Painter and sculptor born at Holywell, near Motherwell in Lanarkshire. She studied at Edinburgh College of Art and RSA School of Painting, where she won the Chalmers-Jervis Prize. She showed at RSA, SSA,

RSW and Royal Glasgow Institute of the Fine Arts. Lived in Edinburgh.

Mary Young HUNTER 1872–1947 Painter and miniaturist, first wife of the artist John Young Hunter. After marrying him she travelled extensively on the continent. She is depicted in her husband's Chantrey Bequest picture My Lady's Garden, held by the Tate Gallery. Lived for some years in Wickhambrook, Suffolk. Showed extensively, mainly watercolours, at Fine Art Society, RA, SWA and elsewhere.

Mercy HUNTER 1910–1989 Teacher, designer, calligrapher, draughtsman and illustrator, born in Belfast, Northern Ireland, real name Martha Saie Kathleen Hunter. She was married to the artist George McCann and was sister of the painter and printmaker John Frederick Hunter. Because her father was a Presbyterian missionary, Hunter grew up in Manchuria, her secondary education taking place in Toronto, Canada, and Belfast. She attended the College of Art there, 1927–9, and won a scholarship to Royal College of Art, 1930–3, taught by the noted calligrapher Edward Johnston. Hunter was a dedicated teacher, for many years at Victoria College, Belfast. She served as president of RUA and of Ulster Society of Women Artists, which she had helped found. Designed extensively for ballet, theatre and opera (Belfast's Grand Opera House holds her work, as does Ulster Museum); completed many calligraphic commissions; and illustrated her husband's 1942 book (written as George Galway) *Sparrows Round My Brow*. Lived in Dungannon, County Tyrone.

Rob HUNTER 1972– Artist whose work employed video and site-specific performance, born in Glasgow. He gained a sculpture degree at Edinburgh College of Art, 1990–4, with a master's in combined media at Chelsea College of Art, 1995–6. Exhibitions included Lux Europae, Edinburgh International Festival, 1992; Paperworks 6, Seagate Gallery, Dundee, 1994; Actual Size, Seagate, 1995; and New Contemporaries at Tate Gallery, Liverpool, and Camden Arts Centre, 1996. In the last show Hunter linked the garage where he worked with the gallery through his image Satellite Employment Piece, 1994–6; surveillance cameras looked in on Hunter's life as a filling station attendant, garage visitors viewing the gallery.

Robert HUNTER 1920–1996 Painter, draughtsman, constructions artist and teacher, born in Liverpool. He attended the College of Art there and after distinguished military service abroad – he won the Military Cross in 1944 – in World War II was again at Liverpool College of Art, 1946–50. In 1957 he was included in Jack Beddington's book *Young Artists of Promise*. Went on to teach at several venues, being head of creative arts at Trinity College, Carmarthen, until retirement in 1983. He was a founder-member of 56 Group Wales, served on WAC art committee and as chairman of the visual arts panel of West Wales Arts Association. Took part in many group exhibitions, including SEA, SWG, Royal National Eisteddfod, where he was a judge for painting, and several shows of Welsh painting and the modern movement in Wales and abroad. At the Royal National Eisteddfod/WAC show An Iconograph of the Mabinogion in 1974 he won first prize. WAC, CASW and National Museum of Wales in Cardiff hold examples. One-man exhibitions included New Art Centre from 1961, later ones York University, 1987, and Pembroke Dock Library, 1988. Hunter said that Byzantine art, especially icons, Paul Klee, Oriental calligraphy and teaching drawing and painting were main influences on his works which were "a synthesis of what I have seen, read or heard."

William HUNTER fl. from 1910–1967 Painter, mainly in oil, born and lived in Glasgow, where he studied at the School of Art under Fra Newbery and Maurice Greiffenhagen. Also studied on the continent, helped by a scholarship. Exhibited extensively at Royal Glasgow Institute of the Fine Arts and ROI, also RSA, Paris Salon and elsewhere overseas. Glasgow Corporation bought his work.

Jeremy HUNTER HENDERSON 1956– Painter, influenced by Vincent Van Gogh and Philip Guston, whose brightly coloured images drew on television and advertising. He studied at Hull College of Higher Education, 1976–9, later working in London. Was included in 10 Hull Artists at Lincolnshire & Humberside Arts Area Centre, Hull, 1980, and Summer Show 3 at Serpentine Gallery, 1982. Solo exhibitions included Acme Gallery, 1981.

Dennis HUNTLEY 1929– Sculptor, printmaker, draughtsman and teacher, born in Weybridge, Surrey. He attended Wimbledon School of Art, 1947–51, teachers including Gerald Cooper, then London University, 1951–2. Went on to become head of Sir John Cass School of Art. Guildford Cathedral and Henry Thornton School in Clapham have examples of Huntley's work. He was made a fellow of RBS in 1970. Lived in Sutton, Surrey.

Moira HUNTLY 1932– Painter, writer and teacher, born in Motherwell, Lanarkshire. She attended Harrow School of Art under Christopher Sanders, 1948–53, then Hornsey College of Art, 1953–4. Huntly taught art, 1954–60, then freelanced as a painter. Group shows included Adam Gallery, Bath; Fosse Gallery, Stow-on-the-Wold; NEAC; Société des Pastellistes de France, Paris; Mystic Maritime Museum, Connecticut, in America; and FCA Gallery, Vancouver. She was a member of RSMA, RI and PS. Solo exhibitions included Theatr Clwyd, north Wales, and Alma Gallery in Bristol. She won a number of awards, including Winsor & Newton, 1985; Laing Painting Competition, 1986; and Manya Igel Fine Arts Award, 1992. Commissions and collections holding works included Clwyd County Council, Alcoa International, CWS Ltd and Nuclear Electric. Huntly was a prolific writer on painting whose books were published internationally. They included *Imaginative Still Life*, *Painting and Drawing Boats* and *Learn to Paint Gouache*. She lived in Willersey, Broadway, Worcestershire.

Nancy HUNTLY 1890– Painter, notably of portraits, born in Nasirabad, India. She was educated in Edinburgh and Düsseldorf,

Germany, where she studied art and at Royal Academy Schools. She also showed as Nancy Weir and under her married name Nancy Sheppard at RA, ROI, RP, New Grosvenor Gallery, Royal Glasgow Institute of the Fine Arts, Paris Salon and in Düsseldorf. Many writers were among her portrait subjects, including the romantic novelist Berta Ruck, Ben Travers the playwright and the novelist E M Forster. Lived in Welwyn Garden City, Hertfordshire. Her daughter Faith Sheppard was also an artist.

Robert HURDLE 1918– Painter and teacher, born in London. He studied at Richmond School of Art, 1935–7, then Camberwell School of Arts and Crafts, 1946–8, under William Coldstream after six years' military service. In 1950 he moved to Bristol to take a teaching post at West of England College of Art. He was senior lecturer in the faculty of fine art at Bristol Polytechnic until 1980 and lecturer in art history in the extra-mural department of Bristol University. For several years Hurdle taught drawing at Barry Summer School, Glamorgan. Hurdle began showing in LG shows in 1949 until 1965; also showed RWA, 1959–75, resigning his membership in 1976; other mixed shows including RA, New Art Centre, Frost and Reed Gallery in Bristol and Pelter/Sands Gallery, Bristol. Hurdle had a one-man show at University College, Swansea, in 1969, others including Albany Gallery, Cardiff, 1974, New Ashgate Gallery in Farnham in 1978, Farnham Maltings Kiln Gallery in 1983 and RWA in 1995. RWA, Bristol Corporation, Bristol and Bath Universities and Hong Kong Arts Centre hold his work. Lived in Bristol.

Charles HURFORD 1907–1974 Technical draughtsman and illustrator. Apprenticed originally as an engraver, he studied at Harrow School of Art. Eventually moved to the art department of Hulton Press. Although Hurford showed at RA, his best-known work was the exploded drawings in the centre spreads of the children's comic *Eagle*. He also illustrated for *Farmers Weekly* and as a freelance drew for books by round-the-world sailors such as Alec Rose and Francis Chichester. He lived at Harrow Weald, Middlesex.

John Bruce HURN 1926– Painter, designer and teacher, born in Spalding, Lincolnshire. He studied at Birmingham College of Art, 1942–6, a year later winning the Worshipful Company of Goldsmiths' design prize. Went on to hold a number of teaching posts in the Midlands, including Moseley School of Art. Showed in London and the Midlands, notably at RBSA, of which for a time he was treasurer. Lived for many years in Moseley, Birmingham.

Peter HURN 1942– Artist in oil, crayon, ink and lino-cut, born at Patchway, near Bristol. He studied in Australia at Perth Technical College with Percival Hunt and Ivor Hunt and in England at St Martin's School of Art; Birkbeck College, 1975–6, with Peter Murray; and in Italy, Switzerland and France. Showed at RA, John Moores Liverpool Exhibition, Guildhall and widely abroad. Two oil paintings, Circus of Life and The Gallery, are among his main works. British and continental private collections hold examples. Lived in London.

Harold HURRELL 1940– Conceptual artist and teacher, one of several artists – the others being Terry Atkinson, Michael Baldwin and David Bainbridge – who formed the influential exhibiting and publishing group Art & Language in 1968. Atkinson met Hurrell at grammar school and kept in touch. After Sheffield School of Art, in 1963 Hurrell moved to London to pursue a year's course at the Institute of Education, then was appointed as a technician at St Martin's School of Art, where Bainbridge had enrolled in the sculpture department. In 1967, the year that he took up a teaching post at Hull College of Art, Hurrell with Bainbridge held the Hardware Exhibition at the Architectural Association. Frustrated at the lack of exposure for their works in Britain, in 1968 Hurrell and friends founded Art & Language, Hurrell contributing to the allied magazine *Art-Language*.

Eric HURREN 1922– Painter, draughtsman, printmaker and teacher, born in Staffordshire, who aged nine moved with his family to Whitstable, Kent. In 1939 Hurren began studies at the Sidney Cooper School of Art, Canterbury, interrupted in 1942 when he was conscripted into the Army. He served in Germany, where he met his future wife Ingrid (they married after correspondence in 1951). In Iserlohn, with the Army of Occupation, Hurren was befriended by the artist Wilhelm Wessel, who "gave me a sense that art was worthwhile … that to be an artist was something quite precious." Demobilised in 1947, Hurren completed his final diploma year in painting at Canterbury. He found part-time teaching at St Edmund's School and at renamed Canterbury College of Art, where, inspired by his contact with Wessel, he went on to study lithography part-time for two years. He obtained a full-time post there, retiring as head of foundation studies in 1988. Hurren proved an adventurous tutor, interested in developments from the continent and America, notably impressed by the work of Estève and Diebenkorn. Exhibited work in Britain and abroad and had a retrospective at Herbert Read Gallery, Kent Institute of Art & Design, Canterbury, in 1996.

Leslie HURRY 1909–1978 Stage designer and painter, born in London, where he died. In 1925 joined St John's Wood Art School, where he remained two years, then won five-year scholarship to Royal Academy Schools. His early professional work involved murals in his father's house and decorative schemes for a firm of brewers in their public bars. Then painted landscapes in Britain and Ireland which led to a first one-man show at the Wertheim Gallery in 1937. Subsequently Hurry worked in France and produced two books of automatic drawings, *The Journey* and *Book of the Seven Eagles,* which had his own text. Redfern Gallery exhibitions led to Hurry's work being seen by Robert Helpmann, the ballet dancer, which led to their collaboration on a production of *Hamlet*. Hurry became closely associated with Sadler's Wells and the theatre, while showing at galleries in London and abroad. Victoria & Albert Museum holds his work, which has a strong Neo-Romantic flavour. Lived in Hundon,

Suffolk. In 1996 Marina Henderson held a retrospective of Hurry's stage designs.

Dora HURST 1925– Painter and artist in mixed media, born in Worcester. She attended Cardiff College of Art, 1956–61, then began teaching, returning to Cardiff College in 1968–9 to gain a diploma in art education. In the early-1970s began lecturing there. Took part in group shows including the WAC show Structure 66, SEA, SWG and Cardiff Artists Exhibition, at Oriel Contemporary Art, 1996, where Hurst exhibited landscapes employing bold shapes and colours. Education authorities in Cardiff, Glamorgan and Oxford hold her work.

Stephanie HURST 1952– Painter and illustrator, born in Wimborne, Dorset, who studied at Bournemouth and Poole College of Art, 1970–1, Hornsey College of Art, 1971–4, Byam Shaw School, 1976–77, and Royal Academy Schools, 1981–4. Showed at RA, Camden Arts Centre, Jonathan Poole Gallery and Royal Festival Hall, winning several prizes. Lived in London.

Martin HURSTHOUSE 1945– Artist in various media, notably a printmaker, born in Mansfield, Nottinghamshire. He studied painting and drawing at Chesterfield and Coventry Colleges of Art. Hursthouse was concerned with "the halting and capturing of a momentary sensation or recollection". He showed with Northern Young Contemporaries in 1968, widely in the north and Midlands, in America and shared an exhibition at The Studio, Dorchester. Settled for some years in Bournemouth, Hampshire, an area which influenced his work.

Eric HUSON 1930– Landscape painter born in Mitcham, Surrey. After Alleyn's School, Dulwich, he attended Camberwell School of Arts and Crafts, 1945–7, his teachers including John Minton and William Townsend, then Shrewsbury School of Art, 1947–8. Showed at Trafford Gallery and elsewhere.

Kabir HUSSAIN 1960– Sculptor, installations artist and photographer, born in Nara, Pakistan. Studied at Jacob Kramer College, Leeds, 1979–80; South Glamorgan Institute of Higher Education, Cardiff, 1980–3; and Chelsea School of Art, 1983–4. Awards included Henry Moore Foundation Prize, 1984, and Setting-up Grant in 1985 and a Travel Grant, 1988, both from WAC. Showed with LG in 1984; Lower Machen Festival, 1987; and in South Bank Centre's The British Art Show 1990. Solo exhibitions included National Eisteddfod, Newport, and Llanover Hall, Cardiff, both in 1988, and Bute Park installation, Cardiff, 1989. Lived in Cardiff.

Henry James HUSSEY 1913– Sculptor and stonemason, born and lived in London. He was self-taught as an artist after attending elementary school. Showed at RA, Leicester Galleries, Ash Barn Gallery in Petersfield and Tryon and Moorland Galleries. University of London Senate House was decorated with figures by Hussey.

John HUSSEY 1928– Sculptor and teacher born in Slough, Buckinghamshire, who studied at Goldsmiths' College School of Art, 1946–9. He later obtained a research diploma at Bristol Polytechnic, 1969–70, and became principal lecturer and director of studies there, retiring in 1983. Hussey was an associate of RBS and a member of RWA, also showing at RA. Lived in St Osyth, Essex.

Tom HUTCHESON 1924– Mixed-media artist and teacher, born in Uddingston, Lanarkshire. He studied at Glasgow School of Art, 1941–2 and 1946–9, teachers including Stanley Spencer, Benno Schotz, Hugh Adam Crawford and David Donaldson. Was for long a Glasgow Art Club member, showing at Royal Glasgow Institute of the Fine Arts as a member, RSA, SSA, in the English provinces and elsewhere. HM The Queen, HRH The Duke of Edinburgh and Scottish education authorities held his work. Lived in Glasgow.

Hilda Edith HUTCHINGS 1890-c.1950 Painter, printmaker and teacher, born in Grantham, Lincolnshire. She studied at Bristol Municipal School of Art, where she became a teacher. Moved to London in the mid-1920s and taught at West Ham School of Art. Showed at RA, RWA, Walker Art Gallery in Liverpool and with Chicago Society of Etchers and was a member of the Print Society of California. Bristol City Art Gallery and Los Angeles National Museum hold her work.

George HUTCHINS 1925– Painter and teacher, born in London. Studied at Brighton College of Art where his teachers included Charles Knight. Showed with RA, RBA and with Brighton and Essex Art Clubs. He completed a number of school murals. Lived in Romford, Essex, then in Meopham, Kent.

John HUTCHINSON 1884–1972 Botanical book illustrator who signed his work J H. Was born at Wark on Tyne, Northumberland, and rose to be keeper of museums at the Royal Botanical Gardens, Kew, Surrey, where he lived. Hutchinson produced many books on British and foreign – mainly wild – flowers, principally published by Penguin Books.

Louisa HUTCHINSON 1954– Gestural abstract painter, born in Wolverhampton, where she studied at the Polytechnic, 1972–3, then at Bath Academy of Art, Corsham, 1973–6. Mixed shows included 55 Wapping Artists, 1979; Tolly Cobbold Eastern Arts, 3rd National Exhibition, 1981; and Wapping Artists Open Studios Exhibition and RA Summer Exhibition, both from 1982.

Norman Douglas HUTCHINSON 1932– Painter, draughtsman and sculptor, notable for figure studies and portraits, born in Calcutta, India, who studied at an English boarding school at Kalimpong, where the Himalayas "gave to me a passion for landscape". Hutchinson later wrote that the disease and deprivation of Indian city life "became the haunting imagery of my painting. A darkness covered my pictures, a predilection for earthy colours, a sadness in every face and figure I painted, and shadow became the principal factor." In 1959 Hutchinson moved to London, and was able to study Western masters. He was largely self-taught, although he benefited from knowing two good artists in India, and in Europe met with Pietro Annigoni and some of his disciples. In 1963 a book, *Ten Drawings of Gloria*, appeared, featuring his wife who, with his daughters, were important models. Having business interests, Hutchinson did not depend on painting for a living. He carried out portrait commissions, and painted leading members of the royal family, including HM The Queen, HRH The Duke of Edinburgh and HM Queen Elizabeth The Queen Mother. Meticulous preparation was a feature of Hutchinson's work. Showed at RA, RP and other London mixed exhibitions. After a first solo show at Upper Grosvenor Galleries in 1964, did not exhibit one-man again until Mayfair Fine Art in 1991. In 1992 had a show with his daughter Rebecca, a pastellist, at Doncaster Museum & Gallery, in 1994 a solo exhibition, A Shift in the Concept of Beauty, at Archeus Fine Art. In that the theme of Lucretia, an important one, was evident. Sometimes signed his work Norman or N Douglas H. Lived latterly in France and Spain.

Peter HUTCHINSON 1932– Creator of landscape-oriented works in photography, montage and boxed form, born in London, who moved to America in 1953. His works confronted the viewer with thoughtful, teasing and amusing images. In America, Hutchinson developed alongside Robert Smithson and other land artists, and he went on to show extensively there and on the continent, but not in England until the Mayor Gallery retrospective of works, 1969–1996, held in the latter year. By then he had had around 50 solo exhibitions, including Landscapes, John Gibson Gallery, New York, 1969; Gallerie 20, Amsterdam, 1971; Stedelijk Museum, Amsterdam, 1974; American Art Company Gallery, New York, 1987; Bugdahn-Kaimer Galery, Düsseldorf, 1993; The Narrative Art of Peter Hutchinson: A Retrospective, Galerie Blancpain Stepczynski, Geneva, 1994; and Retrospective Exhibition & New Work, Holly Solomon Gallery, New York, 1995. Museum of Modern Art in New York, Museum Boymans in Rotterdam, Georges Pompidou Centre in Paris, Museum of Art in Sydney and other international collections hold examples.

Rebecca HUTCHINSON 1961– Painter, born in London, who studied at Byam Shaw School of Art, 1981–4. Exhibitions included Fieldborne Galleries from 1983; PS from 1986; Birch and Conran, 1989; and Phoenix Gallery from 1989. Among her portrait commissions was the actor Steven Berkoff. Her self-portrait was held by Doncaster Museum and Art Gallery.

Rosamund HUTCHINSON 1905– Painter, initially educated in Monmouth and Burnham-on-Sea. Studied with Marcus Holmes, Monmouth, 1923–4, then at the Slade School of Fine Art, where her teachers included Henry Tonks and Tancred Borenius. Lived in Ashfield, Herefordshire, and showed mainly in that area.

Suzanne HUTCHINSON 1957– Versatile artist using a bright palette, born in Lincolnshire. Her home was moved to Hong Kong, 1967–70; she attended Bath Academy of Art, Corsham, for a foundation course, 1975–6; undertook frequent visits to parental home in Baghdad, Iraq, 1976–8, while gaining a fine art honours degree at Brighton Polytechnic, 1976–9; and received her master's in painting at Chelsea School of Art, 1979–80. In 1989 she visited Australia and Malaysia. Set/costume designs and installations included *Petrushka*, Arts Council, 1981, and *Ghost Train*, installations for Hangleton Festival in Sussex, 1988. Group shows included British Drawing, Hayward Gallery, 1982; Off the Wall, Gardner Arts Centre, Brighton, 1991; and What is Jewellery?, Crafts Council, 1994. Had a solo show at Brighton Polytechnic, 1982, later ones including Lure, in 1997, at Museum & Art Gallery, Brighton, Sussex, where she lived.

Isabel HUTCHISON 1958– Largely self-taught artist, born in Hertfordshire, who after leaving school went into interior design, where she developed expertise as a mural painter. After being widowed in 1982 she travelled extensively, painting murals to earn a living. On her return completed courses at Chelsea College of Art under Peter Fleming. Her first solo show, in 1996, in the walkways of Tower Bridge, was the outcome of a three-year project to "paint the portrait", in tempera and mixed media on board, of all 20 of London's road bridges from Hampton Court to Tower Bridge.

Shand HUTCHISON 1920– Painter and teacher, born in Dalkeith, Midlothian, son of the painter Thomas Shand Hutchison. After North Berwick High School attended Edinburgh College of Art where his teachers included William Gillies, John Maxwell and Leonard Rosoman, and was there for two periods – 1939–40 and 1946–9 – interrupted by the war. Showed with RSA, SSA, Scottish Arts Club and elsewhere. Lived in North Berwick and had a studio in Edinburgh.

William Oliphant HUTCHISON 1889–1970 Portrait and landscape painter and influential teacher, born in Kirkcaldy, Fife. He studied at Edinburgh College of Art, 1909–12, then in Paris. James Gunn painted Hutchison several times, one a strikingly dandyish portrait as a young man. Hutchison became director of Glasgow School of Art, 1933–43, was elected RSA in 1943, becoming its president seven years later. He was made an Hon. RA in 1950 and was knighted in 1953. Exhibited widely, including RA, RSA, NEAC, Royal Glasgow Institute of the Fine Arts, Walker Art Gallery in Liverpool and RBA. He has work in several Scottish collections. Lived for a time in London.

David HUTTER 1930–1990 Painter, draughtsman and teacher, born in London, where he died. He studied at St Martin's and Hornsey Schools of Art. Hutter's reputation was established by the late 1960s, mainly on the basis of his landscapes in oil, but it was his watercolours, of the male nude and of flowers, that excited the critics in the early 1980s. The Japanese influence on his technique, using stretched wet paper, combined with an Oriental simplicity were notable features of Hutter's work. As well as writing for *The Artist*, Hutter organised life class groups, conducted other artists around Europe and lectured in prisons. Group exhibitions included RA, RP, RWS and RI. He had solo shows at John Whibley Gallery in 1969–72; Off Centre Gallery, 1979; Ebury Gallery, 1982; Mateloos Gallery, Rotterdam, 1986–7; and St Jude's, 1988; that gallery organised a memorial show in 1990.

Clarke HUTTON 1898–1985 Painter, lithographer and book illustrator, born and lived in London. Studied at the Central School of Arts and Crafts in the late 1920s. Hutton's figures and landscapes were exhibited, under the initials C H, at the RA, LG, RI, Redfern Gallery and elsewhere. The British Museum and Victoria & Albert Museum hold his work. He illustrated about 50 books, for publishers in Britain and America. Some of Hutton's later pictures were of a Surrealist type, rather in the manner of John Tunnard.

Dorothy HUTTON 1889–1984 Artist, especially of flowers, and calligrapher, Hutton was born in Bolton, Lancashire, and studied art at the Central School of Arts and Crafts under F Ernest Jackson and Graily Hewitt. Hutton exhibited at the RA, NEAC, Walker Art Gallery in Liverpool and at other venues. She was an official artist to the Crown Office and among her works was a memorial to General Dwight B Eisenhower. She was a member of the Art Workers' Guild from 1964 and lived in London.

John HUTTON 1906–1978 Painter especially of murals, glass engraver and teacher, he originated in New Zealand and was a self-taught artist. Initial education at Wanganui Collegiate School. For a time he taught mural painting at Goldsmiths' College School of Art and was chairman of the Society of Mural Painters. Although he showed at LG and Arts Council he was mainly known for permanent works in public places. This included murals and glass engravings respectively on the Orient Line ship *Orcades* and Cunard liner *Caronia*, a screen for Coventry Cathedral and doors for Guildford Cathedral. Victoria & Albert Museum bought his work. Joined the Art Workers' Guild in 1975. Lived in London.

John HUTTON 1948– Painter whose work included geometrical abstracts, born and based in London, who studied at Watford School of Art, 1967–70. Mixed shows included Dun Laoghaire School of Art, Dublin, 1975; RA from 1977; Yamaki Gallery, Osaka, Japan, 1981; and Wapping Artists Open Studios from 1982. Solo exhibitions included Middlesex Polytechnic, 1981, and St James' Church, Piccadilly, 1983. London Borough of Camden holds his work.

Sarah HUTTON 1962– Artist in various media, notable for colourful landscapes, born in Haworth, West Yorkshire, where in 1988 she founded Hutton van Mastrigt Art. She attended Bradford College, 1980–1; Central School of Art & Design, 1981–4; Syracuse University, New York, 1983; Leeds University, Bretton Hall, 1987–8; and Leeds Metropolitan University, 1993. In 1984–6 set up Haworth Artists' Field Study Centre. Many mixed shows included Cartwright Hall, Bradford, from 1989; Ilkley Manor House, 1992; and Manchester International Art Fair, 1993. Had a solo show at Albany Gallery, 1990, later ones including Harrogate Exhibition Centre and Ling House, Keighley, both 1993.

Bethan HUWS 1961– Artist born in Bangor, Caernarvonshire. Studied at Middlesex Polytechnic, 1981–5, then Royal College of Art, 1986–8. Participated in South Bank Centre's touring The British Art Show 1990. Solo exhibitions included Institut Sainte-Marie, Brussels, 1987; Rivington Street and Anthony Reynolds Gallery, 1988; Riverside Studios and FRAC des Pays de la Loire, Garenna Lemot, Clisson, 1989. Lived in London.

Richard HUWS 1902–1980 Sculptor, designer and teacher, born in Anglesey, north Wales, as Richard Hughes. As a young man he flirted with the Welsh national party Plaid Cymru, of which he was a founder-member, designing its logo, and changed his name to the Welsh version Huws. He later left the party, always being uncomfortable in organisations. After Beaumaris Grammar School Huws was an apprentice at Cammel Laird's, Birkenhead, then was an Armstrong Whitworth scholar reading naval architecture at Liverpool University, graduating in 1925. He then roamed Europe, sketching – Huws was a superb draughtsman – and studying sculpture in Vienna's Kunstgewerbeschule. Returned to England in 1930, flirted briefly with the early Fascists, then attacked them with cartoons. During World War II fostered his interest in mechanical systems by working on Spitfires. Became a fellow of the Society of Industrial Artists. Huws returned to Liverpool University, being on the staff of the School of Architecture 1955–69 (full-time from 1957, a senior lecturer from 1966), where his grasp of the problems of production design proved invaluable. Teaching commitments forced him to turn down design commissions. Huws created his Water Mobile for the Festival of Britain in 1951. It ejected lumps of water at unexpected intervals and gradually shook itself to pieces. "I spent most of my time repairing it, but it was a breakthrough in fountain design," Huws said in 1967, when his fountain near the Pier Head, Liverpool, was opened, commissioned by Merseyside Civic Society. He also created one for British Petroleum for a British Fair in Tokyo and exhibited in Glasgow and New York. While at Liverpool Huws lived near Llanrwst, Anglesey, developed an interest in landscape design and was an associate of the Institute of Landscape Architects. His wife was also an artist.

Juliette HUXLEY 1896–1994 Sculptor and writer, born in Auvernier, Switzerland, who moved to England in 1915 and became governess to Lady Ottoline Morrell's daughter. She married the biologist Julian Huxley and with him travelled widely. Studied sculpture at Central School of Arts and Crafts under John Skeaping and showed at RA. Her collection included works by artist friends Henry Moore, John Piper, Henry Lamb, Duncan Grant and Julian Trevelyan. In 1986 she published her autobiography *Leaves from the Tulip Tree*. Died in London.

Paul HUXLEY 1938– Painter, draughtsman and teacher whose work used simple geometrical shapes and serpentine forms. He was born in London and studied at Harrow School of Art, 1953–6, and Royal Academy Schools, 1956–60. From 1959 Huxley showed several times with Young Contemporaries, then in 1963 had the first of his one-man shows at Rowan Gallery where with Mayor Rowan Gallery and Juda Rowan Gallery he was a frequent exhibitor. Huxley was a prizewinner at The New Generation Whitechapel Art Gallery show in 1964; at Paris Biennale, 1965; won Linbury Trust Award, 1977; and in 1985 first prize, Athena Award. In 1965 Huxley gained a Harkness Fellowship which took him to America, where he lived in New York until 1967. Among his overseas shows were one-mans at Kornblee Gallery, New York, in 1967 and 1970. Huxley was a Tate Gallery trustee, 1975–82. During the period 1984–87 he was engaged in designing tiling for London Transport's revivified King's Cross underground station. Huxley taught at Royal College of Art from 1976, gaining professorship in 1986. Arts Council holds a wide selection of his work. Elected RA in 1991. Lived in London.

Thomas Bayliss HUXLEY-JONES 1908–1969 Sculptor in a variety of materials who studied at Wolverhampton School of Art under Robert Emerson, 1924–9, and at the Royal College of Art, 1929–33, under Richard Garbe and Gilbert Ledward. Married to the sculptor Gwynneth Holt. He exhibited RA, NEAC, RSA, SSA and RBSA. Huxley-Jones' sculpture is generally smooth and simple in profile, as depicted in Arthur T Broadbent's monograph *Sculpture Today in Great Britain 1940–1943*, and in Eric Newton's companion volume *British Sculpture 1944–1946*. Huxley-Jones completed a large volume of public work, at the BBC Television Centre, London, in Chelmsford Cathedral and in London's Hyde Park. Aberdeen and Wolverhampton Art Galleries hold his work. Was a member of Chelsea Arts Club. Lived in Chelmsford, Essex.

Sidney Edwin HUXTABLE 1905–1992 Painter and teacher, born in South Molton, Devon. He studied at Clapham School of Art and St Martin's School of Art, teachers including Iain Macnab. From 1925 lived and taught in London, occasionally working in Devon. Between 1966–84 he travelled on the continent, the British Museum holding a collection of his illustrated diaries. Showed at RA, NEAC, RBA and elsewhere. In 1993 a group of his pictures was shown at The Jerram Gallery, Salisbury. Huxtable was a member of the Ridley Art Club.

Martin HUXTER 1960– Painter, born in Great Wakering, Essex. He studied at Southend Technical College, 1977–9, then Trent Polytechnic, 1979–82. He won a purchase prize at Leicestershire Exhibition, 1983, and a prize in 1989–90 John Moores Liverpool Exhibition with his metaphorical picture Man on Stilts. He took part in Artists in Essex, at Epping Forest Museum, 1988–9, and had solo shows in Southend and Westcliff-on-Sea, 1988–9, where he lived.

Derek HYATT 1931– Landscape painter, draughtsman, teacher and writer, born in Ilkley, Yorkshire. He studied at Leeds College of Art, 1948–52, then Royal College of Art, 1954–8, where he edited *Ark* magazine, the issue on colour symbolism selling 3,000 copies in three days. From 1959–64 Hyatt was visiting lecturer at Kingston College of Art, then returned to Yorkshire. He was a lecturer at Leeds College of Art, 1964–8, then senior lecturer at Leeds Polytechnic, 1968–84. Hyatt had many solo exhibitions. There was a string from 1960–6 at New Art Centre, others including University of York and Manor House, Ilkley, 1966; Arthur Gallery, Tampa, America, 1967; a series at Goosewell Gallery, Menston, 1969–76; Waddington Gallery, 1975; Waddington and Tooth's Gallery, 1977; Austin/Desmond Fine Art, 1989; and Dean Clough Contemporary Art Gallery, Halifax, 1991–2. Ruskin was a major influence on the work of Hyatt, having been "a star in my sky since student days". His main subject was the Yorkshire landscape, especially from one vantage point high above Bishopdale, and he believed that "the landscape enters our bodies ... we dance its life." Hyatt's work is held by Museum of Modern Art in New York; Contemporary Art Society; Nuffield Foundation; and many British provincial galleries. Lived at Collingham, Yorkshire.

John HYATT 1958– Versatile artist and teacher, born in Wolverhampton, Staffordshire, who attended the Grammar School there, then University of Leeds, 1977–81, gaining a first-class honours degree. Hyatt had considerable teaching experience, beginning at Rochdale College of Art, 1981–4, eventually, after being head of the department of fine arts at Manchester Metropolitan University from 1991, in 1994 being conferred a professorship. Hyatt's publications, of which he was author and illustrator/designer, included *Art Wars*, 1984; *Bashir Makhoul*, 1993; and *Saint Jerome's Disappearing Cat*. He also published (low-noise music) over 50 musical pieces, released in Britain and abroad. Wrote and recorded a four-part radio serial for the BBC, designed and illustrated for record covers and posters and was the regular cover artist for *Psychology News*. Mixed shows included The British Art Show, 1984, Arts Council tour. Later solo shows included Cornerhouse Gallery, Manchester, 1991–2. Lived in Alderley Edge, Cheshire.

Catherine HYDE 1960– Artist in oil and pastel whose pictures, including animals, birds and figures in landscapes, had a strong Symbolist element. She did a foundation diploma course at Medway College of Design, Rochester, 1978–9, then won an honours degree in fine art, painting, at Central School of Art, 1979–82. Mixed exhibitions included Easton Rooms, Rye, from 1989; Gift of Life Competition at The Imagination Gallery, 1993; and Artists of Fame & Promise, Beaux Arts, Bath, 1995. She had solo exhibitions there in 1995 and 1996.

Monair HYMAN 1955– Artist using such materials as oil, ink and gold leaf on paper, born and lived in Leeds, Yorkshire. She graduated from the Leeds Metropolitan University in 1992 with a first-class honours degree in painting. The following year she embarked on an ambitious series of pictures called Constructions of the Spirit, inspired by churches and chapels seen during a study trip to Florence. A picture called Nocturne II, related to the series, is in the Provident Financial Art Collection. Hyman's work was shown in many survey exhibitions of young artists in Britain; was included in a touring show put on by Ikon Gallery, Birmingham; and in 1994 was shown at Dean Clough Contemporary Art Gallery, Halifax.

Timothy HYMAN 1946– Painter, draughtsman, writer and teacher, born in Hove, Sussex, but brought up in London. He attended Slade School of Fine Art, 1963–7. From 1980–1 Hyman was visiting professor at University of Baroda, India; in 1983–4 was artist-in-residence at Lincoln Cathedral; the following year occupied a similar position at London University's Westfield College. From 1987–8 Hyman worked in Ahmedabad, India. Hyman wrote on a wide number of topics for magazines and other publications, including William Blake, John Cowper Powys, R B Kitaj and James Ensor. His own work was strongly autobiographical, tinged with humour, with an Expressionist distortion. In 1979 Hyman mounted the controversial show Narrative Paintings at Arnolfini Gallery, Bristol, which toured. Among mixed shows he appeared in were RA Summer Exhibitions; The Younger Generation of Figurative Painters, at Ashmolean Museum, Oxford, 1984; Portraits at Flowers East, 1988; and Twin Images, Fine Art Society, 1990. Had solo shows at Blond Fine Art in 1981–3; Usher Gallery, Lincoln, and tour, 1984–5; Westfield College and Blond Fine Art, 1985; Contemporary Art Gallery, Ahmedabad, 1988; and Austin/Desmond Fine Art, 1990. Arts Council, British Museum and other public collections hold his work.

Gladys HYNES 1888–1958 Painter, sculptor and draughtsman, born in Indore, India. She studied with Stanhope Forbes in Cornwall and at London School of Art. Among her more notable works were illustrations to Ezra Pound's *Cantos*, published by John Rodker. She showed at RA, RI, IS, LG and at Paris Salon. Lived in London.

Joanna HYSLOP 1956– Versatile painter and draughtsman, born in Haverfordwest, Pembrokeshire. She studied at West Surrey College of Art, Farnham, 1972–4; at Portsmouth Polytechnic, 1974–7; and Chelsea School of Art, 1977–8. Showed in London, where she lived, and the provinces in group exhibitions. These included the 1983 Cleveland Drawing Biennale, the Leicester Exhibition, 1984, and John Moores Liverpool Exhibition, 1985 and 1995–6, in which she won a prize. Had solo exhibitions at Aspex Gallery, Portsmouth, 1986, and in 1987–8 one at the Atkinson Art Gallery, Southport, toured. Walker Art Gallery holds her work.

I

Charles I'ANSON 1924– Sculptor working in rust-proofed steel and glass fibre, born in Birmingham. He studied at Birmingham College of Art and Bradford University, obtaining his Master of Science degree in 1980. I'Anson was elected a member of RBSA in 1966 and a fellow of RBS in 1967. Group exhibitions included RWA, LG, Alwin Gallery, New Vision Centre, SSA and abroad. He took part in many open air exhibitions, including London and the provinces. Solo shows included New Vision Centre, Alwin Gallery, Kidderminster Art Gallery, Leeds City Art Gallery and Midlands Art Centre in Birmingham. The Centre has his work, also held by Birmingham, Bradford and Wakefield public galleries and University of Leeds. Lived in Ilkley, Yorkshire.

Graham IBBESON 1951– Sculptor and draughtsman, born in Barnsley, Yorkshire. Ibbeson studied at Leicester Polytechnic, 1972–3, Trent Polytechnic, 1973–5, and at Royal College of Art, 1975–8, under Bernard Meadows. In 1977, while still at the College, he won Commonwealth Institute and London Symphony Orchestra Commissions, in 1978 gaining the Madame Tussaud Award for Figurative Art. Ibbeson's realistic, painted figurative sculptures were amusing with a strong North Country bent. He showed at Nottingham Castle Museum in 1975, at Royal College of Art Gallery in 1977 and in 1979 at Olanda Kelly Gallery, Chicago. By that time he was well established as an exhibitor with the Nicholas Treadwell Gallery in Britain and extensively abroad in group shows, and later showed solo with Treadwell. Was included in the 1980 show Bernard Meadows at the Royal College of Art 1960–1980, held at the College.

Peter IBBETSON 1909– Painter, printmaker, draughtsman and teacher, brought up in Yorkshire. He came of a farming family and was privately educated, then attending Oxford University. Studied art at Bradford College of Art, 1929–32, Central School of Arts and Crafts, 1932–4, then for about two years in France and Spain. Showed with Senefelder Club, at public galleries in Sheffield and Bradford, did a mural for the science section of the 1951 Festival of Britain and had one-man shows in London and Oxford. Lived for some years in Oxford.

Diane IBBOTSON 1946– Painter and teacher, born in Colne, Lancashire. Between 1964–71 Ibbotson attended University of Reading and Royal Academy Schools, then returned to Lancashire and taught, some time at Blackpool College of Art. Between 1974–8 she taught at the School of Art in Falmouth, Cornwall, where she settled. Was included 1989 Newlyn Orion Galleries exhibition A Century of Art in Cornwall 1889–1989, represented by the typically large landscape All that Glitters, which took five years to complete.

Jill IBROM 1942– Artist in oil, egg tempera and watercolour, born in London, who studied at Watford College of Art, was a draughtswoman for 10 years, then while bringing up her son found more time to paint. The natural history artist John Wilkinson was an influence, teaching her how to use egg tempera. In 1982 was accepted by Medici Society; she produced a series of nativities which they published, one a best-seller. Natura Designs and Polytint also published Ibrom's work. At various times was a member of Hesketh Hubbard Art Society and Watford and Bushey Art Society. Showed in mixed exhibitions at Medici and Mall Galleries, Jane Marler Gallery in Ludlow and Barbican Centre. Had solo shows at Watford Central Library and Chapel Art Centre, Oswestry. Lived in Bushey, Hertfordshire.

Peter IDEN 1945– Painter who studied at West Sussex College of Art & Design, Worthing, 1962–4. Iden freelanced as a topographical watercolourist from 1967, but a serious illness in 1993 prompted him to give up commercial work to concentrate on oil painting, which he had taken up in 1992. He specialised in studies of the South Downs and was a member of the Society of Sussex Painters, Sussex Watercolour Society and the Society of Architectural and Industrial Artists. Showed regularly at RI until he turned to oils. Held many solo shows in Sussex, and in 1979 in Cambridge, and exhibited elsewhere in England and in Chartres, France. Worthing Art Gallery holds examples. From 1969 lived in Chichester, Sussex.

Rudolph IHLEE 1883–1968 Painter and draughtsman, born in London. He was apprenticed to Ferranti as an engineer in 1902, but entered Slade School of Fine Art, 1906–10, where he proved a brilliant student, winning many prizes. After two solo shows at Carfax Gallery, 1912–14, Ihlee worked as an engineering draughtsman in Peterborough during World War I. The year after he became a member of NEAC, in 1921 Ihlee had a successful show at Leicester Galleries, but then settled in Collioure, in the south of France. Although he had a solo exhibition at Chenil Gallery in 1926, between the wars his life and exhibiting career was in France; his second wife, Isabelle, was French. He returned to England when World War II broke out, working in a factory in Leicester, settling eventually in West Deeping, Lincolnshire. He had a solo show at St Peter's College Hall, Peterborough, with Arts Council support, in 1951, and another in Sleaford in 1968. There was a show seven years after he died at Rutland Sixth Form College, Oakham, then in 1978 a retrospective at Graves Art

Gallery in Sheffield and Belgrave Gallery. Victoria & Albert Museum, Manchester City Art Gallery and Cecil Higgins Art Gallery, Bedford, hold work. (The family pronunciation of Ihlee is Eelay, although Ighly is common.)

David IMMS 1945– Painter who studied at Derby College of Art and Central School of Art. He was strongly influenced by the work of the writer Thomas Hardy, the prehistoric culture and landscape of Wiltshire and Dorset. Myths such as Demeter and Persephone and The Paradise Garden were themes in Imms' work. He won a number of awards, including Llewellyn Smith Scholarship and the Northern Arts Purchase Award. Had solo exhibitions at University of Stirling, 1974; Queen Mary College, London, 1976; Thomas Hardy Festival, Dorchester, 1978; Southwark Cathedral, 1981; Central Museum and Art Gallery, Northampton, 1983; and several at New Grafton Gallery from 1987. Victoria & Albert Museum holds his work.

Sax IMPEY 1969– Artist using a variety of media, born in Penzance, Cornwall, who returned to the county in 1994, having gained an honours degree in fine art at Newport, 1988–91, from 1992–4 undertaking film, theatre and performance projects and travels in East Africa. In 1995 was elected a member of the Newlyn Society of Artists. In 1997 he was joint editor of the St Ives-based review *Starts*. Exhibitions included a solo at Plymouth Arts Centre Celtic Festival, 1996, and a shared one with Richard Nott, Common Ground, at The Book Gallery, St Ives, 1998, where Impey showed abstracts dominated by vertical forms in which tone, grain and colour were important.

Charles INCE 1875–1952 Prolific landscape painter and businessman, born in London where he ran the printing and publishing firm Chas F Ince and Sons. He studied at King's College and art with the landscapist Henry Moon. He was a member of RI and RBA, in which he held senior positions, and of Chelsea Arts Club. Also showed at ROI, RWS, Fine Art Society, Goupil Gallery, Royal Glasgow Institute of the Fine Arts and elsewhere. Lived latterly in Purbrook, Hampshire.

Peter INCHBALD 1919– Painter, notably of murals, born in London. After Winchester College he studied at Oxford University, then at the Royal Academy Schools, 1946–51. Sometimes signing his work P I, he showed at RA, LG, NEAC and elsewhere. Some of his work was reproduced by Shell-Mex and BP Ltd for advertising purposes. Inchbald completed a series of murals in England and Northern Ireland, including Southwell Minster in Nottinghamshire. Lived in London.

Marjorie INCLEDON 1891– Painter and stained glass designer who studied at Birmingham School of Art, 1911–14 and again 1941–2. Also studied at Central School of Arts and Crafts, 1917–18, and at Brighton College of Art with Dorothy Coke and Charles Knight, 1942–5. Exhibited RA, ROI, RBA and Society of Sussex Artists, signing her work with a monogram. Lived at Ditchling, Sussex.

Harold ING 1900– Commercial artist who specialised in marine pictures, born in London. Among commissioned work was that done for P&O Group and for Cable and Wireless. Member of Essex Art Club and showed in Home Counties. Lived at Upminster, Middlesex.

Andrew INGAMELLS 1956– Painter and printmaker who had a special interest in depicting buildings. He studied at St Albans School of Art, 1975–6, then London School of Printing, 1976–9. He exhibited at RA, at Blackman Harvey Gallery in 1989, in Architectural Views of Britain at CCA Galleries, 1990, and in the same year in The Broad Horizon, at Agnew. In 1993–4 he shared an exhibition at Galerie Valerie, showing architectural etchings, with a solo show at Grosvenor Gallery, 1994. Had a studio in London.

Alan INGHAM 1920– Sculptor, printmaker and teacher, born in Christchurch, New Zealand, where he studied part-time at the local School of Art early in World War II. He obtained a sculpture diploma, studying under Lyndon Dadswell, at East Sydney Technical College, in Australia, 1946–8; moved to London and attended the Central School of Arts and Crafts with a RA grant, 1949; and was assistant to Henry Moore, 1950–3, whose work remained an influence on Ingham's. While in England, Ingham showed at the first Australian Artists' Association exhibition at the RWS Conduit Street gallery, 1953. He exhibited solo in London and extensively in Australia in the coming years. Returned to New Zealand in 1954, Ingham set up a bronze foundry, establishing a studio and settling in Sydney, New South Wales, 1956. He taught part-time at the National Art School there, and elsewhere. Ingham won the Mildura Prize for sculpture in 1964 and 1967 at the Mildura Art Gallery/Arts Centre. He carried out a series of large-scale commissions, clients including the Snowy Mountains Authority; Phoenix House, Sydney; and Australian Libraries Association. Auckland City Art Gallery in New Zealand holds his work.

Alan INGHAM 1932– Watercolourist and teacher, born in Skipton, Yorkshire. He joined the Royal Navy at an early age, specialised in hydrographic surveying and retired in 1965 as a lieutenant-commander. He founded the Hydrographic Society and lectured at London Polytechnic before becoming a full-time artist, settling in the Cotswolds. Painted that area, Cumbria, Yorkshire and Derbyshire with meticulous care, rather in the style of Victorian watercolourists. Showed with John Noott Twentieth Century in Broadway. Ingham's pictures were also reproduced as prints, greetings cards and calendars; W H Smith used them for its 1990 *Countryside Calendar*. His book *Under a Watercolour Sky*, with an autobiographical introduction, was published in 1996, with a launch show at Phoenix Gallery, Selfridges.

Bryan INGHAM 1936–1997 Painter, sculptor, collagist and etcher, born George Bryan Ingham in Preston, Lancashire. He studied at St Martin's School of Art, 1957–61, with Frederick

Gore and Archibald Ziegler, then Royal College of Art, 1961–4, under Carel Weight, with a stay at British Academy, Rome, 1966. An Italian Government Scholarship and a Leverhulme Postgraduate Research Award were won by Ingham. Group exhibitions included Lords Gallery from 1964; Wills Lane Gallery, St Ives and New Ashgate Gallery, Farnham, from 1976. Had a solo show at Graffiti Gallery, 1980, others in Germany, then a series at Francis Graham-Dixon Gallery from 1988. Showed at the Book Gallery, St Ives, in the 1990s. Department of the Environment, Dartington Hall and Ashgate Trusts and Print Collectors' Club in Washington, America, commissioned Ingham, whose work is held by Arts Council, Ashmolean Museum in Oxford, Victoria & Albert Museum and many other public collections in Britain and abroad. Ingham was a prodigiously talented and hardworking artist whose output followed on from the early Cubists. His declared aim was "to beg, borrow, consolidate and synthesise; to add even to the classical tradition of harmony and contained chance". For 25 years he lived at Jollytown, a remote and primitive cottage on the Lizard, Cornwall, with sustained periods in Germany.

Gillian INGHAM 1951– Abstract painter, born and lived in London, where she continued to work. Studied at Ravensbourne College of Art, 1970–4, then Chelsea School of Art, 1974–5. Took part in many mixed exhibitions, including Stowells Trophy, 1974; LG from 1975; Air Gallery, 1976; Wapping Artists Open Studio Exhibition, 1980; 16 Artists at Battersea Arts Centre, 1982; and 9 Artists from Wapping British Tour, based at DLI Museum & Arts Centre, Durham, 1983. Arts Council and Kettle's Yard, Cambridge, hold her work.

Margo INGHAM 1918–1978 Charismatic gallery owner, artist and collector, notably of L S Lowry, who was a primary school teacher in Manchester where she studied in the evenings under Ian Grant at the local School of Art. From 1946–51 Ingham ran the Mid-Day Studios exhibition space in Mosley Street, which had previously been used by dealer Lucy Wertheim. It became an important gathering place for the Manchester Group and more advanced northern artists, some of whose works had been refused by MAFA. Ingham painted extensively abroad. She was married first to the local artist Ned Owens; she ran a gallery at her home in Rusholme; next was married to painter Geoffrey Lintott, living in Tunbridge Wells; her third husband being advertising executive Bert Drake. Died in Southport, Lancashire.

Mark INGHAM 1960– Painter, draughtsman, sculptor, installations artist and teacher, born in Trinidad, who did a foundation course at Cambridgeshire College of Arts and Technology, Cambridge, 1979–80; gained an honours degree in sculpture at Chelsea School of Art, 1980–3; and took the same subject for a higher diploma in fine art at Slade School of Fine Art, under Richard Deacon, 1983–5. From 1985–6, Ingham was Henry Moore Fellow at Camberwell School of Art. He was schools co-ordinator, Whitechapel Art Gallery, 1990–4; in 1995 began a doctorate on installations, making/teaching, London Consortium; and held a number of residencies. Ingham researched and made work dealing with the relationship between art and mathematics, and in 1997 worked for a time at Acland Burghley School on a mathematics project, part of the education and training programme of the Institute of International Visual Arts. Kingsway College and University of North London architecture department were among Ingham's teaching venues. Group exhibitions included New Contemporaries (slide show), ICA, 1983; New British Sculptors, Air Gallery, 1986; and Whitechapel Open, Spitalfields Market, 1992. Solo exhibitions included Urban Constructs, Unit 7 Gallery, 1986. Lived in London.

Jean INGLIS 1884–1959 Painter, born in Kensington. Studied at the Slade School of Fine Art under Henry Tonks and Philip Wilson Steer. Painted landscapes widely in England. Exhibited RA, NEAC, RP, RSA and Paris Salon, where she gained an Hon. Mention in 1928. Took part in the Pilgrim Trust *Recording Britain* project and had work reproduced in *La Revue Moderne* and *Scots Observer*. She carried out government commissions to copy state portraits of HM King George V and Queen Mary. Sometimes just signed work Jean. Lived at Amberley, near Stroud, Gloucestershire.

John INGLIS 1953– Painter and collage artist noted for his often complex pictures based on memories of coast and landscape. Born in Glasgow, he studied at Gray's School of Art, Aberdeen, 1970–5, and Patrick Allan-Fraser School of Art, Hospitalfield, Arbroath. Inglis won two travelling scholarships, the Keith Prize in 1975 and gained two Scottish Arts Council Awards. Showed in mixed exhibitions at RSW, of which he was a member from 1984, winning an award three years later; RSA; SSA; and Royal Glasgow Institute of the Fine Arts. Had solo shows at Aberdeen Art Centre, Aberdeen University, Compass Gallery in Glasgow and Taurus Gallery, Skipton. Scottish Arts Council holds his work. Lived in Larbert, Stirlingshire.

Judy INGLIS 1952– Draughtsman, artist in oil on gesso ground on paper and teacher, born in Cornwall. She studied at Falmouth School of Art, 1970–1; Exeter College of Art and Design, 1971–2; graduated in fine art with honours from Sheffield City Polytechnic, 1980–3; then gained her master's degree in painting at Royal College of Art, 1984–7, notable teachers there including especially Peter de Francia, also John Golding, Ken Kiff, Alan Miller and Jenny Durrant. In the mid-1980s Inglis won several awards, in 1985 being an exchange student to Athens Academy, Greece. In 1987–8 she gained a fellowship in painting at Gloucestershire College of Art & Design, from 1989 being a senior lecturer at Birmingham Polytechnic, and she was a visiting lecturer at many other centres. Inglis was a powerful draughtsman who said that her work was "figurative, as my concerns are essentially humanist … I use the autobiographical as a core and then incorporate myth, allegory, ritual and metaphor and literary association to enrich and extend the personal." Inglis had a solo show at Mappin Art Gallery, Sheffield, in 1984. She also exhibited at Birch and Conran Gallery, 1987; Groucho Club, 1988; Ikon

Gallery Touring Exhibition, Birmingham, and Paton Gallery, both 1991; and Victoria Art Gallery, Bath, 1992. Sheffield and Birmingham City Art Galleries hold her work. Lived in Stroud, Gloucestershire.

Reece INGRAM 1963– Sculptor in wood, stone, fur and feathers, and teacher, who trained as a taxidermist, 1980–1, at the Booth Museum of Natural History, Brighton, and Snowdonia Taxidermy Studios, Llanrust. After a foundation course in art and design at Wrexham College of Art, 1981–2, Ingram gained an honours degree in fine art, sculpture, at Brighton Polytechnic, 1982–5, then his master's in site-specific sculpture at Wimbledon School of Art, 1990–1. Notable teachers at Brighton included James Tower, Peter Randall-Page and Anthony Gormley, and at Wimbledon, Lee Grandjean. In 1986 Ingram was assistant to Randall-Page. Teaching posts included Open College of the Arts, 1991–2. Ingram's residencies included Booth Museum of Natural History, Brighton, 1988; Towner Art Gallery, Eastbourne, which holds his work, 1990; and The Beacon School, Crowborough, 1995. Group show included Insights, Arundel Gallery, 1991; Maidstone Library Gallery, 1993; and Rye Art Gallery, 1994. Later solo exhibitions included Hannah Peschar Gallery, Ockley, 1993. Among Ingram's many commissions were Three Otters, Bourton Park, Buckingham, 1991; Whalebones, Herne Bay (winner of Rouse Award for public art), 1993; and The Garden of St Jerome, The Princess Alexandra Hospital, Harlow, 1995. Lived in Brighton, Sussex.

Henry INLANDER 1925–1983 Painter and teacher, born in Vienna, Austria, as Heinz Inlander. Lived in Trieste, 1935–8. Settled in England 1938 and became a British subject in 1947. Attended St Martin's School of Art, 1939–41, Camberwell School of Arts and Crafts part-time from 1945, becoming full-time in 1949. In 1950 went to the Slade School of Fine Art, where he won the summer composition prize, in 1952 a Rome Scholarship. First one-man show at Galleria La Tartaruga, Rome in 1953, his first in London being at Leicester Galleries in 1956. Awarded Premio Acitrezza, Sicily, 1958, and a Harkness Commonwealth Fellowship to America in 1960–61. Taught at Camberwell 1957–79 and had many group and one-man shows in Britain and abroad. Tate Gallery, Contemporary Art Society, Arts Council, provincial and overseas galleries hold his work. Lived in London.

Callum INNES 1962– Artist, born and lived in Edinburgh, who studied in Aberdeen. Innes' early canvases were figurative. Then he painted abstract works tending towards Minimalism, although he still saw his pictures "as having a figurative element". Was included in the British Art Show, 1990; Kunst Europa – Kunstverein Freiburg, Germany, and Artisti Invitatial Premio Internationale, Milan, Rome, London and America, 1991; and New Voices, a British Council Exhibition, Brussels, 1992. Innes' solo shows included Frith Street Gallery from 1990; Jan Turner Gallery, Los Angeles, 1990; Gallery Patrick de Brock, Belgium, 1991; ICA, 1992; and Scottish National Gallery of Modern Art, Edinburgh, 1992–3. Won the NatWest Art Prize, 1998.

George INNES 1913–1970 Sculptor, born in Glasgow who studied for four years at School of Art there, in 1936 showing at McLellan Galleries. Two years later he showed stone figures at Glasgow Empire Exhibition. After damage to his hands sustained in the Army in World War II Innes found it hard to carve, so produced little work on return to civilian life. This was doubly regrettable. His post-World War II sculpture took an exciting turn with the adoption of Pre-Colombian monumentality combined with cube-like forms. Kirkcaldy Museum and Art Gallery's Seated Figure, in white sandstone, is a prime example. Innes' final years saw his reputation diminish to obscurity, although he was featured in Scottish National Gallery of Modern Art's Scottish Art since 1900 show in 1989–90, and tour.

William INNES 1905– Artist in oil and pastel, born and lived in London. He painted from the time he was a child and first showed when with Royal Air Force during World War II. Innes was a painter of seascapes and landscapes and was "particularly interested in the effects of light on water". He was a member of PS and UA, also exhibiting with RA, NEAC, ROI and elsewhere, having several solo shows in London. Local authorities held his work.

INNOTT 1899– Flower painter in oil, born in London, whose full name was Alfred Richard Innott Barnes. Studied at Camberwell School of Arts and Crafts, 1910, with J Harvey Bloom. Exhibited RA, Croydon Art Society and Contemporary Arts Group. Lived in Carshalton, Surrey.

David INSHAW 1943– Painter and teacher, born in Staffordshire, of idyllic landscapes depicted with much atmosphere and in minute detail. He studied at Beckenham School of Art, 1959–63 then Royal Academy Schools, 1963–6, a French Government Scholarship in 1964 enabling him to work in Paris. In 1966 Inshaw organised Young Contemporaries show, the year he began teaching at West of England College of Art, in Bristol, a position he held until 1975, when he joined Trinity College, Cambridge. Inshaw had first one-man show at Arnolfini Gallery, Bristol, where he had moved, in 1969, with another at Dartington Hall, in Devon. Three years later with Graham and Ann Arnold he formed the Broad Heath Brotherhood, and this trio with four others went on to create The Brotherhood of Ruralists in 1975. In that year Inshaw had a solo show with Waddington Galleries, which went on to represent him. In John Moores Exhibition, Liverpool, 1991–2, Inshaw was represented by Portrait of Silbury Hill: May 1989. Arts Council holds his work.

John Henry INSKIP fl. from c.1885–1947 Landscape painter who also completed some interiors, born and lived in Scarborough, Yorkshire. He was a member of RBA and Fylingdales Group, also showing with RA, Walker Art Gallery in Liverpool and ROI. Sussex Cottages and The Bridge at Brandon were among his notable works. Rochdale Corporation acquired views of Whitstable and Walmer.

Jeff INSTONE 1941– Artist notable as a draughtsman, who was featured in Woodlands Art Gallery 1981–2 touring show of Greater London Arts Association award winners. Also exhibited at Summer Show 2, Serpentine Gallery, 1976, House Gallery in 1979, Riverside Studios in 1980 and Galeria Akumulatory 2 Poznan, Poland, 1981.

IONICUS 1913–1998 Illustrator, painter and teacher, born and lived in Hoylake, Cheshire, real name Joshua Charles Armitage. He studied at Liverpool School of Art, 1929–36, then taught for almost 15 years apart from Royal Naval service during World War II. His teachers included Will Penn. For a time after the war he was on the staff of Wallasey School of Art. Exhibited RA, RCamA and elsewhere in the provinces. From the early 1940s Armitage contributed to *Punch* magazine, also doing humorous drawings for *Lilliput*, *Radio Times* and *Financial Times*. Ferens Art Gallery, Hull, holds his work. Illustrated a number of books, especially humorous titles such as R G G Price's *How to Become a Headmaster*, 1960, Ogden Nash's *The Untold Adventures of Santa Claus*, 1965, and several dozen titles by P G Wodehouse. President of Deeside Art Group.

Anne IRBY CREWS 1927– Versatile printmaker, watercolourist, teacher, maker of garden sculpture in stoneware and terracotta who was born in Sandgate, Kent. She was at the Central and Camberwells Schools of Art at various times between 1946–51, teachers including Rodrigo Moynihan, Claude Rogers, Richard Eurich and William Roberts. She gained a diploma in printmaking from Leamington Art School in 1990. Irby Crews was engaged in film and theatre work for some years and taught, including King Edward's School in Handsworth and at Solihull College of Technology. She was interested in "the visible and invisible world ... landscapes, and interiors of quiet, sacred and haunted places". She illustrated *Solid Citizens*, the study of public sculpture in Birmingham, 1983, and took part in workshops at Hereford and Dudley Museums, Lancaster Polytechnic and Birmingham University. Irby Crews was a member of the Birmingham Print Workshop and Birmingham Artists' Group as well as LG. Showed in RA Summer Exhibition, RCamA, and widely in the West Midlands. Solo shows included Birmingham University, Midland Arts Centre in Birmingham and Harlequin Gallery, Sutton Coldfield, 1992. Leicester University and Worcester Museum and Art Gallery hold examples. Lived in Edgbaston, Birmingham.

Sydney Joseph IREDALE 1896–1967 Painter, born and lived in London, son of the scenic artist Henry Iredale. Studied at Richmond School of Art, 1915, under T M Smith. Exhibited RA, LG, RI, ROI, PS and Richmond Art Circle, of which he was a member.

Helen IRELAND 1961– Painter who attended Central School of Art and Design, 1982–5, then gained her master's degree at Chelsea School of Art, 1986. She was involved in many group shows, including Warwick Arts Trust, 1986–7, Axiom Gallery in Cheltenham and the Royal Over-Seas League annual exhibition, and she also participated in (dis)parties, held at Mappin Art Gallery, Sheffield, in 1992 and in 1993 at Herbert Art Gallery, Coventry. In 1990 she shared a show with Mary Mclean at Pomeroy Purdy Gallery. Pattern was a strong element in Ireland's work, and Indian miniatures, Aboriginal bark paintings and English tapestries were cited as parallels. Lived in London.

Mary IRELAND 1891– Watercolour painter, stained glass artist, fabric designer, illuminator and writer. Born at Stockingford, Warwickshire, she went on to exhibit at the RA and elsewhere. Dover Town Hall, Bruges Cathedral, in Belgium, and various churches contain her work, such as altarpieces and reredos decorations. Lived at Folkestone, Kent.

Christopher IRONSIDE 1913–1992 Painter, sculptor, draughtsman, designer and teacher who studied at Central School of Arts and Crafts. During World War II he served in the Directorate of Camouflage and worked for the Air Ministry in Leamington Spa. After the war Ironside, a sociable, flamboyant character, worked for the Ministry of Town and Country Planning, then as education officer for the Council of Industrial Design, 1946–8. Taught at Maidstone School of Art and Royal College of Art. Ironside was a painterly painter who shared two exhibitions with his brother, Robin Ironside, at Redfern Gallery in 1944 and Arthur Jeffress in 1960. Also with Robin he collaborated on theatrical designs and postage stamps, including Frederick Ashton's production of the ballet *Sylvia* for Sadler's Wells Ballet at Covent Garden in 1952 and one of the 1964 Shakespeare commemoration issues. Ironside also did much of the designing of decorations for Pall Mall for the Coronation in 1953; designed the obverse side of Britain's decimal coinage; new coinage for Tanzania, Brunei, Qatar, Dubai and Singapore; and the memorial for the Earl and Countess Mountbatten in Westminster Abbey. His first wife was the fashion designer and teacher Janey Ironside, their daughter being the journalist Virginia. Died in Winchester, Hampshire.

Robin IRONSIDE 1912–1965 Painter, theatre designer and writer on art, born and lived in London, studied at Courtauld Institute of Art and overseas. Ironside became assistant keeper at the Tate Gallery, 1937–46, then Contemporary Art Society assistant secretary. Self-taught painter, often of Surrealist pictures, who shared a show with his brother Christopher at Redfern Gallery in 1944, having an initial one-man show at Durlacher Brothers in New York eight years later. Also showed at Hanover and Arthur Jeffress Galleries. Tate Gallery and Leicester City Art Gallery hold his work. While painting, Ironside was developing parallel careers as a stage designer and writer on art. He designed for *Sylvia* at Covent Garden in 1952 and *A Midsummer Night's Dream* at the 1957 Edinburgh Festival. As well as writing for periodicals such as *Horizon*, Ironside wrote the short survey of *Painting Since 1939*, published in 1947, a good introduction to the Neo-Romantic movement; other books include *Wilson Steer*, 1944, and *David Jones*, 1949. Retrospective New Art Centre, 1966.

Albert IRVIN 1922– Painter, printmaker and teacher, born London, which remained his base. Studied at Northampton School of Art, 1940–1, and after five years in Royal Air Force studied at Goldsmiths' College School of Art. Irvin taught for some years from 1960, including Hornsey College of Art, Goldsmiths' College, 1962–83, and gave lessons in Wandsworth Prison. He had his first one-man show at 57 Gallery, Edinburgh, in 1960, and from 1961 held a series at New Art Centre. In 1968 he won an Arts Council Travel Award to America, seven years later gaining an Arts Council Major Award. Also exhibited with LG; had a number of solo exhibitions in Germany; and with Gimpel Fils. In 1990 a retrospective of his paintings, 1960–89, was shown at Serpentine Gallery. Arts Council and other important public collections hold his work, which was abstract, brightly coloured and showed a joy in the manipulation of paint.

Jaki IRVINE 1966– Artist who was born in Dublin where a bachelor's degree was obtained at the National College of Art and Design, 1984–9, with a master's at Goldsmiths' College, 1992–4. Group shows included Emerging Artists Exhibitions, Dublin, 1991; Sonsbeek International, collaboration with Blue Funk, Arnhem, 1993; The Curator's Egg, Anthony Reynolds Gallery, 1994; and in 1995 a show at Project Art Centre in Dublin and submission *Star* (a three-minute film projection) at Venice Biennale. Had a solo show Margaret Again at Anthony Wilkinson Fine Art, 1995. Lived in London.

Olivia IRVINE 1960– Artist and teacher producing abstract work such as Update, oil on canvas, at Royal Over-Seas League Open, 1994. Born in Kilwinning, Ayr, Irvine studied medicine at Aberdeen University, then attended Edinburgh College of Art and Les Beaux-Arts de Montpellier, France. Taught widely, including privately in Edinburgh and as a visitor at Winchester School of Art. Awards included Stuart Prize at RSA, 1986; Spanish Government Scholarship, 1987; a Scottish Arts Council Small Assistance Grant, 1989; and the Hope Scott Trust Award, 1992. Took part in many mixed shows, including The New Generation in Scotland, Mercury Gallery, Edinburgh, and tour, 1985–6; Chicago International Art Exposition, in America, 1988–9; Modern Masters, City Arts Centre, Edinburgh, 1992; and Solitude and Isolation, Royal College of Physicians, Edinburgh, 1993. Scottish Arts Council; Paintings in Hospitals, Scotland; BBC Scotland; and Eastern General Hospital, Edinburgh, hold examples.

Robert Scott IRVINE 1906–1988 Watercolour painter and teacher, son of an art teacher, Robert Irvine. He was born in Edinburgh, where he settled, studying at the local College of Art, 1922–7. Eventually became principal art master at George Watson's College and was a member of the Scottish Arts Club, being its president in the early 1950s. Showed with RSW of which he was a member, SSA and in North America. Had several solo exhibitions in Edinburgh, including Scottish Arts Club in 1978. Aberdeen and Dundee Art Galleries hold his work.

Laurence IRVING 1897–1988 Painter, stage and film designer, theatrical producer, book illustrator and writer, son of the actor and writer H B Irving. Born in London. During World War I served in Royal Naval Air Service and won the Croix de Guerre. Studied at Byam Shaw School of Drawing and Painting, 1919, and Royal Academy Schools. In 1928 helped with production of John Masefield's play *The Coming of Christ* in Canterbury Cathedral; about the same time worked with Douglas Fairbanks Senior on the classic films *The Man in the Iron Mask* and *The Taming of the Shrew*, with Mary Pickford. There were 50 major film and stage production designs over the next 40 years. There were also over 40 stage productions, including *Hamlet* and *The Good Companions*. In 1951 published a biography of his grandfather the noted actor-manager Sir Henry Irving. A series of volumes – *The Successors*, *The Precarious Crust*, *Great Interruption* and *Abiding Curiosity* – later appeared on his family and life. He exhibited at Fine Art Society, Agnew, RA, Royal Glasgow Institute of the Fine Arts and Barton Art Gallery, Tenterden, 1987. Books illustrated, often black-and-white with sharp contrasts, included his own *Windmills and Waterways*, 1927; Joseph Conrad's *The Mirror of the Sea*, 1935; and Richard Church's *Dog Toby*, 1953. He had strong associations with many bodies concerned with advancing the theatre. Lived at Wittersham, Kent.

Flavia IRWIN fl. from 1940s– Artist and teacher, born in London, who studied at Chelsea School of Art with Henry Moore and Graham Sutherland and at Ruskin School of Drawing in Oxford. She was married to the painter Roger de Grey. She worked as a freelance designer and later became senior lecturer and head of department of decorative arts at City and Guilds of London School of Art. Group shows included Zwemmer Gallery, RA Summer Exhibitions, RWA, Curwen and Phoenix Galleries. Had a solo show at Ansdell Gallery. Carlisle City Museum and Art Gallery and Department of the Environment hold examples. Elected Senior RA, 1996. Lived in Meopham, Kent.

Gwyther IRWIN 1931– Painter, designer, collagist, relief artist and teacher who worked in a variety of materials, born in Basingstoke, Hampshire, but spent his youth in north Cornwall. For several years in the mid-1950s he studied illustration at Goldsmiths' College School of Art and design at Central School of Arts and Crafts, having first solo show at Gallery One in 1957. This was followed in 1958 with a one-man show at ICA, followed by a string of shows at Gimpel Fils during 1960s. Also went on to exhibit at Marlborough Fine Art, New Art Centre and abroad. In 1965 gained commission for bas relief in Portland Stone for British Petroleum. Held series of teaching posts at Hornsey College of Art, Chelsea School of Art and Brighton Polytechnic. Irwin has said that he "wrote" his pictures, the equivalent of Persian carpets with their own iconography. Tate Gallery and Arts Council hold examples.

Bert ISAAC 1923– Painter, printmaker and illustrator, especially of landscape, and teacher. He was born in Cardiff where he attended the College of Art. Then started a teaching career that took him to a number of schools and colleges in Wales and England, including heading the art department at Battersea College of Education. Was elected RWA in 1994, at various times being a member of Society of Industrial Artists, WSW and The Welsh Group. Had many solo exhibitions including Howard Roberts Gallery in Cardiff, Richmond Hill Gallery in Surrey, Jablonski Gallery, University of Birmingham, and public galleries in Lincoln and Hull, in 1992 having a retrospective of paintings and prints at Circle Gallery, Pontypridd, with another at Brecknock Museum, Brecon, 1996. Took part in extensive mixed shows, including Leicester Galleries, RA, SEA, SWG, WAC and National Eisteddfod of Wales, where he shared the Gold Medal for Painting in 1989. Also showed at Hill Court Gallery, Abergavenny, run by his wife Joan, where he was latterly artist-in-residence. Illustrated several books, including his own *The Landscape Within*, 1992. National Museum of Wales in Cardiff, CASW, the Universities of Oxford and London hold examples. Lived in Abergavenny, Gwent.

John ISAACS 1968– Sculptor, born in Lancaster, who studied for a science degree in biology at Exeter University, 1987–8; obtained a fine art degree from Cheltenham College of Art, 1988–91; and his master's in sculpture at Slade School of Fine Art, 1991–3. Isaacs was a fan of science fiction whose work superficially could appear amusing but had more serious implications, as seen at Young British Artists VI, Saatchi Gallery, 1996. Lived in London.

James Lawrence ISHERWOOD 1917–1988 Painter who was born and lived in Wigan, Lancashire, where he ran The Isherwood Gallery. He studied at the local Technical College, 1934–53. Isherwood travelled extensively and had over 200 shows, including colleges at Oxford and Cambridge Universities. He painted a number of celebrities, including the singer Gracie Fields, the round-the-world yachtsman Sir Francis Chichester and Lord and Lady Weymouth. Some portraits were issued in signed, limited editions. Churchill and Pembroke Colleges in Cambridge hold his work. Isherwood was an eccentric, controversial character whose work was uneven, often garish and awkward, but who could occasionally produce a telling image, as seen when a large body of it was included in The Northern Art Show, Mall Galleries, 1994.

Graham ISOM 1945– Painter in oil and lithographer, and teacher, specialising in equine art, born in Kent. Studied at Ravensbourne College of Art, 1960–5, then taught painting and sculpture at a grammar school in Dorset until turning freelance in 1973. Became a member of the Society of Equestrian Artists and American Academy of Equine Art. Took part in group shows at Osborne and Tryon Galleries and Rubicon Studios, having solo exhibitions at Michael Stewart and Equus Art Galleries and in America at Klausner/Cooperage Gallery. Won many awards in Britain and America. Commissions included a painting of the Grand Military Gold Cup for the officers' mess of the Household Cavalry and a large-format calendar of 13 pictures for Spillers UK Ltd. Kentucky Derby Museum holds his work. Lived in Baltonsborough, Somerset.

Milan IVANIČ 1947– Painter in oil on canvas, mainly of landscape, born in Czechoslovakia, who studied at Prague's Academy of Fine Arts, 1967–70, then moved to England, settling in Lancaster. Exhibited in mixed shows at Ash Barn Gallery, Petersfield; Terrace Gallery, Worthing, New Ashgate Gallery, Farnham; and Cowfold Gallery, Cowfold. Solo shows included Keele University; Aston Arts Centre, Birmingham; Wolfson College, Oxford, and Clyde Bertrand Gallery, Stockton, California, America.

Jocelyn IVANYI 1900–1993 Naive painter who took up art aged 77. Thrice married and twice divorced with a son by her first husband, she made a living as a dressmaker and designed and made hats. During World War II the Ministry of Defence employed her to collect iron around the country. Her third marriage was to the Hungarian art historian and writer Bèla Ivanyi Grünewald, whose father was a notable painter. They settled from London to Alphamstone, Essex, where she created a beautiful garden. This and her animals featured often in Ivanyi's pictures. Later work was less detailed, due to cataracts. Ivanyi was a woman of strong beliefs: liberalism, pacifism and anti-racism. She died in Suffolk and there was a memorial show at Gainsborough's House, Sudbury, 1994.

Pamela IZZARD 1929– Artist in mixed media and teacher, born and lived in London. She was married first to the artist Keith Lucas, then to Jack Millar. Izzard studied at Beckenham and Bromley Schools of Art under Carel Weight and Ruskin Spear. She taught at Harrogate and Walthamstow Schools of Art, North-East London Polytechnic and Royal Academy Schools and elsewhere. Izzard showed regularly in RA Summer Exhibitions, also with NEAC, LG, David Paul Gallery in Chichester and Curwen Gallery. Solo shows included Ashgate Gallery in Farnham, Linton Court Gallery and Abbot Hall Art Gallery, Kendal. Several public authorities hold examples.

J

JABIR: *see* **Dave BERRY-HART**

Richard JACK 1866–1952 Painter, born in Sunderland, County Durham, who studied at York School of Art, winning a National Scholarship to Royal College of Art in 1886. Two years later a Travelling Scholarship took him to Paris where he worked at Académie Julian and Atelier Colarossi, his teachers including such academic perfectionists as Adolphe Bouguereau. Returning to London he worked for some time as a black-and-white artist for several magazines, including *The Idler*. He painted a number of royal portraits and interiors; won a silver medal at Paris Salon; was a member of RP and RI; and was elected RA in 1920. In his latter years he worked in Canada, dying in Montreal.

Bill JACKLIN 1943– Painter, draughtsman, printmaker and teacher, born in London. After studying graphics at Walthamstow School of Art, 1960–1, then working as a graphic designer, Jacklin returned to Walthamstow in 1962 to study painting and was then at Royal College of Art, 1964–7. Jacklin then taught for eight years, at Chelsea School of Art, Hornsey and Royal Colleges of Art and at schools in Kent and Surrey. Jacklin's reputation started to be established in 1970 when he began exhibiting in group exhibitions at Museum of Modern Art in New York and also had the first of a series of solo shows at Nigel Greenwood Inc. After appearing in mixed company at Marlborough Fine Art in 1978, the following year Jacklin had a one-man exhibition there, and continued to show with Marlborough. Jacklin's work went through a number of changes, although underlying it were preoccupations with geometry and light. Environmental Art, Pop Art and Minimalism claimed him for a time, then he worked representationally, being noted for his American townscapes in which strong draughtsmanship and a distinctive palette were evident. In 1986 moved from London to New York, which then featured in his pictures, a sample being included in a fiftieth birthday survey at Museum of Modern Art in Oxford, 1992–3. Arts Council holds Jacklin's work. Was made RA in 1991.

Florence F JACKMAN 1892– Painter in oil who specialised in flowers and portraits. Brought up in Essex, she studied with Frederic Whiting and married the painter Charles Jackson. Member of the Arts Club. Exhibited RA, NEAC, RP and in America. Lived in London.

Andrzej JACKOWSKI 1947– Painter and teacher, born in Penley, North Wales. He studied at Camberwell School of Arts and Crafts, 1966–9, Falmouth School of Art, 1972–3, and Royal College of Art, 1974–7. During his last two years as a student he produced the magazine *Eleven 32* with David Drain, also winning an Abbey Minor Travelling Scholarship and the Rodney Burn Award and John Minton Scholarship. Jackowski became artist-in-residence at the University of Surrey in 1978–9, two years later being a prizewinner at Tolly Cobbold Eastern Arts. Jackowski was first prizewinner at the John Moores Exhibition, Liverpool, in 1991–2 with his picture The Beekeeper's Son. He had a major show at Marlborough Fine Art in 1986, and in 1988 was represented in the Royal College of Art's Exhibition Road show, by which time he had been on its staff for three years. Jackowski drew on personal experience, films, poetry and art to produce haunting and intense works, examples of which are held by Arts Council. Lived in Brighton, Sussex.

Albert Edward JACKSON 1873–1952 Illustrator, black-and-white artist and painter. Born in London, he studied at Camden School of Art under Francis Black. From 1893–1947 he worked as an illustrator for Amalgamated Press, working on such periodicals as *Little Folks*, *The Quiver* and *The Strand Magazine*. Also illustrated a number of children's books. Exhibited RA, London Sketch Club and RBA. Bristol City Art Gallery holds his work. Member of East Sussex Arts Club, and lived in Hastings. His daughter was the artist Muriel Amy Jackson.

Arthur JACKSON 1911– Mainly abstract painter, principally in oil, also in watercolour and scraperboard, born in Rotherham, Yorkshire, of a Dewsbury family. He attended St Martin's School of Art, 1929–31. Jackson's full name was Arthur Jackson Hepworth. He was the first cousin of the sculptor Barbara Hepworth and although as an architect he worked as Hepworth he adopted his mother's maiden name Jackson for painting to avoid confusion. When he was a young painter Hepworth and her first husband John Skeaping took Jackson "under their wing", then when Ben Nicholson "took Barbara over he took me over as well". Jackson was a pupil of Ben Nicholson, 1931–5. In 1937 Jackson met the architects Leslie and Sadie Martin and was offered a place at the School of Architecture in Hull. At the outbreak of World War II Jackson had partly qualified and was working in the office of Martin, who encouraged Jackson to keep painting. Jackson transferred to war construction work, then from 1943–6 was with Royal Engineers in Britain and the Middle East, in 1948 being elected an associate of RIBA. Until 1957 Jackson worked on various projects including the Royal Festival Hall, then moved to Somerset, settling in Glastonbury, building factories and private houses. Prior to World War II Jackson exhibited with 7 & 5 Society, 1934–5, at Leicester and Zwemmer Galleries; Leicester Museum and Art Gallery, 1936; and London Gallery,

1937. He was included in Art in Britain 1930–40 at Marlborough Fine Art, 1965, and the *Circle* show at Kettle's Yard, Cambridge, 1982. In 1991 Tate Gallery displayed the work Painting 1937 to mark Jackson's eightieth birthday.

Ashley JACKSON 1940– Watercolourist, teacher and writer, born in Penang, Malaya. He studied at Barnsley School of Art, 1955–60, and went on to teach in Yorkshire. He was a founder-member of Yorkshire Watercolour Society and a member of UA. Also exhibited with RWS and RI and had many solo shows, starting with Grosvenor Gallery, 1969. Here's to You Dad!, at Doncaster Museum and Art Gallery, 1995, was a tribute to his father, who died as a prisoner of the Japanese in Borneo. There was a retrospective at Salford Museum & Art Gallery, 1997. Jackson presented several series of television programmes on painting, wrote instructional books and published his autobiography, *My Brush with Fortune*, in 1982. *Yorkshire Post* Newspapers; 2nd Battalion, Parachute Regiment; and British Gas hold examples. Ashley Jackson Galleries were at Holmfirth, Yorkshire.

Charles d'Orville Pilkington JACKSON 1887–1973 Sculptor in stone, wood and metal. Born at Garlenick, Cornwall, Jackson studied at Edinburgh College of Art, 1905–10, and the British School in Rome, 1910–11. Exhibited RA, Royal Glasgow Institute of the Fine Arts, RSA, RBA and Walker Art Gallery, Liverpool. Work illustrated in Eric Newton's *British Sculpture 1944–1946*. Jackson's work is to be found in public in Scotland and abroad, including an equestrian statue of Robert the Bruce, Bannockburn, in the Scottish United Services Museum and Imperial War Museum, in Paisley Abbey and in the chapel of Stowe School. Lived in Edinburgh.

Davina JACKSON 1971– Painter, born and lived in London, who did a foundation year at Central St Martins School of Art. Jackson gained a degree at Byam Shaw School, then in themid-1990s studied for a postgraduate diploma at the Royal Academy Schools. She won the Mercers' Company and Leverhulme Scholarship in 1994, David Murray Travel Scholarship (Landscape Prize) in 1996, and the RA Gold Medal, 1997. Exhibited widely, including Mall Galleries, RA Summer Exhibition, Ben Uri Open Exhibition (in which she twice won first prize, once jointly), and Boundary Gallery, 1998. Jackson's picture The Angry Sea, painted from imagination, was included in Chevron UK Ltd's 1997 calendar, and she was featured in the oil company's show that year at the ICA.

Dilys JACKSON 1938– Artist in bronze, wood and stone, and teacher, born in Badulla, Ceylon, who until 1986 worked under the name of Dilys Vibert. She attended Cambridgeshire High School for Girls, 1945–56, then studied at Slade School of Fine Art, 1956–60, and Swansea College of Art, 1961–2, obtaining her master's degree in fine art from South Glamorgan Institute of Higher Education in Cardiff, where she lived, 1987–9. Jackson was art instructor at Coed Ffranc Youth Centre in south Wales, 1965–6; was teacher/head teacher, special schools, for South Glamorgan Education Authority, 1966–92; from 1994 being environmental artist, Ogwr Groundwork Trust, Ogmore Valley. Among her commissions was the Stackpole Centre Sight Garden, Pembroke, 1993. War and landscape were leading themes in Jackson's works, which were shown in many group exhibitions, including Young Contemporaries, 1960; Pictures for Welsh Schools, National Museum of Wales, Cardiff, 1975; All Women Work 88, Chapter Arts Centre, Cardiff, 1988; Festival Exhibition 91, Collective Gallery, Edinburgh, 1991; and Oriel Contemporary Art, 1996. Had a solo show at Galleri Brinken, Stockholm, 1960, later ones including St David's Hall, Cardiff, 1995. Galleri Brinken, Coleg Harlech in Harlech, Vaughan College in Leicester and Mid-Glamorgan Education Authority hold examples.

Elizabeth D JACKSON 1928– Painter, illustrator and editor, born in Edinburgh. She studied at Edinburgh College of Art, 1945–9, with John Kingsley Cook. Mainly worked for the printed page, acting as art editor for Unilever Ltd in the early 1950s; also illustrated for Oxford University Press. Showed at RA and lived in London.

George William JACKSON 1914– Painter, printmaker and teacher, born in Leeds, Yorkshire. He studied at Leeds College of Art under Douglas Sharpus Andrews, 1931–5, then at Royal College of Art with Percy Hague Jowett and Ernest Tristram, 1935–8, and Central School of Arts and Crafts, 1936–8. Illustration and industrial design were leading features of Jackson's work, which was shown in London and the provinces. He was vice-principal of Chesterfield College of Art, 1949–79, living in the Derbyshire town.

Herbert John JACKSON 1938– Printmaker who was by profession an advertising design studio manager. He was born in King's Lynn, Norfolk, and studied at the School of Art in Norwich, 1954–8, where he settled. Was a member of SWE and RE and took part in mixed shows in Britain and abroad, as well as having solo exhibitions.

John JACKSON 1938– Sculptor and teacher, born in London. He studied at Walthamstow School of Art, Hornsey College of Art, then Central School of Art and Design. Jackson was head of sculpture at Batley School of Art; also taught at Maidstone College of Art, West Ham College, Loughton College of Further Education; then Homerton College, Cambridge and at the School of Art there. From 1969–70 and in 1976 he was visiting artist at University of Wisconsin, and this was followed by a series of similar posts at Maidstone College of Art, the Universities of North Michigan, Mississippi and South Dakota in America, as well as the Wesleyan University of South Dakota there, and at Chesterfield School of Art. Showed with LG; at Leeds and Essex University Arts Festivals in 1966; with East Anglian Artists Today, at Royal Institute Galleries, 1969; and with East Anglian Sculptors Exhibition, Ipswich Civic Centre, 1976. Solo shows included Minories, Colchester, 1977. Dynamic triangular shapes were a strong element in Jackson's work, which was described as "constructionalist ... with an extremely organic quality". Commissions included Mississippi State College and Israel Museum, Jerusalem.

Joseph Arthur JACKSON 1889–1962 Painter in oil and watercolour, born in Hull, Yorkshire, who attended the School of Art there, his fees being paid by the local Member of Parliament T R Ferens. During World War I Jackson served with the 1st South Staffordshire Regiment in Italy, where he was able to study Italian art. After demobilisation in 1919, he was given an ex-serviceman's grant to study for three years at Nottingham School of Art. Jackson painted landscapes, flowers, portraits of local dignitaries and panoramas in the Wollaton Hall Natural History Museum. Exhibited in Nottingham and Eastbourne, Sussex, where he died.

Kevin JACKSON fl. from 1970s– Printmaker and teacher who studied at Plymouth College of Art, 1971–2; Sunderland College of Art, 1972–5; and Chelsea School of Art, 1975–6. Teaching included City Literary Institute, Sir John Cass School of Art and Maidstone College of Art. Mixed appearances included Sunderland Arts Centre, 1974; Bradford Print Biennale, 1976; 55 Wapping Artists, 1979; Wapping Artists Open Studios from 1980; and 2nd National Exhibition of Modern British Prints, Blackpool, 1981.

Kurt JACKSON 1961– Painter, mixed media, born in Blandford, Dorset, who had brief periods at Hertfordshire College of Art and Ruskin School of Drawing in Oxford, under Jane Greenham, but who was essentially self-taught. Jackson graduated at Oxford, 1980–2, then spent a year painting and travelling in Africa. He moved to Boscastle, Cornwall, in 1984 to paint full-time, settling in St Just, Penzance, in 1989. He was a member of RWA and Newlyn and Penwith Societies of Artists. Jackson's work was "rooted in the Cornish landscape, seascape and communal psyche, and the natural, human and industrial interventions in the landscape". Group appearances included Rye Art Gallery, 1994; Leicester Art Gallery, 1995; and in 1996 the Celtic Festival at Plymouth Art Centre and Now & Then at David Messum Gallery. Had a solo show at Robinson College, Cambridge, in 1984, then exhibited prolifically, later shows including Lancashire Mining Museum, Salford. For this, Jackson went under ground to paint alongside miners at South Crofty, the last working tin mine in Cornwall. Exeter University holds Jackson's work.

Marguerite Betha JACKSON fl. c.1930–1955 Painter who studied at Heatherley's School of Fine Art with Henry and Gertrude Massey. Exhibited RA, elsewhere in London and in the provinces. Lived for some time at Leatherhead, Surrey.

Marie Blanche JACKSON fl. c.1920–1955 Painter, brought up partly in France. Lady Jackson, who was married to Sir Arthur Jackson, studied at Westminster School of Art, Slade School of Fine Art and at Académie Julian, Paris. Exhibited RA, RI, RWS, NEAC, Cooling Galleries and Walker Art Gallery, Liverpool. Lived at Stonegate, Sussex.

Mark JACKSON 1970– Artist in oil and mixed media on canvas, born and lived in Bolton, Lancashire. He studied at the local Institute of Higher Education, 1988–9, where he later taught part-time, and at Leeds Polytechnic, 1989–92, graduating with a first-class honours degree in graphic design. Jackson's work was "essentially concerned with religious iconography". Group show appearances included Doppelganger Art, at County Arcade, Leeds, and NEAC, both 1992; and Off Course, at Leeds Metropolitan University Gallery, 1993. In 1993 Jackson had a solo show called Towers of Silence at Dean Clough Contemporary Art Gallery, Halifax.

Mary JACKSON 1936– Painter, born in Sussex. She studied as a mature student at Southampton College of Art and part-time at Winchester College of Art. Won a number of prizes, including the Thomas Agnew, Brandler and Patterson Prizes, and New English Critics' Prize in 1990, three years after she was elected a member of NEAC. Also showed at RA, RWA and Kingfisher Gallery during 1990 Edinburgh Festival. She shared shows at Theatre Royal in Winchester, Hallam Gallery and Waterman Fine Art Ltd in 1991. Was painter-in-residence at Glyndebourne for the opera festival in 1991–2. Travelled in India and Australia to paint. National Trust holds her work. Lived in Hurstbourne Tarrant, Hampshire.

Mel JACKSON fl. from 1980s– Sculptor who studied at London College of Printing, 1986–7, Byam Shaw School of Art, 1987–90, and Royal College of Art, 1990–2. He had a residency in Poland in 1988, and in 1993 a London Arts Board award to develop new work and an Oxford Sculpture Project commission and bursary. Showed in 3D '89 at Waterman's Art Centre, 1989; in 1992 at Royal College of Art master's degree graduation show; and in 1993 in Drawing Towards Sculpture at Isis Gallery, Leigh-on-Sea.

Mihangel JACKSON 1940– Painter and illustrator who studied at Twickenham College of Art, then worked as a freelance illustrator. Did work for General Post Office, telephone directory illustrations, and took part in WAC 1969 show: Recording Wales, Chapels. WAC holds work.

Muriel JACKSON 1901– Painter, notably of portraits and murals, and printmaker. She was the daughter of the architect A Blomfield Jackson and was born in London. After private education she attended the Central School of Arts and Crafts under Noel Rooke and F Ernest Jackson. She showed RA, NEAC, Redfern Gallery, widely in the provinces and in America. Art Institute of Chicago holds her work. Lived in London.

Muriel Amy JACKSON 1902–1989 Painter and black-and-white illustrator, daughter of the artist Albert Edward Jackson. After Berkhamsted High School she studied with Philip Cole and others at Hastings School of Art, with her father and in London between 1915–22, and went on to work as an illustrator for Amalgamated Press and other firms. She was noted for her flower pictures, illustrations for children's books and magazines and architectural subjects. Jackson was a member of East Sussex Art Club. Showed with Highgate Artists' Society and Battle Arts Group. Lived in Hastings, Sussex, for many years, latterly suffering from Parkinson's Disease which prevented her working.

Philip JACKSON 1944– Sculptor, born in Scotland. He studied at Farnham School of Art and worked for Henry Moore. He became a fellow of RBS and in 1990 its vice-president. In that year he won the Society's silver medal and in both 1991–2 the Sir Otto Beit Medal for Excellence in Sculpture. In 1991 Jackson won the Mozart Bicentenary Sculpture Competition, London's first sculpture of the composer whose *Don Giovanni* inspired Jackson's Masked Figure series. One of Jackson's more notable works was The Yomper, a unique casting by The Morris Singer Foundry for the Royal Marines Museum, Portsmouth, commemorating the men of 45 Commando's epic march in the Falklands in 1982. Jackson's powerful group The Struggle for Peace and Freedom, 1987, is in St Peter's Square, Manchester, and London, Geneva and Monte Carlo also have examples.

Robert Griffiths JACKSON 1891–1961 Painter in oil and watercolour. Born in Darlington, Yorkshire, Jackson carried on the family painting, decorating and signwriting business. He was a self-taught artist who exhibited with the Barnard Castle Art Society and Shipley Art Gallery, Gateshead. Lived at Barnard Castle, County Durham.

Stanley JACKSON 1917– Painter and illustrator who studied at St Martin's School of Art. Exhibited RA, UA, RBA and in provinces. Lived in Crawley Down, Sussex.

Vanessa JACKSON 1953– Abstract painter who studied at St Martin's School of Art and Royal College of Art. She went to New York on the Yaddo Fellowship in Fine Art in 1985 and taught at Winchester School of Art. Jackson was included in the South Bank Centre 1988–9 touring show The Presence of Painting. She had solo exhibitions at Air Gallery in 1981 and Vortex Gallery three years later. Although Jackson was a painter notably concerned with a painterly surface, colour and texture, her pictures always had a strong underlying geometry. In 1993–4 John Moores Liverpool Exhibition she won a prize with her canvas So Much Depends. Lived in London.

Arthur JACOB 1916– Painter and teacher, born in Garndiffaith, near Pontypool, Monmouthshire. He attended Newport College of Art and Caerleon College of Education and took in courses at the Colleges of Art at Exeter and Cardiff. Went on to teach at various schools in Wales. A founder-member of Pontypool Arts Society, he showed in group exhibitions at WAC and SWG. One-man exhibitions included Syracuse University in America and Llantarnam Grange Arts Centre, Cwmbran. University College, Cardiff, holds his work.

Romy JACOB 1926– Artist in various media who lived in Woodbridge, Suffolk, and travelled to paint in Spain, France and Italy. Anna Airy and Cecil Collins were influences. Jacob's interest in the effects of light was shown in watercolours at Clarges Gallery, 1996, an exhibition shared with Jenny Spencer. Jacob also exhibited at CCA and Drian Galleries and at Galleria Numero in Rome.

Ruth JACOBSON 1941– Artist and teacher, born and settled in London, who studied painting and etching at Slade School of Fine Art under Peter Brooker and Andrew Forge, 1959–63, gaining awards, notably first prize in figure drawing in 1961. In 1963–4 did a postgraduate teaching course at Manchester University and Art College, subsequently teaching in adult education. After marriage and a move to Reading she studied sculpture at Berkshire College of Art, 1965. She had shown at Agnew in 1963, and further exhibitions followed at Camden Arts Centre and Mall Galleries. Solo exhibitions included Gallery Petit, 1972, and Seldown Gallery, Poole Arts Centre, 1985. Music was a key element in her work, which often involved quick, vivid sketches of people involved in a skilled activity. Etchings took longer to develop, sometimes inspired by a book or operatic performance. From 1989–91 Jacobson studied stained glass at Central St Martins, obtaining a fellowship. Ben Uri Art Society holds her work.

Robin JACQUES 1920–1995 Illustrator, painter, designer and teacher, born and died in London. Lived in France for some years from the mid-1960s and travelled widely in several continents. After attending the Royal Masonic Schools at Bushey, in Hertfordshire, Jacques worked for an advertising agency, then served in the Army in World War II. He had no formal artistic training but held several art school teaching posts, in Brighton, Harrow and Canterbury, after three years as art editor of *Strand Magazine* from the late-1940s. Although he showed in provincial art galleries and Victoria & Albert Museum, which holds his work, Jacques made his reputation as a magazine and book illustrator. Worked for *The Listener*, *Radio Times* and other publications and illustrated several dozen books, where he was noted for his attention to historical detail and meticulous draughtsmanship. Author of *Illustrators at Work*, 1963. Jacques' sister was the humorous actress Hattie Jacques.

Ivy G M JACQUIER 1890– Painter, born in Lyons, France, her married name was Ivy G M Skinner. She studied art in Lyons, Eastbourne, Dresden and Paris, her teachers including J D Fergusson and Jacques-Emile Blanche. Showed in France and at Redfern Gallery, RP and RA. British Museum holds her work. She illustrated a number of books, including André Maurois' life of Shelley: *Ariel* and James Thomson's *The Seasons*. Latterly signed her work with just her surname. She detailed her early life in *The Diary of Ivy Jacquier 1907–1926*, published by Gollancz in 1960. Latterly lived in Broomfield, Essex.

J A D 1909– The working name of Alexander William Davies, born in Glamorgan, who employed charcoal, pencil and watercolour. He was a self-taught artist who retired to St Ives, Cornwall, in 1970, attending St Ives School of Painting under Leonard Fuller. Davies had been a science and mathematics teacher, 1930–5, then entered business in 1947, developing marketing and advertising companies, retiring in 1960. His lifetime hobby was sketching the faces of notable personalities in all fields, mostly autographed, of which he built up a huge collection. Many were published in the national press and other journals. Was a member of RBSA Friends, St Ives Society of Artists, Cartoonists' Club of Great Britain and Sutton Coldfield Art Society. Showed widely in the St Ives and Birmingham areas, where he finally lived at Erdington.

Maurice JADOT 1893–1983 Painter and sculptor, born in Brussels, Belgium, studied art at Académie des Beaux-Arts there, also architecture under Victor Horta. Jadot, who was chairman of the Belgian Cultural Centre in Britain and a founder-member of the Society of Free Painters and Sculptors, exhibited in several countries on the continent as well as at the ICA, in 1979 having a retrospective at the National Museum of Wales, Cardiff. Public collections holding his work include the Museum of Modern Art, Brussels, the National Museum of Wales and the Nalecz Collection, Museum of Warsaw, in Poland. Leinster Contemporary Art held a review show in 1987. Lived in London.

Lois JAFFÉ 1918– Artist, born in Axminster, Devon, who attended St Martin's School of Art in 1939, having won Royal Drawing Society medal five years before. Went on to show at Victoria & Albert Museum, Guildhall, PS, Mall Galleries and elsewhere. She lived at Bellair, Charmouth, Dorset.

Margaret Leah JAGGAR 1908– Muralist, wood engraver and commercial artist, born in Wallasey, Merseyside, who attended Cheltenham Ladies' College, then Liverpool School of Art. She worked as a commercial artist and painter of decorative murals, then was a housewife and practising artist living in Anglesey at Rhydwyn, near Holyhead. Her murals included the Cunard liner *Caronia*, National Trust and Blackpool's Fun Park. She was a member of RCamA, also exhibiting with SWE and Walker Art Gallery in Liverpool. Her solo shows included Sandon Studios, Liverpool, 1930, and Holyhead Library, 1971.

David JAGGER 1891–1958 Versatile painter, born in Kilnhurst, Yorkshire, brother of sculptor Charles Sargeant Jagger and of the artist Edith Jagger. He was a leading member of ROI and belonged to RP, also showing at RA, RBA, Walker Art Gallery in Liverpool and elsewhere. In 1940 his work was included in The Art of the Jagger Family at Mappin Art Gallery, Sheffield. Lived in London.

Edith JAGGER 1896–1975 Painter, sister of the sculptor Charles Sargeant Jagger and of the artist David Jagger, who settled in Sheffield, Yorkshire. She showed at RA, RI, ROI and elsewhere. In 1940 her work was included in The Art of the Jagger Family at the Mappin Art Gallery, Sheffield. Edith contributed designs to the Sheffield firm Painted Fabrics, which in the inter-war years employed ex-servicemen and was the subject of a Mappin exhibition, 1997–8.

Alan Gosset JAMES 1875–1950 Architect and landscape painter, born in Prestbury, Gloucestershire, near Cheltenham where he was articled to a firm of architects. After practising and working as a correspondent in South Africa James joined the department of architecture at London University, 1903–8, working with Edwin Lutyens. He was almost 50 before he began serious painting, studying at Cheltenham and Chelsea Schools of Art. His first work shown at RA, where he appeared for just over 30 years from 1911, was principally architectural designs. Also showed NEAC and Goupil Gallery. Tate Gallery has his Winter on the Windrush, depicting a scene not far from his home in Gloucestershire at Stow-on-the-Wold.

Andrew JAMES 1958– Sculptor, born in Oxford, who attended Chelsea School of Art, 1979–81, gaining his master's degree at Slade School of Fine Art, 1987–9. Group exhibitions included Nicola Jacobs Gallery, 1981; Into the Nineties, Mall Galleries, 1989; New Identities at Camden Arts Centre, 1990; Counterpoint at Gimpel Fils, 1991; and Whitechapel Open Studios, 1992. His solo show Host was held at Hales Gallery, 1993, the Japanese dealer Rumiko Torii staging one at Entwistle Gallery in 1994. James created his own unique worlds populated by toy figures the size of real children who acted out fictional dramas. Lived and worked in London.

Elizabeth Campbell JAMES 1923– Painter, printmaker and teacher, born in London, daughter of the designer Norman James. She studied at Hornsey School of Art with John Moody and Norman Janes and went on to teach at Enfield County School for Girls after World War II. Exhibited RA and SGA, of which she was a member. Lived in Enfield, Middlesex.

Hywel JAMES 1944– Artist, teacher and administrator, born in Brighton, Sussex, where he studied at the College of Art, 1962–6, teachers including Jennifer Dickson, Charles Knight and Ian Potts. He showed at RE, RI and Hastings and Bedford public galleries, but latterly did not paint due to administrative responsibilities. Became vice-principal, director of academic studies, at Bournemouth and Poole College of Art and Design, Poole, Dorset.

Kim JAMES 1928– Sculptor and teacher, who studied at the Borough Polytechnic, 1948–54, under David Bomberg and Tom Eckersley, and at the Royal College of Art. Took part in group exhibitions at RBA, 1959; Wildenstein, 1961; Arthur Jeffress and Grosvenor Galleries, 1963; AIA, 1963–4; and RA, 1967–9. James' figurative-towards-abstraction pieces were given a solo exhibition at Hanover Gallery, 1966. Carried out commissions for the Churches of St Nicholas at Hayes, Middlesex, and St Matthew's at Bethnal Green; a crucifix for the Franciscan Brothers in Dorset; and sculpture and relief work for Hoveringham Gravels Ltd, Nottingham. James gave up art in

1969, having been head of art therapy at what became the University of Hertfordshire. He retrained as a scientist and became a successful management consultant in cybernetics. His sculptures were acquired by a number of public collections, including one in Brussels. James was born and eventually settled in Wollaston, Wellingborough, Northamptonshire.

Lisa JAMES 1949– Artist, designer and illustrator, born in Hamburg, West Germany, who studied at Edinburgh College of Art, 1967–72. She taught at Barnfield College in Luton and did freelance design and illustration. Mixed shows included RA Summer Exhibition from 1980; Alpine Gallery, 1983; Whitechapel Open Exhibition and Berry Street Open Studios, both 1984. Had a solo show at Dryden Street Gallery, 1980.

Louis JAMES 1920– Painter, born in Adelaide, South Australia, who had no formal training. After World War II he began to paint seriously and eventually established a reputation as an abstract and a figurative artist. For about 15 years he worked and showed in Europe, based in London, but from 1964 lived in Sydney, although in 1978 he revisited London and continental Europe and visited New York. Exhibited widely, especially in Australia, where in 1949 he had a one-man show at John Martin's Gallery, Adelaide. In England showed in the 1950s and 1960s at Redfern Gallery, also at Stone Gallery in Newcastle upon Tyne. Had a retrospective show at Bonython-Meadmore Gallery, Adelaide, in 1986. Tate Gallery holds a self-portrait drawing, Ferens Art Gallery in Hull and Towner Art Gallery in Eastbourne also holding examples.

Maggie JAMES 1956– Painter in oil and gouache "entirely from observation", born in Cardiff, where she returned to live in 1985, the year she joined 56 Group Wales. Studied at Newcastle Polytechnic, 1975–8, graduating from Royal College of Art in 1982. Gained a John Minton Scholarship, 1982; Jacob Mendelson Scholarship and WAC Award, both 1984; Oppenheim-John Downes Memorial Trust Award, 1987; and was one of the first WAC Bursary winners when scheme began, 1994–5. Showed at RA Summer Exhibition, 1982; National Portrait Gallery, John Player Award, 1983; Interiors, Andrew Knight Gallery, Cardiff, 1988; and was a prizewinner, Royal National Eisteddfod, 1990. Contemporary Art Society for Wales owns her work.

Margaret Calkin JAMES 1895–1985 Designer, printmaker, calligrapher, illustrator and painter, who grew up in Hampstead, north London, where she lived much of her life. She trained at the Central School of Arts and Crafts, being taught calligraphy by Graily Hewitt. During World War I she oversaw the art department of the central London Young Men's Christian Association, after hostilities designing under her own Rainbow Workshops sign. In 1922 she married C H James and closed her workshops, then living in a house he designed at 1 Hampstead Way and setting up a new workshop there. An impressive stream of banners, book jackets, posters, illuminated books and watercolours followed, clients including Lloyd's of London, RIBA, London Transport, Shell and the General Post Office. In 1969 James had a stroke which deprived her of speech and the use of her right hand, and she was encouraged to take up needlework. She showed at RA and had three solo exhibitions: at Cooling Galleries, St Mary Abbots Place and the St George's Gallery under Basil Jonzen. In 1996 there was a touring show based on Burgh House, Hampstead.

Merlin JAMES 1960– Painter, draughtsman, printmaker and writer on art, born in Cardiff. He studied at the College of Art there, 1978–9, Central School of Art, 1979–82, and Royal College of Art, 1983–6. He wrote critically for *London Magazine*, *Times Literary Supplement*, *Burlington Magazine* and other publications, and in 1992 his *Engaging Images: Practical Criticism and Visual Art*, was published. James was critic-in-residence at Kingston University, 1995, and painter-in-residence at Glasgow School of Art in 1996. In that year James gave The Stanley Picker Lecture at Kingston, in which he questioned supposed oppositions between the traditional and avant-garde, through an examination of failures in art criticism and of the tendency towards literalism in contemporary art. James' own work included figurative and abstract elements. Guest lectureships included Tate Gallery, New York Studio School, Royal College of Art, National Museum of Wales in Cardiff and provincial galleries and art colleges. Later group shows included Kapil Jariwala Gallery, 1994, and Whitechapel Art Gallery, 1996. Had a first solo exhibition at Albemarle Gallery, 1991, later ones including Kettle's Yard Gallery in Cambridge, 1996, and in 1997 Critical Pictures, Andrew Grant Gallery in Edinburgh, Francis Graham-Dixon Gallery and Kingston University.

Owen JAMES 1934– Painter and teacher, born in Yorkley, Monmouthshire. He studied at Lydney School of Art, 1951–3, then Camberwell School of Arts and Crafts, 1953–5, under Karel Vogel. He went on to teach at South-East London College. James was a member of SGA, also exhibiting at RA, NEAC, ROI and RBA. Solo shows included Fairfield Halls, Croydon. Lived in London.

Richard JAMES 1937– Painter in acrylic on canvas, and acrylic and gouache on paper, born in Thorne, Yorkshire. Studied at Doncaster School of Art, 1957–9; St Martin's School of Art, 1959–60; Slade School of Fine Art, 1960–4, where Keith Vaughan was his tutor; then gained Prix de Rome in painting, 1964–5. James lived and worked in London for 23 years, teaching part-time in various art schools. Moved to Norfolk in 1982, settling in Norwich, and was head of painting at the School of Art there, 1983–91, leaving to concentrate more fully on painting. He said that his work "is about colour, movement, rhythm, contrast – the interaction between the energies of the natural world and the man-made world, between the random and the controlled. Painting makes vivid the meltdown between one moment and the next." Group shows included Serpentine Gallery, 1973; John Moores Liverpool Exhibition, 1974, and in that year British Painting '74, at Hayward Gallery; British Painting 1952–1977 at

RA, 1977; Hayward Annual, 1989; and Beardsmore Gallery, from 1992. Later solo shows included Gallery 49, Norwich, 1981, and Studio Exhibition, 1994. Between 1984–93 James was member of faculty for the award of Rome and Abbey Major Scholarships. Albright Knox Museum in America and Eastern Arts hold examples.

Shani Rhys JAMES 1953– Painter, born in Melbourne, Australia, who moved to London in 1962, settling in Wales in 1984. Studied at St Martin's School of Art, 1973–6. Group shows included Whitechapel Open and RA Summer Exhibition from 1982; Wales Open, Aberystwyth, 1989, first prize; Mostyn Open, first prize, 1991; Royal National Eisteddfod, Aberystwyth, gold medal in fine art, 1992; and Hunting/*Observer* first prizewinner, Mall Galleries and tour, 1993. Had solo exhibition with Martin Tinney Gallery, Cardiff, 1993, another of self-portraits, strongly painted in whites and reds, at Oriel Mostyn, Llandudno, 1997. Was married to the artist Stephen West and lived at Llangadfan, Powys.

Stephanie JAMES 1957– Artist in varied media, notably a sculptor, who studied at Concordia University, 1974–7, then Hull College of Art, 1977–80, followed by Newcastle University, 1980–2. Among workshops participated in were a Workshop for the Blind, Harris Museum & Art Gallery in Preston, 1988. Mixed exhibitions included Hull Drawing Show, 1979; Northern Young Contemporaries at Whitworth Art Gallery, Manchester, 1981; Brighton Festival, 1984; and Sculpture at Canterbury from 1986. She showed solo at Morley Gallery; Commonwealth Institute; and Christchurch Mansion, Ipswich, 1991.

Thomas K JAMES 1906– Part-time painter and professional railwayman, born in Nottingham, where he continued to live. He acquired his painting knowledge mainly at Nottingham Society of Artists, of which he was a member. Showed with the Society, at the Nottingham 1951 Festival of Britain, at Mansfield Art Gallery and throughout the provinces at shows organised by British Rail.

Frank JAMESON 1898–1968 Painter in oil, born in London. Became an insurance salesman, in the evenings studying at Birmingham Art School. Commissioned in the Worcestershire Regiment in World War I he was responsible for building bridges and blockhouses. After demobilisation he lived in Redditch and travelled around the county camping and painting landscapes, eventually doing the same in Dorset, Brixham in Devon and St Ives, Cornwall, where he rented the Loft Studio and joined the Society of Artists. Also showed at RWA, RA, RBA, RHA, ROI and Paris Salon. Was a member of Bournemouth Art Club while living there, then moved to Glenovar, near Dublin, in Ireland, in the late-1940s returning to St Ives and then settling in Falmouth. His studio commanded a fine view of the River Fal. As well as harbour scenes filled with extensive colour and reflections, Jameson was noted for his paintings of nudes and portraits of notabilities and the Cornish aristocracy. In 1994 the Penzance auction rooms W H Lane sold Jameson's studio collection.

Joan JAMESON 1892–1953 Painter, born in London, daughter of the baronet Sir Richard Musgrave. She was presented at court, then studied at Académie Julian, in Paris, for two years. After marriage to Captain Thomas Jameson she lived extensively in Ireland, latterly at Ardmore. Painted consistently from 1930, having her first solo show at Leicester Galleries in 1933. Over the years was to exhibit often there, with RHA, French and Wertheim Galleries and at Goupil Salon. Also showed at Dublin Painters Society, where in 1936 her portrait of Lady Charles Cavendish, formerly Adele Astaire, sister of the singer and dancer Fred Astaire, attracted much publicity. Irish country houses were a favourite subject. RHA Gallery in Dublin held a show of Jameson's work in 1989, which indicated a wide range of styles including Cubism. "Competent but derivative" was the judgement of *Irish Times* critic Brian Fallon, who said that Jameson "rarely put a personal stamp on anything she did."

Kenneth JAMESON 1913– Painter, draughtsman and teacher, born in Blackwell, Worcestershire, married to the artist Norma Jameson. He studied at Birmingham School of Music, Leicester College of Art and Bath Academy of Art. Held a series of teaching appointments, eventually being an art inspector for London County Council and Inner London Education Authority. He wrote a number of books, including *You Can Draw* and *Painting: A Complete Guide*. Jameson lectured extensively on child development through art and painting and drawing with an emphasis on aiding adults. He was also responsible for BBC Television programmes on art. Jameson was a member of RCamA, showed at Royal National Eisteddfod, RA, RBA and Paris Salon, where he gained an Hon. Mention. Had several shows with his wife in London and the provinces. Public gallery in Birkenhead holds his work, as do educational authorities. Lived in Beckenham, Kent.

Norma JAMESON 1933– Painter and teacher, born in Burslem, Staffordshire, married to the artist Kenneth Jameson. She studied at Bath Academy of Art, 1951–5, Liverpool University, 1955–6, then in 1978 gained advanced textile diploma at Goldsmiths' College School of Art. Her books included *Batik for Beginners*. She was a member of ROI and RBA, also showing with RA, RCamA, had several shows with her husband and solo exhibitions in London and elsewhere. Inner London Education Authority and provincial education authorities held examples. Lived in Beckenham, Kent.

Susan JAMESON 1944– Printmaker, born in Cumberland, who studied at Carlisle College of Art, 1960–4, gaining a travelling scholarship to Italy, 1963. Attended Goldsmiths' College School of Art, 1964–5, then Central School, 1971–3, for advanced printmaking studies. Mixed shows included Modern Art Gallery, Naples, 1966; Serpentine Gallery, 1973; South West Arts Association travelling exhibition, 1974–5; and ICA, 1977. Solo shows included Tenterden House Gallery, Kent, from 1973 and Graffiti Gallery, 1977.

Robert Kirkland JAMIESON 1881–1950 Painter and teacher, born at Lanark, Scotland. He studied at Glasgow Training College for Teachers, then in Paris. For most of the 1930s he was head of Westminster School of Art, taking over as principal of St Martin's School of Art in 1945. He was married to the artist and potter Dorothea Selous. He showed at RA, LG, NEAC, Redfern Gallery and extensively at RBA. Galleries in Oldham, Worthing, Belfast and Glasgow hold his work. Lived at Burford, Oxfordshire.

Victor JAMILLY 1927– Painter and art dealer who studied at St Martin's School of Art. He showed at RSBA, NEAC and at Euston Gallery. The Jamillys ran the gallery for some years in a large house near Euston Road. Their aim was trying "to educate the public to appreciate and buy original paintings instead of prints and posters". Lived in London.

Lin JAMMET 1958– Painter, designer, illustrator and animator, educated in England and France and of Anglo-French parentage. His mother was the sculptor Elisabeth Frink. He trained at Chelsea School of Art, 1975–7, then for three years founded and ran the rock group AngleTrax, touring England and releasing several records. In 1980 returned to drawing and began to freelance as an illustrator, designing greetings cards, posters and book covers and working for magazines such as *City Limits* and *Tatler*. Did animation work for television commercials, programme titles and promotional videos, clients including Halifax Building Society, London Transport and Weetabix Ltd. Central Office of Information, the Welsh Office and Department of Trade and Industry employed Jammet for animated information films. Had exhibitions at Beaux Arts Gallery, Bath, and St Jude's, 1990.

JANARDAN 1941– Painter, full name Janardan Bhatt, who was born in Nairobi, Kenya. He was educated in England, studying art at Regent Street Polytechnic School of Art, 1959–61. Was associated with ICA and Federation of British Artists. Signed his work Janardan and lived in London.

Alfred JANES 1911– Painter, draughtsman, printmaker and teacher, born in Swansea, who was especially associated with portraits of his friend the poet Dylan Thomas; National Museum of Wales, Cardiff, holds a fine example, of 1934. Janes attended Cardiff School of Art, then Royal Academy Schools. From 1936–40 taught at Swansea School, then after military service returned to Swansea College of Art, 1946–63, later teaching at Croydon College of Art. He was a founder-member of SWG, showed at Mayor, St George's and Redfern Galleries, widely with WAC and CASW and took part in Dylan Thomas Country at Upper Grosvenor Galleries, 1971. WAC gave him a retrospective, with tour, 1974, Attic Gallery, Swansea, one in 1995. Cubism, Paul Klee and American abstraction of the 1960s all attracted Janes' interest, although his portraits and figurative paintings, stylised and sometimes rather disquieting, are his most notable works. Salome, a CASW purchase, is a good example. Lived in London.

Norman JANES 1892–1980 Etcher, wood engraver and painter, noted for his stylish line and sense of design. Born at Egham, Surrey, Janes studied at the Slade School, Central School of Arts and Crafts and Royal College of Art. Exhibited at RA, RWS, NEAC, SWE, RSMA, in the provinces and widely abroad. Two one-man shows at the Beaux Arts Gallery. Married the artist Barbara Greg. His work is extensively held in public collections including the British Museum, British Council, London Museum, in the provinces and in New Zealand and the USA. Lived in London.

Violeta JANES 1917– Artist in oil, pastel and watercolour, and teacher, born in Buenos Aires, Argentina. She studied at Regent Street Polytechnic School of Art, Watford School of Art and City and Guilds of London Art School, her teachers including A R Middleton Todd, Stuart Tresilian, Edward Osmond and Robin Guthrie. Janes held a position in an advertising studio, did a substantial volume of freelance design work including children's illustrations and directed art studies at Alma College in Ontario, Canada. Portraits, landscapes and flower paintings were features of her output, main works including The Fiddler, Red River in New Mexico, Pink Flowers, The Old Shepherd, The Cockney Character and Rosemary Cottage. Janes was a member of UA, Milldon Art Society and Harpenden Art Club. She also showed with PS, RA, RP, at Paris Salon and elsewhere. Had a solo exhibition at Broomfield Museum, Broomfield Park. Lived in Harpenden, Hertfordshire.

Gavin JANTJES 1948– Printmaker, painter, designer and teacher, born in Cape Town, South Africa. Classified as a Cape Coloured, this had a marked effect on him and the direction of his art against racial oppression worldwide. He studied at the School of Fine Art at the University of Cape Town, 1966–9, and won a scholarship to the Hochschule für Bildende Kunst, in Hamburg, Germany, 1970–2. Worked with the Poster Collective in London in 1976 during a short visit, settling in Britain in 1982. He went on to become senior lecturer at Chelsea School of Art. Was also a member of the Arts Council from 1986. Took part widely in group shows in Britain and abroad, solo exhibitions including ICA, 1976, a series at Edward Totah Gallery from 1980 and Herbert Art Gallery and Museum, Coventry, 1988. Victoria & Albert Museum, Wolverhampton Art Gallery and overseas galleries hold his work. Participated in The Other Story, Hayward Gallery, 1989–90, and touring.

Darsie JAPP 1883–1973 Painter, born in Liverpool into a shipping family. Japp was educated at Oxford University and worked in the family office in London, 1904–7, attending Lambeth School of Art in the evenings. As a student at Slade School of Fine Art, 1908–9, he was a contemporary of Stanley Spencer, whom he introduced to the painter Henry Lamb. In 1926 Lamb completed Darsie Japp and Family, owned by City of Manchester Art Galleries, one of his most notable such groups. During commissioned Army service in World War I Japp won the Military Cross and his picture The Royal Field Artillery in Macedonia is in the Imperial War Museum collection. However, Lamb dissuaded him from becoming a full-time artist, and Japp chose to farm and breed racehorses for a living. For many years Japp and his family lived on the continent as well as in England, and he died in Caxias, Portugal.

Norman Clifford JAQUES 1922– Painter, draughtsman, printmaker and teacher. He was born in Manchester and studied at the College of Art and Technology, 1937–42. Among his awards were a Royal Manchester Institute Award; Proctor Travelling Scholarship to Italy and France, 1948; and he was a Giles Bequest Prize winner in blockprinting, Victoria & Albert Museum, 1954. Jaques held a senior lectureship in the faculty of art and design at Manchester Polytechnic, 1950–82. He was president of MAFA, 1984–90. He worked in the field of prints, in which he specialised, illustration and book design. Solo and group shows included Peterloo Gallery and City Art Gallery, both in Manchester; Manchester and Salford Universities; Senefelder Group; Nebraska University Art Gallery; and RA. Victoria & Albert Museum and public galleries in Manchester, Oldham and Stockport hold examples. Lived in Sale, Cheshire.

Tess JARAY 1937– Painter and teacher who studied at St Martin's School of Art, 1954–7, then Slade School of Fine Art, 1957–60. In 1960 she gained an Abbey Minor Travelling Scholarship, the following year winning a French Government Scholarship. Had her first solo show at Grabowski Gallery in 1963. Jaray taught at Hornsey College of Art, 1964–8, then at Slade School of Fine Art. Further solo shows included Graves Art Gallery, Sheffield, in 1972, and the same year at Bristol City Art Gallery; Angela Flowers Gallery in 1976; and key shows at Whitworth Art Gallery, in Manchester, and Ashmolean Museum, Oxford, in the mid-1980s. Jaray's work was abstract, concerned with suggestive interactions of colour and form in complex patterns. Examples are held by Tate Gallery, Arts Council and other major collections in Britain and abroad. Married to the artist Marc Vaux and lived in London.

Alex JARDINE 1913–1987 Painter and draughtsman in colour and black-and-white with a special interest in plastics, born in Essex, where he attended Brentwood School. Jardine was at St Martin's School of Art and studied in Brussels. He was responsible for a river fish series of stamps for the General Post Office, also completing commissions for Imperial Chemical Industries, Bakelite Ltd, Swedish Travel Bureau and publishers such as Collins, Eyre & Spottiswoode and Hutchinson. He was a member of SWLA and Society for Wildlife Art of the Nations and showed widely internationally. Lived in Chislet, Kent.

George JARDINE 1920– Painter, printmaker, collagist, scraperboard artist and teacher, born and lived in Wallasey, Cheshire. He attended Wallasey School of Art, 1936, and Royal College of Art, 1939–43, teachers including Paul Nash, Stanley Spencer, Percy Horton and Edward Bawden. During World War II Jardine moved to Cumbria, becoming absorbed in the landscape of the Lake District. From 1944–80 he was a lecturer in graphics at Liverpool College of Art. Jardine's own pictures, usually on a small scale, were early influenced by Indian miniature painting and Surrealism, especially Max Ernst, collages using pieces of newspaper, sweet wrappers and advertisements. Jardine also painted many portraits. He showed with Sandon Studios Society and Liverpool Academy both of which he was a member, RA, RCamA and elsewhere. Had several solo exhibitions at Portal Gallery; also Williamson Art Gallery, Birkenhead; Bluecoat Gallery, Liverpool; in Belgium and America. The Williamson, Arts Council, Walker Art Gallery in Liverpool and the University there hold examples.

Derek JARMAN 1942–1994 Artist in many media, stage designer, film-maker, photographer and writer, full name Michael Derek Jarman (he showed as Michael Jarman until 1966). He studied at London University, 1960–3, then Slade School of Fine Art, 1963–7. Jarman had a solo show at the True Lovers' Knot public house in Northwood, 1960, and won first prize, amateur class, at University of London Art Exhibition in 1961. He took part in notable mixed shows, including Young Contemporaries, Tate Gallery, 1967, winning a Peter Stuyvesant Foundation Prize; Drawing, at Museum of Modern Art, Oxford, 1972; and he was nominated for the Turner Prize, Tate Gallery, 1986. Jarman was an exhibitor at Lisson Gallery from its opening in 1967, also showing with Richard Salmon Ltd. Retrospectives included ICA, 1984; Dom Kulture Studenski Grad, Belgrade, 1988; and Accatone, Paris, 1989. In 1993 Jarman showed Aids-related pictures at Karsten Schubert (Jarman was diagnosed HIV-positive in 1986). Such later works were notably Expressionist, fiery, colourful and cathartic. Jarman said: "I've got wilder and ruder." Jarman was a notable creator of films, including *Jubilee*, 1977; *Caravaggio*, 1986; *The Last of England*, 1987; *The Garden*, 1990, which won a prize at the Berlin Film Festival; *Wittgenstein*, 1992; and *Blue*, 1993. The book *Modern Nature: The Journals of Derek Jarman*, appeared in 1991. Arts Council and Tate Gallery hold examples. Died in London. There was a major retrospective at Barbican Art Gallery, 1996.

Douglas JARMAN 1902– Painter and designer for industry who attended Croydon School of Art, 1917–20, and continued to live in area. Showed at local Art Society, RI and elsewhere.

Michael JARMAN: *see* **Derek JARMAN**

Nesta JARMAN fl. from early 1930s– Portrait miniaturist, full name Anne Nesta Jarman, born in Sutton, Surrey. After Bedales School she studied at Cardiff School of Art and Heatherley's School of Fine Art and miniature painting with Alfred Praga. She showed at RA, RMS of which she became an honorary member in 1981, RWA and SWAS. Apothecaries' Hall holds her work. Lived in Weston-super-Mare, Avon.

Barbara Anne JARRETT 1934– Painter, born in Liverpool. She attended Horsham School of Art and Central School of Art. A member of Free Painters and Sculptors, she showed at Mall

Galleries, Loggia Gallery and in Surrey and Sussex, where she lived in Pulborough.

Gloria JARVIS fl. from 1950s– Artist in oil, gouache, brush and wash with Chinese ink, pastel and charcoal; teacher, born in Acton, west London. She attended St Martin's School of Art, 1942–50, under James Bateman, Barry Craig, James Guthrie and others, in 1961–2, studying history of art at University of Florence. From 1950–63 taught history of costume and costume drawing at Regent Street Polytechnic. Jarvis showed at RA, NEAC, NS and at Leicester Galleries in the Artists of Fame and Promise shows, having solo shows in Brussels, 1970–83. Several Belgian collections and Abbot Hall Art Gallery, Kendal, hold examples. Among her main works were The Thames Frost Fair 1740 and L'Ommegang, both in private collections. A number of eighteenth-century artists, including Gainsborough and Hogarth, as well as Degas and Daumier were cited as influences. Lived in Canterbury, Kent.

Henry C JARVIS 1867–1955 Landscape painter in watercolour. Studied at Goldsmiths' College School of Art under Percy Buckman and Frederick Marriott. Exhibited RA, RI and RWS. Northampton Corporation bought his work. Lived at Sevenoaks, Kent, where he was a member of the Arts and Crafts Society.

Roland JARVIS 1931– Painter, draughtsman, clockmaker and teacher, born of a French mother and English father, who spent his first nine years in France and was bilingual. Attended Guildford Technical College, 1945–8, then read for a degree in electrical engineering at King's College, 1948–51. After military service training in radar, 1951–3, Jarvis was a research engineer for Morgan Carbon before opting to pursue painting, his tutors at Chelsea School of Art, 1954–6, being Ceri Richards and Robert Medley. From 1956–9 Jarvis lived in Paris, partly on a French government scholarship, then a British Council grant, working at L'Académie de la Grande Chaumière and studying etching in Friedlander's studio. From 1959–91 – apart from a year in India, 1961–2 – Jarvis taught widely, including Watford, Camberwell and Kingston Schools of Art and Brighton Polytechnic. In 1960 BBC Television had made a programme on Jarvis' work, directed by Alex Jacob. Exhibited widely including RA, Victoria & Albert Museum, St George's Gallery, Towner Art Gallery in Eastbourne, solo shows including a retrospective at Brighton Polytechnic Gallery, 1992. Victoria & Albert Museum, New York City Library and National Gallery of Western Australia, Perth, hold examples. From 1972 Jarvis designed and built astronomical clocks, and was elected a fellow of the British Horological Institute in 1992. His work was shown extensively at the Science Museum and Hastings Museum, which bought a large clock in 1995, on permanent display. Lived in Hastings, Sussex.

Catherine JAUSLIN 1958– Painter, born and lived in London, who studied at St Martin's School of Art, 1980–3, then Chelsea College, 1983–4, in the latter year gaining a two-year Rome Scholarship. Showed widely in mixed exhibitions and solo shows in London from 1981 and was represented in John Moores Liverpool Exhibition, 1993–4.

Lallitha JAWAHIRILAL fl. from late 1980s– Painter, born in Ladysmith, Natal, South Africa, who travelled widely, but whose work remained infused with the scenery and colour of her own country. She gained a first-class honours degree at Camberwell School of Arts and Crafts, 1984–7, then her master's degree in painting at Royal College of Art, 1987–9. Awards and scholarships included Africa Education Trust Scholarship, 1987–9, Africa Education Trust Award, London, 1989–90, and Pollock-Krasner Award, 1992. Among her residencies was Casa Manilva, Spain 1992, and Tripura Yoga Ashram, Hardwar, Himalayas, 1993. Had many group shows, latterly including shared exhibition with Rob Olins at New Academy Gallery, 1994. Solo shows included 198 Gallery, 1990; Galerie Trapez, Berlin, 1991; and New Academy Gallery, 1996. South African National Gallery in Cape Town holds her work. Lived in London.

JAY: *see* **Elsbeth JUDA**

JEAN: *see* **Jean INGHAM**

Kathleen Mary JEBB 1879–c. 1950 Black-and-white artist, printmaker, watercolourist and teacher, born in Liverpool. She lived in Bristol from 1903 and taught part-time at Municipal School of Art. The landscape of the West Country and Welsh borderland area were key subjects of her work, which was shown at RA, RWA, RSA and Walker Art Gallery in Liverpool. Bristol City Art Gallery holds prints by her.

Kathleen Grant JEFFERIES: *see* **Kathleen HARTNELL**

Wilfred Avalon JEFFERIES 1907– Painter, printmaker, theatrical designer and teacher, born in Bristol. Educated at Bristol University, at the city's Municipal School of Art, 1920–6, at Académie Julian in Paris, 1928–9, at Geneva Academy, 1930–1, and in Rome at the British Academy on two occasions, in the 1920s and 1930s. He showed at RA, RBA, RWA, SGA of which he was a member, and widely in the provinces. Bristol University has murals by him and National Maritime Museum in Greenwich holds his work. Taught for a time at Portsmouth, Winchester and Basingstoke Schools of Art and lived for many years in Southsea, Hampshire.

Alan JEFFERSON 1918– Artist in a variety of media and teacher, born in London. He studied at Wimbledon School of Art, 1934–7, then Royal College of Art, 1937–9 and 1946–7 with a break for war service. Notable teachers included Gilbert Spencer, Paul Nash, Patrick Heron and Harry Thubron. Jefferson gained a Royal Exhibition Scholarship in painting, 1947. He joined Portsmouth College of Art in that year and taught painting and printed textiles, eventually retiring from department of fine art at Portsmouth Polytechnic as senior lecturer in painting in 1983. Group shows included RA, Redfern and Leicester Galleries,

Southampton City Art Gallery and elsewhere. Had solo shows at Bear Lane Gallery, Oxford, 1965; Portsmouth College of Art, 1968; Hiscock Gallery, 1971; and Portsmouth City Art Gallery, 1974. Portsmouth Museums Collection holds his work. Jefferson's pictures, as shown at Bear Lane, were apparently simple: a disc of colour, surrounded by other colours in a geometrical arrangement, but they were also very complex, containing a multiplicity of pictorial events apparent only after tranquil observation. Lived in Cosham, Hampshire.

Ralph JEFFERY 1920– Painter mainly in oil, born in London. He attended Plaistow Grammar School, then Goldsmiths' College School of Art. Showed at RA, LG and NEAC. Lived in Rogate, Petersfield, Hampshire.

Edward JEFFREY 1898–1978 Painter and illustrator, born on Tyneside. He studied at King's College and then entered the studios of a Newcastle firm of commercial artists, Philipson and Sons, where he stayed for 11 years; then did similar work in London and Huddersfield. In 1944 he was asked, with the writer Sheila Hodgetts, to create a new character for children and the pig Toby Twirl was the result. It ran as a cartoon strip in a Yorkshire paper and appeared in annuals. After this Edward Jeffrey turned to inn signs in the Lake District, where he lived at Ravenstonedale, and when he was not painting these he become noted for his pictures of the area. Showed RSA, NS, RI, RBA, with local art societies and widely abroad.

Gary JEFFREY 1966– Painter of landscapes and townscapes whose vigorous brushwork was compared with that of Kokoschka. Worked a lot in London. In 1984 he gained the Munnings Painting Prize. Jeffrey exhibited at Kingston Heritage Museum in 1988, with RWS, Southwood Brown Fine Art, 1989–90, Llewellyn Alexander Gallery in 1990 and in 1991 shared a show there.

Edward Grover JEFFREYS 1897– Painter, industrial and commercial artist. Studied at Ealing School of Art and Bournemouth School of Art. Exhibited RA, NS, RBA and PS. Lived at Ashford, Middlesex.

Neil JEFFRIES 1959– Sculptor, born in Bristol, who studied at St Martin's School of Art, 1978–82, then Slade School of Fine Art, 1982–4. In 1984 he gained a Boise Travelling Scholarship. Among his mixed exhibitions was The Self Portrait: a Modern View, which toured from Artsite Gallery, Bath, 1987, in which Jeffries showed work in oil on riveted metal sheet. It had a quirky quality, like his Winter Levitation, 1985, held by the Arts Council. Jeffries had a first solo show in Bristol in 1985 and after that in London, Blond Fine Art and Angela Flowers Gallery both handling his work.

Roger JEFFS 1942– Artist, born in Nuneaton, Warwickshire, who gained a national diploma in design, painting, at Coventry College of Art, 1958–62, then attended Slade School of Fine Art, 1962–4. At Coventry and the Slade a fellow-student was John Bowstead, and together they had a show, A New Kind of Brightness, at the Umbrella Club, Coventry, in 1961. In 1964, Jeffs, Bowstead and two other Slade students, Terry Atkinson and Bernard Jennings, formed the group Fine Artz which collaborated on a work called Action Chair. The group presented a project and sound show called *Miss Misty and the Tri-Cool Data* at Birmingham Polytechnic in 1966. After Fine Artz, Jeffs and Bowstead continued to work together until 1968–9 in Light-Sound Workshop, a research unit based at Hornsey College of Art. According to Jeffs, "we made films and experimental audio-visual presentations. We also collaborated with Archigram, the radical architectural group based at the Architectural Association." The Arts Council holds Jeffs' three oil on board portrait panels Vittis, bought from Young Contemporaries, 1963. Jeffs settled in London.

Colin JELLICOE 1942– Painter mainly in oil, but later in acrylic, and art gallery director, born and lived in Manchester. Jellicoe studied art at Heald Place Secondary Modern in the mid-1950s with Keith Pepper; was at the Regional College of Art, Manchester, in 1959; then in the early-1960s was influenced by the painter Geoffrey Key. After leaving college Jellicoe opened his own art gallery which was moved to 82 Portland Street after the formation of a partnership with Alan Behar in 1968. From the mid-1960s Jellicoe began painting figures influenced by Vaughan and Bacon, mainly abstracted in nature, but by the early 1970s the work was more realistic. Comics and film books, mainly on the Western, were other influences, and he used several female models. Jellicoe took part in numerous group shows, early on including Preston's Gallery, Bolton, 1964, and Haworth Art Gallery, Accrington, 1965. Others included Harris Museum and Art Gallery, Preston, from 1974; RA Summer Exhibition, 1981; two-man show with Michael Goddard, Royal Exchange Theatre, Manchester, 1985; and 30-year retrospective at Colin Jellicoe Gallery, 1990.

Ann JENKINS fl. from 1950s– Painter, especially of exuberantly colourful oils of flowers, daughter of the artist Elizabeth Tuke Jenkins. She graduated from the Slade School of Fine Art, winning the Wilson Steer Landscape Prize. For some years she served as an examiner in art for London University's teacher training programme. Work was commended at Paris Salon. Held several solo shows in London, including paintings of Australi at Queensland House in 1991. Work in private collections throughout world. Lived in the family home at Jordans, Buckinghamshire.

Brian JENKINS 1964– Artist using photography, drawing, performance and film "to try to explore questions of space and environment which are not normally associated with … someone with a physical handicap such as my own." An example was Elevation II in South Bank Centre's touring The British Art Show 1990. Jenkins was born in Falkirk, Stirlingshire, and studied at its College of Technology, 1982–4, then Glasgow School of Art,

1984–8. He gained a BP Education Trust Scholarship Award, 1984–8. Other group shows he appeared in included Joint Artist Book Exhibition, RSA, 1987; Open Land, Portfolio Gallery, Edinburgh, 1988; and Through Photography at Third Eye Centre, Glasgow, 1989. Lived in Falkirk.

Elizabeth Tuke JENKINS 1906–1968 Painter in oil and watercolour and lino-cut artist, born in Elsenham, Essex. She was educated at the Sorbonne, Paris, where she also studied art in Montmartre, then at the Central School of Arts and Crafts under Robert Jamieson. Her lino-cuts are distinctive, often of wartime subjects such as refugees, and she worked with Edith Lawrence and Claude Flight. Showed at LG, NEAC, RBA, Leicester Galleries, WIAC of which she was a member, and RSA, and had a one-man show at Beaux Arts Gallery. Won gold medal at Paris Salon. Ministry of Works bought her work. For many years she was chairman of Buckinghamshire Art Society. The painter Ann Jenkins was her daughter. Elizabeth Tuke Jenkins' favourite subject in her oil paintings and watercolours was the garden and especially the trees at her home at Jordans, Buckinghamshire, designed in the Bauhaus style.

Eveline A JENKINS 1893–1976 Artist in various media, but mainly an illustrator. After studying at University College, Aberystwyth, she studied art in her own time. She earned her living as a botanical artist with the National Museum of Wales, Cardiff. Exhibited with the SWG and locally in Cardiff, where she lived.

Heinke JENKINS 1937– Printmaker and teacher, born in Heilbronn, Germany, where he attended the local grammar school. Studied at Stuttgart Academy of Arts and its College of Graphic and Illustration. Both Heilbronn and Stuttgart Galleries hold his work, which was shown in England at RBA and RBSA both of which he was a member. Lived for some time at Sutton Coldfield, Warwickshire.

Henry JENKINS 1906–1975 Artist who trained as a barrister, although his first love was art. During World War II he took up his pencil again and after the war abandoned law and attended Heatherley's School of Fine Art. He became a familiar and popular figure in Westminster and Whitehall, rapidly sketching life in the streets, soldiers and occasions such as viewings at Sotheby's. Ireland was another subject. Had a number of solo shows in Boston and in London and was shown by the dealer Martyn Gregory, who held a one-man exhibition in 1995.

Lawrence JENKINS 1944– Artist in wide variety of media, born and lived in Sevenoaks, Kent, who studied at Maidstone College of Art, 1962, teachers including William Bowyer and David Hockney. He said that his work was "like a diary and can be about anything that interests or concerns me." Showed regularly in RA Summer Exhibition, also with West Kent Open Studios '97. National Museum of Wales in Cardiff and the Belgian National Library hold examples.

Lincoln Pugh JENKINS 1901–1988 Artist in oil, watercolour and various graphic media, and teacher, born in Presteigne, Radnorshire. He attended Leicester College of Art. Became member of staff at Birmingham School of Art, 1925, in 1939 moving to Harrogate as principal, retiring in 1961. Moved to Bangor, Caernarvonshire, in 1970, in 1977 losing his sight. Was a member of the National Society for Art Education. Jenkins' work comprised objective landscapes and work strongly influenced by Cubism, later pieces concentrating on sunlight, patterns and windows. Group shows included RA, City Art Gallery in Leeds and elsewhere widely in the north of England. Solo shows included Oriel Gallery, Bangor. His son was a potter, Christopher Jenkins.

Marjorie JENKINS 1905– Painter, who studied at St Martin's School of Art in 1920s under Stafford Leake, like her husband Reg Jenkins. She was for a time a fashion artist with the Court dressmaker Callista, but the care of parents and the need to look after a family prevented her development as a painter. She was particularly influenced by the Australian painter John Passmore, a colleague of her husband's at Lintas, the advertising agency, who for 10 years from 1939 lived with the Jenkins at their cottage in Suffolk. Passmore encouraged her to a new light palette, and she became absorbed by the interrelationship of form, light and colour. Her oil paintings of 1940–60 were given a solo show at Abbott and Holder, 1989.

Geoffrey JENKINSON 1925– Artist and craftsman in various media, born in Leeds, Yorkshire. He was an apprentice glass-cutter and leaded window maker, 1941–6; worked as a tradesman in Bradford, 1946–50; then from the early-1950s began working as an assistant furniture designer in America, living for some time at Tubac, Arizona. From 1941–8 Jenkinson attended evening art classes at Pudsey Grammar School, becoming a member of RCamA in 1947, later a member of Arizona Artists' Guild. Exhibitions included RA, RBA and Bradford City Art Gallery, and he showed solo in America. Leeds City Art Gallery holdshis work.

Bernard JENNINGS 1942– Artist, brought up and who eventually settled in southeast London. He attended Colfe's Grammar School, 1954–60, then studied for a fine art diploma at Slade School of Fine Art, 1960–4. In 1964 with Terry Atkinson, John Bowstead and Roger Jeffs, Jennings formed the group Fine Artz and produced a work called Action Chair. In 1966 Fine Artz presented a projection and sound show, *Miss Misty and the Tri-Cool Data*, at Birmingham Polytechnic. Jennings became a Buddhist monk in Sri Lanka and Japan, eventually returning to England.

Charlotte JENNINGS 1935– Artist in oil, acrylic and sand, etching and animated film, born and lived in London, although she spent several childhood years as an evacuee in New York and from 1982 had seven years in Australia. She was the younger daughter of the artist Humphrey Jennings. She won a Major County Award to the Slade School of Fine Art, 1955–8, having spent 1953–4 at Hammersmith School of Arts & Crafts, and

1954–5 at Chelsea School of Art. She won several prizes at the Slade, and gained a Boise Postgraduate Scholarship. Studied at Atelier 17 in Paris, 1965, and London International Film School, 1976. Jennings' teachers included William Coldstream, Anthony Gross, William Townsend, Ruskin Spear, S W Hayter, Ernst Gombrich and David Sylvester. Group shows included Young Contemporaries, LG, New Vision Centre, Gardner Centre at University of Sussex and abroad. Had a solo show at Brown Thomas, Dublin, 1965, later ones including Gardner Arts Centre, 1991, and Chequers, London, 1992. Jennings produced several films, including *The Big Hit*, an animated space odyssey, 1980; she was manager of etching production for Editions Alecto; taught art; and did interior design. Commissions included murals for Associated Electrical Industries; fabrics for Courtaulds; and graphics for British Transport Films. University College, London, and Bibliothèque Nationale, Paris, hold examples.

E Owen JENNINGS 1899–1985 Painter, etcher, engraver and illustrator. Jennings attended Skipton School of Art, Yorkshire, followed by Leeds College of Art and the Royal College of Art, where he was a silver medallist. He became principal of the School of Art at Tunbridge Wells, in Kent. Stained glass at Staplehurst Church, in Kent, is his work. Jennings exhibited at the Paris Salon, in New York, Melbourne and Chicago and participated in British Council shows in Belgium, Poland, China and the Soviet Union. *Etchings of Today* and *Fine Prints of the Year* include his work and official purchases were made by the British Museum, Victoria & Albert Museum, and many other British and foreign collections. Lived in Tunbridge Wells.

Humphrey JENNINGS 1907–1950 Artist in oil, pencil, pastel, film and photography, born in Walberswick, Suffolk, father of the artist Charlotte Jennings. Jennings read English at Cambridge University and never went to art school. He worked in theatre design in Cambridge and as a painter, 1929–34, then until 1950 in documentary film, based in London. He was a member of International Surrealist Group, showing with it in 1936. Solo shows were held at London Gallery, 1938; ICA, 1951; and Riverside Studios, 1982. Jennings is best known for work in wartime documentary film: *Spare Time*, 1939; *Listen to Britain*, 1941; *Fires Were Started*, 1943; and *Diary for Timothy*, 1945–6. Tate Gallery holds his work. Jennings' landscapes and portraits, as shown at Mayor Gallery, 1993, were similar to works by the Italian Futurist painters. Died in Poros, Greece.

Leonard JENNINGS 1877–1956 Sculptor, born and lived in London. He studied at Lambeth and Glasgow Schools of Art and at the Royal Academy Schools. Whilst working for the Indian government for several years before World War I he completed a number of statues of members of the British royal family, including King Edward VII. Exhibited RA, RP, RI, Royal Glasgow Institute of the Fine Arts and elsewhere.

Philip Oswald JENNINGS 1921– Painter, printmaker and teacher, born in London. Studied at Harrow School of Art and Royal College of Art, 1940–5, where he was a postgraduate student, 1950–1. After a short period as an illustrator, in 1952 he joined the staff of Cardiff College of Art. As well as a one-man show at Iolo Gallery, Cowbridge, in 1974, Jennings took part in many group exhibitions, including RA, UA, Brighton Art Gallery, AEB tours, Howard Roberts Gallery, Cardiff, RWA and elsewhere. Welsh Arts Council, with which he has exhibited, holds his work. Lived in Pinner, Middlesex, later in Whitchurch, Glamorgan. Was a founder-member of the WSW and belonged to SWG, with which he frequently exhibited. In 1953 he participated in the American Society of Graphic Artists American tour. Sometimes only signed work P O J with date.

Walter Robin JENNINGS 1927– Mainly self-taught artist, born in Old Hill, Staffordshire. He worked in oil and watercolour and was a self-employed painter from 1960. Jennings was noted as a painter of the English countryside. He showed with RCamA, NEAC, ROI, RBSA, The Game Fair and elsewhere in mixed exhibitions. Had a series of solo exhibitions in London and the provinces, also exhibiting in America and on the continent. Royle, Medici, Solomon and Whitehead and other publishers reproduced his work. Valentine's of Dundee published a painting chosen by HM Queen Elizabeth the Queen Mother as her personal Christmas card. Jennings also helped restore early stained glass windows, including some in the House of Commons; made a video on oil painting for Optical Image Ltd; and painted a mural for Fortox of Kidderminster depicting 300 years of family history. Lived near Kidderminster, Worcestershire.

David JEREMIAH 1940– Painter and lecturer, born in Clayton-le-Moors, Lancashire. He studied at King's College, University of Durham, 1958–63, completing his doctorate in art history at Reading University, 1968–72, after which he became senior lecturer at Manchester Polytechnic. Wrote on art and showed in group exhibitions at Young Contemporaries, Bear Lane Gallery in Oxford, SWG and WAC. University of Surrey, Guildford, gave him a solo show in 1972.

Ron JESTY 1926– Watercolourist, graphic designer and teacher, born in Weymouth, Dorset, who had no formal training. He freelanced as a graphic designer, 1947–78, from that time concentrating on watercolour painting and part-time teaching. Jesty was "influenced by J S Cotman" and strove "for purity of colour, formal design structure in composition". Elected RBA in 1982, he also exhibited at RA Summer Exhibition, with RWS, RI and RWA. Solo shows included Bristol City Art Gallery, Brewhouse Arts Centre in Taunton, Yeovil Arts Centre, Alpha Gallery in both Yeovil and Swanage and The Gallery, Dorchester. Somerset County Council holds his work. Lived in Yeovil, Somerset.

Dick JEWELL 1951– Versatile artist in whose work photographic images were important. Postcards, record covers and photographic books took him out of the gallery system for periods. He was born in Worthing, Sussex, and after working on Brighton Marina, 1973–4, studied for his master's degree in prinmaking at Royal College of Art, 1978, the year he published his book *Found Prints*. Group exhibitions included Waddington Galleries and National Museum Art Gallery, Singapore, both 1976; Lives, at Hayward Gallery, 1981; and Summer Show I at Serpentine Gallery, 1983. Solo shows included Chapter Arts Centre in Cardiff, 1980. Arts Council, Whitworth Art Gallery in Manchester, The Open University and several other provincial collections hold examples. Lived for a time in London.

Mary JEWELS 1886–1977 Painter of Cornwall whose work has a primitive charm, her maiden name was Mary Tregurtha (her husband Albert Jewels was killed in World War I). She was born in Newlyn, her sister Cordelia being the first wife of the sculptor Frank Dobson, who made a fine bronze head of Mary. She was encouraged by the painter Cedric Morris, when he was staying in Newlyn in 1919; he gave her a canvas, four tubes of paint and told her to cover the canvas by the evening. She was later encouraged by Christopher Wood and Augustus John, although she claimed she was "influenced by nobody and entirely self-taught, a true Celt loving my Cornwall". Was a member of the St Ives Society and a founder-member of Penwith Society, 1949. Had solo show at Dorothy Warren's Gallery, 1927; 50 years later her work was featured at the Newlyn Gallery.

J M C: *see* **Josephine McCORMICK**

Pat JOBSON 1919– Artist in pastel, watercolour, oil and black-and-white, born in Ilford Essex. Jobson was the fourth generation of painters in his family, and he studied with his father, Frank Mears Jobson, 1924–30, with Alfred Hayes in 1930–8, and with Frank Brangwyn at intervals, 1934–50. Jobson was a noted marine artist, a founder-member of RSMA, being a member until 1954. He was also a founder-member and president of Wapping Group of Artists and a member and president of Langham Sketch Club. He was a prolific book illustrator from 1947–59, notably of titles by Peter Dawlish and Frank Knight, and completed many pub signs from 1947. Jobson showed with RBA, RI, PS and SGA and had solo shows in Hitchin and Croydon from 1974. National Gallery in Adelaide, Australia, holds his work. Lived in North Wembley, Middlesex.

Richard Henry JOBSON 1910–1977 Untrained painter in watercolour and pastel, and photographer, born in Urmston, Manchester. He studied at Manchester University and served as a general medical practitioner in New Radnor from 1937–70. Exhibited RCamA, elsewhere in Wales, in Spain and America. Also made working model locomotives. Lived in Presteigne, Radnorshire.

Natasha JOBST 1934– Painter, draughtsman and teacher, born in Vienna, Austria, but brought up and educated in England. Graduated from Slade School of Fine Art, 1954, where she was well regarded by her teacher William Coldstream, in that year winning a life painting prize and John Nash Scholarship for landscape painting. Worked in Paris, 1954–5, then moved to what is now Zimbabwe, where she brought up a family, taught art and ceramics to children and adults and worked as a freelance artist and journalist. After returning to England in 1962, taught for Inner London Education Authority and for Surrey, started adult and children's art workshops in Richmond and at Hampton Court and for eight years was art tutor to the physically handicapped. Group shows included several in southern Africa, Commonwealth Institute and Academicians' Choice at Mall Galleries, 1990. Had a solo exhibition at The Boathouse Gallery, Walton-on-Thames, 1994, near where she lived at East Molesey, Surrey. The Rhodes National Gallery, Harare, and United Biscuits hold Jobst's work.

John JOEKES fl. from mid-1970s– Sculptor who studied with George Kennethson; at Camberwell School of Art; worked in Paris as a typographer; and then as a stone carver in Chichester Cathedral. Using both stone and wood, carvings explored figurative and abstract forms, often combining the elements. Joekes said that his work "attempts to arrest a moment, to cause reflection upon an object". He took part in many exhibitions, including Feeling to See, at Arnolfini Art Gallery, 1987; Art & Computers, Cleveland Arts touring show, 1989; and Abbot Hall Art Gallery and Museum, Kendal, 1990. His solo shows included Artsite, Bath, and Harris Museum & Art Gallery, Preston, both 1990. In 1985 he conceived and organised the Sculpture Competition in Bath, where he lived.

Chantal JOFFE 1969– Painter, born in London, notably of figure studies using a light palette, who attended Camberwell School of Arts and Crafts, 1987–8; Glasgow School of Art, 1988–91; and Royal College of Art, 1992–4. She gained a Haldane Trust Travelling Scholarship, NatWest 90s Prize for Art and John Kinross Travelling Scholarship, all in 1991; a TI Bursary, 1992–4; Paris Studio Award, 1993; and Delfina Studios Award, 1994–6. Group exhibitions included 369 Gallery Group Show, Edinburgh, and the first of a string of appearances at National Portrait Gallery, both 1991; Whitworth Young Contemporaries, Manchester, 1993; Into the Nineties at Mall Galleries and Group Show at Brewery Arts Centre, Kendal, both 1994; and 30 minus at Paton Gallery, 1996. NatWest and TI Group hold examples.

Alan JOHN 1927– Artist in painting, sculpture, dance and film and teacher. He was chiefly self-taught as a painter, but studied at Hornsey College for Film. His work was "mainly about the human predicament of everyday living, fusing Surrealism with Cubism". Included in John's career were teaching art with Inner London Education Authority, 1961–82, during which he founded Art Basement, in Hackney; a period, 1978–88, when he founded and directed The Arts Factory Gallery; costume and set design, including *Nettle City*, *Creepy Dub* and *Drunk Albert*, 1983–5; and in 1986 costume and set design for Rubberneck Dance Company. John was a member of Penwith Society of Arts and in 1952 was awarded freedom of the Worshipful Company of Painter-Stainers. Exhibitions included RA Summer Exhibitions, RP, LG, NEAC, Leicester Galleries,

Woodstock Gallery, New Contemporary Portrait Painters and elsewhere. Solo shows included Alwin Gallery, 1971; Phoenix Gallery, 1991; and Islington Arts Factory, 1993. Lived in Mount Hawke, Cornwall.

Anthony JOHN 1905– Artist in oil, gouache and watercolour, born in Wales, notable for marine pictures. He studied at Chelsea School of Art with Percy Hague Jowett and in Paris. John said that he "always painted for myself … I am very lazy, and do not paint if I can avoid it when there is nothing that I *have* to say." At times he was a member of Natal Society of Artists, South African Society of Artists and AIA. Showed with Wertheim, Bloomsbury and Redfern Galleries, UA and elsewhere and had several solo exhibitions. Lived in London.

Augustus JOHN 1878–1961 Painter mainly in oil, draughtsman and printmaker. Born in Tenby, Wales, brother of the artist Gwen John, he attended the Slade School of Fine Art, 1894–8, winning a Scholarship in 1896 and the Summer Composition Prize two years later. John's prodigious natural ability as a draughtsman won the admiration of Henry Tonks, and he soon established himself as a star student and an art world character. Became professor of painting at Liverpool University art school, 1901–4. John started an association with gypsies, learning their language and painting them. Began his wide travels in Britain and on the continent, sometimes travelling by caravan. Over several years painted with J D Innes and Derwent Lees. Started to exhibit widely, having his first one-man show at the Carfax Gallery in 1903. Also showed at the Chenil Galleries, NEAC, Alpine Gallery, Independent Club, RA and elsewhere over the coming years, where he became noted for drawings and paintings of his second wife, Dorelia, his children, his sister Gwen, personalities such as George Bernard Shaw, T E Lawrence, W B Yeats and Dylan Thomas, and for his landscapes and romantic scenes of peasant life. Although sometimes out of fashion, John is assured a place as one of the great figures of British painting in his lifetime. His work is in many galleries, including the Tate Gallery and National Portrait Gallery. Elected RA 1928, resigned 1938, re-elected 1940. Awarded Order of Merit 1942. Autobiographical reminiscences *Chiaroscuro* were published in 1952, *Finishing Touches*, 1964. Retrospectives included one at National Portrait Gallery, 1975, another at National Museum of Wales, Cardiff, and tour, 1996. Lived at Fordingbridge, Hampshire.

Eira JOHN 1919– Painter in oil, mostly of still life and figurative works, married to the artist Michael Boycott-Brown. She was born in Durham and studied at Westminster School of Art with Mervyn Peake, Mark Gertler and Blair Hughes-Stanton, then did some part-time work at Storran Gallery. After initial artistic activity, she resumed painting only in her later years, taking part in group shows at Heffer Gallery in Cambridge where she lived, Fermoy Arts Centre in King's Lynn and School House Gallery, Wighton. In December 1996 she and her husband shared a show at Cambridge Arts, Fordham.

Samuel JOHN 1935– Painter, writer and businessman, born in Newport, Monmouthshire. He studied art at College of St Mark and St John, qualifying as a teacher in 1957, gaining a London University bachelor's degree in 1958. Showed with Chenil Galleries, 1956; Oxford Art Society from 1977; Barclay Gallery, Chester, 1980; and Royal Over-Seas League, of which he was a member, 1983. Among his books was *The Sacred and The Profane*, 1980, the year he won the Koestler Prize for Verse.

Vivien JOHN 1915–1994 Painter, daughter of the artist Augustus John and his second wife Dorelia. She was born in Dorset and had a wild childhood, not going to school. Attended Slade School of Fine Art, 1932–4, but was forbidden by Augustus to take instruction. For several years in the late 1930s she studied at Euston Road School with William Coldstream and Victor Pasmore. Having visited her aunt, the artist Gwen John in Paris, in 1944 she returned to study at L'Académie de la Grande Chaumière, in 1945 entering Chelsea School of Art, then married the haematologist Dr John White. With her father she visited Jamaica, Italy and Provence and with her husband lived in Russia, Malaysia and Papua New Guinea, which added colour to her palette. She had a series of solo shows with a first at Cooling Gallery in 1935; others included Upper Grosvenor Gallery and Phoenix Gallery, Lavenham; and in 1987 she was included in an exhibition of Slade Contemporaries at Sally Hunter Fine Art, which gave her a memorial show in 1995. Other mixed exhibition appearances included WIAC, LG and RA. Died in London.

William Goscomb JOHN 1860–1952 Sculptor of figures, portraits, memorials and other public works. Born in Cardiff, he studied at the School of Art there, at the City and Guilds of London School of Art and the Royal Academy Schools. There he won a gold medal and Travelling Scholarship. John also worked with Rodin in Paris in the early 1890s, which left an impression on his classically oriented sculpture. Examples are shown in the volume *RBS: Modern British Sculpture*, published in 1939. John won the RBS gold medal and several Paris Salon awards, including a gold medal. Showed at the RA from 1884 and was elected RA in 1909, in 1911 being knighted for his work. The fact that his father had been a stonemason and that in his youth Goscombe John had aided him in the restoration of Cardiff Castle fitted him for the large body of public sculpture he was to complete, including statues of Viscount Wolseley in Horse Guards Parade, London, the Marquess of Salisbury in Westminster Abbey and King Edward VII in Liverpool. He also designed the regalia for the investiture of the Prince of Wales at Carnarvon in 1911 and the King George V Silver Jubilee Medal of 1935. National Museum of Wales in Cardiff held a major show in 1979. Lived in London.

Ewart JOHNS fl. from 1950s– Painter, muralist, draughtsman and teacher, born in Barry, Glamorgan. A major formative influence was the teaching of Ceri Richards at Cardiff College of Art. Johns later combined a university career with work as a freelance artist. His academic research, mainly at Exeter, was in urban design, and led to a book on British townscape. He became the first head of department of visual arts at University of Lancaster. Showed widely in mixed exhibitions in Britain and America. Had a series of solo shows at Grabowski Gallery from 1961, and elsewhere in London and the provinces, and in 1981 a retrospective at University College of Wales, Cardiff, and University of Lancaster. This was in three parts, with a strong drawn image approach in common: work of the 1950s, subdued in colour, with form influenced by Cubist ideas; freer paintings of the 1960s; and oil pastels of the 1970s, with a special intensity, luminosity and density and strong emphasis on the figure. Johns carried out a number of public murals, and WAC holds his work.

Allan JOHNSON 1907–1994 Architect and artist, born in Leeds, Yorkshire. Trained at the school of architecture at Leeds College of Art from 1925, cramming five years' study into four. Obtained his diploma in 1930. Went into private practice in 1930, the Kingston, Surrey, swimming baths one of the jobs he worked on. An RIBA scholarship in 1935 took him to America, where he met his future wife. In 1936 returned to Lanchester & Lodge, where he had done his practical training. During World War II served in the Army, achieving the rank of captain. From 1945–72 was a partner in Lanchester & Lodge. Did much work at Leeds University, where a glass-reinforced polyester wall decoration of 1963, called A Celebration of Engineering Sciences, was completed by him. Retired to Trebetherick, Cornwall, where he died.

Annette JOHNSON fl. from 1960s– Painter and printmaker, born and settled in London, who started painting while living in Boston, America. She subsequently studied at Sir John Cass School of Art and Morley College. "The feeling of solitude" was important in her work, which was figurative, landscape and seascape. Johnson was a member of SWA, Greenwich Printmakers' Association, The Printmakers' Council, Blackheath Art Society and the South-East London Group. She showed in many exhibitions, including NS, RA, RI, Woodlands Art Gallery, Royal Festival Hall and in the provinces.

Audrey JOHNSON 1919– Painter in oii of still life and wild flowers, small and in meticulous detail. She was married in 1947 to the artist Claude Harrison, their son being the potter Tobias Harrison. Johnson studied at Harris Institute, Preston, and at Central School of Arts and Crafts. She exhibited with the Lake Artists' Society of which she was a member and regularly at RA Summer Exhibition. In 1991 she shared a show with her husband at Phoenix Gallery, Highgate. Lived in Cartmel Fell, Cumbria.

Beatrice JOHNSON fl. from late 1930s–1988 Watercolourist and teacher, who studied at Birmingham School of Arts and Crafts in the late-1930s with Douglas Hamilton Holden, who became her husband (she was known as Trixie Holden). After World War II, they were at the Royal College of Art, 1946–7. Beatrice Johnson taught at the Central School of Arts and Crafts, then at Croydon College of Art almost until her death. She was elected an associate of RWS in 1957 and RWS in 1969. Lived in London, then after Douglas' death in 1972 settled in Hastings, Sussex. In 1988 work from her studio, and from the studios of Douglas and his father Harold Henry Holden, was included in a sale at Burstow & Hewitt, Battle.

Ben JOHNSON 1946– Painter and printmaker, born in Llandudno, Caernarvonshire. He attended Wrexham and Chester Schools of Art, 1961, then Royal College of Art, 1966–70. Exhibited at ICA and Europalia, Palais des Beaux-Arts, Brussels, 1973; in 1974 at Bradford Print Biennale and John Moores Liverpool Exhibition; in 1977 International Print Biennale, Cracow; and in 1982 participated in Peter Moores Liverpool Project 6: Art into the 80s, at Fruitmarket Gallery, Edinburgh. Johnson's work theme then was the closed door, the undulations in wood grains and colour modulations beautifully and meticulously painted. Also showed at RA Summer Exhibition and elsewhere.

Carl JOHNSON 1946– Painter and graphic artist, born in Solihull, Warwickshire. He studied fine art at Newport College of Art, 1968–71, then did a postgraduate course at Ateliers 63, Haarlem, Netherlands, 1971–3, followed by Goldsmiths' College School of Art, 1974–5. Mixed show appearances included Gallery Zwart, Haarlem, 1973; LG, 1978; Eastleigh Museum, 1988; and SGA, 1989, the year he was elected a member. Johnson designed original art T-shirts which were marketed in Europe, America and Japan. Had many one-man shows including Battersea Arts Centre, 1977; The Showroom, 1985; and Bedford Central Library, 1989. In 1990 Johnson shared a three-man show at Woodlands Art Gallery, exhibiting strident figurative work.

Charles JOHNSON 1896–1964 Watercolourist, draughtsman in ink and lecturer, born in Cambridge into an academic background. He graduated from university with a Master of Arts degree and lectured at the National Gallery from 1926–62, from 1939 as an official lecturer and initially, it seems, as a freelance. He wrote a series of books including *English Painting*, *The Growth of Painting* and *Memlinc*. His art tuition was obtained at Regent Street Polytechnic School of Art under George Percival Gaskell. Went on to show at a number of venues, notably Leicester Galleries. Lived in London.

Charles G JOHNSON 1902–1983 Artist in oil, pastel, watercolour and black-and-white, born and lived in Stansted, Essex. Johnson was a self-taught painter and draughtsman who passed on his skills in his *Introduction to Sketching*. Exhibited widely in Britain, at the NS, PS and Russell-Cotes Art Gallery and Museum, Bournemouth. Had a solo show in Bishop's Stortford, near where he lived.

Christopher JOHNSON 1961– Painter, born in Bulawayo, Southern Rhodesia. He studied fine art at Rhodes University in South Africa, where he acquired a master's degree in 1985. Exhibited in mixed shows in South Africa, notably at Everard Read Gallery, Johannesburg, and in London at The Bloomsbury

Workshop, Hurlingham Gallery and Sally Hunter Fine Art, as well as at Fruitmarket Gallery, Ediburgh. In 1992 had solo show at The Scottish Gallery, Edinburgh. Hiscox Holdings Ltd, Anglo-American and Johannesburg Stock Exchange hold his work.

Colin Trevor JOHNSON 1942– Artist in oil, watercolour, pencil, ink, monoprint and collage, born in Blackpool, Lancashire. He studied at Salford School of Art, 1957–9, then Manchester College of Art, 1959–60, teachers including Harry Rutherford and Terry McGlynn. Johnson painted full-time from leaving college. He cited Ben Nicholson and Braque as influences, main themes being "the British coastline, Venice architecture, street markets and glass". He visited and painted Cornwall for the first time in 1959, continued painting in St Ives most summers, then moved to St Ives from the north in 1986 and to Teignmouth, Devon, in 1991. Among Johnson's many activities was direction of the first Bolton Festival, 1979; he was artist-in-residence at Manchester Festival, 1980; and at Wigan International Jazz Festival, 1986–7. Johnson completed a mural for Broadcasting House in Manchester and was a member of MAFA. He took part in many mixed shows. His solo shows included a series at Monks Hall Museum and Art Gallery, Eccles, from 1961; he had a retrospective at Bolton Art Gallery, 1979; and later exhibitions included Maclaurin Art Gallery in Ayr and Salford University, both 1990. Public galleries in Salford, Derby and Southport hold his work.

David JOHNSON 1948– Sculptor whose work included assemblages of objects such as boxes and annotated blackboards. He said that his work was "not formalist, it is about the basic conjunction of matter and meaning, the imaginative relation of the self to the material world and time". Johnson studied at Bartlett School of Architecture at University College London, 1968–71. After living in Australia in 1974–6 he was at Byam Shaw School of Art, 1976–80. His shows included Goldsmiths' exhibition at Woodlands Art Gallery in 1983.

Elaine JOHNSON 1945– Painter, printmaker and teacher who studied at University of Newcastle department of fine art, 1965–70, then did a postgraduate course at Chelsea School of Art, 1970–1. From 1971–2 she was awarded the John Brinkley Fellowship in Painting at Norwich School of Art, and her solo exhibitions included one in its gallery, 1972. Teaching included Brighton and Portsmouth Polytechnics and Bath Academy of Art, Corsham. Mixed shows included several appearances at British International Print Biennale and Northern Young Contemporaries, the Museum of Modern Art in Oxford and Sunderland Arts Centre.

Ernest Borough JOHNSON 1867–1949 Painter, draughtsman, printmaker and teacher, born in Shifnal, Shropshire, who was married to the artist Esther Borough Johnson. He attended Slade School of Fine Art under Alphonse Legros and the Herkomer School at Bushey, where he was a star student. Was professor of fine art at Bedford College, London University and was for many years head of the art department at Chelsea Polytechnic. Borough Johnson, as he signed himself, exhibited prolifically at RA, RBA, ROI, Paris Salon, where he won several awards in the 1920s, and at many other venues. British Museum, Victoria & Albert Museum, National Portrait Gallery, provincial and foreign galleries hold his work. *The Art of the Pencil* and *The Technique of Pencil Drawing* were two of his several books on draughtsmanship. Lived in London.

Esther Borough JOHNSON fl. c.1895–1950 Painter and draughtsman, born in Sutton Maddock, Shropshire. She studied at at Birmingham School of Art, Chelsea School of Art and the Herkomer School, Bushey. Married to artist Ernest Borough Johnson. Among her several books on painting is *Flower Painting in Oil*. Exhibited RA, RI, RMS, Goupil Gallery and Paris Salon. Signed work E B J in monogram form. Lived in London.

Frank JOHNSON 1917– Painter, draughtsman and teacher, born in Leicester. Johnson worked as a commercial artist, 1935–40, served in the Royal Air Force in World War II, then after a period as a commercial artist again, 1946–7, studied painting, 1947–51, at Leicester College of Art. From 1952–80 he taught in the department of advertising at Bradford's Regional College of Art. Johnson showed frequently at RA from early-1950s, also in the provinces, notably Yorkshire. His work was included in Four Yorkshire Artists at Bradford City Art Gallery in 1961; loan exhibition works by Yorkshire artists at the Museum of Modern Art, Skopje, Yugoslavia, 1964; and Face to Face, portraits by Yorkshire artists at Sports Centre Gallery, Huddersfield, 1981. Public galleries in Bradford, Leeds and Glasgow hold his work, noted for its tenderness and compassion.

Holly JOHNSON 1960– Song composer, performer, writer and artist, originally William Johnson and born in Wavertree, Liverpool. He attended Liverpool Collegiate Grammar School for Boys; discovered Marc Bolan, David Bowie, Andy Warhol, Derek Jarman; and made his first performances as a soloist and as a member of the New Wave combo in 1977. In 1978 Johnson began to make screenprints and art T-shirts and decided he was a multi-media artist. Eventually formed and was lead singer of the group Frankie Goes To Hollywood which in 1983, as he was about to start at Liverpool Art College, had a hit record, *Relax*, which concentrated his energies into music. In 1984 Johnson met his future manager and partner, the art collector Wolfgang Kuhle, who had a notable collection of Bloomsbury art and with whom he eventually lived. In 1986–7 Johnson started drawing and painting again, became dissatisfied with the musical direction of Frankie Goes To Hollywood and left the group. In 1989 his first solo album, *Blast*, was hugely successful. Three years later Johnson disclosed that he had an HIV infection. Now he was concentrating on writing and painting again, starting to make his 20th Century Icons, a series of collages, using gold leaf and found objects, inspired by Jarman. In 1994 Johnson's autobiography *A Bone in My Flute* was a best-seller and he showed icons and paintings at The Art Show at Alexandra Palace. The building of Sky studios, a multi-media art facility, followed in 1995, along with illustrations for *Details* magazine and writing for *Modern*

Painters. Johnson's first solo show, The House of Holly, was held at The Gallery in Cork Street in 1996, curated by Kate Chertavian. His paintings were notable for their vibrant style, bold colours and witty social comment.

Joy Alexandra JOHNSON 1958– Painter, born in Hull, Yorkshire. She studied at Newcastle upon Tyne Polytechnic, 1977–80, graduating with honours, then was at Slade School of Fine Art, 1982–4. As well as several solo shows she was in mixed exhibitions including RA Summer Exhibition, Northern Young Contempories and at Mappin Art Gallery, Sheffield. Lived in London.

Kate JOHNSON 1963– Painter, creator of sculptural paintings, sculptor, draughtsman and teacher, of British nationality, born in Ottawa, Canada. Studied under Norman Adams at Newcastle upon Tyne University, graduating in fine art – painting, 1981–5; gained a postgraduate diploma in Quattrocento Italian Art History at Oxford University, as a British Academy Scholar, studying with Christopher Lloyd and Francis Haskell, 1985–6; then as a Fulbright Scholar gained her master's degree in fine art, painting, under James McGarrell, at Washington University, St Louis, 1988–90. In 1991 lived in the Amazonian rainforest, Tambopata, Madre de Dios, Peru, in 1992 being adjunct professor in the department of fine art at Webster University, St Louis. Had an open studio exhibition in Oxford, 1988; mixed exhibitions included Pertinent Dissimilarities: The Figure, at Webster University, 1992 and The Tesmer Collection, Gallery 1616, Chicago, 1994; solo exhibitions including Gallery 1616, 1993, and A View of Peru, South Grand (Gallery), St Louis, 1994. In 1995 settled in Yorkshire.

Les JOHNSON 1957– Artist in various media, lecturer and writer, born in Jamaica. He moved to Manchester when young, but his black background and culture heavily influenced his work, as did an early passion for playing church music. Left Manchester Polytechnic in 1977 after foundation work, spending a year on graphic design at London College of Printing. Continued degree work at Camberwell School of Art, then from 1980 attended Royal College of Art, extending his interests in illustration photography, audio visual, painting and design. From 1983 worked professionally in several fields, including architecture and object making. Among his exhibitions was a three-man show at Woodlands Art Gallery, 1988.

Maurice JOHNSON 1920– Painter and teacher, initially educated in Southport, Lancashire. He attended Liverpool City School of Art under Will Penn and Henry Huggill, 1936–40. Showed at Liverpool Academy, Anglo-French Art Centre, UA, RBA and elsewhere. Liverpool Public Libraries bought his work. Lived in London.

Michael JOHNSON 1954– Sculptor in stone and metal, born in Berwick-upon-Tweed, Northumberland, who studied at Sheffield and Nottingham Schools of Art. Exhibited in Garden Exhibition 2 at Camden Arts Centre, 1978. Lived for a time in London.

Nerys JOHNSON 1942– Artist noted for her drawings of flowers on paper, born in Colwyn Bay, Denbighshire. She studied fine art at King's College, Durham University, 1961–5, and settled there. Exhibitions included Durham's DLI Museum and Arts Centre, Abbot Hall Art Gallery in Kendal and Arts Council's 1981–2 tour Fragments Against Ruin. Arts Council holds several examples.

Nowell Hewlett JOHNSON 1906–1983 Artist in oil, black-and-white and watercolour. Born at Crossens, Lancashire, wife of Hewlett Johnson, sometimes known as the "Red Dean" of Canterbury, because of his political views. Studied at Southport School of Art and the Royal College of Art. Occasionally signed work Nowell Johnson. Exhibited RA, East Kent Art Society and Artists for Peace. Contributed illustrations to *The Socialist Sixth of the World*, the international bestseller by her husband. Lived in Canterbury, Kent.

Pete JOHNSON 1948– Artist and teacher, born in Manchester, who studied at Camberwell School of Arts and Crafts, 1967–70, and Royal College of Art, 1970–3. He went on to live and teach in London. Group exhibitions included Selected Space Artists at Harlow Gallery, 1974, Air Gallery in 1975 and Summer Show 2 at Serpentine Gallery, 1980, where he exhibited works in boxboard, paint and paper. Solo exhibitions included Universities of Sussex and Essex, both 1977.

Stephen JOHNSON 1953– Sculptor using a range of materials, born in Whitstable, Kent. He studied at Goldsmiths' College School of Art, then obtained his master's degree in fine art, sculpture, at Chelsea School of Art, 1981–2. He said that his work was "concerned with images of transition. A threatened object with the threat exorcised. An object of burden without burden." Exhibitions included Summer Show 2, Serpentine Gallery, 1980; The British Art Show, Arts Council tour, 1984; Conceptual Clothing, Ikon Gallery, Birmingham, and tour, 1986; and Second Wave, Bluecoat Gallery, Liverpool, 1988.

Tim JOHNSON 1967– Born in Newcastle upon Tyne, Johnson studied painting, photography, sculpture and installation at University of Reading, graduating in 1989. He moved to Ireland in 1990 and showed widely north and south of the border. In 1994 he appeared in both Works on Paper and Beyond the Partitions, put on by Queen Street Studios, Belfast, with which he was associated.

Alan JOHNSTON 1945– Draughtsman in pencil and sculptor, born in Scotland, he eventually settled in Edinburgh. He attended the College of Art there, 1967–70, then concentrated on life drawing at Royal College of Art, 1970–2. Johnston lived in Germany for a time, having a first solo show at Konrad Fischer Gallery, Düsseldorf, in 1973. Johnston went on to show regularly, at the Graeme Murray Gallery in Edinburgh, at Oxford's Museum of Modern Art and the Pier Arts Centre, Stromness, Orkney, held a touring exhibition. The 1980s saw his work shown widely abroad. Johnston's work was delicate and Minimalist, influenced

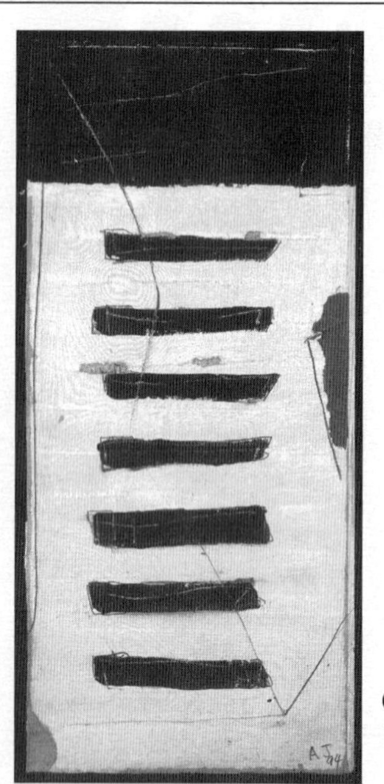

Andrew Johnstone, *ILIAD series*
"Black-walled ships" – 17" x 8"

Roger Cecil – *"Not Seeing is Believing"* – 22" x 18"

by Zen Buddhism. Scottish National Gallery of Modern Art's From the Mountain to the Plain is a good example. In 1998, Norwich School of Art and Design's Norwich Gallery invited Johnston to make one of his wall drawings on a specially constructed wall, giving visitors an opportunity to view and discuss its progress over seven days.

Arnrid JOHNSTON 1895–1972 Sculptor, illustrator, designer and writer, born of English father and Swedish mother in Sweden. Between 1913–20 studied at Slade School of Fine Art, gained a Slade Scholarship for two years in 1915 and learned sculpture under James Havard Thomas. The continuing theme in Johnston's work was a love of animals. As a sculptor her work was compared with that of Henry Moore, Barbara Hepworth, Maurice Lambert and John Skeaping, but its popularity faded. Notable among her output were Cats on Chimney Cowl and Squirrels in an exhibition organised by LG in 1930, in Selfridges' roof garden; and Horses, a carved relief, and cast iron zodiac tiles at 50th Anniversary Exhibition of the Arts and Crafts Exhibition Society at RA, 1938. Her poster for the New Zoological Society in 1930 was a great popular success. She wrote and illustrated *Pigwiggen*, the story of a flying pig, in 1938; *Animal Families*, in 1939; and illustrated a number of other books such as Kathleen Foyle's *The Little Black Calf*, 1952. Her *Fables from Aesop and Others* appeared in 1944, but failing eyesight prevented her finishing *La Fontaine's Fables*. Morley College owns the tapestry The Orchestra which was shown in an exhibition of Johnston's work at Sally Hunter & Patrick Seale Fine Art, 1985.

Brenda JOHNSTON 1930– Artist in various media, born in London. She attended Epsom School of Art, 1948–9 and 1955–60, teachers including the watercolourist Leslie Worth, then Reigate School of Art, 1961–5, with Eric Waugh. She was a member of Free Painters and Sculptors and several local art clubs near where she lived in Ashtead, Surrey. Had a series of solo exhibitions and also showed at RA Summer Exhibition, RBA and abroad.

Duncan JOHNSTON 1924– Sculptor in a variety of materials, notably lignum vitae, and teacher, born in Liverpool. Johnston trained in commercial art at Liverpool School of Art, then served as a physical training instructor in the Royal Marines in World War II. By demobilisation in 1946 he had resolved to be a sculptor; was self-taught while teaching, then chose to work in isolation to avoid influences. In 1956 he began to exhibit in mixed annual exhibitions, notably Royal Glasgow Institute of the Fine Arts, RSA and at Paris Salon. Had a first solo show, 1960, in Leatherhead, Surrey, near where he settled at Ashtead, then was associated with O'Hana Gallery until its closure in 1975. Johnston continued to sculpt despite several operations on his wrists, 1978–81, to relieve arthritic pains. Had a retrospective at Exhall Grange School, Coventry, 1981, and a notable show at The Barbican Centre, 1987. Johnston was especially interested in sculpture as it related to handicapped, partially sighted and blind people. Among his commissions was Celebration Dance for Worcester College for the Blind, 1990. Johnston's sculpture had great vitality, with a sinuous line. Jacob Epstein's *Let There Be Sculpture* prompted his choice of career, and he wrote that "Epstein's life and work has probably been the greatest influence on my work." Michelangelo Museum, Italy, and Tel-Aviv Museum of Modern Art, Israel, hold examples.

Frederick JOHNSTON 1916–1984 Artist in oil, pastel, watercolour, pen and ink. Born in London, he studied art at Hornsey School of Art and London University. Johnston became a noted art instructor, teaching at summer schools as well as writing a number of books for beginners in sketching and painting. In the 1970s he edited *Leisure Painter* for several years. As well as one-man exhibitions, he showed at the RBA, RI, ROI, NS and at the Paris Salon. His work is in private collections throughout the world. Lived in Potters Bar, Hertfordshire.

George JOHNSTON 1933– Painter, teacher and art adviser, born in Edinburgh. He studied at the College of Art there, 1951–6, teachers including William Gillies and Robin Philipson. Johnston then taught for two years, was commissioned in the Army, 1958–60, lectured for three years, was an adviser on art and design until 1991, then painted full-time. He was a member of RSW, also exhibiting at RSA and Royal Glasgow Institute of the Fine Arts, having solo shows in Edinburgh, Dundee, Glasgow, Kirkcaldy, London, Paris and elsewhere. Dundee University, Dundee College of Further Education and several other Scottish public collections hold examples. Lived at Barnhill, Dundee, Tayside.

Roy JOHNSTON 1936– Painter, relief artist and teacher, born in Pomeroy, County Tyrone, Northern Ireland. He studied at Stranmillis College, Belfast, 1957–9, then after three years teaching art in a school in the city was at Belfast College of Art, 1962–6, and after various posts taught for many years at Ulster College. His abstract works included contoured canvases and modular reliefs such as that on the Cross and Passion School, Belfast. Arts Council of Northern, Bank of Ireland and New University of Ulster in Coleraine hold examples. Exhibitions included Arts Council of Northern Ireland Gallery; Richard Demarco Gallery in Edinburgh; David Gallery and David Hendriks Gallery, both in Dublin.

Andrew JOHNSTONE 1933– Sculptor and painter who was educated at Strasbourg and Oxford Universities and at Oxford's Ruskin School of Drawing. Johnstone served in the Foreign Service, 1956–73, continuing to paint while mainly in the Middle and Far East, then on taking early retirement in 1973 moved to Cornwall, settling in the Lizard. After showing at RUA and Living Arts Exhibition in Belfast in 1972 Johnstone concentrated on sculpture. The Queen of Sheba and Johnstone's friendship with Sherif Hussein when he was in Aden in the late-1950s were notable influences. Johnstone's later spare, abstract paintings followed on from the sculpture, with Arabia and Homer's *Iliad* as key inspirations. Gordon Hepworth Gallery, Newton St Cyres, showed his work.

Anne Grahame JOHNSTONE 1928–1998 Versatile artist and illustrator, daughter of the artist Doris Zinkeisen and twin sister of Janet Grahame Johnstone. They trained at St Martin's School of Art after World War II, then collaborated to illustrate many books, including The Bible, children's classics and modern successes including Dodie Smith's *The Hundred and One Dalmatians*. Other projects included artwork for BBC Television programmes, such as *Andy Pandy*; work for the National Maritime Museum; and designs for a projected but aborted theme park in Denmark called Andersen's World. After Janet died following an accident in 1979, Anne – a keen horsewoman – took over the animal drawing which had been Janet's special role, and in 1998 was elected to the Society of Equestrian Artists. Other aspects of her solo work included Christmas cards for Royle's and jigsaw puzzles for Waddington's; writing and illustrating her own books on Santa Claus; and heraldic work on the Post Office's restored mail coach. Died in Badingham, Suffolk.

Dorothy JOHNSTONE 1892–1980 Painter and teacher, born in Edinburgh. Her father was the painter George Whitton Johnstone, her uncle the artist James Heron and she married the painter Douglas Macbeth Sutherland. She enrolled at Edinburgh College of Art in 1908 and in 1910 gained a travelling scholarship to Italy, and also studied in Paris. In 1914 she was appointed to staff of Edinburgh College of Art, having to relinquish her teaching post, as a married woman, in 1924. She exhibited at RSA regularly for many years from 1912, at RA, with Edinburgh Group, jointly with Cecile Walton in 1924, and elsewhere. In 1983 Aberdeen Art Gallery gave her a major memorial show which toured, then in 1987 Bourne Fine Art in Edinburgh and London held a joint Johnstone and Sutherland exhibition. Johnstone was a sensitive painter of women and young girls. She died at Glanclwyd Hospital, north Wales.

Gwyneth JOHNSTONE fl. from 1940s– Painter brought up in Norfolk and London who studied painting with André Lhote in Paris and at Central School of Arts and Crafts under Cecil Collins. Her work mixed gentleness, innocence and a subtle colour sense, but was strengthened by an awareness of the output of painters such as Christopher Wood, Paul Klee and the Cubists. Her love of working in Spain, where she owned a small house in the hills above Alicante, and France fed the rural idyll aspect of her paintings. Showed in group exhibitions with Young Contemporaries, LG, WIAC (of which she was president for a time) and at Roland, Browse & Delbanco. Solo exhibitions included Portal Gallery, Woodstock Gallery, Carter Gallery in Los Angeles, Galeria Arrabal in Spain and Sally Hunter & Patrick Seale Fine Art, 1985. Contemporary Art Society, Nuffield Trust and Ferens Art Gallery, Hull, hold her work. Lived in Norfolk and London.

John JOHNSTONE 1937– Painter and teacher, born in Falkirk, Stirlingshire. He studied at Edinburgh College of Art, 1956–60, then a travelling scholarship took him to the West Indies and Latin America. Johnstone won a number of awards including an Arts Council Award in 1970 and an RSA Lothian Region Award in 1981. From 1963 he taught at Edinburgh College of Art. Johnstone showed regularly at RSA and SSA and participated in other group exhibitions in Britain and abroad. Solo exhibitions included Mercury Gallery and Compass Gallery, Glasgow. Arts Council, Scottish Arts Council and other British and foreign collections hold his work. Johnstone's work was hard to define, and at various times he was included in shows of New Symbolist and Poetic Realist painters. Lived in Lauder, Berwickshire.

Mary JOHNSTONE 1918–1988 Embroiderer and watercolourist, also known by her maiden name Mary Bonning, was the second wife of the artist William Johnstone. She studied under him at Royal School of Needlework and was a member of the Scottish branch of the Embroiderers' Guild, being chairman in the Borders area where she lived in the mid-1980s. Hampton Court Palace holds her work. She was also a watercolourist with a strong sense of design, work being shown at Broughton Gallery in Peebles, and Ancrum and Mainhill Galleries, both in Ancrum. Died in Melrose General Hospital. She appears in William Johnstone's autobiography *Points in Time*.

William JOHNSTONE 1897–1981 Painter and teacher, born in Denholm, Roxburghshire, into a farming family. A youthful friendship with the painter Tom Scott led to Johnstone's taking up painting and he attended Edinburgh College of Art, 1919–23; he then taught there part-time for two years. In 1925 Johnstone won a Carnegie Travelling Scholarship which enabled him to study in Paris with André Lhote at the Académie de la Grande Chaumière and the Atelier Colarossi. In 1927 married the American sculptor Flora MacDonald. For a few years their lives were unsettled, including periods in America and Scotland, finally settling in London in 1931. Johnstone, whose work had shown Cubist and Surrealist elements, took a series of teaching posts and had his first one-man show at the Wertheim Gallery in 1935. Johnstone now got to know such important figures as the poet T S Eliot and the artist Wyndham Lewis. Was influential principal of Camberwell School of Art, 1938–46; from 1947–60 he was principal of the Central School of Arts and Crafts. Retired to be a full-time sheep farmer in 1960, in the Scottish borders area, settling at Crailing, near Jedburgh, in 1970. Johnstone's later work was rather Orientally calligraphic in manner, as seen in his Hayward Gallery show of 1980, the year when Johnstone published *Points in Time: An Autobiography*. His second wife, Mary, also an artist, survived him until 1988. He was given a centenary show at Talbot Rice Gallery, University of Edinburgh, 1997.

Ben JOINER 1952– Sculptor working in such materials as patinated mild steel and rubber. Among his exhibitions were ICA New Contemporaries, 1980; Camden Annual, 1986; Whitechapel Art Gallery, 1989; and Canterbury Sculpture Exhibitions from 1990, with a solo exhibition at Harriet Green, 1997. He won a Greater London Arts Award in 1983 and a commission for Brent Magistrates Court and one for Leamington Spa in 1990. Arts Council and Contemporary Art Society hold his work.

Leon JOINER 1905– Painter and textile designer, born in Watford, Hertfordshire. He attended the local School of Art, 1920–3, and had further tuition in London and Paris, notably with the portrait painter T C Dugdale. Showed at RA, MAFA and elsewhere and lived for many years at Carshalton Beeches, Surrey.

Mabel JOLIN 1898–1959 Painter, born at Newcastle upon Tyne. A self-taught artist, she exhibited at RSA, Shipley Art Gallery, Gateshead, and at the Laing Art Gallery, Newcastle upon Tyne. Lived at Corbridge, Northumberland.

Nicholas JOLLY 1962– Artist born in Bebington, Cheshire, who studied at Gloucester College of Art, 1981–4, then Royal Academy Schools, 1985–8. He exhibited in Threshold of Meaning at Plymouth City Art Gallery, 1990, at Paton Gallery, 1993, and at that gallery's show at *The Economist*, 1994. Metropolitan Museum of Art in New York holds Jolly's work.

Harry Maude JONAS 1893–1990 Artist and restorer, son of a cigar merchant, who was educated at St Paul's School and St John's Wood Art School, where he started a lifelong friendship with the painter John Armstrong (Jonas' portrait of Armstrong is in the National Portrait Gallery). "To avoid an ostentatious lifestyle" Jonas left home and set up as a painter, notably of portraits, with some landscapes and religious pictures. He had a number of patrons, and his subjects included his friend the writer John Davenport, film actress Elsa Lanchester, cricketer Percy Fender and Lady Iris Mountbatten. Jonas acted for the silent screen, playing The Boy in *Love, Life and Laughter*, with Betty Balfour, 1923, and working as art director on *Reveille*, 1924, both directed by George Pearson. After sharing a studio with Armstrong, Jonas occupied one in Maple Street, Fitzrovia, a ramshackle affair where Leigh Hunt had entertained Thackeray and Dickens. During World War II Jonas served in the Home Guard. He was an old-fashioned bachelor bohemian, a member of the Fitzrovia group, who appears in Clifford Bax's memoir *Rosemary for Remembrance*; a devout Roman Catholic; a lover of talk, mysteries and the predictions of Nostradamus; and a discoverer of pictures, including one by Holbein, an alleged portrait of William Shakespeare and what he claimed was a self-portrait by John Constable, which for years he worked to restore in his Myddleton Square studio (he had to be rehoused there when the Post Office Tower dislodged his old studio). Jonas' style was traditional and he was not prolific. His only solo show was at the Matthieson Gallery, 1939, which he said was killed by the outbreak of World War II.

Allen JONES 1937– Painter, draughtsman and printmaker, sculptor and teacher, born in Southampton. He studied at Hornsey College of Art, 1955–9, then was at Royal College of Art until 1960 when "excessive independence" led to his expulsion. From the early-1960s Jones appeared frequently at the Paris Biennale (winning a prize in 1963) and John Moores Exhibition, Liverpool, and he also showed at Documenta 3 and 4 in Kassel, at Tokyo Biennale several times and at São Paulo Bienal in 1967. In 1963 Jones had the first of several solo shows at Arthur Tooth and Sons, and from 1964 showed with Richard Feigen Gallery in New York and later in Chicago and in 1965, by which time he had been living in New York, at Feigen/Palmer Gallery, Los Angeles. Jones' international exhibiting career was now well under way. His reputation was consolidated from the early 1970s with shows at Marlborough Fine Art and Waddington Galleries. Retrospectives included Walker Art Gallery, Liverpool, 1979, and Barbican Centre, 1995, both touring. Jones was famous for his Pop Art images, his glossy female forms owing something to American advertising of the 1960s. The artist designed posters, did stage and film work and produced a calendar for Pirelli. In addition to his three-dimensional fibreglass and aluminium sculptures made from the 1960s, in the early 1980s Jones created freer, silhouette-like coloured images. Public commissions included Red Worker, at Perseverance Works, Hackney, and the huge Acrobat, at Chelsea and Westminster Hospital, both in steel. Jones' work is held by Tate Gallery and Arts Council. Lived in London and was made RA in 1986.

Alwyn Dempster JONES 1949– Painter, designer, illustrator and teacher, born in Chester, son of the artist Thomas Dempster Jones. He was brought up in north Wales, where he settled at Mold, Clwyd, having attended Manchester College of Art & Design to gain an honours degree, then his teaching diploma from University College Cardiff school of postgraduate art education. Was appointed art master at Ysgol Dinas Brân, Llangollen, and worked as a graphic designer at Peter Carlyle Designs, Wrexham. Along with his full-time occupation as a designer, Jones worked as a freelance painter and illustrator, having artwork reproduced by *The Sunday Times*, *The Observer*, *The Times Educational Supplement* and many periodicals; advertisements for Yorkshire Television; and publications for The National Trust, BBC and others. He was further education art tutor for Deeside College. In 1993 Jones was made a member of the North Wales Society of Botanical and Fine Watercolour Artists. His paintings were made on location, especially on walks in the mountains of north Wales, and were predominantly in pastel. Showed in London, Manchester, Cardiff and Bristol.

Aneurin M JONES fl. from mid-1950s– Painter, draughtsman and teacher, born a farmer's son at Cwm Wysg, on the border of Brecon and Carmarthen. Country shows, markets and sheepdog trials were sketched for later working up into the country pictures for which Jones became famous in the principality. Graduated in fine art from Swansea College of Art, 1950–5. Then spent two years with Celtic Studios, designing stained glass windows for churches in Britain and abroad. Was head of the art department at Ysgol y Preseli in Crymych, Pembrokeshire, until he took early retirement to concentrate on his own work. Jones exhibited widely in Wales, elsewhere in Britain and in America, with work in British and foreign public collections. He gained the Rotary Award for outstanding service to art in 1978. Five years later he had an important solo show at the Gregynog Gallery, National Library of Wales, Aberystwyth. Lived in Cardigan, Dyfed.

Ann JONES: *see* **Ann Louise ROE**

Anthony Edward JONES 1944– Painter, sculptor, designer film-maker and teacher, born in Mountain Ash, Glamorgan. He attended Goldsmiths' College, 1961–2, Newport College of Art, 1962–6, for painting and sculpture, then in 1963 Swansea College of Art for stained glass. He then held a number of teaching positions in Britain and America including directorship of Glasgow School of Art, 1980–6, and from the latter year president of the school of art at Art Institute of Chicago. His films included *Pershing Rifles*, 1968, commissioned by Loyola University, New Orleans, and he did extensive research on Welsh chapel architecture, partly incorporated in his 1963 book *Chapel Architecture*. In 1971 he and others renovated and redesigned the interior of The Muscular Arms, Glasgow. Many group shows in Britain and America and solo exhibitions included Loyola University.

Barbara JONES 1912–1978 Painter, mural designer and writer. Studied art at the Royal College of Art. Work held by the Victoria & Albert Museum. She completed murals for the Commonwealth Institute, London, Cheshire County Police Headquarters, in Chester, and wrote a number of books, which she illustrated, on diverse subjects such as follies and grottoes, the Isle of Wight, watercolour painting and furniture. One of the strongest contributors to the World War II Pilgrim Trust *Recording Britain* project. Lived in London.

Ben JONES 1947– Sculptor, painter, writer and teacher, born in Builth Wells, Breconshire. He studied sculpture at St Martin's School of Art, setting up a studio in London in 1971. Began writing about sculpture, and was a founding editor of the magazine *Artscribe*. At the end of the 1970s he turned mainly to painting, also becoming a lecturer in art department at Bristol Polytechnic. In 1981 Jones moved back to rural Wales, settling in Llanwrtyd Wells, Powys, taking a studio in a former church hall. Revalued his work, turning to a figurative, vigorously expressive sculpture, using a variety of materials. Was a member of the Welsh Sculpture Trust, a founder of the Powys Sculpture Trail and was included in the Glynn Vivian Art Gallery & Museum, Swansea, 1986 show Seven Sculptors Working in Wales. In 1985 his sculpture commemorating the poet T Harri Jones was unveiled at Wyeside Arts Centre. Lived in Llanfoist, Abergavenny, Gwent.

Bryan JONES 1938–1997 Artist, teacher and administrator, born into a mining family in Rhymney, south Wales. He completed his National Service in the late-1950s and was employed as a steelworker before enrolling at art college in his early twenties. Became an artist and teacher, and around 1970 was a founder of, and rolled up his sleeves to help build, the innovative Chapter Arts Centre, Cardiff. This brought contemporary arts under one roof, then an unusual notion, from which groups across Europe took inspiration. When he left Chapter, Jones moved to the Caribbean for three years, returning to settle in west Wales. He taught part-time at Carmarthen College of Art, with a special interest in helping mature students. He also exhibited his own work internationally. Died at his home in Pencader, Dyfed, shared with fellow-artist Christine Kinsey who, with Mik Flood, had helped him establish Chapter.

Bryn JONES 1927– Painter, born in east London of Welsh parents. After formal education at Cambridge he worked in the arts faculties of Cairo and Hong Kong Universities. Began to paint in 1955, showed pictures, which included bold abstract shapes, in several London galleries and had a first solo exhibition at Drian Galleries, 1962.

Christopher JONES 1958– Artist born in High Cross, Hertfordshire, producing paintings, prints and collages in which the imagery could be fragmented and oblique. The studio interiors of Georges Braque and the early work of Willem de Kooning were influences. Jones gained an honours degree in fine art at the University of Newcastle upon Tyne, 1977–81 (he later became studio demonstrator in painting there), studying for his master's at Chelsea School of Art, 1982–3. He was fellow in fine art at Gloucester College of Art and Technology, Cheltenham, 1983–4, in the latter year winning a Boise Scholarship to Spain; was artist-in-residence, Humberside College of Higher Education, Hull, 1986–7; won a Monbusho Scholarship, Kyoto University of Arts, Japan, 1987–9; and Northern Arts Travel & Training Grant to Germany, 1992. Group shows included John Moores Liverpool Exhibition, 1982; Northern Young Contemporaries, Whitworth Art Gallery, Manchester, 1983; Show, Kyoto University, 1989; and Gallery Gerulata, Bratislava, Czechoslovakia, 1992. Had a solo exhibition at Nottingham University Art Gallery, 1985, later ones including Reg Vardy Arts Foundation, University of Sunderland, and Hatton Gallery, University of Newcastle, both 1992.

Colin JONES 1928–1967 Painter, restorer and teacher, born in Newport, Monmouthshire, where he attended the College of Art, 1944–6. After completing his National Service Jones was at Cardiff College of Art, 1948–51, then began teaching. He was on staff of National Museum of Wales, Cardiff, 1961–3, then until his death was HM Inspector for art in Wales. Having been converted to Roman Catholicism 10 years before he died, Jones completed restoration in a number of churches. He took part in group shows at SEA, Piccadilly Gallery, Whitechapel Art Gallery, John Moores Exhibition, Liverpool, and RP, being noted for his portraits and figure studies. One-man shows included Bristol Arts Centre, 1966. CASW holds his work.

Colin JONES 1934– Constructivist sculptor who attended Goldsmiths' College School of Art and studied with Kenneth Martin. Exhibitions included AIA Gallery and Düsseldorf International Art Fair. Jones' Relief Structure No 2, of 1964, in wood, Formica and polyurethane, was acquired by the Arts Council. His Relief Construction, of 1983, in aluminium, mild steel and cellulose paint, adorns the Charles Wilson Building at University of Leicester.

David JONES 1895–1974 Painter, draughtsman, printmaker and writer and maker of inscriptions, born in Brockley, Kent, son of a Welsh printer. Drew as a child, then studied with A S Hartrick at Camberwell School of Art, 1909–15. Between 1915–18 served with Royal Welch Fusiliers during World War I, being wounded and invalided home after action in France. The war, Welsh myth and landscape, his Roman Catholic faith, poetry and legend were some of the themes that threaded their way through Jones' writings and pictures, usually watercolours rich in layered imagery. From 1919–22 Jones studied under Bernard Meninsky and Walter Bayes at Westminster School of Art, then joined Eric Gill's Guild of St Joseph and St Dominic, in Sussex, 1922–4, also working with Gill in Wales, 1925–7. First one-man show at St George's Gallery in 1927. Was a member of SWE and the 7 & 5 Society and was exhibited widely abroad. Became an accomplished engraver, working for the Golden Cockerel Press and illustrated Douglas Cleverdon's 1929 edition of *The Rime of the Ancient Mariner* with 10 superb engravings on copper. His book *In Parenthesis*, of 1937, won the Hawthornden Prize and *The Anathemata*, 1952, the Russel Loines Award. Tate Gallery and many other public collections hold his work. Made Companion of Honour, 1974. Lived at Harrow-on-the-Hill in modest circumstances for many years.

Deborah JONES 1921– Self-taught painter of still life, trompe l'oeil and old backstreet antique shops in a style described as part imagery, part reality, Jones overcame family opposition to her career choice. After working as a lathe operator in World War II, Jones moved to London, living with several members of the International Ballet Company, painting friends in the ballet world and sketching people in pubs to make a living. Became immersed in the theatre, designing and painting sets, producing props and costumes for the Royal Opera House; worked as Oliver Messel's assistant; was engaged in television, films, opera at Glyndebourne, the Edinburgh International Festival; had a season working at Stratford; and helped Bernard Miles start the Mermaid Theatre. Painted and drew in places as far apart as Positano, Italy, and New York, showing her paintings in Greenwich Village there in 1952. An exhibition at Liberty's in 1957 established her name as a popular painter. Settled in Bristol, painting several Lord Mayors, being represented by the Alexander Gallery. Showed regularly at Florentine Gallery, Brighton, later exhibitions including Harrods, 1994.

Edward Scott JONES 1922– Painter, graphic artist and illustrator, and printmaker, born and lived in Liverpool. He studied at the College of Art there, 1936–7; worked in an advertising agency as a trainee artist, 1938–41; served in the Royal Air Force as aircrew, 1941–6; then served "in the galleys" as a graphic artist and illustrator in advertising, 1946–62, becoming a freelance painter and illustrator from then on. He was a member of RCamA and Acrylic Society. Showed at RI, RSMA, Paris Salon, Liverpool Academy, Hanover Gallery in Liverpool and elsewhere in mixed exhibitions. Solo exhibitions occurred at Williamson Art Gallery in Birkenhead, Bluecoat Gallery in Liverpool, Salford and Bootle Art Galleries, Liverpool Playhouse Theatre and elsewhere. Royal Liverpool Hospital; Bolton, Salford and Williamson Art Galleries; Liverpool Public Libraries; and Liverpool Pilots' Society hold examples.

Elis Gwyn JONES 1918– Painter, teacher, writer and broadcaster in Wales on art, born and lived in Llanystumdwy, Carnarvonshire, sometimes known as Elis Gwyn. He realised only slowly that he should be an artist, influenced by seeing the work of modern English painters and that of Brenda Chamberlain and John Petts, who became a friend and who first urged him to show at Royal National Eisteddfod in 1951. Attended University College of North Wales, Bangor, 1936–40. From 1948 was art master at Pwllheli Grammar School for 31 years, also teaching evening classes for a decade for the University. Was a regular BBC Television and radio broadcaster and wrote on art, including a bilingual book on Richard Wilson, published in 1973. Also showed at SEA and NWG and at Tegfryn Gallery, Menai Bridge. WAC holds his work.

Enaid JONES 1888–1978 Painter and draughtsman, notably of portraits. She studied at London New Art School, Waterdownes Studio, Grosvenor Road Studio and with Philip de Laszlo, then enrolled at Slade School of Fine Art, 1912, under Fred Brown, Philip Wilson Steer and Henry Tonks. She carried out portrait commissions and showed at RP, London Salon and IS. One of her models was her daughter Julia Lang, famous for the BBC radio *Listen with Mother* programmes. A show of Jones' work was held at Fry Gallery in 1984.

Eric Stephen JONES 1904–1962 Painter, printmaker and teacher, born in Romford, Essex, twin brother of the artist Harold Jones. Studied at Camberwell School of Arts and Crafts and from 1925 at Royal College of Art under William Rothenstein and Randolph Schwabe, being a Rome Scholar in the late-1920s for engraving. Taught at Sheffield College of Art from 1931 until his death. Showed at NEAC and was president of Sheffield Society of Artists. Illustrated for Cresset Press. British Museum, Victoria and Albert Museum and Sheffield hold his work. Lived in Sheffield, where Graves Art Gallery held a memorial show in 1964.

Ernest Yarrow JONES 1872–1951 Painter and sculptor, born in Liverpool, who qualified as a barrister but decided to pursue art as a career. He studied at Westminster School of Art and South Kensington Art School and in Paris at Académie Julian and Atelier Colarossi. Travelled widely, latterly living in Exmouth, Devon. Showed at Leicester Galleries, RA, London and Paris Salons and elsewhere. A group of his watercolours was shown at The Jerram Gallery, Salisbury, 1993.

Fred Cecil JONES 1891–1956 Painter, especially in watercolour, and etcher, principally of townscapes; teacher. Studied at Bradford and Leeds Colleges of Art. Jones was the son of a painter, Maud Raphael Jones, and he married an art teacher, Ethel

Mary Kitson. Exhibited RA, RSA, RBA, RWS and in northern provincial galleries. His work is held by the Tate Gallery as well as galleries in Bradford and Huddersfield. He and his wife taught at Pudsey Technical and Grammar School. Jones was a meticulous draughtsman whose work was illustrated in several books on the English countryside, and *Apollo* and *Studio* magazines. Was a member of Bradford Arts Club. Memorial shows in Bradford, 1956, and Keighley a year later. Lived in Leeds.

Geoffrey JONES 1909–1993 Painter, notably of flowers, creator of meticulously crafted, poetic and jewel-like works, sometimes on Perspex and on a small scale. He was born in Melbourne, Victoria, Australia, where he studied with Arnold Shore and George Bell, at the George Bell School, distinguishing himself by painting on glass. Jones had seen work by Bell's students at the Athenaeum Gallery, which had an immediate appeal, and he worked unsociable hours as a wharf clerk to fund his tuition. Leaving Australia as a deckhand in 1939 intending to continue studies in Europe, Geoff Jones on arrival in England enlisted in the British Army, was sent to Libya with the historian Philip Guedalla and illustrated a posthumously published book by him. Repatriated to Melbourne, Jones resumed his clerking, but had a show in 1947 which was well received. Returned to England in 1950, Jones on a stay in Paris studied at L'Académie de la Grande Chaumière and also made working trips to the south of France and to Italy. In 1953, the year of his return to Australia, Jones exhibited in the first exhibition in London of the Australian Artists' Association, at the RWS Conduit Street gallery. Among his later exhibitions was an eightieth birthday retrospective at Australian Galleries, Collingwood, Victoria, in 1989. National Gallery of Australia in Canberra, National Gallery of Victoria, Melbourne, Adelaide University and other collections hold examples.

Glyn JONES 1936– Painter, printmaker and teacher, born in Tynewydd, Glamorgan. He attended Cardiff College of Art, 1953–7, and the Slade School of Fine Art, 1957–60. Took up several teaching posts, meantime in 1961–2 being co-director of the Image Gallery, Leamington Spa, from 1972 head of the department of fine art at Cardiff College of Art. A member of the 56 Group, he also showed with Young Contemporaries on several occasions, Howard Roberts Gallery in Cardiff, SEA and WAC. One-man show at Elizabeth Gallery, Coventry. University College, Aberystwyth, holds his acrylic Upfront. Lived in Cardiff, south Wales.

Graham JONES 1956– Painter and draughtsman. He studied at Newport College of Art and Royal Academy Schools. His sensitive study Sir Edmund Fairfax-Lucy at Charlecote Park, Warwickshire which appeared in the exhibition The Long Perspective, Agnew, 1987, was bought by the National Trust's Foundation for Art. Jones also showed at the same gallery, in 1990, in The Broad Horizon.

Harold JONES 1904–1992 Painter and book illustrator and teacher, born in Romford, Essex. After an abortive attempt at a career in farming Jones returned to London where he attended Goldsmiths' College School of Art, 1921, under Edmund J Sullivan. Then he worked as a clerk while attending evening classes at Camberwell School of Arts and Crafts, his teachers including Albert Rutherston. A scholarship took him to the Royal College of Art full-time, 1924–8, where he studied design, draughtsmanship and engraving under Randolph Schwabe and William Rothenstein and sold his first picture to Lady Ottoline Morrell. Having begun teaching at Bermondsey Central School for Boys, 1930–4, Jones was introduced to the book publishing world by Barnett Freedman, and his reputation was given a lift with the publication of Walter de la Mare's *This Year: Next Year*, in 1937, one of the illustrations, The Black Door, being acquired by the Tate Gallery. Victoria & Albert Museum also holds his work along with several public collections in America. Jones went on to teach at the Working Men's College. Ruskin School of Drawing in Oxford, 1937–40, and after Army cartographic service in World War II, at Chelsea School of Art, 1945–8. Illustrated many books, including several of his own for children, winning several awards, and showed at Leicester Galleries, NEAC, Sally Hunter Fine Art and elsewhere. Lived in London.

Harold Harris JONES 1908–1991 Painter, notably of portraits, who studied at the Grammar School in Preston, Lancashire, where he settled, then Reading University, obtaining a Bachelor of Science degree. Studied at Southport School of Art, 1933, Harris Art School in Preston, 1934, and locally with Albert Woods, 1935–40, also in St Ives. Showed with RA, NS, RP, ROI and elsewhere.

Helen-Ann JONES 1965– Sculptor and teacher, Welsh-speaking, who attended schools in Mold and Sandbach, then South Cheshire College, Crewe, 1985–6. She did a foundation course at Mid-Cheshire College of Further Education, 1986–7, gained an honours degree in fine art from Bath Academy of Art, 1987–90, then did a postgraduate course at University of Wales, 1992–3, to obtain a teacher's certificate. Among activities over the next few years were a community sculpture project in Bristol, 1989, also assisting with Bath Contemporary Arts Festival; assisting Michael Watts in big commission for Cardiff Bay Development, 1991; being an artist-in-residence at Sully Hospital, South Glamorgan, 1992; and part-time tutoring for South Glamorgan County Council, 1992–3. Group shows included Cardiff Bay Arts Trust Gallery and Artworks at Rudry Church, Lower Machen Music Festival, both 1992. Had a solo show at Sully Hospital, 1992. Lived in Pontcanna, Cardiff.

Henry Conway JONES 1903– Sculptor, born in Llanfairpwll, Anglesey. After attending Friars' School in Bangor, Jones was apprenticed as a general mason, then in 1924–8 worked in London for the marble sculptors Farmer and Brindley. Also studied at City and Guilds of London School of Art, where he gained prizes for modelling, figure work and design. Jones then went freelance, notable commissions involving Portsmouth and Canterbury Cathedrals. Was a member of

RCamA and showed with it for about 30 years from 1936. Was a founder-member of West Middlesex Art Club.

Howel Clayton JONES 1897–1970 Artist in oil, watercolour and black-and-white. After studying at the Normal College, Bangor, Jones studied art in the studio of Tim Evans. He went on to exhibit at the RCamA, SGA, PS and elsewhere and illustrated books on north Wales and its mountains. His work also appeared in *La Revue Moderne*. Lived in Llandudno, Wales.

Huw JONES 1956– Figurative painter, born in Denbigh, who studied at Preston Polytechnic, 1976–80, and Chelsea College of Art, 1982–3. Exhibited at Cooling Gallery, 1993; Oriel Contemporary Art and Welsh National Eisteddfod, both 1995; and in John Moores Liverpool Exhibition at Walker Art Gallery, 1995–6. Lived in Llanfairfechan, Gwynedd.

Ian JONES 1947– Figurative and abstract painter, born in Birmingham, where he attended the Polytechnic, 1975–8, then Royal College of Art, 1979–82. He gained the Whitworth Wallis Award, 1976; John Minton Award, 1982; Greater London Arts Association Major Award, 1983; Athena Award, short list prize, 1988; and Unilever Prize, Portobello Festival, 1989. Group exhibitions included Drawings, Foyle Gallery, Birmingham, 1975; John Moores Liverpool Exhibition, 1982; Nicola Jacobs Gallery Summer Exhibition, 1984; Images of Paradise, Harewood House, Yorkshire, 1989; and The Discerning Eye, selected by Tim Hilton, Mall Galleries, 1991. Had a solo exhibition at Chapter Arts Centre, Cardiff, 1984, with a series at Anderson O'Day Gallery from 1989. Unilever, British Airports Authority and Nordstern in Cologne acquired works.

Idris Phylip JONES 1905– Painter, born in Nebo, Penygroes, Caernarvonshire, to which he eventually retired. Having attended Penygroes County School, Jones was apprenticed as a fitter, ran a taxi service, then in late-1930s embarked on a career as an aircraft fitter and inspector. Much of his life was spent with the Air Ministry, travelling widely in the United Kingdom. It was in the late-1950s that his exhibiting career gained pace, and he showed with Royal National Eisteddfod, in 1968 winning a second prize for painting; CASW; and Penygroes Art Club. In 1972 he participated in the WAC touring show An Alternative Tradition.

Jack JONES 1922–1993 Painter, teacher and writer, born poor and illegitimate in Hafod, Swansea, south Wales. He won a place at Dyneford School and went on to teach French and English, becoming head of English at Barnes Grammar School, London. Jones became interested in art in Paris in his late-twenties and published a life of Van Gogh: *The Man Who Loved the Sun*. Began painting in 1953, soon after returning to England from the University of Paris, and continued virtually untaught. His main subjects were the mining and industrial areas of his childhood. Although he was called "the Welsh Lowry", Jones denied Lowry's influence, terming himself "the Leonardo of the slag heap". Had many years of grave illness, including six operations for cancer and two coronaries, and by the age of 63 was an alcoholic in a mental hospital. In 1985 became a Roman Catholic, gave up drink and worked with alcoholics and drug addicts in Chelsea. His later work was more colourful, partly due to visiting Spain. Exhibitions included Stephen Bartley Gallery from 1988; Taliesin Arts Centre, Swansea, 1991; and Glynn Vivian Art Gallery there, which holds his work, 1993. Lived finally in Putney, southwest London.

Jo JONES 1894–1989 Painter and draughtsman, born in Knebworth, Hertfordshire, as Violet Madeline Josette Jones. She began painting as a young girl in Jamaica, and her studies included Paris and Zurich in the late-1930s. In 1933 the director of the Tate Gallery, J B Manson, introduced Jones to Wildenstein Gallery, which gave her her first solo show in 1935, from which Contemporary Art Society bought Still Life with Green Peppers. In 1938 she had a show at Galerie Zborowski, Paris, with another at Wildenstein in 1939. In that year she moved to London, where she was thereafter based, although she had a cottage and studio in Dorset. During the war worked as a land girl in Dorset and in Intelligence. There were four distinct working periods as a painter: in Paris and London before the war, in Spain in the 1950s, Morocco in the 1960s and after that mainly in Dorset with occasional journeys abroad, especially to Vevey and Zürich. For some years Jones lived with the Sacro Monte gypsies in Granada, and related pictures by her are in the Gypsy Museum at Leeds University. In 1969 *The Gypsies of Granada* was published, with text by Augustus John, Sacheverell Sitwell, Walter Starkie, Laurie Lee and Marguerite Steen. Showed regularly in Britain and abroad, having a retrospective at Alpine Gallery, 1985. The Michael Parkin Gallery had a memorial exhibition in 1992.

John Edward JONES 1926– Artist in all painting media, draughtsman, film-maker, teacher and writer, born near Bristol. He studied at West of England College of Art, Bristol, with George Sweet, 1942–4 and 1948–52, with Army service intervening; then in 1952–4 at Slade School of Fine Art under Claude Rogers and William Coldstream. Several teaching appointments included a senior lectureship in fine art department of Leeds University. It holds his work. Jones wrote a book *Wonders of the Stereoscope* and made several Arts Council/Arts Foundation films, including *Claes Oldenburg hanging a picture* and *Matisse: A sort of Paradise*. He was president of Leeds Fine Art Club and a member of RWA. Also showed with LG and had solo shows in Buenos Aires in Argentina, in Harrogate and Leeds, where he lived.

Jonah JONES 1919– Sculptor, letterer, teacher and writer, born in East Boldon, County Durham. He was educated at Jarrow Secondary School and managed to snatch part-time instruction at King Edward School of Art in Newcastle upon Tyne. After war service he suffered from pulmonary tuberculosis. In 1949 Jones worked in Eric Gill's workshops, about two years later setting up on his own in northwest Wales. He used slate as his principal medium and believed that fine art should be practised as a craft in a local community. For a while he was director of the National College of Art and Design in Dublin and he lectured in sculpture at the British School in Rome, but was mainly a working sculptor participating in a range of group shows, including RCamA, WAC and NWG. A few one-man shows were held, but much of Jones' work appeared in public locations, such as the depictions of Mercy and Justice on the Law Courts in Mold and his sculpture on the theme of Peace for the Emrys ap Iwan School at Abergele. Among his major inscriptions are those to David Lloyd George and Dylan Thomas in Westminster Abbey. His portrait busts included the architect Clough Williams-Ellis and the writer John Cowper Powys. Jones scripted several television films; his novel *A Tree May Fall* was published in 1980 and a book on *The Lakes of North Wales* in 1983. CASW holds his work. Lived at Minffordd, Penrhyndeudraeth, Gwynedd, later in Cardiff.

Joy JONES 1933– Artist in oil, tempera and watercolour, who also worked under her maiden name of Joy (Joyce) Mellor, born in Bangalore, south India. She studied at Regional College of Art, Manchester, 1955–7, then St Martin's School of Art, 1957–9. She was a freelance artist who worked for *Encyclopaedia Britannica*, Cambridge School Classics, Nature Conservancy Wales and the Overton Studios Trust. Her main works were miniature portraits, flowers and animals, and she specialised in still lifes in tempera. The Indian Army holds portraits by her. She showed with Clwyd Open, in Mold; Rhyl Museum and Art Gallery; and Tegfryn Art Gallery and had several two-man shows, including Oriel Bangor. Also showed in Canada. Lived in Colwyn Bay, Clwyd.

Justin JONES 1961– Painter and draughtsman. He studied at Leeds Polytechnic, 1981–4, at St Martin's School of Art, 1986–7, then in 1988 at Warsaw's Academy of Art under a British Council Scholarship. His work was included in many mixed exhibitions in Britain, notably The Broad Horizon, at Agnew, 1990, as well as at Wroclaw International Drawing Triennial, in Poland, and in Italy at Centro d'Arte Verrochio, Siena. In 1990 he had a solo show at Merz Contemporary Art.

Leslie JONES 1934– Printmaker, painter in acrylic and teacher, born in Tremadoc, Caernarvonshire. He attended the Regional College of Art in Manchester, 1951–5; Royal College of Art, 1955–8, tutors John Nash and Julian Trevelyan; was a Rome Scholar, British School at Rome, 1958–60; and a visiting student at Belgrade Academy of Fine Art, 1959. Jones was on the staffs of Kingston School of Art, Hornsey College of Art and St Martin's School of Art, 1961–7; was an HM Inspector for art and design, 1967–83; was a freelance artist and designer; then from 1987–9 was acting head of Gwynedd Art & Design Department. He was also fine art advisor for S4C Television. Jones was a member of RE. He held a number of one-man exhibitions including Oriel Henry Thomas, Carmarthen; Rhyl Museum and Art Gallery; Oriel Bangor; and Tegfryn Art Gallery. He worked for University of Wales Press, Cambridge University Press and others. Victoria & Albert Museum, WAC and CASW hold examples. Lived in Colwyn Bay, Clwyd.

Lucy JONES 1955– Painter and teacher, born and lived in London. She studied at Byam Shaw School of Drawing and Painting, 1975–7, Camberwell School of Art, 1977–9, and Royal College of Art, 1979–82, a Rome Scholarship in painting taking her to British School in Rome, 1982–4. By then she had begun to collect a number of awards and prizes, including the Cubitt Award for Painting, 1980, Anstruther Award for Painting, 1982, Oppenheim–John Downes Memorial Trust, 1986, and RA Summer Exhibition Daler-Rowney Award for the best work in oil, 1989. In 1984 she began teaching at Ruskin School, Oxford, and West Surrey College of Art and Design, Farnham, further teaching posts including Chelsea College of Art and Design, 1984–91. Jones overcame the problems of cerebral palsy to paint her disarming self-portraits and views of London, with an exuberance and rich, singing colour. Showed widely in group exhibitions in Britain and abroad and had solo shows at Angela Flowers Gallery and Flowers East. Arts Council, Museum of Modern Art in New York and other public collections hold her work.

Maggie JONES 1944– Artist in various media, designer and teacher who studied at Liverpool College of Art, Chelsea School of Art and Royal College of Art. Interiors and childhood memories were features of her mixed-media boxes, as shown at England & Co, Art in Boxes, 1992. She also showed at White Space Gallery and Fouts & Fowler. Jones worked for a time on the art publication *Raw Vision*.

Malcolm JONES 1949– Painter, born in Wallasey, Cheshire, who studied at Reading University, gaining a first-class honours degree in fine art. In 1982 won a prize in Sainsbury's Images for Today exhibition. Much of his work concentrated on London's East End, townscapes tending towards abstraction. Showed at Whitechapel Open, elsewhere in London, in the provinces and abroad. In 1983 Malcolm Jones Paints Limehouse was held at the library there.

Nicholas JONES 1965– Painter, born in Bristol, who studied at Bristol Faculty of Art and Design, 1983–8. He went on to exhibit widely in the southwest of England, winning the South West Arts Fine Arts Award in 1990. Exhibitions included RWA, 1988; Crane Kalman Gallery, from 1992; Manchester Contemporary Art Fair, 1994; and Gordon Hepworth Fine Art at 23 Smith Street, 1997. Arthur Andersen and Lloyds TSB hold Jones' work.

Olwen JONES 1945– Painter, printmaker and teacher, wife of the artist Charles Bartlett. She studied at Harrow School of Art, 1960–5, and Royal Academy Schools, 1965–8, and her engraving teacher was Gertrude Hermes. She was a part-time lecturer at Harrow School of Art. Took part in many mixed shows, including A Survey of Influential East Anglian Artists, Chappel Galleries, Chappel, 1991. Was a member of RE, 1978. Had a solo show at Zaydler Gallery, 1971. National Museum of Wales, Cardiff; Reading Museum; and Nuffield Foundation hold her work. Jones was a notable watercolourist, her work having a translucent quality. Lived in Fingringhoe, Essex.

Patrick JONES 1948– Painter who studied at Birmingham College of Art, 1970–1, then MFA Maryland Institute, Baltimore, America, 1973–5. He gained a Greater London Arts Association Award, 1979, then a John Brinkley Fellowship in Painting at Norwich School of Art, 1981. Group shows were many, including Platform '71 at Museum of Modern Art, Oxford, 1971; British Painting at Hayward Gallery, 1974; Henri Gallery, Washington, America, 1975; Tolly Cobbold Eastern Arts Touring Exhibition, 1981; and British Artists at Cyprus College of Art at Woodlands Art Gallery, 1983. Solo shows included Nicola Jacobs Gallery, 1981.

Peter JONES 1917– Painter, artist in collage and designer of reliefs, born in London, was by profession a frame-maker. Showed widely in the London area, including RA, Grosvenor Galleries, Camden Arts Centre, RBA, Redfern Gallery and elsewhere. His work can have much wit and verve and is held by Victoria & Albert Museum and South London Art Gallery. Lived in Twickenham, Middlesex.

Peter JONES 1968– Painter and teacher, whose work included a multi-coloured imaginary landscape of shapes, Series No. 5, oil on canvas of 1992, in the collection of Conoco UK, Warwick. Jones obtained a foundation diploma at Bournemouth & Poole College of Art and Design, 1986–7, then an honours degree in fine art from Coventry Polytechnic, 1987–90. He settled in that city, taking a studio in a canal basin warehouse. From 1990–1 he was a part-time lecturer at Coventry University's foundation department, also being resident artist at the basin, funded by Coventry City Council's arts panel. Reflections, work completed during the residency, was shown at Coventry's Herbert Art Gallery in 1992.

Philip JONES 1933– Painter, born in London, educated at Malvern College, where he was taught art by Henry Fabian Ware, studying at Slade School of Fine Art, 1953–6. Jones' subject was landscape, Malta, Sardinia and Norfolk, where he lived at Little Cressingham, being key themes. His work verged on abstraction as he abstracted the essential elements of a scene, using both subtle shades and occasionally unexpected, muted bursts of colour. He showed with RA Summer Exhibitions; Young Contemporaries, RBA Galleries, 1954; Artists of Fame and Promise, Leicester Galleries, 1955–6; AIA Gallery from 1964; Norwich Group Show, Castle Museum in Norwich, 1978; Chicago International Art Exposition, America, 1988–90; and Eastern Arts Open, King's Lynn, winner of Best Painting and Best in Show awards, 1993. Had a solo show at Galerie Bleu, Stockholm, 1965; Maddermarket Theatre Gallery, Norwich, from 1978; Louise Hallett Gallery, from 1986; Vanessa Devereux Gallery, 1990; retrospective at Malvern College, 1991; and Michael Parkin Gallery, 1994. Contemporary Art Society, Nuffield Foundation and galleries in Newport and Plymouth hold examples.

Philip JONES 1971– Figurative painter, born in Manchester, whose film still-realistic oil on canvas Bullitt, of 1995, was included in New Contemporaries at Tate Gallery, Liverpool, and Camden Arts Centre, 1996. Jones gained a fine art degree at Central St Martin's, 1991–4, and his master's in painting, Royal College of Art, 1994–6. Jones won a TI Group Scholarship to the Royal College for his period there and a travel award to RCA Studios, Morocco, 1995. Exhibitions included Art Viva, Senigallia, Italy, 1994, and MI-Art Fair, Milan, 1995.

Robert JONES 1943– Artist mainly on paper, and teacher, born in Newquay, Cornwall. He attended Falmouth and Manchester Schools of Art, did teacher training in Brighton, then took a design and craft course in Bristol. Held several teaching posts. Jones showed in Bath, Taunton, Oxford and Newlyn, being a member of Newlyn Society of Artists. He was included in the 1989 Newlyn Orion Galleries show A Century of Art in Cornwall 1889–1989, also in Falmouth Connections at Falmouth Art Gallery, 1994, and Porthmeor, A Century of Images, at Tate Gallery, St Ives, 1995. His first London show was organised by Thomas Henry Fine Art at Gallery 27 in 1997.

Royston JONES 1947– Painter, printmaker and photographer, and teacher, born in Wolverhampton, Staffordshire. He studied at Birmingham College of Art and Design, 1965–8, teachers including Trevor Halliday and John Walker, gaining his master's degree at Illinois University, 1969–71. Went on to teach at Southport College of Art and Technology. Jones showed in the Southport area, elsewhere in Britain and in America.

Sarah JONES 1959– Artist employing photography, born in London. She gained a fine art degree at Goldsmiths' College, 1978–81, and her master's there, 1994–6. Exhibitions included Nobby Stiles, Vandy Street, and Sick, 152c Brick Lane Gallery, both 1995; and New Contemporaries at Tate Gallery, Liverpool, and Camden Arts Centre, 1996.

Selwyn JONES 1928– Painter, illustrator and teacher, born in Llanberis, Caernarvonshire. After serving with Royal Naval Air Service in 1945–8, Jones attended Regional College of Art in Manchester, 1948–53. Had a period in London as a freelance illustrator. Several teaching positions followed, including from 1970 head of the art department at Normal College, Bangor. Had a series of solo exhibitions at Howard Roberts Gallery in Cardiff and took part in group shows at that gallery, Bangor Art Gallery, NWG, RCamA and Royal National Eisteddfod. WAC and CASW hold his work.

Stan JONES 1930– Painter, teacher and artist in ceramics, born in Dinas Cross, Carmarthenshire. Studied at Trinity College, Carmarthen and Cardiff College of Art, then went on to teach. He broadcast on BBC radio and television in Wales, completing a series on pottery for children. Was for a time chairman of WSW, and also showed widely in group shows including Thomson House, Cardiff, as well as SEA, SWG and Royal National Eisteddfod. One-man shows included County Library in Haverfordwest.

Stanley JONES 1927– Painter, printmaker and muralist, born in Birmingham, where studied at the College of Arts and Crafts, 1942–5 and 1948–50, teachers including Harold Smith, and at Royal Academy Schools with Henry Rushbury and Bernard Fleetwood-Walker, who had also taught him in Birmingham. He showed with Young Contemporaries, RA, RBSA, widely in Scotland and elsewhere in the provinces. The painter and collector Edward Le Bas and Graves Art Gallery in Sheffield, where Jones settled, held examples.

Stanley JONES 1933– Printmaker and lecturer, born in Wigan, Lancashire, full name John Stanley Jones, who attended the School of Art there, 1950–4, then the Slade School of Fine Art, 1954–6. Jones was awarded the Slade Scholarship in 1955 and the Robert Ross Scholarship in 1956. From 1956–8, he worked at the École des Beaux-Arts in Paris and with the help of S W Hayter joined the staff of Atelier Paris, where he met and worked with many School of Paris artists, including Giacometti, Severini and Braque. In 1958 Jones, prompted by his London dealer Robert Erskine, returned to England to set up a lithographic studio to be run by Curwen Press. This gained an international reputation, handling work by the most distinguished British and foreign artists. Among Jones' innovations was development of the continuous tone process. From 1959, he lectured in lithography at the Slade School. Jones was a founder-member of the Printmakers' Council in 1964, being for many years its president, and in 1965 helped found Curwen Gallery, which showed his own and others' work. He was a participant in the 1977 Artists at Curwen show at the Tate Gallery which, with Pat Gilmour, he helped organise and which celebrated the gift of Curwen's archive to the Tate. In 1989, Curwen Studio moved to Chilford Hall, near Cambridge, was renamed Curwen Chilford Prints and added screenprinting. Jones' book *Lithography for Artists* appeared in 1966.

Stephen JONES 1944– Artist in tempera, born at Brockett Hall, Hertfordshire. He studied at Hornsey College of Art, 1960–2, then ran the picture framing firm Stephen Jones Art Services, 1963–79. In 1980 he began painting again, using tempera, full-time. Exhibitions included Contemporary Portrait Society and RP, 1983; RA Summer Exhibition from 1987; Hunting National Art Competition, 1990. Lived in Twickenham, Middlesex.

Sydney Robert JONES 1881–1966 Painter, illustrator, designer, architect and writer. Born in Birmingham, he studied at the School of Art there for about four years at the turn of the century, then travelled extensively in England and on the continent. Exhibited RA, RI, Walker Art Gallery, Liverpool, Royal Glasgow Institute of the Fine Arts, Paris Salon and elsewhere abroad. Work held by Victoria & Albert Museum, Mappin Art Gallery, Sheffield, and Guildhall Library and Art Gallery, London. Jones did an extensive amount of industrial work and illustrations for publications such as *The Times*, *Illustrated London News* and *The Studio*. His many books concentrated on the English countryside, such as *Old English Country Cottages* and *English Village Life*. Was a member of the Authors' Club. Lived at Wallingford, Berkshire.

Terry JONES 1938–1992 Painter, teacher, enameller and draughtsman, born in Abersychan, Monmouthshire, son of a miner. He attended Newport College of Art, 1955–60, under Thomas Rathmell, then Royal College of Art, 1960–3, where Carel Weight was a strong influence. Taught at Medway, Canterbury and Kingston Colleges of Art part-time, 1963–7, then was a much-liked teacher full-time at Kingston, 1967–92, from 1973 senior lecturer in fine art. He painted extensively in Portugal from 1962 and America from 1980. Showed at Young Contemporaries, RA, LG and Society of British Enamellers, of which he was a founder-member, and solo at Rowan Gallery, 1962 and 1964. There was a retrospective at Watermans Art Centre/Kingston University, 1994, and tour. Jones was a prizewinner at Royal National Eisteddfod in 1976, WAC buying an enamel by him. Lived in London.

Thomas Dempster JONES 1914–1993 Painter, photographer and restorer, born in Harlech, Merionethshire. From 1929–36 Jones worked in Dinorwic Slate Quarries, attended Coleg Harlech, 1937–8, then was employed at aircraft production until training as a photographer in the Royal Air Force, 1942–6. He settled in Buckley, Clwyd, working as a professional photographer, then taught himself to paint from the early 1960s. Jones showed with Buckley Art Society of which he was president, AIA, RA, De Souza Gallery in Chester, RCamA, Royal National Eisteddfod and at Paris Salon, where he gained an Hon. Mention in 1967, a gold medal three years later. First of several solo shows was at New Civic Centre, Connah's Quay, 1968. Coleg Harlech holds his work. His father was the artist Alwyn Dempster Jones.

Thomas Salisbury JONES 1882– Painter and illustrator who was employed by the General Post Office, working in Wales, where he finally lived at Penmaenmawr. Attended Crewe School of Art, 1907–10. He wrote short stories, which he illustrated. Exhibited RCamA and in London.

Tim JONES 1950– Artist, sometimes known as T(imothy) M(artin) Jones, who studied at Berkshire College of Art, 1967–8; High Wycombe College of Art, 1968–9; St Martin's School of Art, 1969–72; Central School of Art, 1976; and Royal College of Art, 1977–80. Among awards won were Mark Rothko Memorial Trust Award, 1980, and Calouste Gulbenkian Printmaker Award, 1982. Was artist-in-residence, Borough of Lewisham, 1982–3. In 1981 gained a commission for Brunel University Music Room, in 1983 one for Lewisham's Ladywell Baths. Mixed shows included RA Summer Exhibition from 1979; John Moores Liverpool Exhibition, 1980, at the Walker Art Gallery, prize winner; Contemporary Artists in Camden, 1981, at Camden Arts Centre; and 10 London Printmakers, St Pancras Library, 1983. Took part in five-man exhibition at Ikon Gallery, Birmingham, 1983. Had a solo show at John Holt Gallery, 1978, later ones including ICA,

1983. British Council, Contemporary Art Society and other public collections hold examples. Lived in London.

Trevor JONES 1945– Painter, printmaker and teacher who produced abstract works. He was born in Stourbridge, Worcestershire, attending the College of Art there, 1960–3; Birmingham College of Art, 1963–5; and Royal College of Art, 1965–8. Taught from 1974, including Birmingham Polytechnic, Camberwell School of Arts and Crafts and the London Institute, where he was senior lecturer in fine arts. Group exhibitions included RA student exhibition, 1967; New British Painting, ICA, 1969; and 1974 John Moores Liverpool Exhibition. Had a series of solo shows at New Art Centre from 1969 and an exhibition of prints and drawings at Cinema Gallery, Aldeburgh, for the Festival, 1990. Also showed on the continent and in America. Worked in London and Suffolk.

T M JONES: *see* **Tim JONES**

Wilfred Emmanuel JONES 1890– Landscape painter in oil and printmaker. Brought up in Birkenhead, Cheshire, Jones taught himself to paint. He painted widely in England and showed at RA, RCamA, Walker Art Gallery, Liverpool, and RBA. Lived at Edgbaston, Birmingham, later in Broadstairs, Kent.

William Henry JONES 1900–1964 Sculptor, born in Menai Bridge, Anglesey. After leaving school aged 14 he served in Army in World War I, then was in Cardiganshire police for 18 years. In the early-1950s he opened Ye Olde Tea Gardens and Café at Menai Bridge, then from mid-1950s showed his cement sculptures there. Appeared in WAC 1972 exhibition An Alternative Tradition.

Wynn JONES 1939– Painter, draughtsman and teacher who was born in Wales, attending Cardiff College of Art, 1957–62, and was Jubilee Fellow at Byam Shaw School of Art in 1963. From the early-1970s he taught at Byam Shaw, from 1980 as senior tutor, and was a tutor at Royal College of Art, 1985–6. His work drew on diverse sources, ranging from cartoon strips to Picasso, sometimes commenting on the bizarre aspects of modern life. Mixed appearances included John Moores Liverpool Exhibition, 1995–6. Had a first solo exhibition at University of Wales in 1974, others being at House Gallery, 1978 and 1981, Artspace Gallery in Aberdeen, 1983, and Concourse Gallery, 1993. Arts Council holds his work. Lived in London.

Zebedee JONES 1970– Painter, born and based in London, who did a foundation course at Camberwell College of Art, 1988–9; gained an honours degree, Norwich School of Art, 1989–92; then a master's honours degree at Chelsea College of Art & Design, 1992–3. Took part in group show at Slade School of Fine Art, 1993; Affective Light at Rear Window, 1993–4; Unbound: Possibilities in Painting, Hayward Gallery, 1994; and Real Art, Southampton City Art Gallery, 1995. In that year had a solo exhibition at Karsten Schubert, with one at Waddington in 1997.

Michelle JONES-HUGHES 1944– Painter, born in Deganwy, Caernarvonshire, married to the artist Selwyn Jones-Hughes. She studied at Liverpool College of Art and exhibited at Liverpool University, Liverpool People and Places, Royal National Eisteddfod and elsewhere. Gained a WAC Award, 1967. Was commissioned to paint a mural for George Rowney & Company, Bracknell.

Selwyn JONES-HUGHES 1943– Painter and teacher, born in Dolgellau, Merionethshire. He attended Liverpool College of Art, 1962–6, then Royal College of Art, 1966–9, going on to teach at St Helens School of Art. Completed a mural for George Rowney & Company in Bracknell as well as decorative work for the London store Harrods. Showed at WAC Celtic Triangle show in 1970, the 1974 An Iconograph of the Mabinogion exhibition of Royal National Eisteddfod/WAC, SWG and RA. Won Merseyside People and Places first prize in 1965 and several Manchester Academy open awards in 1970s and in 1986–7 was included in Walker Art Gallery, Liverpool, touring exhibition Merseyside Artists 3. Had a solo show at Prescote Gallery, Oxford. Lived for some years at Rainhill, Prescot, near Liverpool. He was married to the artist Michelle Jones-Hughes.

Madeleine de JONG 1958– Painter and draughtsman, born in Joure, Friesland, in the Netherlands, who went to school in Brussels, Belgium and studied graphic art at Atelier Met de Peninghem/École Supérieure d'Art Graphique, Paris, 1976. Lived and painted in Venice, 1979, spent another year in Paris in 1980, then settled in London. Cafés, bars and the circus were favourite subjects of de Jong's work, in which the influence of seventeenth-century Dutch genre painters was evident. She carried out a number of portrait commissions, including Viscount David Linley and Lady Florence Hardinge and had work in British and foreign collections. Among her exhibitions was Links of Affinity, Knapp Gallery, 1989.

Leonie JONLEIGH fl. from c.1950–1974 Painter in oil who studied privately with Carel Weight. Born in London. Exhibited RA, LG, RBA, RSA, SEA, Leicester Galleries, New Grafton Gallery and other venues. One-man show at Zwemmer Gallery, 1959. She was a member of the council of the RBA and directed and showed in exhibitions for the Guildford Festival of the Arts, 1969–71. She was interested in art and education, and her work was bought by both the London County Council and Hertfordshire education committees. Lived at Wonersh, Guildford, Surrey, where the Leonie Jonleigh Studio and Jonleigh Gallery were both established.

Basil JONZEN 1913–1967 Painter of landscapes, flowers and portraits, and art dealer. He studied with Bernard Meninsky at the Central School of Arts and Crafts. Showed very successfully with Redfern Gallery, which sent him to Spain, France and the Canary Islands to paint. Also exhibited at NEAC, Tooth and RBA. During World War II Jonzen was involved in camouflage, service including Norway and Nigeria, lecturing on it in

Edinburgh. Married the sculptor Karin Jonzen, as she became known, their son being the artist Martin Jonzen. After the war they renovated Sir Hugh Lane's studio house in London's South Bolton Gardens and ran a Weekend Art Gallery there, which attracted many distinguished clients. Later, Basil Jonzen was involved in the St George's Gallery. Arts Council holds his work.

Karin JONZEN 1914–1998 Sculptor and teacher, born in London of Swedish parents, and continued to live there. Her husband was the artist and dealer Basil Jonzen, and their son the artist Martin Jonzen, and after Basil's death she married the Swedish poet Åke (pronounced Orker) Sucksdorff, whom she had met in the late-1920s. She studied at the Slade School of Fine Art, 1933–6, winning both painting and sculpture prizes; gained a scholarship in 1936 for a fourth year, and attended the City and Guilds Art School, Kennington; also studying at the Royal Academy in Stockholm. In 1939 won the Prix de Rome, but war – during which she served as an ambulance driver – prevented her from going to Italy. After the war Jonzen was elected a fellow of RBS and won the Feodora Gleichen Memorial Fund award as well as a series of international gold and silver medals. She lectured at Camden Arts Centre and in art appreciation at London University extra-mural classes. Took part in Battersea Park open-air sculpture exhibitions. LG member who showed at RA, Wildenstein, Agnew and Roland, Browse & Delbanco. Among her portraits were the writer Sir Alan Herbert, the architect Sir Hugh Casson and the ballerina Dame Ninette de Valois. Jonzen completed a large number of public commissions including the bronze group Beyond Tomorrow, at Barbican Centre, a bronze torso for the World Health Organization building in Geneva and a Madonna and Child for St Mary-le-Bow Church. Tate Gallery, provincial and foreign collections hold Jonzen's work. Nude terracotta examples of her work in Eric Newton's monograph *British Sculpture 1944–1946* were typical.

Ann JOPE 1945– Painter and printmaker, born in Corfe Mullen, Dorset, who grew up in south Devon. She studied at Ealing School of Art, 1966–7; Central School of Art and Design, 1967–70, gaining an honours degree in painting; then did a post-graduate printmaking diploma at the Central, 1980–2. Jope was made a fellow of RE in 1984, was an artist member of Printmakers' Council of Great Britain and of Oxford Art Society. She gave a number of demonstrations, lectured occasionally including Farnham College of Art and West Dean College, and made several television appearances. In 1986 she was artist-in-residence at King Henry VIII School, Abergavenny. Illustrations included the Folio Society Shakespeare, *King John* and *Much Ado About Nothing*; Julian Barnard's *The Song of the Reeds*; and Leslie Norris' *Ransoms*, for Gregynog Poets. Jope's numerous group appearances included RA, RBA, British Crafts Fair, St David's Hall in Cardiff and Morley Gallery. She had a solo exhibition at 5 Dryden Street Gallery in 1976, later ones including Ashridge Management College, 1990, and West Dean, 1991. Lived at Hardwick, Witney, Oxfordshire.

Janet JORDAN fl. from 1960s– Painter and teacher who studied at Sutton Art School and Central School of Arts and Crafts, concentrating on theatre design. She taught at an independent school in Gloucestershire for 21 years at secondary level, also teaching art-related subjects to teachers in training. Jordan was especially interested in the Goethe Theory of Colour and the use of watercolour. Mixed exhibitions included Long Street Gallery in Tetbury and Patricia Wells Gallery, Thornbury, and she had a solo show at Parnham House, Beaminster, in 1985. Was commissioned to paint five pictures of cooling towers for Central Electricity Generating Board's headquarters in Gloucester. Lived in Brookthorpe, Gloucestershire.

Joan JORDAN 1923– Painter, miniaturist and teacher, born in Heckingham, Norfolk. After private education Jordan studied at Tasmanian School of Art, 1966–8. She went on to teach further education classes, was a member of UA and president of the Pastel Society of Western Australia. She showed at Mall Galleries, Royal Exchange and elsewhere in mixed exhibitions and had a number of solo shows. Lived latterly at Duncraig, Perth, Western Australia.

Zee JORDAN fl. from 1980s– Artist in various media, including collage, born in Manchester. She studied at Tameside College with Bill Clark and at Manchester Polytechnic. Exhibited at RA Summer Exhibition, 1992, at Colin Jellicoe Gallery in Manchester, elsewhere in the city and in Cheltenham. Jordan's work strongly emphasised colour and decoration, the human figure and cultural symbols being notable features. She wished "to bring solace through art". Lived in Chorlton, Manchester.

Amy JOSEPH 1876–1961 Painter in watercolour, especially of townscapes. Studied at the Slade School of Fine Art under Henry Tonks, Fred Brown and A W Rich. Exhibited widely, including RA, NEAC, Goupil Gallery, RBA, SWA, RSA and RI. Lived in London.

Andrew JOSEPH 1963– Painter and teacher whose output included enigmatic, small, figurative pictures such as Two, at Royal Over-Seas League Open, 1994. He was born in Bristol and studied at Bournemouth College of Art; Bath Academy of Art in Corsham; and London University's Institute of Education. He was assistant to the artist Stefan Knapp, 1985. Later taught art at Rokeby School, Stratford. Participated in Whitechapel Open Studios from 1986.

Jane JOSEPH 1942– Draughtsman, painter in watercolour and oil and etcher, born in Surrey. She studied at Camberwell School of Arts and Crafts, 1961–5, teachers including Robert Medley, Frank Auerbach, Euan Uglow, Frank Bowling and R B Kitaj. She won a Leverhulme Travelling Award, Europe, 1965–6; travelled in America, 1968; gained an Abbey Award in Painting, working at the British School at Rome, and elsewhere in Italy, 1991; and continued with a further Abbey Award in 1995. Took part in extensive group exhibitions, including SWG from 1971; LG from

1982; Small is Beautiful, Angela Flowers Gallery, from 1983; Beardsmore Gallery, from 1992; and Marking Presence, ArtSway, Sway, 1997. Had a solo show at Morley Gallery, 1973, with a retrospective of drawings and prints, 1980–97, there in 1997. This exemplified Joseph's traditional manner of working from direct observation on site, images being worked up on a larger scale in the studio. Urban locations and the river (her studio was near the Thames) were important. WAC, Government Art Collection, British Museum and Ben Uri Art Society held examples.

Peter JOSEPH 1929– Painter and teacher, born in London, where he continued to work. Self-taught, Joseph taught at Portsmouth College of Art 1969–72. He was awarded a prize at John Moores Exhibition, Liverpool, 1979. Joseph was included in many group shows in Britain, including 1969 environmental work Triple Yellow at Kenwood and the 1970 Yellow Wall at Camden Arts Centre. In 1988 Joseph's geometrical abstract acrylic Eggshell Blue and Black was included in A Disquieting Suggestion at the University of Southampton's John Hansard Gallery, and in 1988–9 he was in the South Bank Centre touring show The Presence of Painting. Joseph exhibited solo at Lisson Gallery from 1971, other shows including Galerie Meert Rihoux, Brussels, 1993, and Paintings and works on paper, Museum of Modern Art, Oxford, 1994. Tate Gallery, Victoria & Albert Museum, Arts Council and important foreign collections hold examples. Lived in Gloucestershire and worked in London.

Laurence JOSEPHS 1913– Sculptor in wood, engraver and painter, and teacher, born and lived in London. Studied at St Martin's School of Art, 1932–5; in the studio of Leon Underwood; learned drawing with R V Pitchforth; and worked as assistant to Underwood in his Brook Green School. Taught in secondary schools for 25 years and "lectured on art theory, when it was possible to do so". Josephs' work was generally figurative, "concerned with truth to material in sculpture". He was a member of the group involved in the short-lived publication *The Island*, conceived in 1931, and of Ben Uri Art Society, 1945–9, being on the committee of its gallery. Showed at many galleries including Ben Uri, and had solo exhibitions at Queenswood Gallery, 1952–3, and October Gallery, 1989 and 1993.

Lawrence JOSSET 1910–1995 Versatile printmaker, born in Croydon, Cambridgeshire. He attended Bromley and Beckenham Schools of Art, 1930–1; was with Waterlow's, 1930–1, working on banknotes and other productions; then studied at Royal College of Art, 1932–5, with Malcolm Osborne and Robert Austin. In 1932–3 Josset was art master at Red Hill School. Josset was a member of RE, 1951, and Art Workers' Guild. He also showed with RA and had prints published by Thomas Ross of Binfield. Josset produced mezzotints after such artists as Boucher and Fragonard as well as sporting prints. He considered "subject matter all-important". He lived at Detling, Maidstone, Kent.

Percy Hague JOWETT 1882–1955 Painter, especially of landscapes in watercolour, and teacher, who in 1912 married Enid Ledward, sister of Gilbert Ledward the sculptor. He was born in Halifax, Yorkshire, and studied at Leeds and Royal Colleges of Art, latterly under Gerald Moira, winning the Prix de Rome which took him to Italy. he taught first at Beckenham School of Art and after World War I service in the Army returned there. He was also principal at Chelsea, the Central School of Arts and Crafts, 1930–5, then the Royal College of Art, 1935–48, where he was influential, making shrewd appointments such as Henry Moore and Gilbert Spencer. Exhibited at RA, RWS, NEAC, Redfern Gallery, Fine Art Society and had a series of solo shows at St George's Gallery in the 1920s. His work is in many British and overseas galleries. Jowett's watercolour Boats, illustrated in Percy V Bradshaw's book *Water-colour*, is typical of the artist's loose and fresh style. Lived in London. Michael Parkin Gallery had a show of his work in 1995.

John JOWITT 1904– Painter in oil and watercolour and teacher, born in Leeds, Yorkshire. After Uppingham School he attended Yeovil Art School, 1935–9, under George Mitchell. He "taught at five art classes, three of which were further education classes." Although he painted landscapes his main work was portraits. Jowitt was exhibited at RA Summer Exhibition and ran his own Jowitt Art Group. Lived at Chideock, Bridport, Dorset.

Steve JOY 1952– Painter, born in Plymouth, Devon. After service in Royal Air Force, 1968–75, studied at Cardiff College of Art, 1975–6, Exeter College of Art, 1976–9, and Chelsea School of Art, 1979–80. Painting fellowships held included Gloucester College of Art and one sponsored by the Japanese government at Kyoto University of Arts. His work included geometrical abstract works, although Joy said that he was "indifferent to any distinction between abstraction and representation". He wanted his works "to act as triggers to stimulate the mind of the spectator into moving onto a different level". Group shows included Spacex Gallery, Exeter, 1979; Theatre Zuidplein, Rotterdam, 1980; and Serpentine Gallery Summer Show 1, 1981. Had a solo show at Riverside Studios, 1978. Lived for a time at Chalford, Gloucestershire.

Henry Stanley JOYCE 1882–1961 Artist mainly in watercolour and pen and ink, lecturer and teacher, born at White Mill, Wimborne, Dorset, a National Trust property open to the public since 1995. Joyce was educated at Wimborne grammar school and developed a special interest in natural history. He was prolific, work being reproduced in many publications such as *The Field* and *Country Life*. His illustrated books include *I Was Born in the Country* and *Holidays with a Rod*. Birds were Joyce's favourite subjects, but he lectured on all aspects of plant and animal life, using his own detailed works as illustrations, many now held in Bristol University library. During retirement, he taught art for several years at Belmont College, Barnstaple, showing regularly at Burton Gallery, Bideford. Throughout his life, Joyce worked on an unpublished, three-volume collection of British wild flower studies. Died at home in a wooded valley near Barnstaple, Devon.

Mark JOYCE 1966– Painter, born in Dublin, Ireland. He studied at National College of Art and Design in Dublin from 1984, gaining a first-class honours degree in fine art, then his master's degree at Royal College of Art, 1991–3. Among his awards were a British Council Scholarship and Arts Council Postgraduate Award, 1991. Joyce was a member of Artists' Association of Ireland. His exhibitions included Limerick Soviet, Limerick City Gallery, 1989; GPA Emerging Artists Show, 1990, where he gained an award; Riverside Studios, 1992; and Europaprijs 93, Ostende, 1993.

Peter JOYCE 1964– Painter and teacher, born in Poole, Dorset. Joyce studied at Bournemouth and Poole College of Art and Design, 1980–2, then Stourbridge College of Art, 1982–5. He lectured at both. Was involved in film-making involving several notable artists, including Gillian Ayres, Elisabeth Frink and Henry Mundy, and was himself the subject of a film by Grove Films. Joyce was notable for his coastal paintings tending towards abstraction, rather in the manner of St Ives artists, with black, grey and white much in evidence. Showed from 1987 with RWA, also at Poole Art Centre and Anthony Hepworth Fine Art, Bath, where he had a solo show in 1992. Lived in Wimborne, Dorset.

Elsbeth JUDA 1911– Artist, photographer, teacher and collector of contemporary art, born in Darmstadt, Germany. She went to live and work in Paris, 1929; in 1931 married Hans Juda, financial editor of *Berliner Tageblatt*, and moved to Berlin; in 1933 settled in London and studied photography with Lucia Moholy, of the Bauhaus, and became a fashion photographer, working as Jay. As associate editor and photographer for *Ambassador Magazine*, founded by Hans Juda, she travelled the world. In 1963 set up a design studio to teach industry practice to graduates. Her private work included paintings, murals and witty collages, a large show of which was given at England & Co, 1994, touring to Germany. Elsbeth Juda's *Ambassador* archive is held by the Victoria & Albert Museum.

Gerry JUDAH 1951– Sculptor, born in Calcutta, India, who studied at Goldsmiths' College School of Art and Slade School of Fine Art. In 1978 took part in 3 Garden Exhibitions at Camden Arts Centre. In 1990 conceived a huge sculpture, dedicated to human rights, which comprised a pair of wooden wings supported on an inclined column, and inset with rows of niches, each containing fibre-optic candles that would have glowed in the wind. It was destined for Potters Fields Park, on the south bank of the River Thames, opposite the Tower of London. Despite heavy support it was refused planning permission by the then environment secretary, John Gummer.

James JUDGE 1958– Gestural painter, draughtsman and etcher born in London, who studied drawing/painting at Frobisher Institute and drawing/etching at Morley College, both 1974–82, and at Byam Shaw School of Art, 1982–5. In 1985, Judge was winner of the RA's Richard Ford Award, with a travelling scholarship to the Prado, Madrid. Group shows included South London Art Gallery, from 1986; RWS and RBA, both Mall Galleries, 1991; Beecroft Gallery, Westcliff-on-Sea, 1993; and Adam Gallery, The Gallery in Cork Street, 1998. Had a solo exhibition, The Studio Gallery, 1998.

Rod JUDKINS 1956– Figurative artist, born in England, who studied at Bath Academy of Art, Corsham, 1976–7, Maidstone College of Art, 1977–80, and Royal College of Art, 1980–3. In 1981 he won the Wilfrid Sirrell Award, in 1982 the Herbert Read DRU Award and in 1983 the Sioux River Annual. Took part in many group shows, including Imperial Tobacco at National Portrait Gallery and Spirit of London, Greater London Council, both 1981; The Music Show, Thumb Gallery, 1983; The Self Portrait – A Modern View, Artsite Gallery, Bath, from 1987, and tour; RA Summer Exhibition, 1991; and Art94 (Jill George Gallery), Islington, 1994. Showed solo at Thumb Gallery from 1983, at Jill George from 1991. Public and private collections hold examples. Lived in London.

Betty JUKES 1910– Sculptor in various materials and teacher, born in Shillong, Assam, India, educated in London. She studied at Royal College of Art, 1928–32, teachers including Henry Moore, Herbert Palliser and Richard Garbe. She qualified as a state registered nurse in 1945 at St Bartholomew's Hospital, then taught sculpture at Sir John Cass School of Art and City of London Polytechnic, 1946–75. Showed at RA and elsewhere. Jukes was a fellow of RBS from 1948 and a member of the SPS. Lived in London.

Mary Victoria JUMP 1897–1989 Watercolourist, brought up in the Liverpool area where she attended the School of Art, also Birkenhead School of Art and obtained City and Guilds Technological Certificate. She settled at Bebington, Wirral, Merseyside and exhibited with the main local public galleries and RCamA and was a member of Wirral Society of Art and Wirral Craft Exhibiting Society.

Hannaford JUNIOR: *see* **Charles Arthur HANNAFORD**

Brigitte JURACK 1962– Sculptor born in Düsseldorf, West Germany. She studied at Kunstakademie Düsseldorf, 1982–8; Glasgow School of Art, 1989–90; and Chelsea College of Art and Design, 1990–91. In 1992 was Henry Moore Sculpture Fellow. Took part in East at Norwich Gallery, 1991, and had show at Winchester Gallery, Hampshire, 1993. Lived in London.

Anne P JURY 1907– Painter, born in Dunmurry, near Belfast, Northern Ireland, her father an architect. She studied at Belfast School of Art, in England and on the continent. Was elected RUA, showed at RHA, in London and Edinburgh and had solo exhibitions at Magee's and Rodman's Galleries in Belfast and with Victor Waddington, Dublin. Limerick Municipal Art Gallery holds her work.

JUSTICE: *see* **Terry SCALES**

K

Norman KADISH 1916–1988 Painter, draughtsman and teacher who was born in London. He had a special interest in portraiture and illustrative art, favouring strong colour. Kadish studied at Regent Street Polytechnic School of Art, 1936–40, interrupted by war service, 1940–6; then in 1946–7 gained his art teaching diploma at London University's Institute of Education. Taught art at school and adult education level. Became a member of Hesketh Hubbard and Ben Uri Art Societies and showed at RA, RSMA, UA and elsewhere, having solo exhibitions at Burgh House, Hampstead, 1984, and Ruislip Library, 1988. Main works included The Lambeth Walk and Belshazzar's Feast. Lived in Edgware, Middlesex.

Menasche KADISHMAN 1932– Sculptor, creator of abstract stone compositions, born in Israel. He studied under R Lehmann in Jerusalem, then from late-1950s at St Martin's School of Art. He showed in Ten Years of Sculpture at Israel Museum, Tel-Aviv, 1958; with Young Contemporaries and LG, 1959–61; in France and Italy in 1961; and in 1965 in Fifty Years of Sculpture at Grosvenor Gallery and in The Visual Arts, at Harlow Arts Festival.

Erich KAHN 1904–1980 Painter, draughtsman and printmaker, born in Stuttgart, Germany. Studied at the State School for Arts and Crafts, 1922–5, in 1926 working with Fernand Léger in Paris. Arrived in England in 1939, shortly after release from Nazi concentration camp. Was interned in Isle of Man in World War II, but went on working in the Expressionist style to which he remained faithful. Settled in London, living in poverty, his life being eased by the arrangement of a pension and marriage. In the 1920s and 1930s Kahn had showed in Stuttgart and Berlin, and although he did exhibit in Paris, Bruges and other continental capitals after World War II, he showed mainly in London, in group shows at Leger and Whitechapel Art Galleries and elsewhere. Redfern, Drian and Molton Galleries gave him solo exhibitions in the 1950s and 1960s and John Denham Gallery gave him a retrospective in 1980. Kahn was a serious, retiring man, a prolific artist whose works are held by the Tate Gallery and Tel-Aviv Museum, Israel.

Peter KALKHOF 1933– Painter and teacher, born in Stassfurt, Germany, working in acrylic on canvas, hardboard, paper and plywood. He attended an evening class at School of Arts & Crafts, Braunschweig, 1952–5; was at Academy of Fine Arts, Stuttgart, 1956–60; did a postgraduate course at Slade School of Fine Art, 1960–1; then was at École des Beaux-Arts, Paris, 1962. Went on to teach at Reading University. Kalkhof said that his main concern was "the abstract phenomena of colour and space". Ancient cities, museums and nature with its climates and seasons were of key importance. In 1987 Kalkhof was commissioned to carry out a mural for the Treaty Centre, Hounslow, for Taylor Woodrow Group. Kalkhof's many mixed exhibitions included Galerie am Bohlweg, Braunschweig, 1962; University of East Anglia, Norwich, 1971; Towner Art Gallery, Eastbourne, 1972; British Painting'74, Hayward Gallery, 1974; Camden Arts Centre, 1981; and The Seventies, Brixton Art Gallery, 1985. He had a solo exhibition at Galerie in der Garage, Stuttgart, 1964, then showed often with Annely Juda Fine Art from 1970. There was a 25-year retrospective at Landesmuseum Oldenburg, Germany, in 1988. Arts Council and other public collections in Britain and abroad hold examples.

Panayiotis KALORKOTI 1957– Artist and teacher, born in Cyprus, who moved to England aged nine. He was noted for his wry and satirical coloured etchings, which employed a firm graphic line, areas of unusually subtle flat or patterned colour and a wide range of subjects. Images were meticulously constructed. Kalorkoti gained a first-class honours degree from Newcastle upon Tyne University, 1976–80, completing a master's degree in printmaking at Royal College of Art, 1982–5. As well as being a part-time visiting lecturer at a number of art schools, Kalorkoti was artist-in-residence at Leeds Playhouse, 1985; won a Netherlands Government Scholarship, 1986–7; was Bartlett Fellow in the Visual Arts at Newcastle, 1988; and artist-in-residence for Cleveland County, 1992. Commissions included Imperial War Museum, 1988; Boroughs of Darlington and Hartlepool, both 1989; and National Garden Festival, Gateshead, 1990. Took part in many group exhibitions, winning the Granada Prize at Northern Young Contemporaries, Whitworth Art Gallery, Manchester, 1983. His solo shows included Imperial War Museum and National Garden Festival, both 1990; and Design Works, Gateshead, 1992. Imperial War Museum, British Council and Laing Art Gallery, Newcastle, own his work.

Annette KANE 1955– Painter, mainly a watercolourist, designer and teacher, born in Birmingham. She studied fine art at Reading University, graduating in 1978. For six years she was a freelance graphic artist, then began to train as a teacher of art and design in 1985. After four years' teaching in Yorkshire she decided to devote more time to painting. She had her first solo show in 1990 at Finegold Contemporary Art Gallery, Hebden Bridge, another following at The Catto Gallery, 1992. Also showed at NEAC, RI and in 1990 won Catto Gallery award for Best Newcomer at RWS. Lived in London.

George MacDowell KANE 1889–1954 Portrait draughtsman, painter and sculptor who spent most of his life in Belfast, Northern Ireland. After attending Belfast Mercantile Academy, Kane was for a time with architects Blackwood and Jury; won a scholarship to Metropolitan School of Art, Dublin; taught at Royal Belfast Academical Institution; then in Edinburgh helped the sculptor James Pittendrigh MacGillivray with the Gladstone Memorial. Kane was associated with the Ulster Literary Theatre and many of his subjects were theatrical people. Showed with Rodman's Gallery and RSA and Ulster Museum holds his work.

Ian KANE 1951– Artist creating installations and abstract wall pieces using a variety of found objects and man-made materials, as in New Art in Scotland, Centre for Contemporary Arts, Glasgow, 1994. He was born and lived in Inverness, attended Edinburgh College of Art, 1975–80, and had a Scottish Arts Council Amsterdam Residency, 1986–7. Was one of four artists showing at Transmission Gallery, Glasgow, 1984; also in Federation of Scottish Sculptors show, Talbot Rice Gallery, Edinburgh, 1985; and Outdoor Sculpture, Crawford Arts Centre, St Andrews, 1988. In that year Discovering the Familiar was a solo exhibition at Moving Space Gallery, Ghent, Belgium, with another, Presence, in 1993.

Paula KANE 1970– Painter, born in Glasgow, who studied at Blackpool College of Technology and Art, 1988–9; Kent Institute of Art and Design, Canterbury, 1989–92; and Goldsmiths' College, 1994–6. Exhibitions included Small Objects of Desire, City Gallery in Leicester, 1994; Whitechapel Open, 1996; Plastic Domestic at The Tannery, 1997; and John Moores Liverpool Exhibition, 1997–8, where she was represented by the meticulous oil on canvas Bobbles. Lived in London.

Raymond KANELBA 1897–1962 Painter who studied at Warsaw Academy of Fine Arts, in Vienna and Paris. Exhibited RA, RP, Lefevre Gallery and in Paris in mixed shows, as well as having one-man exhibitions in London, Glasgow, Edinburgh and in several places on the continent. His work included royal portraiture. Lived in London.

Raghav KANERIA 1936– Sculptor, born in Anida, India. After attending Sagramji High School, Condal, 1950–5, Kaneria studied at the Faculty of Fine Art, Maharaja Sayajirao University of Baroda, where he obtained a diploma in sculpture, 1955–9. Between 1964–8 attended Royal College of Art by way of a Commonwealth Scholarship, working with Bernard Meadows. A Sainsbury Scholarship followed in 1967. As well as showing in India, was included in the Commonwealth Art Exhibition in 1962 and in the Royal College of Art's 1980 exhibition Bernard Meadows at the Royal College of Art, 1960–1980. Arts Council holds Watercarrier, of 1967, in steel.

Rachael Anna KANTARIS fl. from late 1980s– Artist noted for colourful, witty etchings, and teacher, born in Brisbane, Australia. She did a foundation diploma in art and design at Falmouth School of Art, 1985–6; gained an honours degree in visual and performing arts at Brighton Polytechnic, 1986–9; then her master's in fine art printmaking at Brighton University, 1990–2; studying lithography for artists at London College of Printmaking, 1992–3. In 1990 Kantaris worked at Tapestry Studios of Australia, in Melbourne, designing and weaving large tapestries, including work for Parliament House, Canberra; she had a four-month residency at Bethanien Kunstlerhaus, Berlin, in 1993; helped set up Trevor Price Studios in St Ives, Cornwall, 1994; and from 1995 oversaw the running of the Porthmeor Print Workshop in the town. Teaching included the Print Workshop, the School of Painting and Tate Gallery in St Ives and Newlyn Art Gallery. Exhibitions included National Print Exhibition, Royal Festival Hall, 1988; Fresh Art, Barbican Centre, 1991; RA Summer Exhibition, 1992; Three Printmakers, Salt House Gallery, St Ives, 1993; Open Print Exhibition, RWA, 1994; and St Ives Now, Collyer-Bristow Gallery, 1996.

Anish KAPOOR 1954– Sculptor, draughtsman and teacher, born in Bombay, India. He studied at Hornsey College of Art, Middlesex Polytechnic, 1973–7, then Chelsea School of Art, 1977–8. He was a teacher at Wolverhampton Polytechnic, 1979–82, then was artist-in-residence at Bridewell Studios, Liverpool. During a visit to India in 1979 Kapoor noticed mounds of pigment on sale outside temples. On his return to England he began to make forms out of ground chalk or plastic which he placed on the floor and covered with powdered pigment, which became an instantly recognisable feature of his work, which had an elegant, harmonious quality. He participated in individual shows in Britain and abroad including Objects and Sculpture at Arnolfini Gallery, Bristol, 1981; British Sculpture in the Twentieth Century (part II), at Whitechapel Art Gallery, 1982; represented Britain in the 1982 Paris Biennale, with Stephen Farthing and Bill Woodrow; participated in Objects & Figures at Fruitmarket Gallery, Edinburgh, 1982–3, and tour; showed at Lisson Gallery, 1989; represented Britain at Venice Biennale, 1990; in 1991 won the Turner Prize; and in 1998 had a major show at the Tate Gallery. Arts Council and other leading collections have his work. Lived in London.

Edmond Xavier KAPP 1890–1978 Painter and draughtsman, Kapp was a masterly caricaturist, as shown in a series of now-scarce books such as *Personalities*, published by Martin Secker. Born in London, Kapp was educated at Christ's College, Cambridge, and in Paris and Rome. He had several dozen one-man shows in London and provincial galleries as well as on the continent, in Canada and America. A 50-year retrospective was held at Whitechapel Art Gallery in 1961. In World War II Kapp was an official war artist. Kapp's work is in many distinguished private collections, as well as the National Portrait Gallery, Imperial War Museum, the Fitzwilliam in Cambridge and the Ashmolean, Oxford. During the final 20 years of his life Kapp often worked in an abstract style. He was the brother of Helen Kapp and in 1932 married the sculptor, painter and illustrator

Polia Chentoff, who died of a cerebral tumour the following year. Kapp lived in London.

Helen KAPP 1901–1978 Painter, illustrator, wood engraver and curator, born in London, the sister of the artist Edmond Xavier Kapp. She studied at the Slade School of Fine Art, Central School of Arts and Crafts and in Paris. Showed RA, AIA, LG and SWE and had solo shows at Nicholson's Gallery and in Haifa, Israel, with the British Council in 1946. Wrote *Enjoying Pictures* and illustrated many books. Was director of Wakefield City Art Gallery, Yorkshire, 1951–61, then for six years until her retirement in 1967 was first director of Abbot Hall Art Gallery, Kendal, where she established the nucleus of a fine collection. As a curator in Wakefield she organised exhibitions that drew attention to artists such as Alan Davie and Patrick Heron then not very well known, in Kendal showing the painters Joan Eardley, Anne Redpath and Sheila Fell. Finally lived at Leiston, Suffolk.

Chintamoni KAR 1915– Sculptor, painter and teacher, born in Bengal, India. Attended University of Calcutta, 1929–31, then the Indian Society of Oriental Art School there and was at L'Académie de la Grande Chaumière, in Paris, 1938–9. Showed at RA, RBA and Victoria & Albert Museum. Indian Embassy in Paris holds his work. Lived in London.

Olga KARCZEWSKA fl. from 1950s– Painter who was born in Craków, Poland, where she attended university, also attending the Sorbonne, in Paris. She studied art in London at London School of Art and Chelsea School of Art and in Paris at L'Académie de la Grande Chaumière. She showed at Grabowski Gallery, Walker's Galleries and elsewhere and had a solo exhibition at New Vision Centre Gallery in 1964. Was a member of the Association of Polish Artists in Great Britain and the Free Painters and Sculptors. Signed work with initials only. Lived in London.

Stanislawa de KARLOWSKA 1876–1952 Painter in oil, born in Czeliewy, Poland. She studied in Warsaw, Craców and from 1896 at Académie Julian in Paris where she met her future husband, the Camden Town Group painter Robert Bevan. She settled in England in 1898, two years later beginning to show at WIAC and in 1908 with Frank Rutter's AAA. She became well known as a hostess to the artists and clients of the Camden Town, Cumberland Market and LG shows, noted for her sweet nature. Had first solo show at Adams Gallery in 1935, which gave her a memorial exhibition 17 years later. Her interiors and landscapes can at their best be comparable with her husband's in strong construction, also showing a delightful colour sense and often a naive charm. Tate Gallery holds several examples. Died in London.

Josef KARPF 1900–1993 Painter and draughtsman, born in Galicia, Poland, who moved to Britain after World War II, during which he had spent time in a Siberian labour camp. Having graduated in economics at University in Vienna, studying in the evening at the School of Art, Karpf eventually settled in London. There he studied at Regent Street Polytechnic and Camden Arts Centre, exhibiting in the capital. He was closely involved with Ben Uri Art Society, which holds his work.

Linda KARSHAN 1947– Draughtsman and painter, born in Minneapolis, Minnesota, in America, who studied at Skidmore College, Saratoga Springs, New York, in 1965–6 with the architect Robert Reed, a former student of Joseph Albers. In 1967 Karshan worked at the Walker Art Center, Minneapolis, under the direction of Jan van der Maarck; studied art history at the Sorbonne in Paris, 1967–8; read art history at the Slade School of Fine Art; and earned a master's degree in humanistic psychology from Antioch University in 1983, the year she set up a studio in London. Group exhibitions included ASB Gallery, 1986; Runkel-Hue-Williams, 1990; and Grammercy Park Fair, New York, 1995. Had solo shows at Clarendon and ASB Galleries in 1984, later ones including Montgomery–Glasoe Fine Art, Minneapolis, 1995, and Redfern Gallery (drawings), 1996. British Museum and Staatliche Graphische Sammlung, Munich, hold examples.

John KASHDAN 1917– Painter, draughtsman, printmaker and teacher, born in London. He early decided to be an artist, but had to leave school at 14 to work, attending evening classes at the Working Men's Institute. Joined Royal Academy Schools, 1936–9, winning Gold Medal, Travelling Scholarship and many other scholarships. Rejected chance to study at Royal College of Art, preferring freedom of Royal Academy. From 1940, living in Cambridge, became friendly with Henry Moore, John Lehmann, Arthur Koestler and Wolf Mankowitz. Had solo show at Redfern Gallery, 1945. Jankel Adler introduced him to Robert Colquhoun, Robert McBryde and John Minton. In 1946 began teaching at Royal Naval College, Dartmouth, in 1951 moving to Guildford School of Art, in 1972 to Epsom School of Art, retiring in 1982. Had several prestigious shows of monotypes – much admired by Adler – in America, but in 1950 decided to withdraw from exhibiting. Continued to work, however, and his reputation was revived when in 1989–91 England & Co had exhibitions. British Museum made extensive purchases.

Aaron KASMIN 1963– Painter, born and based in London, son of the art dealer John Kasmin. He studied at Chelsea School of Art, 1981–5. Kasmin's works, some three-dimensional, employed delicate colours, scraping away and repainting, resulting in abstracts with landscape affinities. They showed "a debt to primitive, tribal art in its rawness and pattern-like qualities", he wrote on the occasion of his solo show at Harriet Green Gallery in 1996. Other solo shows were at Gallery 24, 1987; Albemarle Gallery, 1988 and 1989; and Groucho Club, 1995. Group exhibitions included Artist of the Day, Angela Flowers, 1986; Cooling Gallery, 1992; and Small is Beautiful, Flowers East, 1993.

Cyril KATKOV 1905–1995 Painter, muralist, architect and icon expert, born in Moscow, Russia. He fled the revolution there in 1921, moving to Prague, Czechoslovakia, for five years, where he studied at the Academy of Fine Art and won first prize, in

1925, for the design of the Cathedral of Ushgorod. Then went to Paris where he studied Byzantine art at the Sorbonne, showing his own paintings. From 1939 in Argentina continued to create murals and develop his own style of paintings in irregular frames, shown in Oxford in 1962. From 1965 Katkov was advisor to the auctioneer Sotheby's in New York on icon restoration, while completing church work in Canada. In 1988 his paintings of Greenwich, southeast London, were included in four-man show at Woodlands Art Gallery. Died in New York.

Elias KATZER 1910– Painter, illustrator and maker of puppets, born into a middle-class family, who was educated in Berlin, Germany. Although he had some art lessons, he was substantially self-taught. Earned his living as an illustrator for newspapers and magazines in Prague, Czechoslovakia, in the late-1930s, then settled in north London. Was noted as an illustrator of children's stories, but showed widely in London, on the continent and in America. Sometimes signed work KA–, alternatively with his full name.

Edward McKnight KAUFFER 1890–1954 Poster designer who also did some textile and theatrical work, painted and illustrated books and magazines. Born in America at Great Falls, Montana, Kauffer grew up in Evansville, Indiana, where was assistant scene painter in the opera house. His early training as a painter was in San Francisco and at the Art Institute of Chicago, where he saw the controversial Armory Show of modern European art. A patron assisted him to study in continental Europe where in Paris he was influenced by Van Gogh's work. Resolved to support himself by poster design, at the outbreak of World War I he had to flee to London where he associated with painters such as Harold Gilman and Charles Ginner and gained commissions for the Underground Electric Railways Company. For the next quarter-century he was the main designer of posters for London Underground under Frank Pick's patronage. Did work for Roger Fry's Omega Workshops, helped to found Group X with Wyndham Lewis and early in the 1920s returned for a while to New York, where he designed for the Theatre Guild. Showed at Goupil Gallery, Arthur Tooth and Son and NEAC. Illustrated for periodicals such as *Radio Times* and *Fanfare* and books such as Arnold Bennett's *Elsie and the Child*, 1929, T S Eliot's *Triumphal March*, 1931, and Edgar Allan Poe's *Complete Poems and Stories*, 1946. However, his reputation rests mainly on his outstanding contribution to modern British poster design, inspired by Cubism and Vorticism, working for such clients as Shell-Mex and BP, the General Post Office and Imperial Airways. His *Soaring to Success – the Early Bird* poster, used by the *Daily Herald*, epitomised Kauffer's aspirations as a designer. After the outbreak of World War II Kauffer, who married the designer Marian Dorn, returned to New York. Victoria & Albert Museum travelling exhibition in 1973.

Pat KAUFMAN 1950– Artist born in Chicago, Illinois, America, who worked in London from 1987. She gained an honours degree in fine arts from Goldsmiths' College, 1989. Group exhibitions included The Crypt, 1988; New Contemporaries, ICA, 1989; Flaxman Gallery and Whitechapel Open at Whitechapel Art Gallery, both 1990; Victoria Miro Gallery, 1992; and Sweet Home at Oriel Mostyn, Llandudno, and tour, 1994. Solo shows included Palazzo Ruini, Reggio Emilia, Italy, and Flaxman Gallery, both 1991. Doris Lockhart-Saatchi Collection and Caldic Collection, Rotterdam, hold examples.

Permindar KAUR 1965– Sculptor using a variety of materials such as cloth, iron, fabric and steel, born in Nottingham. Obtained a degree in fine art from Sheffield City Polytechnic, 1986–9, with a master's from Glasgow School of Art, 1990–2. Awards included a Visual Arts Grant from the British Council, 1994, and one from Banff Centre for the Arts, Calgary, 1995. Group shows included Starting Points, Mappin Art Gallery, Sheffield, 1991; Asian Arts Festival at Worcester City Art Gallery, 1993; Panfletos de Agricultura poster project organised by Transformadors, Barcelona, 1994; Veins, Galeria dels Angels, Barcelona, 1995; and British Art Show 4, and tour, 1995–6. Had a solo exhibition Red Earth at Harris Museum & Art Gallery, Preston, 1993, others including a series in Sweden, among them Hidden Witnesses, Galleri Amidol, Gothenburg, 1994.

Jim KAVANAGH 1960– Painter of romantic landscapes, born in east London, and teacher, who gained a fine art honours degree at Middlesex University, majoring in painting and printmaking, 1981–5. Taught foundation at West Thames College, but gave it up to paint full-time, being represented by Fine Art Promotions. Commissions included five pictures for Planet Designs Ltd, 1995, five more for the VWJ Building, 1996. Group exhibitions included Gagliardi Gallery, 1993; Beatrice Royal Gallery, Eastleigh, 1995; and Coombs Contemporary, 1997. Had a solo show with Black Bull Gallery, 1992, later ones including Lamont Gallery, 1997.

John F KAVANAGH 1903–1984 Portrait sculptor, born in Birr, King's County, Ireland. He studied at Liverpool School of Art, 1920–1, winning a scholarship to the Royal College of Art in 1925. He studied there, 1925–30, under Henry Moore, winning the Rome Scholarship in sculpture in 1930, living at British School in Rome, 1930–3. While teaching at Leeds College of Art, 1934–9, was made a member of RBS in 1935. Kavanagh's bronze Russian Peasant is held by Tate Gallery and his sensitive Wanda Tiburzzi is illustrated in the volume *RBS: Modern British Sculpture*, published in 1939. Notable among Kavanagh's public sculpture are the corner figures and reliefs for Walthamstow Town Hall. In 1951 he was appointed senior lecturer at Elam Fine Art School at New Zealand's Auckland University. Showed at RA and RHA.

Witold Grcjan KAWALEC 1922– Sculptor in various materials, born in Winlo, Poland. He served with the Polish forces in France and the Middle East, then as a fighter pilot with the Royal Air Force. Studied sculpture in Poland and Romania and after World War II at Nottingham University College and College of Art, where he became a visiting teacher. From 1951 he was a freelance sculptor, with well over 100 solo exhibitions in England. Kawalec's work was both figurative and abstract, notable for its spiritual intensity. He was a member of Free Painters and Sculptors, Exeter Art Society and the Kenn Group. Among venues shown at were Castle Museum, Nottingham; RA; Drian Galleries; Edinburgh Festival; and abroad. Kawalec was appointed sculptor to St Christopher's Hospice, Sydenham. He settled at Barnstaple Cross, Crediton, Devon, where there was a permanent display of his work at Dewsmoor Art.

Bob KAY 1907–1994 Painter who was born and bred in the Manchester area who worked first as an electrical engineer, later as an industrial designer. Even while serving in the Middle East with the Royal Air Force Kay continually sketched and painted. In the 1940s he was a member of Manchester Art Society, later joining and becoming patron of Manchester Graphic Club. Engineering equipment and dockyard scenes around the Manchester Ship Canal, trains and the city's back streets, many since demolished, were favourite subjects, as shown in a memorial exhibition at Salford Museum and Art Gallery, 1996.

Emma KAY 1968– Figurative artist who studied at Wimbledon School of Art, 1987–8; Glasgow School of Art, 1988–91; and with Maggi Hambling, Morley College, 1995–7. Also studied film-making, ceramics and sculpture. She gained an Elizabeth Greenshields Award; a Glasgow Film and Video Production Award, 1992; and was commended in the BP Portrait Award Exhibition, 1994. Varied film work, between 1991–3, included *Voyeurs, Persuasion* and *The Patient*. In 1990, Kay was commissioned to paint the Wimbledon football team after it won the Football Association cup in 1987. Solo exhibitions included Drawings from Life, Gallery M, 1997.

Nora KAY fl. from 1930s– Artist, designer, potter and teacher, working in a wide variety of media. After Wycombe High School she studied at St Martin's School of Art, where she also taught, and Royal College of Art, teachers including Ernest Tristram and Eric Ravilious. London Transport, book and ephemera publishers used her designs and she also produced children's books. Kay was a member of the Chartered Society of Designers and exhibited with NEAC, RBA and elsewhere. Lived for many years in Gerrards Cross, Buckinghamshire.

Pamela KAY 1939– Painter and draughtsman – notably still life and portraits – designer, illustrator, teacher and writer on art, born in Isle of Sheppey, Kent. She studied for four years at Canterbury College of Art under Christopher Alexander, Alec Vickerman and Eric Hurren, while working part-time for two years as studio assistant to John Ward (she was the model for his illustrations for Laurie Lee's *Cider with Rosie*). While at Canterbury she exhibited at RA in 1960. Concentrated also on textile design, winning a Sanderson wallpaper competition and having work shown at the Design Centre, and studied design at Royal College of Art for three years. After graduation she launched a freelance practice, producing paper and fabric designs. In mid-1970s, after marriage and children, Kay resumed painting and was eventually elected to RWS, RBA and NEAC. She had a series of solo shows, galleries including Medici, Chris Beetles, Catto and Richard Hagen in Broadway. Fantin-Latour, Chardin and Ingres were key influences. Taught part-time at School of Architecture, Canterbury, and wrote for *Leisure Painter* magazine. From 1988 Kay illustrated books, notably for children. Lived in Cliftonville, Kent.

Violet MacNeish KAY 1914–1965 Painter in oil and watercolour; teacher of art and crafts. Born in Glasgow, daughter of the artist James Kay, she studied at Glasgow School of Art, 1936, under William Somerville Shanks and W O Hutchison. Exhibited RSW, Paisley Institute, RSA and Glasgow Lady Artists' Club. The Pilgrim Trust and Paisley Corporation bought her work. Lived at Garelochhead, Dunbartonshire.

Marcus M KAYE 1898–1984 Sculptor, who gained a first-class degree in mechanical engineering at Cambridge University, simultaneously studying at Cambridge Municipal Art School, 1919–22. On graduating, Kaye joined Shell-Mex to specialize in industrial lubricants, staying until retirement. From 1927–30 Kaye studied with Bernard Meninsky at Westminster Art School. Showed regularly, notably with SPS, NS and at Summer Salon. Among his many commissioned works were a portrait sculpture for the Royal Air Force Club of Sir Barnes Wallis, inventor of the bouncing bomb, which breached the Ruhr dams in World War II. Phillips sold several of Kaye's works at auction in 1998.

Margaret KAYE 1912– Designer, collagist and teacher, born in Yorkshire. She trained at Croydon College of Art, where she studied textile design and stained glass. From 1937 she started a 38-year teaching career and began to show her collages. Exhibited around England, notably at Roland, Browse & Delbanco, and shared a show at Canon Gallery, Chichester, in 1991. In retirement continued to experiment with new techniques and materials, her work mixing reality and abstraction.

Mary KAYE: *see* **Mary WOODS**

Tony KAYE 1952– Conceptual artist and commercial film-maker, born in London. After a one-year course at St Albans School of Art, 1967–8, Kaye was a messenger boy at Horney Blowcox Freeman Advertising and John Camp Studios, 1969, did a two-year graphic design course at Medway School of Design, 1970–2, in 1973 painting as a fine artist and travelling abroad. In 1991 Kaye moved to Los Angeles, California, to set up Tony Kaye Films Inc, a re-emergence of The Wandering Jew, which he had run briefly in 1983. Since the early 1970s he had held a series of designing and art direction posts in England with various organisations, including being art director of Collett Dickenson Pearce, 1978–81. Kaye's list of international advertising awards from the early-1980s ran into several hundreds, including many golds, ranging from the Channel 4 Award for the Best Commercial in the

United Kingdom in 1986 to the British Television Awards Lifetime Achievement Award, 1997. Alongside his advertising work, Kaye pursued a vigorous career as a conceptual and fine artist at museums and alternative exhibition spaces in Europe and America in which he took "issues of widespread social concern – and hypocrisy – reframing them into new formats." Such was their shock value (they covered issues such as domestic violence, racism, homelessness and prejudice) that they elicited strong responses. Roger, a London tramp, was exhibited in and in front of such institutions as the Tate Gallery, National Gallery in Washington, The Louvre, Paris, and San Francisco Museum of Modern Art. With Don't be Scared, held in a Los Angeles hotel and an abandoned warehouse in London, Kaye presented an installation of four naked women and men living with Aids. For several years Kaye was immersed in a multimedia project addressing the topic of abortion. Kaye set up his own large art gallery in Los Angeles. In 1997, he was the subject of a Channel 4 Television *Arthouse* programme.

John KEANE 1954– Painter and printmaker, born in Hertfordshire. He studied at Camberwell School of Arts and Crafts, 1972–6. Keane was artist-in-residence at Whitefield School, 1985–6; completed a screenprint for Greenpeace, 1988; had a commissioned exhibition about Ollerton mining community for Nottinghamshire County Council, 1990–1; and a set of murals was painted for Salsa Celestina, Palace Theatre, Watford, 1993. He became popularly known as the result of his commission by Imperial War Museum in 1991 to cover the Gulf War as an official artist with the British Army. The pictures were shown in 1992 at the Museum, which acquired Mickey Mouse at the Front. Keane's many group appearances included Whitechapel Open from 1983; Artists Against Apartheid, Royal Festival Hall, 1986; Chicago Art Fair, 1987; Silkesborg Kunstmuseum, Copenhagen, 1988; and Lannon Cole Gallery, Chicago, 1991. After a solo show at Minsky's Gallery, 1980, he exhibited frequently in Britain and abroad, with Angela Flowers Gallery/Flowers East from 1985. Contemporary Art Society, provincial galleries and The Detroit Institute of Fine Art hold examples.

Tina KEANE 1946– Film and video artist, born in London, who studied at Hammersmith College of Art, 1967–70, and at Sir John Cass School of Art. Took part in extensive number of international film festivals. Was included in Women's Own at ICA, 1980; had a five-year retrospective at Third Eye Centre, Glasgow, 1982; video performance Bedtime Story was staged at St Paul's Gallery, Leeds, 1983; Circus Diver was put on at Spectrocolour Screen, Piccadilly, 1989; in 1990 was included in Signs of the Times at Museum of Modern Art, Oxford; and in 1996 in Freezeframe at Lamont Gallery.

Brian KEANY 1945– Artist in oil, acrylic and watercolour, and teacher, born in Forfar, Tayside. He attended Edinburgh College of Art, 1963–7, teachers including William Gillies, Robin Philipson, John Houston, Elizabeth Blackadder and William J L Baillie. Keany went on to teach art and design in the Fife region, settling in Glenrothes. He was elected a member of RSW in 1977. Mixed shows included RSA and Royal Glasgow Institute of the Fine Arts. Keany had a series of solo shows at Loomshop Gallery, Lower Largo, from 1976 and one at Fair Maid's House Gallery, Perth, 1987. The artist was commissioned to design a large tapestry for The Carnegie Trust, Dunfermline, in 1986, which involved lengthy weaving. Glen Pirie's The Kingdom of Fife included his work, which is in collections in Britain and abroad. Keany was commissioned by Velux UK to paint one of the fiftieth anniversary series it sponsored from each country in which it operated.

Joseph KEARNEY 1939– Painter, printmaker and teacher, born and lived in Glasgow, where he was a leading member of the Art Club. Kearney studied at Glasgow School of Art, 1957–61, teachers including Philip Reeves and John Miller. Exhibited at Royal Glasgow Institute of the Fine Arts, RP and RSA. Solo shows included Ewan Mundy Fine Art. Glasgow Museums and Art Galleries holds his work.

John KEATES 1915– Painter and teacher, born in Birkenhead, Cheshire. After attending the Birkenhead Institute he studied at Liverpool College of Art, 1933–8, then Central School of Arts and Crafts, teachers including Bernard Meninsky, 1946–7. In 1958 he gained a Liverpool Council for Education travel award. Keates was a principal lecturer at Liverpool Polytechnic until 1978. He was a member of the Liverpool Academy, also exhibiting at Free Painters and Sculptors, Manchester City Art Gallery, with Arts Council, Walker Art Gallery in Liverpool and elsewhere in the north of England. Had several one-man shows in 1960s. Walker Art Gallery and Southport's Atkinson Art Gallery hold examples. Lived in Southport, Lancashire.

John KEATING 1889–1977 Figure, portrait and landscape painter, born in Limerick, Ireland, where he received his first art training. Studied at the Dublin Metropolitan School of Art; won the Taylor Scholarship; then worked with William Orpen in London until 1916. Returned to Ireland, the base for most of his painting career. Exhibited RA, RSA, RHA – he was made an Hon. RA and Hon. RSA – Walker Art Gallery, Liverpool, and Royal Glasgow Institute of the Fine Arts. Became president of the RHA for a time. Is represented in many public collections in Ireland and overseas. Lived in Dublin, where he was professor of anatomy at the National College of Art.

Tom KEATING 1917–1984 Painter, draughtsman, restorer who gained notoriety as a faker/copyist of artists ranging from Rembrandt and Rubens to Constantin Guys and Degas, and especially Samuel Palmer. Born in London into poverty, Keating left school at 14 to become a house painter, yet nurtured a desire to paint. Invalided out of the Royal Navy, he eventually obtained a grant to study art at Goldsmiths' College, but failed his final diploma. Keating became a restorer, working on the epic frescoes at Marlborough House, perfecting his knowledge of style and technique. The sale of a batch of Keating fakes in a country auction room in the mid-1970s led to his exposure and a book about him and he was tried at the Old Bailey in 1978. But the case was dismissed when Keating had a motor cycle accident and was found to have a serious heart complaint. Keating became an art celebrity as the man who had fooled the experts, and a folk hero. He made two television series, had a successful exhibition of his own work at the Barbican and his work's value rose. After his death Keating's copies of famous pictures continued to fetch record prices. Lived in Dedham, Essex.

Helen KEATS 1947– Printmaker, born and lived in London, who gained an honours degree in fine art followed by postgraduate printmaking studies, attending Harrow School of Art, 1977–9, Wimbledon School of Art, 1979–84, then West Thames College, 1994. She was made a fellow of the Printmakers' Council in 1985. For a time she was a visiting artist at Wimbledon School of Art. Took part in numerous group exhibitions, including Stowells Trophy at RA, 1981; ROI at Mall Galleries, 1983; Open Exhibition at RE, from 1984; Royal Festival Hall, from 1986; Five Printmakers, National Theatre and Korean Gallery in Chicago, both 1989; Chelsea Arts Club Centenary, Smith's Gallery, 1991–2; and Battersea Contemporary Art Fair, 1993. Solo exhibitions include two at Ben Uri Art Society, which holds her work, 1987 and 1990, work in other collections including London University Institute of Education, Curwen Archives and Scarborough Art Gallery. Bomberg and the Slade were noted as influences.

Harry KEAY 1914– Painter in oil who studied at Dundee College of Art, 1930–7, under James McIntosh Patrick, then with James Cowie at Patrick Allan-Fraser School of Art, Hospitalfield, Arbroath, 1937–8. Keay exhibited RSA, Royal Glasgow Institute of the Fine Arts, SSA, RBSA and elsewhere. Lived in Dundee, Angus.

John E KEAY 1907– Artist, designer and illustrator, born in Birmingham. He attended the School of Art there on a scholarship for four years from the age of 13, did a two-year course in London and was then apprenticed to a Birmingham studio. Joined a studio in Toronto, Canada, drawing as a commercial artist and illustrator for magazines, in 1945 moving to New York, America, for similar work. Returned to England in 1962 and set up a studio in Chiswick, operating through Thompson Artists and Linden Artists. Keay's extensive client list included RCA, Listerine, Goodyear, Guinness and Black & Decker. The Kew Gardens dealer Peter Bennett handled the work of Keay, who in the late-1990s entered a nursing home.

V KEBBELL fl. c.1915–1955 Painter and draughtsman whose full name was William Francis Vere Kebbell. He studied at Byam Shaw and Vicat Cole School of Art. Was a portrait specialist and a member of PS, where he exhibited, also at RA, ROI, IS and Walker Art Gallery, Liverpool. Lived in London.

Graham KEDDIE 1958– Artist and teacher, whose work included constructions in various materials, including pigment. He did a foundation course at Ipswich School of Art, 1975–7; gained an honours degree in fine art at Camberwell School of Art, 1977–80; then did postgraduate studies at Brighton Polytechnic in art and design, 1982–3. In 1982 gained a Lloyds sponsorship to study southwest America and Mexican Indian reservations. Held a series of lectureships from 1980, latterly including Croydon College, 1986; Southend College, 1987; and Tresham Institute, Kettering, from 1988. Group exhibitions included South London Gallery, 1980; Alfred East Gallery, Kettering, 1986; David Holmes Gallery, Peterborough, 1992; and The Table Studio Group, The Living Room, 1996. Solo exhibitions included Sutton Place Heritage Trust, 1986, and Green Dragon, Brigstock, 1993. Lived in Kettering, Northamptonshire.

Eric James KEDWARDS 1905– Painter and teacher, born in Bridlington, Yorkshire. After private education he attended Birmingham College of Arts and Crafts, 1924–9, his teachers including B J Fletcher. Did book illustrations, especially of birds. Showed in the Birmingham area and lived at Walsall, Staffordshire, where he taught art at Queen Mary's School.

Arnold KEEFE 1911– Artist in oil, watercolour and egg tempera, and teacher, born in London, who studied at Chelsea School of Art, 1928–30, and Royal College of Art, 1930–4, teachers including Eric Ravilious, Edward Bawden, Malcolm Osborne, Percy Jowett, M C Oliver and Graham Sutherland for etching. Was art master at Battersea Grammar School; senior lecturer in art and craft at Wandsworth and Hampton Colleges of Education; head of department of graduate art teacher training at Goldsmiths' College of Art; then district inspector of art for Inner London Education Authority. He also lectured in adult institutes and was a university examiner. Was a member of Reigate Society of Artists and Royal College of Art Society, showing at RA, NEAC, RP and UA. Had a retrospective show in Woking, 1980, with a solo exhibition at Westcott Gallery, Surrey, 1990. His portrait commissions included the chairmen of Thermos Ltd and Mercantile Marine Credit Company. Lived in Wotton, Abinger Hammer, Surrey.

Rita KEEGAN 1949– Artist in a wide range of media, lecturer and administrator, in America born in the Bronx where she attended the New York City High School of Art & Design, 1964–7, gaining a degree in fashion illustration and costume design; obtained a diploma in early childhood development from Bronx Community College, 1968–9; then a fine arts degree from San Francisco Arts Institute, 1969–72. Lived in England from 1979, settling in London, where she lectured in historical and cultural studies at Goldsmiths' College from 1995, having from 1988–92 co-ordinated the Women Artists Slide Library, from 1992–4 being director, African and Asian Visual Artists Archive. Keegan said that in "exploring issues of identity and representation, the use of family narrative and autobiography featured strongly in my work." Exhibitions included Women's Work, Brixton Artists' Gallery, 1983–6; Trophies of Empire, Bluecoat Gallery, Liverpool, and tour, 1992; Time Museum, British Museum, 1994–5; also showing with 198 Gallery.

Geoffrey KEEN 1962– Gestural abstract painter, born in Bristol. He studied at the Polytechnic there, 1985–6, then Humberside College of Higher Education, 1986–9. In 1989 showed in winter exhibition at Ferens Art Gallery, Hull, and in European Art Schools Biennale, Antwerp. His canvas Inner City was included in John Moores Liverpool Exhibition, 1989–90. Lived in Hull, Yorkshire.

Walter Monckton KEESEY 1887–1970 Painter, printmaker, teacher and architect, born in Croydon, Surrey. Studied at Royal College of Art, where he finished in 1911. From 1913 was art master at the Architectural Association for a dozen years, apart from a period in Royal Engineers during World War I, winning the Military Cross. Keesey was a banknote and exhibition designer. Chelsea Arts Club member. Exhibited RA, RE, RSA and Walker Art Gallery, Liverpool. Lived in Edgbaston, Birmingham, and later in Cheltenham.

Moy KEIGHTLEY fl. from 1950s– Painter, notably a watercolourist, draughtsman and teacher, who studied at Chelsea School of Art, where she was awarded the Morland Lewis Travelling Scholarship. Went on to teach at Central St Martins College of Art & Design, was a tutor with the Open College of the Arts in 1988 and a consultant to the BBC Television series *Look, Look and Look Again*. Keightley said that her interest lay "in reconciling representation and abstraction ... The balance of marks and nuances of tone, colour and edge become critical in order to establish poetic qualities beyond topographical identity." Mixed shows included Browse & Darby, LG, Leicester Galleries, RA and RWS. Had a series of solo exhibitions at AIA Gallery from 1965, New Grafton Gallery from 1979 and Barbican Centre, 1994, where landscapes of Iceland, a favourite subject, were featured. Iceland Embassy, Nuffield Foundation and Westminster School hold examples.

Sam KEIL 1965– Figurative-Expressionist sculptor in bronze, whose work was inspired by classical dance and music, to which she worked, and the horse. She graduated with first-class honours from the City and Guilds Art School in 1991, where she won the Best Sculpture Award. She also gained a first prize in the Madame Tussaud Sculpture Competition and The Beckworth Travel Scholarship. After graduating, Keil worked in the scenery departments of leading theatre companies in Canada and America. She exhibited throughout Britain and North America and had a solo show at The Catto Gallery in 1997.

Bridget KEIR 1883–1954 Prolific watercolourist, born in London, daughter of an Army officer and cousin of the artists G A and A D Fripp. She began drawing and painting early; was educated in London, Paris and Boulogne; and was recommended for painting lessons to Claude Hayes, 1905. During 1911–13 Keir spent part of each year in Italy and she was especially fond of Venice, where she was taken up by the painter Clara Montalba. In 1913 she held her first London show, The Lagoons of Venice, spent six months in Egypt painting and had an exhibition in Paris at Galerie Georges Petit, 1914. During World War I Keir was in a concert party raising money for war hospitals, in 1917 spent some months drawing at Heatherley's School of Fine Art and began her Thames series. After the war she took a studio in Cheyne Walk, Chelsea, which remained her base although she travelled extensively. Mixed shows included SWA as a member, also RSW, RI, RHA, RSA, Royal Glasgow Institute of the Fine Arts and Dudley Gallery and she had a series of solo exhibitions at Walker's Galleries. After a period in Onslow Square Keir was moved to a nursing home in Surbiton in June 1954, where she died. Queen Mary was among owners of her pictures.

Harry KEIR 1902–1977 Painter and draughtsman, based in Glasgow, who left school at 14 to become a house painter and signwriter, attending evening classes at the School of Art. He painted the working-class areas of the city in sombre style and also sketched gypsies and travellers. Keir made illustrations for Edward Gaitens' *Gorbal Novels*, recording a fast-disappearing aspect of the city. Showed at RSA, Royal Glasgow Institute of the Fine Arts and elsewhere. He is featured in the sculptor Benno Schotz's autobiography *Bronze in my Blood*. The People's Palace and Kelvingrove Art Gallery in Glasgow hold Keir's work.

Isabella KELENY 1914– Painter born in Woking, Surrey. Brought up in Huntingdon, she was mainly self-taught as an artist, although she did attend schools part-time in Hampshire and Wiltshire. Showed at RI, SWA and NS and lived in London.

Charlotte KELL 1944– Artist in various media, and poet. She studied at Berkeley University, California; North London and Oxford Polytechnics; and University of London. She had a number of mixed show and solo appearances in Britain and America. In 1991 her mixed-media construction The Way Out was included in Art in Boxes at England & Co.

Lorna Beatrice KELL 1914– Painter of still life and abstracts, printmaker and textile designer, born in London. She studied at Hornsey School of Art, 1930–3, teachers including Russell Reeve, Frank Winter and Norman Janes. She joined Henry Lorraine Kell shortly after he began Lorraine Designs in 1935, married him and became sole proprietor in 1956. The firm specialised in commemorative scarves for Liberty of London, the Oxford Collection and others. Kell was elected to SGA in 1959, becoming its president, was a founder-fellow of the Society of Botanical Artists and a fellow of the Royal Horticultural Society, winning its Grenfell Medal. She produced botanical drawings for the *Junior Encyclopaedia Britannica*. Showed at RA, RE, London Guildhall, Paris Salon and in the provinces. Lived in Barnet, Hertfordshire.

Stephen KELLETT fl. from 1980s– Painter of landscape and abstracts using a wide range of media, born in Totnes, Devon. His extensive travels in several continents influenced his work. Kellett gained a diploma in art and social content at Dartington College of Arts, 1983–5, an honours degree at Exeter College of Art, 1985–7, and a postgraduate diploma in art therapy from St Albans College of Art and Design, 1990–1. Exhibitions included Birdwood House, Totnes, and Fulham Gallery, both 1988; The Heifer Gallery from 1989; and Chapel Gallery, Plymouth, 1989. From 1988 Kellett had a series of solo exhibitions at Lamont Gallery.

Diarmuid KELLEY 1972– Figurative painter, born in Scotland, who gained an honours degree in fine art at University of Newcastle, 1991–5, his master's at Chelsea School of Art, 1996. Awards included John Christie prize, at Newcastle, 1994; in 1995 he won the Annabel Walker prize there, first prize in the National Westminster Bank Young Artist Competition (the Bank holds his work) and was runner-up, BP Portrait Award, National Portrait Gallery. Group exhibitions included Northern Graduates, Royal College of Art, 1995; Art and Academia, Christie's, 1996; and in 1998 Modern British Art at Offer Waterman & Co, which later that year gave Kelley his first solo show.

Anthony-Noël KELLY 1995– Artist in mixed media, and teacher, nephew of the Duke of Norfolk, who made legal history in 1998 when he was sentenced to nine months' imprisonment (on appeal cut to three) at Southwark Crown Court, London, where he lived, the first time anyone had been charged with stealing a body or its parts. These were smuggled out of the Royal College of Surgeons, to which they had been donated. Silver-coated sculptures by Kelly, based on casts of such parts, were offered during the Art97 contemporary art fair, at the Business Design Centre, Islington, early in 1997. Kelly's agent was the dealer Jibby Beane. Kelly taught sculpture at the Prince of Wales Institute of Architecture. He had early developed an interest in human anatomy. As well as training as a butcher, working in an abattoir, he had studied as an artist at Heatherley's School of Fine Art. Kelly was apprenticed to a restorer, and spent several years working for private clients. To improve his knowledge, he sketched operations in North Hampshire Hospital, Basingstoke.

Brian KELLY 1946– Artist and teacher, born in Renfrewshire, who studied printmaking and painting at Glasgow School of Art from 1973. He taught lithography at Glasgow Print Studio, 1977–9; was in London, painting, 1980; then for a time was a technician in silkscreen at Glasgow School of Art from 1981. Kelly took part in a number of group shows around this time, including Scottish Print Open Three, 1983, organised by Dundee Printmakers' Workshop.

Deirdre KELLY 1962– Artist, notably a printmaker, and teacher who studied at Wimbledon School of Art, 1984–7, earning a master's degree in printmaking. She gained a Sericol Purchase Prize in 1986, an Atlantis Purchase Prize in 1987 and a Whatman Paper Prize in 1988. As well as mixed shows, including In Piper's Footsteps, at New Academy Gallery, 1993, had solo shows at Bristol Polytechnic, 1987, and Intaglio Printmaker Gallery the same year. Was a member of RE, a screenprinting tutor for Islington Adult Education Centre and a visiting lecturer at South Thames College and Middlesex Polytechnic. King's College School and Sedgwick Group International hold her work.

Felix KELLY 1916–1994 Painter in oil, book illustrator, set designer and muralist. His work had a strong Neo-Romantic flavour. Kelly was born in Auckland, New Zealand, and moved to London, where he eventually settled, in 1935. He worked for the advertising agency Lintas as a layout man until 1939, served in the Royal Air Force during World War II, then returned briefly to Lintas. While still in the Air Force he had begun to paint seriously and in 1943 Lefevre gave him the first of a series of solo shows. A commission prompted Kelly to become a professional painter in 1947 and he worked for a time in America, exhibiting there successfully. Kelly then had series of shows with Leicester Galleries, Arthur Jeffress Gallery, Tooth and Partridge (Fine Arts). He became known as a painter of country houses in England and America, travelled extensively and had a special interest in all types of floating craft and waterways. Among Kelly's book illustrations were Herbert Read's *The Green Child*, 1945, and a series by Elizabeth Burton starting with *The Elizabethans at Home*, 1958. His play sets included *A Day by the Sea*, by N C Hunter, with Sir John Gielgud, and *The Merchant of Venice*, by Shakespeare, for The Old Vic Company. Murals included notable liners such as Union Pacific's *Windsor Castle*, the Royal Palace at Katmandu, Nepal, and Queen's Ice Skating Club. The Earl of Dalkieth, Sir Herbert Read and Viscount Leverhulme owned his work. Read published a monograph on *Paintings by Felix Kelly* in 1946.

Fleur KELLY 1950– Versatile artist and designer notable for fresco murals and egg tempera panel painting, and teacher, born in New Jersey, America, of British nationality. Kelly had a special interest in authentic materials as used in historical art works because of their aesthetic and lasting qualities. She did a pre-diploma course at Somerset College of Art, Taunton, 1968; typographic design at Camberwell College of Arts and Crafts, 1969; followed by painting and pottery at High Wycombe College of Art, 1970–2; then in 1987 undertook an intensive course in fresco technique with Leonetto Tintori at his school in Prato, Italy. Teaching included Workers' Educational Association at Soundwell Technical College, Bristol; being artist-in-residence, Verulamium Museum, St Albans; and fresco technique at Centro d'Arte Verrocchio, Siena. Although many have since studied the technique, Kelly was one of the later pioneers in the fresco revival in Britain. Works included an apsidal dome in egg tempera and two wooden panels for St Augustine's, Swindon; reconstruction fresco project from Romano-British fragments at Verulamium; reconstruction of paintings at St Thomas' Tower in the Tower of London; two domes in buon fresco for new Rural Economy buildings at St John's College, Oxford; plus many private commissions. Lived in Bath, Avon.

Francis KELLY 1927– Painter, conservator and writer, born in St Paul, Minnesota, America. After serving in United States Navy, 1944–8, entered Art Centre School, Los Angeles. During 1951–2 Kelly lived in Paris, attending L'Académie de la Grande Chaumière; in 1953 he went to the University of Hawaii, Honolulu; then to University of California, Los Angeles, where he was graphic laboratory assistant to John Paul Jones. Awarded a Fulbright Grant in 1955 Kelly entered the graphic department of Central School of Arts and Crafts. In 1958 Kelly was awarded the Stacey Grant for painting, in 1966 being appointed art organiser for the American Embassy's Festival of Arts and Humanities. His paintings were shown in the subsequent exhibition Five American Artists in Britain, his etchings having been introduced at St George's Gallery in the mid-1950s. During 1976 Kelly helped Winsor & Newton with a show of American artists for the bicentennial. Kelly studied conservation at the Courtauld Institute and in 1967 he was sent by the Italian Art and Archives Rescue Fund to Florence to restore flood-damaged paintings. He published *Art Restoration* in 1971, then *The Studio and the Artist* in 1975. The lesser-known British landscape, rivers and waterways were key features of Kelly's pictures, which were shown at several dozen British museums and in many galleries. Ashmolean Museum in Oxford, Glasgow University, Los Angeles County Museum and New York Public Library hold examples. Lived in London.

Gerald KELLY 1879–1972 Painter in oil of portraits and landscapes. Born in London, he was educated at Cambridge, then lived and studied art in Paris for several years. Whistler was an early influence. Kelly was an enthusiastic traveller, visiting among other countries Spain, America, South Africa and Burma, where he painted some of his most characteristic and charming figure studies. He became known as a sound academic painter of attractive children and elegant women, untroubled by psychological insight, reliable. Represented in many public collections, including the Tate Gallery. He had retrospective exhibitions at the Leicester Galleries in 1950 and in 1957 at the Royal Academy. He was elected RA in 1930, was its keeper 1943–5 and president, 1949–54. Kelly held a number of official positions, such as his membership of the Royal Fine Arts Commission, 1938–43, and was knighted in 1945. Lived in London.

Kenness George KELLY: *see* **FOWOKAN**

Mary KELLY 1941– Artist working in mixed media, born in America. After studying at the College of St Teresa, Minnesota, 1959–63, then at Pius XII Institute, Florence, 1963–5, Kelly taught fine art at the American University in Beirut, Lebanon, after which she moved to England, undertaking postgraduate study at St Martin's School of Art 1968–70. In 1973, the year she received the Greater London Arts Association Fellowship, Kelly began work on her key work *Post-Partum Document*, which aimed to "expose the fetishistic function of representation". *Footnotes and Bibliography, Post-Partum Document* appeared in 1977, when Kelly gained an Arts Council Award. The Lina Garnade Memorial Foundation Award followed in 1978. Kelly took part in a number of exhibitions with sociological themes. She had a solo show at ICA in 1976, two more soon after at Museum of Modern Art, Oxford, and Leeds University Gallery. Taught at Camberwell School of Art and at Goldsmiths' College School of Art. Arts Council holds her work. Lived in London.

Maurice KELLY 1920– Representational painter, born in Bournemouth, Hampshire, who studied at Royal College of Art. He was a member of The Suffolk Group and showed with Young Contemporaries, Gallery 44 in Aldeburgh, Digby Gallery in Colchester and Warwick University Arts Centre. Kelly's work is held in the South African government's World War II collection, by several education authorities and in many British and foreign private collections. Lived in Walberswick, Suffolk.

Mick KELLY 1949– Painter of domestic scenes who was born in Wallasey, Cheshire. He studied at Camberwell School of Arts and Crafts, 1969–71, Goldsmiths' College School of Art, 1976–77, returning there in the early-1980s for his master's degree. Among Kelly's shows was a solo exhibition at Woodlands Art Gallery, 1981. Much of his work was in private collections.

Percy KELLY 1918–1993 Painter, draughtsman, printmaker and teacher, born in Workington, Cumberland, into a strongly religious background, his father a carpenter. He could "draw with a pencil before I could talk". From 1932 became a telegraph messenger in 1934 postal and telegraph officer for Kendal. In the Army in World War II drew maps and diagrams and was influenced by the work of Paul Klee, Graham Sutherland, Stanley Spencer and C F Tunnicliffe, seen in exhibitions. In 1946 he resumed Post Office duties, showing at RA, RI, RBA, RSA and elsewhere. Kelly resigned from Post Office in 1958, taught part-time and took up printmaking. From 1961–5, having raised £500, studied lithography and printed textiles at Carlisle College of Art and Design, obtaining distinctions, in 1964 gaining a travel scholarship to Brittany. Worked on commission for Sir Nicholas Sekers' silk mills at Hensingham, Whitehaven, having a solo show there at Rosehill Theatre in 1966, another at Fermoy Gallery, King's Lynn, in 1969. From 1970 Kelly's life was unsettled, with two divorces, health and financial problems. In 1980 settled in Attleborough, Norfolk, dying in hospital. A show of his landscapes was held at Castlegate House, Cockermouth, Cumbria, in 1994.

Roger KELLY 1973– Painter, born in Nottingham, who won a fine art degree at Wimbledon School of Art, 1993–6, attending Chelsea College of Art, 1996–7. Had a residency at Royal Court Theatre, 1994, the year of the exhibition Coming on Strong, at the Theatre with tour. Also appeared in Cooltan Summer Exhibition at Cooltan Arts, 1993; New Contemporaries, at Tate Gallery in Liverpool and Camden Arts Centre, and Nerve, at Jason and Rhodes Gallery, both 1996; and in the 1997–8 John Moores Liverpool Exhibition.

Steve KELLY 1952– Sculptor and teacher who attended Doncaster College of Art, St Martin's School of Art and Goldsmiths' College School of Art. He was an art teacher, 1976–81, a part-time lecturer in sculpture at North Essex School of Art, 1981–7, and from then lectured in sculpture full-time at South-East Essex College of Arts & Technology. Showed in New Contemporaries, 1974; Saffron Walden Corn Exchange from

1977; Beecroft Gallery, Southend-on-Sea from 1988; and in Drawing Towards Sculpture at Isis Gallery, Leigh-on-Sea, 1993.

Robert KELSEY 1949– Painter in oil notable for his lively, colourful landscapes of Britain and France. Born in Glasgow he studied at the School of Art there and went on to exhibit with Glasgow Art Club, Paisley Institute of Fine Arts and Royal Glasgow Institute of the Fine Arts. In 1993 completed five landscapes of the Turnberry course used for the 1994 British Open Golf Championship, for hanging in the clubhouse. Was included in Contemporary Art From Scotland at Thompson's Gallery, 1993, and had a solo exhibition at John Martin of London, 1996.

Kalman KEMENY 1896–1994 Artist, critic and teacher, born in Nagykanizsa, Hungary, his daughter being the artist Lydia Kemeny. He was mainly a portrait, landscape and still life artist in oil, but also made pottery. Studied at the Academy of Art, Budapest, 1913–14; was an official war artist to the Austro-Hungarian Army in World War I; and attended Academy of Creative Arts, Vienna, 1920–3, followed by a two-year post-graduate course. Between 1925–38 Kemeny lived in Pilsen, Czechoslovakia, moving to London in the latter year. During World War II while practising as an artist he worked in an aircraft factory and at fire-watching. From 1947–79 Kemeny taught at Hammersmith College of Art and for some years was advisor to the House of Commons Fine Art Committee. Took part in mixed shows at Cooling and Leger Galleries and at Roland, Browse & Delbanco. Had a retrospective in 1991 at Ben Uri Art Society which, like Imperial War Museum, holds his work.

Lydia KEMENY fl. from 1940s– Designer, illustrator, artist and teacher, daughter of the painter Kalman Kemeny, who studied design – fashion/textiles at St Martin's School of Art, 1942–4, then at Royal College of Art, 1944–7. While at College she won the *Vogue* Talent Contest, joining the magazine after graduation, working as an illustrator of fashion reports from London and abroad. Concurrently, Kemeny was invited to teach at St Martin's School of Art, where from 1976 she was head of department fashion/textiles; the department acquired an international reputation. Kemeny was in 1988 made reader in fashion at The London Institute and from 1989–90 was fashion tutor at Middlesex Polytechnic. She was fashion consultant to the television series *The House of Elliot* in 1993. As an artist she showed at RA, LG, NEAC, the Leicester, Savage and John Whibley Galleries and at Paris Salon. Paintings were acquired by the Ministry of Education, Greater London Council, Hertfordshire County Council and were reproduced by the New York Graphic Society and Medici Gallery. Lithographs were commissioned by Curwen Press for Collectors Guild. Lived in London.

David KEMP 1945– Sculptor and assemblage artist, born in London, who spent his childhood in Canada and attended a boys' grammar school in England. He joined the Merchant Navy for four years, then studied painting at Farnham and Wimbledon Schools of Art. In the early 1970s he moved to west Cornwall and pursued sculpture. He scouted the countryside for old farm machinery and industrial scrap and from this created strange beasts and insects. The Arts Council's The Beetle and its The Electro-Griffin are good examples. Northern Arts and public galleries in Glasgow, Manchester, Sheffield and Wolverhampton hold Kemp's work. Kemp was artist-in-residence at several sites where he would construct his witty creations "as a future archaeologist reconstructing the machines and artefacts of a distant past". Among notable group shows were the Welsh Sculpture Trust's Margam exhibition Sculpture in a Country Park, 1983, and A Quality of Light, at The Tate at St Ives and other venues, 1997. Solo shows included Graves Art Gallery, Sheffield; Manchester City Art Gallery, Glynn Vivian Art Gallery, Swansea; and McLellan Galleries, Glasgow. Kemp had a major setback in 1995 when vandals broke into his workshop, started a fire and destroyed nearly 20 years' work. Notable public sculptures by Kemp are The Iron Horse, for Four Lane Ends Metro Station, Newcastle upon Tyne; The Navigators, Hays Galleria, London Bridge; The Old Transformers, Consett; and Old King Coal, Pelton Fell.

Jeka KEMP 1876–1967 Watercolourist and woodcut artist, born in Bellahouston, Glasgow; she hated the name Jacobina given her, shortening it to Jeka. Details of her early life are vague, but she probably studied painting in Glasgow and London, about 1903–4 attending Académie Julian, Paris. She embarked on wide travels to paint, including Europe and North Africa, but showed at first in Scotland from about 1907, having solo exhibitions at Macindoe's Gallery, Glasgow, 1912–14. Several of her pictures were bought by the French government. During World War I Kemp worked as a nurse-masseuse in Paris hospitals. Further shows included Marcel Bernheim, Paris, and Warneuke's Galleries, Glasgow, 1920, and Galerie de la Librairie de la Presse, Nantes, 1922. Kemp continued to live in France until she returned to England in 1939, living with her sisters in Dorset, finally in Eastbourne, Sussex. She had given up painting in 1927, but her reputation was revived by a show at Belgrave Gallery and Wellington Fine Art, Glasgow, in 1977.

Richard KEMP 1958– Abstract painter, born in Croydon, Surrey, where he studied at the College of Art and Design, 1974–6, then Ravensbourne College of Art and Design, 1977–80. Among group show appearances were New Contemporaries, at ICA, 1979; LG, 1985; Carpenter's Road Open Studios from 1988; Pomeroy Purdy Gallery from same year; and John Moores Exhibition, Liverpool, 1991–2. He had a solo show at Greenwich Theatre Art Gallery in 1984. Lived in London.

Jake KEMPSELL 1940– Sculptor and teacher, born in Dumfries, Scotland, who remained close to his Scottish roots. He studied at Edinburgh College of Art and from 1965–75 lectured in sculpture there. He later lectured at Duncan of Jordanstone College of Art, Dundee. Kempsell did much to promote sculpture in Scotland, being a director of Workshop and Artists' Studio Provision; in 1978 he was one of the founders of the Scottish

Sculpture Trust. He showed widely in Scotland and Britain, being featured in Small Sculpture from the Collection of The Scottish Arts Council, 1978, and in the Welsh Sculpture Trust's 1983 show Sculpture in a Country Park, at Margam. Kempsell found his organic materials – wood, slate, stone and feathers – on the shore of the North Sea and in the fields and woodyards of Angus. These were arranged in enigmatic forms, such as his Love Child of the Butterfly that Ravished an Elephant, on the ski slopes of Glenshee.

Kim KEMPSHALL 1934– Printmaker, painter and teacher, full name Hubert Kim Kempshall, signing work K K, who was born in Manchester. Studied at the College of Art there, 1951–5, then Royal College of Art, 1957–60. Went on to teach fine art at Birmingham Polytechnic. Showed RA, RSA, Arts Council and held solo exhibitions. Scottish National Gallery of Modern Art and a number of provincial public collections hold his work. Lived in Harborne, Birmingham.

William KEMPSTER 1914– Painter and mural artist, notably in tempera, born in London. Studied at Wimbledon School of Art under Gerald Cooper and William Sullivan, 1937–9, then Royal College of Art, 1939–42, where his teachers included Ernest Tristram. He did a great deal of exhibition work for Central Office of Information and Festival of Britain in 1951, illustrating aspects of British life and work. Lived in London.

Lucy KEMP-WELCH 1869–1958 Painter, illustrator and teacher, outstanding for her pictures of horses. Was born in Bournemouth, Hampshire, older sister of painter Edith Kemp-Welch, who died in 1941. After attending the local School of Art, the sisters from 1891 studied with Hubert von Herkomer at his school in Bushey, Hertfordshire, where she settled. She ran it from 1905–26, initially as Bushey School of Painting and, after it moved to her house, as the Kemp-Welch School of Animal Painting. From 1928 her friend and assistant Marguerite Frobisher continued under the name The Frobisher School of Art. Kemp-Welch had early success with her student work Gypsy Drovers taking Horses to a Fair, hung at RA in 1895. She was a prolific exhibitor, notably at Fine Art Society, RCamA of which she was a member, as she was of RI, ROI, RBC and RBA; in 1914 she was president of the Society of Animal Painters. Refused permission to be a war artist in World War I, Kemp-Welch responded with the famous recruiting poster *Forward!* Kemp-Welch was an expert horsewoman and in her late-fifties began her travels with Sanger's Circus. Had a solo show at Arlington Gallery, 1938. Tate Gallery, Russell-Cotes Art Gallery and other public collections hold Kemp-Welch's pictures, which were latterly extensively sold by David Messum. Illustrated several books, notably Anna Sewell's *Black Beauty*, using Baden-Powell's horse Black Prince as a model. Died in Watford, Hertfordshire.

Margaret KEMP-WELCH fl. from 1890s–1968 Painter, printmaker and teacher, born in London, cousin of the artists Lucy and Edith Kemp-Welch. She studied with Frank Short and Hubert von Herkomer at his school in Bushey, Hertfordshire, from 1891. Went on to teach at Clapham High School. She showed with Ridley Art Club, RA, RE and elsewhere. Lived in London for many years, then at Throwleigh, Devon. Bushey Museum holds good examples of her prints.

KEN: *see* **Kenneth AITKEN**

Alice KENDALL 1896–1955 Painter and musician, born in Little Hulton, Lancashire. She studied at Manchester College of Music; and art in New York and at Edinburgh College of Art, where her teachers included David Foggie and Gerald Moira. Showed at UA and SEA, of both of which she was a member, SSA, RBA and RI. Mrs Kendall, who painted in several European countries, was the mother of the artist Alice Rebecca Kendall. Died in Cyprus, where she painted.

Alice Rebecca KENDALL fl. from early 1940s– Painter, muralist, illustrator and writer, daughter of the artist Alice Kendall, born in New York. She studied at Edinburgh College of Art. Kendall was a member of SWA and Royal Glasgow Institute of the Fine Arts as well as Royal Zoological Society in Scotland. Her published work included a book for children, *Funny Fishes*, and contributions to *Punch* and *Poetry Review*. Showed at RA, NEAC and Paris Salon and shared several shows with her mother at Cooling Galleries in 1940s and 1950s. Completed murals for British Council and Ministry of Labour. Lived in London for many years.

Dinah Roe KENDALL 1923– Painter and printmaker, born in Bakewell, Derbyshire. Her output included Biblical scenes in a bright palette updated to the present day, influenced by Stanley Spencer, as in her solo show at Duncan Campbell Contemporary Art, 1995. During World War II, Kendall nursed for the Red Cross. Attended Sheffield School of Art, 1946–8, then the Slade School of Fine Art, 1948–51, teachers including A H Gerrard and William Coldstream. Family needs stopped her painting until 1968, then she studied printmaking, 1968–72 with Anthony Gross and Stanley Jones. She returned to Sheffield, Yorkshire, in 1993, having bought a house in Cyprus and lived there from 1988. Group exhibitions included Graves Art Gallery, Sheffield, from 1962; Beecroft Art Gallery, Southend-on-Sea, 1971; and CCA Gallery, Cambridge, 1995. In 1976 she shared a show with her daughter, Emma Chandler, at the Bury St Edmunds Gallery. Later solo exhibitions included Oundle School, Oundle, 1996.

Kay Thetford KENDALL fl. from 1970s– Sculptor and sculptural jewellery creator working in a variety of precious and non-precious materials, notable for her cats and mythical creatures. She was born in Manchester and studied at Malvern and Tunbridge Wells Colleges of Art and at Hertfordshire College of Art and Design, 1976–9. Was for a time in charge of design firm KTK Ltd. She was a member of SWA and RMS, in 1986 winning RMS's Bidder and Borne sculpture award; also exhibited at SPS; and had a series of solo exhibitions in Welwyn Garden City, Hertfordshire, where she lived, elsewhere in south of England and in Italy.

Alistair KENDRY 1957– Painter who studied at Hereford College of Art, 1979, Bath Academy of Art, 1980–3, and Slade School of Fine Art, 1986–8. He gained a Southern Arts Award in 1987, a Barclays Bank Award in 1988. Took part in many group shows from early-1980s, including Whitworth Art Gallery, Manchester, 1981; Stowells Trophy at RA, 1982; York Festival, 1984; and Six of the Best at Christopher Hull Gallery, 1989.

David KENNARD 1953– Painter, printmaker and teacher, born in Beaconsfield, Buckinghamshire, who studied at Marlborough College, 1967–71, winning a travel scholarship for arts studies in 1972, using it for travel to Italy, 1974. After language studies at the Sorbonnne, Paris, and travelling and painting in France, 1971, Kennard did a foundation course at Gloucestershire College of Art and Design, 1972–3; gained a first-class honours degree from Bristol Polytechnic, 1973–6, fine art specialising in painting; then did postgraduate studying in printmaking, City and Guilds Art School, 1980–1; with a study period in Paris in 1987, in the studio of Patrick Betaudier, concentrating on the science and practice of oil painting from van Eyck through to the early Renaissance. In 1976 Kennard was awarded first prize in South Western Regional Competition, for art students, Winsor and Newton Award. Teaching experience included Harrow School, Symondsbury College and School of Art. Travelled extensively, including Albania, East Africa and French West Africa. As well as many mixed show appearances, Kennard held a steady stream of solo exhibitions, starting with a studio show at Guiting Power, 1978. Later ones included Archeus Fine Art from 1994, and Jerram Gallery, Salisbury, 1995. A deft and colourful impression of a scene characterised Kennard's work. Lived in Dorset.

Alexander Grieve KENNEDY 1889–c.1962 Painter, illustrator and writer, born in Liverpool. Studied at Liverpool School of Art and Royal College of Art. Exhibited widely in the provinces and did animal illustrations for books published by Blackie. Usher Gallery, Lincoln, holds his work, sometimes signed A Maculric. Lived in Lincoln and exhibited with the Lincolnshire Artists' Society.

Cecil KENNEDY 1905–1997 Painter in oil, noted for his meticulous pictures of flowers, based on arrangements by his wife Winifred, a ladybird being a common feature. He was the grandson of an artist who had worked alongside Corot in France, Cecil's father was the painter and designer Thomas Robert Kennedy, his brother the artist Thomas Kennedy. He was born in Leyton, Essex, and studied art in London, Paris, Antwerp and Zürich. During Army service on the continent in World War II, Kennedy was able to meet Flemish painters and study their and Dutch painters' work first-hand. He showed at RA, RSA, RHA, Fine Art Society, Paris Salon (where he won a Silver Medal in 1956, a Gold in 1970), the provinces and elsewhere abroad. Queen Mary, the Duke of Windsor, the Astors and newspaper magnate Lord Thomson of Fleet were among his patrons. Public galleries in Rochdale and Merthyr Tydfil hold examples. Owing to advanced age, Kennedy finished painting around 1993. Lived in St Albans, Hertfordshire.

Cedric KENNEDY 1898–1968 Landscape and portrait painter and teacher, born in Exeter, Devon, educated at Rugby School. Served in the Royal Flying Corps in World War I (completed a series of aerial pictures), was shot down and made a prisoner of war. Studied under Richard Jack at London School of Art, Florence School of Art in 1923 and Royal Academy Schools with Charles Sims, 1925–8. After teaching at Rugby, Kennedy taught at Cheltenham College and nearby at Dean Close School, served in camouflage during World War II, then returned to Dean Close, 1945–62. Exhibited at RA, NEAC, extensively at Walker's and Cooling Galleries. There was a big memorial show at Cheltenham, 1969; one at Mannings, 1972; another at Sally Hunter Fine Art, 1997. Victoria & Albert Museum, Ashmolean Museum in Oxford, Imperial War Museum and various provincial collections hold examples.

Chris KENNEDY fl. from 1980s– Mixed media artist who exhibited widely in the northwest of England. He was an artist-in-residence at Walker Art Gallery in Liverpool for a period in 1990 and several years later completed his master's degree at Winchester School of Art. In 1992 he was included in Bluecoat Artists '92, work by members of the Bluecoat Artists' Association in Liverpool, at Williamson Art Gallery & Museum in Birkenhead.

Richard KENNEDY 1910–1989 Painter, draughtsman and writer, born in Cambridge. He was educated at Marlborough School, left at 16 and joined the Hogarth Press as apprentice, the story of which he told in the volume of autobiography *A Boy at the Hogarth Press*, 1972; in 1977 he followed this with *A Parcel of Time*. After a period in an advertising agency and as an illustrator for *Strang's Weekly News* and brief studies including Central School of Arts and Crafts, during World War II service in Royal Air Force commenced his career as a book illustrator which was to encompass dozens of volumes, chiefly for children. Exhibitions included Gallery Edward Harvane, 1972, and King Street Gallery, 1981, with additional shows at his home in Maidenhead, Berkshire. He was influenced by the work of Henri Gaudier-Brzeska and Henri Matisse.

Thomas KENNEDY 1900–1982 Painter in oil and watercolour, born in Leyton, east London, who made a successful living by his brush from 16 to 80. His brother was the flower painter Cecil Kennedy, their father the artist Robert Thomas Kennedy, and grandfather Thomas Kennedy of Edinburgh. As well as studying at art school in London, for many years Thomas worked in the British Museum, Turner, Constable and Italian and Dutch Old Masters being special influences. His work was often reproduced and he showed at RA, RSA, RBSA and with Frost & Reed. HM Queen Elizabeth The Queen Mother bought Kennedy's work, which is in many private collections in Britain and abroad. Lived in Chingford, Essex, and died in Whipps Cross Hospital, Leytonstone.

George R KENNERLEY fl. from 1950– Naturally talented self-taught painter and collector with a strong enthusiasm for art which he combined with an active business career in Liverpool, being a director of Vernons Pools. He was a friend of John Moores and assembled a collection that included works by Vuillard, Bonnard, Bomberg, de Staël and his friend William Scott, with whom he painted at Corsham School of Art and St Ives, Cornwall. Kennerley also made collages, as in his Crane Kalman solo show, 1970, from which Walker Art Gallery acquired one of its works by him. Williamson Art Gallery in Birkenhead and House of Commons also hold examples. Kennerley had a solo show at Cadogan Contemporary in 1993, mixed exhibition appearances including RA Summer Exhibition, Leicester Galleries and Browse & Darby. Lived in Caldy, Wirral, Cheshire.

George KENNETHSON 1910–1994 Sculptor, born in Richmond, Surrey, as Arthur George Mackenzie. Was married to the painter Eileen Guthrie, one of their five children being the photographer Nicholas Mackenzie. Kennethson studied painting at Royal Academy Schools, 1928–34, turning to sculpture in 1937. Kennethson carved stone directly, using only simple sculptural drawings. The nature of the stone influenced his idea of what the finished work would be. His constant subject matter was birds, plants, heads, sky and sea, and his style, influenced by Gaudier-Brzeska and Brancusi, changed little. Much of his work was modest in size. He was an infrequent exhibitor, but had retrospectives at University of Birmingham, 1974; New Art Centre, 1988; and Pallant House, Chichester, 1993. From the mid-1950s Kennethson lived in Oundle, Northamptonshire, in a Victorian house next to a former brewery which contained more than 300 sculptures made over 40 years. Kettle's Yard in Cambridge and the Scottish National Gallery of Modern Art, Edinburgh, hold examples.

James Smyth KENNETT 1915– Painter and draughtsman, by profession a harbour official. Born and lived in Belfast, where he graduated in commercial science after studies at Queen's University. Studied art in London in mid-1940s and at RUA and exhibited in Belfast.

John KENNEY 1911–1972 Painter and book illustrator who specialised in hunting and sporting scenes. After being educated in Leicester and attending the School of Art there Kenney became a commercial illustrator. It was after World War II that Kenney turned to sporting art, drawing on hunting scenes from his locality. Towards the end of his life he lost the sight of one eye, which added problems to years of ill-health, but he kept on working. He showed at Gadsby Gallery, Leicester, 1963, a posthumous exhibition being held in 1980. In the year of his death Abercrombie and Fitch, New York, held a show. The Royal Artillery Museum, Woolwich, holds sketches by Kenney completed during his Army service.

Eric KENNINGTON 1888–1960 Sculptor, draughtsman and painter. Born in London, son of the artist T B Kennington, he studied at Lambeth School of Art and the City and Guilds School. Exhibited from 1908 at the RA; also showed at Leicester Galleries, Fine Art Society, Goupil Gallery, ROI and RP. Kennington was an official war artist, 1916–19, after being invalided out of the Army. The experience was to have a marked influence on his work, his first one-man show at the Goupil Gallery, 1916, of the Kensingtons at Laventie creating a great impression and identifying him in the public mind with depictions of men of action. Soon after the war he travelled in Arabia to illustrate T E Lawrence's *Seven Pillars of Wisdom*, and he was to draw memorable studies of Lawrence over many years. During World War II a book of Kennington's portraits, *Drawing the RAF*, 1942, including his typically incisive studies, further linked him with the forces, as had his sculptures, the memorial to the 24th Division at Battersea Park and the British memorial at Soissons, France, after World War I. Also completed a head of T E Lawrence in St Paul's Cathedral, London, and carvings on the Royal Shakespeare Memorial Theatre, Stratford-upon-Avon. Signed work E H K. Elected RA, 1959. Died at Reading, Berkshire.

Sue KENNINGTON 1955– Painter, born in London, who gained an honours degree in humanities from Middlesex Polytechnic, 1979–82, then was at Chelsea College of Art, 1989–94. Exhibitions included Summer Exhibition at University Gallery, Newcastle upon Tyne, 1993; Small Works at Argile Gallery and Spirit of Place, Piece Hall Gallery in Halifax, both 1994; Tricycle Gallery and Pacesetters at Peterborough Museum and Art Gallery, both 1995; and New Contemporaries, at Tate Gallery, Liverpool and Camden Arts Centre, 1996.

Jenny KENNISH 1944– Self-taught sculptor in porcelain of wild flowers and animals, born in Ewell, Surrey. From 1965–90 she was a schoolteacher, then was self-employed as an artist. Was a member of RMS and SWA and a founder-member of the Society of Botanical Artists, showing at Mall and Westminster Galleries. Kennish said that her "chief influence has been my surroundings. I have always been fortunate and lived in a rural environment." Lived in Little London, Hampshire.

Chris KENNY 1959– Painter, creator of artist's boxes and books and collage "poetry", and teacher, born in Fleet, Hampshire. He studied at Courtauld Institute of Art, 1979–82, then became an artist and part-time teacher. Surrealism was one influence on Kenny's work, psychology-mythology being notable themes. Produced a record cover for The Fall, 1986. Mixed shows included Riverside Open from 1985; London art fairs from 1990, the year when he was main prizewinner at LG annual exhibition; Six Young British Painters, toured Spain, 1991–2; Art in Boxes, England & Co, from 1992; and British Surrealism 1935–95, same venue, 1995. Had a solo show at Birch & Conran in 1989, 1994 venues including Brighton Marina, High Wycombe Museum and Aylesbury Museum. Baker & McKenzie, National Westminster Bank in Madrid and University of South Australia's book collection hold examples. Lived in London.

Mary KENNY 1959– Sculptor, teacher and artist involved in performance-related and community arts work. She attended Bournville School of Arts and Crafts, Birmingham, 1975–7; graduated from Bath Academy of Art, 1977–80; and did apprentice training with a stone-carver and mason in Bristol, 1980–1. Her mixed appearances included British Women Artists' Diary exhibition at York Festival, 1988, and she also showed on a number of occasions at Cleveland and Central Galleries, Bath. Had a solo show at Cross Community Centre, Pontardawe, sponsored by WAC, 1985. In 1985 completed Big Grinning Fish, at Skyros, Greece, and Flying the Kite, Portland Sculpture Park, and in 1986–7 Souvenir of Tomorrow at Sculpture Park, Villany, Hungary, sponsored by British Council. She taught at a school for maladjusted children for a time, and also lectured at Gloucester College of Art and Design and North Staffordshire College of Art. Worked in Edinburgh, where she was involved in Theatre Workshop arts resource team.

Michael KENNY 1941– Sculptor and creator of painted wood reliefs, draughtsman and teacher. He was born in Liverpool where he attended the College of Art, 1959–61, then Slade School of Fine Art, 1961–4. He won a sculpture prize at John Moores Liverpool Exhibition, 1964; a Sainsbury Award, 1965; then a series of Arts Council Awards. Elected RA in 1980. He taught at Goldsmiths' College School of Art, 1966–8, and Slade, 1981–2. Kenny fulfilled a number of public commissions, including Bank of Switzerland in London and Addenbrooke's Hospital, Cambridge. In his work, which can be monumental in concept and scale yet light and airy in conception, it has been said that Kenny alludes to the human presence but it is never fully described. He participated in many mixed shows in Britain and abroad and had solo exhibitions at Bear Lane Gallery, Oxford; Hanover Gallery; Annely Juda Fine Art; a retrospective show at Wilhelm-Lehmbruck Museum, Duisburg, in 1984; Hansard Gallery, Southampton, 1990; The Poussin Series at Dulwich Picture Gallery, 1994, after a residency there, 1992–3; Lamont Gallery, 1996; and Coram Gallery, 1997, touring to RWA, 1998. Arts Council, British Council, British Museum and many other British and foreign collections hold his work. Lived in London.

Christopher KENT 1950– Painter and teacher who studied at Watford School of Art and Bath Academy of Art, Corsham. Worked for a time as a designer, from 1974 teaching part-time in south London. Among his shows was Five at Woodlands Art Gallery, 1982.

Colin KENT 1934– Watercolourist, born in London, who studied painting and architecture at Walthamstow College of Art. Worked for some years as a qualified architect. Was elected RI in 1971. Kent was noted for his watercolours of marshland and waterside, often imbued with an atmosphere of isolation. Showed regularly at RI as well as RA, RWA, Guildhall and elsewhere in Britain and America. In 1990 shared a show at Linda Blackstone Gallery, Pinner. Had a solo exhibition at Adam Gallery, Bath, 1995–6. Lived in Essex.

Ian KENT 1944– Designer and painter who studied design at Stoke-on-Trent College of Art. He began painting in early-1980s. Mixed show appearances included Stoke's City Museum and Art Gallery, Portal Gallery and Art in Boxes at England & Co, 1991.

Jo KENT 1946– Artist and poet; her artworks were characterised by dense lettering, as in Hopscotch Box, included in Art in Boxes at England & Co, 1991. Also appeared in group shows at Stoke-on-Trent City Museum and Art Gallery, Worcester City Museum and Art Gallery and Centre Gallery in Staffordshire, where she lived.

Leslie KENT 1890–1980 Oil painter, mainly of marine and coastal scenes. After education at Bedales and Leeds University he studied painting under Fred Milner, in St Ives, 1918–20. Exhibited widely at RA, NEAC, Goupil Gallery, RBA, ROI, RSA, at the Paris Salon and in the provinces. Was a global traveller. His work has a simple, colourful directness. Lived at Radlett, Hertfordshire.

Mary KENT 1915– Painter in oil whose full name was Mary Kent Harrison. During most of the 1930s she studied at Kingston School of Art, the Slade School of Fine Art and Academy Schools. Exhibited widely in the provinces as well as RA, NEAC, RP, RSA, UA and Leicester Galleries. Had a special interest in dancing. Work reproduced in *People of Britain* and *Britain in Pictures*. Lived at Bolton-le-Bowland, Clitheroe, Lancashire.

Sarah KENT 1941– Painter and teacher, using acrylic on canvas and creating geometrical abstracts. She was born in Rugby, Warwickshire, and attended Slade School of Fine Art, 1960–6. Teaching included Southend School of Art, City Literary Institute and Hornsey College of Art. Kent was included in Camden Arts Centre's 1967 Survey '67 Abstract Painters, her pictures consisting of layers of paint applied between masking tape in the form of narrow stripes, these being built up into a low relief. From this show the Arts Council acquired Orthian 1, of 1966. Also exhibited at Young Contemporaries, Free Painters and Sculptors and Ben Uri Gallery.

William KENTRIDGE 1955– Graphic artist, printmaker, film- and video-maker and teacher, born in Johannesburg, South Africa. From 1973–6 attended University of the Witwatersrand, graduating in politics and African studies. During that time he helped found the Junction Avenue Theatre Company. From 1976–8 studied under Bill Ainslie at Johannesburg Art Foundation, teaching etching there, 1978–80. From 1981–2 Kentridge studied mime and theatre at École Jacques Lecoq, Paris. After this for two years was an art director on television series and feature films. Kentridge had begun showing solo, 1979–81, at Market Gallery, Johannesburg. From 1987 had a series of shows at Vanessa Devereux Gallery, London. In 1990 his work was featured in the Museum of Modern Art, Oxford, touring exhibition Art from South Africa. The year following, Kentridge won the Rembrandt Gold Medal at the Cape Town

Triennial. This was for *Sobriety, Obesity & Growing Old*, one of a number of films and videos in which Kentridge was involved; such work was often imbued with compassion and emotional intensity. Kentridge has been described as “one of South Africa’s most impressive political artists”.

John Dalzell KENWORTHY 1858–1954 Mainly a portrait painter, Kenworthy was born in Whitehaven, Cumberland, where he died, having lived for many years at St Bees. Exhibited RA, RCamA and Walker Art Gallery, Liverpool.

Ley KENYON 1913–1990 Painter, illustrator, designer, teacher and diver, born in London where he lived for much of his life, but died in New Mexico. After Marylebone Grammar School Kenyon studied at Central School of Art and Crafts, 1931–4, where his teachers included Bernard Meninsky and William Roberts. Although during World War II he volunteered for submarine duty he was placed in the Royal Air Force, manned the rear gun turret of a bomber on 45 missions and won the Distinguished Flying Cross. Was imprisoned in Stalag Luft III prison camp where he was involved in the famous Great Escape tunnel project, forging identity passes and papers and making an invaluable record of the burrowing, later used as material for films. After the war he became a keen diver and his subsequent career included helping Jacques Cousteau with underwater filming; being a British Commonwealth lecturer; publishing several classic reference works on the underwater world; and teaching young people on scientific expeditions. Member of London Sketch Club and chairman of Chelsea Arts Club, 1967. National Gallery bought a war drawing by him.

Gerry KEON 1942– Artist, born in London, who attended Hornsey College of Art, 1959–62, and Byam Shaw School of Art, 1962–3. Keon did a variety of jobs – ranging from school and foundation course teaching through bus conducting – which led to a lapse in his wish to paint. This he took up again in 1988, which led to several exhibitions in the early 1990s. In 1994 was included in Kerb Scrawlers at The Living Room, Greenwich, in 1996 having a solo show at Francis Kyle Gallery.

Jan KĘPIŃSKI 1907– Designer and sculptor, one of the Polish paper sculptors who made such an impact in Britain after World War II. After studying at Lvov Institute of Technology, he graduated from the Academy of Fine Arts in Warsaw and became involved in designing for a heavy industry firm including exhibition stands for international trade fairs. Imprisoned in Germany in World War II, he designed posters, stamps and arranged art exhibitions. Released and in Meppen, Kępiński managed the Polish section of the Young Men’s Christian Association’s decorative studio and was noted for his monumental eagles created from one sheet of paper for the 1st Polish Armoured Division’s canteen. He continued such work with the Association throughout Britain after the war. Kępiński then worked with the important Diana Studio; with Antoni Dobrowolski designed for many industrial clients; produced stage designs for *The Nutcracker* with Margot Fonteyn; and created scenery for television productions. In 1959 Kępiński opened his own studio and worked with Mieczyslaw Malski on producing metal relief sculptures in heavy-gauge steel, copper and aluminium until the mid-1980s. Working with the Central Office of Information, Kępiński created emblems and heraldic elements for pavilions at international fairs. Another important client was the Leeds Permanent Building Society. He was included in Polish Paper Sculpture at Polish Cultural Institute and had a solo show of photographs there, both 1995.

Jessie KEPPIE fl. from c.1890–1951 Watercolourist, born in Glasgow. She attended the School of Art there with Fra Newbery and James Dunlop among her teachers. Exhibited extensively at RSW and Royal Glasgow Institute of the Fine Arts, RSA, Walker Art Gallery, Liverpool, and elsewhere in the provinces. Member of Glasgow Lady Artists’ Club. Lived in Prestwick, Ayrshire.

Roma KERFOOT 1905– Watercolourist, draughtsman and teacher, born in Swinton, Lancashire. Studied at Manchester School of Art, 1923–7, with John Willock, then at Royal College of Art, 1927–31, with Reco Capey and Ernest Tristram. Taught for a period at Bolton School of Art and did some book illustration. Lived at Harrow Weald, Middlesex.

Judith KERLANDER fl. from 1960s– Artist in many media and teacher, wife of the sculptor Leonard Kerlander. She studied at Camberwell School of Arts and Crafts, 1960–4, specialising in sculpture; Hamersmith College of Art and Building, 1970–1, concentrating on welding; then Thomas Huxley College, 1975–8, for a Bachelor of Education degree course. In 1969 she went to modelling and sculpture workshop at Shepperton Film Studios, working on the films *Anne of a Thousand Days* and *Oliver Cromwell*. From 1980–4 she was involved in fashion-oriented silkscreen design and printing, clients including Liberty and Norman Hartnell. She also designed and made hats for The Hat Shop, Benny Yong and John Lewis. From 1983 Kerlander taught silk painting and miniature painting at Chiswick. Showed at RA from 1968; Royal Glasgow Institute of the Fine Arts, 1971; Woodstock Gallery, 1973; Whitechapel Art Gallery, 1975; Camden Arts Centre, 1979; and Greenwich Theatre Gallery, 1987. Lived in London.

Leonard KERLANDER 1940– Sculptor and teacher, born and lived in London, husband of the artist Judith Kerlander, who studied under Karel Vogel at Camberwell School of Arts and Crafts between 1954–60. In the early-1960s Kerlander was involved in film work: *Cleopatra* at Pinewood Studios, and at Metro-Goldwyn-Mayer modelling for *Satan Never Sleeps*. Around the same time Kerlander taught for a period at Camberwell; helped cast a monument for the Caribbean Athletics Stadium in Kingston, Jamaica; did portrait-casting work for the sculptor Archibald Ziegler; taught sculpture to physically handicapped people in Islington; and taught art to adults at Woolwich Art Centre. In 1964 Kerlander began teaching sculpture, drawing and painting at what became the City College of Further

Education. In 1966 he carried out life-size figures for Expo '67, in 1968 showing at Camden Arts Centre.

Patricia KERLEY 1919– Painter and teacher, born in Hove, Sussex. After attending Brighton and Hove High School she studied at Brighton College of Art, 1947–51, her teachers including Charles Knight and Charles Morris, then the Royal Academy Schools, 1951–5, where she learned from Bernard Fleetwood-Walker and Henry Rushbury. Exhibited RA, RP, SBA, Association of Sussex Artists and Arts Council. Lived in Hove, Sussex, then in Marlborough, Wiltshire.

Ingrid KERMA 1942– Abstract artist and teacher, born in Eberswalde, Germany, who gained an honours degree under Terry Frost at Reading University's fine art department, 1972–6, winning the Owen Ridley Prize. Gained her master's degree in fine art from Goldsmiths' College, 1990–2. Taught for many years: at Reading, also at Falmouth and St Martin's Schools of Art. Exhibitions included New Contemporaries at Camden Arts Centre, 1975; John Moores Liverpool Exhibition, 1976; Whitechapel Open at Whitechapel Gallery from 1981; New Acquaintances at Fabian Carlsson Gallery, 1986; Chisenhale Studios, 1988; and Bedford Gallery, 1995, as well as extensively in Germany. Arts Council, Portsmouth City Art Gallery and Reading University hold examples. Lived and worked in Berlin and London.

Lesley KERMAN fl. from mid-1960s– Versatile artist, teacher and writer on art, who gained an honours degree in fine art at University of Durham, 1964. From then she lectured in art and art and design history, latterly as head of the department of humanities performance and media at the University of Plymouth. Among her publications was *Graham Rich, The Search for Form, a Memoir*, 1997. Mixed exhibitions included Young Contemporaries, from 1962; Spacex Artists Drawing Show, Spacex Gallery, Exeter, 1984; and Push the Boat Out, Swansea Arts Workshop Gallery, Swansea, 1997. Solo exhibitions included Paintings, Gallery 273, Queen Mary College, 1967; Paintings, Exe Gallery, Exeter, 1985; and Fair Play, University of Exeter Conference on Women in the South West, 1996. Lived in Topsham, Devon.

Doreen KERN 1931– Sculptor in bronze. Technical knowledge was acquired while working at The Morris Singer Foundry, and she also studied at The Hampstead Garden Suburb Institute. Showed at Bristol Cathedral; London University; Brighton Museum & Art Gallery; Waterloo Fine Arts; and widely abroad. Did consultancy work for British Museum. Lived in Edgware, Middlesex.

Theador KERN 1900–1969 Painter, sculptor and stained glass artist, born in Salzburg, Austria. He worked in England from 1938 and taught at Luton School of Art. His oil painting Manifest, showing a pronounced Eastern European influence in its strong colours and brushwork, is in St Paul's Church, Bedford. Lived in Hitchin, Hertfordshire.

Elizabeth Lamorna KERR 1904–1990 Painter, driftwood sculptor and teacher, daughter of the painter Samuel John Lamorna Birch, she was his model, and sat for the circle of painters including Augustus John, T C Gotch and Laura and Harold Knight. She was born and died at Flagstaff Cottage, Lamorna Cove, Cornwall. After working in London as a milliner she moved to Cornwall in the late-1930s with her husband, James Lennox Kerr, who as Peter Dawlish wrote books for boys. Mornie, as she was known, exhibited at the RA, 1939–51; promoted her father's work; and taught and showed with her own group of artists. Her still life and landscape studies are notable for their handling of light.

Helen KERR 1936– Artist in Batik and Batik-embroidery, and teacher, married to the artist Richard John Croft. She studied textiles at Belfast College of Art in the 1950s and at Brighton College of Art, in 1981–2 gaining a diploma in embroidery and textiles at Goldsmiths' College. Between 1970–87 she was head of the art department at Bloomfield Collegiate School, Belfast; gained a fellowship in creative embroidery at Belfast College of Art, 1977; and in 1978 was featured in Ulster Television's *Portrait of the Artist*. From 1987 she worked full-time at a studio in Dundrum, County Down. Showed regularly with RUA and RHA and in Dublin and Belfast at the Irish Exhibition of Living Art. Group shows included Material Evidence at Camden Arts Centre, 1985, and Stitched Textiles, at Commonwealth Institute Gallery, 1989. Solo shows included Ulster Arts Club, 1990, and Cavehill Gallery, 1991, both in Belfast.

Judith KERR 1923– Painter, draughtsman and designer of textiles who was born in Berlin, Germany. She was educated in Germany, France and England and then studied at Central School of Arts and Crafts with John Farleigh, Bernard Meninsky and Ruskin Spear. Showed RA, LG and elsewhere and lived in London.

Nora Jean KERR 1908–1956 Painter and designer, born in Peking, China. She was educated at Benenden School, then studied art at Byam Shaw School of Drawing and Painting, Central School of Arts and Crafts, during World War II in India, then Heatherley's School of Fine Art. She moved to Newport, Monmouthshire, around 1950 and had a solo show there in 1953 at Cheltenham Hall. Also showed SEA, SWG and WAC. It holds her work, as do CASW and Newport Art Gallery and Museum.

Susan KERR 1944– Self-taught artist, born in London. She was a member of Free Painters and Sculptors, also exhibiting with Woodstock Gallery and at Gray Art Gallery & Museum, Hartlepool. Lived in Shepperton, Middlesex.

Suzy KERR 1957– Systems-based artist, born and lived in London, who studied at Bath Academy of Art, 1975–9, then at Brighton Polytechnic, 1980–1, with a Polish Government Scholarship to Warsaw, 1982–3. Group exhibitions included

Sally East Gallery, 1979; 3 Constructivists, Building Design Partnership, Preston, 1980; House Construction Show, House Gallery, and 9 Printmakers, Brighton Polytechnic, both 1981; 7th British International Print Biennale, Bradford, 1982; and Series, Quay Arts Centre, Newport, Isle of Wight, 1983. Kerr then said that her "interest is in revealing process; not only movement in time, as in the mobiles, but also in the form-making power of time, time as expressed by repetition and change, by sequence and seriality." Kerr (pronounced Carr) later worked at the Photographers' Gallery.

Walter KERSHAW 1940– Painter and muralist, born in Rochdale, Lancashire. He was educated at De la Salle College, Salford, 1951–8, and graduated from department of fine art at Durham University, 1958–62, with honours, after which he was self-employed as an artist. In 1972 Kershaw made his home at Littleborough, in the Pennines, where a large studio enabled him to create on a panoramic scale. From the age of 13 he painted the Lancashire landscape and he was to be a pioneer of industrial murals in Britain. From 1977–9 he was awarded a major grant, jointly financed by the Gulbenkian Foundation and North West Arts, to establish external mural painting in the Lancashire area. His mural at Trafford Park, Manchester, was claimed to be the world's largest industrial painting of its type and it took him four years to finish. He worked extensively abroad, notably in Brazil. Major group and solo shows included Bear Lane Gallery, Oxford, 1962; Salford Art Gallery, from 1969; House of Commons, 1972; and Lancashire South of the Sands, which toured from County and Regimental Museum, Preston, 1988. Victoria & Albert Museum, The British Council, Salford University and overseas collections hold examples.

James KESSELL 1915–1978 Painter, mainly in oil, born in Coventry where he continued to live, son of the watercolourist James Everett Kessell. Studied at Coventry School of Art, 1928–34 and 1945–52. Exhibited RA, NS, ROI, RBA and RSMA. Towards the end of his life he ran his own art school. Kessell, who also showed abroad, had a series of one-man shows, including Herbert Art Gallery, Coventry, and Coventry Cathedral, in 1973. He painted portraits of a number of senior figures in the Anglican church. Herbert Art Gallery holds his works One up for the Sky Blues and Cardiff Docks.

Mary KESSELL 1914–1977 Painter, designer, draughtsman and teacher, born in London, where she continued to work. She was married to the designer Tom Eckersley. Kessell studied at Clapham School of Art, 1935–7, and the Central School of Arts and Crafts, 1937–9. In 1937 she was commissioned to illustrate Osbert Sitwell's book *Mrs Kimber*, then shortly after she began painting, in 1939, she executed the Judith and Holofernes mural at Westminster Hospital. In 1945 she travelled through Germany as an official war artist, visiting Belsen and Berlin; her journal and the resulting pictures are often harrowing, extracts from the diary being published in *The Cornhill* magazine in 1946. Had her initial solo show at Leicester Galleries in 1950, the first of a series, also showing at New Grafton Gallery in 1969. From 1952–6 Kessell lectured in jewellery design at Central School, from 1957–76 being a visiting teacher at London College of Printing. She also executed two big murals for ICI; went on an assignment for Oxfam in India in 1967; and did graphic work for Shell, London Transport, *Vogue* magazine and others. Imperial War Museum, Tate Gallery and other public collections hold her work.

Morris KESTELMAN 1905–1998 Painter, stage designer, muralist, book illustrator and teacher, born in London, where he settled, of parents emigrated recently from eastern Europe. He studied at Central School of Art, 1922–5, with Bernard Meninsky, then at Royal College of Art, 1926–9, where he developed an interest in theatre design. Among his theatrical work was Sadler's Wells production of *Carmen*, for Tyrone Guthrie, 1940, and Laurence Olivier's *Richard III* and *The Alchemist* at The Old Vic in the following years. Kestelman did murals for Victoria & Albert Museum exhibition in 1946 and was included in Mural Art To-Day there in 1960. From 1951–71 Kestelman was Central School's head of fine art. Was elected LG, and Senior RA, 1996. Had a solo show at Upper Grosvenor Gallery, 1961, later ones including Sally Hunter Fine Art, 1987, and Boundary Gallery from 1989. In 1983 Kestelman won an Abbey Major Award in Painting Prize. Arts Council, Contemporary Art Society and Victoria & Albert Museum hold his work.

Jean KETCHER 1955– Painter and teacher, born and lived in Ipswich, Suffolk, where she studied at the School of Art, 1971–3, graduating from Maidstone College of Art, 1973–6. She was an Ipswich Art Club member who showed in East Anglia, notably at the Corn Exchange in Ipswich and at Halesworth Gallery.

B KEVILL DAVIES 1954– Painter, born in Dorset. She studied at Bournemouth and Poole College of Art and Design, 1973–7. Was interested in how a painting could become part of the surrounding architecture, working on board on a small scale, creating "studs of colour". She showed in Contemporary Art Society Market, RA Summer Exhibition and was included in John Moores Liverpool Exhibition in 1987. Lived in Sapperton, Gloucestershire.

Geoffrey KEY 1941– Painter, sculptor and teacher, born Manchester, who attended the Regional College of Art there, 1958–61. He was head of art at Broughton High School, 1962–74, then was a full-time artist. Key's main subject themes were the figure, landscape and the horse. He was a member of the Manchester Academy, gaining first prize there in 1971. Key showed at Salford Art Gallery from 1966; Sheffield University and abroad in 1974; other exhibitions including Harris Museum and Art Gallery, Preston, 1983, Blackheath Gallery from 1989 and Barn Gallery, Cheshire, 1991. Public galleries in Salford, Manchester and Bolton hold his work. Lived in Pendleton, Salford, Lancashire.

Joan KEY 1948– Artist and teacher, whose output included Minimalist painting and experimental prints, born in Lancashire, who studied at Liverpool College of Art, 1967–8; Maidstone College of Art, 1968–71; and Royal College of Art, 1971–4. Lecturing included Maidstone, 1975–89; Goldsmiths' College, 1979–94; and Kent Institute, Canterbury, from 1994; subjects included fine art, printmaking, textiles and art and critical theory. Key curated a number of exhibitions, including WaterColour and Surface Tensions, 1993 and 1994, both at Curwen Gallery; and three more, with Paul Heber-Percy, Richard Salmon Gallery and tours, during 1996 and 1997; Plastic, Light and Craft. Group and mixed exhibitions included Seven Painters, Kettle's Yard, Cambridge, and tour, 1980; Printing in Camden, Camden Arts Centre, 1984; Identities, Chisenhale Gallery, 1988; Modern British Prints, Curwen Gallery, 1991; and Contemporary British Drawings, Sandra Gearing Gallery, New York, America, 1997. Later solo exhibitions included Richard Salmon, 1996, and Galerie Hollenbach, Stuttgart, Germany, 1997. Arts Council, Tate Gallery, Kettle's Yard and other public collections hold examples.

Paul KEYSELL 1954– Painter and draughtsman whose figurative work had a strong dramatic content, born in Liverpool. He gained an honours degree in illustration at Maidstone College of Art in 1977, then worked as a freelance illustrator for a wide range of clients including IPC Magazines, Virgin Records and Barrie and Jenkins. Had work in the Best of British Illustration Exhibition. In the 1980s he sought to develop more personal work and undertook postgraduate studies at University College of Wales, Aberystwyth. Showed with MAFA, East Midlands Open and was in Aberystwyth Artists at The Deffett Francis Gallery, Swansea Institute of Higher Education, 1993.

KHAN 1952– Painter and artist in mixed media and found objects, born in Ranpur, India. He was an engineer who began studying art at Camden Arts Centre in 1976, showed in a mixed exhibition there two years later, then continued studying at Middlesex Polytechnic, 1978–9, and North-East London Polytechnic, 1979–82. His initial major exhibition showing was at John Moores Exhibition, Liverpool, in 1991–2, with Virgin of the Radiator. Lived in London.

Balraj KHANNA 1940– Painter and writer, born in Punjab, India. He received his Master of Arts degree in English literature from Chandigarh University and was down for Oxford University, but a mishap prevented this, and he turned almost by chance to art. After a convalescent visit to France, he had first one-man show at New Vision Centre Gallery in 1965, but continued to lead a diverse life. He was a foreign correspondent in the India-Pakistan War, 1971–2; won the Royal Society of Literature's Winifred Holtby Prize for his novel *Nation of Fools* in 1984; and was part-author of the report *Art on the South Bank*, commissioned by the Greater London Council in 1986. Khanna did some figurative work, but made a notable impact with colourful, kaleidoscopic abstract works, witty and original, which have been compared to those of Klee and Miró but which are unique. Participated in many international exhibitions. Solo shows included Serpentine Gallery, 1979; Horizon Gallery, 1987; and The Museum of Modern Art, Wales, in Machynlleth, 1994. Ashmolean Museum in Oxford, provincial galleries and National Gallery of Modern Art, New Delhi, India, hold his work. Participated in The Other Story, Hayward Gallery, 1989–90, with tour. Lived in London.

Bharti KHER 1969– Artist producing brightly coloured figurative pictures such as Misappropriate Functions, which won a prize in Royal Over-Seas League Open, 1996. Kher was born in London and studied at Middlesex and Newcastle upon Tyne Polytechnics. Other mixed shows included Squires Gallery, Newcastle, 1989; Aspects of British Figurative Painting (1988–93), Milton Gallery, 1993; and Of Women – Icons/Stars/Feasts, Eicher Gallery in New Delhi, India, where Kher was based from 1993, held 1996. Solo shows included Art Heritage, New Delhi, 1995.

James KIBART 1912– Painter, designer and teacher, born and lived in Leicester, where he attended the College of Art, 1928–35, teachers including A R Middleton Todd and J F Pettinger. For a time he was a consultant to the Graphic Art Studio. Kibart held senior positions in Leicester's Sketch Club and its Society of Artists. He showed at the public gallery there and in Nottingham, elsewhere in the Midlands and in Edinburgh.

Michael Alan KIDD 1955– Artist notable for his portraits, working in oil, acrylic and silkscreen, born in Balham, south London. Studied at Slade School of Fine Art, 1976–82, graduating with honours, then completing a postgraduate course. Kidd said that "although dependent on portraiture, I have been an experimentalist with the contemporary side of my work." Latterly, he worked on "a completely original method of representation, involving silkscreen usage, the possibilities of which, I believe, were under-exploited by the Pop Art movement". Group appearances included RA Summer Exhibition, 1978; National Portrait Gallery, 1981–2; RP, 1982–3; ROI, 1983; RBA, 1983–4; Laing Landscape Competition, 1983–4; Athena Art Competition, 1985; and British Painters' Open, Mall Galleries, 1989. Later solo shows included Pump House and Hyde Park Galleries, both 1992. Notable works included portraits of HRH The Princess of Wales and the Pop singer David Bowie. Dulwich College and Y Tabernacl, The Museum of Modern Art, Machynlleth, which has his Self-Portrait and a portrait of Iwan Llewelyn-Jones, are among public owners of Kidd's pictures. Lived in London.

Helen KIDDALL 1888–1980 Painter and keen amateur musician. She entered Royal Academy Schools in 1912 for the five-year course where she was a friend of the painter Beatrice Lithiby. She later did a striking portrait of Miss Lithiby in the uniform of a chief commander of the Auxiliary Territorial Service. She exhibited at RA and elsewhere, producing many pictures of black children and flower still lifes. A devout Anglican, she is described as having had "a strong sense of humour, delighting in telling stories against herself". Miss Kiddall was a keen violinist who used to be accompanied by her sister, with whom she lived at Felixstowe, Suffolk.

Robert KIDDEY 1900–1984 Sculptor, artist and teacher, born in Nottingham. Kiddey came to prominence in the 1930s when he showed frequently at RA and Salon des Beaux-Arts, Paris. In 1932 examples of his work were exhibited at Goupil Gallery alongside pieces by Augustus John, Eric Gill and Picasso. Kiddey taught at a technical college in Newark-on-Trent and much of his work is to be found in the Nottinghamshire area, sometimes sculptures and bas reliefs on a large scale.

Hilda KIDMAN 1891– Painter and illustrator, born near Hitchin, Hertfordshire. She was especially noted for her pictures of flowers and children and won an Hon. Mention at Paris Salon. Kidman studied at the Slade School of Fine Art under Henry Tonks, Philip Wilson Steer and Walter Westley Russell, Frank Calderon's School of Animal Painting and St John's Wood School of Art. Her pictures occasionally appeared on the covers of women's magazines. Exhibited RA, RP, SWA and RSA. Lived in Hitchin.

Michael KIDNER 1917– Systems-oriented artist who was included in the key Systems Exhibition at Whitechapel Art Gallery in 1972 and in Systems II at Polytechnic of Central London in 1973. For Kidner the canvas was "a sort of laboratory", and he was variously concerned with such features as shape as an ingredient for colour sensation, wave forms and curved or warped planes. Born in Kettering, Northamptonshire, Kidner was at Cambridge University, 1936–9, after which he was during 1940–1 at Ohio State University. After five years in Canadian Army was at Goldsmiths' College, taking up painting full-time in 1953. Lived in Paris for a while, studying for several months at Atelier André Lhote. Kidner held a number of teaching posts, notably at Bath Academy of Art, 1964–84. He had his first solo show at St Hilda's College, Oxford, in 1959; there was an Arts Council retrospective, 1959–84, at Serpentine Gallery, 1984; and later solo shows included Centre for the Philosophy of the Natural and Social Sciences, 1994, and Galerie Emilia Suciu, Ettlingen, Germany, 1995. Tate Gallery, Arts Council, British Council, Contemporary Art Society and other leading collections held examples. Lived in London.

Susanne KIELY 1962– Artist and teacher who produced complex prints such as Cleansing, of 1995, shown at Royal Over-Seas League Open, 1996. She was born in Carshalton, Surrey, and studied at Warwick University, Colchester Institute and Chelsea and Camberwell Colleges of Art & Design. Work exp rience included several teaching posts, part-time assistant with the dealer Lumley Cazalet from 1994 and in 1995–6 associate guest artist at Camberwell. She was given a commission for St Matthew's Church, Ipswich, 1987 and won 1st Prize, London Lighthouse, 1995. Took part in many group exhibitions, including Ulster University, Belfast, 1991; The Sea, The Sea!, Y Tabernacl, Machynlleth, 1994; and Cover to Cover, London Print Workshop, 1996. Chelsea & Westminster Arts Project, Marakon Associates and Manchester Metropolitan University Library hold examples.

Ken KIFF 1935– Painter, illustrator and teacher, born in Dagenham, Essex. He studied at Hornsey School of Art, 1955–61. Taught at Royal College of Art from 1979. Kiff's pictures were in many mixed shows and in 1986 he was included in Royal College of Art's Exhibition Road show. Solo exhibitions were at Nicola Jacobs Gallery and Fischer Fine Art; he had a retrospective at Serpentine Gallery in 1986; and in 1993–4 Kiff's work done as the result of a prolonged residency, was shown at National Gallery. The artist was noted for lush, apparently naive pictures. The Arts Council holds a number, such as Man Greeting Woman, of 1965–6, and A Knife and Fork Jumped Up from the Dresser, of 1977. He illustrated *Folk Tales of the British Isles*, edited by M Foss, published in 1977. Was elected RA, 1991. Lived in London.

John KIKI 1943– Painter and printmaker, born in Famagusta, Cyprus, whose family – involved in the restaurant business – settled in London in 1946. He attended Camberwell School of Arts and Crafts, 1960–4, then Royal Academy Schools, 1964–7. Kiki's pictures were often on a large scale, figurative, vigorous, using high-pitched and unconventional colours and reflecting his Mediterranean background. Group exhibitions included Young Contemporaries, Mall Galleries, 1966; British Painting '74, Hayward Gallery, 1974; and Viriamu Jones Gallery, University College, Cardiff, 1986. Later solo shows included Art Space Gallery, from 1991. Saatchi Collection holds his work. Lived in Great Yarmouth, Norfolk.

Joyce KILBURN 1884–1972 Miniaturist and watercolourist on ivory, born in London, daughter of the painter The Hon. John Collier. She studied at the Slade School of Fine Art with Fred Brown and Henry Tonks among her teachers. Exhibited RMS, Arlington Gallery, SWA, extensively in the provinces, in Canada, Australia and New Zealand. Signed her work J K in monogram form. Lived in London. Her daughter was the designer and artist Jill Greenwood.

Bruce KILLEEN 1926– Painter, lecturer, writer on art and film-maker, born in Warwickshire. His work was based initially on observed reality, but varied considerably between figuration and abstraction. From 1969–80 he was senior lecturer at Colchester School of Art, later part-time tutor at Royal Academy Schools. Killeen was regional art correspondent for *The Guardian*; wrote articles for art and literary journals; and in 1978 and 1980 won two Arts Council Awards to make art films, after which he concentrated entirely on painting. Was a member of AIA and RWA. Many group appearances included RA, Bruton Street Gallery, Minories in Colchester, Victoria Art Gallery in Bath and Chappel Galleries, Chappel. Solo shows included three at The Minories; others in London, Chelmsford, Bath and Bristol; and one at Alpha House Gallery, Sherborne. Killeen has works in public and private collections in Britain and abroad. His wife, the potter Angela Killeen (1929–1997), had a memorial show at Chappel Galleries in 1998.

Ian KILLEN 1960– Artist working in various media who studied at Liverpool and Leeds Polytechnics. His group exhibition appearances included War of Images, at Transmission Gallery, Glasgow; State of the Nation, at Coventry City Museum and Art Gallery; and Art in Boxes at England & Co, 1991, which featured two Untitled works by him.

Ann KILVINGTON 1944– Painter and teacher who studied at York School of Art, 1960–4, then Royal Academy Schools, 1964–7. She taught at Putney School of Art and in 1982 was included in Artists in Adult Education at Woodlands Art Gallery. Other shows included RA Summer Exhibition from 1967; South London Art Gallery, 1979; and Wells Centre, Norfolk, 1981.

Patrick KILVINGTON 1922–1990 Painter, born in Surrey, educated at Eltham College and Bromley School of Art, who did not take up painting professionally until he was 49. After Army service in World War II, during which he was responsible for arresting Adolf Hitler's successor Admiral Doenitz, Kilvington contracted tuberculosis and after two years in hospital emigrated to Australia in 1951, where he did many jobs. A suspected recurrence of the tuberculosis in 1970 prompted him to resume painting, which led to a first, sell-out show in Brisbane in 1972. Submitted three pictures for the Horse Painters of the World show at Tryon Gallery, London, in 1979; all sold and two years later he was commissioned to do a polo picture as a wedding present for the Prince and Princess of Wales. By this time his pictures of horses and bushmen were popular in Australia, and he produced several thousands for shows there, in New Zealand and the United Kingdom. Died in Southport, Queensland.

Coralie KINAHAN 1924– Painter and writer, born in Bletchingley, Surrey. She was the sister of the artist Lydia de Burgh and sometimes painted under the name de Burgh. Married Sir Robin Kinahan. She studied art with the noted poster artist John Hassall who for a time ran his own school; at Chelsea School of Art, 1943–6; and in the studio of Sonia Mervyn, 1947–9. She was a member of RUA, for a time on its council, and of Ulster Women Artists. Also exhibited at RA, RP, SWLA and elsewhere and held a series of solo shows in Britain and Ireland. In 1985 opened her own gallery in Templepatrick, County Antrim, Northern Ireland, where she lived. Lady Kinahan was active in Ulster public life, being Lady Mayoress of Belfast, 1959–62. Ulster Museum, Belfast, holds her work. Among her historical novels was *You Can't Shoot the English*, 1982.

Agnes Marie KINDBERG 1906– Painter and artist in fabric collage, born in Hartlepool, County Durham. She studied at the local School of Art, principal Alfred Josiah Rushton, also in Newcastle and London, winning her art teacher's diploma. She showed at RSA, SSA and Scottish Craft Centre and exhibited solo regularly for many years at Edinburgh International Festival from 1970. Completed a series of works in public places, such as restaurants and churches. Lived in Edinburgh.

Joan KINDER 1916– Artist, born in Thornton-le-Dale, Yorkshire. After Bridlington High School for Girls Kinder attended Scarborough College of Art, 1932–6. She was a member of the Free Painters and Sculptors and SGA, on whose council she sat. Showed in London, provinces and abroad. London County Council bought her work. Lived latterly in Kenley, Surrey.

John KINDNESS 1951– Versatile artist, born in Belfast, Northern Ireland, who settled in Dublin, in the Irish Republic. Among awards and commissions were a Major Arts Council of Northern Ireland Award, 1988; A Waterfall of Souvenirs: Ulsterbus, Northern Ireland major public sculpture commission, 1991; and in 1992 Romulus & Seamus, Arts Council of Northern Ireland sculpture garden commission. Projects included Skybreaker, advertising panels on Belfast City Bus, 1984, and Big Shoe Dog, sculpture made from shoes, Dublin Airport, 1989. Took part in many group and other shows in Ireland and abroad. Solo exhibitions included A Monkey Town Besieged By Dogs, at Grapevine Arts Centre, Dublin, and tour, 1985; Douglas Hyde Gallery, Dublin, 1990; and Treasures of New York, Kerlin Gallery, Dublin, and tour, 1991. Victoria & Albert Museum, British Council, Boston Museum of Fine Arts in America and Irish Museum of Modern Art in Dublin hold examples.

Andrew KING 1956– Watercolourist and painter in oil on gesso, born in Bedford. He graduated in 1978 in fine art, painting, at Hornsey College of Art, painting full-time from then. He was made a member of NS in 1984, an associate of ROI in 1987. King had an interest in atmosphere, light and mood in landscape, the twentieth-century East Anglian landscapists being an influence. He worked "in true watercolour, on handmade paper in the traditional manner." Exhibited RWS, RI, NEAC and elsewhere in mixed shows. Had a first solo show at Luton County Council Library in 1978; from 1982 showed annually at Thompson's Gallery, Aldeburgh. Local authority collections hold examples. Lived in Colby, Norwich.

Cecil KING 1921–1986 Artist, born in County Wicklow, Ireland. In the early-1950s he ended his business career to become a painter. He was soon showing at RHA and went on to participate in numerous group exhibitions in Ireland, Britain and on the continent. His first show outside Ireland was at New Charing Cross Gallery, Glasgow, in 1964. Other solo exhibitions took place at Compass Gallery, Glasgow; Angela Flowers; Oliver Dowling Gallery in Dublin, in 1984; and Hugh Lane Municipal Gallery, Dublin, 1981, which was a retrospective. Many public collections hold King's work, including Contemporary Irish Art Society; Museum of Modern Art in New York; Ulster Museum, Belfast; Victoria & Albert Museum; and Tate Gallery.

Dave KING 1946– Abstract sculptor, especially in wood, and teacher, born in West Midlands. He attended Leeds College of Art from 1965 and Slade School of Fine Art from 1968. He was a visiting lecturer at Bath Academy of Art, Norwich School of Art, Canterbury College of Art and elsewhere. King was included in The British Art Show, an Arts Council touring exhibition, 1980, chosen by critic William Packer. Solo exhibitions included

Serpentine Gallery, 1970; Angela Flowers Gallery, 1978; Rochdale Art Gallery, 1983; and William Paterson Gallery, New Jersey, 1991.

Dorothy KING 1907–1990 Painter, draughtsman, curator and teacher, born and lived in London. She studied at Hornsey School of Art under J C Moody, then was briefly at Slade School of Fine Art with Randolph Schwabe. During World War II she worked first as a welfare officer, later as a supervisor at East End rest centres. Took up painting professionally after the war; in 1947 was elected RBA; in 1959 was temporary keeper of its Galleries in Suffolk Street; then from 1961–74 was keeper of the South London Art Gallery. She left to spend all her time painting, although for a while she continued teaching art classes in Southwark. Showed at RA, NEAC, SWA and elsewhere. Metropolitan Museum of Modern Art, New York, holds her work, which was given a memorial show at Mall Galleries in 1992.

Geoffrey KING 1941– Artist in a variety of media, born in Pin Mill, Suffolk, where he continued to live. King studied at Ipswich School of Art, 1956–7, then left to run the family boatbuilding business while continuing to draw and paint, boats and the estuary being key themes. His teachers were Colin Moss and Bernard Reynolds. King was a member of Ipswich Art Society and won the Anna Airy Award. He showed in its mixed exhibitions, also with John Russell and Haste Galleries in Ipswich, St Gregory's in Norwich and the Clockhouse, Snape. Had solo shows at the Haste, John Russell and Pin Mill Galleries.

Gordon KING 1939– Watercolourist and illustrator, born in London. He spent the war years in Fife, his father's home, then settled with his family in Reading, where he studied life drawing and painting at Reading University School of Art. After training as an illustrator with Carlton Studios at 22 he went freelance, working for magazines and advertising agencies, illustrating books and developing his portraits and paintings. As well as solo exhibitions King showed at RA Summer Exhibitions, RI and sold his prints in limited and signed editions. Among his favourite subjects were girls in a floral garden, his daughter and friends being the models. Lived in Chalfont St Peter, Buckinghamshire.

Graham Peter KING 1930– Designer, printmaker and writer, born in Adelaide, South Australia. He attended the University there and South Australian School of Art. Showed with Contemporary Art Society, 1950, and elsewhere in Australia. Wrote *Snaps as Art: the aesthetics of the snapshot*, 1978. Lived latterly in London.

Jessie Marion KING 1875–1949 Painter and mural artist, illustrator, designer and teacher, born at New Kilpatrick, Dunbartonshire, she was married to the artist E A Taylor. She studied at Glasgow University and Glasgow School of Art, where she was influenced by Charles Rennie Mackintosh. A travelling scholarship took her to Italy. She began to work for the printed page and by 1902 was teaching book cover design at Glasgow School of Art. Won a gold medal at Turin's International Decorative Art Exhibition. After marrying Taylor in 1908 they moved in 1911 to Paris, where for two years they ran the Atelier Shealing and King came under the influence of Bakst and the Ballets Russes. King now developed a greater freedom of colour and style and matured as a mural painter and designer of fabrics, jewellery and costumes. When World War I broke out she and her husband returned to Scotland and established a modest artistic colony in Kirkcudbright, while retaining a Paris studio until the late 1920s. She exhibited extensively at RSA, Royal Glasgow Institute of the Fine Arts and elsewhere. An exhaustive exhibition of her work was held at Scottish Arts Council in 1971. Scottish National Gallery of Modern Art holds her work.

Mary KING 1926 Painter, collagist, artist in mixed media and teacher, born in Streatham, south London. She qualified as a teacher at Whitelands Training College and Chelsea School of Art, also studying at Central School of Arts and Crafts. Teachers included Carel Weight and Ceri Richards, painting; Francis Spear, stained glass; and Henry Moore, clay modelling. Travelled extensively, including Peru, Egypt, India and Burma. Taught at North-East Surrey College of Technology and Surbiton Adult Education Centre. King joined SWA in 1979, Free Painters and Sculptors in 1980 and NS in 1984. Took part in mixed shows at RA Summer Exhibition, Westminster and Mall Galleries, RBA and elsewhere. Solo exhibitions included Fairfield Halls in Croydon, Loggia Gallery and Farnham Maltings. King's work always related to nature, but she was mainly concerned with non-representational images in an Abstract Expressionist manner, as in her Loom of Life series. Lived in Ewell, Epsom, Surrey.

Michael William KING 1928– Watercolourist, born in Croydon, Surrey, who was self-taught apart from assistance from Arthur Mills. King was elected to WSW in 1983, the year he began participating in mixed shows at Turner Gallery, Penarth. Also exhibited with RCamA, Aberystwyth Art Centre and Museum, Glynn Vivian Gallery in Swansea, at Swansea University and elsewhere. His solo shows included Arlington Gallery, Cardiff, 1965; Dyfed Gallery, New Quay, from 1980; and Newport Caringli Gallery from 1989. In 1981 he was community artist in Llandysul. Lived at New Quay, Dyfed.

Peter KING 1928–1957 Sculptor, born in London, who studied at Wimbledon School of Art. He worked for a time under Henry Moore and in 1956 was engaged on stone carving on the House of Commons. His works were shown in galleries in Paris and Rome and he was represented at the Holland Park Exhibition, 1957; Middelheim Exhibition, 1959; and in 1960 his oak Figure with Cloak was shown at Battersea Park. British Council, Arts Council and Contemporary Art Society acquired his work.

Phillip KING 1934– Sculptor and teacher, born in Kheredine, Tunisia, arriving in England in 1946. Studied modern languages at Cambridge University, 1954–7, and was at St Martin's School of Art, 1957–8. After a year as Henry Moore's assistant, King taught at St Martin's, 1959–80. He was at Bennington College, Vermont, in 1964 and at Hochschule der Künste, Berlin, 1979–80, becoming professor of sculpture at Royal College of Art, 1980. In 1964 King had his first one-man show at Rowan Gallery, the first of a long series there. One-man shows at Richard Feigen Gallery, New York and Chicago, and the Isaac Delgado Museum of Art, New Orleans, followed in 1966. King soon established a solid exhibiting reputation in group and one-man shows in Britain and overseas, work using a variety of materials from fibreglass and metal to wood and slate. In 1969 King won first prize at Socha Piestanskych, Czechosovakia, the year after his retrospective at Whitechapel Art Gallery. Further retrospectives included Hayward Gallery, 1981. Tate Gallery, Arts Council and Ulster Museum, Belfast, hold King's work which although abstract was heraldic and symbolic in character. He was a trustee of the Tate Gallery, 1967–9. Among King's commissions was Expo '70, Tokyo. Elected RA in 1991. Retrospective at Yorkshire Sculpture Park in 1992 which showed that King, originally a figurative sculptor, had after a long period of abstraction moved back to figuration in the late 1980s. In 1997 King had another retrospective at Forte di Belvedere, Florence, only the second English sculptor given this honour (the first was Henry Moore). Two notable sculptures by King are outside C & J Clark's shoe factory at Street, Somerset. Lived near Dunstable, Bedfordshire, and in London.

Robert KING 1936– Painter and printmaker, born and lived in Leicester, where he attended the College of Art, 1956–8. He was a member of Leicester Society of Artists from 1960 and RI from 1970 and was noted for his marine paintings. Showed at RA, RSMA, ROI and elsewhere. From 1970 had a series of solo shows at Gadsby Gallery in Leicester, later ones including Medici Galleries, 1980. Leicester University holds his work.

Ronald KING 1932– Printmaker, painter and teacher, born in São Paulo, Brazil, who studied at Chelsea School of Art, and won a Biddulph Scholarship for Painting, a Monsanto Painting Award, 1957, and a Forrester Painting Award, 1960. King was art director for a publishing company in Canada, 1957–60, and lectured at Farnham School of Art, 1961–5. Mixed shows included Zwemmer's, Bear Lane in Oxford, RA, Heal's Mansard, Medici, Redfern and Curwen Galleries, and he was one of the London Artists shown at Shrewsbury School, 1968. British Museum, Victoria & Albert Museum, Washington's Library of Congress and a series of British and foreign university collections hold King's work. Lived for a time in Hayes, Middlesex.

Simon KING 1951– Printmaker and maker of books, born in Markyate, Hertfordshire. He attended Central School of Art & Design, 1971–5, being an etching technician on its staff, 1978–80. In 1981 he moved to Cumbria and set up a studio, mainly to print his own work. Between 1985–95 printed several projects for Paragon Press, including *Scottish Bestiary* and Bill Woodrow's *Periodic Table*. Exhibitions included The Forgotten Medium, Graffiti Gallery, 1980; Prints & Paintings at Collingwood College, Durham (repeated in 1985 at Gateway Gallery, Windermere); RA Summer Exhibition from 1984; and 3rd International Biennial Print Exhibition, Taiwan. In 1996 there was a show of Simon King's work at Abbot Hall Art Gallery/Bookshop, Kendal.

William Charles Holland KING 1884–1973 Sculptor. Born in Cheltenham, he attended the Royal Academy Schools, where he won the Landseer Scholarship. From 1910 he exhibited at the RA, also at the RSA, in Scotland, the provinces and abroad. Doncaster Museum and Art Gallery owns his work. King, who specialised in portrait sculpture, in 1954 won the gold medal of the RBS, of which he was president, 1949–54. A sculptor in the classical tradition, King is represented by several examples of his work in the volume *RBS: Modern British Sculpture*, 1939. Lived in Ventnor, Isle of Wight.

Hazel KING-FARLOW fl. from mid-1930s–1995 Painter of colourful, extravert works, maiden name Hazel Guggenheim, who showed under her married name of Hazel King-Farlow, later after remarriage as Hazel McKinley. Studied at Euston Road School in 1938, having had a solo exhibition in 1937 at Cooling Galleries, also exhibiting at SWA and at Goupil and Redfern Galleries. From 1939 lived in America, although she was in Paris in the 1950s and showed again in England in the 1960s. American exhibitions included Harry Salpeter Gallery, New York, 1947. English collections holding examples include Leeds and Manchester City Art Galleries and Ferens Art Gallery, Hull. Notable American collectors included Colorado Springs Fine Arts Centre Collection, The Staude Collection in Hollywood, Greer Garson and Mrs Benny Goodman. King-Farlow's daughter Barbara Shukman was also an artist. Wakefield Art Gallery holds fine examples of work by Henry Moore and Victor Pasmore, presented by King-Farlow.

Joan Beeby KINGSFORD 1883–1974 Artist, designer of theatrical costumes and curator, married to the painter Wilfrid R Wood. She studied at Central and other schools of art in London, learning manuscript illumination and lettering under Graily Hewitt. She began by making maps, engravings and drawings for the printing firm of Emery Walker, then for 25 years was curator of the Charles Beatty Collection of Persian and Indian manuscripts, books and paintings. In 1975 her husband helped stage a retrospective show of her work at Upstairs Gallery, Stamford. British Museum and Fitzwilliam Museum in Cambridge both hold examples. Lived at Barnack, Lincolnshire.

Harry KINGSLEY 1914– Painter and teacher, born in Manchester, where he studied at the School of Art. Joined the Army in 1933 and served abroad from 1934–45 in Palestine, India and the Far East. Became an art teacher at a Manchester secondary school. Showed with RA, Royal Glasgow Institute of the Fine Arts, RSA, MAFA and Manchester Graphic Club. Manchester City Art Gallery holds Kingsley's oil The Green Fence, Hulme, of 1960, typical of his northern townscapes and industrial scenes.

John KINGSLEY 1956– Painter, collagist and teacher, born in Glasgow of cultured English parents. Kingsley became a talented flautist as well as a painter who originally worked in the manner of Walter Sickert, later abandoning that artist's tonality for Fauve-like colour, seen to advantage in his French landscapes. He studied at Glasgow School of Art, 1973–7, under James Robertson, Geoffrey Squire and David Donaldson. He taught part-time at a Glasgow secondary school. Kingsley showed at RSA, Royal Glasgow Institute of the Fine Arts and at Paisley Art Institute, of which he was a council member. In 1991 he won the William Bowie Landscape Prize and in 1992 the Mary Armour Award at Paisley. Argyle and Bute District Council and Royal College of Physicians and Surgeons, Glasgow, hold his work. In 1993 John Kingsley's Provence was held at The Contemporary Fine Art Gallery, Eton.

Angela KINGSTON 1936– Botanical watercolourist, born in Mumbles, near Swansea. She studied at Bath Academy of Art, 1955–8, where she was awarded a travelling scholarship. She was a founder-member of the Society of Botanical Artists, a member of Welsh Group and was for a time chairman of WSW. Also showed widely elsewhere in England and Wales. Her solo shows included The Library, Cowbridge, 1975; University College, Cardiff, 1979; The Coach House Gallery, Caerphilly, 1989–92; and in 1992 shared show at Mistral Galleries. Glynn Vivian Art Gallery, Swansea, holds her work.

Caroline KININMONTH 1907–1978 Painter in oil of landscapes and flowers. Lady Kininmonth studied art at Edinburgh College of Art, 1926–30, under D M Sutherland and David Alison. She was married to the distinguished Scottish architect Sir William Kininmonth. She exhibited at the RSA and SSWA and her work is held by Edinburgh University and the Scottish Arts Council. Lived in Edinburgh.

Peter KINLEY 1926–1988 Painter of abstract and near-abstract figure and landscape pictures, born in Vienna, Austria, but arrived in England in late-1930s. After several years in Army he studied at Düsseldorf Academy, 1948–9, and at St Martin's School of Art, 1949–53. First showed with Young Contemporaries in 1951, having first solo exhibition at Gimpel Fils in 1954, followed by a series. Went on to show widely in Britain, in New York at Paul Rosenberg & Co and in India. In 1982 had a retrospective at Museum of Modern Art, Oxford; and in 1986 a solo show at Kettle's Yard Gallery, Cambridge, which toured. Among his teaching posts were sessions at St Martin's, 1954–64, and Bath Academy of Art and Bath College of Higher Education, 1971–88. Tate Gallery and Arts Council hold his work. A dominant influence on the work of Kinley was the 1953 exhibition in London of the French painter Nicolas de Staël.

Shona KINLOCH 1962– Sculptor who studied at Glasgow School of Art, gaining an honours degree, then completed a post-graduate course in sculpture. Exhibitions included Glasgow Garden Festival and Compass Gallery and Ewan Mundy Fine Art, both in Glasgow. Commissions included Thinking of Bella at Italian Centre, Glasgow, and Scottish Nuclear, East Kilbride. Kelvingrove Art Gallery in Glasgow, Lillie Art Gallery in Milngavie and Flemings Bank hold examples.

David KINMONT 1932– Artist in various media and teacher, born in Westgate-on-Sea, Kent. He studied at the Regional College of Art, Manchester, and Cambridge University. He was head of the art department at Rhyl Grammar School, then held a series of teaching posts, becoming senior lecturer in the history of art at Bristol University. Mixed shows included RCamA of which he was a member and Royal National Eisteddfod. Had a series of solo exhibitions including retrospectives at Ferens Art Gallery, Hull, in 1963, and St John's, Cambridge, his old college, 1969; later ones included University of Durham, 1981, and Bristol University, 1983. Lived in Flax Bourton, Bristol.

Linda KINSELLA 1914– Miniaturist and teacher, born in Teddington, Middlesex. She studied at Ealing School of Art and Isleworth Polytechnic and showed at RA, RI, elsewhere in London and at Paris Salon. Sometimes signed work with initials. Lived in Wraysbury, Berkshire.

Christine KINSEY fl. from 1960s– Artist in a wide range of media, teacher and administrator, born in Pontypool, Monmouthshire. She studied at Newport College of Art and University of Wales, Cardiff. Between 1968–76 Kinsey was co-founder and director, Chapter, Workshops and Centre for the Arts in Cardiff, a co-founder of Artists and Designers in Wales Association and artistic advisor to Cardiff City Council for redevelopment of the city centre. She lectured in art and design at graduate and postgraduate level at University of Wales, 1975–6, from 1976–80 being artist and teacher, Foundation for Professional and Vocational Training, St Maarten, Netherland Antilles. A number of part-time and visiting lectureships in Wales, America and Italy followed. Kinsey also took part in many workshops and master-classes. In 1982 she won a print-making prize at the National Eisteddfod of Wales, Swansea. Mixed shows included Group 75, Muse Gallery in Philadelphia, Roy Miles Gallery, Oriel in Bangor and Inverness Museum and Art Gallery. Later touring shows included National Library of Wales, Aberystwyth, and other Welsh venues, 1990. Her work is held by Victoria & Albert Museum and Glynn Vivian Art Gallery, Swansea as well as the National Library. Lived in Pencader, Dyfed.

Kay KINSMAN 1909– Watercolourist and draughtsman, born in Los Angeles, California, her correct name being Katherine Kinsman. She was educated in Cuba, Jamaica and in New York, then studied painting at Parsons School Applied Art, Paris, and Montreal Museum of Fine Arts. SGA member who also showed widely in the Cotswolds and west Midlands area and in Canada. Was an accomplished pianist and produced the books *Montreal Sketchbook* and *Broadway Sketchbook*. Lived in Pershore, Worcestershire.

The KIPPER KIDS Performance, film, video, photography and installation artists, formed in 1970 by Brian Routh and Martin von Haselberg. Routh was born in Gateshead, County Durham, in 1948, von Haselberg in Buenos Aires, Argentina, in 1949. They both attended the E.15 Drama School in London, von Haselberg also the American Film Institute, Los Angeles. The Kipper Kids performed all over Europe and North America, venues including Stedelijk Museum, Amsterdam; Kunstalle, Basel; Maalersaal, Hamburg; and ICA. Sometimes they were joined by others, such as the British performance artist Anne Bean. Latterly, Routh and von Haselberg (who was married to the American actress, singer and comedienne Bette Midler) lived and worked in New York and California. The Whitney Museum, New York, planned a Kipper Kids show in 1998. Von Haselberg also showed solo, venues including P.S.1 Contemporary Art Center, New York, 1997–8.

John KIRBY 1949– Painter, born in Liverpool. He was a shipping clerk, 1965–7, a bookshop salesman, 1967–9, then assistant to the director of Boys' Town of Calcutta, 1969–71, after which he did various social work jobs until in 1982–5 he was at St Martin's School of Art. The Royal College of Art followed, 1986–8. Kirby's figure paintings had a disturbing, Surrealist element; symbols and objects and the painter's own face frequently recurred, and there were references to his Catholic upbringing. Kirby showed in many mixed exhibitions from John Player Portrait Exhibition at National Portrait Gallery in 1984. As a solo artist he showed with Angela Flowers, in Ireland and London, from 1988.

John Kynnersley KIRBY 1894–1962 Mainly a figure painter, he was born in the Nottingham area, was educated at Sedbergh School and then at the Slade School of Fine Art. Kirby showed extensively in mixed exhibitions, including RA, NEAC, ROI, Chenil and Goupil Galleries and in Nottingham. In the 1940s he developed arthritis, which around the end of World War prevented him from painting, about which he became bitter. Although he had been left some money, he is said to have died virtually penniless. Lived from 1929 at Stansted, Essex, building a studio at his cottage, where he completed much locally commissioned work. In 1980 Sparrow's Gallery, in Bishop's Stortford, showed Kirby's work, part of a local characters exhibition. Kirby's picture Old Regent Street was included in Christie's NEAC centenary exhibition in 1986, lent by Bradford Art Gallery and Museum. Kirby was a popular member of the Chelsea Arts Club, remembered by another as "very handsome, rather like Clark Gable, who loved sporting checks, waistcoats and bow ties, who fell in love with glamorous blondes and who drove a dashing car. He was always known as Dick Kirby."

Josh KIRBY 1928– Artist in oil, watercolour and occasionally gouache, born in Waterloo, Liverpool, as Ronald William Kirby. He attended Liverpool City School of Art, 1942–9, teachers including Martin Bell, Will C Penn, George Jardine, Alfred Wiffen and Allan Tankard. Kirby's influences "were Brueghel, Bosch and Brangwyn. I aim to continue the classical tradition and avoid the fads and fashions of the moment. I would like to preserve a sense of wonder in a world obsessed with materialism." This found expression in his The Voyage of the Ayeguy, latter-day altar-pieces in science fiction mode. Kirby had periods painting in a film poster studio in London and freelanced briefly in Paris. Was a member of the Association of British Picture Restorers. Group exhibitions included Portal Gallery, Bluecoat Chambers in Liverpool, ICA and Brighton Art Gallery. Solo shows included DLI Museum & Durham Art Gallery, 1995. Duke of Bedford at Woburn Abbey holds Kirby's work. Lived at Shelfanger, Diss, Norfolk.

Michael KIRBY 1949– Painter and restorer who was born in Farnham Common, Buckinghamshire. He studied at High Wycombe School of Art, 1967–71, teachers including Eric Smith and Romeo di Girolamo. Kirby was a member Free Painters and Sculptors, also exhibiting with RBA and elsewhere. Lived in Hedgerley, Buckinghamshire.

Sarah KIRBY 1903–c.1980 Painter in oil, full name Kathleen Sarah N Kirby, born in London. She studied at King's College, London University, obtaining her Master of Science degree in 1928, also attending London Day Training College. By profession Kirby was a lecturer, and she published *Nature Study for Schools* in 1957. Self-taught, she joined Free Painters and Sculptors in 1972, showing at Loggia Gallery, RA and at Paris Salon. Had a solo exhibition at Bristol Arts Centre in 1967. Lived latterly in Bath, Avon.

Barry KIRK 1933– Painter, draughtsman and teacher, working in a variety of media, born in Deal, Kent. After Westminster School he studied Canterbury College of Art, 1950–4, then Royal College of Art, 1956–9, gaining a Travelling Scholarship in the latter year, teachers including Julian Trevelyan, Edwin La Dell and Alistair Grant. Taught at Canterbury from 1959, becoming principal, 1987–8. Showed in RA Summer Exhibition and had a series of solo shows, including Alwin Gallery. Victoria & Albert Museum holds his work. Lived at Bridge, Kent.

Douglas KIRK 1949– Painter and teacher, born in Edinburgh. He attended Duncan of Jordanstone College of Art, Dundee, 1967–71, then was at Royal College of Art, 1971–4. Kirk worked for several months at Cité des Arts, Paris, in 1973. He gained a British Institute Award in 1971, the Burston Award at the Royal College three years later, in the same year getting a Scottish Arts Council Award. From the early-1970s Kirk showed with SSA as well as taking part in Christmas exhibitions at Compass Gallery, Glasgow, where he shared a show in 1974. Scottish Arts Council holds his work, which could be decorative and abstract. Went on to teach at Sir John Cass School of Art and City of London Polytechnic. Lived latterly at Gravesend, in Kent.

Eve KIRK 1900–1969 Painter and decorative artist, born in London. She studied at Slade School of Fine Art, 1919–22, then travelled widely on the continent. Had first solo exhibition at

Paterson Gallery in 1930, to which Augustus John contributed. Her work at its best had some of the juicy, painterly qualities found in that of John, who painted Kirk's portrait. Kirk went on to show at Leicester, Lefevre Galleries and elsewhere and in the mid-1940s decorated the Catholic church in Newtown, Wales. About a decade later she went to live in Italy and gave up painting. Tate Gallery and Arts Council hold her work.

Joanna KIRK 1963– Artist, notably in pastel, born in Cheshire. She studied at Goldsmiths' College School of Art, 1981–4. In 1987 she gained joint first prize, 1987 Artist Award, Whitechapel Art Gallery. Her group shows included Christie's Inaugural Exhibition and Riverside Studios, 1984; Richard Pomeroy Gallery, 1987; and Norwich School of Art Gallery, 1988. Her work in Contemporary Art Society collection, Cardinals, was shown in South Bank Centre tour The British Art Show 1990. Kirk's solo shows began with Third Eye Centre in Glasgow, 1987, the year she began exhibiting with Nicola Jacobs Gallery. Also showed at New Gallery at Whitechapel Art Gallery in 1988 and at Carine Campo Gallery, Antwerp, 1989. Kirk worked from photographs and wanted pictures to be "well-drawn, highly finished, to be decorative, full of pattern, delicate". Lived in London.

Mick KIRKBY-GEDDES 1966– Sculptor, mostly in junk sheet-metal, born in Sheffield, Yorkshire. He studied at Mansfield College of Further Education, 1984, fine art at Leeds Polytechnic, 1985–8, then became a self-employed sculptor. Kirkby-Geddes' work was "influenced by cartoons, television, life, and so on. It is light-hearted and colourful, employing visual puns, some automata and lots of dogs." Group shows included Rufford Sculpture Park, 1987; Camden Arts Centre, 1989; Galerie Goetz in Basel, Switzerland, 1992; and Benchmarks, Tatton Park, Cheshire, 1993. Had solo shows with Leeds Art Company, 1990; Treadwell's Art Mill, Bradford, 1992; and Crescent Arts, Scarborough, 1993. Lived in Holmfirth, Yorkshire.

Edward Todd KIRKHAM 1947– Sculptor and teacher who did a foundation course at Blackpool College of Art, 1976–8, graduated in sculpture at Leeds Polytechnic, 1978–81, then completed his master's degree at Royal College of Art, 1981–3. Among his teaching experience was Royal College of Art, Royal Academy Schools, Central School and in the provinces. A Leeds Polytechnic Travel Award took him to France in 1981, in 1984 he gained the Royal College Sculpture Prize, in 1988–9 being Rome Scholar in Sculpture. He researched the cult and rituals of Dionysus. Among his exhibitions were Leeds 80, at Lancaster University, 1980; Sculpture in the Landscape, Portland Clifftop Sculpture Park, 1983; as artist-in-residence, 1984, Mostyn Art Gallery, Llandudno; and Sculpture at Canterbury, 1992.

Norman KIRKHAM 1936– Artist, designer and lecturer, working in oil, watercolour, gouache and pastel, born and lived in Glasgow, where he attended the School of Art, 1953–8, taught by David Donaldson. Worked as a designer, 1960–75, began painting then and was in 1977 a part-time lecturer at Glasgow School of Art. He was president of Glasgow Art Club, 1988–91, and honorary secretary of Royal Glasgow Institute of the Fine Arts from 1991. Won many prizes at the Institute. Also showed at RA, RSA, RP, Fine Art Society, Seen Gallery and elsewhere in group exhibitions. Later solo shows included Barclay Lennie Fine Art, Glasgow, from 1986. HRH The Duke of Edinburgh, Arthur Andersen and Fleming's hold examples.

Alison KIRKPATRICK fl. from early 1990s– Sculptor working in a variety of materials, born in Kendal, Westmorland. She moved to Scotland aged two and graduated from Edinburgh College of Art in 1990, then studied for her master's degree. She was an artist who pondered over notes and made sketches over long periods before creating the final work from materials she had "an instinctive response to … The kind of shapes I come up with are accidental." She took part in Danger Artists at Work, a City Art Centre, Edinburgh, touring show in 1991. The city's collection holds her work.

Ian KIRKWOOD fl. from late 1960s– Painter who said that his pictures were "intended as haptic fictions, studio-formed but grounded in experience". He studied at Leicester Polytechnic, 1968–9; St Martin's School of Art, 1969–72; and University College, London, 1972–5. Exhibitions included Yarrow Gallery, Oundle, 1982; Museum of Modern Art, Oxford, and Aspex Gallery, Portsmouth, both 1983; D H Lawrence's Landscape, at Nottingham Playhouse and Leicester Museum, 1985; and Art '87 at Peterborough's Lady Lodge Arts Centre, 1987. Peterborough City Museum, Eastern Arts and Leicestershire Education Authority hold Kirkwood's work.

John Sutherland KIRKWOOD 1947– Artist working in mixed media, printmaker and photographer, born in Edinburgh where he continued to live. After George Watson's College he attended Duncan of Jordanstone College of Art, Dundee, 1965–70, doing a large number of jobs ranging from school teaching to labouring. Elected SSA in 1972 and took part in many mixed shows. Gained Scottish Arts Council Award in 1973, with Council Bursaries in 1976 and 1980, and was included in the Council's show Scottish Art Now in 1982. Kirkwood said that his work was "about trying to communicate with people". He was influenced by Dada and much of his subject matter was industrial and took a pessimistic view of militarism. Solo shows included New 57 Gallery, Edinburgh, in 1972 and 1976; Printmakers' Workshop Gallery, Edinburgh, 1974; and Talbot Rice Art Centre, Edinburgh, 1981. Scottish Museum of Modern Art is among several public collections holding his work.

Dorris KIRLEW 1906– Painter and teacher, born in Bath, Somerset, where she attended the School of Art, then the Royal College of Art. Taught at Grantham Girls' School before moving to Brighton, Sussex, where she taught at the College of Art, also at Lewes Boys' Grammar School and at Hove Girls' Grammar School. Showed early in her career at public gallery in Nottingham, later at RA. In her final years she concentrated more

on collage and tapestry than on painting. Brighton Art Gallery holds several works.

Ronald Brooks KITAJ 1932– Painter, printmaker and teacher, born Cleveland, Ohio. Studied at Cooper Union in New York, and Akademie der Bildenden Künste, Vienna, 1950–2; at Ruskin School of Drawing in Oxford, 1958–9; then Royal College of Art, 1959–61. Kitaj was an important influence on fellow-students at the Royal College, such as David Hockney. Although labelled initially as a Pop Artist, Kitaj's work was more complex, autobiographical, drawing on many, often arcane, sources of inspiration. After a period in the early 1960s painting in England and Spain, Kitaj from 1962–6 taught at Camberwell School of Art, while having a one-man show at Marlborough Fine Art in 1963. He was an infrequent exhibitor, but gradually built up an international reputation from the 1960s, with important exhibitions in America, Germany, Italy and France. In 1967–8 was invited to teach at the University of California, Berkeley. There was a retrospective at Hirshhorn Museum and Sculpture Garden, Washington, 1981, another at the Tate Gallery, 1994. The harsh critical reception of this and the death of his wife Sandra Fisher, also a painter, events which Kitaj saw as related, spurred him to resettle in Los Angeles in 1997. About the same time a huge tapestry, produced at Dovecot Studio and based on Kitaj's picture If Not, Not (in the Scottish National Gallery of Modern Art, Edinburgh), was unveiled in the entrance Hall of the New British Library. Works by Kitaj, who was elected RA in 1991, are also held by the Arts Council, Tate Gallery and other collections.

Bert KITCHEN 1940– Painter, designer, illustrator and teacher, born in Liverpool, who gained a diploma in design at Central School of Arts and Crafts. He was a part-time lecturer there, 1961–4, and at City of London Polytechnic, 1964–92. Kitchen was noted for his versatility, completing textile designs for Edinburgh Weavers; animation films for BBC and London Weekend Television; background paintings for feature and television films; illustrations for Cape, Collins, Kestrel and other publishers; artwork for advertising agencies; and regular illustration for *Private Eye* magazine, 1969–93. Awards included the Chicago & Illinois Cassandra Foundation Award (Painting), 1969; International Graphics, First Prize, Fiera di Bologna, and included in honours list of the Critici in Erba, Bologna, both 1988; and Gold Medal for Illustration, Society of Illustrators, New York, 1991. Mixed shows included Beaux Arts Gallery, 1961; Der Geist des Surrealismus, Baukunst Gallery, Cologne, 1971; First Tokyo Biennale, New Image in Painting, 1974; Deck of Cards, JPL Gallery, 1976; and Surrealism Unlimited, Camden Arts Centre, 1978. Had a solo show at Archer Gallery, 1973, later ones including a retrospective at Smith's Gallery, 1991. From 1984 Kitchen wrote and illustrated a series of his own books. Lived in London.

Myfanwy KITCHIN 1917– Ceramic sculptor, artist in various media on paper, book illustrator and art critic, born in Newbury, Berkshire, who sometimes signed work Myf. She attended Hornsey School of Art, Slade/Ruskin Schools (evacuated to Oxford in World War II), the department of fine art at Reading University under J A Betts and Walsall College of Art. For 15 years Kitchin was art critic for *The Guardian* newspaper in the Midlands area. She also illustrated books for Phoenix House and Duckworth. Her ceramic sculptures stemmed from the slab pottery technique, developed from on-the-spot sketches. The subjects were originally industrial workers in the Midlands and later farmers and animals in Gwynedd, where she lived at Barmouth. Kitchin was a member of RCamA. She also showed with RBSA, Ombersley Gallery at Ombersley and galleries in Birmingham, Walsall and Lichfield, and she had a solo exhibition at Y Tabernacl, Machynlleth, 1997.

Roy KITCHIN 1926–1997 Sculptor and teacher, born in East Anglia. He was brought up in industrial Birmingham and studied at the School of Arts and Crafts there. After working as an architectural sculptor from 1954–60 Kitchin taught at Wolverhampton College of Art for 10 years. He settled to work in Cannock, Staffordshire, teaching at the University of Newcastle upon Tyne. Kitchin showed in mixed exhibitions at Landmark Park in Scotland, at the Yorkshire Sculpture Park and was included in the Welsh Sculpture Trust Margam Sculpture Park show Sculpture in a Country Park, in 1983. Kitchin also held several solo shows, including Whitworth Art Gallery, Manchester. Although Kitchin's early work was normally bronze and concerned with such subjects as landscape and fertility, in the early 1960s he became interested in materials such as steel and cast concrete and industrial topics. The later works, often imbued with humour, could be large and designed to heighten visual awareness.

Robert KITCHINER 1907– Painter, draughtsman and printmaker, born in London, who studied at Slade School of Fine Art, 1928–31, under Henry Tonks and Philip Wilson Steer. Showed at RA, NEAC and in the provinces. Lived at Sawbridgeworth, Hertfordshire.

Arthur KITCHING 1912–1981 Painter, draughtsman and curator, born in Sheffield, Yorkshire. He went into the steelworks as a clerk at 16 and began painting two years later. Financial reasons prevented his taking a place offered at Royal College of Art. Thus he taught himself, apart from a year at Sheffield College of Art in 1934. He never became a professional artist, but did a number of mundane jobs until he became, in 1961, first curator of Manor House Museum and Art Gallery, Ilkley, and then exhibitions officer for Bradford Metropolitan Council. He did not show his own work until he was 53. At times there were Wyndham Lewis- and Matisse-like elements in Kitching's pictures in which, he said, "representation took second place to overall abstract design." His book *Pavements and People* was published in facsimile and after his death Leeds City Art Gallery gave him a commemorative show.

Paul KITCHINGMAN 1947– Artist who was self-taught, painting in oil and watercolour from early youth. His main interest was landscape, and he did conservation work with the National Trust and cultivated bonsai grown from seed collected on foreign trips. From the early 1970s Kitchingman travelled extensively on the continent, notably Mediterranean countries and Turkey. He sold much of his work there, English exhibitions including The Heifer Gallery.

Roger KITE 1947– Painter and teacher, born in Bath, Somerset. Studied at Hornsey College of Art, 1970–4, then Chelsea School of Art, 1974–5. From 1977 he taught at Trent Polytechnic. Among his shows were Athena Awards, 1987; Kettle's Yard, Cambridge, 1988; and John Moores Liverpool Exhibition, 1989–90. He had a solo exhibition at Café Gallery, 1989. Arts Council holds his geometrical abstract picture Diagonal 1, of 1976, bought from Acme Gallery. Lived in Ilford, Essex.

Linda KITSON 1945– Painter, draughtsman and teacher, born and lived in London. She studied at St Martin's School of Art, 1965–7, then Royal College of Art, 1967–70. Kitson was chosen as the official war artist to accompany the Falklands Islands Task Force in 1982, which she found a searing, indelible experience. The three-month tour resulted in 400 works, often done at speed in uncomfortable, hostile conditions. Work was taken into the collection of the Imperial War Museum, which toured a show, and a book was published called *The Falklands War, a Visual Diary*. Kitson also exhibited at RA, Workshop Gallery and elsewhere.

Robert Hawthorn KITSON fl. from c.1920–1947 Watercolour landscapist who became a member of RBA in 1925. Lived for a time at Taormini in Sicily, eventually settling in Leeds in the 1920s. Showed extensively at Fine Art Society, Redfern and Goupil Galleries, also at RA and Walker Art Gallery in Liverpool.

Barry KITTS 1943– Painter, graphic designer, teacher and writer, born in Bath, Somerset. He had early tuition while still at school from the printmaker George Mackley, then studied at Kingston School of Art, 1959–61, teachers including Donald Pavey, and Wimbledon School of Art, 1961–4, under Gerald Cooper. Went on to do visiting lecturing at Ravensbourne College of Design and at London College of Printing. Showed at NEAC, RBA and elsewhere. Was part-author of a book on graphic design sources. Lived in London.

Meyer KLANG 1880–1948 Artist who produced portraits and still lifes, based in London's East End, who showed at RBA, RA, Walker Art Gallery in Liverpool and elsewhere. Ben Uri Art Society holds his oil on canvas Flowerpiece.

Anita KLEIN 1960– Artist in oil on board, charcoal, drypoint etching and ceramic, born in Sydney, Australia. Powerful groups of colourful, stylised figures were a key feature of her output. She studied at Chelsea School of Art, 1978–9; gained an honours degree in fine art from Slade School, 1979–83; then did a postgraduate diploma in printmaking at the Slade, 1983–5. Her teachers included Paula Rego, Mick Moon and John Hoyland. Klein was a member of RE, Greenwich Printmakers and the Printmakers' Council. Group exhibitions included New Contemporaries, at ICA; British Drawing, at Hayward Gallery; Blond Fine Art; RWA; ROI; and Bradford Print Biennale. Solo shows included Creaser Gallery, 1986; Victorian Artists' Society, Melbourne, 1992; and Woodlands Art Gallery, 1993. Arts Council, Ashmolean Museum in Oxford and London University hold examples. Lived in London.

Leo KLIN 1887–1967 Painter born in Grodno, Russia, where he studied at the Imperial Academy of Fine Arts, St Petersburg. In England he exhibited widely, including RA, RP, UA, NEAC and throughout the provinces. Sunderland Museum and Art Gallery and Russell-Cotes Art Gallery, Bournemouth, hold his work. Lived in London.

Clara KLINGHOFFER 1900–1970 Painter, printmaker and draughtsman, born near Lemberg, Austria. She grew up and studied in London, having her first one-man show at 19, which was a triumph. She studied at Slade School of Fine Art and Central School of Arts and Crafts and in the late-1920s married the writer J W F Stoppelman. She went on to show widely through Britain, the continent and North America, living latterly in London and New York. Klinghoffer was noted for her portraits, especially of children, and was a masterly draughtsman, in the Old Master tradition. Jacob Epstein considered her "an artist of great talent, a painter of the first order … in the very first rank of draughtsmen in the world." Venues showing her work included RA, Belgrave Gallery, NEAC and Venice Biennale. Travelled widely and painted many notable people, including Dame Sybil Thorndike the actress, the writer Isaac Bashevis Singer and the politician Sir Barnett Janner. Tate Gallery, Victoria & Albert Museum and Manchester City Art Gallery are among many holding her pictures.

Christiana KLITGAARD: *see* **Christiana Brix MAY**

Olivier KLOMPKES 1972– Painter, designer and illustrator producing colourful, decorative work, born in Belgium. He trained at Stockport College of Art, 1992–4, winning the R J Brown top student award. As a designer Klompkes gained prizes from Royal Doulton and Sundour Fabrics, and exhibited at international trade fairs in New York, Frankfurt and Brussels. Work was shown in mixed exhibitions at Format Studios, Macclesfield, 1995; NaveDiez Art Gallery, Valencia, Spain (with a solo show there in 1997); and Gordon Hepworth Fine Art at 23 Smith Street, 1997.

Margarete KLOPFLEISCH 1911–1982 Sculptor, painter, draughtsman and printmaker, born in Dresden, Germany. She was throughout her life dogged by ill-health, after a deprived youth. Leaving school at 14, she had to mother the family and do menial jobs, but managed to teach herself the violin, went to modelling classes and became involved in left-wing politics. Modelled for Otto Dix's life class at Art School. When Hitler came to power

Gretel joined her future husband, Peter Klopfleisch, in Prague, where she was taught by the artist Käte Schaffner. Joined the Oskar Kokoschka Club in 1937. Through it and AIA, of which she became a member, was able to emigrate to England. Attended sculpture classes at Reading University, but setbacks intervened, and she was interned in Isle of Man, where she was seriously ill, and Peter was sent to Australia. When reunited she worked again as a sculptor, showing in London, Maidenhead, Cookham, Eton, Glasgow, Windsor and Reading. In 1960 returned to Dresden with her two daughters, where her husband eventually joined her, but artistic recognition came slowly. Became a member of Dresden Artists' Union and a year before she died had successful exhibition at Galerie Comenius, Dresden. In 1987 John Denham Gallery had a substantial show of her work.

Stefan KNAPP 1921–1996 Painter, born in Bilgoraj, Poland, who settled in England after World War II. Studied at Slade School of Fine Art, 1947–50, after initial education in Poland. Had first solo show at London Gallery in 1947, then exhibited widely, including France, Germany, America and Brazil. He was given a retrospective at Warsaw Gallery of Zacheta in 1974. Although he established a reputation for subtle spraygun pictures, Knapp was also noted for his painting in glass on steel and for his paintings on enamel, fired in a kiln developed by him. Work held by many international museums, including Victoria & Albert Museum and Museum of Modern Art in New York. Also fulfilled many commissions for large murals, one for the Alexander Stores, in New York, being roughly 100 feet long; it had to be assembled in an aircraft hangar. Lived in London, then in Wormley, Surrey.

John KNAPP-FISHER 1931– Painter in watercolour, oil and mixed media, born in London. He studied at Maidstone College of Art, 1949–52, concentrating on graphic design. Knapp-Fisher then designed in the theatre and painted and exhibited from a sea-going home for five years. He moved to Wales in 1965, settling in Haverfordwest, Pembrokeshire, opening a studio/gallery in 1967. As Trevigan Gallery he published postcards and limited edition reproduction prints of his paintings. Knapp-Fisher's subjects were landscape, seascape, buildings, boats, figures, animals and fish. He aimed "to produce pictures that are exciting, have strong compositional form and powerful visual imagery". Showed at many venues, including RA, Agnew, the Marjorie Parr, Upper Grosvenor, Bankside and Business Art Galleries, RWA, WAC, Beaux Arts in Bath and elsewhere. HRH The Prince of Wales, National Library of Wales in Aberystwyth and Swansea University hold examples.

Bryan KNEALE 1930– Sculptor, painter and teacher, born in Douglas, Isle of Man. He studied at Douglas School of Art, 1947, then Royal Academy Schools, 1948–52, being a Rome Scholar in painting, 1949–51. Kneale began making sculpture at the end of the 1950s, a move which he later described as inevitable, because of his preoccupation with form. At first it was welded steel sculptures, but he later added other materials. Kneale was an abstract sculptor who drew on such inspirations as anthropomorphic and vegetal forms. Teaching included Royal Academy Schools and Royal College of Art, where he was first professor of drawing until 1995. Was made RA in 1973. His work appeared in group shows such as John Moores Exhibition Liverpool, 1961; the 1966–7 Sculpture from the Arts Council Collection show; and 1977 Silver Jubilee Contemporary British Sculpture Exhibition in Battersea Park, London. Kneale's first solo show of paintings at Redfern Gallery in 1954 was followed by many others there. He had a retrospective at Whitechapel Art Gallery in 1966 and at RWA in 1995. Helped organise two big sculpture exhibitions: British Sculptors '72, at Burlington House, London; and the Battersea Park show. His work is in many international collections including Arts Council, Contemporary Art Society, Museum of Modern Art in New York and Tate Gallery. Lived in London.

Howard KNEE 1889–1971 Watercolour painter, born in London, who studied at the School of Art, Dublin. Exhibited at the RA and RHA and had his work reproduced by several British and Irish publishers. Lived in Dublin.

Cecily KNEESHAW 1883– Watercolourist, full name Cecilia Margaret Kneeshaw, who sometimes signed her work C K. She was privately educated, partly as a musician. Was a member of BWS and UA, with which she last showed in 1956. Also exhibited at RI, RCamA, RSA and Walker Art Gallery, Liverpool, and had a solo show at Arlington Gallery in 1935. Lived in Lyndhurst, Hampshire.

Frank KNELLER 1914– Painter of horses and dogs in the manner of Stubbs, born in Bangor, Caernarvonshire. He studied at University College of North Wales and obtained a Bachelor of Science degree. In Edinburgh, studied at the College of Art under John Murray Thomson and dissected horses at a local veterinary college. Exhibited RSA, RCamA, RSW and UA and published some cartoons. Was a member of the Ski Club of Great Britain. Latterly lived in Eastbourne, Sussex.

Bonnie KNICKERBOCKER 1943– Painter, born in Chicago, Illinois, America, whose childhood was spent in Charlottesville, Virginia. She gained her bachelor's degree in fine arts from George Washington University Corcoran School of Art in 1965, then travelled the world for a year, living in Sydney, Australia, 1967–9. She moved to London in 1969, attending Camden Art School, 1969–71. Knickerbocker painted in Madrid, Spain, 1971–2; Mill Valley, California, 1972–4; and Santa Fe, New Mexico, 1974–90. She then worked variously in London, Washington and Tucson, Arizona. A creator of colourful, vibrant images, Knickerbocker showed at Camden Arts Centre from 1970; Festival of the Arts, Santa Fe, from 1976; and Mariposa Gallery, Albuquerque, New Mexico, from 1982. She took part in a three-man show at Tricycle Gallery, 1984, solo exhibitions including Carol Thornton Gallery, Santa Fe, New Mexico, 1986.

Alick KNIGHT 1903–1983 Painter, printmaker, designer, illustrator and teacher, born in Ifield, Sussex, as Sidney Alick

Knight. Studied at Central School of Arts and Crafts, 1919–22, with Bernard Meninsky and A S Hartrick. From 1922–4 Knight did his design training at Carlton Studios, joined the advertising agency Alfred Pemberton in 1924 and from 1926–45 was its art director-designer. Although rejected as an official war artist during World War II, Knight did a body of war work, as shown at Abbott & Holder in 1990. From 1939, Knight assisted with a range of government propaganda, then from 1942 he was in the Army, involved in camouflage and cartography; was attached to the Royal Army Medical Corps, making anatomical drawings in hospital and the operating theatre; then was appointed art instructor at the Army School of Education, Park Hall, Shropshire. After the war Knight resigned from Pemberton's to devote himself to painting, although he also worked freelance for publishers and advertisers and taught in art schools. Knight was a member of the Society of Industrial Artists, Senefelder Club and London Sketch Club, showing at galleries including Leicester and Redfern. Lived in London.

Charles KNIGHT 1865–1948 Landscape watercolourist, by profession an accountant, father of the artist Charles Knight. He was born in Slinfold, Sussex, became a member of Brighton Arts Club and painted extensively in the county where he showed, also depicting other parts of England and Wales. Brighton Art Gallery, which holds his work, gave him a memorial exhibition in 1949.

Charles KNIGHT 1901–1990 Painter, especially of landscape, and teacher, born in Hove, Sussex, the county which he often depicted and where he settled in Ditchling. Encouraged as a child by an amateur painter father, Knight entered Brighton College of Art soon after World War I, remaining there for four years much influenced by his teacher, Louis Ginnett. Then studied for two years at Royal Academy Schools and etching at Royal College of Art. At college Knight won the Turner Medal and Landseer Scholarship; his prize composition, Llangollen, was bought for the Tate Gallery. In mid-1920s was impressed by the work of John Sell Cotman, and this left a lasting influence on Knight's watercolours. Taught at Brighton College of Art, being vice-principal from 1959–67. Showed regularly at RA and was a member of RWS and ROI. In World War II Knight completed 40 watercolours for the Pilgrim Trust *Recording Britain* project, making an invaluable record of the Brighton area. Was married to the illustrator Leonora Vasey. Towner Art Gallery, Eastbourne, held an exhibition of Knight's work in 1997 in conjunction with Chris Beetles.

Clifford KNIGHT 1930– Painter in a variety of media and teacher, born and lived in Kempston, Bedfordshire. He studied at Central School of Arts and Crafts, 1955–7, teachers including William Roberts, Merlyn Evans and Blair Hughes-Stanton. For a dozen years he taught at Bedford College, also Bedford Prison. Neo-Romantic artists including Paul Nash, John Piper and Graham Sutherland influenced Knight's work, which featured ruin and decay in derelict buildings and the landscape. From 1955 Knight was a member of UA. He had solo shows at Upper Street Gallery, Gordon Maynard Gallery in Welwyn and at galleries in Luton, Northampton and Letchworth. The Crown Commissioners, Luton and Letchworth Art Galleries hold examples. Wrote for *Leisure Painter* magazine.

Esmond KNIGHT 1906–1987 Actor, singer and recreational painter, born in East Sheen, Surrey. He was educated at Westminster School and made his first appearance professionally at the Old Vic in 1925. He made his first film appearance in 1931 and then established a career in television. Notable among Knight's numerous appearances was his one-man show *Agincourt – the Archer's Tale*. During World War II Knight was in the Royal Navy, and while serving on the *Prince of Wales* was hit in the face by molten metal and blinded. He underwent rehabilitation at a St Dunstan's training school and was able to resume acting, partially recovering his sight in 1943, but at best it was "like looking through clouds", and it eventually deteriorated. Even so, Knight developed as a competent painter and had several shows, including New Town Gallery, Uckfield. Died in Egypt.

Harold KNIGHT 1874–1961 Painter of sensitive portraits, especially of women, and interiors, born in Nottingham. In the mid-1890s he studied at the local School of Art; also studied in Paris at Académie Julian, his teachers including Jean-Paul Laurens and Benjamin Constant. Knight married Laura Johnson – later to become Dame Laura Knight – the painter, in 1903, having known her in Nottingham and in Staithes, Yorkshire, where he painted on his return from France. With her he studied the Dutch masters in the Netherlands, then from 1908 they lived for a decade in Newlyn, Cornwall, eventually settling in London. Knight was a steady exhibitor at RA from 1896, being elected RA in 1937. Also showed Leicester Galleries, IS and elsewhere. His reticent work and personality were overshadowed by Laura's ebullient, more colourful nature and painting, but his pictures' real qualities have been more appreciated in recent years. Tate Gallery and Hove Museum and Art Gallery hold his work. Died in Colwall, Herefordshire.

Joseph KNIGHT 1870–1952 Painter, printmaker and teacher, born in Bolton, Lancashire, who studied in Paris. He settled in Bury, Lancashire, where he was head of the School of Art. Showed at RA, RCamA, Walker Art Gallery in Liverpool and at Manchester City Art Gallery which holds his still life Chinese Pottery, oil on canvas, of 1931.

Laura KNIGHT 1877–1970 Figure and landscape painter in oil and watercolour, draughtsman and etcher. Born at Long Eaton, Derbyshire, she studied art under Wilson Foster at Nottingham School of Art, where she met her husband, the painter Harold Knight. Together they painted at Staithes, near Whitby, where there was a small colony of artists. Between 1908–18 they lived in Cornwall. Laura Knight exhibited first at the RA in 1903 and had a first exhibition with Harold at the Leicester Galleries three years later. She then began to exhibit widely in Britain and abroad. The Tate Gallery, British Museum and Imperial War Museum hold her work. She was elected RA in 1936, having become Dame Laura Knight in 1929. Laura Knight was a powerful Colourist and a prolific and strident draughtsman. She was especially fond of drawing scenes from the circus, ballet, music-hall, racing and gypsy life. She worked for the War Artists' Advisory Committee during World War II, completing some excellent pictures, and then drew the war crimes trials at Nuremberg. Her autobiography is *Oil Paint and Grease Paint*, published in 1936. A retrospective was held at the Upper Grosvenor Galleries in 1969 and a large show at the Nottingham Castle Museum in 1970. Lived in London.

Lawrence John KNIGHT fl. from 1925–1950 Illustrator. Studied at Leicester College of Art, 1926–37, under John Pettinger and Sydney Watson, and was a member of Leicester Society of Artists and Leicester Sketch Club. After World War II service in the Royal Air Force Knight became art director for a design group. He exhibited at public galleries in Nottingham and Leicester and in Egypt and Palestine, the Egyptian Museum of Modern Art buying his work. Lived in London.

Lionel John KNIGHT 1901– Painter, born in Romsey, Hampshire. Showed at RWA, RBA, Arts Council and elsewhere and had one-man show at Bridgwater Art Gallery, Somerset, in 1968. Lived for some years in Penzance, Cornwall.

Loxton KNIGHT: *see* **Edward LOXTON KNIGHT**

Mervyn KNIGHT 1956– Painter, notably of landscape in sunlight, who trained at Reigate School of Art in the mid-1970s. His mixed show appearances included ROI, 1989; Anthony Sidgwick Gallery, 1990; RBA in 1991; Alberti Gallery, 1992; and Anna-Mei Chadwick, 1993, where he shared an exhibition. After a solo exhibition at Dance Attic Studio, 1989, and Outlines Gallery in same year, in 1991 Knight had one at Matt's Café. His work, largely done in London, Dorset and Surrey, is held in private collections in Britain and widely abroad.

Paul KNIGHT 1950– Painter and teacher who studied at Hammersmith College of Art and Royal Academy Schools, in 1984 gaining a Richard Ford Award, which took him to Spain to work. In that year he had a studio space in Wapping, east London. Taught at Chelsea College of Art and Chelsea & Westminster Institute. Showed at RBA and elsewhere in London.

Robert KNIGHT 1921–1987 Artist in fibreglass and mixed media, born in Leicester. He studied at the College of Art there, 1936–7, then worked in a small commercial studio until 1940. After Army service 1940–5, Knight was at the Royal Academy Schools, 1946–50, then for 20 years he did a variety of jobs, such as handyman and gardener. From the late 1960s he showed busily, including LG; John Moores Exhibition, Liverpool, from 1969; Nicholas Treadwell Gallery, from 1970; and extensively abroad. In 1981 Nicholas Treadwell gave Knight a sixtieth birthday exhibition. Knight's work accorded with Treadwell's interest in Superhumanism. He created three-dimensional works, sometimes erotic, amusing, touching, or cruelly real, which he said were "taken from the Tragi-Comedy of day-to-day life with its preoccupation with sex, love, religion and violence etc."

Sophie KNIGHT 1965– Painter, especially in watercolour. She attended Hertfordshire College of Art, 1982, Camberwell School of Arts and Crafts, 1983–6, and Royal Academy Schools, 1986–9. She gained a number of awards, including the David Murray Scholarship for Landscape, 1988, the Eric Kennington Prize for the Encouragement of Good Academic Drawing and the Hunting Group Student Prize, both in 1989. In 1991 Knight was on the judging panel for the Hunting Group Art Prizes. She began showing at South London Gallery, 1985, following shows including RA, NEAC, Boundary Gallery and Cadogan Contemporary, which gave her a solo show in 1991. British Museum held a picture by her on loan from RWS Diploma Collection.

William KNIGHT 1872–1958 Painter, designer and teacher, born in Leicester, one of 14 children. Attended Leicester College of Art, where he later taught. After working for his father as a painter and decorator, ran off to London – where he studied at Heatherley's School of Fine Art – and Paris to pursue a career as an artist, despite family disapproval. At first he concentrated on figure studies in watercolour, but after 1908 painted only in oil. First important show RBSA, 1901. Also exhibited RA, ROI, RI as well as extensively in Europe and North America. The Victoria & Albert Museum holds designs for printing; Leicester Museum and Art Gallery his oil paintings Autumn Evening and Russet and Gold, typical pastoral scenes. *La Revue Moderne*, 1924, and *The Studio*, 1927, carried articles on Knight, who lived in Leicester.

Arthur Henry KNIGHTON-HAMMOND 1875–1970 Landscape painter, especially in watercolour on a large scale, and etcher; born in Arnold, Nottinghamshire. Studied at Nottingham School of Art under Herbert Wilson Foster, at Westminster School of Art, in France and Italy. Knighton-Hammond was a member of leading watercolour societies in France and America, and was the only English artist to have been elected to the American Watercolour Society, New York, apart from Sir William Russell Flint. In Britain showed at RA, ROI, NEAC, RCamA, RBA, Fine Art Society and RSW. Tate Gallery, Musée du Jeu de Paume, Paris, galleries in New Zealand, South Africa and Yugoslavia as well as many British provincial galleries hold his work. He found watercolour a "nervy" business and disliked being overlooked while painting, yet Knighton-Hammond established an international reputation, described by Augustus John as "the greatest English painter in watercolour of our time". Like John he was a romantic, who travelled extensively to paint. Finally returned to live in Seaborough, Devon. Retrospective at Upper Grosvenor Galleries, 1971.

Winifred KNIGHTS 1899–1947 Painter and draughtsman, born in London, married to the artist Walter Thomas Monnington. She studied at the Slade School of Fine Art, 1915–17 and 1918–20. Her teachers included Henry Tonks and Fred Brown and she personified the Slade School tradition under their reign, her Composition: Mill Hands on Strike, for which she won a shared first prize for summer composition in 1919, having that firm draughtsmanship for which the Slade was then famous. She won a Rome Scholarship the following year, worked in Rome 1920–5 and returned to the Slade in 1927. One of her principal works was The Marriage at Cana for the British School in Rome, now in the National Gallery of New Zealand, in Wellington. Tate Gallery also holds her work. The British School and Fine Art Society put on exhibitions in 1995. Knights died in London.

Tony KNIPE 1942– Painter who employed a drip technique to create abstract pictures which were related to such subjects as lichen, water and graffiti. He was born in Swansea, studying at the College of Art there and in Paris. He gained a Government Research Fellowhip in 1967–70, involving Finnish Academy of Art and Helsinki University. A Henry Moore research grant took him to America in 1987. Knipe showed extensively in groups, including Glynn Vivian Art Gallery and tour in Welsh Artists 2; Jarrow: Impressions of a Town, Bede Gallery, Jarrow, 1986; and in the Newcastle Group 1990 show The Northern Lights, at DLI Museum & Arts Centre. Solo exhibitions included British Council, Helsinki, 1969; Octagon Theatre, Bolton, 1972; and Prudhoe Library Art Gallery, 1986. East Sussex Education Authority and University College in Swansea hold his work. Lived in Newcastle upon Tyne.

Gertrude KNOBLOCK fl. c.1906–1969 Sculptor in lead and bronze, born in New York, who studied art under George Barnard at the Art Students' League there, at the Académie Julian, Paris, then at the Royal College of Art, 1902–7, under Édouard Lantéri. In England exhibited at RA, RSA and SWA. Lived in London.

Joan KNOBLOCK 1917– Portrait and figure painter and draughtsman in ink and pencil, born and lived in London. She studied part-time at Hornsey School of Art, but was largely self-taught. Her early work included fashion drawing and she was influenced in her plant form pictures by those of Graham Sutherland. Knoblock was a member of Free Painters and Sculptors and Hesketh Hubbard Art Society. Mixed show appearances included RI and RP. Solo shows included Commonwealth Institute, Thames Gallery in Henley-on-Thames, the Hendon, Hampstead and North Finchley Libraries and abroad, where Knoblock travelled extensively.

Eardley KNOLLYS 1902–1991 Painter, administrator and collector, born in Alresford, Hampshire. He was educated at Winchester College and Oxford University, where he helped to found the Uffizi Society. After an abortive attempt to become a film director in Hollywood Knollys became part-time secretary to Viscount Hambledon, chairman of the booksellers W H Smith, then in 1935 founded the Storran Gallery, which promoted leading French and British artists, and started to assemble a fine personal collection. After World War he continued to work for the National Trust and became a committee member for the Contemporary Art Society. Took up painting, having his first solo show in 1960 at Minories Gallery, Colchester, others taking place in England and New York, including latterly Southampton City Art Gallery and Parkin Gallery. Knollys (pronounced Noles) painted landscapes in bright colours, often in Spain and France. Lived in London.

Gertrude M KNOPP 1875– Painter born in Kilninver, Argyllshire. After private education in Brighton, Sussex, she attended Slade School of Fine Art, 1899–1904 under Henry Tonks and Fred Brown. Married the Hungarian artist Imre Knopp, who died just after World War II, which led to part of her exhibiting career occurring in Hungary. Thus she showed in Budapest, where the Museum of Fine Arts holds her work; also exhibited widely elsewhere on the continent. In Britain she showed at WIAC, of which she was secretary for several years before World War I, RA, NEAC, ROI and elsewhere. Finally lived in London. Early in her career she exhibited under her maiden name Gertrude M Curtis.

Karen KNORR 1954– Artist using photography, born in Frankfurt, West Germany. She lived in Puerto Rico, 1958–72. Graduated from Polytechnic of Central London in 1980 and went on to do research there. In 1981–2 she was included in Woodlands Art Gallery show of Greater London Arts Association award winners. Also showed at ICA, 1981, having had solo show in 1980 in Paris at La Remise du Parc. Arts Council holds her work.

Martin KNOWELDEN 1943– Wildlife sculptor, born in Hertfordshire. He studied at Watford School of Art, specialising in printmaking. Went on to work on a number of wildlife and field sport publications, notably with the writer D Brien-Plummer. Exhibitions included Ivor Giblin Gallery; Coach House Gallery, Guernsey; San Francisco Art Expo; Bath Festival; and Toronto Art Fair. Lived for a time in Cambridgeshire.

Emma KNOWLES 1967– Figurative painter, draughtsman and teacher, born in Liverpool, who studied at Gwynedd Technical College and Norwich School of Art. Held a number of teaching posts from 1990, including Edge Hill and Blackburn Colleges of Higher Education, St Helens Community College, Wirral Metropolitan College and HM Prison, Risley. Knowles gained a Nöel Spencer Award for Life Drawing, 1989; Elizabeth Greenshields Foundation, 1991; Michael Gourley Award, 1993; and Edward Oldham Trust Award, 1995. Group shows included Portraits North, Harrogate Art Gallery, 1989; MAFA, Manchester City Art Gallery, from 1993; and Royal Over-Seas League Open, 1996, where she showed Before the Game I, one of a series of small studies of the crowd at Old Trafford, her local football ground.

Justin KNOWLES 1935– Self-taught sculptor, painter and printmaker, born in Exeter, Devon, educated at Kelly College, Tavistock, who after National Service, 1955–7, worked in industry and advertising, travelling extensively on the continent and in

Africa. After a visit to New York in 1965, Knowles taught for a time at Bath Academy of Art, Corsham, living near Chudleigh, Devon. Knowles was part of Camden Arts Centre's Survey '67 Abstract Painters in 1967, work including the free-standing shapes which, he said, "remain paintings rather than sculpture in that the painted form works across the physical form rather than following it, as in most painted sculpture." Arts Council acquired two such shapes: Bayaka, 1967, and Steel with Brown, Version I, of 1967–8. Mixed exhibitions also included John Moores Liverpool Exhibition of 1965. Solo exhibitions included Plymouth City Art Gallery, 1967. Museum of Modern Art in Oxford, Arts Council of Northern Ireland and University of Warwick hold examples.

Mike KNOWLES 1941– Painter and teacher, born in Warrington, Lancashire. He studied at Liverpool College of Art, 1959–63, then at Slade School of Fine Art, 1964–6. There he won the Tonks Drawing Prize and Landscape Painting Prize. Landscape remained a main preoccupation, with the countryside around his home in Anglesey, Gwynedd, an inspiration, as in his entry for John Moores Exhibition, Liverpool, 1991–2: Mynydd Eilian, Windy Day, Summer. Other mixed exhibition appearances included The Native Land: Welsh Landscape Painting since 1699, Llandudno, 1979, and The Probity of Art, WAC, 1979–80. His first solo show was at Bluecoat Gallery, Liverpool, 1967, and he had a retrospective at Mostyn Art Gallery, Llandudno, 1992. Knowles taught at Liverpool Polytechnic from 1967, in 1991 being elected professor emeritus in fine art.

Stuart KNOWLES 1948– Painter noted for near-abstract, gestural landscapes in oil inspired by his native Cornwall, to which he returned in 1988 after a period in London. Settled at Plain-an-Gwarry, in the southwest, his ancestors having been miners. Archetypal figures from Kabuki and Noh theatre also featured in his pictures. Studied at Farnham and Winchester Schools of Art, 1964–9, then Slade School of Fine Art until 1971. Exhibitions included City of London Festival, 1971; Arts Council at Hayward Gallery, 1982; Artists from Cornwall, RWA, 1992; and Demarco's Choice, Newlyn Art Gallery, 1993. Solo shows included Newlyn Art Gallery, 1991, and Austin/Desmond Fine Art, 1996. Shaw Theatre held his work.

Charlotte KNOX 1951– Painter and illustrator, born in London, who studied art at Ruskin School in Oxford before attending a one-year postgraduate course in illustration at St Martin's School of Art. Her first solo show was held at Hammond Lloyd Gallery in 1975, featuring watercolour landscapes of Italy and England. From that time Knox worked as a freelance illustrator specialising in natural subjects. She joined with the writer Jane Grigson to produce the book *Exotic Fruits and Vegetables*, illustrations for which were shown at Chris Beetles Ltd in 1986, the year of its publication.

Harry Cooke KNOX 1905– Painter, notable for his portraits and murals, born in Newtownbutler, County Fermanagh. He attended Belfast College of Art, 1924–30. In 1953 was made an associate of RUA, also exhibiting with RHA and ROI. Knox was a prominent member of Ulster Arts Club, being its president in 1955. Lived for many years in Belfast.

Jack KNOX 1936– Painter, draughtsman and teacher, born John Knox at Kirkintilloch, Dunbartonshire. He studied at Glasgow School of Art, 1953–7, where his teachers included William Armour and David Donaldson. In 1958 won a travelling scholarship which enabled him to study in Paris under André Lhote. Knox painted in a variety of styles, being influenced by the American Abstract Expressionists for a time, although on occasion creating still lifes in the manner of the Dutch Old Masters. From 1965–81 Knox taught at Duncan of Jordanstone College of Art, Dundee, in 1981 becoming head of painting at Glasgow College of Art. Took part in many group shows in Scotland and abroad and had a series of one-man exhibitions, including 57 Gallery, Edinburgh; Serpentine Gallery in London; and Civic Arts Centre, Aberdeen. In 1983 a solo show was toured to a number of Scottish venues by the Scottish Arts Council. Was elected RSA and has work in many public collections, including Scottish National Gallery of Modern Art, Edinburgh. Lived for some time in Carnoustie, Angus.

Madeline KNOX 1890–1975 Painter, draughtsman and embroiderer, originally from Grantham, Lincolnshire. She moved to London in 1906 and attended Lambeth School of Art briefly, was then with Sickert at Westminster School of Art, joined his etching class, helped him to set up an etching school and then the Rowlandson House school, but withdrew in 1910. Travelled in France and Canada, then returned to London early in World War I, marrying Arthur Clifton who ran the Carfax Gallery. Settled in Mersham, Kent, in 1925 and gave up painting to concentrate on embroidery. The altar frontal at Burghclere Chapel, decorated by Stanley Spencer, is by Knox. She had a show at Carfax Gallery in 1916, also showing pictures at NEAC and London Salon. In 1976 the Fine Art Society included her work in Camden Town Recalled.

Lay-Ngo KOAY 1975– Painter, often using acrylic on paper, producing richly coloured, gestural images, born in Malaysia. Studied with Hock Aun Teh, then from 1994 at Glasgow School of Art. Exhibited in Salon Glasgow, Centre for Contemporary Art in Glasgow, 1992; Contemporary 1992/93 at Art Gallery & Museum in Kilmarnock, 1992–3; at Royal Over-Seas League Open from 1994; and Paisley Art Institute Exhibition, Paisley Art Gallery, 1995. Manchurian Restaurant, Glasgow, holds work.

Ghisha KOENIG 1921–1993 Sculptor and draughtsman, born and lived in London, daughter of the writer and art critic Leo Koenig. After a poor scholastic start, Koenig won a scholarship to Hornsey School of Art, 1939; left it in 1942, serving four years in the Army; studied under Henry Moore at Chelsea School of Art, 1946–8; and at Slade School of Fine Art, 1948–9. Koenig created modest-size bronzes and terracottas, specialising in high relief.

She stained the terracottas with dark ink prior to burnishing them, to restore the clay's richness. Most of Koenig's work was based on watching factory workers over 30 years. She was conerned with "the dignity of man" and "the trapped nature of human beings". Mixed exhibitions included RA; Jewish Artists in England, Whitechapel Art Gallery, 1956; SPS; AIA; and 10th Sculpture Biennale, Middelheim, Belgium, 1969. Had a solo show at Grosvenor Gallery, 1966, later ones including Serpentine Gallery and tour, 1986. Boundary Gallery held a memorial show in 1994. Tate Gallery and public galleries in Manchester, Sheffield and Stoke-on-Trent hold examples.

Heidi KOENIG 1964– Artist, notably a printmaker, born in Heilbronn, West Germany. She did a foundation course at Walthamstow College, 1990–1; obtained a first-class honours degree in fine art from Brighton University, 1991–4; and gained a postgraduate diploma in fine art printmaking from Slade School of Fine Art, 1994–6. Koenig won a number of awards at the FBA National Print Exhibition, Mall Galleries: in 1995, the Artichoke Print Workshop Award for the most outstanding print; in 1996 the Zenith Gallery Purchase Prize, Galleries Magazine Award and St Cuthberts Paper Mill Award. Group shows included Images in Edition, Maze Gallery, Brighton, 1992, and RA Summer Exhibition, 1996. From 1996 showed solo with Enid Lawson Gallery. Strang Print Room at University College and Whipps Cross Hospital hold her work.

Robert KOENIG 1951– Sculptor and creator of coloured reliefs in wood, born in Manchester. In 1973–6 studied at Brighton Polytechnic for first-class honours degree in fine art, in 1976–8 gaining higher diploma for sculpture at Slade School of Fine Art. Exhibitions included Serpentine Gallery summer show, 1980; Bluecoat Gallery, Liverpool, and Paton Gallery, both 1984; Middlesbrough Art Gallery, 1986; Huddersfield Art Gallery and Milton Keynes Exhibition Gallery, both 1992. Koenig worked in Milton Keynes, Buckinghamsire, and in London and had work in public and private collections.

Hilde KÖHLY 1955– Sculptor born in Warmbaths, South Africa, where she attended Johannesburg School of Art, 1974–6, then St Martin's School of Art, 1977–80. Gained the Afrox Student Prize and New Signatures Sculpture Prize in 1976, in 1980 The Sykes Prize (2nd). Showed in Cannizaro Park, Wimbledon, 1982, and was included in Woodlands Art Gallery 1983 show Have You Seen Sculpture from the Body? Lived in London.

Oskar KOKOSCHKA 1886–1980 Painter, teacher and writer, born in Pöchlarn, Austria. He was educated at Vienna School of Industrial Art, and was early a member of the Jugendstil movement, writing Expressionist plays many found offensive. Badly wounded in 1915 in World War I, after a long recovery Kokoschka settled in Dresden and taught at the Academy and was influenced by the Brücke, notably in choice of colour. Kokoschka had established himself as a painter of psychologically perceptive portraits and in the 1920s he travelled extensively through Europe, North Africa and Asia Minor completing singular landscapes. In 1931 he settled again in Vienna but in 1934, with a politically uncertain future hanging over Austria, Kokoschka moved to Prague, then England in 1938. Became a British subject in 1947, but from 1953 lived mainly in Switzerland. In Salzburg founded the International Academy of Fine Arts and taught there, 1953–63. Had a Tate Gallery solo show in 1962 and showed several times with Marlborough Fine Art from 1967. He was made an Hon. RA in 1970. His autobiography *My Life* was published in 1971, and *London Views, British Landscapes* in 1972. Many international collections hold his work.

Matthew KOLAKOWSKI 1956– Abstract painter who used stencilled shapes and a bright, attractive palette; teacher. He was born in London and studied at Watford School of Art, 1974–5, then gained a first-class honours degree at Ravensbourne College of Art, 1975–8, followed by his master's degree at Chelsea School of Art, 1978–9. Was at Garnett College, 1984–5. Kolakowski showed with New Contemporaries in 1977, other mixed shows including LG of which he was elected a member in 1990, South London Gallery, 1992, and Duncan Campbell Contemporary Art, where he had a solo show in 1993. Kolakowski held a number of teaching posts in the London area, beginning with Ravensbourne in 1980–2, other appointments including St Martin's College of Art, 1985, and Wolverhampton Polytechnic, 1991–2.

Gideon KOLB 1913–1984 Kolb combined careers in industry, acting and art, as a portrait painter and sculptor. Born in Vienna, he was educated there and in Paris before studying art at the Regent Street Polytechnic and Chelsea College of Art. He took part in mixed shows in Munich and London, notably at the Redfern Gallery, and had a series of one-man exhibitions at the Camden Institute and Drian Gallery. The *Financial Times* and Loggia Gallery purchased his work. Lived in London.

Masakatsu KONDO 1962– Painter, born in Nagoya, Japan, where he had a solo show at the Kohji Ogura Gallery, 1996. He studied at Chelsea College of Art, 1988–9, and Slade School of Fine Art, 1989–93. Won the Granada Foundation Prize in Young Contemporaries at Whitworth Art Gallery, Manchester, 1993, and a prize at John Moores Liverpool Exhibition, 1997–8. Other group shows included Annihilation, 1993, and Gallery Artists, 1994, both at Victoria Miro Gallery; British Artists, at Shoshana Wayne Gallery, Los Angeles, in the Biennale there, 1995; Whitechapel Open, 1996; and East, at Norwich Gallery, Norwich, 1997. Lived in London.

Henry KONDRACKI 1953– Painter, born and settled in Edinburgh, who studied at Byam Shaw, 1981–2, then graduated with first-class honours at Slade School, 1982–6. Wryly humorous and imaginative work drew on his childhood and used costumes and other memorabilia. In Whitworth Young Contemporaries, 1983, he gained a Granada Foundation Prize, in 1987 a South Bank Board Prize, then in 1991 a

Spectator Art Prize. Group appearances included Blond Fine Art, 1985; Vanessa Devereux Gallery, 1989; and City Art Centre, Edinburgh, 1993 exhibition Polish Roots – British Soil. Solo shows took place at Traverse Theatre Club, Edinburgh, 1979, and The Collective Gallery there, 1984–92; Michael Wardell Gallery, Melbourne, 1988; and William Jackson Gallery from 1991. Arts Council, British Council and Manchester City Art Gallery hold his work.

Frederick KÖNEKAMP 1897–1977 Painter, lecturer and writer, born in Offenburg, Baden, Germany. After World War I military service was a prisoner of war in Scotland. He then studied mathematics and philosophy at Universities of Basle, Freiburg and Berlin. For most of the 1920s he lectured in mathematics and as a journalist was concerned with advocating school reform. Being a Socialist, he decided to leave Germany in 1933 and travelled widely, began painting and was converted to Roman Catholicism. Settled in Britain in 1935 and after World War II internment in Canada returned to Britain in 1945, in 1949 settling at Cotllwyd, Dyfed, where he founded the Cotllwyd Group, a group that went on to show in England and Germany. Took part in SWG, WAC and Royal National Eisteddfod mixed shows and had many solo exhibitions, including Wilton and Drian Galleries, Albany Gallery in Cardiff and abroad. Had a retrospective at National Library of Wales, Aberystwyth, in 1965. National Musuem of Wales in Cardiff, WAC and German collections hold his work.

Nigel KONSTAM 1932– Sculptor and teacher, born in London. He studied sculpture at Camberwell School of Arts and Crafts with Karel Vogel and briefly at the Royal College of Art. He lectured at many art colleges on art historical subjects; from the early-1980s ran the Verrochio Art Centre in Tuscany with his wife Janet; and produced *The Save Rembrandt Campaigner*, part of a long effort to save the artist from the experts whose effect he felt was diminishing a reputation. Konstam showed at RA, LG, NEAC and at John Moores Liverpool Exhibition. His solo exhibitions included Architectural Association in 1971; Kreisler Gallery (Madrid, Barcelona and Salamanca), 1980; The Orangery, Holland Park, 1984; and in 1993 he shared a show at Cadogan Contemporary. Among musicians who sat for him were the conductor Otto Klemperer, the violinist Manoug Parikian and the composer John Ireland.

Harold KOPEL 1915– Painter in oil and teacher, born in Newcastle upon Tyne, Northumberland. He attended University College in London and Central School of Arts and Crafts. Became a secondary school art master and a senior lecturer in further education. The spirit of a place was a key element sought after in Kopel's pictures. He was a member of ROI and took part in many mixed exhibitions, including RA Summer Exhibition and RWA. He won a Silver Medal at Paris Salon and the Cornelissen Prize at 1990 ROI annual show. Had a series of solo exhibitions. University College and Nuffield Foundation hold examples. Lived in London.

Heinz KOPPEL 1919–1980 Painter, draughtsman and teacher, born in Berlin, Germany. He studied and worked in Germany, Czechoslovakia, Italy, Belgium and England before moving to Wales in 1940, in the mid-1940s settling in Dowlais, Glamorgan. For 15 years he taught art to children and adults at the Art Centre there, worked and taught in London and then went on to teach at Liverpool Polytechnic. Showed in the WAC 1968 show Art in Wales 1900–1956, with 56 Group of which he was a founder-member, SWG, SEA and elsewhere. Had a number of solo shows at Beaux Arts Gallery, also at Glynn Vivian Art Gallery, Swansea. A fine draughtsman-painter, witness his Head, in Arts Council collection.

Adam KOPS 1956– Artist who studied life sculpture and drawing at Camden Arts Centre, 1980–1; did a foundation course at St Martin's School of Art, 1981–2; and sculpture courses at Wimbledon School of Art, 1982–3, and St Martin's, 1984–7, gaining his degree. Mixed shows included Royal Festival Hall, 1986, and Ben Uri Gallery from 1990. Had solo shows at Camden and Kingsgate Galleries from 1988. His work was steel and usually figurative. Lived in London.

Henry KORDA 1957– Painter and draughtsman, notable for figure paintings and portraits. Born in London and studied at City and Guilds Art School, 1975–9, in 1979–81 doing a postgraduate course at Royal Academy Schools. In the following year travelled in Africa. From 1984 showed in RA Summer Exhibition. After sharing a show at Scribes Gallery in 1983 had two solo exhibitions in 1984–5 at Cylinder Gallery. Further one-man exhibitions included Cadogan Contemporary, 1991. From 1988 lived for a time in Scottish highlands.

Fred KORMIS 1896–1986 Sculptor and portrait medallist in bronze, born in Frankfurt, Germany. He studied at Kunstschule there, served in the Austrian Army during World War I, was captured and imprisoned in Siberia for several years, escaping and returning to Frankfurt. Worked as a portrait sculptor until Hitler came to power, when Kormis moved to the Netherlands and then in 1934 settled in London. There he established a reputation as one of the most distinguished medallists of his time, producing effigies of dozens of distinguished figures, including Winston Churchill, Golda Meir, Charlie Chaplin, Michael Tippett and J B Priestley. Showed at Beaux Arts Gallery, Fieldborne Galleries and abroad. His work is held by British Museum, Imperial War Museum, Fitzwilliam Museum in Cambridge and the Royal Air Force Museum in Hendon. Among his public commissions were the Shield Bearer in Corn Exchange in Stratford-upon-Avon, the Prisoner of War Memorial in Gladstone Park, Willesden, and The Everlamenting Harp at Kiryat Gat, Israel.

Halina KORN 1902–1978 Sculptor and painter in oil, born in Warsaw, Poland. She was a self-taught artist who had studied to be a singer and who married the painter Marek Zulawski. Settled in London early in World War II. Showed at RA, LG, WIAC and AIA, had solo shows in Warsaw and New York and a series in

London, including Mayor Gallery, 1948, Beaux Arts Gallery, 1953, and Camden Arts Centre, 1981. Ben Uri Art Society holds her work.

Nathaniel KORNBLUTH 1914– Pen and ink draughtsman and etcher, born of Polish Jewish parents as Naphtali Kornbluth in London's East End. The area was his main subject, and his work remains a valuable record of much that has disappeared as well as capturing its particular atmosphere over several decades. Kornbluth's family did not approve his artistic interests, and he stayed in the wholesale menswear business all his life. Studied in the evenings at Hackney Technical School under Norman Janes, 1933; with W P Robins, Paul Drury and James Fitton at Central School of Arts and Crafts, 1934–7; and at Sir John Cass School of Art in 1970s. Kornbluth showed in the East End Academy from the mid-1930s at Whitechapel Art Gallery, solo exhibitions including Campbell & Franks, 1980; Sir John Cass, 1986; and Lamont Gallery, 1988. His main works included Demolition of Waterloo Bridge, etching 1936; Regents Canal Dock, etching, 1936; and the 1939 lithograph Return from Spain, depicting Major Clement Attlee's section of the International Brigade proceeding along Vauxhall Bridge Road. British Museum, Guildhall Library, Bibliothèque Nationale in Paris, Brooklyn Museum, National Maritime Museum, New York City Library and Ben Uri Art Society hold examples. Lived latterly in northwest London.

Leon KOSSOFF 1926– Painter of portraits and views of the dingier parts of London, where he was born of Russian-Jewish parentage and continued to work, and teacher. Kossoff's sometimes large pictures, in an impastoed, Expressionist style, hard-worked and based on careful drawing, were a contrast to their sensitive, retiring creator. After World War II Army service Kossoff studied at St Martin's School of Art, 1949–53; also at the Borough Polytechnic in the evenings with David Bomberg, which had a lasting influence, 1950–2; and at the Royal College of Art, 1953–6. He had his first one-man show at Helen Lessore's Beaux Arts Gallery in 1957. He taught at Regent Street Polytechnic and Chelsea School of Art, 1959–64, and St Martin's, 1966–9. Was represented in important group exhibitions and had a string of solo shows at venues such as Marlborough Fine Art, Whitechapel Art Gallery and Anthony d'Offay. In 1995 had a first solo exhibition on continent, at Venice Biennale and in Amsterdam, with a retrospective at Tate Gallery in 1996. The Tate, Royal College of Art and Saatchi Collection hold examples.

Adam KOSSOWSKI 1905–1986 Religious artist of major stature who also completed significant secular works. Kossowski worked in many media, but was notable for his use of sgraffito, scratch-through drawing employing two differently coloured coats of plaster. Born in Nowy Sacz, Poland, Kossowski studied architecture at Warsaw Technical University, 1923–5, then painting at Cracǒw Academy of Fine Arts, 1925–8. Began exhibiting and taught mural painting at Warsaw Academy of Fine Arts, 1934–8. In late 1930s studied and worked in Italy and France, then returned to Warsaw. Suffered hardship as a prisoner in Soviet Union in World War II, in 1942 joining Polish Army, serving in Middle East; arrived in Britain and in 1943 was working in London for Polish Ministry of Information. In 1944 had a solo show Polish Soldier's Journey. Started to show extensively, including Guild of Catholic Artists and Craftsmen. From 1950 for about 20 years Kossowski completed 100 works at Aylesford Priory, Kent. Other notable works were the 1,000-square foot Camberwell Public Library Old Kent Road ceramic and the ceiling of the Chapel of St Benet at Queen Mary College. Was buried at Aylesford.

David KOSTER 1926– Artist mainly in etching and aquatint but also relief, watercolour and oil, teacher, born in London. He studied at Slade School of Fine Art with Randolph Schwabe as principal, 1944–7. Taught at Folkestone Art School, 1966–70; Medway School of Design, 1970–5; New Metropole Arts Centre, 1975–6; then part-time at Medway College, 1976–91. Koster was a founder-member of SWLA and among influences on his work were Thomas Bewick, Eric Ravilious and Allen W Seaby for birds. Koster aimed to produce work "with a wide appeal but also with authenticity". He created a mural for Royal Veterinary College and completed wood engravings for John Stewart Collis's *Down to Earth.* Participated in many group shows, including RA Summer Exhibitions from 1960; New Metropole Arts Centre from 1961; Bear Lane Gallery, Oxford, from 1964; John Nevill Gallery, Canterbury, from 1975; and Daler Gallery, Bournemouth, 1990. Had a series of solo shows at Everyman Foyer Gallery from 1958, later ones including Zella 9, 1989. Many public collections hold examples, including galleries in Aberdeen, Belfast, Eastbourne and Southend. Lived in Folkestone, Kent.

Lesley M KOSTER 1927– Painter and draughtsman who was partly educated in England, partly in New York where she attended the School of Interior Design. In 1966–8 studied there at 5th Avenue School of Art, having been at Cheltenham College of Art, 1960–2. Showed widely in America, also at RA, UA, Clarges and Chenil Galleries. Lived in London.

Zygmunt KOWALEWSKI 1913–1982 Artist, designer and sculptor, one of the group of Polish paper sculptors who made an impact in Britain after World War II. He was deported to Siberia, having studied at Warsaw Academy of Arts. After release, joined the Polish Army and went with it to the Middle East, where he was chief of graphics for the Polish Information Centre, preparing exhibitions, designing posters and publications. Demobilised in Britain he set up his own studio, the men's outfitter Austin Reed being an important early client. Others included British Overseas Airways Corporation, Air India, Swiss Air and Ford Motor Company. Perspex, mirrors and moving lights as well as paper sculpture were some techniques Kowalewski employed. He was included in Polish Paper Sculpture, at Polish Cultural Institute, 1995.

Christine KOWAL POST 1951– Sculptor, printmaker, ceramist, draughtsman and teacher. Born and lived in Ibadan,

Nigeria, and Ghana, 1951–3. Attended Accademia di Belle Arti, Florence, 1972–3, from 1970–4 studying at University College of Wales, Aberystwyth; graduated with joint honours in fine art and Italian. After working as a graphic artist in Canada and Europe, 1975–82, Kowal Post worked as an artist on Merseyside; in 1986 she was a visiting lecturer at Bristol Polytechnic. Other features of her career were Artists in Industry, Lever Brothers Ltd, Merseyside; Woodcut Print Workshop at Cornerhouse, Manchester; and Liverpool Disablement Resources Unit tutor, all in 1986. The artist showed at SGA; Mall Galleries; Hanover Gallery, in Liverpool; Contemporary British Woodcuts, at Worcester City Art Gallery; and John Moores Exhibition, Liverpool, in 1987, where she was a prizewinner. Had a solo show at Hanover Gallery, 1985, another at Williamson Art Gallery and Museum, Birkenhead, in 1987. That gallery holds her work. Lived in Wirral, Merseyside.

Elaine KOWALSKY 1948– Printmaker and teacher, born in Winnipeg, Manitoba, Canada, who attended University of Manitoba School of Art, 1967–71; did a postgraduate printmaking course at St Martin's School of Art, 1973; and her master's in visual theory, University of East London, 1992–4. Kowalsky worked independently at Islington Print Workshop, 1972–3, then took part in a specialist printmaking group at the Brighton Polytechnic faculty of design, 1974–5. Among Kowalsky's many awards was a Henry Moore Fellowship in Printmaking at Leeds Polytechnic, 1987. She held numerous lecturing and workshop appointments from 1975, later ones including posts at Universities of East London and Brighton and Birkbeck College. Also held senior appointments with the Printmakers' Council (1982–5) and Designer and Artist Copyright Society (1985–97) and from 1990–3 was adviser to The Prince's Youth Business Trust. As well as participating in many group shows such as the Whitechapel Open, RA Summer Exhibition and LG, Kowalsky had a series of solo exhibitions, from 1976 at Axis Gallery, Brighton, later ones including Anna Bornholt Gallery, 1996. In 1990, Kowalsky was commissioned to create banners for Dover Castle. Public collections holding her work include Victoria & Albert Museum, Smithsonian Institution in Washington, Australian National Gallery in Sydney as well as British provincial and Canadian sites. Lived in London.

Magda KOZARZEWSKA 1952– Painter in oil of landscapes, figures and still life, born in Warsaw, Poland. Originally intended to study in Warsaw, but instead was accepted by Chelsea School of Art, 1974–7, then Slade School of Fine Art, 1977–81, where she was taught by Euan Uglow. She was a bold, rich Colourist, with echoes of Matisse, Cézanne and Derain in her work, which showed a strong design. She had a solo show at Polish Cultural Institute, 1975, another in 1991. Other one-man exhibitions took place at Sue Rankin Gallery, 1988, Petworth House in 1990 and Thackeray Gallery, 1991. Among group shows her work appeared in were Hayward Annual Drawing Exhibition, 1982, and John Player Portrait Award, 1986. Works were held by private collections in several continents.

Helen KOZICH 1958– Versatile artist, designer, illustrator and teacher, notable for paintings, relief prints and collographs, born in Connecticut, America, and resident in Britain from 1974. She gained an honours degree in fine art, printmaking, at the University of Leeds, 1976–80, tutors Terry Atkinson and Griselda Pollock, then her master's in European fine art from the Winchester School of Art in Barcelona and England, 1992–3. Work experience included graphic design and illustration for Leeds City Council, 1981–4; freelance work in the city, 1984–7; teaching fundamental design skills to trainee hairdressers at Thomas Danby College of Further Education in Leeds, 1985–6; working in New Zealand, Australia and Indonesia, 1987–8; then self-employment as an artist from 1989. Kozich was a founder-member of The Pavilion Women's Art Centre, Leeds, 1982–5. In 1996 she had a printmaking residency at Lowick House Print Workshop, Ulverston, developing work from sketches made in Eritrea that year. Kozich's work was "primarily figurative and Expressionist, using the human form metaphorically to deal with themes of birth, death and transformation, notions of identity, and so on. Bold drawing and use of chiaroscuro and movement predominate more than colour." Group exhibitions included Wales Open Art Show, Aberystwyth Arts Centre, 1990; British International Miniature Print Exhibition, Leicester City Art Gallery and tour, 1994–6; Oriel 31 Open, Davies Memorial Gallery, Newtown, where she was first prizewinner, 1995; and Showcase Wales, Y Tabernacl, Machynlleth, 1996. Solo exhibitions included Birdwoman & Other Stories, Station Café, The Railway Station, Aberystwyth, 1995. Lived in Machynlleth, Powys.

Fritz KRÄMER 1905– Painter, especially portraits of juveniles, and teacher who was born in Vienna, Austria. Studied at Vienna School of Fine Arts and in Germany. For a short time towards end of World War II he taught painting at King's College, Durham University. Showed in Vienna and in England in Newcastle, RA and Storran Gallery. Finally lived in London. Tate Gallery archive holds his self-portrait in charcoal.

Jacob KRAMER 1892–1962 Painter, draughtsman and printmaker, born in Klincy, Ukraine. His father Max was a court painter, as was his uncle Boris. Kramer arrived in England in 1900, settling in Jewish colony in Leeds, and he was to remain faithful to the city. After a period at sea and working in northern towns, where he attended evening classes at Manchester School of Art, in 1907 Kramer returned to Leeds, attending similar classes at its School of Art. From 1908–11 he studied there full-time on a scholarship, Sir Michael Sadler becoming his patron, then from 1913–14 studied at Slade School of Fine Art. In 1915 Kramer had a solo show with Mathews & Brooke, Bradford, was invited to show with Vorticists in London and was elected LG. Kramer's sister Sarah married the artist William Roberts. Kramer began to create a name as a Yorkshire-based artist, showing with Fred Lawson at Leeds School of Art in 1916, also having a solo show at Bradford Arts Club. The inter-war years saw Kramer consolidating his reputation with shows in Yorkshire and London. In 1959 he was elected president of Leeds Fine Arts Club, in 1960 having a retrospective at Leeds City Art Gallery. Six years after his death the City of Leeds Branch College of Art was renamed Jacob Kramer College of Art. Later shows included Parkin Gallery, 1973, Belgrave Gallery, 1990, and centenary show at Leeds University Art Gallery. Kramer was a fine draughtsman and was capable of producing memorable, hieratic images. The sculpture of him by Epstein is in Tate Gallery, which also holds Kramer's work, as do Victoria & Albert Museum and British Museum.

Joseph KRAMER 1887– Painter, draughtsman, printmaker and typographer. Brought up in Czechoslovakia, he studied art in Vienna. During World War II he was registered as an alien, which restricted his ability to paint freely. Showed with RCamA and in East Anglia. Lived near Mold, Flintshire.

Jiří KRATOCHVÍL 1946– Sculptor, carver, designer and teacher, born in Vizovice, Czechoslovakia. He worked as a commercial photographer, 1967–8, in 1969 moving to England, working with mentally subnormal children at Bethlem Royal Hospital. From 1972–4 was assistant designer at 401½ Workshops, then studied sculpture at Ravensbourne College of Art and Design, 1975–9. Went on to teach sculpture and woodcarving at adult classes at Bromley Centre for Arts and Crafts and Orpington Adult Education Centre from 1982. Kratochvíl took part in sculpture show at Camden Lock, 1983, at The Showroom in 1984 and in that year participated in a four-man exhibition at Woodlands Art Gallery, showing abstract work.

Marian KRATOCHWIL 1906–1997 Painter and writer, born in Kosow, Poland, whose early training was in the studio of Stanislaw Batowski. He read philosophy and history at University Lwow. After active service in World War II he painted in Scotland, then London, chronicling the life of the city, also painting widely in Spain. In 1961 he married the artist Kathleen Browne, assisted in the running of her school and late in life published a perceptive monograph on her work. British Museum, Victoria & Albert Museum, Scottish National Gallery of Modern Art and several foreign collections hold his work. He shared a retrospective with his wife at Polish Cultural Institute in 1994, showing his drawings of life and places on Poland's pre-war eastern borders.

Roberta KRAVITZ 1944– Artist whose output included performances, and teacher, born in New Jersey, America. She graduated in philosophy from University College in London, 1965–8, in the mid-1970s teaching it at Polytechnic of North London. Studied at City & Guilds of London Art School, 1969, then Slade School of Fine Art, 1969–71. Solo performances included Motherhood at 1st Bracknell Performance Festival, South Hill Park Arts Centre, 1983; group performances Government of the First and Thirteenth Chair, by John Latham, Riverside Studios, 1978. Mixed shows included Wapping Artists Open Studios from 1980. Lived in London.

Marianne KREEGER 1929– Painter, born in Frankfurt, Germany, who attended St Martin's School of Art in 1946. Showed with Hampstead Artists' Council, LG and RA and had a series of solo exhibitions. Lived in London.

Anthony KRIKHAAR 1940– Painter, born in Almelo, Netherlands, who moved to Britain to study art in 1959 and settled in London. After the Deva-Vak School of Art, Almelo, he was at Byam Shaw and St Martin's Schools of Art. He was a landscape, genre and portrait painter, employing bright colours, who applied thick pigment to the canvas, the result being almost sculptural. Exhibitions included Gallery 10 and Galerie Krikhaar, Amsterdam, both from 1987; RVS Fine Art, Southampton/New York and Links of Affinity at Knapp Gallery, both 1989. Singer John Lennon, comedian Danny la Rue, actor Richard Chamberlain and a number of corporate collections in Britain and abroad held examples.

Tamara KRIKORIAN 1944– Video artist, born in Bridport, Dorset. Group appearances included The Video Show at Serpentine Gallery, 1975; Acme Gallery, 1979; Arnolfini Gallery in Bristol, 1981; and Signs of the Times, Museum of Modern Art, Oxford, 1990. Solo exhibitions included An Ephemeral Art, Third Eye Centre, Glasgow, and Eye to Eye, Scottish Arts Council, Fruitmarket Gallery, Edinburgh, both 1979; The Heart of the Illusion, at Ikon Gallery, Birmingham, 1981, and Air Gallery, 1982. Arnolfini, Brighton Polytechnic, British Council and Museum of the Moving Image all hold examples.

KROME: *see* **Krome BARRATT**

Rineke KROON 1945– Artist noted for watercolours and prints of landscapes in Netherlands, where she was born in Hoogezand, and Scotland, where she moved in 1976. Spent a period of each year based at Strathcarron, Wester Ross, part of it in Maastricht. Her wet-into-wet watercolour technique was apt for catching changing weather effects, large skies and damp landscapes. Exhibitions included Haagse Kunstkring, The Hague, 1976; Pier Arts Centre, Stromness, fom 1980; Inverness Museum and Art Gallery, 1982; Gallery Verenigde Spaarbank, Amsterdam, 1986; and Links of Affinity, Knapp Gallery, 1989.

Ansel KRUT 1959– Figurative painter, born in Cape Town, South Africa. He studied fine art at University of Witwatersrand, 1979–82, then for his master's degree in mid-1980s at Royal College of Art. In Johannesburg had a solo show with Shell Gallery. In England exhibited with LG, in Camden Annual and in 1985 was a prize winner in John Moores Liverpool Exhibition. Arts Council holds his picture Restless Tonight, 1986, bought from Fischer Fine Art, Harris Museum and Art Gallery in Preston owning The Ventriloquist's Convention, 1988. Lived for a time in London.

Christopher KU 1957– Painter, born in Hong Kong, who studied at Gray's School of Art, Aberdeen, and at Royal College of Art. In 1987 Ku won the Maclean/Watters Gold Medal and Latimer Award for Painting, in 1989 the John Minton Scholarship at the Royal College. Group shows included Mall Galleries and Scottish Gallery, Edinburgh, both 1989; Paper Work '90, Seagate Gallery, Dundee, 1990; Whitechapel Open, 1994; and Journeys West, University of Essex tour, 1995. Had a solo exhibition at Aberdeen Royal Infirmary, 1989, others including Henrietta House, 1994.

Judith KUEHNE fl. from 1940s– Painter and draughtsman, born in Detroit, Michigan, America, who studied at the local Society of Arts and Crafts, 1946–9, then at College of Architecture, University of Michigan, graduating with an honours degree from Ann Arbor, Michigan, 1954. From 1954–79 Kuehne's work was mainly representational, some being commissioned by University of Lexington, Kentucky, where she then lived, having a solo show at Transylvania University in 1983. In 1979 Kuehne moved to London for a decade, her work turning to Abstract Expressionism. From 1991 she lived in Cabrieres, in the south of France, where she again adopted representation, strongly influenced by abstraction. Kuehne appeared in a group show at Minsky Gallery, 1982; had two solo exhibitions at Usiskin Gallery, 1989–90; then showed solo at Nicholas Bowlby Gallery, Tunbridge Wells, 1995.

Peter KUHFELD 1952– Painter and teacher, born in Cheltenham, Gloucestershire. He studied at Leicester Polytechnic, 1972–6, then at Royal Academy Schools under Peter Greenham, 1977–80. He taught at Rugby School of Art, 1976–8. Among his awards was the David Murray Landscape Prize, 1978–9; RA Silver Medal for Drawing, 1979; Royal College of Surgeons Dooley Prize for Anatomical Drawing, 1980; Elizabeth Greenshields Foundation Scholarship, 1980–1; and Richard Ford Award, 1981. In 1978 Kuhfeld was made a freeman of the Worshipful Company of Painter-Stainers. Kuhfeld showed widely in mixed exhibitions, including RA Summer Exhibitions from 1978, RWA from 1982, at Jonleigh Gallery, Guildford, from 1983, and New Grafton Gallery, from 1983. One-man shows included Highgate Gallery, 1983–5, and New Grafton Gallery, 1986. He was one of the New Grafton's Portrait Centre artists. Kuhfeld accompanied HRH The Prince of Wales on trips to Africa and Japan, some of the resulting pictures being included in a notable Kuhfeld show at Agnew, 1991. The Prince also owns a portrait of him by Kuhfeld. Lived in London.

Andrzej KUHN 1930– Painter and printmaker, born in Poland. He was deported when Russia invaded in 1940 and after privations in exile in the Middle East arrived in England in 1947 where, after six years as a labourer and service in the Merchant Navy, he gained a scholarship to Chelsea School of Art. Postage stamps from Tanna-Tuva, the drawings of Aubrey Beardsley and Sumerian sculpture were some influences, leading to a personal iconography including sellers of moons and stars, travellers and fantastic cities. Kuhn saw art as a consolation in times of trouble. Showed in Lincolnshire where he lived near Boston and had a solo exhibition at Goldmark Gallery, Uppingham, 1994.

Lara Nita KULKARNI 1967– Painter who did foundation studies at Worthing College of Art & Design, 1985–6; gained a first-class honours degree in fine art (painting) from Maidstone College of Art & Design, 1986–9; winning a higher diploma fine art (painting) from Slade School of Fine Art, 1989–91. Awards included Boosey and Hawkes Art Prize (commissions), 1991–2; Boise Travel Scholarship, to China, 1992; Travel to East and Southern Africa, 1993; and a South East Arts Major Award, 1995. Showed at Sandra Drew Gallery, Canterbury, 1989; Metropole Arts Centre, Folkestone, Routes – Four Women Artists Through the Slade, 1991; Bernard Jacobson Gallery, show of seven commissioned paintings, 1992; and Diverse, Kent Institute of Art & Design, 1996. Shared an exhibition at Phoenix Gallery, Brighton, 1995. South East Arts, Boise Collection and Boosey and Hawkes hold examples. Kulkarni from 1992 "explored Chinese concepts of nature in relation to art and philosophy." Her paintings began "by making a small gestural mark, and from my response to it I create a veil-like woven surface of light and colour."

Yuri KUPER 1940– Printmaker, especially of colour lithographs, born in Moscow, in the Soviet Union, where he studied at the Academy of Art. In 1972 he emigrated to Israel and then moved to London. He went to Paris in 1975 and returned to London at the start of the 1980s, becoming a British citizen in 1983. After that he divided his time between the two capitals. Although he had a show in Cambridge in 1973 and at the Sainsbury Centre, Norwich, in 1993, his first exhibition in London did not take place until 1996, at the William Weston Gallery. By that time he had had over 50 one-man shows around the world. Using soft, muted colours, Kuper depicted simple objects, such as a plate with an apple or a mug with a sprig of flowers, making the maximum use of the light and space around them. The use of old lithographic stones with traces of the original text enhanced the surfaces created. Many public collections, including the Museum of Modern Art and Metropolitan Museum of Art in New York, the Pushkin Museum in Moscow and National Gallery in Oslo, as well as the Sainsbury Collection, University of Norwich, hold Kuper's work.

Sylvia KUS 1950– Artist and teacher, born in Chester. She studied at the College of Further Education there, Leicester Polytechnic and Goldsmiths' College School of Art. Taught in Woolwich. Group exhibitions included Aerial Structures, Sunderland, 1973; Twin Towns Art, Reinickendorf, Berlin, and Blackheath Gallery, both 1976. She had a solo show at Maggie Petrie Gallery, 1975, another at Woodlands Art Gallery, 1977. That consisted of wall pieces and constructions using a variety of materials. The collages were "concerned with spatial qualities seen in landscapes", the constructions being "abstract ideas creating new spatial effects".

Georgina Moutray KYLE 1865–1950 Painter, initially in pastel and watercolour, later in oil, daughter of George Wilson Kyle, she was born in Craigavad, County Down, Northern Ireland, afterwards living in Belfast. Studied at Atelier Colarossi in Paris. She was a member of RUA and a prolific exhibitor, including RHA, ROI, RSA, Royal Glasgow Institute of the Fine Arts and Paris Salon. Ulster Museum has several works by her, including Le Marché, Concarneau.

Kathryn Marie KYNOCH 1942– Painter, born in Edinburgh. After attending grammar school in Leicester she returned to Scotland to study under David Donaldson at Glasgow School of Art, 1959–64. In the early-1960s she also studied for short periods at Patrick Allan-Fraser School of Art, Hospitalfield, Arbroath, under James Cumming. She showed widely in Scotland, including RSA, Blythswood Gallery in Glasgow and Royal Glasgow Institute of the Fine Arts. Edinburgh University holds her work. Lived in Glasgow.

George KYRIACOU 1940– Sculptor and teacher who settled in London. He qualified as a teacher in 1959, studied sculpture on a Cyprus government scholarship at Chelsea School of Art, 1961–4, then after working as a teacher and sculptor in Cyprus, 1964–9, was appointed cultural officer at the Ministry of Education responsible for visual arts. In 1972 Kyriacou gained a French Institute Scholarship to study museology in Paris and in 1976–7 studied arts administration at Polytechnic of Central London. He undertook public commissions in Cyprus and exhibited widely, including Biennale des Jeunes de Paris, 1967, Venice Biennale, 1968, and with Gallery K at Art95, 1995. Kyriacou's sculptures employed everyday objects and debris.

L

Rachel LABOUCHERE 1908–1996 Botanical artist, who inherited a collection of flower paintings and studied with John Nash and Mary Grierson; and writer. She was born Rachel Hamilton–Russell, a descendant of the Darbys of Coalbrookdale, the Christy Millers of Adcote and the Wolryche Whitmores of Dudmaston. She had no formal education, although she had wished to go to Oxford University, but during World War II worked for the Admiralty where she met her second husband George Labouchere, knighted in 1955, a collector of modern French and Spanish pictures. With him she travelled extensively, then when he retired as a diplomat in 1966 they settled at her family home, Dudmaston Hall, near Bridgnorth, Shropshire. The house was refurbished by Lady Labouchere and made over to the National Trust in 1978. She also did extensive family historical research, which earned her an honorary doctorate from the University of Birmingham in 1993. Two books on the Quakers from family diaries and a political diary of Adelaide Whitmore were among her writings.

Bruce LACEY 1927– Performance artist, painter, film-maker, sculptor and robot constructor, born in London. He studied at Hornsey School of Art, 1949–51, winning the Knapping Prize in the latter year. Was then at Royal College of Art, 1951–4, gaining an Abbey Minor Travelling Scholarship in the latter year. At the College Lacey established a reputation as a performance artist and creator of happenings sufficient for Ken Russell to make the film *Preservation Man* on him in 1961. Two years later Lacey had a one-man show at Gallery One, another following at Marlborough New London Gallery two years later. By 1975 he had a retrospective at Whitechapel Art Gallery. Lacey believed that the artist should not be constricted to any narrow means of expression, and in the 1970s with his wife Jill Bruce he began performing a series of rituals at various outdoor locations in homage to mysterious and elemental forces. In 1977 he was elected a member of the British Astronomical Association. His work was included in The 1960's at England & Co, 1993. Lived in Silfield, Norfolk, for some years.

Mary Elliott LACEY 1923– Artist in gouache, oil, pencil and conté and teacher, born in Birmingham. She attended Birmingham College of Art, 1939–44, under Bernard Fleetwood-Walker. Went on to teach for seven years at Mansfield School of Art, then two years part-time at Wolverhampton College of Art. Lacey was a founder-member of SWLA. She exhibited at Mall and Tryon Galleries, at Slimbridge Wild Fowl Trust, elsewhere throughout Britain and in Paris. Had a series of solo shows at Fairfield Halls, Croydon. She illustrated regularly for Hamlyn, Balberry Publishing, National Parks of America and designed several jigsaws for James Hamilton. Medici, Royle and World Wildlife Fund reproduced Lacey's pictures and she was commissioned to produce nine for the Sultan of Oman. Lived at Sudbourne, Woodbridge, Suffolk.

Barbara Dacia LACK fl. from 1940s– Artist in many media including textile design who attended Perse School in Cambridge, then the College of Art there, followed by Royal College of Art. Showed at RA, in the provinces and abroad. Continued to live in Cambridge for many years, latterly at Temple Sowerby, Penrith, Cumbria.

Henry Martyn LACK 1909–1979 Etcher and teacher, born in Bozeat, Northamptonshire. He studied at Leicester College of Art and gained a Royal Exhibition to the Royal College of Art, where he remained for five years. Joined the Sakkarah expedition in Egypt to record tomb paintings and carvings, after two years returning to England to be art master at Christ's Hospital, Horsham, from 1937–46. After Army service he was briefly at Northampton School of Art before becoming a tutor in the engraving school at the Royal College of Art. Was then at Hastings School of Art, 1953–68, latterly as acting principal. Then Egypt called him again and until his retirement in 1976 he was a member of a Chicago University team at Luxor for six months of the year, the rest of the time being spent in Hastings. Showed widely in Britain and abroad, including RA and RE. British Museum, British Council and Hastings Museum and Art Gallery hold his work.

Suzanne LACKNER 1908– Sculptor in wide variety of materials, born in Berlin, Germany, where she studied architecture at the Technical University, then studied in France and London. Was a member of Free Painters and Sculptors, also showing at Camden Arts Centre, elsewhere in London where she lived, and abroad.

John LACOUX 1930– Painter, born with an English mother and French father, whose work was inspired greatly by ecclesiastical architecture, the sea and Venice. He used a technique of glazes which exploited effects of light, as in his show at Nicholas Bowlby, Tunbridge Wells, 1996. Other solo exhibitions included Trafford and Madden Galeries, Tib Lane in Manchester, elsewhere in the north of England and in America. Mixed exhibitions included RA Summer Exhibition, RP and Business Art Galleries at Burlington House.

Marek LACZYNSKI 1925– Printmaker, illustrator and teacher, born in Warsaw, Poland. He was a member of the Polish

Home Army in 1941, took part in Warsaw Uprising in 1944, was a prisoner of war in Germany, 1944–5, joined the Polish forces in Italy in 1945 and arrived in England in 1946. Studied book illustration at Borough Polytechnic, 1949–52, then etching and lithography at Central School of Arts and Crafts, 1962–4. Had first show of prints at Redfern Gallery, 1959. Other appearances included Grabowski Gallery, 1959; Giles Bequest Exhibition at Victoria & Albert Museum, 1962; and in same year Prints of the World at Cincinnati Museum, America. From 1964 taught at Exeter College of Art, being appointed head of printmaking in 1979. Published a book of poetry, *Faces of Fear*, in 1973. Was a member of Printmakers' Council of Great Britain from 1965, of the World Printmakers' Council from 1978. Victoria & Albert Museum, Universities of London and Exeter and a number of overseas museums hold his work. Lived in Exeter, Devon.

Roger LADE 1960– Artist in various media, including models and puppets, who was involved in Little Angel Marionette Theatre, Islington. Was born and lived in London, in his teens becoming interested in the theatre and stage management. Did a foundation course at Sir John Cass School of Art, 1979–80, then honours degree in fine art at Wolverhampton Polytechnic, 1980–3. Exhibited at Wrekin College, Telford; Stowells Trophy at RA; Woodlands Art Gallery, and elsewhere.

Edwin LA DELL 1914–1970 Painter, lithographer and teacher. Born in Coventry, he studied art at Sheffield College of Art and the Royal College of Art under Gilbert Spencer and Barnett Freedman. He was the son of Thomas La Dell and Ellen La Dell, both still life painters. Edwin went on to become senior tutor in charge of printmaking at the Royal College of Art. There he was an influential teacher, his vibrantly coloured lithographs gaining inspiration from French models such as Vuillard, Denis and Bonnard. His organisation of the *Coronation Suite*, in 1953, brought together a number of artists connected with the College. He wrote and illustrated *Your Book of Landscape Drawing* and illustrated Wilkie Collins' novel *The Moonstone*. Lived near Maidstone, Kent.

Thomas Sherwood LA FONTAINE 1915– Portrait and animal painter and draughtsman in black-and-white. He studied at Regent Street Polytechnic School of Art, 1934–6, teachers including Harry Watson and Stuart Tresilian; City and Guilds of London Art School, 1936–9, with A R Middleton Todd and James Grant; then Spenlove School, 1939, with Reginald Eves. Showed at RP, RA and elsewhere and lived in Malmesbury, Wiltshire, for many years.

Phillip LAI 1969– Installations artist, born in Kuala Lumpur, Malaya, who graduated from Chelsea College of Art & Design, 1990–3, gaining his master's degree, 1993–4. Group exhibitions included Sweetrice, Unit 219, Elephant & Castle Shopping Centre, 1992; Whitworth Young Contemporaries, Whitworth Art Gallery, Manchester, 1993; Fresh, London Film & Video Umbrella touring show, from 1994; Institute of Cultural Anxiety: works from the collection, ICA, 1994–5; and Deep Signal, Gasworks, 1996. In 1997, The Showroom, in collaboration with the Institute of International Visual Arts, commissioned a new installation by Lai which explored the idea of fluid states: one a working soy sauce fermentation unit, the other a room of automatic drawings on the gallery walls. Lai worked in London.

Annie Rose LAING 1869–1946 Figure painter who lived variously in Glasgow, Frascati in Italy and in London, married to the artist James Garden Laing, who predeceased her by 31 years. Showed extensively at Royal Glasgow Institute of the Fine Arts, also at RSA, RA and Walker Art Gallery in Liverpool. Kelvingrove Art Gallery in Glasgow holds her oils The Mirror and After Rehearsal.

David LAING 1954– Artist, born in Suffolk, who studied medical biology and worked for the Medical Research Council before travelling extensively. He experienced the Iranian Islamic Revolution first-hand before returning to England to pursue art studies, settling in London. Attended Middlesex Polytechnic, 1980–3, École des Beaux-Arts in Paris, 1986, and Royal College of Art, 1985–7. Exhibited in British Council Invited Section, Ljubliana Biennale, Yugoslavia, 1991; Whitechapel Open Exhibition at Whitechapel Gallery, 1992; Artists' Books, South Bank Centre, 1993; and Lannon Gallery, New York, 1995. Solo exhibitions included Harriet Green Gallery, 1995, where Laing showed dark paintings scattered with forms that reflected his biological background.

Gerald LAING 1936– Artist, notably a sculptor in bronze, and teacher, born in Newcastle upon Tyne, Northumberland. Also known as Gerald Ogilvie-Lang. He attended Royal Military Academy, Sandhurst, 1953–5, then after a short Army career attended St Martin's School of Art, 1960–4. Lived in New York for five years, being artist-in-residence at Aspen Institute for Humanistic Studies, Colorado, in 1966. Initially Laing was a Pop Artist and by the late–1960s was known as a sculptor of minimal forms. In 1969, during a period of disillusionment, he acquired Kinkell Castle, on the Black Isle, in Scotland and restored it, in 1977 setting up a substantial bronze foundry there to handle his own work. By this time Laing had rejected abstraction for figuration, returning to the mainstream, but continually experimenting within it. Laing's teaching posts included visiting professor at University of New Mexico, Albuquerque, 1976–7; and professor of sculpture at Columbia University, New York, 1986–7. In 1978–80 he was on the art committee of the Scottish Arts Council, in 1987 being appointed commissioner on the Royal Commission for Fine Art for Scotland. Laing showed widely internationally, having a one-man show at Laing Art Gallery, Newcastle upon Tyne, 1963, another at ICA, 1964, then the first of a string at Richard Feigen Gallery, New York, 1964, and with Richard Feigen in Chicago, 1965, Whitford Fine Art in 1996 holding an exhibition of 17 silkscreen prints made in 1968. The Cincinnati Center for Contemporary Art gave Laing a retrospective in 1971, others following at Herbert Art Gallery, Coventry,

1983, and Fruitmarket Gallery, Edinburgh, 1993. In 1995 Laing was commissioned to make eight dragons for Bank tube station, in 1996 four bronze rugby players for Twickenham Stadium. Tate Gallery, National Portrait Gallery, Victoria & Albert Museum, Scottish Art Gallery and many other public collections in Britain and abroad hold Laing's work.

Arthur Robert LAIRD 1881–c.1957 Lithographer who studied at Camberwell School of Arts and Crafts under Herbert Cole and Francis Jackson, then at the Westminster School of Art under Walter Sickert and Harold Gilman. He exhibited at the Senefelder Club, RA, RBA, SGA, in the provinces, in Belgium and America. The British Museum and Victoria & Albert Museum hold his work. Laird, who worked for a time in local government, became secretary of the Camberwell School of Arts and Crafts and vice-president of the South London Group. Lived at Ewell, Surrey.

Antony LAKE 1905–1956 Painter and illustrator, born at Chalfont St Giles, Buckinghamshire. Studied at St Martin's School of Art. Exhibited at NS and RBA. Worked for the *Illustrated London News*, did posters for London Passenger Transport Board and illustrated a number of books. Belonged to Hoddesdon Art Club and lived near Waltham Abbey, Essex.

Evelyn Frances Coote LAKE 1885–1979 Painter, especially of birds and cats, in various media, born in London, where she continued to live. She studied at Camden and Hornsey Schools of Art and on the continent. Exhibited very widely in London as well as RCamA, RWA, in the provinces and at Paris Salon. She was a prominent member of a number of art clubs, including RWS and Ridley Art Club. Was also involved in a variety of organisations such as the Cats' Protection League and Folk-Lore Society.

John Gascoyne LAKE 1903–1975 Painter and museum curator, educated in Seaford, studied painting at Eastbourne School of Art, 1918–25, and the Royal College of Art, 1925–9. Lake did a variety of work, ranging from figure studies through views of Sussex to later more abstract pictures. Exhibited LG, NEAC and in the provinces. Was curator of the Towner Art Gallery, Eastbourne, 1947–58. Lived at Hailsham, Sussex, but emigrated to Spain after his retirement from the gallery, which held a memorial show in 1975.

Maria LALIĆ 1952– Painter committed to non-figurative work associated with Minimalism and Concrete art. She was brought up in her home town, Sheffield, Yorkshire, completed a master's degree in fine art at Chelsea School of Art, 1977, the following year having a fellowship at the Academy in Bath, Somerset, where she settled. American artists such as Robert Ryman, Brice Marden, Eva Hesse, Agnes Martin and Carl André were influences. She came into prominence in the 1990s through solo exhibitions in London and Munich as well as several group shows: drei Frauen konkret?, Munich, 1995, and Mostly Monochrome, Dublin, 1996. The Lead Fall series was important in her output. She was one of the Jerwood Painting Prize selections at the Central St Martins College of Art and Design, 1997.

Richard LALLY 1928– Painter and restorer, born in London, who attended Hammersmith College of Art and Building under Leon Underwood and Dennis Gilbert, 1955–9. Appeared in mixed shows at UA, SWLA and ROI and had solo exhibition at Manolette Gallery, Richmond, and abroad. Lived at Drumbeg, Lairg, Sutherland.

Charles LAMB 1893–1964 Painter and teacher who was born in Portadown, Armagh, Northern Ireland. Initially he followed his father's trade as a house painter and studied at the local Technical School, but attended evening classes at Belfast School of Art. After gaining a scholarship to Dublin's Metropolitan School of Art, 1917–21, where he won gold and silver medals, Lamb settled in Carraroe, County Galway, where he lived simply and became noted for his studies of peasant life. In the mid-1930s he built a house at Carraroe and ran a summer painting school there. Travelled extensively in Ireland, working in the North extensively from the early 1940s, also in Brittany. He was a member of RHA and RUA and exhibited widely in Ireland and abroad, including RA, America – including Olympic Art Exhibition, 1932, in Los Angeles – and was given a show by CEMA in Belfast in 1947. Municipal Gallery of Modern Art held a memorial show in 1969. Ulster Museum and most Irish public collections hold examples.

Christine Margaret LAMB 1930–1971 Portait and landscape painter in oil and medical illustrator, born in Portsmouth, Hampshire. She studied at the College of Art there, 1945–7; Bromley Art College, 1947–9; and Royal Academy Schools, 1949–51. In addition to exhibiting at NEAC and RP and having work in *The Artist* magazine, Lamb was assistant medical artist at the Central Middlesex Hospital and illustrated medical publications. Before that, in 1949–51, she had taught at Sevenoaks Art Centre. Lived in Rickmansworth, Hertfordshire.

Elspeth LAMB fl. from late 1960s– Printmaker, paperwork and mixed-media artist, and teacher, who attended Glasgow School of Art, 1969–73; did postgraduate studies in printmaking at Manchester Polytechnic, 1973–4; then studied stone lithography at Ruskin School of Drawing, Oxford, 1976. After lecturing in etching in Glasgow, from 1978 taught printmaking, drawing and painting at Edinburgh College of Art. She won many awards, including several from Scottish Arts Council, and took part in a string of international print biennales and art fairs. Mixed shows included New Scottish Prints Tour in New York, 1983; The Mini Print Competition in Cadaques, Spain, 1984; and Amsterdam, Culture City Prints, 1987. Had a solo show at Glasgow School of Art, 1974, later ones including Compass Gallery, Glasgow, 1992, where Lamb's interest in ancient civilisations was evident. British Council, Scottish Arts Council and public galleries in Glasgow, Leeds, Bradford and Perth hold examples. Lamb was unusual in tackling the onerous job of making her own paper, which she saturated with rich, dense pigment.

Henry LAMB 1883–1960 Painter and draughtsman, especially of portraits and figure groups. Born in Adelaide, Australia. Family returned to Manchester in 1886. Lamb studied medicine at Manchester University, but after election as a student for 1904–5 at MAFA moved to London and in 1906 enrolled at Chelsea Art School, run by Augustus John and William Orpen, afterwards attending L'École de la Palette, Paris. Prior to World War I he became involved with Euphemia (Nina Forrest), whom he married, Dorelia John and Lady Ottoline Morrell; painted in Brittany and Ireland; and exhibited with the AAA, Camden Town Group and NEAC. In World War I after further studies he served as a medical officer and as an official war artist abroad. In the 1920s Lamb's reputation grew; he exhibited at RA from 1921 (elected RA in 1949); first one-man show at Alpine Gallery, 1922; married Lady Pansy Pakenham, 1928; and began a long association with the Leicester Galleries, 1927. Official war artist in World War II. Lamb was a fine draughtsman and a painter whose palette was muted, but unmistakeable. He finished a number of pictures which are a key part of modern British painting: Death of a Peasant, Lytton Strachey and Evelyn Waugh. Work in many public collections, including Tate Gallery and National Portrait Gallery. Retrospective exhibition at Manchester City Art Gallery, 1984, and touring. Lived at Coombe Bissett, Wiltshire.

Lynton LAMB 1907–1977 Lithographer, wood engraver, book illustrator and painter. Born in India, he studied at the Central School of Arts and Crafts under William Roberts and Bernard Meninsky, 1928–30. Shared a studio with Victor Pasmore in the 1930s, is featured in Pasmore's picture The Parisian Café and was associated with the Euston Road School. Exhibited RA, RBA, LG, Leicester and Redfern Galleries and widely abroad. One-man show at the Storran Gallery, 1937. On the staff of the Slade School of Fine Art, 1950–71, and the Royal College of Art, 1956–71. Lamb was an exemplary book illustrator; produced the lorry bill *Reaping* for Shell in 1951; and wrote a number of books, including *The Purpose of Painting* and *Preparation for Painting*. Lived at Sandon, near Chelmsford, Essex.

Sue LAMB 1943– Sculptor, draughtsman and Batik artist who began sculpting as a remedial exercise after leaving a career with British Airways. Studied at Sidcup Art Centre for eight years and became assistant to the sculptor John Ravera. Lamb's chief interest was animal sculpture, especially dogs, as evidenced in the four-man show she shared at Woodlands Art Gallery, 1981. She was commissioned to make competition trophies, including a golden Cruft's award, and exhibited annually at major championship shows where her work was bought by internationally known dog breeders and exhibitors.

William LAMB 1893–1951 Sculptor, printmaker and watercolourist, born in Montrose, Angus, where he eventually settled. For several years before World War I Lamb was apprenticed as a monumental sculptor to his brother James and attended evening classes at Montrose Academy. In 1912 he began work for an Aberdeen granite merchants, continuing to study at Gray's School of Art. During the war he lost a hand while engaged in trench warfare, but began using his left hand and during 1918–21 attended classes at Montrose Academy again, changing to full-time study at Edinburgh College of Art, 1921–2, where his teachers included David Foggie. After studying in Paris, 1922–4, at École des Beaux-Arts, Lamb did a cycle tour of France and Italy lasting 3,000 miles, returning to Montrose in 1924 where he established a studio. He now began to exhibit seriously at RA and RSA, at the latter winning the Guthrie Award in 1929. In 1945 he established a stone-carving business. The William Lamb Memorial Studio in his home town houses his output as an artist. Lamb was noted for his heads of the royal family modelled in the early-1930s, but his fame rests on his powerful, Expressionistic depictions of fisherfolk.

Juginder LAMBA 1948– Sculptor in wood, notably bog oak, producing mainly figurative work on themes such as mothers and children and lovers. He was born in Nairobi, Kenya. After four years in India until 1962 the family moved to England. In 1969 Lamba graduated from University of Lancaster. For eight years he was involved in New Plant Arts Workshop and Earthbound Theatre, a touring performance art unit, in 1978 becoming Lancaster's first town artist. Then did work for many arts organisations and schools, eventually based in London. After a solo show on Edinburgh Festival fringe in 1976 others included Abbot Hall Art Gallery, Kendal, 1977; Liverpool University, 1979; Westbourne Art Gallery, 1984; and Commonwealth Institute, 1986. From 1983 he held a series of shows at Woburn Fine Arts, which in 1986 published an illustrated monograph on him.

Peter LAMBDA 1911–1995 Sculptor and writer, born in Budapest, Hungary, to professional parents, his mother a psychoanalyst, a student of Sigmund Freud who later sat to Lambda for the portrait in the Freud Museum. Lambda studied medicine; sculpture in Paris and Prague; then after some success exhibiting moved to London in 1938. During World War II he worked for the Crown Film Unit and wrote propaganda scripts for the BBC. After the war joined Imperial Chemical Industries, engaged in industrial design, notably with the new material Perspex, in which he sculpted. Made a fine head in bronze of the Labour politician Aneurin Bevan, then concentrated on theatrical personalities, including Laurence Oliver, Claire Bloom, Christopher Fry, Terence Rattigan and Wendy Hiller. His work is in the National Portrait Gallery, National Museum of Wales in Cardiff and University College, Swansea. Lambda's last bust was of the actress Liz Robertson, 1981, then eye trouble made sculpting difficult. Lambda married his second wife, the actress Betty Paul, in 1958. By then he had written for the theatre and with her he scripted episodes for television series; they created their own, *Weaver's Green*, for Anglia. Continued writing until 1993, having in 1987 moved from London to Tibberton, Gloucestershire, where he died.

Philip Agnew LAMBE 1897–1968 Painter in oil who over a long period studied privately with Charles Buchel, Charles

Simpson, Arthur Hayward and Bernard Adams, with a period at Heatherley's School of Fine Art. Travelled extensively. Exhibited NS, RP and Paris Salon, where he won a gold medal, sometimes signing work with initials only. Lived in London.

Alison LAMBERT 1957– Artist who was notably a draughtsman, sometimes on a large scale, heads and horses as favoured subjects. Born in Kingston, Surrey, she studied at Leek School of Art and Design, 1978–9, gained a bachelor's degree in fine art at Coventry Polytechnic, 1981–4, then took a studio with Coventry Artists Group. Group shows included Coventry's Herbert Art Gallery, 1984; Oriel Gallery, Welshpool, 1987; Nerlino Gallery, New York, 1990; and Cleveland International Drawing Biennale, 1991. Solo shows included Long & Ryle, 1995. London headquarters of Cité Nationale Bank of France commissioned work, which was held also by Coopers & Lybrand Deloitte, Birmingham collection.

Claire LAMBERT 1936– Painter, draughtsman, printmaker and ceramist, born in Ipswich, Suffolk, settling nearby at Shotley. She was largely self-taught, but did attend part-time and evening classes at Académie des Beaux-Arts in Brussels under Roger Somville, Atelier des Céramiques de Dour with Fernand Wery and Suffolk College. "The human figure and expression, simplicity and feeling" were important aspects of her work. Lambert was a member of Suffolk Craft Society and Ipswich Art Society. Group exhibitions included Peter Pears Gallery in Aldeburgh, Guy Taplin's Gallery in Woodbridge, Falcon Gallery in Boxford and extensively on the continent and in Canada. Solo shows included Gallery 44, Aldeburgh; John Russell Gallery, Ipswich; and Christchurch Mansion there. It and Musée de Verviers, Belgium, hold examples.

Isabel LAMBERT: *see* **Isabel RAWSTHORNE**

Maurice LAMBERT 1901–1964 Sculptor, draughtsman and teacher, born in Paris. His father was the Australian painter George Lambert, his brother the musician Constant Lambert. Educated in London, Lambert was apprenticed, 1918–23, with the sculptor Derwent Wood; assisted his father briefly in his studio; and attended part-time life classes, 1919–27, at Chelsea Polytechnic. Although he worked on Wood's Machine Gun Corps monument at Hyde Park Corner, Lambert's own sculpture, while remaining largely figurative, took a much more modern turn. He was prolific, between 1925–34 exhibiting nearly 150 works, having his first solo show at the Claridge Gallery in 1927. His fourth and final one-man show in his lifetime was at Reid and Lefevre in 1934, and it was left to the Belgrave Gallery to give him a posthumous exibition in 1988. Lambert was a member of NS and a fellow of RBS and was elected RA in 1952. From 1950–8 he was master of sculpture at the Royal Academy Schools. A physically tough and intellectually adventurous man, Lambert undertook a large number of commissions, often of hefty size. They included an equestrian statue of King George V for Adelaide, South Australia; work in the liners *Queen Mary* and *Queen Elizabeth*; fountains for Basildon; and work in the presidential palace, Baghdad. Tate Gallery holds his work. Died in London.

Alan LAMBIRTH 1959– Painter of landscapes and interiors, simplifying the images and often including a single female figure. He studied at West Sussex College of Design, Epsom School of Art and Royal Academy Schools. From 1981 showed in RA Summer Exhibitions, from 1983 with RBA and from 1986 at NEAC. He gained the RA Gold Medal in 1982, the year he won an Edward Travelling Scholarship, winning a David Murray Studentship in 1983. Elected RBA three years later. Had two solo shows at Odette Gilbert Gallery, 1984–6, one at the Solomon Gallery, 1988, and at Sheila Harrison Fine Art, 1989. In 1991 shared an exhibition at Llewellyn Alexander Gallery. Lived in Horsham, Sussex.

George LAMBOURN 1900–1977 Artist, born in London, who early showed an aptitude for drawing and mathematics. In 1916 he was chosen to join Royal Air Service Corps, training as a rear gunner. After World War I he was asked to plan a factory in Bruges for English Electric Light Bulb Company and during that time discovered a natural talent for painting, which then became his dominant interest. He studied at Goldsmiths' College School of Art, the Royal Academy Schools, 1924–7, and briefly in Paris. During World War II he worked with an ambulance unit in France, then as an official war artist, later running a unit which decorated canteens for the 8th Army in Africa and Italy. Before the war Lambourn had shown in London, having a solo exhibition with Matthiesen Gallery in 1938. After the war Lambourn – a multi-talented man of strong views, a black belt at judo, an intellectual, an enthusiast for amateur dramatics – decided to settle in west Cornwall, having years before fallen in love with Mousehole. He was commemorated by a show at Gordon Hepworth Gallery, Exeter, in 1991. Imperial War Museum and Tate Gallery hold his work.

Nigel LAMBOURNE 1919–1988 Draughtsman, printmaker, book illustrator, designer and teacher, born in Croydon, Surrey. He studied, 1934–7, at Regent Street Polytechnic School of Art and Central School of Arts and Crafts, then from 1937–9 at Royal College of Art with Robert Austin and Malcolm Osborne. After Army service in World War II completed his degree course at Royal College of Art. While still at College he taught at Isleworth Evening Institute, later appointments being at Guildford College of Art, 1951–61, and Leicester Polytechnic, 1962–72. In the late-1940s began to establish a name as an illustrator of books and magazines and for leading advertising agencies. Soon became a member of Senefelder Club and RE. Had his first solo exhibition at Kensington Art Gallery in 1949, later one-man exhibitions including Wilton and Zwemmer Galleries. In 1950–1 worked on Festival of Britain South Bank Exhibition. Lambourne was a masterly draughtsman, with a taut, springing line, shown to great effect in his drawings of low life and the female figure. He died at Oakhill, near Bath, Avon, and in 1992 Victoria Art Gallery, Bath, held a show of his work. Arts Council, Contemporary Art Society and Museum of Modern Art, New York, hold examples.

Edie LAMONT 1896–1983 Artist in pen and ink, watercolour and oil, and collector, born in Carnoustie, Angus. In the mid-1930s she studied at St John's Wood Art Schools under Patrick Millard, fellow-students being Robin Treffgarne and John Minton, whom she helped and collected and whose work influenced her own. She showed with St John's Wood Group at Wertheim Gallery, also with Leicester Galleries and LG. Lamont was married to businessman Newton Lamont, who died in 1960. Lived at Chart Sutton, near Maidstone, Kent, a neighbour and friend of Harold Nicolson, in whose diaries she appears, and Vita Sackville-West, whose white garden she painted. Interested in gardening, Edie indexed Sackville-West's articles about it and she was the dedicatee of Vita's 1961 novel *No Signposts in the Sea*. In the year she died Anthony Dawson, of Barnes, organised an exhibition of Lamont's work.

John Charles LAMONT 1894–1948 Painter who studied at Glasgow School of Art under Maurice Greiffenhagen and Fra Newbery. Exhibited RSA, Walker Art Gallery, Liverpool, and Royal Glasgow Institute of the Fine Arts. Lived in Kirkcudbright, Scotland.

Francesca LA NAVE 1954– Artist, art psychotherapist and teacher, born in Florence, Italy, where she matriculated from scientific secondary school in 1973. Joined the Quatenary Era Institute, a scientific research project, concerned with studying prehistoric ecosystems and graffiti, with which she travelled to several national parks and the Algerian Sahara. Moved to London, in 1982 she graduated with credit in fine arts at Chelsea School of Art. Was a founder-member of Pyramid Arts Development, multicultural arts group in Hackney, between 1984–5 co-ordinating community projects for Borough of Islington. She supported her art with teaching, translation and market research. In 1989, La Nave became artist-in-residence at Homerton Hospital psychiatric department. Having studied art psychotherapy at Goldsmiths' College, 1992–6, she worked as an art psychotherapist in adult psychiatry and special education. Took part in group exhibitions in London and Edinburgh, also Unquiet Voices, Doncaster Museum & Art Gallery, 1997. Had solo exhibitions in Verona and London. From 1995, La Nave's work changed dramatically to include writing, video and sound, evolving towards multiples and multimedia installation. Lived in London.

Brian Christy LANCASTER 1931– Painter, illustrator and designer, born in Atherton, Lancashire, with a special interest in steam locomotives. Studied at Bolton School of Art, 1946–9, with John Gauld; Southport School of Art, 1949–52; and Manchester School of Art. Showed RI, RBA, RWA, Atkinson Art Gallery, Southport, and elsewhere. Bristol Museum holds his work. Lived at North Nibley, Gloucestershire.

Edward Purser LANCASTER 1911–1954 Painter, printmaker, designer, mural artist and teacher. Studied at Southport, Liverpool and Chelsea Schools of Art. Eventually taught at London School of Printing and Graphic Arts. Exhibited Goupil Gallery, Atkinson Art Gallery, Southport, elsewhere in the north of England, in London, Paris and New York. General Post Office and Southport Corporation bought his work, which was also reproduced by the London Passenger Transport Board. Lived in London and Bognor Regis, Sussex.

Mark LANCASTER 1938– Painter, printmaker and teacher, born Yorkshire. Studied and later taught at department of fine art at Newcastle University. He also lectured at Bath Academy of Art, Corsham, won the Purchase Prize at the Second British International Print Biennale, Bradford, and was artist-in-residence at King's College, Cambridge, 1968–70. His exhibitions included Rowan Gallery and Magdalene Street Gallery, Cambridge. Lancaster's work is in many collections, including Tate Gallery, Victoria & Albert Museum, Museum of Modern Art in New York and British Council.

Osbert LANCASTER 1908–1986 Cartoonist and social satirist, painter, theatrical designer and writer, born in London. After attending Oxford University, 1926–30, he was at Byam Shaw School of Drawing and Painting, 1925–6, the Ruskin School of Drawing, in Oxford, 1929–30, then the Slade School of Fine Art, 1931–2. In 1932 and 1934 he showed at NEAC, but then forsook easel painting for murals, book illustrations and writing, from 1934–9 being on the staff of the *Architectural Review* while doing some university lecturing. Wrote authoritatively but wittily on architecture in such books as *Homes, Sweet Homes* and *Drayneflete Revealed*. In 1939 was appointed cartoonist on the *Daily Express*, where he chronicled the adventures of the Littlehamptons in his Pocket Cartoon. Designed for all the major British opera and ballet companies. Tate Gallery holds his work. Knighted in 1975.

Percy LANCASTER 1878–1951 Landscape, painter and etcher, born in Manchester. Originally trained as an architect, but turned to art and attended Southport School of Art. Exhibited prolifically, especially RI, RBA, Walker's Galleries and RCamA. Had solo show at Walker's Galleries. Medici Society prints were made of his pictures, which are in public galleries in Manchester, Oldham, Preston and Rochdale. Lived in Southport.

Marjorie LANCE 1900– Versatile painter brought up in Hatfield, Hertfordshire, who married the miniature painter H Carlyon Webb. She studied at the Slade School of Fine Art with Henry Tonks, Philip Wilson Steer and John Wheatley, 1920–3. Exhibited Goupil Gallery, NEAC, RBA, PS and in the provinces. Showed solo at St George's and Woodstock Galleries. Lived in Stanmore, Middlesex.

Colin LANCELEY 1938– Painter, construction artist, printmaker and teacher, born in Dunedin, New Zealand. He studied at National Art School in Sydney, 1956–60, teachers including John Passmore and John Olsen. He first appeared at Annandale

Imitation Realist show at Museum of Modern Art, Melbourne, 1962. Work early showed influence of American Pop Art, from which he moved into junk and assemblage art. Lanceley was awarded the Contemporary Art Society Sydney Young Contemporaries Award in 1963, in 1964 gaining the Helena Rubinstein Scholarship. Lanceley made prints for Marlborough Fine Art in mid-1960s which were well received. He taught for a time at Chelsea School of Art, then returned to Australia. Museum of Modern Art in New York, Tate Gallery and a number of Australian and continental European galleries hold examples. Lived latterly in Sydney.

Audrey LANCEMAN 1931– Artist noted for her watercolour depictions of London, was born and lived there. Studied at Nottingham College of Art and Heatherley's School of Fine Art. She lived in Canada, 1960–5. Won the Lord Mayor's Art Award for two consecutive years; took part in a four-man show at Thackeray Gallery, 1977; and had a series of solo exhibitions in Britain, France, Canada and Sweden.

Reginald LANDER 1913– Artist and designer in gouache, watercolour and black-and-white, Lander was born and lived in London. Studied at Hammersmith School of Art, was during the 1930s chief designer and manager of the Ralph Mott Studio. After World War II went freelance. Government ministries and British Railways used his work.

William LANDLES 1923– Sculptor, born in Hawick, Roxburghshire, whose early exhibited work prompted an Andrew Grant Bequest for studies at Edinburgh College of Art under Eric Schilsky, 1951–6. After his diploma, Landles developed abstracted work in a range of materials, from 1977 changing course to produce figurative bronzes. He was elected a professional member of SSA in 1986 and of SSWA in 1994. Also showed at RSA, Royal Glasgow Institute of the Fine Arts, Aberdeen Artists' Society, Scottish Sculpture Workshop and Scottish Art Exhibition at Gatwick Airport, 1986. In 1996 was included in a three-artist show at Kingfisher Gallery, Edinburgh. Commissions included portraits and the Scottish Junior Rugby Trophy for the Royal Bank of Scotland. The Will H Ogilvie Memorial near Ashkirk, Roxburghshire, was completed in 1994, the Ogilvie Memorial at Bourke, New South Wales, Australia, in 1995.

Alex LANDRUM 1955– Painter, born in Wallasey, Cheshire, who studied fine arts at Leeds Polytechnic, 1984–7; at Chelsea College of Art, 1987–8 and 1989–90, where he gained the Burston Award and received his master's degree in history of art and sculpture; and at Goldsmiths' College, 1990–2. Landrum's works included Minimalist diptychs in household paints, the artist considering his pictures mainly objects, "images of sculpture". He was included in Young British Artists, Saatchi Gallery, 1992; Mandy Loves Declan 100%, Mark Boote Gallery, New York, 1993; Moby Dick, John Hansard Gallery, Southampton, 1996; and John Moores Liverpool Exhibition, 1997–8. Had a solo show at Lisson Gallery, 1992, later ones including Perfect Accident, The Tannery, 1996. Lived in London.

Michael LANDY 1963– Artist who employed photography, born in London. He studied at Loughton College of Art, 1979–81, Loughborough College of Art, 1981–3, then graduated with honours from Goldsmiths' College, 1985–8. Took part in many mixed shows, including Showroom, 1987; Show and Tell, Riverside Studios, 1988; and Multiples, Hirschl & Adler Modern, New York, 1990. Had solo show at Gray Art Gallery, New York, and Karsten Schubert Ltd, both 1989; Studio Marconi, Milan, and Tanja Grunert, Cologne, both 1990. In 1992 Landy's installation Closing Down Sale, at Karsten Schubert, used the paraphernalia of low selling to reflect the recession in the art market with a garish wit.

Abigail LANE 1967– Sculptor, born in Penzance, Cornwall. She studied at Bristol Polytechnic, 1985–6, then Goldsmiths' College School of Art, 1986–9. Participated in the group show Freeze in 1988, then others in Britain, continental Europe and America. In 1993–4 she was part of the Arts Council's touring exhibition Recent British Sculpture. Had a solo show at Karsten Schubert Ltd in collaboration with Interim Art, another at Victoria Miro, 1998. Lived in London.

Christopher LANE 1929– Sculptor, ceramist and teacher, born in Gloucestershire, who studied at Reading University and Royal College of Art. He taught at Berkshire and St Alban's Colleges of Art, then at Reading University. Exhibited at Woodstock, Bear Lane in Oxford and Reading Municipal Galleries, at ICA, AIA, Wadham College in Oxford and University of Wales, Bangor. Some of Lane's work shown in London Artists, Shrewsbury School, in 1968 was "concerned with an interest in the power of recreation in nature".

Richard LANE 1926– Painter, teacher and photographer, born in Mwanza, Tanganyika, who studied at Oxford University, 1948–51, after the Royal Navy. Lane attended Slade School of Fine Art, full- and part-time, 1952–5; taught at Haileybury public school for three years; developed fine art photography for three years; then taught at Christ's Hospital, 1961–85. From 1961–9 he worked with Nell Todd at the art school there, "a genius of a teacher of all ages". His exhibitions included Young Contemporaries, RA, Christ's Hospital Arts Centre in 1970s and Woodstock Gallery, 1982. Latterly lived at Falstone, Hexham, Northumberland. His work is in private collections in Britain, France and America.

Richard Patrick LANE 1922– Painter, notably of landscape, who studied at Shrewsbury Art School and Anglo-French Art Centre. Took part in mixed exhibitions including RA and London Artists at Shrewsbury School, 1968. Lived for a time in London.

Daniel LANG 1935– Painter who was born in Tulsa, Oklahoma, in America. He was educated at the North-Western

University, the University of Tulsa and University of Iowa. He showed at William Hardie Gallery in Glasgow. Work is represented in many public collections, including the Metropolitan Museum and the Museum of Modern Art, New York, and the Hunterian Art Gallery, Glasgow. Lang was a frequent visitor to Scotland, dividing his time between New York and his home in Montone, Umbria.

George LANG 1902– Self-taught painter and illustrator, a perfectionist for detail, born in London where he lived for many years. Showed RMS of which he was a member, RI, RWS, RCamA, PS, widely elsewhere in England and at Paris Salon, where he won an Hon. Mention in 1951. From 1959 Lang lived in South Africa, initially based in Cape Town, but otherwise a nomad. He showed generally with The Everard Read Gallery in Johannesburg; it included Lang in its Eric Heilbronner exhibition in 1981, about the time that it lost touch with Lang. Lang's wife Madge executed the sculpture of a gold prospector in front of Corner House, Johannesburg.

Margaret LANG 1936– Printmaker and teacher who studied at Oldham School of Art, 1952–4, St Martin's School of Art, 1954–6, and Manchester College of Art, 1956–7, becoming a lecturer in art and design at Wirral Metropolitan College. Showed in northwest of England, including Artists of Wirral at Williamson Art Gallery, Birkenhead, and in Etching at the Bluecoat, Liverpool, both 1984; and Merseyside Artists 3, toured by Walker Art Gallery, Liverpool, 1986–7.

Wharton LANG 1925– Sculptor in wood, son of Faust Lang, also a wood sculptor, and born in Oberammergau, Bavaria. He was educated at Newquay Grammar School, then attended St Ives School of Painting with Leonard Fuller, 1946, and privately with his father, 1946–9. Eventually took over father's studio at Mount Zion, St Ives, Cornwall. Was a member of RSMA and SWLA and was included in Artists from Cornwall, RWA, 1992. Ulster Museum in Belfast and National Maritime Museum in Greenwich hold his work.

Beatrice LANGDON 1898–1986 Painter who was educated at St Paul's Girls' School. Miss Langdon was a student at Vicat Cole and Byam Shaw Schools of Art. She showed at RA, ROI, RBA, in the provinces and at Paris Salon and had a solo show at Arlington Gallery. She painted in the St Ives area of Cornwall and lived for some time in London.

David LANGDON 1914– Cartoonist and advertising draughtsman who came to prominence during World War II as an officer in the Royal Air Force, holding various positions on Air Force publications. Was also cartoon adviser to Kemsley Newspapers, 1943–5. Educated in London and a member of a number of clubs there, such as the London Sketch Club and Savage Club. Exhibited in provinces, Switzerland and America, but best known for numerous cartoons in many publications, ranging from *Punch* and *Lilliput* to *New Yorker* and *Evening Standard*. His publications include *Home Front Lines* and *The Way I See It*. Lived at Southgate, Middlesex.

Edgar Mortimer LANGDON 1892–1972 Painter in oil, pastel and watercolour and lecturer by profession. He was born in Hampstead, north London, and studied at Clifton College, Bristol. Showed at RBA, RI, NS, SGA, MAFA and Paris Salon and lived at Watford, Hertfordshire.

Rembert LANGHAM 1941– Painter, sculptor, model-maker, designer and teacher, born in Somerset. Trained at Bristol Technical School, 1955–60; Birmingham College of Art, 1968–9, Falmouth School of Art, 1969–72, and Goldsmiths' College, 1972–3. In 1977 he gained a postgraduate scholarship to Skowhegan School of Painting and Sculpture in Maine, America. Langham had a varied career. He designed and built an adventure playground in Ealing, 1973; taught at Yaba College of Technology, Lagos, Nigeria, 1980; designed for a number of trade exhibitions, such as the Sea Trade Fair, Barbican, 1983; and in that year worked on the film *Indiana Jones and the Temple of Doom*, creating a mechanical model of a Megasoma Elephas Beetle, also working on television commercials. Fine art exhibitions included St Helens National Sculpture Competition, Lancashire, 1974; Wapping Artists Open Studios from 1979; and Talent Store Gallery, 1981.

Mary LANGHORNE 1909– Painter, designer and teacher, born and lived in Exeter. She studied at Royal Albert Memorial School of Art there, 1928–30, then Central School of Arts and Crafts, 1930–2, and showed at RI, RWA, RSA and in the provinces. RWA and a number of West Country churches and Exeter Cathedral hold her work.

LANGLANDS & BELL Artists in various media. Ben Langlands was born 1955 and Nikki Bell in 1959, both in London. Graduated with honours from Middlesex Polytechnic, 1977–80. Took part in many mixed shows, including Red Ashes, University of Reading, 1978; Sainsbury Centre for the Visual Arts, Norwich, 1980; Bookworks from 1986; Interim Art, 1990, and widely overseas. Solo shows began with Traces of Living, Interim Art, 1986; later appearances including same venue and Valentina Moncada, Rome, both 1991, and Serpentine Gallery, 1996. Saatchi Collection holds their work.

Jane LANGLEY 1959– Painter, teacher and printmaker, born in London. She did a foundation course at Chelsea School of Art, 1977–8, graduating with an honours degree in fine art from Camberwell School of Art, 1978–81. Between 1982–5 she obtained her master's degree in painting from Royal College of Art, along the way being artist-in-residence at Battersea Arts Centre, 1982, and winning the Henry Moore Prize for painting in 1984. She taught at Byam Shaw School of Art, 1990–1 and in 1991 gained a Sotheby's Fellowship from Central Saint Martins College of Art. From 1980 she exhibited in a wide range of mixed shows in Britain and abroad, including Camden Annual, 1985;

Galerie Hilger, Vienna, 1986; Peter de Francia and his students, Camden Arts Centre, 1987; The Discerning Eye, Mall Galleries, 1991; and Bruton Street Gallery, 1992. Solo shows began with Battersea Arts Centre, 1982, later ones comprising Central Saint Martins and Etchings and Monotypes, Le Chat Noir Art Exhibitors, 1991. While in Langley's work a figure or townscape may be discerned, it is reinvented with the freedom of abstraction, vigorous brushwork and gently modulating colours conveying energy and poetry.

Winifred Norah LANGLEY 1906–1991 Painter and printmaker, educated at St Andrew's, Eastbourne. She studied at Bolt Court, 1943–6, with Sidney Tushingham; at Camberwell School of Arts and Crafts 1946–9, teachers including Victor Pasmore and William Coldstream; Brighton College of Art, 1955–7; then Brighton Polytechnic, 1958. Showed with PS; LG; Leicester, Redfern and Wertheim Galleries; and had a series of solo exhibitions. Died in Hove, Sussex.

Rowland LANGMAID 1897–1956 Painter and printmaker specialising in marine subjects, commissioned in the Royal Navy, rising to lieutenant-commander. He studied with the sea painter W L Wyllie. Showed extensively at Abbey Gallery, RA and Walker Art Gallery in Liverpool. Among prints of his pictures published by W R Deighton & Sons were *HMS* Victory *in Portsmouth Harbour* and *HMS* Victory *Under Sail*. Accuracy of detail was a characteristic of Langmaid's work. Lived in London.

Dorothie LANGRIDGE: *see* **Dorothie FIELD**

Sonia LANGRIDGE 1923– Painter, printmaker and teacher, born in Derby. She studied at Hornsey School of Art, 1938–9, Derby School of Art, 1939–43, then Slade School of Fine Art, 1943–4, where her teachers included Allan Gwynne-Jones and George Charlton. She went on to teach, in the 1940s and 1950s holding positions at Loughborough College School of Art, then at Croydon High School. Showed at Nottingham Castle Art Gallery and Museum, Blackpool's Grundy Art Gallery and elsewhere. Lived in London.

Lionel LANKESTER 1904– Watercolourist and draughtsman who was by profession a physician. Born in Little Bookham, Surrey, was educated at Haileybury and Cambridge University, then studied medicine at St Thomas's Hospital, in London. Just after World War II while serving in the Army in Palestine he became interested in painting, but had little formal tuition. Showed RWS and with Guildford Art Society. Lived in Milford-on-Sea, Hampshire.

Richard LANNOY 1928– Painter, photographer and writer, born in Surrey, whose main works were large figurative paintings and triptychs in oil. In these he sought "to recreate past experiences of particularly heightened reality, especially from years spent travelling the world as a reportage photographer in the 1950s and 1960s, in a visionary style". Lannoy was taught by Paul Feiler at school; then attended Guildford Art School under Frederick Brill and Heatherley School of Art. He was on the founding staff of ICA, 1950–2, initiator of the Independent Group in the latter year. Was then a freelance photographer for magazines in Europe, the Middle East, Africa and India, publishing several books of his photographs. His *The Speaking Tree*, a study of Indian culture and society published in 1971, long remained in print. In 1984 Lannoy resumed his professional career as a painter, living in Bath, Avon. Showed solo at Bath International Festival in 1994, in 1995 contributing to John Moores Liverpool Exhibition.

Andrea LANSLEY 1960– Painter, born in Manchester. She studied at Wirral College of Art and Design, 1987–8, and Liverpool Polytechnic, 1988–91. As a student prizewinner at Wirral she held a solo show at Williamson Art Gallery, Birkenhead, 1988. She was also a prizewinner in John Moores Exhibition, Liverpool, 1991–2. Other appearances included Whitworth Young Contemporaries, 1989, and Fresh Art Fair, Islington, 1991. Lived in West Kirby, Merseyside.

Erica Faith LANSLEY 1961– Painter of abstracts, born in Salford, Lancashire, who gained a first-class honours degree in fine art, painting, at St Martin's School of Art, 1979–82. Mixed shows included New Contemporaries at ICA, 1981; John Moores Liverpool Exhibition, 1982–3, at Walker Art Gallery; LG Open, Royal College of Art, 1987; Boundaries, Museum & Art Gallery, Brighton, 1995; and Cross Currents, Reed's Wharf Gallery at Barbican Centre, 1996, where Lansley showed paintings done in Ireland. These used an organic or calligraphic figure laid pattern-like across the surface or selectively obscured by a simplifying veil or screen.

Andrew LANYON 1947– Artist in oil, film and photography and producer of books, born in Cornwall, son of the painter Peter Lanyon. After an early enthusiasm for photography Lanyon studied at London School of Film Technique in 1966. He worked with film and photography and then turned to painting and making books, the first being *Snap*, in 1970. Other titles included *The Vanishing Cabinet*, *Paul Feiler*, *Peter Lanyon 1918–1964* and an Art-Fi series: *Deadpan*, *Second Nature*, *The Loose Connection*, *The Unjustified Text* and *The Quick Change Act*. Lanyon's pictures were often on a small scale, with a wry quality, as in his entries for Artists from Cornwall, at RWA, 1992. The Book Gallery, St Ives, held exhibitions, including 1998, of paintings and hollow books. He was a Newlyn Society of Artists member. British Council, Contemporary Art Society and St Ives Museum hold examples. Lived in Newlyn, Penzance, Cornwall.

Deborah LANYON 1958– Painter and draughtsman, bornand lived in London, who worked with acrylic, collage and mixed media and who travelled in Italy, France and Greece, which "challenged fresh ways of seeing". Lanyon's landscapes indicated her interest in music and dance and "a need to express rhythm". They were richly coloured, with a leaning towards abstraction. Studied at St Martin's School of Art, 1977–8; under Geri Morgan at Byam Shaw School of Art, 1979–81, which underlined Lanyon's commitment to drawing; then, after work in the BBC design department, 1982–6, at Putney School of Art, 1986–90; working in Oliver Bevan's studio, 1991–4. Had a solo show at Milne & Moller, 1993, later ones including Pike Gallery, 1995, and Archeus Fine Art, 1996.

Martin LANYON 1954– Artist mainly in college and gouache, son of the painter Peter Lanyon; their paintings shared a strong gestural quality. Born in Redruth, Cornwall, Martin Lanyon was a self-taught painter, obtaining Bachelor of Science degree in physics at Queen Mary College, 1976. Went on to teach physics, eventually lecturing at Truro College. He shared shows at Gordon Hepworth Gallery, Newton St Cyres in 1991–2, then had a first solo exhibition there in 1993. Lived in St Agnes, Cornwall.

Peter LANYON 1918–1964 Painter of landscapes leaning heavily towards abstraction, making some constructions, pottery and collage; also a teacher. Born in St Ives, Cornwall, which remained his base, Lanyon after school had lessons in painting from Borlase Smart in 1936, in 1936–7 attending Penzance School of Art, had lessons for a time at the Euston Road School in 1938, and was encouraged or taught by Ben Nicolson, Adrian Stokes and Naum Gabo. Made first constructions 1939–40, then from 1940–5 served with Royal Air Force. First one-man show at Lefevre Gallery, 1949. He was to exhibit internationally in mixed exhibitions, including West Country Landscape, Arts Council tour, 1953; Metavisual, Tachiste, Abstract, Redfern Gallery, 1957; and British Painting in the Sixties, Tate Gallery, 1963. Also extensive one-man shows in Britain and abroad. Founder member of the Crypt Group, 1946; Penwith Society, 1949; taught at Bath Academy of Art, 1950–7; elected member of the Newlyn Society, 1953; and ran the St Peter's Loft Art School, St Ives, with William Redgrave, 1955–60. Lanyon's first one-man show in New York in 1957 was well received, brought him the friendship of Mark Rothko and made Lanyon impatient with the restricted world of St Ives. But he took up gliding in 1959 to get to know better the Cornish landscape, and this brought to his work a greater feeling of sea and air and brightened his palette. Died in Taunton, Somerset, as the result of injuries received in a gliding accident; his death was a severe blow to Cornish painting. Lanyon's work is in many public galleries, including the Tate. Retrospective at Whitworth Art Gallery, Manchester, 1978, and South Bank Centre, 1992, both with tour. The artists Andrew and Martin Lanyon were his sons.

George LARGE 1936– Painter in watercolour and oil and teacher, born in London. He studied at Hornsey College of Art, 1958–63, teachers including Maurice de Sausmarez, John Titchell and Alfred Daniels. Large spent some time in the display department of Simpson's, Piccadilly, was part-time at Hornsey College of Art, then head of department at St Julian Comprehensive School in St Albans. Large showed 1963–87 with SWE, being vice-president in 1972 and treasurer in 1984; with RE, 1963–5; with RI from 1983, becoming a member in 1986 and its archivist; and was winner of the Winsor & Newton Award, 1989. He had a solo show at Mall Galleries in 1980, later one-man exhibitions including Duncan Campbell Fine Art from 1990. Edward Burra and Stanley Spencer were the main influences on Large's work, which always had people as its theme, at work or leisure, linked to their surroundings. It was an easily recognisable, colourful form of Cubism. He completed a mural for British Rail for the King's Cross Thameslink Station. Large had a house in Malta, as well as Woburn, Buckinghamshire, and his work is held by National Gallery and British Consulate in Malta.

Roger LARGE 1939– Artist born in Wallasey, Cheshire, who began painting during National Service in the Royal Air Force, then studied at Liverpool College of Art, 1960–4, and Royal College of Art, 1964–7. After working as a teacher, carver and letter cutter, Large painted full-time from 1983, based in Watchet, Somerset. While at the Royal College Large won a landscape prize, the year after winning a life painting prize at RA. Mixed exhibitions included Piccadilly Gallery, 1967; Eye Gallery, Bristol, 1987; Bruton Street Gallery, from 1991; White Lane Gallery, Plymouth, 1992; and David Holmes Contemporary Art, Peterborough, 1996, where in a St Ives show Large exhibited pictures partly collaged with thick paint, forming blocks of discordant colour. Showed solo with Salt House Gallery, St Ives, from 1986, later exhibitions including University of Surrey, 1992, and Plumbline Gallery, St Ives, 1995.

Patrick LARKING 1907–1981 Painter, notably of portraits, and teacher, born in Rudgwick, Sussex. He attended Christ's Hospital and worked briefly in an engineering draughtsman's office before gaining the Christopher Head Scholarship to Royal Academy Schools, 1923, studying under Charles Sims and F E Jackson. He later studied at Académie Julian in Paris before returning to London to become a pupil of Sir John Lavery. The economic depression prompted Larking to move to Canada in 1930, where he showed regularly with the Royal Canadian Academy, married Betty Burnham in 1935 and then returned to England. Larking was a keen teacher, at Heatherley's School of Fine Art and from 1949–67 at Sir John Cass School of Art. He then retired and moved to Colyton, Devon, where he lived in a small thatched cottage and held some classes, painting local characters and the landscape. Larking died shortly after his wife. A convivial man, he was a stalwart of the Chelsea Arts Club for over 50 years, being elected a life member in 1972. Larking was made a member of NS in 1947 (honorary member, 1971), ROI in 1951 and RP in 1965. Also showed at RBA and RA. A studio sale of Larking's work was held at Christie's, South Kensington, in 1982.

William Martin LARKINS 1901–1974 Printmaker, painter and teacher who was educated at Bishop's Stortford College, having been born in east London, subject of much of his work. Studied at Goldsmiths' College School of Art and was a visiting teacher at Croydon School of Art. In the 1930s worked for the advertising agency J Walter Thompson; during World War II formed a company to make films on aircraft and tank recognition; after the war for over 20 years working for *Reader's Digest* Association. Showed at RE, RA, NEAC and abroad. In 1979 Garton and Cooke held an exhibition of his etchings, which are held by British Museum and Fitzwilliam Museum in Cambridge. Lived in London for many years.

Eric LARMONT 1943– Painter in oil, printmaker, sculptor in metal and teacher, born in South Shields, County Durham. He studied at Sunderland College of Art and Goldsmiths' College School of Art, 1961–6, then at National School of Architecture and Visual Arts in Brussels, 1968–9, teachers including Anton Ehrenzweig. Those postgraduate studies were on a Belgian Government Scholarship. Larmont went on to teach part-time at Sotheby's and Putney School of Art. Group exhibitions included Sunderland Art Gallery, 1965; Ikon Gallery, Birmingham, 1976; Liverpool Academy, 1978–80; and RA Summer Exhibitions, 1981–2. Larmont had a solo show at 273 Gallery, 1968; later ones included Galerie Blankenese, Hamburg, Germany, 1984. There was a two-man show at Jonathan Poole Gallery in 1985. Carlisle Corporation holds Larmont's work. In late-1980s Larmont began working in seclusion for several years without showing, while continuing to sell prints privately in England and to make sales in Germany. Lived in London.

Gerald LARN 1932– Painter, draughtsman, designer and teacher who studied painting at Farnham School of Art for three years, obtaining a scholarship to Slade School of Fine Art. From 1960–3 showed at Temple and Redfern Galleries and Selfridges Art Gallery, then became resident artist/designer at Shepperton Film Studios, where he contributed to the production of over 40 feature films, including Roman Polanski's *Macbeth* and Charles Chaplin's final film, *The Freak*. Larn taught from 1983–91 at Leicester Polytechnic, from 1988 as part-time head of department. Enduring influences on his work were Turner's late paintings, German Expressionism, Max Ernst and the work of some early French Surrealists. Exploration of forms drawn with a pen were a key part of Larn's 1978–93 retrospective at Gagliardi Gallery, 1994. Lived in Thames Ditton, Surrey.

Dirk LARSEN 1951– Painter, sculptor and teacher, born in Copenhagen, Denmark. He studied at Birmingham College of Art, 1969–72, and Royal College of Art, 1972–5. For some years he taught alternative studies at South Glamorgan Institute for Higher Education. His mixed show appearances included Documenta 6, Kassel; John Moores Exhibition, Liverpool, 1991–2, where his picture Friday 7 pm used a singular personal imagery; and he also did sculptural work for the Stuttgart Garden Festival, in 1992. He had solo exhibitions in Germany, the Netherlands and America. Lived in Bristol, Avon.

Marthe LARSON 1954– Painter, born in America, who studied at Ruskin School of Drawing, Oxford, 1971–3. She was represented in the 1985 John Moores Liverpool Exhibition and held a series of solo shows in London, where she lived.

Karolina LARUSDOTTIR 1944– Painter and printmaker, born in Reykjavik, Iceland, whose work included stylised figures in landscape. She studied at Ruskin School of Drawing, Oxford. Was a member of RE who also showed at RA Summer Exhibitions. Had solo shows in Iceland and Denmark, ones in England including Chenil and Drian Galleries, Church Street Gallery in Saffron Walden and Phoenix Gallery. Lived in Bishop's Stortford, Hertfordshire.

Jennifer LASH: *see* **Jini FIENNES**

Susie LASSAM 1875– Painter of miniatures, born in Dulwich Village, southeast London. She studied at Lambeth School of Art, Central School of Arts and Crafts and Royal College of Art. Showed at RA, SM, of which she was a member, RMS, extensively at RI and at Paris Salon. Lived near Brixham, Devon.

Marie Walker LAST 1917– Painter and printmaker, born as Mary Walker in Scholes, Yorkshire. After private education and boarding school and a visit to New Zealand, during World War II she served in Women's Land Army, then as a driver for Young Men's Christian Association. From 1946–53 lived at home painting when possible, in latter year attending course in Bruges led by Jack Merriott. From 1954–6 went to summer painting courses where tutors included Robert Medley, Terry Frost and Andrew Forge, from 1955–6 attending Chelsea School of Art under Vivian Pitchforth and Edward Wakeford. She worked at New Vision Centre Gallery, 1958–60, and began abstract painting, in 1959 having first solo show at Univision Gallery, Newcastle upon Tyne. First monoprints, to become a key feature of her output, were shown. She joined WIAC, became a member of Free Painters and Sculptors and worked at Molton Gallery. In 1961 married Tom Last. Subsequent years saw Marie Walker Last travelling widely in Europe; having a first solo show in Yorkshire at Manor House, Ilkley, 1964, near where she was to live; producing series of pictures with themes such as Wing Form, Sentinel Rock and *Mary Rose* warship raising; and in 1988 winning first prize in the Druce Constable Award at Camden Arts Centre. A major exhibition was held at Leighton House in 1991 as well as a first retrospective at Dean Clough, Halifax. Her work is held by Bank of England, Bradford Art Galleries and Museums and University of Leeds.

Glenys LATHAM 1946– Sculptor and draughtsman, born in Atherton, Lancashire. She did a foundation course at Bolton College of Art, then a sculpture and life drawing diploma at Wolverhampton College of Art and a Certificate in Education at Manchester College of Art. Latham said that for her drawing had "a central and sustaining activity in my artistic endeavours – it is as relevant to my sculpture as eating is to staying alive." She took part in Drawing Towards Sculpture at Isis Gallery, Leigh-on-Sea, in 1993. Other group shows included Turnpike Gallery, Leigh, 1979; Drumcroon Education Art Centre, Wigan, 1981, and MAFA Open annually from that year; Blackheath Gallery, 1988, and elsewhere. Solo shows included Rochdale College of Art, 1983.

John LATHAM 1921– Artist and teacher, born in Africa, who studied at Chelsea School of Art, 1946–50. From 1966–7 he taught at St Martin's School of Art. Latham was regarded as a pioneer of Conceptual Art and developed his Time-Base Theory, said to contain the seeds of human salvation, and this he proselytised for many years. Latham was sceptical about the value of books, which he called Skoob. While at St Martin's he and a group of students chewed pages from the art critic Clement Greenberg's book *Art and Culture*, spat the result into a bowl, the contents being fermented in acid and distilled into a phial. Latham was dismissed, as the book had come from the School library. Latham designated the phial and his dismissal documents a work of art, acquired by Museum of Modern Art, New York. Latham had first one-man show at ICA in 1960. Began steadily to exhibit overseas, in mixed and solo shows, notably in America, his work continuing in an iconoclastic vein. Retrospective at Museum of Modern Art, Oxford, 1991. In Freezeframe at Lamont Gallery, 1996, relief sculpture and films by Latham were included. Lived in London.

Wilde LATHAM 1931– Landscape painter, born in Worcester, born Harold Victor Latham. He studied with Harry Adams at Worcester College of Art and at Malvern College of Art and settled in Malvern Link, Worcestershire. Showed with Malvern Art Club of which he was a member and elsewhere in the Midlands.

William LATHAM fl. from 1980s– Creator of computer-generated forms, married to the artist Belinda Channer. Latham started painting at 13, won a scholarship to Stowe School, a first-class degree in fine art at Oxford University and a Henry Moore Scholarship to Royal College of Art, 1982–5. Having started to create on paper a huge family tree of shapes, Latham applied to IBM for help and was made a research fellow, 1987–94. One spin-off was Mutator, a sophisticated computer programme with many potential applications. Latham had touring shows in Japan, Germany, Australia, France and Britain. In 1995 had an exhibition of works on cibachrome and in videos at Harriet Green Gallery which coincided with establishment of Latham's company Computer Artworks Ltd. Lived in London.

Kwai LAU 1967– Artist, born in China, who attended Wolverhampton School of Art and Royal Academy Schools. Her art, tending towards abstraction, took her "into unknown places … a journey towards a magical space that I am yet to discover". Awards included André Dunoyer de Segonzac Scholarship; Celia Walker Drawing Prize; Leverhulme Trust Award; and *The Antique Collector* Prize. Group exhibitions were New British Art, Mall Galleries, and RA Summer Exhibition, from 1990, in London, where the artist lived; Beyond Chinese Takeaway, Chinese Arts Centre, Manchester, 1992; Tricycle Gallery and University of Essex touring exhibition, both 1995.

Carl LAUBIN 1947– Painter and architect, born in New York, America, who gained his architecture degree from Cornell University College of Art, Architecture and Planning in 1973, the year he moved to England. Joined the architectural and civic design firm Douglas Stephen and Partners; then Jeremy Dixon/BDP in 1984; produced paintings of the Royal Opera House project for Dixon, and began painting full-time in 1986. When Laubin had his exhibition at Wigmore Fine Arts in 1997, Gavin Stamp described him as "without doubt, the most accomplished and imaginative architectural artist working in Britain today". As well as taking part in group shows, such as RA Summer Exhibitions; National Trust Exhibitions; A Vision of Britain, Victoria & Albert Museum, 1989; and La Ville Moderne en Europe, organised by Centre Pompidou in Tokyo, 1996, Laubin completed an impressive list of commissions. These included Château Pichon Longueville; Museum of Scotland; Museum of London (purchase); Royal Armouries; and for Linklaters and Paines his singular panorama The Square Mile. Lived in Hitchin, Hertfordshire.

Kenneth LAUDER 1916– Painter in oil and watercolour, notable for landscapes, and teacher, born in Edinburgh. He studied at Chelsea School of Art and Royal College of Art, 1933–9, teachers including Robert Medley, Graham Sutherland, Gilbert Spencer and Percy Horton, serving as a pilot in Royal Air Force, 1939–45. Painted and taught in the Isle of Man and Gloucestershire, being senior lecturer in art, Liverpool, 1963–9. Earlier influences on Lauder's work were the later work of Turner in watercolour, while in oil his influence was Braque. Interest in Klee and Kandinsky came later and a visit to Australia in 1986 was important. Earlier themes were concerned with the horizontal and individual isolation, later work leading on to the duality of imagine and interpretation. Mixed exhibitions included Agnew, Scottish Gallery in London and Edinburgh, Harris Museum and Art Gallery in Preston, RA, RWA, Liverpool Academy and elsewhere. Had a solo show at Broadway Gallery, Worcestershire, 1965, later ones including Scottish Gallery, 1990, and Galeries Christiane Cloots, Brussels, 1995. Rhode Island School of Design in America holds his work. Lived in Herefordshire.

John LAURIE 1916– Painter and teacher, born in Shrewsbury, Shropshire. He was educated in Glasgow, then attended the School of Art there, 1933–6, and at Patrick Allan-Fraser School of Art, Hospitalfield, Arbroath, 1938–40, with James Cowie. Won RSA Carnegie Travelling Scholarship in 1939. He was for periods a lecturer at Glasgow School of Art and a lecturer for the Arts Council. Exhibited RSA, SSA, Royal Glasgow Institute of the Fine Arts and elsewhere. A number of his works, including a portrait of James Cowie, were reproduced. Lived in Glasgow.

Kathleen Frances LAURIE 1900– Painter and English teacher who was for some years involved in psychiatric social care work. She was brought up in Ceylon and was educated at London University and London School of Economics. Only in 1946–7 did she attend Oxford Art School, then 1947–9 Ruskin School of Drawing there, her teachers including Peter Greenham, Albert Rutherston and Percy Horton. Favouring watercolour and wash drawings, Laurie exhibited widely, including Oxford Art Society, RWA, RA and ROI. Lived in Beckenham, Kent.

Simon LAURIE 1964– Maker of wooden constructions, watercolourist and collagist, born in Glasgow. He studied at the School of Art there, 1983–8, gaining his fine art degree and completing postgraduate studies. In 1990 he was prize winner at the Royal Glasgow Institute of the Fine Arts. Laurie's great preoccupation was with the sea and man's relationship with it over thousands of years. From 1987 he began to show in many group exhibitions: at New Generation at Mercury Gallery in London and Edinburgh; Sue Rankin Gallery; in 1989 at New Scottish Art at Barbizon Gallery, Glasgow, and Fruitmarket Gallery, Edinburgh; and in 1990 at Surrealist Tendencies at Open Circle, Glasgow. In 1991 Laurie had a one-man show at Mercury Gallery.

William LAURIE 1921– Painter, printmaker and teacher, born in Birmingham. He studied at the College of Art there under Harold Holden, 1937–41, then in 1948 at University of Florence. Showed at Archer Gallery and elsewhere. Lived in London.

Alfred J LAVENDER 1899–1966 Painter, illustrator, printmaker and teacher, born at Gosforth, Northumberland. He was educated at Bede College, Durham University, and at Newcastle University Art Department. From 1927–64 was a teacher at Swansea Grammar School and part-time lecturer at Swansea College of Art. Showed at RCamA, SWG, London Sketch Club and with Swansea Art Society, of which for a time he was secretary. Illustrated the book *A Guide to Gower*, by J M Williams, published in 1965. Lived in Swansea for many years but died in Cambridge.

Cyril LAVENSTEIN 1891–1986 Painter and teacher, born in Birmingham, who was especially noted for his watercolours and pastels of Cornish coastal scenes. At the age of 11 he entered Birmingham School of Art, then strongly under the influence of the Arts and Crafts Movement, where his studies included subjects such as stained glass and where fellow-students included Gerald Leslie Brockhurst and Henry Rushbury. Lavenstein was among the most distinguished students, winning a bronze medal in 1908 and a silver in 1910. Went on to teach at Kidderminster School of Art, having served as a driver in Salonika in World War I, remaining at the School until 1954. Exhibited RA, NEAC, RSA, Paris Salon and elsewhere. In 1930 was elected a member of RBSA, which in 1938 exhibited his works. A second Birmingham exhibition in 1984 led to a television documentary about his life and work. Lived in Kidderminster, Worcestershire.

Barbara LAVERY fl. from early 1990s– Mixed-media artist and organiser of workshops in England and Ireland, Lavery completed her foundation certificate at University of Ulster, Belfast, in 1988. After gaining a degree in fine art from Newcastle upon Tyne Polytechnic in 1991 she won her master's in fine art from Birmingham Institute of Art and Design in 1994. In 1993 she received the Great Britain and Northern Ireland Humanities Bursary. Showed in the northeast of England, in London and Ireland. Appearances included No Access at Ross' Court, Belfast, 1992; Vessels at Eagle Works Gallery, Wolverhampton; and in that year Works on Paper and Beyond the Partitions, both put on by Queen Street Studios, Belfast, with which she was associated.

Andrew LAW 1873–1967 Painter and teacher, born in Kilmaurs, Ayrshire. Studied at Glasgow School of Art, 1890–6, under Fra Newbery, then in Paris for a year. He continued to live in Glasgow, taught for many years at the School of Art and was a member of Glasgow Art Club. Exhibited RSA extensively, also at Royal Glasgow Institute of the Fine Arts, Paris Salon and in the English provinces. Art galleries in Southport, Paisley and Glasgow hold his work.

Bob LAW 1934– Designer, painter, draughtsman, poet and teacher, born in Brentford, Middlesex. He was apprenticed as an architectural designer, 1949–52, studying subjects such as geometry, perspective drawing and ornithology at night school. After two years' National Service, in 1955 Law began painting in watercolour. He moved to St Ives, Cornwall, in 1957, where he learned to pot, began writing poetry and made the first of his field drawings and paintings, paralleling American Minimalist art. Encouraged by the critic Lawrence Alloway he showed at ICA in 1960 in a two-man exhibition with Peter Hobbs; was in New London Situation at Marlborough Fine Art in 1961; then in 1962 had first solo show at Grabowski Gallery. A French Government Scholarship took Law to France in 1961–2, after which he returned to England and designed furniture, began his black series of paintings and became a visiting lecturer at Exeter School of Art, 1964–7. Law began to extend his exhibiting internationally and won a series of awards, including several from Arts Council. Selected solo exhibitions included a series at Lisson Gallery, from 1971; Museum of Modern Art, Oxford, 1974; Whitechapel Art Gallery, 1977; and Karsten Schubert, 1989. Tate Gallery and Arts Council hold his work. Law lived in Twickenham, Middlesex, in a house built to his own design.

John LAW 1941– Abstract sculptor in various materials, and teacher, born in London. He studied at Bath Academy of Art, Corsham, 1960–3, then at Royal Academy of Fine Art, The Hague, Netherlands Government Scholarship, 1963–4. Returned to teach at Bath Academy, and was a visiting lecturer at Reading University and Leeds Polytechnic. Exhibitions included Constructions, Unit-Series-Progressions, Arts Council Gallery, Cambridge, 1967; Biennale de Menton, Menton, and Kunstmesse, Düsseldorf, both 1974; Constructive Rationale, Polytechnic of Central London, 1978; and Non-Standard Constructions, Museum of Modern Art, Oxford/Gardner Centre Gallery, University of Sussex, Brighton, 1980.

Roger LAW 1941– Artist and designer, born in Cambridgeshire who in the 1960s studied at Cambridge School of Art. He was included in Situation at RBA Galleries in 1960, worked on *The Observer* as a cartoonist, then on *The Sunday Times* colour magazine. Was involved in forming the Luck and Flaw partnership and the Spitting Image satirical puppet show on television. Lived in London.

Ruth LAW: *see* **Ruth WOODBRIDGE**

Jo LAWRANCE 1965– Sculptor and draughtsman who studied at St Martin's and Central Schools of Art, 1985–8, gaining a fine art first-class honours degree. Was at Royal Academy Schools, 1988–9, then did a higher diploma in fine art at Slade School of Fine Art, 1989–91. She produced a series of small, detailed drawings of cranes, lines and flying machines with regard to their vulnerable, comic and possibly contradictory aspects. Won a Duveen Travel Scholarship in 1990, a Cyril Sweet Award in 1991 and a Delfina Trust Residency in Spain in 1992. Exhibitions included Nine Outstanding Graduates of 1988, at Oxford Gallery, 1988; Serpentine Gallery, 1992; and Drawing Towards Sculpture, at Isis Gallery, Leigh-on-Sea, 1993.

Alfred Kingsley LAWRENCE 1893–1975 Painter of pictures and murals and draughtsman, born in Lewes, Sussex. He studied at King Edward VII School of Art in Newcastle upon Tyne under Richard Hatton, at Royal College of Art with William Rothenstein and then in Italy as a Prix de Rome winner, 1923. Elected RA in 1938. Lawrence was a fine figure painter and a RA stalwart for many years, his work having a strong underlying draughtsmanship. Also showed RP of which he was a member and widely abroad. Among Lawrence's notable murals are ones in Laing Art Gallery and Museum, Newcastle; Palace of Westminster; and Bank of England. Lived in London.

Barbara LAWRENCE 1928–1994 Watercolourist, printmaker, illustrator and teacher, born on the Isle of Wight. She studied at Portsmouth College of Art followed by teacher training at London University, also learning printmaking under Edwin La Dell at Central School of Arts and Crafts. Lawrence became head of the art department in Rochester and Tonbridge Technical Schools, and after moving to Guildford in 1956 taught adult education classes. Was an exhibiting member of the Guildford Art Society for many years, also exhibiting often at RA, RE, RBA, RWS and SWLA. Also showed at CCA Gallery in Farnham, Wintershall Gallery and University of Surrey. Landscape, buildings in landscape, wildlife and flowers were Lawrence's main subjects. She wrote and illustrated articles on wood engraving for *Artist* magazine. Guildford Borough collection holds two of her etchings. Lived in Burpham, Surrey.

Cyril James LAWRENCE 1926– Painter, printmaker, commercial artist and teacher, born in Grimsby, Lincolnshire. Attended Luton School of Art, 1949–52. Showed at NS, UA and RMS. Lived in Grimsby, later in Luton, Bedfordshire.

Dez LAWRENCE 1970– Artist born in Swindon, Wiltshire, who attended Glasgow School of Art, 1988–93. Mixed shows included In a Sense, at Brewery Arts Centre, 1993; and in 1994 BT New Contemporaries tour, Modern Art at Transmission Gallery in Glasgow, and also in Glasgow New Art in Scotland, Centre for Contemporary Arts. Lawrence's paintings in that show drew on the manuscripts of Modernist authors. Settled in London.

Edith LAWRENCE 1890–1973 Painter, printmaker, designer and teacher, born in Surrey, who attended Queen's College, London, until 1908. From 1910–14 she was at Slade School of Fine Art, a prizewinning student; after a period in St Ives she returned to Slade in 1916 and also studied under Percyval Tudor-Hart. Had begun showing at RA and NEAC. In 1917 began teaching art at Runston Hill School. In 1920 met the printmaker Claude Flight, in 1925 moving to his studio. The following year they had a joint show at Redfern Gallery and in Scotland, in 1927 forming an interior decorating business, experimenting with lino-cuts, textiles, picture panels and wall hangings. Shared a show at French Gallery, 1935. After bomb damage in 1943 Flight and Lawrence moved to Donhead St Andrew, Wiltshire, and when Flight had a stroke in 1947 Lawrence nursed him until 1955. After cataract removal Lawrence resumed painting, having a solo show at University of Hull, 1973. After living for about a dozen years at Worth Matravers Lawrence in 1973 moved to a nursing home in Salisbury, where she died. Shortly after, Parkin Gallery held a memorial show for Flight and Lawrence.

Eileen LAWRENCE 1946– Artist working in paint and college on a handmade paper support. She was born in Leith, Midlothian, and studied at Edinburgh College of Art, 1963–8. She had her first solo show at 57 Gallery, Edinburgh, in 1969, the year she moved to London for three years. In 1972–3 she lived in Germany, then returned to Edinburgh. Lawrence found items such as feathers, twigs and shells and depicted them with geometrical exactness in an attempt to establish a cohesion between herself and nature. The works were likened to Tibetan prayer-sticks. Had several shows at Fischer Fine Art and exhibited at Bath Festival, 1986. Scottish National Gallery of Modern Art holds her work. Retrospective at Usher Gallery, Lincoln, 1992.

G R LAWRENCE 1930– Painter, draughtsman and teacher. Born in Glasgow, where he settled. Attended the School of Art there, 1947–51, his teachers including William Armour and Ian Fleming, in 1951 attending the School of Art at Hospitalfield, Arbroath; added studies followed in the early 1960s in Italy and Greece. Showed SSA, RA and RSA and widely on the continent. Glasgow School of Art holds his work. This was sometimes signed only with initials.

John LAWRENCE 1934– Sculptor and painter, born in London, married to the artist Susan Lawrence. He studied at Bromley College of Art and showed at Trafford Gallery, with the Free Painters and Sculptors of which he was a member, in France and America. Manchester City Art Gallery and Walker Art Gallery, Liverpool, hold his work. Signed this with initials.

Richard LAWRENCE 1955– Sculptor and teacher, born and worked in London, who studied at Hertfordshire College of Art and Design, 1978–9, then Wimbledon School of Art, 1979–82, from 1983 being a part-time lecturer there. In 1984 he won a Boise Travelling Scholarship to Italy. He was artist-in-residence at the Bath Festival in 1986 and at Christchurch Park, in Ipswich, 1988, when he showed in Carving in Christchurch. Other group shows included New Contemporaries at ICA, 1980, the year he began exhibiting at Cannizaro Park, Wimbledon; Figures in a Garden, Yorkshire Sculpture Park, 1984; and Made in Greenwich, The Living Room, 1994. Had several solo exhibitions in London and Eastbourne, including Sir Hugh Casson Gallery in the Sussex town, 1988.

Ronald LAWRENCE 1929– Sculptor, painter and teacher, born in Hopkinstown, Pontypridd, Glamorgan. Studied teacher training at St Luke's College, Exeter, then did National Service in Royal Air Force. Went on to teach, becoming head of craft and technical department at St Ilan Comprehensive School in Caerphilly. In 1965 won the Dunlop Semtex Mural Competition for a mural in Brynmawr. Showed in group exhibitions at Royal National Eisteddfod, SEA, SWG and with WAC, RA and New Art Centre. CASW bought his copper sculpture Standing Figure.

Tory LAWRENCE 1940– Painter, notable for farm animals and sheep studies, born in London, who began painting in 1982, having brought up a family. Mixed exhibitions included RA Summer Exhibition from 1984, Angela Flowers Gallery from 1985, Lumley Cazalet Gallery, 1986, and extensively elsewhere. Had an open studio show in 1985, later solo exhibitions including Montpelier Studio in 1994. She lived and worked in Berkshire and London.

Charlotte LAWRENSON 1883–c. 1971 Painter, notably of murals, and draughtsman in pencil, born in Dublin. She attended Slade School of Fine Art and Byam Shaw School of Drawing and Painting. Showed at RA, RP, Paris Salon and elsewhere abroad. Public galleries in Brighton and Bradford hold her work, which often featured domestic subjects. Lived for many years in East Africa, latterly in Nakuru, Kenya. Sometimes signed work C L.

Fred LAWSON 1888–1968 Painter, printmaker and illustrator, born in Yeadon, Yorkshire. He studied at Dewsbury Technical College, won a scholarship to Leeds School of Art, then went to South Kensington College of Art where he gained silver and bronze medals for drawing. On a painting trip to Yorkshire in 1910 Lawson chose to settle in Wensleydale, the inspiration for much of his work. He travelled extensively on the continent. Illustrated for *The Dalesman* magazine as well as a number of books, including *Dale Folk*, 1927, and is noted for his Romany drawings. Showed in his own area as well as RA, RI, Walker Art Gallery in Liverpool and Royal Glasgow Institute of the Fine Arts. Public galleries in Bradford, Leeds and Wakefield hold examples. A major retrospective was held at Middlesbrough Art Gallery in 1969 and in 1989 Lawson's work, along with that of his wife Muriel Metcalfe and his daughter Sonia Lawson, was included in A Family of Artists arranged by Wakefield Art Gallery. Died at Castle Bolton.

Michael LAWSON 1944– Artist who studied at Liverpool College of Art, 1960–3, Royal College of Art, 1963–6, then University of Washington, in America, 1967. His exhibitions included Atkinson Art Gallery in Southport and Gordon Woodside Galleries in Seattle and he was represented in Merseyside Artists 3, toured by Walker Art Gallery, Liverpool, 1986–7, and a mixed show at The Living Room, 1994. Surreal distortions, humour and fantasy were aspects of Lawson's work, which incorporated comic illustrations. Liverpool University holds it in its collection.

Phyllis LAWSON 1927– Painter who was born in London and studied at Willesden School of Art. After travelling in North and South America, in the mid-1960s she settled in Brussels, Belgium, although she retained a base in Kent. Showed on the continent and in London, having shows at Ben Uri Art Society, which holds her work, in 1969, and at Fieldborne Galleries, 1975.

Sonia LAWSON 1934– Painter, printmaker and teacher, born in Darlington, County Durham, who was brought up in the Yorkshire Dales. She studied at Doncaster College of Art and then Royal College of Art, 1956–9, under Carel Weight, gaining first-class honours, a postgraduate year and a travelling scholarship to France. She lectured at the College and Royal Academy Schools. Lawson made many mixed-show appearances, including RA, Midland Group, Tolly Cobbold and John Moores Exhibition, Liverpool, 1991–2, with a powerful canvas, Grieving Women. Held her first solo show at Zwemmer Gallery in 1960, other major exhibitions including a retrospective at New City Gallery, Milton Keynes, and tour, 1982–3; Manchester City Art Gallery, 1987; and Wakefield and Bradford, 1988; and a 30-year retrospective at Dean Clough Galleries, Halifax, 1996. In 1989 with her parents Fred Lawson and Muriel Metcalfe she was included in A Family of Painters, organised by Wakefield Art Gallery. Arts Council, Open University, Imperial War Museum and many provincial galleries hold examples. Was elected RWS in 1988, RA in 1991. Lived in Leighton Buzzard, Bedfordshire.

Thomas LAWSON 1922– Painter and draughtsman, born and lived in Newcastle upon Tyne, Northumberland. Lawson spent much of his life involved in window display, having studied it at the local College of Art and Industrial Design. Later he studied art in the evenings at King's College, University of Durham, 1951–3, in the latter year winning the John Christie Prize for life drawing. He was a member of Newcastle Society of Artists and Wallsend Art Club and exhibited widely in mixed shows in the northeast, including Laing Art Gallery, Newcastle.

Winifred LAWSON DICK 1890–1978 Painter in oil who was born in London. Studied at Chelsea School of Art, 1950–5, with Brian Robb and Julian Trevelyan. Showed LG, ROI, and elsewhere in London and had solo shows at Walker's Galleries through the 1950s. Her work was featured in a number of women's magazines. She was a freeman of the Worshipful Company of Painter-Stainers and lived at Penshurst, Kent, and in London.

Brian LAWTEY 1945– Painter and teacher, born in Hull, Yorkshire, whose family settled in Oreston, Devon, 1947. Aged seven, Lawtey took up art seriously after developing asthma. Moved to St Austell, Cornwall, he attended Redruth Technical College; from 1962–5 was apprenticed to The St Austell Brewery as a pictorial inn sign painter and signwriter; and attended Plymouth College of Art part-time, exhibiting and selling work. Between 1965–72 Lawtey painted in London and Dorset and did various jobs, including technical author and illustrator. From 1973–4 he studied at Walthamstow School of Art; gained a first-class honours degree in fine art, painting, at Central School of Art, 1974–7; then pursued postgraduate studies at Slade School of Fine Art, 1977–9. Settled in north London, Lawtey was variously employed, including visiting and guest lecturing at colleges and universities. Lawtey was involved with several groups which followed on from the Systems Group, such as Group Proceedings and Series, producing his own geometrical abstracts. In 1986 he contributed theoretical studies to the publication *Constructivist Forum*. Group and collaborative exhibitions from 1970 included Claude Rogers Gallery, Bournemouth, 1970–1; House Gallery, 1981; Pallant House in Chichester and University of Leeds, both 1982; Exhibiting Space, from 1985; and A Disquieting Suggestion, John Hansard Gallery, University of Southampton, 1988. Arts Council holds his work.

Emma LAWTON fl. from 1980s– Versatile artist and teacher who gained a fine art diploma with distinction at Byam Shaw School of Art, 1983–6; was an Open University associate student in modern art and Modernism, 1991; gaining her master's in fine art at Cardiff Institute of Design & Technology, 1992–4. Awards included several WAC grants, including a travel and exhibition grant, Lodz, Poland, 1990. She was a founder-member of the Artists' Project, Cardiff, where she was based. Her teaching experience included working individually with adults who had learning problems, from 1992. Commissions included set design, Dance Alive Theatre Company, Cardiff, 1989; Avexco stands at Montreux Film Festivals, 1990 and 1993; and mirror and lass sculptures/installation, Theatre y Bryd, Cardiff, 1993. Exhibitions included Ffoto Gallery, Cardiff, 1989; Fine Art Society, painting works, 1990; and installation at Oriel, WAC Gallery, Cardiff, 1996.

Sue LAWTY 1954– Textile artist who used such materials as silk, linen, wool and raffia to create her landscape tapestries; these sought to give an impression visually and in texture of what it is like to be exposed to wild and barren areas. Lawty was born in Derbyshire and studied at Leeds Polytechnic. Showed widely in Britain and North America and was included in Images of the Yorkshire Landscape, organised by Sheeran Lock at Leeds Civic Hall in 1991. She lived in west Yorkshire. The British Embassy in Amman, Jordan; British High Commission in Accra, Ghana; and the Bank of the West, Texas, hold commissioned hand-woven tapestries by Lawty.

Cecil Howard LAY 1885–1956 Architect, painter, printmaker and poet, born in Aldringham, Suffolk, where he lived a countryman's life. Was educated at Ipswich School before going to the Architectural Association, but was self-taught as an artist. Was elected to RIBA in 1912, becoming a fellow in 1925. Travelled to Belgium and the Netherlands and became a friend of the painter Frank Brangwyn, who influenced Lay's work. Was a prize winner in the *Daily Mail's* Village Sign Competition. Published seven volumes of verse, books including *Grotesques and Arabesques*, 1928. Showed at RA, NEAC, RBA, RSA, AAA, extensively in the provinces and with Ipswich Art Club and Sole Bay Group. Work was included in A Look at British Printmakers 1860–1940, at Parkin Gallery, 1981. Christchurch Mansion, Ipswich, holds his Forecasting A Loss No 2, of 1933.

Allan LAYCOCK 1928– Commercial designer and painter, born in Sutton-in-Craven, Yorkshire. He attended Keighley School of Art, 1944–6 and 1948–9, then Sheffield College of Art, 1949–50. Showed in London and at various provincial centres, being an enthusiastic member of Keighley Art Club, Norwich Art Circle and the Twenty Group in that city. Lived in Norwich, Norfolk.

Norman LAYCOCK 1920– Painter in oil and teacher, born in Dewsbury, Yorkshire. He studied at the local Technical College, then the School of Art and Crafts, 1934–9, and Royal College of Art, 1946–9. Went on to teach at Harrow School of Art and Isleworth Polytechnic. Laycock joined ROI in 1979, gained the Cornelissen Prize in 1985 and showed four pictures at the annual ROI show in October 1985. Also exhibited at RA, SEA, RBA and widely in the provinces. Had a solo show at Walker's Galleries in 1960. Lived in Stanmore, Middlesex.

Peter LAYTON 1937– Artist in mixed media and teacher, born in Prague, Czechoslovakia, of British parents. He attended Bradford College of Art, 1960–2, then Central School of Art, 1962–5, taught in America, then at Hornsey College of Art. He was included in Lane Gallery, Bradford, 1965; Berkeley Gallery, California, 1967; Commonwealth Institute and Richard Demarco Gallery, Edinburgh, both 1972; and the Hampstead Artists' Council/Scottish Arts Council 1973 show Photography into Art.

Florence LAYZELL: *see* **Florence RUSHBURY**

Richard LAYZELL 1949– Sculptor, happenings artist and lecturer, born and lived in London, who studied at Ealing School of Art and Slade School of Fine Art. His earlier appearances included Garden Exhibition 3 at Camden Arts Centre, 1978. By the mid-1990s Layzell had become noted for his happenings and performances, for the Tate Gallery and many other national museums and galleries, with young people, for the mentally ill, in nightclubs, in the street and in industry. *Jumbo Rumba*, to celebrate Colchester's water tower, took place in 1996; in that year (and in 1995) 100,000 people explored *Tap Ruffle and Shave*, his interactive installation for the sensory-impaired in Glasgow and the South Bank Centre; and in 1997 *Aggravation*, a video installation in collaboration with the University of the Third Age was held at the Bluecoat Gallery, Liverpool, *Infiltration*, a series of impromptu events, was based around the Warwick Arts Centre, and *Ventilation* was staged at the De La Warr Pavilion, Bexhill-on-Sea. At that time Layzell was artist-in-residence with AIT plc and a senior lecturer at Wimbledon School of Art.

Carl LAZZARI 1934– Artist and teacher, born in Newcastle upon Tyne, Northumberland, where he was mainly based. He was head of painting at Leicester Polytechnic, 1975–84; head of the department of visual and performing arts, Newcastle Polytechnic, 1984–9; from 1989 was visiting fellow and artist-in-residence at Newcastle University, from 1993 artist-in-residence at St Alban's Roman Catholic Primary School, Newcastle. Other residencies included Magdelen College, Oxford University; a period with its Aid to Bosnia, in Croatia; and Michigan State University, in America. Magdelen College holds Lazzari's sensitive portrait, oil on canvas, of Sabina Alkire. He was art director for Coventry and Brecon Cathedral Youth Theatres. Group exhibitions included Young Contemporaries, RA Summer Exhibition, British Council in Hong Kong and Brighton Museum and Art Gallery, plus regular appearances at Laing Art Competition from 1993. Solo shows included a retrospective at Leicester Polytechnic and Hatton Gallery, Newcastle University.

Frank Marsden LEA 1900– Portrait painter and commercial artist who attended Nottingham School of Art, 1916–17, after initial education in the city, then Manchester School of Art under Adolphe Valette. Most of Lea's work was commercial, but it included some magazine illustration.

Sheila LEA 1901–1992 Sculptor, born in London, who studied with Hermon Cawthra at the School of Art in Bournemouth, where she settled, also under Harold Brownsword at Regent Street Polytechnic School of Art. She exhibited at RA, until 1982–3 with Bournemouth Arts Club of which she was a member, at Paris Salon and elsewhere. Lea was noted for her portrait studies. Russell-Cotes Art Gallery and Museum in Bournemouth holds her bronze Slugs and Snails, of a kneeling woman holding up a small child.

Bernard LEACH 1887–1979 Artist and potter, born in Hong Kong, studied art at the Slade School of Fine Art, 1903, and the London School of Art. Practised etching, then went to Japan – to which he was to return on a number of occasions through his life – where he studied pottery. Returned to England where he founded and directed The Leach Pottery, at St Ives, from 1920. He exhibited widely throughout the world and was an influential teacher, conducting several lecture tours in America, sponsored by the Contemporary Art Society. His pots are in many galleries and museums. Made Companion of Honour, 1973. Wrote several books, including *A Potter's Book*, 1940, *A Potter in Japan*, 1960, and his autobiography *Beyond East and West*, published posthumously in 1985. Crafts Council held a Leach exhibition in 1998. Lived in St Ives, Cornwall.

Richard LEACROFT 1914– Architect, illustrator and designer for the stage. Born in London, he studied at the Architectural Association and at the London Theatre Studio. Exhibited RA, Arts Council, in provinces and in the Middle East. Leicester Museum and Art Gallery bought his work. Published a number of books on aspects of the theatre. Lived for some time in Leicester.

Alexandra LEADBEATER 1956– Painter, born in Cheshire, who gained an honours degree after studies at Bath Academy of Art, Corsham, then Preston Polytechnic (Lancaster Annexe). Her mixed show appearances included 1981 Summer Show at Serpentine Gallery; Anne Berthoud Gallery, 1982; and 1989 East Midlands Arts touring exhibition. Solo shows included Mappin Art Gallery, Sheffield, 1982; Anne Berthoud Gallery and tour, 1983; and 1989–90 Wilson Hale. In 1991 shared a show at Wilson Stephens Fine Art.

Christine LEADBETTER 1957– Painter, draughtsman and printmaker noted for her exuberant brushwork and colours. She was educated at Preston Polytechnic (Lancaster Annexe), 1975–6, then in the fine art department of Liverpool Polytechnic, 1976–9. She appeared in the Merseyside Artists exhibitions from 1983, toured by Walker Art Gallery, Liverpool, having shown in Stowells Trophy Exhibition at RA in 1979. Gained a Unilever Artists in Residence placement in 1986 and took part in educational activities such as a schools project at Bromborough Pool. Had a first solo show at Williamson Art Gallery and Museum, Birkenhead, 1989–90, and it holds examples, including Aviary – Ocean Park, Hong Kong. Lived at Great Asby, Appleby, Cumbria.

Patience LEADER 1928– Painter and modeller, born in Dromagh, County Cork, Ireland. Studied at Belfast College of Art, 1949, at Chelsea Polytechnic School of Art, 1951, then portraits with Sonia Mervyn, 1949–51, who ran her own classes. Showed at RUA and lived in Armagh, Northern Ireland.

Lily LEAHY: *see* **Lilian HAWTHORN**

Amber LEAMAN 1973– Painter whose work could show strong Cubist influence, as shown at Cadogan Contemporary in 1996 when she exhibited with Ruth Stage and Liz Hough. Leaman studied at Falmouth Art School. She appeared in Cadogan Contemporary's New Year and Summer Exhibitions in 1995 and her work is held by the TSB Collection. Bridget Leaman, the artist, was her mother. Lived in Cornwall.

Bridget LEAMAN 1948– Painter who lived in Cornwall, which was the subject of her work, with strong Cubist overtones. She studied at Bournemouth College of Art and West Surrey

College of Art & Design in Farnham. Mixed shows included RI from 1982, winning a medal in 1988; RWA, 1988; and RA Summer Exhibition, 1992. Solo shows included Salisbury Playhouse, 1981, and Cadogan Contemporary, 1993. Her daughter was the artist Amber Leaman.

Dora LEAMAN 1897– Painter, born in Torquay, where she studied at the Grammar School, then the School of Art. Also attended St John's Wood School of Art and Regent Street Polytechnic School of Art in the 1930s, the latter under George Percival Gaskell. Exhibited RA, RSMA, UA and NEAC. Returned to Torquay, but finally moved to Bournemouth.

Jonathan LEAMAN 1954– Painter in oil on canvas, draughtsman and teacher, born in London, his parents actors and related to the artistic Salaman family. As a boy Leaman drew compulsively, so instead of Oxford University he chose to study at Camberwell School of Arts and Crafts, 1973–7, teaching there, 1977–83. In 1992 Leaman was a featured artist at the London Contemporary Art Fair, chosen by Paula Rego; at the 1997 Fair his picture Strongly, Wrongly, Vainly had crowds jostling to view it. It was typical of Leaman's style and subject-matter: minutely detailed, with a mystery narrative element, in the manner of the Pre-Raphaelites, whose work he admired, plus Surrealist associations. Had a first solo exhibition at Beaux Arts, 1994, another in 1997. Leaman spent years on a canvas, dividing his time between London and Gloucestershire.

Landreth LEAPER 1947– Self-taught artist mainly in watercolour, also pencil, born in Horsham, Sussex. He was elected an associate of RWA in 1979 and favoured mixed exhibitions, showing extensively throughout the south and west of England. Leaper's work "often explored tonal ranges not usually employed in watercolour – of special emphasis and interest is work on skies." Lived in Ashton, Bristol.

David LEAPMAN 1959– Painter, born and lived in London, who was first prize winner at the 1995–6 John Moores Liverpool Exhibition with Double-Tongued Knowability, a mix of hard-edge abstraction and graffiti-like imagery. He studied at St Martin's School of Art, 1977–8; Goldsmiths' College School of Art, 1978–81; and Chelsea College of Art, 1988–9. Took part in Figuring Out The Eighties, Laing Art Gallery in Newcastle upon Tyne, 1988; Aperto Venice Biennale, 1990; and Arts Council tour Recent British Painting, 1993. Had a series of solo exhibitions at Todd Gallery from 1988. Arts Council holds acrylic on canvas Past Behaviour, 1990.

Edwina LEAPMAN 1934– Painter and teacher, born in Hampshire who studied at Slade School of Fine Art and Central School of Art and Design, 1951–7. For a dozen years from 1963 she taught in several art schools, in 1974 having a solo show at New Art Centre. In the same year she was included in the Scottish Arts Council's show Post-Minimal Painting and in John Moores Exhibition, Liverpool, two years later winning a prize there. In 1976, too, she won an Arts Council Major Award and showed solo at Annely Juda Fine Art. Took part in several group shows in Switzerland. Arts Council holds Untitled '77 No. 6, of 1977, and Untitled No. 5, of 1978. Edwina Leapman gave a good statement about her abstract work in the catalogue of the South Bank Centre 1989 touring show The Experience of Painting. Had solo show at Annely Juda Fine Art, 1993. Lived in London.

Noel Harry LEAVER 1889–1951 Watercolourist and teacher, born in Austwick, Yorkshire. He studied at Burnley School of Art, graduating in 1910. Gained a Travelling Studentship in 1911 and an RIBA Owen Jones Studentship in 1912. Leaver then taught at Halifax School of Art. He travelled widely abroad, producing such works as In Sunny Algiers and In Morocco. Showed at a wide range of galleries and had works bought by Burnley Corporation, settling in the town.

Damian LE BAS 1963– Artist using paint, pencil, pastel and collage, born in Sheffield, Yorkshire, into a tinker family. His wife Delaine Le Bas was also an artist. Le Bas had a troubled childhood, finding consolation in his toys, which he drew constantly, along with football crowds. Aged about 10, he and his mother moved to Sussex, where he eventually settled at East Preston, Littlehampton. After leaving school in 1979 without qualifications, Le Bas did various labouring jobs, then was encouraged to attend West Sussex College of Art & Design, Worthing, 1980–5. He gained his master's degree in textiles from the Royal College of Art, 1985–7, although the non-academic nature of his pictures prompted his tutors to let him follow his own direction. After graduation, Le Bas worked in a kettle factory, as a roofer, then sold flowers during the day to enable him to paint at night. At the Royal College students had directed him to the Outsider Archive, where its director, Monika Kinley showed and acquired his work. This was characterised by rich colours, textile-like patterning, bizarre faces and strong linear contouring (Van Gogh was an influence). Group shows included Outsiders, Dean Clough Contemporary Art, Halifax; Art Brut/Outsider Art, Café Gallery, 1990; Singular Imagination, Phyllis Kind Gallery, New York, 1994; and Outsiders & Co, England & Co, 1996. Later solo shows included Courtauld Galleries, 1995.

Delaine LE BAS 1965– Painter, mixed-media artist, collagist and embroiderer, born in Worthing, Sussex, married to the artist Damian Le Bas. She was born into a gypsy/Romany background, spending her early years in caravans and trailers. What she called "the freedom of my Romany spirit" showed in her clothes and highly decorative work. She studied textiles at West Sussex College of Art & Design, Worthing, 1981–6, and St Martin's School of Art, 1986–8. By 1990 Le Bas found the restrictions of fashion design too much for her, and concentrated on picture-making, producing large collages and collage books, drawing on family history and photographs. Lived in a small house full of folk art objects in East Preston, Littlehampton, Sussex. Group shows included Alex Gellard Fine Art, Battle, and Rona Gallery, and solo exhibitions one at Islington Arts Factory, 1993.

Edward LE BAS 1904–1966 Painter and collector, born in London, brother of the sculptor Molly Le Bas. He took a degree in architecture at Cambridge University, studied art briefly in Paris, then from 1924 studied at the Royal College of Art. The Le Bas steel business provided him with private means which enabled him to paint abroad, both on the continent and in North Africa, also to indulge his taste for collecting modern French and English painting. He had superb judgement, buying many English painters when they were young or still underrated. A selection, A Painter's Collection, was shown at the RA in 1963, the critic Jack Wood Palmer commenting that "no collection in England can compare with Edward Le Bas' in size, consistency and quality". Le Bas was a fine painter, a Colourist with a special talent for interiors and flowerpieces who exhibited at RA, LG, Redfern and Goupil Galleries, Arthur Tooth and Son and NEAC. He had a first solo show at Lefevre Gallery in 1936. In 1997, the Michael Parkin Gallery held Edward Le Bas – Painter and Collector. The Tate Gallery, provincial galleries and others in South Africa and Australia hold examples. He was elected RA in 1953. Lived in London and Brighton.

Julian LE BAS 1958– Painter and draughtsman, closely connected with Sussex. He studied at Brighton Polytechnic, 1978–81, completing a postgraduate course at Cyprus College of Art, 1983–4. Took part in many group shows, and had solo exhibitions at The Collective Gallery, Edinburgh; Haileybury College, Hertfordshire; Charleston Farmhouse, Firle, Sussex; and at Towner Art Gallery, Eastbourne, 1990. His Source to Sea was a Rye Art Gallery commission. Represented in David Bomberg and his followers show at Towner, 1991. Lived in Brighton, Sussex.

Molly LE BAS 1903– Sculptor, born in London, sister of the painter Edward Le Bas, daughter of Edward Le Bas the steel magnate. She was educated at Broomfield Hall and in Paris and with her sister Gwen was launched into society. Showed at RA, Walker Art Gallery in Liverpool, Royal Glasgow Institute of the Fine Arts and Paris Salon. Lived in London and in Angmering, Sussex.

Philip LE BAS 1925– Painter and teacher, born in St Quentin de Baron, Gironde, France, cousin of the artist Edward Le Bas. He worked in enamel paint. Studied at Regent Street Polytechnic School of Art, 1948–51. From 1952–66 taught art at various schools, 1968–77 lecturing at King Alfred's College. Was made a member of RBA in 1953, then NEAC in 1955, but both lapsed. Showed with Young Contemporaries, 1950; RA for many years; RBA 1952–60; Walker's Galleries between 1953–7; RP 1953; NEAC 1955–60; Some Young Painters, Camberwell, 1956; and Pictures for Schools, Camberwell, 1965. Solo shows included Heffer Gallery, Cambridge, 1955–7; Trafford Gallery, 1956 and 1958; Piccadilly Gallery, 1960; and Portal Gallery from 1965. HM Government, Methodist Church and a number of private collections with theatrical connections held his work. Lived at Hinton Ampner, Alresford, Hampshire.

Rachel Ann LE BAS 1923– Painter and printmaker, born in Camberley, Surrey. She studied at the City & Guilds of London Art School under A R Middleton Todd, Henry Wilkinson and Rodney Burn. Among awards were the annual Drawing Prize and she twice won the annual Prize for Engraving. Le Bas always worked freelance and undertook commissions which included the National Trust Foundation for Art, Bishop of Bath and Wells and Royal Academy Graphics. She was elected a member of Somerset Guild of Craftsmen in 1962, of the Art Workers' Guild in 1969 the year she joined RE, and was elected a member of NEAC in 1972. She held senior positions in several of these. Ashmolean Museum in Oxford and several other public collections in Britain hold examples. She was not related to other Le Bas artists, her family having fled from France at the revocation of the Edict of Nantes in 1598. Lived in Winsford, near Minehead, Somerset.

Edith LE BRETON 1912– Artist born in Salford, Lancashire, who painted as a child, taking private lessons. Aged 12 she won a scholarship and then a studentship to Royal School of Art, Salford, 1928–32, and was encouraged by the director of the Salford Art Gallery, Albert Frape. Had her first solo show there in 1937 and it bought her work. Le Breton was urged on by L S Lowry and like him believed in "painting the people about you". Showed with MAFA of which she was made a member in 1952, RCamA and Lancashire Artists Group and had several solo shows at Medici Gallery in the mid-1970s. A limited edition of her picture *The Old Street Market* was produced by Mellor Hall Fine Art Reproductions. Le Breton claimed to be the first artist to show and discuss her work on experimental colour television. Lived for a time at Dunham Massey, Altrincham, Cheshire.

Louis LE BROCQUY 1916– Painter, mural and tapestry designer and teacher, born in Dublin and married to the artist Anne Madden. He studied chemistry at Trinity College, Dublin, 1936–7, and worked in the family oil refining business in the late-1930s. In 1938 decided to paint full-time, but was self-taught, studying in London and continental galleries. Returning to Dublin in 1940, he worked on a series of tinker paintings, stained glass, theatre designs and murals, then settled in London in 1946, producing his first tapestries two years later. Had first solo show at Gimpel Fils in 1947, at Esther Robles Gallery, Los Angeles, in 1960 and in Switzerland at Galerie Charles Lienhard in 1961. Notable among later shows was a retrospective at Irish Museum of Modern Art, Kilmainham, 1996–7. Taught at Central School of Arts and Crafts, 1947–54, and Royal College of Art, 1955–8, and was director of the Kilkenny Design Workshops, 1965–71. After destroying much of his work in 1963, Le Brocquy in 1964 began a series of human heads; his figures are often in isolation, sinister, or seen through the mist of memory. Became RHA in 1949, a Chevalier, Légion d'Honneur, 1974, and Hon. RHA in 1983. Tate Gallery, Victoria & Albert Museum and Municipal Gallery of Modern Art, Dublin, hold his work. Lived in Carros, France. The sculptor Melanie le Brocquy was his sister.

Melanie LE BROCQUY 1919– Sculptor, born in Dublin, sister of the artist Louis le Brocquy. She attended the National College of Art, Dublin, the Royal Hibernian Academy School and École des Beaux-Arts, Geneva. While she was at National College le Brocquy knew that she had made a mistake and did not want to be a painter or teacher, then discovered the sculpture department, run by Peter Grant and Peter Brennan. Her first sculpture, Head of a Cat, was accepted by RHA. A Taylor Scholarship took her to Geneva. She had a joint exhibition with her brother in 1942 in Dublin and appeared in the Irish Exhibition of Living Art in 1943, but then marriage preoccupied her until she relaunched her career in the 1960s. In the early 1970s the Dawson Gallery in Dublin took up her work, giving her shows with William Scott and Patrick Heron, the Taylor Galleries in Dublin giving her a small retrospective in 1986. Her sculpture of the period 1938–90 was shown at Austin/Desmond Fine Art, 1990. Most of her mature output is mainly constructed around small-scale and usually full-length human figures. The critic Brian Fallon called her "the best Irish sculptor of her generation".

Christopher LE BRUN 1951– Painter, printmaker and teacher, born in Portsmouth, Hampshire. He studied at Slade School of Fine Art, 1970–4, then gained his master's degree at Chelsea School of Art, 1974–5. Le Brun was a visiting lecturer at Brighton, Wimbledon and at the Slade, 1976–83, from 1989 resuming teaching at the Slade. He was a prizewinner at John Moores Liverpool Exhibitions, 1978–80, and won a Calouste Gulbenkian Foundation Printmakers' Commission Award in 1983. In 1984 he did designs for a revival of the *Ballet Imperial* at Royal Opera House, Covent Garden, produced in 1985; was guest of the Berlin Artists' Programme of the DAAD in 1987–8; and in 1988 gained the Snowdonia Commission, Artists in National Parks, organised by the Victoria & Albert Museum. From 1975 Le Brun took part in numerous mixed shows in Britain and abroad. He showed with Nigel Greenwood Gallery from 1980, also extensively in America. Arts Council, British Council and British Museum hold his work, which when shown in America was described as grand, melancholy and highly romantic. Was elected RA, 1996.

Janet LEDGER fl. from early 1970s– Painter and printmaker whose work was reproduced as popular limited edition prints by Fine Art Editions, and who was noted for subjects such as nuns on beaches, red telephone boxes and people at the seaside. These were photographed or sketched, then worked up in the studio. Born in Northampton, Ledger studied at its School of Art, taught by Henry Bird, her mother's cousin; Horace Colby; and she did an intensive lettering course with Thomas Wrigley. Soon had a number of shows and was a founder-member of the Young Contemporaries student group in the town. Marriage, children and illness interrupted her painting, then in 1972 she painted several pictures as a therapy which set her on course again. HRH Princess Margaret bought a Thames view from Ledger's London '77 show at Somerset House in 1977. Two Curwen Press lithographs are held by the Tate Gallery. Ledger was part of a The Best of Britain exhibition in Dallas in 1985 and in 1987 had a solo exhibition with Linda Blackstone Gallery, Pinner. A puckish humour and charm characterised Ledger's pictures. Latterly lived on the Isle of Wight.

Gilbert LEDWARD 1888–1960 Sculptor of monuments and portraits in metal and stone. Born and lived in London, son of the Sculptor Richard Ledward, he studied for over 10 years prior to World War I at Chelsea Polytechnic, Goldsmiths' College School of Art, the Royal College of Art and the Royal Academy Schools. In 1913 he won the Royal Academy Gold Medal and Travelling Studentship and the first British School in Rome Scholarship in Sculpture. Ledward became professor of sculpture at the Royal College, 1926–9, a year later being made member of the faculty of sculpture and of the council of the British School at Rome. Ledward exhibited at the RA from 1912, being elected RA in 1937 and a trustee, 1956–7. He was president of the RBS, 1954–6. As well as advising the Royal Mint, Ledward completed the Guards Division Memorial, in St James' Park, London, other war memorials in the provinces and overseas and the fountains in Sloane Square, London. The Tate Gallery holds his work, which can be both graceful and majestic.

Colette LEE fl. from late-1980s– Painter and sculptor who gained a diploma from Great Yarmouth College of Art and Design in 1985. In 1988 Lee won a degree in fine art from Gloucestershire College of Art and Technology, obtaining her master's from University of Ulster, Belfast, 1989. She was commissioned by Gloucestershire County Council to make a bronze plaque in 1989 and by the Plaza Hotel, Belfast, to make a sculpture, 1990. Showed in England, Ireland and Germany, appearances including Galerie Hausgeist, Berlin, 1992; Young Contemporaries at One Oxford Street, Belfast, 1993; and in 1994 Beyond the Partitions and Works on Paper, put on by Queen Street Studios, Belfast, with which she was associated.

Dick LEE 1923– Painter and teacher, full name Richard Dale Lee, born in Bulawayo, then Southern Rhodesia. He was initially educated there, then attended Camberwell School of Arts and Crafts, 1947–50, under William Coldstream, Claude Rogers, Victor Pasmore and other Euston Road School-associated artists, whose style left a strong influence on his work. Primarily a landscape and interior painter, he chose to work on the spot, his pictures retaining a freshness and spontaneity. He was awarded an Abbey Major Scholarship in 1951, then two years later began teaching at Camberwell, where he remained until 1982. Took part in many mixed shows, including LG, RA, Leicester Galleries, AIA, New Grafton Gallery and elsewhere. Had show with Francis Hoyland at Galerie de Seine in 1958, a solo series at New Grafton Gallery in 1970s and 1980s, and Cadogan Contemporary. Works purchased by the Arts Council, RA, the Beaverbrook Foundation and others. Lived in London for many years, later in Norfolk with a house in Normandy, France.

Erica LEE fl. c.1925–1980 Sculptor in terracotta and clay, especially of portraits. Born in Manchester, Lee studied under Sir

William Reid Dick and E Whitney-Smith. Exhibited widely, including RA, RSA, Royal Glasgow Institute of Fine Arts, Walker Art Gallery, Liverpool, and Paris Salon. Work held by the New Museum and Art Gallery, Newport. Was a fellow of the RBS and lived in London.

Godfrey LEE fl. from 1980s– Painter, born in St Thomas, Jamaica. After leaving school in 1969 and being unemployed for two years he joined the Army for three years. In 1974 went to live with relatives in America. Returned to Britain where he did various jobs, was unemployed, began to draw, had an exhibition in his local library and then did two years at a further education college. Completed foundation course at St Martin's School of Art and a bachelor's degree in fine art at Newcastle Polytechnic. Lee's work addressed social issues, notably the treatment of mentally ill people who were black. He was included in the 1991–2 Norwich Gallery touring show History and Identity. Lived in London.

Helen C LEE 1951– Painter, born in Southport, Lancashire. She was educated in Scotland and attended Edinburgh College of Art, 1970–6, where her teachers included Robin Philipson. She won a number of prizes and was a postgraduate travelling scholar who showed at Scottish Gallery, Edinburgh; Walker Art Gallery in Liverpool; RA and elsewhere. Lived in Edinburgh.

Joseph LEE 1876– Painter and illustrator who attended Heatherley's School of Fine Art, then the Slade School of Fine Art under Henry Tonks and Walter Westley Russell. Work done during World War I was officially purchased and he published a number of books with war themes, such as *Ballads of Battle* and *Captive at Carlsruhe*. Lived in Dundee, Angus.

May Bridges LEE fl. c.1905–1967 Painter and miniaturist, especially of portraits, born in Lahore, India. After education in England she studied at Lambeth School of Art. The architect, surveyor and engineer Sir Philip Stott's first wife Hannah having died in 1935, Lee married him shortly before he died in 1937, becoming Lady Stott. Stott's home was Stanton Court, Broadway, but Lee continued to maintain a studio in London. Her sitters included her barrister father John Bridges Lee, Sir Jeremiah Colman, Lords Burnham and Cornwallis and The Earl Manvers. She was a member of RMS, SWA, and SM, also showing at RSA, Walker Art Gallery in Liverpool and elsewhere.

Moses LEE 1950– Abstract artist using a rich palette whose sources of influence "are diverse and always expanding", ranging over modern Western artists; music including jazz, dance and Indian classical music; Eastern mysticism; natural forms and the cinema. Studied at Hull College of Art and Liverpool Polytechnic. Group exhibitions included Salford City Art Gallery, 1984; Castlefield Art Gallery, Manchester, 1986; New Art North West, Bluecoat Gallery in Liverpool, 1991; and Journeys West, University of Essex travelling show, 1995. Had solo exhibitions in 1991 at Chinese Arts Centre in Manchester and Stockport City Art Gallery, another at Skelmersdale Arts Centre, 1992. BBC, the Stockport City Art Gallery and private collections hold his work.

Peter LEE 1937– Painter, notably working in tempera, and printmaker. He attended Bournemouth College of Art, 1981–2, then Camberwell School of Art, 1982–5, with an added year's study of printmaking. Showed at RA from 1987 and in many other group exhibitions, including The Broad Horizon, Agnew, 1990.

Robert LEE 1915– Maker of boxed constructions, painter, draughtsman, printmaker and teacher, born in Bingley, Yorkshire, where he was finally based. Attended Bradford College of Art, 1932–7, then won place at Royal College of Art, 1937–40, where he studied graphic design, illustration and printmaking, his teachers including John Nash, Edward Bawden and Percy Horton. Served widely overseas in World War II in Army, 1940–6. In latter year returned to Royal College of Art on fourth-year scholarship, gained 1940. After teaching part-time at Hammersmith College of Art in 1947, Lee took job as art master at Heckmondwike Grammar School, in 1949 being appointed to Batley School of Art, in 1957 deputy head. From 1969 Lee taught variously at Bingley College of Education, Huddersfield Polytechnic, Bretton College and Bradford and Ilkley College. Lee showed regularly in Yorkshire exhibitions from the 1950s. In 1965 he shared an exhibition at Manor House, Ilkley, and a number of two-man exhibitions followed until a solo exhibition at Bishop Grosseteste College, Lincoln, 1978. There were others, then Lee had a retrospective at Bretton Hall, Yorkshire, in 1991. By this time he had been engaged on three-dimensional work for 25 years and his meticulously crafted boxes had become collectors' items.

Rosa LEE 1957– Painter, born in Hong Kong. She completed a degree in intellectual history and German at Sussex University in 1979. Her subsequent fine art training was at Brighton Polytechnic, 1982–3, St Martin's School of Art, 1983–6, and Royal College of Art, 1986–8. Between 1988–9 was visiting fellow at Winchester School of Art, having a solo show there in 1989. In that year she was an Artist of the Day at Flowers East and she also had a prizewinning canvas, Matrix, of 1989, in John Moores Liverpool Exhibition, 1989–90. In 1992 she appeared in (dis)parities at Mappin Art Gallery, Sheffield, which toured to Herbert Art Gallery, Coventry, 1993. University of Liverpool holds her work, which included abstract pictures with a strong sense of design. Lived in London.

Rosie LEE 1935– Artist in oil on canvas, wood or paper, born in Rotterdam, Netherlands. She studied at Sheffield College of Art, 1953–5, then Slade School of Fine Art, 1955–7. She said that her best work was "an exploration of self and awareness". Mixed exhibitions included Fine Arts for Industry, Royal College of Art, 1969; RA Summer Exhibitions from 1970; Basel International Air Fair, from 1973; The Minories, Colchester, 1980; and Nicholas Treadwell's Art Mill, Bradford, from 1988. In 1985–6 she was a prizewinner in Tolly Cobbold Eastern Arts Fifth National Exhibition and tour. Had a solo show at Mansard Gallery, 1968; a series at Piccadilly Gallery from 1969; and widely abroad, especially in Germany, including Galerie Im Kunsthaus Shaller, Stuttgart, 1984. Department of the Environment and Coventry's Herbert Art Gallery hold examples. Lived in Sheffield, Yorkshire.

Rupert LEE 1887–1959 Painter, sculptor, critic and teacher. Born in Bombay, India, Lee studied at the Royal College of Art and the Slade School of Fine Art, where he became friendly with Paul Nash, who describes him in detail in his autobiography *Outline*. Lee did a notable drawing of Nash. Was an enthusiastic amateur musician. From early in the 1920s Lee was associated with the Friday Club and LG, of which for a decade from the mid-1920s he was president. He was chairman of the International Surrealist Exhibition in London in 1936. As well as acting as art critic for several publications, such as *The New Statesman* and *The New Age*, Lee lectured at Westminster School of Art. His sculpture can be found in a number of English provincial churches and at the cathedral in Gibraltar. Towards the end of his life he lived in San Roque, Spain.

Sara LEE 1956– Painter and restorer who studied at Byam Shaw School of Art, 1975. Next she gained an honours degree in chemical physics, 1975–9, from Sussex University, then worked at Hamilton Kerr Institute at Cambridge University, 1980–4, to gain certificate and diploma in the conservation of easel paintings. After four years in London engaged as a restorer, lived in Paris from 1989–91, which was the subject of some of her most atmospheric work. Sara Lee showed in 1980 at Clare College, Cambridge; in 1983 at Trumpington Gallery there; from 1982 at RA Summer Exhibition; in 1986 at Addison Ross Gallery; in 1991 having a solo show at Cadogan Contemporary.

Sydney LEE 1866–1949 Landscape painter and printmaker, born in Manchester. Studied at the School of Art there and Atelier Colarossi, Paris. Painted extensively on the continent, being especially fond of mountainous scenery. Exhibited RA – elected RA, 1930 – and extensively at Cooling Galleries, RE and NEAC; also at Fine Art Society, IS, RBA and elsewhere. He held several official positions, being RA treasurer for some years and a member of the Council of Art and Industry. Included in a number of public collections, notably Tate Gallery. Lived in London.

Terry LEE 1932– Painter and teacher, born in Sheffield. He attended the College of Art there, later returning to teach, and Slade School of Fine Art, 1955–8, under William Coldstream. Showed in north of England, RA Summer Exhibition and in 1980 was included in The British Art Show, Arts Council touring exhibition chosen by critic William Packer. Had a series of solo shows at New Art Centre from 1960 and at Agnew from 1973. Arts Council holds Lee's oil The Spider's Debris, 1962, other examples being held by public galleries in Coventry, Liverpool, Hull and Oldham. Lived for a time in Beeley, Derbyshire.

George William LEECH 1894–1966 Painter and etcher. After initial study at Lambeth and Putney Schools of Art, won a three-year London County Council scholarship which enabled him to study at South Kensington. Worked for some years as a magazine art editor. Exhibited widely, including RA, RI, Fine Art Society and ROI. Lived in London.

Gwyneth LEECH 1959– Painter, draughtsman and printmaker, born in Philadelphia, Pennsylvania, America, who in 1981, the year she moved to Britain, graduated from the University of Pennsylvania in anthropology and French. From her arrival, Leech studied painting at Edinburgh College of Art, funded by a three-year Pennsylvania Thouron Scholarship; studied wood engraving with Kathleen Lindsley; and gained a postgraduate diploma in 1985. In 1983 she was included in Scottish Print Open Three, organised by Dundee Printmakers' Workshop. Was elected president of SSA. Exhibitions included University of Pennsylvania, 1986; Aberdeen Art Gallery and Museum, 1988; Theatre Royal, Glasgow, 1990; and Boundary Gallery, 1995, a show based on sketches made during through Africa and Asia, 1991–3. The American Museum in Bath, BBC, Edinburgh City Art Galleries and Strathclyde University hold examples.

William John LEECH 1881–1968 Painter, born in Dublin, Ireland, who studied at St Columba's College, Royal Hibernian Academy Schools, Metropolitan School of Art and in Paris at Académie Julian. He was elected RHA in 1910 and showed several hundred works there. Also exhibited prolifically at Goupil Gallery, RA, NEAC, Fine Art Society, Baillie Gallery and elsewhere. Had a studio in London, then settled in Clandon, Surrey.

Theyre LEE-ELLIOTT 1903– Artist born in Sussex whose work had a strong fantasy element. Lee-Elliott studied at Central School of Arts and Crafts, 1925–7. Appeared in a four-man show at Thackeray Gallery, 1977. Solo shows included Pulchri, The Hague; Iolas, New York; Redfern Gallery; Chatham Gallery in Hong Kong; and Miyuki, Tokyo. Was chosen to contribute three works to the British section at Musée d'Art Moderne, Paris, International Exhibition of Religous Art, 1965.

William LEE-HANKEY 1869–1952 Painter and printmaker, born in Chester, who was married to two artists: first Mabel Lee-Hankey (Hobson), then Edith Garner. He studied at Chester School of Art under Walter Schroeder, at the Royal College of Art and in Paris. From the early-1890s Lee-Hankey exhibited at the main London galleries, especially Fine Art Society, RWS, Leicester and Lefevre Galleries; also RA, Goupil Gallery, Ridley Art Club, ROI, RE and Walker Art Gallery, Liverpool. During World War I he served with the Artists' Rifles. British Museum and Victoria & Albert Museum hold his work, as do British provincial galleries and galleries as far apart as Budapest, Belfast and Vienna. For some time Lee-Hankey lived in France, where he produced a body of work. He is notable for his paintings of French harbour scenes and paintings and etchings of English country life, often of great sensitivity. Won a gold medal at the

Barcelona International Exhibition and a bronze medal in Chicago, was vice-president of the RWS in the late 1940s and chairman of the Empire Art Council. Lived in London.

Norah LEE-JONES 1911– Artist in many media, designer and teacher, born in Denbigh, north Wales. Aged 16 she attended Halifax School of Art for two years, then Huddersfield School of Art and Leeds College of Art, notably under Frank Simpson. She then taught in a series of Yorkshire grammar schools; spent a year at Prince's Theatre, Leeds, directing their lighting, designing costumes and backcloths; then returned to teaching. Miss Lee-Jones produced landscapes covering a wide area of Britain, as well as Italy, as shown in a solo exhibition at Dorset County Museum, Dorchester. She was a member of the Art Club in Dorchester, where she lived, also showing with groups in Bournemouth and Poole and SWLA. For a time she had her own gallery at King's Arms, Dorchester, shared with Val Buckland, showing many artists' work. Lee-Jones cited as her strongest influences those "from nature, overwhelmingly trees and skies from my earliest days".

Stewart LEES 1926– Artist born in Auchtertool, Fife, who studied at Edinburgh College of Art, 1947–52. He gained an Arts Council Sabbatical Year in 1968. Showed at Bluecoat Gallery, Liverpool; Traverse Gallery, Edinburgh; RA Summer Exhibition, and abroad. Universities of Glasgow and Nottingham hold examples. Lived in Nottingham.

Laurence LEESON 1930– Painter, printmaker and teacher, born in Leeds, Yorkshire. He studied at Shrewsbury Art School, 1948–9, then Birmingham College of Arts and Crafts, 1949–53, teachers including Bernard Fleetwood-Walker and Harold Smith. Showed with Young Contemporaries, Leicester Galleries, Keele University, Piccadilly Gallery and elsewhere. He held a Gulbenkian Fellowship at Keele, 1963–4. Victoria & Albert Museum and other public collections hold examples. Lived in Market Weighton, Yorkshire.

Gerald LEET 1913–1998 Painter and teacher, born in London. He studied painting at Goldsmiths' College School of Art, 1929–34, at Royal College of Art, 1934–7, then again at Goldsmiths' and Courtauld Institute, 1937–8. While at Goldsmiths' and sharing a studio with the artist Carel Weight Leet was asked to recommend a college for Denton Welch, later to become noted as a writer and painter; he befriended Welch, who attended his evening classes. Leet then taught at Ealing School of Art and after service in World War II was appointed an official war artist resident at Viceroy's House, New Delhi, 1945–6. After the war returned to teaching at Ealing, then went to Eton College as a drawing master, where he remained until 1949, then moved to Windsor Castle, teaching at Brighton part-time. He was commissioned by HM Queen Elizabeth the Queen Mother to complete portrait drawings in 1948. Leet had solo exhibitions at Eton Art Gallery and Isobar Gallery, as well as showing in public galleries in Manchester and Halifax.

Peter LEFTWICH 1913– Painter, born in London, notably of fresco and in tempera. After private education he studied at Durban School of Art and at the Michaelis School of Fine Art, University of Cape Town, with both John and Grace Wheatley, 1932–6. Showed widely in South Africa, at Paris Salon and at RA, RI, RP and elsewhere. South African National Gallery in Cape Town holds his work. Arts Club member. Lived in Eston, Natal.

Owen LEGG 1935– Artist, notably in lino-cut and producer of limited-edition books and prints, born in London. He was a medical practitioner from 1959, having studied in London, in 1961 obtaining a diploma in obstetrics at Guy's Hospital. Legg studied art at Tunbridge Wells Adult Education Centre. He was a member of Free Painters and Sculptors, also showing at book fairs: Oxford, 1990, and in 1991 in Mainz and Verona. He had a series of solo shows in Sevenoaks, Croydon and Greenwich, the library there holding his work, as does Kent County Library Service. Among books he produced were *The Garden*, by Vita Sackville-West, and the *Rubayyait of Omar Khayyam*. In 1992, when he went as a medical officer with a British Schools Exploring Society trip to Iceland, Legg's Woodcraft Press published William Morris' *On First Seeing Iceland*. Lived in Tonbridge, Kent.

Jeremy LE GRICE 1936– Painter, born of a Cornish family. Although he travelled as far away as Provence and America, the sea, coast, weather and landscape of Cornwall continued as a preoccupation. Le Grice attended Guildford Art School, 1953–4, was at Lanyon Summer School, 1955–6, then in 1957–61 was at Slade School of Fine Art. For a decade Le Grice was then based at St Just, Cornwall; then after 11 years in the Cotswolds in Gloucestershire, 1972–83, he returned to St Buryan, Cornwall. As well as showing at RA and with LG, Le Grice had a series of one-man shows, the first at Newlyn Gallery, 1962. After a solo show at Cadogan Contemporary in 1989 he had another in 1991, in 1990 having a retrospective at Penwith, St Ives. His wife was the stenciller Lyn Le Grice.

LEHARCA: *see* **Lewis Edward HEATH**

Olga LEHMANN 1914– Painter and designer, born in Chile. She won a scholarship to Slade School of Fine Art, studying under Allan Gwynne-Jones and Vladimir Polunin. She worked for five years at Covent Garden Opera House, then was in costume design and was art director for Rank Advertising, which led to work in Hollywood, her film credits including *Laughter in Paradise*, *The Inn of the Sixth Happiness* and *Witness for the Prosecution*. She painted the portraits in the background of the *Dynasty* television series, her other thespian portrait credits including Dirk Bogarde, Peter Sellers and Ralph Richardson. Lehmann painted landscapes near her Essex homes in Great Sampford and Saffron Walden which were likened to those of John Nash and Rowland Suddaby. Was a member of NS and SGA. Fry Art Gallery in Saffron Walden holds her work.

Damon LEHRER 1967– Figurative painter, born in Boston, Massachusetts, America, who graduated in fine art from Amherst College, 1989, obtaining his master's degree in painting at Boston University, 1994. Exhibitions included Tsai Performance Center, Boston, 1994; Pepper Gallery, Boston, from 1995; and Summer Exhibition, Beaux Arts, Bath, 1998. Lehrer was based in London from 1997. American collections holding his work include New York and Boston Public Libraries, Dartmouth College rare book library, and Fogg Art Museum, Harvard University.

Timo LEHTONEN 1953– Artist, notably a printmaker, and teacher, born in Helsinki, Finland, who attended Falmouth School of Art, 1972–3; Sheffield Polytechnic, 1973–6; and Royal College of Art, 1976–9. Awards included *The Observer* Royal Silver Jubilee Printmaking Prize, 1977; finalist, Sainsbury's Images for Today, 1983; Lowick House Printmaking Residency, 1986; Royal College of Art Printmaking Fellowship, 1987; and Museum of London artist-in-residence, 1994. From 1982 Lehtonen held a number of visiting and sessional lectureships, including Camberwell and Chelsea Schools of Art; Gloucestershire and Royal Colleges of Art; Leeds Polytechnic; Middlesex, Westminster and Hertfordshire Universities, Surrey Institute of Art & Design; and Lambeth College, where in 1993 he was external moderator. Group shows included Royal Over-Seas League Open, 1984; South Bank Picture Show at Royal Festival Hall, 1987 and 1988; and National Print Exhibition, Mall Galleries, 1994. Had a solo show at Eton College 1984, later ones including Museum of London, 1994. Victoria & Albert Museum, Mappin Art Gallery in Sheffield and Northern Arts hold examples.

Sylvia LEIBSON 1915–1989 Sculptor in clay, stone and silver, and painter in oil, born and lived in London, married to Dr Michael Leibson. She was largely self-taught, but studied sculpture with Mosè Tamburrini. Leibson's main work was portrait sculpture, also some small abstracts. She was a member of SPS and was prominent in the Islington Art Circle. Group shows included London Artists at Shrewsbury School, 1968; Upper Street Gallery, 1971; Hemel Hempstead Arts Trust Festival, 1973; Rotunda Gallery, 1974; and Manor House Society, Art in Jewish Ritual, 1984. Leibson ran a gallery in her home (58 Aberdeen Park, Highbury) where she had many solo shows and exhibited about 70 other artists' works.

Emily LEICESTER fl. c.1905–1960 Painter of portraits and miniaturist, born in Northwich, Cheshire, where she attended the High School and the School of Art. Also studied at Manchester School of Art. Exhibited RA, RCamA, Paris Salon and extensively at Walker Art Gallery, Liverpool. Lived in Hartford, Cheshire.

Roger LEIGH 1925– Sculptor, architect, artist in photomontage and teacher, born in Broadwell, Gloucestershire. Served in Royal Air Force during World War II, then attended Liverpool University. He was trained in architecture and town planning, 1947–53, but in late-1940s began abstract sculpture. Was assistant to the sculptor Barbara Hepworth, 1953–4, in the latter year joining Penwith Society of Arts. After working as an architect for London Country Council, 1954–7, sculpting in his spare time, Leigh returned to St Ives, Cornwall, in 1957, serving for some months with Hepworth again and working part-time as an architect in Truro in the early-1960s for two years. Moved to Aldbourne, Wiltshire, in 1966, the year he began teaching at Exeter School of Art. Organised the Sculpture in Landscape show in Aldbourne in 1969. From 1964 held a series of one-man shows, including New Vision Centre Gallery, Arnolfini Gallery in Bristol and Portsmouth City Art Gallery. Lived at Erlestoke, near Devizes in Wiltshire.

Molly LEIGH-HUNT 1912– Painter and film actress who also studied music, born and lived London, daughter of the painter Gerard Leigh-Hunt. Her married name was Molly Loftus-Paton. Studied privately in London, then art at Byam Shaw School in 1930s, working with Ernest Jackson. She won a number of Royal Drawing Society medals. Exhibited UA, of which she was a member, and East Dorset Art Society. Lived in London.

John LEIGH-PEMBERTON 1911– Painter, designer and illustrator, born and lived in London, studying art there for about four years from 1928 after education at Eton College. Leigh-Pemberton showed with ROI and NS of which he was for a time a member, RA, NEAC, at leading London galleries and abroad. He illustrated many books, notably for children and on natural history, including *Shell Guide to Wild Life* and *A Book of British Wild Flowers*. Leigh-Pemberton did much distinguished advertising work for companies such as Midland Bank, British Petroleum and Shell, being included in the "That's Shell – that is!" exhibition at Barbican Art Gallery in 1983. Imperial War Museum and National Maritime Museum in Greenwich hold examples. Leigh-Pemberton retired in 1982.

Katherine LEIGH-PEMBERTON: *see* **Kaff GERRARD**

Clare LEIGHTON 1898–1989 Primarily a wood engraver, but also a writer, designer, artist in mosaic and stained glass, born in London into a literary family. Studied at Brighton School of Art, the Slade School of Fine Art under Henry Tonks, 1920–2, and the Central School of Arts and Crafts, 1923–4, with Noel Rooke. As a result she became a wood engraver at a time of the craft's resurgence in England and was the first woman to publish a book on the technique, in 1932; *Wood Engraving and Woodcuts*. Although she exhibited RE, RA, Redfern Gallery, RHA and elsewhere, her work was primarily for the printed page. She was one of the finest wood engravers of her time, producing strong and vigorous images. Among books illustrated were Thomas Hardy's *The Return of the Native*, 1929; her own *The Farmer's Year*, 1933; and Gilbert White's *The Natural History of Selborne*, 1941. As an author-artist her titles *Four Hedges* and *Country Matters* were notable. In 1939 she emigrated to America, where she lectured and became vice-president of the Society of American Graphic Art and fellow of the National Academy of Design. Designed 33 stained glass windows for St Paul's Cathedral, Worcester,

Massachusetts. Clare Leighton was a pacifist with strong social convictions, evident in her written work. Ashmolean Museum, Oxford, held a major exhibition in 1992.

Tanya LEIGHTON 1970– Artist, born in Guildford, Surrey, who for New Art in Scotland, Centre for Contemporary Arts, Glasgow, in 1994, created wall pieces made with coloured matches. She attended West Surrey College of Art and Design, Farnham, 1988–9, then the School of Art, Glasgow, 1989–95. Exhibitions included The Maltings Student Show, Maltings, Farnham, 1989, and Forum II, Stills Gallery, Edinburgh, 1993.

Robert LEISHMAN 1916–1989 Painter, draughtsman and teacher, born in Inverkeithing, Fife. Leishman graduated from Edinburgh College of Art, a member of the notable generation which included Alan Davie, William Gear and Robin Philipson. After war service, 1940–6, in the Army Leishman taught in Germany, Edinburgh, Fife and Dundee, but in 1972 gave up teaching to paint full-time. He was elected SSA and RSW and won the May Marshall Brown Award in 1987. Showed widely in Scottish group shows and his solo exhibitions included McClure Gallery, Glasgow, several at the Scottish Gallery in Edinburgh, a retrospective at Roseangle Gallery, Dundee, in 1981, and William Hardie Gallery, Glasgow, in 1990. Work held by Scottish Arts Council, Dundee City Art Gallery and elsewhere. Leishman's pictures are colourful, imaginative and witty, a reflection of the artist's own character. Lived in Dundee, Angus.

James LE JEUNE 1910–1983 Painter, born in Saskatoon, Canada. Initially he was educated in Northamptonshire. His art education included Heatherley's School of Fine Art, Byam Shaw School of Drawing and Painting and Art Students' League of New York. Exhibited NEAC, UA, RP, RBA and RSMA. HRH The Duke of Edinburgh bought his work. Lived in London, later in Dublin.

Hendrik LEK 1903–1985 Painter, born in Antwerp, Belgium. His father did not want him to become an artist so he went into the diamond business, studying part-time at Antwerp Academy with Lucien de Jaegher. Fleeing from Germans he moved to Britain in 1940 and after the war became an antique dealer, having always collected, painting in his spare time. In 1946 he restored a 15th-century building called the Tudor Rose in Beaumaris which became an obsession, his shop and the subject of many of his pictures. When he ceased dealing it became a gallery in which his and his son Karel's pictures were jointly shown. Showed at RCamA and other venues in Wales, as well as in Canada, Netherlands and America. Anglesey Art Collection holds his work. Lived in retirement in Anglesey, Gwynnedd, north Wales.

Karel LEK 1929– Artist in a wide variety of media, designer and lecturer, son of the artist Hendrik Lek, born in Antwerp, Belgium. He was educated at Friars' School, Bangor, then Liverpool College of Art, 1946–52. Notable teachers included Karel Vogel and Geoffrey Wedgwood. Lek said that "the country of my birth, regarding my mode of expression, which is emotional," was important to his output. "My concern is humanity. I very often see beauty in what is often neglected." Lek was a member of RCamA. He also showed at RA, Whitechapel Art Gallery, SWE, Woodstock Gallery, RI, ICA and public galleries in Amsterdam and Llandudno. Solo shows included RCamA, Woodstock Gallery, Oriel Bangor, and Tegfryn Gallery in Menai Bridge. Contemporary Art Society for Wales, The Football Association, National Library of Wales in Aberystwyth and overseas collections hold examples. Lived at Beaumaris, Gwynedd.

Francis LE MARCHANT 1939– Artist mainly in oil and watercolour, born in Hungerton, Lincolnshire, full title Sir Francis Le Marchant, Bart. There was an artistic tradition in most branches of his family, notably Fanny Le Marchant, the bird painter. He studied at Byam Shaw School of Drawing and Painting, 1959–62, then Royal Academy Schools, 1962–6. He was offered an extra year in the sculpture school. Teachers included Charles Mahoney, Peter Greenham, Bernard Dunstan, Edward Bawden and Anthony Eyton. In 1968 Le Marchant spent four months at Hornsey College of Art in textile department to study tapestry design. Landscape and architecture were two key themes in his paintings, traditional and realistic in approach. Group shows included RA Summer Exhibitions, Upper Grosvenor Galleries, Leicester Galleries and Oscar and Peter Johnson. Showed with Agnew from 1969 in solo shows, later ones including Sally Hunter and Patrick Seale Fine Art, 1986, and Roy Miles Gallery, 1996. Department of the Environment holds his work.

Helen LEMPRIERE 1907–1991 Painter, printmaker and artist in mixed media, with a strong interest in Australian Aborigine mythology. She was born in Melbourne, Victoria, into a cultured, wealthy family, niece of the singer Dame Nellie Melba, after whom she was named. From 1930 she studied first with the tonal painter Archibald Colquhoun, then for many years with Justus Jorgensen, being a member of his Mantsalvat bohemian circle. After marriage to Keith Wood in 1945 Lempriere's life changed, and from 1950–8 she lived in Paris, studying with Fernand Léger and Fred Klein, father of the artist Yves Klein, and exhibiting in mixed shows. In 1953 she participated in the first Australian Artists' Association exhibition at RWS Conduit Street gallery; she settled in London, 1958–65; and in the latter year showed solo at the Leicester Galleries. The year after, she and her husband settled in Sydney. Lempriere exhibited widely internationally, but tended to be neglected in Australia, although a retrospective at Woolloomooloo Gallery, Woolloomooloo, in 1993 did much to rehabilitate her reputation. A debilitating illness blighted her later years. Lempriere is well represented in public collections in Australia and America, including the Australian National Gallery in Canberra and Miami Museum of Modern Art, Florida, and the *Daily Mirror* Newspapers and *Financial Times* holdings.

Brenda LENAGHAN fl. from early 1960s– Painter, designer and teacher who studied at Glasgow School of Art. She obtained a diploma in commercial and graphic design and obtained a job with Bernat Klein, a Galashiels-based fabric designer. For 15 years from then on taught art in Glasgow, married, studied with the Open University and travelled, but did little painting. In 1978 she exhibited at Peter Potter Gallery, Haddington, with a one-man the following year, in 1980 sharing a show at Stirling Gallery. Then showed regularly in Scotland, including RSW of which she was a member, RSA and Royal Glasgow Institute of the Fine Arts. She gained the Anne Redpath Prize in 1975 and 1983 and the SSWA Special Award in 1980. Later exhibitions included Christopher Hull Gallery, 1988, and Duncan Campbell Fine Art and William Hardie, Glasgow, 1991. Her work is in collections worldwide. She travelled to countries including Russia, Tibet, China, Greece, Italy and Nepal, and they and their mythologies inspired her work.

Patricia LENAGHAN 1958– Artist who obtained an honours degree from Glasgow School of Art, 1977–81, gaining her master's from Chelsea School of Art, 1981–2. Group shows included SSA, 1979; Glasgow Print Studio, 1980; New Generation Artists at Compass Gallery, Glasgow, 1981; Christie's Inaugural Show and Minsky's Gallery, both 1982; and Scottish Print Open Three, 1983, organised by Dundee Printmakers' Workshop.

Barbara LENG-SMITH 1922– Artist in oil, watercolour and pastel, notable for portraits, born in the Isle of Man. She studied at Manchester with Harry Rutherford. Leng-Smith was a member of the Société des Artistes Français. She received an Hon. Mention at Paris Salon in 1969, the Silver Medal in 1972, and a Diplôme d'Honneur twice at Salon International, 1970–1. Showed with RP, RSA, Manchester Academy and in France and had a solo show at Tib Lane Gallery, Manchester. Lived in Hale, Cheshire.

Robert O LENKIEWICZ 1941– Portrait painter and muralist, born of Jewish parents who moved to London in 1939 from Russia and Germany. His mother's father was court painter to mad King Ludwig of Bavaria. Lenkiewicz attended St Martin's School of Art and Royal Academy Schools. He painted on a large scale, one picture at St Martin's being 360 feet long, 17 feet high. Later work was based on a series of themes, including the Jewish Holocaust. Settling in Plymouth, Devon, Lenkiewicz formed a large, valuable library, rooms having themes such as death, magic and metaphysics. Had his first commercial exhibition, organised by The Halcyon Gallery in association with Arthur Andersen, at International Convention Centre, Birmingham, 1994. The retrospective, of over 300 pictures, was aimed at raising up to £500,000 to buy properties adjacent to his studio. There was another retrospective at the Art Gallery, Wolverhampton, 1998.

Dennis LENNON 1918–1991 Architect, artist and designer, who attended Merchant Taylors' School and University College. During Army service, 1939–45, during which he was mentioned in dispatches and won the Military Cross, was captured in France and later escaped, Lennon served in North Africa and Italy. From 1948–50 he was director of the Rayon Industry Design Centre, then went successfully into private practice. Main works included Jaeger shops, London Steak Houses, co-ordination of the interior of the liner *Queen Elizabeth II*, Chalcot Housing Estate in Hampstead, the unusual boat-shaped central dining room at Harrow School and refurbishment of the Ritz Hotel. Was a member of RIBA and of Society of Industrial Artists and Designers and of the Savile Club, where he showed and sold work. Abbott and Holder also sold examples, after his death. Lennon designed the set for Richard Strauss's opera *Capriccio* at Glyndebourne and a number of state galas at Royal Opera House. Lived in Watford, Hertfordshire.

LENSMAN: *see* **Humphrey SPENDER**

Charmian LEONARD fl. from 1950s– Artist in oil and drawing media, and teacher, who also used her maiden name Charmian Leondopoulos to exhibit. Was married to the sculptor Keith Leonard, their son Mark being a painter. She was born in London and studied for her diploma at Chelsea School of Art, 1953–5, and for an art teacher's diploma at Bournemouth School of Art; her teachers included Ceri Richards, Prunella Clough and Vivian Pitchforth. Taught at Newcastle and Sunderland Schools of Art and at several adult education establishments. Leonard's pictures, inspired by "the infinite variety, order and precision of existence", by plants, stars, tides and so on, had a simplicity of approach bordering on the childlike, and drew on the landscape near home in St Ives, Cornwall. Shared shows with her husband at Limited Editions and Artisan Gallery, and Vision Gallery, Sheffield. Mixed exhibitions included Penwith Gallery in St Ives, Ashgate Gallery in Farnham and The Living Room. Had solo shows at Amalgam Gallery in Barnes and Brown's Gallery, Penzance.

Keith LEONARD 1921–1993 Sculptor, painter and teacher, born in Birmingham, husband of the artist Charmian Leonard, their son being the painter Mark Leonard. Keith Leonard studied at Birmingham College of Arts and Crafts; from 1949–52 at Slade School of Fine Art under A H Gerrard, whom he termed a "marvellous teacher"; and with Ossip Zadkine, in Paris, 1953. He was an assistant to Barbara Hepworth, 1955–9. As well as a period teaching at Stourbridge School of Art, Leonard was head of sculpture at Sunderland School of Art, 1959–62, and at Farnham School of Art, 1964–7. Mixed exhibitions included Tate Gallery, 1958; New Art Centre, 1986; and Artists from Cornwall at RWA, 1992; he was a member of the Penwith Society in St Ives, where he lived. Solo shows included Drian Gallery, 1958, and a retrospective at Penwith Gallery, St Ives, 1994. The bronze Pavlova, 1992, in the RWA show was a good example of the grace and elegance of Leonard's abstract style. Barbara Hepworth and Ben Nicholson acquired Leonard's work, which is also held by Birmingham City Museum and Art Gallery and Farnborough Library.

Michael LEONARD 1933– Painter and illustrator, full name Douglas Michael Leonard, born in Bangalore, India. He was educated at Stonyhurst College, then St Martin's School of Art, where he studied graphic design, 1954–7. For 15 years Leonard worked as an illustrator. From 1972 he worked mainly as a painter, appearing in many group shows at Fischer Fine Art, which went on to represent him and where he had a series of solo shows. Also exhibited one-man at Harriet Griffin Gallery in New York, in 1977–8 had a retrospective at Gemeentemuseum in Arnhem, Netherlands, and in 1993 a solo show at Thomas Gibson Fine Art which made clear Leonard's fine abilities as a painter of the nude in the classical tradition. Showed widely in mixed exhibitions on the continent and in America. The Boymans Van Beuningen Museum, Rotterdam, holds his work, as do Victoria & Albert Museum and National Portrait Gallery. It has Leonard's portrait of HM The Queen, commissioned by *Reader's Digest* to celebrate her sixtieth birthday. Lived in London.

Charmian LEONDOPOULOS: *see* **Charmian LEONARD**

Anne LEONE fl. from early 1980s– Painter and teacher, married to the artist Daniel Ludwig, who obtained a bachelor's degree in fine arts at Boston University, 1981, her master's degree at University of Cincinnati in 1985. She showed extensively in America in group and solo shows, being represented by galleries in New York, Kentucky and New England. In England she had a series of solo exhibitions at Cadogan Contemporary from 1988. Taught at UMass Dartmouth and lived in Newport, Rhode Island.

Dante LEONELLI 1931– Sculptor, painter, collagist, creator of optical and kinetic works, and teacher, born in Chicago, Illinois. He studied at the School of the Art Institute of Chicago, 1949–53. After two years in the United States Army Leonelli moved to London where he was a research student at Courtauld Institute of Art, 1955–9. In London he painted, made collages, became involved in kinetic and optical sculptures and helped organise the Continuum Group with Michael McKinnon and Robert Janz. In 1968 Leonelli became head of the plastics research unit at Royal College of Art and from 1969 was director of fourth-dimensional studies at Middlesex Polytechnic. In 1979–80 he visited America and Japan. Leonelli showed at Matthiesen Fine Art in 1959 and 1961 and in 1981 was included in Four Sculptors at University of East Anglia. Among his commissions was the Argon Ice Bridge at Iowa City, 1978–9, and he gained a prize in the Holborn Station Competition, 1980. He was included in British Sculpture in the Twentieth Century at Whitechapel Art Gallery, 1981–2.

Kim C LEONG fl. from 1950s– Versatile painter, born in Malaya, who was educated there and later studied modern languages in England and the Netherlands. From 1960–85 she travelled extensively on the continent, in North America, Mexico and Southeast Asia, where meeting with other artists influenced her work. This had an underpinning of traditional Chinese education and the practice of calligraphy. Chinese brush and silk painting were notable features of her work. Between 1952–67 she took part in the Annual Exhibition in Malaysia, winning first prizes in 1953–4. British appearances included Aron College, Wales, 1972; East & West Art Exhibition, Lauderdale House, 1990; and Primrose Hill Gallery, 1993, where she shared a show. She was also known as Leong Shao Ling.

Zbigniew LES 1914– Sculptor, woodcarver and artist in paper, brought up in Poland, his original name being Leszczyński. Service with Polish Army in Britain during World War II. He was a son of the Polish artist Konstanty Leszczyński, with whom he studied, and also taught himself in Britain and in several countries on the continent. Also studied at Warsaw and Edinburgh Universities, finally settling in Edinburgh. Exhibited RSA, SSA and elsewhere.

Cecil Mary LESLIE 1900–1980 Painter, sculptor, illustrator, printmaker and furniture designer. She was the daughter of Sir Norman Leslie and was born in London. Studied at Heatherley's School of Fine Art, 1919, at the London School of Photolithography and Engraving and at the Central School of Arts and Crafts. In the mid-1920s she taught at Grosvenor School of Modern Art. Served as a nurse in both World Wars. Showed at RA, RSA, Royal Glasgow Institute of the Fine Arts, RCamA, in the provinces and overseas. Illustrated several dozen books. British Museum and National Portrait Gallery hold her work. Lived finally in Blakeney, Norfolk.

Frederick LESSORE 1879–1951 Sculptor and painter, born in Brighton, son of the artist Jules Lessore. Studied art in Paris and London, in 1906 gaining a medal at the Royal Academy Schools. Member of the Art Workers' Guild. Exhibited RA, Walker Art Gallery, Liverpool, and elsewhere. Major Lessore modelled many statues and busts in England and abroad. He founded the Beaux Arts Gallery which his wife, the painter Helen Lessore, took over after his death. Lived in London.

Helen LESSORE 1907–1994 Painter, gallery owner and writer, born and lived in London. She was educated at the Slade School of Fine Art, 1924–8, under Henry Tonks and Tancred Borenius, and in 1931 began working as secretary at the Beaux Arts Gallery, founded by her husband, the sculptor Frederick Lessore. She married him in 1934, John Lessore the artist being their son. Helen Lessore took over running the gallery from 1952–65, then became a full-time painter. Under her direction the semi-moribund Beaux Arts was revitalised, and she gave first exhibitions to Auerbach and Kossoff, showed Freud, Aitchison and Uglow and championed the Kitchen Sink School painters such as Middleditch, Greaves and Jack Smith. She exhibited in Marlborough Fine Art's Helen Lessore and the Beaux Arts Gallery, 1968; at 12 Duke Street in 1981; and had a retrospective at Fine Art Society in 1987. Her book *A Partial Testament* was published in 1986, the year she was elected RA.

John LESSORE 1939– Painter and teacher, born in London where he continued to live. He studied at Slade School of Fine Art, 1957–61, gaining an Abbey Minor Travelling Scholarship to Italy in the latter year. In 1965 he had a one-man show at Beaux Arts Gallery, run by his mother, the painter Helen Lessore. Other one-man shows included Ashgate Gallery in Farnham; New Art

Centre; and Nigel Greenwood Gallery, 1990, where Lessore's brand of Expressionism concentrated on the subject of artist and model. Lessore was an exhibitor in RA Summer Exhibition. In 1965 he took a post teaching at Royal Academy Schools, from 1978 teaching at Norwich School of Art. Arts Council holds his work.

Thérèse LESSORE 1884–1945 Artist, daughter of the painter Jules Lessore and sister of the sculptor Frederick Lessore. She was the third wife of the painter Walter Sickert, who described her as "a Persian miniature", having previously been married to the artist Bernard Adeney. She was born in Brighton and after attending the South-Western Polytechnic Art School was at Slade School of Fine Art, 1904–9, where she won the Melville Nettleship Prize for Figure Composition. She showed at LG, NEAC and Goupil Gallery and had first solo exhibition at Eldar Gallery, with a catalogue preface by Sickert. She married him in 1926, shared a love of the music-hall and circus with him, which was reflected in her work, and nursed him until his death.

Michal LESZCZYŃSKI 1906– Painter, mural artist and draughtsman, born in Dolina, Poland, specialising in ships and the sea. As well as studying at nautical and musical colleges in Warsaw, he studied art at the State Academy in Cracow, anatomy at the University there and privately in England, in which he settled for some years. In England was for a period a navigation officer in the Admiralty, having sailed professionally while in Poland. Was an expert on sailing ships and published, among other books, *How to Draw Sail and Sea*. Exhibited in England at RA, NS and RI and had several one-man shows in London and New York. Polish Embassy in London and Port of London Authority hold his work. Lived for a time in Copnor, Hampshire, later in Montego Bay, Jamaica.

Arthur LETT-HAINES: *see* **Lett HAINES**

John LETTS 1930– Sculptor, son of the designer Joseph Letts, born in Birmingham, where he studied at the Birmingham School of Art under the head of sculpture William Bloye, 1945–9. Showed in London and widely in the Midlands. In 1985 he completed a statue of the novelist George Eliot for the centre of Nuneaton, Warwickshire, near where she had lived. Public gallery in Stratford-upon-Avon also holds Letts' work. He lived at Astley, near Nuneaton.

Marian LEVEN 1944– Painter in oil and acrylic of mostly landscape-based work, born in Edinburgh, married to the artist Will Maclean. She studied at Gray's School of Art, Aberdeen, 1962–6. Was a member of RSW, also showing at RSA, Royal Glasgow Institute of the Fine Arts, with the Aberdeen Artists and at various Scottish galleries. Fife Regional Council holds her work. Lived in Tayport, Fife.

Ben LEVENE 1938– Painter and teacher, born in London. He studied at Slade School of Fine Art, 1956–61, gaining the Boise Scholarship which enabled him to work in Spain, 1961–2. From 1959 Levene began appearing in group exhibitions at Beaux Arts Gallery, RA, LG and abroad. After sharing a show with Olwyn Bowey at New Grafton Gallery in 1969 he had the first of several solo exhibitions at Thackeray Gallery in 1973. Also showed regularly with Browse & Darby. Usually signed work with a B L monogram. Taught part-time at Camberwell School of Art and Royal Academy Schools and was elected RA in 1986. Work in many public collections. Levene was a rich Colourist, handling genre, landscape and still life in oil and watercolour.

Rosie LEVENTON fl. from 1970s– Artist who studied Chinese language and archaeology at London University, 1974–5. Then attended Croydon College of Art, 1976–9, followed by post-graduate course at St Martin's School of Art, 1980–1. Maggi Hambling, Eddie Wolfram, Barry Martin and John Bellamy were cited as influences on her career, which included teaching in Birmingham and at Byam Shaw School of Art. Her False Floor (4), an object measuring 192 inches × 312 inches × 4 inches and created from copper briquettes, was a notable feature of the 1992 East & South Norwich Gallery/Kent Institute of Art and Design show. Other group shows included LG from 1981; Eaumages, Festival of Installations, Villedieu Cultural Centre in Paris, 1984; and Manchester City Art Gallery, 1987. Had series of solo shows from LYC Museum & Art Gallery, Cumbria, 1983, later ones including Serpentine Gallery, 1987 and Woodlands Art Gallery, 1989. Held a sculpture residency at Glasgow Garden Festival, 1988.

Joan LEVER 1925–1997 Artist in oil, watercolour and gouache (she worked latterly as Joan Lever Gibbings, being married for a time to the son of artist and writer Robert Gibbings). Born in London, she was educated there, then in South Africa, where she lived for almost 12 years from 1937 and was involved for a time in hospital and social work. Obtained a diploma from Continental School of Art in Cape Town under Maurice van Essche, 1947–9, a Belgian who had worked under Matisse, whose pictures, with those of Cézanne, greatly influenced Lever's output. This was distinguished by clarity and simplicity of form and colour, representational and abstract styles which evolved throughout her life. In England, from 1949–52 she studied under Kenneth Martin, Peter de Francia, Frederick Gore, John Napper, Vivian Pitchforth, Harold Workman, James Bateman, Barry Craig and John Wheatley at St Martin's School of Art. She was one of a post-diploma group of 10 artists working for a year under the principal Edward Morss. She also spent time at the Anglo-French Summer School, 1949. In the mid-1950s she worked for the Bolton Theatre Club's productions. Mixed exhibitions included The Castle, Cape Town, tercentenary exhibition, 1952; Young Artists from the Commonwealth, Imperial Institute, 1953; the first Gainsborough's House Society Exhibition, Sudbury, 1959; with Tuesday Painting Group, Guntons Coffee Shop, Colchester, 1974; and Colchester Art Society from 1979. Had a first solo exhibition at Alpine Gallery, 1978. Died in Ovington, Suffolk.

David LEVERETT 1938– Painter, printmaker and teacher, born in Nottingham, who studied at the College of Art there, 1957–61, then Royal Academy Schools, 1962–5. In the latter year Leverett had the first of a series of shows at Redfern Gallery and exhibited in Young Contemporaries, in 1967 at John Moores Liverpool Exhibition and in 1968 in Britain Painting and Sculpture at Whitechapel Art Gallery and the RA bicentary exhibition. Other one-man shows were held at Bear Lane Gallery, Oxford; Ikon Gallery, Birmingham; ICA and overseas; and Jill George Gallery, 1995. Leverett taught at Slade School of Fine Art and Reading University. He produced both abstract and landscape pictures, sometimes large and epic in conception, as with his Sacred Gardens shown at Redfern in 1990. Arts Council holds his work. Lived in London.

Anthony LEVETT-PRINSEP: *see* **Anthony PRINSEP**

Margaret LEVINSON 1926– Artist who was born and educated in Bournemouth, Hampshire, where she studied at the College of Art, teachers including the sculptor Hermon Cawthra and etcher Leslie Ward. She went on to specialise in coloured etching and aquatints of Wessex and evolved unique and watercolour techniques. Hampshire Museum Service commissioned her to create 50 etchings of water-mills in the area. Was a member of the Printmakers' Council. Mixed exhibitions included Ben Uri Gallery from 1974; Russell-Cotes Art Gallery, Bournemouth from 1978; and Printmakers' Council, Leighton House, 1982. Solo shows included Poole Central Library, 1974, later one-mans comprising Medici Galleries and Dean Galleries, San Jose, California, both 1986. Ben Uri Art Society and many other collections worldwide hold examples.

Rachel LEVITAS 1964– Painter and printmaker who gained her foundation diploma and honours degree at Camberwell School of Art, 1982–6; studied advanced printmaking part-time at Central St Martins School of Art, 1988–90; then gained a postgraduate diploma from Royal Academy of Art, 1990–3. Awards included John Purcell Print Prize and W H Patterson Prize for Objective Painting, both 1991; Turner Gold Medal, 1992; and in 1993 Trent Bridge Travelling Scholarship and David Murray Landscape Award. Group shows included Fresh Art at Barbican Centre, 1987; RA Summer Exhibition, from 1990; Royal Over-Seas League Open, 1992; and Whitechapel Open Studios, 1994. Had a solo show, Half Light, at Rebecca Hossack Gallery, 1989, another at The Cut Gallery, 1996.

Emmanuel LEVY 1900–1986 Painter, draughtsman, collagist and teacher, born in Manchester, with which his career was closely associated, and where he first showed, in 1924. He studied art in Manchester, London and Paris. Went on to teach in Manchester and at Stockport College. Although for a time he was interested in Cubism and Surrealism, Levy discarded them for a more naturalistic style, although within it his range was wide. His central theme was the human condition, in which he produced some powerful works. Was also a fine portrait draughtsman. Had six solo shows in Manchester between 1925–63 plus a number in London. There was a retrospective at Salford City Art Gallery, 1948; another at Fieldborne Galleries, 1976; and one at Stockport Art Gallery, 1982. National Portrait Gallery, Ben Uri Gallery and galleries in Manchester, Stockport and Salford hold his work. Latterly lived in Alicante, Spain.

Mervyn LEVY 1914–1996 Writer, lecturer, broadcaster and painter, born in Swansea, south Wales. He attended the Grammar School and School of Art there, then Royal College of Art under Sir William Rothenstein and Gilbert Spencer. From childhood was a friend of Dylan Thomas, his portrait of the poet held by the National Portrait Gallery. At the Royal College Levy won the Herbert Read Prize for Drawing at the 1935 annual students exhibition. Exhibited at RWA and elsewhere, solo shows including Glynn Vivian Art Gallery, Swansea. During World War II attended Royal Military College at Sandhurst, becoming a captain in the Royal Army Educational Corps. After the war he was an overseas arts lecturer to the War Office, with the honorary rank of lieutenant-colonel. Held a series of teaching posts, including adult education department at Bristol University, then Royal West of England Academy in Bristol, and he also taught at London University's extra-mural studies department; appeared on *The Critics* programme on BBC radio and for several years had his own television series *Painting for Housewives*; he was associate editor of *Art News and Review* and features editor of *The Studio*. Wrote many books, including *Painter's Progress*, monographs on L S Lowry, Henri Gaudier-Brzeska and Scottie Wilson, and in 1982 published autobiographical fragments *Reflections In A Broken Mirror*. Chelsea Arts Club member who lived in London.

Simon LEVY 1963– Painter, born in Johannesburg, who spent his formative years in South Africa, moving to England in the early 1980s. He studied painting at St Martin's School of Art, winning the Cartier Foundation Prize in 1988. Spent a period as artist-in-residence at Foundation for Contemporary Art at Jouy-en-Josas, France. Levy showed in many mixed exhibitions, including Whitechapel Open; had a first London solo show, Between Location and Identity, curated by Rear Window, in 1992; and in 1995 his show Alchemy, based on travels in Mexico and South Africa and an interest in jazz and modern music, was put on by Austin/Desmond Fine Art.

Viv LEVY fl. from late 1970s– Sculptor, painter and draughtsman who studied at St Martin's School of Art, 1977–80, then after a year in Space Studios, Wapping, was at Royal College of Art, 1981–4. Was Henry Moore Fellow at Wimbledon School of Art, 1989–90. Painted murals as part of Islington Schools Project in 1977, in 1987 gaining a commission for London Borough of Newham. Wrote *Life Drawing: A Beginner's Guide*, 1993. Mixed shows included Art at Work, RIBA, 1988; Artist's Choice at Angela Flowers Gallery, 1992; and 1st RWA Open Sculpture Exhibition, 1993. Solo exhibitions included Castlefield Gallery, Manchester, 1991. Lived in London.

Aletta M LEWIS 1904– Painter and medical artist, born in Orpington, Kent, married to the sculptor Denis C Dunlop. She studied at Beckenham School of Art and the Slade School of Fine Art under Henry Tonks. Taught for a while in Sydney Art School, Australia, and showed there. Also exhibited NEAC, LG, Goupil Gallery and in Paris. Published the book *They call them Savages*. Lived in London.

Alfred Neville LEWIS 1895–1972 Painter, born in Cape Town, South Africa, who divided his life mainly between that country and England. Studied at Slade School of Fine Art, 1914, then served during World War I in several countries on continent. Lewis was a prolific exhibitor, being a member of NEAC, NS and RP, also showing at Leicester Galleries, Goupil Gallery, Redfern Gallery and elsewhere. He had his first solo show at Carfax Gallery in 1920. During World War II he was an official war artist with the South African forces. A number of public collections including Tate Gallery hold his work, which is notable for its portraits and figure studies, often of low life.

Ann LEWIS 1962– Artist in mixed media, lino-cut and etching, born in St Asaph, Flintshire, who gained an honours degree in graphic design from Exeter College of Art & Design, 1985–8. Was a member of RCamA and its hon. secretary. Lewis' special interest was the "interpretation of Welsh landscape, in particular its waterfalls". As well as RCamA, took part in group shows at Tegfryn Gallery, Anglesey; Exchange Theatre, Manchester; Arts Centre, Aberystwyth; and Theatr Clwyd, Mold. Shared a show at Hanover Galleries, Liverpool, 1996. National Library of Wales in Aberystwyth holds her work. Lived in Gerlan, Bethesda, Gwynedd.

Brian LEWIS 1947– Artist who moved to Norfolk in 1980, where he depicted with humour and pathos the lives of people and the architectural oddities of the county's coastal region. Lewis did a foundation course at Epsom School of Art, 1963–4; gained a diploma pass with honours at Guildford School of Art, 1964–7; attended the Royal Academy Schools, 1967–70, winning various prizes, including a bronze medal for painting; then gained a pass with distinction on the advanced printmaking course at Croydon School of Art, 1979–80. Mixed exhibitions included RA Summer Exhibition, Goldmark Gallery in Uppingham, Wells Centre at Wells-next-the-Sea, and Morley Gallery. Solo shows included James Colman Fine Art, 1996.

Charles LEWIS 1916– Sculptor and teacher, born in Southsea, Hampshire. He studied at Portsmouth College of Art, 1932–6, then at Royal College of Art, 1936–9, with Richard Garbe. In 1946 Lewis gained a Royal Exhibition and Continuation Scholarship. Went on to become head of sculpture at Kingston College of Art and Polytechnic, 1947–78. Lewis completed commissions for private architects, Greater London Council and Ministry of Public Building and Works. He was a fellow of RBS and a member of Art Workers' Guild. Lived latterly in New York, where the Weston Press Gallery gave him a retrospective in 1983.

Daniel LEWIS 1908– Painter and draughtsman, born in Trefenter, Cardiganshire, a locality where he spent all his life, finally living in an old people's home in Aberystwyth. He began to draw at classes organised by the Red Cross when he was aged about 60. Chapels were his chief subject and he took part in the WAC 1972 An Alternative Tradition exhibition.

David LEWIS 1955– Painter and teacher, born in Wigan, Lancashire. He studied at Manchester Polytechnic, 1973–4, at Leeds Polytechnic as a scholar, taught at Thomas Danby College, Leeds, 1978–82, and was artist-in-residence in Swansea, 1990. Lewis was some time a visiting lecturer in France and Australia. Lewis' group appearances included St Paul's Gallery, Leeds, and Elizabethan Gallery, Wakefield, 1981; Huddersfield City Art Gallery, 1982; Leeds City Art Gallery and Bankside Gallery, 1984; Ginnel Gallery, Manchester, 1987; and Gainsborough's House, Sudbury, 1990. He had a one-man show at Bridge Arts Centre, Widnes, in 1980, others including a series at Christopher Hull Gallery from 1985. Also had a solo exhibition at Glynn Vivian Gallery, Swansea, 1991. His work is in private and public collections, including those of Calderdale, Sunderland, Huddersfield and Bradford. Lewis' work included pictures tending towards abstraction with landscape references, in muted earth colours.

Dennis LEWIS 1928– Painter and advertising director, born in Bristol, where he continued to live. He began studying art during Army service, continuing at West of England College of Art, Bristol, in 1948–52. Showed locally and was for a time president of the Bristol Savages.

Ffiona LEWIS 1964– Versatile artist and architect, whose works, which involved "a lengthy process of engagement with the subject" using a limited range of colours, quietly explored familiar domestic icons in still lifes and landscapes. After spending her formative years in Devon, Lewis gained an honours degree in architecture at The Polytechnic of Central London, 1983–7, obtaining her architecture diploma there, 1988–90. She then studied at Central St Martins School of Art before turning to painting professionally, balancing this with architectural work and scenic painting for the Royal National Theatre and English National Opera. Mixed shows included Fine Art Consultancy, at various venues, from 1993; Kate Chertavian Fine Art, from 1995; and The Wills Lane Gallery, St Ives, 1996. Had solo shows at The Royal National Theatre and The Wren at St James', both 1993, later ones including Gordon Hepworth Fine Art, Newton St Cyres, 1996. Signed work with initials and date.

Garth LEWIS 1945– Painter, designer and teacher, born in Coventry, Warwickshire. He studied at Hornsey College of Art, 1964–7. After studying and teaching for two years at University of New Mexico Lewis studied and taught during 1969–71 at Queens College at the City University of New York. He returned to England to teacher at Hornsey College of Art and Liverpool Polytechnic from 1972, from 1974 at Central School of Art and

Design, then from 1978 at Slade School of Fine Art. Lewis had had solo shows at both New Mexico University and Queens College. Lewis' work was initially figurative, then abstract. In New York he had studied colour theory with the artist Herb Aach and the use of colour as a pictorial language remained a key preoccupation in his work.

Gomer LEWIS 1921– Painter, sculptor and teacher, born in Caerphilly, Glamorgan. He attended Monmouthshire College of Education and began to draw in the Far East during World War II as a prisoner of war. For a decade on his return he concentrated on painting with the war in mind, then studied sculpture at Cardiff College of Art. In 1963 he moved to London, where for a time he taught art at Shoreditch College, although he continued to paint in South Wales. Showed with groups at SWG, WAC, SEA, Towner Art Gallery in Eastbourne, Bourne Gallery in Reigate and elsewhere. One-man shows included 1951 Festival of Britain, Glamorgan and Gwent; and Chapter Arts Centre, Cardiff. CASW holds his drawing Orpheus – Study for Sculpture, and Towner Art Gallery has his work.

Jane LEWIS 1953– Painter, printmaker, draughtsman and teacher, born in London. After a foundation course at Hornsey College of Art, 1970–1, she studied fine art there, 1971–4, then printmaking at Slade School of Fine Art, 1975–7, in the latter year winning the Slade Prize. After working part-time as a lecturer at Watford College of Art, 1977–9, Lewis worked for the BBC as a scenic artist. She then taught at the Slade, 1980–3, was a visitor to Byam Shaw School of Art, 1983, artist-in-residence with Kent Opera, 1985, and also lectured part-time at Harrow College of Art, 1983–6, in the following two years acting as vistor at the Slade and Reading University. From 1986 she was able to concentrate more of her attention on painting, showing internationally in numerous group shows. Was also a busy solo exhibitor from 1986, when she showed at Metropole Arts Centre, Folkestone; Trinity Arts Centre, Tunbridge Wells; Derngate Theatre Gallery, Northampton; and Royal Museum, Canterbury. Other galleries shown at included Gardner Centre, Brighton, 1987, the year when she also exhibited at RWA and Nicholas Treadwell Gallery; Cartwright Hall, Bradford, 1991; and Collins Gallery, Glasgow, 1991–2. Also completed paintings for Bloodaxe Books. University College London, Manchester City Art Galleries and other public collections hold her work, which looked back to Renaissance and Venetian painters and in which themes such as music, the castrated male and female sexuality played a part.

John LEWIS 1933– Painter of landscapes with a visionary quality, born in Abergavenny, Monmouthshire, raised in the Usk Valley, later establishing a studio in the Hertfordshire countryside in Watton at Stone. Lewis studied at Ruskin School of Drawing, Oxford, 1963–4, and Byam Shaw School of Art, 1965–70. In 1986 won a major prize at Watford Museum Open Exhibition, in 1988 was a Drawing For All prizewinner at Gainsborough's House, Sudbury. Group exhibitions included RA Summer Exhibition from 1967; New Art Centre, 1974; Goldmark Gallery, Uppingham, 1990; and Roy Miles Gallery, 1994. Had a solo show at Upper Street Gallery, 1973, later ones including Oriel Contemporary Art, 1995. Watford Museum, CASW and Hertfordshire, Bedfordshire and Leicestershire County Councils hold examples.

Kit LEWIS 1911– Painter, born in Lichfield, Staffordshire. She was married to the painter Morland Lewis, then to Sir J M Richards, who edited *The Architectural Review*, and her full name was Kathleen Margaret Lewis. Studied at Chelsea School of Art and took part in mixed exhibitions including LG, Sally Hunter Fine Art, in the provinces and in America. She had two solo exhibitions at Leicester Galleries, 1953 and 1971. Arts Council holds her oil Amphytrion, of 1951. Lived in London.

Mary Priestley LEWIS 1870– Painter educated at Trinity College, Southport, noted for her still lifes. She studied at Chelmsford School of Art under Charles Baskett, 1911, Bideford School of Art and worked privately with Sylvester Stannard and Wycliffe Egginton shortly before World War II. Exhibited UA, BWS, of which she was a member, RI and in the provinces. Russell-Cotes Art Gallery and Museum, Bournemouth, holds her work. Lived at Southbourne, near Bournemouth.

Michael LEWIS 1925– Painter, draughtsman and teacher, born in Cheltenham, Gloucestershire. He studied at Regent Street Polytechnic School of Art, his teachers including Patrick Millard, and went on to hold a number of teaching posts in the south of England, eventually becoming senior lecturer in fine art at Croydon College of Art. Showed LG, Young Contemporaries, RA, SEA and elsewhere, having one-man shows at Trafford Gallery and Scunthorpe Art Gallery. That gallery holds his work. Lived in Croydon, Surrey.

Peter LEWIS 1939– Sculptor and teacher, born in Cheshire, who attended Carmarthen School of Art, St Martin's School of Art, 1957–9, then Royal College of Art, 1961–4, for a time teaching part-time at St Martin's in the 1970s. Solo shows included Serpentine Gallery, 1977. Charing Cross Hospital holds his work and his Untitled, 1982, an abstract construction in wood, stone and slate, is sited at South Hill Park Arts Centre, Bracknell.

Simon LEWIS 1945– Non-representational painter and sculptor, born in Okehampton, Devon, working in various media. He studied from 1964–8 at Bath Academy of Art, Corsham, then gained his Master of Fine Art degree at University of Reading, 1970–2. Howard Hodgkin, Adrian Heath, Gillian Ayres, Henry Mundy, Terry Frost and Michael Kidner were among Lewis' teachers. After part-time teaching and various commissions, 1972–5, Lewis taught sculpture full-time at Hull, 1975–81, was head of fine art at North-East London Polytechnic, 1981–5, then head of the art and design department of the University of East London. Commissions included Ford of Europe; Watney, Courage and Whitbread Breweries; and the interior designer John Rogers Ltd. Lewis' exhibitions included Museum of Modern Art,

Oxford, from 1971; LG exhibition at The Showroom Gallery, 1984; Bede Gallery, Durham, 1987; and Portobello Open, 1990. Solo shows included University of Reading, 1972; Ferens Art Gallery, Hull, 1981; Jersey Arts Council Gallery, St Helier, 1987; and Shin Gallery, Seoul, South Korea, 1989. Ferens Art Gallery and the Universities of Reading and Cardiff hold examples. Lived in London.

Stanley C LEWIS 1905– Painter, teacher and museum curator, born in Cardiff. He attended Newport College of Art, 1923–6, and the Royal College of Art, 1926–30, teaching at Newport College in the 1930s. After war service he became principal of Carmarthen School of Art for 22 years from 1946, then retired and with his wife founded the Pram and Toy Museum at Beckington, Somerset. He illustrated newspaper articles by his wife Min Lewis and her book *Laugharne and Dylan Thomas*, in 1967, and had one-man shows at various Laugharne Festivals. Showed for many years with Gwent Art Society, SWG and elsewhere and with Michael Ayrton and Enzo Plazzotta shared a three-man show at Bruton Gallery, Somerset. Newport Museum and Art Gallery holds his work.

Stephen LEWIS 1959– Abstract sculptor, working mainly in mild steel but sometimes using found objects, and draughtsman. He was born in Lancashire and graduated from Manchester Polytechnic in 1980. Showed with New Contemporaries at ICA in 1979, the Jan Van Eyck Annual Exhibition in Maastricht, in 1982, and with Francis Graham-Dixon Gallery. He had a solo show at John Holden Gallery, Manchester, in 1990. Lived in London.

Tim LEWIS 1961– Sculptor, painter and draughtsman, born in Kingston upon Thames, Surrey, who studied at Middlesex Polytechnic, 1980–3, and Royal College of Art, 1984–7. Group exhibitions included New Contemporaries, ICA, from 1982; RA Summer Exhibition, 1988; Now for the Future, Hayward Gallery, and Chicago International Art Fair, both 1990; Frankfurt Art Fair, 1994; and British Abstract Art Part 2: Sculpture, Flowers East, 1995. Showed solo with Flowers East from 1989. Arts Council, British Council and TI Group hold examples.

Wyndham LEWIS 1882–1957 Painter, draughtsman, writer and polemicist, born in Amherst, Nova Scotia. Educated at Rugby School, 1897–8, he was at the Slade School of Fine Art, 1899–1901. For about six years from 1902 Lewis travelled extensively on the continent, vital to his early artistic training, which included six months at the Heimann Academy, Munich. Began to exhibit, with Camden Town Group, Roger Fry's Second Post-Impressionist Exhibition, 1912, and with LG, 1913. Worked with Fry's Omega Workshops, then broke away to form Rebel Art Centre and Vorticist Group, 1914, editing its publication *Blast*. During World War I was seconded to Canadian Corps Headquarters at Vimy Ridge as a war artist, an exhibition called Guns occurring at Goupil Gallery, 1919. Following year organised Group X show at Heal's Mansard Gallery. Lewis' first novel, *Tarr*, was published in 1918, and during the inter-war years he mixed his work as an artist with editing art reviews such as *The Tyro* and *The Enemy*, additional fiction like *The Apes of God* and critical works such as *Wyndham Lewis the Artist*. His group of portrait drawings, Thirty Personalities, in 1932, prompted Walter Sickert to term Lewis the "greatest portraitist of this, or any other, time". Lived in Canada and America, 1940–8. Retrospective exhibitions at Redfern Gallery, 1949, and Tate Gallery, 1956, followed by Arts Council Tour. Wyndham Lewis had lost his sight in 1951. Work in many public collections, including Tate Gallery and Imperial War Museum. Died in London.

Jan LE WITT 1907–1991 Painter, designer, typographer and poet, born in Czestochowa, Poland. Early menial jobs gave Le Witt a hatred of the impersonal factory machine, the "Mechanical Molloch" as he put it, and by 1925 he had embarked on extensive travels through Europe. Back in Warsaw he began a successful career as a self-taught designer, in 1933 teaming up with George Him with whom, after arrival in London in 1937, as Lewitt-Him he produced classic wartime posters. The remarkable Festival of Britain clock of 1951 was their work. A meeting with Paul Klee at the Dessau Bauhaus and sight of work by Braque, Picasso and Cézanne in Paris in the early 1930s encouraged Le Witt to paint, and in England he became a friend of Henry Moore and Herbert Read. Had first one-man show at Zwemmer Gallery in 1947, which was the forerunner of an international exhibiting career, involving much travel. Le Witt was against obscurantism in painting; was a believer in the effectiveness of organic form; painting was "the calligraphy of feeling". From the late 1950s he was out of fashion in England and it was left to the Musée Grimaldi in Antibes, the Museum of Modern Art in Warsaw and the Sala Napoleonica in Venice to give him large retrospectives, although his last show was of small oils at the Fitzwilliam Museum, Cambridge, in 1989. Died in Cambridge.

Margaret LEWTHWAITE 1907–1990 Painter and occupational therapist, born in New York. After education at fashionable schools Peggy Lewthwaite went to the École des Beaux-Arts in Paris, after which she returned to New York to become a textile designer. During a visit to England in the 1930s she met Ray Lewthwaite, a Scots Guards officer. Early in World War II she was one of the first Americans to be appointed Member of the British Empire for her therapy work with Allied troops in Cairo, involving needlework and embroidery. In Paris, and much influenced by the work of Augustus John, after the war she began painting seriously, completing many portraits of the famous and running her own atelier. In the 1970s she painted in Hong Kong and China, Communist leaders and landscapes. Continued to work at her husband's home in Broadgate, west Cumbria, after his retirement. Died in London.

Simon LEWTY 1941– Artist and teacher, born in Sutton Coldfield, Warwickshire. He studied at Mid-Warwickshire School of Art and Hornsey School of Art. Between 1964–81 lectured at Mid-Warwickshire School, then worked full-time as an artist. There were many influences on Lewty's work, including

Surrealism, especially André Breton; theories of automatic writing; the use of text in pictures from the Cubists; Paul Klee; William Blake; and especially medieval graffiti. Lewty showed widely in Britain in mixed shows, being a John Moores Exhibition, Liverpool, prizewinner in 1985; he also won a prize at Cleveland 8th International Drawing Biennale in 1987. After a one-man show at Woodstock Gallery in 1968 Lewty exhibited at Ikon Gallery, Birmingham, 1984, then had the first of a series with Anne Berthoud Gallery in 1985, the year he showed at Serpentine Gallery. In 1992 there was a show at Austin, Desmond & Phipps in association with Anne Berthoud. Arts Council, Victoria & Albert Museum and other public collections hold work. Lived in Leamington Spa, Warwickshire.

Liz LEYH 1943– Artist who was born in New York, America, and studied there at Pratt Institute and at Syracuse University. Between 1974–8 she worked in Milton Keynes as a community artist, initially on a bursary from the Arts Council, then being employed by the Development Corporation in the city. Her The Owl and the Pussycat and Tin Man, both in concrete, were sited there in 1977–8. Leyh's concrete black-and-white Cows, made using scrap materials from building sites with the help of local children, gained much press publicity and became recognised as a landmark. A project in Cambridge with Free Form Arts Trust in 1986 won the RIBA award for community design. Leyh lived latterly in Israel.

Thyrza Anne LEYSHON fl. from 1960s– Miniaturist, born and settled in Swansea, south Wales, who studied with the Southall-based miniature painter Ethol Court. She was a member of SM, also exhibiting at RA, RMS, Castle Gallery in Ilkley and Glynn Vivian Art Gallery, Swansea, in Belgium, France and America. Among awards won were a Silver Medal at Paris Salon in 1968, a Gold Medal in 1973.

LIAM: *see* **William CONOR**

Richard LIBBY 1948– Painter and teacher, born in Banstead, Surrey, who in 1965–70 trained at Reigate School of Art and completed mural commissions in central London. Between 1970–80, Libby kept alive with a succession of temporary jobs, including art teaching, but in isolation continued to review his own style and technique. From 1980–96, while continuing to lecture, Libby showed at the Kevin Platt Gallery and Pendragon Gallery, Cornwall; when he took part in a mixed show at Lamont Gallery, 1996, his work received good critical response. Libby was an assiduous innovator in style and subject, concerned with the darker and unusual aspects of life, the allegorical and metaphysical. Independent Art Promotions began selling him internationally in 1997.

Val LIDDALL 1898– Painter and teacher. He studied at St Martin's School of Art and in Paris. Held a number of teaching positions in private schools, from 1935 at Bradfield College. He was partly a sporting artist and exhibited ROI and elsewhere. His full name was Frederick Val Liddall. Lived at Sulhamstead, Berkshire.

John LIDDELL 1924– Relief printmaker, watercolourist and teacher, born in London. He studied at Hornsey College of Art, 1941–6, teachers including Norman Janes, Russell Reeve and John Moody. He taught part-time at Bournemouth and Poole College of Art, living in Bournemouth. Liddell was a member of the Printmakers' Council and SWE, also showing at RA, RWA and in America. Completed a mural in Poole Art Centre. Topographical themes were a key feature of Liddell's work. From 1991 he ran a co-operative workshop, Poole Printmakers.

Peter LIDDELL 1954– Painter and teacher, born in Bolton, Lancashire. He studied at Goldsmiths' College School of Art, 1982–4, then two years later became a visiting teacher there. His mixed shows included Riverside Studios, 1988; in 1989 Ways of Telling, held in Llandudno and Cardiff, and Critics, Space V, Air Gallery; and in 1989–90 John Moores Liverpool Exhibition. Lived in London.

John LIDZEY 1935– Watercolourist (notable for interiors of his Victorian house in Suffolk), designer, teacher and writer. Lidzey studied typographic design at Camberwell School of Arts and Crafts; worked in advertising studio; and was employed by art studios and design groups for 10 years, during which time he became a member of the Society of Industrial Artists, winning awards. In the late-1960s he returned to Camberwell to lecture on typographic and graphic design. He would sketch for an hour in the London streets before teaching, opting to take up painting full-time in the late-1980s. Lidzey won the Daler-Rowney Award at the 1990 RWS Open, in 1992 winning a prize in the Singer & Friedlander/*Sunday Times* Watercolour Competition at the Mall Galleries. His books included *Watercolour Workshop* and *Mix Your Own Watercolours*, in which his fresh, loose style was demonstrated. Showed with The John Russell Gallery, Ipswich.

Pamina LIEBERT-MAHRENHOLZ 1904– Sculptor, painter and draughtsman, born in Berlin, Germany, who studied sculpture at the Vereinigte Staatsschule am Steinplatz there. She was so highly thought of that she merited her own studio. Exhibited work at the Staatliche Akademie der Künste. She won the Prix de Rome but was unable to to take it up because of the political situation. Although by 1939 Liebert-Mahrenholz was an established sculptor in Germany she decided to emigrate to England, where for many years she worked as a china restorer. She began to concentrate on painting and drawing, working independently and at the Camden Institute in London, where she had settled. Showed at RA. Other exhibitions included Woodstock Gallery, 1958; German Embassy, 1978; major retrospective at Camden Arts Centre, 1983; and Ben Uri Art Society, which holds examples, 1988.

Susan LIGHT 1954– Painter, born in Zimbabwe. She studied at Central School of Art and Design, 1972–3; Leeds Polytechnic, 1973–6; and San Francisco State University, 1981–3. From 1983 she showed widely in Britain and abroad in group exhibitions, including Sacramento State Fair, California, 1983, where she won an Hon. Commendation; Camden Arts Centre, 1987; RAG to the USSR, Riverside Artists' touring show of Soviet Union, 1988–9; Hunting Art Prizes at Mall Galleries, 1991; and Contemporary Art Fair, 1992. In 1989 she was artist-in-residence at Moscow Artists' Union House of Creativity. After a solo show at Kingsgate Gallery in 1984 there was one at Tricycle Gallery in 1985, at 39 Steps Gallery, 1987, and Cadogan Gallery, 1992. Exotic locations and a skilled use of light and shadow were features of her pictures.

Liliane LIJN 1939– Sculptor who was concerned with light and motion in her work, born in New York. In 1958 she studied archaeology and art history in Paris, then while living in New York again at the start of the 1960s began experimenting with movement and light, which led to first solo show in Paris at La Librairie Anglaise, in 1963. After living in Greece in the mid-1960s she settled in London in 1966, where she continued to work. Other shows followed in Britain and abroad, including a key one-man at Serpentine Gallery in 1976 and an individual Arts Council touring show in 1977. Later exhibited with Fischer Fine Art. Arts Council holds her work, which was created with a variety of materials. Milton Keynes Development Corporation commissioned her Circle of Light, sited in 1980 in the Shopping Building, Midsummer Arcade.

David LILLEY 1962– Sculptor, born in Kettering, Northamptonshire, a feature of whose work was small constructions in balsa wood. He studied at Sir John Cass School of Art, 1985–6; Central St Martins College of Art & Design, 1986–9; and Royal Academy Schools, 1990–3. He was awarded a Landseer Scholarship in 1991, a Royal Academy Turner Gold Medal for Sculpture, 1992. Group exhibitions included Portobello Open Sculpture Show and Feast, at Mall Galleries, both 1991; Six Sculptors, City of Plymouth Museum, 1992; and Interventionists' Installation, Whitechapel Art Gallery, 1996. Had a solo show at Bernhard Baron Gallery, 1990, later ones including The Cut Gallery, 1996.

Geoffrey Ivan LILLEY 1930– Artist, illustrator and writer of books and articles on art, born in Cambridge, who studied at local Technical College. Lilley was a member of UA, also exhibiting at NS, RSMA and in the provinces. Lived at Golden Cross, Chiddingly, Sussex.

Gordon LILLFORD 1919–1992 Painter in oil, born in Doncaster, Yorkshire, older brother of the artist Ralph Lillford. He served as a constable in Bournemouth's police force, 1949–74, studying intermittently at the local College of Art. Lillford took part in mixed exhibitions with RA, RWA, Wessex Artists and at the Selldown Gallery, Poole, and Salisbury Galleries. Had solo shows with Peppin-Brown Gallery in Whittlesford and Red House Gallery in Christchurch, Dorset, where he lived.

Ralph LILLFORD 1932– Painter, draughtsman and teacher, born in Hexthorpe, Doncaster, Yorkshire. He attended Doncaster School of Art and Royal College of Art, 1954–7, after National Service in the Army in the Suez Canal Zone, 1952–4. Teachers included John Minton, Leonard Rosoman and Carel Weight. Began teaching at Barnes Secondary School, 1957–60, after several appointments lecturing at Richmond College from 1983. He also lectured part-time at Victoria & Albert Museum and Royal College of Art. Dr Lillford drew and painted in Crete, Russia, Egypt, America, Ireland and on the European continent. Showed at RA, RBA, Brunel University, Imperial College, Gloucester College of Art and elsewhere. The Hermitage and Pushkin Museums in Russia, National Army Museum, Victoria & Albert Museum and Imperial War Museum hold examples. In 1992 Lillford had an exhibition of drawings and paintings of work on the Channel Tunnel at Imperial College. Lived at Osterley, Middlesex.

Marjorie LILLY 1891–1980 Painter, printmaker, lecturer and writer, born and lived in London. Studied at Slade School of Fine Art prior to World War I under "Professor (Henry) Tonks the Terrible", as she described him in her memoir *Sickert The Painter and His Circle*, 1971. In this she writes of Sickert's working methods and the group of artists around him, such as Harold Gilman, Charles Ginner and Robert Bevan. Lilly showed at Walker's Galleries, NEAC, RBA, ROI, Redfern Gallery and elsewhere. She was an Arts Council lecturer during World War II. Was included in The Sickert Women and The Sickert Girls in 1974 and Sladey Ladies, 1986, both at Parkin Gallery.

Kim LIM 1936–1997 Abstract sculptor, photographer and printmaker, born in Singapore, married to the sculptor William Turnbull. She studied at St Martin's School of Art, 1954–6, then Slade School of Fine Art, 1956–9. Took part in many group exhibitions in London, Paris and Tokyo, later ones including Journeys West, tour organised by University of Essex, 1995. Had two solo exhibitions at Axiom Gallery in 1966 and 1968. Several others followed at Waddington Galleries; Museum of Modern Art in Oxford; Felicity Samuel, Tate and Round House Galleries. Later ones included Yorkshire Sculpture Park, Bretton Hall, 1995, by which time Kim Lim favoured stone for her simple and serene works. Arts Council, Tate Gallery, Nagaoka Museum of Modern Art in Japan, National Museum of Art in Singapore and many British provincial galleries hold examples.

Hsiao Mei LIN 1971– Painter who described her work as Abstract Expressionist. After Fu Hsin School of Art, Taipei, Taiwan, 1987–90, gained an honours degree in fine art – painting at University of Brighton, 1991–4, with a postgraduate diploma course in painting at Royal Academy Schools, 1994. Awards included Winsor & Newton Young Artist Award, David Murray Travel Award, Crabtree & Evelyn Scholarship and Tony Smith Prize. Her painting After the Storm was included in Chevron UK Ltd's 1997 calendar. Exhibitions included Hunting Art Prizes at the Royal College of Art, Christopher Hull Gallery and finalist,

The Alasdair Gilchrist Fisher Memorial Award 1998, at Cadogan Contemporary.

Richard LIN 1933– Painter and designer in metal and plastic, working in a Minimalist style, born in Formosa, Taiwan. For a time he worked as Lin Show Yu. Studied at Millfield School, Somerset. In the mid-1950s studied architecture for four years at Regent Street Polytechnic. Had first of a series of one-man shows in 1959 at Gimpel Fils, then began to show internationally in the Netherlands, America, Germany and elsewhere, winning several prizes. Was taken up by Marlborough Fine Art. Tate Gallery, Arts Council, Walker Art Gallery in Liverpool and many overseas galleries hold his work. Lived for a time in Wales, including Aberystwyth, Dyfed.

Kenneth LINDLEY 1928–1986 Printmaker and watercolourist, teacher and writer, born in London, who studied at Ealing and Hornsey Schools of Art. Lindley went on to become principal of Herefordshire College of Art until 1986. He was a member of SWE and of the Society of Industrial Artists and Designers/Chartered Society of Designers and a fellow of RE. He had a series of solo shows in London and elsewhere and after his death a retrospective was held in Hereford. Lindley wrote, printed and illustrated work under the imprint of the Pointing Finger Press. He was responsible for many books, some handled by other publishers, including *Coastline*, 1967; *Chapels and Meeting Houses*, 1969; and *Woodblock Engravers*, 1970. Lived in Hereford.

Doris LINDNER 1896–1979 Sculptor in stone, concrete and bronze, specialising in animals. Modelled them for Royal Worcester Porcelain Company. Born at Llanyre, Radnorshire, where she early developed an interest in animals and wild life, Lindner studied under the School of Animal Painting, South Kensington, then at the St Martin's School of Art and the British School, Rome. Exhibitions included RA, Royal Glasgow Institute, RBA and LG. Lived at Broad Campden, Gloucestershire, for some years, but died in Kent.

Moffat LINDNER 1852–1949 Landscape and marine painter in watercolour and oil, whose full name was Peter Moffat Lindner. Born in Birmingham, he studied at Slade School of Fine Art, 1877, under Alphonse Legros, and at Heatherley's School of Fine Art. Was married to the artist Augusta Baird Lindner. He exhibited prolifically at RWS, RA, Ridley Art Club, ROI, NEAC and Fine Art Society and at many other galleries. Work in British galleries, such as Bradford, Hull and Liverpool, as well as in a number overseas. Moffat Lindner's pictures often featured wind and cloud and large expanses of water, having a singularly breezy appearance, as in the examples shown in G S Sandilands' Studio monograph *Artists' Country*. Fond of painting on the continent, as well as in Britain. Lived at St Ives, Cornwall.

Alan LINDSAY 1918– Painter and designer, born in Ludlow, Shropshire. Attended Birmingham College of Arts and Crafts, 1934–6, under Bernard Fleetwood-Walker, then at Royal College of Art, 1938–9 and 1946–8, under Charles Mahoney and Barnett Freedman. His work was illustrated in *Penguin New Writing*. Exhibited RA, Leicester Galleries and NEAC. Lived in London.

Daryl LINDSAY 1889–1976 Landscape painter in oil and watercolour and administrator. Born at Creswick, Victoria, Australia, brother of the artists Norman and Lionel Lindsay. After initial education in Australia he worked as a bank clerk, served in World War I, then attended the Slade School of Fine Art, London, 1919. Returned to Australia where he painted for 20 years. Then became keeper of prints at the National Gallery of Victoria for two years and its director, 1941–56, when he was knighted. Exhibited RA, Cooling Galleries, RWS, Arthur Tooth and Son and widely in Australia. Work in the collection of the Victoria & Albert Museum and many Australian galleries. Lived at Baxter, Victoria, Australia.

Kathleen M LINDSLEY fl. from 1970s– Printmaker, born in Gibraltar, who was educated in Australia, Singapore and England. Studied fine arts at Leeds University and Newcastle Polytechnic, gaining an honours degree in 1976, having begun engraving with Leo Wyatt in 1975. From 1970 travelled extensively in Britain, for some years dividing her time between Edinburgh and Skye. Did illustrations for *Sunday Times* travel guide and a guide to Oxford. Engraved 250 designs for pub signs for Samuel Websters' Brewery through Pentagram Design, which took over two years. Showed at Thumb Gallery; Mill House and Scottish Galleries, Edinburgh; Print Sellers, Plymouth; and Leeds Playhouse.

Vincent LINES 1909–1968 Painter, printmaker and teacher, born in Dulwich in southeast London. Studied at Central School of Arts and Crafts under A S Hartrick and Royal College of Art, where he gained a Travelling Scholarship in 1932. He took part in the Pilgrim Trust's *Recording Britain* project, was principal of Hastings School of Art and wrote several books, including *Mark Fisher and Margaret Fisher Prout*. Exhibited RA, NEAC, RWS, Leicester Galleries and elsewhere. British Council bought his work. Lived in Hastings, Sussex.

John LINFIELD 1930– Painter who was born in Carshalton Beeches, Surrey. He studied at Wimbledon School of Art and Royal College of Art. In 1982 he was elected NEAC, also showing at RA, RP and elsewhere. He had solo shows at Trafford Gallery in the early-1960s, later exhibitions taking place with Halifax House in Oxford and John Noott Twentieth Century, in Broadway. Winsor & Newton Ltd and Spink & Son Ltd were among the commissioners of his work. Lived in Wells, Somerset.

Alan Carr LINFORD 1926– Painter of realistic landscapes in Britain and abroad, born in Doncaster, Yorkshire, where he studied at the local School of Art, 1940. He attended the Royal College of Art, 1943–7, gaining the Prix de Rome which took him to British School in Rome, 1947–9. After an introduction by the artist Edward Halliday, Linford was commissioned to do a lot of work for the royal family. He completed 24 works of the River Thames for HRH Prince Philip which were hung on the Royal Yacht *Britannia*, other pictures hanging in the private apartments in Windsor Castle and in family homes including Baden-Baden and Salem. In the 1980s further commissions stemmed from the cities of Düsseldorf, Cologne and Achen and from the Sultan of Oman. Was elected a member of RE, 1948, RWS in 1953. Had a solo show of Parisian paintings in 1993 at Mistral Galleries. HM The Queen, Shell and ICI also hold his work.

Leong Shao LING: *see* **Kim C LEONG**

Rita M LING 1922– Sculptor and teacher, born in Wolverhampton, where she studied at the College of Art, then from 1946–50 at Royal College of Art, where her teachers included John Skeaping and Frank Dobson. Ling taught at Farnham School of Art, 1950, and at the Royal College of Art, where she was first woman tutor in sculpture, 1955–60. The year before, she worked with Skeaping on carvings for the Dutch Church, Austin Friars, in the City of London. Showed RA and elsewhere. Tate Gallery holds her limestone sculpture Galway Cow. The artist was partly of Irish parentage and was deeply attached to southern Ireland.

Simon LING 1968– Painter born in Bradford, Yorkshire, who studied at Carmarthen College of Art, 1987–8, and Chelsea College of Art, 1988–91. His picture Side A was included in John Moores Liverpool Exhibition, 1991–2. He lived in Neyland, Dyfed.

Simon LINKE 1958– Minimalist artist, born in Benalla, Victoria, Australia. He studied at St Martin's School of Art, graduating with honours, 1977–81, then Royal College of Art, 1983, and gained his master's degree at Goldsmiths' College, 1985–6. Group exhibitions included Tolly Cobbold, Fitzwilliam Museum, Cambridge, 1983; Air Gallery, 1986; Cornerhouse, Manchester, 1988; Tony Shafrazi Gallery, New York, 1989; and at Lisson Gallery, 1990. Had solo show at Gray Art Gallery, New York, 1986; Lisson Gallery and Tony Shafrazi, both 1987; Stichting De Appel, Amsterdam, 1988; and Kohji Ogura Gallery, Nagoya, Japan, 1989.

Barbara LINLEY-ADAMS 1923– Sculptor and teacher, born in London, who signed her work LA, intertwined. She was initially educated in England and Switzerland, then studied at Central School of Arts and Crafts, 1948–50. In 1958 lectured on sculpture at University of Utah, in America. Showed RA, at the Festival of Britain in 1951 and with Arts and Crafts Exhibition Society, of which she was a member, also at Victoria & Albert Museum. Lived in Bath, Somerset.

Judith LINNELL 1948– Watercolourist and teacher who graduated with an honours degree in fine art, 1966–70, from Leeds University, under Quentin Bell and Lawrence Gowing, in 1970–1, studying there for a postgraduate certificate in art education. Taught art and art history in Leeds and Cambridge schools; English to Italian students in Florence and Rome; settled in St Albans, Hertfordshire, from 1982 taught adults watercolour painting at Oaklands College of Further Education; and from 1996 was a tour leader for Simply Travel, watercolour painting in Corsica and Crete. Showed with local groups and widely in the provinces, also with Westminster and Mall Galleries, including RI 1997 Spring Exhibition. Had a first solo exhibition in 1995 at Walter Rothschild Zoological Museum, Tring. Contributed to several books on watercolour and flower painting techniques.

LIN SHOW YU: *see* **Richard LIN**

Robert LINTON 1930– Painter, sculptor and teacher, born in County Donegal, Ireland. He studied at Belfast College of Art and Central School of Arts and Crafts. Linton won a CEMA Travel Scholarship to Italy in 1955, in 1968 a Northern Ireland Arts Council Travel Grant to the Netherlands. He lived in Limavady, County Londonderry, Northern Ireland, and was head of the art department at its Grammar School. Linton was an associate of RUA. He showed in Belfast and Dublin and had a series of solo exhibitions.

Flora LION 1876–1958 Painter in oil. Born and working in London, she studied at the St John's Wood School of Art, Royal Academy Schools and at Académie Julian, Paris. Married to the painter Rudolph Lion, who took her name. She exhibited widely, including RA, ROI, SWA, Fine Art Society and Goupil Gallery, as well as at several venues in France (she was of Anglo-French parentage). Awarded the silver medal of the Société des Artistes Français in 1921 and the gold medal in 1949. The Tate Gallery, British Museum and Victoria & Albert Museum hold her work.

Rudolph Louis LION fl. c.1920–1960 Painter and printmaker who married the painter Flora Lion, whose name he adopted. Studied privately and exhibited RA and in the provinces, signing his work with a monogram. Lived in London.

Gerald Royston LIPMAN 1929– Painter, commercial and pen and ink artist, son of commercial artist James Lipman. Studied at Harrow School of Art with John Platt, 1943–4, then with Robin Guthrie at St Martin's School of Art. He worked for periods as a layout artist at Unilever Ltd and the advertising agency Lintas. Exhibited RA and NEAC. Lived for a time near Westcliff-on-Sea, Essex.

Lippy LIPSHITZ 1903–1980 Versatile artist, mainly a sculptor, and teacher, born Israel-Isaac Lipshitz in Plungian, Lithuania, brother of the painter Ada Lipshitz-Wolpe and father of the printmaker Toni Lipshitz-Caspi. Lipshitz studied at Cape Town Art School, 1922–5; at Michaelis School of Fine Art, 1925–6; at L'Académie del la Grande Chaumière, Paris, under Antoine Bourdelle, 1928–9. He was a founder-member of the New Group and of Art Club of South Africa, where he lived from 1908–78. Among his teaching posts was Michaelis School, where he eventually became associate professor of fine art, 1964–8. Took part in extensive international exhibitions and had many solo shows in

South Africa and London, where he lived, 1947–8. Tate Gallery archive has his Self Portrait, ink on paper, 1948. Retrospectives included South African National Gallery, Cape Town, 1976. It and many other South African galleries hold his work. Died Kiryat Tivon, Israel.

Tadeusz LIPSKI 1905–1987 Artist and designer, a notable figure in the promotion of paper sculpture as an art in Britain from the 1940s pursued by a number of fellow Poles. In 1928 Lipski graduated from Warsaw Academy of Arts, six years later being offered a post as assistant lecturer. Designed posters, advertisements, interior decorations for commercial premises and shop windows using paper sculptures. His sculptures were incomparably cut, with minute attention to detail. During World War II he served in Poland's forces in the West. Lipski's heraldic arms for a wall of the Council for Industrial Design pavilion for the Britain Can Make It exhibition in 1946 so impressed King George VI, who opened it, that he mistook the paper for marble, then asked to see the artist who had fashioned the work. In 1947 Lipski published his key book *Paper Sculpture*. Was granted fellowship of the Society of Industrial Artists. In the 1940s settled in New York, opened his own studio and devoted himself to screen-printing. His wall decorations commissioned by Ford Motor Company and Waldorf Astoria can be seen in New York as well as in Brook Alexander and Pace Galleries and private collections. Lipski was featured in Polish Paper Sculpture at Polish Cultural Institute, 1995.

Walter LISHMAN fl. c.1925–1985 Etcher and wood engraver, born at Wolviston, Stockton-on-Tees, County Durham. After education at Armstrong College, Durham University, Lishman studied art at King Edward VII School of Art, Newcastle upon Tyne, under E M O'R Dickey. Showed work at NS and SGA. Lived in Sunderland, Tyne & Wear.

Frank LISLE 1916–1986 Painter, draughtsman, mixed-media artist and teacher, born in Leeds, Yorkshire, husband of the artist June Lisle. He studied at Leeds College of Art, 1930–6, then Royal College of Art, 1937–40. Cézanne, Victor Pasmore, Fibernacci and Sufism were important influences on his work. Lisle served in the Army in 1940–6, attaining the rank of captain, and suffered the loss of an eye during time in France. He eventually became principal of Jacob Kramer College in Leeds, 1970–7. Several fine portraits and large abstract or semi-abstract constructions were among Lisle's major works. He showed with Yorkshire Artists, RA, NEAC, RBA and RP and was included in The Teaching Image at Leeds City Art Gallery, 1964. Solo shows included Playhouse Gallery, Leeds, 1973, and Hambledon Gallery, Blandford, 1986. Was a member of RBA and president of Leeds Art Club. Died in Shillingstone, Dorset.

Caroline LIST 1964– Painter and teacher, born in Nottingham, who studied at West Nottinghamshire College of Art & Design; Portsmouth Polytechnic; and Chelsea School of Art & Design. Between 1986–91 List held part-time teaching posts at Derby College of Further Education, Heatherley's College of Art and Essendine Adult Education Centre. Between 1992–3 she taught painting and drawing for beginners at Westminster College of Further Education, then in 1993–4 was tutor in new art theory and practice at Chelsea School of Art. She won an East Midlands Starter Grant 1987, and a Herbert Read Scholarship, 1988. Group shows included Apex Gallery, Portsmouth, 1985; The New Generation, Bonhams, 1990; Contemporary Young Painters, Nigel Greenwood Gallery, 1991; and in 1995 she was first prize winner at Royal Over-Seas League Open, having a solo show there in 1996. Department of Health; Contemporary Art Society; and Arthur Andersen & Company hold List's work, which was "concerned with decoding existing layers of visual language, and unravelling these signs and signifiers which are full of hidden metaphors".

Edward D'Arcy LISTER 1911– Painter and printmaker. Born at Horsforth, Yorkshire, he studied at Leeds College of Art, 1928–33, then at the Royal College of Art for four years under Gilbert Spencer. Became a lecturer at Bournemouth and Poole College of Art. Exhibited RA and provincial galleries, his work being held by the Victoria & Albert Museum and Southampton City Art Gallery. The latter's picture Saturday Night is a good example of the artist's ability to depict provincial urban low life. He also painted several murals. Lived in Broadstone, Dorset.

Henrietta LISTER 1895–1959 Painter in oil and watercolour, born at Manor Park, London. Studied at the Byam Shaw and Vicat Cole School of Art, 1912–14, under Rex Vicat Cole and David Murray Smith. Exhibited extensively at RA, WIAC, UA and in the northern provinces. Work held by Darlington Art Gallery and Laing Art Gallery and Museum, Newcastle upon Tyne. Also drew for the magazine *The Dalesman*. Lived near Leyburn, Yorkshire.

Raymond LISTER 1919– Miniaturist, illustrator and writer, born and lived in Cambridge, where he attended the University. Dr Lister was a noted art historian, specialising in British romantic art, a fellow of Wolfson College and a syndic of the Fitzwilliam Museum, Cambridge, 1981–90. Among his many books were *Samuel Palmer and his Etchings*, 1969; *The Letters of Samuel Palmer*, 1975; *George Richmond*, 1981; and *Catalogue Raisonné of the Works of Samuel Palmer*, 1988. Lister studied privately with the miniaturist Albert Cousins. He was elected RMS in 1947 and was its president, 1970–80. He had several solo shows at RBA Galleries and in Cambridge and made many illustrations, often hand-painted, for the Golden Head Press. New York Public Library, Fitzwilliam Museum and Russell-Cotes Art Gallery and Museum, Bournemouth, hold examples of Lister's miniatures which he said were "mainly imaginative landscapes … which endeavour to explain moods and "atmosphere".

Walter Llewellyn LISTER 1876–1951 Watercolourist and printmaker. After Bristol University, went to Westminster School of Art and St Martin's School of Art, 1900–4. Exhibited with St

Ives Society of Artists and the Society of Graver-Printers in Colour, of which he was an associate, RBA and ROI. British Museum holds his work. Lived in Bodmin, Cornwall.

Beatrice Ethel LITHIBY 1889–1966 Painter and designer, especially of church furnishings and stained glass. She studied at the Royal Academy Schools and eventually settled in Wantage, Berkshire, her studio where she lived being in the grounds of St Mary's Convent, an Anglican order; she was a devout Christian. Miss Lithiby began sketching as a young girl and went on to exhibit at RA, RBA until her final illness, Walker's Galleries, SWA, RI and in the provinces. In her later years she concentrated on landscapes in oil and watercolour, in her youth painting portraits, too. Her ecclesiastical work found its way abroad, to South Africa and Japan. Miss Lithiby, known as Bel to her friends (an acronym of her initials), of commanding appearance, served in the Army in both World Wars, reaching senior rank in World War II. Wrote a historical guide to Wantage parish church. The artist was to have become engaged to a fellow Royal Academy Schools student, Frank Skinner, on his return from the Western Front, but he was killed on the Somme in July 1916. She put a memorial notice in the *Daily Telegraph* each year and died on the 50th anniversary of his death.

Maurice LITTEN 1919–1979 Portrait painter in oil, son of the artist Sydney Litten. Maurice Litten was born in Hammersmith and studied art under James Bateman at Goldsmiths' College School of Art, then under Frank Barrington Craig at St Martin's School of Art. Exhibited at RA, NEAC, RBA and RP. Lived in London.

Doris LITTLE 1895–1977 Painter and draughtsman, born in Lee Green, southeast London. After Bromley High School attended Bromley, Beckenham and Goldsmiths' Schools of Art. She served on the land in World War I, in the Red Cross Ambulance Service in World War II, resuming painting in 1950s. Was a member of Free Painters and Sculptors, Paddington and Blackheath Art Societies. Showed with RBA, PS, at Greenwich Theatre Gallery, Leighton House and elsewhere. Had a memorial show at Woodlands Art Gallery, 1981.

George LITTLE 1927– Painter and teacher, born in Swansea where he attended the College of Art, 1944–51. After World War II service was at Ruskin School of Drawing in Oxford, 1951–3. A series of teaching posts followed, including lecturing in fine art at University College of Swansea. Took part in SEA, SWG and WAC group shows and had several solo exhibitions at University College in Swansea. WAC and CASW hold his work. Little was fond of painting landscapes in the Swansea area, especially industrial subjects such as his oil Old Hafod Works, 1989–92, held by the National Library of Wales, Aberystwyth.

Margaret Isabel LITTLE 1901– Artist, notably in mosaic, born in Bedford, by profession a medical practitioner and psychoanalyst. She was educated at Bedford College, St Mary's Hospital and the Institute of Psycho-Analysis and was for a time on the staff of the London Clinic of Psycho-Analysis. Studied art privately during World War II and at Sir John Cass College, 1957–65. Became a member of Free Painters and Sculptors in 1963, also showing at RBA, SWA and elsewhere. Lived at Dunton Green, Sevenoaks, Kent.

Michael LITTLE 1939– Artist in oil, watercolour and acrylic, and teacher, born in Rhayader, Radfordshire, who grew up in the west of Ireland. Moved to London aged 17 and studied at Chelsea School of Art, 1957–61, and Royal Academy Schools, 1961–4. Became a lecturer in drawing and fine art at Northampton School of Art, later Nene College. Little was a member of East Midlands Arts who claimed as influences Edward Hopper, Balthus and Queen Victoria's portrait painter, Josefine Swoboda. Group shows included Basle Art Fair, Switzerland; Kenny Gallery, Galway; Rufford Craft Centre in Nottingham; and in 1993 Little was included in People and Places at Gagliardi Gallery. Had a series of one-man shows at National Theatre from 1981 and one at Commonwealth Institute, 1994. In 1991 Little won the celebrity's prize in the Anglia Television *Moving Art* series, presented by George Melly. Leicestershire County Council Braunstone Underpass murals are by Little, who lived in Northampton.

William LITTLEJOHN 1929– Painter and teacher, born in Arbroath, Angus, where he eventually settled. He studied at Duncan of Jordanstone College of Art, Dundee, 1946–50, and won the RSA Guthrie Award in 1961; the Cargill Award of the Royal Glasgow Institute of the Fine Arts followed in 1966 and 1990. Littlejohn also won the Sir William Gillies Award of RSW in 1980. In 1966 Littlejohn joined the staff of Gray's School of Art, Aberdeen, of which he became head. From 1963 he had a series of solo exhibitions at Scottish Gallery, Edinburgh; others included University of Leeds, 1976; and Loomshop Gallery, Lower Largo, Fife. Littlejohn's work is in the collection of HM The Queen, Scottish National Gallery of Modern Art, Scottish Arts Council and other Scottish galleries. The artist was noted for his still lifes in which the elements were distorted or abstracted in the interests of a felicitous pattern. Was deputy president of RSA.

John LITTLEJOHNS 1874–c.1955 Painter, illustrator, writer and teacher, born at Orchard Hill, near Bideford, Devon, and married to the artist Idalia Blanche Littlejohns. For some time they occupied 2 Orchard Studios, in Brook Green. Littlejohns was a member of the Arts Club, also of RBA, RWA and RI, with which he exhibited until 1954. He was a prolific artist, also exhibiting with Fine Art Society RCamA, Walker's Galleries and elsewhere. His own books included *Art in Schools, Sketching from Nature in Line and Tone* and with Leonard Richmond wrote *The Technique of Watercolour* and *The Art of Painting in Pastel.*

Wilfred E LITTLEWOOD 1899–1977 Painter in oil and restorer, born at New Mill, Huddersfield. He attended the School of Art in Huddersfield, was a part-time teacher, 1927–38, and continued to live in Huddersfield. Showed RA, in the Yorkshire area and at Paris Salon.

William LITTLEWOOD 1893–1985 Illustrator and artist of realistic work, in a variety of media, born in Scarborough, Yorkshire, where he was brought up by an aunt. She was persuaded to let William attend evening classes at the local School of Art, under the tutelage of Albert Strange, the principal, and Richard E Clarke. Two sponsors paid for the lessons, and Littlewood worked during the day for an architect, then a printer. When war broke out, he volunteered for Queen Alexandra's Own Regiment, seeing most of his contemporaries killed. After the war, with Eric Marshal Hardy and David Woolard, Littlewood ran an advertising agency in Bradford. Plagued by a weak heart, Littlewood became so unwell that in 1936 he had to move south to a cottage in rural Berkshire with his wife Kathleen, herself for many years an invalid, who was the focus of much of his output. Littlewood worked as a government cartographer during World War II, then was a freelance artist, especially an illustrator of children's classics, notable for intensely researched work. Although he showed at RA and RBA, Littlewood was reluctant to exhibit his pictures, which were given a retrospective in 1989 at Scarborough Art Gallery. It holds 15 of his works. The artist Katie Sowter was his daughter.

William Bernard LIVERMORE 1890– Painter, draughtsman and printmaker who was by profession an accountant, born in London. He continued to live in the Hornsey area and studied at Hornsey College of Art from 1938 with John Charles Moody and Norman Janes and at Central School of Arts and Crafts, 1944–8, with William Palmer Robins. Exhibited RA, RI, SGA, RBA and elsewhere. Hastings Art Gallery holds his work.

Thomas Alfred LIVERTON 1907–1972 Watercolourist, commercial designer and teacher, born in Barnstaple, Devon. Liverton studied at Bromley and Beckenham Schools of Art, 1924–8, under Percy Hague Jowett and Henry Carr, then for a similar period at the Royal College of Art under Randolph Schwabe and A K Lawrence. Liverton worked on illustrations and designs for textiles and posters. He taught at St Martin's School of Art, Camberwell School of Arts and Crafts, London College of Printing and the Borough Polytechnic, but retired at a comparatively early age to paint full-time. For many years lived near Rye, Sussex, and was well-known for his masterly evocations of seascapes and the Romney Marsh area in a wash technique similar to that of the better known RV Pitchforth. Exhibited RA, RBA, NEAC and in New York. A memorial show was held by Agnew in 1972. London County Council and provincial museums hold his work.

John LIVESEY 1926–1990 Painter, born in London into the well-known theatrical family. He studied at St Martin's School of Art under Ruskin Spear. Showed widely overseas, with many solo exhibitions in Switzerland and several in Netherlands, Germany and America. After his death an exhibition was held at Linda Blackstone Gallery, Pinner, 1990.

Di LIVEY 1946– Artist and teacher, born in Surrey, who created constructions from materials such as canvas stretched or folded over a frame of wood, covered with many layers of acrylic paint. Although apparently abstract, titles were "keys to the ideas behind the works". She studied at Guildford School of Art, 1962–4, Chelsea School of Art, 1964–7, and Royal College of Art, 1967–70. Taught widely, including St Martin's School of Art, Middlesex Polytechnic and Royal College of Art. Showed at ICA, at several John Moores Liverpool Exhibitions at Walker Art Gallery and in Summer Show 2, at Serpentine Gallery, 1981. Lived in London, where Arts Council held her work. Among her solo shows was Project Arts, Dublin, 1978.

George David LIVINGSTON 1920– Primarily a commercial artist in watercolour and black-and-white, he was born in Belfast, where he continued to live. Attended the Belfast Technical College, also the College of Art there, 1936–8. Showed UA, RUA and elsewhere.

Nan LIVINGSTON 1876–1952 Artist whose talents included landscapes in oil, sewing, tapestry and music, younger daughter of a timber merchant from Haddington, East Lothian. In the 1890s her father paid for trips to Paris to study painting and Germany for music, then in 1897 she married and settled in Edinburgh. East Lothian countryside was the main subject of her early pictures, reached by bicycle carrying her paints and a folding stool. Later she worked more in her studio, notably flower paintings, finally exclusively resorting to a palette knife. Exhibited RSA, RSW, Walker Art Gallery in Liverpool and Royal Glasgow Institute of the Fine Arts. Malcolm Innes Gallery, Edinburgh, put on a retrospective in 1995.

Michael LIVINGSTON-BOOTH 1946– Artist in mixed media and teacher, born in Cambridge, who studied at Falmouth College of Art, 1965–9, then Royal College of Art, 1969–71. Teaching included Portsmouth, Chelsea and Wimbledon Schools of Art. Group exhibitions included Festival at the Serpentine, Serpentine Gallery, 1972, and Electric Theatre, at ICA. When his work was shown in 6 Times at the Serpentine in 1976 Livingston-Booth said that his pieces The Attic, 1975, and View of Victoria, 1976, had "grown out of a belief that at any time, historically, an artist should be working as closely as possible to his present time … Photography, film, television, electronic amplification, etc, have usurped certain aspects of all art forms."

Neil LIVINGSTONE 1952– Sculptor, born in Dundee, Angus, who after Dollar Academy studied at Duncan of Jordanstone College of Art in Dundee, 1971–5, as well during holidays on the continent. Had early success when in 1975 he beat 28 other sculptors to win the City of Glasgow sculpture competition with his abstract conception Kentigern which had a soaring, bird-like shape. The Arbroath-based sculptor also did restoration work on Dunkeld Cathedral.

Julie LIVSEY 1951– Sculptor and creator of assemblages; teacher. She was born in Oxfordshire, was for a while an apprentice jockey, then went to Swindon College of Art and Bristol Polytechnic to study sculpture, completing her master's degree at Newcastle University in 1978. As well as teaching in Britain and at School of Art in Lisbon Livsey held an extensive number of residencies, including Preston Hospital, the National Museum of Horse Racing in Newmarket and Lisnave Shipyard, Portugal. Her exhibitions included Buddle Art Gallery, Tyne and Wear, 1981; Carlisle Art Gallery, 1989; and the Newcastle Group show The Northern Lights at DLI Museum & Arts Centre and tour, Durham, 1990. Public sculptures are sited around Britain and in Portugal.

LI Yuan Chia 1929–1994 Conceptual artist, photographer, gallery owner and teacher, born in Guangxi, China, who moved to Taiwan in 1949 following the Chinese Communist revolution. Enrolled at Taipei Normal College, where a classmate was Hsiao Chin, a crucial figure in Li's artistic development. Li was dissatisfied with the conservative curriculum, and Hsiao introduced him to the studio of Li Chun-shan, legendary precursor of the modern movement among Chinese artists. After graduating, Li taught art to elementary schoolchildren and then, with Hsiao's help, moved to Bologna, Italy, where in 1962–5 he worked for the furniture maker Gavina. In 1957 Li had founded the Ton-fan Group, the first abstract movement in Chinese art. Four years later Hsiao recruited Li as co-founder of the international Punto/Point art movement, a turning point in Li's career, from which time he adopted points/circles in his works. After the 3+1 exhibition at Signals Gallery in 1966 in London, in which Li took part, he decided to remain in England, where Marlborough New London Gallery signed him up. He participated in the Lisson Gallery's Cosmic Point, 1967, and Cosmic Multiple, 1968, exhibitions; in the Hyde Park All or Nothing show in 1967, and in Pavilions in the Park, 1968. Photography became important to him, and was incorporated in mixed media works. In 1968, after a visit to Cumbria, Li settled there and bought a farmhouse from the artist Winifred Nicholson, which opened as the LYC Museum and Art Gallery in 1972. It showed international artists and organised workshops for local people, but was forced to close in 1982 because of financial reasons. Latterly Li concentrated on his own art, which was included in the Hayward Gallery 1989–90 touring show The Other Story. Li's design of a circle equally shared into three parts, with the words Time-Life-Space inside them, became the logo for his museum. It is engraved on his tombstone at Lanercost Priory, Brampton. In 1997 Beatrice Gijsen-Hsieh, former curator at the Taiwan Museum of Art, organised a memorial show for Li there, which corrected many misconceptions about his life. Tate Gallery, Hirshhorn Museum in New York and other international collections showed or hold work by Li, who died in Carlisle.

Julie LLEWELLYN 1954– Artist, notably a draughtsman and printmaker, whose work had abstract tendencies, born in Swansea, south Wales. She studied at Barnsley School of Art, 1972–3, Bristol Polytechnic, 1973–6, and Slade School of Fine Art, 1976–81. Her exhibitions included Stowells Trophy at RA, 1976–8; Graffiti Gallery, Three College Show at Royal College of Art and Barnsley Library, all 1978; and in 1980 a solo show at Woodlands Art Gallery. Worked and lived for some years in southeast London.

Owen LLEWELLYN 1927– Painter, draughtsman and bookbinder, born in Watford, Hertfordshire, whose full name was Owen John Llewellyn Williams. Studied at St Martin's School of Art, 1943–7, his teachers including James Bateman and Robin Guthrie, then Camberwell School of Arts and Crafts and the London University Institute of Education, 1948–9. Taught in Nottingham, where he lived, and showed in the Midlands and London.

Charles LLOYD 1930– Painter, originally a printmaker, and teacher, born in Sydney, Australia. He studied at Julian Ashton Art School there with John Passmore; at London College of Printing and Regent Street Polytechnic School of Art; then did postgraduate study at Atelier 17 in Paris with S W Hayter. In 1967 Lloyd gained a Norwegian government stipend at Atelier Nord, Oslo. From 1966–85 Lloyd lectured at Goldsmiths' College School of Art and also was a visiting teacher at Brighton Polytechnic, after which he drew and painted full-time. Group exhibitions included AIA, Printmakers' Council, Brighton Printmakers and RE, of which he was an associate. Also showed at Salon des Réalités Nouvelles, Paris, 1965–6; Richard Demarco Gallery, Edinburgh, 1966; Bradford Biennial, 1968–72; and Marine Artists, Mall Galleries, 1989–90. Solo shows included Reading University, 1967; Belgravia Art Gallery, 1973; and Amalgam in 1983–9. National Maritime Museum, in Greenwich, the Bibliothèque Nationale, in Paris, hold examples. Lived in London.

Elizabeth Jane LLOYD 1928–1995 Artist in oil and watercolour, mural and film-set painter, writer and teacher. Born into an artistic family in London, she attended Chelsea School of Art from 1946, then from 1952 the Royal College of Art, studying under Ruskin Spear and specialising in mural design. When she left in 1952 she married a fellow-student, Jeffrey Hoare and began teaching. Taught in various art schools in Britain and America, including the Central School of Art, St Martin's School of Art, Cambridge School of Art and Yehudi Menuhin School. Also taught from own studio and took painting groups to India. In 1953 had first one-man show in foyer of Royal Festival Hall, followed by others in Barbican Centre, Sally Hunter Fine Art and Austin/Desmond Fine Art, Sunninghill. Regular RA exhibitor who created several murals, including Chelsea Pensioners' Rest Hall, National Farmers Union and Dundee University; painted scenery for the films *Flash Gordon* and *Chariots of Fire*; and wrote a book on *Circles and Gardens*. Nuffield Foundation and Gulbenkian Trust hold her work which commonly features informal still life in strong sunlight and saturated with colour. Lived in London.

James LLOYD 1905–1974 Painter, principally in gouache using a Pointillist style, consisting of tiny dots. Born at Alsager, Cheshire, until 19 Lloyd assisted on the family farm, then joined the police force. He subsequently worked as a gasworks stoker, bus conductor, builder's labourer and lamplighter. In 1950 he and his family moved to Yorkshire; he lived at Skirpenbeck, where he became a cowman. By this time he was painting seriously, producing about a picture a week in his spare time, having been encouraged by the art critic Sir Herbert Read. In 1965 began full-time painting, his first, 1964, show, at the Portal Gallery, having been acclaimed. He had other exhibitions there in 1966, 1968 and 1971. L S Lowry owned Lloyd's work, in 1968 calling him "the most important British naive painter of today". The Tate Gallery, Leeds City Art Gallery and York Art Gallery acquired Lloyd's pictures. Died in the Purey Cust Nursing Home, York.

Katherine Constance LLOYD fl. from early 1920s– Painter in oil of portraits and flowers; artist in pastel. Studied at Slade School of Fine Art under Philip Wilson Steer and Henry Tonks. Exhibited RA, NEAC, SWA, RP and extensively at Cooling Galleries. Lived at Hartley Wintney, Hampshire.

Marilyn LLOYD fl. from mid-1970s– Artist and designer, who studied at Epsom School of Art from 1967 and St Martin's School of Art from 1969, graduating in art and design (fashion) in 1972, with an advanced certificate in painting and film-making, 1974. Group shows included Gimpel Fils. Solo exhibitions included National Theatre; South Hill Park, Bracknell; Open studio in Guildford; and landscape and still life at Century Galleries, Henley-on-Thames, 1997.

Nick LLOYD 1951– Sculptor, draughtsman and teacher who was born in Wolverhampton. He studied at Newcastle University, gaining a Rome Scholarship in Sculpture, 1975. Among his teaching appointments was Leicester Polytechnic. Lloyd was noted as a stone carver, his work abstract in tendency but related to landscape. He took part in many group shows, including Northern Young Contemporaries, Whitworth Art Gallery, Manchester; Sculpture in the Park, Rufford Country Park, Nottinghamshire, 1987; National Garden Festival, Gateshead, 1990, and in same year the Newcastle Group show The Northern Lights at DLI Museum & Arts Centre and tour. Solo shows included Hatton Gallery, Newcastle, 1978, and Bede Gallery, Jarrow, 1988. Arts Council holds his work. Lived in Blackhall Mill, County Durham.

Norman LLOYD 1894–c.1980 Landscape painter, born in Hamilton, New South Wales, Australia. He studied at Sydney Art School with Julian Ashton; was wounded during World War I military service, after which he began painting again during recovery; then exhibited in Sydney with Ashton's group in the mid-1920s. Lloyd moved to study in France and Italy, settling eventually in St John's Wood, London, becoming a member of ROI in 1935, the Royal Society of Arts in 1938 and the Savage Club and London Sketch Club. He showed with ROI, RA and RI and extensively in Paris. In the mid-1960s Lloyd moved to the Indre region of France. Art Gallery of Western Australia, Perth, holds Lloyd's oil on canvas Morning, Middle Harbour, Sydney, of 1925 (some sources give Lloyd's birth year as 1895 or 1897, but the biographical details supplied by the artist to Perth state 1894).

Reginald James LLOYD 1926– Artist in wide variety of media, born in Hereford, although he was associated with the West Country from the age of two when his family moved to Dawlish, Devon. Was largely self-taught, although after Army service he attended part-time classes at Exeter School of Art, from 1956 living in Bideford. Lloyd was a member of RI from 1992, having been awarded its bronze medal in 1989. His work went through various metamorphoses, but a strong Neo-Romantic streak and an interest in such subjects as Silbury, Stonehenge, Avebury and Maiden Castle were key features. Lloyd contributed to many mixed shows in London and the provinces. Had a solo exhibition at Dawlish, 1950, later ones including Burton Art Gallery, Bideford, 1991, and Waterside Art Gallery, Instow, 1993. Lloyd's commissions included a painted rood for the Church of the Assumption, Walkern, 1954; a 70-foot mural for Salesian College, Battersea, 1965; and an iron lectern for St Boniface's Church, Adler Street, 1980, which contains several other commissions by him, including a 1963 stained glass west window. Lloyd also illustrated books by the poet Ted Hughes, including *What is Truth*, 1984, and *The Mermaid's Purse*, 1993. Victoria & Albert Museum, Tate Gallery and British Embassy, Paris, hold examples.

Sarah J LLOYD 1896– Painter, born in Laugharne, Carmarthenshire, an area which was the subject of her pictures and where she always lived. A self-taught artist, she exhibited in Women's Institute shows, on one occasion winning a gold medal, and took part in WAC An Alternative Tradition show, in 1972.

Selwyn LLOYD 1967– Painter, born in Doncaster, Yorkshire, who studied at the local College of Art, 1985–6, then Loughborough College of Art and Design, 1986–9. Among his appearances was John Moores Liverpool Exhibition, 1989–90, with the enigmatic canvas The Irradiation Ceremony. Lived in Newquay, Cornwall.

Ulrica LLOYD 1911–1987 Sculptor, printmaker, illustrator and letterer, born in Longworth House, Berkshire. She was married to Professor Seton Lloyd, in charge of Western Asiatic Archaeology at London University; her maiden name was Fitzwilliams Hyde, which led to her pet name Hydie. She studied at the Royal College of Art and in Paris; worked as an apprentice to a sculptor; then to a stonemason, for although she had taken a diploma in design and engraving sculpture remained her main business. In between accompanying her husband on digs, Ulrica Lloyd worked mainly on religious sculptures, latterly in metal-filled polyester fibreglass. These she described as "Medieval, straightforward and representational". Her work is distributed widely through England, examples being in churches in Slough, Wantage,

Barnstaple and Ashbury, and she also made a memorial to the writer Agatha Christie in Moulsford. Lived for many years at Woolstone, Berkshire.

Vincent LLOYD 1960– Painter, draughtsman and teacher, born in Folkestone, Kent, who studied at Medway College of Design and Camberwell School of Art. He taught at Marlborough College and for the Open College of the Arts four years after winning a David Murray Studentship, RA, 1984. Took part in the South Bank Picture Show, Royal Festival Hall, from 1984; Café Gallery Open, from 1986; Small Works Open, at Square Gallery, 1988; and Royal Over-Seas League Open, 1995, where he showed the amusing acrylic on board Exotic Dancer With Pink Fringe. Had a solo exhibition, Figures in the Landscape, at Mounthouse Gallery, Marlborough, 1988, later ones including Camden Arts Centre, 1989. South East Arts holds his work.

Wyndham LLOYD 1909– Painter, notable for his landscapes which had a strong pattern element. He exhibited widely in group shows: NEAC in 1942, ROI from 1950, NS and RBA from 1952, UA from 1953 and elsewhere. Was a member of Colchester Art Society from 1960. Although Lloyd's exhibiting career was strongly concentrated in the Essex area in later years, his first three were in Sri Lanka. In 1976 he had a one-man at Mercury Theatre Gallery, Colchester; further shows included one there in 1989 and another nearby at Chappel Galleries, 1992.

Audrey LLOYD JONES 1902–1989 Painter and draughtsman born in Cambridge, where she settled. She studied art privately with A C Amerasekara early in World War II for a short period. Contributed to scientific publications and exhibited with PS, RBA, RCamA and in the provinces, showing solo locally. She sometimes hyphenated Lloyd-Jones.

Mary LLOYD JONES 1934– Painter, textile artist and teacher, born in Devil's Bridge, Cardiganshire. She was educated at Cardiff College of Art, then began a career in teaching which included experience in London, at Swansea College of Art and in Dyfed. In the mid-1970s with her husband she began a summer school in the visual arts at Felinfach Art Centre and College of Further Education, Dyfed. She did television work in Welsh. A member of the 56 Group, she also took part in group shows at Howard Roberts Gallery in Cardiff, Royal National Eisteddfod and elsewhere. Solo shows included WAC, Oriel, Cardiff. Lived in Llandysul, Dyfed.

Peter LLOYD-JONES 1956– Painter of interiors and landscapes notable for their subtle use of colour, delicacy and restraint. After a foundation course at West Surrey College of Art and Design at Farnham, Lloyd-Jones gained his diploma from the Ruskin School of Drawing, Oxford, 1977–9, then did a postgraduate diploma at Royal Academy Schools, 1980–3. He showed at RA Summer Exhibitions from 1982, other mixed exhibitions including Agnew Young Contemporaries in 1988, Lee Ann Lester Gallery in Los Angeles, 1990, and Critic's Choice at Beaux Arts Gallery, Bath, 1991. In 1979 Lloyd-Jones gained the David Murray Award for Landscape Painting, and again in 1982; in 1981 he won the Winsor and Newton Award, and in 1983 the Elizabeth Greenshields Foundation Award for Drawing and Painting. From 1983 he had a series of solo shows at Cadogan Contemporary. Lived in Wotton-under-Edge, Gloucestershire.

John Hodgson LOBLEY 1878–1954 Painter, born in Huddersfield, Yorkshire. After Huddersfield Technical College, went to Royal College of Art, Slade School of Fine Art and the Royal Academy Schools, winning several medals. During the latter part of World War I he was an official war artist. Exhibited RA, RI, RBA, ROI, RP, RIBA, Goupil and Leger Galleries (had a solo at Leger 1934) and Ridley Art Club. Imperial War Museum holds his work. Member of the Art Club in Bournemouth, Hampshire, where he lived.

Brad LOCHORE 1960– Painter, born in New Zealand, who did a fine art diploma at Byam Shaw School of Art, 1986–9; studied at Kunst Akademie in Düsseldorf, 1989–90; then gained his master's degree at Goldsmiths' College, 1990–2. After studying at film and television school, for five years Lochore designed and made film-sets. At Young British Artists IV, Saatchi Gallery, 1995, Lochore showed a group of large, highly atmospheric Shadow Paintings in which refined grey lines, the shadows of windows, were displayed on a white ground. The large oil on canvas Ladder Shadow was in the 1995–6 John Moores Liverpool Exhibition. Lived in London.

Anton LOCK 1893–1971 Painter, printmaker and draughtsman specialising in country scenes, especially of working horses. Studied at Westminster School of Art under Walter Sickert, 1910–12, then Bolt Court School, where he specialised in lithography and worked under Walter Bayes, 1912–14. Illustrated several books with outdoor and hunting themes. Exhibited RA, RWS, ROI and Paris Salon, having one-man shows at Leger Galleries. British Museum and British Council bought his work. Lived in London.

Donald LOCKE 1930– Painter, artist in ceramics, sculptor and teacher, born in Stewartville, Guyana. His initial art education was obtained in a working people's art class, a British Council Scholarship taking him to Bath Academy of Art, in 1954, to study painting, sculpture and ceramics. Five years later a Guyana government grant enabled Locke to attend Edinburgh University, where he took a degree in fine art. From 1964–71 he taught at Queen's College, Georgetown, in Guyana, where he gradually began to concentrate on ceramics. In 1971 he set up a studio in London and also taught, in Chester and London. Exhibited widely internationally and eventually moved to teach and work at Arizona State University, living in Phoenix. Locke's work has been said to scan Modernism and his personal history, with strong sexual allusion. He participated in The Other Story show at Hayward Gallery, and touring, 1989–90.

John LOCKETT 1952– Painter, printmaker and teacher who also worked as John Luce Lockett, born and lived in Northampton. He studied at the local School of Art and Byam Shaw School of Drawing. Lockett was a representational artist who also taught life drawing and artistic anatomy and from 1986 with his wife ran a private studio gallery, holding regular spring and Christmas shows. He showed with RP and was a council member of the Northampton Town and County Art Society. Solo shows included Four Seasons Gallery, Northampton, 1977; Hurlingham Gallery, 1989; and The City Gallery, Leicester, 1992. Weston Hall, Shropshire; Franciscan Novitiate House, Manchester; and St Crispin's Hospital, Northampton, hold examples.

Eva LOCKEY 1952– Abstract sculptor who studied on fine art diploma course at North-East London Polytechnic, 1973–6, then did postgraduate work at St Martin's School of Art, 1976–7. Exhibitions included Young Contemporaries at RA, 1977; Cannizaro Park Sculpture Show, from 1979; Whitechapel Art Gallery, 1981; and in same year Painters + Sculptors from the Greenwich Studios at Woodlands Art Gallery.

David LOCKHART 1922– Painter, teacher and muralist, born in Leven, Fife. He studied at Edinburgh College of Art, 1940–6, with Joan Hassall, John Maxwell and William Gillies, finally for postgraduate work. He was principal teacher of art at Ballingry Junior High School, 1959–84. Lockhart was a member of SSA, 1959–79, and of RSW from 1969. He painted a large mural, Many Mansions, in Benarty Primary School, Lochore. Showed at Douglas & Foulis, Edinburgh, in two-man exhibition in 1963; Fife Group, at English Speaking Union, Edinburgh; RSA, and elsewhere. Solo exhibitions included Loomshop Gallery, Lower Largo, 1989, and Small Gallery, Anstruther, 1991. West Riding of Yorkshire and Dunbartonshire Education Authorities and Scottish Arts Council hold his work. Lived in Hillend, Fife.

Gavin LOCKHEART 1961– Painter, printmaker and teacher, notable for his colourful and imaginative depiction of landscape, born in Staffordshire. Group exhibitions included St Martin's School of Art Degree Show, 1983; Physical Chemistry, Queen Elizabeth Hall, 1985; Five London Painters, Eilat Gordin Gallery, Hollywood, California, 1986; Wild, Ikon Gallery, Birmingham, and Harris Museum & Art Gallery Preston, 1993; and Beaux Arts, 1996. In 1987, Lockheart had solo shows at Carlile Gallery in London and in Italy at Studio d'Arte Lanza, Verbania, and he shared an exhibition with Peter Randall-Page at Houldsworth Fine Art, 1997. The year before, Lockheart had gained an Arts Foundation/Barclays Private Banking Fellowship in Painting. From 1990–4, he was a part-time lecturer in painting and printmaking at Stourbridge College of Art.

Dorothy LOCKWOOD fl. from 1930s– Watercolourist, born and lived in Birmingham, where she studied at Birmingham College of Arts and Crafts, Moseley Street, under Bernard Fleetwood-Walker and Harold Smith. She was elected RBSA in 1959 and RWS in 1974, also showing elsewhere.

Kenneth LOCKWOOD 1920– Designer, illustrator and teacher, born in Huddersfield, Yorkshire. He studied at Leeds College of Art, 1946–9, then Huddersfield School of Art, 1949. As well as doing book-jacket work, illustrations for magazines and commercial designs, Lockwood exhibited in London, the English provinces and in Guernsey, Channel Islands, where he settled in St Peter Port. Had a strong interest in art education.

Diana LODGE 1906–1998 Painter, born Violet Uppington in Tredegar, south Wales, her father a headmaster. After studying English at Bristol University, she taught in Leeds for two years, then moved to London, changing her name to Diana. Worked as a Tiller Girl; modelled for Eric Gill and Duncan Grant; in 1932 married literary scholar and poet Oliver Lodge, eldest son of the physicist and psychical researcher Sir Oliver Lodge; and, having lived for periods in France, Canada and America, and having had three children, in 1946 settled in Gloucestershire. This home became a gathering point for artists and writers, and there she began painting seriously. After her husband's death in 1955 she wintered for some years in Puerto Rico, oil paintings of its landscape selling well; had exhibitions in Washington, America, also in London. Black Mountains watercolours and the interior of her home were other notable subjects. Van Gogh, Samuel Palmer and Odilon Redon were cited as influences on work that had a strong emotional and spiritual content. Prayer and mysticism were important to Lodge, who converted from Anglicanism to Roman Catholicism and who lived finally, still painting, at a retreat centre near Stroud.

George LODGE 1860–1954 Artist, writer and traveller, noted for his atmospheric and meticulous depictions of birds. He was born in Horncastle, Lincolnshire. At Lincoln School of Art Lodge gained 14 prizes for drawing, later becoming an expert wood engraver. As a young man Lodge travelled to Ceylon, Japan, the West Indies and elsewhere. A great sportsman, he enjoyed annual trips to Scotland and the salmon rivers of Norway, gathering material for his work on birds of prey. Lodge himself flew falcons. He had stuffed his first bird, an owl, at the age of 12 and said that it was impossible to draw a bird's appearance correctly without an intimate knowledge of its inside. Eventually Lodge built the Hawk House at Camberley, Surrey, where he settled. His plates for Beebe's *A Monograph of the Pheasants* and his several hundred illustrations for Bannerman's 12 volumes of *The Birds of the British Isles* are classics. Aged 85 Lodge wrote his only book: *Memories of an Artist Naturalist*. The Tryon Gallery showed Lodge's work.

Jean LODGE 1941– Painter, printmaker and teacher, born in Dayton, Ohio, America, who graduated from Miami University of Ohio in 1963, then moved to Europe; in 1964 studying at the Kokoschka School, Salzburg; in 1965 at Ruskin School of Fine Art, Oxford; worked with S W Hayter at Atelier 17, Paris, 1965–9; and helped set up a printmaking workshop in Paris with A Caporaso, 1969. From 1978–96, Lodge was head of printmaking at the Ruskin School, then became a full-time artist and freelance teacher. She was a member of the Printmakers' Council, RE, and in France of Le Trait and Xylon. Mixed exhibitions included Oxford Art Society. Had many solo shows, later ones including Praxis International Art Gallery, University of South Florida, Sarasota, 1994; and in 1996 Galerie Schweitzer, Luxembourg, and Broughton House Gallery, Cambridge. Took part in many international print biennales, latterly including Taipei, Taiwan, from 1987, and Kochi International, Japan, 1993. Work held by many public collections internationally, including Ashmolean Museum in Oxford; Bibliothèque Nationale, Paris; Bibliothèque Royale, Bruxelles; and Museo della Xilografia, Venice. Lodge was a fellow of New College, Oxford, living in the city at Headington, and in Paris, France.

Hermione Thornton LOFTHOUSE fl. from 1940s– Painter and teacher who studied at Heatherley's School of Fine Art under Iain Macnab, 1946–50, and at Académie Julian and L'Académie de la Grande Chaumière, both in Paris, gaining a history of art certificate from the Courtauld Institute. She went on to teach at Moor Park College, 1968–82, and at adult education classes. Lofthouse was a member of NS, UA and Ridley Art Society. Showed also at RBA, ROI, at Walker Art Gallery in Liverpool and elsewhere and had many solo exhibitions. Surrey University holds her work. Lived in Farnham, Surrey.

Andrew LOGAN 1945– Versatile and enterprising designer and sculptor, born in Witney, Oxfordshire, who graduated with a diploma in architecture from Oxford School of Architecture, 1964–70. He "experienced Flower Power" in America in 1967. Did a hologram course at Goldsmiths' College, 1982. Logan was noted for projects carried out with a showbiz flair, who to some dressed weirdly, producing camp sculptures, costumes and jewellery out of mirror and lurid plastic, but who was undeniably dedicated and persistent. He said that his aim was "to bring joy and happiness to the world". Logan was most famous as the inventor and impresario of *The Alternative Miss World*, which began in 1972, the series continuing periodically at various venues. The first showing of the film *The Alternative Miss World* was held at the Odeon, Leicester Square, 1979, followed by the Cannes Film Festival, 1980. Logan had his first solo show at New Art Centre, 1973. Other events in his multi-faceted career included *Egypt Revisited*, sound and light spectacular in a tent on Clapham Common, 1978; decorations for Zandra Rhodes' fashion show, 1980; Snow Sculpture World Championships, Finland, 1982; piece in Holographic Show, York Arts Festival, 1984; debut as a theatre designer, *Wolfy*, Ballet Rambert, Big Top, Battersea, 1987; retrospective, Museum of Modern Art, Oxford, 1991, with tour; and Jewels Fantasy Exhibition, Victoria & Albert Exhibition, 1992. In 1991 the Andrew Logan Museum of Sculpture opened at Berriew, Powys. In 1993 the National Portrait Gallery bought two portraits. Was based at The Glasshouse, Melier Place, where he also held exhibitions.

Gladys LOGAN: *see* **Gladys BARRON**

Johanna LOGAN 1972– Painter of portraits, figures and still lifes, often predominantly in white against sombre backgrounds and with a still, concentrated quality. Born in Glasgow, Logan gained a fine art honours degree at the city's School of Art, 1990–4, awards including RSA Sir Robin Philipson Memorial Award, 1994. Group shows included Compass Gallery, Glasgow, New Generation Show, 1994; Edinburgh Gallery, Edinburgh, 1995; and Glasgow Art Fair, 1997. Had a solo show at Art Bank, Glasgow, 1996, then Offer Waterman & Co Fine Art, 1998. Murray Johnstone, Glasgow, holds Logan's work.

Peter LOGAN 1943– Sculptor and teacher, born in Oxfordshire. He studied at Camberwell School of Arts and Crafts and Slade School of Fine Art and taught at Wimbledon School of Art, Reading University and Goldsmiths' College. Logan's sculptures were shown at Milton Keynes, Buckinghamshire, in 1986 at the Energy World exhibition, then Guardian Royal Exchange commissioned his Javelin I, which was erected in 1988 at Wolverton Mill. Arts Council holds his O for a Ballerina, of 1979, in aluminium with electric motors and computer control. Lived and worked in London.

Renos LOIZOU 1948– Painter, notable for his highly structured and colourful landscapes, born at Paleometochon, near Nicosia, Cyprus, the family moving to London in 1955, later to Cambridge. Loizou studied at Cambridge School of Art from 1963. Took part in many mixed shows, including ICA, 1974; RA from 1980; Chicago International Art Exposition, 1987; and Richmond Gallery, 1992. After a solo show at Fitzwilliam College, Cambridge, 1969, Loizou's others included series at Christopher Hull Gallery from 1982. Kettle's Yard, in Cambridge, holds his work.

John LOKER 1938– Painter, photographer and designer, born in Leeds. He studied design at Bradford College of Art and Design, 1954–8, then painting at Royal College of Art, 1960–3, gaining an Abbey Minor Travelling Scholarship in the latter year. After holding a solo studio show in 1969 Loker had a one-man at Angela Flowers Gallery and ICA the following year. The 1970s saw him showing at John Moores Exhibition in Liverpool on several occasions, another key appearance being in New British Prints in New York and touring in 1974, yet another Arts Council Collection 1975–6 at Hayward Gallery in 1976. After that Loker exhibited abroad in France, Netherlands and Norway. He continued to show with Angela Flowers and in 1981 his Ten Years' Work Exhibition was at Arnolfini Gallery, Bristol and tour. Loker's work was both abstract and abstract with environmental references. Lived in London.

LOM: *see* **Alfred LOMNITZ**

Josephine LOM fl. from c.1945– Painter, sculptor, designer, illustrator and teacher, born in Poland, also known by her married name of Azdia Josephine Lomnicka. She was educated in Poznan, studying art partly in Kassel and in England at Liverpool School of Art in 1946. She went on to teach at Digby Stuart College of Education in southwest London and wrote the book *Step-by-Step Collage*. Took part in group shows at Commonwealth Institute and in the provinces. Lived in London.

Jean LOMAS 1926– Painter, born in Norton, near Malton, Yorkshire. Brought up in the Liverpool area she was educated at Huyton College. Studied at Liverpool College of Art, then Royal Academy Schools. Belonged to Sandon Studios Society Club. Showed at RA, AEB tours and NEAC. Lived in Lymington, Hampshire.

Tom LOMAX 1945– Sculptor and painter, born in Warrington, Lancashire, who studied at Central School of Art and Design, 1971–4, then did postgraduate painting at Slade School of Fine Art, 1974. Commissions included a fountain for Birmingham Centenary Square and work for Urban Learning Foundation. Later shows included Kettle's Yard in Cambridge, Camden Arts Centre and Pomeroy Purdy, 1987, Tokyo International Art Fair, 1992, and Artist of the Day at Angela Flowers Gallery, 1994, chosen by Eileen Cooper.

Azdia Josephine LOMNICKA: *see* **Josephine LOM**

Alfred LOMNITZ 1892–1953 Painter, printmaker, draughtsman and writer, born in Eschwege, Germany, whose early years are vague. He graduated from the Weimar Art School, studied with Henri Van de Velde and ran the Litz design studios in Berlin in the 1920s and 1930s. In 1933, being Jewish in Nazi Germany, he decided to move to England, his family following. Lived in Aston Rowant, Oxfordshire. Worked as a commercial artist for London stores, such as Simpson and Swears and Wells. He was interned early in World War II, in 1941 publishing his experiences of this as *Never Mind Mr Lom* (he signed some work LOM, a name used by his friends). Showed at Ryman's in Oxford, 1934; had a memorial show at Ben Uri in 1954; and was given a solo show at John Denham Gallery in 1986. Lomnitz latterly suffered from Parkinson's Disease and his work became looser and more mystical. At times his pictures showed the influence of Paul Klee, the Expressionists and other Post-Impressionists. British Museum, Ben Uri and Museum of Modern Art in New York hold examples. Lomnitz lived finally in London.

John LONG 1964– Painter and draughtsman, born in Portadown, Northern Ireland, who did a foundation course at Ulster Polytechnic, Belfast, 1983–4, then graduated in painting from the Slade School of Fine Art, 1984–8; the measured style of that school and such artists as William Coldstream and Euan Uglow was present in Long's work. Awards included Elizabeth Greenshields, Canada, 1989; Taylor De Vere, Dublin, and Arts Council of Northern Ireland, both 1993; and Arts Council again in 1994. Long was artist-in-residence at Byam Shaw School of Art, 1990–1. Group shows included Spring Contemporary, Albany Gallery, 1990; RHA from 1992 (he was elected an associate, 1995); and 20th Century British Art Fair, Royal College of Art, 1996. Solo shows included Theo Waddington Fine Art, 1998. Haverty Trust Collection holds the work of Long, who lived in Dublin, Ireland.

John Kenneth LONG 1924– Painter, sculptor and teacher, born in Liverpool. Studied at Manchester School of Art, his teachers including Ian Grant. Showed RA, ROI, RBA, NEAC and in the provinces. Lived in Darton, Yorkshire.

Mike LONG 1951– Sculptor and teacher with a special interest in figures in movement. He was born in Chatham, Kent. After attending King's School in Bruton, Long studied sculpture at Goldsmiths' College School of Art, 1971–4. From 1978 he was head of the art department at King Edward VI School, Southampton. Long began observing dancers while still at Goldsmiths', an interest fostered later at Ballet Rambert and the London Contemporary Dance Group. He was a keen sportsman, which reflected another aspect of his output. From 1984 Long held regular summer shows at New London Theatre and in 1989 had a solo exhibition at Century Gallery. The Morris Singer Foundry cast his work.

Richard LONG 1945– Sculptor, born in Bristol, where he continued to live. He studied at the local School of Art, 1962–6, then at St Martin's School of Art, 1966–8. Long was not a conventional sculptor making gallery objects but adopted landscape as his material. He went on a series of walks, including Ireland, the Himalayas and the Rio Grande, and recovered his impressions of them and identification with an area in photographs, maps and words. His Gobi Desert Circle was a photograph of a circle of stones made in Mongolia in 1966. He sometimes brought material from a walk into the gallery, as in his Delabole Bristol Slate Circle, 1997, commissioned by Bristol City Art Gallery. Other works included River Avon Mud Drawing, of which the artist said, "It was made by mud and water and gravity. Part of the intellectual excitement is that it is a drawing but not actually made by my hand." Long had a one-man show at Whitechapel Art Gallery in 1971, the year he appeared in Guggenheim International Exhibition at Guggenheim Museum, New York, and the following year had a show at Museum of Modern Art there. Later shows included his representing Britain at Venice Biennale in 1976 and a series at Anthony d'Offay Gallery from 1979. Considered by many to be the outstanding British artist of his generation, Long's work is not easily interpreted. He was Turner Prize winner in 1989. Tate Gallery, Arts Council and Bristol City Art Gallery hold his work.

Sheila LONG 1925– Painter, designer and teacher, born in Leeds, Yorkshire, where she attended the College of Art. Held a number of art teaching posts in Leeds and Hertfordshire, before becoming a full-time artist in the early 1960s. Lived for a time in Feltwell, Norfolk.

Charles LONGBOTHAM 1917– Painter in oil and watercolour, father of the artist Claire Dalby, born in Carlton,

Nottinghamshire. Longbotham was self-taught. From 1934–45 he was an apprentice, a ship's officer in the Merchant Navy then in Naval Reserve during the war. From 1946–69 he was a model-maker and dioramist, specialising in landscape models, also painting, from 1969 being a full-time painter. Longbotham was a member of RWS from the same year, also being a member of Art Workers' Guild. His subjects were landscapes, industrial and pastoral, and marine paintings. He had showed watercolours at RSA in 1942 and had his first solo exhibition at Federation of British Artists galleries in 1965, after which he had many more one-man and group showings in London and the provinces. Victoria & Albert Museum, Imperial War Museum, Fitzwilliam Museum in Cambridge and other public collections hold examples. Lived for many years in Cambridge.

Julian LONGCAKE 1964– Painter, notably in watercolour, who studied at Cumbria College of Art and Design and Falmouth School of Art. In 1988 he was commissioned by the National Trust's Foundation for Art to paint at Stourhead, then at Claremont, 1989. He showed in The Secret Garden at Colegate Gallery, Cockermouth, and in the same year, 1989, at Oriel Gallery, Welshpool. In the following year Longcake participated in Agnew's show The Broad Horizon.

Stanislaus Soutten LONGLEY 1894–1966 Watercolour painter, born at Aylesbury, Buckinghamshire. Studied at Regent Street Polytechnic School of Art under Harry Watson and George Gaskell. During World War II served as a camouflage officer. Exhibited Fine Art Society and RBA especially, RA, RI and Paris Salon. He took part in the Pilgrim Trust *Recording Britain* project and his work was reproduced by Medici Society and Raphael Tuck. Lived in Bournemouth, Hampshire.

Tony LONGSON 1948– Artist who employed computers, born in Stockport, Cheshire, who studied at Reading University, 1967–71, then worked in Holland on a Royal Netherlands Government Scholarship, 1971–2. He began to use computers to organise visual ideas in 1973, from 1974–7 doing research using computer facilities at Hatfield Polytechnic, backed by Arts Council funds. Exhibitions included Space, at Abbot Hall Art Gallery, 1976; The Constructive Context, Arts Council tour, 1978; and Non-Standard Constructions, a three-man show at Museum of Modern Art, Oxford/Gardner Centre Gallery, Brighton, in 1980. Research Machines of Oxford made equipment available for Longson's works there. Arts Council, Reading University and several Dutch collections acquired examples.

James LONGUEVILLE 1942– Artist in oil, pastel and watercolour, born near Chester; he settled in the county at Malpas. After a career in journalism Longueville began to paint professionally in 1972. He said that he "learned much from the fine North Country artist Angus Rands". Longueville was influenced by Boudin, Constable, Wilson, Steer and Seago, was "an admirer of the East Anglian School" and spent many years painting in Norfolk. He was made a member of PS in 1983 and RBSA in 1989, also showing with ROI, RI and elsewhere. Later solo shows included Ringstead Gallery, Ringstead, Hunstanton, 1990; Omell Gallery, Windsor, and at Sarah Samuels, Chester, both 1991.

Bernard LORD 1940– Painter, draughtsman and teacher, born in Cardiff. He studied at Coleg Harlech, 1961–2, Newport College of Art and Design in 1963–7, then having won a Tyler Scholarship was at Tyler School of Art, Rome, 1967–8. Won a Temple University Fellowship which took him as a university fellow to Tyler School of Art, Temple University, Philadelphia, in 1968–9. In 1970 Lord began teaching, including periods in Newport, Cardiff and at Luton School of Art. Showed at Philadelphia Artists' Annual Exhibition in 1969, winning first prize, also with SWG and at Royal National Eisteddfod. Had several one-man shows, including Caerleon Community Centre.

Elyse LORD fl. from 1915–1971 Watercolourist, sometimes working on silk, and colourprint artist. She was elected RI, 1922, and was also a member of the Society of Graver-Printers in Colour. Favoured exotic and Far Eastern figure subjects, treated in delicate and imaginative colours. Her work was published by the London dealer Alexander Reid & Lefevre. Showed at that gallery, RA, RI, RSA, Fine Art Society and Paris Salon, where she gained a silver medal for colour prints. In 1990 Cyril Gerber Fine Art held an exhibition of her work. Lived in Bexley, Kent.

Harry LORD 1915–1966 Painter in oil and watercolour, full name Henry Bennett Lord, born in Seaham, County Durham. His family fled the Depression, so he was educated in America and Canada, returning in time to serve in World War II. Became a civil servant, studying painting in his spare time. He also wrote on art and was a co-director of the Univision Gallery, in Newcastle upon Tyne, where he lived. It showed modern international painters, such as Joan Miró and Sam Francis, and Lord had a solo exhibition there. Also exhibited at RI, ROI, RBA, Redfern Gallery, Newcastle Society of Artists and the local West End Art Club, of which he was secretary. Lord was increasingly an abstract artist, an exponent of Tachism.

Mary LORD 1931– Painter and teacher, born in Birstall, Yorkshire. In 1943 she won a late-developer's scholarship to Batley Grammar School. From 1948–50 attended Dewsbury and Batley College of Art, where Robert Lee was an influential teacher, then going to Leeds College of Art, 1950–3, under Richard Macdonald and Tommy Watt. Worked in Batley Library, 1953–5, and as a museum assistant at Bankfield Museum, Halifax, continuing to paint in her spare time, 1955–60. For about the next 30 years Mary Lord taught at venues such as Swarthmore Adult Education Centre, Leeds College of Art and Leeds College of Technology, ceasing in 1991 so as to concentrate on her own painting. Her first important show was at Batley Art Gallery in 1957. Also showed widely in mixed shows such as West Riding Artists, Northern Young Artists, Goosewell Gallery in Menston and in Four Women Artists, at Wakefield City Art Gallery, in 1961. In 1985 had solo show of importance at Bankfield Museum;

in 1991 was included in Images of the Yorkshire Landscape, organised by Sheeran Lock, which toured to Leeds, Bradford and York; and in 1992 had first exhibition in London at Leighton House. The *Yorkshire Post* art critic WT Oliver said of Lord that "there is no more sensitive painter of the Northern landscape." Her work is held by Leeds City Art Gallery, Bradford Art Galleries and Museums, Ferens Art Gallery in Hull and other public collections. Lived in Leeds.

Sarah LORD 1964– Painter, born in Folkestone, Kent, who studied at Canterbury College of Art and Cheltenham School of Art. Group shows included Young Painters South-East, from 1987; RA Summer Exhibition, from 1990; Interiors, Towner Art Gallery, Eastbourne, 1993; and Royal Over-Seas League Open, 1994. Had a solo show, In Haven, University of Kent, Canterbury, 1989, later ones including Stormont Studio, Rye, 1993. South East Arts and Kent County Council Arts & Libraries hold examples.

Amanda LORENS 1969– Sculptor, born in Gibraltar, who attended Cornwall College, 1985–7, then Winchester School of Art, 1987–90, gaining an honours degree. As well as sculpture, she specialised in ceramics and printmaking. She was joint first prize winner at Southampton City Art Gallery's Not Just Another Statue Competition. Mixed shows included Tower Arts Centre, Winchester, 1989; Women Artists from the South-West, Spacex Gallery, Exeter, 1991; Newlyn Site-Specifics, Newlyn, 1993; and The Edge of Beyond, Belgrave Gallery, 1995, where she showed brightly coloured abstract sculptures. Solo shows included Wolf at the Door, Penzance, 1993, and Rainy Day Gallery, Penzance, 1994. Was based in Cornwall.

Hew LORIMER 1907–1993 Sculptor and administrator, born in Edinburgh, son of Sir Robert Lorimer, the architect. Although he began to study at Oxford University in 1928, Lorimer moved to Edinburgh College of Art to study architecture and sculpture under Alexander Carrick, who was keen on direct stone carving. An Andrew Grant Travelling Scholarship took Lorimer to France and Italy in the early 1930s, then a Fellowship enabled him to work with Eric Gill. Gill's influence and that of Romanesque French church carving profoundly affected Lorimer's output, as did Gill's belief that the artist collaborated with God in the creative effort. During World War II Lorimer helped the British Council put on fine exhibitions at the National Gallery of Scotland. After the war with Maxwell Allen he worked on major monumental sculptures which included figures on the front of the National Library of Scotland. An important show of his work was held at Talbot Rice Art Centre, 1988. Lived finally at Pittenweem, Fife.

Albert LOUDEN 1943– Painter and draughtsman, notably in pastel, born in Blackpool into a working-class family during evacuation from London's East End, to which it returned in 1945. Although he toyed over the years with higher mathematics and left-wing politics, from about 1962 Louden decided to concentrate on art while working as a lorry driver. To give more time to painting, from 1979–84 Louden worked part-time, from 1985 painting full-time. Louden was discovered in 1979 by Victor Musgrave, co-organiser of the Outsiders show at Hayward Gallery. In 1985 he had a sell-out exhibition at Serpentine Gallery, in 1986 having a solo show in New York at Rosa Esman Gallery. Later shows included Boundary Gallery, 1990. Louden's pictures comprised heavily distorted figures in urban settings and situations observed with wit and using a unique palette. Arts Council and Collection L'Art Brut, Lausanne, hold his work.

Stanley LOUNDS 1906–1980 Painter and artist in black-and-white and sepia. He was the son of Arthur Lounds, coachbuilder, and was born in Grantham, Lincolnshire. As well as still life, portrait and landscape work he was noted for his architectural pictures, done in Britain and abroad. Signed work S L. Lounds trained for the Anglican priesthood at the former St Paul's College, Burgh, being ordained in Lincoln in 1929. As well as serving for various periods in Lincolnshire and briefly as a Royal Air Force chaplain Lounds was for a time in South Africa. Soon after World War II he joined the Community of the Resurrection in Mirfield, Yorkshire, where he was known as Samuel. Most of his time was then spent there. He continued to paint, but suffered from constant ill-health. Exhibited with Huddersfield and Cardiff Art Societies and illustrated religious publications.

Nicky LOUTIT 1943– Painter, born in London, her mother being the artist Janetta Parladé. From 1961–4 studied at Chelsea School of Art under Lawrence Gowing, then until 1967 at Slade School of Fine Art under William Coldstream. Travelled extensively, returning to England in 1970 where she had a show at Bramante Gallery. In 1977 she and her husband left to join a religious community in India, staying with it through a period in America, but returned disillusioned in 1983, moving to Norfolk, where she settled in Binham, married to the writer Jonathan Gathorne-Hardy. As well as showing at CCA Galleries from 1988 and Michael Parkin, 1989, in mixed shows, from 1989 exhibited solo with Stephen Bartley Gallery, from 1993 showing one-man at Sally Hunter Fine Art. Loutit was an artist keen on depicting people, with a real feeling for paint.

Roelof LOUW 1935– Sculptor, painter, installations artist and teacher, born in Cape Town, South Africa. He studied at the university there, emigrated to England in 1961 and adopted British citizenship, 1967. Worked in an architectural office in London and studied under Anthony Caro at St Martin's School of Art, 1961–5. He taught at St Martin's, Maidstone School of Art and Royal College of Art between 1967–71; settled in New York, 1973; was a visiting lecturer, Victoria University, British Columbia, 1976–7, and visiting artist, Rhode Island School of Design, Providence, 1977–8. Louw showed at Young Contemporaries from 1964; Kasmin Gallery, 1967; Stockwell Depot Show and Survey '68: Abstract Sculpture, at Camden Arts Centre, both 1968; also abroad. In a project at Art Laboratory in 1967 Louw made a pyramid of 5,800 oranges and a cone of 9½ tons of black granite chippings. The oranges were reduced over two weeks as the public removed parts of the exhibit. Solo shows also included Museum of Modern Art, Oxford, 1969; and Nigel Greenwood and Whitechapel Art Galleries, 1971. In 1981 he received a prize in the sculpture competition Waterfront Project, Jane Street Pier, New York. Louw established a firm concerned with art in public places. His own work continued, examples held by Tate Gallery and Victoria & Albert Museum.

Hazel LOVE 1923– Painter in oil and watercolour, born at Hinton St George, Somerset. Attended West of England College of Art, 1946–52, exhibited RWA, AIA and locally in Somerset. The RWA holds her work. Lived at Bexhill-on-Sea, Sussex, and at Sutton Scotney, Hampshire.

James LOVEGROVE 1922– Painter, draughtsman and printmaker, born in Hong Kong into a military family. He was himself an Army officer who retired in 1945. Studied at Woolwich Polytechnic's school of art, 1945–9, then at Royal College of Art, 1949–52. Exhibited at RA, RE, Walker's Galleries and in the area of Winchester, Hampshire, where he settled, having lived a bachelor life in a succession of digs in south London for some years. In 1952 one of Lovegrove's etched plates was bought by the Print Collectors' Club, and the Victoria & Albert Museum and Aberdeen Art Gallery hold his work. A man of many interests, Lovegrove was among other things a bank manager, seaman, postal and local historian and director of finance and administration for the *Mary Rose* Trust. Had a solo exhibition, On The River, at Greenwich Theatre Art Gallery in 1996, partly drawn from the time when he served as mate on a Thames barge. Many of his river studies had been lost when the barge he worked on was cut down by a steamer off Greenhithe in 1953.

John LOVELESS 1943– Painter and printmaker, born in Bristol. Studied there at Royal West of England College of Art, 1963–5, where his teachers included Robert Hurdle and John Epstein. He showed at Camden Arts Centre, Grabowski Gallery and with the Arts Council at Serpentine Gallery; and in west of England at Arnolfini Gallery, Bristol, and at Dartington Hall, Devon. South Western Arts Association and Arnolfini Gallery Trust hold his work. Lived at Rookham, Somerset.

Margaret LOVELL 1939– Creator of abstract sculpture with figurative allusions, printmaker, draughtsman and teacher, born and lived in Bristol area. She studied at West of England College of Art there, 1956–60, with Ernest Pascoe, then at Slade School of Fine Art, 1960–2, under A H Gerrard. Learned techniques in a foundry. Lovell gained an Italian State Scholarship, 1962–3, and a Greek Government Scholarship, 1965–6. Taught at Portsmouth College of Art, 1963–5. Miss Lovell was "interested in and influenced by natural forms, movement and structures". She used "colours and all qualities of materials, notably bronze, stone, marble and slate". She was elected RWA in 1972 and a fellow of RBS in 1973. Lovell's main works included silver trophies for the John Player sailing championships; a six-foot bronze for Barclays Bank, Embassy House, Bristol; and a 16-foot bronze for Grafham Water reservoir scheme, Huntingdonshire. Took part in many mixed and group shows, including Arnolfini Gallery, Bristol; Mignon Gallery, Bath; Wills Lane Gallery, St Ives, and abroad. Showed solo with Marjorie Parr Gallery from 1965, having a first retrospective at Plymouth City Art Gallery, 1972. Arts Council, Plymouth and Bristol public galleries hold examples.

Eleanor Selwyn LOVETT 1917– Painter and sculptor in terracotta, latterly noted for her horse pictures. She was born in Bromley, Kent, and studied at Goldsmiths' College School of Art, Epsom School of Art and Royal Academy Schools; her teachers included Hans Tisdall. She was a member of Hesketh Hubbard Art Society, also showing with Leicester Galleries, NEAC, ROI, at Whitechapel Art Gallery and at RA Summer Exhibition. Robert Fleming & Company, the merchant bank, bought her work. Lived in East Croydon, Surrey.

Bet LOW 1924– Painter, born in Gourock, Renfrewshire. She studied at Glasgow School of Art, 1942–5; at Patrick Allan-Fraser School of Art, Hospitalfield, Arbroath, with James Cowie; and Jordanhill Teachers Training College. She worked for a time as an art therapist and designed sets for Unity Theatre. In the mid-1950s the shortage of exhibitions space for young painters prompted Low to help start the railings exhibitions at Botanic Gardens in Glasgow. In the early 1960s she was founder and director of New Charing Cross Gallery, Glasgow. Redevelopment closed it in 1968, but it was succeeded by Compass Gallery in 1969. Low painted abstracts in the 1960s, but later her work was inspired by frequent trips to the Orkneys, in which landscape is simplified towards abstraction to convey the essence of the place. In addition to many mixed shows Low showed solo in 1961 at 57 Gallery, Edinburgh, as well as David Hendriks Gallery in Dublin and Richard Demarco Gallery in Edinburgh, Compass Gallery in Glasgow and Scottish Gallery, Edinburgh. She was a member of RSW and Royal Glasgow Institute of the Fine Arts. Scottish Arts Council and other Scottish galleries hold her work.

David LOW 1891–1963 Political cartoonist and satirist and writer, born in Dunedin, New Zealand. He grew up in Christchurch and taught himself to draw for the press, inspired by comic papers. By 1903 had published first cartoon strip in *The Big Budget* and he began to work for Christchurch publication *The Spectator*, eventually becoming its full-time political cartoonist. Next big steps were his move in 1911 to Australia to work on the *Bulletin*, Sydney; then eight years later he journeyed to London. There he worked on the *Star*, 1919–27, *Evening Standard*, 1927–50; *Daily Herald*, 1950–3, and *Manchester Guardian*, 1953–63. Low met and befriended the famous in many fields: Arnold Bennett, H G Wells, Lord Beaverbrook, David Lloyd George and Winston Churchill. His wit could be barbed, his drawings powerful, and he invented unique images such as Colonel Blimp and the Trades Union Congress carthorse. Low's work was syndicated throughout the world and he published books such as *British Cartoonists, Caricaturists and Comic Artists* and in 1956 his entertaining *Low's Autobiography*. Knighted in 1962. Tate Gallery holds his work. Died in London.

Diana LOW 1911–1975 Artist in oil, pastel, lithography and etching. Born in London, she was educated at Francis Holland School and Cheltenham Ladies' College, where her art mistress was Charlotte Epton, who married Edward Bawden. Spent a short time at the Slade under Randolph Schwabe after study at Académie Ranson, in Paris, but her greatest influence was William Nicholson, who painted excellent portraits of her and her brother, Oliver Low. Exhibited RA, NEAC, RP, SSWA, Leicester Galleries and in Paris. Married Richard Tuely and lived at Stone-in-Oxney, near Tenterden, Kent. The artists Jane and Mary Tuely were related to her. Work owned by Stoke-on-Trent City Museum and Art Gallery.

Jack LOW 1903– Painter, carver, designer and teacher, born in London, who studied at City and Guilds of London Art School, 1941–2, then with Adrian Ryan at Goldsmiths' College School of Art, 1946–50, during which time he taught for London County Council. Showed at RA, Leicester Galleries, Redfern Gallery, AIA, RBA and elsewhere. Lived for many years at West Stourmouth, Kent.

Stewart LOWDON 1932– Painter, born in Edinburgh, who in 1944 began painting out of doors; by 1948 was showing with SSA. After attending Edinburgh College of Art, 1950–4, in 1955 added a teaching diploma to his diploma in drawing and painting. After National Service in Army Educational Corps embarked on a dozen years in advertising and photography, but continued to paint and exhibit. In 1975 decided to leave for Cornwall and paint full-time. Between 1979–83 made a series of painting trips to Greece as a consequence of which, through Greek Embassy, he took part in Lykion Ton Ellinidon, Kensington, 1983. Other working trips were made to Portugal and Provence. Showed widely, especially in west of England. Later appearances included Eye Gallery, Bristol, 1988; Westside Gallery, 1989; Stable Gallery and Heifer Gallery, 1991.

Adam LOWE 1959– Painter and printmaker, born in Oxford. He studied at Ruskin School of Drawing, 1978–81, then Royal College of Art, 1982–5. Among his group appearances were Kettle's Yard, Cambridge, 1985; Smith's Gallery, 1986; and John Moores Exhibition, Liverpool, 1991–2, where he was a prize winner with a large abstract painting in homage to Robert Motherwell, called The Homely Protestant. Lowe had solo shows at Pomeroy Purdy Gallery, 1989–91.

Jeff LOWE 1952– Sculptor and draughtsman, born in Lancashire. He produced abstract drawings in acrylic and graphite of great strength and presence, as in Isis Gallery's 1993 exhibition Drawing Towards Sculpture, in Leigh-on-Sea. Attended Leicester College of Art, 1970–1, then St Martin's School of Art, 1971–5. Gained a Sainsbury Award in 1975, a Greater London Arts Association award and an Arts Council Award in 1976; he was artist-in-residence at Mermer Stone Quarry, Yugoslavia, 1977, and in 1987 at Prahran College, Melbourne, Australia. Exhibitions included Leicester Galleries, 1974; Laing Art Gallery, Newcastle upon Tyne, 1977; and a series at Nicola Jacobs Gallery from 1981. Arts Council holds his work.

Peter LOWE 1938– Maker of constructions and reliefs, and teacher, born in London where he continued to live. Lowe studied with Kenneth and Mary Martin at Goldsmiths' College School of Art, 1954–60. In 1962 Lowe and Colin Jones showed their first reliefs in the Geometric Environment show at AIA Gallery, the following year taking part in Construction England, a touring show put on by Arts Council, which holds several examples of Lowe's abstract work. Lowe progressively exhibited in Britain and abroad, being associated with the Systems Group, which came together in 1969 and put on the Systemi show at Amos Anderson Museum, Helsinki, Finland. In 1977 he was included in Dilworth, Hughes, Lowe and Steele at Annely Juda Fine Art.

Ronald LOWE 1932– Painter, mural artist, printmaker and teacher, born in Skipton, Yorkshire. He studied at Leeds College of Art, 1949–55, with Richard Macdonald and Keith Lucas, and in London. After serving as an education officer in the Army, taught 1959–71 at Haverfordwest Grammar School, then became Her Majesty's Inspector, Art, Wales, meanwhile lecturing for many years on history of art, part-time, at University College of Wales, Aberystwyth. Took part in many group shows, including RA, SEA and SWG, AIA and Howard Roberts Gallery, Cardiff. Many one-man shows, starting with Dillwyn Gallery, Swansea, mainly in Wales but also in America. Has work in many public collections, including WAC, CASW and University College, Swansea. Lived for a time in Abercrave, Breconshire.

May LOWEN 1903– Painter and miniaturist, born in London. She attended Camden Art School and showed at RA, City of London Guildhall, RMS and elsewhere. Was a member of the Hampstead Artists' Council and lived in London.

Victor LOWER 1887– Commercial artist, born at Hove, Sussex. Studied at the School of Art there, 1900–3, then for four years at Brighton School of Art. He exhibited with Croydon Art Society and published several books on flags, signals and ships, work also appearing in *Boy's Own Paper*. Lived at Merstham, Surrey.

Alex LOWERY 1957– Painter who was born in London and took a bachelor's degree in fine art at Central School of Art and Design, 1979–82. From then he painted continuously, moving to Dorset in 1989. Showed there, in London and with Gordon Hepworth Gallery, Newton St Cyres, Devon.

Thomas Esmond LOWINSKY 1892–1947 Painter, book illustrator, designer of papers and textiles, and collector, born in India, where his father was financial consultant to the Sultan of Hyderabad. Back in England he lived in luxurious surroundings, an introverted and artistic boy who attended Eton College, read English at Oxford University, then studied at Slade School of Fine Art, 1912–14. As a commissioned officer in Army during World War I he saw active service in France. Between the wars, at Garsington Manor and later at The Old Rectory, Aldbourne, Lowinsky and his wife lived with exquisite taste, entertaining the eminent and cultivated. He was a founder-member of the Double Crown Club, a member of NEAC and showed in various mixed exhibitions. Had only one solo show during his life, at Wildenstein in 1926; after his death Graves Art Gallery, Sheffield, had a small show in 1981, and Tate Gallery, which holds some of his limited output, a larger one in 1990. As well as scenes of fantasy Lowinsky painted a body of superb portraits, singular images which owe much to Renaissance example.

Alan LOWNDES 1921–1978 Painter in oil of the industrial north of England, using a bright palette. He was born in Stockport, Cheshire. Left school at 14 and became apprenticed to a decorator. After several years in the Army in World War II Lowndes studied painting in the evenings at Stockport College, then started painting full-time in the late-1940s. He was early on taken up by the Crane Gallery in Manchester, where he had a number of one-man shows, later showing at Crane Kalman, London. Also showed solo at Osborn Gallery in New York; Curlew Gallery, Southport; and had retrospectives at Stockport Art Gallery and tour, 1972, and Crane Kalman, 1995. From the early-1950s Lowndes began to work in St Ives, Cornwall, settling in the area for just over a decade in 1959. He later settled at Dursley, Gloucestershire, but periodically returned to Stockport to work.

Rosemary LOWNDES 1937– Painter, designer, writer and illustrator, born in Cheshire. She studied at Liverpool School of Art, then lived in Paris, working with interior designers. Showed work at Salon des Artistes Français and Salon des Indépendants and had solo show at Galerie Ror Volmar. On return to England worked as graphic designer, examples being selected by Design Centre. Wrote and illustrated over 40 children's books, published internationally. Showed at Moreton Street Gallery, Hurlingham Gallery, Phoenix Gallery in Lavenham and Highgate, Mina Renton Gallery and Charlotte Lampard Gallery. Lived in London.

Laurence Stephen LOWRY 1887–1976 Painter and draughtsman, mainly of industrial landscapes, with figure studies and seascapes. Born in Manchester, Lowry became famous as the painter of northern industrial and backstreet urban scenes populated with "matchstick" figures, and as a reclusive character. But he was no primitive artist, devoting many years to the study of art while working full-time as a rent collector and clerk. After private lessons with William Fitz in Manchester, from 1905–15 Lowry attended painting and drawing classes at the Municipal College of Art under Adolphe Valette, whose urban scenes foreshadowed Lowry's. From 1915–25 Lowry attended Salford School of Art, a period when he established his style and subject matter. In 1919 exhibited two paintings at MAFA, then in the 1920s began to show regularly in open exhibitions including the Paris Salon. An Accident was bought by the City Art Gallery, Manchester, in 1930, the first publicly acquired Lowry. Two years later he exhibited at the RA for the first time. In 1938 A J McNeill Reid noticed his work, leading to his first one-man show in London, at Lefevre Gallery, the following year. By 1945 Lowry was receiving serious critical attention, and his slow climb to fame and many honours was gaining pace. A major retrospective exhibition at the RA followed his death, in 1976. Lowry's work is widely held in public collections, including the Tate Gallery. Lived at Mottram-in-Longdendale, Cheshire, where he had moved in 1948.

Peter LOWRY 1914– Watercolourist who studied at St Martin's School of Art, 1933, and at Bolt Court, 1935–7. Showed at RA, NEAC, RBA and elsewhere. Lived in London.

Edward LOXTON KNIGHT 1905–1993 Painter in watercolour and tempera, printmaker and poster designer, born and lived in Long Eaton, Nottinghamshire/Derbyshire. At Long Eaton Grammar School Loxton Knight (he signed work with this, his surname; he is sometimes wrongly listed in reference books under Knight) was taught and greatly influenced by Samuel Clegg, grandfather of the actor Richard and broadcaster/naturalist David Attenborough. Then studied under Joseph Else at Nottingham School of Art, 1924–9. Was elected a member of the Colour Gravure Society, RBA, PS and RI and exhibited with the New Group and extensively elsewhere in Britain and abroad. Solo exhibitions included Brook Street Gallery, Chapel Bar Gallery in Nottingham and Carl Fischer Gallery, New York. Nottingham Castle Museum and public collections in Wanganui, New Zealand, Derby, Hull and Bolton hold examples. Died in Vicarage Nursing Home, Long Eaton. A memorial show at Erewash Museum in 1994 resulted in a large oil being bought for the collection with support from Victoria & Albert Museum.

Clarisse LOXTON PEACOCK 1928– Painter, notable for her still lifes, a native of Budapest, Hungary. She studied at Budapest University, was for four years at Chelsea School of Art, then did a two-year postgraduate course at St Martin's School of Art followed by two more at Central School of Art. She sold early pictures from Young Contemporaries to Walker Art Gallery in Liverpool and to San Francisco Museum of Art. Also showed at RA, RBA, Leicester Galleries, Lefevre Gallery and Paris Salon, where she gained Gold and Silver Medals and an Hon. Mention. Her second husband was Sir Anthony Grover. Had many solo exhibitions, including Cadogan Contemporary, 1988. Lived in London.

Jan LUBELSKI 1922– Sculptor, noted for portraits and animals, born in Poznan, Poland, son of the sculptor Mieczyslaw Lubelski. He was partly educated in Poland, in Germany and in Scotland, where he worked under the sculptor Benno Elkan, 1940–1. He was included in a War Artists' Exhibition at National Gallery. Studied at Regent Street Polytechnic School of Art, 1945–6; at Slade School of Fine Art, 1946–9, under A H Gerrard, the sculptor; then at London University's Institute of Education,

1950–1. Showed at RA, Fine Art Society, Walker's Galleries and elsewhere. Lived in London.

Mieczyslaw LUBELSKI 1886–1965 Sculptor in varied materials, including bronze, sandstone and marble, born in Warsaw, Poland, father of the sculptor Jan Lubelski. He studied at School of Fine Arts, Warsaw, under Dunikowski, and in Berlin at Akademische Hochschule für Bildende Künste and Meisterschule. He gained the silver medal of the Academy of Fine Arts, Berlin, 1914; gold medal at National Exhibition in Poznan, 1928; and Polish Air Force Medal, 1949. After World War II he spent some years in England, living at Kew Gardens, Surrey. Lubelski specialised in religious statues, but his works also included the Kosciuszko Monument in Lodz, Poland, 1931; Saper Monument in Warsaw, 1933; and the Polish War Memorial, London.

Caroline LUCAS fl. c.1930–1967 Painter, sculptor and printmaker. Studied art in Paris, Rome and London, John Skeaping being one of her teachers. Showed in Paris, paintings at the Lefevre Gallery in 1934 and sculpture at the Leicester Galleries in 1939. With her sister Frances Byng-Stamper, Caroline Lucas had been closely associated with the founding of the CASW in the 1930s. In the 1940s and 1950s they ran Miller's Gallery and Press in Lewes, Sussex (featured in an exhibition at the Towner Art Gallery, Eastbourne, 1989). At Miller's these formidable ladies showed Caroline Lucas' work as well as that of the Bloomsbury artists Duncan Grant and Vanessa Bell, David Jones and the Roberts Colquhoun and MacBryde. Among prints published by the Miller's Press was a portfolio of six lithographs of Lewes and Brighton, some of Caroline Lucas' most accomplished work. Cedric Morris painted a singular portrait of the two sisters which he nicknamed "The Upper Classes". They died within a few months of each other, in retirement at Shelley's Hotel, Lewes.

Denis LUCAS 1918– Painter and teacher, brother of the artist Keith Stephen Lucas. He studied at Beckenham School of Art and Royal College of Art and gained a travelling scholarship in 1949. Taught at Ravensbourne, St Martin's School of Art and Royal Academy Schools. City of Plymouth Museums & Art Gallery holds his work and a portrait of Lucas by Stephen Bullard was included in Belgrave Gallery's exhibition Camberwell Artists of the 40s and 50s, 1988. Lived in Beckenham, Kent.

Keith Stephen LUCAS 1924– Painter, draughtsman, teacher and administrator, born in Beckenham, Kent. He studied at Beckenham School of Art and the Royal College of Art, his teachers including Henry Carr, Carel Weight and Kenneth Rowntree. After teaching at Liverpool and Leeds Colleges of Art, 1951–7, Lucas became involved with design for film and television, 1957–65, returning to Royal College of Art, 1965–72, where he was professor of film and television. From 1972–9, he was director of the British Film Institute, then from 1980–8 was head of the school of film and television for Christ Church College, Canterbury, after this painting full-time. Exhibitions included Sally Hunter Fine Art, Metropole Arts Centre in Folkestone and Neville Gallery, Canterbury. Lucas worked in the traditional English landscape style, having a special concern with light. His brother was the painter Denis Lucas. Lived at Bishopsbourne, Kent.

Marjorie Ashworth LUCAS 1911– Artist in copper and wood engraving and silk drawing (embroidery), and teacher, born in Yorkshire. She studied at Royal College of Art engraving school, teachers including Malcolm Osborne and Robert Austin. Until her marriage Lucas made entomological drawings for the Natural History Museum, did book illustration for Methuen and part-time teaching. After marriage in 1938 she lived in Scotland, first in Galloway, then Edinburgh, her husband being the artist Murray Tod. She showed with him at the Scottish and Hanover Galleries in Edinburgh and at the Dumfries Arts Festival. She was a member of Society of Artist Printmakers from 1935 and of SSA from 1946, also taking part in group shows at RA, RSA, Walker Art Gallery in Liverpool and elsewhere, including overseas. Had several solo exhibitions at Scottish Gallery, also showing one-man at Torrance Gallery, Edinburgh. City of Liverpool Public Libraries holds bookplates by her.

Sarah LUCAS 1962– Artist, born in London, who studied at London College of Printing, 1983–4, graduating with honours from Goldsmiths' College, 1984–7. Took part in group exhibitions at The Showroom, 1986; Freeze, at PLA Building, 1988; East Country Yard, Surrey Docks, 1990; Karsten Schubert and Barbara Gladstone Gallery, New York, both 1992; and Young British Artists II, Saatchi Gallery, 1993, which holds her work. Solo shows included The Whole Joke, 1992, at 8 Kingly Street. The female body as a subject of popular culture, slang and graffiti were features of Lucas' art.

Suzanne LUCAS 1915– Painter and miniaturist in watercolour, born in Calcutta, India. She was of English and French nationality. Lucas attended Roedean School, then travelled extensively in Europe. Studied at universities in Grenoble, Edinburgh and Munich and at Reimer Schule art school in Berlin, 1935. Lived in Egypt – where she began painting on ivory – and France for long periods. Returned to England in 1954, having a first solo show in that year at Cooling Galleries. Developed a passion for toadstools, discovering new varieties, becoming a noted expert and writing on them. In 1992 published a lavish volume, *In Praise of Toadstools*, with her own illustration. Lucas was founder-president of the Society of Botanical Artists, president of RMS and a fellow of the Linnean and Royal Horticultural Societies, winning that Society's Gold Medal over a dozen times and the Grenfell Medal several times. Franklin Mint and Post Office commissioned her work. Showed at RA, RI, Paris Salon and elsewhere. Solo exhibitions included two at Mall Galleries, 1975–9, and Liberty's, 1977. British Museum and Natural History Museum hold examples. Lived at Mere, Warminster, Wiltshire.

Paul LUCKY 1956– Stained glass artist who was born in London and studied at Swansea College of Art. In 1982 he formed the Stained Glass Design Partnership with Susan Bradbury which completed windows in public buildings throughout the United Kingdom. He was a fellow of the British Society of Master Glass Painters and was based in Kilmaurs, Kilmarnock, Ayrshire.

Leila LUDDINGTON fl. c.1930–1965 Watercolourist, born in Aldershot, Hampshire, of a military family. She studied under Henry Tonks at Slade School of Fine Art and at Académie Julian, in Paris. Showed at SWA, Arts Council, NEAC, RI, WIAC and elsewhere. Lived near Saffron Walden, Essex.

LUGOW: *see* **Lucienne GOW**

John LUKE 1906–1975 Painter, born in Belfast, where he finally lived. Luke was fond of working in tempera with a resin-oil varnish; his pictures are often highly coloured with a dramatic and unusual quality. Studied at the School of Art, Belfast, with the mural painter Ivor Beaumont, 1923–7, at the Slade School of Fine Art, 1927–30, under Henry Tonks, and at the Westminster School of Art, 1930–1, with Walter Bayes. Luke won a number of prizes and scholarships and continued his studies privately in museums and galleries in London and Paris. Exhibited Leger and Redfern Galleries, UA, RHA and in America. Queen's University, Belfast, and Belfast Museum and Art Gallery hold his work. Arts Council of Northern Ireland retrospective in 1978.

Edna LUMB 1931–1992 Painter, draughtsman, printmaker and teacher, born in Leeds, Yorkshire. Won a scholarship to Leeds Junior Art School aged 14, another taking her to Leeds College of Art, 1948–53, during which she won a travelling scholarship to France, 1951. Taught unenthusiastically, 1953–64, then – with typical steely determination – decided to paint full-time, buying a van for her trips. She found her own subject in industry, depicting machinery technically meticulously, but tinged with poetry. She believed "the excitement I feel about mills, factories, quarries, machinery, sewers and industrial constructions can enable people to see beauty in the drama of components and power." Her 1973 Bradford Industrial Museum show Components of Power won much acclaim. Commissions poured in from such bodies as Laing Properties, National Audit Office, Sir Alfred McAlpine & Company and the Science Museum, where a solo show was running when she died. Lumb made three trips to West Africa: in 1969 Joint Church Aid asked her to record the Biafran airlift; in 1976 Catholic Relief Services commissioned her to record drought relief in Upper Volta; and in 1977 she worked in Nigeria recording Caterpillar Tractor Company's land development. Her pictures always sold rapidly, and many private and public collections – including Bradford Art Galleries and Museums, Science Museum, Manchester City Art Galleries and National Railway Museum, York – hold her work. Bradford Industrial Museum held a retrospective in 1991, Leeds City Art Gallery a memorial show in 1992–3. Lived in London.

Patrick LUMB 1966– Painter and teacher, born in Bournemouth, Hampshire, who studied at Central School of Art & Design; Falmouth School of Art; and Art Institute of Chicago school of art. He was a founder-member of Woodend Studio Association in Manchester, 1987; was head painter and art director for Too Cute in Los Angeles, 1989–90; then taught at Oakham School, Rutland, in 1994 being exhibition organiser for the Oakham Festival. In 1989 Lumb was a prize winner at MAFA Open. Group exhibitions included Young Contemporaries at Whitworth Art Gallery in Manchester, 1987; Mercury Art Gallery, 1989; The New Van Straaten Gallery, Chicago, 1992; and Leicester City Art Gallery and Royal Over-Seas League Open, both 1994.

Alexandra LUMLEY 1958– Painter, notably of landscape and seascapes, usually in a mix of watercolour and gouache; graphic and theatre designer; and teacher. She studied at Camberwell School of Arts and Crafts, 1977–80, becoming a lecturer at Camberwell College of Arts. Completed a mosaic sign for Homerton Hospital commissioned by the Public Art & Development Trust. Took part in numerous group shows, including Thackeray Gallery, 1983; Laing Competition, Mall Galleries, 1985; and RWS Open, Bankside Gallery, 1989. Solo shows included Austin/Desmond Fine Art, 1982, and New Grafton Gallery from 1986.

Alan LUMSDEN 1937– Artist, notably a printmaker, and teacher, born in Aldershot, Hampshire, as Richard Alan Lumsden. He attended the Technical High School in Cheltenham, 1949–53, then the art school there, 1953–7, and after National Service in the Middle East was at London University Institute of Education, 1959–60. Teaching included Chester School of Art. Exhibitions included Nottingham and Leeds Playhouses, Pictures for Schools at RA and WAC tour The Probity of Art, 1980. Many public galleries, including Dudley, Doncaster, Hull, Nottingham and Sunderland, hold examples. Lived in Bersham, near Wrexham, Clwyd.

Ernest LUMSDEN 1883–1948 Printmaker, painter, teacher and writer, born in London, he married the artist Mabel Royds. Because of poor health Lumsden had to abandon an ambition to go to sea, so aged 15 he entered the University College art department at Reading, five years later studying briefly at Académie Julian, Paris. Back in London he taught himself to etch so well that in 1907 examples were shown at the Paris Salon; a year later he had his first solo exhibition at Arcade Studio, Reading. A 1908 summons from Frank Morley Fletcher to teach at Edinburgh College of Art started his lifelong association with Scotland. Lumsden began to exhibit widely and to travel in several continents, so that in 1912 he left teaching and travelled to India, a country which he loved and which he depicted wonderfully in etching and aquatint. Lumsden and his wife lived and worked in India, 1917–19; he had gone there to join the Indian Army, but was rejected and got a military post censoring telegrams. Returned to Edinburgh, Lumsden made a good living from etchings until the slump, when he set up as a portrait painter, noted for his unwillingness to flatter sitters. In 1925 he published *The Art of Etching*, a standard text. Lumsden was elected RE in 1915, in 1929 became president of the Society of Artist Printmakers and became RSA in 1933. His work is in the Tate Gallery, Scottish National Gallery of Modern Art, British Museum, Victoria & Albert Museum and many foreign holdings.

James LUMSDEN 1964– Artist, designer and illustrator, born in Inverness, who studied graphic design at Cardonald, Glasgow, 1983–5; was an illustrator and graphic designer in Glasgow, 1986–8; from 1989 working in WASPS Studios, Edinburgh. Awards included Hope Scott Trust Award, 1992 and 1994, and Edinburgh District Arts Council Award; and The Scottish International Education Trusts Award, 1996. Group shows included Scottish Drawing Biennial, Paisley Art Gallery, from 1989; 12 Scottish Artists, Payne Gallery, Bethlehem, Pennsylvania, 1993; and the Gulbenkian Suite, Highland Printmakers, Inverness, 1995. Had a solo exhibition, Dilemma, at Citizens Studios, Edinburgh, 1992, later ones including Seduction, Compass Gallery, Glasgow, 1996. An exploration of the nature of symbols was a key feature of Lumsden's work, which was in the Highland Regional Council, Inverness Museum & Art Gallery and Gulbenkian Foundation collections.

Augustus LUNN 1905–1986 A key figure in the revival of tempera painting in Britain, muralist, draughtsman and teacher, H Augustus Lunn became a student of Kingston School of Art, winning a scholarship to Royal College of Art when William Rothenstein was principal. Won the Edward Abbey Mural Scholarship. Lunn joined the staff at Kingston, but also restored murals – for example, at Marlborough House – and carried out commissions for original murals. As an easel painter his output was small but of high quality. He showed at NEAC, Cooling Galleries, LG, RA and elsewhere, but did not have a solo show until that at Michael Parkin's Gallery in 1985. Lunn admired the work of Giorgio de Chirico and Fernand Léger, and a strongly Surrealist element is present in much of his output, as well as a tendency towards abstraction. He said: "I am never interested in recording a scene. I want to reconstruct."

Dora LUNN: *see* **Dora HEDGES**

Lewis Frederick LUPTON 1909–1996 Painter, designer and illustrator, born and lived in London. He attended Sheffield College of Art, 1923–30, with Anthony Betts and Eric Jones, then at Westminster School of Art with Bernard Meninsky and Mark Gertler. Lupton was employed as an illustrator, 1933–40; from 1941–50 worked on exhibition design; from 1950–60 being engaged on Christian literature for the Scripture Union and others. From 1960 Lupton's main interest was the self-publication of a multi-volume *History of the Geneva Bible* in his own calligraphy and with his illustrations. Oxford University Press, Odhams Press and the publisher Macmillan all reproduced his work. He showed at RA, LG, Leger and Redfern Galleries. With his artist wife Joan, Lupton held exhibitions at their own gallery and in the provinces. At Lupton House he completed a large painted ceiling. Bradford City Art Gallery holds his work.

Peter LUTHER 1926– Figurative painter, much admired by his peers, such as Conroy Maddox, born in Sussex. He studied at Hammersmith School of Art and the Working Men's College. Had a series of solo exhibitions at John Whibley Gallery, the fourth being in 1972.

John M LUXMOORE 1912– Carver in wood who studied at Cambridge University. Exhibited RA and in the provinces in the north of England. Lived at Altrincham, Cheshire.

Doris E LUXTON 1908– Painter and teacher, born in Exeter, Devon. She attended Truro Art School under Arthur Jackson and taught there for several years in the late 1920s. Showed widely in the West Country and had a series of one-man shows at Burton Art Gallery in Bideford, Devon, where she lived.

Henry LUYKEN 1892– Painter, architect and printmaker, born in London. After education at Northern Polytechnic he studied at Camden School of Art and Southend-on-Sea School of Art where his teachers included Emerson Groom the etcher and the engraver and watercolourist Charles William Taylor. RWS Club member. Showed mainly in London. Lived in Leigh-on-Sea, Essex.

Len LYE 1901–1980 Film-maker, kinetic sculptor, painter, genetic theorist and experimental writer, born in Christchurch, New Zealand. Lye moved to Sydney, Australia, in 1921, where he acquired animation techniques working for a commercial film company. After time on Pacific islands, he worked his sea passage to England where he met the artists Eric Kennington and Ben Nicholson and writers Robert Graves and Laura Riding. Lye lived on a barge on the Thames, 1927–30, in 1928 being elected a member of the Seven and Five Society, contributing sculpture, constructions and Batik paintings until 1934. Graves' and Riding's Seizin Press published *No Trouble*, a selection of Lye's letters, in 1930; he designed book covers for Seizin and Hours Press (Paris), 1930–1. Lye's first film, *Tusalava*, had been screened in 1929, and four years later he began experiments with direct techniques of painting and scratching on film, using such implements as a hairpin. *Colour Box*, his first such production, was released by the G(eneral)P(ost)O(ffice) Film Unit in 1935, one of several Lye films they sponsored. In World War II Lye directed films for the Ministry of Information and directed for the *March of Time* documentaries. Emigrated to America in 1944. There until his death he continued work to develop a theory of art, a concern since 1936; in 1951 Lye returned to experimental film-making, using shadowgraph techniques; and in 1958 took up kinetic sculpture. His Tangible Motion Sculpture was presented at the Museum of Modern Art in 1961, the first of many inclusions in major sculpture and kinetic art shows. In 1965 Lye had his first solo exhibition at Howard Wise Gallery, New York. Lye resumed painting in 1977, the year he returned to oversee installation of an exhibition of his work at Govett-Brewster Art Gallery, New Plymouth, New Zealand. It holds a repository of Len Lye's output, as do American public galleries, and The Len Lye Foundation is based in New Plymouth. He died in Warwick, New York.

Francis LYMBURNER 1916–1972 Painter and draughtsman, notable for his delicate drawings of animals. He was born in Brisbane, Australia, and died in Sydney. Studied at Brisbane Central Technical College under Martyn Roberts, won the Mosman Prize in 1951 and showed widely in Australia. For about a decade from the early 1950s Lymburner was based in England, where he exhibited with the Australian Artists' Association. Australian state galleries hold examples.

John Langtry LYNAS 1879–1956 Painter, sculptor and illustrator, born in Greenock, Renfrewshire, his parents having Ulster origins. They moved there when he was still small. He attended the Model School in Belfast, spent a short time at Belfast School of Art and in his mid-twenties, without adequate resources, embarked on a trip through Europe and was later said to have studied art in London and Paris. In Belfast did a variety of jobs such as building and signwriting to support self and family. Exhibited at RHA, RUA and at Belfast Museum and Art Gallery. Magee's Gallery gave him a solo show in 1939, CEMA in 1952. Among books illustrated by Lynas was *Why*, published in 1935. Ulster Museum holds his self-portrait. The Ulster critic John Hewitt remembered Lynas as "that diminutive rowdy … forever creating a scene and stumping out in a temper" at exhibitions, "his few pictures in conté crayon the aborted sprouts of his vast imaginings."

James LYNCH 1956– Artist, born in Hitchin, Hertfordshire, who grew up in Devizes and gained a graphic design diploma at Swindon, 1974–6, then began painting professionally. His wife was the artist Kate Lynch. In 1983 was awarded a bursary by the Elizabeth Greenshields Foundation, of Canada, and in 1986 won Pimms Prize for watercolour or drawing. He was well known for his paintings of farm animals, other themes being landscapes and interiors. Lynch's mixed exhibitions included Festival Gallery, Bath, and Portal Gallery, 1981; International Contemporary Art Fair, 1984–5; and The Broad Horizon, Agnew, 1990. Had a solo exhibition at Linfield Galleries, Bradford-on-Avon, 1982, later solo shows including Maas Gallery, 1993. In 1989 he was commissioned by National Trust to paint Bonnie, a prizewinning cow, for the Wimpole Hall Collection; in 1993 Folio Society commissioned Lynch to illustrate Kenneth Grahame's *The Wind in the Willows*. Notable private collections holding his work include Chatsworth and Longleat. Lived in North Cadbury, Somerset.

Kate LYNCH 1949– Artist and teacher, married to the painter James Lynch. Gained an honours degree in the history of art at Essex University, 1975; did a postgraduate certificate in education and an art teacher's diploma at Bristol University, 1976; then a post-graduate diploma in fine art at Bristol Polytechnic, 1992. Lynch taught at Devizes School and Bath High School, was a residential course tutor at Urchfont Manor and conducted adult and children's groups. She was involved in promoting exhibitions and art events near her home at North Cadbury, Somerset, and in 1985 designed and co-ordinated a group embroidery for the Frome 1300 celebrations. It is permanently exhibited in Frome Museum. Shows included Whittox Gallery, Frome; Nevill Gallery, Bath; Bath Contemporary Art Fair; RWA; and Beaux Arts, Bath.

Kaye LYNCH 1949– Draughtsman, watercolourist and designer. She studied at Exeter College of Art and Glasgow School of Art and went on to run a small craft business, for which she did designs. She also found time to make intricate drawings based on her own domestic circumstances. Lynch won a number of awards: in 1972 the Benno Schotz Travel Award; 10 years later the Glasgow Lady Artists' Trust Fund Award and a Scottish Arts Council Major Bursary. She took part in many group shows, including Royal Glasgow Institute of the Fine Arts; Project Arts Centre, Dublin; and Talbot Rice Art Centre, Edinburgh. Solo shows included Arts Council Gallery, Edinburgh; Carlisle Museum and Art Gallery; and Skelmersdale Art Gallery. She was included in The Compass Contribution, Tramway, Glasgow, 1990.

Michael LYNE 1912–1989 Sporting artist in oil, watercolour and line, and writer, full name Charles Edward Michael Lyne. He was born in Upton Bishop, Herefordshire, son of a country parson. Rejected the idea of becoming a vet or a farmer, instead studying for short time at Cheltenham School of Art. Initially he worked in watercolour and body colour, but between late 1940s and 1970s concentrated on oils, producing hunting subjects in rich colours, culminating in notable series on Grand National. Hunted his own pack of beagles, the United Cotswold, also with otterhounds and with over 40 packs of foxhounds in England, Ireland and America. Wrote and illustrated a number of books, including *Horse, Hounds and Country*; *A Parson's Son*; and *From Litter to Later On*. Lived near Fairford in Gloucestershire.

Peter LYON 1926– Sculptor, designer, writer and teacher who attended Bryanston School, where he studied sculpture with Willi Soukop; Oxford University; and Edinburgh College of Art, studying sculpture with Eric Schilsky. After service in Royal Navy minesweepers became a freelance sculptor and designer in 1953. Was married to the artist Toby Lyon. Was a senior lecturer at Central School of Art & Design, 1969–85, also teaching at other schools including West Sussex College of Art part-time. Published *Design in Jewellery* and wrote articles for *The Observer, The Guardian, Yorkshire Post, Apollo* and other publications. Was also consultant design director to the Bonas Group, 1969–74, design consultant for films on gold and silver work and did judging, including Hunting Group national art competition in 1988 and 1991. Solo exhibitions included Upper Grosvenor Gallery. Did much commissioned work, including sculptures for Kingsway Hall; Stevenage New Town centre and Park Town Gardens, Oxford, both competition winners; Cambridge University engineering department; entrance sculpture for Churchill College, Cambridge; and sculpture beside Gertrude Jekyll water garden, Vann, Surrey. Had a London studio and lived in Lymington, Hampshire.

Robert LYON 1894–1978 Artist, mural painter and teacher. Born in Liverpool, he studied art at the Royal College of Art and the British School at Rome, 1924. He became lecturer in fine art and master of painting at King's College, Newcastle upon Tyne, 1932. For eight years from 1934 Lyon was tutor to the Ashington Group of spare-time Northumberland miner artists, one of the most remarkable of such groups to emerge in the inter-war years. From 1942–60 Lyon was principal of Edinburgh College of Art. He exhibited RA, RBA, RP and in the provinces. Also painted murals for Western General Hospital, Edinburgh, and King's College Hospital dental department. Lived at Rushlake Green, Sussex.

Toby LYON 1926–1990 Painter, born into a peripatetic military family in Birmingham. Aged 14, as Colleen McCormick, she enrolled at the St Ives School of Painting. Exhibited at Portal Gallery, in the Netherlands and Germany and was widely collected in America. She was married to the sculptor Peter Lyon, her daughter Charlotte and son Jasper also being artists. Her childhood spent partly in Bexhill-on-Sea, the Sussex seaside resort, was a great inspiration for her gently humorous, naive pictures. Died in Cambridge.

Elizabeth LYONS 1937–1994 Painter and draughtsman whose work was figurative with strong abstract elements; teacher. Born in London, she had a lifelong ambition to go to art college, attending evening classes in life drawing and painting. She founded a company making and designing horse-drawn carriages for world-class driving, winning a gold cup at Windsor for excellent design and craftsmanship. Lyons studied at Ravensbourne College of Art, 1977–8, then gained a first-class honours degree at Falmouth College of Art, 1978–81. From 1988–91 she was artist-in-residence and visiting lecturer in Tuscany, Falmouth and Goldsmiths' Colleges of Art; in 1990–2 was at New York International School of Art, Todi, Italy; and in 1992 at Geoffrey Humphries Studio, Venice. She took part in group shows at RA and Falmouth Art Gallery, 1982; Jablonski Gallery, 1986; LG from 1989, and elsewhere. Had a solo show at Ripley Art Centre in 1983, later ones including Woodlands Art Gallery, 1986–8, and Art Space Gallery, 1989–92, with a memorial show in 1996.

John LYONS 1933– Painter, poet, writer and teacher, born in Port of Spain, Trinidad. Moved to London and studied at Goldsmiths' College School of Art, 1959–64, and at the University of Newcastle upon Tyne's art department, 1964–5. Myths and folklore were a feature of Lyons' pictures, as seen in The Caribbean Connection, at Islington Arts Factory, 1995. Other mixed shows included Edison Galerie, The Hague, 1982; Art Works, Manchester Polytechnic, 1985; and Harris Museum & Art Gallery, Preston, 1991. Solo exhibitions included Huddersfield Art Gallery and tour, 1992. Lyons' paintings were conditioned to an extent by his work as a poet and writer, which was included in many anthologies and which won literary prizes. Lyons was appointed external purchaser for the Arts Council Collection, 1987–9, and was a selector for a number of exhibitions. Taught art at Manchester University.

Michael LYONS 1943– Sculptor and teacher, born in Bilston, Staffordshire. Studied at Wolverhampton College of Art, 1959–63, Hornsey College of Art, 1963–4, and University of Newcastle, 1964–7. Became head of sculpture at Manchester Polytechnic, 1989. Exhibitions included Welsh Sculpture Trust's exhibition Sculpture in a Country Park, Margam, 1983, and 1st RWA Open Sculpture Exhibition, 1993. Many of Lyons' works were in welded metal, designed for an outdoor setting where changing light was of key importance. Had a solo show at Hatton Gallery, Newcastle, 1982, later ones including Beaux Arts Gallery, Bath, 1986, and Wingfield College, Eye, 1990. Was elected an associate of RBS in 1992. Commissions included Peace for Manchester City Council, 1985–6, and Portsmouth Polytechnic bronze, 1990. Arts Council and Whitworth Art Gallery in Manchester hold examples. Lived in Cawood, Yorkshire.

William LYONS-WILSON 1892–1981 Self-taught painter, notably in watercolour, and teacher, born in Leeds, Yorkshire (surname originally Wilson, although he signed work Lyons Wilson, later adopting the hyphenated form). He was strongly influenced by Cotman, Constable and Cézanne. After service in World War I with a West Riding field ambulance unit in France, in 1918 Lyons-Wilson returned to Leeds, taking painting holidays with Jacob Kramer, in 1919 marrying and taking up art full-time. Based in Wensleydale, Lyons-Wilson exhibited throughout Yorkshire and became acquainted with the writer J B Priestley and artists Philip Naviasky, Fred Lawson and Richard Eurich, who called Lyons-Wilson the best watercolourist of his time. In 1930 Lyons Wilson was asked to teach art appreciation, drawing and painting at Sedbergh School, eventually settling there. He was invited by the Cunard Line to supply paintings for their new liner *Berengaria.* In 1938 Lyons-Wilson moved to teach at Blundell's School, sharing his time with King's College, Taunton, retiring from both in 1968. From 1944 Lyons-Wilson developed an interest in abstract and Surrealist paintings, which he showed at the Redfern Gallery. He also exhibited at RA, NEAC, Plymouth Society of Artists, was president of the Somerset Society of Artists, East Devon Art Society and Phoenix Art Club in Tiverton, and vice-president of Tiverton Art Society. Lyons-Wilson was remembered as an inspiring art teacher, an independent spirit and witty raconteur, who had a keen insight into the works of Klee and Miró. Imperial War Museum and Exeter Museum hold his pictures. Lived at Ash Thomas, Devon, dying in Tiverton Hospital.

Anthony LYSYCIA 1959– Artist and photographer, born in Chorley, Lancashire. He studied at Preston Polytechnic, 1978–81; Royal College of Art, 1981–4; then in 1984–5 was Rome Scholar in Printmaking at British School in Rome. Lysycia took part in a number of group shows in London and elsewhere, including The Self Portrait: a Modern View, which toured from Artsite Gallery, Bath, in 1987.

Neville LYTTON 1879–1951 Painter, writer and collector, born in Calcutta, India, became the Third Earl of Lytton. After education at Eton College, Neville Lytton attended L'École des Beaux-Arts, Paris, also working in the studio of Léon Bonnet. He exhibited extensively at Alpine Club Gallery, Carfax Gallery and Beaux Arts Gallery, also RA, NEAC, RP and elsewhere. Among the subjects of portraits by him were Bernard Shaw and the poet Alice Meynell. Lytton wrote a number of books on subjects as varied as the English country gentleman, France and his monograph *Water-colour*, originally a lecture to the Art Workers' Guild in 1907. Lytton was a friend of the noted collector of English pictures Eddie Marsh, introducing him to traditional watercolours, although he disapproved of Marsh's later inclination towards modern British works. Lived in London.

M

M: *see* **Michael David MOODY**

Mary MABBUTT 1951– Figurative painter and teacher, born in Luton, Bedfordshire. She studied at the School of Art there, 1970–1; Loughborough College of Art and Design, 1971–4; and Royal Academy Schools, 1975–8, then gained a junior fellowship in Cardiff in 1979. Taught at the School of Art from that year in Falmouth, Cornwall, where she lived with the artist Joe Coates. Was a member of Newlyn Society of Artists. Group shows included John Player Portrait Award, 1984; TSWA 1984, where she was a prizewinner; A Century of Art in Cornwall 1889–1989, Newlyn Orion Galleries; and John Moores Liverpool Exhibition, 1995–6, prizewinner with her sensitive oil on canvas Big World, Small World. Had a first solo show at New Grafton Gallery in 1980, later ones including Paton Gallery, 1995.

Caroline McADAM CLARK 1947– Versatile artist and teacher (sometimes incorrectly listed as Clark), born and lived in London, who had a French mother and Scots father. Between 1965–70, McAdam Clark gained a fine art master's honours degree at Edinburgh University and her diploma in art and design from Edinburgh College of Art. In the 1970s she illustrated educational books; from 1970–1 worked in Paris for the United Nations Educational, Scientific and Cultural Organization (UNESCO)'s department of mass communication; from 1975 lecturing on the history of art at the London Day School. During the 1980s and 1990s McAdam Clark, while painting, mixed restoration of works on paper, writing for art magazines, designing and decorating furniture, painting murals, teaching at the University of East London's illustration department and co-directing the Piers Feetham Gallery. She was a member of the Printmakers' Council, mixed shows including Barnes Gallery and Open Eye Gallery in Edinburgh, both 1994; Easton Rooms, Rye, and Aldeburgh 100 Exhibition, both 1995. Had a solo show at Aldeburgh Festival, 1972, later ones including Thackeray Gallery, 1996. A strong draughtsmanship underlay McAdam Clark's paintings, memorable for scenes of quiet mystery achieved with a muted palette.

Jane McADAM-FREUD 1958– Sculptor, medallist, draughtsman and teacher, born and lived in London, father the painter Lucien Freud, mother fashion designer Katherine McAdam. McAdam-Freud did a foundation course at Wimbledon School of Art, 1976–7; graduated from Central St Martins School of Art, 1978–81; Goldsmiths' College, 1981–2; Scuola dell'Arte della Medaglia, Rome, 1986–9; and Accademia di Belle Arti, Rome, 1987–9, gaining a postgraduate diploma in sculpture; then her master's degree at Royal College of Art, 1993–5, project tutor Eduardo Paolozzi. McAdam-Freud gained a large number of awards, including a Royal Society of Arts Bursary Award, 1981; a British Art Medal Scholarship in Rome, sponsored by The Royal Mint and Worshipful Company of Goldsmiths, 1986; Italian State Mint Prize, 1991; Erica O'Donnell Medal commission competition winner, and Worshipful Company of Tin Plate Workers research competition, 1st prize, both 1994; and Dollis Hill Underground Subway commission prize, 1995. She was made a member of the British Art Medal Society, 1982; was a founding fellow of the Society of Numismatic Artists/Designers, 1991; and was elected an associate of RBS, 1994. Had a Lisbon Studios Residency at Royal College of Art, 1995. McAdam-Freud was made an engraver/sculptor to The Royal Mint, 1990–2, and master sculptor, Perth Mint, Australia, 1992. Was a visiting lecturer to the Royal Academy, Antwerp, 1994–5, at the same time to the Royal College of Art, 1992–6. Exhibited widely, including Design Centre, 1981; Recent Acquisitions, Goldsmiths' Hall, 1985; Scottish Gallery, Edinburgh, 1986; In The Round, British Museum, 1992; Sculptors' Drawings, Sladmore Gallery, 1994; and 2nd RWA Sculpture Open Exhibition, 1996. British Museum, Goldsmiths' Hall, Berlin State Museum in Germany and Rijksmuseum, Leiden, Netherlands, hold examples.

Violet McADOO 1896–1961 Painter, especially in watercolour, and teacher, born in Cookstown, County Tyrone, full name Annie Florence Violet McAdoo. She studied at School of Art in Belfast, where she lived, and Royal College of Art. Was a member of RUA, also showing at RHA, SWA, UA and elsewhere. Belfast Museum and Art Gallery holds her work.

Clement McALEER 1949– Painter in oil on canvas, born in County Tyrone, Northern Ireland. He studied at Canterbury College of Art, 1972–5, then Royal College of Art, 1975–8. Although he travelled and worked for periods in Italy, Ireland, France and America, McAleer was based at Bluecoat Studios, Liverpool. He was a prizewinner in John Moores Liverpool Exhibition in 1978, also showing there in 1985. Other appearances included Arts Council, Belfast, 1979; Art and the Sea, ICA, 1981; Paton Gallery, 1982; Bluecoat Gallery, 1985; Kerlin Gallery, Dublin, 1988; and Fenderesky Gallery, Belfast, 1991. He also took part in British and foreign art fairs. Arts Council, Ulster Museum in Belfast and European Parliament in Brussels hold examples.

Miles McALINDEN 1937– Painter and teacher who studied at Leeds College of Art and Slade School of Fine Art. He was included in numerous mixed exhibitions, including The Teaching Image, 1964 show of work by staff of Leeds College of Art at the local City Art Gallery. Later moved to Oslo, Norway.

Helen MacALISTER 1969– Artist and teacher who after Trinity Academy Secondary School, Edinburgh, 1980–6, did a portfolio course at Stevenson College of Further Education there, 1986–7, then gained a first-class honours degree in fine art, drawing and painting, Duncan of Jordanstone College of Art, Dundee, 1987–91. On occasions from 1992 she was a visiting lecturer there. From 1991–2 MacAlister lived and worked Cité Internationale des Arts, Paris, further studying printmaking and at the Sorbonne. Among prizes and scholarships won were a Hospitalfield Scholarship, 1990; a bursary to study Italian at Siena University and the Rome Scholarship in Painting at the British School at Rome, both gained 1993; and a scholarship/residency at the MacDowell Colony, Peterborough, New Hampshire, 1995–6. In Rome MacAlister was assistant to the artist David Tremlett. MacAlister's many shows included Demarco Gallery, Edinburgh, 1989; RSA from 1990; Royal Glasgow Institute of the Fine Arts from 1992; and RSW, 1994. Highland Regional Council organised a touring show of her work, 1994–5. MacAlister wrote of her work that her major concern had been "with the uses and origins of imagery in communication". She endeavoured to express how imagery could "convey the significance of time and space". MacAlister's work is held by Scottish Arts Council, RSA and San Francisco Museum of Modern Art. Lived in Edinburgh.

Jane MACALLISTER 1953– Artist, teacher and gallery administrator who graduated in fine art from Sheffield College of Art. She went on to teach at Carlisle College of Art and Design, 1975–9. In 1980 was a visiting tutor at Gordonstoun School, and from that year onwards was involved in Edinburgh Arts Summer Schools and was deputy director of Richard Demarco Gallery in the city. Among special projects involved in was the Demarco Festival Theatre Programme from 1981. Macallister gained a Guild of Master Craftsmen award in 1987. From mid-1980s won a series of British Council Travel Awards, three times to Poland, and to Yugoslavia. She gained the Polish Order of Cultural Merit in 1990. Showed at Design Centre in 1969, with SSWA, SSA, at the Scottish Postal Board Exhibition, 1989, and Ash Gallery, Edinburgh, 1990.

Patricia McALLISTER 1932– Sculptor, born in Rhodesia, who studied in South Africa, gained a travelling scholarship to England, attending Goldsmiths' College sculpture school, later having a year in Rome. In 1958–60 she worked with the African sculptor Lazarus Khumalo at the Sculpture Centre for Africans, Bulawayo, where she exhibited, also in Johannesburg, Rome and London. Work exhibited in London Artists, at Shrewsbury School, 1968, was typical. McAllister was concerned with human relationships in sculpture. She worked with polyester resins and fibreglass, reinforcing built up over a welded rod frame, and using aluminium powder, metal scrapings and coloured glass.

Terry McALLISTER fl. from c.1990– Painter and draughtsman whose work included geometrical abstracts, McAllister graduated in fine art from University of Ulster, Belfast, in 1990. He gained the Silver Medal of the RUA in 1990, and was selected for the Claremorris Open Competition in that year. In 1992 he took part in a slide presentation with three colleagues and members of Voices Northern Ireland which was held at five venues in Belfast and participated in the No Access group show at Belfast Youth and Community Centre. Took part in Trasna, a Belfast/Glasgow Exchange, in 1993, his work being shown at Transmission Gallery, Glasgow. In 1994 McAllister took part in Works on Paper and Beyond the Partitions, put on by Queen Street Studios, Belfast, with which he was associated. His first solo show appeared at New Plaza, Belfast, 1994.

Jean MACALPINE 1953– Printmaker and photographer, born in Lancashire. She gained a bachelor's degree in fine art at Bristol Polytechnic, 1973–6, then did extended studies in printmaking at Camberwell College of Art & Design, 1976–7. Took part in many group shows, including Pelter/Sands Gallery, Bristol, 1976; Photo-Op '85 at Fermoy Centre, King's Lynn, where she was a prizewinner, 1985; Scils Gallery, Stowmarket, 1988; Louise Hallett Gallery, 1989; RA Summer Exhibition, 1992, and On Line Gallery, Southampton, in the same year. Had a solo show at Hampstead Theatre Foyer in 1991, and in that year at Flowers East, with a studio show in Islington arranged by The Hart Gallery, Linby, in 1993. Contemporary Art Society bought her work for Imperial Chemical Industries.

Andrew MACARA 1944– Painter with a rich sense of colour, born in Ashbourne, Derbyshire. Apart from a brief period with Leonard Fuller at St Ives School of Painting he was mainly self-taught. Macara first showed at Derby Museum and Art Gallery in 1976, at RA Summer Exhibition from 1977 and was a member of RBA and NEAC. He was included in Royal Academy Exhibitors at Fosse Gallery, Stow-on-the-Wold, 1987. Had a first solo show at Upstairs Gallery, RA, 1985. Lived in Derby.

Christine McARTHUR 1953– Artist and teacher, notable for studies in pastel, who also worked in embroidery and collage, born in Kirkintilloch, near Glasgow, where she settled. She attended the School of Art, 1971–6, under David Donaldson, gaining a post-diploma and travelling scholarship to Paris, then lectured part-time at Glasgow University from 1986 and at Glasgow School of Art, 1990–2. From 1990 was a member of the Glasgow Institute of the Fine Arts. Had a solo show at Peter Potter Gallery in Haddington, 1984, later ones including Roger Billcliffe Fine Art, Glasgow, from 1992. Won a series of awards, including Scottish Arts Council, Glasgow Society of Women Artists, Lauder and N S Macfarlane. Scottish Arts Council and various corporate collections hold examples.

Paula MacARTHUR 1967– Painter, born in Enfield, Middlesex, who studied at Loughborough College of Art and Design, 1987–90, then Royal Academy Schools, 1990–3. Showed in Northern Young Contemporaries at Whitworth Art Gallery in Manchester, 1989, and RA Summer Exhibitions from 1991. In 1989 MacArthur was joint first prizewinner in John Player Portrait Award, leading to a National Portrait Gallery commission, and she won a prize in 1993–4 John Moores Liverpool Exhibition with a jokey multi-portrait acrylic on canvas. Lived in London.

Ronald MacARTHUR 1914– Painter and teacher, born and lived in Edinburgh, where he attended the College of Art, 1933–7, teachers including David Foggie and William MacTaggart. Went on to teach art at Portobello High School, 1952–79. MacArthur was elected RSW in 1982 and was a member of the Scottish Arts Club.

Thomas McARTHUR 1915–1993 Painter and teacher, born in London. He attended Tottenham Grammar School, then Hornsey School of Art, 1930. Was a founder-member of Wood Green Art Society who went to teach in Somerset, settling in Crewkerne. Was a member of NS, also showing at RBA, RSMA and RP.

Sylvia MACARTNEY fl. from c.1940s– Painter, draughtsman and musician. After private education she studied at Royal College of Music, in London, Chelsea Polytechnic and Atelier Colarossi. Took part in group shows at RI, AIA, NEAC and elsewhere and had several one-man exhibitions at Jack Bilbo's Modern Art Gallery. Lived in London.

Duncan MacASKILL 1944– Versatile artist, born in Clydebank, Scotland, studying at Glasgow School of Art, 1963–7. MacAskill worked in "multi-media, everything/anything" and described himself as "househusband, painter who also designs for dance, sculptor, performance and mail art." Conceptual games and puns were a feature of MacAskill's mail art, the rigours of the postal journey contributing essentially to the final object. For his 1998 solo show at Milton Gallery, St Paul's School, MacAskill mailed to himself daily for six months. Previous one-mans included Reed's Wharf Gallery, 1993; Djanogly University Gallery Nottingham, 1996; and Wapping Pumping Station, 1997. Also did work for Dance House Films, for BBC2 Television, 1990; Almeida Theatre, 1993; Royal Court Theatre, 1994; and Queen Elizabeth Hall, 1995. Lived in London.

Karen MACAW 1960– Versatile artist, born in Lower Hutt, New Zealand, who studied at Canterbury School of Fine Arts in Christchurch, then at Gesamthochschule für Kunst, Kassel, West Germany. Macaw carried out commissions for heraldic paintings for The Sign of the Takahe, at Christchurch, and outdoor sculpture for Diwan Science & Information Technology Ltd. Group shows included Mini Print Exhibition, Joan Miró Foundation, Barcelona, and the Drawing Beinnale there, both 1984; East End Open Studios, from 1990; Paperworks IV, Seagate Gallery, Dundee, 1993; and Royal Over-Seas League Open, 1995. Had a solo show, Minding The Threads, Gingko Gallery, Christchurch, 1984, later ones including Amorc Kunst Kabinett, Baden Baden, 1987.

Henry MACBETH-RAEBURN 1860–1947 Painter and printmaker, son of the artist Norman Macbeth. He studied at Edinburgh University and art at Royal Scottish Academy Schools and at Académie Julian, Paris. He became a member of RE in 1905 and of RA in 1933 and served on their councils. Also showed at ROI, RSA, Walker Art Gallery in Liverpool, RI and elsewhere. He was an Arts Club member and a keen golfer, one of his houses, in Stroud Green, being called Wentworth House. Later settled in Dedham, Essex.

James McBEY 1883–1959 Painter and etcher, born at Foveran, Aberdeenshire, who began work in a bank. He attended evening classes at Gray's Art School, Aberdeen, taught himself etching, built his own press and by 1906–7 was showing at RSA and Royal Glasgow Institute of the Fine Arts. In 1910 he left the bank, worked on the continent and held his first one-man show at Goupil Gallery in 1911 which was very successful. Having travelled in Morocco in 1912, during World War II McBey was appointed official war artist in Egypt. When the etching boom declined in the 1920s McBey, who had already painted some good portraits, including one of T E Lawrence of Arabia, diversified into oils, watercolours and drawings and established a market for his work among American collectors, having a good show at Knoedler Gallery, New York, in 1929. Early in the 1930s McBey returned to Europe and bought a second home in Tangier, where he died. Aberdeen Art Gallery has a large collection of his work.

Alexander MacBRIDE 1859–1955 Watercolourist, born in Cathcart, Lanarkshire, who studied at Glasgow School of Art and at Académie Julian, Paris. He was elected RSW, RI and to Royal Glasgow Institute of the Fine Arts, at all of which he exhibited extensively. Also showed at RA, Walker Art Gallery in Liverpool and elsewhere. He settled in Cathcart, was notable for his Scottish landscapes and was a member of Glasgow Art Club.

Christina McBRIDE 1963– Artist using mixed media, such as photography/film, resin and wax, born and lived in Glasgow, where she attended the School of Art, 1986–90, then the Slade School of Fine Art, 1990–2. She was included in Out of Context, Hallam Fine Art, 1991; Projecting the Gorbals, part of Fotofeis, Glasgow, and A Sense of Place, installation at Chatham Historic Dockyards, Kent, both 1993; and New Art in Scotland, Centre for Contemporary Arts, Glasgow, 1994.

Denis McBRIDE 1939– Artist and teacher, born in Belfast, who studied at the College of Art there, 1958–63, then was at Hornsey College of Art, 1964. He taught for many years at Ulster College of Art and Design. McBride's work showed a strong sense of pattern allied with a notable emotional content. Commissioned works included several for Arts Council of Northern Ireland, which with Ulster Museum holds examples of McBride's output. A two-dimensional assemblage for Strabane County Secondary School was undertaken in 1975. Exhibitions included Brooke Park Gallery in Londonderry, Ritchie Hendriks Gallery in Dublin and Tom Caldwell Gallery, Belfast.

Robert MacBRYDE 1913–1966 Painter, printmaker and theatrical designer who was born in Maybole, Ayrshire. After five years working in a factory, MacBryde entered Glasgow School of Art, 1932–7, where he met his then lifelong companion, the painter Robert Colquhoun. When Colquhoun was awarded a travelling scholarship the School found the money for MacBryde to accompany him to France and Italy, 1937–9. "The Roberts" then returned to Scotland; Colquhoun spent a short time in the Army, although MacBryde was exempt because of his health; then in 1941 they moved to London, becoming associated with Neo-Romantic artists such as John Minton, with whom they lived, Jankel Adler and Wyndham Lewis. The latter two influenced MacBryde's work, still life with some figures. This has generally been rated below Colquhoun's, although MacBryde was a fine picture-maker with a unique colour sense. In 1943 MacBryde had his only one-man show at Lefevre Gallery. After World War II he worked with Colquhoun on prints for Miller's Press in Lewes and they jointly designed sets and costumes for Massine's ballet *Donald of the Burthens*, in 1951. MacBryde also painted murals for the liner *Oronsay* and a large picture, Figure and Still Life, for the Arts Council for the 1951 Festival of Britain. Colquhoun's death shattered MacBryde, who was killed by a car in Dublin, where he had then moved. Tate Gallery, Scottish National Portrait Gallery and other public collections hold his work.

McC: *see* **Otway McCANNELL**

H G McC: *see* **Herbert Graham McCULLOCH**

Gladys MACCABE 1918– Painter, teacher and writer, born in Randalstown, Northern Ireland, married to the artist Max Maccabe. She was educated at Brookvale Collegiate School, Belfast, then at the College of Art there, 1934–8. She was a member of the Watercolour Society of Ireland, ROI and was a president of the Ulster Society of Women Artists. Also exhibited at RUA, RSA and widely abroad. The American statesman Adlai Stevenson, the Irish actor Cyril Cusack and the actress Beatrice Lillie owned Maccabe's work, which is also held by the Imperial War Museum, Ulster Museum in Belfast and Arts Council of Northern Ireland. For a time she taught at Glens of Antrim School of Art and for Carnegie United Kingdom Trust. Had a solo show at The Bruton Street Gallery, 1995. Lived in Belfast.

Max MACCABE 1917– Painter, teacher and art critic, born in Belfast, Northern Ireland, where he continued to live, married to the artist Gladys Maccabe. He was a self-taught artist who was educated at the Royal Belfast Academical Institution. Maccabe went on to teach at the Carnegie United Kingdom Trust and Irish School of Landscape Painting. He was a member of the Watercolour Society of Ireland, also showing in London and widely abroad. Allied Irish Banks holds his work.

Angela McCAFFREY 1962– Painter and teacher, born in Dumfriesshire, Scotland. She did a foundation studies course at Preston Polytechnic, 1983, then gained an honours degree in fine art at Stourbridge College of Art, 1984–7. Was married to the artist John McCaffrey. She went on to lecture at Wolverhampton as a visitor and taught part-time at Stafford College. Taught part-time at Northbrook College, Worthing, 1990–2. She showed with Whitworth Young Contemporaries, 1987; Pacesetters 8, Peterborough, 1988; in East, at Norwich Gallery, 1991; East & South, at Norwich Gallery/Kent Institute of Art and Design, 1992; and in that year she shared a show with her husband at Mina Renton Gallery. Lived in Worthing, Sussex.

John McCAFFREY 1961– Painter and teacher, born Townhead, Glasgow, married to the artist Angela McCaffrey. He did foundation studies at Preston Polytechnic, 1983, then gained an honours degree in fine art, Wolverhampton Polytechnic, 1984–7. In 1987–90 was a visiting lecturer at Birmingham and Wolverhampton Polytechnics; taught part-time at Stafford College; then from 1990–2 lectured in art and design at Northbrook College, Worthing. His exhibition venues included Whitworth Young Contemporaries, 1987; Art Company, Leeds, 1989; East, at Norwich Gallery, 1991; East & South, at Norwich Gallery/Kent Institute of Art and Design, 1992; and joint show at Mina Renton Gallery, 1992. Lived in Worthing, Sussex.

Charles James McCALL 1907–1989 Painter, mainly in oil, especially of small, intimate interiors, and street scenes in London and France. His work has a strong sense of colour, painterliness and an awareness of French influences such as Vuillard. Initially educated in Edinburgh, McCall at first worked for a law firm, studying in the evenings at Edinburgh College of Art. At 23 he won a scholarship to Edinburgh College, sponsored by his teacher D M Sutherland, obtaining his diploma in two years instead of the usual four. Other teachers were David Foggie and S J Peploe. Scholarships in the mid-1930s took McCall extensively around Europe, and for much of 1937 he studied in Paris under Othon Friesz at the Atelier Colarossi. On his return he was awarded a two-year fellowship in Edinburgh. After commissioned service in the Royal Engineers in World War II, mainly working on camouflage, McCall resumed painting and gradually built up an impressive series of one-man shows in England, North America, Canada and Ireland, venues including Leicester Galleries; Waddington Gallery, Dublin; and Belgrave Gallery. Christie's held a large retrospective in 1995. Lived in London.

Rod McCANCE 1950– Artist in oil, acrylic and pen and ink, and sculptor in metal, whose work was tinged with a wry humour. He was born in Hamilton, Lanarkshire, great-nephew of the artist William McCance, who was an influence. Studied textiles at Clydesdale College, Glasgow, then went into the retail trade, buying and selling cloth. After a period as a professional stiltwalker and working for engineering firm Glynwed International as "a troubleshooter on the heating and cooker side", McCance was made redundant in the mid-1980s, and began painting seriously, eventually full-time. Occasionally he toured Scotland as a demonstrator for Winsor & Newton artists' materials. McCance had a strong affiliation with the industrial past of Glasgow and was accused of being a "Vorticist of sorts". He called himself "the bendy artist", reference to his tendency to put compositional curves on straight objects. Group shows included Trinity Gallery, Albert Hall in Stirling and Solstice Gallery, Edinburgh. Solo exhibitions included MacRobert Centre in Stirling and Perth Theatre Gallery. Lived in Strathyre, Perthshire.

William McCANCE 1894–1970 Painter, typographer, sculptor, teacher and writer, born in Cambuslang, Scotland. Studied at Glasgow School of Art under Robert Anning Bell and Maurice Greiffenhagen, winning a Travelling Scholarship. Married Agnes Miller Parker, the wood engraver. In 1920 they exhibited with other Scottish artists at the McLellan Galleries, Glasgow, the year they moved to London. Through the 1920s McCance produced advanced works with a strong Cubist influence. He also engaged in magazine illustration, taught, showed in London galleries and drew for C M Grieve's Scottish Nationalist journal *The Free Man*. In 1930 McCance moved to Newtown, Montgomeryshire, where he worked for three years with the Gregynog Press, designing and illustrating fine books. McCance lived in England in the late-1930s, producing terracotta and fireclay sculpture while writing for the *News Chronicle* and *Reynolds News*. From 1943 for 14 years McCance was lecturer in typography and book production at Reading University School of Art, during this time creating wax-resist watercolours and lino-cuts, inspired by a visit to the Lascaux caves in France, as well as monotype overlay drawings using printer's inks. McCance returned to Scotland in 1960, having separated from his wife, later marrying Margaret McCance and settling in Girvan, Ayrshire. She helped organise a number of exhibitions of his art, including one at Cyril Gerber Fine Art, Glasgow, 1989.

Brian McCANN 1952– Sculptor, draughtsman, installations artist and teacher, born in Glasgow. He studied at Duncan of Jordanstone College of Art in Dundee, 1976–80, and Royal College of Art, 1980–3. Was a Prix de Rome Scholar, 1984–6. In 1988 McCann became a tutor at Kingston Polytechnic, the year following gaining a Tate Momart Fellowship at Tate Gallery, Liverpool. His work was included in Sculpture & Sculptors' Drawings at William Jackson Gallery, 1991. Solo shows included Towards the Fire, at Salisbury Art Gallery and Festival, 1988; Bournemouth Sculpture Festival in 1991; in the same year Watermans Art Centre, Brentford; and Harriet Green Gallery, 1996. Lived in London.

Ellen J W McCANN 1954– Sculptor and teacher, born in Aberdeen, where she studied at Gray's School of Art, 1972–7, including a postgraduate year, in which she gained a Travelling Scholarship to Italy. McCann also won the RSA Meyer Oppenheim Prize and Ottillie Helen Wallace Scholarship Fund Prize, both 1978; Scottish Arts Council Award, 1978; and RSA Benno Schotz Award, 1979. Taught art at Peterhead Academy, 1978–80, also being a temporary lecturer at Gray's School. Showed in various group and national exhibitions in Aberdeen, Edinburgh and Glasgow, and was included in 10 North-East Artists, Artspace Aberdeen Edinburgh Festival show and tour, 1981–2. Lived for a time in Kirriemuir, Angus.

George MacCANN 1909–1967 Sculptor, painter, designer and teacher, born and lived in Belfast, son of the monumental sculptor David MacCann. He was married to the artist Mercy Hunter, whom he met while studying from 1926–9 at Belfast School of Art. A scholarship took him to Royal College of Art, 1929–32. Among teaching appointments on his return was Belfast College of Art, 1938–9, prior to war service in Far East in Army. In 1942 he published short stories, *Sparrows Round My Brow* under the pen-name George Galway (Galway being his middle name). MacCann returned briefly to teaching, then was involved in commissioned work for the Festival of Britain, 1951, in Ulster and London. MacCann had a solo show at New Gallery, Belfast, 1965, and Queen's University there gave him a memorial exhibition in 1968. Arts Council of Northern Ireland holds his work. MacCann was a lifelong friend of Louis MacNeice, sharing the poet's love of talking, art, poetry, rugby football, stout and Irish whiskey. He made MacNeice's death mask and appears in Jon Stallworthy's biography of him.

Otway McCANNELL 1883–1969 Figure and landscape artist in most media, and teacher, born in Wallasey, Cheshire. McCannell was educated in New Zealand, where his family had sailed, and where a football accident left him lame. Began studying at Bournemouth School of Art, 1899, then won a Royal Scholarship to Royal College of Art in 1900, where studied under Gerald Moira. Began teaching at Harrow Art School in 1919; from 1928–45 principal of Farnham School of Art; taught part-time at St Martin's School of Art, 1946–60. Was regarded as an inspiring teacher, many students going on to the Royal College. His daughter Ursula McCannell studied at Farnham. Often signing his work McC, he began exhibiting at the RA in 1915, also showing at Leger and Redfern Galleries, RI, ROI, RBA and Paris Salon. Between 1946–69 one-man exhibitions at Jack Bilbo's Modern Art Gallery, Gallery One, Obelisk Gallery, AIA, New Vision Centre, Drian Gallery and elsewhere. Included in show of three generations of McCannell family at England & Co, 1989. Illustrated several books. McCannell's work went through phases: traditional, then romantic pictures of the 1920s and 1930s, symbolic and satirical works in the 1940s, his later pictures being abstract/Cubist and finally Symbolist. His work is held by several provincial galleries. Lived at Farnham.

Ursula McCANNELL 1923– Painter, born in London, daughter of the artist Otway McCannell. She was married to the artist Peter Rees Roberts, their three sons – Tristan, Marcus and Lucien – all being artists. Ursula studied at Farnham School of Art, 1939–42, then at Royal College of Art, 1942–4, where she transferred to the school of design under Ernest Tristram, leaving with a diploma in mural painting. As early as 1934 had shared a show with her father at Wertheim Gallery. Over the years she had many further shows, including Jack Bilbo's Modern Art Gallery, Ashgate Gallery in Farnham, Thackeray Gallery, Seen Gallery and Clifton Fine Art. Also appeared in mixed shows at Redfern Gallery, RA, Leicester Galleries and Gimpel Fils. In 1989 England & Co included her in a three generations of McCannells show. She had a great love of Spain, visited India in 1972 and in that year bought a remote farmhouse in Ireland. Her work sometimes had a strong romantic flavour. Manchester City Art Gallery holds her early self-portrait, bought by Contemporary Art Society in 1940. Lived in Farnham, Surrey.

Keith McCARTER 1936– Sculptor in wide variety of materials and teacher, born in Edinburgh, where he studied at the College of Art, 1956–60, under Eric Schilsky and Helen Turner. Was awarded an Andrew Grant Scholarship which permitted extensive travels through continental Europe and Scandinavia, 1960–1. McCarter in 1961–3 lived in America, worked as a designer for Steuben Glass, studied materials used in construction which might be employed in art forms and travelled; was a visiting lecturer at Hornsey College of Art, 1964–8; began to work full-time as a sculptor; and in 1969–73 lectured on the aesthetics of concrete at the Cement and Concrete Association, working as a member of the design team for government project at Vauxhall. McCarter was further to travel in Brazil and work on constructions in Scotland, Washington and Galveston. He made a large number of two-dimensional works in concrete and commissioned sculptures included Jupiter for British High Commission, Lagos, Nigeria; Encounter, Guy's Hospital; Embrace, Regent's Park; and Challenger, Abbey Road. He was elected to RBS in 1991. McCarter had a first group of small bronzes taken by Marlborough Fine Art in 1976, and went on to show at RA, 1979, at Alwin Gallery, 1985, and Norwich Cathedral Triennial Festival in 1991. He had a first solo show at Burleighfield, 1978. Lived in Great Plumstead, Norfolk.

Cornelius McCARTHY fl. from 1950s– Painter, in oil and gouache, and draughtsman. He studied under Sam Rabin at Goldsmiths' College School of Art in 1950s when figurative painting was unfashionable. The Keith Vaughan exhibition at Whitechapel Art Gallery in 1962 reinforced McCarthy's desire to concentrate on painting the male nude. After, in 1990, the artist moved into a remote house in the Fens – the first time he had lived outside London – his work became less claustrophic and angular, more relaxed and pastoral. Exhibitions included two solo shows at St Jude's, 1989–91. A collection of McCarthy's paintings was published in 1987 as *Interiors*, with an introduction by Emmanuel Cooper.

Clive McCARTNEY 1960– Painter, notably of landscapes, and teacher, born in New Delhi, India, who later lived in Bahrain until his parents returned to England. McCartney trained at Central and Chelsea Schools of Art, in his degree studies at Chelsea, where he received a distinction, studying under Cecil Collins, Patrick Caulfield, Ken Kiff and Anthony Whishaw. Vuillard, Morandi, Sickert and Matisse were influences on his work. After graduation, McCartney travelled extensively, including India, Arabia, Turkey, North Africa and Spain, strong contrasts of light and shade being of special interest. On his return McCartney taught at Dulwich College, in 1991 was awarded a residency at Sutton Valence School in Kent for two years, then became a full-time painter. Mixed shows included Young Contemporaries at ICA, 1983; Graham Gallery, Duncan Miller Contemporary and RA Summer Exhibition, all 1994; and in 1996 he shared an exhibition at Duncan Miller with Anne Gordon. Had a first London solo show at New Grafton Gallery in 1995. Lived in south London.

Alistair McCHEYNE 1918–1981 Painter, teacher and critic. Born in Perth, Scotland, McCheyne studied art in Edinburgh, under the portrait and interior painter David Alison, in the late 1930s; also studied in London and at L'Académie de la Grande Chaumière, Paris, after World War II. He won a number of scholarships. He became principal art teacher at George Heriot's School, Edinburgh, and taught painting and life drawing at Lauder Technical School, in Dunfermline. His work appeared in *The Scotsman* and *The Listener*. Exhibited at RSA, SSA and with the AEB. Lived in Edinburgh.

John Robert Murray McCHEYNE 1911– Sculptor and teacher, he studied at Edinburgh College of Art, 1930–5, with Alexander Carrick, then from 1936–8 in Copenhagen, Athens and Florence. Became master of sculpture at Newcastle University. As well as exhibiting at RSA, SSA and widely in the provinces, McCheyne completed a number of ecclesiastical commissions. Lived in Gosforth, Northumberland. Laing Art Gallery has McCheyne's Family Group, 1959, in the manner of Henry Moore.

Louise McCLARY 1958– Painter in acrylic, born in Penzance, Cornwall, where she settled in St Ives. She studied at Penzance School of Art, 1975–6. McClary said that her work was "about relationships. Themes include human vulnerability, fragility, tenderness and celebration of life." McClary was a member of Newlyn Orion in Newlyn and an associate of Penwith Gallery, St Ives. Her mixed shows included Eye Gallery, Bristol, and Brewhouse Open, in Taunton, both 1988; Summer Show at Salt House and Penwith Galleries, St Ives, both 1990; Spacex Gallery, Exeter, and Gordon Hepworth Gallery at Newton St Cyres, both 1991; and Marsden Fine Art at Smith's Galleries, 1993. She had a solo show at Penzar Gallery, Penzance, in 1987, later ones including Beaux Arts, Bath, 1991 onwards.

Sheila McCLEAN 1932– Painter in oil and teacher, born in Moville, County Donegal, Ireland. She studied with John Luke and Colin Middleton at Belfast Art College, 1951–6, then taught at grammar and secondary schools in Londonderry, where she lived, 1956–60 and 1969–80, eventually giving up teaching to paint. She was an associate of RUA. Commissions included Stations of the Cross for St Pius X, Moville, and the *Belfast 1991 Calendar*. Participated in many group shows throughout Ireland, later solo exhibitions including Gordon Gallery, Londonderry, 1991, and Cavehill Gallery, Belfast, 1994. Department of the Environment, Belfast, and The Haverty Trust hold examples.

George McCLELLAND 1931– Artist, dealer and expert on modern Irish art. He was an art dealer in Belfast from 1960s for many years. Having begun to paint in 1950s, he studied at National College of Art, Dublin, 1977–9, and showed at annual Oireachtas Exhibition in Dublin, the Irish Exhibition of Living Art and at Art in Boxes at England & Co, 1991, his Waiting for Godot being a mixed-media assemblage. Represented in Ulster Museum, Belfast. Lived in Kerry, Ireland.

Daphne McCLURE 1930– Painter and designer, born in Helston, Cornwall, to which she returned in 1976, living many years at Porthleven. She studied art at Redruth, then at Hornsey School of Art under John Platt. For many years she was a costume and set designer at Royal Opera House, Covent Garden. Became a member of Newlyn Society of Artists and Penwith Society of Arts. Showed at Some of the Moderns, Belgrave Gallery, 1990; and was included in Artists from Cornwall at RWA, 1992. Had a solo show called Aspects of Hayle at Newlyn Orion Gallery, Penzance, 1990; another called Shorelines at Wolf at the Door Gallery, Penzance, 1991. She gained awards at Newlyn Contemporaries exhibitions, 1989–90. A strong sense of pattern was present in her work.

David McCLURE 1926–1998 Painter, teacher and writer, born in Lochwinnoch, Renfrewshire. He was educated at Queen's Park School in Glasgow and Edinburgh University, and attended Edinburgh College of Art, 1947–52, winning a travelling scholarship in 1952–3, then becoming an Andrew Grant Fellow, 1955–7. Between 1957–85 he taught painting at Duncan of Jordanstone College of Art, in Dundee. Wrote monograph on the painter John Maxwell. McClure's painting occasionally adopts the slightly mystical qualities of Maxwell's work, but he is instantly recognisable as a rich Colourist. Elected RSA in 1971 and showed widely in group shows in Scotland and elsewhere. One-man exhibitions began in 1957 with Circolo di Cultura, Palermo; others included Scottish Gallery, Edinburgh; and Thackeray Gallery, London. In 1988 Fine Art Society, Glasgow and Edinburgh, gave him a retrospective. Work in many public collections including Aberdeen and Dundee Art Galleries. For years lived in Dundee.

Emma McCLURE 1962– Painter, born in London, whose flat, decorative compositions were cited as being "like the jazz improvisations which provide one of her most characteristic motifs". She studied at Falmouth School of Art, 1980–1, then gained at honours degree in painting at Winchester School of Art, 1981–4, her master's degree from Chelsea School of Art, 1984–5. Group exhibitions included Royal Over-Seas League and Contemporary Art Society Art Market at Smith's Gallery from 1985; Vanessa Devereux Gallery from 1990; and Marsden Fine Art from 1992. Vanessa Devereux gave her a series of solo shows from 1986, when she was also Artist of the Day at Angela Flowers Gallery, later ones including Cadogan Contemporary, 1994.

Ramsay Dyke McCLURE 1924–1981 Artist in various media. He was one of Keith Vaughan's students at Central School of Arts and Crafts, 1948, eventually becoming Vaughan's lifelong companion and lover. Their relationship was sometimes difficult, but McClure provided some domestic stability. McClure's father had been a political cartoonist, as Dyke White, on a Glasgow newspaper. McClure served in the Royal Navy, but got into trouble for a homosexual offence and served a prison sentence for failing to return to ship. In the mid-1960s Vaughan exiled McClure to a cottage at Toppesfield, near Halstead, although he periodically lived with Vaughan in London, as described by Malcolm Yorke in *Keith Vaughan His Life and Work*, 1990. He finally settled in Sudbury, Suffolk, being a beneficiary of Vaughan's will. McClure had a talent for small collages, models and still life pictures, but his work was overshadowed by Vaughan's.

David MACCOBY 1925– Artist in oil, pastel and charcoal, born in Sunderland, County Durham. He pursued "lyrical Romantic Expressionism with a hint of Surrealism in abstract work". Maccoby studied at Sunderland College of Arts and Crafts, 1941–3; served in the Royal Navy in Europe and the Far East; then continued his studies after demobilisation at Chelsea School of Art, 1946–9, under Raymond Coxon, Ceri Richards, Robert Medley and Vivian Pitchforth. Maccoby's work was portraits, landscapes and figurative in the 1950s; it tended towards Abstract Expressionism in the 1960s; in the 1970s he travelled widely to complete portraits in oil and pastel; then failing sight prevented him from continuing his career. Mixed shows included RP, AIA, LG, NEAC, NS and Drian and Alwin Galleries. Portraits included Bertrand Russell and J B Priestley. Had many solo shows in Britain and America, including Ben Uri Art Society from 1951, with a retrospective, 1975, and an exhibition of work from 1948–75 at Sternberg Centre for Judaism, 1992. Ben Uri holds his oil on paper Spring Equinox. Lived in London.

Malcolm McCOIG 1941– Painter, printmaker, designer and teacher, born in Greenock, Renfrewshire. He studied at Glasgow School of Art, with postgraduate work. In 1964 he was appointed head of the textile department at Gray's School of Art, Aberdeen. McCoig was artist-in-residence at Soulesquoi Printmakers, in Orkney, and in 1988 was visiting lecturer at the University of Nigeria. Among the awards he won was a Scottish Arts Council Award in 1975 and an Arts Council Bursary to Madison, Wisconsin. McCoig's solo shows included New 57 Gallery, Edinburgh, and in 1980 a retrospective in Scotland which included Glasgow School of Art. He was in the first show held by Compass Gallery, Glasgow, and in The Compass Contribution at Tramway, Glasgow, 1990. Scottish National Gallery of Modern Art holds his work.

Dugald Sutherland MacCOLL 1859–1948 Watercolourist, writer, teacher and curator. Born in Glasgow, D S MacColl studied at London and Oxford Universities, then at the Westminster School of Art and Slade School of Fine Art under Alphonse Legros, 1884–92. During his art student days he travelled widely in Europe. From 1896 he was a member of

NEAC and during long stints as art critic of *The Spectator* and *The Saturday Review* he consistently advocated acceptance of Impressionism. He was to write the life of his Impressionist painter friend Philip Wilson Steer. MacColl's own watercolours, signed D S M, have a pale, Impressionist quality. Exhibited extensively at NEAC, Goupil Gallery and Carfax Gallery, also at Fine Art Society, RSA and elsewhere. British Museum, Tate Gallery and Victoria & Museum hold his work. MaColl was keeper of the Tate Gallery, 1906–11, and keeper of the Wallace Collection, 1911–24. Among his other writings are poems and *Confessions of a Keeper*, which contains some fine analytical writing. Memorial show at Tate Gallery, 1950. Lived in London.

Leonard McCOMB 1930– Sculptor in various materials, painter, printmaker, draughtsman and teacher, born in Glasgow. He studied at Manchester School of Art, drawing with Harry Sutcliffe and Ted Roocroft for sculpture, then at Slade School of Fine Art with A H Gerrard for sculpture, 1956–60. He taught at various art colleges, 1960–89, including Royal Academy Schools, Slade School, Goldsmiths' and Sir John Cass. McComb (pronounced comb) was awarded the Jubilee Prize at RA in 1977, gained its, Korn Ferry Prize in 1988 and was elected RA in 1990, its keeper in 1995. He said that his work, signed with the monogram L M, was "sometimes to me a kind of singing in shapes and colours, sometimes light, sometimes dark. Life contains many opposites." McComb destroyed most of his work up to 1976. He was first shown in London at Human Clay, selected by R B Kitaj for Arts Council, 1976. Was also in British Painting 1952–1977, at RA in 1977; British Sculpture in the Twentieth Century, Whitechapel Art Gallery, 1981; Representation Abroad, Hirshhorn Museum, Washington, America, 1986; Towner Art Gallery, Eastbourne, 1990; and The Discerning Eye, Mall Galleries, 1992. There was a solo touring show by Museum of Modern Art, Oxford, and Arts Council, 1982, later ones including Browse & Darby, 1993. Arts Council, British Council, Tate Gallery and other public collections hold examples. Lived in London.

John McCOMBS 1943– Landscape painter, born in Manchester, where he attended the Art School, then St Martin's School of Art, 1962–7, teachers including Leon Kossoff and Frederick Gore. McCombs was a member of ROI, also showing at Tib Lane and Portland Galleries in Manchester, Chenil and Mall Galleries and at several public galleries in the north, where he lived at Delph, Oldham, Lancashire. Salford Art Gallery and Manchester City Art Gallery hold examples.

Charles McCONNELL 1897–1983 Painter of marine subjects, landscapes and portraits, educated at Ardingly College, Sussex. Exhibited RSMA, UA, Fine Art Society and in the provinces. Lived in London's dockland, later in Deal, Kent.

Claire McCORMACK 1953– Artist, garden designer and teacher, born in London. She studied at Royal Botanic Gardens, Kew, 1973–6, then Chelsea School of Art, 1977–81. She gained a prize in Art into Landscape 3, in 1980. Taught at Central Institute of Adult Education. Exhibitions included Pitsea Studios Open Day, 1981; Albany Neon Sculpture Competition Exhibition, 1982, in which she was a finalist; and a four-man show at Woodlands Art Gallery, 1985.

Josephine McCORMICK 1960– Printmaker and teacher, born in Belfast, Northern Ireland, also worked as JMC and Real vivid, who did a foundation course at Preston Polytechnic, 1978–9; graduated at Liverpool Polytechnic in fine art, 1980–2; then gained her master's degree in printmaking, 1991–3. Went on to teach graphic design at University of Central Lancashire and printmaking at John Moores University, Liverpool. She did a variety of work for poetry magazines, record and compact disc covers and for the Camberwell College of Arts' prospectus. Group exhibitions included The Art of the Printmaker, Royal Festival Hall, 1990; Glasgow Print Studio, 1991; Seventh Miniature Print International, New York, 1992; and Hatton Gallery, University of Newcastle, 1994. Had a solo show at Art & Research Exchange, Belfast, 1981, later ones including Tricycle Gallery, Tricycle Theatre, 1994. Ulster Museum in Belfast holds her work. Lived in Chester.

Jane McCOURT fl. from 1980s– Versatile artist who after the North London Collegiate School did a foundation course in art and design at Harrow School of Art, 1980–1; gained an honours degree in fine art at West Surrey College of Art & Design, Farnham, 1981–4; obtained her master's degree at Academia de San Carlos, Mexico City, 1985–7, also completing advanced Spanish at Universidad Nacional Autonoma de Mexico; then studied printmaking at Morley College, 1990–6. Group shows included The Collective Gallery, Edinburgh, 1985; Portobello Open Print Show, 1990; Fisher Gallery, from 1993; and Seven Printmakers, The Gallery at Architecture Ltd, 1997. She had a solo show there in 1997, previous ones being at Freuds, Covent Garden, 1996, and Vic Naylors, 1992. Commissions included pantomime scenery for *Cinderella*, Chester Gateway Theatre, 1989; Ten Years of Covent Garden, mural, Covent Garden Piazza, 1990; Visuals for *Echo City*, musical performance at ICA Stratford Town Hall, Red Rose Club, 1991; and a Stained Glass Mosaic, 1993.

David McCRACKEN 1925– Watercolourist who was by profession a veterinary surgeon, born in Glasgow. He studied professionally at the Veterinary College there. For a time he lived in Hereford, then moved to Perth, Scotland, exhibiting locally.

Bridget McCRUM 1934– Sculptor in stone and painter, born in Yorkshire. She studied painting at Farnham College of Art, 1951–5, then carved stone with John Joekes, 1980–2. From mid-1970s showed in many mixed exhibitions, including RA, RSA, Eton College, Lynne Stern Associates, Phoenix Gallery in Lavenham and Vanessa Devereux Gallery. She had a solo show at Vanessa Devereux in 1986, at Phoenix Gallery in 1988, then in 1990 at School of Architecture, Plymouth. Lived near Dittisham, Dartmouth, Devon.

Herbert Graham McCULLOCH 1883– Artist who began his career in farming. Born in Woolton, near Liverpool, McCulloch attended Chester School of Art under Walter Walter Schroder, then Liverpool School of Art. Exhibited with Liver Sketching Club, of which he was a member, RCamA and at several locations in the north of England. Sometimes signed work H G McC. Lived at Wallasey, Cheshire.

Ian McCULLOCH 1935– Painter, muralist, printmaker and teacher, born in Glasgow, where he studied at the School of Art, 1953–7, and was awarded a RSA Travelling Scholarship. He gained Scottish Arts Council Awards in 1967 and 1972. McCulloch was artist-in-residence at the University of Sussex, 1976, and won 1st Prize Stirling Smith Biennale, 1985. He was elected a member of SSA, 1964, and an associate of the RSA, 1989. McCulloch was commissioned to paint murals for the Italian Centre, Glasgow, 1989, and was winner of the Glasgow International Concert Hall Mural Competition, 1989–90. In 1991–2 he lost a fight to prevent his work being suppressed, leaving him with a "sense of outrage and futility engendered by ... philistinism". McCulloch was a creator of powerful images with a hint of German Expressionism. His prints were directly cut with a range of tools in materials including driftwood, ceiling panels and laminates. For him, "art has a social function ... to contribute to the on-going debate within society about the nature of the times we live in." From 1967, McCulloch was lecturer in fine art at the University of Strathclyde in the department of architecture and building science. Took part in many group shows. Had a solo exhibition at Blythswood Gallery, Glasgow, 1959, later ones including Peacock Printmakers, Aberdeen, 1994. Scottish Arts Council; Saatchi Collection; Universities of Glasgow, Liverpool and Strathclyde; Kelvingrove Art Gallery, Glasgow, and other collections hold his work. Lived in Glasgow.

Jeanette McCULLOCH 1959– Artist in a variety of media and lecturer who studied textiles at Manchester Polytechnic and tapestry at Royal College of Art. She worked as a teacher and illustrator and her exhibitions included Contemporary Design Show, Islington Business Centre, 1990, and Art in Boxes, at England & Co, 1992.

Peter McCULLOCH 1926– Painter, printmaker and teacher, born in Liverpool. Studied at Watford School of Art, Regent Street Polytechnic School of Art where he was a silver medallist and finally at West of England Art College, in Bristol. Showed at Young Contemporaries and elsewhere. Taught for some time in Bristol, where he lived.

George McCULLOUGH 1922– Painter, draughtsman and teacher, born and lived in Belfast, Northern Ireland. He studied at the College of Technology and College of Art there, 1940–7. Went on to run the Donegal School of Landscape Painting. Showed at RUA, Bell Gallery in Belfast, Cambridge and Oriel Galleries in Dublin and in North America.

Joseph McCULLOUGH 1893–1961 Draughtsman, watercolourist, printmaker and teacher, born in Leeds, Yorkshire, and educated at Brudenell School. He studied at the local College of Art, then gained his diploma from the Royal College of Art in 1912. Taught at Ipswich School of Art, 1922–5, then life drawing at Goldsmiths' College of Art, 1941–50, where he was remembered with affection. McCullough's speciality was pictures of public houses, over which he would site a barrage balloon; he favoured the long bar at Victoria Station after teaching evening classes. Eventually the pop of a cork and the gloop-gloop of the contents in the classroom at Goldsmiths' forced Clive Gardiner to sack McCullough, who came to a sad end. He occupied one of the Stamford Bridge Studios and was a member of Chelsea Arts Club, but was latterly reported on the street selling papers or matches. McCulloch was a member of RBA and NS and an associate of RWS. He also exhibited at RA, NEAC, and Redfern, Chenil and Leicester Galleries. Public galleries in Huddersfield, Leeds and Wakefield hold examples.

Adrian McCURDY 1953– Painter, draughtsman and sculptor, born in Kendal, Westmorland. He studied fine art at Nottingham College of Art, where he concentrated principally on sculpture. Settled in the Borders area, he worked partly in the building trade, partly on his art. Took part in group shows and was a contributor to The Compass Contribution at Tramway, Glasgow, 1990. He had had a solo show at Compass in 1982.

John McCUTCHEON 1910– Painter and draughtsman in pen and ink, born in Dalmellington, Ayrshire, settling in Ayr, where he was a member of the Sketch Club. After Ayr Academy he studied at Glasgow School of Art, 1929–33. He became a member of ROI in 1970, also exhibiting at RSA, Royal Glasgow Institute of the Fine Arts and at Paris Salon, where he gained an Hon. Mention. Glasgow's Kelvingrove Art Gallery holds his work.

Brendan McDERMOTT 1924–1989 Painter and teacher, born in Spennymoor, County Durham, who initially studied at Sunderland College of Art. During World War II he served in the Desert and Italy. McDermott was an ex-service student at the Royal College of Art, where he went to study illustration. He gained a John Knox Scholarship and painted in Brittany and Paris, where he developed his interest in etching, exploring the printing studios. Taught in West Hartlepool, then at Liverpool College of Art for most of his career. A key theme of McDermott's output was reminiscence of his childhood in the northeast, which a colleague remembered as "a mixture of Bonnard, Chagall and Carel Weight". Subject to depression, McDermott destroyed many of his pictures.

Carol McDERMOTT 1961– Painter, whose work tended towards abstraction, who studied at Newcastle, Woolwich, Southwark and Goldsmiths' Colleges and City & Guilds, sponsored by Christie's. She was included in many mixed shows throughout the United Kingdom and had a series of solo exhibitions at Christopher Hull Gallery from 1994.

Alan MacDONALD 1962– Figurative artist, who painted "entirely from my imagination" and who endeavoured "to capture a real, but enigmatic atmosphere", as in Dare-Devil, shown at Royal Over-Seas League Open, 1996. He was born in Nyasaland and studied at Duncan of Jordanstone College of Art, Dundee, and Cyprus College of Art, Paphos. Other group shows included Gloria Gallery, Nicosia, 1985; Compass Gallery, Glasgow, from 1986; Merz Contemporary Art, 1993; and The Discerning Eye, Mall Galleries, 1995. Had a solo show at Bruton Street Gallery, 1995. The Leeds Education collection has his work. Lived in London.

Alastair James Henderson MacDONALD 1934– Miniaturist, decorative artist and calligrapher, born in Tighnabruaich, Argyll. Studied at Woolwich Polytechnic School of Art with Heber Mathews and Joan Dawson. He showed with RMS of which he was a member, RI and elsewhere and lived in North Mymms, Hertfordshire.

Bridget MACDONALD 1943– Painter and draughtsman, born in the Isle of Wight, who, as a mature student, did a foundation course at Stourbridge College of Art & Technology, 1983–4, then gained a fine art honours degree at Wolverhampton Polytechnic, 1984–7. Macdonald's concern with the finer techniques of painting, composition and draughtsmanship, unfashionable in the mid-1980s, were important features of her brand of realism. A series of themes ran through her work, including her roles as wife, mother and artist, the poetry of Sylvia Plath, the life of Ezra Pound, and his and her own interest in the Italian Renaissance. Group exhibitions included The Leicestershire Collection Annual Exhibition, from 1988; Women's Images, Wolverhampton Art Gallery, 1989; Inner Language, an Ikon Gallery, Birmingham, tour, 1989–90; 10th International Cleveland Drawing Biennale and tour, 1991–2; and Re-Visions: Barber Institute of Fine Arts & Midlands Arts Centre, Birmingham, where she worked on a commission, 1996. Had a solo show in the New Art Wolverhampton series, Bilston Art Gallery, 1989, later ones including Quay Arts Centre, Newport, Isle of Wight, and Art First, both 1996. Public galleries in Birmingham, Wolverhampton and Worcester, The Leicestershire Collection and several corporate collections hold examples.

Bryan MACDONALD 1932– Sculptor and teacher, born in Singapore. He was educated at Elgin Academy, in Morayshire, then in 1954–6 was at Bretton Hall College of Education, in Yorkshire, followed in 1958–61 by studies at the fine art department of King's College, Durham University. Began lecturing on abstract sculpture at Salford School of Art in 1961, was Gulbenkian Fellow at Keele University, 1964–5, further posts following at Newport College of Art and Sheffield Polytechnic. Took part in many group shows, including LG, Bear Lane Gallery in Oxford, Grosvenor Gallery and Mappin Gallery, Sheffield. One-man show at Keele University, 1965. In 1970 he was joint first prize winner at WAC show Towards Sculpture. Commissions include a commemorative sculpture for Milford Haven, unveiled by HM The Queen in 1968. Keele University holds his work.

Frances MACDONALD 1914– Painter, draughtsman, printmaker and teacher, born in Wallasey, Cheshire, where she attended the Art School, 1930–4, under William Green and Gordon MacPherson, then Royal College of Art, 1934–8, under Barnett Freedman, whose work she always admired. She married the painter Leonard Appelbee. A portrait of Stanley Morison in Oliver Simon's magazine *Signature* led to Macdonald becoming an official war artist, 1940–6, her painting of the building of a Mulberry Harbour being accepted by the Tate Gallery. Also worked for the Pilgrim Trust's *Recording Britain* project. Macdonald taught at Goldsmiths' College School of Art, 1946–8; at Beckenham, 1957–69; Byam Shaw School, 1963–4; and Ruskin School, Oxford, 1964. She showed at Leicester Galleries, Wildenstein, the Festival of Britain 60 Paintings for '51 show and elsewhere. Had a solo show at Alfred Brod Gallery, 1961. Macdonald was a strong advocate of sound draughtsmanship, campaigning against what she believed to be the lack of it in major art schools from 1963. Victoria & Albert Museum and Imperial War Museum also hold examples. Lived in Kincardine-on-Forth, Fife, latterly in Aberdeen.

Frances MACDONALD 1940– Artist in watercolour and oil, born in Glasgow, who studied at St Martin's School of Art and Glasgow School of Art, evening classes. Macdonald was influenced by the Scottish Colourists and Fauve painters. She was known for her landscapes and pictures of fishing boats around the Crinan area of Argyll, where with her husband she ran an hotel, later developing a special interest in interiors and still life. She was a professional member of the SSWA and of Scottish Arts Club, also showing with Royal Glasgow Institute of the Fine Arts and RSW. Had a solo show at Gallery Paton, Edinburgh, 1975, later ones including Sue Rankin Gallery, 1989, and The Kelly Gallery, Glasgow, 1993.

Helen MacDONALD 1968– Painter who did a foundation course at Gamble Institute in St Helens, 1984–6, then studied at Sheffield Polytechnic. She showed in Art & Industry at Gamble Institute in 1986 and in 1986–7 was included in Merseyside Artists 3, Walker Art Gallery, Liverpool, touring exhibition.

Helen McDONALD 1968– Painter, born in Bournemouth, Hampshire, who studied at Kensington & Chelsea College, then Chelsea College of Art & Design. Group shows included King Sturge Art Prize, The London Institute of Higher Education, and Royal Over-Seas League Open, both 1996. There McDonald showed the acrylic on canvas A Way. She hoped in her work that "people may find their own associations", by leaving "an openness for interpretation".

Ian MACDONALD 1946– Artist, photographer and teacher, born in Middlesbrough, Yorkshire. He studied graphic design and printmaking at Teesside College of Art, 1968–71, painting and photography at Sheffield School of Art, 1971–4, and photography and graphic design at Birmingham Polytechnic, 1974–5. Did a variety of jobs, including labouring in industry and photographic technician, took a graduate certificate in education at Lancaster University, 1976–7, and taught in a comprehensive school, for a time living at Grosmont, North Yorkshire. Mixed shows included Stowells Trophy at Mall Galleries, 1975; Northern Art Exhibition at Shipley Art Gallery in Gateshead, 1978; and Summer Show 3 at Serpentine Gallery, 1981. Solo exhibitions included Quoits at Side Gallery in Newcastle, 1980. Arts Council, Birmingham Libraries and Sheffield City Art Galleries hold examples.

James McDONALD 1956– Painter and printmaker, born in Stirling, Scotland. He was noted for his meticulous depictions of piles of old books. Attended Edinburgh College of Art, 1974–8, having a postgraduate year, 1978–9. From 1980 McDonald exhibited in numerous mixed shows, including Lothian Printmakers, Edinburgh City Arts Centre, 1981; New Scottish Prints, at New York City Gallery, 1983; New Art from Scotland, Warwick Arts Trust, 1986; 1987 Humberside Print Biennal, where he wasa prizewinner; and Consumenta Art Fair, Nuremberg, 1990. Among the artist's awards was the Andrew Grant Travelling Scholarship to Paris, 1978; British Council Travel Grant to Belgium, 1985; the IBM Purchase Prize, 1986; the Falkiner Award, 1987; and the N S Macfarlane Charitable Trust Award, 1990. Had a solo show of prints and drawings at Cumbernauld Theatre in 1982, later exhibitions including Glasgow Print Studio, 1989; Cormund Gallery, Glasgow, 1991; and Long & Ryle, 1996. Victoria & Albert Museum and other public collections hold examples.

John McDONALD 1949– Sculptor, by profession a civil servant, born in Denton, Lancashire. He was self-taught as an artist and showed in Manchester at the Portland Gallery and with North West Arts.

Minette Bell MACDONALD 1956– Painter, born in London, who was brought up in southwest Scotland and later had a studio there. Obtained a first-class honours degree in fine art from Cumbria College of Art and Design, 1992–5. Group shows included Westwalls Group Show, William Howard Centre, Carlisle, 1995; Young Blood South West Scotland Graduate Show, Gracefield Arts Centre, Dumfries, 1996; and Clachenmoor Gallery, Dumfries and Galloway, 1997. Had a solo exhibition at Bartley Drey Gallery, 1998, pictures "exploring and celebrating the historical and classical human relationships which develop between man and horse through war." Dumfries and Galloway Art Society holds her work.

Patricia MACDONALD 1945– Graphic designer and photographer, born in Edinburgh. She made aerial photographs with her husband Angus Macdonald, and was "very concerned about how people relate to the landscape". Her work was widely shown in Britain and on the continent and several books of it were published. She was included in the 1991 show Danger Artists at Work, a City Art Centre, Edinburgh, touring show. The city's collection holds her work.

Richard MACDONALD 1919–1993 Painter, film designer and teacher, born in Yeovil, Somerset. He studied at Dauntsey's School, then attended West of England College of Art, Bristol, 1937, and Royal College of Art, 1939, with Gilbert Spencer. For a time he was senior assistant in the school of painting at Leeds College of Art and taught at Camberwell School of Arts and Crafts, 1951–5. Exhibited RA, NEAC, RBA and LG and had a one-man show at Maltzahn Gallery, 1971. From the mid-1950s he became active in the film world, working with the director Joseph Losey and on films such as *The Servant* and *Far From the Madding Crowd.* Lived in London, later in Los Angeles. RWA holds his work, which was signed R M.

Robert MACDONALD 1935– Painter, printmaker and writer, born in Spilsby, Lancashire. He trained first as a journalist in New Zealand, but returned to Britain in 1958 to study painting. As he was not eligible for a grant, went back to work as a journalist after a year at the Central School of Art in 1958; was at the Central again, 1971–2; then at Royal College of Art as a mature student, 1976–9, under Peter de Francia; finally returning to the Central, 1980–2, for more printmaking studies. Notable teachers at the Central were Mervyn Peake, Cecil Collins, Keith Vaughan and Merlyn Evans. Macdonald said that he "combined landscape painting with the exploration of personal fantasy, based on an interest in mythology and Jungian psychology." He showed with RA, LG, New Contemporaries, RWS, Hull Print Biennale and elsewhere. Solo shows included Brixton Gallery, Work-of-Art Gallery, Brunel University Gallery, New Zealand House, Portfolio Gallery in Auckland in New Zealand, Herbert Read Gallery in Canterbury and Kilvert Gallery, Clyro. Had a retrospective at Brecknock Museum, Brecon, in 1997. Among his books was the much-praised *The Fifth Wind*, 1989, about New Zealand and the Maoris. Victoria & Albert Museum and Ferens Art Gallery, Hull, hold his work. Worked in London and in Penpont, Brecon, Powys.

Stuart Wyllie MacDONALD 1948– Painter and teacher, born in Dundee. He attended Gray's School of Art in Aberdeen under Robert Henderson Blyth; Patrick Allan-Fraser School of Art, Hospitalfield, Arbroath; and Aberdeen College of Education, winning an Italian Government Scholarship in 1971. Showed SSA, RSA and elsewhere in Scotland, Scottish Arts Council holding his work. Taught for some time at Mackie Academy, Stonehaven, Kincardineshire. Lived in Montrose, Angus.

Tom MACDONALD 1914–1985 Painter, stage designer and lecturer, born in Glasgow, where he continued to work. Macdonald trained as a marine engineer. Although he was mainly self-taught in art, completing only one session at Glasgow School of Art, Macdonald was a close friend of the painters J D Fergusson and Josef Herman, whose studio he took over in the early 1940s. It was in that decade that he began his association with the stage, directing and designing sets for Unity Theatre, later paintings sets for Scottish Opera. Macdonald was a versatile artist, sometimes working on a large scale. As well as painting abstracts, under the influence of Herman he painted a series of Expressionist pictures drawing on Glasgow working-class life, other paintings taking up themes such as Clowns and Cowboys which explored human behaviour. For some years Macdonald also gave extra-mural lectures on art for Glasgow University. Macdonald took part in inaugural exhibition of Compass Gallery, Glasgow, in 1969, and showed with RSA, SSA and Scottish Arts Council tours. He had a series of solo exhibitions with Compass Gallery, and Third Eye Centre, Glasgow, held his memorial exhibition. Scottish National Gallery of Modern Art holds his work.

Flora McDONNELL fl. from late 1980s– Painter, draughtsman and illustrator who graduated from City and Guilds of London Art School in 1989 with first-class diploma with distinction in the illustrative arts. Soon after, she was commissioned by Savoy Hotel to do a series of pictures about their chefs and kitchens, later hung in Grill St Quentin, Knightsbridge. Other commissioned work, in 1991, included a record cover for Rykodisc; *Sheep*, a Walker Books Ltd title; and an Ulster Television commission to capture life behind the scenes. Had a first solo show at Kerlin Gallery, Belfast, in 1991; another in 1992 at Cadogan Gallery.

Hector McDONNELL 1947– Painter, etcher and draughtsman in pencil and ink, born in Belfast. The Hon. Hector McDonnell's mother was the painter Angela Countess of Antrim. After education at Eton College and Oxford University, McDonnell studied painting in Munich and sculpting in Vienna, 1964–5. He showed at Hamet Gallery in 1972, thereafter in London at Fischer Fine Art, but also extensively overseas. Had a retrospective in Darmstadt in 1981. Depictions of Ulster shops were a feature of McDonnell's work, a notable example of this style being Billingsgate Market in the Fishmongers' Hall, London. Belfast Museum and Art Gallery and the Museum of Art in Darmstadt hold his work. Was a member of RUA.

John McDONNELL 1933– Painter who had no formal artistic training and began painting in oil from 1962. His subjects were drawn from experiences until then: an orphanage where he was brought up, fairgrounds where he had worked and especially scenes of London. In 1975, about two years after he began painting virtually full-time, had a solo exhibition at Camden Arts Centre. Also showed in a number of mixed exhibitions at Agnew.

Lily Martha Maud McDOUGALL 1875–1958 Painter almost exclusively of flowers, born in Glasgow, into an artistic and musical family. She was encouraged to paint by her father, W H McDougall, founder and first president of the SSWA. After five years at the Royal Institution, Edinburgh, she continued her studies at the Hague School of Art and in Antwerp, where she also began modelling. While in the Netherlands in 1900 her first two paintings were accepted for the RSA and hung on the line. Other mixed show venues included Royal Glasgow Institute of the Fine Arts and RSW. From 1904–6 McDougall lived in Paris, studying at the Carrière Académie and Jacques-Emile Blanche studio, where Lucien Simon and Walter Sickert occasionally taught. Had her first solo show at Redfern Gallery, 1947, a retrospective at Scottish Gallery, Edinburgh, 1955, with a memorial show there, 1959. Scottish Arts Council, Kelvingrove Museum and Art Gallery and Kirkcaldy Art Gallery hold examples. Later for some years McDougall lived in Dalkeith, Midlothian.

Carole McDOWALL fl. from 1970s– Painter of large, gestural abstracts, sometimes including collage, which made reference to the landscape of Cornwall, where she lived at Porthleven from 1989. She studied sculpture and etching part-time at Putney Art School, 1970–80, then for a fine art diploma at Sir John Cass College, 1985–8. She was elected a full member of Newlyn Society of Artists, 1990, of Penwith Society of Arts, 1993. Showed at RA Summer Exhibition, 1975; Greater London Council Jubilee Exhibition, 1977; Six Porthleven Painters at Porthmeor Gallery, St Ives, 1990; and in The Edge of Beyond, Belgrave Gallery, 1995. Had a solo show at Rainy Day Gallery, Penzance, 1993.

William McDOWALL 1905–1983 Painter who was educated at St Mary's Cathedral Choir School in Edinburgh. He studied drawing and painting at Edinburgh College of Art, 1932–5, under S J Peploe and William Gillies and won an Andrew Grant Scholarship. After a year in a commercial studio in Edinburgh he worked in London as a commercial artist and painter. From 1948–69 he was a graphic artist for the *Sunday Times*, but continued with his own painting, showing in major exhibitions. These included RA, ROI, RSA, RBA and Royal Glasgow Institute of the Fine Arts. Eventually he settled in Suffolk and was a member of Ipswich Art Club, showing mainly landscapes done in Britain and abroad from 1977 until he died.

Leo McDOWELL fl. from 1970s– Artist in mixed media, born and educated in the north of England, his early moorland landscapes reflecting his background. After studying modern languages at Manchester and Cambridge Universities and art history at Innsbruck University, McDowell spent eight years teaching in the Middle East and working with archaeological research teams in North Africa, Turkey, Cyprus and Jordan. He painted extensively, his work remaining influenced by early Greek and Byzantine art. McDowell was made a member of RI in 1985, joining its council in 1991. In 1990 he won the Winsor & Newton RI Award, in 1992 the Blackstone Gallery Award. Showed at Mall, Mistral and Phoenix Galleries, with James West Fine Art, at Adam Gallery in Bath and Linda Blackstone Gallery, Pinner, as well as widely abroad. Lived in Essendon, Hatfield, Hertfordshire.

Martin McDOWELL 1956– Painter, born in Manchester. Most of his childhood was spent in southern Ireland until his family moved to Jersey when he was 15. His formal education took place at Aravon School, County Wicklow, St Columba's College in

County Dublin and De La Salle, Jersey, culminating in a design foundation course at Ravensbourne College of Art. McDowell's work was in the manner of Klee and Miró, with some Australian aborigine influence. He believed that art was a co-operation between rational and intuitive ways of thinking. In 1987 was winner of J J Fox inter-island painting competition. Also showed with Selective Eye Gallery in St Helier, where in 1990 had a solo show at Arts Centre. Lived in St Helier.

Henry Kennedy McELWEE fl. c.1910–1965 Painter and draughtsman. Born at Rathmelton, County Donegal, he studied at Westminster School of Art and Royal College of Art before World War I, then at the Slade School of Fine Art, 1923–7, under Philip Wilson Steer and Henry Tonks. Became an art teacher and exhibited at the RA, Goupil and other galleries. Lived in London.

Lindsay McEWAN 1965– Painter who studied at Rotherham and Kingston University. McEwan's imagery was hyper-real while remaining ambiguous, the palette having much in common with Pop Art. Showed at Nuan Naang Art Gallery, Bangkok, 1991; Business Design Centre, 1992, in Fresh Air; and at 33 Mossop Street Art Gallery in 1993 in Two Plus Two.

Elizabeth A McEWEN 1937– Painter in watercolour and teacher, born and based in Belfast, Northern Ireland. She studied there at the College of Art, 1956–60, teachers including Romeo Toogood and Tom Carr, then at Reading University, 1960–1. Taught for 13 years, then painted full-time from 1974. She was a member of the Society of Botanical Artists, Ulster Watercolour Society, Ulster Women Artists and RUA and was in its permanent collection. She gained its Gold Medal in 1991. Showed elsewhere in Northern Ireland in mixed exhibitions, and had solo shows at Bell Gallery, Belfast; Seymour Gallery in Lisburn; and Priory Gallery, Holywood.

Rory McEWEN 1932–1982 Painter; constructor of boxes and free-standing sculptures using collage and various materials, born into landowning family at Polwarth, Berwickshire. McEwen was educated at Eton College and Cambridge University, worked as a professional musician, then became a full-time artist at the beginning of the 1950s. In the early 1960s he had several solo exhibitions at Durlacher Bros, in New York, of his meticulous botanical watercolours. He then changed direction, becoming an abstract painter initially working in acrylic on glass and acrylic sheet, then making sculptures, some being mass-produced, which were shown at Richard Demarco Gallery, Edinburgh, in 1969. Two years later a trip to India revived his interest in botanical illustration. He had a show at Nihonbashi Gallery, Tokyo, in 1980; Royal Botanic Garden, Edinburgh, showed his botanical pictures in 1988; and in 1989–90 he was included in Scottish Art since 1900 at Scottish National Gallery of Modern Art, which holds abstract work by him.

Elizabeth MACFADGEN 1923– Painter, mural artist and draughtsman, born in Sevenoaks, Kent, as Elizabeth Macfadgen, daughter of Sir Eric Macfadgen, but she also painted under her married name of Elizabeth Fitzherbert. Studied at Beckenham School of Art and Royal College of Art, 1946–8. Did book illustration, including work for Folio Society, and exhibited RA, AIA, RHA and elsewhere. Lived in Abbeyleix, County Laois, in the Irish Republic.

Jock McFADYEN 1950– Painter and teacher, born in Paisley, Renfrewshire. He studied at Chelsea School of Art, 1973–7, going on to teach part-time at Slade School of Fine Art. McFadyen won a major Arts Council Award, an award from the same source for a film project and in 1981 was artist-in-residence at National Gallery. McFadyen's raw, colourful and sometimes gauche-looking pictures are in fact a serious comment on life in the modern urban environment. His group shows included the Whitechapel Open; the Arts Council tour Fragments Against Ruin; and New British Painting at Cincinatti Arts Centre, and tour. The artist had many solo shows, including Acme Gallery; Bede Gallery, Jarrow; Compass Gallery, Glasgow; Blond Fine Art; and Scottish Gallery, London, 1989. McFadyen's work is held by Arts Council, Scottish Arts Council, Contemporary Art Society and Amnesty International. Lived in London.

David McFALL 1919–1988 Sculptor in stone and bronze, born in Glasgow. After attending the Junior School of Arts and Crafts, Birmingham, 1931–4, McFall was at the College of Arts there for five years from 1934. In London he attended the Royal College of Art, 1940–1, the City and Guilds of London Art School, 1941–5, then worked with Epstein in his studio for around 15 years to the late 1950s. Was elected RA in 1963, having exhibited at RA from 1943. Tate Gallery owns his stone carving Bull Calf, completed when McFall was working as a farm labourer in Buckinghamshire. From 1956–75 McFall was master of sculpture at City and Guilds School, Kennington. Among his commissions are a bronze portrait bust of the composer Ralph Vaughan Williams for the Royal Festival Hall, London, the stone group Oedipus and Jocasta for Norbury Library and a bronze portrait of HRH The Prince of Wales for Buckingham Palace. McFall's work often has a hieratic quality, like Epstein's. He claimed the female form and face as a principal inspiration. Lived in London.

Emily MacFARLANE 1975–1995 Draughtsman, painter and printmaker, born in London, who spent most of her childhood in Cumbria before moving to Felixstowe with her family. Studied art at Ipswich, where she was respected for her outstanding ability, commitment and strong views. She died when crewing the *Maria Asumpta*, wrecked off the Padstow coast. A memorial exhibition was held at Artworks Studio, Felixstowe, in 1995.

John Foster MACFARLANE 1948– Watercolourist and theatre designer, born in Glasgow, where he attended the School of Art from 1966. From 1970 Macfarlane travelled, studied and worked in Italy and Greece. In 1973 he became resident designer at Young Vic Theatre, later designing sets in wide range of theatres, including Royal Court Theatre, Kohn Opera House and

Zürich Opera House. His solo shows were international, including Gallery la Colonna, Milan, 1972; Galerie Hilger, Vienna, from 1977; and Oriel Gallery, Cardiff, 1979. In 1980 Macfarlane was included in Arts Council touring exhibition The British Art Show, chosen by critic William Packer.

Sheila Margaret MacFARLANE 1943– Painter, printmaker and teacher, born in Aberdeen, married to the designer Michael Green. She studied at Edinburgh College of Art, 1960–4, then with S W Hayter at Atelier 17, Paris, 1967–8. Went on to teach printmaking at Duncan of Jordanstone College of Art, Dundee, 1970–6. MacFarlane created the Printmakers' Workshop at Kirkton of Craig, Montrose, Angus, where she lived for some years. Showed with RA, RSA, SSA, Scottish Arts Council Gallery and elsewhere. Solo exhibitions included Printmakers' Workshop, Edinburgh, 1970. Scottish Arts Council holds her work.

Susan MACFARLANE 1938– Artist working in pencil, charcoal and oil, born in Hove, Sussex. She studied at Winchester School of Art, 1954–7, under David Pare and with John Dragoumis, in Greece. She lived there, in Sri Lanka and Hong Kong and in a remote area of France for 20 years "where I developed very much on my own". From returning to Britain in 1986 her choice of subjects included people at work, as at the woollen mills, Stroud; the ancient culture of prehistoric Wiltshire; and people working in hospitals. Her exhibition A Picture of Health stemmed from this, toured the United Kingdom from the Barbican Centre, 1995–6, and America in 1997. Ideas from the sea were another late interest. A large area of stained glass in Holy Trinity Church, Cannes, France, was among her main works. Showed at RWA. Other solo shows included Archaelogical Museum Gallery, Devizes, and The Guildhall Gallery, Gloucester. Settled in Brimscombe, Stroud, Gloucestershire.

John Thoburn McGAW 1872–1952 Watercolour painter, born near Hay, New South Wales. After attending Cambridge University he studied art with Felix Andrews. Showed at RA, RWS, RBA, Ridley Art Club, in the provinces and at Paris Salon. Was a member of Ridley Art Club and lived at Horsham, Sussex.

Anderson James McGEOCH 1913– Painter, sculptor and draughtsman, born in Paisley, Renfrewshire. Studied at Glasgow School of Art under W O Hutchison, 1932–7, then spent the next year in personal tuition in Paris. Exhibited RSA, SSA, Arts Council travelling shows and Royal Glasgow Institute of the Fine Arts. When signing sculpture he reversed the order of his christian names. Lived in Paisley.

Kirsty McGHIE 1959– Sculptor and teacher who used materials such as wire netting and plastics. She was born in Edinburgh and studied at Glasgow School of Art, 1980–5. A scholarship in 1985 enabled her to study in Japan. Two years later she won a Scottish Arts Council Artists in Industry Scholarship, the year she began teaching in the sculpture department of Edinburgh College of Art. McGhie began her extensive exhibiting career in Scotland in 1983, having a solo show at Collective Gallery, Edinburgh, in 1985. In 1989–90 she was featured in Scottish Art since 1900 touring show staged by Scottish National Gallery of Modern Art.

T G McGILL DUNCAN 1896–1978 Painter, especially of landscape in oil and watercolour, who signed his work McG Duncan. He was born in Elie, Fife, and educated at Trinity Academy, Edinburgh, studying art at Edinburgh College of Art before World War I, and at Trinity College, Oxford, after the war. Showed at RSA, RSW, Royal Glasgow Institute of the Fine Arts and SSA and was a member of the Scottish Arts Club. Much of his work was reproduced in postcard form, an idea acquired from the painter William Mervyn Glass. Lived in Edinburgh, where he painted Portobello beach scenes, but died in Kirkcudbright, his favourite part of Scotland, the countryside, shore and hills around Gatehouse of Fleet providing most of his subjects.

Ian McGILLVRAY 1964– Painter of sporting subjects, born in Inverness, who worked mainly to private commission. His work, which owed something to the tradition of Stubbs and Landseer but with an Impressionist flavour, gave a strong sense of having been there. Did a foundation course at Derby Lonsdale College of Further Education, 1982–3, then gained an honours degree in fine art at Maidstone College of Art, 1984–7. Exhibited at Highland Field Sports Fair, 1989; Tryon and Swann Gallery with Musée de la Chasse, Paris, 1994; Holland and Holland Fine Art, 1995; and Diverse, Kent Institute of Art & Design, Canterbury, 1996. In 1992 McGillvray won first prize BASC Wildlife Art competition.

Larry McGINITY 1956– Painter and draughtsman, born Tunbridge Wells, Kent, who mixed Fauve and naive styles. Was a pupil at Priory School, Lewes, until 1975, then studied politics and modern history at Manchester University. After working with the sales teams of several publications, including *The Guardian* and *The Field*, in 1985 he went to Italy, settling as a teacher of English in Siena before returning to England in 1986 when he began to paint seriously. After showing with Margaret Fisher Gallery had a series of solo shows in London, then one in his home town of Lewes, Sussex, at Albion Gallery, 1991. Lived in Needham Market, Suffolk.

Martin McGINN 1955– Painter, born in Gillingham, Kent, who studied at Blackpool College of Technology and Art, 1973–4; Bristol Polytechnic, 1974–7; and the Royal College of Art, 1978–81. From 1980 exhibited in London at Curwen Gallery, in America and Germany, latterly showing in mixed exhibitions at Anna Bornholt Gallery, 1995; Hales Gallery, 1996; and in John Moores Liverpool Exhibition, 1997–8. Had a solo exhibition at Hales in 1997. Lived in London.

James McGLADE 1948– Artist employing a variety of materials, such as pencil, paper, collage and fibreglass, born in Falkirk, Stirlingshire. He studied at Edinburgh College of Art, followed by a postgraduate scholarship at Patrick Allan-Fraser School of Art,

Hospitalfield, Arbroath. McGlade had a one-man show at the 1969 Hospitalfield Summer School, other appearances including New 57 Gallery and Richard Demarco Gallery in Edinburgh. Scottish Arts Council and The Law Society of Scotland hold his work.

Archibald McGLASHAN 1888–1980 Painter, especially of portraits in oil, born in Paisley, Renfrewshire. He studied at Glasgow School of Art under Fra Newbery and Maurice Greiffenhagen. Showed at RSA, to which he was elected in 1939, RA, Lefevre Gallery, Walker Art Gallery, Liverpool, and Royal Glasgow Institute of the Fine Arts. Member of the Society of Eight. McGlashan's portraits, especially of women, have at their best a painterly assurance and sparkle. Member of Glasgow Art Club. McGlashan's work is in the collections of Glasgow University as well as galleries in Glasgow, Aberdeen, Dundee and Paisley. Lived in Glasgow, then later in Rothesay, Isle of Bute.

Barry McGLASHAN 1974– Painter, educated and based in Aberdeen, Scotland, where he attended Gray's School of Art, 1992–6, as an outstanding student. In his final year he gained the RSA's Macallan Award and the John Kinross Travel Scholarship, with plans to pursue postgraduate studies at the Slade School of Fine Art. Aberdeen Art Gallery acquired McGlashan's Scene from an Imaginary Play, 1996, a dreamy, surreal picture recalling the work of Alexander Fraser and Joe Fan, tutors at Gray's. McGlashan's exhibitions included Sketchclub, Peacock Gallery, Aberdeen, 1994; Aberdeen Artists, Aberdeen Art Gallery, 1995; and New Generation Exhibition, Compass Gallery, Glasgow, 1996. In that year McGlashan was commissioned by the Grampian Hospitals Art Trust.

Terry McGLYNN 1903–1973 Landscape watercolourist, industrial mural painter and designer. Educated in Leyburn, Yorkshire, he studied at Manchester School of Art under John Willock. For a time McGlynn produced murals for mill interiors in the Manchester area, and after World War II he became a stalwart of the Manchester Academy. Was a member of the Manchester Group which showed at the Mid-Day Studios. Participated in Arts Council exhibition Some Lancashire Artists. Had a number of one-man shows. McGlynn painted widely, in the north of England, Wales and Scotland, critics describing his watercolours as having a "quiet sparkle" and a "lively and expressive freedom of touch". His Two Figures, completed in 1966 and in Manchester City Art Gallery, shows a later moving towards abstraction. Lived at Stockport, Cheshire.

Paul McGONIGLE 1959– Sculptor, born and lived in London. He attended Central School of Art, 1977–8, and Wimbledon School of Art, 1978–81, taking an advanced sculpture course at St Martin's School of Art, 1981–3. Among McGonigle's group appearances were Cannizaro Park, 1980, and in 1983 at Woodlands Art Gallery in Have You Seen Sculpture from the Body?

Colin McGOOKIN 1958– Painter, born in Belfast, Northern Ireland, who graduated with honours from Ulster College of Art, 1976–81, studying with Alastair MacLennan, eventually having a studio in Lisburn, County Antrim. He was a founder-member of the Artists' Collective of Northern Ireland and of Queen Street Studios, was an associate member of RUA from 1989 and a board member of Crescent Arts Centre, Belfast. McGookin painted on three-dimensional forms, from 1990 using fragments of timber found during a sojourn at Tyrone Guthrie Centre, Annaghmakerrig, Ireland's premier artists' retreat. McGookin's subjects embraced symbolism and iconography of both local and international ethnic or religious groups. The Distant Woodworks, Inside the Kerbstones and Outside the Labyrinth were key works from the 1990s. Took part in numerous group exhibitions, including Irish Exhibition of Living Art, Douglas Hyde Gallery, Dublin, from 1980; Four Voices, at Grapevine Arts Centre, Dublin, 1983; Four Painters, Galloway Arts Festival, Stranraer, and tour, 1987; Living Landscape, Skibbereen Arts Centre and tour, 1990; and Cease-Fire, Wolverhampton Art Gallery, 1994. Later solo shows included The Distant Woodworks, Peacock Gallery, Craigavon, 1994. Arts Council of Northern Ireland and Monaghan County Museum hold examples.

Richard McGOWAN 1950– Painter who to support himself at times taught and worked as a fine art librarian. He was born in Yorkshire and studied at Sheffield College of Art and Design, 1969–70; Hull College of Art, 1970–3; and Birmingham Polytechnic, 1974–5. McGowan disclaimed figurative content in his work. His many group appearances included Ferens Winter Exhibition at Ferens Art Gallery, Hull, from 1971; Northern Printmakers' Exhibition, Sunderland Arts Centre, from 1973; Midlands Open Exhibition at Dudley Art Gallery, 1976; and Summer Show 2 at Serpentine Gallery, 1983. Solo shows included Birmingham University, 1976, and Westill College, Birmingham, where McGowan lived, 1983.

Raymond McGRATH 1903–1977 Architect, watercolourist, illustrator and printmaker, born in Sydney, Australia. Attended University of Sydney and Cambridge University, England, studying at Westminster School of Art under Frank Medworth. From 1930 practised privately as an architect, but in a versatile career did aircraft drawings for the Ministry of Information as well as illustrating for the printed page. His watercolours are often landscapes of England and Ireland. Publications include *Twentieth Century Houses*. Lived in Dublin, Ireland.

David Roy MacGREGOR 1925– Artist and writer with a strong interest in marine subjects, architect, born and settled in London. He attended Eton College and Cambridge University, gaining his master's degree, studying art with the marine painter George F Bradshaw. MacGregor was an associate of RIBA. He exhibited at RSMA, ROI and NEAC and had a series of solo exhibitions including Woodstock Gallery, 1974, and Mercury Theatre in Colchester, 1976. He wrote and illustrated a number of books on sailing craft, notably the three-volume *Merchant Sailing Ships*, 1984–5.

Kerstin McGREGOR 1962– Artist who relied "almost completely on my imagination and memory" and who was included in Merseyside Artists 3, 1986–7, toured by Walker Art Gallery, Liverpool. McGregor gained a first-class honours degree at Liverpool Polytechnic in 1986. Also showed at Cannon Hill Arts Centre, Birmingham, 1979, and Liverpool Garden Festival, 1984.

Mhairi McGREGOR 1971– Painter, who gained an honours degree in fine art at Glasgow School of Art, 1989–93. Awards included John Kinross Scholarship, 1993, and in 1997 she was a finalist for the Alastair Salvesen Scholarship and was Under 25 Regional Winner, Laing Art Competition. Exhibitions included RSA, 1994; John Martin of London, 1996; Art 97, Business Design Centre, Islington, 1997; and finalist, The Alasdair Gilchrist Fisher Memorial Award 1998 at Cadogan Contemporary.

Neil McGREGOR 1963– Painter, born in Nottingham. He studied at Norwich School of Art, 1982–5, Cyprus School of Art, 1985, then settled in Doncaster, Yorkshire, to paint. He shared a three-man show at Doncaster Museum and Art Gallery in 1983 and Hanover Gallery, Liverpool, 1986, the year he showed at Mappin Art Gallery, Sheffield. Also showed in 1988 at Northern Academy, Manchester City Art Gallery; RA Summer Exhibition, 1990; and shared a four-man exhibition at Linton Court Gallery, Settle, 1992. Showed solo at Church View Gallery, Doncaster. Manchester and Doncaster public galleries hold his work.

Sylvia MacGREGOR 1938– Painter and teacher, born in Burnley, Lancashire, daughter of the artist Clifford Astin. She studied art at Burnley Municipal College of Art, 1959–62. She was made a member of SWA in 1977, also exhibiting with RMS and in the north of England and America. Lived in Blackpool, Lancashire.

MacGREGORY 1934– Painter and teacher, full name Malcolm Gregory. He was born in Stony Stratford, Buckinghamshire, and studied at Cambridge School of Art, 1951–5; Swindon School of Art, 1958; Chelsea School of Art, 1958–60; and Goldsmiths' College, 1960–61. He was made a member of UA in 1975. Showed at Portal, Piccadilly and South London Galleries, RA and RBA. Had a number of solo exhibitions included Heffer Gallery in Cambridge and J Hutton Gallery in Peterborough where Gregory taught and lived for a while. Greater London Council, several education committees and firms owned examples.

Ian McGUGAN 1932– Painter, born in Toronto, Canada, who studied at Ontario College of Art, in America and England. Showed widely in mixed exhibitions in and around London. His solo shows included Harcourt Gallery, Toronto, 1965; Ansdell Gallery, 1973; Bourne Gallery, Reigate, 1974; and M Ayres, 1975. In 1976 he shared an exhibition at Woodlands Art Gallery. Canada's Arts Council holds his work.

Bernard McGUIGAN fl. from 1970s– Self-taught sculptor, born and brought up in Essex, who began carving aged 16. McGuigan worked mainly in stone, and he used material from demolished buildings as well as from quarries around Britain. Work was mainly figurative, influenced by primitive African sculpture. Showed at Bruton Street Gallery, Barbican Centre, Hornbeam Environmental Centre and The Gallery, Manchester. Was based in a studio in Hackney, east London.

Johnny McGUINNESS 1955– Painter and assemblage maker, who studied at Duncan of Jordanstone College of Art. McGuinness was notable for his singular assemblages of plastic toys and fragments to create sinister objects often painted in black. They were given such titles as Max, Time Hub and Apocalyptic Horseman and a number were displayed at The Compass Contribution, Tramway, in Glasgow, 1990. Compass gave McGuinness a solo show in 1986, which toured, and he also had a one-man exhibition at Harbour Arts Centre, Irvine. McGuinness showed with SSA, RSA, Glasgow Group and elsewhere in Scotland.

Norah McGUINNESS 1901–1980 Oil and watercolour painter, costume designer and illustrator. Born in Londonderry, Northern Ireland, she studied art in Dublin, at Chelsea Polytechnic and with André Lhote in Paris. Exhibitions included Leicester Galleries and galleries in Ireland. The Irish Arts Council and Trinity College, Dublin, hold her work. Illustrated books by W B Yeats and Elizabeth Bowen, and designed for the Abbey Theatre, Dublin. Lived at Dun Laoghaire, Dublin, Ireland.

David MACH 1956– Sculptor and creator of performance-type constructions, born in Methil, Fife. From 1974–9 he studied at Duncan of Jordanstone College of Art, Dundee; then from 1979–82 he pursued a postgraduate course in sculpture department of Royal College of Art. Settled in London. Mach had a one-man show at Lisson Gallery in 1982. The following year he was commissioned to create his huge Polaris Submarine as part of The Sculpture Show at the Hayward Gallery, for which he used old car tyres. Mach went on to travel the world creating many such objects using the cast-offs from consumer society, as his comment on it. His belief was that "If it's a good idea then it shouldn't matter how long it lasts, five minutes or forever." In 1996 Jason & Rhodes exhibited pictures by Mach, incorporating reconstructed colour photographs, which took a wry look at icons of British culture. Scottish National Gallery of Modern Art holds his work. Elected RA, 1998.

Nicki McHARG fl. from late 1970s– Printmaker who trained at Gray's School of Art, Aberdeen, winning her diploma in 1978, post-diploma, 1979. In 1980 she set up her own print studio. Was included in Scottish Print Open Three, 1983, organised by Dundee Printmakers' Workshop, also exhibiting at RSA, SSA and Royal Glasgow Institute of the Fine Arts. Solo exhibitions included Kenya, Huddersfield and Aberdeen, near to where she settled at Crathes.

Arnold MACHIN 1911– Figure sculptor, often in terracotta, born at Trent Vale, Stoke-on-Trent. He came from a family of potters and studied initially at Stoke School of Art, after which he worked at Minton China Works. After a period at Derby School of Art studying sculpture from 1934 Machin attended Royal College of Art, 1937–40, where he was a prizewinner. He went on to advise the Wedgwood pottery company and was eventually made a fellow of RBS and elected RA in 1956. Tate Gallery holds several examples of his work. Lived in Eccleshall, Staffordshire, married to the artist Patricia Machin.

Frank McHUGH 1954– Painter, born in Manchester. He studied at Stafford College of Art, Manchester Polytechnic and Chelsea School of Art. Showed with 3 Artists at The Showroom, 1986, and Brewhouse Open in same year, then John Moores Liverpool Exhibition, 1987. First solo show was at Senate House, Liverpool University, in 1977. Others included Margam Country Park, 1984, and Horsham Arts Centre, 1985. Although events and things inspired paintings by McHugh, he said that his work was "essentially non-figurative". Lived in Bristol.

Otto MACIAG 1918– Artist in oil, watercolour and ceramics, and teacher, born in Sopron, Hungary. He studied while in the Polish Army, 1938–45, in Dundee and Edinburgh, 1940–3, with Winifred and Alison McKenzie, then at Liverpool College of Art, 1945–7, under William Penn. From 1947–78 was art master at Monmouth School. Among his main works were two large ceramic murals, based on designs by Adam Kossowski, at Monmouth School Chapel; two paintings for the church in Wroclaw, Poland; an altar painting at St Briavels Chapel; Stations of the Cross for the church in Otford, Kent; Madonna at Aylesford Priory, Kent; and Madonna at St Gregory Church, Cheltenham. Had solo shows in Monmouth, Oxford and London, showing widely in the provinces. With his brother Ludwik and daughter Anna exhibited at the International Arts Festival, Llangibby, in 1995. A bilingual book of the family's work was published in Poland in 1996. Lived in Monmouth, Gwent.

William MacILRAITH 1961– Abstract artist and teacher, born in London, who studied at Camberwell School of Arts and Crafts, 1980–3, gaining a teaching scholarship to Syracuse University, New York, 1986–8. His mixed shows included Whitechapel Open, at Whitechapel Art Gallery, 1985; Munson-Williams Proctor Institute, Utica, New York, 1988; and Critics' View, Royal Festival Hall, 1991. Had a solo show of drawings at Sanders Gallery, Syracuse University, 1988, then the first of a series at Connaught Brown, 1988.

Finlay McINALLY fl. from 1980s– Painter, draughtsman and printmaker, brought up in the Isle of Skye. His work could be highly mannered, drawing on images of Skye and his imagination. He studied at Gray's School of Art, Aberdeen, 1981–5, then obtained his master's degree at Chelsea College of Art, 1986. Large pastel drawings were a feature of his work, which was included in Scottish Art in the 20th Century, at RWA, 1991. McInally had his first solo show at Arnolfini Gallery, Bristol, in 1987.

Jock MacINNES 1943– Painter and constructions artist whose work was notable for its enigmatic quality. He gained his diploma at Glasgow School of Art, 1962–6, followed by postgraduate studies, 1966–7, and a travelling scholarship to the continent, 1967–8. Among his awards was the Colquhoun Memorial Painting Competition 1st Prize, 1978; 1st Prize at Scottish Drawing Competition, Paisley Art Institute, 1988/91; and in 1991 The Cargill Award at Royal Glasgow Institute of the Fine Arts, of which he was elected a member, 1992. In 1988 he became a professional member of SSA, joining its council in 1993. Exhibited at Compass Gallery from 1969; Quadrangle Gallery, Dallas, 1982; Richard Demarco Gallery, Edinburgh, 1989; and Roger Billcliffe at Art95, Islington, 1995. Solo exhibitions included Glasgow Arts Centre, 1989. Scottish Arts Council and Glasgow and Strathclyde Universities hold examples.

Archibald Dunbar McINTOSH 1936– Artist, born in Glasgow, who attended the School of Art there, 1953–7. Prizes included the Torrance, May Marshall Brown, Latimer, Guthrie, Glasgow Civic Art and Scottish Arts Club Awards. McIntosh was a member of RSW and Royal Glasgow Institute of the Fine Arts, also showing at RA,SSA, Cyril Gerber Fine Art in Glasgow, Thompson's Gallery and Ainscough Contemporary Art. Lived in Dunfermline, Fife.

Iain McINTOSH 1945– Sculptor in various materials, born in Peterhead, Aberdeenshire. Studied at Gray's School of Art, Aberdeen, 1962–7, settling at Powmouth, By Montrose, Angus. McIntosh became a member of the Guild of Master Craftsmen. He was also an associate of RSA and RBS and showed elsewhere in Scotland. Lived in Cupar, Fife.

Alistair MACINTYRE 1958– Versatile artist whose contribution to the Royal Over-Seas League, 1994, Open was the fire and charcoal on paper abstract Phalanx I. He was born in Macclesfield, Cheshire, and studied at Gloucestershire and Exeter Colleges of Art & Design and South Glamorgan Institute of Higher Education. Residencies included English Bridge Workshops, Shrewsbury, 1992, and Reykjavik Municipal Art Gallery, Iceland, 1995. Awards included Best Fine Art Student in Wales Award, National Eisteddfod, 1990; a prize at Earthscape International in Hastings, 1991; and North West Arts Board Individual Artist's Grant, 1994. Mixed shows included Jaavenpaa Forest Sculpture Trail, Finland, 1983; Young Contemporaries, Whitworth Art Gallery, Manchester, 1989; and Rexel Derwent National Drawing Open, Cheltenham, 1994. Solo shows included To the Surface, English Bridge Gallery, Shrewsbury, 1992, and Negative/Positive, Macclesfield, 1993.

Donald McINTYRE 1923– Landscape and coastal painter, born in Leeds, Yorkshire, who attended Scarborough College and Skipton Grammar School. He studied art with James Wright and developed a style in the Scottish Colourist tradition. McIntyre was a member of RCamA, also exhibiting at Phoenix Gallery in Lavenham, NWG, CASW and Royal National Eisteddfod. Had a long series of solo exhibitions starting at Howard Roberts Gallery in Cardiff, 1965–6, later with Thackeray Gallery from 1969. There was a retrospective at Oriel Ynys Mon, Llangefni, 1996. WAC, National Library of Wales in Aberystwyth and public galleries in Birkenhead, Newport, Merthyr Tydfil and Southport hold examples. Lived in Tregarth, Bangor, Gwynedd.

Hugh McINTYRE 1943– Painter and teacher, noted for landscapes capturing strong sunlight and using a rich palette. He was born in Coalsnaughton, Clackmannanshire and, after secondary education in America, attended Rhode Island School of Design, 1961–3, gaining his diploma at Edinburgh College of Art, 1964–8. In 1974 was tutor for Dumfries' Community Arts Workshop. In late-1980s spent several years at sea, part of the time with the Scottish Fishery Protection Squadron. Commissions included work for British Linen Bank, Bank of Scotland, Dumfries Educational Trust and Glasgow Hilton International. Mixed shows included Scottish Wallhangings, a Scottish Arts Council tour, 1968; Dumfries and Galloway Fine Arts Society, from 1974; RSA Summer Exhibitions, from 1977; Royal Glasgow Institute of the Fine Arts, from 1981; and Four Scottish Painters at The Contemporary Fine Art Gallery, Eton, 1992. It gave him solo shows from 1994. In later years McIntyre travelled widely on the continent and Brazil. TRH The Prince and Princess of Wales, Brunel University and a number of international corporate collections hold McIntyre's work.

James MacINTYRE 1926– Self-taught painter, designer and illustrator, born in Coleraine, Northern Ireland. Having had a solo show at 55a Donegall Place, Belfast, in 1952, MacIntyre won a scholarship from CEMA in 1955 which took him to Paris. For several years in London he was a prolific book illustrator. He showed there with Piccadilly Gallery and RA, in Northern Ireland with RUA and in Dublin at RHA. Had several solo shows with Bell Gallery, Belfast. Trustee Savings Bank commissioned murals for their branches drawing on Ulster themes. Ulster Museum holds MacIntyre's work. Lived in Greenisland, County Antrim.

Jean Douglas McINTYRE 1889–1967 Painter who studied with Walter Sickert prior to World War I at Westminster School of Art, later at Rowlandson House. Her sister Lesley married William, later Earl, Jowitt; they collected pictures and owned a fine group of Sickerts. Jean McIntyre painted in the Sickert manner, as shown in her Cumberland Market, exhibited in Camden Town Recalled at Fine Art Society, 1976, and The Painters of Camden Town, at Christie's, 1988. McIntyre also showed her urban landscapes at London Salon and NEAC.

Keith McINTYRE 1959– Artist with a special interest in theatrical presentations. Born in Edinburgh, he studied at Dundee College of Art, 1978–82, with a postgraduate year at Patrick Allan-Fraser School of Art, Hospitalfield, Arbroath. In 1983 he studied papermaking at Laurence Barker Paper Workshop in Barcelona. Among his several awards were the RSA Guthrie Award and the Greenshields Award, both in 1983. McIntyre took up a number of themes in his work, such as the Arbroath fishing industry and male pretensions and vanities. He was visual director of the Communicado Theatre Company's Jock Tamson's Bairns Project, 1989–90. He participated in a series of influential group shows, including The Vigorous Imagination, at Scottish National Gallery of Modern Art, 1987. Solo shows included 369 Gallery, Edinburgh, 1984; Compass Gallery, Glasgow, 1985; Tramway Gallery, Glasgow, and Raab Gallery, 1990; and Glasgow Museums and Art Galleries, Kelvingrove, 1991. Scottish National Gallery of Modern Art and other Scottish galleries hold his work.

Patricia McINTYRE 1953– Artist and teacher, born in Edinburgh, who gained her diploma from Gray's School of Art in Aberdeen, 1971–6. Went on to lecture in the art department of Aberdeen Technical College. Exhibitions included Scottish Print Open, 1983, organised by Dundee Printmakers' Workshop.

K McK: *see* **Keith MACKENZIE**

MACK: *see* **Hamilton MACK**

Peter MacKARELL 1933–1988 Painter, illustrator, teacher and writer, born in Liverpool, son of a shipwright, he studied at the College of Art, joining the teacher training department. While there he produced a series of battle pictures, described in John Willett's Liverpool study *Art in a City*, 1967. MacKarell also wrote unpublished novels and wrote and drew for *The Times Educational Supplement*. Eventually became head of a department of initial teacher training at Goldsmiths' College. In 1980 MacKarell developed multiple sclerosis. Charting and recording the effects in visual terms of his deteriorating sight and its recovery became a leading theme of his work. He completed his doctoral thesis working closely with the medical profession (Goldsmiths' and the Institute of Education at London University, where he also taught, have copies). After he died the National Society for Education in Art and Design, Corsham, produced a book which includes artwork produced by MacKarell during his final years. Guy's Hospital and Moorfields Eye Hospital acquired some of the pictures. Running parallel with this work was MacKarell's output as a watercolourist in which he was preoccupied with the interpretation and conveyance of mood and character in the people and places depicted. Hard Travelling, 1988–9, was an exhibition at the Dixon Gallery, at the Institute of Education, with a tour. Public, academic, commercial and private collections hold MacKarell's work, which covered a range of media.

Alan MACKAY 1943– Painter and sculptor, born in Filey, Yorkshire, working in a wide variety of materials including stone, wood, flint and modelling compound. He attended Camberwell School of Arts and Crafts, 1960–4, teachers including Robert Medley, Michael Salaman, Lesley South, Frank Auerbach and Henry Inlander. Mackay said that his works were "made with the intention of realising a sense of monumentality. There is also the element of sensual or erotic expression, particularly in the female nude figures." Mixed shows included South London Gallery, 1976; Blackheath Gallery, 1982; Garden Gallery, 1987; and Roy Miles Gallery, British Month, 1991. He was second prize winner in the French Mint Search for Sculptor of the Nude Figure, 1990. Had a solo show at St Catherine's College, Oxford, 1973. St Catherine's College and the French Mint, Paris, hold examples. Lived in London.

Arthur Stewart MACKAY 1909– Painter, poster artist and teacher, born and lived in London, who studied at Regent Street Polytechnic School of Art and Hornsey School of Arts and Crafts, where he was a bronze medallist. Mackay was a keen sportsman and musician who lectured at Hammersmith College of Art and Building. Showed at RA, RBA, ROI of which he became a member in 1949, RSA and Paris Salon.

Eric McKAY 1907– Painter and draughtsman, notably in pastel, and interior decorator, born in London. He attended his local School of Art in Hampstead, then a London County Council art school and also studied in Italy. For much of the 1930s he ran a studio – the Carmelite Studio – in Fleet Street. Showed ROI, NEAC, in North America and in Eastbourne, where he settled, and was a prominent member of the Arts Club. The Towner Art Gallery, Eastbourne, holds his work.

Helen Victoria MACKAY 1897– Sculptor in various materials, born in Cardiff, educated at Cheltenham Ladies' College. Studied art at Regent Street Polytechnic School of Art under George Gaskell. Exhibited RA, RSA, Walker Art Gallery, Liverpool, SWA and Royal Glasgow Institute of the Fine Arts. Mackay won a series of medals at the Polytechnic and went on to become a versatile sculptor, in both the human figure and animal subjects. She was a fellow of the RBS, her spare, economical Torso being illustrated in the volume *RBS: Modern British Sculpture*, published in 1939. See also Eric Newton's monograph *British Sculpture 1944–1946*. Lived in London.

John MACKAY 1937– Painter, born in London, who served in the cavalry and in the 1960s began working as a professional painter despite having no formal training. He had a first London show at Jessop Gallery, 1967, later showing at Furneaux Gallery and London Fine Art Exchange, but from the early 1970s did not exhibit for some time. Until 1975 Mackay painted in an abstract style, up to 1985 in a realistic manner, from then on as a Surrealist. A group of large Surrealist oils was auctioned at Christie's South Kensington in 1997.

Deirdre MACKAY CLARK 1937– Artist and teacher, born in Ilford, Essex, her father being a restorer and craftsman. She studied at Hornsey College of Art, 1954–9, teachers including Norman Janes and Alfred Daniels. She had a wide range, including ceramics and fine art cards, and showed at RA Summer Exhibition, Minories in Colchester and RWS. Lived at Brierley, Herefordshire.

Lorne McKEAN 1939– Sculptor, married to the sculptor Edwin Russell, who studied at Guildford School of Art and Royal Academy Schools, winning a Leverhulme Scholarship. Was elected a fellow of RBS, gaining a Feodora Gleichen Memorial Fund Award. Completed a range of commissioned portrait work, including members of the royal family (HM The Queen's silver wedding gift to her husband and a sculpture of HM The Queen commissioned by The Drapers' Company in 1985); the bear cub Winnie at London Zoo; and a 27-foot-high bronze, Flight, for the new Norwich Union building, Leeds. Exhibitions included Sixteen Sculptors at Sladmore Contemporary, 1997. Lived in Polecat Valley, Hindhead, Surrey.

John MACKECHNIE 1949– Printmaker, who gained his diploma in drawing and painting from Glasgow School of Art, 1967–71, and who then joined the specialist printmakers' group at Brighton Polytechnic, 1971–2. Mackechnie was a part-time print making assistant there, 1972–3; full-time printmaking assistant at Newcastle Polytechnic; and from 1978 was with Glasgow Print Studio, becoming its general manager. Exhibitions included Scottish Print Open Three, 1983, organised by Dundee Printmakers' Workshop.

Robert MACKECHNIE 1894–1975 Painter and draughtsman, who produced representational and abstract works, born in Glasgow, where he studied at the Academy, then at Fettes College, Edinburgh. After a long-debilitating bout of rheumatic fever Mackechnie was privately tutored, attended Oxford University, then gained his diploma at Glasgow School of Art. He married a fellow-student, Margaret Barnard, in 1923 and they lived in Italy, where Mackechnie had a first solo exibition in 1924. Eventually returned to London where Mackechnie joined the RBA and Seven and Five Society and showed at RWS. From 1934 the Mackechnies lived in Rye, Sussex (where in 1977 the Art Gallery gave him a memorial show), although in World War II in London he spent time in munitions – this had been his job in World War I, in Coventry – and from 1948 with his wife he rented a cottage annually above Positano, southern Italy, a benefit in coping with the asthma which had prompted his leaving London. Following a break in painting after loss of memory in 1972, with his wife's encouragement he returned to work during his final months, producing unusual abstract watercolours.

Susan MACKECHNIE 1953– Artist, born in North Yorkshire, who attended Middlesbrough College of Art, 1969–71, then Brighton Polytechnic, where from 1971–4 she studied for an honours degree in painting and drawing. Exhibitions included Stowells Open; Glasgow Print Studio Mixed Shows; and Scottish Print Open Three, 1983, organised by Dundee Printmakers' Workshop.

Ian McKEEVER 1946– Sculptor, painter, draughtsman, photographer and teacher, born in Withernsea, Yorkshire. In 1965 he began studying at Avery Hill College of Education but, opting for a career in fine art, instead took a Space studio in St Katharine's

Dock which brought him in touch with artists including Mark Boyle, Albert Irvin and Bridget Riley while he did manual work to support himself. After showing in Berlin in 1971 he was invited to teach part-time at Slade School of Fine Art and had a first solo show at Cardiff Arts Centre, 1971. In 1980–1 McKeever spent a year in Liverpool as a guest of Walker Art Gallery at Bridewell Studios; worked on a scholarship in Nuremberg in 1981; in 1982 published his manifesto, *Black and White ... or how to paint with a hammer*; and from 1984–9 was senior lecturer in painting at Camberwell School of Arts and Crafts. McKeever's work ranged over Perspex reliefs, sculptural assemblages, large landscape-based canvases, out-of-doors installations, photographic work on site, drawings and a tape-slide called Swedish Lapland and a series of diptychs. He had extensive group and solo shows, notably in Germany. In 1987 had a major exhibition at the Kunstverein, Braunschweig. Later shows included Whitechapel Art Gallery, 1990; Bernard Jacobson Gallery, 1994; and a 15-year retrospective of works on paper at Terrace Gallery, Harewood, 1996. Lived in Hartgrove, Dorset.

Robert McKELLAR 1945– Painter and teacher, born in Gravesend, Kent, where he attended the Technical School for Boys, 1957–62. Emigrated to New Zealand, 1964, returning to England on the death of his father in 1966. Did a foundation course at Medway College of Design, 1969–70, then a degree course at Camberwell School of Arts and Crafts, 1971–3. Gerald Norden and John Ward were among his teachers. From 1977 taught part-time at Hastings College of Art, reducing hours to paint more, ceasing all teaching in 1984. McKellar had a solo show at Marlowe Theatre, Canterbury, in 1976. Afterwards exhibited widely, including Southover Gallery, Lewes, from 1979; Easton Rooms, Rye, from 1980; RA Summer Exhibitions from 1982; Omell Gallery from 1986; Merrifield Studios from 1988; and Touchstone Gallery, Hong Kong, 1990. This was a solo show of abstract work, McKellar having already built a reputation for still life. Work held in many international private collections. Lived at Ringinglow, Staplehurst, Kent.

Frank McKELVEY 1895–1974 Portrait and landscape painter in oil and watercolour. Born in Belfast, he studied art at Belfast Municipal School of Art, 1912–17. Exhibited widely, including RHA, Fine Art Society, Royal Glasgow Institute of the Fine Arts as well as in New York, Brussels and Belfast. His work is in several collections in Ireland, America and the National Maritime Museum, Greenwich. Lived at Holywood, County Down, Northern Ireland. His eldest son, Frank (1925–1979), who sometimes used his mother's unmarried name Murphy, was also an artist.

Donnagh (sometimes Donagh) McKENNA fl. from early 1960s– Expressionist painter and teacher, born in the northwest of England of Irish parents. He studied at Manchester College of Art, at extra-Mural Department of Manchester University and at the Slade School of Fine Art. Taught in London art schools, 1962–70. Group shows included Peterloo Gallery in Manchester, AIA Gallery, Contemporary Artists in Camden at Camden Arts Centre, 1981, and The Joy of Paint, at Warwick Arts Trust and Bede Gallery, Jarrow, 1985. Had a solo show at Warwick Arts Centre, 1986. It acquired McKenna's work, as did Irish Export Board and a number of corporate collections.

Laurence McKENNA 1927– Artist in oil, watercolour and pastel, born and lived in Belfast, Northern Ireland. McKenna was a Post Office official until he retired in 1987. He was mainly self-taught, although he studied life drawing under John Luke, 1965–6. McKenna showed in commercial galleries in Belfast, Dublin and Cork, having a solo exhibition in Belfast in 1958.

Stephen McKENNA 1939– Painter and teacher, born in London, who studied at Slade School of Fine Art, 1959–64. His still lifes, figure studies and landscapes had about them the solidity of Old Master pictures. Group exhibitions included British Art, 1940–80, Hayward Gallery, 1980; Documenta 7, Kassel, Germany, 1982; 100 Years of Art in Britain, Leeds City Art Gallery, 1988; and works acquired by Contemporary Art Society, Camden Arts Centre, 1992. From 1964 McKenna had several dozen solo shows in Britain and abroad, later ones including Edward Totah Gallery, 1988; Kerlin Gallery, Dublin, 1990; and Reed's Wharf Gallery, 1995, The Sea Paintings. He taught at Goldsmiths' College.

Tracy MACKENNA 1963– Sculptor using manufactured materials and found objects to created floor- and wall-based sculptures. Was born in Oban, Argyll, and studied sculpture at Glasgow School of Art from 1981–6. In 1987 she worked at the Artists' Collective Studio in Budapest, Hungary. As well as showing in Hungary she had a solo exhibition at Collective Gallery, Edinburgh, 1986, and at Glasgow Print Studio in 1989. She was a co-founder and director of Glasgow Sculpture Studios and in 1989–90 was featured in Scottish Art since 1900 at Scottish National Gallery of Modern Art, which holds her metal and elastic bands sculpture: Objects 8, 9, 10 in a Row. Mackenna's creations direct the viewer's attention to the character of the materials she employed. Lived in Glasgow.

Alexander MACKENZIE 1923– Painter of abstracts and teacher, born in Liverpool. After Army service in World War II he attended Liverpool College of Art, 1946–50, then moved to Newlyn, Cornwall. He taught in Penzance, 1951–64, then for 20 years was head of the department of fine art at Plymouth College of Art and Design. Became a member of Penwith Society in 1952, exhibiting there, and in group shows at Whitechapel and Bradford Art Galleries, New Art Centre, in the provinces and abroad. Had a series of one-man shows at Waddington Galleries, the City Art Gallery in Plymouth, Durlacher Gallery in New York, and at other venues in Britain. Arts Council, Gulbenkian Foundation and provincial galleries hold his work. Lived in Callington, Cornwall.

Alison McKENZIE 1907–1982 Watercolourist, engraver, designer and teacher, sister of the artist Winifred McKenzie, born in Bombay, India. Studied at Glasgow School of Art, 1926–9, gaining the Fra Newbery medal. From 1930–42 she worked in London and studied under the noted engraver Iain Macnab at the Grosvenor School of Modern Art. In 1942 she moved to St Andrews, Fife, and in 1946 joined her sister as part-time lecturer at Dundee College of Art. She retired in 1957 after the sisters had established the printmaking department there. Showed RSA, RSW and NS of both of which she was a member and SSWA and had two-man shows with her sister at Cork Street Gallery and English Speaking Union Gallery, Edinburgh. McKenzie, who was especially influenced by the work of Braque, did railway posters and other ephemera, all marked with an exquisite sense of design and apt colour.

Clarence V MACKENZIE 1889–1948 Painter in oil and watercolour, mainly of landscapes, and museum curator. He studied at Brighton School of Art under Louis Ginnett and at Regent Street Polytechnic School of Art with Harry Watson. Went on to become curator of Dudley Art Gallery, 1933, and was a founder-member of both the Dudley Art Circle and the SEA. Exhibited RA, RWS, RSW, NEAC, RBSA and elsewhere. Art galleries in Dudley and Kidderminster bought his work, which often featured Black Country scenes. Lived at Halesowen, near Birmingham.

Donald MacKENZIE 1944– Printmaker, born in Glasgow, Scotland. His inspiration was the character and incidents of humdrum life of the modern town. He studied at Dundee College of Art, 1963–8, later at Atelier 17, Paris. His exhibitions included Scottish Young Contemporaries, Edinburgh, and Painters and Printmakers of Dundee, in Glasgow, both 1968; Aspects of Printmaking at Dundee Museum, 1969; with Islington Studio, 1973; and William Weston Gallery. Scottish Arts Council and Victoria & Albert Museum hold examples.

Helen MACKENZIE fl. from c.1905–1966 Painter in oil, born in Elgin, Morayshire. Studied at Royal College of Art under Gerald Moira, gaining her diploma in 1906. Nine years later married the artist Herbert Ashwin Budd. She exhibited widely, including RA, ROI, Cooling Galleries, Royal Glasgow Institute of the Fine Arts and in America. She painted a large number of London, country and genre subjects and the Harris Museum and Art Gallery, Preston, holds her work. Lived in London.

Ivor MACKENZIE 1880– Painter, notably in watercolour, born in Grasmere, Westmorland. Educated at Dartmouth Royal Naval College and attained the rank of commander. Self-taught as a painter, he nevertheless has work in the Imperial War Museum and exhibited widely, including RI, PS, Royal Glasgow Institute of the Fine Arts and in America. Finally lived in Southbourne, Hampshire.

Keith MACKENZIE 1924–1983 Humorous artist and illustrator who used watercolour, lithography and etching. Born in London, where he continued to live, he studied art under James C Tarr in the early 1940s, then at Slade School of Fine Art under Randolph Schwabe. Exhibited Walker Art Gallery in Liverpool, RA and Senefelder Club. University College, London, holds his work, which was sometimes signed K McK. Mackenzie drew for the *Evening Standard* for many years and was later cartoon editor of Associated Newspapers. He was a founder-member and secretary of the British Cartoonists' Association. As such he was largely responsible for the successful Drawn and Quartered cartoon exhibition at the National Portrait Gallery in 1970. He was married to the artist Zelma Blakely.

Lucy MacKENZIE 1952– Painter and artist using assemblages, embroidery and notebooks; teacher. She was born in Sudan and studied at Bristol Polytechnic, 1970–3; at Royal College of Art, 1973–6, with a Princess of Wales Scholarship; gaining a fellowship at Gloucestershire College of Art in 1976–7. She taught part-time from 1977 at the College. In 1971 MacKenzie was a Westward Television Exhibition prizewinner, and six years later she was commissioned to paint two miniatures by the Royal College of Art as a Silver Jubilee gift for HM The Queen. MacKenzie began exhibiting in mixed shows in west of England in 1970s. In 1979 she had a solo show at Fischer Fine Art, another following seven years later at Coe Kerr Gallery, New York. MacKenzie's pictures were small, meticulously painted with fine sable brushes on gesso panels. Ordinary objects were transformed by her intense, affectionate and wry perception. Settled in Gloucestershire although her home was in the Isles of Scilly, which influenced her subjects.

Mitchell MACKENZIE 1908– Commercial artist and painter who spent part of his time designing for industry. Studied at Heriot-Watt College, Edinburgh, then at the College of Art there under DM Sutherland and David Foggie, 1931–6. Exhibited Laing Art Gallery, Newcastle, and elsewhere. Lived in Edinburgh.

Phyllis MACKENZIE 1911– Painter and draughtsman in a wide range of media who studied at Cheltenham Ladies' College and Slade School of Fine Art and in Belgium. Took part in mixed shows at RA, SWA and PS. Had a series of solo exhibitions, including widely overseas, at Marjorie Parr Gallery and at Century Galleries in Datchet and Henley-on-Thames. Lived in Pangbourne, Berkshire.

Winifred McKENZIE 1905– Printmaker and painter in oil and teacher, sister of the artist Alison McKenzie. Born in Bombay, India, she studied at Glasgow School of Art under Maurice Greiffenhagen and wood engraving with Iain Macnab at the Grosvenor School of Modern Art. Shared a studio with her sister and a lectureship at Duncan of Jordanstone College of Art, Dundee, as well as several exhibitions, including Loomshop Gallery, in Lower Largo, Fife. Also showed at Blond Fine Art, SWE, SSWA, RSA and elsewhere, being a member of SWE, SSWA and other societies. Claimed she was influenced by Japanese prints as a student, later Italian and French art. Public galleries in Liverpool, Perth and Cork and HRH The Duke of Edinburgh hold her work. Lived in St Andrews, Fife.

James MacKEOWN 1961– Painter, notably of portraits, who was educated at Gresham's School, Norfolk. His drawing and painting were early encouraged by his father, Martin McKeown, and his grandfather, Tom Carr, both artists. Upon leaving school James MacKeown began painting seriously for exhibition, having a first solo show in Haverfordwest in 1978. His entry for the National Portrait Gallery portrait competition in 1981 was highly commended. MacKeown gradually secured a number of portrait commissions in England and France, where he lived in Normandy. In 1989 he showed with Normandy painters at Gisors and gained first prize and the Medaille d'Honneur. Held solo shows throughout Britain, including Phoenix Gallery, Lavenham, 1986; Fermoy Centre, King's Lynn, 1987; Bury St Edmunds Art Gallery, 1988; and Phoenix Galleries, 1989–91. He shared a show with his father and grandfather at Phoenix in 1990. CASW holds his work.

Martin MacKEOWN 1931– Painter, illustrator and teacher, son-in-law of the artist Tom Carr and father of the painter James MacKeown. From Campbell College, Belfast, he attended the city's College of Art, his teachers including John Luke, Romeo Toogood and Tan Donald. From there he won a scholarship to Edinburgh College of Art, where his teachers included William Gillies, Robin Philipson and Leonard Rosoman. On graduation he gained a travelling scholarship which took him widely across Europe. MacKeown went on to work as a teacher and illustrator. He showed with RUA, SSA, Fermoy Gallery in King's Lynn, Austin/Desmond Fine Art and elsewhere. In 1990 he took part in a show with Tom Carr and his son James MacKeown at Phoenix Galleries. Martin MacKeown's works are held widely in Britain and on the continent.

Robin MACKERTICH 1921–1993 Painter and muralist, born in Lucknow, India. After education in an Epsom convent she studied at Wimbledon School of Art, 1937–9; her studies at the Slade School of Fine Art, 1939–41, and 1946–8, were interrupted by Army service in World War II. Mackertich was a member of the RBA and NEAC, with a richly coloured palette, who discontinued painting to raise a family, but resumed in 1975. Her mentor was Carel Weight, who introduced her to Duncan Campbell Contemporary Art, which gave her three solo shows. When she died of cancer around 500 works made a studio sale there in 1993. Plymouth City Art Gallery holds Mackertich's work. Lived in Cambridge.

Charlie MACKESY 1956– Artist, educated at Radley College, who had no formal art education, although he studied in Paris and London with several leading artists. He had a strong interest in jazz, and limited-edition serigraphs were produced from paintings which caught the performance atmosphere. Mackesey worked as a cartoonist for *The Spectator* magazine; illustrated periodical, book and album covers; and produced a series of works for a leading Hollywood restaurant. Had a series of solo shows in London, Edinburgh, New York and in New Zealand. Lived in London.

Jim McKEVITT 1963– Artist in a wide range of media who graduated from the University of Ulster, Belfast. His work was shown extensively through Northern Ireland, Scotland, in London, Germany Japan. He was chosen to appear in New Artists at Fenderesky Gallery, Belfast, 1991, and at Ash Gallery, Edinburgh, in that year. In Germany he showed at Galerie Martin Schmitz, Kassel, 1992, and Galerie Pigment, Kassel, 1993. From that year his work was featured in I am History Now, a touring show which was exhibited widely in Northern Ireland before travelling to the Itami Museum of Contemporary Culture in Japan. Took part in Works on Paper and Beyond the Partitions, exhibitions organised by Queen Street Studios, Belfast, 1994, where McKevitt worked. Lived in Belfast.

Flory MACKEY fl. from mid-1920s– Portrait and flower painter in gouache and oil. Studied at Birmingham School of Art and in Paris. Exhibited SWA, WIAC, RP and ROI. Lived in Birmingham and London.

Hayden Reynolds MACKEY 1883–1979 Painter, illustrator, printmaker and teacher, born in King's Lynn, Norfolk. He studied at the Slade School of Fine Art and Langham School of Art. At outbreak of World War I was offered commission as a war artist, but declined because of his pacifist views. However, after a period as a stretcher-bearer he accepted the commission, and examples of his work are in the Imperial War Museum. He travelled widely and was a close friend of many well-known artists and literary figures, such as Sir Frank Brangwyn, Austin Osman Spare, Dylan Thomas and G K Chesterton. Exhibited RA, RHA, ROI, in the provinces and at Paris Salon, where he won a gold medal in 1973 for Susannah and the Elders, a silver medal following two years later for The Jazz Drummer, a picture which shows Mackey's liking for strong design, picaresque and slightly bizarre subjects. These traits are evident in his work for private presses, such as the Mandrake Press; among his books were illustrations for his own *La Grande Ducasse Drolatique*, 1922, and Thomas Nashe's *The Unfortunate Traveller*, 1930. Mackey taught for a time at Walthamstow School of Art. A substantial part of his studio was sold at Christie's South Kensington, 1989. Lived in London.

George MACKIE 1920– Painter, designer, illustrator and teacher, born in Cupar, Fife. He was married to the artist Barbara Balmer. Mackie studied at Dundee College of Art, 1937–40, then after a World War II break at Edinburgh College of Art, 1946–8. He went on to become a graphic designer to Edinburgh University Press and head of design at Gray's School of Art, Aberdeen, his work appearing in a number of graphic magazines such as *Graphis*. Also illustrated books on Scotland. Showed with RSW of which he was a member, SSA, Richard Demarco Gallery and elsewhere. Scottish Arts Council and Aberdeen Art Gallery hold his work. Based in Aberdeen and in Edinburgh.

Hamish MACKIE 1973– Sculptor, notable for his small bronzes of domestic and wild animals. He began sculpting at Radley College; completed a foundation diploma at Falmouth

School of Art; then gained an honours degree in furniture and product design at Kingston University. Sculpture to fit a specific environment was a feature of his work. A five-month study trip to Zimbabwe and Kenya enhanced a knowledge of animals nurtured by growing up on a farm in Cornwall Exhibitions included Ainscough Contemporary Art. Commissions included Merill Lynch, Royal Cornwall Agricultural Association, and Holkham, Tregothnan and Trewithen Estates.

Helen MACKIE fl. from c.1920–1957 Illustrator and artist who studied at Lambeth School of Art and went on to work on *Bystander* magazine. She also illustrated for *The Sphere* and *The Graphic* and several books, including P C Wren's *Beau Geste*. Showed at Walker's Galleries extensively, also Brook Street Art Gallery, SWA and RHA. Her work was bought by HM Queen Mary. Lived in London.

John MACKIE 1953– Painter and draughtsman whose work owed much to the Impressionists, oils and pastels focussing on French and Italian landscape. Mackie studied for an honours degree at Glasgow School of Art, 1972–6, winning the W H Shanks award for drawing in the latter year. David Donaldson called him the most talented student of his graduating year. In 1976–7 Mackie gained a travelling scholarship from Scottish Arts Council and worked in America. Completed a number of portrait commissions including D M Kelly, Lord Provost of Glasgow, 1982. Showed with Royal Glasgow Institute of the Fine Arts from 1974; RSA from 1975; Torrance Gallery, Edinburgh, 1982; Duncalfe Galleries, Harrogate, from 1987; Walker Galleries, Harrogate, from 1992; and Thompson's Gallery, 1993.

Sheila Gertrude MACKIE 1928– Painter, draughtsman and teacher, born in Chester-le-Street, County Durham, where she later lived for many years. She studied at King Edward VII School of Art at Durham University, graduating in Fine Art; her teachers, during 1945–50, included Lawrence Gowing and Robin Darwin. Was for many years art mistress at Consett Grammar School. Exhibited widely in group shows, including RA, Festival of Britain touring exhibition, RBA and RSA; had one-man show at Foyles Gallery. Ministry of Works and Shipley Art Gallery, Gateshead, bought her work.

Donald McKINLAY 1929– Artist employing a wide range of media, and teacher, born in Bootle, Liverpool. Although McKinlay produced some abstract work, he was mainly a figurative artist with a wide range; portraits of his friends, a period in India, autobiographical subjects, constructions in wood and photojournalism's impact all featured in his output. He attended Liverpool School of Art, 1946–50, Martin Bell and Karel Vogel being important teachers. From 1953–8 he painted scenery at Liverpool Playhouse, being assistant designer there, 1958–60. From 1960 held a number of full- or part-time teaching posts in the northwest of England, from 1970–91 being a senior lecturer at Manchester Polytechnic. Public work included Tagore Theatre at Ahmedabad, India; Royal Liverpool Hospital mural; and visiting artist at Cammell Laird Shipyard, 1993. McKinlay was a member of MAFA. Also showed in groups at Walker Art Gallery, Liverpool, from 1960, conducting an artist's workshop called Face to Face there in 1995; Bede Gallery, Jarrow, 1983; Liverpool Academy, 1991; and Tib Lane Gallery, Manchester, 1993. Had a long series of solo shows at Bluecoat Gallery in Liverpool from 1973, later ones including Salford Art Gallery, 1995. Lived in Cloughfold, Rossendale, Lancashire.

Miguel MACKINLAY 1895–1958 Artist, born in Guadalajura, Spain, father a Scottish engineer, mother a local woman. Had early modelling tuition in Valencia. After Mackinlay's mother died the family moved to Perth, Australia, about 1909, and when he was 17 Mackinlay – known locally as Mike – began work for a printer, studying at Perth Technical School with Jimmy Linton in the evenings. With other students Stan Cross and Frank Goulding Mackinlay held a show in Perth, raised money and they moved to Chelsea, London, to further their careers. After World War I Army service Mackinlay studied at the Slade School of Fine Art. Between the wars he made a good living, showing at RA, NEAC, Walker Art Gallery in Liverpool and Royal Glasgow Institute of the Fine Arts, illustrating books and handling poster and advertising work, clients including Bovril, the Fifty Shilling Tailors, Nestlé's chocolate and Bournville cocoa. He travelled extensively through England and on the continent to complete landscapes. Moved to Bushey, Hertfordshire, in 1928, where he was one of a colony occupying the famous Meadow Studios. Bushey Museum Trust published a booklet on Mackinlay's life and hold his work.

Hazel McKINLEY: *see* **Hazel KING-FARLOW**

John McKINNEY 1934– Painter, printmaker and teacher, born and lived in Bournemouth, Hampshire. He studied at the College of Art there, 1953–9 and went on to teach at St Peter's School. McKinney was a member of SGA, showing with RA, SWE and RE.

Sine MACKINNON 1901–1996 Painter, especially of French landscapes and some pictures with a Surrealist tinge, using a distinctive palette. She was born in Newcastle, County Down, Northern Ireland, and was a star pupil of Henry Tonks at the Slade School of Fine Art, 1918–20 and 1921–4, her early work showing its influence. Muirhead Bone admired her pictures, and his son Stephen and his wife, Mary Adshead, were friends. Sine (pronounced Shawna) was encouraged to move to Paris by her mother, where she lived in Montparnasse, encountered such painters as Matisse, Utrillo and Dufy, studied at the École des Beaux-Arts and exhibited. Returned to London periodically where she was a prolific exhibitor, having a first solo show at Goupil Gallery in 1928, was taken up by Reid and Lefevre and also exhibited at Tooth, Fine Art Society, Redfern Gallery, NEAC and elsewhere. She married a small-time art dealer and unexhibited painter called Rupert Fordham, whose money came from the family brewery, and they travelled extensively in Europe, staying England during World War II. Tate Gallery holds her picture

Farm Buildings in Provence, other public collections in England and France owning examples. Mackinnon latterly lived near Paris, suffered for several years from Alzheimer's Disease and was nursed by her daughter.

Cherith McKINSTRY 1928– Artist in oil on canvas, paper and board, and sculptor, born Cherith Boyd and married to the architect and artist Robert McKinstry. She was born in Powick, Worcestershire, and attended Belfast College of Art, 1945–7 and 1950–3, in 1953 gaining a CEMA travel scholarship to France and Italy. Her work was concerned with humanity and human values, as well as exploring religious themes. She completed four commissions for her husband, and commissioned work included Church of St McNissi, Magherahoney, County Antrim, 1967, Stations of the Cross; Grand Opera House, Belfast, 1979, six ceiling panels; and Queen's University, Belfast, 1986, a painting, Students. Mixed shows included RHA in Dublin, with solo exhibitions latterly at Ulster Museum, Belfast, 1980, and The Gordon Gallery, Londonderry, 1991. In 1987 she gained an honorary master's degree from Queen's University, Belfast. Arts Council of Northern Ireland, Ulster Museum in Belfast and Bank of Ireland hold examples. Lived in Lambeg, Lisburn, County Antrim.

Robert James McKINSTRY 1925– Architect, artist in pen and ink and watercolour wash and photographer, born in Banridge, County Down, Northern Ireland. He studied at Liverpool School of Architecture, 1942–8, his tutor for the final year being F X Velarde. Became a member of RIBA and Royal Society of Ulster Architects and practised solo and in partnerships. He specialised in conservation work, his most important job being the restoration of the Grand Opera House in Belfast, 1980. Photographs of architectural work were shown in architectural exhibitions. Initially, McKinstry thought he would become a theatre designer. Walker Art Gallery, Liverpool, has a picture by him for a Recording Merseyside exhibition, completed when a student. Lived in Lambeg, Lisburn, County Antrim, with his wife the painter Cherith McKinstry.

George MACKLEY 1900–1983 Printmaker, painter and teacher, born in Tonbridge, Kent, where he settled. Studied at Goldsmiths' Training College, 1918–21, to become a teacher, where he became interested in art. Later while teaching obtained private tuition in wood engraving from Noel Rooke at Central School of Arts and Crafts, which persuaded him to concentrate on this medium rather than on oils and watercolours, which he had shown at RA. Inspired by the work of Agnes Miller Parker, he concentrated on views of the riverside, his engravings having a crispness and economy of line. Member of SWE, RE and Art Workers' Guild. Published *Wood Engraving* in 1948, *Engraved in Wood* in 1968 and *Confessions of a Woodpecker*, 1981. Victoria & Albert Museum and Ashmolean Museum in Oxford are among many holding his work. Blond Fine Art had a show in 1995.

Richard MACKNESS 1956– Sculptor and teacher, born in Ipswich, Suffolk, who studied at York Art School and Bristol Polytechnic, teaching including Portsmouth Polytechnic. Exhibitions included Options, Cardiff, 1978; Waterloo Gallery 1979; and Ikon Gallery in Birmingham and Clay Sculpture at Yorkshire Sculpture Park, both 1980.

Dorothea F MACLAGAN 1895–1982 Painter, born in Greenock, Renfrewshire. She studied at Byam Shaw School of Art, 1914–17, and Royal Academy Schools, 1917–22, where she won silver and bronze medals. Was married to the painter Philip D Maclagan. Exhibited RA, NEAC, ROI and elsewhere and had a one-man show at Dartington Hall, Devon, in 1975. Campden Hill Art Club member who signed work D F M and lived at Meadle, Buckinghamshire, and finally at Bridgetown near Totnes, Devon.

Peter McLAREN 1964– Painter whose work was notable for its exciting sense of movement, light and exhilaration. He was born in Edinburgh and studied at the College of Art from 1982, graduating with a first-class honours degree in painting. Postgraduate studies were completed in 1987. McLaren won many awards; among these were the Richard Ford Award, RA in 1986; the Andrew Grant Travelling Scholarship, to New York: and British Airways Most Promising Artist and the John Murray Thomson Award at the RSA, both in 1989. McLaren exhibited in mixed shows at RSW, Mercury Gallery, SSA, Fruitmarket Open show in Edinburgh and the Morrison Portrait Competition at RSA. He showed often at Compass Gallery in Glasgow and was included in The Compass Contribution at Tramway, Glasgow, in 1990. City Arts Centre in Edinburgh and other British and foreign collections hold his work. A man on a bicycle was a favourite subject, as in Robert Fleming Holdings' picture Rainbow Man, another key theme being a young couple in a car.

Sally McLAREN 1936– Printmaker, painter, artist in mixed media and teacher, born in London. She studied at Ruskin School of Art, Oxford, winning two painting prizes, Rodrigo Moynihan as visiting teacher; then studied at Central School of Art, under Merlyn Evans, Hans Tisdall and Alan Davie. McLaren gained a French Government Scholarship to study printmaking with S W Hayter at Atelier 17 in Paris and returned to teach at Goldsmiths' College of Art. Post-war American painters, notably Rothko and Diebenkorn, post-war French artists and Ivon Hitchens and the English landscape painters influenced McLaren. She was a fellow of the Printmakers' Council of Great Britain and of RE. Her many group shows included St George's Gallery, WIAC, RA, Octagon Gallery in Belfast and overseas exhibitions. Solo exhibitions included Bear Lane Gallery in Oxford, Studio Prints and Pitlochry Festival Theatre. New York Public Library, Scottish Arts Council, several provincial galleries and foreign collections hold examples. Landscapes and seascapes with a strong abstract element were key features. Lived in East Knoyle, Wiltshire.

Robert MACLAURIN 1961– Painter, born in Yorkshire who settled in Edinburgh and who studied at the College of Art there, 1979–83. In the latter year he won an Andrew Grant Scholarship and made his first trip to Turkey; he later won a Turkish

Government Scholarship, which cemented his ongoing relationship with the country. He won other grants, scholarships and bursaries which enabled him to travel widely in Europe. Maclaurin began to show in 1983, having a first solo exhibition in 1984 at Edinburgh University Staff Club. Other solo shows included Mercury Gallery, Edinburgh, 1987; St Catherine's College, Cambridge, 1988; and 369 Gallery, Edinburgh, and Turberville Smith, London, 1989. Scottish National Gallery of Modern Art holds his work. Maclaurin's richly surfaced oils commonly dealt with the vulnerability of an individual dwarfed by an overwhelming landscape.

Bruce McLEAN 1944– Painter, printmaker, sculptor, performance artist and teacher, born in Glasgow. He studied at Glasgow School of Art, 1961–3, from 1963–6 attending the postgraduate sculpture course at St Martin's School of Art, led by Anthony Caro and William Tucker. McLean reacted against what he considered the pomposity of some modern sculpture through his humorous performance art, sculptures made from rubbish and exhibitions such as his first solo show in London, in 1971, at the Situation Gallery, entitled There's a Sculpture on my Shoulder. This followed a solo exhibition in Düsseldorf in 1969. Meanwhile, McLean had taken up teaching posts, at Croydon School of Art in 1966, also at Maidstone College of Art and Epsom School of Art. For a time he gave up art, concentrating, during 1971–5, on Nice Style: The World's First Pose Band. In the late-1970s McLean turned to more traditional forms of art, producing prints and paintings. He began to acquire an international reputation, having a major solo show at Kunsthalle, Basel, and another a year later at Whitechapel Art Gallery, but McLean continued to mock the art world and even himself within it. McLean designed the bar at Arnolfini Gallery in Bristol in 1988; the set and costumes for Ballet Rambert's *Soldat* in 1989; and in the early 1990s was painting in gloss on stove-enamelled metal. Arts Council and Scottish National Gallery of Modern Art hold his work. Had show at Arnolfini with tour, 1990. Lived in London.

Diane MACLEAN 1939– Sculptor of figurative and abstract works, born in London. She obtained an honours degree in modern languages at London University, 1959; lived abroad, chiefly in Africa, 1961–76; then gained a degree in fine art at Hertfordshire College of Art & Design, 1985. Took part in a number of international symposia, group exhibitions including Sculpture in the Park, Essex University, 1990; Jesus College, Cambridge, 1992; and Merseyside Maritime Museum, Liverpool, 1993. Had a solo show at The Crypt Gallery, Bloomsbury, 1990, later ones including Helsinki Festival, Finland, 1994. In that year she shared a three-man exhibition at Morley Gallery. Public sculpture includes The Seated Hand, London Zoo, 1990; Time Beam II, Stansted Airport, 1991; and The Great Wave, Sovereign Centre, Eastbourne, 1992.

Donna McLEAN 1963– Painter and printmaker, born in Lancashire, who was notable for night scenes of the city. She studied at City and Guilds of London Art School, in 1990 having a solo show at Albemarle Gallery; another followed at Beaux Arts, 1994, which was very successful. McLean's work appeared in BP National Portrait Competition at National Portrait Gallery in 1990, and again in 1991 when she was included in The Discerning Eye, at Mall Galleries, winning the Llewellyn Alexander Award. In 1992 she was featured in Just Art 91 Award Winners, at Barbican Centre. Although McLean lived in London she travelled each winter overseas, producing new work.

John McLEAN 1939– Painter of abstracts, including distinctive lozenges, strokes and swirls of colour, and teacher, born in Liverpool. He studied at St Andrews University, 1957–62, and at Courtauld Institute of Art, 1963–6. Awards included Arts Council Award, 1974; its Major Award, 1980; British Council Travel Awards, 1981 and 1984; and The Lorne Award, 1994. After the Courtauld, McLean went on to teach at Chelsea School of Art, Goldsmiths' College, Canterbury School of Art and University College. McLean's numerous group exhibitions included RSW, 1962; AIA Gallery, from 1963; LG, 1970; British Painting 1952–1977, RA, 1977; John Moores Liverpool Exhibition, 1989–90; Lancashire Contemporaries, Harris Museum & Art Gallery, Preston, 1992; and Ten Years After, Kapil Jariwala Gallery, 1997. Had a first solo exhibition at Talbot Rice Gallery, Edinburgh, 1975, then showed regularly, with a series at Francis Graham-Dixon Gallery from 1988. His work was widely reviewed in newspapers and the art press. McLean's pictures are in several dozen public and corporate collections, including Arts Council, British Council, Contemporary Art Society, Scottish Arts Council, De Beers, Wellcome Foundation and elsewhere.

Mary MACLEAN 1962– Painter, draughtsman and teacher. Studied at Bath Academy of Art for a foundation course, 1981–2; gained a first-class honours degree from Glasgow School of Art, 1982–5; did postgraduate studies at Amsterdam Rijksacademie, 1985–6; completing a master's degree at Royal College of Art, 1986–8. Among a string of awards was a British Institute travel award in 1984; the John Kinross Scholarship to study in Florence in 1985, the year she also gained a Dutch Government Scholarship for study in the Netherlands; and John Minton Award for travel, 1988. Went on to teach part-time life drawing at Glasgow School of Art, 1985, being a guest lecturer there, 1987–9. Mixed shows included Sue Rankin Gallery, 1984; Boundary Gallery, Glasgow Girls, 1987; and Artist of the Day at Flowers East, 1989. Had a solo show at Scottish Gallery, Edinburgh, 1989. Collections holding her work include Napier College, Edinburgh, and Sheraton Caltrust.

Talbert McLEAN 1906–1992 Painter, illustrator and teacher who attended Duncan of Jordanstone College of Art in Dundee, 1923–7. He was an illustrator in London and Liverpool until World War II, during which he served and after which he taught at Arbroath High and Arbroath Academy until 1972. He was noted for his assured and economical abstract paintings, sometimes on unconventional supports, with landscape allusions. He showed at RSA, SSA, Glasgow Group, Royal Glasgow Institute of the Fine Arts and New Charing Cross Gallery, Glasgow. Was represented in The Compass Connection, Tramway, Glasgow, in 1990. Scottish National Gallery of Modern Art and other Scottish collections hold his work. A retrospective was held at Talbot Rice Art Centre, Edinburgh, in 1991.

Will MACLEAN 1941– Painter, maker of constructions and sculptures, and teacher, born in Inverness, Scotland. Studied at Gray's School of Art, Aberdeen, 1961–7, including a period at Patrick Allan–Fraser School of Art, Hospitalfield, Arbroath. Then won a scholarship to British School of Art in Rome. Maclean came from a fishing family, and on his return from Rome he worked as a fisherman off Scotland. Meanwhile, he was showing in solo exhibitions, at 57 Gallery, Edinburgh, in 1968; and at Richard Demarco Gallery there, in 1970. When the Scottish International Education Trust commissioned Maclean to make a visual survey of ring-net fishing in 1973 it led to a creative burst of activity; the project was shown at Third Eye Centre, Glasgow, in 1978, eventually being acquired by Scottish National Gallery of Modern Art. From mid-1970s Maclean also worked on sculptures and constructions which reflected his interest in the sea, fishing, Scottish history and folklore. After a period teaching at Bell-Baxter High School, Cupar, in 1981 became a lecturer at Duncan of Jordanstone College of Art, Dundee. Maclean is represented in many public collections including Aberdeen, Dundee, Hull, Perth, British Museum and Scottish Arts Council. Retrospective at Talbot Rice Gallery, Edinburgh, 1992. Was elected RSA. Lived at Tayport, Fife, married to the artist Marian Leven.

Phoebe McLEISH: *see* **Phoebe STABLER**

Alexander Matheson McLELLAN 1872–1952 Painter, muralist and stained glass artist, born in Greenock, Renfrewshire, who studied at Royal Academy Schools, then at École des Beaux-Arts, Paris. In 1900 McLellan had success at the Paris International Exhibition with his stained glass Field of the Cloth of Gold, and Kelvingrove Art Gallery in Glasgow, where he settled, acquired his work. He was elected RBA and RSW, also showing extensively with RSW and ROI and RA.

Malcolm MacLELLAN 1908– Painter of still life and landscape, born in Dunfermline, Fife. As a youth he spent some years in Canada, settling in Glasgow in 1927. He later served as a police officer there, retiring in 1958, the year after he ceased showing at Royal Glasgow Institute of the Fine Arts, where he first showed in 1938, then regularly. His formal studies were mainly at evening classes at the Glasgow School of Art, with some day classes. Also exhibited at RSA. Glasgow's Kelvingrove Art Gallery holds his Lochermill, Near Bridge of Weir, painted in 1957.

Alastair MacLENNAN 1943– Performance artist, painter, sculptor, printmaker and teacher, born Blair Atholl, Perthshire. He attended Duncan of Jordanstone College of Art, Dundee, 1960–5; Patrick Allan-Fraser School of Art, Hospitalfield, Arbroath, 1965; Dundee College of Education, 1966–8; and Institute of Chicago School of Art, in America, 1968–73. MacLennan taught at Wayne State University, Detroit; Eastern Illinois University, Charleston; Acadia University, Wolfville, Nova Scotia, in Canada; Nova Scotia College of Art and Design, Halifax; then returned to teach at Blackpool College of Technology and Art, in England. He took part in many group exhibitions in Canada, his first solo show, in 1971, consisting of 32 one-man performances in Halifax. Was included in A Choice Selection at Fruitmarket Gallery, Edinburgh, in 1975. Vancouver Art Gallery and other Canadian collections early acquired his work.

Duncan MACLEOD 1952– Artist in various media, born in Glasgow where he graduated from the School of Art in 1974. He was elected to RSW in 1980 and showed widely in group and mixed exhibitions, including Thompson's Gallery 1993 show Contemporary Art From Scotland. Clydesdale Bank and Bank of Scotland hold his work, noted for its delicacy of colour.

Flora MacLEOD 1907– Painter, notably of watercolours, born and lived in Forres, Morayshire. After private education she studied for a few years after World War II with the painters Wycliffe Egginton and Jack Merriott. She was at various times a member of BWS, Glasgow Society of Lady Artists, SSWA and SWA. Also showed with RI, Ridley Art Club, Royal Glasgow Institute of the Fine Arts and elsewhere in Scotland.

Ian McLEOD 1939– Painter and teacher who left school at 15 and worked seven years at Burntisland Shipbuilding, Fife, serving a five-year apprenticeship, entering Edinburgh College of Art, 1961–5, on the strength of his portfolio. He had been a shop steward, chairman of a strike committee and was an active Socialist. Also studied at Regent Road Institute of Further Education, Edinburgh, 1965–6, and at Moray House College of Education, 1966–7. From 1990 taught at Duncan of Jordanstone College of Art in Dundee. He was elected a professional member of SSA in 1968. Had a solo show at New 57 Gallery, Edinburgh, 1970. McLeod was included in the 1971 Scottish Realism show of Scottish Arts Council, which holds examples. He was then described as "a balanced erotic classicist" and was noted as a polished craftsman. In 1987 Colin Jellicoe Gallery in Manchester gave McLeod a retrospective.

Margaret Henderson MACLEOD 1922– Painter in oil, pen and wash and watercolour, born in Barnet, Hertfordshire. After education at Elgin Academy she studied art at Edinburgh College of Art, her teachers including William Gillies and David Alison, 1940–4. Showed at RSA and SSA. Lived for some years in Elgin, Moray.

Peter Robert MACLEOD MACKIE fl. from 1890s–1959 Painter and designer who studied in Edinburgh and Paris. Spent much of his life working in Scotland and exhibited at RSA extensively, and at Royal Glasgow Institute of the Fine Arts, in

London, Belfast and on the continent. Sometimes just signed work PM. Lived in Edinburgh.

William Douglas MACLEOD 1892–1963 Painter, printmaker and cartoonist for the *Glasgow Evening News* in the 1920s, born in Clarkston, Renfrewshire. After initial education at Greenock Academy he attended Glasgow School of Art, 1919–23, under Maurice Greiffenhagen and David Forrester Wilson. He exhibited RSA, Royal Glasgow Institute of the Fine Arts, Walker Art Gallery, Liverpool, and Paris Salon. Glasgow Art Gallery and Museum holds his work. Lived at Lenzie, Dunbartonshire.

Hector McLUSKY 1923– Painter, illustrator and cartoonist and teacher, born in Glasgow. He studied at Leeds College of Art, 1939–40, and Slade School of Fine Art, 1945–8. For a couple of years he taught art at Highgate School, also lecturing for London County Council, then developed a varied career including poster and book work, drawing the James Bond strip for the *Daily Express* and exhibiting at RA, RBA and elsewhere. Lived for many years at Datchworth, Hertfordshire.

John Rayment MACMARTIN 1925– Designer, teacher, sculptor and painter, born in Glasgow, where he was educated and where he was a student at Glasgow School of Art, 1946–50, his teachers including the sculptor Benno Schotz and Hugh Adam Crawford. Was for a time president of the Glasgow School of Art Graduates' Association. Clydesdale Bank holds his work. Lived in East Kilbride, Lanarkshire.

William McMECHAN 1929– Painter, especially in watercolour, born in Downpatrick, County Down, in Northern Ireland. Studied at Belfast College of Art, 1944–8, then at National College of Art in Dublin, 1948–9, his teachers including John Keating and Maurice McGonigal. Showed RUA, in Paris and had a series of one-man exhibitions in Belfast. Lived in Newtownards, County Down.

Pádraig MACMIADHACHÁIN 1929– Painter in oil, gouache and watercolour, born in Downpatrick, Northern Ireland, married to the artist Bonnie Brown. Macmiadhacháin (pronounced Macmeeahon) studied at Belfast College of Art, 1949–52; National Art College in Dublin, 1952–3; won a travelling scholarship to Moscow in 1957 and Poland in 1960; then studied at Academy of Art, Craców, 1960–1. He early settled on the Isle of Purbeck, Dorset, and he and Bonnie Brown opened their White Yard Studios in Swanage to the public. He painted widely in Ireland, Cuba, Mexico, North America, North Africa, the Middle East, Central Asia and elsewhere. Macmiadhacháin's work varied widely in style, and he often employed a richly coloured palette. He took part in numerous mixed shows, including RA, RUA, RWA, Royal Glasgow Institute of the Fine Arts, elsewhere in the provinces and abroad. New Academy Gallery showed his work solo from 1990. Irish Arts Council, Sussex University and HM King Juan Carlos, of Spain, hold examples.

Ethel MACMILLAN fl. c.1945–1970 Painter in oil and watercolour. Born in Richmond, Surrey, daughter of the artist W H Webb, she studied at the Royal Academy Schools. Exhibited RA, RBA, NEAC, ROI and NS. Lived in London.

Ian Douglas McMILLAN 1946– Painter and constructions artist, born and lived in Glasgow where he attended the Art School, 1964–8. He became director of the Glasgow League of Artists. Showed in group exhibitions at Aberdeen Art Gallery, at Edinburgh Festival and Project Gallery, Dublin. His solo shows included several in mid-1970s at Fruitmarket Gallery in Edinburgh and Third Eye Centre in Glasgow. Scottish Arts Council holds his work.

Sheila MACMILLAN 1928– Painter in oil and acrylic, born and lived in Glasgow, where she studied at the University, going on to teach geography. She studied painting with her uncle, Iain Macnab, showing widely from 1975. Was a professional member of SSA. Macmillan won the Eastwood Publications Award at Royal Glasgow Institute of the Fine Arts and the Anne Redpath and Lily McDougall Awards at SSWA. Group shows included Vicarage Cottage Gallery, North Shields, and the Macaulay, Ancrum, Torrance and Edinburgh Galleries. Several of these gave her solo exhibitions, plus the Kingfisher Gallery in Edinburgh, John D Kelly Gallery in Glasgow and Atholl Gallery, Dunkeld. Strathclyde University holds Macmillan's work.

William McMILLAN 1887–1977 Monumental and figure sculptor, born in Aberdeen, where he studied at Gray's School of Art, then at the Royal College of Art, 1908–12, under Édouard Lantéri. He showed at the RA from 1917, being elected RA in 1935, and being master of the Academy's sculpture school, 1929–40. McMillan was elected a fellow of the RBS in 1932 and his Syrinx and Mother and Child appear in the volume *RBS: Modern British Sculpture*, published in 1939. Although there is this graceful side to McMillan's work, he was noted for his public statues, such as Admiral Earl Beatty, in Trafalgar Square, of 1948; George VI, in Carlton House Terrace, of 1955; and Alcock and Brown the aviators, at Heathrow Airport, 1966. Represented in several public collections, including Tate Gallery, and lived in London.

Wendy McMURDO 1962– Artist in various media, including cibachrome, and teacher, born in Edinburgh. She studied at Edinburgh College of Art and the Pratt Institute, New York. In 1989–90 she was artist-in-residence at City Art Centre in Edinburgh, where in 1991 she participated in the travelling show Danger Artists at Work. Showed widely elsewhere and taught part-time at Dundee and Edinburgh Colleges of Art. Edinburgh's city art collection holds her work.

Elizabeth Hyde MACMURRAY 1891–1982 Painter who was born in Banchory, Kincardineshire. She graduated from University of Aberdeen, obtaining her master's degree in 1915, and married the legal academic Professor John Macmurray. Studied art privately with the painters Martin Bloch and Roy de Maistre. Showed at RSA, SSWA and elsewhere. Lived latterly in Edinburgh.

Iain MACNAB 1890–1967 Wood engraver, etcher and painter. Born at Iloilo in the Philippines, Macnab was educated in Edinburgh and studied art at Glasgow School of Art and Heatherley's School of Fine Art. From 1919–25 he was principal of Heatherley's, a position he then held until 1940 at the Grosvenor School of Modern Art (it was subsequently occupied by the Warwick Arts Trust), which he founded. He thus influenced a generation of printmakers with his spare, boldly designed engravings. After World War II Macnab returned to Heatherley's as director of art studies, until 1953. His influence was further extended in his books *Figure Drawing* and *The Student's Book of Wood Engraving*. He exhibited widely, including RA, ROI – of which he was president, RE, RSA and Royal Glasgow Institute of the Fine Arts. The Victoria & Albert Museum, British Museum, Ashmolean Museum and galleries and museums abroad hold his work. Lived in London.

Tiffany McNAB 1964– Watercolourist and printmaker who created vibrant, intricate pictures with a rich palette. She was born in Australia and studied fine art and printmaking at Royal Melbourne Institute of Technology. Selected exhibitions included Royal Melbourne Institute, two artists, 1985; RA Summer Exhibition from 1991; and Greenwich Printmakers' Gallery, selected artist, 1993, the year she had a solo show at Intaglio Printmakers Gallery. Lived in London.

Caroline McNAIRN 1955– Painter and draughtsman, notable for oils and pastels, born in Selkirk, Selkirkshire. She studied at Edinburgh University, 1972–8. McNairn's pictures drew on her knowledge and memory of the city, her images often being expressive and bold and owing something to early-twentieth-century French art. Her first one-man show was in 1980 at Calton Studios, Edinburgh; this was followed by a series of exhibitions from 1981 at Scottish capital's 369 Gallery. Other shows included Bourne Fine Art, Edinburgh, 1997. Among group shows was the major Scottish Art since 1900 exhibition, 1989–90, at Scottish National Gallery of Modern Art, and touring. Scottish National Gallery of Modern Art in Edinburgh, Glasgow Art Gallery, The Pushkin Museum of Fine Arts in Moscow and City of Edinburgh hold examples.

John McNAIRN 1910– Painter whose work showed a strong Fauve influence, born in Hawick, Roxburghshire, where his father, also a painter, published the local newspaper. After Edinburgh College of Art, 1926–30, where his teachers included William Gillies and D M Sutherland, in 1933 McNairn studied with Othon Friesz at Académie Scandinave, Paris. After World War II McNairn settled in Selkirk, and showed in Scotland. Robert Fleming Holdings has his work.

Kathy McNALLY 1950– Artist, born in Northampton, who studied art there and at Byam Shaw School of Art. Moved to St Ives, Cornwall, in 1973, exhibitions in the area including Craftsman Gallery there. An instinctive artist, McNally sought the basic elements of a figure, building or landscape, using colour to describe landscape.

Louis George McNALLY 1963– Artist and teacher born in Inverkip, Renfrewshire, who was educated at St David's Roman Catholic School in Dalkeith, then did a variety of jobs, before and after formal art education (honours degree in drawing and painting at Gray's School of Art, Aberdeen, 1989–90) involving children and the handicapped.Group shows included RSA Student Exhibition, 1989; Aberdeen Artists, 1996; and John Martin of London and Ainscough Contemporary Art, both 1998. Solo exhibitions included Edinburgh International Festival, Royal Lyceum, 1996.

Nicolette MACNAMARA: *see* **Nicolette DEVAS**

James McNAUGHT 1948– Painter and teacher, born in Glasgow. He studied at Glasgow School of Art, 1966–70, including a session at Patrick Allan-Fraser School of Art, Hospitalfield, Arbroath, in 1969 under Jack Knox. McNaught went on to teach in a Glasgow school while showing in mixed exhibitions such as Royal Glasgow Institute of the Fine Arts, Portal Gallery and Galerie Hannsler, Munich. Had a first solo show in 1979 at Galerie Petit, Amsterdam, with one at Portal Gallery, 1982. Two were held at Galerie Hannsler, 1983–6, followed by one at Barclay Lennie Fine Art, Glasgow, 1990. In 1992 shared an exhibition at Ewan Mundy Fine Art, showing stylised salacious girls, often with gateaux or ice-cream confections, mixed with a dash of humour. Extensive collections in Britain and abroad hold his work.

Robert Russell MACNEE fl. from c.1884–1952 Painter, born in Milngavie, Dunbartonshire, who studied at Glasgow School of Art. He was an extensive exhibitor at Royal Glasgow Institute of the Fine Arts and RSA, also showing at RA, RHA, RSW and Walker Art Gallery in Liverpool. Was a member of Glasgow Art Club who lived Barnhill, Angus.

Kitty McNEILL 1914– Painter who was educated privately. She showed at Kensington Art Gallery and Paris Salon and had a one-man show at Walker's Galleries in 1952. Lived in London.

Alexander McNEISH 1932– Painter and teacher, born at Bo'ness, near Linlithgow, Scotland. Studied at Edinburgh College of Art with John Maxwell, and in Salzburg, Austria. Went on to teach in Wolverhampton, living nearby at Penn, Staffordshire. Showed with Arts Council, which holds his work, and elsewhere.

Andrew McNIVEN 1963– Artist, born in Scotland, who studied at St Martin's School of Art, 1981–2, then Goldsmiths' College School of Art, 1984–7. Appearances included Whitworth Young Contemporaries, Manchester, 1985, and in 1990 he was Richard Wentworth's choice as an Artist of the Day at Flowers East.

Peter McNIVEN 1952– Painter and teacher, born in Edinburgh, who gained a diploma in art and design from Manchester Polytechnic, 1973. Became director of art at Cranleigh School, Cranleigh, Surrey, where he lived. Mixed shows included RP at Mall Galleries, 1981; Military Portraits at National Army Museum, 1984; Portrait Award (prizewinner), National Portrait Gallery, 1991; NEAC, Mall Galleries, 1993; and Chichester Open Art Exhibition, Chichester, 1996. Later solo shows included A Painter's Progress, 72–87, Guildford House, Gallery, Guildford, 1987, and Canon Gallery, Petworth, from 1994. Imperial War Museum and Queen's Collection, Windsor, hold examples.

Stephen McNULTY 1950– Abstract artist and teacher, born in Bradford, Yorkshire. Studied at College of Art there, 1968–70, Newcastle upon Tyne Polytechnic, 1973–6, then Royal College of Art, 1976–9. From 1978 had a busy teaching career in the northeast of England and London including Newcastle and Sunderland Polytechnics, Hull College of Higher Education and Chelsea School of Art. From 1981–3 was print workshop organiser at Sunderland Arts Centre. His group shows included 9 Printmakers, at Richard Demarco Gallery, Edinburgh, 1979; Inter-City Prints, Glasgow, 1980; Engelsk Grafikk, at Gallery F15, Norway, 1982; and Six Artists from the Coast, Laing Art Gallery in Newcastle and Scandinavian tour, 1983. Had a solo show at Calouste Gulbenkian Gallery, Newcastle, 1976, later ones including Dovecot Arts Centre, Stockton, and Sunderland Arts Centre, both 1983. Arts Council, Northern Arts and Imperial College hold his work in which McNulty divided "the paper up into a series of horizontals, verticals and diagonals, adhering to a rigid proportion theory … I like the idea of working within a very tight structure."

John McPAKE 1943– Printmaker, painter, draughtsman and teacher, born in Burnley, Lancashire. He studied at Wirral College of Art, 1961–5, Liverpool Polytechnic, 1965–6, Birmingham Polytechnic, 1966–7, and Leeds Polytechnic, 1977–8. Went on to become head of foundation course at Barnsley College of Art. He was a member of RE, also showing in RA Summer Exhibitions and abroad. McPake aimed to synthesise images and create a feel for "contemporary experience of the whole of life", as in his 1985 mixed media with pencil on paper work Wakefield in the Eighties, held by Wakefield Art Gallery. Lived in Thurlstone, near Sheffield, Yorkshire.

Alan McPHERSON 1943– Painter, graphic designer and teacher, born in Braunton, Devon, but brought up in Sussex where he attended Brighton College. Studied philosophy and aesthetics, was at University College of North Wales in Bangor as a student and as a part-time lecturer, also teaching at Gwynedd Technical College. Eventually became a freelance artist, showing at David Cross Fine Art Gallery in Bristol, Liverpool Academy, Royal National Eisteddfod and elsewhere. One-man shows included Bangor Art Gallery and Bluecoat Gallery, Liverpool. WAC holds his work.

Alex MACPHERSON fl. from c.1930–1970 Artist mainly in watercolour, some oil, mostly painting boats and some flowers. He was elected to RSW in 1932 and SSA in 1946, also showing at Royal Glasgow Institute of the Fine Arts. In the 1940s and 1950s his works were thought well enough of to be illustrated in catalogues. Macpherson further showed at RSA, RA and Walker Art Gallery in Liverpool and worked until his death, living for a time in Paisley, latterly in Johnstone, Renfrewshire.

Douglas MacPHERSON 1871–1951 Illustrator and artist, born in Abridge, Essex, son of the watercolourist John MacPherson. After private education he attended Westminster School of Art. From 1890–1913 MacPherson was staff artist for the *Daily Graphic* and *Graphic*, from 1913 on the *Sphere*. Events covered by him included the Spanish-American War in Cuba, 1898, the coronation of Edward VII, 1902, revolt in St Petersburg, 1905, and the opening of Tutankhamen's tomb, Egypt, 1923–4. Showed at RA and SGA. Was a member of St John's Wood Arts Club, Langham Sketch Club and Art Workers' Guild from 1941. Lived in London.

George A MacPHERSON 1935– Painter and teacher, born in Invershin, Sutherland. He studied at Edinburgh College of Art, 1954–8. In the latter year he was winner of the RSA's Stuart Prize. Between 1958–60 MacPherson was occupied with a postgraduate year and an Andrew Grant Travelling Scholarship. In 1966 he won the RSA's Latimer and Guthrie Awards. MacPherson went on to lecture at Edinburgh College of Art. As well as taking part in group shows at Douglas and Foulis, Demarco and 57 Galleries in Edinburgh, where he lived, MacPherson had solo exhibitions at 57 and Scottish Galleries. Scottish Arts Council holds his work.

George Gordon MacPHERSON 1910–1984 Painter in oil and watercolour and sculptor in clay, wood and metal. Born in London, he studied at Liverpool College of Art, 1927–32, under William Charles Penn, then at the Central College of Arts and Crafts, London, 1936–8 under Sir Alfred Turner and William Roberts. MacPherson became head of the department of sculpture in Liverpool from 1954–71. Exhibited at the Walker Art Gallery, Bluecoat Gallery and Liverpool Academy, Bradford Art Gallery, the Royal Cambrian Society and elsewhere in Britain. Lived at Llannefydd, Denbighshire, Wales.

Hamish MACPHERSON 1915– Sculptor, industrial designer and teacher, born in Hartlepool, County Durham, but educated in New Zealand, where he attended Elam School of Art, 1930–2, then in London studied at Central School of Arts and Crafts, 1934–9. Macpherson taught for periods at Central School and at Sir John Cass School of Art between 1948–53. He was an associate of RBS. Macpherson completed work for British pavilion at

Paris Exhibition of 1937, also for Festival of Britain in 1951. Showed with LG, NS and abroad and had a number of solo exhibitions. Lived latterly at Monmouth, Gwent.

Neil MacPHERSON 1954– Painter, born in Elgin, Moray. He studied at Glasgow School of Art and Jordanhill College of Education. He soon went on to win a number of awards, including the Shell Expo Award in 1983 and 1984; RSA's Young Artist; Royal Over-Seas League Commonwealth Premier Award in 1986; and Scotland on Sunday Mayfest Award three years later. He showed in mixed groups at RSA, Aberdeen Art Society and elsewhere. His first solo show was at Compass Gallery, Glasgow, in 1986. In 1987 his work was at Boundary Gallery; in 1989 he had a show at Glasgow Print Studio. Scottish Arts Council, Courtauld Institute and Contemporary Art Society hold his work. This has been described as "idealisations of people, of the land around him and their animals", rich and animated surfaces using "varied textures of painted collage".

Sophie MACPHERSON 1957– Painter employing a subtle colour range who had a strong interest in sea- and shore-based pictures. They often featured industrial relics and sometimes had a Surrealist tinge. Although she settled in London, visits to her family home on Scotland's west coast remained an inspiration. Macpherson studied at St Martin's School of Art and Camberwell College of Art and became a professional artist in the late 1970s. Her first major show was at Richmond Gallery, 1989, further exhibitions including Portland Gallery, 1994.

William McPHERSON 1905– Painter and draughtsman, noted for his landscape watercolours of Scotland, born and lived in Glasgow. He was educated at Queen's Park High School, where he won a gold medal, and at Glasgow School of Art, taking a landscape prize. He was a keen sailor and walker, which provided many subjects. Was a prolific and regular exhibitor at Royal Glasgow Institute of the Fine Arts from 1927–54, also showing at RSA, RSW and Walker Art Gallery, Liverpool.

Charles MacQUEEN 1940– Painter and teacher, born in Glasgow, who attended the School of Art there, 1958–62. He used a rich palette and was especially interested in tabletop arrangements and board games. Went on to teach at Callender Park College of Education, Falkirk, 1970–82, and Moray House Institute of Education, 1982–95, becoming head of department. MacQueen was elected to the Royal Glasgow Institute of the Fine Arts, 1983, and RSW, 1984, becoming its vice-president, 1994. He also showed at RSA, SSWA, Scottish Arts Club, Mall Galleries and elsewhere. MacQueen won a string of awards, including the Glasgow Civic Art Prize, 1971; Royal Glasgow Institute Torrance Award, 1974; RSW David Muirhead Memorial Fund, Debenham's Award for outstanding work by a Scottish Artist and Post Office Award for a Painting by an Artist living and working in Scotland, between 1984–9; RSW Scottish Arts Club Award, 1992; and the Royal Glasgow Institute's Teachers Whisky Travel Scholarship, 1994. Later solo shows included Roger Billcliffe Fine Art, 1996. RSA, Paisley Museum and Art Gallery, the British Consulate in Lille, France, and several Scottish education authorities hold examples.

Steve McQUEEN 1969– Film and video artist, born in London, who attended Chelsea School of Art, 1989–90, Goldsmiths' College, 1990–3, and in 1993–4 Tisch School of the Arts, New York University. Group shows included Acting Out at Royal College of Art, 1994; Mirage, ICA, 1995; and British Art Show 4, and tour, 1995–6.

John McQUIRK 1933– Artist who was brought up in a Catholic orphanage, because of a disruptive family background. For years did a variety of dead-end jobs, then when he gave up work was able to indulge a long-cherished ambition to draw. Using pastel crayon on thick paper he created a world of bizarre humanoids which stemmed from his unsettled upbringing. McQuirk, a productive but self-critical artist who destroyed much of his output, was included in Three Outsiders at Belgrave Gallery, 1995.

Jennifer McRAE 1959– Artist in oil on wood panel and mixed media on various papers, born in Cheshire, but lived most of her life in Scotland, especially Edinburgh. She attended North Berwick High School, then did various jobs for a decade until 1985. From 1986–7 studied art at Stevenson College, Edinburgh; obtained a first-class honours degree at Gray's School of Art, Aberdeen, 1987–91; did postgraduate studies there, 1991–2; in late 1992 attending evening classes in printmaking at Edinburgh College of Art. In 1992 joined Edinburgh Printmakers' Workshop. McRae's awards included Cornwall Steele Award, 1989–90 and 1990–1; she was a runner-up with a special commendation in Morrison Scottish Portrait Award, 1991; and won second prize at Hunting/*Observer* Competition, 1992. In 1991 she gained a John Kinross Travelling Scholarship to Florence. McRae said that her daughter appeared in many paintings. "Her head repeatedly inspires me. I make copious notes about reality and then attempt to paint the reality in a symbolic way. I prefer 'clues' rather than obvious statements." Mixed exhibitions included Aberdeen Artists' Exhibition from 1988; RSA Student Exhibition, Edinburgh from 1990; and Compass Gallery, Glasgow from 1991. Solo shows included Anthony Hepworth Fine Art, Bath, from 1992, and Open Eye Gallery, Edinburgh, 1993.

Dale Pring MacSWEENEY 1949– Painter, born and lived in London, who attended Wimbledon School of Art in 1966, then Waltham Forest College in 1967–70, obtaining her diploma in art and design. A Chelsea Arts Club member, she showed at RA, Henry Wyndham Fine Art, NEAC and elsewhere in London.

John McSWEENEY 1952– Painter and printmaker, born in London, who gained a degree in aeronautical engineering at City University, 1970–3, then was at Camberwell School of Arts and Crafts, 1980–4, with a postgraduate year in printmaking, 1984–5. Selected exhibitions included Stowells Trophy, RA, from

1983; Surrey University, 1984; Bruton Street Gallery, 1991; and Artist of the Day, Angela Flowers Gallery, 1994, where he was chosen by Trevor Jones. Solo exhibitions included Camden Arts Centre, 1989.

Tony McSWEENEY 1953– Illustrator and box maker, who studied at Liverpool College of Art and Royal College of Art. He carried out many commissions for various publications, for advertising and editorial. Among his showing venues were Association of Illustrators' Gallery and England & Co, 1991, in Art in Boxes.

William MacTAGGART 1903–1981 Painter, mainly in oil, especially of landscapes. Born in Loanhead, Midlothian, in 1918 he began studies at Edinburgh College of Art, under David Alison and David Foggie, later studying in France and Italy. MacTaggart, grandson of the Scottish Impressionist William M'Taggart, first exhibited at the RSA in 1921, was elected a member of the SSA the following year, when he was a founder-member of the 1922 Group. The first of many annual visits to France took place in 1923, and in 1924 MacTaggart had a one-man show in Cannes. Joined the staff of Edinburgh College of Art in 1933. Over the years MacTaggart exhibited with Connells, in Glasgow, and there with T & R Annan and Sons, at Aitken Dott, in Edinburgh, and with the Stone Gallery, Newcastle upon Tyne. MacTaggart was an able administrator, organising a number of exhibitions and being elected president of the RSA in 1959. Knighted for his services to art in Scotland in 1962. His pictures are in the collections of the Tate Gallery, Arts Council of Great Britain, Scottish Arts Council and Scottish Royal Academy and in many other British and foreign collections. MacTaggart was a rich Colourist in the Scottish tradition whose work was given its first significant exhibition for 30 years at the Scottish National Gallery of Modern Art, in Edinburgh where he had lived, in 1998.

A MACULRIC: *see* **Alexander Grieve KENNEDY**

Michael McVEIGH fl. from early 1980s– Painter, printmaker and muralist, born in Dundee. After working for a firm of postcard publishers and on a public building mural under the Job Creation Scheme McVeigh joined drawing classes at Duncan of Jordanstone College of Art, enrolled for the drawing and painting course, graduated in 1982 and then went to Ireland on a Scottish Education Department Scholarship. There he was attracted by the slow pace of rural life and the world of the folk musician, influences which affected his maturing work. He returned to Edinburgh in the mid-1980s and was for a time artist-in-residence at the Craigmiller Festival Society. He took part in the Scottish Print Open Tour in 1982, the Dundee Print Workshop Tour in 1988 and participated in mixed shows at Compass Gallery, Glasgow. He had solo exhibitions at 22 Gallery, Coupar, in 1986; Glasgow Tron Theatre Bar in 1988; and Compass Gallery, 1989, and was included in that gallery's The Compass Contribution show in 1990. Dundee City Art Gallery and People's Palace, Glasgow, hold examples.

McW: *see* **Frederick Edward McWILLIAM**

Ishbel McWHIRTER fl. from 1940s– Painter, notably of portraits, who was a pupil at A S Neill's experimental school Summerhill, 1939–45. From 1945–54 she received tuition from the painter Oskar Kokoschka. McWhirter exhibited solo with Victor Waddington in Dublin and Arcade Gallery, Hampstead Artists' Council and Anthony Mould Contemporary, 1996. She was a member of New Grafton Gallery's Portrait Centre and painted many notable sitters, including A S Neill, the actor Tom Conti, the sculptor Dame Barbara Hepworth and Lord Longford.

Frederick Edward McWILLIAM 1909–1992 Sculptor in various materials, born in Banbridge, County Down. McWilliam studied drawing at the Slade School of Fine Art, 1928–31, then worked in Paris for a year, beginning sculpture in 1933. Five years later he showed with the British Surrealist Group, having his first one-man show at the London Gallery the following year. After five years' service with the Royal Air Force, partly in the Far East as an intelligence officer, he resumed sculpture, teaching at the Slade, 1947–68. Joined LG in 1949, RBA in 1950 and was elected an RA associate in 1959, but he resigned four years later. Among McWilliam's many commissions were The Four Seasons for the Festival of Britain, 1951; Father Courage for Kent University at Canterbury, New Zealand, 1960; and Hampstead Figure at Swiss Cottage, London, 1964. Tate Gallery holds his work. Retrospectives at Arts Council of Northern Ireland, 1981, and Tate Gallery, 1989. Signed work McW and lived in London.

Joe McWILLIAMS 1938– Artist and teacher working in various media, born and lived in Belfast, Northern Ireland, where he attended the College of Art, 1958–64. He was also associated with the Open University, 1973–6. Lectured in art education at Ulster College. McWilliams was co-founder of the Troubled Image group in 1973 and in his work took a wry look at the troubled political scene in the province; his pictures could have a strong element of pattern, employing symbols such as the chevron and the rainbow. Exhibitions included Municipal Gallery of Modern Art in Dublin, Tom Caldwell Gallery in Belfast and Playhouse Gallery, Leeds. Queen's University, Belfast, holds his work.

Simon McWILLIAMS 1970– Painter who was educated at the University of Ulster, then gained an honours degree in fine art with postgraduate studies at the Royal Academy Schools. Group exhibitions included RUA, from 1991; Belfast Young Contemporaries, from 1992; RA Summer Exhibition, from 1996; and he was winner of The Alasdair Gilchrist Fisher Memorial Award 1998, at Cadogan Contemporary. Had solo shows at Cavehill Gallery, Belfast, from 1993. Arts Council of Northern Ireland, University of Ulster, Department of the Environment Northern Ireland, Unison and Guinness hold examples.

John MADDISON 1953– Painter, teacher and curator, born in Fife, who studied art history at the University of Manchester. He taught it in Leeds in the 1970s and between 1981–92 had curatorial responsibility for National Trust houses in East Anglia, where he settled at Aylsham, Norfolk. Between 1988–92 Maddison studied with Dick Lee, other influences being Chardin and Sickert. Maddison's rich, intimate work was in the Camden Town Group tradition. From 1992, when he began painting full-time, Maddison showed at the RA Summer Exhibition; in 1995 The National Trust commissioned panels from him for Felbrigg Hall; and there was a solo show at The Jerram Gallery, Salisbury, in 1998.

Conroy MADDOX 1912– Painter, teacher and writer committed to Surrealism, born in Ledbury, Herefordshire. Although he refused to show at the 1936 International Surrealist Exhibition in London, Maddox made contact with the Surrealists in Paris the following year and in 1938 joined the British Surrealist Group. Showed at the Wertheim Gallery, London Gallery, AIA and in the provinces and contributed to Surrealist publications. In 1945 he lectured in modern art at Birmingham University. Associated with the Chicago Surrealist Group in 1970. Had several one-man shows at Hamet Gallery in 1970s and retrospectives at Camden Arts Centre, 1978, and Stoke-on-Trent City Museum and Art Gallery, titled Surreal Enigmas, in 1995. Maddox's pictures can be disquieting and may "smash repose", in his own phrase. Tate Gallery, Victoria & Albert Museum and other public collections hold examples. In 1974 published his illustrated study *Salvador Dalí*. Lived in London.

Reginald MADDOX 1900– Watercolourist, potter, metalworker and teacher, brought up in Shropshire. He attended Coalbrookdale Science and Art School, 1915–20, then Royal College of Art, 1920–3, under William Rothenstein. Became senior art master at Bradford Grammar School, living at Guiseley, Leeds. Exhibited at the public art galleries in Bradford and Leeds. Later lived in Bridgnorth, Shropshire, and Wilton, Wiltshire.

Ronald MADDOX 1930– Illustrator, designer and painter, born in Purley, Surrey. He attended St Albans School of Art, 1945–8; Regent Street Polytechnic, 1949–51; and London School of Printing & Graphic Art, 1951–2; his tutors included Christopher Sanders, Raymond Sheppard and Henry Trevick. After serving with the Air Ministry Design Unit/National Service, 1949–51, Maddox worked as an art director with London advertising agencies, 1953–62, then freelanced. Between 1972–89 carried out stamp designs for the Post Office. He was elected a member of the Society of Industrial Artists & Designers in 1956 and RI in 1959, in 1989 becoming its president, was a member of PS and a fellow of Chartered Society of Designers. Maddox won the Winsor & Newton/RI 150th Anniversary Award in 1981 and the Members' Award in 1991 and was a Hunting Group Finalist several times. He said that he was "influenced by the works of John Piper, Eric Ravilious, John Nash and Edward Burra (landscapes). Paintings and drawings are mainly topographical, exploring the shapes and design of landforms, the textures and patterns of buildings." As well as many mixed shows in London and regional galleries, including RA, RWS and RWA, in 1992 Maddox shared a show at the 1992 Lichfield Festival with Sir Hugh Casson. HM Queen Elizabeth the Queen Mother, the Sultanate of Oman, Barclays Bank, BBC, British Rail, Post Office and other collections held examples. Lived in Digswell, Welwyn, Hertfordshire.

Arthur K MADERSON 1942– Painter, notably of landscapes, in the Impressionist manner, born in London. He attended Camberwell School of Arts and Crafts and continued to paint while teaching, being a tutor at British Institute for Brain Injured Children. Worked especially in France, West Country and around his home in Cambrian Mountains. Exhibited RA, Alpine Gallery and RWA where in 1986 a figure painting by him won the Cornelissen Award.

Clive MADGWICK 1934– Self-taught artist in oil, acrylic and watercolour, born in London, who was educated at Epsom College and London University. He took up painting in 1972 "and progressed from landscapes to genre, figure and sporting scenes". Madgwick was elected to UA in 1976, RBA in 1986 and was also a member of the Society of Equestrian Artists. He won a number of prizes, including the Royale Landscape Prize in 1978 and 1991 and in 1987 a Higgs and Hill Bursary and the Daler-Rowney Award, Equestrian Society of London. Abbey National commissioned him to paint abbeys in the United Kingdom and its Baker Street headquarters, Calor Gas products in use. Mixed shows included Blackheath Gallery, Webster Gallery in Eastbourne and galleries in America and on the continent. Solo exhibitions included a series at Haste Gallery, Ipswich, from 1975; Phoenix Gallery, Lavenham, from 1976; and Files, Rochester, from 1978. HM The Queen owns Madgwick's Buckingham Palace from St James' Park, in the Windsor Castle collection. Lived in Sudbury, Suffolk.

Margo MAECKELBERGHE 1932– Painter and teacher, born in Penzance, Cornwall. She studied at Bath Academy of Art, Corsham, 1949–52, her teachers including Peter Lanyon and William Scott. Her landscapes show influence of both teachers, tending towards an abstract simplicity. She taught in London before marriage. Showed at Leicester Galleries, RSA, Plymouth City Art Gallery, abroad, and was included in RWA Artists from Cornwall exhibition in 1992. Had solo exhibitions at Newlyn Orion Gallery, Penzance, 1974; The Queen's Gallery, Penzance, 1988; and Lanigan Fine Arts, 1990. Cornwall County Council holds her work.

Lee MAELZER 1964– Painter and teacher, born and lived in London, who studied at St Martin's School of Art, 1985–9, and Royal College of Art, 1989–91. From 1991 was a visiting teacher at Winchester School of Art. Showed at Paton Gallery, 1991; Art for a Fairer World in Glasgow and elsewhere in 1992, the year she won a Painter-Stainers prize; and 1993–4 John Moores Liverpool Exhibition.

Daniel MAFÉ 1957– Painter, figurative but tending towards abstraction, born in London. He studied at City and Guilds of

London Art School, 1980–3, then Royal Academy Schools, 1983–6. Showed with LG; RA Summer Exhibition, winning the Daler-Rowney Acrylic Prize, 1985; Whitworth Young Contemporaries, 1985; New Contemporaries, 1986; and was first prizewinner in Europe Prize for Painting, Ostend. In 1987 Mafé was a prizewinner at John Moores Liverpool Exhibition. Lived in Cheltenham, Gloucestershire.

Siobhan MAGEE 1961– Sculptor and teacher who did a foundation course in art and design at University of Ulster, Belfast, 1986–7, then graduated with first-class honours in fine art from Kent Institute of Art & Design, Canterbury, 1987–90. In 1990–1 she was assistant to Patrick Crouch at Lee Priory Sculpture Studios, in 1991 teaching at the Studios and at Dover College. Exhibitions included Seven Sculptors, Kent University, 1989; Transitions, Slaughter House, Smithfield, 1990; Gallery Restaurant, Banbridge, County Down, 1991; and Sculpture at Canterbury, 1992.

Frederick MAGER 1882–1961 Painter who worked as a civil engineer in the Federated Malay States for a decade from 1917. Studied with Romilly Fedden in France, 1924–5, at Southampton School of Art, 1927–31, under Percival Moore, then with Bertram Nicholls, 1935–7. Began exhibiting in the late-1930s, signing work F M, at RSA, ROI, NEAC, RA and Paris Salon. Elected UA in 1949. In 1945 Mager presented five watercolours to Southampton, several of which recorded wartime there; they are now in the possession of the City Museums. On his death Mager left all the books from his studio to Southampton. Lived in retirement at Brockenhurst, Hampshire.

Anne MAGILL 1962– Painter, draughtsman and illustrator, born in Millisle, County Down, Northern Ireland. She studied at Liverpool Polytechnic and St Martin's School of Art, 1981–4, graduating with a first-class honours degree and a Design Council prize. Magill worked as a courtroom artist for the BBC and Independent Television News, also illustrating for *The Sunday Times*, *The Observer* and *Today* newspapers. Her client list included The Body Shop, Saatchi & Saatchi, Marks & Spencer, J Sainsbury, Penguin and W H Smith. Her work appeared frequently in *Images, The Best of British Illustration* and *European Illustration* annuals and exhibitions. She won the Benson & Hedges Gold Award for Illustration. Magill's work was in many corporate collections, including British Airways, Nike, Wrangler and Forte. Commissions included a major work for the headquarters of Co-operative Retail Services and portraits of the abbots of Douai Abbey, Berkshire. Exhibitions of her paintings included Royal Festival Hall, Mall and Smith's Galleries and she had a solo show at Hybrid, 1997. This comprised acrylics using strong directional light sources, performing artists in opera and theatre being favourite topics.

Elizabeth MAGILL 1959– Painter and draughtsman, born in Ontario of a Northern Irish immigrant family. After the early death of her father she went to Northern Ireland with her mother and grew up in Cushendall. Studied at Belfast College of Art, 1979–82, her teachers including Roy Johnston and David Letcham. Then was at Slade School of Fine Art, 1982–4, under Lawrence Gowing. Among her awards were Arts Council of Northern Ireland Bursaries in 1982–6–9, a Boise Travel Scholarship in 1984 and The Jacob Mendelson Trust Grant, 1985. In that year she was artist-in-residence at Portsmouth College of Art. Mixed shows included Stowells Trophy Exhibition, RA, 1983; David Hendriks Gallery, 1984; and South Bank Centre's tour The British Art Show 1990. Showed solo with Kerlin Gallery, Belfast and Dublin, from 1987, and with Arnolfini Gallery, Bristol, 1989. Lived in London.

William Laurence MAGOR 1913– Watercolourist and teacher, born at Mountain Ash, Glamorgan, Wales. After initial education in Gloucester he studied at the School of Art there, 1932–6, then at Royal College of Art, 1936–9, under Edward Bawden and Paul Nash. Exhibited RA and RBSA. After World War II he taught at Wolverhampton School of Art and was principal of Berkshire College of Art, 1960–74, finally living at Hardwicke, Gloucestershire.

Marianne MAHLER fl. from 1920s– Designer, commercial artist and book illustrator, brought up in Vienna, Austria, where she had her initial art education. In England in 1930s attended Royal Academy Schools. Exhibited in Vienna, New York, Paris and London, drew for magazines such as *Studio* and *Vogue* and published children's books. Occasionally just signed work Marian. Lived in London.

James MAHON 1919– Painter, printmaker and teacher. He was born in Belfast, brought up in Birkenhead, Cheshire, and attended the School of Art there, 1935–9 and 1947–51, his teachers including Harry Hoodless. In 1951–2 attended Liverpool School of Art where he was taught by W L Stevenson. Did some commercial published work and taught for a time at St Anselm's College, Birkenhead, living nearby at Claughton. Showed mainly in the Merseyside area.

Phyllis MAHON 1953– Draughtsman in pastel, printmaker, born in Ireland. She studied at University of Ulster and went on to show widely in group exhibitions in Britain and Ireland. Women were a key theme of her work. Octagon Gallery, Belfast; Angela Flowers Gallery; and England & Co, Art in Boxes, 1991, all included examples.

Charles MAHONEY 1903–1968 Painter, muralist, draughtsman and teacher. Born Cyril Mahoney in London – his fellow-student Barnett Freedman rechristened him "Charlie" at the Royal College of Art, which he attended 1922–6, after a period at Beckenham School of Art under Percy Jowett – he early established a reputation as a conscientious teacher. He was at the Royal College 1928–53, from 1948–53 as a painting tutor, where he was noted for his concern for academic discipline. From 1954–63 he taught at the Byam Shaw School of Drawing and Painting and from 1961–8 at the Royal Academy Schools. He did mural work at Morley College, 1928–30, with Eric Ravilious and Edward Bawden, but this was destroyed during World War II. The work led to further murals: at Brockley School, Kent, with Evelyn Dunbar; and at Campion Hall Chapel, Oxford. His oil paintings are frequently of a religious nature. His drawings are often of his garden, at Wrotham, Kent, for he was a skilled botanist. Exhibited at NEAC and RA, being made an RA elect in 1968. Represented in the Tate Gallery and other public collections. Memorial exhibition at the Parkin Gallery and Ashmolean Museum, Oxford, 1975.

Rosanna MAHONY 1952– Printmaker, draughtsman and teacher, born in Hampshire. Her studies included Byam Shaw School of Art, Bernard Dunstan among her teachers, and Florence. Exhibited at RI, in the provinces and widely abroad. Ran her own etching studio in Cirencester, Gloucestershire.

Kenneth MAHOOD 1930– Cartoonist, painter and box maker, born in Belfast, Northern Ireland. After school he worked for a lithographic designer, painting and drawing in his own time. He had two solo shows with Waddington, 1955–8, by which time he was establishing a reputation as a cartoonist with *Punch*, to which he contributed regularly. He also drew for *The New Yorker*, *Financial Times* and *Daily Mail*; was art editor of *Punch*, 1960–5, and political cartoonist for *The Times*, 1966–9. He illustrated a series of his own books, including *The Laughing Dragon*, 1970, and *Losing Willy*, 1977. In the late 1980s he resumed painting and made boxes, some included in England & Co's 1991 show Art in Boxes. Lived for a time in London.

MAIDA 1915– Sculptor in stone and wood, full name Maida Crowe, born in Axminster, Devon. After private education she studied at City and Guilds of London Art School, 1957–62. Became a member of Free Painters and Sculptors and also showed at RBA and in the provinces, having solo exhibitions at Loggia and Cockpit Galleries. Lived in London.

Thomas MAIDMENT 1871–1952 Landscape painter who devoted about 40 years in Cornwall to depicting life and scenery there. He was born in London and studied at Royal College of Art, winning a diploma and travelling scholarship. Before World War I he moved to Newlyn, then lived in Penzance, St Ives and Helston and in his final year in Torquay, Devon. Showed at RA, Walker Art Gallery in Liverpool, elsewhere in the provinces and was included in A Century of Art in Cornwall 1889–1989, Newlyn Orion Galleries, 1989. Brighton Corporation and St Ives Town Council hold his work.

Irene Lesley MAIN fl. from mid-1970s– Painter, born in Glasgow. She studied drawing and painting at the School of Art there, 1976–80, her teachers including David Donaldson and Duncan Shanks. Won a scholarship to Patrick Allan-Fraser School of Art at Hospitalfield, Arbroath, and studied in Italy. A strong influence on her work was that of the Scottish Colourists, notably J D Fergusson, with their liking for sensuous handling of paint and emphasis on light and shade and rich colours. She travelled extensively in Europe and America and had studios in Glasgow and Athens. Showed widely in Europe and America and was regularly on exhibition at Main Fine Art, Glasgow. Warwick Arts Trust, Bank of Ireland, Allied Irish Bank, Robert Fleming Holdings and Scottish Arts Council are some owners of her work. Among awards won were the Hiram Walker and Lauder Awards.

Allan Douglass MAINDS 1881–1945 Painter, designer and lecturer on art history, born in Helensburgh, Dunbartonshire, son of the artist William Reid Mainds. He studied at Glasgow School of Art, gaining a travelling scholarship and diploma, further studying on the continent. Taught at Glasgow, then at Durham University. He was a member of Glasgow Art Club and an associate of RSA, also showing at Royal Glasgow Institute of the Fine Arts, RA, RSW and Walker Art Gallery in Liverpool. Lived at Gosforth, Northumberland.

John MAINE 1942– Sculptor and draughtsman, born in Bristol. He studied at the West of England Art College in the city, then from 1964–7 at Royal College of Art. In the early 1970s Maine principally used wood and galvanised steel, but then chose to carve stone. Maine was interested in geometry as the origin of architectural forms, considered the act of carving important, as was the play of light on his structures and their siting in landscape. He was the first sculptor to have a one-man exhibition at the Yorkshire Sculpture Park, in 1978, the year after he participated in the Battersea Park Silver Jubilee Exhibition. In 1983 he was included in the Welsh Sculpture Trust show at Margam: Sculpture in a Country Park. Maine won several awards and exhibited or worked on commissions as far away as Japan and Australia. Many public collections, including Arts Council, hold his work. Was elected RA, 1995. Lived in East Knoyle, Wiltshire.

Roy de MAISTRE 1894–1968 Painter in oil of figures and still life. Born at Bowral, New South Wales, Australia, de Maistre – who until 1930 used the name Roi de Mestre – studied music and painting in Sydney from 1913. He was at the Royal Art Society of New South Wales under Datillo Rubbo and Norman Carter, later at the Sydney School of Art with Julian Ashton. After initially exhibiting in Australia and World War I service with the Australian Army, de Maistre in 1923 won a scholarship which took him to Paris, where he exhibited in the Salon in 1924. Represented in the Australian section of the Venice Biennale 1926. For the next few years de Maistre was variously in France, Australia and London, where in 1934 he opened a painting school with Martin Bloch. For several years during World War II de Maistre did not paint. De Maistre had his first one-man show in London in 1929 in the studio of his friend Francis Bacon, followed by other exhibitions at the Mayor Gallery, Calmann Gallery, Temple Newsam, Leeds, the City Art Gallery, Birmingham, the Adams Gallery and Hanover Gallery, with a retrospective at the Whitechapel Art Gallery in 1960. The Tate Gallery holds several examples of his work and the City Art

Gallery, Leicester, a Crucifixion. De Maistre had a special interest in the nature of colour in art, designing a disc to enable harmonious colour schemes to be chosen from a scale using a standard principle. His pictures show a strong sense of design, with an obvious debt to Cubism. Lived in London.

John MAIZELS 1945– Artist who studied at Chelsea School of Art. He began exhibiting in mid-1960s at Young Contemporaries, then showed widely, later venues including Fouts & Fowler, 1990, and Art in Boxes at England & Co, 1992. He was involved in the publication of the art periodicals *Zombic News* and *Raw Vision* and was a researcher into Art Brut.

Julie MAJOR 1964– Artist in mixed media who was born and lived in London. She studied at Croydon College of Art, 1980–3, Kingston Polytechnic, 1983–6, and Royal Academy Schools, 1987–90. Awards included Stanley Picker Travelling Scholarship to Italy, 1985; Bolton House Trust Awards, 1988 and 1990; and Sculpture Prize, British Institute Fund, 1990. Her mixed show appearances included Mall Galleries, RA Summer Exhibitions from 1989, Berkeley Square Gallery and Art in Boxes at England & Co, 1992. In 1991 she had a solo exhibition at Paton Gallery, also taking part in Paton's show at *The Economist*, 1994, where abstract sculptures including mauve spiral tips in waxed felt were a feature. EMI in Paris holds her work.

Mary Jo MAJOR 1949– Printmaker and painter, born in Edmonton, Canada, attending the University of Calgary, 1971, and Concordia University, Montreal, for painting and printmaking, 1976. In 1970 she gained a World University Students Travel Award, in 1977 a Northern Arts Printmaking Grant. Mixed shows included Air Gallery, 1977; British Print Workshops, Crescent Art Gallery, Scarborough, 1981; and Wapping Artists Open Studios from 1982. Solo exhibitions included Alberta House, Mount Street, 1983. British Petroleum and Universities of Alberta and Michigan hold examples.

Michael MAJOR 1951– Painter and draughtsman, born in Egypt. He attended West Sussex College of Art & Design at Worthing for foundation studies, 1968–9, then was at Birmingham College of Art & Design, 1969–72, obtaining his master's degree at Royal College of Art, 1972–5. Major showed with Northern Young Contemporaries, 1971–2; in John Moores Liverpool Exhibition, 1974; and Artists against Apartheid at Graves Art Gallery, Sheffield, 1983. In 1980 had a solo show at House Gallery, another at Woodlands Art Gallery, 1984, and at Bird and Davis, 1995. That illustrated Major's move from abstraction to landscape painting in the mid-1980s, pictures giving an impression of huge distances, uncluttered space filled with light. Public and private collections hold his work.

Theodore MAJOR 1908– Painter, draughtsman and teacher, born in humble circumstances in Wigan, Lancashire, settling near there from 1950 with his painter wife Kathleen at Appley Bridge. Major's first job in a tailor's shop undermined his always precarious health and he was made unemployed. He attended the local Art School, 1927–32, and taught, 1930–50, while insisting that he was self-taught. Major was a fervent Lancastrian, against materialism, the commercial gallery system and the sale of his pictures to rich collectors. He retained about 3,000 of his pictures, which he said were painted for ordinary people, not money, and he lived in straitened circumstances. Art critic John Berger called Major's pictures "among the best English paintings of our time". Major admired Michelangelo, Rembrandt, Blake, Van Gogh and Rouault and painted in a wide range of styles "to *disturb* and extend consciousness in the mind of the viewer". He drew cartoons for the *Daily Mail* and *Manchester Guardian* and was president of Wigan Art Club, which he founded in 1952. Major shared two-man shows in Nottingham and Bolton and at Crane Gallery, Manchester, and had Arts Council-sponsored solo exhibitions at Carlisle and Blackburn Art Galleries and in 1984 at Salford Art Gallery, which holds his work.

Kum-Siew MAK 1940– Artist using oil, acrylic and Chinese ink, born in Singapore. He studied at St Martin's School of Art, 1961–4, under Frederick Gore, then Royal College of Art, 1964–7, with Carel Weight. He taught at various art colleges and schools in England and Wales, 1969–88, then resumed full-time painting in 1989. Group shows included Whitechapel Art Gallery, ICA, Arnolfini Gallery in Bristol, elsewhere in the provinces and abroad. Solo exhibitions included Arnolfini, Royal College of Art, Commonwealth Institute, Compass Gallery in Glasgow and Singapore. Tate Gallery, National Art Gallery in Singapore and Museum of Modern Art in Hyogo, Japan, hold Mak's work; the several examples in Arts Council collection are all abstracts. Lived in Mortimer, Berkshire.

Trevor MAKINSON 1926– Painter and teacher, born in Southport, Lancashire. He attended Hereford School of Art and Slade School of Fine Art. Went on to lecture at Glasgow's School of Art and the University. Professor Makinson, who was a member of Glasgow Art Club, showed in mixed exhibitions at RA, RP, RSA, UA and elsewhere. He had strong connections with Hereford, being a member of the Farmers' Club there, showing with Herefordshire Arts and Crafts and Wye Valley Art Society and having a series of solo shows at Hereford Art Gallery from 1944; it holds his work. There were other one-man shows in the provinces. Public galleries in Buxton, Glasgow, Newport, Salford and elsewhere hold examples. Lived in Glasgow.

Raphael MAKLOUF 1937– Sculptor in clay, bronze and plaster, painter and teacher, born in Jerusalem. He studied at Camberwell School of Art, 1953–8, teachers including Karel Vogel, Richard Eurich and Gilbert Spencer. Maklouf lectured at Camberwell, 1958–68. He was a fellow of RBS and showed at RA and elsewhere. His main works included HM The Queen; HRH Prince Philip, Duke of Edinburgh; the politician Lady Thatcher; the actress Joan Collins; the broadcaster Michael Parkinson; and the footballer Bobby Moore. Lived in Richmond, Surrey.

Bronwen MALCOLM 1963– Painter and teacher, born and lived in London, a subtle Colourist whose work contained a strong element of fantasy. She studied at Wimbledon School of Art, 1981–2, then St Martin's, 1982–5, graduating with an honours degree in fine art, painting. After teaching part-time at London College of Furniture in 1989 she travelled and painted in Asia, returning to work in London. Carried out painting commissions for Merrill Lynch Ltd and Cardinal Beer, in Germany. Began showing in mid-1980s with Anderson Woods Fine Art, then with Long and Ryle Art International, Mall Galleries and in a mixed show with Sue Rankin Gallery, having a solo exhibition there in 1992, another at Thackeray Gallery in 1996.

Ellen MALCOLM 1923– Painter and teacher, born in Grangemouth, Stirlingshire, married to the artist Gordon Cameron. After Aberdeen Academy she studied at Gray's School of Art in Aberdeen, 1940–4, teachers including David M Sutherland and Robert Sivell. In 1952 she gained the RSA's Guthrie Award, becoming an Academy member in 1976. Showed in Scotland and has examples in Perth Art Gallery & Museum and Lillie Art Gallery, Milngavie. Lived at Invergowrie, Perthshire.

Mary MALENOIR 1940– Printmaker and painter, born in Surrey, where she settled in Farnham, married to the artist Michael Fairclough. She studied at Kingston School of Art, 1957–61; Royal Academy Schools, 1961–4, gaining her diploma; and printmaking at S W Hayter's Atelier 17, in Paris. She was a Rome Scholar in Engraving, 1965–7. Malenoir was elected to RE in 1984. Showed at RA Summer Exhibitions, at Hunting and Humberside Printmaking Competitions and elsewhere. Her abstract work was given a solo show at The George Rodger Gallery, Kent Institute of Art & Design, Maidstone, in 1997. Ashmolean Museum, Oxford, and Graves Art Gallery, Sheffield, hold her pictures.

Leopoldo MALER 1937– Artist in a variety of media, film-maker, writer, teacher and administrator, born in Buenos Aires, Argentina, who studied social sciences at the New School for Social Research, New York, 1957–8; graduated in law from the University of Buenos Aires, 1960; worked for the BBC Latin American Service from 1961 and was a postgraduate student in law at University College, further studying law in Helsinki, 1962–4. Thereafter was involved in numerous artistic, theatrical, film, musical and choreographic events in many countries. In Britain these included *Listen here now*, at the Arts Laboratory, 1968; directing a programme of six choreographic works with dancers, fork-lift trucks and objects, entitled *X-IT*, at The Place, 1969; joint authorship with N F Simpson of *Playback 625*, at the Royal Court Theatre, 1970; the tableau, *Silence*, at Camden Arts Centre, 1971; teaching at Hornsey College of Art and Leeds Polytechnic, with additional work for BBC, 1975; Mortal Issues, Whitechapel Art Gallery, 1976; and Hayward Annual, Hayward Gallery, 1978, to which Maler contributed installations. He then said that he would "like to travel the world organising big celebrations, weddings, birthday parties, staging farewell and welcoming ceremonies ... those things that, if enjoyed totally in a spirit of communion with other human beings, remove all meaning from the term 'artist' as an isolated manifestant in society." Lived latterly in Santo Domingo, Dominican Republic.

Guy MALET 1900–1973 Painter, wood engraver and writer. Malet came from a military background and after attending Downside School he went to the Royal Military Academy, Sandhurst. Part of Malet's artistic training was with John Hassall, then in the late-1920s he studied with Iain Macnab at the Grosvenor School of Modern Art, which marked his style as a wood engraver. This was his strongest medium. Exhibited RA, Redfern Gallery, NEAC, SWE, of which he was a member, and abroad. British Museum, Victoria & Albert Museum, British provincial and Commonwealth galleries hold his work. Wrote on wood engraving for *The Artist* magazine. Lived in London and later at Ditchling, Sussex.

Suzi MALIN fl. from mid-1970s– Portrait painter, especially in tempera. After education at Badminton she studied at Slade School of Fine Art, 1969–75, notable teachers including John Aldridge. She rapidly established a career as a portrait painter, mainly male sitters, spending several months concentrating on one subject. Solo shows included JPL Fine Arts, 1977, and Gimpel Fils, 1982. Her sitters included the actor Peter Sellers, the singer Sir Elton John and the politician Sir Alec Douglas-Home, Baron Home of the Hirsel, the last two in the National Portrait Gallery. Lived in London.

Antoni MALINOWSKI 1955– Abstract artist, born in Warsaw, Poland, who studied at Academy of Fine Art there, 1974–9, then Chelsea College of Art, 1981–2. His spiritually inspired creations were shown widely in group exhibitions in Britain and abroad, including Placed/Displaced (installation), Chisenhale Gallery, 1986; Whitechapel Open from 1989; Todd Gallery, 1992; and he represented Britain in EC Young Painters, The Arts Centre, Seoul, 1993. After a solo exhibition at Künstlerhaus, Hamburg, 1985, later ones included Galeria Dziekanka, Warsaw, 1991, Galerie Marie-Louise Wirth, Zürich, and Gimpel Fils Gallery, both 1993. After 1980 Malinowski lived in London.

John MALLCOTT-MILLS fl. from mid-1970s– Painter whose work had strong surreal, fantastic elements. He studied at West Sussex College of Art and Design, 1971–2, Manchester Polytechnic, 1972–5, Birmingham Polytechnic, 1975–6 and London University Institute of Education, 1976–7. He showed at Radio Brighton and Manchester City Art Gallery from 1974 Portland Gallery, Manchester, 1975; and Ikon Gallery, Birmingham, 1977. In 1980 had solo show at Woodlands Art Gallery.

Linda MALLETT 1949– Artist, born in London, whose paintings derived "their primary inspiration from the landscape – particularly the wilder and more marginal land of the coasts and the uplands". She used a range of media to produce very small and large works "in a fairly loose and expressive way". Mallett gained a fine art and design diploma (sculpture) from West of England College of Art, Bristol, 1967–71, and moved to work in Galloway, 1977, settling in Kirkcudbright, where she ran painting holidays. Was elected a professional member of SSWA in 1995. Also exhibited at SSA, RSW and Royal Glasgow Institute of the Fine Arts. Later solo exhibitions included Firth Gallery in Edinburgh, Cree Gallery in Gatehouse of Fleet and Chatton Gallery, Northumberland, all 1997. BBC Scotland, Dumfries & Galloway College, Stewartry District Council (for presentation to HM The Queen) and Paintings in Hospitals hold Mallett's work.

Violet Sanders MALLET: *see* **Violet SANDERS**

Pat MALLINSON 1930– Artist who studied at Regent Street Polytechnic School of Art, 1946–51, later at Goldsmiths' College School of Art and City and Guilds Art School, learning her etching from Richard Beer. Until marriage in 1958 she taught art, did illustrative work and worked for Patrick Reyntiens' stained glass studio. Eventually returned to printmaking with a studio in north London. Showed in many London and provincial galleries, with work in collections worldwide.

Andrew MALONE 1965– Sculptor creating abstract works in a variety of materials. He attended Hertfordshire College of Art and Design for a foundation course, 1984–5, then obtained first-class honours degree at St Martin's School of Art, 1985–8, followed in 1988–9 by an advanced sculpture course. His exhibitions included Hochschule der Kunst, Berlin, a six-week exchange to make steel sculpture, 1987; Lumsden Sculpture Walk, Aberdeenshire, 1989; Spirit of Wood Sculpture, at Herbert Read Gallery, Canterbury, 1991, and in same year Sculpture at Canterbury.

Martin MALONEY 1961– Artist, born in London, who attended University of Sussex, 1980–3; London College of Printing, 1984–5; Central St Martins School of Art and Design, 1988–91, with time at the the School of Visual Arts, New York, America, 1990, and Nova Scotia College of Art and Design, Halifax, Canada, 1991; and Goldsmiths' College, 1991–3. Group exhibitions included Neo-Naive, one of a series at Lost in Space, all 1995; Die Yuppie Scum, Karsten Schubert, 1996; and the Saatchi Collection-related Sensation, RA, 1997. Had a solo show, Sex Shop, at OO Gallery, Halifax, Nova Scotia, 1991; Portraits, Habitat, King's Road, 1996, and Genre paintings, Robert Prime, 1997.

Kathleen MALTBY: *see* **Kathleen GUTHRIE**

Eric MALTHOUSE 1914–1997 Painter, muralist, printmaker, illustrator and teacher (in the 1940s some work were signed E James Malthouse), born in Erdington, Birmingham. Studied under Bernard Fleetwood-Walker at Edward VI Grammar School there and at Birmingham College of Art, 1931–7. Helped Fleetwood-Walker with his mural for Chelmsford Town Hall, 1937. Other murals included Wales Gas Board and University Hall, both Cardiff and 1963. Malthouse lectured at Cardiff College of Art, 1944–73. He was a founder of SWG, 1949, founder of the 56 Group in 1956, associate of RWA from 1959 and was elected to the Printmakers' Council in 1971. Malthouse showed his first picture at RBSA in 1931, other group appearances including AIA, WAC and Royal National Eisteddfod. His work went through various Surrealist, figurative and, from 1959, entirely non-figurative phases. Solo shows began with Civic Playhouse, Bradford, 1938, later ones including Oriel, Cardiff, and Sherman Theatre, Cardiff, both 1981. National Museum of Wales and WAC in Cardiff hold examples. Lived in Barry, South Glamorgan.

Hale MAN 1969– Abstract painter, born in the United Kingdom with a Chinese background. She felt it was "essential to understand the fundamental principles and intrinsic attributes of one's cultural origins", having experienced "a constant bombardment of images of Western ideals". She studied at Doncaster Art College, Kingston Polytechnic and the Royal College of Art. Group shows included Fresh Art at Business Design Centre, 1990; Into the Nineties, Mall Galleries, 1993; and Journeys West, the University of Essex touring show, 1995. Samaritan Hospital holds her work.

Maurice MAN 1921–1997 Artist and designer, especially in pastel, who was born in northwest London, his funeral taking place nearby at Golders Green Crematorium. Although he lived in Hampstead for many years, from the early 1970s Man lived in the Hastings area, dying of a heart attack in St Leonards-on-Sea. He studied at Willesden and St Martin's Schools of Art and in Paris at L'Académie de la Grande Chaumière. Was engaged on propaganda work during World War II. Man disliked the commercialization of art and was known as a volatile, retiring and eccentric personality. Primarily a figure and portrait painter, notably of women and children, his subjects included the actresses Joan Collins, Shirley Ann Field, Georgina Hale, Julie Andrews, Sylvia Syms and Natalie Wood. Prominent personalities worldwide and the Ben Uri Art Society hold his work. Exhibitions included Kensington Art Gallery, 1958, and Mount Gallery, 1964.

George MANCHESTER 1922–1996 Painter, especially of landscape, in Impressionistic style, mural artist and teacher. Studied at Beckenham Art School with Thomas Freeth, 1946–50, then at Royal College of Art, 1950–3, where his teachers included Ruskin Spear and John Minton. Exhibitions included RA, Young Contemporaries, Beaux Arts Gallery, Leicester Galleries and one-man shows which included Redfern Gallery in 1950s. Lived in London.

Melanie MANCHOT 1966– Artist whose output included photography-related work, and lecturer, born in Witten, West Germany, who studied at the Sorbonne, Paris, 1987; International Center of Photography, New York, and the University there, both

1988–9; City University, 1989–90; then Royal College of Art, 1990–2. She was shortlisted for the Darwin Award and won the Speyhawk Award, both 1991; and in 1992 won the Chesterton Award and was joint winner of the Fuji Award. Manchot held many part-time and visiting lectureships in Britain and Portugal, latterly including Middlesex University and Royal College of Art. Group shows included Treading a Fine Line, at Zelda Cheatle Gallery, 1991; South Bank Photo Show at Royal Festival Hall, 1994; and John Kobal Photographic Portrait Award, National Portrait Gallery and tour, 1995–6. Later solo shows included Well Cured at The Cut Gallery, 1996, in which, merging photographic techniques with those of painting and using her mother as model, Manchot offered a new way of seeing the ageing female body. Saatchi Collection holds her work.

Anita MANDL 1926– Sculptor in wood, stone and bronze, born in Prague, Czechoslovakia. After moving to England she trained as a zoologist and did biological research for 18 years, during much of that period attending evening classes at Birmingham College of Art. In 1965 Dr Mandl married, gave up her readership at University of Birmingham and concentrated on sculpture. Her bronzes were made from carvings, not from clay models, and featured wildlife subjects. The surface of her work was highly polished and she experimented with two-tone effects. In 1967 she became a full member of Devon Guild of Craftsmen; in 1971 was elected a sculptor-member of RSMA; in 1978 RWA made her a full member; and in 1980 she was raised to a fellowship of RBS. She showed at RA, Royal Glasgow Institute of the Fine Arts, Phoenix Gallery in Lavenham, Coach House in Guernsey, RWA and Rooksmoor Gallery, Bath. In 1985 the Zoological Society of London commissioned bronze casts of her Young Hippo for the Stamford Raffles Award. Lived in Budleigh Salterton, Devon.

Stephen MANGAN 1964– Painter, born in Edinburgh, whose figurative pictures could be dark, with a strong fantasy element. Mangan gained an honours degree in drawing and painting from Duncan of Jordanstone Art College, Dundee, 1984–8, with a postgraduate diploma, 1988–9. RSA awards included Saltire Society Purchase Award, 1995, and John Murray Award, 1996. His many group shows included Compass Gallery, Glasgow, from 1988; Paisley Art Gallery, from 1989; St Andrews Fine Art, from 1991; and Aberdeen Artists' Annual, 1996. Had a solo show at Loretto Gallery, Musselburgh, 1990, later ones including Flying Colours Gallery, 1996. RSA and East and Midlothian National Health Service Trust Art Fund hold examples.

Julia MANHEIM 1949– Jeweller, installations artist and lecturer, born and worked in London, who did a foundation course at Hornsey College of Art, 1968–9, then a diploma in jewellery design at Central School of Art & Design, 1969–72. After setting up a jewellery workshop in Covent Garden, 1973, established her own studio in north London, 1975. Held a number of residencies, including Newcastle Polytechnic, 1980–2; in Australia, 1988; Galerie Ra, Amsterdam, 1990, with gallery and British Council funding; and Ballroom Blitz Residency, South Bank Arts Centre, 1993. In 1994 she was consultant artist for Braintree Public Library, funded by Essex County Council. Took part in numerous international exhibitions, solo shows including Abbot Hall Art Gallery & Museum, Kendal, 1978; Aspects Gallery, 1983; Galerie V & V, Vienna, 1985; and Paper Works, Galerie Ra, 1990. Manheim consistently used discarded materials, to avoid their loss, because of their complex associations from a previous life and because she disliked the waste of potentially useful substances. For installations at Galerie Ra and at Reading Visual Arts Week in 1992 she incorporated several tons of newspapers, choosing them carefully. Victoria & Albert Museum, Crafts Council, public galleries in Kendal, Gateshead and Southampton and many other collections hold examples.

Debra MANIFOLD 1961– Artist and teacher, born in London. She studied at Harrow School of Art and Central School of Art and Design. Her work, included in several books on the technique of pastel painting, was shown at Barbican Centre, National Theatre, AOI Gallery, UA and in Paris. In 1992 her work was featured in Linda Blackstone Gallery, Pinner, exhibition Interpretations of Town, Land & Sea. Shared a show there in 1995, when she was elected a member of PS.

Wolf MANKOWITZ 1924–1998 Writer and collagist, born in London, who gained his master's degree in English at Cambridge University. His East End Jewish background was depicted in novels such as *Make Me an Offer* and *A Kid for Two Farthings*, which were successfully filmed, and Mankowitz collected a number of awards for other screenplays, such as *The Day The Earth Caught Fire* and *The Hireling*, as well as writing a series of stage musicals. He also published *An Encyclopaedia of English Pottery and Porcelain* in 1957, four years after publishing the history of Wedgwood. In the 1980s Mankowitz taught English and theatre arts at University of Mexico. Latterly he took up collage as a relief from writing and had a show at Davis Gallery, Dublin, 1990, then was included in a five-man exhibition at Grosvenor Gallery, 1994. Lived in Ahakista, County Cork, Ireland.

Edna MANLEY 1900–1987 Sculptor, born in Cornwall, the fifth of nine children of an English Methodist missionary and his Jamaican wife. While studying art in London she married her first cousin Norman Manley, and after his graduation from Oxford University they returned to Jamaica. He became its president and their son Michael was another. After Regent Street Polytechnic and St Martin's School of Art Edna Manley developed into a power figurative sculptor, a member of LG who also showed with RSA. "I know I am a minor artist," she wrote, "but no-one is a better wood-carver. No-one can bully, cajole, coax, batter or trick wood like I can." Her diaries, covering the period 1939–87, were edited by her grand-daughter Rachel Manley and published in 1989 as *Edna Manley, The Diaries*. Graves Art Gallery, Sheffield, holds her figure Eve. Lived in Kingston, Jamaica.

Jim MANLEY 1934– Watercolour landscape painter, born in St Helens, Lancashire, who moved to Northern Ireland in 1971, settling in Killough, County Down. His sensibility to landscape was conditioned by experiences during National Service, the pit and the Forestry Commission. The watercolours of Peter De Wint, J S Cotman and J M W Turner and the modern artists Ivon Hitchens, Paul Nash and Graham Sutherland were influences. Won a number of awards, including the McGonigal Prize, Oreachtas, 1979; Percy French Watercolour Competition, 1984; and Walker Art Gallery, Liverpool, 1993. Manley was elected an associate of RUA in 1983. Group shows included Abbot Hall, Kendal, 1977; Ulster Way travelling show, 1987–8; and Cruinniu, Sligo, 1995. His many solo shows included a series at Duncan Campbell Contemporary Art from 1992. Arts Council of Northern Ireland and Stormont Castle, Belfast, hold examples.

Alex MANN 1923– Painter and sometime art gallery director, born in Ayr, Scotland. He was educated in Scotland but studied art at Sidcup School of Art. Showed in Midlands and elsewhere and Leamington Spa Art Gallery holds his work. Lived for some time in Stratford-upon-Avon, Warwickshire.

Cathleen MANN 1896–1959 Painter. Daughter of the painters Harrington Mann and Florence Sabine Mann; the Tate Gallery holds a family group by Harrington which includes Cathleen and Sabine. Cathleen studied at the Slade School of Fine Art and in Paris. She went on to exhibit her strong portraits and still lifes at the RA, Goupil, Lefevre and Leicester Galleries, NEAC, PS and widely elsewhere. Her work is held by the Victoria & Albert Museum, in British provincial, French and American galleries. Lived in London.

Cyril MANN 1911–1980 Painter in an Expressionist/ Impressionist style, sculptor and teacher, born in London, who moved with his family to Nottingham in 1914 where in 1923, aged 12, he was the youngest boy to win a scholarship to the School of Art. In 1925 he left school, worked as a clerk, then in 1927 went to Canada to be a missionary; did a variety of jobs; began painting again; and after travelling through America in 1933–4 settled in London. He was in 1935 sponsored to attend the Royal Academy Schools for several years, then for a while in Paris. Served in the Army in World War II, then from 1947–9 taught at Central School of Arts and Crafts, in 1950 teaching at Kingsway Day College and Sir John Cass College. Mann took part in mixed shows at Wildenstein, Park Row Gallery, East End Academy and Archer Gallery. He had a series of solo exhibitions, including St Martin's Gallery, 1963; Rawinsky Gallery, 1964; and Alwin Gallery from 1965. In final years Mann suffered health and mental problems. Piano Nobile Fine Paintings, Richmond, held a tribute show in 1992.

Dale MANN 1959– Artist in a variety of media who studied graphic design and illustration at Suffolk College of Art and Design but was largely self-taught. Showed at Royal Over-Seas League Annual Exhibition, 1986; Essex Open Exhibition, 1988; and England & Co, 1991, Art in Boxes. Work bought by Epping Forest District Museum. Had a first solo show at Chappel Galleries, Chappel, 1993.

Edna MANN 1926–1985 Painter, born in London, where she lived for some years. Attended Romford County High School. Studied art at South-East Essex Technical College, 1942, and won a scholarship to Royal College of Art, 1945. However, opposition to David Bomberg's ideas there prompted Mann to leave after a year because of a conflict of loyalties. From 1946 she studied at Borough Polytechnic under Bomberg, being a founder-member of the Borough Group. Exhibited with it at Arcade, Archer and Bookworm Galleries. Was included in The Visual Arts, Harlow Arts Festival, 1965, the year that she had a solo show at Drian Gallery and, in collaboration with Frank Hitchcock, had a first play broadcast by BBC. Lived in Harlow, Essex.

Frances MANN 1949– Painter and teacher. She studied at Camberwell School of Arts and Crafts, 1973–7, then went on to lecture in the drawing class there in 1979, teaching the degree course in 1982. Design was a strong feature of her work, stemming from her training as a textile designer at Camberwell. She shared a show at Ripley Art Centre, in Bromley, 1979, then showed at Cadogan Contemporary from 1987, sharing a show there in 1990.

James Scrimgeour MANN 1883–1946 Marine painter and poster artist whose work was widely reproduced, born in Dundee, Scotland. He attended Liverpool School of Art and served in Army in World War I. Settled in Liverpool where he was a member of the Academy and drew inspiration for his pictures from the port around him. These included Tide Time, The Coming of the Westerlies and The Great Days. Mann showed at Walker Art Gallery, Liverpool, which holds his canvas Tide Time, was a member of RI and RCamA, and also showed with RBA, RA and Royal Glasgow Institute of the Fine Arts. He died at Caldy, Wirral.

Paul MANN 1907– Painter who experimented with cellulose colours, born in Kettering, Northamptonshire. Studied art at Wellingborough Technical College. Took part widely in mixed shows and had a series of one-man exhibitions in England and America, including Lyall Watson's Woodstock Gallery. Lived for some years near Newport Pagnell, Buckinghamshire.

Sargy MANN 1937– Painter and teacher, born in Hythe, Kent. Originally he was an engineer, studying at Oxford Technical College, 1953–8. Then studied at Camberwell School of Arts and Crafts, 1960–4, with postgraduate studies, 1967. Taught at Camberwell, 1969–88, paralleled by teaching at Camden Arts Centre. Light was a predominant consideration in Mann's pictures, in which forms and places were suggested rather than exactly delineated. From 1979 began to have trouble with sight, being later left with only peripheral vision in one eye. He had a one-man show at Salisbury Festival of Arts in 1973. Other noteworthy landmarks in his exhibiting career were a second prize in the 2nd International Drawing Biennale in 1975; a second prize in the Spirit of London show on the South Bank in 1983, with a first prize in 1985; the Daler-Rowney Prize at RA Summer Exhibition in 1988; and solo exhibitions at Cadogan Contemporary from 1991. Arts Council and Contemporary Art Society hold his work.

Norman Egmont MANNERS 1905– Painter, printmaker, draughtsman and teacher, born in Shoreham, Kent. Studied at Chelsea School of Art, where his teachers included John Revel, 1921–4; won a scholarship which took him to Patrick Allan-Fraser School of Art, Hospitalfield, Arbroath, 1924–7. Showed RA, Senefelder Club, Victoria & Albert Museum and elsewhere. He held a number of teaching posts in the south of England. Lived in London and Quendon, Essex.

Charles MANNING 1952– Artist and teacher, born in Middlesex. He studied at Uxbridge College, Middlesex, 1973–5, Chelsea School of Art, 1975–6, and Ravensbourne College of Art, 1976–9. In 1982 he was included in Artists in Adult Education at Woodlands Art Gallery. Other shows included Artists' Meeting Place, 1976, Brunel University, 1979, and Fulham Society of Artists, 1982.

Jeni MANNING 1967– Artist and teacher who gained an honours degree in fine art printmaking then her master's at Royal College of Art. In 1994 she had a residency at Edna Manley School of Art, Kingston, Jamaica. From 1988 did a number of administrative jobs, in 1995 teaching primary printmaking techniques at Willesden Library Centre, in 1997 holding workshops for various ages around London boroughs. Group shows included Exhibit A, Rotunda Gallery, 1991; Degree Show, University of East London, 1993; and Henry Moore Gallery, Royal College of Art, 1995. Had a solo exhibition at 198 Gallery, 1997. Victoria & Albert Museum holds her work

Michael MANNING 1931– Painter, printmaker, illustrator and teacher who also sang in opera at Glyndebourne, Covent Garden and elsewhere, including continental opera houses, in the late-1950s. He was born Michael Bernard Louis Manning in Berlin, Germany, his birth registered in London (on the continent he also exhibited as Bernard Montaigu). Studied at St Martin's School of Art, Regent Street Polytechnic, Beaux-Arts in Paris, Guildhall School of Music, London University and in Rome, teachers including Blair Hughes-Stanton, Clifford Webb, Frederick Gore, Nigel Lambourne and John Piper, for many years a friend, also John Farleigh and John Ward. As well as teaching at St Martin's, Eastbourne and Medway Schools of Art and elsewhere, Manning worked in advertising as an illustrator and in television. Among his main works were posters for London Transport, the Post Office and Iraq Petroleum. Group shows included RA, RBA, RI, Bourne Gallery in Reigate, Premier Gallery in Eastbourne, Little Gallery in Arundel, Leicester Galleries, on the continent and in North America. Little and Premier Galleries gave him solo exhibitions, as did Pantiles Gallery at Tunbridge Wells and Far Gallery, New York. Several continental and American collections, such as Ulrich Collection in Hamburg and MacGowan Collection in Savannah, Georgia, hold examples. Lived in Eastbourne, Sussex, and Richmond, Surrey.

William Westley MANNING 1868–1954 Painter and printmaker, born in London. He studied initially at University College School in London, at Académie Julian, Paris, 1892, where his teachers included the rigid academic painter Alphonse Bouguereau, then Central School of Arts and Crafts under Malcolm Osborne. He exhibited extensively at RA, RBA, ROI and Royal Institute of the Fine Arts in Glasgow as well as many other venues in Britain and overseas. A large number of foreign and British galleries hold his work, including British Museum and Victoria & Albert Museum. Manning painted widely in Europe and North Africa but lived finally in London.

John MANSBRIDGE 1901–1981 Artist, inspirational teacher and author, educated at Manchester Grammar School and the Slade School of Fine Art under Henry Tonks. His father was Albert Mansbridge, founder of the Workers' Educational Association, and many pioneers of adult education, such as Bishop Charles Gore, William Temple (later Archbishop of Canterbury) and Professor R H Tawney, influenced John's childhood. In 1929 he joined the staff of Goldsmiths' College School of Art, after World War II being senior lecturer in painting there until his retirement in 1966. He also lectured in the history of art and architecture for London University extra-mural department. In 1969 Mansbridge published his well-received *Graphic History of Architecture*, resulting from 10 years' research. His panels of classical historical events decorated ships of the Blue Funnel Line. Mansbridge was a noted portrait painter, exhibiting at RA, RP, RBA and NEAC. He made portraits of the first Labour cabinet of 1924; Battle of Britain fighter pilots; and society figures, Anglican prelates, politicians and writers. Mansbridge's pictures are owned by the Imperial War Museum and National Portrait Gallery, whose holding includes his depictions of his father, Tawney and the writer Sir John Squire.

Andrew MANSFIELD 1953– Painter, born in Leicester, who studied at Loughborough College of Art and Design, 1970–3, and Portsmouth Polytechnic, 1976–9. In 1987 he was an artist-in-residence in Lisbon. His mixed show appearances included Serpentine Gallery, 1984; The Flower Show, Stoke-on-Trent and tour, 1986; and John Moores Liverpool Exhibition, 1987. His solo shows included Spacex Gallery, Exeter, 1984; Winchester Gallery in Winchester, 1985; Midland Group, Nottingham, the same year; and Anthony Reynolds, 1986. Arts Council holds his canvas Nature Morte, of 1985.

Edgar MANSFIELD 1907–1996 Bookbinder, sculptor, draughtsman, potter and teacher, born in London, full name James Frank Edgar Mansfield, his father being a colourman for Reeves. In 1911 Mansfield's family settled in Hastings, New Zealand, which remained his home, although he spent much time in England, dying at Bearsted, Kent. After matriculation, Mansfield from 1924–5 was a pupil teacher, studying drawing part-time with Roland Hipkins; attended Dunedin Teachers' Training College, 1926–7, being taught art by Robert Don; then in 1928 studied various arts and crafts at Otago School of Art. While teaching at Feilding Agricultural High School, 1929–33, Mansfield developed his interest in abstract art, which was to influence his sculpture and bindings, although at this stage he was still mainly a potter. Mansfield travelled to England in 1934 to study at Central and Camberwell Schools of Arts and Crafts, existing in penury in a shed on £1 a week. Continued to study part-time while teaching at a boys' school at Welling, Kent, where he developed a binding class. His interest in abstraction was fostered in 1936 when taught by Elsa Taterka at the Reimann School of Art. After service in the Army in England and India and repatriation to New Zealand in 1946, in 1947 Mansfield returned to London, teaching design and colour at the London School of Printing, 1948–64. During this period Mansfield galvanized bookbinding design; from 1966, *Modern Design in Bookbinding, The Work of Edgar Mansfield*, became a key text. Mansfield was a consummate draughtsman and sculptor (he called his sculptures Animisms), notable for spare, dancing, allusive forms. He turned to these mediums from binding in his later years as his sight faltered. Mansfield was elected a fellow of RBS in 1980. His sculpture was shown at Mercury Gallery, Goldsmiths' College, Oxford Polytechnic and New Zealand House and in 1994 an exhibition of bindings realised by James Brockman and seven Mansfield sculptures was held at the British Library.

Donald MANSON 1948– Painter, notably of still life, born in Ayr, Scotland. He studied at Glasgow School of Art, working as an artist from the time he left in 1971. Showed in mixed exhibitions, such as Cadogan Contemporary and Brian Sinfield Gallery in Burford, and had many solo shows in Glasgow and Edinburgh. Lived in Bridge of Weir, Renfrewshire.

James Bolivar MANSON 1879–1945 Painter, writer and curator, born in London, where he died. After studying at Alleyn's School Manson did clerical work, in 1896 beginning to study painting part-time at Heatherley's School of Fine Art, then Lambeth School of Art. In 1903 he married the violinist Lilian Laugher and together they went to Paris where he studied at Académie Julian, returning in 1904, where Manson set up as a professional painter. In the few years before World War I Manson met Lucien Pissarro, whose work he championed and who influenced his own Impressionistic style; became secretary of the Camden Town Group and acted as its secretary; joined the Tate Gallery as an assistant; and was made secretary of LG. In 1919 with Pissarro he formed the short-lived Monarro Group, inspired by the work of Claude Monet and Camille Pissarro, Lucien's father. Had first one-man exhibition at Leicester Galleries in 1923. Was made director of Tate Gallery, 1930–8, where he did much to build up its Impressionist and Post-Impressionist collection. Painted until he died and had a memorial exhibition at Wildenstein and Ferens Art Gallery, Hull, 1946. Retrospective at Maltzahn Gallery, 1973. Manson was a prolific writer on art, his books including titles on Degas, John Singer Sargent, Rembrandt, Dutch painting and The Tate Gallery, 1930. That gallery and many provincial and foreign galleries hold the work of J B Manson, as he was generally known.

Ruth MANTLE 1925– Artist in all drawing media, mainly buildings and botanical subjects, and teacher, born in Newbury, Berkshire. After war service in Women's Royal Naval Service, studied at Ruskin School of Drawing, Oxford, 1946–50, teachers including Albert Rutherston and Muirhead Bone. She taught private classes, at Queen Anne's girls' school in Caversham, 1966–9, and from 1984 adult education classes for Shropshire County Council, as well as lecturing on history of art as a free-lance, 1960–75. Was elected a member of SGA in 1984, also belonging to Ludlow and Shropshire Art Societies. She carried out a number of commissions to draw buildings, drawings also being used by BBC, conferences, hotels and businesses. Showed in the provinces and won the Rexel Derwent Drawing Prize, 1990. Holdsworth House, Halifax, holds her work. Lived in Church Stretton, Shropshire.

MAO WEN BIAO (sometimes written as Wenbiao Mao) 1950– Artist in oil and watercolour and teacher, of Chinese nationality, born in Singapore. He was educated at PLA Art Academy, Beijing; at Wimbledon School of Art, under William Furlong; then gained his master's degree at Royal College of Art with Paul Huxley. From 1974–89 he was a full-time artist working for the Peking Naval and Military Museum, in 1986 being a tutor for the Peking Movie Academy. In 1987 Mao was vice-professor for the Bei Lee College, China, in 1989 artist for the Museum of Chinese Anti-Japanese War. Among commissions were designs for China's National Olympics from 1975; The Ancient Sailings, an oil painting for the Chinese Scientific Station at the South Pole, 1985; The Opium War, an oil for The Museum of Canton, 1986; and artistic consultancies in Singapore, 1988–90. Among many awards were a series in 1992: The Worshipful Company of Painter-Stainers' Prize; The Delfina Trust 1992–4 Award; The Great Britain-China Education Award; and The Most Popular Work of the Year (Department of Transport Art Competition). In 1993 Mao was artist-in-residence at Museum of London. He was a member of the Association of Chinese National Artists. Mao took part in The State Exhibition of China from 1977. Showed at Royal College of Art, Cooling Gallery and Mall Galleries, 1992, and a first solo exhibition at Christopher Hull Gallery in 1995. Royal College of Art and Department of Transport hold examples. Lived in Chislehurst, Kent.

John MAPP 1926– Painter, illustrator, designer and teacher, born in Northampton. He studied at Northampton School of Art, 1941–5, then Royal College of Art, 1945–8, with Gilbert Spencer and Barnett Freedman. Went on to teach at Grey Court Comprehensive School at Ham, Surrey, near where he lived in Wimbledon, southwest London. Showed at RA and other galleries.

Louis MAQHUBELA 1939– Painter and printmaker, born in Durban, South Africa, when it was almost inconceivable to be a black professional artist. Studied part-time under Cecil Skotnes at Jubilee Centre, Johannesburg, having further guidance from Guiseppe Gattaneo. Began showing in Artists of Fame and Promise, Johannesburg, 1959, in 1968 winning the Grand Award there, which enabled him to work in Europe, mainly in St Ives, Netherlands and France. Had had first solo show at Adler Fielding Galleries, Johannesburg, in 1967, and from 1968 had series of exhibitions at Lidchi Art Gallery in Johannesburg and Cape Town. In 1973 left to work in Spain, in 1976 moving to United Kingdom. Attended Goldsmiths' College School of Art, 1984–5, in 1985–8 attending Slade School of Fine Art for postgraduate diploma in printmaking. Maqubela was originally a figurative painter, depicting scenes in Orlando West shanty town; later his work included animals and birds of an African type with Klee and Miró associations; then he moved into abstraction, rich colours sometimes being applied with a roller, as in printmaking. Was included in Art from South Africa at Museum of Modern Art, Oxford, in 1990. Had solo shows at Vanessa Devereux Gallery, 1989–91, then a series at Art First. Lived in London.

Tim MARA 1948–1997 Printmaker and teacher, born in Dublin, Ireland, who attended Epsom & Ewell School of Art, 1968–70; Wolverhampton Polytechnic, 1970–3; and Royal College of Art, 1973–6. Prizes and awards included Stowells Trophy winner, 1972; British Airways Art Award, 1973; Major Travelling Scholarship, Royal College of Art, 1976; Greater London Arts Association Award, 1978; and British International Print Biennales, 1982 and 1984. Mixed exhibitions included Northern Young Contemporaries, Whitworth Art Gallery, Manchester, 1973; Humberside Printmaking Competition from 1980; and Ties that bind the family, Collins Gallery, Strathclyde University, Glasgow, and tour, 1987, plus many overseas venues. Had a solo show at Birmingham Arts Lab, 1974, later exhibitions including a retrospective at Flowers East, 1996. Arts Council, Tate Gallery, Victoria & Albert Museum and many other public collections hold examples. When Alistair Grant retired from the chair of printmaking at the Royal College in 1990, Mara, who had been his student, succeeded him. University of East London put on a memorial show in 1997. Mara lived in London.

Leonard MARCHANT 1929– Painter, draughtsman, artist in etching and mezzotint and teacher, born in Cape Town, South Africa. Marchant studied at St Martin's School of Art, 1956, and Central School of Arts and Crafts, 1960–3. He went on to teach etching at Central School of Art and Design for 20 years, having reintroduced the technique of mezzotint engraving, at which he was an expert, in the 1960s, it having suffered a decline since the early part of the century. His work was reproduced by Christie's Contemporary Art and in 1986 Marchant won Christie's prize at the exhibition of RE, of which he was a fellow. He had previously won the Stet Prize, Florence Biennale, 1970, and the Grocers' Fellowship, British School at Rome, 1975. Took part in many mixed shows, including RA Summer Exhibitions. Had a solo show at Argus Gallery, Cape Town, 1950, others including Lidchi Gallery, Johannesburg, 1957; Angela Flowers Gallery, 1975; Hogarth Galleries, Sydney, Australia, 1983; Pretoria Museum and Michaelis, University of Cape Town, both 1988; Ludlow Assembly Rooms, 1994; with a retrospective at RE in 1998. Victoria & Albert Museum; British Council; Ulster Museum in Belfast; Museum of Fine Art in Boston; and several South African public collections hold examples. Lived latterly in Shrewsbury, Shropshire.

MAREK 1908–1985 Painter of pictures and murals and book illustrator, born in Rome, full name Marek Zulawski. He studied at Warsaw University and at Warsaw Academy of Fine Art, 1927–33, then in Paris, 1934–5, settling in London in 1936. Was married to the sculptor Halina Korn. As well as exhibiting in Poland, where he is represented in a number of public galleries, Marek showed at RA, AIA, RP, provincial galleries and widely overseas. Did a mural for the homes and gardens pavilion at Festival of Britain, 1951, one for Durham University 10 years later and mosaics for Burnley Chamber of Commerce. Victoria & Albert Museum and Arts Council bought his work. Illustrated many books including *Poland*, 1944; *Warsaw in Poetry*, 1947; *Dawn, Noon and Night*, 1958, and *From Hogarth to Bacon*, 1973. In 1993 Marek's work was included in the City Art Centre, Edinburgh, exhibition Polish Roots – British Soil. Lived in London.

Jerzy MAREK 1925– Self-taught artist, oil on board or canvas, born in Grudziadz, Poland. Marek lived in England from 1948, latterly in Edinburgh, as Jerzy Murray. Began to paint in 1970, mainly at night, after work as a civil engineer who designed bridges. After early retirement in 1981 he devoted all his time to painting. Living for a time in Preston he spent much time encouraging self-taught artists in the north-west; they became known as The Marek Circle and they included his mother-in-law, Margaret Baird. Marek worked slowly on a small scale, deriving most of his ideas from tiny doodles. After sporting and pastoral scenes lush Victorian interiors followed, all showing a characteristic velvety technique, then close-ups of animals and people. He favoured "weird and enigmatic expressions on faces of animals rather than pleasing ones". About 60 of his cards were published, plus illustrations in books. Showed at Rona and Portal Galleries and widely on continent. Solo exhibitions were held in Amsterdam and Lancashire. Public galleries in Salford, Manchester, Lancaster and Kendal hold examples.

MAREVNA 1892–1984 Painter, draughtsman, designer and writer, born in Tcheboksary, Russia, as Marie Vorobieff. After studying art in Tiflis and Moscow, in 1910 went to study in Italy, where she met the writer Maxim Gorki, living at his house in Capri. He christened her Marevna, daughter of the sea. In 1912 Marevna moved to Paris, where she studied at Académie Zuluaga, Académie Russe and Atelier Colarossi. Became acquainted with a group of artists including Picasso, Modigliani, Kisling and Soutine, as she described in her 1972 autobiography *Life with the Painters of La Ruche*. During ensuing years she travelled in Europe; exhibited at such venues as the Salon d'Automne and

Salon des Tuileries; and had a daughter by the Mexican painter Diego Rivera, with whom she lived. Continued to work and live in France until in 1949 she moved to England, where she began to exhibit. In 1963 published her early autobiography *Life in Two Worlds*, in 1979 *Memoires d'une Nomade*. In 1980 showed at Lyric Theatre, to coincide with her daughter Marika's solo show about the painters of Montparnasse. After Marevna's death there was a retrospective organised by Musée Bourdelle, Paris; a show of her works on paper took place at England & Co, 1989; and in 1992 Wildenstein put on Marevna and Montparnasse, a centenary tribute. Lived in London.

MARIAN: *see* **Marianne MAHLER**

Richard MARIENTREU: *see* **Richard von MARIENTREU**

Saša MARINKOV 1949– Printmaker, draughtsman and teacher, born in Belgrade, Yugoslavia. Gained an honours degree in fine art from Leeds University, 1967–71, then did specialist printmaking course at Central School of Art and Design, 1975–6. From 1972 taught, including art history at Middlesex Polytechnic and graphics at Kingsway Princeton College. Group appearances included Printmakers' Council Gallery; Clare College, Cambridge; Northern Young Contemporaries; 2nd International Mini Print, Cadaques, Spain; and 1985 Spirit of London Painting Competition, print prize. Solo shows included Printmakers' Council Gallery, 1981, and Clare College, Cambridge, 1985. Leeds and London Universities hold her work. Lived in Twickenham, Middlesex.

Brenda MARK 1922–1960 Painter, draughtsman and teacher, born in Hull, Yorkshire, although she was brought up and died in Edinburgh, where she attended the College of Art, 1939–43. Mark was influenced by John Maxwell. Like his work hers has a lyrical quality, with cool colours and a strong decorative sense. Her pictures can have an atmosphere of time suspended, with people in windows, waiting. Mark taught art successfully in primary schools, for four years was attached to Moray House as a crafts lecturer, also in the art department, followed by a period at St Denis School and a return to Moray House. She married Robin Philipson the artist in 1949, his first wife. Mark was a prominent exhibitor at SSA of which she was a member and RSA. She received the RSA Award and its Guthrie Award. Philipson reckoned Mark's work underrated. She was a slow worker who filled many sketch-books, travelled in France, Italy and Germany, was a close friend of the artist Anne Redpath, with whom she often painted, and was fond of icons.

MARKEY 1918– Sculptor and primitive painter, born and lived in Belfast, Northern Ireland, son of a house painter, who studied at Belfast College of Art. His work early gained notice at Northern Ireland Civil Defence Art Exhibitions in 1943–4 at Belfast Museum and Art Gallery. His first solo show was at Cottar's Kitchen in 1950, later ones including Oriel Gallery in 1977. Markey – full name Markey Robinson – has works in Ulster Museum and Arts Council of Northern Ireland collections.

Danny MARKEY 1965– Painter in oil on board, born in Cornwall at Falmouth, where he studied at the School of Art, 1983–4. Then obtained a first-class honours degree for fine art (painting) at Camberwell School of Art, 1984–7. Markey travelled in France, Italy and Switzerland in 1987; painted in Cornwall in 1988; lived in Tokyo, Japan, 1990; then settled in London. Markey won first prize in the South Bank Picture Show at Royal Festival Hall, 1986–7, winning the Richard Chamberlain Memorial Prize Camberwell School of Art Painting Exhibition, South London Art Gallery, 1987. Group shows included Royal Over-Seas Annual Open Exhibition, 1987; Sue Williams Gallery from 1987; Newlyn Society of Artists Summer Exhibition, 1989; and in 1991 Summer Exhibition at Redfern Gallery, where he had his first solo show in 1992. Markey's small landscapes were notable for their understated charm, finely judged tones and right sense of mark. The artist Peter Markey was his father.

Peter MARKEY 1930– Creator of animated models, painter and teacher, father of the artist Danny Markey. He was born in Swansea, where he studied at the College of Art. Later moved to Falmouth, Cornwall, where he taught in a local school. Showed in the Recording Wales – Chapels WAC exhibition in 1969 and at Royal National Eisteddfod. Solo shows included Studio 17 in Bristol and in 1995 Cheltenham Art Gallery & Museum, where he was artist-in-residence. WAC holds his work. Markey's models, cut out of wood and brightly coloured, were cranked into life by turning a handle, and included kissing couples, footballers, argumentative politicians and a classroom of children. He also made wave machines. Later lived in Powys.

Ray MARKEY 1946– Sculptor, born in London, who did a prediploma course at Camberwell School of Art, 1962–4, then at the Slade School of Fine Art, 1964–9, gained his diploma in sculpture and postgraduate diploma. Markey won an Elephant Trust grant in 1991. Markey's exhibitions included a first solo show at House Gallery, 1979; Anniversary Exhibition, Sainsbury Centre for Visual Art, University of East Anglia, 1987; Camberwell College of Arts Foundation Staff Exhibition, Morley Gallery, 1991; Kohler Gallery, 1993; and Foundations for Fame, London Institute, 1997, where Markey showed figurative work in bronze.

Michael Adrian MARKHAM 1921– Painter, draughtsman and teacher, born in London, where he lived. Attended Battersea Polytechnic, St Martin's School of Art, 1936–8, then Malvern School of Art, 1940–5, under Victor Moody. For several years after World War II Markham designed for a West End dress firm, then taught in a secondary school. He exhibited RA, RBA, RP, Leger Gallery and elsewhere.

Herbert MARKIEWICZ 1900– Portrait painter and draughtsman, born in Berlin. Studied art in Berlin and Rome, 1933–9. Exhibited RA and RP. Lived in Godalming, Surrey.

Claude MARKS 1915–1991 Painter and draughtsman, theatre designer, art historian and lecturer and writer, born in London. Trained in Paris as stage designer and worked extensively for the theatre in Britain and America. Was noted for his sketches and portraits of famous thespians, such as Glenda Jackson, John Gielgud, Ralph Richardson and Laurence Olivier. In 1991 the Royal National Theatre put on his show Theatre People and Places and in 1982 *Theatre Sketchbooks* was published. Also published *Pilgrims, Heretics and Lovers* as well as *Sketch Books of the Great Masters*. Lectured extensively at Metropolitan Museum in New York and was a noted linguist.

Gerald MARKS 1921– Painter and teacher, born in London. Studied at Central School of Arts and Crafts, 1938–41, then 1946–8 after war service. From 1948–61 was a visiting lecturer at Camberwell, at Morley College, Heatherley's School, South-East Essex Technical College School of Art and for Workers' Educational Association. Was from 1962–86 on staff of Croydon College's fine art department, from 1985–7 being a visiting tutor at Stourbridge School of Art. Marks was a Marxist, a man of strong convictions who believed art was a socially purposeful activity. As a member of the central committee of AIA, 1946–57, he aligned himself with Social Realism, yet he later produced Abstract Expressionist pictures, his Madeleine Series, of a quite different kind. In 1957 Marks was one of Jack Beddington's *Young Artists of Promise* in the publication of that name. Had extensive group appearances from late 1930s, including LG; Redfern, Piccadilly, Leicester and Ben Uri Galleries; and Warwick Arts Trust. Had solo shows at Drian Gallery, 1962; Faroe Road Studios, 1988; and William Jackson Gallery, 1991. Gained an Arts Council Major Purchase Award, 1980. Arts Council and Warwick Arts Trust hold his work. Lived in London and France.

Laura MARKS 1954– Painter, draughtsman, event organiser, papier mâché sculptor and teacher, born in Toronto, Ontario, Canada. In 1963 she gained a scholarship to study at Art Gallery of Ontario children's classes for a year; attended Central Technical School arts course, 1971; then studied with Paul Young for a decade, from 1972. Marks had a first solo show, of papier mâché sculptures, at Evans Gallery, Toronto, in 1973. In 1982 had a solo show at October Gallery, in London, and another at Alberta House there. An Elizabeth Greenshields Foundation grant in 1982–3 enabled Marks to stay in England. After this Marks showed widely in England, Canada and on the continent, including a solo exhibition at John Denham Gallery, 1991. Ontario House holds her work, which includes landscapes and interiors of great exactness which sometimes have a fantastic element. Lived for a time in London.

Margret MARKS 1899–1990 Painter, ceramist and teacher, born in Cologne, Germany, as Margarete Heymann. Marks early determined to be an artist. She was trained at the Kunstgewerberschule Koln and Kunstakademie Düsseldorf as well as the Weimar Bauhaus, 1920. After a period teaching, in 1923 with her husband Gustav Loebenstein she set up a ceramic factory which was forcibly sold when the Nazis came to power in 1933. In 1935 Marks emigrated to England. After more teaching she established a factory in Stoke-on-Trent, moving her operations to London just after World War II. In the period leading to the war she had turned more to painting and in the early 1950s started to work in oil, showing in summer exhibitions at the Redfern Gallery. Marks travelled widely over the years, in England, around the Mediterranean, in East and West Africa and in the south of India. Further teaching included experimental work and tuition in a mental hospital. Solo exhibitions of paintings included a series at Ben Uri Gallery from 1960; Cardiff University, 1978; and John Denham Gallery, 1992. Victoria & Albert Museum, National Portrait Gallery, Bauhaus Archiv in Berlin and Stoke-on-Trent's art Gallery hold examples.

Peggie MARKS 1914– Sculptor, born in Oldham, Lancashire. She studied at Manchester Regional College of Art and exhibited at the public galleries in Manchester, Oldham and Salford, as well as in France. Early work was signed Peggie A E Bethel, her maiden name. She was a member of the Society of Artists in Oldham where she lived, and several other local groups.

Stella Lewis MARKS 1889–1985 Portrait painter and miniaturist, born in Melbourne, Australia. Studied at National Gallery School of Art, Melbourne, her teachers including Frederick McCubbin. She exhibited in Australia, America and in Britain at RA, NEAC, RSA and RMS, on whose council she sat; she was also a member of the American Society of Miniature Painters. She completed miniatures of notable people in America and England, including HM The Queen and HRH The Duke of Edinburgh. Lived in London.

Penny MARLER 1955– Sculptor who practised cold casting in ciment, plaster and bronze resin, born in Birmingham. After qualifying as a physiotherapist in 1976, was self-taught as a sculptor, also attending night classes with Helen Collis, 1989–90. Was a member of Society of Sussex Sculptors, exhibiting with them at Hove Museum and Art Gallery, 1993, Charleston Farmhouse, Firle, 1994–5, Worthing Museum and Art Gallery, 1995, and elsewhere. Solo exhibitions included Neale House, East Grinstead, 1993 and 1994. After working figuratively, later tried "to abstract my work down to essential elements, concentrating on planes of movement and simplification". Lived in Hove, Sussex.

Brigid MARLIN fl. from mid-1960s– Painter, writer and teacher, born in Washington, America. She studied at the National College of Art, Dublin; the Centre d'Art Sacré and Atelier André Lhote, both in Paris; at Beaux-Arts, Montreal; and the Art Students' League of New York. Early in her career she also studied the Mische technique with Ernst Fuchs in Vienna, an oil and egg tempera process which she later taught in England, where she settled. Marlin founded the Inscape group of painters and craftsmen; was in 1982 artist-in-residence at Dorland Mountain Colony; in 1985 holding a similar post at Carl Rogers Centre,

University of California. Group and solo shows included Molesworth Gallery, Dublin, 1964; Festival Hall, 1967; Drian Galleries from 1972; Jubilee Festival for Mind and Body, Olympia, 1977; Arts Club, 1980; Alpine Gallery from 1986; and John Bonham, Murray Feely Fine Art, 1993. Marlin's portraits included the writer J G Ballard, in National Portrait Gallery.

Leslie MARR 1922– Painter in oil and watercolour and photographer, born in Durham. Trained as an engineer, Marr spent World War II in the Royal Air Force, starting to paint in Palestine. In 1947 enrolled at a private art school in London and was introduced to David Bomberg by Dinora Mendelson, Bomberg's step-daughter, whom he married in 1948. Marr joined Bomberg's classes at the Borough Polytechnic, was a member of the Borough Group and its secretary, 1948–9. Took part in several Bomberg-related shows, including Spirit in the mass, Fine Art Associates, 1989. Solo exhibitions included Everyman Gallery from 1959; Laing Art Gallery, Newcastle upon Tyne, 1965; Maddermarket Theatre Gallery, Norwich, from 1976; Wells Centre, Norfolk, 1981; and Catto Gallery, 1990. *From my point of view*, photographs of Norfolk churches, was published in 1979. Public galleries in Newcastle and Sheffield hold examples. Lived latterly on Isle of Arran, Strathclyde.

Michael MARREN 1959– Sculptor, born in Hertfordshire. He attended Watford School of Art, 1977–8, then Wimbledon School of Art, 1979–81, and St Martin's School of Art, 1981–3. Marren showed with New Contemporaries at ICA, 1979, at Cannizaro Park from that year and in 1983 at Woodlands Art Gallery in Have You Seen Sculpture from the Body? Worked in London.

Padraig MARRINAN 1906–1973 Largely self-taught painter interested in religious and mythological subjects who was born in Belfast, Northern Ireland. Because he contracted infantile paralysis as a small child he was privately educated. Showed regularly with RUA of which he was a member and had a solo show at 55a Donegall Place, Belfast, in 1951. His pictures are in a number of Irish churches, notably The Madonna and Child of Loreto in the convent school, Omagh, County Tyrone, where Marrinan finally lived.

Alan MARRIOTT 1952– Painter, born in Reading, Berkshire. He studied at the University of Newcastle upon Tyne, 1970–4, and at Chelsea School of Art, 1975–6. As well as showing at various venues in London he was represented in the John Moores Liverpool Exhibition, 1987, with the two-panel abstract acrylic on canvas Torch Song. Marriott's aim was "to make paintings that have an emotional as well as visual impact … by working as directly as I can". Lived in London.

Charles MARRIOTT 1939– Painter and photographer who studied painting at Cambridge and Kingston Schools of Art. In 1976 he worked with Joseph Beuys and Albrecht D, ICA/Barnet College. His photographic work was represented for a time by Ace Photo Agency. Photographic exhibitions included Young Photographers at Oxford University; The Quality of Life, National Theatre; and Primrose Hill, House, 1977. As an artist he showed with Cambridgeshire Artists, Arts Council Gallery in Cambridge, and East Anglian Artists at King Street Gallery there; LG at RBA Galleries; John Moores Liverpool Exhibition; and Paintings for Welsh Schools, Cardiff. Took part in the Islington Festival, 1974, and in 1981 appeared with Contemporary Artists in Camden at Camden Arts Centre.

John MARRIOTT 1921– Painter, born in London, who attended Eton College. He studied at Chelsea Polytechnic School of Art, 1948, then privately with the painter Oskar Kokoschka. Signed work with initials. Showed at Trafford Gallery and elsewhere.

Michael MARRIOTT 1940– Abstract sculptor and teacher, born London. Studied at St Martin's School of Art, 1956–60, under Anthony Caro, Elizabeth Frink and Eduardo Paolozzi. He assisted Phillip King and Franta Belsky part-time, 1970–1. Teaching appointments included Sir John Cass School of Art and Richmond Adult College. Was made fellow of SPS. Marriott had work in many exhibitions, including RA, 1960; SPS from 1961; Birmingham University, 1970; Marjorie Parr Gallery, 1973; Sculpture Center, New York, from 1974; Victoria Art Gallery, Bath, 1977; and Barbican Arts Centre, 1981. Commissions included stone carvings for London Assurance Building, Croydon, and Gateway Building Society, Worthing, and polished aluminium sculpture for New Welsh College of Music and Drama, Cardiff.

Rosemary MARRIOTT-TRESTINI 1948– Painter, born in Surrey, who studied at Sutton Junior Art School, gained a diploma at St Martin's School of Art, then won a scholarship to Royal College of Art, where she gained her master's degree in fine art under Carel Weight. Showed at RA Summer Exhibitions, Royal College of Art, RWA and Gagliardi Gallery in People and Places, 1993. Her pictures were also commissioned by Pike Print Patrons, Cumbria, for the National Trust, and Atkinson Art Gallery, Southport, holds her work.

Diana MARSDEN 1943– Painter in oil, born in Preston, Lancashire, where she attended Harris School of Art, 1959–63. In 1967 she moved to Suffolk, settling in Eastbridge, Leiston, in Aldeburgh meeting her mentor, Mary Potter, who encouraged her semi-abstract interpretation of landscape. Marsden's preoccupation with light and colour were also evident in her still lifes. Was a member of the Suffolk Group, also showing in mixed exhibitions at Harris Museum & Art Gallery in Preston; Fermoy Gallery, King's Lynn; Grape Lane Gallery, York; Dennis Taplin Gallery, Woodbridge, and elsewhere. Solo shows included John Russell Gallery, Ipswich, 1994.

Ray MARSH 1936– Painter who began working in St Ives, Cornwall, after moving there in 1958, influenced by Roger Hilton, Peter Lanyon and Anthony Benjamin, his brother-in-law. For the next 17 years Marsh lived and worked in St Ives, Bristol and

London, where he eventually settled in 1975, with frequent trips to Cornwall. A natural reticence and the experimental nature of his work prompted Marsh not to exhibit for many years. In the 1970s he was encouraged to contribute to group exhibitions in Bristol, then had a first solo show at South London Book Centre in 1991. Others followed at Porthmeor Gallery, St Ives, 1993, and The Living Room, Greenwich, later that year. Marsh said of his later works that they were "fragments abstracted from the Cornish landscape. The fragments are taken from my own experience and are used to create in each painting a landscape of its own." Other works mixed figuration and abstraction. Marsh's son Simon was also an artist.

Robert MARSH 1950– Painter and teacher, in oil on canvas or board, sometimes known as Robert Burkall Marsh. His output included strong figurative metaphysical, allegorical and thematic series, the style moving from Photo-Realist to Expressionist. Born in Cardiff, he graduated in fine art from the Elam School of Art at Auckland University, in New Zealand, 1967–70, studying with Colin McCahon and Garth Tapper; and obtained his master's in painting at the Royal College of Art, 1975–8, teachers including Peter Blake, Anthony Green, Ruskin Spear and Donald Hamilton Fraser. Was a prizewinner at John Moores Liverpool Exhibition, other mixed shows including Northern Young Contemporaries, Athena Art Awards, RA Summer Exhibition, LG, Lamont Gallery and elsewhere. Solo exhibitions included Merz Contemporary Art, Atlantis Art, Royal College of Pathologists and Southwark College, where he taught. Granada Foundation and National Theatre hold examples. Lived in London.

Simon MARSH 1961– Artist who did a foundation course at Chelsea School of Art, 1979–80, then gained an honours degree in fine art from Central School of Art & Design, 1980–3. In 1981 he won a bursary to study painting in Quimper, France, in 1987 the Lloyds Young Printmakers Award. Publications included *Almond Fields*, 1989; and in 1991 *Theatre*, a set of 26 etchings, and *Three Stages*. From 1988 Marsh held a number of exhibitions with Benjamin C Hargreaves, who sponsored his 16-month walk around the coast of England and Wales starting in July 1991. This led to a number of exhibitions in which Marsh brilliantly caught the spirit of place using pencil, oil-sticks, watercolour and gouache. Victoria & Albert Museum and Imperial Chemical Industries own examples. His father was the artist Ray Marsh.

Elaine MARSHALL fl. from 1950s– Printmaker, draughtsman, painter and teacher, born and worked in southeast London. She studied at Goldsmiths' College School of Art until 1956, gaining David Murray Landscape Scholarship, 1954. Then won a Slade School of Fine Art postgraduate course, 1956–8. She was a founder of Greenwich Printmakers' Association and became a member of the Printmakers' Council, 1984. Exhibited widely in mixed shows, including RA Summer Exhibition from 1976, RE from 1977 and Rye Art Gallery from 1978. In 1985 shared a four-man exhibition at Woodlands Art Gallery. Also exhibited solo on the *Cutty Sark* during Greenwich Clipper Week, 1978, and in 1979 at Lantern Gallery, Manchester. Private and public collections in Britain and abroad hold her work.

Francis MARSHALL 1901–1980 Illustrator and author who studied at University College in London and Slade School of Fine Art. During World War II he was a camouflage officer with the Admiralty, having been educated on HMS *Worcester*. Marshall was noted for his witty, elegant drawings allied to the world of fashion. In later life he was a prolific cover illustrator for the novels of Barbara Cartland. Among periodicals illustrated by him were *Vogue*, *Woman's Journal* and *Harper's Bazaar*. His books included *Fashion Drawing*, *Magazine Illustration* and *The London Book*, about aspects of London. Victoria & Albert Museum textiles and dress collection holds his work. Exhibited at Walker's Galleries and elsewhere. Lived latterly at New Barnet, Hertfordshire.

John J MARSHALL fl. from 1950s– Painter of romantic landscapes, born in Colchester, Essex, who attended Rugby School, art tuition coming from the landscape and portrait painter Cedric Kennedy, on whom he wrote. Had a series of solo shows at Leicester Galleries from 1956. Of the second, in 1959, John Russell wrote in *The Sunday Times*: "His watercolours should be noted for their richness and concision of style; the strength and power of his colours have won him many admirers." Castle Museum in Norwich and several American collections hold examples. Lived in London.

Maria MARSHALL 1964– Sculptor who completed her degree at Wimbledon School of Art. She worked mainly in steel. By searching scrap metal yards she was able to assemble material for often very large sculptures, such as her commissioned work for Argent Estates, Knightsbridge, of a goddess 15 feet high, completed in 1990. Marshall exhibited widely in solo and mixed exhibitions in London and abroad, including Munich, Geneva, Chicago and Los Angeles. In 1990–1 she had a solo show at Odette Gilbert Gallery, in 1996 one at *Economist* Plaza.

Olga MARSHALL 1921– Artist in watercolour, pen and ink and pencil, and writer, born in Yorkshire. She studied at Hull Art College. She married the marine biologist N B Marshall and travelled extensively with him in America, Canada and Australia, helping with his collecting, then with photographing and illustrating specimens. Her illustrations to his first book, *Aspects of Deep-Sea Biology*, in 1954, prompted *The Times* to call it "perhaps the most beautifully illustrated scientific book so far produced this century". This led to Olga Marshall writing and illustrating such children's books as *Along the Edge of the Sea* and *Down to the Pond.* For children's book illustration she used the name Jill Norman. Showed at RA from 1974, including frontispieces of her husband's books. Oceanographical Institute, Godalming, holds her work. Lived for many years in Saffron Walden, Essex.

Richard MARSHALL 1943– Painter in oil and pastel, and part-time teacher, born in Goring, Sussex. He studied privately,

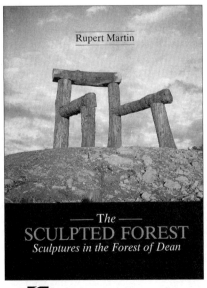

1969–71, with William Cartledge and, 1973–89, with Gyula Sajó. Was a member of PS from 1983, also showing at Atelier Art Group in Worthing, Sussex, and with International Pastel Exhibition, France, main works being still life and landscapes. Had solo shows at Fairfield Halls, Croydon, and Little Gallery, Arundel. Influenced by the Impressionists, Post-Impressionists and Kokoschka, Marshall was "mainly a colourist experimenting in mixed media, with emphasis on design".

Rita MARSHALL 1946– Abstract painter, born in Birmingham, who attended the local College of Art, 1962–4, then St Martin's School of Art, 1964–7. Between 1967–71 had a studio at Stockwell Depot, from 1969–73 being assistant to Bridget Riley. Group exhibition appearances included Stockwell Depot, 1969, and in 1974 both Virtual Image at Romford Library and Arts Council's British Painting '74. By that time Marshall was involved in the Transcendental Meditation movement. By the mid-1990s she had long given up her art, was part of a Transcendental Meditation community of about 300 adults and 150 children in Skelmersdale, Lancashire, and was involved in advanced practices such as Yogic Flying. If she resumed painting she would not start where she had left off, as she had herself changed, she said.

Stuart MARSHALL 1949– Performance, installation, video and film artist, born in Manchester. He studied fine art at Hornsey and Newport Colleges of Art, 1968–71, gaining his bachelor's degree with first-class honours; then studied with Alvin Lucier at Wesleyan University, Middletown, Connecticut, in America, with a teaching fellowship, obtaining his master's degree in new music composition and ethnomusicology. Took part in many international group exhibitions, including Signs of the Times, Museum of Modern Art, Oxford, 1990. Solo appearances included Sound track for Cambrian Theatre Company, Wales, 1970; Performances and video tapes, Lucy Milton Gallery, 1974; Slide projection installation, Robert Self Gallery, Newcastle upon Tyne, 1977; and Videotapes, London Video Arts, Acme Gallery, 1980. Gained a number of Arts Council major bursaries and Channel 4 Television commissions.

DUNBAR-MARSHALL-MALAGOLA 1918– Artist using oil and metal foil, born in Florence, Italy, as Dunbar Marshall. He attended Westminster School of Art prior to World War II, under Mark Gertler and Bernard Meninsky, then Chelsea School of Art, 1948–52, with Ceri Richards and Robert Medley. He did some teaching, 1954–67, then from 1967–86 was with UNESCO as secretary-general of the International Association of Art. He was a member of the RBA and Salon d'Automne and friendships with Miró, Vasarely and Alexander Calder were cited as important. Showed with RA, Free Painters and Sculptors and elsewhere in mixed exhibitions, having solo shows at Grabowski Gallery, 1961 and 1964; UNESCO, Paris, 1985; and Prévôt Gallery, Paris, 1986 and 1992. Contemporary art museums in Bihać and Skopje, Yugoslavia; Lodz, Poland; Japan Artists' Association; and other collections hold examples. Lived in Vanves, France.

Geoff MARSTERS 1929– Figurative artist living in East Anglia in whose work light and colour were important; it sometimes focused on a particular element and used a degree of abstraction. He studied at Bath Academy of Art, then L'École des Beaux-Arts in Paris. Marsters' work was reproduced in several books, including *Pastel Masterclass*, by Judy Martin; *The Complete Drawing Course*, by Ian Simpson; and *Pastels Workshop*, by Jackie Simmonds. Exhibitions included Clare Hall, and the Conservatory and Heffer Galleries, Cambridge; PS; and The John Russell Gallery, Ipswich. The Forestry Commission and many corporate collections hold Marsters' work.

Freda MARSTON 1895–1949 Painter and printmaker, born in London, who was married to the artist Reginald St Clair Marston. Studied at the Regent Street Polytechnical School of Art, 1916–20, under Terrick Williams and Harry Watson. Exhibited RA, RBA, Fine Art Society, ROI and elsewhere. Medici Society reproduced her work, which is in public galleries in Eastbourne and Stoke-on-Trent. Lived at Robertsbridge, Sussex.

Anne MARTIN 1936– Artist and teacher, working in two- and three-dimensional media, born and lived in London, wife of the artist David Methuen Campbell. She studied at Royal College of Art painting school, 1956–9, being awarded an Abbey Minor Travelling Scholarship to Rome, 1959, then a French Government Scholarship, 1960. Taught at Central School of Art/Central St Martins from 1966 and at Architectural Association, 1984–6. Martin pursued research "into the Surrealist roots of Abstract Expressionism". Group shows included Young Contemporaries at RBA Galleries, 1958–9; Arts Council Travelling Exhibition, 1958; Space at St Katherine's Dock, 1970; and The Sixties Art Scene in London, Barbican Art Gallery, 1993. Martin had a solo show at Courtauld Institute, 1967, and one for Vidal Sasson Company, 1984. She was a member of AIA and Royal College of Art holds her work.

Barry MARTIN 1943– Painter, sculptor and kinetic artist, born in Amersham, Buckinghamshire. He studied at Goldsmiths' College School of Art, 1961–6, from the mid-1960s showing with Young Contemporaries and LG, then studied sculpture at St Martin's School of Art, 1966–7. In 1968 Martin had a solo show, Pavilions in the Parks, in Chelsea, the following year sharing a show at Compass Gallery, Glasgow. Further exhibitions included a one-man at Serpentine Gallery in 1970; at Studio International Gallery and Newcastle Polytechnic Gallery, in 1977; and at Goya Gallery, Zaragosa, and in Barcelona, Spain, in 1980. Arts Council holds his work. Lived for some years in Ramsgate, Kent.

David G MARTIN 1965– Artist, born and lived in London. He studied at St Albans College of Art, 1984–5, Sheffield Polytechnic, 1985–8, and in the mid-1990s at Royal College of Art. In 1989 Martin was first prizewinner at MAFA; he won the Young Artist of the Year prize at Hunting/*Observer* Awards; and was included in the 1995–6 John Moores Liverpool Exhibition with an abstract oil and acrylic on canvas The Tyranny of Impressionism. Shared a show at Tricycle Gallery, 1993.

David McLeod MARTIN 1922– Artist in oil, gouache and pastel, and teacher, born in Glasgow, settling in the area later at Eaglesham. He studied at Glasgow School of Art, 1940–2 and 1946–8, interrupted by war service in the Royal Air Force, teachers including David Donaldson, Hugh Adam Crawford and Ian Fleming. He taught in the Glasgow and Lanarkshire area, latterly 10 years as principal teacher of art at Hamilton Grammar School until 1983, when he retired early to paint full-time. Martin was a member of RSW and Royal Glasgow Institute of the Fine Arts. Among awards won was the Robert Colquhoun Memorial Art Prize, 1974; the RSW's May Marshall Brown Award in 1984; and the Royal Glasgow Institute's Mabel Mackinlay Award, 1990. Martin said that "work derived from landscape explores the rhythmic lines and related shapes which are sometimes echoed in other areas of the painting. This sometimes leads to a simplified statement bordering on abstraction, which is the quality of landscape that interests me." Showed in mixed exhibitions at RSA, RA and Compass Gallery, Glasgow. Had a solo show at Stone Gallery, Newcastle, 1965; several more in Scotland, including Kingfisher Gallery, Edinburgh, 1991; and a first one-man show in London at Thackeray Gallery, 1992. Scottish Arts Council, Scottish Television, City of Edinburgh Art Collection and other notable collections hold his work.

Dorothy MARTIN 1882–1949 Botanical painter and teacher of art at Roedean School, in Sussex and during evacuation to Keswick during World War II. She was described by a former pupil as coming "from one of those battalions of eccentric English women, dressed in an arty-frumpy style, with Fair Isle cardies and long socks". When she died she was more than halfway through a satisfactorily representative British flora, her paintings revealing a delicacy of handling and lightness of touch while being close and careful studies of the plants. The headmistress of Roedean allowed her one day off a week to go to London to make paintings for the Royal Horticultural Society. A large selection of her work was included in its 1993 diary. Martin studied at Wolverhampton Municipal School of Art and Royal College of Art. She held a number of teaching posts before Roedean and was an enlightened teacher of etching, pottery, embroidery and illumination. Showed at RA, RI and elsewhere.

Ethel MARTIN 1873– Painter, born in Sevenoaks, Kent, sister of the watercolourist Beatrice Martin. She studied with Harriet Halhed in Sevenoaks, then in Paris, 1892–1900, with Louis Deschamps. Showed at RA, ROI, NEAC, SWA and Royal Glasgow Institute of the Fine Arts. Lived in London.

Francis Patrick MARTIN 1883–1966 Painter, notably of genre scenes, born in Anstruther, Fife, by profession a General Post Office telegraphist. Studied at Glasgow School of Art, settled in the city at Bearsden and had work acquired by its public gallery as well as General Post Office. Showed frequently at Royal Glasgow Institute of the Fine Arts, RSA and with Walker Art Gallery in Liverpool.

Frank MARTIN 1914– Sculptor and teacher, born in Portsmouth, Hampshire. After a technical school education there he attended the local School of Art, then the Royal Academy Schools. Went on to become head of the sculpture department at St Martin's School of Art during the key 1960s period when the emphasis was on abstraction rather than figurative work and when many notable modern British sculptors studied there. Was a fellow of the RBS. Lived in Hayling Island, Hampshire.

Frank MARTIN 1921– Printmaker, illustrator and teacher, born in Dulwich, southeast London. Studied at St Martin's School of Art, where his teachers included Gertrude Hermes, also studying etching privately with John Buckland-Wright. Prior to this he had read history at Oxford University. After Army service in World War II Martin gradually established himself as a freelance artist, although he taught at Camberwell School of Arts and Crafts, 1953–80, ending as head of the department of graphic arts. Had several one-man shows and his work is held by the Victoria & Albert Museum and Fitzwilliam Museum, Cambridge. Editions Graphiques gave him a 50-year retrospective in 1998. Member of RE and SWE. Illustrated many books, including *Charles Lamb's Essays*, 1963, and *William Hazlitt's Essays*, 1964. Lived in London.

Gerald Trice MARTIN 1893–1961 Painter in oil of portraits and still life. Born in Clifton, Bristol, he studied in Newlyn with Stanhope Forbes and at the Royal Academy Schools, 1920–3. Exhibited RA, PS and Paris Salon and had one-man shows in Bristol and London. Lived in London.

Jason MARTIN 1970– Painter, born in Jersey, Channel Islands, who studied at Chelsea School of Art, 1989–90, then gained an honours degree at Goldsmiths' College of Art, 1990–3. Group exhibitions included Contemporary Artists at Feigen Incorporated, Chicago, 1992; Wonderful Life at Lisson Gallery, 1993; Surface Tensions, Curwen Gallery, 1994; and in 1995 Four Paintings, Papf Gallery, Tokyo, and Real Art at Southampton City Art Gallery, both 1995. Had a solo show at Lisson, 1997, in which experiment with sumptuous colour and texture, a range of materials and a variety of size, shape and support were evident. Martin's were abstract, rather Minimalist works, with carefully selected, iconic titles. Lived in London.

John MARTIN 1957– Painter, notably of interiors and landscapes, who studied at Hornsey College of Art, 1975–6, then Exeter College of Art, 1976–9, gaining a first-class honours degree, followed by Royal Academy Schools, 1980–3. Among his awards was Route Cézanne, 1979, a European Economic Community-sponsored project to paint in France; David Murray Landscape Scholarship, 1982–3, and Winsor & Newton Student Prize, 1983. Mixed shows included Chagford Gallery, Devon, 1979; RA Summer Exhibition, from 1982; Highgate Gallery,

1988; and NEAC Open, 1989. Shared a show at Waterman Fine Art, 1993. Solo shows included Blenheim Gallery, 1987, and Milne & Moller, 1988. Norwich County Collection holds his work.

Kenneth MARTIN 1905–1984 Painter, constructions and kinetic artist, draughtsman and teacher, born in Sheffield, married to the artist Mary Martin. Martin began work as a designer, studying part-time at Sheffield School of Art, 1921–3 and 1927–9. A Royal Exhibition took him to Royal College of Art, 1929–32. He taught at St John's Wood School of Art and was a visiting lecturer at Goldsmiths' College School of Art, 1946–67. Martin was a highly cerebral artist, originally painting in a naturalistic style. After World War II his work moved towards abstraction; he studied developments in art outside England, and science and mathematics relative to art; and with his wife began to make reliefs and he, too, explored kinetic possibilities. The guiding principle was to build "from a nucleus outwards" rather than the traditional contours. First one-man show was at Leicester Galleries, 1943. As Martin and his wife began to lead a new Constructivist movement in England after World War II and exhibit in allied shows, his reputation grew internationally. He was given a retrospective exhibition at the Tate Gallery in 1975; a two-man show with Henry Moore at Scottish National Gallery of Modern Art in Edinburgh, the following year; a one-man Arts Council travelling exhibition in 1977; and there was an Arts Council touring show, with Mary Martin, Annely Juda Fine Art, 1987. Tate Gallery and Arts Council hold his work. Lived in London.

Leigh MARTIN 1964– Painter producing abstract works, systematically applied marks in bands and grids, as in New Art in Scotland, Centre for Contemporary Arts, Glasgow, 1994. Born in Hamilton, New Zealand, Martin studied there at Christchurch Polytechnic, 1983–4, then in Britain at Brighton Polytechnic, 1989–90, and Glasgow School of Art, 1990–95. Exhibitions included Paperworks, Seagate Gallery, Dundee, 1992, and RSA Student Exhibition in Edinburgh from 1993.

Mabel L I MARTIN 1887–1978 Painter, miniaturist and teacher who was born and lived in Dover, Kent, where the Museum holds her work. She studied at the Regent Street Polytechnic School of Art under Harry Watson, 1922–4; at Bolt Court; Hornsey College of Art, 1932–4; Westminster School of Art, 1938; and privately in Paris. Exhibited at RA, ROI, SWA, Walker's Gallery and The East Kent Art Society of which she was a member.

Mary MARTIN 1907–1969 Abstract artist in painting and constructions. Born at Folkestone, she studied at Goldsmiths' College School of Art, 1925–9, and at the Royal College of Art, 1929–32. Married the artist Kenneth Martin, 1930. Four years later she began exhibiting at the AIA using her maiden name, Mary Balmford, boldly coloured landscapes and still lifes. She moved towards geometric abstraction in the 1940s. She taught drawing, design and weaving at Chelmsford School of Art, 1941–4. Painted her first abstract picture in 1950, made her first reliefs in 1951 and her first free-standing construction five years later. First one-man show, with her husband, at the Heffer Gallery, Cambridge, in 1954, six years before her first major show, at the ICA. Another notable exhibition occurred at the Tate Gallery – it holds her work – in 1984. Arts Council touring exhibition (with Kenneth Martin), Annely Juda Fine Art, 1987. Also participated in exhibitions in Germany and Japan. Commissions included reliefs for the Orient Line's S S *Oriana* and Stirling University, Scotland. Lived in London.

Mary MARTIN 1951– Painter in oil and watercolour, born in Cornwall, where she settled at St Dominic, Callington. Almost all of Martin's work was done out-of-doors, where she worked swiftly to capture changing effects of light, flowers " being a special feature. She did her pre-diploma studies at West of England College of Art in Bristol, diploma at Cheltenham College of Art and postgraduate work at Royal Academy Schools which she left in 1975 to paint full-time. She was the subject of a BBC Television film in the *Look, Stranger*! series, *Daffodils, Bullions and Steam*. Martin showed in mixed exhibitions including RA from 1975; New Grafton Gallery, from 1979; Interceltic Festival, Lorient, France, 1982; and Oliver Swann Galleries, 1988. She was a frequent solo exhibitor, showing at St Dominic Parish Hall, 1976; Plymouth City Museum and Art Gallery, 1978; later ones including Oliver Swann, 1989, and St Dominic Parish Hall, 1990. National Trust, National Maritime Museum in Greenwich and Plymouth's Art Gallery hold examples.

Nicholas MARTIN 1957– Artist in paper collage, monoprints, mosaic and Formica, born in Edinburgh, where he attended the College of Art, 1975–80, gaining an honours degree after studies under Robin Philipson and Denis Peploe. His work was influenced by "Greek and Roman art, Japanese erotic art (Shunga), Roman mosaics, pop music videos, poster art of the 1920s, computer art, 1950s cartoons and Kitaj". Martin moved to Brighton, Sussex, in 1982, and had a number of artist-residencies in the south, including Royal Pavilion, Brighton, and Towner Art Gallery, Eastbourne, kitemaking, both 1983; Ramsgate Library, 1989; and Broadstairs Library, 1991. Among a series of public commissions were a painting of the Royal Festival Hall, 1984; banner for Canterbury Festival, 1987; Alban Park Mosaic, St Albans, 1990; and St George's Hospital, Tooting, mosaic, in collaboration with Marion Brandis, 1991. As well as group shows in Kent and Sussex, Martin had a solo show at Gardner Arts Centre, Brighton, 1983, later ones including Royal Festival Hall, 1986, Ramsgate Library Art Gallery, 1989, and Ramsgate Art Gallery, 1994. Towner Art Gallery, Eastbourne, holds his work.

Patrick MARTIN 1958– Artist, born in Glasgow, who studied at Edinburgh College of Art, at Fleisher Institute in Philadelphia and at Goldsmiths' College. Group exhibitions included Whitechapel Open at Whitechapel Art Gallery, 1989; Leicester Schools Exhibition, Beaumanor Hall in Leicester, from 1990; and

Royal Over-Seas League Open, 1996, where Martin showed part of a series of 100 heads made in preparation for larger-than-life sculptures. Solo shows included Horsemen At An Obelisk, Queen's Hall, Edinburgh, 1984. Leicester Education Department holds his work.

Pierre Noël MARTIN 1920– Artist in various media, including kinetic sculpture, born and lived in London. Studied engineering at Hackney Technical Institute. Was for a time a Hampstead Artists' Council member, also showing with Free Painters and Sculptors and with Chelsea Artists.

Ronald MARTIN 1904–1989 Designer, printmaker, painter and writer, born in Eastbourne, Sussex, full name Arthur Ronald Martin. He studied at the local School of Art, 1921–4, under A F Reeve-Fowkes, then at London County Council School of Art and Graphic Reproduction, having aged 19 "to help my widowed mother got a job in a London advertising studio." He designed everything from posters and book jackets to Mars' confectionery wrappers. During the war Martin worked for the Ministry of Supply, handling secret material. Until poor health forced his retirement Martin ran a commercial art firm, then moved from Bromley to live near the Sussex county ground at Hove, where as a keen fan he painted many cricket pictures. He painted the local Alfred Waterhouse-designed town hall two months before it was burned down, then was commissioned by Hove Museum & Art Gallery to paint the demolition. Martin was a fellow of the Society of Industrial Artists and a member of SGA, also showing with RA, RI, RBA and in the provinces. He was a member of Sussex Artists' Club and had a solo show at Gentle Gallery, Steyning, in 1977. He published *Illustrating with the Airbrush.* Died in Royal Sussex County Hospital, Brighton.

Teresa MARTIN 1961– Sculptor in a variety of materials, and teacher, born and lived in Shoreham-by-Sea, Sussex. Gained her diploma at Worthing College of Art and Design, 1978–9; after marriage in 1981 obtained an honours degree in sculpture at Winchester School of Art, 1979–83; further studying at University of Brighton under Henry Clyne, 1983–4. Taught art at Steyning Grammar School, 1985–6, then sculpture at Chanctonbury Centres, Steyning, and Brighton College of Technology from 1987. Martin said that she abstracted "material from a world rich in exciting forms ... building up form using designed units". Was a member of the Society of Sussex Sculptors and showed at Star Gallery, Lewes, 1992; Hove Museum, 1993; The Grange, Rottingdean, 1994; and Worthing Museum and Art Gallery, 1995.

Timothy Stuart MARTIN 1908– Artist in line and watercolour and teacher, born in Bolsover, Derbyshire. He was educated at University College, Nottingham, gaining distinctions in art and crafts. Studied also at Chesterfield Pupil Teacher Centre under H T C Simmonds, Chesterfield College of Art with F W Mounsell and Nottingham College of Art. Martin lectured at Mansfield School of Art and was arts and crafts master at Queen Elizabeth's Grammar School for Boys, 1931–73. He was an examiner in drawing for national boards and a City and Guilds adviser for teacher examinations for 21 years. He illustrated many journals and newspapers and was editor of *Junior Craftsman* and *Boys' Practical Aid.* Was a judge for the Federation of Midland Art Societies. Showed in Mansfield, Derby, Leicester, Nottingham and Chesterfield and has work in Mansfield Art Gallery. Lived in Mansfield, Nottinghamshire.

William MARTIN 1899–1988 Amateur painter who made a valuable record of Cornish country life early in the twentieth century. He was born in Falmouth, Cornwall, was apprenticed as a gardener, his lifelong occupation apart from service in France in World War I. After the war Martin was a successful part-time student at Redruth Art School. Showed in Truro area and in London. In 1970 he was elected a Bard of the Cornish Gorsedd for services to art. He was included in A Century of Art in Cornwall 1889–1989, Newlyn Orion Galleries, 1989.

Toni MARTINA 1956– Artist and teacher, born and lived in London with southern Italian antecedents, whose interest in architecture stemmed from three years in civil engineering between school and college. He attended Harrow College of Art for foundation studies, 1974–5; gained a first-class honours degree in fine art at Kingston Polytechnic, 1975–8; then did post-graduate studies in advanced printmaking at Central School of Art & Design, 1986–7, where he later lectured. Sometimes worked on a large scale, following the Central studies. Teaching also included an associate professorship at Rhode Island College of Art, America, in 1989. Cityscapes and street life were strong features of Martina's output. Influences included Frank Brangwyn, Muirhead Bone, Anthony Gross, Graham Sutherland and Stanley Spencer's shipyard scenes; German Expressionist printmakers; Masaccio; Edward Hopper; Mexican muralists including Diego Rivera; and the Italian Neo-Realist film movement. Among awards were Prix de Rome Scholarship in Fine Art, British School in Rome, 1987–8, and first prize winner, Department of Transport national competition, 1992. Elected RE, 1992. Took part in many group shows, including RA Summer Exhibition from 1985; Hunting Group Art Prizes, Mall Galleries, from 1986; Cleveland College of Art, 1991; LG from 1992; and Kerb Scrawlers, The Living Room, Greenwich, 1994. Ashmolean Museum in Oxford, Cambridge Libraries; and public museums in Plymouth, Rochdale and Oldham own examples.

Raymond MARTINEZ 1937– Painter who was born in Barry, Glamorgan. He studied at Cardiff College of Art, 1955–9, Slade School of Fine Art, 1959–61, then had a postgraduate year at the Slade. A 1962 Abbey Major Scholarship took him to Rome, where he contined to live. In 1963–4 he won a Gulbenkian Foundation Purchase Award. Lefevre Gallery gave him a series of solo exhibitions. CASW holds his work.

Enid MARX 1902–1998 Designer, painter, writer, printmaker, illustrator and teacher, born and lived in London. An interest in art and crafts was fostered at Roedean School, after which she attended Central School of Art for a year, then in 1922 went to Royal College of Art, where Paul Nash and Leon Underwood were influences. Joined Barron and Larcher textile printing studio, in 1927 starting own workshop, her moquette being used for many years on Underground trains. In 1931–3 taught wood engraving at Ruskin School, Oxford; in the 1960s she was head of the department of dress, textile and ceramics at Croydon College of Art. Marx wrote and illustrated children's books; contributed to the Pilgrim Trust *Recording Britain* project; was a member of the Board of Trade Utility Furniture team; was elected a Royal Designer for Industry; worked on furnishing fabrics for Morton Sundour; and designed for Penguin Books, Festival of Britain, General Post Office, Shell and London Transport. With Margaret Lambert wrote *English Popular and Traditional Art*, 1946, and *English Popular Art*, 1951. Showed widely in Britain and abroad. In 1979 Camden Arts Centre held a major show and Sally Hunter Fine Art gave her a solo exhibition in 1988. Arts Council and Victoria & Albert Museum hold examples.

Pam MASCO 1953– Artist painting still life, interiors and landscapes using a rich palette, and illustrator, married to the artist John Heseltine. She was born in Springfield, Massachusetts, America, and studied at School of the Boston Museum of Fine Arts, graduating in 1976. Was involved in drawing, painting, technical painting courses, watercolour and graphic design, 1978–9. Illustrated for major British and American publishers until 1988, authors including Bruce Chatwin, Daphne du Maurier and V S Pritchett. She exhibited in a number of mixed shows, including Bourne Gallery, Reigate, from 1984; Clarendon Gallery, 1986; and RBA and RWS, both 1992. Solo exhibitions included David Messum, 1990. Lived in Petworth, Sussex.

Denis MASI 1942– Sculptor, installations artist, designer, printmaker and lecturer, whose preoccupations included man's yearning for territorial expansion, the means of conflict, surveillance and imprisonment. Born in West Virginia, America, Masi graduated in history and philosophy from Seton Hall University, New Jersey, 1960–4; then studied sculpture, Marino Marini studio, Brera Academy, Milan, 1964–6; etching in Paris at S W Hayter's Atelier 17, 1966–7; postgraduate printmaking at Slade School of Fine Art, 1967–8; and gained his master's degree in sculpture at Chelsea School of Art, 1981–2. His many teaching posts included colleges of art in London, Bradford, Croydon and Wimbledon. In 1984 Masi was artist-in-residence at Imperial War Museum, in 1984–5 designing sets and costumes for Hidden Grin/Rational Theatre Company at ICA. Commissions included an outdoor sculpture at St James' Church, Clerkenwell, for Edge 88, 1988; a plinth for Imperial War Museum, 1989; and an installation work for the show Civil War at Angel Row Gallery, Nottingham, 1992. As well as many mixed exhibitions, Masi had extensive solo shows, starting with Il Cenobbio Galleria, Milan, 1966, later ones including Imperial War Museum and Serpentine Gallery, both 1988, and Anderson O'Day Gallery from 1991. Arts Council, Victoria & Albert Museum, Tate Gallery and a number of foreign galleries hold examples.

Jeanne MASOERO 1937– Painter, born and based in London, although her parents were Italian and she spent her early childhood in Italy. From 1957–63 attended Goldsmiths' College and Slade School of Fine Art under Kenneth Martin, a notable teacher, and Mary Martin. Masoero said that she regarded herself "as an abstract painter first and foremost". A series of tiny portraits or head paintings, while being an important aspect of her work had "*grown* out of my abstract painting quite naturally". Painters of light were a significant influence, notably "the early Italians and Giotto, Zurbaran and Goya". Group shows included Young Contemporaries, 1964; British Painting '74, Arts Council at Hayward Gallery, 1974; Portraits & Paintings at Warehouse Gallery, 1978; and Critics' Choice – New British Art, Christie's, 1993. Showed solo with Angela Flowers Gallery from 1971, later exhibitions including Mall Galleries, 1993, and *The Economist*, 1995.

Arnold MASON 1885–1963 Landscape and portrait painter, born at Birkenhead, Cheshire. Studied at Macclesfield School of Art, Royal College of Art and Slade School of Fine Art, 1918–19, also in Paris and Rome. He helped Sir William Richmond with decorations to the Old Bailey, London, 1906–8. Served in the Artists' Rifles, 1915–18. Exhibited RA from 1919, being elected RA, 1951; also showed NEAC, RP, Leicester Galleries, Goupil Gallery and ROI. Work in the collections of the Tate Gallery, Manchester City Art Gallery and Wakefield City Art Gallery. Lived in London.

Barry MASON 1952– Abstract sculptor who after working as a photographer studied at Reading University's fine art department, 1970–4, in the former year winning a travel scholarship to Italy. Then did postgraduate work at Slade School of Fine Art, 1974–6, gained a year's fellowship at Gloucester College of Art and was assistant to the sculptor William Pye, 1977–80. Exhibitions included Yorkshire Sculpture Park, 1979–80. Among Mason's publicly sited works is the dramatically positioned Tetra, 1974, in wood, steel and stone, at Glenshee Sculpture Park, Tayside.

Bateson MASON 1910–1977 Painter and teacher, born in Bradford. He studied at the College of Art there, 1927–32, with Henry Butler, then at Royal College of Art, 1932–5, with Sir William Rothenstein. Exhibited LG, NEAC, Leicester and Redfern Galleries and in the provinces. Galleries in Manchester and Wakefield hold his work, which was often closely related to architecture and the landscape. Travelled widely on the continent, which provided subject material. His Fulham by Moonlight, a typical example of 1949, is illustrated in Herbert Read's *Contemporary British Art*, 1951. Taught at Ravensbourne College of Art, lived in London. Sometimes signed work F Bateson Mason.

Christopher MASON 1928– Painter, film-maker and teacher who attended Chelsea School of Art, 1948–52. A prize enabled

Mason to move to Paris. After 11 years on his return to England he taught at Ravensbourne College of Art. There he experimented with animation film and during the 1970s produced a number of films, including one on Alfred Wallis, the Cornish primitive painter, another on the Bloomsbury artist Duncan Grant. After his one-man show at Redfern Gallery when he returned to England in 1963 Mason showed at NEAC, RA, RWS and elsewhere. He had a joint exhibition with his wife Joanna Carrington at New Grafton Gallery in 1991, shortly after two shared shows with her at University of Amiens and in Avranches. Mason's work was in oil, acrylic and watercolour, landscape done in France and England, colourful and highly structured. Lived mainly in Normandy.

Frank Henry MASON 1876–1965 Marine painter, illustrator and printmaker. Born at Seaton Carew, County Durham, into a naval family, he was educated on HMS *Conway* and spent some time at sea before taking up art, having had a period in engineering in the north of England. Exhibited RA, RBA, RI and elsewhere. Work in several public collections, including National Gallery of Victoria, Melbourne, Australia. Member of Royal Thames Yacht Club. Lived in London.

Gilbert MASON 1913–1972 Painter, draughtsman, printmaker and teacher, born in Newport, Monmouthshire. He studied at Newport College of Art, 1930–4, and Royal College of Art, 1934–7, working in the school of engraving under Robert Austin and Malcolm Osborne. From 1938–40 taught at Leeds College of Art. From 1940–3 served in Military Police, then transferred, 1943–5, to Royal Air Force Central Photographic Unit Model Making Section, returning to teach at Leeds, 1945–9. Next moved to Eastbourne College of Art as deputy principal, 1950–2, then going to Birmingham College of Art and Design, 1952–70, where he was eventually appointed head of the school of painting. Mason was a member of RBSA. His exhibitions included Ikon Gallery, Birmingham; John Moores Exhibition, Liverpool; RA; a solo show in Eastbourne; various group shows in Birmingham, Bradford, Leeds and London; RP; and Hexagon Gallery, Midlands Arts Centre, Birmingham. Although he often did highly stylised portraits and landscapes, Mason was a superlative draughtsman with a great feeling for atmosphere. WAC and Towner Art Gallery, Eastbourne, hold his work. A memorial exhibition was held in 1974 at Ikon Gallery, Birmingham.

Maxine MASON 1967– Painter whose work was reminiscent of the American artist Edward Hopper's, being concerned with suspended incidents. She was born in London and studied at Ravensbourne College of Art & Design, 1986–7, Coventry School of Art & Design, 1987–90 and Royal College of Art, 1992–4, and was included in Five RCA Painters at Paton Gallery, 1994. Previously had shown at Beaumanor Hall, Leicester, 1991, and Herbert Art Gallery & Museum, Coventry, 1992. Gained a John Minton Travel Award to Barcelona and Darwin Scholarship, both 1993, and Delfina Studios Award, 1994–6.

Michael MASON 1930– Painter and teacher, born in Brooklands, Cheshire. He was educated in Devon and studied art there at Exeter College of Art, 1947–51 and 1953–5, going on to become art master at Colyton Grammar School for many years. He showed at Roland, Browse and Delbanco, at several British universities, in America and was given a retrospective show at the University of Exeter in 1963–4. Plymouth City Museum and Art Gallery holds his work. Lived in Exeter.

Michael MASON 1935– Sculptor and teacher, born in Ashton-under-Lyne, Lancashire, attending the local School of Art from 1952 and Manchester College of Art and Design from 1954. From 1957 taught part-time at Ashton-under-Lyne, later appointments including Cheshire School of Art and Manchester College of Art and Design. Mason had many solo exhibitions, including Zaydler Gallery, 1969; Peterloo Gallery, Manchester, 1977; and Whitworth Art Gallery, Manchester, outdoor sculpture, with Michael Lyons, 1978. In 1980 Mason was included in the Arts Council's touring exhibition The British Art Show, selected by critic William Packer.

Paul MASON 1952– Sculptor, draughtsman and teacher, born in Bolton, Lancashire, who said of his work that it "centres on the way we perceive and describe the natural landscape. The way in which we objectify the landscape and use artificial conventions as a means of understanding common experiences." He did a foundation course at Bolton College of Art & Design, 1970–1; gained an honours degree in fine art at Wolverhampton Polytechnic, 1971–4; then did postgraduate studies at Royal Academy Schools, 1974–7, winning the Gold Medal in 1976. Did an extensive amount of teaching, part- and full-time, later appointments including principal lecturer, Staffordshire University, head of sculpture, 1989–91; visiting lecturer at Royal Academy Schools, postgraduate work, 1990–3; and fine art course leader at degree level, University of Northumbria, Newcastle, 1993. Among a series of British and foreign residencies was Tate Gallery, St Ives, 1996. Mixed exhibitions included Redfern Gallery, 1978; RIBA, 1984; Midlands Contemporary Arts, Birmingham, 1993; and Pitt-Rivers Museum, Oxford, 1995. Had a solo show at North-West Arts Centre in Manchester, 1978, later ones including RIBA Sculpture Court, 1992, and Tate, St Ives, 1996. Mason carried out extensive commissions, which included Vertex, Harlow New Town, 1980; Slate, straddled & splayed, Northern Arts Association, Grizedale Forest, 1981; Valley Wing, St Albans Grammar School, 1987; Waterhead, Nottingham County Council, at Beeston, 1989; and North Star, Edinburgh City Council, 1994. Public galleries in Bolton, Lincoln and Nottingham hold examples. Lived in Long Eaton, Nottingham.

Raymond MASON 1922– Sculptor in bronze and epoxy resin and stage designer, born in Birmingham. The son of a motor mechanic brought up in a poor part of Birmingham, Mason wanted to be a research chemist, but his art master persuaded him to study at the city's School of Arts and Crafts, 1937. After being invalided out of the Royal Navy Mason was briefly at Royal College of Art, 1942, then at Ruskin School of Drawing in Oxford, 1943, and Slade School of Fine Art, 1943–6. In the latter year Mason decided to settle in Paris, where he continued to work, being granted a French State Scholarship to École des Beaux-Arts. After mounting a first show of coloured abstract sculptures at Galerie Maeght, Mason went figurative under the influence of Giacometti. His first important work was Man in the Street, of 1952. From this solo figure he moved on to Barcelona Tram, of 1953, with over 20 figures; then in 1975 his 99-figure Crowd was installed in the Jardin des Tuileries. Another powerful work, The Departure of Fruit and Vegetables from the Heart of Paris 28 February 1969, was in 1975 installed in the Chapel of St Joseph in the church of St Eustache. In 1959 Mason had been commissioned to design the set and costumes for *Phèdre* at Théâtre du Gymnase. Mason believed that "realism is the common language of everybody and everybody thus has an entry into my work", but critical plaudits were slower in coming. In 1989 Birmingham Museum and Art Gallery, which holds Mason's work, staged a major exhibition, which toured.

Robert MASON 1923– Painter in oil and teacher, born in Newport, Monmouthshire. He studied at Camberwell School of Arts and Crafts, 1939–42, then at Goldsmiths' College School of Art, 1947–8, his teachers including Victor Pasmore and R V Pitchforth. Showed at RA, ROI, UA, Royal Glasgow Institute of the Fine Arts and RBSA and lived in Gillingham, Kent. Signed work R M.

Robert MASON 1946– Collagist, painter, draughtsman and teacher, born in Leeds, Yorkshire. He studied at Harrogate School of Art, 1963–5, then Hornsey College of Art, 1965–8, receiving an Italian Government Scholarship in latter year, working at British School in Rome, 1968–70. Mason's first one-man shows were at Galleria d'Arte, Rovigo, and Galerie Asinus, Hamburg, in 1970. Mason taught at University of Florida, 1970–1, then part-time at Chelsea School of Art from 1977. That was the year he had a one-man show at University of Sheffield, others soon following at ICA and Hester van Royen Gallery. Later exhibitions included Eastbourne Clarke Gallery, Florida; Hal Katzen Gallery, New York; and Yale Center for British Art, Connecticut. Mason won Arts Council Awards in 1977 and 1979. His work drew on various sources of inspiration, ranging from North Africa and London's East End to the writings of André Gide. British Council, Arts Council and Fitzwilliam Museum in Cambridge hold his work. Lived for some time in London.

Robert MASON 1951– Painter, illustrator and teacher, born in Kent. Studied at Maidstone College, 1970–3, and Royal College of Art, 1973–6. Went on to teach at Norfolk Institute of Art and Design, in Norwich, where he lived. Mason's picture St Paul of the Cross was included in the 1992 Norwich Gallery/Kent Institute of Art and Design East & South show. Sue Coe, Kahlo, Masereel, Spencer and Balthus were cited as principal influences. Mason worked on his saints series for many years.

Robin MASON 1958– Painter and draughtsman, born in Porthcawl, Glamorgan whose work could be rich in colour and metaphor. He attended Cardiff College of Art, 1976–7; Wolverhampton Polytechnic, 1977–80; and Royal College of Art, 1981–4. Awards included first prizes in: Northern Young Contemporaries, 1979; Cleveland International Drawing Biennale, 1989; and Royal Over-Seas League, 1989, and trophy winner. Participated in extensive group shows, with a series of solo exhibitions in Britain and England including Lamont Gallery from 1995. Government Art Collection, Leicestershire Education Authority, London Underground and a number of corporate collections hold examples.

Gertrude MASSEY 1868–1957 Painter and miniaturist, born and lived in London, married to the artist Henry Massey. She was privately educated. Showed at RA, RMS, Fine Art Society, Walker Art Gallery in Liverpool and at Paris Salon, also having several solo exhibitions. Her work was widely reproduced and included miniatures of King Edward VII, Queen Alexandra and the Dowager Empress of Russia.

Jane MASTERS 1954– Painter and teacher who studied at Plymouth College of Art and Camberwell School of Arts and Crafts. She exhibited in London mixed shows, including Park Walk Galleries and Figurative Painters at Woodlands Art Gallery, 1985. Taught at Southwark Adult Education Institute. Lived in London.

Fortunino MATANIA 1881–1963 Painter, draughtsman and miniaturist who specialised in historical subjects. Born in Naples, Italy, the son of the artist Edward Matania, he studied with his father. Aged only 14, he went to Milan to draw for an illustrated magazine, taking up similar work in Paris a few years later. He also worked on *The Graphic* and *The Sphere* in London. During World War I he was active as a war artist and was honoured by the Italian government. Exhibited extensively in England, including RA and RI, and Italy. Queen Mary bought his work. Lived in London.

Franco MATANIA 1922– Artist in all media, though mainly in conté and pastel, born in Naples, Italy, who became a British subject in 1935. He was a pupil of the related artist Fortunino Matania and worked in Paris and southern Spain until 1958. Matania was a member of UA, SGA and the Society of Equestrian Artists. His awards included a first prize for a pastel at Mall Galleries, 1984, and Society of Equestrian Artists awards at Mall Galleries in 1986 and Westminster Gallery, 1988. Also showed at NS, ROI, RA, RI, at Tanisia Gallery in New York and elsewhere. Personal exhibitions included Alpine Gallery, Campbell & Franks, Christie Gallery in Bedford and abroad. Industria Marmo Design, of Italy, commissioned designs in 1985. Lived in London.

Beryl MATCHWICK 1907– Miniaturist, painter of flowers in watercolour, musician and teacher of music, born in London.

After private education she attended Reigate and Redhill Schools of art, teachers including William Todd-Brown. Became a member of RMS and won Royal Horticultural Society Grenfell Medal several times for botanical paintings. Showed at RA, RSA, RI, in the provinces and at Paris Salon. Lived latterly at Ramsbury, Wiltshire.

John MATHERS fl. from late 1980s– Artist in a variety of media producing figurative and abstract images who gained a degree in fine art from the University of Ulster, Belfast, in 1988. In 1990 Mathers travelled through America, visiting many galleries and studying the paintings of Edward Hopper. In 1992 he had a residency at Bristol Artspace Studios for several weeks. Group exhibitions included Artists' Collective Open Exhibition at Laganside Galleries, Belfast, 1990; Four Belfast Artists at Artspace Gallery, 1992; the Arts Council tour Still Lives in 1993; and in 1994 Works on Paper and Beyond the Partitions, organised by Queen Street Studios, Belfast, with which Mathers was associated. In the city he showed solo at Harmony Hill Arts Centre in 1991.

Gertrude A MATHESON fl. c.1935–1985 Animal, figure and landscape painter in pencil and watercolour and oil. Matheson was born in Edinburgh and studied for five years there at the College of Art. She exhibited extensively in Britain and on the continent, including the Paris Salon, RSA, SSA, RBA and at the Cooling Galleries. One-man shows included Edinburgh and London. Lived at North Berwick, East Lothian, Scotland.

Ben MATHEWS 1889–1975 Painter, born in Duston, Northamptonshire. He began painting when he was about eight years old, encouraged by the Northampton watercolourist T L Shoosmith. Had a nautical education and in World War I served in Army and Royal Flying Corps, then qualified as an architect in the early 1920s. In 1923 went to Paris where he studied at the Académie Moderne, his teachers including Fernand Léger and Othon Friesz, and became interested in modern European art. In 1939 he settled in Northampton, where he lived until his death. Mathews was a member of the Chelsea Arts Club and he was a president of NS and an honorary secretary of ROI. He held a one-man show in Northampton in 1922 and his last major exhibition was held at Mall Galleries, London, in 1973.

Binny MATHEWS 1960– Painter and teacher who studied at Bournemouth and Poole College of Art, West Surrey College of Art and Design, then Brighton Polytechnic. Was artist-in-residence at Oakland School, 1982–5, also teaching at London College of Printing and at Cornwall College. Showed with National Portrait Gallery from 1981, with NEAC from 1984 and in 1990 was included in The Broad Horizon, at Agnew. Mathews had a solo show at Cadogan Contemporary in 1988. In 1989 Mathews won an Elizabeth Greenshields Foundation Award. Was noted for portraits and pictures of everyday subjects employing a rich palette as seen in her shared show at Anna-Mei Chadwick in 1993.

Denis MATHEWS: *see* **DENIS**

Henry MATHEWS 1912–1991 Artist in a variety of media, full name David Henry Joseph Mathews, who was born in Berlin, Germany, but who moved to England in 1938. He served in the Army in World War II and became a British citizen. Mathews was by profession a dress designer and manufacturer. He studied at art school for three years in Berlin, attended the City Literary Institute in London and became a keen amateur musician. His work, of a decorative nature, combined images and music. Had an exhibition in Germany at Haus am Kleistpark, Berlin-Schöneberg, 1979. Others took place at Harrow Arts Centre, Wealdstone, 1980; Queen's Hall, Edinburgh, 1984; with a retrospective at Library Gallery, Poole, 1991, one of a series there. Ben Uri Art Society holds his work. Lived for many years in Bournemouth, where he died, although he kept a studio in Hampstead, north London.

Richard George MATHEWS 1870–1955 Draughtsman, printmaker and illustrator, born in Montreal, Canada, father of the artist Denis Mathews. Until the mid-1890s Mathews worked for Canadian Pacific Railway, and began to publish drawings in various journals, including some in New York where he lived for a time, the Railway's president, Sir William van Horne, being an early patron. Joined the *Montreal Star* as a reportage artist, became known for his adept portraits of visiting personalities and showed regularly at Royal Canadian Academy. Moved to London in 1907, sending back work for the *Star*, and gained a regular income by making weekly portraits of theatrical stars for *The Graphic* and *The Bystander*. In 1912 he married the actress Lily Nanton and during World War I he was commissioned into the Canadian Expeditionary Force. After the war Mathews published more etchings for various print dealers, gradually moving to landscape and architectural subjects. Wrote and illustrated *Sailing Craft*, 1933, a travelogue about English waters. From 1935 he regularly contributed to *The Tatler* drawings of London life, and during World War II he recorded devastation in the city and Hampstead area where he lived. In 1996 Bartley Drey Gallery held a show of Mathews' topographical and portrait drawings and prints, subjects including Arnold Bennett, Rudyard Kipling, Marie Lloyd and Sir Hugh Walpole.

Anthony MATTHEWS 1925– Painter and teacher, born in Cheltenham, Gloucestershire. He attended the College of Art there and Reading University department of fine art. In 1954 began a series of teaching appointments, including head of School of Art in Rugby. Was art representative on the West Midlands Regional Council and honorary secretary of that area's Art Principals' Council for some years. Showed RA, RWA, Young Contemporaries, SEA, RCamA of which he was a member, LG and elsewhere. One-man shows included Gordon Waller Gallery, Coventry.

Laura MATTHEWS 1964– Painter of vivid, dramatic pictures who studied at Slade School of Fine Art, 1983–9. She gained a number of awards, including the David Bailey Travelling Scholarship, Catherine Maude Pearse Postgraduate Award, Rosa Morrison Award, Elizabeth Greenshields Award in 1987 and 1992, Boise Travelling Scholarship and Cyril Sweet Award for outstanding figurative work. In 1989 she was elected freeman of the Worshipful Company of Painter-Stainers. Taught at Slade Summer School. Mixed shows included Abbott and Holder, Austin/Desmond Fine Art, Heffer Gallery in Cambridge and New Grafton Gallery where she had a joint show in 1995 with Henrietta Young.

Les MATTHEWS 1946– Painter in oil, gouache, egg tempera and watercolour, illustrator and teacher. Born in Bristol, educated at the local Cathedral School and at Gloucester College of Art 1964–7 and Royal College of Art 1968–70. Worked in conservation department, National Gallery, for four years, then head of art in schools, including Churchill School, Somerset, from 1984. Solo and many mixed shows included RA Summer, RWA, Bath Society of Artists, Bristol Savages of which elected artist member 1990, Bristol Guild, BWS, Erotica, Kaleidoscope and *Sunday Times*, Mall Galleries. Illustrated for OUP and notably Transworld Corgi. His wide subject range included the female nude, Egyptology and mythology, chivalry and science fiction. Lived latterly in Clevedon, north Somerset.

Peter MATTHEWS 1942– Artist, notably a printmaker, and teacher, born in London. He studied at Ealing School of Art, 1957–62, later becoming senior lecturer in printmaking at Wimbledon School of Art. Exhibitions included Scottish Print Open Three, 1983, organised by Dundee Printmakers' Workshop. Matthews' work is held by Victoria & Albert Museum; Arts Council of Northern Ireland; Scottish College of Textiles; Bibliothèque Royale, Brussels; Albertina Museum, Vienna; and Free Library, Philadelphia.

Peter MATTHEWS 1948– Painter, born in Prittlewell, near Southend-on-Sea, Essex. He studied at Farnham College of Art, in Surrey, 1967–70; at Bristol Polytechnic, 1970–73; then Reading University, 1973–5. Was for a time attached to Gloucestershire College of Art. Showed at Bath Festival Gallery and elsewhere. Lived in Stroud, Gloucestershire.

Philip MATTHEWS 1916–1984 Painter and influential teacher, born in Belfast as H Philip Matthews. After education in the west country Matthews attended Maidenhead School of Art under the landscape painter Bernard Casson, was next at Reading University, then studied with Victor Pasmore and William Coldstream at Euston Road School, 1939. Matthews' work of that period shows a strong Coldstream influence; later the colour was richer, the paint thicker, although he remained an artist in the Euston Road tradition. He early made an impression, being included in the 1948 Euston Road School exhibition at Wakefield City Art Gallery and in notable collections such as that of Edward Le Bas. He exhibited at LG, NEAC, RA and at other venues, but justifiably felt later in life he had not been given the recognition he deserved. Joined the staff of Camberwell School of Arts and Crafts in 1946, retiring only a few years before his death. Lived in Maidenhead, Berkshire, and in Devizes, Wiltshire.

Rodney MATTHEWS 1945– Versatile artist, illustrator and designer, born in Paulton, Somerset, who studied at West of England College of Art, Bristol, teachers including Anthony Rossiter. From 1962–70 he designed for a Bristol advertising agency, then worked mainly as a freelance illustrator of fantasy and science fiction, with diversions into factual bird illustration and the design of fibreglass drum kits. Matthews' illustrations of prophetic scenes from *The Bible*, especially Revelations, were important to him. Participated in many joint exhibitions and had solo shows including Langton Gallery and Y Tabernacl, Machynlleth, Chris Beetles Ltd permanently stocking his pictures. Media celebrities John Cleese and Terry Jones owned examples. In addition, Matthews illustrated dozens of record covers, including those by Thin Lizzy, Magnum and Rick Wakeman (his *Tiger Moth* album cover won first prize at The Music Trade Association Awards in 1984); in 1992 Matthews released a three-track compact disc, on which he played drums, with Rudi Dobson and Tony Clarkin; his full-colour posters, in many designs, sold several million copies; he also produced jigsaw puzzles, calendars and postcards; and operated his own animation company, Yendors Images. Lived at Llancycil, Bala, Gwynedd.

Feliks MATYJASZKIEWICZ 1913– Versatile artist and designer, one of the group of Polish paper sculptors who made an impact in Britain after World War II. He graduated from Warsaw Academy of Arts in 1936 and early practised paper sculpture. In 1936 his design for stained glass windows for St Ladislau Church at Pruszkow, near Warsaw, won first prize. He also worked as a book illustrator for Biblioteka Polska publishing house. After extensive and hair-raising travels through Europe in World War II he eventually reached Britain, served in the Polish forces and settled in London. For many years designed scenery for the Polish theatre. He was noted as a designer for his crisply constructed paper heads and figures, produced for exclusive clubs, such as Curzon, Palm Beach and Mayfair, and for major airlines such as KLM, SAS and Qantas. Was included in Polish Paper Sculpture at Polish Cultural Institute, 1995.

Sue MATHERS 1945– Printmaker and artist in acrylic, born in Lancashire, who studied at Barnsley College of Art, 1979–80; Hereford College of Art 1981–4 and 1989–91; afterwards studying for her master's degree at Wolverhampton University while working as a fine artist and printmaker in her Herefordshire studio at St Owen's Cross. Maud said that her "life and love is sailing, and because of this major influence most of my work is connected with the sea." Group shows included Bankside Gallery and RWA from 1992; Dudley Museum and Art Gallery, 1993; Y Tabernacl, Machynlleth, from 1994; Beatrice Royal, Eastleigh, 1995. Had a solo show at Wakefield District College of Art, 1992, then at Upstairs Downstairs, St Albans, from 1994. Hartlepool Renaissance, which gave Maud an award in 1995, holds her work.

Alice MAUDE-ROXBY 1963– Artist employing objects, photography, film, video and performance, born in London. She was educated at Queen's College, 1975–81, did a foundation course at Brighton Polytechnic, 1981–2, then a fine art degree course in sculpture school at Newcastle upon Tyne Polytechnic, 1982–5. Maude-Roxby then gained a Leverhulme Trust Scholarship to Trondheim, Norway, 1986–7; an Eastern Arts Photography Bursary, 1989–90; and a DAAD stipend to Berlin, 1990–1. She was involved in collaborative projects, such as Giroux's *A Bigger Trap*, as video-maker, in 1993. Exhibitions included Bridge Lane Theatre Gallery, 1985; Trondheim Fort, Norway, 1987; Bookworks, Sandra Higgins Fine Arts, 1990; Nachtbogen, Berlin, 1991; Cleveland Gallery, 1992; and Plymouth Arts Centre, 1993. Victoria & Albert Museum holds her work. Lived in Berlin and London. She was the daughter of Roddy Maude-Roxby.

Jean MAUDE-ROXBY 1915– Sculptor in wood, clay, plaster and papier mâché, born in London, full name Dulcie Jean Maude-Roxby. Her main interest was animal sculpture. She started "at the age of 10 with Dorothy Doughty, the great ceramic sculptor of birds", her studies including Vita Studio, Bexhill, then had three years with Henry Moore at Chelsea Polytechnic, other teachers being Willi Soukop and Atri Brown. Showed at RA, RSA and in several international shows of sculpture as well as in local exhibitions near her home in Burwash, Sussex. She also "started a small guild of artists for painting and sculpting nativity sets in Southwark Cathedral, crucifixes and saints in many churches." Jack Beddington included Maude-Roxby in his 1957 book *Young Artists of Promise*.

Roddy MAUDE-ROXBY 1930– Actor and artist, born and lived in London, one of several artistic Maude-Roxbys. Studied at Royal College of Art, editing *ARK* magazine in 1958 and being president of the College's Theatre Group. He shared a show with Peter Blake at Portal Gallery in 1960, exhibited elsewhere and was included in The Sixties Art Scene in London, Barbican Art Gallery, 1993, but became best known as a character actor on the stage and in television. Appearances in N F Simpson's *One Way Pendulum*, 1959, and Albert Bermal's *One Leg Over the Wrong Wall*, 1960, both at Royal Court Theatre, were typical of the zany parts Maude-Roxby became known for. Later appearances included the 1993 film *Shadowlands*, based on the writer C S Lewis' life. In that year Maude-Roxby was included in England & Co's celebration of 1960s art.

Karl MAUGHAN 1964– Representational painter, as in his oil on canvas Plume, at John Moores Liverpool Exhibition, 1997–8. Maughan was born in Wellington, New Zealand, and studied at The Elam School of Fine Arts, Auckland, 1983–7. Exhibitions included Waikato Museum of Art, Hamilton, 1993; Blind Field at Coventry Gallery, London, where Maughan latterly lived, 1995; and Undergrowth at Holly Street Studios, 1997.

Moshe MAURER 1891–1971 Painter whose work has a naive charm, sometimes with fantastic elements, born in Brody, Russia, near Lvov and the Polish border. Moved to Antwerp, Belgium, around the start of World War I, settling in England in 1940. He began painting 10 years later. Maurer wrote that "only my dear wife understood and encouraged me, and after she died in 1962 I was unable to touch a brush for many months ... Then suddenly I woke up in a paradise of painting and through it have found rest, consolation, relaxation and inner satisfaction." As well as Britain, Maurer showed widely abroad. Had a solo show at St George's Gallery, 1956; Ben Uri Art Society, which holds his work, 1957; and Mercury Gallery, 1970 and 1971. Died in London.

John MAXWELL 1905–1962 Painter, draughtsman and teacher, born and died in Dalbeattie, Kirkcudbrightshire. A superlative draughtsman, Maxwell's still lifes, landscapes and imaginative compositions have a distinctive colour range and a unique lyrical, fantastic quality. Very self-critical, he left only just over 200 works. Maxwell studied at Dumfries Academy and from 1921 at Edinburgh College of Art. In 1927 a travelling scholarship enabled him to study under Léger and Ozenfant in Paris; visited Spain and Italy, where he discovered the primitives. After a teacher-training course at Moray House in 1928 he began his teaching career at Edinburgh College of Art which lasted until 1946, when he retired to Dalbeattie to paint full-time. In 1955 W G Gillies invited him to Edinburgh College as senior lecturer in composition, and he only gave up teaching finally because of ill-health. He was a member of SSA, being elected RSA in 1949. A memorial show was held at the Scottish National Gallery of Modern Art in 1963.

Christiana Brix MAY 1876–1954 Painter and miniaturist. Born in British Honduras as Christiana Klitgaard (a name sometimes used in early work), she studied art at Durham College, in Copenhagen and elsewhere on the continent. Exhibited RA, RI, RMS, ROI, Paris Salon and elsewhere abroad. Royal Academy Schools hold her work, which also appeared in *Colour* magazine and the *Christian Science Monitor*. Lived at Axminster, Devon.

Fred MAY 1891–1976 Caricaturist and artist, born in Wallasey, Cheshire. He attended the local Liscard School of Art and Reading University. Exhibited at Middlesbrough Art Gallery but was chiefly known as a caricaturist for the *Liverpool Daily Post & Echo*, in Fleet Street and for *Tatler* and other magazines. Retired in 1953, but continued to work part-time. Served with the Green Howards in World War I and Territorial Army in 1939 and was noted for his military cartoons, which are to be found in many regimental museums. Was a nephew of the cartoonist Phil May. Lived in Reading, Berkshire.

Gwen MAY 1903–1992 Watercolourist and printmaker, born and lived in London, who studied at Hornsey School of Art. In 1930s worked as an heraldic artist at College of Arms. May had a great interest in the theatre, being a member of the Arts Theatre Club, also RE and SGA. Showed at RA, NEAC, RBA and elsewhere. Public galleries in Bradford and Nottingham hold her work.

Nicholas MAY 1962– Painter, born in County Londonderry, Northern Ireland. He studied at Bath Academy of Art, 1981–4, gaining an honours degree, then obtained his master's degree at Goldsmiths' College School of Art, 1988–90. Was included in New Contemporaries at ICA, 1989–90, and in 1991 at Barclays Young Artist Award at Serpentine Gallery. Had a solo show at Frith Street Gallery, 1991. In 1992–3 May was included in Twelve Stars at Arts Council Gallery, Belfast, with tour, his work Alluvion 2, of 1992, being acquired for the European Parliament Collection. This was described as "the quintessence of gestural painting, combining European eroticism with post-war American abstract painting."

Charlotte MAYER 1929– Sculptor in various materials, including steel and concrete, born in Prague, Czechoslovakia. She studied at Goldsmiths' College School of Art, 1945–9, teachers including Ivor Roberts-Jones and Harold Wilson Parker, then Royal College of Art, 1949–52, with Frank Dobson. Showed at RA, Young Contemporaries, Bear Lane Gallery in Oxford, Gallery Pangolin in Chalford, RWA, Sladmore and Belgrave Galleries and elsewhere. She was a fellow of RBS and gained its silver medal, 1991. Solo exhibitions included Iveagh Bequest, Kenwood; St John's, Hampstead; and Coombs Contemporary. Major commissions included Care, at Lord Mayor Treloar Hospital, Hampshire; Ascent, Barbican, City of London; King, British Petroleum; and Bison, for Concrete Ltd. Mayer's work created forms which were often fluid and sinuous, apparently abstract, but implying links with living things. Lived in London.

Eric MAYER 1903–1971 Interior designer and teacher. Born in Wigan, he studied at Manchester Municipal School of Art, 1920–7. He taught in Manchester in the 1930s, becoming principal of Ipswich School of Art in 1949. Exhibited locally. Lived at Stowmarket, Suffolk.

Hansjörg MAYER 1943– Graphic artist, publisher and teacher, born in Stuttgart, Germany. In 1959 he studied philosophy with Max Bense and music at the University of Stuttgart, and graphics at the School of Painting, in 1962 attending the School of Painting in Zürich. Contacts with such artists as Ian Hamilton Finlay, John Furnival and Dom Sylvester Houédard fostered Mayer's interest in concrete poetry, and he participated in an exhibition at ICA in 1965. Taught at Bath Academy of Art, 1966–71, while basing himself in London. After 1971 he occasionally lectured at Corsham, devoting his time to publishing and working with such artists as Dieter Rot and Richard Hamilton. Mayer was included in the show devoted to the Academy at Michael Parkin Gallery in 1989.

Michael MAYER 1932– Artist and teacher, born in Kent. He attended Exeter College of Art in 1955, from 1965 lecturing there. In 1980 he was included in The British Art Show, a touring exhibition chosen by the critic William Packer and put on by the Arts Council, which holds Mayer's work. The 1980 show included Telegraph, of 1978, and The Aura of Joseph "Cornbread Thomas", abstracts constructed of small lines and patterns, oil on canvas. Solo shows included Gimpel Fils, 1978.

William MAYER 1910– Artist and architect, born in Heaton Mersey, Cheshire. He was mostly self-taught, although spent a short period with Terry McGlynn at Stockport. Mayer latterly concentrated on watercolour, having between 1950–70 also painted in oil and acrylic. Mayer qualified as an architect, taking his finals in Edinburgh in 1944, and was still practising in his eighties. He was a fellow of RIBA. Mayer showed landscapes, some semi-abstract, in group exhibitions at National Theatre, Chenil Gallery, John Moores Liverpool Exhibition and elsewhere. Had many solo shows, including public galleries in Lancaster and Salford, Vernon Gallery in Preston, Theatre in the Forest at Grizedale and Crane Gallery in Manchester. Manchester City Art Gallery and Salford Art Gallery hold works. Lived at Whittle-le-Woods, Chorley, Lancashire.

George MAYER-MARTON 1897–1960 Painter, artist in mural and mosaic, illustrator and teacher, born in Gyor, Hungary. After service in World War I in the Austro-Hungarian Army, Mayer-Marton in 1919 began training as an art student in Vienna at the Academy of Arts, later in Munich. From 1924 he fast established a reputation in Vienna, where he held senior positions in the Hagenbund, a leading society of artists. Works by him were acquired by the art galleries of Budapest, Vienna, Brussels, Prague and Rome, and he won a number of prizes and awards. In 1932 he illustrated two books from the Chinese and in 1936 helped to arrange a show of British watercolours in Vienna. Mayer-Marton emigrated to England in 1938, taking a post at the St John's Wood School of Art, but his studio was hit by an incendiary bomb in 1940, which destroyed most of his life's work. During the 1940s and 1950s he lectured, but continued to paint, mainly in watercolour. In 1952 he left London to settle in Liverpool, where he became senior lecturer at the College of Art, a post held until his death. He began to make use of knowledge acquired before World War II in Ravenna in the field of mosaic and mural painting, carrying out work in churches and other public buildings. Derby Museum and Art Gallery, the National Museum of Wales, Cardiff, and the Walker Art Gallery, Liverpool, are among British galleries holding his work. A memorial show was held at the Walker in 1961. Sometimes signed his work M M.

Anna MAYERSON 1906–1984 Sculptor and painter, brought up in Austria. She initially studied art in Zürich and at the Vienna Academy, then at the Slade School of Fine Art. Signing her work A M, she showed extensively in Europe. Mixed shows in Britain included AIA, Arts Council, LG, Leicester Galleries, Hanover Gallery and the provinces. Also had a number of one-man shows, including Leger Gallery and Modern Art Gallery. Ben Uri Art Society holds Untitled, a gestural abstract by her. Lived in London.

Reginald MAYES 1900–1992 Painter, poster artist and illustrator who was born and schooled in Great Yarmouth, Norfolk. His career began in design studio of *Eastern Daily Press*, Norwich, where he learned to grind colours with a pestle and mortar. Moving to London, he designed watermarks for paper-makers and studied at Regent Street Polytechnic with Harold Brownsword and Harry Watson and at Goldsmiths' College School of Art under Clive Gardiner. From 1936–46 was chief staff artist for London, Midland and Scottish Railway. His poster *In War and Peace We Serve* was shown at Science Museum's poster exhibition in 1985. Victoria & Albert Museum and National Railway Museum, York, hold examples. Mayes became art director of West One Studios. His work was noted for its bright and bold designs. In retirement lived at Westbrook, Margate, Kent, painting landscapes.

Chris MAYGER 1918– Marine artist and illustrator who was educated at South-East London Technical College and Camberwell School of Arts and Crafts, 1934–8, with Cosmo Clark and Eric Fraser. He became a member of RSMA in 1976, also exhibiting at Guildhall Art Gallery, elsewhere in Britain and in America. National Maritime Museum in Greenwich holds his work. Lived in Hildenborough, Tonbridge, Kent.

Alister MAYNARD 1903– Painter and designer, born and worked in London. Studied at Chelsea School of Art. Did a volume of commercial work, but also showed at RBA and RI.

Anthony MAYNARD 1937– Painter, illustrator and sculptor dealing with wildlife subjects, sometimes in precious metals, born in Ruislip, Middlesex. Attended Harrow Grammar School. Showed with RA, SWLA of which he was a member and illustrated natural history books. Lived in London.

Eileen MAYO 1906–1994 Painter of pictures and murals, illustrator, printmaker, writer and teacher. She was born in Norwich, Norfolk. Attended Clifton High School, Bristol. Studied variously full-time and part-time with Henry Tonks at the Slade School of Fine Art, 1924–5; lino-cutting with Claude Flight; at the Central School of Arts and Crafts with Noel Rooke and John Farleigh; Chelsea Polytechnic, 1936; and with Fernand Léger in Paris, 1948–9. She was an artists' model for a time. Taught at St Martin's School of Art and Sir John Cass School of Arts and Crafts and later in Sydney, Australia, and Canterbury, New Zealand, living in Christchurch from the early 1960s. Exhibited Redfern Gallery, RA, LG, in the provinces and extensively abroad. British Museum, Victoria & Albert Museum, Whitworth Art Gallery in Manchester and a number of overseas galleries hold her work. She was a fine animal illustrator, combining accuracy with liveliness on the printed page, her books including *The Story of Living Things*, 1944, and *Animals on the Farm*, 1950. Mayo was the second wife of Dr Richard Gainsborough, who founded *Art News & Review*, and she designed the first issue when it appeared in 1949. In Australia and New Zealand Mayo carried out commissions for coins and postage stamps, including the Captain Cook bicentenary issue in 1969. In 1993–4 a retrospective touring show was organised by the National Library of New Zealand. Mayo was created a Dame of the British Empire in the 1994 New Year's Honours List.

Hannah MAYOR 1871–1948 Painter who was born in Sheffield, Yorkshire, and educated at the High School there. She studied at the Royal Female School of Art and Westminster School of Art. In 1895 one of her watercolours, a still life, was bought by Queen Victoria. Mayor often exhibited flower and still life pictures at Goupil Gallery, RA, RI, RBA, SWA and elsewhere. She met her husband, the painter Fred Mayor, while she was a member of the Staithes group – with Laura and Harold Knight – and they married in 1902. They settled in Montreuil-sur-Mer, in northern France, spending summer months at Cassis, in the south, only returning to England when their eldest child was of school age. Lived at Whitchurch, near Aylesbury, Buckinghamshire. Fred died during an operation in 1916. The eldest son, Fred, founded the avant-garde Mayor Gallery. Latterly, Hannah Mayor lived at Leigh, near Reigate, in Surrey.

Patti MAYOR 1872–1962 Painter and draughtsman, notably of portraits. She was a native of Preston, Lancashire, where she mostly lived. Was educated at Slade School of Fine Art and in Paris. She was a keen amateur musician who lived with her sister, Amy Mayor, a concert pianist who died in 1964, their home being a local artistic salon imbued with liberal Victorian values. Miss Patti Mayor was a keen Christian Scientist. She exhibited widely in Lancashire, in 1959 was given a retrospective at Grundy Art Gallery in Blackpool and in 1963 a memorial show was held at Harris Art Gallery, Preston. Those galleries and Walker Art Gallery, Liverpool, hold her work. Died at Ashton-on-Ribble, Lancashire.

Douglas Lionel MAYS 1900–1991 Illustrator and painter, born in Kingston upon Thames, Surrey, where he died. Studied at Goldsmiths' College School of Art, after Army service in Germany, his notable teacher being Edmund J Sullivan. Mays followed in the tradition of versatile black-and-white men, going on to draw for magazines such as *Punch* and *John Bull* as well as Royle Publications. His speciality was family life, with his own family as models. Mays was a reclusive, reflective man who later in life made thoughtful studies in oil, shown at RA.

Jeanne MAZE 1955– Painter with a strong decorative sense, born in London. Was early influenced by her grandfather, the Post-Impressionist Paul Maze. After Byam Shaw School of Art studied Chinese art forms at Victoria & Albert and British Museums. In 1976 she began to paint Chinese murals and until 1990 carried out a large number of commissions in traditional Oriental styles. She also had an interest in Scottish wildlife, as indicated in her first solo show in London, at Cadogan Gallery, in 1992.

Paul MAZE 1887–1979 Painter, born in Le Havre, France, who grew up with a family background of art and music. Educated in France and England, he was meant to enter his father's firm and early experience of business life took him to Liverpool, London and Hamburg, but his enthusiasm for painting determined that he moved to Perugia, Italy, to paint in 1914. World War I interrupted and Maze went to the front with the Royal Scots Greys where he met Winston Churchill with whom he stayed close friends. Churchill wrote a preface to Maze's 1934 book *A Frenchman in Khaki*. The several-times-decorated Maze in 1918 rented a studio in Paris, where he became a notable member of the art scene, his immediate neighbours Derain and de Segonzac. Eventually Maze settled in England, at Treyford, Sussex. He was a regular exhibitor in Paris, London and widely in America, notable for pictures with a Dufyesque lightness of touch. Among later exhibitions was a series at Browse & Darby from 1983. Tate Gallery, Fitzwilliam Museum in Cambridge and Glasgow Art Gallery hold examples.

Dino MAZZOLI 1935– Painter in oil and watercolour, born in Terni, Italy. Dino (Leopoldo) Mazzoli was the son of Gino, artist and teacher, and after education at Oriani College, Rome, studied at Villa Massimo there, 1953–4, with Renato Guttuso, at Villa Medici, 1954–6, at Eastbourne College of Art under Peter Berrisford and with Dorothy Swain. He was a member of the Eastbourne Group and as well as showing in Italy exhibited at Brighton Museum and Art Gallery and Star Gallery in Lewes, with a permanent exhibition at La Charbonnière, St Laurent en Grandvaux, Jura, France. Lived in Eastbourne, Sussex.

Anna MAZZOTTA 1970– Artist whose work was shown in Five RCA Painters, at Paton Gallery, 1994, and was said to "update the world of steamy female sensuality earlier exploited by Degas, Delacroix and Ingres". Born in Swindon, Wiltshire, Mazzotta studied at Wimbledon School of Art, 1989–92, and Royal College of Art, 1992–4. She gained a Henderson & Parker Award in 1994. Anthony Hepworth Gallery, Bath, showed her work in 1992 and in 1993 she was in Preface at Royal College of Art.

MEA: *see* **Mea ANGERER**

Neil MEACHER 1934– Artist, illustrator and teacher working in a variety of media, born in Sandwich, Kent. He attended Canterbury College of Art, 1951–5, then Royal College of Art, 1957–60, teachers including Edward Ardizzone, Humphrey Spender and Alistair Grant. He was a member of the Association of Illustrators and RI, exhibiting with John Nevill Gallery in Canterbury, New Ashgate Gallery in Farnham and Rye Art Gallery, Sussex. Taught at Ealing College of Higher Education and lived in Shepperton, Middlesex.

Dorothy MEAD 1928–1975 Painter, draughtsman and etcher, born in London, where she continued to live for some years. Studied at South-East Essex Technical College, Dagenham, with David Bomberg, then followed him to the City Literary Institute (where she met Cliff Holden, with whom she was closely associated for many years) and the Borough Polytechnic, 1945–51. Attended Slade School of Fine Art as a mature student, 1956–9; had a strong influence on many students, including Mario Dubsky; gained the Steer Medal, 1958, and several major prizes; but left without a diploma because of her refusal to attend lectures and examinations on perspective, which she considered outdated. As a founder-member of the Borough Group Mead participated in Group shows and did much to disseminate Bomberg's ideas in Britain and abroad, notably through her association with Andrew Forge. Mead was president of Young Contemporaries, 1958–9. She showed with LG from 1947, was elected in 1959 and was its first lady president, 1973–4, resigning in 1975 due to cancer. Worked extensively in Spain. London dealers showed no interest in Mead's pictures, which were strongly influenced by Bomberg, and she never had a solo exhibition. A drawing of Dorothy Mead by David Bomberg and Richard Michelmore and three etchings by her were in a Borough Group show at Fine Art Associates, 1989; she was included in David Bomberg and his followers at Towner Art Gallery, Eastbourne, 1991. Arts Council, London University and Tate Gallery hold her work.

Philip MEAD 1948– Painter, born in Lincoln. He took a fine art honours degree at Gloucestershire College of Art, 1979–82, gaining his master's in painting, 1983–4. Mead then had an artist-in-schools residency, at Hartshill School, Nuneaton, 1985, followed in 1985–6 by another residency at Porthcawl School, Wales. After Greek Government Scholarships, 1986–7, Mead was artist-in-residence at The National Gallery, 1987–8, then in 1992 at Pennsylvania Academy of the Fine Arts. Among his many awards and prizes were an Arts Council Award, 1977, and a WAC Travel Award in 1989. His many shows included Stowells Trophy Exhibition, RA, 1982; one-man show at British School at Athens, 1986; solo show at Winchester Gallery, 1988; and the first of a series of one-mans at New Academy Gallery, 1989. National Gallery and Gallery of Modern Art, Oslo, hold his work. His later landscapes tended more towards abstraction.

Rose MEAD 1867–1946 Born Emma Rose Mead, she was a painter in oil and watercolour of portraits and personalities in Bury St Edmunds, Suffolk, where she was born and lived. Mead attended Lincoln School of Art around 1888–92, gaining several awards; was briefly at Westminster School of Art, under Fred Brown; then, after nursing her father until he died, joined the studio of Auguste-Joseph Délécluse in Paris, 1895. Took a studio in London, then returned to Bury to nurse her mother. Began to show at Paris Salon and RA and in 1907 produced 12 watercolours commemorating the Bury Pageant, printed and sold as commemorative postcards. Mead was a fiery-tempered feminist who in the 1890s indignantly refused an offer of £500 (then a considerable sum) from a cooker manufacturer if she would add its name to a stove in one of her pictures. Also showed with a local photographer and framer Harold Jarman and at RP, RCamA and SWA. A retrospective was organised by Bury Art Society in 1955, another show by the local Manor House Museum, which holds a collection of her pictures, occurring in 1996.

John Edward MEADE 1909–1982 Restorer and painter. After a period in Intelligence in World War II in Egypt, working for

War Office, Meade in 1946 joined Ministry of Works as an artist restorer. Among ceilings restored were the the Thornhill in the Painted Hall at Royal Naval College, Greenwich, and in 1960, working by himself, the Queen's Audience Chamber at Windsor. In his spare time Meade continued to produce watercolours, oils and pastels, landscape and figurative, and a first show of these was held by Moss Galleries in 1991. In 1967 Meade was made a fellow of the Royal Society of Arts.

Bernard MEADOWS 1915– Sculptor, mainly in bronze, draughtsman and teacher, born in Norwich. He studied at the School of Art there, 1934–6; at Chelsea School of Art, 1936–7, while serving for several years as studio assistant to Henry Moore; then was at Royal College of Art, 1938–40 and 1946–8, spending intervening years in Royal Air Force. Meadows had his first one-man show at Gimpel Fils in 1957 and in New York at Paul Rosenberg Gallery, 1958–9. During the 1950s he was represented in a number of influential shows, including Venice Biennale in 1952 (again in 1964), Antwerp Sculpture Biennale in 1953 and 1959 and São Paulo Bienal in 1958. He was an influential teacher, at Chelsea School of Art, 1948–60, then for many years at Royal College of Art as professor of sculpture, as the exhibition Bernard Meadows at the Royal College of Art 1960–1980, at the College in 1980, clearly indicated. His commissions included Festival of Britain in 1951. Meadows' sculpture was both abstract and abstract with figurative allusions, in which dynamic energy can be concentrated. There was an eightieth birthday show at Yorkshire Sculpture Park, Wakefield, in 1995, with a retrospective at Gimpel Fils. Tate Gallery and many other public collections hold examples. Lived in London.

Stuart MEALING 1946– Artist and teacher, born in Epsom, Surrey. He attended Goldsmiths' College and Cardiff College of Art where he later became a lecturer in fine art. Was interested in brain research, computer arts and artificial intelligence. In 1970 Arts Council commissioned Participation Print from Mealing, who showed in Liverpool, Cardiff, Swansea and elsewhere and was a consultant in 1974 to Kidsplay II at Tate Gallery. Had one-man show at Serpentine Gallery, 1971. WAC holds his work.

Gerald A MEARES 1911–1975 Sculptor, woodcarver and painter, born in Woodford, Essex. Studied at Regent Street Polytechnic School of Art, 1945–7, under the sculptor Geoffrey Deeley. Meares eventually set up in business as a monumental mason and carver. Showed in RA, RBA and Young Contemporaries. Lived in Tenterden, Kent. Judy Hines' Gallery 45, Norwich, also handled his work.

David MEASURES 1932– Natural historian and artist, born in Warwick, who attended Leamington Spa Art College, Bournemouth College of Art and Slade School of Fine Art. Measures was a pioneer of the movement to change the study of natural history from collecting and killing towards observation and conservation. He was noted for his rapid sketches of subjects such as butterflies in flight, as in the Arts Council 1981–2 tour Fragments Against Ruin. In 1976 his work was published in *Bright Wings of Summer*, and in 1980 he organised an exhibition for the 1980 York Festival, The Artist-Naturalist in Britain.

David MEDALLA 1942– Sculptor, performance artist, writer, gallery owner and teacher, born in Manila, Philippines, as David Cortes de Medalla. He was a youthful prodigy, at the age of 12 years translating major international poets into his native language, at 15 being admitted as a special scholar at Columbia University, New York. It was there that he began painting seriously. After extensive travelling Medalla arrived in London in the early 1960s. Among his activities over the following years were the founding of the Signals London gallery; the co-founding of the Arts Council of the Philippines; organisation of the First Festival of Performance Art at Bracknell, in 1983; and participation in a number of exhibitions and performances worldwide. He staged performances for the Paris Bicentenaire, in 1989, and took part in The Other Story, Hayward Gallery, and touring, 1989–90. Was for a time artist-in-residence for New York Port Authority. Medalla was fond of bubble-creating machines, such as Cloud Canyons, of 1963; Cloud Windows, of 1966; and Cloud Discourse, of 1971. They were a feature of Mondrian in Excelsis, staged at 55 Gee Street on New Year's Eve, 1994, a happening which celebrated the founding of the Mondrian Fan Club, of which Medalla was president, a year earlier. Medalla was then living at Bracknell, Berkshire, as artist-in-residence at the South Hill Park Arts Centre. Milton Avery, Franz Kline, Jackson Pollock, Willem de Kooning, Marcel Duchamp and Man Ray were met by Medalla and were influences. Arts Council holds examples.

Gina MEDCALF fl. from late 1960s– Abstract painter born in Llandudno, Caernarvonshire, who eventually settled in America. She studied at St Martin's School of Art, 1965–6, then Central School of Art and Design, 1966–9. In America held National Endowment for the Arts and New York State Council for the Arts Grants, 1983–4. Among group show appearances were John Moores Liverpool Exhibition, 1989–90. Later solo shows in America were at Sound Shore Gallery, Port Chester, 1987, and Smith-Jariwala Gallery, New York, 1990. Lived in London for a time.

Ruth MEDFORTH 1961– Painter and teacher. Between 1981–6 she studied at Wimbledon School of Art and Slade School of Fine Art, gaining a bachelor's degree and higher diploma. In 1986 won the Slade Prize and the David Bayley Scholarship to travel and paint. From 1987 she lectured part-time at Wimbledon School of Art and at Byam Shaw School of Art. Showed in group exhibitions at Robertson Mort Gallery, Bedford, in 1987; at Hertfordshire College of Art and Design, St Albans, 1988; and she was one of seven figurative artists in The Prose of Painting at Austin/Desmond Fine Art, 1991. Worked in London and St Albans, Hertfordshire.

Philip MEDLEY 1962– Sculptor, born in Chester, who studied sculpture at North Staffordshire Polytechnic, 1981–4, gaining an honours degree. Exhibitions included Greenwich Open Studios, 1985–93; Whitechapel Open, 1988; Kepler Gallery, 1992; Roche Court Sculpture Garden, Wiltshire, from 1993; and Made in Greenwich, at The Living Room, 1994, when he showed welded steel work reminiscent of sculpture by the American David Smith, provocative in profile, with interesting spaces between the metal.

Robert MEDLEY 1905–1994 Painter, printmaker, theatre designer, teacher and writer, born in London, where he lived for much of his life. Studied at Byam Shaw School, 1923–4, briefly at Royal Academy Schools in 1924, then at Slade School of Fine Art, 1924–6, and in Paris, 1926–8. In the period 1929–34 assisted Duncan Grant and Vanessa Bell. Showed with LG from 1929, becoming a member in 1937, and helped establish AIA the year before. Had first solo show at London Artists' Association, 1932. Also in that year became associated with Rupert Doone, director of Group Theatre, and designed plays by W H Auden, Christopher Isherwood and T S Eliot, a period well described in Medley's *Drawn from Life*, published 1983. For part of World War II was involved in camouflage work in Middle East. He taught at Chelsea School of Art, 1932–9, and 1946–50; taught stage design and painting at Slade, 1950–8; was head of fine art department at Camberwell School of Arts and Crafts, 1958–65; and was chairman of faculty of painting at British School in Rome, 1967–77. In 1980 published limited edition of screenprints for Milton's *Samson Agonistes*, "one of the best things I have done". After that he returned to painting the figure after a period in which pictures had been "metaphors for actual visual experience". Retrospective exhibition at Whitechapel Art Gallery, 1963. Represented in Tate Gallery and other public collections.

Reuben MEDNIKOFF 1906–1976 Surrealist artist and writer, sometimes known as Ricky Pailthorpe, born in London. After studying at St Martin's School of Art from 1920, Mednikoff worked in advertising, 1923–35, then met the much older Freudian analyst Grace Pailthorpe, who invited him to join her research into psychoanalysis and art at Port Isaac, Cornwall. Their collaboration released a flood of inspiration in Mednikoff. He and Pailthorpe, whom he married, showed at the International Surrealist Exhibition in 1936 as well as subsequent Surrealist shows. Their work appeared in *London Bulletin*. In 1939 they shared an exhibition at Guggenheim Jeune Galleries. During World War II Mednikoff and Pailthorpe worked in North America before returning to England. A Mayor Gallery show in 1998 celebrated their achievements. He died in Bexhill-on-Sea, Sussex.

Sarah MEDWAY fl. from early 1990s– Artist who gained a modern art diploma at ICA, 1984–5; then attended Chelsea School of Art, 1989–90; Heatherley's School of Fine Art, 1990–1; and Byam Shaw School, 1991–4. Group exhibitions included Ben Uri Art Society, 1994; Candid Gallery, 1995; Kunsthandlung, Heidelberg, Germany, 1996; and Schwetzingen Castle, Germany, 1997. Showed solo with Lamont Gallery from 1996. Paintings in Hospitals holds Medway's work.

Henry MEE 1955– Painter in oil on canvas, born in Bishop's Stortford, Hertfordshire, noted for his portraits. He studied at University of Leeds, 1975–9, teachers including Lawrence Gowing, Tim Clark, Griselda Pollock, Francis Fraschina and Terry Atkinson. Mee considered himself "a figurative painter in the English tradition, working from life and drawing being of paramount importance". He made a big impression with his British Eminences solo show at Sotheby's in 1990, which was also exhibited at the Hop Exchange, 24 Southwark Street. Group exhibitions included nudes at Browse & Darby, 1994. His main works included HM The Queen and former prime ministers Margaret Thatcher, Harold Wilson and Alec Douglas Home, all in the Palace of Westminster collection. HRH The Princess Royal is in HM The Queen's Collection, and many university collections hold examples. Other eminencies depicted included HRH The Duke of Edinburgh, HRH The Prince of Wales, The Princess of Wales, Lord Carrington, Sir Peter Hall, Anthony Powell who wrote the catalogue for his Sotheby's show, Sir Hugh Casson and Sir Roger de Grey. Lived in London.

Margaret MEE 1909–1988 Painter of botanical subjects, born in Chesham, Buckinghamshire, who studied under Victor Pasmore at Camberwell School of Arts and Crafts, 1947–50. With her artist husband Greville she moved to São Paulo, Brazil, in 1952 and was captivated by the tropical flora of the forests and coastal mountains. Worked for a period as official artist at the Botanical Institute of São Paulo, moved to Rio de Janeiro in 1968 and then became a freelance botanical artist. Her 15 long, arduous journeys to the Amazon forests were described in her book *Margaret Mee – in search of flowers of the Amazon Forest*, 1988. Mee completed over 400 folio gouache compositions, 15 diaries and about 25 sketchbooks packed with detailed drawings in the field. A small display was staged at Camden Arts Centre, 1995, loaned by the Royal Botanic Gardens, Kew. Her work is best known through two superb folio books: *Flowers of the Brazilian Forests*, 1968, and *Flores do Amazonas – Flowers of the Amazon*, 1980. Mee's sister was the artist Dora Prower.

Charlie MEECHAM 1950– Artist who used photography to study the changing nature of urban and natural environments in Britain and abroad. He was born in Oxfordshire and studied photography at Manchester Polytechnic, 1971–4. Group exhibitions included British Landscape, Maryland Institute in Baltimore, America, 1988, and New North, Tate Gallery Liverpool, 1990. After solo exhibitions at the Museum of Modern Art in Oxford and Whitechapel Art Gallery, both 1974–6, had many others, later ones including Landscape for the Car, Posterngate Gallery, Hull, 1989. Arts Council holds examples. Lived in West Yorkshire.

Dora MEESON fl. from c.1905–1955 Painter, born in Melbourne, Australia, who worked under her maiden name of Dora Meeson. She married the artist George Coates, of whom she wrote a memoir. She began to study art while living in Melbourne, then in England attended the Slade School of Fine Art, under Henry Tonks, going to Paris to study at the Académie

Julian. Exhibited ROI, RA, RSA, SWA and Paris Salon, where she gained an Hon. Mention. The National Maritime Museum, Greenwich, Port of London Authority and many Australian galleries hold her work. Lived in London.

Marjorie MEGGITT 1906– Sculptor, born in Sheffield. She attended the College of Art there under the sculptor Francis Jahn, then the Royal Academy Schools, her teachers including Sir William Reid Dick and William McMillan. In 1930 she won the Schools gold medal and Travelling Scholarship and the Prix de Rome for Sculpture, enabling her to study at the British School in Rome, 1932–5. Exhibited RA, Royal Glasgow Institute of the Fine Arts and in the provinces. Among a variety of public commissions was the children's shelter in Guilford Street in Bloomsbury, London. Lived in London.

Else MEIDNER 1901–1987 Painter and draughtsman, born in Berlin, where she studied at the Kunstgewerbe Museum's teaching department, 1918–25, with Adolf Meyer. She also studied at Lewin-Funke art school under the Expressionist Ludwig Meidner, whom she married in 1927. He influenced her work, as did her friend, Käthe Kollwitz. After some success in Germany, with the advent of the Nazis Else Meidner moved to London in 1939 with her husband, who returned to Germany in 1952. She remained in London, visiting him until his death in 1966. She showed at Ben Uri and with Margaret Fischer. In 1990 John Denham Gallery included her in a show of exiled artists. Ben Uri Art Society holds her work.

Ludwig MEIDNER 1884–1966 Artist and teacher, born in Bernstadt, Germany, who from the early years of the century studied first in Breslau, then Berlin and Paris. He went on to develop an Expressionist style and work at Lewin-Funke art school, where he taught his artist wife Else whom he married in 1927. They moved to England in 1939, but while she remained he returned to live first in Frankfurt, then Darmstadt, where she continued to visit him. They shared a show at Ben Uri Art Society, which holds his work, in 1949; he later showed in Italy and in 1985 Kunstverein Wolfsburg, Germany, commemorated him.

Jean MEIKLE: *see* **Jean OSBORNE**

Alicia MELAMED 1927– Artist, mainly in oil, born in Borystaw, Poland, also known as Alicia Melamed Adams. Married at 16, she and her husband left Poland in 1950, settling in Paris for two years where she attended the Alliance Française. In London she studied at St Martin's School of Art, 1960–3, and Sir John Cass School of Art, in Paris at L'Académie de la Grande Chaumière. Her teachers included Harold Workman, Vivian Pitchforth, David Graham and John Pelling. Melamed's pictures were richly coloured and romantic, flowers and figures featuring strongly. Her ideas were "usually triggered by a photograph, and when I don't have any I paint flowers and fruit with a cup with a heart on it. This has become almost a signature." She was a member of UA and Ridley Art Club. Exhibitions included RA Summer Exhibition, Foyles Gallery and abroad. Later solo shows included Mermaid Theatre, 1991, and Leicester City Gallery, 1993. Lived in London.

Colin MELBOURNE 1928– Sculptor and teacher, born and lived in Newcastle-under-Lyme, Staffordshire. After a period with Josiah Wedgwood attended Royal College of Art, 1948–51. After teaching at Stoke-on-Trent College of Art was on staff of the North Staffordshire Polytechnic, then freelanced. His effigy of a steelworker in steel and a bronze of Sir Henry Doulton were both completed for Hanley.

George MELHUISH 1916–1985 Painter and writer of a philosophical nature, born in Bristol, where he lived, somewhat mysteriously, until his death. Bristol City Council declined to accept conditional bequest of his fine neo-Gothic house, which he had filled with art treasures, because it was impracticable to open to the public. Studied art in London and Paris and showed at RA, in war artists exhibitions at National Gallery during World War II, Arts Council, RWA, in galleries in the West of England and had series of one-man shows. Public galleries in Bristol, Bournemouth, Walsall, Worcester and elsewhere hold his work, as does Imperial War Museum. Melhuish wrote *The Paradoxical Universe*, 1959, and *The Paradoxical Nature of Reality*, 1973.

Sylvia MELLAND 1906–1993 Printmaker and painter, born in Altrincham, Cheshire. She studied at Manchester College of Art; Byam Shaw School, 1925–8, with Ernest Jackson; Euston Road School, 1937–9, with William Coldstream; and the Central School, 1957–60, under Merlyn Evans and Tony Harrison. Travelled extensively, including South Africa, 1930–2, and then to France, Poland, Czechoslovakia, Denmark and Sweden. In Paris in 1934 Cubism was an influence. During World War II Melland was actively involved with Civil Defence Artists' Group. She exhibited regularly with RE and WIAC; joined Roter Treiter Group of Printmakers in Munich in 1961; in 1970 joining Free Painters and Sculptors. She showed solo with Wertheim and Jackson Galleries, Manchester; Zwemmer Gallery; and in Italy and Switzerland. Many public collections hold her work, including Victoria & Albert Museum and Manchester City Art Gallery. Boundary Gallery held a retrospective in 1997. Lived in London.

Margaret MELLIS 1914– Painter, maker of reliefs and collages and sculptor, born in Wu-Kung-Fu, China, of Scottish parents. Moved to Britain as a baby, was educated in Edinburgh and attended the College of Art there, 1929–33, her teachers including Hubert Wellington and S J Peploe. A postgraduate award and scholarship enabled her to study and travel on the continent, where she was taught in Paris by André Lhote. From 1935–7 she held a fellowship at Edinburgh College of Art. Then studied at Euston Road School and in 1939 with her first husband, Adrian Stokes (she later married Francis Davison), moved to St Ives where they became key figures in the artists' colony. There she was influenced by Ben Nicholson and Naum Gabo and adopted a Constructivist style, making reliefs, returning to painting after the war, when she lived for two years from 1948 in the south of France. Returning to England in 1950 she went to live in Suffolk, settling in Southwold, where found objects and driftwood were employed in her work. Exhibited widely in group shows and had many solo exhibitions, including AIA Gallery, Bear Lane Gallery in Oxford, Redfern Gallery and a retrospective at City Art Centre, Edinburgh, 1997. Victoria & Albert Museum, Ferens Art Gallery in Hull and other public galleries hold examples.

Campbell A MELLON 1876–1955 Painter in oil, especially of East Anglian beach and coastal scenes. Having studied painting privately with Carl Brennir in Nottingham, Mellon went to to settle in Gorleston-on-Sea, Norfolk, at the end of World War I, where he had tuition for three years from Arnesby Brown. Their styles are similar, and Mellon became noted for his small, uncomplicated, breezy panels of the Norfolk seaside. His pictures are in public collections in Bristol, Yarmouth, Sheffield and elsewhere. He exhibited Fine Art Society, RA, ROI, RBA, Walker Art Gallery, Liverpool, and in other galleries.

Eric James MELLON 1925– Artist in a variety of media, including prints and ceramics, who studied at Watford, Harrow and Central Schools of Art. He was married to the painter Martina Thomas (1924–95), and his show Living with Angels, in 1996 at Pallant House, Chichester, was dedicated to her. Mellon's other shows included Victoria & Albert Museum, 1972 and 1994; David Paul Gallery, Chichester, and British Craft Centre, both 1978; Solomon Gallery, Dublin, 1983; and Gainsborough's House, Sudbury, 1988. Lived in Bognor Regis, Sussex.

Dawn MELLOR 1970– Artist, born in Manchester, who attended Central St Martins College of Art and Design, 1993–4, then Royal College of Art, 1994–6. Her paintings had a strong theatrical feel, with unusual lighting effects. Selected exhibitions/ performances included, 1995, Collaborative performances with Esther T Performance Company: *Careful* ... Title of performance, *Baby's Got a Gun*, performed at Queer Circus, Pride Arts Festival, Ministry of Sound; Torture Garden, The Brix Theatre; Summer Exhibition, ICA; Fist Substation South; Naive Madame JoJo's; Come Market Tavern. And in 1996: *30 minus*, Paton Gallery.

Joy MELLOR: *see* **Joy JONES**

Oscar MELLOR 1921– Self-taught artist in oil, photographer, publisher and teacher, born in Manchester. Mellor said that his themes "generally were figures in an environment, closely allied to the Surrealists". He was a photographer from the 1930s, teaching it at Exeter College of Art, 1969–81; began painting about 1946; and from 1952 was a publisher of poetry under the imprint Fantasy Press. His work was included in extensive group and solo shows in Oxford, Paris, Cheltenham, Didcot, London, Exeter and Birmingham. He was represented in The Birmingham Seven show at John Bonham, Murray Feely Fine Art in 1991. Arts Council holds examples. Lived in Clyst St Mary, Exeter, Devon.

Pam MELLOR fl. from 1940s– Painter and writer, born in Sydney, Australia, sister of the artist Deirdre Henty-Creer. She showed with RWS, RMS, Chelsea Art Society and Artists of Chelsea, Qantas Gallery, Ridley Art Club and Armed Forces' Art Society of which she was a committee member. Wrote *The Mystery of X5*. HRH The Prince of Wales holds her work. Lived in London.

Avram MELNIKOV 1892–1960 Sculptor, writer and composer, born in Bessarabia, Russia (sometimes known as Abraham, also as Melnikoff). He was the creator of the Trumpeldor Memorial at Tel Hai, Israel, national monument and place of pilgrimage (although a zealous Zionist, Melnikov's antecedents are believed to have been non-Jewish). The statue of Edmund, 1st Viscount Allenby, the British soldier, which stands in Beersheba, was also by Melnikov, who sculpted Sir Winston Churchill, Ernest Bevin and Gilbert Murray. After briefly studying medicine in Vienna, Melnikov went to America where he was a prizewinning student at the Chicago Art School. When World War I broke out he moved to Canada, joined the Army (in which he was a boxing champion), then travelled to England for training. Served under Allenby in the Middle East and joined the Jewish Brigade. After the war he helped form a Jerusalem Art School and during the 1921 riots commanded the Jerusalem section of Hagana to counter Arab riots. Settled in London in 1933, returning to Israel in 1957 and dying in Haifa. In 1944 Melnikov's novel *Mooshka* was published, an idyllic picture of pre-revolutionary Russian life which revealed his mastery of English. Exhibitions included Beaux Arts Gallery, 1936, and University of Haifa, 1982. Ben Uri Art Society holds examples.

Janet MELROSE 1964– Painter, draughtsman and teacher, born in Edinburgh, where she studied at the College of Art. From 1987 she taught art at Daniel Stewart's & Melville College in the city. In that year Melrose gained an Andrew Grant Bursary. Group shows included Summer Exhibition, Peter Potter Gallery, Haddington, 1986; Wildlife Exhibition, Kingfisher Gallery, Edinburgh, 1989; Aberdeen Artists' Society Summer Exhibition, Loomshop Gallery, Lower Largo, 1992; and Royal Over-Seas League Open, 1996. Had a solo show at Kingfisher Gallery, 1996, Journey of the Birds. The Line Partnership holds her work.

Stephen MELTON 1964– Sculptor, foundry manager and teacher. He did a foundation course at Barnsley College of Art, 1983–4, then an honours degree in sculpture at Camberwell College of Art, 1984–7. In 1987–8 gained a foundry diploma at Royal College of Art, in 1988 gaining The Angeloni Award for Best Founder at the College. In that year he studied casting techniques with Tuareg tribes in Sahara, and in 1990 foundry techniques in Sri Lanka and kiln building in Japan. In 1989–90 he opened the Melton Bronze Foundry in Ashford, then Canterbury. He also participated in some performances, such as White Wing at Museum of Modern Art, Oxford, 1989. Taught, notably at South Kent College of Technology and at Kent Institute of Art & Design. In 1989 he was personal sculptor to Sir Eduardo Paolozzi.

Commissions included Royal Festival Hall, 1986, and in 1997 Melton's depiction of a young City of London trader was sited outside the Liffe building in Walbrook. Showed widely in group exhibitions from 1983–6 at Ardsley Gallery, other venues including Yorkshire Sculpture Park, 1987, and Sculpture at Canterbury, 1992.

Harald MELVILL fl. from 1930s– Painter, playwright, stage designer and teacher, educated in London and Brighton. Although he showed at several venues, including Chester, Dowdeswell and Maddox Street Galleries, Melvill was mainly noted for his association with the stage. He was a scenic designer and painter; lectured on the subject in the 1960s at Manchester University; and wrote a series of books with titles such as *Theatrecraft* and *Historic Costume for the Amateur Theatre*. Lived in London and St Agnes, Cornwall.

John MELVILLE 1902–1986 Painter, born in London, but moved with his family in childhood to Birmingham where he continued to live. Largely self-taught, Melville towards the end of the 1920s became associated with the Modern Group in Birmingham. By the early-1930s he was connected with the Surrealists in London and had acquired a valuable patron in Birmingham, a civil servant, Enoch Lockett. In 1938 some of Melville's works were banned from an exhibition in Birmingham by local councillors as being "detrimental to public sensibility". Just before World War II, during which Melville worked for the Ministry of Food in Birmingham, the artist published a series of pieces in the Surrealist publication *London Bulletin*. From the 1950s Melville taught for a time in the extra-mural department of Birmingham University. For many years, however, he remained a largely neglected painter working away in provincial obscurity, his reputation getting a revival with the fiftieth anniversary of the International Surrealist Exhibition. He had exhibited widely from the 1930s at St George's Gallery, Wertheim Gallery, RBSA and elsewhere and was featured in international shows of Surrealist and Dada art. Blond Fine Art had a retrospective show in 1986, Gothick Dream Fine Art a memorial exhibition in 1987. His brother was the writer Robert Melville.

Derek MENARY 1943– Painter who studied at Belfast College of Art, 1962–5, then worked in production design with BBC. Was at Dartington College of Arts, 1970–2, then at Rolle College, Exeter University, 1972–3. Group shows included RA, RUA, RWA and Curwen Gallery. Had a solo show at Upper Street Gallery in 1975, two at Oxford Gallery in Oxford, 1976–81, later shows including Salt House Gallery in St Ives and Studio Gallery in Bristol both 1991. In 1992 he shared a show at Sweet Waters Gallery. Arts Council of Northern Ireland holds his work.

Adrien de MENASCE 1925–1995 Painter and collagist for whom painting was a daily passion, despite the resulting poverty. Menasce (pronounced Menash) was born in Alexandria, Egypt, into a cultured upper-class Jewish family, his father being Baron Edmond de Menasce. Adrien was bilingual in French and English. The family had connections, directly or through relations, with Proust, Cavafy and Lawrence Durrell. Although in 1947 Adrien studied briefly in Paris in the studio of André Lhote and with pupils of his in Alexandria, he claimed that "my main source of study has been the countless hours I have spent in museums". Balthus and Jungian analysis were important influences. In 1966 he settled in London and adopted British nationality. Although he had had an exhibition at the important Charles Lienhard gallery in Zürich with help from Herbert Read, with another at Fischer Fine Art in 1972, which the critics chose to ignore, Adrien worked in obscurity, apart from the support of a few keen collectors. His output ranged from paintings of the crucifixion to witty collages based on newspaper photographs of English footballers. He would spend years on a canvas and for a long time was working towards a major exhibition. Many of the canvases, in muted colours and in which parts of bodies and hats hovered, were included in a memorial exhibition at The Mayor Gallery, 1996.

Renée MENDEL 1908– Sculptor, notably of figures, and ceramic artist, born in Elmshorn, Germany, who studied at university in Berlin, Frankfurt and Paris and art in Berlin and Paris. Showed at RA, Salon d'Automne in Paris, Camden Arts Centre and Heal's and had a solo exhibition with Royal Copenhagen Porcelain. National Portrait Gallery holds her sculpture of the writer James Joyce. Lived for many years in London.

Anne MENDELOW 1947– Artist in oil, watercolour, pastel and monoprint, and gallery owner, born in South Africa, who emigrated to Scotland in 1977, founding The Gatehouse Gallery in Glasgow, 1988, where she showed. Studied at Glasgow School of Art, life drawing under John Boyd, Norman Edgar and Parick Dorrian. Began painting and drawing in 1968, and was a professional member of SSWA, and a member of Glasgow Society of Women Artists and Royal Glasgow Institute of the Fine Arts. The female form was her favourite subject, still lifes being inspired by those of the Scottish Colourist S J Peploe. Solo exhibitions included Tron Theatre, Glasgow, 1984.

Dinora MENDELSON 1924– Painter in a rich palette, notable for portraits, life studies and remote, mountainous landscapes. She was the stepdaughter of David Bomberg, the daughter of Lilian Holt by her first marriage to Jacob Mendelson and was at one time married to the artist Leslie Marr. She studied with Bomberg at Borough Polytechnic, 1947–53, and was a member of Borough Group and Borough Bottega. Was included in Borough Group show at Fine Art Associates, 1989. Also showed with LG, NS, at Archer, Arcade, Bookworm and Berkeley Galleries and elsewhere. Ben Uri Art Society holds her work. Lived in Sunbury on Thames, Middlesex.

Theo MENDEZ 1934–1997 Artist in oil, acrylic and collage, muralist and teacher, born and lived in London. He studied at Camberwell School of Art, 1950–4 and 1956–7, and at London University, 1957–8. Teachers included Martin Bloch and Michael Rothenstein. Mendez taught at Camberwell part-time, 1958–63, then full-time until 1984 when he took early retirement to paint full-time; from 1976 he was head of department, textiles. In the mid-1970s Mendez was the tutor in charge of about 40 big murals produced for Southwark Borough Council by students. In his own work Mendez believed with Picasso that "nothing is produced without solitude". He took part in group shows at Redfern Gallery, Victoria & Albert Museum, Bear Lane Gallery in Oxford and Arnolfini Gallery, Bristol, and in the 1972 and 1979 John Moores Liverpool Exhibitions. Had own-studio solo exhibitions, 1987–9–92.

Anthony MENDLESON 1915– Costume designer and painter, born in London where he continued to live. After education at St Paul's School he studied art at Chiswick Polytechnic, France and Italy. Although he showed at Redfern and Piccadilly Galleries and elsewhere, he was primarily known as a costume designer, working for Ealing Studios for about a decade from 1947.

June MENDOZA fl. from 1960s– Portrait painter, born in Melbourne, Australia, into a musical family. Following education there she studied briefly at St Martin's School of Art, having from childhood been interested in portraiture. After a period involved in illustration for magazines, books and record sleeves Mendoza concentrated on portraits internationally, based in London, to both public and private commission. Was a member of RP, ROI and Contemporary Portrait Society and was an honorary member of SWA. Portraits included HM The Queen, TRH The Prince and Princess of Wales, HM Queen Elizabeth the Queen Mother, the politician Lady Thatcher and other international government figures. A series of musicians included the conductor Sir George Solti and Dame Joan Sutherland, the opera singer. Group portraits included the House of Commons in Session, for the House, and the House of Representatives, Canberra, Australia.

Bernard MENINSKY 1891–1950 Painter, draughtsman and teacher, born in Karotopin, Ukraine, father of the artist Philip Meninsky. A few weeks after birth he was taken to England and was brought up in Liverpool, where he attended the School of Art in 1906 after attending evening classes in art. In 1911 left with King's Medal, having in the meantime studied briefly at Royal College of Art and Académie Julian, Paris. With a scholarship he entered the Slade School of Fine Art, 1912–13. In 1913 worked for Edward Gordon Craig at his theatre school in Florence, returning to teach at the Central School of Arts and Crafts. After several years in the Army, in 1918 was naturalised a British citizen, had a nervous breakdown and was discharged from service after six months as a Ministry of Information war artist. In 1919, having returned to Central School, Meninsky had first solo show, at Goupil Gallery. In 1920 he began teaching at Westminster School of Art, where he was an influential tutor in life drawing, being a superb figure draughtsman. Later Meninsky was to teach at Oxford City School of Art, 1940, and again at the Central, 1945. A highly sensitive man, Meninsky had periodical mental trouble, finally committing suicide. He had shown with LG and NEAC both of which he was a member; had published *Mother and Child: 28 Drawings by Bernard Meninsky*, 1928, and illustrated Milton's *L'Allegro* and *Il Penseroso*, 1946; and had designed sets and costumes for the ballet *David* for the Markova-Dolin Company in 1935. Arts Council memorial exhibition, 1951–2, and retrospective show at Adams Gallery, 1958. A retrospective touring Museum of Modern Art and elsewhere was held in 1981. Tate Gallery and provincial galleries hold his work. Lived in London.

Philip MENINSKY 1919– Figurative painter and draughtsman, born in London, younger son of the artist Bernard Meninsky. After education in Hertfordshire Meninsky joined the Army in World War II, was taken prisoner by the Japanese, worked on the Siam-Burma railway and made drawings for the Australian medical authorities. They were used at war crime trials, and the Imperial War Museum has a collection. HRH The Duke of Edinburgh and the Lillie Art Gallery, Milngavie, also hold Meninsky's work. After the war Meninsky lived in Scotland, where he met William and Mary Armour and became associated with Glasgow School of Art. He showed with RSA, SSA, RSW and the Royal Glasgow Institute of the Fine Arts. His first solo show was under the auspices of Scottish Arts Council in 1961, his first London one-man exhibition at Leighton House in 1975. In 1982 Meninsky began to paint dancers, was appointed artist to English National Ballet School, 1990, and his World of Dance exhibition was held at Dillon Gallery, Barnes, 1995. In 1996 there was a 50-year retrospective at Kingston Museum, Kingston upon Thames.

John MENNIE 1911–1983 Painter, printmaker and teacher, born in Aberdeen, who studied at Gray's School of Art there and at Westminster School of Art under Blair Hughes-Stanton and Mark Gertler. He was an associate of RMS, also showing with RA and RP and solo with Medici Society. Imperial War Museum has a group of works by Mennie, including drawings and lino-cuts and depictions Japanese prisoner-of-war camps. Lived in London where he taught for the Inner London Education Authority.

Gordon MENZIES 1950– Artist in pastel, aquatint, engraving and ceramic, born in Motherwell, Scotland. He attended Duncan of Jordanstone College of Art, Dundee, 1969–73, teachers including Ron Stenberg, James Morrison and Sheila Green; then with S W Hayter, at Atelier 17, in Paris, 1974. Menzies won the Josef Sekalski Award for Printmaking. He showed at RSA, SSA, Compass Gallery in Glasgow and Potter Gallery, Haddington. In 1982 he established the Ion Pottery/Gallery, where he showed his work year-round. Lived on Isle of Iona, Argyll.

Llewelyn Frederick MENZIES-JONES 1889–1973 Painter, etcher, pastellist and potter, born in Carshalton, Surrey. Menzies-Jones studied at Eton College and Oxford University, the Slade School of Fine Art and Royal College of Art. He returned to Eton, teaching in the drawing schools and developing a pottery school. He was known as Mones and appears in Wilfrid Blunt's memoir

Slow on the Feather, where he is described as "a tall, courtly, middle-aged, well-to-do, eccentric Welshman, a bachelor of course, gaunt as Don Quixote". Blunt chronicles his mental decline and how "finally he faded away to a remote village in Oxfordshire where he died". Menzies-Jones was a member of the Arts Club who exhibited at RI, Walker's Galleries, NS and Paris Salon.

Moelwyn MERCHANT 1913–1997 Academic, writer, sculptor, poet and priest, born in Port Talbot, Glamorgan, full name William Moelwyn Merchant. He graduated in English and history at University College in Cardiff and began teaching at Carmarthen Grammar School in 1935. Held a series of academic posts, including professor of English at University of Exeter, 1961–74. Was ordained to Anglican Orders, 1940. Wrote a number of books, including *Wordsworth's Guide to the Lakes*, illustrated by John Piper, 1952; *Breaking the Code*, poems, 1975; a novel, *Fire from the Heights*, 1989; and *Fragments of a Life*, his autobiography, 1990. His career as a sculptor began in 1964, influenced by Barbara Hepworth. Merchant's sculptures were often erect, their subjects ranging from the human to natural forms and symbolic images. Had several dozen solo shows, in Exeter, Cardiff, Swansea, Plymouth, London and elsewhere from 1971. Was included in the Welsh Sculpture Trust's 1983 Sculpture in a Country Park, at Margam Park. In later years Merchant was closely involved with Eton College, which holds his manuscripts and correspondence. Lived in Leamington Spa, Warwickshire.

Julian MEREDITH 1952– Printmaker, painter, draughtsman and teacher, born in Bath, Somerset. He studied at Exeter College of Art, 1971–4. Travelled in Zambia, Malawi and Botswana, 1977. Meredith until 1988 worked a smallholding in Norfolk, then moved to the north of England. In 1992 he ran two workshops for Royal Academy Schools, then in 1993 again spent time in Zambia, the year he received a Cleveland Arts Grant. Took part in mixed exhibitions, including RA, RE, RWA and Marlborough Graphics, winning several prizes. Meredith enjoyed working with wood and Oriental paper, producing large prints; one, of a humpback whale, was 30-feet long. Favoured subjects were plants, fish, birds and animals, as in his Scarborough Art Gallery touring show, 1993–4. Victoria & Albert Museum and Cartwright Hall, Bradford, hold examples.

Norman MEREDITH 1909– Artist born in Liverpool, working in pen and ink and Normatone, from 1976 in full colour and bodycolour, full name Eric Norman Meredith; teacher. Meredith studied at Liverpool City Art School, 1925–31, and Royal College of Art, 1931–4, a Travelling Scholar under Sir William Rothenstein and Stanley Spencer. Lectured in art at University College, Aberystwyth, 1935, during World War II being technical illustrator for Ministry of Aircraft Production at Farnborough, then was a visiting lecturer at St Martin's School of Art, 1947–74. Meredith worked for *Punch, Tatler, Bystander, Sketch*; was a texile designer for Moygashel; and illustrated over 100 books, specialising in historical subjects. From 1984 showed regularly at Chris Beetles, having a first solo exhibition in 1985. Humorous animals in bodycolour were a feature of Meredith's later output. Lived at Stoneleigh, Epsom, Surrey.

Morris MEREDITH WILLIAMS 1881–1973 Painter, stained glass artist and illustrator, born in Cowbridge, Glamorgan. Was married in 1906 to the artist Gertrude Alice Meredith Williams, who died in 1934. He studied at Slade School of Fine Art and in Italy and France. During World War I he served in the Army in France and completed work based on his Somme front experiences. Work by Williams and his wife is at the Scottish National War Museum in Edinburgh. He painted widely in France and showed in Liverpool and elsewhere, sometimes signing as M M Williams.

Jack MERRIOTT 1901–1968 Painter, poster designer, illustrator and teacher. Studied at Croydon School of Art and St Martin's School of Art. He was a member of the Wapping Group of Artists, of which for a time he was vice-president; Croydon Art Society; Langham Sketch Club; and St Ives Society of Artists. Exhibited RA, ROI, RI, RWA and RBA. Bradford City Art Gallery and Sunderland Museum and Art Gallery hold his work, which is characterised by a breezy freshness, crisp, with well-controlled colour. Lived at Polperro, Cornwall, an area he often painted.

Christine MERTON 1925– Sculptor, painter and teacher, born in Germany, who studied painting at Chelsea College of Art, 1959–62, then ceramics at Sir John Cass College of Art, 1972. Taught at Sir John Cass and at Camden Arts Centre. Exhibitions included WIAC, 1975; National Museum of Wales in Cardiff and Whitechapel Art Gallery, both 1976; British Crafts Centre, 1978; City of London Polytechnic, 1979; and Oxford Gallery in Oxford and Clay Sculpture at Yorkshire Sculpture Park, both 1980.

John Ralph MERTON 1913– Artist craftsman, working to commission in his own form of tempera, silverpoint, pencil and charcoal. He was born in London, son of Sir Thomas Merton, and studied at Eton College, Oxford University and Ruskin School of Drawing, notable teachers including Kenneth Clark. Had a solo exhibition at Colnaghi, 1938, and showed regularly at RA Summer Exhibition from 1948. Merton served in air photo reconnaissance research in World War II, attaining the rank of lieutenant-colonel, 1944. He was especially noted for his meticulously crafted portraits, many of which were illustrated in *A Journey Through An Artist's Life*, published privately in 1994, a sumptuous volume costing £250. Among his sitters were The Countess of Dalkeith, at Drumlanrig, 1958; Sir Charles Evans, 1973; Triple Portrait of Sir David Piper, 1984, in National Portrait Gallery; Triple Portrait of HRH The Princess of Wales, for Cardiff City Hall, 1987; HM The Queen, at Windsor Castle, 1989; and Paul H Nitze, in Johns Hopkins University, 1991. There was a loan exhibition of portraits at Christopher Wood Gallery, 1995. Lived in Oare, Wiltshire.

Sonia MERVYN 1893–1977 Painter and teacher, notable for portraits. She won a scholarship to the Royal College of Music but after getting her degree decided to pursue art, winning a scholarship to the Regent Street Polytechnic School of Art where she trained under Ralph Middleton Todd. During the early years of World War II she worked on the land and was then invited to teach at Maidstone Art School, 1943–5. After the war she started private classes and completed many commissions throughout Britain. Her students included many famous people, such as the actor Terry-Thomas and the pianist Eileen Joyce. Exhibited at all the leading London galleries, including Beaux Arts and Leicester Galleries, RA, NEAC and had pictures toured by AEB and Arts Council. Her work drew admiring letters from Sir Alfred Munnings, Sir Stanley Spencer, Dame Ethel Walker, Philip Connard and other painters. Southampton City Art Gallery had a show of her work in 1990. Lived at Milford-on-Sea, Hampshire.

Édouard Léon Théodore MESENS 1903–1971 Artist in collage, art dealer, poet, writer, editor and collector, born and died in Brussels, Belgium. He studied music at the Conservatoire there for several years from 1919, met the composer Erik Satie and visited Paris, where he mixed with the artistically avant-garde. Back in Belgium, Mesens promoted Surrealism; he was Belgian representative at the International Surrealist Exhibition in London in 1936. Ran the London Gallery, set up in Cork Street with the financial support of Roland Penrose, 1938–51, editing *The London Bulletin*, 1938–40, in 1944 producing the publication *Message from Nowhere*. During the war, Mesens worked for the Belgian service of the BBC at Bush House. After hostilities he reformed the London Gallery with a financial struggle, with George Melly, then an aspiring jazz singer, as one of his assistants. Mesens showed artists such as Magritte, whom he especially promoted and collected, Klee, Masson, Severini and Max Ernst alongside Conroy Maddox, John Banting and Eileen Agar, who gives memories of him in her autobiography *A Look at My Life*. Following the collapse of the London Gallery, Mesens put on a number of scholarly exhibitions in Belgium. Mesens' collected poems were published in 1959. His collection of pictures was impressive and valuable in his later years and his own work, carried out spasmodically, is in galleries in Belgium and elsewhere. A tribute to the London Gallery was held at John Bonham, Murray Feely Fine Art in 1992. The best account of his quirky personality is in George Melly's *Don't Tell Sybil, An Intimate Memoir of E L T Mesens*.

Isabel Beatrice MESHAM 1896– Painter and printmaker. Born at Gorey, County Wexford, Ireland, of a British Army family. Exhibited RA, other London galleries, at the Paris Salon and in Lisbon. Had several English and foreign one-man shows. Lived at St Marychurch, Torquay, Devon.

Yair MESHOULAM: *see* **YAIR**

Oliver MESSEL 1904–1978 Theatrical and film designer and decorator and painter, born in London, his father Lieutenant-Colonel Leonard Messel, his mother Maud the daughter of the black-and-white artist Linley Sambourne. Attended Eton College, 1917–21, leaving early for the Slade School of Fine Art. By the early 1930s he was one of Britain's principal stage designers, having had great success with productions such as the Cochran Revues; his baroque style raised standards and attracted its own public. Operatic, ballet and film productions and royal command performances followed. In World War II Messel served as a captain in the Army. His books included *Stage Designs and Costumes*, 1933; *Designs for A Midsummer Night's Dream*, issued by The Folio Society, 1957; and designs for Adrianne Allen and Marjorie Salter's *Delightful Food*, 1958. Messel's exhibitions included Portrait Paintings at Leicester Galleries, 1938; Paintings and Designs, Redfern Gallery, 1951; and O'Hana Gallery, 1962. The Oliver Messel Suite at the Dorchester Hotel was popular; he designed for the reconstruction of Flaxley Abbey in Gloucestershire, 1958–65; worked on Queen's Park Theatre, houses and garden at Bridgetown, Barbados, 1967–75; and did extensive designs for buildings on the island of Mustique, 1968–75. Messel's final years, plagued by ill-health, were spent in St James, Barbados. In 1982 his nephew, the Earl of Snowdon, lent for an indefinite period to the Victoria & Albert Museum a large archive of Messel's production material.

Tony MESSENGER 1936– Artist and teacher who was born and lived in London where he studied at London College of Printing and Royal College of Art. During the 1960s he worked as a designer for *Ambassador* magazine and produced illustrations for the BBC. He taught painting at Wolverhampton Polytechnic and Camberwell College of Arts. Showed at RA, LG and Young Contemporaries and had his first solo exhibition at Trafford Gallery in 1957. In 1991 Messenger was included in England & Co's Art in Boxes, with Paint Box, as well as the same venue's The 1960's, in 1993.

Charles MESSENT 1911–1971 Painter, notably in enamel, born in Felixstowe, Suffolk. He studied at the Regional College of Art in Manchester and privately in Egypt. Museum of Modern Art, in Cairo, holds his work. Messent exhibited widely, especially in the north of England, and was a founder-member of the Manchester Group. Among venues where he exhibited were Manchester City Art Gallery, which holds his work; Whitechapel Art Gallery; NEAC; and Paris Salon. Lived at Hassocks, Sussex.

Roi de MESTRE: *see* **Roy de MAISTRE**

Muriel METCALFE 1910– Artist, born in Leyburn, Yorkshire, who early developed a gift for painting and drawing. Aged 14 she gained the Hatton Scholarship to attend Newcastle School of Art, but had to wait two years before she was able to join classes because of the rules. In 1933 she married the artist Fred Lawson and their work and that of their daughter Sonia Lawson was featured in A Family of Artists, organised by Wakefield Art Gallery in 1989; it holds her work. Contributed to Yorkshire Artists shows at Leeds, Bradford and Scarborough; showed at Royal Glasgow Institute of the Fine Arts; and in 1957 exhibited jointly with her daughter at Dewsbury Art Gallery. St Margaret's Church, Preston-under-Scar, commissioned a mural from Metcalfe in 1932. She continued active into the 1960s despite poor health and lived on in the cottage at Castle Bolton, Yorkshire, which she had shared with Fred Lawson.

Sidney METEYARD 1868–1947 Painter, notably in tempera, and stained glass artist. Meteyard studied at the Birmingham School of Art under Edward Taylor and was one of the original members of the Birmingham Group of Painters and Craftsmen, which included Joseph Southall, Arthur Gaskin and Henry Payne. He married the artist, jeweller and illuminator Kate M Eadie. Meteyard exhibited at the RA, RBSA, Walker Art Gallery, Liverpool, and at the Paris Salon. Illustrated the poet Henry Longfellow's *The Golden Legend.* Sometimes signed work with a monogram, but usually it remained unsigned. Lived in Birmingham.

Lord METHUEN 1886–1974 Landscape and figure painter, real name Paul Ayshford, born in Corsham, Wiltshire. Methuen took a degree in natural science at New College, Oxford. While there he studied painting under Sir Charles Holmes, later under Walter Sickert, whose influence remained. Methuen became assistant at the Transvaal Museum, Pretoria, 1910–14. After World War I Army service he was at first livestock officer and then marketing officer to the Ministry of Agriculture; all his life he remained a countryman, interested in scientific farming. He now gradually established himself as a painter, having a first one-man show at the Warren Gallery, 1928. He had many solo exhibitions at the Leicester Galleries and at Colnaghi's and showed at RA and NEAC. Tate Gallery and Victoria & Albert Museum hold his work. Methuen held a number of official positions in the art world, including presidency of the RWA and trusteeship of the National Gallery and Tate Gallery, 1938–45. He was elected RA in 1959. His World War II Army service was recalled in *Normandy Diary*, 1952. After the war he offered part of the family home, Corsham Court, to the Bath Academy of Art, run by Clifford and Rosemary Ellis. Methuen had a retrospective in 1973 and a memorial show in 1975 at the Fieldborne Galleries.

David METHUEN CAMPBELL 1929– Painter in oil and teacher, born in Glasgow, husband of the artist Anne Martin. He studied at Bath Academy of Art, Corsham, 1950–1, with William Scott; in Paris in 1951–2, with Fernand Léger and Arpad Szenecs; then at Royal College of Art, 1952–6. Methuen Campbell worked in Britain, Norway and France, being a visiting lecturer at Maidstone College of Art, 1967–8. His main works were yellow Dune and The Gower Series, and The Nabis were an important influence. Group shows included RA Summer Exhibition, 1956–8; Howard Davies Gallery, Cardiff, 1957; Bradford City Art Gallery from 1957; LG, 1965; and Stubbing Studio, Sagaponack, America, 1989. He had solo shows at Eton College Drawing School, 1960, and Sandford Gallery, 1980. Lived in London.

Graham METSON 1934– Artist and teacher involved in painting, drawing, photomontage, collage and video, born in London. He studied at Cambridge School of Art, at College of St Mark and St John, Chelsea, 1957, and gained his master's degree at London University Institute of Education, 1965. His teachers included Henry Moore and John Heartfield, whom he met in 1956 as a five-artist delegation to East Germany, the year Metson had his first solo and group exhibitions in England and on the continent. In 1960 he began creating performance pieces with Richard Hamilton and other Pop Art artists. After visiting America for a solo show at Georgia Museum of Art in 1967, in 1968 Metson emigrated there, was visiting artist at 30 universities, art galleries and museums and created art events and exhibitions. After a solo show at ICA in 1972 Metson went to teach at Nova Scotia College of Art and Design, taking Canadian citizenship. He moved his studio to Montreal in 1986, teaching at Concordia University and the University of Ottawa. Metson moved his home to Gloucester, Ontario, in 1995, but retained a flat in London, which he visited regularly. Later solo exhibitions included Playhouse Gallery, Harlow, 1988; a retrospective of smaller works at Gallery 78, Fredericton, 1992; and Immolation, Beaverbrook Art Gallery, Fredericton, and tour, 1992–4. Many public collections hold Metson's work, including Beaverbrook Art Gallery, Essex University, Harlow Development Corporation, Manchester City Art Gallery and University of Kentucky.

Graham Peter METSON 1950– Draughtsman, painter and printmaker who studied at Edinburgh College of Art, 1970–74, then did a postgraduate certificate, art and drama, at Bretton Hall College (Leeds University), 1975–6. Among awards were an Andrew Grant Award, 1974–5; Daniela Jesson Fine Art Prize for Landscape Study, Artists in Essex, 1990; and Most Promising Artist's Award, Eastern Open, 1991. Metson said that "the content and subject matter of my works are particularly the natural energies of the planet relevant to ecological issues." Group exhibitions included Scottish Young Contemporaries, Edinburgh, 1973–4; and Printmakers' Workshop there, 1975; Usher Gallery, Lincoln, 1984; RA Summer Exhibition, 1991; and International Print Exhibition, Yokohama, Japan, 1995. Had a solo exhibition at Gallery 20, Brighton, 1978, later ones including Loughton Central Library, 1995. The Grant Institute of Geology at Edinburgh University, Cambridgeshire Libraries and Epping Forest District Museum hold examples. Lived in Chelmsford, Essex.

Gustav METZGER 1926– Artist and theorist, born in Nuremberg, Germany, who emigrated to Britain in 1939. Studied at Sir John Cass Institute, at the Borough Polytechnic under David Bomberg, at the Anglo-French Art Centre, Antwerp Academy and Oxford School of Art. Was a founder-member of Borough Bottega with Bomberg and others, taking part in its first show at Berkeley Gallery, 1953; within a few years became dissatisfied with painting and began to theorise about auto-destruction. Had a first solo show at 14 Monmouth Street, 1959. Metzger was secretary for the Destruction in Art symposium in 1966, then was editor of *Page*, bulletin of the Computer Arts Society, 1969–72.

His Earth Minus Environment project, with 120 cars and motor car exhaust in plastic tubing, originally appeared at Documenta, Kassel, in 1972. Metzger lived for some years in Amsterdam, returning to London late in 1994, in the following year having a solo exhibition at Workfortheeyetodo in which his second version of Earth Minus Environment was shown. By then Metzger had taken part in many international events and symposia, having spoken on auto-destructive art at University of Frankfurt, 1981; had displayed documents, lectured and demonstrated at University of Sussex, 1983; had begun work on research for a monograph on Vermeer in 1990 (gave several papers on Vermeer in 1994); and in 1993 had drawn up plans for an Elements Centre on Amsterdam's waterfront. Metzger's brother Max was also involved with Bomberg, but gave up art to study agriculture in Paris.

Betty MEWS 1890–1982 Artist in oil, pastel, charcoal, lithography, wood engraving and lino-cutter. Born in Warwick, she studied at the Slade School, 1919–21, under Henry Tonks, and at Chelsea School of Art, 1926–32, under Harold Sandys Williamson. Exhibited at RA, RBA, NEAC and UA. Lived at Pitsford, Northampton.

Klaus MEYER 1918– Relief printmaker, painter and teacher, born in Berlin, Germany, who moved to London as a refugee in 1938. He studied graphics at Central School of Art, where he also attended drawing classes under Bernard Meninsky and Morris Kestelman. After the war he studied painting with Henryk Gotlib and from 1956–8 printmaking under Anthony Gross and Ceri Richards at Slade School of Fine Art. In his mid-thirties Meyer felt an urge to cut images into wood rather than paint, although his approach remained that of a painter. He held teaching posts at Hornsey College of Art and Kilburn Polytechnic and was an examiner in art for Cambridge University Syndicate. From 1945 Meyer was a member of the Hampstead Artists' Council, also belonging to SWE and Printmakers' Council. Numerous mixed shows included LG, Camden Arts Centre and Campbell & Franks. Later solo shows included Camden Arts Centre, 1988, and Primrose Hill Gallery, 1991. Victoria & Albert Museum, the Getty Center in Santa Monica, Yale Center for British Art, Harvard and Princeton Universities have examples.

Sally MEYER 1961– Artist, born in Windsor, Berkshire, who studied at St Martin's School of Art & Design and Central School of Art. Group shows included South-West Open, Plymouth City Museum, 1990; Print Open, RWA, 1991; Demarco's Choice, Newlyn Orion Gallery, Newlyn, 1993; and Royal Over-Seas League Open, 1995, where she showed the oil on canvas The Evelyn Cabinet, The Geffrye Museum. Museums were a key theme for Meyer, whose solo shows included Museum Interiors, Plymouth City Museum and tour, 1993–5; Recent Paintings, St David's Hall, Cardiff, 1994; and Rooms Within, Geffrye Museum, 1995. The Geffrye and The Philpott Museum, Lyme Regis, hold her work.

Wolfgang MEYER-MICHAEL 1890–1976 Sculptor, painter, draughtsman, ceramist, illuminated glass mosaic-maker and teacher, born in Berlin into a cultured family where his talents were early encouraged. Attended progressive boarding school, Haubinda, then aged 16 returned to Berlin where enrolled at Berliner Kunstgewerbeschule to study sculpture for three years, also studying engraving with Hermann Struck. Before entering Hochschule für die Bildenden Künste he worked for six months as a stonemason with Engelhardt; graduating after three years he was offered an in-house studio in Berliner Akademie as a master pupil of Louis Tuaillon. After World War I Army service Meyer-Michael launched his career as a multi-talented artist, but was notable as a sculptor. His bronze statue Dream of Zion, exhibited in Palestine pavilion at 1939 World Exhibition, was eventually renamed Zippia and was acquired by city of Haifa, Israel. In 1935 Meyer-Michael emigrated to Palestine, later Israel, between 1942–55 teaching at faculty of architecture of Haifa Technion. After his wife died in 1963 Meyer-Michael moved to London to join his daughters, at the age of 73 enrolling at Central School, where he studied stained glass work. He developed shallow boxes to give each glass mosaic its own light source. Meyer-Michael's work had been shown at Ben Uri Gallery in 1953. In 1954 he showed with Piccadilly Gallery, and other shows included one of his glass mosaics at Pilkington Gallery, St Helens, in 1970. A centenary show of his work was held at John Denham Gallery in 1990. Died in London.

Joyce Jessie MEYERS 1933– Painter and illustrator, born in London. She studied at South-East Essex Technical College and St Martin's School of Art, teachers including William Dring and Phyllis Legge. For many years Meyers worked as a fashion illustrator; she was also a picture restorer and ran the Meyers Gallery in Ingatestone, Essex. Showed there and at Beecroft Art Gallery, Westcliff-on-Sea and with Brentwood Art Society, of which she was a member. Her landscapes and still lifes were notable for their free brushwork and subtle colours.

MIA 1935– Draughtsman, artist in collage and teacher, actual name Maureen Parsons-Irwin. She was born in Guildford, Surrey, and studied at Hastings School of Art, 1951–5, with Vincent Lines. Held a number of teaching posts, including Brighton College of Art. Work shown with RA and had several one-man shows. Lived in Hastings, Sussex.

Peter MICHAEL 1964– Artist and architect, born in Singapore and educated in Dublin, Ireland, who graduated in architecture in London, obtaining a diploma in advanced architectural studies in Aberdeen. Michael trained with, and worked for, the Morrison Partnership for two years until 1991, from then painting full-time, notable for delicate watercolours of buildings. His awards included Sir John Kinross Award and Sir Robert Lorimer Memorial Award. Showed at RSA, 1991; Open Eye Gallery, Edinburgh, from 1992; Roger Billcliffe Fine Art, Glasgow, 1993; and with Flying Colours Gallery. RSA, Renfrewshire District Council, Royal Lyceum Theatre in Edinburgh and corporate collections hold examples.

Meraud MICHAEL: *see* **Meraud GUEVARA**

Michael MICHAELEDES 1927– Artist notable for figurative and abstract works created with cotton duck on stretchers, born in Egypt. He studied art and architecture in Italy and England and in 1954 won the Philadelphios Panhellenic poetry competition in Athens. Took part in many group shows, including Leicester Galleries, 1960; John Moores Liverpool Exhibition, 1967; Europe Prize, Palazzo Reale, Milan (Silver Medal), 1971; Scottish Arts Council tour, 1976; and Homage to the Square, Flaxman Gallery, from 1988. Had a solo exhibition at Leicester Galleries, 1959, then showed frequently after that, notably with Annely Juda Fine Art. Arts Council; Israel Museum, Jerusalem; Municipal Gallery, Dublin; and National Museum of Modern Art, Seoul, and other international collections, have examples. Lived and worked in London and Florence, Italy.

Richard MICHELMORE 1928– Architect and painter who was educated at London University, then Kingston School of Art. He met David Bomberg, who remained a lasting influence on his work, at Bartlett School of Architecture where the older man was holding an evening drawing class. This led to Michelmore attending Borough Polytechnic classes. He showed with Borough Group, Borough Bottega, Bookworm and Tate Galleries and organised the 1986 exhibition Bomberg the Teacher in South Kensington. Was included in Borough Group exhibition at Fine Art Associates, 1989.

Alastair MICHIE 1921– Painter and sculptor, son of the artist Anne Redpath and brother of the artist David Michie, born in St Omer, northern France. He studied architecture in Edinburgh and after war service as a pilot in the Royal Air Force had a career as a freelance graphic artist. In the early 1960s became deeply involved in painting and sculpture, eventually concentrating on acrylic and mixed media. Was elected RWA in 1984, joining its council, also showing at RA, RSA, RSW, SSA, Paris Salon and elsewhere. In 1964 Michie was a finalist in the Arts Council Open Painting Competition; he was one of 15 British painters chosen to show at Museum of Modern Art, Warsaw, in 1967; and a solo exhibition at Richard Demarco Gallery, Edinburgh, in 1971, led to an invitation by the Brazilian Embassy to give a series of major shows in that country in 1972. Had major show of sculpture at Alwin Gallery, 1979. The Museums of Modern Art in Rio de Janeiro and São Paolo, British Aerospace, City Art Gallery in Cleveland, Ohio, and Sultanate of Oman hold examples. Lived in Wareham, Dorset.

David MICHIE 1928– Painter and teacher, born in St Raphael, France, son of the artist Anne Redpath. Studied at Edinburgh College of Art, 1946–53, under William Gillies, in 1953–4 visiting Italy with a travelling scholarship. Michie (pronounced Miki) lectured in painting at Gray's School of Art, Aberdeen, 1957–61; he then joined the staff of Edinburgh College of Art, being appointed head of drawing and painting, 1982–90, and to a personal chair at Heriot-Watt University in 1990. In 1979 he was visiting professor of painting at the Academy of Fine Art, Belgrade. He was a member of Royal Glasgow Institute of the Fine Arts, a president of SSA and was elected RSA in 1972. Was a regular exhibitor in one-man shows at Mercury Gallery. Work held by HM The Queen, Scottish Arts Council and many other public collections. Lived in Edinburgh.

Krysia Danuta MICHNA-NOWAK: *see* **Krysia NOWAK**

Edwin MICKLEBURGH 1946– Photographer, painter, film-maker and writer who in 1963 worked on a Grimsby trawler and sailed the Arctic seas, polar regions thereafter inspiring his artistic work. Studied painting at West of England College of Art, Bristol, 1964–8. Mickleburgh was then with the British Antarctic Survey, as a meteorologist and film-maker, 1968–71; cameraman, *Survival*, Anglia Television, 1971–2; expedition cameraman/photographer for International Library of African Music, 1972–3; widespread filming, including work for BBC *Wilderness*, series, 1973–6; then with grants undertook filming and photography in Lapland and South Georgia, 1979–80. He further travelled in Finland, Norway, America, Israel, the Himalayas, North Greenland and the Canadian Arctic. Mickleburgh's books included *Antarctic Adventure* and *Beyond the Frozen Sea*, which was shortlisted for The McVitie Prize for the 1988 Scottish Writer of the Year. Films included, in 1981–2, *Island at the Edge of the World*, which won the Gold Medal, International Maritime Festival, France, and Bronze Award, London Film Festival. Exhibitions included Another World, Commonwealth Institute and tour, 1977–8; North & South, Aberdeen Art Gallery, 1981–2; and Ultima Thule, Peacock Printmakers, Aberdeen, 1988.

Robert MICKLEWRIGHT 1923– Illustrator, designer and painter in oil and watercolour, born in Staffordshire. He studied at Croydon School of Art in 1939; during World War II served with the Army in North Africa, Italy and Greece; was at Wimbledon School of Art, 1947–9; then at Slade School of Fine Art, 1949–52. Micklewright became a freelance, a prolific illustrator for *Radio Times* and book publishers, also designing Post Office stamp books, painting for major industrial companies such as Shell and Gulf Oil and completing posters for London Transport. He was a Sunday painter, a member of RWS and exhibitor at RA Summer Exhibition, being included in *Royal Academy Illustrated.* Lived at Mogador, Tadworth, Surrey.

Edward MIDDLEDITCH 1923–1987 Painter, draughtsman and teacher, born in Chelmsford, Essex. After several years in the Army, when he won the Military Cross, Middleditch studied at Regent Street Polytechnic School of Art and Royal College of Art, 1948–52. From 1954 he had a series of solo shows at Beaux Arts Gallery, where he was included among the Kitchen Sink realist group. Represented Britain at Venice Biennale, 1956. Graduated later to sombre and poetic landscapes. There was a particularly fine series of paintings and drawings based on Sheffield Weir, of which Tate Gallery has an example. After a number of important mixed shows in the 1960s, the winning of a Gulbenkian Foundation

Scholarship in 1962 and an Arts Council Bursary in 1964, with another in 1968, Middleditch had a series of solo exhibitions from 1969 at New Art Centre. Middleditch was head of fine art at Norwich School of Art, 1964–84. He was elected RA in 1973 and was keeper of the Royal Academy Schools, 1984–86. Was included in The Forgotten Fifties, Graves Art Gallery, Sheffield, and tour, 1984. Retrospective Arts Council exhibition, Castle Museum, Norwich, and tour, 1987–8. Lived in Boxford, Essex.

Fred MIDDLEHURST 1918– Painter, designer, engraver and teacher who studied at Blackburn School of Art, 1932–9, under George Reed, then at Royal College of Art, 1943–6, with Malcolm Osborne and Robert Austin. Middlehurst had begun exhibiting as a child in Preston, where he later showed, also at RA, RE and in the provinces. Harris Museum and Art Gallery, Preston, holds his work. Lived in London.

Alan James MIDDLETON 1926– Architect, painter and draughtsman, born in Coventry, his father being an artist and teacher, James Middleton. He attended Liverpool University and studied architecture with the Architectural Association School. Showed RA, RBA, PS and elsewhere. Medici Society Ltd reproduced his work. Lived in London, then in Chislehurst, Kent.

Colin MIDDLETON 1910–1983 Restlessly experimental artist and teacher whose work often has a magical intensity. He was born in Belfast, Northern Ireland, son of a linen damask designer who had many artist friends. Middleton reluctantly followed his father into the family business instead of going to art school, took it over on his father's death in 1935 and did not relinquish it until 1947. After leaving Belfast Royal Academy Middleton attended the College of Art part-time, getting good tuition from Newton Penprase in the design department. Van Gogh and James Ensor were early influences. Middleton's pre-war work had two main strands: Expressionist scenes in Belfast and Surrealism. In 1934 he first exhibited with Ulster Unit, inspired by Unit One, then in 1943 had an initial solo show at Stranmillis Museum and Art Gallery. An association with the Victor Waddington Galleries in Dublin did much to promote his name, and many one-man and group appearances followed, noteworthy being Ulster Museum, Belfast, and Municipal Gallery of Modern Art, Dublin, 1976. They and many other public collections hold examples. Middleton worked widely in Northern Ireland, often living in a caravan and cycling around the province, but eventually settled in Bangor, County Down. In the mid-1950s he was forced into part-time teaching at Belfast College of Art; in 1955 taught full-time at Coleraine Technical College; then in 1961–70 taught at the Friends' School, Lisburn. In 1972 Middleton went on a world cruise; it, an interest in religion, philosophy, writing poetry and making music all fed his art. He was elected RHA in 1970. There was a studio sale of Middleton's work at Christie's, London, in 1985. His son was the artist John Middleton.

James Charles MIDDLETON 1894–1969 Painter and teacher, worker in metals and engraver. Born in Redruth, Cornwall, studied at the School of Art there, 1910–15, and Birmingham School of Arts and Crafts, 1920–5. Was a member of Croydon Art Society and the Wapping Group of Artists, of which he was honorary treasurer. Exhibited RA, RI, PS, ROI and elsewhere. Middleton taught art in a boys' secondary school and acted as a tutor for Galleon Painting Holidays. Lived in Wallington, Surrey.

John MIDDLETON 1945–1981 Artist, designer and teacher, born in Belfast, Northern Ireland, son of the artist Colin Middleton. He studied at Belfast College of Art, 1963–6, then Royal of Art, 1966–9. Taught in London and Belfast, where he also worked as a graphic and exhibition designer. A strong clue to his output was the yin and the yang, antagonistic and complementary forces which are reckoned to operate in the universe, centrifugal force away from the centre and centripetal towards the centre. Shows included New Gallery in Belfast; Arts Council of Northern Ireland Gallery – the Arts Council holds his work; David Hendriks Gallery in Dublin; and Third Eye Centre, Glasgow. Died in Perth, Western Australia.

Marion MIDDLETON fl. c.1915–1950 Painter and draughtsman, born in Dodford, Northamptonshire, whose full name was Agnes Marion Middleton. After private education she studied at Frank Spenlove-Spenlove's Yellow Door School of Art. Showed at RA, in Nottingham and 1948–50 with Norfolk and Norwich Art Circle, her special interests being Norfolk scenes and flower studies. Lived at Aylmerton, near Norwich.

Max MIDDLETON 1944– Artist in various media, born in Staffordshire, who studied at Goldsmiths' College School of Art and St Martin's School of Art, 1961–5, and who went on to teach. Lectured at Furzedown College of Education, 1972–6, then part-time at Thurrock School of Art. In 1970 he published *Etching and Intaglio Printing*, having been engaged in opera design for two years, in 1972 carrying out a mural for the French government. Took part in group shows in Britain and France. His solo exhibitions included Greenwich Theatre Gallery, 1967; Versailles Salon des Arts, 1975; Salon de la Porte d'Italie, Paris, in 1976; and in the same year he shared a show with Frederick Palmer at Woodlands Art Gallery. Middleton's work included highly stylised figure studies.

Renée MIDDLETON 1920– Pen and ink artist, educated in Croydon, Surrey. She was a member of SGA, Society of Botanical Artists and societies in Sussex, where she settled at Thakeham. Gained the Rexel Prize in 1984.

Barry MIDGLEY 1947– Sculptor in mixed media, stone and bronze, and teacher, who attended Bradford Regional College of Art, 1966–7; Wolverhampton Polytechnic, 1967–70, under John Paddison and Louise Kim; then Chelsea School of Art, 1970–1, under George Fullard and Geoff Dudley. Taught at Wolverhampton Polytechnic, 1971–2; Harris Institute, Preston, 1972–4; then University of Central Lancashire from 1974, where he was head of sculpture. Land, sea, air, tragedies and disasters

were cited by Midgley as themes in his work, which was influenced by Rembrandt, Bugatti, George Fullard and Joel Shapiro. He was a member of the Yorkshire Sculpture Group. Exhibitions included Bluecoat Gallery in Liverpool; Holden Gallery, Manchester; Turton Tower, Bolton; and Dean Clough Contemporary Art Gallery, Halifax, 1993. Also showed at 2nd, 3rd and 4th International Shoebox Sculpture Exhibitions, Hawaii, and Hawaii State Foundationfor the Arts holds his work. Lived in Todmorden, Yorkshire.

Peter MIDGLEY 1921–1991 Painter, constructor of abstract reliefs, printmaker, draughtsman and teacher, born in Berlin, Germany, as Fleischmann, adopting the surname Midgley after the family who took him in in Manchester. Midgley had a tough childhood in Germany in an orphanage, attending the Berlin Art School before arriving in England for a period of internment in the Isle of Man. He was released into the care of two painters who found him a place at Beckenham School of Art, 1947–51, attended Royal College of Art, 1951–3, winning a travelling scholarship to Rome, 1953–4. In 1955 Midgley began teaching at Beckenham School of Art, becoming a tutor at Ravensbourne College of Design and Communication, 1966–86. He was elected to Society of Mural Painters in 1956, joining the Chartered Society of Designers in 1958. He showed with LG, RA, Victoria & Albert Museum, Camden Arts Centre, Royal Festival Hall and Greenwich Theatre Gallery. In 1978 he gained a retrospective show in Berlin, Woodlands Art Gallery giving him a memorial exhibition in 1992. Was a member of Printmakers' Council. Had work in public and private collections in Britain and abroad.

Laimonis MIERINS 1929– Painter, draughtsman and teacher, born in Latvia, who settled in Yorkshire as a political refugee in 1947. For many years he was an agricultural and textile worker, attending evening classes at Bradford College of Art. In the early-1960s Mierins studied at Leeds College of Art and Goldsmiths' College, then started teaching at Leeds College of Art & Design in 1966, retiring in the mid-1990s. In 1995 there was a retrospective at State Art Museum in Riga, which was also featured at Cartwright Hall in Bradford and at Barbican Centre. Mierins was there shown to be a powerful figure draughtsman and abstract painter. Bold colours, jostling shapes and intersecting forms were features of his work. Lived in Shipley.

Christopher MIERS 1941– Painter of landscape and still life, born into an Army family. Although showing an aptitude for painting, he left Wellington for Sandhurst where he passed out with the sword of honour. Then served in the Royal Green Jackets in Britain and widely overseas, the Imperial War Museum acquiring his pictures done in Northern Ireland, Borneo and Cyprus. Left Army in mid-1980s as a lieutenant-colonel and became secretary of the Arts Club. Began to show at RA, added to a string of solo exhibitions and was elected RBA in 1986. Working on a small scale, Miers painted widely in Britain and continental Europe, as indicated in his one-man show at Sally Hunter Fine Art, 1990. Lived in London.

Elise MIERS 1920– Painter, notably of murals, and teacher, born in Cirencester, Gloucestershire. After private education she studied at Slade School of Fine Art, 1946–50, with Vladimir Polunin specialising in stage design; then at Camberwell School of Arts and Crafts with Claude Rogers and Victor Pasmore. Taught at St Ursula's School for Girls, in Blackheath. Showed at LG, AIA, UA, Paris Salon and had one-man show at Kensington Art Gallery in 1949. ICA member and lived in London.

Harry Robert MILEHAM 1873–1957 Painter, born in London, who attended Dulwich College, Lambeth Art School and Royal Academy Schools, where he won a Gold Medal and travelling studentship. Mileham's decorative work is found in a number of churches, such as Foleshill Church, Coventry; St Thomas', Hove; Chapel Royal, Brighton; and Wakefield Cathedral. He was a keen organiser of pageants, reflected in a body of historical paintings. Settled in Hove, Sussex, and was a leading member of Brighton Art Club as well as a long-standing member of the Art Workers' Guild. Showed at RA, Royal Glasgow Institute of the Fine Arts, RCam A and elsewhere. There was a retrospective at Leighton House in 1995. Hove Museum & Art Gallery holds Mileham's work, that of a natural and belated Victorian.

Arthur MILES 1905–1987 Painter, especially of landscape in watercolour, born in Faversham, Kent, a self-taught artist. Miles did many jobs throughout his life, including labouring, working as a process artist, a signwriter and painter of scenery, then self-employed designer and painter. He was able to paint full-time from the late 1960s, working in Gwaelod-y-garth, Glamorgan. A member of RI from 1949, also of SWG, and in 1985 president of both WSW and SWAS, Miles showed in group exhibitions with Royal National Eisteddfod and SEA, and at RA in the early 1950s. Solo shows included Howard Roberts and Albany Galleries, Cardiff; Clarges Gallery; and Welsh Gallery in Abergavenny. He did a considerable amount of commissioned work for the National Museum of Wales in Cardiff, murals, drawings and dioramas; also the Welsh National Union of Mineworkers' banner. National Museum of Wales, CASW and WAC hold his work. Died in Torquay, Devon.

Gordon E MILES 1947– Artist, mainly known as a printmaker with a distinctive palette, born in Maidstone, Kent. From 1963–8 he studied photolithography at London College of Printing, then did a vocational illustration course at Harrow Art School, first-class pass, 1968–71. His commissions included two editions for Cadw Historic Monuments, 1987, one of Strata Florida, one of Conway Castle. Took part in extensive group shows, including RE from 1969, RA from 1973, Attic Gallery in Swansea from 1981, and Open Eye Gallery, Edinburgh, 1986. Later solo shows included Harrogate British Craft Trade Fair from 1985 and Goldsmiths Gallery, Lenham, 1987. Lived for a time at Lampeter, Dyfed.

John Francis Beverley MILES 1944– Painter, artist in ceramics and teacher, born in Cardiff, but moved to St Agnes,

Cornwall when still small. From 1961–6 attended Newport College of Art, then Cardiff College of Art, 1966–7. Held a number of teaching appointments, including a period at Torquay School of Art. Won major Arts Council prize. IBM Computers in London and National Westminster Bank in Torquay both commissioned works from him. Took part in group shows at Howard Roberts Gallery in Cardiff, South London Art Gallery, SWG and SEA. WAC and CASW hold his work.

June MILES 1924– Painter in oil and teacher, born in London. She studied at Slade School of Fine Art under Randolph Schwabe, 1941–3; worked in an Admiralty drawing office, 1943–5; studied at West of England College of Art, Bristol, 1946–8; and taught at Bristol Polytechnic faculty of art and design, 1966–76. She married the painter Paul Feiler, 1946, and until her divorce from him in 1967 painted as June Feiler, changing to her maiden name of June Miles after that. She married the sculptor Paul Mount in 1978. Miles was a member of RWA, Penwith Society of Arts and Newlyn Society of Artists. She participated in many mixed shows, including RA, RP, LG, RBA, John Whibley Gallery, Women's International in Paris, where she gained a bronze medal in 1968, and in Cornwall. Had a long series of solo shows, including Van Mildert College, Durham University, 1970; RWA, 1977; Beaux Arts, Bath, 1983; Penwith Gallery, St Ives, 1985; and Coach-House Gallery, Guernsey, 1988. RWA, Plymouth and Bristol City Art Galleries hold examples. Lived at St Just, Penzance, Cornwall.

Graham MILESON 1949– Artist in a variety of media and teacher, born in London where he settled from 1976. Mileson studied sculpture, painting and drawing at Gloucester College of Art, 1965–7; did foundation studies at Coventry College of Art, 1968–9; gained his diploma at Coventry Polytechnic, 1969–72; then teacher training at Goldsmiths' College, 1976–7. He was a visiting lecturer at Stourbridge College of Art, 1974; taught at Goldsmiths', 1977–88; was a visiting lecturer at Coventry Polytechnic, 1991, and at Wimbledon School of Art, 1992. Exhibitions included mixed at Warwick Arts Trust, 1986; Artexpo, Los Angeles, 1990; Gimpel Fils, 1991; and The Gallery at John Jones, 1992. Had a solo show at Goldsmiths' Gallery, 1986, later ones including The Living Room, 1995. Shaped canvases, three-dimensional works, site-specific and conceptual pieces were all featured in Mileson's output. He said that he aimed "at richness and depth. It doesn't matter how they are done or what is made; what matters is creating an expressive content."

Raoul MILLAIS 1901– Painter of horses, son of the artist John Millais and grandson of Sir John Everett Millais. He studied at Royal Academy Schools and Byam Shaw School of Drawing and Painting. His knowledge of horses was first-hand, as he was a keen huntsman. Millais was commissioned to paint a number of notable successful racehorses and his work is included in the collection of HM The Queen.

Jack MILLAR 1921– Painter and teacher, born and lived in London. He studied at Clapham School of Art, 1939; St Martin's School of Art, 1941; and at Royal College of Art, 1947–50, gaining a first-class pass and the Andrew Lloyd Scholarship for landscape painting, 1950. Was married to the artist Pamela Izzard. Millar was elected to RBA in 1954. He was a visiting lecturer at Royal Academy Schools from 1964; was head of fine art at Walthamstow School of Art, 1966–73; then was head of fine art at Kingston Polytechnic, 1973–86. Showed widely in mixed exhibitions, including Leicester and Piccadilly Galleries; RA; Roland, Browse & Delbanco; Odette Gilbert and Fieldborne Galleries; Royal Glasgow Institute of the Fine Arts; Whitechapel Art Gallery; and the provinces. Solo shows included Rumbold Gallery, Linton Court Gallery, Linfield Galleries and Duncan Campbell. Among prizes won were Greater London Council Spirit of London Painting Competition, Rowney Prize, 1979; RBA 1st prize, Daler-Rowney Award, 1986; and De Laszlo Medal, 1989. RA holds his work.

Jane MILLAR 1964– Painter, draughtsman, collage-maker and teacher who gained an honours degree in fine art at Canterbury College of Art, 1984–7, then her master's degree in painting (tapestry) at Royal College of Art, 1987–9. From 1989 held several visiting lectureships, including Winchester School of Art; University of West England, Bristol; and Kent Institute of Art and Design, Canterbury. Dissatisfied with conventional perspective and narrative space, Millar created pictures from disparate images, giving them a heightened significance, "trying to grasp in painted form a sense of mystery". Mixed shows included Whitechapel Open, Cable Street Studios, 1989; East Meets West, Smith's Gallery, 1991; and Brick Lane Gallery, 1994. Later solo shows included England & Co, 1995.

Patrick MILLARD 1902–1977 Painter and teacher, born in Aspatria, Cumberland. He studied at Liverpool School of Art, then at Royal Academy Schools, 1921–5, under Charles Sims and Ernest Jackson, winning a gold medal in 1925. A travelling scholarship took him to France, Italy and Spain the following year. He was principal of the St John's Wood Art Schools, 1931–8, taught at Shoreditch Training College, 1944–50, then served as headmaster of Regent Street Polytechnic. Published the *Students' Book of Life Drawing*, 1938. Exhibited extensively at RBA, also at RA, LG, NS and NEAC. Lady Lever Art Gallery, Port Sunlight, holds his work. Retrospective show at Christopher Hull Gallery in 1987. Lived in London.

Alain MILLER 1961– Painter, born in London, where he later worked. Miller studied at Maidstone College of Art, 1979–80, Brighton Polytechnic, 1981–4, Chelsea School of Art, 1984–5, and Goldsmiths' College School of Art, 1985–7. Among group exhibitions he appeared in were Kettle's Yard, Cambridge, and Anthony Reynolds Gallery, both 1985, with subsequent appearances at Anthony Reynolds, including solo shows from 1987. Miller also showed in the 1990 Whitechapel Open; John Moores Exhibition, Liverpool, in 1987, 1991–2 and 1997–8; and in About Vision, Museum of Modern Art, Oxford, and tour, 1996–7.

Alan MILLER 1941– Painter, draughtsman and teacher. He was born in Warrington, Lancashire. Miller studied at Bath Academy of Art, 1959–63, and Slade School of Fine Art, 1963–5. Showed with LG, Whitworth Art Gallery in Manchester, in Sweden and Germany, in Arts Council's British Painting '74 and in John Moores Exhibition, Liverpool, where he was a prizewinner in 1974 and 1976. He had his first solo show at Serpentine Gallery in 1971. The year following he joined staff of Royal College of Art, becoming a fellow in 1982 and senior tutor in painting from 1989. Millar had a retrospective at Ikon Gallery in Birmingham in 1984. Other shows included Lanchester Gallery, Coventry Polytechnic, 1990. Miller was a Greater London Arts Association Award winner in 1985. He was originally an abstract painter, but later moved into representational work. His pictures could be complex, sombre and with an atmosphere of foreboding. Arts Council, Victoria & Albert Museum, Wakefield City Art Gallery and other public collections hold his work. Lived in London.

Alec MILLER 1879–1961 Sculptor, draughtsman and teacher, born in Glasgow. Studied at the School of Art there, 1900–2, and in Italy six years later. He was a member of the Art Workers' Guild and taught at Campden School of Arts and Crafts, 1902–14, then from 1919–23 at Oxford City School of Art. Exhibited RA, RSA, RMS, Walker Art Gallery, Liverpool, and widely in America. He did war memorial work in England and had work in a number of galleries in America, including Canton in Ohio and Savannah, Georgia. Published *Ruskin Reconsidered*, 1929, and *Tradition in Sculpture*, 1949. Sometimes just signed work A M. Miller's marble head Charlotte Heberden Wilgress is illustrated in Eric Newton's monograph *British Sculpture 1944–1946*. He lived in Campden, Gloucestershire, and Monterey, California. Died in Thanet, Kent.

Andrew MILLER 1969– Artist using everyday items as the inspiration for works employing photographs and installations/wall pieces, as in New Art in Scotland, Centre for Contemporary Arts, Glasgow, 1994. He was born in Dartington, Devon, and studied at Torquay Technical College, 1985–8, then in 1988–93 at the School of Art, Glasgow, where he lived. Exhibitions included Fresh Art '91, Business Design Centre, Islington, 1991; Invisible Cities, Fruitmarket Gallery, Edinburgh, 1992; and BT New Contemporaries tour, 1994.

Archibald Elliot Haswell MILLER 1887–1979 Painter and curator, born in Glasgow, where he studied at the School of Art under Maurice Greiffenhagen and Jean Delville, 1906–9, then for a year in Munich. Was married to the artist Josephine Miller. Miller taught at Glasgow School of Art for 20 years from 1910, apart from World War I, then was keeper and deputy director of the National Galleries of Scotland, 1930–52. He also held positions with the Royal Fine Arts Commission, National Buildings Record and Scottish Council. Wrote, especially on military uniforms. Sometimes signing his work H M, he exhibited at RSW, of which he was a member, and RSA, also RA and Royal Glasgow Institute of the Fine Arts. Imperial War Museum and Glasgow Museum and Art Galleries hold his work. Lived for many years in Edinburgh but latterly in Gillingham, Dorset.

Betty MILLER fl. from 1960s– Sculptor, ceramist and teacher, brought up in Royston, Yorkshire, who gained her diploma from Borough Polytechnic, sculpture and modelling, with honours, then studied for a diploma, specialising in ceramics and embroidered design, at Goldsmiths' College. She taught in state and private secondary schools; lectured in ceramics at Hastings College of Further Education; and was artist-in-residence, Perth College of Art and Clairmont College of Art, both in Perth, Western Australia. Miller said that "my theme is the human condition," and within that brief her work was diverse, being mainly in clay for casting or firing. A major project was My Village, a narrative in bronze of images from her childhood in a coalmining area where her father was a photographer. A selection of these bronzes, with their flattened, illusory sense of perspective, and her father's photographs were shown at Kent Institute of Art & Design, Rochester, in 1996. Miller also showed at RA Summer Exhibition, Towner Art Gallery in Eastbourne and elsewhere. Her work also included commissioned portraits of the writers Malcolm and Kitty Muggeridge and J B Priestley, the footballer Gordon Banks, the cricketer Fred Trueman and Sir David Brand and John Tonkin, former premiers of Western Australia. She also completed a nativity scene for Chichester Cathedral. Lived in Sussex.

Clive Beverley MILLER 1938– Painter and teacher, born in Bexley, Kent. He attended Sidcup School of Art, 1955, and Bromley College of Art, 1956, then after Royal Air Force Service was at Royal College of Art, 1960–4. He won Rome and Abbey Scholarships. After teaching at Sheffield College of Art and Medway College of Design Miller ran a private school. Showed with RA Summer Exhibition, Swansea Art Society of which he was a member and elsewhere. WAC holds his work. Lived latterly at Cheriton, Gower, south Wales.

David Thomson MILLER 1931– Sculptor in stone, wood, metal, resins and clay, draughtsman and teacher, born in Bo'ness, West Lothian. He attended Gray's School of Art, Aberdeen, 1948–50; gained an Andrew Grant Scholarship to Edinburgh College of Art, 1950; and in 1953 a scholarship to Paris and Villauris, spending some time working in a pottery. Teachers included T B Huxley-Jones and Eric Schilsky. Miller, known to friends as Dusty, was a carver rather than a modeller. After National Service in the Army he attended Jordanhill College of Education, 1956–7, then taught, becoming senior lecturer in sculpture at Moray House College, 1961–81, retiring early to concentrate on architectural stone carving. After open-heart surgery in 1989 he was limited to smaller pieces. Miller's main themes were the torso and the bird. He was elected to SSA in 1960 and was made a fellow of RBS in 1970. In 1961 he won the RSA's Latimer Award. Had his first solo show at Paperback Gallery, Edinburgh, 1963, a retrospective at Peacock Gallery, Aberdeen, 1991. Scottish Arts Council holds Miller's impressive Portsoy Marble Torso, 1975. Lived in Pathhead, Midlothian.

Eirene MILLER 1898– Painter in oil, born in London and educated in Bristol. Although she studied art at Stratford-upon-Avon School of Art, she was mainly self-taught. Showed at LG and SWA. Lived in London.

Gary Fabian MILLER 1957– Artist, born in Bristol, whose father was a professional photographer and who taught him how to use a camera. He was influenced by the work of artists such as Ben Nicholson and Barbara Hepworth; a Nicholson picture seen at the age of 13 made him realise that a work of art could, "like a stone or a piece of wood", assume its own identity. Miller was a Quaker and gave his works quasi-religious titles. From 1984, he worked without a camera, using such techniques as passing light through flowers and leaves direct onto cibachrome paper or filters of water and oil, creating mysterious combinations of colour and light. Worked in Lincolnshire, 1980–88, then on Dartmoor. Had the first of many solo shows at Arnolfini Gallery, Bristol, 1979, later ones including Michael Hue-Williams Fine Art and De La Warr Pavilion, Bexhill-on-Sea, both 1997. Victoria & Albert Museum, Usher Gallery in Lincoln, Bibliothèque Nationale in Paris, Metropolitan Museum in New York and other overseas public gallery and corporate collections hold examples.

Geoffrey MILLER 1904–1992 Printmaker, born in South Park, Reigate, Surrey, where he settled at 29 Allingham Road. Attended Reigate Grammar School, then studied painting at Royal Academy Schools, although he often slipped away to the engraving studios. From late 1930s and through the 1940s Miller illustrated for *Radio Times* and book publishers. In the immediate post-war years he worked as an artist for a firm making film-strips and preparing training films for the Ministry of Defence. During the 1950s he produced large lino-cut black-and-white posters for Joan Littlewood's Theatre Workshop at Stratford. Two series of engravings of scientists were commissioned by Imperial Chemical Industries and were featured at the Brussels International Trade Exhibition, 1958, and at the 1960 New York Trade Fair. Miller was chairman of the Reigate Society of Artists in the early-1970s (it gave him a tribute show at the Old Town Hall in 1992; another was held at Miller's home). He was involved in the Reigate Pageants and founded the local Arts Council in 1972, serving as its chairman and establishing an annual arts festival in the town. Pallant House, Chichester, has a print of Reigate Grammar School, made in 1961, by Miller.

Hilary MILLER 1919– Artist, teacher and illustrator who married the painter Hubert Hennes. She studied at Blackheath School of Art, 1936–40, then at Royal College of Art, 1940–3. She held a number of teaching appointments, including Oxford School of Art, and illustrated books with gardening themes. Exhibited at RA and lived in Oxford.

James MILLER 1893–1987 Painter in oil and watercolour of Scottish descent. Studied at Glasgow School of Art under Maurice Greiffenhagen and Robert Anning Bell and went on to exhibit at the RSA and RSW. The *Studio* magazine and *The Scotsman* newspaper reproduced his work, which is in the collections of the Arts Council of Great Britain as well as galleries in Bradford, Edinburgh, Glasgow and Melbourne. Lived on the Isle of Skye.

John MILLER 1911–1975 Painter and draughtsman. Born in Glasgow, Miller studied art at Glasgow School of Art under William Oliphant Hutchison. Miller was to return to the School as a senior lecturer in painting and drawing. From Glasgow Miller continued studying at the School of Art, Hospitalfield, Arbroath, under James Cowie. Miller went on to exhibit at the RSA, SSA, RSW and Royal Glasgow Institute of the Fine Arts. His work is owned by public galleries in Glasgow and Dundee. Lived at Rhu, Dunbartonshire.

John MILLER 1931– Painter and architect, born in London. After National Service he studied architecture and was articled to the church architects Milner and Craze. In 1958 he moved to Cornwall, settling in the Penwith peninsula, and becoming a member of the Newlyn Society of Artists in 1961, serving as chairman for some years. He had a retrospective at Newlyn Orion Gallery in 1978. Miller showed with David Messum from 1982, the gallery publishing his autobiography *Leave Tomorrow Behind* in 1989. Miller has work in public and private collections around the world. His pictures employ a rich and imaginative palette.

Josephine MILLER 1890–1975 Painter in oil, tempera and watercolour, and etcher. Born in Glasgow, she studied art at Glasgow School of Art under Robert Anning Bell and Maurice Greiffenhagen. Exhibited RA, RSA, in the provinces and in America. Glasgow Corporation and the RSA bought her work. She was married to the artist A E Haswell Miller and lived in Scotland for some years, later settling in Gillingham, Dorset.

Kenneth MILLER 1915– Sculptor, painter and printmaker, educated in London. He attended St Martin's School of Art, 1935–9. Exhibited with Free Painters and Sculptors, Fermoy Gallery in King's Lynn and elsewhere. Lived in Great Massingham, Norfolk.

Marjory (Kusha) MILLER: *see* **Kusha PETTS**

Marmaduke MILLER 1900–1973 Painter of landscape, especially in watercolour, and printmaker, born at Arncliffe, Yorkshire. Studied part-time at Skipton School of Art, then painted while doing a number of jobs, such as running the Falcon Inn, Arncliffe, where he continued to live. Showed at RA and in the provinces and illustrated for *The Dalesman* magazine. City Art Gallery in Bradford holds his work.

Michael MILLER 1942– Artist working in a wide range of media, and teacher, born in Derby. Studied at Joseph Wright Secondary School of Art, 1955–9, with John Fineran, and at Derby & District College of Art, 1959–63, under Keith Richardson-Jones. He was a fellow of the Digswell Arts Trust,

1966–73, teaching full-time until retirement. Did some book illustration. Showed with Young Contemporaries, in the 1961 and 1963 John Moores Liverpool Exhibitions and with Derby Group travelling shows. Lived at Wheathampstead, Hertfordshire.

Nick MILLER 1962– Artist born in Ireland in 1962, moving back there in 1984 after studying at University of East Anglia, 1981–4. He gained a National Portrait Award, Ireland, subsidiary award in 1989 and an open award, 1991, winning Irish Arts Council Visual Arts Bursaries in 1992 and 1994. Had a solo exhibition at Temple Bar Gallery in Dublin in 1986; later ones included Irish Museum of Modern Art, Kilmainham, 1994, and Fenderesky Gallery, Belfast, 1996, the year he took part in a three-man exhibition, Drawing, at Fine Art Society.

Stuart McAlpine MILLER 1964– Painter, born in Irvine, Ayrshire, who took an honours degree at Dundee School of Art, 1986–90. He created a world of hard-edged, sometimes distorted figures inhabiting a world with its own peculiar symbolism. Group exhibitions included Byzantine Gallery, Edinburgh, 1990; Gallery Albion, Cannes, 1991; and O'Hara Gallery, New York, 1994. Had a solo show at Trinity Gallery, 1991, later ones including Connaught Brown, 1994.

William Ongley MILLER 1883–1960 Painter and teacher, born in Haywards Heath, Sussex, son of the artist Fred Miller. He studied at Brighton College of Art, 1900–6, and Royal College of Art, 1906–11, and went on to hold a number of art school teaching posts, being principal of Gravesend School of Art, 1924–9. Showed RA, Walker Art Gallery in Liverpool and elsewhere in provinces. Manchester City Art Gallery holds his picture The Artist's Daughter. Lived in Gravesend, Kent, then in Canonbury, north London.

Paul MILLICHIP 1929– Painter, printmaker and teacher, born in Harrow, Middlesex. Studied at Leeds College of Art, 1948–50, where his teachers included Maurice de Sausmarez, then at Brighton College of Art, 1952–54, with George Hooper; at Leeds he won a travelling scholarship. Went on to teach for some years at Great Yarmouth School of Art. Showed at Gallery One, with Young Contemporaries, LG, *Daily Express* Young Artists Exhibition and elsewhere. Lived in Great Yarmouth, Norfolk.

Frances Jane Grierson MILLIGAN: *see* **Peggy WATKINS**

Terence MILLINGTON 1942– Artist, notably a printmaker, and teacher, born in Birmingham. He attended the College of Art there, 1958–63, Manchester College of Art, 1965–6, and later taught at Birmingham College, 1963–5, Leeds College of Art, 1966–7, and St Albans School of Art, 1972–4. Millington's work was shown in extensive mixed shows in Britain and abroad, including British International Print Biennale from 1970; Ljublana Biennale, Yugoslavia, 1973; Angela Flowers Gallery, 1974; Norwegian and Craców Biennales, 1976; and 1977 British Printmakers' Artcurial, Paris, 1977. Solo shows included Boadicea Gallery, 1972, and Woodlands Art Gallery, 1977. Victoria & Albert Museum, Arts Council and British Council, provincial and foreign galleries holds Millington's work.

Teddy MILLINGTON-DRAKE 1932–1994 Painter, draughtsman and traveller, born in London as Edgar Louis Vanderstegen Drake, his father Sir Eugen Millington-Drake, eccentric diplomat, his mother Lady Effie, daughter of the 1st Earl of Inchcape, a notable heiress. He travelled extensively when young, settling in London in 1940. Attended Eton College where the art tutor Wilfrid Blunt was an influence, and Oxford. After National Service in the Rifle Brigade, during which he was posted to Egypt during the Suez Crisis, Millington-Drake travelled widely in the Near and Middle East, then lived near Venice, where Freya Stark, Barbara Hutton, Peggy Guggenheim and Daisy Fellowes were friends. Finally settled in Patmos, Greece. Millington-Drake produced landscape and abstract works, the latter influenced by Jung. He showed in New York and London, notably at Eyre & Hobhouse, 1982. Although posing as a languid aesthete Millington-Drake produced several thousand drawings of India and the Middle East. His art collection included Edward Burra, Malcolm Morley and Cy Twombly, of whom he was an early admirer. The Lefevre Gallery held a memorial show, 1996.

Arthur MILLS 1897–1968 Etcher and wood engraver, who after Cambridge studied at Goldsmiths' College School of Art. Taught art and was a member of the SWE. Exhibited RA, RE, SWE, in the provinces and abroad. Lived at Steep, near Petersfield, Hampshire.

Enid MILLS fl. from 1940s– Painter, notably of portraits, miniaturist and calligrapher. She studied at St Martin's School of Art and Central School of Arts and Crafts, teachers including Walter Bayes and Bernard Meninsky. Was elected a member of RMS in 1961, also exhibiting at RI, RWS and abroad. Lived in Alderley Edge, Cheshire.

Ernestine MILLS fl. from c.1900–1959 Worker in enamel and metal, watercolour painter. Studied enamelling at Finsbury Technical College and art at the Slade School of Fine Art. Won several medals abroad for her enamelling, including one at the Paris Salon in 1950, silver medal 1955. Exhibited widely, including RA, RMS, Walker Art Gallery, Liverpool, SWA, in several Commonwealth countries and in America. She completed memorial tablets for Brook Hospital, Woolwich, and the Ethical Church, Bayswater, London. Among her publications was a life of the Victorian painter Frederick Shields. Sometimes signed her work E M. Lived in London.

John FitzMaurice MILLS 1917–1991 Painter, restorer, art historian, writer, lecturer and broadcaster, born Cheam, Surrey. He was educated at Bryanston School and the Architectural Association, his studies of painting, restoration and painters' techniques being done privately. He was the author of over 30 books on art, many for children, and a novel called *Top Knocker*. Was a prolific television and radio broadcaster, scripting or appearing in over 800 programmes, and lectured internationally. Was a chief examiner on the history of art for London University. Showed at RI, RBA, NS, elsewhere in Britain and overseas. Had a special interest in conservation and was one of the British team sent to Florence after flooding in the 1960s. Finally lived in Brecon, Powys.

John W MILLS 1933– Sculptor in bronze, writer, born in London. Studied at Hammersmith School of Art, 1947–54, with Leon Underwood and Keith Godwin, then Royal College of Art, 1956–60, under John Skeaping, Robert Carruthers and Ralph Brown. Became a fellow and president of RBS. Among several works on the technique of sculpture were *Sculpture in Concrete*, *The Technique of Casting for Sculpture*, and *Modelling the Figure and Head*. Showed at AIA; Pollock Gallery, Toronto; Alice Simsar Gallery, Michigan; Madden Gallery; Robin Gibson Gallery, Sydney; Galerie Cassiope, France; Alwin Gallery; Beaux Arts Gallery, Bath; King Street Gallery; Minories, Colchester; and Jonathan Poole Fine Art, Oxfordshire. Main works included Memorial to William Blake; Jorrocks; Blitz, St Paul's; and St George, New Orleans. HM Queen Elizabeth The Queen Mother; London Fire Brigade; Chicago Institute of Fine Art; and Universities of Cambridge, Oxford, Manchester and Michigan held examples. Lived in Hinxworth, near Baldock, Hertfordshire.

Pippa MILLS 1962– Painter, noted especially for still life in oil, but who later worked in gouache, born in Brighton. She did a foundation course at Worcester Technical College, 1978–80, winning an honours degree in fine art at Gloucestershire College of Art, Cheltenham, 1981–4. In 1987 she gained the Young Artist's Prize at Hunting Group Art Prizes, also showing at NEAC. In 1991–2 exhibited with RWA and at Turtle Fine Art, Cheltenham, also with Richard Hagen at Broadway in 1994.

William MILLS 1923– Painter and teacher, born in Hampshire. He served in the Royal Air Force, 1941–5, then studied painting at Goldsmiths' College School of Art, 1945–9. Taught part-time at Goldsmiths' in 1950, later full-time in Hertfordshire, part-time at Chelsea School of Art from 1978, giving up all teaching in 1988. The development of rheumatoid arthritis in 1970, which later became more acute, and several heart attacks were problems for Mills, but he continued a prolific painter. Early on he was influenced by Klee and de Staël and later the American Expressionists. Painted abstracts, but these developed into gestural, juicy landscapes. Spain was a favourite subject after a visit to Ronda in 1980 as was the countryside around his home at Knighton, Powys. Bill Mills had many shows in London and Wales, sharing an exhibition at Alpha House Gallery, Sherborne, 1992. Work held by several public collections.

David Wynn MILLWARD 1944– Versatile artist and teacher, born in Shrewsbury, Shropshire, who trained as a lawyer while painting and exhibiting. After a time working in advertising and several years as a freelance artist, studied at Royal Academy Schools under Peter Greenham and Edward Bawden, 1971–4. Was awarded the Griffin Prize, 1972; Print Prize for Screenprinting and Etching, 1972 and 1973; Landseer Scholarship and Connoisseur Prize for Painting, both 1973. From 1974–5 obtained art teacher's certificate, at Goldsmiths' College. Exhibited widely in America and Britain, including RA Summer Exhibition and RWA, solo shows including Newtown Memorial Gallery, 1976. Lived with his wife, the children's writer Jenny Nimmo, in a water-mill at Llangynyw, Welshpool, Powys, where a summer school of painting and drawing was held. National Museum of Wales, Cardiff, WAC and Bolton Arts Council hold Millward's work.

John MILNE 1931–1978 Sculptor in bronze, wood, aluminium and stone. Born in Eccles, Lancashire, Milne studied electrical engineering at Salford Royal Technical College in 1945, then transferred to the art school at the College, specialising in sculpture, until 1951. In the following year he attended the Académie de la Grande Chaumière, in Paris. For two years he was then a pupil of the sculptor Barbara Hepworth and her assistant. Although some of Hepworth's assistants later moved away from her style, Milne's work continued to bear some relation to it. Milne from the early 1960s visited Greece regularly, an influence which showed itself in works such as Gnathos, owned by the Tate Gallery. Milne participated in many group exhibitions, including Penwith Society and Newlyn Society, in Cornwall, Plymouth City Art Gallery and Genesis Galleries, New York. One-man exhibitions included several at Marjorie Parr Gallery, Lad Lane Gallery, Dublin, and a retrospective at the City Art Gallery, Plymouth, in 1971. Lived at St Ives, Cornwall.

John Maclauchlan MILNE 1885–1957 Painter, mainly of landscapes, who worked on the continent as well as in Scotland. Exhibited extensively at RSA, also at Royal Glasgow Institute of the Fine Arts and Walker Art Gallery, Liverpool. Elected RSA in 1937. Lived in Dundee, Angus.

Malcolm MILNE 1887–1954 Artist, especially in pen and ink and watercolour, born in Cheadle, Cheshire. Educated at Sedbergh School, he was articled to Thomas Worthington & Sons, architects, in Manchester, but ill-health prevented his following a professional career, so encouraged by his amateur painter father he turned to art. From 1908–11 studied at Slade School of Fine Art with Henry Tonks and at Westminster School of Art with Walter Sickert. After World War I service in First British Ambulance Unit in Italy, in 1919 resumed professional artist's life and joined NEAC, where he showed regularly. In 1928 elected member of Manchester Academy, where he showed until 1952. Milne travelled widely in Britain and on the continent, producing work of singular delicacy. In 1947 shared show with Robin Ironside at Redfern Gallery. Died in Oxford. A show of his early work was held at Maltzahn Gallery in 1971. Tate Gallery, British Museum and Victoria & Albert Museum hold his pictures.

Peter MILNE 1912– Part-time painter who worked in local government, born in North Shields, Northumberland. A self-taught artist, he showed at Shipley Art Gallery in Gateshead and the Laing

Art Gallery in Newcastle upon Tyne, as well as with Wallsend Art Club with which he was long associated. Lived in Newcastle.

Susan MILNE fl. from late 1950s– Artist, designer, illustrator and teacher with a strong interest in natural history environment, born in Sussex, who trained at St Martin's School of Art, 1954–9, specialising in book illustration. After working in London design studios she freelanced, clients including Liberty's and periodicals. In 1975 she moved to Surrey, with her husband Michael Bowers, and began illustrating gardening books for Blandford Press, other publishers and the Woodland Trust. Michael Bowers Editions was set up in 1979, to produce texts and illustrations for books from major publishers, and two years later the Bowers family moved to the Black Mountains, Wales. Milne's teaching included Inner London Education Authority schools; University of Greenwich; Hereford College of Art; International Agarische Hogeschool, Netherlands, and elsewhere. Development Board of Rural Wales commissioned two paintings from her. In 1994, Milne gained a WAC Travel Grant to work in the Netherlands, the year she had a solo show at Brecknock Museum, Brecon, a retrospective following at Rye Art Gallery, 1995.

Allan MILNER 1910–1984 Painter whose output included abstract and Surrealist works, born in Castleford, Yorkshire. He attended the local Grammar School, where his art teacher also taught the sculptor Henry Moore, then went to Leeds College of Art and the Royal College of Art. Exhibited in 1932 at Mayor Gallery, having a portrait bought by the artist Edward Wadsworth. In World War II served in the Royal Navy. Exhibited in mixed exhibitions at Redfern Gallery and Gimpel Fils and had solo shows including E L T Mesens' London Gallery, 1949, and Woodstock Gallery, 1967. Salford Art Gallery bought an oil, Abstraction, in 1956. Settled in Ramsey, Isle of Man, where he was a founder-member and became vice-president of the Mannin Art Group, where he was a prolific exhibitor. The Manx Museum, Douglas, holds an abstract watercolour and a Manx landscape by Milner. The artist was described by one friend as a "stout bohemian fellow, competent with both brush and corkscrew". He was an able piano and organ player whose "hero was Bach", and was also said to be "a red-hot Communist". Later in life Milner was reported suffering from dizziness, finally from senile dementia, and he died in Ballymona Hospital.

Donald Ewart MILNER 1898–1993 Painter, stained glass designer, typographer and teacher, born in Huddersfield, Yorkshire. He was the son of artist James Milner and husband of artist Mildred Milner. Donald Milner studied at Camberwell School of Arts and Crafts and Royal College of Art, 1919–23. He became principal of the West of England College of Art, Bristol, after teaching at art schools in Birmingham and Gloucester. Milner did typographical design for several publishers, including Bibliographical Society and Sidgwick and Jackson. He was president of RWA 1974–8 and showed at RA, NEAC, Arts Council and Cooling Galleries. Bristol Courts of Justice and the University and Ivy Hatch Church, in Kent, have Milner's stained glass windows. Victoria & Albert Museum and public galleries in Bristol and Gloucester hold works by him. Lived latterly at Wotton-under-Edge, Gloucestershire. Died of leukaemia. RWA gave him a memorial show in 1995.

Elizabeth MILNER 1861–1953 Engraver of coloured mezzotints and early in her career a painter, born in Stockton-on-Tees, County Durham. She studied at Lambeth, St John's Wood and Royal Academy Schools and at Hubert von Herkomer's School at Bushey, gaining a silver medal at South Kensington. She settled in Bushey, Hertfordshire, and showed at RA, SWA, ROI, Walker Art Gallery in Liverpool and elsewhere. The Duke of Sussex and Lady Castlereagh were among many portraits.

James Hiley MILNER 1869–1954 Painter, printmaker noted for his colour woodcuts and teacher, born in Huddersfield, Yorkshire, father of the artist Donald Milner. He studied at Huddersfield School of Art, in Manchester, at City & Guilds of London Art School and at Atelier Colarossi, Paris. He sometimes signed his work H M. Milner was an associate of RWA and a leading member of the South London Group, showing at RA, NEAC, LG and widely in the provinces. Borough of Camberwell obtained his picture Grand Surrey Canal, Peckham. Lived in London.

John MILNER 1876–1951 Painter and draughtsman, born in Nottingham, who studied at the School of Art there, 1897–1905, under Wilson Foster, Joseph Harrison and Thomas Barrett. In 1904 won a bronze medal at South Kensington for life drawing. Father of the artist Vernon Milner. Went on to exhibit Nottingham City Museum and Art Gallery, RCamA and Midlands galleries. Morning Glory and Bridlington Harbour are among his most notable works. Member of Colwyn Bay Sketch Club and lived at Trefriw, Caernarvonshire, north Wales.

Marion MILNER 1900–1998 Freudian psychoanalyst who obtained a science degree in psychology and physiology, but had an interest in painting persisting from childhood. In 1947 she began attending a holiday painting school run by Cedric Morris and Arthur Lett-Haines (Benton End, near Hadleigh, Suffolk); from 1953 for four years studied at the weekend painting classes at the exiled University of Vilno, in London, run by Marian Bohusz-Szyszko; and attended several of Harry Thubron's Boxford Summer Courses. Milner went on to exhibit in England and France and had a first solo show at Drian Galleries in 1971. She also contributed articles to learned journals within her specialisation and wrote books, mainly under the pseudonym Joanna Field, including *A Life of One's Own*, 1934; *An Experiment in Leisure*, 1937; *On Not Being Able to Paint*, 1950; and *The Hands of the Living God*, 1969. Her brother was the atomic physicist and Nobel prizewinner P M S Blackett.

Mildred G MILNER 1896–1982 Mainly a landscape artist and draughtsman, she studied at Brunswick Road School of Art in Gloucester. married the painter Donald Ewart Milner. She was a prolific exhibitor at RWA, of which she was an associate, 1934–57, also showing at RA. Lived for many years at Wotton-under-Edge, Gloucestershire.

Stuart MILNER 1909–1969 Painter and interior designer who studied at Central School of Art and Regent Street Polytechnic School of Art, 1926–9. Exhibited RA, RSA, RHA, RBA, RI, widely in the provinces and Paris Salon. Northampton Central Museum and Art Gallery bought his work. Member of Essex Art Club. Lived for some time at Woodford Green, Essex.

John MILNES-SMITH 1912– Painter and collagist, notably of abstract work, born in Middlesex. From 1934–8 Milnes-Smith studied at the Architectural Association, specialising in historic buildings, qualifying in 1939. From 1940–4 war service took Milnes–Smith to the Far East. His painting in the late-1940s was representational, although he fast moved towards abstraction, in 1951 being represented in British Abstract Art at Gimpel Fils, the first of many group appearances in the 1950s. In 1959 he had his first solo show at New Vision Centre, four years later beginning a long association with Drian Galleries. In 1988 he shared a show called Reflections of the Fifties at England & Co, and in 1990 was given a retrospective at Austin/Desmond Fine Art. National Gallery in Gdansk, Poland, holds his work. Lived in London.

Keith MILOW 1945– Painter interested in architecture who created two-dimensional and three-dimensional images in a variety of materials, employing symbols such as crosses and cenotaphs, often in sustained series. He was born in London, but eventually settled in New York. Milow studied at Camberwell School of Art, 1962–7, and Royal College of Art, 1967–8. He did experimental work at Royal Court Theatre in the latter year, and after teaching at Ealing School of Art, 1968–70, was Gregory Fellow as artist-in-residence at University of Leeds, in the early 1970s having two years in New York under a Harkness Fellowship. Returned to teach at Chelsea School of Art for a time. Milow won a Calouste Gulbenkian Visual Arts Award, 1976; First (equal) prize at Tolly Cobbold/Eastern Arts, 1979; and Arts Council Major Award in the same year. Showed widely internationally and solo with Nigel Greenwood Inc. Arts Council holds his work.

Jack MILROY 1938– Artist, notable for torn paper works, and teacher, born in Glasgow. Taught at West Surrey College of Art and Design, in Farnham. He was included in The British Art Show, organised by Arts Council with tour, 1980, chosen by the critic William Packer. Solo shows included Hester van Royen Gallery, 1977, and Glen Hanson Gallery, Minneapolis, 1979. Lived in London.

Lisa MILROY 1959– Painter, noted for her minute depiction of similar objects, as in Lightbulbs, shown in South Bank Centre's tour The British Art Show 1990, and Handles, with which she won first prize at John Moores Exhibition, Liverpool, 1989–90. Milroy was born in Vancouver, Canada. Attended Banff School of Fine Art, 1976; L'Université de la Sorbonne, Paris, 1977–8; St Martin's School of Art, 1978–9; and Goldsmiths' College School of Art, 1979–82. Participated in many mixed shows after Charterhouse Gallery in 1983, including John Moores from 1985; Sixth Sydney Biennale, 1986; Current Affairs, Museum of Modern Art, Oxford, and Eastern Europe tour, 1987; Art of the '80s, from the Collection of Chemical Bank, Montclair Art Museum, New Jersey, 1989; and About Vision, Museum of Modern Art, Oxford, 1996–7, and tour. Showed solo with Nicola Jacobs Gallery from 1984, later solo exhibitions including Galerie Patrick de Brock, Belgium, 1996. Lived in London.

Geoffrey MILSOM 1917– Sculptor, born in Castleford, West Yorkshire, who settled in Cardiff. He was at Leeds College of Art, 1934–6, then Royal College of Art, 1936–9. Was one of Jack Beddington's *Young Artists of Promise* in the 1957 book of that title. His Torso in Portland stone therein depicted found its way into the Arts Council's Welsh collection. Cardiff Corporation commissioned work by him and he showed in group exhibitions at Howard Roberts Gallery, Cardiff; Dillwyn Gallery, Swansea; SWG and elsewhere. In latter years Milsom was an infrequent exhibitor.

Frith MILWARD 1906–1982 Painter in watercolour and oil and teacher, full name Frank Frith Milward, born in Worcester Park, Surrey, married to the artist Lydia Peggy Rogenhagen. Both were keen gardeners. He studied at Wimbledon Art School under Gerald Cooper, then Kingston Art School with Anthony Betts and at the Royal College of Art under William Rothenstein. Milward went on to teach at Abbotsholme School, Rocester, then at Burslem Art School, part of Stoke-on-Trent College of Art, until retirement. Showed with Kingston Group and LG, Manchester Art Club and Staffordshire Art Society, also in Buxton. Died in Stoke-on-Trent City General Hospital and was buried at Newtown Longnor, near Buxton, Derbyshire, where he lived, a funeral attended by many artists including John Piper. His wife, who painted in the manner of Chagall and exhibited locally, is also buried at Newtown Longnor, having died in 1986.

Neil MINERS 1931– Painter and printmaker, born in Redruth, Cornwall, full name Samuel Arthur Neil Miners. Studied drawing at Falmouth School of Art, 1948, under Jack Chalker, and painting privately. The Cornish coast, landscape and seascapes were common features of Miners' work, shown at ROI, RI and in a series of solo exhibitions, notably at Falmouth Art Gallery, 1985–88–92. In his late-fifties Miners suffered a stroke, but was able to resume work after two years. Royal National Lifeboat Institution, HRH The Prince of Wales and Trinity House hold examples. Lived in Falmouth, Cornwall.

Tim MINETT 1947– Sculptor who specialised in work for the silversmith trade, born in Greenwich, southeast London. He trained at Royal College of Art and undertook many commissions for private companies and individuals, including Milton Keynes Development Corporation. Lived in Hebron, Dyfed.

Bill MING 1944– Artist in various media, teacher and curator, born in Bermuda, who settled in England in 1971. For a time he was a merchant seaman. Ming studied at Mansfield College of Art, 1975–6, gaining a degree in sculpture and creative writing from Maidstone College of Art, 1979. Went on to act as an advisor to the Arts Council, East Midlands Arts and Angel Row Gallery in Nottingham. In 1992–3 Ming won the Henry Moore Fellowship in Sculpture at Liverpool University. By then he had taken part in a variety of projects, including carving and mask-making workshops widely throughout the Midlands; had been a part-time lecturer at Loughborough College of Art and Leicester Polytechnic; had finished a mural at Chesterfield Youth Club; and had completed a series of commissions, including Appleton Gate Mural at Newark-on-Trent, and Paging the Oracle at Beaumont Leys Library, Leicester. In addition to group shows held solo exhibitions at Crucible Theatre, Sheffield, and Gold Frame Gallery, Leicester, 1982, later ones including Mappin Gallery, Sheffield, 1989, and Sculp/Lages at Commonwealth Institute in 1993. A strong African element ran through Ming's work, which is held by the African Archive. Lived in Newark-on-Trent, Nottinghamshire.

Michael MINNIS fl. from mid-1980s– Painter who gained a first-class degree in painting from Manchester Polytechnic in 1986, then his master's in fine art from University of Ulster, Belfast, in 1989. He received the Prince's Trust Award in 1990, in 1993 the Victor Treacy Award at Butler Gallery, Kilkenny. Took part in numerous exhibitions and tours, including British Telecom New Contemporaries, 1989–90; Shifting Borders, commissioned by Laing Art Gallery, Newcastle, as part of a European Arts Festival, 1992; and in 1994 Beyond the Partitions, organised by Queen Street Studios, Belfast, with which he was associated. Minnis was co-founder and secretary of FlaxArt Studios, where he was based. In 1993 he was invited to put on a solo show at Werkstatt Galerie, Bremen, in Germany.

John MINTON 1917–1957 Painter, illustrator and teacher, born near Cambridge. Studied art at St John's Wood Art Schools, 1935–8, under Patrick Millard and Kenneth Martin. During the following year he stayed in Paris, where French Neo-Romantic painting made a strong impression. Was a conscientious objector during World War II. Designer for John Gielgud's production of *Macbeth*, 1941. Shared a studio with Robert Colquhoun and Robert MacBryde, 1943–6, and with Keith Vaughan, 1946–52, which reinforced his association with the English Neo-Romantic movement. From 1943–6 Minton taught at Camberwell School of Arts and Crafts, at the Central School of Arts and Crafts, 1946–8, and at Royal College of Art, 1948–57. He was a popular, charismatic teacher and personality, who in later years continued to be a cult figure. Minton's work has an assured linear quality, seen in his illustrations to Alain-Fournier's *The Wanderer* and a number of other books. He also painted on a large scale with a distinctive palette, work stemming from travels in Corsica, Spain, the West Indies and Morocco in the late 1940s and early 1950s. Minton exhibited at the RA, LG, RBA and Lefevre Gallery, and had a first one-man show at Redfern Gallery in 1945. Lived in London and committed suicide. Arts Council memorial exhibition, London and touring, 1958–9, with retrospectives at Reading Museum & Art Gallery, 1974, and Royal College of Art, 1994, and tour.

Julian MINTON 1945– Artist and teacher. Attended Camberwell School of Arts and Crafts and Royal Academy Schools. He was awarded the Landseer Prize, David Murray Studentship and Etching Prize. Minton went on to teach in London and to show widely there and overseas. In 1980–5 was included in Woodlands Art Gallery show Figurative Painters, a series of exhibitions which he had originally organised in association with the Opix Gallery. Solo shows included London University, 1971; Allfarthing Gallery, 1976; and Opix Gallery, 1978.

Wladyslaw MIRECKI 1956– Painter, born in Chelmsford of Polish parents. He was self-taught, having painted all his life including periods spent gaining a science degree, as an industrial designer and then as co-proprietor of Chappel Galleries, at Chappel, in Essex. He showed there from 1986. Other mixed shows included NEAC, 1988; Epping Forest District Museum, Artists in Essex, 1989; and Southend-on-Sea 31st Open Exhibition, 1989, where Essex County Council bought his work. Had a first solo show at Chappel Galleries in 1990, another at Foyles Art Gallery, 1991, and in 1996 an exhibition of his watercolours marked the tenth anniversary of Chappel Galleries. The Chappel Viaduct and Essex countryside were strong features of Waj's work.

Quddus MIRZA 1961– Painter, born in Lahore, Pakistan. He was trained in the art of Indian miniature and drew inspiration from Dubuffet and Klee and the art of children. He obtained an honours degree with distinction at National College of Arts, Lahore, 1986, completed a miniature painting course in Jaipur, India, in 1988, then obtained master's degree in painting at Royal College of Art, London, in 1991. From the start of the 1990s appeared in group shows in Britain and abroad, and had a solo exhibition at Mina Renton Gallery, 1992. Won a number of awards, including British Council Award for postgraduate studies, 1989–91; Royal College Award for Studio Cité Internationale des Arts, Paris, and Maclennan Prize, 1990; and Punjab Painting Prize, 1991. National Art Gallery, Islamabad, holds his work.

Lionel MISKIN 1924– Painter, ceramist and teacher, born in Cannes, France, who attended Oxford University. He studied at St Martin's School of Art, printmaking at Central School of Art and Oskar Kokoschka's classes in London. Went to Cornwall in 1949, living in Mevagissey, then moved to Falmouth in 1967 where he was principal lecturer in art history and complementary studies at the School of Art until 1981, on retirement moving to Paphos, Cyprus. Early in the 1990s returned to settle in Devon. Exhibited widely throughout Britain, Ireland and Cyprus, notably Woodstock Gallery and Dartington Hall; in 1989 was included in

Newlyn Orion Galleries show A Century of Art in Cornwall 1889–1989; then in 1994 in Falmouth Connections at Falmouth Art Gallery.

Dhruva MISTRY 1957– Sculptor whose work fused Indian and European elements, received and invented forms, and who worked in a wide range of styles. He gained his master's degree at Maharaja Sayajirao University of Baroda, India, 1974–81, obtaining another at Royal College of Art under a British Council scholarship, 1981–3. He was artist-in-residence at Kettle's Yard, Cambridge, 1984–5, having his first British show there in the latter year. In 1991 Mistry was the youngest RA to be elected since Turner. He showed in RA Summer Exhibition, represented Britain in the 3rd Rodin Grand Prize Exhibition, Japan, 1990, and was in the Arts Council's Recent British Sculpture, 1993–4. In 1996 Dhruva Mistry Unmasked, a show of wooden masks, inaugurated the Meghraj Gallery and an exhibition at the Yorkshire Sculpture Park, West Bretton, surveyed his previous six years' output. At this time Mistry was planning his return to India. Commissions included National Museum of Wales in Cardiff, Birmingham City Council for Victoria Square in Birmingham and Hunterian Art Gallery, University of Glasgow. Lived in Ingatestone, Essex.

Betty MITCHELL 1927– Weaver, artist in gouache and teacher, sometimes known by her married name of Betty Randles. Born in Wakefield, Yorkshire, she was educated at King's College, Newcastle upon Tyne, Durham University, where she obtained a Bachelor of Arts degree studying with Robin Darwin, 1947–8, and Lawrence Gowing, 1948–50. Showed at Wakefield City Art Gallery and elsewhere. Lectured on textiles, at Carlisle College of Art, then Bradford Regional College of Art, 1955–9. Lived in Holmfirth, Yorkshire.

Bob MITCHELL 1930– Abstract sculptor in various materials, and teacher. He became head of sculpture at Kennington School of Art, having studied there under David McFall and before that under Karel Vogel at Camberwell School of Arts and Crafts. He was a fellow of RBS. Shows included Alwin Gallery; Guildford Art Gallery; New York Exhibition and Basle Arts Fair both from 1979; and RA. Bolton Art Gallery, Cambridge University and Trades Union Congress hold his work. Lived at Hinxworth, Hertfordshire.

Brenda MITCHELL 1933– Painter of landscape in an Impressionistic style. She showed at many galleries in Britain, notably in the West Country, including Northcott Theatre and Barnfield Theatre, Exeter, Chapter House at Exeter Cathedral, Red House Art Centre in Crediton, Boundary Gallery in Framlingham, PS and at Linda Blackstone Gallery, Pinner. Cards & Prints by Art Marketing published her work.

Chuck MITCHELL fl. from c.1960– Artist in a variety of media who studied at Glasgow School of Art, 1958–63, graduating in printed textiles and doing a post-diploma year. He joined the School's staff, working in the textile department until 1988, after which he worked full-time on exhibitions and commissions. Mitchell's work sometimes had a fantastic, highly imaginative element. He developed a technique for painting on slates and showed these in his solo shows at Compass Gallery, Glasgow, in 1969–71, and at Broughton Gallery in 1980. He also showed at Qantas Gallery, 1977, in London, in other mixed shows in Britain and participated in the Compass Gallery's The Compass Contribution in 1990.

Crawford MITCHELL 1908–1976 Printmaker and teacher, born and lived in Belfast, Northern Ireland, who gained a scholarship to the city's School of Art, spending another three at Royal College of Art. On return to Belfast in 1935 he began teaching, most of his career being spent at Grosvenor High School, 1950–70, as head of art. Showed at RUA of which he was made an associate in 1975, the year he won its silver medal. Victoria & Albert Museum holds his work. Rupert Stanley College, Belfast, held a memorial show, 1977.

Denis MITCHELL 1912–1993 Sculptor, painter and teacher, born in Wealdstone, Middlesex. When a baby his family moved to Mumbles near Swansea, where he grew up. In 1930 he attended evening classes at Swansea School of Art, then moved to the St Ives area of Cornwall in 1938. A series of jobs followed over the years, such as running a market garden and tin mining, and while doing them Mitchell pursued his painting seriously. Started to sculpt in wood when became assistant to Barbara Hepworth, 1949–59. He began Porthia Textile Prints, 1957–60, his first sculptures in bronze being done in 1959. Taught part-time at Redruth Art School and Penzance Grammar School, 1960–7, then was able to become full-time sculptor, living and working in Newlyn. Mitchell's sculpture is elegant and beautifully finished, abstract with figurative references. In 1968 the Foreign Office commissioned a bronze sculpture for the University of the Andes, Bogota, Colombia, where Mitchell lectured briefly two years later. He participated in many group exhibitions and had a lot of solo shows, including Britain and overseas. Glynn Vivian Art Gallery, Swansea, gave him a retrospective in 1979; Penwith Galleries, St Ives, 1992; and Flowers East, 1993, during which he died at Newlyn, Cornwall. In 1996, Penwith Galleries held a two-man show of Mitchell and his old friend, Tom Early. For many years he had shared a studio complex there with the painter John Wells. Arts Council, Tate Gallery and many public collections hold Mitchell's work.

Enid MITCHELL fl. from 1960s– Sculptor of figures and portraits in a variety of materials, including ceramic, who studied at Ealing School of Art, teachers including Robert Thomas and Tom Bailey. She was a fellow of RBS and a member of SPS. Leamington Spa Art Gallery and Museum holds her ciment fondu figure Hodie, of 1971. Lived in London, then Swindon, Wiltshire.

Frederick James MITCHELL 1902–1982 Painter, artist in black-and-white, teacher and designer, born and lived in London.

He studied at Willesden School of Art, 1917–20, then Royal College of Art, 1920–4, under Robert Anning Bell, Edward Johnston and Eric Kennington. Taught at Hornsey School of Art, 1932–47. Was a member of Art Workers' Guild from 1957, and of Chelsea Arts Club. A roll of honour for Wakefield Cathedral was one of a number of public commissions. Exhibited RA, NEAC, RBA, RP and elsewhere.

Gordon Kinlay MITCHELL 1952– Painter and muralist working in oil, acrylic and watercolour, producing Surrealist pictures, born and lived in Edinburgh. He attended the College of Art there, 1970–4, under Sir Robin Philipson, won a Postgraduate Scholarship, 1974–5, then a Travelling Scholarship to Ireland, 1975–6, after which he was a professional artist. Mitchell was a member of SSA and SSWA. Completed murals for Royal Navy, Edinburgh University and National Westminster Bank. He exhibited at RSA, RSW and Royal Glasgow Institute of the Fine Arts. Also had a series of solo shows, including Henderson Gallery, Edinburgh; other appearances included Traverse Theatre and Open Eye Gallery, Edinburgh; Dorothy Quinn Gallery, St Andrews; Blue & White Gallery, Jerusalem, and Roger Billcliffe Fine Art, Glasgow, 1995. Scottish Arts Council and corporate collections hold examples of work that was often quirky and witty.

Helen MITCHELL 1924– Self-taught artist in pastel, born in Nottingham, who began painting in 1990. Her husband was the 1978 Nobel Prize-winning chemist Dr Peter Mitchell, who died in 1992. He ran his own laboratory, with which his wife was involved. She showed with J L W Bird, her solo shows including Camelford Museum Gallery (in Cornwall, where she lived at Glynn, Bodmin) and Workshop Design, Cambridge.

John MITCHELL 1937– Watercolourist, printmaker and teacher, born in Glasgow. He studied at Edinburgh College of Art, 1956–61, and exhibited in Scotland, notably at SSA and RSW of which he was a member. Scottish Arts Council holds his work. Lived at Lower Largo, Fife.

John MITCHELL 1942– Painter and teacher who studied at Kingston College of Art. He taught at Coventry College of Art, 1964–71, where he was associated with the founder-members of Art & Language. After that he taught at Stourbridge College of Art. Was Gregory Fellow at Leeds University, 1978–80, and taught at Birmingham College of Arts and Crafts. Mitchell was interested in the nature of colour and form and in the way spaces or shapes geometrically identical can deceive the eye by the manner in which they are related on paper or canvas. Arts Council holds such a work: Gate, of 1976. Mitchell was well thought of on the continent, showing often at Galerie Swart, Amsterdam. Had a major one-man show at Ikon Gallery, Birmingham, 1987, and was included in the South Bank Centre 1988–9 touring exhibition The Presence of Painting.

John MITCHELL 1953– Artist working in variety of materials including found objects, born in Glasgow. He attended Edinburgh College of Art, 1974–8, with a Summer School at Yale University, 1977; Goldsmiths' College School of Art, 1979–80, returning for his art teacher's certificate, 1984–5; then attended Institute of Education, 1989. He showed with Printmakers' Workshop, Edinburgh, 1977; New Contemporaries, ICA, 1980; Woodlands Art Gallery, 1986; and in South Bank Centre's The British Art Show 1990 and tour. Shared shows at Mercer Union Gallery, Toronto, 1981, and in a John Hansard Gallery exhibition, The Gantry, Southampton, 1986, with tour. His solo exhibitions included Riverside Studios, 1986, and Seagate Gallery, Dundee, 1987. Lived in London.

Jonathan MITCHELL 1960– Painter who gained a bachelor's degree and higher diploma in painting at Slade School of Fine Art, 1979–85. In 1988 won the Elizabeth Greenshields Award. Group exhibition appearances included Pick of the Graduate Shows, Christie's, 1983; Robertson Mort Gallery, Bedford, 1987; and The Prose of Painting at Austin/Desmond Fine Art, 1991, one of seven figurative artists. Lived in St Albans, Hertfordshire.

Madge Y MITCHELL 1892–1974 Painter and teacher, born in Uddingston, near Glasgow. She studied at Gray's School of Art, Aberdeen, then for a short time in Paris. Mitchell taught portrait painting at Gray's from 1917–53, then pursued a career as a portrait painter. Lord Boyd-Orr and the children of Lord Airlie were among her sitters. She showed widely in group exhibitions, including Aberdeen Artists' Society, of which she was a member. Aberdeen Art Gallery and the public gallery in Auckland, New Zealand, hold her work. Lived in Aberdeen.

Maggie MITCHELL fl. from c.1905–1953 Sculptor, noted for her figurative work, born in London, married to the artist George J Mitchell. She studied at Goldsmiths' College School of Art and Royal College of Art, was an associate of RBS and a member of RBA. Also exhibited at RA, RSA, SWA, Royal Glasgow Institute of the Fine Arts and Walker Art Gallery in Liverpool. Mitchell's powerful study Chloe is illustrated in the 1939 volume *RBS: Modern British Sculpture*. From the early-1920s she lived in Somerset, settling eventually at Norton sub Hamdon.

Sheila MITCHELL fl. from 1940s– Sculptor in a variety of materials, married to the artist Charles Bone. She was educated in Farnham, Surrey, near where she settled at Puttenham, and studied at the School of Art there, 1946, with Charles Vyse. Also attended Guildford School of Art, 1947, with Willi Soukop, and Royal College of Art, 1948–51, teachers including John Skeaping and Frank Dobson. Royal Worcester Porcelain commissioned her designs. Mitchell was a fellow of RBS and a member of SPS, becoming president. Showed also at RA, NEAC, Ashgate Gallery in Farnham and Furneaux Gallery. Had a series of solo shows, including Ashgate Gallery, Gainsborough's House, Sudbury, and University of Surrey, Guildford, 1994.

William George MITCHELL 1925– Sculptor and designer, born in London, where he continued to live. Studied at Southern

College of Art in Portsmouth, at Royal College of Art and at British School in Rome; was an Abbey Award-winner. Went on to lecture widely and was a member of the design advisory board, Hammersmith College of Art and Trent Polytechnic. Also did work for Concrete Society and completed a frieze for Swiss Cottage Library.

Louise MIZEN 1961– Painter, draughtsman and printmaker, born in Okehampton, Devon. She was an experienced horsewoman who was an associate of the Society of Equestrian Artists and who was noted for her depictions of the horse and human figure in action. In 1979 Mizen did an art foundation course at Brighton Polytechnic, gained an honours degree in fine art at Norwich School of Art, 1980–3, then worked as a freelance professional artist. Took part in mixed shows at Hamilton, Richmond Hill and Walton Galleries and at the Guards Polo Club and in 1994 was runner-up in the Spinal Injuries Association Competition Art and the Racehorse. Had solo exhibitions at 15 Pembridge Road, Notting Hill, from 1991. Commissions included Royal Berkshire Polo Club, Bob Champion Cancer Appeal and Matador, winner of the Volvo Dressage World Cup final. Lived in London.

Jan MLADOVSKY 1946– Artist whose output comprised installations and performance art, and teacher, born in Prague, Czechoslovakia. He studied at Slade School of Fine Art, 1968–72, going on to teach at Croydon School of Art. Mixed shows included Studio Marconi, Milan, 1977; Ikon Gallery, Birmingham, 1980; and in 1981 Art and the Sea at Sunderland Arts Centre and tour, and Summer Show 3 at Serpentine Gallery, where Mladovsky and Simon Desorgher performed *La Mer*. British Council and London Borough of Camden acquired examples. Lived for a time in London.

Piotr MLECZKO 1919–1995 Painter, born in Poland, who became a prisoner of war in Nazi Germany in 1939 and for five years was forced to watch the horrors of nearby concentration camp life. Art became the outlet for his experiences, and he produced haunting, moving pictures. After settling in England in 1946, Mleczko studied at Sir John Cass School, 1950–4, later being influenced and encouraged by the artist Marian Kratochwil. Mleczko was a committee member of the Association of Polish Artists in Great Britain and a member of the Lewes & District Visual Arts Association, in Sussex. Had two exhibitions with Grabowski Gallery, 1961 and 1963, later ones including Lewes Gallery, in Lewes, and Posk Gallery, both 1989. There was a retrospective at the Polish Cultural Institute, 1997.

Harold MOCKFORD 1932– Mainly self-taught artist. He showed with LG, RA Summer Exhibitions and in Arts Council travelling shows. In 1993 won overall prize for outstanding work in the Sussex Open, Brighton, and was included in The Sussex Scene, Hove Museum of Art/Towner Art Gallery, Eastbourne. Had two solo shows at Towner, 1970 and 1987; a solo show at Thackeray Gallery in 1978; two more at Hove, 1980 and 1985; with a retrospective at Newport Museum and Art Gallery, 1995. Hove, the Government Art Collection, the Chantrey Bequest at Tate Gallery hold his work. Mockford painted in and around Eastbourne, Sussex, where he lived for many years.

Halina MODELSKA 1910– Painter and wood carver of Polish origin who attended university in Wilno. During the 1930s she exhibited in Poland, then in England at RI, SWA and with Catholic Guild of Artists and Craftsmen of which she was a member. Lived in London.

Alexander MOFFAT 1943– Painter, notably of portraits of his artistic contemporaries; teacher, writer and curator of exhibitions. He was born in Dunfermline, Fife, and studied at Edinburgh College of Art, 1960–4. For the next decade he worked in an engineering factory and as a photographer. From 1968–78 Moffat was chairman of 57 Gallery, Edinburgh, and he went on to select several shows of contemporary painting. From 1979 Moffat taught at Glasgow School of Art, where he became senior lecturer and was influential as a teacher, breathing new life into the School's tradition of hard-edged figurative painting. Among Moffat's exhibitions was one of his portraits at Scottish National Portrait Gallery, Edinburgh, 1973; a travelling show of portraits of Scottish poets, organised by Third Eye Centre, Glasgow, 1981–2; and portraits of young artists at Scottish National Gallery of Modern Art, 1988. That gallery holds his work.

Helen MOGGRIDGE fl. from 1930s– Painter and draughtsman who studied at Slade School of Fine Art, teachers including Henry Tonks, Walter Westley Russell and Philip Wilson Steer. She exhibited in mixed shows at RA, NEAC, Leicester Galleries, Towner Art Gallery in Eastbourne and with Free Painters and Sculptors, of which she was a fellow from 1972, and Eastbourne Group. Drian and Woodstock Galleries gave her solo shows. Lived in Piddinghoe, Sussex.

Gerald MOIRA 1867–1959 Painter, mural decorator and teacher, born in London. He studied at Royal Academy Schools, 1887–9, winning several prizes, having been earlier tutored and encouraged by his father, a miniature painter who had served in the Portuguese diplomatic service. Moira failed to win the Royal Academy gold medal only by the casting vote of its president, Sir Frederick Leighton. On leaving the Schools Moira immediately set up a studio in London and received a number of important portrait commissions. Showed at RA from 1891 and IS from 1899. Was to become a member of NPS and RWA and hold senior positions in ROI and RWS. Moira went on to become professor of mural and decorative painting at Royal College of Art, 1900–22, then principal of Edinburgh College of Art, 1924–32. In addition to teaching he carried out a formidable number of large commissions, including decorations for the old Trocadero Restaurant, in Shaftesbury Avenue; ceiling for the boardroom of Lloyd's Register; a frieze for the Passmore Edwards Free Library, in Shoreditch; work at the Central Criminal Court; as well as work in private houses, church decorations and many easel pictures. His output had a grand manner feel about it and his colours were rich. Tate Gallery holds his work Washing Day. Died in Northwood, Middlesex.

Victoria MOISEIWITSCH fl. from 1960s– Sculptor and painter who studied painting at St Martin's School of Art. Became interested in modelling abstract forms around 1975, using materials such as concrete and bronze resin, then worked mainly in this medium. Moiseiwitsch showed in a variety of group and mixed shows including Loggia Gallery, 1974; International Art Centre, 1975; Paperpoint Gallery, 1976; and South London Art Gallery, 1978. Shared a show at Ben Uri Gallery in 1979 and was part of a four-man exhibition at Woodlands Art Gallery, 1984.

C Allen MOLD 1905–1952 Painter of watercolours and pastellist. He studied in the evenings at Chiswick Polytechnic with Hubert Schroder and William Cubitt Cooke, 1929–33. His work was often reproduced on calendars. Percy V Bradshaw in his book *Water-colour: A Truly English Art* illustrates examples of Mold's broadly brushed landscape and portrait work. Mold was a member of the Chelsea Arts Club, Langham Sketch Club, PS and RI, with which he showed until 1951, also exhibiting at RA, ROI and in the provinces. Lived in Clavering, Essex.

Sally MOLE 1965– Painter and printmaker who did foundation course at Shrewsbury College of Arts, 1984, then graduated at Bristol Polytechnic with an honours degree, 1987, taking a postgraduate diploma at Royal Academy Schools, 1988–91. Among her many awards were David Murray Landscape Studentship, 1989–90–91, and in 1991 Sir Frank and Lady Short Print Prize and André de Segonzac Travelling Scholarship. Showed at Gateway Arts Centre, Shropshire, and RA Summer Exhibition, from 1990; The Orangery and New Grafton Gallery, 1991; NEAC and The Casson Gallery, 1992; and in 1993 she shared a show at Cadogan Contemporary.

Sylvia MOLLOY 1914– Artist in various media, including stained glass, who studied at Armstrong College, Durham University, 1932–6, teachers including Robert Lyon, then at Johannesburg College of Art, 1949–52. She obtained her master's degree. Molloy was a member of Free Painters and Sculptors and NS, also showing with RA, RBA and SWA. Had a series of solo shows in London and Hertfordshire, including Letchworth, where she lived and where the Art Gallery holds her work.

Jessica MONCKTON 1896–c.1981 Sculptor in wax and clay. Born at Hokstad, South Africa, she studied art with John Erland. Lived in London.

Jane MONCUR 1890–1983 Painter, born in Kirriemuir, Angus. Pre-1914 she studied at Stafford School of Art with Hubert Wellington, then about 1916–18 at Westminster school of Art and with the Camden Town Group member Harold Gilman. These two with Charles Ginner were influences, as was her husband, Herbert William Palliser the sculptor, whom she married in 1921. She showed with LG, NEAC, RA and at Yoxford Art Gallery and died at Yoxford, Suffolk.

Michael MONK 1954– Abstract painter, born in Essex, who attended Thurrock Technical College, 1970–2, then Bath Academy of Art in Corsham, 1972–5. He was included in 55 Wapping Artists, 1979, Whitechapel Open in 1980, then frequently in Wapping Artists Open Studios from that year.

Percy MONKMAN 1892–1986 Artist who was born in Bradford where he studied at the College of Art and at Bradford Arts Club, of which he became chairman. He showed at RI, RBA and extensively in the north of England. He also contributed cartoons and caricatures to *Yorkshire Evening Post, Bradford Telegraph and Argus* and other regional publications. Bradford's Cartwright Hall Art Gallery holds his work. Lived finally at Baildon, Shipley, Yorkshire.

John MONKS 1954– Painter of heavily impastoed interiors and still lifes, printmaker, born Manchester. He graduated from Liverpool College of Art, 1972–5; gained a John Moores Scholarship, Liverpool, 1975–6; then earned his master's degree at Royal College of Art, 1977–80. Group exhibitions included New Contemporaries, where he won a prize, ICA, 1976; New British Painting, Cincinnati Contemporary Art Center, America, and tour, 1988–9; and Monotypes from the Garner Tullis Workshop, Persons Lindell Gallery, Helsinki, 1989. Solo shows included Hull College of Art, 1981; a series at Paton Gallery, from 1985; and Manchester City Art Galleries, 1994. Monks held a number of artist's residencies in America, Yugoslavia and Spain and in 1992 made a sustained lecture tour in America starting with Yale Center for British Art, New Haven. Metropolitan Museum of Art, New York; Yale Center, Manchester City Museum, Contemporary Art Society and many other public and private collections hold examples. Lived in London.

Margaret Arnold MONNAIE 1890– Painter and draughtsman, born in Maidenhead, Berkshire, where she studied at the School of Art, at several schools in London, then in Sussex. She taught and sang for periods professionally. Showed in London and extensively in West Sussex where she was a co-founder of the Arun Art Society. Lived in Ferring, Sussex.

Susie MONNINGTON 1967– Painter, born in Lewes, Sussex, settling nearby at Glynde. She studied at St Martin's School of Art, 1987–90, with Anthony Whishaw, then worked near the Sussex Downs which were "a main influence on my work. I work from the landscape in an intuitive way, without being specific to it." Forms carved into chalk hills were an important element. Showed at NEAC and at 33 Mossop Street in 1990. Had solo exhibitions in 1993 at Mermaid Gallery and Horsham Arts Centre. Tread Softly Because You Tread On My Dreams, of 1991, and Summer Splash, of 1993, were notable works.

Walter Thomas MONNINGTON 1902–1976 Painter, especially of murals. Born in London, he studied at the Slade School in 1918–23, Rome Scholar 1923–6. Married the artist Winifred Knights, 1924. Among his public works are a decoration for St Stephen's Hall, Westminster, 1928, and the new Council House, in Bristol, 1956. Monnington taught drawing at the Royal Academy Schools 1931–9, in 1949 joining the staff of the Slade, whose strong linear tradition marked his own work. Monnington is represented in a number of public galleries, including the Tate. He was elected RA in 1938, became its president in 1966 and was knighted in 1967. There was a memorial exhibition at RA, 1977, another travelling from the British School at Rome to the Royal Albert Memorial Museum in Exeter and the Fine Art Society in 1997. Tom Monnington lived at Groombridge, Kent.

Alfonso López MONREAL 1953– Painter, muralist, printmaker, lecturer and restorer, born in Zacatecas, Mexico, whose country of origin was evident in his colourful work. He spent seven years at Guanajuato University, then moved to S W Hayter's Atelier 17 in Paris in 1976. He lectured in printmaking in Barcelona, 1978–9; at Dublin's National College of Art and Design, 1987–8; and at the University of Ulster, Belfast, 1988–9. During his period as director of restoration for the Musea Pedro Coronel in Zacatecas, from 1981 Monreal also lectured in fine art there. From 1990 he worked as an artist full-time, winning major prizes at open competitions in Mexico and Ireland. He also gained notable commissions for prints and murals in both countries. Monreal was a prolific exhibitor. In 1994 his work was chosen for the Chicago International Art Expo and he was included in Beyond the Partitions, organised by Queen Street Studios, Belfast, with which he was associated. There was a constant string of shows in Mexico, North America and Europe, among them Fenderesky Gallery, Belfast, from 1984; Taylor Galleries, Dublin, from 1987; and Prospectus Gallery, Chicago, 1993.

Nicholas MONRO 1936– Sculptor and teacher, born in London. He studied at Chelsea School of Art, 1958–61, then taught at Swindon School of Art, 1963–8, and Chelsea. Specialised in the life-size figure, modelled and cast in fibreglass. They were realistic and witty, and featured such subjects as Morris Dancers and the comedian Max Wall. A year after his first one-man show at Robert Fraser Gallery, in 1968, Monro received an Arts Council Award, then in 1972 he was featured in Peter Stuyvesant Sculpture Project, in Birmingham, under commission. Monro's work early found favour in Germany, and his shows in that country included Galerie Thelen, at Essen, in 1969. Further British exhibitions included Waddington Galleries, City Art Gallery in Bristol and Felicity Samuel Gallery. Southampton City Art Gallery holds his work. Lived for some years at Newbury, Berkshire.

Lucile Christine MONTAGUE 1950– Painter, born and worked in London, educated at Flying Hall School, Whitby, then studied at Plymouth College of Art, 1967–9, and Byam Shaw School, 1971–4. Showed at RA, LG, Ikon Gallery in Birmingham touring show and elsewhere. Solo exhibitions included Mario Flecha Gallery. Tower Hamlets Picture Loan Scheme holds her work.

Bernard MONTAIGU: *see* **Michael MANNING**

Felicity MONTAIGU 1944– Painter and teacher who studied at Kingston School of Art, 1966–9, winning a French Government Scholarship, 1969–70. Appeared in John Moores Liverpool Exhibition, 1973, in Figurative Painters at Woodlands Art Gallery, 1985, and abroad. Taught widely in London, where she lived.

Fernando MONTES 1930– Painter in egg tempera, born in La Paz, Bolivia. He studied under Vicente Puig in Buenos Aires, in 1959 gained a scholarship from the Spanish government to study at the San Fernando School of Fine Arts in Madrid and in 1960 moved to London, attending St Martin's and Central Schools of Art. Montes' first professional arts activity was in films, as one of a three-man pioneering group that made some of the first Bolivian films. In 1959 he represented Bolivia at the 5th São Paulo Bienal and in 1977 was awarded the first prize in painting at the 2nd IMBO Bienal. In 1993 he was elected academician of the Accademia Archeologica Italiana, Rome. Montes said that his work was inspired by "the relationship of Man and Earth as you see it in the High Andes". He was widely reviewed in the international press and on television and radio, and was included in many mixed shows. Over two dozen solo exhibitions included Galeria Municipal, La Paz, from 1956; St Martin's Gallery, 1965; Upper Grosvenor Galleries, 1968; Madden Galleries, 1975; and among later ones Azabu Museum in Tokyo and Awano Sato Forum, both 1994. National Museum in La Paz; Bolivian Embassy; and Museum of Modern Art, Austin, Texas, hold examples. Lived in London.

Marian Alice MONTFORD 1882– Painter, miniaturist and draughtsman who was married to the sculptor Paul Montford. Studied at Chelsea Polytechnic, Royal Academy Schools and privately with several painters including Sir Arthur Cope. Showed at RA, RMS and in Australia, where she lived for a time. Later lived at Sutton, Surrey.

Amanda MONTGOMERY 1968– Artist known especially for sculpture, and teacher, who did a foundation course at University of Ulster in Belfast, then graduated with a first-class degree in fine art from Coventry University's school of art and design in 1991. She taught sculpture at Ulster University in 1992 and in 1992–3 was artist-in-residence at Share Centre in County Fermanagh. Group shows included Fresh Art Fair, Islington, 1991; No Access at Ross's Court, Belfast, 1992; and Works on Paper and Beyond the Partitions, organised in 1994 by Queen Street Studios, Belfast, with which she was associated. Her solo show Sense ... was shown in the Ardhowen Theatre in Enniskillen and at the Crescent Arts Centre, Belfast, 1993.

Elizabeth MONTGOMERY 1902–1993 Stage designer and painter, born in Oxfordshire. Was so precocious at drawing that her parents sent her to art classes from age of six. Began selling work to *Good Housekeeping*, *Tatler* and *Illustrated London News*, and aged 18 studied at Chelsea Illustrators school, where she met Sophie and Margaret (Percy) Harris. They began to design for the theatre and formed Motley, the leading stage designer of the 1930s and beyond. In New York after World War II Montgomery was responsible for the costumes for the musicals *South Pacific*, *Oklahoma!*, *Can Can* and *Paint Your Wagon* and worked for the Metropolitan Opera House. Settled in England from 1966, then from mid-1970s decided to concentrate on her painting. Her portraits included John Gielgud, Peggy Ashcroft and Edith Evans, as well as stage personalities in America. Died in London.

Kate MONTGOMERY 1965– Painter in casein tempera on wood, and teacher, whose work had a strong pattern element, alluding to medieval painting and the miniaturist tradition of the Moghul Empire. She studied painting at Ruskin School of Drawing and Fine Art, Oxford, 1985–8; taught art history in the city and learned to make furniture, 1988–90; then studied visual Islamic and traditional art at the Royal College of Art, 1990–2, gaining her master's degree with distinction. Won a number of awards including the Prince of Wales' Institute of Architecture Prize, Royal College of Art Degree Show, 1992, in 1992–3 being artist-in-residence at the Prince's Institute. Montgomery taught cultural studies and painting at Central St Martins, 1992, also being a visiting lecturer at the Prince of Wales' Institute. He holds her work. Mixed shows included Contemporary Art Society, Smith's Gallery, 1992; Royal Over-Seas League Open Exhibition, 1994; RA Summer Exhibition and LG Biannual, Barbican Centre, both 1995. Had a solo exhibition at St James' Church, Piccadilly, 1990, later ones including Cadogan Gallery, 1996.

Donald MOODIE 1892–1963 Painter, draughtsman and teacher, born in Edinburgh, where remained, studying at the College of Art, winning the Guthrie Award in 1924 and then joining its staff from 1919 for 36 years. He was a fine Colourist as well as being an excellent draughtsman. Moodie was president of the SSA for several years from 1937 and later was secretary of the RSA for a few years from 1959, having been elected a full member in 1952. Also exhibited at Royal Glasgow Institute of the Fine Arts and at Walker Art Gallery in Liverpool.

Catherine Olive MOODY 1920– Painter and teacher, born in London, daughter of the artist Victor Hume Moody. She studied under him at Malvern School of Art, at Royal College of Art with Gilbert Spencer and at Birmingham College of Art under Bernard Fleetwood-Walker. She taught at Manchester College of Art, then was head of Malvern School of Art, 1962–80. Was a designer for Dent Allcroft and wrote *Silhouette of Malvern*, 1953, and *Painter's Workshop*, 1982. Catherine Moody produced pastel interiors, compositions and portraits. She was a member of PS and president of Malvern Art Club. Showed at PS and RP. Worcester City Art Gallery and Malvern Festival Theatre hold her work. Lived in Malvern, Worcestershire.

Eric MOODY 1946– Artist notable for coloured reliefs with city and suburb as their theme; teacher. He was born in Sedgefield, County Durham, his artistic career being prompted by his father's work as a stone carver. Studied fine art at Sunderland College of Art and Goldsmiths' College School of Art. Also formative for Moody were periods in North America in the 1960s and two separate years at London University, studying aesthetics and the sociology and psychology of art. Went on to teach with the arts policy and management department at City University. Showed at Air, Whitechapel, Royal College of Art, RA Business Art and Curwen Galleries. Also exhibited at Tolly Cobbold/Eastern Arts Fifth National Exhibition and Woodlands Art Gallery, where he had a solo show in 1986.

John Charles MOODY 1884–1962 Painter, printmaker and teacher, born in Walton-on-Thames, Surrey. He studied art in London and in several centres on the continent, eventually becoming principal of Hornsey School of Art, 1926–47. Was president of SGA and Society of Sussex Artists, in 1954. Exhibited at RA, RI, RE, ROI and Royal Glasgow Institute of the Fine Arts, as well as provincial, continental and American galleries. His work was exquisite and academic, mainly of architectural subjects, although he was fond of nature study watercolours. Moody's coloured drawings are reminiscent of the work of George Clausen. Lived in Burpham, Sussex.

Michael David MOODY 1946– Administrator, designer and artist in mixed media, born in Newcastle upon Tyne. He attended the College of Art and Industrial Design there, 1962–7. Went on to work at Imperial War Museum, where he mounted a number of exhibitions; did set designs for film *Overlord*; and wrote on World War I. Sometimes just signed work M. Lived in London.

Ronald MOODY 1900–1984 Sculptor and writer, born in Kingston, Jamaica. He left to study dentistry in England in 1923, but decided to give up practising to sculpt, learning by trial and error. Moody was in 1929 inspired by Egyptian sculptures in the British Museum, and primitive sculpture greatly influenced his work, which was preferably in wood, although periods of ill-health were later to curb his ability to handle large sculptures. Moved to Paris in 1936 and had outstanding early success with one-man exhibitions: in Paris in 1937, and in Amsterdam in 1938. World War II forced his return to England in 1941, which then remained his base. Although he had some success, he was not taken up by the art establishment. Showed often with SPS, of which he was a member, and exhibited solo at Woodstock Gallery in early 1960s. Leicester Museum and Art Gallery and National Gallery in Jamaica, where he was several times honoured, hold his work. Was represented in The Other Story, Hayward Gallery and touring, 1989–90.

Victor Hume MOODY 1896–1990 Artist in oil, pencil and charcoal, and teacher, born in London. He studied at Battersea Polytechnic and at Royal College of Art under William Rothenstein. Became headmaster of Malvern School of Art, 1935–62, succeeded by his daughter, Catherine Olive Moody. Showed at RA, RP and RBSA and had a solo show at Goupil

Gallery, 1939. Moody produced classical compositions and portraits. Harris Museum & Art Gallery in Preston, Bolton and Worcester Libraries and Worcester Cathedral hold examples. Lived in Malvern, Worcestershire.

Jeremy MOON 1934–1973 Painter, sculptor and teacher, born in Cheshire. Studied law at Cambridge University, 1954–7, being the son of a lawyer. He had early thought he would become a classical dancer and drew and painted as a hobby. After National Service in the Far East Moon worked for an advertising agency. When he saw the RBA Situation exhibition, in 1960, it was "like getting the whole message of what modern painting was about suddenly fresh on your doorstep", so he enrolled for a short time, in 1961, at Central School of Art and Design. The following year Moon was awarded the Associated Electrical Industries Prize for Sculpture. He taught at St Martin's School of Art, 1963–8, and Chelsea School of Art, 1963–73. As well as taking part in many group exhibitions Moon had a series of solo shows at Rowan Gallery from 1963. Late in 1973 he was killed in a motorcycle accident, and the following year there was a memorial show at Rowan. In 1976 Arts Council toured a show of his paintings and drawings based on the Serpentine Gallery. Moon's allegiance was to hard-edge abstract painting in which everything was stated unambiguously, and he denied any attempt at representation. Tate Gallery, British Council, Victoria & Albert Museum and many other public collections hold his work.

Liz MOON 1941– Painter and draughtsman whose natural talent produced figurative works of grace and felicity. She was born in Ootacamund, India, and gained her bachelor's and master's degrees in engineering from Oxford University. Worked as a structural engineer in Malaysia and San Francisco. Attended San Francisco Art Institute and Redland College, Bristol University, gradually developing a career as a professional artist. Was a member of SWA, also exhibiting with RWA, RBA, RSMA, Old Fire Engine House in Ely, Solent Gallery in Lymington and at Clare Hall, Cambridge, where she lived. Solo exhibitions included Broughton House Gallery in Cambridge, Heifer Gallery and from 1991 The John Russell Gallery, Ipswich.

Mick MOON 1937– Artist, born in Edinburgh, who painted on plastic strips, later using calico and acrylic to create pictures which had characteristics of monoprints and collage. Braque and Cubism were key inspirations. Moon studied at Chelsea School of Art, 1958–62, then at Royal College of Art, 1962–3. For a decade he then taught at Chelsea, from 1973 at Slade School of Fine Art. He had a series of one-man shows at Waddington Galleries from 1969. Appeared in British Painting '74 at Hayward Gallery in that year and in British Painting 1952–1977 at RA in the latter year. Had a one-man at Tate Gallery in 1976, later ones including Alan Cristea Gallery, 1996. Elected RA, 1994. Arts Council holds his work.

Tennant MOON 1914– Artist in pencil, chalk, watercolour and wash, and teacher, born in Penarth, Glamorgan, full name Alan George Tennant Moon. He was at Cardiff School of Art, then at Royal College of Art, 1933–7, under William Rothenstein and Gilbert Spencer. He became a lecturer in the school of painting at Leicester College of Art, 1946–9; principal of Gravesend School of Art, 1949–57; then from 1957–78 principal of Cumbria College of Art & Design. He was chairman of the Association of Art Institutions and a member of the National Society for Art & Design Education, being its president in 1972. Moon showed at Leicester Galleries, Glynn Vivian Art Gallery in Swansea and National Museum of Wales, Cardiff, which holds his work, as does Newport Art Gallery. Lived in Cheltenham, Gloucestershire.

Jim MOONEY 1955– Painter, draughtsman and teacher, born in Glasgow, who was brought up in a mining community in Scotland. Initially his Socialist outlook affected what he painted, influenced by Cubism and the work of French painters such as Léger; later experiences in Italy and Venezuela prompted a broader, less polemical art. Mooney attended Edinburgh College of Art, 1973–8. After he was at Royal College of Art, 1978–81, a Rome Scholarship took him to the British School in Rome, 1981–3. He was at Escuela Campo Alegre, in Caracas, in 1986 under a travel scholarship. He had his first solo show at Edinburgh College of Art in 1981 and was represented in the Royal College of Art's Exhibition Road show in 1988. In 1991 Mooney's mixed-media drawing Mapping Desire was included in the show East at Norwich Gallery. He taught painting at Royal College of Art and was head of painting at Middlesex Polytechnic. Lived in both Edinburgh and London.

John MOONEY 1948– Artist and teacher, born in Edinburgh where he attended the College of Art, 1966–70. In 1970–1 he had a postgraduate year, a 1971 Andrew Grant Travelling Scholarship taking him to Greece, Turkey and Spain. Mooney went on to teach at Edinburgh College of Art. Mooney's prints and paintings from the mid-1960s appeared in such exhibitions as Printmakers' Workshop, Scottish Young Contemporaries and the Pernod Competition, all in Edinburgh, and he was represented in A Choice Selection at Fruit Market Gallery in the city in 1975. Had a first solo show at New 57 Gallery in Edinburgh in 1973.

Martin MOONEY 1960– Painter of landscape and still life in a traditional manner, using warm colours such as olive greens and umbers. He was born in Belfast, Northern Ireland, studying at University of Ulster faculty of art and design, 1979–80; gained an honours degree in fine art at Brighton Polytechnic, 1980–3; then did postgraduate studies at Slade School of Fine Art, 1983–5. In 1986–7 he was a part-time tutor at Brighton College of Art. Among his awards was the Richard Ford Award, RA, 1985. Mixed exhibitions included Stowells Trophy Exhibition at RA, from 1983; NEAC, 1990; and RHA, from 1991. Had a series of solo shows at Solomon Gallery, Dublin, from 1988, and exhibited at Waterman Fine Art, 1995. Government Art Collection, Durban Museum in South Africa and Harvard University in America hold examples. Lived in Donegal, Ireland.

Robert James Enraght MOONY 1879–1946 Painter, born in Athlone, Ireland, who studied art at Académie Julian, Paris. He settled in Mount Hawke, Cornwall, and was a member of the Newlyn Society of Artists as well as an honorary member of the Sheffield Society of Art. Showed prolifically at RBA of which he was also a member, and at RA, NEAC, Royal Glasgow Institute of the Fine Arts and at Carnegie, in Pittsburgh, the public art gallery in Chicago acquiring his picture The Kite.

Alan MOORE 1923– Painter in watercolour and oil, born in Leicester, settling nearby at Oadby. He studied at the Gateway School, affiliated to Leicester College of Art, 1936–9, under Hugh Collinson. Showed at Leicester Society of Artists of which he was a member, Leicester Sketch Club and the local Crown Hills Art Society, and at Nottingham Castle Open Exhibition. University of Leicester holds his work.

Alice MOORE 1909– Embroiderer, illuminator and teacher, born in Honolulu, but moved to Cornwall in 1913, settling in Lelant. She attended Penzance School of Art, 1928–31, specialising in industrial design/illumination, gained her art teacher's diploma at Brighton College of Art, 1931–2, taught in Devizes, Wiltshire, 1932–5, then studied at Royal College of Needlework, 1938–9. Moore brought a modern feel to her embroidery work, with the sea and its creatures key themes. Was a member of Devon Guild of Craftsmen, Penwith Society, Red Rose Guild of Craftsmen and Crafts Centre and was included in the Tate Gallery's 1985 show St Ives 1939–64. Among her solo exhibitions was Penzance Public Library, 1971.

Brenda MOORE fl. from c.1930– Painter and sculptor, she began specialising in art at the age of 14. Scholarship awards gave her six years at Brighton School of Art and three at Royal Academy Schools. In 1935 she married the artist Leonard Campbell Taylor; her portrait head of her husband is the frontispiece of Herbert Furst's 1945 study of him: *Leonard Campbell Taylor, RA, His Place in Art*. After 26 non-painting years Moore launched into portraiture, and her work included flowers and landscapes in oil, watercolour and line. Showed at RA, Fermoy Art Gallery for the King's Lynn Festival, the Radlett Gallery in Hertfordshire and Suffolk Street Galleries. Had a solo show of flower pieces at Barbican Centre. Her drawing of Campbell Taylor is in National Portrait Gallery.

Bridget MOORE 1960– Painter, born in Whitstable, Kent, who studied at Epsom School of Art, then Royal Academy Schools. In 1985 she was an Elizabeth Greenshields Foundation scholar. Showed at RA, RBA and elsewhere. Lived in London.

Charlotte MOORE fl. from late 1960s– Painter who studied at Chelsea School of Art, 1965–6, then Falmouth College of Art, 1966–9. She held several short-term artist's placements, including Staffordshire College of Agriculture, 1984, and in 1985 gained a painting commission for GKN Steelstock under the West Midlands Arts Artists and their work scheme. Group exhibitions included The Brewhouse, Taunton, 1982; Peterborough City Museum & Art Gallery, 1983; and Worcester Museum & Art Gallery, in Selected Birmingham Artists, 1985. Midlands Art Centre, Birmingham, gave her a solo show in 1980, later ones including Woodlands Art Gallery, 1985.

Conchita MOORE fl. from 1950s–1996 Versatile artist, teacher and critic, born in Rio de Janeiro, Brazil, mother Dutch, father Italian. She was educated in France, Belgium and the Netherlands and was a puppeteer at the Marionette Theatre, The Hague, for two years. Her first love was music, and she served as a critic of it for a Dutch national newspaper. In the early 1950s she moved to England and attended St Martin's School of Art. After marriage, she lived in India for five years and brought up a family and worked on set and costume design as well as painting. She returned to London in the early 1960s, soon to be self-supporting doing graphic design and book illustration. After part-time teaching at Wormwood Scrubs, gained her teaching certificate at Roehampton Institute and worked for many years in prison education. Married in 1973, taught art part-time at St Benedict's School, Ealing, for 10 years and in 1988 gained an honours degree in fine art and critical studies from St Martin's. For two years she was an artist at The Small Mansion Arts Centre, Gunnersbury, setting up a home and studio at Hastings, Sussex, just before she died. Group shows included Camden Arts Centre, Piccadilly Gallery, RA Summer Exhibition, LG and Royal College of Art. Among solo shows was a retrospective at Hastings Museum and Art Gallery, 1997.

C Rupert MOORE 1904–1982 Stained glass and heraldic artist, painter and lecturer, born in Doncaster, Yorkshire, who married the artist Gwen White in 1934. He attended Doncaster School of Art, gaining a major scholarship to Sheffield College of Art, 1922, and Royal College of Art, 1925–9. There he transferred from the painting to the stained glass school, under Martin Travers, and studied a range of crafts, twice winning the Anning Bell prize. His first of many exhibits at the RA Summer Exhibition was a tempera painting of aircraft. Moore had a detailed knowledge of them, having modelled as a boy. He designed his own method of powering them; went on to produce many covers for *The Aeromodeller* magazine, to which he contributed articles; helped with aircraft recognition and camouflage during World War II; was made a companion of the Royal Aeronautical Society in 1946; and has paintings in the Royal Air Force Museum, Hendon. From 1950 Moore was a prolific designer of stained glass windows for James Powell & Sons, later for Chapel Studios. He became a member, then a fellow and finally honorary vice-president of The British Society of Master Glass Painters. As well as designing dozens of windows in churches in England and Wales, Moore is well represented in New Zealand, which appreciated his traditional standards of drawing and painting. Ely Cathedral; Shaftesbury Abbey; Huyton College; Elizabeth Garrett Anderson Hospital Chapel; Royal Holloway College; and Chequers have work by Moore. The College of Arms rated him the finest heraldic artist of his day; his over 300 coats of arms for Lincoln's Inn took about four years. For a time, Moore lectured on the history of Art at St Albans School of Art, where his wife also taught. A long series of strokes hampered Moore's later years. Lived in Radlett, Hertfordshire.

Elsie Matley MOORE 1900–1985 Painter, born in Wilmslow, Cheshire. She specialised in ecclesiastical paintings, copying stained glass and monument restoration. Much of her work was done in Worcester and Wells cathedrals, and she aptly chose to live in Worcester. Restored wall paintings in churches. Victoria & Albert Museum and the National Buildings Record hold her work.

Gabrielle MOORE 1949– Painter, etcher and teacher, born in Worcestershire and educated in London. After a dozen years working in Britain and abroad she returned to study at Byam Shaw School, the Royal Academy Schools and City and Guilds of London Art School, where she later taught part-time. She won the Chadwyck Healey Painting Prize and the Rodney Burn Drawing Prize in 1981, the Richard Ford Travel Scholarship, Madrid, 1983, and 1st Prize, Wimbledon Lawn Tennis Centenary Poster, 1986. Open-air activities were an important aspect of her art. Showed at RA regularly from 1978, NEAC, RP, Agnew and elsewhere. Had a solo show at Spink & Son, 1991. Lloyd's of London and Museum of Jerusalem commissioned works by her.

Gerald MOORE 1926– Painter, muralist, sculptor and author, born in London at Guy's Hospital where he graduated 20 years later in dentistry. He qualified in medicine in 1954 and later took his master's degree. Dr Moore practised in Harley Street, retiring in 1985. Moore painted prolifically, attending Bromley College of Art for two years' evening classes. He showed at Whitechapel Art Gallery, 1950; Woodstock Gallery, 1960; Rowan Gallery, 1961; and was a prizewinner in Spirit of London open, 1981. Solo shows included Harlequin Gallery, Bath, 1981, and Italian State Tourist Board, 1984–5. His work was brightly coloured, often humorous, with distorted figures. He was commissioned to do two canvases for Italian State Tourist Board in 1981. Moore's work was included in the Sotheby's sale in May 1993 of the contents of Heathfield Park, Sussex, which also contained works by other painters Moore had collected. He wrote poetry and his autobiography, *Treading in Treacle*, was published in 1983. Lived latterly in north Devon.

Gerald John MOORE 1938– Painter in oil and watercolour and teacher, born in Ratby, Leicestershire. He was a student at Loughborough College of Art, 1955–8, did a year at Manchester University, 1958–9, then taught art in Taunton and the Midlands. From 1966–9 studied theology at University of Exeter, gaining an honours degree. After a period teaching, notably at King Edward VI Grammar School, in Nottinghamshire, in 1974–5 Moore began to prepare for a thesis on Constable at Exeter University, but instead decided to practise as a professional artist. Moore was an artist whose work looked back to "the Great Tradition, from Leonardo to the Pre-Raphaelites". Notable pictures were Bosworth Field, The Brass Pan, Teign-Valley Farm, Grove Hall, The Brownings with the Hunt and Pintails on West Sedge Moor. He showed widely in the west of England and lived at Stoke St Gregory, Taunton, Somerset.

Harry MOORE 1883–1979 Painter and draughtsman, born in Derby, where he studied under Thomas Simmonds. Moore was a captain in the 11th Sherwood Foresters during World War I. He acted as personal topographical assistant to the British commander-in-chief, Douglas Haig, and won the Military Cross, awarded for his work in going ahead of the front line to draw German trenches. A qualified art teacher, Moore showed with the Derby Sketching Club, of which he became secretary. Lived latterly in Swanage, Dorset, and died in a Bournemouth nursing home.

Henry MOORE 1898–1986 Internationally renowned sculptor in stone, wood and and bronze, mainly of figure subjects, Moore was born in Castleford, Yorkshire, the son of a miner. After attending Leeds School of Art from 1919, Moore then studied at the Royal College of Art 1921–4. He went to France and Italy on a travelling scholarship in 1925, returned to teach at the Royal College until 1932, after which he taught at Chelsea School of Art until 1939. He was then able to live off his own work. He had his first one-man show at the Warren Gallery in 1928 and from his early exhibiting years was bought by discriminating collectors such as Sir Michael Sadler. His first public commission, for a relief on the London Underground Building, over St James' Park tube station, was in 1928–9. Eventually his monumental sculptures were to be purchased by galleries throughout the world and several retrospective exhibitions were held, with a memorial show at the RA in 1988. During his career Moore was to participate in a number of forward-looking groups, such as the 7 & 5 Society, Unit One and the International Surrealist Exhibitions in London in 1936 and Paris in 1938. During World War II his talents found new outlets in drawings of miners working and groups of Londoners sheltering in the underground, published in *The Shelter Sketch-Books*. Moore was internationally honoured, became a Companion of Honour in 1955 and was awarded the Order of Merit in 1963. The Henry Moore Centre for the Study of Sculpture exists in Leeds. Moore lived at Much Hadham, Hertfordshire, where his house and grounds helped form The Henry Moore Foundation.

Joan MOORE 1909–1996 Sculptor working in many media, but specialising in steel and enamelled steel, born in Eltham, southeast London. She married the sculptor Kenneth Armitage in 1940. Had a private school education and a year in domestic college. She studied under A H Gerrard at Slade School of Fine Art, gaining her diploma in 1935. She also studied under A J Ayres at a carving school in Kensington and at Purbeck Quarries, Dorset. During World War II worked in a plastics factory in Camberley. Also did some part-time teaching. Moore said that her early figure carving was "influenced by Epstein and studying Egyptian work at the British Museum. Most work materialises from drawings, many made at the Zoo." Her work is included in Eric Newton's monograph *British Sculpture 1944–1946*. Moore showed in numerous galleries in Britain and on the continent, including John Moores Liverpool Exhibition, 1961–63–68; Galeria Creuze and Musée d'Art Moderne, Paris; City of London, 1969. She was given a gold medal for sculpture by city of Athens, 1979. Completed a bronze group for Burnley town centre, 1961; bronze group for Little Angel Marionette Theatre; and steel sculpture of Three Swans, for British Petroleum at Britannic House, 1981. She was a member of ICA, was a committee member for Hampstead Artists' Council and AIA and vice-chairman of WIAC. Lived in London.

Ken MOORE 1923– Painter, born in Melbourne, Australia, son of the artist and teacher Albert Moore. He studied at St Martin's School of Art, teachers including Kenneth Martin and Derrick Greaves. Moore travelled and exhibited widely, at various times living in Britain, Canada and France. In 1963 he was director of the London-based Commonwealth Biennale of Abstract Art. Universities of Sydney and Melbourne, the American Legation in Tangier and a number of American collections hold examples.

Leslie MOORE 1913–1984 Painter and teacher, born in Cardiff, where he attended the College of Art, 1932–6. Moore then began teaching in Cardiff, to which he returned after World War II Army service abroad. From 1950 he was an art adviser in the Glamorgan area for many years. He was a leading figure in the Barry Summer School, SWAS and SWG and was at one time on the WAC art committee. Showed widely in Welsh group shows, notably Royal National Eisteddfod and WAC. He also had solo exhibitions at Howard Roberts Gallery in Cardiff, Dillwyn Gallery in Swansea and in his own home at Barry, Glamorgan. National Museum of Wales, Cardiff, and many education authorities hold his work, which could have strong Neo-Romantic tendencies. His daughter was the painter Sally Moore.

Leslie Lancelot Hardy MOORE 1907– Watercolourist and illustrator, born in Norwich, Norfolk, who studied at Reading University and Norwich School of Art. Showed at RA, Edwin Pollard Gallery, RI of which she was a member and in the provinces. Among books illustrated was *Norwich Inns*. Lived in North Walsham, Norfolk.

Michael D L MOORE 1927– Painter, printmaker, notably of coloured lino-cuts, and teacher. Born in Tonbridge, Kent, he was educated at Bradfield College, then Brighton College of Arts and Crafts, his teachers including Raymond Cowern and Charles Morris. Showed at RA, Young Contemporaries, SGA and elsewhere. Taught for some time at Sidcot School in Winscombe, Somerset, where he lived.

Mona MOORE 1917– Illustrator and designer, born and lived in London. She studied at St Martin's and Central Schools of Art, 1931–9. Her work was reproduced in many popular publications, including *Good Housekeeping*, *The Listener* and *Radio Times* and she also worked for Ministry of Information and Pilgrim Trust *Recording Britain* project. Tate, Leicester and Whitechapel Art Galleries showed her pictures. Victoria & Albert Museum and National Museum of Wales in Cardiff hold examples.

Nicholas MOORE 1958– Painter and printmaker, fond of still lifes of fruit using a rich palette, born in London. He studied printmaking at Colchester Technical College, 1980, etching at Heatherley's School of Fine Art, 1990, then painting next to John Craxton in Xania, Crete. From 1991 Moore was based in London, although he maintained a studio on the Greek island of Syros. Had solo exhibitions at Christopher Hull from 1986, with the British Council in Athens, 1987, and with Gallery K, 1994. Showed at RA Summer Exhibitions from 1981.

Percival MOORE 1886–1964 Painter and illustrator, born at Oakworth, Yorkshire. Studied at Royal College of Art, 1906–11. Became principal of Wakefield School of Art, 1920–7, and of Southampton, 1927–44. Exhibited RA and has works in collection of Southampton Art Gallery. Lived in Southampton.

Raymond MOORE 1920–1987 Artist, photographer and teacher, born in Wallasey, Cheshire, his father an architect. In 1937 he attended the School of Art in Wallasey, developing an interest in photographing architecture. After war service with Royal Air Force, 1940–6, Moore studied painting at Royal College of Art. From 1949 spent nine summers with painter Ray Howard-Jones on Skomer, an island off the Welsh coast, having met her in 1948. Moore taught lithography part-time at Watford School of Art from 1950, in 1956 becoming a teacher of photography there. In 1959 Moore was commissioned by Gordon Fraser to produce postcard studies of buildings of historic interest in Britain. After taking up a teaching appointment at Trent Polytechnic, Nottingham, in 1975, in 1977 Moore gained a major busary from Arts Council, then resigned his teaching post and moved to Carlisle to concentrate on his own work. This he did, along with freelance lecturing, settling in Canonbie, Dumfriesshire, in 1983. By that time Moore had become one of the most important photographers of his generation, whose work was informed by painterly considerations. He referred to his subject as "the no-man's land between the real and the fantasy – the mystery of the common place – the uncommonness of the commonplace". There was a retrospective of his work at Hayward Gallery in 1981, and a touring retrospective in 1990 organised by Ffotogallery, Cardiff, and WAC. The Raymond Moore Archive is based in Castle Douglas, Galloway.

Sally MOORE 1962– Portrait and genre painter in a meticulous style whose pictures featured women and animals. She was born in Cardiff, south Wales, did foundation studies, 1980–1, at South Glamorgan Institute there, then attended Ruskin School of Drawing in Oxford, 1981–4, and did a master's degree in fine art at City of Birmingham Polytechnic, 1986–7. Among Moore's many awards were a travelling scholarship, Somerville College, Oxford, 1983; WAC Grant, 1986; Abbey Memorial Scholarship at British School, Rome 1992–3; and prizewinner, National Eisteddfod, Wales, 1994. In 1988 she had a residency at Delfina

Studios Trust for two years. In addition to many group exhibitions had a series of solo shows, later ones including Long & Ryle Art International, 1991, and Martin Tinney Gallery, Cardiff, 1995. Contemporary Art Society and Sunderland Art Gallery hold examples. The artist Leslie Moore was her father.

Theo MOORE 1879– Landscape painter and teacher, born in Birmingham, who studied in St Ives; at Frank Spenlove-Spenlove's Yellow Door School of Art, Beckenham; in Paris, and privately. She became principal of the Cathcart School of Modern Art for some years. Showed RA, ROI, RI, SWA and at Paris Salon. Miss Moore lived in London.

William Stanley MOORE 1914– Painter in oil and watercolour and theatre designer, born in London. He was mainly self-taught, although he attended Shrewsbury School of Art, 1929. Ran a firm called Stage Decor Ltd which was very active in the 1950s and 1960s. He showed at the Redfern Gallery, RBA, RWS and widely in the provinces, had solo exhibitions at Lyric and Embassy Theatres and a retrospective at Mall Galleries in 1973. Shrewsbury Art Gallery and Technical College and Kensington Palace hold examples. Lived in Purley, Surrey, then in Ashton, near Helston, Cornwall.

Blanche MOORHOUSE 1885– Artist in pastel and watercolour, she married the artist George Mortram Moorhouse. She studied at Leeds School of Art and exhibited RSA, RCamA, RWA, Lake Artists' Society, of which she was a member, and Walker Art Gallery, Liverpool. Sometimes signed work B M. Lived at Helsington, Westmorland.

George Mortram MOORHOUSE 1882– Painter, especially of figures, and printmaker, who was married to the artist Blanche Moorhouse. He studied at Lancaster School of Art and privately, among his teachers being Frank Brangwyn, J M Swan and Augustus John. A native of the lakeland area, he became president of the Lake Artists' Society, showing there and at RA, RCamA, RHA, RWA and elsewhere. Lived at Helsington, Westmorland.

Andrew MORAN 1957– Artist, born in Manchester, who did a foundation course at Tameside College, 1976–7; was at Falmouth School of Art, 1977–8; and graduated from Goldsmiths' College in fine art, 1978–80. While working as a postman at Victoria (South-West) Office Moran made a series of drawings about working in the Post Office that culminated in two commissioned triptychs which were put on permanent show at Victoria and Swindon District Offices. Mixed shows included Red Lion Group, Conway Hall, 1986; and Kerb Scrawlers, The Living Room, Greenwich, 1994. Showed solo at Dryden Street Gallery, 1987.

Truda MORDUE 1909– Painter, miniaturist and teacher, born in Hursley, Hampshire. She attended Poole School of Art, Bournemouth College of Art and Camberwell School of Arts and Crafts. She wrote and illustrated a number of children's books, including *Timothy Finds a Playmate* and *The Lonely Kitten* and taught at Isleworth Polytechnic in the 1960s. Became a member of RMS in 1957 and SWA in 1965 and showed at RA, RWS and elsewhere in London. Lived for a time at Sherborne, Dorset.

Harry MORE GORDON 1928– Painter and muralist, textile designer, illustrator and teacher, born in Farnborough, Hampshire, of Scottish parents. He trained as a commercial artist at Edinburgh College of Art, 1949–53, then did a postgraduate course at Central School of Arts and Crafts, 1954. He was then a freelance illustrator and art editor for several magazines before returning to Edinburgh College of Art where for 25 years until 1988 he was in charge of graphic design, retiring early to paint. Textile designs were created for Liberty; he illustrated books, newspapers and magazines, ranging from *The Times* to *Lilliput*; and created a huge mural for 200 Summers in the City. In addition to mixed shows More Gordon had solo exhibitions including Richard Demarco Gallery and the Scottish and Henderson Galleries, all in Edinburgh, near where he lived at Inveresk. Scottish Arts Council and Robert Fleming Holdings own his work.

Herbert MOREL 1925– Artist in watercolour, some oil and mixed media, by profession an architect, born in Croydon, Surrey. He studied at Architectural Association School, teachers including Harold Workman and Hugh Cronyn, graduating with honours in 1950. In 1983 he gained a diploma in landscape architecture. Was elected a fellow of RIBA in 1960. After working for James Cubitt and Partners and other London practices Morel began his own in 1953, after winning a *News Chronicle* national house competition, and schools, children's homes, homes for the elderly and many private houses followed. Morel taught at Architectural Association and Thames Polytechnic. His main works were landscape paintings in watercolour of Britain, continental Europe, Turkey and North Africa. Showed, usually with Susan Horsfield, at Elan Gallery, Ide Hill; Halesworth Gallery; Digby Gallery in the Mercury Theatre, Colchester; Linton Court Gallery, Settle; and with Architect Artists at RIBA, which holds drawings of many early houses by him. He was based in Bessels Green, Sevenoaks, Kent.

Alice Bertha MORETON 1901– Sculptor and artist in black-and-white, born in Liverpool where she attended the School of Art after Bootle School of Art. Then attended Royal Academy Schools under William Reid Dick, 1924–7, winning three silver and three bronze medals, followed by studies in France and Italy. Member of Sandon Studios Society Club and RCamA. Sometimes signed work with maiden name, A B Tippin. Exhibited RA, the galleries in Liverpool, Manchester and Southport and at Paris Salon. Lived at Hooton, Cheshire.

Nicolas MORETON 1961– Sculptor and teacher, born Watford, Hertfordshire. Studied at Nene College School of Art and Design, Northampton, in 1981–2. He was at Wolverhampton Polytechnic, 1982–5, graduating with an honours degree in fine art (sculpture). From mid-1986 Moreton freelanced as a sculptor, teaching for a term part-time at Weston Favell Upper School, Nottingham, in that year, in 1988 being resident sculptor at Manorbier Castle, Dyfed. He took part in many group exhibitions, including Scottish Sculpture Workshop, Lumsden, 1983; Maclean Gallery, from 1987; Fenny Lodge Gallery, Milton Keynes, 1988; and Northamptonshire Artists, at Savage Fine Art, Northampton, in 1989. Solo exhibitions included Abington Park Museum, Northampton, 1983; Arts Barn, Wellingborough, 1986; was offered first London solo at Mall Galleries, 1989; others included a series at Lamont Gallery from 1992. His sculpture was used in the film *The Rachel Papers*, by Martin Amis, 1989. Weston Favell Upper School commissioned a public sculpture for a 25th Jubilee and Moreton completed private commissions including one for the art critic Brain Sewell in 1992. In 1995 was elected an associate of RBS and gained first prize, Northamptonshire Contemporary Art Award. The male and female form were a constant theme in Moreton's carvings. Lived at Courteenhall, Northampton.

Colette MOREY de MORAND 1939– Artist, born in Paris, France, who gained a science degree at University of Toronto, Canada. Studied painting and printmaking, attending Wellington Polytechnic in New Zealand and Queens University in Kingston, Ontario. Her frequent group exhibitions included Vancouver Art Gallery, 1969; Winchester School of Art, 1979; Berry Street Open Studio Exhibition from 1981; and Triangle Artists' Workshop, New York State, 1983. Showed solo extensively in New Zealand from 1969, London one-man exhibitions including Air Gallery, 1980, and Commonwealth Institute, 1981. Awards included an Elephant Trust Grant, 1983. Lived for many years in London.

David MORGAN 1964– Painter who was born in Woodmansterne, Surrey. He studied at Croydon College of Art and Design, 1982–3, then Winchester School in Art, 1983–6. Between 1988–91 worked as artist-in-residence at North Kingston Centre. During this time he took part in the Roy Miles Gallery's British Month and the 10th Cleveland International Drawing Biennale. In 1992 he shared a show at Woodlands Art Gallery. Lived in East Grinstead, Sussex.

Gerald MORGAN 1922– Painter, born in Merthyr Tydfil, Glamorgan, who trained for Royal Air Force air crew during World War II, but for health reasons had to become a Bevin Boy coal miner. Studied to be a pharmacist, but gave it up to paint. After spending only two months at art school chose to sell insurance to support himself, also working as a part-time crooner. In the 1950s, influenced by the work of Jackson Pollock, Morgan changed from painting "competent mediocre trad paintings" towards abstraction. Despite artistic changes of fashion Morgan, at his home in Mumbles, near Swansea, for years pursued his twin theme: precise stripe pictures, chromatic and created with masking tape; and a pebble shape-type series, against a black background. Exhibitions included Alwin Gallery, 1966; Raymond Duncan Gallery, Paris, 1967; Woodstock Gallery, 1971; Swansea Art Workshop, 1981; and West Wharf Gallery, Cardiff, 1989. Abulafia Gallery, Llandeilo, represented him.

Geri MORGAN 1926– Painter, draughtsman and teacher who attended St Martin's School of Art, 1944, then Camberwell School of Art, 1948–51, that School's measured and restrained style leaving its mark on the artist's work, as seen in a joint exhibition with Joan Gillespie at Duncan Campbell Contemporary Art, 1998. Morgan taught at Hornsey College of Art, 1958–68; Camberwell, 1964–70; New York Studio School from 1989; and was principal of Byam Shaw School of Art, 1970–91. Mixed shows included RA Summer Exhibition from 1967; Hayward Annual British Drawing, 1982; and John Moores Liverpool Exhibition, 1983. Lived in north London.

Glyn MORGAN 1926– Painter and teacher who grew up in Pontypridd, Glamorgan, where he took part in exhibitions which Esther Grainger organised along with art classes. In 1943 was introduced to the artist Cedric Morris and from 1944 for 38 years for varying periods attended Morris' East Anglian School of Painting and Drawing. In 1951 Morgan, who was a member of the Society of Botanical Artists, worked in Paris. He obtained a Goldsmiths' Company Fellowship to work in Crete in 1968, in 1973 lecturing at Aegina Art Centre, Greece. In 1985 he organised The Benton End Circle, a tribute to Morris' school, at Bury St Edmunds Art Gallery and in 1994 had his work shown with Morris' in Master & Pupil at Chappel Galleries, Chappel. Morgan showed in many mixed exhibitions, including Edinburgh International Festival, 1952; Leicester Galleries, 1962; John Whibley Gallery, 1970; RA from 1987; and The Broad Horizon, Agnew, 1990. Had a solo show at Drian Galleries, 1969, others including a retrospective at The Minories, Colchester, 1981, Chappel Galleries, 1991, and The Simon Carter Gallery, Woodbridge, 1995. WAC and Contemporary Art Society hold examples. Lived in Hadleigh, Suffolk.

Gwenda MORGAN 1908–1991 Wood engraver, born and spent most of her life in Petworth, Sussex, whose countryside she loved and depicted frequently in her work. She attended Brighton and Hove High School and then Goldsmiths' College School of Art until 1929, after that the Grosvenor School of Modern Art under Iain Macnab. During World War II she worked in the Women's Land Army, doing a great variety of jobs, then returned to wood engraving. She exhibited RA, Redfern Gallery and RE of which she was a member, but became best known for her book and other illustrations, especially Gray's *Elegy* for the Golden Cockerel Press, of 1946, and *Grimm's Other Tales*, 1956. In 1985 the Whittington Press published *The Wood-Engravings of Gwenda Morgan*. Victoria & Albert Museum and Ashmolean Museum, Oxford, hold her work, which was given a review show at 20th Century Gallery in 1996.

Gwynydd Ruth MORGAN 1904– Painter, printmaker and teacher, born on Ascension Island, in the Atlantic. Was educated at a convent in Weymouth, Dorset, then studied at Chelsea Polytechnic School of Art with John Revel, Maidstone School of

Art and Birmingham School of Art where her teachers included Bernard Sleigh. She held a number of teaching posts in England from the mid-1930s, then taught in Southport, Queensland, Australia, in the mid-1950s. Showed in the English provinces and abroad. Lived in Southport and in Cranleigh, Surrey.

Howard MORGAN 1949– Painter, notably of commissioned portraits, born in north Wales. He studied at Newcastle University's fine art department, 1967–73, moving to London in 1974 to establish himself as a portrait painter. Also became noted for watercolour interiors and landscapes, working in Britain and abroad. Was elected RP, 1986. Showed at RA, Anthony Mould Ltd, Agnew, Richmond Gallery and elsewhere. Had a series of solo shows at Cadogan Contemporary. In 1978 Morgan was commissioned by the Carlton Club to paint Lord Home of the Hirsel, the former prime minister. Many other commissions included the composer Herbert Howells, the playwright Tom Stoppard and the poet Philip Larkin, as well as members of the British and foreign royal families.

Hugh MORGAN 1967– Painter using bold, colourful, figurative images, as in Inner City Blues, oil on canvas shown at Royal Over-Seas League Open, 1994. He was born in London and was a self-taught artist, although he obtained an honours degree in architecture from South Bank University, and worked as an architectural assistant, 1989–91. Among commissions was a mural for London Weekend Television, 1993. Group shows included South Bank Picture Show, Royal Festival Hall, 1992; Art vs Architecture vs Art, Lewisham Art House, 1993; and Black Men Don't Cry, Brixton Art Gallery, 1994.

Jeffrey MORGAN 1942– Painter, teacher and illustrator, born in south Wales. He attended Cardiff School of Art, 1960–2, then Central School of Art, 1962–5. Morgan taught in art schools in Hornsey, Colchester and Winchester, then Maidenhead School of Art and Design. He contributed work to many periodicals, including *The Observer*, *The Independent*, *The Times* and *The Daily Telegraph*. His work appeared at Portal Gallery; The Minories, Colchester; Third Eye Gallery, Athens; Peggy Wynne, New York; John Moores Liverpool Exhibition; and Woodlands Art Gallery. Morgan and his wife, the writer Patricia Craig, lived in southeast London.

Richard MORGAN 1942– Painter who spent his early years in London's East End. He gained his initial training as an illustrator while working in advertising. In 1966 left London to concentrate on painting. His work was in the tradition of the English mystical romantics and drew inspiration from the Suffolk landscape. One-man shows included Read's Gallery, Aldeburgh; Deben Gallery, Woodbridge; Magdelene Street Gallery, Cambridge; The Maddermarket, Norwich; Pottergate Gallery, Norwich; and Buxton Mill Galleries, Norfolk.

Robert MORGAN 1923– Painter, printmaker, writer and poet, and teacher, born in Penrhiwceiber, Glamorgan, south Wales. For some years he was a miner, then attended Fircroft College in Birmingham, 1949–51, and Bognor College of Education, 1951–3, under Charles Woolaston. Morgan settled in Denmead, Hampshire, but his subject continued to be "the mining landscape of South Wales". He was a schoolmaster for 20 years, but retired early to paint and write. His mixed show appearances included Cumberland House, Portsmouth, from 1958; Southampton Art Gallery, 1960; and WAC, 1960, Industrial Wales. Had a solo show at Mermaid Theatre, 1965, with many more following in London, Wales, Portsmouth and elsewhere. Morgan first published poems and short stories in the early 1960s, to which he frequently added. His autobiography, *My Lamp Still Burns*, appeared in 1981.

Ronald MORGAN 1936– Painter, illustrator and teacher, born in Landywood, Staffordshire. He was self-taught as a painter, but spent two years at Walsall School of Art studying graphic design. He became a draughtsman in Tower Hamlets' planning department. Joined RBA and ROI in 1984 and was also a member of Chelsea Art Society. Showed at RA, RI, NEAC, RSMA, Paris Salon, Guildhall Art Gallery, National Museum of Wales in Cardiff, Whitechapel Art Gallery, Royal Festival Hall and many provincial galleries. In 1974 won first prize at Lord Mayor of London's Art Award Exhibition and won several other awards. Graves Art Gallery in Sheffield holds his work as well as London Boroughs of Islington and Tower Hamlets. Lived in London.

Corrado MORGANA 1969– Artist using video, born in Port Talbot, Galmorgan, who gained a fine art degree at Bath College of Higher Education, 1991–3, then a master's at Chelsea College of Art, 1994–5. Exhibitions included Fringeworks, Bath, 1994; Out of the Nineties, Mall Galleries, 1995; and New Contemporaries at Tate Gallery, Liverpool, and Camden Arts Centre, 1996.

David MORGAN-JONES 1900–1978 Painter in oil, born in London. Dr Morgan-Jones qualified at Middlesex Hospital in 1924 and eventually became a surgeon, specialising in mental care, but retaining his appointment to the Mid-Herts Hospital until his retirement in 1963. He studied at St Albans School of Art under William Lismore and with the Royal Academician Christopher Sanders in the late 1930s. Signed work with his own name or as David Voel. Exhibited at RA, ROI of which he was a member but more widely in France. Lived at Hemel Hempstead, Hertfordshire.

Paul MORIARTY 1961– Artist, born and worked in London, who gained a first-class degree in fine art at Goldsmiths' College, 1979–83, took a studio in Wapping from 1983–5, then did his master's degree at Chelsea School of Art, 1985–6, after that returning to paint. Mixed exhibitions included Stowells Trophy at RA from 1982; Fringe Exhibition at Windsor Arts Centre, 1985; Celtic Vision at Bank of Ireland Exhibition Centre, Dublin, 1988; and 22nd Festival of Painting at Cagnes-sur-Mer, France, 1990, when he was British Council representative. Had a solo show at

Drian Gallery, 1984, from 1988 exhibiting with Rebecca Hossack Gallery, his first show there inaugurating the gallery.

Francis MORLAND 1934– Sculptor and teacher, born in Munsley, Norfolk, who attended Rudolf Steiner School, 1941–7, King Alfred's School, 1947–51, Central School of Art, 1951–2, then after two years' National Service in the Army was at Slade School of Fine Art, 1954–6. A number of teaching appointments from 1963 included head of sculpture at Norwich School of Art, 1968–9. Group shows included Battersea Park annual open-air sculpture exhibition from 1963; New Generation, Whitechapel Art Gallery and tour, 1966; Arnolfini Gallery in Bristol, 1968; and Bath Festival, 1970. Solo exhibitions included New Vision Centre Gallery in 1963, Axiom Gallery, 1969, and ICA, 1970. Several university collections hold his work, as do British Council and Arts Council, which has his abstracts Cork Float Figure, in bronze, of 1961; and Inside Green, in fibreglass, of 1966. Morland later lived in America.

John MORLEY 1942– Painter and teacher, born in Beckenham, Kent, married to the artist Diana Howard. Studied at Beckenham School of Art and Ravensbourne College of Art, 1957–62, then Royal Academy Schools until 1966, winning several scholarships. In 1974 he gained a further scholarship from Arts Council. Morley was a visiting lecturer at Epsom School of Art and Design and taught at Westminster School. He took part in mixed shows at RBA and NEAC of both of which he was a member, RA, Paris Salon and elsewhere. Showed solo regularly at Piccadilly Gallery. Like his wife he was included in that gallery's 1985–6 exhibition The Brotherhood of Ruralists and Friends. In 1982 John Read made an *Omnibus* BBC Television film about Morley. Sometimes signed work J M. Lived in Stoven North Green, Suffolk. In 1990 Morley was elected a brother of the Art Worker's Guild.

Malcolm MORLEY 1931– Painter, born in London. He worked on transatlantic and North Sea barges and took a correspondence course in art, then attended Camberwell School of Arts and Crafts, 1952–3, and Royal College of Art, 1954–7. Moved to New York in 1958 where he initially worked as a waiter, getting to know leading avant-garde Americans in the Cedar Bar. Influences noted in Morley's paintings were many, ranging from English artists such as Sickert to de Kooning, Matisse, Pollock and Soutine. After an early period of Abstract Expressionist-influenced abstraction Morley returned to figuration in the mid-1960s, gaining a reputation for his Super-Realistic works. Later work was rich and exotic, drawing on his wide travels. Had a major retrospective in 1983–4, organised for the Whitechapel Art Gallery, with international tour. Won Turner Prize, 1984. Showed with Anthony d'Offay, 1990, also with Pace Gallery, New York. Saatchi Collection holds his work. Lived in Long Island.

Simon MORLEY 1958– Painter, lecturer and writer, born in Eastbourne, Sussex, who gained his master's degree in modern history at Oxford University, 1977–80. Between 1981–87, when he settled in London, Morley lived in Milan, Paris (where in 1982 he studied at École des Beaux-Arts) and New York (there in 1985 attending the Art Students' League). Morley was artist-in-residence, Open House, Mind, in Tower Hamlets, 1989–90, and between 1989–95 completed residencies and workshops for the Tate, Hayward and Whitechapel Galleries and the Camden Arts Centre. From 1989 he lectured and led courses at the Tate, Birkbeck College, London University and Sothebys. Exhibited in London and in 1996 was included in Cross Currents, Reed's Wharf Gallery at Barbican Centre, showing abstract works, with a preponderance of black, on irregularly shaped supports.

Ken MORONEY 1949– Self-taught artist who was born and then lived in London. He specialised in small oil studies which were swiftly executed, and which were compared with those of Sir Alfred Munnings and Edward Seago. Appeared in many mixed exhibitions in London and the provinces and had a series of solo shows, including Duncan Miller Contemporary Arts, 1991.

Jacqueline MORREAU 1929– Figurative artist and teacher, born in Milwaukee, Wisconsin, America, who over the years "mined a number of fairly nameable subjects like Identity, Desire, Memory, Creation, Choice". From 1972, she produced several large cycles of mythic figures. From 1943–7 Morreau attended the Susan Miller Dorsey High School and Chouinard Art Institute, Los Angeles; 1946, began studying with Rico Lebrun at Jepson's Art Institute; 1947–9, was at Jepson's and Los Angeles City College; 1949, travelled to Paris and New York; 1950; returned to Los Angeles City College and Jepson's; 1953, moved to Berkeley, where she was a research assistant at the University of California for about seven years; in 1958, gained a diploma in medical illustration there; postgraduate studies in etching followed, at Berkeley and San Francisco Art Institute; 1967, moved to Massachusetts, in 1969 making lithography studies with Herb Fox in Boston, then moved to London in 1972. Morreau took theatre design at the Royal Academy of Dramatic Arts, from that year being a visiting lecturer in drawing at Oxford Brookes University and professor of art at Regent's College. From 1995 was a visiting lecturer in drawing at the Royal College of Art. Took part in many group shows in Britain and abroad. Had a series of solo exhibitions, later ones including Themes and Variations at Ferens Art Gallery, Hull, 1996.

Peter MORRELL 1931– Painter and teacher, born in Newton Abbot, Devon. He was married to the artist Helene Halstuch. He attended Kingston College of Art, 1952–6; Royal College of Art, 1956–9, where his teachers included Ruskin Spear, Carel Weight and John Minton; and he was the winner of a British Institute Prize in 1955, Arts Council prize in 1959, and in that year the Prix de Rome in Painting. Was made a member of RWS in 1983; also showing from 1955 onwards at RA Summer Exhibition; at John Moores Liverpool Exhibitions, 1961–7; and was a Hunting Group Prize finalist, 1986–7. Took part in a three-man show at New Art Centre, 1962; two-man at Ben Uri Gallery, 1987; and four-man at

Woodlands Art Gallery, 1989. Had a solo exhibition at New Art Centre, 1964. Taught at Central School of Art and Maidstone College of Art. Arts Council and Science Museum hold his work. Lived in London.

Jane MORRICE 1965– Painter and teacher who did a foundation course at Cambridge College of Art and Technology, 1984–5, gaining an honours degree in fine art, 1985–8, with studies in France 1987, completing her postgraduate diploma at Edinburgh, 1988–9. Was part-time art tutor at Casterton Community College and Stamford School from 1990. Residencies and awards included British Council-funded collaboration with Catalan artists, Barcelona, 1992; St Hugh's Foundation Henrietta Bowder Travel Bursary for study of Renaissance art in Italy, 1993; and an Eastern Arts grant for research work in Iceland, 1995. Group exhibitions included Table Studio Group, Leicester City Art Gallery, 1995, previous shows including Performance, Richard Demarco Gallery, Edinburgh, 1989, and On Show 4, Usher Gallery, Lincoln, 1991. In 1996–7 Morrice participated in New Territories, a touring show based on Stamford Arts Centre which stemmed from work done in Iceland. Solo shows included Clare Hall Gallery, Cambridge, 1990; Stamford Arts Centre, 1990–1; and Guildhall Centre, Grantham, 1991.

Adrian MORRIS 1929– Painter, draughtsman and teacher, born in London, where he settled. He was educated at Putney School, Vermont, 1941–7, and from 1947–8 attended the Anglo-French Art Centre, where a number of distinguished painters, including André Lhote, taught. Morris served in the Royal Horse Guards, 1948–50, then attended L'Académie de la Grande Chaumière, Paris, 1950–1, gaining his diploma from the Royal Academy Schools, 1951–5. From 1957 he taught at various London secondary schools, including Dick Sheppard School, Tulse Hill. Morris was a slow worker who showed rarely, although the painter Michael Wishart, who met him at the Anglo-French Art Centre, later wrote: "*I am convinced* he is the most important painter of my generation in the UK." In America Morris thought highly of pictures in the Guggenheim gallery Art of this Century, especially those of de Chirico. On his return to England, where he worked in isolation, he was impressed by paintings by Francis Bacon and Lucien Freud. Morris showed at Leicester Galleries' Artists of Fame and Promise and had a solo exhibition at the St George's Gallery in 1955; in 1957 he was in the Leicester Galleries' winter show; in 1969 was in The Poetic Image at Hanover Gallery; then was in the Hayward Annual at Hayward Gallery, 1978. At this time he said that: "For me painting has been an attempt to create an environment in which life could exist." After a fallow exhibiting period, early drawings by Morris were included in a show of André Lhote's pupils at Michael Parkin Fine Art, 1996.

Anthony MORRIS 1938– Multi-media artist, born in Oxford, who attended the College of Art there, then Royal Academy Schools under Peter Greenham and Bernard Fleetwood-Walker. He was awarded a Leverhulme Scholarship. Was made a member of RP in 1975, was a regular at RA Summer Exhibitions and had a solo show at Medici Gallery. Morris' subjects were portraits and English country landscapes. He lived at Talyllyn, Brecon, Powys.

Cedric MORRIS 1889–1982 Painter, teacher and plantsman, born in Sketty, Swansea, into a local industrial family. Sir Cedric succeeded his father as 9th Baronet in 1947. After Charterhouse School Morris worked in Canada, studied singing in London, then in 1914 attended Académie Delacluse in Paris. After a time working in Cornwall, Morris in 1921 moved to Paris where he studied at the Académies Moderne, Suédoise and La Grande Chaumière and Atelier Colarossi, his teachers including André Lhote, Othon Friesz and Fernand Léger. During 1920s travelled extensively in Europe and North Africa. Returned to Britain in 1927 where he worked in London; was elected to LG and 7 & 5 Society; and worked in Wales to promote Welsh art. In 1937 he opened The East Anglian School of Painting and Drawing with the artist Arthur Lett-Haines, situated mainly at Benton End, near Hadleigh, which became notable for its garden and distinguished students, including Lucian Freud. In the early 1950s Morris lectured at Royal College of Art. Had many one-man shows and in 1984 was commemorated in a major exhibition at Tate Gallery. Morris is noted for his colourful still lifes, portraits and landscapes, which are in many public collections.

Charles Alfred MORRIS 1898–1983 Painter in oil and watercolour, especially of Sussex scenes, who was born in Portsmouth, Hampshire. He studied at Brighton College of Art and the Royal Academy Schools. Later became principal of Worthing School of Art and head of drawing and painting at Brighton College of Art. Was for a time president of the Society of Sussex Painters. Morris exhibited RA, RWS and RBA, of which he was a member, and elsewhere. Eastbourne, Brighton and Worthing galleries hold his work. Lived at Kingsley, Bordon, Hampshire.

Desmond MORRIS 1928– Writer and broadcaster on animal and human behaviour and Surrealist painter, born in Purton, Wiltshire. Morris graduated with a science degree from Birmingham University, gained his doctorate at Oxford University and did post-doctoral research at the Department of Zoology at the University, 1954–6. He went on to hold a number of notable academic and media positions, including curator of mammals at Zoological Society of London, 1959–67; director, ICA, 1967–8; and research fellow at Wolfson College, Oxford, 1973–81. He made a national name with the book *The Naked Ape*, 1967, and appeared on television programmes such as *The Animals Roadshow*. Among his books were *The Biology of Art*, 1962. The book *The Secret Surrealist*, 1987, coincided with a Mayor Gallery show of his work. He also showed on the continent and in America and was included in The Birmingham Seven at John Bonham, Murray Feely Fine Art, 1991. Swindon Museum and Art Gallery gave him a retrospective in 1976 and Mayor Gallery another in 1997. Lived in London.

Elizabeth MORRIS fl. from 1950s– Printmaker and painter, brought up in Hampshire. She studied at Southern College of Art,

Bournemouth, 1949–53, Central School of Art and Crafts, 1953–4, and Goldsmiths' College School of Art, 1954–5, attending Morley College for printmaking, 1975–8. Morris in 1979 helped to set up the Greenwich Printmakers' Association, being chairman, 1982–4, and was a member of the Printmakers' Council. Among her mixed shows were Greenwich Theatre Gallery, 1984, RE from 1985 and Royal Festival Hall, 1986. Solo shows included Scribes Cellar, 1986; Royal Exchange Theatre, Manchester, 1985–7, and Woodlands Art Gallery, 1987.

Gerard MORRIS 1955– Painter and draughtsman who created pictures full of bold figures in intensive colours in the Glasgow tradition. Born in Scotland, he studied at Glasgow School of Art, 1974–8. In 1986 he won a travel bursary to Madrid, Old Master pictures seen there influencing his work. He was a prizewinner in the Leigh Gallery competition. Morris' mixed show appearances included Moose Gallery, Miami, 1987; Compass Gallery, 1988; Barbizon Gallery in Glasgow and Fine Art Society, Edinburgh, 1989; Olympia International Art Fair, 1990; and New York Print Fair, 1991. His solo exhibitions included Francis Graham-Dixon Gallery and Odette Gilbert Gallery, 1988; Agnew, 1990–1; and Beaux Arts, Bath, 1992. Agnew, BBC in Scotland and University of Tennessee hold his work, which used what was claimed to be a unique form of drawing: hand-made senelier pastel and Lascaux fixative liquid was put on a gesso ground, which in turn was on Fabriano paper from Italy. Oil on heavy cotton paper, then varnished, was also employed. Lived in London.

John MORRIS 1922– Watercolourist and teacher, born in Deiniolen, Caernarvonshire. He attended Bangor Normal College, 1955–7, then studied with Press Art School, Forest Hill, 1958–60. Retired from headship of Ysgol Llandfynydd, Clwyd, in 1979 to concentrate on professional art career. He was a member of WSW and an associate of NS as well as a member of Nantlle Vale Art Circle. Held regular solo shows and exhibited widely at National Museum of Wales in Cardiff, Albany and Sherman Theatre Galleries there, at Royal National Eisteddfod, RI, widely elsewhere in Wales and in America. In 1982 and 1985 designed a Christmas card for Council for the Protection of Rural Wales. National Library of Wales in Aberystwyth and Royal Welsh Agricultural Society hold examples of his work, which concentrated strongly on Welsh landscape. Had a studio gallery at Mold, Clwyd.

John Meirion MORRIS 1936– Sculptor, draughtsman and teacher, born at Llanuwchllyn, Bala, Merionethshire. He worked in a variety of materials, his sculptures amalgamating natural, human and other forms with a strong literary or spiritual content. Morris obtained his diploma from Liverpool College of Art, 1955–9; did a postgraduate sculpture year there, 1959–60; qualified as a teacher at Liverpool University, 1960–1; then in 1989 gained his Master of Philosophy degree from University of North Wales, Bangor, research on Celtic La Tène art. Morris lectured at Mid-Warwickshire School of Art, Leamington Spa, 1964–6; at the University of Kumasi, Ghana, 1966–8; and at University of Wales, Aberystwyth, 1968–81; from 1981–5 being a sculptor and researcher; then took early retirement to be a professional sculptor in 1990 after five years as head of art at the Normal College, Bangor. In 1962 Morris completed five big relief panels in Lanuwchllyn's village hall. Portrait commissions included the Welsh writers Marion Eames and T Llew Jones, bought by National Library of Wales, Aberystwyth, and educationalist Jac L Williams, for the University of Wales, Aberystwyth. Exhibitions included National Eisteddfod of Wales, Bluecoat Chambers in Liverpool, Piccadilly Gallery, 1994, Invited Artists at RCamA, 1996, and Artwork Wales at National Eisteddfod of Wales, Bala, 1997. Had a solo exhibition at Y Tabernacl, Machynlleth, 1998. Lived in Caernarvon, Gwynedd.

Locky MORRIS 1960– Artist in all media, but mainly sculpture and installations, born in Londonderry, Northern Ireland. He studied at Ulster Polytechnic, 1978–80, and Manchester Polytechnic, 1980–3. Won a series of Visual Arts Awards from Arts Council of Northern Ireland from 1988. Group exhibitions included Irish Exhibition of Living Art, Guinness Hop Store, Dublin, 1985; GPA Awards for emerging artists, Douglas Hyde Gallery, Dublin, 1988; Kunst Europa, Mannheimer Kunstverein, Germany, 1991; and Clean and Dirty, Ikon Gallery, Birmingham, 1994. Had a solo exhibition at Orchard Gallery, Londonderry, 1985, others including Comm at Cornerhouse, Manchester, 1992. Morris' steel sculpture Navvy's Dinner was sited near the Rochdale Canal, Castlefield, in 1985.

Mali MORRIS 1945– Painter, born in north Wales. She was educated at Caernarvon and Llandudno Grammar Schools. Studied from 1963–8 at Department of Fine Art, University of Newcastle, then did postgraduate studies at University of Reading, 1968–70. In 1970 went to be lecturer in extra-mural studies at Sunderland College of Art, four years later beginning to paint in London. Showed at Hatton Gallery, Newcastle, in mid-1960s, winning the Hatton Scholarship in Painting in 1967. Also showed at LG, Reading University and with Space Studios Group Show, Francis Graham-Dixon Gallery and in South Bank Centre touring show of 1989 The Tree of Life. Had solo exhibitions at Ikon Gallery, Birmingham, 1979, and Nicola Jacobs Gallery from 1980. Vibrant abstract paintings using bands of saturated colour were characteristic of Morris' output, some inspired by travels in Spain, Cyprus and Canada. WAC and University of Newcastle hold her work. Lived in London.

Margaret MORRIS 1891– Miniaturist and watercolourist, born in Lisbon, Portugal, who after Manchester High School spent periods at Southport and Manchester Schools of Art. Lived in Brazil, then settled for a time at Virginia Water, Surrey, later in London. The Lancashire-based watercolourist and miniaturist Eva Noar was an influence. Morris was a member of the Weybridge Society of Arts in Surrey (also, a keen golfer, of the Wentworth Club), also being an associate of RMS and showing with RA and London Salon.

Margaret MORRIS 1891–1980 Dancer, choreographer, artist and writer, daughter of the artist William Bright Morris and wife of the artist J D Fergusson. She was a child stage prodigy who did ballet training at Theatre Royal in London, later studying with Raymond Duncan, the dancer Isadora's brother. Keen to extend the expressive power of dance, she invented her own technique which she began teaching prior to World War I in her own Margaret Morris Movement school, staging her own shows. In 1913 during a Paris tour she met Fergusson and they formed a creative partnership. Between the wars more Margaret Morris Movement schools opened in France and Britain and the Morris-Fergusson artistic circle widened enormously. After returning to Glasgow on the outbreak of World War II the pair played a big role in forming the New Art Club and New Scottish Group of painters, and Morris founded the Celtic Ballet which in 1960 developed into the Scottish National Ballet. Fergusson encouraged his wife's artistic talents and she emerged as a clever, decorative painter and draughtsman, adept at catching a likeness in movement. Among her books was *The Art of J D Fergusson*, 1974. The first comprehensive show of her work occurred at Cyril Gerber Fine Art, Glasgow, 1984, which held a centenary show in 1991. After Morris' death her dance work continued through the International Association of Margaret Morris Movements in many countries.

Roy MORRIS 1890–1967 Painter, etcher and teacher, son of the sculptor Albert Morris. He was born in Chester and studied at the School of Art there, Slade School of Fine Art and Central School of Arts and Crafts. Moved to Derby, where he taught art from 1920–57, including the School of Art. Showed RA, NEAC, RBA and had a number of shows at Derby Art Gallery. It holds his picture A Suffolk Water Mill, and other provincial galleries, the Victoria & Albert Museum and British Museum have Morris's work. Lived in Derby.

Stanley MORRIS 1922– Artist and teacher who studied at Birmingham College of Arts and Crafts. He was a member of Free Painters and Sculptors, an associate of RBSA and showed with ROI, NEAC and at Paris Salon. Midlands Arts Centre holds his work. Taught at Madeley College of Further Education and lived latterly at Abbots Bromley, Staffordshire.

Anne MORRISON 1966– Painter and teacher who studied at Glasgow School of Art and Royal College of Art. She went on to lecture at Kent Institute of Art and Design, Canterbury, and Glasgow School of Art. In 1988 Morrison won the Elizabeth Greenshields Award; in the follow year she worked in Paris at Cité Internationale des Arts; then in 1990 she was awarded the Ensign Award and first prize from the British Institution Fund. Appeared in mixed shows at Pittencrieff House Museum in Dunfermline, in London and Switzerland and in 1992 she was included in Somatic States at the Quicksilver Place Gallery, Middlesex University. Had a solo show at 369 Gallery in Edinburgh. Scottish Arts Council holds her work.

James MORRISON 1932– Painter and teacher, born in Glasgow. He studied at the School of Art there, 1950–4, then taught part-time, 1955–8. In 1962–3 he was visiting artist at Patrick Allan-Fraser School of Art, Hospitalfield, Arbroath. In 1965 he joined the staff of Duncan of Jordanstone College of Art, Dundee, becoming head of department from 1979–87, when he resigned to paint full-time. He then made an extended painting trip to Canada, having in 1968 won an Arts Council Travelling Scholarship to Greece. Was keeper of RSA, a council member of SSA and a member of RSW. Morrison was a frequent broadcaster on the arts on television. One of his most notable achievements was the series of paintings of disappearing and decaying Glasgow which he made over many years, featured in an exhibition at William Hardie Gallery, Glasgow, 1990. Frequent one-man shows also included a series at Scottish Gallery, Edinburgh. HRH The Duke of Edinburgh, Glasgow and Edinburgh Universities and a number of Scottish galleries hold his work. Lived in Usan, Montrose, Angus.

Joseph Albert Colquhoun MORRISON 1882– Painter and artist in black-and-white. He studied at Cambridge University in the opening years of the century, then at New Art School with Richard Jack and John Hassall. Between 1911–20 he made four contributions to *Punch* magazine. Exhibited RA, NEAC, Goupil and Chenil Galleries and Paris Salon. Lived in Chalford, Stroud, Gloucestershire.

Robert Boyd MORRISON 1896–1969 Painter, designer and teacher, born in Belfast, Northern Ireland, where he worked for a lithographer, studying part-time at Belfast School of Art. After being wounded in the Army in France during World War I, Morrison studied under Henry Tonks for three years at Slade School of Fine Art, where he was a prizewinner. Among Morrison's achievements between the wars were: furniture decoration; writing articles for *Apollo* and *Artwork*; modelling for the Ulster Pavilion at the 1924 Wembley British Empire Exhibition; theatrical design, and co-editing, with the designer and artist George Sheringham, the lavishly illustrated costume book *Robes of Thespis*, 1928; and teaching art in school and as principal of the Well School of Drawing and Painting, Hampstead, north London. He was a member of NS and of the Grubb Group (see Michael Parkin Gallery exhibition, 1992), also showing at RA, RHA, PS and Goupil Galleries. Returned to Bangor, County Down, soon after World War II, where he also taught. Victoria & Albert Museum and Ulster Museum, Belfast, hold examples.

Alberto MORROCCO 1917–1998 Painter and teacher, born in Aberdeen of Italian parents. He studied at Gray's School of Art there, 1932–8, the following year travelling and studying on the continent. In 1942 he won the RSA's Guthrie Award. From 1946–50 Morrocco was a part-time teacher at Gray's School, becoming head of painting at Duncan of Jordanstone College of Art, Dundee, from 1950. Won the Medaglio d'Oro, San Vito, Italy, in 1957. Morrocco was a member of Royal Glasgow Institute of the Fine Arts and RSW and was elected RSA in 1962.

As well as being a still life, portrait, figure and landscape painter he illustrated Lockhart's *Anatomy* and painted murals for St Columba's Church, Glenrothes, and Liff Hospital, Dundee. Morrocco was a decorative artist of great felicity, using a rich and varied palette. He had a British Council show in Aberdeen in 1949, others following at Compass Gallery in Glasgow, a retrospective at Dundee Art Gallery in 1981, and a series at Thackeray Gallery. RSA, Scottish Arts Council and many Scottish galleries hold his work. The painter Leon Morrocco was his son. Lived in Dundee, Angus.

Leon MORROCCO 1942– Painter, draughtsman and teacher, born in Edinburgh. His work was colourful and witty and adept at catching the spirit of a place. He studied at Duncan of Jordanstone College of Art in Dundee, Slade School of Fine Art, Edinburgh College of Art and Accademia di Brera, Milan. From 1965–8 he lectured at the Edinburgh College of Art, taking a similar post at Glasgow School of Art, 1969–79. In the latter year he moved to Australia as head of the department of fine art at Chisholm Institute in Melbourne, resigning in 1984 to paint full-time. After eight solo shows in the United Kingdom Morrocco had a series of one-mans in Melbourne and Sydney, his first British show for a dozen years being held at Portland Gallery in 1991. Scottish Arts Council, Leeds City Art Gallery and Nuffield Foundation hold his work. The painter Alberto Morrocco was his father. Lived in London.

George MORROW 1869–1955 Illustrator, born in Belfast, brother of the artists Albert and Edwin Morrow. After studying art in Paris, George exhibited a little in London, at RA and RBA. But he was principally known as a magazine and book illustrator. His children's illustrations were early on found in books published by Seeley Service and his humorous drawings were used in *Punch* magazine for about half a century and reflected his own jolly character. Was art editor of *Punch* for five years from 1932. Lived at Thaxted, Essex.

Colin MORSE 1942– Painter, draughtsman, printmaker and illustrator, born into a farming family in north Pembrokeshire at Priskilly Fawr, Hayscastle, where he continued to live. He farmed until, aged 30, he was unable to continue due to an accident. His father had been a good amateur artist and during a long convalescence Colin's own interest in drawing was reawakened, and he attended Dyfed College of Art for four years. After this he worked as a freelance illustrator and designer and undertook painting commissions. He published his own limited-edition prints sold in galleries throughout the United Kingdom and from his farmhouse studio. Was a member of the Chartered Society of Designers.

Dorothy MORSE-BROWN 1900–1995 Artist and teacher, born in Bristol, who moved to Tenby, Pembrokeshire, in 1939, where she had a studio in the former mortuary. She was ateacher at the School of Art in Carmarthen, lectured at Tenby Art Club and was a founder-member of the Friends of Tenby, which later became the Tenby Civic Society. Tenby Museum, which holds a collection of works which she donated in 1968, sold Morse-Brown's pictures and prints. She left Pembrokeshire in 1979 and went to live with her son in the west Midlands, where she died.

Sydney MORSE-BROWN 1903– Portrait painter, born in Ernakulam, Kerala, in southwest India. Studied at Bristol School of Art and showed at RP, of which he was a member, ROI, NEAC and elsewhere. He had many distinguished sitters, including HRH The Duke of Edinburgh, General Sir Gerald Templer, the boxer Jimmy Wilde and King Umberto of Italy. Lived near Lewes, Sussex.

Arminell MORSHEAD 1889–1966 Painter and printmaker, noted for her horse and polo pictures, born in Tavistock, Devon. She studied at Slade School of Fine Art and etching with Malcolm Osborne and Frank Short at Royal College of Art. She was an athletic woman, keen on travelling, and among her notable works are Canadian Timber Team and New Forest Staghounds. Showed at RA, RP, ROI, RCamA, Walker Art Gallery in Liverpool and abroad. Lived for a time in Guildford, Surrey.

Edward MORSS 1906– Painter and teacher, born in Exeter, Devon, eventually settling in Exmouth. He studied at Sheffield College of Art, then Royal College of Art, 1927–31, and after being in charge of Colchester School of Art and Maidstone College of Art became principal of St Martin's School of Art, retiring in early 1970s. Showed at RA Summer Exhibition, elsewhere in London, the provinces and abroad.

Marjorie MORT 1906–1988 Painter and teacher, born in London. Studied at Manchester School of Art from 1924, Slade School of Fine Art from 1934 and then with Walter Bayes at Westminster School of Art. After wartime teaching settled in Mousehole, Cornwall, in 1945 and with Charles Breaker and Eric Hiller founded the Newlyn Holiday Sketching Group which lasted until mid-1960s. She showed with Manchester City Art Gallery and Walker Art Gallery in Liverpool and in Cornwall, where she finally lived in Penzance. She was included in A Century of Art in Cornwall 1889–1989, Newlyn Orion Galleries, 1989. It had held a 50-year retrospective of Mort's work in 1985.

Carey MORTIMER 1962– Artist in a range of media who in 1981–2 attended first year of architecture degree course at Manchester University; studied decorative arts at City & Guilds of London Art School, 1984–6; studied fresco at Il Laboratorio per Affresco at Prato, Italy, 1989; then gained a Master of Philosophy degree at Duncan of Jordanstone College of Art, Dundee, studying public art and design, 1990–1. Won a South West Arts Craft Award, 1989. Exhibitions included Paper Works, Ruskin Craft Gallery, Sheffield, 1989; Sue Rankin Gallery, 1994; and a joint exhibition with Jamie Owen at Thackeray Gallery, 1995. Commissions included murals in orphanages, Transylvania, Romania, 1990; designs for external decoration of St Mary Le Port church, Bristol, 1992; and designs for Temple Jazz Club,

Bristol, 1992. In 1993 went on a three-month expedition to Guyana as artist with Raleigh International.

Justin MORTIMER 1970– Painter in oil on canvas, born in Shropshire. After Wells Cathedral School, 1981–8, he attended Slade School of Fine Art, 1988–92. He had won first prize in Cadbury's National Exhibition of Children's Art, 1986, and after graduation mixed show appearances included BP Portrait Award, 1991, which he won with Three Seated Figures. His portrait of the playwright and actor Harold Pinter is in National Portrait Gallery collection. Had a solo show at Beaux Arts Gallery, Bath, 1993, another at The Blue Gallery, 1995. Lived in London.

Alastair MORTON 1910–1953 Abstract artist, born in Carlisle, Cumberland, to which he eventually returned after some years in Edinburgh, the family textile firm Morton Sundour being based in both places. Morton joined it aged 21, having studied mathematics for a year at Edinburgh University and been briefly at Oxford University. In 1928 his father, James Morton, founded Edinburgh Weavers, to which Alastair was eventually appointed artistic director. This brought him into contact with many contemporary artists who used the firm, notably Barbara Hepworth and Ben Nicholson. From the mid-1930s Morton began to work in a manner similar to Nicholson's, exhibiting in group shows. An exhibition on Morton's involvement with Edinburgh Weavers was held in 1978 at Scottish National Gallery of Modern Art, which holds his work.

Cavendish MORTON 1911– Painter, designer and printmaker, born in Edinburgh, son of the artist Cavendish Morton with whom he studied and twin brother of the artist Concord Morton with whom he produced joint work. Cavendish Morton was a member of RI, ROI, SGA and NS whose subjects included notable aeroplanes and ships. For a time he was art therapist to Hartismere Hospital in Eye, Suffolk, where he lived. Showed at RA, RBA, in the provinces and abroad and had a number of solo exhibitions. British Museum, Contemporary Art Society and several provincial collections hold examples. Settled in Bembridge, Isle of Wight.

Dorothy MORTON 1905– Painter in oil, watercolour and gouache, and teacher, born in London, who attended Art Teachers' Training College in Clapham and studied with A S Hartrick and Dora Billington at Central School of Arts and Crafts. Taught for 10 years, then in the late 1960s studied painting in oils at Benton End with Cedric Morris and Lett Haines. Became a member of Cambridge Drawing Society, Colchester Art Society, Sudbury Art Society and Gainsborough's House Print Workshop. Group shows included The Minories in Colchester, Arts Theatre and Barge on the Cam in Cambridge and elsewhere. Solo shows included a retrospective at Bury St Edmunds Art Gallery, 1983. The Leys School, Cambridge, holds her work. Lived in Cromer, Norfolk.

Victoria MORTON 1971– Painter, who graduated from Glasgow School of Art, 1989–93, gaining her master's there, 1993–5. Group exhibitions included Modern Art, Transmission Gallery, Glasgow, 1994; Swarm, The Travelling Gallery (Scottish Arts Council), tour, 1995; Insane Stoopid Phat Fuct Pervert, Concrete Skates, Glasgow, and Cubitt Gallery, 1996; and Satellite City, Catalyst Arts, Belfast, 1997. Had a solo show at Gallery Wilkes, Glasgow, 1995, later ones including Gallery Tre, Stockholm, and Dirty Burning at Andrew Mummery, 33 Great Sutton Street, both 1997.

Isobel MORTON-SALE 1904–1992 Illustrator, publisher and painter, born in London, the wife of the artist John Morton-Sale and mother of the book illustrator Roysia Romanelli. From a cultured family, she attended Ramsgate and Margate Schools of Art and the Central School of Arts and Crafts, where her teachers included A S Hartrick, Noel Rooke and Gerald Spencer-Pryse. There she met John Morton-Sale, marrying him in 1924. He specialised in landscape, she in sensitive portraits and they did much illustrative work together. For over 20 years until 1977 the Morton-Sales ran the Parnassus Gallery, bringing out many beautiful works such as enamels, paintings and stained glass from notable museums and private collections as well as their own creations. Isobel Morton-Sale admired the work of Gwen John and Winifred Nicholson. She showed at RP for several years from late-1970s and a retrospective of her and her husband's work was held at Maas Gallery, 1984, another exhibition at Chris Beetles Ltd, 1996. Lived at Moretonhampstead, Devon.

John MORTON-SALE 1901–1990 Artist and publisher, born in London, who was married to the artist Isobel Morton-Sale, his daughter being the book illustrator Roysia Romanelli. He attended Putney School of Art and Central School of Arts and Crafts, his teachers there including A S Hartrick and Gerald Spencer-Pryse. He married Isobel Morton-Sale in 1924 and they collaborated on many book illustrations, a number by their friend Eleanor Farjeon, including *Cherry Stones*, 1942 and *The Mulberry Bush*, 1945, and Beverley Nichols' *The Tree that Sat Down*, 1945; in 1933 Lewis Carroll's *Alice's Adventures in Wonderland* as well as *Through the Looking-Glass* appeared with John Morton-Sale's illustrations only. For over 20 years until 1977 the Morton-Sales ran the Parnassus Gallery, bringing out their own and many beautiful works from notable collections. In 1984 a retrospective of the two artists' works was held at Maas Gallery, with an exhibition at Chris Beetles Ltd in 1996. Lived at Moretonhampstead, Devon.

Richard MOSEK 1961– Painter whose work included abstract pictures, such as the oil on canvas Ledger, in Royal Over-Seas League Open, 1994. Born in Mansfield, Nottinghamshire, Mosek studied at Bristol Polytechnic and the Royal Academy Schools. Awards included prize at South Bank Picture Show, 1987; Landseer Scholarship, 1988; David Murray Landscape and de Segonzac Travelling Scholarships, both 1989. Completed commissions for Unilever and ICA. Group shows included Artists at Work, Collectors Gallery, 1990; Whitechapel Open Studios, 1991; and Contemporary Art Society, Towner Gallery, Eastbourne, 1992–3.

Malcolm MOSELEY 1947– Painter, draughtsman, printmaker and lecturer, born in Birmingham, who after the Five Ways Grammar School did a foundation year at Birmingham School of Art, 1965–6. He then attended Winchester School of Art, 1966–9; Central School of Art, 1969–70; and gained his master's degree at Royal College of Art, 1970–3. After etching at the Central and a year at the Royal College, Moseley knew that "I urgently needed to paint and draw … and I was encouraged. From that time I have tried to move forward, gradually becoming concerned with the adventure of colour. The attempt to place one colour next to another successfully remains a constant challenge," he wrote on the occasion of his retrospective of works on paper, 1969–1995, entitled Along the Road, at Christchurch Mansion, Ipswich, 1996. Moseley won a Royal College Travel Scholarship, 1972. He was administrator for the RA, 1977–84, eventually becoming drawing lecturer at the school of art and design at Suffolk College. Moseley was a member of Ipswich Art Society committee and of Suffolk Group. Mixed shows included RA Summer Exhibitions, NEAC, LG, RSW, New Academy Gallery and widely elsewhere. Solo exhibitions included Quay Theatre at Sudbury, Opixfilm Studio, and John Russell Gallery and Wolsey Theatre, both in Ipswich. P&O Shipping (*Royal Princess* liner), Hammersmith and Fulham Council, Ipswich Borough Council Museums and Galleries and many private collections held his work, which was sometimes signed with initials only. Lived in Ipswich, Suffolk.

Oswald MOSER 1874–1953 Figure painter and illustrator, born in London. Moser was a mature man before he pursued art seriously, studying at St John's Wood School of Art. He exhibited extensively at RI, of which he was a member, as well as RA, RSA, Walker Art Gallery, Liverpool, and Royal Glasgow Institute of the Fine Arts. Won a silver medal at Paris Salon in 1922. Moser's work has a strong emphasis on religious themes. Glasgow Corporation bought his picture Girl in Red. Lived in Bournemouth, Hampshire, later at Rye, Sussex.

Rosemary MOSLEY 1928–1992 Painter, born Rosemary Salmond, who came from an aristocratic background. From an early age she wanted to study art, but her family discouraged this. She married the writer Nicholas Mosley in 1947, from whom she was divorced in the early 1970s, and after her children had grown up would periodically study art in Paris. For 20 years she lived in the north of the Isle of Man, painting prolifically and travelling to Australia, New Mexico and California. Although she had several shows in London in the 1960s she later was reluctant to exhibit her work, which pursued several themes, such as *Alice in Wonderland* and *Red Riding Hood*. In 1981 an operation on her back led to her spending much of her time in bed or a wheelchair. An exhibition of her pictures was held shortly after death at The Gallery, 74 South Audley Street, in 1992.

Helen MOSLIN 1956– Painter, born in Manchester. She studied at Liverpool Polytechnic, 1974–9. Mixed show appearances included Serpentine Summer Show 2, 1981; John Moores Liverpool Exhibition from 1983; and Edward Totah Gallery's Nature Morte exhibition in 1985. She had a solo show at Original Picture Shop, 1985. Lived in London.

Colin MOSS 1914– Painter, draughtsman, printmaker and teacher, born in Ipswich, Suffolk, where he settled, teaching at the School of Art, 1948–79. During the war he had been engaged in camouflage for the Ministry of Home Security. Moss studied at Plymouth College of Art, 1930–4, then at Royal College of Art, 1934–8, under Barnett Freedman and Gilbert Spencer. In 1961 he studied under Kokoschka in Salzburg, and like this teacher he was an Expressionist, employing strong, rich colours and tones and forceful brushwork. In 1958 Moss was a founder-member of New Ipswich Art Group, in 1976 a founder-member of Six in Suffolk Group and from 1980–2 chairman of Ipswich Art Club. He took part in many mixed shows from Britain in Watercolour at RWS Gallery in 1953. After a solo exhibition at Kensington Gallery in 1951 and Zwemmer Gallery in 1955, Moss's one-man appearances were mainly in East Anglia. Later shows included John Russell Gallery, Ipswich, in 1992, and in the same year he had a retrospective of works on paper at Chappel Galleries, Chappel. Tate Gallery and Imperial War Museum hold his work.

Hugh MOSS 1904–1986 Watercolourist, calligrapher and teacher, born in Uxbridge, Middlesex, who attended Harrow School of Art, 1921–3, then Royal College of Art, 1923–7. After Medway School of Art and Wakefield College of Art, Moss was principal of Gloucester College of Art, 1945–68. From a small enrolment of a few hundred, while he was there it grew to thousands of students. Calligraphy by him is held by Gloucester Cathedral. Late in life Moss travelled in Tuscany and to Australia. Lived for many years at Westbury-on-Severn, Gloucestershire.

Joanna MOSS 1959– Versatile artist, born in Liverpool, who studied at Universities of St Andrews and Bristol, 1978–83; Liverpool Polytechnic, 1985–9; and Goldsmiths' College, 1990–2. In the 1990–1 BT New Contemporaries Moss won an award; and was artist-in-residence at John Hansard Gallery, Southampton, 1991–4, BT and that Gallery sponsoring her 8-day World Tour performance in 1991. Other mixed shows included John Moores Liverpool Exhibition, 1997–8. Solo exhibitions included Items, Dean Clough, Halifax, 1993. Lived in Sedgeford, Norfolk.

Marlow MOSS 1890–1958 Painter and sculptor, born in Richmond, Surrey. After private education she studied at St John's Wood School of Art, 1916–17, with Leonard Walker, at the Slade School of Fine Art, 1917–18, where her teachers included Henry Tonks, then in the late 1920s in Paris with Amedée Ozenfant and Fernand Léger. Exhibited internationally, in Switzerland, Netherlands and France, and was a member of a number of advanced groups such as Abstraction-Création, of which she was a founder-member. Was the friend of the artists Max Bill and Piet Mondrian and was totally committed to her aesthetic ideals. Finally lived at Lamorna, near Penzance, in Cornwall, virtually a recluse. She was known as an eccentric, dressing like a jockey and driving a pony and trap. The exhibition catalogue produced by Gimpel and Hanover Galerie, Zürich, in 1973–4, contains a good account of Moss's life. Florette Dijkstra's Marlow Moss Reconstructed was held at Tate Gallery St Ives, 1997.

Nicola MOSS 1960– Medallist, sculptor, printmaker, painter and jeweller, born in Buckinghamshire, who was educated at the Intaglio Glass Engraving Workshop, 1978, with Peter Dreisser; Hertfordshire College of Art and Design, St Albans, 1978–80; gained an honours degree in fine art from Canterbury College of Art and Design, 1980–3; and attended International Medallic Workshop, Pennsylvania State University, with John Cook, 1984, under that University's scholarship. In 1988–9, Moss had a 12-week residency at the Royal College of Art's jewellery and metalwork department, sponsored by the Royal Mint. Moss was a member of the Féderation Internationale de la Médaille, British Art Medal Society and the American Medallic Sculpture Association. Among her exhibitions were Contemporary British Medals, British Museum tour, 1986–7; The Horse: Art Medals and Coins of the British Museum, Negishi Equine Museum, Yokohama, Japan, 1990; Whistling to the Moon, solo show at Circa Gallery, Mineapolis, 1993–4; and a retrospective, American Numismatic Society, 1996. Its catalogue drew attention to Moss's "outstanding adaptation ... of age-old subjects and motifs into forms which are at once personal, modern and evocative of traditional artifacts." Lived in Shepherd Shield, Northumberland.

Roger MOSS 1949– Sculptor and teacher, born in Lancaster, who studied at Central School of Art, subsequently working as studio assistant to sculptors Brian Wall and Barry Flanagan. In 1974 he moved to Wales to work as lecturer at Dyfed College of Art, Carmarthen, being appointed head of sculpture in 1982. He showed widely around Wales, at Artsite Gallery in Bath and in 1986 was included in the Glynn Vivian Art Gallery & Museum, Swansea, show Seven Sculptors Working in Wales. That gallery bought his work Caryatid in 1984. Moss's works were often small and used found objects such as sandstone pebbles.

Sidney Dennant MOSS 1884–1946 Painter, born in Ipswich, Suffolk, who was a member of RBA, Suffolk Artists and Brighton Arts Club. Many of his landscapes were of Sussex, as he lived originally in Tunbridge Wells, Kent, then in Sussex at Pevensey, and he was given a memorial exhibition at Brighton Art Gallery in 1947. His work was also shown at RA, RI, Fine Art Society, in the provinces and at Paris Salon.

Max MOSSCROP 1963– Painter, born in Lancashire, who studied architecture at Liverpool John Moores University, winning the John Rankin Prize for Architecture in 1984. He went on to study fine art at Royal Academy Schools, winning the Silver Medal in 1996. In 1997, Mosscrop won The NatWest Art Prize, was featured in Chevron U K Ltd's calendar (using a computer to obtain random, abstract shapes for his water picture Surface), and appeared in the oil company's show at the ICA. Other mixed exhibitions included Fresh Art, at Islington's Business Design Centre, 1994; RA Summer Exhibition, from 1995; and 8th Mostyn Open, Oriel Mostyn, Llandudno, 1996–7. Solo exhibitions included Chora: Paintings by Max Mosscrop, The Lyceum, Liverpool, 1994–5. Lived in London.

Stephen MOSS-HORTON 1965– Assemblage-painting artist, sculptor and teacher who received "the highest degree ever awarded by the departments of art history and theatre design at the Institute of Art and Design, Birmingham Polytechnic" (later the University of Central England). While undertaking post-graduate studies at the Slade School of Fine Art Moss-Horton was invited to return to teach in Birmingham, where he was responsible for stage design and the history of theatre at degree level. Influenced by Rauschenberg, Kienholz and Schwitters among others, Moss-Horton's work included many personal symbols. His first major show, House of Cards, was staged by The Halcyon Gallery at Selfridges, 1993, and London and Birmingham exhibitions were sell-outs. His work was also issued as limited-edition prints.

Anna MOSSMAN 1963– Artist in various media, born and lived in London. She studied at Camberwell School of Art, 1981–5, and Goldsmiths' College School of Art, 1986–8. In the latter year she gained a Rome Award at British School in Rome. Was included in exhibition there in 1989 and in 1989–90 John Moores Liverpool Exhibition showed ink on plastic drawing Interior. Shared a show with John Murphy at Lisson Gallery, 1996.

Marjorie MOSTYN 1893–1979 Painter, daughter of the artist Tom Mostyn, especially noted for her flower pictures. She was married to the artist Leonard Fuller. After private education she attended the St John's Wood School of Art under Leonard Walker, then the Royal Academy Schools, 1912–15, where her teachers included John Singer Sargent and George Clausen. She won silver and bronze medals and gained a British Institution Scholarship for painting in 1915. Settled with her husband in St Ives, Cornwall, in 1938, where he opened the St Ives School of Painting, which he ran until his death in 1973, when she took it over. She was a founder-member of the Penwith Society of Arts in 1949 as well as being a member of the St Ives Society of Artists and the Newlyn Society. Exhibited RA, RCamA, of which she was a member, RP and elsewhere. Lived in St Ives.

Marie-Louise von MOTESICZKY 1906–1996 Painter, notable for her fine self-portraits, born in Vienna, Austria. She studied there before going to Frankfurt in 1923, where she met Max Beckmann, a major influence, as was Oskar Kokoschka. Beckmann invited her to join his classes at the Stadel, where she stayed until 1928 before returning to Austria. Because of the political situation in 1938 she left for the Netherlands, where she first showed her work in The Hague in 1939, that summer moving to England, settling in London after World War II. She had a first solo exhibition at Beaux Arts Gallery in 1960, but otherwise rarely showed. There was a solo exhibition at the Goethe Institute in 1985, and after one in Vienna in 1994 a selection was shown at Manchester City Art Gallery. Fitzwilliam Museum in Cambridge, Tate Gallery and National Portrait Gallery hold examples.

Toby MOTT 1964– Artist in a wide range of media and styles, work tinged with humour and enigma. He was born and lived in London. From 1983 was a founding member of the Grey Organisation, showing with it in over 20 exhibitions until 1990. Group exhibitions included Riot Furniture, Furniture of the Twentieth Century, New York, 1991; Candy Man II, Building C, Tower Bridge, 1994; Greatest Hits, Tri Gallery, Los Angeles, 1995; and Flag, Clink Street, 1996. Had several solo exhibitions in America and at Interim Art from 1995.

Tony MOTT 1950– Sculptor, photographer and teacher. He was at Goldsmiths' College School of Art, 1969–72, and Slade School of Fine Art, 1972–4. Won a number of awards including Sainsbury Award and Boise Scholarship, both 1974, Italian Government Bursaries in 1979–82 and in 1985 he was a Camden Open Prizewinner. Went on to teach at Kent Institute of Art & Design, Canterbury, and was director of studies at Heatherley School of Art. Group shows included Northern Young Contemporaries, 1973, LG from 1974, RA in 1977, Camden Annual in 1985 and Sculpture at Canterbury, 1992. From 1979 Mott had a series of solo shows of photographs, at Istituto Italiano de Cultura London and Dublin; University of Swansea in 1980; RIBA, 1986; and elsewhere.

Pauline Patricia MOTTRAM 1920– Painter, designer and teacher, born in London. She studied at Bromley School of Art and at the Art Schools of Canterbury and Tunbridge Wells, there with E Owen Jennings. Widowed during World War II, she later taught in Kent, where she exhibited. Lived in Tunbridge Wells, Kent.

Romanos MOUKARZEL 1965– Painter, born in Lebanon, who graduated from Manhattanville College with a degree in liberal arts. He continued his studies in Florence, Italy, at an academic painting school, in 1991 moving to London, where he set up as an independent artist. As well as solo exhibitions in London and Beirut, in 1997 he shared a show with David Bachmann at The Edith Grove Gallery.

Alan MOULDING 1943– Printmaker, painter and teacher who studied at Waltham Forest Technical College & School of Art until 1966, then painting at Royal College of Art until 1969. Taught for a year on art foundation course at York University in Canada, where he lived for eight years. On his return in 1978 he joined Bristol Printmakers' workshop. Went on to establish own workshop in Coleford, Gloucestershire, where he lived. Among Moulding's shows were Ontario Now, Art Gallery, Hamilton, 1976; Gallery One, Ann Arbor, Michigan, 1977; and in 1980 Stroud Festival Print Exhibition, Spacex Gallery, Exeter, and South West Arts touring show Seven Print Makers. In 1986 he won a prize at Ninth International Print Biennale, Bradford. Showed at España 88, Malaga, Spain, in 1988.

George Frederick MOULES 1918–1990 Printmaker, designer and painter who was married to the artist Noël Slaney. He studied at Glasgow School of Art, his teachers including Hugh Adam Crawford and Ian Fleming. Exhibited RA, RSA, Royal Glasgow Institute of the Fine Arts, Society of Artist Printmakers, of which he was a member, and Walker Art Gallery, Liverpool. He was a member of RSW and of Arts Club in Glasgow, where he lived. Glasgow Museums and Art Galleries hold his work.

Kevin MOUNT 1951– Artist, notably in collage, born in Nottingham. After attending Bath Academy of Art, 1969–73, Mount was for about a dozen years a journalist in Nottingham and Wiltshire. From 1985 he was for some years at Dartington Hall in Devon, where he lived. In 1991 his collage From The Voyage of the Desire: "Delving Deep" was included in the Norwich Gallery's show East.

Paul MOUNT 1922– Sculptor, painter, draughtsman and teacher, born in Newton Abbot, Devon, married to the painter June Miles. Studied at Paignton School of Art, 1937–40, under the sculptor Alexander Sutcliffe, then at Royal College of Art, 1940–1 and 1946–8, with Gilbert Spencer, Percy Horton and others. During World War II Mount served in the Friends' Ambulance Unit attached to the Second French Armoured Division. Mount taught drawing and painting at Winchester School of Art, then in 1955 went to Nigeria to open and run an art department at Yaba College of Technology. While there he was introduced to architectural sculpture and began three-dimensional work. He experimented with new materials and worked on a large scale, but when Mount returned to England in 1962 for lack of architectural outlets he turned to smaller pieces in fibreglass, cast iron and bronze. Learned to weld with local blacksmith, began to use stainless steel extensively and joined Penwith Society of Art, with which he had much in common. First London show at Drian Gallery in 1964; later showed with John Whibley Gallery, Marlborough Fine Art, New Art Centre and Beaux Arts, in Bath. Mount's work can be found in most West European countries, in America and Nigeria. His sculptures and mobiles are abstract with themes frequently suggested by the natural world, sometimes alien and strange, charged with energy. Lived at St Just, Penzance, Cornwall.

Duncan MOUNTFORD 1954– Artist who studied at Liverpool Polytechnic, 1972–3, then Lancaster Polytechnic, Coventry, 1973–6. Showed with Walker Art Gallery, Liverpool, touring exhibitions Merseyside Artists from 1985, and at RA Summer Exhibition and Winter Exhibition, Blond Fine Art, both 1986. Had a solo show at Hanover Galleries, Liverpool, 1985.

John Herniman MOWELS 1889–1953 Sculptor, designer, critic and administrator. A native of Brighton, Sussex, Mowels studied at the School of Art there. After Army service abroad in

World War I Mowels taught at Varndean School of Art, Brighton, in Salford and Carlisle, from 1930–49, with a break for war service, being principal of Southport School of Art and curator of the Atkinson Art Gallery. Wrote criticism for the *Manchester Guardian*. Lived in Sale, Cheshire.

Geoffrey MOWLAM fl. from 1970s– Gestural abstract painter, born in Weymouth, Dorset, who studied at Bournemouth College of Art and Bristol Polytechnic. In 1988 he attended a Triangle Artists' Workshop in New York and in 1993 was invited to take part in the Mbile International Artists' Workshop in Zambia. Group exhibitions included New Contemporaries at ICA (*Artscribe* Prize, 1979), and Made in Greenwich, The Living Room, 1994. Solo exhibitions included Pike Gallery, 1993. Was based in London.

James MOYES 1937– Artist, musician and teacher who, after a grammar school education on Tyneside, attended Dartmouth Royal Naval College and then studied electrical engineering at St Andrews University. Moyes worked as a BBC recording engineer from 1959; studied at Chelsea School of Art, 1962–6; and by the early 1970s was teaching at Bath Academy of Art, Corsham. Group exhibitions included Axiom Gallery, 1967; Critic's Choice, Tooth, 1970; Matrix, at Arnolfini Gallery, Bristol, 1971; and Systems, Arts Council, Whitechapel Art Gallery and tour, 1972–3, for which Moyes wrote at length about his contribution, A vibration tent, involving both sound and light. Moyes' interest in music – such as Indian ragas, "a type of system in themselves" – now took over. He studied guitar at the Guildhall School of Music and composed for the instrument, but by the mid-1990s had "returned to painting".

Rodrigo MOYNIHAN 1910–1990 Artist in oil, watercolour, charcoal and chalk, and teacher. He was born in Santa Cruz de Tenerife, Canary Islands, of Irish-Spanish descent, spent part of childhood and youth in England, America and Italy, where he began to study art in Rome, later attending the Accademia Rosso, in Florence. From 1928–31 was at the Slade School of Fine Art. Exhibited with LG from 1930, between 1933–6 being a leading member of the Objective Abstractions Group with Geoffrey Tibble and Graham Bell. In the late 1930s he was associated with the Euston Road School, painting portraits, still life and figure groups typical of it. Was married first to Elinor Bellingham-Smith, then Anne Dunn, both painters. After serving in camouflage in World War II became an official war artist in 1943. Elected RA in 1954, resigned 1957, then re-elected 1979. From 1948–57 professor of painting at the Royal College of Art. Retrospective at the RA in 1978. First one-man show at the Redfern Gallery in 1940, after which many followed in London, New York and elsewhere. The Tate Gallery, Arts Council, RA, British Council and Metropolitan Museum of Art, New York, are among the many public collections containing his work. Moynihan travelled widely to paint and his work defied easy categorisation. Portraits, abstracts, clinically precise studio still lifes and searching self-portraits were all undertaken at periods, and all with a rare technical adroitness. Lived in London.

Ursula MOYNIHAN 1912– Painter, married to the sculptor Percy Brown. She studied at Royal College of Art and exhibited RA, UA, RBSA and elsewhere. Leicester Museum and Art Gallery bought her work. Lived at St Margaret's on Thames, Middlesex.

Arthur MOYSE 1914– Watercolourist, draughtsman and writer, born and lived in London. Moyse was a self-taught artist of Irish working class stock who did "every drear job to earn a living, including six years in the Army" in World War II. His main works were large watercolours which mixed Hogarthian morality and Surrealism. Showed extensively in London galleries, including Angela Flowers, but latterly did not sell his work. Publications included *Zero One* and *Revolutionary Manifesto* and he was art critic for Freedom Press.

Charles MOZLEY 1914–1991 Illustrator, printmaker, painter and teacher, born in Sheffield, Yorkshire. He attended the College of Art there while still a schoolboy and had an exhibition at the Hibbert Brothers' Gallery in 1933 which made him a local celebrity. Won a scholarship to Royal College of Art which he went to in 1934, having taught for a year in Sheffield; he also taught briefly at Camberwell School of Arts and Crafts in the late-1930s. After war service, during which he was in camouflage and intelligence, Mozley became a prolific artist, a master of many techniques. He finished hundreds of book jackets; did film posters for Alexander Korda; completed Festival of Britain murals in 1951; and illustrated a number of books, including work for the Folio Society and Limited Editions Club. In 1979 his drawings and paintings of Venice were exhibited at Somerset House, to aid the Venice in Peril fund, and he had a restrospective show at the King Street Gallery. Mozley was noted for his deft figure studies and caricatures, which he could complete at great speed. Died in Kew, Surrey.

Ron MUECK 1958– Creator of hyper-realistic sculptures modelled in clay, then cast in fibreglass or silicone and resin, the resulting figures sometimes being eerie and disturbing. Mueck was born in Melbourne, Australia, where he worked on and with puppets for television. In the mid-1980s he was engaged on the children's television series *Sesame Street* and in films including *Labyrinth* after which he was self-employed making models for advertising, then turned to sculpture. The painter and printmaker Paula Rego used his 1995 Little Boy/Pinocchio figure in a series of pictures. Mueck's meticulously detailed yet child-size model of his late father, Dead Dad, was one of the most remarked-upon exhibits in the Saatchi Collection-related exhibition Sensation at the RA, 1997. Solo show Anthony d'Offay, 1998.

Max MUELLER 1901– Painter in oil and watercolour, by profession a lithographer, who studied art in Leipzig, Germany. Moved to England after World War II, settling in Swaffham,

Norfolk, and that county became his main subject. Mueller was noted for washy landscapes, often in earthy browns and greens, sometimes with a thin pen line for detail. His wife, Winifred, was a flower painter. She showed with him at Assembly House, Norwich, in 1971, one of several solo exhibitions by him there. Also showed at RA Summer Exhibition, 1969.

Anne Davidson MUIR fl. from c.1910–1951 Painter of flowers and portraits, born in Hawick, Roxburghshire. After education at George Watson's Ladies College, Edinburgh, she studied at Edinburgh College of Art and Heriot-Watt College Art School, her teachers including John Campbell Mitchell and James Riddel. Exhibited RA, RSA, RSW, SSA and elsewhere. Kelvingrove Art Gallery, Glasgow, holds her work. Lived in Edinburgh.

Jane MUIR 1929– Artist in mosaic, watercolour and etching, and teacher, born in London. Gained her master's degree in modern history at Oxford University, 1947–50. Then studied painting and sculpture at Middlesbrough College of Art, 1960–5, from 1965–8 gaining a diploma in architectural decoration, specialising in mosaic under Joan Haswell, from Teesside College of Art, having become interested in mosaic from 1950 with a travel bursary to Italy. Set up own studio in 1968 at Weston Turville, Buckinghamshire. Was a fellow of Art Workers' Guild, Society of Designer Craftsmen and Chartered Society of Designers. Participated in numerous group shows, later solo exhibitions including Milton Keynes Art Gallery, 1991, and St John's, Smith Square, 1993. Was a tutor at West Dean College, 1976–82, and elsewhere. Muir was "concerned with imaginative works, often based on landscape, including rocks, found objects and glass". St Anne's College, Oxford; Open University, Milton Keynes; and Oxfordshire County Museum hold examples.

Keiko MUKAIDE 1954– Installations and glass artist, born in Tokyo, Japan who graduated in visual communication design at Musashino Art University there. Worked as a graphic designer; 1982–7 periodically made hot glass and kiln work studies in America; attended Royal College of Art for her master's in ceramic and glass, 1989–91; with further studies in France and Germany, 1993–4. In the 1990s she held a number of residencies, including Westminster Adult Education Institute and the College of Art in Edinburgh, where she lived. Mukaide's International Festival show there in 1996, including her Japanese garden installation, prompted *The Glasgow Herald* to call her "the most unusual and gifted glass artist to appear in the 1990s." City Art Gallery, Manchester, showed an installation in 1998. Victoria & Albert Museum and other international collections hold examples.

Nanny MULDER 1948– Painter, printmaker and teacher, born in Leiden, Netherlands, who moved to Edinburgh in 1976. Career moves included being a visiting lecturer at Glasgow School of Art and lecturing at Edinburgh College of Art; a period living and working in Dublin, and lecturing at Dun Laoghaire School of Art and Design and at the University of Ulster, Belfast; then a return to Edinburgh in 1987, where she started the Buccleuch School of Drawing and Painting and was a visiting lecturer at Edinburgh College of Art. Mulder studied at the Gerrit Rietveld Academie, Amsterdam, 1967–72 and 1973–4, winning a scholarship to concentrate on the mezzotint at Academii Sztuk Pienknych, Craców, Poland, 1972–3. The concentration needed for such printmaking was reflected in her paintings, in which her main subject, sea shells, were enlarged, transformed and overlaid with new significances by a type of Surrealism or Hyper-Realism. Exhibitions included Grafton Gallery, Dublin, from 1985; Traditional and Innovation in Printmaking Today, Rank Xerox touring show, 1986; 6 Women Artists, Scottish Gallery, 1988; and Links of Affinity, Knapp Gallery, 1989. Scottish Arts Council, Aberdeen Art Gallery and a number of Dutch and Polish collections hold examples.

Jane MULFINGER 1961– Sculptor and installations artist who employed everyday objects such as spectacle frames in her work. She was born in California, America, attending Stanford University, 1979–83, Pasadena Art College of Design, 1980, Stanford University in Florence, Italy, in 1980–1, then Royal College of Art, 1987–9. Mulfinger's work was included in Sculpture & Sculptors' Drawings at William Jackson Gallery, 1991. Her solo shows included an installation at Oriel Mostyn, Llandudno, and one at Newcastle, both in 1989; installations at Carignano, Italy, and in Paris, in 1991, and Lost for Words, in same year at Flaxman Gallery. Lived in London.

Carolyn MULHOLLAND 1944– Sculptor, noted for her portraits, born in Lurgan, Armagh, Northern Ireland. She attended Belfast College of Art, 1962–6. Although she taught for a time she had no desire to continue. Mulholland modelled in clay or wax as she "hadn't the mentality for stone or wood, that needs patience and physical strength". Exhibitions included Kenny's Art Gallery in Galway, New and Tom Caldwell Galleries in Belfast, and Oireachtas in Dublin, Belfast and Letterkenny. She carried out a considerable amount of commissioned work including Figures, in fibreglass bronze, for The Forum, Antrim; Man on a Trestle, Wilton Place in Dublin, for New Ireland Assurance Company; and Tree, for Jefferson Smurfit headquarters at Clonskeagh. Her portrait heads included the poet Seamus Heaney and his wife Marie. Arts Council of Northern Ireland holds her work. She was based in Belfast and Dublin.

Craig MULHOLLAND 1969– Painter, draughtsman and etcher, born in Glasgow, where he attended the School of Art, 1987–91. He won the Armour Prize at the Art School, 1992, and Elizabeth Greenshields Scholarship. Group exhibitions included Van Gogh Self-Portrait Competition, Burrell Collection, Glasgow, 1991; Bath International Art Fair, Edinburgh Art Fair and Royal Glasgow Institute of the Fine Arts, McLellan Galleries, all 1992; and Scottish Master Prints, Scottish Gallery, Edinburgh, 1993. Solo shows included Compass Gallery, Glasgow, 1992; Scottish Gallery, Edinburgh, 1993; and Paton Gallery, 1994. Mulholland was an artist capable of working at ambitious subjects on a large scale, as his diptych Pier, 1993, at Paton showed. Unilever and Robert Fleming & Company hold examples.

Kathleen MULLANIFF 1957– Painter producing strongly gestural canvases, born in County Longford, Ireland. Moved to London with her family at the age of six, living in a single room in Camden Town, where she, her mother and brother on the wallpaper drew "paradisal landscapes ... and the creatures which inhabited them ... In my paintings I try to create an equivalent day dream." She gained an honours degree in painting at Camberwell School of Art, 1974–8, then her master's degree at Goldsmith's College School of Art, 1983–5. Among her exhibitions were new Contemporaries at RA, 1976; South London Art Gallery, 1978; Woodlands Art Gallery, 1985, and in same year Whitechapel Open; and in 1986 The Spirit of London Competition and, at the Minories, Colchester, 4 London Artists. Mullaniff has work in collections of Basildon Arts Trust and Leicestershire County Council.

Sybil MULLEN GLOVER fl. from 1950s–1995 Artist, mainly in watercolour, born in Cheshire. After private education she studied at St Martin's School of Art and with private tutors, notably R V Pitchforth. She was elected RI 1962, RSMA 1964 and RWA 1965 and exhibited at RA, RSA, ROI, NEAC and at Paris Salon, where she gained gold and silver medals. Shared shows with Sir Hugh Casson and Francis Russell Flint and her solo exhibitions included Plymouth City Museum and Art Gallery in 1979. It holds her work, as do National Maritime Museum in Greenwich and public galleries in Brighton and Walsall. Lived at Stoke, Plymouth, Devon.

John MULVEY 1939– Self-taught sculptor, born in Manchester, who spent some years as a sheet metal worker which he reckoned influenced his work, helping him "to achieve the essence of his subject with a simplicity of form and an economy of line". Mulvey worked in bronze, figure and animal subjects, the forms sometimes bordering on abstraction. He showed at Expositions Annuelles des Beaux-Arts, Paris, bronze medallist 1974, silver 1976; Robert A Young Gallery, New York; Lad Lane Gallery, Dublin, and elsewhere. Solo exhibitions included Beauford Art Centre, Devon, 1971; Edinburgh International Festival, 1974; National Exhibition Centre, Birmingham, 1979–81; and Foyles Gallery, 1983. The sculptures were cast by Westley Brothers Ltd, of Cradley Heath. Municipal galleries hold Mulvey's work, which was commissioned by Rolls-Royce Ltd, the Parachute Regiment and Trust House Forte. His wife was the painter Mary Mulvey and they ran a studio gallery at Willesley, Tetbury, Gloucestershire.

Matilda MULVEY 1882– Flower and portrait painter, born in London, who studied under Frederic Whiting at Heatherley's School of Fine Art. She exhibited widely, notably at RBA, SWA, NEAC, RP, ROI, in the provinces and abroad, and gained an Hon. Mention and silver medal at Paris Salon. Lived at Barnet, Hertfordshire.

Stephen MUMBERSON 1955– Versatile artist, notably a printmaker, and teacher, who studied at Brighton Polytechnic, 1974–7; Royal College of Art, 1979–81; was a printmaking fellow there, 1989; and was elected an associated of RE, 1991. From 1982 held a number of teaching posts, including visiting and sessional lectureships at West Surrey College of Art & Design, at Farnham; London College of Fashion; Middlesex University; Bournemouth & Poole College of Art & Design; Brighton Polytechnic, where he was acting head of printmaking, 1990; and Brixton College. Awards included a residency at Westminster University, 1992. Group exhibitions included Post Cards, Gardner Arts Centre, 1977; LG, Camden Arts Cente and tour, 1982; Spirit of London, Royal Festival Hall, 1987; and the Great Print Show, Bankside Gallery, 1993. Two- and three-man exhibitions included the Cut Gallery, 1994. Had a solo exhibition at the Young Vic Theatre, 1982, later ones including Art Now from 1988.

Lucy MUMFORD 1970– Painter, born in Harpenden, Hertfordshire, who studied at St Albans Art School and Cheltenham Art College. Showed at Fresh Art, Business Design Centre in Islington, and Painting Today, Bonhams, both 1992; Axiom Centre, Cheltenham, 1994, winning an Axiom Open Minor Award; and The Discerning Eye, Mall Galleries and Brown's Restaurant, and Royal Over-Seas League Open, both 1995.

Claude MUNCASTER 1903–1974 Painter in oil, pastel, watercolour and draughtsman in pen and ink of landscapes and marine pictures; etcher and illustrator. Born at West Chiltington, Sussex, as Grahame Hall, son of the Royal Academician Oliver Hall, who launched his son on a career as a landscape painter at 15. Although early works were signed Grahame Hall, he changed his name to Claude Muncaster to overcome any suggestion that he gained from his father's name. They had the same ideal, "to carry on the best traditions of English painting." Muncaster painted conventional landscapes and some large, meticulous panoramas of the Thames and Bradford, commissioned by firms. He travelled widely, was a good speaker in public and broadcaster. As a young man he sailed as a deckhand on a windjammer around the Horn,which gave him an expert knowledge of ships. *Rolling Round the Horn* was one of several books by him; he also illustrated John Masefield's *Bird of Dawning*. During World War II Muncaster served as a camouflage expert with the Royal Navy. He had his first purchase accepted by the RA in 1920, exhibited widely throughout his life and accepted royal commissions. Many of his 5,000 pictures hang in galleries around the world, including the Tate Gallery. Lived at Sutton, near Pulborough, Sussex.

Henry MUNDY 1919– Painter and teacher, was born in Birkenhead, Cheshire, where he attended the Laird School of Art, 1933–7, then Camberwell School of Arts and Crafts, 1946–50, with Victor Pasmore and William Coldstream. Was married, later divorced the painter Gillian Ayres. Had first one-man show in 1954 at Gallery One in London. others following in England and abroad, including Gallery KB, Oslo, Norway; Stone Gallery in

Newcastle upon Tyne; Kasmin Gallery; Hoya Gallery; and Nigel Greenwood Gallery. In 1981 shared a show with Colin Cina and Dennis Creffield at Serpentine Gallery. Showed widely in group exhibitions and won a number of prizes including first prize at John Moores Liverpool Exhibition in 1961. Taught at St Martin's School of Art and Bath Academy of Art, Corsham. Tate Gallery, Arts Council and many other galleries in Britain and abroad hold his work. Mundy was known for his brightly coloured, often witty abstracts. Lived in London, later in Devon.

William Percy MUNDY 1936– Artist in watercolour, oil and pencil, born in Wokingham, Berkshire. He served a five-year apprenticeship as a lithographic artist and designer in Reading, but was essentially a self-taught painter. specialising in meticulous trompe l'oeil pictures and portraits. Mundy spent most of his National Service drawing maps for jungle forces in the Malayan Emergency. From 1960 he held senior positions with advertising agencies in the Far East, retiring to England to paint full-time in 1978. He was a member of RMS, winning its Gold Memorial Bowl in 1986; Miniature Artists of America; Hilliard Society; and a fellow of Chartered Society of Designers. Showed at RA Summer Exhibitions from 1977, RP, Paris Salon where he won a Silver medal in 1982, and in 1991 had a solo show, under royal patronage, at Oriental Hotel, Bangkok. Portrait subjects included HRH The Duke of Edinburgh and HRH The Sultan of Johor, the comedian Spike Milligan and actor Rodney Bewes. Victoria & Albert Museum holds his work. Lived in Henley-on-Thames, Oxfordshire.

Shirley MUNGAPEN 1933– Wood engraver, graphic artist and painter, born in Boston, Lincolnshire, studying at Nottingham College of Arts & Crafts and Portsmouth College of Art. She gained her National Diploma in Design in 1961, her teachers having included the wood engraver Gerry Tucker. Mungapen qualified as a State Registered Nurse in 1959 and become an art therapist in several hospitals. She was made a member of SWE in 1976, is mentioned in books on wood engraving and illustrated for Folio Society Shakespeare as well as doing private press work. She liked "to use curved lines in engraving as these represent movement and life". Showed at RE, Ferens Art Gallery in Hull, Bear Lane Gallery in Oxford and elsewhere. Lived in Fawley, Southampton.

Frank MUNGER 1920– Self-taught artist, born in Buckinghamsire, who in 1945 joined Iliffe Press as an editorial artist. Exhibited his first paintings in London, 1966, and worked in all media but mainly watercolour, also showing in the provinces and having solo exhibitions local to West Hallam, Derbyshire, where he lived. Was a member of the Royal Aeronautical Society, the Guild of Aviation Artists and was a founder-member of the Guild of Motoring Artists. Wildlife and landscapes were also painted. Won a number of awards, including Aviation Painting of the Year, 1991. Numerous magazines and books included Munger's work, which was held in public and private collections.

Alfred MUNNINGS 1878–1959 Painter, mainly in oil, of landscapes and equestrian scenes. Born at Mendham, Suffolk, he remained closely associated with that part of England, living finally at Dedham. For five years towards the end of the nineteenth century Munnings worked for a lithographer in Norwich, studying part-time at Norwich School of Art. Travelled widely on the continent. In 1899 Munnings won a gold medal at the Poster Academy at Crystal Palace, London; began exhibiting at the RA; and lost the sight of one eye. But this did not deter him from further study at the Académie Julian, 1903–4, in Paris. First one-man show at Leicester Galleries in 1913. Towards the end of World War I he was attached to the Canadian Cavalry Brigade in France, painting for the Canadian government. After the war Munnings steadily built his reputation as a painter and a character. Was elected RA 1925, was knighted in 1944 and became president of the RA, 1944–9. He was a controversial president, gaining much publicity for his forthright criticism of modern art. His three volumes of autobiography, published early in the 1950s, were entitled *An Artist's Life*, *The Second Burst* and *The Finish*. Several retrospective exhibitions were held in his lifetime, including one at the RA Diploma Gallery, in 1956. Many public galleries around the world hold his work, including the Tate Gallery, Walker Art Gallery, Liverpool, and Aberdeen Art Gallery. Munnings' dashing colourful scenes of riding and racing life have retained public popularity despite changes in artistic fashion. An exhibition was held at Victoria Art Gallery, Bath, in 1998.

Alexander Graham MUNRO 1903–1985 Painter, draughtsman and teacher, born in Midlothian, who in 1932 married the artist Ruth Morwood. He was educated at George Heriot's School, in Edinburgh, and attended the RSA life school. In 1925 he won the Chalmers-Jervis Bursary Prize, Keith Prize and Carnegie Travelling Scholarship, which took him to Paris to study with André Lhote. In the 1920s and 1930s Munro travelled extensively in Europe and North Africa, producing a large body of work. Became art master at Loretto School, near Edinburgh, later Trinity College, Glenalmond. He was elected RSW in 1960, by then an established exhibitor at RSA, and Royal Glasgow Institute of the Fine Arts. William Hardie organised a first solo exhibition of Munro's work at Edinburgh College of Art in 1984 during the International Festival and was involved in a show of Munro's pictures with those of Majel Davidson at Portland Gallery in 1989.

Charles MUNRO 1913–1990 Designer and artist, who attended Ealing College of Art, 1929–31. He then worked in advertising and publishing in India, being art editor and political cartoonist of Rudyard Kipling's old paper the *Civil and Military Gazette* of Lahore, then served in Indian Army, rising to rank of major. After World War II he was involved in exhibition design, for the Central Office of Information and in private practice. He designed Section I of the British Pavilion for the World Fair, Expo '70, held in Osaka, Japan. He worked widely abroad. The Dodington Carriage Museum was designed by him and he did an enormous amount of artwork for International Chemical

Innocent fine art

Black Moon Sir Terry Frost RA

Twentieth Century British painting, prints and sculpture.

Gallery artists include –

SIR TERRY FROST RA, ROSE HILTON, MARY STORK, NEIL MURISON RWA, JAMES SCRASE, JOHN CODNER RA, CHARLES HOWARD, SYLVIA EDWARDS, BEN HARTLEY, DOUGLAS PORTWAY

Framing and restoration

Contact: Carole Innocent, Deirdre Hardwick

Monday – Saturday 10am – 5.30pm

7a Boyces Avenue, Clifton, Bristol, BS8 4AA Tel: 0117 973 2614 Fax: 0117 974 1425

Classical Still Life *oil, 1968*

Doris Brabham Hatt

MICHAEL WRIGHT FINE ART

4 Boyces Avenue, Clifton, Bristol BS8 4AA

Tel/Fax: 0117 974 1998

Specialising in 20th Century British Art

Institute of International Visual Arts Library

inIVA's reference library has an up-to-date, growing collection of monographs, catalogues, periodicals, slides and other media on visual arts and cultural studies. The collection focuses on contemporary art from Africa, Asia, Latin America and on the work of British artists from different cultural backgrounds: over 3,000 catalogues, 700 monographs covering cultural, political, gender and media studies, and 150 periodicals worldwide.

Opening Hours: 10:00am – 5:00pm
Monday to Friday (by appointment).
A scale of charges operates for users.

For further information and regular updates on new acquisitions, see inIVA's website: www.iniva.org/library

inIVA Library
Kirkman House
12/14 Whitfield Street
London W1P 5RD
Tel. +44 171 636 1930
Fax: +44 171 636 1931
e-mail: ariede@iniva.org

Registered Charity number: 1031721

Company's corporate ethical advertising. Showed at RA and elsewhere and was a London Sketch Club member with a special interest in marine activities. Lived in Walhampton, Hampshire, for some years, where was a maroon-firing authority for the Royal National Lifeboat Institution, also an auxiliary coastguard, later moving to Isle of Wight.

James MUNRO 1925–1990 Sculptor and teacher, born in Musselburgh, Midlothian, working in a wide variety of materials. Studied at Edinburgh College of Art, sculpture with Eric Schilsky, 1947–52. Went on to lecture on visual arts at Moray House College, Edinburgh. Munro was a member of SSA, RSA and Royal Glasgow Institute of the Fine Arts and an associate of RBS. He several times won the RSA's Sculpture Award. Showed extensively in Scotland, also at Swansea University and in France. Lived at Loanhead, Lothian, then returned to Musselburgh.

Elizabeth MUNTZ 1894–1977 Artist and teacher, born in Toronto, Canada, who studied at Ontario College of Art, at L'Académie de la Grande Chaumière in Paris under Antoine Bourdelle and then privately with Frank Dobson. She exhibited in London at Cooling Galleries, LG and elsewhere, widely on the continent and North America. Was an exhibiting member of the 7 & 5 Society, being included in the commemorative touring show arranged by Michael Parkin Fine Art in 1979–80. Betty Muntz was given a big retrospective of sculpture and drawings in 1971 at Dorset County Museum in Dorchester and a smaller show of paintings, many Canadian landscapes, in 1973. She bought a cottage at Chaldon Herring, Dorset, in 1929 and settled there permanently in 1932. Muntz taught at Bryanston School, her pupils including the painter Patrick Symons. Her work is held by the City Art Gallery in Manchester and by Bristol City Art Gallery, which has her head of the writer T F Powys.

Nina MURDOCH 1970– Painter who graduated the Slade School of Fine Art, 1993, gaining a postgraduate diploma from the Royal Academy School in 1996. In 1993, Murdoch gained 1st Prize, Sir William Coldstream (Slade competition) and Landscape Award, David Murray Studentship (Royal Academy); in 1994 the British Institution Fund Award; and in 1996 an Aneas Travel Award to Italy. Exhibitions included RA Summer Exhibition, from 1994; a two-man show at Cadogan Contemporary, 1995; and Serpentine Gallery, 1996. Had a solo exhibition at Portland Gallery, 1997. The Slade and a number of corporate collections hold examples. Lived in London.

Michael MURFIN 1954– Painter, draughtsman and teacher, born in St Neots, Cambridgeshire. He studied at Leicester Polytechnic, 1972–3; Trent Polytechnic, Nottingham, 1973–6; and Birmingham Polytechnic, 1976–7; then worked in a timber yard in St Neots. During the 1980s Murfin participated in Artist in School schemes in Cambridgeshire and nearby counties, in 1983 gaining a major award from Eastern Arts Association. In 1990 he was visiting lecturer at University of Guelph, Ontario, Canada, and artist-in-resident at Oundle School. Murfin was a realistic painter with a wide range of subjects who took part in many mixed showed, including Tolly Cobbold/Eastern Arts 2nd National Exhibition, 1979; 2nd International Drawings Triennale, Nuremberg, Germany, 1982; Drawings for All, Gainsborough's House, Sudbury, 1986; and British Council touring show Picture People, 1989–90. Had a solo show at Huntingdon Public Library, 1978, later ones including a series at Piccadilly Gallery from 1984. Contemporary Art Society, British Council and Government Art Collection hold examples.

Neil MURISON 1930– Painter and teacher, born in Bath, Somerset, who attended West of England College of Art in Bristol, where he settled. He taught at Queen Elizabeth's Hospital School for nine years and was course co-ordinator for the department of foundation studies at Bristol Polytechnic until 1987. Was made a member of RWA in 1979. Had a long series of solo shows, including Bear Lane Gallery, Oxford, from 1963; Oxford Gallery, from 1970; and Park Street Gallery, Bristol, from 1978; later ones including Albany Gallery, Cardiff, 1991. Bank of America, London and Amsterdam; Museum of Modern Art, Skopje; and Oxford and Bath Universities hold examples.

Milika MURITU 1965– Sculptor and installations artist, born in Portsmouth, Hampshire. Attended Central St Martins College of Art and Design, 1984–7, and Royal College of Art, 1987–90. Was included in William Jackson Gallery's show Sculpture & Sculptors' Drawings in 1991. Other later exhibitions included installation Ducking Stool at Air Gallery, 1988; installation Murmur at The Crypt Gallery, 1989; and Battersea Arts Centre, 1991. Lived in London.

Diana MURPHY 1906–1976 Painter, especially in line and wash, and embroiderer, born in London. She was married to the artist A E Poulter. Studied at Clapham School of Art and Royal College of Art. Exhibited RA, RI, NEAC, WIAC of which she was a member, NS and widely in the provinces. Whitworth Art Gallery in Manchester and Carlisle Art Gallery and Museum hold her work, which commonly featured actors and dancers and had a strangely dreamlike quality. A small retrospective was held at Parkin Gallery, 1985. Lived for some years in Richmond, Surrey.

Francis MURPHY 1951– Painter and draughtsman who attended Camberwell School of Arts and Crafts under Philip Matthews, 1972–6, after working as an interior decorator, 1967–72. After graduating with an honours degree Murphy studied at Royal Academy Schools, 1976–9, under Peter Greenham. He participated in many mixed exhibitions, including Royal Over-Seas League, 1978, where he won first prize; Ash Barn Gallery, Petersfield, 1979; Imperial Tobacco Award at National Portrait Gallery from 1981, winning a prize in 1983; and Cadogan Gallery, 1984. In that year he had a solo show at Woodlands Art Gallery. Lord Gowrie owned his work. Lived in London.

John MURPHY 1945– Painter and teacher, born in St Albans, Hertfordshire. His work, produced with thin layers of paint, contained figurative and non-figurative images, was Minimal and metaphorical in style, establishing moods of lyricism, tension and fear. He studied at Luton School of Art, 1962–4; Chelsea School of Art, 1964–7, in the latter year winning a Boise Scholarship to France; had a postgraduate painting year at Chelsea, 1967–8. Living in London, he taught at Brighton College of Art for a time. Mixed shows included Young Contemporaries from 1965, and Space at the Midland Group Gallery, Nottingham, 1971. Early solo shows included Arts Council Serpentine Gallery, 1971, and Museum of Modern Art, Oxford, 1972; later ones included Lisson Gallery, 1985, and Whitechapel and Arnolfini, Bristol, 1987–8. Arts Council holds Murphy's work.

Myles MURPHY 1927– Painter, especially of figures in interiors, born in Bury, Lancashire. He studied at Slade School of Fine Art, 1951–4, doing a postgraduate year in 1954–5, then receiving an Abbey Travelling Scholarship in 1955. Murphy taught at Slade during 1958–9, then from 1960 at Chelsea School of Art. He showed with Young Contemporaries and LG, and in 1974 in John Moores Exhibition, Liverpool, gaining a first prize, also Hors Concours in 1978. In 1973 he had won the Lorne Award. Arts Council holds his Yellow Nude, of 1963. Lived in London.

Peter MURPHY 1942– Artist in carved and painted wood bas-relief, born in Goole, Yorkshire. Studied at Leeds College of Art, 1961–6, Harry Thubron head of painting, Harry Phillips head of sculpture. Murphy taught at Wallasey College of Art, 1966–7, Sutton Coldfield and Walsall Schools of Art, 1967–8, then from 1968 at West of England College of Art/Bristol Polytechnic/West of England University. As well as working as a fine artist, Murphy worked for television, advertising and publishing and was a member of the Chartered Society of Designers. Murphy rediscovered his interest in carving in West Country churches, especially Wells Cathedral. Influences were Paul Gauguin, Ernst Barlach, the writers Henry David Thoreau and Ralph Waldo Emerson and Oriental and medieval painting. Group shows included Sweet Street Gallery, Leeds, 1965; RWA from 1969; and Portal Gallery from 1981. Had a solo exhibition at Festival Gallery, Bath, 1979. Lived in Nailsea, Bristol.

Peter CURRAN MURPHY: see Peter CURRAN

Sandy MURPHY 1956– Painter in acrylic and oil, notably of landscape and still life, using an imaginative palette, born in Irvine, Ayrshire, eventually settling at Seamill, West Kilbride. He studied at Glasgow School of Art, 1976–80, under Duncan Shanks and James Robertson and in 1979 won a scholarship to the Patrick Allan–Fraser School of Art, Hospitalfield, Arbroath. Was highly commended in the Laing Competition on several occasions from 1989, being a national prizewinner in 1994 and 1995, and won the Mary Armour Award at Paisley Arts Institute, 1994. Murphy was a member of RSW, also showed annually with the Royal Glasgow Institute of the Fine Arts and took part in group exhibitions including Harbour Arts Centre, Irvine; Dick Institute, Kilmarnock; Courtyard Gallery, Crail; in Glasgow at Collins, Blythswood, Michael Main and Gatehouse Galleries; at Open Eye Gallery, Edinburgh; and at Catto Gallery. Main Fine Art and Blythswood, Gatehouse and Open Eye all gave Murphy solo shows.

Stephen MURPHY 1962– Artist, born and worked in London, who obtained an honours degree in fine art, painting, at St Martin's School of Art, 1984–7, gaining his master's degree at Goldsmiths' College, 1990–2. He was included in Young British Artists II at Saatchi Gallery, which holds his work, in 1993; there, by computer-doctoring photographs, Murphy examined such ideas as personal and collective memory and information control.

Tom MURPHY 1924– Artist whose work in ink The Card Players was included in Merseyside Artists 3, toured from Walker Art Gallery, Liverpool, in 1986–7. Murphy was an exhibitor at 5th and 6th Cleveland International Biennales, 1981–3; was a Warrington Biennale Prizewinner, 1981 and 1985; took part in Lancashire Art Exhibition at Harris Art Gallery, Preston, 1983; and in BBC North West Art Competitions, 1984–5. Had a solo show at Neptune Theatre, Liverpool, 1976.

Andrew MURRAY 1917– Painter, born in Tientsin, in the north of China. In England he attended Eltham College, where his favourite subject was art, but turned to writing when he left, publishing fiction while at Oxford University. During World War II he served in the Royal Navy, then went to South Africa where he worked as a journalist. He resumed painting aged 39 and after several shows in Cape Town returned to England in 1969 to become a full-time artist. Showed widely abroad in group shows and had a series of one-mans at Portal Gallery, which specialised in naive painters. Murray was a painter of Biblical subjects, classical mythology and cities, especially London, where he settled. His pictures twinkled with colour, people and incidents, as featured in *Andrew Murray's London*, published in 1980.

Charles MURRAY 1894–1954 Painter and printmaker whose work sometimes has religious overtones. Born in Aberdeen, Murray studied at Glasgow School of Art for about three years from around 1908. From 1918–22 he served in Russia, then won a Prix de Rome for etching which enabled him to work at the British School there, 1922–5. Among Murray's wide travels was a visit with an archaelogical expedition to Iceland. Had first one-man show at Leicester Galleries in 1946, another following at Batley Art Gallery in 1950. Memorial exhibition at Temple Newsam House, Leeds, 1955, and an Edinburgh International Festival show at The Merchant Company Hall in 1977. Tate Gallery and Scottish National Gallery of Modern Art hold his work. Died in London.

Dawson MURRAY 1944– Artist and teacher, born in Glasgow, who studied at the School of Art there; at Patrick Allan-Fraser

School of Art, Hospitalfield, Arbroath; and at L'Accademia, Venice. Went on to become head of art at Boclair Academy, Bearsden. Exhibitions included Stirling Gallery, 1980; Henderson and Hawick Galleries, 1981; Printmakers Drawing, Printmakers'Workshop, Edinburgh, 1982; and in 1983 both Galleria del Cavallino in Venice and Scottish Print Open Three, organised by Dundee Printmakers' Workshop. Murray was a member of RSW and showed at RSA. Scottish Arts Council and Dumbarton Burgh Council hold examples. Lived in Kilbarchan, Renfrewshire.

Donald MURRAY 1940– Designer, painter, calligrapher and teacher, born in Edinburgh, attending the College of Art there, 1958–63, teachers including Stuart Barrie. Went on to become head of art at Robert Gordon's College, Aberdeen. He was a prolific book-jacket illustrator for publisher Oliver & Boyd. Murray for a time belonged to SSA, also showing with RSW, Aberdeen Artists' Society and elsewhere in Scotland. Heriot-Watt University, Edinburgh, holds his work. Lived in Insch, Aberdeenshire.

Elizabeth MURRAY 1961– Artist in various media, and teacher, born in Southall, Middlesex. She studied at Chelsea School of Art, 1980–1; Camberwell School of Arts and Crafts, 1981–4, gaining an honours degree; then Blackheath School of Art, 1985. Won a Thames & Hudson Drawing Prize, 1984. Murray's shows included Intaglio Printmakers, 1983; South London Art Gallery, 1984; Ladywell Baths, 1985; New Moon Group Show, Woodlands Art Gallery, 1987; and in 1995 The Abstract Landscape, The Milton Gallery, and the Royal Over-Seas League Open. She was a visiting lecturer at Chelsea School of Art, 1992–4, and also showed as Liz Murray.

Liz MURRAY: *see* **Elizabeth MURRAY**

Mary MURRAY fl. c.1920–1955 Painter of landscape in watercolour. Studied privately with Walter Severn. Exhibited RSA, BWS, of which she was a member, and held a number of one-man shows for charity. Lived at Polmaise Castle, Stirling, Scotland.

Val MURRAY 1944– Artist, born in Edinburgh, who was a member of TEA (see separate entry). Studied at Stockport College of Technology, 1979–80, and Manchester Polytechnic, 1980–4. Lived in Manchester.

William Grant MURRAY 1877–1950 Landscape and figure painter, teacher and curator, born in Portsoy, Banffshire. He studied at Blairgowrie School of Art, Royal Institution and School of Art in Edinburgh, Royal College of Art and Académie Julian, Paris. He was principal of Swansea School of Art, 1910–43 and director of the Glynn Vivian Art Gallery there, 1910–50, that gallery giving him a memorial show in 1952. Showed RA, RI, Swansea Artists with WAC and SWG. Also had a series of solo shows. Aberdeen Art Gallery holds his work. Died in Swansea.

William Staite MURRAY 1881–1962 Potter, painter, printmaker, draughtsman and teacher, born in London. From 1893–5 he studied with his cousins William Fisher and Hettie Staite, further studies taking place on continent in late 1890s while working as a bulb and seed farmer. After extensive travels in North America, Europe and Africa, before World War I he attended pottery classes at Camberwell School of Arts and Crafts, about 1915 joining Cuthbert Hamilton at Yeoman Pottery. After World War I Army service, in 1919 set up own pottery and began to exhibit in mixed exhibitions, including Leicester Galleries, Red Rose Guild and Arts League of Service, having a first solo exhibition at William B Paterson's Gallery in 1924. In 1925 was appointed to Royal College of Art staff, in 1926 becoming head of the pottery department. Joined 7 & 5 Society in 1927. Had a series of solo shows in 1930s with Lefevre in London and Glasgow. In 1939 Murray visited Rhodesia, where he and his wife settled, only visiting England. In 1958 he was given a solo exhibition at Leicester Galleries and his work continued to be included in important mixed shows. A monograph, *William Staite Murray*, 1984, by Malcolm Haslam, was published to coincide with a Cleveland Gallery/Victoria & Albert Museum exhibition. That Museum holds his work.

Jim MURRELL 1934–1994 Conservator and artist who studied at Maidstone College of Art, 1955–60, then qualified, 1960–1, to teach at London University Institute of Education. He entered the Victoria & Albert Museum in 1961; gained a permanent post in 1964; and was conservation department deputy keeper, 1980–5, valued especially for his work on wax sculptures and portrait miniatures. As an artist did a great deal of book illustration work and jackets, especially for Penguin. In 1994–5 Courtauld Institute Galleries put on a celebration show for Murrell included his drawings and printed page work including wood engravings, pottery and sculpture; he was noted for his bizarre, witty figures. A project involving the dress designer Jean Muir was a key later part of his output.

Richard MURRY 1902–1984 Painter, etcher, illustrator, teacher and administrator, born in London, brother of the writer John Middleton Murry. Unsuited to printing for which he was initially trained, Richard Murry was encouraged by his brother and his sister-in-law the writer Katherine Mansfield to attend the Central School of Arts and Crafts, which he entered in 1922 with a London County Council scholarship, to study book production. Then attended Slade School of Art, where he gained a Robert Ross Scholarship, in 1925. Was NEAC secretary for three years, in 1928 becoming assistant art master at Architectural Association, in 1930 leaving to teach at Surbiton Grammar School for eight years. Was then offered the position of librarian at the Central, at which he stayed – apart from service in the Royal Marines and Royal Naval Film Unit – until retirement in 1967. Was for many years secretary of the Art Workers' Guild, from 1962. Murry continued to paint, even during the war. Showed at Goupil and Leger Galleries, LG, NEAC, RBA and ROI; posthumous exhibition at Sally Hunter Fine Art, 1988. Lived for many years in London.

Jack MURTON 1958– Painter who attended Christopher Wren School, 1970–1, but then for much of the 1970s was at various Borstals. A "crimulum" vitae prepared for his solo show at Eva Jekel Gallery, 1992, said that "the only time I ever went to an art class at school was to disrupt it." During a 12-year prison sentence for armed robbery, for which he served 1984–91, Murton was in 1988 sent to Blantyre House experimental prison. "It was there that I started to paint. I was encouraged to attend formal art classes, but decided against it so that I would develop my own style rather than that of my tutor." Murton's resulting work was in what is termed the naive style, graphic and richly coloured, featuring jungle scenes and cityscapes.

Barbara MUSGRAVE 1937– Sculptor, born in London, who studied at Regent Street Polytechnic School of Art, 1955–9, under sculptor Geoffrey Deeley. She was a member of NS, also exhibiting with Harrow Art Society and elsewhere in the London area. Lived in Ruislip, Middlesex.

Olivia MUSGRAVE 1958– Sculptor, born in Dublin, Ireland, her father Irish, her mother Greek, who studied sculpture at the City & Guilds of London Art School under Allan Sly. Her work was often witty, including female figures. She worked from life and the imagination, pieces frequently inspired by Greek mythology in a style influenced by twentieth-century Italian sculptors, Marini and Manzu. Showed at RA Summer Exhibition and was included in Sixteen Sculptors at Sladmore Contemporary, 1997. Lived in London.

Eve MUSKE 1962– Artist in mixed media, born in Belfast, Northern Ireland. She moved to London in 1983 to study at St Martin's School of Art, 1983–6, completing a master's degree at Chelsea School of Art, 1986–7. Among her mixed show appearances was (dis)parities, at Mappin Art Gallery, Sheffield, in 1992, and at Herbert Art Gallery, Coventry, in 1993. Of her work there it was said that it confronted "questions of feminist theory, and in particular issues of authorship and identity".

Joan MUSKER: *see* **Joan GILBERT**

Rachel MUSKER 1928– Painter specialising in large wall decorations, born in India but educated at Badminton School. She studied at St Martin's School of Art. Showed SEA, Arts Council, RA and elsewhere in group exhibitions, having solo shows at Thackeray and Travers Galleries. Nuffield Foundation and Inner London Education Authority were among public bodies holding her work. Lived in Bathwick, Avon.

Alicia Frances MUSPRATT 1902–1986 Painter and portrait miniaturist, born in Freshfield, Lancashire. She studied at Liverpool School of Art and privately with Garnet Wolseley. Exhibited RA, RBA, RCamA, SWA, RP, Cooling Galleries and Paris Salon. During World War II was commissioned in the Women's Royal Naval Service. Lived in Enfield, Middlesex, then at Slindon, Sussex.

Leszek Tadeusz MUSZYNSKI 1923– Painter, draughtsman, printmaker and teacher, born in Halicz, Poland. After education there he studied art at Edinburgh College of Art, 1946–9, under William Gillies, John Maxwell and William MacTaggart. A travelling scholarship took him to France and Italy, then he did a postgraduate year, teaching at the College. He also taught at Gray's Art School in Aberdeen and at West Surrey College of Art and Design, taking early retirement as head of the painting school in 1984. He settled in Liphook, Hampshire, but also worked around his second home in Ibiza. Muszynski's richly coloured paintings were shown extensively in solo exhibitions in London, the provinces and abroad, later shows including Pallant House and Canon Gallery, both in Chichester, and a retrospective in Poznan and at the Polish Cultural Institute, London. National Portrait Gallery and Victoria & Albert Museum hold examples.

MUSZYNSKI: see also **Tadeusz ZNICZ-MUSZYNSKI**

Gil MUTCH 1955– Painter and draughtsman whose output included landscapes tending towards abstraction. Studied at Lowestoft College, 1983–4, then Camberwell School of Art, 1984–7. Awards included Thames & Hudson Drawing Prize, first prize, 1987; East Anglian Artists Open Exhibition, first prize, 1988; and winning the Norwich City Council Commission, 1991. Mixed shows included South London Art Gallery, from 1987; The School House Gallery, Wighton, from 1988; RA Summer Exhibition, from 1990; and The John Russell Gallery, Ipswich, from 1994. Later solo shows included Stables Gallery and Lowestoft Art College, both 1995. Public collections holding work included City of Hope Duarte, California; City Hall, Norwich; and Castle Museum, Riga, Latvia.

Hyam MYER 1904–1978 Painter and teacher of Rumanian extraction, born in Manchester, who studied at Slade School of Fine Art with Henry Tonks, then in Paris, living in France between the wars. After World War II he taught at Central and St Martin's Schools of Art and Royal College of Art. He was a member of LG and Chelsea Arts Club and exhibited at Lefevre, Goupil and Alpine Club Galleries. Lived in London. Ben Uri Art Society holds several examples.

Bernard MYERS 1925– Painter, printmaker and teacher, born and lived in London. He studied at St Martin's School of Art, 1947–9, Camberwell School of Arts and Crafts, 1949–51, and Royal College of Art, 1951–4. Taught at Royal College of Art, and other London art schools and travelled extensively abroad, including India and the Middle East, although from taking a studio on the Thames at Hammersmith in 1987 he said that his work "was dominated by the river", as shown in his solo exhibition at New Grafton Gallery, 1991. Also showed at RA, RWA and in other mixed exhibitions and had many solo shows including a series at New Art Centre, 1969–83. Arts Council, Carlisle City Art Gallery and other public and corporate collections hold examples.

Mark Richard MYERS 1945– Self-taught artist, born in San Mateo, California. He gained a bachelor's degree in history and art from Pomona College, California, 1967. Between 1965–70 Myers had extensive service in sailing ships which he alternated with periods of painting, then moved from California to Devon in 1971 and to Cornwall in 1974, settling at Woolley, Bude. Myers was made a member of RSMA in 1975, in which he held several senior positions; was made a fellow of American Society of Marine Artists from 1979; and a member of Canadian Society of Marine Artists in 1983. He illustrated various maritime books. *Seamanship in the Age of Sail*, by John Haland, pictures by Myers, appeared in 1984. Participated in many group shows in Britain and abroad. Had his first solo show at San Francisco Maritime Museum in 1967, followed by a string of exhibitions in that area, in North Devon and in Seattle, America. National Maritime Museum, Greenwich, and other notable official and royal collections hold examples.

MYERSCOUGH 1908–1984 Painter, designer, printmaker, writer and architect, full name Raymond Myerscough-Walker. He was born in Knaresborough, Yorkshire, and studied at the Architectural Association; he was expelled for extravagance but readmitted because of his talent, being a Victory Scholarship and Prix de Rome finalist. He admired such modern architects as Avar Aalto, Le Corbusier and Frank Lloyd Wright and worked for luminaries like Edwin Lutyens and Berthold Lubetkin, being notable for producing perspectives to order. By the late 1930s, however, he became disillusioned with the state of British architecture and after World War II went to live in a gamekeeper's cottage on the Sussex Downs. He had met Surrealism through Paul Nash and John Tunnard, with whom he shared a love of jazz drumming, and his own work, as Myerscough, was both Surrealist and abstract. He wrote for architectural and building press and published *Stage and Film Décor*, *Choosing a Modern House* and *The Perspectivist*. Showed at RA, RIBA, Yorkshire Artists and elsewhere. There was an exhibition of his work at Architectural Association, 1984–5, and he was included in The Surrealist Spirit in Britain, Whitford and Hughes, 1988. Finally lived in a caravan at Chilgrove, West Sussex.

Ishbel MYERSCOUGH 1968– Painter in oil on canvas and board of meticulous figurative and still life pictures, born and worked in London. Her mother was Betty Fraser Myerscough, an artist working with fabric, embroidery and weaving. Ishbel gained a fine art honours degree from Glasgow School of Art, 1987–91; worked in a Glasgow studio for two years, having a first solo show; then gained a higher diploma in fine art with distinction at Slade School of Fine Art, 1993–5. Travelled in America, returned to Britain and had a second one-man show; went to America for the studio programme run by Robert and Susan Summers in Connecticut, then returned to England early in 1997. Awards included John and Mabel Craig Bequest, 1990 and 1991; National Portrait Gallery Portrait Award, commended in 1991/1993, third prize, 1992, first prize, 1995; Elizabeth Greenshields Foundation, 1991/1993; Hunting/*Observer* Prize for Art (under 24), 1992; and a Rootstein Hopkins Travel Scholarship, 1995. Group exhibitions included Treasures of the National Portrait Gallery, tour of Japan, 1995–6; and British Figurative Art, Flowers East, 1997. Had solo shows with Anthony Mould Ltd Contemporary, Turtle Quay Studios, 1992 and 1996. Was commissioned to paint actress Helen Mirren for National Portrait Gallery. Robert and Susan Summers, National Westminster Bank and Christie's hold examples.

Raymond MYERSCOUGH-WALKER: *see* **MYERSCOUGH**

MYF: *see* **Myfanwy KITCHIN**

Noel MYLES 1947– Artist in a range of media, latterly known especially for photographic collages, born and lived in London. He studied painting and drawing at Hornsey College of Art, 1966–7, then Waltham Forest School of Art, 1967–70. Took part in numerous exhibitions and won a number of prizes. His career included exhibiting big abstract paintings, mainly at House, in 1970s–1980s; in 1980s also working on small paintings and etchings, with several years concentration on sea and wave images in Cornwall; in 1984 began making photographic panoramas which soon developed into collages; in 1987 Murphy was awarded first prize by David Hockney at the Open College Competition at The National Museum of Photography, Film and Television, Bradford, and was commissioned by 3i to make a portrait of Bob Worcester, chairman of the opinion poll firm MORI. In 1988–9 Myles began a long association with Rowe & Maw, when Citigate Design commissioned him to make four big collages for them; in 1989–92 his French Forest Project involved 12,000 photographs to make 16 collages, shown at the Royal Photographic Society in 1992; then in 1994–5 Rowe & Maw commissioned four large collages to celebrate their centenary, with a show at The Gallery in Cork Street, 1995. In the same year Myles held a show of cyanotypes at Alliance Française, with a dozen purchases by the Contemporary Art Foundation in Limousin. Victoria & Albert Museum also holds Myles' work. Myles won the McNaughton Prize for Illustration in 1995.

Andrew MYLIUS 1935– Sculptor, born in London. After studying agriculture in Edinburgh, in 1959–62 Mylius was at Camberwell School of Arts and Crafts and Slade School of Fine Art. After living in America in 1968 and for several years designing racing cars, in 1974 Mylius was the winner of a joint competition for sculpture at the Regional Centre at Livingston, Scotland. The following year he was commissioned for Fife County Council by Scottish Arts Council at Lochore Meadows. Mylius showed with Young Contemporaries in 1961–2, with LG in 1962 and several times in mid-1960s with Richard Demarco Gallery, Edinburgh. In 1978 he was included in Scottish Arts Council's Objects and Constructions show. Mylius' first solo show was with Gallery West, in Los Angeles, in 1968. Later exhibitions included Angela Flowers Gallery, 1973, and St Andrews University, 1975. Dundee Art Gallery and Universities of Edinburgh and Strathclyde hold his work. Mylius was involved in the formation of the Scottish Sculpture Trust in 1978 and he started the Sculpture Park at Carrbridge, Invernesshire. Lived at Newport on Tay, Fife.

Nicholas MYNHEER 1958– Artist in oil and stone, born in Oxford, settling in the county at Horton-cum-Studley. "All my painting and sculpture is on Biblical themes or themes from Christian iconography." Mynheer graduated with honours from Hornsey College of Art, 1976–80, then spent a few years in advertising before turning full-time to art. He was a member of Oxford Art Society, group shows including Museum of Modern Art in Oxford, 1992; Bath, Manchester and Isle of Man Contemporary Art Fairs, all 1993; and Glasgow Contemporary Art Fair from 1995. Solo exhibitions included Lady Margaret Hall, Oxford, 1992; Marsden Fine Art from 1993; and Ca'si Gallery, Richmond, Virginia, 1995. St John's College, Oxford, holds his work. Two public commissions were important: 14 Stations of the Cross, St Matthew's Church, Birmingham; and Triptych, The Assumption, Church of the Assumption, Beckley, Oxford. His work appeared in Edward Robinson's book *Icons of the Present.*

Derek MYNOTT 1925–1994 Painter and printmaker, born and lived in London, husband of the artist Patricia Mynott and father of the artists Lawrence, Gerald and Katherine Mynott. He studied at Slade School of Fine Art, 1946–50, with Randolph Schwabe and William Coldstream. Was a member of RBA and NEAC, also showing in mixed exhibitions at RA. Had a solo show at RBA Galleries in 1953, later ones including RA's Business Art Galleries from 1983. Won Lord Mayor of London's Annual Art Award, 1972; Silver Medal at Paris Salon, 1974; and Worshipful Company of Painter-Stainers' Award, 1987. Tate Gallery holds his work.

Gerald Philip MYNOTT 1957– Painter, calligrapher and printmaker, born in London, son of the artists Derek and Patricia Mynott and brother of the artists Lawrence and Katherine Mynott. He studied at Reigate College of Art, College of Arms and at Vienna Kunstlerhaus, Austria. Was a member of the Society of Scribes and Illuminators. Did work for BBC and Victoria & Albert Museum and exhibited regularly with Francis Kyle Gallery. Tate Gallery holds his work. Lived in Brighton, Sussex.

Lawrence MYNOTT 1954– Painter, illustrator and lecturer, born in London, son of the artists Derek and Patricia Mynott and brother of the artists Gerald and Katherine Mynott. He studied at Chelsea School of Art, 1972–6, then Royal College of Art, 1976–9, gaining his master's degree. He was a member of the Society of Scribes and Illuminators and showed in mixed exhibitions at RA and elsewhere. Had solo exhibitions at Cale Art. National Portrait Gallery holds his work. Lived for a time in Richmond, Surrey.

N

Hazel NAGL fl. from 1980s– Painter, born in Glasgow who studied at Glasgow School of Art and who worked very much in its tradition. She went on to work for the School at Cargill Art School Hostel. Nagl showed in group exhibitions at Fine Art Society in Glasgow, with Glasgow Group, RSA, Royal Glasgow Institute of the Fine Arts and Glasgow Art Club. She won the Alexander Stone Prize at Royal Glasgow Institute in 1987 and 1990 and was elected RSW in 1988. Had a solo show at Open Eye Gallery, Edinburgh, 1989. Glasgow University holds her work. Lived at Bridge of Weir, Renfrewshire.

Richard NAISH 1912–1988 Artist and teacher, a devout and active Quaker, educated at Bootham School, York, where he studied at the local School of Art. Went to Royal College of Art in 1932, then Ruskin School of Drawing in 1934, his teachers including Albert Rutherston, Gilbert Spencer and Percy Horton. On a trip to America, where he painted intense oils of the Arizona Desert, he met his future wife, Martha Anson, a writer under the name Anne Vernon. After World War II moved to Lewknor, Oxfordshire, the countryside which featured in his pictures, shown with Oxford Art Society and NEAC. Became Ruskin Master of Drawing, 1964–71. A classical painter, fond of working in contact with the direct visual experience, often in the open air.

Eva NAJMAN 1923– Painter, printmaker and illustrator, born in Berlin, Germany. Part of her education was on the continent, part in Farnham, Surrey, where she then attended the School of Art, 1939–40. After World War II she went to the Central School of Arts and Crafts, 1946–9, her teachers including Clarke Hutton, Rodrigo Moynihan and Anthony Gross. As well as doing a volume of book-illustrative work, Najman exhibited at Leicester and Redfern Galleries, NEAC, RWS and elsewhere. Lived in London.

Nobuo NAKAMURA 1950– Sculptor working in a variety of materials, born in Tokyo, Japan. In 1972 graduated from Meiji University, Tokyo, with a degree in law. Travelled to Britain in 1975. Two years later studied at Royal College of Art's school of furniture design, transferring to the sculpture school to work under Bernard Meadows. Was included in the College's 1980 show Bernard Meadows at the Royal College of Art 1960–1980.

Halima NALECZ 1917– Artist in oil and mixed media, gallery director, born near Vilnius, Poland, married to the writer Zygmunt Nalecz. She studied art in Poland and Paris, moving to England in 1946. Was a founder of the New Vision Centre Gallery, in 1957 starting the Drian (based on name Mondrian) Gallery with Constructivist Art 1950–1960. Well over 200 artists were launched at Drian, including John Bellany and William Crozier. In 1976 Nalecz donated 180 works from her collection to the National Museum in Warsaw, in 1983 387 to the National Museum in Gdańsk. Nalecz's own work was abstract in the 1950s, changing to richly coloured fantasy landscapes. Showed widely in Britain and abroad, including AIA, WIAC, Free Painters and Sculptors all of which she was a member, RA and LG. Had a series of solo shows, including Polish Cultural Institute, 1993. Nalecz's pictures are in St John the Evangelist, Hyde Park Crescent.

Robert MORTON NANCE 1873–1959 Painter, illustrator and ship modeller who attended Cardiff Art School, and was at the Herkomer School in Bushey for several years in the mid-1890s. He married twice, both fellow-students at Bushey: first Beatrice Michel, secondly Maud Cawker, who survived him to 1961. Despite being a star student at Bushey, Nance's exhibiting career only lasted until about 1910. As a small boy he had lived a while in St Ives, Cornwall, where his grandfather had taught him a love of ships, which resulted in highly skilled drawings and paintings of them. In his middle years Nance's enthusiasm for sailing ships and Cornwall took over from art and he settled in the Carbis Bay area. Among his publications was *Sailing Ship Models*. He became the editor of *Old Cornwall*, was Grand Bard of the Cornish Gorsedd, 1934–59, and was president of several other institutions concerned with Cornish affairs. Showed at RA, New Gallery and Walker Art Gallery in Liverpool. In 1991 he was included in Three Bushey Artists by the Bushey Museum Trust, which holds his work.

Charles NAPER 1882–1968 Landscape and coastal painter, born in Devon, who briefly studied architecture, attended Royal Academy Schools, returned to the family home and met his future wife Ella. She was a jeweller and potter who, after extensive study in London, was to show at RA, SWA and Walker Art Gallery in Liverpool. They settled in Cornwall, building a house at St Buryan, where Naper fished, gardened and kept bees. He showed at RA and Walker Art Gallery but, after criticism, soon before he died burned the contents of his studio. Naper was represented in Painting in Newlyn 1880–1930 at Barbican Art Gallery, 1985.

Charles NAPIER 1889–1978 Painter, especially in watercolour, sometimes on pottery, black-and-white artist, born in Edinburgh. He studied initially at George Watson's College, Edinburgh, then at the College of Art, 1911–14. Showed extensively at RSA, RSW and Royal Glasgow Institute of the Fine Arts. First London show at Brook Street Art Gallery in 1934. Scottish National Gallery of Modern Art, Edinburgh, holds his work. After living near Oxford for some years, eventually returned to Edinburgh.

David NAPP 1964– Artist and teacher, born in Lewisham, southeast London, notable for his use of chalk pastel on paper. He studied at Canterbury College of Art, 1981–5, then lectured there, 1988–91. Was twice a winner of the Elizabeth Greenshields Foundation, 1986–90. Contributed to *The Artist* and *Artist and Illustrator* magazines. Showed at RWS, RBA, PS, Weald of Kent Preservation Society, Neville Gallery in Canterbury, Sally Hunter Fine Art and elsewhere. In 1991 had a show at Bourne Gallery, Reigate, of work done in France, displaying his love of rich colour in still life and landscape. Lived in Hove, Sussex.

Heda NAPPER: *see* **Heda ARMOUR**

Helen NAPPER 1958– Painter, printmaker and teacher. She studied at Colchester School of Art, Wimbledon School of Art where she obtained a first-class honours degree in fine arts, completed her master's degree at Reading University, was then at London University and the Central School of Art and design where she did postgraduate advanced printmaking. Her teaching posts included Kingston Polytechnic; Colchester, Braintree, Ipswich and Norwich Schools of Art; and Trent Polytechnic. Napper was noted for her depiction of nude female figures, inspired by Etruscan art, for an emotional attitude to anatomy and for her powerful colour. She showed widely in group exhibitions, including New Contemporaries from 1980; Printmakers at Reading Museum, 1982; Essex University, 1984; and Minories Gallery, Colchester, 1989. She had several solo shows at Sue Rankin Gallery from 1989. At her studio in Suffolk she also painted furniture to commission.

John NAPPER 1916– Painter and teacher, born in London, son of John Napper, painter and illustrator. He studied at Royal Academy Schools, 1933–4, then was a pupil of Gerald Kelly, 1936–8. After being a war artist to the Ceylon Command, 1943–4, Napper taught life painting at St Martin's School of Art, 1949–57, then lived in France until 1968. From 1968–9 Napper was visiting professor of fine arts at University of Southern Illinois, Carbondale, then in 1971 he moved to Shropshire, settling at Bromfield, near Ludlow. Napper said that his work was about understanding space and the organisation of spatial relationships. Notable among his later works was a series based on an Aga stove and utensils around it. Napper showed at RA from 1942, in British Painting 1925–50, Arts Council in 1951, and abroad. His long series of solo exhibitions began with Leicester Galleries from 1949 and included a series at Larcada Gallery, New York, from 1967. There were retrospectives at Walker Art Gallery, Liverpool, 1959; Oldham Art Gallery, 1984, and Colnaghi, 1996. Agnew gave him a watercolour first show in 1986. Among his awards was a Silver Medal at Paris Salon, 1947; Moscow, International Exhibition of Fine Arts, 1957; and Critics' Prize, International Association of Art Critics, London, 1961. British Museum, Walker Art Gallery and many other public galleries in Britain and abroad hold examples.

Peter NARDINI 1947– Painter, teacher, playwright, song writer and performer, born in Glasgow. Studied at Glasgow School of Art, 1970–5, doing a postgraduate year in printmaking. In 1980 was given a grant to use Scottish Arts Council studio in Amsterdam, winning a Council Award in 1987. Was a regular exhibitor at SSA, RSA and Royal Glasgow Institute of the Fine Arts and had a one-man show at Compass Gallery, Glasgow, in 1986. Produced several record albums of his own words and music and wrote a number of stage plays. Much of Nardini's work was figures in landscape, with a strong imaginative element. Lived for some time in Hamilton, Lanarkshire.

William NARRAWAY 1915–1979 Painter and sculptor of portraits, working in oil, pastel; also landscapes and genre scenes. Educated in Yorkshire, Narraway went on to exhibit widely, including RA, RP, RBA, NEAC, PS, Paris Salon and provincial galleries. One-man show at Guildford House gallery, in Surrey. Narraway became noted for his highly professional portraits of celebrities, including HM The Queen (several versions in the 1970s), the musicians Ralph Vaughan Williams and Sir Malcolm Sargent, the actress Susan Hampshire and actor Tony Britton – in all, over 600. His pictures are in collections throughout the world. Lived at Holmbury St Mary, Dorking, Surrey.

David NASH 1945– Artist in wood, and teacher, born in Esher, Surrey. He studied at Kingston College of Art, 1963–7. Then became visiting lecturer at art colleges and universities, including Newcastle Polytechnic, Royal College of Art and Newport and Dublin Colleges of Art. Between 1969–70 Nash attended Chelsea School of Art. Nash's decision in 1967 to base himself in Blaenau Ffestiniog, north Wales, was of key importance to the development of his work. In 1969 he took over an old chapel and there and in the surrounding woods he created his sculptures. At first these were painted and stained, but he abandoned this in favour of the natural colour and shape of the wood. His work, often witty, was in the form of clams, pods and tables, sometimes in series. Among Nash's projects was the establishment of a field centre at Blaenau Ffestiniog and he also took part in events away from the area. In 1975 he was awarded a Major Bursary from the Welsh Arts Council. Took part in mixed shows. One-man exhibitions included York Festival, in 1973; Air Gallery, 1978; Arnolfini Gallery, Bristol, 1976–9; and Serpentine Gallery, 1990. Arts Council and WAC hold his work.

John NASH 1893–1977 Painter, mainly of landscape, in oil and watercolour, wood engraver and illustrator, especially of humorous subjects and plants. Born in London, the brother of the painter Paul Nash, he worked initially as a local journalist. Encouraged by Paul he turned to art, remaining self-taught. Exhibited with his brother at the Dorien Leigh Galleries, 1913, first one-man show at the Goupil Gallery, 1921. By that time Nash was established as a member of the Friday Club, LG and Cumberland Market Group. In 1914 he had begun to paint in oil and this combined with his experience with the Artists' Rifles led to some fine pictures when he was made an official war artist in 1918. Oppy Wood, Evening, and Over the Top: The 1st Artists' Rifles at Marcoing, both in the Imperial War Museum, are good examples. Nash was also an

official war artist attached to the Admiralty in World War II. Between the wars Nash established himself as a sympathetic painter of the English landscape using a style that was less dramatic than his brother Paul's, yet building up a steady following. This painting was interlarded with forays into diverse fields, such as acting as the *London Mercury's* first art critic; much book illustration; and painting a big mural for the 1937 Paris Exhibition. Nash taught at Ruskin School, Oxford, 1922–7, and for two long periods before and after World War II at the Royal College of Art. Demobilised in 1944, he lived in a country cottage near Colchester where he developed his expertise as a plantsman and painted the East Anglian countryside. The Tate Gallery among many public galleries holds his work. In 1951 elected RA, where a major show of his work was held in 1967.

Pamela NASH 1925– Painter and ceramist, born in London, who studied at Willesden School of Arts and Crafts. She was a member of WIAC, also appearing in mixed shows at Federation of British Artists, Whitechapel Art Gallery, AIA Galleries, Smithsonian Institution in Washington and Gallery Numero, Florence, and London Artists at Shrewsbury School, 1968. Solo shows included Mount and Foyer Galleries. Many companies and schools commissioned Nash's ceramics.

Paul NASH 1889–1946 Painter, designer, illustrator, photographer, writer and teacher, born in London, brother of the artist John Nash. Studied at Chelsea Polytechnic, 1906–7, then at Bolt Court, Fleet Street, 1908–10, and Slade School of Fine Art, 1910–11. Was given early encouragement by William Rothenstein and Sir William Richmond, who urged Nash to develop his landscape work, evident in Carfax Gallery first solo show in 1912. The next few years saw Nash work with Roger Fry at Omega Workshops, become a member of Friday Club and LG, NEAC and SWE. Serving with Artists' Rifles during World War I, the success of his Ypres Salient show at Goupil Gallery, 1917, led to his appointment as an official war artist. Ministry of Information commissioned his important picture The Menin Road, painted back in England in 1918 working with his brother. Taught at an Oxford art school run by Albert Rutherston, 1920–3, and Royal College of Art, 1924–5 and 1938–40. The inter-war years saw Nash illustrate books such as Sir Thomas Browne's *Urne Buriall* and *The Garden of Cyrus*; become president and chairman of the Society of Industrial Artists; helped found Unit One; exhibit at International Surrealist Exhibitions in London in 1936 and in Paris two years later; and edit the *Dorset Shell Guide*, 1936. During World War II Nash was an official war artist to the Air Ministry and Ministry of Information, leading to such major paintings as Totes Meer. Not long after painting probably his last oils, Eclipse of the Sunflower and Solstice of the Sunflower, Nash died on holiday at Boscombe, Hampshire, of pneumonia. By then he was established as one of Britain's greatest landscape painters of the century, whose influence on younger artists continues. His book of photographs, *Fertile Image*, was published in 1951, and his uncompleted auto-biography, *Outline*, in 1949. Tate Gallery, which with many public galleries holds his work, held a major exhibition, which toured, in 1975.

Thomas Saunders NASH 1891–1968 Painter of figure, rural and Biblical subjects, born in Walton on the Hill, Surrey. He studied at the Slade School of Fine Art, 1909–12, where he met such artists as Wadsworth, Nevinson and Stanley Spencer, who influenced his work, then attended government art classes at Reading, 1912–13. Nash married Mabel Emery, 1914; in 1920 moved to Ackworth School, Yorkshire; shared a house with Gilbert Spencer; and married Frances Gurr in 1929. Showed with NEAC, RA, Goupil Gallery and especially Redfern Gallery, his pictures being bought by discerning collectors such as Sir Michael Sadler and Thomas Balston. In 1979–80, there was an exhibition at the Museum and Art Gallery at Reading, Nash having spent periods in or near the Berkshire town. Lenders included British Museum, Russell-Cotes Art Gallery in Bournemouth, Harrogate Art Gallery, Whitworth and City Art Galleries in Manchester, Laing Art Gallery in Newcastle and Ashmolean Museum, Oxford. Nash died at Wareham, Dorset.

Tom NASH 1931– Artist and teacher working in a wide range of materials including retroflective plastics, born in Ammanford, Carmarthenshire. He studied at Llanelli School of Art and Swansea College of Art, 1949–54, working in north Wales slate quarries, 1954–5. A travelling scholarship in 1963 took him through France. Later lived and worked in Llandeilo, Dyfed, teaching part-time at Dyfed College of Art, Carmarthen. Nash was long a member of RCamA, showing extensively with groups in Wales and abroad. Had a solo show at Woodstock Gallery, 1962, later ones including Howard Roberts Gallery, Cardiff, 1964, Redfern Gallery, 1967, University of Bradford, 1974, and abroad. National Museum of Wales in Cardiff and many other academic and corporate collections hold examples.

Claire NASH-WILLIAMS 1970– Designer, illustrator and artist, who won first prize in the Anglia Building Society Christmas Card design competition, 1981. In 1992 she gained an honours degree in graphic design/illustration from Kingston University, excused the need to take a foundation course. She became a graphic designer for the *Newbury Weekly News* Group. Nash-Williams won Chevron U K Ltd's Young Artist Award in *The Artist* magazine's Art in Nature competition in 1993, and was commissioned by the oil company to illustrate its 1994 calendar with watercolours. She was an animal illustrator for Friends of the Earth's *Earth Matters* magazine in 1995, and expedition artist for a Raleigh International Chile expedition in 1996. Exhibitions included the 1997 Chevron calendar artists show at the ICA. Lived in Ascot, Berkshire.

Janet NATHAN 1938– Maker of constructions, born in London where she continued to work. She studied at St Martin's School of Art. Nathan took the sea, river and shoreline as her subjects, creating her constructions from found objects and discarded wood, painted wood and resin. Although apparently abstract at first glance, references to a dock, jetty or mudflat become evident on perusal. She participated in many mixed exhibitions from the late 1970s, including RA Summer Exhibition from 1980; Art and the

Sea, at Third Eye Centre, Glasgow, 1981, and LG and Wapping Artists at Space Studios from the same year; Whitechapel Open from 1983; John Moores Exhibition in Liverpool, 1987; and The Discerning Eye, 1990. After a solo show at Newcastle Polytechnic Art Gallery in 1979 she exhibited solo regularly, later examples being Warwick Arts Trust, 1988, and The Gallery at John Jones, 1992. Walker Art Gallery in Liverpool holds her work.

Robert NATKIN 1930– Painter of abstracts, frequently using recurrent symbols in soft, pastel colours, born in Chicago. He studied at the Art Institute of Chicago's Art School, 1948–52. Married the artist Judith Dolnick. Natkin had extensive solo exhibitions in America and abroad after beginning with Wells Street Gallery, Chicago, in 1958. In Britain he showed at Festival Gallery, Bath, 1974; with Gimpel Fils from 1977; and at Art in Boxes, England & Co, and Winchester Cathedral, both in 1992. Natkin's work is in many American collections, including Museum of Modern Art, New York. Lived in Redding, Connecticut, and New York City.

Philip NAVIASKY 1894–1983 Portrait and landscape painter, born and lived in Leeds, of Polish extraction. Studied at Leeds School of Art. Was then admitted as a student of painting at Royal Academy Schools at 18, said to have been the youngest ever. He also gained a Royal Exhibition award from Board of Education for three years at Royal College of Art. Naviasky was a fluent artist who worked widely in Yorkshire as well as abroad in Spain, the south of France, Morocco and elsewhere. Among his portraits were Lord Nuffield the industrialist, the politicians Ramsay Macdonald and Philip Snowden and many Dales characters. Showed at RA, RP, RSA and had a series of solo shows. In the late-1960s had to stop painting because of failing sight. Galleries in Leeds, Newcastle, Preston and Stoke-on-Trent hold his work.

Clifford NAYLOR 1953– Painter and multi-media artist, brought up in Derbyshire where he settled at Ripley. Studied at Derby College of Art, 1971, then Birmingham College of Art, 1972–4, where his teachers included Richard Gear. Showed at Derby Museum and Art Gallery and elsewhere in the area.

Francis Ives NAYLOR 1892– Painter, printmaker and stage designer, whose principal career was in local government, born in Bickley, Kent. Studied at Hornsey College of Art, his teachers including Norman Janes, 1937–9 and 1946–8. Showed RA, SGA of which he was a member, RI and with Islington Art Circle. Islington Libraries hold his work. Lived in London and Norwich.

Martin NAYLOR 1944– Sculptor and creator of assemblages, born in Morley, Leeds, Yorkshire. After a period at Dewsbury and Batley Technical and Art School, 1961–5, Naylor was at Leeds College of Art, 1965–6, and Royal College of Art, 1967–70. From 1966–7 he was art advisor to Leeds University's psychology department. In 1971 Naylor gained an Arts Council Award, the year before his first major solo show, at Serpentine Gallery, and two years after a Peter Stuyvesant Award. Further prizes included John Moores Exhibition, Liverpool, in 1978, and the year later he gained an Arts Council Major Award. Naylor had the first of a series of one-man exhibitions at Rowan Gallery in 1974; other key shows were Leeds City Art Gallery in 1975 and Museum of Modern Art, Oxford, in 1976. He also showed overseas. From the 1970s Naylor taught at Royal College of Art and Hornsey College of Art, in 1976 was visiting professor at École Nationale des Beaux-Arts, at Bourges, France, and from 1977 was head of sculpture at Middlesex Polytechnic. Loxley Hall, in Warwickshire, and Arts Council are among public collections holding his work.

Stephen NAYLOR 1957– Abstract sculptor, born in Newcastle, New South Wales, Australia. He moved to England in 1965 and studied at Reading University, 1976–80. Among his shows was Painters + Sculptors from the Greenwich Studios at Woodlands Art Gallery, 1981.

Paul NEAGU 1938– Sculptor in various materials, painter and draughtsman, environment and performance artist and teacher, born in Bucharest, Romania. He studied at the Institute Grigoresco there, 1959–65, and had a solo show at Amphora Gallery, Bucharest, and at Demarco Gallery, Edinburgh, in 1969, the year he settled in Britain. He was naturalised in 1976 and lived in London. In 1970 Neagu showed in John Moores Exhibition, Liverpool, the first of several appearances, the following year having the first of his solo shows at Compass Gallery, Glasgow. Other solo exhibitions included Museum of Modern Art in Oxford, Leeds Polytechnic Gallery, Third Eye Centre in Glasgow and with Elise Meyer Inc., New York, who became his dealer. Neagu won many awards, including Arts Council Awards in 1973, 1975 and 1978, and Northern Arts Fellowship, 1979–81. Taught for various periods at Hornsey College of Art, Chelsea School of Art and Middlesex Polytechnic. Neagu pursued a series of themes in his abstract art, in which he sought to express complex ideas in simple form. Arts Council holds his work.

Arthur NEAL 1951– Painter, printmaker and teacher who studied at Camberwell School of Arts and Crafts, 1969–73. Neal then had a varied life, being a shepherd and farm worker for five years until 1978. From 1980–3 he taught at the New Metropole Arts Centre, in Folkestone; for five years he worked on pub signs and murals; then he taught at Maidstone College of Art, 1983–6. Neal was fascinated by the work of the poet Edward Thomas, in 1973 publishing *Eight Poems* illustrated with a suite of etchings, in 1978 working on a limited-edition centenary volume, again illustrated with etchings. His mixed group appearances included Hunting Group exhibitions from 1987, RA Summer Exhibitions and Discerning Eye, at Mall Galleries, 1990. He had several solo shows at Cadogan Contemporary from 1989. Lived in Deal, Kent, the county where he was born, and where his garden was a constant preoccupation. Elected NEAC in 1992.

James NEAL 1918– Painter and draughtsman, born in London, who studied at St Martin's School of Art and Royal College of Art. He showed at RA, RSA, NEAC, LG and Redfern Gallery and after settling in Hull in the 1950s was a founder-member of the Avenues Group. Solo shows included Trafford Gallery and Wildenstein and in 1983–9 Ferens Art Gallery, Hull, gave him a two-part retrospective. It and public galleries in Beverley, Nottingham, Sheffield and Wakefield hold examples.

Maud Hall NEALE fl. c.1890–1960 Portrait painter, born at Waterloo, near Liverpool, married to the painter George Hall Neale. After initial education in Liverpool she studied art in Paris. Exhibited RA, SWA and Walker Art Gallery, Liverpool, prolifically, also ROI and RP. Lady Lever Gallery, Port Sunlight, holds her portrait of Lady Lever. Lived in London.

Clare NEASHAM 1965– Abstract artist, born in Stockton-on-Tees, County Durham, who gained an honours degree in printmaking at Newcastle University, 1984–8, then a master's degree with distinction at Royal College of Art, 1991–3, where Richard Wentworth was an "absolute inspiration". He understood "where my ideas came from – that we have an openness to look at everything." Forms such as the dovetail, lozenge and wedge were important to Neasham, as in her solo show at Francis Graham-Dixon Gallery, 1994.By then she had appeared in mixed exhibitions, including Fourth Oriel Mostyn Open, Llandudno, 1992, and Bradford Open Print exhibition, Cartwright Hall, 1993, and had won a series of awards, including John Christie, Northern Arts, Abraham & Lillian Rosenberg Foundation and Augustus Martin Award. Worked in London.

Norman NEASOM 1915– Painter, draughtsman and teacher, born in Tardebigge, Worcestershire. Studied at Birmingham College of Art, 1931–5, notably watercolour with Bernard Fleetwood-Walker. Went on to teach art for 34 years. He was a member of RBSA, RWS and Stratford-upon-Avon Art Society. Neasom wrote that his aim was "only to express my feelings about a subject". He did a lot of on-the-spot drawing and "cannot work from photographs". The Vet, Oddingly; Crowle Old Barn; Little Comberton Church; Meon Hill at Dawn were among his main pictures. Wrote a number of illustrated articles for *Leisure Painter*. Lived at Redditch, Worcestershire.

Edward NEATBY 1888–1949 Portrait painter and draughtsman, born in Leeds, son of the mural painter W J Neatby. Studied art at the Royal College of Art under Beresford Pite, W R Lethaby and Gerald Moira, then at the Slade School of Fine Art under Henry Tonks, Philip Wilson Steer and Walter Russell. Member of Chelsea Arts Club. He exhibited RA, RMS, RP and extensively in the provinces. Victoria & Albert Museum has his work. Lived in Harrogate, Yorkshire.

Alice Headley NEAVE 1903–c.1980 Painter in oil, born at Hastings, Sussex. She studied art at the Slade School of Fine Art under Sir Walter Westley Russell and Henry Tonks, winning the Landseer Prize. Headley Neave became a prolific exhibitor, including the RA, NEAC, WIAC, RP, RBA, RSA and Paris Salon. She lived at Etchingham, Sussex.

Philip Gregory NEEDELL 1886–1974 Painter in oil and watercolour and printmaker, born and lived in north London. After school Needell worked for Westminster Bank, taking part-time lessons in drawing at Regent Street Polytechnic. Served in the Navy, several of his World War I sea pictures being held by Royal Naval Museum, Portsmouth. He had married Anne Fairey, daughter of the aviation pioneer Sir Richard Fairey, in 1912; although they had three children, they divorced after 1926. One grandson was the racing driver Tiff Needell. As a landscape painter he worked often in France, from 1925–63. Needell's early scenes show the influence of notable watercolour painters such as Cotman and Turner, but later they are simplified, with more abstract tendencies. Needell also investigated the art of the Japanese print, cutting his own wood blocks for colour printing. He donated a series to the British Museum. Needell was a member of the Colour-Woodcut Society, Society of Graver-Printers in Colour, SGA, Wapping Group of Artists and Langham Sketch Club. Also showed at ROI and Walker Art Gallery in Liverpool. Much of his work went on to the market when he died. Had exhibitions at Galerie R Tuffier, Les Andelys, France, 1978 and 1982, and at Alexander Gallery, Bristol, in 1979.

Victor NEEP 1921–1979 Painter, sculptor and teacher, born in Nottingham. After World War II Army and Royal Air Force service Neep between 1945–8 attended Liverpool College of Art, Blackpool School of Art and Chelsea Polytechnic. The late 1940s and early 1950s saw Neep teaching and doing freelance artistic work, including industrial design. After a year at Bath Academy of Art, 1954–5, Neep did a variety of teaching and painting, living in Gwynedd. Showed in mixed exhibitions at University College of North Wales, Bangor; LG; Redfern Gallery and elsewhere; and showed solo at Howard Roberts Gallery in Cardiff and at University College of North Wales. Various commissions were carried out, including television play design for independent companies and sculpture for the Indian government. WAC and CASW hold his work. Lived for some time at Rhosgadfan, Caernarvon, Gwynedd.

Angus NEIL 1924–1992 Painter, born in Kilbarchan, Renfrewshire. In 1950–3 he studied at Glasgow School of Art, gaining the Chalmers Jarvis Prize and the RSA Award. Neil seems to have been a rare exhibitor, although Scottish Arts Council and Aberdeen Art Gallery are among several Scottish public collections holding his work. He was included in Painters in Parallel at Edinburgh College of Art, 1978. Lived near Montrose, Tayside.

Brendan NEILAND 1941– Painter and printmaker, born in Lichfield, Staffordshire. He attended Birmingham College of Art, 1962–6, then Royal College of Art, 1966–9, winning the John Minton Scholarship in the latter year. In that year, too, he showed at ICA, with Young Contemporaries and in North America, in 1970 making the first of several appearances at Bradford Print Biennale, in 1971 having the first of a series of exhibitions at Angela Flowers Gallery. In 1973 Neiland gained a solo show at Victoria & Albert Museum, which toured. Won a prize at John

Moores Exhibition, Liverpool, in 1978. Neiland went on to show with Fischer Fine Art, where he was noted for his sophisticated cityscapes which dwelt on reflections and refractions of light. Arts Council and Banque Arabe et Internationale d'Investissement, Paris, hold his work. Lived in London and was elected RA in 1992.

Anna Dudley NEILL 1935– Painter, born in London. She studied at Winchester School of Art, 1950–4, then Slade School of Fine Art, 1954–7. Was elected RI in 1980, also exhibiting at RBA and abroad. She was also known as Anna Dudley, her maiden name. Lived in Winchester, Hampshire.

Henry Echlin NEILL 1888–1981 Painter, printmaker, designer and teacher, born and lived in Belfast, Northern Ireland. He studied at the city's School of Art, then became a lithographic artist, working for several firms including S C Allen & Company. Showed at RHA, Belfast Art Society of which he was long a member and RUA, of which he was made honorary academician. Ulster Museum holds his work.

Hylton NEL 1941– Potter, painter and teacher, whose productions were notable for their wit and colour. He was born in Northern Rhodesia and brought up on a farm in the Northern Cape, studying painting and art history at Grahamstown, South Africa, and ceramics at the Royal College of Art in Antwerp, Belgium. In the early 1970s Nel lived in England, showing with the Crafts Centre of Great Britain. After returning to South Africa he taught in art schools in Port Elizabeth, Cape Town and Stellenbosch, all the time working with clay. In 1991 he moved to a small village, Bethulie. From the early 1990s Nel showed around the world, having his first London solo exhibition in 1996 at the Fine Art Society.

John NELLIST 1923– Painter, teacher and writer who attended the Schools of Art in Hull and Harrogate, Yorkshire, where he settled. After Royal Air Force service in India and the Far East, 1942–6, from 1950–82 Nellist was head of the art department, later of the general studies department, at Ashville College, Harrogate. In 1957 he was included in Jack Beddington's book *Young Artists of Promise*, Neo-Romantic country scenes. Soon after, Nellist wrote that he "became dissatisfied and disillusioned with both my own painting and the general trend that painting seemed to be taking, towards abstraction". He turned to architectural history and wrote *British Architecture and its background*, published in 1967. As a result he gave lectures for many years to the extra-mural department at Leeds University. A lecture tour to Europe for American students took Nellist to Venice, "a reaffirmation of the value of painting and colour, and I began painting with renewed vigour." Much of his best work was commissioned. Also showed at RA, RSA, Paris Salon, at university centres, Percival Guildhouse in Rugby and at London galleries including the Belgrave. A 40-year retrospective was held at Fairbairn House, University of Leeds, 1991.

Edmund NELSON 1910– Painter, especially of portraits, and illustrator, born in London. Studied at Goldsmiths' College School of Art with James Bateman and Clive Gardiner, 1927–30. Chelsea Arts Club member. Showed RA, RP, NEAC and RBA. Trinity College, Cambridge, has his portrait of the historian G M Trevelyan, who was its master, 1940–51. Lived in London, then in Wembley, Middlesex.

Harold NELSON 1871–1946 Designer, painter and illustrator, born in Dorchester, Dorset, who studied at Lambeth School of Art, then Central School of Arts and Crafts, etching with Luke Taylor. He went on to become a member of Art Workers' Guild from 1912, was one of its committee, 1917–19, and its honorary secretary, 1936–48. Designed commemorative stamp for the British Empire Exhibition in 1924 and the £1 Postal Congress Commemorative Stamp, 1929. He was an expert designer of bookplates, *Harold Nelson: His Book of Book-Plates*, 1904, being one of a number of volumes appraising them. W H Thoms' three-volume *Early English Prose Romances*, 1903, was one of several books illustrated by Nelson, whose work also appeared in magazines including *The Bookplate, The Graphic* and *Sphere*. Showed at RA, RI, Walker Art Gallery in Liverpool and elsewhere. Lived for many years in London, later at Carshalton, Surrey.

Stephen NELSON 1961– Sculptor, painter and teacher, born in Liverpool. He studied at South Glamorgan Institute of Higher Education, 1980–3, and Birmingham Polytechnic faculty of art, 1983–4, in 1984 being appointed junior fellow in painting at Cheltenham College. Group exhibitions included Whitechapel Open, Whitechapel Art Gallery, from 1990; Curator's Egg, Anthony Reynolds Gallery, 1994; and Konard Lorenz's Duck, Ex Lanificio Bona, Turin, 1995. Had solo exhibitions at Adam Gallery from 1992; at Mario Flecha Gallery, 1993; and Camden Arts Centre, 1996. There his large, totemic, coloured sculptures were based on the remote, mysterious Tepuis mountains of South America. Lived in London.

Oscar NEMON 1906–1985 Sculptor, born in Osijek, East Croatia, who when young began modelling clay in local brickworks, also exhibiting. He applied unsuccessfully to enter Akademie der Bildenden Kunst, Vienna, but eventually gained a bursary to study at Académie des Beaux-Arts, Paris, where he won a gold medal for sculpture. While in Paris Nemon shared a home with the Surrealist painter René Magritte and he showed, including solo exhibition at Palais des Beaux-Arts. Under threat from the Nazis, Nemon settled in England just before World War II, living in Oxford. He was befriended by John Rothenstein, whose bust by Nemon is in Tate Gallery, and began to establish a reputation as a portrait sculptor, notable for his ability to catch likenesses and a typical pose. He modelled busts of Queen Elizabeth II, the Queen Mother, Earl Mountbatten of Burma and notable statesmen and politicians, including some large figures of Winston Churchill. Ashmolean Museum held an exhibition of his work in 1982.

Coral NERELLE 1909–1986 Portrait painter in oil who was born in Sydney, Australia. She was married to the painter John Gordon Bill. Attended Sydney College of Art, Johns Hopkins

University in America and Byam Shaw School of Art, in London. Her tutors included Peter Greenham. She was elected RWA in 1986, just before she died. Her work, which included medical illustration, is in the RWA permanent collection, Cheltenham Art Gallery and Museums, Johns Hopkins University and Westminster Abbey. Lived in Northleach, Gloucestershire.

NERO: *see* **Harry BLACKER**

NERYS 1913– Painter and potter, born in Holyhead, Anglesey, North Wales, whose full name was Nerys Prys Williams. She studied at Slade School of Fine Art, 1932–6. Showed RA, Arts Council, RCamA and elsewhere. Lived in Oxshott, Surrey, then in Glyn Ceiriog, Denbighshire.

Anne NESS 1910– Painter and art director, born in Fife, Scotland. She attended Edinburgh College of Art in late 1920s under Gerald Moira, during her postgraduate year being taught by Hubert Wellington and winning a travelling scholarship. After starting in advertising in Jenner's, the Edinburgh department store, she moved to London, had a short time in the Women's Land Army and then took a job with the Lintas advertising agency, later moving to Notley's. She continued to paint, with a studio in Hammersmith, later living in Saffron Walden, Essex, and showing locally. Was included in the Lintas Beyond the Horizon show at Agnew, 1988.

Walter NESSLER 1912– Versatile artist, notable for landscapes and townscapes influenced by the School of Paris, whose media included oil-sand and polyester resin. He was born in Leipzig, Germany. Studied at Castelli Italian Art School in Dresden, 1933–5, but learned much in galleries of London and Paris. In 1937 Nessler emigrated from Nazi Germany to England, was interned when World War II broke out, then served in British Army until 1946, settling in London from 1947. Nessler showed at RA, RBA and elsewhere in mixed company. Had solo shows at Leger Gallery, 1943 and 1947, later ones including a series at John Denham Gallery from 1984. Latterly Nessler gained recognition in Germany. In 1990 the Bund-Verlag produced an edition of Toller's *Das Schwalbenbuch* using Nessler's 1937 illustrations, Dresden Academy made him an honorary fellow and Galerie Berlin gave him a solo exhibition which toured. Contemporary Art Society and Royal Air Force Museum in Hendon hold examples.

Ray NESTOR 1888– Painter and draughtsman who spent much of his life working for the Kenya civil service, but eventually settled in London. In addition to education at the City and Guilds School and Imperial College of Science and Technology, Nestor studied art at Heatherley's School of Fine Art under Henry Massey. He exhibited in Kenya, also at RBA and RI.

Florence NEUMEGEN: *see* **Florence ENGELBACH**

Ernst NEUSCHUL 1895–1968 Painter, born in Aussig, Bohemia. He studied at the Academies of Prague, Vienna and Cracow, winning the Rome Prize at the Berlin Academy in 1918. Through the 1920s he obtained solo shows in many European capitals and in America. In 1935 he gained a one-man exhibition at Museum of Western Art, Moscow, and in 1936 received an official invitation to portray Stalin. Although the Soviet press acclaimed him as a leading Socialist Realist painter, it was pointed out that his work retained remnants of an idealist dreamworld. Shortly – disillusioned – he left Russia for Prague and in 1938 fled to Britain with his family, where he continued to paint, anglicising his name to Ernest Norland. He was given shows in Swansea, Cardiff, London and, in 1959, Jerusalem. Died in London where, in 1981, his work was shown by Wylma Wayne Fine Art. Glynn Vivian Art Gallery, Swansea, has Neuschul in its collection. He had lived in the area at Mumbles, 1940–5.

Heather NEVAY fl. from late 1980s– Painter and illustrator whose work included a strong element of fantasy. Graduated with honours from department of printed textiles at Glasgow School of Art, in 1988. After participating in the Scotfree Designs Exhibition and Betty Jackson Fashion Show at Olympia, Nevay began a busy career as an illustrator. Book cover commissions included Robin Jenkins' *Fergus Lamont*; Neil Gunn's *Wild Geese Overhead*; and Edwin Muir's *Collected Poems*. As a painter she showed at RSA, SSA, Royal Glasgow Institute of the Fine Arts and Compass Gallery, Glasgow. Cyril Gerber Fine Art, Glasgow, gave her a solo show in 1995.

Margaret NEVE 1929– Painter, mainly in oil, and teacher, born in Wolverhampton, Staffordshire. She was educated privately, then studied at local School of Art, Birmingham College of Art, 1946–50, under Bernard Fleetwood-Walker, won a scholarship to study in Florence, then was at Royal Academy Schools, 1950–3, gaining a Leverhulme Scholarship. Neve used a Pointillist technique and her pictures had a strong pastoral and visionary quality. She showed at RA, Young Contemporaries, Leicester Galleries, WIAC, Redfern Gallery and was included in an exhibition of sacred paintings at St Botolph's Church in 1991. Had solo show at New Art Centre in 1962, later ones including series at Montpelier Studio from 1987. Birmingham City Museum and Art Gallery holds her work. Lived in London.

Alison NEVILLE 1945– Artist, notably a printmaker and draughtsman, born in Rhodesia. She studied at Gloucestershire and Portsmouth Colleges of Art and University of London, 1962–8, then Boston University School of Arts in America, 1974–6. Exhibited at RA Summer Exhibition; Camden Annual from 1984; Whitechapel Open from 1986; Print Anthony Dawson at the Barbican, 1990; and In Piper's Footsteps, at New Academy Gallery, 1993. Made two drawing trips to India and one to Egypt, 1988–90. Had a solo show at John Curtis & Partners, The Drawing Room, Pershore, 1984, later ones including Royal National Theatre, 1991. The Museum of Leicester, Laing & Cruikshank and Citibank hold her work. Lived in London.

Anne NEVILLE 1900–1981 Portrait and landscape painter in oil, she was born and lived in London. She went on to study at the

Central School of Arts and Crafts, 1917–21, under Bernard Meninsky and James Grant. Her real name was Elsie Farleigh, being married to the artist John Farleigh. Showed at a number of venues, including Redfern Gallery, LG, Leicester Galleries and in the provinces. Arnold Haskell's book *Black on White* includes her work. Lived in London.

Jane NEVILLE 1949– Watercolourist, born in Richmond, Yorkshire, educated in Stratford-upon-Avon, who attended Loughborough College of Art, 1967–70. She joined SWLA, also showing with William Marler Gallery in Ludlow and elsewhere. Lived in Aslockton, Nottinghamshire.

Pete NEVIN 1952– Painter and printmaker who studied at Mid-Cheshire College of Art, 1978–9; Leeds Polytechnic, 1979–82; and Royal College of Art, 1982–5. Group exhibitions included Art Fair at Warwick Arts Trust, 1985; Print Show, Angela Flowers Gallery, 1986; Fiona Whitney Gallery, Los Angeles, 1991; and Contemporary British Graphic Fine Art, South Hill Park, Bracknell, 1996. Had a series of solo shows at Vanessa Devereux Gallery, 1986–9, then at The Cut Gallery from 1995. Public galleries in Huddersfield and Leeds hold examples.

Christopher Richard Wynne NEVINSON 1889–1946 Painter of landscapes, figures and interiors, printmaker and writer, born in London, son of the writer H W Nevinson. He studied painting at St John's Wood School of Art, after leaving Uppingham School, with the intention of going to Royal Academy Schools; then abandoned that aim for Slade School of Fine Art, 1908–12; after which he went to Paris and studied at Académie Julian and Matisse's Cercle Russe. Nevinson's entertaining autobiography, *Paint and Prejudice*, of 1937, is very good on these bohemian years. He also studied lithography at Central School of Arts and Crafts under Ernest Jackson. Was closely associated with Marinetti and Futurism and was represented in Vorticist Exhibition in 1915, as well as showing with Friday Club, AAA and was a founder-member of LG. Nevinson was invalided out of Army during World War I but become an official war artist in 1917, producing some of the starkest images of the conflict, which have Vorticist/Futurist overtones. His first one-man show of war paintings, at Leicester Galleries, in 1916 was a great success. After the war Nevinson found a suitably modern subject in the cityscape of New York. He continued to travel; joined the RBA, RI and NS; and became a Chevalier of the Legion d'Honneur in 1938. Died in London and had memorial show at Leicester Galleries, 1947. Tate Gallery and Imperial War Museum hold his work.

Keith NEW 1926– Painter, draughtsman, illustrator, designer, stained glass artist and teacher, born in London. Studied at Sutton and Cheam School of Art, 1942–5, then in the stained glass department of Royal College of Art, 1948–53. After working in New York for Steuben and Corning Glass, 1953–4, taught in the stained glass department of Royal College of Art, 1955–68, then became principal lecturer in foundation studies at Kingston Polytechnic. As well as doing book-jacket design for the publisher Michael Joseph and designs for John Cranko's ballet *Reflection* at Sadler's Wells, New handled a number of stained glass commissions including three nave windows for Coventry Cathedral, a south choir window in Bristol Cathedral plus a rose window in Christ Church, Calgary, Canada. He was a fellow of the British Society of Master Glass Painters. New's paintings had a strong Neo-Romantic element mixed with a slight Surrealistic menace in his unpopulated landscapes. Mixed shows included RA Summer Exhibition, John Moores Exhibition in Liverpool and Austin/Desmond Fine Art, Sunninghill, where he had a solo show, 1991.

Vincent NEW 1906–1994 Draughtsman, printmaker and painter, born in Bromley, Kent. As a young man New went to Australia, studied art full-time at Bromley and Beckenham Schools of Art, 1925–9, teachers including Herbert Ashwin Budd and Rowland Gill, then became a freelance artist, working for Kent papers. Attended Camberwell School of Art, 1931. New was an illustrator from 1943–67 in the Admiralty's Naval Intelligence Division, in 1944 working on Normandy invasion plans. New was elected a member of the Art Workers' Guild, 1938, and showed in Kent and Surrey. Had solo exhibitions in Belfast, 1927, and Otford, 1989. Lived in Brasted, Kent, and was noted for topographical pictures of that county.

John NEWBERRY 1934– Watercolourist, who painted widely on the continent with a special interest in architecture, and teacher. He was born in Horsham, Sussex, and after National Service read architecture at Cambridge University, but changed courses, moving to King's College, Newcastle upon Tyne, where under Lawrence Gowing and Victor Pasmore he graduated in fine art in 1960. After that he lived in Oxford or the immediate area, teaching at Ruskin School of Drawing between 1963–89, retiring as acting head, although between 1986–88 he had taught landscape painting at a school in Umbria. Showed at RA, NEAC, RI, annually in Oxford and at RWS, where in 1989 he won the Watercolour Foundation Prize. From 1990 had several solo shows at Chris Beetles Ltd.

Evan NEWBERY 1904– Painter, calligrapher and teacher who studied at Borough Polytechnic, Hammersmith School of Building and Arts and Crafts, Spring Grove Polytechnic and Harrow School of Art. Exhibited RA, in the provinces and in America. Lived at Woodbridge, Suffolk.

Francis H (Fra) NEWBERY 1855–1946 Teacher and painter, born in Membury, Devon, who in 1889 married the embroiderer and artist Jessie Rowat, their daughter being the painter Mary Newbery Sturrock. Fra Newbery trained at Bridport and South Kensington Schools of Art and in 1885 was appointed director of Glasgow School of Art. Under his direction it was transformed, staff and students were encouraged to look and show abroad and Charles Rennie Mackintosh's notable building to house the art school was designed and constructed. Around the end of World War I Newbery and his wife retired to Corfe Castle, Dorset. Newbery was a member of the Glasgow Art Club, IS and RWA and was a prolific exhibitor, also showing at RSA, Royal Glasgow Institute of the Fine Arts, Walker Art Gallery in Liverpool, RA and NEAC. Public galleries in Venice, Udine, Turin, Magdeburg, Munich, Santiago, Paisley, Exeter and Newcastle upon Tyne acquired examples.

Jessie NEWBERY 1864–1948 Embroiderer, artist and teacher, born in Paisley, Renfrewshire, who in 1889 married the noted director of Glasgow School of Art, Fra Newbery, having studied there, 1884–8. Their daughter was the painter Mary Newbery Sturrock. Between 1894–1908 she was on the staff of the School, transforming the teaching of embroidery. Her own work was marked by an interest in flowers and foliage, and she showed at Royal Glasgow Institute of the Fine Arts, RSA and RSW. In 1918 she and her husband retired to Corfe Castle, Dorset.

Thomas NEWBOLT 1951– Painter, draughtsman and printmaker, born in London. He attended Camberwell School of Arts and Crafts, 1970–4, gained a first-class honours degree in painting. Won Italian Government Scholarship, 1974–5, then French Government Scholarship, 1977–8. Was a Fellow Commoner in Creative Arts at CambridgeUniversity, 1979–81; gained a Harkness InternationalFellowship, University of Virginia, visiting scholar, 1981–3; then was a visiting artist at University of Wisconsin-Milwaukee, 1983. Newbolt won an Eastern Arts Purchase Grant then a Materials Grant in early 1980s. Showed at Browse & Darby solo from 1986, other exhibitions including Tatischeff Gallery, New York, from 1988, and Belloc Lowndes Gallery, Chicago, 1995. University of Surrey, Churchill and New Hall Colleges in Cambridge, Dayton Art Institute in Dayton, Ohio, and several corporate collections hold examples.

Frank NEWBOULD 1887–1951 Poster and black-and-white artist, born in Bradford, who studied at the local College of Art and won several silver and bronze medals in national competitions. During and after World War I he was a black-and-white artist, working for such publications as *Passing Show*, but more profitable poster work attracted him, and he became one of the most prolific and distinguished practitioners in the inter-war period. Initially he worked for Morton Studios in Fleet Street, then set up his own studio. His posters for Orient Lines and London North Eastern Railway were notable, especially landscapes studied on location. Exhibited Chenil Galleries and lived in London.

Barbara NEWCOMB 1936– Printmaker, born in Arlington, Virginia, America. Studied at Syracuse University, 1954–8, Central School of Arts and Crafts, 1960–2, and at Stanley William Hayter's Atelier 17 in Paris, 1962–3. Exhibited widely, her work being held by Victoria & Albert Museum, Arts Council and by collections in America and France. RE member, also a member of the Printmakers' Council, who lived for some years in London.

Mary NEWCOMB 1922– Painter in oil and watercolour, wife of the potter Godfrey Newcomb and mother of the artist Tessa Newcomb, born in Harrow on the Hill, Middlesex. She gained her bachelor's degree in natural sciences at Reading University, 1940–4, also studying pottery at Bath School of Art. She taught for a time, married in 1950 and then farmed and painted. Showed at Beaux Arts Gallery, Wildenstein, with Norwich Twenty Group and Norfolk and Norwich Art Circle both of which she was a member, and elsewhere. From 1970 showed solo with Crane Kalman Gallery in London, also abroad. Her work is in public and private collections. Newcomb's landscape and other pictures had a lyrical, undemonstrative charm and quirkiness. Lived at Newton Flotman, Norwich, Norfolk.

Tessa NEWCOMB 1955– Painter in oil on board or on furniture, and illustrator, born in Suffolk, daughter of the artist Mary Newcomb. Studied at Norwich School of Art, 1972–3; gained an honours degree from Bath Academy of Art, 1976, doing a year's advanced printmaking at Wimbledon School of Art, 1977. The Suffolk countryside or country events were features of her work. Mixed exhibitions included Crane Arts and Mercury Gallery in London and Edinburgh. Had two solo shows at Annexe Gallery, Wimbledon, 1979–80, later ones including Christopher Hull Gallery from 1987, and Chappel Galleries, Chappel, 1996 (with Hein Bonger). Completed jacket illustrations for Julia Blackburn's *Daisy In The Desert* and the paperback of *The Emperor's Last Island*, both 1994. Bradford Metropolitan Museum, Whitworth Art Gallery in Manchester, Strawberry Hill College and Ocean and Transport hold examples. Lived at Wenhaston, Halesworth, Suffolk.

William NEWCOMBE 1907–1969 Versatile artist, born in Victoria, British Columbia, Canada, where he attended King Edward High School, Vancouver. Although he had some lessons from F H Varley he was mainly self-taught, his early career encompassing commercial art, cartooning and being staff artist for the *Province*, Vancouver. In 1941 enlisted in Royal Canadian Air Force, flew as an air-gunner in many missions over Europe, broke his leg while parachuting after his plane was shot down, was discharged back to Canada and began to show there and in America. From 1946 lived for a year in Mexico. Returned to Europe in 1955 and settled in England, although he paid a visit to Canada in 1958. Took part in many group shows, including Nicholas Treadwell Gallery, 1965, and held extensive solo exhibitions in Britain and abroad, including London, where he lived. There was a series at Obelisk Gallery from 1956 and New Vision Centre Gallery from 1958, others including Manchester City Art Gallery, 1961, and Elizabethan Manor House Gallery, Ilkley, 1962. There *The Manchester Guardian* critic W E Johnson compared Bill Newcombe's work with that of Sam Francis, mentioned the bent matches and pieces of rope that were sometimes included and praised its rightness, evoking "a sensual pleasure somewhere midway between the coldly clinical pure mathematics of the Constructivist and the passionate heat of the Fauve". Whitworth Art Gallery in Manchester, Boston Museum of Fine Art in America, National Gallery of Israel in Tel-Aviv and many other international collections hold examples. Newcombe's Abstract Expressionist works were shown at Obelisk Gallery, 1988.

John NEWICK 1919– Modeller, printmaker, but primarily a lecturer and writer on art, born in Bristol. Studied at the Grammar School there, then at West of England College of Art with Donald Milner. Held a number of lectureships, specialising in art education, notably at University of London Institute of Education from the late 1960s. His exhibiting was mainly didactic, and he wrote and illustrated several teaching books, including one on lino-cuts: *Making Colour Prints*.

Mary Jane NEWILL 1860–1947 Painter of landscape and figure subjects, stained glass designer, book illustrator and teacher, based in Edgbaston, Birmingham. She studied at Birmingham School of Art and taught needlework there for nearly 30 years from 1892. She was an original member of the Birmingham Group, was strongly associated with the Arts and Crafts Movement and was made RBSA in 1926. Took time off from teaching to study tempera painting in Florence. Showed at Fine Art Society and in 1900 her wall hangings of *The Faerie Queene* were exhibited at Paris International Exhibition. Among her book illustrations were some for Tennyson's *The Passing of Arthur*, 1894. William Morris inspired much of her stained glass, which was produced for domestic and ecclesiastical clients. Saints Mary and Ambrose, Edgbaston, has a two-light window by Newill, of 1906. Birmingham Museums & Art Gallery holds examples.

Charles NEWINGTON 1950– Painter, printmaker and teacher, born in Kent. He studied at Byam Shaw, Camberwell and Central Schools of Art. Worked as an etching technician and teacher at Central School for three years, leaving in 1976 to become director of etching studio at Editions Alecto. In 1979 he set up an independent studio in London, but after three years moved to Warehorne, Kent to live and work as a full-time painter and etcher. Newington made extensive working trips through Europe, North Africa, India and the Far East. For much of 1987 he worked in France on a series of commissions, painting chateaux, and he held two solo shows at Le Chateau de la Batie, Beaujolais. He also had a special love of Venice, showing Venetian work at Londra Palace there. CCA Galleries published his etchings of Venice. Newington had first London solo show at the Newburgh Street Gallery in 1989.

Barry NEWIS 1939– Painter and draughtsman, born in Bromley, Kent. He studied at Beckenham and Bromley Schools of Art. Showed with Young Contemporaries, LG, South London Art Gallery, Richard Bradley and Buxton Mill Galleries, University of East Anglia and elsewhere. In 1990 had solo show at Cadogan Contemporary. Newis' pictures were frequently on a large scale, depicting city industrial scenes in a gritty way.

Anne NEWLAND 1913– Painter in oil and teacher, born in Wiltshire. She studied at Byam Shaw School, 1936–8, under Ernest Jackson, in 1938 gaining an Edwin Abbey Major Scholarship. During World War II she was involved in camouflage, then taught in Scotland. Signed her work, which was mainly large, decorative canvases, A N. Was influenced especially by the work of Andrea Mantegna. Showed at RA, RSA and elsewhere. Lived in London.

John NEWLING 1952– Sculptor, draughtsman, installations artist and teacher, born in Birmingham. He gained a first-class honours fine art degree at North Staffordshire Polytechnic, 1971–4; his master's degree in sculpture at Chelsea School of Art, 1974–5; and his Master of Philosophy degree at Wolverhampton Polytechnic, 1975–8. He was the first Fulbright Fellow in Visual Art, 1984. Went on to teach installation sculpture at Nottingham Trent University. Mixed shows included Peter Moores Exhibition, Fruitmarket Gallery, Edinburgh, 1982; Crammond Sculpture Park, Edinburgh, 1989; and Printed Matter Gallery, New York, 1994. Had a solo exhibition at Midland Group, Nottingham, 1980, later ones including Cornerhouse, Manchester, 1995. The catalogue documented the exhibition and all of Newling's work over the previous 20 years. Spectacular in scale and content, this was based on symbols and emblems from church and state. Themes running through Newling's work included spirituality, absences, belief, courage and choice. His Settlement History Line, 1983, in gun-metal and gauze, is sited at Rufford Country Park, Ollerton.

Abraham NEWMAN 1907– Painter in watercolour and gouache in a Pointillist style "not to intensify the colour, but to control and enrich the form". Newman was born in Bootle, Lancashire, and settled nearby in Liverpool, practising as a solicitor. He had studied at Liverpool at the School of Art, 1927–32, then Royal College of Art, 1932–5, in the sculpture school, his strongest influences being Epstein, Gill and Mestrovic. For economic reasons Newman in 1936 entered Liverpool University, gaining his bachelor's degree in law in 1939; qualified as a solicitor in 1941; and while in the Royal Air Force, where he served in Tunisia, was awarded his master's degree. Oriental, opera and ballet subjects were important to Newman, who showed at Walker Art Gallery in Liverpool, with Liverpool Academy and had a series of solo exhibitions including Galerie Mouffe, Paris, 1969; Galerie Vallombreuse, Palm Beach, Florida, 1973 and 1974; Serpentine Gallery, 1978; and Ben Uri Art Society, which holds his work, 1982.

Andrea NEWMAN 1957– Figurative draughtsman and painter, born in Belfast, Northern Ireland, who studied at Gloucestershire College of Art and Design, then obtained an honours degree at Brighton Polytechnic. Group exhibitions included Eastern Open, Fermoy Centre, King's Lynn, from 1987; Artists in Essex, Epping Forest District Museum, 1989; and Drawings for All, Gainsborough's House, Sudbury, 1994. Solo exhibitions included Christchurch Mansion, Ipswich, 1993; Gallerie Thaysen-Heyduck, Wuppertal, Germany, 1994; and Chappel Galleries, Chappel, 1996.

Avis NEWMAN 1946– Artist in mixed media who was born and lived in London. Took part in many group exhibitions, including British Drawing at Hayward Gallery, 1982; The British Art Show, Arts Council 1984 and tour; Sixth Biennale of Sydney, Art Gallery of New South Wales, Sydney, 1986; Excavating the Present, Kettle's Yard, Cambridge, 1991; and Worlds in a Box, Arts Council tour, 1994–5. Had a solo show at Matt's Gallery,

1982, later ones including Ikon Gallery, Birmingham, 1995. Arts Council holds her work.

Beryl NEWMAN 1906–1991 Painter and draughtsman, born in St Albans, Hertfordshire, married to the Reverend Canon Rupert Newman. She also showed under her maiden name, Beryl Trist. She studied with Rowland Wheelwright at Herkomer School, Bushey, then at Regent Street Polytechnic School of Art. Exhibited extensively at Goupil, Little Burlington and Kensington Galleries in solo exhibitions, also in mixed shows at RA, RP, RBA and elsewhere and was a member of UA. Lived for many years at Lustleigh, Newton Abbot, Devon, going into a retirement home in Moretonhamstead for her final year, dying in Moreton Hospital.

Colin NEWMAN 1923– Painter, draughtsman and printmaker, born in Chipping Sodbury, Gloucestershire. After World War II Army service, partly as a cartographic draughtsman, and during which he did a correspondence course with Percy Bradshaw's Press Art School, Newman studied at Florence College of Art in Italy, with particular regard to architecture. After returning to England Newman was an artist designer and lithographic artist designer while continuing his studies at the West of England College of Art, Bristol. In 1973 be became a full-time artist, showing in West Country galleries and having several one-man shows with John Noott Galleries, Broadway. He was a founder-member of the Society of Botanical Artists. Gardens and flowers were key features of Newman's meticulous pictures, reminiscent of Victorian watercolours. They were reproduced as greetings cards and calendars by Camden Graphics, the Medici Society and others, and are in private collections throughout the world. Lived in Frenchay, Bristol.

Gerald NEWMAN 1945– Artist, notably using sound tapes and slides, born in Marlborough, Wiltshire. He studied at Slade School of Fine Art, 1964–70, winning the Walter Neurath Prize in 1965 and a Boise Travelling Scholarship to Germany and Netherlands, 1970. In 1975 gained an Arts Council Major Award, Arts Council holding his work. Took part in Linguistic Structures at Arts Council, 1979, and was in Woodlands Art Gallery's 1981–2 touring show of Greater London Arts Association award winners. Solo shows included Lisson Gallery, 1970, Robert Self Gallery in Newcastle and London, from 1975, and Ikon Gallery, Birmingham, 1981.

Hayley NEWMAN 1969– Video and performance artist, who obtained a fine art degree at Middlesex Polytechnic, 1989–92, then a postgraduate diploma in fine art media at Slade School of Fine Art. She obtained a DAAD Scholarship to the Hochschule für Bildende Künste, Hamburg. Also held a residency with an exhibition at Western Front, Vancouver, Canada, 1996. Other exhibitions included a performance, Bild Me Bild You, at Galerie KM235, Hamburg, and The Tingle Factor, performance, AVE, Arnhem, Netherlands, both 1995; and Urbane Aboriginale, Festival of Experimental Music in Britain, and New Contemporaries at Tate Gallery in Liverpool and Camden Arts Centre, both 1996.

Ian David NEWMAN 1953– Artist in charcoal, pastel and oil, born in Brighton, Sussex. He studied at Eastbourne College of Art, 1970–71, then at Brighton Polytechnic's faculty of art and design, 1971–5. Showed at Brighton Festival, Hove Museum and with South East Arts Travelling Exhibition of winners. Solo exhibitions included Gallery 20 in Brighton, Canterbury Museum, Brighton Polytechnic Gallery, Cootes Gallery in Lewes and Stables Theatre Gallery, Hastings. Lived in Epsom, Surrey.

Peter NEWMAN 1969– Conceptual artist in a variety of media, born and working in London, who studied at Goldsmiths' College, 1987–90. Group shows included Laure Genillard and Henrietta House, both 1993; Photoworks, *The Economist*, 1995; and Art Node, Stockholm, and Out of Space at Cole and Cole, Oxford, both 1996. In 1990, Newman had a solo show at Fred's. In 1997, Newman followed a 1995 exhibition at Entwistle, called In the Sky with Diamonds, with a second called God's Speed. The title-piece was a 10-minute video of a 1994 storm off California, when surfers tried to ride 30-foot waves. As in previous explorations of human aspiration by him, Newman drew out the iconic aspects of the film, created wall-pieces and a sculpture using aluminium rods.

Thomas NEWMAN 1906–1980 Painter in oil, born in London, son of the director of the Bank of England. Studied art under Jack Merriott and exhibited at the Alpine Gallery and Qantas Gallery. Was president of the Association of Devon Art Societies. Newman was a notable naive artist, who sold over 200 pictures, one of which was chosen to illustrate the 1976 calendar of the United Nations Children's Fund (UNICEF). Lived in Kingsbridge, Devon.

Victor NEWSOME 1935– Painter, sculptor, draughtsman and teacher, born in Leeds. He studied painting at Leeds College of Art, 1953–5, returning there, 1957–60, after National Service. In 1960–2 he was a Rome Scholar in painting at the British School in Rome, after which he returned and took to sculpture, returning to painting in the early 1970s. Between 1962–70 Newsome taught at Leicester and Nottingham Schools of Art and Hull College of Art, then until 1977 was variously at Camberwell School of Arts and Crafts, Goldsmiths' College, Brighton Polytechnic, Canterbury College of Art and Wimbledon and Chelsea Schools of Art. Among his awards was a Peter Stuyvesant Travel Bursary to America in 1966. From 1962 Newsome participated in many important group shows, even though he was by nature a slow worker. He had his first solo exhibition, of sculpture, at Grabowski Gallery in 1966, showing later with Hester van Royen Gallery; the Ikon Gallery in Birmingham; Anne Berthoud Gallery; Ferens Art Gallery, Hull; and in 1987 he had a key one-man show at Marlborough Fine Art. That showed his continuing preoccupation with the female head and figure, accompanied by detailed drawings, exact yet enigmatic, calm and hieratic. Newsome's work is held by Arts Council, Victoria & Albert Museum and other public collections. Lived in London.

Algernon NEWTON 1880–1968 Painter of townscapes and landscapes, mainly in oil. Born in London, Newton studied at

Cambridge and then attended Frank Calderon's School of Animal Painting and the London School of Art, Kensington. He began exhibiting at the RA from 1903, 40 years later being elected RA. His first one-man show was at the Leicester Galleries in 1931. Also exhibited at the NEAC, Royal Glasgow Institute of the Fine Arts and the Cooling Galleries. Although he worked in Cornwall and Yorkshire, Newton is especially noted for his views of inner suburban London and its canals, such as The Surrey Canal, Camberwell, in the Tate Gallery. Still, empty streets are a characteristic of his work, giving them a slightly unreal quality. He is well represented in provincial and overseas galleries. The RA held a major exhibition of his work in 1980. Lived in London. The artist Nigel Newton was his son.

Eric NEWTON 1893–1965 Artist in mosaic, designer, recreational painter, art critic, teacher and historian. Born near Manchester, he studied at Manchester University and from 1913–14 and 1918–33 worked as a mosaic designer and craft-men with L Oppenheimer Ltd, Manchester. Commissioned in Army during World War I. He became art critic for the *Manchester Guardian*, 1930–47, and for the *Sunday Times*, 1937–51. Several lecture tours in North America. Slade Professor of Fine Art, Oxford, 1959–60, and art advisor to the Commonwealth Institute, 1960–63. Exhibited RA. Newton was one of the most perceptive, concise, sympathetic and lucid critics of his time, with a keen following. Wrote a number of books, including *The Artist and his Public*, 1935, *Christopher Wood*, 1938, *The Meaning of Beauty*, 1950, *In My View* (a collection of his newspaper articles), 1950, and *The Romantic Rebellion*, 1962. Lived in London, where the step of his house in Cumberland Gardens, Finsbury, has a mosaic by him.

Herbert H NEWTON 1881–1959 Landscape painter who studied at London University. He was a prolific exhibitor, showing work at the RA, Alpine Gallery, Goupil Gallery, NEAC, LG and in the provinces. One-man shows in London, Paris, New York and elsewhere on the continent. Work in many international collections, including Fitzwilliam Museum, Cambridge, British Museum, Victoria & Albert Museum and Imperial War Museum. Wrote *An Artist's Experience*, an autobiographical notebook, a new edition of which appeared six years before he died. Lived in London.

Irene Margaret NEWTON 1915– Textile designer, painter, draughtsman and teacher, educated in Truro, Cornwall, where she studied at School of Art, 1934–8, with W P Hodgkinson. Went on to teach in Manchester at Elizabeth Gaskell College of Education after positions in Hereford and Stourbridge. Showed at RBA, RBSA, UA, at Paris Salon and elsewhere. Lived latterly in Southport, Lancashire.

Joanna Dawson NEWTON 1958– Painter and draughtsman, born in Oxford, who studied at Byam Shaw School of Art, 1979–82, teachers including Nicholas Volley and Paul Gopal-Chowdhury. Showed at RA Summer Exhibition, Whitechapel Open, National Portrait Gallery in John Player Award and elsewhere. Lived in London.

Nigel NEWTON 1903– Painter in oil, son of the artist Algernon Newton. Studied at St John's Wood School of Art and Royal Academy Schools, 1922–3, with Charles Sims. Showed at RA, LG, RHA and elsewhere. Lived at Dursley, Gloucestershire.

Stephen NEWTON 1948– Painter, draughtsman, lecturer and writer who gained an honours degree in fine art at Leeds University, 1971, his master's in fine art at Nottingham Polytechnic, 1986, and after research in the psychiatry department of the University of Sheffield, in 1991, his master's with distinction in art and psychotherapy there, 1993. He followed this with doctoral research into psychoanalysis and creativity at University of Sheffield, in 1995 publishing the acclaimed study *The Politics and Psychoanalysis of Primitivism.* Newton was a visiting lecturer at Exeter College of Art, 1989–92, and at University of Plymouth, 1993. Exhibitions included Wolfson 25 at Wolfson College, Oxford, 1991; Miart, Milan, from 1995; and Art's Hidden Order, Mappin Art Gallery, Sheffield, 1996. Had a solo show at Art96, and Documents of a Decade, at University of Northumbria, Newcastle, and Stanley Picker Gallery, University of Kingston, both 1998. Newton said that his painting dealt "with unconscious form .... My subject matter is abstract and minimal. In the end, Art can say absolutely nothing outside its own intrinsic dialogue." Worked in north Lincolnshire and London.

Diana Elizabeth NEWTON-DAVIES 1942– Watercolour miniaturist, born in London, whose art studies included Accademia di Belle Arti, Florence, 1959–60, and Camberwell School of Arts and Crafts, 1961–2. Showed at RA, RMS, Westminster and Medici Galleries. Lived in Chailey, Sussex.

Colin NICHOLAS 1949– Abstract sculptor and teacher, born in Bacup, Lancashire. He attended Rochdale College of Art, 1966–8; Ravensbourne College of Art, 1968–71; and Slade School of Fine Art, 1971–3. Gained an Arts Council Minor Award, 1976. From 1973 Nicholas held a number of part-time lectureships, including Goldsmiths' College and Kingston Polytechnic. Took part in many mixed shows, including Sculpture in the Park, Ealing, 1972; LG from 1973; Ikon Gallery, Birmingham, 1978; Annely Juda Fine Art from 1979; and Wapping Artists Open Studios from 1982. London Borough of Tower Hamlets picture library holds his work. Lived for a time in London.

Isabel NICHOLAS: *see* **Isabel RAWSTHORNE**

Peter NICHOLAS 1934– Sculptor, draughtsman and teacher, born in Ebbw Vale, Monmouthshire. Studied at Cardiff College of Art, 1951–6, then after Royal Navy National Service, in 1956–8, was at the Royal College of Art, 1958–61. In 1996 Nicholas won a Major Arts Council Bursary. He was head of foundation studies at Newport College of Art until 1980, then head of school faculty of art at Swansea until 1988. Nicholas was a founder-member of the Welsh Sculpture Trust, was elected a fellow of RBS in 1993 and was sculptor-director of Sculpture at Margam. Group shows included 56 Group, Royal National Eisteddfod and WAC, Sculptors' Drawings at Sladmore and Pangolin Galleries, both 1994, and Wales Art Fair, Cardiff, 1994 and 1995. He was represented by Compton Cassey Galleries, Withington, and internationally by Poole Fine Art. WAC and CASW hold Nicholas' work, which was figurative in bronze and marble, sometimes with a tendency towards abstraction. Commissions included Guto The Running Man, a bronze at Mountain Ash, 1991, and Mother Sea, in Portland stone, for Porthcawl, 1993.

Gordon NICHOLL 1888–1959 Painter, born in London, who was initially educated at Swinton's School, Southampton. Studied at Hornsey School of Art, 1911, under Frank Swinstead. During World War II spent several years engaged in camouflage for the Air Ministry. Chelsea Arts Club and London Sketch Club member who showed at RA and RI, to which he was elected in 1935. Lived in West Byfleet, Surrey.

Bertram NICHOLLS 1883–1974 Landscape painter, especially in oil, whose pictures owe much, according to his biographer Frank Rutter, to "diligent study of our own eighteenth-century masters", having an old-fashioned stillness and high degree of finish. Born in Didsbury, Manchester, Nicholls studied at the Slade School of Fine Art, 1901–4, although he said that it took him some years to unlearn much of what he had been taught there. In 1904 went to Madrid and devoted several months to study of Velasquez, and on his return studied with Fred W Jackson in Yorkshire. Disillusioned with modern art ideas in London, went to Montreuil in 1911 where he met his wife who introduced him to Frank Mura, who painted in Sussex where Nicholls settled, and who "initiated him into the secrets of finer craftsmanship" of the earlier Dutch painters. First exhibited at RA in 1912, afterwards regularly. During World War I was enrolled in Kite Balloon Service of Royal Flying Corps and made panoramic drawings in France. After the war made extensive research into methods used by Sir Joshua Reynolds and technique of Richard Wilson. His painting Drying the Sails was bought by Tate Gallery in 1921, his first public recognition. Nicholls exhibited widely in Britain and abroad, having first one-man show at Barbizon House in 1924. Work in many public galleries. Was president of MAFA, 1921–31 and of RBA, 1931–47. Lived at Steyning, Sussex, and died in Worthing.

Howard NICHOLLS 1950– Painter, draughtsman, mixed-media artist and teacher. He studied at Camberwell School of Arts and Crafts, 1972–5, then Royal Academy Schools, 1975–8. Was made a member of RBA in 1983, also showing at RA. Taught at Epsom School of Art, 1979–84. Lived in London.

Lorna NICHOLLS 1889–1953 Portrait painter and miniaturist, born in Twickenham, Middlesex. She studied art at Academia das Bellas Artes, Oporto, Portugal, where the family home then was and remained while she did a fine arts course, under her maiden name Lorna Frances Wiltshire, at Slade School of Fine Art, 1908–10. Studied with Henry Tonks and Philip Wilson Steer and won four certificates in drawing, perspective, fine art anatomy and painting. Exhibited RA, RMS and at Paris Salon and was a member of the Art Society in Exeter, where she settled.

Patricia NICHOLS 1923– Miniaturist and portrait painter who studied at Central School of Arts and Crafts, teachers including William Roberts, John Minton and Ruskin Spear. Was a member of SWA and RMS, being on its council for a time. Showed at RI, Westminster and Mall Galleries and elsewhere and worked to commission. Lived in Old Hunstanton, Norfolk.

Alice Hogarth NICHOLSON fl. c.late 1890s–1950 Figure and landscape painter in oil and pastel, born in Manchester where she studied at the School of Art and Atelier Colarossi, Paris, 1900–01. She showed RA, SWA, RSA in the provinces and America. Gray Art Gallery and Museum in West Hartlepool bought her picture Idleness. Lived at Hindhead, Surrey.

Anne NICHOLSON 1956– Sculptor, notable for carved work, born in London, who studied at Camberwell School of Arts and Crafts, 1974–9, then did Slade School of Fine Art postgraduate studies, 1980–2. She worked for periods in quarries in Carrara, Italy, and at Purbeck, Dorset. Took part in mixed shows including Digswell Art Gallery in Welwyn Garden City and London Sculpture Exhibition. Her abstract work Pend, in Portland stone, 1983–4, is on London's South Bank near the National Film Theatre.

Ben NICHOLSON 1894–1982 Painter, draughtsman, printmaker and artist in low relief, of abstract persuasion but often using still life and landscape motifs. He was born in Denham, Buckinghamshire, son of the painter William Nicholson; his first wife was the painter Winifred Nicholson, his second the sculptor Barbara Hepworth; the artists Kate, Simon and Rachel Nicholson were his children. Studied at Slade School of Fine Art, 1910–11, then travelled in Europe in 1911–14; further travels, partly because of his health, took him to Madeira, America, Italy and France. First one-man show at Adelphi Gallery, 1922. Seven and Five Society member. First visit to Cornwall with Christopher Wood, where they discovered the painter Alfred Wallis, 1928. This was a key influence on his work, as were meetings in Paris with Arp, Brancusi, Picasso, Miró and Mondrian in the early 1930s. In 1933 he joined Abstraction-Création and made his first reliefs. Co-editor of *Circle* in 1937. From 1939–58 lived in St Ives, Cornwall, being a founder-member of Penwith Society of Arts. In the 1950s began to consolidate his international reputation, exhibiting widely abroad, winning a number of prizes and having a series of retrospective exhibitions. Order of Merit, 1968. Lived in Switzerland for many years from 1958, but returned to England in the early 1970s, dying in London. Nicholson's pictures and reliefs are distinguished by their deceptive simplicity and meticulous employment of colour and shape. Tate Gallery, which holds his work, gave Nicholson a major retrospective in 1993–4.

Charles Herbert NICHOLSON 1900–1960 Marine artist, mainly in watercolour, born in Blyth, Northumberland. During a career at sea he taught himself to draw and paint, exhibiting at the Laing Art Gallery and Museum, Newcastle upon Tyne, RA, RSA and RSMA, his work also being reproduced on calendars. Member of the Newcastle Society of Artists. Lived at North Shields, Northumberland.

E Q NICHOLSON 1908–1992 Designer, printmaker and painter, born Elsie Queen Myers in London, where she died. She was the daughter of the writer L H Myers and wife of the architect Kit Nicholson, son of the painter William Nicholson, whose work she assisted. She grew up in artistic circles, studied for a year in Paris concentrating on Batik, and then practised it and designed rugs and wallpapers. Nicholson worked with Marion Dorn, E McKnight Kauffer and Cole & Son. In the 1940s and 1950s she made fabric designs for Edinburgh Weavers. Nicholson's designs were elegant and witty. She was interested in the natural motion of bird and animal life and plant forms. Her painting career lasted 15 years from 1941 and she had one solo show at Hanover Gallery, in 1950. Tate Gallery holds her Still Life with Mirror, of 1949, which shows the influence of Braque, who was revered by her.

Greer NICHOLSON fl. c.1915–1960 Painter who studied at Cambridge University and South Kensington Schools. Exhibited RA, Walker Art Gallery, Liverpool, RCamA, of which was a member, and extensively in provinces. Member of Liver Sketching Club, and lived at Great Crosby, near Liverpool. Work bought for Liverpool permanent collection.

Jim NICHOLSON 1924–1996 Artist and graphic designer, born in Otley, Yorkshire. After Prince Henry's Grammar School there Nicholson succumbed to parental pressure and followed his father into banking, which he loathed, but in 1941 he was conscripted into the Royal Air Force, was commissioned in Bomber Command and took part in the bombing of Dresden. In 1945 he returned to the bank but, after attending evening classes at Leeds, joined a Leeds advertising agency as a graphic artist. Moved to Edinburgh in 1955 to work with McCallum Advertising and after nine years persuaded the National Trust for Scotland that it needed an artist-designer, retiring as art director in 1983, when he began painting full-time. He became noted as a painter of the Scottish landscape, showing in group exhibitions with the National Trust for Scotland, at Haddo House in Aberdeenshire and at English-Speaking Union, Edinburgh. Had solo shows at The Scottish Gallery, Edinburgh, from 1982, and Macaulay Gallery, Stenton, from 1985. His work was in the collections of HM Queen Elizabeth the Queen Mother, Tate Gallery and Imperial Chemical Industries. Died in Edinburgh.

John Hobson NICHOLSON 1911– Self-taught artist and designer, teacher, born in Douglas, Isle of Man. He ran his own art gallery and was on the staff of Douglas School of Art. Designed a number of Manx stamps and banknotes. Nicholson was president of the Isle of Man Art Society, and was made a member of BWS in 1939, UA in 1947, a fellow of the Institute of British Decorators and Interior Designers in 1948, RI in 1951 and PS in 1975. Manx Museum and Art Gallery and public galleries in Blackpool and Wolverhampton hold examples. Lived latterly in Port Erin, Isle of Man.

Kate NICHOLSON 1927– Artist and designer, born in London, who trained at the Royal College of Art as a textile designer. For many years she worked for the textile and wallpaper industries. Her Bead Screen was commissioned by Milton Keynes Development Corporation and was sited in 1979 in Trinity Centre, Fishermead, there. Lived in St Albans, Hertfordshire.

Kate NICHOLSON 1929– Painter, especially of still lifes and flower pieces; teacher. Was born at Bankshead, Brampton, Cumberland, the only daughter of the artists Ben and Winifred Nicholson. She attended Bath Academy of Art, 1949–54, after which she taught for two years at Totnes High School. She had visited Cornwall and in 1956 settled in St Ives. She worked there, at Bankshead and regularly visited Greece. As well as showing with Penwith Society from 1956, Kate Nicholson was included in the Arts Council tour Six Young Painters in 1961 and The Nicholsons, Crane Kalman, 1983. Solo shows included Waddington Galleries, Marjorie Parr Gallery and LYC Museum and Art Gallery, Brampton, 1981. Arts Council holds her work.

Phillida NICHOLSON 1924– Painter and tapestry designer. After private school education in Yorkshire went to Liverpool College of Art, the Academy of Fine Art in Florence and Académie André Lhote in Paris. In 1970s worked for degree in history of art at London University. Nicholson's career included extensive travel and painting in continental Europe, North Africa and the Middle East, including work as an artist with British and American archaeological expeditions. Many group show appearances included Redfern and Piccadilly Galleries, AIA, Leicester Galleries, The Minories in Colchester and WAC, which holds work by the artist.

Rachel NICHOLSON 1934– St Ives, Cornwall-based painter of landscape and still life, daughter of the artists Barbara Hepworth and Ben Nicholson, by whom her work was influenced. Showed in mixed exhibitions at Milton Keynes Exhibition Gallery and Beaux Arts Gallery, Bath, both 1981; and Crane Kalman Gallery, The Nicholsons, 1983. Had a series of solo shows at Montpelier Studio from 1980.

Roger NICHOLSON 1922–1986 Painter, especially in pastel and watercolour, designer and teacher. He was born in Australia but spent most of his life in Kent. Originally lived at Sissinghurst and studied at Rochester Art School and Royal College of Art under Gilbert Spencer, qualifying in 1947. He had seen war service in Africa and Italy. Became a full-time lecturer at St Martin's School of Art for 10 years, then served as professor of textile design at Royal College of Art, 1958–84. Although he was always painting Nicholson, a very shy man who spurned self-promotion, did not show his work; a memorial show was held at the Royal College, which included a large number of Japanese and Spanish views. His work showed a strong sense of design and command of colour. As a designer Nicholson worked on the Festival of Britain in 1951, also for Wallpaper Manufacturers Ltd and the Cotton Board. Completed murals for Caledonian Hotel, Edinburgh, British Insurance Association and other clients. National Gallery and Imperial War Museum hold his work.

Simon NICHOLSON 1934– Sculptor who used a large range of mass-produced or found objects to create abstract works; teacher, born in London, one of the triplets of artists Ben Nicholson and Barbara Hepworth. After studying at Royal College of Art sculpture department, 1953–4, Nicholson attended Cambridge University, where he read archaeology and anthropology, 1954–7, followed by a research year. He lived in St Ives, Cornwall, in the early 1960s, then was visiting professor of sculpture at Moore College of Art, Philadelphia, 1964–5; taught at University of California, Berkeley, 1965–71; then joined the staff of the Open University in 1971. One-man shows included McRoberts and Tunnard Gallery, 1964, and York University, 1978. Arts Council holds his work. Lived in Oxford.

Thomas Edward NICHOLSON 1933– Painter and commercial artist, born in Dunfermline, Fife. He studied at the Regional College of Art in Bradford, was a member of Bradford Arts Club and showed in Yorkshire and Lancashire. Lived for a time in Shipley, Yorkshire.

William NICHOLSON 1872–1949 Painter, printmaker and poster and theatre designer, born in Newark-on-Trent, Nottinghamshire. After showing promise at school in Newark, Nicholson attended Herkomer's School in Bushey, 1888–9, where he met the painter James Pryde. Nicholson married Pryde's sister, Mabel, also a painter, their son being the painter Ben Nicholson. Prior to marriage Nicholson studied at Académie Julian, Paris, 1889–90. The next decade was a busy one, with Nicholson and James Pryde designing successful posters under the name J & W Beggarstaff; Nicholson's memorable series of woodcuts, which appeared in such books as Nicholson's *An Alphabet* and W E Henley's *An Almanac of Twelve Sports*; and early in the new century his designing of sets for J M Barrie's *Peter Pan* and other plays; and his becoming a foundation member of the Society of Twelve, 1904. Seven years later he helped to found the NPS. Nicholson had his first one-man show at Paterson Gallery in 1906 and thereafter he travelled and consolidated his reputation as a true little master, in portraits such as Walter Greaves and Diana Low; still life, as in The Lowestoft Bowl and The Gold Jug; his landscapes of the Sussex Downs, Spain and France; and set pieces such as Sports on the Cedric and Armistice Night. Several retrospective shows were held in Nicholson's lifetime, including National Gallery, 1942, six years after he was knighted. Exhibition at Towner Art Gallery, Eastbourne, and tour, 1995–6. Tate Gallery, Manchester City Art Gallery and Fitzwilliam Museum, Cambridge, hold his work. Latterly Nicholson lived with the novelist Marguerite Steen, who published his biography, *William Nicholson*, 1943. Died at Blewbury, Berkshire.

Winifred NICHOLSON 1893–1981 Painter in oil, watercolour, gouache and pencil, especially of flowers and landscapes. Born in Oxford, she attended the Byam Shaw School of Art, then studied art in Paris, Lugano, India and the Hebrides. Participated in extensive mixed exhibitions throughout her life, initially as Winifred Roberts, her maiden name. She married the painter Ben Nicholson in 1920 and had her first one-man show at the Mayor Gallery as Winifred Nicholson in 1925. Was a member of the 7 & 5 Society 1925–35 and the NEAC 1937–43. Was the mother of the painter Kate Nicholson. Contributed to *Circle, International Survey of Constructive Art*, in 1937, designed a "constructive" fabric for Alastair Morton's Edinburgh Weavers in the same year, as Winifred Dacre, and under the same name showed four abstract works in an Exhibition of Constructive Art at the London Gallery. Until late in life she travelled widely, showing pictures of Morocco, Greece, Cornwall and Cumbria. Her later work was concerned with prismatic colour experiments. Exhibited internationally, and her pictures are held by many public galleries including The Tate Gallery, Bristol, Bradford, Adelaide and Melbourne. Lived at Brampton, Cumbria. A major exhibition toured from the Tate in 1987–8.

Graham NICKSON 1946– Painter, draughtsman and teacher, of Lancastrian background. He studied at Camberwell School of Arts and Crafts and Royal College of Art. His winning of the Prix de Rome – one of many prizes and awards – led to membership of the painting faculty of the British School in Rome. In 1976 Nickson moved to America and became Harkness Fellow at Yale and later a Howard Foundation Fellow in Fine Art at Brown University. Was eventually made dean of the New York Studio School. Nickson's work was included in many museum group shows in Europe and America and he had one-man exhibitions ranging from the William Benton Museum of Art, Connecticut, to Hirschl and Adler Modern, New York. His strikingly bold beachscapes with figures were featured in a show at Albemarle Gallery, London, in 1989. Nickson's work is held by many public collections, including Metropolitan Museum of Art, New York, where he lived.

Philip NICOL 1953– Painter and teacher, born in Caerphilly, Glamorganshire, who attended Cardiff Art College, 1972–6. Was lecturer in fine art at South Glamorgan Institute of Higher Education, Cardiff, 1979–82; lectured at Limerick School of Art in Ireland, 1983–4; had a residency at Kunststiftung, Stuttgart, West Germany, 1984; and, based in Cardiff, taught in a range of other art schools. Nicol was elected a member of 56 Group Wales in 1984. Group exhibitions included Prints for Proclamation, Cardiff, 1977; Paint, Presence, Other Stories, Ikon Gallery in Birmingham, 1983; Arts Council British Art Show with tour, 1984; and Mid-Wales Open (second prize), 1989. Had a solo show at Spacex Gallery, Exeter, 1985, later ones including Glynn Vivian Art Gallery, Swansea, 1995. National Museum of Wales in Cardiff and other public collections hold examples.

NICOLE 1960– Painter and draughtsman, full name Nicole Wakefield, born in Manchester. She studied with Garth Edwards at Blackburn College of Art and Design and then with Norman Rowe at Wolverhampton Polytechnic, obtaining an honours degree in fine art. Engaged in youth work, being leader at Bethesda Youth Theatre in Wales where she lived for a time at Bangor, Gwynedd. She was an associate of RCamA, also showing at Tettenhall Gallery in Wolverhampton and elsewhere.

Gordon NICOLL 1888–1959 Painter, born in London. Studied initially in Southampton, then at Hornsey School of Art under Frank Swinstead. During World War II served for several years as a camouflage officer with the Air Ministry. Was a member of the Savage Club and the London Sketch Club. Exhibited RA, RI, in other London galleries and at the Royal Glasgow Institute of the Fine Arts. Lived in Totton, Hampshire.

John NICOLL 1925– Painter, mainly in tempera, draughtsman, printmaker, textile designer and teacher, born in Edinburgh. He studied at Duncan of Jordanstone College of Art in Dundee, under James McIntosh Patrick and Alberto Morrocco, 1947–53, with a travelling scholarship in his final postgraduate year. During that time he also studied with Ian Fleming at Patrick Allan- Fraser School of Art, Hospitalfield, Arbroath. He taught at Camden Institute and Camden Arts Centre, 1965–89; at Camden School of Art, 1989–94; then was tutor in life drawing and painting at Hampstead School of Art. Was a member of Hampstead Artists' Council. Took part in extensive group exhibitions, including RA, LG, SSA, AIA, at Beaux Arts, Leicester, Redfern and Whitechapel Galleries. Showed solo from 1953, later ones including Camden Arts Centre, 1989, Dome in Hampstead, 1990, and Square Gallery, 1992. Nicoll was a figurative artist whose work was included in Hans Schwarz's *Figure Painting*, 1967. Newport Museum and Art Gallery holds a 1949 watercolour by him. Lived in London.

John NICOLSON 1891–1951 Painter, illustrator and printmaker, born in London, son of the artist Alec Nicolson. Studied at St Martin's School of Art. Was a prolific exhibitor, including RSW, RE and RSA especially, Royal Glasgow Institute of the Fine Arts, RA, NEAC and Paris Salon, where he won a silver medal in 1946. Member of the Chelsea Arts Club and lived in Streatham, south London.

Stanislaw NICZEWSKI 1910– Sculptor and designer, one of the group of Polish artists who successfully promoted paper sculpture in Britain in post-war years. Niczewski graduated from the architectural department of Warsaw Institute of Technology. Was a prisoner of war in Grossborn camp where he was active in stage design and producing a newspaper. Arrived in England in 1947, and with the help of the singer Richard Tauber's wife Diana set up Diana Studio in 1948, which served many important industrial clients. Two years later Niczewski established his own studio, whose clients included the British Tourist Board, British Overseas Airways Corporation, Hoover, Dolcis, Mullard and the Ideal Home Exhibition. Nizcewski was noted for the strength of his architectural designs and his search for new materials. In addition to traditional paper sculpture he employed anodised aluminium sculpture and macroetched aluminium. He was included in Polish Paper Sculpture at Polish Cultural Institute, 1995.

Gudrun NIELSEN 1951– Abstract sculptor who studied at Reykjavik College of Crafts, Iceland, 1971–3, graduated at The Icelandic College of Art and Crafts, 1985–9, then studied mural design at Chelsea College of Art and Design, 1990–2. Between 1970–85 she had practical experience as a ceramist and draughtsman in industry. Showed at Kjarvalsstadir Exhibition Hall in Reykjavik, 1989; Sir Norman Foster & Partners Gallery and Design Museum, both 1992; and 1st RWA Open Sculpture Exhibition, 1993. Lived latterly in London.

Paul NIETSCHE 1885–1950 Painter and draughtsman, born in Kiev, Ukraine, of German parents. He had a wandering life, and was said to have studied art in Germany and France before arriving in England in the 1920s, moving on to Belfast, Northern Ireland, which became his base, although he was to travel further, on the continent and in North America. He was interned on the Isle of Man during World War II and on returning to Belfast had several shows at the CEMA gallery, 55a Donegal Place. Ulster Museum holds his self-portrait and other works. Arts Council of Northern Ireland held a retrospective in 1984.

Nell NILE 1948– Artist in chalk pastels and teacher, born Glastonbury, Somerset. Studied art at Somerset College of Art, Taunton, 1965–7 and School of Art, Yeovil, 1968, receiving a South West Arts visual award, 1990. Teaching included school and adult workshops and visits, while undertaking commercial design work and illustrations for Boomerang Publishing and Women's Press. Her own work notably explored myth and storytelling, using intense colours on a large scale to illustrate gods, animal deities and masked figures, described as "colourful and witty, with sinister undercurrents". Her first solo show Some Times with Anubis at Arnolfini, Bristol, in 1988 sold out; she later showed solo in West Country and Rebecca Hossack, 1990. Mixed shows included Saatchi & Saatchi, Rebecca Hossack, municipal galleries in Bristol and Leicester, Innocent Fine Art and One Off Gallery, both in Bristol in 1997, and in USA at Eleanor Jeck Gallery, Tucson, and Stetter Gallery, Phoenix, both in 1992. Lived in Bristol.

Uli NIMPTSCH 1897–1977 Sculptor in bronze, especially of busts and figurative subjects. Born in Berlin, Nimptsch studied at the Applied Art School there, 1915–17, and at the Academy, 1919–26. For most of the 1930s he lived in Rome, latterly being in Paris, then settled in Britain in 1939. He had a first English solo show at Redfern Gallery in 1942, showed at RA from 1957 and was elected RA in 1967. There were a number of public commissions, including a bust of David Lloyd George for the House of Commons, 1962–3. Had several retrospectives, including RA, 1973. Tate Gallery and Arts Council hold his work.

Bernard NINNES 1899–1971 Landscape painter in oil. Born at Reigate, Surrey, Ninnes studied at the Slade School of Fine Art, 1927–30, under Henry Tonks and Philip Wilson Steer, and in Paris. He exhibited RA, RBA, ROI, NEAC, RWA, provincial galleries and the Paris Salon. Ninnes lived in St Ives, Cornwall, and was a member of the St Ives Society of Artists. In 1951 his painting Cornish Village won a prize in the St Ives Festival of Britain art competition and was reproduced in *Cornish Review*. His work is held by several provincia public galleries, including Hereford, Leamington Spa and Stoke-on-Trent.

Alex NISBET 1952– Artist, born in Lauder, Berwickshire, who studied drawing and painting at Edinburgh College of Art, 1974–8, in the latter year gaining a travelling scholarship to Sri Lanka, with postgraduate studies at the College, 1978–9. In 1982 he became a member of SSA, also showing, in 1983, in Scottish Print Open Three, organised by Dundee Printmakers' Workshop. Edinburgh University and Bank of Scotland hold examples.

Eileen NISBET fl. from mid-1960s–1990 Sculptor and teacher, born in London, who studied at Central School of Art and Design, 1960–5, then began her workshop. Taught part-time at Central School and Harrow Art School. Exhibitions included Midland Group, Nottingham, 1977; Graham Gallery, New York, 1978; and Clay Sculpture, Yorkshire Sculpture Park, 1980.

Noel Laura NISBET 1887–1956 Painter and illustrator, whose work is often of a highly decorative type, born at Harrow, Middlesex. Father was the painter and writer Hume Nisbet, and she married the artist Harry Bush. Nisbet studied at Royal College of Art, where she won three gold medals and the Princess of Wales' Scholarship, established in 1863 to reward the most distinguished female art student in the United Kingdom and what is now the Republic of Ireland. She exhibited RA, RI extensively, ROI, Walker Art Gallery, Liverpool, in the provinces and abroad. Newport Museum and Art Gallery holds her work. She also illustrated a number of books, including several of Russian fairy tales. Lived in London.

Grizel NIVEN 1906– Versatile artist, working in a variety of materials, abstract and figurative styles, born in London. Miss Niven discovered a talent for woodcarving at school and, after studying at the Royal Academy of Dramatic Art and a short time on the stage, in the mid-1930s attended Chelsea School of Art under Henry Moore, whose influence was apparent in some of her abstract figures. Black-and-white paintings and drawings (entitled Catoptrics, her description of reflected light); three-dimensional wall hangings, made of fibreglass, called fissures; spray paintings; and experimental metal shapes set on bases of Perspex and hardboard were features of her work. Niven was the only British entry to reach the final five in the international competition for the Dachau Memorial, and she was one of the 20 finalists in The Unknown Political Prisoner competition, in 1953, won by Reg Butler. Group shows included RA, Paris Salon, the Hanover, Goupil and Redfern Galleries and elsewhere abroad. Solo exhibitions included The Place and Edith Grove Gallery, where she had a retrospective in 1996 which included a bust of her brother, the actor David Niven. The Courtauld Institute holds details of Niven's work.

Margaret Graeme NIVEN 1906– Painter, notably of flowers, born in Marlow, Buckinghamshire. She studied at Heatherley's School of Fine Art under Bernard Adams. Was elected a member of NS in 1932, ROI in 1936, also showing at RA, Leicester and Wildenstein Galleries and elsewhere and having a series of solo exhibitions. Bradford City Art Gallery holds her work. Lived in Godalming, Surrey.

Julie NOAD 1955– Painter and illustrator, born in Essex, who moved to Suffolk in 1979. She studied at Camberwell School of Art, 1975–8, and its gentle, considered, painterly style influenced her work. Noad created illustrations and covers for poetry books and magazines, including *Agenda* and *PN Review*. She had a solo exhibition of oils at Chappel Galleries, Chappel, in 1998. Other venues included South London Gallery and a series in Suffolk, among them Westleton Chapel, Aldeburgh Cinema, Yoxford, John Russell and Coach-House Galleries.

Michael NOAKES 1933– Artist in oil and pencil, notable for portraits and landscapes, born in Brighton, Sussex. He was educated at Downside School, gained his national diploma from Reigate School of Art, also attending Royal Academy Schools. He was for a time president of ROI and a member of RP. Also exhibited at RA, NS, Young Contemporaries, Contemporary Portrait Society, Grosvenor and Upper Grosvenor Galleries, New Grafton Gallery and widely abroad. Noakes made a reputation as a painter of most members of the British royal family together with other leading figures from many aspects of national life. Notable collections holding examples are HM The Queen, for the Royal Collection, Windsor; HRH The Prince of Wales, portrait studies of The Queen and HM Queen Elizabeth the Queen Mother and drawings of the Prince of Wales; British Museum; National Portrait Gallery; the House of Commons; and numerous Oxford and Cambridge colleges. In 1968 Noakes published *A Professional Approach to Oil Painting*. Many of his pictures were reproduced as book jackets, in magazines and newspapers. Lived in London.

Eva NOAR fl. c.1905–1960 Miniaturist and painter in oil and watercolour, born in Swinton, Lancashire. Studied privately and at Salford School of Art. Member of MAFA. She exhibited extensively at RMS, of which she was a member, also at RA, Walker Art Gallery, Liverpool, and widely overseas. The art gallery in Toronto, Canada, holds her work. Lived for some years in Manchester, later at Penrhyndeudraeth, Merionethshire.

Dora NOBLE 1920– Portrait sculptor who studied at Regent Street Polytechnic with Howard Bate. She was a member of SPS and showed with SWA; at casino in Knokke, Belgium; Mall Galleries, and elsewhere. Her main works were portrait heads, on commission. Ben-Gurion University, Israel, holds Noble's work. Lived in London.

Guy NOBLE 1959– Painter, born in Kent, where he studied at Medway College of Art, 1976–7, and then in London at Byam Shaw School, 1977–80. He gained a Spanish Government Scholarship in 1981–2, and was a National Portrait Gallery Portrait Award winner in 1981 and in 1984. In 1991 he was the Singer & Friedlander/*Sunday Times* first prize winner. For four years from late 1980s Noble lived in Italy, and shortly after he returned his picture The Suicide was featured in John Moores Exhibition, Liverpool, 1991–2; he had also appeared there in 1985. Other showings included Jablonski Gallery, 1987; Lamont Gallery, 1987–91; and Piazza D'Azeglio, Florence, 1989. Noble said that "The type of painting that interests me most is that which seems to intensify reality." Lived in London.

James NOBLE 1919–1989 Painter and draughtsman, born in Hounslow, Middlesex. His real name was Edgar Holloway and his earlier work was so signed, also E H. He was largely self-taught, although before World War II he attended the Grosvenor School of Modern Art under Iain Macnab, then from 1946–8 Regent Street Polytechnic School of Art under Clifford Hall. Showed at RA, RBA, NS, NP, ROI and Paris Salon. Noble's pictures were regularly exhibited at E Stacy-Marks Ltd in Eastbourne, where he had several solo shows, and at Mandell's Gallery in Norwich, Norfolk, where finally he lived. From the early 1950s Noble was inspired by Dutch Old Master flower paintings. He became noted for his informal rose pictures. The Greeting Card and Calendar Association commissioned him to paint Elizabeth of Glamis roses to be presented to the Queen Mother on her eightieth birthday, a special greetings card being made for sending to her and other ladies who were 80 on the same day.

John Rushton NOBLE 1927– Painter, commercial artist and designer and teacher, born in Gateshead, County Durham, where he eventually taught for some years at the Technical College. Noble studied art at King Edward VII School of Art at the University of Durham in 1944–6, his teachers including Robin Darwin. He did a volume of illustrative material for magazines in the north of England and showed at RBA, RI, in Scotland and America. Lived for many years at Newfield, County Durham.

Melvyn NOBLE 1937–1989 Painter, printmaker, draughtsman and teacher, born in Huddersfield, Yorkshire. From 1953–61 he worked for a display firm specialising in screen printing while attending day release classes at Huddersfield College of Art. Graduated in painting and ceramics from Bath Academy of Art, 1961–4. From 1964–80 taught in Yorkshire and London, in 1968 doing a postgraduate course in printmaking at Leeds College of Art and in 1979 becoming a founder-member of Crescent Arts Workshop. From 1980–3 Noble was exhibition organiser at Scarborough Art Gallery, organising the visual arts festival in the town, 1984–5. In the mid-1980s Noble was a visiting lecturer at the University of Wisconsin and at Museum School, Boston, in America. Noble was an intellectually probing, experimenting artist. He showed widely in group exhibitions in London and Yorkshire and won several awards. His solo shows included Camden Arts Centre, 1975; a retrospective at Scarborough Art Gallery and Crescent Arts Workshop in 1990; and another at Huddersfield Art Gallery, 1991.

Tim NOBLE 1966– Artist using video, who gained a fine art degree at Nottingham Polytechnic, 1986–9, and his master's degree in sculpture from Royal College of Art, 1992–4. Exhibitions included Fête Worse than Death, Hoxton Square, 1994, the year Noble won a Royal College of Art commission, Absolut Art; Ideal Standard Summertime, and Postscript, both Lisson Gallery in 1995; and New Contemporaries at Tate Gallery in Liverpool and Camden Arts Centre, 1996.

Camilla NOCK 1944– Painter and teacher, born in Gloucester, who trained at Cheltenham College of Art, with postgraduate studies at Goldsmiths' College. For some years she combined teaching at Salisbury, Southend and Bristol University with a career as a figurative painter, from the early-1990s producing a series of more austere pictures. These linked her spiritual development from early days of convent education to a later exploration of religious philosophies and traditions. Exhibitions included Three Women Painters, Eye Gallery, Bristol, 1986; LG, Barbican Centre, Millfield Open (where she won a prize), and Breakthrough at Victoria Art Gallery, Bath, all 1995; and in 1997 Festival of Light in St Ives and Gordon Hepworth Fine Art at 23 Smith Street.

Roy NOCKOLDS 1911–1979 Self-taught aviation and motor racing artist, born in London, who was attracted to motor sport on his first visit to Brooklands in 1924. He contributed to *Motor Sport*, *Autocar* and *Motor*, was noted for his mechanical detail, atmosphere and accurate depiction of each driver's position at the wheel, as in one of his masterpieces, Finesse en Vitesse, Louis Chiron driving a Grand Prix Bugatti. His interest in flying in the 1930s led to a commission to paint the authoritative picture of the Battle of Britain for Royal Air Force Fighter Command. During World War II Nockolds served in the Air Force, developed a revolutionary camouflage for Mosquitos and was a war artist. He was chairman of the Guild of Aviation Artists, 1975, and of The Brooklands Society, 1976. Nockolds also experimented; he produced excellent drypoints, published by *Autocar*, using a school compass and a sheet of copper; a series of abstracts of science and technology for Mullard; sporting prints for Frost & Reed; and specially commissioned portraits of gun dogs. Showed at RA, RP, Guildhall Art Gallery and elsewhere, and there was a memorial exhibition at Qantas Gallery, 1980. Lived near Farnham, Surrey.

Laurence NOGA 1961– Abstract painter, born in London, who attended Wimbledon School of Art, 1980–1, then Byam Shaw School of Art, 1990–1; in 1991 he won the Award of Merit for Painting there. Group shows included Eggison Daniel and Whitworth Young Contemporaries, Manchester, both 1991. Had two solo shows with Grabowski Gallery, 1987–8, then from 1992 a series at Le Chat Noir Gallery, which represented him. It described Noga's pictures as "personal narratives, emotional commentaries on people, places and events … Noga's paintings are organic in their ability to issue a sense of living, breathing matter."

Lucia NOGUEIRA 1950–1998 Creator of constructions in a variety of materials such as steel, gloss paint and iron; the work Black, of 1994, employed 6,000 pieces of chandelier. Studied at Chelsea School of Art, 1976–9, and Central School of Art, 1979–80. Had a residency at Fondation Cartier, Paris, 1993. Group shows included Gulliver's Travels, Galerie Sophie Ungers, Cologne, 1991; Spit in the Ocean, Anthony Reynolds Gallery, 1993; Here and Now, Serpentine Gallery, 1995; and British Art Show 4, and tour, 1995–6. Had a series of solo exhibitions at Anthony Reynolds from 1992, others including Ikon Gallery, Birmingham, 1993, and Camden Arts Centre, 1994.

Sidney NOLAN 1917–1992 Painter, draughtsman, printmaker, book illustrator and theatre designer, born in Melbourne. He studied part-time at Prahran Technical College, Melbourne, 1932–4, then full-time at National Gallery School, 1934–6. After World War II service in Australian Army Nolan worked as a designer and as an illustrator, emerging as a full-time painter in Sydney at the start of the 1950s, after which he moved to Europe to paint. He participated in numerous mixed exhibitions worldwide. First one-man show was in his studio in Melbourne in 1941, since when there have been many globally, in Britain notably at Redfern Gallery, Marlborough Fine Art, Ashmolean Museum in Oxford, Tate Gallery and ICA. Was knighted in 1981, gained Order of Merit, 1983, elected RA, 1991. While in England Nolan visited Australia for special projects, such as the series of pictures connected with the film *Burke and Wills*. In addition travelled widely, including Africa, Greece and Antarctica. A retrospective exhibition of works on paper done over 40 years toured Australia in the early 1980s, a vast retrospective visited state galleries there in 1987–8 and there was a review exhibition from the estate at Agnew, 1997. Nolan has been called a painter's painter, whose work often took the form of a personal diary. He was able to work intensively over short periods and was noted for series of pictures with a single theme, such as the Ned Kelly paintings and drawings, among his most memorable images. Died in London.

Erna NONNENMACHER 1889–1988 Sculptor, born in Berlin, Germany, studying there and in Brunzlau. In 1919 she married the artist Hermann Nonnenmacher. They shared a studio in Berlin-Zehlendorf until 1938, when because Erna was Jewish they had to move to London. Early in World War II they were interned in the Isle of Man. Ben Uri Art Society holds several examples.

Hermann NONNENMACHER 1892–1988 Artist and teacher, born in Coburg, Germany, who studied wood-carving at Dresden's Royal Academy of Arts. After World War I service, which led to hearing damage, Nonnenmacher in 1919 married his wife Erna, a sculptor, worked in porcelain factories and with her shared a studio in Berlin-Zehlendorf. Because she was Jewish they had to leave for London in 1938, being interned for a time in World War II in the Isle of Man. Nonnenmacher taught modelling and pottery at Morley College, 1948–70. He showed widely, including RA, Royal Glasgow Institute of the Fine Arts, Leicester and Berkeley Galleries and with RBS. Solo shows included Geffrye Museum, Heal's Mansard Gallery and King's College, University of London, 1973; in 1986 he was included in Art in Exile in Great Britain 1933–45, at Camden Arts Centre. Carried out many public commissions, including Church of St John, Waterloo Road; Boulton & Paul, Norwich; and works now in Morton College, Oxford. In 1982 Nonnenmacher gained Germany's Federal Cross of Merit. Nonnenmacher's achievement was commemorated in a 20-minute colour film made in 1971 by his nephew, George Powell.

Edward NOOTT 1965– Painter of flowers, still life, landscapes and figure studies. He was educated at Cheltenham Boys' College, then studied art at Nottingham Polytechnic and at the State University of New York, graduating with a degree in fine art, 1988. Spent some time painting in Spain before returning to England. Showed at John Noott Twentieth Century, Broadway, and had flower paintings used by several greetings card publishers.

Gerald NORDEN 1912– Painter, writer and teacher, born in London. He studied at Royal College of Art, gaining his diploma in 1937, notably under Gilbert Spencer. Went on to teach at Sidney Cooper School of Art, Canterbury, 1942–7; was acting principal of Maidstone School of Art, 1947–8; then principal of Dover and Folkestone School of Art, 1948–71. As well as articles in art magazines he wrote *A Practical Guide to Perspective*. Norden was a regular RA exhibitor and had a series of one-man shows at Trafford Gallery, King Street, Newburgh Street and Catto Galleries. He was known for his still lifes in oil, usually small and painted with great precision. Lived in Folkestone, Kent.

Edgar NORFIELD fl. from c.1935–1977 Illustrator and painter, especially of humorous brush drawings, signing himself E N. He studied at Cambridge School of Art, in London and Paris. Showed at RI. Illustrator of children's books, including titles by Lewis Carroll and Paul Gallico. Also drew for various magazines including *Punch*, to which he contributed 75 illustrations between 1937 and 1954. Lived in Lewes, Sussex.

Ernest NORLAND: *see* **Ernst NEUSCHUL**

NORMAN: *see* **Norman Douglas HUTCHINSON**

Anne NORMAN 1937– Painter, born in London, where she continued to work. Influenced by Monticelli, Norman was notable for claustrophobic, uneasy pictures of suburban gardens, as shown in the Norwich School of Art Gallery 1986–7 touring show A Reputation Among Artists. Norman studied Heatherley's School of Fine Art and Académie Julian, Paris, 1953–4; then at Slade School of Fine Art in 1954–8 to painting and drawing she added sculpture and printing. Was included in Serpentine Summer Show 1 in 1982 and mixed exhibitions at Stoppenbach and Delestre and

Brixton Art Gallery in 1984 and 1985 respectively. Had a solo show at Theo Waddington Fine Art in 1996.

Jill NORMAN: *see* **Olga MARSHALL**

John Henry NORMAN 1896–c.1982 Painter in oil, born in Nottingham, who settled in Coventry aged 13. Joined the Army in 1915, served in France and gained the Military Medal in 1917. Norman spent his early years in Coventry at the Rover works as a crankshaft balancer, moved to Standard Motor Company for 20 years and shortly before retirement was a showroom supervisor for Armstrong Whitworth Aircraft. In World War II he worked in an ammunition factory. Attended evening classes under William Henry Milnes at Coventry School of Art, 1919–24. He was a founder of Coventry Art Circle, of which he was chairman for many years; from 1934 was a member of ROI, also exhibiting at RA, Paris Salon, RBA, UA, RBSA and elsewhere in the provinces. Coventry's Herbert Art Gallery & Museum gave him a solo show in 1962. Harry Norman first attracted attention for his romantic landscapes, rooted in the tradition of George Clausen and JMW Turner, but in the middle-1930s he moved towards greater formal abstraction and freedom, devising his Golden Mean charts, a series of geometrically constructed radiations and relationship. He urged fellow-artists to "guarantee your relativities". Herbert Art Gallery holds three works by Norman.

Keith NORMAN 1935– Theatre designer and artist in ink and gouache, born in Beckenham, Kent, where he attended the School of Art; was then at Slade School of Fine Art, studying stage design with the artist Robert Medley. Showed at Roland, Browse and Delbanco and elsewhere. Whitworth Art Gallery in Manchester and Geffrye Museum, London, hold his work. Lived in Kingston upon Thames, Surrey.

Michael NORMAN 1933– Artist-modelmaker who worked in line and watercolour, born in Ipswich, Suffolk, settling in Woolverstone. He studied at Bournemouth School of Art and Regent Street Polytechnic School of Art. Began paintingfull-time in 1970 and was elected to RSMA in 1976. Showed annually at Aldeburgh Festival from 1978 and had over 60 solo exhibitions in East Anglia. Norman's work was featured in several books on marine painting and he said that "John Sell Cotman, Turner, Towne, Ravilious and John Nash have influenced me considerably." Department of the Environment holds his work.

Walter NORMAN 1912–1994 Artist and teacher who trained at Winchester School of Art, Royal College of Art and Goldsmiths' College School of Art. After being principal of Ryland Memorial School, an art school in West Bromwich, in 1949 Norman took over from Richard Ray as principal of Sunderland School, shortly to become College, of Art, eventually taking up a similar post at Liverpool Regional College of Art. Norman exhibited in the north of England and was included in an exhibition connected with the local College at Sunderland Museum and Art Gallery in 1995. It has one oil by him, Wear Tugs, of 1954. A tall, upright figure, Norman was known in Sunderland as The Captain.

Douglas NORRIE 1970– Sculptor and constructions artist, born in Ipswich, Suffolk. He was educated at Dalbeattie High School until 1987; did a portfolio course at Dumfries Technical College, 1990–1; and graduated in sculpture with honours from Gray's School of Art, Aberdeen, 1992–6. Exhibitions included RSA Students' Exhibition at The Mound, Edinburgh, and Gray's Sketch Club Exhibition, Aberdeen Arts Centre, both 1996. Aberdeen Art Gallery acquired Norrie's Untitled Wallpiece, of 1996, a wooden construction with coloured lights of purity and beauty. Norrie lived at Palnackie, By Castle Douglas, Galloway.

Claire NORRINGTON 1969– Artist in charcoal, pen and ink and watercolour, and sculptor in bronze who graduated in fine art from Winchester School of Art, 1991, gaining the Principal's Award. In that year she also won the P & O Ferries National Students' Competition. She was noted for her depictions of birds and animals, captured with a fluid, vigorous line. Carried out many private commissions and showed solo with The Jerram Gallery, Salisbury, 1996.

Arthur NORRIS 1888– Painter and teacher who after attending Lancing College studied at Slade School of Fine Art under Henry Tonks, 1908–10. Went on to become art master at Repton School, Derbyshire. Norris exhibited RA, RP and extensively at Fine Art Society. Member of Chelsea Art Club and the Arts Club. Lived in London.

David NORRIS 1940– Sculptor in bronze, born in São Paulo, Brazil, son of Sir Alfred Norris. He studied at Guildford School of Art and Royal Academy Schools, 1961–4. Elected a fellow of RBS and became its vice-president for a time. Showed at RA, Mall Galleries and elsewhere. Among his commissions was Sir Barnes Wallis, inventor, for the Royal Air Force Museum in Hendon. His Women and Doves was awarded the Sir Otto Beit Medal for the best sculpture of 1981. Norris' Mother and Child, bronze, 1983, is sited at the Great Portland Street Hospital for Women and Children. Lived in Cranleigh, Surrey.

Dom Charles NORRIS 1909– The Reverend Louis Charles Norris entered Buckfast Abbey in 1930 and began work as a stained glass artist with traditional techniques in 1933. His particular study was the work of the twelfth and thirteenth centuries in the cathedrals of Canterbury and Chartres. In 1937–8 he worked under E W Tristram in the design school of the Royal College of Art, specialising in mural painting, fresco, tempera and mosaic. Service as an Army chaplain in World War II enabled him to study classical, Egyptian and Byzantine work in the Middle East and Italy and after the war he extended his range. In addition to windows at Buckfast and at The Friars, Aylesford, he completed dozens of commissions in Roman Catholic and Church of England churches plus some domestic decorations and constructions.

Edith NORRIS fl. from 1940s– Stained glass and mosaic artist, born in Bolton, Lancashire, where she continued to live. She studied with the Manchester-based artist Ernest Hartley and showed at RA, with the Red Rose Guild of which she was a fellow, and widely in Lancashire.

Hector Claude NORRIS 1926– Sculptor in a variety of materials and teacher, born in Bristol, where he settled in Clifton. His father having worked in wood to some extent influenced his career. Studied at West of England Art College in Bristol, his teachers including Paul Feiler, George Sweet and Donald Milner; Norris was there for two periods, 1943–4 and 1947–52, interrupted by the war. Went on to teach at Weston-super-Mare School of Art and showed in his home area.

Norman Norris 1932– Painter, draughtsman and teacher, born in London, who studied at Slade School of Fine Art, 1953–6, Rome Scholar, 1956–8. Norris' teaching included West of England College of Art, Bristol; Chelsea School of Art; Cambridge School of Art; and the Slade. In the 1979 Hayward Annual exhibition Norris showed portraits in the manner of William Coldstream, head of the Slade when he was there, commenting that his "main consideration is drawing. I think of my painting as coloured lines." Lived in Coggeshall, Essex.

Tom NORRIS 1960–1997 Painter and teacher who obtained a bachelor's degree and higher diploma in painting at Slade School of Fine Art, 1978–84. In 1982 gained the Troughton and Boise Scholarships to travel and paint, working for a time in Italy. From 1989 lectured part-time at Slade. His group appearances included Pick of the Graduate Shows, Christie's, 1983; Burgh House, 1986; Robertson Mort Gallery, Bedford, 1987; Whitechapel Open, 1989; A New Perspective, Leighton House, 1990; The Prose of Painting, Austin/Desmond Fine Art, 1991; and RA Summer Exhibition, 1992. Lived in London.

John NORRIS WOOD 1930– Artist in a variety of media, naturalist and teacher, born in London but grew up in Essex. He was educated at Bryanston School, where the collector Charles Handley-Read taught and was a great influence. He attended Goldsmiths' College School of Art, East Anglian School of Painting and Royal College of Art, winning a silver medal for zoological drawing, teachers including Edward Bawden, Sam Rabin, Betty Swanwick, Adrian Ryan, Cedric Morris and Lett Haines. He became a freelance illustrator, working for publishers in Britain and America, including BBC, Hamlyn, Collins, *Reader's Digest* and Golden Books. Designed a series of bird stamps for the Post Office, as well as working for London Zoo and Natural History Museum.Went on many natural history expeditions throughout the world and ran his own small nature reserve, living in Wadhurst, Sussex. Became a senior tutor at Royal College of Art, responsible for department of natural history illustration and ecological studies, and started the Environmental Group with Professor Christopher Cornford. He was also consultant for David Attenborough's television series *Life on Earth*. Norris Wood said that "almost all my work reflects my passion for the natural world and directly or indirectly its conservation." He showed at Victoria & Albert Museum, RA Summer Exhibitions, Natural History Museum, Fine Art Society and abroad. Fry Art Gallery in Saffron Walden holds his work.

Kitty NORTH 1963– Painter and teacher, born in Lancashire, who studied at Chelsea School of Art, 1980–1; gained a fine art honours degree from Brighton University, 1982–5; and her master's degree with honours at Manchester University, 1986–7. She worked in Indonesia, Thailand, Burma, Malaysia, Hong Kong and China; taught at Victoria College of Arts and Geta South School, Victoria, Australia, 1988–9, then variously after that. North's work was both figurative and impastoed landscape-cum-abstract. Mixed shows included Manchester City Art Gallery, 1985; Alvin Gallery, Hong Kong, 1987; Christopher Hull Gallery, 1994; and Cross Currents, Reed's Wharf Gallery at Barbican Centre, 1996. Solo exhibitions included Naive Gallery, Melbourne, 1988; Cadogan Contemporary, 1992; Rebecca Hossack Fitzrovia, 1994. Many private collections hold examples.

Suzanne NORTH fl. from early 1990s– Sculptor who was inspired to carve her own works as a result of seeing an exhibition by Zimbabwean sculptors at Yorkshire Sculpture Park. Self-employed, she worked part-time for Narey Art Stone, Halifax, carving architectural pieces from which silicon moulds were made for dry-casting stone, doing her own work at a studio in Dean Clough Industrial Park. Serpentine, slate and limestone were especially favoured and Barbara Hepworth, Ben Nicholson, Alfred Wallis and David Hockney were among artists admired. Was a member of Yorkshire Sculptors Group, mixed exhibitions including Portland Gallery, 1993; Tenants' Auction Centre, Leyburn, 1994; and The Gallery, Manchester, 1995. Had a first solo exhibition at Design Innovation Centre, Leeds, 1992. Lived in Huddersfield, Yorkshire.

Jack Ludlow NORTHEAST 1909–1968 Painter and illustrator, born in Leytonstone, East London, he attended King Alfred's College, Winchester, 1928–30. Also studied art at Winchester School of Art and the Southern College of Art, Southampton. He began teaching and in 1940 became art master at Peter Symond's School, Winchester, not far from where he lived at Crawley. During World War II was commissioned in the Royal Air Force, serving mainly in the Middle East. A keen sportsman and painter of the countryside. Exhibited RBA, Bladon Gallery at Hurstbourne Tarrant, at Winchester Art Club and had a one-man show at King Alfred's College. Wrote and illustrated *With an Artist in Winchester*.

Maureen Joan NORTON 1928– Painter who sometimes worked on ivorine, born and lived in Norwich, Norfolk. She was an associate of UA and RSM and a member of SM and had several solo shows at Ancient House in Holkham.

Paul NORTON 1946– Painter, born in Bournemouth, Hampshire, who was an engineering craft apprentice, 1962–7; then attended Trent Polytechnic, Nottingham, graduating as a teacher, 1975–8; and Croydon College school of art and design, 1978–9. He was a prizewinner at Amateur International Exhibition, 1973; showed at RA Summer Exhibition from 1974; with ROI, 1978; and Wapping Artists Open Studios from 1982. Lived for a time in London.

Peter NORTON 1913–1995 Artist, teacher, writer and naval officer, notable for his landscapes in pastel of England and France. Norton was influenced by the Impressionists, Cézanne and his friend Paul Maze. He was educated at Winchester College and studied under R M Y Gleadowe, then Slade Professor of Fine Art. After serving as a deckhand on commercial sailing craft Norton joined the Royal Navy in 1931, achieving the rank of captain. He saw action in the battle for Crete in 1941, for which he was decorated. While stationed in Alexandria Norton met and married Olive Deacon, a soloist with the Ballet Russe de Monte Carlo and a former principal ballerina with Sadler's Wells. Norton became a knowledgeable balletomane, painting a portrait of his friend Dame Margot Fonteyn. While based at Simonstown, South Africa, after World War II Norton and his wife ran the local ballet company, for which he designed set and costumes. In 1958 Norton chose to leave the Navy and until 1968 taught painting and history of art at Guildford School of Art, being dismissed with 40 members of the faculty when they sided with students seeking more say in the syllabus. The Nortons restored a dilapidated farmhouse at Cubertou in the Lot region of southwest France and for over 25 years ran a summer painting centre noted for its relaxed atmosphere. Norton had many exhibitions in London, South Africa and the Middle East. Among his books were *The End of the Voyage*, about sailing craft, and *The Special Train*, for children. For many years his wife ran an infant school at their home in Sussex, at Compton.

Ann Louise NOSWORTHY 1929– Artist in oil, gouache, oil pastels and charcoal, born in Stonehaven, Kincardineshire. She studied at Harrogate Art School, 1948–52, gaining her national diploma in design, specialising in book illustration; then Leeds College of Art, obtaining her teacher's diploma in 1953. Nosworthy was concerned with "the nature of reality" in her work, which was exhibited at Yorkshire Artists for several years. She also had solo shows at Castle de Vide in Portugal and in Redcar and Northallerton, Yorkshire. Street of the Jews, Portugal; Whitby Harbour; Square of Philip V, Portugal; Large Green Still Life; and Market Scene, Helmsley, were among her main works. Lived at Lealholm, Whitby, Yorkshire.

Richard NOTT 1963– Painter producing abstract work in mixed media, as in the show Common Ground shared in 1998 with Sax Impey at The Book Gallery, St Ives. Nott was born in the county at St Eval. Obtained a first-class honours degree in fine art at Lancashire Polytechnic, 1982–5; was assistant to the sculptor Andy Goldsworthy, 1985; gallery assistant, Royal Academy, 1986–7; gained his fine arts master's degree, Reading University, 1987–9; and in 1991–2 was assistant at Oldham Art Gallery, running schools workshops. In 1994, won a Visual Arts and Photography Award from South West Arts and was made an associate member of Newlyn Society of Artists. Mixed shows included Tom Thumb Gallery, 1991; Rainy Day Gallery, Penzance, 1994; and Inaugural Open Exhibition John Jones Gallery, 1995.

Krysia NOWAK 1948– Painter and designer, working in mixed media, full name Krysia Danuta Michna-Nowak. She was born in Halesworth, Suffolk. Studied at Ealing College and Garnett College, her teachers including Marian Bohusz-Szyszko and Marek Zulawksi. From 1975–87 was art education officer for Sheffield City Art Galleries; from 1987–8 was exhibitions organiser for Salama-Caro Gallery in London; in 1989–90 was company secretary of Hertfordshire firm Sportorama; then in 1991 became a design consultant and interior designer. The artist said that "Polish history, especially human suffering and isolation, has influenced my work," which is held by a number of collections including Worksop Town Hall and Gray's College, Durham. In 1987 won second prize from Dulux in a national competition for mural designs at Royal Hallamshire Hospital, Sheffield. Solo shows included Drian Galleries, Waterloo Gallery in Stoke-on-Trent, Crucible Theatre in Sheffield, and Sheffield University Gallery. Lived in Worksop, Nottinghamshire.

Margot NOYES 1939– Figurative artist, mainly in oil, teacher, born in London, married 1960–84 to the artist Leo Austin. She studied at Camberwell School of Art, 1956–60, teachers including Robert Medley, Anthony Eyton, Patrick Symons and Henry Inlander. Her teaching included adult classes, Lowestoft and Ipswich Schools of Art and a special school. Had many mixed show appearances including The Suffolk Group, of which she was a founder-member in 1990, RA Summer Exhibitions, Piccadilly Gallery and New Art Centre. Solo shows included a series at Southwold and Halesworth Galleries. Noyes painted many pictures for films and television productions, including *A Month in the Country*, 1986; *A Hazard of Hearts*, 1987; *Kremlin Farewell*, 1989; and *Forever Green*, from 1990. Lived in Halesworth, Suffolk.

Basil NUBEL 1923–1981 Landscape painter in oil and watercolour. Born in Great Yarmouth, Norfolk, Nubel studied art at Leeds College of Art under Alfred Daniels and Maurice de Sausmarez, then at the Royal College of Art under Carel Weight, Robert Buhler and Rodrigo Moynihan. Mixed exhibitions included RA and RBA. Nubel had a number of one-man shows, including the Woodstock Gallery, Gallery Petit and Argonaut Gallery. He was one of Jack Beddington's *Young Artists of Promise*, in the 1957 book of that title. Leeds Education Committee holds his work, which is in many private collections. Lived in London.

Harold NUTTALL 1896– Watercolourist and caricaturist, born in Oldham, Lancashire, who was educated at the local Municipal Secondary School. He was a member of BWS, also showing at Mansfield Art Gallery and with RBA. Lived in Hartford, Cheshire.

Richard NUTTALL 1941– Abstract painter, born in Wallasey, Cheshire, who attended the local Art School, 1955–6, and Liverpool

College of Art, 1962–3. He studied again at Wirral Metropolitan College, 1987–9, Liverpool University, 1989–90, and Liverpool John Moores University, 1990–3. He was included in group exhibitions at Liverpool University, Morley Gallery and Hanover Gallery in Liverpool and participated in the John Moores Exhibition there, 1995–6. Had a solo show at Birkenhead Priory in 1993. Lived at Heswall, Wirral.

Ralph NUTTALL-SMITH 1898–1988 Sculptor, painter, draughtsman and teacher, born in Abbeyleix, Ireland, married to the illustrator Peggy Fortnum. After education in South Africa and England Nuttall-Smith took an honours degree in chemistry at Oxford; taught, worked in America at many jobs, including milk roundsman and chemistry teacher at Yale; was a gasworks chemist in Montreal, Canada, while studing at the École des Beaux-Arts; then returned to England, working at the School of Rural Economy and studying at the Ruskin School in Oxford with Sydney Carline. Next he attended the Central School of Arts and Crafts with Bernard Meninsky; studied painting for a year at Slade School of Fine Art, teachers including Henry Tonks; learned sculpting for 18 months with Alfons Magg, in Switzerland, further studying in Paris for four years with Charles Despiau; then returned to London where he became secretary of the Euston Road School. In World War II in Oxford he held the same post with the Slade, teaching there 1941–65. He also taught at Camberwell School of Arts and Crafts and in retirement, spent in West Mersea, Essex, at Colchester Art School. Showed with RA, LG, Salon des Tuileries in Paris and elsewhere and in 1970 had a retrospective at The Minories, Colchester, which holds his work.

Henning NYBERG 1903–1964 Painter, of Swedish origin, who lived in Canada for a while. He studied art at the Byam Shaw School and Royal Academy Schools, then became an apprentice at Alec Johnston's Scenic Paint Room, where he met Charles Ricketts, the artist, whose companion he became. Also acted as Ricketts' studio assistant and went on two trips to Italy with him. After Ricketts' death Nyberg married and lived in Uckfield, Sussex. He exhibited abstract watercolours and drawings there and elsewhere.

O

Brenda OAKES 1947– Sculptor, collagist and administrator who did an Open University foundation course, 1972–3, a foundation course at Wrexham College of Art, 1978–9, an honours degree in fine art at Manchester Polytechnic, 1979–82, then gained her master's degree part-time at Newcastle Polytechnic, 1984–5. Went on to work as an assistant arts and exhibitions officer in Wrexham. Oakes said of her work that "I often need to have it explained to me. When I start to draw as an investigation, an end in itself, anything can happen." She was a prizewinner in the Wrexham Open in 1984, showed at RIBA in 1986 and was included in Merseyside Artists 3, toured by Walker Art Gallery, Liverpool, in 1986–7. Oakes gained a WAC grant in 1984 and had a solo show at The Brick Studio, Manchester, 1984–5.

Alfred James OAKLEY 1878–1959 Sculptor and teacher, born into a woodworking environment in High Wycombe, Buckinghamshire. Studied in the provinces and at City and Guilds of London Art School, 1903–8 and 1910. He later taught in several London schools. Showed at RA, RSA and in the provinces. Was elected a fellow of RBS in 1938, from which he retired in 1952. Tate Gallery holds his pearwood sculpture Mamua. Oakley lived for some years in the famous Mall Studios, Hampstead, but left in 1941 to become a monk, and most of his later work is for churches. Finally lived in Newbury, Berkshire.

Ann OAKLEY 1929– Artist in a wide range of media, born in London, who eventually settled in Chediston, Halesworth, Suffolk. Originally she attended Morley College evening classes on the history of art; in the 1970s sculpted at Inner London Education Authority adult groups in Greenwich and worked with Gerda Rubinstein's open studio group; in the mid-1980s pursued printmaking, sculpture, painting and life drawing at Audrey Pilkington's Clock House Studios, Bruisyard; and in the 1990s concentrated on oils and prints, with some collage. As well as being a member of Clock House Art Association, was also with Suffolk Open Studios. Exhibitions included Woodlands Art Gallery and South London Art Gallery, both 1977; St Julians, Sevenoaks, 1980; Halesworth Gallery, Halesworth, and Snape Maltings, Snape, both 1991; Maddermarket Theatre Gallery, Norwich, 1993; and Strand Gallery, Aldeburgh, 1997. In 1992 Oakley was artist-in-residence for sculpture workshops at Gwyn Jones Primary School, Leytonstone, the year Stowupland School bought an etching of hers from Amnesty International Art Exhibition. Oakley often worked in series from representation towards abstraction.

Charles OAKLEY 1925– Painter and teacher, born in Manchester, whose work had a Surrealist tinge. He was interested in ruins and derelict machinery. Oakley attended Queen's University, Belfast, 1943–4, then Slade School of Fine Art, 1948–52, in 1951 winning the Wilson Steer Medal, the year after he was at the British School in Florence. After teaching in Cumberland he was senior lecturer in painting at Ulster College of Art and Design, 1962–74, then joined staff of Newcastle upon Tyne Polytechnic. Exhibitions included Crane Gallery in Manchester, Carlisle Art Gallery, Tom Caldwell Galleries in Dublin and Belfast and University Theatre, Newcastle. Brighton and Carlisle Art Galleries and Arts Council of Northern Ireland hold examples.

Peter OAKLEY 1935– Artist, notably a printmaker, and teacher whose work led him "to explore those areas of the urban environment which have fallen into disuse and where discarded articles of human use have been abandoned." An example was his collograph print Wasteland Victim in Merseyside Artists 3, toured by Walker Art Gallery, Liverpool, in 1986–7. Oakley studied at Stafford College of Art, 1952–6, then Leicester College of Art, 1958–9. Went on to teach at Edge Hill College of Higher Education, Ormskirk. Other appearances included Atkinson Art Gallery, Southport, 1984, Lancashire Open at Harris Art Gallery in Preston, 1985, and Hanover Galleries, Liverpool, 1986. Was for a time president of MAFA and lived in Southport, Merseyside.

Barbara A OATEN 1899–1966 Painter of miniatures, born and lived in London. She was educated at Queen's College, Harley Street, 1908–17. Exhibited RMS, RI and SWA, signing her work B A O.

Bennett OATES 1928– Painter in oil, especially of flowers, born in London, who studied at Wimbledon School of Art, 1943–6, with Gerald Cooper, then at Royal College of Art, 1948–51, with Ruskin Spear and Carel Weight. Was a member of Guild of Norwich Painters and showed elsewhere widely, notably E Stacy-Marks Ltd. Later work included Impressionist landscapes. Lived at Little Plumstead, Norwich, Norfolk.

Christine Tate OATES 1913– Painter, illustrator and teacher, born in Bradford, Yorkshire. She attended the Regional College of Art there, 1930–5, then Royal College of Art, 1935–9. Began teaching at Ely High School, taught in Lancaster, then was at Truro High School, 1945–70. Wrote and illustrated *Truro City Trail*, 1983, and illustrated a number of other publications on the Cornish city, where she lived. Victoria & Albert Museum holds examples.

Damian O'BRIEN 1969– Painter who was educated at John Fisher School, Trent Polytechnic and Middlesex University, from which he graduated with first-class honours, obtaining a master's degree with distinction at Royal College of Art. From 1991 O'Brien exhibited in mixed shows, including the Henry Moore Gallery, solo exhibitions including Michael Parkin Gallery and Jorn Langberg, Langham Fine Art. Stimulating colour was a feature of his work, which included commercial textile designs.

Kevin O'BRIEN 1956– Painter, draughtsman and teacher who studied at North Staffordshire Polytechnic, 1974–7, and Royal College of Art, 1978–81. During 1983–4 he was artist-in-residence at the National Gallery, at which time he was praised for figurative allegories. Then he decided to withdraw from exhibiting for a while, during which time he developed his own iconographic language as seen in his solo show of Spanish Chapel Pictures at Art Space Gallery, 1994. He had begun showing solo at New Art Centre, 1983. Group exhibitions included Consort Gallery, 1981; Castlefield Gallery, Manchester, 1987; and Albertina Museum, Vienna, 1993. O'Brien became senior lecturer in painting at Leeds Metropolitan University.

Robert O'BRIEN 1939– Painter in oil, born in Southampton, Hampshire. He studied at Central School of Art and Design, gaining his diploma in 1961. Lived in Greece for two years. Showed in London and the provinces in group exhibitions and had one-man shows at Benet Gallery, Cambridge, and at Grabowski Gallery, London. Lived in London.

Breon O'CASEY 1928– Painter, jeweller and relief construction maker, born in London, son of the Irish dramatist Sean O'Casey. In 1939 the family moved to Devon, where Breon attended Dartington Hall School and was taught metalwork by the ex-Bauhaus teacher Naum Slutski. After studying three years at the Anglo-French Art Centre, O'Casey moved to St Ives, becoming assistant to the sculptor Denis Mitchell, then Barbara Hepworth. Mixed shows included the RWA's Artists from Cornwall, 1992; Shining Through, Crafts Council, 1995; and Gordon Hepworth Fine Art, Newton St Cyres, 1997. Had many solo exhibitions, including Victoria & Albert Museum Craft Shop, 1985; The Oxford Gallery, Oxford, from 1985; Taylor Galleries, Dublin, 1988; and Collier/Campbell, 1990. Arts Council; Kettle's Yard, Cambridge; Plymouth Museum and Art Gallery; Trinity College, Dublin; and Victoria & Albert Museum hold examples.

Humphrey OCEAN 1951– Painter and teacher who studied at Tunbridge Wells School of Art, 1967–9, Brighton College of Art, 1969–70, and Canterbury College of Art, 1970–3. In 1976 Ocean was artist-in-residence on an American tour with the singer Paul McCartney. In 1979 he obtained a commission for the Artistic Records Committee of the Imperial War Museum. From 1978 showed at RA Summer Exhibition. Other exhibitions included Whitechapel Open Exhibition at Whitechapel Art Gallery, from 1980; Imperial Tobacco Portrait Award at National Portrait Gallery from 1980, Ocean being a winner in 1982. In that year he wrote, illustrated and published *The Ocean View*. In 1983 Ocean was included in the Woodlands Art Gallery show British Artists at Cyprus College of Art and in 1986–7 his selection of work from the collections of Ferens Art Gallery, Hull, toured from that gallery with a group of Ocean's own drawings and paintings. National Portrait Gallery holds Ocean's portrait of the poet Philip Larkin. Ocean taught at Oxford Polytechnic, 1974–6, and part-time from 1979 at Oxford Polytechnic, Canterbury College of Art, City & Guilds of London Art School and Cyprus College of Art. Lived in London.

Kathleen OCKENDON 1913– Watercolourist, illuminator, calligrapher and teacher, born in London. Studied at Ealing School of Art, 1931–4, where her teachers included the watercolourist Thomas Lightfoot, then at Hornsey School of Art. She went on to hold several teaching posts, being at Ealing School of Art and Ealing Technical College in all for over 30 years. Published practical books on calligraphy and modelmaking. She exhibited RA, NEAC, UA, Heal's Mansard Gallery and elsewhere. Lived in Northolt, Middlesex.

Deirdre O'CONNELL 1956– Artist and teacher, born in London, who taught widely in British and Irish art colleges. She received a first-class honours degree from North Staffordshire Polytechnic in Stoke-on-Trent in 1978, gaining her master's in fine art from University of Ulster, Belfast, in 1980. In 1991 O'Connell won the Studio Scholarship for the PSI Studio Residency in New York. She was a regular contributor to *Circa* and on its editorial panel. She showed at the Irish Exhibition of Living Art, Guinness Hop Store, Dublin, 1985; The Fifth Province, Edmonton Art Gallery and Canadian tour, 1991–3; and in 1994 in Beyond the Partitions, organised by Queen Street Studios, Belfast, with which she was associated. Had a series of solo shows in Northern Ireland, including Arts Council Gallery, Belfast, 1990.

Eilis O'CONNELL 1953– Sculptor, born in Londonderry, Northern Ireland. Attended Crawford School of Art, Cork, 1970–4; Massachusetts College of Art, Boston, 1974–5; then Crawford School, 1975–7. In 1991 obtained commissions for Cardiff Bay Art Trust at Gateway, Cardiff, and Phoenix Park, Dublin. Was included in William Jackson Gallery show Sculpture & Sculptors' Drawings in 1991. Later solo shows included Riverrun Gallery, Limerick, 1988–9, and Artsite Gallery, Bath, 1990. Lived in London.

John O'CONNELL 1935– Landscape painter and teacher, born in Londonderry, studying at St Mary's College, Belfast, 1953–7. He went on to teach at Our Lady and St Patrick's College, Knock, Belfast. Showed from 1975 with RUA and from 1983 with RHA. Had a one-man show with Keys Gallery, Londonderry, 1981; other solo exhibitions included Narrow Water Gallery, Warrenpoint, 1989, and Eakin Gallery, Belfast, 1990, and in 1992 shared a show at Mistral Galleries. Work is held in many private collections throughout the world.

Michael O'CONNELL 1898–1976 Mural, collage and Batik artist and teacher, noted for innovative design and use of colour. He was born in Dalton, Lancashire, of Irish parents. After uncompleted studies to be a priest at Ushaw Hall, Durham, and service in an Irish regiment during World War I, when he was taken prisoner, O'Connell farmed, then in 1920 emigrated to Australia. There he built a house at Port Phillip Bay, became involved in the arts and crafts movement in Melbourne, set up a business to make concrete pots, garden ornaments and church fonts and held exhibitions of his paintings. Around 1930 O'Connell married Ella Moody and they settled in Perry Green, Much Hadham, Hertfordshire, where he built another house, The Chase, in 1936. As textile designer O'Connell was interested in primitive African, Australian and Pacific area art which influenced designs made for Heal's store and displayed in businesses, canteens, public buildings, theatres and churches around Britain. O'Connell developed drawing techniques using paste resists which lent a special freedom to his work. Was a member of the Society of Industrial Artists. Among venues where he showed were the 1937 Paris Exhibition; Australian Artists' Association, 1953; Beaux Arts Gallery, 1953, and abroad. O'Connell's work is held by Victoria & Albert Museum and University of Reading (its Rural History Centre has his huge hanging for the Country Pavilion at the 1951 Festival of Britain). He completed murals for the Technical College at Corby New Town and the new St Martin's Church, Baguley Hall, Wythenshawe. Depressed by failing eyesight, O'Connell committed suicide by shooting himself.

Denis O'CONNOR 1959– Sculptor and teacher, born in Dublin, Ireland, who attended Limerick School of Art and Design and Birmingham Polytechnic. He used a wide range of materials to create works, often with a wide public in mind, sometimes enigmatic, with a strong humorous streak. O'Connor held a large number of residencies, notably in the Midlands, and gained a string of awards which included West Midlands Arts, 1986; East Midlands Arts, 1986; Arts Council of Ireland, 1987; and Nottinghamshire County Council, 1988. Live work included Ikon Gallery, Birmingham, 1983, and Bridges Dance Company, 1987–9. Showed in mixed exhibitions at Ikon Gallery from 1983, others including Castle Museum, Nottingham, 1985; Sculpture at the National Garden Festival, Stoke-on-Trent, 1986; and Loseby Gallery, Leicester, 1987. Solo exhibitions included Herbert Art Gallery, Coventry and Castle Museum, Nottingham, both 1985, and Derby Museum & Art Gallery, with a residency, 1991. Taught extensively from 1983, being a visiting tutor at St Martin's School of Art, 1986–8, and part-time at Derby School of Art and Design, 1988–90. Leicester City Council and Derbyshire County Council hold examples.

Edward Dominic O'CONNOR 1896–1958 Painter and printmaker. O'Connor studied at Leicester College of Art and Leicester School of Architecture. He exhibited RHA, in the provinces and in America. Lived at Desford, Leicestershire.

John O'CONNOR 1913– Painter, printmaker, illustrator, writer and teacher, born in Leicester where he attended the College of Art, 1931–4, then Royal College of Art, 1934–7, where his teachers included Eric Ravilious and John Nash, long a friend. After service in the Royal Air Force, 1941–6, O'Connor continued his teaching career, begun at Birmingham College of Art, 1937, then Bristol College of Art, 1938–41, by becoming principal of Colchester School of Art, 1948–64. Visiting lectureships included St Martin's School of Art, 1964–74. O'Connor's own written and illustrated books included *Canals, Barges and People*, 1950; *Landscape Painting*, 1967; *The Technique of Wood Engraving*, 1971; *Introducing Relief Printing*, 1973; and *A View of Kilvert*, 1981. His illustrated books included some for the Golden Cockerel Press and were notably about the countryside. O'Connor was a member of RWS and was a regular exhibitor at RA. Had many solo shows, including a series at Zwemmer Gallery, 1955–68; New Grafton Gallery from 1970; and Markswood Gallery, Great Bardfield, 1987. He wrote in 1989 that he retained "a search for timelessness in subject matter and in mood of painting with avoidance of material that dates or humanises the picture. Also, I seek unusual weather conditions." Arts Council, Tate Gallery, British Museum and many other public collections hold examples. Lived latterly at Parton, Castle Douglas, Kirkcudbrightshire.

Marcel O'CONNOR 1958– Painter who was born in Lurgan, Northern Ireland. He studied at Brighton Polytechnic and Cyprus College of Art, in Paphos. His works were almost totally abstract, but retained hints of objects; the paint surface was rich and textural. Had his first major solo show in Edinburgh, where he lived, at City Art Centre in 1993.

Martin O'CONNOR 1953– Artist in a range of media who studied at Wigan School of Art, 1970–2, North Staffordshire Polytechnic, 1972–5, and Birmingham Polytechnic, 1976–7. He was included in 6 Young Contemporaries at Bluecoat Gallery and New Work by Merseyside Arts, Liverpool Academy, 1980. Of work included in Merseyside Artists 3, toured by Walker Art Gallery, Liverpool, in 1986–7, O'Connor said that he "formulated and articulated ideas directly onto a surface. Concepts and emotions rise out of the subconscious from a wealth of source material."

Michael O'CONNOR 1944– Sculptor and teacher, notable for big architectural reliefs in multi-layered plywood, born in Seven Kings, Essex. Studied art at Shoreditch College of Education, Egham, 1963–6. Held a number of teaching posts, including Eton College and Carmel College, Wallingford, and was Granada Arts Fellow, York University. That University, Brighton College of Art and the Home Office hold his work. Lived for some time in Wallingford, Oxfordshire.

Patricia O'CONNOR 1971– Painter and draughtsman, born in Hertfordshire, who studied at Kent Institute of Art and Design, 1990–3, then Royal College of Art, 1994–6. She won a John Purcell Drawing Prize, 1993, a Mario Dubsky Travel Fund, 1995. O'Connor said that her work embodied "a world of fantasies by using the images of glossy magazines … comfort, sex and stardom … The people I paint are momentarily caught in ambiguous acts."

Group shows included Recent Works, Natfhe Exhibition Centre, 1992; Concourse Gallery, Barbican Centre, 1995; and Cheltenham Open Drawing Competition, 1996. Had a solo show, Fluff, at Paton Gallery, 1997.

Terry O'CONNOR 1939– Artist and teacher who studied at Gloucestershire College of Art and Design, 1967–70, and the Institute of Education, 1970–1. He taught art and history of art at North Gloucestershire College of Technology. Took part in group exhibitions Shared Experience/Critical Views, at Cheltenham Art Gallery and Cockpit Theatre, 1978, and Figurative Painters at Woodlands Art Gallery, 1980.

Liam O'CONOCOHAIR: *see* **William CONOR**

Sachiko ODASHIMA 1962– Painter whose work included singular and colourful imagery, as in Trouble in Mind, at John Moores Liverpool Exhibition, 1993–4. She was born in Japan and studied at Heatherley's School of Fine Art and at Chelsea College of Art, 1989–93. In 1993 she gained first prize in the Transport Art Exhibition at Mall Galleries, having in 1992 had a solo show at Sadler's Wells. Lived in London.

Henry ODLING 1921– Painter and teacher, born and lived in Sheffield, Yorkshire, where he studied at the College of Arts and Crafts and at Royal College of Art. Exhibited RA, RSA and in the provinces.

Mowbray ODONKOR 1962– Painter and draughtsman, born in London, where she continued to work. She studied at Wimbledon College of Art, 1984–7. Odonkor's articulate drawings were included in the 1991–2 Norwich Gallery travelling show History and Identity. Of her work she said that she wished "by juxtaposing certain images which have symbolic references … to challenge prevailing attitudes and conventions". Other exhibitions in which Odonkor's work appeared included Creation for Liberation open shows in 1985–7 and The Image Employed, at Cornerhouse, Manchester, 1987. Arts Council holds her work.

Hugh O'DONNELL 1950– Painter, artist in ceramics and teacher, born in London, where he worked for much of his life. He attended Camberwell College of Art, 1968–9, Falmouth School of Art, 1969–72, then Birmingham School of Art, 1972–3. Among his awards was First Prize, Sir Whitworth Wallace Trust, Birmingham, 1973, and an Arts Council Award in 1978. After a fellowship at Gloucestershire College of Art, 1973–4, O'Donnell gained a Japanese Government Scholarship to Kyoto University of Arts, 1974–6. From the mid-1970s he taught extensively at colleges and universities in Falmouth, Birmingham, Reading, Bath, Wimbledon, Croydon and Brighton. In 1979 he gained an installation commission for Bognor Regis Arts Centre. As a painter O'Donnell was greatly influenced by what he saw in Japan, other influences being Bulgarian icons, the introduction of wooden frames as an active part of the image, the sea and its light. He took part in mixed shows in Britain and abroad and solo exhibitions included Air Gallery and Ikon Gallery, Birmingham. Arts Council holds his work.

John O'DONNELL 1948– Painter of portraits and landscapes, teacher, born and lived in London. He studied at Camberwell School of Arts and Crafts, 1967–72, Royal Academy Schools, 1972–5, and Middlesex Polytechnic, 1976–7. He gained a number of awards, including Rotary Italian and David Murray Travelling Scholarships. As well as being a visiting teacher at Slade School of Fine Art, O'Donnell taught youth and adult education classes. He had a solo show at National Theatre in 1976. Mixed exhibitions included South London Art Gallery, 1969; RA Summer Exhibition, 1975; Wapping Artists at Crane Wharf, 1981; and Summer Show I at Serpentine Gallery, 1982.

Michael O'DONNELL 1946– Draughtsman, sculptor, designer and teacher, born in Penzance, Cornwall. Attended Bath Academy of Art, Corsham, 1964–7, then taught in Sussex for two years, from 1969–71 designing furniture in London. Eventually joined staff of Falmouth School of Art. St Michael's Mount, stars and the sky were key subjects in the work of O'Donnell, who was included in the 1989 Newlyn Orion Galleries show A Century of Art in Cornwall 1889–1989. Lived in Marazion, Cornwall.

Ron O'DONNELL 1952– Artist noted for his creative photography, born in Stirling. He was a trainee photographer at Stirling University, 1970–6, studying photography at Napier College, Edinburgh, 1970–3. O'Donnell's work was wide-ranging, progressively becoming less illustrative, more allusive. His images reflected his humorous, ironical outlook and Scottish and Catholic upbringing. They included a series of studies of Scottish sculptors, made in 1981 as a documentary commission, and works particular to locations abroad, such as Israel and Canada. As well as building up a body of potential images in a sketchbook, O'Donnell would gather random materials on site to achieve the effect he wanted. Group shows included Masters of Photography, Victoria & Albert Museum, 1986; The Vigorous Imagination, Scottish National Gallery of Modern Art, Edinburgh (installation), 1987; Anima Mundi, Canadian Museum of Contemporary Photography (exhibition and installation), 1989; and New North, Tate Gallery Liverpool, 1990. Solo shows included Stills Gallery, Edinburgh, where he lived, 1985. Arts Council holds his work.

Bernadette O'DONOGHUE 1958– Artist in mixed media, including collage and prints, born in Greenwich, southeast London. She studied at Ravensbourne School of Art, 1978–9, Wolverhampton Polytechnic, 1979–82, then did a one-year part-time extended printmaking course at Camberwell School of Art. Exhibitions included Humberside Printmaking Competition, 1982; a solo show at Woodlands Art Gallery, 1983; and in 1984 Pandora's Box, tour including Rochdale Museum and Art Gallery, organised by Women's Images.

Hughie O'DONOGHUE 1953– Draughtsman and painter whose work tended towards abstraction, born in Manchester. He gained his master's degree at Goldsmiths' College School of Art, 1980–2. Among his awards were the Artist's Award, Lincolnshire and Humberside Arts Association, 1977–8–9; Artist in Industry Fellowship, Yorkshire Arts Association, 1983; and he was artist-in-residence at National Gallery, 1984. Among his group shows were Surfaces, at Posterngate, Hull, 1979; Galleria Carini, Florence, 1986; and John Moores Liverpool Exhibition, 1995–6. Had a solo show at Ferens Art Gallery, Hull, 1979, later shows including Galleria Carini and Woodlands Art Gallery, both 1987. Arts Council, National Gallery and public galleries in Hull and Huddersfield hold his work. Lived in Bromley, Kent.

Eleanor O'DONOVAN 1967– Artist capable of producing singular and slightly disturbing images in a range of media, who completed a course in visual education at Limerick's College of Art in 1987, graduating in fine art from University of Ulster, Belfast, in 1990. In 1991 she was invited to take a residency at Langholm Studios in Ayrshire, the year she was commissioned to create her sculpture Talking North for Liverpool. Took part in many Irish group shows, including That's A Good Question and That's Another Good Question, Harmony Hill Arts Centre, 1989–90; Monaghan Open Exhibition, 1993; and in 1994 Works on Paper and Beyond the Partitions at Queen Street Studios, Belfast, with which she was associated.

Monika OECHSLER 1957– Artist using video installation, born in Munich, West Germany, who gained a fine art degree at Goldsmiths' College, 1987–90, and her master's there, 1994–6. Oechsler won an Arts Council New Technologies Award in 1994, the year she took part in Festival International de Arte Electronica, SESC, São Paulo, Brazil. In 1995 Oechsler took part in and curated Nobby Stiles, Vandy Street, 1995, in 1996 participating in both Pandaemonium at ICA and New Contemporaries at Tate Gallery in Liverpool and Camden Arts Centre.

Adrian OFFICER fl. c.1955–1985 Artist and teacher, born in Belfast, Northern Ireland, full name David Adrian Officer. He studied art at King Edward VII College of Art and Faculty of Fine Art, Durham University, and at Edinburgh University. Officer, who signed his work Adrian and Adrian Officer, exhibited in Britain, France, Australia and Canada. He taught at Harrow School of Art and was later head of the art department at Rhyl Grammar School, in North Wales. He lectured on television in Northern Ireland, Australia and Canada and his publications include *Painting for Pleasure*. Lived in Hessle, Yorkshire.

Chris OFILI 1968– Artist born in Manchester who studied at Tameside College of Technology in Ashton-under-Lyne, 1987–8; Chelsea College of Art, 1988–91; and Royal College of Art, 1991–3. Had a solo exhibition at Kepler Gallery in 1991, followed by travel awards to Berlin and Zimbabwe, where he also exhibited, with a major exhibition at City Art Gallery, Southampton, 1998. Other shows included Tokyo Print Biennale, 1993, where he won second prize; Take Five at Anthony Wilkinson Fine Art, 1994; and in 1995–6 British Art Show at Manchester City Art Gallery and tour and John Moores Liverpool Exhibition. Lived in London, where the Arts Council holds his 1993 series of etchings The Visit.

Geoff OGDEN 1929– Painter, mainly self-taught, born in Ashton-under-Lyne, Manchester. He began painting in the Pennines, where he grew up, but moved to Cornwall in 1965 and then became noted for depictions of its landscape. Ogden favoured a figurative style and completed a number of domestic scenes based on his own home and family. He was included in RWA's Artists from Cornwall, 1992, and had solo exhibitions in London, Newlyn, Exeter, Falmouth and Penzance, as well as showing in the north of England, including Atkinson Art Gallery, Southport, and Liverpool University. Ogden was a member of Newlyn Society of Artists. Work by Ogden is held by Y Tabernacl, Machynlleth, in its permanent collection.

Kirsty OGG 1967– Artist using a variety of media such as embroidery and fine draughtsmanship (see her drawing Kate Moss, New Art in Scotland, Centre for Contemporary Arts, Glasgow, where she was born and lived, 1994). Studied at Edinburgh College of Art, 1986–90. Exhibitions included Contact 552 4813, Transmission Gallery, Glasgow, 1992; Left Luggage, Rencontre dans Couloir, Paris, and tour, 1993; and Difficult Relationships, 99 Gallery, Glasgow, 1994.

Clare M OGILVIE: *see* **Clare M CLIFFORD**

Elizabeth OGILVIE 1946– Draughtsman, especially in pencil in monochrome, who was originally a sculptor and who employed collage and various materials in work of great restraint, sometimes on a huge scale. The sea, Oriental art and the isle of St Kilda were among her inspirations. Born in Aberdeen, Ogilvie studied sculpture at Edinburgh College of Art, 1964–9, with Eric Schilsky, from 1969–70 producing plaster reliefs. Eventually she returned to lecture at her old College. First solo show was in 1974 at 57 Gallery, Edinburgh. In 1981 she had an exhibition at Serpentine Gallery. Won several Scottish Arts Council awards and was president of SSA, 1981–3. Lived in Leith, Lothian.

Mervyn O'GORMAN 1871–1958 Engraver, lacquer worker and administrator, born in Brighton, Sussex, who after Downside College studied at University College, eventually obtaining his science doctorate. Lieutenant-Colonel O'Gorman was at one time superintendent of the Royal Aircraft Factory at South Farnborough. He was a member of a number of professional bodies such as the Institutes of Mechanical and Electrical Engineers and was from 1930 a member of the Art Workers' Guild. He exhibited at Spring Gardens, with British Engravers in Paris, 1928, and elsewhere, among his main works being Seven Swans and Alsatian Dog. British Museum holds his work. Lived in London.

Tony Ó GRIBÍN fl. from late 1970s– Artist, born in Belfast, Northern Ireland, who completed a foundation course at Ulster Polytechnic in Jordanstown, 1975, graduating in fine art from Exeter College of Art in 1978. In that year he moved to Paris to live for a year, from 1981 living in West Germany for an extended period. Was represented in many group shows in Britain and Ireland, including Works on Paper and Beyond the Partitions, both put on in 1994 by Queen Street Studios, Belfast, with which he was associated. Works in many private collections.

Suzanne O'HAIRE 1968– She studied at West Surrey College of Art and Camberwell College of Arts. O'Haire was noted for her witty constructions using pieces of metal as seen at England & Co's Art in Boxes, 1991. Also showed in Storm in a Teacup at Association of Illustrators' Gallery and in Festival Hall's Recycled Art show, 1991.

Kay OHSTEN 1935– Painter, printmaker and teacher. She studied at Norwich School of Art and taught design there. Showed widely, including RI and Nina Zborowska Fine Paintings, Painswick. Lived in Norwich, Norfolk.

Jenny OKUN 1953– Artist in sculpture, film and photographs, teacher, born in America, who moved from New York to London in 1971. She did a foundation course at Wimbledon School of Art; was at Chelsea School of Art, 1972–4, gaining a painting degree; then did postgraduate experimental media work at Slade School of Fine Art, 1975–7. Okun co-ran the London Filmmakers' Co-op Workshop; co-selected Film/London International Avant-Garde Festival; taught four years at Central School of Art, and three years, painting, at Chelsea School of Art. Okun took part in many group shows including Centre Pompidou, Paris, 1978; National Film Theatre, 1984; Hartje Gallery, Frankfurt, 1990; and John Jones and Tate Gallery, both 1991. Solo shows included Yehudi Menuhin School, Cobham, 1986; Special Photographers' Company, 1989; and Rebecca Hossack Gallery, 1995. Commissions included British Waterways Board, Central Electricity Generating Board and Derby/Inglehart (Bowater House). Okun's work is held by Victoria & Albert Museum, Brooklyn Museum and many other public and corporate collections. She began her sculptures – which were geometrical – in 1989, and used photographs as "working drawings". The sculptures were "intended as a fusion of the disciplines of painting, sculpture and architecture".

Leon OLIN 1939– Artist and illustrator in oil, watercolour and ink and pencil, gallery owner and teacher, married to the painter Sylvia P Gainsford. He was born in Leicester and studied at the College of Art there and in Brighton. Olin was head of fine art at Southampton College of Further Education to 1974, when he went freelance full-time, for two years travelling the British Isles in a mobile studio. After living in Kent he moved to Fishguard, Dyfed, where he set up studio and ran Gallery One. Olin was a founder-member of Group South. Mixed shows included Albany Gallery, Cardiff; Cross Keys Gallery, Beaconsfield; Frances Iles Gallery, Rochester; and Library Gallery, Haverfordwest. Showed solo with Hamwic Gallery, Southampton. Illustrated books for Angus and Robertson, Bell and Hyman, Bishopsgate Press and Rosedale Publications. Portsmouth City Museum and Art Gallery holds his work. Olin's main themes were landscape and seascape featuring traditional sailing craft, architecture and old farm machinery, with a strong underlying draughtsmanship.

Rebecca OLINER 1959– Outstanding draughtsman in pencil of still life, born in London, who studied at Camberwell School of Arts and Crafts, 1978–82. Had a first solo show at Agnew, 1993, which exhibited her work at Art95, in 1995, in Islington. Also showed in Images from my kitchen, William Joll at Christopher Hull Gallery, 1996.

Marie-Paule OLINGER 1952– Painter, draughtsman and teacher, born in Luxembourg, producing works saturated in light, tending towards abstraction, with a strong mystical element. After studying commerce and languages in Lausanne, Switzerland, Olinger took up painting in 1977. She studied life drawing in Britain and Germany, 1984–7; was taught by Maggi Hambling at Morley College, 1988-93; attended a printing workshop there, 1993–4; and a Dali Workshop at St Martin's, 1994–5. Taught students privately in her studio. Exhibited in group and solo shows on the continent, especially in Luxembourg, British groups including Art for Youth, Mall Galleries, 1990; Women Celebrate Europe, RIBA, 1993; Christmas Show, Chelsea Arts Club, 1996; and Celebration of Europe, York City Art Gallery, 1998. Later solo shows included Traces of Timeless Energies, The Gallery in Cork Street, 1997. Musée de la Ville du Luxembourg, Luxembourg, and many corporate collections hold examples. Lived in London.

Rob OLINS 1956– Sculptor, designer and teacher who did a foundation course, 1976–7, at Barnet College, gained a first-class degree at the Polytechnic in Wolverhampton, 1977–80, a certificate in adult education at the City Lit, 1985–6, and in 1986 a course on metal casting at Poplar College. Olins' sculptures were noted for their contrast and tension; they used a variety of materials and were delicately held together, from sometimes friction, gravity and even balance by magnetism. They were abstract and a number were kinetic. Took part in many group shows in England and abroad, later solo exhibitions including New Academy Gallery, 1994, and Galerie Glasnost, Munich, 1995. Olins obtained a large number of awards and residencies, including Columbus Art League, prizewinner, 1993, and in 1994 Symposium in St Lamprect, Austria. Commissions included a set of four sculptures for Unilever and an award for a wall feature in the Rutherglen Centre, Sunderland, both 1994. Lived in London.

David OLIVANT 1958– Artist, notably a draughtsman, born in Watford, Hertfordshire, into a working class family. Started drawing aged four, with a strong interest in animals. While attending Watford Boys' Grammar School began to study the world of ideas, at 14 reading the Existentialist writings of Albert Camus, which led to an interest in the work of George Berkeley and idealism. Did a one-year foundation course at Hertfordshire College of Art and Design in St Albans, then read for his bachelor's degree at Falmouth School of Art and his master's at Royal College of Art. Lived for a time in India and Italy, then settled in Darlington, County Durham. A substantial show of Olivant's works on paper, ranging from figurative to non-representational, was held at The Center for International Contemporary Arts, New York, 1990.

Charles William OLIVER 1911– Painter, printmaker and teacher, born in Youngstown, Ohio, America. After education in Lancashire he attended Liverpool City School of Art under Will Penn, then Royal College of Art, 1930–4, under William Rothenstein. Went on to teach at Laird School of Art, Birkenhead, for many years, becoming vice-principal. In 1972 he published *Anatomy and Perspective*. Oliver joined the Liverpool Academy in 1938, also exhibiting at RP, RSA, RCamA and Senefelder Club. Williamson Art Gallery, Birkenhead, near where he lived at Oxton, Cheshire, holds his work.

Edith OLIVER fl. from c.1910– Portrait miniaturist, born in Newcastle upon Tyne, where she eventually settled. She studied with the miniaturist Alfred Praga at his school in London and went on to become a member of RMS, with which she showed, also at RA, Fitzwilliam Museum in Cambridge, Walker Art Gallery in Liverpool and Laing Art Gallery and Museum in Newcastle. Oliver painted a number of members of the royal family including HM Queen Mary.

Julia OLIVER 1966– Artist in various media. She studied at Gray's School of Art, Aberdeen; Scottish College of Textiles, Galashiels; and Royal College of Art. She exhibited at Liberty in Interior Spaces and in 1992 in Art in Boxes at England & Co.

Ken OLIVER 1948– Painter and teacher, born in Yorkshire. Studied at Sheffield College of Art, 1965–70, then Royal College of Art, 1971–4. Took part in many mixed shows, including Sheffield Open (National), at Graves Art Gallery, 1973; LG from 1977; Recent Work by Young British Painters, Dallas, Texas, 1979; Maidstone Staff Show, at Maidstone College of Art, 1980; Whitechapel Open, 1982; and in 1983 9 Artists from Wapping British Tour, based at DLI Museum & Arts Centre, Durham. Oliver's solo shows included Air Gallery, 1977, and Atlantis Gallery, 1982. Arts Council, Victoria & Albert Museum and Sheffield City Art Galleries hold his work. Originally an abstract painter, Oliver later moved towards representation, although his approach remained in many ways abstract, as evidenced in his work at Peter Moores Liverpool Project 6: Art into the 80s, at Fruitmarket Gallery, Edinburgh, 1982. Oliver visited China and lectured on British painting in 1988. He won the Rome Award in Painting, British School in Rome, 1990–1. Lived in London.

Kenneth Herbert OLIVER 1923– Printmaker, watercolourist, draughtsman and teacher, born in Norwich, Norfolk, married to the artist Joyce Beaumont. He attended Norwich School of Art, 1939–42, under Charles Hobbis, then Royal College of Art, 1947–50, with Robert Sargent Austin. Taught at Cheltenham College of Art/Gloucestershire College of Arts and Technology, living at Pitchcombe, near Stroud. He was a member of RWS, RE and RWA, which holds his work. Also exhibited with Norfolk and Norwich Art Circle, Cheltenham Group of Artists, RA and elsewhere.

Patrick OLIVER 1933– Gestural painter of landscape in oil, using a limited palette and employing elements of abstraction. Oliver was born in Leeds, Yorkshire, studying at the College of Art there and in St Ives Cornwall, teachers including Peter Lanyon. Cornwall, the west of Ireland and the Yorkshire Dales, where he often stayed, were important subjects. Oliver was included in Images of the Yorkshire Landscape, organised by Sheeran Lock at Leeds Civic Hall in 1991.

Peter OLIVER 1927– Painter, born in Jersey in the Channel Islands. He began painting when ill and went on to study at Exeter School of Art, continuing with postgraduate studies in Liverpool. While a student he showed at RBA and at Redfern Gallery, further mixed show appearances including New Art Centre, with LG; Hamet Gallery; and City Art Gallery, Salford. Between 1955–63 Oliver had five solo shows at Redfern, one of Keele University in 1964, another at Mercury Gallery, 1965. In 1992 an exhibition of his earlier work was given at Anthony Hepworth Fine Art, Bath, with a retrospective in 1994. His work is held by notable British collections, including Tate Gallery, Courtauld Institute and Manchester City Art Gallery.

Raymond OLIVER 1933– Painter in watercolour and oil, interiors and still life being leading themes, Sickert and Bonnard two influences. Oliver was born in Hemsworth, Yorkshire, eventually settling in the county at Thorpe Audlin, Pontefract. He studied commercial art at Wakefield School of Arts and Crafts, 1946–50, and after National Service embarked on a career in engineering with De Havilland Aircraft Company, meanwhile studying technical illustration and interior design. Began painting in watercolour and oil in 1983 and from 1985 was a regular exhibitor in Ferens Art Gallery, Hull, winter show, also at RA Summer Exhibitions, ROI, NEAC, RWS Open, Laing competition and other mixed shows in London and the provinces. He was a member of Leeds Fine Art Club. In February 1991 Oliver's paintings of the interior of Castle Howard were featured in *House & Garden* magazine. Corporate and private collections in Britain and the continent hold Oliver's work. Oliver gave up engineering in 1987 to be a full-time painter.

Herbert Arnould OLIVIER 1861–1952 Landscape and portrait painter, born at Battle, Sussex. Entered the Royal Academy Schools in 1881 and won Creswick Prize the following year. From 1883 exhibited at RA, sometimes signing work just HAO, having other showings at RP, RBA, Ridley Art Club, RHA, and one-man exhibitions at RI, Fine Art Society and Grafton Galleries. Silver medal at Paris Salon, 1922. Was an official war artist during World War I. Lived in London.

Tim OLLIVIER 1971– Painter of lyrical, allusive abstracts, born in London, who attended Norfolk Institute of Art & Design, 1991–4, then Royal College of Art, 1994–6. He gained The

Worshipful Company of Painter-Stainers Award in 1994 and 1995; a Paris Studio Award, Cité Internationale des Arts, 1995; and in 1996 the Jardine Insurance and Daler-Rowney Awards. Group shows included Norwich Gallery, Norwich, 1993; The Queen Elizabeth II Conference Centre, 1995; Midhurst Gallery, Sussex, 1996; and New Abstraction, Paton Gallery, 1997. Essex County Council and Aberdeen Art Gallery hold Ollivier's work.

Kate Elizabeth OLVER fl. from 1907–1960 Painter in oil and watercolour, educated at the Royal Academy Schools. She exhibited at the RA, SWA, RP, Royal Glasgow Institute of the Fine Arts and at the Paris Salon. Ferens Art Gallery, Hull, holds her work. She illustrated a number of books, including Robert Louis Stevenson's *A Child's Garden of Verses*. Lived in London.

Deirdre O'MAHONY 1956– Artist and teacher, born in Ireland. Studied at Regional Technical College, Galway, 1974–6, then St Martin's School of Art, 1976–9. She showed frequently in Ireland and London from 1980, being included in Art in Adult Education at Woodlands Art Gallery, 1990. In 1987 O'Mahony co-founded Livia, an association of Irish artists based in London, which held many exhibitions.

Jane O'MALLEY 1944– Painter, born in Montreal, Canada, married to the artist Tony O'Malley. She attended Sir George Williams University Art School in 1962. Between 1963–9 she travelled extensively, including Europe, Australia, Russia, Japan and Switzerland, in 1969 attending Leonard Fuller's St Ives School of Painting, in Cornwall. She married O'Malley four years later, settling in St Ives. Painted the local landscape, the Canaries and the West Indies. Was a member of Newlyn Society of Artists and Penwith Society of Arts and was represented in the 1989 Newlyn Orion Galleries exhibition A Century of Art in Cornwall 1889–1989.

Tony O'MALLEY 1913– Painter whose work from the early 1960s tended towards abstraction, born in Callan, County Kilkenny, Ireland. He worked in a bank, 1933–58, apart from Army service at the beginning of the 1940s. He produced his first oil painting in 1945. Ten years later, while painting on holiday in St Ives, he became acquainted with Peter Lanyon, Bryan Wynter and other notable artists. After O'Malley was forced to retire from the bank because of ill-health in 1958, in 1960 he settled in St Ives and worked there for many years before eventually returning to Ireland. In 1981 was awarded the Douglas Hyde Gold Medal by Irish Arts Council. O'Malley had early one-man shows at Sail Loft Gallery, St Ives, 1961 and 1962. After a string of British and Irish exhibitions, in 1984 had an Ulster Museum, Belfast, retrospective which toured to Dublin and Cork, with a retrospective of paintings 1950–95 at Coram Gallery, 1996. Was married to the painter Jane O'Malley.

Julia Trevelyan OMAN 1930– Designer and photographer, married to the former director of the Victoria & Albert Museum Sir Roy Strong, 1971. She was educated at Royal College of Art as a Royal Scholar, 1953, in 1955 gaining a Silver Medal. She designed for BBC Television, 1955–7, then was engaged in designing for the theatre, opera, ballet, films, television and exhibitions. Her credits included the play *40 Years On*, 1968; a number of operas for Covent Garden, including *La Bohème*, 1974; the ballet *A Month in the Country*, 1976; the film *Alice in Wonderland*, 1966; the television production *Separate Tables*, 1982; and the exhibition Samuel Pepys, at National Portrait Gallery, 1971. Lady Strong gained the Designer of the Year award in 1967. With her husband she produced a number of books including *The English Year*, 1982, and *A Celebration of Gardens*, 1991. She was the director of Oman Productions Ltd and lived at Much Birch, Hereford.

Yoko OMOMI 1971– Artist whose work showed a strong calligraphic element, as in her solo exhibition at Christopher Hull Gallery, 1997. Of Japanese nationality, Omomi was born in Madagascar. She did a pre-foundation course at Heatherley School of Art, 1991; a City and Guilds of London Art School foundation course, 1991–2, gaining a diploma with first-class honours there in 1992–5, with summer school experience at the Slade School of Fine Art, 1993. She won a Philip Connard Travel Award, 1994, with several more awards in 1995, including the Christopher Hull Prize. Gained her master's degree with distinction from Winchester School of Art, 1995–6, with a Barcelona Exchange, in 1996 winning a Gold Medal (City and Guilds Senior Award). Exhibitions included Tallers Obert, Barcelona, Spain, and Oriel Mostyn Open Exhibition, Llandudno, both 1996, and Mall Galleries (National Print Exhibition) and Morley Gallery, both 1997.

Bernard O'NEIL 1919– Sculptor, painter and restorer, brought up in western Canada. Although he did have a period at Edinburgh College of Art, he was largely self-taught as a painter. He exhibited at a number of venues in Canada, and at RSA and SSA and had a solo exhibition at Mathieson's Gallery, Edinburgh, where he lived for some years.

Daniel O'NEILL 1920–1974 Painter whose works show a rich imaginative streak, born and died in Belfast, Northern Ireland, although between 1958–71 he was based in London. After an elementary school education O'Neill had a short time at Belfast College of Art and in the studio of Sidney Smith, worked as an electrician for several years painting part-time, then with the encouragement of the dealer Victor Waddington became a professional artist. After a solo show with Waddington in Dublin in 1946, O'Neill's work began to be widely seen, including in Dublin at the Irish Exhibition of Living Art shows; RHA; Tooth; and with CEMA at Belfast Museum and Art Gallery in 1952. There was an important show in Belfast at McClelland Galleries in 1970. Ulster Museum and other public collections hold examples.

Mary O'NEILL fl. c.1935–1955 Painter, artist in black-and-white and teacher, born in Carisbrooke, Isle of Wight. Initially educated in a convent in Bruges, Belgium, she went on to study at Slade School of Fine Art under Henry Tonks and at Royal

Academy Schools. Among books illustrated by her was the Irish writer Kate O'Brien's *Farewell Spain*, 1937, and her book on *Teresa of Avila*, 1951. Exhibited RBA, NEAC and elsewhere and lived in London.

Shirley O'NEILL 1947– Painter, draughtsman and collagist, born in Warwickshire. She studied at Nuneaton School of Art, Walthamstow College of Art and Royal Academy Schools, graduating in 1972. From 1970s exhibited in a number of group shows as a member of the Wapping Studio Collective of Artists, with Francis Graham-Dixon Gallery and in second Summer Show at Serpentine Gallery in 1982. A characteristic technique of O'Neill's was deployment of strips or slabs of colour on a stained ground of glowing acrylic paint. Lived in London.

Toni ONLEY 1928– Painter and mural artist, born in Douglas, Isle of Man, full name Norman Antony Onley. Probably Canada's most-travelled modern artist, Onley's speciality was the lean landscape of the frozen north. After working for a printer he was articled to an architect, attending part-time classes at Douglas School of Art under John Hobbs Nicholson, 1942–8. With his family he emigrated to Canada in 1948 and studied at Doon School of Fine Arts, Ontario, 1949–50. He won a scholarship to Instituto de Allende, Guanajuato, Mexico, in 1957 and stayed there until 1960, although he had his first one-man show at Vancouver Art Gallery in 1958. He showed his abstract work widely elsewhere in Canada, as well as being represented at Paris Biennale in 1961, the year he completed a big mural for Queen Elizabeth Playhouse, Vancouver. Two years later he was first winner of the Zacks Prize. It was through the Zacks Award that Tate Gallery acquired Onley's picture Polar No. I. Several dozen other public collections in Canada and abroad hold Onley's work. He became a prolific worker and rich enough to learn to fly and use his own flying boat to explore the Canadian Arctic, a favourite subject. Vancouver Art Gallery gave him a retrospective in 1978.

Glen ONWIN 1947– Painter, born in Edinburgh, where he studied at the College of Art, 1966–71. Onwin while still a student became interested in salt as a medium to create images, and in 1973 discovered a large salt-marsh near Dunbar which inspired him to create works charting the evolution of nature. Salt was seen as a life-giver and as a destroyer, and Onwin went on to use it and other natural substances to make works which warned of the dangers of industrial pollution. Scottish National Gallery of Modern Art has his three-panel work Salt Room Crystal, of 1977. Onwin's show Saltmarsh appeared in 1975 at Scottish Arts Council Gallery, Edinburgh, and Serpentine Gallery; other shows included Revenges of Nature, at Fruitmarket Gallery, Edinburgh, and Third Eye Centre, Glasgow, 1988–9, and in 1997 The Quality of Light, The Tate at St Ives. Lived in Edinburgh.

Julian OPIE 1958– Sculptor, born and lived in London, who studied at Goldsmiths' College School of Art, 1979–82. Opie depicted objects drawn from daily life. To do this he drew the object on a steel sheet, cut it out, shaped it and painted it with its leading characteristics. The Tate Gallery's Making It, of 1983, an assembly of mock tools, is a good example. Later, Opie created clear and opaque partitions, as found in some modern architecture. Showed solo with Lisson Gallery and soon acquired an international reputation. He also took part in many group shows in Britain and abroad, including Art Gallery of Western Australia, Perth and Australia/New Zealand tour, 1985; Stedelijk Museum, Amsterdam, 1986; Lia Rumma Gallery, Naples, 1989; and South Bank Centre's The British Art Show 1990. Arts Council holds work and included him in its 1993–4 touring show Recent British Sculpture. Hayward Gallery put on an ambitious show of Opie's work in 1993–4.

Duncan OPPENHEIM 1904– Painter and printmaker who showed his first watercolour at Walker Art Gallery, Liverpool, in 1923. He later exhibited at LG, RA and had a first solo exhibition at Upper Grosvenor Gallery in 1971. Other solo shows, mainly watercolours, were at Spink & Sons in 1980–3, and at New Grafton Gallery from 1985. As well as working in oil and watercolour, he also showed screen prints. After retirement in 1974 Oppenheim was able to give more time to painting and he travelled in England, on the continent and in Egypt.

Mary OPPENHEIM fl. c.1939–1969 Painter in oil who studied art privately and at the Euston Road School. Was a member of the WIAC, with which she exhibited, along with LG, Leicester Galleries and the Arts Council. One-man shows at Temple Gallery, Medici Society Gallery and Bear Lane Gallery, Oxford. Lived in London.

Charles OPPENHEIMER 1875–1961 Landscape painter, born in Manchester, who studied at Manchester School of Art under Walter Crane and Richard Willis, and in Italy. Exhibited RA, RSA, RSW, Fine Art Society and widely abroad, including Paris Salon. His work is owned by Manchester City Art Gallery and the Whitworth Art Gallery there, many other British provincial galleries and in America and South Africa. Lived in Kirkcudbright, Scotland.

Emily OPPENHEIMER 1968– Painter, notably of richly coloured still lifes, who studied at City and Guilds of London Art School; after a foundation course, 1986–7, she completed her fine art diploma, 1987–90. She showed in 1988 with BBC *Children in Need*, a portrait of the actress Rula Lenska; and in 1991 at Lamont Gallery and Bonhams, Auction for Cancer. In 1992 had solo show at Cadogan Gallery. Sir Roger de Grey, RA president, wrote of her "sumptuous evocations of the delights of living" in that show.

Francis OPPENHEIMER 1870–1961 Diplomat, mediaevalist and watercolourist, born in London, he was early educated in Frankfurt, Germany, where his father was British consul-general. In 1890 Oppenheimer went to Balliol College, Oxford, thereafter reading for the Bar in the chambers of Rufus Isaacs. After being called by the Middle Temple in 1895 he decided to sacrifice his career and the financial support of his family to study at Académie Vitti, Paris, maintaining himself for part of the time by designing for the art publisher Lemercier. After three years at Vitti he was recalled to Frankfurt by the illness and death of his father, whom he succeeded as consul-general in 1900. For 20 years he displayed outstanding ability as a negotiator, especially on international trade, around Europe. Oppenheimer was knighted in 1907. During the war he was the subject of hysterical attacks by parts of the press because of his German-Jewish origins. After his Paris studies he was never without a studio, but he refused to exhibit during his life. A small exhibition at O'Hana Gallery in 1961 was prompted by Oppenheimer's wish for a posthumous show. After publishing *Frankish Themes and Problems* in 1952 and *The Legend of Ste Ampoule*, 1953, in 1960 Oppenheimer produced *Stranger Within: Autobiographical Pages*. Lived latterly in London and Rye, Sussex.

Joseph OPPENHEIMER 1876–1966 Painter, draughtsman and teacher, born in Würzburg, Bavaria, Germany, who was a child prodigy, a well-known portrait painter by the age of 20. His drawing of the German chancellor Bismarck, done at 13, was presented to him. Studied in Munich and Rome and moved to London in 1896, teaching at the London School of Arts. By 1900 he was in New York but returned to London where he was married, before returning to Germany in 1908, where he immersed himself in the Berlin Secession and other contemporary art movements. By 1933 the Nazis had driven him back to England, where he took British nationality and spent most of his life apart from long periods in Canada, from 1949, where he died in Montreal. Oppenheimer was a frequent exhibitor at RA from 1905–53 and for long a member of RP. He was a member of Chelsea Arts Club, knew Whistler, Sargent and Epstein and was a great sketcher of London as he walked around it. His huge collection of portrait sitters included Albert Einstein, Otto Klemperer, Yehudi Menuhin, Leonid Pasternak, Harold Macmillan, James Mason and Deborah Kerr. As well as Canadian exhibitions, one-mans were held at O'Hana Gallery, 1957 and 1963, and David Bathurst, 1990. Ben Uri Art Society holds his picture Piccadilly Circus.

Ann ORAM 1956– Painter and teacher who studied at Edinburgh College of Art, 1976–82. She taught at the College, 1983–5; taught privately for two years; lived and painted in Spain, 1987–8, Spain continuing as a strong theme in her work; was a visiting lecturer at Newcastle Polytechnic in 1988; then a part-time teacher at Edinburgh College of Art, 1991. She won a number of awards, including a Carnegie Travelling Scholarship in 1980; the Andrew Grant Travelling Scholarship to New York, 1981; the Andrew Grant Major Award, in 1981–2, which took her to France and Italy; and the May Marshall Brown Award, 1991, at RSW, five years after she was elected to the Society. Showed widely in Scotland. She had solo exhibitions at Scottish Gallery, Edinburgh, 1985–90; Macaulay Gallery, Stenton, 1986–8; and Thackeray Gallery, 1991. Her work is in Bank of Scotland, Heriot-Watt University and other collections.

Colin ORCHARD 1935– Painter and designer, born in Ewell, Surrey, who trained as a typographer and layout artist with *The Times* newspaper. He joined Letraset in 1962 as art director, from 1972 was a freelance graphic designer and moved to St Ives, Cornwall, in 1983 to develop his painting, which he eventually did full-time. Later mixed exhibitions included Wills Lane Gallery, St Ives; New Grafton and Medici Galleries; RA Summer Exhibitions; and Courcoux & Courcoux, Stockbridge. Had a series of solo shows with Porthmeor Gallery, St Ives, in the 1990s, later ones including The Book Gallery there, 1997.

Brian ORD 1946– Sculptor and teacher, born in Byker, Newcastle upon Tyne, an area where he continued to live. He studied at Chelsea School of Art and eventually became lecturer in sculpture for the foundation course at Newcastle College. Among his awards was a travel award to America and a Northern Arts Major Travel Award, 1989. Among his many group shows were Ten Sculptors, Laing Art Gallery, Newcastle, 1980; Smith's Gallery, 1987; Richard Demarco Gallery, Edinburgh, 1988; and the Newcastle Group show The Northern Lights, DLI Museum & Arts Centre and tour, 1990. His solo shows included Bede Gallery, 1979, and Washington Arts Centre, Tyne and Wear, 1990. Ord's work was abstract, recycled from debris. Several public collections hold examples.

Faith O'REILLY 1938– Painter, artist in multi-media and teacher, born in Boston, Massachusetts, America, who also worked under the name Faith Gibbon, an adoptive name. She studied at West Hartlepool College of Art with James Crowther; Berkshire College of Art with Carl Cheek; at Royal Academy Schools, with Peter Greenham and Charles Mahoney, 1961–4; and at Hornsey College of Art, with Keith Kennedy and Robert Ferguson, for film. Had "a very influential friendship with Stanley Spencer, 1957–9". Taught at Brighton Polytechnic. Figurative work, landscape, fairgrounds and music were key elements in O'Reilly's output. She was a member of Free Painters and Sculptors and ROI and had many solo shows, Cookham, 1959–60; Midland Group Gallery, Nottingham, 1966–7, and elsewhere. Many private collectors, including Lord Astor and Gilbert Spencer, held examples. Lived in Brighton, Sussex, and Le Vernet, Lamalon-les-Bains, France.

Joseph O'REILLY 1957– Painter, notable for meticulous still lifes, especially of flowers, in acrylic. Studied at Batley School of Art and Design, 1976–7, then graduated with a first-class honours degree from Sheffield Polytechnic faculty of art and design, 1977–80, teachers including Terry Lee and Brian Peacock. Awards included J J Lloyd Fine Art Prize and Yorkshire Arts Award, 1981; an Artist in Industry Fellowship, 1985; and MAFA's – to which he belonged – People's Prize, 1991–2. Took part in many mixed shows, including Huddersfield Open Art Exhibition, 1977; Batley New Gallery, 1981; International Contemporary Art Fair, Basel, from 1987; and Leeds Fine Art Club at Leeds City Art Gallery, from 1988. Had a solo show at Leeds Playhouse Gallery, 1983, later ones including Yorkshire Television, Leeds, 1992. Public galleries in Calderdale, Kirklees and Sheffield and Boston University in America hold examples. Lived in Mytholm, Hebden Bridge, Yorkshire.

Philip O'REILLY 1944– Artist and lecturer, born in Leamington Spa, Warwickshire, who studied at Coventry College of Art, 1959–64, and Slade School of Fine Art, 1964–6, winning a Boise Travelling Scholarship in the latter year. Was technician at Wimbledon School of Art, 1966–7, then after a series of lectureships returned there in 1979. Group shows included LG, FBA Galleries, 1969; RA Summer Exhibition, from 1972; and Browse & Darby, 1980. Had a solo show at Angela Flowers Gallery, 1973, later ones including paintings, drawings, prints and wall hangings at Newport Museum and Art Gallery, Newport, 1997.

Bryan ORGAN 1935– Painter and teacher, full name Harold Bryan Organ, born in Leicester. He studied at College of Art, Loughborough, and Royal Academy Schools, teaching at Loughborough College, 1959–65. He had a first one-man show at Leicester Museum and Art Gallery, 1959, having the first of a series at Redfern Gallery, his dealer, in 1967. Further solo shows followed in New York, Cologne and Turin. Organ early established himself as a painter of notabilities, including the composer Sir Michael Tippett, the writer and broadcaster Malcolm Muggeridge, HRH Princess Margaret, HRH The Duke of Edinburgh and HRH The Prince of Wales. His work is in public collections in Britain and abroad.

Robert ORGAN 1933– Painter, draughtsman, architectural designer and teacher, born in Hutton, Somerset, his father being an architect, Edward Organ. He studied at West of England College of Art in Bristol and Slade School of Fine Art, George Sweet and Claude Rogers being notable teachers. Taught painting and drawing at Falmouth School of Art and elsewhere and architecture at Architectural Association and Bristol and Cambridge Universities, eventually becoming a full-time painter. Was a member of RWA and Newlyn Society of Artists. Solo exhibitions included Beaux Arts Gallery, Bath, and Newlyn Orion Gallery from 1983; Browse & Darby from 1984; and Exeter Museum, 1987. Public collections in Brighton and Exeter and University of Illinois in America hold examples. Lived in Wambrook, Chard, Somerset.

Tim O'RILEY 1965– Painter and teacher who studied at Leicester Polytechnic, 1985–8, and Chelsea College of Art, 1991–2. From 1994–7, he held a research studentship in fine art and computing at Chelsea, and became a visiting tutor. Mixed shows included into the Nineties at Mall Galleries, 1992, and in 1997–8 John Moores Liverpool Exhibition, where he exhibited the acrylic on linen Three Windows, initiated using a computer. Solo shows included Adam and Diorama Galleries, London, and Arthouse Gallery in Dublin, all 1996, and Home Ideals FAT/Islington Festival, 1997. Lived in London.

Simon ORMAN 1960– Sculptor, born in Manchester. He attended Rochdale School of Art, 1978–9, then St Martin's School of Art, 1980, returning for advanced sculpture, 1982–3. Orman attended the Kornarija Symposium of Sculpture in Yugoslavia, 1980. Among his group exhibitions were The Compilation Show at Rochdale Art Gallery, 1982, and in 1983 Have You Seen Sculpture from the Body?, at Woodlands Art Gallery. Worked in Yorkshire.

Stanley Horton ORMEROD 1918–1983 Painter, lithographer, engraver, etcher and graphic artist specialising in wildlife topics. Born in Morecambe, Lancashire, he studied art at Accrington School of Art and Cottingen, Germany. Exhibited widely all over Britain, including SWLA, RE, NS, and in New York. Work reproduced in *La Revue Moderne* in 1969. Produced a wide range of lithographs for vintage car museums and wildlife parks. Lived at Aultbea, Achnasheen, Wester Ross.

Susan ORMEROD 1955– Artist working in a variety of media, born in Eastbourne, Sussex. She studied at Trent Polytechnic in Nottingham, 1974–7, then Slade School of Fine Art, 1977–9. Mixed exhibitions included Summer Show 3 at Serpentine Gallery, 1981. Arts Council holds her work. Lived in London.

OROVIDA: see **Orovida PISSARRO**

Burnett Napier Henderson ORPHOOT 1880–1964 Etcher who was an architect by profession. Born in Peebles, Scotland, he attended Rugby School and Edinburgh University, then the School of Applied Art there and in Paris. Exhibited RA, RSA, Royal Glasgow Institute of the Fine Arts and Walker Art Gallery, Liverpool. Elected RSA in 1942. Lived in Edinburgh.

Arthur Anselm ORR 1868–1949 Church glass designer, born in London, his father Thomas Orr being an ecclesiastical designer and furnisher. Orr was educated in Dublin, then studied art in Birmingham, at Westminster School of Art and Royal College of Art. Showed extensively at RA from 1896, also at Whitechapel Art Gallery, Victoria & Albert Museum and Grosvenor Gallery. Windows were completed for St James Church, Twickenham; St Mary Magdalen, Regents Park; St Mary and St Michael's, Commercial Road; in a number of English and foreign cathedrals and in parish churches. Lived in Harrow, Middlesex.

Chris ORR 1943– Printmaker and teacher, born in London, who attended Ravensbourne College of Art, 1959–63, Hornsey College of Art, 1963–4, and Royal College of Art, 1964–7. Then went on to teach part-time for several years at Cardiff College of Art. Additional teaching posts mixed with freelance work included Winchester, Liverpool, Glasgow, Newport, the Ruskin School of Drawing in Oxford and Royal College of Art. In 1973 published his book *Chris Orr's John Ruskin*. Many group show appearances and solo exhibitions including Gorner and Millard, Bear Lane Gallery in Oxford and Glasgow School of Art. In 1993–4 Orr shared a show with Norman Ackroyd at the Bankside Gallery, where Orr had an exhibition in 1996. Socially Surrealistic was one term used of his work. Victoria & Albert Museum and other major collections hold examples. Orr was elected RA in 1995.

James ORR 1931– Painter in oil and acrylic, born in Glasgow, who was 25 years in the distributive trade before painting full-time.

He studied part-time at Glasgow School of Art under William Crosbie. Was a member of the Royal Glasgow Institute of the Fine Arts, also showing in groups at Richard Hagen Gallery, Broadway; Gatehouse Gallery in Glasgow; and Contemporary Fine Art Gallery, Eton. Solo shows included the Gatehouse; Macaulay Gallery, Stenton; and Gallery 41, Edinburgh. HRH The Duke of Edinburgh holds his work. Lived in Prestwick, Ayrshire.

James R Wallace ORR 1907–1992 Painter, printmaker and teacher, born in Glasgow, where he attended the Academy and its School of Art, gaining his diploma from Royal College of Art, 1933. Then trained as a teacher at Moray House, Edinburgh, and after a brief period teaching in Birmingham joined the staff of Glasgow Academy where, apart from war service, he stayed until retirement in 1967. During the war he served first in the London Fire Brigade during the Blitz before enlisting with Royal Air Force Bomber Command. He took part in 30 active operations as a rear gunner in Lancasters, winning the Distinguished Flying Cross. Orr built a house to his own design at Kippen, near Stirling, where he lived from 1960. He was an elder of the church there, which has some of his pictures. Wallace Orr found especial inspiration from the quality of light and variety of colour he saw over mountains beyond the Carse of Forth. Showed at RA, RSA and Royal Glasgow Institute of the Fine Arts and had solo exhibitions in Glasgow, Edinburgh, Dunblane and Falkirk. There was a retrospective at Kelly Gallery, Glasgow, in 1995. Imperial War Museum and Worthing Museum and Art Gallery hold examples.

Cecil OSBORNE 1909–1996 Artist in oil, watercolour, scraperboard and mosaic, born in Poplar, east London. He studied in the evenings at John Cooper's Bow and Bromley Evening Institute classes, showing with the East London Group at Lefevre Gallery, also with NEAC, RA and Civil Defence Artists' Association at Cooling's Gallery. About 1933 Cooper became interested in mosaic and new materials for wall and other decorations; arranged classes at Central School of Arts and Crafts, with Osborne as his technical assistant; with a studio in Camden Town they carried out several commissions. Later Osborne went into town planning with St Pancras Borough Council and completed three large wall panels in oil dealing with its history. Retired to Jimena de la Frontera, Cadiz, Spain, eventually dying there after a stroke left him helpless.

Christopher OSBORNE 1947– Painter of landscape, born in Kent, who was self-taught. For 11 years he lived in East Anglia, later living in Sussex, where he concentrated on painting the Downs, Weald and marshland. Alfriston Gallery, Sussex, and Clairmonte Gallery, Brighton, handled his work.

Dennis Henry OSBORNE 1919– Painter in oil and watercolour, and teacher, born in Portsmouth, Hampshire, married to the artist Jean Osborne. He studied at Camberwell School of Arts and Crafts, 1946–50, on a London County Council grant, teachers including William Coldstream, Victor Pasmore and John Minton, gaining his diploma in 1950. Also attended Heatherley's School of Fine Art. In 1952 he emigrated to Canada, settling in St Catharines, Ontario, conducting evening art classes at St Catharines Collegiate and at Smithville High School and courses in portraiture and landscape for Lakehead Area Art Association. Showed widely in Canada and his 10-foot mural of a central scene of Welland, in the Sundy-Macmillan Chiropractic Clinic there, was completed in 1959, the year he returned to Britain to head the art department at Portadown Technical College. For many years prior to retirement he taught at Lisnagarvey High School, Lisburn. Was an associate of RUA. Mixed shows included NEAC, RA and Queen's University, Belfast, Festival Exhibition from 1987. Solo shows included Art Centre, Newtownards, County Down, where he lived, 1988.

James Thomas Armour OSBORNE 1907–1979 Painter, illustrator, printmaker and teacher, born in Battle, Sussex. He was married to the sculptor Charlotte Gibson. He studied at Hastings and Sussex School of Art, 1912–15, at the Royal College of Art, 1925–30, under Malcolm Osborne and William Rothenstein, then had a year in Rome as a Prix de Rome Scholar at the British School. Also studied in Greece. He went on to teach at Regent Street Polytechnic School of Art for some years before and after World War II. Showed with RA, Redfern Gallery, NEAC, Arts Council and elsewhere. Barton Fine Art had an extensive exhibition in 1987. Lived in Orsett, Essex.

Jean OSBORNE 1926–1965 Artist, married to the painter Dennis Henry Osborne. She was born in County Antrim, Northern Ireland, and studied at Camberwell School of Arts and Crafts on a four-year Ministry of Education grant, graduating in 1951. In 1953 she emigrated to Canada, settling in St Catharines, Ontario. Showed with LG, NEAC, Young Contemporaries, at Hamilton Art Gallery annual shows in Canada, with the Ontario Society of Artists and the Colour & Form Society, of which she was a member. In 1958 shared a show with her husband at Thielsen Gallery, London, Ontario. Sometimes worked under her maiden name Jean Meikle.

Malcolm OSBORNE 1880–1963 Etcher and engraver. Born at Frome, Somerset, he studied art in Bristol before attending the Royal College of Art under Frank Short and W R Lethaby. Elected RA in 1926. Osborne was an influential teacher who was head of the engraving school at the Royal College of Art for many years. Exhibited widely, including RA, Fine Art Society, Leicester Galleries, RE, RSA and Royal Glasgow Institute of the Fine Arts. Lived in London.

Nick OSBORNE 1948– Artist who studied at Kingston School of Art and then Reigate. After leaving art school he worked in acrylic and oils, then concentrated mainly on watercolour. Founded a jewellery design partnership called Cicada with his wife Pat Thornton. Later Osborne moved into silkscreen printing, influenced by such artists as Matisse, Klee and Hockney. Sold his work through Belgravia Contemporary Arts and elsewhere.

Philip OSBORNE 1926–1994 Painter. He was originally a journalist who was a compulsive spare-time painter, then in 1962 entered Exeter College of Art for five years under Clifford Fishwick, where he was influenced by the teacher John Epstein. Osborne was a slow, painstaking worker, creating highly mannered figurative compositions with recurrent male characters. He had a solo show at Dartington Hall in 1970, then sold occasionally to private buyers, having a 20-year retrospective at St Jude's in 1990. Lived in London and died of cancer of the oesophagus.

Stuart OSBORNE 1925– Sculptor, wood carver and teacher, born in Weston-super-Mare, Somerset, son of an artist, Margaret Cole. He studied at West of England College of Art, Bristol, 1948–53, and at Royal College of Art, teachers including John Skeaping and Frank Dobson. Went on to teach sculpture at the College of Art/College of Further Education, Stafford, Staffordshire, where he lived. He was a member of Free Painters and Sculptors and showed with RBS, SPS, RWA, Galerie Salammbo in Paris and elsewhere abroad.

A OSCAR 1919–1994 Artist in paint and mixed media, including such elements as found ceramic fragments, and art critic, born in Cork, Ireland, as Peter Sheldon-Williams. He came from a long line of painters. As a critic for the *International Herald Tribune* and as a broadcaster he wrote as Sheldon Williams (omitting the hyphen). He hated his English public school, regarded himself as an outsider and through Eric Gill's recommendation studied with John Cooper and John Skeaping at Central School of Arts and Crafts, 1935–6; at the Académie Julian, Paris, 1936; École des Beaux-Arts, Epinal; and Lemmel-Schule, Berlin. Showed extensively in mixed exhibitions, including Wertheim Gallery, Leicester Galleries, Kaplan and Brook Street Galleries. One-man shows included Galerie Zak, Paris, 1936; Wertheim Gallery, 1937; Chiltern Gallery, from 1958; International Arts Festival, Harlow, 1965; and Windsor Arts Centre, 1986; retrospectives at Beatrice Royal Gallery, Eastleigh, and Belgrave Gallery, 1995. Leicestershire Education Committee plus several museums in continental Europe and America hold his work, which in later years could be rather in the manner of Nicolas de Staël. André Masson and Joan Miró were cited as earliest influences. He was a colourful and witty man. As a critic he was cosmopolitan, interested in contemporary art of Australia, Brazil and central Europe; his book *Voodoo And The Art of Haiti* is a key work. Lived in London.

Grace OSCROFT 1903–1970 Painter, notable for roofscapes and street scenes in London, where she was born and died. She attended John Cooper's Bow and Bromley Evening Institute classes and exhibited with East London Group at Lefevre Gallery. In 1935 she and her family, who ran a cycle repair business, moved to north London, when Grace's interest in painting lessened. She did a variety of jobs, including doctor's housekeeper and in a glove factory. Died in a hospice in Hackney.

Stefan OSIECKI 1904–1977 Architect, designer, sculptor and film-maker, one of the group of Polish artists who successfully promoted paper sculpture in Britain after World War II. After obtaining his master's degree in architecture from Warsaw Institute of Technology Osiecki was engaged in commercial and display art, then held several positions in the film industry, twice as a cameraman in the Andes. Then did extensive exhibition work throughout Europe and at the New York World Fair, 1939. After serving in the Polish Army he escaped to Britain where he made many films for the Polish Film Unit, doing similar work after the war for Concaen Productions. Also worked as a graphic designer at Studio 2 before, in 1956, becoming an architect again. Osiecki was one of the masters of paper sculpture and was included in Polish Paper Sculpture at Polish Cultural Institute, 1995.

Edward OSMOND 1900– Painter, illustrator and teacher, born in Suffolk, married to the sculptor and painter Constance M Osmond, known as Laurie. He taught at Regent Street Polytechnic School of Art. A Carnegie Award winner, Osmond showed at RA, Walker Art Gallery in Liverpool and RBA. Lived latterly at Seaford, Sussex.

Ozi OSMOND 1942– Artist, teacher, also worked in films, who was born in Wattsville, Gwent. He attended Newport College of Art, 1959–64, then Cardiff College of Art, 1964–5 and 1975–6. For several years he was involved in films, including the 1976 prizewinning documentary *Above us the Earth*, also in promoting theatrical and musical events in west Wales. Teaching experience included being visiting lecturer at Dyfed College of Art and teaching foundation studies at Carmarthen College. Was in Six Young Painters, Newport Art Gallery, 1963; Fishguard Festival, St David's Cathedral, 1977; and had a series of solo shows, including Glynn Vivian Art Gallery, Swansea, 1996.

Cicely OSMOND-SMITH 1917– Painter, printmaker and teacher, born in Llandaff, Glamorgan, who studied painting at Worthing and Brighton Colleges of Art, followed by art teacher training. Was a member of Oxford Art Society and Oxford Printmakers' Co-operative. Exhibited at Pictures for Schools Exhibitions in London and Cardiff, with Sussex Artists, New Academy Gallery, Forum Gallery in Manchester, Museum of Art in Oxford and in France. She had exhibitions at Halifax House in Oxford, The Old Gaol Gallery in Abingdon, The Oxford Graphics Centre, and at St Giles' Church, The University Church and The Museum of Oxford, in 1996. Lived at Waterstock, Oxford.

Gerald OSOSKI 1903–1981 Landscape, portrait and decorative painter in various media and draughtsman, born and lived in London. He studied at St Martin's School of Art, 1917–22, then under William Rothenstein at the Royal College of Art, 1922–6. During the difficult years of the 1930s Ososki helped found the firm of Roffe Ltd, which specialised in cinema and theatre interior decoration. In World War II he worked as a camouflage artist, after which he turned his firm's attention to the restoration and conservation of historic buildings. St James' Palace, Clarence House and Buckingham Palace were among commissions. Exhibited in mixed shows at RA, RBA, NEAC and other London galleries and overseas. One-man shows at the Claridge Gallery, 1930, and Mall Galleries, 1973. *Colour* magazine and *The Times* reproduced his work, which is in the collection of the Ben Uri Art Society, whose gallery held a retrospective in 1987.

Roy OSTLE 1930– Artist in various media, teacher and antique dealer, born in Chester. He attended the local School of Art, 1946–50, and Liverpool College of Art, 1950–1. After teaching in London he held a range of appointments, latterly St Mary's College, Bangor, and the University College of North Wales there. Ostle was a council member of RCamA, also showing in mixed groups at New Art Centre, Royal National Eisteddfod, WAC and Peterloo Gallery, Manchester. A series of solo shows included Edinburgh Festival, 1963, where he gained first prize for the best one-man exhibition. The parish church at Pwllheli, Gwynedd, commissioned his painting of the crucifixion. Lived in Gwynedd at Nant Ffrancon, near Bethesda.

Jiro OSUGA 1968– Painter, born in Tokyo, Japan, who studied at Chelsea School of Art, 1987–90, and Royal College of Art, 1990–2. His appearances included East & South at Norwich Gallery/Kent Institute of Art & Design, 1992; Off Site at Cooling Gallery and Flowers East, both 1995; and John Moores Liverpool Exhibition, 1995–6. Lived in London.

Denis O'SULLIVAN 1953– Artist in various media, born in London. He lived in New York, 1964–71. Did a foundation course at Croydon College of Art, 1971–2, then was at Ravensbourne College of Art & Design, 1975–8. His group exhibitions included Off Centre Gallery and Crane Arts, 1980; Nicholas Treadwell Gallery and RA, 1981; Woodlands Art Gallery's touring exhibition of Greater London Arts Association award winners, 1981–2; and Bradford Print Biennale, 1982. Had solo shows at Galerie Jurka, Amsterdam, from 1979, and Riverside Studios, 1981.

Barbara OTLEY: *see* **FIENNES-FOSTER**

Thérèse OULTON 1953– Painter, born in Shrewsbury, Shropshire. She studied at St Martin's School of Art 1976–9, and Royal College of Art, 1980–3, gaining a Boise Scholarship in the latter year. In that year, too, she made an impression in the College's Diploma Show, which soon led to widespread appearances in mixed exhibitions in Britain and abroad. Oulton worked on a large scale in thick impasto but in subdued colours, her pictures mixing mystical elements which alluded to figuration but were on first glance abstract. Among her solo exhibitions were Gimpel Fils and later Marlborough Fine Art. Was included in Exhibition Road at Royal College of Art, 1988. Arts Council holds Oulton's works Dispossessed, of 1983, and Counterfoil, 1987. Lived in London.

Harry OUSEY 1915–1985 Painter and draughtsman, born in Manchester and brought up in Lancashire, who studied art in the late 1930s/early 1940s, teachers including Ronald Allan. While working for an architect in London during the early 1930s Ousey saw a show by Paul Nash, which determined him to become an artist. Ousey's work progressed slowly from figurative landscapes towards abstraction, with large watercolours and gouaches a feature. Eric Newton gave Ousey critical recognition in 1947 when he was showing in Salford, an exhibition called The Lancashire Scene. Solo exhibitions included Peterloo Gallery, Manchester, 1968; Hamet Gallery, from 1970; a series in France and Sweden from 1976; and Tib Lane Gallery, Manchester, 1997. Ousey travelled widely in Britain, but died in Marseilles, France. Museum of Modern Art, Skopje, Yugoslavia, where he showed in 1966, acquired his work.

Annie OVENDEN 1945– Painter and graphic designer, born in Amersham, Buckinghamshire, married to the artist Graham Ovenden. She was one of the seven founders of The Brotherhood of Ruralists in 1975, taking part in the first show in 1976 at RA. She studied at High Wycombe School of Art, 1961–5, working as a graphic designer, 1966–9. Lived for many years at Barley Splatt, near Mount, in Cornwall, from 1973. Began painting full-time in 1975, showing in group exhibitions from that year at Bodmin Fine Arts and Piccadilly Gallery from 1980.

Graham OVENDEN 1943– Artist and writer, born in Alresford, Hampshire. He studied at Southampton School of Art, 1960–4, then at Royal College of Art, 1965–8. In 1969 he had one-man show at Gallery 200, in Amsterdam, then from 1970 had series of shows with Piccadilly Gallery. In 1970 also exhibited with Peter Blake in the *Alice* exhibition at Waddington Galleries. In 1975 Ovenden had his solo show *Lolita* – Drawings and Prints at Waddington, the year he co-founded with six other artists The Brotherhood of Ruralists. It had its first show appearance at RA in 1976, after which Ovenden was a frequent exhibitor with the Brotherhood. The co-founders were artists who had moved from London to the West Country who believed that Modernism had swamped certain important elements in British art: the romantic, linear, mystical and literary. Ovenden was a photographer who had a show of his work at Olympus Gallery in 1984, and he was co-author of a number of books on nineteenth-century photography. His own work, both landscape and figurative, had a strong erotic element. Lived at Mount, near Bodmin, Cornwall, his wife being the artist Annie Ovenden.

Edward OVERTON-JONES 1889–late 1950s Artist and designer whose father Horace and uncle were both artists. He was educated at Stoke Grammar School and Rhos College, Wales, then began his artistic training in Stoke-on-Trent followed by periods of study at South Kensington Museum. From 1910 spent much time in Paris, where he met the artist Majel Davidson, encouraging her interest in pottery and its designs. Overton-Jones served in the Artists' Rifles in France in World War I, was twice slightly wounded and like Majel was decorated for bravery. After the war Overton-Jones hoped that his friendship with Majel, which lasted throughout their lives, might result in marriage, but their paths diverged. Overton-Jones joined the family pottery firm near Stoke, George Jones & Son, which was in the 1950s to be absorbed into the Coalport and then the Wedgwood groups. Eventually he chose to emigrate to America, where he married, had a family, earned his living and died. William Hardie Gallery, Glasgow, included Overton-Jones' French and American views in a 1989 mixed show.

Fiona OWEN 1957– Painter and illustrator, born in Wales, married to the artist John Owen. She obtained an honours degree in illustration at Newport College of Art and went on to a postgraduate course at London University, finished in 1979. She then settled in the Cotswolds to paint. Had a successful first exhibition at Medici Galleries in 1981, shared a show with her husband there in 1982 and the Society published several of her works as greetings cards. The main influences on her work were the detailed mediaeval manuscripts of Persia, India and France, notably the work of the Limbourg brothers.

George Elmslie OWEN 1899–1964 Painter and printmaker. Studied at Edinburgh College of Art, 1921–3, with Gerald Moira, then at L'Académie Moderne, Paris, 1923–5, with Amadée Ozenfant and Fernand Léger. Exhibited RA, LG, NEAC, RBA and RSA. Was a member of the Society of Sussex Painters. Lived in Steyning, Sussex.

Hermione OWEN 1951– Painter and printmaker, born in Lossiemouth, Scotland, brought up in Midhurst, Sussex. In 1968, she studied art and music in Florence, followed by two years' travel overland to India and on to Australia, then attended Byam Shaw School, 1970–4. Group shows included NEAC, RA Summer Exhibition, ICA and Andrew Colvin Contemporary Art. Had a solo show at The Coln Gallery, 1980; two at Clarendon Gallery, 1982–8; Hurlingham Gallery, 1989; and Sally Hunter Fine Art, from 1993. Owen painted extensively in India and on the continent.

Jamie OWEN 1966– Sculptor who attended École des Roches, France, 1982–3; Grenoble University, 1983–4; then City & Guilds of London Art School, 1990–4, with a three-year scholarship award. In 1994 gained first prize in sculpture at Alexandra Palace, then Grand Prix (overall prize) there. Showed at Portobello Art Festival, 1991; had a solo exhibition at Kilburn Business Centre, 1993; was on-site sculptor in Richmond, 1994; and in 1995 shared an exhibition at Thackeray Gallery with Carey Mortimer.

Janet Patricia OWEN 1965– Artist in oil on panel, charcoal and paper, and teacher, born and lived in London. Was notable for her heads of women, paintings being signed with initials. Owen studied at Central School of Art and Design, 1983–4, under Cecil Collins, then at Canterbury College of Art, 1984–7, with Dennis Creffield, Kevin Sinnott and Iain Biggs. A wide range of influences affected her work, from Paula Rego, Vermeer and Russian icons through Angela Carter and the great Victorian novelists to Hollywood musicals. Gained a Delfina Studios Trust two-year residency in 1992. Solo shows included Merz Contemporary Art from 1990 and Beaux Arts, Bath, from 1994. In 1995 Owen taught at Ohio State University, America, then moved to Los Angeles for two years. Lord Rothermere held her work.

John OWEN 1955– Painter and illustrator, born in Wales, married to the artist Fiona Owen. He achieved an honours degree in illustration at Newport College of Art and settled in the Cotswolds, painting pastoral scenes influenced by Victorian genre painters. In 1978 he won second prize in the International Mural Competition; was a prizewinner in the International Watercolour Competition twice in 1979–81; and won first prize in 1981 in the Rural Church Preservation Competition, judged by John Piper. Showed at RA, Mall Galleries, widely in the West Country and with his wife at Medici Galleries in 1982.

Mark OWEN 1963– Painter of landscape who chose to work out of doors around the year. He studied at Grimsby School of Art, 1981–2, then at Royal Academy Schools, 1982–5. After concentrating on product design at Chelsea School of Art, 1985–7, he worked for some years with a London consultancy. He showed in Japan in 1986, shared an exhibition at Clarendon Gallery in 1987 and had a solo show at Cadogan Contemporary in 1993. Royal Surrey Hospital, Guildford, holds his work.

Marjorie Nevshehir OWEN fl. from 1930s– Painter, born in Uxbridge, Middlesex, who studied with Henry Carr at Beckenham School of Art. Showed at UA of which she was a member, RBA and elsewhere, the Walker Art Gallery, Liverpool, holding her work. Lived in Garelochhead, Dunbartonshire.

Maurice OWEN 1947– Sculptor, printmaker and lecturer, born in Surrey, who attended Portsmouth College of Art, 1965–8; was a Japanese government scholar at Tokyo University's department of fine art, 1970–2; and gained his Master of Philosophy degree for studies in metaphysical perspective, 1983. Owen lectured at Liverpool College of Art, 1969–70; Hornsey College of Art, 1973–5; was artist-in-residence at Trent Polytechnic, Nottingham, 1975–8; then was in the fine art department at Portsmouth Polytechnic, 1978–84. In 1988 he gave the Giorgio de Chirico Centenary Lecture at the British School, Rome, and Portsmouth City Library. Ran a department at Southampton Institute involved in "Artresearch, employing art strategies as a scientific method", and had solo exhibitions including Aspex Gallery, Portsmouth, 1988; Southampton City Art Gallery, 1990; and 21st Century, 54–5 Slaidburn Street, Chelsea, 1996. Portsmouth City Museum and Art Gallery, Southern Arts Association and Nottingham City Council hold examples.

M E OWEN 1927– Painter, modeller and teacher, born in Penistone, Yorkshire; her full married name was Margaret Elizabeth Griffith-Owen. Educated in Barnsley at the Girls' High School, she studied art at Leeds College of Art, her teachers including Maurice de Sausmarez. She went on to teach art for many years at her old school and showed in Yorkshire. Lived at Redbrook, Barnsley.

Muriel OWEN fl. from 1950s– Watercolourist and teacher, born in Welwyn Garden City, Hertfordshire. She studied at St Albans School of Art, 1946–50, with Christopher Sanders and

Gwen White, then at London University, 1951. She was head of art and deputy principal, Dixon & Wolfe Tutors, 1969–82; was a designer for the firm Accraform; travelled widely abroad selling and exhibiting her work from 1968; and operated painting holidays in the Isle of Wight and abroad from 1984. Was a member of UA, SWA in which she held senior positions, and Thames Valley Arts Society. Also showed in mixed exhibitions at RI and had a series of solo shows, including Fine Art Trade Guild and Fairfield Halls, Croydon. Public commissions included two large watercolours of the Bank of England, one of the Queen Elizabeth Military Hospital in Woolwich and another of the Atomic Energy Commission's London headquarters. English Heritage bought 30 of her pictures for permanent summer exhibition at Yarmouth Castle. Lived at Totland, Isle of Wight.

Pat OWEN: *see* **Patience Sandra OWEN**

Patience Sandra OWEN 1949– Painter and draughtsman, who sometimes worked as Pat Owen, born in Glanaman, Carmarthenshire, into a mining family. Went to Carmarthen School of Art, 1967–8. Showed with RP, UA of which she was made an associate in 1983, RCamA and elsewhere. Lived for a time in London.

Peter OWEN 1956– Artist who studied at City of Birmingham Polytechnic, 1975–6, then Leicester Polytechnic, 1976–9. He gained awards from Yorkshire Arts in 1980 and Merseyside Arts in 1982 and 1985. Owen took part in a three-man show at Bakehouse Gallery, 1980, the RA exhibition Human Figure, 1986, and the Walker Art Gallery, Liverpool, touring show Merseyside Artists 3 in 1986–7. Solo exhibitions included Atkinson Art Gallery, Southport, 1982.

Will OWEN 1869–1957 Humorous black-and-white illustrator and poster artist. Born in Malta of a Naval family, he studied at Lambeth School of Art. Exhibited at Royal College of Art, RCamA and extensively at the Brook Street Art Gallery. He illustrated a number of books by the popular novelist W W Jacobs, as well as his own titles *Alleged Humour*, 1917, *Old London Town*, 1921, and *What's the Dope?*, 1944. Among the many periodicals he drew for were Jerome K Jerome's *The Idler*, *Sketch*, *Strand* and *Temple* magazines. Lived in London.

Ned OWENS 1918–1990 Artist, cartographer and teacher, working in a wide variety of media, born James Edward Owens in Newcastle upon Tyne, Northumberland, where he attended the local art school in the late 1930s. From 1945–58 Owens taught part-time at Manchester School of Art, also painting as a freelance. With his first wife Margo Ingham he was joint owner of the Mid-Day Studios, an important exhibition and gathering place for more advanced artists in Manchester. From 1959–75 Owens was staff cartographer for the *Manchester Guardian*. Sickert, Daumier and Rembrandt were influences on Owens, whose own work encompassed the female nude, figures in landscape, industrial scenes, single figures, the poor and deprived materially and emotionally. Owens showed at Manchester's City Art Gallery and elsewhere in the north, and Salford and other regional galleries hold examples. Well-known actors and Manchester dignitaries were frequent subjects. Died in Milnthorpe, Cumbria.

Thomas Bernard OXENBURY 1904– Watercolourist, born in Totnes, Devon, who was by profession a town planning consultant. He studied art at King Edward VI Grammar School in Totnes and exhibited only with Ipswich Art Club, of which he was a member, but not in later years. Also practised marquetry, but not did not exhibit. Lived latterly in London.

Roy OXLADE 1929– Painter in oil, born in London. He attended Bromley College of Art, 1950–5, and David Bomberg's Borough Polytechnic classes, 1950–3. He took part in Borough Bottega Group shows at Heffer Gallery, Cambridge, 1954, and Walker's Galleries, 1955. Oxlade's mixed show appearances also included Young Contemporaries, 1952–4; Winnipeg Biennale, first prize for drawing, 1960; John Moores Liverpool Exhibitions, 1964 and 1991; LG, 1965–8; RA Summer Exhibition, from 1984; and Jan Turner Gallery, Los Angeles, 1988. Had a period in Canada, with a solo show at Vancouver Art Gallery, 1963, later ones including Odette Gilbert Gallery, 1985–7–8. Lived in Newnham, Sittingbourne, Kent.

Joan OXLAND 1920– Painter and teacher, born in Cardiff, where she attended the School of Art. Also studied at Wimbledon School of Art and London University Institute of Education. Some years of teaching followed, then attended Académie Julian in Paris, 1962–3, before returning to teaching in Wales. In early 1970s retired to write, paint and teach for Workers' Educational Association. Showed at RWA, RA, Royal National Eisteddfod, SWG and elsewhere, including Abergavenny Art Group. Solo exhibitions included Chapter Arts Centre, Cardiff, 1974. WAC holds work.

Martin OXLEY 1961– Painter who studied at Ruskin School of Art, in Oxford, then Royal Academy Schools, 1983–8. His work could be stylish, using an unusual palette, as seen in his picture The China Pond at Wallington, included in The Broad Horizon, Agnew, 1990. Oxley's drawing of Temple of Apollo, Stourhead, had been commissioned by National Trust's Foundation for Art and was included in the Agnew show The Long Perspective, in 1987.

Ursula OXLEY 1918– Artist in watercolour, pen and ink, pastel and conté, born in Ealing, west London, who attended Winchester School of Art, 1935–9, and studied oil painting with Basil Gotto. She taught art to children, did secretarial work in ordnance during World War II, then married. Was known mostly as a child portraitist, but then turned to topography, cat paintings and flowers. Her father was the portrait painter Lawrence Deller. Oxley exhibited with RI, Guildford Art Society, PS, NS, SWA and in the Hampshire area, where she lived in Alresford and belonged to its Art Society. Illustrated A J Robertson's *History of Alresford*.

David OXTOBY 1938– Painter, printmaker and teacher. Was born in Horsforth, Yorkshire. He studied at Bradford Regional College of Art, 1950–7, with John Fleming, then at Royal Academy Schools, 1960–4, under Sir Henry Rushbury. Then became visiting professor at Minneapolis College of Art in America, from 1966–72 teaching at Maidstone College of Art. Learned etching from his friend Norman Stevens. Oxtoby's great interest was popular music of the 1950s–1970s, Oxtoby's Rockers being the subject of a show at the Redfern Gallery in 1977, a publication also appearing with that title. Had many international solo exhibitions. Work held by Tate Gallery, Museum of Modern Art in New York, Victoria & Albert Museum and Cartwright Hall, Bradford, which in 1990 staged his exhibition Oxtoby's Oxtobys. Lived in London.

Judith A A OYLER fl. c.1935–1985 Watercolour painter of landscapes, Oyler was born at Wychbold, Worcestershire. She studied at Grimsby School of Art and Leicester College of Art under George Scott Ingles, John Pettinger and Sydney Robert Watson. Oyler taught at Harrogate School of Art, then at Christ's Hospital Girls' High School. Exhibited at RA, RBS, RI, SWA and Goupil Gallery. Lived in Lincoln.

P

P: *see* **Charles PIERCE**

Martin PACE 1949–1997 Sculptor (notably of abstract works using found materials), draughtsman, painter and teacher, born and died in York, son of the distinguished ecclesiastical architect George Pace. Martin did a pre-diploma course at York Art School, 1968–9, studied at Cheltenham College of Art, 1970–3, under the influential Antanas Brazdys, then declined postgraduate study to return to his beloved Yorkshire. From 1974–97 taught at York Art School under Denis Donn, latterly as head of sculpture, emphasizing the need for sound drawing and technical skills. As well as siting his work in locations near to where he lived, Pace took part in Vera Russell's Artists Market shows as well as other surveys of contemporary sculpture, and had solo exhibitions at Newcastle Polytechnic Art Gallery, 1977, and Ikon Gallery, Birmingham, 1979. Although Pace was prominent as an exhibitor from the late 1970s to the mid-1980s, he continued developing new ideas until he died. Modernist abstraction, formal Japanese sculpture, Ernst, de Chirico, Carra, poetry, science fiction and Surrealist film were key interests and influences. Martin Ackerman Collection, Connecticut and New York, holds his work.

Ana Maria PACHECO 1943– Sculptor, printmaker, draughtsman, painter and teacher, born in Brazil, producing powerful and sometimes disturbing work in which death, magic and sexuality were important elements. Between 1960–4 Pacheco worked for degrees in sculpture and music at University in Goias, in 1965 studying music and education at the University of Brazil, Rio de Janeiro. After teaching sculpture and art at University in Goias, 1966–1973, from 1973–5 Pacheco was at the Slade School of Fine Art on a British Council Scholarship, taught by Reg Butler. She was head of fine art at Norwich School of Fine Art, 1985–9, where she was noted for her rigorous standards. Group shows included Women's Images of Men, ICA and tour, 1980; Hayward Annual, Hayward Gallery, 1982; Stockholm Art Fair, Sweden, 1985; 5th Biennale of European Graphic Art, Baden-Baden, West Germany, 1987; and 9th Norwegian International Print Triennale – Prize Winners Exhibition, 1989. Had a solo exhibition at Ikon Gallery, Birmingham, 1983, then showed widely in Britain and abroad, including Artsite Gallery, Bath, and tour, from 1989, and Wrexham Arts Centre, Wrexham, 1997. Victoria & Albert Museum, British Museum, Arts Council, and other public collections in Britain and abroad hold examples.

Antonio PACITTI 1924– Painter, designer, ceramist and teacher, born in Monte Cassino, Italy, his family moving to Glasgow as political refugees in 1928. He won a Gold Medal for Drawing at Glasgow School of Art, 1941–3; worked as a scenic artist for Ambassador Studios, Lambeth, in 1948; from 1949–51 attended Sir John Cass School of Arts and Crafts; from 1951–4 Slade School of Fine Art. In 1972 Pacitti obtained a double honours degree in Italian and history of art. He was head of art and design at Southwark Adult Education Institute and South Lewisham Adult Education Institute, 1972–87. Pacitti said that his temperament was "basically intuitive, though it's based on rationality and experience". Rembrandt, Turner and Van Gogh were key influences. He showed at RA Summer Exhibitions, Bedford College, Keele University, Gagliardi Design and Contemporary Art and elsewhere. Had solo shows at Accademia Italiana and West Soho Gallery, 1993. British Museum owns his work. Lived in London.

Jack PACKENHAM 1938– Painter, poet, writer and teacher, born in Dublin, Ireland, who in 1959 graduated from Queen's University, Belfast, in French, Spanish and philosophy. After writing and painting on Ibiza and then living in Dorset, 1959–60, from 1961–90 taught English in a secondary school in Belfast, Northern Ireland, where he settled, then painted full-time. Pakenham published several collections of poetry, including *The Last Day*, 1980. He won a number of Arts Council of Northern Ireland awards, gained the RUA's Conor Prize in 1985 and its Silver Medal in 1986, in 1987 being elected an academician. Took part in group and mixed shows, including Group 63, 1963–73; 4 Ulster Painters at Lurgan Arts Festival, 1966; Art for Society, at Whitechapel Art Gallery and Ulster Museum in Belfast, 1978; and 5 Artists, Wyvern Gallery, Dublin, 1991. Had many solo shows, later ones including Selected Works, 1975–91, at Wyvern Gallery, Dublin, 1991.

Frederick PACKER 1925– Artist in various media and teacher, born in London. Studied at College of Rhine Army, 1946, and Chelsea School of Art, 1947–51, in latter year winning a Morland Lewis Travelling Scholarship. After teaching at various schools and colleges of art taught at Central School of Art and Design. Showed with RA, Young Contemporaries, LG and elsewhere. Lived latterly in Hastings, Sussex.

Jennifer Maskell PACKER 1944– Painter and designer, born in Knowl Hill, Berkshire, her father a farm worker. She studied at Berkshire College of Art, 1960–4, and began designing and printing fabrics for the Landmark Trust. Influences on her painting included country lore and the work of the painters Chardin, Vermeer and Paula Rego. It had a strong pattern element and a sometimes uneasy atmosphere. She shared a show at Sally Hunter Fine Art in 1992. Continued to work in Berkshire.

Lilian PACKER 1903– Watercolourist and miniaturist, born in Hove, Sussex. Studied at Brighton School of Art. She showed at RA, RMS, West Sussex Art Club of which she was a member, and Worthing Museum and Art Gallery, which also owns her work. Sometimes signed this only with initials. Lived at High Salvington, Sussex.

William PACKER 1940– Art critic, painter, draughtsman and teacher, born Birmingham. Was at Wimbledon School of Art, 1959–63, Brighton College of Art, 1963–4. From 1974 was art critic of the *Financial Times*. Was the author of *The Art of Vogue Covers*, 1980; *Fashion Drawing in Vogue*, 1983; and – with Gemma Levine – *Henry Moore*, 1985. Showed in group exhibitions at Angela Flowers, Camden Arts Centre and elsewhere and in 1992 took part in a three-critics show at Cadogan Contemporary, showing work done in England, France and Italy. Held a solo show of drawings at Piers Feetham Gallery, 1996. Graves Art Gallery, Sheffield, holds his work. Lived in London.

John PADDISON 1929– Sculptor and teacher who studied at Wolverhampton College of Art, 1945–7, returning there after National Service in the Army from 1949–52. At the Royal College of Art, 1952–6, Paddison studied under Frank Dobson and John Skeaping. From 1965 Paddison lectured in Wolverhampton Polytechnic's sculpture department, having from 1956 until then been a freelance sculptor working with the Birmingham sculptor Thomas Wright on some of his architectural commissions, also teaching part-time. Paddison tended to work in seclusion rather than exhibiting widely. Mixed shows included Cannizaro Park, Wimbledon, 1983, and Yorkshire Sculpture Park, Bretton Hall, 1984, as well as other London and Midlands exhibitions. Had solo exhibitions at the Hatton Gallery in Newcastle upon Tyne, and at Ikon Gallery, Birmingham. Public gallery in Birmingham, Hereford Public Library and Coventry Cathedral hold Paddison's work. Lived Llanidloes, Powys.

Philip PADWICK 1876–1958 Landscape painter, born in Horsham, Sussex. He studied at Slade School of Fine Art. Was an extensive exhibitor, including RBA and ROI of both of which he was a member, Fine Art Society, RA, RHA and Paris Salon. His Littlehampton Front, painted in 1923, owned by Astley Cheetham Art Gallery, Stalybridge, was included in a tribute to the dealer Lucy Wertheim, who showed him, Salford Museum and Art Gallery and tour, 1991–2. Padwick's work looked back in subject and technique to the eighteenth century. Lived in Fittleworth, Sussex.

Kathleen PAENSON fl. from 1940s– Painter, decorative artist, draughtsman in ink and teacher, born in London. Studied at Sidcup School of Art, where her teachers included Ruskin Spear and Robin Guthrie, then at Slade School of Fine Art under George Charlton. Showed at RA, RBA, AIA, in Switzerland where she lived for some time, and in Paris where she also lived. Contemporary Art Society member. United Nations building in Geneva holds her work, which was signed K P inside a circle.

Albert Schiller PAGE 1905– Painter, industrial designer and printmaker, born and lived in London, whose art education was wide, including South Hackney Technical Institute, 1922–4; St Martin's School of Art, 1928–9; Edinburgh College of Art, 1942–3, under Adam Bruce Thomson; and Central School of Arts and Crafts; he also studied alone on the continent for a period after World War II. Page did a volume of industrial design and illustrative work, also showing at RSA, Heal's Mansard Gallery, Whitechapel Art Gallery and elsewhere.

Carole PAGE 1955– Painter, designer, illustrator and teacher who attended the Slade School of Fine Art. After working as a graphic designer and illustrator she settled in Cornwall and developed work which took the landscape and natural structure and colour as themes. Taught at summer school at Marlborough College, was a member of the Arts Centre Group in London and Newlyn Society of Artists and was represented by the oil A Garden Enclosed in the 1989 Newlyn Orion Galleries show A Century of Art in Cornwall 1889–1989. Lived in Newmill.

Claude PAGE fl. from 1940s– Artist and illustrator, born in Handsworth, Warwickshire, attending the School of Art there, then Birmingham College of Art. During 1940–6 Page served in the Royal Engineers, for much of the time at the School of Military Engineering, Ripon. He was an illustrator for military training manuals and a recognised war artist, producing over 200 air battle pictures. Page joined the National Trust, making over 850 drawings and paintings of its properties, was information officer for Wales and retired in 1978. His work appeared in a number of publications, including the *Daily Telegraph*, *Western Mail*, *Country Life* and *Reader's Digest*. Page was made an honorary life vice-president of the Museum in Tenby, Pembrokeshire, where he lived, and which holds his work.

David Michael PAGE 1935– Artist in oil, pastel and mixed media, and teacher, who studied English literature at Oxford University and at Ruskin School, when Percy Horton was head, 1953–9. After two years at Marburg, Germany, 1959–61, then a year painting in St Ives, 1961–2, Page taught at Hornsey College of Art and North East London Polytechnic, taking early retirement in 1985, after which he painted on the Norfolk/Suffolk border full-time. His pictures were "about people, places and things, using whatever pictorial devices seem appropriate at the time". Group shows included Young Contemporaries; Penwith Gallery, St Ives; Fermoy Art Gallery, King's Lynn; Schoolhouse Gallery Open, Bath; and Drawings for All, Gainsborough's House, Sudbury, and tour. Solo shows included Greengate House, E 13, 1981; Adnams Wine Warehouse, Aldeburgh, from 1989; The Gallery, Pentonville Road, from 1990; and South Norfolk House, Long Stratton, 1997. Lived at Starston, Norfolk.

Dennis PAGE 1926– Watercolourist, notable for his depiction of urban architecture across Europe. Born in London, he studied at Harrow and Central Schools of Art, teachers Ruskin Spear and Mervyn Peake. He then travelled and painted widely for two years.

After National Service, Page developed a successful career in advertising, while continuing to paint, oil company publicity a speciality. His Esso tiger campaign was seen worldwide. Retired in 1989 to paint full-time, showing regularly at Bankside and Mall Galleries and in the provinces, in 1991 gaining the RWS Beautiful Britain Award. Page's Travels was a one-man exhibition at The Linda Blackstone Gallery, Pinner, 1996.

Dione PAGE 1936– Artist and teacher. Her still lifes and landscapes had a rich, colourful quality, often employing red, and she worked in materials claimed to be exclusive: a mix of gouache, wax pastel and lumigraph pencil. Page trained at Colchester School of Art, 1953–6, leaving to work as a graphic designer in publishing and advertising. She went on to become an Essex County Council adult education art tutor and was a selection committee member for Colchester Art Society. Won a series of awards, later ones including East of England Art Exhibition Special Award and Bury St Edmunds Art Society Best Newcomer, both in 1996. She was elected a full member of SWA in 1992, RWA in 1993. Showed at RA Summer Exhibition from 1957 and widely elsewhere in the provinces in mixed exhibitions. Solo shows included The Minories, Colchester; Gainsborough's House, Sudbury; Digby Gallery, Colchester; Phoenix Gallery, Lavenham; and Chappel Galleries, Chappel, from 1992. National Library of Wales, Aberystwyth; Nuffield Foundation; Ernst & Young; Essex County Council; and other public and corporate collections hold examples. Lived at Weeley, Clacton-on-Sea, Essex.

James PAGE-ROBERTS 1925– Artist in various media, born in Silchester, Hampshire. He studied with Bernard Meninsky at Central School of Arts and Crafts and at Old Vic School of Theatre Design with Margaret Harris. Showed solo with Galerie de Seine, Reid and Qantas Galleries and abroad. Ministry of Works bought his work. Lived in London.

E Willis PAIGE 1890–1960 Printmaker, draughtsman and teacher whose early life is a mystery. He joined Bristol's Municipal School of Art as assistant principal in the early-1920s and stayed until his retirement in 1950. He was an active and popular member of the Bristol Savages and showed in Chicago, at RA and RWA, of which he was a member. A notable etcher, he specialised in topographic views throughout England and travelled widely in northern Europe. Bristol City Art Gallery holds his work. Lived in the city.

John PAIGE fl. from 1960s– Wildlife artist, graphic designer, illustrator and teacher who left Birmingham College of Arts and Crafts in the 1960s. Previously he had been a regular soldier for 15 years in the Armoured Corps and a warden in Uganda National Parks for a year. Paige was a member of the Chartered Society of Designers and of SWLA, and was included in Dorset County Museum's show for Dorset Naturalist Trust, 1982–3. Lived in King's Cliffe, Peterborough, Cambridgeshire, where he had a studio gallery and taught with Jane Paige.

Grace PAILTHORPE 1883–1971 Surrealist artist and writer, born Sussex, married to the painter Reuben Mednikoff, also known as Ricky Pailthorpe. She served as a surgeon in World War I, worked as a district medical officer in Western Australia, 1918–22, returned to England to study psychological medicine, published books on delinquency and set up what eventually became the Portman Clinic, for its treatment. Met Mednikoff in 1935, and they embarked on a life study of psychological art research. Automatism was the key to their art theory and practice. In the 1930s Pailthorpe contributed to main Surrealist shows, but she fell out with the British Surrealist Group in late 1930s, having published *The Scientific Aspect of Surrealism* in 1938, being expelled two years later. Continued to paint and research until her death. Was included in Women Artists of The British Surrealist Movement, 1930–1990, at John Bonham, Murray Feely Fine Art, 1992. Leeds City Art Gallery held a a retrospective of Dr Pailthorpe's and Mednikoff's work, Sluice Gates of the Mind, 1998, the exhibition being opened by veteran Surrealist Conroy Maddox.

Ken PAINE 1926– Pastel draughtsman and painter, notable for his portraits, born in London. He studied at Twickenham Art College, 1942, and served an apprenticeship as a commercial artist. After four years in Army from 1948 Paine travelled the world in the Merchant Navy, in 1958 emigrating to America where he earned his living drawing portraits and exhibiting in the San Francisco area. In 1968 returned to England and set up studio in Hampton Hill, Middlesex. Showed with PS of which he was a member, RP, Omell Gallery and elsewhere. In 1987 gained first prize at International Pastel Exhibition, Lille, France. Had solo exhibition at Jablonski Gallery, 1988, sharing one at The Linda Blackstone Gallery, Pinner, 1995.

Ula PAINE 1909– Painter, born in Surbiton, Surrey. Studied with Lettice MacMunn at Queen Anne's Studio, 1929–31, then nearby at Chelsea Polytechnic School of Art, 1930–1, qualifying as a teacher in the latter year, Harold S Williamson being among her teachers. She showed at RI, RBA, WIAC, NS, UA and Phoenix Gallery in Lavenham, and had a one-man show at Galerie de Seine in 1958. Lived in London.

Graham PAINTER 1947– Painter, born and brought up in east London, who moved to country aged 12 and immediately felt at home. After a varied career, aged 29 he decided to study art and completed a one-year foundation course at Braintree College, followed by three years at Sheffield City Polytechnic, where he gained an honours degree in fine art. Painter showed in a number of mixed exhibitions, including Sheffield National Open, 1980; RI, ROI and RA; Wade Gallery, Los Angeles, 1986; and John Laing, Mall Galleries, 1989. He had two solo shows at Deben Art Gallery, Woodbridge, 1986–7; Rye Art Gallery, 1988; Lion & Lamb Gallery, Farnham, 1988; and Markswood Gallery, Great Bardfield, 1990. Painter's work was still life and landscape in the mainstream English tradition.

Joan PAINTER 1913– Artist in a wide range of media, including collage, and teacher, born in Bristol, where she studied with Gwen Pallin, also at Reigate College of Art. She was married to George D Painter, biographer of Proust and Chateaubriand. Joan Painter taught art at Friends' Centre, Brighton, and Dupont Arts, Hove, where she lived in Sussex. She showed at International Congress for Art in Education, aged 15, also with Reigate Society of Artists' annual exhibitions – she was a member – from 1965; other mixed shows included South East Arts Touring Exhibition, 1974–5; Worthing Museum and Art Gallery, 1975; Alpine Gallery, 1985; and Albion Gallery, Lewes, 1990. Later solo shows included Trinity Arts Centre, Tunbridge Wells, opening exhibition, 1983, and Hove Museum and Art Gallery, 1994. Worthing Museum and King's College, London, hold examples. Painter's work was noted for its rich, vibrant colour.

Tom PAINTER 1918– Sculptor in various materials and teacher, married to the artist Muriel Painter. He was born in Wolverhampton, Staffordshire, and studied with Robert Emerson at the local College of Art, 1932–40, then with Frank Dobson at Royal College of Art, 1946–9, and in Italy. Taught at Ravensbourne College of Art. Painter was a fellow of RBS and a member of RBA, also exhibiting at RA. Lived in London.

Rhonda PAISLEY: *see* **RHONDA**

Herbert William PALLISER 1883–1963 Sculptor, born in Northallerton, Yorkshire. After time as a pupil with an architect in Harrogate, he studied at Central School of Arts and Crafts, 1906–11, then with J Havard Thomas at the Slade School of Fine Art, 1911–14. Taught at Royal College of Art. Showed at RA, NEAC, Walker Art Gallery, Liverpool, and Royal Glasgow Institute of the Fine Arts. His commissions included the Calcutta War Memorial, 1924; Cobra Fountain, New Delhi, 1932; and Roosevelt Memorial, Westminster Abbey, 1946. Palliser was a fellow of the RBS. Examples of his work are illustrated in Arthur T Broadbent's *Sculpture Today in Great Britain 1940–1943*, and in Eric Newton's *British Sculpture 1944–1946*. He was married to the painter Jane Moncur and lived in London.

Joyce PALLOT 1912– Painter, designer and teacher, born in Brightlingsea, Essex, married to the artist Henry Collins. She was educated at Colchester County High School and the local and Southend School of Art. After World War II she taught part-time in a private school and adult education centre in Colchester, as well as the School of Art. With her husband she worked on a large number of murals and exhibition designs, including the Brussels Exhibition; Expo '70, in Japan; Ind Coope Ltd, Philips Business Systems and British Home Stores. Exhibited widely in the provinces and in 1984 and 1995 with her husband had retrospectives at The Minories, Colchester. Was a member of the Colchester Art Society and the Society of Industrial Artists and Designers. Pallot's later work frequently embraced dockland and industrial scenes, emphasising the angular nature of structures.

Albert Harold PALMER 1911–1985 Artist and teacher, born in Northamptonshire, who studied art part-time, then full-time at Grimsby School of Art, 1923–9; worked in a London commercial art studio, 1929–33; then attended Royal College of Art, 1933–6. In 1938 he received a Travelling Scholarship from the College, also a Gold Medal. After copying House of Commons murals for the World Trade Exhibition in New York, 1938–9, Palmer from 1939–45 served in the Camouflage Corps, then spent 1947–9 in a tuberculosis sanatorium in Switzerland. He was on the staff of Maidstone Art School, 1950–4; from 1954–62 was lecturer in painting at Gravesend Art School, then acting principal; and was head of art and craft at Gravesend Adult Education Centre, 1962–77. From 1977–85 painted full-time at his own studio gallery in central London. Exhibitions included Leysin, Switzerland, 1949; Football and the Fine Arts, Football Association tour, 1953; NEAC from 1953; RA Summer Exhibition from 1959; Posterngate Gallery, Hull, 1990–1; Grimsby Central Library, 1991; and latterly Sally Hunter Fine Art. Ferens Art Gallery, Hull, holds Palmer's work and the Tate Gallery archive his papers.

Alfred PALMER 1877–1951 Painter in oil and watercolour, sculptor and draughtsman, landscapes, portraits and figure subjects. Studied art at the Royal Academy Schools, where he came under the influence of John Singer Sargent, and at the Académie Julian, for several years around the turn of the century. Maintained a studio in Paris and travelled regularly to Italy, Germany and Spain, where he was influenced by Velasquez. He had a fine bass singing voice, which was trained while living in Florence. In 1906 married the artist Mary Croom, with whom he settled in Kent. Palmer continued his travels in North Africa, and his ability as a linguist led to his doing secret service work in World War I. He was showing extensively, including RA, RBA, ROI, RI, Paris Salon and elsewhere on the continent. In 1925 made first visit to southern Africa, where he won the Natal Society's Goldfinger Award in 1929 for his depiction of Bantu life. During World War II lived in Dorset, but returned to South Africa for several years in 1947, returning to England in 1950, finally living in Swanage, Dorset. Palmer's travels contributed to his becoming a powerful Colourist. He was a pupil at Dulwich College, which held an exhibition of his work in 1987.

Anne PALMER 1932– Painter, designer and teacher, born in Hythe, Kent, married to the artist James Palmer. She originally studied as a textile designer and gradually turned to painting, being influenced by Paul Klee. After Canterbury College of Art she was at the Central School of Arts and Crafts, her teachers including Mervyn Peake, Eduardo Paolozzi and Gordon Crook. She taught textiles at Bromley College of Art and at Dover and Canterbury Grammar Schools. A member of East Kent Art Society, Palmer showed at New Art Centre, RA, at John Moores Exhibition in Liverpool, New Ashgate Gallery in Farnham and elsewhere in the provinces. Lived at Lower Hardres, Kent.

Eugene PALMER 1955– Painter and teacher, born in Kingston, Jamaica. He experimented with both abstract and figurative images and spoke from a black perspective. After a foundation course at Sutton Coldfield, 1974–5, Palmer obtained his bachelor's degree from Wimbledon School of Art, 1975–8; after gaining a teaching certificate from Garnett College, 1982–3, he obtained his master's degree at Goldsmiths' College School of Art, 1983–5. Palmer showed in many group exhibitions from Young Contemporaries in 1977, including the Whitechapel Open in 1988. After a solo show at Bedford Hill Gallery in 1988 he had another at 198 Gallery in 1990, and in 1997 one of a series at Duncan Campbell Contemporary Art. Palmer had a wide-ranging teaching career, appointments including Wolverhampton Polytechnic, Open University and Slade School of Fine Art. In 1990 he completed an Aid for Romania project in Bucharest.

Frederick PALMER 1944– Painter, teacher, theatre designer and writer, born in Blackpool, Lancashire. Studied at Goldsmiths' College School of Art from 1954, being a part-time lecturer there, 1956–7. After various teaching appointments became principal lecturer in art at Furzedown and Philippa Fawcett Colleges. Among Palmer's ventures were *Poems*, published by The Kit Kat Press, 1958; editorship of *3 Arts Quarterly*, published by Woodstock Gallery, 1960; design of several productions for Questors Theatre in mid-1960s; a series of television programmes, including *Images*, Thames Television, 1973; and books, including *Monoprint Techniques*, published by B T Batsford, 1975. From 1958 Palmer took part in a series of mixed and solo shows. In 1976 he shared an exhibition, including landscapes in Britain and abroad, at Woodlands Art Gallery.

Garrick PALMER 1933– Illustrator, printmaker, painter, photographer and teacher, born in Portsmouth, Hampshire. He was educated at St John's College, Southsea, and studied at Portsmouth College of Art and Design, 1951–5, then the Royal Academy Schools, 1955–7, where he won a series of awards including the Gold Medal and Edward Stott Travelling Scholarship, 1958. Showed in London and the provinces. Cumberland House Museum and Art Gallery, Portsmouth, and public galleries in Eastbourne, Brighton and abroad hold his work. A fine draughtsman, Palmer illustrated a number of books, notably a series of novels and stories by Herman Melville, to which his dramatic style was suited. RE member. Taught at Winchester School of Art and lived in Cowplain, Portsmouth, for some years.

James PALMER 1917– Painter and teacher, born in Sunderland, married to the artist Anne Palmer. He studied at Clapham School of Art, 1934–8, then Royal College of Art, 1938–40 and 1946–7, his teachers including Percy Hague Jowett. From 1947 Palmer taught at Canterbury College of Art, Camberwell School of Art and then Bromley/Ravensbourne College of Art, part-time 1947–61, full-time 1961–81. An East Kent Art Society member, he showed at RA from 1946 as well as with the LG, NEAC, John Moores Exhibition in Liverpool and at Leicester Galleries and exhibited solo on several occasions at Drew Gallery, in Canterbury. A rich Colourist, Palmer's earliest influences were Bonnard and Matisse, then Paul Klee, his later Dream Sequences series having slightly Surrealist elements. Lived at Lower Hardres, Kent.

Juliette PALMER 1930– Artist mostly in watercolour, illustrator and writer, teacher, born in Romford, Essex. She studied at South-East Essex School of Art, 1946–50, illustration under William Stobbs and Alan Wellings, life with Bernard Carolan, then was at University of London Institute of Education, 1950–1. She taught in Essex secondary schools, 1952–7; was a display designer for Metal Box, 1957–8; worked for a com- mercial art studio, 1958–9; freelanced as a children's book illustrator, 1959–80, during part of that period writing and designing children's books. From 1969 was a prolific exhibitor, mixed show appearances including RA Summer Exhibition, RI, RWS, RWA, NEAC, ROI and abroad. Solo shows included Crane Gallery, Chichester, 1988, and Phyllis Court, Henley, 1992. Leicestershire County Council and Barking, Essex, Library hold examples. Lived in Cookham, Berkshire.

Kate PALMER 1966– Painter of abstracts, born in Norwich, Norfolk. She studied at Oxford Polytechnic, 1985–6, St Martin's School of Art, 1986–9, and Royal College of Art, 1989–91. In 1991 won The Burston Prize. Showed in 2nd Biennale of European Art Schools, Antwerp, 1989; Into the 90s III, Mall Galleries, 1992; and in 1993 shared a show at Paton Gallery. This featured her Cabot Series, employing cool, dark colours.

Margaret PALMER 1922– Painter and illustrator, born in London, who studied at Hornsey School of Art, 1938–9; Salisbury School of Art, 1939–41; then Bournemouth College of Art, 1941–2. She was a member of NS and PS, also showing with ROI and RP, being noted for her portraits. These included Dame Alicia Markova the ballerina; Susan Hampshire the actress; and two Lord Mayors of London, Sir David Rowe-Ham and Sir Greville Spratt. Palmer illustrated J B Priestley's first children's book, *Snoggle*. Her work is held by Guildford Borough collection. She lived at Wonersh, Surrey.

Marjorie PALMER: *see* **Marjorie PROCTER**

Ralph H PALMER 1916– Sculptor in various materials, painter and teacher, whose real name was Herbert Ralph Palmer. Born in Richmond, Surrey, but educated in South Africa, attending Johannesburg Art School, with a scholarship, 1932–6. Returned to England where he studied with Percy Hague Jowett, head of the Royal College of Art. Worked for Victoria & Albert Museum and taught art part-time. Took part in many group shows in England and abroad, had several one-man exhibitions and carried out a series of sculptural commissions for South African and British clients. South Africa House, in London, has a bronze Mother and Child by him and the Imperial War Museum has his work. Eric Newton in his monograph *British Sculpture 1944–1946* illustrates Palmer's life-size bronze Head of Basuto Boy. Lived in London.

Robert PALMER 1927– Painter, born in Cambridge where he studied at its School of Art part-time, 1951–8. He was elected ROI in 1978, also showing at RA, RBA and RWA. Palmer's solo exhibitions included Fermoy Gallery, King's Lynn, 1980. Lived in Bournemouth, Dorset.

Simon PALMER 1956– Visionary painter and printmaker, inspired by the work of Paul Nash, Samuel Palmer and Edward Bawden, born in Doncaster, Yorkshire. Although they drew on the familiar world, Palmer's places and characters had a peculiarity all their own. He studied at Reigate School of Art & Design, 1973–7, concentrating on illustration, graphics and various printmaking processes, although tutors encouraged him to paint landscape. In 1977 Palmer sold a first set of etchings to Christie's Contemporary Art. Exhibitions and solo shows included Lombard Gallery, Bromley, 1977; Alexander Gallery, Bristol, 1984; RA Summer Exhibition, 1987; Dreamers of Landscape at Bohun Gallery, Henley-on-Thames, 1992; and with James Huntington-Whiteley at Gallery 27, in 1997. After his studies in the south of England, Palmer returned to live in Yorkshire, and in 1995 was commissioned to write and illustrate the verse book *Saltaire: a picture story book*, about the model industrial village. In 1989 he had written and illustrated his first, privately printed publication, *Pebbles on a beach.*

William John PALMER-JONES 1887–1974 Versatile artist and architect, born in Hartford, Huntingdonshire, originally as William John Jones. After Dulwich College, 1900–4, he studied at the Architectural Association Schools, 1906–8, gaining a Banister Fletcher Bursary, and printmaking at Central School of Arts and Crafts. During the period 1908–12 he was attached to the Metropolitan Museum of Art, New York, as staff artist for excavations in Egypt, also taking part in British archaelogical work at Sparta and Melos. World War I saw Palmer-Jones serving in the Royal Naval Volunteer Reserve and Royal Naval Air Service; he was commissioned in the Egyptian Labour Corps, serving in Sinai and Palestine, and designed a war memorial for the Egyptian Expeditionary Force at Jerusalem, 1919, not built for lack of funds. After the war he resumed practice in London, also designing furniture and being involved in book illustration and stage work. He won a silver medal at the first *Daily Mail* Ideal Home Exhibition. During World War II Palmer-Jones was engaged in passive air defence in the Ministry of Supply. He was a fellow of RIBA and had work reproduced in such publications as *Studio, Colour, Building News, Cabinet Maker* and the *Architectural Review*. Showed at RA, Walker's Galleries, Walker Art Gallery in Liverpool and abroad. Lived in London.

Shanti PANCHAL 1951– Artist, notably on paper, born in India. he studied at Sir J J School of Art, Bombay, 1971–7, then Byam Shaw School of Art, 1978–80. Showed widely in Britain and India, figurative pictures reflecting his Indian background. Exhibited at RA, at John Moores Liverpool exhibition from 1987, winning a prize in that year, other group shows including John Player Awards at National Portrait Gallery, Whitechapel Open exhibitions, and London Paper Works, at Square Gallery, 1989, where he was first prize winner. In 1988–90 a major solo tour of his work was based at City Art Gallery, Bradford. Arts Council holds a typical watercolour, Veil, of 1984. Lived in Harrow, Middlesex.

Robert PANCHERI 1916– Sculptor in wood and stone, born in Bromsgrove, Worcestershire, where he settled. He studied at Birmingham School of Arts and Crafts, 1934–9, with William Bloye and Bernard Fleetwood-Walker. Established a workshop in Bromsgrove in 1934 and apart from a period in the Army, 1939–46, sculpted there. Pancheri was made an associate of RBS. He completed statues in Winwick church, Malvern Priory and elsewhere and a Portland stone relief for Sheldon Fire Station.

Denis PANNETT 1939– Watercolourist, born in Hove, Sussex, son of the artist Juliet Pannett and brother of the artist Liz Pannett. He was "mainly self-taught, but with help from my mother and Edward Wesson". After commissioned National Service with the Devon Dorset Regiment Pannett worked for 20 years with the diamond firm De Beers in Britain, on the continent and in Africa, becoming a full-time painter in 1982. He was mainly involved in landscape, marine and aviation art, although latterly he was heavily engaged in golf prints with Rosemary Young Fine Art. He also did covers and illustrations for several Richard Binns travel guides and cards and calendars for Royle's. Pannett was a member of the Guild of Aviation Artists, on the committee of the Wapping Group of Artists and was president of Arun Art Society. Mixed exhibitions included RI, RS, MA, Royal Festival Hall, National Maritime Museum in Greenwich and Royal Air Force Museum, Hendon. He took part in a number of family shows, including Brotherton Gallery; Southover Gallery, Lewes; River Gallery, Arundel; Arun Art Centre, Arundel; and Pacific and Fringe Clubs, both in Hong Kong. The Fine Art Gallery, Dower House Gallery in Berkhamsted and Warwick Gallery, Beaconsfield, Buckinghamshire, where he lived, gave Pannett solo exhibitions.

Juliet PANNETT 1911– Career portrait painter working in oil, watercolour, charcoal and sanguine, born in Hove, Sussex, mother of the artists Denis and Liz Pannett. She studied at Brighton College of Art, teachers including Louis Ginnett, Charles Knight and Morgan Rendle. She showed at RA, RP and elsewhere. Solo and family exhibitions included Brotherton and Cooling Galleries, galleries in New York and Cleveland in Ohio, and at Coventry Cathedral Festival; and in 1986 in Hong Kong with her children. Pannett was special artist to the *Illustrated London News*, 1957–64. She was a freeman of the Painter-Stainers' Company, with a prize in 1960, and a freeman of the City of London. Her main works included two portraits of HM The Queen as well as other members of the royal family. National Portrait Gallery holds many pictures by her, as do Oxford and Cambridge University colleges. Lived in Angmering Village, Sussex.

Ben PANTING 1964– Sculptor who studied at Central School of Art, 1984–7, then Royal College of Art, 1988–91. Awards included

Phoebe Lewellyn-Smith Scholarship, 1986; Fleur Cowles Award and Korn Ferry Award, both 1990; Madame Tussauds Award, 1991; and Morris Singer Foundry Scholarship, 1993. Among Panting's commissions were the Clare Foundation, 1991; Chelsea Harbour sculpture, 1993; Bolesworth Castle Commission, 1995; and Tattenhall Business Park Commission, 1996. Group shows included South Bank London Institute Show, 1986; RA Summer Exhibition, from 1989; and Foundations for Fame, London Institute, 1997, where he exhibited figurative work. Among his solo shows were Odette Gilbert Gallery, 1991, and in 1992 Glasgow Print Studio in Glasgow and a studio show in London.

John PANTING 1940–1974 Sculptor and teacher who created abstract sculptures in glass fibre and steel. He was born in New Zealand and studied at Canterbury University School of Art, 1959–62, then at Royal College of Art, 1964–7. He taught at Royal College and Central School of Art and Design, 1972–4, being head of sculpture at Central for final two years. Painting's work covered a wide range and was often of considerable grace and simplicity, as several examples in Arts Council collection show. As well as taking part in British and overseas group shows, Panting had two solo exhibitions at Galerie Swart, Amsterdam, 1967–8, and memorial retrospective at Serpentine Gallery, 1975. He gained a New Zealand Arts Council Award in 1963 and a Bickert and Widdowson Scholarship, New Zealand, 1969. Commissions included Peter Stuyvesant Sculpture Project, Plymouth, 1972.

Lawrence PANTON 1894–1954 Artist in oil, gouache and tempera, born in Egremont, Cheshire. After initial education in England, he studied art at the Ontario College of Art, Toronto, of which he eventually became principal. He exhibited extensively in Canada, also in Britain and other Commonwealth states, venues including RSW. Lived in Toronto.

Eduardo PAOLOZZI 1924– Sculptor, draughtsman, designer, printmaker and teacher, born in Leith, Midlothian, of Italian parents. Studied at Edinburgh College of Art, 1943, and Slade School of Fine Art, 1944–7. After Army service he worked in Paris, 1947–50, his work being shown at Galerie Maeght in 1948. His first one-man show was at Mayor Gallery, 1947 and in New York at Betty Parsons Gallery, 1960. By then Paolozzi had been represented at Venice Biennale in 1952, São Paulo Bienal in 1957, Documenta II, Kassel, 1959, and in various touring shows. After then Paolozzi's work was shown internationally, including Tate Gallery retrospective, 1971, and seventieth birthday show, Yorkshire Sculpture Park, Wakefield, 1994. Was an influential teacher, including St Martin's School, 1955–8, where he taught sculpture; Royal College of Art, where he lectured in ceramics, 1968–89, from which time he was visiting professor; and at schools in Hamburg, Cologne and Munich, Germany, starting in 1960, teaching ceramics and sculpture. Winner of many awards. Produced several films and books. Among his commissions was a cast iron sculpture to Bruckner the Austrian composer, in Linz, 1977; four cast-aluminum doors for Hunterian Gallery, Glasgow, 1976–80; Master of the Universe, a bronze for Kowloon Park, Hong Kong, 1987–88; and Newton after James Watt, bronze for Design Museum, London, 1989–90. Elected RA, 1979; knighted in 1988. Lived in London.

Aristide PAPAGEORGE 1899–1983 Painter and draughtsman, born in Alexandria, Egypt, of Greek parentage. He went to Paris in 1920s to study art at several schools, including Atelier Colarossi, Académie Julian and L'Académie de la Grande Chaumière. He showed at Salon des Tuileries, Salon des Indépendants and Salon d'Automne. Went back to Egypt as a professional painter and then returned in 1962 to Paris. Held solo shows in Alexandria and Cairo and in Athens in 1958. Showed extensively in Paris, then married in England and settled in 1973. Papageorge appeared in mixed exhibitions at John Whibley Gallery in 1965, Mercury Gallery, 1966, O'Hana Gallery from 1973 and RA from 1974. In 1982 a show of his drawings was held at Woodlands Art Gallery, in 1986 a memorial exhibition being organised by Ethniki Pinakothiki and Alexandros Soutzos Museum in Athens. Papageorge was a rich Colourist and fluent draughtsman whose work owed much to early twentieth-century French influences. His wife Marjorie was also a painter.

Bohdan PARASZCZUK 1950– Artist in oil and watercolour who studied in "living room/kitchen/museums", noted for portraits, "especially figures known as down-and-outs". Showed at Colin Jellicoe Gallery in Manchester, Salford University, Bolton Little Theatre and elsewhere. Helped with stage set design at the Theatre, which holds the artist's work, sometimes signed Bohdan. Lived in Bolton, Lancashire.

Kathleen Ophir Theodora PARBURY 1901–1986 Sculptor who was born at Boreham Wood, Hertfordhire. From 1920–4 studied at Slade School under Henry Tonks and Havard Thomas. As well as making portrait sculpture, Parbury worked extensively in churches throughout the world. Examples are in London, Salisbury, Southampton, Sutton Coldfield and County Durham, Ireland, Canada and Nigeria. Museums in New Zealand and Ohio, in America, also hold her work. Wrote a book on the Lindisfarne saints. Was made a fellow of RBS in 1966. Signed work K O T P. Lived latterly in Beadnell, Northumberland.

William Francis PARBURY 1889–1957 Watercolour painter and draughtsman, born at Rusper, Sussex. Although he studied at evening classes at Chelsea Polytechnic, he was mainly self-taught. Exhibited RBA, UA and RWS. Lived in London.

David PARE 1911– Painter and teacher, born in Nottingham, where he attended the School of Art, then Slade School of Fine Art, 1935–7. Taught at Scarborough School of Art, 1937–9, Portsmouth College of Art, 1946–52, and was principal of Winchester School of Art, 1953–76. Exhibited at RA, NEAC, Ash Barn Gallery in Petersfield and elsewhere. Randolph Schwabe and Allan Gwynne-Jones were influences. Lived latterly at Hampstead Norris, near Newbury, Berkshire.

David Alexander PARISH 1941– Painter, sculptor in various materials including precious metals, and teacher. Born in Southend-on-Sea, Essex, Parish attended the local College of Art, 1965–7, later having some private tuition in sculpture. Showed Chenil Gallery, International Art Centre and in Canada and America. Lived in Westcliff-on-Sea, Essex.

Alfred PARK 1921– Sculptor and teacher, who studied art at King's College, Newcastle upon Tyne. He was included in The Teaching Image, 1964 show of work by staff of Leeds College of Art at the local City Art Gallery.

Alistair PARK 1930–1984 Painter and teacher, born in Edinburgh, where he studied at College of Art, 1949–52, his final year accommodating work under an Andrew Grant Postgraduate Scholarship. After National Service, from 1955 Park taught part-time at his old College, then for six years from 1957 taught at a secondary school in Edinburgh. In 1963 he moved to teach at Bradford College of Art, four years later taking up a post at Newcastle upon Tyne's College of Art until he died. Park had a solo show at 57 Gallery, Edinburgh, in 1957, another the year later and the 1960s saw his showing widely throughout Britain. He had several solo exhibitions at Richard Demarco Gallery, Edinburgh, the last in 1983. Park's work moved from figurative to abstract, although human images remained a strong inspiration.

Andrew PARK 1971– Figurative painter, born in London, who studied at Central St Martins College of Art & Design and Kent Institute of Art & Design. His work contained allusions to popular culture, as in his oil on canvas Ted and Vincent, Royal Over-Seas League Open, 1996. Other group shows included Almost a Football Team, Cubitt Gallery, 1994.

Emma PARK 1950– Sculptor and teacher, born in Yorkshire, who studied at Chelsea School of Art, 1968–72, then Slade School of Fine Art, 1972–4. Went on to teach at Wimbledon School of Art and Portsmouth and Leicester Polytechnics. She was noted for her abstract wood reliefs, as in the Serpentine Gallery/South Bank Centre's The Sculpture Show, 1983. Park favoured abstraction because of the way it made its own internal values independent of anything outside. Arts Council has several examples, including work from the Sally East Gallery, 1980. Lived for a time in London.

John Anthony PARK 1880–1962 Painter, especially in oil of seascapes and harbour scenes in Cornwall, born in Preston, Lancashire. He moved to St Ives in 1899 and studied there under the seascape specialist Julius Olsson and in Paris at Atelier Colarossi. Chelsea Arts Club member. Park spent most of his life in St Ives, but left in the early 1950s to live for a short time in Brixham, Devon, ultimately moving back to Preston, where he died. By this time he had established a solid reputation as a painter of fishing boats and West Country scenes, such as the Tate Gallery's Snow Falls on Exmoor. Exhibited RA 1905–49, Paris Salon, where he won a bronze medal in 1924, and St Ives Society of Artists; one-man shows included Ruskin Gallery, Birmingham, and Penwith Gallery, St Ives, 1983. Preston Art Gallery, Manchester City Art Gallery and Salford Museums and Art Galleries are among the many provincial and overseas holders of his work.

Agnes Miller PARKER 1895–1980 Painter in oil and tempera, teacher, but chiefly a wood engraver. Her engravings involve a subtle use of light and shade, springing forms and very delicate hatching. She was born in Irvine, Ayrshire, and was married to the painter William McCance. Parker studied at Glasgow School of Art, 1911–17, teachers including Maurice Greiffenhagen and Forrester Wilson, won a Haldane Travelling Scholarship, then taught at the School for two years. She and her husband then moved to England where she taught for eight years, at schools in Gerrard's Cross, Buckinghamshire, and in Clapham, at the same time studying wood engraving with Gertrude Hermes and her husband Blair Hughes-Stanton. In 1930 the McCances went to Wales to run the Gregynog Press. She exhibited at SWE of which she was a member, RE, Society of Artist Printmakers, RSA, Redfern Gallery and in America. Illustrated books for Gregynog, Golden Cockerel Press and Limited Editions Club of New York. She separated from McCance in 1955; the marriage was dissolved in 1963, when she again used her maiden name; lived for a time in Glasgow, but then settled at Lamlash on the Isle of Arran. Parker died in Ravenscraig Hospital, Greenock. A centenary exhibition took place at Scottish National Gallery of Modern Art, Edinburgh, 1995, and Cyril Gerber Fine Art held a show in Glasgow, 1996.

Alan PARKER 1965– Painter and draughtsman, born in Woodsetts, Yorkshire. He studied at Barnsley College of Art and Design, 1985–6, gained an honours degree from Brighton Polytechnic, 1986–9, then did a postgraduate diploma at Royal Academy Schools, 1989–92. For 1993–5 he was appointed Fellow Commoner in the Creative Field at Trinity College, Cambridge. Parker was interested in English folk songs, nursery rhymes, fairy tales, Morris Dancers and similar subjects "to emphasize and satirize the social ills of his time". Group exhibitions included Brighton Polytechnic, 1987; RA Summer Exhibition, 1990; The Sussex Scene, Towner Art Gallery, Eastbourne, 1993; and Trinity College, Cambridge, 1994. Had a solo show at Piccadilly Gallery, 1994. British Council holds his work.

Brynhild PARKER 1907–1987 Painter and teacher, full name Margaret Brynhild Parker, brought up in Letchworth, Hertfordshire. Her father was a craft teacher at St Christopher School, which she attended, her mother was Swedish and her uncle was Barry Parker, architect responsible for much of the early development of the Garden City. Studied at Slade School of Fine Art, 1925–8, where she won a number of prizes, gaining her diploma. Exhibited at Goupil Gallery, NEAC, with the East London Group and had a solo exhibition at Lefevre Gallery, 1938. Parker taught art at Letchworth Grammar School for several years in early 1940s, then went to live in France with a younger French artist, a follower of Picasso, who influenced her style towards abstraction for a while, although it did not suit it. In the 1950s she left him and settled in Antibes in the south, where she let out rooms. She illustrated a book for Penguin on pond life. Manchester City Art Gallery holds her striking oil on canvas The White Hat, which indicates what a fine painter she might have become with more application.

Constance-Anne PARKER 1921– Painter, sculptor and printmaker, born and lived in London. She studied at Regent Street Polytechnic School of Art and Royal Academy Schools, teachers including A R Middleton Todd, Bernard Fleetwood-Walker and William Dring. Won a number of awards and scholarships. She became assistant librarian at RA in 1974, and eventually lecturer, archivist and travelling exhibitions organiser. Showed at RA, NEAC, RP and in the provinces and was a fellow of RBS. Among her books were *Mr Stubbs the Horse Painter*, 1971, and *A Picture of the RA*, 1985.

Cornelia PARKER 1956– Creator of installations, notably of objects suspended from a ceiling, and sculptor. She was born in Cheshire and attended Gloucestershire College of Art and Design, 1974–5, Wolverhampton Polytechnic, 1975–8, and Reading University, 1980–2. Won a Wolverhampton Polytechnic Travel Scholarship, 1978, a Southern Arts Award in 1983 and a Greater London Arts Award in 1985. She was artist-in-residence at Crewe and Alsager College, 1979–80, with a Sculpture Residency and Commission, Forest of Dean, 1988. Undertook a number of commissions, including National Garden Festival, Stoke-on-Trent, 1986, and Ikon Gallery, Birmingham, commission, 1988: Thirty Pieces of Silver. This was the installation featured in the South Bank Centre's touring The British Art Show 1990, one of many group shows the artist joined. Her solo shows began with Alsager Arts Centre Gallery, 1980; later ones included Cornerhouse, Manchester, 1989, and Avoided Object, Chapter Arts Centre in Cardiff, 1996. Arts Council holds her work and included it in 1993–4 touring show Recent British Sculpture. Lived in London.

Harold Wilson PARKER 1896–1980 Sculptor and medal-maker in bronze, wood and stone. Born in London, he studied art at Walthamstow School of Art, St Martin's School of Art, Central School of Arts and Crafts, Sir John Cass School of Art and the Royal College of Art, in the mid-1920s. Exhibited RA and the Royal Glasgow Institute of Fine Arts. Parker's sensitive sculptures of a Nightjar and Study of a Lamb are illustrated in Arthur T Broadbent's monograph *Sculpture Today in Great Britain 1940–1943*. The Ministry of Works commissioned Parker to create a memorial to the Labour politician George Lansbury; the Nuffield Orthopaedic Centre, Oxford, has a bronze by him; and he made many medals, including the Indian General Service Medal and the Civil Defence Medal. Parker was a fellow of the RBS and its vice-president at one time. Lived in London.

Herbert PARKER 1908– Artist in watercolour and teacher, born in Buckley, Flintshire. He was mainly self-taught in watercolour, but obtained his teacher's certificate at Normal College, Bangor, and attended short courses at Liverpool and Chester Schools of Art and elsewhere. Parker was art master at St Margaret's Technical and Commercial School in Liverpool, deputy head of Colomendy Hall Boarding School and Environmental Study Centre and an adult education tutor elsewhere. He was a founder and president of Clwydian Art Society, also showing with RI, RCamA, RWS and Paris Salon. Had several solo shows, including Oriel Community Gallery, 1991. Lived in Llanferres, Mold, Clwyd.

Jayne PARKER 1957– Film and video artist, born in Nottingham. She did a foundation course at Mansfield College of Art, 1976–7; gained and honours degree in fine art at Canterbury College of Art, 1977–80; then obtained a higher diploma in fine art in the experimental media department, Slade School of Fine Art, 1980–2. Exhibitions included Installation and films, Ikon Gallery, Birmingham, 1980; Arts Council, British Art Show, 1984, with tour; I Dish, Georges Pompidou Centre, Paris, 1987, and widely elsewhere in the 1980s; and in 1990 Retrospective, international film fair, Arnsenal, Riga, Latvia, and Signs of the Times, Museum of Modern Art, Oxford. In 1983–4 Parker held a video fellowship at North-East London Polytechnic.

Lorraine PARKER 1958– Artist and teacher who studied at Falmouth School of Art, 1978–80, and Helsinki Academy of Fine Art, Finland, 1980–1, having gained a British Council Scholarship in 1980. Showed at Swedish Institute in Stockholm, 1983, Ayling Porteous Christmas Show, 1985–6, and 1986–7 touring exhibition organised by Walker Art Gallery, Liverpool, Merseyside Artists 3.

Walter F PARKER 1914– Watercolourist, printmaker and teacher, born in Carlisle, Cumberland. He studied at the local School of Art, 1930–5, then won a major award to attend Royal College of Art, 1935–9, under Ernest Tristram and Stanley Spencer, specialising in illustration and textile design. After a period as a freelance designer he attended London University and Courtauld Institute in 1938, gaining his art teacher's diploma. Was appointed art master at Rutherford College of Art, Newcastle upon Tyne, 1940, prior to service in Royal Air Force. From 1946–53 taught at Preston College of Art then Hastings School of Art, then joined Hartlepool College of Art, being principal from 1954–78. Parker was elected a member of Society of Industrial Art and Design in 1947 and was a member of the Lake Artists' Society from 1964, its president in 1989. He cited as main influences "art of the Far East and the works of Stanley Spencer and Eric Ravilious". Parker exhibited in Carlisle, Manchester and Hartlepool, living at Seaton Carew, County Durham.

Molly PARKIN 1932– Writer, painter and media personality, born in Pontycymmer, Glamorgan. She won a scholarship to study at Goldsmiths' College School of Art and Brighton College of Art and gained a travelling scholarship to study in Venice. She had early success, showing with Young Contemporaries, ROI, NEAC and WIAC and in 1961 having a sell-out solo show in London. In 1964 her painting Spring in New York was bought by

Contemporary Art Society, but then she had a painting block until 1987. In the meantime she was a Chelsea boutique and restaurant owner, a fashion editor for magazines and the *Sunday Times*, television personality and novelist. After she resumed painting Parkin had several shows in London and Wales, returning in 1990 to St Ives, where she had lived with her second husband, the painter Patrick Hughes (her first husband was Michael Parkin, who became a noted art dealer), and worked up a Cornish show which was held late in the year at England & Co. It featured pictures as exuberantly colourful as their creator. Her autobiography *Moll, The Making of Molly Parkin*, was published in 1993. Lived in London.

Trevor PARKIN fl. from c.1950– Painter, illustrator and teacher, born in South Normanton, Derbyshire. He studied at Derby College of Art. Had solo shows in Suffolk and Nottinghamshire, but was mainly known for illustrations in children's and educational books. Lived in Pinchbeck, Lincolnshire.

Geoffrey PARKINSON 1944– Printmaker, born in Newcastle, New South Wales, Australia, who gained his diploma in art and design at Chelsea School of Art. Contributed etchings and woodcuts to London Artists, Shrewsbury School, 1968.

Gerald PARKINSON 1926– Painter who was born in Shipley, Yorkshire, studying at Bradford College of Art, 1951–4. Was a member of AIA, exhibiting at RA, SEA and RWA, having solo shows in London, the provinces and abroad. Public galleries in Brighton and Glasgow hold examples. Lived in Polegate, near Eastbourne, Sussex.

Ti PARKS 1939– Artist and teacher, born in Sevenoaks, Kent. His work ranged across painting, three-dimensional pieces, large-scale installation works and books. Parks began exhibiting in the early-1960s at Young Contemporaries, LG and AIA. In 1964 he went to live in Australia and over the next decade exhibited solo with Frank Watters Gallery, Sydney, and Bruce Pollard's Pinacotheca, Melbourne, as well as in group exhibitions, public collections acquiring examples. Was appointed lecturer in sculpture at University of Auckland, New Zealand, 1974, in 1975 returning to England but continuing to show in Australia. In 1978 the Acme Gallery sponsored a long-unfinished work of found or ready-made sculpture. Another project was a large exhibition of Mail Art from around the world at Greenwich Theatre Gallery. An ongoing work, 10,000 Collages, was shown as variable-size wall installations at Air and Dartington Hall Galleries, the London College of Printing and South London Book Centre. Parks' Artists Books, a venture begun in 1992, were shown at various locations and were bought by many national and international library collections, including Museum of Modern Art in New York. The Living Room, Greenwich, held a large exhibition in 1993.

William PARKYN 1875–1949 Marine and landscape painter, born in Blackheath, London. Much of his art training was undertaken at Newquay and St Ives, Cornwall, with Louis Grier. Member of the St Ives Art Society, Arts Club and London Sketch Club. Exhibited RCamA especially, also RA, RI, RWA, PS and elsewhere. Lived at the Lizard, Cornwall.

Janetta PARLADÉ 1921– Artist in watercolour and gouache, mother of the artist Nicky Loutit, born in London. As a young girl she lived for a while in Spain and eventually settled there at San Pedro de Alcantera, Malaga, living partly in London. Left school at 16 and drew from life at Chelsea School of Art and by outbreak of World War II was a member of London's literary and artistic world, wearing a cloak over a corduroy trouser suit and carrying a long stick. During the war she worked in a munitions factory, illustrated books and worked on Cyril Connolly's review *Horizon*. In 1971 married Jaime Parladé, having helped him create and run an hotel in Marbella. Eventually took up painting after a lapse of some years, mostly drawing on Spanish themes. Solo shows included Pigeon Hole, Chelsea, 1981–2; Rodeo Gallery, Marbella, 1984; and Sally Hunter Fine Art, 1993.

Adrian PARNELL 1952– Figurative and landscape painter, born in London, who studied at St Martin's School of Art and Slade School of Fine Art, 1970–77. Was an associate member of Penwith Society in St Ives, also exhibiting at RA Summer Exhibition, Mall Galleries, New Grafton Gallery and Gordon Hepworth Fine Art at 23 Smith Street, 1997. Later solo exhibitions included White Lane Gallery, Plymouth; Dartington Hall; Exeter Arts Centre; and Plymouth Theatre Royal.

Eva PARNELL-BAILEY 1894–1990 Painter in oil and teacher, born in Camberwell, southeast London. She studied with Harold Workman, Walter Sickert and Herbert Holt. Taught at Holloway Prison and several special schools for London County Council, including handicapped children. She was a founder-member of the Philosophical Society of England, 1937, a member of RBA and UA and an associate of RCamA. Views of Devon, the River Thames and dockland were exhibited at RA, RSA, ROI, NEAC, SWA and in the provinces, and she had a solo show at Chenil Galleries. Lived latterly at East Molesey, Surrey.

D Lynn PAROTTI 1968– Painter, notable for well-defined, brilliantly coloured landscapes, born in Nassau, Bahamas. She graduated in painting, State University of New York, 1987–90, gained her master's degree (like her bachelor's, summa cum laude), at Virginia Commonwealth University, Richmond, Virginia, 1991–3, then undertook a Training for Artists in Schools course at London University Institute of Education, 1995–6. In 1992, Parotti held a residency at Skowhegan School of Painting & Sculpture, Skowhegan, Maine. Group shows included Fresco Barn, Skowhegan, 1992; Nine Northumbrian Fields, Tallentyre Gallery, Morpeth, 1994; Celebrating Women Through the Millennium, Contemporary Art Gallery, 1996; and A Sense of Place, Collyer-Bristow Gallery, 1997. Solo shows included 23rd Anniversary of Independence Celebration for the Commonwealth of the Bahamas, Britannia Intercontinental Hotel, Grosvenor Square, 1996. Had a studio in London.

Denis William PARROTT 1931– Painter, printmaker and teacher, born in Dewsbury, Yorkshire, who studied at local School of Art; 1948–51, Camberwell School of Arts and Crafts, 1951–3; then Leeds College of Art, 1957–8. Went on to teach at Nene College, Northampton. Showed at RA, Mall Galleries, Galerie Salammbo in Paris and in America, where he was a Fulbright Scholar, 1970–1. Lived in Kettering, Northamptonshire.

David PARRY 1942– Wildlife watercolourist, born in Liverpool, who attended Tunbridge Wells School of Art, having been educated locally, then Central School of Art. Was a member of SWLA, showing in the provinces, notably Cornwall, where he settled at Lostwithiel.

Jacki PARRY 1941– Painter, printmaker, draughtsman, teacher and handmade paper artist, born in Wonthaggi, Victoria, Australia. After studying in Melbourne, from 1961 she spent almost a decade teaching and travelling in Australia, Europe and Asia. In 1974 she graduated in printmaking at Glasgow School of Art, completing a postgraduate year in textiles. During this period she was a founder-member of Glasgow Print Studio. Parry worked in Poland in 1975 on a Cargill Scholarship and a Glasgow Lady Artists' Club Award took her to Japan in 1988. Meanwhile, she had become interested in the making of paper, studying the techniques at Barcelona Paper Workshop. So skilled did she become that during the period 1981–5 she was put in charge of the papermaking department of Glasgow School of Art; she had a show of related works at Compass Gallery in 1984; and two years later she opened her own papermaking workshop. She was artist-in-residence at several colleges in Australia and in Orkney. Parry showed her work internationally, in 1988 having a big show at Third Eye Centre, Glasgow. In 1996 she was included in the three-man exhibition Sculpting at the Fine Art Society, where the works titled Ways of Editing and the book *Visible Traces* explored ways that information is created and edited, exposed and concealed. They stemmed from her attempts to make sense of evidence and theories surrounding the disappearance of her brother James off the coast of Northern Australia in 1986. British Council, Scottish Arts Council and Scottish National Gallery of Modern Art hold Parry's work.

Leigh PARRY 1919– Artist in black-and-white, pastel and watercolour, related to the sporting artist Walter Parry Hodges. Studied at Cambridge University, obtaining master's degree in 1946, and St Martin's School of Art. Parry's subjects were landscapes and townscapes, interiors, people and places and horses. Was made a member of PS in 1966, being its president, 1983–88; a member of Society of Equestrian Artists, 1983; and an associate of RBA in 1987. Served on board of Federation of British Artists, 1983–6. Showed widely at RA, RCamA, NEAC, New Grafton Gallery, Paris Salon and abroad. Solo shows included Alpine Club Gallery, provincial galleries and in Canada. Also did book illustration and work for private patrons. Midland Bank, Singer & Friedlander Bank, Lincolnshire Museums and Essex County Council hold examples. Lived in Stamford, Lincolnshire.

Sheila Harwood PARRY 1924– Painter and miniaturist, born in Salford, Lancashire, settling in same county at Southport. She attended Salford Technical College, 1937–9, then the College of Art, 1940–2, with Leslie Reid. She was made a member of SM in 1969 and RMS in 1971. Showed at RA, RWS and abroad including Paris Salon. Atkinson Art Gallery, Southport, holds her work.

Beatrice PARSONS 1870–1955 Painter, chiefly of landscapes and gardens, born in London. After studying at King's College, London, she attended the Royal Academy Schools. Exhibited RA, ROI, SWA and extensively at Dowdeswell Galleries. Victoria & Albert Museum holds her work. Lived in Watford, Hertfordshire.

Huw PARSONS 1954– Painter and printmaker who established a reputation for lively illustrative work, much of it inspired by the landscapes and events in Breconshire, Herefordshire and Pembrokeshire. He was born in Llyswen and was educated at Brecon Boys Grammar School and Chelsea School of Art. For many years he worked in the printing industry as a graphic designer, draughtsman and photo-lab technician, but from 1992 was able to paint full-time. Had work commissioned by two Welsh language magazines, *Barn* and *Prentis*, and by the Welsh Development Agency. Had shows at Abergavenny and Hereford Museums and at Wyeside Arts Centre and showed in groups in Aberystwyth, Leddfa and Cardiff. In 1995 had a solo exhibition at Brecknock Museum in Brecon, where he lived.

Jonathan PARSONS 1970– Artist who did a foundation course at West Surrey College of Art and Design, Farnham, 1988–9, gaining an honours degree at Goldsmiths' College, 1989–92. Parsons took part in many group exhibitions. Appearances included Coventry Open, at Herbert Art Gallery, 1992–3; Every Now & Then, Richard Salmon, 1994; Plastic, Arnolfini Gallery, Bristol, 1996–7; Building Site, Architectural Association, 1997; and in 1997–8, Pictura Britannica: Art from Britain, Australian and New Zealand tour, and the Saatchi Collection-related show Sensation, at the RA. Solo exhibitions included Heber-Percy Gallery, Warwickshire, 1994, and Richard Salmon, 1996.

Maureen PARSONS-IRWIN *see* **MIA**

Peter PARTINGTON 1941– Painter, maker of clay constructions, printmaker, illustrator, teacher and writer, born in Cambridge. He attended Bournemouth College of Art and Design, 1960–6, then Hornsey College of Art, 1967–8. Before freelancing Partington taught painting and drawing to art students for 15 years. Among his commissions was illustrating *Down by the River*, by H E Bates, 1987, and in 1989 he published *Learn to Paint Birds*, one of his favourite subjects. Partington was elected a member of SWLA in 1985 and was a keen supporter of game conservancy and the Royal Society for the Protection of Birds. Exhibited widely in London and the provinces, including Tryon Gallery. Museum of Wildlife Art, Gloucester, holds his work. Lived in Gravesend, Kent.

Brian PARTRIDGE 1953– Notably an artist working in pen and ink, who did not often exhibit. He did show at Wraxall Gallery, 1981, and Victoria Art Gallery, Bath, 1983, and in 1985–6 was included in the Piccadilly Gallery show The Brotherhood of Ruralists and Friends. Partridge's creations sometimes had a fantastic quality, as in in his 1989 drawing Mr A's Big Green Hat, in which the hat is an idyllic landscape. He illustrated Simon Rae's *Great Tew*, 1988, published by the Brotherhood of Ruralists Press. Lived in Cheltenham, Gloucestershire.

David PARTRIDGE 1919– Painter, printmaker, sculptor and teacher who was notable for his creations using nails, which he termed nailies. Was born in Akron, Ohio, in America. He lived in England for seven years from 1928. Moved to Canada, becoming a Canadian citizen in 1944. He studied at University of Toronto, 1938–41; served in Royal Canadian Air Force for four years; then attended University of Kingston. Studied painting variously in Canada, at Art Students' League of New York, at Slade School of Fine Art and at Atelier 17, Paris. Taught at several venues in Canada, 1958–61. Produced his first nail pieces in 1958 and in 1962 won the Montreal Spring Show sculpture prize. The roof restaurant at Royal Garden Hotel, London, 1965, was one of his commissions. Showed widely in England, including LG. From 1962–74 lived in London, then settled in Canada. His many Canadian commissions included murals for Toronto City Hall and he exhibited widely in Canada, later shows including Moore Gallery, Hamilton, 1987, a retrospective, and Nancy Poole's Studio, Toronto, 1986–8. Numerous collections hold Partridge's work including Tate Gallery and Victoria & Albert Museum and in Canada the National Gallery in Ottawa. Rock formations and fossils and his experience as an ultralight aircraft pilot influenced Partridge's imagery. Lived in Toronto for some years.

Josh PARTRIDGE fl. from 1960s– Painter, printmaker and teacher who grew up on a farm near Cardigan, west Wales, which remained her strongest source of inspiration. She used richly textured watercolour and pastels to suggest rough pasture, bracken and gorse. Partridge trained at Bath Academy and Slade School of Fine Art, 1959–65, then woodblock printing in Kyoto, Japan, 1966–7. In 1973–4 she painted in the Australian Bush, in 1988–90 studying greyhounds at Hackney Wick Stadium and in County Kerry, Ireland. Teaching included London University Institute of Education, North London Polytechnic architecture department and in Italy. Partridge had a solo show at Stanhope Institute Gallery, 1972, later ones including Cadogan Gallery, 1993, The Ice House, 1994, and West Wales Arts Centre, Fishguard, 1995. British Museum, Greater London Council and CASW acquired examples.

Roger PARTRIDGE 1959– Sculptor, born in London, who attended Chelsea School of Art, 1977–8; Camberwell School of Arts and Crafts, 1978–81; and Slade School of Fine Art, 1981–3. He was a carver of large blocks of stone, as included in the Serpentine Gallery/South Bank Centre's The Sculpture Show, 1983. Partridge said that in his work "there is a good deal of understatement as well as a kind of Victorian desire to emellish."

Ahmed PARVEZ 1926–1979 Painter and draughtsman, born in Rawalpindi, Pakistan, dying in Karachi. In 1952 he was awarded Punjab University's highest art prize, had five one-man shows in Pakistan and took part in the 3rd Bienal, São Paulo, Brazil, in 1955, the year he moved to London. There he was a founder of the Pakistan Group and was appointed honorary secretary of the Council of Commonwealth artists. His first one-man show was at the New Vision Centre Gallery in 1959 and he had a retrospective at the Commonwealth Institute in 1963. In 1967 he left England finally, lived in New York for two years, then returned to Pakistan. He had shown in New York and was to continue showing in his own country. Parvez's painting took Abstract Expressionism as its springboard. His life was spent in turmoil. He could be difficult to deal with, was involved with drugs, sometimes lived in squalid circumstances and suffered from a sense of failure. His work was included in The Other Story, Hayward Gallery and touring, 1989–90.

Ernest PASCOE 1922–1996 Sculptor, painter and teacher who studied at Carlisle School of Art, 1937–41; served in the Royal Air Force; then was at Slade School of Fine Art, 1945–8, winning the Robert Ross Scholarship, Wilson Steer Medal and Tonks Drawing Prize. Pascoe became head of fine art at Bristol Polytechnic. He was a fellow of RBS and a member of RWA, holding several senior positions including chairman; was also a member of the British School at Rome's faculty. Showed at RA, RBA, LG, AIA, with Arts Council and in the provinces. Bristol City Art Gallery and RWA hold examples. He was father of the artist Jane Pascoe. Lived latterly at Weston-in-Gordano, Bristol.

Jane PASCOE 1955– Painter, printmaker and teacher, daughter of the artist Ernest Pascoe, born in Bristol where she studied at the Polytechnic, 1974–7. She was elected RWA in 1988, also exhibiting at Michael Parkin Fine Art; Victoria Art Gallery and Beaux Arts Gallery, both in Bath; Eye Gallery, Bristol; and Swindon Museum and Art Gallery. RWA holds her work. Lived in Wilton, Wiltshire.

David PASKETT 1944– Painter, notably a watercolourist, and teacher, born in Potters Bar, Hertfordshire. He studied fine art at Hornsey and Exeter Colleges of Art and did his teacher training at Liverpool College of Art, 1961–7, gaining a Queen's Award to study in Italy, 1965. From 1967–70 Paskett was a member of the Norwich Twenty Group, taking part in group exhibitions at the Castle Museum and Maddermarket Gallery. During his period as a lecturer in fine art in Bristol, 1970–85, Paskett took part in mixed shows at RWA, Croft Gallery and elswhere, having several solo exhibitions, including Bristol Arts Centre and The Pump Room, Bath. During 1986–90, he lived and exhibited in Hong Kong. In 1990–2 Paskett worked at London's Science Museum on a series of pictures for a show there; had another solo show at the Pitt-Rivers Museum in Oxford, resulting from a year's residency, 1993, the year he made a painting trip to China, the first of several in ensuing years; was a visiting lecturer at Oxford University, 1994; and worked on the Oxfordshire Museums

Reserve Collection, with a studio at Woodstock Museum, 1995. He took part in many mixed exhibitions in Britain and abroad, winning several prizes, his solo exhibitions including David Paskett's China, The Catto Gallery, 1997. Commissions and collections included Hong Kong's Jockey Club, its University and Tourist Association, Time-Life, Lord and Lady Wilson and a number of corporate holdings.

Victor PASMORE 1908–1998 Painter, collagist, construction-maker and teacher, full name Edwin John Pasmore, married to the artist Wendy Pasmore, who appeared in some of his early work. He was born in Chelsham, Surrey, and for a decade from 1927 worked in local government at County Hall, London, until with the help of Sir Kenneth Clark he was able to cease being a Sunday painter, painting full-time and in 1938 helping to form the Euston Road School with William Coldstream and Claude Rogers. He had attended Central School of Arts and Crafts part-time and had begun showing with London Artists' Association, having his first solo show with it in 1933; was showing with LG, becoming a member in 1934; and had shown with Objective Abstractions group at Zwemmer Gallery, 1934. Pasmore was also to teach at Camberwell School of Art, 1943–9, from 1949–53 being visiting professor at Central School of Art and Design. Around 1948 Pasmore's work shifted from the atmospheric, representational Euston Road style to abstraction, the course he thereafter pursued. In the period 1951–63 began to work on relief constructions. From 1954–61 was director of painting at Department of Fine Art, University of Newcastle; between 1954–77 was consulting director of urban design at Peterlee New Town. Pasmore's international reputation grew from 1960s, including a retrospective exhibition at Tate Gallery and touring, 1965, with a one-man British Council travelling show and a special display at the Tate Gallery, both in 1980. The Tate, Arts Council and other leading collections hold his work. Pasmore, who was made a Companion of Honour in 1981 and was elected RA in 1984, latterly lived in Gudja, Malta, and London.

Wendy PASMORE 1915– Artist and teacher, born in Dublin, Ireland. She studied art privately and at Chelmsford School of Art, 1933–4. Married the painter Victor Pasmore. She taught at Sunderland College of Art, 1955–8, and Leeds College of Art, 1958–67. Showed with WIAC and LG, being a member of both. Retrospective show at Molton and Lords Galleries in 1963; in 1997 there was a 30-year one of free-flowing abstracts, limited-edition prints and collages at Air Gallery. Tate Gallery, Arts Council and Leeds Education Committee hold Pasmore's work. Lived latterly in Gudja, Malta, and London.

Derek PASS 1929– Ceramist and watercolourist, born and lived in Newcastle-under-Lyme, Staffordshire. He attended Burslem School of Art and Stoke-on-Trent College of Art, 1942, with Reginald Haggar and Gordon Forsyth. Went on to work for Royal Doulton Tableware and Coalport China. Pass was a member of the Society of Ceramic Artists and Free Painters and Sculptors, also showing at NS and elsewhere.

Donald PASS 1930– Artist in oil, watercolour and pastel, and teacher, born in Congleton, Cheshire. He studied at Stoke-on-Trent College of Art, 1947–51, with Arthur Berry and Arnold Machin, then Royal Academy Schools, 1951–4, under Henry Rushbury, William Dring and Gilbert Spencer. Went on to teach in Liverpool, Manchester, Carlisle and Birmingham Colleges of Art. In his own work Pass was "from 1957–69 concerned with landscape in a semi-figurative way. From 1969 onwards I was concerned with the transfiguration of landscape being motivated by the resurrection, with vast numbers of figures and black space with bands of gold." He took part in mixed shows at Drian Galleries, New Art Centre, John Whibley Gallery, Graves Art Gallery in Sheffield, the University of Keele and Gallery of Art, Lissone, Milan. Had a series of solo shows at Drian Galleries from 1957 and one at New Art Centre, 1962. Yorkshire Education Committee, Keele University and Sir John Rothenstein held his work. Lived in Wheatley, Oxford.

John PASSMORE 1904–1984 Painter, draughtsman, designer and teacher, born in Sydney, Australia. Leaving school at 13, Passmore was apprenticed to a signmaker, moved on to a lithographer's, then during the early 1920s began work as a commercial artist with an advertising agency. For about 15 years from 1918 Passmore attended night classes at Sydney Art School. After moving to London in 1933, working at the Lintas agency, Passmore attended Westminster School of Art in the evenings, studying with Bernard Meninsky and Mark Gertler. Passmore was for long a friend of Keith Vaughan, was an introspective, analytical personality and like Vaughan was greatly influenced by Cézanne. For many years he lived in Suffolk with Lintas colleague Reg Jenkins and his artist wife Marjorie. After Royal Air Force service in World War II, Passmore left for Australia in 1950, was a charismatic teacher in the Sydney area, painted a lot and began – reluctantly – to show more of his work. The Helena Rubenstein Travelling Scholarship took him to England again in 1960, but after ill-health he returned to Australia. He had a major retrospective at Art Gallery of New South Wales, Sydney, which holds his work, in 1984–5; in 1988 Passmore was included in Agnew's Lintas show Beyond the Horizon.

Sunil PATEL 1959– Indian painter, born in Nairobi, Kenya, who was taken to England when he was 15. He travelled extensively through India and won the Boise Travelling Scholarship in 1986 to continue this journey. Between 1982–6, he studied at the Slade School of Fine Art. Using the Indian miniature as a starting point and maybe a verse from Hindu scriptures, Patel's small acrylics on canvas, as in his solo show at Long & Ryle, 1998, were almost devotional works. They comprised a continuous narrative of a paradisical world.

Alexander Nisbet PATERSON 1862–1947 Architect, draughtsman and painter, a member of the distinguished Scottish Paterson painting family and father of the artist Viola Paterson. He was born in Glasgow, gained his master's degree from the University there, then moved to the Atelier Jean-Louis Pascal at the École des Beaux-Arts in Paris, 1883–6. In 1897 he married the painter and embroiderer Maggie Hamilton, having commenced practice in Glasgow a few years before as an architect. For almost 40 years he showed architectural drawings at RSA, of which he was an associate, being a member of RSW. Also showed at Royal Glasgow Institute of the Fine Arts and elsewhere. He designed his own house, The Long Croft, Helensburgh, as well as the National Bank of Scotland, St Enoch Square, Glasgow, and the nearby Liberal Club. He was included in the Belgrave Gallery's The Paterson Family show in 1977. Died in Helensburgh, Dunbartonshire.

Anda PATERSON 1935– Painter and administrator, born in Glasgow, married to the artist James Spence. With him she founded the Glasgow Group in the late 1950s, which did much to promote an interest in contemporary art in the west of Scotland and elsewhere. Paterson studied at Glasgow School of Art, in Spain and Portugal. She was elected RSW in 1966 and to Royal Glasgow Institute of the Fine Arts in 1978, and was a winner of the Anne Redpath and Latimer Awards. She showed in mixed exhibitions in Scotland and abroad and had a solo show at Compass Gallery, Glasgow, in 1971, being included in The Compass Contribution at Tramway, Glasgow, in 1990. Paterson was noted for her unusual pictures of ordinary people, often old, lonely and hard-up, which she treated with sympathy. Her work is held by Scottish Arts Council, Arts Council of Northern Ireland and New York Print Workshop.

G W Lennox PATERSON 1915–1986 Painter, printmaker and teacher, son of the architect George Andrew Paterson. He attended Glasgow Academy and the Glasgow School of Art where he later taught graphic art, eventually becoming deputy director. He exhibited RSA, where he gained the Guthrie award in 1946, granted for best painting by a young Scottish artist at the annual exhibition. Also showed RE of which he was a member, Society of Artist Printmakers, Royal Glasgow Institute of the Fine Arts and elsewhere. War Artists' Advisory Committee bought several works by Paterson. In 1996 Ewan Mundy Fine Art, Glasgow, had an exhibition of his colour woodcuts. Paterson lived in Glasgow, then in Helensburgh, Dunbartonshire.

Hamish Constable PATERSON 1890–1955 Painter, notable for his portraits, son of the artist James Paterson, cousin of Viola Paterson and thus a member of the distinguished Scottish painting family. After an unhappy period in an architect's office he was appointed to the stained glass designer James Valentine and in 1910 at the same time began studying at Edinburgh College of Art. During Army service in World War I injuries threatened his painting career, but although he recovered physically his experiences left a lasting mental mark, and he suffered from depressions. His uncle William Bell Paterson gave him a show in Bond Street in 1922 which included portraits of the former prime minister David Lloyd George and many titled people, but instead of pursuing portraits Paterson chose to live in France painting landscapes. Showed at RSA, RSW, RA, Royal Glasgow Institute of the Fine Arts and was included in The Paterson Family at Belgrave Gallery, 1977. Two years before he died Paterson returned to the family home at Moniaive, Dumfriesshire.

Viola PATERSON 1899–1981 Painter, draughtsman and printmaker, born in Helensburgh, near Glasgow. Viola was a member of the distinguished Paterson family of artists and she was equally talented as a Colourist in oil, in watercolour and as a lithographer and engraver. As a teenager at a finishing school in London, around 1917–18, she studied with Henry Tonks at the Slade School of Fine Art, from 1919–23 attending the Glasgow School of Art under Maurice Greiffenhagen. In 1924–5 she studied in Paris at L'Académie de la Grand Chaumière with Lucien Simon Besnard and then with André Lhote and thereafter continued to paint in Paris, although she also travelled widely in Europe. At the outbreak of World War II she moved to the south of France, but returned to Britain in 1941. During the war she worked for several years for the Admiralty in Oxford, after the war living in Chelsea, returning to Helensburgh in 1955. The family home, The Long Croft, had been designed by her architect father, and it embodied the last 100 years of Scottish art. A woman of private means and great vitality, Viola Paterson was a keen gardener and expert cook as well as being a prolific artist. She exhibited RA, RSA, Royal Glasgow Institute of the Fine Arts, SSA, Society of Artist Printmakers, Belgrave and Parkin Galleries. A retrospective was held at The Round House, Havering-atte-Bower, 1983.

Anne PATERSON WALLACE 1923– Painter and teacher, born in Montrose, Angus, a member of the Paterson family of artists and grand-daughter of James Paterson. His work was a great influence from her childhood. War interfered with her ambition to paint, then after demobilisation from the Women's Royal Naval Service she was awarded a grant to study at Chelsea School of Art, 1946–9. After marriage settled in Butley, Woodbridge, Suffolk, where "the play of light on landscape exerted a continual fascination." She was a member of Free painters and Sculptors and BWS, chairman of Ipswich Art Club and a founder-member of the group Eight Plus One. Showed widely in East Anglia and elsewhere in the provinces in solo and mixed exhibitions. Was included in The Paterson Family, Belgrave Gallery and tour, 1977. From 1960–9 she ran an art gallery in Woodbridge and she also taught adult education classes.

Avril PATON fl. from 1980s– Painter of detailed figurative works which can have a slightly Surrealist element, whose father Hugh Paton and grandfather Donald Paton were both painters from the Isle of Arran. She spent many years there before returning to Glasgow, where she depicted the lives of ordinary people, its houses and street scenes. Her father gave her rudimentary lessons and taught her perspective, to which was added an abortive year at Glasgow School of Art. Had a first solo show in 1985, the year Glasgow Museums bought Paton's work The Barras for the People's Palace. Windows in the West, measuring four feet by five feet and in watercolour, was shown at Paton's solo exhibition at The Gatehouse Gallery, Glasgow, in 1994, on loan to the Royal Glasgow Concert Hall. Several hundred prints of this depiction of a typical Glasgow tenement had sold within a year or so. Scottish Power, Clydeport Authority and the Royal Navy also own Paton's works.

Mary PATON 1920–1990 Painter, full name Frances Mary Richmond Paton, born in Hareshawmuir, Ayrshire. Was educated in England and on the continent. She studied before and after World War II at Edinburgh College of Art, gaining her diploma in 1947 and undertaking post-diploma work, 1948. Teachers included William Gillies, William MacTaggart and Leonard Rosoman. She was a member of SSA and Aberdeen Art Society, also showing with RSA and Royal Glasgow Institute of the Fine Arts. Lived at Rathen, Aberdeenshire.

PATRICK: *see* **John BYRNE**

Ann PATRICK 1937– Painter in oil and pastel/gouache, daughter of the artist James McIntosh Patrick and wife of painter Richard Hunter from 1960. She was born in Dundee, Angus, and studied at Duncan of Jordanstone College of Art there and at Patrick Allan-Fraser School of Art, Hospitalfield, Arbroath, 1954–8, her teachers Alberto Morrocco and David McClure. Although she lived in Arbroath, Angus, she frequently painted abroad. Her work "reflected my surroundings, giving formal permanence to ephemera such as fruit, flowers, aspects of the sea and landscape." Solo shows included Roseangle Gallery, Dundee from 1958; Fine Art Society, Edinburgh, 1974; Fine Art Society, Glagow, 1981; Rendezvous Gallery in Aberdeen and Open Eye Gallery, Edinburgh, both from 1985; and Isetan Gallery, Tokyo, and Gallery Tokitsu, Nagoya, both in Japan in 1994. Public galleries in Aberdeen and Dundee, HRH The Duke of Edinburgh and a number of corporate collections, such as Robert Fleming and Scottish Television, hold examples.

Emily PATRICK 1959– Painter of portraits, domestic subjects and still life who grew up on a farm in Kent and graduated in architecture at Cambridge University. In 1987 she was commissioned to paint HRH The Princess of Wales by The Royal Hampshire Regiment. Had a series of solo exhibitions at Agnew, and in 1997 at both Gallery 27 and Hanover Square Gallery, New York City, America.

James McIntosh PATRICK 1907–1998 Painter, printmaker and teacher, born in Dundee, Angus. At Glasgow School of Art from 1924 he was very successful, winning many prizes and gaining a post-diploma scholarship. His meticulous landscape etchings caught the attention of a London print dealer, and in 1928 he acquired an important contract for editions of prints. With the collapse of the print market in the early 1930s Patrick turned to oil painting, but his attention to detail in landscape remained his trademark. He also taught part-time at Dundee College of Art. From 1928 showed at RA and from 1934 at Fine Art Society. During World War II served in Camouflage Corps. Patrick continued to live in Dundee and depict the surrounding area. Was elected RSA in 1957. Key solo shows were held at Dundee City Art Gallery in 1967 and at Dundee, Aberdeen and Liverpool in 1987 and there was a ninetieth birthday celebration at Scottish National Gallery of Modern Art, Edinburgh, in 1997. Tate Gallery holds his work. His daughter was the artist Ann Patrick.

Marion PATRICK 1940– Painter in oil on board, born in Liverpool. She studied at Burnley Municipal School of Art and showed at Mall Galleries and widely in the provinces. Bristol University holds her work. Lived in Gravesend, Kent.

Iain PATTERSON 1946– Artist and teacher, born in Ayr, Ayrshire. He studied at Edinburgh College of Art, 1964–9, in 1969–70 winning an Andrew Grant Travelling Scholarship which took him to Czechoslovakia and the Balkans. Two years later he gained a Scottish Arts Council Award. After studying at Moray House College of Education, 1972–3, Patterson taught in Edinburgh while also being a committee member of the New 57 Gallery. He later settled in Edinburgh, teaching at the College of Art. In the 1960s and 1970s Patterson began to establish a reputation at group shows in Scotland, such as the New 57 Gallery and Edinburgh Printmakers' Workshop. He had a first one-man show in 1970 at New 57 Gallery, others following at Richard Demarco Gallery in Edinburgh and abroad. Scottish Arts Council holds his work.

Jane PATTERSON 1955– Painter and teacher. She won a diploma in painting at Slade School of Fine Art, 1973–7, in the latter year gaining the Steer Prize for drawing and Boise Scholarship to travel and paint. From 1988 lectured part-time at Slade. Patterson appeared from 1977 in mixed shows at Browse & Darby; from 1979 at RA Summer Exhibition; in 1983 at Ogle Fine Arts, Cheltenham, in Painting the Nude; in 1985 in Three Gloucestershire Painters at Axiom Gallery, Cheltenham; and in 1991 in The Prose of Painting at Austin/Desmond Fine Art. Solo exhibitions included Lionel Wendt Gallery, Colombo, Sri Lanka, 1978; Egypt Mill, Nailsworth, 1983; and Nicoll Centre, Cirencester, 1987. Worked in Gloucestershire and London.

Janet PATTERSON 1941– Painter and teacher, born in Edinburgh. She trained at Slade School of Fine Art. A French Government Scholarship enabled her to extend her studies, and a Churchill Fellowship in 1987 provided six months travelling and painting in Australia. Lectured at Liverpool and Wallasey Colleges of Art and then at Edinburgh College of Art, later moving to London. She said that her painting was "about the passage of life, how I react to situations and atmosphere". Group exhibitions included Sheffield Open, Liverpool Academy, LG, National Trust and Fine Art Society, Edinburgh. Solo shows included Petter Potter, Haddington; Scottish Gallery, Edinburgh; and Camden Arts Centre, 1982. Was included in Scottish Art in the 20th Century at RWA, 1991.

Richard PATTERSON 1963– Painter, born in Leatherhead, Surrey, who attended Watford College of Art & Design, 1982–3, then Goldsmiths' College, 1983–6. His picture Minotaur, 1996, in About Vision, Museum of Modern Art, Oxford, 1996–7, and tour, prompted fellow-exhibitor Fiona Rae to comment that Patterson's "protagonists have a strong physical presence". Group shows also included Freeze, Surrey Docks, 1988, and Portrait of the Artist, Anthony d'Offay Gallery, 1996, which in that year gave Patterson a solo exhibition, Project Space, with another in 1997. Photo-Realist images with popular culture features were part of Patterson's output. Lived in London.

Simon PATTERSON 1967– Artist, born in Leatherhead, Surrey, whose work included type and word patterns. He studied at Hertfordshire College of Art & Design, 1985–6, then graduated with honours from Goldsmiths' College, 1986–9. Group exhibitions included London University Institute of Education, 1987; 1789–1989 – Ideas and Images of Revolution, Kettle's Yard Gallery, Cambridge, 1989; and Milch Ltd, 1990. Had a solo exhibition at Third Eye Centre, Glasgow, 1989, Chisenhale Gallery, 1994, and Lisson Gallery, 1996.

Thomas PATTISON 1894–1993 Painter, notably of architectural watercolours and portraits, and teacher, born in Cardiff, south Wales. He studied with Richard Hatton at Armstrong College, Newcastle (later King's College and Newcastle University) until World War I interrupted, when he served with the Army in France, where he continued to sketch. Returned to Armstrong College, where he qualified with distinction, teaching on the staff of King's College and nearby in Hexham before becoming a full-time artist. Showed at RA, RSA and at Laing Art Gallery in Newcastle which gave him a big exhibition in 1942. It holds a lunette by him of the building of Newcastle plus a series of lively watercolours of street scenes. Lived finally in Gosforth, Northumberland.

Marcus PATTON 1948– Largely self-taught artist in pen and ink and watercolour, born in Enniskillen, County Fermanagh. He studied architecture and worked as an architect, planner, second-hand bookseller and artist. Was a fellow of the Society of Architectural Illustrators and an associate of RUA. Solo shows included Octagon Gallery, Belfast, where he lived, from 1980; Peacock Gallery, Craigavon, 1985; and Ulster Arts Club, Belfast, 1990; also appeared in travelling exhibitions in Northern Ireland. Belfast City Council, Ulster Television and Down Museum hold examples.

Lin PATTULLO 1949– Painter brought up in Ayrshire who qualified as a sick children's nurse. After studying drawing and painting part-time at Glasgow School of Art took up painting full-time, exhibiting in mixed shows and having a first Glasgow solo exhibition in 1993, the year she appeared in Thompson's Gallery show Contemporary Art From Scotland. Also showed at Royal Glasgow Institute of the Fine Arts and lived at Giffnock, Glasgow.

Celia PAUL 1959– Figure and portrait painter and draughtsman, born in Trivandrum, India. From 1976–81 attended Slade School of Fine Art. Group exhibitions included The School of London: Works on Paper, at Odette Gilbert Gallery, 1989; Contemporary Art Society Market, Royal Festival Hall, 1994; Art95, The Museum of Women's Art exhibition, Business Design Centre, 1995. Had a solo show at Bernard Jacobson Gallery, 1986, showing with Marlborough Fine Art from 1991. British Museum, Fitzwilliam Museum in Cambridge, Saatchi Collection and Metropolitan Museum, New York, hold examples. Lived in London.

Jeremy PAUL 1954– Artist interested in painting wildlife in its natural surroundings, born in Accrington, Lancashire. He attended Queen Elizabeth's Grammar School in Blackburn, then took a degree in marine biology at Liverpool University and gained his doctorate for work in the Isle of Man. He settled there after some years on Scotland's west coast. Paul was a self-taught artist whose work was sold in limited-edition prints by Halcyon Gallery, Birmingham.

Raymond Hodges PAUL 1910–1988 Artist and teacher, born in Canterbury, Kent, who moved to Margate when his father became headmaster of a school there. Attended Margate School of Art then Royal College of Art, graduating in early 1930s. After teaching at Selby Grammar School, moved to Worthing College of Art around 1938. Served in signals in the Royal Artillery in England, North Africa and then returned for the Second Front. Taught briefly in Germany at end of the war, then became head of the graphics department at Worthing College of Art. Was art critic for the *Worthing Herald* and drew cartoons for two local papers. Imperial War Museum accepted Hodges Paul's illustrated war diary and Worthing Museum and Art Gallery holds two works by him, both of 1947: View from a Shoreham Beach Pillbox and Church of the Good Shepherd, Shoreham Beach.

Robert PAUL 1949– Printmaker, born in Glasgow, who studied at Glasgow School of Art, 1967–71, then became a technician there. His various group shows included Photography in Printmaking at Glasgow Print Studio; New Scottish Prints, in New York; and Scottish Print Open Three, organised by Dundee Printmakers' Workshop, all in 1983.

George Henry PAULIN 1888–1962 Sculptor, born at Muckhart, near Dollar, Scotland, where he attended the Academy, then studied at Edinburgh College of Art under Percy Portsmouth. Also studied in Rome, Florence and Paris, 1911–14. Brother of the painter Jeanie Wright Ellis. Paulin exhibited RA, RSA, Royal Glasgow Institute of the Fine Arts, RI and in the provinces. Among his notable works are a statue in Hampstead, London, to the ballerina Anna Pavlova and a bronze bust of the artist Sir John Lavery. Paulin's work could often be witty, in a classical style, examples being Fountain Group for a Bird Bath and The Chase, pictured in the volume *RBS: Modern British Sculpture*, published in 1939. Paulin was a fellow of the RBS. Lived in London.

Helen PAVEL 1964– Painter who studied at Kingston Polytechnic, 1982–6, and Royal College of Art, 1987–9. Although an abstract artist, her work was reminiscent of places and the natural world, using subtle, poetic colours. Gained several awards, including the Picker Travel Scholarship and in 1989 first prize in the Barclays Young Painters' Award. Exhibited widely in group shows such as New Contemporaries, Into the Nineties at Mall Galleries, LG and in (dis)parities at Mappin Art Gallery, Sheffield, in 1992, and in 1993 at Herbert Art Gallery, Coventry. Contemporary Art Society and Leicestershire Education Authority hold her work.

Don PAVEY 1922– Artist in oil, alkyd and computer art, writer and teacher, born in Wimbledon, southwest London, settling nearby at Sheen. He studied at Royal College of Art under Gilbert Spencer, 1943–6; did five years' extra-mural work with London University, 1954–9, in art history and psychology, concentrating on colour; and spent a year in the Royal College of Art department of design research, 1976–7. He was senior lecturer at Kingston Polytechnic, 1969–82, then retired to work as a film producer and director of the Micro Academy video unit. Pavey was co-founder of the National Art Education Archive at Bretton Hall, Wakefield, and of the Royal College of Art's colour reference library. Colour was Pavey's main interest, but he was also involved "with the irrational and game theory as a creative instrument in art". Bretton Hall holds paintings and 100 group murals by Pavey; St Lawrence College, Kent, 10 portraits; and St John's, St Leonards, Sussex, stained glass. Pavey's publications include the Methuen *Handbook of Colour and Colour Dictionary*, 1963–67–78, and *The Artists' Colourmen's Story*, 1984.

Sydney Herbert PAVIÈRE 1891–1971 Painter, etcher and curator, born in Oxford, son of the artist F Leslie Pavière. After private and convent education, he attended Oxford University, then studied art in Oxford and overseas. He held a series of posts in public art galleries in England, eventually becoming art director and curator of the Harris Museum and Art Gallery, Preston, in Lancashire. Among his many interests were the collecting of coins and antiques. Writer on art, especially prints, being a member of the Print Collectors' Club. Exhibited works, with an inclination towards architectural subjects, at Alpine Club Gallery, Goupil Gallery, RHA and widely in the provinces. Pavière's proudest achievement was in recognising the merits of the Preston artists Arthur and Anthony Devis, whose works he began collecting in the 1930s when they could be obtained for as little as 15 shillings a watercolour; he also wrote about their work. On retiring from the Harris in 1959 he became honorary curator of the National Trust showplace Rufford Old Hall. Lived in Preston.

John PAWLE 1915– Painter in oil and watercolour. He was a businessman who studied briefly with Mark Gertler at Westminster School of Art before World War II, who was able to paint full-time only on retirement, when he became a prolific exhibitor. There was a ready private-client and corporate-collector market for his richly coloured landscapes and still lifes. Was fond of painting in North Africa. Showed in group exhibitions at Leicester Galleries, 1941; NEAC, 1957; City of London Art Fair, 1989; and elsewhere. Had a solo show at Dallas Gallery, London, 1981; the first of several with Parkin Gallery, 1983; and James Hunt Baker Gallery, Palm Beach, in America, 1985. Allied Lyons, Charterhouse Group and Robert Fleming & Company hold his work.

Peter R PAY 1945– Sculptor and lecturer, born in Folkestone, Kent, who worked in wood, steel and bronze. He studied at Canterbury College of Art, 1964–5, with Michael Kenny, then at Exeter College of Art, 1965–8, under Robert Adams and Roger Leigh. Pay was assistant to Robert Adams, 1970–1, from 1972 lecturing in sculpture at University of Plymouth. In the mid-1990s his doctoral studies concerned the language of sculpture exemplified by the work of Tony Cragg. Mixed shows included RWA, RA, Newlyn Orion Gallery in Newlyn and elsewhere. 2nd RWA Open Sculpture Exhibition included sculpture by Pay based on household electrical adaptors "re-presented and valued as aesthetic furnishings". Pay had solo exhibitions at Spacex and Exe Galleries in Exeter, Granary Gallery in King's Lynn and at Trumpington Gallery, Cambridge. Lived in Chulmleigh, Devon.

Barrie PAYNE 1945– Painter who studied at Southampton School of Art, 1961–3, Camberwell School of Arts and Crafts, 1963–5, and Royal Academy Schools, 1965–8. He won the David Murray Studentship, S J Solomon Prize (silver medal) and Simon Elwes Prize. He was included in Figurative Painters at Woodlands Art Gallery, 1980.

Charles Johnson PAYNE 1884–1967 Painter in watercolour and gouache and printmaker, writer, born in Leamington Spa, Warwickshire. Charlie Payne was not a great draughtsman but he became a very popular one among sporting and military types for his captioned and hand-coloured lithographs published under the name of Snaffles. He illustrated for periodicals such as *The Graphic*, *The Field*, *Punch* and *The Illustrated Sporting and Dramatic News*. Also produced a number of popular books, including *'Osses and Obstacles*, 1935, and his autobiography *A Half Century of Memories*, 1949. He began his artistic career while serving in the Royal Garrison Artillery, sketching officers. In World War I he was a lieutenant in the Royal Naval Volunteer Reserve and was employed on camouflaging ships by the dazzle method. Also worked a lot in Ireland and in India, where he depicted the final sporting days of the British Raj. Member of Fine Art Trade Guild, publishing his own work. Showed at Alpine Gallery, Sporting Gallery in 1936 and was included in The British Sporting Art Trust shows in 1981 and 1983 at Alpine Club. Malcolm Innes with The Berkeley Studio had an exhibition in 1996. Lived in Guildford, Surrey, and at Tisbury, Wiltshire.

David PAYNE 1928– Painter in oil and watercolour, notable for his triptychs, and teacher, born in Dover, Kent. He studied at Canterbury, Farnham and Brighton Colleges of Art until 1954, and had a sabbatical year at Royal Academy Schools, 1980–1. For a time he was senior lecturer in painting at Bedford College of Higher Education. Payne said that his pictures combined "imagination and observation. Places made significant by history or association are often featured in landscape settings. In still life objects hint at other levels of meaning. A heightened reality is present with an undercurrent of Surrealism." Was a regular exhibitor at RA Summer Exhibition from 1976. Also showed at Ash Barn Gallery, Petersfield; Bedford School; Portal Gallery and elsewhere. Solo exhibitions included New Ashgate Gallery, Farnham, 1987. Bedfordshire County Council Education Loan Service holds his work. Lived in Bedford.

Edith PAYNE 1875–1959 Painter of miniature studies of nature and craftsman in various media. She was the sister of the artists Charles March Gere and Margaret Gere; the sisters, known as "the masterful Miss Geres", attended Birmingham's School of Art in the 1890s. She was a member of the Birmingham Group of Painters and Craftsmen with Henry Payne. After marrying him she moved to the Cotswolds in 1909. She assisted projects in which Group members were involved, gesso-moulding and gilding frames. Showed at RA, NEAC, RBSA and Fine Art Society. A show of her work was held at Birmingham City Museum and Art Gallery, 1979.

Edward Raymond PAYNE 1906–1991 Painter and stained glass artist, born in Birmingham into a family closely assocated with the Arts and Crafts Movement and the teachings of William Morris, his father being the stained glass creator Henry Payne, his mother, Edith, a watercolourist. Studied at Royal College of Art, 1924–7, under William Rothenstein, then returned to Gloucestershire to help his father with glass commissions. Showed RA and NEAC. Work held by Imperial War Museum and Cheltenham Art Gallery and Museum, but is best seen in Gloucestershire churches, including Randwick, Box, Edge and Minchinhampton, where he died.

Freya PAYNE 1968– Artist and teacher, notably a printmaker, who studied at Falmouth Art School, 1986–7; Manchester Polytechnic, 1987–90; did a diploma in book binding, Newcastle College, 1991–2; and attended Royal College of Art, 1992–4, having a one-year printmaking fellowship there, 1994–5. She was a visiting lecturer at Humberside, Manchester and Coventry University and Brookes University, Oxford. Commissions included a mural at Babooshka, 1993, and a painted relief construction, Barking & Dagenham Council, 1994. Showed at Young Printmaker of the Year, CCA Galleries, 1990; Intaglio Arts, Manchester, 1991; and in 1994 at both Zenith Gallery and Flowers Graphics, which gave her solo exhibitions from that year. Payne's outstanding figurative and abstract prints were noted for their technical accomplishment, imaginative imagery and ravishing colour. *The Economist* and Westdeutsche Landesbank, London hold her work.

Margaret PAYNE 1937– Artist whose work included computer graphics and teacher, born in Southampton. She studied at Harrow School of Art, 1955–9, gaining her national diploma in design; then obtained art teacher's certificate from Goldsmiths' College, 1960. Later added an honours degree in history of art, 1981, and a master's degree in art education, 1983. Was elected RE in 1975, also showing at RA, RI, SWA and at Paris Salon. Taught at Digby Stuart College, Roehampton, and lived in southwest London at Sheen.

David PAYNTER 1900–1975 Painter and teacher, son of a British missionary and a Sinhalese mother. He studied at Royal Academy Schools, 1918–22, then in Italy, 1922–3. Between the wars he lived in London and showed at RA, NEAC, London Salon and Cooling Galleries. In 1965 he was teaching in the College of Art, Colombo, Sri Lanka, where he latterly spent some years farming. Brighton Art Gallery and Museum holds Paynter's sensitive, richly coloured picture L'Après-Midi.

Hilary PAYNTER 1943– Wood engraver and teacher, born into a naval family, spending most of her early years abroad before studying sculpture and wood engraving under Gerry Tucker at Portsmouth College of Art. She also attended London University Institute of Education and added a master's degree in the psychology of education while running departments of special educational needs in inner city comprehensives. She was elected RE and was honorary secretary of SWE, which she relaunched in 1984 after a quiescent period. Illustrated books for a variety of publishing houses. Solo shows included The Garden Gallery, Kew Green, 1985. Ashmolean Museum and Hereford City Art Gallery hold examples. Lived in East Twickenham, Middlesex.

Colin PAYNTON: *see* **Colin SEE-PAYNTON**

Sheila PAYTON 1932– Painter, draughtsman and teacher of art at secondary level, born in Henley-on-Thames, Oxfordshire. She studied art at Reading University with Anthony Betts, then at Bath Academy of Art where teachers included Peter Lanyon, Bryan Wynter and Jack Smith. Showed at RA, NEAC, Campbell and Franks, SWLA and in the provinces. She was interested in wildlife and conservation, which was reflected in her subjects. Lived in Appleshaw, Hampshire.

David PEACE 1915– Glass engraver and designer, born in Sheffield. He attended the University there and studied art with Clarence Whaite. He eventually became a liveryman of the Glaziers Company and was for a time master of the Art Workers' Guild, as well as being first chairman of the Guild of Glass Engravers and later its president for several years. Had a large number of solo exhibitions, his work being in the collections of Victoria & Albert Museum and Fitzwilliam Museum, Cambridge. Engraved screens and windows are also to be found in Westminster Abbey, Manchester Cathedral and a number of churches. From the mid-1980s Peace formed a partnership with the artist Sally Scott to carry out decorative architectural glass commissions. He lived in Hemingford Abbots, Cambridgeshire.

Roger PEACH 1907–1964 Designer of metalwork and jewellery. Studied at Leicester College of Art and exhibited with the Arts and Crafts Exhibition Society in 1946. Lived in Leicester.

Brian PEACOCK 1935– Painter and teacher, born in London, who studied at Royal College of Art, 1957–60. He gained a Silver Medal there in 1960 and Prix de Rome, 1960–1. He was a part-time lecturer at Ravensbourne and Hornsey, 1961–2, senior lecturer in painting at Manchester College of Art, 1962–7, then for many years was principal lecturer in charge of painting at Sheffield Polytechnic from 1967. Mixed exhibitions included Young Contemporaries, John Moores Liverpool Exhibition, RA, Arts Council touring exhibitions and elsewhere, including one of four painters at Mistral Galleries, 1992. Had a series of solo shows with Piccadilly Gallery from 1962, Mappin Art Gallery in Sheffield in 1978 and several at John Davies Fine Art from 1989. Peacock was noted as an atmospheric painter of landscape. As well as living in Sheffield he latterly lived and worked in Cognac region of France. Government Art Collection, Nuffield Foundation and Contemporary Art Society hold examples.

Herbert PEACOCK 1910– Painter, miniaturist and glass engraver, born in Heacham, Norfolk. He studied at Cambridge University but was largely self-taught as an artist, having some private tuition and for part-time lessons attending Hornsey School of Art. Was a member of UA, also showing at PS, RMS, RWA and in Canada. Lived in London.

Percy PEACOCK 1953– Sculptor, draughtsman and teacher, born in York, who studied at the Art School there, 1970–2; at Bristol Polytechnic, 1972–5; and Royal College of Art, 1975–7. Taught at Sheffield and Portsmouth Polytechnics, then was a fellow in the Hull College of Higher Education department of fine art. Exhibitions included Midland Group in Nottingham and State of Clay at Sunderland Arts Centre and tour, both 1978; Portsmouth Museum and Art Gallery, 1979; and Clay Sculpture, Yorkshire Sculpture Park, 1980. Arts Council holds examples.

Ralph PEACOCK 1868–1946 Painter, born in London, where he died. Entered Royal Academy Schools, where he won a gold medal and Creswick Prize, 1887. Showed at RA from 1888; 10 years later he won a gold medal in Vienna and in 1900 a bronze at Paris Universal Exhibition. Noted for his paintings of women, of which the Tate Gallery holds good examples.

Fabian PEAKE 1942– Artist mostly in oil on canvas, also gouache, and teacher, son of the artists Mervyn Peake and Maeve Gilmore. He was born in Rustington, Sussex, attending Chelsea School of Art, 1958–63, and Royal College of Art, 1963–6, winning several prizes. Then taught and lectured extensively, from 1977 at Manchester Polytechnic/Metropolitan University. Mixed shows included Young Contemporaries, 1964; LG, 1965; John Moores Liverpool Exhibition, 1972; RA Summer Exhibition, from 1983; Vortex Gallery, 1986; and Brick Lane Open, 1993. Had a series of solo shows at Francis Graham-Dixon Gallery from 1987. Peake also played the saxophone and wrote poetry. His work is held by Arts Council, Liverpool University and Bedfordshire Arts Loan Collection. The artist's output presented odd, compelling images, sometimes based on apparently unpromising sources such his 1987 series related to word processors. Lived in London.

Mervyn PEAKE 1911–1968 Author, poet, artist, illustrator and teacher, born in Kuling, China. He was the husband of the artist Maeve Gilmore and father of painter Fabian Peake. He was educated at Tientsin Grammar School, Eltham College and Royal Academy Schools, where he won the Hacker Prize, 1931. After two years in an artists' colony Peake taught life drawing at Westminster School of Art where he met Gilmore, marrying her in 1937. During Army service in World War II had a nervous breakdown, then was for two years attached to the Ministry of Information. Was appointed a war artist, then in 1946 returned to live on the tiny Channel Island of Sark for three happy years. Taught at Central School of Art, but eventually had to give this up, as he had Parkinson's disease. Published *Titus Groan*, 1946, *Gormenghast*, 1950, and *Titus Alone*, 1959, all set in a fantasy world. He illustrated Lewis Carroll's *The Hunting of the Snark*, 1941, the *Alice* books, 1946–54, and Coleridge's *The Rime of the Ancient Mariner*, 1943, his own books including *The Craft of the Lead Pencil*, 1946. Peake's work was widely exhibited, including RA; in 1991 there was a joint show of his and Gilmore's work at Littlehampton Museum. Died at Burcot, Berkshire, and like his wife was buried at Burpham, Sussex. A Mervyn Peake Society was formed in 1975.

Ashley PEARCE 1962– Painter, born in London. Studied at High School of Art in Manchester, then graduated from Lancashire Polytechnic after further studies at Manchester Polytechnic. Group exhibitions included 1985 Whitworth Young Contemporaries, at Whitworth Art Gallery, Manchester; Five Painters at Peterborough Museum & Art Gallery, 1987; and Art 89 and Art 90 at Olympia. His solo shows included Bury Metro Arts Association, Manchester, and tour, 1987; and Sue Williams Gallery from 1987. In 1991 shared a show at Wilson Stephens Fine Art. Pearce employed collage on occasions and there were elements of the fantastic in his work.

Bryan PEARCE 1929– Painter who through childhood illness contracted brain damage. He was born in St Ives, Cornwall, where he lived all his life, the town being the subject of many charming depictions in a naive style. Began painting in 1953, the following year beginning three years' study at Leonard Fuller's St Ives School of Painting. Started painting in oil in 1957, the year he joined the Penwith Society, two years later joining the Newlyn Society. In 1959 also he had a solo show at Newlyn Gallery, then showed regularly, including a retrospective at Penwith Gallery, St Ives, in 1966; a series of exhibitions at New Art Centre in 1960s and 1970s; later shows including Stoppenbach & Delestre, 1982; Plymouth Art Centre, 1984; and a retrospective at RWA, 1995. Arts Council holds his work.

Charles Maresco PEARCE 1874–1964 Painter and draughtsman, especially of architectural subjects. Born in London, son of Maresco Pearce a solicitor and artist and father of the architect

John Ricardo Pearce. Studied at Oxford University, then at Chelsea School of Art under Augustus John and William Orpen, 1904, two years later in Paris with Jacques-Emile Blanche, and with Walter Sickert, who left an imprint on his style. Blanche records in his memoirs how Pearce was one of a group of artists, friends of Sickert, who congregated in the Dieppe area before World War I, among them Max Beerbohm, Marie Tempest and Percy Grainger. Pearce's training as an architect and his love of France are reflected in pictures by him illustrated in *Artists' Country*, by G S Sandilands. Pearce was a prolific exhibitor, including RA, LG, of which he was a member, as he was of the NEAC, Leicester Galleries and Goupil Gallery. British Museum, Victoria & Albert Museum, Ashmolean and Fitzwilliam Museums hold his work. Lived in London and at Graffham, Sussex.

David PEARCE 1963– Self-taught painter and draughtsman, whose work, apparently abstract, drew on landscape and other sources for inspiration. Pearce was "interested in the warm, naive presence which comes from children's art. I try to reproduce this." An example was the acrylic on canvas Towan Farm Garden, in Royal Over-Seas League Open, 1996. Born in Buckinghamshire, Pearce attended Camborne Technical College in Cornwall, where he settled at Padstow. Other group shows included The Studio, Padstow, from 1986; Newlyn Orion Gallery, Penzance, 1993; and in 1996 Salt House Gallery in St Ives and David Holmes Contemporary Art, Peterborough, in A Continuity of Vision. Later solo exhibitions included Salthouse Gallery, 1993 and 1996, and Plymouth Arts Centre, 1996.

Edward Holroyd PEARCE 1901– Painter who was educated at Charterhouse and Oxford University, became a barrister and judge, and was married to Erica, daughter of the Royal Academician Bertram Priestman. Among his appointments were Lord Justice of Appeal, 1957–62, and Lord of Appeal in Ordinary, 1962–9. He was made independent chairman of the Press Council, 1969–74. Was knighted in 1948, was made a Privy Councillor in 1957 and Baron Pearce of Sweethaws, Sussex, 1962. Showed at RBA of which he was made a member in 1940, RA (he was an Hon. RA), NEAC and elsewhere. Had a series of solo shows in Britain and abroad, including Alpine Gallery, 1983. In 1995 Nicholas Bowlby in Tunbridge Wells had an exhibition of Pearce's pictures to mark the publication of Philip Mould's book *Sleepers: In Search of Lost Old Masters*, which revealed how for nearly 50 years Pearce, a shrewd collector, had kept the bronze The Dancing Faun by Adrien de Vries in the garden of his house in Crowborough, Sussex, and how, in 1989, "it became the most expensive sculpture ever sold at auction."

Frederick Thomas PEARCE 1889–c.1970 Artist in oil, pastel and watercolour, born at Aldershot, Hampshire. Studied art at Putney School of Art, 1905–6 and privately with several teachers, including David Murray. Exhibited RI, Walker Art Gallery, Liverpool and Russell-Cotes Art Gallery and Museum, Bournemouth, where he lived.

John PEARCE 1942– Painter in oil and watercolour, teacher, born and continued to live in north London. Pearce was notably a landscape painter, on a fairly large scale, who worked on the spot. He studied painting and stained glass at Hornsey College of Art from 1960, latterly at University of Newcastle through to 1964, and taught full-time 1964–84. His work was included in the 1962 Young Contemporaries show at RBA; was the subject of three solo shows while teaching between 1972–6; in 1980 was a prizewinner in the Greater London Council Spirit of London Exhibition, one of his pictures being bought for Guildhall collection; and in 1982 his painting of Barry Hall was chosen for the John Player Award Exhibition at National Portrait Gallery.

John Allan PEARCE 1912– Painter who was by profession a solicitor, born in Sidcup, Kent. He was educated at Charterhouse School, graduated from Oxford University and studied art privately. Signing his work AP, he showed with RBA, ROI, NS, NEAC and Chelsea Art Society and lived in London.

L A D'Arcy PEARCE 1903– Painter, commercial artist in black-and-white and animator, born in London. He studied at Ealing and Hammersmith Schools of Art, Chelsea School of Art, Bolt Court School under Sylvan Boxsius and privately. Showed PS, London Sketch Club of which he was a member, and in the Home Counties. Lived at Taplow, Buckinghamshire.

Pat PEARCE 1912– Painter and draughtsman who after seven years in Chelsea moved with her family to Natal, South Africa. Aged 16 she enrolled at Ruskin School of Drawing, Oxford, then moved to Royal College of Art; her teachers included Gilbert Spencer, Albert Rutherston, Paul Nash and Eric Gill. After World War II she married and moved to Rhodesia, farming and creating a weaving co-operative. From 1971 she lived in England, but continued to travel in Europe and Africa. A 20-year retrospective was held at The Anderson Gallery, Broadway, 1993.

Charles PEARS 1873–1958 Marine painter and lithographer, born at Pontefract, Yorkshire. Pears worked initially as a black-and-white artist for magazines from the late 1890s, serving as a theatrical caricaturist for *Pick-Me-Up*. During World War I he was an official war artist for the Admiralty, a position he repeated during World War II, and he gradually established a reputation as a sound marine painter with a strong sense of design. He was founder and first president of the RSMA and his work found its way into the National Maritime Museum, Greenwich, and the Imperial War Museum. However, as a versatile draughtsman he also did many posters and illustrated Lewis Carroll's *Alice's Adventures in Wonderland*, 1922, and the works of Charles Dickens. He wrote a number of books, such as *From the Thames to the Seine*, 1910, and *South Coast Cruising from the Thames to Penzance*, 1931. Exhibited widely, including RA, ROI and Fine Art Society. Lived at St Mawes, Cornwall.

Phyllis PEARSALL 1906–1996 Artist, writer and cartographer, born in London of Anglo-Hungarian parents. Her father was a noted Hungarian map publisher, her brother the artist Anthony Gross. She was educated at Roedean School and the Sorbonne, in Paris, where she took up painting, encouraged by the artist James McBey. Travelled extensively in eastern Europe. Returned to London in late-1920s, she originated the A-Z London street map. During World War II she worked in Ministry of Information, her company producing maps of Europe – such as the Maginot Line – to aid the war effort. In 1965, the company having gone through a bad patch while she was helping her father in America, she founded the Geographers' Map Trust to safeguard her colleagues' jobs and to prevent a takeover of the business. She had continued to paint and from the mid-1960s had many solo shows. One, of her early work, was held at Sally Hunter Fine Art, 1989. Lived in Shoreham, Sussex.

Norah PEARSE 1885–c.1980 Watercolourist, printmaker and teacher, born in Exeter, Devon, settling in the county at Exmouth. She attended Exeter School of Art under Nathaniel Baird and R Kirkland Jamieson and went on to teach art at St Margaret's School in the city. She exhibited at RA, SWA, SGA, RBA, RWA, RI, Paris Salon and elsewhere. Fountain Picture Gallery, Tiverton, held a show of her work in 1983. Royal Albert Memorial Museum & Art Gallery, Exeter, holds a picture Coverack, Cornwall, by Pearse.

Cath PEARSON 1965– Artist using photography, born in London, who graduated from Staffordshire Polytechnic in 1990. She worked as Goldsmiths' College as a visual arts photography technician for several years. Pearson said that her works examined such themes as "pregnancy, isolation, escapism, sex and the human condition", pictures of her own pregnancy being described as significant for their reintegration of humour and candid sexuality. Took part in many group shows, including 9th Mostyn Open, at Oriel Mostyn, Llandudno, 1997, and Ikon Gallery, Birmingham, 1998. Shared an exhibition, Space at the Centre, Curtain Road Arts, 1996. Had a solo show, Photofusion Photography Centre, 1997. Pompidou Centre, Paris, holds her work. Lived in London.

David PEARSON 1937– Artist in a variety of media and teacher who studied at St Martin's School of Art and Royal Academy Schools. Group exhibitions included Serpentine Gallery, 1973, Arts Council's British Painting '74, in 1974, and abroad. Had a solo exhibition at New Art Centre in 1961; in 1972 at Liverpool's Bluecoat Gallery and the Academy's Gallery; at Bede Gallery, Jarrow; and in 1989 at University of Liverpool's Senate House Gallery. Began lecturing in visual studies department of Manchester Polytechnic, 1974, later being senior lecturer at its Medlock Fine Art Centre.

Kathleen Margaret PEARSON 1898–1961 Portrait and equestrian painter in oil, born in Knutsford, Cheshire. She studied at the Slade School of Fine Art, 1920, then at the Royal Academy Schools, 1921–6. Exhibited RA, ROI, RSA, SWA, Cooling Galleries and elsewhere. Was a member of the Ridley Art Club. Her work is held by Russell-Cotes Art Gallery and Museum, Bournemouth, and Sunderland Museum and Art Gallery. Lived at Broadway, Worcestershire.

Frank PEARSONS 1920– Watercolourist, draughtsman and designer for industry. He was born in Ipswich, Suffolk, where he continued to live. Mainly a self-taught painter, he did study for several years with the landscape and portrait painter Cor Visser. Pearsons showed with RI, Ipswich Art Club of which he was a member and elsewhere in the provinces.

Margaret PEART 1948– Artist and teacher who studied at Sheffield College of Art, 1968–9, then Falmouth School of Art, 1969–72. She went on to become head of art at Stanley High School, Southport. For 1987 Peart was offered a senior visiting lectureship at British School, Rome. Exhibitions included a joint one with Clement McAleer at Bluecoat Gallery in Liverpool, 1981; Williamson Art Gallery, Birkenhead, 1984; and the Merseyside Artists touring shows organised by Walker Art Gallery, Liverpool, from 1985–6. Solo shows included Washington Arts Centre, 1984.

Tony PEART 1961– Painter and teacher, born in Darlington, Yorkshire. He studied at Cheltenham College of Art, 1979–80, then Leeds Polytechnic, 1980–3, winning a travelling scholarship there in 1982. The following year he gained a Northern Arts Award. Was at Newcastle upon Tyne Polytechnic, 1984–6, teaching at North Tyneside and South Tyneside Colleges, 1984–9, also at Cumbria College of Art from 1986. Peart, whose work is linked to the English countryside and rural pursuits, with an element of fantasy present, participated in many group shows from the early 1980s. These included Sheffield Open, at Mappin Art Gallery, 1983; Portraits North, at Abbot Hall Art Gallery, Kendal, 1985; New Grafton Gallery, 1987; Laing Exhibition at Newcastle Polytechnic Gallery, 1990; and Carlisle Open, Carlisle Museum and Art Gallery, 1992. Had a solo show at Myles Meehan Gallery, Darlington Arts Centre, 1984, later exhibitions including Piccadilly Gallery from 1990. Carlisle Museum and Art Gallery holds his work.

Bill PEASCOD 1920–1985 Artist, mountaineer and writer, born in Maryport, Cumberland, son of a miner, a job which he took up. In 1952 Peascod emigrated with his first wife and child to Wollongong, Australia, attending the National Art School in Sydney. In 1971, the year he won an art prize, Peascod, who had shown in Sydney, Melbourne and Brisbane, visited Japan, where he met his second wife. Wollongong City Art Gallery put on a key exhibition of Peascod's work in 1980, the year he retired to the English Lake District. Five years later he died of a heart attack while climbing in north Wales. In that year Peascod's book *Journey After Dawn* was published, and in 1989 *Women Climbing*, co-authored with Bill Birkett, appeared. In 1995 Castlegate House Gallery, Cockermouth, held an exhibition of Peascod's work.

Arthur PEAT 1888–c.1963 Painter in oil and watercolour who was by profession a farmer. Born at Galgate, Lancaster, into a farming family, Peat studied at Lancaster School of Art under

Charles Ripper. He exhibited with the Preston Society of Artists and elsewhere in the provinces. Lived at Scorton, near Preston.

Enid PEATE 1883– Watercolourist and craftsman in various materials who studied at Willesden School of Art and Oswestry School of Art. She showed at Liverpool Academy, Walker Art Gallery, Liverpool, and with Liver Sketching Club. Walker Art Gallery holds her watercolour Winter Sunshine. Lived at Portmadoc, Carnarvonshire.

Alec Maurice PECKER 1893–1975 Painter, draughtsman and printmaker specialising in portraits and figure studies. Studied art at St Martin's School of Art and the Central School of Arts and Crafts under William Palmer Robins and Malcolm Osborne. Exhibited RA, RI, RBA, RP, Leicester Galleries and widely abroad. The British Museum holds his work. Lived in London.

Michael PECKHAM 1935– Doctor, scientist and painter. He was educated at Cambridge University and University College Hospital medical school, going on to hold a number of important posts. He was a specialist in cancer, with a special interest in cancers afflicting young adults, and was from 1991 director of research and development at the Department of Health. He was at various times president of the Federation of European Cancer Societies, deputy chairman of the Imperial Cancer Research Fund, founded the Bob Champion Cancer Trust and founded and co-founded several national and international cancer associations. Professor Peckham showed in mixed exhibitions, and his solo shows included Bear Lane Gallery, Oxford, 1964; Woodstock Gallery, 1970; Upper Street Gallery, 1976; Consort Gallery, 1982; and Christopher Hull Gallery from 1983. His work is in private and public collections throughout Europe and America. Lived in London.

Sophie PECKO 1961– Painter in oil of still life, interiors and portraits, born and lived in London of Polish parents, reflected in her work's rich, Expressionistic colour. She studied fine art at Manchester Polytechnic, 1983–6, and Middlesex University, 1992–3. Exhibitions included Sackville and Posk Galleries, and Graham Gallery in Tunbridge Wells, all 1997, as well as venues in France.

Beatrice Stella PEDDER 1875– Painter, born in Clevedon, Somerset, who after private education studied art under William Mouat Loudan at Westminster School of Art. She showed extensively at Arlington Gallery, also RA, ROI, RBA, SWA and NEAC, Kensington and Chelsea Borough Councils buying her work. Lived in London.

Archibald PEDDIE 1917– Painter, draughtsman and teacher, born in Helensburgh, Dunbartonshire. He studied at Glasgow School of Art, 1935–9, under Hugh Adam Crawford. Exhibited RSA, SSA, Royal Glasgow Institute of the Fine Arts and Glasgow Art Club, of which he was a member. Lived at Rumbling Bridge, Perthshire.

Michael PEEL 1940– Printmaker and teacher, born in Singapore, who studied at Scarborough School of Art. His teaching appointments from 1965 included Chesterfield School of Art, Epsom School of Art and Design and part-time at Maidstone College of Art. A first solo show of his screenprints was given at William Weston Gallery in 1970. For that Peel wrote that he was "basically interested in space; either in the illusion of space on a two-dimensional surface, or real physical space or the association of shape, colour, surface, in relationship to space and environment." Peel was included in The British Art Show, organised by the Arts Council in 1980, chosen by the critic William Packer. Group appearances included New Art Centre, Woodstock Gallery and Richard Demarco Gallery, Edinburgh.

Misomé PEILE 1907–1983 Painter, printmaker, writer and teacher, born Marjorie Mary Misomé Peile in Southsea, Hampshire, into a naval family. She was initially educated in Seaford, Sussex, lived in Malta from 1936–8, then studied art in Rome and with Leonard Fuller at St Ives School of Painting, 1939–43. From 1945–8 Peile (pronounced Peel) worked officially with the Royal Marine Commando, 29th United States Infantry Division, the Ballet Rambert and Alan Carter Ballet. In 1947–8 she toured the Midlands with the Adelphi Guild Theatre under Arts Council auspices. She was an invited member of Newlyn Society of Artists and in 1949 a founder-member of Penwith Society of Arts. In 1947 Peile showed in St Ives with the Crypt Group in New Gallery, with St Ives group at Heal's Mansard Gallery, 1951, was a founder-member of Taurus Artists and exhibited with RWS, RBA, RBSA and abroad, notably in South Africa. Miss Peile was a devout Anglican. After moving to St Ives as a traditional painter, in the mid-1950s she changed to abstraction, having done hundreds of action drawings of Carbis Bay to acquaint herself with the Cornish landscape. She returned to G'Mangia, Malta, in 1969, and while there had shows at The National Museum, Valletta, in 1973–7. Ill-health and old age prompted her return to Cornwall. In 1985 there was a tribute show at Newlyn Art Gallery, which contains archive material on her. Cornwall Education Committee and P&O Group hold her work.

Ernest PEIRCE 1886–1961 Landscape painter in oil and printmaker. Studied painting privately, then exhibited extensively in London and the provinces; one-man shows at Greatorex Galleries, London, and at Harrogate Art Gallery. Harrogate Corporation holds his work. Lived at Ludgvan, Cornwall.

Robert PELL 1928– Artist in oil, gouache and crayon, and teacher, born in Northampton. He studied at the School of Art there, 1944–9, then at Camberwell School of Art, 1964, with Michael Podro. Went on to teach at North Oxfordshire Technical College and School of Art, Banbury. Pell said that his paintings were "concerned with light and water, the intangibles of objective painting. The changing relationships between sky and sea and the abstracted reflections of forms between interest me." Pembrokeshire and Cornwall were favourite sketching places. Showed at Leicester and Piccadilly Galleries, RBA of which he was made a member in 1958 and Warwick University. Solo shows included Canaletto Gallery,

Bear Lane Gallery in Oxford and Century Art Gallery, Nottingham. Balliol and University Colleges, Oxford, hold his work, as do public galleries in Northampton and Coventry. It holds his Boats in a Misty Light; The Ferry, Evening Light is another main work. Lived in Brackley, Northamptonshire.

Claughton PELLEW 1890–1966 Watercolourist, draughtsman and printmaker, born in Redruth, Cornwall, son of William Pellew-Harvey, a mining engineer, and Elizabeth Hitchens, an artist. After childhood spent in Vancouver, returned to England about 1900 and attended Merchant Taylors' School and Slade School of Fine Art, 1907–11, where his teachers included Henry Tonks and Fred Brown. Dropped Harvey from his surname. Shortly before World War I Pellew became closely associated with the artists Paul and John Nash. Pellew became a Roman Catholic in 1914 and was a conscientious objector in World War I. Having married the artist Kechie Tennent in 1919, in the mid-1920s he bought land at Southrepps, in remote Norfolk and built a house there, where they lived in seclusion. Most of his work was done in the 1920s and 1930s, was strongly based on the English countryside and had a visionary, Arts and Crafts quality. He showed with English Wood Engraving Society; Society of Artist Printers, Edinburgh; Society of Artist Printers, London; did illustrations for *The Reward of Faith*, by Elizabeth Goudge, 1950; among other work. A small memorial show was held at Assembly House, Norwich, 1967; a show of wood engravings at Ashmolean Museum, Oxford, 1987; and a centenary exhibition was at Hove Museum and Art Gallery, with a tour, 1990. It holds his work.

Kechie PELLEW: *see* **Kechie TENNENT**

John PELLING 1930– Painter in oil and Church of England clergyman, born in Hove, Sussex. He studied at Royal College of Art, 1951–5, teachers including Rodrigo Moynihan, John Minton, Roger de Grey, Colin Hayes, Carel Weight and Ruskin Spear. Pelling then studied at Chichester Theological College, 1955–8, being ordained in 1959. From 1979–81 was chaplain to Nice and went on to paint mostly in the south of France, living at Monte Carlo. A friend of Francis Bacon, Pelling admired his work along with that of Munch, Balthus and Beckmann. "Tension between spirit and flesh and vulnerability are present in my own work." Showed at RA Summer Exhibition. Solo exhibitions included Drian Galleries, 1965; Moyan Gallery, Manchester, 1966; and University of Sussex, Brighton, 1967. Among his portraits was Graham Greene, the novelist, 1989. Nuffield Foundation holds his work, as does National Collection of Modern Art, Gdansk, Poland.

Frances PELLY 1947– Sculptor, mainly in stone, wood, clay and plaster, and teacher, born in Edinburgh. She studied at Duncan of Jordanstone College of Art, Dundee, 1965–71, teachers including Scott Sutherland, for diploma and post-diploma work. Lectured at Gray's School of Art, Aberdeen, 1979–83, then went self-employed on her own and commissioned work, including letter-cutting, although in 1988 she was appointed a tutor for the Open College. Pelly was a member of RSA and SSA. In 1987 she was appointed artist-in-residence at Highland Park Distillery, Orkney, and settled there in 1988, living at Evie. Pelly said she was "strongly influenced by early traditional training and working from the figure and by the environment, island living and the north." This was evident in her show Nousts at Pier Arts Centre, Stromness, with tour, 1992. Other exhibitions included a retrospective at Crawford Arts Centre, St Andrews, 1987. Pelly's main works included a bronze panel for Glasgow Royal Concert Hall and stone sculpture for Rose Terrace, Perth, both 1991, and stone carving in Banff, 1992. RSA, Scottish Arts Council, Aberdeen and Inverness Art Galleries hold examples.

PELOUSE 1913– Painter in oil and watercolour and printmaker, born at Gargrave, near Skipton, Yorkshire. Ann Ginsbury, originally christened Nancy, adopted the painting name Pelouse, a French translation of her maiden name, to avoid being confused with a painter brother-in-law. Originally a pianist, she studied art at Skipton Art School, then at Central School around the late 1950s under Victor Pasmore, Keith Vaughan and Mervyn Peake. Showed at RA, with Young Contemporaries, with East Kent Art Society and had a series of solo shows, including Liberty's, Fieldborne Galleries and Deal Library Gallery, 1995. Her work was in private collections including the writer Julian Symons, Archdeacon Michael Brown and Sir Kenneth and Lady Robinson. Lived in Walmer, Kent.

Lois PELTZ 1936– Painter who was by profession a graphic designer and illustrator, born in Wallasey, Cheshire, where she studied at the School of Art. Moved to London where her exhibitions included David Tilleke Fine Art, 1991–3. Was closely connected with the Ben Uri Art Society, which holds her gouache On the Bus.

Alex PEMBERTON 1957– Painter of landscapes, townscapes and interiors who attended Camberwell School of Arts and Crafts, 1977–8, then Chelsea School of Art, 1978–81. He won a number of awards, including Magnolia National Landscape Competition, second prize in 1980 and first prize in 1981; a British Council Scholarship to work in Seville, Spain, 1981–2; and Elizabeth Greenshields Foundation grant to work in Mexico, 1983–4. Among his group appearances were Constable Art Competition at Camden Arts Centre, 1988; RA Summer Exhibition, 1989; UA, 1990; and Austin/Desmond Fine Art, Camberwell Painters II, 1991. After a solo show at Novo Ltd, 1983, others followed regularly, later ones including Morley Gallery, 1988, and Cadogan Contemporary, 1992. International Mexican Bank holds his work.

Christopher PEMBERTON 1923– Painter, draughtsman and teacher. He was educated at Eton College, where he began painting under Robin Darwin. Then read history at Oxford University, going on to Camberwell School of Arts and Crafts, 1948, for four terms. Was art master at Bryanston School, taught and painted in London for three years, became art master at Shrewsbury School, and eventually taught foundation and degree courses at Camberwell School for 27 years. In 1957 was included in show of

Camberwell-trained painters at South London Art Gallery. Also showed at John Moores Exhibition in Liverpool, 1958; Hayward Annual, 1982; and had a series of solo shows including Woodlands Art Gallery, 1982; Quay Theatre, Sudbury, 1987; and in 1988 shared a show at Gainsborough's House, Sudbury. Returned to live in Suffolk, where he had been brought up, in 1983.

Muriel PEMBERTON 1909–1993 Fashion designer, draughtsman, painter and teacher, born in Tunstall, Staffordshire, into an artistic family. She studied at Burslem School of Art – its youngest student – 1925–8, with Gordon Forsyth, then with a scholarship and major award at Royal College of Art, 1928–31, with William Rothenstein and Ernest Tristram. Although initially in the school of painting she was allowed to devise her own course and obtained the College's first-ever diploma in fashion. Began teaching part-time at St Martin's School of Art, where she became head of the fashion/textile faculty, and at the Katinka School of Cutting; and drew fashions for magazines and advertisements. An exotic personality, Pemberton designed cards for Fortnum's, fabrics for Liberty and stage costumes for C B Cochran. In 1941 she married the head of St Martin's graphics department, John Hadley Rowe. She was fashion artist for the *News Chronicle*, 1945–52, and *Vogue*, 1952–6. After retirement to Hastings, Sussex, the year her husband died, Pemberton taught in Brighton and Hastings part-time and did more painting. Was elected RWS in 1984, also exhibiting at RA and Beaux Arts Gallery. Solo shows included a retrospective at Chris Beetles Gallery, 1993. Arts Council and public galleries in Hanley and Worthing hold examples.

Tom PEMBERTON 1925– Painter in oil, sculptor in welded steel, fibreglass and plastic and teacher, born and lived in Leeds, Yorkshire, husband of the artist Jean Bell. Pemberton was a mature student at Leeds College of Art, 1957–62, under Tom Watt and Harry Thubron, having been in the Fleet Air Arm, 1943–7, at Leeds University, 1948–50, in the chemical industry, 1950–3, then in boat-building, 1953–7. After lecturing at Leeds College of Art, 1962–6, Pemberton was at Canterbury College of Art, 1966–85, becoming principal lecturer in sculpture and deputy head of the school of fine art. He had worked as studio assistant part-time to Hubert Dalwood at Leeds University, 1959–61, while doing his diploma in painting, and at Canterbury raised sculpture from foundation to degree status. Showed paintings with Yorkshire Artists from 1961–90 and took part in many sculpture shows in Canterbury. Solo shows included Canterbury College of Art, 1974.

Joanne PEMBERTON-LONGMAN 1918– Painter in oil and tempera with a special interest in wildlife subjects. Studied at the Byam Shaw School of Drawing and Painting under F E Jackson, 1934–8. Went on to exhibit widely, with the RA, RHA, NEAC, ROI, SWA, NS and at the Paris Salon, where she won a silver medal in 1961. Sometimes signed work only with initials J P L. One-man show at RWS in 1949. Was a member of the St Ives Society of Artists and Society of Painters in Tempera. Lived in London.

Oliver PEMSEL 1910–1989 Artist and teacher who early worked in oil, later lithography, etching and watercolour. Pemsel's graphic work portrayed his love of the northern scene. He was born in Hornsey, north London, son of the artist George Pemsel. After education at the Moravian School at Fulneck, where his art master was Fred Jones, Pemsel studied at Hornsey School of Art, 1927–32, under Robert Lyon and Norman Janes, then did a year's pedagogic course directed by Douglas Percy Bliss. He designed and executed murals for Muswell Hill Public Library, irreparably damaged in the Blitz. In 1934 Pemsel married Mary Coffey, a fellow-student at Hornsey, their son Christopher being a television designer and Michael a painter and printmaker. After periods as art master at grammar schools in Cleckheaton and Harrogate, from 1940–5 Pemsel was commissioned in the Army, pen drawings of service life ending in the Royal Artillery Association headquarters, Woolwich. After demobilisation Pemsel joined the staff of Harrogate School of Art, retiring in 1974, after which he did part-time teaching. Experimented with light-colour projection, some designs being used on the television series *Top of the Pops*. An ambitious series of murals for Richard Bentley at Pannal Hall was a major feature of Pemsel's later output. Pemsel exhibited at RA, with Yorkshire Artists in Leeds and Wakefield and at many other galleries in the north. Showed solo at Hawksworth Gallery, Ilkley. Mercer Art Gallery in Harrogate and Stoke-on-Trent City Art Gallery hold examples.

João PENALVA 1949– Painter and designer, born in Lisbon, Portugal. He studied at Chelsea School of Art, graduating in 1981. He exhibited in group shows, including Francis Graham-Dixon Gallery, and abroad in Portugal, Spain and Japan. In 1990 held a major solo show at Centre de Arte Moderna, Calouste Gulbenkian Museum, Lisbon. Penalva was for a time a dancer with Pina Bausch Dance Theatre and worked as a set designer. Dance and the theatre continued to attract him as an artist, each picture being a bravura performance of dots, stripes and other devices. Lived in London.

Jack PENDER 1918–1998 Painter and teacher, born in Mousehole, Cornwall, to which he returned to live permanently in 1956. His pictures, usually oil on board, representational but sometimes near-abstract, are mostly concerned with Cornwall's sea and ships. Pender began painting in 1936, then studied at Penzance School of Art, 1938–9. He was in the Army, 1939–46, from 1945–6 attending Athens School of Art; then had three years at Exeter School of Art under Clifford Fishwick and John Skeaping; and gained his teaching diploma with a year, 1949–50, at Bristol's West of England College of Art. Taught at Plymouth Art School, 1950–4, and Royal Naval College, 1954–6. Pender showed with the Penwith and Newlyn Societies from late 1940s. His other group show appearances including New Art Centre and Chenil Gallery. Had a solo show at Arnolfini Gallery, Bristol, in 1963. More recent solo exhibitions included Leon Suddaby Fine Art, Penzance, 1989, and Belgrave Gallery, 1990. Plymouth Art Gallery and United Nations Building in New York hold his work.

Susan PENDERED 1925– Artist in watercolour, paper collage and mixed media, born in London, who sometimes signed work S P. After leaving school during World War II trained as a physiotherapist, pursuing her interest in art when children left home. Did non-vocational studies at Brighton Polytechnic under Norma Weller, 1975–82. Was made a member of RI in 1983 and gained the Winsor & Newton RI Award, 1988. Also belonged to Sussex Watercolour Society and Association of Sussex Painters and showed at RA Summer Exhibition, RWS, RWA and elsewhere in south of England. Lived in Hurstpierpoint, Sussex.

Peter PENDREY: *see* **Peter STRAUSFELD**

Audrey PENN 1897–1992 Watercolourist, born in Staffordshire, who was still working to her ninety-fifth year. She was a keen student of *The Artist* magazine, also taking summer lessons from Jack Merriott and Frank Egginton. Disliked publicity and considered herself "someone who painted" rather than an artist. Penn was noted for her views of Suffolk, done on the spot accompanied by a basket containing a paintbox, picnic lunch and a bottle of Malvern Water, also used for painting. She was especially fascinated by windmills and caravans. Showed in group exhibitions at Snape Maltings Gallery, solo shows being heldat Reid's Gallery in Aldeburgh; Deben Gallery, Woodbridge, 1964–93; and Gainsborough's House, Sudbury, 1994. British Museum holds her work. Died at Bawdsey, Suffolk. The proceeds from her last Deben Gallery show were used to fund repairs to Bawdsey Church organ, originally given by the Penn family.

William Charles PENN 1877–1968 Painter and influential teacher at Liverpool School of Art, 1911-post World War II, born in London. He studied at Lambeth and City and Guilds Schools of Art from 1895, winning medals and a scholarship to Royal Academy Schools, 1900–5, then studied at Académie Julian in Paris, 1908, and in following year in Netherlands and Belgium. As well as being a member of Sandon Studios Society and Liverpool Academy, belonged to ROI from 1908 and RP from 1952. Also exhibited with RA for many years, Royal Glasgow Institute of the Fine Arts and in Liverpool Autumn Exhibitions. Walker Art Gallery in Liverpool holds several examples. Lived for many years in Birkenhead, but died in Brampton, Cumberland. As an artist in oil Penn was noted for his sparkling, luscious technique.

Michael PENNIE 1936– Sculptor, printmaker and teacher, born in Wallasey, Cheshire. Pennie studied at Sunderland College of Art, 1953–7, then Royal College of Art, 1957–61, in the latter year attending British School in Rome. He was a teacher at Bath Academy of Art and Bath College of Higher Education from 1962, moving to Corsham in 1964. In early 1970s was appointed a Gregynog Fellow at University College of Wales in Aberystwyth. Participated in many group shows, solo exhibitions including Angela Flowers Gallery, Demarco Gallery in Edinburgh and elsewhere. In 1983 involved in Making Sculpture at Tate Gallery; in 1984 had a sabbatical to work on three commissions; and in 1985–6 was included in British Artists in Italy, 1920–80, touring show. Had a solo exhibition at Artsite, Bath, 1989. Collections holding Pennie's work include Arts Council, which has his abstract sculptures Ziggurat and 4 Spheres and 4 Cubes.

Edwin PENNY 1930– Wildlife watercolourist, notably of birds, who attended Bath College of Art from 13 and, after further studies at Royal West of England Academy, took up an apprenticeship in 1947 as a lithographic engraver. Born in Bristol, and continued to live near there. During Army National Service, in 1953 Penny was posted to Hong Kong, where, as the only European entrant, he won a government art competition with a landscape. As a result he gained six months' tuition with a Chinese master. He reckoned that technically he could teach Penny no more about watercolour; instead, he helped him understand the principles of Eastern composition, which Penny blended with Western ideas. Penny also admired the illustrations of Thorburn and Audubon, and Edwin Alexander's hedgerow birds. Had regular solo shows from the early 1960s at Frost & Reed, his sole agent.

Giles PENNY 1962– Sculptor, stage designer and film animator, born in Dorset, who attended Heatherley's School of Fine Art, Bournemouth College of Art and Design and Newport College of Art. He was a creator of witty and original sculptures, exhibited extensively in England and France, and included in Sixteen Sculptors at Sladmore Contemporary, 1997. In 1994, Penny was elected an associate of the RBS.

Kate PENOYRE fl. from mid-1970s– Painter, designer and illustrator who studied at Bristol College of Art, 1973, then graduated in graphic design at Canterbury College of Art, 1974–7. Penoyre began as a freelance graphic artist and illustrator, working for such publishers as Heinemann, Pan Books and Macdonald Publishing. In 1990 she shared an exhibition at John Hunt Galleries, of Brightling, also showing there in mixed exhibitions, and at Rye Society of Artists, 1991, and Hastings Art Gallery & Museum in 1992.

Newton PENPRASE 1888–1978 Painter, sculptor and teacher, born in Redruth, Cornwall, where one version of the family name was Penpraze. While still a student at Redruth School of Art, which he entered in 1903, he helped his father, who restored churches, and had drawings bought by Victoria & Albert Museum. For over 40 years from shortly before World War I Penprase taught at Belfast's College of Technology and showed at RUA and Ulster Arts Club, of which he was president. Ulster Museum holds a range of sculpture, painting and drawings by him.

Frances PENROSE 1896–1986 Painter, printmaker and draughtsman working on a small scale, interested in the countryside and flowers. She studied at Bournemouth Municipal College of Art under Sir Leslie Ward, the illustrator and caricaturist known as Spy. Much of her work was done while looking after a chronically invalid mother. Frances Penrose came from a distinguished family, among her ancestors being Archbishop Thomas Cranmer; Elizabeth Penrose, who as Mrs Markham wrote a children's history of England; and Dame Emily Penrose, head of both Royal Holloway College and Somerville College, Oxford. Frances Penrose was a major benefactor to the Cecil Higgins Art Gallery, Bedford, giving it notable pictures by J M W Turner and R P Bonington.

Roland PENROSE 1900–1984 Painter, writer, collector, exhibition organiser and advocate of modern art. The son of painter James Doyle Penrose, Roland Penrose was brought up a Quaker. He graduated from Cambridge University in 1922, went to Paris in that year and stayed there until 1934, during which time he painted his Surrealist picture Captain Cook's Last Voyage, now in the Tate Gallery. Penrose married the Surrealist poet Valentine Boué in 1925, his second wife being the American photographer Lee Miller. During the Paris period Penrose began to collect Cubist and Surrealist works, of which he became a lifelong advocate in Britain and abroad, being involved in the seminal International Surrealist Exhibition in London in 1936. During World War II he lectured to the Home Guard, then served in camouflage with the Army. In 1947 he helped found the ICA, remaining its chairman until 1969. Organised there landmark exhibitions: Forty Years of Modern Art, then Forty Thousand Years of Modern Art. Also organised a series of big exhibitions at the Tate Gallery for the Arts Council, such as Picasso in 1960, Max Ernst in 1962 and Miró in 1964. Penrose had met Picasso in 1934, which led to his fine book, in 1958, *Picasso his Life and Work*. Knighted 1966. Penrose showed widely, but his own painting was rather overshadowed by his other activities. In 1995 Scottish National Gallery of Modern Art, Edinburgh, showed Dada & Surrealist Masterpieces from the Penrose Collection which it had acquired. Penrose lived in London.

Mary Denise Nym PEN-SYMONS, 1923– Painter in oil, born in Melbourne, daughter of the Victoria Cross-winner Lieutenant-Colonel W I Pen-Symons. She was educated in Dublin, then studied art at Leicester School of Art, 1938, Royal Academy Schools, 1940, with Sir Walter Westley Russell, then 1946–9 with Philip Connard and William Dring, also Art Students' League of New York in 1947. At Royal Academy Schools won Hacker and Landseer prizes. Showed at RA, National Portrait Gallery and elsewhere. Lived variously in London; Goathurst, Somerset; and Skibbereen, County Cork, in Ireland.

Hilary PEPLER 1878–1951 Fine printer, carver, puppeteer and creator of mimes, brought up a Quaker and educated at Bootham School, York. His early life was diverse, spent running a small manufacturing firm in London. He then did land surveying, work for London County Council and was joint founder of Hampshire House working men's club. Eric Gill taught Pepler stone carving and engraved illustrations for his satire *The Devil's Devices*. In 1916 Pepler set up St Dominic's Press in Ditchling and became a key member of the Guild of St Joseph and St Dominic, but eventually fell out with Gill. Pepler's mercurial energy was finally directed into work with marionettes and dramatic mime, examples being shown in the early days of television and toured on the continent and in America. In 1937 the press was renamed The Ditchling Press and was later run by Pepler's son Mark. He lent material to Pepler's Puppets, an exhibition at Hove Museum & Art Gallery, in 1996.

Clothilde PEPLOE 1916–1997 Painter, born and died in Florence, Italy, where her father, the American Harry Brewster, owned a magnificent palace, bought from his father-in-law, the German sculptor Hildebrand. Educated privately, Clothilde grew up with painters, writers and musicians (her brother Harry's book *The Cosmopolites* tells the family's history), and she maintained through her life strong aesthetic and intellectual interests along with a devout Catholicism. With her brother and husband Willie Peploe, son of the Scottish Colourist S J Peploe and co-founder of Lefevre Gallery, she travelled widely in Europe and had a love of Greece, especially the Cycladic islands, the peace and isolation of which she campaigned to preserve. Shortly after World War II she was for a time in London, but the life did not suit her, and she returned annually to work in the Mediterranean. Although she began painting at 16, it was 40 years before she had her first exhibition of landscapes, at the New Grafton Gallery in 1971, several more following until 1982.

Denis PEPLOE 1914–1993 Painter and teacher, a native of Edinburgh, son of the artist Samuel John Peploe. After leaving Edinburgh Academy in 1931 Peploe was five years at Edinburgh College of Art, then studied in studio of André Lhote in Paris. In pre-war years travelled widely in countries around the Mediterranean Sea, wartime service, 1940–6, including a period in the Special Operations Executive and a serious motorcycle crash in North Africa. Taught drawing and painting at Edinburgh College of Art 1955–79, then was made a governor, 1982. He was elected RSA in 1966. Solo shows included a series at Scottish Gallery from 1947, with a major memorial exhibition in 1995. National Portrait Gallery, Edinburgh City Arts Centre and public galleries in Glasgow, Kirkcaldy and Perth hold examples. An independently minded, ironic and rather taciturn man, Peploe was scornful of fashionable trends in art. Among his interests was seeking and sketching wild fungi.

Mark PEPPER 1957– Figurative painter, born in Belfast, Northern Ireland. He graduated from the University of Ulster there in 1985, gaining his master's in fine art in 1986. In 1984 Pepper was a prizewinner in the Guinness Peat Aviation Awards for Emerging Artists, his work on show at RHA Gallery, Dublin. In 1985 he was chosen for the Claremorris Open Competition, where he also won a prize. Other appearances included Artists Endeavour, Otter Gallery, Belfast, 1987; Gateway to Art, Aer Rianta Arts Festival, Dublin Airport, 1993; and Works on Paper and Beyond the Partitions, put on in 1994 by Queen Street Studios, Belfast, with which he was associated.

Rhoda PEPYS 1914– Painter and teacher, born in Port Elizabeth, South Africa, mother of the artist Sandra Pepys. She studied at Collegiate School of Arts and Crafts in Port Elizabeth, winning the

Silver Medal in 1934. She was notable for her portraits, which included one of her husband, Professor Jack Pepys, for London University. Showed with Hampstead Artists' Council, Leicester Galleries, RP, RA and elsewhere in Britain in mixed shows, as well as in South Africa, also having solo exhibitions, including Barbican Centre, 1982. Lived in London.

Sandra PEPYS 1942– Painter, born in Cape Town, South Africa, daughter of the artist Rhoda Pepys, and like her a teacher. She studied at Slade School of Fine Art and with the artist Zdzislaw Ruskowski. Showed at RA Summer Exhibition, Accademia Italiana, Society of Landscape Painters of which she was chairman and Small Paintings Society of which she was vice-president. She was twice awarded the University of London Art Prize and was commissioned by British Rail to paint British woodlands in the four seasons. Solo shows included Duncan Campbell Contemporary Art, 1994. Lived in London.

Maurice Marshall PERCIVAL 1906–1981 Painter, muralist, designer and teacher who had a special knowledge of the Shakespearian theatre, illustrating books on the subject by Ronald Watkins and Jeremy Lemmon. After education at Hurstpierpoint College, he studied at Central School of Arts and Crafts and Royal College of Art. Became art master at Malvern College, 1940–5; head of art at Harrow School, 1945–54; then taught at Downside School, 1962–9. While at Harrow Percival was close to the artist David Jones, a fellow Catholic. Entered a religious house near Seville, Spain, where according to his friend Wilfrid Blunt, in his book *Slow on the Feather*, "the austerity of the life eventually killed him." This was not true. Percival became disillusioned with the religious life and retreated to England. Italian landscape and people were favourite picture subjects. Showed at RA.

Robert PERCIVAL 1924– Painter, printmaker and designer, born in Chesterfield, Derbyshire. Studied at Liverpool School of Art, 1941–5, under Will Penn and in Paris at L'Académie de la Grande Chaumière. He exhibited St James' Art Society in London, otherwise mainly in the north of England, at public galleries in Salford, Liverpool (where he was a member of the Academy), and Manchester. Walker Art Gallery, Liverpool, where he lived, holds his work.

George PERCY 1935– Painter and teacher, born in Hertfordshire. He studied at St Albans School of Art, 1955–8, then Academy of Fine Arts, Munich, 1958–9. Went on to teach fine art at North-East London Polytechnic. Among his shows was one at Woodlands Art Gallery, 1988, of which he said that his pictures were "intended to be specifically abstract. I am an old-fashioned Modernist in that I am challenged and excited by the philosophy of early abstraction, and by that of the later Abstract Expressionists." Arts Council holds several examples. Lived in southeast London.

Irene Rice PEREIRA 1902–1971 Painter, born in New York, America, where she attended the Art Students' League, 1927–31. After studying briefly at L'Académie Moderne, Paris, in 1931, she travelled in North Africa, then returned to New York, having a first solo show at the ACA Gallery, 1933. Pereira was associated with several artists' groups; was on the staff of the Works Progress Administrational Federal Art Project Design Laboratory; worked in the early 1940s at the Museum of Non-Objective Painting; and was associated with Peggy Guggenheim's Art of This Century Gallery, having a solo exhibition there in 1944. Nine years later she was given a retrospective at the Whitney Museum of American Art, New York. By then she had been married about three years to George Reavey (her third husband; the first was Humberto Pereira), the Irish-Ukrainian poet with Surrealist connections, who taught Russian at Manchester University. He and Irene had a flat in Salford decorated with some fine Surrealist pictures, which Irene rarely left because of her distaste for the climate and where she produced her transparent-layered abstracts. Reavey introduced Irene to mysticism. This, aspects of the Bauhus style, Jungian psychoanalysis, alchemy, other ideas and motifs found their way into Pereira's pictures and writings, which included *The Nature of Space*, 1956, and *The Lapis*, 1957. She divorced Reavey, lived latterly mainly in New York and died a few weeks after moving to Marbella, Spain, at the end of 1970.

Ed PERERA 1936– Painter and graphic designer, born in Kandy, Ceylon, who moved to London in 1962. He studied in the largest studio in Colombo, later working there, 1956–61, at the Central School of Arts and Crafts for painting, 1963, and at London College of Printing for graphic work, 1964. Went on to work as an art director with three agencies and a design group, 1966–72, painting in his spare time, then painted full-time from 1972. Perera showed in many mixed exhibitions in London and quickly held a series of one-man shows, his first solo in America taking place in 1976 at Genesis, New York. In that year he shared a show at Woodlands Art Gallery. Perera's work, in public collections in the United Kingdom and Germany, as well as many private collections, was figurative and decorative.

Peter PERI 1899–1967 Sculptor in concrete and polyester resin, printmaker and architect, born in Budapest, Hungary, where he first worked as a stonemason. Studied art there and architecture in Berlin. Just after World War I produced Expressionist drawings and was member of the artists' group MA with Moholy-Nagy. In the early 1920s took part in an art congress in Düsseldorf, visited Russia and Paris and then moved to Berlin where the Constructivists left a lasting impression. Exhibited abstract linocuts at Sturm Gallery, but shortly returned to realism during the mid-1920s when he worked for several years in Berlin City Architects' Department. In 1933 moved to London, where he settled, to escape Nazi persecution; in 1939 was granted British citizenship, changed his name to Peter from Laszlo and joined the British Communist Party, having been a member of the German one from the early 1920s. In 1936 participated in From Constructivism to Realism show at Foyles Gallery. From late 1930s very active as an etcher. From 1948 developed method of making figures in polyester resin and carried out commissions for schools, colleges and churches. Active AIA member. Exhibitions included St George's Gallery, 1958; Herbert Art Gallery, Coventry, 1960; The Minories, Colchester, 1970; and Gill Drey Gallery, 1989. Retrospective Leicestershire Museum and Art Gallery, 1991. Tate Gallery and British Museum hold his work.

Ivan PERIES 1921–1988 Painter, born in Deriwala in what is now Sri Lanka, whose art training initially was with Harry Pieris. He emerged as a leading figure in Sri Lankan art circles after World War II, being a founder-member of the 43 Group of painters, set up to show independent work. A government scholarship took him to London in 1946 to study at the Anglo-French Centre. Although he returned to Sri Lanka in 1949, he was back in England in 1953, settling eventually in Southend-on-Sea, Essex. He continued to show widely in England and Sri Lanka, including AIA, South London Art Gallery, Bear Lane Gallery in Oxford, having solo shows at Commonwealth Institute in 1966; Newman Room, Oxford, 1979; and Grayshott Art Gallery, 1980. Imperial War Museum, Victoria & Albert Museum and galleries abroad hold his work. Peries' pictures have a dreamlike quality, with a hard-to-interpret symbolism, often using a motif of two trees of unequal size. He was represented in The Other Story, Hayward Gallery and touring, 1989–90.

Alexander Georgiou PERIFIMOU 1916– Painter and draughtsman of imaginary narrative scenes in a naive style, born in Cyprus into a large family. He had little education and left school aged 11, working on the land and as a blacksmith; emigrated to Britain in 1935; worked as a chef and a tailor; then served abroad in World War II. After this, a skin disease prevented Perifimou from taking up his old work, and he was unemployed until he was offered jobs as a warder, 1973–81, at the RA, then the Tate Gallery. To relieve boredom at work, aged 59 he began to draw on his knee, sometimes producing larger versions, but usually on a small scale. Exhibitions included In Another World, Outsider Art From Europe and America, South Bank Centre, 1987, and Outsiders & Co, England & Co, 1996. Perifimou's work is held by the Outsider Collection and Archive.

Angelo PERINI: *see* **William Francis BURTON**

Muriel Kathleen PERKES 1898–1988 Painter, born in Newton-le-Willows, Lancashire, and initially educated in Southport. She attended Clapham School of Art and showed at RCamA and RI. She painted landscape and still life in watercolour and wrote and illustrated two books for small children, *The Little Green Door* and *The Secret of the Sundial*, as well as writing poetry. Lived for many years at East Horsley, Surrey, latterly near Pontesbury, Shropshire.

Christopher PERKINS 1891–1968 Painter and draughtsman, born in Peterborough, Huntingdonshire, who studied at the Slade School of Fine Art. From 1929–34 he lived in New Zealand, where his work was keenly sought in later years. He also lived in Suffolk and Jersey for a time. Exhibited at RA, ROI, London Salon and RP. He was a fine portrait draughtsman, subjects including the artists Adrian Allinson and Harry Jonas, included in a group of Perkins' works sold at Phillips in 1996, provenance Perkins' family.

Gary PERKINS 1967– Versatile artist, born in Manchester, who gained a fine art degree from Liverpool School of Fine Art, 1985–8, then a master's in sculpture from Chelsea College of Art, 1995–6. Exhibition included House, at John Moores University, Liverpool, 1994; New Potatoes, Gallery ON, Poznan, Poland, and Padded Wallpaper, Gallery II, Bradford, both 1995; and New Contemporaries at Tate Gallery, Liverpool, and Camden Arts Centre, 1996. In that show, Perkins' work The kind of prizes money just can't buy, of 1995, used a 1/20 scale kitchen, CCTV cameras and a 12-inch picture monitor.

Stuart PERKINS 1935– Painter – notably in watercolour – potter, sculptor and teacher, who studied under Albert Pountney at Leicester College of Art, 1952–6, winning first-class honours in his diploma, then gained his teaching certificate at the University of Leicester, 1957–8. From part-time lecturing at Nuneaton School of Art, 1956–7, until 1976 Perkins held a number of teaching posts. He was then a self-employed craftsman potter until 1985, after which he combined his own work with teaching the mentally handicapped at Stepping Stones, Broadoak. Following a lecture tour in America, Perkins became interested in painting miniatures, and from 1986 showed regularly in the United States, winning many awards at the four major East Coast societies. He was a member of RMS, 1990, a signature member of the Miniature Artists of America, 1991, also being a member of the Hilliard Society, of the Miniature Art Societies of Florida and Georgia and of the Miniature Society of Painters, Sculptors and Gravers, Washington. Also showed with RWA and RWS. Lived in Scowles, Coleford, Gloucestershire.

Suzanne PERLMAN fl. from 1960s– Painter of vibrant landscapes and townscapes that owe much to the influence of Oskar Kokoschka. Born in Hungary she went to live in the Netherlands, then settled in Netherlands Antilles for over 20 years. From early 1980s she lived in London. She studied art at Columbia University, New York; St Martin's School of Art; and San Miguel de Allende in Mexico. Perlman participated in shows on continent and exhibited one-man internationally; these included Carsons Pirie & Scott Department of Fine Art, Chicago, 1962; Upper Grosvenor Gallery, 1969; Municipal Museum, Gouda, Netherlands, 1970; Sternberg Centre for Judaism, 1986; and Boundary Gallery, 1993, in an exhibition titled London Observed. That gallery gave her a solo show in 1997. Perlman's works are in the collections of the Jewish Museum, Amsterdam, and Municipal Museum of Curaçao.

Brian PERRIN 1932– Artist in etching and watercolour, and teacher, born in Streatham, south London, who attended Croydon School of Art, 1948–51, and Royal College of Art, 1951–4, in the latter year winning the Rome Scholarship. Taught at Ealing School of Art, 1956–63; Hornsey College of Art, 1960–4; Royal College of Art, 1963–4; and was head of printmaking at Wimbledon School of Art after that. Was a senior fellow of RE. Mixed exhibitions included Galeria Bucholz, Brazil, and Graven Image at Whitechapel Art Gallery, both 1959; Cincinatti Biennale, 1962; Bradford City Art Gallery, 1964; National Museum of Wales, Cardiff, 1978; and British Prints Moscow and Leningrad, both 1988. Had a solo show at St George's Gallery, 1961, later ones including Sussex University, 1968 and 1970, and Burnaby Art Gallery, British Columbia, 1975. Metropolitan Museum in New York; Library of Congress, Washington; Glasgow University; Leeds City Art Gallery; Victoria & Albert Museum; and British Council are among many public collections holding Perrin's work. Lived in Kingston upon Thames, Surrey.

Ernest PERRY 1908–1976 Painter of portraits, and teacher, born in Belfast. He studied at Heatherley's School of Fine Art and at the Royal Academy Schools under F E Jackson and Sir Walter Westley Russell. Prior to World War II he was co-principal of the St John's Wood Art Schools with P F Millard, then by himself. After the war he taught at the same place, by then the Anglo-French Art Centre. Exhibited at RA, RP, LG and NEAC, signing his work E P. In later life Perry took up making stringed instruments, some of which he sold. Lived in London.

Julian PERRY 1960– Painter, notably in oil of the landscape around his home in Leyton, east London, who was born in Worcester. Studied at Berkshire College of Art & Design, 1977–8, then gained an honours degree in fine art at Bristol Polytechnic, 1978–8. Won many awards and prizes, including Jeffrey Archer Prize, Royal Festival Hall, 1987; British Council Exhibition Award, 1992; and its Travel Award, 1993. Group exhibitions included The New Painting at Artsite Gallery, Bath, 1984; Whitechapel Open at Whitechapel Art Gallery, 1987; Three Invited Artists, Madler Passage Galerie, Leipzig, 1992; and Towards The Millenium, Museum of London, 1995. Solo exhibitions included Tom Allen Centre, 1987, and Austin/Desmond Fine Art, from 1995. Luminous light and an intense concentration of detail were characteristics of Perry's pictures. The Museum of London, Cleveland County Council and London Transport and London Guildhall Collections hold examples.

Raymond George PERRY 1918– Sculptor who was brought up in Staffordshire and attended Birmingham University, but was self-taught in art. Settled in Lamorna, Penzance, Cornwall, where he was elected to join Penwith Society of Arts shortly after its foundation in 1949. Exhibited in Cornwall, sometimes signing work Cae Einion.

Richard PERRY 1960– Sculptor in a wide range of materials who was born in Nottingham. Perry studied at Leeds Polytechnic, 1978–81, and gained a first-class honours degree. From then he practised as a full-time artist. Among his many public commissions were Quartet, four over-life-size figures in bronze, commissioned by Nottingham City and County Councils, sited in the Old Market Square, 1986; four carved oak doors for Newark Library, 1988; Tree, a carved Portland stone sculpture commissioned by Northampton Borough Council for the new Guildhall extension, 1991–2; and in 1992 Conventions, a carved-oak relief for Birmingham City Council. The Morris Singer Foundry cast Perry's work, which called for much attention to detail. Showed widely in Britain from 1984–5, later exhibitions including The Palace of Culture in Poznan, Poland, and Contemporary Art Society Market, both 1992; and 1st RWA Open Sculpture Exhibition, 1993. British Museum, Derby Museums Service and Milton Keynes Development Corporation hold examples. Lived in Mapperley, Nottingham.

Roy PERRY 1935–1993 Artist in watercolour, gouache and acrylic, born in Liverpool. He was educated at the John Lyon School, 1948–53, then read economics at Southampton University, after which he "masqueraded as a chartered accountant". While working in industry Perry began to exhibit in mixed shows in the Camberley, Surrey, area, having his first solo in the local library. By the time he was offered redundancy in 1971 Perry was successful enough to paint full-time, and he moved to Dorset, where he settled at Donhead St Mary in a converted water-mill. Perry was made a member of RI in 1978, the year he won its Gold Medal. He also showed at RA, RBA and RSMA and had many solo exhibitions, including Linda Blackstone Gallery, Pinner, 1986, and a memorial show, Century Galleries, Henley-on-Thames, 1994. Perry travelled widely in Europe, China and North America and had several shows in Barbados. A soft blend of light and shade were hallmarks. He did a large amount of commissioned work, including regimental pictures for The Parachute Regiment, the Gurkhas and Royal Artillery; industrial pictures, including refineries and chemical works, clients including Davy Corporation; and paintings of cricket, Perry's passion, limited-edition prints being made of famous grounds. TRH The Prince of Wales and The Duke of Edinburgh were patrons.

Margot PERRYMAN 1938– Abstract painter, born in Plymouth, Devon, who also taught. She attended Harrow School of Art, 1953–6, and Slade School of Fine Art, 1956–9. In the mid-1960s she lived for a short time in New York, returning to London. Perryman's earlier works were ragged, flat-colour shapes, but by the time of the Camden Arts Centre's 1967 Survey '67 Abstract Painters her shapes gave slight suggestions of depth. Also exhibited at John Moores Liverpool Exhibition in 1965, LG and New Art Centre, from which Arts Council acquired Octave No 3, 1969, acrylic on canvas. She had had a solo show there in 1965. Leicestershire Education Committee also holds Perryman's work.

Robert PERSEY 1951– Sculptor and teacher, born in London. He attended Bulmershe College of Art, Reading, 1971–5, then St Martin's School of Art, 1976–7. From 1977 worked for some years in Greenwich Studios. He taught at Norwich School of Art and was a visiting lecturer at St Martin's. Persey's group appearances included New Contemporaries at RA and St Martin's on the South Bank, both 1977; 12th Annual Stockwell Depot Exhibition, 1979; and Have You Seen Sculpture from the Body?, at

Woodlands Art Gallery, 1983. Berkshire Education Authority holds his work.

K M PERSSE 1899– Painter, draughtsman and teacher, born at Loughrea, County Galway. After education at Heathfield School, Ascot, Mrs Persse studied at the Byam Shaw and Vicat Cole School of Art and with Margaret Kemp-Welch. After marriage lived for some time in Uganda, where she taught in Church Missionary Society schools and was a director for the Red Cross, also examining in Kenya under the Froebel method. Exhibited Beaux Arts Gallery, PS, in Uganda, at Paris Salon where she won a silver medal in 1965 and with UA, resigning in 1977. Lived in Hythe, Kent.

Eric PESKETT 1914– Sculptor and teacher, born in Guildford, Surrey. Studied at Brighton College of Art, 1929–35, with E A Sallis Benney, then Royal College of Art, 1935–9, teachers including Richard Garbe and Percy Hague Jowett. Exhibited at RA, LG and elsewhere in mixed shows, having a solo show at Paul Alexander Gallery in 1950. Peskett went on to become head of sculpture at Ravensbourne College of Art and a fellow of RBS in 1961. He worked in a range of materials and was noted for sculpture in architectural settings, completing a big volume of public work. Australia House, wood carvings; Austin Reed, Regent Street, mural; Congress Theatre, Eastbourne, brick reliefs; and crucifixes, Church of the Holy Cross, Eccles, are a few examples. Lived in Whyteleafe, Surrey.

PETER (in mirror-writing style): *see* **Peter SAMUELSON**

Robert Charles PETER 1888–1980 Painter and printmaker, born in London. Studied at Bolt Court and the Central School of Arts and Crafts. Exhibited widely, including RE, of which he was a member, RA, Goupil and Chenil Galleries and Ridley Art Club. Chelsea Arts Club member. His work is held by British Museum and Fitzwilliam Museum, Cambridge. Lived in Kew Gardens, Surrey.

Robert PETERS fl. from mid-1980s– Painter, muralist, draughtsman and administrator who gained a degree in fine art at University of Ulster in 1984. He was commissioned to paint several big murals, including The Royal Victoria Hospital and Hilltown Hospital in Northern Ireland. He was closely involved in the founding of Catalyst Arts in Belfast. Took part in group exhibitions including Crescent Arts Centre, Belfast, 1985; also in the city in 1994 he was included in Beyond the Partitions, organised by Queen Street Studios, with which he was associated. Had a solo exhibition at the Crescent, 1985.

David PETERSEN 1944– Sculptor, model maker and teacher, born in Cardiff. After Taunton School, in Somerset, he worked for a year as an architectural draughtsman, 1960–1, then was at Newport College of Art and Design, 1961–5, and London University Institute of Education, 1965–6. In the latter year he was engaged in model and special effects work on the film *2001, A Space Odyssey*. Then freelanced and held several teaching posts, including his old college at Newport. In 1970s worked to convert Usk Priory, in Gwent, to workshops and studios and a gallery. Showed at WAC Structure '66 exhibition, ICA and Royal National Eisteddfod, where he was a joint prizewinner in 1974. Carried out commissions for Harrow Public Library and a series of murals for Welsh Brewers Ltd in several locations.

Peter PETERSON 1934– Painter and teacher who took his diploma in painting at Hornsey College of Art. He began his teaching career in the visual research department of Chesterfield College of Art, was on staff of Epsom College of Art and a visiting lecturer at Falmouth College of Art, 1986. He was elected to RBA in 1978, becoming its vice-president in 1988. Showed at RA Summer Exhibitions from 1968, also exhibiting at NEAC and Southwell-Brown Gallery, Richmond. He had a one-man show there, also Portal Gallery and in the provinces. Peterson won the Daler-Rowney Prize in 1983 and a first prize, 1988. Lived in London.

David T PETHERBRIDGE 1950– Painter of geometrical abstracts, and teacher, born in Hull, Yorkshire. He studied at Nottingham College of Art, Bath Academy of Art and Whitelands College. Went on to teach in south London. Among his exhibitions was Five, at Woodlands Art Gallery, 1982.

Deanna PETHERBRIDGE 1939– Artist, writer and teacher, born in Pretoria, Transvaal, South Africa. Studied at University of Witwatersrand, Johannesburg, 1956–9, leaving South Africa shortly after. Travelled to England to live by way of Italy, then for the next few years travelled extensively in Balkans, Middle East and North Africa. First one-man show at Angela Flowers Gallery in 1973; also showed Whitechapel Gallery, Warehouse Gallery and abroad. From mid-1970s wrote for various magazines on art and architecture. Continued travels through India in late 1970s and in 1982 was artist-in-residence at Manchester City Art Gallery. That gallery, Arts Council and Museum of Modern Art in San Francisco hold her work, which includes shaped canvases, sculpture in various media and especially drawings, sometimes of an abstract, mathematical or architectural nature. In 1995 Petherbridge was made professor of drawing at Royal College of Art. Was based for a time at Holmbury St Mary, Surrey.

Arthur Leonard PETIT 1919–1954 Painter and architect specialising in architectural subjects. Born Guernsey, Channel Islands, where he continued to live. Studied art at Reading University and at the Regent College of Art. Exhibited at City Art Gallery, Bradford, and was a member of Bradford Arts Club, which holds his work.

Roy PETLEY 1951– Painter and draughtsman, notable for sunlit landscapes with figures, born in Norfolk, whose parents separated when he was an infant. By the time he was five his mother was unable to handle him and he was placed in a children's home and school for 10 years, where he began to draw. At Brighton

School of Art in 1967 Petley's request for a transfer from the commercial to the fine art course was refused, so he left in the first term. He spent a year on the continent studying art in museums and galleries, earning his living with instant sketches, which honed up his draughtsmanship. Back in Britain, Petley supported himself partly with various jobs while showing in small galleries, influences on his work including Constable, Turner, Sargent, Sickert, Lavery, Campbell Mellon and Seago. After rejection by West End dealers in London, Petley was discovered by royalty when showing at the Hyde Park railings (at his 1996 Century Galleries, Henley-on-Thames, solo exhibition works by the Duchess of Norfolk, who opened it, were included), and a television programme drew attention to him, West End exhibitions following. Petley was also commercially successful in America. Lived in the Dordogne area of France.

Llewellyn PETLEY-JONES 1908–1986 Painter and teacher, born in Edmonton, Alberta, Canada, father of the artist Nancy Petley-Jones. Worked for a bank for three years, then turned to painting and teaching at his studio in Edmonton, where he became a member of the Art Club and Alberta Society of Artists. Moved to London in 1934, studied in Paris and had some success showing in both capitals. After a brief time in Italy left for London again because of outbreak of war and had first solo show at Matthiesen Gallery. After further travels settled in Richmond, Surrey. In 1955 was commissioned by Alberta government to paint portraits of HM The Queen and HRH The Duke of Edinburgh for Alberta Legislative Building. By 1958 Petley-Jones was producing abstract pictures, holding a show at Waddington Galleries. Further solo shows included St George's Gallery, Wildenstein, Gimpel Fils and University of London. In 1989 Richmond Antiquary Gallery held a show of his work. Petley-Jones' flower paintings and landscapes were often in the manner of the Scottish Colourists.

Nancy PETLEY-JONES 1953– Painter, designer and illustrator, born in Vancouver, British Columbia, daughter of the artist Llewellyn Petley-Jones. From an early age she lived in Richmond, Surrey, where she attended the County School for Girls and her father's drawing classes. In 1976 graduated from Kingston Polytechnic with an honours degree in graphic design. Started her professional life working as a freelance illustrator in publishing and for BBC Television, including such programmes as *Play School* and *Merry-Go-Round*. Later she concentrated on landscape painting while still doing some work for television, showing locally in St Margarets. In 1990 her work was shown with her father's at Richmond Antiquary Gallery.

Gladys PETO 1890–1977 Versatile illustrator, designer and writer, born in Maidenhead, Berkshire, who studied at local School of Art, 1908, then London School of Art, 1911. She married Major Cuthbert Emmerson and lived in Malta, Cyprus and Egypt, 1924–8, as a result of which she published *Malta and Cyprus* and *Egypt of the Sojourner*, with her own illustrations. She also produced children's books, such as *Bedtime Stories* and *Sunshine Tales*, her illustrative style being reminiscent of Aubrey Beardsley's. Designed for the stage, furnishings and posters. On her travels completed many watercolours and showed at Abbey Gallery. Lived latterly in County Londonderry, Northern Ireland.

James PETO 1928– Painter, mainly in watercolour, full name Michael James Peto, who was born in Jaffna, Ceylon. He was educated in England and studied art at Canterbury School of Art, 1944–5, his teachers including Gerald Norden. Then attended Bartlett School of Architecture, London University, 1945–51. Showed in Canterbury and elsewhere in England and in Salisbury, Rhodesia, where he lived for some years.

Rosemary PETO 1916– Painter, born in London. Came from and married into a family of painters and collectors. She studied drawing at Westminster School of Art, 1931–2, and at Royal College of Art, 1953–6. A pre-medical course fostered her interest in plant structure, and flower studies were a feature of her first London show, at Sally Hunter & Patrick Seale Fine Art, 1985.

Claudia PETRETTI 1965– Painter and teacher of Italian-Scots background in the Scottish Colourist tradition. Notable for landscapes painted in Britain and on the continent in which a tendency towards greater abstraction emerged in late 1980s. Born in Edinburgh, she attended the College of Art there, 1983–8. In 1987 she gained the John Kinross Travelling Scholarship to Florence as well as the Richard Ford Travelling Scholarship to Madrid. In 1988 won the Adam Bruce Thomson Award at RSA in the student competition. From 1989 she was tutor of drawing and painting for the 369 Gallery education programme. Group shows included Young Contemporaries, 1989; Painting the Forth Bridge, 1990, 369 Gallery in Edinburgh and tour; and Scottish Colourists Old and New, at Kirkcaldy Museum & Art Gallery, 1991. She had solo shows at 369 Gallery and Italian Cultural Institute, Edinburgh, 1990, then shared an exhibition with James Skelton Smith at Mina Renton Gallery, 1991.

Wilfred Stanley PETTITT 1904– Painter of landscapes and commercial artist, born in Great Yarmouth, Norfolk. He was the son of an art dealer, Charles Pettitt. Attended Great Yarmouth and Norwich Schools of Art. The Medici Society reproduced his work and he showed at RA, RCamA and Norwich Twenty Group, of which he was a founder-member. His speciality was views of East Anglia. Lived in Norwich, Norfolk.

John PETTS 1914–1991 Multi-talented artist, sculptor, teacher and publisher, born in London. Although the glass engraver and writer Laurence Whistler ranked Petts alongside Henry Moore, Graham Sutherland and Stanley Spencer as an artist dealing with Christian themes, Petts remained an outsider, relatively unknown. Studied at Hornsey College of Art, 1930–2; then 1933–4 was at Royal Academy Schools and Central School of Arts and Crafts. In 1934 he moved to Llanllechid, in a remote part of Wales, where with his first wife, the artist and writer Brenda Chamberlain, he founded Caseg Press which published popular prints with

Snowdonia themes. After World War II, during which Petts was a pacifist non-combatant, the artist resumed life in Wales with his second wife, the artist and writer Marjory (Kusha) Miller. He was for periods associated with the Welsh Committee of the Arts Council and a teacher at Carmarthen College of Art, but from the early 1960s was mainly preoccupied with stained glass design. Among his most notable commissions were windows for the 16th Street Baptist Church, in Birmingham, Alabama; and the 40-foot windows for the Brighton and Hove Synagogue. As a painter, sculptor, designer, artist in mosaic and craftsman Petts exhibited widely. Work in many public collections, including National Library of Wales, Aberystwyth; Derby Art Gallery; and the University of Hong Kong. Died in Abergavenny, Monmouthshire.

Kusha PETTS 1921– Painter, craftsman–artist and writer, born Marjory (Kusha) Miller in London, and was the second wife of the artist John Petts. She studied fine art at University of Reading, 1939–44. Then she taught, including St Paul's Girls' School, 1945–7. In the latter year she married John Petts and helped him with his mosaic and stained glass work. In 1967 she began writing, publishing the book *Necklace for a Poor Sod* in 1970 and, living in Llanstephan, Dyfed, also made commemorative plates. Exhibited Howard Roberts Gallery in Cardiff, Royal National Eisteddfod and SEA and had a one-man show at Thomson House, Cardiff.

Anthony PETTY 1918– Artist in watercolour, ink, pencil, crayon, gouache and mixed media, born in Southampton. He attended the Southern College of Art, 1934–8, with William Dring, then Architectural Association School, 1946–8, under Gordon Brown. He was by profession an architect and planner and a part-time painter, showing at RA Summer Exhibitions, with Sussex Artists at public gallery in Brighton, with Arts Council and in other provincial galleries. Lived in Lindfield, Sussex.

Helmut PETZSCH 1920– Painter and teacher, born in Berlin, Germany. After education in Hamburg and London he attended Edinburgh College of Art, 1947–51, where his teachers included William Gillies. For a time taught at Castlebrae High School, in Edinburgh, where he lived. Wrote a book on *Architecture in Scotland* and showed at RSA, SSA and elsewhere in Scotland.

John PEZARE 1911– Painter, illustrator and teacher, full name Walter John Pezare, born in Portsmouth, Hampshire. Studied at Southern College of Art, 1926–32, at Royal College of Art, 1932–6, under William Staite Murray and Ernest Tristram, and Central School of Arts and Crafts, 1933–6. Exhibited RA, Worcester Art Gallery and elsewhere in provinces. Did poster work for Air Ministry. Pezare held a number of teaching posts, joining Bromley College of Art shortly after World War II. Victoria & Albert Museum and British Museum hold his work. Lived in Tatsfield and in Bromley, Kent.

Vong PHAOPHANIT 1961– Installations artist, born in Laos, educated in France to 1985, when he moved to Britain. Attended École des Beaux-Arts, Aix-en-Provence, 1980–5. Was shortlisted for the Turner Prize, 1993. Stephen Friedman Gallery gave Phaophanit a solo show in 1996. Lived and worked in Bristol.

Julia PHELPS 1948–1993 Painter and teacher, born in Blandford Forum, Dorset. She studied at Harrow School of Art with Ken Howard and Charles Bartlett, then at Royal College of Art under Ruskin Spear and Carel Weight. The Phelps family were boat-builders and river men on the Thames, and Julia adopted the river as her subject. She showed at SWA, in the Open show at RWS, won prizes at the Spirit of London exhibitions put on by the Greater London Council and carried out a number of commissions, notably for the Dyers' Company and Fishmongers' Company. Died in London.

Jackie PHILIP 1961– Painter and teacher, born in Edinburgh, who studied at Gray's School of Art, Aberdeen; Wimbledon School of Art; and Royal Academy Schools. Awards included an Italian Government Scholarship and British Institute Award, both 1986–7. Lectured at Newham Community College & Eastham Centre, 1987–90, then was head of painting at Hungry Creek Art School in New Zealand, 1990–4. Group shows included South Bank Picture Show, Royal Festival Hall, and RA Summer Exhibition, from 1985; Six of the Best, Cadogan Contemporary Art, 1988; Waterman Fine Art, 1989; Abbott & Holder, 1990; Studio of Contemporary Arts, Auckland, 1994; and in 1995 The American Club, Hong Kong, and Royal Over-Seas League Open.

Wogan PHILIPPS 1902–1993 Farmer and painter, born in Wales, who attended Eton College and Oxford University. He began painting in his twenties, studying briefly at Ruskin College, Oxford, with John Nash and Gilbert Spencer, and at Euston Road School. Philipps turned politically left with the 1926 General Strike, driving an ambulance in the Spanish Civil War, 1936, in 1937 joining the British Communist Party. He became the second Lord Milford in 1962, was married to the novelist Rosamond Lehmann, 1928–44; Cristina, Countess of Huntingdon, 1944–53; and from 1954 to Tamara, widow of Bill Rust, founder of the *Daily Worker*. In the 1940s Philipps took up farming in the Cotswolds which he combined with painting. How man changed the landscape was his dominant theme, and he said that the only thing he wanted to leave behind was "a few good pictures". A penniless farmer neighbour paid for one picture with a load of hay. Later paintings, when he had retired from farming, had an internationally political slant. Showed with AIA, Leicester and Brook Street Galleries, RWA and abroad, and had several solo exhibitions with Woodstock Gallery. Died in London.

Robin PHILIPSON 1916–1992 Painter and teacher, born Robert James Philipson in Broughton-in-Furness, Lancashire. After attending Edinburgh College of Art, 1936–40, Philipson served in a Scottish regiment during World War II, then joined the staff of Edinburgh College of Art in 1947. Was appointed head of the school of drawing and painting in 1960, a post held until retirement in 1982. His work was deeply influenced by that of Oskar Kokoschka. It had great Expressionistic attack and vitality. He took up themes such as cock-fighting, kings and queens, cathedral interiors and zebras, which gave him opportunities for jewel-like painting. Was elected SSA in 1948; RSA in 1962, being president for 10 years from 1973; RSW in 1965; Royal Glasgow Institute of the Fine Arts in 1980; in 1981 he was elected RA. Philipson was knighted in 1976. He served on the Scottish Advisory Committee of the British Council and was a member of the Royal Canadian Academy of Fine Arts. Had a major retrospective at Edinburgh College of Art in 1989. Scottish National Gallery of Modern Art, in Edinburgh where he lived, and other public galleries hold his work. Philipson's first two wives were the artists Brenda Mark and Thora Clyne.

Albert PHILLIP 1915– Painter, printmaker and teacher, born in Skipton, Yorkshire, where he attended the local Art School from 1934, teachers including Dan Binns, then Royal College of Art from 1937, gaining his associateship in 1940, winning several awards, teachers including Frank Dobson, Malcolm Osborne and Robert Austin. He was made an associate of RE in 1956, also showing with RA, in the provinces and abroad. Phillip taught at Lancaster and Morecambe College of Art, living in Lancaster.

Agnes PHILLIPS 1917– Painter and wood engraver, born and lived in Rugby, Warwickshire, where she attended the High School. Studied at Birmingham College of Arts and Crafts, 1933–9. Showed with RA, Rugby Art Society and elsewhere in Midlands.

Aubrey R PHILLIPS 1920– Artist, noted for his pastels and watercolours of Malvern Hills and Black Mountains areas, and teacher, born in Astley, Worcestershire, married to the artist Doris Phillips. He studied under Ernest Dinkel at Stourbridge School of Art and at Kidderminster School of Art, his teachers including Cyril Lavenstein. Became a part-time lecturer at Malvern and Bournville School of Art, wrote two books on the art of pastel and contributed to art magazines. Was a member of RWA, PS, WSW and Armed Forces Art Society, also showing at city art galleries in Hereford, Worcester and Gloucester and Patricia Wells Gallery, Thornbury. Gained gold medal at Paris Salon, 1966. Solo shows included National Library of Wales, Aberystwyth. Aubrey Phillips lived in Malvern, Worcestershire.

Doris M PHILLIPS 1921–1993 Painter and collagist, born in Stourport, Worcestershire, married to the artist Aubrey Phillips. She studied at Malvern School of Art and showed at UA and PS. She lived in Malvern, Worcestershire, where a tribute show was held at the Church of the Ascension in 1994 as part of the Flower Festival.

Harry PHILLIPS 1911–1976 Figurative sculptor and teacher, born in London, who spent his formative years as a wood-carver, furniture-maker, blacksmith and potter, in St Albans and at Dartington Hall, then from 1935 as a teacher, including time at Blundell's School. In 1950, Phillips was appointed head of sculpture at the College of Art in Leeds, where he was long-settled. In 1958, he was awarded the Herbert Baker Travelling Scholarship for Sculpture. He was a regular exhibitor at RA Summer Exhibitions until 1963; in 1959, he showed The Risen Christ for St John's Church Westminster, under the name H Raines Phillips; and he was represented in The Teaching Image, 1964, a Leeds College of Art staff show at Leeds City Art Gallery. Where possible, he believed, "the artist should carry out every stage of the work himself and this applies particularly to bronze sculptures." Phillips completed a series of large public sculptures for locations in London and the provinces. They included Miner, 1960–3, at Richborough Power Station, Kent; Crucifix, 1962, at St Francis', Leigh Park, Havant; Christ Triumphant, 1964, at St George's, Letchworth; and St Christopher, 1975, at St Christopher's Hinchley Wood, Surrey. There was a retrospective at Temple Newsam, Leeds, 1976, the year Phillips died, by which time he was living in Lewes, Sussex, where his St Michael, a late work, was chosen for St Michael's Church. Phillips said that he was "strongly influenced by Bernard Leach and Eric Gill with whom I worked for a short period in the thirties." He felt "some depression when confronted with the totality of the visual arts during the past fifty years".

H Raines PHILLIPS: *see* **Harry PHILLIPS**

John PHILLIPS 1920– Painter and teacher, born in Horsham, Sussex. Studied at Cardiff College of Art in 1930s with Evan Charlton and William Pickles. From 1947 taught at grammar schools in Luton, Ramsgate and Romford, retiring from the administration side of University of London's School Examinations Department in 1980. Showed with Ramsgate and New Hertfordshire Art Societies. Lived in Harold Hill, Essex.

John PHILLIPS 1936– Sculptor and teacher, born in London, but educated at Penarth County School, in Wales. He attended Cardiff College of Art, 1952–6, then Slade School of Fine Art 1956–7 and 1959–61 with a two-year break for National Service in Royal Air Force. Then began teaching in Bristol, although in the mid-1960s he briefly ran the Mechanical Theatre with the composer Martin White. Among a series of further teaching posts was senior lectureship at Manchester Polytechnic, then Hertfordshire College of Art and Design. Participated in many group shows, including Arnolfini Gallery in Bristol where he was an open exhibition prizewinner, also Howard Roberts Gallery in Cardiff and SEA. In 1967 was Donald Miller Memorial Prize winner for WAC and United Nations Association. Solo show at Forum Gallery, Bristol, others at Wadham College in Oxford and Abbot Hall Art Gallery in Kendal. WAC holds Phillips' work and his Blodewedd (The Flower Girl), 1967, mainly in coloured concrete, is sited at University College of Wales in Aberystwyth.

Patrick Edward PHILLIPS 1907–1976 Portrait and landscape painter in oil and watercolour, and teacher. Studied at Byam Shaw School of Drawing and Painting under F E Jackson, Glyn Philpot and Charles Shannon, 1926–30. He became principal of Byam Shaw, 1946–55. Phillips exhibited at RA, RP, RWS, NEAC and

Cooling Galleries. Tate Gallery holds his portrait of Mrs Carter Gifford. Lived in Maldon, Essex.

Peter PHILLIPS 1939– Painter and teacher, born in Birmingham, where he attended the College of Art, 1955–9, exhibiting for first time in Young Contemporaries in latter year. While he was at Royal College of Art, 1959–62, showed in John Moores Exhibition, Liverpool. While at Royal College Phillips transferred from painting to television school due to some disagreements with his teachers. He early established a reputation as an uncompromising Pop Artist who produced mixed-media collages. From the early 1960s he was appearing in important group exhibitions, then the Harkness Fellowship in 1964 took him to New York, 1964–6. He had a first one-man show there at the Kornblee Gallery in 1965, with several more to follow. He later moved to Zürich, Switzerland, and showed in Germany and elsewhere abroad, teaching at Hochschule für Bildende Kunst, Hamburg, in the late 1960s. Touring retrospective, Walker Art Gallery in Liverpool, 1982, then a show at Thomas Gibson Fine Art, 1998. Arts Council holds his work.

Tom PHILLIPS 1937– Witty and erudite artist and teacher, a Renaissance man whose interests included painting, graphics, making books, musical composition and performance. Interviewed on the BBC2 Television programme *The Artist's Eye* in 1989, Phillips reckoned that he had many small talents rather than one big one, hence his diversification. He included among his inspirations childhood memories, the Victorian writer W H Mallock's novel *A Human Document* (metamorphosed by Phillips into the multi-volume *A Humument*), and graves seen in Crete, which prompted his tombstone-shaped World War II sculpture for the Imperial War Museum. His opera *Irma* stemmed from his quest for the ideal woman, like Dante's Beatrice (Dante's *Inferno* inspired the Phillips book which he translated, designed and printed). Phillips was born and worked in London. He attended Oxford University, 1957–60, obtaining a degree in Anglo-Saxon literature, from 1961–3 studying at Camberwell School of Arts and Crafts. By 1964 he was exhibiting in Young Contemporaries. A year later he had a solo show at AIA Gallery. He taught at Bath Academy of Art, 1966–7. Showed at Venice Biennale, 1971. Phillips' work was widely exhibited in group and solo exhibitions. He had an early retrospective at Marlborough Graphics, 1973; others followed in Britain and abroad. There was a major show at the RA in 1992, with sixtieth birthday exhibitions at South London Gallery and Dulwich Picture Gallery, 1997. Phillips was elected RE in 1987, RA in 1989. Arts Council holds his work.

Tony PHILLIPS 1952– Artist in various media, born in Liverpool. He studied mural design at Lancaster Art College, Preston. He was a major contributor to the 1991–2 Norwich Gallery touring exhibition History and Identity with a series of pastel drawings charting the history of Benin Bronzes taken from Nigeria. Phillips moved to Shrewsbury, Shropshire, in 1978 and began painting full-time. He worked on a number of community arts projects throughout Britain, including residencies and workshops in schools and galleries. He tended to work in series, such as Jazz, 1988, and Icarus, 1988–91. Shows of his pictures were held at Harris Art Gallery, Preston, 1979, Commonwealth Institute, 1983, People's Gallery, 1984–8, Africa Centre, 1986–9, Graves Art Gallery in Sheffield and Rochdale Art Gallery, both 1987. Victoria & Albert Museum and a number of provincial galleries hold his work.

Leonard PHILPOT 1877– Painter, architect and designer, born in London. Studied architecture at South Kensington Schools and practised in Britain, China and America. Also designed rooms and furniture. Took up painting and exhibited RA, RI, Fine Art Society, Walker Art Gallery, Liverpool and abroad. Galleries in Brighton, Preston and Worthing hold his work. Lived at West Moors, Dorset.

Howard PHIPPS 1954– Printmaker, painter in oil and watercolour and teacher, born in Colwyn Bay, Denbighshire. He studied at Gloucestershire College of Art, Cheltenham, 1971–5, then Brighton Polytechnic, 1975–6. He taught in Devon for four years until 1980, then was established in Salisbury, Wiltshire, as a painter-printmaker, best known for wood engravings. Phipps showed at RA Summer Exhibitions from 1985, in that year winning a Christie's Contemporary Print Award; other group shows included Fremantle, Australia, and tour, and New Ashgate Gallery, Farnham. Had solo shows at Salisbury Playhouse Gallery from 1987, with one of wood engravings at Cheltenham Art Gallery & Museum, 1997. Phipps was from 1982 a member of RWA and SWE. He was particularly known for his illustrations to Whittington Press, Folio Society and other presses' books.

Adrian PHIPPS-HUNT 1940– Artist in wide variety of media, specialising in three-dimensional work, photographer and lecturer, born in Pevensey, Sussex. He attended Brighton College of Art and Design, 1957–61, sculpture school with Arthur J Ayres. In 1970 gained a research fellowship, Nottingham College of Art. Phipps-Hunt, who sometimes signed work A P-H, listed among his main works a 1969 floor tile configuration sponsored by Dunlop Semtex Ltd; 2 x 2 ton drops into concrete, at Art Spectrum London, 1971; and Down the grass, over the wall and into the Thames, 1972, at St Mary's Churchyard, Putney. Phipps-Hunt said that most of his studio works he saw "as experiments towards my visions for large environmental creations – layouts, sculptural placements to be created in-situ for specified situations". Group shows included Survey '68: Abstract Sculpture, at Camden Arts Centre, 1968; Photography into Art, same venue, 1972; Umbrella Experiment 4, Midlands Group Gallery, Nottingham, 1975; and Open House Gallery, Brighton Festival, 1986 and 1991. Solo shows included County Town Gallery, Lewes, 1964; Arnolfini Gallery, Bristol, 1976; and Atrium Gallery – Art Locate, Derwent Business Centre, Derby, 1993. Lived in London.

Johannes PHOKELA 1966– Painter, born in Johannesburg, South Africa, who studied at Fuba Academa, 1983–6, St Martin's School of Art, 1987–8, Camberwell College of Art, 1988–91, and

Royal College of Art, 1991–3. In 1993 he took up a Delfina Studios Award in London, where he lived. Phokela was a prizewinner at 1993–4 John Moores Liverpool Exhibition. He also took part in BP Portrait Award at National Portrait Gallery in 1990 and in 1992 had a solo show at Harlequin Gallery.

Charles PIBWORTH 1878–1958 Sculptor, painter and designer. Born in Bristol, he studied at the School of Art there, at the Royal College of Art, where he won two gold medals, and at the Royal Academy Schools under Onslow Ford, George Frampton and Thomas Brock. Exhibited RA, ROI, RBA, Royal Glasgow Institute of the Fine Arts, IS and Paris Salon, where he won a bronze medal in 1947. He finished a large number of public commissions, including a bust of Sir Johnston Forbes-Robertson, for Drury Lane Theatre, the Turf Club war memorial and twenty-one life-size figures for Bristol's Central Library. Several British galleries hold his work, including Leicester's Museum and Art Gallery and Aberdeen Art Gallery. Was a fellow of the RBS. Lived in London.

PIC: *see* **Charles HIGGINS**

Roland PICHÉ 1938– Sculptor and teacher, born in London, who studied at Hornsey College of Art, 1956–60. After a period working with the sculptor Gaudia in Montreal, Canada, Piché was at Royal College of Art, 1960–4. During this time he gained the Walter Neurath Prize, worked as an assistant to Henry Moore and showed with Young Contemporaries in 1963. From 1964 Piché taught sculpture at Maidstone College of Art. After a Peter Stuyvesant Foundation Travel Bursary in 1965 the artist had a one-man show at Marlborough New London Gallery in 1967, the year following gaining a commission prize in the Moorgate Sculpture Competition. Among other important showings were Silver Jubilee Contemporary British Sculpture Exhibition in Battersea Park, in 1977. Piché created sculpture from a variety of materials, his work having both organic and geometric forms. Arts Council holds his Garden Without a Ceiling, of 1967. Lived for some years in Tollesbury, Essex. Made a fellow of RBS in 1993.

George PICKARD 1929–1993 Sculptor, architect, painter and teacher, born in Syston, Leicester, settling nearby at Rearsby. He attended Leicester School of Architecture, 1945–52, becoming an associate of RIBA in 1953. In 1952–4 did his National Service in the Royal Artillery as regimental artist engaged in camouflage design. From 1957–66 practised as an architect, interested in interior design and sculptural components in building. From 1966–88 Pickard was senior lecturer in interior design at Leicester Polytechnic, in 1986 being granted a sabbatical to study advanced design and methods in flat glass related to sculpture. Was a founder-member of the Architectural Sculptors Group in 1972, was a member of Leicester Society of Artists and showed widely in Britain. Many sculpture commissions included Tube Investments, Coalville; Leicester and Loughborough Universities; United Reform Church, Groby; and Beaumont Leys, Leicester. Pickard was a non-representational artist whose work had "strong references to forms in nature and designed artefacts". He explored the potential of a huge range of materials. There was a memorial show at his studio in 1994, when an illustrated monograph on his work was published by his estate.

Beryl Mary PICKERING 1918– Painter, illustrator and teacher, born in Cambridge, where she continued to live forsome years. Studied at Cambridge School of Art, 1935–9, where she later taught; Leicester College of Art, 1941–2; and Chelsea Polytechnic School of Art, 1949–51. Publishers using her work included London University Press. Exhibited RA, RBA, RI, NEAC, RSA and elsewhere. Later lived at Buchlyvie, Stirlingshire.

John PICKING fl. from 1960s– Painter and teacher who studied at Wigan School of Art, 1956–60; Edinburgh College of Art, 1960–3, gaining a postgraduate scholarship; and Goldsmiths' College School of Art, 1965–6. Went on to teach at Manchester Polytechnic and was a member of MAFA. Showed in the city with Colin Jellicoe Gallery, also at Scottish Gallery in Edinburgh, Mercury Gallery and abroad. Peasant communities were a special interest.

Cherry PICKLES 1950– Painter in oil on canvas, and teacher, whose main works were self-portraits, views through car windscreens and landscapes, especially of Greece and Wales. Pickles was born there in Bridgend, later settling at Trefin, Haverfordwest, Dyfed. She gained a degree in mathematics from the New University of Ulster, 1973; obtained a first-class degree in painting from Chelsea School of Art, 1973–7, teachers Patrick Symons, Myles Murphy, Norman Norris and Craigie Aitchison; with a postgraduate diploma from the Slade School of Fine Art, 1977–9, taught by Lawrence Gowing, Patrick George and Euan Uglow. Won many prizes and scholarships, including Boise Travelling Scholarship, Italy, 1980; WAC Travel Grant, Jordan, 1986; Greek Government Scholarship, 1992–4–5; and WAC Travel Grant to America, 1993. In 1994 Pickles had a Ragdale Foundation Residency, Chicago. Was a member of 56 Group and mixed show appearances included RA Summer Exhibition, 1986; John Player Award, National Portrait Gallery, 1987 and 1989; Cleveland Drawing Biennale, 1989; and Intimate Portraits, Glynn Vivian Gallery, Swansea, and tour, 1995. Later solo exhibitions included Smith Jariwala Gallery and St David's Hall, Cardiff, both 1994, and Jill Yakas Gallery, Athens, 1995. Pickles' extensive teaching experience included part-time posts at Falmouth, Bath, Chelsea, Slade, Byam Shaw and Cardiff Schools of Art. National Museum of Wales in Cardiff, Brunel and St Andrews Universities and Royal Jordanian Gallery hold examples.

David PIDDOCK 1960– Artist who studied at Ruskin School of Art, Oxford, 1979–82, then at Royal Academy Schools, 1983–6. He went on to exhibit widely in Oxford and London. In 1983 he was included in Focus on Drawing at Museum of Modern Art, Oxford. He was also represented in the Agnew show The Long Perspective, in 1987, and in the gallery's The Broad

Horizon, 1990, where Piddock's Ham House Fantasy – one of a series based on the building – showed well the artist's ability to make a pleasing, colourful pattern from landscape. Piddock saw his work as a reaction against "bucket and slosh abstract and installation art" when he was at college. For his first major solo show in London, at The Gallery in Cork Street, 1996, where he exhibited oils on gesso, he "spent hours examining the surfaces of Old Masters". Lived in London.

Peter Paul PIECH 1920–1996 Graphic designer, printer, printmaker and teacher whose stark images supported humane and libertarian causes. Born in Brooklyn, New York, America, of Ukrainian parents, Piech studied there at the Cooper Union College of Art. In 1937 he began work as a graphic artist at Dorland's Advertising Agency under its notable Austrian art director Herbert Bayer. During World War II Piech served with the United States Army Air Force, based in Cardiff; married a local nurse in 1947; then studied at Chelsea School of Art on a Government Issue (GI) grant. Between 1951–68 Piech worked as an artistic director for W S Crawford, the advertising agency. In 1959 he set up his own Taurus Press, which disseminated a series of hard-hitting political texts and images. The Library of Congress bought his poster of American president Richard Nixon with Dicktator printed above his head. From 1968 Piech was a freelance graphic artist, teaching at Chelsea College of Art, London College of Printing and elsewhere. His many mixed exhibitions included National Eisteddfod, Aberystwyth, 1992. Peter Paul Piech's Jazz Collection was shown at Brecknock Museum, Brecon, just after his death, in 1996, in conjunction with the Jazz Festival. Lived in Porthcawl, Mid Glamorgan.

Charles PIERCE 1908– Artist in oil, watercolour, pastel, pen and ink, scraperboard, engraver and etcher. Born in Edinburgh, Pierce studied art at Edinburgh College of Art and the RSA Schools. Sometimes signed work with initial P only. It was reproduced in magazines such as *The Studio* and *The Artist*. Pierce showed with the RA, RSA and the Royal Glasgow Institute of the Fine Arts. Lived in London.

Lucy Elizabeth PIERCE fl. from 1910–1950 Painter and miniaturist in watercolour and enamel, born and lived in Enfield, Middlesex. After attending Hackney Technical Institute, studied at Slade School of Fine Art under Henry Tonks and Fred Brown. Exhibited extensively at RMS, of which she was a member, and Walker's Galleries, also at RA, ROI, in the provinces and overseas. The Wellcome Foundation Medical Museum bought her work. Lived in Enfield.

Norman PIERCE 1915– Sculptor, modelling and carving, and teacher, born in London. He studied at Reading University fine art department, 1931–5, with Allen Seaby, then at Royal College of Art, 1935–8, under Richard Garbe. He taught at Colchester School of Art, 1945–7; Winchester School of Art, 1947–66; then in adult education in Winchester, where he lived, 1966–86. Pierce was a fellow of RBS. He showed at RA, Mall Galleries, in the provinces and at Paris Salon. Main works included figure in Portland stone of Christ in Benediction, at Highcliffe, Hampshire; eight heraldic coats of arms for New County Offices, Winchester; Sir Seretse Khama, Botswana; and works for Madame Tussauds.

PIERRE: *see* **Peter SAMUELSON**

Simon PIERSE 1956– Painter and teacher who attended Saturday classes at Camberwell School of Arts and Crafts, 1973–5, and Slade School of Fine Art, 1975–9. He won a Boise Scholarship and Melville Nettleship Prize, both 1979. In 1980–1 gained an Italian Government Scholarship. Pierse taught for a time in Essex. He showed at Opix Gallery from 1979 and Woodlands Art Gallery from 1980, in 1985 being included in Figurative Painters there. In 1992 Pierse joined the visual art department at University College of Wales, Aberystwyth, as tutor in studio studies and art history, the following year being included in Aberystwyth Artists at The Deffett Francis Gallery, Swansea Institute of Higher Education. Lived at New Cross, Aberystwyth, Dyfed.

Rosalind PIERSON 1954– Artist with an interest in wildlife subjects who was born and worked in Tavistock, Devon. She studied at Ruskin School of Drawing, Oxford. Pierson was a member of RMS, Hilliard Society and Montana Miniature Art Society. She showed at RA, in the provinces, at Paris Salon where she won gold and silver medals and abroad.

Allanah PIESSE 1946– Painter who studied at Camberwell School of Arts and Crafts, 1963–8, and Royal Academy Schools, 1968–71. Showed at RA Summer Exhibition, Opix Gallery, 1979, and in 1980 was in the Figurative Painters show at Woodlands Art Gallery. Lived in London.

Jack PIESSE 1945– Painter in a detailed style who studied at Camberwell School of Arts and Crafts, 1963–7, and Royal Academy Schools, 1967–70. Lived and showed in London, including Figurative Painters at Woodlands Art Gallery, 1980.

Heinz-Dieter PIETSCH 1944– Abstract artist working in a variety of media, born in Glogau, Silenia. From 1966 he attended State Academy of Fine Art in Stuttgart, West Germany, also State Academy of Fine Art in Karlsruhe and Stuttgart University. Having been awarded a scholarship by the German Academic Exchange for postgraduate studies in London, in 1974 Pietsch joined students at St Martin's School of Art, in 1975 attending the Royal College of Art, in 1977 gaining a fellowship at Gloucestershire College of Art. Pietsch was included in the 1980 touring exhibition The British Art Show, chosen by the critic William Packer and organised by the Arts Council, which holds Pietsch's work. As well as solo shows in Germany Pietsch exhibited one-man at Riverside Studies and Pigeonhole Gallery, 1978.

PIF: *see* **Philip FORTIN**

John PIGGINS: *see* **John REDVERS**

Hadrian PIGOTT 1961– Sculptor and ceramist, born in Aldershot, Hampshire. He obtained a Bachelor of Science degree in geology at Exeter University, 1980–3, then gained his master's degree in sculpture/ceramics from the Royal College of Art, 1990–3. Pigott was included in Young British Artists V, at Saatchi Gallery, 1995, his exhibits being a series of objects associated with washing and personal hygiene with a wry twist: a lavatory sealed tight, frustrating any attempt to lift the seat; and bars of soap, labelled for parts of the body. In 1997 Pigott appeared in the BBC2 Television series *Date with an Artist*, in which he created a sculpture based on a saxophone.

Bernard PIKE 1908– Painter, draughtsman and teacher, born in Barnet, Hertfordshire. After Highgate School, Pike studied at Byam Shaw School of Drawing and Painting where he was awarded an annual scholarship and where he won several prizes. Pike held several art teaching jobs, including Harrow School and Byam Shaw. He showed at RA, RP and elsewhere and was a member of the Old Cholmelian Society. After World War II he is believed to have devoted himself mainly to Quaker humanitarian work, living in London.

Jonathan PIKE 1949– Painter and printmaker, born in Leatherhead, Surrey, who attended Central School of Art & Design, 1967–8, and Falmouth School of Art, 1968–71, teachers including Robert Organ and Francis Hewlett. Group shows included RA Summer Exhibition from 1980; Waterman Fine Art from 1991; Michael Parkin from 1992; and Barney's in Greenwich, Connecticut, America, from 1994. Had a solo show with Michael Parkin, 1992, others with Gavin Graham Gallery from 1994. Greater London Council and The Clothworkers' Company hold examples. Lived in London.

Joseph PIKE 1883–1956 Watercolourist and draughtsman, born in Bristol. He studied art at Ampleforth College with William Boddy, leaving in 1901. Showed at RA, SGA of which he was a member, and PS, specialising in architectural subjects. Lived in London.

Leonard PIKE 1887–1959 Painter of pictures and murals, interior decorator and designer. Born in London, he studied at Worcester School of Arts and Crafts, where he later taught for some years. Exhibited RA, RBA, RI, PS and Paris Salon. Pike was a collector of watercolours. His own work is held by the City Art Gallery, Bradford, Worcester City Art Gallery and Cheltenham Art Gallery. Pike lived in a caravan, used a caravan as a studio and died at Powick, near Worcester.

Richard PIKESLEY 1951– Painter and teacher, born in London. Studied at Harrow School of Art, 1969–70, Canterbury College of Art, 1970–3, and University of London, 1973–4. Went on to teach at Budmouth School, Weymouth. Pikesley was elected to NEAC in 1974. He was a finalist for the Hunting Group Prize in 1981 and 1989; gained the E F Hutton Group Prize, 1987; and the W H Patterson Prize, 1988. Mixed exhibitions included RA, RWA, Henry Wyndham Fine Art and abroad. Solo shows included New Grafton Gallery, 1990. St John's College, Cambridge, holds his work. Lived in Bothenhampton, Bridport, Dorset.

Wieslaw PILAWSKI 1916– Oil painter, born in Mscislaw, Russia. He studied art in Poland and at the Regent Street Polytechnic under Harold Brownsword. Took part in many mixed exhibitions, including RA, ROI, RBA, NS, Leicester and Piccadilly Galleries and at Roland, Browse & Delbanco. One-man shows were held at Wilton and Leicester Galleries. Lived in London.

Martin PILCHER 1948–1992 Painter, photographer and diver, born in Düsseldorf, Germany. After education at Aiglon College in Switzerland and at Cirencester Agricultural College he farmed for 15 years with his father in Hampshire before deciding to become a full-time photographer, experimenting with infra-red film. As a keen yachtsman and diver he turned to marine and then underwater photography, doing work on commission. This in turn led to underwater painting on prepared wood panels, weighted and lowered into the water along with weighted oil paints. Styling himself Pilcher of Poole he had shows in London and Poole, and an exhibition of his underwater painting was to have begun days after an accident caused his death, but had to be cancelled, at Century Galleries, Henley-on-Thames. In addition to these interests Pilcher was an adept rural sportsman, who had shot moose in Canada; he was also keen on the art and culture of Japan, visiting the country twice, and he had begun learning Japanese. Died in Poole, Dorset.

Thomas PILCHER 1908– Watercolourist, born at Old Basing, Hampshire, educated at Uppingham School and Cambridge University. He studied art at City and Guilds of London Art School under A R Middleton Todd, 1946–7, and in 1947 at Heatherley's School of Art with Iain Macnab. Exhibited at many venues, including RA, RBA, RI, RWA, RWS, Paris Salon and elsewhere. Had one-man shows at Walker's Galleries in the early 1950s. Was a member of Winchester Art Club and lived at Twyford, Hampshire.

Albert Thomas PILE 1882–1981 Painter, lithographer, etcher and illustrator, born in London. He studied art at the Central School of Arts and Crafts under William Palmer Robins, at Camberwell School of Art under Randolph Schwabe, Roland Pitchforth and Ian Strang, Goldsmiths' College School of Art with Stanley Anderson and James Bateman and Bournemouth College of Art with Leslie Ward. Pile went on to exhibit widely, landscapes and architectural subjects, at the National Gallery, RSA, RHA, RWA, at Paris Salon and in the provinces. Leeds University holds his work. His topographical illustrations were included in a number of books, especially on Yorkshire, where he latterly lived in Whitby. During World War II he was an official artist for the Ministry of Information.

Herbert Francis PILGRIM 1915– Painter and photographer, born in London, with a special interest in animal subjects. Studied at Gravesend School of Art with Job Nixon and at Yellow Door School of Art with Reginald Eves. Showed in London and elsewhere and lived in Chatham, Kent.

Audrey PILKINGTON 1922– Artist in pastel, oil, watercolour, gouache and collage, and teacher, wife of the artist Patrick Heriz-Smith and mother of sculptor Bridget Heriz. She studied from 1938–9 at Lancaster Art School, then 1939–41 at Slade School of Fine Art, teachers including Allan Gwynne-Jones, William Roberts and Albert Rutherston. As well as practising as an artist, for many years she ran an independent art school with her husband. Showed with Redfern Gallery, Swansea University, New Ipswich Art Club and elsewhere, having solo exhibitions in Lancaster, Southport, Barrow-in-Furness, London, Florence and Hamburg. Lived latterly at Resolven, near Neath, West Glamorgan.

Cathie PILKINGTON 1968– Sculptor, jeweller and teacher, born in Manchester. She did a foundation course at North Chester College of Art, Northwich, then in 1986 sculpture department of Edinburgh College of Art, transferring to the jewellery department in 1988. She graduated with first-class honours from Edinburgh in 1991, having had teaching experience in America and India in 1989–90. In 1991 was awarded the first John Watson Prize for Art during Edinburgh Festival. Showed with Bruton Gallery, Bath, from 1992, and was in 1st RWA Open Sculpture Exhibition, 1993.

Margaret PILKINGTON 1891–1974 Watercolourist and wood engraver. Born in Salford, Lancashire, she studied at the Slade School of Fine Art and Central School of Arts and Crafts. Exhibited SWE. For many years she was closely associated with the running of the Manchester public galleries and founded the Red Rose Guild of Craftsmen. Whitworth Art Gallery, Manchester, holds her work. Lived at Alderley Edge, Cheshire.

Ruth Jane PILKINGTON 1924– Artist, mostly in oil, born in Manchester. She studied at Johannesburg Technical College, in South Africa, 1947–8, then at Macclesfield College of Further Education, 1962–5. Pilkington was made a member of ROI in 1976 and of SWA in 1985. She showed with MAFA, RBA, UA, Paris Salon and with groups in Jersey, Channel Islands, where she settled in Grouville. Barreau Art Gallery, St Helier, which holds her work, gave her a solo show in 1976.

Lena PILLICO 1884–1947 Artist who was married to the painter of Jewish people and genre scenes, Leopold Pilichowski. Born in Poland, Pilichowski moved to England in 1914, settling in London, where he was president of the Ben Uri Art Society, 1926–32, dying in 1933. It holds his work and that of Pillico, who was an active member of the Seven and Five Society in the 1920s. In Michael Parkin's exhibition on the Society, which toured, 1979–80, an oil and a handprinted scarf by Pillico were shown. Died in Oxford.

Lynn PILLING 1960– Artist, born in Bolton, Lancashire, who was a member of TEA (see separate entry). Studied at Mid-Warwickshire College of Further Education, Leamington Spa, 1979; Manchester Polytechnic, 1980–3; and Hertfordshire College of Art and Design, St Albans, 1985–6. Lived in Manchester.

Lorna PILLOW fl. from 1940s– Artist, designer, illustrator and teacher who studied at Leeds College of Art, 1934, Hull College of Art, 1935–40, and Royal College of Art for periods between 1940–6. Went on to teach, latterly at West Surrey College of Art and Design in Farnham. Showed at RWS, Ferens in Hull and Beverley Art Galleries, Design Centre, Victoria & Albert Museum and elsewhere. Lived in Maidenhead, Berkshire.

Geoff PIMLOTT 1946– Artist in acrylic, watercolour and lino-block printing, born in Croydon, Surrey. He studied at Reigate School of Art, 1965–8, teachers including Stanley Ayres, Michael Noakes, Denis Lucas, Francis Spear and Eric Waugh. He was a member of Free Painters and Sculptors, Reigate Society of Artists and the National Society for Education in Art & Design. A series of acrylics on paper and block prints from Papua New Guinea and landscapes of north-east Surrey, acrylic on canvas, were among Pimlott's main works, influence on which included Ivon Hitchens, George Hooper, Frances Hodgkins, Kandinsky, Degas and Matisse. All imagery was "derived from my sketchbook observations, which are a record of my travelling experiences". In 1991 Pimlott gained second prize, Nina Hosali Award, at the Free Painters; in 1992 a Rome Study Bursary, British School at Rome/Art Historians' Association. Solo exhibitions included Fairfield Halls, Croydon, 1969; Arts 38 Gallery, from 1976; Heriot-Watt, Edinburgh, 1980; Harlequin Theatre Gallery, 1987, in Redhill, Surrey, where he lived; and Loggia Gallery, 1997.

John PIMLOTT 1905– Painter and illustrator, son of the artist E Philip Pimlott. He studied at Goldsmiths' College School of Art under Edmund J Sullivan and showed at RA, RI and in the provinces. Pimlott became a member of the Art Workers' Guild in 1946. He was born in London and finally lived in Bromley, Kent.

Joseph Frank PIMM 1900–c.1975 Watercolourist and printmaker. Studied at Birmingham College of Art under Bernard Fleetwood-Walker. Exhibited RA, RWA, RHA, RE, RCamA, RI, RSA and Paris Salon, where he gained a silver medal in 1948; also widely in the provinces. Bilston Art Gallery, Staffordshire, bought his work. Lived at Handsworth, Birmingham.

Diana PINE 1915– Artist in watercolour, pastel and oil, teacher and film director, born in London. In late 1930s she studied at Regent Street Polytechnic School of Art with Clifford Ellis, also at Chelsea School of Art with H S Williamson, at Central School of Arts and Crafts and was an apprentice art director for films, teachers including Edward Carrick. She became a documentary film director, working for Crown Film Unit, 1942–51, with Wessex Films and BBC. Was a teacher for many years from 1977 in Surrey adult education. Was a member of SWA, Association of Sussex Artists and Dorking Group of Artists. Also showed with RI, and PS. Lived in North Holmwood, Surrey.

Michael PINE 1928– Architect and sculptor, full name John Michael Pine, born in Wolverhampton, Staffordshire. He studied at Birmingham School of Architecture, 1948–54. Showed with LG, ICA and in St Ives, Cornwall, where he lived for} some years.

Austen PINKERTON 1951– Painter, sculptor, draughtsman and printmaker, born in North Harrow, Middlesex. Pinkerton began studying architecture at Oxford School of Architecture in 1970; took a year out from course as a draughtsman with Oxford Regional Hospital Board, 1972; resigned from his course, becoming a hospital porter, 1973; then until 1976 studied at Goldsmiths' School of Art, teachers including Jon Thompson. obtaining his bachelor's degree in fine art (painting). From then on Pinkerton did a variety of jobs, including part-time positions with several architectural firms, mixing in work as designer, model-maker, joinery specialist and illustrator as a freelance. In 1986 joined the Air/Space studio organisation, with his own studio in Deptford. Principal works were listed as Hangliders, Sunset Landscape, Trouble in Paradise and Quo Vadis. Pinkerton took part in many mixed and group shows, including Blackheath Gallery; Casa Pupo Gallery; South London Open Show, at South London Gallery; and Interior Space. Had a solo exhibition at Oxford Playhouse Gallery, 1973, later ones including Horniman Museum, 1991. Lived in London.

Richard PINKNEY 1938– Artist, teacher, businessman and administrator, born in Ipswich, Suffolk, who studied painting and printmaking at Ipswich School of Art and education at West of England College, Bristol. He taught at Ipswich, Colchester, Walthamstow, Winchester, St Martin's and Kingsway Colleges of Art; founded and ran a tool and equipment hire company; worked as an engineering contracts manager, designing and building timber-frame houses in Britain and America; and in the mid-1980s directed the Lady Lodge Arts Centre, Peterborough. His graphics and mail art were included in many group shows in several continents, galleries in Colchester, Leicester, Peterborough and Ipswich displaying his pictures and sculptures. Had solo shows in London and Edinburgh, Christchurch Mansion in Ipswich giving him a retrospective, Words and Images, in 1995. Pinkney wrote then that he had "flirted more or less continuously with making and distributing ephemeral works", consuming "a wide menu of delights: prayer flags and comics, broadsheets and timetables, commercial stationery and Japanese woodcuts, native American iconography and Dada texts, trade catalogues, tattooing, Celtic decoration and so on". Was a member of The Suffolk Group and Ipswich Arts Society. Tate Gallery, Victoria & Albert Museum and British Museum hold examples. Pinkney's wife was the artist Judith Foster. They lived at Bramford, Ipswich.

Gladys A PINKS 1890– Portrait painter, especially of children. Studied at the Grosvenor Studio under Walter Donne, 1909–12, then in Paris with Lucien Simon, 1912–13. Showed at RA, SWA, RI, RP, WIAC, Société des Artistes Français and in Canada. Lived in London.

Christopher PINSENT 1922– Painter in oil, draughtsman and teacher, born in Birmingham. He studied at The Downs School, Colwall, 1931–5, with Maurice Feild; was a private pupil of William Coldstream, 1940; then was at Camberwell School of Arts and Crafts, 1946–8, under Coldstream, Claude Rogers, Victor Pasmore, Lawrence Gowing, John Dodgson and others. Sir Christopher, who succeeded to the baronetcy in 1978, was an assistant at Charterhouse, 1949–52; taught drawing and painting at Camberwell, 1962–86; and at the Centro d'Arte Verrocchio at Casole d'Elsa, 1985. Pinsent listed Portrait of Jo Higson and The Southwold Railway among his main works. "The use of geometry in sustaining the subject of pictures" and "synthetic perspective in connection with drawing and painting from nature" were cited as key features of his paintings. Group shows included The Euston Road School and Others, Wakefield City Art Gallery and tour, 1948; Camberwell Artists of the 40s and 50s, Belgrave Gallery, 1988; and Homage to Claude Rogers, RWA, 1993. Lived in Guildford, Surrey.

Edward PIPER 1938–1990 Painter, photographer and graphic designer, son of the artist John Piper, from whom he absorbed the technique and a love of watercolour. After Lancing College Piper spent a year at Bath Academy of Art at Corsham, studying drawing under Howard Hodgkin, followed by four years at Slade School of Fine Art. He first worked as a Pop Artist and showed at ICA in 1965, then as a freelance photographer and graphic designer. For 20 years worked on *Shell Guides* with his father. In latter years he concentrated more on his painting, a delicate sense of colour and felicitous line being especially employed on landscape and female nudes. Memorial show at Catto Gallery, 1991.

John PIPER 1903–1992 Painter, notably of architecture and landscape, designer of stained glass and for the theatre, and writer, born in Epsom, Surrey. His first wife was the artist Eileen Holding, his second the writer Myfanwy Evans, and his son the artist Edward Piper. From 1921–6 studied law and worked in his father's solicitor's office before studying at Richmond and Kingston Schools of Art and Royal College of Art, 1926–9. In mid-1930s after a visit to Paris concentrated on abstract painting, but then reverted to representational work. First solo show, of collages and drawings, at London Gallery, 1938. Member of LG in 1933 and 7 & 5 Society, 1934–5. Piper was a prolific writer, working for *The Athenaeum*, *New Statesman*, *Nation* and *Architectural Review*, publishing his first guide book in 1938. With his wife he produced the influential *Axis – a Quarterly Review of Contemporary "Abstract" Painting and Sculpture*, 1935–7. From 1940 for about 20 years had one-man shows with Leicester Galleries. His ballet designs included *The Quest*, 1943 and *Job*, 1948, as well as operas for Benjamin Britten. Piper was an official war artist in World War II. In 1942 he published his best-selling monograph *English Romantic Artists*. Was on several occasions a trustee of Tate Gallery, member of the Arts Council panel and a member of Royal Fine Art Commission. Stained glass window designs included Coventry Cathedral and Christchurch College Chapel, Oxford. Made Companion of Honour, 1972.

Retrospectives were held at Museum of Modern Art, Oxford, 1979, and Tate Gallery, 1983. The Tate, Arts Council and many provincial galleries hold his work. Died at Fawley Bottom, Oxfordshire.

Keith PIPER 1960– Painter, draughtsman and artist in slides, photomontage and text, born in Birmingham. Studied art at Lanchester Polytechnic, Coventry, 1979, and Trent Polytechnic, Nottingham, 1980–3, followed by an environmental media course at Royal College of Art, 1984–6. At Coventry he met the artist Eddie Chambers, with whom he organised a show with a Black Art theme at Wolverhampton Art Gallery in in 1982, with the first Black Art Convention at the same venue in that year; and several other events. Piper was committed to the role of art as a way of putting over ideas, his Black Assassin Saints being an example of blacks as victims. Participated in a number of radical black art group shows; was included in The Other Story, Hayward Gallery and tour, 1989–90; and had a major solo exhibition at Royal College of Art, 1997. Manchester and Sheffield City Art Galleries hold examples.

Raymond PIPER 1923– Painter, sculptor, draughtsman, illustrator and teacher, born in London. Studied in Belfast and London and settled in Belfast. Piper taught for a while in Dungannon, Northern Ireland, at the Royal School. He showed with CEMA in Belfast, where he lived, also at RWS, RHA and at Belfast Museum and Art Gallery which holds his work. In 1950 he was awarded a CEMA Travelling Scholarship. Piper, who later divided his time between Belfast and London, was keenly interested in natural history and did illustrations for books and magazines on it, also on Ireland. An exhibition of flower drawings was held at the Ulster Museum, which holds his work, in 1975, the year after he was awarded the John Lindley Medal of the Royal Horticultural Society for his illustrations of Irish orchids. He was also made a fellow of the Linnaean Society. Piper painted a series of portraits of Lord Mayors of Belfast, held in the City Hall.

J E PIPKIN 1945– Artist whose work included abstract paintings, born in Middlesex, who studied at Bideford School of Art, 1960–4. Pipkin showed at Flint Eisteddfod, sponsored by WAC; worked on animating a film sequence produced for a large computer company; and in November 1969 exhibited works in the ICA Play Orbit show at Nash House. Solo shows included Woodstock Gallery, 1969; Hampstead Artists' Council/Camden Arts Centre, 1979; and Knapp Gallery, 1995.

Stephen PIPPIN 1960– Sculptor, born in Redhill, Surrey, who gained an ordinary national certificate in mechanical engineering, Charles Keene College, Leicester, 1976–8. Took a foundation course in art and design at Loughborough College, Leicester, 1981–2; gained his bachelor's degree in fine art sculpture at Brighton Polytechnic, 1982–5; and his master's at Chelsea School of Art, 1986–7. Pippin's interests included Englishness and class, and potting sheds; he was a creator of mechanical objects with an aesthetic appeal, full of metaphors. Group shows included New British Sculpture, Air Gallery, 1986; Twelve British Artists, Staine Gladstone Gallery, New York, 1992 (the year before he had been appointed artist-in-residence at Sculpture Space, Utica, there); Venice Biennale, 1993; Minky Manky at South London Art Gallery and Brilliant!: New Art From London, The Walker Art Center, Minneapolis, both 1995. Solo exhibitions included Introspective, ICA, 1993; Work from the Recession, Victoria Miro Gallery, 1994; and Study in Time and Motion, FRAC Limousin, Limoges, France, 1995. Contemporary Art Society and Museum of Modern Art in New York hold examples.

Monika PIRCH 1966– Artist using video and film, born in Braunschweig, West Germany. After studying for a diploma in photography and film design in Dortmund, 1986–92, Pirch obtained her master's degree in fine art combined media at Chelsea College of Art, 1994–5. Exhibitions included Into the Nineties, Mall Galleries, 1994, and New Contemporaries at Tate Gallery, Liverpool, and Camden Arts Centre, 1996. Participated in Scholarship, German-French Youth Organisation, in 1996.

George PIRIE 1863–1946 Painter of animals and birds, born in Campbeltown, Argyllshire. He studied painting in Paris at Académie Julian. In early 1890s lived in Texas, America. Served in Army during World War I. Pirie was a prolific exhibitor at Royal Glasgow Institute of the Fine Arts and RSA, also exhibiting at RA, Fine Art Society and elsewhere. His Mother Duck was a Chantrey Bequest purchase in 1940, now in Tate Gallery. Was elected RSA in 1923, becoming its president, 1933–44; was made an Hon. RA in 1933; was knighted four years later. Died in Glasgow.

Litz PISK 1909–1997 Artist, stage designer, choreographer, writer and teacher, born in Vienna, Austria. She studied stage architecture and kinetism at State Art and Crafts School, and was for a time a guest student of the producer Max Reinhardt. In 1932 Pisk designed Berthold Brecht and Kurt Weill's first production, *The Rise and Fall of the City of Mahoganny*. In the mid-1930s Pisk taught at the Royal Academy of Dramatic Art, in London, settling permanently in England in 1937. After World War II Pisk was further involved in theatre school teaching, including the Royal Shakespeare Company, and did film and television work. From 1953–6 taught drawing and movement at Bath Academy of Art. Pisk had a one-man show at Redfern Gallery in 1947, others following at New Art Centre in 1980 and 1982. A retrospective exhibition was held at Newlyn Art Gallery in 1986. In 1989 Pisk was included in the Bath Academy show at Michael Parkin Gallery. She died in Edward Hain Hospital, St Ives, Cornwall, having lived at Trencrom.

Lélia PISSARRO 1963– Painter in the Impressionist manner, teacher and restorer, born in Paris, great-grand-daughter of the French artist Camille Pissarro. She studied with her grandfather Paulémile Pissarro and father Hugues-Claude; her grandparents brought her up until the age of 11; her mother Katia was an art dealer. Aged 16, Lélia enrolled at the École des Beaux-Arts,

Tours, having already exhibited at the Salon de la Peinture and sold her first canvas to a New York dealer. In Paris, she taught art at the Moria School, studied restoration with an expert from the Louvre and had a solo show at Galerie du Marais. Lélia married the art dealer David Stern and they settled in London. She exhibited internationally, in 1993 was included in Four Generations of the Pissarro Family at Portland Gallery and in 1997 showed solo at Catto Gallery.

Orovida PISSARRO 1893–1968 Printmaker and painter, often on linen and silk. Born at Epping, Essex, the daughter of the artist Lucien Pissarro and grand-daughter of Camille Pissarro, Orovida studied with her father. In 1914 in France she started experimenting with etching, then on return to England "bought a press and a book on the technique of etching and set to work". A big exhibition of Chinese painting in 1914 left an indelible impression, and some of Orovida's most memorable etchings are of Oriental subjects, especially animals. She exhibited at the RA, RBA and had one-man shows in London and North America. In 1969 the Ashmolean Museum, Oxford, held a memorial show of her etchings, paintings and drawings and published a catalogue of her etchings and aquatints. Signed her work Orovida. Of singular appearance, Orovida was the subject of two remarkable portraits by Carel Weight, one in the Ashmolean, the other in the Tate Gallery. The British Museum, Victoria & Albert Museum and many other British and foreign galleries and museums own her work. Lived in London.

Mabel Kincaid PITCAIRN fl. c.1895–1950 Painter of flowers in miniature whose actual name was Mary Mabel Kincaid Pitcairn. She was educated in Brighton, Sussex, then in Paris at Atelier Colarossi in the mid-1890s. Exhibited at SM, of which she was a member, RSA, Walker Art Gallery, Liverpool, and at Paris Salon. Lived in Greenock, Renfrewshire.

Elsie PITCHERS 1910– Watercolourist and teacher, born in Bradford, Yorkshire. After Morecambe Grammar School she studied art at Lancaster School of Art, 1936–40, then in 1940–1 at Liverpool School of Art under Henry Huggill. She went on to teach art for many years at Lancaster Girls' Grammar School. Showed extensively in the major towns and cities of Lancashire and Yorkshire, notably with Lancaster Art Group, of which she was a member. She lived in Morecambe, Lancashire.

Roland Vivian PITCHFORTH 1895–1982 Landscape and predominantly seascape painter in watercolour and, before 1945, oil. Born at Wakefield, Yorkshire, Pitchforth studied at Wakefield School of Art in 1912–14, Leeds College of Art 1914–15 and 1919–20, his studies being interrupted by war service. He was then at the Royal College of Art 1920–5, and also visited Paris. Pitchforth's first one-man show was at the London Artists' Association in 1928, and the year later he exhibited with the LG. Was an official war artist 1940–5. Pitchforth began exhibiting at the RA in 1941 and was elected RA in 1953, his first retrospective having been held at Wakefield 10 years earlier. From 1945 Pitchforth travelled extensively, in Ceylon, Burma and South Africa. On return from there in 1948 he took up a teaching post at Chelsea polytechnic, Camberwell, St Martin's School of Art, Clapham and the Royal College of Art also drawing on teaching skills at various times. Pitchforth's delicately washy watercolours became a feature of RA Summer Exhibitions after World War II. His work is in the Tate Gallery, Victoria & Albert Museum, in many provincial galleries and abroad. Lived in London.

Thomas Baron PITFIELD 1903– Artist, composer, writer and teacher, born in Bolton, Lancashire. He worked in watercolour, pen and wash and lino-cut. Pitfield left school at 14 and served an engineering apprenticeship, attending Bolton School of Art and becoming a National Registered Designer. He showed at RA, MAFA and had several dozen solo shows, including West Park Museum, Macclesfield, 1990, on his life's work. Taught in schools of art and public schools. Main works included *The Poetry of Trees* (hand-lettered text and lino-cuts). Pitfield also at 21 enrolled in the Royal Manchester College of Music and in 1947 joined its staff. He became professor of composition, stemming over to the Royal Northern College of Music until his retirement aged 70, with many compositions to his credit, including two piano concertos. His autobiography was published in two parts: *No Song, No Supper* and *Song After Supper*. Lived at Bowdon, Altrincham, Cheshire.

Primrose Vera PITMAN fl. from 1940s– Designer, painter and printmaker, based in Exeter, Devon, where she attended the Royal Albert Memorial School of Art, teachers including James Sparks. She was made a member of SGA in 1953, also showing with Exeter Art Society and Kenn Group both of which she was a member, RWA and elsewhere in the provinces. She was noted for her pencil drawings of Exeter, where the Royal Albert Memorial Museum holds her work.

Barry PITTAR 1880–1948 Painter, printmaker, architect and artist in ceramics, brought up in Kent. Studied at St John's Wood School of Art and Royal College of Art with George Frampton. He acted as technical adviser to several firms on ceramics and art colours. Exhibited extensively at RBA, of which he was a member, and Fine Art Society, also at RSA, ROI and Paris Salon. Victoria & Albert Museum, Bethnal Green Museum and galleries in Australia and South Africa hold his work. Lived in Dunstable, Bedfordshire.

Osmund PITTMAN 1874–1968 Painter, born in London, who studied at Royal College of Art and Royal Academy Schools, winning the Turner Gold Medal and Creswick Prize. He was elected ROI in 1916, also showing at RA, Ridley Art Club and Royal Glasgow Institute of the Fine Arts. Pittman was a Chelsea Arts Club member who lived in several parts of England and was notable for his landscapes. Latterly had a studio in Hampstead, north London.

Douglas Frederick PITTUCK 1911–1993 Painter, notably of landscapes in oil, and teacher; born in London. Studied at Ruskin

School of Drawing, Oxford, part-time in 1931–9, then from 1946–8 full-time, his teachers including Percy Horton and Barnett Freedman. Showed Cooling Galleries, RBA, at public galleries in Gateshead, Newcastle upon Tyne and Darlington and had several one-man shows. Ashmolean Museum in Oxford holds his work. Lived in Barnard Castle, County Durham, where Glaxo Laboratories commissioned a mural by him.

Carl PLACKMAN 1943– Sculptor making assemblages with a variety of objects, born in Huddersfield, Yorkshire. He was apprenticed as an architect, 1959–60, then studied mathematics and history in Bath, 1960–2, attending West of England College of Art in Bristol, 1962–7, and Royal College of Art, 1967–70. In 1967 Plackman worked with Lynn Chadwick. He won the Walter Neurath Prize for drawing in 1968 and the sculpture drawing prize at the Royal College in 1970. From 1972 he taught at Goldsmiths' College School of Art, having the year before begun teaching at Ravensbourne College of Art. Plackman was a prizewinner at Young Contemporaries in 1969 and soon established a reputation for disturbing assemblages in which mundane and abstract elements were mixed. He had a one-man show at Serpentine Gallery in 1972, contributed to many influential exhibitions of modern British sculpture overseas and had further solo shows at Arnolfini Gallery in Bristol, Chapter Arts Centre in Cardiff and Felicity Samuel Gallery, which became his dealer. Arts Council and Arnolfini Gallery hold his work.

Andy PLANT 1955– Mechanical sculptor, born in Sheffield, Yorkshire, who studied at the local and Wolverhampton Colleges of Art. His two main areas of work were large outdoor theatrical props and sets and civic mechanical clocks, such as the Water Clock, Covent Garden; World Clock, Accrington; and Collapsible Clock at Newport, Gwent. Worked in Hebden Bridge, Yorkshire.

Mary PLANT 1943– Painter and teacher, born in Famagusta, Cyprus, who graduated in painting from Chelsea School of Art, 1976–80, winning a Morland Lewis Scholarship in the latter year; did her master's degree at Chelsea, 1980–81; and later was a visiting tutor there. Her work included abstract paintings on a large scale, as in her Berry Street Open Studios showing in 1984. Other mixed exhibitions included Stowells Trophy at RA, from 1978; Northern Young Contemporaries at Whitworth Art Gallery in Manchester, 1981; and Woodlands Art Gallery, 1983. Had a solo show at Jenny Stein's House in 1983.

Eric PLATT 1915– Artist mainly in watercolour latterly, but also a printmaker, draughtsman, painter in oil and cut-card relief, and teacher, born in Cudworth, Yorkshire. He studied at Royal College of Art, 1937–40, teachers including Malcolm Osborne and Robert Austin. Platt gained a Silver Medal, travelling scholarship and continuation scholarship (engraving school). After war service, 1940–6, Platt entered teaching, retiring in 1980, positions including vice-principal of Doncaster College of Art. He was an honorary member of Doncaster Art Club, also showing with RA, Arts Council, Brighton Museum & Art Gallery and elsewhere in the provinces. Had several solo shows. Lived in Bessacarr, Doncaster, Yorkshire, where the public gallery holds his work.

John Edgar PLATT 1886–1967 Wood engraver and painter, born at Leek, Staffordshire. Studied at the Royal College of Art, 1905–8. Father of the artist Michael Platt. John Platt went on to become principal of both Leicester College of Art and Blackheath School of Art. During World War II he was an official war artist. Won gold medal at the International Print Makers' Exhibition, 1922. Exhibited RA, NEAC, RE and with the British Council. His work is held by the British Museum, Imperial War Museum and Victoria & Albert Museum, he wrote for a number of publications including *The Studio* and *The Artist* and produced several books on the art of the colour woodcut. Tate Gallery holds his work. Lived in Eastbourne, Sussex.

John Gerald PLATT 1892–1976 Painter, wood engraver and etcher, born in Bolton, Lancashire. He studied art at King Edward VII School of Art, Armstrong College, Newcastle upon Tyne, then at Leicester College of Art, 1919–20, and the Royal College of Art, 1920–4. Exhibited at RA, RP, in the provinces and widely abroad. Platt was a noted teacher, holding posts at Kingston School of Art, Goldsmiths' College School of Art, Harrow Technical and Art School, 1930–47, as principal, a post he also held at Hornsey College of Art, 1947–57. His work is owned by the Victoria & Albert Museum, Bolton Museum and Art Gallery, elsewhere in Britain and in America. Lived at Flushing, Falmouth, Cornwall.

Lorraine PLATT 1962– Painter, born in Cheshire, who graduated with honours in fine art from London University. She painted exuberant still lifes which were "simply a hedonistic impulse to celebrate the beautiful". Washington Green Fine Arts Publishing and Athena published some of her work, which was shown in mixed exhibitions including McGrath Gallery, 1988; Anna-Mei Chadwick, 1990; and Catto Gallery, 1992. Solo shows included Gaku Gallery, Tokyo, 1991, and Sue Rankin Gallery, 1993.

Michael PLATT 1914– Painter, potter and teacher, born in Leek, Staffordshire, son of the artist John Edgar Platt and married to the artist Joan Dickson. He studied at Blackheath School of Art and Royal College of Art, gaining a Royal Exhibition (painting), 1935, and his associateship in 1938. From 1945 held positions at Southampton and Birmingham Colleges of Art, finally teaching at Mayfield School, Putney, 1960–3, then at North-West Polytechnic, 1967–9. Showed with RA, LG, NEAC, Arts Council and elsewhere. London County Council bought his work. Lived latterly at Burton, Dorset.

Russell PLATT 1920– Painter, draughtsman, muralist, printmaker and teacher, born in Wallasey, Cheshire, youngest son of a butcher. He served in the Royal Navy in World War II, then was at Wallasey School of Art, 1946–8, and Royal College of Art, 1948–52, becoming an associate in 1951, when he gained a Silver

Medal for Work of Special Distinction and the Research Scholarship for the School of Painting. Platt was awarded the Evelyn Prize by York City Art Gallery in 1956. From 1952 Platt taught at York and Harrogate Schools of Art, became lecturer in painting at Leeds College of Art in 1964, then senior lecturer in fine art at Leeds Polytechnic until retirement in 1985. Mixed shows included Whitworth Art Gallery, Manchester, 1947; Whitechapel Art Gallery, 1952; The Teaching Image, at Leeds City Art Gallery, 1964; Wakefield Art Gallery, 1973; and Stonegate Gallery in York, where he settled, from 1988. Of his later solo exhibitions The Bar Convent Museum, York, was 1990, Ally Capellino, 1991. The former comprised Platt's rich and impressive series of York Minster paintings, the latter work being more irreverent: portraits to picnics, fornication to football. Murals were completed for The National Aeronautical Collection, ICI Terylene and Royal College of Art.

Stella PLATT 1913– Painter and draughtsman who specialised in painting the industrial north of England, born in Bolton, Lancashire, where she studied at the School of Art. She exhibited ROI, SWA, RI, Paris Salon and elsewhere. She is extensively represented in the collections of northern public galleries, including Manchester City Art Gallery, Salford and Oldham. A member of MAFA, with which she regularly exhibited. Lived for many years at Garstang, Lancashire, later at Pooley Bridge, Ullswater, Cumbria.

Theo PLATT 1960– Portrait, nude and still life painter in the representational tradition, born in York. He did a foundation course at York College of Art, 1979–80, gaining an honours degree in fine art, painting, at St Martin's School of Art, 1980–3. Group exhibitions included RP, John Player Awards at National Portrait Gallery and St James' Art Group. Had a solo show at Jonathan Wylder Gallery, 1996. Commissions included Viscount Whitelaw. The Argyll & Sutherland Highlanders Collection holds Platt's work.

Enzo Mario PLAZZOTTA 1921–1981 Sculptor in marble and bronze, Plazzotta was born at Mestre, Venice, Italy, and became an artist with an international reputation. He studied sculpture with Giacomo Manzu and architecture at the Politecnico in Milan, 1938–46. He did an enormous volume of commissioned work, including the Catholic University, in Washington, and the Boys' Town Monument, Nebraska, both in America; and Nippon Television Headquarters in Tokyo, Japan. He held extensive one-man shows, including Marjorie Parr Gallery, Edinburgh Festival, Hogarth Gallery, New Orleans, and Queensland Art Gallery, Brisbane. Several open-air exhibitions were staged. Lived in London. The Bruton Street Gallery held a retrospective in 1995.

Donald PLENDERLEITH 1921– Painter, printmaker and teacher, full name Thomas Donald Plenderleith, born in Peebles, Peeblesshire. Studied at Ealing School of Art, 1937–9 and 1945–6, his teachers including Thomas Lightfoot; then Hornsey School of Art, 1946–7, with John Gerald Platt. Plenderleith went on to hold a number of teaching posts in the London area, including St Nicholas Grammar School, Northwood. Exhibited RA, RE and elsewhere. Lived at Hatch End, Middlesex.

Vangelis PLIARIDES 1964– Artist born in Thessaloniki, Greece, who studied at Aristoteliou University School of Fine Art, 1984–9, and Royal College of Art, 1992–4. Group shows included A Question of Drawing, Atlantis, 1993; BT New Contemporaries, Camden Arts Centre and tour, 1994; and John Moores Liverpool Exhibition, 1995–6, with an enigmatic oil on canvas, Untitled. Had a solo exhibition at Strandgalleriet, Södertälje, Sweden, 1989. Lived in London.

J Richard PLINCKE 1928– Artist in a range of media, and architect, born in Woldingham, Surrey, who gained his Architectural Association diploma in London, then was a partner in a practice in Winchester, after which he became a professional artist. At Southampton Institute of Higher Education he gained a higher certificate in painting with distinction. Plincke (pronounced Plinkee) worked mainly in watercolour and mixed media. Early influences were Matisse and Christopher Wood. Plincke's concern was with "attention to structure within the confines of a flat surface, in largely semi-abstract work, coupled with a continuing preoccupation with colour". He was elected RI in 1985, also exhibiting at RA, RWA, RSMA, ROI, PS, The Society of Architect Artists and widely in the provinces. Had a solo show at Guildhall Gallery in Winchester and was a gallery artist with Linda Blackstone Gallery in Pinner and Shell House Gallery, Ledbury. He carried out a mural at Shakespeare June School, Eastleigh; an installation of stained glass windows at St Mark's Church, Kempshott; and latterly worked on tapestry designs. British American Tobacco, The Institute of Directors, Price Waterhouse, other corporate collections, David Tovey and the writer Lord Archer held examples.

Robert PLISNIER 1951– Painter, born in Brussels, Belgium. He was educated at Eton College, then studied fine art at L'Académie des Beaux-Arts in Paris, 1969–72. He showed in mixed exhibitions at Fosse Gallery, Stow-on-the-Wold, RBSA and Bath Contemporary Art Fair. Plisnier had a solo show at Alpine Gallery, 1989, later ones including Leighton House, 1991, and Nomadic Zone Gallery, 1993. It was said of Plisnier's pictures that they were "strong and strident", possessing "a uniquely quite and disquieting power". Lived in Gloucestershire.

John PLOWMAN 1953– Sculptor who studied at Leicester Polytechnic and Goldsmiths' College, where he gained his master's degree in fine art. Exhibitions included White-chapel Open, Whitechapel Art Gallery, 1983; New British Sculpture, Air Gallery, 1986; Sculpture in Scarborough at Scarborough Art Gallery, 1987; and Second Wave, Bluecoat Gallery, Liverpool, 1988. In 1987 had a solo show at Mario Flecha Gallery, then exhibited Monumental Works at Crypt Gallery, 1988.

John PLUMB 1927– Painter and teacher, born in Luton, Bedfordshire. He studied at the local School of Art, 1942–5, Byam

Shaw School, 1948–50, and Central School of Art and Design, 1952–4, his teachers including Victor Pasmore, Keith Vaugham and William Turnbull. From 1955–68 taught at Central School, with periods teaching at Luton College of Technology and Maidstone College of Art. Plumb was for some years an abstract painter, often employing vinyl and cloth tapes in his pictures, but in the late 1970s he moved to figurative pictures. He had been represented in the AIA abstract shows in the 1950s and Situation exhibitions of the 1960s. Early one-man exhibitions were at Gallery One and the New Vision Centre Gallery. In the 1960s he began to show widely internationally and taught from 1968–9 at Bennington College, Vermont, in America, resuming at the Central College on his return. Later shows included The Plough Arts Centre, Torrington, 1995. Tate Gallery holds his work. Lived in London.

Alan PLUMMER 1931– Artist in various media and teacher. He studied at Leicester College of Art and Royal College of Art. Became senior lecturer in fine art at University of Reading. Among his mixed shows were Midland Artists at Ikon Gallery, Birmingham, 1967; Arts Council Open in Belfast, 1968–70; Didsbury College, Manchester, 1976; and British Artists at Cyprus College of Art at Woodlands Art Gallery, 1983. Had a solo show at Midlands Arts Centre, 1966, others including University of Reading 1976.

Brian PLUMMER 1934– Artist in watercolour and paper relief, with major works in acrylic on board relief, and teacher. He was born and lived in London where he studied at Hornsey College of Art, 1954–7, then Royal Academy Schools, 1957–60. Became director of foundation studies at University of Westminster. Group exhibitions included Barcelona Biennale, 1979, where he won a prize; Riverside Gallery, 1983–4; International Contemporary Arts, Tokyo, 1989; and Bruton Street Gallery, 1991. Had a solo show at Drian Galleries, 1965, later ones including Abbot Hall Art Gallery, Kendal, 1984, and Macquarie Galleries, Sydney, Australia, 1988. Abbot Hall, Lancaster University, Mobil Oil and other public and corporate collections hold examples.

Robin PLUMMER 1931– Artist, born in London, where he continued to live for some years. Studied at Royal College of Art with Rodrigo Moynihan, being a Rome Scholar in 1958. Showed at LG, Gimpel Fils, with Young Contemporaries of which he was secretary in the late 1950s, in Rome and at the New Vision Centre Gallery, where he shared a two-man show in November 1968. Was included in The 1960's at England & Co, 1993, and had a solo exhibition at Coombs Contemporary in 1996: Heroes and Heroines, Victims and Villains. These and landscape paintings were more typical of Plummer's later works than his Two-Way Construction, a relief in wood of 1966, in the Arts Council collection.

Jenepher POCKLEY fl. from 1990s– Artist who graduated in fine art from Kent Institute of Art and Design, 1994, then studied for a postgraduate diploma in painting at Royal Academy Schools. She was awarded the David Murray Studentship for Landscape Painting by the RA in 1995, exhibited in its Summer Exhibition and had several shows of her work. Pockley's seascape Forecast was chosen for the Chevron UK Ltd calendar in 1997, the year she appeared in the oil company's exhibition at the ICA.

Geoffrey Buckingham POCOCK 1879–1960 Painter and teacher, born in London, who was married to the artist Anna Airy. Studied at the Slade School of Fine Art, where he obtained first class certificates for painting and drawing. He gained a number of other prizes and became a life master at the London County Council School of Photo Engraving and Lithography. Was for a time life master and teacher of etching at Battersea Polytechnic School of Art. Exhibited RA, RI, NEAC and ROI, and a small selection of his work was shown during the Anna Airy retrospective at Christchurch Mansion, Ipswich, in 1985. Lived at Playford, near Ipswich.

Horace George William POLAINE 1910–1971 Painter of portraits, landscape, still life and miniatures in oil, tempera watercolour. Born in Walthamstow, he studied at West Ham Technical College, 1927–32, exhibiting at RA and RI. In the 1940s he worked in a design studio, then taught commercial art and design at his old College from 1947–50. Taught at City of London College, 1954–6. Lived at Woodford Green, Essex.

Sylvia POLLAK 1912– Painter and designer, exhibition specialist and writer on art. Studied at London University, the Bartlett School of Architecture, the Slade School of Fine Art and in Paris and Vienna. Exhibited AIA, Arts Council and widely in the provinces. Wrote in *The Studio* and *Architectural Design*. Lived in London.

Ingrid POLLARD 1953– Artist employing photography and installation, born in Georgetown, Guyana, who settled in London. She gained an honours degree in film and video from the London College of Printing, 1988; was photographer-in-residence, Lee Valley Park, 1993–4; then obtained her master's at Derby University, 1995. Group shows included Celebration of Black Women, Southall, 1984; The Black Experience, Black Art Gallery, 1986; Through the Looking Glass, Barbican Gallery, 1989; Documentary Dilemmas, British Council tour of Europe and the Americas, 1993; Boxer, Walsall City Museum and Art Gallery, 1995; and British Art Show 4, and tour, 1995–6. In the late 1980s she was nominated for Sun Life Photography and Athena Arts Awards. Had a solo show, Seaside Series, Watershed Gallery, Bristol, 1988, later ones including Hidden Histories, Heritage Stories, Lee Valley Park, 1994. Victoria & Albert Museum and National Museum of Film, Photography and Television, Bradford, hold examples.

Roger POLLEY 1948– Artist in mixed media, writer and teacher, born in Wallingford, Oxfordshire. He studied at High Wycombe School of Art, concentrating on fashion design, 1969–72, gained his degree after studying sculpture at St Martin's

School of Art, 1972–5, obtained his art teacher's certificate at Goldsmiths' College, 1976–7. Went on to be a freelance writer/designer and part-time teacher of art in Reading and London. Among his books was *Making Wooden Toys*, 1978. Exhibitions/installations/performances included Polygon at Nettlebed Gallery, Henley-on-Thames, 1970; Games at Oxford Playhouse Gallery, 1974; and in 1983–4 his joint show Ritual/Landmarks with John Woodman toured from South Hill Park, Bracknell.

Sally POLLITZER 1945– Painter and stained glass artist, born in Oxford, who studied at Central School of Arts and Crafts and Byam Shaw School, 1968–72. She moved into the medium of glass in the 1970s, undertaking domestic, ecclesiastical and public commissions while continuing to paint and exhibit. Was a member of The British Society of Master Glass Painters and of the Art Workers' Guild. Group shows included Whitechapel Open, 1979, Barbican Centre, 1984, and RIBA, 1986, with a solo exhibition at Sue Rankin Gallery in 1989. House of Lords holds her work. Lived in London.

Sigmund POLLITZER 1913–1982 Artist and designer, born in London, where he was educated, and in Switzerland. Pollitzer began his career as an industrial art designer, becoming chief designer for one of Europe's biggest glass-makers. After World War II he concentrated on the graphic arts, showing frequently in London, mainly at the Hanover and Redfern Galleries. In 1948 Pollitzer visited Cyprus, fell in love with the Mediterranean area, stayed there for eight years, then moved to Italy. As well as cultivating his garden at Positano he produced a long series of ink and wash drawings: classical buildings and studies of the human figure, living and in statue form, noted for their sensual qualities. He had solo shows at Galleria 88, Rome. Sally Hunter Fine Art included pictures by Pollitzer in her 1996 summer show.

Fred POLLOCK 1937– Painter and teacher, born in Glasgow. He studied at the School of Art there, 1955–9, then spent a year working in St Ives, Cornwall. From 1974–5 Pollock taught at Brighton Polytechnic, then at Canterbury School of Art, 1979. Pollock was an abstract artist who had a first solo show at New Charing Cross Gallery in Glasgow, another occurring at Garage, London, in 1974. He was in mixed shows at the Stockwell Depot from the mid-1970s and was included in the RA's important show British Painting 1952–1977, in 1977, where he exhibited typical works employing vertical coloured bands. Pollock later showed with Vanessa Devereux Gallery from 1986; at Talbot Rice Gallery. Edinburgh, 1993; Rebecca Hossack Gallery, 1994; and in 1995 shared a three-man exhibition with Douglas Abercrombie and Gabriel Flynn at The Living Room, Greenwich. Scottish Arts Council holds his work.

Helen POLLOCK 1945– Multi-media textile artist, painter in acrylic and teacher, born in Limavady, County Londonderry, Northern Ireland, wife of the artist Laurence Roche. She studied at Edinburgh College of Art, 1963–7, teachers including Robin Philipson, Elizabeth Blackadder, John Houston and James Cumming, from 1989 attending creative embroidery classes. Was a practising artist from 1967, an art teacher, 1968–89. Pollock was an associate member of the Guild of Gloucestershire Craftsmen. "Christian faith, colour and light and the use of an infinite variety of materials" were cited as key features of her work. Showed with John Whibley Gallery, SSA, Ogle Gallery in Cheltenham, SSWA, Reading Museum and Art Gallery and elsewhere in mixed exhibitions. Solo shows included Chepstow Art Centre and Fiery Beacon Gallery, Painswick. Lived in Stroud, Gloucestershire.

Ian POLLOCK 1950– Artist, illustrator and teacher, born in Cheshire, who studied illustration at Manchester Polytechnic, 1969–73, and at Royal College of Art, 1973–6. His illustrated books included Brian W Aldiss' *Brothers of the Head*, 1977, drawings also being done for magazines and colour supplements. Showed at Mall Galleries and Redfern Gallery, which sold two drawings of low life, a favourite subject of Pollock's, to Arts Council. His work appeared in the Council's 1981–2 tour Fragments Against Ruin.

Stephen POLLOCK 1958– Sculptor and framer, born in Greenford, Middlesex. After Berkhamsted School and Aylesbury College, he did a foundation course at Watford College of Art, 1980–1, then gained an honours degree in sculpture at Canterbury College of Art, 1981–4. Between 1984–9 was framer and manager at Frame Express branches in London. Pollock was noted for abstract sculptures in metal, as shown at Sculpture at Canterbury, 1991. Other exhibitions included a two-man exhibition at Kent University Library, 1984; a two-man show at The Crypt Gallery, 1989; and four-man show, called Mixed Steel, at Camden Galleries, 1989.

Nicole POLONSKY 1962– Artist whose work ranged from printmaking to sculpture and multi-media events. She studied at Ruskin School of Art, Oxford, then obtained her master's degree in printmaking from Royal College of Art. She aimed "to express my political beliefs" using "materials that are familiar to people for the symbolic meanings they have". Exhibitions included New Contemporaries, ICA and tour, 1986; Installation at Riverside Studios, 1987; and International Screen Print Exhibition at New Mexico University in America and Second Wave at Bluecoat Gallery, Liverpool, both 1988. Lived in London.

Elizabeth POLUNIN 1877–1950 Painter and designer, born in Ashford, Kent, who aged 17 went to Paris to study art, mainly at Atelier Colarossi, with Lucien Simon and at École des Beaux-Arts, later with Léon Bakst in St Petersburg and with Walter Sickert at Westminster School of Art. In 1907 in Russia she married the artist Vladimir Polunin (pronounced Pol*oo*nin), they moved to England and in 1918 she joined her husband in his work for Sergei Diaghilev's Russian Ballet. She produced portraits of Diaghilev and of the singer Chaliapin. During this period of collaboration with Braque, Derain, Picasso and others her outlook broadened, and she wrote that "about 1924, it was with new enthusiasm" she "restarted her own work in portraiture and landscape." In 1933 Polunin designed the scenery and costumes for *The Snow Maiden* at Sadler's Wells and some of her other designs were bought by the Victoria & Albert Museum. Had a series of solo shows in London from 1925. Early on she exhibited in Paris with Salon d'Automne and Salon des Indépendants, then added NEAC, RP, LG, Goupil and provincial galleries, North America and Greece and elsewhere abroad. Manchester City Art Gallery holds Polunin's portrait of the ballet dancer Anna Pavlova. The artist died in London.

Vladimir POLUNIN 1880–1957 Designer, artist and teacher, born in Moscow, Russia, who turned from forestry to art, which he studied in St Petersburg, Munich and Paris. Picasso painted sets for him when he worked for Sergei Diaghilev's Russian Ballet, and he was also employed by the Beecham Opera Company. After his arrival in London, just before World War I, he taught stage design at the Slade School of Fine Art, and exhibited a little in the 1930s at the Beaux Arts and Redfern Galleries. Polunin's wife was the artist Elizabeth Polunin. Their sons were all distinguished scientists: the botanist and environmentalist Nicholas, the botanist and plant geographer Oleg and the medical anthropologist Ivan.

Fay POMERANCE 1912– Artist in a wide range of media, born in Birmingham, who studied at School of Arts and Crafts there, 1929–32. She worked as a freelance commercial artist in the early 1930s and began exhibiting in mixed shows including Sheffield Society of Artists, of which she was a member; Ben Uri, Archer, Leicester, Molton and Redfern Galleries; RBSA and elsewhere widely in the provinces. She had several dozen solo shows. Main works included The Sphere of Redemption cycle, panels in tempera. Pomerance designed a stained glass window, Rebirth of the State of Israel, for Birmingham Synagogue. Ben Uri Art Society, Batley Art Gallery and Staffordshire Education Committee hold examples. Lived in Sheffield, Yorkshire.

Jacqui PONCELET 1947– Artist in various media, including sculpture and ceramics, and teacher, born in Belgium. She attended Wolverhampton College of Art and Royal College of Art, where she studied ceramics. In 1978 was granted a British Council Arts Fellowhip to America and in 1981 a major show of her ceramic work was organised by the Crafts Council. Also showed at ICA and had solo exhibitions of sculpture at Whitechapel Art Gallery, 1985; Max Protetch in New York, 1986; and Riverside Studios, 1988. In 1992 participated in Somatic States at Quicksilver Place Gallery, Middlesex University. Victoria & Albert Museum, Stedelijk Museum in Amsterdam and Museum of Modern Art in New York hold her work. Taught part-time at Camberwell School of Art.

Kate PONSONBY 1944– Printmaker who worked "mostly from landscape", born in Suffolk. She studied at Guildford School of Art, Goldsmiths' College, Chelsea School of Art and at Atelier 17, in Paris. Exhibitions included Prints '68, AIA Galleries and London Artists at Shrewsbury School, 1968.

Sarah PONSONBY 1943– Sculptor of realistic bronzes, often of horse, riding and hunting themes. She grew up in Ireland, but was educated in England and France, to which she returned to live in 1989. Her art education included Accademia di Belle Arti, Florence, 1960–1, and Brera, Milan, 1963. In 1969, she won an award from the Elizabeth Greenshields Memorial Foundation, Montreal. Gained many commissions in Britain and America; had a first solo show at Tryon Gallery in 1967, and continued to show there regularly until 1980. In 1981, she invented, designed and eventually published and marketed herself a successful board game: *The Garden Game*. Returned to sculpting and was included in Sixteen Sculptors at Sladmore Contemporary, 1997.

Susan PONTEFRACT 1947– Painter and teacher, born in Stalybridge, Cheshire. She was noted for her colourful, detailed domestic still lifes of fruit and flowers. After Stourbridge College of Art for a foundation course, 1966–7, Pontefract was at Birmingham College of Art, 1967–70, then studying for three years at Royal College of Art, obtaining her master's degree. Taught at Rochdale College of Art, 1973–86. She had solo exhibitions at Rochdale Art Gallery in 1975 and Bolton Art Gallery in 1977, later appearances including Duncan Campbell Contemporary Art, 1992.

A John POOLE 1926– Sculptor, letter-cutter and teacher, born in Birmingham, where he attended the Moseley Road School of Art, studying industrial design at Birmingham College of Art, 1938–9. He completed his diploma there, 1949–51, having studied letter-cutting with William Bloye for two years during World War II. Poole taught sculpture part-time at Mid-Warwickshire College of Art and Walsall School of Art, 1952–61. Established his own studio in 1949, working in stone, wood, concrete and metal. He was elected a fellow of RBS in 1969, winning the Otto Beit Medal in that year and in 1974, was chairman of the Society of Church Craftsmen and a member of the Arts League of Great Britain. Commissions included Life and Times of Liverpool, 1965; High altar and ambo, St Helen's Cathedral, Brentwood, 1974; and Brunel and Slade Memorial Tablet, University of Aston, 1976. Lived in Bishampton, Worcestershire.

Jonathan POOLE 1947– Artist and art dealer, born in London. He studied commercial design at Hertford College, then at City & Guilds of London Art School. Was a studio assistant for the sculptor James Butler and for Bernard Kramer and Robert Mitchell, also working in the studios of Madame Tussauds, the waxworks museum. From 1970 Poole organised shows of leading sculptors. His own exhibitions included RA; Edinburgh Festival; Playhouse Gallery in Harlow; widely abroad; and Cadogan Gallery, where he had a solo show in 1993. Lived in Ipsden, near Wallingford, Oxfordshire.

Monica POOLE 1921– Wood engraver, born in Canterbury, Kent, settling in the county at Tonbridge, daughter of the writer C Reginald Poole. She studied at Central School of Arts and Crafts, 1945–9, teachers including John Farleigh. In 1985 she published

The Wood Engravings of John Farleigh. Poole was a fellow of RE and a member of SWE and the Art Workers' Guild. Exhibitions included RA; International Exhibition of Botanical Art, Pittsburgh, America, 1972; and Xylon 8 and 9, International Society of Wood Engravers' Exhibitions, 1979–83. Solo shows included Studio One Gallery, Oxford, 1981; Andrew Knight Gallery, Cardiff, 1984; Bluecoat Gallery, Liverpool, 1987; and Duncan Campbell Contemporary Art, 1989. In 1993 Duncan Campbell held a major retrospective exhibition to coincide with one at Ashmolean Museum, Oxford, which with Victoria & Albert Museum and other public collections in Britain and abroad hold examples.

Walter G POOLE 1916–1988 Versatile painter and gallery owner, originally from Swindon, Wiltshire, where his father worked for the Great Western Railway and was a talented amateur artist. Poole briefly studied lithography at Swindon School of Art; at the outbreak of World War II enlisted in the Royal Air Force Volunteer Reserve and was posted to Northumberland, where he gained special leave to attend Newcastle School of Art under Robert Lyon; was discharged on medical grounds in 1943; then worked as a machine shop inspector for Short Brothers and Vickers Armstrong, painting when he could. Poole had shows at Leger and Burlington Galleries, to which he added a controversial Expressionist picture at Swindon Art Gallery in 1943, Redfern Gallery and RA and a solo exhibition at Peter Jones Gallery, 1944. Henry Moore won him a place at Chelsea School of Art, where he studied life drawing under Ceri Richards for four years. Became associated with the Neo-Romantics, such as John Minton and the Roberts Colquhoun and MacBryde, and in 1952 opened the Fimbarrus Gallery, showing contemporary art, in Bath, where he settled. Later solo shows included University of Bath, 1974, and in London Road Gallery there, 1988. From the 1970s Poole did not paint and led a reclusive, wheelchair-bound life.

Vanessa POOLEY 1958– Sculptor in clay, ceramic and bronze, born in Norwich, Norfolk. She did a foundation course at the local School of Art, 1977–8; gained an honours degree in fine art, sculpture, there, 1978–81; then did a postgraduate diploma, City & Guilds of London School of Art, 1981–2. She was a member of RBS. Botero, Laurens and Picasso were influences on the work of Pooley, which distorted the female figure to reinvent its form. Group exhibitions included Austin/Desmond Fine Art, 1988; The Discerning Eye, Mall Galleries, prizewinner, 1990; Gillian Jason Gallery, from 1991; and The Castle Show, Norwich Castle, 1993. Had solo shows at Southwark Cathedral, 1985; Café Gallery, Southwark Park, 1987; and The Orangery, Holland Park, from 1989. Lived in London.

Hilda Chancellor POPE 1913–1976 Painter, muralist, puppet-maker and teacher, born in London. Studied at Bromley School of Art, 1928–32, under Herbert Ashwin Budd, with Henry Carr at Beckenham School of Art, then at Royal College of Art, 1932–5, under Sir William Rothenstein. Was a prolific, regular exhibitor at RA, 1950–68, also showing at Goupil Gallery, AIA and widely in the provinces. Graves Art Gallery in Sheffield holds a collection of landscape sketches and watercolours by her, presented by the Sheffield Print Club, 1936. Lived near Woking, Surrey.

Nicholas POPE 1949– Sculptor in various materials, born in Sydney, Australia. He studied at Bath Academy of Art, 1970–3. He won a Southern Arts Association Bursary in 1974; a Romanian Government Exchange Scholarship, 1974–5; a Calouste Gulbenkian Foundation Visual Arts Award, 1976; he was a British Council Visitor to Romania in 1977; and in 1979 he was an Australian Council Visitor to Australia. In 1978 Pope won a Commonwealth Games Commission for Edmonton. Pope settled in Alton, Hampshire, where he rejected topical content in his work, choosing to employ conventional materials such as wood and stone. His sculptures were abstract and classical in form. Showed in important travelling group shows and had one-man exhibitions at Garage Gallery, City of Portsmouth Museum and Art Gallery in 1976, Anthony Stokes Gallery and abroad. After suffering a severe viral infection, Pope was unable to work for some years. As part of his rehabilitation he began building tall, hollow ceramic shapes. In 1996–7 his installation The Apostles Speaking in Tongues, based on such shapes, was shown at the Tate Gallery. The Arts Council holds Pope's wood and chalk sculpture Tall Chalk, of 1975.

Perpetua POPE 1916– Landscape artist in oil and watercolour, notably of Hebridean scenes, teacher, born in Solihull, Warwickshire. She studied at Edinburgh College of Art, teachers including William Gillies, William MacTaggart, James Cumming and Leonard Rosoman. She taught in primary and secondary schools and at Moray House College of Education in Edinburgh, where she settled, retiring early to paint full-time. Pope was a member of SSA, Scottish Arts Council and Aberdeen Artists, also exhibiting at RA and RSA. Had a series of solo shows at The Scottish Gallery from 1956–82; Loomshop Gallery, Lower Largo, 1979; Peter Potter Gallery, Haddington, 1980; then from 1983 at Macaulay Gallery, Stenton. Scottish Arts Council, Nuffield Foundation, Royal Bank of Scotland and HRH The Duke of Edinburgh hold examples.

Ronald POPE 1920– Sculptor, painter and teacher, born in Westbury-on-Severn, Gloucestershire. He was educated at Derby College of Technology, gaining an engineering degree in 1941 that led him to the tool design office at Rolls-Royce. Studied at Derby College of Art, 1943–5, then Slade School of Fine Art, 1945–8. His teachers included A H Gerrard, Randolph Schwabe and for ceramics Heber Mathews. Won a prize for stone carving. Part-time lecturing in art at Lonsdale College of Higher Education, Derby, and University of Nottingham allowed Pope to handle many architectural commissions in the Midlands. In 1966 he was commissioned by Basil Spence for a figure of St Catherine on a church in Sheffield, other commissions including a large abstract sculpture for Cathedral of All Saints, Derby, and a wall relief in the entrance to the Museum and Art Gallery: Family of Man. The human figure, alone and in groups, was a preoccupation of Pope, who often sculpted in bronze using oxy-acetylene welding. Showed at Alwin Gallery, Yew Tree Gallery in Ingleby and Ninety-Three Gallery, Derby. The public gallery there, county council and public company collections hold his work. Pope lived in a house and studio he designed in Melbourne, Derbyshire.

Terry POPE 1941– Sculptor and maker of constructions, born in Cornwall. He studied at Bath Academy of Art, 1959–62, obtaining a Royal Netherlands Government Scholarship in the latter year, enabling him to study at Royal Academy of Fine Art in The Hague, 1962–3. Pope went on to teach at University of Reading from 1968 and at Chelsea School of Art from 1975. He was interested in the rules of perspective and their modification and extending his experience of space, to which end he invented experimental spectacles which altered the way we see.His work was included in Axiom Gallery's Constructions '66 show in 1966, and three years later he showed in John Moores Exhibition, Liverpool. Pope gained Arts Council Awards in 1974 and 1976 and a British Council Award in 1977. He had his first solo show at Lucy Milton Gallery in 1974. Other important mixed shows including his work, of which the Arts Council has several examples, were the Hayward Gallery's Hayward Annual in 1978 and Non-Standard Constructions at Museum of Modern Art, Oxford, in 1980.

George POPESCO 1962– Painter, born in Paris. He attended West Surrey College of Art and Design, in Farnham, 1981–4, graduating in painting with an honours degree. He then studied at Royal Academy Schools, 1984–7. Showed at RA Summer Exhibition and shared a first London exhibition with Suzanne Balchin at Hyde Park Gallery in 1991, another in 1992. Attention to detail and a rich palette were features of his work.

James POPHAM 1884– Painter, born at Farningham, Kent, educated at Nottingham High School. Arts Club member. For some time honorary treasurer of PS, with which he exhibited, also ROI, Ridley Art Club, RA and RBA. Wrote *How to Use Pastels*. Lived in Chelmsford, Essex.

Roy PORRITT 1942– Artist in paper collage and oil paint, and teacher, born in Bury, Lancashire, settling at Tottington, Bury. He studied at Bolton College of Art and Liverpool University, where he gained his art teacher's diploma in 1982. Held a fellowship at St Martin's College, Lancaster, and in 1986 had a year's secondment from teaching in Middleton to do research into art education; lectured in various art colleges. Porritt developed a great interest in gardens as a subject and visited many owned by the National Trust. The changing pattern of light and its qualities were important in his work, key influences cited being Claude Monet and Ivon Hitchens. Group shows included Lancashire South of the Sands, which toured from the County and Regimental Museum, Preston, in 1988; Salford Open Exhibition; and Blackburn Museum & Art Gallery, an exhibition of works by artists employing waste material, 1995. Showed solo at Bury Art Gallery from 1964; at Blackburn Museum & Art Gallery from 1989; and at Paperpoint, Covent Garden, 1994. A 1996 show at Blackburn included studies of the Balata Rain Forest Gardens, Martinique, done during the previous year. Yorkshire Television held Porritt's work.

Roland John PORTCHMOUTH 1923– Painter, teacher and writer, born in London. Studied at Harrow School of Art, 1946–50, then Hornsey College of Art. Portchmouth had a varied career, holding a number of art teaching posts, broad-casting and running an art gallery, living in Coalbrookdale, Shropshire; Wingham, Kent; and Peebles, Scotland. Exhibited RA, ROI, RBA, Whitechapel Art Gallery and elsewhere, having one-man shows in Bath and Bristol. RA and National Trust bought his work. Published a number of volumes on practical art and craft work and some poetry. Eventually took Nonconformist holy orders and lived in Avoch, Black Isle, Ross-shire.

Michael PORTER 1948– Landscape painter, born in Derbyshire. He studied at Chelsea School of Art, 1968–72. Was artist-in-residence at National Gallery, 1982–3. Among his group show appearances were The Romantic Tradition in Contemporary British Painting, Murcia in Spain with Spanish and English tour, 1988; Landscape Now at Stoke-on-Trent Museum and Art Gallery, 1989; and John Moores Liverpool Exhibition, 1989–90. His solo shows included Anne Berthoud Gallery, 1985; Galeria Akumalatory 2, Poznan, Poland, 1986; and Fabian Carlsson Gallery touring show Derbyshire Woods, 1988. Lived in London.

Alex PORTNER 1920– Artist, born in Berlin, Germany. He claimed to have invented organic wood painting in which the picture subject is painted translucently into planed timber. Of Polish-Russian parents, Portner studied art in Amsterdam, Paris and Berlin before serving in the British army during World War II. After the war he began to exhibit extensively, mixed shows including the RA, Wildenstein's and the ROI, as well as one-man exhibitions at the Walton Gallery, New Art Gallery, Madden Gallery and in South Africa and America. St John's College, Oxford, and private collections in Britain and America hold his work. Lived in London.

Delia PORTSMOUTH 1939– Self-taught painter, born in Mottram, Cheshire, who spent much of her life in Bala, Gwynedd, where she attended the grammar school. Showed at ROI, Hesketh Hubbard Society and elsewhere, solo exhibitions including Oldham Art Gallery & Museum and Usher Gallery, Lincoln. National Museum of Wales in Cardiff and National Library of Wales, Aberystwyth, hold examples.

Percy Herbert PORTSMOUTH 1874–1953 Figurative sculptor in a traditional style, born in Reading, Berkshire. He was educated at University College in Reading and at Royal College of Art, where he was a Royal Exhibitioner, teachers including Édouard Lantéri. He was elected RSA in 1922 and a fellow of RBS in 1927, was a member of Scottish Arts Club and head of sculpture at Edinburgh College of Art. Showed at RA, Paris Salon, Royal Glasgow Institute of the Fine Arts and Walker Art Gallery in Liverpool. His Fountain Group and In Remembrance (Buck Memorial, Edinburgh) are illustrated in the 1939 volume *RBS: Modern British Sculpture*. Lived latterly in Rushden, Hertfordshire.

Douglas PORTWAY 1922–1993 Painter, draughtsman and designer, born in Johannesburg, South Africa, who had a poor, unsettled childhood. Became a window-dresser; drew in his spare timeand attended art schools including Witwatersrand Technical Art School, 1943–4, but was dissatisfied with the instruction; for several years taught at Witwatersrand and at University of Johannesburg; and in 1945 had his first solo show at Constantia Gallery, Johannesburg. In 1948 Portway married art student Rosalind Hertslet (they were later divorced), and they designed murals, tapestry and stained glass windows and exhibited together. In 1952 Portway gained a travel grant, spending several months in America. Five years later Portway left South Africa for good, travelled extensively in Europe, from 1959–66 living in Ibiza, in 1967 settling in St Ives, Cornwall, moving to Bristol in the early-1980s. Had regular annual periods working in France, at Razac d'Eymet, Dordogne, where he died. Portway took part in numerous group shows, including international art fairs in Basel, New York and Chicago, winning the European Painting Prize Bronze Medal, 1969, Gold Medal, 1971; he gained the Cornelissen Prize in 1992. The signing of a contract with Drian Gallery in the late 1950s cemented a long association, and Portway also held some of his many solo shows with Marjorie Parr and Gilbert–Parr Galleries. He was a prolific loner whose figurative and abstract works showed technical mastery, having an erotic element and being influenced by Klee, Zen and Jung. He said that his painting "suggests a meaning at many levels". Tate Gallery, Victoria & Albert Museum and many foreign collections hold examples. Memorial retrospectives at Gallery Gilbert, Dorchester, 1997–8.

Peggy POSTMA 1962– Painterand teacher, born in Montreal, Canada, who lived in Singapore and the Netherlands until 1983, when she moved to Britain to continue her art education, settling eventually in London. Postma studied at the Academy of Art, Rotterdam, 1980–3; gained an honours degree at Exeter College of Art, 1983–5; and her master's degree at Birmingham Polytechnic, 1985–6. A fellowship in painting at Gloucestershire College of Art, 1986–7, was followed by a part-time lectureship in painting at Stourbridge College of Art, 1987–91, and she was a visiting lecturer on other fine art degree courses around Britain from 1986. Gained several awards from South West Arts and in 1989 was a finalist in British Airways' Most Promising Artist Award. Music was a strong source of inspiration for Postma's work, which tended towards Abstract Expressionism, using a rich palette. Group exhibitions included Stowells Trophy Awards at RA, 1984; Ikon Gallery, Birmingham, 1986; Knapp Gallery, 1989; and Pittville Gallery, Cheltenham, 1992. Had a solo show at Government Buildings, The Hague, 1982, later ones including Plymouth City Museum & Art Gallery, 1993, Victoria Art Gallery in Bath, 1994, and Netherlands Embassy, 1995. In 1996 she shared an exhibition with Marcelle Hanselaar at Collyer–Bristow Gallery.

Donald POTTER 1902– Sculptor in a variety of materials, born in Newington, Kent, a pupil of the sculptor Eric Gill. He was elected a fellow of RBS. Among his works were a figure of St Sebastian at Winchester College and a statue of Robert Baden-Powell, founder of the Boy Scout movement, in Queen's Gate, Kensington. Lived finally at Bryanston, Dorset.

Frank POTTER 1885– Painter and printmaker who studied at Académie Julian, Paris, 1910. Chelsea Arts Club member. Exhibited RA, ROI, NEAC, RSA and Paris Salon. Rotherham Corporation bought his work. Lived in London.

Frank Hayden POTTER 1896– Painter who was by profession an art teacher and examiner, born in Sutton, Surrey. Studied at Heatherley's School of Fine Art, Slade School of Fine Art under Henry Tonks, Philip Wilson Steer and Randolph Schwabe and at Central School of Arts and Crafts with Walter Bayes. Potter did a typography course with H W Thomas at the Baynard Press. Exhibited widely, including RA, NEAC, RP, LG and Paris Salon. Lived in Reigate, Surrey.

Mary POTTER 1900–1981 Painter in oil and watercolour of landscapes and still life. Born at Beckenham, Kent, she studied at the Slade School of Fine Art 1918–21, winning a Slade Scholarship in 1919. Began exhibiting with the NEAC from 1922 (under her maiden name of Mary – originally Marian – Attenborough), having her first one-man show at the Bloomsbury Gallery in 1931. Was married to the writer and humorist Stephen Potter 1927–55. From the 1930s through to the 1980s there was a stream of one-man exhibitions, including the Redfern Gallery, Leicester Galleries and New Art Centre. There was a retrospective at the Whitechapel Art Gallery in 1964, with a selective retrospective at Davies Memorial Gallery, Newtown, 1989–90, which toured. Potter's essentially English, beautifully composed pictures, with their muted but distinctive colours, won her a loyal following. Represented in many public collections, including Tate Gallery, Arts Council, Contemporary Art Society and galleries in America, Canada and Australia. Lived in Aldeburgh, Suffolk.

Mary POTTER 1920– Artist in Batik and collage, born in Udimore, Sussex, where she later set up a studio gallery in Laughton. Potter attended Hastings and Folkestone Schools of Art, 1937–41 and 1949–51, including teacher-training. Following a general art education she began experimenting with Batik. She was a member of Art and Architecture, Batik Guild and Guild of Sussex Craftsmen. Textures of rocks, patterns of waves, Greek landscapes and simple grasses were used by her and she was interested in designing for public interiors. Exhibitions included Trinity Arts Centre in Tunbridge Wells, Brighton University Gallery, Knapp Gallery and Towner Art Gallery, Eastbourne.

Frank POTTINGER 1932– Sculptor in wood and ceramics, and teacher, born in Edinburgh. Graduated in 1963 from Edinburgh College of Art; visited Greece and Turkey on a travelling scholarship; then returned to Moray House Training College and began teaching in Edinburgh and Fife. From 1973–85 lectured in art at Aberdeen College of Education, then became full-time artist. Work included large wooden abstract sculptures, ceramic pieces generally being smaller. Visited Oakland, California, International Sculpture Conference on Scottish Arts Council grant and won a Council award, William J Macaulay Award and the IBM Award in 1986. Was elected a member of RSA and SSA and took part in group shows such as Glasgow Group. Also showed at 57 Gallery, Edinburgh, and Compass Gallery, Glasgow. Hunterian Gallery, Glasgow; Paisley Art Gallery; and Dundee University hold his work.

Ian POTTS 1936– Artist and teacher who studied at Sunderland College of Art and Royal Academy Schools. Taught for a time at Brighton Polytechnic, living nearby in Lewes, Sussex. He showed in the Polytechnic Gallery, in Guildford Summer Exhibition and elsewhere including Arts Council tour Fragments Against Ruin, 1981–2. The Council holds several watercolours by him of Greece and Italy.

Peter POTWOROWSKI 1898–1962 Painter in oil, born in Warsaw, Poland. After initial architectural studies at Warsaw Polytechnical School, transferred to the Painting School in 1921, then studied at Cracǿw Academy of Fine Art, 1923–4. Travelled extensively in Europe and Scandinavia for about 20 years, then in Scotland and London, where he arrived in 1943. From 1946 for about a dozen years he visited Wookey Hole, Somerset, initially and then regularly Sancreed, Cornwall. In London he had met Jankel Adler, and now in Cornwall he mingled with St Ives painters. In the 1950s he made a number of trips to the continent, in 1950 touring Spain with the sculptor Kenneth Armitage. Armitage was one of his colleagues when he taught at Bath Academy of Art, Corsham, 1949–58, others being William Scott, Peter Lanyon, Terry Frost and Adrian Heath. When he visited Poland in 1958 it was meant to be a one-year stay, but he decided to remain permanently, and was appointed professor at Gdańsk and Poznan art colleges. In the early 1960s he designed for theatrical productions in Poznan and Warsaw, where he died. Potworowski was an influential teacher and a rich Colourist who created a uniquely patterned private world. Showed throughout Britain, the continent and North America, notably in 1960 at the Venice Biennale. One-man shows included Claridge Gallery, 1928, Redfern Gallery, 1946, National Museum in Poznan, 1976–7, RWA and Institute of Education, 1984.

Albert POUNTNEY 1915– Sculptor in stone, metal, wood and clay, and teacher, born in Wolverhampton, Staffordshire. He studied at the local School of Art, 1931–5, under R J Emerson; at Royal College of Art, 1935–8, with Richard Garbe; then was a Rome Scholar, attending British School at Rome, 1938–9. He was head of sculpture at Leicester College of Art, 1947–60, and on retirement was head of the school of fine art at Leicester Polytechnic, where he was on the staff 1960–78. Pountney was a fellow of RBS and a member of the Society of Rome Scholars. He showed at RA and elsewhere but worked mainly on commission from architects, notably in Leicestershire, where he settled at Saddington. The Royal Infirmary carries a 10-foot carving in Portland stone. Pountney believed "in the traditional training of sculptors, fast disappearing, and that sculpture is about volume and space, structure and spatial relationships, not about ideas in words."

Jack POUNTNEY 1921– Painter, especially of the Thames and southeast London, who was born and lived there. He showed at RA, RBA, International Boat Show, Lord Mayor's Art Award, Bexley Arts Council, Blackheath Art Society and RSMA. Had solo shows at The Room, Greenwich, 1972, and Court Lodge Gallery, Horton Kirby, 1974, and in 1975 shared an exhibition at Woodlands Art Gallery. Guildhall Art Gallery holds his work.

Monica POUNTNEY fl. from 1950s– Painter and draughtsman, born and lived in London, who studied with Ruskin Spear and Carel Weight at Hammersmith School of Arts and Crafts, then Central School of Arts and Crafts with John Farleigh. Did some book illustration. Was a member of UA, also exhibiting with RI, NS and elsewhere.

Ed POVEY 1951– Painter and muralist, born in London, who began painting aged eight. After comprehensive school he became an office boy at 16, but emigrated to Canada in 1969, where he became a member of the Baha'i Faith, sang in clubs and toured with his band Synergy and lived with the Blackfoot Indians. Working at a kibbutz in Israel in 1971 Povey painted the first of the many murals he became noted for, Abraham and Isaac, before returning to England and from 1972–3 doing a foundation course at Eastbourne College of Art and Design. From 1974 Povey lived in north Wales, engaged on a four-year graduate teacher-training course at University of Wales while painting many shopfront murals. Povey moved to Grenada, West Indies, in 1982, selling to American collectors and returning to Britain for occasional commissions. In 1989 Povey moved to Cleveland, in northeast England, in 1991 buying a house in Guisborough. In that year the Laguna Gloria Museum of Art, Austin, Texas, bought a Povey picture and the University of Wales awarded a major commission. Meridian Gallery of Hay-on-Wye; Art Gallery Gerard in The Hague, Netherlands; and Midtown Payson Galleries, New York, latterly showed Povey's work.

Bernard POWELL 1924–1957 Painter and draughtsman. He had his first one-man exhibition at Cooling Galleries in 1952. Among his portraits were Yvonne Mitchell the actress and the conductor George Weldon. Member of the ICA. Lived in London.

Cynthia POWELL 1933–1977 Painter, born in London, who studied at Camberwell School of Arts and Crafts. Showed at Beaux Arts Gallery, 1955. Her oil Girl on a Sofa, 1954, was included in The Forgotten Fifties, Graves Art Gallery in Sheffield and tour, 1984.

John POWELL 1911– Artist in oil, watercolour and pastel, and teacher, born in Nottingham. After six years apprenticed as a lithographic artist Powell left industry and studied at Nottingham College of Art, 1932–5, then Royal College of Art, 1935–9, under Gilbert Spencer. He taught at Sutton and Cheam School of Art, then at Manchester Regional College of Art, as head of foundation studies; Nottingham as head of fine art; then Portsmouth College of Art as principal. Powell took part in numerous mixed and group exhibitions, including RA, Victoria & Albert Museum, Whitechapel Art Gallery, National Maritime Museum in Greenwich, Archer Gallery and elsewhere. Had solo shows at New Ashgate Gallery, Farnham, in 1981, and Bosham Walk Art Gallery, Bosham, 1990. Bristol Education Authority holds his picture Harbour, Tenby, and Manchester Education Authority Fair at Twilight and Child at Breakfast. Lived in Fishbourne, Sussex.

Richard POWELL 1958– Sculptor, poster artist, printmaker and teacher, born in London. He studied at Chelsea School of Art in 1977 and graduated from Cardiff College of Art, 1981. His teaching experience included part-time at Portsmouth College of Art, 1986, and Humberside College of Art, 1988. Dick Powell set up the Starless Cast Media Group in 1982; in 1983 gained a WAC grant for the film *Dog Lake*; in 1984 helped set up 13 Amp Press to aid miners; in 1986 bought warehouse premises for studio space and accommodation; worked with Welsh National Opera in 1988; held a residency at Glynn Vivian Art Gallery, Swansea, 1989, and was commissioned in 1992 to create a sculptural fountain for Margam Sculpture Park. Powell showed with Young Contemporaries at ICA, 1980; with Nine Sculptors, Lower Machen Festival, 1989; and took part in South Bank Centre tour Wild Creatures, 1991.

Roy POWELL 1934– Painter and teacher using a rich palette, who studied at Cardiff College of Art, 1953–6 and 1958–9. He taught art in schools, 1959–90, from 1974–90 at Brecon High. Had a large show at National Library of Wales, Aberystwyth, 1997, others including Llanover Hall, Cardiff, 1998. Lived in Brecon, Powys.

Stephen POWELL 1955– Painter in oil, printmaker and teacher, born in Hartlepool, County Durham. He studied at the College of Art there; Leicester Polytechnic; and Hornsey School of Art, graduating with honours in 1988. Teachers included John Loker for painting, Simon Reed for photography/installations and Kevin Atherton, sculpture. From 1989 Powell was a part-time lecturer in painting and print at Southampton Institute of Higher Education. "The analogy between artist and performer" was important in his work. Group shows included University of Ulster Gallery, 1987; and Aspex Gallery, Portsmouth, 1990. Had a solo exhibition at Phoenix Art Centre, Leicester, 1988; two at 5 Dryden Street, 1989–90; and The Town Quay, Southampton, 1992. He was artist-in-residence at Town Quay in that year. Among commissioned works were illustrations for Thames Television's *This Week*, February 1991. Associated British Ports, Southampton, hold Powell's work. Lived in Southampton, Hampshire.

Terry POWELL 1944– Sculptor and teacher, born in Birmingham. He attended the University of Auckland in New Zealand, 1962–5, then was a tutor in fine art there, 1968–9. Between 1970–3 Powell studied at Royal College of Art under Bernard Meadows. Between 1971–5 he was at various times teaching at Lanchester Polytechnic, Coventry; Central School of Art and Design; and Maidstone College of Art; lecturing from 1975–9 at Royal College of Art. In 1974 won Sainsbury Award. In 1976 Powell was a visiting lecturer at Auckland University, New Zealand. Powell produced abstract sculptures in a variety of materials. His shows included John Leech Gallery, Auckland, 1964; New Zealand House and Central Gallery, both in London, 1973; New Art Centre, 1979; and the Royal College of Art 1980 show on Bernard Meadows 1960–1980, 1980.

Virginia POWELL 1939– Painter and printmaker, born in Henley-on-Thames, Oxfordshire. She studied at Chelsea School of Art in late 1950s with Fred Brill. Her watercolours, lithographs and etchings dealt with country and domestic subjects. Selected exhibitions included Traverse Theatre, Edinburgh, 1967; Green and Abbott from 1969; Parkin Gallery from 1976; Maclean Gallery from 1981; and Austin/Desmond Fine Art, Sunninghill, 1988, and Rose Street Gallery, 1991.

Cyril Edward POWER 1872–1951 Printmaker, architect, watercolourist, writer and lecturer, born in London. Trained as an architect with his father's firm; won RIBA's Soane Medallion in 1900; then continued practising as an architect until World War I, when served with Royal Flying Corps. In 1912 he published *English Mediaeval Architecture*, in two volumes. After the war he left his wife and children and with the artist Sybil Andrews enrolled at Grosvenor School of Modern Art, where he eventually taught. He had done some teaching at University College and Goldsmiths' College before the war. By now Power was busy as a printmaker and watercolourist, showing at pioneering Redfern Gallery print exhibitions in 1930s. Also exhibited RA, RBA, Goupil Gallery and Royal Glasgow Institute of the Fine Arts during his career. Power's association with Andrews petered out by World War II, and eventually he returned to his family. His work was shown at Parkin Gallery in A Look at British Printmakers 1860–1940, in 1981, and at British Museum in Avant-Garde British Printmaking 1914–1960, in 1990–1.

Alan POWERS 1955– Artist in watercolour, lithography and intaglio, muralist and writer on architecture and art, born and lived in London. He obtained his doctorate in the history of art at Cambridge University and learned lithography from Stanley Jones at Curwen Studio. Powers was an illustrator for publications including *The Spectator* and did work for The Twentieth Century Society. He was a member of the Art Workers' Guild. Showed in the RE Open from 1990 and had a series of solo exhibitions at Heffer's Bookshop in Cambridge from 1979–84, at Judd Street Gallery, 1985–9. Powers "worked in emulation of the English topographical tradition", latterly being "more concerned with the figure". National Trust Foundation for Art and HRH The Prince of Wales hold examples.

Val POWNALL 1917–1981 Artist in oil and watercolour, born in Penworthan, studied art under Charles Oliver at Laird School of Art, Birkenhead. Exhibitions include Zadler Gallery and Gorstage Gallery, Weaverham, Great House Gallery, Rivington, PS, ROI and Portico Library Gallery, Manchester. Bowater House, London, holds her work. Lived in Chester.

Gertrude Mary POWYS 1877–1952 Artist in various media, notable for her portraits of members of the literary Powys family, including John Cowper Powys and Llewelyn Powys. Between 1910–23 she lived at Montacute Vicarage, Somerset, then in Paris. *Earth Memories*, 1934, *Rats in the Sacristy*, 1937, and *A Baker's Dozen*, 1941, all by Llewelyn Powys, were illustrated by her. She also showed at RWA and an exhibition of her work was arranged in conjunction with the conference of The Powys Society in Bath in 1986.

Malcolm POYNTER 1946– Sculptor, born in Reading, Berkshire. Poynter studied vocational graphics at Goldsmiths' College School of Art, 1969–70, then at the Royal College of Art, 1970–3, with Bernard Meadows the sculptor. Poynter's work used such materials as fibreglass and consisted of realistic figures, life size and sometimes with sadistic or humorous over tones. Showed extensively abroad, at RA and with Nicholas Treadwell Gallery and was included in British Sculpture in the Twentieth Century at Whitechapel Art Gallery, 1981–2.

Philip POYSER 1912–1988 Painter, muralist and therapist who lived in Isleworth, Richmond and Twickenham, west of London, and who studied at Willesden and Richmond Schools of Art, later studying in Paris and Antwerp. During a long career as an art therapist Poyser showed often at Redfern, Leicester and other London galleries. He was encouraged by Augustus John, who admired his work. After his death The Hampton Hill Gallery, Hampton Hill, exhibited Poyser. There are murals by the artist in Grove Road Hospital in Richmond, the West Middlesex, Isleworth, and at Dartford.

Michael PRAED 1941– Painter and teacher, born in Hayle, Cornwall, whose subject was the local landscape, notably around Newlyn where he had a studio. Attended Falmouth School of Art and Brighton College of Arts and Crafts, 1960–4, then returned to Cornwall to teach in Penzance, in 1980 becoming head of art at Humphry Davy School. Was a member of Newlyn Society of Artists and Penwith Society of Arts, showing widely inCornwall, London and Brittany. His painting Approaching the Scillies was included in the 1989 Newlyn Orion Galleries exhibition A Century of Art in Cornwall 1889–1989.

Sophia Rosamond PRAEGER 1867–1954 Sculptor and illustrator, born and eventually settled in Holywood, County Down, Northern Ireland. She attended the School of Art in Belfast under George Trobridge and Slade School of Fine Art under Alphonse Legros, winning a silver medal for drawing. She illustrated a series of children's books to help make a living, some written by her. Her most famous sculpture, The Philosopher, made her name when shown at RA in 1920; she gave a copy to Belfast Museum and Art Gallery and many others were sold worldwide. Praeger was an honorary member of RHA and a member and president of RUA. Also exhibited at Belfast Art Society and at Walker Art Gallery in Liverpool. In 1976 Holywood's Business and Professional Women's Club held a commemorative exhibition.

Alfred PRAGA 1867–1949 Painter, notably of portraits, and miniaturist, born in Liverpool, who studied art in London, Paris and Antwerp. He was one of the founders of SM, became its president and a member of RBA. Among a string of portraits of titled and notable people were Father Bernard Vaughan and Princess Marie Louise. He was also a member of Savage Club, which owned his portrait of King Edward VII, and Chelsea Arts Club. Praga was a prolific artist, showing at RI, RA, ROI and elsewhere. Lived in London.

Valerie PRAGNALL 1942– Sculptor, born in Worthing, Sussex. After doing various jobs in London and Paris in her twenties, Pragnall moved to Glasgow in the early 1970s, from 1981–5 studying in the mural and stained glass department at the College of Art there. In 1988 she was artist-in-residence at the Glasgow Garden Festival. Pragnall showed in mixed exhibitions in Scotland from the mid-1980s, although sometimes her works were specifically designed for a site, being created from natural materials. Tree Pods and Storm were featured in the Scottish National Gallery of Modern Art 1989–90 Scottish Art since 1900 show. Pragnall worked in Glasgow.

Bertram PRANCE 1889–1958 Illustrator and artist, born in Bideford, Devon, where his father skippered his own fishing vessel. Bertram left school aged 12, was employed by a solicitor, but soon became a pupil at the local School of Art and Science. A fellow-student and lifelong friend, whose books he was to illustrate, was B C Hilliam, Flotsam of the radio singing duo Flotsam and Jetsam. Prance took a local studio and became a prolific producer of humorous drawings for dozens of publications, including *Bystander*, *John Bull, Punch*, *Tit Bits* and national newspapers. Moved to the London area and was a member of Savage and London Sketch Clubs, in 1948 the latter's president. During World War II worked on mechanical drawings for the Admiralty. Health concerns prompted him and his wife to spend a period at Menton, in south of France, then in 1952 he settled at Leith Hill, Surrey. Because Prance's style of humour and meticulous black-and-white draughtsmanship became out of fashion in the popular press, he concentrated on book illustration, advertising work and his own landscape gouaches and oil paintings. Burton Art Gallery and Museum, Bideford, gave Prance a retrospective in 1998.

Sista PRATESI 1966– Painter, born in Aberdeen, who studied at Byam Shaw School of Art and Slade School of Fine Art. Pratesi sought to create "claustrophobic, alien interior spaces, using synthetic green and yellow colours which, on account of their luminosity, create unsettling barriers and blockages". An example was the oil on canvas Leatherhead, in 1996 Royal Over-Seas League Open, which won a prize. Pratesi gained a Space Studio Award in 1994. Other group shows included D Ward, The Metropolitan Gallery, 1993; Fresh Art, Business Design Centre, Islington, and Out of the Nineties, Mall Galleries, both 1994; and Fitzrovia Open, Venezuela Cultural Centre, 1996.

David Ellis PRATT 1911–1988 Wildlife and natural history artist and writer, born in Kobe, Japan. He was a member of SWLA and Federation of British Artists and showed at Mall Galleries and elsewhere. Lived in St Austell, Cornwall.

Derrick Edward Henry PRATT 1895–1979 Painter, printmaker and teacher, born in Walsall, Staffordshire, son of the painter Edward Derrick Pratt. Studied at Leeds College of Art, 1911–15, then at Royal College of Art, 1919–23. Served in Royal Artillery in World War I. From 1923–60 he was principal of Llanelli School of Art, in Wales. Showed RA, SWG and with Llanelli Art Society, being given a retrospective at Parc Howard Mansion, Llanelli, in 1969. CASW bought his work. In 1971 he moved to Harpenden, Hertfordshire, but was recorded as dying in St Albans.

Kate PRATT 1967– Sculptor of animals and birds in a variety of materials, noted for her ability to capture character, movement and humour, who studied fine art and history of art at Tudor Hall, Banbury, but who was essentially self-taught as an artist. In her early twenties moved to London to work in interior design, but gave this up to concentrate on sculpture. Mixed and solo shows included Oxford Art Week, the Sue Rankin, Thackeray and Mossop Street Galleries, Ainscough Contemporary Art and John Martin of London. Had a studio in Warwickshire.

Lucy PRATT 1970– Painter born in Banbury, Oxfordshire, who in 1988 began training at local School of Art, moving to study at Loughborough and Cheltenham. In 1990 painted under Sarah Spackman, of Camberwell School of Art, and Peter Samuelson, Paris Conservatoire, while working at Museum of Modern Art, Oxford. Exhibitions included Antony Sidgwick and Swan Gallery, Burford, both 1991, and she shared a show at John Davies, Stow-on-the-Wold, 1994. This included energetic and colourful views completed during a year-long trip to India, Nepal and Thailand, sponsored by Pure Art, 1992–3.

Nick PRATT 1952– Sculptor in wood and stone of human and animal figures which sensitively exploit the nature of the material, its knots, cracks and abstract shapes. Born in London, Pratt studied at Kingston and Guildford Schools of Art and West Surrey College of Art and Design, Farnham. He showed with Norwich Artists, 1984; Steeple End Gallery, Halesworth, 1985; Orwell Bookshop, Southwold, 1987; Binotti Gallery, Glasgow, 1989; The Collection Gallery, 1990; and Chappel Galleries, Essex, 1992.

Daniel PREECE 1970– Painter, draughtsman and teacher, who studied drawing at Camberwell School of Art, trained at Chelsea School of Art, 1988–9, and gained an honours degree in painting at the Slade School of Fine Art, 1989–93. Awards included the William Coldstream Prize, 1990; second prize, Slade Summer Competition, 1991; Slade Project Award, 1992; Henry Tonks Prize, 1993; finalist, The Alasdair Gilchrist Fisher Memorial Award, 1994 (and again in 1998); and Boise Scholarship, 1995. Preece taught at the Slade Summer School. His group exhibitions included Cadogan Contemporary, 1995, and Contemporary Art Society Art Market, Royal Festival Hall, 1996. Had a solo show at the Slade, 1997. Collections include Stoves, Liverpool, and Peat Marwick Accountants.

Lawrence PREECE 1942– Painter and teacher, born in Shepton Mallet, Somerset. Studied ceramics at Brighton College of Art, 1958–63, after which he taught. In 1971 he was a visiting lecturer at University of Washington, and he later taught at Middlesex and Brighton Polytechnics. His exhibitions included New Chelsea Gallery, 1962; Clytie Jessop, 1970; John Moores Liverpool Exhibition from 1972; Art into Landscape at Serpentine Gallery, 1977; and in 1979 Basle Art Fair, Israel Observed, sponsored visit to Israel to work. Had a first solo show at Redfern Gallery in 1972, followed by others, and one of fantasy paintings at Woodlands Art Gallery, 1979. Lived in London.

Patricia PREECE 1894–1966 Painter, born into a peripatetic military family, who became Lady Spencer, second wife of the painter Stanley Spencer, In 1917 entered the Slade School of Fine Art, studying under Henry Tonks, there meeting her lifelong companion Dorothy Hepworth. They became members of the Bloomsbury Group circle and shared a studio. She spent four years in Paris on the urging of Roger Fry and studied in André Lhote's studio, Dorothy Hepworth attending the Atelier Colarossi. Returning to England in 1925 they rented a number of cottages in the west of England, in 1927 settling in Cookham, Berkshire. There Patricia Preece met Stanley Spencer, modelled for him and entered into the bizarre marriage of 1937 recounted in her autobiography as told to Louise Collis; after the marriage she did not live with Spencer. Although Augustus John thought highly of her work and she exhibited at Warren, Leicester, Lefevre and Leger Galleries and has work in public galleries in Cardiff and Swansea, how many paintings can be firmly attributed to Patricia Preece and how many to Dorothy Hepworth, who appears to have done much of her work, is unclear. Towards the end the two led a reclusive life in Cookham.

Kathy PRENDERGAST 1958– Sculptor and draughtsman, born in Dublin, Ireland, who studied there at National College of Art & Design, 1976–80 and 1982–3, and as a studio camera operator, 1980–1, moving to Royal College of Art, 1983–6. Prendergast worked in a variety of materials. Her sculpture Land, one of a series of tent-like structures, was bought for the Arts Council collection in 1991 from the Strongholds show at Tate Gallery, Liverpool, and in 1993 was the subject of a Spotlight exhibition at Landau Forte College, Derby. Other solo shows included Henry Moore Foundation Fellowship Exhibition, Camberwell School of

Arts and Crafts and Unit 7, 1987; and Douglas Hyde Gallery, Dublin, and tour, 1990. Land's successor, Range, was shown at Camden Arts Centre, 1992, and she was in Art Now at Tate Gallery, 1997.

Peter PRENDERGAST 1946– Painter and teacher, born in Abertridwr, Glamorgan, son of a miner. He attended Cardiff College of Art, 1962–4, Slade School of Fine Art, 1964–7, and Reading University for a postgraduate course, 1968–70. Gomer Lewis and Frank Auerbach were influential teachers. Taught Liverpool College of Art, 1971–4. He was later a part-time lecturer at Gwynedd Foundation Course. In 1970 Prendergast moved to Bethesda, the North Wales village most like a mining village in South Wales, near the huge Penrhyn Slate Quarry. He painted a long series of craggy, colourful quarry panoramas, as shown in WAC's The Dark Hills, The Heavy Clouds show of 1981. Prendergast showed at Royal National Eisteddfod, SWG and SEA and had solo exhibitions at Bluecoat Gallery, Liverpool, 1973; WAC, Cardiff, 1975; The Road to Bethesda, Mostyn Art Gallery, Llandudno, and tour; and Paintings from Wales, National Museum of Wales at Penarth, and tour, 1993–4. In 1992 Prendergast was awarded a travel scholarship by WAC to visit America. Tate Gallery, British Museum and WAC hold his work. Lived at Carnarvon, Gwynedd.

David PRENTICE 1936– Artist and teacher, born in Solihull, Warwickshire. He studied at Moseley School of Art in Birmingham, 1949–52, then the College of Art and Design, 1952–7. Prentice was co-founder and director of the Ikon Gallery in Birmingham, 1965–71. From 1971–82 he was senior lecturer in charge of the experimental workshop at City of Birmingham Polytechnic, taking over the honours degree course direction, 1982–6. He was visiting artist for various times at Trent Polytechnic, Ruskin School of Drawing in Oxford and Birmingham Institute of Art and Design and was artist-in-residence at Nottingham University, 1986–7. Had a long series of solo shows including RBSA from 1961, Ikon Gallery from 1965 and latterly Cowleigh Gallery, Malvern, from 1990, Nevill Gallery in Canterbury, 1991, and Art First, 1997. In 1990, Prentice won first prize in the Singer & Friedlander/*Sunday Times* Watercolour Competition. Arts Council; Birmingham Museum and Art Gallery; Whitworth Art Gallery, Manchester; Victoria & Albert Museum; and The Art Institute of Chicago hold Prentice's works. Lived in Malvern, Worcestershire.

Lawrence PRENTICE fl. from late 1980s– Printmaker and painter who studied fine art printmaking at Newcastle Polytechnic, 1989–92. Prentice said that in his work he enjoyed narrative and "[I] begin to build stories or tales into the pictures. Many are about fictional journeys made from dreams, television, film and books. Repeat motifs occur and characters or personalities evolve that I can develop in a fresh series of prints." Exhibitions included Clayton Gallery, Newcastle, 1992; Zillah Bell Gallery, Thirsk, 1993; Gateshead Library, 1994; Norwich Print Fair, 1995; and David Holmes Contemporary Art, Peterborough, 1996. Prentice had a printmaking fellowship at Newcastle Polytechnic, 1992–3, then set up a studio in Norwich, Norfolk, where he pursued experimental etching and lithographic work.

Frances PRESS 1941– Painter, born in Lancashire, who studied at St Albans College of Art, 1987–91. Exhibited in Fresh Art at Business Design Centre, Islington, and Connecting Lines, Het Rietveld Paviljoen, Amsterdam, both 1992; and in 1995–6 at John Moores Liverpool Exhibition showed one of her Banners series, oil on cotton duck. The series was begun at the International Workshop at the Polish Centre for Sculpture, Oronsko, in 1992–3, where Press made several site-specific works. Lived in Bushey Heath, Hertfordshire.

PRESTON: *see* **Preston GODDARD**

Lawrence PRESTON 1883–1960 Artist and teacher, born in Leeds, Yorkshire. After working with his father as a lithographic artist studied at Leeds College of Art, then Royal College of Art, serving as a topographical artist with Army in France in World War I. Preston taught for 25 years at Brighton College of Art and Crafts, living in the town. Exhibitions included RA and Sussex Arts Club, of which he was for a time president. He was a distinctive figure, tall, with an erect almost military bearing and a small moustache.

Susan PRESTON 1943– Painter producing abstract work, oil on canvas or linen, gouache on paper, born in Liverpool. She graduated with an honours degree in fine art from West Surrey Institute, Farnham, teachers including Pete Nevin, Bev Brennan and Paul Butler. She was a member of the Women's Art Library. Mixed shows included RWA Open, 1988; Maltings, Farnham, 1993; Anthony Hepworth Fine Art in Bath and Tabernacle Gallery, both 1995; and Logos Gallery, 1996. Had a first London show at The Studio, 130 Percy Road, and another at Mount House Gallery, Marlborough, both 1997. The former stemmed from the wrappings and bindings of mummified birds, the canvases being worked over and scraped back many times, surfaces becoming richly but delicately layered, like an archaeological site. Lived in Marlborough, Wiltshire.

Peter PRETSELL 1942– Printmaker, draughtsman and teacher, born in Edinburgh, where he attended the College of Art, 1960–5. He lectured at Nene College, Northampton, 1966–85, then at Edinburgh College of Art. Pretsell was a member of SSA, Printmakers' Council and Edinburgh Printmakers. He showed with Thumb Gallery; and New 57 Gallery and Printmakers' Workshop, both in Edinburgh. Victoria & Albert Museum and Scottish Arts Council hold his work. Lived in Loanhead, Midlothian.

Arthur PRETYMAN: *see* **Arthur Pretyman WALLER**

Bill PRICE 1921– Painter and teacher, born in Swansea. He studied at the College of Art there, Royal College of Art where he won the Rome Scholarship and Bournemouth College of Art briefly during World War II service. Went on to teach at Swansea College of Art. Showed SWG, WAC and Glynn Vivian Art Gallery in Swansea, which holds his work.

E Jessop PRICE 1902– Painter, born in Ashby-de-la-Zouch, Leicestershire, educated locally and in France. She studied with Leonard Fuller at the St Ives School of Painting, at St Martin's School of Art with Archibald Ziegler and with Iain Macnab at Heatherley's School of Fine Art. She was married to the Reverend A Jessop Price and lived for many years in Kent, latterly in Hythe. Was a member of SWA from 1951, also exhibiting at Bradford City Art Gallery, ROI and elsewhere. In 1957 gained freedom of the Worshipful Company of Painter-Stainers.

Joanna PRICE 1956– Painter, born in Ireland, who studied at City and Guilds of London Art School, 1979–82, gaining a scholarship to New York Studio School, 1982–3. In 1991 she won the Grand Prix at Cagnes-sur-Mer, France, International Festival of Painting, and was invited to be British representative there in 1993. Her singular image Small Blue Executive World, part of a series called Golden Handshake, was included in 1993–4 John Moores Liverpool Exhibition. Showed solo at Anna Bornholt Gallery. Lived in London.

Leslie PRICE 1915– Portrait painter, commercial artist and critic who studied at Birmingham College of Art, 1930–4. Exhibited RBSA and elsewhere in Birmingham, where he lived and wrote criticism for the *Birmingham Gazette*.

Rebecca PRICE 1966– Artist who gained an honours degree in fine art, Slade School of Fine Art, 1984–8, then an advanced diploma in film/video from Central St Martins, 1993–4. Awards included The Audrey Wickham Prize, 1985, and a South East Go and See Grant for research in Germany, 1995. She had a South East Arts residency, St Andrew's First School, Cobham, 1992; in 1993 she held residencies at Snape Maltings Concert Hall and William Cobbett School, Farnham, again South East Arts. Group exhibitions included Blenheim Gallery, 1988; Diorama Gallery, from 1990; LG, Barbican Centre, 1992; and Electric Lives at Lethaby Gallery, 1994. Later solo exhibitions included Windsor Arts Centre, 1993, and Morley Gallery, 1996. Examples held by Robert Holmes à Court Collection, Perth, Australia, and Leicester County Collection. Lived in Esher, Surrey.

Trevor PRICE 1966– Printmaker, born in Redruth, Cornwall, later diving his time between the county and London. Price used a wide range of printmaking techniques. Abstract works were influenced by years of living by the sea, his more figurative, narrative pieces being a reflection of his life. Price gained a foundation diploma from Falmouth School of Art, 1984–5, then an honours degree in fine art/printmaking from Winchester School of Art, 1985–8. Was elected an associate of RE in 1995. Showed at Christie's Contemporary in Bath, Honor Oak Gallery, Lamont Graphics and elsewhere in two- or three-man shows, later solo exhibitions including Zella Gallery, 1998.

James PRIDDEY 1916–1980 Painter in watercolour and printmaker. Born in Handsworth, Birmingham, Priddey was educated at the Moseley School of Arts and Crafts there and at Birmingham College of Art, 1931–5, with Harold Holden and Arthur Edward Harvey. Priddey was a tireless exhibitor at many venues, including RBA, RBSA, RCamA, RWA, RE and Paris Salon, where he won a bronze medal in 1948 and silver medal in 1949. He had a one-man show at Bilston Art Gallery in 1967. Priddey's illustrated work ranged from the Birmingham telephone directory to the *Birmingham Post* newspaper. South London Art Gallery holds his work. Lived in Harborne, Birmingham.

Phyllis Elsie PRIDE fl. c.1938–1978 Portrait painter and musician, who studied at the Royal Academy of Music. She also studied at Heatherley's School of Fine Art, in 1938, and at the Yellow Door School of Art with Reginald Grenville Eves. Showed RA, ROI, NEAC, RP, and at SWA and RCamA, both of which she was a member. As well as winning an Hon. Mention at Paris Salon, she won a silver medal in 1955 and a gold one five years later. Lived in London.

Margaret PRIEST 1944– Painter, draughtsman and teacher, born in Tyringham, Buckinghamshire. She studied at South-West Essex School of Art, 1963–4, Maidstone College of Art, 1964–7, and Royal College of Art, 1967–70, being among other things a John Minton Scholarship winner. Showed at Tate Gallery, Garage Art Ltd, Arnolfini Gallery in Bristol, Theo Waddington in New York and Toronto, Albemarle Gallery and elsewhere. From 1970–4 taught at Harrow School of Art, then St Martin's School of Art, 1972–6, when she went to live in Toronto, Canada. Her teaching posts there included Guelph University, Toronto, from 1983. Arts Council, British Council and Tate Gallery are among many public collections in Britain and North America holding her work.

Philip Collingwood PRIESTLEY 1901– Painter, especially notable in watercolour, illustrator and teacher, born in Leicester. Studied at the Art College there under John Frederick Pettinger and George Ingles, 1915–20. Priestley went on to teach at Maidenhead College of Art and drew cartoons for *Maidenhead Advertiser*, his local paper in Berkshire. Showed at Nottingham Art Gallery and Museum, RBA, RI, Leicester Museum and Art Gallery and elsewhere.

Andrew PRIESTMAN 1953– Versatile artist and potter, born in London, who did a foundation course at Kingston College of Art, 1971–2, in 1973 moving to southwest Scotland. From 1973–92 Priestman worked as a potter while painting and sculpting, from 1993 concentrating on paintings and collages. He said that what he produced was "concerned with object and space: juxtaposition. I am inspired by landscape, still-life, surface, old buildings, doorways and the patina of age. Sculpting and building with wood, concrete, stone. Heraldry and road signs." England & Co showed Priestman's work.

Bertram PRIESTMAN 1868–1951 Landscape painter in oil, born in Bradford, Yorkshire, studied at the Slade School of Fine Art. Travelled extensively in Europe. Exhibited frequently at RA, also RBA, Goupil Gallery, ROI, Walker Art Gallery, Liverpool, and widely elsewhere in the provinces. His pictures were reproduced by the Medici Society and Frost & Reed. Priestman is noted for his painterly, rather breezy landscapes, which left their mark on the work of his notable pupil Edward Seago. Priestman's pictures are in many provincial galleries in Britain, including Liverpool, Bristol, Birmingham and Manchester, as well as a large number of overseas holdings. Won a series of international medals and was elected RA, 1923. Lived in Crowborough, Sussex.

Kathleen PRIMMER fl. c.1935–1960 Painter, costume designer and illustrator. Born in Palmerston North, New Zealand, and was educated there, Switzerland and France. Studied art at Royal Academy Schools, Central School of Arts and Crafts and in Paris at L'École Nationale des Arts Décoratifs. She was involved in stage work for the Westminster and Scala Theatres before and after World War II, during the war served as a camouflage artist for the Ministry of Civil Defence and also taught for several years in London schools. Published a book on Scandinavian peasant costume. Exhibited RA, RP and elsewhere. Lived in London.

Jean PRIMROSE 1910– Painter who was born in Glasgow. She studied painting under Ralph Middleton Todd at the City and Guilds School of Art, Kennington. Exhibited RA, RBA and at Bradford Art Gallery, occasionally just signing work J P. Lived in London.

Nigel PRINCE 1963– Sculptor and lecturer, born in Wolverhampton. He studied at Stourbridge College of Art, 1981–2, then fine art at Liverpool Polytechnic, gaining a first-class honours degree, 1982–5. He was a John Moores Fellow, 1985–6. Went on to work as a visiting lecturer at Tate Gallery, City College, Bluecoat Gallery and Polytechnic in Liverpool and Birmingham Polytechnic. Showed at Nicholas Treadwell Gallery from 1985; in touring exhibition Merseyside Artists 3, Walker Art Gallery, Liverpool, 1986–7; and his work Between the Arch and the Dome was included in the Norwich Gallery/Kent Institute of Art and Design 1992 East & South show. Had a solo show at Bluecoat Gallery, 1986. Prince's work used a number of materials and dealt with various sculptural concerns, ranging from the sensual and organic to geometric and architectural, surface being a key interest. Lived in Edgbaston, Birmingham.

Sybil Norah PRINGLE 1913– Artist with a special interest in metalwork who was born in Barrow-in-Furness, Lancashire. She studied at Edinburgh College of Art from 1939–43 and 1946–7, interrupted by the war, her teachers including Hubert Wellington and Robert Lyon. Showed SSA, SSWA and elsewhere in Scotland. Lived in Newcastle upon Tyne, Northumberland.

Anthony PRINSEP 1908– Sculptor, painter and illustrator, born in Shenstone, Staffordshire. Although he attended the Royal Military Academy, Sandhurst, and also studied for a period as a veterinary surgeon, Prinsep in 1931–5 studied at the Central School of Arts and Crafts, as well as attending other art schools. Took part in group shows at Leicester, Wildenstein, Mayor and St George's Galleries and had solo shows at Beaux Arts Gallery and Drian Gallery. During World War II Prinsep lived in West Africa, later settling at Snekkersten, Denmark. Tate Gallery archive holds his Self-Portrait, 1951, under the name Anthony Levett-Prinsep.

Arthur PRITCHARD 1927–1993 Painter, born in Llanystumdwy, Carnarvonshire. He became an articled pupil in county surveyor's office, Carnarvon, qualified as a chartered surveyor and was promoted eventually to area engineer in Gwynedd County Council's highways department. Began painting seriously in the mid-1950s. Was made an associate of RCamA in 1969. Showed with NWG, Royal National Eisteddfod, David Griffiths Gallery in Cardiff, Heal's Mansard Gallery, Tegfryn Gallery in Menai Bridge and elsewhere. WAC holds his work. Lived in Bodffordd, Anglesey. His brother was the artist Gwilym Pritchard.

Gwilym PRITCHARD 1931– Painter in oil and tempera, notable for landscapes and still life, born at Llanystumdwy, Carnarvonshire. He was married to the artist Claudia Williams, his brother being the painter Arthur Pritchard. Studied at Normal College, Bangor, and Birmingham College of Art, 1960–4, where he did little painting, concentrating on ceramics and weaving. Held several teaching posts, latterly at Friars' School, Bangor, settling at Anglesey, an area of key importance to his painting. Decided to become a full-time artist in 1973, settling near the border with England, commissioned work including some for British Army in Belfast. In 1978 an East Midlands Arts Association bursary funded a record of National Trust properties in the St Davids area of Pembrokeshire. In 1979 Pritchard returned to north Wales, where he became a part-time teacher with University College, Bangor's extra-mural department, also teaching at Plas Tanybwlch, Maentwrog. Pritchard was a member of RCamA, also exhibiting with Royal National Eisteddfod, WAC, SEA and NWG. Had regular solo shows, starting with Howard Roberts Gallery, Cardiff, in 1961, other venues including New Art Centre and Heal's Mansard Gallery. St Michael's Church, Ruabon, Clwyd, has a mosaic by Pritchard, whose work is in many public collections, including University College of Wales, Aberystwyth, WAC and CASW.

Ivor Mervyn PRITCHARD fl. from c. 1925–1948 Etcher and architect, born at Beaumaris, Anglesey, Wales. After university in north Wales and the Architectural Association in London, Pritchard attended the Royal Academy Schools and Central School of Arts and Crafts. Exhibited RA, Paris Salon and in Austria. Lived in London.

Dora PRITCHETT 1878– Painter and miniaturist, born in Folkestone, Kent. She studied at Goldsmiths' College School of

Art under Frederick Marriott, Camberwell School of Arts and Crafts and Redhill School of Art under William Todd-Brown. Showed at RA, SWA and with St Ives Society of Artists. Lived in Mousehole, Cornwall.

Peter PROBYN 1915–1991 Cartoonist, teacher and wine buff, son of Frank Probyn, professor of horn at Royal College of Music. His talent for drawing emerged early at Imperial Services College, Windsor, after which he went into advertising. This career was terminated early when he developed tuberculosis, but by then he was placing work with magazines such as *Punch*, *The Tatler* and *Lilliput*. After teaching art in a school soon after World War II, Probyn went to live in Thaxted, Essex, where he developed as a successful artist and designer, then settled in Hassocks, Sussex. In 1962 was appointed art advisor to East Sussex Education Authority, became a governor of Brighton College of Art and then retired in 1980 to resume freelance work. Was a keen member of The Wine Society, illustrating its publications.

Patrick PROCKTOR 1936– Painter, printmaker and stage designer, notable for fluent watercolours, who travelled extensively abroad. He was born in Dublin, Ireland, his father dying in 1940, so was brought up in England by his mother and maternal grandparents, his grandmother being a talented amateur painter. After Highgate School, where his art master was the painter Kyffin Williams, Procktor worked for a builders' merchants, 1952–4, then was conscripted into Royal Navy as a student of Russian. Graduated from Slade School of Fine Art, 1958–62, teachers including William Coldstream, whose old London flat he later lived in for many years. With scholarship aid, 1962, travelled in Italy and Greece. In 1963 the first of a long series of solo shows at Redfern Gallery fully sold before opening. Foreign exhibitions included Galerie Biedermann, Munich, 1976. In 1978 Procktor's prints for *The Rime of the Ancient Mariner* by Samuel Taylor Coleridge were published as a book. There was a retrospective of aquatints at Birmingham Museum and Art Gallery in 1985 and a touring show of paintings, 1959–89, from Davies Memorial Gallery, Newtown, in 1989–90. In 1984, the year his wife Kirsten died, Procktor painted a reredos for Chichester Cathedral. Many public collections hold his work. His autobiography *Self-Portrait* was published in 1991. Procktor was elected to RWS, 1981, RE in 1991, and RA, 1996.

Anthony PROCTER 1913–1993 Painter in oil and pencil draughtsman, born in Cheadle Hulme, Cheshire, educated at Bootham School in York and at Manchester University. As a schoolboy in York Procter spent much time sketching the Minster, the many churches and tortuous streets of the city; northern English and Scottish landscapes and the skylines of big cities remained favourite subjects. Having studied electrical engineering Procter went into industry, from 1936–71 being with George Angus Oil Seal Division, eventually as managing director; because of a takeover by Dunlop he left, and was managing director of Newall's Insulation Company, 1971–6. Formal art school training was limited to two nights a week for over a decade at Newcastle University, where he obtained a certificate in fine art. Travelled extensively in Europe, America, Mexico, India, Australia and Japan, using the experiences in his paintings. Mixed exhibitions included RA, RSA, ROI, NEAC, UA, RBA and Royal Glasgow Institute of the Fine Arts; at Paris Salon gained an Hon. Mention, 1967, Silver Medal, 1978. Had a solo show at Laing Art Gallery, Newcastle upon Tyne, 1971, then exhibited regularly, with a memorial show at Vicarage Cottage Gallery, North Shields, 1994. It, Procter & Gamble and other collections hold examples. Lived at Ponteland, Northumberland.

Brenda PROCTER 1948– Artist in mixed media and teacher, born in Manchester. She studied at the fine art department of the University of Newcastle upon Tyne, 1966–71, and in Italy. From 1971–5 she managed the Portfolio Gallery in Scunthorpe, then farmed with her husband at Waterbeck, Lockerbie, Dumfriesshire. She was a gallery artist with Colin Jellicoe Gallery, Manchester. Also exhibited at Howarth Gallery, Accrington; Laing and Hatton Art Galleries in Newcastle; and elsewhere in Lincolnshire and Scotland. "In my work I want to express awareness, spontaneity and intimacy. Main influences are Chagall, Picasso, Schwitters and a meeting with John Heartfield when a student. Teaching is very important to me."

Dod PROCTER 1892–1972 Painter, born in London, married to the artist Ernest Procter. She studied art with Stanhope Forbes in Newlyn around 1907–8 and at Atelier Colarossi, Paris. Was a prolific exhibitor, at RA, to which she was elected in 1942; member of NEAC; Fine Art Society, where she had a joint show with her husband in 1913; Leicester Galleries; Barbizon House, and elsewhere. In 1920 she helped her husband to decorate the Kokine Palace in Rangoon, Burma. The 1920s were the high point of her career, her 1926 picture Morning, now in Tate Gallery, being acclaimed picture of the year at RA in 1927. Dod Procter went on to live in Newlyn, Cornwall, and is most associated with pictures of the people and countryside in that area. In 1990 a show at Laing Art Gallery, Newcastle upon Tyne, paid tribute to both Dod and Ernest Procter, having originated as a Dod-only exhibition in Liverpool and Penzance.

Kenneth PROCTER 1909– Artist in oil, pastel and gouache, and teacher, born in New Brighton, Cheshire, who was married to the artist Majorie Procter. He studied at Liverpool City School of Art, 1935–7, under Will C Penn, then at St Martin's School of Art, 1945–7, under James Bateman. He taught at Ealing School of Art, 1947–74. Showed with RA, RBA, RI, PS and RSMA and had a solo exhibition at Temple Gallery, Llandrindod Wells, 1968. Lived at Woonton, Herefordshire.

Marjorie PROCTER 1918– Painter, draughtsman and teacher, born in Birmingham but educated in Widnes, Lancashire. She studied at Liverpool City School of Art, 1935–40, and taught for a period during World War II in Liverpool, eventually joining the staff of Ealing School of Art. Showed RA, NS, RSMA, Liverpool Academy and elsewhere. She originally exhibited under her maiden name Marjorie Palmer, but changed after marrying the artist Kenneth Procter in 1964. Lived in Ealing, west London, latterly in Woonton, Herefordshire.

Cecile A PROCTOR 1897– Artist, notably in pastel and pen and ink, born and lived in London. She studied at Chelsea School of art with William Wood, also at St John's Wood and Byam Shaw Schools. Showed extensively in London area, notably with RA, LG, NEAC, ROI and SWA. Campden Hill Club member.

Oleg PROKOFIEV 1928–1998 Artist and writer, born in Paris. From 1936–71 he lived in Moscow, then moved to England, settling in southeast London, becoming a full-time artist. Studied at Moscow Art School, 1944–7, from 1949–52 working in the studio of the painter R Falk. He later studied the history of art in India and Southeast Asia and published two books on the subject in 1964–7. Meanwhile he painted, showing twice, at exhibitions of young artists, in 1958–64. Obtained a Gregory Fellowship in Painting at Leeds University, 1972–4, lived in Paris, 1977–8, then after a visit to America's east coast turned to Constructivist-style sculpture, sometimes painted, using wood. Prokofiev showed in groups at ICA, Pratt Institute in New York and Institut Audio-Visuel, Paris. Had a solo show at Leeds City Art Gallery in 1974, then showed in Britain and abroad, later exhibitions including Woodlands Art Gallery, 1985. Prokofiev, son of the Russian composer Sergei Prokofiev, was married to Camilla Gray, author of the pioneering study *The Russian Experiment in Art 1863–1922*.

Jane PROPHET 1964– Artist, teacher and speaker, who gained a first-class honours degree, fine art, at Sheffield City Polytechnic, 1984–7; her master's in electronic graphics at Coventry Polytechnic, 1988–9; and her doctorate in arts education at Warwick University, 1990–5. Between 1987–91, Prophet was visiting lecturer in performance, digital media and video at various colleges of education, then was principal lecturer in media, 1991–5, University of Westminster, head of digital media research and video (school of design and media). Prophet was a member of Cutting Edge, National Research Group for Women in Design & Media. Exhibitions, papers and presentations included Sheffield Media Show, 1992, speaker on An Art-Historical Approach to Computer Images; Circles of Light, 1994, Westminster Arts-funded interactive installation combining live-action video with computer-generated backgrounds; European Media Art Festival, Osnabrück, Germany, where she spoke on TechnoSphere: artificial Life on the Internet, 1995; and Video Positive 97, Manchester Museum of Science & Industry, 1997, where she took part in CD Forest.

Marsden PROPHET 1933–1989 Painter, born in St Ives, Cornwall. He settled in Penzance and studied with E Bouverie Hoyton at the School of Art there, 1944, at Huddersfield School of Art, 1950, and in the following year in Germany, also having lessons from the illustrator Heath Robinson. William Harry Marsden Prophet specialised in murals and was well known in west Cornwall for his pirate and smuggling scenes. The Meadery restaurants, St Ives Guildhall and The Pirates Rugby Clubroom featured his work, which was also reproduced in print form. Prophet had a tragic end, committing suicide days after being arrested on suspicion of indecent assault and gross indecency; he was found dead in a car with a pipe leading from the exhaust. Was a member of the Penzance Club.

Helga PROSSER 1932– Sculptor and teacher who was born in Natal, South Africa, studying fine art in Cape Town from the mid-1950s. In 1959 she lectured for a short time at Port Elizabeth Technical College, then lived in London and Cambridge in 1959–61, moving to Cardiff in 1961 and five years later to Michaelston-y-Fedw, Newport, in south Wales. In early 1970s left for Ahmadu Bello University, Nigeria, to teach sculpture. Apart from South African exhibitions showed at RA, Paris Salon, SWG, WAC and had solo show at Woodstock Gallery.

James Stanley PROSSER 1887–1959 Artist, notably of watercolours and spacious landscapes, born in Manchester, but who grew up and was based in Belfast, Northern Ireland. Prosser studied at Belfast School of Art and was apprenticed as a lithographer. He was a member of RUA and Ulster Arts Club and was briefly president of the Ulster Society of Painters. Also showed with RHA, New Irish Salon and 1924 British Empire Exhibition at Wembley. The Linen Hall, Belfast, which holds Prosser's work, held a show of his pictures in 1986.

Alastair PROUD 1954– Artist and naturalist with a special interest in birds of prey and game birds. Was educated in Dublin at St Andrew's College. After leaving art college in 1979 painted widely for galleries and publishers. Was a member of SWLA. Also did work for Henry Brett Galleries, Royal Society for the Protection of Birds and Patricia Wells Gallery, Thornbury. Settled in Wales at Carmarthen, Dyfed.

Alexander PROUDFOOT 1878–1957 Sculptor. Born in Liverpool, he studied at Glasgow School of Art under Johan Keller. He was to become head of sculpture at the School, 1912–28. The Scottish National Portrait Gallery, Edinburgh, and Kelvingrove Art Gallery, Glasgow, hold his work. He was to complete war memorials at several sites in Scotland. Exhibited RA, RSA, Walker Art Gallery, Liverpool, and the Royal Glasgow Institute of the Fine Arts. Sometimes signed work A P. Lived in Glasgow.

James PROUDFOOT 1908– Painter, especially of portraits, and artist in black-and-white, born in Perth. Studied at Perth Academy, then Heatherley's School of Fine Art, Goldsmiths' College School of Art and in Paris. Arts Club and Chelsea Arts Club member. He exhibited RP and ROI, being a member of both, RA, RSA and NEAC. Lived in London.

M Eyre PROUDMAN 1906– Painter, illustrator, printmaker and designer of many objects, born in Oxton, Cheshire, whose correct name was Maureen Patey Proudman (Eyre was her maiden name). She graduated in art in Rome, also studying at Royal College of Art under Ernest Tristram and William Rothenstein. Exhibited in Italy, India, Leicester Galleries, Walker Art Gallery, Liverpool, and elsewhere in the provinces. Lived in London and later in Romsey, Hampshire.

Rod PROUSE 1945– Watercolourist and printmaker, born in England, but his parents emigrated with him to Toronto, Canada, when he was only two years old. He studied at Ontario College of Art, then worked in the commercial art world before going freelance and travelling widely. His first solo show at Canadian Fine Arts Gallery, Toronto, was extremely successful, with others following. John Noott Twentieth Century, Broadway, gave him a shared show in 1990. Prouse's work was deft, colourful and witty, reminiscent of Dufy. Lived near Halifax, Nova Scotia.

Margaret Fisher PROUT 1875–1963 Painter and teacher in the Impressionist style of figures, landscapes and still life. Born in London, only daughter of the artist Mark Fisher. Studied with her father and at the Slade School of Fine Art, 1894–7, under Fred Brown, where she was considered an outstanding student. Being rather diffident, she did not push to exhibit, although she eventually taught life classes at the Hammersmith School of Art. Married a farmer, John Prout, and living in the country and with him creating gardens provided subjects for her work. After World War I became frequent exhibitor at London galleries, RA, NEAC, RWS, RWA and extensively abroad. Her watercolours became noted for their brilliance. She employed unconventional techniques such as washing out work under the tap, using chinese white and charcoal in unusual ways. Often made oil studies for watercolours, reversing the normal process. British Museum, Contemporary Art Society and Chantrey Bequest bought her work, which is in many foreign galleries. Lived at Pett Level, Sussex. She was given a retrospective at Worthing Art Gallery, 1961, memorial exhibition RWS, 1966, retrospective Blond Fine Art, 1979.

Dora PROWER 1907–1996 Versatile painter, draughtsman and ceramist, sister of the artist Margaret Mee, she was born in Chesham, Buckinghamshire. Spent several years at Watford School of Art. Prower travelled to much of Europe, especially to the Mediterranean countries, Asia, Africa and South America. For many years she had a house at Molini-di-Triora, in the Ligurian Mountains of north Italy. Sketches made on her travels were worked up into larger oils at her studio in Hampstead, north London, where she had a kiln and made ceramics and held annual shows. Exhibitions also included Collectors' Gallery, 1962; John Whibley Gallery, from 1963; St Albans Gallery, in St Albans, from 1965; Gordon Maynard, Welwyn Garden City, from 1968; and Burgh House.

Gidleigh PROWZ: *see* **Roger HALLETT**

Dunstan PRUDEN 1907–1974 Sculptor and craftsman in a variety of materials, including silver and ivory. He was born Alfred Charles Pruden in London, changing his name to Dunstan upon conversion to Catholicism. After private education he studied at Central School of Arts and Crafts, learning silversmithing from Onslow Whiting; was then assistant to the London goldsmith F Morton Crookes. An early a disciple of Eric Gill, Pruden was recommended by Gill to make a new altar cross for Exeter College, Oxford, which established his reputation as a consummate craftsman. In 1934 became a full member of the Gill-inspired Guild of St Joseph and St Dominic in Ditchling, Sussex. St Dominic's Press published his book *Silversmithing*. Taught at Brighton College of Art for over 30 years. Pruden carried out hundreds of ecclesiastic commissions, the climax being the gold chalice for the Metropolitan Cathedral, Liverpool. When he was finally crippled by multiple sclerosis his second wife, the writer Winefride Wilson, took over the running of his workshop. Lived latterly at Burgess Hill, Sussex.

Coela PRYCE HARRISON fl. c.1920–1955 Watercolourist, born in Thorpe, Norfolk, into a military family. She was educated at St Felix's School, Southwold. Studied art with Leonard Fuller at the St Ives School of Painting, at Heatherley's School of Fine Art with Iain Macnab and with David Cox in East Anglia. As well as exhibiting overseas she showed in England with RWS, RI and in Norfolk. Lived at Dedham, Essex.

Tim PRYKE 1966– Artist, born in Hassocks, Sussex, who studied at Northbrook College, Worthing, 1989–90, and Coventry University, 1990–3. His work was included in Art on The Move, Coventry, 1992, the Sussex Open in Brighton, 1993, and the 1993–4 John Moores Liverpool Exhibition. Had a solo exhibition at Tower Bridge Piazza, 1993. Lived in Stoke, Coventry, Warwickshire.

Gerald Spencer PRYSE 1881–1956 Watercolourist, printmaker and poster designer who studied art in London and Paris. Was commissioned in the Army and completed war posters. Exhibited extensively at Alpine Gallery, also at RA, RSA, Leicester Galleries and Royal Glasgow Institute of the Fine Arts. British Museum and Victoria & Albert Museum hold his work. Lived in London and was a member of Art Workers' Guild, 1911–14. His daughter was the artist Tessa Spencer Pryse (see entry under Spencer).

Ieuan Meirion PUGH 1939– Painter, graphic artist and teacher, born in Aberystwyth, CardiganshireAttended Swansea College of Art, 1958–62, and Cardiff College of Art, 1962–3. Later teaching appointments included Birmingham, Manchester, London and Salisbury College of Art. Group shows included Glynn Vivian Art Gallery, Swansea, and Polytechnic of Central London, which holds his work. Among solo exhibitions were The Red Noise at Salford City Art Gallery; Written Treeforms and Other Poems at Compendium 2; and Bangor Art Gallery.

Peter Rose PULHAM 1910–1956 Painter and photographer, born in London. He studied at Architectural Association School of

Architecture, 1927–8, then at Oxford University. Was a member of the Association for five years from 1926. During the 1930s Pulham made his name as a photographer, working for *Harper's Bazaar*, but his association with Surrealist art circles in Paris led to his taking up painting full-time in 1938. Late in World War II Pulham returned to Paris, but he had one-man shows at Redfern Gallery in 1947, and Hanover Gallery, 1950. Two years later his work appeared in Recent Trends in Realist Painting at ICA. Died in poverty at Conives, Indre, France, where he was reduced to painting on roof slates as he could not afford canvas or wood, related in Theodora FitzGibbon's autobiography *Love Lies A Loss*, 1985. The Surrealist André Masson was a keen collector of Pulham's work, also held by the Tate Gallery.

Margaret Ida Elizabeth PULLAN 1907– Painter, born in Saharanpur, Uttar Pradesh, India, her father being a member of the Indian Civil Service. She schooled in England and studied art privately. Showed with RBA, RP, UA, in the provinces and at Paris Salon, where among awards she gained Gold and Silver Medals. Rugby Art Gallery holds her work. Lived latterly at Tunbridge Wells, Kent.

Tessa PULLAN 1953– Sculptor. She served a three-year apprenticeship in France with the sculptor John Skeaping, 1971–4. From 1974–7 Pullan did a diploma course at City and Guilds of London Art School, then from 1977–80 undertook postgraduate studies at Royal Academy Schools. She then worked at her own studios in Sandwich, Kent, and Aberystwyth, Wales. Pullan carried out a number of commissions, including a bronze statue of a horse for Lloyds Bank, Cambridge, and several items for Paul Mellon, including a bronze portrait of him, 1984. Animals were a major feature of Pullan's work, in various materials, which could be directly representational or highly stylised. She showed at Guildhall, 1976; at RA from 1978; with Cork Street Fine Arts from 1982; with Quinton Green Fine Art from 1984; and at John Hunt Redchurch Galleries, 1996. Pullan's work is in a number of international private collections. She was a member of the Society of Equestrian Artists and an associate of RBS.

Edward PULLÉE 1907– Artist mainly in oil and watercolour, although earlier work involved printmaking, and teacher. He was born in London, his wife was the artist Margaret Pullée, his son the artist Michael Pullée and his full name was Ernest Edward Pullée. Studied at Dover School of Art, 1922–6, then Royal College of Art, 1926–30. First taught at Cheltenham School of Art, 1930–4, was then principal of Gloucester School of Art until 1939, when he went to Portsmouth. In 1945 was appointed principal of Leeds College of Art for 10 years, moving to Leicester College of Art where he was increasingly involved in art education nationally and internationally. From 1967–74 was chief officer of the Summerson Council. Pullée first showed at RA and NEAC, of which he was a life member, in 1931, also exhibiting in various London and provincial galleries. Leeds City Art Gallery holds two oils by him and he is in collections in Wakefield and Leicester. Lived in Chichester, Sussex.

Margaret PULLÉE 1910– Artist mainly in oil and gouache, born in New York, America, full name Winifred Margaret Pullée. She was married to the painter Edward Pullée and mother of the artist Michael Pullée. She studied at Chelsea School of Art, 1927–8, then Royal College of Art, 1928–32. She exhibited widely in provincial and London galleries, notably RA and NEAC of which she was a member for many years, and was notable for amusing pictures of shops. Leeds City Art Gallery holds her gouache The Opening of an Exhibition, 1948. Lived in Chichester, Sussex.

William PULLEN 1961– Artist working in oil, pure egg tempera, watercolour and silverpoint, born in Alton, Hampshire, settling in the county at Liss. He gained his first-class honours/master's degree from Edinburgh's University and College of Art, 1979–84. Teachers included John Johnstone and David Evans. In 1984 won the John Kinross Travelling Scholarship to Florence, awarded by RSA, and most of his work remained "based on subject matter drawn from Italian expeditions". Pullen was given basic instruction on making gesso panels by John Busby at the College, but otherwise taught himself egg tempera technique. His tempera work was "based structurally on the ideas of later American abstract painters, such as Diebenkorn, Marden and Motherwell". Larger oil paintings from the late 1980s took "years to complete". Group exhibitions from 1984 included Ancrum Gallery, Scotland; RA Summer Exhibitions, from 1986; Hunting Group National Art Competition, 1987, winning first prize, and Piccadilly Gallery from that year; and Bohun Gallery, Henley-on-Thames, 1991. Also in 1991 had a solo show at Bedales School, Petersfield. For several years was a committee member of Fry Art Gallery, Saffron Walden, which holds his work.

Wynn PULLEN: *see* **WYNN**

Phyllis Mary PULLING 1892–1951 Painter, poster artist and printmaker, born and lived in London. Studied at the London School of Art, St John's Wood School of Art and the Royal College of Art. Exhibited RA, SWA, Goupil Gallery and Walker Art Gallery, Liverpool, often views in southern Europe. Was a member of the Ridley Art Club. Pulling was a versatile artist, producing posters for the British Empire Exhibition at Wembley, 1924, also providing decorations for bomb-damaged shop fronts in London during World War II.

Charles PULSFORD 1912–1989 Artist and teacher, born in Leek, Staffordshire, married to the stained glass artist Bronwen Gordon. Pulsford studied at Edinburgh College of Art, 1933–6. In 1937 he attended the Patrick Allan–Fraser School of Art, Hospitalfield, Arbroath, had a postgraduate year in 1938, in 1938–9 gaining a travelling scholarship. His fellowship at Edinburgh College of Art, 1939–47, was interrupted by two years' war service. He was elected an associate of the RSA in 1959, the first abstract artist so honoured. Pulsford taught at Edinburgh College of Art, 1947–60, then for four years was initially a teacher at Loughborough College of Art before being made vice-principal and head of fine art at Wolverhampton

Polytechnic. He retired in 1972 after a period as a visiting lecturer at the University of Edinburgh's architecture department. That was the year he published his collection of theoretical writings, *The Creative Cell*. As well as group shows he exhibited widely in solo shows, initially at French Institute, Edinburgh, 1951; shared several shows at Gimpel Fils; had one-mans at Stirling and Cambridge Universities; and was given a studio show of works on paper at William Hardie Gallery, Glasgow, in 1992. Scottish Arts Council holds his work. Lived in Cambridge.

Michael PUNT 1946– Sculptor, draughtsman and teacher in whose work allusion and wit played an important role. Born in London, he studied at Bath Academy of Art, 1964–8, then after working as a toy designer he taught from 1974, being senior lecturer in sculpture at Newport College of Art. Mixed shows included National Eisteddfod, 1969; National Museum of Wales, Cardiff, from 1975; Arts Council tour Six Sculptors, 1979; St Paul's Gallery, Leeds, 1982; and Aspects of Gaia, Ars Electronica, Linz, Austria, 1989. Had a solo show at Ikon Gallery, Birmingham, 1970, later ones including Hull College of Art Gallery, 1981, and Ikon, 1984. Punt also contributed to commercial videos. Lived at Aylburton Common, near Lydney, Gloucestershire.

Lesley PUNTON 1969– Artist using photography, born in Falkirk, Stirlingshire, who studied at the School of Art, Glasgow, where she continued to live, 1986–92. Exhibitions included Speed, Transmission Gallery, Glasgow, 1991; Love at First Sight, 1992; Home and Away, Intermedia Gallery, Glasgow, 1993; and in 1994 both Revisions, Fotomuseum, Munich, Germany, and New Art in Scotland, Centre for Contemporary Arts, Glasgow.

Alice PURCELL 1959– Designer, painter, sculptor and artist in mixed media. She studied at Edinburgh College of Art, Edinburgh University and Royal Academy of Dramatic Art for theatre design and scene painting. Took part in exhibitions which included animated boxes and objects and performances. In England & Co's 1992 Art in Boxes show she exhibited Tomb I.

Keith PURSER 1944– Painter, born in Bromley, Kent, who attended Sidcup School of Art, 1960–2. Travelled on the continent and the Middle East. He spent some years in Cornwall and Lincolnshire, but was mainly based near Rye, Sussex, where he was a member of the Rye Society of Artists and where the Art Gallery holds his work. Purser said that finding ways of depicting landscape where it meets the sea, "self-renewing, as regularly variable as the English weather", was a key theme of his work, as in his solo show at Jonathan Clark Fine Art, 1997.

Rodella PURVES 1945– One of Britain's leading botanical artists, Purves was born in Paisley, Renfrewshire, studying at St Margaret's School, Edinburgh. In that city she won a diploma in agricultural botany from East of Scotland College of Agriculture, 1962–4, and another in seed testing from the National Institute of Agricultural Botany, Cambridge, in 1967. Purves was employed by the Department of Agriculture for Scotland, 1964–8; Department of Agriculture, Palmerston North, New Zealand, 1968–9; and Royal Botanic Garden, Edinburgh, 1969–76. As an exhibit designer for the Chelsea Flower Show she won a silver medal, with gold medals for similar work at the Royal Highland Show. Her work was included in specialist and consumer publications as well as several books. Group exhibitions included International Exhibition of Botanical Drawings, The Hunterdon Art Center, Clinton, New Jersey, 1977; The Plant in 20th century Botanical Illustration, a Scottish Arts Council touring show, 1980; and in flower picture exhibitions at Broughton Gallery, Biggar, from 1987. In 1996 City Art Centre, Edinburgh, gave Purves a 20–year retrospective.

Tom PURVIS 1888–1959 Poster designer and painter, born in Bristol, son of a master mariner turned artist who was assisted by Tom. Purvis' father financed a first term at Camberwell School of Art, scholarships keeping him there for three-and-a-half years. He also studied with Degas and Sickert. Spent six years with the advertising agency Mather & Crowther, then two at The Avenue Press to learn practical lithographic printing while freelancing. In World War I served in Flanders as a captain in the Artists' Rifles and was wounded. Then worked for *Pan* and *London Magazine* and developed his distinctive poster style – flat areas of brilliant adjacent colour with no dividing line – that earned him much money and the title The King of the Hoardings. Did his finest designs for London North Eastern Railway, Shell, Yardley, Aquascutum, London Underground and Austin Reed. Purvis said: "I loathe the word artist. Personally I am proud of being called a Master Craftsman." In 1930 he helped form the Society of Industrial Artists; became one of the first Royal Designers of Industry in 1936, and in 1939 was elected Master of the RDI Faculty. During World War II he was an official artist for the Ministry of Supply and firms such as Pilkington, Rolls-Royce and Cammell Laird. After the war Purvis turned to portrait painting and, having become a Roman Catholic, religious works. He was buried at Buckfast Abbey, Devon. In 1990 the National Railway Museum, York, held an exhibition of posters by Purvis from its extensive collection.

Doris PUSINELLI fl. from c.1918–1976 Portrait, figure and flower painter, notable as a watercolourist. Pusinelli was a member of RI and PS, who also showed at RA, RBA and SWA. In 1927 she shared a show with William Milner at Dover Gallery. Pusinelli did commissioned work for such companies as Goodyear and Dubarry and in mid-1930s published a series of articles on watercolour painting in *The Artist*. Lived in Bosham, Sussex.

Salliann PUTMAN 1937– Painter in oil and watercolour and teacher, born in London, who studied at Redland Teacher Training College, Bristol, 1955–7, then obtained a fine art honours degree from West Surrey College of Art and Design, Farnham, 1988–93. Taught in her own studio and elsewhere, including Philipps House, Dinton. Putman painted still life, interiors and landscapes and admired Bonnard, Morandi and Vuillard. Although she preferred not to accept commissions, she chose to paint a number of watercolours for REME at Arborfield, 1990. Awards included PS Willi Hoffman Guth Award, 1989; RWS Open Exhibition Chris Beetles Award, 1990; and RWS Award, 1994. Mixed exhibitions included RA, RI, NEAC, ROI and RBA and many provincial galleries. Had a solo show at Compton Gallery, Windsor, 1986, and Wykeham Gallery, Stockbridge, 1989. Lived in Sunningdale, Berkshire.

Lyn PYATT 1946– Painter, printmaker and teacher, born in Bedford, whose Zen beliefs led her to seek the ordinary and miniscule in landscape. She attended Luton School of Art, 1946–67, completing her studies at Coventry College of Art with a degree in fine art, 1969. She taught at W R Tuson College in Preston, Lancashire, where she lived, also Lancaster College of Adult Education and Lancaster and Morecambe College of Further Education. Showed widely and was included in Lancashire South of the Sands, which toured from the County and Regimental Museum, Preston, 1988. Work in many private collections in Europe, North America and Australia.

Susan PYE 1942– Artist and designer, born in London, who studied at Wimbledon and Brighton Schools of Art, 1958–62. Marriage and family commitments delayed Pye in fulfillin g her early promise, the acquisition of a suitable studio in themid-1980s allowing her to work more expansively. Expressionist, abstracted studio still lifes were a key theme. Group shows included Another Pair of Eyes, Michael Parkin Gallery, 1984; Cleveland International Drawing Biennale, 1989; Small is Beautiful, Flowers East, 1992; and The Discerning Eye, Mall Galleries, where she was a prize winner, 1996. Later solo shows included Art Space, 1997. Later commissions included a carpet design for Mercury House atrium, Cable & Wireless; and a painting for Sutton House, National Trust Foundation for Art.

William PYE 1938– Sculptor, artist in film, musician and teacher, born in London, where he continued to live. He studied at Wimbledon School of Art, 1958–61, then Royal College of Art, 1961–5, under Bernard Meadows. Pye taught at Central School of Art and Design, 1965–70, at Goldsmiths' College School of Art, 1970–5, the following year being visiting professor at California State University. As well as taking part in group shows in Britain and abroad Pye had his first solo show at Redfern Gallery in 1966, the first of several, other notable shows being at Great Hall and City Museum, Winchester, 1979, and University College, Aberystwyth, 1980. His commissions included King's Cross House, Pentonville Road, in London, 1974, and Eastgate Mall, Cincinnati, Ohio, 1978. In 1971 his film *From Scrap to Sculpture* documented the making of the Zemran sculpture, for the South Bank, London. Pye began sculpting aged 12 and his work passed through several phases: sculpture inspired by Greek classical forms; modelled organic forms; work with highly reflective surfaces; forms inspired by the chemical industry; and more ephemeral work employing curtains and shafts of tensioned steel cables. Arts Council, Museum of Modern Art in New York and many British provincial galleries hold Pye's work.

Jessie PYM 1868–1946 Painter who studied at Slade School of Fine Art and in Paris late in the nineteenth century; she also travelled widely on the continent. She was fond of agricultural and horse subjects, notably based on the South Downs. Showed RBA, RI and SWA and lived for some time at Selmeston, Sussex.

Mary PYM 1935– Artist and teacher born in The Hague, Netherlands, who studied at Winchester School of Art, 1954–8, did a postgraduate experimental painting course at Southampton College of Art, 1974–8, and was a part-time teacher from 1985. Took part in mixed shows, including RA Summer Exhibition, Mall Galleries, Thompson's and Llewellyn Alexander Galleries and widely in Hampshire, Surrey, Sussex and Wiltshire. Had a solo exhibition in Southampton, 1965, and in a four-man show at Hambrook Gallery, Chichester, 1997, exhibited small landscapes and seascapes. Lived in Hamble, Hampshire.

Doris PYNE 1910– Artist in wide variety of media, illustrator and teacher, born in Wealdstone, Middlesex. She attended Hornsey School of Art, 1930–4, studying with Douglas Percy Bliss and Norman Janes; then Slade School of Fine Art, with Randolph Schwabe and Adrian Hill. During a long freelance career she accepted commissions for portraits, murals, book illustrations and designs for civic plate. She was a member of SGA, Blackheath and Bromley Art Societies. Also showed with RI, SWA and in France and had a number of solo exhibitions in Norwich and elsewhere. Lived in Chislehurst, Kent.

Q

Jane QUAIL 1936– Sculptor in stone and wood, married to stained glass artist Paul Quail. She was born in India, where at an early age she was influenced by temple carvings, in 1954 spent a year carving at Natal Technical College, Durban, South Africa, then worked at the Cyrene Mission Art School, Harare, in what is now Zimbabwe, moving to England in 1960. Until 1982 Quail mostly made small carvings, then worked mainly on church commissions, including National Shrine, Walsingham; Parish Church, Shipdham; St John the Baptist, Harleston; St Paul's Church, East Ham; and Catholic Church, Queensway. Lived in Gunthorpe, Norfolk.

Paul QUAIL 1928– Stained glass artist, born in Langley, Buckinghamshire, husband of the sculptor Jane Quail. Studied at Chelsea School of Art, 1946–52, teachers including Ceri Richards and Robert Medley, then gained his art teacher's certificate at Brighton College of Art, 1952–3. In 1954 Quail started training in stained glass at the studio of Francis Spear, worked in the studio of J E Nuttgens, 1954–7, then with the firm Lowndes and Drury until 1959, when he went freelance, establishing a studio in Gunthorpe, Norfolk, in 1974. He was a fellow of both The British Society of Master Glass Painters and of the Society of Designer-Craftsmen. Quail carried out extensive commissions, including Ardingly College, Sussex; St Mary's Cadogan Street; Carmel of Our Lady of Walsingham, Langham; Cirencester Agricultural College; and St Anthony Claret Chapel, Buckden Towers, Cambridgeshire.

Michael QUANNE 1941– Painter, born in Surrey, whose family moved to Bethnal Green in London's East End when Quanne was one. During World War II he was evacuated for a time to Torquay. Quanne failed his eleven-plus and aged 16 was arrested for attempted larceny. By the time of his key Camden Arts Centre show in 1985, the longest period he had been out of prison was three years. To accompany that first major show, which was a sell-out, the critic John Berger, a continuing champion of Quanne's, wrote an introduction to his book *Prison Paintings*. Although he has been described as a primitive artist – Quanne was self-taught – the pictures are adept, full of haunting images, wit and irony. Quanne won the Koestler award for prisoners' paintings in 1975. In 1994–5 he had shows at Bruton Street Gallery. Lived in London.

George QUARMBY 1883–1957 Painter. Studied at Holmfirth and Huddersfield Schools of Art, at the Royal College of Art under Édouard Lantéri, Beresford Pite and Gerald Moira and at the Royal Academy Schools under George Clausen, followed by further study in France, Italy and South Africa. Exhibited RA, RBA, NEAC and ROI. The War Artists' Advisory Committee bought his work. From 1946–50 he was on the staff of Goldsmiths' College School of Art. Lived at Blewbury, Berkshire.

Marjorie QUENNELL 1883–1972 Artist in oil, watercolour and black-and-white, writer and mother of the author Sir Peter Quennell. She studied art at the Crystal Palace Studio, in Beckenham and Westminster. Exhibited RA, SWA, Walker Art Gallery in Liverpool and NG. In 1904 she married the architect Charles Henry Bourne Quennell and after his death in 1935 until 1941 was curator of the Geffrye Museum. With her husband she published and illustrated a series of educational books, the first and most popular being *A History of Everyday Things in England*, 1918–34, in four volumes. The others included *Roman Britain*, 1924, and *Classical Greece*, 1932. Lived in Lewes, Sussex.

Bob QUICK 1939– Abstract painter who, after studying accountancy and National Service, attended Croydon and Brighton Colleges of Art. Group exhibitions included Midland Group Gallery, 1971; First International Drawing Biennial, Teesside, 1973; and National Museum of Wales, Cardiff, 1974. WAC holds his large vitreous enamel on steel, Tab, of the same year. From early 1970s had a series of solo shows at Grabowski Gallery, when he was living in London.

Marc QUINN 1964– Sculptor, born in London, who graduated from Cambridge University and was assistant to the sculptor Barry Flanagan. Group exhibitions included Hands, at Grob Gallery, 1991; London, at Karsten Schubert Gallery, 1992; and in 1993 Young British Artists II, at Saatchi Gallery, which holds his work. What constitutes an individual or the life force? were the type of subjects which preoccupied Quinn, as in his Saatchi showing, where the 1991 sculpture Self constituted a head made from nine pints of the artist's blood. Solo exhibitions included Bread Sculpture, Galerie Marquardt, Paris, and Middendorf Gallery, Washington, both 1990; Out of Time, Grob Gallery, 1991; and a major one at South London Gallery, 1998.

Tom QUINN 1918– Painter of romantic landscapes and figurative pictures, in soft colours, son of a commercial lithographer, sometimes known as T W Quinn. He was initially apprenticed to his father's firm, served in World War II in the Royal Air Force and then studied at Camberwell School of Arts and Crafts in the late 1940s. Teachers included Victor Pasmore and Lawrence Gowing. Showed in London and had a solo exhibition at Century Galleries, Henley-on-Thames, 1992. A further one in 1997 reflected the influence on his work of painting in the French studio of his friend Roy Petley.

Michael QUIRKE 1946– Atmospheric painter of townscapes and landscapes in oil and acrylic, who studied at St Martin's School of Art, 1972–5, then worked under Maurice Feild, 1978–88. Had a first solo exhibition at Ophelos Gallery, 1989, later ones including Highgate Fine Art, 1998. Lived in St Ives, Cornwall.

QUIZ: *see* **Powys EVANS**

R

Olivier RAAB 1955– Painter, born in Paris. He studied at École des Arts Decoratifs before spending two years at Chelsea School of Art in London, 1976. On his return to Paris he attended the École des Beaux-Arts, while starting to paint in his studio for a first exhibition at Galerie Étienne de Causans, 1980. Raab went on to show regularly at International Paris Art Fair; Gallery La Gabbiano, Rome; Gallery Fred Lanzenberg, Brussels; and at Robertson's Gallery, Los Angeles; also with CCA Galleries. Raab's first works were influenced by American realist works such as those of Edward Hopper. In Paris he worked on large watercolours depicting interiors in New York and other industrial buildings, light playing an import role. Artists' studios and the Leviathan series were later developments. Raab had the first of several solo exhibitions at Cadogan Contemporary in 1987, the year before he settled in London.

Sam RABIN 1903–1991 Draughtsman, sculptor, printmaker, teacher, actor, wrestler, boxer and singer, born in Cheetham, Manchester, as Samuel Rabinovitch, son of Russian-Jewish exiles. As a schoolboy he aspired to be the world's strongest man and built a powerful physique as well as taking wrestling lessons. Aged 11 he won a scholarship to Manchester School of Art, its youngest-ever pupil, studying with Adolphe Valette. From 1921–4 was at Slade School of Fine Art under Henry Tonks, which helped develop his belief in primacy of drawing. After a study year in Paris, Rabin returned to London and gained a reputation as a sculptor, working on the London Transport headquarters and *Daily Telegraph* building. After in 1928 winning a bronze medal for wrestling at Amsterdam Olympics, Rabin funded his artistic career by professional wrestling, and took part in several feature films. William Roberts' picture Sam Rabin versus Black Eagle was a result of this. Rabin also trained his bass baritone voice, entertaining the troops in World War II and singing for the BBC Light Programme in the late 1940s. In 1949 Rabin was appointed teacher of drawing at Goldsmiths' College School of Art, in 1965 moving to Bournemouth College of Art for 20 years, then teaching at Poole Art Centre. While at Goldsmiths' in 1955 Rabin designed an Underground poster for London Electricity Board. His boxing pictures were first shown at Wildenstein in a mixed show in 1951. Other notable career events were in 1969, winning drawing prize in second International Biennale of Sport in Fine Art, in Madrid; 1974, British Museum acquiring his work; 1977, winning drawing prize at sixth International Biennale of Sport in Fine Art, Barcelona; and 1979, designing the memorial for the boxer Freddie Mills. Rabin's drawings have been compared with those of Degas. He used coloured wax crayon on paper and board, but was secretive about his methods. Died in Poole, Dorset.

Pamela RACHET 1923– Sculptor, painter and illustrator, born in London. Attended Roedean School, studying art with Dorothy Martin, in 1939 having painting lessons from Laura Knight. In 1940 she studied sculpture at Farnham School of Art with the potter Charles Vyse, in 1942 winning a scholarship to Royal College of Art. After wartime service in Women's Royal Naval Service, 1943–5, was at Royal College of Art, 1945–7. Showed at RA from 1942–6 under her maiden name Pamela Ascherson, Contemporary Art Society buying her terracotta Jersey Bull in 1943. Rachet had a solo show at Berkeley Galleries in 1953. During 1958–68 her paintings of circuits and racing cars were bought by the Donnington Park Racing Museum. After marrying in 1947 Rachet had moved to Provence. A year after she wrote and illustrated *C'était Hier – St Rémy de Provence*, in 1988, her self-portrait was bought by the museum there. Rachet's sculptures were exhibited at Duncan Campbell Contemporary Art in 1993 and 1998.

Paul RADCLIFFE 1907– Artist in various media, born in Stourbridge, Worcestershire. He studied at Grimsby School of Art, gaining his diploma in 1927, and Central School of Arts and Crafts. Originally an industrial designer, he became a landscape and portrait painter. He was a founder-member of Saddleworth Art Group and appeared in its show at Woodlands Art Gallery, 1973, among other exhibitions. His works are in public and private collections.

Matthew RADFORD 1953– Painter and teacher, born in London who continued to work there and in New York. Radford was notable for his pictures of urban crowds in movement. He studied at St Albans School of Art, 1971–2, then Camberwell School of Art, 1972–5, when he gained a first-class honours degree. He taught at Camberwell, 1979–83, Drawing Center in New York, 1985–6, then at New York Studio School, 1989–93. Group exhibitions included Royal Festival Hall and RA Diploma Galleries, both 1980; New York Art Now, at Helander Gallery, Palm Beach, 1989; and Mostyn Open Exhibition, Llandudno, 1993. Had solo shows at Letchworth Museum and Art Gallery, 1980, and Kettle's Yard Gallery, Cambridge, 1984; then after extensive showings in New York an exhibition at Houldsworth Fine Art, 1994. Metropolitan Museum of Art in New York, the Public Library there, Morgan Grenfell Ltd and other corporate collections hold examples.

Celeste RADLOFF 1930–1994 Artist without formal training, who painted in the naive style. She was born in Pretoria, South Africa, and married the painter Edward Bishop in 1956, having moved to London, where she settled, in 1952. Showed regularly at RA Summer Exhibitions, also at Grosvenor Gallery, Roland, Browse & Delbanco and elsewhere. Walker Art Gallery in Liverpool holds her work.

Sara RADSTONE 1955– Sculptor, ceramist and teacher, born and lived in London, who attended Hereford College of Art and Design, then Camberwell School of Arts and Crafts, 1976–9. Among her many awards was a Sainsbury Trust Award, 1981, Unilever Prize, 1988, and an Arts Foundation Fellowship, 1993. Had a show with Angus Suttie at Contemporary Applied Arts, 1990, also showing at Galerie L, Hamburg, 1991, and Osiris Gallery in Brussels and Artist of the Day at Angela Flowers Gallery, where she was chosen by Jennifer Lee, both 1994, with a major exhibition at Aberdeen Art Gallery, 1997. Taught widely in Britain and abroad. Victoria & Albert Museum, Contemporary Art Society and British Council hold examples.

Barbara RAE 1943– Painter and teacher, born in Stirlingshire. She studied at Edinburgh College of Art 1961–5 concluding with postgraduate study, in 1966 using a travelling scholarship to work in France and Spain. In 1966–7 was at Moray House College of Education, then taught in Edinburgh Schools until appointments 1972–4 at Aberdeen College of Education, then from 1975 at Glasgow School of Art. In 1984 she was an exchange teacher at University of Maryland. Won a number of awards and prizes, including Arts Council Awards and RSA Guthrie Award and Medal. In 1985 she gained a Scottish Arts Council Grant which permitted her to paint in Spain and New Mexico. Rae was an extremely prolific exhibitor internationally and from 1967, when she had her first solo show at New 57 Gallery, in Edinburgh, was regular at venues including Aberdeen Art Gallery; Scottish Gallery, Edinburgh and London; and Glasgow Print Studio. Her work is in several dozen collections, including Aberdeen Art Gallery, University of Glasgow and British Museum. Rae was a striking landscape painter with a rich palette, yet her pictures sometimes have an intense, brooding quality. Was elected RSA, and RA in 1996.

Fiona RAE 1963– Painter, born in Hong Kong. She studied at Croydon College of Art, 1983–4, and Goldsmiths' College School of Art, 1984–7. The first appearances of this abstract painter were Freeze, London Docklands, 1988, and Promises Promises at Serpentine Gallery, 1989. Other mixed show participations were British Art Show, Glasgow, 1990, the year she had a solo exhibition at Third Eye Centre there. She had another at Waddington Galleries in 1991. Fiona Rae also took part in John Moores Exhibition, Liverpool, 1991–2, and in 1991 was shortlisted for the Turner Prize, at the Tate Gallery. Lived in London.

John RAE 1931– Artist in a wide range of media, architect and teacher, born in Devonshire. He studied painting with W Lyons-Wilson and sculpture with Willi Soukop, and architecture at University College London. As an architect he worked with Maxwell Fry on West African and Indian projects. Taught at Hornsey College of Art, at Architectural Association and University College. Rae was a prizewinner in a competition to redevelop the central area of Dumbarton in the 1950s. Group shows included RWA, Mall Galleries and in Australia. Also held solo shows in Australia, New Zealand and Sweden, and widely in the English provinces and Scotland, with an exhibition for the National Trust Centenary at Petworth House, Sussex. His illustrated *Sketchbook of the World* was privately published in a limited edition. Lived in St Albans, Hertfordshire.

Nicola RAE 1961– Artist in a variety of media, born in Reading, Berkshire, who studied at Kingston Polytechnic; Canterbury College of Art; City of London Polytechnic; and Dieppe Workshop, 1989. She was artist-in-residence, Ashmanor School, Aldershot, 1990; and Atelier des Mouches, Gueberschwihr, France, 1993. Awards included a Special Award, Johnson Wax Kiln Gallery, Farnham, 1991, and gallery prize at Eva Jekel Gallery, 1992. Rae took part in numerous mixed exhibitions, including First Showing, The Showrooms, Wolverhampton, 1985; Woodlands Open, Woodlands Art Gallery, from 1987; ROI Open, Mall Galleries, 1990; RE Open, Bankside Gallery, 1992; and Royal Over-Seas League Open, 1994. Among her solo shows were Battersea Contemporary Art Fair, 1993–4.

Patricia RAE 1933– Portrait sculptor. She studied at Bournemouth School of Art and in Cape Town, South Africa, at Michaelis School of Fine Art, and at Royal College of Art. Rae showed at RA and SPS and was a member of New Grafton Gallery's Portrait Centre. Among her notable sitters were the writer George Mikes, the Sultan of Oman and General Sir Hubert Gough, in the collection of National Portrait Gallery.

Robin RAE 1928– Figurative and abstract artist and teacher, born in London, who worked in oil, etching and three dimensions. He studied at Ealing School of Art and Royal College of Art, teachers including John Nash, Francis Bacon, Rodrigo Moynihan and Edward Bawden. Rae showed considerable early talent, exhibiting at RA in 1946 and by the age of 21 he had held two successful London solo shows, which gained critical appreciation. He taught etching at Edinburgh College of Art and three-dimensional design at Liverpool College of Art, where younger artists found his approach sympathetic. Much of Rae's early painting was destroyed, the fate of most of his sculpture made between 1970–80, when he began painting again. Rae retired from teaching to settle in Bradpole, Bridport, Dorset, where the local landscape was an influence on his work, as were Bacon and Balthus. In the mid-1990s he wrote that he was "painting more at present than at any other time, but avoid the art world and am glad to be quite out of touch." Mixed shows included Aitken Dott in Edinburgh, LG and Young Contemporaries. Showed solo twice with Little Gallery, other one-man exhibitions including Ashmolean Museum in Oxford and Dorchester's Museum & Art Gallery, 1994. Walker Art Gallery, Liverpool, holds his work.

Ronald RAE 1946– Sculptor on a huge scale working in granite, draughtsman and cartoonist, born in Ayr. He produced a weekly cartoon strip for *Ayr Advertiser*, 1960–1, starting to carve granite in the latter year. He attended Glasgow School of Art, 1964–6, staying as technical assistant until 1968. Rae lived in America for a time. His drawings of down-and-outs and alcoholics there and miners formed the subjects of notable exhibitions at Compass Gallery, Glasgow, the first being in 1980; he was included in The Compass Contribution, Tramway, Glasgow, 1990; and in 1997 Cyril Gerber Fine Art, Glasgow, reviewed Rae's work back to the 1970s. Energy, integrity, physical strength combined with gentleness, dedication, sincerity and intensity were attributes of Rae cited in that catalogue. Rae showed in numerous galleries and open spaces in Britain and has sculptures on public sites. His carving The Deposition is in Rozelle Park, Ayr. He was an associate of RBS.

Susan RAE fl. from early 1970s– Painter who studied, 1972–3, at Berkshire College of Art and Design, graduating with an honours degree in fine art from West Surrey College of Art and Design, Farnham, 1973–6. Travelled extensively, including India and Morocco. She showed in mixed exhibitions at Commonwealth Institute, 1979; Bohun Gallery, Henley-on-Thames, from 1983; and Christopher Hull Gallery, 1987. After a solo show at Bohun Gallery, 1986, she had another at Niccol Centre in Cirencester; one at Upton Lodge Galleries, Tetbury, 1989; and Thackeray Gallery, 1991. Stroud District Council holds her work.

Agnes RAEBURN fl. from c.1890–1955 Painter, born and lived in Glasgow, where she studied at the School of Art under Fra Newbery. She was president of the Lady Artists' Club of Glasgow, 1940–3, a member of the council of the RSW, 1948–51, and a member of the SSWA. Exhibited extensively with RSW, also with Royal Glasgow Institute of the Fine Arts, RSA, Walker Art Gallery, Liverpool, in the provinces, on the continent and in America.

Kenneth RAEBURN 1942– Sculptor and teacher, born in Haddington, East Lothian. He studied with Eric Schilsky at school of sculpture, Edinburgh College of Art, graduating in 1966, having a postgraduate scholarship, 1966–7. Travelling scholarships took him to Amsterdam and Greece. Taught in a comprehensive school. Raeburn was a figurative sculptor who was early influenced by Schilsky, Aristide Maillol and Giacomo Manzu. Although he worked in a range of materials, wood was his preferred medium. Raeburn was elected to SSA in 1968. Also showed at RSA, New 57 Gallery and Saltire Gallery, both in Edinburgh, Atholl Gallery in Dunkeld and in France and Switzerland. In 1972 he gained the Saltire Society Award, commendation for a relief mural commissioned by West Lothian County Council. He completed woodcarving for St Columba's Church, West Lothian and a sculpture of a seal with her pup in the open at South Queensferry. Lived in Linlithgow, West Lothian.

Emanuel RAFT 1938– Versatile painter, sculptor, jeweller and teacher, born as Emanuel Raftopoulos (changed to Raft in 1964) in Suez, Egypt, of a Greek father and Italian mother. After a period in Greece, Raft matriculated from the British School, Suez, in 1955, then his family moved to Australia, arriving in Sydney in 1956. From 1956–9 Raft attended the Bissietta Art School; worked as an industrial draughtsman; attended Brera Academy, Milan, 1959–60, studying sculpture with Luciano Minguzzi, and travelled extensively through Europe; then back in Sydney, in 1960 becoming an industrial designer. He became an Australian citizen in 1962, the year before his first solo show at Max Hutchinson's Gallery A, commencement of teaching at Sydney University's school of architecture and a commission to make panels for Wollongong Teachers' College. In 1965, Raft participated in the Helena Rubinstein travelling scholarship, travelling to England/Europe in 1966. He taught at Croydon and Birmingham Colleges of Art, returning to Australia in 1969 via America, where he took part in Sculpture 69 at the Byron Gallery. Between 1970–8 Raft lived in London, became known as a British jeweller and showed internationally. He taught at Sutton College of Liberal Arts and West Sussex College of Art and Design and had his first solo show in London at Electrum Gallery. Back in Sydney, Raft became head of sculpture at the City Art Institute, 1984–90, gained a master's degree in 1986, and was twice resident at Cité Internationale des Arts, Paris. Between 1990–6 Raft was senior lecturer, College of Fine Arts, University of New South Wales. He set up a studio in southwest France in 1992, eventually living between Sydney, France and Greece. Raft had extensive solo shows in Australia, group shows including Cross Currents, Reed's Wharf Gallery at Barbican Centre, 1996, where he showed rectangular abstracts in muted colours. Major Australian collections, including the National Gallery, Canberra, hold examples, as does Goldsmiths' Hall, London.

Robert E RAGG 1922–1953 Painter, potter and teacher, educated in Belper, Derbyshire. He studied at Derby School of Art, 1939–41, then at Edinburgh College of Art, 1941–5, under David Alison and William Gillies. In 1944–5 obtained postgraduate scholarship and travelling scholarship. Taught adult classes in Truro, near which he lodged at a farm at Idless for almost 12 years. He showed at RA, LG, NEAC, Roland, Browse & Delbanco and Leger and Lefevre Galleries, at the County Museum and Art Gallery in Truro with the St Mawes Group; and some of his pottery was exhibited in the International Museum of Ceramics at Faenza, Italy. Leicester and Derbyshire Schools Museum Services held his work. Ragg, who was unmarried, died tragically, being found hanging from a tree in Treworgan Woods, St Erme, after a police search.

Sarah RAINE 1967– Artist, born in London, who studied printed textiles at Liverpool Polytechnic, 1986–9, then held a series of residencies: at Walker Art Gallery in Liverpool and Oldham Art Gallery, both 1993, and Oviedo, Spain, 1994. Group exhibitions included Tricel at The Design Centre, 1989; Plymouth City Art Gallery, 1992; Liverpool meets Melbourne at Grand Central Gallery in Australia, 1994; and Making It at Tate Gallery in Liverpool, where she lived, 1995, with a work called Splanchnology, created from human hair, plaster, pigment and velvet. Had a number of Liverpool-based solo exhibitions, including Lesser Gods, Waterstones, 1993, and Nice, Not Nice, at Arena House, 1994.

Clifford RAINEY 1948– Sculptor working in a variety of materials, notable draughtsman and teacher, born in Whitehead, Antrim, Northern Ireland. He had a chequered early career. Had three years as a linen damask designer in Belfast; was at Hornsey College of Art, 1968–9; and after touring North America in 1969–71 was at North-East London Polytechnic, in 1970 touring Norway with a circus; after working at a glassworks in Denmark, was in 1971–3 at Royal College of Art, in 1972 a travelling scholarship taking him to a glassworks in Finland. The mid-1970s were to see Rainey travelling widely in Greece, Turkey and Africa. He was a visiting lecturer at Royal College of Art. Exhibitions included Ulster Museum, Scottish Arts Council Gallery in Edinburgh, Arnolfini Gallery in Bristol and Arts Council of Northern Ireland Gallery, that body and Ulster Museum holding examples. In 1976 Victoria & Albert Museum commissioned Rainey to create a sculpture to celebrate Queen Elizabeth II's silver jubilee.

Tristram RAINEY 1910– Versatile painter in oil, whose full name was Francis Tristram Rainey. He was educated at Blundell's School, then attended Slade School of Fine Art under Henry Tonks and Philip Wilson Steer. Rainey exhibited RA, Redfern Gallery, where he had a one-man show in 1939, RP, RBA and in Warsaw, Poland, where he worked for a time in the 1930s. Member of Chelsea Arts Club. Lived at South Godstone, Surrey.

Christopher Jasper RAINHAM 1966– Painter, born in Rainham, Kent. He attended Canterbury College of Art, 1984, Gillingham Adult Education Centre, 1984–5, Medway College of Design, 1985–6, and Wolverhampton Polytechnic, 1986–9, obtaining an honours degree in fine art. Among his exhibitions were Joe Binns Trophy, Gillingham, 1984; Manchester Academy, 1989; Laing Landscape Exhibition, at Salford City Art Gallery, in 1991; and Fisher Gallery, Covent Garden, 1991–2.

Peter RAINSFORD 1921– Artist in oil and gouache, born in Tavistock, Devon, who studied law as a solicitor, passing his examinations up to intermediate, 1940–4, then was at Chelsea School of Art, 1950–4, under Robert Medley, Raymond Coxon and Fred Brill. From 1967 he became an antiquarian bookseller, but continued to paint and draw. Rainsford was a member of Penwith Society in St Ives, showing at Newlyn Art Gallery, John Whibley and Comedy Galleries and with Cornish Painters at Plymouth in 1960. Had a solo show at Newlyn Art Gallery in 1960, at St Martin's Gallery, 1962, and Penwith Galleries, St Ives, 1979. Lived in Bath, Avon.

Basil RÁKÓCZÍ 1908–1979 Painter, stage designer, illustrator and writer, born in London, father of the artist Anthony Rákóczí. He sometimes worked as Basil Beaumont. He studied at Worthing, Brighton School of Art, the Académie de la Grande Chaumière in Paris and privately with the sculptor Ossip Zadkine. His father was Hungarian, a musician and artist, his mother from County Cork. Rákóczí lived and worked in southern Ireland from 1939–46, where he was leader of the White Stag Group along with artists such as Mainie Jellett, Kenneth Hall and Stephen Gilbert. Later lived in London, then Paris. He was an eclectic, subjective artist, interested in such subjects as myths, magic and folklore and contributed to publications on these topics. Founded the Society for Creative Psychology and was a member of the Gypsy Lore Society and Folk Lore Society. He was associated with Lucy Wertheim's Gallery and his work appears in her autobiographical book *Adventure in Art*. Exhibited widely in England, Ireland and on the continent. Retrospective at European Modern Art Gallery, Dublin, 1991.

David RALPH-SIMPSON 1963– Painter, muralist and installations artist, born in Plymouth, Devon, who gained a fine art honours degree at Newcastle upon Tyne Polytechnic, 1982–5. He won a South West Project Art Award in 1988; a South West Arts Marketing Grant in 1989; and a three-month studio placement award with Delfina Studios Trust, Bristol, in 1993. In 1989 he carried out a mural for Television South West, followed in 1995 by murals for Exeter City Council. Group shows included Laing Landscape and Seascape Painting, at Pelter Sands Gallery, Bristol, where he was a prize winner in 1990 (he won the South West Regional Prize in 1994); Gordon Hepworth Gallery, Newton St Cyres, from 1991; and High Point Fair, North Carolina, America, 1996. Solo exhibitions included Gallery Gilbert, Dorchester, 1997.

Jean RALSTON 1928– Sculptor in many materials born in Birkenhead, Cheshire. Studied at Kingston School of Art, 1947–52. Showed at RA and elsewhere and signed work J R. Lived for a time at New Maldon, Surrey.

Adrian RAMOS 1963– Painter in oil using a rich palette, born in Portugal, who moved to London in 1969 where he studied at Chelsea School of Art. Ramos often focused on the relationship between man, technology and the environment and made expeditions to the Amazon rainforest and the coral reefs of Thailand. Showed in Switzerland and Germany and in London had exhibitions at Fiell, 1989, and the Gallery in Cork Street, 1994 and 1996.

Theodore RAMOS 1928– Painter in oil noted for his portraits, muralist, illustrator and teacher, born in Oporto, Portugal, of Spanish parents, who became a British subject. He attended Royal Academy Schools with postgraduate studies, 1949–54, under Sir Gerald Kelly. For various periods between 1959–68 he was a visiting lecturer at Brighton College of Art, Harrow School of Art and Royal Academy Schools. Showed at RP, RA Summer Exhibitions, 20th Century Portraits at National Portrait Gallery, 1980 and 1989, and elsewhere. Commissions included a Distillers Company mural The Transfiguration, 1979. Carried out many boardroom and domestic portraits, subjects including HM The Queen, HRH The Duke of Edinburgh and HM Queen Elizabeth the Queen Mother. National Portrait Gallery, RA, Guildhall Chamber in Windsor hold examples. Ramos cited "the combined influences of Spanish and English portraiture" as important. Lived in London. His son was the painter Tod Ramos.

Tod RAMOS 1956– Painter in oil of horse racing, born in London, full name Adrian Henry Ramos. Other family members were painters, his father being Theodore Ramos, his mother Julia, daughter of Sir Henry Rushbury. He studied at Brighton Art School, Gloucestershire College of Art & Design in Cheltenham, taught by Colin Lanceley, and Royal Academy Schools, 1979–82, teachers including Ruskin Spear, Robert Buhler and Peter Greenham. Ramos was a member of the Contemporary Portrait Society and Chelsea Arts Club, group shows including RSA and NEAC. Had a solo show at Stephen Bartley Gallery in 1983, a series at Richmond Gallery from 1984, later ones including Swiss Derby Club in Zurich, Switzerland. Ramos said that he admired "Stubbs and Degas, the most important influence being Lautrec". RA and Chelsea Arts Club hold examples. Lived in Bromsberrow, Ledbury, Herefordshire. Ramos rode for a time as a gentleman jockey in France, having developed the interest while at Cheltenham.

Alexander RAMSAY 1947– Gestural abstract painter and teacher who attended Chelsea School of Art, 1964–9, He won a Greater London Arts Association award in 1978 and taught at St Martin's School of Art. Was included in British Painting 1952–1977 at RA, 1977; Small Works, at Newcastle Polytechnic, 1978; LG at South London Art Gallery, 1981; RA Summer Exhibition, 1982; and Wapping Artists Open Studios, 1983. Solo shows included Hatton Gallery, Newcastle upon Tyne, 1976, and Bradford City Art Gallery, 1983. Lived in London.

Graham RAMSAY 1968– Artist, born in Kirkcaldy, Fife, who gained an honours degree in fine art at University of Leeds, 1987–91. Until early in 1993 Ramsay worked as a partnership with Gavin Bird as Ramsay Bird. They gained the British Telecom Enabling Award, 1990, and publications included the *Ramsay Bird Book*, 1991. Mixed shows included British Telecom New Contemporaries, Arnolfini Gallery, Bristol, and tour, 1990–1, and Fresh Art, Business Design Centre, 1991. They had a solo show at Church View Gallery, Doncaster, 1989, later ones including Gimpel Fils, 1992, which had a jokey quality; it was described as Post Neo Avant-Garde-ism and included small sculptures made from bits of brightly coloured plastic toys and colour photographs printed on to industrial carpeting.

Lady Patricia RAMSAY 1886–1974 Painter of flowers and-landscapes who travelled widely. She was the daughter of the Duke and Duchess of Connaught and grand-daughter of Queen Victoria. Her full name was HRH Princess (later renounced) Victoria Patricia Helena Elizabeth; she married Admiral The Hon. Sir Alexander Ramsay in 1919. As well as being a member of RWS, RWA and NEAC, she showed extensively at Goupil Gallery, also at RA, Fine Art Society and elsewhere. HM Queen Elizabeth the Queen Mother lent Dans le Midi by Ramsay to the NEAC centenary exhibition at Christie's in 1986. Lived at both Clarence House and Windlesham, Surrey.

Meredith RAMSBOTHAM 1943– Painter, glass engraver and illustrator, born in Palestine, was educated in Melbourne, Australia, and then at Cranbourne Chase, entering Slade School of Fine Art, 1965. Her main teachers were Anthony Gross and Frank Auerbach. For a time she took up glass engraving, encouraged by Laurence Whistler, then teaching it at Marlborough College where her husband taught, and although she had examples bought by public collections she returned to painting. She was notable for her still life pictures, in the quiet English tradition of Allan Gwynne-Jones and William Nicholson. Another aspect of her talent was the illustration of Pope's *Imitations of English Poets*, for Libanus Press, 1987. As well as showing at Parkin Gallery and RWA in mixed exhibitions, solo exhibitions included New Art Centre and Sally Hunter Fine Art, 1990. Arts Council holds her work. Lived in Marlborough, Wiltshire.

Charlotte RAMSDEN: *see* **Charlotte CHEVERTON**

Elisabeth RAMSDEN: *see* **Elisabeth COLLINS**

Eric RAMSDEN 1927– Printmaker, painter and designer, born in Runcorn, Cheshire. He studied at Liverpool College of Art for periods between 1943–50, teachers including Will Penn and Geoffrey Wedgwood. Became chief designer for Portals Ltd, the papermakers. Ramsden was a fellow of SWE and an associate of RE, also exhibiting at RA and in the provinces. Lived at Freefolk, Whitchurch, Hampshire.

Alma RAMSEY 1907– Carver in alabaster and other stones and draughtsman in chalk, married to the artist Hugh Richard Hosking. She was born in Tunbridge Wells, Kent, and studied at Bournemouth School of Art and Royal College of Art, her teachers including Gilbert Ledward and Henry Moore; also studied ceramics with William Staite Murray. Was a prolific exhibitor until late in life, in mixed shows, and in a long series of solo exhibitions including Herbert Art Gallery, Coventry, 1969; Southwell Minster, 1972; Stoke-on-Trent City Art Gallery, 1980; and Warwick Museum, 1989. Herbert Art Gallery and Leamington Art Gallery are among several public owners of her work. Commissions included the first Coventry crib for Coventry Cathedral and Christ in Glory for St Francis of Assisi, Elmdon Heath, Warwickshire. Lived in Warwick.

Peter RANDALL 1950– Watercolourist and graphic designer, born in Leeds, Yorkshire. He studied graphics at Leeds College of Art, 1967–70, then worked for about a decade as a graphic designer and illustrator for advertising agencies. In 1981 Randall moved to the Scottish Highlands to concentrate on painting, in 1983–87 appearing in a number of mixed shows. In 1988 he had a solo exhibition at South Bank Gallery, Hebden Bridge, in 1989 showing watercolours of the Highlands and Lowlands at Torrance Gallery, Edinburgh.

Terence Donovan RANDALL 1923– Stained glass designer and craftsman, born in Leytonstone, east London, his father being a metal craftsman. Studied at Chiswick School of Art, Twickenham School of Art and part-time at Central School of Arts and Crafts. Contributed to Festival of Britain in 1951, took part in the Art in the Service of the Church exhibition at Lambeth Palace and showed at the Usher Gallery, Lincoln, in 1954. Did a large amount of work for churches. Lived in Worcester Park, Surrey.

Peter RANDALL-PAGE 1954– Sculptor, draughtsman and teacher, born in Essex, but spent his childhood in Sussex. He studied at Bath Academy of Art, 1973–7, then after graduating in 1977–8 worked with the sculptor Barry Flanagan and in 1979 with Robert Baker on conservation at Wells Cathedral. In 1980 as a Winston Churchill Fellow he visited Carrara quarries in Italy to study carving. Back in London, Randall-Page was a visiting lecturer at Brighton Polytechnic, 1982–9, moving eventually to Drewsteignton, Devon, where he established a workshop to handle major pieces of sculpture with associates. Randall-Page had exhibited widely in mixed shows from the On Site exhibition at Arnolfini Gallery, Bristol, in 1977. He had solo exhibitions at Gardner Centre Gallery, Brighton, 1980; another followed at Anne Berthoud Gallery, 1985; then in 1992 a major retrospective was based on Leeds City Art Gallery and Yorkshire Sculpture Park, which toured. Randall-Page carried out a large volume of commissioned work, such as Scales and Horizons, at Leicester Royal Infirmary; Cuilfail Spiral, Lewes; "…and Wilderness is Paradise Enough", at St George's Hospital; and Three Fruit, at The Barbican. Was one of several artists commissioned to help rejuvenate the war-Blitzed Castle Park area of Bristol in 1990s. He was also a formidable draughtsman on a large scale, as in Fruiting Bodies, at Leeds City Art Gallery. Randall-Page was influenced by the sculptors Brancusi and Noguchi and fruit and fossil shapes were an important inspiration. Some of his works were positioned in rural sites where they became part of the landscape. He saw each sculpture as "a vessel for life". Lived in Crockernwell, Exeter, Devon.

Betty RANDLES: *see* **Betty MITCHELL**

Angus RANDS fl. c.1960–1985 Landscape painter in pastel and watercolour. Born in Ilkley, Yorkshire, he studied pharmacy but had no formal art training. Showed at the Mall Galleries in 1970s and at many northern public galleries. Contributed to *The Artist* magazine and *Leisure Painter*. Lived in Harrogate, Yorkshire.

Ian RANK-BROADLEY 1952– Sculptor, draughtsman, medallist and teacher who studied sculpture at Epsom School of Art, 1970–4, winning a Major Award in Sculpture from the British Institution Fund, 1973; in 1974–6 he did postgraduate studies at Slade School of Fine Art, then in 1976–7 was awarded a Boise Travelling Scholarship, studying in Rome and elsewhere. Rank-Broadley was assistant to Reg Butler, 1977; visited the Greek islands to study Cycladic sculpture in 1980; was visiting lecturer in life studies at Heatherley's School of Fine Art, 1982; and was assistant to Ralph Brown, 1986. He was elected an associate of RBS in 1989 and a fellow of the Society of Numismatic Artists and Designers, 1990. Commissions included University of Surrey, 1977; British Art Medal Society, 1989; and London Library, 1990. Exhibitions included Lyric Theatre, 1981; University of Surrey, 1989; and 1st RWA Open Sculpture Exhibition, 1993. British Museum Royal Mint, National Portrait Gallery and many other important collections hold examples. Lived at Rodborough, Stroud, Gloucestershire.

Beryl RANKIN 1942– Painter and teacher who lived mostly in Newcastle upon Tyne where she trained at the local University's fine art department, 1960–5. Became head of art and design at Central Newcastle High School. Group shows included Myles Meehan Gallery in Darlington and Tyne Tees Open at Sunderland Art Centre. Solo shows included University of Northumbria, 1994. Rankin's work was richly coloured, "frozen moments of time and place that are dredged up from my memory bank", with a strong imaginative element.

Catherine Geraldine RANKIN fl. from c.1910– Painter and draughtsman who after education widely throughout Britain studied at Royal College of Art and the School of Art in Manchester, where she lived. For a time was honorary secretary of MAFA, exhibiting locally, in London and at RCamA.

Stella RANKIN 1915– Painter, born in London, who gained her diploma at Goldsmiths' College School of Art in 1960, studying there, 1959–61, and previously under Kenneth Martin at St Martin's School of Art, 1958–9. She become a member of Free Painters and Sculptors and of the West Wales Artists' and Designers' Group. Jackson Pollock, Naum Gabo and Malevitch were at times all influences on Rankin's work; latterly it alternated between the abstract and semi-realistic with a Surrealist touch. Group shows included LG, AIA, Royal Festival Hall, RA Summer Exhibition and abroad. Solo exhibitions included Chappel Galleries, Chappel, 1991. Lived in Essex.

Joan Elizabeth Margaret RANSOME 1928– Painter born in Tunbridge Wells, Kent. She was educated in Malvern, Worcestershire, then studied at Malvern School of Art under Victor Hume Moody and Royal Academy Schools where her teachers included Bernard Fleetwood-Walker and William Dring, 1950–4, and where she gained several silver medals. Exhibitions included RA, RBSA, NEAC and Brighton and Worcester Art Galleries. Lived in London.

Sarah RAPHAEL 1960– Painter and draughtsman, born in Suffolk, daughter of the writer Frederic Raphael. In 1981 she obtained a first-class honours degree from Camberwell School of Art and gained the Iraqi Cultural Award. Participated in group shows at Whitechapel Art Gallery, Morley Gallery, National Portrait Gallery, and the Gillian Jason and Albemarle Galleries. She had a solo show at Christopher Hull Gallery in 1985, others at Agnew in 1989 and 1992. Raphael was a portrait and landscape painter; her scenes including animals and figures sometimes have a strange, other-worldly quality.

Catherine Margaret RASCH 1891–1983 Artist in oil and pastel, born in London. She was educated privately, then studied at Byam Shaw School and Slade School of Fine Art. Lady Rasch was married to Colonel Sir Frederic Carne Rasch and showed at PS, ROI and Paris Salon. She lived for a time at Danebury, Essex, also in London.

Peter RASMUSSEN 1927– Pastel artist and teacher, notable for his child and animal portraits. He studied at Brighton College of Art, then taught in several schools, finally becoming head of fine art at Chesterfield College of Art. In 1964 resigned to paint full-time. Elected PS, he exhibited regularly there, at RWA and RP. In 1990 he shared a show at John Noott Twentieth Century, Broadway. Notable sitters included Terry Biddlecombe, Chris Bonington and Lady Frances Lloyd George. Lived in Brighton, Sussex.

John RATCLIFF 1914– Architect and painter, born in Mirfield, Yorkshire, who studied at Architectural Association, 1932–7, being made a fellow of RIBA in 1955. Four years later he was made a fellow of Free Painters and Sculptors, became its president and had a major show at Loggia Gallery in 1994. Also exhibited at RA and John Moores Exhibition in Liverpool. British Council holds his work. Lived latterly in Swanage, Dorset.

Andrew RATCLIFFE 1948– Painter, notable for portraits, born in Colne, Lancashire, who studied at Burnley College of Art, 1965–7, and Canterbury College of Art, 1967–70. He was included in John Moores Liverpool Exhibition from 1978, in that year winning a prize. Exhibitions also included Liverpool University, 1989, and Brewery Arts Centre, Kendal, 1992. Appeared in John Player Portrait Awards at National Portrait Gallery, for which he completed a commission. Lived in Temple Sowerby, Penrith, Cumbria.

Anthony RATCLIFFE 1954– Printmaker, mostly woodcuts, and lecturer, born in Mexborough, Yorkshire, who attended the local Grammar School, where he produced his first print, a linocut. Did a foundation course at Manchester Polytechnic, graduated with honours from Wolverhampton Polytechnic, 1973–6, returning to Manchester as prints technician for the foundation course. Eventually became a full-time lecturer in the fine arts department of Manchester Metropolitan University. Ratcliffe was a member of MAFA and exhibited widely in group shows. These included Stowells Trophy, at ICA, 1975; Lake District Landscapes, Abbot Hall Art Gallery, Kendal, 1980; Tradition and Innovation in Printmaking Today, Yorkshire Arts Exhibition, 1986; Van Gogh A Requiem, Bede Gallery, Jarrow, 1990; and St Helens Open, St Helens College, 1995, where Ratcliffe was a prizewinner. Later solo exhibitions included, in 1995, Stoke-on-Trent City Museum and Art Gallery and Manchester: City on the Move, at The British Council, Manchester, commissioned by Sheeran Lock Fine Art Consultants. That show included six large colour woodblock handprints, a record of Manchester at the end of the twentieth century that took two years to complete. Ratcliffe's work is held by the British Council, Sheffield and Astley Cheetham Art Galleries and several corporate collections. Lived in Mossley, Lancashire.

Henry Barwick RATCLIFFE 1913– Painter, textile designer, teacher and curator, born in Keighley, Yorkshire. Studied at Keighley School of Arts and Crafts and at Royal College of Art under Percy Hague Jowett. He held a number of teaching posts in the north of England, finally being principal of Southport School of Art and curator of the Atkinson Art Gallery there. Showed mainly in the north of England. Chelsea Arts Club member who lived in Southport, Lancashire.

Margaret RATCLIFFE 1925– Painter of miniature country landscapes working in watercolour and pastel, a teacher of arts and crafts, born in Leicester. She studied at the College of Arts there, 1943–5; later did refresher courses with Pitman's, pastels with Ernest Savage and watercolour with John Blockley. Showed with RMS, SWA, at Patricia Wells Gallery in Thornbury and extensively in America, where awards were gained, and at The British and Commonwealth Women's Club, in Brussels, and Malvern Art Club. Lived in Berrow, Malvern, Worcestershire.

William RATCLIFFE 1870–1955 Painter, printmaker and designer, born at Churchwater, Norfolk. Studied at Manchester School of Art, then spent almost 20 years designing wallpaper. Met the painter Harold Gilman in 1908, who persuaded Ratcliffe to paint. Studied briefly part-time at the Slade School of Fine Art, 1910. Attended Fitzroy Street meetings, exhibited at AAA, was a member of the Camden Town Group just before World War I and a founder-member of the LG. Painted in Dieppe with Walter Sickert and in Sweden, encouraged by Gilman. From the early 1920s Ratcliffe concentrated on watercolours and wood engravings. Although he exhibited at the Carfax Gallery, NEAC, Goupil Gallery and in America, Ratcliffe had to wait for his first one-man show until 1946, at Roland, Browse and Delbanco. Another was held in Letchworth, where he lived much of his life, in 1954. Ratcliffe was a shy man who lived a frugal, nomadic life, staying with friends or his brother, the lecturer and freelance journalist, S K Ratcliffe. The painter William Townsend, who met him late in life, recalls a "tiny old man … like a wise old carpenter … sad thinking of the huge bill for framing" after the London show that was "a failure". Tate Gallery holds his work. Died in London.

Thomas RATHMELL 1912–1990 Painter and teacher, notable for portraits and figure compositions, born in Wallasey, Cheshire, who attended Liverpool School of Art and Royal College of Art. He worked in industrial and naval camouflage, Ministry of Home Security, London and Leamington Spa, 1940–5. Taught at Newport College of Art as head of fine art and vice-principal, 1949–72, then until his death lived at Caerleon, Gwent. Rathmell was a member of the Welsh Group and WSW and participated in numerous mixed shows from late 1940s, including RA Summer Exhibitions, SWG, Howard Roberts and Albany Galleries in

Cardiff and RP. A one-man show toured south Wales in 1956, he had a series of exhibitions at Howard Roberts from 1956, and there was a WAC retrospective in 1982. Among Rathmell's commissions was Investiture of the Prince of Wales, Welsh Office, 1969. WAC, National Museum of Wales in Cardiff and public galleries in Newport and Swansea hold examples.

Mike RAVEN: *see* **Churton FAIRMAN**

John RAVERA 1915– Sculptor and teacher, born in Surrey, who worked figuratively in a wide range of materials. He studied at Camberwell Junior School and then Camberwell School of Arts and Crafts between 1954–62, teachers including Karel Vogel. Ravera's teaching included Woolwich Adult Education Institute and Sidcup Art Centre. He became a prominent member of SPS and RBS. Among his exhibitions were RA, Woodlands Art Gallery and Alwin Gallery. He completed a bronze of dolphins for the Barbican and an abstract work for Elstree plus other public sculptures. Lived in Bexleyheath, Kent.

Gwen RAVERAT 1885–1957 Wood engraver, illustrator, painter, designer and writer. She was the daughter of the Cambridge University professor of astronomy Sir George Darwin, and described her early life in the city with great charm in *Period Piece*. Studied painting, 1908–11, at the Slade School of Fine Art under Henry Tonks, Fred Brown and Philip Wilson Steer. From an early age she had admired the wood engravings of Thomas Bewick, so she took instruction in engraving from her cousin by marriage Elinor Monsell, then was self-taught. Married the artist Jacques Raverat, 1911, and they lived in France; when he died from illness in 1925 she returned to England and eventually to her Cambridge home. In 1931 she designed scenery and costumes for Ralph Vaughan Williams' ballet *Job, a Masque for Dancing*; she was art critic for *Time and Tide* magazine, 1928–39; and during World War II she served as a draughtsman in Naval Intelligence. She exhibited NEAC, Redfern Gallery, RSA, RHA; was a founder-member of the SWE and a member of the RE. Illustrated many books, including Frances Cornford's *Spring Morning*, 1915, Laurence Sterne's *A Sentimental Journey*, 1932, and Charlotte M Yonge's *Countess Kate*, 1948. British Museum holds her work, which she signed G R.

Darsie RAWLINS 1912– Sculptor in various materials, born in remote Kentmere, Westmorland, son of a metal craftsman. After Bembridge School he studied at Royal College of Art, 1930–4. Was a member of the Guild of Memorial Craftsmen, for a time being its master, and a fellow of RBS. Showed at RA and in the provinces and completed a number of public commissions, including work for Denbighshire Technical College, Wrexham; the Municipal Offices, Staines; and Tewkesbury Abbey. Lived for many years at Penn, Buckinghamshire.

Ethel Louise RAWLINS fl. c.1900–1962 Painter who studied at the Slade School of Fine Art and in Newlyn, Cornwall. She settled in Sussex in the early 1920s, about a dozen years later making her home in Ditchling, where she continued to live. Was a prolific exhibitor, being a member of WIAC and SWA, also showing at RA, RBA, RE, RHA, Walker Art Gallery in Liverpool and elsewhere.

Janet RAWLINS 1931– Illustrator, designer, muralist, painter, collagist and teacher, born at Horsforth, Leeds, Yorkshire. Studied at Leeds College of Art, then taught widely in England. Showed at RA; Walker's, Heal's and Foyles Galleries; and in the provinces, especially the north of England. Public galleries in Batley, Bradford and Leeds hold her work, as do National Coal Board and Imperial Chemical Industries. Illustrated a number of children's books. Lived latterly at Askrigg, Yorkshire.

William Thomas RAWLINSON 1912–1993 Wood engraver, painter in oil and teacher, born in Liverpool, where he attended the City School of Art, 1929–35. He held the Senior City Art Travelling Scholarship, 1932, studying widely on the continent. Rawlinson was in the Royal Air Force in 1941–6, as an official war artist in North Africa, Sicily and Italy, 1943–4, and in England, 1945–6. The Air Ministry commissioned 14 oil paintings depicting the history of radar. Plants and cats were among his own favourite subjects. Rawlinson began teaching in Liverpool in 1935. Among other appointments was one as an inspector of schools, and he was finally head of art at Stratford-upon-Avon High School for Girls, 1966–77. Rawlinson was a member of SWE from 1972, showing at RA, RBA, RE, RSA, Royal Glasgow Institute of the Fine Arts and Paris Salon, where he won Gold and Silver Medals for engraving. Royal Air Force Museum in Hendon, Imperial War Museum and Ashmolean Museum in Oxford hold extensive examples. Lived in Harvington and died in Redditch, Worcestershire. There was a celebratory show at Williamson Art Gallery & Museum, Birkenhead, in 1994.

Philip RAWSON 1924–1995 Writer, teacher, curator and artist, son of a Middlesbrough, Yorkshire, industrialist, he was educated at Winchester College. After being invalided out of the Fleet Air Arm and a short wartime course at Oxford University, Rawson taught himself Sanskrit to enter London University's School of Oriental and African Studies. His master's thesis, published as *The Indian Sword*, remains a standard work. After an assistant curatorship at the Ashmolean Museum, Oxford, in 1960 Rawson became founder-curator of the Gulbenkian Museum of Oriental Art at Durham University, staying 15 years. Among his 25 books were *The Art of Tantra*, 1978, which appeared five years after he had organised the exhibition Tantra at the Hayward Gallery; and *Ceramics*, 1984. Taught painting, sculpture and ceramics at the Royal College of Art – he was a full-time senior tutor, 1977–80, becoming dean of the faculty of arts at Goldsmiths' College, 1981–4. After then retiring to Dorset, Rawson was able to concentrate on his own figurative and abstract two- and three-dimensional work, little shown in his lifetime. Another side of this Renaissance man's interests was his appearance as a tenor with the London Ensemble Singers in the 1940s, having studied composition with Egon Wellesz and Karl Rankl and singing with Jani Strasser.

Isabel RAWSTHORNE 1912–1992 Painter and stage designer, born in London as Isabel Nicholas. She married in succession Sefton Delmer, foreign correspondent of the *Daily Express*; the conductor and composer Constant Lambert; and the composer Alan Rawsthorne. She attended Liverpool School of Art, then at 18 went to the Royal Academy Schools, in 1934 going to Paris to study at L'Académie de la Grande Chaumière. She had modelled in London for the sculptor Jacob Epstein and in Paris she financed her studies by sitting for André Derain, the sculptor Giacometti and others. A striking Derain portrait of her is in the Fitzwilliam Museum, Cambridge; a later portrait by Francis Bacon is in the Tate Gallery. After World War II, during which she helped Delmer with his black propaganda work at Bletchley Park, she held an exhibition at Hanover Gallery, as a result of which the choreographer Frederick Ashton invited her to design the ballet *Tiresias* for Covent Garden. She was to design other productions there, as Isabel Lambert. Her studies of Dancers in Action were shown at October Gallery in 1986. She travelled in Africa and Australia in the 1960s and 1970s and was keen on wildlife conservation. Died at Little Sampford, Essex. Memorial exhibitions at The Woods Gallery, Leicester, 1992, and The Mercer Art Gallery, Harrogate, 1997–8.

Peter RAWSTORNE 1930– Water sculptor, born in Cape Town, South Africa, who studied architecture at University of Natal under Paul Connell. Rawstorne also worked as a journalist for among other outlets the BBC, *The Observer* and *News Chronicle*, as art critic. Rawstorne was much influenced by research into primitive and natural art in the 1960s, an environmental artist committed to design-build sculptural forms. He co-founded Virbela Flowforms Partnership in 1980, which became Rawstorne Associates in 1985, which persisted "with the ideal of artist/industry collaboration". Showed at Salon d'Art Sacré in Paris, 1974. Was based in Forest Row, Sussex.

RAY: *see* **Ray HOWARD-JONES**

Edith RAY 1905– Painter, printmaker and teacher who studied at Hastings High School, gained her art master's certificate in 1925 and attended Portsmouth College, 1925–7. She studied art with the Sussex artist Philip William Cole, was a member of East Sussex Arts and SWA, also showing at RE, RI, RSA, in the provinces and at Paris Salon. Lived for many years at Tenterden, Kent.

Geo. RAY: *see* **George Ray BURTENSHAW**

Karen RAY 1932– Painter and teacher, wife of the artist Stuart Ray, she was born in Townsville, Queensland, Australia. She studied at Queensland Technical College, 1949–51, Walthamstow School of Art, 1952–4, and the Royal Academy Schools, 1954–6, her teachers including her husband, Robert Greenham, Clifford Hall and John Titchell. Was for a time a member of NEAC and at 1989 show won the Worshipful Company of Painter-Stainers Award. As well as showing in Australia, she had a series of one-man exhibitions at Phoenix Gallery, Lavenham, as well as at Drew Gallery, Canterbury, also showing for many years at RA; Roland, Browse and Delbanco; and elsewhere. Ray worked in oil, watercolour and coloured pencils, painting "white pictures, and beds, and my studio and presents from friends". Lived in London.

Richard Archibald RAY 1884–1968 Teacher, painter and sculptor, born in London, who studied at Brighton School of Art and Royal College of Art, qualifying in 1914. Became chief assistant art master of the School of Art in Sunderland, County Durham, where he lived; from 1919–49 Ray was an energetic and enterprising head of the School, overseeing a period of rapid expansion. He also lectured at the local teachers' training college and was involved in examinations and syllabus formation. Ray was president of Stanfield Art Society in the 1920s and a member of Sunderland Art Club, showing elsewhere in the north. He carried out many commissions for local authorities and societies to design insignia, war memorials and plaques, being best known for his war memorial in Mowbray Park, Sunderland, where the Museum and Art Gallery holds examples.

Roy RAY 1936– Painter in acrylic, collagist and teacher, born in Feltham, Middlesex. He was self-taught, producing depictions of landscape in rich, earthy colours, as seen from the air, focusing on essentials. He moved to Cornwall in 1974 and was principal of St Ives School of Painting from 1977 for many years. Ray was a member of Newlyn Society of Artists, Penwith Society of Arts and a founder member of Porthmeor Printmakers. Regularly lectured at Tate Gallery on aspects of painting in St Ives and was part-author of *Art About St Ives*, 1987. He organised a number of shows at Penwith Gallery and the Crypt in St Ives, where he lived. Residencies included Falmouth School, 1983, Mere Oaks School in Wigan, 1986, and Richard Lander School, Truro, 1987 and 1992. Took part in many mixed exhibitions, especially in Cornwall, and had first solo show at Salt House Gallery, St Ives, 1981, later ones including St Ives Pottery Gallery, 1994, with potter John Bedding. St Thomas' Hospital, Falmouth School and Allied Irish Bank hold examples.

Stuart RAY 1916–1985 Painter, printmaker, draughtsman and teacher, born in London, husband of the painter Karen Ray. Ray studied at Regent Street Polytechnic School of Art, 1937–9, Royal College of Art engraving school, 1939–40, and, after being invalided out of the Army in India, Royal College painting school, 1945–8, his teachers including Gilbert Spencer and Percy Horton. In 1951 he was appointed head of the art school at South-West Essex Technical College, Walthamstow, retiring in 1983. Among staff he employed were Peter Blake, Clifford Hall, Fred Cuming, Olwyn Bowey and Ken Howard. Showed in England and abroad: Roland, Browse and Delbanco and Phoenix Gallery, Lavenham, solo exhibitions and group shows at RA and NEAC. Queensland Art Gallery, Brisbane, holds his work. Lived in London.

Terry RAYBOULD 1940– Artist in oil, charcoal and watercolour, and teacher, born in London. He studied at Camberwell

School of Arts and Crafts, 1958–62, winning first prize in the Ana M Berry Awards, teachers including Frank Auerbach, Dick Lee and Euan Uglow. Taught at Camberwell, 1963–75; at West Surrey College of Art in Farnham, 1965–70; then was head of art at Northampton School for Boys from 1975. Raybould was a member of The Town and County Art Society in Northampton, where he lived. Group shows included LG, RA Summer Exhibitions, Camden Arts Centre, South London Art Gallery, East Midlands Arts Council Touring Exhibition, Cadogan Contemporary and elsewhere. Had a series of solo exhibitions including Woburn Abbey, Northampton Museum and Leicester University. His work is held by Durham University, Leicester University and London Press Exchange. Raybould usually worked from nature.

Ruth RAYMOND 1897– Painter, calligrapher, weaver and teacher, born in Greenwich, in southeast London. Studied at Camberwell School of Arts and Crafts, 1914–17, at Woolwich Polytechnic, 1917–19, and Royal College of Art, 1919–21, where her teachers included Robert Anning Bell and Edward Johnston. She taught at Gloucester School of Art and exhibited widely in the Cotswold area. Gloucester Cathedral holds her work. Lived in Brookthorpe, Gloucestershire.

Desmond RAYNER 1928– Self-taught artist, born in London, working in gouache, charcoal and wash. Kandinsky, Klee, Miró, Sonia and Robert Delaunay, Mondrian and Vasarely were cited as influences. Rayner's pictures were hard-edged abstracts and landscapes. Exhibitions included Embankment Gallery, 1976; Lombard Gallery, 1977; Talent Store, 1980; Barbican Centre, 1983; Wylma Wayne Fine Art, 1985; and Building Centre, 1992. Rayner was a member of SGA. First National Securities and Allied Lyons own examples. Lived in Harrow on the Hill, Middlesex.

Donald Lewis RAYNER 1907–1977 Watercolourist, born in Halstead, Essex, who after private study attended Manchester School of Art part-time. He was by profession a textile designer, working for Tootal Broadhurst Lee until 1966, after that for a furnishing fabrics firm. Was for many years secretary of MAFA and also showed at RI, RBA, RSA and Paris Salon. Was noted for his landscapes and canal scenes, work being in several permanent collections including Manchester and Stoke-on-Trent. Lived in Marple, Cheshire.

Gilly RAYNER 1948– Portrait artist working mainly in pencil, occasionally in other media but not professionally, born and lived in London. She was not formally trained as a portrait artist, although she studied history of art at Villa de L'Assomption, Paris, and was taught privately to paint for some years by Matt Bruce. Rayner "started drawing portraits when I used friends as models and they wanted to buy, then their friends wanted portraits, and so on." Worked in the Far East and America, but principally in Britain, mainly on commission, although she exhibited at RP and PS. "I feel the most important factor is to get a likeness, and I only let the clients have the work if *they* are fully satisfied." Portraits included Lady Thatcher the politician, the actor Stewart Granger, the dancer Anthony Dowell and the actress Sarah Miles, as well as many society people.

Martin RAYNER 1946– Mainly a sculptor and artist in mixed media, Rayner did not enter Dundee College of Art until he was 29, graduating in drawing and painting five years later. Prior to that he was a journalist for a dozen years, had worked in New Zealand in tourism and on a cargo ship. From the late 1970s Rayner acquired many awards. These included one Major Scottish Arts Council Award in 1983, a second two years later; not long after, he had one of the Council's Artist in Industry placements; then in 1988 he won a £10,000 sculpture commission from the Scottish Development agency for Dundee waterfront. Ships and the sea are a key theme in Rayner's work. This he showed widely in Scotland and had a solo exhibition at Compass Gallery, Glasgow in 1982, another at 369 Gallery in Edinburgh in 1983. Among Rayner's public work was a glass mural for Rosyth Health Centre. After spending 18 months in the mid-1980s at the Scottish Sculpture Workshop, Lumsden, in 1987 he was artist-in-residence on Blair Atholl Estate in Scotland.

Trevor Samuel RAYNOR 1929– Painter and designer, notable for flower pictures, born and lived in Oldham, Lancashire. He studied at the local School of Art, 1942–5, then Manchester School of Art, 1945–9. Was an associate of Société des Artistes Français, showing at Paris Salon, also in the Lancashire area including solo exhibition at Salford Art Gallery.

Sheila RAYNS 1923– Painter in oil and teacher who was brought up in St Albans, Hertfordshire, attended the School of Art there and St Martin's School of Art and was a pupil of Ruskin Spear. Exhibited RA and NEAC. Taught in South Croydon, Surrey, where she lived.

Betty REA 1904–1965 Sculptor, painter, draughtsman and teacher, born in London, who studied with Ernest Cole and Henry Moore at the Royal College of Art, 1924–6. Marriage and bringing up a family interrupted her output in the 1930s. Serious production of sculpture began in 1949, chiefly in terracotta, work remarkable for its personal style and strong humanist sympathies. Rea (pronounced Ree) was closely associated with the AIA and was featured in the touring show around it organised by the Museum of Modern Art, Oxford, in 1983. In 1955 Rea originated the exhibition Looking at People, in collaboration with Paul Hogarth and Carel Weight; it was first shown at the Whitworth Art Gallery, Manchester, afterwards touring the provinces; with the work of five other artists it was sent to Moscow in 1957, the first showing of English art in Russia since the 1917 revolution. In 1960 Rea was featured in Three Humanist Sculptors at Zwemmer Gallery, with a retrospective of her work there in 1965. In the same year, the RA Summer Exhibition gave a memorial show of three of her sculptures. London County Council, a number of training colleges and education authorities and Harlow Development Corporation hold Rea's work; her bronze Kore was erected in High Street, Old

Harlow, a decade after she died. Lived latterly in Cambridge, and was for many years companion of the artist Nan Youngman.

Edwin Alfred READ 1918– Painter, born in south London, who studied commercial art at Wimbledon School of Art, 1938–9, and became a stonemason. He showed in Valletta, Malta; Naples, Italy; in London; and in south Wales, where he was for a time a member of Wye Valley Art Society. For some years was foreman in charge of masons working on Laugharne Castle. Retired and lived at Tonna, Neath, Glamorgan.

Herbert READ 1908– Painter, draughtsman, printmaker and teacher, born in London. After studying at Regent Street Polytechnic School of Art, Read attended Ealing School of Art and Heatherley's School of Fine Art, his teachers including Iain Macnab. Showed ROI, UA, RBA of which he was a leading member, and elsewhere. Was a notable figure in organisation of City of London Art Exhibition. Lived in Pinner, Middlesex.

James READ 1965– Painter and printmaker, producing enigmatic works, born in Hampshire, where he studied at Winchester School of Art; then Gwent College of Higher Education and Chelsea College of Art & Design. He was resident artist at Essendine Arts Centre, 1990, then gallery attendant, Museum of Modern Art, Oxford, 1991. He won a Julian Trevelyan Printmaking Prize, 1990, and a gallery prize at Johnson Wax Kiln Gallery, Farnham, 1991. Group shows included National Student Printmaking Show, Bristol, 1989; RE Printmaking Open, Bankside Gallery, 1992; Wolfson College, Oxford, and Royal Over-Seas League Open, from 1994; and Beatrice Royal Art Gallery, Eastleigh, 1995. Had solo shows at Windsor Arts Centre, 1992, and Museum of Oxford, 1995. Wolfson College holds Read's work.

Joseph Stanley READ 1915– Draughtsman, watercolourist, commercial artist and teacher, born in Leicester, where he settled and attended the College of Art, 1942–4. Also studied elsewhere, including Percy Bradshaw's Press Art School, 1945–6. Showed at RBSA, NS, RI and in the Leicester area, where he held senior positions in the Sketch Club and Society of Artists. Local public art gallery holds his work.

Simon READ 1949– Artist employing imaginative phot graphy, ink, pencil and gouache; teacher. He was born in Bristol and studied at Somerset College of Art, 1968–9, University of Leeds, 1969–73, and Chelsea School of Art, 1973–5. Read won an Arts Council Major Award in 1978. He went on to teach at venues such as Slade School of Fine Art, Chelsea School of Art, North-East London Polytechnic, Reading University and Bath Academy of Art. Read was a portrait artist who chose to record his subjects in an unconventional fashion. It was said that he reinvented the camera and questioned "the very nature of reality and our perception of that reality". Exhibited in mixed shows in London and abroad, solo exhibitions including Acme Gallery, Wakefield Art Gallery and Anthony Stokes Gallery. Arts Council holds his work. Lived in London for some years.

Sue READ 1941– Still life painter, mainly of porcelain, born in Slough, Buckinghamshire, who studied at High Wycombe School of Art and West of England College of Art, Bristol. She "worked closely from observation using pure watercolour". Read was a member of RI, also showing at RA Summer Exhibitions, RWS, NEAC and at The Linda Blackstone Gallery, Pinner. Her work was featured in Angela Gair's book *Letts Practical Art: Watercolour*. Lived in Buckingham.

Peter READING 1933– Artist in watercolour and pastel and industrial designer, born in London, who attended Hornsey School of Art and London School of Printing. Spent over 30 years in industrial design, then settled in Gunnislake, Cornwall, to paint. The Tamar Valley, Dartmoor and frequent trips to the Vendée region of France were main inspirations. Showed regularly in galleries and at art fairs in the West Country, Gloucestershire, Hampshire, France and in London, where in 1995 had his first major exhibition at The Gallery in Cork Street.

REAL VIVID: *see* **Josephine McCORMICK**

Cyril REASON 1931– Painter and teacher, father of the artist Sophie Reason. He studied at Royal College of Art, 1951–4. He won a travelling scholarship to Spain, held a fellowship in fine art at Nottingham University, 1959–62, and was director of art at Morley College, 1972–9. Mixed exhibitions included LG, RA Summer Exhibitions and New Grafton Gallery. Solo exhibitions included Beaux Arts Gallery from 1958 and latterly Brighton Museum and Art Gallery, 1986, with a retrospective at Morley Gallery, 1995. Arts Council holds his work. Lived at Tregaron, Dyfed, Wales.

Sophie REASON 1957– Painter in oil on canvas or board, draughtsman in charcoal, born in Sussex where she settled in Brighton, attending the Polytechnic there, 1976–7, Falmouth School of Art, 1978–80, and Aix-en-Provence School of Art in 1979. Her father was the painter Cyril Reason and a notable influence on her work was Bomberg's former student Dennis Creffield. She was "obsessed by the subject of heads, mine or others dead or alive", examples being the writers Thomas Hardy and Charles Dickens and Romanesque sculpture in France. Mixed shows included LG at Camden Arts Centre, 1982; Red Herring Gallery, Brighton, 1987; and The Crypt Gallery, a shared exhibition, 1992. Solo exhibitions included Falmouth School of Art Gallery, 1979; Food for Friends, 1982; and East Anglian Film Co-op, 1984.

John REAY 1947– Painter and draughtsman who trained at Brighton School of Art and Norwich School of Art. He lived in Lowestoft, Suffolk, and was noted for his beach scenes with figures. From the late 1970s Reay appeared in many mixed exhibitions, including Piccadilly Gallery, 1978; Aberbach Fine Art, 1980–1–2; Crane Kalman, 1982–4–6–8; Thackeray Gallery, 1983–5–7–8–9, where in 1990 he shared a show; and Fieldborne Gallery, 1988–9–90. Reay had a solo show at Alwin Gallery in 1978; Bohun Gallery, Henley-on-Thames, 1982; Bury Art Centre,

Bury St Edmunds, 1988; Phoenix Gallery, Lavenham, 1988; and Chappel Galleries, Chappel, Essex, from 1989.

Rachel RECKITT 1908–1995 Artist in mild steel, wood, stone, paint and wood engraving, born in St Albans, Hertfordshire. She studied at the Grosvenor School of Modern Art in late 1930s under Iain Macnab, and in 1970–5 at the Roadwater Smithy, Somerset, with Harry and Jim Horrobin. After training Reckitt worked from home in west Somerset at Rodhuish, Minehead. Carried out commissions for pub signs; wood-engraved book illustrations and single prints; and did sculpture in five Somerset churches and for private commission. She was an honorary member of the Somerset Guild of Craftsmen and SWE and a member of British Artist Blacksmiths' Association. Other group shows included Wertheim Gallery and LG. Had solo exhibitions at Duncan Campbell Contemporary Art and Bridgwater Arts Centre. Public collections in Salford and Bridgwater hold examples, as do Withycombe, Old Cleeve and Leighland.

Jean M REDDAWAY 1923– Painter and teacher, who gained her Ministry of Education diploma in 1944. Studied at Slade School of Fine Art under Randolph Schwabe, 1940–3. Exhibited RA and lived in London.

Peter REDDICK 1924– Wood engraver, woodcut artist, watercolourist and teacher, born in Ilford, Essex. He studied at South-East Essex Technical College, 1941–2; Cardiff School of Art, 1947–8; Slade School of Fine Art, 1948–51; and London College of Printing, 1959–60. From 1951–6 was visiting tutor at Regent Street Polytechnic; taught commercial design at Kumasi University of Science and Technology, Ghana, 1960–2; lectured at Glasgow School of Art, 1963–7; then was senior lecturer in illustration, Polytechnic, Bristol, where he lived at Redland, 1967–89. For periods between 1956–63 Reddick freelanced and was design assistant to Willy de Majo and Peter Hatch. In 1979–80 Reddick was Gregynog Arts Fellow. He did advertising work and illustrated for the Folio Society and Gregynog Press. Reddick was at various times a fellow of RE and a member of SWE and RWA. He was a founder-member of both Artspace Bristol studio scheme and Bristol Printmakers' Workshop. Took part in many shared shows in the provinces and solo exhibitions included 1988–90 retrospective at Rhyl, part of a tour. Victoria & Albert Museum, Bristol City Art Gallery and National Library of Wales in Aberystwyth hold examples. Continued to live in Bristol.

David REDFERN 1947– Painter and teacher, born in Burton upon Trent, Staffordshire. He attended Reading University Fine Art Department, 1965–9, then Slade School of Fine Art, 1969–71. From 1971–83 he worked at the Serpentine Gallery, then did part-time lecturing in drawing at Croydon College. Appeared at John Moores Liverpool Exhibition, 1974; Tolly Cobbold/Eastern Arts National Touring Exhibition from 1977; Whitechapel Open from 1982, and in many other group shows. Had a solo exhibition at Guildhall, Thetford, 1980, later ones including Woodlands Art Gallery, 1986. Arts Council and Wolverhampton and Southampton public galleries hold Redfern's work.

June REDFERN 1951– Painter and teacher, born in Fife, Scotland. She studied at Edinburgh College of Art, 1968–72, winning first prize in Scottish Young Contemporaries in the latter year. Ten years later she won Scottish Arts Council awards. She taught part-time at Preston Polytechnic from 1982–3, in the latter year becoming a junior fellow at Cardiff College of Art. In 1985 she was artist-in-residence at London's National Gallery, the year following being guest artist at the University of Minnesota and visiting tutor at Goldsmiths' College in London, also in Canterbury, Watford, Newcastle upon Tyne and Glasgow. Redfern had a solo show at Scottish Arts Council in Edinburgh in 1976, then exhibited regularly, latterly at Trinity Gallery, Compass Gallery in Glasgow and Bohun Gallery in Henley-on-Thames. Early in the 1980s Redfern became disillusioned with her broadly realist style and worked in collage, but in a short time she had resumed oil painting, working in an Expressionist manner, with strong colours and brushwork. Her work is in many public collections, including Scottish Arts Council, Scottish National Gallery of Modern Art and Contemporary Art Society. Lived in London.

William REDGRAVE 1903–1986 Artist in various media and teacher who was for a time a clerk with London Transport. He attended Central School of Arts and Crafts and West Clapham School of Art and eventually settled in Cornwall. With Peter Lanyon and Terry Frost he founded the St Peter's Loft summer school in St Ives, 1955–60. He was a Penwith Society of Arts member and showed at RA and when the Sail Loft Gallery was opened in St Ives in 1960 he was in the first mixed show. His vigorous bronze The Call of the Sea, 1980, is in Lowestoft. The actor Lord Olivier and the conductor Sir Adrian Boult were among his many bronze portrait subjects. Commemorative show at Roy Miles Gallery, 1998.

Simon REDINGTON 1958– Artist notable as a printmaker, born and lived in London, who graduated in fine art from Goldsmiths' College, 1976–80, teachers including Michael Craig-Martin and John Bellany; then did postgraduate diploma in art therapy at Hertfordshire College of Art, 1984–5. Also studied advanced printmaking at Central St Martins where the work of Ken Campbell and other makers of books were influences. Redington came from a theatrical background and produced a series of thespian portraits. These included Sir John Gielgud, Theatre Museum, 1988; and Peter O'Toole, Shaftesbury Theatre, 1991. In 1993 Redington founded the Kamikaze Press, the year before he won a scholarship from The Charitable Trust of the Stationers' and Newspaper-Makers' Company, The Francis Mathews Award, a travel award to study book arts in America. Exhibitions included The Spirit of London, Royal Festival Hall, 1986; RWA, 1991; Worcester City Museum and Art Gallery, 1992; and Kerb Scrawlers, which he curated, The Living Room, Greenwich, 1994.

REDO: *see* **Anthony HILL**

Anne REDPATH 1895–1965 Painter in oil and watercolour, born at Galashiels, Selkirk, daughter of Thomas Redpath, tweed designer. She was the mother of the painters Alastair and David Michie. She studied at Edinburgh College of Art and Moray House College of Education from 1913, qualifying as an art teacher in 1917. In 1919 won a travelling scholarship which took her to Belgium, France and Italy, where she took a special interest in the Trecento painters. After marrying James Beattie Michie, an architect, in 1920, she settled in France and painted little until returning to Edinburgh in 1934. First one-man show there 13 years later, her first in London, at the Lefevre Gallery, 1952. By this time Redpath was showing with such groups as the SSA, SSWA, RBA and RSA, of which she was elected an academician in 1952, one of many honours she was to receive. Later in life she travelled extensively in Spain, Corsica, the Canary Islands, Portugal and to Venice. One of the pre-eminent Scottish women painters and Colourists of the century, her work is to be found in many public galleries in Britain and abroad, including the Tate Gallery and RA, Aberdeen Art Gallery and Scottish National Gallery of Modern Art, in Edinburgh, where she lived, which gave her a retrospective, 1996–7.

Barbara REDPATH 1924– Painter and teacher born in London. Educated Streatham, then studied at Edinburgh College of Art, where she was an Andrew Grant Scholar, 1942–4 and 1945–7, her teachers including William Gillies and John Maxwell. In 1948 a travelling scholarship took her to Italy. She went on to work for a time in the education department of Kelvingrove Museum and Art Galleries, in Glasgow, where she settled. Showed widely in Scotland, including SSA, RSA and elsewhere, having a number of solo shows in Edinburgh and Glasgow. The Universities of Glasgow and Strathclyde hold her work.

John REDVERS 1928– Portrait painter, until 1979 exhibiting as John Piggins, born in Birmingham. He studied at Slade School of Fine Art, 1945–8, teachers including Randolph Schwabe, then Ruskin School of Drawing in Oxford, 1950, with Albert Rutherston. Showed at PS of which he was a member, RP, out of London and abroad. Lived in Hartpury, Gloucestershire.

William Josiah REDWORTH 1873–1947 Landscape painter, born in Slough, Buckinghamshire. After education at Upton he attended Chelsea School of Art. Showed at RA, Royal Glasgow Institute of the Fine Arts, IS and several groups of which he was a member: PS, RI and ROI. Lived in Slough for some years, later moving to Cornwall.

Alan REECE 1938– Illustrator, printmaker and craftsman, born in London, where he settled. After education in Taunton, Somerset, Reece studied at Central School of Arts and Crafts, 1954–6, the School of Fine Arts in Madrid, 1962–3, and Sir John Cass College, 1968–9. RMS member who showed at Mall Galleries and elsewhere in London.

Alan REED 1961– Artist and teacher, notable as a watercolourist of urban views with people, born in Corbridge, Northumberland, who settled nearby at Ponteland, Newcastle upon Tyne. His father was Kenneth Reed, well known as a golf artist. Alan Reed studied at the College of Arts and Technology, Newcastle, gaining a diploma in applied design. After a year as a graphic artist at the Hancock Museum, Newcastle, he chose to freelance as a illustrator/painter and to teach part-time. Experience included Derwentside College, Consett, 1984–92; Cleveland College of Art, Middlesbrough, 1986–7; then Newcastle and Tyneside Colleges. Some work was produced as limited-edition prints, Di Rollo Gallery, Edinburgh. Exhibitions included Ponteland Library, 1981; Gallery 7, Newcastle, 1984–8; Merton Gallery, Ponteland, and Gulbenkian Gallery, Newcastle, both 1992; and Malcolm Innes Gallery, Edinburgh, from 1993. Watercolours by Reed were several times chosen for the Singer & Friedlander/*Sunday Times* Watercolour Competition from 1992. Newcastle City Libraries used a series of greetings cards employing Reed's images.

John REED 1933– Artist and teacher who studied at London of College of Printing and went on to teach at Maidstone College of Art. He showed at RA, ICA, Gallery 47 and was included in England & Co's Art in Boxes, 1991, with a series of mixed-media boxes.

Stanley REED 1908–1978 Painter, notably of portraits, born in Ullock, Cumberland, who studied from 1926–32 at Liverpool School of Art with Will Penn, gaining a scholarship to Italy, 1930. He showed at RCamA, of which he became a member in 1932, RA, MAFA, RP and extensively in the north. Completed many commissioned portraits of leading church and academic figures in the Liverpool area, where he lived. Public galleries in Blackpool, Liverpool, Manchester and Southport hold examples.

Carlyle REEDY 1938– Born in Virginia, America, Reedy described herself as a self-taught collage/detritus/object/performance/installation artist, although she did attend La Grande Chaumière in Paris and was a guest student at Royal Academy Schools. Graduated in 1960, and for four years was writing Pop poetry and for film and theatre, in the late 1960s reading Pop poetry around Britain. Other career highlights included Destruction in Art Symposium, 1966, and work with John Latham, Stuart Brisley and Peter Dockley on interface arts events; theatre of dream in the Netherlands and Royal Court Theatre appearances, 1969–71; establishment of Monkey Enterprises, Inc, a performing artists collective, participants including Paul Burwell and David Toop, 1971–7; the start of K'un films with Joanna Jones, 1975; performance and new structures, Franklin Furnace Gallery, New York, 1980–1; performances, Mainz Festival of Theatre, Mainz, Germany, and Rotterdam, Netherlands, mid-1980s; solo show of collages, Peter Biddulph Gallery, 1986; and performance work at Chisenhale Dance Theatre, 1987. Reedy taught her own Living Human Sculpture techniques and published poetry in anthologies from Corgi, Penguin and Virago. Lived in London.

William Maxwell REEKIE 1869–1948 Businessman and painter, born in Manchester of Scottish parents. As a young man he joined the textile merchants Robert Barbour and Brother Ltd, was appointed a director in 1910 and remained on the board until 1942. For several years he was a director of Manchester's Chamber of Commerce and of Manchester Athenaeum, where he was much interested in its educational work; he served on the Library committee; and in 1938 he received the Heywood Medal for 30 years' service with Royal Manchester Institution, of which he had been president. Art was Reekie's principal enthusiasm. When Sickert taught in Manchester in the 1920s he was one of his pupils, and he also studied under one-time president of MAFA Tom Mostyn, himself showing often at the Academy. Painted widely in Britain and abroad. Manchester City Art Gallery holds works by Reekie, one, A Convoy in the Mediterranean April 1918, stemming from active service in World War I, which was presented in 1920. Died in Didsbury, Manchester.

Brian REES 1930– Painter, graphic artist and printmaker, born in Neath, Glamorgan. Attended Swansea School of Art, 1947–9 and 1951–4, with an intervening year at Camberwell School of Arts and Crafts. He later resumed his studies after several jobs including teaching, studying at University College, Swansea, 1957–8, and Central School of Arts and Crafts, where he studied book production and relief printing. Afterwards worked for several publishers and handled a large number of commissions, including a book jacket for Dylan Thomas' *Under Milk Wood*, for J M Dent, in 1958, graphic work for British Railways and other outlets as diverse as Shell and *Melody Maker* magazine. Group shows included Royal National Eisteddfod, SEA and South London Group.

Bromfield REES 1912–1965 Painter and draughtsman, full name John Bromfield Gay Rees, he was born in Llanelli, Carmarthenshire. While suffering from acute eczema as a small boy he developed an artistic talent, so that aged 13 he won first prize in the drawing and design category at National Eisteddfod junior section. Aged 14 enrolled at School of Art and Craft, Llanelli, where the headmaster D E H Pratt encouraged him to show at Swansea public gallery. Pratt recommended him to Royal Academy Schools where he was a brilliant student from enrolment at the end of 1932, a friend of Alfred Janes and William Scott. Illness in 1935 prompted surgery and this led to a nervous disorder which affected the rest of his life. Although his work was praised by Sir William Rothenstein, Rees was now confined to his home and did not show. In the early 1940s he worked frenetically on a series of stream-of-consciousness watercolours which exhausted him. The critic Jack Wood Palmer became a supporter, arranging for Rees to visit Paris in 1948, where Cubism made a great impact. In 1951 Arts Council included Rees' work in a Festival of Britain Contemporary British Painting touring show. Lived finally at Richmond Surrey, dying in Brompton Hospital of cancer of the lungs. In 1989 Michael Parkin Fine Art held a tribute show.

Gladys REES: *see* **Gladys Rees TEESDALE**

Michael REES 1943– Printmaker, mainly screenprinter, whose work had a strong personal-nostalgia element. He was born in Neath, Glamorgan, and studied at Sutton Coldfield, Maidstone and Brighton Colleges of Art. Had many exhibitions, especially in London, Midlands and southern provinces, including a shared show at The Studio, Dorchester, also exhibiting in Sweden and America. Lived for a time in Bournemouth, Hampshire.

Michael REES 1962– Versatile artist who studied at Suffolk College of Art and Design and eventually settled in Cornwall. His small pictures could be witty and quirky, odd and enigmatic titles being used; or more serious, as in his solo exhibition at Austin/Desmond Fine Art, 1997, based on Seamus Heaney's poetry. Rees took part in a three-man show at Quay Gallery, Sudbury, 1986; Christmas Show at Wolf at the Door, Penzance, 1988; Rainy Day Gallery, Penzance, 1992; The Edge of Beyond, Belgrave Gallery, 1995; and Gordon Hepworth Fine Art, Newton St Cyres, 1996. Other solo exhibitions included Salt House Gallery, St Ives, 1989, and Southgate Gallery, Launceston, 1990. The Anthony Petullo Collection, Milwaukee, Wisconsin, holds Rees' work.

Richard REES 1900–1970 Painter in oil and watercolour. Born in Oxford the son of Sir J D Rees, MP, Sir Richard Rees studied watercolour technique with Fred Lawson in 1936, a year later moving to the St John's Wood Art School. In 1945–6 he studied at Camberwell under William Coldstream, Victor Pasmore and Claude Rogers. Lived in London.

Ronnie REES 1945– Artist, born in Kilmarnock, Ayrshire, who studied at Coventry College of Art, 1962–7, then did postgraduate study in New York, 1967–9. Mixed shows included Arts Council show British Painting '74, in 1974. From that year lived in London.

Victoria REES 1955– Painter who studied at Ruskin School of Drawing, Oxford, 1976–9, then Royal Academy Schools, 1982–5. She gained the Goghill Landscape Award in 1979; The Jack Goldhill Scholarship to the Royal Academy Schools, 1982; David Murray Landscape Award, 1985; and *The Spectator* and Adam & Company Award in 1990. Took part in a number of group shows, including RA from 1983; Sue Rankin Gallery from 1985; and New Grafton Gallery from 1986. Had a solo exhibition at Christ Church Picture Gallery in Oxford, 1988, another following at Cadogan Contemporary, 1990. She was a painter in the restrained English tradition of Mary Potter and Elizabeth Vellacott.

David REES DAVIES 1953– Painter, printmaker, illustrator and teacher, born in Bridgend, Glamorgan, who studied at Manchester Polytechnic, 1972–5, gaining his master's degree at Royal College of Art, 1976–9. Rees Davies produced both figurative work and figurative with abstract elements, and his pictures could be richly coloured. Taught widely at art colleges and universities in Britain, South Africa and Australia; in the mid-1990s he was research fellow at the University of Portsmouth, engaged on a collaborative project with the musician and composer Ron Geesin exploring sound, image and poetry. In the late 1970s Rees Davies won first and second prizes in the Folio Society Competition;

gained the Hugh Dunn Award at Royal College of Art, 1979; and among his Eastern Arts Association Awards in the early 1980s was one for *Grasping the Nettle*, a limited-edition book of etchings, 1984. From 1979–82 he was a regular contributor to *Private Eye* magazine, from 1979–86 doing book covers for Picador, Penguin and Hutchinson Books. In 1990 he was artist-in-residence, Union of Artists, Senej, Moscow, in 1996 completing a limited-edition print, Moscow Studio. Group exhibitions included 8th International Print Biennale, Bradford, 1984; Glasgow Print Studio, 1989–92; Alive and Printing, McLellan Gallery, Glasgow, 1993; and Works on Paper, Seagate Gallery, Dundee, 1994. Had a solo show, Satire and Caricature, Riverside Gallery, Norwich, 1980, later ones including A3 Gallery, Moscow, and East West Gallery, both 1996. King's College, Cambridge; Castle Museum & Art Gallery, Norwich; Scottish Arts Council; and Kharkov Museum in Ukraine hold examples.

Lucien REES ROBERTS 1952– Painter and architect, born in Farnham, Surrey, son of the artists Peter Rees Roberts and Ursula McCannell. In 1968 began attending life drawing classes at Farnham Grammar School. During the 1970s he studied architecture at Cambridge University, finishing his degree in 1976; during the intervening period he had travelled extensively in several continents and had continued to paint and exhibit. In 1981 he moved to New York, hoping to give up architecture and paint full-time, which he managed to do in 1986. From mid-1980s showed at Civilisation Gallery and Red Studio Gallery, Surrey University, Lance Lappin Gallery, John Davies Gallery and Ashgate Gallery, Farnham. Periodically worked in Europe. He developed a method of cut-out oil paintings made from bolted wood which as a result had a novel sculptural quality. Was noted for his portraits. Included in a three-generation show of McCannells at England & Co in 1989.

Marcus REES ROBERTS 1951– Printmaker, teacher and painter, born in Farnham, Surrey, son of the artists Peter Rees Roberts and Ursula McCannell. He read English at Cambridge University, 1970–3, then for two years studied film theory at Slade School of Fine Art, with a special interest in German Expressionist cinema, and began to etch. From 1975–7 studied postgraduate printmaking at the Slade, won the Slade Prize and began to show widely in Europe and Britain. From 1977–9 was an assistant in the Slade's printmaking department; was in 1980 made a lecturer at Edinburgh College of Art; and in 1982–3 was visiting professor of fine art at University of Central Florida. Went on to exhibit including a 1984 show of Scottish prints which toured northern Europe; in 1985 gained Hon. Mention at Hull Print Biennale, and had solo exhibition at Glasgow Print Studio; and had a one-man show at Edinburgh Printmakers' Workshop in 1987. In 1989 was included in a three-generation show of McCannells at England & Co, which gave him a one-man in 1995. Victoria & Albert Museum and Scottish Arts Council hold examples.

Peter REES ROBERTS 1923– Painter, muralist, designer, sculptor and teacher, born in Mitcham, Surrey. He was married to the artist Ursula McCannell, their sons Tristan, Marcus and Lucien all being artists. He studied drawing and illustration at Wimbledon School of Art, 1939–41, and mural painting at Royal College of Art while at Ambleside. In 1945, having married, he taught at Farnham School of Art. From 1947–64 was involved in magazine and newspaper illustrative and advertising work, while continuing to paint, travel, take out patents for inventions and exhibit at LG, Modern Art Gallery, Arcade Gallery and in Spain, where he bought a house in 1963. In 1964 restarted teaching at Farnham School of Art; he also taught for a time at Brighton College of Art until 1970. The ensuing years saw Rees Roberts busy on a plenitude of projects, including murals for Marlborough Hotel, Lloyd's Bank in Cambridge, the SS *Goya* and Guildford Hospital; nine big exterior wall sculptures; and designs for Allied Breweries. In 1989 he was included in a three-generation show of McCannells at England & Co. Lived in Farnham, Surrey.

Tristan REES ROBERTS 1948– Architect and painter, born in Farnham, Surrey, son of the artists Peter Rees Roberts and Ursula McCannell. While at Farnham Grammar School he concentrated heavily on his painting, then at Cambridge University, 1967–70, studied architecture. After a period in India, he returned to Cambridge to do an architectural diploma course, 1971–3. He was in 1982 to form an architectural practice in Cambridge which trimmed his painting time, but he continued to work figuratively, with exotic influences on his pictures. Was included in a three-generation McCannell show at England & Co, 1989.

Marion REEVE 1926– Painter who was born and lived in Watford, Hertfordshire, for many years. She studied at Watford College of Technology art school with Alexander Sutherland, 1947–53, gaining her national design diploma, then worked for the Building Research Establishment. Became a member of Free Painters and Sculptors, 1968, and was a member of Watford and Bushey Art Society, also showing with Young Contemporaries, in the provinces and abroad. Had a solo show at Loggia Gallery, 1974. St Michael and All Angels Church in Watford contains Stations of the Cross by her.

Russell REEVE 1895–1970 Watercolour and oil painter; etcher. Born at Hethersett, Norfolk, Reeve studied at the Norwich School of Art, at the Slade School under Philip Wilson Steer and Henry Tonks and at the Royal College of Art. He exhibited at the RA, NEAC, Goupil Gallery, RBA, LG and in the provinces. His pictures The Concrete Mixer and Unloading Timber are typical of the industrial scenes he favoured. He also worked abroad painting conventional landscapes, such as his picture of Cadaques, Port Algue, in Spain, illustrated in *Artists' Country*, by C Geoffrey Holme and G S Sandilands. Reeve's work is in many public collections, including the Victoria & Albert Museum, Guildhall Art Gallery and Imperial War Museum. A retrospective was held at Christchurch Mansion, Ipswich, 1992. Lived in London.

Amy Constance REEVE-FOWKES 1886–1968 Painter, especially in watercolour, born in Bournemouth, Hampshire, where she studied at the School of Art. Married the artist Arthur Reeve-Fowkes. She exhibited at RA, RBA, RI and widely in the provinces. The Towner Art Gallery in Eastbourne, Bolton Museum and Art Gallery and Russell-Cotes Art Gallery and Museum in Bournemouth hold her work, which was widely reproduced. Lived in Eastbourne, Sussex.

Arthur Fred REEVE-FOWKES 1881–1965 Portrait painter, notably working in pastel, and teacher. He studied at Leicester College of Art and the Royal College of Art, 1903–8. Married the artist Amy Constance Reeve-Fowkes and was the father of the artist David Fowkes. Was for a time principal of Eastbourne School of Art and curator of the Towner Art Gallery, Eastbourne, where he lived from 1923–47.

Aimie REEVES 1971– Painter, born in Grimsby, Lincolnshire, who studied at Chelsea College of Art & Design. Her brightly coloured abstract oil on canvas, This is the picture which tells a heart-warming story of faith in the human will to survive, won a prize in the 1996 Royal Over-Seas League Open. Other group shows included Blaffer Gallery, Houston, Texas, 1992; Top Marks, The London Institute of Higher Education, 1993; and Dad, Gasworks Gallery, 1994. The London Institute holds her work.

Daniel REEVES 1948– Creator of videos, and site-specific and time-based installations such as Eingang, in New North, Tate Gallery Liverpool, 1990. He was born in the District of Columbia, America, and graduated from Ithaca College, New York, with a degree in cinema studies and anthropology in 1976. Time spent in Vietnam was drawn on for Reeves' film essay *Smothering Dreams*, of 1981. Moved to Scotland in 1985, settling in Argyll. Group exhibitions included D-Vision Video Awards Festival, 1st prize, San Francisco Video Festival, 1981; Video Culture Canada Festival, Toronto, 1st Prize Video Art, 1983; Documenta 7, Kassel, West Germany, 1985; 3rd International Video Biennial, Ljublana, Yugoslavia, Grand Prize, 1987; and San Francisco International Film Festival, San Francisco, Golden Gate Award, 1988. Solo shows included An Artist's Perspective, Rochester Memorial Art Gallery, Rochester, New York, 1983.

Keith REEVES 1947– Abstract sculptor in various materials and draughtsman, born in London, where he remained based. He studied at Goldsmiths' College School of Art, 1969–71. Won a Boise Travelling Scholarship to Italy, 1971–2, an Arts Council Minor Award in 1976 and in 1980 an Arts Council Purchase Award and British Council Award. Took part in many mixed shows in Britain and abroad, including Young Contemporaries, 1970–1; LG from 1974, being elected a member in 1976; XIth Paris Biennale, 1980; Whitechapel Open, 1982; and in 1983 9 Artists from Wapping British Tour, based at DLI Museum & Arts Centre, Durham. After 1970 solo show at Kingston, later ones included Spectro Gallery, Newcastle, in 1982, and Galleria Katarina, Helsinki, 1983. Arts Council holds his work.

Philip REEVES 1931– Printmaker, painter and teacher, born in Cheltenham, Gloucestershire. He studied at the School of Art there, 1947–9, and Royal College of Art, 1951–4. Was one of Jack Beddington's *Young Artists of Promise*, in the 1957 volume of that title. From 1954 was lecturer at Glasgow School of Art, becoming senior lecturer in 1970. As head of department he influenced many printmakers. Elected RE, RSW and RSA in 1976. Reeves had a one-man show at Douglas and Foulis Gallery in 1962. In 1980 there was a print retrospective tour organised by Peacock Printmakers at Aberdeen Art Gallery; Edinburgh; and in 1997 Glasgow Print Studio ran a retrospective of monoprints and etchings, 1972–97. Public collections holding works include Scottish Arts Council, Scottish National Gallery of Modern Art and other Scottish galleries. Reeves was a founder-member of the Edinburgh Printmaking Workshop and of the Print Studio in Glasgow, where he lived.

Paula REGO 1935– Painter and teacher, born in Lisbon, Portugal. Married the artist Victor Willing. Rego became resident in London permanently from the mid-1970s, having studied at Slade School of Fine Art, 1952–6. She had numerous group and solo exhibitions in Britain and abroad. From 1986 Rego taught at Royal College of Art and was included in its Exhibition Road show in 1988. In that year, too, she had a key retrospective exhibition at Gulbenkian Foundation in Lisbon and at Serpentine Gallery. An exhibition called Tales from the National Gallery was held at the Gallery in 1991–2 following Rego's term as the first associate artist there. She was a narrative painter, often drawing on fairy tales and childhood recollections, who produced images that could be apparently innocent and yet fundamentally disturbing, with underlying sexual and psychological implications. Latterly showed with Marlborough Fine Art, and Arts Council holds her work.

Mark REICHERT 1948– Painter, film-maker and writer, born in Long Island, New York, son of the portrait painter and sculptor Rex Reichert. He studied at Rhode Island School of Design and lived and worked in America until moving to England in 1980. He settled in Northumberland, but kept a base in North Carolina. In addition to painting, sometimes using collage, Reichert wrote and directed films and wrote plays. His play *Tenderly* was staged in London in 1988. He had a retrospective at Hatton Gallery, Newcastle upon Tyne, in 1990 and a solo show at Christopher Hull Gallery, 1991.

David REID 1972– Sculptor, born in Manchester, who did a foundation course at Cheltenham and Gloucester College of Higher Education, 1990–1, gained a visual arts first-class honours degree at Lancaster University, 1991–4, then his master's in sculpture at Winchester School of Art, 1994–5. Awards included an Enzo Raines County College travel scholarship to Barcelona, 1992, and a Very Special Arts (Ireland) Award, 1995. Reid's sculpture proposal for Lancaster Chaplaincy Centre was accepted with support from Pilkington Glass in 1993. In 1996 he gained a residency at the Tyrone Guthrie Centre, Annamakerrig, County

Monaghan, Ireland. Exhibitions included Stepping Out at Atlantis Gallery, 1995, and 2nd Open Sculpture Exhibition at RWA, 1996. Lived at Woodmancote, Cheltenham, Gloucestershire.

Elspeth Mary REID 1930– Sculptor in stone, wood and bronze, teacher, born in Blackheath, Kent. Studied at City & Guilds of London Art School, teachers including Sydney Harpley, David McFall and James Butler, later at Hammersmith College of Art, winning second prize for sculpture in 1958 and the Beckwith Scholarship in 1961. Miss Reid gained the City and Guilds Certificate of Merit in 1961 and the London Certificate of Art and Design from Hammersmith in 1976. She became a member of RBS and of Free Painters and Sculptors. Taught sculpture for London Borough of Hillingdon adult education classes. Reid showed at RA, Royal Exchange, SPS and RBA and held several solo exhibitions. Her commissioned work included a portrait of HM King George VI, a figure of St Alban for the Catholic church of that name in St Albans and a crucifix for the new Church of the Resurrection, Sydenham. Lived in Northwood, Middlesex.

Nina Winder REID 1891–1975 Painter of seascapes and landscapes, born in Hove, Sussex. Studied at St John's Wood School of Art. Showed at ROI, RSMA, of which she was a founder-member, SWA, Walker's Galleries, extensively at Arlington Gallery, Paris Salon and elsewhere. Kidderminster Art Gallery and Museum bought her work. Lived for a time in London, finally in Eastbourne.

Norman REID 1915– Curator, administrator and painter, born in London, who in the 1930s studied at Edinburgh College of Art and Edinburgh University, served in the Army in World War II and joined staff of Tate Gallery, 1946. Rose to become director, 1964–79. Among many appointments were British representative on the International Committee on Museums and Galleries of Modern Art, Contemporary Art Society Committee, Paintings in Hospitals Advisory Committee, University Board of Studies in the History of Art, Advisory Council of the Paul Mellon Centre and Trustee of the Graham and Kathleen Sutherland Foundation. He was knighted in 1970. Exhibitions included RA Summer Exhibition and Montpelier Gallery. Tate Gallery and Scottish National Gallery of Modern Art in Edinburgh hold examples. Lived in Park Langley, Beckenham, Kent.

Stephen REID 1873–1948 Painter, notably of historical subjects, and illustrator, born in Aberdeen. Studied at Gray's School of Art, Aberdeen, and Royal Scottish Academy Schools in Edinburgh. Exhibited RA, RBA, RSA and in the House of Commons. Aberdeen and Reading art galleries hold his work, which is also in several American collections. He was life master at King's College, in Kensington, London. Lived in London.

David REID-HENRY 1919–1977 Painter of wildlife, notably birds, born near Kandy, Ceylon, son of the painter and naturalist George Henry and brother of the wildlife artist Bruce Henry. He began painting aged six. After school he did an office job in London for a while, then was conscripted into the Royal Tank Corps in 1940, becoming an officer cadet at Sandhurst. During the North Africa campaign Reid-Henry became ill, then served in India and the Far East as an officer in the military police, where he cultivated his interest in wildlife painting. Apart from lessons with his father and help from the noted bird painter George Lodge, Reid-Henry was self-taught. In 1948 he married and settled in Woodford Green, Essex, where he set up a studio as an artist and falconer. Although he illustrated many books and magazines, and produced several stamp series, his fees were low and living was hard. In 1960 Reid-Henry was commissioned to paint in Rhodesia, where he stayed two years, acquiring his famous African crowned eagle Tiara, with which he hunted rabbits. The bird was so fierce that on occasion Reid-Henry had to enter hospital because of talon lacerations. Reid-Henry emigrated to Rhodesia where, after a divorce, in 1976 he married the botanist and ornithologist Louise Westwater. Reid-Henry was a founder-member of SWLA. He did commissioned work, but his main sales were through exhibitions which he planned in southern Africa and Britain. Reid-Henry regarded himself as a naturalist, who hated deadlines that impeded study, sketched from life and scorned those who used photographs. He kept a collection of live birds and bird skins for authenticity. Reid-Henry consorted more with ornithologists and museum men than with painters. He died of cancer at his home in what is now called Harare, Zimbabwe, having, according to his brother, left "a legacy of skill and excellence in wildlife art which few have attained". In 1979 the National Gallery of Zimbabwe put on a show of Reid-Henry's bird sketches.

Adèle REIFENBERG 1893–1986 Artist and teacher, born in Berlin, Germany, who studied with Lovis Corinth, 1911–15; then, during a brief period at the Weimar Academy she won its prize for landscape painting. In the 1920s and 1930s her work appeared in many mixed and several solo shows, the Jewish Museum of Berlin, later destroyed, buying two oils. From 1927–39 Reifenberg taught in various schools in Berlin, and at the Jewish Teachers' Training College. In 1930 she married the artist Julius Rosenbaum, moving to London with him in 1939. From 1948–56 they ran a private painting school and it showed as The Belsize Group. With Rosenbaum's death Reifenberg concentrated on her own career. She showed at Camden Arts Centre, Burgh House and elsewhere in mixed company; in 1950 with her husband and Ruth Collet she exhibited at Ben Uri Art Society, which holds her work, and at the same venue in 1961 with two others; in 1983 Margaret Fischer gave her a show. Haifa Museum in Israel and the New Berlin Gallery, in Berlin, also hold examples.

Freda REILLY fl. c.1930–1978 Artist in pastel, educated at Pinner, Middlesex, and in Geneva, Switzerland. Exhibited PS and UA. Lived at South Ledaig by Connell, Argyllshire.

Michael REILLY 1898– Landscape artist and commercial painter who sold most of his work direct to publishers for reproduction. He studied at Central School of Arts and Crafts, in Birmingham, 1923–6, living for a time in the Sutton Coldfield area where he had been brought up. Exhibited RA, RBSA and Paris

Salon. Public galleries in Leeds and Dudley, Worcestershire, bought his work.

Simon REILLY 1960– Painter, born in Dublin, Ireland, who completed a foundation course in 1979 at the College of Marketing and Design, Parnell Square. Graduated in fine art in 1985 from University of Ulster, Belfast. In 1989 Reilly won the Arts Council Scholarship to the British School in Rome for a year; his work was shown there and was subsequently chosen for the Ten years of the British School in Rome show in 1990, in London. Among many other group appearances were Works on Paper and Beyond the Partitions, organised by Queen Street Studios, Belfast, with which he was associated, in 1994. Solo exhibitions included Arts Council Gallery, Belfast, 1988 and 1992, and Temple Bar Gallery, Dublin, 1992.

Victor REINGANUM 1907–1995 Illustrator, painter and designer, born Edward Victor Reinganum in London. He studied at Heatherley's School of Fine Art, Académie Julian in Paris and was a private student of Léger. From mid-1920s worked for over 40 years for *Radio Times*, other clients including Shell, London Transport, Ministry of Works and British Rail. In 1928 he was appointed art director of Elstree Studios. Two years before that, with the cartoonist Nicolas Bentley, Reinganum had formed the Pandemonium Group, which showed at Beaux Arts Gallery. His work was also shown at Mayor Gallery and in 1992–3 Oriel Gallery, Mold, held a solo exhibition of his pictures, which could be savage and powerful. Reinganum was drawn to the work of the Surrealists Yves Tanguy, Jean Arp and Max Ernst and his superbly crafted pictures have been a feature of many exhibitions associated with Surrealism. From 1962–6 he passed on his graphic design skills at Croydon College of Art. York Art Gallery owns his picture Torso. Lived finally at Tunbridge Wells, Kent.

George Francis REISS 1893–1973 Wood engraver, born at Kendal, Westmorland, and educated in the northwest of England. Exhibited RA, RSA, RCamA, RHA and RUA, also with SWE, UA and widely abroad, including bronze medal at Paris Salon, 1958. His work was reproduced in *The Studio* and in the form of Christmas cards which for years were used by the royal family. Continued to live at Kendal and was a member of the Art Society there, Lake Artists' Society and Lancaster Art Group. Abbot Hall Art Gallery, Kendal, holds a collection of Reiss's meticulously detailed studies, which belie his largely self-taught status.

Gerald REITLINGER 1900–1978 Writer, collector and painter, born in London. He attended Westminster School and graduated in literature from Oxford University, studying art at Slade School of Fine Art and Westminster School of Art. His work owed much to the Impressionists. Showed at LG, NEAC, Redfern and Goupil Galleries. Reitlinger was perhaps best known for his articles and books on the history of taste, the contemporary world and the archaeology of Iraq and for his important collection of ceramics, given to the Ashmolean Museum, Oxford. Reitlinger's multi-volume study *The Economics of Taste* was a pioneering work. A show of his pictures was held at Bowmoore Gallery, 1990. Lived for some years near Rye, Sussex.

Lottie REIZENSTEIN 1904–1982 Artist and teacher, born in Nuremberg, Germany, sister of the composer and pianist Franz Reizenstein. She studied in Nuremberg and Berlin, then after settling in London in 1936 was taught by Oskar Kokoschka. Reizenstein was a great traveller, and when she was not teaching in her studio in Hampstead was seeking subjects in France, Spain, North Africa, Mallorca and especially Yugoslavia and its Adriatic coast. Shared a number of exhibitions at Ben Uri Art Society, which holds several examples, notably 1987, with Iris Blain. Others included Italian State Tourist Office, 1960; Galerie Trojanski, Düsseldorf, 1966; and Margaret Fischer, 1976.

David REMFRY 1942– Painter, notably of watercolours of young girls and trendy party life, born in Sussex. He studied at Hull College of Art, 1959–64, after which he lived in London. Was elected RWS in 1987. Showed widely abroad and had many solo exhibitions, notably from 1975 at Old Fire Engine House, Ely; Mercury Gallery and Bohun Gallery in Henley-on-Thames, from 1978; at Galerie de Beerenburght, Netherlands, from 1979; Ankrum Gallery, Los Angeles, from 1980; and Zack Schuster Gallery, Florida, from 1986. Victoria & Albert Museum, National Portrait Gallery, provincial English and American galleries hold his work.

Mary REMINGTON 1910– Painter in oil, born in Reigate, Surrey. She studied with William Todd-Brown, principal of Redhill School of Art, then at Royal College of Art, 1930–3, on a scholarship under William Rothenstein, later in Paris at L'Académie de la Grande Chaumière. She was elected a member of NEAC in 1954 and ROI in 1962. Also exhibited at RA, RBA and in the provinces. Public galleries in Blackpool and Brighton hold examples of her work, which was representational. Had a studio for many years in Sutton, Surrey. Her son Roger was also an artist.

Percy RENDELL 1872–1955 Painter and teacher, son of the potter James Rendell, full name Joseph Frederick Percy Rendell. He studied art with Walter Wallis and Julius Olsson, the notable sea painter. Rendell also was noted for his marine pictures, being a keen sailor. He became chief of staff at Croydon School of Art, 1897–1932. Was a member of Chelsea Arts Club and showed widely including RCamA of which he was an associate, RA, RSA, RWA, ROI, Goupil Gallery, Paris Salon and in America. Lived in Croydon, Surrey.

Morgan RENDLE 1889–1952 Painter, teacher and administrator, born in Bideford, Devon. Attended the School of Art there, Brighton College of Art, then Royal College of Art. Became vice-principal of Brighton College of Art, having joined its staff in 1924. Exhibited RA, RI, ROI, in the provinces and abroad, the South Downs, near his home in Hove, being a frequent subject for his pictures. Medici Society and Frost & Reed reproduced his work, which is in galleries in Hove, Eastbourne, Southport and Brighton. Member of Brighton Arts Club.

Mary RENNELL 1901–1981 Painter, daughter of the 1st Lord Bicester, she married Francis Rennell Rodd, Lord Rennell of Rodd, diplomat, banker and explorer. After studying at Slade School of Fine Art, 1918–22, with Henry Tonks and Philip Wilson Steer, she became a professional painter. During 1940–5 she lived in America and for some time did not paint, resuming in 1960s. When arthritis prevented her working in oils outside she worked in Chinese ink on rice paper. In 1975 Fowler-Wright Books Ltd produced *The Paintings of Mary Rennell*, some hand-coloured by the artist, in a limited edition. She was widely travelled overseas, showing in solo exhibitions in America and Australia and in Britain at Howard Roberts Gallery in Cardiff, WAC, National Book League, RA and RP. WAC and National Library of Wales in Aberystwyth hold her work.

Alasdair RENNIE 1973– Figurative painter who was educated at Haileybury, 1986–91; Anglia Polytechnic University, 1992–3; and the City and Guilds of London Art School, 1993–6. Gained a Richard Ford Travel Award, 1996, which enabled him to work in Spain, other awards in that year including The David Wolfers Prize and Sir Roger de Grey Memorial Prize for Drawing. Had a first solo show at New Grafton Gallery, 1997. Magdalene College, Cambridge, holds his work.

Edward RENNIE 1966– Artist in various media, including collage, whose work included geometrical abstracts. He was born in Sunderland, County Durham, and studied at Trowbridge Technical College, 1985–6, Liverpool Polytechnic, 1986–9, and Royal College of Art, 1989–91. In 1991–2 he was fellow in painting at Cheltenham College of Art. Showed at Art London 91, Olympia, 1991; Five Abstract Painters, Montreal, 1992; and 1993–4 John Moores Liverpool Exhibition. Had a solo show at XO Gallery, 1992. Lived in North Bradley, Wiltshire.

Bill RENNISON 1932– Artist in watercolour, pastel and oil, born in Boroughbridge, Yorkshire, educated at Knares-borough Grammar School, settling in the county at Harrogate. He made his career in the Royal Air Force and in building services. Was a member of Harrogate and Nidderdale Art Club, showing at Mercer Art Gallery, Harrogate, and Barrowby House, Kirby Overblow, with a solo exhibition in Knaresborough.

Philip Brian RENNISON 1922– Watercolourist, draughtsman and teacher, born in York. Studied at the School of Art there under the painter and sculptor Reginald Cotterill, then at Leeds College of Art. Did some book illustration and showed with Northern Artists, Barnsley Art Society and at Laing Art Gallery and Museum in Newcastle upon Tyne. He taught for some years at the High School in South Shields, County Durham, where he lived.

Joan RENTON 1935– Watercolourist and teacher, born in Sunderland, County Durham. She studied painting at Edinburgh College of Art, 1953–8, teachers including William Gillies, John Maxwell and William MacTaggart. After a post-diploma scholarship year, in 1959 was awarded a travelling scholarship with which she went to Spain. In 1960 she took a teaching diploma at Moray House, Edinburgh, then until 1980 taught art in Edinburgh schools. Renton was elected a member of SSA in 1960, SSWA in 1972 and RSW in 1977. SSWA gave her a special award in 1985. Group exhibitions also included Contemporary Art from Scotland, Arts Council tour, 1965; The Knightsbridge Gallery, Wichita, America, 1979; Ancrum Gallery, Ancrum, 1984; and National Trust for Scotland, 1985. Had a solo show at Douglas & Foulis Gallery, Edinburgh, 1965, later exhibitions including Macaulay Gallery, Stenton, 1985–6, and Sally Hunter Fine Art, 1987. HRH The Duke of Edinburgh, Edinburgh Schools Collection and Royal College of Physicians hold examples. Lived in Edinburgh.

Leonard C RENTON 1920– Painter, a Londoner who studied at St Martin's School of Art, 1936–8, and Royal College of Art, 1938–9 and 1947–9, where he was an outstanding student. Showed with LG, Young Contemporaries, RA Summer Exhibition and elsewhere in mixed shows and in the 1960s had solo exhibitions at High Hill Gallery; Seaford Gallery, in Sussex; and at North Finchley Library. As well as rather mannered figurative pictures Renton completed some abstract work. Hertfordshire County Council bought his work.

Stanislaw REPETA c.1913– Sculptor and designer, one of a group of Polish artists who promoted paper sculpture in Britain in post-war years. After studying art in Poznań, Repeta graduated with honours in sculpture from Warsaw Academy of Arts. He won first prize in a competition for a monument to Marshal Josef Pilsudski, the Polish soldier and statesman. Repeta was in the Polish Army and took part in the Warsaw Uprising, was a prisoner of war in Germany, was assigned to the Young Men's Christian Association there and arrived in Britain in 1948. As a commercial designer of paper sculpture he was noted for his witty and immaculately cut figures, as shown in the exhibition Polish Paper Sculpture at Polish Cultural Institute, 1995. Its catalogue noted that Repeta later was "diagnosed as suffering from a severe mental disorder".

Albert REUSS 1889–1975 Painter and sculptor. Born in Vienna, Reuss was self-taught. He first showed in Vienna in 1926 at the Wurthle Gallery and again in 1930. He was included in the Chicago Exhibition in 1933, five years later emigrating to England, later taking British citizenship. Reuss and his wife moved to Mousehole, Cornwall, in 1948 where they had a small studio-gallery showing various artists' work and local crafts, but Reuss kept apart from the Cornish art world centred on St Ives. Had regular one-man shows at O'Hana Gallery, London, as well as solo exhibitions in municipal galleries in Birmingham, Cheltenham and Penarth. Several such provincial galleries hold his work, as do the Victoria & Albert Museum, the Fitzwilliam Museum, Cambridge, British Museum and the Albertina Museum, Vienna. There was a big show of Reuss at Newlyn Orion Gallery in 1980, and a retrospective at The Stable Gallery, Long Ashton, Bristol, 1989.

John REVEL 1884–1967 Painter, decorative designer, architect and administrator. Born in Dundee, he attended the Royal College of Art, 1906–12, under Gerald Moira. Was married to the artist Lucy Revel. He became the head of Chelsea School of Art, 1913–25, and of Glasgow School of Art, 1925–32. Exhibited RA, ROI, RSA, Chenil Galleries, the Royal Glasgow Institute of the Fine Arts and in the provinces. Manchester City Art Gallery and Paisley Museum and Art Gallery hold his work. Was a member of Chelsea Arts Club. Lived at Blewbury, Berkshire.

Lucy REVEL 1887–1961 Painter of portraits, figures and flowers, married to the artist John Revel. She showed with SWA of which she was a member, RSA, RA, Royal Glasgow Institute of the Fine Arts and elsewhere and settled in Blewbury, Berkshire.

Stanislas REYCHAN 1897– Sculptor and potter whose father was an artist. He studied in schools in continental Europe, then attended St Martin's School of Art under Walter Marsden and Central School of Arts and Crafts with Dora Billington. Showed at RA, NS, elsewhere in Britain and at Paris Salon, where he won Silver and Bronze Medals. Leicester Museum and Art Gallery holds his work. Lived in London.

Ian David REYNARD 1942– Painter and teacher, born in Leeds, Yorkshire. Studied at Lancaster and Morecambe College of Art, 1960–5, and in 1963 won Guinness Travel Prize. Showed in London and the provinces. Lived in Barton, Lancashire.

Alan REYNOLDS 1926– Painter of landscapes and abstracts, maker of constructions and reliefs, and teacher. He was born in Newmarket, Suffolk. Studied at Woolwich Polytechnic School of Art, 1948–52, then won scholarship to Royal College of Art, 1952–3, receiving a medal for painting. Had first one-man show at Redfern Gallery in 1952 and at Durlacher Gallery in 1954. He was one of three prizewinners at Giovani Pittori show in Rome the following year, one of several awards he won. Taught at Central School of Art and Design, 1954–61, then at St Martin's School of Art. Although Reynolds' work until 1958 had Neo-Romantic overtones, he was aware of trends in modern European art from 1946 and his early landscapes have a strong geometrical underpinning. From 1958 he was moving into abstraction, creating paintings, reliefs and constructions, often in white to maximise "the play of light and shadow". Retrospective of relief constructions and drawings at Annely Juda Fine Art, 1991. Tate Gallery and Arts Council hold his work.

Bernard REYNOLDS 1915– Sculptor, draughtsman, printmaker and teacher, born in Norwich where he studied at the School of Art and Westminster School of Art, 1932–7. From 1938–47 worked as an engineer. He went on to teach sculpture, retiring from Suffolk College. Reynolds' art was wide-ranging, his sculpture including portraits of children, an Amanita figure series with elegant, purposeful distortions, Mycomorphs which were based on fungi and some pure abstractions. The nude was a constant theme of his drawings over 50 years. Reynolds showed widely in East Anglia. A survey of his work was shown at Chappel Galleries, Essex, in 1991. His commissions included a pair of 20-foot pylons for Suffolk College and a fountain sculpture for Ipswich Civic Centre which won the RBS's Sir Otto Beit Award in 1972. Reynolds was a fellow of RBS. Lived in Barham, Suffolk.

Daphne REYNOLDS 1918– Artist, born in Yorkshire, who briefly studied at Huddersfield School of Art. Between the wars Reynolds helped her father, Thomas Dent, run his ailing photographic business in Huddersfield. In 1941 she moved with Civil Defence to London and started to exhibit in mixed shows in the 1950s. During the 1960s Anthony Gross taught her printing at the Slade School of Fine Art. Her work appeared in many mixed exhibitions, including Arts Council's New Painting, 1958–61; The Mezzotint Rediscovered, Colnaghi, 1974; 80 Prints by Modern Masters at Angela Flowers Gallery, 1982; and NEAC, 1992. When her husband Graham Reynolds retired from being keeper of paintings, prints and drawings at the Victoria & Albert Museum in 1974, they moved to Suffolk. Thus Daphne Reynolds was included in A Survey of Influential East Anglian Artists, at Chappel Galleries, Chappel, 1991, which gave her a solo show in 1996, the first of many one-mans since having been at Everyman Gallery, 1958. From 1951 Reynolds was a member of the Hampstead Artists' Council; was chairman of the Women's International Art Club, 1964–7; was a founder-member of Gainsborough's House Print Workshop and its first chairman, 1978–9; and a fellow of the Printmakers' Council. Arts Council, Victoria & Albert Museum, National Gallery of Victoria in Melbourne, Auckland City Art Gallery in New Zealand and other collections hold examples.

Frank REYNOLDS 1876–1953 Illustrator and watercolourist, born in London into an artistic family. He studied art privately and at Heatherley's School of Fine Art. Exhibited extensively at Walker's Galleries, also at RA, Walker Art Gallery, Liverpool, and RI, of which he was a member. Reynolds was, however, most known for his work on the printed page. He illustrated for magazines such as *Pearson's*, *Illustrated London News* and *Pick-Me-Up*; was on the staff of several publications like *The Sketch* and *Punch*, of which he was art editor for many years. He illustrated a number of books by Charles Dickens and wrote an excellent guide to *Humorous Drawing for the Press*, 1947. Member of the London Sketch Club. Lived at Thames Ditton, Surrey.

Mabel REYNOLDS fl. c.1955–1980 Painter, sculptor and teacher who studied at Manchester School of Art, where she won a number of medals and prizes. She showed at RA, RBA, with the Free Painters and Sculptors and at Paris Salon, having solo exhibitions at Loggia and Woodstock Galleries and at Plymouth City Museum and Art Gallery. Lived for some time at St Agnes, Cornwall.

Maureen REYNOLDS 1926– Painter in oil and watercolour, born in Thames Ditton, Surrey. She studied at St Martin's School of Art under James Bateman. Exhibited RA and Horniman Museum. St Martin's School bought her work. Lived in London.

Michael REYNOLDS 1933– Artist using oil, watercolour, pastel, chalk, pen and pencil, but not acrylic, born in Brighton, Sussex, where he studied at the College of Art, 1951–6, under Alan Sorrell, R T Cowern, Charles Knight and Alfred Fairbank. He was a Rome Scholar, engraving, 1962–4. Rubens, Velazquez and Vermeer were cited as influences. Reynolds was a member of RP and RBA, also exhibiting at RA and elsewhere in group shows. Had solo exhibitions including Fermoy Gallery, King's Lynn. Reynolds listed as his main works a mosaic in Stevenage, portraits of the critic Brian Sewell and actors Cyril Cusack and Paul Eddington, and watercolours contributed to the Singer & Friedlander/*Sunday Times* Watercolour Competition, where in 1996 an atmospheric Italian landscape by him won a runner's-up prize. He said that his work was "traditional and totally out of fashion", maintaining that "drawing is the foundation of everything."

Ruth REYNOLDS 1915– Sculptor and painter in oil and watercolour, born in Wellington, Madras, India. She was the daughter of and married to Army officers. After education overseas and in England Reynolds, who sometimes signed her work with initials, studied with painter and illustrator Victor Burnand at Guildford School of Art, 1932–3; High Wycombe School of Art, 1959–75; and with Arthur Pan at Académie Authentique, Budapest, Hungary, 1969–70. She was a member of Contemporary Portrait and Buckinghamshire Art Societies and Ridley Art Club, also showing with Amnesty International. Solo exhibitions included English-Speaking Union, 1967, Loggia Gallery, 1982, and Century Galleries, Henley-on-Thames, 1987. Royal Air Force at Halton in Buckinghamshire and Guinness Brewing, Park Royal, are among collections holding examples. Latterly Reynolds had a stroke, making use of her right arm difficult. Lived in Princes Risborough, Buckinghamshire.

Vicki REYNOLDS 1946– Painter, sculptor and draughtsman, born in Portsmouth, Hampshire. She studied with John Thompson at Goldsmiths' College School of Art, 1972–6, then with Peter Greenham at Royal Academy Schools, 1976–9, graduating with honours. Among her awards were British Institution and Richard Ford Scholarships and the Simeon J Solomon Silver Medal for Painting. Showed in RA Summer Exhibition, New Contemporaries, Vortex Gallery and elsewhere. Lived in London.

Patrick REYNTIENS 1925– Painter and artist in metal, but he is mainly known for his contribution to stained glassmaking. Born in London; married to the painter Anne Mary Bruce. After education at the Catholic public school Ampleforth College, Reyntiens studied at Regent Street Polytechnic School of Art and Edinburgh College of Art and won an Andrew Grant Fellowship. Exhibited with Arts Council and elsewhere, but is principally shown in places of worship throughout the British Isles. Many examples are listed in Mark Angus's monograph *Modern Stained Glass in British Churches*: Ampleforth Abbey, Clifton School Chapel in Bristol, and in many parish churches. Wrote a standard book, *The Technique of Stained Glass*, and had a one-man show at Fine Art Society, 1990. Lived for many years in Loudwater, Buckinghamshire.

Geoffrey Hamilton RHOADES 1898–1980 Painter in oil, watercolour, pen and ink and sepia, and teacher. Born in London, Rhoades studied painting at Clapham Art School 1915–7, then after World War I service in the Mercantile Marine attended the Slade School of Fine Art under Henry Tonks 1919–23. His landscapes, figure studies and flower paintings reflect his love of natural history and interest in the classical world. When Rhoades left the Slade Tonks said: "You've something I haven't – imagination," and Rhoades' inner life did nourish his work throughout his career. His pictures are unmistakeably English in their understatedness. In the mid-1920s Rhoades completed murals and other work for the owners of Stoke Rochford House, in Lincolnshire. He then held a series of teaching posts, notably at the Ruskin School of Drawing, Oxford, 1953–72. He exhibited at the NEAC, RI and Goupil Gallery and had one-man shows at Maltzahn Gallery, Ashmolean Museum, Mall Galleries and Sally Hunter Fine Art, 1987. The Tate Gallery, Ashmolean Museum, Victoria & Albert Museum and provincial galleries hold his work. Lived at Cuddington, Aylesbury, Buckinghamshire.

Marjorie Field RHOADES 1904– Painter, designer and teacher, born in Gosport, Hampshire. She studied art in Liverpool, at Regent Street Polytechnic School of Art and in Paris. Showed at Cooling Galleries, at the 1937 Paris International Exhibition and elsewhere. Her work was reproduced widely in fashion magazines and she lectured on fashion at the Royal College of Art, 1948–54. Lived near Hartfield, Sussex, and in London.

Carol RHODES 1959– Painter in oil of modern landscapes in which she said "there is a feeling of unease and the absence of people is marked", as in New Art in Scotland, Centre for Contemporary Arts, Glasgow, 1994. Medieval painting and modern science fiction were cited as influences. Other exhibitions included a three-man show at Transmission Gallery, 1984, and Recent Paintings, Intermedia II Gallery, 1994, both in Glasgow, and A Different View, Andrew Mummery, 1997. Rhodes was born in Edinburgh and settled in Glasgow, having attended the School of Art there, 1977–82. In 1995 she had a residency in Slovnia and gained a Scottish Arts Council Award. British Council, Arts Council, Saatchi Collection and Unilever hold examples.

Marion RHODES 1907– Painter, black-and-white artist and printmaker, born in Huddersfield, Yorkshire. She studied at Huddersfield School of Art, Leeds College of Art and Central School of Arts and Crafts. Showed at RA, RSA, Walker Art Gallery in Liverpool and elsewhere in the provinces and in Paris at the Salon, where she won Gold, Silver and Bronze Medals. Was elected SGA in 1936 and RE in 1953. British Museum, Victoria & Albert Museum and Bradford, Brighouse and South London Galleries hold examples. Lived for many years in London.

RHONDA 1959– Artist in mixed media, work often on a small scale, brightly coloured still lifes and landscapes, born and lived in Belfast, Northern Ireland. Influences were Matisse, Paul Henry, Matthew Baumgardner and Lorraine Edwards. She attended Bob

Jones University, Greenville, South Carolina, 1977–81, gaining a bachelor's degree in fine art, teachers Emery Bopp and Carl Blair. Until 1983 did graphic design and taught part-time. Rhonda Paisley was the daughter of Ulster politician and minister, Reverend Ian Paisley. She was active as a youth worker, fund-raiser, journalist and Democratic Unionist Party councillor and from 1989 spoke for the Party on arts matters. In 1988 she published *Ian Paisley, My Father*, in 1994 *Kids Under Construction*. Solo shows included Emer Gallery, Belfast, 1990 and 1992, and Duke Street Gallery in Dublin, 1990.

May RIACH: see **Mary BRYSON**

Albert Charles RIBBANS 1903–1967 Watercolourist and muralist, born and lived in Ipswich, Suffolk where he attended the School of Arts and Crafts. He completed decorative panels for the Dorchester Hotel. Was a member of Ipswich Art Club, also showing at RA, RI and Royal Glasgow Institute of the Fine Arts. Ipswich Art Gallery acquired his picture The Edge of the Wood.

Ian RIBBONS 1924– Painter and illustrator, born in London as Harold Ian Ribbons. He studied at Beckenham School of Art and the Royal College of Art, 1947–51, with John Nash and Edward Bawden. He did a body of magazine illustrative work, also working for publishers such as Oxford University Press. Showed RA, Whitechapel Art Gallery and Young Contemporaries. Lived in London.

Lancelot RIBEIRO 1933– Painter, born in Bombay, India. He started painting seriously in 1955, becoming a full-time artist in 1958. Showed in many group exhibitions in India and London, including Nicholas Treadwell Gallery. British solo exhibitions included Everyman Gallery, Hampstead, 1965.

Eugène RIBOULET 1883–1972 Painter and sculptor, born at Tarare, near Lyons, France, where he studied at the École nationale des Beaux-Arts, 1902–6, winning a gold medal for anatomy. Appointed art teacher at the École municipale de Dessin et d'Art industriel in Tarare, later becoming principal, a post held until 1952. In that year he married Elizabeth Brown, a French teacher, from Belfast and went to live there, where he died. After World War I service Riboulet had studied sculpture in Paris and in the 1920s completed a number of French war memorials, one in Tarare. In 1937 won a gold medal at Paris International Exhibition. Showed widely in Ireland, was elected RUA and had several solo shows, including a retrospective at Queen's University in 1972. In 1971 he received the Ordre du Mérite from the French government but died before it could be officially conferred. Riboulet was an eclectic artist, taking elements from Neo-Impressionism and Surrealism.

Anne Estelle RICE 1877–1959 Painter and draughtsman born at Conchohocken, near Philadelphia, in America. After briefly studying at Philadelphia Academy of Fine Arts, she worked as an illustrator for magazines such as the *Saturday Evening Post* and for books. Rodman Wanamaker of the Philadelphia Department Store commissioned her in 1906 to go to Paris, and two years later she completed eight big murals in the style of Watteau for his shop. She took a studio in Paris and was soon elected sociétaire of the Salon d'Automne, was made a member of the jury and her picture The Egyptian Dancers was given the place of honour one year. Had a solo show in 1910 at Baillie Gallery, London, so successful she was asked to hold another the following year. In Paris she was associated with production of the magazine *Rhythm* and was friendly with numerous artists including Picasso, J D Fergusson and S J Peploe. In 1913 married the critic O Raymond Drey and settled in London. There she designed for Arts Theatre and Savoy Theatre, illustrated poems by Robert Nichols and D H Lawrence and showed regularly at Leicester Galleries and at Wildenstein. Rice was noted for her landscapes and still lifes in rich colours and with strong design, in the manner of the Fauves. National Art Gallery of New Zealand holds her portrait of the writer Katherine Mansfield. After her death a major show was held at University of Hull, 1969; others occurring at Annexe Gallery, 1978; Browse & Darby in 1980; Fosse Gallery, Stow-on-the-Wold, 1986; and Emscote Lawn Gallery, Warwick, 1995.

Bernard RICE 1900–1998 Designer, printmaker, sculptor, painter of frescoes, born in Innsbruck, Austria. His father, also Bernard Rice, was a stained glass artist, his mother, Marion Bateman, a painter. Rice between 1919–26 studied at Westminster School of Art, Royal Academy Schools and Royal College of Art. He early developed a reputation as a wood engraver, also designing furniture and making posters of cars. Showed at Chenil and Redfern Galleries and in 1980 Amberley Fine Arts Centre exhibited a selection of his work. British Museum, Victoria & Albert Museum and Cairo Modern Art Gallery hold examples.

Brian RICE 1936– Painter, printmaker and teacher, born in Yeovil, Somerset, who obtained his diploma at the local School of Art, 1952–6, then his teacher's certificate at Goldsmiths' College, 1958–9. From 1959 Rice held many teaching appointments including Central, St Martin's and Slade Schools of Art and Brighton, Croydon, Hornsey and Royal Colleges of Art, later appointments including Yeovil College and University of Brighton from 1991. From 1961 Rice took part in numerous group shows, including those of the Printmakers' Council of Great Britain, of which he was chairman, 1974–7. In the 1960s and early 1970s work by Rice seemed to be everywhere: at advanced galleries such as the New Vision Centre; in national newspapers and colour supplements; in *Tatler*, *House and Garden*, *Woman* and *Peace News*; and in advertisements for White Horse Whisky, furniture, carpets and gas fires. Rooms at the Geffrye Museum and at the Ideal Home Exhibition in 1970 contained Rice's pictures, which were also evident in films such as *Morgan, A Suitable Case for Treatment*, *The Untouchables* and *The President*. American companies filming Swinging London included Rice on their circuit. His work was linked with that of the Op-Art movement. In 1972 with Tony Evans Rice published *The English Sunrise*, an influential and successful book which won several awards. After a two-man exhibition at Fimbarrus Gallery, Bath, in 1961, Rice had a series of solo and shared shows until one of collages at Paperpoint Gallery, 1979, by which time he had returned to the West Country, involving himself in sheep-farming, building conversion and archaeology. The changed environment and his discoveries influenced Rice's work, and after a lull he began showing again, having solo exhibitions at The David Hall Gallery, South Petherton, and The Meeting House Gallery, Ilminster, both 1995. Rice's work is held by Victoria & Albert Museum, Universities of Cardiff, Aberystwyth, Bristol and Lancaster, the British Council and many other public and corporate collections in Britain and abroad. Lived in Hewood, Chard, Somerset.

Elizabeth Helen RICE 1947– Watercolourist and illustrator, born in Canterbury, Kent. She studied at Exeter College of Art and Design and City & Guilds College of Art & Design, with a bursary to study wallpaper design with Arthur Sanderson & Sons, 1963–70. She became a freelance artist and illustrator, a member of SWLA and Society of Botanical Artists. Her main work was most of the illustrations to Collins' *Field Guide to the Crops of Britain and Europe*, and she also contributed to *Collins' Gem Guide to Herbs*, *Reader's Digest A Field Guide to Butterflies and Other Insects in Britain* and other volumes. Rice took part in group shows at National Trust, Cotehele; Pawsey and Payne; and Medici Gallery. Had a solo exhibition at Sadler's Wells Theatre, 1969. HRH The Princess of Wales and the National Trust at Sissinghurst held examples. Lived at Seaton, Devon.

Marion Sutherland RICE 1902–1961 Painter, draughtsman, printmaker and teacher, born in London, although she was brought up in Hastings, Sussex, where she won a three-year scholarship to School of Art, 1919–22. Then attended Royal College of Art, 1923–6, after which she travelled in Italy, Yugoslavia and Albania. From 1928–45 Rice lived and worked in Egypt, working notably on portraits. During the early years of World War II she taught drawing to King Farouk's three sisters, then from 1943–5 taught design and decoration in the Higher Institute of Women Teachers, Cairo. After leaving Cairo in 1945 Rice settled in London, teaching variously at Camberwell School of Arts and Crafts, London County Council evening classes and at the Royal School of Needlework. Showed at NEAC, SEA and RWS. British Museum, Victoria & Albert Museum and Cairo Modern Gallery hold her work. Sally Hunter Fine Art gave her a show in 1991.

Mary Elizabeth RICE 1934– Sculptor, printmaker, painter and poet, born in Pontycymmer, Glamorgan. Studied art at London School of Adult Education, Lewisham, 1965–9, with a year's course in ceramic sculpture at Goldsmiths' College, 1968. From 1988 studied for some years at Kent Institute of Art & Design, latterly for an honours degree in fine art, and at Canterbury Technical College. Teachers included Roland Piché, David Thompson, Patrick Crouch, Peter Nevin and Tim Fagan. Group exhibitions included Blackheath Art Society, 1967–9; Riviera Gallery Hastings, 1991; and St Augustine's Gardens, Canterbury, 1992–3. The family and pleasures and pain were cited as leading themes of her work, and William Turnbull the sculptor as an influence. Lived in Deal, Kent.

Seán RICE 1931–1997 Sculptor in bronze and non-ferrous metals, painter in watercolour and oil, and teacher, born in London. He attended Brighton College of Art, 1947–51; Royal Academy Schools for sculpture, 1951–3; then won the Prix de Rome, working at the British School there, 1953–5. His teachers included Maurice Lambert and James Woodford. Rice taught at West Sussex College of Art, 1956–9; Nottingham College of Art, 1959–63; was a lecturer and head of sculpture at Liverpool College of Art/Liverpool Polytechnic, 1963–80; then head of 3D design, Wrexham College of Art, 1985–9. From 1970 had a studio/foundry in Liverpool. Solo exhibitions began with Bluecoat Gallery, Liverpool, and Midland Group, Nottingham, both 1966; others included eight at Alwin Gallery, 1968–84, then work was continuously shown at Art Scene Gallery; and there was a series of solo shows of paintings at Carrara Massa, Italy, from 1984. Atkinson Art Gallery, Southport, holds Rice's work. From the mid-1960s he carried out many major commissions. These included steel crucifix at St Margaret's, Anfield, Liverpool, 1966; fountain for Atlantic Tower Hotel, Liverpool, 1972; Constance Fund, national competition winner, fountain for London Zoo, 1972; two figures for Myrtle Gardens (Minster Court) redevelopment, 1983; and the Stations of the Cross for Liverpool's Metropolitan Cathedral, installed shortly before Rice's death. He lived in Walton, Liverpool.

Graham RICH 1946– Imaginative, inventive artist who lived most of his life on the River Exe, Devon, a keen sailor whose work was closely associated with ships and the sea. He obtained an honours degree in fine art at Exeter College of Art, 1967; qualified as a teacher with distinction at the University of Bristol, 1968; and gained his Master of Education degree with distinction at the University of Exeter, 1993. Rich created pictures by adding his own depictions of ships to found objects: a plank from a ship, a tin can or chunk of foam, using the existing texture or worn colour to indicate weather or physical features such as rocks. The process could take years, as described in Lesley Kerman's memoir *Graham Rich, The Search for Form*, published for an exhibition of Rich's work by Gordon Hepworth Fine Art, Newton St Cyres, at The Lower Air Gallery, in 1997. Group shows included Spacex Gallery, 1986; Cairn Gallery, Nailsworth, from 1992; and Contemporary British Painting, Exeter Quay Centre, 1995. Victoria & Albert Museum holds Rich's work.

John RICH 1931– Painter, born in Dorking, Surrey. Showed at LG, Leicester Galleries, Redfern Gallery and other principal London venues, having a one-man exhibition at Rowan Gallery. His work is in the permanent collection of the Museum of Modern Art in Haifa, Israel. Lived for some time at Chiddingstone Hoath, Kent.

Laura RICHARD-TRONCY: *see* **Laura Anning BELL**

Alan John RICHARDS 1932– Printmaker, painter and teacher, born in St Agnes, Cornwall, although when he was still a child his family moved to Mold, Flintshire. Attended Chester School of Art and Liverpool College of Art. After National Service, 1955–7, he began a number of teaching appointments, including Exeter College of Art. A member of both RCamA and Newlyn Art Society, he showed also at Margaret Fischer Gallery and University College in Swansea in mixed exhibitions and solo at Grabowski Gallery, Newlyn Gallery and Bristol University. In 1966 formed the Bartholomew Print Workshop and he also undertook commissions, including work for Harvey's of Bristol, in 1972. That firm and Plymouth and Exeter City Museums and Art Galleries hold his work.

Ceri RICHARDS 1903–1971 Painter, draughtsman, maker of relief constructions and teacher, born in Dunvant, south Wales, into a family where music and poetry – always influences on his work – were encouraged, he left school in 1919 to be apprenticed to a local electrical engineering firm, but attended art classes. Studied at Swansea School of Art, 1921–4, then at the Royal College of Art, 1924–7. First experience of Picasso and Matisse, who remained influences. Worked as an illustrator for the London Press Association, 1927–8; in 1929 married Frances Clayton, met at the Royal College; in 1930 had first one-man show at Glynn Vivian Art Gallery, Swansea. During the 1930s Richards was associated with the Objective Abstractions Group, Surrealist Group and LG. First one-man show at Leger Gallery, 1942. While head of painting at Cardiff School of Art, 1940–4, he was commissioned by the Ministry of Information to draw tinplate workers. During the 1950s and 1960s Richards was involved in diverse projects, such as his painting Trafalgar Square for the 1951 Festival of Britain; décor and costumes for the opera *Ruth*, by Lennox Berkeley; the design of two stained glass windows for Derby cathedral; and lithographs to accompany poems by Dylan Thomas. He taught at Chelsea Polytechnic, 1947–57, the Slade School, 1955–8 and the Royal College of Art, 1958–60. Among his awards was the Einaudi Prize for Painting at the Venice Biennale, 1962. The Tate Gallery, which holds his work, put on a major exhibition in 1981. Lived in London.

Elsie Margaret RICHARDS 1918– Painter in oil and watercolour, and etcher, who early in her career worked as Peggy Turner. She was born in Kingston upon Thames, Surrey, attending the School of Art there, 1935, under Reginald Brill, then gained an exhibition to Royal College of Art, 1939–40, with Gilbert Spencer. Won a Royal College Drawing Prize, 1943. Was a member of Free Painters and Sculptors, also showing with RA, LG, NEAC, ROI and elsewhere, abstract and representational work. Lived in Horsell, Woking, Surrey.

Frances RICHARDS 1903–1985 Painter, notably in tempera, book illustrator, pottery designer and teacher. Born in Burslem, Staffordshire, she married the painter Ceri Richards in 1929. Studied at Burslem School of Art, then the Royal College of Art. She taught at Camberwell School of Art 1928–39 and Chelsea School of Art 1947–59. Her first one-man exhibition was at the Redfern Gallery in 1945, other venues being the Hanover Gallery, Leicester Galleries, the Oriel Fach Gallery at St Davids and Howard Roberts Gallery, Cardiff, as well as the Aldeburgh Festival. Many mixed shows, in Britain and France. Commissions include illustrtions for *Acts of the Apostles* and *The Book of Revelation* and decoration for the P & O liner *Orcades*. The Tate Gallery, Victoria & Albert Museum, Leicestershire and Hertfordshire Education Authorities hold her work. Lived in London.

Patricia RICHARDS 1935– Painter, draughtsman and teacher, born in New Malden, Surrey. She studied under Reginald Brill at Kingston School of Art, 1950–5, and went on to teach, including elderly and handicapped students. Showed at RA, Royal Festival Hall, at Boathouse Gallery in Walton and Parkshot Gallery, Richmond. Solo exhibitions included Free Painters and Sculptors. Lived in East Molesey, Surrey.

Paul RICHARDS 1949– Painter, draughtsman, performer and teacher, educated at St Martin's and Maidstone Schools of Art, who went on to teach at Slade School of Fine Art. Richards' vivid portraits, based on an initially tight and realistic image, emerged from sweeps and flecks of brilliant pigment. His mixed exhibitions and performances included the performance *Deep Freeze*, Hanover Grand, 1973; Collazione Inglese, Venice, 1982; Nicola Jacobs Gallery, 1985; and the performance *Vital Statistics* at Donmar Warehouse, 1987. Had a solo show at Robert Self Gallery, 1967, later ones including a series at Connaught Brown from 1985 and Denis Hotz Fine Art in Johannesburg, 1991. Contemporary Art Society and Arts Council hold examples. Artist Bruce McLean and composer Michael Nyman collaborated with Richards in performance work.

Paul RICHARDS 1951– Painter, draughtsman and potter, born in Penzance, Cornwall, where he settled in St Ives. Studied at Falmouth School of Art, 1969, with Ray Exworth as tutor. Was at Pendeleath Pottery, 1974; Porthleven Pottery, 1976; and Porthmeor Pottery, 1979–90. Exhibited pottery in Cornwall, including Penwith Gallery, of which he was an associate; Trelissick Gallery, Truro; Cornwall Crafts Association. In 1991 Richards started painting and abandoned pottery. Exhibitions included Penwith Gallery from 1993; New Craftsman, St Ives, and The Living Room, both 1994, and elsewhere. Korean and Japanese potters, notably Hamada, were influences on Richards, also Constable's sketches, Vlaminck and Van Gogh. He was "intoxicated by landscape painting".

Adrian RICHARDSON 1950– Abstract painter, whose images could be rich and strident, as in Bassarta, his entry for John Moores Exhibition, Liverpool, 1991–2. He was born in Birkenhead, Cheshire. Richardson followed studies at the Architectural Association School, 1969–71, with others at St Martin's School of Art, 1971–4, and Slade School of Fine Art, 1974–6. Later lived in Cairo, where he exhibited, and London, where his appearances included Zoo, 1988, and Black Bull Gallery, 1990.

Albert RICHARDSON 1880–1964 Architect and architectural watercolourist, born in London. He attended London University, studying architecture at Birkbeck College and abroad, eventually becoming professor of architecture at University College, 1919–46, and at the Royal Academy Schools from 1947. Was made a fellow of the RIBA, was an RIBA gold medallist, was president of the RA, 1954–6, being knighted in 1956. Exhibited RA and wrote several books on architecture. Lived in London and at Ampthill, Bedfordshire.

Frances RICHARDSON 1965– Artist born in Leeds, Yorkshire, who did a foundation course at Jacob Kramer, Leeds College of Art, 1983–4, then an honours degree in fine art sculpture at Norwich School of Art, 1984–7, establishing a studio in London. In 1987 gained a Robin Walpole Purchase Prize, a Norfolk Contemporary Arts Society Purchase Prize and a Noël Spencer Award for work from the life model. Exhibitions included Drawings for All '86, Gainsborough's House, Sudbury, 1986; New Art in Yorkshire, Leeds City Art Gallery, 1987; and in 1988 Contemporary Portrait Society at Alpine Club Gallery, New Prints from Norwich at Bloomsbury I Gallery and Carving in Christchurch at Christchurch Park, Ipswich.

Geoffrey Philip RICHARDSON 1928– Painter and printmaker who sought "to promote the East Anglian landscape". He was born and lived in Woodbridge, Suffolk, and studied at Ipswich School of Art, 1940–4, teachers including Archibald Ward and Alan Bellis. Richardson was a member of Ipswich Art Club who also showed at RI, NS and Summer Salon. Solo exhibitions included Haste Gallery in Ipswich and Deben Gallery, Woodbridge.

Gordon RICHARDSON 1939– Creator of free-standing abstract sculpture, and teacher, born in Oxford. He studied at Goldsmiths' College School of Art, 1962–6, then Slade School of Fine Art, 1966–8. Went on to lecture at Winchester School of Art. His mixed shows included Sculpture 65 at AIA Gallery, 1965; Young Contemporaries at both Tate and Piccadilly Galleries, 1967; LG from 1975; and Winchester Open, from 1979. He had a solo show at Serpentine Gallery, 1971, and in 1981 shared a three-man exhibition at Woodlands Art Gallery.

Ian RICHARDSON 1964– Sculptor who in the mid-1990s studied for an honours degree in fine art, sculpture, at University of the West of England. Work experience included teaching sculpture skills to children, vehicle mechanic and heavy goods driver, care nursing, forestry and quarrying. Richardson's abstract sculpture, as in the 2nd RWA Open Sculpture Exhibition in 1996, was "inspired and informed by a broad-based experience in mechanics, general fabrication and industrial construction." Lived in Littledean, Cinderford, Gloucestershire.

Ilana RICHARDSON fl. from 1970s– Watercolourist who was born in Haifa, Israel. Studied at Batzalel Academy of Arts, Jerusalem, 1963–7, and Hornsey College of Art, 1967–8. Did design work in Tel-Aviv, 1969–70, moving to London in 1974. Showed in group exhibitions in Britain and abroad. Had a solo show with Christopher Hull Gallery in 1983, then with CCA Galleries from 1986 and at other venues. Crisp draughtsmanship and a light, sunny palette were characteristics of Richardson's work.

John Frederick RICHARDSON 1912– Painter, draughtsman and teacher, born in London, who attended Camberwell School of Art, 1928–31, teachers including Cosmo Clark and Randolph Schwabe, then the London Day Training College, 1931–2. Richardson taught in the London area and Hove from 1934, finally at Emanuel School, 1951–74 as head of art. Was at various times a member of Croydon Art Society, London Sketch, Langham Sketch and Ridley Art Clubs. Showed also at RA, RSMA, NEAC and PS. Lived in Sanderstead, Surrey.

Kathleen R RICHARDSON 1900– Oil painter and teacher who studied at Reading University. She exhibited at RA, AEB and Oxford Art Society, living in Oxford.

Martin RICHARDSON 1958– Holographic artist, born and worked in London, who gained an honours degree in fine art at Hornsey School of Art, 1979–82; his master's Royal College of Art, 1983–5; and received the first Doctor of Philosophy degree for creative holography there, 1985–8. Awards included artist-in-residence, Museum of Holography in New York, 1984; Madame Tussauds and Pilkington's Major Sponsorship Awards, both 1985; a further residency New York Holography Museum, 1986; and the Keith Johnson and Pelling Cross Excellence Award, 1988. Published a series of articles in holographic and photographic publications. Commissions included work for Tiffany & Co, British Airways, British Railways, Tetra Pak and University of Wales. Group exhibitions included New Contemporaries at ICA, 1983; The Thinking Image, Royal Photographic Society, The Octagon, Bath, 1988; World of Holography '93, The Tokyo Shimbun, Japan, 1993; and Freezeframe, Lamont Gallery, 1996. Later solo shows included Vacant Solitudes, Nogizaka Arthall, Tokyo, 1991. In 1993 Richardson founded The Holographic Image Studios, which claimed "the largest collection of hol graphic images in the world". Science Museum, Royal College of Art, Madame Tussauds and American, Italian and Japanese collections hold examples of Richardson's work.

Paul RICHARDSON 1967– Figurative sculptor in various materials, especially steel, born in Barking, Essex. Richardson did an art and design foundation course at Loughton College of Further Education, 1983–6, then obtained a fine art honours degree at University of Central England, 1986–9. Among Richardson's public commissions were the tightrope walker Blondin, for Ladywood Middleway, Birmingham, and Ahoy, a spaceship sculpture, a New Works Trust Commission, Midlands Arts Centre. Exhibitions included Food is Art, Café des Artistes, Custard Factory, Birmingham; Undercurrents, a Network Touring Exhibition; and 3F Studios Show, Leamington Spa Art College. In 1996 Richardson was given a solo exhibition at The Lawns, Christchurch Mansion, Ipswich, of his Reception steel figures, amusing depictions of real people, but larger than life. Reception was "an ever-expanding piece as new characters evolve", a "look at the way we dress and interact with each other in social situations".

Philip RICHARDSON 1951– Painter, born in Harpenden, Hertfordshire, who did a foundation course at St Albans College of Art, 1970–1, gaining an honours degree at Liverpool College of art, 1971–4. From 1974–5, Richardson painted a series of London landscapes; from 1976–9 worked exclusively on still lifes; in 1979 moved to Milan, Italy, to paint landscapes; then from 1981 produced landscapes around San Rocco a Pilli, Siena. Group exhibitions included Stephanie Knight Gallery and Francis Iles Gallery, Rochester, both from 1990; Coventry Gallery, 1993; Logos Gallery, 1994; and New Academy Gallery, 1995. Later solo shows included Fairfax Gallery, Tunbridge Wells, 1996, and Enid Lawson Gallery, 1997. Richardson's works are in private collections in several continents.

Ray RICHARDSON 1964– Painter who was educated at St Martin's School of Art and Goldsmiths' College School of Art, where he gained a fine art degree with honours. He went on to paint full-time, although occasionally he did voluntary work with children on projects and murals. Richardson gained a British Council Award in 1989, then won a Special Commendation in BP Portrait Award at National Portrait Gallery in 1990. Richardson's pictures were like snapshots and commonly featured bruiser and brutish types, sometimes accompanied by aggressive-looking dogs. Showed in Greenwich Open at Woodlands Art Gallery from 1983, other mixed show appearances including John Player Portrait Award, 1988, and Contemporary Art Fair, Islington, 1991. After a solo show at Greenwich Theatre Gallery in 1985 exhibited often, later shows including Gallery 31 in Lille, France, 1990, and Beaux Arts, Bath, 1991.

Juliet RICHARDSON GOODDEN 1957– Painter, born in Suffolk. She studied at Falmouth School of Art, graduating in 1977. She appeared in a number of mixed exhibitions, including Francis Graham-Dixon Gallery and widely in Cornwall and had a solo show at Commonwealth Institute in 1985. Her interiors, still lifes and landscapes suggested details without being merely literal, the brushwork reminiscent of that of Ivon Hitchens. Lived in London.

Keith RICHARDSON-JONES 1925– Painter, construction artist, printmaker and teacher, born in Northampton. In 1950s studied at Royal Academy Schools, then went on to teach from mid-1960s at Newport College of Art. He was a Midland Group Gallery Open Competition first prize winner in 1968. Group exhibitions included LG, AIA, Experiment in Form at Grosvenor Gallery, John Moores Exhibition in Liverpool and Third British International Print Biennale in Bradford. One-man shows include Lisson Gallery and a 25-year retrospective toured by Wrexham Library Arts Centre, 1996. Public collections including Arts Council hold examples of his abstracts. Lived at Tintern, Chepstow, Gwent.

Elizabeth RICHES 1931– Painter in oil, born in London. She was a medical student for four years, during which time she painted scenery and carried out medical art commissions, then studied at Byam Shaw School of Drawing and Painting, 1955–9, teachers including Charles Mahoney, Bernard Dunstan and Peter Greenham, followed by part-time studies at City & Guilds, 1961–3. She showed at NEAC, 1958, and at RA, 1962–3 and then from 1989, her painting being interrupted by bringing up a family. Riches' meticulously constructed pictures concentrated on portraits, mainly of the elderly, and on industrial scenes; a brickyard in Bridgwater pre-occupied her from 1958 until its closure in 1965. Lived in Chichester, Sussex.

Don RICHMOND 1929– Painter, theatrical designer and teacher, born in Ilford, Essex. He studied at South-West Essex Technical College, Walthamstow, 1946–8 and 1950–2, then at Brighton College of Art, 1952–3. Went on to hold a number of art teaching positions, from 1966 being senior lecturer in stage design at West Midlands College. His theatre design work included productions at Morley College, London, in the 1960s. Showed with RBA and was closely involved in organisation of Young Contemporaries in the 1950s. Lived in Potters Bar, Hertfordshire.

Douglas RICHMOND 1911– Oil painter and draughtsman. Born in Chesterfield, Derbyshire, Richmond studied art in Chesterfield and at the Slade School of Fine Art under Randolph Schwabe. Exhibited RP and NEAC. Richmond held a number of teaching posts in Derbyshire and Yorkshire before World War II, after then moving to the London area. Between 1949–73 he was head of the art and crafts department at Trent Park College, Barnet. Lived at Potters Bar, Hertfordshire.

Leonard RICHMOND fl. from c.1910–1965 Painter, teacher and writer who studied at Taunton School of Art and Chelsea Polytechnic. He was a prolific exhibitor at Fine Art Society, RA, Cooling and Walker's Galleries. Also showed widely overseas, winning a number of awards. These included the Tuthill Prize at Chicago International Watercolour Exhibition, 1928, and in 1947 silver medal at Paris Salon. Having carried out war commission work for Canadian government in World War I, Richmond went on to paint and lecture in Canada in mid-1920s and several years later in America. Was a member of PS, RBA, RI and ROI. Wrote instructional books, including *The Art of Landscape Painting* and *The Technique of Oil Painting*, as well as travel books such as *Devon and Cornish Days*, produced for Southern Railway, and *The Enchantment of Canada*, done for Canadian Pacific Railways. Lived in London.

Miles Peter RICHMOND 1922– Painter and teacher, born in Isleworth, Middlesex. He studied at Kingston upon Thames School of Art, 1940–3, teachers including Raymond Coxon; in 1946–50 with David Bomberg at Borough Polytechnic, which markedly influenced his style; and in 1946 was a foundation-member of the Borough Group. Between 1947–9 Richmond, who then painted as Peter Richmond, participated in Borough Group exhibitions at Archer and Arcade Galleries and regularly at the Group's own gallery in Little Newport Court. Early in the 1950s he moved first to

France, then Spain, in 1954 joining Bomberg as assistant in his school. In 1970 Richmond became director of art at the International School, Spain. From 1979 Richmond lived in East Rounton, North Yorkshire, becoming a foundation member of Rounton Design. He had continued to exhibit often and in 1992 contributed to Homage to David Bomberg at South Bank University, in 1993 having a joint show with his wife Susanna Richmond at the same venue. A major retrospective was toured by Middlesbrough Art Gallery, 1994–5.

Oliffe RICHMOND 1919–1977 Sculptor in wood and metal, born in Old Beach, Tasmania. Studied at East Sydney Technical College, 1946–8, then worked in the studio of Henry Moore, 1949–50. Became visiting sculpture tutor at Chelsea School of Art. Exhibitions included Molton Gallery and Commonwealth Institute, plus shows in Australia and America. Sometimes signed work O R. Work held by National Gallery of New South Wales, Sydney, and Arts Council, which has his bronze Twisting Man, of 1960. In working his figures Richmond was interested in energies or dynamic forces, in the potentialities of movement. Lived in Grayswood, Surrey, later in London.

Peter RICHMOND: *see* **Miles Peter RICHMOND**

Robin RICHMOND 1951– Painter, writer and illustrator of children's books and teacher, born in America, educated in Rome. She was at Chelsea School of Art, 1969–74, then went on to lecture at Universities of London and California. In 1990 she illustrated Mozart's *The Magic Flute* for children, *Introducing Michaelangelo* for children and an adult book *Michaelangelo and the Creation of the Sistine Chapel*. From 1980 made many group appearances, including ROI, Boundary Gallery and Bratislava International Biennale. After a solo show at Galleria Ariete, Rome, in 1971, and Ben Uri Gallery, 1976, others included Boundary Gallery, 1987, Mercury Gallery from 1989 and Barbican Art Gallery, 1992.

Herbert Davis RICHTER 1874–1955 Painter, mainly in oil, especially of elegant interiors and of flowers. Born in Brighton, Sussex, he initially studied furniture design at Bath School of Art, and he continued to practise as a designer and architect there for about 10 years from the mid-1890s. Then in London studied painting with J M Swan and Frank Brangwyn. Exhibited prolifically, including RA, RBA, ROI, RSW, Goupil Gallery and Leicester Galleries. At the Paris Salon won a silver medal, having won both gold and silver medals for furniture design at the Paris International Exhibition, 1900. Was for a time president of the PS, as well as the Bath Society of Artists. Represented in Victoria & Albert Museum and in many British provincial and overseas galleries. His work is well shown in *Paintings and Poems*, which he published, with poems by Lady Margaret Sackville, in 1944. Although Richter is today thought of mainly as a producer of decorative work, he could outstrip this image, as in his powerful pastel Building the Great North Road, in the manner of Brangwyn. Lived in London.

Irma Anne RICHTER 1876–1956 Painter, born in Paris, who studied there and at the Slade School of Fine Art. She later taught at Rosemary Hall, at Greenwich, Connecticut, in America, finally living in London. Exhibited Goupil Gallery and NEAC.

Tony RICKABY 1944– Artist, notably a draughtsman, who studied at Portsmouth College of Art and St Martin's School of Art. He was included in Woodlands Art Gallery's touring show of Greater London Arts Association award winners, 1981–2. Other group exhibitions included Art from the British Left, at Artists' Space, New York; The Open & Closed Book, at Victoria & Albert Museum; and Cleveland Drawing Biennale. Solo shows included Franklin Furnace and Printed Matter, both in New York, and Pentonville Gallery. Arts Council holds his 1980 drawing Law and Order: Army and Police.

Stephen RICKARD 1917– Sculptor and glass engraver, born in Carshalton, Surrey. He studied at Kingston School of Art, 1936–9, teachers including Reginald Brill and Harold Wilson Parker, then Royal Academy Schools, 1939–40 and 1946–8, with William McMillan. Rickard was a fellow of RBS, of the Society of Designer-Craftsmen and of the Guild of Glass Engravers. Victoria & Albert Museum and University College Library hold examples. Lived in Newark, Nottinghamshire.

George RICKEY 1907– Sculptor with a strong interest in kinetic works, born in America. His family moved from New England to Scotland, and from 1914 he was educated at Helensburgh, Dunbartonshire. Went to Oxford University and the Ruskin School of Drawing in Oxford, lived in Paris, taught in America, then during engineering work in the Royal Air Force developed a liking for sculpting. Scottish National Gallery of Modern Art, Edinburgh, holds his mesmeric, wind-blow sculpture Three Lines Fixed, Two Moving, of 1970. His 1972 piece Three Squares Gyratory, again wind-driven, is held by Hunterian Art Gallery, Glasgow, and Three Right Angles Horizontal, of 1982, is sited in water at the Highland Sculpture Park. Rickey latterly lived in America at East Chatham, New York.

Philip RICKMAN 1891–1982 Watercolour painter, especially of birds. Born at Richmond, Surrey, he studied with George E Lodge, the bird and animal painter. Rickman painted widely in Scotland and Sussex, his work being reproduced in *Birds of Sussex* and *Game Birds*. Among his books is *Notes from a Bird Painter's Journal*. The Glenbow Foundation, at Calgary, in Canada, holds his work. Lived at Wilmington, Sussex.

Huseph RIDDLE 1912– Painter in oil, especially of portraits, born in Beaconsfield, Buckinghamshire, whose full name was Hugh Joseph Riddle. He was educated at Harrow School and Cambridge University, then studied at the Slade School of Fine Art under Henry Tonks and Randolph Schwabe and the Byam Shaw School of Art. Exhibited RP, of which he was a member, RA and ROI. Chelsea Arts Club member. Lived in London.

Stephen RIDDLE: *see* **BIGGLES**

Jim RIDDOCK 1926– Artist in many media and teacher, born in London. He studied in Kent colleges and at Royal College of Art, teachers including Ruskin Spear, John Minton, Carel Weight and Robin Guthrie. Riddock taught mainly in Surrey and London where he was "head of art at a vast school for 35 years". His work themes were constantly changing. He had solo and group shows widely in Britain, including Woodlands Art Gallery, near where he lived in Blackheath, and abroad.

John RIDGEWELL 1937– Painter and teacher, born in Halstead, Essex. He studied at Colchester School of Art, 1954–8, then Royal College of Art, 1958–61. Taught at Scarborough School of Art, 1961–6, then gave up to concentrate on painting. English landscapes meticulously depicted but with the occasional unusual feature or viewpoint were Ridgewell's speciality. Mixed shows included New Art Centre, Piccadilly Gallery and RA Summer Exhibition, but in addition there was a string of solo shows from 1963, at Austen Hayes Gallery, York. Later ones included Grape Lane Gallery, York, 1990, and Mistral Galleries, 1993. From late 1980s Ridgewell did much commissioned work.

Harold RIDING fl. from c.1925– Painter who studied at Manchester School of Art. He exhibited Manchester City Art Gallery, Walker Art Gallery, Liverpool, and MAFA, in 1952 helping to hang the spring exhibition there. Stockport Art Gallery holds his work. Lived in Grange-over-Sands, Lancashire.

Edward RIDLEY 1883–1946 Painter of portraits and figures, stained glass artist and teacher, born in Birmingham. While working on stained glass studied part-time at Birmingham Municipal School of Art. Obtained gold medal in stained glass design. After working for Birmingham Education Committee and Cheltenham Ladies' College joined Central School of Art, becoming head of new department of fashion design. Was art critic for *Birmingham Mail*. Showed at RA but mainly at RBSA, becoming a member in 1944. Retired to Beddgelert, Caernarvonshire, in 1944, where he died.

Uwe RIEK 1964– Artist, notably a draughtsman, born in southern Germany, who studied at Staatliche Akademie der Bildendun Kunst, Stuttgart, 1985–90. His drawings sought a reference and relationship to landscape. Riek lived in Durness, Sutherland. Exhibitions included SSA from 1992; and in 1994 both Grafinnova 94, Vaasa, Finland, and New Art in Scotland, Centre for Contemporary Arts, Glasgow.

Christa van RIEL 1963– Sculptor, painter, theatrical designer and teacher, born in The Hague, Netherlands, then settled in London in the late 1960s. Studied for a diploma at Epsom School of Art, 1981, then gained an honours degree in fine art from Wimbledon School of Art, 1984. She handled a number of commissions during 1983–6 while helping the mentally ill and handicapped and teaching art. The commissions included work for Sacks Wine Bar, Manchester, 1984; paintings and collages for Blinkers public house, Kempton Park; and a design on plastic for a Unipart calendar. From 1987 she worked as a scene painter on a string of productions, including *The Hooded Fang* at the Unicorn; *Dick Whittington*, at the Gordon Craig, Stevenage; and a set for *Prince Lovesexy* concert in Oslo. The sculptural people she created could be super-real and unnerving. Exhibitions included Art at the Showroom, which she shared with Steve Odlum, Bethnal Green, 1987; Art to Go, Sue Arnold Gallery, 1988; and Links of Affinity, Knapp Gallery, 1989.

James RIELLY 1956– Painter, born in Wales, who attended Deeside College there, 1974–5; Gloucestershire College of Art and Design, Cheltenham, 1975–8; and Belfast College of Art, 1980–1. He was fellow at Artescape Trust in Lincoln, 1983–4; at The Fine Arts Work Center, Provincetown, America, 1984–5; at Kunstlerhaus Bethanien, Berlin, 1988–9; and in 1995 was Momart Fellow at Tate Gallery, Liverpool, where he contributed to Making It with a series of figure paintings with some subtle deformation. Other group shows included Douglas Hyde Gallery, Dublin, 1983; Ferens Art Gallery, Hull, and The Usher Gallery, Lincoln, both 1984; Christopher Hull Gallery from 1986; and Galerie Wittenbrink, Munich, 1995. Had a regular programme of solo exhibitions in Britain and abroad, latterly including Laurent Delaye from 1994. Lived in London.

Dolf RIESER 1898–1983 Printmaker and teacher, born in King William's Town, South Africa. As a small boy was educated in Germany and Switzerland. In 1917 he studied at École Polytechnic, Zürich, obtaining a diploma in agricultural engineering, then from 1918–22 obtained doctorate in science at University of Lausanne, in 1923 researching in science at Munich University while studying art with Hans Hoffman. After settling in Paris in 1928 Rieser studied at Atelier 17 with S W Hayter and Joseph Hecht. Having moved to England to join war effort in 1940, in 1945 Rieser settled to civilian life there, lecturing in biology, liberal studies and art, also giving private tuition in printmaking. In 1960 he was invited to Cape Town and Johannesburg Universities to lecture on that subject. Rieser was elected to RE. He took part in group shows widely throughout Europe and America, including Peggy Guggenheim Gallery, 1939; Atelier 17, New York and San Francisco, 1954; AIA from 1955; RE from 1956; and RA from 1965. His solo shows were international, including Galerie Bonjean, Paris, 1936; Zwemmer Gallery, 1956; Lumley Cazalet, 1968; and David Paul Gallery, Chichester, 1979. Victoria & Albert Museum, Arts Council and New York Public Library hold his work, which commonly used bird themes, stylised and realistic. His son Martin was also an artist. Dolf lived in London and had a house at Zennor, Cornwall, for about 30 years.

Martin RIESER 1951– Artist, photographer and teacher, son of the printmaker Dolf Rieser, born in London. He was introduced to etching at the age of three and inherited a strong sense of biological form from his father. Took an English degree at Bristol University, studied printmaking in Paris with S W Hayter and then at postgraduate level at Goldsmiths' College. The combination of his own verse and imagery remained a recurrent concern. From the early 1970s taught at various schools and colleges, eventually becoming lecturer in charge of printmaking and graphics at Sir John Cass School of Art, with a home and studio in Suffolk. Did illustrations for Roger Harris' *Islands*, 1973, and wrote articles and reviews for *The Artist* magazine. Mixed shows included Cité des Arts, Paris, 1972; RE, from 1974; Lumley Cazalet, 1975; and Kingsgate Gallery, from 1978, where he had an exhibition of photographs, 1980. Just before his father died, in 1983, they shared a show at Salt House Gallery, St Ives.

Adrian RIGBY 1962– Artist who specialised in wildlife, born in Lancashire, working mainly in watercolour and gouache. Brought up in wood and moorland landscapes he was early on a keen artist and amateur naturalist, but it was not until leaving college that he was able to combine the two to make it his career. After studying at Blackpool College of Art he was for a time a commercial artist. His work was shown widely, including America, and in 1992–3 his exhibition Call of the Wild was held at Warrington Museum & Art Gallery.

Geoff RIGDEN 1943– Artist working in a variety of media, including abstract paintings and constructions with found objects. He was born in Cheltenham, Gloucestershire, and studied at Somerset College of Art, 1960–3, and Royal College of Art, 1963–6. Was artist-in-residence at Cyprus College of Art, 1979, and a visiting lecturer at Winchester School of Art and Canterbury College of Art in 1982. He was a prizewinner at John Moores Liverpool Exhibition in 1965, and at Tolly Cobbold Exhibition in 1977. Other group shows included second Summer Show at Serpentine Gallery in 1979, Hayward Annual in 1980–2, British Artists at Cyprus School of Art, at Woodlands Art Gallery in 1983, and Whitechapel Open in 1989. Had solo shows at Studio, Greenwich, and Spacex Gallery, Exeter, in 1981, in 1993 having a one-man at Francis Graham-Dixon Gallery. Rigden's brightly coloured pictures were said to owe something to his love of music, notably jazz, having singular rhythmic qualities. Gained Greater London Arts Association Awards in 1979–82. Arts Council holds his work. Lived in London.

Ernest Higgins RIGG 1868–1947 Painter, born in Bradford, Yorkshire, where he studied, also at Académie Julian, in Paris. His pleasant open-air scenes were in the manner of French late-nineteenth century painting. Showed at RA, RBA, Walker Art Gallery in Liverpool and elsewhere, working in many parts of England. He was a member of the Staithes Group and was included in Phillips & Sons' Marlow show of group work in 1983. Lived for a time in Letchworth, Hertfordshire.

Bridget RILEY 1931– Painter, stage designer and teacher, born and lived in London. She studied at Goldsmiths' College School of Art, 1949–52, and Royal College of Art, 1952–5. Taught children for two years, then taught at Loughborough School of Art and Croydon and Hornsey Colleges of Art. For a time she was adviser to the J Walter Thompson advertising agency. She had her first one-man show in 1962 at Gallery One, was a prizewinner at John Moores Liverpool Exhibition in 1963, then took part in a series of overseas shows in 1964 which consolidated her growing international reputation. There were Arts Council touring shows in 1973 and 1984, the year after she designed sets and costumes for Ballet Rambert's *Colour Moves*. She had a number of retrospectives, including a European tour in 1970–1, a multi-continent British Council tour in 1978–9 and a retrospective of the previous decade at Hayward Gallery, 1992. The British Council and Tate Gallery hold her work. Riley experimented with a number of styles, including Impressionism and Pointillism, until 1960 when she began producing the Op-Art images for which she became famous.

Harold RILEY 1934– Artist, born and based in Salford, Lancashire, where he attended the Grammar School. Won a scholarship to Slade School of Fine Art aged 17, did a postgraduate year at London University and two travel scholarships took him to study in Italy and Spain. After returning to Salford in 1960 Riley decided to concentrate his talents depicting the area and its life. In 1975 Greater Manchester Council commissioned Riley to work for three years recording the older areas of the county and its people in a variety of media for eventual exhibition. Riley said afterwards that such an area could not be "considered in a vacuum; you must smell it, hear it, and be touched by it day and night … A person's view is most valid when it relates to the things he feels closest to." In addition to this work Riley reckoned to paint two commissioned portraits each year. They included HRH Prince Philip, The Duke of Edinburgh; HRH Prince Alexander of Yugoslavia; His Holiness Pope Paul; the conductor Sir John Barbirolli; and the American president John F Kennedy. Although he showed great early promise as a footballer Riley rejected the career in favour of art, but leading players were among his painting subjects. Showed at RA, MAFA, Salford Art Gallery and elsewhere. In 1996 The Old Fire Station, Salford, put on a retrospective, 1941–96, of Riley's photographs. Examples of his pictures are in public and private collections throughout the world.

Harry RILEY 1895–1966 Painter, commercial artist, cartoonist and lecturer. Born in London, he attended Bolt Court, under Walter Bayes, 1910–15, then St Martin's School of Art. Exhibited RA, RBA, RI and ROI, being elected RI in 1939. Was a member of the London Sketch, Chelsea Arts and Savage Clubs. Percy V Bradshaw in his book *Water-colour: A Truly English Art* gives examples of Riley's briskly done watercolours, having seen him at the Savage Club "complete a portrait in oils – and frame it – in under *four minutes*." Riley was a versatile entertainer, being a member of the Concert Artistes' Association; and a tutor with Galleon Painting Holidays. Lived in London.

Paul RILEY 1944– Painter, muralist, printmaker and teacher, born Warwickshire. Showed a talent for watercolour at grammar school, where his father was art master. He studied at Kingston College of Art and aged 16 showed at RA. In the following two years he had a first solo show at Richmond Art Gallery and won an Elizabeth Greenshields Award. During the 1970s Riley worked as an architectural painter. He moved to Devon in 1979 and after five years' lecturing opened Coombe Farm Studios, a centre for teaching arts and crafts. Latterly showed at RI and RWS, had solo show at Chris Beetles Ltd in 1990 and published *Flower Painting: how to paint free and vibrant watercolours*.

Paul RILEY 1963– Painter, notably of still life, and teacher. He studied at Bournemouth and Poole College of Art and Design, 1981–2, Gloucester College of Art and Technology, 1982–5, and Royal Academy Schools, 1986–9. Went on to teach part-time at Salisbury College of Art. Riley appeared in mixed shows at RA, Curwen Gallery and Bankside and Berkeley Square Galleries. In the late 1980s he gained a Landseer Scholarship, Fred Elwell Award for Still Life Painting, a Richard Ford Award and the Humphrey Brooke Award. In 1990 he was one of three painters given a show at New Grafton Gallery, which gave him the first of a series of solo exhibitions in 1991, with one at The Blue Gallery, 1996.

Reginald RILEY 1895– Landscape painter in oild and watercolour. Riley studied at St Albans Art School with the Royal Academician Christopher Sanders. Exhibited RA, RI and Paris Salon.

John RIMMER 1962– Painter, born in Salford, Lancashire, who settled in Manchester, with a studio in Levenshulme. He gained an honours degree in philosophy, Polytechnic of North London, 1980–3; an honours degree and his master's in fine art at Manchester Metropolitan University, 1990–4; followed shortly after by a postgraduate certificate in further/higher education at Bolton Institute of Higher Education. Group shows included Fresh Art, Business Design Centre, Islington, 1994, and John Moores Liverpool Exhibition, 1995–6, with his oil on canvas Removal. Rimmer said that in his paintings "autobiography and appropriation are two main constituents". Referencing material included "amateur photography, found diagrams, sketches, doodles, and also my son's drawings and paintings". Had a solo show, Familiar Snaps, Winsford Arts Centre, 1994.

Edith RIMMINGTON 1902–1986 Surrealist painter, mainly in watercolour, relatively neglected in her lifetime. Born in Leicester, she studied at Brighton School of Art, and was married for a time to the fellow-artist and teacher John Baxter. In 1937 she moved from Manchester to London and through the intervention of Gordon Onslow Ford was accepted enthusiastically into the Surrealist circle around the formidable dealer E L T Mesens. Was much admired and encouraged by better-known artists such as Edward Burra and her close friend John Banting. Her work is delicate and precise yet poetic, notable elements being sex, death and the sea. Died at Bexhill-on-Sea, Sussex.

Eric RIMMINGTON 1926– Painter, draughtsman and teacher, noted for his still life paintings of meticulous exactness. He studied at Slade School of Fine Art, then went on to teach in art schools in Britain and America. His mixed show appearances included Four Artists at Bradford City Art Gallery and John Moores Exhibition in Liverpool, both in 1961; British Painters in Skopje, Yugoslavia, 1964; Angela Flowers Gallery, 1984; and in 1985 Still Life/New Life, an Arts Council touring show. Had a solo show at Lane Gallery, Bradford, 1963, from 1983 showing one-man at Mercury Gallery. Bradford City Art Gallery, Gulbenkian Foundation, Leeds and Wisconsin Universities hold his work.Lived in London.

Peter RIPPON 1950– Artist and teacher, born in Essex, who attended Colchester School of Art, 1969, St Martin's School of Art, 1971, and Royal Academy Schools, 1973. From 1976 taught part-time at Colchester as well as Central, Chelsea and Winchester Schools of Art and Newcastle Polytechnic. Had a first solo show at RA Diploma Gallery in 1975 and was also exhibited by Nicola Jacobs Gallery. In 1980 Rippon showed a number of wax/pastel on paper geometrical abstracts in the Arts Council touring exhibition The British Art Show, chosen by the critic William Packer.

Paul RISOE 1945– Painter and part-time teacher, born in Calcutta, India, whose work was "based on landscape themes". He studied at Epsom School of Art, 1963–5, then Chelsea School of Art, 1965–8, under Brian Young and Jeremy Moon. He showed at Young Contemporaries, RA, and had a series of solo exhibitions including London, Middlesbrough and Newbury. BP International and Leicester Education Authority hold examples. Lived in Newbury, Berkshire.

David RITCHIE 1914– Painter, draughtsman and architect by profession, born in Lanark, Scotland. His father was a builder and he decided to study architecture at Glasgow School of Architecture, 1931–8, but was self-taught as a painter. Showed at Heal's Mansard Gallery, RI and in the provinces. Lived in Hemel Hempstead, Hertfordshire.

Eric RITCHIE 1934– Painter, mural artist, stage designer, illustrator and teacher, born in Aberdeen. He studied at Edinburgh College of Art, winning the Andrew Grant Major Travelling Scholarship to Italy in 1956–7. Ritchie early on established a name as a mural painter, among his commissions being the Diaghilev Exhibition at Edinburgh Festival in 1955; the Military Tattoo in 1959 and 1970; and then in 1985 the Epstein Exhibition. During the late 1950s and early 1960s Ritchie taught at Edinburgh College of Art as well as Dewsbury and Batley Technical Art College. Then after seven years teaching secondary school, in 1973 he gave this up to teach art privately. Meanwhile, Ritchie had designed a range of stage sets, from *Nabucco* to *HMS Pinafore*. He also did book illustration as well as work for magazines such as *Scottish Field*. His solo shows included Scottish Gallery, Edinburgh, 1978 and 1981, and he was included in The Compass Contribution at Tramway, Glasgow, 1990.

Louise RITCHIE fl. from late 1980s– Expressionist painter using a rich palette, and teacher, born in Lanarkshire, who studied at Duncan of Jordanstone College of Art, Dundee, gaining a fine art honours degree followed by a postgraduate diploma in drawing and painting in 1991. She won a three-month scholarship at

Hospitalfield School of Art in Arbroath. Spent seven months painting in Andalucia, Spain, after completing her studies; taught at her old College and at Glasgow College of Commerce; was artist-in-residence at the Charlie Reid Centre, Glasgow, connected with the National Schizophrenic Society; and was engaged on design commissions as far apart as Bon Accord Centre, Aberdeen, and an arts and crafts shop in Torre del Mar, Spain. Exhibitions included touring show of Scottish artists, Denmark, 1988; RSA Student Show, Edinburgh, 1989; New Generation Show, Compass Gallery, Glasgow, 1991; SSA, Edinburgh, 1995; and Richard Demarco Foundation, Edinburgh, 1996. Solo show at Compass, 1996.

Paul RITCHIE 1948– Printmaker, born in Chatham, Kent. He studied at Manchester Regional College of Art, then advanced printmaking at Croydon College of Art. He won a number of awards, including first prize in the Hull Print Open. Ritchie's etchings were noted for their versatility of colour and tone, and he made the handmade paper for them. He helped set up the etching department of Peacock Printmakers in Aberdeen and in 1978 established Manchester Etching Workshop, which he continued to run. Exhibitions included RA, RSA, MAFA, 7 Artists at Whitworth Art Gallery in Manchester and Oldham and Rochdale Art Galleries. Arts Council, Scottish Arts Council and Victoria & Albert Museum hold examples. Lived in West Didsbury, Manchester.

Trekkie RITCHIE 1902–1995 Artist and illustrator, born in Natal, South Africa, of English and Scottish parents. Moved to England during World War I and was accepted for Slade School of Fine Art when 18, meanwhile attending Edinburgh College of Art for several months. Slade studies lasted 1920–4, and she was taught by Henry Tonks, Philip Wilson Steer, Walter Russell, John Wheatley, Ethelbert White, George Charlton and James Wilkie. Showed at NEAC, Goupil and Leicester Galleries and latterly had a string of solo exhibitions at Southover Gallery, Lewes. When paper was scarce in World War II she invented the Midget Books for children, which sold several hundred thousand copies at tuppence each, having learned printing at Central School; these were lithographed at Chiswick Press and published by Chatto & Windus. Ritchie also did posters for London Underground and prints for Baynard and Curwen Presses. In the 1950s Ritchie set up her press at Monk's House, Rodmell, the home of Leonard Woolf, whose close companion she had become. They travelled extensively abroad and she inherited Monk's House and Woolf's papers, which she immediately gave to Sussex University. Ritchie also designed book jackets for Hogarth Press and Chatto, and among books illustrated were *Flower of Cities A Book of London*, 1949, and *Cooking for Mother*, 1958. Her real name was Marjorie Tulip Ritchie. Her first husband was Peter Brooker, a fellow Slade student, her second, from 1932 until his death in 1980, was Ian Parsons, who became Chatto's chairman. She lived at Kingston, Sussex, dying nearby at Lewes.

Walter RITCHIE 1919–1997 Sculptor in most media, born in Coventry, Warwickshire, who settled in the county at Kenilworth. He determined "to work in Warwickshire only a few miles from where I was born and try, through my work, to identify with local society." Ritchie studied at Coventry School of Art under Victor Candey, lessons supplemented by a former pupil of Rodin; then gleaned rudimentary techniques and carving and moving stone from local masons, an education carried on at Hornton Quarries; and completed his early training as a pupil of Eric Gill, learning about wood with Donald Potter, Gill's former assistant. The work of Lewis Mumford and Patrick Geddes were of importance to Ritchie who for five years was interested in society and environment through town survey and social planning. Ritchie "never thought of art in isolation but always as part of a social or architectural scheme." Much of his output was done for Warwickshire County Council on schools, fire stations and other civic buildings and it showed his liking for direct carving. Herbert Read also obtained many commissions for Ritchie, including work for the Design Research Unit and Festival of Britain. Ritchie worked closely with the Brick Development Association to develop the technique of carving bricks. He was keen for his work to be on public display in the street rather than in art galleries. Examples of his sculptures are in the new shopping precinct in Coventry; Our Lady of the Wayside Roman Catholic Church, Shirley; St Joseph's Roman Catholic Church, Whitnash, Leamington; and Caldecotte Lake Business Park, Milton Keynes. Style, a flowing line, wit and a truth to material are some characteristics of Ritchie's versatile work.

Claire RITSON: *see* **CLAIRE**

Elizabeth RIVERS 1903–1964 Wood engraver and painter who was born in Hertfordshire. She studied at Goldsmiths' College School of Art, 1921–4, at the Royal Academy Schools, 1925–30, and in Paris, 1931–4, with Gino Severini and André Lhote, devoting some time to the study of fresco painting. Exhibited RA, SWE, NEAC, LG and had one-man shows at the Wertheim Gallery, 1933, Nicholson Gallery, 1939, and in Dublin. Rivers was a member of Lucy Wertheim's Twenties Group and Wertheim illustrates a mural design by Rivers in her book *Adventure in Art*. Rivers wrote several books, including *Stranger in Aran*, 1946. The British Museum and Belfast Museum and Art Gallery hold her work. Died at Dalkey, near Dublin, where The Gorry Gallery held a retrospective in 1989.

Hugh Goldwin RIVIERE 1869–1956 Portrait painter, born in Bromley, Kent, son of the artist Briton Riviere. Studied at Royal Academy Schools. Exhibited RA and RP especially, also at Ridley Art Club, Fine Art Society and Walker Art Gallery, Liverpool. Lived at Midhurst, Sussex.

Jacqueline RIZVI 1944– Painter and muralist, born in Dewsbury, Yorkshire, who worked as an illustrator and lecturer before painting full-time. She studied at Regent Street Polytechnic School of Art, 1962–3, then at Chelsea School of Art, 1963–6, teachers including Norman Blamey and Patrick Symons. Showed at RA Summer Exhibitions from 1978, widely abroad and was a member of NEAC from 1982 and RWS, 1986. Although she was especially noted as a watercolourist, commissions included a large mural for St Mary's Medical School, Paddington. Had a solo show at Sallyport Tower, Newcastle upon Tyne, 1970, later ones including New Grafton Gallery, 1983, and a series at The New Academy Gallery and Business Art Galleries from 1985. London Underground Ltd; Shell, Amoco and Davy Corporation; and London Clubs Ltd hold examples. Lived in London.

Michael RIZZELLO 1926– Sculptor, born in London into an Italian family. After military service with the Indian Army in World War II, Rizzello studied at Royal College of Art, winning a drawing prize and a Major Travelling Scholarship which in 1950–1 enabled him to study in France and Italy. Award of the Prix de Rome for Sculpture took him to Rome until 1953. Rizzello was noted for a series of heroic bronzes, his work being cast by The Morris Singer Foundry. The earliest was the Welsh National Memorial in Cardiff to David Lloyd George; others include Sir Thomas Beecham, at Royal Opera House, Covent Garden, and at the Royal Festival Hall; and Nelson Mandela, at Trades Union Congress headquarters. Rizzello also designed an impressive series of medals and portrait medallions, including the double medallion of HM The Queen and His Holiness Pope John Paul II, marking the Papal visit to Britain. Rizzello was elected fellow of the RBS in 1961, being its president for 10 years, 1976–86. In 1977 he was elected fellow of the Chartered Society of Designers, having in 1968–73 been president of the SPS. Lived in London.

Andrew ROBARTS 1956– Sculptor who said that his work "reinvents the products of industry and commerce through containers and packaging. The containers are distorted to reveal not their contents but their consequences." He obtained his bachelor's degree in fine art, sculpture, at Manchester Polytechnic. Exhibitions included New Art from Manchester, Salford City Art Gallery, and Forms in the Shadows 2, Turton Tower, Bolton, both 1985; City Life, Cornerhouse, Manchester, 1986; Market Force, Art & Research Exchange, Belfast, 1987; and Marginalia, Turin, Italy, and Second Wave, Bluecoat Gallery, Liverpool, both 1988.

Alan ROBB 1946– Painter and teacher, born in Glasgow, who attended Gray's School of Art, Aberdeen, 1964–8, in the summer of 1968 studying at Hospitalfield House, Arbroath; gained a postgraduate scholarship 1968–9; attending Royal College of Art, 1969–72. Teaching appointments included Oundle School and Crawford School of Art, Cork, Ireland. Robb's work was difficult to classify, having at times a Pop Art element, indicating a liking for classical Italian art and architecture, and a Surrealist component, as in the landscapes in his first London show at East West, 1997. Group shows included RA and RSA. Public and private collections held his pictures.

Alexander Rhynd ROBB 1950– Artist in oil, pastel and gouache, born in Kirkwall, Orkney, who dealt with "traditional subject matter, treated in a realistic manner with a strong emphasis on contrasting colour and bold pattern". He studied at Glasgow School of Art, 1968–72, taught by David Donaldson, Alexander Goudie, James Robertson, Duncan Shanks and Leon Morrocco. Robb taught art in secondary and primary schools until in 1989 he gave up to concentrate on his own work. Was a member of SSWA. Group shows included RSA, RSW, Royal Glasgow Institute of the Fine Arts, Kingfisher Gallery in Edinburgh, 1990, Gatehouse Gallery in Glasgow, 1992, and Catto Gallery, 1996. Had a solo exhibition at Gatehouse, 1994. HRH The Duke of Edinburgh, Gracefield Art Gallery in Dumfries and the Dumfries and Galloway Educational Trust hold examples. Lived in Auldgirth, Dumfriesshire.

Brian ROBB 1913–1979 Illustrator, painter and teacher, born in Scarborough, Yorkshire. He studied at Malvern College, Chelsea School of Art, 1930–4, then Slade School of Fine Art, 1935–6. He taught at Chelsea, 1936–62, with a break for World War II service, then headed Royal College of Art's illustration department, 1963–78. Robb did publicity work for Shell and Guinness; worked for magazines such as *Punch* and *Night and Day*; and illustrated many books, including his own *My Middle East Campaigns*, 1944. He was a member of LG and in 1962 held a solo show of paintings at Arthur Jeffress Gallery. Arts Council and Contemporary Art Society hold his work. Lived in London.

Karen ROBBIE fl. from late 1980s– Abstract artist who studied at Duncan of Jordanstone College of Art, Dundee, 1986–90, then Royal College of Art, 1990–2. She gained an award that took her to Paris in 1988, and in 1989 a Hospitalfield Summer Scholarship. Robbie showed in the RSA Student Exhibition in Edinburgh in 1988, and its Annual Exhibition in 1989. Other shows included Compass Gallery Christmas Exhibition, Glasgow, 1989, and Printmakers' Workshop Exhibition, Edinburgh, 1990. In that year she was Barbara Rae's Artist of the Day choice at Flowers East, where she showed solo in 1997.

Bruce ROBBINS 1946– Painter and artist in collage and Letraset on paper who worked individually and collaborating with Jo Baer. Starting in Ireland in 1978 they worked together until 1984, Robbins settling in Ashton-under-Lyne, Lancashire. Their collaborative appearances included 112 Workshop, New York, and Galerie Rolf Ricke, Cologne, both 1980; and Lisson Gallery and Riverside Studios, 1982. Robbins' solo shows included Jack Wendler Gallery, 1973; Museum of Modern Art, Oxford, 1974; Robert Self, 1976; Barry Barker Gallery, from 1977; and Oliver Dowling Gallery, Dublin, 1978. Arts Council holds several examples.

Richard ROBBINS 1927– Painter, sculptor, draughtsman and teacher, son of Lord Robbins, author of the *Report on Higher Education*, 1963. After education at Dauntsey's, studied English at New College, Oxford, and part-time at Goldsmiths' College and Slade School of Fine Art, his tutor Clive Gardiner (he helped organise the Gardiner memorial show at South London Art Gallery, 1967). Following part-time preparatory school, Camberwell School of Art and Hornsey College of Art teaching, 1952–71, was then full-time at Hornsey/Middlesex University until 1993, when he retired as honorary fine art professor. His many group exhibitions included RA Summer Exhibition, John Moores Liverpool Exhibition and LG. From 1960 held many solo shows, later ones including The Studio, Bruton Place, and Peter Nahum, both 1996; Gallery 26, Highgate Literary and Scientific Institution and Town Mill, Lyme Regis, all 1997. In 1988, The Hon. Richard Robbins published *Moment*, an illustrated book of poems connected with an exhibition in 1987. Among works in British collections are sculptures in the London School of Economics and Stirling University, 1990; and in foreign collections three large paintings in the Hainan Mandarin Hotel, Haikow, China, 1997. Lived in London.

Arthur Spencer ROBERTS 1920–1997 Painter, draughtsman and teacher, noted for exotic wildlife and sporting subjects subjects, born in Cork, Ireland. When he was 10 he developed tuberculosis and his father, an Army musician, took him to Hastings, Sussex, to benefit from the sea air; he eventually settled nearby at Fairlight. Spencer Roberts recovered sufficiently to become an outstanding swimmer, training with the Olympic team. After Hastings Grammar School he studied at the local Art School, but in 1939, when he was serving in the Territorial Army, he was called up, preventing his taking up a scholarship to the Royal College of Art. Transferred to the Royal Air Force, Spencer Roberts qualified as a navigator and taught at flying schools in North America, but after a flying accident returned to the Army. Serving in Burma, he developed an enthusiasm for sketching animals, using improvised materials. After the war he returned to Hastings School of Art, in 1949 gaining a teaching diploma from Brighton College of Art. Teaching experience included Vancouver University, and with his wife Mavis he taught remedial classes at Down County Secondary School, Bexhill. From 1968 Spencer Roberts painted full-time, exhibitions including Harrods and elsewhere in London and he was offered shows widely in America. In 1985 the zoo owner John Aspinall asked him to decorate Port Lympne House; the Spencer Roberts Room took three years and includes over 220 species of Oriental animals. The Royal Artillery, Woolwich, and Star and Garter Home, Richmond, also hold his work.

Bruce ROBERTS 1918– Painter, designer, illustrator and teacher who was born in Southport, Lancashire. Studied at Liverpool School of Art, 1936–8, St Martin's School of Art and Chelsea Polytechnic, 1938–9. Showed at RA, LG, Redfern Gallery, Portal Gallery and New Grafton Gallery, in Paris and New York. Finished murals for firms such as Unilever, Shell, Silver City Airways and Shannon Airport. Taught at Central School of Art and Design and at the London College of Printing. Lived in London.

Chris ROBERTS fl. from 1960s– Versatile artist who studied at Chelsea Art School, teachers including Ceri Richards, later working in Julian Trevelyan's print studio. She did commissioned work for American, Australian and Dutch papers and had graphics syndicated by Camera Press worldwide. Exhibited paintings and etchings in various mixed exhibitions, including RE and at West Wales Art Centre, Fishguard. Her rich colours and strong shapes were reminiscent of the work of Matthew Smith.

Cyril ROBERTS 1871–1949 Portrait painter and draughtsman who also painted some landscapes. Born in Uxbridge, Middlesex, he studied at the Royal College of Art, 1889–92, at the Slade School of Fine Art under Henry Tonks, 1892–4, and at the Académie Julian, Paris, 1894–6. Exhibited prolifically at the RBA and Walker's Galleries, also at RA, RP and in the provinces. Member of the Arts and Chelsea Arts Clubs. Lived in London.

David ROBERTS 1954– Painter and teacher, born and lived in Chester, where he taught at the School of Art, which he attended, 1973–4, also Royal Academy Schools, 1977–80. Exhibitions included Stowells Trophy, 1977; RA Summer Exhibition from 1979; and Summer Show I, Serpentine Gallery, 1982.

Derek ROBERTS 1947– Painter, born in Berwick-upon-Tweed, Northumberland. He studied at Edinburgh College of Art, 1966–71, after which he lived in the Pentland Hills. Although Roberts' work was abstract, in it he strove to find an equivalent for the harmony of nature around him. He had a solo exhibition at New 57 Gallery in Edinburgh in 1977; others included a show at Laing Art Gallery in Newcastle upon Tyne in 1988, in which Four Seasons was the theme, and exhibitions at Francis Graham-Dixon Gallery, 1990 and 1992. Arts Council, Scottish Arts Council and Scottish National Gallery of Modern Art hold his work.

Diana ROBERTS 1941– Painter and teacher, born in Worcester. From 1957–62 studied at Birmingham College of Art, then went on to several teaching posts, including Dyfed College of Art in Carmarthen. In 1970 was Royal National Eisteddfod prizewinner. Also showed in groups at SWG and WAC, which holds her work. Solo exhibitions included Swan Theatre in Worcester, University College in Swansea.

Diane ROBERTS 1956– Painter, born in Dorset, whose work had a strong pattern element. Her Elizabeth I Series, shown at Woodlands Art Gallery in 1988, drew on the rich allegory and symbolism of that period. She attended Bournemouth College of Art, 1973–7, then Bretton Hall College, Yorkshire, 1977–8. Group exhibitions included 1979–80 Wessex Artists, Southampton Art Gallery; Out of Isolation, Wrexham Art Gallery and tour, 1986; and Southampton Art Gallery, 1987. Roberts had a solo show at Goya Art Gallery, Christchurch, 1979, later ones including Gillingham Gallery, 1986. Imperial War Museum and Russell-Cotes Art Gallery, Bournemouth, hold her work.

Elspeth ROBERTS 1963– Artist, born in Dundee, who studied at Gray's School of Art, Aberdeen. Exhibitions included RSA and Scottish Print Open Three, organised by Dundee Printmakers' Workshop, 1983. Lived in Glasgow.

Gilmore ROBERTS 1906– Painter, sculptor and teacher. Studied at Blackheath and Westminster Schools of Art before himself teaching at a series of art schools. Was eventually principal of Heatherley's School of Fine Art and then of the London School of Film Technique until 1958. Showed at public galleries in Brighton and Kingston and wrote about stage and screen décor. Lived for many years in London.

Gladys ROBERTS fl.from 1950s– Painter and teacher, born in Rhyl, Flintshire. She was educated at Pendre School in Prestatyn and studied art at Bangor Technical College, 1959–63. Was a member of RCamA, also showing at NWG, ROI, Anglesey Art Group and Tegfryn Gallery in Menai Bridge. Lived in Bangor, Gwynedd, for many years.

Howard ROBERTS 1922– Painter, teacher and gallery director, born in Cardiff. He attended the College of Art there in 1938–41, then did World War II service abroad for five years, returning to Cardiff College, 1946–7. After several years teaching at Tiverton Art School and two years painting full-time in Cardiff, Roberts was director of the Howard Roberts Gallery in Cardiff, 1957–70. He had several solo shows there, showing in group exhibitions at RCamA of which he was a member, CASW which holds his work, SWA, RA and RP.

Hugh Lloyd ROBERTS 1900– Self-taught painter, born in Bangor, Caernarvonshire. After leaving school aged 13 he became an apprentice joiner and served in HM forces overseas. From the early 1920s he worked on the railways, then as caretaker at Friars' School in Bangor, but on retirement in 1965 was able to paint full-time. Was featured in the WAC exhibition An Alternative Tradition in 1972.

John ROBERTS 1923– Painter, graphic artist and teacher, born in Tredegar, Monmouth. He studied at Cardiff School of Art, 1939–42, served with the South Wales Borderers and Indian Signal Corps, 1942–7, then attended Royal College of Art, 1947–51, under Robert Austin. Several teaching appointments concluded with his being head of faculty of art and design at Liverpool Polytechnic. Roberts was a member of RWS, RE and RCamA. He illustrated for publishers and did advertising work. Also showed at SWG, Liverpool Academy of Arts of which for a time he was treasurer, and elsewhere and had a series of solo shows. WAC and National Museum of Wales, Cardiff, hold examples. Lived in St Davids, Dyfed.

Julie ROBERTS 1963– Painter in oil and acrylic on canvas, born in Flint, Wales. Won a higher national diploma at Wrexham School of Art, 1980–4; attended St Martin's School of Art, 1986–7; gaining a master's degree at Glasgow School of Art, 1988–90. Participated in many group exhibitions, including Speed, Transmission Gallery, Glasgow, 1991; Aperto, Venice Biennale, 1993; Redefining the Art Icon, Pamela Auchincloss Gallery, New York, 1994; and in 1995–6 both SWARM Scottish Arts Council Travelling Gallery and British Art Show 4, and tour. Had solo shows at James Hockey Gallery, Farnham, and Centre for Contemporary Art, Glasgow, both 1992; Interim Art, 1993; and in 1995 both Interim Art and Galerie Ghislaine Hussenot, Paris. Roberts had a keen interest in medical subjects, which was reflected in her appearance on the 1997 BBC2 Television programme *A Date with an Artist*, in which she produced commissioned pictures for three Glasgow doctors. Aberdeen Art Gallery holds her work.

Keith ROBERTS fl. from 1990– Painter who studied at Camberwell School of Arts and Crafts, 1986–7, Newcastle upon Tyne Polytechnic, 1987–90, and then Royal College of Art, 1990. His exhibitions included NEAC Annual Open, 1990; Salon der Debutanten, Holland, and The Discerning Eye, at Mall Galleries, and tour, 1991, where he was a prizewinner. Had a first solo show at The New Academy Gallery & Business Art Galleries, 1993.

Kenneth ROBERTS 1932–1995 Painter and teacher, born in Applegate, Arbroath, Angus, noted for his depictions of that area, who enrolled at Dundee College of Art, 1950, under Alberto Morrocco. After National Service he taught 1958–93, being principal teacher of art at Harris Academy, Dundee, from 1973. In *The Scotsman*, Duncan Macmillan termed Robers "the supreme painter of the Scottish winter...one of the finest landscape painters of his time." Showed regularly at RSA and Dundee Art Society and was given a first show in Edinburgh in 1998 at Bourne Fine Art.

Lancelot ROBERTS fl. from c.1910–1950 Painter, signing himself L R and noted for his dashing style, based for some years in Manchester, where the City Art Gallery holds his work. Was a frequent exhibitor at RCamA of which he was a member, Walker Art Gallery in Liverpool and RA.

Laura Staniland ROBERTS 1906–1994 Miniaturist and painter who was especially keen on depicting wild flowers, and teacher, born in Brighton, Sussex, where she studied at the College of Art, then St Martin's School of Art. Worked in the studio of *Vogue* magazine, also for Cecil Beaton, retouching many of his works. After 20 years in London in 1952 Roberts moved to St Ives, Cornwall, occupying Zelah Studio near Porthgwidden beach, for many years holding an open studio during carnival week. Roberts was an associate of RMS, also belonging to SWA and St Ives Society of Artists. Travelled extensively, including Europe, Australia and New Zealand, completing many portraits and landscapes. Roberts gave private lessons in miniature painting. Exhibited prolifically, including RA, Paris Salon, Royal Glasgow Institute of the Fine Arts and West of England and Cornish galleries. In 1996 The Book Gallery, St Ives, offered pictures by Roberts and a small archive from her studio.

Luther ROBERTS 1923–1988 Artist in various media, notably as a printmaker, and art teacher, born in Petworth, Sussex, where he settled in Worthing. He was the son of commercial artist Harold Roberts, his older brother being the artist and teacher Bevil, who published a memoir of Luther in 1990. Early Biblical and literary influences were important to Roberts, a bluff, old-fashioned and reclusive man. He attended Worthing Art School aged 17, where he learned a love of wood engraving. While serving in the Army in

World War II he was able to study at Bournemouth Art School. In the Middle East Roberts drew the life of the area with his characteristic tinge of caricature. In 1946 Roberts resumed studies at Worthing, then did teacher training at Brighton School of Art. In 1949 married the ceramist Joan Kirk. The 1950s saw Roberts illustrating for magazines such as *Country Fair* and *London Mystery Magazine*, and in the 1960s he completed many inn signs for Tamplin's Brewery. Taught for 38 years, for last dozen full-time including Brighton College of Art and Brighton Polytechnic. Roberts was a keen exhibitor, with RA and London societies, was a brother of the Art Workers' Guild and showed with Society of Sussex Painters. Hove Museum and Art Gallery holds his work.

Marguerite Hazel ROBERTS: *see* **Marguerite HARRISON**

Perry ROBERTS 1954– Minimalist artist, born in Newcastle upon Tyne, County Durham. He attended the College of Art there, 1973–4; then Bristol Polytechnic, 1974–7, where graduated; gaining a master's degree at Goldsmiths' College, 1987–9. Was artist-in-residence, Rijksakademie, Amsterdam, 1990. Group exhibition appearances included RWA, 1975; LG from 1981; Aspex Gallery, Portsmouth, 1982; Open Exhibition, Whitechapel Art Gallery, 1983; Minimal Means, Showroom Gallery, 1989; and Chisenhale Gallery, 1991. Had solo show at Goldsmiths', 1989, from same year showing with Laure Genillard Gallery.

Phyllis Kathleen ROBERTS 1916– Painter and sculptor, notable for portraits, born in London. She studied at Hornsey College of Art under Jesse Dale Cast. Was elected ROI in 1961, also showing at RA, Contemporary Portrait Society, RP, in the provinces and at Paris Salon, where she won Gold and Silver Medals. Lived latterly at Aldwick, Bognor Regis, Sussex.

Rachel ROBERTS 1908– Printmaker and painter, mainly in watercolour, born and lived in Bristol. Studied at Swindon School of Art and the Royal College of Art, 1930–3. In 1941 she joined the West of England College of Art, Bristol, as assistant in charge of illustration, lithography and wood engraving. Exhibited RA, SWE, RWA and in America.

Sheila ROBERTS fl. from early 1980s– Expressionist and figurative painter in oil on canvas and primed paper whose work stemmed from musical and literary sources. Gained a diploma at the School of Art, Leamington College of Further Education, 1981. Mixed shows included Herbert Art Gallery Open Exhibition from 1983; Solihull Open, 1990; Leamington Open, 1993; and Pacesetters at Peterborough Museum and Art Gallery, 1995. Had a solo show at Rugby Civic Gallery, 1986, later ones including Abbotsholme, Uttoxeter, 1991.

Walter James ROBERTS 1907– Painter and black-and-white artist, by profession a civil servant, born in Doncaster, Yorkshire. He studied at the local School of Art under Frederick Glass. As well as showing with RA, Roberts was a member of Doncaster Art Club, Scarborough Sketch Club, Newcastle Society of Artists, Agricola Art Club, Society of Staffordshire Artists and Crewe Music and Arts Society, holding senior positions in some. National Trust and public gallery in Stoke-on-Trent hold examples. Lived for many years at Wistaston, Cheshire.

Will ROBERTS 1910– Painter, born in Ruabon, Denbigh-shire, but moved to Neath, Glamorgan, where he continued to live, as a child. He was apprenticed to a watchmaker and jeweller in the town, in the 1930s attending Swansea School of Art part-time. After Royal Air Force service, 1940–6, Roberts became a pupil of Josef Herman, who changed a rather tentative watercolourist to a more Expressionist painter in oils. Roberts also painted alongside Martin Bloch and was influenced by the work of the Belgian Expressionist Constant Permeke when shown in London in 1957. This all resulted in rich and forthright paintings of Neath and its area, plus still lifes and religious pictures. Roberts had his first one-man show with Roland, Browse & Delbanco in 1954, also showing with AIA Gallery, Arnolfini Gallery in Bristol, Howard Roberts Gallery in Cardiff and Tegfryn Art Gallery, Menai Bridge. He had a retrospective at Llandaff Festival in 1973 and another at Mostyn Art Gallery, Llandudno, and tour, 1993–4. National Museum of Wales, Cardiff, holds his work.

William ROBERTS 1895–1980 Painter of portraits – especially of himself and of his wife Sarah, sister of the painter Jacob Kramer – writer and teacher, born in London, where he continued to live. In 1909 Roberts was apprenticed to the poster firm of Sir Joseph Causton Ltd, in the evenings attending St Martin's School of Art. In 1910–13 with a London County Council scholarship studied at Slade School of Fine Art. After continental travel joined Roger Fry's Omega Workshops in 1913, the year following joining Wyndham Lewis at Rebel Art Centre. Exhibited as member of Vorticist Group, Group X and joined LG in 1915. Entered Army in World War I and became official war artist. Had first one-man show at Chenil Galleries, 1923; belonged to London Artists' Association 1927–32; and exhibited at RA from 1952, being elected RA in 1966. Roberts published a number of polemical writings, such as *The Vortex Pamphlets* in 1956–8, in response to Wyndham Lewis' show at Tate Gallery. An Arts Council Roberts retrospective was held at Tate in 1965, a further retrospective at Reading Museum and Art Gallery in 1983 and a show of Roberts' family portraits at National Portrait Gallery in 1984. Roberts taught from 1925–60, apart from the war years, at Central School of Arts and Crafts, and during World War II at Oxford Technical School while living in Oxford, but his formalised tube-man style remained distinctively his own.

Winifred ROBERTS: *see* **Winifred NICHOLSON**

Paul ROBERTS-HOLMES: *see* **HOLMES**

Ivor ROBERTS-JONES 1916–1996 Sculptor and teacher, born in Oswestry, Shropshire. He studied at Goldsmiths' College School of Art, 1932–4, and Royal Academy Schools, 1934–8. After wartime service with the Army in Burma the artist taught at

Goldsmiths' from 1946–73. He was elected RA in 1973 and was awarded the gold medal of RBS the year after. Roberts-Jones took part in many group exhibitions in Britain, including the 1977 Battersea Park Jubilee Exhibition. One of his most important sculptures is the huge equestrian work completed in 1983 for Harlech Castle. He had his first solo show with Beaux Arts Gallery in 1954 and carried out a notable series of commissioned portraits of the famous, including HRH The Prince of Wales, the writer Somerset Maugham, Kyffin Williams the painter and the Sir Winston Churchill Memorial in Parliament Square, London. Roberts-Jones modelled in plaster and cast in bronze. Tate Gallery and National Portrait Gallery hold his work. Lived in Cratfield, near Halesworth, Suffolk.

Alexander ROBERTSON 1916–1992 Artist and teacher, born in Tomintoul, Banffshire. He studied at Edinburgh College of Art under William Gillies, Hubert Wellington and Robert Westwater, then at Dartington Hall, teachers including the sculptor Willi Soukop. Shortly after World War II he was a scenic artist with Two Cities Films, then taught art for many years at Acklam College, Middlesbrough, until 1980. Showed with RSA, SSA, LG and abroad. Lived in Linthorpe, Middlesbrough, for many years.

Anderson Bain ROBERTSON 1929– Painter and teacher, born in Bristol. After Ardrossan Academy he was at Gray's School of Art, Aberdeen, 1951–2, under Robert Sivell, then at Glasgow School of Art, 1952–5, to win his diploma, an art teacher's certificate following. In 1981–2 Robertson was again at Glasgow, gaining an honours degree. Teachers at the School included William Armour, David Donaldson and Jack Knox. Robertson was head of art at Prestwick Academy. Showed at RSA, RP, SSA, Royal Glasgow Institute of the Fine Arts and elsewhere and lived at Barassie, Ayrshire.

Barbara ROBERTSON 1945– Printmaker, illustrator and teacher, born in Broughty Ferry, Angus. She attended Blairgowrie High School, then studied at Duncan of Jordanstone College of Art, Dundee, 1965–71, her teachers including Jozef Sekalski. She was awarded a Major Scottish Education Department Travelling Scholarship. Robertson went on to teach printmaking at Duncan of Jordanstone, then worked full-time mainly on lino-cuts. She showed in mixed groups at RSA, Printmakers' Workshop in Edinburgh and at Compass Gallery, Glasgow, where she had a solo exhibition in 1981. Her work is held by public collections in Aberdeen, Glasgow, Leeds and elsewhere. Lived in Douglastown, Forfar.

Carol ROBERTSON 1955– Painter of abstract pictures, born in Berkshire, who obtained a degree in fine art from Cardiff College of Art, 1974–8, then her master's in the same subject from Chelsea School of Art, 1980–1. In 1981–2 Robertson gained a Boise Scholarship to Italy, in 1993 an Edwin Austin Abbey Memorial Award, British School at Rome. Took part in many group and mixed shows, including Sherman Theatre in Cardiff and Stowells Trophy at RA, both 1978; Three Artists, New Art Centre, 1982; Acme Artists, Bethnal Green Library and tour, 1987; Art on Paper, Weatherspoon Art Gallery, Greensboro, North Carolina, 1990; and Contemporary Art Society Market, Royal Festival Hall, 1995. Had a solo show at Howard Gardens Gallery, Cardiff, in 1983, later ones including Galeri Weinberger, Copenhagen, and The Blue Gallery, both 1996. Arts Council, Contemporary Art Society and London College of Furniture hold examples.

Edward W ROBERTSON 1919– Designer for interior decoration and the theatre, illustrator and teacher, born in Edinburgh, where he continued to live, the son of the artist Eric Robertson. After education in Cambridge and George Watson's College in Edinburgh, he studied at that city's College of Art. Showed SSA, Royal Glasgow Institute of the Fine Arts and RSA. For some years lectured at Royal Academy of Dancing in Edinburgh.

Eleanor Moore ROBERTSON 1885–1955 Painter of landscapes and figures in oil and watercolour, born in Northern Ireland, who studied at Glasgow School of Art. In 1922 she married Dr Cecil Robertson, and when he was appointed a public health official in Shanghai three years later she moved to China where she made a valuable record of the country and its people. In the late 1930s fighting between China and Japan prompted her return to Scotland, where some work had been shown in her absence. Ewan Mundy Fine Art, Glasgow, included a group of pictures in Glasgow Boys & Glasgow Girls, 1996.

James ROBERTSON 1931– Painter and teacher, born in Cowdenbeath, Fife. He studied at Glasgow School of Art, 1950–6, then went on to teach at Keith Grammar School, 1957–8, becoming a part-time lecturer at Glasgow School of Art, 1959–66, from 1967 full-time. He was a visiting lecturer in 1970 at Michaelis School of Fine Arts, Rhodes University, Cape Town; in 1986 at Gray's School of Art, Aberdeen, and Duncan of Jordanstone College of Art, Dundee; and in 1987 at Millersville University, Pennsylvania. He was elected RSW, Royal Glasgow Institute of the Fine Arts and RSA in 1989. Among Robertson's solo shows were Douglas and Foulis Gallery, Edinburgh, 1961; Gallery 10; several at Christopher Hull; and Portland Gallery. HM The Queen Mother, Scottish Arts Council and RSA hold his work.

Janet Elspeth ROBERTSON 1896– Printmaker and watercolourist, daughter of the landscape painter David Mitchell Robertson. Brought up in Douglas, Isle of Man, she studied at the School of Art there under her father. She exhibited Redfern Gallery, Royal Glasgow Institute of the Fine Arts, extensively in the provinces and in Paris, Canada and America. Walker Art Gallery, Liverpool, bought her work. Lived for some time at Beckenham, Kent.

Malcolm ROBERTSON 1951– Sculptor, ceramist and relief artist, born in Edinburgh who attended Glasgow School of Art, 1969–74, gaining a sculpture diploma. Showed at RSA from 1976 and two years later became resident artist for Glenrothes Development Corporation, Fife, where he completed a large body of work. His fibreglass figures Tommy and Maggie, completed

1976–9, are dramatically situated in Glenshee Sculpture Park, Tayside.

Michael Ralli ROBERTSON 1915– Painter and teacher, born in Ilkley, Yorkshire. After a period in 1937 studying art privately with W Lyons-Wilson, Robertson in 1938 went to St John's Wood Schools of Art, his teachers including Patrick Millard, in 1939 attending Westminster School of Art under R Kirkland Jamieson. Showed at RA, RWA and in public galleries in Liverpool, Wakefield, Bradford and Leeds. Had a series of one-man shows at Norwich Assembly House in 1950s and 1960s. Lived in Norwich.

Richard Ross ROBERTSON 1914– Sculptor and teacher, born in Aberdeen, where he lived for many years, although latterly at Blairgowrie, Perthshire. Robertson studied at Glasgow School of Art, 1933–4, then at Gray's School of Art, 1934–8, teachers including T B Huxley-Jones and Benno Schotz. He lectured at Gray's, 1946–79. Robertson was elected SSA in 1947, a fellow of RBS, 1963, and RSA in 1977. He showed at RA, Royal Glasgow Institute of the Fine Arts, Kingfisher Gallery in Edinburgh and elsewhere. Aberdeen Art Gallery, Aberdeenshire Education Authority and Princeton University, in America, hold examples.

Sheila Macleod ROBERTSON 1927– Painter and wire sculptor, born in London, who studied at Watford School of Art and Central School of Arts and Crafts. Was made a member of UA in 1956, RSMA and 1969 and of St Ives Society of Artists in 1970. Also showed with SWA and ROI. National Maritime Museum in Greenwich holds her work. Lived in Rickmansworth, Hertfordshire.

Stuart ROBERTSON 1962– Painter and illustrator, born in Sheppey, Kent, who studied at Maidstone College of Art and Wimbledon School of Art. He was a freelance illustrator for Artist Partners, 1984–6, and Sharp Practice, 1986–94, from 1989 working for *Times of India*, reflected in his picture Railway Train Entrance at Royal Over-Seas League Open, 1995. Group shows also included *Reader's Digest* Competition, Association of Illustrators Gallery, 1984; and 30 Years of *New Scientist* Covers, Seven Dials Gallery, 1987. Piccadilly Theatre holds Robertson's work.

Tom ROBERTSON 1850–1947 Painter, notably of landscapes in France, Morocco and Scotland, especially effective in his moonlight scenes and pictures dependent on artificial light. He was born in Glasgow, studied at the Academy there, at the School of Art and in Paris under Benjamin Constant. On return to Glasgow in the late 1880s he began to show in his studio and in main London and provincial exhibitions. In 1898 painted for several months in Morocco, and on his return showed the resulting pictures at Fine Art Society. The year before, his picture Luna Sorgente had been exhibited in Venice and was bought by the King of Italy for his own collection. In 1904 his picture En Ecosse won an Hon. Mention at Paris Salon, he won a gold medal at the Nantes Exhibition in 1910 and the Musée des Beaux-Arts bought The Morning Star in 1928. Was elected ROI in 1912. Robertson's most productive period was now into the early 1920s. He was by then showing as far away as America, Australia and New Zealand. A heart attack in 1922 reduced Robertson's output, but he continued to show into the 1930s. In 1933 moved from London to live in retirement with his daughter in Eastbourne Sussex. Jeremy Wood Fine Art, Cranleigh, held an exhibition of his work in 1977.

Walford Graham ROBERTSON 1866–1948 Painter, illustrator, writer and collector, born in London, where he continued to live, and in Witley, Surrey. He studied art with Albert Moore and attended Eton College and South Kensington. Went on to assemble a large collection of William Blake's work, as well as important pieces by Dante Gabriel Rossetti, Edward Burne-Jones and Moore. He was author and illustrator of *A Masque of May Morning, Old English Songs and Dances* and other works. Plays included *Pinkie and the Fairies* and *Alexander the Great*, and *The Fountain of Youth* was a comic opera. Was a member of RBA, RP and ROI, showing extensively at Carfax Gallery, NEAC, Goupil Gallery, Walker Art Gallery in Liverpool and elsewhere. His memoirs *Time Was*, which went through many impressions after first appearing in 1931, are packed with such characters as Oscar Wilde, Ellen Terry, James McNeill Whistler and Sarah Bernhardt.

Ron ROBERTSON-SWANN 1941– Abstract sculptor, painter and teacher, born in Sydney, Australia. He studied at National Art School there, 1957–9, under Lyndon Dadswell, then travelled, 1960–1, settling in England, where he did postgraduate sculpture course under Anthony Caro and Phillip King at St Martin's School of Art. In 1963 taught part-time at St Martin's; was assistant to Henry Moore, 1963–5; then taught at East and West Ham Technical Colleges and Goldsmiths' College before returning to Australia in 1968. Among his activities there was teaching at National Art School and elsewhere; involvement with Visual Arts Board; helping in 1978 to organise a British Council tour of Caro's work; and in 1986 becoming creative arts fellow at the Australian National University. Robertson-Swann gained a painting prize at John Moores Liverpool Exhibition in 1965 and in 1968 was included in Arts Council touring exhibition Sculpture in a city. Had many solo shows in Australia from 1968, including series at Rudy Komon Gallery, Sydney, as well as winning a number of prizes. His large yellow sculpture Vault, of 1978, for Melbourne's new City Square, prompted endless controversy. Is represented in numerous Australian public collections and that of Leicestershire Education Authority.

David ROBILLIARD 1952–1988 Painter and writer. He showed at Stephen Bartley Ltd, 1984; Van Abbé Museum, Eindhoven, Netherlands, 1987; was an Artist of the Day at Angela Flowers Gallery, 1988; appeared at Friedman-Guinness Gallery, Frankfurt, which represented him, 1989; and was featured in South Bank Centre's touring The British Art Show 1990. Among his printed works were *Inevitable*, a book of poems produced by Gilbert and George, 1984; mailing of monthly poetry cards, published by Birch & Conran, 1987–8; and *Baby Lies Truthfull*, poems published Inanout Press, New York/Rome, 1990. Arts Council holds his work.

Tessa ROBINS 1965– Sculptor, born in Chelmsford, Essex, who graduated with honours, 1985–8, from Middlesex Polytechnic. Appeared in Summer Show, Laure Genillard Gallery, 1990, then in 1991 at Graeme Murray Gallery, Edinburgh, and Victoria Miro Gallery. Showed solo with Laure Genillard, 1989, then in 1990 at Wilma Tolksdorf Galerie, Hamburg, and in 1991 at Modulo, Lisbon.

William Palmer ROBINS 1882–1959 Printmaker, watercolourist and teacher, born and finally lived in London. He gained a silver medal in architecture from King's College in 1899, also winning a number of prestigious medals in Britain and abroad for etching. Studied at St Martin's School of Art, where he later taught, Goldsmiths' College School of Art and Royal College of Art. Eventually became head of etching department at Central School of Arts and Crafts. Wrote the manual *Etching Craft*. He was a member of RE, RWS, NS, Print Makers' Society of California, Chicago Society of Etchers and was an honorary fellow of the Australian Society of Etchers. Showed at RA and widely internationally.

Alan ROBINSON 1915– Painter in oil, especially of figures, born in Toronto, Canada. He was educated at Bryanston School, Dorset, then Bournemouth College of Art under Harold Williamson. Exhibited RA and extensively in the provinces, sometimes signing his work just A R. Lived at Southbourne, Bournemouth, and was a member of Bournemouth Arts Club.

Basil ROBINSON 1909–1992 Sculptor, stained glass artist and poet, son of the cartoonist William Heath Robinson, born in Hatch End, Middlesex. After studies at Royal College of Art he entered Prinknash Abbey in 1932, received the religious name Basil, was professed a monk in 1934 and ordained priest in 1940 (Dom Basil's original name was Alan Heath Robinson). At Prinknash he helped make the pottery a success. In the early 1950s was appointed prior of St Michael's Abbey, Farnborough; in 1958 went to Pluscarden Abbey, Elgin; spent five years in England preaching for Catholic Truth Society; then returned to Pluscarden in 1974, where he resumed artistic work. This included a set of a dozen stained glass windows for the Baptistery of St Mark's, Edinburgh, and sculptures, sacred and secular, in wood, stone, and glass fibre, ranging from abstracts to over-life-size figures. Was invited to north Wales to carve stone sculptures for Garthewin and stayed on as chaplain to Benedictine nuns of Talacre Abbey, eventually taking up residence in parish of St Winefride's, Holywell. Died in Colwyn Bay, Clwyd, following convalescence for leukaemia.

Bay ROBINSON 1898–1983 Painter, illustrator and printmaker, born in London, the daughter of the famous black-and-white artist Charles Robinson. After private education she attended the North London Collegiate School and studied at Hornsey College of Art, going on to teach at several schools, including Downe House in Newbury, Berkshire, not far from where she settled at Cookham Rise. Bay Robinson showed at RA, RI, RBA and SGA and had solo exhibitions at Walker's Galleries. Illustrated several children's books.

Bob ROBINSON 1951– Painter and draughtsman born in Newtownstewart, County Tyrone, Northern Ireland. From 1968–71 he was a drawing office apprentice with Rolls-Royce, then studied fine art at North-East London Polytechnic and at Trent Polytechnic in Nottingham, where he settled and where he studied low life for his subjects, tinged with an element of fantasy. Showed in Midlands, had a solo exhibition at Derby Museum and Art Gallery in 1980 and in 1981–2 was included in the tour Fragments Against Ruin, organised by the Arts Council, which holds several examples.

Christopher ROBINSON 1945– Artist in oil, watercolour and drypoint, born in Watford, Hertfordshire. He studied at Sunderland Art College and then Royal Academy Schools. There he was instructed in the working methods and materials of the Old Masters by Ruskin Spear and Peter Greenham and was trained by Maggi Hambling and Edward Bawden. He won the Armitage Prize for Figure Drawing and the Landseer Prize for Imaginative Painting at the Academy in the mid-1970s. Worked as a mural painter in London, 1975–80, then developed as a portrait and still life painter, with a special interest in musicians. Among his main works were the novelist Dame Catherine Cookson and Aung San Suu Kyi, leader of Burma's National League for Democracy and Nobel Peace Prize winner. Robinson met her while travelling in Burma. For the journey he "became a Buddhist monk and was at great personal risk from the military junta." After that, he considered that Burma would "be my major life interest", and began a lengthy project: Eye of Truth, Impressions of Burma. Exhibitions included Laing Art Gallery, Newcastle, 1971; RA Summer Exhibition from 1973; National Portrait Gallery, 1987; and Leeds Art Fair and RP from 1992. Had solo shows at Yorkshire Television and Lancaster Museum. They, the Laing, South Shields Museum and Provident Financial hold examples. Lived in Low Bentham, Yorkshire.

Geoff ROBINSON 1945– Artist, born in what is now Tanzania, who studied at Bournemouth College of Art, 1962–6, before spending 25 years in the advertising and music businesses, concentrating full-time on his painting from 1990. Later shows included Beatrice Royal Gallery, Eastleigh, and Alpha Gallery, Swanage, both 1996, and Gordon Hepworth Fine Art at 23 Smith Street, 1997, where Robinson showed abstract work. Russell-Cotes Art Gallery & Museum, Bournemouth, holds work in its collection.

George Saunders ROBINSON 1928– Artist in oil, pastel and watercolour. Born and lived in Belfast where he studied at RUA, 1944–8, then through the following four years in Dublin, Paris and Rome. Exhibited widely in Belfast, France, Switzerland, Italy and America.

James Martin ROBINSON 1953– Artist in oil and mixed media and teacher, born in Belfast, Northern Ireland. He studied at

Manchester Polytechnic, teachers including Jack Wright, and Northern Ireland Polytechnic, Neil Shawcross, gaining an honours degree in fine art. Worked as a teacher, part-time postman and youth and community artist. Robinson's work had as its main themes the head and landscape, but was non-figurative. Mixed shows included Octagon Theatre in Bolton and Colin Jellicoe Gallery, Manchester. Lived at Farnworth, Bolton, Lancashire.

John ROBINSON 1935– Self-taught sculptor, in metal, of abstract and figurative work, and tapestry artist, born in London. He was a fourth-generation Australian educated in Australia and England. Robinson lived in Australia 1940–3 and 1952–69, then returned to England, living in Somerset. He became interested in sculpting when farming in South Australia's Ninety-Mile Desert for 12 years. Robinson's work was shown by Freeland Gallery and in Australia by Beaver Galleries, Canberra. Several Australian collections hold examples. Among Robinson's many public commissions were sculpture near Tower of London, 1973; Seattle Opera House, America, 1974; Universe, for Collins-Wales House, Melbourne, 1975; Portsmouth, 1980; The Acrobats, Bruce Stadium, Canberra, 1980, commissioned by National Capital Development Commission; and Soccer Players, also ordered by the Commission, 1983. The Universe Series of sculptures and tapestries emanated from the Collins-Wales sculpture and was donated anonymously to Canberra in 1980 (one item, Bonds of Friendship, is sited in Portsmouth and marks the site where the First Fleet left for Sydney). The Series expressed Robinson's creed that "the universe is the materialisation of a divine idea".

Kate ROBINSON 1965– Artist and teacher, a creator of softly coloured abstracts used "as a vent for complicated passions and paranoias". She said that they were "finished when my conversation with them, or argument with them, is over, and we can no longer inform one another." Robinson did a foundation course at Hastings College of Arts and Technology, 1983–4; gained an honours degree in fine art painting at North-East London Polytechnic (where she was a visiting lecturer in 1990), 1984–7; obtained her master's in fine art printmaking, Brighton Polytechnic, 1990–2; and studied lithography for artists at London College of Printing, 1992–3. Mixed shows included For Art's Sake, Tobacco Dock, 1992; Portobello Open, 1995; and Benjamin C Hargreaves at Art98 at Business Design Centre, 1998. Solo shows included The Leathermarket, 1993. Neville Russell Accountants, BAA and NDL International hold her work. Lived in London.

Lewis ROBINSON 1960– Sculptor and teacher, born in Leicester, who studied at Loughborough College of Art and Design, Hull College of Art and Newcastle Polytechnic. He received Northern Arts Awards, 1988–9. Became associate lecturer in sculpture at Cleveland College of Art and Design. As well as having solo shows in Hull, Newcastle and Cleveland Robinson exhibited widely in mixed shows in north of England and was included in 1st RWA Open Sculpture Exhibition, 1993. Northern Arts Collection holds his work. Lived at Saltburn-by-the-Sea, Cleveland.

Margaret Nancy ROBINSON 1912– Artist in oil, watercolour, ink and pottery. Born in Trowbridge, Wiltshire, she was at Cheltenham School of Art, 1929–33, and then at Royal College of Art until 1936. Exhibited at RA and elsewhere. She sometimes signed her work Nan Robinson, also Nancy Bartlett. Lived finally in Emsworth, Hampshire.

Markey ROBINSON: *see* **MARKEY**

Nan ROBINSON: *see* **Margaret Nancy ROBINSON**

Peter ROBINSON 1945– Painter, printmaker and teacher, born in Leeds, Yorkshire. He attended Harrogate School of Art, 1961–4, and Derby College of Art, 1964–6. Went on to teach at Stockport College of Technology, showing at Portland Gallery in Manchester and elsewhere in area. Lived in Stockport, Cheshire.

Peter ROBINSON 1957– Painter and teacher, born in Mumbles, Swansea. He did a foundation course at local College of Art, 1975–6, then a fine art honours degree at Manchester Polytechnic, 1976–9, in 1979–81 gaining diploma in fine art at Slade School. During the following year Robinson was painting fellow on a fine art degree course at Gloucestershire College of Art and Technology, Cheltenham, followed by part-time lecturing at Waltham Forest College and Great Yarmouth College of Art and Design. Robinson's pictures had a bright, cheerful, jokey quality, the images reduced to flat, cardboard cut-out forms. He exhibited extensively, starting with MAFA in 1978. Other selected exhibitions were Nine Slade Painters, Seven Dials Gallery, 1980; Fitzwilliam Museum in Cambridge and Museum of Modern Art, Oxford, 1983–4; William Morris Gallery, Walthamstow, and Lyric Theatre, Hammersmith, 1985; and The Minories, Colchester, 1986, one of 4 London Artists. Manchester Polytechnic and Boise Collection at University College, London, hold his work.

Sarah ROBINSON 1964– Printmaker and lecturer, born in Wells, Somerset, who gained an honours degree at West Surrey College of Art and Design, Farnham, 1983–7, then her master's at Royal College of Art, 1987–9. Robinson's work drew "upon my inherent interest in the 'Human Condition' and the vulnerability of the human body, combined with my lifelong fascination with anatomy and medical images." Group exhibitions included The Nude, 1918–1989, The Pride Gallery, 1989; Summer Show, Long & Ryle Art International, 1990; Four Women Artists, Mid-Pennine Gallery, Burnley, 1996; and Eye to Eye, Hanover Gallery, Liverpool, 1997. Collections holding her work included Morgan Grenfell Bank, John Purcell Paper Company and Royal College of Art. Lived in Helmshore, Rossendale, Lancashire.

Sheila ROBINSON 1925–1987 Printmaker, designer, illustrator and teacher, born in Nottinghamshire. She was the wife of the artist Bernard Cheese and mother of the artist Chloë Cheese. Robinson studied at Nottingham School of Art, was for a short time in the Women's Land Army during World War II, then became a student at Royal College of Art, where she went on to teach part-time, also working as a freelance printmaker and illustrator. Her illustrations for D H Lawrence's novel *Sons and Lovers* for the New York Limited Editions Club were highly regarded. Among her other jobs were designs for a series of stamps for the Post Office; work for BBC and London Transport; and designing a Noah's Ark for the beach at Blackpool. Showed at RA and had several solo exhibitions at Mel Calman's gallery, Workshop. Fry Art Gallery in Saffron Walden holds her work.

Stephen ROBINSON 1961– Painter, draughtsman and film-maker, who studied fine art at Canterbury College of Art and Farnham School of Art. A long-standing interest in photography and documentaries led to his involvement in film-making. From 1985 he worked as a cameraman for many of Britain's leading documentary film-makers at home and abroad, while continuing to paint and draw. In 1997 he had a solo show of watercolours at The Catto Gallery resulting from a 40-week journey as part of the film crew accompanying Michael Palin to produce the BBC Television series *Full Circle*.

Jim ROBISON 1939– Ceramic sculptor and teacher, born in Independence, Missouri, America. He trained as a jet engine mechanic in the United States Air Force, serving in Germany for three years before returning to America, where he studied liberal arts and took up ceramics, being at Graceland College, Iowa, 1961–5, and Eastern Michigan University, 1968–70. He taught at Ann Arbor, Michigan, and moved to England in 1971. After establishing a studio in Leeds he moved to Holmfirth, Yorkshire, in 1975, and set up Booth House Gallery and his own workshop. Was head of 3D and Ceramics at Bretton Hall College, Wakefield. Served on the visual arts panel of Yorkshire Arts Association and was a member of the Craftsmen Potters' Association. Landscape, rock formations and megaliths were features of his work. Worked closely with architects, murals being included on major buildings in Cambridge, Pontefract, Chepstow and Wilmslow. Exhibitions included White Rose Gallery, Bradford, 1976; Ceramic Sculpture, Leeds City Art Gallery, 1979; and Clay Sculpture at Yorkshire Sculpture Park, 1980; and he also exhibited at Hart Gallery, Linby, and on the continent.

Zsuzsi ROBOZ fl.from 1950s– Painter, draughtsman and printmaker, born in Budapest, Hungary. She moved to London in 1947 and studied at Regent Street Polytechnic School of Art, at Royal Academy Schools with Peter Greenham and Bernard Fleetwood-Walker and in Florence with Pietro Annigoni. In 1956 she had first portrait commissions from Sir Alexander Korda of Claire Bloom and Mary Ure, the actresses, the beginning of a series on his contract artists. Roboz in 1964 painted the final days of the Windmill Theatre backstage; published a first book, *Women and Men's Daughters*, in 1970; published *Chichester 10: Portrait of a Decade*, in 1975; in 1982 painted a portrait of the ballerina Dame Ninette de Valois, in National Portrait Gallery, and portraits of the choreographer Sir Frederick Ashton and Lord Olivier, the actor, for the Victoria & Albert Museum's Theatre Museum; in 1993 completing 52 oils and drawings of 28 British artists, including Francis Bacon and Lucien Freud, which took three years. Had many solo shows, later ones including Royal Festival Hall, 1987; Lincoln Center's Amsterdam Gallery, New York, 1989; and Roy Miles Gallery, 1994. Tate Gallery and public galleries in Bradford and Sheffield also hold examples.

Gavin ROBSON 1950– Painter and teacher, born in Edinburgh, where he studied at the University and at the College of Art, 1968–74. Lectured in painting at University of Newcastle upon Tyne from 1977, from 1992 as head of fine art. Mixed shows included, in 1995, Hatton Gallery in Newcastle and 10 Artists from Great Britain, which toured Slovakia; and in 1995–6 John Moores Liverpool Exhibition. Robson had a first solo show at University of Nottingham in 1975, subsequent exhibitions there including one in 1993, following one at Hatton Gallery in 1992. Lived in Jesmond, Newcastle.

Hugh Mather ROBSON 1929– Artist in oil, gouache and pen and ink, born in Hinckley, Leicestershire. He studied at St Martin's School of Art, 1945–9, teachers including Russell Hall and William Craig, then at Slade School of Fine Art, 1949–53, under Sam Carter and Lucien Freud. Although as a young artist Robson saw many others turning abstract he chose to pursue representational work "using the now almost forgotten techniques which I was fortunate enough to have handed down to me at St Martin's," and most of his output was done on commission "through long-established clients in various countries". Interior decorators including John Siddley, Nina Campbell and Colefax & Fowler employed Robson; he completed murals for Park Lane Hotel, Belfry Club, Crockfords Club and private clients; and showed at Arthur Jeffress and Trafford Galleries, King Street Gallery and elsewhere. Lived in London.

John ROBSON 1931–1987 Sculptor, draughtsman and teacher who studied at Kingston School of Art, and Royal College of Art, 1953–6. Moved to Digswell House, Hertfordshire, and was assistant to Henry Moore, 1957–60. Taught at Bournemouth Municipal College of Art, 1960–4, and at Kingston Polytechnic fine art department from 1961, being senior lecturer, 1970–87. Exhibitions included Homage to Elgar, Chichester, 1984; Piccadilly Gallery's The Brotherhood of Ruralists and Friends, 1985–6; and Exhibition of British Woodcarvers, which toured, 1987–8. Took part in Three Sculptors at Trinity Arts Centre, Tunbridge Wells, 1987. In 1989 Tunbridge Wells Museum and Art Gallery gave him a memorial show.

Julien ROBSON 1955– Constructivist artist, born in Bellshill, Lanarkshire, who studied at Cleveland College of Art, Middlesbrough, 1973–4; Bath Academy of Art, 1974–5; and Slade School of Fine Art, 1977–9. Group exhibitions included 3 Constructivists, Building Design Partnership, Preston, 1980; House Construction Show, House Gallery, 1981; and Series, Quay Arts Centre, Newport, Isle of Wight. For that show Robson wrote that he was "motivated by the conception of order as expressed through pattern and movement". In 1988 he contributed an introduction to the catalogue of A Disquieting Suggestion (work by four abstract artists) at John Hansard Gallery, Southampton University. Robson later moved to Austria.

Catherine ROCHE 1969– Artist and teacher who studied at Carmarthen College of Art & Design, 1988–9 (where from 1994 she became a visiting lecturer); Holloway & Bedford New College, 1989–90; and University of Reading, 1990–4. Group exhibitions included Hexagon, Reading, 1992; Reading Visual Arts Week, 1993; and in 1994 South Hill Park, Bracknell, and First Cut at The Cut Gallery. The Cut gave her a solo show in 1996 following one at Henry Thomas Gallery, Carmarthen, 1995.

Laurence ROCHE 1944– Painter and teacher born in Goodwick, Pembrokeshire, married to the artist Helen Pollock. He attended Swansea College of Art, 1962–5, then Edinburgh College of Art, 1965–8, under Robin Philipson. After a postgraduate scholarship at Edinburgh he qualified as an art teacher at Moray House College there, then taught in schools in Reading and Cirencester before becoming a full-time artist in 1979. Roche was a member of Guild of Railway Artists, and his work was included in two of its books: *The Great Western Collection*, 1985, and *To the Seaside*, 1990. As well as railway subjects Roche specialised in canals and collieries, images of industry past and present, also marine subjects and the rural landscape. Exhibited RWA, RSW, RSA and widely elsewhere, and had solo shows. Early in 1990s was artist-in-residence to Allied Steel & Wire, chronicling its operations. Lived in Stroud, Gloucestershire.

Tobit ROCHE 1954– Painter, born in Manchester, whose work reflected his admiration of romantic and Symbolist pictures. His formative years were spent in Hong Kong, Canada and India. Began painting at an early age, studied at Ontario College of Art, 1974–6, then at Camberwell School of Arts and Crafts, graduating in 1980. Friendship with Duncan Grant, a lifelong friend of Roche's father, was an important influence. Had a series of solo shows in London including one at Maas Gallery, 1996, which featured many Indian works.

Basil ROCKE 1904–1966 Teacher and artist, born in London, full name George Basil Rocke. He joined the family firm of leather factors from 1924 during which he studied part-time at Central School of Arts and Crafts. In Australia and New Zealand he also studied in his spare time, joined the Theosophist movement and resolved to be an art teacher. Attended Reading University school of art, 1927–9. In Vienna, 1929–31 studied art at the Kunstgewerbeschule, observing Franz Cizek's historic children's art classes, and at the Kunst Academie. From 1937–9 studied at Euston Road School under Victor Pasmore, William Coldstream and Claude Rogers and was included in the School's exhibition at Wakefield City Art Gallery, 1948. From 1939–44 was in the Fire Service. Rocke began teaching at Bembridge School, 1932, and was eventually appointed senior art adviser for West Riding County Council in 1946, where he proved an inspiring teacher and put together a valuable collection of pictures. Died at Long Preston, Yorkshire. A retrospective of his pictures was held at Harrogate Art Gallery, 1967, and in 1989 *Basil Rocke Artist and Teacher* was published by his widow, Rosemary Devonald.

Fermin ROCKER 1907– Artist of the naturalistic school, influenced by American painting of the inter-war years. He was born in London's East End, son of Rudolph Rocker, editor of the Yiddish anarchist weekly *Arbeiter Freind*. The Port of London was his first subject, his older half-brother Rudolph his first instructor. At the end of World War I Rocker's family moved to Germany, where he studied at the Berlin School of Arts and Crafts, then was apprenticed as a lithographer for four years. From 1929 went with his father to America, returning to London in 1972. In America he worked nine years in a New York cartoon studio, then as a freelance including a lot of printmaking. Kennedy Galleries handled much of his output, the Library of Congress collecting examples, the Philadelphia Print Club giving him a prize in 1944. In London he showed with Thelma Watt in 1984, then from 1986 with Stephen Bartley Gallery, which gave him a 90th Birthday Tribute in 1998. Simultaneously, Rocker's autobiography *The East End Years – A Stepney Childhood* was published.

Martin RODDA 1955– Sculptor and lecturer, born in Chesterfield, Derbyshire. He studied at Falmouth School of Art, 1974–8, then Slade School of Fine Art, 1978–80. Visiting lectureships included Falmouth School of Art, Exeter College of Art and Design, Trent Polytechnic fine art department and Gloucestershire College of Art and Technology. Rodda was sculpture fellow at Gloucester, 1980–1, then at Winchester, 1982–4, and was included in Fellows of the Winchester School of Art, Winchester Gallery, 1983. He said then that his work, which appeared mechanical or structural, was "to evoke invisible forces and atmospheres contained within constructions of geometric and partially referential forms". Showed at Penwith Gallery, St Ives, 1977; Premises Arts Centre, Norwich, 1979; and Cheltenham Fellows Show, Cheltenham, 1981. Solo exhibitions included October Gallery, 1982.

Jan RODDICK 1937– Painter and teacher, brought up in Derbyshire, who spent six years in a studio as part of her art education, taking a City & Guilds qualification to teach. Roddick enjoyed sketching while travelling, her trips including New Zealand, Canada, Sicily, Greece, Kenya and Nepal, where she trekked. Colour and light were important aspects of her work, which was mainly in watercolour and water-based media. In 1996 she was artist-on-board for a cruise through the Far East, and she taught in her studio and at residential colleges such as Earnley Concourse, near Chichester; Old Rectory, Fittleworth; Urchfont Manor, Devizes; and Penleigh House, Warminster. Exhibited throughout Britain, including Pallant House in Chichester, and the Mall and Westminster Galleries, and had two solo shows for the National Trust at Petworth House, near her studio, in Sussex. Contributed regularly to *Leisure Painter* magazine.

Guy RODDON 1919– Painter and teacher, born in London. After Bryanston School he studied at Goldsmiths' College School of Art with James Bateman and Clive Gardiner, 1937–9, then at the Byam Shaw School of Drawing and Painting, 1939–40, with Ernest Jackson. Taught widely, including Arts Council, Goldsmiths' College and Morley College. Showed at RA, LG, Leicester Galleries, SEA, AIA and elsewhere. Chelsea Arts Club member who lived latterly in London.

Stephen RODEN 1964– Artist in mixed media who studied at Chester College and Central School of Art & Design. He took part in mixed shows, including the touring exhibition Merseyside Artists 6; Boxes & Totems, 1990, and Art in Boxes, 1992, both at England & Co.

Endre RÖDER 1933– Painter, notably of female figures in interiors or in a landscape, and teacher, born in Budapest, Hungary. He grew up in Malta, moving to England in 1949. After National Service in the Army Röder in 1954 trained as a map draughtsman with Ordnance Survey, then studied architecture and finally art, qualifying in 1960. After five years' teaching he was appointed education officer with Sheffield City Art Galleries, leaving this post in 1975 to teach art history to postgraduate level. From 1988 worked as a full-time painter, showing widely, including a shared exhibition at Bourne Gallery, Reigate, in 1993.

Robertson RODGER 1916– Painter and scraperboard artist whose full name was Sidney Bertram Robertson Rodger and who was born at Burgh Heath, Surrey. After Malvern College he attended Byam Shaw School of Drawing and Painting with Ernest Jackson and Patrick Phillips 1934–8. Showed at RI, UA, ROI and elsewhere and War Artists' Advisory Committee bought his work. Lived in Brookland, Kent.

Willie RODGER 1930– Painter, designer, muralist, printmaker and teacher, born in Kirkintilloch, Dunbartonshire. He attended Glasgow School of Art, 1948–52, specialising in graphic design, then after a post-diploma year went on to teach art at Lenzie Academy, later becoming department head at Clydebank High School. Resigned from teaching in 1987 to freelance full-time. Rodgers' talents were very varied, encompassing a set of Scottish historical playing cards; a memorial stained glass window at Kippen Parish Church; and Historic Monuments and Buildings commissions, including a mural, lino-cuts and line drawings about the whisky industry, another being concerned with the history of Rothesay. Illustrated books included Monica Clough's *The Field of Thistles*, 1986, and *Behind the Lines*, 1989. Showed solo at Ewan Mundy Fine Art, Glasgow, and Collins Gallery at Strathclyde University mounted a retrospective in 1986.

Harry Stewart RODGERS 1920– Artist in acrylic and pastel, born and lived in Stamford, Lincolnshire, who sometimes worked as Roger. He studied at Heatherley's School of Fine Art under Iain Macnab, 1951–2. Became a member of UA, and showed solo in Stamford, as well as in mixed exhibitions in London and Dublin, mainly nudes and landscapes. Lincolnshire Arts holds his work.

Marjorie RODGERS 1894–1972 Painter in oil and watercolour; miniaturist. Born in Cambridge, she married the artist Douglas Wray. Studied at Clapham School of Art, 1911, under Leonard Charles Nightingale, then at Royal Academy Schools under Andrew Gow. Exhibited widely, including RA, RI, ROI, RMS of which she was a member, the provinces and Paris Salon, where she won a gold medal in 1939, a silver medal nine years later, for portrait painting. Raymond Lister's book on *The British Miniature* features her work. Lived at Berkhamsted, Hertfordshire.

Roy RODGERS 1935– Painter and teacher who studied at Kingston School of Art and Royal Academy Schools who went on to teach at Harrow School of Art. He gained first prize in the Lord Mayor's Art Award, City of London, 1964, and showed at RA, Piccadilly Gallery, NEAC, RBA, Bradford and Brighton Art Galleries and at Gallery Stockholm, Sweden. Manchester City Art Gallery, Reading University, Rothschild Bank and Leicester and Carlisle Education Authorities hold examples. Lived for some time in Teddington, Middlesex.

Harry Hudson RODMELL 1896–1984 Oil and watercolour painter, especially of marine subjects. Studied at Hull College of Art, his work is owned by the National Maritime Museum, Greenwich. He exhibited at the RA, RBA, RI, SGA and RSMA, out of London and at the Salon de la Marine, in Paris. He illustrated David W Bone's *The Lookoutman*, and his work appeared in a wide range of magazines, such as the *Illustrated London News*. Lived at Hornsea, North Humberside.

Ilsa RODMELL 1898– Painter and linguist, born in Alsace, who was educated at Belfort, France. She began painting at 15, abandoned it at 18 and only resumed 20 years later when living in England. As she was married, there was no financial need to paint, but she liked to convey a personal gaiety and vivacity to her canvases, which were often of children, doll-like with large eyes. Took part in mixed shows at Arcade Gallery, 1954–5, and Chiltern Gallery, 1962, and had a solo exhibition at AIA Gallery in 1950. Rodmell was taken up by the dealer Lucy Wertheim, who opened Rodmell's solo exhibition at The Hotel Alexandra, Hove, in 1965, near where the artist lived in Russell Square, Brighton, Sussex. Pictures by Rodmell were included in Modern English Paintings from the Wertheim Collection, at Worthing Art Gallery, 1958; in The Wertheim Collection, at Hove Museum and Art Gallery, 1960; and in Naive Paintings from the Wertheim Collection, Art To-Day Gallery, Shoreham-by-Sea, 1962.

Ofelia RODRIGUEZ 1948– Artist in mixed media who was born in Colombia and who studied at University of Los Andes, Bogota, Yale University and Pratts Institute in America and in Paris at Atelier 17. She participated in many group shows, including Venice Biennale, 1988, where she represented Colombia, as she did in 20th São Paulo Biennale in the same year; at Gimpel Fils; and in 1992 at England & Co in Art in Boxes. Her exotic creations, which had a strong Latin American folk art and Surrealistic tinge, were also shown in solo exhibitions.

Eric RODWAY 1914– Painter, draughtsman and teacher, born in Birmingham. Student at Wimbledon School of Art, 1933–7, under Gerald Cooper and Robert Baker, then at Royal College of Art, 1937–40, with Gilbert Spencer, Barnett Freedman and Percy Horton. At the Royal College he was a silver medallist and scholarship winner. Exhibited RA, NEAC and RBA. For a short time after World War II he taught at Guildford School of Art, moving to Epsom and Ewell School of Art in 1947. Lived in Puttenham, Surrey.

Ann Louise ROE 1935– Painter, draughtsman and teacher notable for portraits, born into a versatile artistic family in London. She studied at Regent Street Polytechnic School of Art for four years, teachers including Norman Blamey; in France; and for a year at Brighton College of Art. Other influences were the artists Patrick Larking and Zdzislaw Ruszkowski. Roe, also known by her married name of Ann Jones, became head of art and design at the Grammar School, Colyton, Devon, where she lived. She was president of Colyton Leisure Painters, and a member of Seaton Art Society and of the Kenn Group, Exeter. Also exhibited at PS, Mall Galleries and had a solo show at The Market Place Gallery.

Fred ROE 1864–1947 Painter, notable for historical subjects, son of the artist Robert Roe and father of the critic and writer Frederic Gordon Roe. He studied at Heatherley's School of Fine Art and with Seymour Lucas. From 1887 showed at RA, ROI, Walker Art Gallery in Liverpool and with several groups of which he was a member: RBA, 1895; RI, 1909; and RBC, 1920. Among his portrait subjects was King Edward VII. Victoria & Albert Museum, Christchurch Mansion in Ipswich and several other provincial collections hold examples. He spent many years studying old oak furniture and writing about it. An Arts Club member who lived in London.

Helen ROEDER fl. from 1930s– Painter in oil and latterly mainly in watercolour. She studied at Goldsmiths' College School of Art in the early 1930s where she met Carel Weight. They were lifelong companions, marrying in 1990. After College, Roeder worked as a secretary in the Industrial Design Partnership to Misha Black, Milner Gray & Partners. During World War II she worked with the Artists' Refugee Committee, formed under the auspices of the AIA, serving on its central committee with artists such as Muirhead and Stephen Bone, Paul Drury and Richard Carline. After the war Roeder worked for several years at the Warburg Institute, compiling a dictionary of medieval saints. Retirement gave her more time for painting. Her work was included in Four Painters at New Grafton Gallery, 1993. Lived in London.

Herbert W RÖELL 1958– Versatile artist and architect, born at Goma on Lake Kivu in what was the Belgian Congo. From 1959–70 he lived with his family in the Netherlands, Brazil and Uruguay, then, when the family moved to Senegal, Röel went to school in Britain, 1970–6. After a period in Italy, during which he studied art at the Tyler School in Rome, 1976–7, Röel returned to England where he studied architecture at Cambridge University, 1977–80 and 1981–3, gaining an honours degree and diploma, working for the architect David Roberts in the city, 1980–1. He did more architectural work and painted there, 1983–5, then painted in south London for some years, eventually moving back to Italy. Röell took part in the National Children's Art Exhibition, 1974 and 1976; had a show of Sicilian pictures at King's College, Cambridge, 1980; another at Clare College, Cambridge, 1988; and participated in Links of Affinity, Dutch contemporary art in Britain, 1989. In 1988 he won a Three Cities Award for Professional Young Artists.

Peggy ROGENHAGEN 1911–1986 Painter and teacher, full name Lydia Peggy Rogenhagen, born in Epsom, Surrey, married to the painter Frith Millward. She studied at Wimbledon School of Art, 1929–32, with Gerald Cooper, then for three years at the Slade School of Fine Art under Randolph Schwabe. Taught art at Denstone College, 1948–51, near Uttoxeter, Staffordshire, living in Denstone. Showed at RBA, South London and Hove Art Galleries, Arts Council and elsewhere. WIAC member. Lived finally at Newton Longnor, near Buxton, Derbyshire, where she is buried with her husband.

ROGER: *see* **Harry Steward RODGERS**

Anthony ROGERS 1965– Painter, sculptor, conceptual and installation artist, born in Bristol, who worked there and in London. He studied at Goldsmiths' College School of Art and in Lublin, Poland. Showed in Lublin, also at Sheffield Media Show and 1st RWA Open Sculpture Exhibition, both 1993. Giacometti was and influence on his sculpture.

Claude ROGERS 1907–1979 Painter of portraits, landscapes and still life; draughtsman. Born in London, Rogers spent his earliest years there and in Buenos Aires, Argentina. After St Paul's School Rogers studied art at the Slade School, 1925–8. Visited Paris in 1927, then in the early 1930s began exhibiting with the LG and London Artists' Association. Married Elsie Few the painter 1937. At the Slade Rogers had been contemporary with William Coldstream, Rodrigo Moynihan, Geoffrey Tibble and others who were associated with the founding of the Euston Road School in the late 1930s, and he was to remain true to its principles. In Andrew Forge's words: "Whatever was put down had to be shown frankly as evidence of looking and registering … Painting was marking a flat surface in a certain way." In the 1930s Rogers taught at Raynes Park County School for Boys. He lectured at Camberwell School of Art in 1945, was a visiting lecturer at the Slade 1948–63 and was professor of fine art at the University of Reading 1963–72, then became professor emeritus. Rogers' work is in many important collections, including the Tate Gallery. Major retrospective Whitechapel Art Gallery 1973, and Ben Uri Gallery 1992–3, both with tour. Lived in London.

Derek ROGERS 1910– Landscape painter, born in London. He attended Marlborough College, then taught himself to paint. Eventually became curator at Brighton Art Gallery. Exhibited RA;

RI; Leicester Galleries; and Roland, Browse & Delbanco. Lived in London, then Brighton.

Edward ROGERS 1911-c. 1994–5 Self-taught artist, born Wisbech and educated in Ely, Cambridgeshire, who began painting in 1937. Until 1948 he produced mainly portraits and landscapes, then turned to coloured geometric abstract pictures and cut-metal sculptures. Rogers served in the Royal Air Force, 1940–5, and travelled extensively in Europe, India and Egypt. He had solo exhibitions at Drian Galleries, 1966, and Vincintoria Art Gallery, Brighton, 1968. BBC Southern Television made a film on his work, which is held by the Warsaw National Museum, Poland. Belgrave Gallery and Abbott and Holder latterly exhibited Rogers' work.

Eric ROGERS 1902– Sculptor, painter, administrator and teacher, born in Leeds, Yorkshire. After initial education in Leeds he studied at School of Art there, 1918–24, then at Royal College of Art, 1924–8, with Gilbert Ledward, the sculptor. He went on to hold a series of teaching posts, being principal of Oldham School of Art, 1938–46, then becoming Lancashire's county organiser of arts and crafts. Showed in London and provincial galleries and carried out commissions for public buildings in Lancashire, where he lived at Fulwood.

Howard ROGERS 1946– Painter, notable for townscapes with strong abstract tendencies, born in London. He studied at Walthamstow School of Art, 1963–5, Manchester College of Art, 1965–8, and Chelsea School of Art, 1969. Group exhibitions included Northern Young Contemporaries, Whitworth Art Gallery, Manchester, 1969; Four Artists from England, T'Hooght Gallery, Utrecht, Netherlands, 1974; LG, Camden Arts Centre, 1982; Southern Arts touring show, Small Works, 1994–5; and Namibian State Gallery of Modern Art, Windhoek, 1996 (the year that Rogers was invited to Tulipamwe International Workshop). Had a solo show at Museum of Modern Art in Oxford, 1973, later ones including Quay Arts, Newport, Isle of Wight, ArtSway Gallery, Sway, and Art Space Gallery, all 1997. Contemporary Art Society, BP Oil, London Boroughs of Tower Hamlets and Hounslow and several other public collections hold examples.

John ROGERS 1939– Painter in watercolour and oil, born in Cardiff, where he studied at the College of Art, teachers including the watercolourist John Roberts and David Tinker. In 1972 he opened a studio gallery in St Davids, Pembrokeshire, and the west Wales landscape was a key feature of his work. This could be realistic or have a mystical, dreamlike quality. In 1979 Roberts' pictures were featured in the BBC2 feature *Christmas in Saint Davids*, which he also narrated. Roberts gained a WAC grant in 1983 to paint in Morocco, and the exhibition Journey in Morocco toured from WAC in Cardiff. In 1991–2 Henry Thomas Gallery, Carmarthenshire College of Technology and Art, toured a retrospective of Roberts' pictures. WAC and other public collections hold examples.

John Boydell ROGERS 1934– Artist and teacher, born in Leigh, Lancashire, who gained a certificate in education, University of Leeds, Bretton Hall, 1958, obtaining his master's in fine art at Goldsmiths' College, 1979. Between 1958–87, when he took early retirement, Rogers held various posts in education from primary to higher education level, from 1973 being senior lecturer at Goldsmiths' for the postgraduate certificate of education course. He moved to Wales in 1979, settling at St Dogmaels, Dyfed, continuing part-time at Goldsmiths'. He gained a WAC grant in 1981, from 1981–4 being a member of its art committee. From 1982–3 Rogers was chairman of the Association of Artists and Designers in Wales, from 1983–5 a member of South Glamorgan Institute of Higher Education's fine art advisory committee. In 1980 he gained first prize for painting at the Welsh National Eisteddfod, in 1993 third prize at Dyfed Art Show. His work was shown at Arnolfini Gallery in Bristol, Camden Arts Centre, Greenwich Theatre Gallery, Kilvert Gallery in Clyro and at Mappin Art Gallery, Sheffield.

Olive Bousfield ROGERS 1901– Painter who was born in Pembroke Dock, Pembrokeshire, where she was confined as she was partly an invalid. However, as a keen member of the Pembroke Dock United Reformed Church she was able to preach in Pembrokeshire chapels for several decades and to paint. Although largely self-taught she did attend some extramural art classes and she was included in WAC's An Alternative Tradition in 1972.

Paul ROGERS 1944– Printmaker and teacher, born in Bristol. He studied at the West of England College of Art there, 1962–5, then Royal College of Art, 1965–8. From 1968 held various teaching positions at Hornsey and Maidstone Colleges of Art part-time, from 1973 lecturing at Newcastle upon Tyne Polytechnic. In 1976 Rogers won a Northern Arts Print Bursary, with a Major Award from the same source in 1980. In 1982 gained an Arts Council Production Grant as well as a North Tyneside Commission. The fishing boats of North Shields were a key subject for Rogers, as shown in the 1983 exhibition Six Artists from the Coast, Laing Art Gallery in Newcastle and Scandinavian tour. Rogers began showing in mixed exhibitions in 1972 at Bradford Print Biennale, followed by Grenchen Print Triennale in 1973 and Pratt Graphics, New York, 1974. Further shows included Hull Print Open, from 1980, and Hatton Gallery, Newcastle, 1983. After a solo show with Gallery 17, Bristol, 1965, Rogers showed at North Shields Library Gallery, then at Buddle Arts Centre, both 1982. British Council, Northern Arts and other public collections hold his work.

Stanley ROGERS fl. from c.1920s–1961 Painter and draughtsman with special interest in marine subjects. Born in Nottingham, he studied art at Goldsmiths' College School of Art under Edmund Sullivan, Harold Speed and Stanley Anderson, also attended L'Académie des Beaux-Arts, Antwerp. He wrote several dozen books on shipping and marine history, published in Britain and America, where he lived in Bronxville, New York. Also served as a camouflage officer with the Admiralty during World War II.

Exhibited RI, Suffolk Gallery, in provincial galleries and was a member of the RSMA. The Admiralty holds his work.

Will ROGERS 1950– Abstract artist, born in Anglesey, Wales. He attended Northwich College of Art, 1969, Birmingham College of Art in 1970, Slade School of Fine Art in 1973 and British School, Rome, 1975. Rogers had a first solo show at Peterloo Gallery in Manchester in 1979 and in the following year was included in The British Art Show, chosen by the critic William Packer, organised by the Arts Council, which holds his work.

Maurice Mancini ROITH 1900–1958 Born and based in London, Roith was a scene painter at the Royal Opera House in Covent Garden while studying part-time under Westminster School of Art teachers Walter Sickert and Bernard Meninsky. When he went into business he continued to paint, showing variously, having a solo exhibition organised in 1979 by Ben Uri Art Society, which holds a collection of his oils and watercolours.

Sunderland ROLLINSON 1882–1950 Painter, draughtsman and printmaker, born in Knaresborough, Yorkshire. He was schooled in Scarborough, then attended the School of Art there under Albert G Strange, going on to the Royal College of Art under Gerald Moira. Exhibited RA, RI, RSA, Walker Art Gallery, Liverpool, on the continent and in America. Lived in Cottingham, Yorkshire, and was married to the miniaturist Beatrice Malam.

Danny ROLPH 1967– Artist who was born in London and who studied at St Martin's School of Art, 1986–7, Winchester School of Art, 1988–91, and Royal College of Art, 1991–3. In 1991 he gained the Cunningham/Knowler Prize and White & Bowler Award, in 1992 a foreign study award to Lisbon and Jeremy Cubitt Award. Took part in a series of shows at Paton Gallery, including Abstraction II and exhibition at *The Economist*, both 1994, where abstracts in oil on steel employing fossil-like prehistoric shapes were a feature. Metropolitan Museum of Art in New York has work.

Richard ROME 1943– Sculptor and teacher who attended St Albans and Chelsea Schools of Art, completing the post-graduate course at Chelsea in 1966. Went on to teach at many art colleges part- and full-time, including Brighton Polytechnic, Bath Academy, Rinehart School of Sculpture in Baltimore, America, and Canterbury College of Art. He showed regularly from 1966 in group and solo shows indoors and outdoors. Among group exhibitions was inaugural show at Air Gallery, 1975, and Hayward Annual, 1979. Outdoor sculpture was shown at Yorkshire Sculpture Park from 1978; Cannizaro Park, 1983; and Canterbury Cathedral, 1984. In 1985 shared a three-artist show at Woodlands Art Gallery. His solo shows included Serpentine Gallery, 1975, and University of Kent, 1977. Arts Council holds his work. Lived in London.

Caroline Eve ROMER 1955– Painter, born in Braughing, Hertfordshire, daughter of the artist Philippa Romer. After Ware Grammar School for Girls she studied painting and etching at Cambridge College of Arts and Technology, 1973–4, then Byam Shaw School of Art, 1974–7. In 1978 she settled at Gavás, in the Spanish Pyrenees. From 1982 she undertook several journeys to India, where she painted. Showed RA, RBA, NEAC and elsewhere in mixed shows. Her solo exhibitions began in 1982 at Brotherton Gallery and from 1989 exhibited at Thackeray Gallery, also showing in France and Spain.

Philippa ROMER 1929– Portrait painter in oil, born in Hitchin, Hertfordshire, mother of the artist Caroline Eve Romer. She studied at Cambridge School of Art, Byam Shaw School of Drawing and Painting and Royal Academy Schools. She was one of Jack Beddington's *Young Artists of Promise*, in the 1957 volume of that title. Showed at RA, NEAC, SWA, RP and elsewhere. Lived in Braughing, Hertfordshire.

Kenneth ROMNEY-TOWNDROW 1900–1953 Painter, writer on art and teacher, born in Malvern Link, Worcestershire. He studied at Southport School of Art and Heatherley's School of Fine Art. At various times he was: curator of the Ruskin collection, at Coniston; lectured at Southampton University; and, after World War II, held the Leverhulme Research Fellowship in the history of art. He was an authority on the work of Alfred Stevens, the sculptor, writing extensively on him. Lived at West Chiltington Common, Sussex.

Dick ROMYN 1915– Painter, draughtsman and designer, born in London, who studied design in Paris. After war service in Burma he continued his art studies in Rome and Paris, where he lived from 1953–62, when he returned to England, living in Hampton Court, Middlesex. Romyn was much influenced by modern French painters, spent a lot of time in the galleries and museums of Europe and insisted on the importance of keen observation. Music and still life were features of his work, which was figurative, sometimes moving towards abstraction. Showed at Galerie Elysée in Paris in 1956, after which he exhibited widely in the city. Had a showing at Upper Grosvenor Gallery in 1961, then a substantial one at Boundary Gallery in 1994. In 1957 he won the Émile-Othon Friesz Prize.

Alan Ian RONALD 1899–1967 Painter, born in Edinburgh, who after George Watson's College studied at Edinburgh College of Art. He exhibited extensively at RSW, of which he was made a member in 1935, resigning just over 30 years later. Also showed at RSA, Walker Art Gallery in Liverpool and at Royal Glasgow Institute of the Fine Arts. Ronald contributed a series of Scottish subjects to the Pilgrim Trust's *Recording Britain* project, and Victoria & Albert Museum holds work. For many years he lived in Dunfermline, Fife.

Ronald RONALDSON 1919– Painter and draughtsman with a strong feeling for colour, born in Newcastle upon Tyne, Northumberland. Showed early talent for art, but was largely self-taught, apart from studying technical drawing at technical school as a boy. Spent a dozen years in Royal Navy, taking up oil painting. Worked then until retirement as a medical laboratory scientific officer. Showed from late 1940s in mixed exhibitions, including Northern Artists, Bury St Edmunds Art Society, Phoenix Gallery in Lavenham and Gainsborough's House, Sudbury. Was a member of Suffolk Art Society and latterly showed in St John's Street Gallery in Bury St Edmunds and in Laing Competition from 1991. Had first solo show at Chappel Galleries, Chappel, in 1993.

Marcel RONAY 1910– Artist and designer, born in Budapest of a Jewish Romanian father and an aristocratic Roman Catholic mother. When he was small the family moved to Berlin, but at the outbreak of World War I Ronay and family went to Vienna, where he finished formal education aged 14. In 1928 Ronay joined the master class under Eugene Steinhof at the Kunstgewerbeschule, even though he had had no formal art training. He finished his master carver's course in half the normal five years. In 1931 Ronay was nominated for the State Prize for Art, but one of his works was judged too erotic and this cost him the award. After exhibiting and travelling through Italy Ronay arrived in England in 1936, and with his family began designing and making porcelain costume jewellery, shown at the British Industries Fair, 1950. Also showed with RA, ROI and in 1952 at the International Exhibition of Contemporary Sculpture. After World War II Ronay worked as a commercial artist, mainly in Perspex, clients including building societies, breweries and shipping lines. Had a solo show at Ben Uri Art Gallery, which holds his work, in 1986, with another at John Denham Gallery in 1995 which included witty and perceptive drawings. Lived latterly in Essex.

Willi RONDAS 1907–1975 Painter, architect and teacher, born and died in Brussels, Belgium, the details of whose life vary according to accounts, including his own. In essence he was the son of a civil engineer and had an English mother. Studied singing, then after qualifying as an architect in Paris Rondas (pronounced Rondass) practised in the Belgian Congo, but returned to Paris in 1931 and took up painting. Rondas studied at L'École des Beaux-Arts and reportedly at the Slade School of Fine Art. In Paris he worked with Dufy, became disciplined in neglected techniques while doing restoration at the Louvre and assisted the stage designer Christian Bérard. After briefly serving in the Belgian Army at the outbreak of World War II Rondas was evacuated at Dunkirk and served in the British Army. He was to spend most of his painting life in England. He was a reluctant teacher in art schools in Nottingham and Croydon; designed for the textile firm Jacqmar; completed a mural in the Johannesburg Post Office Tower restaurant; and did 12 pictures for the 1972 Sabena airline calendar. Rondas was both a Surrealist and a painter of London suburbs in a realistic style, but transformed by an atmosphere of unease. Solitude, anguish and cruelty were preoccupations. During his life Rondas showed extensively in Europe and America. He had a first exhibition at Galerie Le Centaure, Brussels, 1938. Others included Galerie d'Egmont, Brussels, and Ben Uri Art Society, both 1961; John Whibley Gallery, 1966; and Galerie Rutzmoser, München, 1987. Waterloo Museum in Belgium and Ben Uri hold examples, which were also acquired by the collector of Surrealism Edward James.

Ted ROOCROFT 1918–1991 Sculptor and teacher, based in Cheshire, whose work was tinged with a wry humour. Roocroft began carving with an Army dinner knife in World War II. Studied art in Edinburgh and Manchester and at Slade School of Fine Art, where he won prizes for sculpture. In the early 1950s he joined Manchester School of Art, later part of the Polytechnic, teaching there for almost 30 years. Showed with MAFA as a member and elsewhere. Won an Arts Council major award in 1979. Worked mainly in wood and was especially fond of animal subjects as he "liked animals better than humans". Roocroft believed in truth to his materials, one of his last works, a dead rhinoceros, being chosen "because that's what the shape of the wood told me". Sheep, in Manchester's Castlefield Gardens, is one of his best-known pieces. Others are displayed throughout northwest England and in Ireland, France, Italy, the Netherlands, Zimbabwe and America. Lived at Toft, Knutsford, Cheshire.

Janine ROOK 1959– Artist in various media who studied at St Martin's School of Art and Slade School of Fine Art. Her work was featured in mixed exhibitions including Passing Glances, at New British Library, and shortly after at England & Co's Art in Boxes, 1990.

Noel ROOKE 1881–1953 Printmaker, illustrator, painter and teacher, born and lived in London, son of the painter Thomas Matthews Rooke. After education partly in Chartres, France, Rooke studied at Slade School of Fine Art under Fred Brown, Philip Wilson Steer and Henry Tonks, 1899–1903, then at the Central School of Arts and Crafts with Edward Johnston and W R Lethaby. This set him up well to hold the position of head of book production at the Central, 1930–46. In addition, Rooke was president of the Double Crown Club, chairman of the NS and was a founder-member of SWE. Exhibited RE, NS, NEAC and abroad. He was a noted engraver on wood, whose work appeared in the *Print Collectors' Quarterly*, being held by the British Museum.

Mick ROONEY 1944– Painter and teacher, born in Epsom, Surrey. He studied at Sutton School of Art, 1959–62, Wimbledon School of Art, 1962–4, and Royal College of Art, 1964–7. He won the Rome Scholarship, attending British School in Rome, 1967–8. From then until 1982 he taught at various art colleges, in 1983 being artist-in-residence at Towner Art Gallery, Eastbourne. Among his prizes were Calouste Gulbenkian Printmakers' Award, 1984; John Player Portrait Award, 1985; and Korn/Ferry International Premier Award at RA Summer Exhibition, 1989. The faded café scenes and brilliantly coloured crowd scenes led to Rooney's work being described by one critic as "successive volumes of the Human Comedy". Rooney took part in numerous group exhibitions from Young Contemporaries in the 1960s. Early solo shows were at Fulham Gallery, Galerie Petit in Amsterdam and Seasons Gallery, The Hague. In 1989 a travelling show was based on Metropole Arts

Centre, Folkestone, and he also showed at Mercury Gallery and New Grafton Gallery. Elected RA, 1991.

Paul ROONEY 1967– Painter, printmaker and teacher, born in Walton, Liverpool, who studied at Southport and Edinburgh Colleges of Art. He lectured part-time at Edinburgh, 1990–3; held a fellowship at Cheltenham & Gloucester College of Higher Education, 1991–2; lectured at Staffordshire University from 1993; and in 1995 was artist-in-residence, British School at Rome and Walker Art Gallery, Liverpool. Rooney won a string of awards, including an Andrew Grant Humanities Travel Scholarship, 1988; Andrew Grant Award at Edinburgh College of Art, 1989–91; John Kinross Scholarship to Florence, RSA, 1991; Alexander Graham Munro Travel Award, RSW, 1993; Hope Scott Trust Award, 1994–5; and an Abbey Award for Painting the British School, Rome, 1995. Rooney participated in numerous group shows, including Royal Over-Seas League Open, 1996. Had a solo exhibition at Acorn Gallery, Liverpool, 1986, later ones including Walker Art Gallery, 1995. Edinburgh College of Art, RSA, the British School at Rome, Liverpool John Moores University and corporate collections hold examples.

Leonard ROOPE 1917– Watercolourist, born in London. After elementary education his art tuition was restricted to life classes in the evening at West Ham College of Art and watercolour tuition with Walter Spradbery at Walthamstow. Moved to Cockermouth, Cumberland, in 1966, three years later resigning from clerical work to concentrate on landscape watercolours. From 1971 taught watercolour at local further education classes. Had many solo shows in Cumbria region in public and private galleries, also showing at RI in 1964 and Patricia Wells Gallery, Thornbury, in 1985, in mixed exhibitions.

Frank ROPER 1914– Sculptor and designer in various materials, and teacher. Born in Haworth, Yorkshire, Roper studied at Keighley School of Art and Royal College of Art. He was the son of the sculptor George H Roper, and his wife Nora assisted him with the painting of some of his work. Roper lectured at and became vice-principal of Cardiff College of Art, but eventually worked full-time on his often amazing creations, such as musical sculptures. Also made a lot of sculptures and stained glass windows using aluminium. His casting sometimes employed the lost-polystyrene and dry sand process. Created fabulous beasts and figures from mythology. Exhibited on many occasions at Howard Roberts Gallery, Cardiff, also RBA, Camden Arts Centre, SWG and WAC. Among his commissions was The Stations of the Cross for St Martin's Church, Roath, Cardiff; work for Llandaff Cathedral; and for Durham Cathedral. National Museum of Wales, Cardiff, holds his work. Was the subject of several BBC Television programmes, including *Look, Stranger*, 1976. Lived in Penarth, Glamorganshire.

Geoffrey ROPER 1942– Painter, born in Nottingham, where he attended the College of Art, 1958–60, then Edinburgh College of Art, 1960–2. He was an Andrew Grant Scholar, 1963. Teachers included William Gillies, Robin Philipson, John Maxwell and James Cumming. Was a part-time teacher at the College, 1967–9. Solo exhibitions included William Street Gallery, Douglas and Foulis Gallery, David Letham, Great King Street Gallery and The Fine Art Society, all Edinburgh (and with the Fine Art Society in London and Glasgow); King Street Gallery in Dublin; and Middlesbrough Civic Art Gallery. That gallery, Edinburgh New Town Conservation Committee and New University of Northern Ireland hold Roper's work. Lived in Midcalder, West Lothian.

Michael ROSCHLAU 1942– Printmaker, painter, draughtsman and teacher, born in Sonneberg, Germany. Studied at Hochschulinstitut für Kunst und Werkerziehung, Mainz; Hochschule für Bildende Künste, Braunschweig; and Slade School of Fine Art (German Academic Exchange Service), where he concentrated on printmaking from 1967, winning the Slade prize for lithography in 1968, the year he was appointed lecturer in printmaking at Glasgow School of Art. Won a Scottish Arts Council Major Award in 1971 and the Curwen Prize for Lithography at Bradford Print Biennale in 1972. Richard Demarco Gallery in Edinburgh, Glasgow Print Studio and galleries in Germany and America showed his work. He was featured in Scottish Print Open Three, 1983, organised by the Dundee Printmakers' Workshop, and the 1990 Tramway, Glasgow, exhibition The Compass Contribution. Compass Gallery, Glasgow, gave him a solo show in 1970.

Adrian ROSE 1958– Paper collagist, born in Thundersley, Essex, who obtained his Bachelor of Music degree from the Royal Academy of Music, 1976–80, and his master's from Nottingham University, 1981. His teachers included Lady Evelyn Barbirolli, oboe, and Geraint Jones, harpsichord, and he studied early music privately with members of the Dolmetsch family. Rose had no formal training as an artist. His work was "wholly abstract and intuitive and reflects an interest in the structural potential of colour. Influences include Mondrian, Herbin, Matisse, Sonia Delaunay and Francis Davison", whose wife, the artist Margaret Mellis, owned Rose's work. Rose was a member of the Viola da Gamba Society of Great Britain and the Theosophical Society. Group shows included Aldeburgh Festival and Open Studios at Yoxford Gallery, 1997. In 1995, had solo exhibitions at Martha Stevns Gallery, Fressingfield, and Halesworth Gallery, Halesworth, Suffolk, where he lived nearby at Huntingfield.

Christopher ROSE 1935– Painter, designer and teacher, born in Oxford. After leaving school he worked in design for several years while attending evening classes at Byam Shaw School of Art and St Martin's School of Art where his teachers included Elizabeth Frink and Edouardo Paolozzi. In 1959 he began full-time studies at Bath Academy of Art, Corsham, with Howard Hodgkin and Adrian Heath. In 1964 he gained his design diploma after further studying graphics at St Martin's School of Art under Marcello Minale and Frederick Gore. Rose taught at St Martin's before spending several years as a designer and art editor, becoming a member of the Chartered Society of Designers. He became involved in the protection and restoration of old buildings; in the mid-1970s moved to Exmoor, where he dealt in antiques and pictures and resumed painting; then after travelling the world in the early 1980s established the Cotswold Antiques Centre in Stow-on-the-Wold. He settled not far away at Burford, Oxfordshire, and in 1993 had a retrospective of work, 1959–93, at St David's Hall, Cardiff. Rose's chief concern as a painter was with the figure, particularly the unclothed female figure, sometimes representational, formalised or symbolic.

Colin ROSE 1950– Sculptor, born in Newcastle upon Tyne. He studied at the Polytechnic and University there. His awards included one from the Arts Council, a Northern Arts Travel Award and the Northern Arts Major Bursary, 1985–6. Among his residencies was Woodhorn Museum, Northumberland, 1986. Rose's many group appearances included Small Works Show, Newcastle Polytechnic Gallery, 1982; Steel Sculpture, at Yorkshire Sculpture Park, 1988; and the Newcastle Group show The Northern Lights at DLI Museum & Arts Centre, Durham, 1990. Solo exhibitions included Gulbenkian Gallery, Newcastle, 1978, and Hatton Gallery, Newcastle, 1979, and in 1992 Yorkshire Sculpture Park, where Rose showed tree and ground sculptures. That exhibition marked the culmination of Rose's Henry Moore Foundation Bursary. Rose described his work as Minimal. Arts Council holds it. Lived in West Chevington, Northumberland.

David Thomas ROSE 1871–1964 Watercolourist, brought up in Nairn, Scotland, one of 11 children of a butcher who did not encourage his son's drawing talent. After a detested period in the family firm Rose was articled to a firm of civil engineers, then during his first job in Glasgow attended art evening classes for a year. Worked on construction of the West Highland Line; went to Malta for the building of a breakwater in Valletta harbour, where he met his wife; after he had spent a few unsuccessful months in London as a freelance artist they married. Worked on dockyard construction at Southampton and Fishguard; was at Nidderdale, 1920–35, for the building of Scar House reservoir; then retired, first to Brighton, then Hove, Sussex. On site, Rose had only to draw a quick sketch of a man for him to be instantly recognised, even if his name was not to hand. Showed at RA, RI, Alpine Club Gallery, RWS, RSA and elsewhere. Collections of Rose's work, relating to areas where he was employed, are in Science Museum, Bradford Industrial Museum, Malta Museum, Edinburgh Public Library and elsewhere. In 1995, Nidderdale Museum showed a collection.

Diana ROSE 1921– Painter in oil, born in London, who studied at St Martin's School of Art, 1946–7, under Archibald Ziegler, then part-time, 1948–60, at Southend School of Art with Leo Hardy. Was elected a member of Free Painters and Sculptors, 1976, also exhibiting at Whitechapel Art Gallery, Barbican Centre and in Essex, where she lived in Leigh-on-Sea.

Edna ROSE 1901–1985 Sculptor of animals and wildlife in ceramic and bronze, and teacher, born in Sligo, Ireland, her father Scots, her mother Irish. He was a dentist who early in the century moved his family to Hoylake, Wirral, where Edna remained. One of three sisters, she became known and loved as an eccentric, determined, self-willed and direct. Studied at Liverpool School of Art, returning to teach modelling and sculpture for several years. Rose had an extensive knowledge of wildlife, even travelling to Kenya to study it. From childhood, when she had a one-eyed pony called Hero, her home was full of animals, including many cats, strays and birds. Became a full member of RCamA in 1968, also belonging to Liverpool Academy, Deesside Art Group and showing annually at Crufts Dog Show. In 1970 Chester Zoo accepted her commissioned Otter Fountain in bronze.

Francis ROSE 1909–1979 Painter, stage designer, printmaker and draughtsman, born at Moor Park, Farnham, Surrey. He was partly educated by Jesuits at Beaumont College, partly by private tutors abroad. A baronet, Sir Francis studied art for 10 years in Paris from 1926, mainly with Francis Picabia, by which time he had acquired his taste for travel. This was chiefly in Europe, although he also visited North Africa, America and lived for several years in the Far East. By the time that he had his first exhibition, with Salvador Dali, at the Galerie Marie Cuttoli in Paris in 1930, Rose had already designed scenery and costumes for Diaghilev, and he went on to design for the Lord Berners ballet *Cupid and Psyche* at Sadler's Wells in 1939. Rose exhibited extensively internationally and was given a retrospective at England & Co in 1988. He led a bohemian life which brought him into contact with such people as Gertrude Stein, Cecil Beaton and Christopher Wood, but also included Royal Air Force service as a disciplinary sergeant in World War II. His pictures range from the elegant to the bizarre and cannot be easily classified. Died in London.

Geoffrey Keith ROSE 1889–1959 Watercolourist and draughtsman, born in Oxford, who had early success when he showed in the 1900 Paris International Exhibition Rose was an entrance scholar to Harrow School, 1903–8, by 1907 distinguishing himself as a monitor. He was also a scholar at King's College, Cambridge, first-class history tripos part I. While in London Rose was a member of London Rowing Club, appearing at Henley in 1912, the year he took his Bar finals, becoming a barrister in 1913. In World War I Rose was a major in the Oxford and Buckinghamshire Light Infantry, winning the Military Cross and bar and twice being mentioned in dispatches. He was recorder of Ludlow, 1932–4, then a Metropolitan Police magistrate, and a Justice of the Peace in Essex. Served in the Home Guard in World War II. Rose exhibited at a number of venues and has work in the Imperial War Museum. Lived in Ipsden, Oxfordshire.

George ROSE 1882–1955 Painter of landscapes and etcher. Born at Chipping Ongar, Essex, and privately educated. Exhibited RA, Colnaghi's, NEAC and RSA. Work held by British Museum, Williamson Art Gallery & Museum, Birkenhead, and Grundy House Museum, Blackpool. Lived at Nedging Tye, Ipswich, Suffolk.

Joe ROSE 1915– Artist, born in Woldenberg, Germany, who studied at ateliers there and was imprisoned for anti-Nazi activities, going to concentration camps at Sonnenberg, 1933, and Buchenwald, 1938. In 1939 escaped with his wife to England, volunteered for the British Army and served with the Reconnaissance Corps. After demobilisation gained a diploma from International Correspondence Schools and worked in display, in 1957 emigrating to Australia where he took private lessons with Max Feuerring and decided to become an artist. Rose won several dozen awards, including many first prizes. He was elected a member of the Australian Watercolour Institute and in London, to which he returned in 1971, he joined the Contemporary Portrait Society, Contemporary Art Society and Ben Uri Art Society, which holds his work. From 1979 Rose decided to live and work in London and Sydney, eventually settling in Hobart, Tasmania, where he was a member of Tasmanian Art Society. Rose's Surrealist work could be powerful, disturbing and mesmeric. As well as showing widely in Australia, including an eightieth birthday exhibition at Holdsworth Galleries, Woollahra, 1995, Rose took part in many mixed exhibitions in Britain, solo shows including Ben Uri Gallery, 1977; Obelisk Gallery, 1981; and Wilma Wayne Gallery, 1982. Examples held by Jewish Museum in Berlin; Nuffield Foundation; Art Gallery and Museum of Tasmania; Sydney University and elsewhere.

Kate ROSE 1948– Painter, born in Nottingham, who studied from 1966 at the College of Art there, also at Birmingham and Royal Colleges of Art. She taught at Birmingham and Sheffield. Rose was included in the 1980 exhibition The British Art Show, chosen by the critic William Packer and toured by the Arts Council, which acquired her work. She also showed at Graves Art Gallery in Sheffield and Ikon Gallery, Birmingham.

Matthew ROSE 1971– Artist who did a foundation course at Loughborough College of Art and Design, 1989–90; gained a fine art honours degree, Norwich School of Art and Design, 1991–4; and his master's in painting at Royal College of Art, 1995–7. In 1997 he won The Fatima and Faiza H Alkazzi Award, The *Oriana* Prize and The Daler-Rowney Award. Group appearances included Norwich Contemporaries, Norwich Gallery, 1993, and Long & Ryle, Art98, at Business Design Centre, 1998. TI Group and The *Oriana* Art Collection, P&O Cruises, hold examples. Lived in London.

Muriel ROSE 1923– Artist in oil, pen and ink and ceramics, and teacher, born and lived in London. She was encouraged in art by an amateur painter father. After Forestry Commission and farm work in World War II worked part-time in drawing offices and studied at Richmond, Kingston and St Martin's Schools of Art, teachers including Roman Black, later taking a teaching course in ceramics at Hammersmith School of Art. Taught painting and ceramics to adults until retirement. Landscapes of hot Mediterranean places and plant drawings were features of her own work. Was a member of RBA, ROI, NS, WIAC, a fellow of Free Painters and Sculptors and a member of Campden Hill Club and Fulham Artists. Had a series of solo shows including Canaletto Gallery, London and Surrey Universities and Leighton House. Nottingham and Hertfordshire Education Committees hold examples. Anne Redpath, Redon and Bonnard were cited as influences.

Ismond ROSEN 1924–1996 Sculptor, born in South Africa, where he studied medicine, moving to Britain in 1952. He practised as a psychoanalyst and psychiatrist. Rosen, whose brother Frank was a painter, sculpted from childhood and was self-taught apart from short periods at the École des Beaux-Arts and Académie Julian, Paris. In 1959 he was elected a fellow of SPS. He had a first solo show at John Whibley's gallery in 1972, two years later his key one-man exhibition Genesis: The Process of Creativity taking place at Camden Arts Centre. Rosen's work Civilisation and other works are held by Royal Society of Medicine, of which he was a fellow, as he was of the Royal Society of Psychiatrists, which holds his portraits of Henry Maudsley and Erwin Stengel. Rosen created The Holocaust Chapel for long-term exhibition in St Paul's Cathedral; one part of the triptych, The Revelation, was given in first-cast form by the Council for Christians and Jews to Pope John Paul II on his visit to Britain and is now in the Vatican, Rome. Rosen's work was cast by The Morris Singer Foundry. Lived in London.

Julius ROSENBAUM 1897–1956 Craftworker, painter, printmaker and teacher, born in Neuenburg, Germany, who studied in Paris, Munich and in Berlin like his wife Adèle Reifenberg, whom he married in 1930. Because the Nazis forbade him to paint, Rosenbaum had to teach crafts in Jewish schools until he and his wife left for London in 1939. There he restored houses and porcelain, was able to resume serious painting and with his wife ran a private art school from 1948 until his death, in The Hague, Netherlands. Ben Uri Art Society holds several examples, having given Rosenbaum shows in 1957 and 1968.

Paul ROSENBLOOM 1949– Painter, draughtsman and teacher, born in Manchester. He studied at Lanchester Polytechnic, 1967–8; Leeds Polytechnic, 1968–71, gaining a first-class honours degree; and Birmingham Polytechnic, 1971–2, for a higher diploma. Among Rosenbloom's awards were a fellowship in painting at Gloucestershire College of Art & Design, 1972–3, and artist-in-residence, University of Western Sydney, 1993. Rosenbloom had extensive teaching experience, commencing as a part-time lecturer at Stourbridge College of Art, 1973–6; visiting lectureships including Central School of Art & Design, Chelsea College of Art, Reading University and Goldsmiths' College; Victoria College of the Arts, Melbourne, 1985–6; then acting head of painting at Cheltenham & Gloucestershire College of Higher Education, 1991. Also lectured at Museum of Modern Art in Oxford, Durham University and Whitechapel Art Gallery. Took part in many group shows including Northern Young Contemporaries at Whitworth Art Gallery from 1971; British Painting '74, Hayward Gallery, 1974; British Drawing, same gallery, 1982; Portico Gallery, Manchester, and Ben Uri Gallery, both 1988; and Beatrice Royal Gallery, Eastleigh, 1995. Had a solo show at Durham University,

1977, later ones including Space YZ, Sydney, 1993, and Spacex Gallery, Exeter, and Pittville Gallery, Cheltenham, both 1994. Kingston Polytechnic and Chemical Bank hold examples. Lived in London.

Stanley ROSENTHAL 1933– Artist and lecturer, born in London, whose work was "influenced strongly by the British Neo-Romantics". He worked in oil, watercolour, mixed media, acrylic and oil pastel. Rosenthal studied at Southend and Leicester Schools of Art. As a young artist he "had a pavement exhibition outside the Tate Gallery where the director, Sir John Rothenstein, gave me five shillings and sent out a cup of tea on a silver tray." Rosenthal was "thrown out of various colleges for being naughty", but was a visiting lecturer/artist-in-residence at the Graham Sutherland Gallery near where Rosenthal set up a studio gallery in Saint Davids, Pembrokeshire. Welsh landscapes, especially those of Pembrokeshire, were his main works, shown in mixed exhibitions in London, including the Ben Uri Gallery, and Leicester. Had solo shows in London, Cardiff, Plymouth and Saint Davids. HM The Queen and Tenby Museum and Art Gallery hold his work.

Peregrine ROSKILLY 1947– Painter, designer and illustrator, born in Twickenham, Middlesex, who did a four-year fine art and illustration course at Twickenham College of Technology. As well as periods landscape painting in Dorset, in an ashram in India and working in a commune and in freelance advertising illustration, Roskilly was employed by several advertising agencies, latterly for 10 years at Abbott Mead Vickers BBDO as storyboard illustrator. At various times he was a licentiate of the Society of Industrial Artists and Designers/member of the Chartered Society of Designers/The Designers' and Art Directors' Association. In 1996 Roskilly had a show of his Bio/Dynamics paintings at Gallery Differentiate. The series of highly coloured abstract works, begun in 1993, "came about from a desire to express a positive life energy." The artists Miró, Sutherland, Picasso, Matisse, Cockrill, Fiona Rae, Albert Irvin and John Hoyland were all cited as influences.

Leonard ROSOMAN 1913– Painter, mural artist, illustrator and teacher. Born in London Rosoman basically remained there, although he travelled extensively. He studied, 1930–5, at King Edward VII School of Art, University of Durham, where his teachers included E M O'Rorke Dickey, then at Royal Academy Schools, 1935–6, and at Central School of Arts and Crafts, 1937–8, under Bernard Meninsky. Rosoman taught from 1938–9 at Reimann School, where his subject was perspective, but on outbreak of World War II he was mobilised into the National Fire Service. In 1943 he was seconded to the War Office to illustrate books on firefighting, being appointed an official war artist to the Admiralty in 1944. His depictions of firefighting were among his most outstanding early work. Had first one-man show in 1946 at St George's Gallery. In 1947–8 Rosoman taught at Camberwell School of Arts and Crafts; at Edinburgh College of Art, 1948–56; and at Royal College of Art, 1956–78. He exhibited in RA Summer Exhibition from 1960 and was elected RA, 1970. Showed extensively at Fine Art Society, which gave him a retrospective in 1974. Rosoman carried out a number of important mural commissions, notably for Festival of Britain in 1951 and for Shakespeare Exhibition at Stratford-upon-Avon, 1964. Tate Gallery, Imperial War Museum and other public collections hold his work.

Alastair Robertson ROSS 1941– Sculptor and teacher, born in Perth, Perthshire. Studied at Edinburgh College of Art, 1960, with Eric Schilsky and Norman John Forrest, then Duncan of Jordanstone College of Art, Dundee, 1960–6, teachers including Hugh Adam Crawford, and abroad. Later lectured in sculpture and fine art in Dundee. Was elected to SPS in 1966, was a council member of SSA, 1972–5, and was made a fellow of RBS in 1975, holding several senior positions. Also showed at RSA and Paris Salon, where he won Bronze and Silver Medals. Other awards included RSA's Sir William Gillies Award and RBS's Otto Beit Medal, both 1989. Scottish Arts Council hold his work. Lived in Dundee, Angus.

Ann ROSS 1945– Artist, noted for decorative works on paper, born in Edinburgh, where she continued to work; she was for a time art editor with the publisher W & R Chambers. Ross studied at Edinburgh College of Art, 1962–7. She gained an Andrew Grant Travelling Scholarship to France and Italy in 1967, four years later winning a Scottish Arts Council Award. For many years she was in group shows at New 57 Gallery in Edinburgh, also showing with SSA and with Compass Gallery. New 57 Gallery and Scottish Arts Council gave her solo exhibitions, the Council and Glasgow University of Strathclyde holding her work.

Arabella ROSS 1959– Artist, born in York, who studied at Krishnamurti Educational Centre, Hampshire; Taunton College of Art and Design; Wolverhampton Polytechnic; and Chelsea School of Art. She won a Tim Turner Travelling Scholarship and was artist-in-residence, Arts Centre, Calcutta, India, 1992. Group shows included Battersea Open Drawing, Battersea Arts Centre, 1985; Morley College Gallery, 1988; Cleveland International Drawing Biennial, Cleveland Gallery, Middlesbrough, 1993; and Royal Over-Seas League Open 1994. She had had a solo show there the previous year. Wolverhampton Art Gallery holds her work.

Cyril Joshua ROSS 1891–1973 Self-taught painter in oil, born and lived in London, by profession a businessman. He published *Furs and Furriery* and *Pirate in Striped Trousers*. Was a member of ROI, also showing at RA, RWS and Cooling Galleries. He was a noted figure in Ben Uri Art Society, was shown there in 1968 and 1972 and it holds his work.

Jenepher ROSS 1937– Sculptor in welded metal who studied under Benno Schotz at Glasgow School of Art, gaining her diploma in 1960, doing a post-diploma course under Anthony Caro at St Martin's School of Art. Gained a fellowship in the architectural department at Strathclyde University, 1973, the year she was elected an associate of RBS. In 1992 was president of the Glasgow Society of Women Artists, also belonging to SSWA. Ross's early work was influenced by Giacometti and by Schotz, whose studio assistant she was periodically for 20 years; birds and vintage cars were notable themes. Took part in group shows at 41, Torrance and Open Eye Galleries, in Edinburgh, also at RSA (where in 1986 she gained the Rothman's Purchase Award) and Royal Glasgow Institute of the Fine Arts. Solo exhibitions included Queen's Church and Collins Gallery, Glasgow; Dick Institute, Kilmarnock; Montrose Art Gallery; and Kelly Gallery and Scottish Amicable, Glasgow. Scottish Arts Council and Scottish Television hold her works.

Jeni ROSS 1945– Tapestry, rug and furniture designer, full name Jennifer Ross, born in Cambridge, who studied for her diploma at Farnham School of Art, fine art sculpture, in 1980–2 doing two years' part-time research into woven tapestry. Her tapestries had "a strong feeling of event and movement", subjects being "drawn from poetry, music and the theatre". Group shows included Rye Art Gallery, 1993. Showed solo at Havant Arts Centre, 1984; The Oxford Gallery, Oxford, 1986; Kunstformen Jetzt, Salzburg, 1989; and Karen Haag & Associates, Vienna, 1995. Held a number of artist-in-residencies, including Bishop David Brown School in Woking; Matthew Arnold School, Staines. Commissions and sales included tapestry for Guildford Borough Council Art Collection, 1989, and Conquest Hospital, Hastings, 1993. Lived in Hale, Farnham, Surrey.

Victor ROSS 1899–1963 Painter and illustrator, born in Berlin as Gunther Victor Russ. Attended Berlin University and Munich Academy, 1920–3. He arrived in England shortly before World War II, during which he saw service there and in France in the Pioneer Corps. He exhibited in London and in Germany, but mainly worked for the printed page. Illustrated a number of books, including John Mortimer's *English Fashion*, 1947, and Peter Pirbright's *Off the Beeton Track*, 1949; also worked for periodicals such as *Eagle*, *Lilliput* and *Strand Magazine*. Lived in London.

Sarah ROSSBERG 1952– Artist in various media who was born in Recklinghausen, West Germany, in 1952. She studied at the Academy of Fine Art, Frankfurt, 1971–6, then at Camberwell School of Arts and Crafts, 1976–8. Her first show in Britain was at the RA Summer Exhibition, 1978. Her subsequent shows included Nicholas Treadwell Gallery: group shows in 1982–3 and a one-man, 1987; solo shows at Basle International Art Fair in 1986, Thumb Gallery, 1988, and Newport Museum and Art Gallery with tour, 1989. Rossberg was included in The Self Portrait: a Modern View, Artsite Gallery, Bath, and tour, 1987, and John Player Portrait Award, National Portrait Gallery, 1989, the year she won a prize for her picture Map at John Moores Exhibition, Liverpool. In 1990 she had solo shows at Thumb Gallery and in New York and Los Angeles, in 1992 having a one-man at Warrington Museum and Art Gallery. The artist said that she aimed to "create 'objects made of paint', which convey their content on as many levels as they have pictorial aspects". Lived in London.

Stella ROSS-CRAIG 1906– Botanical illustrator and artist working in watercolour, pencil and pen and ink, born in Aldershot, Hampshire. She studied at Art School in Thanet and botany at Chelsea Polytechnic. Stella Ross-Craig was, like her father, a member of the Linnean Society. She drew for the *Botanical Magazine* and other specialist publications and was for some time based at Kew Gardens, whose reference collections holds several hundred of her watercolours.

Nicholas St John ROSSE 1945– Artist who aged 16 was accepted as a pupil of Pietro Annigoni in Florence. He became known particularly for his oil paintings of children at the seaside, but also completed still lifes, gardenscapes and nude figure studies. He showed at RP, RBA, Grand Prix d'Art in Monaco, the Patrick Seale Gallery, City of London Exhibition, the New Ashgate Gallery in Farnham and RA. In 1992 he shared a show with three artists at Anna-Mei Chadwick.

John ROSSER 1931– Artist in acrylic, oil, gouache and watercolour, born in London. He studied at Regent Street Polytechnic School of Art and Watford School of Art, 1947–52. Rosser, made a member of ROI in 1978, was fond of bright colours and pictures full of light, including landscapes, coastal scenes, gardens, figurative and studio subjects. Group shows included RA Summer Exhibitions, RBA, NEAC, RI and Blackheath Gallery. Had a series of solo shows including Hallam Gallery, Brian Sinfield Gallery in Burford and Chelsea Library. BP Oil and Watford Museum hold examples. Lived in Poole, Dorset.

Carlo ROSSI 1921– Painter and teacher, born in Johnstone, Renfrewshire. He studied at Glasgow School of Art and in Italy, which remained an inspiration to his work, and went on to teach for some years. Rossi appeared in many mixed shows: at Compass Gallery, Glasgow; Glasgow Group; Fine Art Society in Glasgow; and RSW and Royal Glasgow Institute of the Fine Arts, of both of which he was a member. He had many one-man shows, including Compass Gallery, Strathclyde University and more recently at Open Eye Gallery, in Edinburgh. Rossi was a painter, often in mixed media, whose works – especially the still lifes – were coolly ordered and elegant.

Mario ROSSI 1958– Painter and sculptor, born in Glasgow, where from 1975–9 he studied sculpture at the School of Art. From 1979–81 he did a postgraduate sculpture course at Royal College of Art. He was Gulbenkian Scholar at the British School in Rome in 1982–3. Rossi was artist-in-residence at Trinity College, Cambridge, 1988–9. Although trained as a sculptor Rossi became well known as a painter and draughtsman, his work juxtaposing images from classical antiquity with those of contemporary life and society. He took part in many group shows and was featured in the Scottish National Gallery of Modern Art's 1989–90 touring exhibition Scottish Art since 1900. That gallery holds his suite of nine drawings, Charms, Capillaries and Amulets: Suite No. 2, of 1987. Solo shows included Anderson O'Day Gallery, 1993. Rossi was based in London.

Anthony ROSSITER 1926– Painter, writer and teacher, born in London. After Eton College he studied at Chelsea Polytechnic,

1947–51. Rossiter went on to lecture in fine art department of Bristol Polytechnic, 1960–83. In the latter year he formed Dalesford Studio for personal tuition in art, an extension of his own studio. From the mid-1950s Rossiter showed in London and the provinces. His autobiography, *The Pendulum*, was published in 1966, the book being linked to a retrospective show at Reading Museum and Art Gallery. A tour of selected work organised by The Lincolnshire Association in 1969 toured the county. In 1970 he had his first solo show in London to coincide with publication of *The Golden Chain*, which won an Arts Council Award for creative prose. In 1980 Rossiter illustrated Elizabeth Jennings' poems *A Dream of Spring*. Rossiter was elected RWA in 1964 and lived at Litton, Somerset. Victoria & Albert Museum, Ashmolean Museum in Oxford and other public and private collections hold his work.

Betty ROTHENSTEIN: *see* **Duffy AYERS**

Michael ROTHENSTEIN 1908–1993 Printmaker, painter, maker of reliefs, designer and teacher, born in London, son of the artist Sir William Rothenstein (pronounced Rohthenstein). He studied at Chelsea Polytechnic and Central School of Arts and Crafts, 1924–7. Had first one-man show at Matthiesen Gallery in 1938 and during World War II participated in the Pilgrim Trust *Recording Britain* project. In 1954 founded a graphic workshop in Great Bardfield, Essex, home to such artists as Edward Bawden and John Aldridge. Rothenstein won first prize in the Giles Bequest Competition for colour woodcuts and lino-cuts in 1954 and 1956. He went on to teach printmaking at Camberwell School of Art and was Art Fellow at Sheffield University in 1962. Rothenstein published a number of books, including *Frontiers of Printmaking*, 1966, *Relief Printing*, 1970, *Suns and Moons*, 1972, and the folio *Song of Songs*, 1979. Showed in major London galleries and had a retrospective at Stoke-on-Trent City Museum and Art Gallery, and touring, 1989–90. Tate Gallery, Victoria & Albert Museum, British Museum and Museum of Modern Art in New York hold his work. Made Hon. RE and elected RA, 1983. Rothenstein's daughter Anne was a painter. He lived at Stisted, Braintree, Essex.

Pascal ROUSSON 1963– Creator of satirical pictures related to the modern urban landscape, as in New Art in Scotland, Centre for Contemporary Arts, Glasgow, 1994. Rousson was born in Lyon, France, studying at the School of Fine Arts there, 1985–7, then at the School of Visual Arts, Geneva, 1987–91. Exhibitions included Villa Arson, Nice, France, 1990; La Régie, Geneva, Switzerland 1991; Answer Machines, Geneva, 1992; and in 1994 both Seagate Gallery, Dundee, where Rousson lived, and Collective Gallery, Edinburgh.

Brian ROUTH: *see* **The KIPPER KIDS**

David Paul ROWAN 1950– Artist in acrylic, born in Colne, Lancashire, where he lived for a time, then in south London. Studied at Maidstone College of Art, 1969–72, teachers including William Bowyer, then after his diploma did postgraduate work at Royal Academy Schools, 1972–5, with Peter Greenham and Margaret Green. Became a member of RBA in 1979, also showing in the provinces.

Eric ROWAN 1931– Painter, teacher and gallery director, born in Liverpool. He studied at the local College of Art, then at the Academy of Fine Arts, Florence, 1951–57. For two years ran a gallery for the New Shakespeare Theatre Club which was exemplary in showing the work of such artists as Paul Klee, Francis Bacon and Josef Herman. After a year in Italy Rowan returned to teach in Britain, including posts at Liverpool and Cardiff Colleges of Art. Was a member of the 56 Group and also showed at Howard Roberts Gallery in Cardiff, Clark Gallery in New York and elsewhere. Made a number of films, including one on Augustus and Gwen John, in 1975, for BBC Television. CASW, National Museum of Wales in Cardiff and other public galleries hold his work.

Evadné ROWAN fl. from 1940s– Freelance painter, illustrator and printmaker, born in Warsash, Hampshire. She studied at Gloucester School of Arts and Crafts and Central School of Arts and Crafts, teachers including Ernest Pullée, James Tucker and John Farleigh. She was elected a member of AIA in 1949 and the Society of Industrial Artists in 1952, later resigning from them when retired from professional work, which included extensive commissions from BBC, General Post Office, Penguin Books, Methuen, Rupert Hart-Davis and other publishers and publications. Exhibited with Senefelder Club. Lived for many years in London.

Mark ROWBOTHAM 1959– Artist in various media who studied at Epsom School of Art and Design. He showed at RI, ROI, NEAC, PS of which he was a member, and was included Thompson's Gallery, Aldeburgh, 10th Anniversary Exhibition, 1993. He was married to the artist Sherree E Valentine-Daines and lived in Ashtead, Surrey.

Annette ROWDON 1931– Sculptor in bronze, plaster, clay and stone notable for portrait busts, and teacher, born in Berlin, Germany, who grew up in America. She graduated in German literature from Bryn Mawr College, Pennsylvania. Then studied sculpture at Accademia di Belle Arti, Rome; having moved to London attended Central School of Arts and Crafts, 1954–8; but said that "the best training I received was in the marble workshops and foundries in Pietrasanta, Italy." Rowdon held a residency at Wilson College, Chambersburg, Pennsylvania, from 1978; was associate professor of art to Marlboro College students, Vermont, 1980–5; from 1985 did a teacher's certificate course at London Polytechnic, teaching at Chelsea School of Art, Hammersmith Leisure Centre and in Italy and Austria. In 1983 Rowdon gained a DAAD grant to work at Kunstlerhaus Bethanien Centre in Berlin. In 1984 the Royal College of Music acquired Rowdon's bust of Sir David Willcocks; in 1986 Schiller National Museum, Marbach, acquired a bust of the publisher Samuel Fischer; and in 1990 she completed a bust of the Crown Prince of Burma. Took part in many group shows internationally. Shared an exhibition at Ben Uri Art Society, which holds her work, 1986, with another shared exhibition at Medici Fortress, Livorno, 1992.

Cliff ROWE 1904–1989 Prolific and versatile artist and lifelong book illustrator whose work was marked by strong draughtsmanship, vigorous design and careful pictorial organisation, his underlying interests being social concerns and working situations. He was born and lived in London. Attended Wimbledon School of Art, 1918–21, won a scholarship to the Royal College of Art, but was dissatisfied by the teaching and left after a year; was employed by an advertising firm for two years; then went self-employed, to get more time for his own work. This reduced him "to drawing with boot polish on newspapers", and prompted him to question the economic basis of society. Rowe studied Socialist literature, read the *Communist Manifesto*, and in 1932 went on an exploratory holiday to the Soviet Union, where he stayed 18 months, designed book jackets and did commissioned work for the Red Army. Back in London, Rowe, who was a long-term member of the Communist Party, with Misha Black and others launched the AIA in 1933 (he left in the 1950s when it ceased to have a political purpose). In the late 1930s, Rowe came to question the tenets of Socialist Realism, which "I believed to be too limited in its theory and practice", and spent many years striving for a type of art neither photographic nor abstract. Rowe did not exhibit often, and in 1985 donated much of his work to date to galleries and museums including the Science, London and National Railway Museums, Leicester City Art Gallery and National Museum of Labour History (it gave him a solo show in 1995). The Tate Gallery holds work and the Electrical Trades Union College his General Strike and Tolpuddle Martyrs murals. Rowe was included in the AIA touring exhibition, organised by the Museum of Modern Art, Oxford, 1983, and in Fighting Spirits, with Peter Peri, Camden Arts Centre, 1987.

Jane ROWE 1919–1995 Painter in oil, full name Helen Josephine Rowe, born in Kettering, Northamptonshire. She began painting at Thamesside Institute in 1972 and notable among her teachers were George Gault, Steve Shepherd and Peter Clossick. Matthew Smith was cited as one influence. Rowe said that her approach to painting was "totally uncomplicated; I paint what is in front of me and, if I can communicate the absolute joy of colours and shapes of everyday objects, then my work speaks for me." Showed with Blackheath Arts Society, South-East London Art Group, Sweet Waters Gallery, in France and Germany. Had a first solo exhibition at Woodlands Art Gallery, 1988, with a memorial retrospective there in 1995. Lived in southeast London.

Lincoln ROWE 1951– Artist and adventurer who studied drawing and painting at Duncan of Jordanstone College of Art, Dundee, having been born in Scotland and educated in the border country. In 1977 Rowe was asked by the Marine Society to become their sea-going artist, creating a record of the Merchant Navy; he travelled worldwide, including painting the battlefields of the Falklands. In 1985 he joined a British and Royal Nepalese Army expedition in northeast Nepal, an area forbidden to foreigners, and undertook his first major climb, to 22,000 feet. A series of additional expeditions involved climbing Mount Everest. Rowe's solo shows included a series of exhibitions at Marine Society from 1977; Liverpool Maritime Museum, 1985; Royal Geographical Society, 1988; and The Osborne Studio Gallery from 1993. HRH The Duke of Edinburgh was among his patrons.

Liz ROWE 1955– Painter and teacher, born in Portsmouth, Hampshire (around 1990 Rowe, a former transvestite, sought a gender change. Rowe's work sometimes contained items of clothing alluding to her life outside the studio). She studied at Wolverhampton Polytechnic and Reading University and eventually taught at Newcastle Polytechnic. Was artist-in-residence at Tyne Tees Television in 1984. Rowe's mixed shows included Stowell's Trophy at RA, 1977; Hatton Gallery Summer Show, Newcastle, 1986; and the Newcastle Group exhibition The Northern Lights, DLI Museum & Arts Centre, Durham, 1990. Was a prizewinner in Tyne Tees Northern Open, 1985. Later solo shows included Hang Ups, Northern Centre for Contemporary Art, Sunderland, 1987. Was commissioned to paint a ceiling at Theatre Royal, Newcastle upon Tyne, Tyneside, where she lived.

John N ROWLAND 1931– Painter and printmaker who was born in Bradford, where he continued to live and studied at the School of Art. Exhibited RA and elsewhere.

George ROWLETT 1941– Painter, born in Troon, Ayrshire. Rowlett's landscapes and seascapes were singular in their bold brush strokes, sweeps of the palette knife and thick impasto, capturing the essence of a scene. He studied at Grimsby School of Art, 1960–2, Camberwell School of Art, 1962–5, and Royal Academy Schools, 1965–8. At Camberwell he won the Samuel Jones Fellowship, 1965–7, in 1966 gaining the David Murray Travelling Scholarship and Auerbach Criticism Prize. In 1967 a Silver Medal for Painting, First Landseer Prize, Landseer Scholarship and David Murray Travelling Scholarship followed. In 1984 Rowlett gained the Oppenheim–John Downes Memorial Trust Award. Rowlett showed widely, including RA, Camden Arts Centre, Whitechapel Open and overseas. He had a solo show at Cleveland Bridge Gallery in 1989, in Bath, another at Albemarle Gallery, 1990, and at Art Space Gallery, 1993. Grimsby Museum, Northern Arts and Cleveland Museum hold Rowlett's work. Worked in London and Deal, Kent.

Margaret ROWNEY 1908– Painter and printmaker, born in London, her father Walter Rowney, managing director of Rowney's, the artists' colourmen. Studied at St John's Wood Art School and Slade School of Fine Art, 1927–30, with Henry Tonks and Randolph Schwabe. Was a member of SWA, also exhibiting at RA, RE, elsewhere in London and solo abroad. Lived in Pinner, Middlesex.

Kenneth ROWNTREE 1915–1997 Painter, illustrator, artist in collage and murals, draughtsman and teacher, born in Scarborough, Yorkshire. Studied at Ruskin School of Drawing, Oxford, under Albert Rutherston, 1930–4, and at Slade School of Fine Art, 1934–5, with Randolph Schwabe. During World War II participated in Pilgrim Trust *Recording Britain* project and was an official war artist. Had first one-man exhibition at Leicester Galleries in 1946, others following at Ashmolean Museum, Oxford, Zwemmer Gallery, New Art Centre, Laing Art Gallery in Newcastle upon Tyne, with a retrospective at Hatton Gallery there in 1980. In 1992 an Oriel 31 Davies Memorial Gallery, Newtown, retrospective toured. Group shows included NEAC, AIA and RSW. Became a member of Society of Mural Painters in 1943, taught mural painting at Royal College of Art for 10 years from 1948 and received a Ford Foundation Grant to visit America in 1959. From 1959–80 was professor of fine art at Newcastle University. In 1948 illustrated *A Prospect of Wales*. Murals completed include those for Barclay School, Stevenage, 1946, RMS *Orsova* and *Iberia*, 1954, and British Pavilion at Brussels International Exhibition in 1958. Tate Gallery, Victoria & Albert Museum and WAC are among many public owners of his work. Rowntree's pictures reflect the genial and witty nature of the artist, usually being landscapes and townscapes in which the elements have a toy-like neatness and familiar notations are employed. Did some abstract work. Sometimes just signed work K R. Lived at Corbridge, Northumberland.

Hugh Thomas ROWSON 1946– Painter, born in Aberdeen, where he attended Gray's School of Art, 1965–70, under William Littlejohn and Robert Henderson Blyth. Became a member of RSW in 1980, also showing with the University and the Arts Centre in Aberdeen, where he worked as education officer for the Art Gallery and Museums.

Namba ROY 1910–1961 Sculptor and painter, born in Jamaica, son of a native wood-carver who gave Namba Roy tuition. Showed widely in London, including Westminster Cathedral Hall and St Pancras Town Hall, and two one-man shows at the Archer Gallery, early 1950s. Central Office of Information commissioned work, which was widely reproduced in *The Universe*, *Catholic Times*, *Church of England Newspaper*, *The Listener* and *Daily Mail*. Lived in London.

David ROYLE 1947– Painter, born in Manchester, his father a demolition worker, into a culturally deprived background. Went to a secondary technical school, transferring to a grammar school where he studied engineering drawing. Was at Central School of Art and Design, 1966–9. His work there and for some time after that was an exploration of the notation of forms and limits, free and contained movements, geometry and randomness. After this his work went through several stages, interspersed with some teaching and printmaking when money was short. There was a series of paintings from the late 1980s called Wasteland, another called City-River. Royle's work was figurative and abstract, often employing fiery colour. He said that he was interested "in the way that colour can generate what appears to be light". Showed at John Moores Exhibition, Liverpool, from 1967. In 1971 had solo show at Winchester School of Art, later one-man exhibitions including Minories, Colchester, 1989, and Beardsmore Gallery and Woodlands Gallery, 1992. He won a Wingate Scholarship, 1991. Arts Council holds his work.

Herbert ROYLE 1870–1958 Painter, especially of landscapes, born at Patricroft, Lancashire. He trained at the Harris Institute in Preston, Southport School of Art and with John Buxton Knight. He was a member of MAFA, Liverpool Academy and Sandon Studios Society. Showed at RA, RBA, RSA and extensively at Walker Art Gallery in Liverpool, which holds his work, as does Manchester City Art Gallery and other public galleries in Preston, Southport and Bradford. Lived latterly at Ilkley, Yorkshire.

Stanley ROYLE 1888–1961 Landscape painter, chiefly in oil, with a special interest in North of England scenes. Born in Stalybridge, Lancashire, he studied art at Sheffield School of Art under Oliver Senior. Exhibited widely, including RA, RI, RSA, Royal Glasgow Institute of the Fine Arts, Paris Salon, where he won silver and gold medals, at the New York World's Fair and widely in Canada. Royle was director of the school of fine arts at Mount Allison University, Sackville, New Brunswick, 1934–45. His work is held in many British provincial collections, including Sheffield, Derby, Rotherham and Bristol, and widely throughout Canada. Lived at Worksop, Nottinghamshire.

ROYSTON 1954– Artist in various and mixed media and designer, full name Royston du Maurier-Lebek, born in Stoke-on-Trent, Staffordshire. Although recommended at school to take up art, Royston went to catering college, North Staffordshire Polytechnic, 1971–3. Between 1974–80 was in fashion design in London and Brighton, from 1980–2 living in Paris as a fabric designer. Between 1982–90 was a knitwear and interior designer, then became a full-time artist, donating money to charitable causes. Male nudes, flowers and abstracts comprised his main works. Open shows included Pullit Gallery, Ben Uri Gallery and The Pump House Gallery. Solo exhibitions were held at Drill Hall Arts Centre, Bloomsbury Theatre, Almeida Theatre and Body Positive. Lived in London.

Beatrice ROZENBURG: *see* **Benedict DAVIES**

Benedict RUBBRA 1938– Painter and teacher, son of the composer Edmund Rubbra, married to the potter Tessa Rubbra. He was educated at Christ's Hospital and the Slade School of Fine Art. During his early career he taught in England and painted in France and Italy. Had a first one-man show in 1965. In 1970 Rubbra began a career as a portrait painter. His notable commissions included HRH The Prince of Wales, for the Fishmongers' Hall; Lord Hailsham, Sir Colin Davis and family, Sir Ove Arup and Ursula Vaughan Williams. As well as his portrait work he developed an original approach to landscape painting. Three-dimensional models were constructed, based on ideas drawn from landscape, which provided the starting point for final canvases of subtlety and beauty. An exhibition was held at the Barbican Centre in 1991, and in 1992 some were included, with a selection of his wife's pots, at John Bly, Bury Street. Rubbra's *Winter Sunlight Searching for Snowdrops* was produced by Curwen Chilford Press as a limited edition print in 1992. The artist wrote two books on portraiture: *Drawing Portraits* and *Painting Children*. Lived in Speen, Buckinghamshire. The County Museum in Aylesbury held a retrospective in 1998.

Sue RUBIN 1945– Artist in many media, including collage, photograms, monoprints and Hebrew calligraphy, and art therapist. She studied at Hornsey College of Art, 1963–6; Barnet College, 1972–86; Camden Art School, 1981–9; and in St Albans, 1983–5; notable teachers included Elizabeth Hepworth, Jack Yates and Izzy Pludwinsky. Rubin was an art therapist with physically handicapped adults, retirement home residents, hospital patients and children. She was a member of Ben Uri Art Society and several art therapy groups. Her own work was notable for its strong images. Group shows included Camden Arts Centre, Horniman Museum, ROI, NS, RBA and Hesketh Hubbard Art Society. Fitzroy Gallery, Yakar Educational and Cultural Centre and Alfred East Gallery in Kettering gave her solo shows. She had a studio in north London.

Gerda RUBINSTEIN 1931– Sculptor of figures, birds and animals, and teacher, born in Berlin, Germany, who grew up in Amsterdam, Netherlands, from the age of two. Moved to London in 1959, settling in Blackheath from 1960. For many years Rubinstein taught sculpture at the Catford and Greenwich Adult Education Institutes, her classes organised as open studios, based on the Atelier Colarossi, Paris, where she studied with Ossip Zadkine. Rubinstein studied in Wessel Couzijn's studio, Amsterdam, 1948, also at Rijksakademie there and in Paris at L'Académie de la Grande Chaumière, 1949–53. She won the Prix Jeune Sculpture. Group exhibitions included Whitechapel Open, 1983; Sculpture from the Open Studios under Gerda Rubinstein, 1977; Galerie Petit, Amsterdam, 1988; and Links of Affinity, Dutch contemporary art in Britain, Knapp Gallery, 1989. She had a solo exhibition at Holland Park Gallery, 1964, later ones including The Ashdown Gallery, Uckfield, 1987, and Gainsborough's House, Sudbury, 1992. One of her most exciting works is the bronze Arctic Terns water feature at the Merry Hill Shopping Centre, Birmingham.

Bob RUDD 1944– Painter, born in Suffolk, who attended Bath Academy of Art, Corsham, 1969–74, becoming a freelance artist in 1985. Was elected a member of RI in 1995. Group exhibitions included Beaux Arts, Bath; RWA from 1988; Roy Miles Gallery, 1990; Singer & Friedlander/*Sunday Times* Watercolour Competition, 1994; and Flying Colours Gallery, Edinburgh, 1997. Had a solo exhibition at Eye Gallery, Bristol, 1989, later ones including John Martin of London and City Gallery, both 1996. In 1994 Rudd won the St Cuthberts Mill Watercolour Award at RWA; in 1996 the Linda Blackstone Award at RI; and in 1997 he was a regional winner in the Laing Competition. BBC in Bristol, New Parliamentary Buildings at Westminster and a number of corporate collections hold Rudd's work. Lived in Bradford-on-Avon, Wiltshire.

Julian RUDDOCK 1965– Artist in a wide range of media, who spent his childhood in Cheltenham, Gloucestershire, in 1978 moving to Hong Kong for four years, where he developed an interest in painting. Did a fine art foundation course at Gloucestershire College of Arts and Technology in 1985, then moved to Wales, where he settled at Capel Seion, Aberystwyth, Dyfed, in the mid-1990s studying at University College Wales there. On moving to Wales Ruddock spent short periods as a conservation worker on an organic farm and as a graphic artist for the Welsh Traffic Education Programme. The Enterprise Allowance Scheme made it possible for him to concentrate full-time on his painting. This was "strongly influenced by the mid-Wales landscape, its mystery and beauty. It explores our existence in the environment, our impact upon it and its impact upon us." Showed at Ceredigion Museum, Aberystwyth, from 1991; Aberystwyth Arts Centre, 1994; Showcase Wales at Y Tabernacl, Machynlleth, from 1995; and Ashbourne Gallery, Derby, from 1996.

Matt RUGG 1935– Painter, carver in relief and teacher, born in Bridgwater, Somerset. He studied at the University of Newcastle – the department of fine art, King's College – from 1955–61, then from 1962–4 was lecturer in painting there. In 1965 went to Chelsea School of Art to lecture in sculpture. Showed Young Contemporaries, LG, in Sculpture Today and Tomorrow at Bear Lane Gallery in Oxford, in Twenty-Six Sculptors at ICA and had several one-man shows at New Art Centre. Arts Council holds his Relief Construction, 1960, and Relief Painting, 1964, and Tate Gallery and Leeds City Art Gallery also hold his work.

Jeremy RUGGE-PRICE 1940– Painter of landscape, brought up in Suffolk, whose two years in the Merchant Navy gave him a love of travel, sea and ships. The two greatest influences on his work were the pictures of Edward Seago and Matthew Alexander, with whom he drew and painted. Settled in North America, where he exhibited widely. His solo show at Century Galleries, Henley-on-Thames, 1997, included pictures of East Anglia, Brittany and Venice.

Sandrine RUMMELHARDT 1967– Artist using installations and photography, as in New Art in Scotland, Centre for Contemporary Arts, Glasgow, 1994. Work there was described as "an experiment, a series of questions about reality … gestures rather than objects." Born in Forbach, France, Rummelhardt studied there at L'École des Beaux-Arts, Mulhouse, 1986–7, and at L'École des Arts Decoratifs, Strasbourg, 1989, then at Glasgow School of Art, 1992–4. Exhibitions included Des Artistes pour les Droits de l'Homme, Course des Chaines, Mulhouse, 1989; Invitation to a Living Winter Picture, Glasgow School of Art, 1993; and in 1994 both Doppelganger, Gallery Simulakrum, Mainz, Germany, and Titanic, Old Fruitmarket, Glasgow.

Ralph RUMNEY 1934– Painter, writer, publisher, broadcaster and teacher. From 1952 Rumney studied at Halifax School of Art, but left disillusioned and travelled on continent, partly to avoid conscription; he was a conscientious objector. After founding an arts weekly called *Other Voices* Rumney went to Trieste and had his first solo show. In 1956, in Milan, Rumney had another one-man exhibition and made contact with the Movimento Nucleare and Il Movimento Internazionale per un Bauhaus Imaginista, a further one-man show taking place in London's New Vision Centre. Showed in International Exhibition in Tokyo. Promoted by Redfern Gallery, Rumney's picture The Change was used as the cover of the catalogue for the key Metavisual, Tachiste and Abstract exhibition in 1957. He was a founder member of Internationale Situationniste and collaborated in setting up the environmental project Place at ICA in 1959, while busily showing his work internationally, such as at the Paris Biennale. In 1960 was involved in Situation at RBA Galleries. In the early 1960s Rumney became disillusioned with the innovation-quashing aspect of the gallery system. For about the next 16 years he worked as a writer and broadcaster, much of it for French Broadcasting, in the mid-1970s teaching art history and theory and film-making at Canterbury College of Art. Began to create artworks again in 1983. Had solo show at Transmission Gallery, Glasgow, in 1985, in 1989 having a major retrospective at England & Co. Rumney was married for a time to Pegeen, painter and daughter of the art collector Peggy Guggenheim, who had previously been married to the French painter Jean Hélion.

Paul RUMSEY 1956– Artist, notable as a draughtsman of imaginative subjects, born in Essex, who did a foundation course at Colchester School of Art and Design, 1972–4, winning a Munnings Travel Scholarship in the latter year, then gained a bachelor's degree at Chelsea School of Art, 1974–7. Mixed shows included *Spectator* Art Award Show from 1988; Colchester Art Society, The Minories, Colchester, 1991; Art Bus, Fife, Scottish Arts Council tour show to schools, 1994; and Drawings for All, Gainsborough's House, Sudbury, third prize, 1996 (one of a number of prizes gained over the years at various venues). His solo shows included one at Gainsborough's House, another at Chappel Galleries, Chappel, both 1997.

Frank RUNACRES 1904–1974 Painter and teacher who studied at St Martin's School of Art, then the Slade School of Fine Art and Royal College of Art, 1930–3. Exhibited RA, Manchester City Art Gallery, Leicester Galleries and NEAC. Taught for a period at Hornsey School of Art. Lived in Richmond, Surrey.

Albert RUNCIMAN-CUMMINGS 1936– This was the painting name of Albert Arratoon Runciman Cummings, artist in watercolour and egg tempera, born in Edinburgh. He was an apprentice scene painter under William Grason, studied painting with Charles Napier and Robert Jardine and restoration with John Buchanan at Aitken Dott & Son. Was for a while a member of UA, also exhibiting with a series of Edinburgh galleries: Fine Art Society, Scottish Gallery, Open Eye and Edinburgh Gallery. Leeds Education Authority and Edinburgh Hospital Board hold his work. Lived in Aberlady, East Lothian.

William RUSCOE 1904–1990 Ceramist, painter, writer and teacher, born in Stoke-on-Trent, Staffordshire, son of the potter William Ruscoe and married to the designer Olga Harris. He studied at Stoke-on-Trent Schools of Art under Gordon Forsyth, worked in industry as a modeller, sculptor and designer, then taught in Stoke area and as a visiting instructor at Royal College of Art, moving to Exeter in 1994 to lecture at College of Art. He wrote several books on ceramics, including *English Porcelain Figures* and *A Manual for the Potter*. Ruscoe was a member of the Society of Industrial Artists and of the Kenn Group, Exeter. Also showed with Society of Staffordshire Artists and had solo shows including Exeter University, Plymouth Civic Centre and Stafford Art Gallery. The Fitzwilliam Museum in Cambridge and museums in Stoke-on-Trent and Exeter hold examples. Ruscoe's chief ceramic interests were highly fired stonewares of an individual nature with glaze effects peculiar to the high temperature metallic oxides when reduced.

Florence RUSHBURY 1896–1981 Painter, draughtsman, embroiderer and dress designer, born in London, who also worked under her unmarried name Florence Layzell. She was married from 1914 to the artist Henry Rushbury, their daughter Julia also being a painter. In 1924 attended Chelsea School of Art, having begun painting and drawing on marriage, also studying at Westminster School of Art. Rushbury was noted for portraits of people in their own environment, clarity of vision and an immaculate technique being notable characteristics. A self-portrait completed in Caudebec, a portrait of Naomi Fennel and Flowers, bought by Sir Sidney Cockerell, were notable works. Showed at RA Summer Exhibition and NEAC. Brighton Museum and Art Gallery has an embroidered dress made by Rushbury early in her marriage.

Henry RUSHBURY 1889–1968 Watercolourist, draughtsman and printmaker who concentrated on architectural-type subjects. Born at Harborne, near Birmingham, he studied at Birmingham School of Art, 1903–9, where he concentrated on mural painting and stained glass design. He later studied for a short time under Henry Tonks at the Slade School of Fine Art. Before moving to London Rushbury assisted Henry Payne to decorate Madresfield Court, near Great Malvern. Francis Dodd persuaded Rushbury to try engraving and etching. Married the artist Florence Layzell. He became an official war artist during World War I, a role he repeated in World War II. Rushbury's first one-man show was at the Grosvenor Gallery in 1921, and he also showed at such venues as the RA, NEAC, RWS, RE, Fine Art Society and Goupil Gallery. The Tate Gallery holds his work, much of which was done in France and Italy. He was elected RA, 1936, was keeper of the RA, 1949–64, and was knighted, 1964. As a delineator of buildings and complicated structures Rushbury has few equals. Lived at Lewes, Sussex. Rushbury's daughter Julia was also a painter.

Julia RUSHBURY 1930– Painter and muralist, born in Suffolk. She was daughter of the painter Henry Rushbury; her husband was the painter Theo Ramos, her son the artist Tod Ramos. Studied at Lanford Grove under the muralist Hans Feibusch, in 1947 at Chelsea School of Art and at Royal Academy Schools, 1948; she gained the Landseer Prize, RA Gold Medal and Edward Stott Travelling Scholarship, 1950, studying in Italy, 1951. Early Italian methods influenced Rushbury's murals, which were based on accurate drawing but were not a pastiche. A painted room at Asa Briggs' house in Lewes, Sussex, the town where Rushbury lived, was one commission, others being completed for A Stewart-Roberts at Offham, another at Old Bridge, Huntingdon, for John Hoskins. Group shows included Young Contemporaries, Leicester Galleries, RA Summer Exhibitions and Arts Council and British Council exhibitions.

Dorothy Marion RUSHTON 1884–c.1973 Painter of landscapes and architectural subjects, mural designer and etcher. Born in Greenhithe, Kent, she studied painting at Cope's Art School, at the Royal Academy Schools and in Hanover, Germany. Exhibited Walker Art Gallery, Liverpool, RHA, SWA, WIAC, RWS and in France. Lived in London.

George Robert RUSHTON 1868–1948 Painter, decorative and stained glass artist and teacher, born in Birmingham. He studied art there and in London, winning several medals. Taught for a time at Armstrong College in Newcastle upon Tyne, then assumed control of Ipswich Art School, 1906–29, where he was considered an enlightened principal. He was a member of RBSA, RI and RBA and was a prolific exhibitor, also showing at Fine Art Society, RA, Brook Street Art Gallery and Walker Art Gallery in Liverpool. Rushton completed a number of large, decorative projects which led to his being illustrated in architectural publications. Cinemas in Blackpool, Ipswich, Oxford, Slough and Southampton commissioned his work and he finished a big scheme for McGill University, Montreal, Canada. Public galleries in Ipswich and Newcastle upon Tyne hold examples. Lived for a time in Dedham, Essex.

Stephen RUSS 1916– Designer and teacher, born in Sheffield. He was educated at Kingswood School, Bath, then at Royal College of Art, 1935–9, his teachers including Paul Nash, Eric Ravilious and Edward Bawden. Russ went on to work as a freelance designer and poster artist, from 1947 teaching for many years at Bath Academy of Art. He died shortly after retirement when hill walking. Was the author of the primer *Setting up in Screen Printing*. Lived in Melksham, Wiltshire.

Bruce RUSSELL 1946– Painter, draughtsman and teacher, born in London. Studied at Chelsea School of Art for his bachelor's and master's degrees, 1964–9, gaining a fellowship in painting at Gloucestershire College of Art, 1969–70. He was Young Contemporaries prizewinner, 1968, gaining an Art Council Award in 1975 and its Major Award, 1978. Russell began teaching at York School of Art, 1971–4; further appointments followed at Newcastle Polytechnic and St Martin's/Central St Martins; then from 1993 he was professor of fine art at Kingston University. Russell was closely involved in promoting exhibitions at Newcastle, St Martin's and Kingston, from 1997 being director of Kingston's Stanley Picker Gallery. Participated in numerous group exhibitions and showed solo steadily from his exhibition in 1973, at the White Rose Gallery, Bradford. Later one-mans included Venice Biennale, Aperto, and Demarco Gallery, Edinburgh International Festival, both 1995, and Beardsmore Gallery, 1997. Arts Council, British Council, Contemporary Art Society, European Parliament and many other public collections held Russell's work.

Caroline RUSSELL 1962– Sculptor, born in Aldershot, Hampshire. She studied at Ruskin School of Art, Oxford, 1980–3, Goldsmiths' College School of Art, 1986–8, and had a fellowship at Goldsmiths', 1989–90. Took part in New Sculpture in Oxford, at St Paul's Art Centre, Oxford, 1984; Chisenhale Gallery, 1986; and South Bank Centre touring The British Art Show 1990. Solo exhibitions included Anthony Reynolds Gallery, 1988, and Chisenhale, 1989. Lived in London.

Edwin RUSSELL 1939– Sculptor, born in Heathfield, Sussex, married to the sculptor Lorne McKean. He studied at Brighton College of Art and Crafts, 1955–9, then Royal Academy Schools, 1959–63. He won the Academy's Gold Medal and Edward Stott Travelling Scholarship. Was elected a fellow of RBS in 1978, in 1991 winning the Otto Beit Medal for Sculpture. Russell produced a large volume of public sculpture. This included sculpture for churches; crucifix in limewood, 1964, for St Paul's Cathedral, also St Michael, in oak, 1970; also a series of sundials: with a large bronze dial for Parliament Square, Dubai, in 1988, and one for Tower Hill Underground Station, 1992; shopping centre sculpture: including Mad Hatter's Tea Party, Warrington, 1984, and Panda in marble, World Wildlife Fund International Headquarters, 1988. Private collections included Sir Robert McAlpine & Sons, Arup Associates, Worshipful Company of Stationers and City of London Grammar School. Lived in Hindhead, Surrey.

Ena RUSSELL 1906–1997 Painter, illustrator and writer, married to the Member of Parliament Sir Ronald Russell, who predeceased her in 1974. She was born in Cleveland, Yorkshire, maiden name Ena Glen Forrester. Her father was an architect who won a competition to redesign Middlesbrough after War War I, but the recession prevented this and forced the family from their house into a boarding house. The experience, which tinged Ena's character with a lifelong frugality, prompted her to earn money by writing and illustrating fashion articles, as Eva Glen. After marrying her husband, who worked for the Reuters news agency, she concentrated on her painting. She studied at St Albans, Chelsea and Sir John Cass Colleges of Art. Work appeared in *The Artist*, *Leisure Painter*, *The Daily Telegraph* and *The Lady*. She was elected ROI in 1972, also exhibiting in RA Summer Exhibition, at NEAC, RP and in other mixed shows. Solo exhibitions included House of Commons, 1974. In 1968, Lady Russell organised a Wives of Westminster show to support the Artists' General Benevolent

Institution, her favourite charity. She continued to paint into old age, despite poor eyesight, at her studio in Provence, France, and in London, where she lived.

Gyrth RUSSELL 1892–1970 Marine artist in oil and watercolour, etcher and writer, born in Dartmouth, Nova Scotia. He studied art in America and in Paris, 1912–14, at the Académie Julian and Atelier Colarossi. During World War I Russell was an official war artist for the Canadian government. He took part in the Canadian War Memorial Exhibition, in London, in 1919. Group shows included RI, RBA, SEA, SWA and RBC. One-man shows were held at the Howard Roberts Gallery, Cardiff, 1956, and two in Penarth, where he died, held in 1961 and 1966. Russell wrote several books, including *Unknown Devon*, 1927.

Jim RUSSELL 1933– Painter, draughtsman, illustrator and teacher, born in Walsall, Staffordshire, who attended Birmingham College of Art, 1951–5 and 1957–8. Lived in London from 1960, teaching part-time at St Martin's School of Art, and illustrating for major book publishers, BBC Television and magazines such as *Radio Times* and *Punch*. Was a member of RBA and showed at RA from 1959, also at NEAC, RI, Cleveland Drawing Biennale, John Moores Liverpool Exhibition and elsewhere, in 1970 gaining the Lord Mayor's Art Award. Showed solo at William Ware Gallery, 1967–9; from 1978 regularly at Amalgam, Barnes; Nuffield Centre, Southampton, 1993; and Crucible Theatre, Sheffield, 1994. Russell was especially interested in depicting people at work, working in the theatre and landscapes with figures. The boxer Herol Graham, the actress Vanessa Redgrave and playwright Arthur Miller were among his main works.

Joan RUSSELL 1911– Watercolourist and teacher, born in Lichfield, Staffordshire. After education locally and in Eastbourne, she attended Birmingham School of Art, 1930–4, under Harold Holden and Bernard Fleetwood-Walker, then the Royal College of Art, 1934–7, under Percy Hague Jowett and Ernest Tristram. Exhibited RWS, of which she was a member, and RA. Lived in Epsom, Surrey.

Kathleen RUSSELL 1940– Artist in gouache, watercolour, oil, pastel, pen and wash, and teacher, born in Edinburgh, who studied at the College of Art there, 1958–63, teachers including Robin Philipson and William Gillies. She lectured there full-time, 1963–72, then taught part-time in London schools, including Plumstead Manor School, until 1980, when she became a full-time painter. Mixed shows included Woodlands Art Gallery. Had a long series of solo exhibitions, including French Institute, 1965, New 57 Gallery, 1969, and Douglas & Foulis, 1972, all in Edinburgh; Durham University, 1975; and The Scottish Gallery, Edinburgh, from 1981. Durham University, King's College and Royal Botanic Gardens, Kew, hold examples. Was a member of SSWA. Lived in southeast London.

Nicola RUSSELL 1964– Painter who completed a foundation course at University of Ulster, Belfast, in 1983, then gained a degree in fine art at Winchester School of Art, 1986. Russell won a fellowship at British School in Rome, 1993–4, her work being shown there in the latter year. She took part in Hausegeist/Nomade, a Berlin Exchange Scheme, in 1992, and was represented in Still Lives, a travelling group exhibition sponsored by Arts Council of Northern Ireland in 1993. Other mixed appearances included Fenderesky Gallery, Belfast, 1989; Arts Council Gallery in the city, 1992; and in 1994 Beyond the Partitions, organised by Belfast's Queen Street Studios, with which she was associated.

Robert RUSSELL 1948– Sculptor in various materials, and teacher, born in Newport, Shropshire. He attended Shrewsbury School of Art, 1965–7; Central School of Art and Design, 1967–70; and Royal College of Art, 1970–3. From 1973 lectured in sculpture and its history at West Surrey College of Art and Design, Farnham, and elsewhere. Russell gained an Arts Council Award for sculpture in schools and a Granada Foundation Award for Sculpture, in 1973; in 1975–6 Arts Council grant and minor award; in 1979 he was artist-in-residence at Woolmore School; in 1980 obtaining a Greater London Arts Association grant, commission for sculpture, at Woolmore. Took part in many group shows, including Garden Exhibition I, Camden Arts Centre, 1978; Cannizaro Park, 1982; and Whitechapel Open, from 1983. Solo exhibitions included Stoke-on-Trent City Museum and Art Gallery, 1984. Arts Council and London Borough of Tower Hamlets hold examples.

Rodney Fryer RUSSELL 1918– Painter and teacher, born in Bournemouth, Hampshire, and educated at Sherborne School in Dorset. Studied at Bartlett School of Architecture, 1936–9, Central School of Arts and Crafts, 1947–9, then in 1950 in Paris at Académie de la Grande Chaumière. For a time taught art at St Paul's School. Showed RA, RI, PS, Walker's Galleries and elsewhere. Lived in London, near Cranleigh in Surrey and finally in Andraitx, Majorca.

Ron RUSSELL 1923–1994 Painter in oil, born in London, who began painting in Sydney, Australia, studying with G F Bissietta. Returned to London in 1959. Had many shows with New Vision Centre painters in Britain and overseas, also South London Art Gallery, Nicholas Treadwell Gallery, Bear Lane Gallery in Oxford and 1st Commonwealth Biennale. Solo shows included New Vision Centre, Grabowski Gallery, Edinburgh International Festival, St Catherine's College in Oxford and L'Oeil Ecouté Gallery, Lyon, France. The work of Antonio Calderara, of Milan, was influential, as well as Rothko and Piero della Francesca. St Catherine's College and St Edmund Hall in Oxford hold examples. Russell's work was Minimalist, with resonant, jewel-like colours, as seen in his commemorative show at Diorama Arts Gallery, 1995.

Vida RUSSELL 1962– Painter, who studied at Dartington College of Art, 1981–3, Central St Martins College, 1991–4, and earned a postgraduate diploma at Royal Academy Schools, 1994–6. In 1996 she gained first prize at MAFA annual exhibition, the Eric Kennington Award for Best Academic Drawing and W H

Patterson Award for Painting. Russell began exhibiting in 1983, including The Blue Gallery, Contemporary Art Society and at Art '95. In 1995 she had a solo exhibition at Phillips Contemporary Art in Manchester, 1995, with one at Cassian de Vere Cole Fine Art, 1996. There Russell showed paintings of women in baths, influenced by icons, late Titian and Rembrandt, in which she was "concentrating on stillness and contemplation". The pictures emerged "out of an earthy darkness, focusing on surfaces, touch, skin, decay, transience. Like an archeological dig these bodies are uncovered".

Walter RUSSELL 1867–1949 Painter and teacher, born Epping, Essex. Walter Westley Russell studied under Frederick Brown at Westminster School of Art and worked for a time in the early 1890s as a printmaker and illustrator. He was assistant professor at Slade School of Fine Art, 1895–1927. He began showing at NEAC in 1893, becoming a member two years later; he also became a member of IS, 1906, National Portrait Society, 1910 (the year he had his first solo show at Goupil Gallery), and RWS in 1930. Russell showed from 1898 at RA, being elected RA in 1926 and made keeper for 1927–42. During World War I he was for three years in the Army, engaged on camouflage. Was knighted in 1935. Russell was notable for his coastal scenes and portraits of women. Tate Gallery has a good collection of his work. He died in London and there was a memorial show at Beaux Arts Gallery in 1950.

Hugh RUSSELL-HALL 1905– Painter and teacher who studied at Duncan of Jordanstone School of Art in Dundee and then in Paris with Émile-Othon Friesz. Taught painting for 30 years at St Martin's School of Art. Was elected ROI in 1959, also showing at RA, RP and in the provinces. Lived in Halstead, Essex.

Mollie RUSSELL-SMITH fl. from 1960s– Artist and teacher, notably a printmaker, who studied at Beckenham School of Art and East Anglian School of Painting and Drawing run by Cedric Morris. Taught at Bromley Centre for Arts and Crafts. Showed with WIAC, at RBA and Cooling Galleries and was included in Group '77 Printmakers at Woodlands Art Gallery, 1981. Had solo exhibitions at Beckenham Theatre and Fairfield Halls, Croydon.

Agatha RUSSON 1903– Artist in oil, crayon and watercolour. Born in Raymond, Wisconsin, America, she studied art under Bernard Adams, F D Daniels and Mabel Wickham. Exhibited at the Ashmolean Museum, Oxford, RBA, ROI, and in Portsmouth and Southampton. Lived at Chandlers Ford, Hampshire.

Zdzislaw RUSZKOWSKI 1907–1991 Painter and teacher, born in Tomazov, Poland, the son of the painter Waclaw Ruszkowski. Studied at Craców Academy, 1924–9, after showing very early talent, then Warsaw Academy, 1930–2, in the latter part of the 1930s working in France where he knew the English painter Matthew Smith and came under the influence of Cézanne. Moved with the Polish Army to Scotland during World War II, in the mid-1940s settling in north London. Showed widely there and in the provinces, having his first one-man show at Roland, Browse and Delbanco in 1948. There was a retrospective at Leeds City Art Gallery, which holds his work, in 1966. Despite lean times Ruszkowski had several good patrons, such as Tom Laughton, the actor Charles Laughton's brother, and these encouraged him to travel on the continent. His work has a strong lyrical quality and he is a powerful Colourist.

Alexa RUTHERFORD 1952– Illustrator and designer, brought up in Fife, Scotland, the daughter of an architect. She studied at Duncan of Jordanstone College of Art in Dundee, 1969–74. Showed RSA and elsewhere in Scotland and did book and other commercial illustration. Lived in Edinburgh.

Eric RUTHERFORD 1923– Painter, printmaker, designer for theatre and teacher, born in Edinburgh. He was educated at St John's College, Southsea. In 1959 he shared a show of paintings at the New Vision Centre, followed by a number of solo exhibitions at Leicester Galleries in the early 1960s, from one of which the Arts Council bought his abstract watercolour and collage Xenio. Rutherford began to exhibit widely in several continents, especially in North America. The National Museum of Wales in Cardiff and several American galleries bought his work. National Film Archive, in London, holds a pioneering African feature film by him.

Harry RUTHERFORD 1903–1985 Painter, illustrator and teacher. Born at Denton, Lancashire, he was encouraged by his father, William, hatter and keen amateur artist. While still at school Harry attended Hyde School of Art on Saturdays, then after leaving school joined evening classes at Manchester School of Art, supervised by Adolphe Valette, who taught the older L S Lowry. In 1925 joined Walter Sickert's art class in Manchester, in St Mary's Parsonage, taking over the class in 1926 when Sickert gave it up. Rutherford remained a disciple of Sickert, adopting the slogan "Thou shalt be interesting." In the late 1920s, having been head artist at the F John Roe Advertising Agency, and having begun to draw for the *Manchester Evening News*, Rutherford moved to Cornwall to work with Ernest and Dod Procter in Newlyn, supervising their classes for a period. While at Newlyn his picture Penzance became his first accepted for the RA, in 1930. He then drew for the Duke of Devonshire at Chatsworth, moving to London in 1932 where he taught and freelanced for Fleet Street papers. Was associated with television before and after World War II, having his own programme, *Sketchbook*, for children. During the war he was attached to the Royal Air Force. Returned to Hyde in the 1950s; taught painting at the Regional College of Art, Manchester, until 1968; and in 1961 was made president of the MAFA, a position held for eight years. Completed a 30-foot mural for Hyde Town Hall in the late 1940s. Also exhibited NEAC, RBA, RP and Paris Salon. A number of public galleries hold Rutherford's work, typified by northern townscapes and personalities. Astley Cheetham Art Gallery, Stalybridge, which has a big collection of his work, put on a memorial show in 1985.

Iain RUTHERFORD 1953– Artist who did a foundation course at Winchester School of Art, 1970–1; then at Goldsmiths' College gained an honours degree in fine art, 1971–4, his art teachers' certificate, 1976–7, and his master's, 1978–80. Mixed shows included ICA Student Exhibition, 1972; Space Open Studios, 1975; Eleven Artists, Camden Arts Centre, 1980; 14 days, Lewisham Visual Arts Festival, 1986; and Woodlands Art Gallery, 1997. Had a solo show at Art Space Gallery, 1986. Leicestershire Education Authority holds his work. Lived in London.

Jane RUTHERFORD 1967– Painter, born in London. She studied at Edinburgh College of Art, 1985–90, to obtain her master's degree. Group exhibitions from late 1980s included King's College Hospital and Macaulay Gallery, Stenton. In 1990 Rutherford won a McColl Arts Foundation arts travel bursary to travel in Brazil and paint land development in the northern Amazon area. She had a solo show in Brazil at Galleria Cunha, Roraima, in 1991, and in 1992 a show of exuberant Brazilian pictures at Flying Colours Gallery, Edinburgh.

Rosemary RUTHERFORD 1912–1972 Stained glass artist, painter and draughtsman who early in life lived in Broomfield, near Chelmsford, in Essex, where her father was rector for many years. Between the wars she showed at NEAC, after World War II being associated with Cedric Morris' and Lett Haines' East Anglian School of Painting and Drawing at Hadleigh, Suffolk. Rutherford was more known for stained glass than for pictures, but she had a real feeling for richly coloured pigment, as in The Dining Room, Michael and Valerie Chase Collection, Minories, Colchester, 1994.

Albert RUTHERSTON 1881–1953 Painter, poster and stage designer and book illustrator. Born in Bradford, the younger brother of the artist Sir William Rothenstein. Albert and his elder brother Charles, a noted collector, changed their names to Rutherston in 1914, the year World War I began. Albert studied at the Slade School of Fine Art, 1898–1902. His early work was realist, such as Laundry Girls, held by the Tate Gallery, but it later became more decorative, while always retaining a strongly linear Slade influence. Exhibited prolifically and widely, including Leicester Galleries and NEAC especially, also Goupil Gallery, Fine Art Society and RWS. First one-man show at Carfax Gallery, 1910. Served in Palestine during World War I. His connection with the theatre included working with the actor-manager Harley Granville-Barker and writing *Decoration in the Art of the Theatre*, 1919. Illustrated books for the Cresset Press and Nonesuch Press. Was Ruskin Master of Drawing at Oxford, 1929–48. Lived much in Cotswolds and London, but died in Ouchy-Lausanne, Switzerland. Retrospective Max Rutherston, 1988.

Chloe RUTHVEN 1969– Painter, draughtsman and printmaker who attended London College of Printing, 1986–8; did a foundation course at Camberwell School of Arts and Crafts, 1988–9; then gained an honours degree in fine art from Central St Martins School of Art, 1989–92. Mixed shows included Sotheby's, 1994, and Art98 at Business Design Centre, with Eagle Gallery, 1998. She shared a show at Rebecca Hossack Gallery, 1995. Had a solo show, Nostalgie de la Boue, Eagle Gallery, 1996, with another at King of Hearts Gallery, Norwich, 1997.

Robert RUTTER 1909–1955 Painter in oil and tempera. Studied at Hammersmith School of Art under William Washington, 1932–6, then at the Royal College of Art under Percy Jowett, 1936–40. Became painting master at Hammersmith School of Art. Exhibited RA, the provinces and in America. CASW bought his work. Lived in London.

Adrian RYAN 1920– Painter and teacher, born in London, son of the landscape and portrait artist Vivian D Ryan. Adrian Ryan studied at Architectural Association, 1938–9, and Slade School of Fine Art, 1939–40. He taught at Goldsmiths' College School of Art, 1948–83. Over the years he painted in a variety of places, including Cornwall, France and Suffolk, being latterly based in London and Suffolk. As well as appearing in various mixed shows, including LG and RA, he had a number of one-man shows, starting with the first of a series at Redfern Gallery in 1943. Later solo exhibitions included University of West Virginia in 1978, Gallery 10 in 1980, a retrospective at The Minories, Colchester, 1985, with other solos in Atlanta, Georgia, from 1989. Tate Gallery holds his Flowers on a Chair.

David RYAN 1956– Painter, born in Liverpool, who studied at Coventry Polytechnic. In 1980 won a German Scholarship that enabled him to study in several cities there. He showed in Britain and Germany and was included in four-artist show at Woodlands Art Gallery, 1989, where his works were "concerned with the pictorial possibilities of space, gesture, format and focus". Lived in London.

John RYAN 1921– Children's author and illustrator, artist and teacher, working mostly in pen and ink watercolour, creator of many books and of over 80 films for the BBC. He was born in Edinburgh, son of the diplomat Sir Andrew Ryan, and attended Ampleforth College and Regent Street Polytechnic School of Art, 1945–8. Was assistant art master at Harrow School, 1948–54. From 1966 was cartoonist for *Catholic Herald*, but was most famous for his creation Captain Pugwash, also Harris Tweed, Lettice Leefe and Sir Prancelot, his work appearing in the comics *Eagle* and *Girl*. Ryan was a member of Rye Art Society, in Sussex, where he lived, and the Society of Authors. He showed at RA, Round House, Royal Festival Hall and Rye Art Gallery. University of Kent's cartoon archive and The Museum of the Moving Image hold Ryan's work. His aim was "to entertain children of all ages with words and pictures."

Paul RYAN 1955– Artist and teacher notable for his work using handmade paper and paper pulp, born in Burslem, Staffordshire. He gained his teacher's certificate at Crewe and Alsager College, Cheshire, 1973–6; then graduated with an honours degree in fine art at North Staffordshire Polytechnic, 1976–9, gaining his master's degree at Manchester Polytechnic, 1979–80. In 1980 he was a North West Arts Award Winner, in

1982 gaining an award from South West Arts, then in 1983 won a Calouste Gulbenkian Foundation Printmaking Award. Was a commercial printer in Manchester, 1980–1, then held a series of teaching posts, including Rochdale College of Art and Slade School of Fine Art. Exhibitions included Northern Young Contemporaries at Whitworth Art Gallery, Manchester, 1979; Cirencester Craft Workshops, 1982; and Crafts Council, 1983. Had a solo show at Rochdale Art Gallery, which holds his work, 1981; Curwen Gallery, 1983; and at Woodlands Art Gallery, 1984. Lived in London.

Paul RYAN 1968– Painter, born in Leicester, who studied at Chelsea School of Art. Group shows included Compass Gallery, Glasgow, 1989–90; RA Summer Exhibition, from 1991; Christmas Exhibition, England & Co, 1992–3; and Royal Over-Seas League Open, 1994 and 1996. Had a solo exhibition at Red Herring Gallery, Brighton, 1990, later ones including Gruzelier Contemporary Art, 1994, Royal Over-Seas League, 1995, and Australia House, 1996. Ryan gained a Prince's Trust Award, 1991; Brian Ward Trust Fund, 1992; a Royal Over-Seas League Travel Scholarship, 1994; and London Arts Board Award, 1995. Paintings in Hospitals holds his work.

Sally RYAN 1916–1968 Sculptor and painter, born in New York City, who sculpted in the manner of Jacob Epstein, who encouraged her. She attended school in Montreal and while still there first showed a bronze at Royal Canadian Academy of Arts in Toronto, entered under an assumed name, giving the family chauffeur's address. She subsequently studied briefly with the sculptor Jean Camus in Paris, and spent four years as an artist in London before returning to America in 1938. She had a successful solo show at Cooling Galleries aged only 20, her subjects including Arturo Toscanini the conductor, Paul Robeson the singer and actor and Ellen Ballon, the Canadian pianist. Ryan continued to work for periods in Connecticut and London and showed regularly in Europe and America. Her later life was persistently marred by illness, and was spent in London. Like her father and grandfather, the wealthy American railway magnate and financier Thomas Fortune Ryan, Sally Ryan was an avid collector of art. A close friendship with Kathleen Garman, Lady Epstein, led to their forming the Garman-Ryan Collection, now housed in Walsall Museum & Art Gallery. Much of Ryan's own work is included.

Veronica RYAN 1956– Sculptor and draughtsman, born in Plymouth, Montserrat, West Indies. She studied at St Albans College of Art and Design, 1974–5, Bath Academy of Art, 1975–8, Slade School of Fine Art, 1978–80, and School of Oriental and African Studies, 1981–3. Among her awards were a Boise Travelling Scholarship, 1980, and Henry Moore Foundation Award, 1987. Participated in many group exhibitions, including Five Black Women Artists, The Africa Centre, 1983; Sculptors and Modellers, Tate Gallery, 1984; Stoke City Garden Festival, Stoke-on-Trent, 1986; and South Bank Centre's touring The British Art Show 1990. Her solo shows began with Tom Allen Centre, 1984, later ones including Kettle's Yard, Cambridge, and Riverside Studios, 1988. Arts Council holds her plaster and bronze Territorial, of 1986, and included her in its 1993–4 touring show Recent British Sculpture. Lived in London.

Vivian Desmond RYAN 1893–1950 Versatile painter, father of the artist Adrian Ryan. Vivian Ryan was both deaf and dumb. He was brought up at Hintlesham Hall, Ipswich, Suffolk, his father being the baronet Sir Gerald Hemmington Ryan. He studied with Seymour Lucas, was made a member of New Society of Artists in 1921 and an associate of RBA in 1926 and also showed at RA, ROI, Walker Art Gallery in Liverpool and Beaux Arts Gallery. One Summer Morning, Study of a Jester and Lady in Grey are notable works. During World War I he moved to London.

Andrew William RYDER 1950– Artist whose work included wall-mounted sculptures, born in Ruislip, Middlesex. He attended Hammersmith and Winchester Schools of Art, Leicester Polytechnic and Goldsmiths' College. In 1978 gained a South East Arts Award. Exhibitions included an installation at Belmont Hotel, Leicester, 1974; another at Haymarket Theatre, Leicester, 1976; Gardner Centre at University of Sussex and Camden Arts Centre, both 1980; and Berry Street Open Studios, 1984.

Margaret Elaine RYDER 1908– Artist in watercolour, oil and pastel, born and lived in Sheffield, Yorkshire, who studied at the College of Art there with James Betts. She worked for 20 years as a freelance commercial artist. Ryder's own main work was miniatures on ivory and vellum, and she also painted portraits, flowers and landscapes. As well as being vice-president of RMS, she was a member of SWA, SM and Hilliard Society, a founder-member of the Society of Botanical Artists and president of the Sheffield Society of Women Artists. Also showed with RA, RI, RWS, MAFA, Paris Salon and elsewhere abroad. Had several solo shows in Sheffield.

Sophie RYDER 1963– Sculptor, painter, printmaker and collagist who did a foundation course at Kingston Polytechnic, 1980–1, then attended Royal Academy for a diploma course, 1981–4, studying painting. It was in the south of France in 1980 that Ryder watched a friend making a wire fence and realised the material's potential for sculpture. This resulted in such ambitious creations as Ring of Hares, shown in 1992 at Bruton Street Gallery. Ryder's animals have a strong sense of place, give the impression of extreme animation and come into their own in an out-of-doors setting. Other mixed exhibitions in which she appeared included Christie's inaugural Pick of the Graduates, 1984; Zürich Art Fair, Edward Totah Gallery, 1986; Harris Museum and Art Gallery, Preston, 1989; and Art/London 90, Olympia. Had a solo show at Edward Totah in 1987; later individual exhibitions included Yorkshire Sculpture Park, 1991, and Cheltenham Art Gallery & Museum, 1997. Lived in Gloucestershire.

Susan RYDER 1944– Painter, draughtsman and teacher, born in Windsor, Berkshire. She studied at Byam Shaw School of Painting,

1960–4, with Maurice de Sausmarez, Bernard Dunstan and his wife Diana Armfield, and Peter Garrard. Gained the David Murray Travelling Scholarship in 1964. Taught painting at Claygate School, Esher, 1965–6, then concentrated on her own work and commissions. She was a member of RP and NEAC and exhibited regularly at RA Summer Exhibitions from 1964 and at RBA. Had solo exhibitions at Haste Gallery, Ipswich, 1979 and 1982 and had first solo show at W H Patterson in 1989. Themes of work included lamplight, sunlit interiors, space and distance in interiors created by colour rather than perspective and portraits in settings. Van Dyck, Vuillard, Cézanne and Freud were cited as influences. Pears Collection holds her work. Lived in London and Belchester, Coldstream, Berwickshire.

Adolfine RYLAND 1903– Sculptor who was born and eventually settled in Windsor, Berkshire. She had a strong interest in Indian and Oriental sculptural forms. Studied at Heatherley's School of Fine Art, 1920–5. Two years later she began showing at WIAC, becoming a member 1936–54. Tate Gallery holds her limestone relief Isaac Blesses Jacob.

Christopher RYLAND 1951– Painter, muralist, printmaker and teacher, born in Sussex, who, after graduating from Goldsmiths' College School of Art, joined a community of artists and worked on public and environmental arts projects, painting big murals. Began painting from nature in the early 1980s, flower pictures using bold imagery and later introducing a human presence. In 1994, moved to Sudbury, Suffolk, and ran courses from his studio. Was elected a member of the Society of Botanical Artists in 1995. Ryland's flower paintings were published as prints by Felix Rosentiel's and he completed floral plate designs for Wedgwood. Exhibitions included Clarges Gallery, Royal Horticultural Society and Medici Galleries, all 1980; RSBA at Mall Galleries, 1983; Deben Gallery, Woodbridge, 1986; and John Russell Gallery, Ipswich, 1996, with a solo show there in 1997. The Bridgeman Art Library holds his work.

Irene RYLAND fl. from c.1910–1951 Versatile painter who studied initially at Queen's College, Harley Street, in London and in Brussels, then went on to study art at the Grosvenor Life School, founded by Walter Donne, and with William Nicholson at the London School of Art. She exhibited RA, NEAC, in the provinces, Paris and Canada. Was a member of the ROI, SWA and RBA, at which she also showed. Lived in London.

Jenny RYRIE 1957– Artist in watercolour and mixed media on paper, teacher, born in Lincolnshire. On her father's side of the family there were four generations of watercolourists who all taught art at Eton College, the most famous William Evans of Eton. Ryrie studied at Edinburgh College of Art and University, 1975–80, gaining her master's degree in the latter year. Her teachers included Elizabeth Blackadder and David Michie. She studied botantical illustration at the Royal Botanic Garden and in 1982 designed and illustrated the book *Honeybees in Oman*. Natural History Museum of Oman and Durham University hold her work, which had as its main theme "the innate power and forces of the natural landscape. Paintings are semi-abstract/Expressionist." Ryrie was a member of North West Women Artists. Mixed exhibitions included Colin Jellicoe Gallery, Manchester; MAFA; Thackeray Gallery; and Fruitmarket Gallery, Edinburgh. One- and two-person shows included Lamont Gallery and Broekman Gallery, Chester. Lived in Saughall, Chester.

S

Andrew SABIN: *see* **SAM**

Sarah SABIN 1965– Painter who combined collage with Xerox, acrylic painter and other materials. She said that her pictures were "built up layer by layer, and I treat them as maps or areas of land viewed from the air." She completed a foundation course at Colchester Institute, graduating from Sunderland Polytechnic in 1989, settling in Colchester, Essex, to work in Trinity Studios. A trip to Southeast Asia in 1990 influenced her work. In 1993 she shared a show at Gainsborough's House, Sudbury.

Rolf SACHS 1955– Installations artist and designer, born in Lausanne, Switzerland, who studied business administration in London and San Francisco. Began designing furniture in 1984. He lived in Munich until moving to London in 1994. Group exhibitions included Galerie 54, Munich, and Design Galerie, Berlin, both 1990; Neotu, Paris, 1991; Art to Use, Frankfurt, and Abitare II Tempo, Verona, both 1994; and Neues Museum Weserburg, Bremen, 1995. Had a solo show at Wunderhaus, Munich, 1990, then a series in several continental countries, also the London-based Collection Gallery, 1994, and Faggionato Fine Arts, 1997. That exhibition included the installation Silenced, 200 custom-profiled foam panels which wrapped the gallery walls, warm to the touch but visually aggressive.

Gilles SACKSICK 1942– Painter, notably of nudes, and printmaker, born in Paris, France. He was awarded the Grand Prix de Portrait Paul-Louis Weillor, 1979, and was made a Pensionnaire of the Casa Velasquez in Madrid, 1979–81. From 1977 numerous albums of Sacksick's aquatints, engravings and woodcuts were published and tapestries, woven by Monique Créplet, were completed from 1984. Galerie Le Mur Ouvert gave Sacksick a solo show in Paris in 1968, and from the mid-1980s he was exhibited frequently one-man by the Bruton Gallery, in Bruton, Somerset, from 1986; in New York, 1987; and in Paris in 1988.

Richard SADLER 1927– Artist and teacher who studied sculpture at Coventry College of Art and later photography. Went on to lecture in creative photography at Derby College of Art. Exhibitions included Southwell Art Festival, 1969; Midland Group Gallery, Nottingham, 1971; Repton Arts Festival, 1972; and Photography into Art, Hampstead Artists' Council/Scottish Arts Council show, 1973.

Yehuda SAFRAN 1944– Artist and designer, teacher and exhibition organiser. His early experience was in stage design, as resident designer at Alborg in Denmark, 1966–7, then in Israel 1968–9. Safran then studied at St Martin's School of Art, 1969–71, and the Royal College of Art, 1971–3. He became a tutor at the College in 1976 and also taught in his native Israel. In later years Safran's interest shifted towards architecture. He was a trustee and consultant with the 9H Gallery, 1986, and was a regular contributor to its magazine. Safran was enthusiastic about the work of Adolf Loos, organising a touring exhibition of his work for the Arts Council. Safran's Hommage à Adolf Loos, created in 1985–6, was included in Royal College of Art's Exhibition Road show in 1988.

Henry James SAGE 1858–1953 Painter in oil and watercolour and illustrator, born in London, who visited Surrey in the 1890s, marrying Kate Stuart in the Wesleyan Methodist Church, Guildford, in 1898. Illustrated *Some West Surrey Villages*, by E A Judges, 1901. Sage became a well-known figure around Surrey in the first half of the century, standing at his easel in neat suit, hat and bicycle clips. Scenes such as Guildford High Street and Shalford Church were often repeated. From 1911–52 lived at Bramley, finally at Milford with a son. Guildford House Gallery, Guildford, held an exhibition in 1996, the borough owning examples and publishing a booklet on his work. Previous shows included a major one in 1971.

Virén SAHAI 1933– Artist in oil, watercolour and pen and ink, born in Shahjehanpur, India, full name Virendra Sahai. He moved to England after a brief spell working as a draughtsman in Burma, his paintings being first exhibited when he was studying at Central School of Arts and Crafts. Sahai trained as an architect and town planner at Regent Street Polytechnic and was an associate of RIBA. The artist represented India at the Commonwealth Biennale of Abstract Art on three occasions, 1961–5. Solo shows included New Vision Centre and Biggins Gallery, both 1961; Commonwealth Institute, 1967; and Horizon Gallery, 1991. Public collection in Bradford holds his work, which drew its inspiration from landscape, flowers and the human figure. In 1986 he won the Philip Gooding Scholarship, which enabled him to travel in America, Japan and Australia. Lived in Barton, Cambridgeshire.

Anne SAÏD 1914–1995 Painter and draughtsman, born in Hook, Hampshire. She studied at Queen's College, London, 1925–30. During the late 1930s she studied periodically in Paris with Amédée Ozenfant before he left for New York. She designed textiles to pay for these studies. From 1941–55 worked in Egypt with her husband Hamed Saïd, creating a student group which showed in Cairo. In England from late 1950s showed New Art Centre and elsewhere and had first solo show at Beaux Arts Gallery in 1957.

In 1961 settled in Wiltshire. The Flight, about 12 feet by five feet square, was among Saïd's most important works, one of many large drawings. Her work was included in the limited-edition English/Egyptian publication *The Word & The Image*. Early works were signed Anne Cobham. Her daughter was the artist Safaya Salter. Tate Gallery holds Saïd's work.

Loudon SAINTHILL 1919–1969 Theatre designer and painter, born in Tasmania, who established a reputation in Australia where he also exhibited, moved to London in 1950 and in 1951 had great success with his designs for Shakespeare's *The Tempest* at Stratford-upon-Avon. Further Shakespearian designs followed and he also designed for ballet, opera and pantomime, the Old Vic, Royal Opera and Sadler's Wells using his talents. Just before he died his costumes for a New York musical based on Chaucer's *Canterbury Tales* earned him a Tony award. Lived in London.

Marty St JAMES 1954– Artist and teacher, born in West Midlands, who studied at Bournville School of Art and Cardiff College of Art. He taught fine art and graphics at Camberwell College of Art. St James worked on joint projects with Anne Wilson. Their exhibition at Gallery M in 1994 included cibachromes on canvas and a series of video portraits, the faces comprising, for example, one made of waves with sound effects, another a man silently smoking. Video works were broadcast on British and foreign television. Selected exhibitions included Charting Time, Serpentine Gallery, and Video Exhibition, Tate Gallery, both 1986; and Viewing Figures, Camden Arts Centre, 1990.

Peter SAINTY 1943– Sculptor and teacher working in range of materials including plaster, wood and steel, born in Liverpool. He attended the College of Art there, 1960–4, then Slade School of Fine Art, 1964–7. From 1970–3 Sainty taught the pre-diploma course at Liverpool and in Wrexham; worked in the theatre, 1974–80; then as a sculptor and propmaker. Among influences on his work were Henry Moore, Gaudi and Noguchi, John Edkins and Mike Knowles. Took part in group shows at Walker Art Gallery and Bluecoat Gallery, Liverpool, and had solo exhibitions at the Academy there and Liverpool University. His abstract sculpture Reading-Piece, of 1982, in welded steel, was made for Heron House near the River Kennet, Reading, Berkshire. Sainty was based in Cardiff.

Gyula SAJÓ 1918–1989 Painter, graphic artist and teacher, born in Hungary, who remained there until the year of the uprising against Communism, 1956. He studied art and architecture at the Academy of Applied Art, Budapest, 1935–41, teaching in the capital until he left. As well as mixed and solo shows in Hungary, Sajó exhibited at RA, Paris Salon and in the English provinces, one-man shows including University of Surrey, which holds his work. Lived in Worthing, Sussex, from 1959 with his wife Erzsbet, also an artist. He founded the Atelier Art Group there. The *Daily Telegraph* art critic Terence Mullaly wrote that Sajó "was an archetypal master of the Hungarian tradition of painting," with "a sense of colour rare in British art." In 1995 Worthing Museum and Art Gallery displayed works it owns by Sajó, as well as showing an extensive privately made video on his life.

Hana SAKUMA 1970– Versatile artist and designer, born in Osaka, Japan, who graduated in industrial design, fashion and textiles at Kobe Design University, 1993; did a postgraduate diploma in textiles at Goldsmiths' College, 1994–5; and obtained her master's in fine art, sculpture, at Slade School of Fine Art, 1995–7. Among positions held was illustration and book cover design, 1991–2; interior design consultant at Kobe Design University and assistant for an animation design company, 1992; design research for a shoe company, 1992–3; then research into British art education plus translation for a design company. Group shows in England included Beyond the bounds, Maidstone Museum and Art Gallery and Manchester Metropolitan University, both 1996, and in 1997 Between at The Shooting Gallery, University College London, and Cloth, at Norwich Gallery. There she exhibited exquisite tiny chairs set in fields of flour and made from the covers of old hardback books, her subject being the English attitude to landscape. Had a first solo show at Alternative Art Gallery, 1996. Lived in London.

Christopher SALAMAN 1939– Painter and sculptor, son of the artist Easton Salaman, born in Dorking, Surrey. After Bedales School Salaman studied with the sculptor Karel Vogel at Camberwell School of Arts and Crafts. Showed at Woodstock Gallery, Mall Galleries, Upper Street Gallery and elsewhere and lived in High Ongar, Essex.

Merula SALAMAN 1914– Artist, daughter of artists Michel and Chattie Salaman and brother of painter and teacher Michael Salaman. She worked as a riding instructor, trained as a dancer with Ballet Rambert, then turned to acting, her first professional role being in André Obey's *Noah* in 1935 (John Gielgud was in the title role, Alec Guinness, whom she married in 1938, also appearing). After World War II, she studied painting at Chelsea Polytechnic and with Kathleen Browne. Her first book, an ABC for her nephew, *Christopher's Book*, appeared in 1941; she wrote and illustrated three more: *William & Cherry*, 1943; *Christopher's Rainy Day Book*, 1945; and *Christopher's New House*, 1946. She also created needlework pictures, showing in Hampshire where she lived and at Crane Kalman Gallery. Others, and some of her auto-biographical paintings, The Four Seasons, were included in James Huntington-Whiteley's show The Salamans at Gallery 27, in 1997.

Michael SALAMAN 1911–1987 Artist in oil, pen and ink and pencil, and teacher, born in Porlock, Somerset. He came from a family with artistic interests, several members depicted by Augustus John, by whom Salaman had a fine collection of drawings. Salaman studied at the Slade School of Fine Art under Henry Tonks, 1928–31, under Albert Rutherston at the Ruskin School of Art, Oxford, 1930–1, then in 1933–4 in Paris at Académie Ranson. He taught at Camberwell School of Arts and Crafts and at Chelsea for about 30 years from the late 1940s and for a period at Royal

Academy Schools from 1964. South London Art Gallery and Victoria & Albert Museum hold his work. Salaman was granted a Civil List Pension for services to art in 1977, two years after a retrospective at the Morley Gallery. Ben Uri Art Gallery held another in 1996. He stood apart from fashion in the art world, did not court success and in his work was often concerned with loneliness. There can be a strong atmosphere of disquiet, as in his masterpiece La Petite Kermesse, included in James Huntington-Whiteley's 1997 show The Salamans, at Gallery 27. Lived in London.

Kenneth N SALINS 1950– Painter, teacher and administrator, born in Boston, Massachusetts, where he gained his bachelor's degree in fine arts from the University of Massachusetts, 1972, then his master's from South Illinois University in 1975. From 1975–7 was an instructor at that University's continuing education division; was artist-in-residence at Delawater Water Gap National Park in New Jersey; then from 1977–82 was assistant director and then director of Artists for Environment Foundation. In 1990 gained a grant from the British American Arts Association that allowed a residency in Wales, in 1991 moving to Carradale, Kintyre, based in what was the artist William McTaggart's summer residence. Salins early showed in group exhibitions in Philadelphia and New York City and had two solo shows at Mitchell Museum, Illinois, and Sheldon Swope Museum, Indiana, in 1975. In 1994 his Scottish work was shown at Ewan Mundy Fine Art, Glasgow.

Alan SALISBURY 1946– Artist and teacher, born in Preston, Lancashire, who studied at Manchester College of Art, 1965–6, Liverpool College of Art, 1967–70, Royal College of Art, 1970–3 and Cardiff College of Art, 1973–4. He went on to be head of visual art at the University of Glamorgan. Among awards were a Gold Medal for Painting, Stowells Trophy Competition, 1972, the year he won a Royal College of Art Travelling Scholarship to Paris; also gained a John Minton Memorial Scholarship, 1983. Illustrated covers of several volumes of poems by Tony Curtis and Leslie Norris. Mixed shows included Walker Art Gallery, Liverpool, 1969; National Portrait Gallery, 1983; Hill Court Gallery, Abergavenny, from 1986; and Cardiff Arts Festival, 1988. Later solo shows included Hill Court, 1988. Yorkshire, Mid-Glamorgan, West Glamorgan Education Authorities and Cardiff City Council own examples. Lived in Barry, South Glamorgan.

Frank Owen SALISBURY 1874–1962 Painter of historical and ceremonial subjects and portraits. Born in Harpenden, Hertfordshire, Salisbury studied art privately, at Heatherley's School of Fine Art, at the Royal Academy Schools and widely on the continent. His foreign studies contributed to Salisbury's rather grand manner of painting, in the Edwardian tradition. Exhibited RA, RI, RP, Fine Art Society and Walker Art Gallery, in Liverpool, which holds his work. Members of the British royal family, church and military dignitaries and senior politicians were among Salisbury's subjects, along with depictions of state occasions. Member of Garrick Club. Christie's held a studio sale in 1985. Lived in London.

Chris SALMON 1960– Painter, printmaker and musician, born in Dublin, Ireland, but after six months settled in England. Salmon did an honours degree in fine art at Canterbury Art College, 1980–3, in 1992–4 gaining his master's degree with distinction in printmaking at Camberwell College of Art. From 1986–90 Salmon was guitarist with a band called Stump, which had a recording contract with Chrysalis and recorded three albums (*Mud on a Colon, Quirk Out* and *Fierce Pancake*) and two singles (*Charlton Heston Put His Vest On* and *Buffalo*). He was a *Galleries* magazine prizewinner in 1990; a Rotring prizewinner in 1991; won a Daler-Rowney prize in 1992; and in 1993 was Marina Vaizey's Critic's Choice in Art for Sale. Took part in many group shows, including Bankside Print Show, 1990; RA Summer Exhibition, 1991; LG at Barbican Centre, 1992; and Contemporary Art Society, Royal Festival Hall, 1994. Later solo shows included Morley Gallery, 1994, and Lamont Gallery, 1995. Salmon's paintings and etchings had a theatrical quality. "The images do not tell stories," he said. "The stage is set but nothing needs to be explained, and nothing is ever going to happen – but the implication is that it will."

Graeme SALMON 1933– Painter in watercolour and oil, born in Tasmania, Australia. He made frequent trips there and was influenced by the landscape of Tasmania, where there was a long tradition of landscape painting. Salmon first visited England in 1955, moved to America, 1962–4, in 1965 returning to Oxford, which became his home. He studied part-time at Ruskin School of Drawing, 1980–96. Was a member of Oxford Art Society and took part in group shows with it, RI and RWS. He was represented in the exhibition Fifty years of watercolour painting in Tasmania, 1978. Solo shows included Lloyd Jones Gallery, Hobart, 1964; Borlase Gallery, Blewbury, 1973; Salamanca Place Gallery, Hobart, from 1976; Halesworth Gallery, Halesworth, 1980.

James Marchbank SALMON 1916– Painter, draughtsman, printmaker, potter and teacher, born in Edinburgh where he studied at the College of Art, also studying at the Academy of Art, Reimann School and elsewhere in Berlin. Salmon worked as an artist for several years during World War II for the Ministry of Information, then resumed his full-time teaching career which included principalships of Lincoln School of Art and Croydon College of Art. He exhibited RSA, RSW, SSA, RA and in Germany. Lived in South Croydon, Surrey.

Ronald SALMOND 1912– Printmaker, painter and teacher, born in London, who studied at Hornsey College of Art. Went on to teach at Preston Manor High School, Wembley. Was elected a member of SGA in 1967, also exhibiting at RA and RE. 20th Century Gallery gave him a show in 1997. Ashmolean Museum in Oxford holds Salmond's work. Lived in Harrow, Middlesex.

Rebecca SALTER 1955– Artist in acrylic on canvas and mixed media on paper, born in Sussex. In 1977 she graduated from Bristol Polytechnic faculty of art and design, then was a research student at Kyoto City University of Arts, Japan, under a Leverhulme

Scholarship, 1979–81. From 1981–5 she lived in Japan, returning to London in 1985, when she won a Greater London Arts Award. For the next decade Salter's abstract work was "involved with the attempt to capture stillness in movement … a stillness with potential, not a passive quiet." Her pictures employed "the quiet anchor of the grid to give a freedom and independence to the fragmented lines." Salter took part in numerous group exhibitions in Britain, Japan and elsewhere overseas, including Rijeka Drawing Biennale, Yugoslavia, 1982; World Print Council IV, San Francisco, 1983, purchase prize; Chicago International Art Exposition, from 1987; LG, 1990; and Salama-Caro Gallery, 1993. Had a solo show at Gallery Maronie, Kyoto, in 1981, later ones including Jill George Gallery, 1994. British Museum, British Council and San Francisco Museum of Modern Art are among many collections holding examples.

Safaya SALTER 1950– Artist in gouache, illustrator and designer, born in Cairo, Egypt. Her father was the Egyptian artist Hamed Saïd, her mother the painter and draughtsman Anne Saïd. Salter studied initially with her mother, then on her own. She worked as a freelance textile designer for large London firms until 1979, when she started painting. Among influences were Persian miniatures, J M W Turner, Edmund Dulac, Gustav Klimt and Henri Rousseau. Illustrated Rudyard Kipling's *Just So Stories* for Children, 1986, and *Aesop's Fables*, 1989. Exhibited in mixed exhibitions and solo in Gloucestershire, also studio.

J W SALTONSTALL 1873– Painter and draughtsman, educated at Sowerby, Yorkshire. Studied at Halifax School of Art with Arthur Whitehead, 1891–2, then Blackpool School of Art, 1897–8, Preston School of Art with Arthur Burt, 1899–1900, and in Doncaster with William Tindall, 1908–9. Showed at BWS and in Lancashire and Yorkshire. Wakefield City Art Gallery and Museum holds his work. Lived near Halifax, Yorkshire.

Avis SALTSMAN fl. from mid-1950s– Printmaker, painter and teacher, born in Manchester of mainly Welsh ancestry, her paternal grandfather's family moving from Germany to Salford in 1879. An important influence on her was the artist and teacher Terry McGlynn, who ran his home in Stockport as an art centre. Saltsman went on to teach many age groups in schools and adult education centres. Moved to London in 1971 and from 1985 worked full-time as an artist. In the late 1970s she was national librarian of the Artists' Union and for several years was a member of the Printmakers' Council committee. She helped Conway Hall to develop a gallery and had a retrospective there in 1995. Other solo shows included Almeida Theatre, 1990 and 1992, and Manchester Royal Exchange, Art of the Theatre, 1994. Mixed shows included Alpine Gallery, 1987, National Theatre, 1990, and Hatton Gallery, Newcastle upon Tyne, 1994. Manchester University holds her work.

SAM 1958– Sculptor in a range of media and teacher, full name Andrew Sabin, born and lived in London. He studied at Chelsea College of Art & Design, teachers including Richard Deacon, and from 1984 was a sculptor and teacher at Chelsea, Camberwell School of Art and elsewhere. Sabin's solo shows included Chisenhale Gallery, Battersea Arts Centre, Tate Gallery in Liverpool and Salama-Caro Gallery. Chisenhale Installation and The Sea of Sun, the Battersea Art Centre installation, were cited as main works. Arts Council, Contemporary Art Society and Leicestershire Education Authority hold examples.

Helen SAMPSON 1885– Painter and textile designer, born in London. After private education she studied at Byam Shaw School of Art, 1907, then at Central School of Arts and Crafts, 1925–31, where her teachers included John Cooper and Bernard Meninsky. Showed at NEAC, WIAC, AIA, UA, LG and widely in the provinces. Lived in Saltdean, Sussex.

Stephanie SAMPSON 1959– Figurative painter, collagist, printmaker and teacher, using a colourful palette, born in Montreal, Canada. She studied at Bath Academy of Art in Corsham, Carleton University, Ottawa, and the University of Saskatchewan, Saskatoon. She taught at Alta Vista School in Ottawa, 1985; Ottawa School of Art, 1986–8; and University of Saskatchewan, 1989–91. Among awards were a Canadian Artists' Grant, SAW Gallery, Ottawa, 1985, and a bursary, Ionian Cultural Centre, Chios, Greece, 1984. Group shows included Mall Galleries, 1978; Commonwealth Institute, 1980; Athens Odeon Centre, Athens, 1982; Amigo's Cafe and Gallery, Saskatoon, 1990; Islington Arts Factory, 1993; and Royal Over-Seas League Open, 1994. She had a solo show there in 1995. Several Canadian collections and the Greek Embassy, Ottawa, hold examples.

Peter SAMUELSON 1912–1996 Painter, draughtsman and writer, born in Tisbury, Wiltshire, who prided himself on being largely self-taught and who was a sporadic worker. After childhood years on a Kent fruit farm and briefly, disastrously attending a boarding school, at 15 Samuelson moved to the south of France to live with relations for two years. Relocated in Paris he made desultory studies at the New York School of Fine and Applied Arts which was based there, supporting himself as an errand boy. In 1935 Samuelson married a beautiful Dutch woman, by whom he had three children, returned to his English childhood home and began intensive painting. After war service in bomb disposal he lived as an illustrator in the Netherlands, music – a lifelong passion – being a major subject, but after his marriage broke up moved to England to help his stepmother run an hotel in Torquay, eventually running a lodging house in Kensington. In the 1960s he became an expert on Oriental rugs and skilled restorer of them. Having moved with a daughter to an Oxfordshire village in 1982, where he concentrated on his rugs and earned money labouring on a farm, Samuelson was rediscovered as an artist. In the late 1980s he showed at Leighton House and at St Jude's Gallery, in 1991 with Roy Miles. His book *Post-War Friends*, 1987, included portraits drawn from the 1950s. Samuelson also sustained a huge autobiography-cum-diary, which he hoped would eventually be published. Early work was signed Pierre, later pictures Peter, in mirror-writing style. Died in Horton General Hospital,

Banbury. The Brewhouse, Eton College, held a memorial show in 1997.

Carlos Luis SANCHA 1920– Portrait painter, born and lived in London, notable for conversation pieces. He studied at Central School of Arts and Crafts under Rodrigo Moynihan, 1939, then at Byam Shaw School of Drawing and Painting, 1946–8, where teachers included Patrick Phillips. Was elected RP in 1973, also showing at RA. TRH The Prince of Wales, Duke of Edinburgh and Duke of Kent hold examples, which are also in collections across the continent and in America.

Margot SANDEMAN 1922– Artist in oil and acrylic used as watercolour whose work had a lyrical, decorative quality. She was born Mary Margaret Sandeman in Glasgow, where she continued to live and where she studied, under Hugh Adam Crawford, at the School of Art. She was the closest friend of the painter Joan Eardley and later collaborated with Ian Hamilton Finlay. Sandeman, who signed her work with initials plus date, won the RSA's Guthrie Award in 1964; the Anne Redpath and Scottish Arts Council Awards in 1970; and was Scottish Winner of the Laing Competition in 1989. The island of Arran was an influence on her work. Group exhibitions included Scottish Landscapes, Whitechapel Art Gallery, 1960; Robinson Gallery, Houston, Texas, 1985; London Poetry Society, 1989; and The Compass Contribution, Tramway, Glasgow, 1990. Showed with Richard Demarco Gallery from 1974 in Edinburgh, later solo exhibitions including retrospective at The Lillie Art Gallery, Milngavie, 1991. Scottish Arts Council and Contemporary Art Society hold examples. Her father was the artist Archibald Sandeman, with whom she was given a joint show at The Scottish Artists Shop, Edinburgh, 1986, her mother being the embroiderer Muriel Boyd Sandeman.

Muriel Boyd SANDEMAN 1888–1981 Embroiderer, draughtsman and teacher, born in Glasgow as Muriel Boyd, who married the businessman and amateur painter Archibald Sandeman, their daughter being the artist Margot Sandeman. Studied at Glasgow School of Art, 1904–9, where she gained several prizes, teachers including Anne Macbeth. After her diploma she trained to teach, being needlework mistress of Bearsden School, 1910, and of Rosslyn School, 1913, giving up teaching upon marriage in 1916. Exhibited throughout her career, notably in a show of British and Irish decorative artists in the Louvre, Paris, 1914. Also showed at Glasgow Society of Lady Artists' annual exhibitions until 1965, winning the Lauder Award, 1955. Art Nouveau greatly influenced her work, which eventually became almost wholly based on flowers and foliage from her garden. Her last piece was completed when she was 77, then failing eyesight made her stop work. In 1932 she and her husband had a joint show at Bennett Gallery, Glasgow, and Glasgow Museums and Art Galleries, which holds her work, had another of it in 1987.

Bob SANDERS 1945– Artist, printmaker, designer and teacher, born in Leeds, Yorkshire, but went to school in London. He spent six years travelling in America, Australia and New Zealand, studying for a year at University of New South Wales. On return to England studied at Barking College of Art, where for a time he lectured in graphic design. From 1974 worked as a full-time artist, also designing stage scenery. Sanders' work was shown extensively around the world and is in public and private collections there, being sold by CCA Galleries. He was a pioneer in developing the technique and style of blending soft colours in silkscreen printing.

Christopher SANDERS 1905–1991 Painter and teacher, born in Wakefield, Yorkshire. He attended the School of Art there, 1922–4, Leeds School of Art, 1924–6, and the Royal College of Art, 1926–9, where he met his future wife Barbara. Was for some years head of painting at Harrow School of Art. Sanders was a solid journeyman painter whose landscapes were often detailed studies of foliage, grasses and flowers. He exhibited regularly at RA from early 1930s, becoming RA in 1961, six years earlier winning a gold medal at Paris Salon. Was also a member of RP. Sanders, known as Sandy, was a bluff character, keen on sport, who lived for some years in Slough, Buckinghamshire.

Henry SANDERS 1918–1982 Painter of landscapes, figures and animals in oil and watercolour, lithographer and lino-cutter. Born in Dresden, Germany, Sanders studied art at Hornsey College of Art 1935–9, studies which continued in 1945, tutors including Russell Reeve and John Moody. His work was reproduced in *Arts Review* and *Connoisseur* and the Ben Uri Art Society has it in the permanent collection. Lived in London. Sanders' original name was Helmut Salomon.

Jill Cowie SANDERS fl. from 1960s– Sculptor and teacher producing figurative works, commonly with simplified forms, in smooth bronze. She was born in London and studied drawing and painting at St Martin's School of Art, 1948–9, and Chelsea Polytechnic, 1950–2. From 1959–60 she studied and taught art at Cordova Museum, Lincoln, Massachusetts. Won scholarships to study sculpture at Boston Museum School of Fine Arts, graduating with distinction in 1964. She married fellow-student John Sanders and they moved to Spain, where they founded an art colony in the Roman city of Medinaceli. She eventually set up a studio near Tarifa, Andalucia. Jill Cowie Sanders showed solo with Artists Associates, Atlanta, in 1968, after which several dozen international exhibitions followed. From 1984 her bronzes, from miniature to life-size and larger, were shown by Jonathan Poole in Britain, with a solo exhibition at his Compton Cassey Galleries, Withington, in 1995. In 1992 the sculptor's three entries were accepted for the X Biennial of Sport in the Fine Arts, Barcelona, Spain, one being bought for the new Olympic Museum in Lausanne, Switzerland.

Rosanne Diana SANDERS 1944– Botanical watercolourist, born in Stoke Poges, Buckinghamshire, who after Roedean School attended High Wycombe College of Art. Showed at Mall and Westminster Galleries, RA and was a member of Society of

Botanical Artists. Sanders won the Royal Horticultural Society Gold Medal on several occasions from 1981 plus other awards. *The English Apple*, 1988, was among many horticultural books in which her work appeared. Lived in Stokenham, Devon.

Susan SANDERS 1946– Painter who also studied etching and sculpture, she trained at Byam Shaw School, obtaining a scholarship in her fourth year, followed by three years at Royal Academy Schools. Showed at RA Summer Exhibition from 1970, Wye Art Gallery (run by her husband at Wye, Kent), Northern Art Gallery, Cale Art, RWA and Patricia Wells Gallery, Thornbury. Has work in many private collections in Britain and abroad.

Violet SANDERS 1904–1983 Painter, wood engraver, clay modeller, heraldic artist and illuminator. She was born in Mexico City, her father, who was an amateur artist and caricaturist, working for Shell there. She studied at Blackheath School of Art, 1922–3, Harrow Technical School, 1923–5, and Willesden Polytechnic during same period under Ernest Heber Thompson. Exhibited RA, NS, SGA and SWA as well as in the provinces. Signed her later work Violet Sanders Mallet (Mallet being her married name). She was a keen genealogist and during World War II completed maps for the Cabinet and War Office, working on the D-Day landings, but was most noted for her wood engravings. Lived at Perranporth, Cornwall.

Charles J SANDERSON 1949– Artist in wide range of media, including oil, pastel and printmaking, born and lived in London. After Millfield School he attended Byam Shaw School of Art, 1967–71, teachers including Maurice de Sausmarez. Showed at RA Summer Exhibitions from 1970, Ashgate Gallery in Farnham from 1973 and elsewhere, solo exhibitions including Woodstock Gallery in 1974 and Drian Gallery, 1979.

Christopher SANDERSON 1939– Sculptor, born in Jerusalem. He studied at Leeds College of Art, 1955–60, then the Slade School of Fine Art, 1960–2. After working for two years in Rome, Sanderson worked and taught in Yorkshire, visited New York in 1964–5, worked and taught in London, 1966–8, then was again in New York. Among his awards was the Prix de Rome, 1962, a John Moores Travelling Scholarship, 1964, a Peter Stuyvesant Foundation Travelling Bursary to America in 1965, a Harkness Foundation Fellowship to America in 1968 and the International Symposium for Sculpture, Yugoslavia, 1971. Sanderson began showing in group exhibitions at John Moores Exhibition, Liverpool, in 1961, had a one-man show at Axiom Gallery in 1967 and was included in the RA show British Sculptors '72, where he showed abstract works in metal and resin, coloured and with New York as a theme. Arts Council holds his work.

Lesley SANDERSON 1962– Painter, draughtsman and teacher, born in Malaya. The exotic and Oriental featured in Sanderson's work, which she said employed self-portrait quite often "to confront the stereotype, to voice an opinion on racism, generally, personally and from the viewpoint of a woman". An example was her exhibit Point of Contact in the South Bank Centre's touring The British Art Show, 1990. Sanderson studied at West Surrey College of Art and Design, Farnham, 1980–1, and the City Polytechnic, Sheffield, 1981–4, where she settled. Lectured at the University of Central Lancaster, Preston. She showed in many group exhibitions in Yorkshire and elsewhere, including 1986 New Contemporaries at ICA; Black Art: Plotting the Course, at Oldham Art Gallery, with tour, 1988–9; in 1990 North by North West at BBK Gallery, Cologne; and in 1991–2 Norwich Gallery's travelling show History and Identity. Had a solo exhibition at Mappin Art Gallery, Sheffield, and Leeds City Art Gallery, 1994–5.

John S SANDERSON-WELLS 1872–1955 Sporting and portrait artist in oil and watercolour, educated at Woodard Schools, Slade School of Fine Art and at Académie Julian, Paris. He was elected RI in 1903 and in later years was its honorary treasurer. Showed at RBA, Fine Art Society, RA, ROI and at Walker Art Gallery in Liverpool and lived for many years in London.

Lettice SANDFORD 1902–1993 Printmaker, draughtsman, publisher and watercolourist, born in St Albans, Hertfordshire. She studied at the Byam Shaw and Vicat Cole School of Art, then at Chelsea School of Art, 1926–9, teachers including Graham Sutherland. In 1929 she married Christopher Sandford – their son was the writer Jeremy Sandford – and they ran the Boar's Head Press, then the Golden Cockerel Press. Lettice Sandford illustrated several of their fine books; she produced line and wash drawings for two children's books of her own; and after World War II illustrated Folio Society books with pen drawings. Her finest work has a sensuous, sinuous quality. After the Golden Cockerel Press was sold in 1959 the Sandfords ran a small museum at Eye Manor, near Leominster, Herefordshire, displaying corn dollies, on which Lettice became an expert. Sandford published *Decorative Straw Work and Corn Dollies* in 1964. She latterly returned to landscape watercolour painting.

George Sommerville SANDILANDS 1889–1961 Painter and writer on art. Born in Glasgow, Sandilands after university studied art widely on the continent. Exhibited at the RA, NEAC, ROI and elsewhere. Was art critic on the Labour newspaper *Daily Herald*, 1928–39, followed by 10 years as registrar at the Royal College of Art. Wrote a number of books on painting, including titles on the watercolours of J M W Turner, Frank Brangwyn and William Russell Flint and the anthology of pictures *Artists' Country*. Lived at Sanderstead, Surrey.

Michael SANDLE 1936– Sculptor, printmaker, painter and teacher, born Weymouth, Dorset. Studied at Douglas School of Art and Technology, 1951–4, then at Slade School of Fine Art, 1956–9. During 1959–60 Sandle concentrated on lithography in Paris. He then returned to England to teach, initially at Leicester College of Art, 1961–3, during which he formed the Leicester Group, then at Coventry College of Art until 1968. After several years teaching in Canada, in 1973 Sandle became professor of sculpture in Pforzheim, then in 1980 at Akademie der Bildenden

Künste, in Karlsruhe. Sandle participated in many influential group shows in Britain and abroad. He had his first one-man show at Drian Gallery in 1963. Later solo exhibitions included Galerie Suzanne Fischer, Baden-Baden in 1979; Kunstverein, Mannheim; and several with his dealer Fischer Fine Art. There was an important retrospective at Whitechapel Art Gallery, 1988, which toured to Germany in 1989. Mortality and war were key themes in Sandle's work which was often on a large scale and owed something to the monumental output of sculptors such as Sir Alfred Gilbert and Charles Sargeant Jagger. Sandle was an outsider, but was elected RA in 1989. Arts Council, Imperial War Museum and Tate Gallery hold examples. Among commissioned works were Memorial for the Victims of a Helicopter Disaster, Mannheim, 1985, and St George and the Dragon, London, 1988. Lived in Karlsruhe, Germany.

Ethel SANDS 1873–1962 Painter of Impressionist pictures, born in Newport, Rhode Island, America. As a baby she travelled with her family to England, where they settled in London in 1879. With her great friend the painter Nan Hudson Sands studied with Eugène Carrière, 1896–1901, and with Henri Evenepoel, 1897. She exhibited in Paris, and in England with Frank Rutter's AAA, Fitzroy Street Group and NEAC and was a founder-member of LG and a member of WIAC. She had a first London show with Nan Hudson at Carfax Gallery in 1912. Was naturalized British 1916 and died in London. Tate Gallery holds her work, which was included in Camden Town Recalled, at Fine Art Society, 1976.

Frederick SANDS 1916–1992 Painter and teacher, born in Liverpool, where he attended Northway School, studying art with his father, James Sands. During World War II, 1940–5, Sands was a cine cameraman for the Royal Aircraft Establishment, Farnborough. Taught art for many years at De La Salle College in Jersey, Channel Islands, where he lived at St Saviour. Was a member of RI, also exhibiting at RA, Paris Salon, Bihan L'Art Contemporain in Paris where he won a diploma, and was a finalist several times, 1981–4, in Hunting Group Art Prizes, also exhibiting in North America. Department of the Environment holds his work.

Noelle SANDWITH 1927– Painter, draughtsman and printmaker, born in Cape Town, South Africa. She was educated in England and became a State Registered Nurse. Studied art at Kingston, Heatherley's School of Fine Art and in Croydon. Her work reflected extensive travels, including outback of Australia. Was a member of Hesketh Hubbard Art Society, also exhibiting at RA, SWA, in the provinces and abroad. In 1960 had solo show at Foyles Gallery. Royal Naval College in Greenwich holds her work. Lived latterly in London.

Edwina SANDYS fl. from early 1970s– Sculptor in marble and bronze, sometimes producing witty two-dimensional with colourfully delineated features added. She was the daughter of politician Duncan Sandys and was married to the architect Richard D Kaplan. She was born in London, where she began painting in 1970, taking up sculpting five years later. Moved to America in 1978 and then showed on both sides of the Atlantic. Solo exhibitions began with The Spot and Crane Arts, both 1971, later ones including Women of the Bible at Everson Museum of Art, Syracuse, New York, and Cathedral of St John the Divine there, 1986–7. United Nations, New York, Geneva and Vienna; *Der Spiegel*, London; and a number of American collections, including Winston Churchill Memorial Museum, Fulton, Missouri, hold examples.

Sheila SANFORD 1922– Watercolourist, born in Singapore, who studied at St Martin's School of Art. She carried out book-jacket work and magazine illustration. Was a member of RI and RMS and showed with Edwin Pollard Gallery, Llewellyn Alexander (Fine Paintings) and Miniature Art Society of Florida, which holds her work. Lived at Uploders, Bridport, Dorset.

Piero SANSALVADORE 1892–1955 Painter, draughtsman and printmaker, born in Turin, Italy, and self-taught. As well as showing in Italy, he exhibited at the RA, Fine Art Society, RP, Walker Art Gallery, Liverpool, and Royal Glasgow Institute of the Fine Arts. His work – which featured extensive use of the palette knife – was given one-man shows at venues including Fine Art Society, 1938, and the provinces. Was extensively illustrated in publications including *Colour*, *Glasgow Evening News*, *The Times* and *The Observer*. Lived in London. Tate Gallery archive holds his pencil self-portrait.

Anne SAPALSKA 1960– Artist who lived for a time in Kingskettle, Fife, and who studied at Gray's School of Art, Aberdeen, 1978–83, followed by Slade School of Fine Art. Was included in Scottish Print Open Three, 1983, organised by Dundee Printmakers' Workshop.

Prue SAPP 1928– Painter in oil, born in London, educated at Benenden School, Kent, and English School of Languages, Chateau d'Oex, Switzerland. She studied at Epsom School of Art, attending her husband Reg Sapp's portrait class for seven years. They met in Provence on a course directed by Peter Garrard. Prue Sapp was a member of Chelsea Art Society. She first had her work hung in Mall Galleries in a SWA show in 1974 and became a full-time painter in 1986, also exhibiting at Wykeham Galleries, Bourne Gallery in Reigate, NEAC, ROI and RA. Solo shows included Charlotte Lampard Gallery and Hyde Park Gallery, from 1991. Lived in Tadworth, Surrey.

Reg SAPP 1904– Painter in oil and teacher, born in London, husband of the artist Prue Sapp. He studied at Epsom School of Art, where he later taught for many years, his teachers including Will Evans, Bernard Dunstan and Peter Garrard. Showed at RP and ROI and had a solo show at the Thorndike Theatre, Guildford. Lived in Tadworth, Surrey.

Francis William SARGANT 1870–1960 Sculptor, born in London, brother of the artist Mary Sargant Florence. He was educated at Oxford University, then studied at the Slade School of

Fine Art, 1895–6, and on the continent for several years. Lived for many years in Florence. Exhibited RA and IS. Represented in Tate Gallery. Sargant's work, in the Italian Renaissance tradition, is to be found in the war memorial chapel of Oakham School, where he completed stone reliefs. Also finished a memorial to Florence Nightingale in the Church of Santa Croce, Florence. Lived finally in Cambridge.

John SARGENT 1910– Sculptor, born in London, son of Sir Percy Sargent. Was educated at Charterhouse and Cambridge University. Exhibited RA and Paris Salon, gaining a gold medal in 1962. Lived at Great Wilbraham, Cambridgeshire.

Eric SATCHWELL 1926– Painter influenced by Old Masters, especially the Venetian School, in his use of colour, who was born in Northampton, attended the School of Art there and then Institute of Education in London. Served in the Army and spent 18 months in Venice. Was art master at Salford Grammar School and chairman of Salford Arts Committee, 1951–3. Exhibited at MAFA and elsewhere in Lancashire. Manchester City Art Gallery has his oil Playing Fields, 1953, Salford Art Gallery The Chip Shop.

Kenneth James SATERLAY 1932–1983 Painter of miniatures and small pictures "of wild flowers in their natural habitat", as he described them, Saterlay was born in London. He studied at the London College of Photographic Arts in the late 1940s. Early on he worked in pastel and watercolour but latterly favoured oils. Exhibited at RA, NEAC, Paris Salon, ROI and elsewhere and lived in Rayleigh, Essex.

Isabel SAUL 1895–c.1982 Artist in watercolour, tempera and etching, miniaturist and teacher, born and lived in Southbourne, near Bournemouth, Hampshire. She attended Bournemouth Municipal School of Art and went on to specialise in ecclesiastical subjects and portraits. York Minster, Carlisle and Salisbury Cathedrals hold examples. She was a fellow of the Royal Society of Arts until 1981.

Coleman SAUNDERS 1955– Sculptor who worked variously as a prop maker, builder and designer and who was interested in the use of mirrors; he liked their mystery and atmosphere and "differing levels of interpretation". Saunders studied at St Martin's School of Art. Mixed exhibitions included Sculpture on the South Bank, 1977; Space Studios Open Exhibition, from 1981; and Brixton Gallery, 1984.

David SAUNDERS 1936– Painter, constructions artist, teacher and musician, born Southend, Essex. He studied at St Martin's School of Art and Royal Academy Schools, 1956–62, then began teaching, including Liverpool Polytechnic. Saunders produced his first Systematic-Constructive works in 1967, then in 1969 began collaborative work with composers and co-founded the Systems Group of artists. He was artist-in-residence at Sussex University, 1970, and at Stedelijk Museum, Amsterdam, 1972, where he made an intensive study of the works of Piet Mondrian. In 1978 Saunders began investigations into colour functions, in 1985 being co-organiser of the exhibition Colour Presentations, a Clwyd Arts & Exhibitions Service touring show, while living in north Wales. In 1994 Saunders returned to live in London. In Wales he was a member of the 56 Group. Other group exhibitions included Survey '67 at Camden Arts Centre, 1967; Matrix, Arnolfini Gallery, Bristol, 1971; Systems, Whitechapel Art Gallery and Arts Council tour, 1972; Four British Constructivists, Engstrom Gallery, Stockholm, 1983; and Mostyn Open Exhibition 5, Oriel Mostyn, Llandudno, 1994. Had a solo show at AIA Gallery, 1965, later ones including Janus Avivson Gallery, 1995. Arts Council, National Museum of Wales in Cardiff, WAC and Dean Clough Collection, Halifax, hold examples.

Georgina SAUNDERS 1946– Painter, notably in watercolour, born in Colchester, Essex, near where she eventually settled at Copford. Her father was the artist William Francis Burton, her mother the painter Elizabeth Crampton-Gore and for a time she showed as Georgina Williams. Attended Colchester School of Art, having had lessons from her father, but was mainly self-taught. Painted prolifically in Australia, William Russell Flint, Monet and Whistler being influences, but was later influenced by the Symbolists. Showed at Arts Council Gallery, in East Anglia and privately.

Gwen SAUNDERS fl. c.1950–1975 Painter in oil and watercolour, born in Dunedin, New Zealand. She studied at Heatherley's School of Fine Art and showed at RA, ROI, RBA and at Paris Salon. Lived in London.

Helen SAUNDERS 1885–1963 Painter of abstracts and still life, born in Croydon, Surrey. She studied at the Slade School of Fine Art, 1906–7, and Central School of Arts and Crafts. Her early work was abstract, but shortly after World War I she moved towards a naturalistic style. She showed with Frank Rutter's AAA from 1912; LG 1916; and latterly with Holborn Art Society in London, near to where she lived. She was a signatory of the Vorticist Manifesto in *Blast No. 1*, contributed to the Vorticist show in 1915 and was represented in the Twentieth Century Art exhibition at Whitechapel Art Gallery in 1914. Tate Gallery holds several examples of her abstract style. Ashmolean Museum in Oxford held a survey show in 1996.

Kay SAUNDERS 1946– Abstract painter, collagist, sculptor and teacher, born in Blackpool, Lancashire. She went to Australia in 1968 and began painting, attending evening classes in Sydney. Returning to England she did a foundation course at Wimbledon School of Art, 1974–5, then an honours degree in fine art at Kingston School of Art, 1975–8. Began teaching adults in 1982 and later was a visiting artist at Hardingham Sculpture Workshop, Norfolk, and a visiting lecturer at St Albans School of Art/Hertfordshire University, both from 1986; taught at Open College of the Arts from 1989; was artist-in-residence at Stoke-on-Trent Museum and Art Gallery (it holds her work), 1990; and was an artist/teacher at Whitechapel Art Gallery, 1991. In 1982 she won Lambeth Arts Council and Elephant Trust Awards. Took part in many mixed shows, solo exhibitions including Greenwich Theatre Gallery, 1989, and Kepler Gallery, 1992. Lived in London.

Nina SAUNDERS 1958– Sculptor, born in Denmark, who transformed furniture into sculpture, as in Young British Artists VI, Saatchi Gallery, 1996, the critic Sarah Kent commenting that Saunders' sculptures "often encapsulate bitter childhood memories". From 1986–91 she gained an honours degree in fine art and critical studies at Central St Martins College of Art and Design and worked in London. In 1997 Saunders appeared in the BBC2 Television series *A Date with an Artist*, in which she created an artwork on a beekeeping theme.

Peter SAUNDERS 1940– Painter, draughtsman, muralist and teacher, born in Bicester, Oxfordshire. He attended Camberwell School of Arts and Crafts, 1957–61, Slade School of Fine Art, 1961–3, with a postgraduate year in painting in 1963–4, in 1964 going on a private scholarship to Greece. From 1982 he was a teacher at Sir John Cass arts faculty, being a visiting lecturer at Newcastle University. Completed a mural for National Trust. Among his several prizes were a first prize in the Spirit of London show at Royal Festival Hall in 1980, another in The World of Newspapers at Sotheby's in 1982. His other mixed exhibition appearances included Fitzwilliam Museum in Cambridge, Whitechapel Open at Whitechapel Art Gallery and LG and RA. He had a solo show at Cadogan Contemporary in 1990. Arts Council holds his work.

Robert A SAUNDERS 1950– Painter and curator, born in Paisley, Scotland. He studied at Glasgow School of Art and Moray House College in Edinburgh. He twice won the John and Mabel Craig Award as well as a Scottish Arts Council Bursary. Saunders went on to become art director for Paisley Museum and Art Galleries, 1975, then from 1978 deputy director of arts and libraries for Renfrew District Council. He selected and co-ordinated the first big exhibition of Scottish painting in 1983. Saunders' work was described as "unashamedly hedonist", featuring elegant ladies in fashionable interiors or at Ascot, "seductive often sensual, attractive yet unthreatening". He showed at RSA, Glasgow Art Club, Edinburgh Arts Club and Duncan Campbell Contemporary Art, where he had a solo exhibition in 1992.

Roy SAUNDERS 1911– Etcher and teacher, born in Cardiff, where he studied at the School of Art, 1929–34, under the painter Wilson Jagger. Showed RCamA, RWA, SWAS, Swansea Art Society and elsewhere, having a number of one-man shows including Glynn Vivian Art Gallery, Swansea, Pump Rooms in Bath and Royal National Eisteddfod, Wales. Member of SWAS. Lived at Rhiwbina, Cardiff.

Ramiro Fernández SAUS 1961– Artist born in Sabadell, Spain, who graduated from the Facultat de Belles Arts, Barcelona, in 1984. Among his awards was a scholarship to work abroad, Generalitat de Catalunya, Barcelona, 1989, which resulted in a year's residence at Delfina Studios, London. He took part in many group exhibitions in Spain and Venezuela, as well as in Britain, including Paton Gallery, 1989; Olympia Contemporary Art Fair, 1990; and Romantic Spanish Painting, Long & Ryle, and Nature and Reverie, Victoria Art Gallery, Bath, both 1992. Exhibited solo pro-lifically from 1979, with a series at Long & Ryle from 1990, including The garden of Edén, 1997, which included lush paintings and polychromed bronze figures. Several Spanish galleries hold his work.

Rudolf Helmut SAUTER 1895–1977 Painter, printmaker, illustrator and poet, son of the artist George Sauter. He was educated at Harrow School, studying art in London and Munich, his father having come from Bavaria. Sauter had strong literary interests, being a member of the writers' club PEN; he illustrated a definitive edition of works by the novelist John Galsworthy, whom he drew in 1927, Sauter's mother being Lilian Galsworthy. Showed at RA, RI, PS, in the provinces, in Paris at the Salon where he gained an Hon. Mention and widely in America. Had one-man shows in London and New York. National Portrait Gallery, RWA and Ferens Art Gallery in Hull hold his work. Much of Sauter's work was destroyed in a fire in the early 1980s, yet a lot is in private hands in South Africa. A great traveller, he celebrated his eightieth birthday with a glider flight. Although Sauter's work is mainly figurative, late in life he did a series of pastel abstracts. Lived at Butterow, near Stroud, in Gloucestershire.

Francis SAVAGE 1908–1985 Painter, born in Wallasey, Cheshire, partly educated at George Watson's College, Edinburgh. He studied art there and in Bristol. Savage was chairman of Salcombe Art Club, Devon, where he lived, also exhibiting at RA, ROI, RI, at the Paris Salon and elsewhere.

Roma SAVEGE 1907– Artist in various media, especially Plaka gouache, born in Christchurch, New Zealand. She attended the College of Fine Arts there, 1926–8, and studied with Cecil and Elizabeth Kelly and their group. In 1928 moved to England to sing, but instead had three years in the theatre, two at Bristol's Little Theatre, then touring in Middle East. She was a honorary member of NS and a member of Free Painters and Sculptors and the Art Society in Richmond, Surrey, where she settled. Showed solo with Richmond Hill Gallery, also exhibiting with Contemporary Portrait Society, NEAC and elsewhere. Among her main works was a series of six steel figures, The Listeners, The Warners and The Protectors. Colour relationships, the importance of drawing and simplification were cited as key interests.

Ursula SAVILL fl. from mid-1960s– Watercolourist and draughtsman who meticulously recorded the lives of remote peoples, animals and birds. She was taught as a child by Oscar Thompsett, then studied fine art and ceramics at Brighton College of Art, 1959–64. After living in the Far East and Australia, Savill's interests took her, in 1978, to Papua New Guinea. She spent four years among the people of the Southern and Eastern Highlands, learning about their customs and making studies of their dress and decoration and natural environment. After two years in England she moved to Africa and from 1985–90 lived with the Samburu tribe in Northern Kenya, then spent much time with the Turkana and Rendille peoples, engaged in a similar project to that in Papua New Guinea. She was accompanied at all times by guides to protect her from any danger. Savill attended performances and rehearsals of the Royal Ballet when visiting Nairobi, part of a fund-raising drive known as Dances for Elephants. The event was to raise money for anti-poaching activities and protection of the endangered Grevy zebra. The auctioning of her pictures raised $10,000. Saville also sought to publicise the plight of the Turkana people who suffered from Hydatid disease. Showed with World Wildlife Fund Exhibition, 1976; Association of British Illustrators, 1983; RBA, 1984; and SWLA, Mall Galleries, 1991. Solo shows included Royal Geographical Society, 1990. Her home was in Storrington, Sussex.

Jenny SAVILLE 1970– Painter and draughtsman, born in Cambridge, who studied at the School of Art in Glasgow, where she lived, 1988–92. In 1990 she exhibited in the National Portrait Competition at National Portrait Gallery and in the Van Gogh Self Portrait Competition, Burrell Collection, Glasgow; in 1992 she was the critic Clare Henry's selection in Critics Choice at The Cooling Gallery, exhibited in Art Parcels at Frost & Reed and at SSA. Saville's contribution to Young British Artists III at The Saatchi Gallery, 1994, gained much critical coverage for her depictions of huge female nudes, covered with slogans and graffiti. The Saatchi Collection holds her work.

Harold SAWKINS 1888–1957 Publisher and painter, born in Stockton-on-Tees, County Durham, who was educated at Barnard Castle. After 20 years in advertising he became a publisher, his titles including *The Artist* and *Paris Salon Illustrated*. Showed at RI and elsewhere. Lived in London, later Bournemouth, Hampshire.

Fred SAWYER 1907–1976 Artist in black-and-white; draughtsman. Brought up in Leicester, he attended the College of Art there. Showed at Leicester Museum and Art Gallery and widely in Nottingham and Leicester area, where he lived at Oadby.

Dorothy SAWYERS: *see* **Dorothy FULLER**

Richard SAXTON 1909– Painter, commercial artist and teacher, born in Retford, Nottinghamshire. He studied at Stafford School of Art with William Cartledge and with Stanley Smith, 1930–2. Went on to teach at that school, also Wolverhampton School of Art, 1932–3. Showed with NWG, Denbighshire Art Society of which he was a member and elsewhere in north Wales. Lived in Colwyn Bay, Denbighshire.

Harry SAYCE 1918– Artist and teacher, born and lived in London, whose education included Trent Park College. Before and after World War II, during which he spent some time abroad with a Royal Engineers survey unit as a lithographic artist, Sayce was at Harrow School of Art and Colchester School of Art under Edward Morss, also studying art in Florence and at Hammersmith School of Art. Went on to teach at a school in Paddington. Showed at RA, RBA, AIA and in the provinces.

Harold SAYER 1913– Painter, printmaker and teacher, born in Isleworth, Middlesex. He studied at Willesden Art School, 1930–3, Royal College of Art, 1933–6, and Goldsmiths' College School of Art, 1936–7. During World War II was a meteorological officer with Fleet Air Arm. Went on to hold various teaching posts, retiring from St Paul's College of Education, Cheltenham, in 1976. Was a member of RWA and RE, also showing at RA, West Country galleries such as Patricia Wells Gallery, Thornbury, on the continent and abroad. Lived at Sheepscombe, Gloucestershire.

Brian SAYERS 1954– Painter, draughtsman and teacher, born in Kent, who obtained a diploma in fine art from Slade School of Fine Art, 1974–8. Between 1979–81 Sayers was studio assistant to Lawrence Gowing; he was visiting tutor in the drawing schools at Eton College, 1983–4; then taught art part-time at City of Westminster College from 1987. Awards included Winsor & Newton, 1978; Richard Ford, 1979; and The Discerning Eye, Mall Galleries, 1995. Mixed shows included RA Summer Exhibition, from 1986; Riverside Open, Riverside Studios, 1990; The Hunting Art Prizes, London/Glasgow, 1994; and the 6th Oriel Mostyn Open, Llandudno, 1994–5. Had a solo show at Long & Ryle, 1992, another at Hohenthal & Littler, Munich, 1995.

Molly SAYERS 1904– Painter and draughtsman, notably in pastel, born in London, who studied in Paris in 1921–4. Exhibited RA, Paris Salon and elsewhere. Geological Society of London holds her work. Lived in Bramley, Surrey.

Norman SAYLE 1926– Painter mainly in watercolour, and teacher, born in Douglas, Isle of Man, who eventually returned there to live at Onchan. He studied at Goldsmiths' College, qualifying in 1952, taught in Kent, 1952–4, then was head of art at Isle of Man College of Further Education, 1954–89. Was a member of RI from 1995. Sayle was mainly a painter of landscape, strongly influenced by Archibald Knox and J S Cotman. His aim was "to reconcile complexity and simplicity: structure very important." Sayle showed extensively in the Isle of Man. In 1994 and 1995 he won third prizes in the Singer & Friedlander/*Sunday Times* Watercolour Competitions, at Mall Galleries, gaining the first prize in 1997. At the same Galleries in 1995 he won the RI Medal. Also exhibited at Richard Hagen Gallery, Broadway. Isle of Man Arts Council holds Sayle's work.

Edith SCALES 1892– Painter, born in Newark, Nottinghamshire. She studied at Lincoln High School, then went to Nottingham School of Art. She showed at RA, RI, ROI, Paris Salon and at many other venues. Museum of London holds several watercolours of the capital by her. Lived finally at Monks Eleigh, near Ipswich, Suffolk.

Terence SCALES 1932– Painter in oil and watercolour and teacher, born and lived in southeast London. He attended Camberwell School of Arts and Crafts, 1946–52, first as a junior, later taking diploma in fine art. His teachers included John Minton, Susan Einzig, Keith Vaughan and William Coldstream, the last two collecting Scales' early work. Did his National Service in Royal Air Force, 1952–4, then worked in Surrey Docks as a docker before being invited to teach part-time at Camberwell's painting department, where he remained for 32 years from 1960. The Neo-Romantic and Euston Road strains both affected Scales' work, which eventually moved towards a form of urban realism, the Thames being a strong source of pictorial ideas. Mixed shows included Scottish Arts Council, ICA, Ikon Gallery in Birmingham, Whitechapel Art Gallery, Austin/Desmond Fine Art and RA Summer Exhibitions. Solo shows included Greenwich Theatre Gallery, 1968; Woodlands Art Gallery, 1978; Royal Over-Seas League, 1985; Obelisk Gallery, 1988; and Sweet Waters Gallery, 1989. During his years as a docker Scales drew portraits of veteran colleagues in Surrey Docks for the *SURDOC* magazine, aptly signing them Justice. Examples were shown in A Thames Elegy at Café Gallery, Rotherhithe, 1995. Landmark Trust holds his work.

Ann SCAMPTON 1933– Painter and architect, born in Shanghai, China, daughter of an architect. Studied at Royal West of England Academy School of Architecture. Was elected RWA and showed at Waterloo Gallery and elsewhere. Lived at Chew Magna, Somerset.

Robert SCANLAN 1908– Painter, printmaker, mural artist and illustrator, born in Cork, Ireland. Studied art in London and widely on the continent. Worked for Central Office of Information, London Passenger Transport Board and J Lyons & Co. Exhibited Festival of Britain, Leicester Galleries and abroad including North and South America. Imperial War Museum bought his work. Lived in London.

Jo SCANNELL 1925– Painter and teacher who studied painting at Camberwell School of Arts and Crafts, 1946–9. Originally she painted under her maiden name of Higson, which changed when she married the poet Vernon Scannell in 1954, after which there was an interlude, while she brought up her family, until 1982. After leaving Camberwell she taught at Wisbech High School for Girls for a year, then from 1950 at Leeds College of Art. In 1953 gained Abbey Memorial Travelling Scholarship and spent a year in Italy. Showed at LG, in mixed shows in Leeds, Bradford and Wakefield, and RA. In 1988 shared an exhibition at Brunel Gallery, in 1996 having a solo show at Dolphin House Gallery, Colyton. Lived at Nether Compton, near Sherborne, Dorset.

Gerald SCARFE 1936– Cartoonist and designer, sculptor, painter and printmaker who was born and lived in London. He attended the Royal College of Art and then established a wide reputation as a cartoonist with strong satirical and political interests. Publications worked for included *Private Eye*, *The Daily Mail*, *Punch* and *Time* magazine. Was involved with the BBC in animation and film direction; designed and directed animated sequences in the film *The Wall*, 1982; designed for *Who's a Lucky Boy?* at Royal Exchange, Manchester, 1984, and for *Orpheus in the Underworld*, English National Opera, 1985. Books included *Gerald Scarfe's People*, 1966, *Gerald Scarfe*, 1982, the autobiographical *Scarfe by Scarfe*, 1986, televised in 1987, and *Scarfeland*, 1989. Group shows included Violence in Contemporary Art, ICA, 1964, Grosvenor Gallery from 1969, and Expo '70, Osaka, 1970. His first solo show was at Horse Shoe Wharf Club, 1966, later ones including Waddell Gallery, New York, from 1968, National Portrait Gallery, 1971, a retrospective at Royal Festival Hall in 1983, and Chris Beetles, 1989.

Laurence SCARFE 1914–1993 Artist and designer in wide range of media, writer and teacher, born in Idle, Yorkshire. He studied at Shipley Art School, then Royal College of Art, 1933–7, specializing in mural painting. Scarfe lectured at Bromley School of Art, 1937–9, then at Central School of Art, 1945–70, and for about a decade from 1971 at Brighton Polytechnic. His murals included the Regatta Restaurant and Dome of Discovery for the Festival of Britain, Coronation Pavilion for Imperial Chemical Industries and for P&O Orient Lines the liners *Orcades* and *Oriana*. Scarfe designed extensively for print, including the Royal Coat of Arms for Central Office of Information. He was art editor and a contributor to *The Saturday Book* and illustrated for *Radio Times*. Scarfe's books included *Rome: Fragments in the Sun*, 1950, and *Alphabets: History of Calligraphy and Typography*, 1954. He was a member of the Society of Mural Painters and a fellow of the Society of Industrial Artists. He exhibited at RA, RBA and at the Leicester, Zwemmer and Redfern Galleries. Victoria & Albert Museum, Imperial War Museum and Brighton Museum & Art Gallery have holdings of his work. Lived in London.

John SCARLAND 1947– Artist in oil, gouache and charcoal, born in Bletchingley, Surrey. He was mainly self-taught by study of previous painters' work but had a short period working with Charles Bartlett. Scarland's work was originally mainly landscape, then figurative. In late 1980s he moved towards becoming a full-time artist, having worked for many years in landscape design and in the building industry as a carpenter. Scarland's work was exhibited at RWS Open, Mall Galleries, Bourne Gallery in Reigate and Cider House Gallery, Bletchingley; at several London art fairs including The World of Watercolours; and he had a series of solo exhibitions, including studio shows and Horsham Arts Centre, 1997. Limited-edition prints were published by St James' Fine Art. Lived in East Grinstead, Sussex.

Rosa SCHAFER 1901–1986 Painter and teacher, born in Vienna, Austria. Studied at the State Academy there. Exhibited in Vienna and in England with PS, AIA and SEA of both of which she was a member, and Leicester Galleries, having several one-man shows. Member of the Ben Uri Art Society. Signed work RS. Lived in London.

Samson SCHAMES 1898–1967 Artist in a variety of media, born in Frankfurt-am-Main, Germany, who studied painting and the graphic arts there, elsewhere in Germany and in France. From 1920s began establishing a reputation as an artist and stage designer, had several solo exhibitions, but fled to England from the Nazis in 1938. The plight of the Jew and the horrors of war became the core of his output. During the Blitz he created mosaics out of the rubble of buildings. Interned in the Liverpool area for several months and lacking artists' materials, Schames made a brush with his own hair and used home-made dyes to paint on cardboard; pieces of barbed wire from the fences were used for sculptures. On release he became a civil defence worker. A series of solo exhibitions in London gained good reviews as did work shown in mixed exhibitions including RA. CEMA, the Ministries of Information and Supply and prominent private collectors were among his clients. In 1948 Schames moved to New York and became an American citizen. Exhibited with American Watercolour Society, Pennsylvania Academy of Arts, Jewish Museum in New York, Provincetown Art Association and had a series of solo exhibitions, including Este Gallery, also with Marcel Bernheim's, in Paris. In 1986 Schames was included in Art in Exile in Great Britain 1933–45 at Camden Arts Centre.

Pat SCHAVERIEN 1951– Printmaker and painter, born and worked in London. Her work drew strongly on the architecture of urban areas. Gained an honours degree at Hornsey College of Art, 1970–4, then did higher diploma in printmaking at Slade School of Fine Art, 1974–6. In 1976 worked at Crane Studio for a year, then set up with partners new printmaking studio in Clerkenwell Workshops. Gained an Arts Council Award in 1977, in 1979–81 sitting on the committee of Printmakers' Council. Extensive mixed appearances included Stowells Trophy, Mall Galleries, 1974; LG at Camden Arts Centre, 1975; RA Summer Exhibition, 1976; Ben Uri Gallery, 1982; and Eighth British International Print Biennale, Cartwright Hall, Bradford, 1984. Solo shows included Everyman Cinema Gallery, 1977; National Film Theatre, 1979; and Woodlands Art Gallery, 1984. Victoria & Albert Museum and Ben Uri Art Society hold examples.

Irene SCHEINMANN 1933– Printmaker, painter and artist in mixed media, born in Baghdad, Iraq. She had a cosmopolitan upbringing, being educated at a French-Jewish school although her mother tongue was Arabic. After a year in an English boarding school from 1952, she studied languages and literature at Brown University, America, returning to England in 1957 where she married and settled. An interest in the visual arts prompted her in 1967 to attend Regent Street Polytechnic, followed by four years of adult education classes in painting, drawing and printmaking; she spent a year with Joëlle Serve at his Atelier 63 in Paris, improving her printmaking techniques, then for a decade from 1978, until his death, worked in Julian Trevelyan's studio, in 1979 spending another three months at Atelier 63. Was a member of Trace, the Paris printmaking association begun by Serve, and of the California Society of Printmakers. Became a member of the Printmakers' Council in 1984, in that year organising Contemporary Prints at the National Theatre, followed Print Europe at Barbican Centre, 1991. Took part in many other mixed shows in Britain and abroad. Solo exhibitions included Petworth Gallery, Petworth; Salford University; Radann Gallery, New York; and in 1995 she shared a show with Dania Appel at Ben Uri Gallery, which holds her work. Glasgow University, Radcliffe Infirmary in Oxford and University College Hospital in Nottingham are also owners. Lived in London.

Tai-Shan SCHIERENBERG 1962– Painter, notable for portraits and head studies of an Expressionist type, who studied at St Martin's School of Art, 1981–5, then Slade School of Fine Art, 1985–7. He first came to general notice as National Portrait Gallery's John Player Portrait Award first prize winner in 1989. In 1992 the Gallery took into its collection a portrait by Schierenberg of the writer and barrister John Mortimer, commissioned as part of the Award. Showed in mixed exhibitions at Diorama Gallery from 1990; RA Summer Exhibition from 1991; and Flowers East Nudes show at Watermans Arts Centre, 1991. Solo exhibitions were also with Diorama Gallery, then Angela Flowers. Lived in London.

Eric SCHILSKY 1898–1974 Sculptor, draughtsman and teacher, born in Southampton, younger brother of the actor Austin Trevor, from a musical family and deeply interested in music. Schilsky was a figurative sculptor whose work had a strong spiritual quality. He was educated at Haberdashers' Aske's School and then college in Geneva, initially studying art at École des Beaux-Arts, Paris. His sculpture studies at the Slade School of Fine Art, under Havard Thomas, 1914–17 and 1918–19, were interrupted by World War I service abroad in the Gloucester Yeomanry. Schilsky joined the staff of Westminster School of Art around 1932; moved to the Central School of Arts and Crafts in 1939; worked for the government's Directorate of Camouflage, 1940–5; then was head of sculpture at Edinburgh College of Art, 1945–69. He married the model Bettina Fenton in 1928; after she committed suicide in 1944, in 1946 he married the artist Victorine Foot. Schilsky's portraits included the actor Ernest Thesiger, the naval commander Earl Beatty and Modigliani's model Gabrielle de Saone. He was elected RSA in 1956, RA in 1968. His solo exhibitions included Fine Art Society, 1977; Aitken Dott, Edinburgh, 1980; and Bourne Fine Art, 1991. Chantrey Bequest and public collections in Aberdeen, Paisley and Stoke-on-Trent hold examples.

Gerik SCHJELDERUP 1899–1985 Painter, draughtsman, printmaker and actor, born in Dresden, Germany, his father Gerhard Schjelderup being a Norwegian opera composer, his German mother a concert singer. Leaving school in Oslo in 1918, studied scene painting at National Theatre there, in 1919–23 studying painting in Munich, first at the Heymann School, then the Hoffmann School. In Norway was encouraged by the painter Edvard Munch and had first solo show in Oslo. In 1926 visited London for portrait commissions and in 1927 had solo exhibition at Waddington Gallery, Dublin, marrying the Irish actress Natalie Moya Mullally the following year. Travelled widely in Australia and Pacific Islands; in 1931 had first one-man show in London at Cooling Galleries; and worked on scenery for Ballets Russes. In

1930s–1960s he painted; taught at Hampstead Artists' Council; and acted, notably for the BBC, for which he wrote features. Retired in Ireland, he published a biography of his father. Retrospective show at Sally Hunter Fine Art, 1985. Finally lived in West Bantry and in Dublin.

Anne SCHLEE: *see* **ANSCHLEE**

Hans SCHLEGER: *see* **ZERO**

Peter SCHMIDT 1931–1980 Painter, draughtsman, printmaker, designer, performance artist and teacher, born in Berlin, Germany, who emigrated to England in 1938. Schmidt was a thoughtful, versatile artist, his work ranging from abstract programme paintings, based on systems, to a series of later delicate landscapes and still lifes. After internment on the Isle of Wight in 1940, he became a British subject in 1945, starting to paint in 1947. Following National Service, 1949–51, Schmidt studied at Goldsmiths' College, 1951–3; then at the Slade School of Fine Art, 1953–7; with an Abbey Minor Scholarship in Sicily, 1957–8. Began teaching at Watford School of Art, 1959–60, establishing the foundation course there, 1962, the year that BBC Television made a film, *Departure*, about Schmidt's and Ian Stephenson's work. Schmidt held a first solo show at Beaux Arts Gallery in 1961, another at Curwen Gallery in 1966. In 1967 Schmidt was involved in a number of performances including sound, among the venues ICA and Bristol Arts Centre; in 1968 he was musical adviser at the ICA's Cybernetic Serendipity exhibition at Critici Kiezen Grafiek (Holland Festival); and in 1969 assembled the *Electronic Soupmixes* performance at Curwen Gallery, *Filmsoundmixes* at ICA featuring an animated film. Schmidt was involved in a number of projects with Brian Eno, including the *Taking Tiger Mountain* sleeve design in 1974 and Before and After Science, 1977. He had several showings of his work at Lisson Gallery, including Programmed Paintings in 1968 and Autobiographical Monoprints, 1970. Schmidt died on a painting holiday in Tenerife in 1980, the year of a retrospective, including works by Eno, at The Paul Ide Gallery, Brussels. The retrospective Remembered Images took place at Watford Museum in 1987.

Stella SCHMOLLE 1908–1975 Lithographer and painter, born and lived in London who studied and taught at Central School of Arts and Crafts. Showed at RA and elsewhere. The British Museum holds lithographs by Schmolle, including pre-war works The Bandstand, Hyde Park, and Rehearsal at The Old Vic, also a wartime gouache Army Blood Supply, Bath.

Raoh SCHORR 1901–1991 Sculptor and decorative artist, born in Muttenz, Switzerland, as Friedel Schorr. Studied at Hoffmanschule, Munich, then went to Paris in 1923 to complete his studies where he met leading School of Paris painters. Helped Jean Dufy with fabric designs and designed dresses for the couturier Robert Piguet. After establishing a reputation as a decorative sculptor of animals he moved to London in 1936, had a solo show in 1937 at Redfern Gallery, had a bronze – Bengal Tiger – acquired by Tate Gallery and was commissioned by Royal Doulton to design pottery animals. Exhibited bronzes for many years at RA, but was mainly a commercial designer, which made possible elegant life in Chelsea, retiring in early 1960s. Harrods, Elizabeth Arden and Helena Rubinstein had been among his clients. Upon retirement he began producing pottery animals influenced by Chinese ceramics and elegant, botanically accurate flower studies, showed at Cooling Gallery in 1967. Ill-health prompted Schorr's return to his family in Brunnen, Switzerland, where he died.

Bernard SCHOTTLANDER 1924– Sculptor in metal, born in Mainz, Germany. He moved to England in 1939 and two years later began work as a welder and plater, attending evening classes in sculpture at Leeds College of Art. After war service, 1944–8, he studied at Anglo-French Art Centre, 1948–9, transferring to industrial design at Central School of Arts and Crafts, 1949–51. In the latter year Schottlander started his own metal workshop, active as an industrial designer and metalwork maker, engaging in full-time sculpture from 1963. For a time he taught at St Martin's School of Art. Schottlander participated in a number of group shows, including Arts Council's Sculpture in a City, 1968, which toured. He had solo exhibitions at Architectural Association, 1964; Annely Juda (Hamilton Galleries), 1965; and an open-air exhibition at Guinness' Brewery, 1972. Schottlander's sculpture was geometric to 1977, when it became organic, steel plate finished with marine paint. Arts Council, Leicester City Art Gallery, Warwick University, Sackler Foundation in New York and City of Toronto are some of the collections holding his work. Schottlander's large, impressive steel sculpture South of the River stands in front of Ernst & Young's offices in Lambeth Palace Road. Lived in Chipping Norton, Oxfordshire.

Benno SCHOTZ 1891–1984 Sculptor and teacher who was essentially a modeller of portraits. Born in Arensburgh, Estonia, after coming to Britain Schotz initially studied engineering at the Royal Technical College in Glasgow, then decided to study art at the School of Art there. His first one-man show took place at Reid and Lefevre's gallery in Glasgow in 1926, Lefevre giving him his first one-man show in London four years later. He was head of the sculpture and ceramic departments of the Glasgow School of Art from 1938. Schotz was elected RSA in 1937 and was appointed HM Sculptor in Ordinary for Scotland. He exhibited widely, including the RA, RSA, Royal Glasgow Institute of the Fine Arts and Walker Art Gallery, Liverpool. Owners of his work include the House of Commons, Kelvingrove Art Gallery, Glasgow, the National Portrait Gallery, Edinburgh, and Jerusalem and Tel-Aviv art galleries, in Israel. Wrote an autobiography, *Bronze in my Blood*, and lived in Glasgow, where Christie's held a studio sale in 1997.

Randolph SCHWABE 1885–1948 Influential teacher, draughtsman and printmaker, especially of urban subjects, illustrator and designer. Born in Manchester, Schwabe studied briefly at the Royal College of Art, Slade School of Fine Art, 1900–5, and at Académie Julian, Paris, 1906. Official war artist during World War I, making drawings of the Women's Land Army. Went on to teach at

Camberwell and Westminster Schools of Art. Was drawing master at the Royal College of Art, then succeeded Henry Tonks as Slade Professor and head of the Slade School of Art, 1930, an apt choice, as Schwabe's exact draughtsmanship was firmly in the Slade tradition. Schwabe was a prolific exhibitor at NEAC and Goupil Gallery, also showing at Carfax Gallery, Fine Art Society, Leicester Galleries and RWS. Tate Gallery holds his work. Among the books Schwabe illustrated were Walter de la Mare's *Crossings*, 1921, several books by the writer on dance Cyril Beaumont and H E Bates' *The Tinkers of Elstow*, 1946. A large retrospective was held at Chris Beetles in 1994. Lived finally at Helensburgh, Dunbartonshire.

Sue SCHWARTZ 1944– Artist in ceramic, notable for her cats. She was born in Bath but spent her childhood in Newcastle upon Tyne. As a student teacher in the 1960s she specialised in pottery, taught for a short time, then worked in art and antiques and rediscovered ceramics. Each of her cats was made using the coil method and was Raku-fired. Schwartz's cats were included in a Graves Art Gallery, Sheffield, touring show Cat & Mouse. She also exhibited with Schwartzsackin Fine Art and Primrose Hill Gallery, both 1990, and Castlegate House, Cockermouth, 1991. Lived in Ashelton, Coryton, Okehampton, Devon.

Hans SCHWARZ 1922– Artist in oil and watercolour, sculptor, illustrator, teacher and writer, born in Vienna, Austria, where he attended the Art School, 1937–8. He was expelled by the Nazis in 1938 and moved to Birmingham in 1939, working as a labourer, was interned in 1940–1, then attended Birmingham School Arts and Crafts, 1941–3. As well as joining a commercial art studio, 1943–5, Schwarz began teaching part-time and worked in various art schools until 1966. He was a freelance illustrator from 1945, but gave up graphic design in 1964 to paint and sculpt full-time. He published *Figure Painting*, *Colour for the Artist* and *Painting in Towns* for Studio Vista and a series of art books for Pitman. Schwarz was a member of NEAC, RWS RP, RBA and the Contemporary Portrait Society as well as an honorary life member of the Hampstead Artists' Council. Schwarz was awarded the Hunting Group Prize for the best watercolour of the year in 1981. His solo shows included a series at Thackeray Gallery from 1982; Compton Gallery, 1983; Ben Uri Gallery, 1985; Woodlands Art Gallery, 1991; and Sternberg Centre, 1992. His work is in many public collections, including portraits of Sir Nikolaus Pevsner, Lord Soper and Miles Malleson in National Portrait Gallery. His son Julian was also an artist. Lived in London.

Julian SCHWARZ 1949– Artist in wood sculpture and woodcut prints, son of the artist Hans Schwarz, born in Birmingham. He studied at Slade School of Fine Art, 1968–72. Mixed exhibitions included Piccadilly Gallery from 1976; Leeds City Art Gallery, 1987; Printmakers' Council, Barbican Centre, 1989; Galerie La Teinturerie, Paris, from 1992; and National Print Exhibition, Mall Galleries, 1994. Had a solo show with Ian Birksted Gallery, 1980; Camden Arts Centre, from 1984; and Ben Uri Art Gallery and St David's Hall, Cardiff, both 1985. Henry Moore Sculpture Foundation in Leeds; education authorities in Yorkshire and Leicester; and South Glamorgan County Council hold examples. Lived in London.

Anne SCHWEGMANN-FIELDING 1967– Artist who studied at North Essex School of Art, Stourbridge College of Art and Wolverhampton Polytechnic. She took part in group shows including Richard Demarco Gallery, Edinburgh, and England & Co. In that gallery's Art in Boxes show in 1991 Schwegmann-Fielding showed Crushed Consumerism, a typical work created from urban detritus.

Kurt SCHWITTERS 1887–1948 Sculptor, collagist, maker of assemblages, publisher and writer, born in Hanover, Germany. He studied at Kunstakademie, Dresden, 1909–14, Kunstakademie, Berlin, 1914, and at architectural studios in Hanover, 1918. From about that time he created his first Merz works, built up in layers from collaged sections. Was founder and editor of *Merz* magazine, 1923–32. Schwitters was associated with Dada movement and incorporated Constructivist elements. He sometimes employed ephemera and rubbish to create his abstract works, which had themes such as crocus, violin or fish or employed geometric forms, and which were always finely crafted and good to look at. Having visited Norway frequently from late 1920s, under pressure from the Nazi regime Schwitters went to live there in 1937. Schwitters settled in England in 1940, where he was interned, then lived in London, 1941–5. From then until his death he settled in Westmorland where, with help from a Museum of Modern Art, New York, grant he was able to create what was called the Merz Barn. Schwitters showed with Galerie der Sturm, Berlin, in 1920, then built an international reputation. Retrospectives included Museum of Modern Art, New York, 1948, and Marlborough Fine Art, 1972; Tate Gallery, which held 1985 exhibition, owns his work, as do many other public collections. Lived in Kendal.

Gavin SCOBIE 1940– Sculptor, painter and teacher, born in Edinburgh where he studied painting at the College of Art, 1958–62. From 1963–74 he taught art in an Edinburgh school, then left to take up sculpture full-time, settling in Ross-shire. Scobie's sculpture dates from the mid-1960s. He had a first solo exhibition in 1972 at Richard Demarco Gallery, Edinburgh, two years before he won the Invergordon Sculpture Prize. Although at first Scobie worked in metal in a Minimalist tradition, from the early 1980s he employed mainly terracotta. An important Scobie series was the bronze books begun in 1977; the Arts Council collection includes his Untitled Book Sculpture of 1981. A major retrospective was held at Talbot Rice Art Centre, Edinburgh, in 1984, and a show of Scobie's Constructivist sculpture at Reed's Wharf Gallery in 1994.

Arthur SCOTT 1881–1953 Painter, printmaker and teacher, born in Stoke-on-Trent, Staffordshire, son of the potter George Scott. He studied at Burslem School of Art, then Royal College of Art, 1907–13. Held several teaching posts, being for many years head of Watford School of Art. Showed RA, RBA extensively,

Walker Art Gallery, Liverpool, and Paris Salon. Lived in Harrow, Middlesex.

Bernard SCOTT 1918–1990 Painter and printmaker, born in London's East End into an Orthodox Jewish background, who won a London County Council scholarship to study at St Martin's School of Art with Leon Underwood among others. He also studied at Toynbee Hall School of Art. At St Martin's Scott gained first prize in a mural competition, carrying out his winning design on a wall of the school. As a company director Scott was prevented from painting full-time until 1969; then his output was prodigious. It ranged from witty, colourful pictures inspired by folk art to abstracts. His series of lithographs of the 1960s concerned with victims of the Korean and Vietnamese wars is notable. Showed at RA, Whitechapel Art Gallery and Camden Arts Centre, had solo exhibitions at Drian Galleries and Rene Darom Gallery in Tel-Aviv and there was a retrospective at Ben Uri Art Gallery in 1995. Scott's wife, Christine, was also a painter, living at Goring-by-Sea, Sussex.

Bill SCOTT 1935– Sculptor and teacher, born in Moniaive, Dumfriesshire. He studied at Edinburgh College of Art, 1953–9, and École des Beaux-Arts, Paris, 1959–60. He went on to teach sculpture at Edinburgh College of Art. Scott gained the RSA Lothian Region Award in 1978 and travelled widely in Europe in 1981 with a Gillies Bequest Scholarship. He was included in 11 Scottish Sculptors at the Fruitmarket Gallery, Edinburgh, in 1975, and the International Exhibition of Small Sculpture, Budapest, 1981, as well as Virtue and Vision at RSA in 1990. Solo shows included sculpture and drawings at New 57 Gallery, Edinburgh, in 1979, and Kirkcaldy Art Gallery and Museum, 1985. Was elected RSA. Lived in Roslin, Midlothian.

Garth B SCOTT 1931– Painter and teacher whose father was Angus Scott, cartoonist and illustrator. Attended Bromley School of Art and Borough Polytechnic. He took a number of jobs to raise money to continue his art studies, including work with David Bomberg in Spain. Scott trained as a teacher, 1956–8, was a civil servant for a year, then taught until retirement in the late 1980s. He was included in the Borough Group show at Fine Art Associates, 1989. Bomberg remained a strong influence on Scott's work, which was signed G B S.

George SCOTT 1938– Artist, designer and teacher, born in Glasgow, where he attended the School of Art under Philip Reeves, 1958–62. Went on to teach adults part-time. Scott was a member of Coventry Art Guild and Coventry and Warwickshire Art Society, showing elsewhere in the Midlands and the provinces. Had a series of solo shows, mainly in his home area of Coventry.

Gerald SCOTT 1916–1977 Sculptor, painter, draughtsman, potter, printmaker and teacher, born in Hersham, Surrey. After school worked for a firm of Lloyd's brokers for seven years, then served in Army, 1941–6, partly in East Africa. After a period as a potter he studied at Kingston School of Art under Reginald Brill, 1946–9, with some time in 1948 at Burslem College of Art, during which Arnold Machin advised him to take up sculpture. This he did at Slade School of Fine Art, 1949–52, under A H Gerrard. Went on to teach: part-time at Kingston, 1950–2, and Hammersmith School of Art, 1951–2; at Southend-on-Sea School of Art, 1952–8; then from 1958 at West of England College of Art (later Bristol Polytechnic), becoming principal lecturer in the faculty of art and design. Showed at RA, ICA, Festival of Britain, RWS, with RBS of which he was made a fellow in 1970, and at RWA of which he was a member. RWA, Bristol Corporation and London County Council held his work. The bird was a recurrent theme in this. His commissioned pieces included much church work, including a life-size figure for St Edmund the King, Pinner; a memorial panel for 501 Squadron, Royal Air Force, in Bristol Cathedral; and a dove in hemlock for a font cover at Lockleaze Church. Lived in Bristol.

Gordon SCOTT 1918– Painter and teacher who studied at Croydon School of Art and Royal College of Art, winning a Travelling Scholarship there. Went on to teach at Camberwell School of Art. He showed at RA, LG, RBA, Cooling Gallery, Opix Gallery and in 1980 was included in Figurative Painters at Woodlands Art Gallery.

Ian SCOTT 1940– Sculptor in a range of materials and painter, born and settled at Ronaldsay, Orkney Islands. He studied with Leo Clegg at Gray's School of Art, Aberdeen, doing postgraduate work in 1961–2. Among prizes won were the RSA's Latimer Award, 1965, and its Benno Schotz Prize, 1966. Scott was made a fellow of RBS in 1972. Showed at Scottish Arts Council, Graves Art Gallery in Sheffield and abroad and had solo exhibitions. Oxford University and Scottish Arts Council hold examples.

Ian SCOTT 1957– Painter, printmaker and designer, born in North Shields, Northumberland, but from childhood lived in Wick, Caithness. Scott's work, noted for its fine draughtsmanship, had a mystical, challenging and elusive quality in which aspects of the sea were a leading feature. As a student he began to make an impact in exhibitions, participating in Scottish Young Contemporaries in 1984 and the RSA Student Exhibition. In 1985 after graduating he was included in Compass Gallery, Glasgow, New Generation show, followed by Mercury Gallery and again in the following postgraduate year. He completed the album cover and artwork for the music and film *Tree of Liberty*, about Robert Burns. The year 1988 was spent working in Germany and in 1989 Scott had a solo show at Compass Gallery.

Ian McLachlan SCOTT 1943– Painter and teacher, born in Dunoon, Argyll, who studied at Glasgow School of Art, gaining his diploma in drawing and painting, 1966. He won the Newbery Medal, 1966; a post-diploma scholarship, 1966–7; and a Landscape Scholarship from RA, 1967. Taught at Rothesay Academy, Bute, 1968–75; Dunoon Grammar School, Argyll, 1975–8; was art advisor, Tayside Region Education Authority, Perty, 1978–96, then returned to painting full-time. He was president and secretary of the Scottish Association of Advisors in Art and Design; a member of the curriculum award panel of the National Society for Education in Art and Design; and a lecturer and demonstrator for Scottish Arts Council. Exhibitions included Ainscough Contemporary Art.

James SCOTT 1920– Artist in oil, watercolour, pen and wash and metals, born in Londonderry, Northern Ireland, where he settled in Belfast. Studied at the local College of Art under John Turner and John Luke. For 30 years Scott was involved in engineering: mechanical, civil design and research at Queen's University. He was an associate of RUA and took part in many group exhibitions elsewhere throughout Northern Ireland. In 1992 he made and donated a bronze medal, won by the artist Basil Blackshaw, given in memory of William Conor, at RUA. Had several solo shows in the province, including Centre Art Gallery, Belfast, 1976.

Joan SCOTT 1916–1989 Artist in various media and teacher, born in London, who studied at Warrington School of Art under Bernard Statters, 1937–42, also having private tutors. She went on to teach adults and wrote manuals published by Frederick Warne, including *Using Pastels*. In addition to several solo exhibitions showed at SWA, NS, RI, PS and at Paris Salon. Lived in Ickenham, Middlesex.

John SCOTT 1934– Painter and teacher, born in Beckenham, Kent. He studied, 1953–7, at Reading University School of Fine Art and then held a number of teaching posts, including Denbighshire Technical College School of Art, living in Wrexham. Was a member of RCamA and showed in group exhibitions at RBA and Leicester Galleries, having solo shows at New Art Centre and Kensington Gallery.

Judy SCOTT 1939– Painter and draughtsman who studied at Maidstone School of Art, 1956–8, Central School of Arts and Crafts, 1958–61, in the 1970s studied life drawing with Leslie Marr and from 1986 painting with Dick Lee. Her mixed shows included NEAC, New Grafton Gallery and Brian Sinfield Gallery. She had a solo show with Wells Art Centre, in Norfolk, in 1988; began showing at Bacon's Gallery, at Aylsham, Norfolk, in 1989; having a one-man at Cadogan Gallery in 1992. Her work was very much in the Camberwell tradition and included complex and challenging interiors. She also did some commissioned portraits.

Kathleen SCOTT 1878–1947 Sculptor of figures and portrait busts, born at Carlton-in-Lindrick, Nottinghamshire. After initial education in France and Italy, she studied at the Slade School of Fine Art, Atelier Colarossi in Paris, 1901–6, and with Rodin. In 1908 she married the Polar explorer Robert Falcon Scott (Captain Scott of the Antarctic, who died there in 1912), then in 1922 Sir Edward Hilton Young (later Baron Kennet of the Dene). She was the mother of Peter Scott, the naturalist and artist. Lady Kennet exhibited at RA, 1913–47, IS, RMS, SWA and elsewhere; one-man show Fine Art Society in 1934. She was elected a fellow of the RBS in 1946. Memorial exhibition at Mansard Gallery, 1947, and her own *Self-Portrait of an Artist* appeared two years later. Was an extensive traveller. Tate Gallery holds her work, which is illustrated in the volume *RBS: Modern British Sculpture*, published in 1939; also in Eric Newton's monograph *British Sculpture 1944–1946*. Among her notable works are the memorial to Captain Scott in Waterloo Place; Earl of Oxford and Asquith; George Bernard Shaw; and the film actor Sabu. Lived in Great Yarmouth, Norfolk, and London, where she died.

Maggie SCOTT fl. from early 1970s– Painter and artist in collage, born in Enfield, Middlesex, full name Margaret Elspeth Scott, her father was painter Charles Scott. She attended Carlisle College of Art and Design, 1973–4, Loughborough College of Art and Design, 1974–7, then Slade School of Fine Art from 1978, where her teachers included Tess Jaray and Bernard Cohen. NS member who also showed in the provinces. Lived for a time in Selkirk, Scotland.

Mary SCOTT 1912– Sculptor, painter and teacher, born in Bristol where she studied at the local School of Art. Early in the 1930s she attended Slade School of Fine Art, then was at Royal Academy Schools, 1934–7, transferring from painting to sculpture and winning a silver medal. Married the artist William Scott and, after continental travel, early in 1938 settled in Pont Aven where with her husband and Geoffrey Nelson she started the Pont Aven School of Painting. At outset of World War II left for Dublin, in 1941 settled in Radstock, Somerset to run a market garden. From 1946–51 taught initially at Bath Art School, then part-time at Bath Academy of Art. Mary Scott showed with her husband at Bath Society of Artists until early 1950s, having shared a show with him at Leger Galleries in 1945.

Michael SCOTT 1946– Painter, born in Peterhead, Aberdeenshire, whose figurative work often contained an element of fantasy. Studied political science at Liverpool, 1965–8; trained as a teacher in Hull for a year, then settled in Glasgow. Did soci logical research, then lectured at what became Glasgow Caledonian University. Studied for many years with the painter John Boyd, including life classes at Glasgow School of Art. In 1989 won the David Cargill Senior Award at Royal Glasgow Institute of the Fine Arts, in 1991 the Paper Tiger Award 1990. In 1990 was elected a professional member of SSWA. Mixed exhibitions also included Smith Biennial, Smith Art Gallery, Stirling, 1985–7; RA Summer Exhibition from 1988; RSA from 1989; and ROI from same year. Had solo shows at Roger Billcliffe Fine Art, Glasgow, and The Contemporary Fine Art Gallery, Eton, both 1994. Several corporate collections hold examples.

Michael SCOTT 1954– Painter, born in Lisburn, near Belfast, Northern Ireland. He studied at Chelsea School of Art, 1977–81. Among his mixed show appearances were New Contemporaries at ICA, 1979–80, and John Moores Liverpool Exhibition from 1982, when he won a prize. He gained a Northern Ireland Arts Council Bursary for travel in Portugal, 1984, and three years later at John Moores showed the canvas Earthquake of Lisbon, All

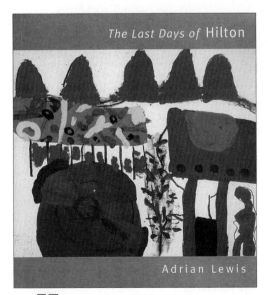

Saints Day 1755. Arts Council acquired this work. Lived for some time in London.

Peter SCOTT 1909–1989 Ornithologist, broadcaster and painter, born in London, son of Robert Falcon Scott the Antarctic explorer whose wife was Kathleen Kennet, the sculptor, as she later became known after her second marriage. Peter Scott was educated at Oundle School and Cambridge University, the Munich State Academy and the Royal Academy Schools. An Olympic Games-class yachts-man and national gliding champion, he was founder of the World Wildlife Fund and campaigned endlessly for endangered species. He lived for many years at Slimbridge, Gloucestershire, in the grounds of the Wildlife and Wetlands Trust, which he founded in 1946. Knighted in 1973, partly in recognition of his prowess as a bird painter and as the author and illustrator of many books on birds. Showed at RA and elsewhere internationally. There was an eightieth birthday retrospective at Cheltenham Art Gallery, 1989.

Richard SCOTT 1938– Painter in oil, sculptor and teacher, born in Bromley, Kent. He studied at Lowestoft School of Art, 1954–6, then Camberwell School of Arts and Crafts, 1956–8, for his diploma, and 1960–1. Taught part-time at Camberwell, 1961–5, also at Suffolk College, 1971–82, then was a full-time lecturer there, 1982–95, when he took early retirement. Scott was a founder-member of the Suffolk Group, and was a member of Ipswich Art Society and Southwold Art Circle, in the mid-1990s being the president of the latter body. Showed at RA Summer Exhibition in 1984 and at NEAC from 1992 and took part in numerous two- to four-man exhibitions in East Anglia from 1961. Had a solo show at Orpington Civic Hall, 1960, and at Belstead Brook Hotel, Ipswich, 1982. Lived in Walberswick, Suffolk. He made researches into the village as an artistic colony, one by-product being a successful exhibition at Christchurch Mansion, Ipswich, in 1994. Although Scott trained as a sculptor, by the mid-1970s he had decided to concentrate on painting. Among his sculpted portraits were Norman Manley, prime minister of Jamaica, 1960, and William Alwyn, the composer, 1980.

Sally SCOTT 1939– Painter, muralist, decorative architectural glass artist and teacher, born and based in London, who studied at Croydon College of Art and Royal Academy Schools. Taught at Birmingham School of Art, 1962–4, and lectured part-time at Middlesex Polytechnic (formerly Hornsey College of Art), 1964–91. Scott's London paintings were mainly still life; pastel landscapes were done in the Languedoc, France; with flower paintings in both countries. Work for films included *The Bliss of Mrs Blossom* and *The French Lieutenant's Woman*, with mural locations including Madame Tussauds; Expo '70 in Osaka, Japan; Farnborough and Paris Air Shows; and Hilton Hotels in Britain and abroad. Group shows included regular exhibitions with Alresford Gallery; Society of Botanical Artists from 1992; and NEAC, 1993. Had a solo show at Richmond Art and Ceramic Gallery, 1976, later ones including JK Hill Gallery, 1993, and Le Mimosa, St Guirand, France. From the mid-1980s Sally Scott with David Peace formed a partnership to make decorative architectural glass, sandblasting and engraving. Among works they produced were chapel doors for Lincoln College in Oxford; a screen for Llandaff Cathedral, Wales; and the east window for St Mary's, Burwell, Cambridgeshire. She also handled independent commissions, including screens for a series of hotels internationally; mirrors for the Royal Albert Hall; murals for the Victoria & Albert Museum; and a fanlight for the Catholic Church of Our Lady and St Michael, Abergavenny, Wales. In 1995 Scott and Peace published *Engraved Glass in Architecture*. Scott was a member of the Guild of Glass Engravers and the Art Workers' Guild.

Tim SCOTT 1937– Sculptor and teacher, born in Richmond, Surrey. He studied at Tunbridge Wells School of Art, Architectural Association, 1954–9, and part-time at St Martin's School of Art, 1955–9. In the late 1950s showed with Young Contemporaries. In 1959–61 lived in Paris and worked at Atelier Le Corbusier-Wegenscky. He much admired Le Corbusier and Brancusi and wrote a thesis on Le Corbusier's Villa Savoye. In 1961 Scott showed at ICA in 26 Young Sculptors. Began to teach 1962 at St Martin's School of Art and other schools, becoming head of the St Martin's sculpture department in 1980. Among his awards were a Peter Stuyvesant Foundation Bursary, 1965, and the position of sculptor-in-residence at North London Polytechnic, 1978–9. His commissions included Peter Stuyvesant Sculpture Project in Liverpool, 1972. He had the first of a string of solo exhibitions at Waddington Galleries in 1966, later showing with Knoedler Gallery. Also exhibited widely abroad. Retrospectives included Whitechapel Art Gallery in 1967, then Museum of Modern Art, Oxford, 1969. Scott was an abstract sculptor using a variety of materials. His work is held by Tate Gallery. Lived in London.

William SCOTT 1913–1989 Painter, printmaker, sculptor and teacher, born in Greenock, Renfrewshire. Was brought up in Northern Ireland, attending Belfast College of Art, 1928–31, then Royal Academy Schools, 1931–5. Lived in France and Italy for three years, helping to run an art school at Pont-Aven, Brittany. During World War II served in the Royal Engineers, a period notable for some outstanding landscape watercolours, having his first one-man show at Leger Gallery in 1942. After the war Scott taught at Bath Academy of Art, 1946–56, where he got to know the St Ives painters. He also taught at Royal College of Art and Alberta University's Banff School of Fine Arts. In America he met Mark Rothko, Jackson Pollock and other leading painters and as well as exhibiting at LG, of which he was a member, and showing at Leicester and Hanover Galleries, he began to establish an international reputation. Exhibited at Venice Biennale in 1958 and São Paulo Bienal in 1961, when he won the Sanbra Prize, as well as in Brussels, Copenhagen, Oslo, Paris, Rotterdam and Zürich. Scott's Scottish-Ulster background is reflected in the rather austere still lifes of pots and pans for which he became famous, although he was capable of employing quite voluptuous colour. Elected RA in 1984, by which time the first symptoms of the Alzheimer's disease, which prevented him from doing much work in his final years, were becoming evident. The 1950s and 1960s had seen a series of retrospective exhibitions in Zürich, Hanover,

Berne and Belfast, and there was one at Tate Gallery, which holds his work, in 1972, another at Bernard Jacobson Gallery, 1997. He was married to the artist Mary Scott.

Bill SCOTT-BROWN: *see* **Walter Graham SCOTT-BROWN**

Walter Graham SCOTT-BROWN 1897–1987 Artist, especially noted for work in pastel, known as Bill Scott-Brown. He was born in London. After Army service with distinction on the continent in World War I he entered Corpus Christi College, Cambridge, as an exhibitioner, proceeding to St Bartholomew's Hospital where he graduated in 1925. He became a distinguished ear, nose and throat surgeon who wrote the classic textbook on this subject. From 1950 he studied with his friend the artist Paul Maze and with Dunoyer de Segonzac and went on to exhibit in London, Edinburgh and abroad. Was for some time honorary secretary of PS. Lived near Alresford, Hampshire.

Melissa SCOTT-MILLER 1959– Painter, noted for highly detailed oils of scenes and interiors in London, where she was born and lived and attended the Slade School of Fine Art. Showed at RA Summer Exhibition, RP, *The Spectator* Art Prize Exhibition and BP Portrait Awards. She won the Lord Leighton Prize and the Lucy Morrison Award at the Royal Over-Seas League and second prize in the South Bank Picture Show. In 1997 was one of Four British Artists at Grosvenor Gallery. Solo shows included Royal Over-Seas League and Acquavella Gallery, New York, in America.

Elizabeth SCOTT-MOORE 1902–1993 Painter and illustrator, notable as a fluent watercolourist, born in Dartford, Kent, as Edith Elizabeth Brier, which she used to illustrate books published by Blackie, Nelson and Oxford University Press. Her mother, born Victoria Carruthers, was an illustrator of children's books. When Elizabeth Scott-Moore's husband died in 1947 she changed to painting. She had trained under Edmund J Sullivan at Goldsmiths' College School of Art in the 1920s, also attending the Central School of Arts and Crafts. In 1957 she was chosen as one of Jack Beddington's *Young Artists of Promise*, in the book of that title. Showed at RA Summer Exhibitions and RP; RI, RWS and NEAC, all of which she was a member; and Paris Salon, where in 1962 her portrait of her artist friend Alfred Hayward won a Gold Medal. Ministry of Works owned her work. Died in Virginia Water, Surrey.

Elizabeth SCOTT-TAGGART 1927– Artist in wood and stone, born in Penge, Kent. She studied at Central School of Arts and Crafts, 1945–8, then St Martin's School of Art, 1948–9. Main works were carved in wood, and favoured subjects were athletes and animals. Scott-Taggart, who signed work est, was a member of Free Painters and Sculptors and Buckinghamshire Art Society. Also showed at RA and RBA and locally and had solo shows at Century Galleries, Henley-on-Thames, 1984 and 1987. Lived in Beaconsfield, Buckinghamshire.

Glen SCOULLER 1950– Painter and teacher, born in Glasgow. He studied at the School of Art there, 1968–72, and as a postgraduate, 1973, in 1972–3 also studying at Patrick Allan-Fraser School of Art, Hospitalfield, Arbroath. For many years he taught at Cranhill School, from 1985–9 also teaching at Glasgow School of Art, then giving up teaching to paint full-time. In 1989 he was elected to the Royal Glasgow Institute of the Fine Arts. He participated in many group shows and had a series of one-mans, including John D Kelly Gallery, in Glasgow; Scottish Gallery, in Edinburgh; Fine Art Society, Glasgow; and Portland Gallery. Scouller won a number of awards, including the Royal Glasgow Institute's Scottish Amicable Award and Glasgow Art Club Lauder Award. Scouller used strong primary colours in his landscapes and still lifes, his palette being especially suited to landscapes of Provence, shown at Portland Gallery in 1992. Scottish Arts Council holds his work.

Audrey SCOVELL 1942– Artist in a variety of media who worked in television production for Independent Television News before starting printmaking, drawing and painting in the early 1970s. She was a member of the Greenwich Printmakers' Association. Showed at RA Summer Exhibition from 1977, RE from1981 and in Whitechapel Open Exhibition, 1986. Took part in four-man show at Woodlands Art Gallery, 1989. After a solo show at Tudor Barn, Eltham, 1982, later one-man exhibitions included Liberty's Picture Gallery from 1985. Lived in Bromley, Kent.

Bob SCRIVEN 1943– Sculptor and teacher, born in London. He studied at St Albans School of Art and Royal Academy Schools and became principal lecturer in charge of sculpture at Liverpool Polytechnic. Robert Scriven used wood and steel, favouring welded steel for the flexibility of form it offered. His sculpture was positive, optimistic, entertaining and anecdotal, and he sometimes used bright colour to add gaeity and even vulgarity to a piece. In 1979 Scriven participated in Sculpture for the Blind at Nottingham Castle and in 1983 his works Locarno Lady and Bingo Bango were included in shows at the Yorkshire Sculpture Park and Landmark Park, Scotland. In the same year he was included in the Welsh Sculpture Trust Margam exhibition Sculpture in a Country Park.

John T SCRIVENER 1907– Painter, printmaker and teacher, born in Little Wratting, Suffolk. Studied at Cambridge School of Art and went on to teach, partly in the Midlands, where he showed widely. Lived in Stafford where, after Army service in World War II, he taught at the County School of Arts and Crafts.

Janet SCRYMGEOUR WEDDERBURN 1941– Sculptor and stained glass designer, born in Winchester, Hampshire. After attending Convent of the Sacred Heart, Bridge of Earn, Perthshire, she studied with the sculptor Alastair Ross in the early-1970s, awards including RSA's Benno Schotz Prize, 1973. She showed at RSA and Paris Salon and was made a fellow of RBS in 1980. The east window of the Episcopal Church of St James the Great in Cupar, Fife, where she lived, was by her.

Louise SCULLION 1966– Artist who used painting, print-making installations and photography, born in Helensburgh,

Dunbartonshire. She showed individually and with Matthew Dalziel as Dalziel & Scullion. She studied at Glasgow School of Art, 1984–8, graduating with a first-class honours degree in fine art (environmental art). Gained the Cargill Travelling Scholarship and went to North America. Between 1989–95 held several residencies, latterly at Banff & Bucan District, 1994–5. Her exhibitions and commissions incuded Reconnaissance Bench, commissioned by Glasgow Garden Festival, 1988; The Lie of The Land, Compass Gallery, Glasgow, 1990; and The Furnished Landscape, Crafts Council Gallery, 1992. Lived at St Combs, near Peterhead in Aberdeenshire.

Sean SCULLY 1945– Painter and teacher, born in Dublin. After Croydon College of Art Scully studied at Newcastle University, 1968–71, from which he graduated and where he taught for a while in the early-1970s. About this time he also studied at Harvard. Scully further taught at Chelsea School of Art. He had a first one-man show at Rowan Gallery in 1973, from which Arts Council bought its picture, Red, of 1972. Scully took part in many group shows, including Northern Young Contemporaries and Young Contemporaries, 1971; Spectrum, North, 1972; the John Moores Exhibition, Liverpool; and abroad. In 1988–9 Scully was included in The Presence of Painting, the South Bank Centre's touring review of British abstraction in 1957–88. In 1989 Scully was given a major show at Whitechapel Art Gallery, with a 20 year retrospective at the Irish Museum of Modern Art, Kilmainham, 1996. Scully worked in stripes, broken up into interlocking squares and rectangles; the picture surface could consist of overlapping canvases. He lived in New York from 1976 and became an American citizen in 1983.

Elliott SEABROOKE 1886–1950 Painter, especially of landscape, and actor, born in Upton Park, Essex (his adopted name combined that of his father, Robert Elliott, with his mother's, Harriet Seabrooke). Seabrooke studied at Slade School of Fine Art, 1906–11, with Henry Tonks, then took a remote shed in Westmorland for £2 a year as a studio, putting in his own windows, door and chimney. In World War I Seabrooke – a pacifist – served in the British Red Cross, won Italy's highest award for gallantry and was an official war artist on the Italian front. He was tall and handsome, with a fine singing voice, which led to a thespian career. Did much work with the directors Theodore Komisarjevsky and J B Fagan, and acted with John Gielgud, Lewis Casson, Sybil Thorndike, Wendy Hiller, Charles Laughton and Ralph Richardson. Also appeared in films, including Gabriel Pascal's *Major Barbara*, 1941, but preferred the stage, which left the day free for painting. He showed at NEAC, LG of which he was vice-president and president during most of the 1940s, having had a first solo show at Carfax Gallery, 1912. Seabrooke was much influenced initially by Cézanne in both style and palette, Italian Futurism and Pointillism being later influences. Travelled widely in England and on the continent for landscape subjects, after 1930 living often in the Netherlands. Died in Nice and had memorial shows at Leicester Galleries, 1951; Arts Council 1952; 1955 at Matthiesen Gallery; and in 1966 at Upper Grosvenor Galleries. There was a show at Blond Fine Art in 1979. Tate Gallery, Imperial War Museum and Arts Council hold examples.

Allen William SEABY 1867–1953 Painter, colour woodcut artist, writer and teacher, born in London. Studied under F Morley Fletcher at Reading University's school of art, where from 1920–33 he was professor of fine art. He exhibited at the Fine Art Society, RSA, Royal Glasgow Institute of the Fine Arts and on the continent. He illustrated a number of books and wrote on a variety of subjects, including *Art in the Life of Mankind*, 1928–31, *British Ponies*, 1936, and *Blondel the Minstrel*, 1951, as well as on *Colour Printing with Linoleum and Wood Blocks*, 1928. Signed work AWS. His son was the painter Wilfred Seaby. Lived in Reading, Berkshire.

Wilfred A SEABY 1910–1991 Curator and watercolourist, born in Reading, Berkshire, son of the painter Allen William Seaby. He studied at Reading School of Art, 1926–7, and was from 1962–70 director of Belfast's Ulster Museum, which holds several works by him. Lived latterly at Solihull, West Midlands.

Harry SEAGER 1931– Sculptor in variety of media including glass, and teacher, born in Birmingham, where he attended the College of Arts and Crafts, 1951–5. Seager settled in Stourbridge, Worcestershire, lecturing at the College of Art. Contemporary Art Society, Leeds City Art Gallery and Department of the Environment hold examples. Had several solo shows at Gimpel Fils from 1965.

Edward SEAGO 1910–1974 Oil and watercolour painter and draughtsman. Despite ill-health as a child and parental resistance, Seago painted from an early age, studying at the Royal Drawing Society and winning a prize when aged only 14. Although substantially self-taught as a painter, he did receive invaluable instruction from the RA Bertram Priestman, who left a mark on his style. As a young man Seago began his association with travelling shows and circuses. Such scenes featured in his first one-man show, at the Sporting Gallery in 1933, where he had an instant success. He was to retain a wide and loyal public following until his death, but did not get much critical favour. He travelled and exhibited widely, showing at the RA, RBA, RHA, ROI, RCamA and in galleries in many countries overseas. Seago was also a lively and entertaining writer. Books by him or illustrated by him include *Tideline, Circus Company, Peace in War, With the Allied Armies in Italy*; he often worked with the poet John Masefield, examples being *The Country Scene* and *A Generation Risen*. Seago was a lover of East Anglia, the Norfolk Broads and sailing, could be a masterly watercolourist and painter of Broadland. His later, more commercial overseas work has tended to overshadow his quieter, early East Anglian work, also his fine flower-pieces. Lived at Ludham, Norfolk.

Barney SEALE 1896–1957 Sculptor and painter, noted for his portrait sculptures in bronze, but also as an architectural sculptor. He worked with the sculptor William Silver Frith, who taught at

Lambeth School of Art and who was also an architectural sculptor. Seale was elected RBA in 1938, also exhibiting at RA, RCamA and RSA and having solo shows in London and New York. He was an associate of RBS. Seale's striking figure I Write for the New Kensington Library, one of a series of three and in stone, is illustrated in Arthur T Broadbent's *Sculpture Today in Great Britain 1940–1943*, published in 1949. In 1986 the Fine Art Society included him in the survey Sculpture in Britain Between The Wars. Seale, a huge, hard-drinking man who was fond of good living, was a noted member of the Chelsea Arts Club. He was commercially astute and produced successful portrait busts of artists Augustus John, Joseph Simpson and C R W Nevinson. Lived in London and Walton-on-Thames, Surrey.

Colin SEALY 1891–1964 Painter, muralist and teacher, born in Cirencester, Gloucestershire, full name Cuthbert Collingwood Sealy. He spent part of his early life in Ceylon, where he was a tea planter for a time. Early in World War I, for which he was medically unfit to serve, Sealy married the artist Doris Vaughan. He worked at the department store Peter Jones in Chelsea, then in the early 1920s studied at the Royal Academy Schools. In 1924 he began teaching life drawing at Camberwell School of Arts and Crafts, about the time that he painted several privately commissioned murals. Cubism and abstraction influenced him, as seen in works shown with the 7 & 5 Society. During World War II Sealy worked as a camouflage officer for the Directorate of Camouflage, in 1944 being appointed to the American government's Office of Strategic Services at Leamington Spa as a modeller. Sealy separated from Vaughan by the mid-1950s, a period when his reputation declined. He died unrecognised living at Mousehole, Cornwall. A joint exhibition of Sealy and Vaughan was held at Belgrave Gallery in 1977.

Adrian SEARLE 1953– Figurative painter, critic and exhibition organiser, born in Welwyn Garden City, Hertforshire. He studied at St Albans School of Art, 1971–2, Trent Polytechnic, 1972–3, and Winchester School of Art, 1973–5. Among exhibitions he organised were ones for Atlantis Gallery in 1982 and Ikon Gallery, Birmingham, 1983. He was included in shows at Arnolfini Gallery, Bristol, and tour, 1979; Serpentine Gallery, 1984; and in 1985 he won a prize in John Moores Liverpool Exhibition. Arts Council holds his picture Hubris, of 1984. Lived for a time in London.

Ronald SEARLE 1920– Artist, notably a humorous draughtsman, and designer, born in Cambridge, where he attended the School of Art and had first work published in the local daily paper and *Granta*, 1935–9. Served in Army, 1939–46, being a Japanese prisoner-of-war, 1942–5. Began freelancing for national publications in 1946, including *News Chronicle*, *Punch* and *New Yorker*. Searle's extensive publications included *Forty Drawings*, 1946; *Hurrah for St Trinian's!*, 1948; *The Rake's Progress*, 1955; *Searle in the Sixties*, 1964; *Searle's Cats*, 1967; *Ronald Searle*, 1978; *Ronald Searle in Perspective*, 1984; and *To the Kwai – and Back*, 1986. Among films designed by Searle were the animation sequence in *Those Magnificent Men in their Flying Machines*, 1965. Five St Trinian's films were produced, the last being *The Wildcats of St Trinian's*, 1980. Searle designed medals for the French Mint and British Art Medal Society and was made a Royal Designer of Industry, 1988. He had extensive international shows, beginning with Batsford Gallery, 1947, a series at Leicester Galleries from 1948, later ones including Imperial War Museum and British Museum, 1986, Fitzwilliam Museum in Cambridge, 1987, and Museum of Fine Arts, San Francisco, 1987–8. Tate Gallery, Imperial War Museum, British Museum, Victoria & Albert Museum and foreign collections hold examples.

Helen SEDDON fl. c.1925–1955 Painter who was born in Chelmarsh, Shropshire. The daughter of a New Zealand sheep farmer, she studied art partly there, but went to school in Worcester. Also studied painting in Edinburgh and Paris and with Charles Simpson and Fred Milner. Settled in St Ives, Cornwall, where she was a member of the St Ives Society of Artists. Exhibited there, at SWA, in Bristol and elsewhere. A keen traveller.

Richard SEDDON 1915– Painter, printmaker, draughtsman, teacher and writer, born in Sheffield, Yorkshire. Studied at the College of Arts and Crafts there, 1932–6, then at Royal College of Art design school, gaining his diploma in 1939. Seddon then volunteered for the Army, but after active service – graphically described in his memoir *A Hand Uplifted*, 1963 – he was released to research history, psychology and aesthetic philosophy at University of Reading from 1943, gaining his doctorate in 1946. Seddon's two main appointments were as director of Sheffield City Art Galleries, 1948–64, and of art history and complementary studies at Buckinghamshire College of Technology and Art, 1964–80. Among commissions undertaken were the design of decorations in 1952 for the main streets and buildings of Sheffield for the Queen's coronation. Seddon's picture subjects were usually British and continental landscapes. Among mixed shows were National Gallery first War Artists' Exhibition and Pilgrim Trust, both 1941; RWS Gallery, Britain in Watercolours, 1952; Leeds City Art Gallery, Yorkshire Artists, 1954; Whitworth Art Gallery, Manchester, Paintings of the North, 1987; and RA, NEAC and RBA. A solo show of his war pictures was held at Graves Art Gallery, Sheffield, 1941. Imperial War Museum, Victoria & Albert Museum and public galleries in Reading, Sheffield and Southport hold examples. Seddon was art critic for *The Guardian*, *The Birmingham* and *Yorkshire Posts* and *The Art Magazine*. Among his books are *The Illustrated Dictionary of Art Terms*, with Kimberley Reynolds, 1981, and *The Artist's Studio Book*, 1983. Lived in London.

Peter SEDGLEY 1930– Artist who besides painting employed audio-visual means and special light effects to achieve his ends. He was born in London and studied architecture at Brixton Technical School, 1944–6. In the mid-1960s he began to make an impact with several exhibitions at McRoberts and Tunnard Gallery and at Howard Wise Gallery, in New York. In 1966 he was a prizewinner at Tokyo Biennale. The 1970s saw Sedgley making a considerable impression at exhibitions in Germany. He was commissioned to provide an audio-visual display for the Donaueschingen Music Festival, in 1972. The following year he had a retrospective at Ikon Gallery, Birmingham. Went on to show with Redfern Gallery. Was included in The Sixties Art Scene in London, Barbican Art Gallery, 1993. Arts Council holds his work. Lived for some years in Berlin, Germany.

Jørgen SEDGWICK fl. from early 1950s– Painter, printmaker and teacher, notable for atmospheric landscapes and seascapes in gouache. He was born in Copenhagen, Denmark, but settled in London in 1946. Studied at Regent Street Polytechnic and Beckenham Schools of Art and went on to become senior lecturer at Croydon College School of Art. Was an extensive exhibitor, including Young Contemporaries from 1950; RA from 1952; RBA, 1952; AIA from 1954; Beaux Arts Gallery from 1955; John Moores Liverpool Exhibition, 1959; Reading University and South London Art Gallery from 1969; Greenwich Theatre Gallery, 1979; and in 1981 he shared a three-man exhibition at Woodlands Art Gallery.

Irena SEDLECKÁ 1928– Sculptor, born in Pilsen, Czechoslovakia. Studied at secondary school there for four years, from 1945–9 attending the sculpture school of the Academy of Creative Arts, teachers including Karel Pokorný. In the years 1945–6–9 she achieved an honorary mention and her final state diploma work was a portrait. Sedlecká has work in Prague's National Gallery and she was also engaged for the Monument for the Victims of Fascism in Moravia at Velke Meziřici. With two other sculptors (one, Ludwig Kodym, became her first husband) she worked on several prestigious projects, including reliefs for the walls of Lenin Museum, Prague, which won the Museum competition. Sedlecká moved to England in 1966. Her second husband, a paediatrician, decided to return after the Prague Spring uprising of 1968, but she stayed; in 1997 the sculptor Franta Belsky became her third husband. Sedlecká joined SPS and became a fellow of RBS, living in London, with a studio in Watford. Actors, singers, musicians and television personalities became her subjects. Among these was a series of portraits of Callas, Gielgud, Olivier, Sutherland and others for the actor and collector Richard Bebb. Her statue of the singer Freddie Mercury overlooks Lake Geneva in Montreux, Switzerland.

David SEEGER 1937– Artist and teacher who studied at Leeds College of Art. He also taught there and was included in The Teaching Image, the 1964 exhibition of its staff's work at Leeds City Art Gallery. Seeger's exhibits included pieces in ciment fondu; Construction, in wood, metal and glass; and Panel, made of tiles and metal. He was also notable as a potter. Took part in group shows at AIA Gallery, 1961, and Gimpel Fils.

Colin SEE-PAYNTON 1946– Painter and printmaker, also known as Colin Paynton, who studied under Henry Bird at Northampton School of Art, 1963–5. Among his printed page work were illustrations for private press publications. He was made an associate of RCamA in 1982 and a full member of SWE in 1984 and of both SWLA and RE in 1986. Also exhibited at RA, RWS and elsewhere and had a retrospective toured by Glynn Vivian Art Gallery, Swansea, in 1996. Lived in Berriew, Powys.

Hyman SEGAL 1914– Painter, sculptor, draughtsman and designer, born in London, who studied at St Martin's School of Art with Leon Underwood and Vivian Pitchforth. Segal was a member of RBA, a National Registered Designer and saw the founding of Penwith Society of Arts in 1949 and its stormy emergence from St Ives Society of Artists, of which he had been a committee member. He showed at RP, Workers' Educational Association, Whitechapel and Truro Art Galleries and elsewhere widely in the provinces plus the Paris Salon. Many solo shows included Bankfield Museum in Halifax, Heffer Gallery in Cambridge and Castle Gallery and The Crypt, both in St Ives, Cornwall, where he lived for many years. Manchester City Art Gallery and National Museum of Wales in Cardiff hold examples.

Doris SEIDLER 1912– Artist, notably a printmaker, born in London, who studied with S W Hayter at Atelier 17, New York, America, where she settled. Seidler received fellowships from Tamarind Lithographic Workshop; The McDowell Artists' Colony; awards from Brooklyn Museum, which has work in its collection; Potsdam Printmakers; Print Club Philadelphia; Audubon Artists; and the Society of American Graphic Artists, of which was a vice-president. She had extensive group and solo shows in America and abroad, including ICA, Redfern and St George's Galleries. In 1955 she showed solo at the Schools of Art in Norwich, Yarmouth and Ipswich, with another at Pallant House, Chichester, in 1991. Seidler gave a series of prints to Pallant House, including some of the Cathedral Series, done during visits of England. British Museum, Library of Congress, several American universities and the Seattle and Philadelphia Museums of Art also hold examples.

Adele SEIGAL 1928– Painter and printmaker, born in South Africa, who moved to England in 1959. Largely a self-taught artist, she concentrated on landscape of Provence, France, where she spent part of the year, also on Little Venice, London, where she made her home. Had a solo show at Coram Gallery, 1995.

Geneviève SEILLÉ 1951– Artist in various media, including performance, and teacher, born in France. She taught in schools in France and England, 1970–6, then did a fine art honours degree course at Wolverhampton Polytechnic, 1978–81, following a two years' foundation course at Stafford College of Further Education. While in Wolverhampton during the period 1979–83 she was engaged in performance work at the Arena Studio. She was also involved in puppet and drama workshops, freelance teaching and was artist-in-residence at Stoke-on-Trent Museum and Art Gallery in 1990, carrying out the same role in schools in Warwickshire in 1990–91 and in a school in Nuneaton in 1991. Seillé took part in many group shows, mainly in the Midlands. She had a solo exhibition at Eagle Work Gallery, Wolverhampton, in 1989, other such shows including England & Co, 1992. Seillé's works on paper and her book-works drew on such sources as graffiti, music, medieval books on anatomy and armour to create her own "cosmology". Victoria & Albert Museum holds her work.

Jozef SEKALSKI 1904–1972 Painter, printmaker, designer, illustrator and teacher, born in Turek, Poland. Studied medicine for several years but gave it up to study, from 1929–34, at Wilno University's faculty of fine art. Then painted church murals until in 1937 he became head of a studio in Lodz. Escaped from occupied Poland in 1940 and travelled to Budapest, where he held a very successful print show depicting the burning of Warsaw. More travels took him to France where he enlisted in the French-run Polish Army, was captured and escaped to Scotland where in 1942 he rejoined the Polish Army. Settled in St Andrews where he became a member of a key wood engraving circle and built up a reputation as a book designer and etcher. From 1957 lectured in printmaking at Duncan of Jordanstone College of Art in Dundee. Showed with SSA, of which he was elected a member, RE, RA, RSA and elsewhere. His paintings can show a marked Cubist influence.

William SELBY 1933– Painter, self-taught, noted for his painterly still lifes and bar scenes. He was born at Fitzwilliam, Yorkshire, son of a miner. He worked in the mines, 1948–55, did his National Service, 1955–7, then worked in engineering and insurance until he became a full-time painter in 1974. He became ROI in 1982, RBA in 1990 and RWS in 1992 and won several awards. Took part in group exhibitions at Hallam Gallery, Century Gallery, Linda Blackstone Gallery in Pinner, Adam Gallery in Bath, Catto Gallery and Anna-Mei Chadwick. Had a solo show at Adam Gallery in 1995. Mappin Art Gallery in Sheffield holds Selby's work. Lived in Byrom-cum-Sutton, Yorkshire.

John SELBY-BIGGE: *see* **John BIGGE**

Colin SELF 1941– Artist who studied at Wymondham College, Norwich Art School and Slade School of Fine Art. He had strong Pop affiliations, his 1960s work being especially influential. The artist Richard Hamilton called Self "the best draughtsman in England since William Blake"; when he "went through a period painting landscape watercolours, it was as though Cotman had come to life again". Had many group shows including Galleria Milano, Milan, 1965; Camden Arts Centre, 1967; Tokyo International Print Biennale, 1969; Museum of Modern Art, New York, 1972–3; China and Hong Kong tour, 1982; Comic Iconoclasm, ICA, 1987; and Chappel Galleries, Chappel, Continuing the Tradition, 1993. Solo shows included Piccadilly Gallery, 1964–5; Alecto Gallery, 1968; Fermoy Centre, King's Lynn, 1979; ICA, 1986, and Tate Gallery, 1995–6. That exhibition, drawing on the Tate's large holding of Self's work in a range of media, indicated how his interests had been redirected since his return to Norfolk in the 1970s, concerned with landscape, his children, the art of the past, politics, money and the unemployed, which the artist termed "works of fusion". Also showed solo in France and Germany. Arts Council also holds examples. Lived in Thorpe, Norwich, Norfolk.

Lawrence SELF 1924– Painter and draughtsman, born in Sutton, Surrey. After Brentwood School and war service, 1944–7, Self was at Wimbledon School of Art, 1947–9, then Royal College of Art, 1949–52, winning a Richards Travelling Scholarship. From 1957 he settled in Suffolk. Selected group exhibitions were Royal College of Art Painting School, at RWS, 1952; East Anglian Painting Competition, 1963, at King Street Gallery, Cambridge, where he was a prize winner; East Anglian Art Today, at Royal Institute Gallery, 1969; and Laing Art Competition, at Mall Galleries, 1989, where he was an East Anglian Regional Prizewinner. Self also showed at RA from 1956 and NEAC from 1988. His series of solo shows, in which he was distinguished by his meticulous draughtsmanship, began at East Anglian Gallery, Ipswich, 1963. Later ones included Gainsborough's House, Sudbury, and Royal Shakespeare Theatre, Stratford-upon-Avon, both 1974; and there was a retrospective at Christchurch Mansion, Ipswich, 1991. Nottinghamshire, Hertfordshire, Carlisle and Coventry Education Committees hold his work. Lived latterly at Rattlesden, near Bury St Edmunds.

Robert Gordon SELLAR 1920– Prolific artist in many media and teacher, born at Berwick, East Lothian. An early influence was his father, a marine engineering draughtsman, who on walks acquainted his son with the Belfast locality; a Christian education also encouraged an interest in its symbolism. Studied at Belfast College of Art, 1939–43, teachers including Ivor Beaumont, Newton Penprase and Edward Mansfield. Teaching included Belfast Royal Academy and its College of Art, then Sellar was an adviser in art education, finally with the North-Eastern Education and Library Board, retiring in 1984. He was a member of RUA, Coleraine Art Society and Pastel Society of Ireland. Later solo shows included a series from 1979 at Coleraine University, Northern Ireland, near which he lived. Arts Council holds his work, and he designed a stained glass window for Ballycastle Presbyterian Church.

Dorothea SELOUS fl. c.1905–1960 Painter and potter, born and lived in London, married to the artist Robert Kirkland Jamieson. After private education she studied at Royal Academy Schools and in Paris. Exhibited RA, RBA of which she was a member, LG, NEAC, SWA and RI. Belfast Art Gallery holds her work.

John SELWAY 1938– Painter and teacher, born in Askern, Yorkshire, although as a baby he moved to his parents' birthplace at Abertillery, Monmouthshire. In 1953–7 he attended Newport College of Art, then after two years' National Service returned to study at Royal College of Art, 1959–62. In 1962–3 a University of London Boise Travelling Scholarship enabled him to paint in Portugal. He returned to teach at Newport College of Art and became a member of 56 Group for many years. Showed extensively, including Young Contemporaries, Café Royal Centenary Exhibition in 1965, Camden Arts Centre, SWG, WAC and International Arts Fairs in Basle and Düsseldorf. Solo shows were at Roland, Browse and Delbanco, Piccadilly Gallery and elsewhere. He was represented in the WAC touring show The Probity of Art, 1980. WAC, Arts Council and National Museum of Wales, Cardiff, hold his work. Lived in Abertillery.

William SELWYN 1933– Painter, especially of watercolours, and teacher. He was born in Caernarvon and attended Bangor Normal College in 1954–6, later teaching in Caernarvon. A member of WSW he showed at Arun Art Centre in Arundel, Albany Gallery in Cardiff, RBA and RWA. Won the Anfield and Everton Prize for Art in 1956; RCamA Saxon Barton Prize in 1961; and was a Royal National Eisteddfod prize-winner in 1974. Albany Gallery and National Library of Wales, Aberystwyth, gave him one-man shows. CASW holds his watercolour A Ferry in Scotland.

John SEMMENCE 1930–1985 Painter, draughtsman and teacher, born in Kincardine O'Neil, Aberdeenshire. He was educated at Robert Gordon's College, Aberdeen, and at Gray's School of Art there, 1947–52, under Robert Sivell. In 1953 a travelling scholarship took him to Rome, then he had several years painting in Paris, returning to Britain in 1957, settling in London. He taught, becoming head of art at St John's Comprehensive School, Newham. In 1982 early retirement gave Semmence the opportunity to paint full-time again. His landscapes, townscapes and interiors were distinctive, with an unusual palette and clearly defined shapes, light and shadow. He was a member of UA and showed in group exhibitions at RSA, NEAC, RBA and elsewhere. Had a series of solo shows, including 6½ Suffolk Street, Edinburgh Festival, Mall Galleries and Commonwealth Institute. Nuffield Foundation holds his work. Lived in Beckenham, Kent.

Gabriel SEMPILL 1945– Versatile artist, born in London, who studied at Colchester School of Art, 1963, taught plant drawing by John Nash. After briefly studying ceramics at Royal College of Art, drew insects for several years at Natural History Museum, specialising in bird lice, but in the early 1980s began to exhibit her own pen and ink drawings and concentrated on book illustration, contributing to *The Celtic Inheritance*, 1985, and in the early 1990s moved into printmaking. Showed at first National Print Exhibition, Mall Galleries, and at New Ashgate Gallery, Farnham, both 1994, and in 1995 had a solo exhibition, Within the Garden Square, at Oriel Contemporary Art.

Carol SEMPLE 1958– Artist whose output included abstract patterned works with some figuration, as in her solo show at Cree Gallery, Gatehouse of Fleet, 1997. She studied at Duncan of Jordanstone College of Art, Dundee, for an honours degree in drawing and painting, 1980–4, gaining her master's there, 1984–5. In the latter year she won a Pollack Travelling Scholarship. Was artist-in-residence, Dumfries and Galloway Arts Association, 1988. Commissions included Dundee District Council and Dundee University, both 1985; Standard Life, Kirkcaldy, 1986; Edinburgh Book Festival and Scottish Ballet, in Glasgow, both 1989; and Sheraton Caltrust, Belfast, 1990. Group exhibitions included Aberdeen Artists, Aberdeen, 1986; Royal Glasgow Institute of the Fine Arts, 1989; RSA, 1991; Compass Gallery, Glasgow, from 1992; and Paisley Fine Art Institute, 1995. Lived in Glasgow.

Antonio SENA 1941– Painter and printmaker, born in Lisbon, Portugal, where he studied science at the university. In London attended St Martin's School of Art, 1966–7, his teachers including John Latham, obtaining a Calouste Gulbenkian Scholarship. Exhibited in various international mixed shows, winning first prize in the General Motors Art Exhibitions in Lisbon, 1968, including ICA, London. One-man shows included Lisson Gallery. Lived for some years in London.

John SENDALL 1947– Painter of landscapes and the female nude, born in Barnstaple, Devon, who studied under John Wonnacott at the University of Reading. Was included in Four British Artists at Grosvenor Gallery, 1997.

Nadin SENFT 1932– Sculptor in a range of materials, born in London. She studied at Leicester College of Art and City and Guilds of London Art School, gaining her fine art diploma in 1968. Showed at RA, Alwin Gallery, Annely Juda Fine Art, Richard Demarco Gallery in Edinburgh and elsewhere. Among her commissions was Seated Bronze Figures for Guildhall Square, Portsmouth. Lived in Tredington, Warwickshire.

Bryan SENIOR 1935– Artist in oil and acrylic, born in Bolton, Lancashire. He studied at Clifton College, Cambridge University and Chelsea School of Art and lived in London from 1957. In that year he won Clare Prize, Cambridge; other awards included Greater London Council Spirit of London, 1981, and Druce-Constable, 1986. Senior's work covered figures, streets, landscape and still life. He had a wide range of solo shows, including Crane Kalman and Fieldborne Galleries, Architectural Association, Richard Demarco Gallery in Edinburgh, Ashgate Gallery in Farnham and abroad, including Ireland, Italy and America. CASW, Nuffield Foundation, *Financial Times*, Hampstead Museum and Bolton Museum and Art Gallery hold examples. Lived in Tunbridge Wells, Kent.

Gordon SENIOR 1942– Mixed-media artist and teacher, born in Yorkshire. He attended Wakefield College of Art, 1958–60, Leeds College of Art, 1960–3, for diploma and postgraduate studies, and Goldsmiths' College, 1963–4, for a teaching certificate. As well as extensive visiting lecturing experience, Senior taught at Clarendon College of Further Education, 1964–6; Newcastle Polytechnic, 1966–90; then Norfolk Institute of Art and Design. Between 1986–92 Senior took part in exhibitions with the Newcastle Group in Britain and abroad. Other group exhibitions included Tolly Cobbold Eastern Arts 5th National Exhibition, 1985; Nine from Newcastle, Ukrainian Museum of Modern Art, Chicago, 1986; Three Artists from the North of England, RIBA, 1988; and Ten Days, Pyramid Arts Centre, 1991. He had a solo show at LYC Gallery, Brampton, in 1981, later ones including City Art Gallery, Dundee, 1989. Various collections in the United Kingdom hold Senior's work, the main concern of which "is the relationship between humans and earth … Man is an integral part of nature, not over or apart from nature." Lived in Norwich, Norfolk.

William SENIOR 1927– Artist using gouache, and oil with wax medium, born and lived in Glasgow, where he attended non-diploma classes in drawing and painting. Hugh Adam Crawford, his teacher, commented: "Senior, you are a painter's painter." Senior's output of landscapes and still lifes was small; he claimed to be "not only unambitious, but very lazy, a Laodicean, as Thomas Hardy put it." Painting influences were many, and Delacroix's and Gauguin's *Journals*, Sickert's *A Free House*, Whistler's *Ten o'clock* and Pissarro's *Letters to Lucien* were "goldmines". After returning from Paris, 1947–8, Senior "decided not to starve ever again, so I worked in bookshops, was a farm-hand near Mull, became a scene-hand with BBC Television, then went to the Groves of Academe in a television department where I did the graphics and studio sets." Group shows included Skelmorlie Community Centre, Glasgow's Iona Community House, Edinburgh's International House, Royal Glasgow Institute of the Fine Arts and with the New Scottish Group at McClellan Galleries. Had a well-reviewed solo show at Royal Glasgow Institute gallery, 1961, another at John D Kelly Gallery, 1988.

Emma SERGEANT 1959– Painter and draughtsman, born in London. She studied at Camberwell School of Art, 1978–9, and Slade School of Fine Art, 1979–83. In 1981 she won the Imperial Tobacco Award and the National Portrait Gallery Painting Competition. She had a first solo show at Agnew, 1984, with others including Paintings from Afghanistan, 1986, a subject repeated at Mona Bismarck Foundation, Paris, 1987. Commissions included Lord David Cecil for National Portrait Gallery, two po traits for Oxford University Press and Sir William Deacon, for St Anthony's College, Oxford.

John SERGEANT 1937– Painter and illustrator. He studied at Canterbury College of Art and Royal Academy Schools, where he won the Drawing Prize. Among books he illustrated were Charles Dickens' *Oliver Twist* and Richard Church's *Portrait of Canterbury*. Exhibited at RA, Trafford Gallery, New Metropole Arts Centre in Folkestone, London University and New Grafton Gallery. He had solo shows at Waterhouse Gallery. In 1994 Sergeant's drawings, with those of his friends John Ward and Jehan Daly, were featured in Three Contemporary Masters at Hazlitt, Gooden and Fox. Sergeant contributed to the Prince of Wales' book *Vision of Britain* and accompanied him on an official visit to Prague in 1991. Lived in Ashford, Kent.

Terry SETCH 1936– Painter and teacher, born in London. He attended Sutton and Cheam School of Art, 1950–54, then after National Service in Germany, 1954–6, was at Slade School of Fine Art, 1956–60, the final year being postgraduate studies. Setch then went on to teach, at Leicester College of Art, 1960–4; was organising tutor at Barry Summer School, 1963–9; and from 1964 was senior lecturer in painting at South Glamorgan Institute of Higher Education, Cardiff. Among Setch's other appointments was as visiting lecturer at Emily Carr College of Art, Vancouver, Canada, 1981; artist-in-residence at Victorian College of Art, Melbourne, Australia, 1983; and in 1987 he was elected to the faculty of British School in Rome. Setch also did extensive work as an external assessor and examiner for degree courses. For many years Setch combed the beaches along the Severn Estuary and used the detritus of society to create pictures of singular quality. As well as taking part in many mixed shows Setch had an extensive list of solo exhibitions, starting in 1965 at the Grabowski Gallery. More recent ones included Nigel Greenwood Gallery; Andrew Knight Gallery, Cardiff; and in 1992–3 an Oriel Welsh Arts Council show which toured Britain. Setch's work is held by Tate Gallery, Victoria & Albert Museum, Arts Council and other British and foreign collections. Lived in Penarth, South Wales.

Andrew SETO 1966– Painter, born in Edinburgh, who studied at University of Birmingham; St Martin's School of Art; New York School of Drawing, Painting & Sculpture; and Slade School of Fine Art, where he won the Coldstream Prize, 1989. Group exhibitions included Portobello Open IV at Tabernacle Gallery, East London Open Studios, Whitechapel Open at Whitechapel Art Gallery and Royal Over-Seas League Open, all 1994.

Joseph SEVIER 1961– Painter of figures and still life who studied art at University of New Mexico, Santa Fe, where the brilliant, vibrant light left a lasting impression on his work. Moved from America to England and from 1989 lived in Sandwich, Kent, undertaking many portrait commissions. Showed at RA Summer Exhibition and NEAC, both 1993, and at RP, 1994. In 1995 had a solo show at Montpelier Sandelson.

Prudence Eaton SEWARD 1926– Watercolourist and etcher, born and lived in London. She studied at Harrow School of Art, 1945–6, with Ernest Heber Thompson, then at Royal College of Art, 1947–9, with Robert Austin. Exhibited RA, RE and RBA.

Marc SEWELL 1930– Sculptor, painter and draughtsman whose preoccupation was with landscape and the human figure. He was born in Market Deeping, Lincolnshire, was educated at King's School, Peterborough, 1943–7, then studied photography and sculpture at Nottingham College of Art & Craft, 1949–52, gaining his master's in fine art at Goldsmiths' College, 1979–81. In 1984–6 he was appointed moderator for fine and applied art at degree level. Exhibitions included RA Summer Exhibition from 1981; Willis Poole Gallery, New York and Washington and an LG travelling show, all 1983; and Art '87, at Peterborough's Lady Lodge Arts Centre, 1987. Solo shows included one there, 1984. Commissions included Relief Panels, St Vincent House, Glasgow; Sculpture, head office of Walter Lawrence, Sawbridgeworth; Boundary Markers for City of London; and Thiepval War Memorial Model, Arts Council Lutyens Exhibition.

Robin SEWELL 1951– Painter and teacher, born in Leeds, Yorkshire, studying at the Jacob Kramer College there, 1969–70, then at Cardiff College of Art, 1970–3, and Slade School of Fine Art, 1973–5. From 1987 Sewell was senior lecturer at Canterbury School of Fine Art, showing regularly there in the Herbert Read Gallery and elsewhere in the United Kingdom, including John

Moores Liverpool Exhibition, 1997–8. His Castle (2), encaustic on panel, in that show was one of a series "like magnified etchings with dots and lines assembled and disassembled to describe and deny form". Sewell showed solo at The Showroom from 1983, and in 1984 at both Bradford University and The Cut Galleries. Lived in east London.

Eileen SEYD 1907– Painter, born in London, who studied at Central School of Arts and Crafts. Showed at NS, ROI, RA and elsewhere. Had one-man shows at Cooling and Parsons Galleries. Worked as an art therapist in the Middlesex area, where she lived at Hatch End.

Maria SEYDA 1893–1989 Painter of portraits in oil, brought up in Poland, she studied art at L'Ecole des Beaux-Arts in both Geneva and Warsaw and at the Atelier Colarossi, Paris. Her husband was Marian Seyda, minister of foreign affairs and wartime minister of congressional works in the Polish government-in-exile, who died in Buenos Aires, Argentina, in 1967. His wife began exhibiting at RA and RP in the 1940s, and in the English provinces. Lived for a time in London.

Dermot SEYMOUR 1956– Figurative painter, born in Belfast, who graduated from the University of Ulster there in 1978, obtaining his advanced diploma in 1981. His work was widely reviewed and among his awards were the Arts Council of Northern Ireland and An Chomhairle Ealaíon, the Claremorris Open and the Department of Foreign Affairs, Dublin. Group shows included Clean Irish Sea, Ireland and United Kingdom tour, 1989; and in 1994 Works on Paper and Beyond the Partitions, organised by Queen Street Studios, with which he was associated. Solo exhibitions included Art Research Exchange, Belfast, 1978 and 1981; Paula Allen Gallery, New York, 1987–8–9; and Pentonville Gallery, 1988. Latterly lived and worked in Country Mayo, Irish Republic.

Gabrielle King SEYMOUR fl. from late 1980s– Painter and decorative artist who studied at Byam Shaw School of Art, 1985–8, graduating with a diploma honours fine art degree. In 1988 Seymour took up specialist decorating, working for several years for individual clients and design studios in London and Paris. A mural for a Pompeian room setting at the Olympia Antiques Fair won first prize. For about a year from 1991 she worked in a WASPS studio in Glasgow, returning to London in 1992, where she occupied several ACAVA studios. Seymour mostly painted oil on canvas, large and boldly coloured works in which animals, especially dogs, figured repeatedly. She was "interested in the dynamic of the relationship between people and animals". Group shows included Leighton House, 1988; Dumbarton Road Studios, Glasgow, 1991; Chelsea Arts Club, 1995; and A Clear Picture, Collyer-Bristow Gallery, 1997.

Keith SHACKLETON 1923– Painter in oil notable for his interest in wildlife, and writer, born in Weybridge, Surrey. After early years in Australia his education continued at Oundle; served five years in the Royal Air Force; then had 15 years with the family aviation business as salesman and pilot, always painting in his spare time. As a small boat sailor he published two books, *Tidelines* and *Wake*, and represented Great Britain in international dinghy meetings. Gradually relinquishing aviation commitments he joined the BBC Television series *Animal Magic* and illustrated several bird books. Shackleton worked extensively as a naturalist on the ship *Lindblad Explorer*, mainly in the Antarctic, also handling film commentary assignments. In the late 1970s/early 1980s he presented *Animals in Action* for Survival Anglia Television. Shackleton was mainly known for pictures of the sea and seabirds. He was president of RSMA and SWLA, of which he was a founder-member, and was chairman of the Artists' League of Great Britain. In 1983 he was made an hon. Doctor of Laws at Birmingham University. *Wildlife and Wilderness – An Artist's World* and *Ship in the Wilderness* were later books. Showed at Tryon Gallery and Mall Galleries. National Maritime Museum in Greenwich and Nature in Art Museum, Gloucester, hold examples. Lived in London and south Devon.

Frederick SHAEFFER 1932– Painter and draughtsman, of American nationality, who won many awards, including first prize in a national oil painting competition and a year's scholarship to study in San Francisco. Dissatisfied with his studies in New York, because he wished to concentrate on drawing, Shaeffer attended Slade School of Fine Art, 1952, funded by the Kinsman Trust of the English Speaking Union. Utrillo, especially his White Period, was a marked influence on Shaeffer's work. In 1956 he shared an exhibition with Madeleine Pearson at Arthur Jeffress Pictures. Shaeffer travelled widely in Europe, and the show included landscapes of Ibiza, Torremolinos and the Pyrenees. Tate Gallery archive has an ink self-portrait.

Tony SHAFRAZI 1943– Sculptor, painter and art dealer. His work was shown at Camden Arts Centre in Survey '68: Abstract Sculpture, where it was remarked that it was "original in the sense that no-one else has made such a marriage of minimal abstraction with colour". Shafrazi was born in Abadan, Iran, and studied at Royal College of Art. He had a solo show at Galerie Swart, Amsterdam. He settled in New York, originally as a painter, then ran the Tony Shafrazi Gallery, which showed graffiti, sculpture and other art. Shafrazi made news in 1974 when he sprayed the words "Kill Lies All" in red paint on Picasso's Guérnica in the Museum of Modern Art in New York and was charged with criminal mischief. Arts Council holds Shafrazi's abstract sculpture Tablet, in fibreglass, of the late 1960s.

Marjorie Kathleen SHAKESPEARE 1899– Artist working in oil and tempera, who studied under Bernard Fleetwood-Walker at Birmingham College of Arts and Crafts. Went on to show at RA, ROI, RP, RBA and RBSA, of which she was made an associate in 1946. Lived in Enville, Staffordshire.

Manou SHAMA-LEVY 1947– Artist in watercolour, acrylic, oil and lino-cut, born in Alexandria, Egypt. She obtained a degree in French from University of Warwick, 1965–8; lived and worked in Paris with the painter François Imhoff, 1972–81; and attended life classes run by Gerry Calleja at the Working Men's College, 1990–5. Shama-Levy was originally concerned with abstract geometrical shapes, work developing through still lifes and landscapes compressed into flat surfaces of intense colour, portraits and privately commissioned murals. Exhibitions included Corner Gallery, 1972; FIAP, Paris, 1975; Art et Culture, Paris, 1979; Twopence Coloured Gallery, Whitney, 1987; and Studio Show, 1996. Lived in London.

Thomas J SHANAHAN 1945– Sculptor and craftworker who studied at St Hugh of Lincoln School, Venerable English College in Valladolid, Spain, and Oxford and Cambridge Universities, as well as spending some time in Nanjing, China. Shanahan came from several generations of craft iron workers, and studied black- and goldsmithing, jewellery, ceramics and sculpture. He was a member of the Educational Institute of Craft Design and Technology, Oxfordshire Craft Guild and a professional member of the British Artist Blacksmith Association. He worked mainly to commission. Showed at 1st RWA Open Sculpture Exhibition, 1993. Lived in Tintern, Gwent.

John SHANKIE 1957– Video, photographic, painter and performance artist, born in Lanark, who attended Glasgow School of Art 1984–89, then 1992–4. Exhibitions included Gracefield Arts Centre, Dumfries, and Young Glasgow Painters, McLellan Galleries, Glasgow, both 1986; A Gala Celebration, performances with Rotating Dancers at Kelvingrove Museum and Art Gallery and elsewhere, 1987; V: Photography in Fine Art, Glasgow School of Art, 1990; Contact 552 4813, Transmission Gallery, Glasgow, 1992; and New Art in Scotland, Centre for Contemporary Arts, Glasgow, 1994.

Duncan SHANKS 1937– Painter and teacher, born in Airdrie, Lanarkshire, where he continued to live, at Crossford, By Carluke. Shanks was a painter inspired by the river and valley close to his home and as an artist was highly regarded by his peers. He studied at Glasgow School of Art, receiving a post-diploma and travelling scholarship to Italy. He returned to teach at Glasgow School of Art, eventually becoming a full-time painter. Shanks won an Arts Council Award, Royal Glasgow Institute of the Fine Arts Torrance Award and the RSA Latimer Award as well as other awards and prizes. He was elected to the Royal Glasgow Institute in 1982, to RSW in 1987 and RSA in 1990. Shanks was included in a number of notable group shows, having solo exhibitions at Stirling University, Scottish Gallery in Edinburgh, Fine Art Society in Glasgow and Edinburgh and at other galleries. Scottish Arts Council, Arts Council and many Scottish galleries hold his work. Shanks' wife Una was also a painter.

Tom Hovell SHANKS 1921– Artist in watercolour, pen and ink, mixed media; muralist, designer and teacher, born in Glasgow. He left school to become an apprentice carpet designer for Templeton's, first exhibiting with the firm's art club. After war service Shanks took the diploma course at Glasgow School of Art. Upon graduating in 1950 he started on a career as a freelance mural painter; was a designer and printer with Edinburgh Weavers' Dovecot Studios for eight years; stage designer with Rutherglen Rep; and teacher at Glasgow School of Art and in schools in the city and in Renfrewshire, where he settled in Kilbarchan. However, he termed his main occupation "landscape painter", having been in love with the landscapes of the Western Highlands since his parents took him to the Isle of Skye aged seven. These were portrayed in his Scottish Horizons show at Cyril Gerber Fine Art, Glasgow, in 1994, and previously in solo exhibitions throughout Scotland. He was a member of RSW and Royal Glasgow Institute of the Fine Arts, also exhibiting with RSA, Royal Scottish Society and Glasgow Group. Public galleries in Glasgow and Paisley and Lillie Art Gallery, Milngavie, hold examples.

Una Brown SHANKS 1940– Artist in pen and ink and watercolour and teacher, born in Bowhousebog, Lanarkshire, married to the artist Duncan Shanks. She studied in the textile department of Glasgow School of Art, lectured in art at Hamilton College of Education until 1984, then became a full-time illustrator and artist. She was a member of RSW, also showing with RSA, Royal Glasgow Institute of the Fine Arts, Talbot Rice Art Centre in Edinburgh and in Glasgow at both Fine Art Society and Roger Billcliffe Fine Art. Showed solo with Roger Billcliffe, also at Scottish Art Shop, Edinburgh. Lived at Crossford, By Carluke, Lanarkshire.

William Somerville SHANKS 1864–1951 Artist and teacher, born in Gourock, Renfrewshire. He studied part-time at Glasgow School of Art while working as a designer, then in Paris and eventually taught at the Glasgow School between the wars. He was elected RSW in 1925 and RSW in 1933 and was a member of Glasgow Art Club, living in the city but eventually settling in Stirling. Showed also at Royal Glasgow Institute of the Fine Arts, RA, Walker Art Gallery in Liverpool and elsewhere including Paris Salon, where he gained a Silver Medal in 1922. Walker Art Gallery and several Scottish public collections hold examples.

Roger SHANTZ 1944– Shantz began painting while serving in the Army, then left to study at the Ruskin School of Fine Art, Oxford. After a period dividing his time between Spain and London, from 1976 he based himself in a village in the Andalucian region of Spain. Its landscape and that of southern France, providing subjects with strong outlines and contrasting shadow and light, became key themes. Showed at RA Summer Exhibition, RP and NEAC and various London galleries and was one of four artists in the Autumn Exhibition at Jerram Gallery, Salisbury, 1996.

Hermon SHAPIRO 1933– Painter, sculptor and teacher, born in London. He studied at Camberwell School of Arts and Crafts, then from 1956 held various teaching posts including Cardiff College of Art and Bridgend Comprehensive School. Took part in many group shows, including RWA, SEA, Howard Roberts and Albany Galleries in Cardiff, RCamA, SWG, WSW and Royal

National Eisteddfod. From 1970s concentrated on sculpting rather than painting. WAC and a number of Welsh education authorities hold his work.

Edward W SHARLAND fl. from c.1905–1967 Printmaker and painter who worked for some time as cabinet-maker and carver before becoming a self-taught artist. He did some topographical etchings of Bristol, and its City Art Gallery holds his work. Frost & Reed published much of his output, which included coloured etchings. Showed RA, RWA and Walker Art Gallery in Liverpool. Lived in Portishead, Bristol, for many years, finally in Cornwall.

Dorothea SHARP 1874–1955 Painter in oil, especially of flowers and seaside scenes with children. Studied art at Regent Street Polytechnic School of Art after initial education on the continent. Exhibited prolifically at the RA, RBA, ROI, SWA, Fine Art Society and other venues, including Paris Salon and Commonwealth countries. Her small monograph *Painting in Oils* illustrates her work, which in the 1980s gained new popularity. Her pictures, idyllic and sunlit, have wide appeal, and although her range is limited at her best she is an excellent flower painter. Many British and Commonwealth galleries hold her work, including Laing Art Gallery and Museum, Newcastle upon Tyne, and Manchester City Art Gallery. Lived in London.

John SHARP 1954– Artist whose media included oil, monotype and collage, born in Bentham, Yorkshire. He studied at Lancaster College of Art, 1971–2, then Leicester Polytechnic, 1972–6, and supported himself with a variety of jobs including clerical assistant, postman and graphic designer. Solo exhibitions included Phoenix Theatre, Leicester, 1976, and Howarth Art Gallery in Accrington and Nelson and Colne College, both 1979. Wit was an important feature of Sharp's work, as in his Deadly Sins series at Summer Show 3, Serpentine Gallery, 1980. Lived in Blackburn, Lancashire.

Miles SHARP 1897–c.1980 Painter in oil and watercolour and printmaker dealing with landscape and architectural subjects. Born in Brighouse, Yorkshire, Sharp studied art at Bradford School of Art, Leeds School of Art, Royal College of Art and the Central School of Arts and Crafts. He exhibited at RA, RBA, RI, ROI, RBSA and had a number of one-man shows, including Foyles Gallery. He was principal of Nuneaton Art School, 1925–52. Work in about a dozen public collections, mainly in the north of England, including Rotherham Museum and Art Gallery, Yorkshire, and Bootle Museum and Art Gallery. Lived at Exmouth, Devon.

Nancy SHARP 1909– Painter and teacher, born in Cornwall. Her first husband was the artist William Coldstream, her second Michael Spender, brother of the poet Stephen Spender and of the artist Humphrey Spender. She was educated at Cheltenham Ladies' College, then attended Slade School of Fine Art, 1928–31. She showed her work regularly in 1930s, including LG and Leicester Galleries. From 1945–77 taught art at Kinnard Park School, Bromley, then at Archbishop Temple School and the Archbishop Michael Ramsay School in Lambeth. Nancy Sharp was a figurative painter in the mainstream English tradition, noted for her flower paintings and portraits. She also showed at AIA, of which she was a committee member for five years; Wildenstein's; WIAC; National Portrait Gallery, and elsewhere. Government Art Collection and Ashmolean Museum, Oxford, hold her work. Sharp's intimate relationship with Louis MacNeice and her collaboration with him on his 1938 travelogue *I Crossed the Minch* are described in Jon Stallworthy's biography of the poet. Sharp was a central figure in MacNeice's long autobiographical poem *Autumn Journal*, and she appears in *Autumn Sequel* as Jenny. She lived for many years in north London.

Charles William SHARPE 1881–1955 Artist notable for his landscapes in a traditional style, and teacher, born in Liverpool, where he trained at the School of Art. Held a number of teaching posts, from 1930–46 serving as principal of Laird School of Art in Birkenhead. Was a member of Sandon Studios Society, Liverpool Academy, what became RUA and RCamA, of which he was honorary secretary for a time. Showed at Walker Art Gallery, which owns his oil Hilbre, RA, RI and elsewhere. Died in Deganwy, Caernarvonshire.

Leo SHARRATT 1934– Painter and teacher, born in Durham. From 1952–6 studied at department of fine art at King's College, Durham University, then after National Service was at Slade School of Fine Art, 1958–9. He taught for five years, then in 1963 travelled extensively through the Middle East and Asia, returning to teach in Wales in 1964. Also was at Chester School of Art. A member of Liverpool Academy, Sharratt showed with Young Contemporaries, John Moores Exhibition in Liverpool, RCamA and elsewhere. Solo shows included Westgate Gallery in Newcastle upon Tyne and Peterloo Gallery in Manchester. Bertrand Russell Peace Foundation holds his work.

Alfred Burgess SHARROCKS 1919– Painter, writer, ornithologist and teacher, born in Stockport, Cheshire. He attended Stockport College School of Art, 1933–7, the College of Technology in Manchester, 1937–9, then after World War II Naval service and a short period teaching at Stockport School of Art was at Royal Academy Schools, 1946–51. Held a number of teaching positions, including lecturing from 1967 at Llandrillo College of Technology. He was well known as a writer and artist concerned with birds and was in 1957 president of the Cambrian Ornithological Society, in 1962–7 being president of RCamA. Mixed shows included RCamA and NEAC and he had several solo exhibitions. National Museum of Wales, Cardiff, holds his work. Lived near Conway, Gwynedd.

Terry SHAVE 1952– Painter, draughtsman and teacher, born in Suffolk. He studied at Ipswich School of Art, 1971–2; Loughborough College of Art, 1972–5; and Slade School of Fine Art, 1975–7. He taught at North Staffordshire Polytechnic; Harlow College, in Essex; Portsmouth, Manchester and North-East London Polytechnics; and Chelsea School of Art. Shave showed in many mixed exhibitions from mid-1970s, including Loughborough

University, Ipswich Art Gallery, Thumb Gallery, Aspex Gallery in Portsmouth and Gainsborough's House, Sudbury. After a solo show at Framlingham Art Gallery in 1974, he showed at North Staffordshire Polytechnic Gallery and Morley Gallery in 1983 and The Minories, Colchester and tour, 1985. He was included in the South Bank Centre's touring show the Presence of Painting, 1988–9. Shave's pictures had a strong Expressionist element, painted in hot, earthy colours. The theme of the garden was a strong one. He wrote that the main themes running through his work were "order and chaos and the transience of existence which encompasses both biblical and mythical implications as well as the mundane." The Arts Council's example Inferno Storms, of 1986, is a good example. Lived for some time at Newcastle-under-Lyme, Staffordshire.

Varvara SHAVROVA 1968– Painter, muralist and illustrator, born in Moscow, Russia, who attended a special English school there, 1975–85; had private art lessons with Dmitri Lyon, 1983–7; studied painting and book illustration at Moscow Polygraphic Institute, 1987–90, then moving to England and settling in London. Shavrova had a three-year residency at Florence Trust Studios, 1990–3, a European Artists' Award in 1993 permitting travel to Weimar in Germany, then gained a Prince's Trust Go & See Portugal award in 1994. Commissions included a mural at the Leisure Centre, Ross & Cromarty District Council, 1993. After mixed shows in Moscow and elsewhere in Russia, Shavrova showed at Merz Contemporary Art, 1988; Dancefest, City Museum & Art Gallery, Worcester, 1992; Purdy Hicks Gallery, 1995; and Cross Currents, Reed's Wharf at Barbican Centre, 1996. Had a solo show at Original Jazz Café, 1992. Large, atmospheric abstracts were characteristic of Shavrova's output, as in Cross Currents.

Arthur Winter SHAW 1869–1948 Painter of the countryside, born in Kent, who after a private education studied at Westminster and Slade School of Fine Art and in Paris. He was elected RI in 1900. For many years lived in Kent and Sussex, in that county working alongside James Charles, William Estall, Edward Stott and José Weiss. Was a member of Chelsea Arts Club for a time, being a prolific exhibitor at RI, also RA, RHA, Goupil Gallery and elsewhere.

Barbara SHAW 1924– Painter, printmaker and teacher, born in London. She studied under Lionel Ellis at Wimbledon School of Art, 1940–3, also at Hornsey College of Art. She was on the staff of Wimbledon High School for Girls. Medici Society Ltd published her work, which was also shown at RA and NS. Lived in New Malden, Surrey.

Elizabeth SHAW 1920–1992 Artist and writer, born in Belfast, who attended Chelsea School of Art before World War II, studying with Henry Moore and Graham Sutherland. During the war she established a reputation as an illustrator and cartoonist, drawing for *Lilliput* and *Our Time*, the left-wing monthly. In 1942 she married the Swiss sculptor and painter René Graetz and in 1946 they moved to Germany and anticipated a new Communist society in the east. For 20 years she and Bertha Waterstradt produced monthly articles for *Das Magazin* on aspects of East Berlin intellectual life. She also wrote and illustrated children's books. Became disillusioned with the political establishment and turned to books on places she had visited and loved, such as Ireland. There were Arts Council shows of her work in Belfast and Coventry. In 1990 her autobiography *Irish Berlin* was published. Died in Berlin.

Hilary SHAW 1923– Sculptor and teacher, born in Thame, Oxfordshire. She studied at Chelsea School of Art, 1948–51, her teachers including Bernard Meadows and Willi Soukop. Taught for a while at Westonbirt School in Gloucestershire, later living in Machakos, Kenya, where she was at the Training College. Showed in England with RWA, Guild of Catholic Artists and elsewhere.

Kerry SHAW 1967– Painter in oil and teacher, born in Huddersfield, Yorkshire, who studied printed textiles at Manchester Metropolitan University, 1990–3. She taught printed textiles, worked as a freelance designer and artist and was included in Julia Bawden's *The Art & Craft of Fabric Decoration*. Exhibitions included Castlegate House Gallery, Cockermouth. Lived in Shelley, Huddersfield.

Margaret SHAW 1917–1983 Painter and lithographer who was born and finally lived in Sheffield, Yorkshire. She studied at the city's College of Art, 1934–8, then at the Royal College of Art, 1938–41. Taught at King's College, Newcastle and at Sheffield City Polytechnic, where she was senior lecturer in the history of art. Showed at RA, NEAC, RSA and in the provinces in mixed shows, being president in 1960 of Sheffield Society of Artists. One-man shows included Calouste Gulbenkian Gallery, Newcastle, and Mappin Art Gallery, Sheffield. The Graves Art Gallery there and Ferens Art Gallery, Hull, hold her work.

Michael John SHAW 1959– Painter, sculptor and teacher who gained an honours degree in fine art, painting, at Slade School of Fine Art, 1977–81, winning his higher diploma in painting there, 1981–4. He went on to teach at the Slade and at Byam Shaw School of Art. The Islington area of London was a notable feature of Shaw's landscapes and his grandmother a favourite figure subject. Shaw gained a string of awards, including the Troughton Scholarship in Painting and Steer Medal for Painting, both 1981; J Milner Kite Scholarship, 1982; The Jeremy Cubitt Prize, 1983–4; BP Portrait Award Exhibition, National Gallery, and Hunting/*Observer* Prize Exhibition, Mall Galleries, both 1992; and Royal Over-Seas League, 10th Annual Open Exhibition Travel Prize (visited Venice and Florence) and East West Solo Exhibition Prize, 1993. Solo shows included East West Gallery, 1994, and Royal Over-Seas League, Edinburgh and London, 1997. Lived in London.

Robert SHAW 1946– Printmaker, born in Edinburgh, who studied law at the University there, and began printmaking at the original Printmakers' Workshop in Victoria Street. He moved to Kirkwall, Orkney, where he became chairman of the Solisquoy printmaking workshop. Exhibitions included Scottish Print Open Three, 1983, organised by Dundee Printmakers' Workshop.

Rosena SHAW 1917– Painter, mainly in oil, and teacher, born in Glasgow. She taught in the Glasgow area for several years during World War II. Studied at Notre Dame Training College in Glasgow and at the School of Art, 1935–9, under Hugh Crawford. Showed at RUA, in Glasgow and Dublin and lived latterly at Whiteabbey, County Antrim.

Rupert SHAW 1950– Artist who studied at Harrow College of Art, 1973, notable for his etchings. Showed at RA from mid-1970s, also at RE, National Museum of Wales in Cardiff, Sweet Waters Gallery and elsewhere. In 1992 shared a show at Sweet Waters featuring etchings of Cornwall, where he lived for some years from late 1970s.

Samantha SHAW 1967– Painter and teacher. She was in the tradition of English poetic and romantic landscape painters and used a rich palette. She did a foundation course at City and Guilds of London Art School, 1986–7, then from 1987–90 studied for a fine art diploma in painting, gaining first-class honours. Among her scholarships and awards were the Philip Connard Travel Scholarship, 1989; and in 1990 the Royal Academy Richard Ford Award and Haworth Trust Scholarship. From 1991–2 she was visiting lecturer at University of Reading's fine art department and in 1992 she painted a large triptych for Christ the Cornerstone, the City Church of Milton Keynes. She had solo shows at Talent Store Gallery in 1991 and Cadogan Contemporary, 1992.

Sax SHAW 1916– Artist in stained glass, tapestry, watercolour and oil, and teacher, father of the glass painter Christian Shaw, born in Yorkshire. He attended Huddersfield School of Art, teachers including Reg Napier and Nöel Spencer, and Edinburgh College of Art, under Herbert Hendrie and Hubert Wellington; Shaw taught there until 1984 as head of stained glass. He had been a postgraduate scholar. Shaw won a Travel Scholarship to France, studying tapestry at the Gobelin, Paris. He was elected a fellow of the Master Glass Painters in 1979. Shaw's work was exhibited in London, Edinburgh, the English provinces and extensively abroad. There was a show of his watercolours, 1936–83, at Calton Gallery, Edinburgh, in 1984. Among Shaw's stained glass windows were St Andrews, Isle of Bute; Bell's Whisky Reception Centre, Perth; and Scottish Experience, Edinburgh. Mural decorations included Lady Roberts Memorial Mosaic, Aberdeen; and and University Agricultural College, Edinburgh. His many tapestries included Rolls-Royce Guest House, Glasgow; Cappers Guild Chapel, Coventry; and Liverpool University Veterinary College. Shaw was director of Dovecot Studios, Edinburgh Tapestry Company, and had work woven there. Lived in Edinburgh.

Simon SHAW 1961– Artist and teacher who studied at Wirral College of Art and Design, 1978–9, then Braintree College, 1979–80. Went on to become supervisor, arts, drama and music, Birkenhead. Showed at Acorn Gallery in Liverpool, 1985; Williamson Art Gallery in Birkenhead, 1986; and in 1986–7 his Snap, Crackle, Rip – slab-built and using a coarse Raku clay – was exhibited in Walker Art Gallery, Liverpool, touring show Merseyside Artists 3.

Tim SHAW 1964– Sculptor and teacher, born in Belfast, Northern Ireland, full name Stephen Timothy Shaw. He studied the foundation course at Manchester Polytechnic, 1984–5, with a distinction award; then obtained a first-class honours degree in fine art at Falmouth School of Art, 1985–9. Shaw was an associate of the Newlyn Society of Artists. Mixed shows included Otter Gallery, Belfast, 1985–7; Arts Centre, Falmouth, 1986; and One Oxford Street Gallery, Belfast, 1997. Had a solo show at Albemarle Gallery, 1992, later ones including Duncan Campbell Contemporary Art, 1997, with bullfighting the subject. Metaphysical questions were a key theme in Shaw's work. Shaw organised art workshops for the mentally handicapped in Belfast and Falmouth, 1988–91; worked on building and sculpture restoration projects around the south of England, 1989–90; received a Prince's Trust award to set up a studio in 1990; was visiting tutor at Falmouth College of Art, 1994–7; and gained a Delfina Studios Trust Award for Spain, 1996. Lived in Mabe, Penryn, Cornwall.

Neil SHAWCROSS 1940– Painter, draughtsman, designer and teacher, born in Kearsley, Lancashire, who studied at Bolton Junior Art School, 1953–5, Bolton College of Art, 1955–8, and Lancaster College of Art, 1958–60. He went on to lecture part-time there and elsewhere in Lancashire, later teaching at Belfast College of Art and Ulster College of Art and Design. Shawcross was notable as a Colourist and figure painter who was interested in the work of Matisse, Braque and primitive artists, popular art and ephemera. Among his commissions was one from Arts Council of Northern Ireland, which with Ulster Museum holds his work, for a portrait of the painter Colin Middleton. Showed at RUA, Tib Lane Gallery in Manchester, New and Tom Caldwell Galleries in Belfast, RHA and Oireachtas, Dublin. Lived in Hillsborough, County Down.

Stella SHAWZIN fl. from 1950s– Figurative sculptor in a variety of materials, painter, draughtsman and printmaker, born in Ogies, Transvaal, South Africa, sister of the writer Olga Levinson and of the artist Alma Hayden. For a time she acted, danced and sang on the stage and in films in Britain and Africa. In New York she studied at the Art Students' League, teachers including Yasuo Kuniyoshi, George Bridgeman and Du Mond, and at the Pratt Institute with Ponce de Leon; in London she was taught by Martin Bloch and Tony Harrison. In the handling of metals, carving in stone and marble and use of semi-precious stones and wood Shawzin was mainly self-taught. Although she lived in Cape Town and in the south of France, Shawzin spent much time in the marble yards of Carrara, Italy, where she could work with the local artisans. Group exhibitions of paintings and sculpture included many in South Africa, Rhodesia, America, Britain and Italy. Solo exhibitions included Argus Gallery, Cape Town, 1953; Lidchi Gallery, Johannesburg, 1970; Crane Kalman Gallery and Goodman Gallery, Johannesburg, both from 1972; and Kunskamer, Cape Town, from 1977. In 1996 Shawzin was invited to participate in a show of sculpture at Chichester Cathedral cloisters. She is represented in several South African collections, including Willem Annandale Art Gallery, Lichtenburg.

Charles SHEARER 1956– Painter, illustrator, printmaker and teacher, born in Kirkwall, Orkney, who graduated from, and did a year's postgraduate studies at, Gray's School of Art, Aberdeen, 1975–80, gaining his master's at Royal College of Art, 1980–3. In 1984 he won a Major Travel Award to the Philippines. Taught at several art schools in London, where he was based. Illustrated for the literary magazine *Ambit* and for the Cadogan travel guides. In his adapted hearse, Shearer travelled through Ireland, Scotland and Wales, lyrically capturing the lonely landscapes of the Celtic fringe and its inhabitants. Had a series of exhibitions at Kilvert Gallery, Clyro.

Marcelle Dorothy SHEARS 1926–1997 Artist in a variety of media, including watercolour on vellum and silhouette, born in Croydon, Surrey, her father an artist, George Tozer, with whom she studied. She was a member of RMS which holds her work, Hilliard Society, SM and SWA, also exhibiting at RA and in the provinces. Lived at Two Bridges, Yelverton, Devon.

Edyth May SHELDON 1897–1988 Painter, printmaker and teacher, born in Reading, Berkshire. Studied at University College there under Allen Seaby, and like him specialised in colour woodcuts. She taught at several schools and ended up as principal of St Nicholas School, in Earley, near Reading. Exhibited with Archer Gallery, Colour Woodcut Society and extensively with societies in the Reading area. Prints in many galleries in England and abroad.

John SHELLEY 1938– Painter, born in Margate, Kent. He studied at Wimbledon School of Art, 1953–8; won a British Institution Fund Award in 1957; and studied at Slade School of Fine Art, 1958. His teachers included Gerald Cooper. Showed at Trafford Gallery and elsewhere and Tate Gallery holds his work.

Len SHELLEY 1964– Artist in mixed media who had experience of puppet animation film-making. He studied at Maidstone College of Art and film and television at Bournemouth and Poole College of Art and Design, 1986–9. He mainly used found objects from Sussex beaches for his constructions, such as Peter won't go to the Barber, included in the 1992 Norwich Gallery/Kent Institute of Art and Design East & South show. Shelley was also "interested in illustrating stories based on overheard snatches of conversation, chance remarks and people's family legends", as in his solo show at England & Co, 1994. Had a previous one-man exhibition at Booth Museum in Brighton, 1993. Took part in many group shows in London and southeast of England and gained South East Young Artists Award, 1991, at Maidstone. Kent County Council and South East Arts, Towner Gallery in Eastbourne, hold examples. Lived in St Leonards-on-Sea, Sussex.

Harold SHELTON 1913–1994 Teacher, painter, designer and printmaker, born in St Helens, Lancashire. William Green, principal of Wallasey School of Art, discovered Shelton when he was working as a railway station ticket collector and encouraged him to study at Wallasey, 1934–6; from 1936–9 he was under Malcolm Osborne and Robert Austin at Royal College of Art. After World War II he worked for a short time for Grafton Furnishing Fabrics as a designer, then was principal of Carlisle School of Art. As principal of Hornsey College of Art Shelton experienced the 1968 students' sit-in; this was an attempt, supported by some staff, to make the College more democratic and to end academic examinations. Shelton, who retired in 1977 as assistant director of art, the College having become a Polytechnic, was a subtle administrator, seen by some as an empire-builder, who wanted Hornsey to have university status. One of his achievements was the establishment of a visual research department, inspired by his wife Joanna, who had been a popular teacher of plant drawing at Carlisle Art School. She predeceased him. Shelton, who lived for many years in Enfield, finally had a stroke and died in Colchester, Essex.

Elaine SHEMILT 1954– Artist using a wide range of media, notably sculpture and printmaking, and lecturer, born in Edinburgh, who in 1960 moved to Northern Ireland. She studied at Brighton Polytechnic, foundation course, 1972–3; gained a first-class honours degree from the department of sculpture at Winchester School of Art, 1973–6; and gained her master's in printmaking, Royal College of Art, 1976–9. She was artist-printmaker-in-residence, South Hill Park Arts Centre, 1980–2, then was a visiting fellow in fine art–print-making at Winchester, 1982–4. She was a visiting lecturer there, and at Berkshire and Chelsea Schools of Art, at Hull Further Education Centre and at Newcastle and Middlesex Polytechnics. Exhibitions included Serpentine Gallery, video work, 1976; Bradford Print Biennale, 1978; Ikon Gallery, Birmingham, sculpture/photography, 1980; and Fellows of the Winchester School of Art, Winchester Gallery, 1983. Her contribution there, mainly figurative in origin, was influenced by early historical/megalithic and mythological symbolism. She likened her work "to a language where each separate image is carefully selected and placed to form a visual statement".

Mary SHEMILT 1953– Sculptor and teacher, who attended St Martin's School of Art, specialising in sculpture on the advanced course. Went on to teach as a regular and visiting lecturer at various art colleges, including Canterbury, Ravensbourne, Stourbridge, East Ham Technical and Cambridge. Although she worked for some time in London, eventually moved to a studio near Cambridge where she produced abstract works made of forged, cut and welded steel. Group shows participated in included New Contemporaries at RA, Whitechapel Open, Air Gallery and Ikon Gallery, Birmingham. In 1985 she shared a three-artist show at Woodlands Art Gallery. Solo exhibitions included The

Minories, Colchester, 1979. Various private and public collections hold Shemilt's work.

Anwar Jalal SHEMZA 1928–1985 Painter, writer and teacher, born in Simla, India, into a cultured family. He studied at Mayo School of Art, in Lahore, Pakistan, 1943–6, and set up a commercial art studio in Simla, but had to give this up during Indian partition, when he joined his family in Lahore. While conducting career as a writer he worked towards several group shows in Lahore, 1953–6, also founding the Lahore Art Group. British Council scholarship took him to Slade School of Fine Art, 1956–9, after which he did postgraduate research in graphic arts at the Slade in 1960. After a return to Pakistan in that year, where he had several shows, Shemza returned to England, settling in Stafford, where he taught. Grounded in Islamic abstract art Shemza also absorbed Western influences, although he had some problems in establishing a distinct identity along the way. Participated in many international group shows, and one-man exhibitions in Britain included New Vision Centre Gallery, 1959 and Ashmolean Museum, Oxford, 1964. Retrospective at Canberra Playhouse, England, 1987. Bradford Museum and Art Gallery holds his work. Was a participant in The Other Story, Hayward Gallery and touring, 1989–90. Shemza was given a retrospective at Birmingham Museum & Art Gallery in 1997–8.

Ernest Howard SHEPARD 1879–1976 Artist in watercolour, pen and ink and oil; exemplary illustrator of almost 100 books. Born in London, his father was a keen amateur watercolourist, his mother's was the Dicksee family, which produced several painters. Shepard studied at Heatherley's Art School from 1896, then entered the Royal Academy Schools on a scholarship, 1897–1901, and first exhibited at the RA in that year. His painting Followers was bought from the RA by Durban Art Gallery in 1904. *Punch* took his first drawing in 1906, he joined its staff in 1921, became its senior political cartoonist in 1945 and did his last drawings for the magazine in 1958. In 1924 Shepard illustrated A A Milne's *When We Were Very Young*, to be followed by *Winnie-the-Pooh* (1926), *Now We Are Six* (1927) and *The House at Pooh Corner* (1928). In 1931 his status as an illustrator for children was enhanced when he drew for Kenneth Grahame's *The Wind in the Willows*. Shepard was the true professional, whose drawings have a light, sure line and meticulous attention to detail. He wrote two delightful books of reminiscence: *Drawn From Memory* and *Drawn From Life*. Lived at Lodsworth, Sussex. Chris Beetles Ltd and Sally Hunter Fine Art latterly exhibited Shepard's work.

Jean SHEPEARD 1904–1989 Draughtsman and actress whose artistic reputation was revived by an exhibition at Jonathan Poole's Compton Cassey Gallery, Withington, in 1996, after a concealed trunk of work was found after her death. Shepeard trained at the Royal Academy of Dramatic Art and performed in numerous plays at leading theatres along with John Gielgud, Jack Buchanan, Anthony Quayle, Peggy Ashcroft, Sybil Thorndike and Lewis Casson. In 1942 she appeared as Mrs Briggs in the film *Thunder Rock* with Michael Redgrave and went on to make many more films with Boulting Brothers. Such personalities and such artist friends as Vanessa Bell and R O Dunlop were astutely depicted by Shepeard, who in 1929 showed with Francis Bacon in his Queensberry Mews studio, the year she exhibited at the Redfern Gallery with Augustus John, Lucien Pissarro, Paul Nash and Eric Gill. The year before, Shepeard had joined the Emotionist Group, founded by R O Dunlop, consisting of painters, musicians, philosophers, poets and actors. In 1933 the *News Chronicle* art critic Gui St Bernard urged readers "with a few spare pounds" to "rush and buy Jean Shepeard's drawings".

Rupert SHEPHARD 1909–1992 Painter, draughtsman and teacher, born in London, where he continued to live. He studied at Slade School of Fine Art, 1926–9, and began to show with LG, Cooling Gallery and with Euston Road School painters, with whom he shared a style. Had first solo show at Calmann Gallery in 1939, the year he painted two portraits of Dylan Thomas, later bought by National Portrait Gallery. During World War II Shephard worked as a draughtsman in industry. He was appointed an official war artist in 1945, the year he joined NEAC, about this time also showing at Leicester Galleries. Shephard taught part-time at Central and St Martin's Schools of Art, 1945–8, then from 1948–63 held the post of professor of fine art at University of Cape Town, showing there and in Johannesburg. On his return to England Shephard became a full-time painter, struggling to re-establish his reputation, which he did with a long series of solo shows, including Agnew, Patrick Seale Gallery, National Museum of Wales in Cardiff and Sally Hunter Fine Art. In 1972 he was elected RP. By then he had been married seven years to Nicolette Macnamara, widow of the painter Anthony Devas and herself a writer and painter.

David SHEPHERD 1931– Painter in oil and writer, full name Richard David Shepherd, born in London. After failing to become a game warden in Africa, Shepherd moved to painting, but was turned down as "not worth training" by first art school he tried to enter. Then studied privately, 1950–3, with Robin Goodwin and began career as an aviation artist, being a founder-member of Society of Aviation Artists. Began painting African wildlife in 1960; his picture Tiger Fire raised £127,000 for Operation Tiger in 1973; and in 1985 he founded The David Shepherd Conservation Foundation. Shepherd was also known for his portraits, including HM Queen Elizabeth the Queen Mother, 1969. Many military paintings were commissioned by the Royal Navy, Parachute Regiment, Green Howards and Special Air Service. Shepherd bought two mainline steam locomotives, *Black Prince* and *The Green Knight*, in 1967, and founded The East Somerset Railway. Among films on his work was the BBC documentary *The Man Who Loves Giants*, 1971. Shepherd's books included *Artist in Africa*, 1967, and his autobiography, *The Man Who Loves Giants*, 1975. Showed RA, RP and had a series of solo shows in London, Johannesburg and New York. Lived at Hascombe, Godalming, Surrey.

David SHEPHERD 1944– Sculptor, constructions artist and teacher, born in Wigan, where he attended the School of Art,

1961–5, followed by Goldsmiths' College, 1965–6. Then began teaching, a series of appointments including Leamington Spa School of Art and Cardiff College of Art. He was a member of the 56 Group and showed at Chapel Gallery in York; RBSA Gallery in Birmingham; Midland Group Gallery in Nottingham; and John Moores Exhibition in Liverpool. One-man shows included Bluecoat Gallery, Liverpool; Serpentine Gallery, 1971; and Ikon Gallery, Birmingham.

F H S SHEPHERD 1877–1948 Prolific painter, born near Yeovil, Somerset, educated at Rugby School and Oxford University. Studied at Slade School of Fine Art for several years around 1900. He was elected to NEAC in 1912, also exhibiting at RA, Colnaghi, Goupil and Chenil Galleries, RHA, RSA and els where. Settled in London.

James Affleck SHEPHERD 1867–1946 Illustrator and painter, notable for his perceptive, amusing animal studies, born in London as William James Affleck Shepherd. He studied with the draughtsman Alfred Bryan and at Zoological Gardens for several years. From the 1890s he was on the staff of the magazine *Punch* for a long time, and illustrated many books, including a series of his own beginning with *Zig-Zag Fables*, 1897, later ones including *Animal Caricature*, 1936. In 1911 won a gold medal at International Exhibition of Humorous Art held in Rivoli, Italy. Showed at PS, Baillie Gallery and Royal Glasgow Institute of the Fine Arts and had an exhibition of watercolours at Paterson's Gallery in 1928. British Museum holds his work. Shepherd was a keen huntsman who lived for a time at Charlwood, Surrey, also near Cirencester, Gloucestershire.

Richard SHEPHERD 1952– Artist, born in London, who studied at Lincoln College of Art, 1971–2; Liverpool College of Art, 1972–5; and Royal College of Art, 1975–8. Exhibitions included Northern Young Contemporaries, Whitworth Art Gallery, Manchester, 1974; Riverside Open, 1988; and John Moores 1995–6 Liverpool Exhibition, where his oil on calico After Picasso appeared. Lived in Norwich, Norfolk.

Scott SHEPHERD 1892–c.1973 Painter of miniatures, illustrator and sculptor. Born and lived in London, he studied at Heatherley's School of Fine Art. Exhibited at RMS, of which he was for a time president. Also drew for books and magazines.

S Horne SHEPHERD 1909–1993 Painter, printmaker and teacher, born in Dundee, Angus. He studied at Glasgow School of Art, 1927–30, teachers including Maurice Greiffenhagen, and also taught there. Later taught at Shoreditch Training College and St Martin's School of Art. Showed at RSA, SSA, NS, Free Painters and Sculptors and abroad. Victoria & Albert Museum holds his work. Lived latterly at Rudgwick, Sussex.

Clive SHEPPARD 1930–1973 Sculptor and teacher who studied building and architecture and from 1949 worked as an exhibition designer. After National Service Sheppard worked as a designer in natural history section of British Museum and studied sculpture at St Martin's School of Art, 1952–5, working with Anthony Caro. After five years at the Abbey Art Centre Sheppard spent several years acting as assistant to the sculptor Henry Moore, teaching at art colleges in Bournemouth and Hornsey and going as visiting artist at Washington University, in America. He returned to teach in Britain in 1967, finally at Sheffieldm Polytechnic School of Art and Design, whose gallery gave him a retrospective in 1974. Sheppard was an artist primarily concerned with the image, to which surface and material were incidental. He pursued themes periodically through his career, broken forms seen in car crash photographs leading to powerfully brutal bronzes. Arts Council holds his work. He was married to the artist Liz Sheppard.

Faith SHEPPARD 1920– Painter, notably of marine pictures, born in London. She was the daughter of the artist Nancy Huntly, with whom she studied, also at Byam Shaw School of Drawing and Painting, Royal Academy Schools and Chelsea School of Art. Exhibited at RA, ROI, RBA, Chelsea Art Society and at Paris Salon, where she won a Silver Medal, 1975, and a Gold Medal, 1978. Several of her paintings were published as prints and HM Queen Elizabeth The Queen Mother owned her work. Lived for many years in Welwyn Garden City, Hertfordshire.

Liz SHEPPARD 1933– Printmaker, painter in oil and watercolour and teacher, born in Tonbridge, Kent, married to the sculptor Clive Sheppard. She studied at St Albans School of Art, 1950–2, St Martin's School of Art, 1952–55, and London University Institute of Education, 1955–6. Her teachers were Anthony Caro, Derrick Greaves, Peter de Francia, Frederick Gore and Alistair Grant. In 1954 she won the Pratt Bequest scholarship to Italy. From 1976 she held a number of teaching appointments including College of Art Design, Barnfield, Luton; Middlesex Polytechnic; and Mount St Joseph, Connecticut, and Lansdowne College. She worked at Digswell House Arts Trust before moving to Woburn, Milton Keynes. In 1990 she was artist-in-residence at Bedford School. Took part in many mixed exhibitions including Bear Lane Gallery in Oxford, RA Summer Exhibitions and Cartoon Gallery. Later solo shows included Leighton Buzzard Arts Centre and Bedford School, 1990. HRH Princess Margaret, Open University and Bedfordshire Education Committee hold her work.

Maurice SHEPPARD 1947– Painter in oil and watercolour, born in Llangwm, Pembrokeshire. He studied at Loughborough College of Art, Kingston College of Art under Alfred Heyworth and Royal College of Art, where his teachers included Robert Buhler, Carel Weight and Ruskin Spear. Among his awards were British Institution Award, 1970; David Murray Landscape Award, 1971; and Geoffrey Crawshay Memorial Travelling Scholarship, 1973, University of Wales. Showed in mixed exhibitions at RA from 1971; Agnew; New Grafton Gallery; Salon de Mai, Paris, 1975; and West Coast Watercolour Society of America, 1975. Was for a time president of RWS. Victoria & Albert Museum and

National Museum of Wales, Cardiff, hold his work. Lived at Rusthall Common, Tunbridge Wells, Kent.

Nancy SHEPPARD: *see* **Nancy HUNTLY**

Raymond SHEPPARD 1913–1958 Painter and black-and-white illustrator, notably of natural history subjects. Born in London, he studied at the London County Council Bolt Court art school. Exhibited RA, RSA, RBA and elsewhere. Appeared in such magazines as *Lilliput*, *Picture Post* and *John Bull* and produced several books on how to draw animals and birds. Lived at Harrow Weald, Middlesex.

Stephen SHEPPARD fl. from early 1950s– Painter and draughtsman who studied at L'École des Beaux-Arts, Paris, 1946–8, then Camberwell School of Arts and Crafts, 1949–52. Went on to teach art at Greenwich and Frobisher Adult Education Institutes. Sheppard exhibited in a number of leading mixed shows. Had solo exhibitions from 1972 at Court Lodge Gallery, Kent; in 1975 at Galerie d'Ars, St Montan, and Galerie Gigondas, Gigondas, France; in 1977 at Galerie ML, Paris; and in 1979 at Woodlands Art Gallery. His works are in many private collections in England and France.

Sydney SHEPPARD 1905–1991 Sculptor, painter and teacher, born in Cairo, Egypt. After education at Marlborough College he attended the Slade School of Fine Art under Henry Tonks, then briefly studied with André Lhote in Paris, starting what he called his abstract phase, and through his friendship with the sculptor Aristide Maillol became sympathetic to the classical tradition. This made Sheppard hyper-self-critical, reluctant to exhibit. Unfit for military service in World War II, Sheppard began teaching at Lancing College and King Edward's School, Oxford. His great period as a teacher was at Camberwell School of Arts and Crafts, which he joined in 1946, retiring in 1970 as senior lecturer. He continued to develop as a painter, using colour to establish form, and his last pictures were said to be his best. Died in London where a first show of any size was held at Sally Hunter Fine Art in 1994.

Patricia SHEPPERSON 1929– Artist notable for her pictures of animals and birds in pastel, born in London. She studied life and portrait drawing under Patrick Larking, first at Heatherley's School of Fine Art and then at Sir John Cass School of Art, 1959–67, having studied drama at the Guildhall School of Music and drama, 1946–9. Was elected a member of UA in 1978, mixed exhibitions including RA, PS and abroad. Solo shows included Woodlands Art Gallery, 1978. Lived in Norwich, Norfolk.

Clare SHERIDAN 1885–1970 Portrait sculptor, painter and writer. Born in London, she was educated at the Convent of the Assumption, Paris, and in Darmstadt, Germany. Studied art at the Royal College of Art and with John Tweed. Exhibited at the RA and overseas. She produced many portrait busts of famous people, including Lord Oxford and Asquith for the Oxford Union, Lord Birkenhead, Winston Churchill, Mahatma Gandhi and Lenin and Trotsky, for the Soviet government. Among her books were *Russian Portraits*, 1921, *My American Diary*, 1922, *Nuda Veritas*, 1927, and *To the Four Winds*, 1954. Lived at M'cid, Biskra, Algeria, also for a time at Hastings, Sussex.

Rachael SHERLAW-JOHNSON 1938– Artist in oil, watercolour and etching, born in London, whose main themes were "landscape, weather, Oxfordshire places, bells, bell towers and musical instruments". Her mother, Eularia Clarke, and brother, James Kenelm Clarke, were both artists. After studying music, Sherlaw-Johnson switched to painting, studying with Jane Dowling at Ruskin College, Oxford, in the 1970s, then became a member of Oxford Printmakers, where she studied in the 1980s. Was also a member of Oxford Art Society. Among her main works were the *Oxfordshire Sketchbooks* series (she lived in the county at Stonesfield, near Witney), produced by Senecio Press. Showed at RA Summer Exhibitions from 1977; Discerning Eye, Mall Galleries, 1991; Museum of Modern Art, Oxford, 1992; and New Academy Gallery, 1995, as well as in many other group exhibitions elsewhere. Had a solo show at Woodstock County Museum, 1997.

Marjorie SHERLOCK 1897–1973 Painter, etcher and draughtsman in pencil, born in Wanstead, Essex. After early education in Cambridge, Sherlock studied art under Walter Sickert and Harold Gilman, the Camden Town Group painters, shortly before World War I. Also studied with Malcolm Osborne at Royal College of Art in late 1920s and with André Lhote in the late 1930s. She first exhibited at RA in 1917, a powerful picture of Liverpool Street station, and she continued to show at the Academy for over 50 years. She admired continental painters, notably German and Baroque, but could be astringent in her comments on English artists. Although her own painting bore traces of Camden Town influence, that school was reckoned "good, but *very* English, no depth of feeling"; of Osborne, who greatly improved her etching technique, which can be very fine, she remarked: "good, up to a point." Travelled widely after unsuccessful marriage to an Army officer, publishing *Indian Etchings*, 1932, which followed *Egyptian Etchings*, 1925, and *German Etchings*, 1929. Also worked widely in America. For final 30 years of her life lived in obscurity at Oxenways, a rambling house near Axminster, Devon, on little money, keeping chickens, helping to found Axminster Art Society in 1947, and occasionally travelling abroad with her friend Orovida Pissarro. Had no one-man shows during her life, but there was a retrospective at Maltzahn Gallery in 1973. Bristol City Art Gallery, museums in Stockholm, Copenhagen and Amsterdam hold her work.

She She SHERWANI 1970– Painter, born in Dar es Salaam, Tanzania, whose family moved to Wales when she was 11. Her Indian heritage contributed to richly coloured, organically effervescent pictures in which "childhood memories, entrances, new beginnings, journeys and nature's sense of healing" were central themes. Gained a distinction in a foundation course at Swansea

College of Higher Education, 1988–9, obtaining a good honours degree in fine art at University of Newcastle upon Tyne, 1989–93. In 1992 she won the Bartlett Travelling Scholarship for India, in 1993 a prize for the most outstanding graduate at Newcastle. Took part in many art workshops, some with Bahá'í links. Group exhibitions included Khunduchi Gallery, Dar es Salaam, 1986; Welsh National Eisteddfod, 1989; and Christie's, selected graduates, 1994. Solo shows included Duncan Campbell Contemporary Art, 1995.

Frank SHERWIN 1896–1985 Painter in oil and watercolour, born in Derby where he studied at the School of Art, later attending Heatherley's Art School, under Henry Massey, in 1920. Sherwin, a rather military figure, became a member of RI in 1950 and RSMA in 1967, last exhibiting there in 1981. He also showed at RA and elsewhere, the public gallery in Derby holding his work. Sherwin was widely reproduced by Frost & Reed Ltd, British Railways and the Medici Society. He published articles in *The Artist* magazine and lived in Cookham, Berkshire.

Tim SHEWARD: *see* **James WHITE and Tim SHEWARD**

George SHIELD 1919– Sculptor in a variety of materials, and teacher, born in Leicester. Graduated with Bachelor of Science degree from University College, Leicester, then studied at the College of Art there, 1948–52. Held several teaching posts, eventually becoming head of Mexborough Grammar School in South Yorkshire, living at Conisbrough. Showed at RA, RI, SSA and elsewhere, and Paisley Museum and Art Gallery holds his work. Member of Leicester Society of Artists.

Dennis SHIELDS 1947– Sculptor in wood and paper, painter and teacher, born in Liverpool. He attended evening classes at the city's College of Art while he was still at school. Shields emigrated to Canada in 1964 and it was there that he took up his education again to enable him to study full-time at Ontario College of Art until 1973 and his return to Britain, concentrating on sculpture. He gained the Art Directors' Club of Toronto Award for Sculpture for *Time* magazine advertisements and the Governor General of Ontario's Medal for Sculpture in his final year at college. In Britain Shields began to teach, but worked at his abstract wooden and paper sculptures and paintings and had solo shows at Compass Gallery, Glasgow, and Third Eye Centre. Was included in The Compass Contribution at Tramway, Glasgow, 1990.

Mark SHIELDS 1963– Painter and draughtsman, whose acrylic on linen paintings and charcoal drawings, portraits and still lifes, in their attention to detail, craftsmanship and fine finish indicated a debt to the Old Masters. Shields gained a fine arts honours degree at the University of Ulster, 1981–5, adding a teaching certificate, art and design, 1988–9. He won an Ulster Television award for outstanding work by an artist under 30, 1990; was a Winsor & Newton Young Artist Award finalist, 1992; won an Abbey Stained Glass Studios Award, RHA, Dublin, 1994; and in 1995, the year he gained his associated diploma from the RUA, obtained the Anderson's Auctioneers & Valuers Prize there. Group shows included RUA from 1987; Cavehill Gallery, Belfast, from 1990; RI, 1992; ROI from 1992; RA from 1993; and BP Portrait Award Exhibition, National Portrait Gallery, from 1994. Had a solo show at Otter Gallery, Belfast, 1986, another at Grosvenor Gallery, 1997. Ulster Museum in Belfast, Arts Council for Northern Ireland and National Self-Portrait Collection of Ireland, Limerick, hold examples.

Anthony SHIELS 1938– Painter with an interest in Surrealism, born in Salford, Lancashire, who studied with Gilmore Roberts at Heatherley's School of Fine Art, 1954–6. He was a member of AIA and Penwith Society of Arts, also showing elsewhere in the provinces and abroad. Had solo exhibitions at Rawinsky and Mingus Galleries. Settled in Ponsanooth, Truro, Cornwall, later in Ireland.

Alan SHILLINGFORD 1932– Printmaker and teacher, born in London. He studied at Hammersmith School of Art and at Brooklyn Museum in America. From 1966 had regular mixed show appearances, including RA Summer Exhibition, AIA Gallery, Arnolfini Gallery in Bristol and Eastern Region Print Competition, where he won first prize for a screenprint. He was included in Arts Council Far East tour in 1967 and several international print biennales in 1970s. Had a solo show at Gallery 273 in 1966, later ones including a retrospective at Beecroft Art Gallery, Westcliff-on-Sea, 1992. That gallery, Essex University, Smolin Gallery in New York and Tamarind Gallery, Sydney, hold his work. Shillingford retired from South-East Essex College of Arts and Technology in 1992. Latterly lived in Norfolk.

Felicity SHILLINGFORD 1960– Artist in mixed media and teacher who obtained a first-class honours degree in fine art printmaking at Manchester Polytechnic, 1980–3. She was granted a Ford Foundation Scholarship at the School of the Art Institute of Chicago, 1984–6, gaining her master's degree. Had varied teaching and workshop experience in Britain and America. Her many group appearances included John Holden Gallery, Manchester, 1981; Young Contemporaries at Whitworth Art Gallery, Manchester, 1983; Printmakers' Council Members Shows, Manchester, from 1987; and Young Printmakers, Blenheim Gallery, 1989. From 1992 Shillingford had a series of shows with Le Chat Noir Gallery, which represented her. Her 1993 exhibition, The Little Nipper, on the theme of babies, used cast-off pieces of wood upon which she painted, collaged and embellished her ideas.

Claude Percival SHILTON 1887– Painter and commercial artist, born in Stoke Golding, Leicestershire. Attended Leicester School of Art. Showed at RI, PS and elsewhere. Lived in Richmond, Surrey.

Kumiko SHIMIZU 1948– She created art from rubbish, painted and made outdoor murals. Shimizu was born in Osaka, Japan. She came to London in 1975 to learn English as a secretary, discovered modern art through a friend, joined classes at the City Lit which gave her a perspective on the subject and joined Reading University, taking her degree in 1982 in fine art. She was artist-in-residence in Osnabrück, Germany, in her graduation year, which involved a project decorating 200 trees. Participated in group shows, notably at Brixton Art Gallery, and had a number of international solo exhibitions. In 1989 she gained a commission to decorate façade of Manchester City Art Gallery. Participated in The Other Story, Hayward Gallery and touring, 1989–90.

Harold SHIMMELL fl. from 1930s– Landscape painter, printmaker and teacher who studied at Woolwich Polytechnic School of Art and Royal College of Art. He went on to teach at Woolwich Polytechnic, Medway and Sidcup Schools of Art and at North London Polytechnic in the School of Architecture and Interior Design. Showed at Foyles Gallery, 1934; Chas Hammond, Sloane Street, 1964; North London Polytechnic, 1965, Ranger's House, Blackheath, 1972; Park Gallery, Chislehurst, 1973; Court Lodge Gallery; Horton Kirby, 1975; and in that year was one of Four Greenwich Watercolour Artists at Woodlands Art Gallery. Also showed with RA in Summer Exhibition, RBA, NEAC and SWE. Lived for some years at New Eltham, southeast London.

Audrey SHINER 1900–c.1980 Painter, especially of portraits, and teacher, born in Grays, Essex. Studied at Central School of Arts and Crafts and Slade School of Fine Art, her teachers including Henry Tonks and Tancred Borenius. Also studied on continent. Taught at Winterbourne Collegiate School in the early 1950s. Showed RWA and at other venues in the west of England. Lived in Chipping Sodbury, near Bristol.

Michael Lawrence SHINN 1934– Painter and teacher, born in London, where he studied at Wimbledon School of Art, 1951–5, then Slade School of Fine Art, teachers including William Coldstream. Went on to teach at Gloucestershire College of Art and Design/Arts and Technology. Showed at RA, RWA of which he was a council member and elsewhere in west of England. RWA and the Art Gallery and Museum in Cheltenham, near where he lived at Southam, owned examples.

Frank SHIPSIDES 1908– Artist, notable for marine paintings and illustrations of Bristol, born in Mansfield, Nottinghamshire. He studied at the College of Art there, 1923, then with Joseph Else at Nottingham College of Art, 1925. Shipsides was a leading member of Bristol Savages, showing widely in west of England and had a series of solo exhibitions at Alexander Gallery in Bristol, where he lived. His work was popular locally, queues forming on private view nights, which often seemed like rugby scrums. Reproductions of his paintings were widely displayed in Bristol homes and offices. Among many commissions, paintings by him of seven HMS *Bristols* hang in the city's Council House. In 1977, he was invited by the publisher John Sansom to contribute pen and ink illustrations to his *Bristol Impressions*; they later collaborated again in *Frank Shipsides' Bristol*, 1984. Other publications with Shipsides' illustrations were *Bristol Profile, Bristol: Maritime City* and *Quayside Bristol*. His son Pat Shipsides also showed marine subjects locally.

Yuko SHIRAISHI 1956– Abstract painter, born in Tokyo. She studied in Vancouver and at Chelsea School of Art. Was included in a number of mixed shows, including South Bank Centre's 1988–9 touring exhibition The Presence of Painting. Had a solo exhibition at Curwen Gallery in 1984, another at Edward Totah Gallery in 1988. Shiraishi was one of the six finalists for the Jerwood Painting Prize in 1994. Lived in London.

George SHIRLAW 1932– Painter and draughtsman, born in London. He travelled widely, spending several years in the Far and Middle East and for some years lived in Australia. Then settled in Blackheath, southeast London, and had a series of shows in the capital and the provinces, including Woodlands Art Gallery, 1977. Also exhibited in many mixed exhibitions, including RBA and ROI. British Museum and overseas collections hold his pictures.

Ralph Oakley SHIRLEY 1918– Artist in wide range of media and teacher, born in Doveridge, Derbyshire, who studied at Derbyshire College of Art, 1936–40, including basic education there, then at Royal College of Art, 1941–5, where teachers included Gilbert Spencer and Percy Horton. Went on to teach at North Staffordshire Polytechnic. Showed in London and the provinces. Southampton University holds his work. Lived in Foston, Derbyshire.

Raymond SHIRLEY 1930– Self-taught artist, notable for still life, born in Coventry, full name Sidney Raymond Shirley. He was an associate member of Société des Artistes Français, gaining a Silver Medal at Paris Salon in 1981; a member of Coventry and Warwickshire Society of Artists; and showed at RA, ROI, NEAC and elsewhere. Had a series of solo exhibitions at Nuneaton Museum and Art Gallery from 1968 and lived at Bulkington, Warwickshire.

Richard SHIRLEY SMITH 1935– Painter, muralist, collagist, printmaker and teacher, born in London. While at Harrow School he met David Jones, who influenced his own work as an engraver and painter. Was at the Slade School of Fine Art, 1956–60, under Anthony Gross, then studied for two years in Rome. Merivale Editions published his wood engravings. His notable work as a book illustrator included titles for the Folio Society and Limited Editions Club and his *Selected Engravings* were published in 1983 by Cuckoo Hill Press. In 1985 a major retrospective was held by the Ashmolean Museum in Oxford and RIBA Heinz Gallery. As a muralist he handled prestigious commissions for sites such as Kensington Palace and Guardian Royal Exchange. Taught at St Albans School of Art, later being head of art at Marlborough School. In 1992 a wide-ranging exhibition at Maas Gallery in which Shirley Smith's abilities as a creator of Arcadian worlds was highlighted. Whimsical details, visual puns and Surrealism all played a part. Lived in Blewbury, Oxfordshire.

Jack SHIRREFF 1943– Printmaker, designer and teacher, born in Colombo, Ceylon. Studied at Hastings College of Art, where his teachers included Vincent Lines and Henry Martyn Lack, and

Brighton College of Art. Went on to hold several teaching posts, including Bath Academy of Art and Croydon College of Art. Sussex University and Brighton College of Art hold his work. Lived for some years in Punnetts Town, Sussex.

Ernest SHONE-JONES 1899– Sculptor, especially of portraits, son of the artist William Jones. Born in Oldham, Lancashire, he studied at Liverpool City School of Art, 1915–22, under George Marples; Manchester School of Art, 1922–3, Kennington Art School, 1923, under Thomas Tyrrell; at the Royal Academy Schools, 1925–30, with Henry Poole; then finally, in 1931, in the sculptor John Tweed's studio. Showed at RA, RBS, RBA and at Walker Art Gallery, Liverpool. Made fellow of RBS in 1961. Lived in London.

Yinka SHONIBARE 1962– Artist, born and lived in London, who took part in Byam Shaw School of Art final year show, 1989. Other mixed exhibitions included Black Art New Directions, Stoke-on-Trent City Museum and Art Gallery, also 1989; Space Studios Open Exhibition, 1993; The Art of African Textiles: Technology, Tradition and Lurex, Barbican Centre, 1995; Painting, Stephen Friedman Gallery, 1996; Pledge Allegiance to A Flag?, London Printworks Trust, 1996–7; and the Saatchi Gallery-related Sensation, RA, 1997. Had solo shows at Byam Shaw and Bedford Hill Galleries, both 1989, later ones including Stephen Friedman, 1997, and Ikon Gallery, Birmingham, 1998.

Jack SHORE 1922– Artist in various media, including collage, and teacher, born in Ramsbottom, Lancashire. He studied at Accrington and Manchester Schools of Art, 1938–43, when he obtained his art teacher's diploma, teachers including John Holmes. Shore was a prominent member of RCamA, showing elsewhere in north Wales and north of England. Solo shows included RCamA, Conway, 1980, and Oriel Gallery, Bangor, 1984. Bury Art Gallery holds his work. Shore was head of the College of Art in Chester, where he lived, 1960–81.

Denys SHORT 1927– Sculptor and teacher, born in Bideford, Devon. He studied at Goldsmiths' College School of Art, 1948–53. After some years teaching in junior schools Short taught for a while part-time at Goldsmiths' and at Hornsey College of Art, living and working both in London and in Pontypridd, Glamorgan. He won a gold medal at Royal National Eisteddfod and showed at John Moores Exhibition, Liverpool; Serpentine Gallery; and SEA and WAC. WAC, CASW and National Museum of Wales in Cardiff hold his work. In 1974 had solo show with WAC at Oriel, Cardiff.

Tim SHORTEN 1957– Artist in watercolour and acrylic and teacher, born in Bolton, Lancashire, where he settled at Heaton. He studied at Bolton College of Art, 1975–6; Preston Polytechnic, 1976–9; and Leeds Polytechnic school of education, 1979–80. He gained an honours degree in fine art and an art teacher's certificate. From 1980 he taught art in Altrincham, Cheshire. Shorten, full name Edwin Timothy, showed regularly with Colin Jellicoe Gallery, Manchester, also with ICA in New Contemporaries; Whitworth Art Gallery, Manchester, in Northern Young Contemporaries; Grundy Art Gallery, Blackpool; and Haworth Gallery, Accrington. Had a solo show at Octagon Theatre, Bolton.

Arthur Charles SHORTHOUSE 1870–1953 Portrait painter who, after private education in the West Midlands, studied art at Birmingham College of Art and RBSA. From the early 1890s he became a prolific exhibitor at the RBSA, also showing at RA and elsewhere. Lived at Moseley, Birmingham.

Martin SHORTIS 1959– Artist, notably a draughtsman, who studied at Ruskin School of Drawing and Fine Art, Oxford, and Royal Academy Schools. He obtained a Goldsmiths' College teaching certificate. Shortis was one of the artists commissioned by the National Trust's Foundation for Art to show the effects of the Great Storm of October 1987. His work was included in The Long Perspective, Agnew, 1987; in Stormstruck, Petworth House, 1988; and in the Agnew exhibition The Broad Horizon, 1990, where his meticulous style was shown to good effect in drawings of the Great Storm and the storm of February 1990.

Dorothy SHORTLAND 1908– Self-taught painter who was a member of Free Painters and Sculptors and an associate of Société des Artistes Français, showing at Paris Salon, RI, SWA and elsewhere. She had a series of one-man exhibitions, including Mall Galleries, the provinces and in France. Lived in Rothwell, Northamptonshire.

Linda SHORTT 1951– Abstract artist and teacher, born in Berwick-upon-Tweed, Northumberland. Studied at Loughborough College of Art and Newcastle University. Went on to teach painting at Newcastle Polytechnic. Among her awards were a travel award to America and a Northern Arts Award to India in 1986. Her exhibitions included Hatton Gallery, Newcastle, 1976; Four Women Artists at Newcastle Polytechnic Gallery, 1983; Richard Demarco Gallery, Edinburgh, 1988; and DLI Museum & Arts Centre, 1990, the Newcastle Group show The Northern Lights. She lived in Newcastle upon Tyne and its University holds her work.

Jack SHOTBOLT 1948– Painter and teacher, notably of birds and fishes, born in Leicestershire. He said: "Scale, image and metaphor are central to my concern." Shotbolt studied at Loughborough and Hornsey Colleges of Art, 1966–71, and at University of Manchester Institute of Science and Technology, 1972–3. He was a research fellow at Sussex University, 1974–6. Went on to teach at South Glamorgan Institute of Higher Education. His mixed shows included WAC and John Moores 1985 Liverpool Exhibition, where he was a prizewinner. In 1984 he shared a show at Chapter Gallery, Cardiff, and lived locally at Pontcanna.

Ann SHRAGER 1948– Painter of atmospheric landscapes, born in London, who studied at Byam Shaw and Royal Academy

Schools. Showed at RA Summer Exhibition, was elected to NEAC in 1975 and had a series of solo shows at Michael Parkin Gallery. Lived in Richmond-upon-Thames, Surrey.

David SHRIGLEY 1968– Creator of photo-based art, born in Macclesfield, Cheshire, who attended Leicester Polytechnic, 1987–8, then in 1988–91 the School of Art in Glasgow, where he settled. Exhibition and publication projects included Head Shrinker, Glasgow Green, Glasgow, 1990; Guard Dog, Wills Tobacco Factory, Glasgow, and the publication *Slug Trails*, both 1991; In Here, Transmission Gallery, Glasgow, and the publication *Merry Eczema*, both 1992; Billboard, for Tramway, Glasgow, 1993; New Art in Scotland, Centre for Contemporary Arts, Glasgow, 1994; and *Err*, London Book Works, 1995.

Rupert SHRIVE 1965– Figurative painter mainly in oil, sometimes watercolour, born in West Runton, Norfolk. He studied at Norwich School of Art for his foundation course, 1983–4, graduating with honours in fine art from St Martin's School of Art, 1984–7. From 1989 Shrive shared his time in Valencia in Spain, London and Norfolk. He considered himself "in the British figurative tradition, keen to innovate and influenced by School of London painters". Took part in extensive mixed exhibitions in Spain, with solo shows there; also in 1993 at Caleta Palace, Gibraltar, and 1995 at Danan Gallery, International House.

Christopher SHURROCK 1939– Artist in various media, including construction and early in his career printmaking, and teacher, born in Bristol. He attended the painting school at West of England College of Art there, 1955–9, then Cardiff College of Art/University of Wales, 1960–1. Shurrock was art adviser to University Settlement, Bristol, 1961–2, then was a member of Cardiff College of Art staff, 1962–91, directing the foundation course in art and design. Shurrock showed extensively in group exhibitions including Axiom Gallery, National Museum of Wales in Cardiff and Whitechapel Art Gallery. He was variously a member of Printmakers' Council, 56 Group and RWA. Solo exhibitions included Old Hall Gallery, Cowbridge, 1994. National Museum of Wales, WAC, National Gallery of Slovakia in Bratislava and other public collections hold examples. Lived in Rhiwbina, Cardiff.

Omra SIAN 1967– Largely self-taught painter and draughts an whose work, commonly on a large scale, included Surreal, abstract, Dadaist and figurative works. Sian showed exceptional talent when he began drawing aged three. He left secondary school at 16, continued to paint part-time, then full-time. After 10 years, he held his first major exhibition, Diverse Innovation, at The Gallery in Cork Street and Gallery 27 there. Lived in Dartford, Kent.

Matthew SIBLEY 1958– Painter in oil on canvas, born and lived in London, a late developer who did an art foundation course at Middlesex University and his bachelor's degree in fine art, Kingston University, 1982–5. Painted full-time from late 1992 He took part in BP Portrait Award at National Portrait Gallery from 1992, also showing at Royal Over-Seas League and Towner Art Gallery in Eastbourne. Solo shows included Barbican Centre, 1994.

Vera Ethel SIDERY 1916– Artist, notably in pastel, who studied with the portrait painters Leonard and Margaret Boden. She was a member of PS and Enfield Art Society and lived in Enfield, Middlesex.

Dawn SIDOLI 1933– Painter and screenprinter, born in Gosport, Hampshire. She studied at Northampton School of Art, 1949–52, and gained her bachelor of education degree from Manchester Training College. Was elected to RWA in 1981, NEAC in 1990, also being a member of Bath Society of Artists and Clifton Arts Club, Bristol, where she lived. Sidoli was first prize winner in Laing National Painting Competition in 1988. Also showed at RA Summer Exhibitions from 1977, RBA, RI, ROI and elsewhere. RWA, Avon Art for Schools and Cardiff Polytechnic hold examples.

Alice SIELLE 1950– Painter, notably of abstracts, born in London. She attended Bath Academy of Art, Corsham, 1967–9. Received a number of grants, including Southern Arts, Northern Arts and Victoria & Albert Museum purchase grant for Abbot Hall, Kendal. She began to appear in mixed showed from the early 1970s, including Westward Television Open Art Exhibition, Dorchester, RA and Thumb Gallery. Had a solo exhibition at Selwood Gallery, Frome, 1974. Later exhibitions included Half Moon Theatre and Thumb Gallery, 1989, and Austin/Desmond & Phipps, 1992.

Ellis SILAS 1883–c.1975 Painter, stained glass artist and writer, son of the painter Louis Silas, was born in London. He studied painting with his father and Walter Sickert and is notable for his landscapes and marine studies. Was a war artist for the Australian government during World War I, one of his books being *Crusading at Anzac*. Also travelled extensively in Papua, featured in his volume *A Primitive Arcadia*. Member of UA, Ridley Art Club and London Sketch Club; showed with RA, ROI and RI, and had one-man shows at Fine Art Society and Hereford City Museum and Art Gallery, which holds his work, as does the British Museum. Lived in London.

Henry SILK 1883–1947 Painter in oil and watercolour, noted for interiors and still life, who lived in London's East End. Silk was gassed during Army service in World War I. Views done then in France and on holiday and Edinburgh were among his non-London works. He was an unmarried basket-maker who worked for a time for an uncle who had a factory. Silk was the brother of the artist Elwin Hawthorne's mother and lived with the family in Bow. Like Hawthorne he showed at Lefevre Gallery with the East London Group, started by John Cooper through his classes at Bow and Bromley Evening Institute; at Agnew; and he had a solo exhibition of watercolours at Walter Bull & Sanders in 1931. The poet and artist Laurence Binyon was among collectors of Silk's work.

William SILLINCE 1906–1974 Oil painter and illustrator; commercial designer. Born in London, Sillince studied art at Regent Street Polytechnic and the Central School of Arts and Crafts. After a period in advertising in the 1920s and 1930s, Sillince went freelance, drawing for *Punch* and other periodicals. He also began to exhibit widely, including RA, RBA, RWS, NEAC, RSA and on the continent. His work is held by the British Museum, Imperial War Museum, Science Museum and provincial collections. Sillince taught at Brighton College of Art, 1949–52, then until 1971 at Hull Regional College of Art. Lived in Hull, Humberside.

Norman SILLMAN 1921– Sculptor, designer of coins and medals and teacher, born in London, whose family farmed in Australia, 1924–34. Studied under James Woodford at Blackheath School of Art from 1935–40, began studying at Royal College of Art in 1941, but Army service interrupted; during this, in 1946, studied at the Accademia in Florence; then completed Royal College studies under Frank Dobson and John Skeaping, 1946–9. As well as freelancing, 1949–56, Sillman taught part-time, then was on the staff of Nottingham College of Art/Trent Polytechnic, 1956–84. Sillman was a fellow of RBS, a member of Midland Group and joined Fédération Internationale de la Médaille. He exhibited at RA, RBA, SEA, LG, Arts Council Sculpture in the Home and elsewhere. He designed an extensive range of coins, mainly for foreign governments, from 1959, but also including Britain's Empire Games commemorative £2, 1986. There was a similar large range of award/commemorative medals, including a series for RIBA, Prince of Wales investiture, royal jubilee and wedding subjects. Sillman had strong interests in ancient history and mythology and art history, mainly in the ancient and tribal areas. British Museum and Royal Mint hold examples. Lived latterly in Eye, Suffolk.

Howard SILVERMAN 1946– Painter, printmaker and teacher, born in New York, America. Attended the High School of Art and Music and Art there and San Franciso Art Institute, graduating in 1969. Lived and showed in Britain from 1972. He took part in Cleveland International Drawing Biennale from 1981; Brewhouse Open, Taunton, 1983 onwards, winning first prize in 1985; and John Moores Liverpool Exhibition, 1987. Solo shows included Bath University, 1982, Brewhouse, Taunton, 1985, Woodlands Art Gallery, 1986, and Artsite, Bath Festival Gallery, 1987. Lectured part-time at Somerset College of Arts and Technology. Provincial Insurance and the London Boroughs of Hammersmith and Fulham and of Hounslow hold his work. Lived in Clifton, Bristol.

Jack SIMCOCK 1929– Painter, teacher and poet, born in Biddulph, Staffordshire, son of a coal miner. Simcock was for many years noted for bleak, sombre landscapes, which are instantly identifiable. He wrote that he "began to paint in 1945, more seriously in the Army in 1948." He attended Stoke-on-Trent School of Art periodically, 1949–55. "I began painting 'Simcocks' in 1954." Started teaching at a private school, 1953, and was a visiting lecturer at his old art school in 1965, but retired from all teaching in 1967. After showing locally, Simcock began exhibiting at Piccadilly Gallery in 1956, after which it became his agent; he had more than 50 solo shows, including overseas. Because of ill-health, from 1979 Simcock could not paint for a while, then in 1980 he began to produce small, brightly coloured abstracts, "which caused longstanding admirers much confusion". These were exhibited by his new agent, John Hunt, in 1997. Simcock also exhibited in many mixed exhibitions, including John Moores Liverpool Exhibition, 1957, where he was a prize winner. The autobiography, *Simcock, Mow Cop* – the mountain village where he lived for many years on the Staffordshire/Cheshire border – was published in 1975, along with his first volume of poetry, *Midnight Till Three*. Tate Gallery, Contemporary Art Society, many provincial public galleries, education authority collections and foreign art galleries hold examples.

Margaret SIMEON 1910– Designer and teacher, daughter of the ceramic designer Harry Simeon, who studied at Royal College of Art, becoming an associate in 1933 and a travelling scholar the year after. She taught at the College, 1936–40, and at Wimbledon School of Art, 1934–84, her special subjects being textile design, printing and art history. Among her books was *The History of Lace*. Showed for many years with Arts and Crafts Exhibition Society, at Victoria & Albert Museum's Britain Can Make It show of 1946 and five years later in Festival of Britain. Lived for many years at Stoke D'Abernon, Surrey.

Nicholas SIMINGTON 1930– Painter and teacher. He lived for 10 years in Navan, County Meath, and Drogheda, County Louth, in Ireland. He moved to England at the start of World War II and began adult life as a technical draughtsman and worked in industry in Scotland. For about 10 years he painted at home and attended art classes in the evening, then Glasgow School of Art, 1968–72, and went on to teach at Garrion Academy, Lanarkshire, 1973–5. Won an Arts Council Award. From 1970s began to show in mixed exhibitions throughout Britain, including Trumpington Gallery, Cambridge; Norwich School of Art Gallery; and The Minories, Colchester. Had a solo show at Art Centre, Motherwell, in 1968, with another at Buxton Mill, Norfolk, in 1977, and one in same year at Manor Gallery, Royston. Later shows included Fermoy Gallery, King's Lynn, 1988, and Southey Fine Art, Lewes, 1989. Lived in Norfolk.

Dorothy SIMISTER fl. from late 1970s– Artist in various media and teacher. She studied at Chester College of Further Education, 1972–5, graduated with honours from Camberwell School of Arts and Crafts, 1975–8, took an art teacher's certificate at Brighton Polytechnic, 1978–9, then taught handicrafts for four years for Southwark Social Services. After travels in India and South Asia in 1984 returned to a series of teaching posts, including part-time tutor at Putney School of Art. Simister's work was allied to a number of causes, such as anti-apartheid and strike support and she drew on her travel experiences. In 1978 gained the Adrian Trefell Fund Award. Showed at South London Open

Exhibition; New Moon Group Shows, including Woodlands Art Gallery, 1987; and had solo exhibition as part of Lewisham 14 Days Festival.

Connie SIMMERS 1941– Artist in oil and gouache, born and lived in Glasgow, who attended the School of Art there as a non-degree student, 1981–3. She was elected an artist-member of Glasgow Society of Women Artists, 1983 (she won its Scottish Amicable Award, 1994); Glasgow Art Club, 1987; and SSWA, 1989. Held a number of council appointments, including Royal Glasgow Institute of the Fine Arts, 1983–9. Group exhibitions included RSA; Sotheby's, Glasgow, from 1984; Barclay Lennie Fine Art, Glasgow, from 1987; William Hardie, 1992; Green Gallery, Aberfoyle, 1994; and City Gallery, 1995. Had solo exhibitions at Flying Colours, Edinburgh, from 1989, and Macaulay Gallery, Stenton, from 1991.

William George SIMMONDS 1876–1968 Sculptor in a variety of materials, painter of pictures and murals, designer, and carver and operator of marionettes. Born in Constantinople, Turkey, where his father was working as an architect, Simmonds was encouraged to draw and make cutouts from childhood. On leaving school he was trained in his father's office for five years, studying part-time at Windsor School of Art. Then attended Royal College of Art, 1893–9, under Walter Crane, and Royal Academy Schools, 1899–1904. Was an illustrator for a time, then became assistant to the painter Edwin Abbey, at Fairford, carrying out many of the designs for State Capitol at Harrisburg, Pennsylvania, 1905–10. During World War I he worked as a draughtsman engaged in tank and aircraft design. While nursing his father Simmonds began seriously to carve puppets, having earlier made just one, of the comedian Dan Leno as Widow Twankey, and was encouraged to give a performance before village children. Simmonds moved to Gloucestershire in 1919, eventually settling at Far Oakridge. Although he had intended to be a painter, Simmonds now devoted himself to carving marionettes and figures of animals, often on a big scale. Tate Gallery and Gloucester Museum and Art Gallery have good examples of his work. Simmonds became internationally known as an expert on marionettes and their operation. An exhibition celebrating the work of Simmonds and his designer and embroiderer wife Eve was held at Cheltenham Art Gallery and Museum in 1980.

Fay SIMMONS 1938– Sculptor, born in New Zealand, educated in Bideford, Devon, where she studied at the School of Art, also attending Hammersmith College of Art and Royal Academy Schools. She was an associate of RBS and showed at RA, AIA, Nicholas Treadwell Gallery and abroad. Lived in London.

Edith SIMON fl. from 1950s– Artist in wide variety of media, notable for papercut bas reliefs, novelist and historian, addicted to painting and writing from childhood. Studied at Slade School of Fine Art from 15, later Central School of Arts and Crafts from which she dropped out to become a member of AIA. Wrote for *Time-Life* and *Encyclopaedia Britannica*; novels including *The Chosen, The Golden Hand* and *The Great Forgery*; and history: *The Piebald Standard, The Making of Frederick the Great* and *The Anglo-Saxon Manner*. Sculpted and painted full-time from mid-1970s, serious and witty work, showing with SSWA, Glasgow Group and elsewhere. Had a solo show at Galerie Balans, Amsterdam, 1971, and after many others in 1994 at Student Centre, Edinburgh, where she lived and was a frequent International Festival exhibitor.

Jean-Georges SIMON 1894–1968 Painter, sculptor, draughtsman and teacher, born in Trieste. He was the son of an Austro-Hungarian diplomat and served in the Empire's cavalry on the Russian frontier in World War I. Studied in Romania and at Budapest Academy of Fine Art, 1918; in 1919 in Milan; then from 1920 lived in Paris, attending Académie Julian and L'École des Beaux-Arts and being a pupil of Antoine Bourdelle. Between 1923–36 exhibited in Budapest and Switzerland, then moved to London, where in 1937 he married an English wife. Prior to World War II there were further shows in Budapest and Switzerland and a Chelsea studio exhibition in 1939. In 1940 Simon won the Zichy Mihaly Graphical Prize Hungary. From 1942 lived in Yorkshire for the rest of his life, apart from a period in London, 1956–63. He lectured at Harrogate College of Art under Lincoln Jenkins and at Bradford College of Art. There was a solo exhibition at Redfern Gallery, 1943, and later showings included Mercer Gallery, Harrogate. Wakefield City Art Gallery gave him a memorial show in 1973.

Naomi B SIMON fl. c.1895–1965 Painter, miniaturist and artist in black-and-white, born in Sydney, Australia. She was educated in London, partly at King's College for Women, then Hammersmith School of Arts and Crafts and the Byam Shaw and Vicat Cole School of Art. She belonged to Ridley Art Club and Campden Hill Club, for a time being its honorary secretary. Showed at RA, SWA, Cooling Galleries, ROI and elsewhere. Lived in London.

Vera SIMONE 1898– Painter who was by profession a dress designer, born in Petrograd, Russia, her father being a senior government official. Studied at Petrograd Imperial Institute of Art. Exhibited at NEAC, SWA and Paris Salon. Lived in London.

Alan SIMPSON 1941– Marine and landscape artist, born in Basingtoke, Hampshire. Studied for a time at Bournemouth College of Art. Showed extensively in mixed exhibitions including RSMA of which he was a member. Also exhibited at Edwin Pollard Gallery in North America and at Linda Blackstone Gallery, Pinner. He did an amount of commissioned work for Poole Harbour Commissioners, Royle Publications, Abbey National Building Society and Bournemouth Polytechnic. Lived in Wimborne, Dorset.

Alice Mary SIMPSON 1867– Painter, especially of flowers, born in Norwood, Middlesex. Part of her education took place in Dresden, Germany, where she studied music. Showed RBA,

SWA, in Ireland and on the continent. Member of Sussex Women's Art Club and lived in the county at Bishopstone.

Audrey SIMPSON 1946– Painter, draughtsman and teacher, born in London. Her work was figurative, often with a humorous element. She studied at South-West Essex School of Art, Walthamstow, 1962–4, then for a teacher's certificate at Battersea College of Education, 1967–70. After a time at Wimbledon School of Art, 1975–8, Simpson studied for master's degree in fine art at Goldsmiths' College School of Art, 1979–81. From 1978 she taught widely in London area, including Goldsmiths'. Took part widely in group shows from late 1970s including RA Summer Exhibition; Imperial Tobacco Portrait Award at National Portrait Gallery, where she gained a Special Commendation; André Malraux Theatre, Gagny, France; Joe Klaffki Gallery, Minden, Germany; and Look Gallery, York. Undertook portrait commissions. Her solo exhibitions included Woodlands Art Gallery, 1983. Lived for a time at New Malden, Surrey.

Charles SIMPSON 1885–1971 Painter in oil, tempera and watercolour mainly of landscapes, marine pictures, animals, hunting scenes and birds; writer. Born in Camberley, Surrey, a riding accident prevented Simpson from pursuing a military career. Studied art in Paris at the Académie Julian and privately. Married Ruth Alison, a portrait painter. They moved to St Ives, Cornwall, in World War I, where they ran a painting school before moving on to London in 1924, and returning to Cornwall in 1931. Exhibited at RA, RI, Royal Glasgow Institute of the Fine Arts and Paris Salon. His work is owned by the Laing Art Gallery and Museum, Newcastle upon Tyne, and by galleries in Doncaster, Derby, Bournemouth and abroad. In the 1920s rodeo displays at the Wembley Empire Exhibition inspired Simpson's lively book *El Rodeo*. He went on to publish a number of other titles, including *Leicestershire and its Hunts*, *The Harboro' Country*, *Animal and Bird Painting* and an autobiography, *The Fields of Home*. Simpson won a silver medal at the Paris Salon in 1923 and gold medals at the Panama International Exposition at San Francisco, in 1915, and at the exhibition of sporting paintings held in Paris connected with the Olympic Games in 1924. As a painter of wildfowl Simpson can have few rivals. Lived at Alverton, Penzance, Cornwall.

Charles SIMPSON 1952– Designer and artist educated at Alloa Academy, who graduated with an honours degree in graphic design from Glasgow School of Art, 1970–5. He was a graphic designer at Queen Margaret College, 1975–6, then with Terston Design Studios, 1976–7, both in Edinburgh; designed for the medical publisher Churchill Livingstone, 1977–82; was graphic manager with County NatWest, Edinburgh, 1982–90; then moved to the Borders and freelanced as a designer and artist. Mixed shows included RSW; Open Eye Gallery, Edinburgh; Macaulay Gallery, Stenton; and Ancrum Gallery, Ancrum. Later solo exhibitions included Ainscough Contemporary Art, 1997.

Colin SIMPSON 1953– Painter, born in Hertfordshire, who studied at St Albans School of Art, 1971–2, Falmouth School of Art, 1972–5, and Royal College of Art, 1976–9. From 1983–5 he was Harkness Research Fellow at Yale University's faculty of art in America. Smith was joint first prize winner at the Royal Over-Seas League and his canvas Wardrobe 14, one of a series, was included in 1993–4 John Moores Liverpool Exhibition. Had a first solo show at Nicola Jacobs Gallery, 1982, later ones including Anderson O'Day, 1991, and Gallery Three-Zero, in New York, 1993.

Edna Gertrude SIMPSON 1900–c.1955 Painter and qualified art teacher, born in London. She studied at Croydon School of Art under Walter Wallis, 1915–21, then at Goldsmiths' College School of Art under Harold Speed. Exhibited RA, until 1955 at Croydon Art Society of which she was a member, and with Royal Horticultural Society, winning a gold medal. Lived in Coulsdon, Surrey.

Herbert SIMPSON 1907–1972 Versatile artist – especially printmaker – and teacher, born at Hud Hey, Haslingden, Lancashire, who won a scholarship to Accrington Grammar School, attended the local Art School and was its first student to gain a scholarship to Royal Academy of Art. There he transferred from the painting school to the engraving school under Robert Austin, and was outstanding enough to be given a two-year appointment as a junior tutor, showed at the RA and was commissioned by patrons including the Duke of Westminster. After teaching at Leicester College of Art from 1931, from 1934 until his retirement in 1967 Herbie, as he was known, became an inspiring tutor at Sunderland College of Art. Deafness prevented him joining the Royal Air Force in World War II, so he became a dispatch rider with Civil Defence. A love of boats and old Sunderland are apparent in Simpson's work, which is characterised by a sure sense of pattern and line. Showed locally and had work bought by Sunderland Museum and Art Gallery, which gave him an exhibition in 1995. His son was the artist Ian Simpson.

Ian SIMPSON 1933– Artist, writer and teacher, born in Loughborough, Leicestershire. He studied at Sunderland College of Art, 1950–3, then Royal College of Art, 1955–8, in latter year being an Abbey Travelling Scholar. Then taught at several art colleges and was principal of St Martin's School of Art, 1972–88. Was also a course consultant for Open College of the Arts. Simpson wrote for several publications, presented a number of television series on art and published books, including *The Challenge of Landscape Painting*, 1990, in which some of his own pictures appeared. He was a fellow and one-time president of the National Society for Art Education. Showed at RA Summer Exhibitions and elsewhere and had several solo shows. Glasgow Museums and Art Galleries and several education authorities hold examples. Lived at Clare, Suffolk. His father was the artist Herbert Simpson.

Jane SIMPSON 1965– Sculptor, who transformed everyday domestic things into uncommon creations, imparting them with a new presence. She was born and lived in London, where she graduated from Chelsea School of Art in 1988, then attended the Royal Academy Schools. Mixed shows included Some Went Mad, Some Ran Away, Serpentine Gallery, 1994, and Sensation, Young British Artists from the Saatchi Collection, RA, 1997. Had a solo show at Laurent Delaye Gallery, 1996.

Michael SIMPSON 1940– Painter and teacher, born in Dorset. He studied at Bournemouth College of Art, 1958–60, and Royal College of Art, 1960–3. He went on to be associate lecturer in painting at Bath College of Higher Education. Among mixed shows in which he participated were Northern Ireland Arts Council Open, in 1968, when he shared first prize; British Drawing at Hayward Gallery, 1982; and John Moores Exhibition, Liverpool, 1989, and in 1991–2, when he was a prizewinner. His first solo show was at Piccadilly Gallery in 1964, others including Serpentine Gallery, 1986, and Arnolfini Gallery, Bristol, 1996. Lived in Bradford-on-Avon, Wiltshire.

Ruth SIMPSON 1889–1964 Portrait painter and teacher who moved to Newlyn to study at Stanhope Forbes' school shortly before marrying the artist Charles Simpson in 1913. During World War I they went to live in St Ives, where they ran a painting school, moved to London for seven years in 1924, returned to Lamorna in 1931 and finally lived at Alverton, Penzance, Cornwall. Exhibited at SWA, IS and elsewhere, but latterly did not paint due to illness. She was represented in Painting in Newlyn 1880–1930 at Barbican Art Gallery, 1985.

Steve SIMPSON 1946– Artist and teacher born in Mansfield, Nottinghamshire, who attended the Art College there. In 1969, he became assistant lecturer in printmaking at Newcastle Polytechnic, and three-and-a-half years later moved to Wakefield District College, becoming head of visual studies. Wakefield Art Gallery holds his colourful and expressive mixed media on Xerox Russian Altarpiece II, of 1991, bought from his show at Waterside Art Gallery.

Dorothy SIMS-WILLIAMS 1909– Artist in oil and pastel and teacher, born in Disley, Cheshire. She studied 1926–8 at Stockport School of Art under G H James, then Royal Academy Schools, 1928–33, teachers including Walter Russell and F E Jackson. Was for a time a member of SWA, also showing at RP and RWA. Her work was mainly portraiture "influenced by Holbein", and landscapes and still life "influenced by the French Impressionists and Cézanne". Gained an Hon. Mention at Paris Salon and had a series of exhibitions with one or two other artists. St Matthew's Church in Stockport and St John's at Hopwood, Lancashire, hold her work. Lived in East Harting, Petersfield, Hampshire.

Beryl SINCLAIR 1901– Painter, designer, printmaker and administrator, born in Bath, Somerset. Studied at Bath School of Art, then Royal College of Art under William Rothenstein, completing her studies in 1925. In the 1930s and 1940s she was closely involved with the work of AIA, WIAC and Central Institute of Art and Design. Exhibited RA, NEAC, WIAC, AIA, Leicester Galleries and LG. Arts Council and London County Council bought her work. Lived at Amersham, Buckinghamshire.

David SINCLAIR 1937– Painter, printmaker and teacher, born in Glasgow. He studied at the School of Art there, winning a Major Travelling Scholarship and studying in London and on the continent. He then taught in schools and colleges, spending some years in special education, notably with blind children. In 1992 he took early retirement and moved to Paxton, Berwickshire, with his wife, also an artist, to create an art studio and workshop. Sinclair showed at RSA, SSA, Royal Glasgow Institute of the Fine Arts and elsewhere in Scotland. In 1992 he shared an exhibition at Duncan Campbell Fine Art. He also showed with Bourne Fine Art, Edinburgh. Work of the Italian artist Morandi was latterly an influence.

Gillian Ruth SINCLAIR fl. from 1950s– Sculptor, painter and draughtsman whose style evolved from studying painters of the Italian Renaissance, Van Gogh, Picasso and Modigliani and in sculpture especially Lynn Chadwick and Hubert Dalwood. Sinclair's paintings included people during moments of repose and reflection, isolated in their thoughts. The sculptures, in bronze and resin bronze, were figurative and abstract, and she had over a dozen portrait heads commissioned. As well as groups of figures and bird studies, Sinclair produced non-representational works reflecting her interest in classical music. She sponsored many London concerts. Sinclair also published poems, including the volume *The Walnut Tree and other poems*, 1988. Showed between 1959–63 (as Ruth Sinclair) at Leicester Galleries and WIAC. Also exhibited at Century Galleries, Henley-on-Thames, 1982: Osborne Gallery, 1986; and Edith Grove Gallery from 1992, having a solo show there in 1996. Lived in London.

Helen SINCLAIR 1954– Sculptor, born in Llanelli, Carmarthenshire, who studied at Dyfed School of Art, 1972–3, then Wimbledon School of Art, gaining an honours degree in fine art, sculpture, 1973–6. In 1988 she set up Sculpture Culture, designing and making limited-edition pieces and one-off sculptures on commission. She was commissioned to make a series of classical torsos and wall reliefs for the Grand Theatre, in Swansea. Exhibitions included 1990 Chelsea Flower Show, The Heifer Gallery in 1993 and Flying Colours Gallery, 1997. Sinclair's work was exported to the continent and America.

Ruth SINCLAIR: *see* **Gillian Ruth SINCLAIR**

Bernard Ralph SINDALL 1925–1998 Figurative and portrait sculptor and teacher, son of the illustrator Alfred Sindall. Studied at Brighton College of Art, 1946–50, in the latter year winning Prix de Rome. During the next two years in Italy he was much impressed by the work of Manzù and Rosso. On his return to England Sindall taught at City and Guilds Art School, 1953–6, and at Canterbury and Maidstone Schools of Art, 1956–65. Sindall first showed at Palazzo Venezia, Rome, in 1951, later exhibiting solo at Bedford House Gallery in 1972, Birmingham University, 1974, and Rye Art Gallery, 1988; interspersed were solo exhibitions in Switzerland, America and Norway. His group shows included RA and NEAC. Jonathan Clark Ltd also handled his work, which is in the collections of Royal Mint and Birmingham University. Lived in Wittersham, Kent.

Tony SINDEN fl. from mid-1960s– Versatile artist, born in Brighton, Sussex, who in 1985 was a founder-member of Housewatch, a collective using film, video, performance and installation. Sinden began independently to produce experimental films and expanded media events in 1966. In the 1970s and 1980s his installation and time-based work was seen at such galleries as the ICA, Hayward, Serpentine and Arnolfini in Bristol, National Film Theatre and Edinburgh International Festival, as well as events held on the continent and in America. Arts Council, British Film Institute, British Council, Scottish Arts Council, America's National Endowment to the Arts and the Contemporary Music Forum of Kyoto were among funding bodies. Later works included Approaching the Dissolve, Durham Cathedral, 1995.

Amrit SINGH 1966– Artist whose contribution to the Royal Over-Seas League Open, in 1996, Nyrmla's Wedding, used conventional paints plus gold dust on paper, and was in the style of an Indian miniature. It sought "to assert the artist's identity as a British Asian and the value of ethnic cultures against the advancement of global destruction and westernisation" and won the Countess Enid Driscoll-Spalletti Prize. Singh was born in London and studied at University College of Chester and Manchester University. Won a string of awards, and commissions from public galleries/museums in Bradford, Glasgow, Leicester and Liverpool. Group shows also included BBC North-West 6th Annual Art Competition, Salford Art Gallery, 1989; Twin Studio, Bluecoat Gallery, Liverpool, 1994; and An Exhibition of Football, Gallery 27, 1996. Had a solo show at Lancashire Polytechnic Arts Centre, Preston, 1987, later ones including Twin Perspectives, Salford City Gallery and tour, 1995–6, and Blackburn House Women's Centre, Liverpool, 1996.

Sushila SINGH: *see* **SUSHILA**

Kevin SINNOTT 1947– Painter and teacher, born in Wales. He was a natural painter, notable for his often complex figurative compositions and watercolours of great delicacy. Sinnott studied at Cardiff College of Art, 1967–8, Gloucester College of Art, 1968–71, and Royal College of Art, 1971–4. He went on to teach at Ruskin School in Oxford, Canterbury College and St Martin's School of Art. He made notable appearances at John Moores Exhibition, Liverpool, in 1978, 1980 and 1991–2, in the second winning a prize. His first solo show was at House Gallery, 1980, after which he exhibited regularly in Oxford, London and America. In 1990 he had simultaneous exhibitions at Bernard Jacobson and Anne Berthoud. Lived in East Barnet, Hertfordshire.

Francis SISLEY 1921– Painter and sculptor, born in London, who studied art at Woolwich Polytechnic. He showed at Redfern Gallery, AIA and with Free Painters and Sculptors, of which he was a member. Had a series of solo exhibitions at Loggia Gallery from 1974, later ones including Victoria Hotel, Bognor Regis, Sussex, the town where he lived. Sisley's ink and watercolour portrait drawing of the artist Alan Reynolds is held by the Tate Gallery archive.

Pauline SITWELL 1916– Artist and designer in a variety of media, poet and teacher, born in Malta, married to the artist Peter Stebbing. Her early education included training as a dancer and choreographer. Studied at St John's Wood School of Art, 1930, and Royal Academy Schools, 1933–7. Sitwell was a member of SWE, also showing at SGA and RSMA, Paris Salon and elsewhere. A series of solo exhibitions included one sponsored by Westminster City Council in 1973. Her poetry included *Train Journey to Deal and Other Poems*, 1981. Lived in London for many years.

Robert SIVELL 1888–1958 Painter and teacher, born in Paisley, Renfrewshire. Sivell left school at 14 and worked as a Clydeside shipyard apprentice engineer. After two years in North America he attended evening classes at Glasgow School of Art. World War I saw him serving as a ship's engineer, but afterwards Sivell determined to work as an artist full-time, after studying in Paris and Florence. From 1940–55 he was head of drawing and painting at Gray's School of Art in Aberdeen, then returned to Kirkcudbright, where he had painted before World War II. Sivell showed at Royal Glasgow Institute of the Fine Arts and RSA, to which he was elected in 1943. He was noted for his sensitive portraits, of which Elspeth, held by Aberdeen Art Gallery, is a good example. Scottish Arts Council held a memorial show in 1960.

John Rattenbury SKEAPING 1901–1980 Sculptor in wood, stone, terracotta and bronze, draughtsman and teacher, born at South Woodford, Essex. Skeaping – son of Kenneth Mathieson Skeaping, the painter – studied at Goldsmiths' College School of Art, the Central School of Arts and Crafts 1917–19 and the Royal Academy Schools, 1919–20. In 1924 Skeaping married Barbara Hepworth the sculptor, marriage dissolved 1933, and won the Rome Prize. His first one-man show was held, with Barbara Hepworth, at Alex Reid and Lefevre, Glasgow, in 1928. Was a member of the 7 & 5 Society 1932, LG 1928–34 and became an official war artist during World War II. After the war he lived in Mexico for a time, also in France and exhibited widely abroad. First exhibited at the RA in 1922 and was elected RA in 1960. Taught sculpture at the Royal College of Art from 1948 and was professor of sculpture 1953–9. Among his books were *Animal Drawing* and *How to Draw Horses*. Skeaping's autobiography, *Drawn from Life*, was published in 1977. His work is notable for its depiction of animals, in its simplicity of line and elemental quality resembling the prehistoric cave drawings found in France and Spain. Skeaping lived in France and at Chagford, Devon.

Walter M SKEENS 1886–1969 Artist and teacher, born in Portsmouth, Hampshire. For many years he taught in Bristol, latterly at Cotham Grammar School. Showed views of old Bristol at Bristol Savages and at RWA.

Victor SKELLERN 1908–1966 Designer, born at Fenton, Staffordshire. Skellern studied art at Hanley School of Art, Burslem School of Art and the Royal College of Art. He became chief designer and art director for the pottery firm Josiah Wedgwood & Sons, retiring in 1965. Details concerning Skellern and his development of wares and designs at Etruria and Barlaston are detailed in Maureen Batkin's book *Wedgwood Ceramics 1846–1959*, notably his work on freelance design in the 1930s. He exhibited RA, widely overseas and at the Victoria & Albert Museum, which holds his work.

John SKELTON 1923– Sculptor in a wide range of materials, letter-cutter, watercolourist, draughtsman and teacher, born in Glasgow. After Norwich Cathedral Choir School and Bablake School in Coventry Skelton was one of Eric Gill's last apprentices, 1940. In World War II he served in the Army in the Far East. Studied at Coventry School of Art and Architecture under Victor Candey and Walter Ashworth, also studying widely on the continent and in Asia. Skelton set up his own workshop and studio in 1950. He showed at RA, Alwin Gallery, Chichester Museum, elsewhere in England and abroad. His work is in many cathedrals, including St Paul's, Chichester, Hereford, Lincoln and Portsmouth. Bodleian Library in Oxford, Chichester Museum and Herbert Art Gallery in Coventry hold examples. A major retrospective for Skelton's seventieth birthday was held at Streat, Hassocks, Sussex, where he was based, in 1993.

Pam SKELTON 1949– Artist in various media and teacher. She studied at Camberwell School of Art and on English National Opera Theatre Design Course. In 1987 she was a finalist for the Athena Art Award and was joint winner of the City of Birmingham Fine Art Award. From 1990 was a senior lecturer at Central St Martins School of Art, three years after being artist-in-residence at Birmingham Museum and Art Gallery. In 1992 was a member of a team of artists which produced an eight-week experimental workshop for Bauhaus School, Weimar. Skelton showed widely in Britain, France and Germany. Group shows included Somatic States at Quicksilver Place Gallery, Middlesex University, 1992. Solo exhibitions included Groundplans at Ikon Gallery, Birmingham, and Benjamin Rhodes Gallery.

Mary SKEMPTON 1914–1993 Wood engraver, painter, bookbinder and teacher, brought up in Scarborough, attending its School of Art, then Royal College of Art. Exhibited RA, RBA, AIA and in the provinces. Lived in Watford, Hertfordshire, later in London.

Mark SKILTON 1954– Sculptor and teacher, born in London. He attended St Martin's School of Art, 1974–7. Gained a Greater London Arts Association Award in 1979. After teaching at Duncan of Jordanstone College of Art, Dundee, 1979–80, from 1982 Skilton taught at St Martin's. His group exhibitions included New Contemporaries at RA and St Martin's on the South Bank, both 1977; Cannizaro Park, 1979; and in 1983 Have You Seen Sculpture from the Body?, at Woodlands Art Gallery.

Alistair SKINNER fl. from late 1960s– Artist and teacher, studied at Camberwell School of Arts and Crafts, 1965–8, and Royal College of Art, 1968–72. He gained an exchange scholarship to Falmouth School of Art, 1967, and a scholarship to Cité des Arts, Paris, 1971. In 1982 he was included in Artists in Adult Education at Woodlands Art Gallery. Other shows included Polytechnic of the South Bank, 1967; Young Contemporaries at RA, 1970; then a joint project with Horst Reichert and Margaret Maier for redevelopment of Tiergarten Quarter, West Berlin, 1974.

Cyril L SKINNER fl. from c.1930–1970 Artist, notably a printmaker, and teacher who studied at Bristol Municipal School of Art, gaining a British Institute engraving scholarship in 1928. In the mid-1930s he left Bristol for Luton School of Art; became headmaster in 1946 and died just before retirement during a visit to Bristol. He had joined the Bristol Savages in 1930 and retained his membership 35 years. Was from 1931 an associate of RWA, exhibited in Chicago and was a key figure in annual art exhibition in Luton. Showed only once at RA. Bristol City Art Gallery holds his work, his Restoration of Bristol Cathedral being reproduced in *City Impressions: Bristol Etchers 1910–1935*, by Sheena Stoddard.

Freda SKINNER 1911–1993 Sculptor in a wide range of materials, letter-cutter and teacher, born in Limpsfield, Surrey. She studied at Royal College of Art from the age of 17 with Henry Moore and Alan Durst. In the early-1940s began to teach at Kingston School of Art, and after war service, during which she was involved in relief map work, she became head of the sculpture department at Wimbledon School of Art, 1945–71, setting high standards. In 1961 she published a standard book on wood carving. She was a fellow of RBS and a member of SPS' council. Skinner's work was representational and she completed numerous commissions. These included The Risen Christ in Glory, 1960, for St Paul's Church, Southwark, the foundation stone for the Barbican Centre in 1972 and in the same year the Virgin and Child for the Lady Chapel of St Elphege's Church, Wallington. A retrospective was held at Bruton Street Gallery starting just before Skinner died. Lived latterly at West Amesbury, Wiltshire.

Ivy G M SKINNER: *see* **JACQUIER**

John SKINNER 1953– Painter and draughtsman of figurative, near-abstract works, born Chatham, Kent. His group exhibitions included Stowells Trophy at RA and LG at Camden Arts Centre, both 1976; Cyprus Summer School, Paphos, 1977; and North-Eastern Artists' Co-op at Newcastle Polytechnic, 1978. Had solo shows at New Gallery, Haringey Park, 1980, and Woodlands Art Gallery, 1982.

Mark SKINNER 1957– Painter and teacher who said that "the starting point for much of my work is physical and ideological conflict." He was born and lived in Liverpool, studied at the Polytechnic there, 1976–7, then at Birmingham Polytechnic, 1977–80. He taught at Edgehill College and Wrexham College of Art. His shows included Sainsbury Centre, Norwich, 1981; Bluecoat Gallery, 1983 and 1988; Merkmal Gallery, Liverpool, 1991; John Moores Liverpool Exhibition, 1991–2; and Bluecoat Artists, Williamson Art Gallery & Museum, Birkenhead, 1992.

Sabrina SKINNER 1962– Painter whose work contained a strong pattern-making element. She gained an honours degree in history and politics at Exeter University, 1981–4; a fine & decorative arts diploma with distinction from Victoria & Albert Museum, 1984–5; did a foundation course at City & Guilds of London Art School, 1988–9; then obtained a first-class fine art degree there, 1989–92. Won the NatWest Villiers David Travel Award, 1992, and in 1996 the Daisaku Ikeda Award, Tokyo, and the first prize in the Oleum Art Competition, Accademia Italiana. Exhibitions included Art For Youth, Mall Galleries, 1992; Paperworks at Seagate Gallery, Dundee, 1993; PS, Mall Galleries, 1995; and NatWest Art Prize, 1995 and 1996, being a finalist in both years. Had a solo show at 172 Walton Street in 1995 and was included in a four-woman exhibition at Cadogan Contemporary, 1997.

Birgit SKIÖLD 1923–82 Printmaker and teacher, born in Stockholm, Sweden, where she studied at the Konstfackskolan, settling in England in 1948. Studied at the Anglo-French Art Centre; in Paris at L'Académie de la Grande Chaumière; and at Regent Street Polytechnic. In 1957 she started the Print Workshop, providing facilities for artists. Skiöld was a visiting lecturer in printmaking at Bradford, Hammersmith and Wolverhampton Colleges of Art, and a visiting teacher of lithography at University of Wisconsin, 1964. Was a member of the Senefelder Group and its secretary, 1958–60; was a founder-member of the Printmakers' Council; and a member of Grafiska Sallskapet, Sweden, and of AIA. Took part in international mixed shows and had several solo exhibitions, including Curwen Gallery, 1968, and Oxford Gallery, Oxford, 1971. In 1970 her *Chimes*, relief etchings with seven poems by Dante Gabriel Rossetti, won the award of the Aigle d'Or (Prix de la Bibliophilie), published by Circle Press Publications. There was a memorial show at Cartwright Art Gallery, Bradford, 1984. Arts Council holds her work.

Jerzy SKOLIMOWSKI 1907–1985 Sculptor, designer, architect and graphic artist, one of the Polish paper sculptors who made an impact in Britain after World War II. While studying at Warsaw Institute of Technology, from which he graduated in 1935, Skolimowski freelanced as a graphic artist and designer so successfully that he exhibited posters internationally, gained a Diplôme d'Honneur at the Paris Exhibition and eventually had posters on permanent display at Warsaw's Museum of Posters. Saw active service in the Polish Army and Special Operations Executive in the war, for which he was decorated, in 1945 being evacuated to England and demobilised. In 1948, as George Skolli, his *Zoocuts, a Story Book from which Animals come to Life*, was published and patented, having success on television. In London Skolimowski worked as an architect and commercial designer, clients including Science Museum, where he designed the iron and steel gallery, and Farnborough and Paris Air Shows, doing work for British Overseas Airways Corporation. Also had a period in South Africa, designing for De Beers and Anglo-American. He designed tapestries for his wife Stanislawa and with her produced a technique for unusual three-dimensional fibre sculptures. Was included in the exhibition of Polish Paper Sculpture, of which he was an acknowledged master, at Polish Cultural Institute, 1995.

George SKOLLI: *see* **Jerzy SKOLIMOWSKI**

Kim SKOVGAARD 1927– Artist in watercolour, oil and acrylic, architect and teacher, born in Manchester. He followed in the family tradition of at least five generations of artists, some of his pictures being included in the Skovgaard Museum, Viborg, Denmark. Skovgaard studied architecture at Manchester University, 1943–8, eventually obtaining his doctorate. From 1955 he had his own practice as an architect, working in parallel as an artist, lecturing from 1962–90 at Manchester Regional College of Art and Liverpool College of Building and Liverpool Polytechnic. He was a member of the Society of Architect Artists. Showed at RCamA, Manchester City Art Gallery, Colin Jellicoe Gallery in Manchester, Royal Danish Embassy, RIBA and in Paris, Luxembourg and Frankfurt. Solo shows included Skovgaard Museum, Warrington Art Gallery and elsewhere. Skovgaard painted in Denmark, Wales, Italy, Mexico, France, Spain, Cyprus and elsewhere overseas. Lived at Moore, Warrington, Cheshire.

Ian SKOYLES 1964– Artist born in Great Yarmouth, Norfolk, who attended the College of Art and Design there, 1983–5, then Birmingham Polytechnic, 1985–8. Exhibitions included Midlands Art Show at Dudley Museum and Art Gallery and Coventry Open at Herbert Art Gallery, both 1992; Sevenfold Warehouse Exhibition, Birmingham, 1993; Birmingham Museum and Art Gallery, 1994; and Gallery 101 in Ottawa, Canada, and Pacesetters at Peterborough Museum and Art Gallery, both 1995.

Eleanor May SKRIMSHIRE 1886–1978 Painter, draughtsman and teacher, born in Morpeth, Northumberland. She studied with the watercolourist H Dawson Barkas at Reading School of Art, Berkshire, and in London. Lived and taught in the Reading area, notably at the Blue Coat School. She exhibited with Reading Guild of Artists, of which she was a leading member, and in the local art gallery.

Iain SLACK fl. from mid-1980s– Painter, illustrator and teacher who studied at Glasgow School of Art, 1982–6. Among his various positions over the next few years were a period as an illustrator and graphic artist for Strathclyde Regional Council in 1988, following engagements in America working as a general counsellor with mentally handicapped and as an art specialist at Camp Lindenmere, Pennsylvania. From 1989 he began work as a full-time artist, but found time to teach art in Lowmoss Prison.

Among Slack's awards were the Greenshields, James Torrance and Arthur Andersen. He showed at Royal Glasgow Institute of the Fine Arts, RSA, SSA in mixed shows. After solo shows at Langside Galleries, Glasgow and Greenock Arts Guild in 1990, had one at Compass Gallery, Glasgow, 1992. McLean Museum and Art Gallery, Greenock, holds his work, which included fantastic and Surrealist elements.

Richard SLADDEN 1933– Sculptor and teacher, born in Clevedon, Somerset. His mother was a painter, Hilda Scott. Educated in Taunton, he attended the Royal West of England Academy school of architecture in Bristol, but was principally self-taught as a sculptor. Came into prominence in the 1960s with one-man shows at the New Vision Centre Gallery, Alwin Gallery and at Arnolfini Gallery, in Bristol, as well as showing with groups such as LG. From New Vision Gallery in 1965 Arts Council bought his stone sculpture Gangile. Went on to teach sculpture at Croydon College of Art.

Lionel John Charles SLADE 1924– Painter, designer, draughtsman and teacher, born in London. Studied at Camberwell School of Arts and Crafts, 1939–40 and 1948, where his teachers included Victor Pasmore and John Minton; St Martin's School of Art, 1941; and Brighton College of Art, 1948–50. Taught for a time in Sussex and was a member of the Association of Sussex Artists. Showed at UA, RI, RBA and elsewhere. Lived in Hatch End, Middlesex.

Roy SLADE 1933– Painter, notably in acrylic, administrator and teacher, born in Cardiff, where he attended the College of Art, 1949–54. Was at University of Wales, 1953–4. Slade held a number of teaching posts in Britain, then in 1967–8 became professor of painting at Corcoran School of Art, in Washington, when his career took an American direction; became an American citizen in 1975. Wrote for *Studio International* and other art magazines. Took part in many group exhibitions in Britain and America and one-man shows included Howard Roberts Gallery, Cardiff, 1958, several at Jefferson Place Gallery in Washington, and elsewhere. Arts Council, Contemporary Art Society and Westinghouse Corporation hold his work. Lived latterly at Bloomfield Hills, Michigan.

Noël SLANEY 1915– Artist mainly in oil, full name Margery Noël Slaney, born and lived in Glasgow, married to the artist George Frederick Moules. She studied at Glasgow School of Art under Hugh Adam Crawford, gaining her diploma in 1937 and post-diploma in 1939, both with distinction. Was at various times a member of RSW, Royal Glasgow Institute of the Fine Arts, SSA and SSWA, also showing at RA. Lillie Art Gallery in Milngavie and galleries in Glasgow, Aberdeen and Dundee hold her work. In 1992 she had a solo show of drawings, paintings, pastels and Batiks at The College Club, University of Glasgow.

Alison Jane SLATER 1967– Artist and designer, working in gouache on paper, whose main themes were English landscapes and streets in Spain. She was born in Manchester and studied textiles at the Polytechnic there under Alan Holmes, graduating with honours. Slater was a member of the Chartered Society of Designers and showed regularly at Colin Jellicoe Gallery in Manchester, also at Altrincham Library, Llewellyn Alexander Gallery and New Designers Exhibition at Business Design Centre. Lived in Sale, Cheshire.

Humphrey SLATER 1906–1958 Writer, painter and military strategist who spent the early years of his life in South Africa, where his father remained, Humphrey, his mother and brother returning to England. Attended Tonbridge School, then Slade School of Fine Art, 1923–6, leaving mysteriously halfway through a term. Slater was taken up by Lucy Wertheim, who showed him in her first exhibition in 1930 and afterwards, figurative and abstract works. He appears in her memoir *Adventure in Art*, with his work illustrated. Slater joined the Communist Party and is believed to have visited the Soviet Union, but he became disillusioned during the Spanish Civil War, in which he served with the International Brigade, from 1938 as chief of operations, XV Brigade Staff. (During the war Slater took to using Hugh, his third name, instead of Humphrey, as he felt Hugh sounded more proletarian.) Slater's experiences led to his being chosen in 1940 to help form the Home Guard in World War II and to select officers for training. After the war Slater's continuing interest in art had an offshoot in his editorship of the short-lived magazine *Polemic*. Its contributors were distinguished, including George Orwell and Bertrand Russell, reflecting Slater's wide range of intellectual friends. Slater latterly developed a career as a writer, factual books and adventure novels. In 1949 *Conspirator* was filmed, starring Elizabeth and Robert Taylor. The film, which drew on Slater's life with the first of his four wives, Elisabeth Robertson, whom he had met at the Slade, made its author money, which he enjoyed spending at venues such as L'Étoile, although circumstances eventually made him an undischarged bankrupt. Slater was a multi-faceted eccentric and man of secrets; a brilliant talker who invented an ingenious racing game, fondly remembered by friends such as A J Ayer and John Davenport, but never commercially marketed; capable of irrational behaviour, such as firing a revolver through the ceiling of a private house; who had in him a vein of self-destruction. He died in La Linea, Spain, where he had gone to write his autobiography. William Coldstream though him "a very gifted and rare artist".

Richard SLATER 1927– Painter, draughtsman, printmaker, collagist, illustrator and teacher, born in London, who attended Hornsey School of Art, 1944–51, part-time 1951–4. After nine years teaching art in Dagenham and London Schools, and printmaking at the Working Men's College, he was appointed to the College of St Mark and St John, 1960, transferring with it from Chelsea to Plymouth in 1973, retiring as head of department in 1980 to paint full-time. During the 1960s, Slater did book illustrations for Cambridge University Press; made several lithographic editions at Curwen Press for Consolidated Fine Arts, New York; and completed mural and ceramic mural commissions. A romantic, dreamlike quality pervaded much of Slater's work, which often involved figures in landscape. He participated in numerous mixed shows, including RA; RI; RSMA; Alresford Gallery in Alresford; Cowfold Gallery at Cowfold; Savage, St George's and John Whibley Galleries, and elsewhere. Awards included first prize in the Drake 400 competition, sponsored by Plymouth City Council, 1980; first prize in the watercolour competition sponsored by Becton Dickinson, Plymouth, 1982; first prize, South West Open Figurative Art Competition, sponsored by *Western Morning News*, 1991; and RI Medal for most outstanding painting by a non-member, Mall Galleries, 1992. Showed solo with John Whibley, 1974, later exhibitions including Sterts Arts Centre, Cornwall, 1992. Prince Albert Museum in Exeter, Nuffield Foundation and several local authorities hold examples. Lived in Landrake, Saltash, Cornwall.

Rosemary SLATTERY 1927– Artist, notably a printmaker, born in Peru. She studied at Croydon School of Art and with the wood engraver Gertrude Hermes at Central School of Arts and Crafts. Showed at Victoria & Albert Museum which holds her work, RBA, Crafts Centre and elsewhere and lived in London.

James Sinton SLEATOR 1885 (some sources say 1889)–1950 Versatile painter and teacher, born in County Armagh, Northern Ireland. He studied at Belfast School of Art, in 1910 gained a scholarship to attend Dublin's Metropolitan School of Art where William Orpen was among his teachers, went to the Slade School of Fine Art and then worked in Paris. From 1915 taught at Dublin's Metropolitan School, went to Florence in Italy and then in the late 1920s to London, where he became a noted portrait painter. The painters Orpen, John Lavery and Jack B Yeats were among his subjects. Among his pupils was Winston Churchill. In 1941 Sleator settled in Dublin, soon becoming president of the RHA, continuing until he died. Also showed at RA, Royal Glasgow Institute of the Fine Arts and RP. In 1951 Victor Waddington Galleries, Dublin, held a memorial show. Ulster Museum holds his portrait of the novelist Forrest Reid and Dublin's National Gallery of Ireland a self-portrait.

Keith SLEEMAN 1921–1987 Painter and teacher, born in Bristol. Studied at Willesden and Hornsey Schools of Art, at Hornsey gaining his teacher's diploma. Sleeman taught at South Hampstead High, a girls' school, for nine years to 1981, leaving to concentrate on his own work. He was remembered for "his original approach to life at the school" and the "congenial atmosphere" he created. Set up Sleeman Studio where he taught in Hampstead. Showed in mixed exhibitions in London, including Nicholas Treadwell Gallery, and had a solo show at Foyles Gallery, 1961.

Bernard SLEIGH 1872–1954 Wood engraver, painter,stained glass artist, cartographer, muralist and teacher, born in Birmingham. He studied at Birmingham School of Arts and Crafts and then taught there, specialising in wood engraving and book illustration. He was a notable visionary engraver, working for many Birmingham School artists and producing a manual, *Wood Engraving*. One of his major tasks was to cut 100 illustrations by A J Gaskin for the two-volume Hans Christian Andersen edition of 1893. He also worked for *The Quest* magazine and for Essex House Press. Fairies and elves were a feature of his work, as in his 1920 *Faerie Calendar*. Showed RA, RBSA of which he was made a member in 1928 as well as extensively abroad. Birmingham City Museum and Art Gallery holds his work. Lived in Edgbaston.

Sylvia SLEIGH 1916– Painter in oil on canvas and teacher, born in Llandudno, Caernarvonshire, who studied at Brighton School of Art and later settled in New York. She became a member of the Women's Caucus for Art and was on the selection committee for Women Choose Women, New York Cultural Center, 1973. Her teaching posts included Kreeger Wolf Distinguished Professor, Northwesten University, 1977. In 1982 she gained a National Endowment Arts Visual Artists' Fellowship Grant, in 1985 a Pollock-Krasner Foundation Grant. Group shows included American Landscapes, Bryony Gallery, 1965, and Portraits from the American Art World, The New York School of Social Research Center, 1966, both in New York. Had a first solo show at Trafford Gallery, 1962, later ones including G W Einstein, New York, from 1980, and Zaks Gallery, Chicago, 1985. Sleigh's singular portrait of members of the Situation Group was included in The Sixties Art Scene in London, Barbican Art Gallery, 1993. Depicted among the sitters was theoretician and critic Lawrence Alloway, Sleigh's husband.

Kevin SLINGSBY 1950– Artist in various media, born in Guiseley, Yorkshire, who attended Bradford School of Art, 1965–8. He gained Southern Arts Awards in 1986 and 1990 and an Arts Council Award in 1990. Slingsby was a member of LG, also exhibiting in groups at staff exhibition, Ruskin School of Drawing, Oxford, 1982; Oxford Printmakers at Reading City Art Gallery and Five Artists at Oxford Polytechnic, both 1985; Oxford Artweek Billboard Project, 1989; and in East at Norwich Gallery, 1991. Had a solo show at Bradford University Gallery, 1983, later ones including Morley Gallery, 1993. Slingsby said that his paintings "contain a visual vocabulary of symbolic objects. These objects act out visual dramas commenting on social and political conditions." Bradford City Art Gallery, Bradford University, several Oxford colleges and Yorkshire Arts Association hold examples. Lived in Dorchester on Thames, Wallingford, Oxfordshire.

Andrew SLOAN 1954– Abstract sculptor, born in Essex, who worked in steel and cast iron. He studied at Norwich School of Art, 1973–6, under Katherine Gili and David Nash, then worked as assistant to John Foster, 1976–80. In 1985 began working at Foster's studio complex, Hardingham, Norfolk, living in Norwich. Exhibited in Hardingham Workshop Exhibition at Sainsbury Centre, Norwich, 1986; Painting and Sculpture, Audun Gallery, 1987; East, at Norwich Gallery, 1991, and in that year was invited to participate in Thupelo International Artists' Workshop, Broederstroom, South Africa, contributing to a show at Fuba Building, Johannesburg. Several notable private collections in Britain and America hold examples.

Bob SLOAN 1940– Sculptor, based in Portadown, Armagh, Northern Ireland. He took part in numerous group shows, including the Women of Ulster Arts Council touring show, 1975–6; Waterman's Art Centre, Brent, 1986; Fenderesky Gallery at Queen's, Belfast, 1990; and Solomon Gallery, Dublin, 1993. Had a solo show with Tom Caldwell and Arts Council Galleries, Belfast, both 1982, then a touring exhibition in 1991 including Garter Lane Arts Centre, Waterford. Participated in many conferences, seminars and workshops, being on the organising committee of the International Sculpture Conference, Dublin, 1988. Awards included RUA Silver Medal in 1983, its Gold Medal in 1988, elected academician of RUA in 1990 and a member of its council, 1992. From 1988–91 Sloan was director, Sculptors' Society of Ireland. Ulster Museum in Belfast, Northern Ireland Arts Council, Arts Council of Ireland and *Belfast Newsletter* hold examples. Lived in Purdysburn, Belfast.

Victor SLOAN 1945– Artist combining photography, printmaking and painting, born in Dungannon, County Tyrone, Northern Ireland. He studied at Belfast and Leeds Colleges of Art, 1964–9. Took part in many mixed shows, including Kettle's Yard, Cambridge, 1986; Douglas Hyde Gallery, Dublin, 1987; Ulster Art in the Eighties, Gallagher Gallery, Dublin, 1988; Open Eye Gallery, Liverpool, 1991; Bradford Print Exhibition, Cartwright Hall, 1993, and widely abroad. Later solo shows included International Baltic Arts Centre, Ustka, Poland, 1994, and Borne Sulinowo, Orchard Gallery, Londonderry, 1995. Arts Council of Northern Ireland and Ulster Museum in Belfast hold examples. Lived in Portadown, County Armagh.

Mary Annie SLOANE fl. from c.1890–1961 Painter, illustrator and printmaker, born in Leicester, who after initial studies there attended Herkomer's School in Bushey and then Royal College of Art. She was made an associate of RE, a member of SWA and of the Leicester Society of Artists and settled in Enderby, Leicestershire. Also showed with Ridley Art Club, RA, RI and at Alpine Club Gallery. Victoria & Albert Museum holds her work.

Stephen SLOCOMBE 1972– Artist, born in Bristol, who gained an economics degree at Manchester University, in the mid-1990s studied at Central St Martins College of Art & Design after Clifton School of Art. Group exhibitions included King Sturge Art Exhibition, at London Institute of Higher Education, and Royal Over-Seas League Open, both 1996. Slocombe examined popular myths, stereotypes, pre- and misconceptions that hovered around what was popularly known as Art.

Vikki SLOWE 1947– Printmaker, born and lived in London, who studied at London College of Fashion and Camden Arts Centre. She was a member of RE and Printmakers' Council, also exhibiting at RA and in the provinces. Smithsonian Institution in Washington, America, holds her work.

Phyllis Maud SMALE 1897– Painter and teacher, born in Darlington, Yorkshire. She studied at School of Art there and Regent Street Polytechnic School of Art. Showed extensively at ROI, also at RA, SWA, NEAC and elsewhere. Lived in Esher, Surrey.

Anthony SMART 1949– Sculptor and teacher, born in Yorkshire. He attended Hull College of Art, 1967–70, and St Martin's School of Art, 1970–3. He worked at Stockwell Depot, 1973–6, then Greenwich Studios, 1976–8. Smart taught at St Martin's and Wimbledon Schools of Art. Participated in many group exhibitions, including Platform '72, in 1972, at Museum of Modern Art, Oxford; Six Sculptors, at Chelsea Gallery, 1974; The Condition of Sculpture, Hayward Gallery, 1975; Contemporary British Sculpture, Battersea Park, 1977; Cannizaro Park from 1978; and Have You Seen Sculpture from the Body?, at Woodlands Art Gallery, 1983. Arts Council holds his work. Lived for some years in Beverley, Yorkshire.

Douglas I SMART 1879–1970 Watercolourist and printmaker who studied with Frank Short. Exhibited RA, RI, RE, Cooling Galleries, Fine Art Society and Walker Art Gallery, Liverpool. British Museum, Victoria & Albert Museum, Ashmolean Museum, Oxford, and Fitzwilliam Museum, Cambridge, hold his work. Lived in London, then Lee-on-the-Solent, Hampshire.

Jeffrey SMART 1921– Painter and draughtsman, born in Adelaide, South Australia, where he studied at the School of Arts early in World War II. After the war, in Paris he attended L'Académie de la Grande Chaumière and Académie Montmartre, with Fernand Léger in 1948–9. As well as Whitechapel Art Gallery and Tate Gallery Smart had a series of solo exhibitions at Redfern Gallery from 1967. Major Australian galleries including Sydney, Melbourne and Adelaide hold examples. Lived for a time in Arezzo, Tuscany, Italy.

R Borlase SMART 1881–1947 Painter and draughtsman, born in Kingsbridge, Devon. Studied at Plymouth School of Art, 1897–1900, at the Royal College of Art, 1900–01, then privately with Julius Olsson at St Ives, Cornwall, where Smart died. He was art critic for the *Western Morning News* for 10 years from 1903 and while in the Army in World War I drew on the Western Front. After the war settled in St Ives and began exhibiting regularly at the RA, RBA, ROI, Fine Art Society and elsewhere. One-man shows included Penwith Gallery, St Ives, 1949 and 1981, and City Art Gallery, Plymouth, 1950 and 1975. Borlase Smart was closely associated with the St Ives Society of Artists, and the Penwith Society of Arts was founded as a tribute to him in 1949. Although a traditional painter himself, Smart encouraged Peter Lanyon to start painting and some of the more radical artists to exhibit in St Ives. Designed railway posters and wrote *The Technique of Seascape Painting*.

Carlyon SMEDLEY 1901–1993 Artist, designer, craftsman and teacher, brought up in Maidstone, Kent, where his father had a shop involved in the watch and clock trade, an interest Carlyon retained. Smedley studied at the School of Art there and at the

Royal College of Art and was on the staff of Gravesend School of Art, 1927–61, where he became head of design. Although Smedley had a congenital deformity, one hand being merely a stump, he was a superb craftsman, with a special interest in egg tempera, lacquer and stained glass. He was revered as a teacher and old-fashioned gentleman, with impeccable manners. Among Smedley's output was a fine painted, lacquered and gilded fourfold screen (see The Fine Art Society spring 1996 catalogue). The Smedleys were keen churchgoers in Meopham, Kent, for which he designed the British Legion memorial window, installed 1951. Other Kent churches hold his work. In 1938 Gravesend Grammar School for Boys received new library windows designed by Smedley. After retirement, the Smedleys lived in Yopps Green, Plaxtol, then after Bertha Smedley's death in 1982 Carlyon moved to Abbeyfield Trust accommodation in Tonbridge, dying in Plaxtol Nursing Home.

Geoffrey SMEDLEY 1927– Non-representational sculptor and draughtsman, and teacher, born in London, who studied at Camberwell School of Arts and Crafts and Slade School of Fine Art. He was senior lecturer at Portsmouth College of Art, 1956–8; head of sculpture at Portsmouth Polytechnic, 1968–78; visiting artist at Queen's University, Kingston, Ontario, 1977–8; and from 1978 professor, department of fine arts, at the University of British Columbia, Vancouver. Group exhibitions included Experiment in Form, Grosvenor Gallery, and WAC touring show Structure '66, both 1966; Systems, Lucy Milton Gallery, and Systems touring show from Whitechapel Art Gallery, both 1972; Open Field, Reading Art Gallery, 1973; and Nature as Material, Arts Council, 1980. Solo exhibitions included AIA, 1965; Agnes Etherington Art Centre, Queen's University, Kingston, Ontario, 1978; and Vancouver Art Gallery, 1982. Arts Council holds several works by Smedley, in various materials, and his Columns, 1975, in aluminium with a steel base, is in Victoria Park, Portsmouth.

Gordon Owen SMEDLEY 1925– Painter, designer, printmaker and teacher, born in Bournville, near Birmingham. Studied at the School of Art there, 1940–3, then at Birmingham College of Art, 1947–9. He went on to teach at several art schools in the Midlands, eventually becoming vice-principal of Bolton School of Art, then the head of the school of art and design at Tameside College of Technology. Lived in Stalybridge, Cheshire.

Michael SMEE 1946– Painter, scenic artist and theatre designer and teacher who studied at Colchester School of Art, 1961–5. He became scenic artist and resident designer at Birmingham Repertory Theatre, 1965–7; scenic artist at the Royal Opera House, Covent Garden, 1967–8; then had a decade working as a scenic artist for Thames Television, London Weekend Television and various film production companies. From 1978 Smee was senior lecturer and head of visual studies at Colchester School of Art and Design, Colchester Institute. Mixed exhibitions included Bankside Gallery, 1987; Quay Gallery, Sudbury, 1990; and New Grafton Gallery Christmas Show and Artists of Today and Tomorrow, both 1994. Had a solo show at Compendium Gallery, Birmingham, 1966, later ones including Minories Gallery, Colchester, 1987, and New Grafton, 1995.

Lavinia SMILEY 1919–1991 Artist in pen and wash and writer, born in London, grand-daughter of the first Viscount Cowdray. She grew up in a privileged atmosphere, described in her book *A Nice Clean Plate*, inheriting the family shyness but great love of historical buildings. She was educated in London and Paris and after World War II with her husband Major Michael Smiley was given Castle Fraser, in Aberdeenshire, which they restored and in 1977 made over to the National Trust for Scotland. She wrote the Trust's book on the house, a volume called *The Frasers of Castle Fraser,* and published a number of children's books with delightful illustrations. Died in London.

Alan SMITH 1941– Artist and teacher. He employed a range of media, including ceramics and photo-lithographic installations. Born in Biggar, Lanarkshire, Smith studied at Edinburgh College of Art, 1960–4. He was in Nigeria, 1966–7, taught from 1967–9, then from 1969–75 was co-founder and chairman of the Ceramic Workshop in Edinburgh, where he settled after working in Italy for two years. In Italy he had a solo show in 1977 at Studio la Citta and Galleria Ferrari, Verona, and he showed in mixed exhibitions in Italy and Britain. Was included in Painters in Parallel at Edinburgh College of Art, 1988. The Council and Scottish National Gallery of Modern Art, Edinburgh, hold his work.

Alan Partridge SMITH 1922– Painter, born in London. He studied at Hornsey School of Art, 1946–50. In early 1950s showed three pictures at RA Summer Exhibition, landscapes of Essex. Also showed Brighton Art Gallery and RBA, and loaned work to AEB and Arts Council. Lived at Rochford, Essex, and signed his work P S.

Andrew SMITH 1960– Sculptor with a special interest in monumental figurative and decorative carving. He trained under a three-year apprenticeship with W J Laffords as a stonemason carver. In 1989 gained first prize in the National Association of Monumental Masons Sculpture Award for Estate, a marble head and shoulders depicting Summer. Took part in mixed shows at Black Boy Gallery, West Wycombe; Towner Art Gallery, Eastbourne; and Linda Blackstone Gallery, Pinner. His solo shows included Cow Byre, Ruislip, 1989; Uxbridge Library, 1990; and Beck Theatre, Hillingdon, 1991. Public commissions included Mother & Child, 1989, Marlow Churchyard; and 1991, two life-and-a-half-size figures of Adam & Eve, London Borough of Hillingdon.

Bob and Roberta SMITH: *see* **Patrick BRILL**

Bridget SMITH 1966– Artist employing photography, born in Southend-on-Sea, Essex, who attended Central School of Art, 1984–5, and Goldsmiths' College, 1985–8. In 1991 gained a GLA Women's Photography Award. Group shows included Hit & Run, Tufton Street, 1992; Time Out Billboard Project, 1993; Institute of Cultural Anxiety: Works from the Collection, ICA, 1994; Something Cheap, Custard Factory, Birmingham, 1995; and British Art Show 4, and tour, 1995–6. Had a solo show at Entwistle Contemporary, 1995.

Carlton Alfred SMITH 1853–1946 Painter, notably of genre works, born and lived in London, married to the artist Martha Sarah King, who also showed under her married name. His father was the steel engraver Alfred Smith. He studied at Slade School of Fine Art, winning gold and silver medals. For seven years from 1916 he visited India, painting portraits and landscapes. He was a member of RBA, RI and ROI, also showing at RA and Royal Glasgow Institute of the Fine Arts. His pictures such as When Little Ones Grow Weary and The Close of Day were illustrated in magazines including *Illustrated London News*. National Gallery of South Australia in Adelaide bought his picture Dawn and National Gallery of Victoria in Melbourne acquired Christmas Eve.

Charles SMITH 1913– Painter in oil and watercolour, born in Chislehurst, Kent. He attended Brixton School of Building and Architecture, serving for a time in Royal Air Force in World War II. Studied art at Heatherley's School of Fine Art and Camberwell School of Arts and Crafts, teachers including David Ghilchik. Smith's main works were marine pictures. He was a member of Wapping Group of Artists, Chelsea Art Society and Croydon Art Society, and also exhibited in provinces. National Westminster Bank and Sutton and Leamington Borough Councils hold examples. Lived in Peasmarsh, Sussex.

David SMITH 1920– Painter using a richly Expressionist palette, draughtsman, printmaker and teacher, born in Lowestoft, Suffolk, where he attended the Technical School, also Lowestoft and Norwich Schools of Art. From 1939–40 Smith was visiting art master at Framlingham College, then he served in Royal Air Force, 1940–5; a collection of his Air Force pictures toured the country in aid of a forces' charity, finishing at Cooling Galleries, opened by Group Captain Sir Douglas Bader. After the war Smith studied at Slade School of Fine Art, winning Abbey Major Rome Scholarship at British School, Rome, 1949. Further teaching included senior lecturer in fine art, Chelsea School of Art, 1965–79. Smith was elected RE in 1951, also showing at RA, LG, New Art Centre and elsewhere. He had over 60 solo shows in Britain and abroad, later ones including retrospective at Evesham Arts Festival, 1990; a major show at Sogo Art Gallery, Yokohama, Japan, 1991; and a retrospective at Bankside Gallery, 1996. Smith sold well in Japan, where he painted all the major harbours. He was official artist to the British Antarctic Survey, 1975–6, with a second voyage in 1979–80. In 1982–4 he was invited by Trinity House to record the lighthouses of England and Wales. He illustrated Richard Woodman's book *View from the Sea* and Antony Fogg's *The Discovery of Antarctica*. HRH The Duke of Edinburgh, British Antarctic Survey in Cambridge, Barclays Bank and many other corporate and private collections hold examples, as well as public galleries in Blackpool, Lincoln, Portsmouth, Sheffield and elsewhere. Lived in London.

David Henry SMITH 1947– Painter in oil and watercolour, born in Cleethorpes, Lincolnshire, where he settled at Holton, near Wragby. Studied at Grimsby School of Art, 1965–8, and at Royal College of Art, 1968–71, teachers including Carel Weight, where he gained his master's degree. Smith showed with Angela Flowers Gallery, Usher Gallery in Lincoln, Dartington Hall and elsewhere. Solo exhibitions included Fischer Fine Art from 1974. Arts Council bought several landscapes by Smith from that gallery.

David Murray SMITH 1865–1952 Painter and printmaker, notably a landscape watercolourist, born in Edinburgh, where he attended the School of Art, also the Royal Scottish Academy Schools. In the 1890s he moved to London and after that had a number of southern English addresses, especially in the Dorking and Guildford, Surrey, areas. He was at various times a member of RBA, RSW and RWS and was a prolific exhibitor, also with RA, Fine Art Society, Leicester Galleries and elsewhere.

Derek SMITH fl. from late 1980s– Artist who graduated from the University of Ulster, Belfast, in fine art, 1989. Two years before that he had participated in an Exchange Print Exhibition with University of China. Showed extensively in Belfast, including Octagon Gallery, 1987; Laganside Gallery, 1990; and in Beyond the Partitions, organised by Queen Street Studios, with which he was associated, in 1994. In 1992 he had two solo exhibitions of drawings, prints and sculpture in Quebec, Canada, participated in two Snow Sculpture Events in that year and in the International Biennale Print Exhibition there.

Donald SMITH 1934– Painter and creator of abstract constructions and teacher, born in London. After general education in Matlock, Birkenhead and Dartford, Smith attended the Laird School of Art in Birkenhead and Liverpool's Regional College of Art, 1950–5. Worked widely in schools and technical college teaching art, by the mid-1970s being principal lecturer in art and design at Didsbury College of Education in Manchester. Showed in north of England, Manchester City Art Gallery holding his acrylic and gloss paint on wood construction Estate IV, of 1968. Lived for a time at Timperley, Altrincham, Cheshire.

Ed SMITH 1923–1988 Painter and draughtsman, born in Detroit, Michigan, America as Edward Lionel Smith. His father was English, his mother – who died when he was 15 – was half Red Indian and half American. Lived in New York with an aunt and joined the Art Students' League there, resuming after World War II service in the Canadian Army after desertion from the Marines. After a short period in Paris moved to London and had a show at Arts Council, 1948. Joined Royal Academy Schools and St Martin's School for etching in 1949, then went to live in Paris. A roving life followed, included periods in Sweden, Australia and then Afghanistan and Bangladesh as a war artist. After returning to London in 1980 he went to Israel for a time. Additional shows included Obelisk Gallery, 1960, World's End Gallery in 1979 and in 1991 an extensive show was held at John Denham Gallery.

Edwin SMITH 1912–1971 Photographer, architect, writer, painter, draughtsman and printmaker, born in poor circumstances in London, leaving school aged 12. While at a trade school became interested in architecture and won a scholarship to the Architectural Association. Smith became known, however, mainly as a photographer. His name appeared on about 40 volumes published internationally, and many shows of his prints have been held, for example at the Plymouth Art Centre and Brighton Festival in 1985. Edwin Smith also made two films for Samaritan Films, one on Rembrandt, the other on the Pre-Raphaelites. Smith wrote several books on photography and public collections, including Victoria & Albert Museum, hold his work. During his life only a few friends knew that Smith regarded himself mainly as an artist. Although he produced a huge volume of oils, watercolours, drawings and prints, it was after his death that exhibitions began to give some idea of his achievement. Shows included House Gallery, 1978 and 1980, Church Street Gallery in Saffron Walden, 1985, Clare College in Cambridge, 1986, and in 1987 Smith's pictures and photographs were included in A Paradise Lost at Barbican Art Gallery. His wife, the artist and writer Olive Cook, wrote that Smith "captured the joy and immediacy of the fleeting visual experience" in some work, in other "recollected images irradiated by an inner apocalyptic private vision." Smith settled in Saffron Walden, Essex, in 1962 and Fry Art Gallery there holds his work.

Elizabeth Stuart SMITH 1942– Artist in a range of media, notable concerned with paper works, who studied at Liverpool Polytechnic, 1974–7, graduating in fine art; then did part-time postgraduate research there, 1977–82. She was artist-in-residence, Bury Art Galley, 1985, the year she had an Artists in Schools Placement, Astley Park School, Chorley. Stuart Smith gained a North West Arts Award in 1980–2. Was represented at Paton Gallery, 1982; Bluecoat Gallery, Liverpool, 1984; First International Paper Biennale, Leopold-Hoesch Museum, Duren, West Germany, 1986; and in 1986–7 Walker Art Gallery, Liverpool, touring Merseyside Artists 3. Solo shows included Watermans Art Centre, Brentford, 1986.

Erik SMITH 1914–1973 Painter in oil and watercolour, printmaker, stained glass artist and lecturer. Born in Birmingham, he studied art at Willesden School of Art, 1934–6, then at Royal College of Art, 1937–8 and 1945–7. Smith went on to lecture in art history at High Wycombe College of Technology and Art. Exhibited widely, including RA, RWS, RBA, RE, NEAC and abroad. Victoria & Albert Museum, Ashmolean Museum in Oxford and South London Art Gallery acquired his work and he designed a number of stained glass windows for churches. Lived at Princes Risborough, Buckinghamshire.

Frank Sidney SMITH 1928– Painter in oil, self-taught with help from evening classes, born in the Thanet Union workhouse in Minster, Kent, brought up in The Manston Cottage Homes, Ramsgate. He was evacuated to the Midlands during World War II and eventually settled in Small Heath, Birmingham. Smith was in the Army and Royal Marines as a regular, 1946–53, including service in Palestine and Korea, then returned to work in Austin and Rover car factories. His wife and son were both schizophrenic, she dying from overdosing of lithium, the son committing suicide. In 1976 Smith decided that the only way to cope with the traumas of his life was to paint his experiences. Over 400 meticulously detailed pictures, which had a primitive earthy humour and vigour, resulted. He donated much of his output to Kent County Council. As well as showing in the Midlands, notably at RBSA, in mixed exhibitions, Smith had solo shows at the Ramsgate Library Gallery in 1987 and 1993. He had slowly taught himself to read and write and in 1993 his illustrated autobiography *A Brush with Life* was published.

George Herbert Tyson SMITH 1883–1972 Sculptor and carver, born in Liverpool, where he continued to work, son of a lithographic artist. Studied at local School of Art, his teachers including Charles John Allen. Worked in a mason's yard and also attended evening classes at the Art Sheds for several years around the turn of the century. Was a member of Sandon Studios Society, of which he was president from 1956, and showed at Liverpool Autumn Exhibition from 1907. Started own practice in 1912 and became noted for his work on Birkenhead Cenotaph, Fleetwood War Memorial and Liverpool War Memorial. Also designed medals. He was made an honorary instructor to the School of Architecture in 1925 and gained an hon. Master of Arts degree from Liverpool University in 1948. His work is mostly in a neo-classical style and is shown in the volume *RBS: Modern British Sculpture*, published in 1939. Was featured in Walker Art Gallery show The Art Sheds, in 1981.

Gerald E R SMITH 1883–1959 Stained glass painter and ecclesiastical designer. Born in Melbury, Dorset, he studied art at Clapham School of Art. Exhibited RA. Lived in London.

Grainger SMITH 1892–1961 Painter, printmaker and teacher, born in Hull, who moved to Liverpool in 1895 where he studied at the School of Art, becoming art master at Liverpool College. He was a member of Liverpool Academy and a president of RCamA, also showing with RA, RSA, Fine Art Society and elsewhere in the provinces. Walker Art Gallery in Liverpool, Salford Art Gallery and Manchester City Art Gallery hold his work. His full name was George Grainger Smith and he lived at Malpas, Cheshire, retiring to Wales.

Gregor McFarlane SMITH 1944– Painter and teacher, born and lived in Glasgow. Studied at Edinburgh College of Art, 1962–7, his teachers including Robin Philipson. Was awarded a postgraduate scholarship and travelling scholarship to Rome and Florence in 1967. A member of SSA and RSW, the artist participated in many group shows, including Royal Glasgow Institute of the Fine Arts, Compass Gallery in Glasgow and elsewhere, as well as having numerous solo exhibitions, including Glasgow Print Studio; Lillie Art Gallery, Milngavie; and Torrance Gallery, Edinburgh. Scottish Arts Council and a number of other Scottish public collections hold his work, which often features stark, brooding hill and fell scenes in England and Scotland.

Hassel SMITH 1915– Artist in all media, latterly mostly acrylic on canvas, and teacher, born in Sturgis, Michigan, America. Smith studied art history and practice, 1932–6, at Northwestern University, Illinois, then painting, 1936–8, at California School of Fine Arts, San Francisco. Among Smith's awards were one For Distinguished Service to American Art from the National Endowment for the Arts, 1967, and a honorary Doctorate of Fine Arts, San Francisco Art Institute, 1991. Smith taught there, extensively elsewhere in America including Universities of California and Oregon, and in England at West of England College of Art/Bristol Polytechnic and Cardiff College of Art. Had numerous group and solo shows, mainly in America, later one-mans including Cleveland Bridge Gallery, Bath, 1988, and London Contemporary Art Fair, Iannetti-Lanzoni, 1989. Tate Gallery and many American public galleries hold examples. Lived at Rode, near Bath, Avon.

Helen SMITH 1956– Artist and teacher who gained a first-class visual arts degree at Cheltenham & Gloucester College of Higher Education, 1996, in that year obtaining the Student of the Year Award. The College holds her work. From 1997 she became a freelance artist and teacher. Her exhibitions included Locations '96 at Gloucester Docks; degree show at her college (work selected to be featured in *Ceramic Review*); and Cheltenham Group of Artists Open, at Axiom Centre, Cheltenham, all exhibitions in 1996. In 1997 participated in Transports of Light, Stroud, and Unquiet Voices, Doncaster Museum & Art Gallery. Lived in Cheltenham, Gloucestershire.

Ian McKenzie SMITH 1935– Painter and curator, born in Montrose, Angus. He studied painting at Gray's School of Art in Aberdeen, 1953–8, also attending courses at Patrick Allan-Fraser School of Art, Hospitalfield, Arbroath. With a travelling scholarship won in 1958 McKenzie Smith went to Paris. Ten years later he was appointed director of Aberdeen Art Gallery and Museums. He was elected RSA in 1987 and a year later president of RSW. In Paris McKenzie Smith had shown an interest in African and Japanese art, and during the 1970s this Oriental influence strengthened, so that later work by the artist has much in common with Chinese calligraphy. Had a number of solo shows, at 57 Gallery and Scottish Gallery, both in Edinburgh, and Fine Art Society, 1997.

Ivy SMITH 1945– Painter and teacher who studied at Chelsea School of Art and Royal Academy Schools. Went on to teach part-time at Norwich School of Art. Among many venues exhibited at were RA Summer Exhibition and Woodlands Art Gallery, in Figurative Painters, 1985. Awards included Eastern Arts Awards, 1978–83, and Imperial Tobacco/National Portrait Gallery Award, 1981–3. Graves Art Gallery, Sheffield; Sussex University; and Eastern Arts Association hold Smith's work, which included sensitive portraits. Lived at Aylmerton, Norfolk.

Jack SMITH 1928– Painter and teacher, born in Sheffield. He studied at the College of Art there, 1944–6, then St Martin's School of Art, 1948–50, and Royal College of Art, 1950–3. His first one-man show was at the Beaux Arts Gallery in 1953, a series following during the 1950s. Ruskin Spear and Carel Weight had taught him at the Royal College, and at first he worked in a Neo-Realist style known as the Kitchen Sink School, stark and rather drab scenes. But from the mid-1950s he became more interested in the play of light on shapes, and eventually became a meticulous abstractionist. These pictures he termed "diagrams of an experience or sensation". Taught at Bath Academy, Corsham, in the 1950s, in 1963–71 at Hornsey School of Art, then in 1971–4 Chelsea School of Art. Won first prize at John Moores Liverpool Exhibition in 1956, by which time he had begun to show in America, in 1959 having a retrospective at Whitechapel Art Gallery. Other major exhibitions followed at Sunderland Arts Centre and touring in 1977 and Serpentine Gallery in 1978. Smith also completed some sculptures and designed for the Ballet Rambert in 1986. Lived in London, where he latterly exhibited at Angela Flowers Gallery, then in Hove, Sussex. His wife, Susan, was also a painter.

James Skelton SMITH 1961– Painter and draughtsman, born in Hamilton, Lanarkshire. He was an admirer of the painter Cecil Collins and created often disturbing pictures which contain stylised figures and landscapes which can be interpreted on several levels. Smith was a notable Colourist. He studied at Duncan of Jordanstone College of Art, Dundee, 1980–4. In 1989 he showed with the Edinburgh Festival Fringe and at the Wasp Gallery Group Show, Glasgow. In 1990 again showed at Wasp and with Compass Gallery, Glasgow. After his show Dancers in a Dark Wood, at Lomond Centre, Glenrothes, in 1989, Smith had shows in 1990 at Municipal Museum & Art Gallery, Kircaldy; Five Dryden Street and Kenulf Galleries. In 1991 he shared a show with Claudia Petretti at Mina Renton Gallery.

John SMITH 1900–1975 Sculptor, painter and teacher, born in Dagenham, Essex, son of a farmer. He studied at Royal Academy Schools, 1920–3, and was a Prix de Rome scholar. After several years of advertising and graphic work in London Smith moved to Sussex, concentrating first on painting, then only on sculpture. The BBC asked him to carry out preliminary designs for a sculpture for Broadcasting House. Moved to Cambridge in 1939 where from 1948–72 he was head of the sculpture department at the local College of Art. In 1963 Smith completed a bronze wall panel for Trinity Hall. Five years later the Cambridge Society of Painters and Sculptors, in the Arts Council Gallery, included a retrospective of Smith's work in its show, largely figurative pieces in bronze. Smith exhibited in London galleries and in Arts Council touring shows.

John Francis SMITH 1888– Painter, printmaker, illustrator and commercial artist. He was born and worked in Liverpool, attending the School of Art and showing at Liverpool Academy, of which he was a member. Also exhibited at RBA, RCamA and extensively at Walker Art Gallery in Liverpool, where the Corporation bought his work.

John Guthrie Spence SMITH 1880–1951 Landscape and architectural painter, born in Perth, Scotland. He was known to artist friends as Dummy Smith, because as a child an attack of scarlet fever robbed him of speech and hearing. After attended a school for the deaf and dumb in Dundee he went to the College of Art there, eventually moving to Edinburgh to study at Royal Institution. Travelled to France before World War I, but did not go abroad again, although he painted widely in Scotland. Showed at RSA, Royal Glasgow Institute of the Fine Arts, RA, RSW and Walker Gallery in Liverpool. He was a member of the Edinburgh Group and his work was included in the show of that name at City Art Centre, Edinburgh, and tour, 1983. Work held by public collections including Glasgow, Paisley, Perth and Greenock. Lived in Edinburgh.

Kate SMITH 1971– Artist and illustrator who attended Plymouth College of Art and Design, 1989–90; gained an honours degree in graphic design, specialising in illustration, from Norwich School of Art, 1990–3; then her master's in illustration from the Royal College of Art, 1993–5. Although Smith trained as an illustrator, she could be a rich Colourist, with strong abstract elements, as in her work at Cadogan Contemporary's 1997 four-woman show. Other exhibitions included The Hunting/*Observer* Art Prize '93, Mall Galleries, 1993; Marks and Spencer Headquarters Exhibition, 1995; and Railings Gallery, 1996.

Keir SMITH 1950– Sculptor in a wide range of styles and materials, and teacher, who studied at Newcastle University, 1969–73, with postgraduate studies at Chelsea College of Art, 1973–5. Exhibitions included Oriel Gallery, Cardiff, 1973, where he was a Young Contemporaries prize winner, and Ikon Gallery, Birmingham, 1982. Taught part-time for several years in late 1970s at Sheffield College of Art. In 1979–80 was resident sculptor at Grizedale Forest, completing the wood and wickerwork construction The Realm of Taurus, 1980. The Iron Road, 1986, commissioned for the Forest of Dean Sculpture Project, was a series of 20 carved wooden railway sleepers, recalling the original use of the railway line through the Forest, each with an over-reaching symbolic meaning, the images ranging from feather, leaf and water jug to industry, fire and destruction. This work, illustrated and discussed in *The Sculpted Forest*, achieved Smith's ambition "to blur the boundaries between site and sculpture".

Lance SMITH 1950– Painter, born in Bournemouth, Hampshire. He studied at Camberwell School of Arts and Crafts, 1969–73, then Royal Academy Schools, 1973–6. He gained an Arts Council Minor Award in 1980 and first prize in the Tolly Cobbold/Eastern Arts Fifth National Exhibition in 1985. As well as exhibiting in mixed shows in Britain and abroad, he had a solo show at Fabian Carlsson Gallery and Arnolfini Gallery, Bristol, in 1986; at Forum International Kunstmesse, Zürich, in 1987; and in 1988 had a touring show which originated in Turnpike Gallery, Greater Manchester. Smith worked in series, ambiguous paintings using potent symbols. His work is held by Fitzwilliam Museum, Cambridge, as well as private collections in Britain and widely abroad.

Leo Illesley Gibbons SMITH 1919– Painter and illustrator, born in Cobham, Surrey, who attended Hornsey College of Art, 1945–9. He was for some years an art editor, latterly for *Radio Times* magazine. Was a member of SGA and UA, also showing at RP, PS, RBA and elsewhere. Lived in Potters Bar, Hertfordshire.

Leslie SMITH 1948– Painter, born in Bromley, Kent. He did a pre-diploma course at Hornsey College of Art, 1967–8, a painting course at Maidstone College of Art for his diploma, 1968–71, then studied painting as a postgraduate at Royal Academy Schools, 1971–4. Showed at RA, Portal and Piccadilly Galleries and had first one-man show at King Street Galleries, 1980. Published *The Garden of Eden*, 1985, and two years later showed in a National Trust Gardens exhibition, with accompanying detailed catalogue, at Douwes Fine Art. A meticulous painter of landscape, Smith lived in Hertfordshire and was married to the illustrator and fabric designer Lyndel Clarke.

Linda Jane SMITH 1962– Painter who studied graphic design at Bournville College of Art, 1980, six years later gaining a government grant which enabled her to build up a group of works to show publishers. Using tiny dabs of paint, Smith created humorous cat pictures, with musical and stagey settings, which became popular signed and numbered prints. Halcyon Gallery, Birmingham, handled these and she showed at London and other provincial galleries.

Maggie SMITH 1959– Artist, born in Edinburgh, who studied at Glasgow School of Art for an honours degree, 1977–81, gaining her master's at Royal College of Art, 1981–3. Group exhibitions included Folio Society, Royal College of Art, 1983; Rank Xerox Print Collection, United Kingdom tour, 1986; Whitechapel Open at Whitechapel Art Gallery, 1990; Salama-Caro Gallery, 1993; and Cross Currents, Reed's Wharf Gallery at Barbican Centre, 1996. There Smith showed abstracts comprising brightly coloured backgrounds on which contrasting hard-edged discs floated. Rank Xerox, Texaco and Department of Trade & Industry hold her work. Lived in north London.

Marcella SMITH 1887–1963 Painter, notably of flowers, born in East Molesey, Surrey. She studied at Corcoran School of Art in Washington, America, at the School of Design in Philadelphia, and in Paris. She was a member of RBA, SWA of which she was vice-president, RMS and RI as well as the Society of Artists in St Ives, Cornwall. Smith lived for many years in St Ives and acted as curator for Lanham's Art Gallery in the High Street, although she retained a base in London. Also exhibited at RA, NEAC, RCamA and ROI. In 1955 she published *Flower Painting in Watercolour*. Died of natural causes in her bed at 1 Piazza Studios, St Ives.

Marian SMITH 1951– Painter and teacher, born in Kelso, Roxburghshire. After studying at the local High School she attended Edinburgh College of Art, 1969–73, where her teachers included Robin Philipson. She showed at Richard Demarco Gallery, RSA, the 1974 Border Arts Festival and had solo exhibitions at New Edinburgh Gallery and elsewhere. Lived in Edinburgh.

Marion SMITH 1969– Sculptor, who also experimented with media such as printmaking and tapestry, born in St Andrews, Fife, who graduated with honours from Gray's School of Art, Aberdeen, 1987–91, in 1989 attending Hoogeschool voor de Kunsten, Arnhem, Netherlands. She won several RSA awards. Was employed as an artist/technician at Scottish Sculpture Workshop, 1994, becoming workshop manager, Glasgow Sculpture Studios, 1996. Exhibitions included RSA from 1992; Scandex, at Aberdeen Art Gallery, in Aberdeen, 1994; and Cast, Carved and Constructed at Crawford Arts Centre, St Andrews, 1995; she had a solo show there, Corpus, in 1997. Publicly sited work included Gyle Shopping Centre, in Edinburgh, for Edinburgh District Council; Tyrebagger Forest, Aberdeen, for Forest Enterprise; and Peatyards Rehearsal Rooms, Haddo Arts Trust, Tarves, all 1994.

Mary SMITH 1904–1992 Painter in oil, born in Bury, Lancashire, who studied at Slade School of Fine Art, 1923–6, under Henry Tonks and Philip Wilson Steer and was a prizewinner. She married the Assyriologist Professor Sidney Smith, lived in Iraq, 1928–30, London, 1930–55, and Barcombe, Sussex, 1955–82. She painted throughout her life, but part-time only. Her main works included New Street, Baghdad, other tempera pictures in Iraq, still lifes, occasional portraits and landscapes. She was a member of WIAC, also showing with LG, NEAC and regularly with the RA. Public galleries in Bury and Rochdale hold her work. From 1980 Mary Smith suffered from Alzheimer's Disease and lived near her daughter in care in Australia at Dalmeny, New South Wales.

Matthew SMITH 1879–1959 Painter of landscapes, still life and figures, mainly in oil. Born at Halifax, Yorkshire, he worked for several years in his father's factory before going to Manchester School of Art to study design, 1900–4. Studied Slade School of Fine Art, 1905–7. Lived at several places in France for many years, briefly studying with Henri Matisse in 1911. Began exhibiting at the Salon des Indépendants, 1911–12, then went on to exhibit widely, at Leicester Galleries, Redfern Gallery, Arthur Tooth and Son, Goupil Gallery, having his first one-man show at the Mayor Gallery, 1926. Several retrospective exhibitions included Venice Biennale, 1938, and Tate Gallery, 1953, one of many public collections holding examples. He was knighted in 1954 and after his death in London there was a memorial exhibition at RA in 1960, with a major show toured by the Barbican Centre in 1996. Smith was a rich Colourist, uncommon among English painters, whose work owed much to his years in France and the Fauve tradition.

Merilyn SMITH 1942– Artist in all media and teacher, born in Arbroath, Angus. She studied at Edinburgh College of Art, with Californian ceramists and Kathleen Horsman. Smith founded a ceramic workshop in Edinburgh; worked in Britain, Italy and Nigeria; then became professor of fine art at Liverpool School of Art, John Moores University. She was a member of SSA. Group shows included Walker Art Gallery and the Tate Gallery, both in Liverpool; Scottish National Gallery of Modern Art and Scottish Arts Council Gallery, both Edinburgh; and abroad. Solo exhibitions included Third Eye Centre, Glasgow; Richard Demarco Gallery, Edinburgh; and Air Gallery. Her main works included Helix Aspersa Sublima Smith, 1984, and The Cutty Stool, 1995. Smith's works are held by Aberdeen Art Gallery, Scottish Arts Council, St Giles Cathedral in Edinburgh and Liverpool University.

Muriel Constance SMITH 1903– Painter and miniaturist, notable for portraits, born in Gunthorpe, Nottinghamshire. She studied at Nottingham College of Art and with the miniaturist portrait artist Alyn Williams. She was a member of RMS for many years, also showing at RA, Walker Art Gallery in Liverpool and abroad. Won a Silver Medal at Paris Salon, 1935. Showed solo at Walker's Galleries. Castle Museum and Art Gallery in Nottingham, where she lived for a long time, holds her work.

Norman SMITH 1910– Painter in oil and watercolour and teacher, born in Walsall, Staffordshire. He studied at Manchester School of Art under Leslie Robert Baxter; at the Anglo-French Art Centre; City and Guilds School of Art, with Rodney Burn; and at Morley College under Colin Hayes. Smith painted landscapes and did topographical work in watercolour until 1965; at this time he became attracted to the work of Giorgio Morandi and began concentrating on still life in oil, at the same time becoming a visiting teacher of drawing and painting. Smith was elected to NEAC in 1970, also exhibiting at RA, RSA, RWA and Paris Salon. Showed solo at Woodlands Art Gallery and The Lusson Gallery, Ashbourne, both 1980, also at The Honor Oak Gallery, 1987. Main works included Still Life with Globe Artichokes, in a private collection, and Green Still Life with Mandolin, Edinburgh Education Department. Salford Art Gallery and St Marylebone and St Pancras local history collections hold examples. Lived in London.

Percy John Delf SMITH 1882–1948 Painter, printmaker and designer, notably of books. Studied at Camberwell and Central Schools of Arts and Crafts and became master of the Art Workers' Guild, 1941. Worked in America and the Middle East. Produced a number of books of etchings, notably *The Dance of Death* 1914–18 and *The Singing Beggar*. Exhibited RI and Walker Art Gallery, Liverpool, and is included in several public collections. Lived in London.

Peter SMITH 1920– Landscape watercolourist and still life painter in oil, born in New Malden, Surrey. He studied at Reigate Art School in 1960s, teachers including Michael Noakes. Smith painted only "when the time and inclination allows, which is less frequently than in years gone by". He showed with North Weald Group, East Sussex Art Club and elsewhere. Lived in Newdigate, Surrey.

Peter SMITH 1946– Painter, wood engraver and teacher who studied at Birmingham College of Art, going on to become head of art and design at Kingston Polytechnic. Having taken up wood engraving Smith became a member of SWE and his work was included in Agnew's show The Broad Horizon, 1990.

Peter SMITH 1949– Equestrian artist, working in oil, who was born in Lanarkshire, his first drawing as a child being of a horse. Attended Carlisle College of Art, 1967–70 and then Glasgow School of Art for one year. Inspired by Degas, Alfred Munnings and Van Gogh, he lived and worked five miles from Ayr racecourse in Scotland, his models being horses from local stables. Also painted flat racing and steeple chasing from sketches made at Aintree, Hamilton Park, Newmarket and other British racecourses. Showed at Frost & Reed from 1983.

Peter Macdonald SMITH 1945– Painter who attended Falmouth School of Art, 1970–4. His work was abstract, but drew on landscape sources. Smith moved from Leicestershire to the Scillies in 1965 and after a decade in Penzance from the late 1970s returned to the Scillies where he occupied a Duchy of Cornwall Workshop on St Agnes, also a gallery for his work. He was a member of Newlyn Society of Artists and was represented in Newlyn Orion Galleries' 1989 exhibition A Century of Art in Cornwall 1889–1989.

Philip Henry SMITH 1924– Artist in oil, watercolour, ink and chalk, and teacher, born in Cheltenham, Gloucestershire. He studied at Cheltenham School of Art with Gerald Gardiner, 1940–3, then at Royal College of Art with Ruskin Spear and Carel Weight, 1947–50. Smith lectured at Wallasey College of Art, 1950–82. He was a member of Wirral Society of Arts and for a time of Liverpool Academy and the Cheltenham Group. He had a retrospective at Williamson Art Gallery, 1974, another at Cheltenham Art Gallery & Museum, 1996. That was of drawings of Cheltenham, 1942–65, a valuable record of vanished and changed buildings. Both the Williamson and Cheltenham hold Smith's work. Lived at Neston, South Wirral, Cheshire.

Ralph Maynard SMITH 1904–1964 Architect and artist in pen and watercolour. Smith studied architecture in London in the 1920s and became an associate of RIBA in 1927. Later worked on Shell Centre and other buildings. Smith did not promote his personal work, which had something in common with that of Paul Nash, being poetic and visionary. The terrains of Mull and Iona were early influences. Two uncompleted manuscripts, *The Ravine*, volumes 1 and 2, contain many of his ideas in prose and poetry. Lived for some years in Tadworth, Surrey, and in the 1950s was with the architectural practice of Easton & Robertson. Austin/Desmond Fine Art showed his work and an exhibition of his Surreal drawings was held at David Holmes Contemporary Art, Peterborough, in 1993.

Ray SMITH 1949– Versatile sculptor and painter, teacher and editor, who drew on popular and media images in his work, as in prizewinning picture Surface Tension at John Moores Liverpool Exhibition, 1989–90. Smith was born in Harrow, Middlesex, and graduated from Trinity Hall College, Cambridge, 1971. He had his first solo show in Cambridge in 1970. Smith was a self-employed artist from 1974, mainly working to commission. Among his major public commissions were works for Southampton General Hospital, 1985; Tesco Stores, Slough, 1990; Milton Keynes Development Corporation, 1992; and Leeds Development Agency, 1994. Smith had many solo exhibitions, including Spacex Gallery, Exeter, 1987, and Winchester Gallery, 1990. In group exhibitions he participated in Tolly Cobbold Eastern Arts Fourth National Exhibition, 1983–4, and John Moores, 1987. Smith's publications included two award-winning picture books for children and a number of books on art, including *The Artist's Handbook*, and he was consultant editor on the Dorling Kindersley *Art School* series. He was a visiting lecturer at many colleges of art, from 1978–80 was fellow in fine art at University of Southampton and during 1981 was senior lecturer at Hull College of Higher Education. Arts Council, Eastern and Southern Arts and Contemporary Art Society hold examples. Lived in Tintinhull, Somerset.

Rhonda SMITH 1969– Artist, born in Glasgow, where she gained an honours degree in drawing and painting at the School of Art, 1987–91. Awards included runner-up, Young Artist of the Year, Hunting/*Observer* Art Prizes, 1993; and Winsor and Newton Young Artist Award, 1994. Commissions included Hilton International Hotel, Glasgow. Included in group shows at Paisley Art Institute 4th Scottish Drawing Exhibition, Paisley Museum and Art Galleries, 1991; Victoria Art Gallery, Bath, 1993; and ROI, Mall Galleries, 1994. Had a series of solo shows with Flying Colours Gallery from 1994, one at Paisley Museum, 1995. It and several corporate collections hold examples.

Richard SMITH 1931– Painter who was briefly involved with Pop Art. He used shaped canvases and kite-like structures, sometimes aided by metal rods and strings, yet Smith was always a notable Colourist. He was born in Hertfordshire and studied at Luton School of Art, 1948–50. After Royal Air Force service he was at St Alban's School of Art, 1952–4, then Royal College of Art, 1954–7, gaining a Harkness Travel Fellowship in 1959. Smith had the first of several solo shows at Green Gallery in New York in 1961, followed by one at ICA in 1962. In 1963 there was the first of a string of solos at Kasmin Gallery, the year he showed in the Tokyo Biennale. He also showed several times in the Venice Biennale, gaining a prize, and won the Grand Prize at São Paulo Bienal in 1967. From then on Smith's career gained an impressive international impetus. In 1975 he had a retrospective at Tate Gallery. Went on to show with Knoedler Gallery. British Council, Royal College of Art and Arts Council hold his work. He lived in New York.

Robert T H SMITH 1938– Painter and teacher, born in Scotland, settled in Edinburgh. He attended the College of Art there, eventually becoming an assistant principal in higher education. Smith exhibited abstracts in mixed media in many group shows, and had solo exhibitions from 1969 over many years at Scottish Gallery, Edinburgh. Scottish Arts Council holds his work.

Rita SMITH fl. from 1970– Painter and artist involved in a variety of community projects, stage and costume design, textiles, fashions, embroidery, video and dance, as well as teacher. She trained at Harrow and Coventry, graduating 1970. Was involved in secondary and tertiary education. Successful multi-arts projects included work for the English Dance Theatre's *Incommunicado*, 1987; Colour Moves, an exhibition installation for the production of *Going Away* by the Scottish Ballet's Steps Out company, 1987; and In Plaster, 1989. In 1991–2 Semana Santa was a Collins Gallery, University of Strathclyde, touring show.

Sam SMITH 1908–1983 Creator of beautifully crafted, fantastic painted sculptures, born in Southampton. A lonely, introspective child, he "always wanted to be an artist", went to art school, but the 1930s Depression meant that he had to become a handyman and advertising illustrator. Also developed as a craft toymaker, especially of small boats. During World War II illustrated bridge-building manuals. After the war his creations were shown at Royal Festival Hall, prompting an American from Design Research to buy and commission objects from Smith which sold well, so that he could give up advertising work. Smith's objects became bigger, more elaborate and less toy-like, based on childhood memories and colourful characters, witty but a stringent comments on society. Smith had a retrospective at Bristol City Art Gallery in 1972. There was a notable show at the Serpentine Gallery in 1980–1. In 1976 the Arts Council made a film: *Sam Smith.Genuine.England.* Southampton City Art Gallery holds Smith's work. He lived latterly at Dartmouth, Devon.

Sarah L SMITH 1978– Painter, studying at Glasgow School of Art in mid-1990s, producing figurative work. She was "interested in images of women and their own self-image". Exhibitions included Valvona and Crolla Café Bar, Edinburgh, and New Morning, at Maxwelltown Gallery, Dumfries, 1997. Lived in Lockerbie, Dumfries and Galloway.

Sebastian SMITH 1943– Painter, born in London, who moved to Bristol in early 1950s. He was educated at Ludlow Grammar School and studied ceramics at West of England College of Art, with brief studies in Cardiff. In Bristol he set up a graphic and interior design partnership in 1971, in 1973 forming a design-and-build firm. On moving to the country in 1978 he began painting, wide travels abroad influencing his work. From 1985 Smith moved away from figurative painting and began work on bigger, multiple canvases in an abstract style. He said that he was "increasingly involved in the exploration of the complex relationships between space, form and structure" employing a variety of materials, such as industrial paint and adhesive. Showed solo at Cleveland Bridge Gallery, Bath, and the Old Vic Theatre Gallery, Bristol. In the early 1990s produced a series of installation works "based on the global political problems of innocent bystanders caught up in political power struggles". Showed solo, combining installations and paintings at Colston Street Gallery, Bristol, 1993 and Whiteleys Gallery, London, 1994. Moved to the south of France in 1996.

Sidney SMITH 1912–1982 Mural painter and draughtsman, born in Belfast, who studied at the Royal Belfast Academical Institution, attended local College of Art in evenings and had private lessons from R Boyd Morrison. Exhibited at RHA, RUA and RBA, contributed drawings of air raids in World War II to Ulster Museum and gained a name painting portraits of military personnel. He painted a first mural at British Restaurant in Belfast, then shortly after the war moved to London where he established an international reputation as a muralist. In the mid-1960s he completed a huge mural for the Playhouse Theatre in Fredericton, New Brunswick, Canada, under the patronage of Lord and Lady Beaverbrook. Also painted murals in a number of liners, including Canadian Pacific's *Empress of Britain.*

Simon SMITH 1929– Painter and draughtsman, born in Wallington, Surrey. Attended Kingston School of Art, 1946, then the Slade School of Fine Art under Randolph Schwabe. Showed at RA, NEAC and RI. Lived in Tadworth, Surrey.

Stan SMITH 1929– Painter, draughtsman, printmaker, teacher and writer, born in Hull, Yorkshire. He attended St Albans School of Art. Went on to write several art instructional books, became head of Ruskin School in Oxford, also teaching at Royal College of Art and most major art schools in the United Kingdom. Smith was a figurative painter, concerned with the "twentieth-century continuation of the great tradition following Cézanne and Picasso". He was for a time president of LG, and was active in Society of Landscape Painters and RWS. Other group appearances included RA, RI, Whitechapel Art Gallery and John Moores Liverpool Exhibition. Had solo shows which included Gallery 10, Morley Gallery and the provinces. Chantrey Bequest holds his work. Lived in Brighton, Sussex.

Stanley SMITH 1893– Artist in oil and watercolour, born in Halifax, Yorkshire, married to the watercolourist Ethel May Smith. He studied at Halifax School of Art, 1908–13, then Royal College of Art, 1913–19, under Gerald Moira and W R Lethaby. Went on to exhibit at RA, Fine Art Society and widely in provinces. Lived in Stafford.

Stephanie SMITH: *see* **Stephanie SMITH/Edward STEWART**

Stephanie SMITH/Edward STEWART Artists who collaborated for many exhibitions, but who also worked independently. Stephanie Smith was born in 1968 in Manchester, where she did a foundation year at the Polytechnic, 1986–7, graduating from Slade School of Fine Art, 1987–91. Edward Stewart was born in 1961 in Belfast, Northern Ireland; after a foundation year at the University of Ulster, 1984–5, he graduated from Glasgow School of Art, 1985–8, gaining his master's degree there, 1988–90. Smith/Stewart, whose work obtained extensive media coverage in Britain and abroad, held a residency at Tramway, Glasgow, 1995, and gained a Scottish Arts Council Artists Award, 1995–6. They were participating artists (Smith, 1991–3; Stewart, 1990–2) at Rijksakademie van Beeldende Kunsten, Amsterdam, Netherlands. Collaborative exhibitions included Gallery at Rijksakademie, 1992–3; New Visions, International Film & Video Festival, Glasgow, 1994; Video Positive, Tate Gallery, 1995; Biennale d'Art Contemporain, Lyon, France, 1995–6; Video Screening Programme, Anthony d'Offay, 1996; and they took part in Video Positive 97, Green Room in Manchester and Open Eye, Liverpool, both 1997.

Tony SMITH 1953– Painter and printmaker, born in Birmingham. Studied at Loughborough College of Art and Newcastle University. Gained a prize at Northern Arts Exhibition in 1978 and five years later at Tyne Tees Northern Open. Granted a Northern Arts Major Bursary in 1984, a Grizedale Forest Residency in 1985 and two years later was artist-in-residence at Lowick House Print Workshop, Cumbria. His group appearances included Shipley Art Gallery, Gateshead; Newcastle Group at Richard Demarco Gallery, Edinburgh, and Centrum Beeldende Kunst, Groningen, Netherlands, 1988; and DLI Museum & Arts Centre, Durham, 1990, in the Newcastle Group show The Northern Lights. His solo shows included Chester Arts Centre, 1979, and Moira Kelly Gallery from 1980. Arts Council holds his work. Lived in Newcastle upon Tyne.

Wendy SMITH 1946– Artist and teacher, born in Mansfield, Yorkshire. She studied at Nottingham College of Art, 1965–8, Slade School of Fine Art, 1968–70, and University of York, 1975–6. Went on to teach in fine art departments at Norwich School of Art and Manchester Polytechnic, 1970–5, later being visiting artist at Leicester Polytechnic. Group exhibition appearances included Three Artists at Kettle's Yard Gallery, 1979, and in 1980 Summer Show 2 at Serpentine Gallery, where she showed geometrical abstract drawings. Solo shows included Park Square Gallery in Leeds, 1978, where she lived.

Tessa SMITH-AGASSI 1942–1998 Artist, mainly in watercolour and inks, textile designer and teacher, who was born in London. Sister of Sebastian Smith. Educated at St Martin's College of Art, 1959–61 and Central School of Art & Design, 1961–64. Died in car crash with art historian husband Meir Agassi and young son in 1998, when she was principal lecturer/director of studies in design for floorcoverings and interior textiles, Kidderminster College, and external assessor, Shenkar College of Fashion and Textiles, Tel-Aviv, Israel. At Kidderminster, she was an inspirational teacher "who unlocked her students' developing talent", her own work neglected because of the burden of teaching and administration. Smith-Agassi maintained that, with the right encouragement, anyone could draw, and her unrealised ambition was to set up a drawing school. Showed in design exhibitions London, Manchester and Frankfurt and, in 1989, drawings at The Guild Gallery, Bristol, where she lived. As a painter, she specialised in detailed botanical studies, and illustrated *Flowers of Israel,* 1985, text by Avi Eliasaf. At the time of his death husband Meir Agassi, born 1947, had accumulated an immense art historical archive, and was working on a study of "art by non-artists". He had also created a series of "alter egos" whose imaginary work he documented and publicised, a small memorial exhibition of this being held at the Cairn Gallery, Nailsworth, Gloucestershire, 1998. Plans were also made to commemorate his life by establishing a permanent Agassi museum in Israel.

Ronald SMOOTHEY 1913–1996 Painter and teacher, born in Rochford, Essex, who studied at Guildford School of Art and Goldsmiths' College where he obtained his art teacher's certificate first class. For 32 years Smoothey was head of art at the Grammar School in Guildford, Surrey, where he lived. He also pioneered adult classes for 30 years and examined and taught courses in many areas. He was the first British teacher to travel to Hawaii on a Fulbright Award, 1953–4. Won a design competition for the Italian partisan war memorial at Pastorello, near Parma, 1946. Smoothey was president of Guildford Art Society and a member of Midhurst Art Society and showed at NS. Had solo exhibitions at Guildford House Gallery from 1962, also at Universities of Surrey and Leicester, Cranleigh College, Yvonne Arnaud Theatre in Guildford and elsewhere. His marionettes were shown in national exhibitions in London, Manchester and Liverpool. Guildford Borough Council, Cable and Wireless and colleges of education hold his work. Guildford House held a memorial show of abstract work in 1997.

John Frederick SMOUT 1938– Painter, draughtsman and teacher, born in Oldbury, Worcestershire. After studying at the local Grammar School, Smout attended Stourbridge College of Art, 1961–5, then Liverpool College of Art, 1965–6. Showed in group exhibitions in Midlands and Wales and had solo exhibitions, including Coleg Harlech, Wales, several in Chester and Alternative Visions, at Oriel/Gallery, Llangollen, Clwyd, where Smout lived, in 1996. This included his latest work, introducing letter forms and shapes as an integral part of the image.

Montague SMYTH 1863–1965 Painter of atmospheric landscapes, born and based in London, who spent several early childhood years with his mother in New Zealand, returning to live with his grandmother. Was educated at Leamington College and Cambridge University, abandoned the idea of an Army career, then studied art alone on the continent. His only lessons were from Fred Brown at Westminster School of Art and in Italy. Smyth had early success, in 1894 joining the RBA and showing at RA; having a solo show at Dowdeswell Galleries in 1899; in 1904 joining the ROI. He became its president, also of the London Sketch Club of which he was a founder-member in 1898. In 1905 Smyth travelled through China and Japn, resulting pictures illustrating books on the countries and forming the basis of a solo exhibition at Baillie Gallery, 1906. In 1914 Smyth falsified his age and served with the Artists' Rifles. Supported by a small private income Smyth, a keen sportsman, continued active as an artist until he died. His last one-man exhibition was at the Fine Art Society in 1921. Belgrave Gallery organised a touring show in 1978.

Norman SMYTH 1933– Painter mainly in oil and occasionally acrylic, and teacher, born in Belfast, Northern Ireland. He was also known as N W J Smyth. Self-taught as an artist, Smyth gave lessons in private classes and for adult education. His main interests were "light and its effect on colour and form, the human figure in its traditional environment". Smyth was an associate of RUA, also taking part in group shows at RHA; Irish National Portrait Exhibition in Dublin; the Mall, King Street and Oliver Swann Galleries; and Ulster Arts Club, Belfast. Solo exhibitions included Ardowen Arts Centre, Enniskillen; Bell Gallery, Belfast; and Oriel Gallery, Dublin. Department of the Environment in Northern Ireland holds his work. Lived in Hillsborough, County Down.

N W J SMYTH: *see* **Norman SMYTH**

Olive Carleton SMYTH 1882–1949 Artist and teacher, born in Glasgow, where she settled in Cambuslang. She was the sister of the painter Dorothy Carleton Smyth, who predeceased her. Olive, who signed her work O C S, studied at Glasgow School of Art, where she went on to teach, becoming head of design. Her work, in a variety of styles, was shown at Royal Glasgow Institute of the Fine Arts, RSA, RHA, Walker Art Gallery in Liverpool and elsewhere. Miss Smyth was a fresco specialist and had work accepted in several public galleries internationally. Her Pytheas buys Amber was illustrated in the 1923 *Studio* volume *Figure Painting in Water-colours*.

Minnie SMYTHE fl. from c.1895–1955 Watercolourist, daughter of the artist Lionel Percy Smythe, born and lived in London. She was educated in France, living in the Pas de Calais in the mid-1890s. Was elected RWS in 1937 where she showed extensively, also exhibiting at Leicester Galleries, Fine Art Society, SWA, RHA and elsewhere.

SNAFFLES: *see* **Charles Johnson PAYNE**

Olive SNELL fl. c.1910–1955 Painter in oil who was born in Durban, South Africa. In England she studied under Augustus John and Boris Anrep after initial schooling at Wycombe Abbey, in Buckinghamshire. Medici Society reproduced her work, which was exhibited extensively at Fine Art Society and Redfern Gallery, also at RA, NEAC, Paris Salon and elsewhere. Lived in London, then East Ashling, Sussex.

Rosie SNELL 1971– Painter, draughtsman and printmaker, born in Littlehampton, Sussex, who studied at Northbrook College of Art and Design, Horsham, 1988–90; Loughborough College of Art and Design, 1991–4; and Norwich School of Art and Design, 1994–5. Awards included Elizabeth Greenshields Awards, 1994 and 1997; Royal Bath and West Scholarship, 1996; and runner-up at NatWest Art Prize, 1997. Exhibited large, meticulously painted unpeopled landscapes, sometimes including industrial hardware, as in her solo show at Paton Gallery, 1997. Residencies included mentally handicapped art therapy, Park Road Day Centre, Loughborough, 1993, and Florence Trust Studios, Highbury, 1998. Saatchi Collection bought her work, which was partly influenced by Paul Nash.

John SNELLING 1943–1992 Watercolourist, teacher and writer, born in Newcastle Emlyn, Carmarthenshire. He was a self-taught artist who lectured on liberal studies at Maidstone College of Art, 1966–71, then travelled overland to India and Nepal and in the early 1970s on his return to England became a Buddhist, general secretary of the London Buddhist Society and editor of its journal *The Middle Way*. His career as a writer and broadcaster reflected his religious interests. *The Buddhist Handbook* was a major work. Suffering for many years from leukaemia he settled finally at the Sharpham North Community, near Totnes, Devon, showing his watercolour landscapes locally and in London. Died in Totnes.

Chris R H SNOOK 1950– Artist and teacher who studied at Maidstone College of Art, 1970–3, and Royal Academy Schools, 1973–6. Went on to teach at Sir John Cass Art School and was included in Artists in Adult Education, 1982, Woodlands Art Gallery. Also showed at RA Summer Exhibition from 1972, RBA from 1978 and Portrait Award at National Portrait Gallery, 1981. Lived in London.

Harry SNOOK 1944– Artist and teacher, born in Gower, West Glamorgan. He studied at Hornsey College of Art from 1961, from 1968 teaching appointments including Bradford, Watford and Exeter Schools of Art and Birmingham Polytechnic. Had a first solo exhibition at Edinburgh Gallery West, Los Angeles, others including Ibis Gallery, Leamington Spa, 1979. Snook was notable for untitled wood reliefs, as included in The British Art Show, 1980, chosen by the critic William Packer and toured by the Arts Council, which holds his work.

Graham SNOW 1948– Artist whose work included constructions and performances. He studied at Hornsey College of Art, 1968–71, then Slade School of Fine Art, 1971–3. From 1975–7 was Research Fellow at Nihon University, Tokyo; 1979–80, artist-in-residence, Cambridge University; then Gulbenkian Video Fellow, 1980. His performances included Mythologies, at Garage Fine Art, 1974, and Annunciation, St Peter's Church in Cambridge, 1979. Solo exhibitions included Clare Hall, Cambridge, 1978; Kettle's Yard, Cambridge, 1979; 12 Duke Street Gallery, 1983; and Galleria Grafica, Tokyo, 1984. Arts Council holds his work.

Michael SNOW 1930– Artist and teacher, born in Manchester. He was educated at Lawrence Sheriff School, Rugby, worked for three years in Cheshire, then settled in Cornwall in 1952. He was elected to membership of the Penwith Society, became secretary in 1954 and showed regularly until resigning in 1965. Snow was closely associated with Ben Nicholson and other advanced St

Ives-based artists. He was a co-founder of the Peterloo Group in Manchester in 1957 and had a solo exhibition there in 1959. Other solo shows were held in St Ives and at Rowan Gallery in 1964 and he showed widely in group exhibitions in London and the provinces as well as overseas. He taught for some years at Exeter College of Art. Had a retrospective at Gordon Hepworth Gallery, Exeter, in 1993.

Peter SNOW 1927– Painter, designer and teacher, born and lived in London. In 1946 he worked as a journalist for the South London Press and studied at Goldsmiths' College School of Art before joining the Royal Engineers, 1946–8, announcing for the Forces' Broadcasting Service in the Middle East. From 1948–53 Snow studied painting at Slade School of Fine Art, joining its staff in 1957. In 1962 he was commissioned to design an altarpiece for St Mathias Church. His extensive theatre designing experience began in 1951 when he designed *Love's Labours Lost* for Rupert Doone in Southwark. Also designed for the English Opera Group and Joan Littlewood's Theatre Workshop; in 1955 he designed a ballet for Frederick Ashton at the Royal Opera House, also Samuel Beckett's *Waiting for Godot* at the Arts Theatre. Also worked for Ballets Minerva and Western Theatre Ballet Company and in 1971 and 1975 designed and wrote the multimedia *Reflections I* and *Reflections II* in London and Cardiff. He founded The Electric Theatre Company in 1970. In 1979 an exhibition of Theatre Designs was held at Sadler's Wells Theatre. In addition to extensive group shows Snow showed solo from a 1956 exhibition at the Prospect Gallery, having a retrospective at Morley Gallery, 1995.

Hilda Mary SNOWDEN 1910– Artist in wide variety of media, including stone carving and collage, and writer and illustrator, born in Bradford, where she continued to live. Professionally she was in charge of the accounts office for British Rail, Bradford, attending the local College of Art's evening classes for over 30 years, as well as Positano Art Workshop, Italy. She showed at Cartwright Hall, Bradford, in Ilkley, elsewhere in Yorkshire and in London, and was a member of art societies in Bradford and Shipley. After retirement Snowden gained a history honours degree through the Open University, in 1989 publishing *Under Stag's Fell*, the story of Simonstone Hall in the Dales, which she researched for three years, wrote and illustrated.

Michael SNOWDEN 1930– Sculptor, clay modelling using also wax and plaster for bronze, and teacher, born in Billinghay, Lincolnshire. He studied at Camberwell School of Arts and Crafts, 1953–62, under Karel Vogel. Taught anatomy and sculpture at Camberwell, 1956–62, then taught at Edinburgh College of Art from 1964. He was elected RSA in 1985. Took part in numerous group exhibitions, solo shows including Leicester Galleries, 1971; Bruton Gallery, 1973; Lamp of Lothian Gallery, Haddington, 1981; and English Speaking Union Gallery, Edinburgh, 1984. Snowden received commissions for Livingston New Town, Cumbernauld New Town and Royal Bank of Scotland fountain at Kelvingrove, Glasgow. Arts Council holds his work. Lived in Edinburgh.

Corisande Wentworth SOAMES 1901– Mainly a portrait painter in a variety of media, she studied at Chelsea Polytechnic, 1919–20, under John Revel. Sometimes just signing her work C W S, she showed at RA, RP, RBA and in the Midlands. Lived in London.

Maurice SOCHACHEWSKY 1918–1969 Painter and draughtsman, born in London, who in early 1930s gained a scholarship to St Martin's School of Art. Served in the Army in World War II and retired to Kent. In 1949 he visited Israel. Had a show at Ben Uri Art Society in 1969, and it holds his work.

Robert SODEN 1955– Artist in watercolour and gouache on paper and teacher, born in Taunton, Somerset. He did a foundation course at Taunton College of Art, 1974–5; gained a first-class honours degree, fine art painting, from Birmingham Polytechnic, 1975–8; then his master's from Royal College of Art's painting school, 1979–82. Teachers included Alan Miller and Mario Dubsky. Soden wrote that he was "a painter of contemporary and political themes," much work stemming "from a dialogue with the English topographical tradition of landscape painting, in particular Girtin, Cotman and Turner." Among his many awards were, latterly, a Northern Arts Major Print Bursary, Lowick House Print Workshop, Cumbria, 1992; First Prize Open Class, Honiton Festival Art Competition, 1994; and 1st Prize, *The Journal (Newcastle)* Art Competition, 1996, being runner-up in 1997. From 1983 he held a number of visiting lectureships in polytechnic and university fine arts departments in Birmingham, Newcastle, Bristol, Newport, Leicester and Sunderland, and he also held many residencies and placements. Among a string of commissions were London Tourist Board, Silver Jubilee, 1988; National Museum of Science and Industry, Science Museum, 1994; and University of Sunderland, 1995. Among later numerous group showings were Artists' London, Museum of London, 1992–3; British Watercolours, Laing Art Gallery, Newcastle upon Tyne, 1993–4; Drawing Outside, Sunderland Museum and Art Gallery, Sunderland, 1994–5; and City Journeys, London Arts Café, 1996. Had a solo show at Mappin Art Gallery, Sheffield, 1984, others including Walker Art Gallery, Liverpool, and State House, Cologne, 1987; Eye Diary, Bede Gallery, Jarrow, 1992; and Review, Durham Art Gallery and DLI Museum, Durham, 1995. Lived in Sunderland, Tyne & Wear.

Michael SOFRONIOU 1957– Painter of landscapes and still life, notable for rich colour and vigorous handling, born in London. From 1975–8 obtained honours degree in English language and literature at Oxford University. After a foundation course at Wimbledon School of Art, 1978–9, Sofroniou studied at Camberwell School of Arts and Crafts, 1979–82, obtaining a first-class honours degree. Group exhibitions included RI from 1987; Jonathan Poole Gallery, Woodstock, 1989; and Medici Society and Edith Grove Gallery, both 1990. Had a solo show at Westgate Central Library, Oxford, 1987, and during Oxford Art Week in 1989 and 1990 and in 1994 shared an exhibition at John Davies, Stow-on-the-Wold. In 1991–2 Sofroniou was artist-in-residence at

Royal Shakespeare Company, Stratford-upon-Avon. Lived in Gloucestershire.

Themoulla SOFRONIOU 1966– Artist in mixed media who studied at Waltham Forest College and Polytechnic of East London. She exhibited in group shows at Ben Uri Gallery, Smith's Gallery and in England & Co, 1992, in Art in Boxes. In previous year had a solo exhibition at Leytonstone Library. Lived in London.

Tasadaq SOHAIL 1930– Miniaturist and watercolourist, born in India, but during violence caused by partition he and his family fled to Pakistan. Moved to England in early 1960s and attended St Martin's School of Art as an evening student for eight years. Sohail's pictures were full of brightly coloured imaginary creatures in idyllic settings and radiated hope and harmony. Solo exhibitions included Indus Gallery, Karachi, from 1977; October Gallery, 1979; South Bank Centre, 1991; Gallery 2000, Sweden, 1992; and Boundary Gallery, 1993.

Nils SOLBERG 1920–1955 Painter, born in Melmoth, South Africa. Studied art for several years in Natal with Merlyn Evans prior to World War II, then at Regent Street Polytechnic School of Art, 1946–8, with Norman Blamey and Clifford Hall. Showed at RA, RBA and at several venues in South Africa, including a one-man show in Durban, South Africa, 1953, where Solberg lived.

Enid SOLOMON 1910– Painter, printmaker and teacher who studied at St John's Wood School of Art and the Royal Academy Schools, under Ernest Jackson and Walter Westley Russell, winning a scholarship. She had also studied at the Sorbonne, Paris. Married the artist Paul Drury. Was closely associated with the WIAC, being its vice-chairman after World War II. Also showed RA, NEAC, LG, Leicester Galleries and in the provinces.

Gilbert SOLOMON 1890–1955 Painter, who studied at Slade School of Fine Art, 1907–11, and in Paris with René Prinet, 1913–4. During World War II he was involved in civilian camouflage and in his final years was vice-president of RBA, of which he became a full member in 1926. Also showed at RA, RP and in 1959 at Ben Uri Art Society, which holds his work. Solomon, who was fond of rural subjects, is noted for his assured use of watercolour. Lived in London.

Estella Frances SOLOMONS 1882–1968 Painter in oil, born in Dublin, Ireland. She attended the Metropolitan School of Art there, RHA Schools, then Chelsea School of Art. Exhibited Royal Glasgow Institute of the Fine Arts and prolifically at RHA. Well represented in Irish public collections, including Municipal Art Gallery in Dublin, where she lived.

Frederick SOLOMONSKI 1904– Painter, writer on art history and curator, born in Berlin, Germany. He studied at the University there and art with Max Liebermann the Impressionist painter and at the Studienateliers fuer Malerei und Plastik. As well as showing extensively abroad, after he came to England he exhibited at RA, AIA, NEAC, with the Leger and Leicester Galleries and in the provinces. From 1943–6 he was curator of the Ben Uri Gallery, London. Member of the Hampstead Artists' Council. Lived in London and later in America.

Louise SOLOWAY 1962– Artist in a variety of media and teacher, born and lived in London. She did a foundation course at Harrow College of Further Education, 1978–80; graduated in fine arts at Bath Academy of Fine Art, Corsham, 1980–3; in 1984 gaining a Commonwealth Scholarship to the Baroda Faculty of Fine Art, India. In 1987 Soloway had a part-time job writing and drawing on *Spitalfields News*. From 1989 she held a number of teaching and artist-in-residence posts in east London. In 1991 Soloway was commissioned to complete a fibreglass relief sculpture at Oxford House, for presentation to Peter Scott, which depicted life at the Bethnal Green community centre. Group shows included Stowells Trophy at RA, 1982; Art Heritage Gallery, New Delhi, 1986; Whitechapel Open, Whitechapel Gallery from 1988; and South Bank Picture Show at Royal Festival Hall, 1990. Her solo exhibition Working Girls was held at Hillside Gallery, Edinburgh, during the Festival, 1989. British Council in Bombay, Whitechapel Library and Homerton Hospital in Hackney include examples.

David SOMERVILLE 1962– Painter in acrylic of bright, gestural, landscape-based abstracts. He attended Salisbury College of Art, 1978–80; Bath Academy of Art at Corsham, 1980–3; and Chelsea School of Art, 1984–5. Group shows included James Birch Gallery, 1985; The Dub Factor, Arts Council tour, 1992–4; and Royal Over-Seas League Open, 1995. Had a solo exhibition, Submarine Gallery, 1987, later ones including British Council, Barcelona, 1993, and Harriet Green Gallery, 1996. In 1988 *David Somerville – A Video Portrait*, by Karen Alexander, was shown at the Tate Gallery.

Howard SOMERVILLE 1873–1952 Versatile painter and printmaker, noted for his portraits, born in Dundee, Angus. He studied at West End Academy and University College in Dundee and was elected RP in 1917, also being a member of Chelsea Arts Club. Showed at Royal Glasgow Institute of the Fine Arts, NEAC, RA, RSA and at many other venues. He had a studio in The Boltons, London.

Jennifer SOMERVILLE 1928–1994 Landscape and portrait painter, daughter of the composer Horace Somerville and his arts administrator and painter wife Lilian Somerville. Studied at Camberwell School of Arts and Crafts and Slade School of Fine Art, having been revealed as a child prodigy.

Lilian SOMERVILLE 1905–1985 Arts administrator and painter, born in Bolton, Lancashire, as Katherine Lilian Tillard, under which name she continued to paint before World War II, when most of her work was concentrated, even after marriage in 1928. Her husband was the composer Horace Somerville, who died in 1959, their daughter Jennifer also being a painter. Lilian Somerville studied at the Slade School of Fine Art, exhibition venues including Goupil Gallery, RBA, ROI and SWA. In 1941 she joined the British Council, becoming its influential fine arts department director, 1948–70. Won a number of awards, including an honorary doctorate from Royal College of Art, 1972, and fellow University College London, 1973.

Peggy SOMERVILLE 1918–1975 Painter and draughtsman, sister of the artist Stuart Somerville. She was a child prodigy, aged three showing with Royal Drawing Society. By the time she was 14 she had had three solo shows in London, her work being much admired by the artists Walter Sickert and John Lavery, who referred to "the extraordinary genius of the little girl". She learned a lot from her artist-collector father, Charles, and was much encouraged by her writer mother, Rose Anne Chantrey. In 1930 the family moved from Ashford, Middlesex, to mid-Suffolk and Peggy Somerville spent five war years in the Women's Land Army. In 1960 she settled at Middleton, near the coast, dying of cancer 15 years later, by which time she was developing as a notable Colourist, although much of her final work was unexhibited. Three exhibitions followed: at Aldeburgh Festival in 1977; at Norwich Castle Museum, based on the collection held there, in 1985; and at Gainsborough's House, Sudbury, in 1986. Eventually a selling show was held at Stephen Reiss Fine Art, Norwich, 1987, Reiss helping to select a significant exhibition at Christchurch Mansion, Ipswich, in 1997.

Stuart SOMERVILLE 1908–1982 Painter, mainly in oil, of figures, landscapes, still life and figures. Born at Arksey, Yorkshire, he was the son of the artist and collector Charles Somerville and the brother of the painter Peggy Somerville. Studied art with his father, then self-taught. In his early twenties travelled to Africa, where he painted. An exuberant Colourist, Somerville exhibited at the RA, ROI, the Alpine Club Gallery, RHA, RSA, the Fine Art Society and in the provinces. Lived near Woodbridge, Suffolk.

Alex SONNIS 1905– Lithographer, painter and teacher who studied part-time at Central School of Arts and Crafts with Bernard Meninsky, gaining a scholarship to Royal College of Art, 1929–32. Taught at a number of art schools, notably part-time at St Martin's School of Art, 1946–73. Showed with LG, NEAC, RA and elsewhere and had work bought by War Artists' Advisory Committee. Lived in Twickenham, Middlesex.

Erik SONNTAG 1925– Sculptor in wood, bronze, plastic and other materials; painter in oil, acrylic, gouache and watercolour. Born in Marburg, Germany, Sonntag initially studied there, then at Winchester, the Slade School of Fine Art, in 1954, under William Coldstream, Reg Butler, Henry Moore and F E McWilliam, in Birmingham and at the Courtauld Institute, 1975. He exhibited at the Ashmolean Museum, Oxford, RA, ICA, in the provinces and abroad. Sometimes signed work E S. Lived in London and in Minorca, Spain.

Eileen Alice SOPER 1905–1990 Illustrator, printmaker and writer, born in Enfield, Middlesex. She was the daughter of the artist and amateur naturalist George Soper, from whom she learnt etching – so well that at 15 she had two etchings of children accepted by RA. She eventually became illustrator for 35 Enid Blyton books. After her father's death in 1942 her interest in natural history developed and she and her sister Eva, also a gifted artist, created a wildlife sanctuary in their garden at Harmer Green, Hertfordshire. Eileen Soper came to know badgers and deer intimately and her book *When Badgers Wake*, in 1955, was a notable success. A series of natural history books followed and she also wrote several books for children. She was a member of RMS, a founder-member of SWLA and had work accepted by a number of public galleries, including the British Museum. Chris Beetles held a show of both Sopers' work in 1995.

Agatha SOREL 1935– Printmaker, sculptor, watercolourist and teacher, born in Budapest, Hungary, where she attended the Academy of Fine Arts. After arriving in England in 1956 she continued studies at Camberwell School of Arts and Crafts, working with S W Hayter at Atelier 17, Paris, 1958–60. She was awarded a Gulbenkian Scholarship, 1958–60, and the Churchill Fellowship in 1966–7 to work in America and Mexico. Part-time lectureships included Camberwell, Maidstone, Goldsmiths', Canterbury and Royal Colleges of Art, Slade School of Fine Art and Philadelphia Museum of Art. Sorel was a member of RE and of the Printmakers' Council, being its chairman, 1981–3, was on the council of the Royal Society of Printmakers, helped select 8th International Print Biennale in Bradford and found the Studio of Contemporary Art training centre. She took part in many mixed shows, including RA Summer Exhibitions, and had a long series of solo exhibitions starting with Curwen Gallery, 1965, later ones including Intaglio Printmaker Gallery and Trumpington Gallery in Cambridge, both 1990, and Malargalleriet, Stockholm, 1992. Tate Gallery, Victoria & Albert Museum, Arts Council, British Museum, British Council and many other public collections in Britain hold examples, as well as many museums and galleries overseas. Lived in London.

Adrian SORRELL 1932– Sculptor and teacher, born in Salford, Lancashire of Russian and English parents. He studied at local School of Art, 1940–54, in Stockholm in 1957, spent a further three years in Scandinavia and continued to travel and study in Europe until 1959. From 1960–74 lectured at Bolton College of Art and Design, then retired to do his own work. This consisted of bronzes of wildlife, refined and with little detailing. He showed with RA, Sladmore Gallery and John Davies Contemporary, Stow-on-the-Wold. Lived in Whitefield, Manchester.

Alan SORRELL 1904–1974 Muralist, artist in oil, gouache and watercolour, teacher, illustrator and lithographer of landscapes and figure subjects with a strong interest in early history. Born in London, Sorrell studied at Southend School of Art. He worked for several years as a commercial designer, entered the Royal College of Art, 1924–7, then was awarded a scholarship to the British

School at Rome, 1928. Exhibited at RA, NEAC and RWS. Taught at the Royal College, 1931–48, during which time he visited Iceland. During World War II Sorrell served as a war artist with the Royal Air Force for several years, his work – which has a strong Neo-Romantic flavour, typical of its time – being held by the Imperial War Museum. Tate Gallery, Ashmolean Museum in Oxford, London Museum and National Museum of Wales in Cardiff also own examples. In 1947 Sorrell married the artist Elizabeth Tanner, their children being the artists Richard and Julia Sorrell. Completed a series of murals after World War II, including one for the Festival of Britain, 1951. Commissioned by the Ministry of Works to make drawings of ancient monuments. Lived at Daws Heath, near Thundersley, Essex.

Elizabeth SORRELL 1916–1991 Painter, designer and teacher, born at New Skelton-in-Cleveland, Yorkshire, as Elizabeth Tanner. She married the painter Alan Sorrell, their children Richard and Julia also being artists. Studied at Eastbourne School of Art, 1934–8, where her teachers included Frank Archer and Oliver Senior; then at Royal College of Art, 1938–42, in the design department under Ernest Tristram. After the Royal College she taught in several art colleges; worked as a designer of wallpapers and fabrics; and designed for the British Industries Fair and Ideal Home Exhibitions. Showed at NEAC from 1947 and RA from 1948. Her work had a strong decorative element, and subjects such as dolls and plants frequently featured, painted in meticulous detail. Became a member of RWS in 1966. Tate Gallery owns her picture Ferns in the Conservatory. Died at Thundersley, Essex.

Julia SORRELL 1955– Artist mostly in watercolour, pen and ink, pastel and pencil; embroiderer and teacher, born in Essex. She was the daughter of the artists Alan and Elizabeth Sorrell and the sister of Richard. She said that as an artist her parents "had a profound influence," as had "the fact of being a woman, being married and having children." Her first solo show at Maas Gallery, in 1994, featured "wooded glades, with ethereal figures floating through (usually her family)". Sorrell graduated from Goldsmiths' College, 1973–6, where she studied embroidery, then the Royal Academy Schools, 1978–81; Betty Swanwick and Constance Howard were notable teachers. Showed in Sorrell family annual exhibitions, 1970–87, at RA from 1975, RWS from 1983 and Arts Council. In 1981 she came second in Imperial Tobacco Award, in 1982 being commissioned to paint her Portrait of Baron Ramsey of Canterbury, now in National Portrait Gallery. Chelmsford Museum and Art Gallery and Beecroft Art Gallery, Southend, also hold examples. Sorrell taught at Southend College of Art and Technology (where she had studied, 1972–3), 1983–4, Aberystwyth Arts Centre, 1988, and elsewhere. Lived in Snetterton, Norfolk.

Richard SORRELL 1948– Painter, born in Thundersley, Essex, the son of the artists Alan and Elizabeth Sorrell. He studied at Walthamstow School of Art, 1965–6, Kingston College of Art, 1966–9, and Royal Academy Schools, 1969–72. There he won silver and bronze medals. Was elected RWS in 1978, RBA in 1989. Sorrell showed at RA from 1971, RWS from 1975 and RBA from 1988. Other appearances included Sorrell family shows, Hayward Gallery in the Lutyens Exhibition, 1980, and Victoria & Albert Museum, Artists in National Parks, 1988. He carried out a number of commissions, including aerial views for National Trust. Had a solo show at Agnew, 1990, and Cadogan Gallery, 1992. Victoria & Albert Museum and Museum of London hold his work. Lived in King's Lynn, Norfolk.

Willi SOUKOP 1907–1995 Sculptor in a variety of materials, especially of the female figure; draughtsman, teacher. He was born in Vienna, Austria, and studied at the Academy of Fine Art there, 1928–34, after a period as an apprentice engraver and student in the evenings at Vienna Arts and Crafts School. While teaching he met an Englishwoman who invited him to England where he settled at Dartington Hall with his own studio among other artists. Taught at Dartington Art School, 1937–9. After a period of internment in Canada in World War II returned to teach art at Blundell's School, Devonshire, until 1945. Settled in London, he went on to teach at Bromley School of Art; Guildford School of Art; Chelsea School of Art, 1947–72; and became master of sculpture at Royal Academy Schools, 1969–82. He was an examiner for sculpture and was a member of the Faculty for Sculpture at the British School in Rome. Was elected RBA, 1950; fellow of RBS, 1956; and showed often at RA, being elected RA in 1969. Soukop was a carver rather than a modeller with a variety of styles who considered his greatest style debt was to the German sculptor Ernst Barlach. Official commissions and purchases included Dartington Hall Gardens, Hull University Library, St Paul's Cathedral and Westminster Abbey. Tate Gallery and provincial museums hold his work. A substantial review show of this took place at Belgrave Gallery, 1991. Lived in north London, but died in Glasgow.

John Bulloch SOUTER 1890–1972 Painter, draughtsman, printmaker and restorer, born in Aberdeen, Scotland. After showing much promise in art at Gordon's College, Aberdeen, he attended Gray's School of Art there. A travelling scholarship allowed him to work extensively on the continent, where Velasquez, Chardin and Vermeer, especially, much impressed him. During World War I served as non-combatant in Royal Medical Corps, then married and moved to London. By this time he had established himself as an RA exhibitor, and in the period after the war he made a name as a portrait painter, his subjects including stage personalities such as Ivor Novello, Gladys Cooper and Fay Compton as well as notables in public and academic life. In 1926 Souter's picture The Breakdown caused a stir at RA, depicting a negro jazz musician, a naked white girl dancer and a broken classic statue. Souter consolidated his reputation with exhibits at Redfern Gallery, Fine Art Society, RSA and elsewhere. In World War II he worked in the Censorship Department, London, as a translator and restored paintings at Windsor Castle. Returned to Aberdeen in 1952, where he remained.

Joan SOUTER-ROBERTSON 1903–1994 Painter and draughtsman, born in India, who determined to be an artist despite the early death of her father and her mother's straitened circumstances. She studied with André Lhote, at L'Académie de la Grande Chaumière from 1925 and then returned to London, where she established a career as a painter of children and was noted as a decorator of furniture. Charm with an underlying strong draughtsmanship characterised her landscapes and portraits. In 1936, the year that she had a first solo show at the Storran Gallery, she married Jacques Cochemé, a biologist and agroclimatologist, and travelled and showed extensively abroad, including Beirut, Khartoum, Amman and Nairobi, in the 1950s. Her mixed exhibitions included LG, New Burlington Galleries and RA Summer Exhibition. Later solo shows comprised two at the Upstairs Gallery at RA, 1982–3, the second of glass paintings, and a retrospective at Addison-Ross Gallery in 1993. Died in London.

Derek SOUTHALL 1930– Painter and teacher, born in Coventry, Warwickshire. While still at school studied at Coventry School of Art, 1943–6, then as a student there from 1947 for two years; this was followed by two years at Camberwell School of Arts and Crafts and one at Goldsmiths' College School of Art. A Spencer Travelling Scholarship, 1954, allowed him to work for a year with Karl Schmidt-Rottluff and Hans Jaenisch at Hochschule für Bildende Kunst, Berlin. He began teaching at Coventry College of Art from 1955 and at Birmingham Regional College of Art. Later teaching positions included London and Birmingham and a period as artist-in-residence at University of South Carolina. Commissions included work for Department of the Environment, 1972. Exhibitions included Museum of Modern Art, Oxford, a solo show at Herbert Art Gallery and Museum, Coventry, 1971, Arnolfini in Bristol, 1980, and elsewhere. Herbert Art Gallery holds works by him. Lived in London.

Jeanne SOUTHGATE 1930– Painter, born in Bournemouth, Hampshire, where she studied art at the Technical College. Showed in range of exhibitions in the south of England and has work in Russell-Cotes Art Gallery and Museum, Bournemouth.

Francesca SOUZA 1957– Artist and lecturer, born and lived in London, daughter of the painter F N Souza and sister of the artist Karen Souza. She did a foundation course at St Martin's School of Art, 1978–9; gained an honours degree in textiles at Goldsmiths' College, 1979–83; then a postgraduate diploma in painting at Central School of Speech and Drama, 1995–7. Souza was a visiting lecturer at Kingsway and City and Islington Colleges. She said that she was "an autobiographical artist in search of metaphors for my thoughts; to represent my unrepresentable", and to this end employed depictions of domestic objects, cartoon characters and token trophies on exotically coloured grounds. Shows included Women and Textiles, Battersea Arts Centre, 1983; Material Evidence, Camden Arts Centre and Virago Book Shop Gallery, 1985; National Theatre, 1992; Candid Gallery, 1997; and Julian Hartnoll Gallery, Art98, Business Design Centre, 1998.

Francis Newton SOUZA 1924– Painter and draughtsman, born in Goa, India. Studied art in Bombay, 1940, but was expelled for political activities. While in Bombay he founded the Progressive Artists' Group, showed regularly and won the Bombay Art Society Award in 1947. Travelled to London in 1949, where he studied at Central School of Arts and Crafts. Souza suffered poverty and misery until he started showing on the continent. Then he began to get acceptance in Britain, winning a prize at the John Moores Liverpool Exhibition in 1958, the year when he represented Britain in the Guggenheim International Award, New York. He moved to New York in 1967, by which time he had shown widely internationally. Had a number of one-man shows in Britain and abroad and retrospectives in Delhi and Bombay, 1987. Souza was included in The Other Story, Hayward Gallery and tour, 1989–90, and Julian Hartnoll gave him a solo exhibition, 1997. Tate Gallery, National Gallery of Modern Art in New Delhi and other public collections hold Souza's work. This was on occasion marked by narcissism, a strong erotic element, powerful use of paint and assured, incisive and graceful draughtsmanship.

Karen SOUZA 1956– Painter and draughtsman, born and lived in London, daughter of the artist F N Souza and sister of the painter Francesca Souza. She did a foundation course at Hornsey College of Art, 1974–5, then graduated with honours in fine art painting from Ravensbourne College of Art and Design, 1975–8. Mixed shows included Women's Eye Gallery, Lauderdale House, 1985; Portobello Arts Festival, 1989; Making a Mark, Mall Galleries, 1993; and World of Drawings & Watercolours, The Dorchester, with Julian Hartnoll, 1998. Later solo shows included Cherry Orchard Restaurant, 1996.

Brain SOWERBY 1920– Printmaker and teacher, born in Grimsby, Lincolnshire. He worked at Norwich School of Art, including part-time lecturing. Was a member of RE, also exhibiting with Cheshire Homes Foundation and elsewhere in mixed shows. Had a series of solo exhibitions in Norwich, Norfolk, where he lived.

Millicent SOWERBY 1878–1967 Watercolourist and black-and-white artist, full name Amy Millicent Sowerby, daughter of the artist John G Sowerby. She was mostly self-taught, acquiring her technique from the example of her father and the study of other illustrators. She was mainly an illustrator of children's books, notably those of her sister Githa, including *The Wise Book*, 1906, and *The Bonny Book*, 1918. Robert Louis Stevenson was another favourite author, and publishers such as J M Dent, Grant Richards and Oxford University Press employed her, as well as magazines: *The Tatler* and *Illustrated London News*. Showed at RA, RI, Baillie Gallery and Walker Art Gallery in Liverpool. Lived in London.

Katie SOWTER 1944– Representational artist, notable for large pastels, born in Reading, Berkshire, daughter of the illustrator and artist William Littlewood. Still lifes and interiors with a figure, often herself, and coastal scenes with shells were features of her work. She studied at Byam Shaw School of Art, 1965–8, under Maurice de Sausmarez. Was a member of The Suffolk

Group, also showing at RA Summer Exhibition; Drawings for All at Gainsborough's House, Sudbury, and at the Quay Gallery there; in the Eastern Open in King's Lynn; Town Art, Unity Wharf; and with The Monday People, Suffolk. Lived in the county at Rattlesden, Bury St Edmunds.

Basil SPACKMAN 1895–1971 Painter in oil and watercolour, born in Happisburgh, Norfolk, educated at Lancing College. He began his service career as a private in the Norfolk Regiment in 1914, being commissioned in the following year and transferring to the Royal Flying Corps in 1917. He rose to become air vice-marshal, widely experienced in the Middle East in both World Wars and winning a number of decorations, including the Distinguished Flying Cross and bar. In 1950 Spackman retired at his own request, in that year attending Hammersmith School of Art under Frederick Gray. Charles Basil Slater Spackman settled in the Irish Republic, living finally in Cork. He showed with Cork Art Society, Watercolour Society of Ireland and Armed Forces', of all of which he was a member, as well as RSA, RHA, RCamA, RBA, RI and elsewhere.

Cyril Saunders SPACKMAN 1887–1963 Painter, printmaker, sculptor and architect, born in Cleveland, Ohio, America. He studied at King's College architectural department in London and was a pupil of the architect T E Lidiard James. Was a member of many artistic and architectural bodies, including RBA, RMS and SGA. Settled in the Croydon area of Surrey in early 1920s, where he was a member of the Camera Club, also exhibiting with RA, RCamA, Walker Art Gallery in Liverpool and ROI. British Museum print room holds his work.

Sarah SPACKMAN 1958– Painter, born in Reading, Berkshire. She studied at Byam Shaw School of Art in 1977, after a brief time in Liverpool studying for a teaching qualification, where she decided to become an artist full time. In 1978–81 she studied at Camberwell School of Arts and Crafts while Philip Matthews was head of the painting department, and the School left a marked impression on her work. She eventually moved to Oxford, where she had lived in the early 1980s, after a time working in Italy and living in West Yorkshire. Exhibited at Whitechapel Art Gallery, 1979, in the Uses of Drawing show, the following year gaining third prize in the Magnolia National Landscape Competition. Had a series of one-man shows at Henley Exhibition Centre from 1982, later solo exhibitions including Austin/Desmond Fine Art, Sunninghill, from 1989. In 1986 was winner of the Winsor & Newton Young Artists Award, having been a finalist in 1985.

Iola SPAFFORD 1930– Artist in various media, born in Cambridge. She studied at Bristol Art School, 1947, Nottingham School of Art, 1948–50, and Slade School of Fine Art, 1950–4, winning a Travelling Scholarship to Italy. She was a member of MAFA and RCamA and showed at RA, Tegfryn Gallery at Menai Bridge, Pitcairn Gallery in Knutsford and elsewhere. Salford Art Gallery and Manchester City Art Gallery's Rutherston Collection hold examples. Lived in Wilmslow, Cheshire.

Lily SPANDORF 1919– Painter, designer and mural artist, born in Vienna, where she studied at the Academy of Applied Art. Exhibited widely abroad, including Austria, Italy and America, and in England at Sunderland Public Art Gallery, Foyles Gallery and in Hampstead, where she was a member of the Artists' Council. Lived in London.

Mabel Mary SPANTON 1874– Prolific exhibitor, notably of landscape in watercolour, born in Hanley, Staffordshire. She studied at the School of Art there and in Newlyn with Stanhope Forbes. Was elected BWS in 1927, also showing at RA, Walker's Galleries, SWA, Goupil Gallery, RSA and RI. Miss Spanton spent much of her life overseas, using Bourlet and Sons, her framers, as a London address.

Martin SPANYOL 1952– Painter and printmaker, born in Wiltshire, who studied at Bath Academy of Art, 1970–4. His exhibitions included RA Summer Exhibition from 1976; Young British Painters and Young British Printmakers, both Chenil Gallery, 1978; Artisera, Syracuse, America, and LG, both 1982; and Goldsmiths' show at Woodlands Art Gallery, 1983. In 1974 had solo show at Bristol Arts Centre. Lived for a time in London.

Austin Osman SPARE 1888–1956 Draughtsman, painter, designer and printmaker specialising in bizarre subjects, which stemmed from his interest in mysticism and the occult. Born in London, he exhibited in his early teens a drawing at the RA which was highly praised. Studied at Lambeth School of Art and Royal College of Art. After an abortive attempt at editing a hoped-for successor to *The Yellow Book* for the publisher John Lane, Spare had more success in the early 1920s with *The Golden Hind*, which he jointly edited with the writer Clifford Bax. Experimented for a time with automatic drawing. Eventually became a recluse and pauper. Exhibited extensively at Lefevre Gallery and had a number of one-man shows. Lived at Goodmayes, Essex.

Judith SPARK 1965– Installations artist, born and lived in Glasgow, where she attended the School of Art, 1989–93. Exhibitions included New Generation, Compass Gallery, Glasgow, and Spaghetti Junction Project for Fine Rats International, Birmingham, both 1993; and in 1994, all in Glasgow: Modern Art at Transmission Gallery, Titanic (collaboration with Kirsty Stansfield) at Old Fruitmarket, and New Art in Scotland, Centre for Contemporary Arts, with an installation called Continuous Anxiousness.

Claire SPARKES 1970– Painter and teacher, born in Crayford, Kent, whose subject-matter was sometimes domestic, as in All It Took Was A Wish And A Pinch of Pixie Dust, acrylic on canvas in Royal Over-Seas League Open, 1995. She studied at Maidstone College of Art and Liverpool John Moores University, then was a part-time art tutor at adult education centres in Deal, Folkestone and Dover, whose Grammar School for Girls held her work. She won a Daler-Rowney Cryla Award for Modern Art, 1995. Group shows included Fresh Start, Businesss Design Centre, Islington,

1992, and Eurotunnel Celebration 94, Eurotunnel Exhibition Centre, Folkestone, 1994. Was a prolific solo exhibitor, including Hilderstone Adult Education Centre, Margate, 1990; Through the Glass Wall of Sleep, Library Gallery, Maidstone, 1993; Voices of my Household (I & II), Hanover Galleries, Liverpool, 1994; and Voices of my Household – they tell their Secrets Slowly, Library Gallery, Folkestone 1995.

Jean SPARKS 1929– Painter, potter and teacher, born in Nuneaton, Warwickshire, where she attended the High School for Girls. Studied at Leicester College of Art, 1946–51. She went on to teach in a secondary school and became chairman of the Melton Studio Group of Artists and Craftsmen, in Melton Mowbray, Leicestershire, where she lived. Exhibited Young Contemporaries and Under Thirties shows at RBA, as well as locally.

Nathaniel SPARKS 1880–1956 Printmaker and watercolourist, born in Bristol, a cousin of the writer Thomas Hardy. Educated at home, he won a scholarship to Bristol Municipal School of Art, then another scholarship took him to Royal College of Art in 1910. His teachers were Reginald Bush and Frank Short. Whistler employed Sparks to print his plates. Sparks' own work was variable, but he did fine etchings of Bristol, as found in its City Art Gallery and illustrated in *City Impressions: Bristol Etchers 1910–1935*. In later life Sparks made much of his living from topographical watercolours in England and Scotland. Sparks showed at RE from 1905, being elected a full member in 1910, and at RA in 1915 Queen Mary bought Sparks' view of Westminster Abbey. Also showed at Chenil Gallery, Walker Art Gallery in Liverpool, at Paris Salon and in Venice. Late in 1930s Sparks left London and died in Somerton, Somerset. Dorset County Museum, Dorchester, held a centenary exhibition in 1980.

Leslie SPAULL 1914– Painter, illustrator and teacher, born in East Sheen, Surrey. Studied at Richmond School of Art, St John's Wood Art Schools under Patrick Millard and Royal Academy Schools with Walter Westley Russell. He held a number of art teaching posts, including Wrekin College and Westminster School. Did illustrative work for Central Office of Information. Exhibited RA and Brighton Art Gallery. Lived in London.

Ruskin SPEAR 1911–1990 Painter and teacher, full name Augustus John Ruskin Spear, born in Hammersmith, London, where he spent most of his life and which he frequently painted. An attack of polio as a child badly affected one leg, so he attended Brook Green School for crippled children. Aged 15 won scholarship to Hammersmith School of Art, another scholarship in 1930 taking him to the Royal College of Art for four years under William Rothenstein. In 1934 became part-time tutor at Croydon School of Art; he was eventually to teach at St Martin's School of Art, Central School of Arts and Crafts and Hammersmith School of Art, in 1948 becoming tutor at the Royal College of Art, where he remained until 1975. These were years which brought in such movements as Kitchen Sink and Pop Art. Spear was to retain his individuality as an essentially English painter in the Sickert tradition, a reflection of his working-class Cockney background being his pictures of seedy street and bar-room life. He exhibited at the RA from 1932 and for the Summer Exhibition provided talking-point portraits of Winston Churchill, Princess Anne and Margaret Thatcher. His outstanding portraits included fellow-painter Carel Weight, Lord Hailsham and Lord Olivier, the actor. Elected RA in 1954. Painted an altarpiece for the Royal Air Force church St Clement Danes and designed murals for the liner *Canberra*. Retrospective at RA in 1980 was a popular and critical success. Work in many public collections.

Jeffrey SPEDDING 1944– Portrait and landscape painter and draughtsman, and teacher, who acquired his diploma in design (painting special) at Wimbledon School of Art, 1965, and his Sussex University art teacher's diploma, Brighton College of Art, 1966. Taught at several schools, 1966–79; was a part-time lecturer in Wales, 1981–90; was on the full-time staff of Swansea Institute of Higher Education, 1990–5; thereafter being head of division of fine and applied arts at Nene College of Higher Education school of art and design, Northampton, where he lived. Spedding was artist-in-residence at Fishguard Music Festival, 1985; Carmarthen Arts Festival, 1988; and Llanelli Arts Festival, 1990. Had a solo exhibition at The Minories, Colchester, 1976, others including Royal Festival Hall, 1986, St David's Hall, Cardiff, 1988 and 1990, and Philharmonic Hall, Liverpool, 1992. Spedding had a strong interest in classical music and produced many commissioned portraits. Those in private collections included Lord and Lady Menuhin, Sir Michael Tippett, Elizabeth Schwarzkopf and Walter Legge, Leonard Bernstein and Sir George Solti. St David's Hall has a large Igor Stravinsky portrait, and Llandovery College life-sized paintings of composers of the Second Viennese School. The EMI and Conifer recording companies used his portraits on record sleeves. Spedding had a house and studio in Roussillon, France.

Sidney SPEDDING 1916– Sculptor in various materials and teacher, born in Ashington, Northumberland. Studied art at Armstrong College at Durham University, 1932–6, his teachers including Herbert Maryon, then at Edinburgh College of Art, 1936–9, with Hubert Wellington. He held a number of teaching positions, including a spell in Pakistan and a period lecturing in sculpture at Manchester School of Art, 1948–53. Exhibited RSA and in the provinces, signing work with initials in the form of a monogram. Lived for many years near Stockport, Cheshire.

Harold SPEED 1872–1957 Painter and writer on art, born in London. Speed was the son of an architect, Edward Speed, and initially studied architecture at the Royal College of Art, but changed to painting, winning a gold medal for life studies in 1890. He went on to study at the Royal Academy Schools, 1891–6, again winning a gold medal. A travelling scholarship took him to Belgium, France, Italy and Spain, 1894–5. He exhibited at the RA for 40 years from 1893, also at many other venues, including RP, Fine Art Society, Leicester Galleries and RBA. Speed was a consummate draughtsman and portrait painter and wrote *The Science and Practice of Drawing*, 1913, and *The Science and Practice of Oil Painting*, 1924, as well as *What is the Good of Art?*, 1936. He was master of the Art Workers' Guild, 1916, nine years after he had his first one-man show, at the Leicester Galleries. The Tate Gallery, National Portrait Gallery, many provincial and Commonwealth galleries hold his work. Lived at Watlington, Oxfordshire.

Kira SPEISER 1971– Painter in oil on aluminium of urban scenes in which the ugly legacy of development and industry were key features. She was born in Zürich, Switzerland, and was educated at Schule für Zeichnen & Gestalten, Zürich, 1988–90; Kunstgewerbe Schule, Zürich, 1989–91; and Byam Shaw School of Art, 1991–5. Gained several financial awards in Switzerland, 1992–3; a scholarship to Byam Shaw, 1992–4; and while there, in 1994 won joint first prize, drawing competition. Group shows included Conductors Hallway, 1996, and Lamont Gallery from 1997. Solo shows included Salon des Arts, 1995; No Man's Landscape, Galerie Wehrli, Zürich, 1997; and Lamont Gallery, 1998. Lived in London.

Bette SPEKTOROV 1939– Painter and teacher. She gained her master's degree in modern history at Oxford University, 1961, then did postgraduate diploma in art history at Courtauld Institute. From 1966 taught at City University in New York, in 1968 gaining master's degree in fine art, Hunter College, University of New York. From 1981 was senior lecturer in history of art at Middlesex Polytechnic. In 1981 had a studio show with Anthony Gormley, Di Livey and Tim Mara, the New Bagnigge Group. Four years later participated in John Moores Exhibition, Liverpool, later appearances including annual shows at Camden Arts Centre, in 1986, and Ben Uri Art Society, 1987. Had a solo show at Ben Uri in 1989 and in 1992 her exhibition The Mystery of Decoration toured fom Usher Gallery, Lincoln. In that, richly coloured paintings took their inspiration from old objects in the Usher collection.

Michael SPELLER 1958– Sculptor in various materials and pen and ink draughtsman who lived in Greenwich, southeast London, where for a time he ran a catering business. He began by creating pen and ink drawings, then concentrated on sculpting for two years at local evening classes. Speller studied for an honours degree in The Practice and Theory of Visual Arts at Chelsea College of Art. His work is in private collections, especially in Germany. Had a studio in Deptford and received his first London solo show at Paul Hawkins Gallery in 1997.

Annora SPENCE 1963– Artist in mixed media and textile designer who was educated at Itchen Sixth Form College in Southampton. She attended Winchester College of Art and Design, 1981–2; gained an honours degree in printed textiles, Liverpool Polytechnic, 1982–5; and her master's degree in the same subject at Birmingham Polytechnic, 1985–6. For that degree she was sponsored by the Textile Institute. Exhibitions included The Poetry Show, Rebecca Hossack Gallery, 1992; and in 1993 Bruton Street Gallery and a shared exhibition at Thackeray Rankin Gallery.

John SPENCE 1944– Painter notable for small landscapes in a variety of media, and teacher, born near Carlton, near Nottingham, where he was based. He attended the Nottingham College of Art, 1962–7, Slade School of Fine Art, 1967–9, and Leicester Polytechnic school of educational studies, 1970–1. Then went on to hold a number of teaching jobs. Showed in mixed groups in the Midlands, and solo exhibitions included Nottingham Playhouse, 1978. In 1981–2 he was included in Fragments Against Ruin tour by Arts Council, which holds a series of his works.

Robert SPENCE 1871–1964 Printmaker and painter, born in Tynemouth, Northumberland, son of the artist Charles Spence. He studied in Newcastle, at Slade School of Fine Art and in Paris. Was elected RE and was an associate of Société Nationale des Beaux-Arts. Showed at RA, Fine Art Society, Walker Art Gallery in Liverpool and Fine Art Society. Lived in London, where he was an Arts Club member.

T Everard SPENCE fl. from c.1930s–1992 Painter, mainly of landscapes, although he painted many portraits of people he knew, educated at Bootham School in York. He was largely self-taught, but spent about nine months at Belfast College of Art when a young man and took a few lessons from Frank McKelvey. Spence was a knowledgeable collector of miniatures, from which he derived a keen eye for detail in his own work. As a linen manufacturer he travelled widely, always carried his painting gear with him, and painted on the spot, savouring the atmosphere of the scene. Showed at RA, RHA, RBA, RUA and had several solo shows. Lived in Belfast, Northern Ireland, for many years.

Charles SPENCELAYH 1865–1958 Genre and figure painter in minute detail, miniaturist and printmaker. Born at Rochester, Kent, he studied at the Royal College of Art and in Paris. From the early 1890s he began exhibiting at the RA until his death, also showing at RI, RMS, RHA, Royal Glasgow Institute of the Fine Arts, Paris Salon and elsewhere. One-man show at Sunderland Art Gallery, 1936. He was the father of the painter Vernon Spencelayh. Charles Spencelayh's works, sometimes just signed C S, are in many public collections, including Harris Museum & Art Gallery, Preston, the City Art Gallery, Bradford, and the Tate Gallery. His pictures, having great popular appeal, were widely reproduced. Lived at Wellingborough, Northamptonshire.

Vernon SPENCELAYH 1891–1980 Painter and miniaturist, born in Chatham, Kent, who studied with his father, the artist Charles Spencelayh. Exhibited RI, RMS, Walker Art Gallery, Liverpool, and BWS, of which he was a member. On the advice of his father, Vernon Spencelayh made his career in Barclays Bank, retiring after World War II, after which he could concentrate on his painting, which was often in the manner of his father's. He travelled widely in southern Africa, living for some time in South Africa, where he had a number of shows at the Maskew Miller Art Gallery, Cape Town. He also lived in Madeira and the Canary Islands, eventually returning to live in the south of England. A then-child neighbour of Spencelayh, in 1945 when he was living at Verwood, on the Hampshire border in an isolated bungalow, later recalled him as "a to me old man in a straw hat and light-coloured summer clothes in a well-kept garden.... He used a camera obscura in his front-room studio to view his mainly still life subjects."

Gilbert SPENCER 1892–1979 Painter, especially of landscapes, draughtsman, teacher and writer. Born at Cookham, Berkshire, brother of the painter Stanley Spencer. Gilbert studied at Camberwell School of Arts and Crafts, woodcarving at the Royal College of Art, 1911–12, then with Fred Brown and Henry Tonks at the Slade School of Fine Art 1913–20, although between 1915–19 this was broken by Army service. Spencer had his first one-man show at the Goupil Gallery in 1923, also exhibiting at RA (he was elected RA in 1960), NEAC of which he was early made a member, Leicester Galleries, RSA, Redfern Gallery and many other venues. Although he produced notable wall paintings for Holywell Manor, Oxford, 1934–6, Spencer made his name as a landscape artist working mainly in the English southern counties. At various times he taught at Royal College of Art, Glasgow School of Art and Camberwell, serving meanwhile as an official war artist, 1940–3. His book *Stanley Spencer* appeared in 1961 and his *Memoirs of a Painter* in 1974. Retrospective exhibition at Reading, 1964. Tate Gallery and many other public collections hold his work, sometimes just signed G S. Lived near Reading, Berkshire.

Gwen SPENCER 1927– Artist mainly in oil and pastel, full name Violet Gwendoline Spencer, in whose work movement, as in the game of polo, was a key theme. She was born in Buenos Aires, Argentina, and studied at Atelier Josse there, 1944–5, then at Putney School of Art, 1964–80. Became a full member of NS in 1979, acting as treasurer and secretary. She also showed with PS, ROI, Annexe Gallery, Poole Art Centre, Ridley Society and Medici Gallery, Medici Society publishing cards of her pictures. Solo shows were held at Putney School of Art in 1974 and 1976 and at L'Herisson, in Wimbledon, in 1989. Wandsworth Borough Council holds her work. Lived in London.

Jean SPENCER 1942–1998 Artist and teacher, born in Hampshire, who made her first constructed reliefs as a student at Bath Academy of Art, 1960–3, then studied at University of Sussex. She showed widely in Britain and on the continent, including the Systems exhibitions of 1969–73; with the Arbeitskreis from 1977; in 1977–8 she produced *Working Information*, a series of publications and drawings by Systematic-Constructive artists; later worked with the Exhibiting Space project; and was included in Colour Presentations, Gardner Centre Gallery, University of Sussex, and tour, 1986. From 1968–88 she taught at Bulmershe College of Higher Education, where her work included general courses in art for primary teachers, from 1988 being on the staff of the Slade School of Fine Art. Arts Council holds her work. Lived in London. For over 25 years Spencer was the companion of the artist Malcolm Hughes, becoming his second wife in 1997.

June SPENCER: *see* **June BUCHANAN**

Liam SPENCER 1964– Painter and lecturer, born in Burnley, Lancashire, who attended the College of Arts & Technology there and Manchester Polytechnic. Eventually he occupied a studio in Manchester with "a vast panorama of industrial buildings, stretching out to the distant Pennines", from which he painted the oil on board Landscape With Bright Cloud, in Royal Over-Seas League Open, 1996. Spencer was on the exhibition committee of Manchester's Castlefield Gallery, 1987–95, and in 1991 was a visiting lecturer at Manchester Metropolitan University. Commissions included several northern corporate ones and Towneley Hall Art Gallery & Museums, Burnley. Group shows included Wykeham Galleries, Stockbridge, 1992; RA Summer Exhibition, 1994; and Northern Colourists, Kentmere House, York, 1995. Later solo shows included Windows On The City, Towneley Hall and tour, 1996; Royal Over-Seas League tour, 1997–8; and a first London show at New Grafton Gallery, 1998.

Noël SPENCER 1900–1986 Printmaker and artist in black-and-white, born in Nuneaton, Warwickshire. Studied at Ashton-under-Lyne School of Art, Manchester School of Art and Royal of Art. He held a number of teaching positions, notably principal Norwich School of Art 1946–64. Exhibited RA, RBSA, Norwich Twenty Group, NEAC and widely in America. Public galleries in Birmingham, Sheffield, Huddersfield and Chicago hold his work, the Museum of London having a considerable collection. Spencer was interested in depicting townscapes and landscapes, a notable achievement in the 1940s being many pen drawings of Huddersfield, completed while he was head of the Art School there. Finally lived in Norwich.

Pamela Mary SPENCER 1924– Artist in oil, watercolour and pencil, born in Manchester. She studied at St Martin's School of Art, 1945–51, under H A Freeth, James Bateman, Barry Craig and Gilbert Spencer, having served in Women's Land Army, 1943–5. Began exhibiting from 1945 and was a member of Hampstead Art Club, 1952–3. Also showed at RA, NEAC, SWA, NS, RBA, ROI, PS, Russell-Cotes Art Gallery and Museum in Bournemouth, Ashmolean Museum in Oxford and elsewhere. Main works included Fishing Nets. Private collections in Britain and abroad hold her pictures. Lived in Henley-on-Thames, Oxfordshire.

Roy SPENCER 1918– Painter, illustrator and teacher, born in Stamford, Lincolnshire. His career as an architect – he was an articled pupil from 1938 – was interrupted by the war, during which he served in the Army abroad. He travelled widely and met the artist John Ward, an important influence. After leaving the Army in 1946 he studied at Chelsea School of Art under Raymond Coxon while teaching at Wimbledon School of Art under Gerald Cooper. When he finished as a student at Chelsea he became a visitor there, retiring in late 1980s. He was a noted teacher of life drawing. Spencer also did advertising and magazine work for periodicals such as *House & Garden*, freelanced for Shell, illustrated for Bodley Head and showed at RA and NEAC. In 1970s remarried, after divorce, the illustrator Carolyn Dinan. Showed solo at Trafford Gallery, 1950, 1970 Bath Festival and at Sally Hunter Fine Art from 1990. Spencer chose hedonistic subjects, which he drew with grace and felicity.

Sarah SPENCER 1965– Painter who completed a foundation course at Canterbury College of Art, 1984–5; gained a bachelor's degree at Camberwell School of Arts and Crafts, 1985–8; then completed a postgraduate diploma at Royal Academy Schools, 1988–91. She gained the W S Vellum Award in 1986; Gordon Macara Prize in 1988; David Murray Landscape Scholarship in 1989; Richard Jack Prize, Creswick Landscape Prize, Duff Greet Prize and Haite Travel Scholarship were awarded in 1991; Elizabeth Greenshields Award, 1996. Commissions comprised Stanhope Estate Community Mural, 1988; East Kent Equestrian Centre mural, 1989; and a drawing for Hambros Bank, 1991. Had a first solo show with New Grafton Gallery, 1992, later ones including Offer Waterman & Jonathan Cooper, 1997. West Wales Arts Council holds her work.

Stanley SPENCER 1891–1959 Painter of portraits, landscapes and imaginative, visionary, quirky works with a Biblical flavour set in his native Cookham, Berkshire. Studied at the Slade School of Fine Art, 1908–12, where he was awarded a Scholarship in 1910 and won the Summer Composition Prize two years later. Exhibited at Roger Fry's Second Post-Impressionist Exhibition, 1912. During service in the Army in World War I was commissioned to paint a picture for the Imperial War Museum. He was to serve as an official war artist during World War II, painting shipbuilding work at Port Glasgow, Scotland. After the war Spencer travelled on occasion in Europe, although his work remained essentially his own, in the English-eccentric tradition. Was the brother of the artist Gilbert Spencer and was married first to Hilda Carline, then Patricia Preece, who both painted. Decorated the oratory of All Souls, Burghclere, 1926–32, with his memories of the Macedonian campaign. First one-man show at the Goupil Gallery, 1927. Elected RA, 1950, and knighted, 1959. His work is held in many international collections, including Tate Gallery, London, and a Stanley Spencer Gallery was opened in Cookham, three years after he died at Taplow, Buckinghamshire. There have been several retrospective exhibitions, a memorial show was held in Plymouth in 1963 and a major appraisal was staged at the Hirshhorn Museum, Washington, in America, in 1997–8.

Vera SPENCER 1926– Painter and designer, born in Prague, Czechoslovakia, who arrived in England aged 10 and studied at Slade School of Fine Art and Central School of Textile Design. She was included in many important mixed shows of abstract work, including one at AIA, 1951; Collages and Objects, at ICA, 1954; and Groupe Espace at Royal Festival Hall, 1955. She was part of Belgrave Gallery's 1992 survey British abstract art of the 50s and 60s. Spencer's solo shows included Galerie Apollinaire, 1948; Galerie Arnaud, Paris, 1952; Conran Furniture, 1953; and Elizabeth Gallery, Coventry, 1968. Spencer showed three works in Coventry and Warwickshire Society of Artists show at Herbert Art Gallery and Museum, Coventry, in 1963.

Tessa SPENCER PRYSE 1940– Painter of interiors, figures and landscapes direct from the subject, in whose work sunlight was an important element. She was born in Wales, then from the age of 10 lived in the Alps. Her father was the artist Gerald Spencer Pryse (see Pryse), and after his death in 1956 she rebelled against his wishes and studied at the Byam Shaw School of Art; married and moved to the Black Isle, where her work was influenced by the Scottish Colourists; moved to East Anglia in 1981; was elected a member of the RBA; studied printmaking under Richard Bawden, and was invited by the keeper to be guest student at the Royal Academy Schools in 1983; and in 1984 won the Oppenheim Award to pursue printmaking. Mixed shows included RA Summer Exhibition, NEAC, RP, RSA and the Singer & Friedlander/*Sunday Times* Watercolour Competition. Had a first solo show at Craftsman Gallery, Colchester, 1976, then exhibited frequently, later ones including The John Russell Gallery, Ipswich, from 1995. Lived for a time at Wivenhoe, Essex.

Humphrey SPENDER 1910– Painter, pencil draughtsman, photographer, designer and teacher, born in London, full name John Humphrey Spender, brother of the poet Stephen Spender. He was a fellow of the Society of Industrial Artists and Designers and an honorary designer, Royal College of Art. Spender attended Gresham's School, Holt, then in 1928 went to Freiburg in Breisgau (Schwarzwald) University, "for language (under cover of history of art)". From 1928–34 Spender gained his diploma at the Architectural Association School of Architecture. His teachers included Howard Robertson. In 1935–41 Spender took a photographic studio, working for *Picture Post*, Mass Observation and the *Daily Mirror* as Lensman (in 1987 a book of Lensman photographs was published with Spender's introduction). World War II Army service included photo-interpretation of V1 and V2 rocket sites and D-Day invasion maps. Between 1946–56 did varied freelance work, including textiles, carpets, wallpapers and murals, winning Council of Industrial Design awards four times, between 1956–76 adding teaching at Royal College of Art textile school. As well as numerous mixed shows, Spender had solo painting exhibitions including Redfern and Leicester Galleries, New Art Centre and provincial venues. There were also solo photographic exhibitions, including Arnolfini Gallery, Bristol, retrospective, with tour, 1982. Among Spender's widely varied commissions, which included work for Festival of Britain, British Rail and Shell International, was the design of the Maldon Millenium Embroidery, which he finished in 1990. Victoria & Albert Museum, Ministry of Works and many provincial galleries hold pictures by him. Spender hoped that his paintings "might make people see differently". Lived in Maldon, Essex.

Matthew SPENDER 1945– Sculptor, painter and writer, born and brought up in London, son of the poet Stephen Spender. He read modern history at Oxford University before devoting himself to painting, then in 1980 he began sculpting in wood, clay and occasionally stone. In 1967, he married the artist Maro Gorky, and they moved to Tuscany, Italy. Bernardo Bertolucci's film *Stealing Beauty*, released in 1996, celebrated their marriage. Spender's memoir *Within Tuscany* was published in 1992. His exhibitions included Long & Ryle Art International and Berkeley Square Gallery.

Romana SPERSKA 1958– Painter, born and based in London, who attended Canterbury College of Art, 1978–9, then Kingston Polytechnic, 1979–81. Mixed shows included Metro Show at Metropolitan Wharf, Wapping, from 1981; Browse & Darby from 1982; and Wapping Artists Open Studios, 1983. Had a solo show at Galleria Accademia, Milan, 1983.

Renée SPIERDIJK 1957– Painter and teacher whose strong images had autobiographical themes, such as the birth of her daughter. She was born in Amsterdam, Netherlands, where she studied at Academie De Schans, 1976–7, continuing her art at the Camden Institute, 1977–8, Byam Shaw School of Art (where she later taught), 1979–83, then pursuing her master's degree at Goldsmiths' College from 1987. Exhibitions included New Contemporaries at ICA, 1983; Kingsgate Gallery from 1984; John Player Award, National Portrait Gallery, 1986; and Links of Affinity, Knapp Gallery, 1989. Solo shows included Kingsgate Gallery, 1984, and Gallery Tholen, Bergen, Noord Holland.

David SPILLER 1942– Painter, born in Dartford, Kent, whose work drew on popular art icons such as cowboys, Snoopy and Felix the Cat. He studied at Slade School of Fine Art. Took part in many international art fairs, including in 1998 Art98, Business Design Centre, with Beaux Arts, which gave him a solo show in that year. Spiller exhibited widely at fairs and exhibitions in continental Europe and America, later solo shows including a series at Gallery Cotthem, Knokke, Belgium, from 1994. Utrecht Museum of Modern Art, Netherlands; Kunstverein Mannheim, Germany; Stadt Museum, Ratingen, Germany; and Van Bommel Museum, Venlo, Netherlands, hold examples.

Jason SPIVACK 1961– Artist and lecturer, born in Philadelphia, Pennsylvania, America, who attended Tyler School of Art, Rome, 1982–3, and in 1983 the Skowhegan School of Painting and Sculpture, Maine, gaining his fine arts degree from Tyler School of Art in Philadelphia, 1984, with a master's programme at Hunter College, New York, 1985–8. In 1986 and 1989 Spivack obtained a scholarship to the Virginia Center for the Creative Arts, Sweetbriar, Virginia, where he was visiting artist and guest lecturer. In 1991–2 he was granted a Starr Foundation artist-in-residence scholarship to Royal Academy Schools. Group exhibitions included Landscapes, Area X Gallery, New York, 1986; diploma show, RA, 1992; and Art93, Houldsworth Fine Art, 1993. Had a solo show at Seventh Art Gallery, Philadelphia, 1986, and one at Houldsworth, 1993.

Arthur SPOONER 1873–1961 Painter and teacher, born in Nottingham where he made his career. He studied at Nottingham School of Art, eventually becoming life master there. Spooner was a versatile painter, especially adept at atmospheric landscapes, horses and nudes. Worked in the Nottingham area and during painting holidays abroad, although he was unable to work in his final years owing to failing eyesight. Became member of RBA in 1920; joined Nottingham Society of Artists in 1908, being elected vice-president in both 1924 and 1938; also exhibited at RA.

Walter SPRADBERY 1889–1969 Landscape painter in oil and watercolour, poster designer, teacher and lino-cut artist, born in London. Was educated at the William Morris School, Walthamstow, where he studied at the School of Art, but claimed to be mainly self-taught. From 1911 designed posters, working chiefly for London Transport, until 1944. In World War I served in Army. Made sketches on active service which were later worked up into 90 paintings, presented to Imperial War Museum. Spradbery became lifelong pacifist, active in the World War II peace movement. In 1929 married the opera singer Dorothy d'Orsay. He settled in Buckhurst Hill, Essex, where he was one of the founders of the Community Centre. Taught watercolour classes at Walthamstow Education Settlement, 1921–64, and widely elsewhere. A close friend of the artist Frank Brangwyn, he was active in getting the Brangwyn gift of artworks presented to the Borough of Walthamstow in 1935–6, which led to the opening of the William Morris Gallery in 1950. Exhibited RA, Fine Art Society, RHA, Alpine Club and overseas. The William Morris Gallery held a memorial show in 1970.

Ken SPRAGUE 1927– Artist who went to school in Hampshire and studied at Bournemouth College of Art. Worked at many jobs from mining to political cartooning. In 1969 he was granted an award by Council of Industrial Design for poster work and in 1970 the diploma of the Museum of Poster Art, Warsaw. Went on to become a printmaker who developed a method of printing on wood with a view to producing furniture. Among his exhibitions was Seven Print Makers, 1980 South West Arts touring show.

John SPRAKES 1936– Painter and teacher, studied at Doncaster College of Art, then at Edinburgh College of Art, 1954–7, teachers including William MacTaggart, Robin Philipson and William Gillies, where he gained an Andrew Grant Scholarship. Was elected to ROI in 1986, also showing at RA, MAFA, NEAC and Blackheath Gallery. Won a number of awards and had several solo exhibitions. Lived at Long Eaton, Nottinghamshire/Derbyshire.

Derek SPRAWSON 1955– Abstract artist and lecturer, born in Liverpool, who studied fine art at the Polytechnic there; graduated from Newport College of Art; and gained his master's at Reading University. Lived in Nottingham, where he was senior lecturer in fine art at The Nottingham Trent University. Sprawson gained three project awards from East Midlands Arts Board, 1985–92, in 1995 winning a drawing first prize, Biennial International for Sculpture and Drawing, Caldas da Rainha, Portugal. Later group shows included Michael Schultz Gallery, Berlin, 1991; Palace of Culture, Poznan, 1992; 7th Oriel Mostyn Open Exhibition, Llandudno, 1995–6; and winter show, Bernard Jacobson Gallery, 1996–7. At this time Sprawson was exhibiting paintings of simple shapes on grounds using muted colours, a contrast to earlier work which was densely layered and complex, and employed a rich palette.

A B S SPRIGGE 1906–1980 Sculptor in stone, wood and marble, born in London. Miss Sprigge studied art at the Royal College of Art, 1926–7, under William Rothenstein, Gilbert Ledward and

Henry Moore. She exhibited at some of London's principal galleries in the 1930s and after, including Leicester Galleries and Agnew. She had a one-man show at the Bloomsbury Gallery in 1936. Lived at Llanpumpsaint, Dyfed, Wales.

Peter SPRIGGS 1963– Painter and teacher, born in Cardiff, who studied at South Glamorgan Institute of Higher Education and Royal College of Art. He was winner of the Jeremy Cubitt Prize there, 1986, gaining 2nd Prize, National Eisteddfod of Wales, 1990. Spriggs taught adult classes part-time for London Borough of Hillingdon, 1988–90, then was full-time at Carmarthenshire College of Technology & Art from 1990. Group shows included Young Masters, Solomon Gallery, 1986; Arthur Andersen Art Award, 1993; Bayer Earth Art Exhibition, Mall Galleries, 1995; and Royal Over-Seas League Open 1996. Solo shows included Face the Facade, Llandaff Festival, Cardiff, 1986; and Three Paintings, Church of St George's, 1990. Prudential Assurance holds his work.

John SPRINGS 1960– Draughtsman, noted for his depictions of political and other personalities for the printed page. He was born in Yorkshire, son of a Latvian father and Estonian mother who had settled in England after World War II. Dyslexia, a stammer and short sight drove Springs at his preparatory school to pursue solitary interests, notably the nineteenth century. At a tutorial college he was able to develop a talent for drawing, but he was turned down for a place at Jacob Kramer College of Art, Leeds, as his style of draughtsmanship was regarded as too established. Springs then travelled in the Middle East in the wake of his hero Sir Richard Burton. When funds ran out he tried his luck as a freelance illustrator in England, being accepted by *The Literary Review*, *Harpers & Queen*, *The Spectator*, *The Sunday Telegraph* and *The Financial Times*. In 1992 he had a solo show at Sally Hunter Fine Art and a first exhibition of paintings at Rebecca Hossack Gallery, 1998. Lived in London.

Effie SPRING-SMITH 1907–1974 Painter and illustrator, born in Woodbridge, Suffolk, was married to the artist Herbert Cutner. Studied at Ipswich School of Art with George Rushton, then the Slade School of Fine Art, 1925–9, under Henry Tonks, where she won many awards. Exhibited RA, RBA, NEAC, RWA and many other venues. Member Ipswich Art Club. Felix Cobbold Bequest, Ipswich, bought her work, which was latterly signed E Cutner. Lived in London.

Elizabeth SPURR 1912–1987 Sculptor, printmaker and painter who studied at the Central School of Arts and Crafts, where John Skeaping taught. She was one, and "by far the most talented" of several private pupils taken by the sculptor, even helping him, as he recalls in his autobiography *Drawn from Life*, by collecting money when he busked with his accordion. Spurr's early sculptures had Cubist overtones, stylised in the manner of Skeaping and Barbara Hepworth. Her carving, in wood and stone, which often included animals, is notable for its beautiful finish: see examples illustrated in the monographs *British Sculpture 1944–1946*, by Eric Newton, 1947, and *Sculpture Today in Great Britain 1940–1943*, by Arthur T Broadbent, 1949. Spurr was a talented printmaker, producing innovative coloured monotypes, etchings and contributing to Everyman Prints, which the AIA produced by offset lithography for popular distribution. Spurr's paintings, in oil and gouache, were figurative, including London street and market scenes. Although married with children she went on working, but did not often exhibit. Died in London. England & Co latterly showed Spurr's work.

Mabel SPURRIER 1880– Painter in oil and watercolour, born at Moseley, near Birmingham, where she studied at the College of Art. Exhibited until near her death, specialising in animals, figures and architecture. Took part in mixed shows at RA, RBA, RBSA of which she was an associate and elsewhere. Lived in London.

Raymond SPURRIER 1920– Painter, notably a watercolourist, printmaker and writer on art, born in Wellingborough, Northamptonshire. He studied part-time at St Martin's and Central Schools of Art, while working as a town planner. Spurrier was a member of RI and an associate of RWA, also showing at RA. His batch of Australian landscapes in the 1992 RI annual exhibition showed a strong interest in topographical pattern-making. In 1984 Spurrier won the Winsor & Newton Award there. Department of the Environment holds his work. Lived in Halstead, Kent.

Steven SPURRIER 1878–1961 Painter, designer and illustrator, born and died in London. Following his father's profession of silversmith at first, Spurrier studied during the evening at Heatherley's School of Fine Art, then at the Gilbert Garrett School. From 1900 he became a full-time illustrator, working for such publications as *Black and White*, *The Graphic*, *Illustrated London News* and *Radio Times*. During World War I he worked on camouflage of ships for the Admiralty. Exhibited with the RA from 1913, elected RA 1952. Also showed at RBA, ROI, RSA, Goupil Gallery and RHA. He wrote *Black and White* and *Illustration in Wash and Line*. Work held by Tate Gallery, Victoria & Albert Museum and provincial galleries. John Benison, the designer and artist, was his son. In 1993 a show at Paisnel Gallery highlighted Spurrier's interest in circus and theatrical subjects.

Geoffrey SQUIRE 1923– Painter, draughtsman and teacher, born in Cleckheaton, Yorkshire. He studied at Leeds College of Art, 1939–41, then for two periods, 1941–2 and 1946–8, at the Slade School of Fine Art under Randolph Schwabe. Showed at RA, RSA and RBA and had one-man exhibitions at Batley and Brighouse public galleries in Yorkshire. Lectured for a period at Glasgow School of Art. Lived in Batley.

Leonard SQUIRRELL 1893–1979 Watercolour and oil painter and etcher of landscapes and architectural views. Born at Ipswich, Suffolk, Squirrell studied art at Ipswich School of Art, 1908–16, under George Robert Rushton, then at the Slade School of Fine Art, 1921, under Henry Tonks. From just before World War I

Squirrell exhibited at the RA, then throughout a long career his work was regularly seen at venues such as RWS, RE, RI and RSA. Squirrell won a number of medals for his etchings, a technique of which he was a master. Yet his firmness of line did not inhibit his fluency as a watercolourist, his main inspiration being the work of John Sell Cotman. His work is in many public and private collections, including the Victoria & Albert Museum, British Museum and Fitzwilliam Museum, Cambridge. He wrote several books on watercolour and pastel technique. Lived at Witnesham, near Ipswich, Suffolk. His son Martin was also a painter.

Harold STABLER 1872–1945 Sculptor, potter, artist in precious metals and teacher, born in Levens, Westmorland, son of a schoolmaster. He trained initially as a wood and stone carver, then as a metalworker and silversmith. In 1898 was made director of Keswick School of Art, taught at Royal College of Art and from 1907–32 was head of the arts and crafts department at Sir John Cass Institute. Was a member of the Art Workers' Guild from 1903, being on its council, 1910–12; was a founder-member of the British Institute of Industrial Art; and was on the first council of the Design and Industries Association when it began in 1915. In 1906 married the artist Phoebe Stabler and with her worked closely with Poole Pottery after World War I, having fired figures in a kiln in their Hammersmith garden. Other makers, including Royal Doulton, produced them under licence. Stabler was also closely associated with Frank Pick of London Underground and produced the first official seal for the London Passenger Transport Board, a cap badge design, decorative tiles and alloy ventilation grilles for Manor House, Turnpike Lane and Wood Green tube stations. Glazed sculptures for the war memorial in Durban, South Africa; the official war medal for Mercantile Marine; and Royal Victorian Order collars were by Stabler, who showed at Walker Art Gallery in Liverpool, Royal Glasgow Institute of the Fine Arts, RA, RMS, the Arts and Crafts Exhibition Society and elsewhere. The Louvre, Paris, holds an enamelled panel by him.

Phoebe STABLER fl. from c.1908–1955 Sculptor in stone, metal and terracotta, potter and black-and-white artist who early on exhibited under her maiden name Phoebe McLeish. She was educated at Liverpool University and, having won a travelling scholarship, attended Royal College of Art under Richard Garbe, Édouard Lantéri and Augustus John. Exhibited widely, including RA, Royal Glasgow Institute of the Fine Arts, SWA, Walker Art Gallery in Liverpool and RMS and was a fellow of RBS. In 1906 married the artist Harold Stabler. Phoebe developed a series of pottery figures with rich glazes, first fired at a commercial pottery, then in a kiln in their London garden. Royal Worcester, Royal Doulton and especially Poole Pottery in Dorset produced the figures. Phoebe was also involved in war memorials for Durban and Rugby School, garden sculpture for the Paris Exhibition and a fountain for the Bank of England. Phoebe's sister Minnie McLeish was one of the designers the Stablers introduced to Poole Pottery. Walker Art Gallery, Leicester Art Gallery and the Museum in Helsingfors, Finland, hold examples of Phoebe's work.

Aleksander STACHOW 1924– Sculptor, painter and draughtsman, known as Kostia Stachow, one of the Polish paper sculptors who made such an impact in Britain after World War II. In Poland he initially studied painting, early in the war was taken prisoner by the Germans, was freed by the British and joined the Polish Army. After arriving in England in 1946 he worked in an antique shop, eventually enrolling at Sir John Cass College. Did freelance work, notably for Diana Studio, his designs being noted for their classical dignity. Was included in Polish Paper Sculpture at Polish Cultural Institute, 1995.

Albert STAFFORD 1903–1979 Painter, printmaker, designer and teacher, born in Leicester, where he studied at the College of Art, then the Royal College of Art, where he was a Royal Exhibitioner, gaining his diploma in 1927. Stafford was a man of many interests, listing football, chess, billiards and card fortune-telling. He showed at Victoria & Albert Museum, Sketch Club and elsewhere. Was a member of the Art Workers' Guild from 1958 and lived in London.

Paul STAFFORD 1918– Painter, born in Minsterley, Shropshire, who was educated at Worksop College, Nottinghamshire. Exhibited at NS, RI and widely in provinces, including many solo shows. Lived for a time at Ely, Cambridgeshire.

Paul STAFFORD 1957– Sculptor and painter who attended Rochdale College of Art, 1975–6, Coventry College of Art, 1976–9, then Slade School of Fine Art, 1979–81. He was Fellow in Sculpture, Kingston, 1981–2. Stafford won a Boise Travelling Fellowship, 1982, an Elizabeth Greenshields Major Award (Canada), 1981–2, and a Picker Fellowship, for Sculpture, 1982. Among group shows appeared in were Eight Slade Sculptors, at Digswell House, Welwyn Garden City, 1979; Obsessions, at Angela Flowers, 1983; and Whitechapel Open, Whitechapel Art Gallery, 1985. After a solo show at Spacex, Exeter, in 1982, others included Angela Flowers, 1983, and Woodlands Art Gallery, 1989, comprising paintings chronicling Stafford's own life over the previous year.

Julius STAFFORD-BAKER 1904–1988 Painter, draughtsman and printmaker, born in Leigh-on-Sea, Essex. His father, also Julius, was the creator of the Tiger Tim comic strip in the children's comic *The Rainbow*. Julius took this on and meanwhile taught himself to paint. He had a lifelong fascination with the Royal Air Force, which began as a messenger boy for the Royal Flying Corps in 1918, and during World War II he was in the Air Force attached to a radar unit, then became an intelligence officer, serving abroad. The War Artists' Advisory Committee bought hundreds of pictures of planes from him, which found their way into numerous public collections, including Imperial War Museum, British Museum and Victoria & Albert Museum. After the war continued as a children's illustrator and showed at RA, in 1956 winning a Giles Bequest Prize at Victoria & Albert Museum for printmaking. He went on to experiment in various print techniques. In 1989 Sally Hunter Fine Art had a retrospective of his work and that of his brother, Philip.

Philip STAFFORD-BAKER 1908–1955 Artist, notably in watercolour and gouache, fond of seaside and beach scenes, born in Leigh-on-Sea, Essex. He was the son of the illustrator Julius Stafford-Baker, who created the children's cartoon strip *Tiger Tim*, and brother of the artist Julius, with whom he shared a retrospective at Sally Hunter Fine Art in 1989. Philip attended Southend-on-Sea Art School, but his career was diminished by an illness which damaged his heart. Much of his life had to be spent in bed, otherwise he drew from a favourite bench overlooking the sea in Leigh-on-Sea. Chose to exhibit little work.

Ruth STAGE 1969– Painter, especially of views associated with the river and the sea, brought up in Cleveland, where she attended Cleveland College of Art and Design, 1987–8. After Newcastle upon Tyne University, 1988–92, obtained a postgraduate diploma at Royal Academy Schools, 1992–5. Among her awards were Tony Smith Landscape Award and British Institute Fund, both 1994; David Murray Scholarship, National Westminster Bank Art Prize and runner-up, The Hunting Prize, all 1995; and in 1996 at RA Summer Exhibition, prize from M&G for best painter under 35 years. Mixed shows included RA Summer Exhibition from 1993; Redfern Gallery, 1995; and Making a Mark, at Mall Galleries, and three-artist exhibition at Cadogan Contemporary, both 1996. Had a solo show at Trevelyan College, Durham University, 1994, another at New Grafton Gallery, 1997. Was commissioned to illustrate 1996 Chevron UK calendar. Lived in London.

Andrew STAHL 1954– Painter and teacher, born and lived in London. He studied at Slade School of Fine Art, 1973–9, when he won Abbey Major Rome Scholarship. Went on to teach at Chelsea School of Art and Royal College of Art. In 1985 Stahl was a prizewinner at John Moores Liverpool Exhibition, the year he represented Britain at 17th International Festival of Painting at Cagnes-sur-Mer, France. He showed solo with Air Gallery from 1981, at Paton Gallery in 1984, later exhibitions including Flowers East from 1992 and Maidstone Library Gallery, 1994. Arts Council holds examples.

David STAINER 1897–1979 Artist, teacher and writer with a special interest in natural history. Born in Folkestone, Kent, he attended King's School, Canterbury, 1912–14, during World War I serving in the Royal Naval Volunteer Reserve at Gallipoli and in France, including the battle of Passchendale. At the École des Beaux-Arts, Rennes, from 1919, he won the Premier Prix (Painting), then obtained a degree in geography at King's College, 1927–8. Stainer was headmaster and proprietor of Carlisle Preparatory School, 1928–36; art master, Carlisle Boys' Grammar School, 1936–43; doing that job at King's School, Canterbury, 1943–57. In 1947 he founded the Association of School Natural History Studies. As well as having pieces published in *Blackwood's Magazine*, in 1936 he produced an autobiography, *The Road to Nowhere*, using the pen-name John Cropton, with his own illustrations. Showed work with SGA and with the East Kent and Whitstable and Swale Art Societies. Lived latterly at Barley, Hertfordshire.

Geoff STALKER 1948– Painter and writer, born in Whitehaven, Cumberland. He studied at Loughborough College of Art, 1966–7, Sunderland College of Art, 1967–70, and University of Reading, 1970–1. In 1992 he published *Oil Painting Techniques*. In his own work, as in A Brick In A Dark Ditch, at 1993–4 John Moores Liverpool Exhibition, Stalker said that he aimed for "an entirely sensory activity; I try to eliminate ideas and concept." From the early 1980s he exhibited widely, later shows including Gagliardi Gallery, 1993. Lived in Yelvertoft, Northamptonshire.

Constance STALLARD 1870– Painter and writer, born in Kingstown, County Dublin. Went to school in Dublin, then studied at South Kensington Schools, 1888. She exhibited RA, SWA, PS and in provinces and wrote novels, plays and poetry. Her work is held by public galleries including Bristol, Hastings and Worthing. Lived in London.

George Loraine STAMPA 1875–1951 Painter and black-and-white artist normally known as G L Stampa. The son of an architect, Dominic Stampa, he was born in Constantinople but educated in England. Studied art at Heatherley's School of Fine Art early in the 1890s, then attended Royal Academy Schools, 1895–1900. Although he exhibited RA, RI, and in the provinces, and especially at Walker's Galleries, Stampa was primarily an artist of the printed page, associated with the days of the great black-and-white men. He specialised in street and low life, with a humorous bent. Among the books he illustrated were his own *Ragamuffins*, 1916, and *Humours of the Streets*, 1921 – both typical – and he drew for periodicals such as *Punch* and *The Sketch*. Member of Langham Sketch Club and lived in London.

James William STAMPER 1873–1947 Painter, born in Birmingham, who studied at Manchester Technical School and Manchester School of Art, his teachers being the architect Richard Glazier and the painter William Fitz. After a period in business, in the early years of the century he moved to Conway, north Wales, where he painted professionally, setting eventually at Amlwch, Anglesey. Exhibited extensively RCamA, of which he was a member, Walker Art Gallery, Liverpool, and elsewhere in the provinces. Manchester City Art Gallery has Stamper's detailed study Wallflowers.

Mark STANCZYK fl. from c.1980– Ceramist, illustrator and teacher, born in America, who served in the United States Navy at Holy Loch, 1970–4. After three years as a freelance illustrator he graduated from Glasgow School of Art in ceramics, adding a post-graduate year in 1982. Stanczyk held a number of teaching posts, including a year in Nigeria, from the mid-1980s being with Duncan of Jordanstone College of Art in Dundee. He did much to promote an interest in creative ceramics in Scotland, organising and exhibiting in Clay Figures, a touring exhibition of a dozen ceramics artists in Britain. He was also a council member and chairman of the Scottish Craft Centre. He took part in Compass Gallery, Glasgow, New Generation Shows in 1980–81 and participated in its Danish Tour, and was included in The Compass

Contribution, 1990. In 1983 he had solo shows at Dumbarton Museum and Art Gallery and Eire Art Museum, Pennsylvania, in America. Also had several solo shows at Open Eye Gallery, Edinburgh.

Peter STANDEN 1936– Painter in oil and acrylic, etcher and lithographer, born in Carshalton, Surrey. Studied at Nottingham College of Art, 1954–6, then at Edinburgh College of Art, 1956–9, teachers including Derek Clarke and William Gillies. Standen was on the committee of Edinburgh Printmakers' Workshop, 1974–87, and its chairman, 1979–82, having joined in 1972. Six years previously he had been elected a professional member of SSA, and was a council member from 1991. Standen travelled extensively in North Africa, the Middle East, Sudan and East Africa, 1962–4. His work "always had an allegorical/metaphysical character and has always been of a literary nature". Later preoccupations were "imaginary landscapes of the future and allegorical cats". In 1987 Standen had a Scottish Arts Council artist-in-industry placement with Ferranti Professional Components' Dundee factory. Group shows included Art into Landscape, Serpentine Gallery, 1974 and 1979; Artists in Industry, Seagate Gallery, Dundee, 1987; Festive City, Fine Art Society, Edinburgh, 1988; and Inverclyde Biennial, 1992. His Up the Nile solo show was held at Commonwealth Institute, Edinburgh, 1965, later ones including Meet Mr Cat, Traverse Theatre Club, Edinburgh, 1985, and Edinburgh Printmakers' Workshop Gallery, 1988. Scottish Arts Council, City of Edinburgh, Hamilton Art Gallery in Ontario and other collections hold examples. Lived in Portobello, Edinburgh.

Muriel STANES 1914–1966 Painter and illustrator, born in London, also known by her married name of Muriel Stevens. She was educated at Highbury Hill School, where her art teacher was Nan Youngman. Studied at Chelsea School of Art with Graham Sutherland and Harold Sandys Williamson, 1931–4, where she met and later married the painter Geoffrey Howard Stevens. They moved to Wales in 1937 and lived first in Aberporth, then in New Quay, Cardiganshire. Exhibited LG and elsewhere.

Marion Willis STANFIELD fl. from 1922–1965 Sculptor, teacher and decorative metalworker who studied at Goldsmiths' College School of Art, in Paris with Antoine Bourdelle and in Florence. Was assistant art lecturer at Whitelands Training College, Putney, and lectured on sculpture at University of Reading. Miss Stanfield was a fellow of the RBS and exhibited at RA, Leicester Galleries, Paris Salon and elsewhere. Lived in London.

Eric STANFORD 1932– Sculptor in stone, teacher and curator who studied at St Martin's School of Art, where he was taught carving by José Alberdi. While further studying at University of Reading's department of fine art under A C Carter, Stanford met Eric Kennington and after military service, 1955–7, became Kennington's assistant until his death in 1960, finished Kennington's big relief panel for Glasgow University and became a part-time lecturer at Berkshire College of Art. He also worked for the Workers' Educational Association, Reading and London Universities. From 1968–89 Stanford was keeper of art at Reading Museum and Art Gallery, while continuing with his own work. Showed with RA, ICA, SPS, LG, AIA and Woodstock Gallery, was an honorary life member of Reading Guild of Artists and was included in 1st RWA Open Sculpture Exhibition, 1993. Did a large volume of commissioned work, council and university collections in Berkshire and Oxfordshire holding examples. Lived in Devizes, Wiltshire.

Bernard Gareth STANILAND 1900–1969 Sculptor, artist in ceramics and painter. Born in Canterbury, he became a medical practitioner, having studied at the City of London School and London Hospital. Settled in Newcastle upon Tyne, where Dr Staniland showed with local groups and nationally and was a founder-member of the Federation of Northern Art Societies, Newcastle, begun in 1947. he was chairman, 1950–68, and president for a short period before his death. Described by his widow as "an obsessive amateur artist", Staniland had no formal training apart from evening classes at Newcastle University just before World War II. Lived in Newcastle, Tyne and Wear.

Diana STANLEY 1909– Illustrator and painter, born in London. After attending Cheltenham Ladies' College she studied at Regent Street Polytechnic and Byam Shaw Schools of Art, her teachers at the latter, 1929–34, including F Ernest Jackson. Exhibited RA, LG and had a one-man show at Batsford's Gallery in 1945 and in Basingstoke Town Hall, Hampshire, 1966. She lived in Basingstoke, the local council buying her work, an example of which was also on the liner *Queen Mary*. Stanley was most noted as a book illustrator for children, including Mary Norton's *The Borrowers* series, although she also published *Anatomy for Artists* in 1951.

Michael STANLEY 1944– Abstract painter and teacher who studied at Chelsea School of Art, 1963–7, then London University, 1967–8. He went on to teach in London secondary schools and was included in Woodlands Art Gallery show Artists in Adult Education, 1982. Also exhibited at AIA Summer Exhibition, 1965; Arts Council Touring Exhibition, 1966; Surrey University, Guildford, 1975; and Four + Charlie, Bakehouse Gallery, 1981. Worked on mural project for Arndale Centre, Wandsworth, 1971.

Shaun STANLEY 1958– Painter, notably of landscape, born in Cambridge. In 1977–8 completed a foundation course at Heatherley's School of Fine Art, attending Slade School of Fine Art, 1978–82. Stanley travelled and painted in Australia in 1984–5, having pictures on show at Dridane Gallery, Adelaide, in 1985–6. He had a solo show at Thackeray Gallery in 1986, followed by several of Australian paintings after return trips there.

Sidney STANLEY 1890–1956 Painter, woodcarver and designer, born in London. He studied at Clapham School of Art and Heatherley's School of Fine Art under Henry Massey. Exhibited RA, IS, NS, RI, RP and at the Royal Glasgow Institute of the Fine Arts. Stanley was a multi-talented man, designing toys and models, illustrating books and completing murals. His work is to be found in Selfridges store in Oxford Street, London, and the White House, Regent's Park, all finished in the 1930s. Lived in London.

Braida STANLEY-CREEK 1909–1952 Painter, muralist and draughtsman whose home was in Farnham, Surrey. She was educated at Gorse Hill PNEU School, Farnham and Guildford Schools of Art and the Slade School of Fine Art for a part-time fine art course between 1931–5, where she won a certificate in drawing. Stanley-Creek was a member of WIAC from 1933, also showing at RA, NEAC, RBA, RSA and in Canada. During World War II settled in Mousehole, Cornwall, but at the time of her death, "after a short illness", her address was again Farnham. Miss Stanley-Creek's figurative pictures, sometimes in her own decorated frames, have a singular period quality, seen in a group sold by Phillips in 1998.

Henry John Sylvester STANNARD 1870–1951 Watercolour painter of landscape and teacher, born in London, son of the artist Henry Stannard, father of the artist Theresa Stannard. Studied art at South Kensington Schools. Went on to exhibit at RBA extensively, also at RA, RCamA, RHA, RI and elsewhere. His work was bought by several English royal collectors and it is also in a number of provincial galleries, including Wolverhampton and Kettering. Stannard's watercolours were of the traditional cottage garden and hollyhock variety, which have maintained popular appeal. Lived in Flitwick, Bedfordshire.

Frank STANTON 1931– Painter in oil, theatre designer, teacher and gallery owner, born and lived in London, who attended the Slade School of Fine Art, 1949–52, teachers including William Coldstream, Robert Medley and John Piper. Stanton worked and designed for the theatre; designed decorative panels for hotels; started and ran the Leigh Underhill Gallery; and became head of art at St Dunstan's College, Catford. His work was included in Beryl Dean's *Designing Ecclesiastical Textiles*. Geometrical abstracts and plant forms were features of his pictures, which were shown at RA Summer Exhibition, Contemporary Portrait Society, RI and Islington Art Circle. Solo exhibitions included All Hallows-by-the-Tower, Salford City Art Gallery, Canonbury Bookshop Gallery and John Jones Gallery. Private collections in Britain and abroad hold examples.

Fergal STAPLETON 1961– Conceptual artist, born in Tipperary, Irish Republic, who gained an honours degree in fine art at Middlesex Polytechnic, 1987–90, then his fine art master's degree at Goldsmiths' College, 1991–3. Group exhibitions included ADD, Greenwich Festival, 1992; Mind the Gap …, Acud Galerie, Berlin, Germany, 1994; I Beg to Differ, Milch Ltd, 1996; and Craft, Richard Salmon, 1997. Stapleton took part in a number of collaborative exhibitions, mostly with Rebecca Warren, such as The Showroom, 1997. Solo exhibitions included Tonight, The Agency, and Celtic Festival, Riutsu Centre, Tokyo, Japan, both 1996. Lived in London.

Judy STAPLETON 1940– Painter, printmaker and teacher, born in Manchester where she attended the High School for Girls. Studied at Goldsmiths' College School of Art, 1958–61. Was married to the painter Denis Bowen, then the artist Harvey Daniels. WIAC member who showed at a number of venues and had work in British and overseas galleries, including Victoria & Albert Museum and Whitworth Art Gallery, Manchester. Taught for a time at Eastbourne School of Art. Lived in London and then Brighton, Sussex.

Marjorie STARK 1914– Painter, born in Edinburgh, who studied at the College of Art there, then dancing in Edinburgh and London, being a member of Royal Academy of Dancing. Stark nursed in India from 1942–6, then returned to art college, 1949–55. She travelled abroad, especially in Italy, where the buildings of Venice and Tuscany were of continuing interest. Showed at RSW of which she was made a member in 1974, RSA and SSA. HRH The Duke of Edinburgh, Scottish Arts Council and Edinburgh Education Authority hold examples. Lived in Kelso, Roxburghshire.

Walter Percival STARMER fl. from c.1905–1962 Mural painter and artist in stained glass, born in Teignmouth, Devon. Educated in Norwich and studied at School of Art there and at Birmingham School of Art. Exhibited RA, RBA and Paris Salon. His work is to be found in London and provincial churches and Imperial War Museum holds his World War I work. Lived in Bushey, Hertfordshire, where he was closely involved in Watford and Bushey Art Society, being its president 1951–5, later living in Hatch End, Middlesex. Starmer regarded his extensive decoration of Sir Edwin Lutyens' St Jude's Church in Hampstead Garden Suburb as his finest achievement.

Georgina STARR 1968– Artist, born in Leeds, Yorkshire, who employed video, installation and performance in her works, in which she appeared in various guises including herself. She attended Middlesex Polytechnic, 1987–90; Slade School of Fine Art, 1990–2; and Rijksakademie Van Beeldende Kunst, Amsterdam, 1993–4. Among her awards were a British Institute Award for Sculpture and Duveen Travel Award, both 1991, and VSB Bank Award, Leverhulme Trust Award and Uriot Prize, all 1993. Group shows included Through View, Diorama Gallery, 1992; High Fidelity, Kohji Ogura Gallery, Nagoya, 1993; Here and Now, Serpentine Gallery, 1995; and British Art Show 4, and tour, 1995–6. She had the first of a series of solo exhibitions at Anthony Reynolds Gallery, 1992; had several on the continent in the mid-1990s; and in 1996 displayed Hypnodreamdruff at Art Now room, Tate Gallery.

Marion STARR 1937– Painter and decorator, born in Hitchin, Hertfordshire, whose teachers included included Fred Cuming. Showed at RA, ROI, NEAC and elsewhere and lived in Wittersham, Kent.

Norma STARSZAKOWNA 1945– Textile designer, artist and teacher, born in Fife of Polish and Scottish parents, her father having moved to Scotland with the Polish Free Army. She graduated from Duncan of Jordanstone College of Art, Dundee, in 1966 and was the first of its students to be accepted by Royal College of Art, but pregnancy prevented her taking up the place. From 1976 she taught widely throughout Britain including Duncan of Jordanstone, where from 1984 she became head of textiles. In 1977 she gained a Scottish Arts Council Award for research work in surface and three-dimensional treatments of cloth. Her commissions included a large Silk Wall for General Accident Assurance Company headquarters in Perth, in 1982–3. She participated in many group shows in Britain and abroad and had solo exhibitions at Compass Gallery, Glasgow, 1971 and 1979, and Anatol Orient Gallery, 1986. Work held by Scottish Arts Council, Scottish Crafts Collection and Leeds City Art Gallery. Lived in Dundee, Angus.

Peter STARTUP 1921–1976 Sculptor in wood, and teacher, born in London, where he died. He studied at Hammersmith School of Arts and Crafts, 1935–9, Central School of Arts and Crafts, 1943–4, at Ruskin School of Drawing, 1944–5, and at Slade School of Fine Art, 1945–8. It was there that his interest in sculpture developed, and after studying it at the Abbaye de la Cambre, Brussels, in 1948–49, within a couple of years or so he had abandoned painting for it. In 1952 had first solo show at Roland, Browse and Delbanco, gouaches and drawings. Ten years later first sculpture exhibition was part of a three-man show at AIA Gallery. Startup needed to teach, and was at Guildford School of Art, 1949–59, Willesden School of Art, 1954–8, Bath Academy of Art, 1960–2, Ealing School of Art from 1960, and Wimbledon School of Art, 1962–76. He was visiting artist at Minneapolis School of Art in 1968. Startup was fond of using pieces of discarded wood and wooden manufactured objects to create his sculptures, which mix abstraction and figurative allusions. Had a memorial retrospective at Serpentine Gallery, 1977, with one covering 1948–1975 including unseen pieces of the 1940s at Wakefield Pavilion Gallery, Yorkshire Sculpture Park, 1995. Arts Council and Tate Gallery hold examples.

David STATTER 1942– Painter, sculptor, illustrator, printmaker and teacher, born in the north of England. He studied at Liverpool College of Art and went on to teach art at Eltham Green Comprehensive School. Among his commissions were wood engravings for George Lee's poems *A Year of Grace*, Lilac Tree Press; jacket illustration for *The Conveyancing Fraud*, by Michael Joseph; and illustrations for *La Semaine Sante à Seville*, by Juliette Decreus, for Peuple Libre, Appeared in group shows at Ludlow Festival and at Tudor Barn, Eltham. Solo shows included Nelson Gallery, Greenwich; Shrewsbury House, Shooters Hill; and in 1978 Woodlands Art Gallery, Greenwich. Lived in London.

Tim STEAD 1952– Sculptor and craftsman in wood, born in Balsby, Cheshire, who worked mainly on commission. He studied at Trent Polytechnic, Nottingham and Glasgow School of Art, graduating in sculpture. Stead won a travelling scholarship in 1975 and seven years later a Scottish Development Agency Crafts Fellowship. Because of his specially designed furniture and activities such as tree replanting and the establishment of a community plantation on the Scottish Borders, Stead was the subject of several television films. Showed at such venues as Scottish Craft Centre and Collins Gallery in Glasgow; also widely on the continent and in America; and had first sculpture show at Compass Gallery, Glasgow, in 1990, another at Ancrum Gallery, Ancrum, 1992.

Ralph STEADMAN 1936– Cartoonist and artist, designer and writer, born in Cheshire. He studied at East Ham Technical College and London College of Printing and Graphic Arts, was apprenticed to de Havilland Aircraft in 1952, then was cartoonist for Kemsley (Thomson) Newspapers, 1956–9, freelancing for such publications as *Punch* and *Private Eye* in the 1960s, including being artist-in-residence at Sussex University in 1967, was political cartoonist for *New Statesman*, 1978–80, then retired to work on a book on Leonardo da Vinci. Steadman's many book illustrations included Frank Dickens' *Fly Away Peter*, 1961, Daisy Ashford's *Where Love Lies Deepest*, 1964, Lewis Carroll's *The Hunting of the Snark*, 1975, and Wolf Mankowitz's *The Devil in Texas*, 1984. Books written and illustrated included *Sigmund Freud*, 1979, *I, Leonardo*, 1983, and *Near the Bone*, 1990. Retrospective shows included National Theatre, 1977, Royal Festival Hall, 1984; and October Gallery, 1990. Steadman was involved in several cathedral festivals and among awards won were Designers' and Art Directors' Association Gold Award, for illustrative work, 1977, and BBC Design Award, for postage stamps, 1987. Steadman was a creator of bitingly satirical images. He was a Chelsea Arts Club member and lived latterly in Kent.

Philip STEEGMAN 1903–1952 Portrait painter, sculptor, writer and illustrator, younger brother of the writer on art and architecture John Steegman. He studied from 1922–4 at Slade School of Fine Art and then in Rome. He exhibited at ROI and NEAC and in 1931 had a solo exhibition at Claridge Gallery. Included were portraits of the pianist Harriet Cohen, the writers Somerset Maugham and Aldous Huxley and David Horner, close friend of Osbert Sitwell. National Portrait Gallery has the portrait of Maugham, Brighton Art Gallery and Museums that of Horner, lent to the National Portrait Gallery for the Sitwell exhibition in 1995. In 1933 Steegman set up a studio flat in Calcutta, India, where he painted rather stiff, formal portraits of notabilities and was interviewed by the magazine *India* about his experiences. His book *Indian Ink* was published in 1939. Steegman was in America when World War II began, but he returned to England and joined the Navy as an ordinary seaman (he was the son of a naval commander and the grandson of an admiral), narrowly escaping being in the ill-fated HMS *Hood* because he was sent on a course. Steegman was killed in a car accident in New Orleans, where he was living. Although he worked as Steegman, the original spelling of his name was Steegmann.

Charlotte STEEL 1965– Painter and teacher who drew her inspiration from familiar objects and people, domestic interiors and daily places. Studied at Chelsea School of Art, 1983–4, then Royal

Academy Schools, 1984–7. From 1990–1 was assistant to the art therapist for Wiltshire Health Authority, in 1991 being Royal Academy Outreach Tutor. Was included in South Bank Picture Show at Royal Festival Hall in 1987, John Player Portrait Award at National Portrait Gallery in 1988 and NEAC in 1991. Had a show at Cadogan Contemporary in 1992. HRH The Prince of Wales owns her work.

Dorothy STEEL 1927– Painter, born in Glasgow, who attended the School of Art there in 1946–9. Showed SSA, with Greenock Art Club of which she was a member and elsewhere in Scotland. Greenock Art Gallery holds her work. Settled in Gourock, Renfrewshire.

George Hammond STEEL 1900–1960 Painter and stained glass designer, born in Sheffield, son of the artist G T Steel. Studied at Sheffield School of Art, in Birmingham and London. Exhibited RA, RBA, RI, Leicester Galleries and Paris Salon. His work was bought by a number of provincial galleries, including Sheffield. Lived at Ashdon, Essex.

Kenneth STEEL 1906–1973 Watercolour painter, lithographer and engraver of landscapes and urban scenes. Born and based in Sheffield, Yorkshire, he studied at Sheffield College of Art under Anthony Betts and Francis Jahn. Exhibited at the RA, RHA, RCamA, in the provinces and at the Paris Salon. He wrote a number of books on artistic techniques and had his work widely reproduced in such publications as *Arts Review*, *Sphere*, *Studio* and *The Artist*. Galleries in Newcastle upon Tyne, Wakefield, Cambridge and the Irish Republic hold his work.

Anita STEELE fl. from 1950s– Painter and printmaker, born in London. She studied with Iain Macnab at Heatherley's School of Fine Art, 1950–6, then at Byam Shaw School of Drawing and Painting, 1958. A notable feature of her work was colour printing. She showed at RA, RWA SWA, RE, at the Paris Salon, where she gained an Hon. Mention, and in Canada. RWA holds prints by her. She lived partly in London, partly in Hurley, Berkshire.

Jeffrey STEELE 1931– Abstract and Op-Artist involved in kinetics, and teacher, born in Cardiff. Steele's mathematical skills and interest in Cartesian philosophy led him to explore systematic forms of art, initially black and white, from the 1970s using colour. Steele attended Cardiff College of Art, 1948–50; Newport College of Art, 1950–2; also studying at École des Beaux-Arts in 1959–60. Steele held a number of teaching positions including Newport College of Art, Portsmouth College of Art and Portsmouth Polytechnic, and was visiting artist at Sheffield University in 1967. Participated in numerous group shows including Young Contemporaries, John Moores Exhibition in Liverpool, Carnegie International in Pittsburgh, Systems exhibition at Whitechapel Art Gallery and touring, and with CASW, SEA and SWG. Had a solo exhibition at ICA, 1961, later ones including Galerie Swart, Amsterdam, 1978; Galerie Lydia Megert, Berne, 1979; Galleria Seno, Milan, 1989; and work from 1960–1990 at Clare Hall Gallery, Cambridge, 1992. His work is held by extensive public collections, including Arts Council, Victoria & Albert Museum, National Museum of Wales in Cardiff, Fitzwilliam Museum in Cambridge and the Government Art Collection. Lived in Portsmouth, Hampshire.

Tony STEELE-MORGAN fl. from early 1970s– Painter, born in Montreal, Canada, of Welsh parents, who was educated in Haverfordwest and Coventry. For a time he was a librarian and did clerical jobs before attending Newport College of Art, 1967–71. He began to show in the early 1970s, showing in the WAC show Every Picture Tells, in 1972, and having one-man exhibitions at Portal Gallery and 369 Gallery, in Nottingham. WAC and Newport Museum and Art Gallery hold his work.

Gloria STEEMSONNE 1944– Artist, film animator, therapist and teacher who obtained her national diploma in painting at Camberwell School of Arts and Crafts, 1960–4; was at Byam Shaw School of Drawing and Painting, 1964–5, gained the Rowney Award; did a painting course at Royal Academy Schools, 1965–8, gaining the Michael Leverhulme Award for Life Drawing; painted in Aix-en-Provence, 1968–9 under a French Government Scholarship Award; did a master's degree course in animation at Central School of Art & Design, 1979–80; further studies including a Goldsmiths' College one-year foundation course in art therapy, 1986. In 1972 Steemsonne was head of the dyeing and printing department for English National Opera, after the birth of her son continuing to work for opera companies until 1978. From 1982–3 she taught fabric printing and basic printing for Clapham/Battersea Adult Education, in 1987–91 teaching part-time art classes for Holbeach School. Art exhibitions and works purchased included Nuffield Foundation, Birmingham City Art Gallery, Piccadilly Gallery, Sweet Waters Gallery, Portman Hotel Gallery and elsewhere. Lived in London.

Harold STEGGLES 1911–1971 Painter, mainly in oil, notable for his landscapes often on a small scale, brother of the artist Walter Steggles. By profession he was a partner in a firm of solicitors. Studied at Bow and Bromley Evening Institute classes started by John Cooper in the 1920s, other teachers including William Coldstream, Rodrigo Moynihan and Gerald Ososki. Steggles received many commissions to paint country and London houses, shops and restaurants, with a series of meticulously delineated London club views for the collector and artist Villiers David. Showed extensively with East London Group at Lefevre Gallery, sharing an exhibition there with his brother in 1938. Also showed prolifically at Agnew, Arthur Tooth, Manchester City Art Gallery which holds his work and abroad. One critic described his work as "nature with a new skin". Died in Bishop's Stortford, Hertfordshire.

Walter James STEGGLES 1908–1997 Painter, notably of small landscapes in oil, with some watercolours and prints, born in London, brother of the artist Harold Steggles. Attended Charles Genge's classes at the Bethnal Green Men's Institute, then John

Cooper's there from 1925, moving with him to the Bow and Bromley Evening Institute which led to the formation of the East London Group and shows through the 1930s at Lefevre Gallery. Other teachers included William Coldstream, Rodrigo Moynihan and Gerald Ososki. At West Ham Technical College Steggles set about learning engraving and etching, but although encouraged by Colnaghi, the early-1930s slump in the trade thwarted these ambitions. Additional studies took place, 1939–48, at Central School of Arts and Crafts under Kirkland Jamieson, F J Porter and Bernard Meninsky. For some years Steggles was employed in the drawing office of the shipping company Furness Withy, then worked for the Ministry of Transport in World War II. Although he shared a show with his brother at Lefevre in 1938, he favoured mixed exhibitions. Here he was prolific, including Whitechapel Art Gallery; Tate, Redfern, Agnew, Tooth and Mayor Galleries; widely in the provinces and abroad. Lived for many years in East Anglia and was a member of the Norfolk and Norwich Art Circle. Designed posters for Shell. Had three pictures bought by Contemporary Art Society; Manchester City Art Gallery holds two. Lived latterly in Bradford-on-Avon, and briefly at Calne, Wiltshire.

Douglas George STEPHEN 1909– Sculptor in various materials, born in London. He studied at Camberwell School of Arts and Crafts, 1939–41, his teachers including R V Pitchforth, and the City and Guilds School under Edgar Allan Howes. Exhibited RA, Cooling Galleries, LG and elsewhere. Savage Club member. Lived in Lodsworth, Sussex.

Frank STEPHEN 1936– Artist mainly in pastel, born in Stirling Village, Peterhead, Aberdeenshire, where he eventually settled at Ellon. He trained at Gray's School of Art in Aberdeen as a potter/ceramic artist, but switched to painting and drawing on graduating. Was a member of Gordon Forum for the Arts, showed at several venues in Aberdeen and Peterhead and the immediate area and at The Tron Shop, Culross, with work in northeast Scottish museums. His main work, Fittie, is in an American collection.

Dulcie Mayne STEPHENS 1909– Watercolourist, born in Barry, Glamorgan. She studied painting and etching at Cardiff College of Art, continuing at Bath Academy of Art. A member of WSW, she showed in group exhibitions at Royal National Eisteddfod, SEA, RWA and CASW. It and the National Museum of Wales, Cardiff, hold her work.

Ian STEPHENS 1940– Printmaker, designer and teacher, born in north Buckinghamshire. He concentrated on illustration and lettering at Northampton School of Art, then after a short time in industry became an art teacher in Northampton. After leaving teaching in 1978 concentrated on relief printmaking in addition to commissions in illustration and graphic design. Was a member of Northampton and Kettering Art Societies. Also showed at RA Summer Exhibition from 1976, NEAC in 1979 and shared an exhibition with Terry Raybould in Northampton in the same year.

Nicholas Anthony STEPHENS 1939– Sculptor and teacher, born in Nottingham. He studied with William Turnbull at Royal College of Art, 1960–3, having gained his national diploma in design, 1960; won a Harkness Fellowship to America, 1963–5, attending Pratt Institute in New York, 1964, and San Francisco Art Institute, 1965. Held visiting teaching posts in America and Australia in 1981 and 1983 and became principal lecturer in fine art at Gloucestershire College of Art and Technology. Exhibitions included Nicholas Tread-well Gallery, RA Summer Exhibitions, Park Gallery in Cheltenham and St David's Hall, Cardiff. Lived in Bredon, Gloucestershire.

Cecil STEPHENSON 1889–1965 Painter in oil and tempera, originally of representational pictures, later of Constructivist and abstract works; designer and teacher. Born in Bishop Auckland, County Durham, as John Cecil Stephenson. In 1906 Stephenson was a student at Darlington Technical College, then from 1908–12 attended Leeds School of Art, the Royal College of Art and the Slade School of Fine Art. In 1919 took over 6 Mall Studios, Hampstead, from Walter Sickert, where he lived until he died. In 1922 Stephenson was appointed head of art, teaching architectural students, at the Northern Polytechnic, London, a post he held until 1955. His first abstract pictures were painted in 1933. Exhibited with 7 & 5 Society in 1934, then during the 1930s was increasingly involved with abstract painting and exhibitions, one picture being reproduced in *Circle*. Married the painter Kathleen Guthrie in 1942. He had pictures of the Blitz bought by Imperial War Museum and Northern Polytechnic. Stephenson finished 30 pictures for the Festival of Britain in 1951, six years before his Plyglass design on Perspex was used at the Engineering Faculty Building, Queen Mary College, London. In 1958 his mural Plyglass erected for the Brussels International Exhibition won a silver medal. In 1963 the Tate Gallery bought Painting 1937. Memorial show at Drian Gallery, 1966. Retrospectives at Camden Arts Centre, London, and touring, 1975, and Fischer Fine Art, 1976.

Ian STEPHENSON 1934– Abstract painter and teacher, born at Browney, County Durham. He studied at Department of Fine Art, King's College, Newcastle upon Tyne, 1951–6. Not long after he received a John Moores junior prize and was awarded a Boise Travelling Scholarship to Italy. He had his first one-man show at New Vision Centre in 1958. Went on to exhibit in key shows in Britain and abroad and by 1970 had qualified for a retrospective at Laing Art Gallery, Newcastle upon Tyne. His international reputation was consolidated in the 1970s, and in 1977 he had a retrospective at Hayward Gallery and travelling. Taught at Chelsea School of Art, 1959–66, was then director of foundation studies in fine art at University of Newcastle until 1970 when he became principal lecturer in painting at Chelsea. Elected RA, 1986. Arts Council and Tate Gallery hold his work. Lived in London.

Margery STEPHENSON 1929– Noted painter of ornithological and wildlife subjects, and teacher. She was born in Northumberland and attended King Edward VII School of Art and

King's College, University of Durham, 1945–50. From 1950–4 she taught art in Liverpool and Newcastle, then lectured at King Edward VII School of Art, 1954–7, before living as a freelance in Glasgow and Leeds, 1957–66. In 1966–8 was art mistress at Leeds Girls' High School, becoming head of art department there, 1968–81, then taking up a career as a full-time painter. In 1958 she won the Northumberland National Parks Sign Award, in 1961 the National Design Competition of the Chest and Heart Association. Took part in many mixed shows in north of England. Had a solo show at Leeds University, 1975, one at Dunkeld Gallery in Perth in 1983, showed solo at Macaulay Gallery in Stenton in 1988, and had one-man at Duncalfe Galleries, Harrogate, 1989.

Bernard STERN 1920– Artist in oil and mixed media, born in Brussels, Belgium. He studied at Académie Royale des Beaux-Arts there, 1935–7; at Antwerp Académie, 1937–9; moved to England in 1940 and for a short time in 1942 studied at St Martin's School of Art. Took part in many mixed shows internationally, including France, Switzerland, Belgium and America. Solo shows included Archer Gallery, 1970; David Paul Gallery, Chichester, 1975; Tampa Bay Art Center, Florida, and Carlton Gallery, New York, both 1977; Camden Arts Centre, 1981; Galerie Isy Brachot, Paris, 1983; Chicago International Art Exhibition, 1986; a retrospective of works on paper at Galerie Michel Broomhead in Paris, and Leinster Fine Art, both 1987; Sid Deutsch Gallery, New York, and Fuji International Art, Tokyo, both 1989; and Century Gallery, 1993. Among collections holding Stern's work is Ben Uri Art Society. Latterly lived in New York and Provence, France.

Catharni STERN 1925– Figurative sculptor in various materials, and teacher, born in Southsea, Hampshire. After high school she worked on a sheep farm and planned to study to be a vet at Liverpool University, but her family decided aganist it. Eventually enrolled at Chelmsford Art School for commercial art, 1945–6, transferred to Regent Street Polytechnic School of Art, 1946–7, then returned to Chelmsford where she studied sculpture under T B Huxley-Jones, 1947–50, finally studying at Royal Academy Schools, 1950–3, under Maurice Lambert. Won the Feodora Gleichen Award for Sculpture, 1953. After a year at London University Institute of Education, she taught briefly at Great Yarmouth Technical High School, 1954, designed for Poole Pottery, 1954–5, then became assistant sculptor at Bournemouth College of Art, 1955–9. Other posts at St Martin's School of Art, Southend School of Art and Chelmsford College of Further Education followed, and she eventually taught young offenders in Chelmsford Prison. In 1957 she was one of those to be featured in Jack Beddington's book *Young Artists of Promise*. In addition to many mixed show appearances, Stern showed solo with John Whibley Gallery from early 1960s, later shows including Alwin Gallery, 1981, and The Minories, Colchester, 1986. Commissions included a mosaic panel for Eastern Electricity Building, Chelmsford; a lifesize carving in wood of a madonna, Willesden Church; and a group for British Racing School, Newmarket. National Museum of Wales, in Cardiff, and The Minories hold her work. Lived for some years in Maldon, Essex.

Honor STERNDALE BENNETT 1886–1975 Watercolour painter, born in Watford, Hertfordshire. She married John Sterndale Bennett, grandson of Sir William Sterndale Bennett the composer, who was in the Indian Army, and for some years she lived in the sub-continent. Although before World War I she painted landscapes in the south of France, she was primarily a flower painter, especially fond of irises which she cultivated in her garden at Wateringbury, Kent, opened annually to the public. Showed at RA, RBA, RI, Paris Salon and other venues. Honor Sterndale Bennett was remembered by her nephew, the artist Robin Sterndale Bennett, as "a flamboyant character with a great sense of humour". She died in Maidstone, Kent.

Robin STERNDALE BENNETT 1914– Watercolourist, nephew of the artist Honor Sterndale Bennett, born in Uppingham, Rutland, where his father was director of music at Uppingham School. He attended the Royal Naval College, Dartmouth, after which he served in the Royal Navy until retirement as Commander in 1964. From 1969–75 he was secretary of the Royal Harwich Yacht Club, during which time he developed his painting, having some tuition under Michael Norman and at Ipswich Art School. Was on the committee of Ipswich Art Club and was a founder-member of the East Anglian Group of Marine Artists, in 1979. Had several solo shows at Gallery 44, Aldeburgh, and illustrated Geoffrey Morgan's book *East Anglia – Its Tideways and Byways*. Lived in Grundisburgh, Suffolk.

Anthony STEVENS 1928– Sculptor and teacher, born at Shirenewton, Monmouthshire, near Chepstow where he attended the Grammar School. Was at Newport College of Art, 1945–7 and 1949–51, during the intervening period being an Army College teacher of drawing and painting. In 1951–2 was at London University Institute of Education. Then commenced a series of teaching posts including Newport College of Art and a decade from 1959 as a tutor at Barry Summer School. A member of the 56 Group, Stevens showed in group exhibitions at Howard Roberts Gallery in Cardiff, New Vision Centre and SWG at Leicester Galleries, Royal National Eisteddfod where he was winner of the sculpture prize in 1959, and elsewhere. One-man exhibitions include University of Keele and University College of North Wales, Bangor. He carried out a series of commissions including Kate's Bears for St Dials Junior School, Cwmbran, for WAC; a fountain sculpture for Cwmbran Town Centre; and a relief sculpture for the Bateman Supermarket, Ebbw Vale. Newport Museum and Art Gallery and WAC hold his work.

Christopher STEVENS 1961– Painter and teacher, born in Staines, Surrey. He studied at Somerset College of Art, 1976–8, Brighton Polytechnic, 1978–81 and Central School of Art, 1981–2. From 1987 lectured at Brighton Polytechnic. Mixed show appearances included Piccadilly Gallery from 1981; TSWA Competition, 1984, where he won a prize; as he did at John Moores Liverpool Exhibition, 1985. Stevens' picture The Despot in John Moores 1989–90 and his Two Trunked Elephants, in South East Arts Collection, feature children in unusual, memorable poses while at play. Stevens had a solo show at Piccadilly Gallery in 1986 and at Brighton Polytechnic, 1988. Lived in Brighton, Sussex.

Elsie STEVENS 1907– Painter of landscape in oil, born in Brighton, Sussex. Studied and collaborated with Marian Bohusz at Studium Malarstwa Sztalugowego, London, for 15 years. Had solo exhibitions at Alwin, Woodstock, Barrett and Loggia Galleries, being a member of the Free Painters and Sculptors, plus other venues in Brighton, Durham, Eastbourne, Sussex University and Amsterdam. Work held in international private collections. Lived at Barcombe, near Lewes, later moving to St George's Retreat, Wivelsfield Green, Sussex, a nursing home.

Geoffrey Howard STEVENS 1899–1979 Painter, etcher, illustrator and teacher who was married to the artist Muriel Stanes and who until he retired held senior rank in the Royal Navy. After education at Gresham's School, Stevens went on to study at Chelsea School of Art with Graham Sutherland, then at Goldsmiths' College School of Art, 1931–4, with Clive Gardiner and Edward Bawden. Moved to Wales in 1937, living first in Aberporth and then New Quay, Cardiganshire. Exhibited RBA, of which he was a member, NS, RSA, NEAC and in America.

Harry STEVENS 1919– Painter, born in Newton Heath, Manchester, studying at St Augustines, a local school. From age of 14 worked as a designer with a Manchester firm, living for some years at Stretford, studying privately as a painter. From 1939–46 served in the Cheshire Regiment. He was a member of the Society of Modern Painters, showed in the Manchester region; elsewhere in the provinces; in London including Tate Gallery; and at Museum of Modern Art in New York. Had solo exhibitions in Nottingham, Liverpool and Manchester, at Gibb's Bookshop. Manchester City Art Gallery holds his stylised oil, Kite in the Sea, 1949. Stevens lived latterly at Lyndhurst, Hampshire.

Henry STEVENS 1875– Watercolourist who was by profession a chemist, having obtained a Master of Arts degree at Oxford University. Born in London, he finally lived in Beccles, Suffolk. Showed at RA, Colnaghi's and in the provinces.

Meg STEVENS 1931– Painter mainly in oil, some gouache, teacher and illustrator, born in Yorkshire. She gained a Reading University fine art degree in 1954, an external master's from Leeds University, 1956. William McCance was a notable teacher. Taught for two years in a girls' school and part-time at Christ College Boys' School, Brecon, Powys, where she lived, for three years. Freelanced in book illustration and graphics and "started painting seriously in 1975". Was a member of RCamA, also taking part in group shows at Albany Gallery, Cardiff. Margaret Stevens was mainly known for her solo exhibitions all over Wales, several dozen pictures being transported and hung free by herself and her husband. She worked on the spot in all weathers and was noted for her paintings of grass – flowerscapes, trees and a towpath series also being toured. The pictures had a strong conservation message.

Muriel STEVENS: *see* **Muriel STANES**

Norman STEVENS 1937–1988 Printmaker, painter, draughtsman and teacher, born in Bradford. Studied at Bradford Regional College of Art, 1952–7, after three years at Bradford Junior Art School. He also assisted his father, a signwriter. Between 1957–60 was at Royal College of Art, his teachers including Ceri Richards. He won the Lloyd Landscape Scholarship and Abbey Minor Travelling Scholarship. Stevens was later to win the Chichester Arts Festival Prize, in 1975, and awards at British International Print Biennale in 1979 and John Moores Exhibition, Liverpool, 1983. From 1960–7 Stevens taught painting at Manchester College of Art. The year 1965 was significant, for Stevens undertook a 7,000-mile Greyhound Bus tour of America, recording it in photographs and drawings; he also had a one-man show at Mercury Gallery. Stevens taught at Maidstone College of Art, 1967–70, at Hornsey College of Art, 1970–3. In 1974–5 Stevens was Gregory Fellow at University of Leeds. The 1970s saw Stevens' international reputation grow, and he was increasingly admired for his superb technical ability as a printmaker, mastering such difficult and unfashionable techniques as the mezzotint. His The Shadowed Garden plates are in the Victoria & Albert Museum collection, and Tate Gallery and Arts Council also hold his work. Clapboard houses, Venetian blinds, Stonehenge and landscape dappled by light and shadow were typical Stevens subjects.

Philip STEVENS 1953– Landscape painter in oil, born in Plymouth, Devon, where he attended the College of Art, 1972–3. Was then at Wimbledon School of Art, 1973–6, and Royal College of Art, 1977–80. He won the J Andrew Lloyd Landscape Prize, 1979, the Jacob Mendelson Trust Prize, 1982. Appeared in many group exhibitions, including Stowells Trophy at RA, from 1974; Ginle Gallery, 1980; Herbert Read Gallery, Canterbury, 1989; and Hunting/*Observer* Art Competition, Mall Galleries, 1992. In that year he was a prizewinner at Laing Open Landscape Competition at same galleries. Showed solo at Paton Gallery from 1987, in 1993 sharing an exhibition there with Nicholas Jolly. Stevens' work could be sombre and atmospheric, with a preponderance of green.

Bernard Trevor Whitworth STEVENSON: *see* **Trevor STEVENSON**

Jeremy STEVENSON 1958– Artist using video and photography, born in Redruth, Cornwall, who attended Gwent College of Higher Education, 1978–81, and the School of Art in Glasgow, where he continued to work, 1989–92. Exhibitions included The Wolf at the Door Gallery, Penzance, 1987; West Quay Gallery, Cardiff, 1988; Stem, Inverleith House, Royal Botanical Garden, Edinburgh, 1993; and in 1994 both Scottish Open Photography Exhibition, at Stills Gallery in Edinburgh, and New Art in Scotland, Centre for Contemporary Arts, Glasgow, where Stevenson's contribution was "mainly concerned with landscape".

Leo STEVENSON 1958– Artist mainly in oil but also in other painting media, plus various three-dimensional materials including stone, wood and resins. He was born and lived in London and studied at East Ham Art College from 1976, in parallel studying conservation and restoration. Stevenson then worked in industrial design; for over six years in the British Museum's conservation department; then for over three with Plowden & Smith, restorers to the Queen. From mid-1989 Stevenson was a freelance artist and consultant. Most of his work, which included "copies and pastiches of old master paintings or museum-grade one-off replicas of three-dimensional objects has been done to commission". Stevenson was a member of the conservation unit of the Museums and Galleries Commission and The Save Rembrandt Society. Collections holding his works include the British Museum, RA, J Paul Getty Museum, British Library, Foreign Office (Admiralty Building) and English Heritage (Boscobel House and Audley End). Stevenson's work was widely covered in press articles, magazine features and television appearances.

Patric STEVENSON 1909–1983 Painter, teacher and administrator, full name John Patric Leslie Stevenson, born in Wadhurst, Sussex, but educated in Belfast, where he attended the School of Art, 1926–8, under Samuel Taylor, then went to Slade School of Fine Art with Randolph Schwabe. Taught adult education classes in Tring, Hertfordshire, 1946–50, then returned to Northern Ireland, becoming director of the Hillsborough Art Centre which opened in 1971 but had to close because of the troubles. Stevenson was also secretary-administrator of RUA, then its president, having become a full member in 1959. Also showed at RHA, at 55a Donegall Place in Belfast. RI and elsewhere. HRH The Duke of Edinburgh, Ulster Museum and Waterford's public gallery hold examples.

Paul STEVENSON 1926– Artist in oil and pencil on carved and sawn hardboard, and teacher, born in Devonport, Plymouth. He studied at Northern Polytechnic School of Architecture where Cecil Stephenson greatly influenced him, resulting in a change to painting. He sparked Stevenson's lifelong interest in the work of Ben Nicholson, Cecil Stephenson's neighbour in Hampstead. Stevenson then studied for his national diploma in painting at St Martin's School of Art, teachers including Vivian Pitchforth, Frederick Gore and John Wheatley. After gaining his teaching diploma at London University Stevenson began teaching at Medway College of Art, Rochester and from 1960–83 was on the staff of Buckinghamshire College of Higher Education. From 1984 Stevenson devoted himself to painting. He said that "the patching and painting of boats has taught me more about paintcraft than almost anything else", and boats were a key theme. Mixed exhibitions included 1959 John Moores Liverpool Exhibition; Bear Lane Gallery, Oxford, 1963; Park Gallery, Cheltenham, 1985; Malt House Barn Gallery, Aylesbury, 1990; and Anderson Gallery, Broadway, 1992. Showed solo at Michael Parkin Gallery from 1990. Royal Air Force Museum, Hendon, holds his work. Lived in Prestwood, Great Missenden, Buckinghamshire.

Robert Macaulay STEVENSON 1854–1952 Landscape painter, born in Glasgow where he studied at the School of Art. His wife, who died eight years before him, was the artist Stansmore Stevenson, who also worked under her maiden name of Stansmore Dean. Stevenson worked for some time in France, was a member of RSW and IS and also showed at Royal Glasgow Institute of the Fine Arts, Walker Art Gallery in Liverpool, RA and elsewhere. From early 1930s settled in Kirkcudbright.

Trevor STEVENSON 1899–1985 Watercolourist and art critic who was by profession a librarian, born in Nottingham, son of C Bernard Stevenson who became curator of the public gallery in Newcastle upon Tyne. His full name was Bernard Trevor Whitworth Stevenson, and early work was signed this way. After the Royal Grammar School in Newcastle Stevenson was prevented from going to university by military service. From 1920–5 he studied under R G Hatton at King Edward VII School of Art in Newcastle, opened a private gallery, then during the Depression joined King's College library, qualified as a librarian and took his master's degree in honours English, also writing as the art critic for the *Evening World* newspaper in Newcastle. After a library job in Sheffield Stevenson moved to Southport in 1934, becoming chief librarian and curator of the Atkinson Art Gallery. Was for many years secretary of Southport Palette Club and he also belonged to Sheffield Arts Club and showed with Northern Counties and Hallamshire Society of Artists, Walker Art Gallery and elsewhere in the northwest. Lived finally at Haltwhistle, Northumberland.

William Lennie STEVENSON 1911– Painter, printmaker, sculptor and teacher, born in Liverpool. He trained at the Liverpool School of Art, then taught at Liverpool City School of Art and at Architectural Association School of Architecture, London. During World War II he served as a squadron leader and pilot in the Royal Air Force. He was featured in Liverpool Artists in the Fields of War, City of Liverpool Art Gallery Bluecoat Chambers, 1946. He painted a ceiling for the Bluecoat Chambers concert hall and made sculpture for St Monica's Church, Bootle. Walker Art Gallery in Liverpool has several works by Stevenson, including a menu design for the Sandon Studios Society, and he is in Manchester City Art Gallery's collection.

Frank STEWARD 1920– Painter and designer, born and lived in London, who studied at the Royal College of Art with Rodrigo Moynihan, 1946–9. Showed at RA, NEAC, LG and elsewhere. Illustrated for *Punch* magazine.

Allan STEWART 1865–1951 Painter, notably of historical and military subjects, born in Edinburgh. Studied at Edinburgh Institution and RSA Schools, then in France and Spain. Was on the staff of the *Illustrated London News*. Exhibited RSA, RSW, Fine Art Society and RA. He travelled quite widely and illustrated books on travel and history. Among his notable pictures are King Edward Inspects the Royal Archers and Prince Charlie's Last Look at Scotland. His work is in Holyrood Palace, Edinburgh. Lived at Castle Douglas, Kirkcudbrightshire.

Charles William STEWART 1915– Painter, illustrator and teacher, born in Iloilo, Panay, Philippines. After attending Radley

College he studied at Byam Shaw School of Drawing and Painting, 1932–8, teachers including F E Jackson, teaching at the School, 1950–8. Shortly after finishing teaching Stewart returned to the family estate at New Abbey, Dumfries. Although he painted a variety of still life, costume and landscape pictures, Stewart was best known as an illustrator in the British black-and-white tradition. Books illustrated included C Henry Warren's *A Boy in Kent*, 1944; a series of books by Barbara Leonie Picard, beginning with *The Faun and the Woodcutter's Daughter*, 1951; a series by Nicholas Stuart Gray, beginning with *Grimbold's Other World*, 1963; and volumes by Margaret Storey, including *Timothy and the Two Witches*, 1966.

Dorothy STEWART fl. c.1955–1975 Painter, from Sydney, Australia, where she obtained an honours degree in botany from University of Melbourne. She was married to the psychiatrist Dr Randal Stewart. Did postgraduate studies in Britain, settling in London, and became interested in painting. Joined the Hampstead Artists' Council and was taught by the painter Zdzislaw Ruszkowski. Showed in the Council's exhibitions, also with WIAC, Commonwealth Institute, RWS and Parkway Gallery and was a member of Free Painters and Sculptors. Had a first London solo show in 1972 at Gallery Petit.

Edward STEWART: *see* **Stephanie SMITH/Edward STEWART**

Graham STEWART 1956– Artist in various media who studied at Camberwell School of Arts and Crafts, 1975–8, Royal Academy Schools, 1978–81, and School of the Art Institute of Chicago, in America, 1984–7. His series work Image Retrieval III was included in East at Norwich Gallery, 1991. Stewart lived in Norwich, Norfolk.

Ida Lillie STROTHER-STEWART fl. c.1915–1965 Painter and draughtsman, born in Newcastle upon Tyne, to which she eventually returned after extensive travel, her husband being in the colonial legal service. She studied initially at Armstrong College, then won a scholarship to L'Académie de la Grande Chaumière, in Paris, and St John's Wood School of Art. Had extensive showings, including one-man exhibitions, in parts of Africa, Malta and Trinidad, National Gallery of South Africa in Cape Town holding her work until sold in 1947. SWA, RI, Laing Art Gallery in Newcastle and elsewhere gave her exhibitions in England.

Kerry STEWART 1965– Sculptor, born in Paisley, Renfrewshire, who obtained a Master of Arts honours degree in history and German at Edinburgh University 1985–9, did an arts foundation course at Chelsea School of Art, 1989–90, then gained an arts degree with honours there, 1990–3. She was included in Young British Artists V, at Saatchi Gallery, 1995. Her exhibits included a pregnant schoolgirl, twins and a sleeping nun, in plaster and fibreglass, realistic and finished in high-gloss paint. In 1997–8, Stewart was included in Correspondences at Scottish National Gallery of Modern Art, Edinburgh. Lived in London.

Nick STEWART fl. from early 1980s– Artist and teacher who studied biology and environmental science at University of Ulster, Jordanstown, 1970–4, subsquently attending Belfast College of Art and Design where he gained a degree in fine art, 1981. He won many prizes and bursaries, including those of the Irish Exhibition of Living Art, 1985 and 1987; The Canada Council Bursary, for a Residency at the Articule Gallery, Montreal, 1989; and the Irish Arts Council Bursary for Commissioned Installation Work for Diaspora, 1993. Stewart presented many exhibitions of performance, installation and video work as well as drawings in North America, in Ireland, Britain and on the continent. Taught widely at universities and colleges of art, eventually working as an artist and tutor at Sheffield Polytechnic. In 1994 Stewart was included in Beyond the Partitions, organised by Queen Studios, Belfast, with which he was associated. His video installation Reflective Surface appeared at Arnolfini Gallery, Bristol, 1997.

Robert STEWART 1924–1995 Designer, artist and teacher, born in Glasgow, where he studied at the School of Art, 1942–7. After gaining his diploma in design, Stewart won a Travelling Scholarship, which took him to the continent. In 1949 Stewart was appointed teacher of design for printed fabrics at the School of Art; from 1949–78 was head of printed textiles (1955–7 as a visiting member of staff); from 1979–80 head of design; and from 1981–4, when he retired, was the School's deputy director. Stewart was a major designer for Liberty's in the 1950s and 1960s and undertook numerous private ceramics, textiles and painting commissions. Was included in Austerity to Affluence, at Fine Art Society, 1997.

Will A STEWART 1882–1953 Painter, Oriental artefact restorer and teacher, born in Ilkley, Yorkshire. After Bradford Technical College he studied at Royal College of Art under Augustus John, returning to Yorkshire to work as designer for Lister's at Manningham Mills. Continued to paint and was a founder-member of Lofts Arts Club, which became Bradford Arts Club. In 1911 became an inspector of arts and crafts in Egyptian Ministry of Education, setting up the Cairo School of Arts and Crafts and becoming its principal. At end of World War I was seconded to Palestine to advise on crafts and small industries re-establishment, working closely with the architect C R Ashbee. Back in Egypt, from 1927 for three years Stewart worked on restoration of furniture from tomb of Queen Hetapheres, for which he developed his own techniques. His copious papers on this are in the Ashmolean Museum, Oxford. In 1930 Stewart relocated with his family to Jerusalem to become supervisor of technical education in Palestine, during World War II being made controller of light industries, helped by his colloquial Arabic. In 1948 returned to High Wycombe, Buckinghamshire, where he concentrated on painting, revived his association with Bradford Arts Club and became art critic for the *Yorkshire Herald*. Died in High Wycombe. An exhibition of Stewart's work was held at Carlton Gallery, Edinburgh, in 1986, another at Bradford Art Galleries and Museums in 1989.

Carole STEYN 1938– Abstract sculptor working in a wide range of materials, born in Manchester, who studied at Académie

Julian, Paris, in 1953; St Martin's School of Art, 1954–6; then concentrated on sculpture at Camden School of Art, 1968. Had a series of shows at Drian Galleries from 1971; at Jablonski Gallery, 1987; and Galerie Harounoff, 1991. Warsaw and Gdansk National Museums in Poland and Ben Uri Art Society hold examples. Lived in London.

Stella STEYN 1907–1987 Painter, draughtsman, designer and printmaker, born in Dublin, Ireland. The family of her father, a dentist, was of Russian origin. Stella was at Alexandra College until 1924, when, aged 16, she started at the Metropolitan School of Art. Her teacher, Patrick Tuohy, encouraged her first visit to Paris, in 1926, and for the next five years she divided her time between the two capitals, studying at Académie Scandinave and at L'Académie de la Grande Chaumière. Through Tuohy Steyn met James Joyce, producing etchings to illustrate *Finnegans Wake*, published in *Transition* in 1929. Next Steyn studied in Germany, at Stuttgart and at the Bauhaus, Dessau, 1931–2, going there with a personal recommendation to Kandinsky. Although she did some typography-oriented work in the Bauhaus style, the school "made a very dreary impression" on her and she eventually reverted to the painterly precepts of the School of Paris (the British Museum holds some of Steyn's experimental Bauhaus lithographs). Because of her Jewish background, Steyn's mother urged her to leave Germany. She met David Ross, marrying him in 1938, and they lived in England, eventually settling in London from around 1950 when he was appointed professor of French at Birkbeck College. Steyn had shown in Dublin and London between the wars. As well as accepting advertising commissions, she exhibited at the RA, Contemporary Art Society; the Carnegie International, Pittsburgh, 1952; Hampstead in the Thirties, at Camden Arts Centre, 1974–5; and Recent Acquisitions, British Museum, 1976. She showed paintings in two solo shows at Leicester Galleries, 1951 and 1954. After her death Abbott & Holder sold some of Steyn's early prints. There were shows at Gorry Gallery, Dublin, 1995, and Belgrave Gallery, 1996. Hugh Lane Gallery in Dublin, Irish National Portrait Collection in Limerick and Ulster Museum in Belfast hold examples.

John STEZAKER 1949– Artist in photomontage and teacher, born in Worcester. Studied at Slade School of Fine Art, 1967–73. While still a student he began to exhibit, having a solo show at Sigi Krauss Gallery in 1970. Another followed at Nigel Greenwood Inc in 1972, the start of a long association with that gallery. The 1970s saw Stezaker's reputation grow, with one-man shows at Museum of Modern Art in Oxford and at the Photographers' Gallery, the Ikon Gallery in Birmingham and City Museum, Southampton, as well as several on the continent. From 1975 Stezaker was a teacher at St Martin's School of Art. The Arts Council holds examples of his work.

Eric STHYR 1909– Painter in oil and teacher, born Erik Sthyr in Whitley Bay, Northumberland. He studied part-time from 1924–8 at Clapham, Westminster and Chelsea Schools of Art, then full-time from 1928–31 at Slade School of Fine Art. He was a prize winner, his teachers including Henry Tonks, Philip Wilson Steer, Randolph Schwabe and Graham Sutherland. Sthyr taught at St Paul's School, then after war service at Winchester School of Art. Painted still lifes, nudes, ruins and landscapes, with W R Sickert an influence. Showed at RBA, LG, AIA International War Exhibition, New Grafton and Alresford Galleries, and in 1994 shared an exhibition at Winchester Guildhall with the sculptor John Souter. Lived in Winchester, Hampshire.

Jacqueline STIEGER 1936– Painter who turned towards sculpture, jewellery and medals, and teacher, born in London. She studied at Edinburgh College of Art, 1954–9, teachers including William MacTaggart, John Maxwell, William Gillies and James Cumming. She married the sculptor A Gruber and lived and worked in Switzerland, 1964–9. Returning to England she taught drawing at Hull School of Architecture, 1976–88, while continuing with her own work. Stieger was a member of the British Art Medal Society and a freeman of the Worshipful Company of Goldsmiths, Goldsmiths' Hall and the British Museum holding her work. She did a large and varied body of commissioned work in Britain and abroad. This included four windows in etched relief, at Church Ennetbaden, Zürich, 1967; church interior furnishings, St Margaret's, Glasgow, 1972–3; glass and lead madonna, for the same church, 1973; shrine to St Ogilvie, St Columbkille, Glasgow, 1977; William Kent Tercentenary Medal, 1985; T E Lawrence Centenary Medal, 1988; and BBC Africa Sports Star of the Year Medal, 1992. Main works were bronze screen and door panels, Robinson College, Cambridge, 1980; bronze water sculpture, Eastgate, Beverley, 1989; and bronze and stone lectern steps, St Giles Cathedral, Edinburgh, 1991. Later solo shows included Copernican Connection Gallery, Beverley, 1988. Lived in Welton, East Yorkshire.

Christopher STILING 1946– Painter who grew up in Gravesend, Kent, where he attended the College of Art. In 1995 he gave up work as creative director in the advertising industry to paint full-time. Stiling was an enthusiastic sailor, the Thames Estuary was a recurring theme and many of his works were based on sketches, watercolour notes and photographs taken at sea, as in the show Land & Sea which he shared with James Duncan at Gallery Forty Seven in 1997. Other exhibitions included Young European Painters, Château Sceaux, Paris, 1977, and Mosman Galleries, New South Wales, Australia, 1996. He had a solo exhibition at Castle of Park, Banff, 1995. Lived in London.

Myra STIMSON 1961– Artist notable for relief paintings, as shown in a three-man exhibition at Woodlands Art Gallery, 1990. Was born and worked in London, studying at Goldsmiths' College School of Art, 1979–83. Participated in a series of mixed shows and was represented by Rebecca Hossack Gallery. Arts Council holds her work.

Frederick H STINGEMORE 1890–1954 Draughtsman, poster designer, cartographer and photographer, who joined the

Underground Group in 1919, becoming personal draughtsman to its dynamic publicity manager Frank Pick and eventually head of the commercial drawing office. Stingemore did important work on the London Underground map. His design simplified the layout and continued in use until 1933, when the stylised H C Beck design, the basis of today's map, came into use. Stingemore also designed posters for the Underground and contributed illustrations to many publications, such as *London's Country*, 1922, *London*, 1924, and *London Town and Country*, 1928. He was a transport enthusiast, whose photographs, drawings and verse were published in *The Railway Magazine*. Stingemore died in the Watford area of Hertfordshire.

Dilys STINSON 1949– Tapestry designer and weaver, born in America. She studied at Hammersmith College of Art, West Dean College in Sussex and Manufactures des Gobelin, Pris. Worked for eight years at West Dean tapestry studio as a dyer and weaver and eventually joined Lesley Millar, a maker of rugs, in Textiles for Interiors. Stinson's tapestries are in the American Embassy, Bangladesh, South East Arts Collection and elsewhere. She exhibited at Michaelson & Orient, 1988, and World Tapestry Today in Australia, 1988–9. Lived in Tenterden, Kent.

Alison STIRLING 1962– Artist who undertook printmaking course at Glasgow School of Art, 1980–3. Among her exhibitions was Scottish Print Open Three, organised by Dundee Printmakers' Workshop, in 1983, where she showed Don't Have A Mutant, screenprint and lino, 1983.

Dorothy STIRLING 1939– Artist working in acrylic on plaster, with found objects and box constructions, born in Glasgow. She studied at the School of Art there, 1983–7, under Jack Knox, Barbara Rae and Neil Dallas Brown. She was a member of the Scottish Arts Club, SSA and SSWA. Group shows included Art in Boxes at England & Co; Compass Gallery, Glasgow; Open Eye Gallery, Edinburgh; RSA; and Laing Art Competition, Overall Winner in 1993. Had a series of solo shows at Open Eye from 1989, and at Compass, 1994. BBC in Glasgow; Paintings in Hospitals; Stirlingshire Educational Trust; and St John's Hospital, Livingston, hold examples. Living in Stirling.

Mary STIRLING 1948– Self-taught artist in watercolour and gouache, although she did a botanical illustration course with Margaret Petterson at West Dean College and studied landscape with Alastair Paterson. She was born in Windsor, Berkshire, and was the daughter-in-law of the artist Diana Low. Did a variety of jobs, including ski-teaching and was a radionics practitioner. Exhibited at Tenterden Art Gallery and in East Anglia and solo shows included Oliver Swann Galleries, 1984. Lived at Wootton, Woodstock, Oxfordshire.

Helen STIRLING THOMAS 1890–c.1970 Painter who studied widely in Italy and married the artist Henry Winslow. She was made a member of SWA in 1938. Showed with Tempera Society and Ridley Art Club, at RA, RBA, Kensington Gallery and at Russell-Cotes Art Gallery and Museum, Bournemouth. Lived in London for many years.

John STIRLING MAXWELL 1866–1956 Painter, educated at Eton College and Cambridge University, the son of Sir William Stirling Maxwell. Sir John studied painting under Samuel Evans and with A S Cope. Exhibited RSA, RSW and RWS. Signed work J S M. Lived in Glasgow and Edinburgh.

Fred STIVEN 1929–1997 Creator of boxes and constructions, freelance graphic and exhibition designer, book illustrator, typographer, printmaker and teacher, born in Fife, son of a sailor. He was educated there and in Essex. Studied at Edinburgh College of Art, 1947–51, teachers including John Kingsley Cook and Leonard Rosoman, gaining a postgraduate scholarship. Following National Service Stiven was appointed to the art staff of Fife Education Authority in 1954, after which he joined Gray's School of Art, Aberdeen, in 1958. With a chemistry lecturer at Aberdeen University, John Holloway, Stiven created an exhibition called Integration which, based on boxed exhibits, examined the interface between art and science, which was to remain a preoccupation. Stiven was a lecturer in the extra-mural department of Aberdeen University and through the 1970s participated in the Edinburgh-based Demarco Gallery's experimental Summer School and expeditions exploring Scotland's cultural heritage. Stiven was made an associate of RSA, and a member of SSA, the Glasgow Group and the Society of Industrial Artists. He took part in many group shows in Scotland, including the Scottish Arts Council exhibition Inscape in 1976 and Painters in Parallel at Edinburgh College of Art in 1978. Had several solo shows at Demarco Gallery. In 1976 he had a first one-man show in London at Paul Neagu's Generative Arts Gallery, the year before his work was exhibited at the Galleria del Cavallino in Venice alongside advanced Scottish artists. Stiven was made head of the design school at Gray's in 1981, reluctantly retiring in 1987 because of illness. Died in Dundee. Scottish Arts Council and Aberdeen City Art Gallery hold examples.

Jane STOBART 1949– Printmaker and teacher, based in London, who trained at Central School of Art and Design. She taught printmaking, graphic design and computer graphics in several London colleges. She was a member of RE and showed widely, including a solo exhibition at Gainsborough's House, Sudbury, 1994, during which she taught etching in the print workshop. For several years the subject of her work was the Whitechapel Bell Foundry, producing hundreds of drawings to form the basis of etchings.

John STOBART 1929– Painter and illustrator of marine subjects and landscapes, and teacher, born in Leicester. Attended Derby College of Art, 1946–50, where his teachers included Alfred Bladen, then Royal Academy Schools with Henry Rushbury, 1950–6. Was a Landseer Scholarship winner. From the early 1950s he became a frequent RA exhibitor, also RBA and RSMA of which he was a member, and in Canada and New York, which eventually became his primary outlet. Had a series of exhibitions at Kennedy Galleries there and eventually settled in America, where he was vice-president emeritus of the American Society of Marine Artists. Stobart drew on his extensive seagoing experience in his paintings, often of historical harbour scenes in some detail.

Andrew STOCK 1960– Painter, printmaker and sculptor, born in the British Military Hospital, Rinteln, West Germany. Stock left Sherborne School in 1978 and became an artist, self-taught with some encouragement from Sir Peter Scott. Was a member of SWLA from 1983, later being on its council. Had a series of solo shows at Malcolm Innes' London and Edinburgh galleries from 1981, Alpine Gallery from 1989 and at The Gallery in Cork Street, 1994. Sultan of Oman had a large collection of Stock's work, on which the palettes of J M Whistler and Andrew Wyeth were influences. Lived in Beaminster, Dorset.

Alan STOCKER 1949– Artist who was born in London and became addicted to Speed, 1961, between 1966–73 being a heroin addict. Stocker was confined to Campsfield House detention centre in 1963, then Borstal in Rochester, 1965. While on heroin he robbed banks and security vans, in 1973 being sentenced to 14 years for armed robbery, cut to 12 years on appeal in 1974. While he was in Maidstone Prison the then governor, Peter Timms, allowed Stocker to paint full-time, and by 1979 Lawrence Gowing was petitioning the Home Office that Stocker be released to study at the Slade School of Fine Art, which he attended 1979–83. In the latter year Stocker gained the Rodney Burn Prize for the best figurative painting at the Slade and a Boise Scholarship. He had a solo show at Pomeroy Purdy in 1989, was included in a mixed exhibition at Bernard Jacobson in 1990 and by the mid-1990s was being represented by Flowers East. In 1997–8, Stocker's acrylic on canvas Burst Being was included in the John Moores Liverpool Exhibition. By that time he was settled in London.

Guy STOCKER: *see* **GUY**

Neil STOCKER 1925–1969 Sculptor who liked to work in plaster because it "records instantly your emotions and reactions, and stays put". He was born in Sydney, Australia, working for a time as an industrial chemist, then in glass decoration, part-time study at East Sydney Technical School convincing him to be a sculptor. Moved to England in 1952 and studied at Chelsea School of Art, part-time then full-time. In 1958 entered Slade School of Art as a sculpture student, did a year's postgraduate study at Royal College of Art and spent a summer as Henry Moore's assistant, then assisted Bernard Meadows. Stocker tried to avoid external influences in case they might weaken his own ideas, but he admitted Brancusi and Richier were important to him. His biomorphic work showed a concern with the forces of nature, sources and origins and development. From 1958 Stocker was prominently associated with the Young Commonwealth Artists' Exhibitions. In 1961 he won the Susse Prize at Young Contemporaries, later in the year exhibiting in an ICA sculpture show. In 1962 he showed in an AIA sculpture exhibition, in 1963 sharing a show with two painters at Grabowski Gallery. Arts Council holds examples. Taught latterly at Hornsey College of Art.

Alfred STOCKHAM 1933– Painter and teacher, born in London, who after leaving school was in the Royal Navy, 1950–6; at Camberwell School of Art, 1960–3; at Royal College of Art, 1963–6; and was a Rome Scholar, 1966–7, and a Granada Arts Fellow, 1967–8. Was on the staff of Bristol Polytechnic, 1968–88, until retiring, as head of fine art, to paint more. Among Stockham's awards were a Silver Medal for Painting at Royal College and a British Institute 1st Prize, Painting. Working in a Neo-Impressionist style, his mixed exhibitions included Arts Council of Northern Ireland and LG, 1964; Bradford City Art Gallery, 1965; RA Summer Exhibitions from 1976; and Avon Open Exhibition, Arnolfini Gallery, Bristol, 1984. Had a solo show at York City Art Gallery, 1968, later ones including Anthony Hepworth, Bath, 1992. The City Museum and Art Gallery, Bristol, where Stockham lived, and other public collections hold examples.

Jo STOCKHAM 1961– Artist and teacher who worked with a wide range of materials and media, including found objects, photographs, wax, glass and steel in combination with sound, motors, texts and projections. Her works were often made for specific places, using them "as a base for exploring memory and history". She was born in Elstree, Hertfordshire. After a foundation year at Hertfordshire College of Art and Design, 1979–80, she gained an honours degree in fine art from Falmouth School of Art, 1980–3, then her master's from Chelsea School of Art & Design, 1985–6. Won a number of awards, including a Kettle's Yard/Henry Moore Fellowship at Corpus Christi College, Cambridge, 1989, and a Sculpture Research Residency, Warwick University, 1995. She had extensive teaching experience, including Chelsea College of Art, Cambridge University, Central St Martins, Goldsmiths' and the Royal College of Art. Group exhibitions included Recent British Sculpture, Arts Council tour, 1993–4, and Triplicate, Tate Gallery, St Ives, and tour, 1996. Had a solo exhibition, Rest Assured, at The Showroom, 1987, later ones including Mead Gallery, University of Warwick, 1997. Arts Council holds her work. Lived in London.

Henry STOCKLEY 1892–1982 Bus driver who painted in a primitive style on any materials he could afford, including linoleum and old bits of linen; he mixed his own bold colours, having learned from his signwriter father. Having tried every gallery in London, Stockley was about to burn all his work if dealer Lucy Wertheim had not taken him on in 1932. She urged him to illustrate Bunyan's *Pilgrim's Progress*, and gave him a solo show, exhibiting him then as Busdriver Stockley. As Henry Stockley he appeared in mixed shows. He was also exhibited by Jack Bilbo's Modern Art Gallery, with the London Transport Group and in RA Summer Exhibitions, in 1948 being in the Academy's touring show Crowded Out. Stockley's pictures reflect his daily life: work as a bus driver, scenes from his Kent childhood and experiences in the Blitz. His experiences in World War I, during which he ferried ammunition around for Vickers Armstrong, made him a pacifist. Stockley began work as a bus driver in 1924, retiring in 1957, and only then could paint when he wanted. Five years before, he wrote down his reminiscences, published by John Walker in 1994 as *Stockley on the Buses*. Stockley completed 400 paintings, only a quarter known to have survived, many found in his daughter's attic in 1988. In 1996 London Transport Museum put on a show of pictures and memorabilia. Stockley died in a psychiatric hospital in Dartford, Kent, and is buried at Horton Kirby, near Swanley.

Hilda van STOCKUM 1908– Painter in whose work the Dutch still life tradition and an Impressionist feeling for light and form mixed. She was born in Rotterdam of some Irish ancestry, studying at Metropolitan School of Art in Dublin, 1924–7, where her teachers included Sean Keating; Rijks Academie Voor Beeldende Kunst, Amsterdam, under R Roland Holst, 1927–31; at Corcoran School of Art, Washington, with Richard Lahey, 1935–6; and with André Lhote. She showed with RHA of which she was made an honorary academician, RA Summer Exhibition, Montreal Museum of Modern Art and Caldwell Galleries in Dublin and Belfast. Had a series of solo exhibitions including Dublin Painters Gallery, Difar Gallery in Geneva, Moll Gallery and RHA Gallagher Gallery, which gave her a retrospective in 1991. RHA and National Gallery of Ireland hold examples.

Susan STOCKWELL 1962– Versatile artist and designer, born in Manchester, who did a foundation course at Stockport College, 1984–5; gained an honours degree in fine art/sculpture from Sheffield Hallam University, 1985–8; then her master's degree in sculpture from Royal College of Art, 1991–3. From 1987 Stockwell gained a number of commissions, including a bronze for the foyer of Curtins Engineering, Liverpool; carved figures for Tarantella Restaurant, Manchester; and a logo for the London and Scandinavian Metallurgical Company. In 1988 she became a visiting lecturer for Salford Education Authority, and extensive visiting and part-time university appointments followed, latterly including Chelsea and Wimbledon Schools of Art and University of East London. She also held a series of residencies, later ones including Mappin Art Gallery, Sheffield, 1991, and Art Mart, Islington Business Design Centre, 1992. Awards included Visual Artists Award, Yorkshire Arts, 1990, and Osarka Prize, Royal College of Art, 1993. In 1994 she designed and made a set for the opera *The Pillow Song*, Royal Festival Hall Purcell Room, 1994. Group exhibitions included Manchester Open at Manchester City Art Gallery, 1989; New British Art, Pony Park, Slagharen, Netherlands, 1991; and Beyond the Wow Factor, Computer-Generated Works, State University of New York at Purchase, New York, 1993. Had a solo show at Mappin Art Gallery, 1991, later ones including Bernard Jacobson Gallery, 1994, and a sculpture/installation show at Wrexham Library Arts Centre, 1996, in collaboration with Angel Row Gallery, Nottingham, and Battersea Arts Centre. Lived in London.

Rosalind STODDART 1960– Painter and printmaker, who did a foundation course at Byam Shaw School of Painting and Drawing, 1978–9; gained an honours degree in fine art, painting, at Camberwell School of Arts and Crafts, 1979; then did postgraduate studies in art and design at Middlesex Polytechnic, 1982–3. Gained a number of British Telecom commissions from 1986; won a portrait award at British Painters '88, Mall Galleries, 1988; the Curwen Gallery John Purcell Award, 1993. Was artist-in-residence, Gallery Avsenik, Slovenia, 1994. Group shows included Loseby Gallery, Leicester, 1985; Goldmark Gallery, Uppingham, 1989; Open Print Exhibition, Mall Galleries, from 1994; and The Table Studio Group, The Living Room, 1996. Had a solo show at Guild Gallery, 1988, then regularly, later ones including The John Russell Gallery, Ipswich, and Surrey University, Guildford, both 1995. Bedford County Council holds her work. Lived in Brigstock, Kettering, Northamptonshire.

Adrian STOKES 1902–1972 Painter, influential critic and writer and poet, born in London. Between 1920–3 Stokes studied history, philosophy, politics and economics at Oxford University. After a year travelling in India and the Far East he began to study art and to write on it, including the books *Stones of Rimini*, 1934, and *Colour and Form*, 1937. Began to paint and studied at Euston Road School in late 1930s. In 1938 he married the artist Margaret Mellis and shortly before World War II bought a house at Carbis Bay, Cornwall, and began a market garden. His marriage broke up in 1946, then Stokes returned to London and married Margaret Mellis's sister Ann. In the postwar period Stokes consolidated his position as a painter, having a one-man show at Leger Galleries in 1951. Tate Gallery in 1973 showed his work after he died and in 1982 there was a retrospective at Serpentine Gallery, and touring. Stokes was a trustee of the Tate, 1960–7. His later books include *Cézanne*, 1947, *Reflections on the Nude*, 1967, and shortly after that he began to write extensive poetry. Arts Council and Tate Gallery hold still lifes and landscape by Stokes.

George Vernon STOKES 1873–1954 Painter, notably of animal subjects, printmaker and illustrator. Born in London, he was educated privately. Exhibited RA, RBA especially, RI, Fine Art Society and RMS. He drew for children's books, country magazines and illustrated books on dogs. Work held by Carlisle Art Gallery and Museum. Lived near Deal, Kent.

Mel STOKES 1964– Artist, born in London, who studied at Duncan of Jordanstone College of Art, in Dundee, and Chelsea College of Art. Was artist-in-residence at Hospitalfield House, Arbroath, 1993, from 1995 teaching part-time at Duncan of Jordanstone and being a workshop leader in Dundee. Group shows included New Generation, Compass Gallery, Glasgow, 1994; Five East Coast Artists, Eastern General Hospital in Edinburgh, 1995; and in 1996 Drawing the Figure at Mall Galleries and Royal Over-Seas League Open. Solo shows included Mercat Theatre, 1994, and Ubiquitous Chip Restaurant, 1995, both in Glasgow.

Michael STOKOE 1933– Painter, draughtsman, printmaker and teacher, born and lived in London. He was a student at St Martin's School of Art, 1953–7. Was a member of the Printmakers' Council and showed at RA, ROI, Young Contemporaries, Arnolfini Gallery in Bristol and in 1967 John Moores Liverpool Exhibition. Solo shows included Bear Lane Gallery in Oxford, Drian Galleries and Anna-Mei Chadwick. Stokoe taught at Ravensbourne College of Design. Victoria & Albert Museum, public galleries in Hull, Leeds and Liverpool and a large number of educational authorities hold examples.

Bunny STONE: *see* **Cedric Arthur Cuthbert STONE**

Cedric Arthur Cuthbert STONE 1916–1990 Painter and flyer, born in Amritsar, India. He always carried his childhood nickname Bunny, so-called because at birth he was covered with fluffy black hair. Stone was educated at Broadstairs and Charterhouse, spent a year at the College of Aero-Engineering in Chelsea and then went up to Cambridge where he learned to fly with the University Air Squadron, joining the Royal Air Force on a short-service commission in 1937. As a Hurricane pilot in 3 Squadron Stone destroyed three enemy aircraft before the Dunkirk evacuation, gaining the Distinguished Flying Cross. During the Battle of Britain Stone fought with 249 and 254 Squadrons, in late 1940 moving to 607; he was given command of 17 Squadron, which fought courageous actions in Burma, about to be overrun by the Japanese (Stone's logbook sketches are in the Air Force Museum at Hendon); commanded Squadron 135; and was with 222 Group in Ceylon in 1944. After hostilities Wing Commander Stone took a studio in St Ives, Cornwall, where he studied under Leonard Fuller, John Park, Leonard Richmond and others, for a time sharing a studio with painter Terry Frost. With his first wife he then flew in a small Auster aircraft to Cape Town, building a studio at Hermanus, overlooking the Bay of Aughullas, where he worked for 14 years when not travelling throughout Africa and the Rhodesias. His many portraits included Sir Roy Welensky, prime minister of the Federation of the Rhodesias. In 1960 Stone returned to St Ives, where he continued to paint, notably commissioned portraits, landscapes and seascapes. His solo exhibitions included Downing's Bookshop, St Ives, 1947, and The Rose & Crown, Fletching, 1963.

John Christopher STONE 1923– Painter and draughtsman, born in Trinidad, British West Indies. He attended Ontario College of Art under John Alfsen, 1941–4; Art Students' League of New York, under Kenneth Hayes Miller, 1944–5; and in the early 1950s the Royal College of Art under Ruskin Spear, Carel Weight and Rodney Burn, becoming an associate and winning a Travelling Scholarship and the College Drawing Prize, 1952. As well as showing in America and Canada Stone exhibited at RA, RBA, Leicester Galleries, Tib Lane Gallery in Manchester and Ash Barn, Petersfield. Lived for many years in London.

Kirsten Tvilum STONE fl. from mid-1970s– Printmaker, painter and designer, educated in Denmark, where she did a four-year course in Copenhagen at Tegne-og-Kunstindustriskolen. Worked as a graphic designer before moving to England in 1965 to study antique porcelain restoration. Became interested in etching in mid-1970s and attended Morley College. From 1981 was a member of Greenwich Printmakers. Showed at RA Summer Exhibition; took part in four-man show at Woodlands Art Gallery in 1988; and had several solo shows in Denmark. The Jutland peninsula was a favourite landscape subject.

Reynolds STONE 1909–1979 Designer, engraver, letter-cutter and watercolourist. After education at Eton College and Cambridge, Stone studied printing at Cambridge University Press. He worked for a printing house, then became a freelance designer and engraver. Studied lettering and engraving with Eric Gill, 1931. Worked mainly for printers and publishers, but also engraved glass and designed and executed memorial tablets. Carried out the lettering for the Winston Churchill memorial for Westminster Abbey, 1965; official heraldry for HM Stationery Office; designed Bank of England notes; also stamp designs and headings for *The Times* newspaper. Illustrated many books. Exhibitions of watercolours New Grafton Gallery and wood engravings William Weston Gallery, 1975. The Victoria & Albert Museum, which gave him a show in 1982, and the Ashmolean Museum in Oxford hold Stone's work. Stone lived with his wife Janet at Litton Cheney, Dorset. She was a photographer, who died in 1998, who depicted their many friends, including Henry Moore, L P Hartley, John Piper, and David Jones. Her book *Thinking Faces* was published in 1988 and a collection of her prints is held by the National Portrait Gallery archive.

J Gareth STONE-JONES 1925– Painter, teacher and writer on art, born in Pont Yates, Carmarthenshire. After Trinity College, Carmarthen he attended University College in Swansea and then for a dozen years taught English, art and economics, returning to Trinity College to specialise in art teaching. Reviewed for the *Anglo-Welsh Review* and took part in the Royal National Eisteddfod/WAC 1973 show Portraits of Welsh People, the same sponsors' 1974 exhibition An Iconograph of the Mabinogion as well as other Welsh group shows.

Alan STONES 1947– Painter and printmaker, born in Manchester. Trained, 1967–71, at St Martin's School of Art and settled in Cumbria from 1982, living at Blencarn, near Penrith. His oil paintings and lithographic prints reflected a concern with people, labouring on farms, in an urban context or through close study of family or friends. He produced a series of farming lithographs as the result of a bursary from the Gulbenkian Foundation. His oil on linen, Portsmouth, was commissioned for the city's Central Library. National Science Museum, IBM UK Ltd, Lord Devonport and Dista Products also commissioned Stones. Gulbenkian Foundation provided a bursary to fund a series of lithographs.

Angela STONES 1914– Artist in oil, watercolour and gouache, and teacher, born and lived in London. Her teachers included Harold Workman, Jack Merriott and Patrick Larking. She studied at Birmingham School of Art, Heatherley's School of Fine Art and Sir John Cass College. After World War II she was an Inner London Education Authority teacher of adults for 14 years. Was at various times a member of SWA, NS, Chelsea Art Society and

Exmouth Art Group. Showed with ROI, PS and elsewhere and had a solo show at Gallery 19.

Frederick Henry STONHAM 1924– Painter, printmaker, wood-carver and teacher, born in Reading, Berkshire. Attended Oxford School of Art, 1948–52, under Hubert Hennes, then Bournemouth College of Art, 1952–3, with Hermon Cawthra. Showed at RA, RP, NEAC and on the continent. For some years taught art in prisons, including Parkhurst on the Isle of Wight. Lived at Binstead, on the island.

Andrew STONYER 1944– Sculptor and teacher who studied at Northampton School of Art, 1961–3, sculpture at Loughborough College of Art and Design, 1963–7, architecture at the Architectural Association's School of Architecture, then went to Ankara, Turkey for two years. From 1975–8 did doctoral research into The Development of Kinetic Sculpture by the Utilisation of Solar Energy. He gained many awards including travelling scholarships to Germany and Canada and in 1982–9 lectured and undertook research at Concordia University, Montreal, also carrying out sculpture commissions. Stonyer returned to England to teach at Falmouth School of Art and Design as head of fine art in 1989, then from 1993 was reader in fine art and design at Cheltenham and Gloucester College of Higher Education. Showed widely, solo shows including Architectural Association Gallery, 1971, and Leicester Polytechnic, 1978. Exhibited as an associate member of Newlyn Society of Artists at Newlyn Orion from 1991 and was included in Falmouth Connections at Falmouth Art Gallery, 1994.

Len STOPPANI 1919–1989 Artist, teacher and administrator, born in London, who studied at Chelsea and Wimbledon Schools of Art and Royal College of Art school of painting. Served in the Army in World War II. After periods on the staff of Guildford and Bradford Colleges of Art, Stoppani was seven years vice-principal and then 12 years principal of West Surrey College of Art and Design, Farnham, near which he lived. He was elected a member of SWE in 1951 and from 1968 was an honorary member of Farnham Art Society, being its vice-chairman, 1985–8. He was involved in the running of Farnham Maltings arts centre and was chairman of the trustees of the New Ashgate Gallery from 1976. Stoppani was involved in numerous bodies to do with art education in Britain and abroad. In 1984 the annual Stoppani Lecture was founded by the southern region of the National Society for Art and Design Education. In the same year he was made director, honoris causa, École des Beaux-Arts, by the city of Aix-en-Provence, France. Showed at Leicester, Wilton and Piccadilly Galleries, at Victoria & Albert Museum, Bradford City Art Gallery and abroad, as well as in Arts Council touring shows and locally. Victoria & Albert, Skopje Museum of Modern Art, Swedish Lloyd Shipping Line and many private collectors hold examples. Had cancer for a year before he died.

John STOPS 1925– Painter, relief printer and teacher, born in Radlett, Hertfordshire, who attended Northampton School of Art, 1947–51, and Leeds College of Art, 1951–2, teachers including Alicia Boyle, Henry Bird and Lionel Brookes. Teaching appointments included Bristol Polytechnic. Was elected full member of RWA in 1980. Completed landscapes and architectural pictures, Bristol, the west of England and Peak District being favourite subjects. Showed at Guild Gallery in Bristol, solo shows including there, RWA and Patricia Wells Gallery, Thornbury. Lived in Bristol.

Dooze STOREY 1972– Painter, real name Rachel Storey, born in Bury St Edmunds, Suffolk. Her work had a strong abstract element, with landscape allusions, and which also included personal symbols and images. She studied art in Chester and Stoke-on-Trent and from 1992 lived with the artist Kelvin Bowers, in Staffordshire, from 1993 in Languedoc, France, from 1995 in St Ives, Cornwall (initially in the cottage once occupied by the painter Alfred Wallis), then from 1997 in London. Had a solo show at Salt House Gallery, St Ives, 1995; another at Galeria Punkt, Gdansk, Poland, in 1996; and in that year was included in a St Ives exhibition at David Holmes Contemporary Art, Peterborough.

Harold STOREY 1888–1965 Painter, notably a landscape watercolourist of Scottish subjects, who lived for many years in Glasgow, later at Newton Mearns, Renfrewshire. He was a member of Glasgow's Art Club and a regular and prolific exhibitor at the Royal Glasgow Institute of the Fine Arts from 1912–64, also showing at RSA, RSW, RA and Walker Art Gallery, Liverpool. Kelvingrove Art Gallery and Museum, Glasgow, has his oil Symington, Ayrshire, bought in 1944. The Glasgow Institute's Blythswood Gallery put on a memorial show, another being held later in the city at the Armstrong Gallery.

Paul STOREY 1957– Painter and draughtsman, born in London, who early in life worked in an architect's office. Was married to the artist Rose Warnock. Storey did a foundation course at Watford School of Art, 1978–9, an honours degree in painting at Birmingham Polytechnic, 1979–82, then his master's degree at Royal College of Art, 1984–7. From 1987–9 lived and worked in Athens, from 1990 moving to France. He won a WAC Award, 1983–4, and in 1987 the Burston and Madame Tussauds Awards, followed by a Greek Government Scholarship. Storey created strange and haunting worlds of his own, working in thin, transparent layers of acrylic paint; the pictures reflected his deep study of the art of fifteenth-century Italy. Mixed exhibitions included Heritage at Oriel Gallery, Cardiff, 1984; The Spirit of London, Fischer Fine Art, 1989, the year of his first solo show, also at Fischer; and Art London 90 at Olympia, 1990. Had a solo exhibition at Jason & Rhodes, 1994.

Terence STOREY 1923– Painter, notably of marine pictures, born in Sunderland, County Durham. He attended the School of Art there and Derby College of Art. Became a member of RSMA, served on its council and was president, also exhibiting at ROI, NEAC, RBA and elsewhere. HRH The Prince of Wales and National Maritime Museum in Greenwich hold examples. Lived in Derby.

Warren STOREY 1924– Painter, designer, muralist and teacher, born in South Shields, County Durham. He attended the School of Art there, 1941–4, under Ernest Gill, then with a British Institution Scholarship studied under Ernest Blamey at Regent Street Polytechnic School of Art, 1947–50. Settled in Weston-super-Mare, Somerset, where he was head of the School of Art, 1958–84, also teaching at Bristol University. Was elected to RWA in 1976, later becoming its vice-president. Showed at RA, Young Contemporaries and RBA and had a series of solo exhibitions in West Country.

Mary STORK 1938– Painter and draughtsman whose figurative pictures had a strong linear dynamism. She studied at West of England College of Art in Bristol and at Slade School of Fine Art. Raising a family interrupted her painting career, which resumed in the mid-1980s. Showed widely in London, Edinburgh and the provinces and was a member of Penwith Society of Arts and Newlyn Society of Artists. In 1994 she was included in Three Painters from Penwith at David Messum Fine Art. Lived in St Just-in-Penwith, Cornwall.

Greenup STORM 1901– Oil painter, born at Robin Hood's Bay, Yorkshire. Studied painting with Ethel Walker. Exhibited RA, RWA, Walker Art Gallery, Liverpool, and elsewhere in the northern provinces. Fylingdales Group member who lived in Harrogate, Yorkshire.

James STOUPE: *see* **Seamus STOUPE**

Seamus STOUPE 1872–1949 Sculptor, painter, printmaker and teacher, also known as James Stoupe, born in Belfast, Northern Ireland, where he attended the Model School. As well as art education in Belfast he studied lithography at Metropolitan School of Art, Dublin, during World War I. From 1904–38 Stoupe taught modelling at Belfast School of Art. Showed extensively at RHA, was a member of Belfast Art Society and its Arts Club. The Club and the Ulster Museum hold examples.

Rosalind STRACEY fl. from early 1950s– Sculptor who studied at Chelsea School of Art, 1947–52/3, for five years, mainly under Bernard Meadows and for a short time with Germaine Richier. Stracey completed a bas-relief for a gateway to St Luke's Estate, Chelsea. Made many group show appearances, including RA, 1955; Woodstock Gallery, 1961; Walberswick Galleries, Farnham, 1974; Sculptors of Suffolk, 1978; Deepdale Exhibitions from 1984; and Michael Parkin Gallery, 1990. Had solo shows at Fermoy Art Gallery, King's Lynn, and University of East Anglia, Norwich, in 1973, later exhibitions including Gallery 44, Aldeburgh Festival, 1992. Had a studio in Chelsea for many years.

David STRACHAN 1919–1970 Painter, printmaker and teacher, notable for enigmatic, poetic still lifes and landscapes. He was a member of the long-disparaged Sydney Charm School of painters, including Donald Friend, Margaret Olley and Francis Lymburner, influenced by the English Neo-Romantics. Strachan (pronounced Strawn) was born in Salisbury, Wiltshire, and was taken to Australia in 1921, his father, a doctor, wanting his son to follow him into medicine rather than be an artist. Strachan studied at the Slade School of Fine Art, 1936–8, with time at L'Académie de la Grande Chaumière, Paris, 1937; George Bell School, Melbourne, 1938–40; and East Sydney Technical College, Sydney, 1945. During World War II he was assigned to the Civil Construction Corps as a camouflage artist. Between 1948–60, Strachan lived in France, England and Majorca, furthering his studies of past and contemporary artists' work. With a Dutch artist he set up Stramur Presse, in Paris, and turned to etching. He developed an interest in Jungian analysis and studied at the Jung Institute in Switzerland. In 1953, Strachan took part in the first Australian Artists' Association exhibition at RWS' Conduit Street gallery. Strachan returned to Australia in 1960, teaching at East Sydney Technical College, also supporting his art by involvement with friends in real estate renovation, creating his own studio in the Paddington area which his sister preserved intact for many years after he died in a car accident, at Yass, New South Wales. There were retrospectives at Art Gallery of New South Wales, Sydney, 1973, and S H Ervin Gallery there, 1993. National Gallery of Australia, Canberra, holds his work.

Douglas STRACHAN 1875–1950 Stained glass designer, decorator and painter, born in Aberdeen where he attended Robert Gordon's College. He studied at RSA life schools, then widely in continental Europe. His interest in easel painting gradually gave way to more public decorative projects, such as work on the Scottish National War Memorial, Whittington window in the Guildhall and windows which Britain contributed to the Palace of Peace, The Hague. Strachan was an honorary RSA, 1920, who also showed at Royal Glasgow Institute of the Fine Arts. Lived latterly in Lasswade, Midlothian.

Eddie STRACHAN 1940– Painter and teacher, full name David Edward Campbell Strachan, born in Forfar, Angus. He studied at Duncan of Jordanstone College of Art, 1957–62, with Alberto Morrocco, with a period in 1961 under James Cumming at Patrick Allan-Fraser School of Art, Hospitalfield, Arbroath. Until 1978 he taught and painted in Scotland, then moved to Brussels to become professor of design at L'École Européene Woluwe. While in Scotland showed regularly at RSA and participated in Scottish Artists Under 30; also exhibited at SSA and Marjorie Parr and Mercury Galleries, London. One-man show at Compass Gallery, Glasgow, 1977. The human figure is commonly the basis for Strachan's tight, intricate works. Hospitalfield and other Scottish collections hold his pictures, usually in gouache or watercolour.

Matthew STRADLING 1963– Painter, born in Hertfordshire. He studied at St Martin's School of Art, 1982–5, his teachers including Katy Deepwell, Adam Gray and John Kirby; was then at Reading University, 1987–9, taught by Roger Cook, Martin Froy and Mali Morris. Stradling won a British Academy Scholarship, 1987, and a Boise Travelling Scholarship, 1989. His large work

Omphalos was included in the 1992 Norwich Gallery/Kent Institute of Art and Design East & South show, a painting in the manner of the Renaissance masters. Lived in London.

Hilary STRAIN 1884–1960 Portrait painter, born in Alloway, Ayrshire. She married the artist Harold Wyllie and studied for some time with his father, W L Wyllie. Initially studied at Glasgow School of Art with Maurice Greiffenhagen. Exhibited RA, RSA, RP, RSMA and Paris Salon. Lived in Portsmouth, Hampshire.

Robert William Magill STRAIN 1907– He was by profession a physician, lecturer and writer on medicine who studied and taught at Queen's University in Belfast, Northern Ireland, where he practised for many years. Showed with RUA of which he was an exhibiting member, Walker's Galleries and elsewhere. Lived in retirement in Cheltenham, Gloucestershire.

Ian STRANG 1886–1952 Draughtsman, printmaker, black-and-white artist and painter. Born in London, elder son of the artist William Strang, he first studied at the Slade School of Fine Art, 1902–6, with Henry Tonks and Fred Brown, then at the Académie Julian, Paris, with Jean-Paul Laurens, 1906–8. Strang was a fine etcher and draughtsman in the Slade tradition, but with his own slightly austere style. His drawn landscapes often feature continental, especially southern European, locations. Exhibited RA, RE, NEAC, Fine Art Society, Goupil and Leicester Galleries, with a large and consistent output. Imperial War Museum, Victoria & Albert Museum, British Museum, many provincial and overseas galleries hold his work. Wrote *The Student's Book of Etching*, 1938. His work appeared in many publications including *Fine Prints of the Year* and *Print Collectors' Quarterly*. Lived at Wavendon, Buckinghamshire.

Dody STRASSER 1921– Painter and draughtsman who was born in Yugoslavia, where she studied art. She was elected RBA in 1975, also having solo exhibitions at Ben Uri and Thackeray Galleries. Lived in London.

Hilary STRATTON 1906– Sculptor, born in Amberley, Sussex, son of the painter Fred Stratton. He was an apprentice to Eric Gill, 1919–22, then studied at Royal College of Art, 1933–6, under Gilbert Ledward. Chelsea Arts Club member. Exhibited RA, NS, Leicester Galleries and elsewhere. Lived in London, then at Barns Green, near Horsham, Sussex.

Jekabs STRAUPENIEKS 1921–1983 Painter, stage designer and book illustrator. Born in Latvia, Straupenieks studied at art academy there for five years. Moved to England after World War II and, finding it difficult to make a living as an artist, he studied physics and worked at university laboratories in Birmingham, Witwatersrand in South Africa and finally in Sussex. Showed widely in Britain, including NEAC, Paris Salon, RSMA and in New York. His work is held in a number of British and foreign collections. Lived in Peacehaven, Sussex.

Peter STRAUSFELD 1910–1980 Artist in a wide range of media – notably a printmaker – illustrator and teacher, born in Cologne, Germany, where he studied at the Werkschule, 1929–32, under Richard Seewald. He also worked as Peter Strausfield and Peter Pendrey (his wife Peggy's maiden name. She was also an artist, who studied in Cologne). Strausfeld was an anti-Nazi Catholic who helped people escape until he had to flee Germany in 1939. In Cologne he did much work for the church, including murals, stained glass and woodcuts, the annual carnival inspiring many witty, singularly coloured lino-cuts. Interned in the Isle of Man Strausfeld met George Hoellering, who ran the Academy Cinema, for whom he was to provide several hundred graphic Underground posters, original lino-cuts, from the 1940s until his death. After internment, Strausfeld served in the Pioneer Corps, then was seconded to the Ministry of Information to make short propaganda films. Strausfeld, who was a member of the Society of Industrial Artists, also taught the foundation course at Brighton Polytechnic part-time for many years; was responsible for design and art direction for Hoellering's film *Murder in the Cathedral*, made in 1951 (Strausfeld's wife wove fabric for the costumes); and illustrated books for the Folio Society. Latterly reclusive, Strausfeld did not seek exhibitions. There was a retrospective at Brighton Polytechnic, 1978; another at Stadtmuseum, Cologne, 1987; other shows being at Star Gallery, Lewes, 1992 and 1995.

Peter STRAUSFIELD: *see* **Peter STRAUSFELD**

Anne STRAUSS 1902–1988 Figure sculptor, sister of the poet Robert Nichols, daughter of J Bowyer Nichols, of Lawford Hall, Manningtree, Essex. At Lady Margaret Hall, Oxford, she read Modern Greats, then studied sculpture at Westminster Technical School, under Frank Dobson, and at Royal College of Art. Showed at RA. Strauss preferred carving to modelling, liking to use stone and wood; contended that the direction of a sculpture's masses were of primary importance, not the planes on its surface; and was particularly interested in early Chinese, Assyrian, early Greek and Maya sculpture. She married H G Strauss, who became 1st Baron Conesford, of Chelsea. They lived there at 25 Cheyne Walk, the garden containing Lady Conesford's fountain with fishes of Roman stone on a Portland stone base. Her husband died in 1974.

Käthe STRENITZ 1923– Artist, born in Czechoslovakia, who moved to England in 1939, settling in London. She was awarded a British Council Scholarship to the Regent Street Polytechnic School of Art on the recommendation of Oskar Kokoschka. In 1982 was elected a fellow of RE, where she had shown regularly for a decade. Was a contributor to many other mixed shows, including RWA, Industrial Painters' Group at the Guildhall Gallery, Bankside Gallery, Camden Arts Centre, Whitechapel Gallery, Phoenix Gallery in Lavenham and elsewhere, including America, France and Russia. Had a series of solo exhibitions, including Boundary Gallery, 1990. Also exhibited with Ben Uri Art Society, had a solo exhibition there in 1961 and is in its collection, also in the collections of Guildhall Library, Ashmolean Museum in Oxford, Camden Libraries, Greater London Record

Office and Royal Commission on the Historical Monuments of England. In 1973 won the Lord Mayor's Award for her woodcuts of London.

John STREVENS 1902–1990 Painter, born in London, who was primarily self-taught. Although Strevens completed some prints, watercolours and drawings, he was mainly a painter in oil with a rich palette, rather in the manner of John Singer Sargent and Philip Wilson Steer. Strevens painted formal portraits but was especially noted for his pictures of women, flowers and interiors. Showed at RA, Paris Salon where he gained an Honourable Mention and had one-man exhibitions in England, Spain and widely throughout America. Harris Museum and Art Gallery, Preston, holds his work. Retrospective at Epping Forest District Museum in 1991. Lived in Loughton, Essex.

Sarah STRIDE 1921– Painter, born in Bristol. She studied at West of England College of Art, Bristol, then at Chelsea Polytechnic with Raymond Coxon. Exhibited at RA, RBA and SWA, showing solo in Bristol. Lived near the city at Shirehampton.

Madeleine STRINDBERG 1955– Painter and teacher, born in Cologne, West Germany. After an international upbringing arrived in Britain aged 19. She studied at Byam Shaw School of Art, 1977–80, Goldsmiths' College School of Art and Royal College of Art, 1982–5. From 1987 she taught at Brighton Polytechnic. In 1988–9 was artist-in-residence at National Gallery for six months, having a show there. Strindberg was an abstract painter with her own colour symbolism who employed metal sheet lozenges on a menacing black ground. She won awards at 1983 Northern Young Contemporaries and 1984 New Contemporaries shows. Her picture Without End was included in John Moores Liverpool Exhibition, 1989–90. In 1987 she had a Barclays Bank Award solo show at Warwick Arts Trust. Worked in London.

Simon STRINGER 1960– Sculptor, born in Bovey Tracey, Devon, who obtained a distinction in sculpture at Natal Technikon Durban, South Africa, 1978–81, then a national higher diploma in fine art, 1982. Stringer was accepted as a three-year postgraduate student at Royal Academy Schools in 1983, in 1986 for specialist studies at Staatliche Akademie der Bildenden Künste, Karlsruhe, in the same year gaining a Royal Academy Travelling Scholarship. Stringer's figurative work, in steel and bronze, was provocative, challenging and uncompromising, evident in his show at Goldmark Gallery, Uppingham, in 1990. Stringer also showed at Royal Festival Hall, 1985; RA Summer Exhibition and Camden Arts Centre, both 1986; and collaborated in a building project with Howard Constable Partnership and in the musical work Mkultra with Malcolm Poynter and Frank Tovey, both 1987. Had a studio in London.

Jane STROTHER 1956– Artist in various media, and teacher. She studied at Northampton School of Art, 1974–5, then Bath Academy of Art, Corsham, where she took fine art (painting) with printmaking as a subsidiary. In 1980 moved to Cambridge where she taught art in a comprehensive school, meanwhile teaching herself screenprinting. From 1983 Strother moved to part-time teaching, began showing her work in the Cambridge area and in London, where Belgravia Contemporary Arts handled it. In 1985 was a winner of the Lloyds Bank Young Printmakers' Award and exhibited at RA. Latterly developed an interest in illustration. Her work was widely reproduced in popular print form. Lived near Oxford.

Ida Lillie STROTHER-STEWART: *see* **STEWART**

Peter STROUD 1921– Abstract Constructivist artist and painter, born in Ealing, Middlesex. Became a professional soldier in 1938 and was a prisoner of war, 1941–5. Studied for teacher's diploma at London University. Although he pursued part-time studies at Central and Hammersmith Schools of Art, Stroud was mainly self-taught. After being until 1958 a Constructivist artist he decided to expand into colour. Showed in Situation at RBA Galleries in 1960, the year he had his first one-man show at ICA. Stroud's exhibitions included Museum of Modern Art in Oxford, 1969, Ulster Museum in Belfast, 1971, and a number of American showings. Held several teaching posts in America, including professor of painting at Rutgers University in New Brunswick, New Jersey, where he lived. Completed a series of relief paintings and murals, including International Union Architectural Congress Building in London, 1961, and Manufacturers Hanover Trust Company, New York, 1969. Tate Gallery and Guggenheim Museum in New York hold examples.

James STROUDLEY 1906–1985 Painter, printmaker and teacher, born and lived in London. He studied at Clapham School of Art, 1923–7, then Royal College of Art, 1927–30, his teachers including Thomas Monnington, A K Lawrence, William Rothenstein and Allan Gwynne-Jones. Stroudley was a Major Abbey Scholar, 1930–3, which gave him three years travelling in Italy. Thus his main influences were classic Italian painters, notably Giotto and Piero della Francesca. Although Stroudley was noted as a follower in that tradition, and was a fine figurative draughtsman, he did complete paintings showing a Cubist influence and richly coloured. Stroudley became a visiting lecturer at the Royal Academy Schools. Showed at RA, RBA of which he was made a member in 1934, RE and elsewhere and Arthur Tooth and Sons and Apollinaire Gallery gave him solo shows. Posthumously Paisnel Gallery sold work by him. Public collections in Bradford, Brighton, Coventry and Rochdale hold examples.

Sidney STRUBE 1891–1956 Black-and-white artist, cartoonist and advertising designer. Born and lived in London. He was noted for the cartoon work he supplied daily for the *Daily Express*. *Strube's Annual* appeared on several occasions. Member of the Press Club.

Sheila STUART 1905–1949 Painter and draughtsman, born in Edinburgh, where she studied at the College of Art, then in Paris. Exhibited RSA, RSW, SSA and Roland, Browse and Delbanco.

The collector Hugo Pitman owned her work. Lived at Dalkeith, Midlothian.

A STUART-HILL fl. from c.1920–1948 Painter of landscapes and portraits, who completed a series of Thames scenes, included in many years of exhibiting at RA Summer Exhibition. (He is sometimes listed as A Stuart Hill, under Hill.) Among his sitters were notabilities such as Turner Layton, The Duchess of Choiseul and The Countess Cahan d'Anvers, and the Institution of Civil Engineers holds his 1946 portrait of its president F E Wentworth-Shields. Painted views of Switzerland and Italy. Stuart-Hill was made a member of RP in 1931, also showing at Redfern Gallery, NEAC, RSA and Royal Glasgow Institute of the Fine Arts. For around 30 years had a studio in Glebe Place, Chelsea.

Mark STUART-SMITH 1958– Artist who studied at Cambridge University and Royal Academy Schools. Participated in RA Summer Exhibition, also showing at Mall Galleries, at Robinson College in Cambridge and at King's Manor Gallery, York. In 1991–2 was included in the Spanish tour Six Young British Painters.

Tony STUBBING 1921–1983 Painter, muralist, sculptor and ceramist, born in London where he died, his full name being Newton Haydn Stubbing. Was educated at Uppingham School, where he gained his first art prize. After a Newfoundland ornithology expedition, with Royal Geographical Society, in 1938, Stubbing was in the Army, 1939–47, including a period in Iceland, where he painted influenced by the local artist Kjarval. During 1946–7 studied in evening at Camberwell School of Arts and Crafts, his teachers including Coldstream, Johnstone and Pasmore. Stubbing was in Spain from 1947, becoming a founder-member of School of Altamira, studied sculpture and ceramics and from 1951 developed his distinctive hand-print pictures, inspired by cave paintings. In the mid-1950s designed for Marquis de Cuevas Ballet Company, moving in 1957 to Paris where he mingled with advanced artists, in the early 1960s settling in New York where he produced single-colour Minimalist works. Moved back to London in 1963, although later travelled regularly to America. Until his death he painted many murals, including Isle of Man Casino and Findhorn Murals, Scotland; made a sculpture for Pergamon Press, Oxford; designed for Royal Ballet School; and in 1977 was voted Fellow of Lindisfarne Foundation, a cultural think-tank. Showed widely internationally in group exhibitions. Had many solo shows, starting with British Institute, Famagusta, 1943; in 1990 England & Co held a show of his Ritual paintings, 1948–68. Tate Gallery, Museum of Modern Art, New York, and many other public galleries hold Stubbing's work.

Irene Gertrude STUBBINGS 1881–1956 Painter and draughtsman, born in Lowestoft, Suffolk. Studied at Ramsgate School of Art and Ipswich School of Art under George Rushton. Exhibited regularly with the Art Club in Ipswich, Suffolk, where she lived.

Constance STUBBS 1927– Painter, muralist, printmaker and teacher. She studied at Cheltenham College of Art and Royal College of Art, and after graduating worked in the studio of Christos Kapralos. On returning to England taught at a girls' school in Shropshire, then worked in advertising in London. There followed lecturing at Coloma Teacher Training College, in Kent; the painting of a mural for the chapel at St Mary's Teacher Training College, Strawberry Hill; printmaking at Croydon College of Art; then a move to Suffolk in 1981 where she joined Gainsborough's House Print Workshop in 1982. An exuberant Colourist, Stubbs built up her images from torn strips of paper, overlaying them with chalk, gouache and watercolour. She took part in many mixed exhibitions. After a first solo show at Anglo-Hellenic League, Athens, she showed in London at Blenheim Gallery, Brampton Gallery and Brunswick Gallery, later exhibitions including Chappel Galleries, Chappel, Essex, in 1991. Pictures for Hospitals; Christchurch Mansion, Ipswich; and Unilever hold her work.

Richard John STUBINGTON 1885–1966 Stained glass artist, draughtsman and teacher, based in Birmingham. He was a star pupil of Henry Payne at Birmingham School of Arts and Crafts, taking over teaching of stained glass in 1909. He also taught black-and-white illustration, drawing from the antique and life drawing at the school of jewellery and silver-smithing. Stubington showed at RBSA and NEAC. Notable examples of his glass, in which the lettering is exquisite, are in the Hall of Memory, Birmingham, and in Warwickshire at St Giles, Packwood, and St Mary's, Lapworth. Birmingham City Museum and Art Gallery holds his work.

Trevor STUBLEY 1932– Illustrator, notably of children's and educational books, landscape and portrait painter, and teacher, born in Leeds, Yorkshire. He studied at the College of Art there, then Edinburgh College of Art, then spent a year in continental Europe on a travelling scholarship. After National Service he taught at Keighley, Harrogate and Huddersfield Schools of Art. From 1960 became the prolific illustrator of children's titles, with several hundred to his credit. Gordon Boshell, Dick Cate, Nicholas Fisk, Richard Parker and Jenny Seed were especially illustrated. Stubley was made a member of RP in 1974, Society of Industrial Artists and Designers in 1976 and Association of Illustrators in 1979, and in 1986 he was made an associate of RBA. Landscapes of Yorkshire's hill towns, such as Holmfirth, where he lived, were favourite subjects. Exhibited in Britain and abroad and British Library and public galleries in Doncaster, Huddersfield, Leeds, Lincoln, Sheffield and Wakefield hold examples.

John STURGESS 1933– Non-figurative painter and printmaker, born in Northampton, where he attended the School of Art, 1950–4; after National Service studied at Royal College of Art, 1956–9. Commissioned works included National Trust, Oxborough Hall, Norfolk; Sir Gordon Russell, for Lygon Arms Hotel, Broadway; and the setting up of an atelier for research into colour etching at Digswell Arts Trust, 1960–7. A number of themes ran through Sturgess' work, including music; a series based on 16 squares and the idea of a non-hierarchical and never-ending structure with repetition and variety; festive villages in the south of France; the southern landscape; and visual language and how it works. Shared a show with John Brunsdon at New Vision Centre, 1963–4. Many other exhibitions included Bear Lane Gallery, Oxford; New Art Centre; ICA; St George's Gallery; Hull University; Harlow Arts Centre, and abroad. Arts Council, Metropolitan Museum of Modern Art in New York, several education committee and corporate collections hold examples. Lived in Codicote, Hertfordshire.

Christopher STURGESS-LIEF 1937– Self-taught painter and draughtsman who created poetic pictures using a private symbolism. He was born in Berlin, Germany, but was educated at Sherborne School, Dorset. From the early 1960s began showing on the railings in Hyde Park, where his work was spotted by Victor Musgrave, of Gallery One, who gave Sturgess-Lief a solo exhibition in 1962. Also showed at Rye Art Gallery, 1969, and took part in mixed exhibitions at New Vision Centre Gallery, New Art Centre, Leicester Galleries, LG, Arnolfini Gallery in Bristol and elsewhere in the provinces, and abroad. Lived for some years in London. His Red Painting was included in the Belgrave Gallery's 1992 show British abstract art of the 50s and 60s, and in 1997 Julian Hartnoll's Gallery put on a small solo exhibition. By this time Sturgess-Lief had "retreated into the obscurity in which he began."

Jean STURGIS 1931– Painter in oil and watercolour, etcher and teacher, born in Kendal, who grew up in Westmorland. The landscape of the north, especially Cumbria, was important to her. Studied at Goldsmiths' College and the Slade School of Fine Art, winning a Slade etching prize. An Italian Government Scholarship in 1954 enabled her to work in Italy for 18 months. Taught in London, but from the late 1980s was a full-time artist. Took part in mixed shows in London and Edinburgh from the 1950s. Had solo exhibitions at Clarendon Gallery, 1990, and Rebecca Hossack Gallery, 1996, sharing a show with Brian Pike at Linton Court Gallery, Settle, 1997.

Alick Riddell STURROCK 1885–1953 Painter, especially of landscape in oil, born and lived in Edinburgh, where he became a member of the Edinburgh Group. Served apprenticeship with a firm of lithographers and attended Royal Scottish Academy life classes at the Scottish Institution. Served in the Army during World War I. Married the artist Mary Newbery Sturrock, daughter of Fra Newbery. Sturrock especially appreciated the landscape of Galloway and of Dorset, where he and his wife lived for a while, and where his painting style reached its maturity. Returned to Edinburgh in 1938 to become treasurer of the RSA. Was elected RSA in 1937. He was briefly RSA secretary in 1953 before his death on holiday at St Abbs. Sturrock's pictures have a dry, subdued appearance, and the landscapes, usually without animals or figures, are notable for their gaunt trees. Exhibited Royal Glasgow Institute of the Fine Arts, RA, RSA and elsewhere. Paisley Museum and Art Gallery and the Scottish National Gallery of Modern Art, Edinburgh, hold his work.

Mary Newbery STURROCK 1892–1985 Artist in various media, born in Glasgow, the daughter of Francis H Newbery, director of the Glasgow School of Art, her mother being the designer and embroiderer Jessie Newbery. She married the artist Alick Sturrock in 1918. They were both members of the Edinburgh Group, and were included in the travelling show of that name in 1983 based on City Art Centre, Edinburgh. She studied at Glasgow School of Art and became friendly with Charles Rennie Mackintosh and his wife Margaret Macdonald, their influence persuading her to work in brilliant bright wools in bold colours. She filled sketchbooks with exquisite flower and figure drawings and became interested in arts such as ceramics. During World War I worked as a tracer for de Havilland aircraft company. Showed at RSA, Royal Glasgow Institute of the Fine Arts, RSW and elsewhere. In 1950s travelled extensively abroad.

Helen STUTCHBURY 1934– Painter who was taught at school by Helen Lessore, who later ran the Beaux Arts Gallery and exhibited widely. Stutchbury lived in Paris and Florence and later worked in Suffolk by the sea. She showed in open, mixed and solo shows, one being a shared exhibition at Sue Rankin Gallery, 1991. She said that "the quirkiness of human, bird or animal movement in spaces is fundamental to my vision of the world."

Rowland SUDDABY 1912–1972 Painter, mainly of landscapes. Born in Kimberworth, Yorkshire, Suddaby studied at Sheffield College of Art from 1926, winning a scholarship there. In 1931 he married and moved to London with few prospects, but spent two years designing for films in Wardour Street before starting to paint full-time. In 1935 had a first one-man show at the Wertheim Gallery, the next year he exhibited with the Redfern Gallery and with it had a series of one-man appearances. After World War II exhibited solo with Leger Galleries, more recent exhibitions including Austin/Desmond Fine Art. Eventually Suddaby settled at Great Cornard, Sudbury, Suffolk, and became associated with scenes of East Anglia. He illustrated the covers of books by the Essex Marshland writer S L Bensusan and was a founder of the Colchester Art Society, with Edward Bawden, John Nash and Cedric Morris among the exhibitors. Suddaby also did poster work for Shell, designed textiles and prints and participated in the Pilgrim Trust *Recording Britain* project. During his final years he was curator of Gainsborough's House, in Sudbury. Suddaby's work is in many public collections in Britain and abroad, including the Victoria & Albert Museum. His pictures have a spontaneous vitality, a richness of colour, an immediacy which is unmistakeable.

David SUFF 1955– Painter and printmaker, notably of landscape using a meticulous, Pointillist-type technique and rich palette. He was born in Exeter, Devon, and studied at University of Leeds department of fine arts, 1973–7, then at Royal College of Art's school of painting, 1978–81. Gained the Anstruther Award for Drawing in 1980 and Pimm's Award for Drawing or Watercolour, 1987. Group exhibitions included Winsor & Newton Award Finalists, 1977; Mall Galleries from 1978; RA Summer

Exhibitions from 1981; and Basle International Art Fair from 1984. Had a solo show at Parkinson Gallery, Leeds, 1978, then with Piccadilly Gallery from 1983 as well as abroad.

Glenn SUJO 1952– Painter and teacher, born in Buenos Aires, Argentina. He studied at Slade School of Fine Art, 1972–5, then completed a postgraduate degree in the history of art at Courtauld Institute. Sujo's own work, such as his canvas Roma, the Fountain, at John Moores Liverpool Exhibition, 1987, looked back to the classical Italian tradition. He showed in Caracas, Venezuela, where he lived as a child, solo shows including Bluecoat Gallery, Liverpool, and tour, 1982, and Anne Berthoud, 1983. In 1994 Sujo with Harris Museum and Art Gallery, Preston, and Ipswich Museum organised exhibitions of his own work and British drawings. He saw the role of the artist as "history's caretaker" and sought to show "the diversity of drawing as a record of lived experience". Sujo taught at Norwich School of Art for a time from 1985. Lived in London.

John SULLIVAN 1940– Kent-born painter, teacher and sculptor who trained at St Martin's School of Art and Hornsey College of Art. After many summer visits to Provence, France, he settled there, where the bright light and rich colours were reflected in his paintings, often interiors. Solo exhibitions included Architectural Association, 1964; University of Wisconsin, America, 1974; Hilton Gallery, Amsterdam, 1983; British Council, Brussels, 1984; and Montpelier Studio from 1987.

Maud SULTER 1960– Artist using photography, painting, performance and video and the written word to help define the place of black women artists. She was born in Glasgow, and gained her master's degree in photographic studies at the University of Derby, 1990. Among group shows participated in were Creation for Liberation, Brixton Art Gallery, 1984; Whitechapel Open, Whitechapel Art Gallery, 1987; New Contemporaries, ICA and tour (British Telecom Award Winner), 1989; and New North, Tate Gallery Liverpool, 1990. Later solo shows included Plantation, University Gallery Leeds, 1995.

Chris SUMMERFIELD 1955– Artist producing sculpture and works on paper, born in London, who said that his work "is a response to both the 'natural' and the 'man-made' world, and is located between representation and abstraction." He did a foundation course at St Martin's School of Art, 1974–5, gain-ing a degree in sculpture there, 1975–8; attended Newcastle University, 1978–80; then did a bronze foundry course at Royal College of Art, 1981–2, and his master's degree there, 1982–4, in fine art. From 1982–5 Summerfield held a Henry Moore Scholarship, being part-time assistant to the sculptor. He held a Picker Fellowship in Sculpture at Kingston Polytechnic, 1984–5. Exhibitions included New Contemporaries, ICA, Artscribe prizewinner, 1980; Sculptors' Drawings, Ruskin School of Art, Oxford, 1983; Wind and Water, Rufford Country Park, Nottinghamshire, 1988; LG, 1989; Utopias, Galerie Dagmar, 1991; and he shared a three-man exhibition at Norwich Gallery, 1994.

Dora SUMMERHAYS 1883–1955 Watercolour painter and miniaturist. Studied at Birmingham School of Art under Bernard Fleetwood-Walker in early 1930s. Exhibited RA, RMS and Paris Salon, where she won a silver medal in 1938 and a gold medal 10 years later. Lived at Shaftesbury, Dorset.

Gerald SUMMERS 1886–1969 Painter, draughtsman and printmaker, husband of the artist Nora Summers, born into a north country steel manufacturing family. His mother encouraged him to attend the Slade School of Fine Art, 1905–9. With Nora he embarked on a roving, bohemian life, including friendship with August John and gypsy caravanning. After Gerald's World War I service in France, in 1923 the Summers settled at Ferndown, Dorset, where he took up toy- and furniture-making. Showed at NEAC, Chenil and Redfern Galleries and Walker Art Gallery in Liverpool, having a solo exhibition at Paterson Gallery, 1930. Was represented in The Summers Family, at Sally Hunter Fine Art, 1995. The work of his grandson, Gabriel, was also included.

John SUMMERS 1896–1969 Prolific watercolourist and printmaker, who lived in Sunderland, County Durham, noted for his local marine views. Sunderland Museum and Art Gallery holds some examples. Summers served in the Royal Navy in World War I and worked for many years as a timekeeper in the borough engineer's department at Eden Vale. Showed in the 1930s with Stanfield Art Society and with Sunderland Art Club after World War II, during which he served in Civil Defence with artist friends. Summers did artwork for newspapers and magazines. He regularly went on sketching holidays with Sunderland Art School teacher Frank Wood.

Leslie SUMMERS 1919– Sculptor and lecturer, born and lived in London, who worked in bronze and acrylic. His figurative work featured rounded and simplified forms. Summers studied at Chelsea School of Art and Hammersmith College of Art. He was elected a fellow of Free Painters and Sculptors in 1969. Exhibited widely including RA, Royal Glasgow Institute of the Fine Arts, Wills Lane Gallery in St Ives, Vth International Bienal in Barcelona in 1975 in which he was a prizewinner, and elsewhere widely abroad. Work was also shown continuously at Cork Street Gallery from 1967 and then at Alwin Gallery. National Museum of Wales in Cardiff, British Tourist Authority and Brighton Marina contain examples. Summers was an occasional lecturer on sculpture of the Italian Renaissance.

Nora SUMMERS 1892–1948 Painter, born in Bristol, father an engineer, who studied at Slade School of Fine Art from 1907, meeting her future husband, Gerald Summers, there in 1909, marrying in 1912. They were extensive travellers in England, Ireland and on the continent, leading a bohemian life, friends of Augustus John, whose work influenced Nora's. In 1923 settled in Ferndown, Dorset, where Nora bred prize goats and took up photography. Latterly suffered from illness and alcohol. Showed extensively at NEAC, also Walker Art Gallery in Liverpool and was represented in The Summers Family at Sally Hunter Fine Art, 1995, with a solo show there in 1998.

Edward SUMMERTON 1962– Painter and teacher, born in Dundee, Angus, where he studied at Duncan of Jordanstone College of Art, and later taught part-time, also being a visiting lecturer at Edinburgh College of Art. He obtained a first-class honours degree in fine art, 1984, and had a highly commended postgraduate year, 1985. He was accepted for the Stirling Smith Biennale before graduation. Soon after, he participated in the Students' RSA exhibition and the ICA show New Contemporaries. Upon graduation Summerton, fast building a reputation as a creator of striking images with a theme of concern about pollution, participated in Compass Gallery, Glasgow, New Generation show. In 1986 he had a solo exhibition at Compass, other one-man exhibitions including MacRobert Arts Centre in Stirling and Seagate Gallery, Dundee. His work began to be shown in exhibitions of contemporary Scottish painting at key venues in America, London and at the St Andrews Festival of 1989. Summerton was visiting artist at several art schools and universities in Britain and in America; won a number of travelling scholarships; and travelled in China and Japan. RSA and public galleries in Aberdeen and Dundee hold examples.

Harman SUMRAY 1920– Figurative artist, teacher and writer, born in London, twin brother of the artist Maurice Sumray and father of the painter Jason Sumray, with whom he shared an exhibition at Boundary Gallery, 1996. Studied painting at Central School of Arts and Crafts, 1937–9; saw extensive overseas service with the Royal Air Force Volunteer Reserve in World War II; was at Sir John Cass College, 1946–8; studied with Maurice at Goldsmiths' College, 1948–51; gained a teaching certificate at Trent Park College, 1953; doing postgraduate research into aesthetics, philosophy and psychology at London University's Institute of Education, 1970–2. For 40 years from 1953 Sumray held a number of teaching, advisory and writing posts. He gained The Queen's Silver Jubilee Medal for services to Art Education in 1977. Later solo shows included The Playhouse Gallery, Harlow, 1985.

Jason SUMRAY 1962– Painter and muralist, son of the artist Harman Sumray, born in Hertford, who attended Hertfordshire College of Art & Design, 1981–2, then Brighton Polytechnic, 1982–6. Carried out several interior mural commissions, 1987–8. Took part in open studio shows at Cable Street and Southgate Studios, 1991–4; participated in Derwent Open drawing exhibition and showed at Milan Art Fair, both 1994; and in 1996 shared an exhibition of figurative work at Boundary Gallery with his father.

Maurice SUMRAY 1920– Painter and pencil draughtsman, born in London. From 1935–40 studied and practised engraving, with occasional bouts of painting, from 16 showing at Whitechapel Art Gallery. Sumray served with the Ministry of Economic Warfare, 1940–6, from 1942–6 being a member of Hogarth Group with spells of drawing at Toynbee Hall and Sir John Cass College. In 1946–9 set up Sunray Textiles, specialising in hand-printed cottons, then with twin brother Harman gained a scholarship to Goldsmiths' College School of Art, where teachers included Clive Gardiner, Paul Drury, Kenneth Martin and Adrian Ryan. Wyndham Lewis praised Sumray's 1950 Gimpel Fils exhibit Lovers, calling him one of the best painters in England. For about 20 years from this time Sumray was a friend of painters and poets at Muriel Belcher's Colony Room drinking club in Soho. In 1953 Sumray, a slow-working and self-critical artist, ceased painting and destroyed all works in his possession. From 1953–68 he established an engraving studio, developing the flexographic process, in 1968 moving to St Ives, Cornwall, where he returned to painting. He was elected a member of Penwith Society of Arts in 1980 and of Newlyn Society of Artists in 1981. As well as group exhibitions Sumray's showings included a large retrospective at Penwith Galleries, St Ives, in 1984, another at Falmouth Art Gallery, 1997. Sumray's figure studies, featuring clowns and jugglers, were meticulously designed in the manner of early Italian paintings. British Museum holds his work.

Peter SUMSION 1930– Painter, printmaker and teacher, born in Gloucester, son of that cathedral's organist and composer Herbert Sumsion. Studied at Cheltenham School of Art, 1949; Chelsea School of Art, 1950–2; and Royal College of Art, 1952–5, teachers including John Minton and Robert Buhler. Went on to lecture at Glasgow School of Art. Showed at RP and Royal Glasgow Institute of the Fine Arts and solo exhibitions included Eton College, from 1960. Lived in Cairndow, Argyll.

Frances Watson SUNDERLAND 1866–1949 Watercolourist and teacher, born and died in Keighley, Yorkshire, who studied at the local School of Art and Crafts. She later taught there, for 50 years ran her own school and was a member of Keighley Art Club, which gave her a retrospective about three years before she died. She exhibited annually in her studio, at RCamA, RWA, Walker Art Gallery in Liverpool and elsewhere. Cliffe Castle Museum, Keighley, has an extensive collection of Sunderland's work, which comprises a valuable historical record of the town. She also painted Whitby, Hull and the Brontë country.

John Edwin SUNDERLAND 1885–1956 Landscape painter and teacher, born in Keighley, Yorkshire. After studying for four years as an art pupil teacher at the local School of Art Sunderland was at the Royal College of Art, 1904–8, gaining a scholarship. From 1908 he was design master at Shipley School of Art, from 1912 being headmaster. During World War I Sunderland was commissioned in the Royal Garrison Artillery, making a special study of camouflage, lecturing on it at Aldershot. From 1919–27 Sunderland was principal of Keighley, then of Medway School of Art, 1927–8, and finally Sheffield College of Arts and Crafts, 1929–44. Cliffe Castle Museum, Keighley, holds his watercolour Fell Lane, Keighley, 1915. Died in Sheffield, Yorkshire.

Lesley SUNDERLAND 1947–1995 Painter, craftswoman – notably in textiles – and teacher, born in Henley- on-Thames, Oxfordshire, who studied printed textiles at Chelsea School of Art (where until 1984 she taught surface design) and Royal College of Art. There she met her husband, the painter and wood engraver Jonathan Heale, with whom she collaborated and held annual exhibitions. As a member of the Swinging Sixties Sunderland was keen on silkscreen printing, using photo-derived images combined with hand-painting. Pop Art and Surrealism were influences. A series of sculpted, printed and painted gloves was a memorable part of her output. From 1975 she lived in a converted Sunday school in Montgomery, on the Welsh borders, and worked a lot for distinguished private clients.

John SUNG 1951– Artist who did a foundation course at Liverpool College of Art, 1979–80. Exhibitions included Medici Gallery, Val Smith's Gallery and Bluecoat Chambers, all Liverpool, 1986, and 1986–7 touring Merseyside Artists 3, Walker Art Gallery, Liverpool, where his studies Jesus and Christine were shown. Sung said that his art was "an extension of my subconscious, in direct touch with the source of universal life".

Ben SUNLIGHT 1935– Artist and teacher, born in Brighton, Sussex, whose father was a notable Mancunian architect who became a Liberal Member of Parliament in the late 1920s. After Cambridge University Sunlight studied at Central School of Art and Design, teachers including Alan Davie and Harold Cohen, gaining a mural diploma in 1962. Sunlight taught part-time at Hornsey College of Art, 1964–5, and Cranfield Institute of Technology, 1973–4, then was a practising professional painter and printmaker. He was a fellow of Free Painters and Sculptors, 1964–71, for a time being vice-chairman. Showed in mixed exhibitions in Britain and abroad and held a series of one-man exhibitions including Heffer Gallery, Cambridge, 1958; Drian Galleries, 1963 and 1967; John Whibley Gallery, 1969; and Pitcairn Gallery, Knutsford, 1976. French Impressionism and Japanese prints were cited as influences and Sunlight's range of subjects was constantly expanding. "The aesthetic content is paramount. My attempt is to build into the very pigmentation of my paintings an intrinsic quality of light." Sunlight was based in Teddington, Middlesex.

Mark SURRIDGE 1963– Painter, collagist and teacher, born in London, who studied at Maidstone College of Art, eventually becoming a part-time lecturer in art and design, Barnet College. Group exhibitions included Association of illustrators at Smith's Galleries, 1992; Space Open Studios, 1993; Summer Exhibition, Burlington New Gallery, 1994; and Royal Over-Seas League Open, 1995, where Surridge showed the large, brightly coloured landscape with abstract overtones Pond At Lloyd Park. Heinemann Books and The Medicine Group hold his work.

SUSHILA 1904– Painter, notably in tempera, muralist and wood engraver, full name Sushila Singh. She was born in India. Her father, the Queen's Counsel Bawa Dhanwant Singh, retired to England to give his youngest daughter the advantage of an education then not available to girls in India. She was a fellow-student of the artist Arthur Henry Andrews, whom she married in 1930, at Hornsey School of Art and Royal College of Art, where they gained their degrees in 1929. Sushila's early work was Surrealist and her later pictures were more abstract while retaining a dream-like quality. Mixed shows included CEMA in World War II; public galleries in Bradford, Leeds and Wakefield; Wildenstein and John Whibley Gallery; New Art Centre and Rowan Gallery; and Ashgate Gallery, Farnham. Solo shows included Ashgate and John Whibley, Grabowski and Heal's Mansard Galleries and Galerie Niklaus Knoll, Basle. Contemporary Art Society, Atkinson Art Gallery in Southport, Nuffield Foundation, Exeter College in Oxford and Leicester Education Authority hold examples. Lived in Bournemouth, Dorset.

Rosemary SUTCLIFF 1920– Miniaturist who studied at Bideford School of Art, then under the miniaturist Edwin Morgan. Showed at RA, RMS, of which she was made an associate just after World War II, SWA and in the provinces. Lived near Barnstaple, Devon.

Stuart SUTCLIFFE 1940–1962 Figurative and abstract painter, and musician, born in Edinburgh. The family moved to Liverpool in 1943 and Sutcliffe attended Prescot Grammar School, 1950–6. He entered Liverpool College of Art, 1956, where he was encouraged by the teacher Arthur Ballard and was a friend and contemporary of John Lennon. After taking his diploma the College refused to let him continue with a teacher's training course; it contended that he was a painter and not a teacher, having worked with originality and shown with the John Moores Liverpool Exhibition in 1959 (his painting was subsequently bought by John Moores). Sutcliffe in 1959 began playing with Lennon's Rock 'n' Roll group Johnny and the Moondogs as a bass guitarist and travelled with the Beatles Pop group to Hamburg in autumn 1960. Sutcliffe was encouraged to take up painting again and during the Beatles' second visit to Hamburg he enrolled at the city's Staatliche Hochschule für bildende Kunste and left the group. In 1961–2 he studied in Eduardo Paolozzi's master class. Died in Hamburg of a brain haemorrhage. There was a major retrospective at Walker Art Gallery in 1964, followed by many other solo exhibitions and appearances in The Art of the Beatles around the world. In 1995 there was a solo show at Liverpool's John Moores University when the Stuart Sutcliffe Fellowship Award was launched, to be granted annually to a student who successfully combined visual art with sound/music (the first winner was Jonathan Hannah). Walker Art Gallery holds Sutcliffe's Hamburg Painting No 2.

Carol Ann SUTHERLAND 1952– Artist in mixed media, born in Greenock, Scotland. She studied at Glasgow School of Art, 1969–73, travelling in Italy during her final year. In 1973–4 attended Aberdeen Teachers' Training College, then taught, 1974–80, as a peripatetic art advisor in the Scottish highlands. Her mixed show appearances included RA from 1982 and RSA from 1987. In 1986 Sutherland gained the Meyer Oppenheim Prize there. She showed solo at Mercury Gallery from 1983. Her work, which had on occasions Fauve- and Chagall-like elements, is held by Middlesbrough Museum and Art Gallery; Paintings in

Hospitals; and McNay Museum, San Antonio, Texas. Lived in London.

David Macbeth SUTHERLAND 1883–1973 Painter and teacher, born in Wick, Caithness, he married the artist Dorothy Johnstone. He studied at Royal Institution, Edinburgh, 1906, then in Royal Scottish Academy life class, 1906–9, under Charles Mackie, a notable influence. He was the first recipient of Carnegie Travelling Scholarship which enabled him to paint in Paris and Spain in 1911, and he continued to paint in France, at Concarneau, with much success in the early 1920s. Sutherland was appointed head of Gray's Art School, Aberdeen, in 1936, the year he was elected RSA, retiring in 1948. Sutherland lived at Cults, Aberdeenshire, but died at Plockton, Ross-shire, which had long been a favourite painting haunt. In 1973 Aberdeen Art Gallery held a memorial show and in 1987 Bourne Fine Art, Edinburgh and London, held a joint Sutherland and Johnstone exhibition.

Graham SUTHERLAND 1903–1980 Painter of imaginative landscapes, portraits and still life, draughtsman, printmaker, designer of tapestry, textiles and stained glass. Born in London Sutherland for a year was a railway engineering apprentice, which he left to study at Goldsmiths' College School of Art, 1920–5. As an engraver and etcher at this stage he was much influenced by Samuel Palmer, William Blake and Paul Nash, which led to his being grouped with the English Neo-Romantic artists of the 1930s and 1940s, as did his Pembrokeshire landscapes. At various times Sutherland taught at Kingston School of Art, Chelsea School of Art, Ruskin School of Drawing and Fine Art, Oxford, and at Goldsmiths', until after World War II his growing reputation enabled him to paint full-time. Decided to become a painter in 1935, after his first visit to Pembrokeshire, and during the war was an official war artist, painting scenes of bomb damage and workers in mines and foundries. After the predominantly Wales-inspired first period of 1934–6, Sutherland enjoyed a second period, 1947-mid-1960s, when he worked mainly in the south of France, during which his popular international acclaim increased. During a final third period Sutherland returned to Wales as an inspiration and to graphic work, in 1965–80. By this time he had established a reputation as a masterly portrait painter – subjects included W Somerset Maugham, Lord Beaverbrook and Sir Winston Churchill – and as the designer of the Christ in Glory tapestry for Coventry Cathedral. The Picton Castle Gallery, Wales, devoted to Sutherland's work, opened in 1976. He was awarded the Order of Merit in 1960. His work is in many international collections, including the Tate Gallery, which gave him a major retrospective in 1982. Lived at Trottiscliffe, Kent, and near Menton, in southern France.

Scott SUTHERLAND 1910– Sculptor and teacher, born in Wick, Caithness. He studied at Gray's School of Art, 1928–9, Edinburgh College of Art with Alexander Carrick, 1929–33, L'École des Beaux-Arts in Paris, 1934, then for another year in several countries on the continent and North Africa. Held a number of teaching positions, including instructing in sculpture at Dundee College of Art. Lived in Newport-on-Tay, Fife.

Hector McDonald SUTTON 1903– Painter, draughtsman, mural artist, printmaker, teacher and latterly sculptor, born in Walsall Wood, Staffordshire. Studied at Southport and Liverpool Schools of Art and at Royal College of Art where his teachers included Tom Monnington, Randolph Schwabe and A K Lawrence, whom he helped complete the Bank of England murals. Showed at RA, Archer Gallery, Victoria & Albert Museum and in the provinces. Nottinghamshire Education Committee bought his work. Held several art teaching posts, then became the first principal, for 31 years until 1968, of Mansfield College of Art; was art adviser to Nottinghamshire Education Committee. A forthrightly outspoken man of "progressive" views, Sutton had many interests, including the Blake Society, was a founder of the Midland Group of Artists, president of the Mansfield Art Society and helped found the Nottinghamshire Puppetry Guild, which toured the county on a coal cart. There is a painting of St Christopher by Sutton in St Mary Magdalen, Hucknall, and four more pictures in St Mary, the parish church of Edwinstowe. Lived in Linby, Nottinghamshire, later retiring to Surrey.

Helen SUTTON: *see* **Helen EDWARDS**

Keith SUTTON 1924–1991 Artist especially in collage, teacher and writer on art, born in Dulwich. He left Rutlish School at age 16 for Wimbledon Art School until old enough for service in the Navy. Won a scholarship at Slade School of Fine Art, 1948–52. During the 1950s and 1960s Sutton wrote on art for various publications, including *Art News and Review, The New Statesman*, *The Listener, The Times* and *London Life* and taught part-time. His first one-man show was in 1958 at Galerie de Seine, where he showed work in a largely naturalistic style, a contrast to the fairly severe collages – developed after periods on the continent around 1960 – at his Hanover Gallery exhibition of 1962. Its indifferent reception deterred him from another one-man show. After further teaching at Bath Academy of Art and Stourbridge College of Art Sutton's fortunes waned, although he took up painting in the early 1980s with renewed zeal before depression and poor health sapped his impetus. Arts Council holds his collage Still Life, of 1962, the year he published his book on Picasso. Died in London.

Kingsley SUTTON 1907– Painter, notably of portraits, and black-and-white artist. Born in Tunbridge Wells, Kent, into an artistic family, he studied art at Regent St Polytechnic School of Art under Seymour Lucas. Taught art and completed some industrial paintings. Exhibited RA, UA, RBA, ROI, London Sketch Club and Ridley Art Club. Lived at Old Woking, Surrey.

Jake SUTTON 1947– Painter, draughtsman and designer, born in Manchester. Aged seven, Jake won the *Daily Express* National Painting Competition, aged 13 attending Manchester High School of Art, continuing at St Martin's School of Art from 1965. In 1983 Sutton designed a poster for the Bath Festival, had his first solo show in the city and exhibited at RWA. Other mixed shows included RWS, 1984, and Venezia Ancora at the Arts Club, 1987. Commissions included Royal Mail stamps, on the theme of sport,

1988; and Highlights of London, 18 pictures for the House of Commons, and a painting for Bath International Music Festival, for promotion, both 1995. Among Sutton's solo shows in London was one at 27 Cork Street, 1996, organised by Kim Sutton Fine Art: exuberant watercolours on the theme of sailing. In 1988 the Victoria & Albert Museum bought a circus painting.

Linda SUTTON 1947– Painter, printmaker and muralist, born in Southend-on-Sea, Essex. She studied at local College of Technology, 1964–7, Winchester College of Art, 1967–70, then after a year living in Antwerp gained her master's degree at Royal College of Art, 1971–4. In 1972 the College commissioned a 100-foot mural. Appeared in group shows at RA Summer Exhibition, where she was a prizewinner in 1987; Greater London Council Spirit of London shows at Royal Festival Hall, 1979–82, being a prizewinner each year; Contemporary Art Society On the Open Road, 1981, where she gained a first prize; and National Portrait Gallery John Player Award, 1982, getting a third prize. Had a solo show at Galerij de Zwarte Panter, Antwerp, 1971; others including Ikon Gallery, Birmingham, 1979; Royal Festival Hall, 1984; Christopher Hull Gallery, 1988; and Austin/Desmond Fine Art, 1989. Sutton's work was colourful and exotic, drawing on inspirations such as Tristan and Isolde, Shakespeare's plays and Aristophanes' *The Birds*. Lived in London, married to the artist Peter Blagg.

Philip SUTTON 1928– Painter, printmaker and teacher, born in Poole, Dorset, father of the artist and photographer Jake Sutton. He was brought up in London's East End, left school at 14, worked in a drawing office for three years and did his National Service during the Berlin Airlift. Studied at Slade School of Fine Art, 1948–53, where he won the Summer Composition Prize, travelling to Spain, France and Italy on scholarships. Had a first one-man show in 1956, one of many, at Roland, Browse and Delbanco, the year he was elected a member of the LG. Won a special award at John Moores Liverpool Exhibition in 1957 and second prize six years later. Taught at the Slade, 1954–63, then travelled for a year to Australia and Fiji to paint. The environment suited Sutton's style – direct painting in front of the object or model, using bright, clear colours. His wife Heather made a film, *Philip Sutton Working in Fiji*. He had a retrospective at Leeds City Art Gallery, 1960, another at RA in 1977, the year he was made an associate, becoming a full member in 1989, the year he began to paint in Pembrokeshire, settling at Manorbier, near Tenby. Later exhibitions included ceramics at Odette Gilbert Gallery, 1987; an Oriel Theatr Clywd touring exhibition in Wales, 1993–4; and Philip Sutton in Pembrokeshire, to celebrate the opening of the new gallery at Tenby Museum and Art Gallery, 1995. Sutton was noted for his versatility, works including tapestry designs made at West Dean College; a wall of tiles, commissioned by Pentagram, for DNB Bank, Amsterdam; Post Office greetings stamps; a London Transport Soho poster; and colour woodcuts on Japanese paper, working with IM Imprint. Arts Council, Tate Gallery and many other British and foreign collections hold Sutton's work.

Trevor SUTTON 1948– Artist who favoured subtle, refined and apparently simple geometrical abstracts which might employ abutment of a cool, light green with a darker olive, or brown above grey. Born in Romford, Essex, Sutton studied at Hornsey College of Art, 1967–71, and Birmingham Polytechnic, 1971–2. He gained the Sir Whitworth Wallis Award (First Prize) in 1972; an Arts Council Minor Award in 1976; Tolly Cobbold/Eastern Arts 2nd National Exhibition, with tour, equal First Prize, 1979; he was a prizewinner at John Moores Liverpool Exhibition, 1980; and won a Lorne Award, 1989. Many mixed exhibitions included Seven Painters, City Art Gallery, Birmingham, 1973; Annely Juda Fine Art, from 1979; Tongue and Groove, Coracle Press, and tour, 1983; Five New Painters, John Davis Gallery, New York, 1989; Contemporary Prints, Tate Gallery, 1994; and Cross Currents, Reed's Wharf Gallery at Barbican Centre, 1996. Had a solo show at Brighton Polytechnic Gallery, 1985, later ones including White Art Gallery, Tokyo, 1995, and Kapil Jariwala Gallery, 1996. Tate Gallery, Arts Council, Contemporary Art Society, British Council, Government Art Collection and other notable holdings have examples. Lived in London.

Takashi SUZUKI 1948– Sculptor of geometrical pieces born in Hiroshima, Japan. Studied at Architectural Association in 1972–3, was with Denys Lasdun & Partners, 1973–7, then attended Chelsea School of Art, 1978–82. He was included in the Hayward Annual at Hayward Gallery in 1982. Showed from 1984 with Michiko Fine Art, Hiroshima, and with Moris Gallery, Tokyo, from 1985. In 1990 he was chosen by Nigel Hall as an Artist of the Day at Flowers East.

Douglas SWAN 1930– Painter, born in New Britain, Connecticut, America, who was educated at Arbroath High School. He attended Dundee College of Art, where his teachers included the landscape painter James McIntosh Patrick and Hugh Adam Crawford; then was at Patrick Allan-Fraser School of Art, Hospitalfield, Arbroath, under Ian Fleming; and finally in London with William Scott. He won an RSA Scholarship in 1954 and three years later a British Council Italian Government Scholarship. Showed RSA, Young Contemporaries, LG, Gimpel Fils, AIA and had a series of one-man shows in Italy and Switzerland. His work is held by public galleries in Brazil and Germany. Lived for some years in Carnoustie, Angus, Scotland.

Peter John SWAN 1936– London-born painter of landscapes, portraits and still life, working in oil, watercolour, pastel and gouache, sculptor and teacher. He was educated at Somerset College of Art, Taunton, 1953–5; St Martin's School of Art, 1955–7; and London University Institute of Education, for his art teacher's diploma, 1958–9. He was awarded first prize, Saunders Artist in Watercolour Competition, 1975. Swan became senior lecturer in the Bristol Polytechnic faculty of fine art, retiring 1985, then travelled and painted in America, Australia, Arabia and France. Mixed shows included AIA; John Moores Liverpool Exhibition; Bear Lane Gallery, Oxford; Exeter Arts Festival; and RWA, of which he was a member. Had solo shows at

Arnolfini, Bristol, 1961–2–6, and Barrow Court, Somerset, 1976. Work is held in private collections internationally, and Yateley Comprehensive School, Hampshire, commissioned two murals. Lived in Clifton, Bristol.

Robert SWAN 1888–1980 Painter, draughtsman and teacher, born in London, who studied at Putney School of Art and the Royal Academy Schools under Charles Sims, John Singer Sargent, William Orpen and others. From 1920 for a period he taught at St Martin's School of Art. Exhibited RA, RP, NS, Chenil Gallery and elsewhere. He wrote for *The Studio* magazine in the 1940s. National Trust and Pembroke and Jesus Colleges, Cambridge University, hold his work. R J Swan, as he is often known, lived in Pinner, Middlesex, and in London.

R J SWAN: *see* **Robert SWAN**

Marilyn SWANN 1932– Painter in oil and watercolour, born in Crayford, Kent. She studied at Woolwich Polytechnic, then in the evening at Central School of Arts and Crafts with Leslie Cole and Chelsea School of Art with Ruskin Spear. Before taking early retirement Swann had to paint in the evening and at weekends, around a job in commercial art and publicity. She was a fellow of Free Painters and Sculptors and a member of the Association of Civil Service Art Clubs. Solo exhibitions included Brangwyn Studio, Hammersmith; Old Bull Centre, Barnet; University of Surrey; Loggia Gallery; and Orangery Gallery. Main works included Galloping Horse and The Scaffolding. University of Surrey and Queen Mary's Hospital, Sidcup, hold examples. Lived in Bexleyheath, Kent.

Graeme G SWANSON 1957– Artist, born in Aberdeen, who studied there at Gray's School of Art and the College of Education. Mixed exhibitions included New Generation and Christmas Show, both Compass Gallery, Glasgow, 1979; Aberdeen Artists' Society from 1979; RSW and RSA, both 1981; and 10 North-East Artists, Artspace Aberdeen, Edinburgh Festival show and tour, 1981–2. Solo shows included 369 Gallery, Edinburgh, 1981. Scottish Arts Council and Air Écosse hold his work.

Betty SWANWICK 1915–1989 Painter, designer, illustrator and teacher, born in London, daughter of the marine painter Henry Gerard Swanwick. She studied at Goldsmiths' College School of Art, where her teachers included Clive Gardiner and Edward Bawden; the Royal College of Art; and the Central School of Arts and Crafts. Later she taught for some years at Goldsmiths'. Swanwick designed posters and advertisements for London Passenger Transport Board, Shell-Mex and BP and Central Office of Information; she painted murals for Great Ormond Street Children's Hospital and for the 1951 Festival of Britain; and illustrated her own humorous novels as well as for periodicals. Her superb pencil draughtsmanship, often using Biblical themes, was a distinctive feature of RA Summer Exhibitions, and she was elected RA in 1979. Also showed RWS of which she was a member, Little Gallery and in the provinces. Lived in Tunbridge Wells, Kent.

Mary SWANZY 1882–1978 Painter, born in Dublin, Ireland, educated there and in France and Germany. About 1900, having had private lessons in art, she entered the studio of May Manning, attending the Metropolitan School of Art in the evenings. In 1905 began long exhibiting career at RHA, then went to Paris, where her studies included L'Académie de la Grande Chaumière and Atelier Colarossi. Had her first solo show in 1913–14 at Mill's Hall, Dublin, in 1914 first exhibiting at Salon des Indépendants, in Paris. In 1920 she became a committee member. During the 1920s Swanzy travelled widely abroad, including Pacific islands, and showed extensively. Around 1926 she settled in Blackheath, southeast London. After her house was bombed during World War II she had three years in Dublin. Her painting The Message was presented to Municipal Gallery, Dublin, in 1945, and it was to give her a retrospective in 1968. She had a solo exhibition at Dawson Gallery in Dublin in 1974. After her death in London there was a retrospective at Dublin's Taylor Gallery in 1982, Pym's Gallery in London having an exhibition in 1986.

David SWEET 1945– Painter and teacher, born in Lincolnshire. Between 1961–9 he studied at Hull College of Art and Royal College of Art. He went on to lecture extensively in art schools throughout Britain, including Slade School of Fine Art and Newcastle University, for some time being head of painting at Manchester Polytechnic. His paintings were exhibited in mixed shows from 1969, notably Big Paintings for Public Places at RA. Had a solo show at Serpentine Gallery, 1976. He wrote for magazines *Artscribe* and *Art and Artists*. Ferens Art Gallery, Hull, and other public collections hold his work.

George SWEET 1909–1997 Painter and teacher, born in London, who while studying medicine switched to attend the Slade School of Fine Art under Henry Tonks, where fellow-students were William Coldstream and Claude Rogers, for long a friend. Afterwards, Sweet travelled in Europe where he became fluent in French, Spanish and Catalan, returning to England at the outbreak of the Spanish civil war. From 1938–60, Sweet taught at the West of England College of Art in Bristol, where he died, becoming head of fine art. After early retirement he continued to paint, showing his realistic, painterly work at RA, Browse & Darby and elsewhere. Sweet was a passionate ornithologist, became an authority on raptors and wrote about them. On his death Judith Greenbury, a student of his in the 1940s, wrote a memoir, published in 1998, with insights into art teaching of that period.

Agnes SWIFT 1907– Painter and draughtsman, especially known for ecclesiastical portraits, born in Preston, Lancashire. Studied at Hornsey School of Art, 1923–8, under John Henry Willis; at the Royal Academy Schools, 1928–32, notably with Sir Walter Westley Russell and Ernest Jackson, also under Bernard Adams and Ralph Middleton Todd. Showed RA, RP, ROI, RSA at Paris Salon and elsewhere. Member of Chelsea Arts Club and for some time secretary of Chelsea Art Society. Lived in Pinner, Middlesex, later in Bromley, Kent.

Thomas SWIMMER 1932– Painter, designer and draughtsman, born in Dieppe, France. He studied art at Heatherley's School of Fine art with Iain Macnab, 1948–50, then at the Royal Academy Schools, 1950–6, his teachers including Peter Greenham and Bernard Fleetwood Walker. Won a RA Gold Medal in 1955. Showed at RA, Redfern and Piccadilly Galleries and in the provinces. Leicester County Council bought his work. Worked for a time for BBC Television and lived in London.

Ralph Leslie SWINDEN 1888–1967 Painter, decorative and mural artist and teacher, born in Meriden, Connecticut, America. Initially educated in Sheffield, Yorkshire, he attended the College of Art there, 1902–11; the Royal College of Art where his teachers included Gerald Moira and W R Lethaby; and the Slade School of Fine Art under Fred Brown and Ambrose McEvoy. He taught at Torquay School of Art and Portsmouth College of Art before moving to Darlington, County Durham, where he settled in 1928, serving until 1953 as principal art master at the local School of Art. Swinden did church restoration in Torquay and Darlington, where the local authorities bought his work. Showed at RA, Victoria & Albert Museum and extensively in the provinces, being chairman of Teesside Art Association. Swinden's wife Sybil was an art teacher and amateur watercolour painter who, like her husband, has work in Darlington Art Gallery.

Edmund SWINGLEHURST 1917– Painter, carver and writer, born in Chile, who worked in oil, watercolour and wood. He believed that "art has a function as popular entertainment." After education in England, Swinglehurst returned to Chile, became headmaster of an English school, later moving to Buenos Aires to work in advertising. Started painting with John Duguid, and, on his return to England, in Paris was involved with a Spanish exile group and studied with André Lhote, Fernand Léger and at the Beaux-Arts. In London he worked in public relations for the travel agency Thomas Cook, where he became archivist. Wrote several books, including *Scottish Walks and Legends, Britain Land of Contrasts, Cook's Tours, The Victorian and Edwardian Seaside* (with Janice Anderson, his wife) and the *Country Life Book Of Britain Then and Now*. Swinglehurst knew many of the Hampstead painters, including Stanley Spencer. Showed with LG and in mixed exhibitions in Britain and abroad, solo shows including Bath, Autun in France and The Bridewell, 1995. Lived latterly in Marlow, Buckinghamshire.

Eulalia Hillyard SWINSTEAD 1893– Miniaturist and singer, born and lived in north London, daughter of the artist George Hillyard Swinstead and one of a family of painters. She studied music with the singer Liza Lehmann and with Francis Korbay and became an associate of Royal College of Art in 1926. Only sang as an amateur, being a soloist in oratorio in Hampstead where the family had a large house and led a cultivated life. Married late and eventually settled in Dorcas Cottage, Seaford, Sussex, where she died. Exhibited at RCamA and RA.

David SYKES 1949– Landscape watercolourist who was self-taught apart from private tuition from Charles Mussett, art master at Radley College, Oxford. Sykes moved to Yorkshire in 1973, settled at Carleton, near Skipton, and worked mostly in the Dales. He painted in his studio using sketches and notes made during walks, but imagined details were included to express the mood of a particular area. Sykes showed in London and America and widely in Yorkshire, in 1991 being included in Images of the Yorkshire Landscape, organised by Sheeran Lock at Leeds Civic Hall.

Dorcie SYKES 1908– Versatile artist, notable for her watercolours, born in Sheffield, Yorkshire, daughter of the artist John Guttridge Sykes. She was educated at Penzance High School and studied at the Harvey and Procter School of Painting. The British Art Company published reproductions of her works *Dahlias, The Ginger Jar, Reflections* and *Roses* and she showed at RI, RWA, RSA, Walker Art Gallery in Liverpool and at Passmore Edwards Art Gallery in Newlyn, Cornwall, where she lived with her father.

Steven SYKES 1914– Artist, designer and teacher, born in Formby, Lancashire. After education at the Oratory School, Caversham, in Berkshire, he studied at Royal College of Art, 1933–6. Shortly after World War II he began teaching at Chelsea Polytechnic School of Art. Showed at LG, St George's Gallery, Redfern Gallery and elsewhere. Walker Art Gallery, Liverpool, and Ashmolean Museum, Oxford, hold his work. He also did work for companies such as Imperial Chemical Industries and Shell. Sculpture was completed for Coventry Cathedral; the United States National War Memorial, Washington Cathedral; and a water sculpture for the British Pavilion, Expo '67. Lived latterly at Midhurst, Sussex.

Diana SYLVESTER 1924– Painter and teacher, born in Bath, Somerset. She studied at Chippenham Technical College; Bath Academy of Art, Corsham; and Bristol Polytechnic. She was a member of Bath Society of Artists and Corsham Art Society, also showing at RWA of which she became a member in 1986, RA, ROI and elsewhere. Lived at South Wraxhall, Wiltshire.

Lydia SYLVESTRI 1929– Sculptor, born in Sondrio, Italy, who studied with Marino Marini. She collaborated with architects on many buildings in Italy, America, Hong Kong and Japan. Went on to teach at Bath Academy of Art in Corsham and was included in Arts Council's touring show Contemporary British Sculpture, in 1966. Took part in Italian and Japanese group shows and was awarded first prize, Sondrio, 1961, also having a series of international solo exhibitions.

SYLVIA T: *see* **Sylvia TREADGOLD**

Ken SYMONDS 1927– Artist, notably in pastel, well known for his nudes in interiors, but also for portraits and landscapes. He was born in Swindon, Wilshire, studying art at Regent Street Polytechnic School. He did work in Africa for a publisher, then settled in Cornwall in 1960, eventually living in Newlyn. He was an award-winner with PS, of which he was a member, as he was of

Penwith Society of Arts and Newlyn and St Ives Societies of Artists. Also showed on the continent and in America and was included in the 1992 RWA show Artists from Cornwall.

Judith SYMONS 1953– Painter who studied at Gloucester College of Art, 1973–6, then gained a diploma in art therapy at Goldsmiths' College, 1981–2. Symons was first prize winner at Winsor & Newton Award, Mall Galleries, 1976. Also showed at New Gallery, Hornsey, 1978; Picture Gallery, Battersea, from 1980; and Wapping Artists Open Studios, 1983. Lived in London.

Patrick SYMONS 1925–1993 Painter, draughtsman and teacher, born in Bromley, Kent. He attended Bryanston School, where he was taught by Elizabeth Muntz; Goldsmiths' College School of Art; and Camberwell School of Arts and Crafts, 1946–50, under John Dodgson. Symons taught at Camberwell and St Albans School of Art, 1953–9, then at Chelsea School of Art, 1959–86, where he was the admired teacher of the foundation course. In 1957 he was included in Jack Beddington's book *Young Artists of Promise*, his portrait of the painter Tony Eyton illustrated. Symons was a slow, painstaking worker, with an informed interest in botany and music, and was not a prolific exhibitor. He showed at RA Summer Exhibitions from 1969, one painting winning the Picture of the Year Award in 1990, the year before he was elected RA. Also exhibited at John Moores Liverpool Exhibition in 1974 and several times at Hayward Gallery, including Hayward Annual, 1979. Symons' first solo show was at New Art Centre in 1960, followed by one at William Darby in 1975, and two at Browse & Darby in 1982–9, and it held an exhibition after his death, in 1994. Tate Gallery and other collections hold examples. Symons was killed in a street accident in Paris. He lived in London and at Ryme Intrinseca, Dorset.

Dennis SYRETT 1932– Artist in oil, watercolour and pastel, born in Beaconsfield, Buckinghamshire, who settled in the county at Lacey Green, Aylesbury. He was self-taught and in 1960s gave up a career in the city of London to become a professional painter, supporting this with an art shop. Showed at RA, RSMA, ROI, RBA and elsewhere and in 1994 had a solo exhibition at Catto Gallery, it having commissioned him to travel through Israel and Egypt. The subject suited Syrett's bold, vivid palette.

Martin SYRETT 1935– Painter in oil and acrylic, born and lived in London. He was "mainly self-taught but was helped and encouraged by George Gault, Sir William Coldstream, Frank Auerbach and Graham Reid." Syrett showed at Reid Gallery in London and Guildford; Leicester, John Whibley, Marjorie Parr and Mercury Galleries; at Horniman Museum; and Gallery Darboven, Hamburg. His work is in many public and private collections in England and abroad.

Wladyslaw SZOMAŃSKI 1911– Versatile sculptor and collagist, whose trademark was humour, one of the group of Polish paper sculptors who made an impact in Britain after World War II. After studying architecture at Lvov Institute of Technology, Szomański graduated from the Academy of Fine Arts specialising in paper sculpture, which he practised until World War II. Served with the Polish Army in Italy, then after evacution to Britain in 1946 and demobilisation enrolled at Sir John Cass College. After working briefly working for Diana Studio he opened his own studio in 1948. Clients included a series of airlines such as British European Airways and British Overseas Airways Corporation, Alitalia and Aer Lingus, and British American Tobacco. In America he gained gold, silver and bronze medals and extensive private collections hold examples. Was included in Polish Paper Sculpture at Polish Cultural Institute, 1995.

T

SYLVIA T: *see* **Sylvia TREADGOLD**

Barrington TABB 1934– Painter, especially of Bristol, working in heavy, almost encrusted oil pigment. He was born in Almondsbury, near Bristol, and lived in and around the city all his life. Educated at All Saints School, Clifton, he left at 15 to help the family as his father was ill. He finally settled in engineering and worked as an inspector in Bristol Commercial Vehicles. He was self-taught and painted as a hobby, being very interested in the French Impressionists and primitive painting. Was a member of Clifton Arts Club and showed regularly with it and Clevedon Arts Club. Mixed shows included RWA and Nevill Gallery, Bath. Solo exhibitions included Cleveland Bridge Gallery, Bath, 1989–90; Anthony Hepworth Fine Art, Bath, 1993; and RWA, 1998.

Lincoln TABER 1941–1989 Painter, draughtsman and muralist, a native of California, in America, who moved to Paris, France, to study at the Beaux-Arts in 1960; visited Salvador Dalí in Spain; then worked in the atelier of Signorina Simi, in Florence, Italy, where he absorbed sound academic draughtmanship. Helped paint sets for the film about Michelangelo *The Agony and the Ecstasy,* in 1965, the year he first visited England and joined Pietro Annigoni for two years, working on church frescoes in Tuscany. Settled in Essex with his wife Jacqueline, a painter and picture restorer, whom he had met in Florence (with Julian Halsby, in 1998 she published a memoir of her husband, *A Bit of Trompe The Art of Lincoln Taber 1941–89)*. Taber made a career as a portrait painter (among his commissions was Princess Anne, in 1983) and witty, allusive muralist (in 1980 he painted the Thames Foyer in the Savoy Hotel, followed by the Beaufort Rooms, in 1984). Showed still lifes, landscapes and trompe l'oeil pictures at RA Summer Exhibitions and had solo shows at King Street Galleries. Accidents and ill-health dogged Taber's final years. There was a retrospective at Leighton House, 1998.

Len TABNER 1946– Painter, draughtsman and printmaker, born at South Bank, near Middlesbrough, Yorkshire, where his father worked on the river. On leaving school Tabner did a foundation course at Middlesbrough School of Art, then in 1965 transferred to Bath Academy of Art, Corsham, where he met his future wife, the sculptor Helen de Paravicini. Teachers at Corsham included Adrian Heath, Martin Froy, Michael Kidner and Howard Hodgkin. Then did a postgraduate two-year course at Reading University under Claude Rogers and Terry Frost, visiting tutors including Hodgkin, Froy and Heath. From 1970 settled in a cottage he had bought at Boulby, Teesside, on the highest cliff in England, extending the building himself and buying 250 acres of land and coastline to preserve it. Tabner's subjects were man at work and the challenges of nature. He painted wild places, on North Sea oil platforms and on trips with the Royal Navy to the Falklands, South Georgia and the South Atlantic. Agnew had a show of paintings and drawings, 1970–1989 in 1989, and in 1992–3 Laing Art Gallery, Newcastle, and Agnew gave Tabner a retrospective, for which a new book, *A Voyage to the South*, was published.

David TABORN 1947– Abstract painter, born in Birmingham, where he studied at the College of Art, 1966–70, then at Slade School of Fine Art, 1970–2. Awards included Northern Young Contemporaries, where he gained the Stuyvesant Prize, and Southern Young Contemporaries, Arts Council Prize, both 1970; Boise Scholarship, 1972; East Midlands Arts Purchase Award, 1981; and Midland View II, major prizewinner, 1982. Taborn's work, which was richly coloured and densely textured, was shown in group exhibitions including John Moores Liverpool Exhibition, 1980; Aberdeen Art Gallery, 1984; and Courtauld Institute, 1991. Had a solo show at Greenwich Theatre Gallery, 1973, later ones including Grob Gallery/University of Nottingham Art Gallery, 1992 (he was a fellow in fine art at Nottingham, 1979–81). Courtauld, Warwick Arts Trust and Nottingham University hold examples.

Miriam M TACHON 1909– Painter, miniaturist and teacher, born in Guernsey, Channel Islands. By profession a nurse, she settled in Dover, Kent, where she studied at the School of Art, taught at Dover Society of Miniature Painters and was a member of the Art Club. Showed at SM, RMS, Paris Salon where she gained a Silver Medal in 1977, a Gold Medal in 1980, and elsewhere.

Richard TAFFS 1949– Abstract painter, born in Northamptonshire. He attended Rugby School of Art, 1971–2, and Cardiff College of Art, 1972–5. Took part in wide range of group and mixed shows including Penarth Galleries, 1974; 55 Wapping Artists and Rugby Arts Festival, 1979; RA Summer Exhibition, 1982; and 9 Artists from Wapping British Tour, based at DLI Museum & Arts Centre, Durham, 1983. Private collections in Britain, America and Germany held his work. Based in London.

Renny TAIT 1965– Painter, born in Scotland, who studied at Edinburgh School of Art, 1983–8, then Royal College of Art, 1988–90. He won a Yale University Summer Scholarship in 1986, a Richard Ford Award, Prado, Madrid, in 1987, then was a Rome Scholar at British School in Rome, 1990. Among Tait's exhibitions were 1st Year Students at the Royal College in 1989 and Decade Ahead, at Scottish Gallery, Edinburgh, in 1990. In that year he was a Flowers East Artist of the Day, chosen by Michael Rothenstein, having a solo show there in 1993. Tait was notable for his singularly coloured, atmospheric, uninhabited townscapes. Edinburgh and Royal Colleges of Art and Royal Academy's Richard Ford Collection hold examples.

Thomas Scott Elliott TAIT 1982– Painter, commercial artist and draughtsman, born in Granton, Midlothian. He was partly educated in New York, partly in the north of England. Studied art in Carlisle with F W Hodgson, in Edinburgh and at the Imperial Institute, in London. Exhibited with UA of which he was a member, RBA, Chenil Galleries and extensively in the provinces. Lived in London.

Helen TALBOT 1966– Ceramic artist, born in Nottingham, who studied at Loughborough College of Art & Design, 1990–3, when she began to explore the properties of paperclay. With a Setting Up Grant from the Crafts Council in 1995, Talbot examined how paperclay can be printed on and manipulated almost like fabric; it can be wrapped, torn and layered, something beyond most clay bodies. Her creations had a poetic, contemplative quality. Won an Exhibition Prize from the Craftsmen Potters Association, 1996, awarded for Having it all. Exhibitions included New Designers, Business Design Centre, Islington, 1993; Box Art, Castle Museum, Nottingham, 1994; Small Objects of Desire, Leicester Museum & Art Gallery, 1995; Collection Gallery, Ledbury, 1996; and Gordon Hepworth Fine Art at 23 Smith Street, 1997.

Leon TALBOT 1905–1985 Painter, film-maker, writer and teacher with an interest in anthropology and art therapy, born in London. Doctor Talbot was married to the artist Nancy Talbot. He studied at Chelsea School of Art, Brighton College of Art and the Slade School of Fine Art, 1945–8, under Randolph Schwabe. Showed at Herbert Art Gallery, in Coventry; elsewhere in England and in Africa. Talbot wrote under the name of Baroqueon, including some art criticism, and his book *Tomorrow's Television* appeared in 1986. Lived in Ringwood, Hampshire.

Nancy TALBOT 1925– Painter in oil, stage designer and teacher, born in Coventry, Warwickshire, married to the artist Leon Talbot. She studied at Ruskin School of Drawing, Oxford, under Albert Rutherston, 1945; then at Slade School of Fine Art, 1945–8, with Randolph Schwabe and Vladimir Polunin. She acted as a consultant to Talbot Film Productions and provided illustrations for her husband's book *Tomorrow's Television*. Brueghel, Vermeer, Tiepolo and Renoir were influences, her work "celebrating life itself, as an exuberant cabaret". Showed at Kaleidoscope Gallery and had first solo show at Herbert Art Gallery, Coventry, in 1965. Lived in Ringwood, Hampshire.

Neil TALBOT 1943– Sculptor and teacher, born in Durham. He studied fine art at Newcastle University. After a period as visiting lecturer in sculpture in Chicago at the start of the 1980s he went on to be senior lecturer in the subject at Newcastle Polytechnic. He gained a major prize at Tyne Tees Northern Open in 1985. Talbot's group shows included West Hubbard Gallery, Chicago, 1980; Sea Drifts, at Laing Art Gallery, Newcastle upon Tyne, 1986; Richard Demarco Gallery, Edinburgh, 1989; and DLI Museum & Arts Centre, 1990, in the Newcastle Group show The Northern Lights. His solo shows included Serpentine Gallery, 1980; Wolfson College, Oxford, 1987; and University of Texas, 1989, as visiting artist. Eastern Arts and Northern Arts hold his work. This included reliefs in stone in the manner of early Italian artists. Lived in Northumberland.

Chloë Elizabeth TALBOT KELLY 1927– Freelance bird artist and illustrator, picture framer and restorer, born in London, daughter of R B Talbot Kelly and one of a family of artists. She learned from her father and in the bird room of the British Museum National History Museum. She was made a member of the British Ornithological Union, 1960; was a founder member of SWLA, 1964; and a member of Chartered Society of Designers, 1968. Travelled extensively around the world and showed widely in Britain and abroad. Warwick County Museum has her oil Parts of Insect. She was official orchid painter, Royal Horticultural Society, 1953–4. Her illustrations appeared in many books on birds and ornithological magazines, including Longman's six-volume *African Handbook of Birds, 1947–71*, and she part-designed, illustrated and wrote Collins' *Handguide to the Birds of New Zealand*. Lived in Leicester.

Richard Barrett TALBOT KELLY 1896–1971 Painter, draughtsman and modeller, born in Birkenhead, Cheshire, notable for his pictures of birds. He was son of Robert Talbot Kelly and the father of Chloë Elizabeth Talbot Kelly, both artists. Was educated at Rugby School and Royal Military Academy, Woolwich, achieving the rank of major and winning the Military Cross. He became a member of RI in 1925 and in 1964 was a founder-member of SWLA. Exhibited at RA, Brook Street Art Gallery, Walker Art Gallery in Liverpool, elsewhere in the provinces and at Paris Salon. Principal works included Canada Geese, Red Kite and Spring. Corporation of Birkenhead bought his work. Lived for a time in London.

Yiannis TALIOTIS 1964– Abstract artist whose work employed geometric forms, born in Limassol, Cyprus, who studied at Bristol Polytechnic, 1985–91, then Royal Academy Schools, 1991–4. In 1991 he won the Davis Innes Wilkins and Rebecca Smith Awards; in 1992 the Creswick and Vincent Harris Awards; and in 1994 the Dorothy M Morgan Award. Taliotis' mixed show appearances included Eye Gallery, Bristol, 1990; RA Summer Exhibition, 1993; and Aspects of Abstraction, at Paton Gallery, 1995. Had a solo show at Bristol Old Vic, 1993.

Anne TALLENTIRE 1949– Painter and teacher, born in Portadown, County Armagh. She studied art with Kenneth Webb and showed at Mall and Archer Galleries, RBA, Heal's Mansard Gallery and in Ireland, where she lived at Ballinaboy, County Galway.

Harold TAMBLYN-WATTS 1900– Watercolourist and illustrator, born in Settle, Yorkshire, son of the artist Thomas Tamblyn-Watts. Like his father he did a great deal of magazine and book illustration as well as commercial work, being studio manager for Emmett Group, 1935–48. Studied at Southend School of Art. Showed with Fleet Street Artists, at Fairfield Halls in Croydon and with Croydon Art Society. Had a strong interest in natural history, being a fellow of the Zoological Society. Lived for many years in Shirley, Surrey.

Mosè Angelo TAMBURRINI 1905– Sculptor in stone, marble and bronze, and draughtsman of Italian origin. His family travelled to London in 1912 where his father, Nicola, opened a carving business which did much architectural work. Until his death in 1950 Nicola operated the business in England and Italy; Mosè was involved in it from 1935, closing down the company, N Tamburrini, in 1974 on retirement. Mosè studied art and philosophy in Viareggio from 1922, especially the work of the Italian Renaissance sculptors, leaving Italy finally in 1924. In London freelanced as a sculptor, then enrolled at St Martin's School of Art for evening classes, between 1927–39, studying anatomy at Royal Academy Schools as well as African and Egyptian sculpture. During World War II most of his early work was lost. On retirement Mosè began his own work, free of business worries, in 1983 moving to Sussex, settling at Bexhill-on-Sea. It was not until 1988 that the first bronze was cast from his direct-carved sculptures and his work was shown locally in public for the first time. In 1990 Tamburrini had a solo show at John Hunt Galleries, Brightling, with another at John Hunt Redchurch Galleries, 1996. Tamburrini was an international affiliate of RBS.

Bonita TANDY 1946– Painter and teacher who studied at Camberwell School of Arts and Crafts, 1963–8. She went on to teach in adult education in London. Work appeared in Whitechapel Open, 1984; Royal Over-Seas League in the same year; and in 1985 she was included in Figurative Painters at Woodlands Art Gallery. Paintings in Hospitals collection held her work.

Michael TANDY 1942– Sculptor, ceramist and painter specialising in bird subjects, born in Malvern, Worcester, where he attended the College of Art. Showed widely, was an associate of RBS and has work in Worcester City Museum. Lived at Upper Colwall, Worcestershire.

Allan Peel TANKARD 1897–1964 Watercolour painter of topographical views. Born in Hulme, Manchester, he studied art at Manchester, 1913, and Liverpool, 1917–22, Schools of Art. Exhibited RA, was elected RCamA and had work in Walker Art Gallery, Liverpool, and Williamson Art Gallery, Birkenhead. Was noted for his depiction of city of Liverpool. Lived at Wallasey, Cheshire.

Elizabeth TANNER: *see* **Elizabeth SORRELL**

Robin TANNER 1904–1988 Etcher, draughtsman, painter in watercolour, teacher and writer, born in Bristol, but spent most of his life in northwest Wiltshire, which was the main subject of his work. In 1921 he became a student teacher in a local school, then attended Goldsmiths' College and taught at a poor school in Greenwich. Studied at Goldsmiths' School of Art in the evenings, his teachers including Clive Gardiner and Stanley Anderson, was influenced by Blake, Palmer and F L M Griggs and began to show work. In 1928 returned to Wiltshire and married the writer Heather Tanner, who was to supply the text of several joint books; they had a house built at Kington Langley. In the 1929 slump he took a teaching job while continuing his artistic work, in 1934 being elected to the Society of Painters in Tempera. In 1935 Tanner was made a schools inspector, working initially in Leeds, then in Gloucestershire and Oxfordshire, where he advocated liberal ideas in arts and crafts teaching. He retired in 1964, which allowed him to take up etching again after a gap of about 20 years. A painstaking craftsman, he completed only about 40 plates. Tanner was a Quaker who revered the countryside and traditional crafts. Among his books were *Wiltshire Village*, 1939; *Flowers of the Meadow*, 1948; *Woodland Plants*, 1981; and his autobiography, *Double Harness*, 1987. There was a retrospective at City of Bristol Museum and Art Gallery and Ashmolean Museum, Oxford, 1980–1. In 1988 Garton & Co held a memorial show.

Yvonne Rosalind TANNER 1924– Painter and draughtsman who after early education at Dame Alice Owen's School attended Central School of Arts and Crafts and Chelsea School of Art, working under James Grant and John Farleigh, 1941–5. For a time she served part-time working for Mass Observation sociological research unit, with which a number of Euston Road School painters were involved, concentrating on Bolton. She exhibited at the public art gallery there, RA, Foyles Gallery and elsewhere. Lived in London.

Steve TANZA 1962– Multi-media artist, educated in Southport, Lancashire, who did an art foundation course at Hugh Baird College, Bootle, 1981; gained an honours degree in fine art and art history at Goldsmiths' College, 1985, completing a postgraduate diploma in television and video there, 1987. After a one-year course in recording technology, ITEC, in 1991, Stanza gained his teaching certificate at University of Greenwich, 1995, and in 1996 studied Lingo Modules 1 and 2 at Kingsway College, with additional multimedia and Internet courses at Central St Martins. He was a Wolfson first prize winner in 1992, gaining a Department of Trade and Industry Innovation Award, 1997. His later discography included *The State of the Art*, video compilation, 1987; *Schizoid*, cassette, 1991; and *Searches for Naked Forms*, compact disc, 1993. Mixed shows included Eight by Eight, Pallant House, Chichester, 1997, where he exhibited gestural abstract works. Had a solo show at Wolfson College, 1992. Lived in London.

Deborah TARR 1966– Painter whose works on canvas and paper had a powerful presence and spirituality. She graduated from Winchester School of Art in 1988, then continued her studies in Paris and London. Had a show in Winchester Cathedral in 1994,

where two of her murals are in the refectory. Bruton Gallery, Bruton, gave her an exhibition in 1995.

James TARR 1905–1996 Painter, sculptor, printmaker and teacher, born at Oystermouth, Swansea. He attended Cheltenham School of Art, 1921–4, and Royal College of Art, 1924–8, being a Royal College of Art Scholar, 1928–9. Taught at Colchester School of Art, 1929–31, then after art school appointments in Hull and Derby was principal at Lydney and High Wycombe Schools of Art, finally until retirement at Cardiff School of Art, 1946–70. Continued to live in Cardiff, painting, sculpting and making prints until his sight failed. Tarr won first prizes for landscape and portrait at the 1930 Royal National Eisteddfod, adding the first prize for landscape at the 1932 Eisteddfod. Group exhibitions included RA Summer Exhibitions, SEA, SWG, WAC and in London and other provincial galleries. Tarr believed that every child had the potential to be good at something, and his unrealised ambition was to found a student assessment centre.

Margaret Winifred TARRANT 1888–1959 Illustrator and painter, born in London, daughter of the artist Percy Tarrant. After Clapham High School she attended the School of Art there, then Heatherley's School of Fine Art. At first she did routine commercial illustrative work, much for Medici Society, then gravitated towards children's books. These included Robert Browning's *The Pied Piper of Hamelin*, 1912; F J Snell's *The Girlhoods of Famous Women*, 1915; and a series of her own books including *The Margaret Tarrant Nursery Rhyme Book*, 1944. Ridley Art Club member who exhibited extensively at RBSA, also at RA and SWA. Lived in Peaslake, Surrey.

Olwen TARRANT 1927– Painter, sculptor, printmaker and teacher, born in Newport, Monmouthshire. She studied at Sir John Cass School of Art, teachers including David Graham and Clive Duncan. She was a member of ROI and NS, holding senior positions in both; in 1987 she won the Cornelissen Prize at ROI. Also exhibited at Ridley Art Society, RBA and Medici Gallery. Tarrant believed in the links between visual art and music, literature, drama and poetry. She lived and worked in Hutton, Brentwood, Essex, and on Mallorca, where sensations of light and colour influenced her pictures. City of London Polytechnic and the sculptor Sir Charles Wheeler owned examples.

Peter Rex TARRANT 1943– Painter in oil, born in Bridgnorth, Shropshire. He studied at Shrewsbury Art School. He was under contract to The Linney Gallery, Ludlow, and afterwards Compendium Galleries, Birmingham, during the mid-late-1960s and early-mid-1970s. From then on he termed himself "a rural recluse", living in Shropshire, keeping "a low profile, in order to research, and reassess work, while continuing to paint full-time". Tarrant described his work as "individual, uninfluenced, figurative, modern, detailed fantasy woven with hard realism – a jaundiced look at the latter half of the twentieth century with a countryman's eye." He published scientific papers and composed music to broaden his experience. As well as group and one-man shows at Compendium Galleries in London and Birmingham, also showed in Birmingham with Ikon Gallery, with South Shropshire Artists in Ludlow and had a solo exhibition with Maltzahn Gallery. Birmingham City Museum and Art Gallery holds his work.

Barbara TATE fl. from 1940s– Painter in oil, born in Uxbridge, Middlesex, married to the artist James Tate. She studied at Ealing School of Art, 1940–5, teachers including the watercolourist Thomas Lightfoot and John Nicholls; Wigan School of Art, 1945–6; then with Peter Coker, 1957–8. She completed some work with her husband, herself showing in mixed exhibitions with SWA and RMS, both of which she was a member, also UA, Hesketh Hubbard Art Society, NEAC, NS and abroad, including Paris Salon, where she gained a Silver Medal, 1968, a Gold Medal, 1969. Lived in Ealing, west London.

James TATE 1914–1980 Painter, illustrator and writer, born in Chatham, Kent, was married to Barbara Tate, the painter with whom he worked on collaborative pictures, too. He studied at Chatham Polytechnic, 1930–3, Woolwich Polytechnic, 1936–7 and Central School of Arts and Crafts, 1946–8. While serving in Egypt during World War II he was a prolific contributor to Forces magazines and radio stations, as well as drawing for British periodicals such as *The Stage* and *Reveille*. Exhibited RA, ROI, RMS, Free Painters and Sculptors, Paris Salon and elsewhere. Lived in London.

Agnes Clara TATHAM 1893– Painter in oil, tempera and watercolour; illustrator. Born in Abingdon, Berkshire, she studied at the Byam Shaw and Vicat Cole School of Art, then at the Royal Academy Schools, 1915–20, where she received several medals for painting. Exhibited RA, RP, RBA, in the provinces and at the Paris Salon. Illustrated children's books and had work reproduced in *Royal Academy Illustrated*. With the artists Elsie Gledstanes and Alice Mary Burton ran the Unique Studio for Children art school in London. Had a studio there for many years.

Peggy TAUB fl. from late 1960s– Sculptor in a variety of materials such as steel, copper, canvas and hessian; painter and printmaker. She was born in America, daughter of a Russian Jewish immigrant. Studied at The Sculpture Centre, in New York, under Dorothea Denslau, later at Morley College, London, where she settled. Among her exhibitions were Alonzo Gallery, 1968, and in 1969 Chapman and Avanti Galleries, all in New York; Penwith Society of Arts from 1974; Camden Arts Centre and Obelisk Gallery, 1975; RA, 1977; in 1978 RE and New Art Centre; and in 1979 Woodlands Art Gallery.

John TAULBUT 1934– Self-taught sculptor in stone, wood and bronze, who also worked as an architectural draughtsman and teacher, born in Gosport, Hampshire. Taulbut was a member of RWA. His work Seasong, in the 1st RWA Open Sculpture Exhibition, in 1993, was bought by the Porthcawl Civic Trust and is in the Grand Pavilion. Taulbut's Madonna and Child is in the Parish Church, Llanstephan, Carmarthenshire, where he lived. Taulbut was awarded the Jack Goldhill Award for Sculpture at 1987 RA Summer Exhibition. Other mixed shows included RBA and Swindon and Southampton public galleries. Solo exhibitions included Bajazzo Gallery, Marlborough; Swansea Arts Workshop; Oriel, Cardiff; and Swindon Art Gallery. Taulbut believed in "truth to material" and aimed "to symbolise with economy the internal spirit of the subject".

Adrian TAUNTON 1939– Atmospheric landscape watercolourist, from a line of painters stretching back to William Taunton, a pupil of David Cox. Adrian Taunton's father, Edward Seago, the Norwich School and other East Anglian artists were influences. Showed with RSMA, RI, in the provinces and twice reached the finals of the Singer & Friedlander/*Sunday Times* Watercolour Competition. Had a solo show at Century Galleries, Henley-on-Thames, 1997. Lived in Norfolk.

Donald Battershill TAUNTON 1885–1965 Artist in stained glass, born in Birmingham. He studied at the School of Art there and exhibited at the RA. Lived at Radlett, Hertfordshire.

Robert TAVENER 1920– Illustrator, printmaker, designer and lecturer, born in London. He trained at Hornsey College of Art, 1946–50 after six years' war service in the Army. He was art teacher at Temple School, Strood, and at Medway College of Art prior to joining staff of Eastbourne College of Art and Design, where he was deputy principal. He carried out many book illustrations for educational series published by Hamish Hamilton, Longmans Green, Oxford University Press and Methuen and did commissioned work for Central Office of Information, General Post Office, Imperial Chemical Industries and others. Tavener showed widely in group exhibitions and had several dozen solo shows. He was a member of RE and Society of Industrial artists. Over 2,000 of his prints were bought for national collections in Britain and abroad, including National Museum of Wales in Cardiff; Towner Art Gallery in Eastbourne; Victoria & Albert Museum; and Yale University, in America. In 1957 Tavener was chosen as one of Jack Beddington's *Young Artists of Promise* in the book of that title. Lived in Eastbourne, Sussex.

Alan TAYLOR 1942– Artist in acrylic, watercolour and stained glass, born in Kingsbury, Middlesex. From 1988 lived in Calvados, Normandy, France, co-owner and founder of La Chapelle Painting & Drawing, a residential summer school. He studied at Colchester School of Art, 1963–5, with John Nash, John O'Connor and Geoffrey Clarke; at Stourbridge College of Art, 1965–8 and 1972–3; then at Brighton Polytechnic/ University of Sussex, 1973–4. Participated in many exhibitions in London, East Anglia, Birmingham and Devon, 1968–88, latterly working mainly on commission. Urban and rural landscapes were Taylor's leading themes, influences cited being Hockney, Renoir, Monet and fine art in advertising (transport posters, 1920–40).

Albert Jenkins TAYLOR 1918–1987 An etcher and engraver, Albert Taylor was born in Liverpool and worked in business. Having studied art under Geoffrey Wedgwood at Liverpool College of Art and privately with Charles H Clark, Taylor went on to exhibit at the RA, RSA, RCamA, RE and RWA. He was a keen walker and rock climber. The South Bristol Technical College and RWA bought his work. Lived at Wirral, Cheshire.

Anita TAYLOR 1961– Painter, draughtsman and teacher, born in Scholar Green, Cheshire, whose oil on canvas Studio Dialogue I, at Royal Over-Seas League Open, 1996, was one of a series "which deals with issues of reflection, gaze and scrutiny". Taylor studied at Mid-Cheshire College of Art, Gloucester College of Arts & Technology and Royal College of Art. She was artist-in-residence at Durham Cathedral, 1987–8, and at DLI Museum & Art Gallery, in the city, 1988, then was fellow in painting at Gloucestershire College, 1988–9. From 1987 held a number of part-time and visiting teaching posts, including Gloucestershire College; Coventry, Newcastle, Nottingham/Trent, Sheffield and Sunderland Polytechnics; Birmingham Institute of Art & Design; Central St Martins College of Art & Design; Cheltenham & Gloucester College of Higher Education; and Royal College of Art. She gained the John Minton Travel Award, 1987; was a finalist, British Airways Most Promising Artists Awards, 1989; and won the Malvern Award for Drawing, 1993. Her many group show appearances included Whitworth Young Contemporaries, Whitworth Art Gallery in Manchester, 1987; Cleveland International Drawing Biennale, Middlesbrough, and tour, from 1989; Millfield Open, Street, 1994; and Summer Exhibition, Beatrice Royal Gallery, Eastleigh, 1996. Later solo shows included Pittville Gallery, Cheltenham, 1993. Schools Loan Service, Leeds Education Authority; University of Sunderland; and Private Bank & Trust hold examples.

Barbara Austin TAYLOR fl. from 1930–1951 Sculptor who studied at Westminster School of Art, at the Grosvenor School of Modern Art, under Iain Macnab, in Rome and with a monumental mason. Exhibited RA, LG, RBA, NS, RP and in the provinces. Manchester City Art Gallery holds her work. Lived in London.

Brian TAYLOR 1936– Painter of landscape and portraits who studied at Slade School of Fine Art, 1954–9. Shows included Shaw Rimmington Gallery in Toronto, Canada, 1966, where he had other exhibitions; Richard Gray Gallery, Chicago, from 1970; and, after being out of the commercial gallery scene for some years, The Gallery, Manchester, 1994. Museum of Modern Art, New York, holds his work.

Bruce TAYLOR 1921– Sculptor and teacher, born in Yorkshire, who studied at Bath Academy of Art, Corsham. He taught in Hertfordshire, then in Cornwall, living in St Ives. Was a member of the Penwith Society, becoming chairman in 1957. Showed in many mixed exhibitions in Britain and abroad, including 19 Young Sculptors, Hillfield Gardens, Gloucester, 1962, when he was resident at Pitchcombe, Stroud. Had a solo exhibition at Drian Gallery, 1958. Taylor had work in the collections of the Museum of Modern Art in New York and the Leicestershire

Education Authority. He was featured in Belgrave Gallery's 1992 show British abstract art of the 50s and 60s.

Charles William TAYLOR 1878–1960 Watercolourist and printmaker, born in Wolverhampton, Staffordshire. Studied at Wolverhampton School of Art and Royal College of Art. Exhibited RA, RE, RSA and RHA. Several provincial galleries hold his work. Lived at Findon, Sussex.

Donald TAYLOR 1945– Artist and teacher, born in Bury, Lancashire, who settled in Lancaster. A figurative artist, he worked in graphite and tempera on paper and oil and tempera on canvas, signing work with initials and date. Taylor studied at Bolton College of Art, 1963–4; graduated from Newport College of Art, 1964–8; gaining his higher diploma at Slade School of Fine Art, 1968–70, under William Coldstream and Keith Vaughan, "a great help in my career and a major influence". Taylor was a Rome Scholar, British School at Rome, 1970–2. He gained a certificate in education, Manchester College of Education, 1975, with a master's degree in educational research, University of Lancaster, 1986. After Rome and two years working as keeper of fine and applied art at Salford Art Gallery Taylor left to pursue his own work and teaching part-time, from 1981–92 teaching full-time at Bolton College of Art/Institute of Higher Education. Participated in many group exhibitions, including Northern Young Contemporaries, Whitworth Art Gallery in Manchester, 1967; John Whibley Gallery, 1970; Portland Gallery, Manchester, 1974; Rome Scholars Exhibition, South London Art Gallery, 1980; and Paul Fowler Studio Gallery, 1993. Solo and joint shows included ICA, 1974; Osborne Gallery, Winnipeg, 1979; and Gallery Gabrielle, Lancaster, 1985. Workers in the British mining industry were a feature of Taylor's output in the 1990s. Bury, Bolton and Salford Art Galleries and Camden Council hold examples.

Doris TAYLOR 1890–1979 Painter, embroiderer and teacher, educated in Failsworth, Lancashire. In 1905–6 attended Oldham and Manchester Schools of Art part-time, gaining entry to daytime classes at the Manchester School by scholarship in 1907. After a period as a pupil teacher from 1910–13, again by scholarship, attended Manchester full-time, then after winning a Royal Exhibition Scholarship in 1915 went to Royal College of Art, 1916–19. As well as a teaching certificate, Taylor was qualified in stained glass, embroidery and painting, later working as an examiner. From 1919–21 she taught design at Hastings School of Art, eventually returning to Manchester School until retirement. Showed at NEAC, SWA and MAFA. Completed altar frontals, Mothers' Union banners and medical society banners. Manchester City Art Gallery holds two strong still lifes by her.

Eric TAYLOR 1909– Painter, printmaker, sculptor, ceramist and teacher, born in London. Studied at Royal College of Art under William Rothenstein, then was visiting lecturer at Camberwell School of Art, 1936–9; was at Willesden School of Art, 1936–49; at Central School of Art, 1948–9; then was head of design school at Leeds College of Art, 1949–56; was principal there, 1956–69; becoming deputy director of Leeds Polytechnic, 1969–71. Was a member of RE and of Leeds Fine Art Club. Also showed at NEAC, RA, LG and extensively abroad in mixed exhibitions. Solo shows were held at Middlesbrough and Wakefield Art Galleries, at Linton Court Gallery in Settle and at Goosewell Gallery, Menston. Taylor's main work was a 60-foot by 10-foot mosaic mural for Leeds Merrion Centre. He was interested in "the inter-relationship of all media". Imperial War Museum, British Museum, Victoria & Albert Museum, Ashmolean Museum in Oxford, public gallery in Leeds, Art Institute of Chicago and Washington Art Gallery hold examples. A major show of Taylor's work was held at The University Gallery, Leeds, 1994. Lived near Wetherby, Yorkshire.

Ernest Archibald TAYLOR 1874–1952 Painter, printmaker, stained glass and furniture designer, born in Greenock, Renfrewshire. In the early 1900s he worked for the Glasgow cabinet makers Wylie and Lochhead, in 1908 married the artist Jessie M King and moved to Manchester where he managed and designed for George Wragge Ltd, notably stained glass, then for about three years prior to World War I the Taylors lived in Paris. They set up a school there, Atelier Shealing, then when they had settled in Kirkcudbright ran a summer school on the Isle of Arran. Modern French art, the Scottish Colourists and the Ballets Russes all affected Taylor's art. He showed extensively at RSA, also at RSW and Royal Glasgow Institute of the Fine Arts as well as abroad.

Françoise TAYLOR 1920– Artist and illustrator, born in Liége, Belgium, who studied at Brussels Royal Academy, 1937–41. She illustrated books for Belgian and British publishers. Married Kenneth Taylor, a Bolton in Lancashire man, and settled and raised a family there. In 1950, she was awarded the Mastery of Book Illustration, at ENSAAD, in Brussels. Took part in group shows in London and Paris, also at Bolton School (Boys' Division), 1951, and at Bolton Art Gallery (which holds her watercolour Boy and Bicycle), 1959. Had several solo shows in Liége (1946), Brussels (1947 and 1950), Manchester (1961 and 1963) and in Bolton at Prestons Art Gallery, 1964. Le Cabinet des Estampes de Bruxelles and leading provincial Belgian galleries hold examples.

Frank TAYLOR fl. from 1980s– Artist, illustrator, designer and teacher, who studied fine art at Cardiff and Brighton Colleges of Art. He was an illustrator and graphic designer for several years; held senior posts at Amersham School of Art and Salisbury College of Art; then in 1989 left Salisbury College, where he was head of fine art and graphics, to travel and paint. Taylor worked in various media, taking his subjects from observation, memory and imagination. Had many solo exhibitions, also showing at RBA, ROI, RSMA, RI, NEAC and RWS. Taylor was a finalist in the Singer & Friedlander/*Sunday Times*, Hunting, Spink and Laing painting competitions, being chosen for the 1996 and 1997 Laing calendars. Public and private collections hold examples. Lived near Albury, Surrey.

Fred TAYLOR 1875–1962 Painter and poster designer, born in London. Studied at Académie Julian in Paris, Goldsmiths' College School of Art and in Italy, having won a gold medal and travelling scholarship. He did a considerable volume of work for railway and shipping firms and was an official camouflage artist during World War II. Exhibited RI especially, also RA, Fine Art Society, Ridley Art Club and RWA. Public galleries in Liverpool and Bristol hold his work. Lived in London where he was a member of Art Workers' Guild from 1924.

Fred TAYLOR 1947– Liverpool-based artist who studied at the Polytechnic there, 1970–3 and 1982–3 and went on to lecture part-time. Showed with Major Liverpool Artists, 1978, University of Liverpool, 1983, Acorn Gallery, 1985, and in 1986–7 Walker Art Gallery touring Merseyside Artists 3.

James Spencer TAYLOR 1921– Painter of landscapes in oil and watercolour and teacher, born in Burnley, Lancashire, where he settled at Cliviger, married to the artist Joyce Barbara Taylor. He studied at Burnley School of Art, 1935–40, under Noel H Leaver; at Slade School of Fine Art, 1940–1; then at Royal College of Art, 1945–8, under John Nash. Taylor lectured at Bolton College of Art, 1948–79. He was a member of MAFA, also showing in mixed exhibitions at RA, RWS and RI, having solo exhibitions at Accrington, Bolton and Burnley public galleries.

Jo TAYLOR 1969– Equestrian artist, born in Blackburn, Lancashire, who settled in the county at Whalley, Clitheroe. Worked in mixed media and oil. Taylor travelled to studs, yards, horse fairs and moors to watch horses, being interested in "their speed and spirit, using bright, loose and expressive colour. I l ook for inspiration to sculpture – the Greeks, Frink, Marini andReg Butler. I look at painters such as Kokoschka, Schiele and Piper for their energy and vibrancy." She did a foundation course at Blackburn College, then graduated with honours at Leeds Metropolitan University with John Ross as tutor. Showed with Society of Equestrian Artists; at Equus, Newmarket; and Country Living. Solo shows were held at Hencotes, Hexham, and Towneley Hall, Burnley. Main works held by Guinness Gallery in Dublin and by Duchess of Westminster.

Joan D TAYLOR 1915– Hand-printed textile artist, painter and teacher, born in Aintree, Lancashire. She studied at Liverpool College of Art, teachers including Will C Penn, Geoffrey Wedgwood and Allan Tankard. Taught textile printing at Laird School of Art, Birkenhead, 1946–67. Exhibited with Wirral Society of Arts, Liverpool Academy, RA, NEAC and elsewhere in northwest of England. Lived in Birkenhead, Cheshire.

John TAYLOR 1936– Painter, notably in watercolour, gallery owner and teacher, born in Darvel, Ayrshire. Graduated from Glasgow School of Art in 1959, some years later taking a higher diploma in art. Taylor made a big impact on the Scottish gallery scene when in 1963 he opened the New Charing Cross Gallery in Glasgow, giving young artists a chance to exhibit more adventurous work. Taylor's own work could sometimes have a strong polemical element, notably regarding war and the nuclear threat. As well as taking part in many group shows across Europe he was a regular solo exhibitor. Notable among these were Compass Gallery, Glasgow, 1985 and 1987; Richard Demarco Gallery in Edinburgh and Glasgow Print Studio in 1987; and Edinburgh Print Studio Gallery in 1989. He participated in The Compass Contribution, Tramway in Glasgow, 1990.

John H TAYLOR 1921– Expressionist genre painter and printmaker, born in Melbourne, Victoria, Australia, who studied at Footscray Technical College, 1937–9, when war service interrupted. Then, under the Commonwealth Rehabilitation Scheme, attended Melbourne Technical College, 1945–6; Saturday lessons at George Bell School, Melbourne, 1948–50; and Chelsea Polytechnic, 1951–3. As well as European study tours in the early 1950s, there was one in 1979. In 1953, Taylor participated in the first Australian Artists' Exhibition at RWS Conduit Street gallery. He took part in London and Australian group exhibitions and his solo shows included the Athenaeum Gallery, Melbourne, 1970. The National Gallery of Victoria, Melbourne, Benalla Regional Gallery in Benalla and private collections in Australia and abroad hold Taylor's work.

Joyce Barbara TAYLOR 1921– Painter, embroiderer and teacher, born in Burnley, Lancashire, where she settled at Cliviger. Her husband was the artist James Spencer Taylor, their daughter the painter Joanne Taylor Wilson. Studied at Burnley and Manchester Schools of Art, taught full-time for five years, later part-time at Bolton College of Art and the College of Adult Education. Joyce Taylor was a flower and still life painter in watercolour and oil and also a freelance ecclesiastical embroiderer who exhibited at Red Rose Guild of Craftsmen, Whitworth Art Gallery, Manchester, and Embroiderers' Guild, main works including altar frontals for a number of churches in northwest of England. Showed paintings at RWS Galleries and had a solo exhibition at Hyndburn Art Gallery.

Leonard Campbell TAYLOR 1874–1969 Painter, born in Oxford into a musical family. His second wife was Brenda Moore, the sculptor and painter, who modelled a head of Campbell Taylor. He was educated at the Dragon School, Oxford, and Cheltenham College. Then studied at Ruskin School of Drawing, Oxford; St John's Wood School of Art; and Royal Academy Schools, which he entered in 1905. Exhibited at RA (he was elected RA in 1931) from late 1890s and in 1907 painted a large picture, The Rehearsal, now in Tate Gallery, which put him in the forefront of academic painters. Campbell Taylor's pictures are highly finished interiors with figures, often with a period flavour, which owe much to the Dutch Old Masters. He also painted a number of portraits, including Queen Mary, and still lifes which follow in the footsteps of Chardin. However, his picture Herculaneum Dock, Liverpool, of 1919, in the Imperial War Museum, showed that the artist could work in a near-Futurist style. His work is in many other public collections and he exhibited internationally. Lived at Felsham, Suffolk, for some time.

Linda TAYLOR 1959– Painter, draughtsman and sculptor, born in Stranraer, Wigtownshire. Although she studied painting and drawing at Edinburgh College of Art, 1976–80, her reputation after College was made mainly as a sculptor. She won an Andrew Grant Travelling Scholarship in 1980 and three years later gained a Young Artist's Bursary from Scottish Arts Council. Solo shows were held in two Edinburgh galleries: Collective Gallery, 1985, and Graeme Murray, 1987. Her large copper sculpture Unseen Currents, for which Scottish National Gallery of Modern Art holds several drawings, was shown at Glasgow Garden Festival in 1988. She was featured in South Bank Centre's touring The British Art Show 1990. Lived in Glasgow.

Malcolm TAYLOR 1950– Sculptor, draughtsman and teacher. From 1970–5 he trained in civil engineering with British Railways' Special Projects Section. From 1975–6 Taylor was at Chelsea School of Art, from 1976–80 at St Martin's School of Art, obtaining a first-class honours degree. He specialised in figure-based work exploring the relationship of the body to formal and conceptual structures. This was followed by drawing research at Chelsea School of Art, 1988–90. Taylor had extensive teaching experience, beginning with Architectural Association, 1980–1, including Lancashire and Liverpool Polytechnics, St Martin's and Winchester Schools of Art, Bristol Polytechnic and Glasgow School of Art. Was represented in Drawing Towards Sculpture at Isis Gallery, Leigh-on-Sea, 1993.

Marcus TAYLOR 1964– Sculptor, born in Belfast, Northern Ireland, who did a foundation course at Ulster Polytechnic, 1981–2; completed a higher diploma in fine art at Camberwell School of Arts and Crafts, 1983–6; then gained his bachelor's degree in fine art at Slade School, 1986–8. In Young British Artists IV, at Saatchi Gallery, 1995, Taylor showed a series glacial boxes in clear acrylic sheet. Lived in London.

Martin TAYLOR 1954– Painter, printmaker, photographer and teacher, born in Hayes, Middlesex, who studied at Ealing and Wimbledon Schools of Art and Goldsmiths' College School of Art. Showed at RA Summer Exhibition, RI, Mercury Gallery, Chris Beetles Ltd, Linda Blackstone Gallery in Pinner and in the provinces. Solo show at The Catto Gallery in 1995 of pictures meticulously depicting the countryside. Lived in Northampton.

Michael TAYLOR 1952– Figure and still life painter in oil, born in Worthing, Sussex. He studied at Goldsmiths' College School of Art, 1970–3, teachers including Stephen McKenna and Basil Beattie, then painted full-time. Taylor showed in RA Summer Exhibitions, RWA, Beaux Arts in Bath, Florence Art Gallery and elsewhere. Taylor was winner, National Portrait Gallery John Player Award, 1983; winner, Millfield Open, 1989; and gained third prize in the Hunting Group Art Prizes, 1988. Solo shows included Morley Gallery and Quay Arts Centre in Isle of Wight, both 1983; Worthing Museum & Art Gallery, 1984; and Beaux Arts, London, 1993. National Portrait Gallery and Millfield School hold his work. Lived at Child Okeford, Dorset.

Neil TAYLOR 1906– Part-time watercolourist and businessman, born in Workington, Cumberland. Secondary school art tuition only, otherwise self-taught. He showed with RA, RI, RSA, Walker Art Gallery in Liverpool and with the Lake Artists' Society, of which he was a member. Lived in Kendal, Westmorland, where he belonged to the Art Club.

Newton TAYLOR 1911– Printmaker, watercolourist and teacher, born in Normanton, Yorkshire, actual name William Henry Taylor (he was married to Elsie Newton). He studied at Wakefield and Leeds Schools of Art, then gained free studentship to Royal College of Art, 1932, winning his associate rank in 1934. He was a Prix de Rome finalist in engraving in 1935. Became head of Amersham School of Art. Taylor was made an associate of RE in 1957, eventually becoming an hon. retired associate. Showed at RA, RBA and with Yorkshire Artists' Society and Buckinghamshire Art Society, living in the county at Marlow.

Norah Helen TAYLOR 1885– Painter and miniaturist, born in London. She studied at the Slade School of Fine Art under Henry Tonks, Philip Wilson Steer, Walter Westley Russell and Fred Brown, her instructor for miniature painting being Edwin E Morgan. Exhibited widely internationally, including Canada, America, Sweden and Australasia, and in Britain at RA, RI, RMS, SWA and RSA. Won a silver medal at the Paris Salon, 1932, a gold 20 years later. Lived in Stratford-upon-Avon, Warwickshire.

Pam TAYLOR 1929– Sculptor mainly in bronze and resin/bronze, born in Pontypridd, Glamorgan. Studied at Sir John Cass College School of Art, 1947–50, teachers including the sculptors Edward Bainbridge Copnall and Beth Jukes. Taylor became a member of SPS in 1975 and an associate member of RBS in 1980, exhibiting at Mall Galleries and at Scone Palace, University of Swansea, RWA, Guildhall, Royal Exchange and elsewhere. Among her portraits were the actor John Thaw and the actress Sheila Hancock. Public works included bronze portraits of Group Captain Sir Douglas Bader and Marshal of the Royal Air Force Sir Arthur "Bomber" Harris, 1978, and a memorial bronze figure of a World War II air gunner, 1981, all in the Royal Air Force Museum, Hendon; a bronze bust of Shakespeare in Shakespeareplatz, Berlin, given by the City of London Corporation, 1987; a six-foot bronze, The Unknown Airman, for the International Royal Air Force and Allied Air Forces Monument, Plymouth Hoe, 1989; eight life-size Dockside Urchins for Tobacco Dock, 1990; and a life-size bust of Shakespeare, commissioned by the City of London Corporation for the restored Globe Theatre. Lived in South Woodham Ferrers, Essex.

R H Redvers TAYLOR 1900–1975 Sculptor in metal, painter in oil and gouache, born in Brighton, Sussex. Taylor attended Heatherley's School of Fine Art and signed his work R H R T. Took part in a number of group exhibitions, including LG. After World War II he had a series of solo shows at Reid and Lefevre, Gimpel Fils and Kettle's Yard Gallery, Cambridge. Lived at Belchamp St Paul, Sudbury, Suffolk.

Richard TAYLOR 1924– Artist, printmaker, designer and illustrator and teacher, born in London. He attended Newton Abbot Art School, 1939–42, and Royal College of Art, 1946–9. Became head of the graphic design department at Bristol Polytechnic. Exhibited at RWA and completed a number of book-jacket designs. Victoria & Albert Museum, Imperial War Museum and Bristol Education Committee hold examples. Lived at Clevedon, Somerset.

Suzanne TAYLOR 1910–1962 Painter, woodcarver and engraver. Studied at Battersea Polytechnic under Henry Cogle, 1929–33, and at the Central School of Arts and Crafts under Noel Rooke. Much of her work was of a commercial nature: book-jackets, fabric designs and designs for perfume makers such as Yardley and Coty. Lived at Pinner, Middlesex, where she was a member of Pinner Sketch Club.

Walter TAYLOR 1875–1965 Painter, tapestry weaver and teacher, born in London. Studied at East London Technical College (People's Palace), then was accepted as a pupil at Merton Abbey Works in 1890, for six years weaving under the personal supervision of William Morris, eventually becoming chief weaver on the intricate parts of tapestries such as faces. Further art studies included Putney, 1895–6, Westminster School of Art, 1896–7, and Royal College of Art, 1897–1900, with Fred Brown. In 1909, left Merton Abbey to concentrate on his art, being appointed to teach at Beaufoy Institute Senior Technical School, Lambeth. After 10 years, transferred to Central School of Arts and Crafts, retiring in 1940. During World War II, Taylor served as an air raid warden. Exhibited from 1898 at RA, also at RBA and the General Post Office bought his work. After retirement, filled 200 sketch-books, even until his ninetieth birthday sketching the scenery of the Cotswolds, where he had settled, as he was slowly driven about.

Wendy TAYLOR 1945– Sculptor, draughtsman, printmaker and teacher, born in Stamford, Lincolnshire. She studied at St Martin's School of Art, 1961–6, in 1964 winning the Walter Neurath Award. Other awards received included the Sainsbury Award in 1966 and Arts Council Award in 1977, the year she won a gold medal in the Listowel Graphics Exhibition. Taylor's first solo show was in 1966 at Axiom Gallery, and she later exhibited in many group shows and solo at Angela Flowers Gallery, Oliver Dowling Gallery in Dublin and appeared in Hayward Annual at Hayward Gallery in 1978. Taught at Ealing School of Art, 1967–75, and Royal College of Art, 1972–3. Taylor was early on a gardener, which was reflected in her interest in locating sculpture in a natural setting. Using a variety of materials she created abstract forms in which balance, weight and stress were key components. Completed a large amount of commissioned work, including Triad, at Somerville College, Oxford, 1971; Time Piece, Tower Hotel, St Katherine's Dock, 1973; Equatorial Sundial, Bletchley, 1982; and Pharos, East Kilbride, 1986–7. Member of Royal Fine Art Commission. Lived in London.

Wilfred TAYLOR 1915– Painter, draughtsman, teacher, administrator and conservator, born in Gateshead, County Durham, where he continued to live. Studied at King Edward VII School of Art, Newcastle upon Tyne, 1932–7, under the watercolourist Thomas Pattison and Diana Lall. Was for a while assistant curator at Shipley Art Gallery, teaching part-time at Gateshead Technical College, where he later taught conservation. Showed locally, including Laing Art Gallery and Museum, Newcastle.

William S TAYLOR 1920– Painter, teacher, writer, exhibition organiser and film-maker, born in Sheffield. Studied at the College of Art there and at Royal College of Art. Taught at Sheffield College where in 1964 he established the history of art department; he was dean of the faculty of art and design at Sheffield Polytechnic, 1972–5. He held a Master of Philosophy degree in art history from Nottingham University. Organised major shows of Aubrey Beardsley and Edward Burne-Jones at Mappin Art Gallery and made the film *Portrait of Beardsley*. Exhibited RA, NEAC, SBA, at Leicester and Redfern Galleries and in New Zealand and Canada. Taylor's pictures closely identify figure and landscape, with strong Neo-Romantic overtones. Lived latterly at Callington, Cornwall.

Joanne TAYLOR WILSON 1953– Artist in oil, gouache and watercolour, born in Bolton, Lancashire, daughter of the artists James S Taylor and Joyce B Taylor. She studied at Edinburgh University/College of Art, 1972–7, with Robin Philipson as head, then at Royal Academy Schools, with Peter Greenham as head, 1979–81. She was awarded the David Murray Landscape Scholarship and the Elizabeth Greenshields Scholarship, 1981–2. Became a member of MAFA. Her main works were still life and flower paintings in oil and landscapes. She showed at RA, RSA, NEAC, West Midlands College, Netherbow Arts Centre in Edinburgh and elsewhere. Had a solo show at Bolton Art Gallery, 1979, and it holds her work. Lived in Clitheroe, Lancashire.

Sam TAYLOR-WOOD 1967– Artist employing a range of media including video installation, born in London. She studied at North East London Polytechnic, 1987–8, then gained an honours degree in fine art from Goldsmiths' College, 1988–90. Group shows included Show Hide Show, Anderson O'Day Gallery, 1991; Close Up, Times Square, New York, and Annihilation, Victoria Miro Gallery, both 1993; Curator's Egg, Anthony Reynolds Gallery, 1994; and British Art Show 4, and tour, 1995–6. Solo shows included The Showroom, 1994, and Galleri Andreas Brandström, Stockholm, 1995.

Jessica TCHEREPNINE 1938– Botanical watercolourist and draughtsman, born in Sussex, whose interest in plants stemmed from painting flowers in the family garden. Studied with Simi in Florence, moved to America in 1968 settling in New York and extended her subjects to the tropical islands of the Caribbean, which she visited annually. Tcherepnine, sister of art dealer Jonathan Harris, was a board member of the Horticultural Society of New York and a member of the Society of Botanical Artists. Had a solo show at Christopher Wood Contemporary Art, 1994.

British Museum and Royal Horticultural Society, whose Gold Medal she twice won, hold examples.

T E A (Those Environmental Artists) 1987– Four artists made up this collective, which from 1987 set up what they termed "temporary institutions" to make art works. These were said to examine "the forms and formalities of historical, cultural, factual and conceptual commodities". The four artists were Jon Biddulph, Peter Hatton, Val Murray and Lynn Pilling (see separate entries). Among T E A's creations were Homeworks, an exploration of a semi-derelict house in Levenshulme, Manchester, 1987; In Transit, contents of suitcases revealed at bus stations, 1989; Anxiety and Escapism, part of Milennium Festival at Royal Festival Hall, 1994; and Making It, at Tate Gallery, Liverpool, 1995.

Roma TEARNE fl. from late 1970s– Artist producing still life and landscape tending towards abstraction, with a subtle colour sense. She attended London School of Printing, 1975–6. Commissions included London Underground, London Poster Company and Friends of the Earth. Tearne's work appeared in mixed exhibitions at RA Summer Exhibitions from 1989; in an Oxford Printmakers touring show from the same year; Oxford Gallery, 1990; Bankside Gallery, 1991; and in the Tenth Anniversary show at Cadogan Contemporary, 1996. Had a solo show at Peter Dingley Gallery, 1990, and at Bedford Hill Gallery, sponsored by Southern Arts, 1991.

Percy Morton TEASDALE 1870–1961 Painter in various media, wallpaper designer and teacher, described as "the perfect English gentleman". He studied at Herkomer's School at Bushey, Académie Julian in Paris, and in Leeds. Taught at Leeds and Harrogate Schools of Art and was noted for his views of Yorkshire. Showed at RA, RCamA of which he was a member, ROI, Goupil Gallery and RSA. Between the wars lived in Bushey, Hertfordshire, occupying one of the famous Meadow Studios, married late in life and died in Clapham, south London.

Susan TEBBY 1944– Sculptor, draughtsman and teacher who studied at Goldsmiths' College School of Art, 1962–6, then Chelsea School of Art, 1966–7. Taught visual research in School of Three-Dimensional Design at Leicester Polytechnic, 1967–70, then lectured full-time in sculpture there. Exhibitions and commissions included, from 1966, commission for maquette for a sculpture at John Dalton Faculty of Technology, Manchester Polytechnic; Arts Council commission and tour Serpentine Directions II; Themes & Variations, a touring show organised by Wolverhampton Art Gallery; and in 1973 Space from the Quadrangle at Woodlands Art Gallery. Arts Council holds her work.

John TEED 1911–1996 Artist in watercolour, pastel and oil, born in London, who studied at Westminster School of Art with Mervyn Peake and Mark Gertler. He exhibited at RA, PS and in local exhibitions in the Bradford-on-Avon district, Wiltshire, where he lived. National Gallery of New South Wales, Sydney, holds his work.

Gladys Rees TEESDALE 1898–1985 Illustrator, watercolour and oil painter. Born in London, she studied at Chelsea School of Art, 1915; she later taught there, part-time, 1917, full-time, 1920. Prior to the late 1960s she combined painting with illustrative work, then became a full-time landscape watercolour painter. Did poster work for London Under-ground. Sometimes signed work Gladys Rees, her maiden name. Exhibited widely, including RA, NEAC, UA, RI, SWA extensively being a member, and had one-man shows in Lincolnshire, mainly at Stamford Arts Centre. Her grand-daughter wrote a degree dissertation on the artist, who lived at Ryhall, near Stamford.

Simon TEGALA 1973– Conceptual artist, born and lived in London, who graduated from Goldsmiths' College, 1992–5. Group exhibitions included Simona Bordone Gallery in Milan, Electronic Undercurrents at National Gallery of Denmark in Copenhagen, and Men and Masculinities, Waterman's Art Centre, all 1996; Organ Fused, at Woodlands Art Gallery, and A Kind of English, Die Box, Berlin, both 1997. Had solo shows with Laure Genillard Gallery from 1995, with others in Italy, Norway, Poland and Germany. Supported by the Institute of International Visual Arts, in 1998 Tegala staged Anabiosis, in which he monitored his own heart rate and transmitted digital information to an electronic sign in the city of London.

Denis TEGETMEIER 1895–1987 Painter, printmaker and illustrator, born in London, in 1930 he married Petra, Eric Gill's second daughter. After being apprenticed to an advertising agency in 1912 and Army service in World War I, in 1919–22 attended Central School of Arts and Crafts and began to work occasionally for Gill. Was received into the Roman Catholic church and made periodic visits to Gill's Ditchling community, in 1928 moving to join Gill at High Wycombe after freelancing as a cartoonist, 1924–7. Lack of funds eventually made the Tegetmeiers leave High Wycombe, 1962, when they settled at Wardour, Wiltshire. Tegetmeier produced fine quality illustrations for publishers such as The Golden Cockerel Press, J M Dent & Sons and Sheed & Ward. Studio One Gallery made an extensive exhibition of his output, which had a marked religious emphasis, in 1977, Wolseley Fine Arts holding a show in 1996.

Andrew Claude TELEPNEFF 1927– Painter and teacher, born north London. After private education he attended St Martin's, Andover and Winchester Schools of Art and the Royal Academy Schools. Showed at RBA, NEAC, RWS and in the provinces. Lived for some time in Lymington, Hampshire, where he taught.

William TELFER 1907– Painter, printmaker and businessman, born in Falkirk, Stirlingshire, where he was a director of the colour-printing firm Thomas Paul Ltd. Was also president of Falkirk Art Club for about a decade from 1938 and a collector of early Scottish paintings. Exhibited RSA, RSW, SSA and in Canada. Lived latterly for some years at Eggington, Bedfordshire.

Victor TEMPEST 1913– Painter and teacher, born in Swaffham, Norfolk. He studied at Woolwich Polytechnic School of Art, 1927–32, with Herbert Buckley, then Royal College of Art, 1932–6, under William Rothenstein, gaining associate status in 1935. Showed at RA, NEAC, RBA and in Doncaster, Gateshead and Sunderland. Public collections in Leicester and Wolverhampton hold examples. Lived in Plumstead, southeast London, and later in Keston, Kent.

Malcolm TEMPLE 1949– Artist in various media who studied at Southend School of Art, sculpture at Wimbledon School of Art, then at Central School of Art. After working mainly in applied arts he concentrated on painting and sculpture, showing carved wooden objects in England & Co's Art in Boxes, 1990. Fetish, ritual, display and sexuality were features of these objects as of much of Temple's work, which was shown widely in Europe, Australia and Japan.

Nigel TEMPLE 1926– Artist in collage, photographer, lecturer and writer on architecture and garden history, born in Lowestoft, Suffolk. He studied at Farnham School of Art, then received his national diploma in design and art teacher's certificate at Sheffield College of Art. Temple also gained his master's degree in architecture at University of Bristol and doctorate at University of Keele. After serving in Royal Air Force Meteorology, 1944–8, then five years as a full-time art student Temple lectured at colleges of art and education, 1953–78, from 1978–9 having an artist-in-residence secondment at Bristol University. Temple was a council member of the Garden History Society and a member of the Society of Architectural Historians of Great Britain and contributed to learned journals. His books included *Farnham Inheritance*, 1956, and *John Nash and the Village Picturesque*, 1979. He was a member of RWA, also showing with the Cheltenham Group and on the continent. Had a series of solo exhibitions in the provinces including RWA and Cheltenham Art Gallery, both of which hold his work, Bristol and Reading Universities and New Ashgate Gallery, Farnham. Lived in Cheltenham, Gloucestershire.

Kathleen TEMPLE-BIRD fl. from c.1910–1962 Portrait and landscape painter in various media. Born at Ipswich as Kathleen Temple, she was educated in Ipswich and on the continent, then studied art at the Slade School of Fine Art, among her teachers being Henry Tonks and Alfred Rich. For two years just before World War I she taught at Havergal College, Toronto, where she was head of the art department. Exhibited widely including RA, RI, RBA, RP, NEAC and in the provinces, with several one-man shows. For many years honorary secretary of the Ridley Art Club. The Luxembourg, Paris, holds her portrait of Mahatma Gandhi. Lived in London.

Nancy TENNANT 1904–1969 Painter and campaigner, the sixteenth child of the Victorian entrepreneur Sir Charles Tennant. She grew up in a cultured atmosphere, then from 1920 studied at Académie Julian, Paris, where she met many advanced painters and writers, although she chose to paint in a traditional style. Between 1920–47 she showed at Goupil Gallery, RA and NEAC. In 1936 she married Captain (later Sir) Thomas Dugdale, who was Conservative Member of Parliament for Richmond, Yorkshire, for 30 years and held several government appointments, in 1959 being created 1st Baron Crathorne. Nancy Tennant developed a talent for public speaking and affairs and this new life with family matters took her away from painting, her chief interest. Among her later achievements was the restoration of the perfect Georgian theatre in Richmond; from 1963 she put on productions there. In 1974 her book about her family, *Tennant's Stalk*, was published. She was featured in Three Women Painters at Michael Parkin Fine Art Ltd, 1975.

Trevor TENNANT 1900–1980 Sculptor and teacher, born in London the son of the painter C Dudley Tennant. He studied at Goldsmiths' College School of Art and the Royal Academy Schools. He taught at several art schools and Dulwich College, including Hammersmith School of Art, 1946–53. Showed RA, NEAC, LG, IS and elsewhere and had solo shows at Beaux Arts, French, Leicester and Leger Galleries. Contemporary Art Society, Leicester and Stoke-on-Trent public galleries hold his work. He did a large amount of public sculpture, including Durham University library extension, Hatfield Technical College and Welwyn and Hatfield Hospital. Examples of Tennant's highly stylised sculptures, which often featured mothers and children, are in Arthur T Broadbent's *Sculpture Today in Great Britain 1940–1943*, and Eric Newton's *British Sculpture 1944–1946*. Dudley Trevor Tennant, who lived a bohemian life with his artist wife Dorothy Annan, much of it in London and including a period in a double-decker bus, died in Thornham, Norfolk.

John TENNENT 1926– Wildlife and landscape artist, born in Singapore, working in watercolour, oil, acrylic and prints. Tennent developed an interest in birds at his preparatory school, then at Bryanston School was taught by Elizabeth Muntz. He was a Bevin Boy coal miner, then read geography at Oxford University. Followed a career in the Colonial Service and spent 10 years in Kenya, followed by six in the Diplomatic Service, partly in Egypt, having a first solo exhibition at Atelier du Caire, Cairo, in 1967. Having in 1962 studied at St Martin's School of Art, Tennent in 1968 decided to become a full-time artist. He was a member of SWLA, a keen tree planter and conservationist. While an artist Tennent led study trip parties to Africa and wrote travel articles. Worked on calendars for National Trust, Royal Society for the Protection of Birds and Wildlife Conservation Society of Zambia, also providing illustrations for several books. As well as mixed shows including Medici Society and Wildfowl Trust, had series of solo exhibitions at Clarges Gallery and Dorset County Museum, Dorchester, both from 1972; Peter Potter Gallery, Haddington, from 1978, and elsewhere Lived at Wareham, Dorset.

Kechie TENNENT 1888–1968 Watercolourist and printmaker, born Emma Marie Tennent. Although she usually signed her work by her adopted name Kechie, several early watercolours were signed Kechie Pellew, as she married the artist Claughton Pellew. She studied at Slade School of Fine Art. Her work had a marked Japanese influence. For most of her life she lived in seclusion with her husband in Southrepps, in remote Norfolk. Had a show at Goupil Gallery in 1927 and Assembly House, Norwich, 1965. Work was also included in a show of her husband's wood engravings at Ashmolean Museum, Oxford, 1987; and in a touring centenary show of his work based at Hove Museum and Art Gallery, 1990.

Yoko TERAUCHI 1954– Sculptor working in a variety of materials whose work had a strong underlying sense of geometry. It sprang from her notion of unity, which she related to natural unity and to self-perpetuating natural cycles. Born in Tokyo, Japan, she studied at the Women's College of Fine Arts there, 1973–8, then St Martin's School of Art, 1979–81. She was included in the Serpentine Gallery/South Bank Centre's The Sculpture Show, 1983, exhibiting abstract works in torn paper. Was then based in London.

TERRY 1947– Artist and framer, born in Hertfordshire, where he continued to live in St Albans. His full name was Terence Edward Duncan. Studied at St Albans School of Art and Harpenden Art Centre. Was elected a member of the Guild of Master Craftsmen in 1980. Exhibited in the St Albans area and in London.

Edith Blanche TERRY fl. c.1895–1950 Painter, miniaturist and draughtsman in silver and gold point. She studied with Louise Jopling-Rowe and went on to exhibit at RI, NEAC, both SM and WIAC of which she was a member, Friday Club and in Poland. Lived in Bath, Somerset.

Anthony Peter TEWFIK 1955– Painter and miniaturist, initially educated in Cornwall, to which he returned to live in West Looe. He studied at Epsom School of Art, 1975–7 and showed NS and other mixed exhibitions.

Eva THATCHER 1971– Painter and draughtsman who studied at the School of Fine Art in Bulgaria and at Central St Martins College of Art & Design. In 1994 she was commissioned to create the Young Men's Christian Association 150th Anniversary international youth logo. While in Bulgaria she had solo shows at Dodrich, 1985, and Varna, 1986. Mixed shows included The Art Show, Alexandra Palace, and Royal Over-Seas League Open, both 1994.

Harry George THEAKER 1873–1954 Illustrator, designer, painter and teacher, born in Wolstanton, Staffordshire, son of George Theaker, headmaster of Burslem School of Art. Apprenticed to the Doulton pottery as a painter, Harry attended the Burslem School. Then went on to the Royal College of Art, where he won a gold medal for design and a travelling scholarship, which took him to Italy and further studies. For 36 years he was design master and then headmaster, 1931–8, of Regent Street Polytechnic. As a member he showed extensively at RBA, also at RA, RI and Walker Art Gallery in Liverpool. He was a painter of stained glass windows and a prolific illustrator of books for children, notably volumes in colour, titles including R H Barham's *The Ingoldsby Legends*, 1911, Charles Kingsley's *The Water Babies*, 1922, and *Grimm's Fairy Tales*, 1930. Theaker was a member of the Art Workers' Guild from 1921, being one of its committee, 1926–8, and lived in London. In 1996 Jeremy Wood Fine Art, Billingshurst, showed a selected of Theaker's pictures.

Franciszka THEMERSON 1907–1988 Painter, designer, publisher and illustrator, born in Warsaw, Poland, daughter of the painter Jakob Weinles. She attended Warsaw Academy of Fine Art with the highest distinction, 1924–30, lived in Paris, 1937–40, and from then on lived in London. She worked in several fields, collaborating with her husband, the writer Stefan Themerson, on experimental films, illustrated books for children which he wrote and in 1948 with him founded the Gaberbocchus Press, of which she was art director. Her theatre designs included productions of *Ubu Roi* and *Ubu Enchainé*, by Alfred Jarry, and of *Threepenny Opera*, by Berthold Brecht and Kurt Weill. Themerson took part in many mixed exhibitions and major solo shows included Gallery One, from 1957; Whitechapel Art Gallery, 1975; and a Polish tour, 1981–2. In 1993 the South Bank Centre and Royal National Theatre held exhibitions of her work. Arts Council and Victoria & Albert Museum hold examples. Themerson was a brilliant draughtsman with a whiplash line and a sharp sense of humour exposing human oddities. Several collections of her drawings were published as books, including *The Way it Walks*, 1954, and *The Drawings of Franciszka Themerson*, 1991.

Dom THEOBALD 1963– Painter and printmaker, born in Redhill, Surrey, whose work included large and small abstracts. Studied at Camberwell, Norwich and Slade Schools of Art. Awards included an Erasmus Travel Bursary, 1989; MacColl Arts Travel Award, 1990; and Artichoke Print Award, 1992. Group exhibitions included Kunsthochfachschule and Kulturministerium, Kiel, both 1990; Print Europe, Barbican Centre, 1991; RA Summer Exhibition, 1993; and Artists for Nuclear Disarmament at Swiss Cottage Library and Royal Over-Seas League Open, both 1994. Took part in Suffolk Open Studios, 1996. Theobald shared a studio with Anya King at Ditchingham, Bungay, their flat, the former billiard room of the writer H Rider Haggard's house, also being open periodically.

Hilda THEOBALD 1901–1985 Modeller, watercolourist and teacher, born in Soham, Cambridgeshire, who "in my childhood had no art teaching, for which I thank heaven!" Although a watercolourist initially, aged around 30 Miss Theobald attended Saturday morning classes at Norwich School of Art and turned to portraiture in clay, casting almost everything herself, in cold polyester copper, bronze or silver. Showed with Norfolk and Norwich Art Circle from the early 1940s and had several solo exhibitions in Norfolk in 1961 and 1973 in the Dereham area where she lived. As time was limited, she concentrated on heads, with the occasional statue or relief. Her Virgin of the Magnificent is in Great Snoring church; a font which she designed, for which she did the four silver panels, is in the Methodist church at Toftwood; a bronze bust was completed for a store in High Wycombe; portrait heads were acquired for collections in Texas and Kenya; and the education offices in Koblenz, Germany, had another.

Frank THEODORE 1892–1972 Painter and draughtsman, born in London. Studied at Central School of Arts and Crafts, where his teachers included W R Lethaby, and Regent Street Polytechnic. He led a chequered career, working as an ecclesiastical craftsman and in an architect's office. Saw Army and Navy service in two World Wars, achieving high commissioned rank in the Royal Naval Reserve. Travelled extensively. National Maritime Museum, Greenwich, and Victoria & Albert Museum hold his work. Finally lived in Seaford, Sussex.

Amanda THESIGER 1964– Painter of lyrical abstract forms, using a muted palette, born in Surrey, distantly related to the traveller and writer Wilfred Thesiger and the actor Ernest Thesiger. She gained an honours degree in fine art, painting, at Maidstone College of Art, 1983–6, with a postgraduate diploma at the Royal Academy Schools in painting, 1986–9. In 1987 she won the Winsor and Newton Prize, in 1988 the Turner Gold Medal for Landscape and the Creswick Prize for Drawing. Studied painting at the British School at Rome, 1989–90, with an Abbey Major Scholarship. Group shows included Three English Artists, Universita di Pavia, Italy, 1991; Contemporaries I, The Eagle Gallery, 1993; Oriel Mostyn Open, Llandudno, 1995; and Ace! Arts Council Collection new purchases tour, 1996–7. Had a solo show at Aspex Gallery, Portsmouth, 1994; Plymouth Arts Centre, Devon, 1995; with a series at Francis Graham-Dixon from 1995.

Ernest THESIGER 1879–1961 Actor who initially trained to be a painter. Born and lived in London, son of the Hon. Edward Thesiger, he was educated at Marlborough College, then studied art at the Slade School of Fine Art under Henry Tonks and Walter Westley Russell. Made his first appearance on the stage in 1909 under George Alexander. Thesiger, a cadaverous, witty, stylish actor, made a considerable reputation on the stage and in films, working almost until he died. His roles ranged from modern farce through Shaw and Shakespeare. He exhibited as a painter at the RA, Goupil Gallery, Fine Art Society and in the provinces and the Victoria & Albert Museum holds his work. His watercolours can be brilliant, in the manner of John Singer Sargent. He wrote memoirs, *Practically True*, and *Adventures in Embroidery*.

Ronald THEXTON 1916– Oral surgeon by profession who painted in his spare time and retirement. He studied at Birmingham and Edinburgh Universities, art tuition coming from Allan Gwynne-Jones, the Australian Hayward Veal and James Cowie. Showed at RA, SSA, Belgrave Gallery, RWA and elsewhere. Lived latterly at Barnsley, Cirencester, Gloucestershire.

Margaret THEYRE 1897–1977 Painter and potter, born in Northamptonshire, her father a vicar. She studied with Frank Spenlove-Spenlove at his Yellow Door School of Art and in Paris. Theyre spent time there with her sister, the concert pianist Violette Clarence, and in the Pyrenees, where she painted. When bombed out of her studio in Chelsea in World War II, Miss Theyre moved to her weekend cottage in Southwater, Sussex, which became her home. After the war she worked mainly as a potter, having been a prolific painter of landscape and figures, exhibiting at RSA, ROI, RA, RBA, Cooling Galleries, London Salon and elsewhere. Lived finally in a nursing home in Dorking, Surrey, and was cremated at the Surrey and Sussex Crematorium.

Ann THISTLETHWAITE 1944– Landscape painter and draughtsman and teacher, born in Birmingham. She studied with Gilbert Mason at Birmingham College of Art & Design, 1961–6, then taught art and design from 1966–9. Showed with RSMA, PS, ROI, NEAC, RBA, in the provinces and abroad. Had several dozen solo exhibitions. Thistlethwaite won first prize at the Royal Over-Seas League Commonwealth Art Exhibition in 1969, was joint winner of the same award in 1970 and the special prize in 1972. She was a keen conservationist. Lived in Droitwich, Worcestershire.

Morwenna THISTLETHWAITE 1912– Painter of still life, landscapes and figures who studied at Leamington Spa School of Art and Birmingham College of Arts and Crafts, where she was a prizewinner for painting. In 1960s returned to St Ives, Cornwall, where her mother was born and was included in Artists from Cornwall at RWA in 1992. Also showed frequently at RA and had solo shows at New Grafton Gallery and at galleries in Ontario and Toronto, Canada.

THOMAS 1924– Painter in oil, full name Thomas Bartlett, who was born in Gateshead, County Durham. Exhibited at Laing Art Gallery and Museum, Newcastle upon Tyne, and Shipley Art Gallery in Gateshead. Lived at Framwellgate Moor, County Durham.

Annie Margaret THOMAS 1897–1979 Painter, draughtsman and teacher, born in Lympstone, Devon. She studied at Bristol Municipal School of Art under Reginald Bush and obtained the Royal Drawing Society Teacher/Artist's certificate. Went on to teach at The Convent School, Exmouth, and at further education classes. Was an illustrator for *The Bookman* magazine and for publishers, especially of children's books. Was a founder-member of the Exmouth Art Society, serving as its secretary and president. Showed RWA, PS, SWA, Paris Salon and Association of Devon Artists and with other local societies. Lived in Exmouth, Devon.

Bert THOMAS 1883–1966 Humorous illustrator and poster artist, born in Newport, Monmouthshire, son of the sculptor Job Thomas. Educated in Swansea, he was apprenticed after school to a metal engraver and from about 1900 began contributing to periodicals. Joined the staff of *London Opinion* just before World War

I, in which he served in Artists' Rifles. His "Arf a mo', Kaiser!" drawing, which raised £250,000 for a cigarettes for troops fund, made Thomas nationally famous. Member of PS and also showed as a young man with London Salon. Thomas drew more than a thousand cartoons for *Punch*, also working for *Radio Times* and *The Bystander*. Many books of his cartoons were published during the two decades from 1928 and his illustrations for others volumes included W W Jacobs' *Sea Whispers*, 1928, to which his simple, direct style was admirably suited. Lived in Pinner, Middlesex, for many years where he was known as a horsily-dressed character who rode with the Pinner Drag Hounds. Finally lived in Bayswater, London.

Brian THOMAS 1912–1989 Muralist, stained glass designer and writer, born in Barnstaple, Devon. After Bradfield College he attended Byam Shaw School of Painting and Drawing, 1928–34. He was Rome Scholar in Mural Painting, 1934–7. *Vision and Technique in European Painting*, 1952, and the *Master Glass Painters' Directory*, 1972, were among his books. Thomas' own work was held by St Paul's Cathedral, Westminster Abbey, Tower of London, Winchester Cathedral and St George's Chapel, Windsor. He was master of the Art Workers' Guild in 1952 and of the Glaziers' Company in 1976. Lived at Charminster, Bournemouth, Dorset, in a residential care home.

Cecil THOMAS 1885–1976 Sculptor, medallist and occasional painter, born and lived in London. He studied at the Slade School of Fine Art, Heatherley's School and the Central School of Arts and Crafts. Richard Garbe, Edwin Roscoe Mullins and Henry Wilson were among his teachers. Showed at RA, RMS and in the provinces, at the Paris Salon and in America and contributed work to several public collections. Was master of the Art Workers' Guild in 1946 and was awarded a gold medal by the RBS in 1973.

Ceri THOMAS 1958– Painter, draughtsman and printmaker, born in London, son of the sculptor Robert Thomas and the artist Meg/Mary Gardiner. Thomas aimed to produce works that combined tradition and innovation, "a metaphysical realism, notably in figure and still life pieces". He gained a degree at University College in art history and Italian, 1978–82, at the same time attending life classes at Slade School of Fine Art under Lawrence Gowing. This was followed by a master's degree in visual art at University College Wales, Aberystwyth, 1983–7. Significant periods were spent in Italy. For his academic year abroad in 1980–1 Thomas chose Florence where he attended the arts faculty of the University, also frequenting the Accademia and the studios of Pietro Annigoni and his former pupils. In the summer of 1985, having been awarded a scholarship by the Italian Institute, he again went to Florence to collect first-hand material for his post-graduate thesis on Annigoni and post-war Britain. Awarded a Council of Europe Higher Education (Painting) Scholarship for 1989–90, he based himself in Florence, dividing his time between the Accademia and the studio of Luigi Falai. Thomas also taught history of art, art and Italian. He exhibited from 1983, group shows including Euro-Wales '92 Group, of which he was a founder member, at Third Wave Gallery, Cardiff, 1993. He shared a show, Thomas Twice, with his father at Rhondda Heritage Park, Trehafod, which holds his work, in 1991. Later solo shows included Compositions at St David's Hall, Cardiff, 1991, and Golden Prospects, Cardiff Bay Norwegian Church, 1992. Lived in Barry, Glamorgan.

Glynn THOMAS 1946– Printmaker and teacher, born in Cambridge, where he studied at the School of Art, 1962–7, specialising in illustration and printmaking. He taught printmaking at Ipswich School of Art, 1967–79. Thomas was elected an associate member of RE, 1976, in 1983 his picture Honfleur winning a best print prize. His work was commissioned by RE, Christie's Contemporary Art and the Riding for the Disabled Association. Exhibitions included The Craftsman, Colchester, 1977; The Minories in Colchester and RA Summer Exhibition, both 1978; and The John Russell Gallery, Ipswich, from 1984.

Gwilym THOMAS 1914–1995 Ceramist, painter, draughtsman, printmaker and teacher, born in Swansea, south Wales, who gained a scholarship to its School of Art, 1931, studying at the Royal College of Art, 1935–8, where he was attracted by the classes of the potter William Staite Murray, who had a lasting influence on his work. He taught at boys' clubs, at Putney, Bromley and Maidstone Schools of Art, and became full-time head of ceramics at Hammersmith College of Art, 1973–5, where he had taught part-time since 1951. He died at Orpington, Kent, having moved there in 1956 and set up a pottery studio with a gas kiln which catered for reduced firings. Had a exhibition at the Commonwealth Institute, 1970, with a retrospective memorial show at Glynn Vivian Art Gallery, Swansea, 1997.

Gwyther THOMAS 1900– Painter and teacher, born in Pembroke Dock, Pembrokeshire. Around World War I Thomas was apprenticed locally to a shipbuilder, but left to train as a teacher in Chester. For over a quarter of a century he taught, ending up as a headmaster in Birmingham, but in 1949 resigned to pursue farming in Haverfordwest. In the mid-1960s he began seriously to paint and show his work. He appeared at Royal National Eisteddfod and in the WAC 1972 exhibition An Alternative Tradition.

Keith THOMAS 1946– Abstract painter, born in Birmingham, where he studied at the College of Art, 1965–8, then at Chelsea School of Art, 1968–9. In 1974 settled in London. Was included in British Painting '74, 1974, organized by Arts Council, which holds several abstracts bought from the artist.

Leslie Gurwin THOMAS 1914–1975 Painter and teacher, husband of the painter Norma Thomas, born in Fochriw, near Merthyr Tydfil, south Wales. He studied art and architecture at Cardiff School of Art, Welsh School of Architecture, University College of Cardiff, Goldsmiths' College School of Art and at Hornsey. After World War II service he continued teaching, being finally head of the art department at Christ's College, in London. He held over a dozen one-man shows in England and Wales, having a retrospective at Blaenporth Gallery, his own studio and gallery, in 1976. Completed heraldic design and paintings in a number of public buildings and galleries, as well as illumination and works for local authorities in Britain and abroad.

Margaret THOMAS 1916– Painter, born in London, who was privately educated, then attended Sidcup School of Art, under Barry Craig. From 1936–8 she was at Slade School of Fine Art, but then left for Royal Academy Schools, 1938–9, studying with Thomas Monnington and Ernest Jackson. Was a member of NEAC, RWA, and RBA, painting landscapes and still lifes in the mainstrean English tradition, subtle and understated. She was a regular exhibitor at RA and RSA and in 1981 was Hunting Group Award winner for oil painting of the year. Solo shows included Leicester Galleries; Minories, Colchester; Octagon Gallery, Belfast; Sally Hunter Fine Art; and Aitken Dott and Scottish Gallery, Edinburgh, having a major retrospective in 1982. Painted works in the collections of Chantrey Bequest, Arts Council, Ministry of Works and a number of provincial galleries, including Hull, Wakefield, Paisley and Carlisle. For many years worked in London, then moved to Bungay, Suffolk, in 1984, having had a second studio in Edinburgh from 1956.

Marjorie Lilian THOMAS 1897– Painter, illustrator and miniaturist, born in Birmingham. Studied at the School of Art there and at Byam Shaw School of Art. Exhibited RA, RBSA and with Oxford Art Society, of which she was a member. Lived in Oxford and in London.

Norma Marion THOMAS 1922– Painter, mainly in oil, wife of the artist Leslie Gurwin Thomas, born in Hawarden, Clwyd. She studied at Bangor Normal College, Liverpool School of Art, Hornsey College of Art and for short periods at Goldsmiths' College School of Art. Taught for some time, including Wirral Grammar School. Her work was mainly atmospheric landscapes, with some abstracts. Ran own studio gallery at Blaenporth, Cardigan, Dyfed, so declined other exhibiting venues.

Peter THOMAS 1927– Painter, draughtsman and businessman, born in Sydenham, southeast London, where he continued to live. Studied at Camberwell School of Arts and Crafts, 1944–50, where his teachers included Victor Pasmore and Claude Rogers; Goldsmiths' College School of Art in 1950–1, under Paul Drury. Showed RA, LG and elsewhere.

Robert THOMAS 1926– Sculptor in bronze and stone, born in Treorchy, Glamorgan, married to the textile designer Mary Gardiner. Thomas studied sculpture at Cardiff College of Art, 1947–9, having spent the war in the mines; then studied with Frank Dobson at Royal College of Art, 1949–52. As a sculptor he was in a tradition going back to the nineteenth century, truth to the appearance of the model and immaculate craftsmanship. Mostly he was known for his portraits, often larger than life-size, but he also produced images depicting family life. Among his subjects were Aneurin Bevan the politician, Sir Geraint Evans the singer and Lord Gordon Parry. His work can be seen in Birmingham city centre, Blackburn town centre and in London and Cardiff. He won the Sir Otto Beit Medal of the RBS in 1963 and its silver medal three years later. He was president of SPS, 1972–7, and was RBS vice-president, 1979–84. Thomas showed frequently in London and his work was included in several outdoor exhibitions. In 1991 he shared a show, Thomas Twice, with his son, the painter Ceri Thomas, at Rhondda Heritage Park, Trehafod. Lived in Barry, Glamorgan.

Simon THOMAS 1960– Sculptor and lecturer, born in Portsmouth. He attended Plymouth College of Art and Design, 1978–9, Ravensbourne College of Art and Design, 1979–82, then Royal College of Art, 1985–8. Thomas worked in a variety of materials, often on a small scale, with a carver's response to stone, wood and plaster. He had a special interest in the forms of seed and fruit. Some of Thomas' work was placed in a landscape setting, such as the 1985 commission from Common Ground for the New Milestones project at Durdle Door, Dorset. Thomas was assistant to John Maine on the Arena project, at South Bank, 1983–4, in 1984 also being assistant to Phillip King on the Docklands Sculpture Project at Canary Wharf. Other activities included a lecture tour of Finnish Lapland, in 1989, the year after he gained the Madame Tussaud Award for figurative art. Began showing at Toute Quarry, Portland Sculpture Park, and Quarries at Camden Arts Centre in 1983. Later exhibitions included one-man show at Albemarle Gallery, 1989.

Trevor THOMAS 1907–1993 Artist, curator, editor and teacher, born in Ynysddu, south Wales. He took an honours degree in human geography and anthropology at Aberystwyth, at 24 becoming keeper of Liverpool Museums, where his novel display techniques attracted praise. Thomas was a versatile man whose own painting owed much to American Abstract Expressionists; he acted and sang; and collaborated with David Webster, later director of the Royal Opera House, Covent Garden, on T S Eliot's *Murder in the Cathedral*. Among his official posts was directorship of Leicester Museum and Art Gallery, 1940–6; surveyor, regional guide to works of art, Arts Council, 1946–8; director, Crafts Centre of Great Britain, 1947–8; programme specialist for education through the arts, Unesco, 1949–56; professor of art, State University of New York College for Teachers, Buffalo, 1957–8; professor of art history at Buffalo University, 1959–60; and art editor for Gordon Fraser Gallery, 1960–72. Died in Bedford.

Walter THOMAS 1894–1971 Landscape and marine painter in oil and watercolour, illustrator and poster artist. Born in Liverpool, he attended its College of Art, 1912–13, followed by two years studying art in London. He had a varied career, including museum curator, ship interior and exhibition designer. Exhibited RI, RCamA and Walker Art Gallery, Liverpool. Shipping firms commissioned pictures by Thomas for their vessels' public rooms. Lived at Kirk Michael, Isle of Man.

Winifred THOMAS 1910– Painter, designer and teacher born at Pengam, near Bargoed, south Wales. She attended Swansea School of Art, 1929–32, where her teachers included William Grant Murray; Newport School of Art, 1932–5, with William Dudley; and with Stanhope Forbes at his school in Newlyn, Cornwall. She went on to hold a number of teaching posts, latterly lecturing at Carmarthen School of Art. Signing her work W T in monogram style, she showed at SWG, RBA and elsewhere in Wales. Lived in Carmarthen.

Alfred Oscar THOMPSETT 1931– Painter in oil, and teacher, born in Crawley, Sussex, who attended West Sussex College of Art, Worthing, and Brighton College of Art, notable teachers including Alfred Heyworth, Guy Roddon, Bevil Roberts and Ronald Horton. After teaching in schools and lecturing for Southampton Extra-Mural Department/Workers' Educational Association, and part time-teaching at West Sussex College and Brighton Polytechnic, Oscar Thompsett became a full-time lecturer at the Polytechnic in painting, drawing and history of art. Family obligations prevented him from painting as much as he originally intended. Showed at the Polytechnic, at Worthing Art Gallery and elsewhere in Sussex. Held a joint exhibition with Norma Weller at Radio Brighton, another with her, Norman Clarke and David Hopkins at the Polytechnic. Work included portraits and a series of didactic oils on overpopulation, racialism and pollution. Lived in Patcham, Brighton, Sussex.

Brian THOMPSON 1950– Sculptor, draughtsman and teacher, born in Morley, Yorkshire. He studied at Newcastle University. After varied teaching experience he taught at Sunderland Polytechnic. Thompson's sculpture sought to reflect the nature and feelings inherent in various landscapes rather than represent their exact appearance. He showed in groups at Northern Young Contemporaries, Whitworth Art Gallery, Manchester; XI Biennale de Paris, Museum of Modern Art, Paris, and Third Eye Centre, Glasgow, 1980–1; Works on Paper, University of Washington, Seattle, 1983; Gray Art Gallery, Hartlepool, 1988; and DLI Museum & Arts Centre, the Newcastle Group show the Northern Lights, 1990. His solo shows included Norwich School of Art, where he was John Brinkley Fellow in Sculpture, 1977; Spectro Gallery, Newcastle, 1979; and Sunderland Arts Centre, 1983. Northern Arts and Newcastle University hold his work. Lived near Richmond, Yorkshire.

Charles James THOMPSON 1931– Aviation artist in oil, born in Poona, India, educated at La Martiniere College, Lucknow. Thompson had no formal art training, taking up oils in 1979. Trained as a draughtsman with Ford Motor Company – did National Service in Royal Air Force, 1955–6 – staying with Ford for 37 years, styling cars in England, Germany and America, taking early retirement in 1986. Thompson was a full member and chairman of the Guild of Aviation Artists; a founder-member of the Guild of Motoring Artists; an artist fellow of the American Society of Aviation Artists; and a master artist of America's Experimental Aircraft Association. Among many awards were the Wilkinson Sword Poignard, 1983, and Jeffrey Quill Memorial prize, 1997. Also exhibited with ROI and RSMA. Thompson was a lifelong aviation enthusiast, building and flying many models. He was interested in "the look of aircraft, I like to capture the effect of light on surfaces and reflections." Southend Council, Ford Motor and many other collections held examples. Solo shows included Beecroft Art Gallery, Westcliff-on-Sea, 1998. Lived in Rayleigh, Essex.

Constance Dutton THOMPSON 1882– Painter, printmaker, stained glass artist, draughtsman and teacher, born in St Helens, Lancashire. She studied at the Art School there, under John Skeaping, then at Liverpool School of Art. Was a member of Liver Sketching Club, Liverpool Academy, RCamA (discontinuing her subscription in 1950), and the local Art Association in Heswall, Cheshire, where she finally lived, after being some years at Huyton, near Liverpool. Also showed at RA, UA, Walker Art Gallery in Liverpool, RBA and elsewhere. Harris Museum and Art Gallery, Preston, and Williamson Art Gallery and Museum, Birkenhead, hold her work. This was sometimes signed with a monogram.

David THOMPSON 1939– Sculptor and teacher who studied at Carlisle College of Art, 1956–60, then Slade School of Fine Art, 1960–3, for sculpture. Thompson won the Boise Scholarship in 1964, a Sainsbury Scholarship in 1965 and a North Eastern Arts Association Purchase Prize in 1966. Thompson participated in the International Sculpture Symposiums in St Margarethen in 1964 and Portoroz, Yugoslavia, 1969. He was a visiting tutor in sculpture at Canterbury College of Art, 1965, becoming a full-time tutor and senior lecturer in sculpture at Canterbury, 1970–89. In 1972 he was assistant professor at Kokoschka Summer School in Salzburg. His many group appearances included New Metropole Arts Centre, Folkestone; Quatrain Gallery, Los Angeles; Agnew; RA; East Kent School; and Sculpture at Canterbury, 1992. He lived in Canterbury, Kent.

Elaine THOMPSON 1969– Artist and teacher producing a wide range of work who graduated in painting and drawing from Edinburgh College of Art, 1992, gaining her master's degree in European fine art from Windsor School of Art, 1993. In 1991 Thompson received the Ulster Television Award for Young Artists. Visited L'École des Beaux-Arts in Montpelier through the Erasmus Exchange Programme, also working in France at restoration. Lived in Belfast, Northern Ireland, where she was included in Works on Paper and Beyond the Partitions, organised in 1994 by Queen Street Studios, with which she was associated.

Ernest Heber THOMPSON: *see* **Heber THOMPSON**

Estelle THOMPSON 1960– Painter and teacher who studied at Sheffield City Polytechnic to get her bachelor's degree, 1979–82, then Royal College of Art, gaining her master's degree in painting, 1983–6. She won a number of awards, including the Royal Overseas League Travel Award, 1988, and Prudential Awards for the Arts 1990/Arts Council Special Award. She went on to teach part-time at Winchester School of Art, Christie's Fine Art Course, Ruskin School at Oxford and Royal College of Art. Her mixed show appearances included Anderson O'Day Gallery, 1990, and Bruton Street Gallery, 1992. Showed at Pomeroy Purdy Gallery from 1989 as a solo artist and Eastbourne Clark Gallery Florida from same year, in 1992 having a show at Castlefield Art Gallery, Manchester, in 1994 at Towner Art Gallery, Eastbourne. Thompson created iridescent abstractions with layers of size, gesso and glazes of paint. Her work is held by Arts Council, British Council and Contemporary Art Society. Lived in London.

Heber THOMPSON 1891–1971 Painter, draughtsman, printmaker and teacher, born in New Zealand at Dunedin, where he attended the School of Art under A H O'Keeffe, was a commercial artist and a cartoonist for the *Daily Times*. Served with the New Zealand Army in World War I, was badly wounded at Messines and recovered in England. Battle scenes completed alongside George E Butler are in the New Zealand National Archives. An Army scholarship of 1919 enabled Thompson to study at the Slade School of Fine Art with Henry Tonks and Philip Wilson Steer; studying etching with Frank Short at the Royal College of Art, he won first prize; and he also attended the Central School of Arts and Crafts. He was an engraving finalist, Prix de Rome, 1923 (he was a member of its faculty, 1941–66). Heber Thompson travelled widely in Europe and exhibited prolifically abroad, RA, RE, RP, RSA and elsewhere. In 1939 he was elected a full member of RE, 15 years after being made an associate. During World War II Thompson was an air raid warden during the Blitz, and in 1945 he was commissioned to portray members of the police force and civil defence who had won bravery awards. Taught part-time until the 1950s, including Harrow, Willesden, Highgate and Hornsey Schols of Art. A retrospective exhibition was held at Dunedin Art Gallery in 1970. British Museum, Victoria & Albert Museum and Walker Art Gallery, Liverpool, hold examples. Lived at Long Crendon, Buckinghamshire.

Jenny THOMPSON 1940– Painter and draughtsman. She studied at Brighton Polytechnic, 1976–9, completing a fine arts degree. Became a full-time painter, exhibiting in mixed shows at Shaw Theatre, Spitalfields Workspace and elsewhere. In 1991 had solo exhibition with Sue Rankin Gallery. Thompson's early was abstract, but she later concentrated on the human figure.

John THOMPSON 1954– Sculptor in a variety of materials, born in Belfast, Northern Ireland, who studied at Maidstone College of Art, 1973–6. Shows included Matter of Degrees, South East Arts Association tour, 1976; Whitechapel Open Exhibition, 1977; 55 Wapping Artists, 1979; Wapping Artists Open Studios from 1980; and LG, 1981. Lived in London.

Jon THOMPSON 1936– Conceptualist artist and teacher, who attended St Martin's School of Art, 1953–7, and Royal Academy Schools, 1957–60, then was at British School at Rome, 1960–2. Thompson taught at Lancaster College of Art, 1962–5; Leicester College of Art & Design, 1965–8; St Martin's School of Art, 1965–70; and Goldsmiths' College, 1970–92, finally as head of department of fine art and reader in the school of humanities. Early in the 1990s Thompson moved to Antwerp, Belgium, from 1992 being head of postgraduate studies in fine art at Jan van Eyck Akademie, Maastricht, Netherlands. At Goldsmiths', he was closely associated with the Freeze generation of artists, including Damien Hirst. Thompson organised and chaired conferences at Maastricht from 1995, topics including the architecture and ideology of the museum; theory of the image; and crisis in criticism. Exhibitions curated/part-curated included The British Art Show, Birmingham and tour, 1984; Falls the Shadow, Hayward Gallery, 1986; and Gravity and Grace, same venue, 1993. Thompson cited Marcel Duchamp as an influence. Believing that "most of the works I have done have been waste products," Thompson destroyed much. Latterly he overcame what he considered a Calvinistic resistance to using the camera. Believing that "theory has invaded all our conceptions of the world," he chose himself as a principal subject, works of homoerotic power "recognising the sensuality of the body, but also denying it." First showed solo at Rowan Gallery, 1960, later exhibitions including a series at Anthony Reynolds Gallery.

Liam THOMPSON 1956– Painter who studied at Newcastle upon Tyne College of Art, 1974–5, Chelsea School of Art, 1975–8, and City and Guilds of London Art School, 1978–9. He showed in many group exhibitions, including RA from 1983, RWS from 1985 and in The Broad Horizon, at Agnew, 1990. From 1980 he had a series of solo shows, including Belfast, Canterbury and Edinburgh. Lived in Selling, Kent.

Margaret Douglas THOMPSON 1910–1994 Stained glass artist, born in Birmingham, where she studied at the School of Art. In later life lived in Lewes, Sussex, where she mainly painted subjects involving the peace and anti-nuclear movements.

Mary Elizabeth THOMPSON 1896–1981 Draughtsman of the Welsh slate and granite quarries, born in Braunton, Devon. A weak baby, she learned to overcome severe disabilities and developed enough mentally and physically – although a dwarf with severe curvature of the spine – to attend a Quaker boarding school in Darlington. Showing artistic talent there, she then studied at St Albans School of Art, 1913–14; in St Ives with Alfred Hartley; then at the Brussels Academy, Belgium, 1919–22. She returned to settle in north Wales, moving eventually to Bethesda in 1937, painting landscapes. Dislodged by the Army, she began drawing the Penrhyn slate quarry. Drawings of quarrying then became her life's focus, and she learned to speak Welsh to talk with the men to ensure her pictures were accurate. In 1949 she was given a show in the Geological Museum, London, and in 1981 a Welsh Arts Council touring show was accompanied by a booklet: *An Artist in the Quarries*. In 1954 Mary Thompson joined her family in Tunbridge Wells, Kent, and as well as drawing the countryside there she also made trips to Ireland and northern Scotland. Cardiff's National Museum of Wales holds her work.

Phyllis THOMPSON 1927– Painter, modeller and teacher, born in Peshawar, India. Was educated in Australia then studied at the Slade School of Fine Art, 1945–8, under Randolph Schwabe. Showed at RA and Walker Art Gallery, Liverpool. Lived for some time in Chorleywood, Hertfordshire.

Robert THOMPSON 1915–1956 Painter, draughtsman and teacher, son of an iron worker, who was taught by James Cowie at Bellshill Academy, Lanarkshire, 1930–3. Thompson's tight, meticulous style reflected the influence of Cowie, who gave him extra tuition and who persuaded his parents to let him attend Glasgow School of Art and Edinburgh College of Art, where he gained the Andrew Grant Travelling Scholarship. During World War II Thompson spent five years in the Royal Air Force as a radio operator and art tutor. He returned to Glasgow and taught there, including Rutherglen Academy. In 1953, Thompson became head art teacher at Castle Douglas High School and moved to Crossmichael, Kirkcudbrightshire, but soon contracted fatal cancer. Cyril Gerber Fine Art, Glasgow, held an exhibition in 1997, shortly after one at Bellshill Academy.

Tom THOMPSON 1923– Painter, muralist and teacher, born in Narrabri, New South Wales, Australia, who spent his early life in the state's New England district. Studied at National Art School, Sydney, where he returned to teach. In England he was notable as the painter of the Australia House murals, initiated on the advice of the Art Advisory Board of the Commonwealth Government. Thompson painted two panels in Australia (the ones representing the steel industry and mining) and brought them to London, where he began work on the large central panel representing agriculture. He finished the two smaller panels, depicting the arts and science, in Australia. Strong reds and blues are a feature of the murals, commenced in 1959.

Colin THOMS 1912–1997 Painter and teacher, born in Edinburgh. He was early interested in painting through his friendship with the Peploe family, and from 1929–33 studied at Edinburgh College of Art with S J Peploe, William Gillies and D M Sutherland. From 1934–6 more studies followed at Slade School of Fine Art, at several schools in Paris including Atelier Colarossi, then in Italy, Belgium and Germany; he had gained a travelling scholarship from Edinburgh College of Art and an Andrew Grant Fellowship. Began part-time teaching at Loretto School, Musselburgh in 1937, to which he returned, after war service, in 1946, full-time. From 1951–77 he taught at Gray's School of Art, in Aberdeen, then started painting full-time. Thoms was a prominent member of SSA, being its president in 1949; exhibited regularly with RSA from 1928. Thoms' great breakthrough stemmed from his seeing the 1963 Miró retrospective at the Tate Gallery, and his first one-man show at Scottish Gallery, Edinburgh, in 1966 was called "the dreamworld of re-born Thoms". From then on his work strove to emulate the colour and wit of Miró and Klee. Thoms had a retrospective at Artspace Galleries, Aberdeen, in 1984. Later shows included Aberdeen University in 1988 and England & Co, 1989 and 1992. Scottish Arts Council and Aberdeen and Kirkcaldy Art Galleries hold his work. Lived finally in Edinburgh after many years in Aberdeen.

Adam Bruce THOMSON 1885–1976 Painter, printmaker and teacher, born in Edinburgh, where he continued to live. Was for a time on Edinburgh College of Art staff, where he had trained, where he was a notable teacher of etching. Exhibited extensively at RSA and SSA, being president of both for a time; was also a member of RSW and showed at Walker Art Gallery, Liverpool, and Royal Glasgow Institute of the Fine Arts. Member of Scottish Arts Club. Aberdeen Art Gallery holds his work.

Alexander THOMSON 1942– Painter inclined to abstraction, he studied at Glasgow School of Art, 1960–4, Slade School of Fine Art, 1966–8, then gained a John Brinkley Fellowship, Norwich, 1970–1. Among his shows were McLellan Galleries, Glasgow, 1964; John Moores Liverpool Exhibition, 1965; LG, 1970; British Painting, Iceland, 1978; and in 1981 Painters + Sculptors from the Greenwich Studios at Woodlands Art Gallery. Municipal Gallery, Reykjavik, Iceland, and Arts Council hold his work.

Alexander P THOMSON fl. from c.1905–1962 Landscape painter, especially in watercolour, working in a traditional style. Lived in Glasgow but worked a lot in the Scottish highlands. Exhibited widely, notably at RSA, RSW, Royal Glasgow Institute of the Fine Arts and Walker Art Gallery, Liverpool.

Alfred Reginald THOMSON 1894–1979 Portrait, figure and decorative artist, born in Bangalore India. After attending the Royal School for the Deaf and Dumb, Margate, A R Thomson studied at the London Art School, Kensington, then began exhibiting at the RA from 1920. He was elected RA in 1945, after several years as an official war artist with the Royal Air Force. Thomson was a mainstream portrait painter of sensitivity, whose works were a feature of RA and RP shows for many years. He completed murals for the Science Museum, London, and Birmingham Dental Hospital and painted many royal and official portraits. The Tate Gallery and provincial galleries hold his work. Lived in London.

Diana THOMSON 1939– Sculptor in clay, plaster, wood for bronze and ceramic, born in Manchester. She studied at Kingston Polytechnic sculpture department, 1976–9, teachers including Charles Lewis, Annesley Tittensor and John Robson. Thomson said that "the human figure is the best way that I can express myself in my sculpture." Although "this caused quite a lot of debate at art college I kept to my own themes and expressions during training, and beyond in my public commissions." Diana Thomson was elected a fellow of RBS in 1990. She exhibited at Commonwealth Institute, RA, University of Swansea, Alwin Gallery, RWA, New College in Oxford and elsewhere. Commissions included bronze plaque, Woking Market, Network House, Woking, 1981; The Hurdler, bronze life-size, Harmondsworth, West Drayton, 1984; The Swanmaster, seven-foot figure at Staines, 1983; The

Bargemaster, seven-foot bronze at Data-General Tower, Brentford, 1990; and Homage to D H Lawrence, Nottingham University, 1994. Lived in Chobham, Surrey.

Douglas THOMSON 1955– Painter, restorer and administrator, born in Greenock, Renfrewshire. He studied at Glasgow School of Art and at Patrick Allan-Fraser School of Art, Hospitalfield, Arbroath. During the period 1979–81 Thomson was at Hospitalfield as restorer and assistant warden. A strong, figurative painter, Thomson showed at SSA, Glasgow Group, in art fairs in Bath, London and Los Angeles and widely in Germany, having spent a great part of 1989 there. Having participated in Compass Gallery, Glasgow, New Generation show after graduating, Thomson had his first solo exhibition there in 1982, his second occurring in 1987, with others at Glasgow Print Studio.

John Murray THOMSON 1885–1974 Painter of animals and birds who studied at the RSA Schools, gained the Carnegie Travelling Scholarship and went for further studies in Paris. His knowledge of his subjects stemmed from a love of the Scottish countryside, trout and salmon fishing. Was a president of SSA, was also a member of RSA and RSW and showed extensively at Royal Glasgow Institute of the Fine Arts, Walker Art Gallery in Liverpool and Arlington Gallery. With his wife Ellen Frew he wrote and illustrated *Animals We Know*. Polar Bears and Ploughing in Central France were among his main works. Lived in Edinburgh.

Louis THOMSON 1883–1962 Painter, printmaker and draughtsman, she was born in Kandy, Ceylon, as Louise Emily Thomson. Studied art in Rome and lithography in London under Francis Jackson. She exhibited RA, RP, UA, RI, Senefelder Club, in the provinces, at the Paris Salon, in Italy and widely in America. Victoria & Albert Museum holds her work. Lived at East Molesey, Surrey, and in Chelsea, London.

Marion THOMSON 1960– Artist and teacher in many media including wax and raw pigment on canvas, daughter of the artist Mavis Thomson, she was born in Enniskillen, County Fermanagh, Northern Ireland. She graduated in fine art with honours from University of Newcastle upon Tyne, 1979–83, then did a postgraduate diploma at Royal Academy Schools, 1988–91; her teachers included Norman Adams, David Parfitt, Jennifer Durrant, Basil Beattie and John Holden. In late 1980s taught at a number of workshops and residencies, becoming a self-employed artist from 1991. Simplicity of shape and texture were important in Thomson's work, influences on which included Antonio Tapiés, Alberto Burri, Robert Ryman and William Scott. Showed at RA, Lynne Stern Associates, RHA in Dublin, Sligo Art Gallery in Sligo, Ireland, and elsewhere in mixed exhibitions. Had a series of solo exhibitions at Gordon Gallery, Londonderry, from 1989. Lived in Sheffield, Yorkshire.

Mavis Anne THOMSON 1935– Chiefly self-taught artist in oil, watercolour and mixed media, born in Omagh, County Tyrone, Northern Ireland. Her main career was as a medical secretary, although did some art school teaching. Thomson was influenced by a wide range of artists, ranging from J M W Turner through Impressionism to Kurt Schwitters, informed by a large personal art library. She was a member of RUA, Ulster Society of Women Artists, Watercolour Society of Ireland and Ulster Watercolour Society. Extensive mixed shows included Fermanagh Artists, Town Hall, Enniskillen (where she settled), 1971; Shambles Art Gallery, Hillsborough, 1981; Gordon Gallery, Londonderry, from 1984; and Jonathan Swift Gallery, Carrickfergus, 1992. Later solo shows included Gordon Gallery, 1984. Commissions included 39th Field Regiment, Royal Artillery, 1981; Derek Hill, 1983 and 1986; and The Ulster Defence Regiment, 1990. RUA, Department of the Environment, Fermanagh County Museum and Limerick University held examples. Her daughter was an artist, Marion Thomson.

Molly THOMSON 1953– Artist and teacher, born in Perth, Scotland, who gained a master's degree in fine art at Edinburgh University/Edinburgh College of Art, 1971–8; a postgraduate diploma at the College of Art, 1978–9; and her master's in painting at Royal College of Art, 1980–3. Awards included an Andrew Grant Scholarship, 1978; a Catherine Pakenham Award for Young Woman Writers. 1982; and a John Minton Award, 1983. From 1983–91 visiting and part-time teaching included Falmouth School of Art, Ruskin School in Oxford and Cleveland Institute of Art, Cleveland, Ohio, USA; from 1991 was subject leader in painting at Norwich School of Art and Design, whose Norwich Gallery gave her a solo show, Inscription, in 1998. This included works which "could be described as wordless scripts which confirm both the act of painting and the formative power of minute accumulating events."

Peter THOMSON 1962– Painter, muralist and draughtsman, born in Glasgow where he gained an honours degree at the School of Art, 1980–4. Thomson was a keen observer of human behaviour and social attitudes whose work was tinged with a fantastic quality. From 1986–7 he worked as team supervisor for Haringey Health Authority Mural Project. Commissions included Artlink (Edinburgh), mural for St John's Hospital, Livingston, 1993. Group shows included Images of Tottenham, Tottenham Town Hall, 1987; Figure in the City, Mia Joosten Gallery, Amsterdam, and tour, 1992–3; and Scottish Painters, Flowers East, 1993. Had a solo exhibition at Transmission Gallery, 1990, and Compass Gallery, 1995, both Glasgow. Scottish Arts Council holds examples.

Sinclair THOMSON 1915–1983 Painter, draughtsman, potter and teacher, full name Robert Sinclair Thomson, born and lived in Glasgow. While at Allan Glen's School there aged 16 a rugby injury prompted leg amputation, always to cause pain and inconvenience. During World War II served as a dispatch rider – he was obsessed by motorcycles – in 1941 going to Glasgow School of Art to study drawing and painting under Hugh Adam Crawford. While teaching in the High School Thomson, a fine potter who erected his own kiln at home, taught pottery in the evening at the

School of Art. He created large pottery murals for Lanarkshire schools. Thomson also arranged art classes in his home, which brought together students such as Joan Eardley, Margot Sandeman and his first wife Florence, a painter. One of his pottery students, Barbara, became his second wife. Thomson was a well-liked teacher of drawing and painting at the School of Art from 1960 until ill-health prompted his retirement in 1975. He was elected associate of RSA in 1952, four years after winning the Guthrie Award, was a member of RSW and showed regularly at Royal Glasgow Institute of the Fine Arts. For many years he painted in the summer at his cottage at Ballantrae, Strathclyde, where he died. Blythswood Gallery, Glasgow, held a show in 1989. Abbot Hall Art Gallery and Museum, Kendal, holds his drawing of Joan Eardley.

William THOMSON 1926–1988 Painter, etcher and teacher, born in Hamilton, Ontario. He attended McMaster University and Ontario College of Art, Toronto, 1945–7, where he was influenced by John Alfsen and won a gold medal. Left to study with a scholarship at Royal Academy Schools, London, 1948–9, and was then at Royal College of Art, 1949–52. An early influence was Francis Bacon. In 1957 Thomson studied with Oskar Kokoschka, who called him the best painter of his generation. Thomson travelled on the continent and from 1949 he held various teaching posts; from 1973–84 at Central School of Art and Design he kept life classes going when they were unfashionable. Showed at RA and elsewhere in group exhibitions and had numerous solo shows in Britain abroad. Completed a number of BBC Television programmes on art. The female nude was Thomson's primary subject, the "most challenging", he said. At first his style was Post-Impressionist, but by the late 1960s it had tightened up and became quite hard-edged, later becoming an amalgam of the two. At the end his painting gods were Rembrandt, Degas and Cézanne. Museum of Fine Arts, Boston, and several galleries in Canada, including Hamilton Art Gallery, hold his work.

William Hill THOMSON 1882–c.1956 Portrait painter and miniaturist, born in Edinburgh where he continued to live. Studied in Edinburgh, where his teachers included James Riddel and Henry Lintott. Showed at RMS of which he was a member, RSA, RA, SSA and Royal Glasgow Institute of the Fine Arts.

Jan THORN 1937– Painter, creator of photographic constructions and teacher, born in east Yorkshire. Studied at Hull Regional College of Art, 1955–9, in 1960 at Leeds Regional College of Art. For several years Thorn taught in secondary education, from 1966 working in the art department at St Martin's College of Higher Education, Lancaster. The English traditions of the picturesque and the romantic in landscape were important influences. His work was included in Lancashire South of the Sands, which toured from the County and Regimental Museum, Preston, 1988.

Mary Elizabeth THORN 1928– Painter and sculptor, born and educated in Egypt; and England, where she studied art at Amersham College of Further Education. Teachers included Derek Berryman. Thorn was made a member of Buckinghamshire Art Society in 1975 and NS in 1980 and had several solo exhibitions. Lived in Amersham, Buckinghamshire.

Mary THORNBERY 1921– Painter, born in Bredhurst, Kent. She studied at Bromley School of Art under Carel Weight, 1939–41; at Regent Street Polytechnic School of Art, 1946–7; with Thomas Freeth at Beckenham School of Art, 1947–9; then on her own in Italy for two years. Showed with RA, LG, WIAC and RWA, which holds her work. Lived in London and was a member of Hampstead Artists' Council, later living in Brechfa, Carmarthen, Dyfed.

Angela THORNE 1911– Painter, sculptor and illustrator, born in London. She overcame parental opposition to become an artist. Studied at Winchester School of Art, 1921–3; Southover, Lewes, 1924–7; at Académie Julian, Paris, 1928–9; with Bernard Adams, 1947; and Stanley Grimm, 1948–9. Was a member of NS, also showing with RSA, RP, RSMA, PS, ROI, Paris Salon and elsewhere. Had solo show at Midland Bank, Pall Mall. Her first major work was 34 portrait illustrations for a presentation book to HRH The Prince of Wales, in 1933, and she later completed portraits of HM The Queen, HM Queen Elizabeth The Queen Mother and HRH The Duke of Edinburgh as well as the politician Ernest Bevin. Thorne's bust of the Indian politician Indira Gandhi was on loan to India House and that of Ross McWhirter was completed for the McWhirter Foundation. Her father was Gerald Deane, racehorse breeder and owner of Littleton Stud, and early oils of such horses and polo ponies were completed as Angela Deane. Ecclesiastical commissions included a triptych for Winchester Cathedral Festival, 1981. Lived in Andover, Hampshire.

James THORNHILL 1967– Artist producing word- and photo-based conceptual work, as in New Art in Scotland, Centre for Contemporary Arts, Glasgow, 1994. Thornhill was born in Bournemouth, Hampshire, attending the Bournemouth and Poole College of Art, 1988–9; Frei Universitäte für Bildende Kunst, Hamburg, West Germany, 1989–90; and the School of Art in Glasgow, where he continued to work, 1990–3. Took part in a group show at Galerie Hans Hoppner, Hamburg, 1990; Royal Glasgow Institute of the Fine Arts, 1992; and shared a three-man exhibition, Unbuilding, at 99 Gallery, Glasgow, 1994.

Cecil Jeffery THORNTON 1911– Mural painter and decorator, born in Narborough, Leicestershire, where he chose to live. Studied at the College of Art there, his teachers including Ralph Middleton Todd and Hubert Hennes. Showed at RA, RBA and Paris Salon, where he gained a gold medal.

Frederick Charles THORNTON 1898–1978 Painter best known for his portrait miniatures, born in Thorpe, Surrey. In his fifties Thornton, who was for most of his life an engineer, studied with the miniature painter Mrs Ethol Court. He exhibited locally, living in Norwood Green, Middlesex, at RMS, RA and Paris Salon.

Harold THORNTON 1892–1958 Watercolourist and printmaker, born and lived in London. Studied, 1920–4, under Douglas Smart at Clapham School of Art, at the Central School of Arts and Crafts, 1929–33, under William Palmer Robins, and at Hornsey School of Art, 1939–43, under John Moody. Exhibited RA, SGA, Paris Salon and elsewhere overseas. The Ministry of Works bought his work. Taught for almost 20 years at Southwark Central School prior to World War II.

Kathleen THORNTON 1901– Painter in oil, pastel and watercolour and miniaturist. Studied at Heatherley's School of Fine Art with Henry Gibbs Massey as well as with the miniature painter Alfred Praga. Exhibited RSM, SWA, SM of which she was a member, RA and Walker Art Gallery, Liverpool. She did work for Queen Mary and published several volumes of poetry. Miss Thornton occupied one of the famous Meadow Studios at Bushey, Hertfordshire.

Leslie THORNTON 1925– Sculptor and draughtsman, born in Skipton, Yorkshire. He attended Leeds College of Art, 1945–8, and Royal College of Art, 1948–51. Took part in many group exhibitions, including ICA, Portsmouth Art Gallery, São Paulo Biennal in 1957 and abroad. Had a series of solo exhibitions at Gimpel Fils from 1957, Arts Council purchasing several examples, collections in Australia and America also holding his work. Lived in Harrogate, Yorkshire.

Minna THORNTON fl. from late 1970s– Artist and teacher who studied at Portland State University, Oregon, in America, 1973, then Hornsey College of Art, 1974–5, and Goldsmiths' College School of Art, 1975–8. Taught at London College of Fashion and was included in the 1982 Woodlands Art Gallery Exhibition Artists in Adult Education. Also exhibited at Angela Flowers Gallery, 1980; Artists in Adult Education at Camden Arts Centre in 1981; and Fort/Da, Downstairs at Tuttons, Covent Garden, 1982.

Pat THORNTON 1946– Painter, sculptor and teacher, born in Cheshire, married to the artist Oliver Bevan. She obtained her bachelor's degree in fine art at Brighton Polytechnic, 1965–8, then did postgraduate sculpture at St Martin's School of Art, 1969–70, teachers including Anthony Caro, Phillip King and Barry Flanagan. She lectured in sculpture at West Surrey College of Art & Design, Farnham, and at De Montfort University, Leicester. Thornton was a British Airports Sculpture Competition finalist in 1991, gained a John Moores Foundation Sculpture Bursary in 1992 and was elected to RBS in 1993. She started with objects such as a lemon squeezer, a water pistol and an oilcan and "by working exploratively, examining closely and drawing out the qualities that attract me, end up with a sculpture which realises something that I didn't know was there." Mixed exhibitions included Gardner Centre, Brighton, 1969; AIA Gallery, 1971; Bradford Print Biennale, 1975; Blind Machines, Cleveland Gallery, 1991; and LG, Barbican Centre, 1994. She had a solo show at The Orangery, 1987, later ones including Sue Williams Gallery, and Woodlands Art Gallery, both 1993. South London Gallery Print Collection and National Museum of Photography, Bradford, hold examples. Lived in London.

Valerie THORNTON 1931–1991 Etcher and painter, born in London. Was married to the artist Michael Chase, curator of the Minories Art Gallery, Colchester. She studied at Regent Street Polytechnic School of Art, 1950–3, and for eight months in 1954 at Stanley William Hayter's Atelier 17, in Paris, an experience she termed "electrifying". In the 1970s she did a series of etchings of East Anglian churches, later finding her inspiration in Romanesque churches in Italy, France and Spain. Her work can be intensely rich, but strongly delineated and well ordered and she was highly regarded by her peers. Examples were exhibited widely internationally and are to be found in many collections, including Victoria & Albert Museum, Fitzwilliam Museum and Museum of Modern Art in New York. In 1994 Christchurch Mansion, Ipswich, held a retrospective based on an archive collection of Thornton's work donated by her husband; there was an important exhibition at Chappel Galleries, Chappel, in 1998. She lived at Chelsworth, Suffolk.

Paul Hamo THORNYCROFT 1949– Figurative and semi-figurative sculptor who was educated at Maidenhead Grammar School, Dartington Hall and University of Sussex, where he did a degree in biological sciences. After post-graduate research in ecology he served an apprenticeship in aboriculture and tree surgery for about a decade. Taught himself to carve in wood and stone and worked as a mason and carpenter in the restoration of old buildings, which influenced his sculpture. Exhibitions included All Saints Exhibition Centre, Bristol, 1980; Trumpington Gallery, Cambridge, 1986; Studio International, Westbury-on-Trym, Bristol, 1992; and 1st RWA Open Sculpture Exhibition, 1993. Lived in Stroud, Gloucestershire.

Stanley THOROGOOD 1873–1953 Artist, potter and teacher, born in Ripley, Surrey. He became superintendent of art instruction for Stoke-on-Trent, then principal of Camberwell School of Arts and Crafts, after studying at Brighton School of Art and Royal College of Art, where he was a Royal Exhibitioner, gold medallist and travelling scholar. He was one of the first exhibitors of pottery figures at RA, and also showed at Paris Salon and in the provinces. His work is held in public collections in Stoke-on-Trent and Brighton, where he lived for some years.

Selina THORP 1968– Artist using a colourful palette, born in Leeds, Yorkshire. She gained an honours degree in drawing and painting at Edinburgh College of Art in 1990, and a graduate business enterprise qualification from the Universities of Sheffield and Huddersfield in 1991. Won a number of prizes, including NEAC and Laing Art Competition, Harrogate. Flying Colours Gallery and Royal College of Physicians in Edinburgh showed her work, which also appeared at Leeds Art Fair and in Four Yorkshire Artists, Phillips, Leeds, 1996.

William Eric THORP 1901–1993 Painter, designer and model maker, born in London. His father, John Thorp, was an architect and model maker. Studied at City of London School, where Herbert Dicksee was drawing master, and at Royal Academy Schools. He was principally a marine artist and was made a member of PS in 1952 and RSMA in 1958, also being a member of Wapping Group, Langham and London Sketch Clubs and Chelsea Arts Club. Showed at RA, Paris Salon and elsewhere. National Maritime Museum in Greenwich and Guildhall Art Gallery hold examples. Latterly lived in a nursing home, having settled in Nottingham, and did not work.

James THORPE 1876–1949 Illustrator, black-and-white artist, painter and writer. Born in London, he won a scholarship that took him to Bancroft's School, then studied at Heatherley's School of Fine Art in the late 1890s and with Alec Carruthers Gould while earning his living as a schoolmaster until 1902. For the next 20 years he designed advertisements for the London Press Exchange, with a break during World War I when he served with the Artists' Rifles. Thorpe exhibited at RI and Leicester Galleries but was better known for his illustrations for magazines such as *Punch*, *London Opinion* and *The Windmill* and especially for his books about black-and-white men such as Phil May and Edmund J Sullivan and for his excellent study *English Illustration: The Nineties*. Two years before, he had published *Happy Days, Recollections of an Unrepentant Victorian*, a rambling memoir. Lived in Buckfastleigh, Devon.

Mackenzie THORPE fl. from 1970s– Painter who grew up in Yorkshire Dales, settling in Richmond. After various jobs he attended Cleveland College of Art, 1977–9, then Byam Shaw School of Painting and Drawing, 1979–82. After college worked in local government with children, mainly art-based. Thorpe was noted for his colourful pictures of animals, especially sheep, simplified and with an apparently naive charm. Had a solo show at The Halcyon Gallery, Selfridges, 1994.

Michael THORPE 1937– Artist and teacher. He studied at St Martin's School of Art, 1957–61, then the Royal Academy Schools, 1961–4. He won an Abbey Minor Scholarship in 1963; the Leverhulme Prize and a Boise Travelling Scholarship in 1964; an Italian Government Scholarship in 1965; then a Winston Churchill Fellowship, America, 1967–86. Thorpe became a tutor at Royal College of Art in 1976 and was made a fellow four years later. He was also a governor of the London Institute of Art and Design. Thorpe's work was mainly conceptual and formalist, latterly showing a return to figuration after other preoccupations. Arts Council holds. Lived in London.

Harry THUBRON 1915–1985 Artist and teacher. Prior to the mid-1960s Thubron's work was involved with resins, wood and metals, then he tended towards collages often created from rubbish. Visits to America, Mexico and Ronda in Spain, with their revelations of a new light, were important. Born in Bishop Auckland, County Durham, he went to Sunderland School of Art, 1933–8, then Royal College of Art, 1938–40. He began a distinguished and influential teaching career at Sunderland College of Art, 1950–5, as head of fine art. Was then at Leeds College of Art, 1955–64; Lancaster College of Art, 1964–6; and Leicester College of Art, 1966–8, where he was head of the painting school. Was briefly visiting professor at University of Illinois in the mid-1960s and for a time from early 1970s taught part-time at Goldsmiths' College School of Art. Solo shows included Peterloo Gallery, Manchester, in 1976 and retrospectives at St Paul's Gallery, Leeds, 1985; Goldsmiths' College Gallery, 1986; and Gray Art Gallery, Hartlepool, 1987. Although originally a figurative artist, Thubron moved towards abstraction. Arts Council and British Council hold his work. Lived in London. His wife Elma was an artist.

Peter THURSBY 1930– Sculptor in bronze, sterling silver, resin fibreglass and slate, and teacher, born in Salisbury, Wiltshire. He studied at West of England College of Art, Bristol, under Paul Feiler, then sculpture at Exeter College of Art & Design. He held various teaching posts, notably head of art at Hele's Grammar School, Exeter, 1960–71, then head of art and later head of school of art and design at Exeter College, Exeter, 1971–91. Thursby was a member of RWA and a fellow of RBS. Rodin, César Baldaccini, Jean Ipousteguy, Brancusi, Richier, Gabo, Viera da Silva and Tapiés were cited as influences. Thursby said that "both my large and small sculptures embody a sense of architectonic power … The image is invariably vertical … Apart from the early 1960s and 1970s, my two-and three-dimensional work has been distinctly abstract. There is a deep sense of symbolism within." Public commissions included Randolf House, Croydon, 1966; Looking Forward, commissioned by Exeter City Sculpture to commemorate Queen Elizabeth's Silver Jubilee, 1977; Mazda Cars Head Office, Tunbridge Wells, bronze fountain and sculpture, 1982; Designed Growth, bronze relief, Rowan House, Westminster, 1986. Thursby had a solo show at Arnolfini Gallery, Bristol, in 1963, later ones including Alwin Gallery, 1976, and RWA, 1981. Arnolfini, RWA, Plymouth City Museum and Art Gallery and Sheffield Education Committee hold examples. Lived at Pinhoe, Exeter, Devon.

Rosalie Winifred THURSTON fl. from early 1930s–1991 Architectural and landscape artist, born in Plymouth, Devon. She studied at Birmingham School of Arts and Crafts and Central School. Was a member of Society of Mural Painters and WIAC. Exhibited at RA, SWA, RBA and in the provinces. Lived for many years at Aldeburgh, Suffolk.

Frances THWAITES 1908–1987 Painter and draughtsman, born in India. She went to school in Edinburgh and later attended the College of Art there. She studied stained glass at the College and in Paris under a scholarship, but on her return to Edinburgh could not get work so turned to her first loves, drawing and painting. At College she had won several prizes and scholarships. In 1965 spent six months in San Francisco, Tahiti and Australia, from which a body of work stemmed. She had five solo shows at Scottish Gallery, Edinburgh, between 1950–68. Other solo exhibitions included University of Hull, Kettle's Yard Gallery in Cambridge, Talbot Rice Art Centre in Edinburgh, and abroad. Thwaites' was subtle, tonal work, with a strong linear structure; within a small space and using carefully placed highlights she was able to evoke an infinity of space. Memorial show at Scottish Gallery in 1990. Scottish Arts Council holds her work.

Alexander THYNN(E) 1932– Painter and muralist, writer, political campaigner and singer, born in London. He was educated at Eton College and gained his master's degree at Oxford University, studying art in Paris at L'Académie de la Grande Chaumière and Académies Julian and Ranson. He became the 7th Marquess of Bath in 1992, having changed his name from Alexander Thynne to Thynn in 1976 to distance himself from his family. As Viscount Weymouth he had had disagreements with his father and was called "Britain's premier hippie" on succession to the title. There is a permanent exhibition of murals by Weymouth in Longleat House the family home's private apartments, a *Kama Sutra* room depicting varieties of sexual intercourse. They were painted 1964–9, opened to the public in 1973 and in 1974 *Lord Weymouth's Murals* was published. Among his other books were the novels *The King is Dead*, 1976, and *Pillars of the Establishment*, 1981. *A Regionalist Manifesto*, 1975, alludes to his political campaigns as a Wessex Regionalist. In 1974 he made a record, *I Play the Host*, singing his own compositions. Lived at Longleat, Warminster, Wiltshire.

Geoffrey TIBBLE 1909–1952 Painter in oil, born and lived in Reading, Berkshire, where he studied art at the university, then at the Slade School of Fine Art, 1927–9. Between 1933–6 Tibble, with Rodrigo Moynihan, was engaged in abstract painting, and they showed in the Objective Abstractions show at Zwemmer's Gallery in 1934. In 1936 Tibble was also interested in Surrealism, but he was soon to become involved with the Euston Road School, with which he is most strongly identified. In 1938 Tibble participated in Fifteen Paintings of London, an early Euston Road exhibition, at the Storran Gallery. Tibble served in the Royal Air Force in World War II, but was invalided out. In 1946 he held a very successful show at Tooth's Gallery, figures in interiors in the manner of Degas and Vuillard, which prompted the critic Raymond Mortimer to place him "in the front rank of living English painters". Several more exhibitions followed, then Tibble died suddenly. There is work in major collections in Britain and abroad. Retrospective at Manchester City Art Gallery, 1958.

Brüer TIDMAN: *see* **BRÜER**

Roy TIDMARSH 1944– Painter in oil, main works being interiors with figures, born in Birmingham. He studied at Moseley School of Art and Birmingham College of Art, 1956–63. Tidmarsh's father was the woodcarver L C Tidmarsh and like him "devoted a lifetime to the traditional arts employed in realism". Influences cited were Alfred Sisley, Philip Wilson Steer and Sir Alred Munnings. Showed at RA, RBA, ROI and NEAC. Lived in Balsall Common, Warwickshire.

James TIERNEY 1945– Printmaker, teacher and painter, born in Newcastle upon Tyne, Northumberland. He studied at Sunderland College of Art, 1961–6, then did a post-diploma course in printmaking with Jennifer Dickson, 1966–7, at Brighton College of Art. Showed in northeast and south of England and taught printmaking at West Surrey College of Art and Design, Farnham. Lived in Basingstoke, Hampshire.

Robert TIERNEY 1936– Artist and designer, notably of textiles, born and based in Plymouth, Devon. He studied with Joan Lee at Plymouth College of Art, then with Alan Reynolds, 1956–8, at Central School. Showed at Design Centre in London and widely abroad, especially in the Far East, and received many commissions. Victoria & Albert Museum holds examples.

Sheila TIFFIN 1952– Painter in oil, born in Barking, Essex. She was self-taught as an artist. After leaving dance school at the end of the 1960s she toured the entertainment circuit as a chorus girl. Her life was chequered for many years, painting interspersed with office and shop work, a period as a dance teacher, waitress, go-go dancer, helping to run a pet shop and cattery, and eventually a move to Cornwall, where she ran a gallery with a friend in St Ives. Exhibited with RP, Tiffin Studios in St Ives, opened in 1982, and at Tony Sanders' Penzance gallery. In 1991 had solo show Bear Necessities with John Noott Twentieth Century, Broadway, based on her extensive collection of bears, dolls and other toys. From 1990 lived in Penzance, Cornwall.

Lilian TILLARD: *see* **Lilian SOMERVILLE**

Robert TILLING 1944– Artist in acrylic, watercolour and charcoal, illustrator, teacher and writer, born in Bristol. He studied architecture and art education at Bristol and Exeter, 1961–6. Taught art at Tiffin School in London, 1966–8, then was head of art at Victoria College, Jersey, where he lived at St Saviour. Tilling illustrated two books by the Cornish poet Charles Causley; wrote regularly for blues and folk magazines in Britain and America; and lectured on painting and American music at such venues as the Tate Gallery, Polytechnic of Central London and British National Blues Festival. In 1985 at RI Tilling gained the bronze medal for "the most outstanding work by a non-member", being elected a full member later that year. In 1989 he won a major prize at Cleveland International Drawing Biennale. Also showed at RA, RWS, RBA and NEAC. Had many solo exhibitions including Exeter University, Barbican Centre and Polytechnic of Central London. Tilling said that he was influenced "by the Cornish School, Sidney Nolan and Morris Louis". Shell (UK) Ltd, BP Ltd, Lodz Museum in Poland and Cleveland Gallery hold examples.

Edmund TILLOTSON 1941– Sculptor, painter and teacher, born in London, who studied at Chelsea School of Art gaining a Gulbenkian Rome Scholarship in Sculpture, 1964–5. He went on to teach in various colleges, then lectured in sculpture at Sunderland Polytechnic. In 1984 he was artist-in-residence at

Hartlepool Nuclear Power Station. Tilllotson's work, which sometimes had a jokey quality, was exhibited widely in group exhibitions. These included LG; Curwen Gallery; South London Art Gallery, 1981, in Rome Scholars in Sculpture; Quarries, at Camden Arts Centre, 1983; A Place for Art, Vardy Foundation Gallery, Sunderland Polytechnic, 1989; and DLI Museum & Arts Centre, 1990, in the Newcastle Group show The Northern Lights. Solo shows included Acme Gallery, 1976; Spectro Arts, Newcastle, 1982; and Northern Centre for Contemporary Art, 1985. Victoria & Albert Museum holds his work. Lived at Alston, Cumbria.

William TILLYER 1938– Printmaker, painter, ceramist, illustrator and teacher, born in Middlesbrough, Yorkshire. He attended the local College of Art, 1956–9, then studied at Slade School of Art, 1960–2, painting with William Coldstream and etching with Anthony Gross. In 1962 Tillyer gained a French Government Scholarship to study gravure under William Hayter at Atelier 17 in Paris. Taught part-time at Chelsea School of Art, 1963–70, etching at Bath Academy of Art, Corsham, until 1972, and at Watford School of Art, 1970–3. Stopped regular teaching in 1973, although in 1975–6 was visiting professor at Brown University, America. In 1981–2 was artist-in-residence at Melbourne University, Australia. Tillyer travelled widely, in the early 1980s through Europe for the First Grand Tour watercolours; in 1984 through southwestern America; and in 1990 through California and Arizona. Tillyer worked on various projects: hotel room watercolours, mesh paintings, Esk Bridge etchings and Fulham Pottery ceramics. As well as taking part in mixed exhibitions, had several dozen solo shows in Britain and abroad: from 1962 at Middlesbrough Art Gallery; from 1970 at Arnolfini Gallery, Bristol; and in 1971 at Serpentine Gallery. In 1991 showed at Cleveland Bridge Gallery, Bath; Bernard Jacobson Gallery; Wildenstein; and Everard Read Gallery, Johannesburg. Was widely represented in public galleries, including Victoria & Albert Museum, Arts Council and Tate Gallery, as well as Museum of Modern Art, New York, and several Australian galleries. Lived in Yorkshire.

Frederick Colin TILNEY 1870–1951 Painter, writer, teacher and illustrator. After studying at Birkbeck College, London, he attended Westminster School of Art under Fred Brown. Taught at Hornsey School of Art, wrote for magazines such as *The Artist* and *The Studio* and edited *Art and Reason*. Exhibited extensively at Walker's Galleries, also at RA, RI and Walker Art Gallery, Liverpool, and had several one- man shows. Member of the Art Workers' Guild. Lived in Cheam, Surrey.

Jake TILSON 1958– Artist, designer and publisher, son of the artist Joe Tilson. He was at Chelsea School of Art, 1976–9, then at the Royal College of Art, 1980–3. His production of the magazine *Cipher* while at the College continued an interest begun at school, and it presaged other striking little magazines and publications notable for their use of colour. Tilson also designed clothes. His art works, drawing on the legacy of Pop Art and employing such objects as urban junk, began to be exhibited in the early 1980s at key shows such as the Paris Biennale, 1983. Three years later Tilson showed with Nigel Greenwood, who remained his dealer, and in 1988 he appeared in New Forms in Visual Poetry at Guggenheim Museum, in New York, and in Exhibition Road, at Royal College of Art. His Dry Signals No 2 was in the 1993–4 John Moores Liverpool Exhibition. Tilson was born and lived in London.

Joe TILSON 1928– Painter and creator of reliefs in wood, born in London. Tilson was a carpenter and joiner, 1944–6, then served in Royal Air Force, 1946–9. He was a student at St Martin's School of Art, 1949–52, and at the Royal College of Art, 1952–5, where he won the Knapping and Rome Prizes. Between 1955–7 Tilson travelled in Italy and Spain, which had a marked influence on his early work. After winning the Gulbenkian Foundation Prize in 1960, Tilson exhibited in the Paris Biennale and Carnegie International Exhibition, in Pittsburgh, in 1961, and had the first of several appearances at Venice Biennale in 1964. Had first one-man show at New London Gallery in 1961, the 1960s seeing the burgeoning of his international exhibiting career. He became associated with the Royal College's generation of Pop Artists, but was always prepared to experiment with novel subjects, sometimes stemming from his eclectic reading, and materials. Tate Gallery and Arts Council hold his work. Lived for some time in London, later in Wiltshire and Italy. The artist Jake Tilson was his son. Joe was elected RA in 1991.

Eugène TILY 1870–1950 Printmaker and painter, born in Walkern, Hertfordshire, noted for his high-quality stippling work. He studied at Bedford Park School of Art and with Arthur Stocks and Walter Williams, declining to follow his father as a medical practitioner. His work was widely reproduced by Frost & Reed and others and he completed pictures after notable artists such as Meissonier and Raeburn. Showed at RA, Royal Glasgow Institute of the Fine Arts, Connell & Sons, Paris Salon and in America, where at the St Louis International Exhibition he gained a Gold Medal for colour proofs from stipple plates. Lived in Sutton, Surrey.

Robert TIMMIS 1886–1960 Painter, draughtsman and teacher, born in Leek, Staffordshire. He was educated there and at Patrick Allan-Fraser School of Art, Hospitalfield, Arbroath. He taught at Liverpool College of Art and showed at RA, at Walker Art Gallery in Liverpool, which holds his oil The Two Jugs, and elsewhere in the provinces. Died in Liverpool.

Padraig TIMONEY 1968– Artist constructing and painting works in a wide range of materials, born in Londonderry, Northern Ireland, who attended St Martin's School of Art, 1987, and Goldsmiths' College, 1988, in 1991 winning a Nicholas and Andrei Toot Travelling Scholarship. Group exhibitions included Four Sculptors at Laure Genillard Gallery, 1991; Galerie Martina Detterer, Frankfurt, 1994; and Making It at Tate Gallery in Liverpool, where Timoney lived, 1995. Solo exhibitions included

Goldsmiths' and Milch Gallery, both 1992; Laure Genillard, from 1993; and Galleria Raucci/Santamaria, Napoli, 1994. Lived in Liverpool.

David TINDLE 1932– Painter, notably in egg tempera, printmaker and teacher, born in Huddersfield, Yorkshire. Studied at Coventry School of Art, 1945–6. From early 1950s he was featured in RA Summer Exhibition shows and had regular solo exhibitions at Piccadilly Gallery. By 1957 he had a retrospective at Coventry's Herbert Art Gallery. Tindle then began to build up an impressive British and continental exhibitions record, including appearances in John Moores Exhibition, Liverpool, in 1959 and 1961; retrospective at Northampton's Central Museum and Art Gallery in 1972; and appearances in such shows as British Painting '74 at Hayward Gallery in 1974, and British Painting 1952–77 at RA in 1977. Two years later he was elected RA. From 1985 Tindle showed with Fischer Fine Art, in 1996 showing new paintings and prints with The Redfern Gallery. He taught at Hornsey College of Art, 1959–74, and at Royal College of Art, 1972–83, being made a fellow of the College in 1981. Tindle was also for a time Ruskin Master of Drawing at Oxford University and held a professorial fellowship at St Edmund Hall. Tindle's work, sometimes signed D T, was subtle and delicate, portraits and objects in carefully arranged interiors in which surface and texture were important. Tate Gallery, Manchester City Art Gallery, National Portrait Gallery and many other public collections hold. Lived in Leamington Spa, Warwickshire.

Michael TINGLE 1954– Printmaker, draughtsman and painter, born in Skegness, Lincolnshire. He studied at Torquay Art College, 1971–3; gained a degree in fine art from Bath Academy of Art, Corsham, 1973–6; and was a member of Gainsborough's House Print Workshop, Sudbury, 1983–93. Mixed shows included Festival Gallery, Bath, 1976; RA Summer Exhibition, from 1983; Centre International d'Art Contemporain, Paris, 1984; and in 1993–4 7th Mini Print International in Cadaques, Spain, and Brandler Galleries, Brentwood. Had a solo show at Market Cross Gallery, Bury St Edmunds, 1982, later ones including The John Russell Gallery, Ipswich, 1995. Tingle's *An Artist's View of William Blake* was published in 1997. The artist spent most of his childhood in the southwest of England, and its landscape and hill figures were important in his lyrical, witty work, earlier Bacchanalian themes deriving from Poussin and Titian. Lived in Newton Abbot, Devon.

David TINKER 1924– Painter of pictures and murals, designer, draughtsman, sculptor and teacher, born in London. He was brought up in Kent and Hampshire and attended Winchester and Bath Schools of Art, 1941–2, then after several years' service in the Royal Naval Volunteer Reserve went to Slade School of Fine Art, 1946–9. He then began lecturing at Cardiff College of Art, later teaching and holding administrative posts at University College of Wales in Aberystwyth. In 1959 he won a WAC travel bursary to study stage design in several continental European countries and a year later was a WAC prizewinner. Participated in many group shows mainly in Wales, including the Bath Society of Artists; LG; Wales and the Modern Movements at University College of Wales, Aberystwyth in 1973; 56 Group of which he was a founder member; SEA, SWG and Royal National Eisteddfod. His one-man shows included Howard Roberts Gallery in Cardiff and Dillwyn Gallery, Swansea. Commissions included University College of Wales, Aberystwyth, acrylic mural and metal sculpture, and he completed set designs for Welsh National Opera Company. CASW and National Museum of Wales, Cardiff, hold examples of his work. which was included in The 1960's at England & Co, 1993.

Dorothea TINNE 1899–1985 Painter of animals in oil and other media, draughtsman in chalk and scraperboard. She sometimes signed her work E D Tinne (pronounced Tinnah). Was born in Hawkhurst, Kent, and studied at St John's Wood School of Art under Frederick Whalen, also in Amsterdam with Herbert van der Poll. Was a founder-member of SWLA. Had one-man shows in London and Worcester as well as exhibiting widely at Ackermann's, RI, SGA, PS and SWA. With her husband, Lieutenant-Colonel Martyn Strover, she ran a camp site for disabled people and a workshop for disabled women known as Woodlarks Camp Site Trust and Woodlarks Workshop which continued to flourish after her death. She published children's books and outdoor titles such as *Signposts to the Wild* and *Lure of Lakeland*. Lived in Farnham, Surrey.

E D TINNE: *see* **Dorothea TINNE**

Bruce TIPPETT 1933– Artist in various media, working originally in a figurative style, then abstract, born in Boston, Lincolnshire. He attended Leicester College of Art, 1951–4, then Slade School of Fine Art, 1954–7. In latter year was influenced by Japanese films and brush paintings. After a first solo show at Lords Gallery in 1958 was awarded a French Government Scholarship and lived in Paris 1959–62, where he became interested in new American painting and began to roller and pour paint and use experimental fabrics. Worked in Rome, then in America from 1965, in 1966 becoming affiliated with the Betty Parsons Gallery with which he was associated for many years. Designed furniture for Gavina factory in Italy. In late 1960s made a series of works using rubber matting, some calling for audience participation. In 1970 was guest artist at University of Southern Illinois. From 1970s travelled extensively in Kenya, Egypt and India, in late 1980s producing the first of a series of figure-related pictures again. From 1990 Tippett worked mainly in London with part of the year in France. In 1992 England & Co had a retrospective of his works, 1950–80. As well as being held by many private collections globally, Tippett's work is in Arts Council collection, Contemporary Art Society, Museum of Modern Art in New York and elsewhere.

A B TIPPIN: *see* **Alice Bertha MORETON**

Willy TIRR 1915–1991 Self-taught painter and teacher working mainly in watercolour, oil, acrylic and collage, born in Stettin,

Germany. Moved to the United Kingdom in 1938 and began teaching at Leeds College of Art in 1960; from 1968 he held the position of head of fine art until retirement in 1980. Tirr's abstract pictures include subtle biographical references, strong sweeps of colour beckoning and threatening. He appeared in many mixed shows, including The Teaching Image, at Leeds City Art Gallery, 1964. Had several dozen solo shows after New Vision Gallery, 1958, later ones including Leeds University Gallery, 1988; Scarborough Art Gallery, 1989; and Gallery North, Kirkby Lonsdale, 1990. Many public collections hold examples, including Bradford, Durham, Lancaster and Leeds Universities; Bradford City Art Gallery; Ben Uri Art Society; and Wollongong University, Australia, where in the early 1980s Tirr was artist-in-residence. Died in Leeds, Yorkshire.

Hans TISDALL 1910–1997 Painter, designer, teacher and writer, born in Munich, Germany, as Hans John Knox Aufseeser, his father an artist. In 1941 Tisdall married Isabel Gallegos, who in 1964 started her own weaving firm, Tamesa Fabrics, for which Tisdall made many designs. In 1928 he entered the Academy of Fine Art, Munich, in 1929 being apprenticed to Moisey Kogan, the sculptor, living in Paris and Ascona. After only three days in an advertising agency in London Tisdall left to become a full-time painter, designer and muralist. Tisdall joined the Civil Defence Corps in 1940 and worked for the Ministry of Information, in 1947 joining the staff of Central School. Notable in Tisdall's career were: 1935, first big mural pictures for University Settlement, Wapping; 1936, Medal of Honour, International Exhibition, Paris, for work on British Pavilion; 1950, winning competition to design entrance to funfair at Festival of Britain South Bank site; 1956, first designs for Edinburgh Weavers; 1964, large outdoor mural for Manchester University; and 1966, mosaic murals for Manchester College of Science and Technology. In 1942 Tisdall wrote *Balbus – a picture book of Building*, also *Wheels – a picture book of Motion*, with Oliver Hill. Had a first solo show in London at Leger Galleries in 1945, others following in England, France and Germany, including latterly Albemarle Gallery, 1990. Lived in London.

Sarah TISDALL 1938– Artist, born in Dartington, Devon, who trained at Wimbledon College of Art and Slade School of Fine Art. Went on to work as an art teacher and gallery education officer and produced trompe l'oeil works for private and public organisations. Her oil on board Topiary Water Garden was sited in 1988 in Milton Keynes General Hospital, commissioned by the Milton Keynes Development Corporation. Lived and worked in Winchester, Hampshire.

John TITCHELL 1926–1998 Painter who studied at Sidcup School of Art and Royal College of Art, becoming an associate and a professional artist in 1951. Was elected RA in 1991 and lived at Pluckley, near Ashford, Kent. The county's countryside was depicted by Titchell using a personal, colourful, shimmering Pointillism, latterly especially in watercolour.

John TITCOMB 1863–1952 Watercolour painter, notably of landscapes, born in London, brother of the artist William Titcomb. Titcomb, son of the Bishop of Rangoon, went to Westminster School, then studied art under Henry Tonks and Fred Brown at the Slade School of Fine Art. Lived in St Ives, Cornwall, and was a member of the Society of Artists there. Exhibited RA and RI.

Mayling TO 1970– Artist and illustrator, producing strong figurative work, born in Harlow, Essex, who studied at Northbrook College of Design and Technology, 1987–90; gained an honours degree in illustration at Harrow College of Art and Design (University of Westminister), 1990–3; with postgraduate illustration work at Central St Martins College of Art and Design (London Institute), 1993–5. Won the Prince's Trust Award in 1994 and 1996, being a St Cuthbert's Paper Mill Award group winner, 1995. Exhibitions included Ben Uri Art Gallery, 1993; National Print Exhibition at Mall Galleries, from 1994; Links 96 Exhibition, Chinese Arts Centre, Manchester, 1996; and 198 Gallery. Lived in Sidcup, Kent.

John TOBIN 1924– Painter and teacher, educated at King Alfred School, Hampstead. He was a private student of George Mortram Moorhouse and Mary Kendal-Johnson. Spent seven years as a graduate and postgraduate student at Lancaster College of Art, Oxford Art School and Willesden College, teachers including Bernard Meninsky and Walter Bayes. In the early 1950s Tobin set up a studio and summer school in the Lake District and, maybe as the result of five years as a surveyor in the Royal Engineers, produced austere landscapes tending towards abstraction. After his first wife died he moved back to London where he rethought his approach, then recommenced painting in 1961 with great vigour. He quickly produced over 100 large works plus smaller pictures and constructions. Humanistic Expressionism and the relationship between time and people became key elements in his work. Showed at Drian Gallery, Minories in Colchester and in 1965 was included in The Visual Arts at Harlow Arts Festival.

Murray Macpherson TOD 1909–1974 Painter in oil and watercolour, etcher and teacher. He studied at Glasgow School of Art, 1927–31, and at Royal College of Art under Robert Austin, obtaining his diploma in 1935. Was then at the British School at Rome, 1935–7. Married the artist Marjorie Lucas in 1938. After teaching at Dalbeattie High School, 1941–6, Tod taught etching part-time at Edinburgh College of Art, 1949–59, living in the city. Showed at RA, RSA, Royal Glasgow Institute of the Fine Arts, SSA and elsewhere.

Arthur Ralph Middleton TODD 1891–1966 Painter and draughtsman, mainly of figures and portraits, and teacher. Born at Helston, Cornwall, son of the painter Ralph Todd, from 1907 he studied with Stanhope Forbes at Newlyn. After serving in the Army during World War I and first showing at the RA in 1918, from 1920–1 studied under Henry Tonks at the Slade School of Fine Art, for two years after that studying and working on the continent. From 1936–9 Todd was head of drawing and painting at

Leicester School of Art, in 1939 becoming master of the life class at Regent Street Polytechnic School of Art, from 1946–9 tutor at the Royal Academy Schools and from 1950–6 at the City and Guilds School. Was elected RA in 1945. Todd was an artist of great perception, described by Robert Buhler "by far the most sensitive and accomplished painter of his generation … modest and unambitious". The Tate Gallery, Victoria & Albert Museum and Ashmolean Museum, Oxford, hold his work. Lived in London.

Daphne TODD 1947– Painter and teacher, born in York, who studied at Slade School of Fine Art, 1965–71. She became director of studies at Heatherley School of Fine Art, 1980–6. Was elected a member of RP and NEAC in 1985, also showing at RA, Morley Gallery and John Player Award at National Portrait Gallery. That Gallery, University College in London and Lady Margaret Hall, Oxford, hold examples. Lived in Mayfield, Sussex.

Graeme TODD 1962– Artist, born in Glasgow, who settled in Edinburgh having studied at Duncan of Jordanstone College of Art, Dundee, 1979–85. Group shows included Scatter – New Scottish Art, Third Eye Centre, Glasgow, 1990; Collective Gallery, Edinburgh, 1994; Swarm, Scottish Arts Council tour, 1995; and New Found Land Scape, Kerlin Gallery, Dublin, 1997. Solo shows included Andrew Mummery, 1998. Scottish Arts Council and BZW hold examples.

Harold TODD 1894–1977 Painter, born in Leeds, Yorkshire, where he studied at the School of Art under Charles Mayne. Todd concentrated on interiors and landscapes of the Yorkshire coastal area. He showed at RBA and in exhibitions throughout his home county and a number of public galleries there, notably Bradford and Leeds, hold his work. Was at one time secretary of the Yorkshire Society of Artists and honorary secretary of the Fylingdales Group of artists. Was also honorary curator of the Pannett Art Gallery in Whitby for a dozen years until his resignation in 1976. Lived at Robin Hood's Bay, Whitby.

Margaret Gillison TODD: *see* **Margaret GILLISON**

Nell TODD 1909–1976 Charismatic, inspirational teacher and artist, brought up in Milngavie, near Glasgow, who attended Glasgow School of Art, 1927–9, teachers including Robert Anning Bell and Dorothy Carleton Smyth. Unlike her sister Jean, who studied at Glasgow 1927–32, graduating in 1930, Nell did not get her diploma, owing to illness. Nell was still recuperating in the 1930s in London, staying with friends in Campden Hill Square, where her abilities as an exquisite needleworker were useful. When during World War II the friends were evacuated to Dorset Nell went with them, taught at a boys' preparatory school, then at Canford School, where William Coldstream, who Todd later called "my professor", painted the headmaster's portrait. From 1950–69, Todd was head of art at Christ's Hospital school, Horsham, where she transformed a dry, academic art school into a haven of creativity. Her first, symbolic act – with a bucket of dye and a scrubbing brush – was to turn the art school's dull, brown carpet into a vibrant, purple one. After Christ's Hospital, Todd taught for a short time at Hanford School for Girls, near Blandford, then retired to Edinburgh. Todd was an enthusiastic amateur cellist, keen on fishing and a good horsewoman. Her own landscapes, still lifes and portraits had both Impressionist and Post-Impressionist influences, using rich but sensitive colouring. Exhibited at Heal's Mansard Gallery, Richard Demarco Gallery in Edinburgh, in Granton-on-Spey where she fished and elsewhere. Died in her bath in her Edinburgh home about the time she was planning to move to Hampstead, north London. There was a memorial show at Christ's Hospital.

Peter TODD 1921– Painter and teacher, born in Sheffield, Yorkshire. He attended the College of Art there, 1936–40, with Eric Jones, then at the Royal College of Art, 1946–9, with Charles Mahoney. He went on to teach, becoming head of Grimsby School of Art. Showed at RA, NEAC and LG. Lived in Grimsby, Lincolnshire.

William TODD-BROWN 1875–1952 Painter, decorative artist, printmaker and teacher, born in Glasgow. Studied there at the School of Art and at Slade School of Fine Art under Philip Wilson Steer, Fred Brown and Henry Tonks. Exhibited at RA, ROI, NEAC, RE and at the Royal Glasgow School of the Fine Arts. Was principal of Redhill School of Art, 1922–40. Lived finally at Carbis Bay, Cornwall.

Pip TODD WARMOTH 1962– Painter and draughtsman. Studied at Grimsby College of Art, Camberwell School of Art and Royal Academy Schools. Took part in a number of group exhibitions, at New Grafton Gallery, RA Summer Exhibition from 1986 and at Agnew, in 1990, in The Broad Horizon. Lived in London.

Albert TOFT 1862–1949 Sculptor of figures and portrait busts, born in Birmingham. He came from a long line of Staffordshire artists and craftsmen, his brother being J Alfonso Toft and his father Charles Toft. Albert Toft was apprenticed as a modeller to the Wedgwood pottery firm, attending evening classes at Hanley and Newcastle-under-Lyme. In 1880 he won a scholarship to Royal College of Art, where he studied under Édouard Lantéri. He was elected a fellow of RBS in 1938 and two examples of his restrained style are illustrated in the 1939 volume *RBS: Modern British Sculpture*. Wrote the book *Modelling and Sculpture*, 1911. Toft was a prolific exhibitor at RA, Walker Art Gallery in Liverpool, Royal Glasgow Institute of the Fine Arts and elsewhere. War memorials in Birmingham and Cardiff were among his many public commissions. Died in Worthing, Sussex.

J Alfonso TOFT 1871–1964 Painter of landscape whose work often has a peculiar quality of light. He was born in Birmingham, son of the artist Charles Toft and brother of the sculptor Albert Toft, a Staffordshire artistic family. Studied at Hanley and Birmingham Schools of Art, then at Royal College of Art. He was a prolific exhibitor, showing at ROI of which he was a member, Walker Art Gallery in Liverpool, RA, RI and elsewhere. Leighton

House Museum and Art Gallery had a show of his work in 1990, Abbott & Holder in 1997. Lived in London.

Ottilie TOLANSKY 1912–1977 Painter in oil who was born in Vienna, studied in Berlin and at Hammersmith School of Art. She exhibited at the RA, NEAC, WIAC and at other galleries, having several one-man shows in London. *Studio International* and *Arts Review* reproduced her work, which is held by Stoke-on-Trent, Staffordshire, City Museum and Art Gallery. Lived at Richmond, Surrey. Hurlingham Gallery held a retrospective in 1989.

Edward TOLEDANO fl. from 1960s– Artist, born in New York City, America, who studied at Yale University school of fine arts, settled in London in mid-1960s, and attended Sir John Cass School of Art, 1979–82, and St Martin's School of Art, 1983. Took part in extensive mixed shows, including Basil Jacobs Gallery, 1971; Obelisk Gallery and National Museum of Wales in Cardiff, both 1973; Marjorie Parr Gallery, 1976; Camden Arts Centre, 1978; and On the Wall Gallery, 1986. Solo shows included Basil Jacobs Gallery, 1972; Ben Uri Art Gallery, which owns his work, from 1977; Talent Store Art Gallery, from 1979; University of Surrey Gallery, 1987; and Carmel College, Wallingford, 1995. Shortly before that show Toledano had turned to sculpture, first in clay, then in wood constructions and bronze. Under the guidance of Kennet Westmacott he developed a fluid style which ranged over small table models to 10-foot structures, all painted in bright, glossy colours. Victoria Art Gallery & Museum, Bath; Tel-Aviv Museum and Israel Museum in Jerusalem; Tate Gallery; and Smithsonian Museum in Washington all own examples.

Peter TOLHURST 1917– Painter and draughtsman who was by profession a surveyor and valuer, born in Bristol. Studied at Regent Street Polytechnic School of Art, 1934–5, showed at Leighton House and in other mixed exhibitions in London, where he also showed one-man. Lived in London and in Broadstairs, Kent, where he was a keen sailor.

Tim TOLKIEN 1962– Creator of artworks, sculptures and designs, born in Hillingdon, Middlesex. He gained an honours degree in fine art, sculpture, at University of Reading, 1981–5, then worked at odd jobs towards becoming a professional sculptor. In 1985 began collaborating with Nicholas Treadwell Gallery which led to exhibitions at major art fairs worldwide. Other shows included: 1986, Fresh Art, Barbican Centre; from 1990, Marcus & Marcus Gallery, Amsterdam, also Arts Week and Himley Sculpture Trail, Dudley. Workshops included: producing a junk orchestra with borough artist Steve Field, at Wordsley Youth Centre, Dudley, 1990; and scrap plastic robot workshop with sculptor Claire Carter, Dudley Art Week, 1991. Tolkien's commissions included: 1983, pen and ink drawings for Wethered's Brewery, Marlow; 1984, mural for Arthur Hill Swimming Pool, Reading; 1991, Box Office Bertie, mobile kiosk for Alhambra Studio Theatre, Bradford; and 1992, 20-foot sculpture for Equinox Night Club, Leicester Square, for First Leisure. Tolkien said that he had an interest in "the extremes and contradictions of humanity – the happy versus sad, the technology at a cost to the humanity – a mixture of real world and dream world". Lived in Wheelock, Sandbach, Cheshire.

Paul Arnold TOLLER 1921–1977 He was by profession a dental surgeon of distinction, born in Bushey, Hertfordshire, educated at Merchant Taylors' School and Royal Dental Hospital, where he gained several senior prizes. Alongside his career Toller pursued many interests, being a watercolourist who was an RWS member and a researcher into subjects such as the history of the English drinking glass, the migration of the art of the Chinese potter to Phoenicia and the water condition of the fish he caught. He was a council member of the Oriental Ceramic Society, a director of the Oriental Art Magazine and a trustee of the Victor Sassoon Ivories Trust. Lived in Northwood, Middlesex, and Rickmansworth, Hertfordshire.

Sheila TOLLEY 1939– Painter, notably in watercolour, born in Birmingham. She studied at Bournemouth and Poole College of Art, 1972–4. Showed at RWA from 1976, RA from 1978 and in 1988 was included in Some of the Moderns at Belgrave Gallery.

Roger TOLSON 1958– Painter, born in Sheffield, Yorkshire, where he attended the King Edward VII School, 1970–7. After Oxford University, 1978–82, he was at Sir John Cass School of Art, 1986. He showed at RA from 1986, other mixed appearances including Whitechapel Open and NEAC in 1988. In 1990 had solo exhibition at Cadogan Contemporary.

Peter TOMALIN 1937– Landscape watercolourist and architectural illustrator, born in Kettering, Northamptonshire. He gained his RIBA diploma in architecture, Leicester, 1964, was made a fellow of Society of Architectural Illustrators in 1978 and was a member of Northampton Town & County Art Society. Tomalin studied art with Frank Cryer at Nene College, Northampton. He won the BBC Pebble Mill Christmas card painting competition, 1977. Showed at The Studio, Courtenhall; with UA at Mall Galleries; and at Northampton Central Museum and Art Gallery. Kettering Council owns his work. Lived at Overstone, Northampton.

Sarah TOMBS 1961– Sculptor, notably in steel and bronze, who studied at Wimbledon School of Art, 1981–4, Chelsea School of Art, 1984–5 and Royal College of Art, 1985–7, where she was awarded the Henry Moore Bursary. She was appointed artist-in-residence by British Steel in 1986 and by Nicholas Chamberlaine Comprehensive School in 1988, which had a commissioned sculpture installed. Her group shows included Cannizaro Park, Wimbledon, 1981–6; Audun Gallery, 1987; British Coal, Coventry, 1988; and Six of the Best, at Christopher Hull Gallery, 1989.

Bernard TOMLINS 1904–1976 Oil painter and black-and-white artist who was born in Brighton, Sussex. The Tomlins family ran laundries. Bernard was educated as an engineer, but also studied at Heatherley's School of Fine Art, St John's Wood and Willesden Schools of Art. He exhibited at RA, NEAC, NS, SGA and PS. The National Gallery of South Australia, Adelaide, holds his work. Finally lived in Reading, Berkshire.

Martin TOMLINSON 1954– Artist in watercolour, pastel and oil who trained at Lancaster College of Art. In 1969 was made a member of Lake Artists' Society, in 1996 being its vice-president. Tomlinson showed at RA Summer Exhibition, RI and PS. He mainly produced landscapes of Britain, but also worked with Phil Hobbs in Spain and North Africa. Their show Andalucia to Africa was in 1996 held at The Hobbs Gallery, Ambleside, Cumbria.

Reginald Robert TOMLINSON 1885–1978 Portrait painter, pottery designer, etcher and teacher, born in Overton, Hampshire. He studied at Farnham School of Art, then became a pottery painter and designer in the Midlands. Further study followed at Stoke-on-Trent School of Art and Hanley School of Art. From 1913–19 Tomlinson was art director to the Crown Staffordshire China Company. He studied etching under Frank Short at the Royal College of Art and for a time travelled on the continent. Tomlinson was principal of Cheltenham College of Arts and Crafts, 1922–5, and acting principal of the Central School of Arts and Crafts, 1935–6 and 1939–46. His main position was as senior inspector of art for London County Council, 1925–51. Among various official positions with art bodies he was for a time president of the Royal Drawing Society and he was master of the Art Workers' Guild, 1955. He wrote several books on child art and his pottery is in museums in Britain and abroad. He painted a number of portraits and exhibited at the RA, RI, RBA, Cooling Galleries, NEAC, ROI, in the provinces and overseas. Lived in London, later near Chichester, Sussex.

David TONER 1944– Painter, collagist and teacher, born in Glasgow, where he settled. He was educated partly there and partly in Changi, Singapore, and studied at Glasgow School of Art under David Donaldson and James Robertson in mid-1970s. Showed at Royal Glasgow Institute of the Fine Arts, RSW and RSA and had a series of solo shows, including Studio Nis in Lewis, 1977–9, and Corners Gallery, Glasgow, 1982–3. Strathclyde University and Comhairle Nan Eilean hold examples.

Rosemary TONER 1967– Artist using video and film who gained a fine art degree at Central St Martins School, 1992–5. Took part in Showcase, London Film-Makers Co-Op, 1994; Start 1995 Festival, Plymouth; and Pandaemonium, at ICA, and New Contemporaries at Tate Gallery, Liverpool, and Camden Arts Centre, both 1996. There, Toner exhibited her video Why is it that sometimes I feel horny and don't understand why until later?, of 1994.

Paul TONKIN 1951– Painter on canvas, paper or board, and teacher, born Southampton. He studied at the College of Art there, 1969–70, then at Canterbury College of Art, 1970–3, taught by Geoff Rigden and Alan Gouk. He moved to London in 1973, at Space Studios, Wapping Wall, 1974–85, then at Greenwich Studios from 1986. Tonkin said that his pictures were "attempts at orchestrating visual elements by improvisatory means. It is by the eye that they are made and by the eye that they may be understood." He worked as visiting lecturer at Reading University, and at Canterbury, Manchester, Hull and Goldsmiths' Colleges of Art. Mixed shows included Stockwell Public Library, 1974; Stockwell Depot Annual Exhibitions, 1976–9; Serpentine Gallery Summer Show, 1982; Whitechapel Art Gallery Open Exhibitions from 1984; and Merz Gallery, 1989. Had a solo show at Air Gallery, 1980.

Godfrey TONKS 1948– Artist in mixed media and pastel, notable for landscapes using a bright palette. He was born in Yorkshire, distantly related to Henry Tonks, who taught at the Slade School of Fine Art with distinction prior to World War II. Studied at Burnley and Swansea Schools of Art and eventually settled with his family in a remote Pennine farmhouse. Frequently painted abroad, notably in France. Exhibited at Walker Gallery in Harrogate, Zillah Bell in Thirsk, Art Works in Bradford-on-Avon, Jane Neville Gallery in Ashlockton, Mall Galleries and had a major solo exhibition at The Medici Galleries, 1996.

John TONKS 1927– Sculptor and teacher, born in Dudley, Worcestershire. He studied at Birmingham College of Art, 1945–6 and 1951–2, his teachers including the sculptor William Bloye, also at Wolverhampton College of Art, 1948–51. Went on to teach for some years at West Midlands College of Education. Completed a number of commissions for churches and schools, including some abstract work, in the Midlands. Lived at Wall Heath, Staffordshire.

Myles TONKS 1890–1960 Painter and draughtsman who was by profession a surgeon, born at Darley, Warwickshire. Studied at Medway School of Art and with Henry Tonks. Exhibited RA, NEAC, RI, ROI, RHA, PS and elsewhere. Percy V Bradshaw in his book *Water-colour: A Truly English Art* illustrates Tonks' Col de Lauteret mountainscape in which the artist looked for "translucency, an unworried paper-surface", a good example of his work. Lived at Watchet, Somerset.

Romeo TOOGOOD 1902–1966 Painter and teacher, born in Belfast, Northern Ireland, who began his career as a painter and decorator, studied at Belfast School of Art, teaching there part-time, then went to Royal College of Art. He held a series of teaching posts after his return to Ulster, in 1949 joining the staff of Belfast College of Art. Showed at RUA of which he was an associate, RHA, Magee Gallery in Belfast and elsewhere. Ulster Museum holds his work. Arts Council of Northern Ireland put on a retrospective in 1978.

Olwen TOOKEY 1910– Painter and muralist, born in Birmingham where she continued to live at Moseley, studying at the local School of Art under Bernard Fleetwood-Walker and Richard Stubington. She was made an associate of RBSA in 1948, also showing at RA, RP and Paris Salon.

David TOOP 1949– Musician, artist and writer, born in Enfield, Middlesex, who studied fine art/graphic design at Hornsey College of Art and Watford School of Art, 1967–70. Between 1964–8 Toop had played guitar in bands and projected light shows at rock gigs, and between 1970–80 concentrated on improvised and experimental music rather than the visual arts. Among his many-faceted activities were: in the theatre, with Paul Burwell, in 1976, performing music for Steven Berkoff's Greenwich Theatre production of *Agamemnon*; in publishing, co-founding *Musics* and *Collusion* magazines, between 1975–83; in recording, launching the Quartz Publications record label in 1978; in sound recording/research, in 1978, recording in the Amazonas rainforest; in writing, in the 1980s, acting as music critic and columnist for many publications, including *Sunday Times, Arena, Spin, Elle, Tatler, The Independent, The Wire, The Times* and *GQ*; and in books, in 1992, contributing a lengthy biographical essay to the monograph on *Stephen Cripps: Pyrotechnic Sculptor*. In 1993, Toop lectured and performed in Japan and in 1994 released *Buried Dreams* with Max Eastley, with whom he had shared a show at Chapter Arts, Cardiff, in 1976. Lived in London.

Cecil Wotton TOOVEY 1891–1954 Painter and printmaker, born at Berkhamsted, Hertfordshire. He held a commission in the Indian Army, in which he served 1915–47. He was educated at Malvern College and exhibited RA, Guildford Art Society, SWE and Army Art Society, of which he was vice-chairman, 1952. Lived at Godalming, Surrey.

Marianne TOPHAM 1945– Artist and designer, descended from a line of artists, notably Francis William Topham, she was trained at Byam Shaw School of Art under Bernard Dunstan. Worked as a designer for the General Trading Company; freelanced, doing work for David Hicks, Colefax & Fowler and Nina Campbell; then worked with architects on the rebuilding of Windsor Castle. In 1994 had a solo show at Christopher Wood Contemporary Art, meticulously painted interiors.

Feliks TOPOLSKI 1907–1989 Artist and writer, born in Warsaw, Poland. Studied at Warsaw Academy of Art, 1925–30, then travelled in Italy and France in late 1930s. From age of 20 was a prolific contributor to books and periodicals in Poland. Although he had settled in England in 1935 he was an official Polish war artist during World War II, depicting the Battle of Britain but also serving widely overseas. *Britain in Peace and War*, 1941, and *Russia in War*, 1942, were two selections of drawings. Topolski published many sketchbooks, often stemming from trips abroad, such as *Paris Lost*. Also designed for the theatre; drew his huge Cavalcade of the Commonwealth for the Festival of Britain, 1951; drew Labour Party leaders for the 1964 general election; and produced his *Memoir of the Century* from his studio under the arches of Hungerford Bridge. Topolski was a pictorial journalist whose febrile, hectic line is instantly recognisable. Work held by the British Museum, Tate Gallery and Imperial War Museum. Lived in London, which he called "our beautiful black city" before its buildings began to be cleaned up.

Amikam TOREN 1945– Artist working in a variety of paper-type media, born in Jerusalem, Palestine, who was self-taught. He showed at Venice Biennale in 1984 and John Moores Liverpool Exhibition from 1987, in 1989–90 winning a prize for his Minimalist work Of the Times, one of a series created by pulping an issue of *The Times* newspaper. Also took part in On a Plate, Serpentine Gallery, 1987, and Fragments of False Houses at Pomeroy Purdy Gallery, 1988. From 1983 he had regular solo shows in London, notably at Anthony Reynolds Gallery from 1985. In 1990 had one-man show at Israel Museum with tour. Arts Council holds his work.

Peter TOSELAND 1917– Watercolourist, restorer, scribe and teacher, born in Broughton, Northamptonshire. He attended Northampton School of Art, 1931–7, then Royal College of Art, 1937–40, under Ernest Tristram and Dorothy Mahoney. Toseland served in the Army in World War II, 1940–6, as a cartographer, then taught art, 1946–65, being involved in picture restoration, 1965–84. He was a scrivener of the College of Arms. Showed in RA Summer Exhibitions, 1950–1, in Britain in Watercolours, and between 1950–62 had 24 solo shows at Eton College. The Brewhouse Gallery there and Hove Museum and Art Gallery hold examples. Lived in Brighton, Sussex.

John TOULMIN 1911–1967 Artist in gouache and watercolour, studied at Armstrong College, Durham University, eventually becoming a company director. No formal art training. Exhibited at Laing Art Gallery, Newcastle upon Tyne, Shipley Art Gallery, Gateshead, and Sunderland Museum and Art Gallery. Lived at Corbridge, Northumberland, where he was a member of the Art Club. Toulmin was also a fellow of the Royal Geographical Society from 1936 until his death.

Margaret Clarisse TOULMIN 1916– Modeller who did a volume of ecclesiastical work, in England mainly in west of England churches. She was born in Filton, Bristol, and studied there at the West of England Art College under Donald Ewart Milner. Her earlier work is signed with her maiden name, Margaret C Hayes. Westbury Parish Church, Bristol, is one that contains her work. Later she moved to Canada, living for some time in Beaconsfield, Quebec.

Robert Lawton TOVEY 1924– Painter in oil and watercolour and teacher, born in Birmingham, where he studied at the College of Art, 1939–43 and 1946–7, under Bernard Fleetwood-Walker. Tovey taught painting and drawing at Dudley School of Art, 1947–53, and in Birmingham, Coventry and Leamington Colleges, 1958–9, otherwise working in Geneva, Switzerland. Exhibited at RBSA, RBA, AIA, NEAC, ROI, RWA and elsewhere in mixed shows. Showed solo in Geneva from 1957, in Baden from 1973 and at other venues. Dudley Art Gallery and Musée d'Art et d'Histoire in Geneva hold examples.

James TOWER 1919–1988 Artist noted for his ceramic work and teacher, born in Sheerness, Kent. Before studying painting and illustration at Royal Academy Schools, 1938–40, he travelled in the Pacific. After World War II service Tower attended Dora Billington's ceramic classes at Central School of Arts and Crafts, met Clifford Ellis and was invited to join Bath Academy of Art staff, where he stayed 1949–64. At various times Tower was interested in sculpture related to architecture and mosaic, sculptured forms and decorated forms. In 1963 he won a Leverhulme Research Award for terracotta research. From 1966–86 was head of sculpture department at Brighton Polytechnic. Tower's work was shown regularly at Gimpel Fils and he was included in Corsham A Celebration, Victoria Art Gallery, Bath, 1988–9, and tour. His solo shows included Gardner Centre, University of Sussex, 1967, and in America at Art Latitude, New York, 1979. Victoria & Albert Museum and Museum of Modern Art in New York hold examples.

Meriel TOWER 1911– Textile designer, teacher and painter, born in Windsor, Berkshire. She was educated at St Paul's Girls' School, then studied art at Westminster School of Art, 1929–31, and Chelsea School of Art, 1931–4, with Boris Heroys. Well-known as a textile designer from the late 1930s, after World War II she taught in Windsor. Lived Little Marlow, Buckinghamshire, later in Aston Rowant, Oxford.

Norman TOWNE 1915–1988 Painter and teacher, a follower of Keith Vaughan, whom he met in the Army during World War II. Both admired the work of Graham Sutherland. Towne became a Bevin Boy coal miner, and endured a tough time, near Wakefield, in 1942. After the war he studied at Royal College of Art, did commercial work, then taught graphics and typography at Wimbledon College of Art, retiring in 1975. Towne features in Malcolm Yorke's *Keith Vaughan His Life and Work*, 1990, and Peter Nahum showed his work.

Donald Chisholm TOWNER 1903–1985 Painter of landscapes and church works, and writer. He studied at Eastbourne and Brighton Schools of Art and under William Rothenstein at Royal College of Art, 1923–7. Showed at RA, NEAC, Goupil Gallery and elsewhere. As well as studio shows in Hampstead where he lived, also had solo exhibitions at Leicester, Walker's and Beaux Arts Galleries, at Burgh House and at Temple Newsam, Leeds, and in 1979 at Towner Art Gallery, Eastbourne, which holds three oils and four watercolours by him. Public galleries in Carlisle, Leeds and Sheffield also hold examples. Among his ecclesiastical work were reredos at Abbotsbury, Dorset; Plumstead in southeast London; and Sleaford, Lincolnshire. Towner's books included *The Leeds Potter*, 1963; *Creamware*, 1978; and an autobiography, *Reflections*, 1979. Donald Towner's niece was the artist Elizabeth Mary Towner. His father was responsible for establishing and endowing the Towner Art Gallery.

Elizabeth Mary TOWNER 1934–1995 Watercolourist, ceramist/potter and teacher, born in Birmingham. She was niece of the artist Donald Towner, whose father set up and endowed the Towner Art Gallery, Eastbourne. Studied at Royal College of Art, graduating in 1957. Taught art and ceramics at Dover and Folkestone School of Art and until mid-1995 lectured part-time in ceramics at Yeovil College of Art. Towner was a member of the Royal Horticultural Society, which was left three series of botanical paintings by her. At her death she was working on a set of iris, her main works also including series of hellebores, lilies and clematis. Exhibited with the Society, gaining two gold and one silver gilt (Grenfell) medals, also in France. Had solo exhibitions in West Country, including Charlton Adam, Avon, where she lived and had her own studio to produce slipware.

Erin TOWNSEND 1957– Portrait and landscape painter, draughtsman and designer, born in London. Her father was the athlete and academic Roger Bannister, her mother the Swedish painter Moyra Bannister. She was encouraged to paint, her teacher at St Paul's being Victor Pasmore's sister Winifred. Townsend studied at Ruskin School of Art, Oxford, 1975–8, and Royal Academy Schools, 1978–81, with Peter Greenham, Jane Dowling, Leonard McComb and Norman Blamey. She twice won the David Murray Landscape Prize, 1977–9. Mixed shows included Balliol College, Oxford, 1976; RA Summer Exhibition, 1979; Arun Art Centre, Arundel, from 1982; and Art in Business Exhibition, Oxford, 1991. Solo shows included Sally Hunter Fine Art, 1993, the year Townsend completed costumes and designs for Humphrey Carpenter's musical *Diary of a Teenage Health Freak*. Lived in Oxford.

William TOWNSEND 1909–1973 Painter, draughtsman, teacher and writer. Born in London, Townsend studied at the Slade School of Fine Art, 1926–30, under Henry Tonks. He then began to travel extensively in Europe and the Near East. His first one-man show was at the Bloomsbury Gallery, in 1932. In the 1930s became involved in Labour politics, while working as a painter and book illustrator. Among Townsend's contemporaries at the Slade were the painters William Coldstream, Claude Rogers, Geoffrey Tibble and Rodrigo Moynihan, so not surprisingly he became associated with the Euston Road School in the late 1930s, participating in Euston Road exhibitions. During the early days of World War II he made a series of drawings of Canterbury Cathedral – Canterbury was his home – and it remained an important theme in his work, as were the hop gardens and landscape of Kent. After the war, Townsend taught at Camberwell School of Art, 1946–9, and at the Slade School from 1949, on Coldstream's appointment as principal. His association with Canada began in 1951 when he went to teach summer session at Banff School of Fine Arts. He later became visiting professor at the University of Alberta and painted widely in the Edmonton area. Died at Banff. Townsend was a good teacher and excellent writer, publishing *Canterbury* in the *Face of Britain* series and *Canadian Art Today*. His journals, a small selection of which have been published, are an invaluable record of his times. Townsend was a fine draughtsman and painter whose work lost much of his Slade reticence in the Canadian pictures. Work in many permanent collections, including the Tate Gallery, Victoria & Albert Museum and Arts Council.

James TOWNSHEND fl. from c.1880–1949 Versatile and prolific painter who was educated in London, where he eventually settled, and in Paris, teachers including Adolphe Bouguereau and Carolus Duran. There was a strong story element in his pictures, notable examples being Christmas Eve in Shakespeare's Country and The Village Tuck Shop. He was elected RBA in 1897, was a member of the Royal Drawing Society and exhibited at RA, ROI, RI and elsewhere.

Jo TOWNSHEND 1967– Painter and printmaker interested in portraying ideas through the layered use of colour, shape and scale, often large pictures in acrylic. Mixed exhibitions included Antidote, Tower Bridge Piazza, 1992; RA Summer Exhibition, 1993; Print Biennial, Cologne and Berlin, 1994; and Permanent Waves, Hastings Museum & Art Gallery, 1995. Shared a show with Markus Blee at Towner Art Gallery & Museum, Eastbourne, 1997. Had solo exhibitions at Windsor Arts Centre, 1994, and Horsham Arts Centre, 1995. Leicestershire Arts Collection, South East Arts Collection and several corporate collections hold her work. Lived in Cranbrook, Hawkhurst, Kent.

Pamela TOWNSHEND 1920– Artist in oil, watercolour and mixed media, and teacher, born and lived in Cambridge. She studied in India and Switzerland and at Cambridge College of Arts and Technology. Taught at Women's Institute Denman College weekend courses during the 1970s and was president of the Cambridge Drawing Society in 1980–6. Took part in mixed exhibitions at RA, RBA, NEAC, RWA and Gainsborough's House in Sudbury. Had solo exhibitions at the Old Fire Engine House, Ely; Trumpington and Heffer's Galleries, both in Cambridge; Fry Art Gallery, Saffron Walden; and at Markswood Gallery, Great Bardfield. Cambridge and Suffolk Education Authorities hold examples.

Lawrence Leifchild TOYNBEE 1922– Painter and teacher, born in London, son of the historian and social philosopher Arnold Toynbee and brother of the writer Philip Toynbee. He attended Ampleforth College and Oxford University and studied at Ruskin School of Drawing, Oxford, 1945–7, teachers including Randolph Schwabe, Albert Rutherston, Percy Horton, Rodrigo Moynihan and Kenneth Rowntree. Among his teaching appointments were Ruskin, Oxford School of Art and Morley College, where the Gallery under his direction was notable for its exhibitions. Toynbee was a member of Marylebone Cricket Club and was especially fond of painting sportsmen in action. Had a series of solo shows at Leicester Galleries, Mayor Gallery, Agnew and Fine Art Society. National Portrait Gallery, several provincial galleries and Marylebone Cricket Club hold examples. Lived latterly at Ganthorpe, Terrington, Yorkshire.

Norman TOYNTON 1939– Painter, creator of environments and teacher, born in London, who attended Hornsey and Royal Colleges of Art. For several years from the mid-1960s he lectured at Cardiff College of Art after a period at Leicester College of Art and early in the 1970s was at Ohio State University, in America. In the late 1960s he was invited to Germany to create environments. A member of the 56 Group, Toynton showed at Grabowski Gallery's 1962 show Image in Progress and later at Zwemmer Gallery, Galleria Milano in Milan, ICA and WAC.

Virgil TRACY 1964– Visual and performance artist and lecturer, born in Redhill, Surrey. He gained a first-class honours degree in creative arts at Nottingham Polytechnic, 1989–92, post-graduate studies in 1992–3 including a professional practice and business course and the interpretation of society and culture at Nottingham University and Trent University there. Teaching experience included University of Derby, Sunderland University and Nottingham Trent University. Tracy's exhibitions and projects included *Index*, a live art work commissioned for Nottingham's Now '93 Arts Festival, 1993; *A Good Book*, transcripts of speeches by Nottingham evangelist street speakers, published as a Filofax accessory, 1994; *Soccer Skills Wallchart*, 1995; and Welcome, willkommen, bienvenue, again with a soccer theme, Cornerhouse, Manchester, 1996. Lived in London.

Richard TRATT 1953– Wildlife artist, born in Enfield, Middlesex, who studied at Northwich College of Art, 1970–2, and Dartington College of Arts, 1972–4. He was elected to SWLA in 1981 and Society of Botanical Artists in 1987. His work was widely reproduced, notably by Royal Society for the Protection of Birds, Royle Publications and Reynard Fine Art and the Society for Wildlife Art of the Nations includes it in its collection. Showed at RA, Blackheath Gallery and in Greater London Council Spirit of London exhibition and held a series of solo shows. Lived in Fordingbridge, Hampshire.

Dorothea TRAVERS-SMITH fl. from mid-1930s– Painter and printmaker, educated privately in England and Paris, who studied art at Regent Street Polytechnic School of Art and with the miniaturist Arthur Lindsey. Showed at RA, LG, SWA, Paris Salon and elsewhere. Lived for many years in London.

Dinah TRAVIS fl. from 1970s– Printmaker and teacher who studied at Bath Academy of Art, Corsham, and London University Institute of Education. She taught art in secondary schools while printing at Centre for Arts and Crafts in Beckenham, also teaching at Adult Education Institute there. Exhibited in Kent and was included in Group '77 Printmakers at Woodlands Art Gallery, 1981, where she showed geometrical abstract work. Her pictures were held in British and foreign collections.

Walter TRAVIS 1988–1962 Oil painter and lithographer, born in Ashton-under-Lyne, Lancashire. He studied at the Royal College of Art, gaining his diploma in 1915, then went on to exhibit at the RA, NEAC, RBA and in the provinces. Lived in London.

Sylvia TREADGOLD 1918–1987 Artist in pastel, watercolour and black-and-white. Was educated at Haberdashers' Aske's and Bedales, studied art at St John's Wood School of Art, 1935–8, with Patrick Millard and also trained professionally as a medical illustrator. Signed non-medical work Sylvia T. She was art editor of *Medical and Biological Illustration*, published by the British Medical Association, and was attached to several hospitals, including Guy's, in London, as a medical artist. Her work was reproduced in medical magazines and children's books, as well as being used for advertising and in films. The Science Museum, London, holds her work and she designed and carried out a huge mural for Charles Darwin's house at Downe, in Kent. Exhibited RBA and was especially noted for her paintings of cats. Lived at Bishop's Stortford, Hertfordshire.

Frances TREANOR 1944– Artist in pastel and collage and teacher, born in Penzance, Cornwall, whose work was richly coloured, with a strong interest in flowers. The themes "of inaccessibility and distancing which occur between people" were important to her. Treanor won a major country scholarship to study fine art at Goldsmiths' College, where her teachers included Sam Rabin and Betty Swanwick; then did postgraduate studies at Hornsey College of Art, 1966–7, with Kurt Rowland and Peter Green. She gained a diploma in geriatric art teaching, London University, 1972. Was elected a member of PS, 1978, becoming a council member. She taught art in various Inner London Education Authority establishments, including St Joseph's Academy, Blackheath; Guy's Hospital; and the American College. She received the Law Society Art Group Special Prize, 1972–3; Diplôme d'Honneur Salon d'Anthony, 1975; L'Artiste Assoifée Award, 1975; George Rowney Pastel Award, 1982; Frank Herring Award for Merit, 1984; and Conté Award, 1986. Medici Society and United Nations Save the Children Fund reproduced her work. In 1993 Treanor was given a chapter in Judy Martin's book *Pastel Masterclass*, with 10 paintings reproduced. Took part in many mixed shows in Britain and abroad. Solo exhibitions included Hall Place, Bexley, 1979; Paperpoint, 1985; London Weekend Television Centre, 1987; and Coach-House Gallery, St Peter's, Guernsey, 1991. She did the stage set for Oxford University Dramatic Society's production of Shakespeare's *As You Like It*, 1988, which toured in England and abroad. Lived in London.

John TREDGETT 1911– Painter and printmaker who studied at Westminster School of Art. He showed with NS of which he was a member and in other mixed shows. Lived in Farnham, Surrey.

Michael TREE 1921– Painter and draughtsman, born in New York into a wealthy family, moving to England in the 1920s. His mother owned the decorating firm Colefax and Fowler. After education at Eton College and a commission in the Household Cavalry in World War II, Tree studied at Slade School of Fine Art under William Coldstream, where he became a close friend of Lucian Freud, who painted him. Tree became a director of the auction house Christie's, heading the valuation department. Had solo shows with Jacobson/Hochman Gallery in New York, 1981; Fine Art Society, 1984; and Lumley Cazalet, 1995. Contributed illustrations to John Betjeman's autobiographical poem *Summoned by Bells*. Tree's celebrated garden at Shute, Dorset, designed by Sir Geoffrey Jellicoe, was for years important, as were trips abroad, especially to the Greek island of Spetsai. Lived latterly in London.

Robin TREFFGARNE 1916–1976 Artist in oil, ink and watercolour, and teacher, born in London. His full name was Arthur Robert Howard Williams-Treffgarne, but he declined to use this. He was educated at Westminster School, St John's Wood Art School, 1935, under Patrick Millard and at Slade School of Fine Art, 1936–8, where he won the Robert Ross Prize, Design Prize and Diploma. During World War II served with the Middlesex Regiment, was art master at Mercers School, 1943–4, at Oundle, 1944–54, then Harrow School, 1954–76. John Minton, Bryan Wynter, Patrick Heron and Paul Feiler were close friends and the painter and patron Edie Lamont owned his work. Treffgarne was a member of Penwith Society and took part in its Winter Show, 1949. Other mixed show appearances included City Art Gallery, Bristol, Contemporary Painting, 1950; LG, New Burlington Galleries, 1951; Arts Council, Country Life, 1952; Robins Croft Gallery, Chilham, 1967; and Merchant Taylors' School Exhibition, 1968. Had a solo show at The Thames Gallery, Windsor, 1963. Died in Harrow on the Hill, Middlesex.

Suzanne TREISTER 1958– Painter, born in London where she continued to work. She studied at Brighton Polytechnic, 1977–8, St Martin's School of Art, 1978–81, and Chelsea School of Art, 1981–2. She showed in Figuring out the 80s, Laing Art Gallery, Newcastle upon Tyne, 1988, and in same year The New British Painting, Cincinnati and American tour; and 21st Cagnes-sur-Mer International Painting Festival, 1989. In 1989–90 John Moores Liverpool Exhibition she was third prize winner. She was a solo exhibitor at Edward Totah Gallery from 1985 and in 1990 a touring one-man show was based at Ikon Gallery, Birmingham. Arts Council holds her work.

Richard Barrie TRELEAVEN 1920– Artist in oil, alkyd and red crayon, born in London, who specialised in depicting birds of prey. Having always painted and drawn, in late 1940s Treleaven met the bird painter George Lodge, joined the British Falconers' Club, served on its committee and obtained live hawks for models. In the early 1970s Treleaven met the painter Alexander Mackenzie, having settled in Launceston, Cornwall, which broadened the scope of his pictures. In 1977 Treleaven published *Peregrine*; wrote for specialist publications on the falcon and was acknowledged as an authority. Showed with Contemporary Bird Painters Exhibition at Reading, with Sporting and Wildlife Paintings, Moorland Galleries and AEB. Was a founder member of SWLA and British Ornithologists' Union. Showed solo at Tamar Gallery, Launceston, from 1973. T H B Bowles Collection, Retford, holds his work.

Su TREMBATH 1965– Artist, born in Rustington, Sussex, who studied at Bristol Polytechnic, Humberside College of Higher Education, Edinburgh College of Art and Cheltenham & Gloucester College of Higher Education. She gained an Andrew

Grant Bequest Major Award & Travel Scholarship, 1989; Helen Rose Bequest, same year; Winsor & Newton Prize, Edinburgh College of Art, and 1st Prize, Macallan Award, RSA Student Exhibition, both 1990. Group exhibitions included RWA Summer Show from 1984; Glasgow Print Workshop, Glasgow, 1989; Courtauld Institute of Fine Art, 1993; and Royal Over-Seas League Open, 1996. Solo shows included Art First, 1996. Trembath's work was held by Contemporary Art Society and a number of corporate collections.

David TREMLETT 1945– Sculptor and installations artist who employed a variety of materials such as steel, photographs and painted wood. He was born in St Austell, Cornwall, and studied at Falmouth Art School, 1962–3, Birmingham College of Arts and Crafts, 1963–6, and Royal College of Art, 1966–9. He created sculpture installations and from the early 1970s travelled widely, making wall-based artworks related to places visited. Had a show at Grabowski Gallery, 1970; a book-related exhibition at Stedelijk Museum, Amsterdam, 1979; and at John Hansard Gallery, University of Southampton, 1981. The year following he was included in Whitechapel Art Gallery's British Sculpture in the Twentieth Century. In 1992 Tremlett was shortlisted for the Turner Prize at the Tate Gallery. He published a number of books, including *Some Places to Visit*, 1975, and *On the Border*, 1979. Arts Council holds his work.

Geoffrey TRENAMAN 1926– Illustrator, printmaker and typographer, born in London. Studied at Brighton College of Art, his teachers including Leslie Cole. Showed at Senefelder Club and lived in Brighton, Sussex.

Kerry TRENGROVE 1946–1991 Performance artist and creator of object-based installations, born in Penryn, Cornwall. After attending the Grammar School in Falmouth he went to the local Art School, after which he embarked on a singular career. Made his name in late 1970s with a number of time-based works at Acme Gallery, Covent Garden. In Passage he tunnelled his way from the gallery into the street; in Solo he trained four dogs over two weeks. In the 1980s he created object-based installations using video, text and drawings. His Monument XI – The Guardian of Culture was shown in London in 1983, at the Venice Biennale in 1984 and then the Orchard Gallery, Londonderry, in 1985. Despite contracting cancer of the throat he taught himself to speak again so that he could teach in Sheffield, where he finally lived. Memorial show at Chisenhale Gallery, 1992.

David TRENOW 1939– Sculptor in resin and painter in acrylic, born in Woodford Green, north London. He trained as a civil engineer before studying at Hornsey College of Art, teachers including Derek Boshier, David Tindle, Hubert Dalwood and Maxim Adam-Tessier. Group shows included A Blast from the Past, Minories, Colchester, 1992. He had several solo shows in this Essex town, where he lived: at the Minories and the University of Essex, both 1982, and at Trinity Street Studios Gallery, 1990. Main works included Splash, of 1983, in welded, galvanised and painted metal, sited at Nottinghamshire County Council's open-air Rufford sculpture park. Colchester Royal Grammar School also holds Trenow's work.

Newbury TRENT 1885–1953 Sculptor and painter, born in London. Studied at Royal College of Art and Royal Academy Schools. Exhibited RA especially, also Walker Art Gallery, Liverpool, and Royal Glasgow Institute of the Fine Arts. Among his public works is a statue of King Edward VII in Brighton. Lived at Abbots Langley, Hertfordshire.

Jane TRESIDDER 1944– Artist in a range of media, including mixed, oil and gouache, and poet, born in Sutton Coldfield, Warwickshire as Jane Ford, but brought up in Cornwall. In 1978 she was married to the artist B A R (Sam) Carter. She attended Falmouth School of Art, 1964, then Slade School of Fine Art, 1965–8, gaining the drawing and summer competition prizes in 1966, the Boise Travelling Scholarship and Milner Kite Travelling Bursary, 1968. Tresidder painted in Cornwall, 1969–72; from 1974 for 12 years was influenced by the Jungian therapist Buntie Wills; visited Cyprus in 1981, helping on archaelogical sites; and in 1986–9 attended Cecil Collins' drawing groups. Tresidder's work reflected her interest in universal mythologies. Group exhibitions included RA Summer Exhibitions, South London Gallery, Salt House Gallery in St Ives and Norwich School of Art touring show A Reputation Amongst Artists, 1986–7, where she exhibited as Jane Ford. Solo shows included King Street Gallery, Bristol, 1981, and Chapel Gallery, Westleton, Suffolk, 1985. Her poems *In the Mirror of Your Eyes* were published in 1992. Lived in Mousehole, near Penzance, Cornwall.

Stuart TRESILIAN 1891–1974 Painter, illustrator and teacher, born in Bristol. Studied at Regent Street Polytechnic School of Art, teaching there as a pupil teacher, then gained a scholarship to Royal College of Art. During World War I he was taken prisoner at Rastatt, in Germany, made drawings of camp life and is represented in Imperial War Museum. He became a brother of the Art Workers' Guild and was master in 1960; was a member of SGA, being its president, 1962–5; and showed at RA and Royal Glasgow Institute of the Fine Arts. Cecil Stuart Tresilian was principally a graphic artist who illustrated many books, notably a series of children's stories by Enid Blyton and some by Rudyard Kipling. After World War I he returned to teach at Regent Street Polytechnic, living in London, eventually retiring to Winslow, Buckinghamshire. Tresilian had a first solo show at Upper Grosvenor Galleries in 1970 which included illustrations to Kipling's Mowgli stories, based on drawings done in the London Zoo and photographs.

David TRESS 1955– Painter and teacher, born in London, who studied at Harrow College of Art and Trent Polytechnic, Nottingham, where he graduated in fine art. Moved to Pembrokeshire in 1976. Taught art history part-time for the extra-mural department of The University College of Wales, Aberystwyth, and from the early 1980s earned his living as a painter. Worked in a wide variety of media. Early in his career

Tress was an abstract artist in the manner of Ben Nicholson and in Nottingham he had a period working on conceptual and performance themes. In Wales he was strongly influenced by the landscape, producing strongly gestural pictures; also painted widely on the continent and produced a series of nudes in interiors. Showed widely in Wales and England, including RA Business Art Galleries, West Wales Arts Centre in Fishguard, Pelter/Sands Gallery in Bristol, Attic Gallery in Swansea and CASW. Later solo shows included University of Swansea, 1994, and Boundary Gallery, 1995. Commissions included Nature Conservancy Council. Served on WAC art committee. CASW, Pembrokeshire Museums, National Museum of Wales, Cardiff, and National Library of Wales in Aberystwyth hold examples.

Julian TREVELYAN 1910–1988 Painter, printmaker, teacher and writer, born in Dorking, Surrey, son of the poet and scholar R C Trevelyan. Educated at Bedales School and Cambridge University, where he was a member of the Experiments group. For several years in early 1930s studied with S W Hayter at Atelier 17 in Paris. His early work was experimental, his paintings incorporating everyday objects. At university he had written that "to dream is to create" and so it was logical that he became one of the English Surrealist Group in 1936. During service as a camouflage officer in the Royal Engineers during World War II he declared his religion to be Surrealism. His pictures, in a variety of styles, retained a dreamlike, often childlike, fantastic quality. Was married to the potter Ursula Darwin, marriage dissolved in 1950; then from 1951 the painter Mary Fedden. He was a tutor at Chelsea School of Art, 1950–60, and engraving tutor at the Royal College of Art, 1955–63. Made hon. senior RA in 1986. Published his autobiography *Indigo Days* in 1957. Tate Gallery holds his work. Lived in London.

Cecil G TREW 1897–1959 Primarily a medical artist, was born in Clifton, Bristol, studying art at Bristol School of Art, 1913–15. Was during the 1930s for several years head of the art department at the Imperial Service College. Exhibited RWA, Victoria & Albert Museum and abroad. Trew published a large number of books on animals, sailing, flowers and some art instructional titles such as *Elementary Pen and Ink Work* and *Elementary Pencil Drawing*. Lived in Ongar, Essex.

Harold Fletcher TREW 1888–c.1973 Painter in oil, etcher and architect by profession, born in Gloucester, settling finally nearby at Churcham. Trew became a chartered architect, having attended the Crypt School in Gloucester and Sidcot School in Somerset, and after World War I for a few years was engaged in town planning and reconstruction for the Greek government. He was a fellow of RIBA and a member of the Town Planning Institute. Studied art at Gloucester and Cheltenham Colleges of Art and in Paris. Showed at RA, Cooling Galleries, NEAC and elsewhere.

Barbara TRIBE fl. from late 1920s– Sculptor, painter, printmaker and teacher, born in Edgecliff, New South Wales, Australia, married to the artist John Singleman. Studied at Sydney Technical College under George Rayner Hoff, 1928–33; at City and Guilds School of Art with Edgar Frith, 1936–7; then with Regent Street Polytechnic School of Art under the sculptor Harold Brownsword. After working in London in World War II she moved with her husband to Cornwall, settling at Sheffield, Penzance. From 1948 taught at Penzance School of Art. Tribe was made a member of SPS in 1954 and a fellow of RBS in 1957. She regularly travelled to the Far East and Australia and was prolific, being noted for her portraits. Showed at RA, UA, LG, St Ives and Newlyn Societies of Artists, Paris Salon and elsewhere and had several retrospectives, including City Museum and Art Gallery in Stoke-on-Trent, 1979; a sequel there, 1981; also in 1981 a retrospective at Mall Galleries, work by "Australia's most important living sculptress" plus a collection of complementary Aboriginal paintings. Stoke-on-Trent and Royal Air Force Museum in Hendon hold examples. Tribe's Jarrah Maid is illustrated in Eric Newton's monograph *British Sculpture 1944–1946*, published in 1947.

Tony TRIBE 1947– Painter and teacher, notable for landscapes, who studied at Camberwell School of Arts and Crafts, 1963–8. Went on to teach in adult education in London, where he was born and lived. Exhibited widely in mixed shows, including RA Summer Exhibitions from 1969; Greater London Council Spirit of London, 1978; Opix Gallery, 1979; and Woodlands Art Gallery from 1980, in Figurative Painters. Solo shows included Woodstock Gallery, 1972, and Radlett Gallery, 1977. HRH The Prince of Wales bought his work.

John TRIGG 1943– Painter, sculptor, draughtsman and teacher, born in Boston, Lincolnshire. The Fenland landscape long held an attraction for him. Trigg studied carpentry and furniture-making at Rycotewood College, Thame, 1959–60, then gained his national diploma in furniture at High Wycombe College of Art and Design, 1960–4. During 1965–6 Trigg worked on prefabricated housing in Finland, Lapland and Russia; he was to continue travelling widely through his career. After working for London architects, 1966–9, from 1969–71 Trigg lived in Amsterdam and began painting. His wide teaching experience was to encompass Buckinghamshire College of Art and Design, 1971–7; Her Majesty's Prison, Oxford, 1978–92; Berkshire College of Art and Design from 1988; Museum of Modern Art, Oxford, 1989–92; and Thames Valley University, 1993–4. In 1993, the year he moved his studio/workshop to Penzance, Cornwall, Trigg was granted a Churchill Travelling Scholarship to Africa. The totemic nature of the local sculpture influenced his own output. Group shows included Museum of Modern Art, Oxford, 16 Studios, 1986; Piccadilly Gallery, 1988; and Ainscough Gallery, Liverpool, 1996. Among his later solo shows was Falmouth Art Gallery, 1997. In 1987 Trigg was commissioned by the Crown Estate Commissioners to paint five panels, with a theme of The Beach, for Chilterns Shopping Centre, High Wycombe. Arts Council holds drawings by him.

Alker TRIPP 1883–1954 Painter, poster artist, draughtsman, illustrator and writer. Born in London, he followed his father George Tripp into a public service career which curtailed the time he could devote to art. However, he exhibited quite widely at RA, RI, ROI, SMA and Walker Art Gallery, Liverpool. He illustrated for a large number of publications and his work appeared as railway posters. Wrote and illustrated several books with watery themes, such as *The Waters of the Wight* and *Shoalwater and Fairway*. Was knighted, as Sir Herbert Alker Tripp, in 1945. Lived at Thames Ditton, Surrey.

Stella Jane TRIPP 1954– Artist working in mixed media, born in Taunton, Somerset. She studied at Portsmouth Polytechnic, 1973–6; Camberwell School of Arts and Crafts, 1976–7; at Eastern Illinois University in America, 1980–1; in 1982–3 at Southern Illinois University. She showed the construction Untitled at East, Norwich Gallery, 1991, about a decade after abandoning oil paint on canvas as alone too restrictive to express ideas. Lived in Exeter, Devon.

Beryl TRIST: *see* **Beryl NEWMAN**

Sybil TRIST 1907–1991 Portrait painter who was born in St Albans, Hertfordshire. After private education she was taught painting at Slade School of Fine Art, 1923–5, then at the Royal Academy Schools, 1925–7, under Harold Workman. She was married to the physician Sir John Richardson. Noted for her portraits of children, she showed at RA, RI, SWA and UA, of which she was a member. Lived in London.

Ernest William TRISTRAM 1882–1952 Painter, draughtsman, writer and influential teacher, born in Carmarthen, Wales. Studied under W R Lethaby at the Royal College of Art and went on to become professor of design there. Exhibited RA. His four-volume *English Wall Painting* is a standard work, published between 1944–55. Examples of his drawings of such paintings are in the collection of the Victoria & Albert Museum. Lived at Haslemere, Surrey.

Henry TRIVICK 1908–1982 Artist, teacher and writer, great-grandson of the artist Benjamin West. Studied at Central School of Arts and Crafts, later teaching lithography there and at Regent Street Polytechnic School of Art. He was a friend of Stanley Spencer, collaborating with him to produce lithographs from Spencer's drawings. Wrote a number of books, including *Autolithography*, 1960, and *The Craft and Design of Monumental Brasses*, 1969, and illustrated many others. Executed murals for the liner *Queen Elizabeth II*. Was chairman of the Senefelder Group and and a member of RBA, the Craft Centre of Great Britain and The Arts and Crafts Exhibition Society. Exhibited with leading societies and had several solo shows at Leicester Galleries. In 1996 was included in Stanley's Friends at Olivier Foyer, Royal National Theatre, organised by Michael Dickens. Victoria & Albert Museum, Ashmolean Museum in Oxford, Imperial War Museum, London Museum and Luton Art Gallery hold examples. Lived in Bourne End, Buckinghamshire.

Nina TROITZKY fl. from 1980s– Painter whose work showed strong Expressionist influences and an interest in exuberant colour. The daughter of a Russian emigré, she was born in Yugoslavia and moved to England in 1953 where she studied part-time at Leeds College of Art. Then started icon painting with Ira Kvastowctz, undertaking many commissions in Britain and America. Following a period of painting in Dutch still life school manner, Troitzky studied part-time at Chelsea School of Art with John Watson and Jo McGill. She showed with ROI, Society of Botanical Artists and in other group exhibitions. Had a solo show at Chelsea Arts Club, of which she was a member, in 1990, and Hurlingham Gallery in the same year, in 1991 showing solo at The River Gallery, Arundel. Her works were held in many British and foreign private collections.

David TROOSTWYK 1929– Artist and teacher whose output included abstract works, as in Arts Council collection. He studied at Royal College of Art, and was a travelling scholar. Troostwyk was head of painting at Winchester School of Art, 1964–7; head of sculpture at Sydney College of Arts, 1977–9; and was a visiting lecturer at Slade School of Fine Art and Chelsea School of Art. Group exhibitions included Kursaal, Ostend, and Galerie 20, Amsterdam, both 1968; Annely Juda Gallery, 1969; Axiom Gallery, 1970; Objects and Documents, Arts Council, 1972; Biannual, Sydney, 1976; Tate Gallery (which holds his work), books, 1982; and Artspace, Sydney, 1984. Solo exhibitions included University of Southampton, 1966; Kasmin, 1971; ICA, 1974; Felicity Samuel Gallery, 1977; Institute of Modern Art, Brisbane, 1979; Matt's Gallery from 1979; and Akumulatory Gallery, Poznan, 1980. Lived in London.

Peggy TROTMAN 1916– Painter, artist in collage and teacher, born in Swindon, Wiltshire, where she attended the local grammar school. A self-taught artist, she went on to show with RA, RWA and SEA. RWA holds her work, which was also obtained by a number of education authorities, including Oxford and Bristol. Lived in Parkstone, Dorset.

Josephine TROTTER 1940– Painter who studied at St Albans School of Art, 1957–9, then Chelsea School of Art, 1959–61. She participated in mixed shows at Young Contemporaries, Midland Group, Bear Lane Gallery in Oxford, Mercury Gallery and RA. Had early one-man shows at City Gallery from 1971; others included Sloane Fine Art, 1980, Grant Fine Art, in County Down, 1981, and New Grafton Gallery from 1984. Her landscapes in Britain and abroad showed a painterly spontaneity.

E J L TROWELL 1938– Artist who was born in County Durham. He studied at Sunderland College of Art, then gained his diploma at Royal Academy Schools in 1962. Among Trowell's awards was the Landseer Silver Medal for Painting; he also gained the Sir James Knott Travelling Scholarship by the Royal College of Art and painted in Spain and North Africa. Trowell became a member of NEAC in 1986. His mixed exhibitions included New Bauhaus, Cologne; RA; RBA; and in 1993 The Continuing Tradition at Chappel Galleries, Chappel. Solo shows included Brod Gallery, Culham College in Oxford, and appearances in New

York and Australia. Royal College of Art, HRH The Prince of Wales, the University of East Anglia, Imperial College and a number of corporate collections hold examples. He also painted as Jonathan Trowell.

Jonathan TROWELL: *see* **E J L TROWELL**

Herbert TRUMAN: *see* **W Herbert TRUMAN**

W Herbert TRUMAN 1883–1957 Painter of landscapes and figures, known socially and sometimes as a painter just as Herbert Truman, born in Devon, where he was brought up in Dawlish. Studied at South London School of Art and St Martin's School of Art. By 1912, the year he first exhibited at the RA, Truman was in Cairo, where he started an art school and a trades school. The Egyptian government engaged him to help the Secret Service to suppress drug trafficking and two years later Truman joined the Egyptian Intelligence Office, becoming head of the political section of the Cairo Criminal Investigation Department and a friend of T E Lawrence. Later transferred to the British General Staff and rose to the rank of lieutenant-colonel. By the mid-1920s Truman was in St Ives, Cornwall, in 1946 settling in Clifton, Bristol, where he soon joined the Savages, three years later being elected an honorary member of RWA. Also showed with Royal Glasgow Institute of the Fine Arts and at the Walker Art Gallery, Liverpool. Public galleries in Bristol and Plymouth hold examples, as does Bristol's Cathedral and its Lord Mayor's Chapel. Truman was chosen to design and illustrate the dust-jacket of Thor Heyerdahl's account of the *Kon-Tiki* expedition.

Jane TRUZZI-FRANCONI 1955–1993 Sculptor and draughtsman, born in Brixton, south London, who trained as a sculptor at Ravensbourne College of Art and Design and at Goldsmiths' College. Bernard Meadows was persuaded to accept her on the foundry course at the Royal College of Art, where in 1978 she became the first female student. The "charm, skill and dedication to hard work" commemorated by Tissa Ranasinge, then in charge of the foundry, won her the Angeloni Prize. From the early 1980s Truzzi-Franconi spent much time in Suffolk, where she established a foundry at Clock House, Bruisyard, and a studio at Yoxford. Truzzi-Franconi's work, sometimes using the lost-wax process, was notable for the tree and spiral forms of her student days; sculptures of bantams and peacocks, simple in outline; and mysterious, highly abstracted sea and fish forms of her later years. There was a retrospective at The Wolsey Art Gallery, Ipswich, 1996.

Lill TSCHUDI 1911– Lino-cut artist, born in Schwanden, Switzerland, educated in Lausanne, whose early interest in printmaking led her to study with Claude Flight who taught at the Grosvenor School of Modern Art. Also studied in Paris in the early 1930s with André Lhote, Gino Severini and Fernand Léger. During the second half of the 1930s Tschudi lived in Zürich, although she travelled widely on the continent and visited Flight in London. After World War II she returned permanently to Schwanden. Tschudi's work was notable for its bold, modern, sport- and jazz- influenced designs, coloured and black-and-white, which after World War II tended to be softer, more abstract. Showed at Redfern and Ward Galleries, with WIAC and RSA, work being acquired by the British Museum and Victoria & Albert Museum. In recent years exhibitions held by Michael Parkin and the Coram Gallery – notably Lill Tschudi and the Continuing Tradition of the Linocut, 1995 – revived interest in her work.

TSENG Yu 1933– Painter and draughtsman, born in Shanghai, China, into a family of intellectuals interested in European culture. His grandfather translated Victor Hugo into Chinese; his father was a professor at Nanking University and writer; his mother a pianist. Learned English at a Roman Catholic college in Peking and at Yenching University painted incessantly, to the detriment of his academic studies. He copied daily in the Imperial Museum, collected folk art and befriended professional painters. In 1948 travelled with his family from northern to southern China, settling in Hong Kong, where he failed his finals because of art. Huang Yun Yu was an influence and reproductions of work by Picasso and Matisse led Tseng to study in Europe. In 1952 he visited Naples, Florence, Rome and Paris and in 1953 moved to England, studying at Slade School of Fine Art. Had a solo show at Arthur Jeffress (Pictures) in 1955. Tate Gallery archive has his striking ink self-portrait, of that year.

William TUCK 1900– Landscape watercolourist, born in London where he continued to live. Apprenticed to engineering at the age of 14; from about the age of 10 he taught himself watercolour "by copying Birket Foster prints", although he also attended local evening classes. After World War II retired and spent most of his time painting, visiting France, Italy, Spain and Portugal; also painted a lot in East Anglia. Showed at RBA, RI and many other London galleries and "twice had pictures accepted by the RA but not hung". Retrospective at Passmore Edwards Museum, east London, 1974. Favoured transparent washes reinforced by pen and ink, usually spontaneous executed on-site. Became chairman of the South-Eastern Federation of Art Societies.

James Walker TUCKER 1898–1972 Painter and teacher, born in Wallsend, Northumberland. He studied at King Edward VII School of Art, Armstrong College, Newcastle, 1914–22, with Richard Hatton, then at Royal College of Art, 1922–7, under William Rothenstein, for the latter two years acting as his studio assistant. Tucker won a travelling scholarship in his final year. He went on to become head of drawing and painting at Gloucester College of Art, 1931–63. Showed widely, including RA – where his painting The Champion was Picture of the Year in 1941 – RWA and widely in the Midlands. Had a series of solo shows in that area. Chelsea Arts Club member. Lived at Upton St Leonards, Gloucestershire.

Michael TUCKER 1944– Sculptor and teacher using mixed media/found materials, born in Hope Cove, Devon, who studied at Borough Road College under Ralph Lillford. From 1966, Tucker taught in London schools, latterly at Elliott School, Putney. For his master's degree, at Roehampton Institute, University of Surrey, Tucker's dissertation was Adding to Reality, 1994; his retrospective show of that title, in 1989, was held at the George Sko Gallery. Tucker wrote that his "sometimes transient pieces", in urban and rural environments, "propose a complex membrane through which information about the world is modulated and reconstructed." Apart from Adding to Reality, the most significant were Round Britain Sculpture, postal works, 1970–4; On the Flood, constructed sculpture, Otter Estuary, Devon, 1978–85; and Escultura Andaluzas, conceptual work, Madrid, Spain, 1988. In Haiku, 1998, Tucker made "tiny, intimate objects with fragments collected on journeys and constructed to strict syntactical rules." Lived in London.

Patricia Rosa TUCKER 1927– Artist in watercolour and oil producing a range of figurative and abstract work, notably murals, born in London. She studied at Swindon School of Art and West of England College of Art, Bristol. She was a member of UA, Bromley Art Society and Chelsea Artists, also showing with RWS Club, RA and Blackheath Art Society. Had a series of solo shows including Swindon, Gloucester, Bromley, Croydon, Sidcup and in Denmark. John Piper and Walter Sickert for textural work; John Ward, Peter Folkes and Peter Greenham for portraiture; and William Bowyer were cited as influences. Main works included Albert Bridge, St Katharine Dock and Portrait of Churchill. Tucker taught in art schools and London schools, latterly in adult education. Lived in Bromley, Kent.

William TUCKER 1935– Sculptor and teacher, born in Cairo, Egypt, but came to England in 1937. Studied history at Oxford University, 1955–8, then sculpture at St Martin's School of Art, 1959–60. At St Martin's Tucker began to develop his abstract style, being one of the most gifted pupils of Anthony Caro. Brancusi was an important influence, the desire being to divest sculpture of subjective and literary references. Tucker taught at Goldsmiths' College School of Art and St Martin's in the early 1960s, later teaching in Canada and America. First one-man show was at the Rowan Gallery in 1963, and he has also shown at Grabowski Gallery, Kasmin Gallery, Waddington Galleries, Serpentine Gallery and widely abroad. Commissions include Peter Stuyvesant Sculpture Project in Newcastle upon Tyne, 1972, and Livingstone Development Corporation, Lanark, 1976. Tucker later went to live in New York, where his solo shows included David McKee Gallery and Neuberger Gallery, both 1985. Tate Gallery and Arts Council hold examples. Elected RA, 1992.

David TUDOR 1957– Artist and teacher who was born in Mold, Flintshire. He studied at Aberystwyth College of Art, 1975, then Carmarthen College of Art, 1976–80. He taught art in north Wales from 1980. Showed with RCamA, 1981; Brocton Gallery, Lichfield, 1985; Bangor Gallery, 1988; Glyn y Weddw Gallery, Llanbedrog, 1990; National Eisteddfod, Aberystwyth, 1992; and in 1994 he shared an exhibition at Martin Tinney Gallery, Cardiff.

William Desmond Latham TUDOR 1920– Painter, sculptor, potter and teacher, born in Wrexham, Denbighshire. He studied at Chester School of Art, 1938–41 and in 1946; then at Birmingham College of Arts and Crafts, 1946–7. Showed at RA and elsewhere. Taught for some years at College of Further Education in High Wycombe, Buckinghamshire, where he lived in Marlow.

Percyval TUDOR-HART 1873–1954 Teacher, painter, designer and sculptor, born in Montreal, Canada. He originally crossed the Atlantic to France to study medicine, but instead attended École des Beaux-Arts in Paris, where he revered his teacher Gérôme. He showed widely in France winning gold and silver medals at the Paris Salon. But he was best-known as a teacher in Paris, in Meudon and, after World War I, in London. Tudor-Hart was a taskmaster, his methods being outlined by one of his students, R A Wilson, in his privately published *Memoirs of an Individualist*. In England Tudor-Hart showed at RA and Walker Art Gallery, Liverpool. He lived in London but eventually returned to Canada, dying in Quebec.

Jane TUELY 1937– Painter, draughtsman and versatile printmaker, born in Wittersham, Kent, daughter of the painter Diana Low. Tuely (pronounced Tooley) studied at Canterbury School of Art, 1954–8, Central School of Art and Design and additionally in north London, her teachers including Gertrude Hermes. As well as studying graphic design she worked for a year as a typographer, then for nine years as a landscape architect, later returning to printmaking. Hampstead Artists' Council, Islington Art Circle and Printmakers' Council member who showed at Burgh House, Hampstead; Institute of Education; and The Square Gallery, Highgate. London Museum holds her work. All Tuely's work was "based on drawings done from life, usually of places, sometimes of people". Lived in London.

Edward TUERSLEY 1933– Painter, designer and teacher, born in Farnham, Surrey. Studied at Bournemouth Municipal College of Art, 1949–54, under Frederick E Courtney, then at Royal College of Art, 1956–9. Went on to teach at both Hornsey and Hammersmith Colleges of Art, showing in London, where he lived, and elsewhere.

Richard TUFF 1965– Painter and silkscreen printmaker, born in Manchester, who completed a foundation course at Mid-Chester College of Art in 1985, then gained a degree in textile design at Winchester School of Art, showing his final-year work at Smith's Gallery. He sold designs to companies in England and abroad. Moved to Falmouth, Cornwall, in 1988, eventually concentrating on paintings of Cornish towns and harbours; these had an almost-childlike, patterned quality, with rich colours. Mixed shows included RWA, New Ashgate Gallery in Farnham and The Eye Gallery, Bristol. Later solo exhibitions included Beside The Wave Gallery, Falmouth, from 1992.

Phyllis Mary TULL 1886– Painter, born in Norwich, Norfolk, where she studied at the High School. Went on to Lowestoft

Technical School, 1902–3, and attended Heatherley's School of Fine Art, 1933. Mrs Tull signed her work P M T. Exhibited with Norfolk and Norwich Art Circle, 1946–7, based in Sheringham, Norfolk. Also lived in London.

Maurice TULLOCH 1894–1974 Painter and illustrator, born in India, where he served in the Poona Horse and South Wazuristan Scouts. During World War II he commanded the 18th Cavalry and was on active service in North Africa. He contributed to *The Field* and in 1934 illustrated *A History of the Peshawar Vale Hunt*. He studied with the sporting artist Lionel Edwards and took up oil painting on retirement from the Army, being noted for his sporting and racing scenes. Was included in The British Sporting Art Trust exhibition at Alpine Gallery, 1983.

Hilary TULLY fl. from c.1990– Painter who studied at the National College of Art and Design in Dublin, 1986–7, then Limerick School of Art and Design, 1987–90. Tully then concentrated her career in Belfast, Northern Ireland. She was involved in many mixed shows, including Belltable Arts Centre, Limerick, 1989; No Access, at Crescent Arts Centre, Belfast, 1992; and in 1994 Works on Paper and Beyond the Partitions, put on by Belfast's Queen Street Studios, with which Tully was associated.

Joyce Mary TULLY 1933– Painter and teacher, born in Wooler, Northumberland, educated at Duchess Grammar School, Alnwick. She studied part-time at Hammersmith College of Art, and privately with the painter Harold Workman after attending Sunderland Training College, returning to Wooler after 14 years in 1979. She was a member of UA and Ridley Art Society and exhibited at Paris Salon, ROI, RBA, with Chelsea Artists, NS and in travelling exhibitions, including Australia. Main works included pictures of Chelsea Embankment and Bamburgh Castle.

John TUNNARD 1900–1971 Painter, designer and teacher, born in Sandy, Bedfordshire. He was educated at Charterhouse public school, where he distinguished himself in art, then studied textile design at Royal College of Art, 1919–23. During the 1920s he played jazz semi-professionally and was also a textile designer for Tootal Broadhurst Lee, 1923–9. Was also art adviser to the carpet-makers H M Southwell. Married the artist Mary Robertson. Tunnard began painting seriously in 1929, the year that he was a part-time teacher at Central School of Arts and Crafts. In 1930 he moved to Cadgwith in Cornwall and began a hand-blocked printed silk business with his wife. From this time his painting started to take off, with three paintings at RA in 1931 and a first one-man show at Redfern Gallery two years later. Exhibited in Surrealist section in AIA exhibition in 1937. Although Tunnard's work has strong realistic elements, there is usually a Surrealist flavour. After serving in coastguard during World War II Tunnard was art master at Wellington College in 1945, then from 1948 taught at Penzance School of Art for many years. Designed a mural for the Festival of Britain in 1951. Retrospective at RA, 1977. Tate Gallery holds his work.

Charles Frederick TUNNICLIFFE 1901–1979 Painter, printmaker, book illustrator and writer, son of a shoemaker-become-farmer, born at Langley, near Macclesfield, Cheshire. Tunnicliffe was noted for his depictions of birds, animals and the countryside. His pictures were anatomically immaculate yet often, especially the early etchings, had great atmosphere. He won a scholarship to Macclesfield School of Art; then Manchester School of Art, 1915–21, preceding a Royal Exhibition Scholarship to the Royal College of Art, 1921. Gained his diploma in painting, 1923. Tunnicliffe was elected RE in 1934 and RA in 1954. His work was bought by the British Museum, Harris Museum and Art Gallery in Preston and by overseas collections. He won the gold medal of the Royal Society for the Protection of Birds, 1975. Tunnicliffe was a hugely prolific illustrator of books about the country and had a long association with Henry Williamson, author of *Tarka the Otter*, 1932, and *Salar the Salmon*, 1935. Tunnicliffe's own publications included *My Country Book*, 1942, *Mereside Chronicle*, 1948, and *A Sketchbook of Birds*, 1979. He was married to the artist Winifred Wonnacott and lived at Bodorgan, Gwynedd, Wales.

Eric TUNSTALL 1897–1987 Portrait painter and illustrator, born in Stoke-on-Trent, Staffordshire, where he continued to live. He attended art schools in Stoke-on-Trent, Hanley and Burslem and went on to show at RI of which he was a member, Nottingham Art Galley Museum and RP.

Philippa TUNSTILL 1945– Artist, designer and teacher using oil, watercolour and collage, born and lived in London, who studied at Hornsey College of Art, 1964–8, under David Tindle, Michael Tyzack and John Rae. She was an interior designer, 1971–6; course director, interior design department, Croydon College of Art, 1977–87; and from 1989 foundation lecturer at Chelsea College of Art. Miss Tunstill said that her "paintings are journeys through internal and external spaces defined by shapes and forms taken from landscape and architecture. Colour is an all-important factor that tends to take over and direct the outcome." Mixed shows included RA Summer Exhibition, RSW Bankside Gallery, Manor House at Chipping Norton, Pike Gallery and Nine Elms Group. Had solo shows with Square and Harriet Green Galleries.

Gavin TURK 1967– Artist in wide variety of media, born in Guildford, Surrey. He studied at Kingston Polytechnic for foundation work, 1985–6; gained an honours degree in sculpture at Chelsea School of Art, 1986–9; then was at Royal College of Art, 1989–91. Work shown at Young British Artists IV, Saatchi Gallery, 1995, took an ironic view of his position as an artist. His Greater London Council-style blue wall plaque declared: Gavin Turk The Sculptor Worked Here 1989–91; his work Pop presented him as Sid Vicious of the Sex Pistols, holding a gun. Lived in London.

TURKLETOB: *see* **Benedict DAVIES**

Peter TURLEY 1955– Artist, born in London, who studied at Goldsmiths' College School of Art, 1972–3, then Chelsea School of Art, 1974–7. His work was included in Land, at Riverside Studios, 1988, and in South Bank Centre's The British Art Show 1990. Lived in Suffolk.

Roy TURLINGTON 1942– Artist born in Sileby, Leicestershire, who studied industrial design, 1959–65, and began painting in 1970. Studied at Sheffield College of Art, 1974–7, and was for a time artist-in-residence at Nottingham City Hospital, living in the city. In his early work Turlington "was mainly concerned with line, surface and structure"; then after a trip to Italy in 1973 he "became fascinated with frescoes where the surfaces have been changed by time, architectural alterations, deterioration and fragmentation." Group shows included Ammonite Gallery, Leicester, from 1971; Whitworth Art Gallery in Manchester and Graves Art Gallery in Sheffield, both 1975; South Hill Park Gallery, Bracknell, 1978; and Summer Show 3, at Serpentine Gallery, 1980.

Alison TURNBULL 1956– Geometrical abstract painter who was born in Bogota, Colombia. She studied at Academia Arjona, Madrid, 1975–7, West Surrey College of Art and Design in Farnham, 1977–8, and Bath Academy of Art, Corsham, 1978–81. She appeared in Whitechapel Open from 1989; in the British Council show New Voices, Brussels and Luxembourg, 1992–3; and 1993–4 John Moores Liverpool Exhibition. Showed solo with Anne Berthoud Gallery from 1989. Lived in London.

Andrew Watson TURNBULL 1874– Painter, printmaker and stained glass designer. He was educated in Edinburgh, then studied at the Royal College of Art, 1895–6, and Royal Academy Schools, 1897–1902, with Luke Fildes and George Clausen. Exhibited RA, RSA and Paris Salon. Birmingham City Museum and Art Gallery holds his work. For a time Turnbull was a partner in the stained glass designing and manufacturing firm Turnbull and Ochterlony. Lived latterly at Richmond, Surrey.

Peter TURNBULL 1950– Painter, draughtsman and teacher, born at Rockferry, Birkenhead, Cheshire, who studied at Chester College, 1971–3, Nottingham College of Art, 1973–5, then Royal College of Art, 1975–8. In 1976 he won the Rodney Burn Award for figurative drawing. After visiting lectureships at Trent Polytechnic, Cheshire and Chester Schools of Art, 1980–2, in 1982 Turnbull was appointed art department head of Chester College. Group shows included Basle Art Fair in Switzerland from 1978, RA Summer Exhibition from 1981 and he was a prizewinner at The World of Newspapers, Sotheby, 1982, sponsored by *The Daily Mirror*. Had solo shows from 1979 at Piccadilly Gallery, in 1983 exhibiting at Terry Dintenfass Gallery in New York.

William TURNBULL 1922– Sculptor, artist in other media and teacher, born in Dundee, Angus. He was early interested in drawing, and when he left school aged 15 he studied art in the evenings, enabling him to get a job as a magazine illustrator. After World War II service as a pilot in the Royal Air Force Turnbull studied at Slade School of Fine Art, 1947–8, then lived in Paris for several years where he met two artists whose work was to profoundly influence his: Brancusi and Giacometti. Had first one-man show of sculpture at Hanover Gallery in 1950 and of paintings at the same gallery in 1952. In the 1950s Turnbull began to build up an impressive tally of overseas shows. From 1951 for a time taught sculpture at Central School. Turnbull's sculpture went through a range of styles, idols and totemic figures being a leading feature. Retrospective exhibition at Tate Gallery in 1973. That gallery and many of the world's principal museums hold examples. In 1995–6 had first major show for over 20 years at Serpentine Gallery. Lived in London.

Alan TURNER 1942– Artist who described himself as "not a career artist, but a visual addict", working in such media as assemblage, boxes and mail art including rubber stamps, born in Farnham, Surrey. He studied at Hornsey College of Art, 1962–4. To support himself, Turner did a number of jobs including temping at the Prices and Incomes Board, house-painting, heavy goods vehicle driving, exhibition set builder for an electronics business and art moving. From 1991, was engaged in a number of mail art projects, including All Washed Up, 1995–6. Took part in many mixed shows, including Constructions 3, Hornsey and Romford Libraries, 1970–1; LG from 1978; Art in Boxes, England & Co, from 1991; Concern for The Earth, Riviera Gallery, Hastings, 1993; and Haringey Arts Council Open Exhibition, from 1994. Showed solo at Camden Institute, from 1967, later ones including Haringey Arts Council, 1996, and Pleasance, 1997. His work was featured in *Leonardo*, published by Pergamon, 1975, 1976 and 1980. Lived in London.

Clare TURNER: *see* **Clare DUNCAN**

Francia TURNER fl. from 1970s– Painter and illustrator, born in Boston, Massachusetts. After periods in South America, 1964–72, and Australia, 1972–8, lived in England from 1978. Studied at Ruskin School of Drawing and Fine Art, Oxford, 1981–4. She took part in mixed shows at St Hilda's College, Oxford, 1983, and Patricia Wells Gallery, Thornbury, 1985. Her individual exhibitions included two 1985 shows at Fitzwilliam College, Cambridge, and Old Fire Station Arts Centre, Oxford. She illustrated a number of books, including *The Wind Comes*, 1974, commended by Children's Book Council of Australia. Lived in Oxford.

Harry TURNER 1908– Tempera and watercolour artist, born in Halifax, Yorkshire. Studied part-time at Halifax School of Art and Bradford Regional College of Art. Showed at RA, Heal's Mansard Gallery and extensively in Yorkshire, where he lived at Braithwaite.

Harry M TURNER 1912–1979 Painter, mainly in oil, born in Walsall, Staffordshire. He studied at Birmingham College of Art, 1929–34, and declined to take up a scholarship at Royal College of Art in order to continue studies with Harold Holden. Painted still life, landscapes and a few commissioned portraits. A strong draughtsman, he was in his landscapes partly influenced by Cézanne. Held a number of teaching posts and eventually became deputy dean of Wolverhampton Polytechnic. Showed at RBA and ROI of both of which he was a member, RA and at venues in America and Japan. Memorial show of his paintings held at Wolverhampton Art Gallery in 1982. Lived in Upper Ludstone, Staffordshire.

John TURNER 1916– Painter, notable for portraits which reflected his interest in bygone techniques, born in Belfast, Northern Ireland. He studied at the College of Art there, 1935–8, then Slade School of Fine Art, 1938–41, and after returning to Ulster took up teaching, eventually at Belfast College of Art, from 1964–90 full-time. Exhibited at RUA of which he was a member, at 55a Donegall Place in Belfast and at Belfast Museum and Art Gallery. Ulster Museum and Arts Council of Northern Ireland hold examples. Lived in Holywood, County Down.

Ken TURNER 1926– Artist in various media and teacher, born in Pakistan. He studied at Ealing Art School and after war service was at Anglo-French Art Centre and Regent Street Polytechnic School of Art, a British Council scholarship allowing him to paint in Spain. Went on to teach at Central School of Art and Design. Turner from 1968–78 directed Action Space, which promoted art in the community through video, performances and sculpture, and he was also associated with ADBC, an experimental arts workshop. Took part in group exhibitions, including Art in Boxes, at England & Co, 1991. His solo exhibitions included ICA, Heal's Art Gallery and Lords Gallery. Lived in London for some years, later in the country.

Lynette TURNER 1945– Artist in a variety of media, including stained glass and printmaking, born and based in London. She studied at Manchester University, gaining an honours degree in zoology. Studied art at Brighton, City & Guilds of London and Manchester Schools of Art. Showed at RA, Century Galleries in Henley-on-Thames, Margaret Fischer Gallery and elsewhere.

Martin TURNER 1940– Painter, printmaker and muralist, born in Reading, Berkshire. He attended Gravesend Technical School, then studied art at Medway College of Art, teachers including David Graham, 1957–60, passing entrance examination to Royal Academy Schools, 1961. Turner was made a member of ROI, 1975, and NS, 1976. Also showed at RI and RA. He won a number of awards, including Bronze Medal of RI in 1976; a major prize in Artists in Watercolour Competition, 1977; and a major prize, Laing Landscape Competition, 1989. His pictures had three main themes: townscapes and villages, often in an evening light or under snow; landscapes mainly in Kent and Sussex; and river scenes of the Thames and Medway. He also carried out portrait and mural commissions for industrial organisations. Lived in Rainham, Kent.

Michael TURNER 1934– Artist in gouache, acrylic and oil, born in Harrow, Middlesex, as Geoffrey Michael Turner, who specialised in aviation and motor sport, plus military, marine and transport subjects. After a year at Heatherley's School of Fine Art, 1951–2, under Gilmore Roberts in the commercial art department, Turner did his National Service in the Royal Electrical & Mechanical Engineers, then worked in a commercial art studio in London for three years before turning freelance in 1957. His son Graham was also an artist. Turner was a founder-member, twice chairman and then president of the Guild of Aviation Artists, an honorary fellow of the Guild of Motoring Artists and a member of the Guild of Motoring Writers. He flew in a wide variety of military aircraft, held a private pilot's licence and owned a DHC-I Chipmunk, restored in Royal Air Force colours. *The Monaco Grand Prix through the eyes of M T*, 1995, and *The Motor Sport Art of Michael Turner*, 1996, were among his books. Had a series of solo shows at Mall and Carisbrooke Galleries; Watkins Glen, New York; Royal Air Force Museum in Hendon, and elsewhere. Science Museum, Fleet Air Arm Museum in Yeovilton, Brazilian Aerospace Museum in Rio de Janeiro plus club, association, squadron and mess collections hold examples. Lived in Chesham, Buckinghamshire.

Patricia Wyndham TURNER 1923– Painter, draughtsman and teacher, born in London but educated in Sevenoaks, Kent. Studied art at Cambridge School of Art, 1940–1, Tunbridge Wells School of Arts and Crafts and Central School of Arts and Crafts. Worked for a time in Ashford, Kent, as an art therapist. Had a strong interest in art craftwork and showed at Victoria & Albert Museum and elsewhere. Lived in London.

Peggy TURNER: *see* **Elsie Margaret RICHARDS**

Philip TURNER 1918–1997 Sculptor in a range of media, full name John Philip Turner, born in Sussex. He was educated at Marlborough College and studied at St Martin's School of Art and in the studio of Leon Underwood, 1936–8; at Slade School of Fine Art, 1938–40; then after Army service abroad, 1940–6, returned to the Slade, 1946–9, subsequently gaining an art teacher's diploma at London University. Thereafter, Turner taught part-time, first at Farnham School of Art and then at Willesden, Ealing and Harrow Schools of Art until retirement in 1983. Concurrently began experimenting in bronze casting, and exhibited in numerous mixed show. Carved a life-size stone figure and executed an altar-front in bronze, both for Ely Cathedral. Had a first solo show at Reid Gallery, 1964, later ones including Llanelli Festival, 1985, subsequently at Stephen Bartley Gallery. In 1986 was sculptor-in-residence at Swanage Stone Festival, Dorset; carved a stone figure of the Virgin and Child for St Mary the Virgin, Primrose Hill, 1986–7; and was sculptor-in-residence at Castlegate House, Cockermouth, in 1990, where new works were regularly shown. Was a member of Chelsea Arts Club and London Sketch Club. Arts Council holds Turner's work. Lived in London.

Prudence TURNER 1930– Painter in oil on canvas plus some watercolour, born in India, who very early showed a gift for painting. She was mainly self-taught, works being both abstract and figurative, with a special interest in Scottish landscapes. Showed widely, as well as India living in Egypt and France. King Hussein of Jordan owns her work, which was also reproduced as limited-edition prints. Lived latterly in Brentford, Middlesex.

Sheila TURNER 1941– Painter and teacher who lived on Merseyside for most of her life. At school she showed strong art talent, took a job in window display and worked in several stores before in 1974 she chose to become a full-time artist. Group shows included Northwest One and Weaver Galleries, 1976; RA Summer Exhibitions from 1979; Davey Gallery, Liverpool, 1985, where she worked part-time; and The Gallery, Manchester, 1994. Had a solo show at Neptune Theatre, Liverpool, 1975, later ones including BDP Gallery, Preston, 1994. In 1988 Turner taught part-time at Wirral Metropolitan College. Birkenhead and Wallasey Corporations bought work for their local history collections.

Stephen TURNER 1954– Painter and teacher who studied at Leeds University, 1972–6. Gained a fine art honours degree, adding his master's degree, 1977–9, at University of Regina, Saskatchewan. He was a Winsor & Newton Northern England prizewinner, 1976, gained a Canadian Commonwealth Scholarship, 1977, and in 1980 won Lincolnshire and Humberside Arts Association and ATV Network Awards. Turner held many teaching and artist-in-residence posts, including head of visual art department at Gillingham Adult Education Centre, 1984, and in that year visiting professorship at University of Regina, Saskatchewan. Mixed shows included Mappin Art Gallery, Sheffield; Midland Open, at Midlands Arts Centre, Birmingham; Andrew Grant Gallery, Edinburgh; and Metropole Arts Centre, Folkestone. He shared a four-man show at Woodlands Art Gallery, 1986. Solo exhibitions included Exe Gallery and Spacex Gallery, Exeter; Greenwich Theatre Gallery.

William TURNER 1877– Painter, notably of portraits, born in Andover, Hampshire. Studied at Southampton School of Art, 1895, and Andover School of Art, 1900. Showed at RA, UA of which he was a member, RBA and elsewhere, including Royal Glasgow Institute of the Fine Arts, 1954–60. Russell-Cotes Art Gallery and Museum, Bournemouth, holds his work, which was sometimes signed W T in monogram form. Lived in Liskeard, Cornwall.

William TURNER 1920– Painter, draughtsman and teacher, born in Chorlton-on-Medlock, Lancashire, who was noted for his portrayal of the industrial north tinged with a grim romanticism. Turner studied at Derby College of Art and went on to teach for Manchester Education Committee. He was a member of MAFA and RCamA, also exhibiting with RI, RBA, Tib Lane Gallery in Manchester, Pitcairn Gallery in Knutsford, Compton Gallery in Windsor and Boundary Gallery. In 1996 he shared a show at Graham Gallery, Tunbridge Wells. Stockport Art Gallery holds Turner's work, which was also in the collection of the writer and actor Peter Ustinov, the athlete Sebastian Coe and publisher Eddie Shah. Had a studio in Cheadle Hulme, Cheshire.

William McAllister TURNER 1901–1976 Painter, printmaker, restorer, cartoonist, administrator and teacher, born in in Mold, Flintshire. Brought up in Shotton he went to work in the steel industry but was advised by the painter Sir John Lavery to study art, so went to Chester School of Art under Walter Schroder the landscape painter, then Liverpool School of Art and finally to Italy. In 1926 he set up a studio in Chester and after several appointments became county art organiser for Flintshire. Exhibited RCamA of which he was president for a time, RSA, Manchester Salon, RWA and extensively elsewhere. In 1970–1 had a retrospective at Shire Hall, Mold. From 1961–4 was a member of WAC's art committee and in 1962–5 a governor of National Museum of Wales, Cardiff. Lived in Hawarden, near Chester.

Winifred TURNER 1903–1983 Sculptor, born in London, daughter of the sculptor Alfred Turner. She studied at Central School of Arts and Crafts, 1921–4, with her father, and at Royal Academy Schools, 1924–7. Showed at RA from 1924 and was elected a fellow of RBS in 1930. Tate Gallery and Hove Museum and Art Gallery hold her work. Ashmolean Museum, Oxford, held a show of both Turners' work in 1988.

Albert TURPIN 1900–1964 Painter and draughtsman, born and lived in Bethnal Green, east London, where he was a prominent councillor and mayor in 1946. Although he was offered a place at art school Turpin chose to devote his time to the Labour Party. At various times he was in the Royal Marines, seeing service in World War I; worked as a window cleaner; was a prominent anti-Fascist in the 1930s; and was in the heavy rescue squad of the National Fire Service in World War II, also being its official war artist; then was a supporter of Moral Re-Armament, painting a portrait of its leader Frank Buchman's London home in Berkeley Square for presentation on his eighty-first birthday. Turpin had studied with John Cooper, who started classes at the Bow and Bromley Evening Institute in the late 1920s which led to the formation of the East London Group, with which Turpin showed into the 1930s at the Lefevre Gallery. He also exhibited at Guildhall Art Gallery, East London Academy at Whitechapel Art Gallery, RA, Tate Gallery and abroad. Turpin's mission was to record the vanishing East End, and his output was prolific. The Borough of Tower Hamlets holds many examples.

Albert Walter TURPIN 1888–c.1966 Watercolourist, draughtsman and printmaker. Born in London, he studied at the Northampton Institute, 1903–9, under Robert Osmond and Nathan Vanderlyn. Sometimes signed work A W T and exhibited at RA. Lived at Wembley, Middlesex.

Dorothy TURTON fl. from 1960s–1990 Painter, miniaturist and silhouette artist, born in Cape Town, South Africa. She studied at School of Art in Bournemouth, Dorset, where she lived, also with the miniaturist Isabel Saul. She was like Saul a member of RMS, also of Miniature Art Society of Florida whose highest merit award she won in 1978, adding a Silver Medal at Paris Salon, 1979. She showed with UA, at Hunting Group Art Prizes in 1983 where she was a finalist, at Westminster Gallery from 1987 and at Grundy Art Gallery, Blackpool, 1988.

Adam TURYN 1908– Painter and black-and-white artist. Studied in Paris at Académie Julian and École Nationale Supérieure des Beaux-Arts, 1928–34. Showed at RA, RSA, SSA and Paris Salon, having one-man showing in Edinburgh. Lived in London.

Sidney TUSHINGHAM 1884–1968 Painter and printmaker, born in Burslem, Staffordshire, who attended the School of Art there and Royal College of Art, graduating in 1910. He became an associate of RE in 1915, also showing at RA, Connell & Sons, Walker Art Gallery in Liverpool and elsewhere. Public collections in England and America hold examples. Lived in London from just before World War I.

George William TUTE 1933– Printmaker, notably a wood engraver, painter, illustrator and teacher, born in Hull, Yorkshire. After education in Lancashire he studied at Blackpool School of Art, Royal Academy Schools, Courtauld Institute, Regent Street Polytechnic School of Art and Central School, notably with Gertrude Hermes. Tute taught at West of England College of Art and Bristol Polytechnic. Elected RE, first chairman of the revived SWE, was an associate of RWA and showed at RA as well as having a series of solo exhibitions. He worked for major publishers such as The Folio Society, *Reader's Digest* Association, Batsford and Penguin, for firms such as the whisky company Glenmorangie and had prints published by Merivale Editions. Victoria & Albert Museum holds his work. Lived at Westbury-on-Trym, Bristol.

Sophie TUTE fl. from early 1980s– Painter and draughtsman who completed a foundation course at Wimbledon School of Art, 1980–1. She was then at Ruskin School of Art in Oxford, 1981–4, completing postgraduate studies at Royal Academy Schools, 1984–7. Tute gained the David Murray Landscape Award in 1983, getting the Jack Goldhill Scholarship, 1984–7. In 1986 she obtained the Worshipful Company Painters-Stainers' Award, the year after getting the Haite Landscape Scholarship. Exhibited in RA Summer Exhibition from 1986 and showed solo with Cadogan Contemporary from 1988 and Vincent Gallery, Exeter, from 1989.

TUTT 1890–c.1965 Painter and draughtsman who began to work in a primitive style in the mid-1950s. His correct name was Phoebus Tuttnauer, he was born in Austria, studied at University of Vienna and became a plastic surgeon. Moved to Britain in 1938, where he studied art. Mixed exhibition appearances included London Art Gallery, RBA, RA, O'Hana Gallery, Spain and France. He had solo exhibitions at Brod and Arthur Jeffress Galleries and Ben Uri, 1959. Tate Gallery holds his pen self-portrait of that year in its archive. Tuttnauer lived in London, where he was a member of the British Medical Association and a fellow of the Royal Society of Medicine.

Phoebus TUTTNAUER: *see* **TUTT**

Jill TWEED 1931– Sculptor in bronze, married to the artist Philip Hicks, noted for her portraits. She obtained her diploma from Slade School of Fine Art, 1954, teachers including F E McWilliam. Was made an associate of RBS. Was associated with New Grafton Gallery's portrait centre, portraits including HM Queen Elizabeth The Queen Mother, TRH The Prince of Wales and The Princess of Wales, the violinist Iona Brown and the actor Gerald Harper. Had solo shows at Marjorie Parr Gallery, 1967; Compendium Gallery, Birmingham, 1975; Lad Lane Gallery, Dublin, 1978; and Quinton Green Gallery, 1987. HM The Queen holds her work as do a number of corporate and regimental collections. Lived in London.

Jim TWEEDIE 1951– Painter and graphic designer who lived in Glasgow since childhood. He was mostly self-taught, but studied graphic design at Glasgow College of Building and Printing for two years. Was a producer of simple, direct images of strong and immediate appeal. He took part in many mixed exhibitions, including Glasgow League of Artists, SSA, Glasgow Group and abroad. One-man shows included Compass Gallery, Glasgow; and he appeared in The Compass Contribution at Tramway, Glasgow, in 1990. Other solo exhibitions were at Arts Guild, Greenock, and Open Circle, Glasgow, both in 1987.

Arthur H TWELLS 1921– Painter and sculptor, born in Nottingham, where he studied under Arthur Spooner at the local College of Art, 1933–6. Showed at RHA, RUA, Magee Gallery in Belfast, Walker Gallery in Coleraine, Omell Gallery and elsewhere. Lived in Londonderry, Northern Ireland.

Flora TWORT 1893–1985 Painter and illustrator who began painting when she was only four. After South Hampstead High School she attended the London School of Art under Richard Jack, London Polytechnic and Slade School of Fine Art. Moved to Petersfield, Hampshire, after World War I and went into partnership with two other young women selling secondhand books and crafts. She became noted for her illustrations of life in Petersfield and at Langstone, where she had an old mill as a studio. From late 1920s showed with few intervals for over 20 years at RA, also at Walker Art Gallery in Liverpool, NEAC and SWA. In 1985 she bequeathed her studio cottage to Hampshire County Council and in 1991 the Flora Twort Gallery and Restaurant opened. London Library, Southampton Civic Centre and Royal College of Physicians hold her work.

Kit TWYFORD 1936– Sculptor and teacher, born in Sheffield, Yorkshire, who attended King Edward VII Grammar School there, the local College of Art, 1954–7, then Slade School of Fine Art, 1957–60, with a Slade School Postgraduateship in the latter year. After gaining an Italian Government Scholarship through the British Council, 1960–1, Twyford returned to the Slade to complete his studies, 1961–2, in that year winning a British Commonwealth Scholarship to India. A Sainsbury Foundation Scholarship followed in 1963. Teaching included Leeds and Ravensbourne Colleges of Art. Had a first show of sculpture at

Redfern Gallery in 1969. After a long period of not showing in London, had a solo exhibition at Pomeroy Purdy, 1989–90. Lived at Clapham via Lancaster, Yorkshire.

James TYLDESLEY 1947– Artist in oil, and teacher, born in Bolton, Lancashire, who studied at Central School of Art & Design, 1974–7, teachers including John Plumb, Cecil Collins, Bill Turnbull and Adrian Berg. He taught there (later Central St Martins) from 1978, and at other schools for short periods, such as Blackheath and Hornsey (Middlesex Polytechnic). Tyldesley latterly joined The Society of Catholic Artists. He produced "landscape, still life and religious paintings and worked both from direct observation and imagination. For me the power of art is to console." For many years he felt unready to exhibit, and usually did so only when pressed to by others; the Central St Martins staff show at Conway Hall, 1997, was an example. The Inner London Education Authority owned Tyldesley's work. Lived in London.

Philip TYLER 1964– Figurative artist and teacher, born in London, who studied at East Ham College of Technology; Loughborough College of Art and Design, 1983–6; Virginia Commonwealth University in Richmond, America, 1985; and Brighton Polytechnic, 1988–90. Between 1986–8 Tyler was slide librarian at Loughborough College, also lecturing at John Storer House Community Centre, Loughborough; he lectured at Loughborough during 1988 and was a part-time lecturer at Richmond-upon-Thames College, 1988–9; becoming head of printmaking, course co-ordinator and lecturer in advanced art and design there, 1990. His awards included first prize in Young Contemporaries in Paint and Print at Horsham Arts Centre, 1992. Other group exhibitions included University of Creative Arts, Bratislava, Czechoslovakia, 1985; Deepdale Exhibitions, Burnham, from 1989; Grafiki, Warsaw Academy of Fine Arts, Poland, 1990; Pacesetters 12, Peterborough Museum & Art Gallery and tour, 1992; and Royal Over-Seas League Open, 1994. In 1988 had solo shows at Loughborough College and Clock Yard Gallery, Derby. Hove Museum & Art Gallery has his 1995 oil on canvas Wrestlers (after Muybridge).

Derek TYMAN 1962– Sculptor using a variety of materials, born in Stockport, Cheshire. He did a foundation course at Stockport College, 1984–5, then was at Liverpool Polytechnic, 1985–8, and Royal College of Art, 1988–91. He won a Henry Moore Foundation Scholarship in 1990. His submission for the 1992 Sculpture at Canterbury exhibition was Blind, in which a folded and sewn suit, suit material, wood and screws were used. In the same year his installation The Awkwardness of Speech was in the Norwich Gallery/Kent Institute of Art and Design East & South show. In 1989 Tyman was featured in the Channel 4 television series: *Bed, Chair, Table, Lamp*. Lived in London.

Ursula TYRWHITT 1878–1966 Painter who was born in Nazeing, Essex. Was married to the artist Walter Tyrwhitt. She studied at Slade School of Fine Art 1893–4, then again in 1911–12, also in Paris at Atelier Colarossi and at the British Academy in Rome. She was a friend of Augustus John, who drew her and described her as one of the "talented and highly ornamental girl students" at the Slade when he was there. Exhibited extensively at NEAC, of which she was a member, Alpine Club Gallery, Oxford Art Society and elsewhere. Tate Gallery holds her work. She lived for some years in Puerto de la Cruz, Tenerife, Canary Islands, but died in Oxford.

Peter TYSOE 1935– Artist and sculptor using a variety of traditional and modern materials, born in Bedford. He attended Oxford Technical School and Oxford School of Art, 1952–6, then Goldsmiths' College School of Art, 1956–7. He obtained his art teacher's certificate, was a fellow of the Society of Designer-Craftsmen and British Society of Master Glass Painters as well as for a time being chairman of Devon Guild of Craftsmen and Federation of British Craft Societies. Did a substantial amount of commissioned work in Britain and continental Europe, latterly being head of the glass section at Jam Factory Workshops at St Peters in South Australia, living in Adelaide. In 1990 he had a show of sculptural glass at Jam Factory Gallery. Plymouth City Museum & Art Gallery holds his work.

Ian TYSON 1933– Artist in a range of media, born in Wallasey Cheshire, who studied at Birkenhead School of Art and Royal Academy Schools. He founded Tetrad Press in 1970 and organised and wrote the catalogue for the show British Artists' Books 1970–83 with Silvie Turner. Was awarded a Brinkley Fellowship at Norwich School of Art, 1979–80. Group shows included Norwegian Print Biennale, 1980; Printmaking: Four Observations, Newcastle Polytechnic Gallery, 1982; and UEA Collection, Sainsbury Centre, Norwich, 1983. Later solo shows included Bookworks, 1985, and Flowers East, 1994, where Tyson showed paintings and relief constructions based on a simple frame-like motif. WAC, Victoria & Albert Museum, Tate Gallery and many other public collections worldwide hold examples.

Kathleen TYSON 1898–c.1982 Oil painter of landscapes, marine pictures and miniatures. Born at Grimsby, she studied at Hull Art School and the Westminster School of Art. Went on to exhibit widely, venues including RA, NEAC, RBA, ROI, SWA and LG, the provinces and Paris Salon. Her work was reproduced in *The Times* and *Manchester Guardian* and in *Royal Academy Illustrated*. Principal works include The Flower Market, Antwerp, Polperro and Royal Dock, Grimsby. Hull and Southampton Corporations bought her pictures. Lived at Poole, Dorset.

Keith TYSON 1969– Artist working in variety of media, born in Ulverston, Lancashire, who did mechanical, engineering craft studies at Barrow-in-Furness College of Art, 1984–9; was at Carlisle College of Art, 1989–90; then studied alternative practice at University of Brighton, 1990–3. Tyson gained an ICA Arts and Innovation Award, 1996. Group exhibitions included Passive Voyeurs, Stanwicks Theatre Complex, Carlisle, 1990; Institute of Cultural Anxiety, ICA, 1995; In Passing, The Tannery, 1996; and Dissolution, Laurent Delaye, 1997. Solo shows included Anthony

Reynolds Gallery, 1995; David Zwirner Gallery, New York, 1996; and Galerie Georges Philippe Vallois, Paris, 1997. Also in 1997, had a solo exhibition at Anthony Reynolds which included Give us this day in the life, painting/mixed media on 366 breadboards set into a wall drawing.

Nicola TYSON 1960– Figurative artist, born in London, who studied at Chelsea School of Art, 1979–80, and at Central St Martins School of Art 1980–1 and 1986–9. Moved to New York in 1991, where for two years she operated Trial Balloon, an alternative women-only gallery, in her studio loft. Tyson had sell-out solo shows, there in 1993 and elsewhere, producing works compared by some critics to those of Hans Bellmer, Francis Bacon and the Surrealists, with a fluid handling of paint and fine draughtsmanship. Her figures included biological mutations and could be erotic and disturbing. Group exhibitions included Whitechapel Open, at Whitechapel Art Gallery, from 1988; Milch Gallery, 1990, where Tyson showed a range of hybrid creatures made from sectional plaster casts of toy pets; Urban Analysis, Barbara Braathen Gallery, New York, 1993; Identity Crisis, The Puffin Foundation, New York, 1994; and Revealing Desire, Cristinerose Gallery, and Human/Nature, The New Museum of Contemporary Art, both New York in 1995. Other solo shows included Anthony d'Offay Gallery, Entwistle Gallery, and Friedrich Petzel Gallery in New York, all 1995.

Rowell TYSON 1926– Painter, draughtsman and teacher, born in London, who taught for many years at Carlisle College of Art and in adult education. He studied at Tunbridge Wells and Beckenham Schools of Art and at Royal College of Art, becoming an associate in 1949 then staying on for a fourth year. In 1952 was elected RBA. Showed with RA, RI, NEAC, Royal Glasgow Institute of the Fine Arts, RSMA and abroad. Carlisle City Museum and Art Gallery holds his work. Lived in Carlisle and later in Sandwich, Kent.

Marian TYSON EDWARDS 1937– Sculptor in a variety of materials, born in Manchester. She studied at Liverpool and High Wycombe Colleges of Art, gaining her fine art diploma. Showed at Mall Galleries and widely in the Home Counties. Lived in Cookham, Berkshire.

Michael TYZACK 1933– Painter and teacher, born in Sheffield, Yorkshire, who attended the College of Art there, 1950–2. He then went to Slade School of Fine Art, 1952–6, winning a French Government Scholarship in 1956. Began lecturing at Cardiff College of Art in 1964, later appointments including Hornsey College of Art and University of Iowa School of Art in America. Tyzack, who was a John Moores Exhibition, Liverpool, principal prizewinner in 1965, took part in many group shows in Britain and abroad and had a number of solo shows including Axiom Gallery and Demarco Gallery, Edinburgh. His work is in extensive public collections, including Arts Council, which holds his acrylic abstract Praetorius of 1966; CASW; WAC; Victoria & Albert Museum; and City Art Gallery, Manchester.

U

Shafique UDDIN 1962– Painter and draughtsman, born in Bangladesh. The artist's work was heavily autobiographical, drawing on childhood memories of Bangladesh or later recollections in Britain. Appeared in group exhibitions such as Whitechapel Open from 1982; Outsiders, Prema Project in Gloucestershire, 1987; and South Bank Centre's touring The British Art Show 1990. After a solo show at Whitechapel Art Gallery in 1979 others included Salvatore Ala Gallery, New York, in 1986, and Horizon Gallery, 1988. Arts Council holds. Lived in London.

Ernest Boye UDEN 1911– Painter, commercial artist and teacher, born in London. He studied at Camberwell and Goldsmiths' Schools of Art and began showing in early 1930s. From 1941–5 was an official artist with National Fire Service, resulting work being illustrated in *War Pictures by British Artists: Air Raids*, published in 1943. Uden went on to teach at Reigate School of Art. Exhibited at RA, RI, NEAC and abroad. Lived latterly in Sudbury, Suffolk.

Euan UGLOW 1932– Figure and still life painter, and teacher, born in London where he continued to live. He studied at Camberwell School of Art, 1948–51, and at the Slade School of Fine Art, 1951–4. He gained a travelling scholarship to Spain in 1952, an Abbey Minor Scholarship the following year taking him to Italy for several months. Taught at St Albans School of Art, Camberwell and Slade Schools from early 1960s. Uglow joined LG in 1959 and had his first solo show at Beaux Arts Gallery two years later. In 1961 he was a John Moores Liverpool Exhibition prizewinner, and in 1972 won first prize there. Was included in Arts Council travelling show 6 Young Painters in 1964. In 1971 won Edwin Austin Abbey Scholarship. Had shows at Whitechapel Art Gallery in 1974 and 1989, and also exhibited regularly at Browse and Darby. Uglow was a meticulous, considered draughtsman and painter, especially of the female nude and still life subjects, in the tradition of William Coldstream and the Euston Road School. Tate Gallery and Arts Council hold his work.

Fred UHLMAN 1901–1985 Painter in oil of landscape, townscapes and still life with a slightly quirky, naive appearance and employing a distinctive palette. Uhlman was born in Stuttgart, Germany, became a doctor of law and practised as a barrister 1927–33. He left Germany for Paris in 1933 and in 1934 began painting there as a self-taught artist. In 1936 he moved to London, where married, and where he soon established his reputation as a painter. Although he lived in London, he spent summers in the Croesor Valley, Gwynedd, Wales. Uhlman had his first one-man show in 1935 at the Galerie Le Niveau, Paris; his first solo show in London was at the Zwemmer Gallery, in 1938. From then on Uhlman showed regularly, one-man exhibitions and mixed shows throughout Britain. A retrospective was held at Leighton House, London, in 1968. He wrote several books, including his 1960 autobiography *The Making of an Englishman*. His work is in many important public collections, including the Fitzwilliam Museum, Cambridge, and Victoria & Albert Museum.

John UHT 1924– Painter and sculptor in a variety of materials, born in Dayton, Ohio, whose studies included University of Illinois, 1943–7. He was elected RI in 1976, becoming a prolific exhibitor, also showing at RA, Edwin Pollard Gallery and in America. Lived in Weymouth, Dorset.

Rick ULMAN 1940– Painter, printmaker and sculptor, born in America, who studied at the Art Institute of Chicago, Cincinnati Art Academy, University of Chicago, Edinburgh College of Art and Duncan of Jordanstone College of Art, Dundee. In the year that he moved to Scotland, 1963, Ulman had a show at Gerald Bernard Gallery, Chicago. In Britain he quickly began to exhibit pictures rich in imagery, in 1964 showing at the Traverse Gallery, Edinburgh, where he had a solo exhibition in 1965. In that year he was included in Drian Artists at Drian Gallery, soon followed by a solo show, other 1965 solo exhibitions including Dundee Art Gallery and the County Town Gallery, Lewes. Dundee and public and private collections on the continent, in North America and Australia hold Ulman's work.

Ewart UNCLES 1919– Printmaker, potter and teacher, born at Pill, near Bristol. Attended West of England College of Art, 1937–40 and after a World War II break in 1945–6, his teachers including Donald Milner and the painter Evan Charlton. Went to teach art and design at Redland College in Bristol, where he lived, and became chairman of the Twentieth Century Crafts Trust. Chelsea Arts Club and RWA member.

Tony UNDERHILL 1923–1977 Painter, notably of nudes and figure studies, and teacher, born in Sydney, Australia. In 1941 he joined the Australian Army, serving in New Guinea, and while in the Army and at Melbourne Technical College, 1945–6, on discharge studied with William Dobell. Had his first solo show in Melbourne, 1947, with subsequent exhibitions at Sydney and Hobart, then moved to Europe in 1948, settling in London. Travelled on continent and America. Became head of postgraduate painting at Birmingham Polytechnic. Took part in many mixed shows, including LG, Arts Council, and Redfern, Leicester and

Mayor Galleries. In 1958 Underhill had a retrospective sponsored by the German government in Ruhr cities, Bochum, Essen and elsewhere. Other exhibitions followed in Britain and abroad, including Annely Juda Fine Art, 1975. Works by Underhill are held by public collections in Britain, Australia, Germany, France and Spain.

Keith Alfred UNDERWOOD 1934– Sculptor, painter and restorer, born in Portsmouth, Hampshire. He studied at Newport College of Art, 1953–7, teachers including Thomas Rathmell and Hubert Dalwood, then West of England College of Art in Bristol, 1960–1. Showed at Young Contemporaries, WAC, Mall Galleries and elsewhere. Lived at Sedbury, Gwent.

Leon UNDERWOOD 1901–1975 Sculptor, printmaker, painter, designer, writer and teacher, born in London. Studied from 1907–10 at Regent Street Polytechnic School of Art under Percival Gaskell, then a scholarship took him to Royal College of Art, 1910–13, where he was taught painting partly by Gerald Moira. After World War I service in Royal Engineers Camouflage Section, Underwood completed commissioned pictures for Imperial War Museum. From 1919–20 enrolled for year's refresher course at Slade School of Fine Art, almost exclusively life drawing under Henry Tonks. In 1921 opened Brook Green School, started on two years of constant printmaking and began first major painting, Venus in Kensington Gardens. From 1920 Underwood had been teaching life drawing at Royal College of Art, but in 1923 he resigned and went to Paris and Iceland on a Rome Prize grant. By then he had had first one-man show at Chenil Galleries, 1922. The 1920s were busy for Underwood: he travelled extensively, notably in Mexico, studying Mayan and Aztec sculpture, and in Spain studying cave paintings; he illustrated a number of books, including his own novel *The Cat*, with woodcut illustrations; exhibited widely; taught drawing at St Martin's School of Art; and in 1931 founded and published the magazine *The Island*, to which such artists as Henry Moore and Eileen Agar contributed. The 1930s saw intense sculpture activity, and in 1934 he published *Art for Heaven's Sake*. In World War II Underwood served in Civil Defence Camouflage, 1939–42. After the war he visited West Africa, wrote several books on its art and did first oil paintings on African themes. From the 1950s Underwood was very busy with sculpture again and advocating his cycle of style theory and his use of optimistic subject matter. There was a first full-scale retrospective at The Minories, Colchester, in 1969; the exhibition Mexico and After took place at National Museum of Wales, Cardiff, in 1979. Tate Gallery holds his work which has been among the most neglected of twentieth-century British art, especially the sculpture.

Hans UNGER 1915–1975 Designer and mosaicist, born in Germany, where he studied poster design in Jupp Wiertz's Berlin studio, 1934–5, before emigrating to South Africa. Was a freelance designer in Cape Town, moving to London in 1948. Between 1950–74 produced many posters for the London Underground, and did work on the Blackhorse Road tube station. Was a member of the Art Workers' Guild, 1966–9.

Daphne UNITE 1907– Flower and landscape painter, born in London, studied at St John's Wood Art School, 1924–6. Showed Goupil Gallery, ROI, WIAC, SWA and NEAC. Lived in London.

Jim UNSWORTH 1958– Sculptor using scrap metal to produce abstract works, irreverent and slightly battered-looking, which he decorated in bright colours. He studied at the University of Reading, 1976–80, and for a time was assistant to the sculptor Jeff Lowe. Mixed shows included New Contemporaries at ICA, 1980, where he was a prizewinner; Painters + Sculptors from the Greenwich Studios, Woodlands Art Gallery, 1981; Whitechapel Open (Invited Artist, 1992); and The Lewes Sculpture Trail, 1997. Later solo shows included Worcester City Museum and Art Gallery and Air Gallery. Bedford Education Authority, Hertfordshire County Council, Homerton Hospital and Worcester City Council hold examples.

Peter UNSWORTH 1937– Painter and stage designer, born in County Durham. He studied at Middlesbrough and St Martin's Schools of Art. Designed sets and costumes for three productions of the Royal Ballet. Unsworth showed extensively in group exhibitions from mid-1960s, including Camden Arts Centre, Rutland Gallery, The Minories in Colchester and abroad, including the British Council touring show Picturing People, in 1989–90. Had many one-man exhibitions at Piccadilly Gallery from 1963, a number on the continent and in 1980 a retrospective at Middlesbrough Art Gallery. Arts Council, the Government Art Collection and provincial galleries hold his work, as well as several abroad. Lived in London after several years in Ibiza.

Nora Spicer UNWIN 1907–1982 Wood engraver, book illustrator and watercolour painter. After education at Surbiton High School, Unwin studied art with Leon Underwood, at Kingston School of Art and the Royal College of Art, gaining her diploma in 1932. Exhibited at the RA, RE, SWE, Redfern Gallery, in the provinces and America. Her pictures are in many public collections. The Contemporary Art Society, the Library of Congress and New York Public Library made official purchases. Wrote and illustrated children's books. In her final years lived at Peterborough, New Hampshire, in America.

Charles UPTON 1911–1990 Sculptor and teacher, who studied at Birmingham College of Art under William Bloye, Clifford Webb, Nöel Spencer and Ernest Dinkel. With the sculptor Alan Bridgwater Upton was an occasional assistant to Bloye, then the partnership of Bridgwater and Upton of Harborne was formed, which lasted from 1937–46, when Upton became head of sculpture at Portsmouth College of Art, retiring in 1975. Their joint work can be seen on Dudley Police Headquarters, Worcestershire, Upton carving the wooden doors, lion and cubs in a deliberately naive style in emulation of medieval craftsmen. Other work by Upton is in St Swithin's School, Southsea, and Titchfield Parish Church, Hampshire. He was elected an associate of RWA in 1952, a fellow of RBS in 1965 and in 1973 gained the International Award for Sculpture in Biarritz. Also showed at RA, RBSA and

Paris Salon. Bristol City Art Gallery holds Upton's work. Lived in Warsash, Southampton, Hampshire.

John UPTON 1933– Self-taught artist, born in Hastings, Sussex. A colourful personality, he was prolific, producing works which were often large, with popular appeal and a fizzy vitality. Euro-Disney, Paris, was one of his commission venues. Mixed shows included Holborn Artists, Holborn Town Hall, 1957; Lucy Wertheim Gallery, Hove, from 1966; Erotic Art, Kaleidoscope Gallery, 1977; Painting the Town, British Council and foreign tour, 1980; Mystery Trip 90, Warsaw, Poland, 1991. Had a solo show at Hammersmith Gallery, 1958, followed by several dozen more, including latterly Harbour Art Centre, Irvine, 1992. In the 25 years 1966–91 Upton painted around 50 murals, including many works in Brighton, Dudley, Leicester, Irvine, Glasgow, Paisley and Burnley. He held a large number of residencies and produced works for festivals, including Brighton Festival and Glasgow Garden Festival. Victoria & Albert Museum holds his work. Lived at Dreghorn, Ayrshire.

Mark UPTON 1964– Painter, born in Marlborough, Wiltshire. He was noted for his commissioned portraits of horses, dogs and people. The Upton family was strongly connected with the countryside, Mark's father being Roger Upton, the falconer, his mother, Jean Turnell, the daughter of Bob Turnell, a chasing trainer. Mark Upton attended school in Marlborough and began painting young under the tutelage of his uncle Peter Upton. He took a foundation course at Swindon College of Art and embarked on a professional painting career aged 20. His first major show was held in Jeddah, Saudi Arabia, in 1990, after four years' exhibiting in the Middle East. This was followed by an exhibition at William Marler Galleries, Circencester, then in 1992 he showed at Park Grosvenor Galleries. His work is widely held in private collections overseas.

Michael UPTON 1938– Painter, performance artist and teacher, born in Birmingham. He attended the College of Art there, 1954–8, then the Royal Academy Schools, 1958–62. From 1971 he was a visiting tutor and external assessor in painting at various art colleges as well as being a teacher at Royal Academy Schools. Upton won the Leverhulme Scholarship there in 1960; the Abbey Scholarship (Rome Scholarship to Italy) in 1962; a Cassandra Foundation Award (William Copley), New York, in 1971; and 10 years later a South West Arts Major Award. Upton took part in many group shows, mainly in Britain. Had a solo show at Piccadilly Gallery in 1966 and one at Warehouse Gallery 10 years later. In 1980 he was the subject of the inaugural exhibition at Anne Berthoud Gallery, where he later showed on a number of occasions. In 1987 a show arranged by Anne Berthoud toured in Britain, finally going to Yale Center for British Art, in America. Upton generally worked on a small scale, his precisely crafted, muted pictures being concerned with time and change. Arts Council, British Council and Government Art Collection hold examples. Had a studio in Mousehole, Cornwall.

Peter UPTON 1937– Painter, printmaker and writer, born in Dulwich, south London. His mother was a professional artist, Rachel Cain; his uncle Charles Cain the etcher. Charles taught Peter Upton during the time he was studying art and art history at college and university. The Upton family had a long association with the countryside (Peter Upton's twin brother, Roger, was a noted falconer), and Peter became noted for his pictures of Arab horses. He wrote and illustrated *The Arab Horse*, 1992. Upton had many mixed and solo shows in Britain and abroad. He also painted watercolours of the British countryside, as shown at Park Grosvenor Galleries, 1992.

John URBAN 1941–1988 Printmaker, painter and teacher, born in Old Furnace, Massachusetts, America. He attended the University of Massachusetts, 1963–6; courses at Oxford University; and Brighton College of Art, 1967–9, where he concentrated on printmaking with Jennifer Dickson. For a time lectured at West Surrey College of Art and Design. Showed RE of which he was a member, William Weston Gallery, Museum of Modern Art in Oxford and widely abroad. British Museum and RE hold examples. Urban ended up living in London, alcohol leading to a tragic early death. He was a well-read man, interested in artists such as Samuel Palmer and William Blake. Lacked self-confidence, although his etchings, often witty and showing an exquisite technique, were of consistently high quality. They appeared in the *Transatlantic Review* and he completed four bookjackets for Bell of *Persian, Breton, Chinese* and *Russian Folktales*, to which his style was admirably suited.

Joseph URIE 1947– Painter, printmaker and draughtsman of strongly autobiographical and emotional works often featuring animals, richly coloured and with Symbolist, Surrealist and Expressionist undertones. He was born in Glasgow and studied at Duncan of Jordanstone College of Art, Dundee, 1977–81; he won the RSA's Chalmers-Jervis Prize, a Duncan of Drumfork Travelling Scholarship, a Patrick Allan-Fraser Scholarship and a British Institute Prize in 1980, with a Farquhar Reid Travelling Scholarship in 1981. From 1981–4 studied at Royal Academy Schools, in 1982 gaining the Dorothy M Morgan Prize, in 1984 the J van Bueren Wittman Prize and in 1984–5 a fellowship at Cardiff College of Art. Group exhibitions included Forebank Gallery, Dundee, 1978; Dundee Printmakers, Printmakers Workshop, Dundee, 1981; Scottish Drawing Exhibition, Paisley Art Institute, 1985; The Vigorous Imagination, Scottish National Gallery of Modern Art, Edinburgh, 1987; and The Vigorous Imagination – Ten Years On, The Scottish Gallery, Edinburgh, 1997. Solo shows included Roger Francis Gallery, 1985. Worked latterly on Scottish west coast.

Gera URKOM 1940– Artist working in a wide variety of media, including installations work, born in Yugoslavia. He studied at Belgrade Academy of Fine Arts until 1972 when he moved to England on a travelling scholarship, living in London from 1974. Group shows included Richard Demarco Gallery in Edinburgh, 1973; Tokyo Biennale of Prints, Gallery of Modern

Art, Rome, 1979; and Summer Show 3 at Serpentine Gallery, 1980. Solo shows included Museum of Modern Art in Belgrade, which like the Tate Gallery holds his work, 1975, and in the same year ICA.

Donald URQUHART 1959– Painter, draughtsman and photographer, born in Bankfoot, Perthshire. He studied at Edinburgh College of Art from 1978–82. During this period before graduation he won a scholarship to the Patrick Allan-Fraser School of Art, Hospitalfield, and was commended at Stowells Trophy Exhibition at RA in 1980. In addition to travelling scholarships to Paris in 1981 and Belgium in 1982 he was the first Scot to win the Richard Ford Award from RA, enabling him to work in Spain in 1982. From 1983 Urquhart painted full-time in Glasgow, while travelling extensively in Europe, North America and India. He exhibited widely in group and one-man shows in Britain and Europe, including Main Fine Art, Glasgow. In 1990 he painted for three months in Amiens, France, on a cultural exchange programme. The following year he was invited to participate in the International Weeks of Painting at Celje, Slovenia, after which he travelled to Zagreb, Croatia, to work on a series of photographs of a city at war. His work used a limited palette to express his concern and foreboding for the natural world; this was a preoccupation, as was the landscape of his youth.

Jane URQUHART 1947–1983 Painter and draughtsman, who was said to have lived "close to the interface between genius and mental illness" – she was diagnosed by a psychiatrist as suffering from chronic schizophrenia – and whose intense, exact output, notably still lifes of dolls, was concentrated into her early twenties. She was born in a military hospital in Graz, Austria, only daughter of Major-General Ronald "Tiger" Urquhart. She attended Elmhurst Ballet School in Camberley before leaving home to board at Sherborne School for Girls, where she was considered clever, sociable and artistic. Suffered from anorexia nervosa, her health deteriorating so that she was admitted to a London mental hospital for drug treatment and was unable to complete formal education. She had begun to paint and in 1966–7 worked in the studio of the painter John Ward, returning for two months in 1969. Also attended irregular classes at Malvern School of Art, 1967–9, and for a week only was a guest student in Royal Academy Life Class, 1967. After a long period of mental instability she drowned herself near her home in Newent, Gloucestershire. Her most notable works were A Box of Souls and An Hymn to Love, which was shown in RA Summer Exhibition in 1974, was bought by the photographer Norman Parkinson but was destroyed by fire. A memorial show was held at Cheltenham Art Gallery and Museum, 1990–1.

Murray URQUHART 1880–1972 Painter, notably of animals, born in Kirkcudbright. Studied at Edinburgh School of Art, Slade School of Fine Art, Westminster School of Art under Walter Sickert, at Frank Calderon's School of Animal Painting and at Académie Julian, Paris. Exhibited extensively at RBA of which he was a member, also at Lefevre Gallery, Walker's Galleries, RA and NEAC. He completed a portrait of Lord Snell for Chatham House, London. Lived in Meopham, Kent.

Clara URSITTI fl. from late 1980s– Conceptual and installation artist, born in Toronto, Ontario, Canada, who attended York University there, 1988–92, then Glasgow School of Art, 1993–5. Exhibitions included Temagami Wilderness Project, Whitewater Gallery, North Bay, Ontario, 1988; Round Up 90, Vermont Park, Toronto, 1990; Outspoken Red, Student Centre Gallery, Toronto, 1992; and New Art in Scotland, Centre for Contemporary Arts, Glasgow, 1994. In that show, aided by a chemist and perfumier, Ursitti attempted a non-visual self-portrait by "reproducing my body odour chemically".

David URWIN 1937–1988 Versatile artist and town planner, born in London. Urwin started painting and sculpting in 1956, and was "interested in a range of techniques, choosing the medium which best reflects the form envisaged." He studied in Kent with Derek May and with various tutors in Cambridge. After reading geography at Cambridge University and National Service, Urwin joined the town planning department of the London County Council/Greater London Council in 1964, later moving to Cambridge City Council, where he became city planning officer. He took part in a variety of mixed exhibitions, ranging from London Artists, Shrewsbury School, 1968, to The Gallery on the Cam, Cambridge, 1985, and was a member of the East Anglian Potters' Association. Among influences on Urwin's work were music (for a time he was in the Southwark Cathedral choir), especially Bach and Beethoven; characters in Arthur C Clarke's science fiction novel *Childhood's End*; man's desire to fly; painters of the 1950s; potters such as Bernard Leach; and medieval, Renaissance and Yemeni architecture. Urwin died of cancer at home in Cambridge in 1988. In 1988–9 there were posthumous solo exhibitions at Bottisham and Soham Village Colleges. Some of Urwin's photographs are in the Cambridge collection at Lion Yard Library in the city. Ruth Mellanby's booklet *Cambridge in Brief* is illustrated by Urwin. In 1989 his widow, the calligrapher Jenny Urwin, helped set up The David Urwin Heritage Awards.

William UTERMOHLEN 1933– Painter and printmaker, born in Philadelphia, Pennsylvania, who studied at the Academy of Fine Art there, then Ruskin School of Drawing, Oxford. Solo exhibitions included Traverse Theatre Gallery, Edinburgh, 1963; Bonfiglioli Gallery, Oxford, from 1965; and Amherst College, Massachusetts, 1974, where he had been visiting artist for two years. Royal Free Hospital, Hampstead, has a mural by him, completed 1985. Lived in London.

John UTTING 1948– Artist, notably a printmaker, and teacher who studied at Brighton College of Art, 1967–8, at Liverpool College of Art, 1968–72, then fine art at Slade School, 1972–4. As well as part-time lecturing at several colleges and universities, Utting lectured in printmaking at Falmouth School of Art and Design, 1974–85, then was senior lecturer in fine art there from 1987. Showed widely, including Britain, the continent and Japan and was included in Falmouth Connections at Falmouth Art Gallery, 1994.

John UZZELL EDWARDS 1937– Painter and illustrator, born at Deri, Rhymney Valley, south Wales. Uzzell Edwards said that he "avoided art colleges". Between 1962–70 he had studios and a studio gallery in Merthyr Tydfil and Tenby, while working as a technical illustrator. From 1967–8 he was Granada Arts Fellow at the University of York, the following year being spent at the British School at Rome. He began showing from the early 1960s, then participated in many group shows, notably at the National Eisteddfod, where in 1972 he won the Images of Wales competition and in the following year was a winner at Portraits of Welsh People. Solo shows included University of York, Clytie Jessop Gallery, Swansea Arts Festival, West Wharf Gallery in Cardiff and in 1991 Red Square Gallery. The artist said that he went "right back to my Celtic roots for inspiration", which resulted in strong, primitive-looking, highly colourful images. WAC, National Museum of Wales in Cardiff and other collections hold his work. Lived in Swansea, West Glamorgan.

V

Guy VAESEN 1912– Painter, printmaker, muralist and illustrator who was for many years a professional theatre director, born in London. He began work on the *Ilford Recorder*, 1926–8; was in hairdressing, 1928–30; worked for Ilford Borough Council's surveyor's department, 1930–9; during World War II being in British Army Tanks Corps. From 1946 onwards Vaesen directed in repertory theatres, working in Britain and America, and began painting when he joined BBC Radio in 1963, studying with BBC Art Society, then at Central and Camden Institutes. He was elected a member of NS in 1984. Mixed exhibitions included RA, ROI, Colin Jellicoe Gallery in Manchester and Campbell & Franks. Had a solo show at Mercer College, New Jersey, in America, 1977; others including National Theatre, 1981 and 1983; Royal Exchange Theatre, Manchester, 1984; and in 1986 British Council Gallery in Kolonaki, Athens, and in Thessaloniki, both in Greece. Vaesen latterly settled in Milos, Cyclades. Commissions included a mural for a new TSB Bank in Highgate; illustrations for the first edition of Harold Pinter's play *Family Voices*; Paintings of Lady Antonia Fraser's drawing-room; and other commissions from theatrical clients: Vincent Price, Judi Dench, Nigel Hawthorne and Paul Eddington. Beecroft Art Gallery in Southend-on-Sea holds his work.

Lorna VAHEY 1946– Painter in oil and watercolour, born at Pett, Sussex, whose work was strongly autobiographical. Obtained her bachelor's degree in fine art at Brighton College of Art and Design, spending a short time at Manchester College of Art. Was a member of RSA. Settled in Hastings, Sussex, and showed in various mixed local exhibitions, 1967–91. Other appearances included Easton Rooms, Rye, 1992; RA Summer Exhibition from 1993; Hastings Museum, 1994; and Riviera Gallery, Hastings, and The Gallery, Battle, both 1995.

Denise Rooum VALE 1929– Painter, draughtsman and teacher, born in Bradford, Yorkshire. She attended Canterbury College of Art, 1954, under Christopher Alexander. Showed at Keighley and Middlesbrough Art Galleries and in the area around Bradford, where she settled.

Dennis VALENTINE 1935– Artist in watercolour, oil and various drawing media, born in Leicester. He studied at the College of Art there, 1951–4, painting under Donald Carrington, then was an art teacher and lecturer in primary education at Bishop Grosseteste College in Lincoln, 1965–88. Valentine showed with Lincolnshire & South Humberside Artists' Society of which he was a member, in Arts Council regional shows and John Laing Exhibition, Mall Galleries, 1989, and exhibited in his own Gallery in the Garden, Navenby, Lincolnshire. His work drew on "sources in the landscape. It is often close to reality but may achieve an original vision, for example where a decaying tree becomes imbued with animistic energy."

Sherree E VALENTINE-DAINES 1956– Painter, born in Effingham, Surrey, where she settled at Ashtead. She was married to the artist Mark Rowbotham and like him studied at Epsom School of Art and Design, 1976–80, teachers including Leslie Worth. She carried out a wide range of sporting commissions and showed at UA and SWA both of which she was a member, RA, RP and Royal Festival Hall.

John VALLELY 1941– Painter, born in Armagh, Northern Ireland. He had a special interest in music and musicians and the life of the province as seen in aspects such as games and customs. With his wife Eithne he produced a book called *Sing a Song and Play It*. Vallely attended Armagh Technical School part-time in 1958, was at Belfast College of Art, 1959–61, gained a Royal Dublin Society Taylor Scholarship and then went to Edinburgh College of Art, 1961–4, in 1964–5 a major travel scholarship from there taking him to Spain and Morocco. Exhibitions included Ulster Museum – it holds his work, as does Arts Council of Northern Ireland – Magee Gallery in Belfast, Municipal Gallery of Modern Art in Dublin and Tom Caldwell Galleries there and in Belfast.

Saloman VAN ABBÉ 1883–1955 Illustrator, painter and etcher, born in Amsterdam, brother of Joseph Van Abbé, the editor and illustrator who became known as Joseph Abbey. Saloman came with his family to England as a child, attended the People's Palace School, Bolt Court School and Central School of Arts and Crafts. Although at first he worked for newspapers, later he did more book work. Van Abbé was a member of the London Sketch Club, also belonging to the Art Workers' Guild from 1935. Exhibited at RA, RWA, Walker Art Gallery, Liverpool, and elsewhere. Chicago Institute, in America, bought his work. John Galsworthy's *Loyalties*, 1930, and Thomas Hughes' *Tom Brown's Schooldays*, 1951, are among books illustrated. Lived in London.

Anton van ANROOY 1870–1949 Painter, born in the Netherlands, educated at Delft University, who settled in England in 1896 and took British nationality. Interiors in Shelley House and Lansdowne House were important works. He was elected RI in 1915, also showing at RA, Walker Art Gallery in Liverpool, Royal Glasgow Institute of the Fine Arts and Goupil Gallery. Was a member of Arts Club and lived in London.

Nathan VANDERLYN 1872–1946 Painter, printmaker and black-and-white artist and teacher, born in Coventry, Warwickshire. He studied at Slade School of Fine Art and Royal College of Art and became a teacher at Central School of Arts and Crafts. Was a member of RI for some years, also showing at RA, RMS and Walker Art Gallery in Liverpool, in 1937 having a solo exhibition at Brook Street Art Gallery. Lived in London and died in Streatham, Surrey.

William Peters VANNET 1917– Painter, printmaker and teacher, born in Carnoustie, Angus. He studied at Dundee College of Art, his teachers including James McIntosh Patrick, 1935–40. Showed at RSW, Royal Glasgow Institute of the Fine Arts, SSA and elsewhere in Scotland, his work being bought by Arbroath Art Gallery. Vannet was a keen collector and student of etchings by early twentieth-century artists. Lived in Dundee, Angus.

Sarah VAN NIEKERK 1934– Wood engraver and teacher, born in London, who studied at Central School, 1951–4, then Slade School of Fine Art, 1954–5, teachers including Gertrude Hermes. She taught wood engraving at Royal Academy Schools, 1976–86; City and Guilds of London Art School from 1978; and West Dean College, Sussex, from 1980. Van Niekerk was a member of SWE, RE, RWA, Printmakers' Council and Art Workers' Guild. She illustrated for *Reader's Digest* Association, Oxford University Press, Folio Society, Gregynog Press and other publishers. Group exhibitions included RA Summer Exhibition, Museum of Modern Art in Oxford, National Theatre, widely in the provinces and abroad. From 1979 had a series of one- and two-man shows. Her work was widely featured in books concentrating on wood engraving. Victoria & Albert Museum, Fitzwilliam Museum in Cambridge, Ashmolean Museum in Oxford and other notable collections hold examples. Lived in Saul, Gloucestershire.

Arnold VAN PRAAG 1926– Painter in oil and teacher, born in London. He studied at Slade School of Fine Art, 1953–7, then became head of painting at Hertfordshire College of Art & Design, 1970–5, and visiting tutor in painting at Camberwell School of Art & Design, 1975–91. Group shows included Whitechapel Art Gallery, 1967; Art Spectrum, Arts Council tour, 1971; 40 Pictures from the Roland Collection, Birmingham City Art Gallery, 1974; The Subjective Eye, Arnolfini Gallery, Bristol, and tour, 1980; and Summer Exhibition, Redfern Gallery, from 1992. Had a solo show at ICA, 1963; a series at Roland, Browse & Delbanco, from 1965; later ones including Cadogan Gallery, 1991, and Art Space Gallery from 1994. Peter Stuyvesant and Arthur Andersen Collections, Arts Council, Courtauld Institute and University of Keele hold examples. Van Praag's pictures included a number of series: butcher and fishmonger themes, Lautrec at work, Susannah and the Elders and crossing the Red Sea. Lived at Weston Colville, Cambridgeshire.

Cecilia VARGAS 1957– Artist born in Bogotá, Colombia, who studied at Heatherley's School of Art, 1984–5, Chelsea School of Art, 1986–8, and Royal College of Art, 1988–90, gaining its Travel Award, to Paris, in 1989. She also gained an Alkazzi Award in 1990. Exhibitions included Into the Nineties II, Mall Galleries, 1990; Six Colombian Artists, Gimpel Gils, 1991; Abstraction I at Paton Gallery, 1993; and Paton Gallery at *The Economist*, 1994, where abstracts employing coloured rectangles were a feature. Paton held her first London solo exhibition later that year. Consolidated Real Estate, Geneva, holds her work.

José Luis VARGAS 1965– Painter, born in Santurce, Puerto Rico, who studied at Pratt Institute in New York, 1984–8, held a fellowship at Skowhegan School of Painting and Sculpture in Maine, 1991, then attended Royal College of Art. He appeared in group exhibitions in New York and Oxford from 1989 and won a prize in 1993–4 John Moores Liverpool Exhibition. His first one-man show was at the Arts Students' League, San Juan, 1988, and he shared an exhibition, Homage to Zurbarán, at Cubitt Street Gallery, 1994. Lived in Brighton, Sussex.

Eleanor Doris VARLEY fl. from c.1935–1976 Painter, draughtsman in pen and ink and teacher, born in London, daughter of the landscape artist Illingworth Varley and older sister of the painter Mabel Varley. She studied at Willesden and Regent Street Polytechnic Schools of Art and held several teaching posts in East Anglia and the north of England, eventually becoming principal of Lowestoft School of Arts and Crafts. Showed with SWA, RA, widely in Norfolk and Suffolk and elsewhere in the provinces. Illustrator of several books. Lived in Lowestoft, Suffolk.

Emma Louise VARLEY 1966– Printmaker, born in Welwyn, Hertfordshire, who grew up in Ipswich and studied at the College of Art there, Bradford College of Art and Leeds Polytechnic. She gained a first-class honours degree in fine art and two works from her highly praised degree show were bought by the Polytechnic for its collection. Varley often mixed print processes in a single work; used heavy-textured handmade paper which she occasionally made herself; frequently worked on a large scale; might meld over 30 colours into a single image; and incorporated such materials as sand, gold dust, tissues, glue, varnish and string into her prints. Travels in Portugal, North Africa, India and Thailand added exoticism to her colours and forms. Varley's work was included in Images of the Yorkshire Landscape, organised by Sheeran Lock at Leeds Civic Hall in 1991, and reflected her travels and sketching in the county after graduation.

Mabel Illingworth VARLEY 1907–1992 Artist in oil, watercolour, pastel and charcoal, and teacher, born in London, daughter of the artist Illingworth Varley and younger sister of Eleanor Varley. She studied art at Malvern School of Art, 1924–5; Regent Street Polytechnic School of Art, 1925–30; Central School of Arts and Crafts, 1929–30; and London University Institute of Education. She taught at St George's School, San Remo, Italy, as head of art, 1932–3; St James' School, Malvern, 1933–67; and Malvern School of Art, 1943–51. Showed at RBA, PS, NS, ROI and in the provinces. Lived in Malvern Wells, Worcestershire.

VARUNI 1909– Artist, born in Kandy, Ceylon, whose full name was Varuni Brown, and who was married to the sculptor Atri Brown. Studied art privately in Ceylon with the figure and portrait painter David Paynter, then attended Slade School of Fine Art under Randolph Schwabe and the Royal College of Art with Sir William Rothenstein. She also studied in Paris. Lived in London.

VASANT 1934– Painter and artist in collage, full name Vasant Narayan Chinchwadkar, was educated in Indore, Madhya Pradesh, India, where he attended the Art College. Showed widely in India, in London and the English provinces, signing work Vasant. It is in the collection of Trinity College, Oxford. Lived in Maldon, Essex.

Josephina de VASCONCELLOS 1904– Sculptor, born in Molesey on Thames, Surrey, her father being the Brazilian consul-general. Studied sculpture at Regent Street Polytechnic School of Art under Harold Brownsword, in Paris with Antoine Bourdelle, then in Florence. Showed at RA, RSA, Paris Salon and in 1947 shared an exhibition at RWS with her husband, the artist Delmar Banner. Signed her work in a monogram form. Was a founder-member of SPS and a fellow of RBS. National Gallery of Brazil, in Rio de Janeiro, holds her work which is also in Blackburn Cathedral, Lancashire; Hilfield Friary, Dorset; and St Paul's Cathedral. Lived in Ambleside, Westmorland.

Gladys VASEY 1889–1981 Painter, notably of portraits, one of twin sisters born in Blackpool but brought up in Manchester. She studied in evenings with Polish painter William Fitz about 1909, after attending a finishing school in Germany. In 1936 she visited Lamorna Birch's school in Cornwall, meeting Stanley Gardiner. Vasey was elected a member of MAFA in 1934, where she showed extensively, was an associate of RCamA from 1953–6 and was a full member of SWA, 1961–5. She also showed at RP and ROI. In 1938 Vasey's picture Madeleine was accepted by City Art Gallery in Manchester. From 1957 Vasey wrote for *Art Quarterly* magazine. In 1973 she had a show at National Library of Wales in Aberystwyth, where she lived, and it held a commemorative exhibition in 1991.

Andrew VASS 1961– Artist in charcoal, oil, drypoint and watercolour, and part-time lecturer, born in London, who attended Cambridge College of Arts and Technology, 1978–82, teachers including Jon Harris. Group shows included South Bank Picture Show, from 1984; Hunting Group, Mall Galleries, from 1989; and Artwalks, Ipswich, from 1996. Had a series of solo shows at Trumpington Gallery, Cambridge, from 1982, later ones including Amalgam, from 1990, and Christchurch Mansion, Ipswich, 1998. This 1990–7 retrospective included work responding to Vass' home environment around Holbrook, on the Shotley Peninsula, Suffolk. Richmond Borough Council holds his work.

Geoffrey VASSIE 1926– Painter in oil, born in London, who was in the retail footwear and menswear trade in Bristol, eventually settling in Southbourne, Dorset. From 1974–9 studied with Kit Gunton. Had solo studio shows and exhibited in groups at Russell-Cotes Art Gallery and Museum, Bournemouth. Scenes of the New Forest area and Christchurch were among Vassie's favoured subjects. In 1980 he was made a fellow of the Royal Entomological Society.

Elsa VAUDREY 1905–1990 Painter, born as Elsa Dun in Glasgow, who was married for a time to the artist Peter Barker-Mill (whose second name, Vaudrey, she adopted for her work), their daughter being the painter Amanda Barker-Mill. Although Vaudrey was initially an artist of a traditional type, towards the end of the 1950s she developed a distinctive abstract style, vibrantly colourful pictures often being on a large scale. Some were shown in a memorial show at Fine Art Society in 1990. Vaudrey graduated from Glasgow School of Art, 1924–7, taught by Ancell Stronach. After marrying Barker-Mill they settled in Wookey Hole, Somerset. There during World War II she ran a vegetarian maternity home. After the war she showed in Rome and at the Storran, Leicester and Redfern Galleries, de Chirico praising a solo exhibition there in 1959. The image of the Grail and a close friendship with the writer J C Powys were key influences on the work of Vaudrey, who travelled extensively while being based in London.

VAUGHAN: *see* **Michael John Vaughan BEVIS**

Doris VAUGHAN 1894–1975 Painter, notable as a Colourist and follower of her friend Christopher Wood. Little is known of her early life, spent in Cheltenham. Early in World War I she married the artist Colin Sealy, and although financially their early years were not easy, they were eased when Sealy came into an inheritance. In 1927 they acquired a studio in St Ives, Cornwall, and from then Vaughan's work became inextricably linked with the harbours of St Ives and Mousehole. During the 1930s Vaughan showed at Wertheim Gallery, with a series of solo exhibitions in 1934–7–9. Vaughan separated from Sealy by the mid-1950s. She continued to live in London, but had an unsettled life from the early 1970s when the council required her Chelsea flat for demolition. After her death, in 1976 Gallery 10 in Richmond held a show of her work, and in 1977 Belgrave Gallery had a joint Vaughan and Sealy exhibition.

Keith VAUGHAN 1912–1977 Painter, draughtsman, diarist and teacher, born at Selsey Bill, Sussex. Although Vaughan did not have formal art training he gained a good grounding in Italian Renaissance art while at Christ's Hospital, then worked in the Lintas advertising agency, then owned by Unilever, 1931–9, painting in his spare time. During World War II was at first a conscientious objector, then served in the Pioneer Corps, from 1941–6 his fluent German enabling him to be a prisoner-of-war interpreter in Yorkshire. This was the period when he came into contact with the Neo-Romantic painters, such as Graham Sutherland and John Minton, which markedly affected his work. First one-man show of drawings at Lefevre Gallery in 1942, followed by another of oil paintings in 1946. From now on he established himself as a successful artist in Britain and abroad. Painted the Theseus mural decoration in the Festival of Britain Dome of Discovery in 1951. Vaughan taught at Camberwell School of Arts and Crafts, 1946–8; at the Central School of Arts and Crafts, 1948–57; then at the Slade School of Fine Art from 1954. He travelled extensively, being visiting resident artist at Iowa State University, in America, 1959. Vaughan's artistic theme was constant: the male nude in the landscape, although in his later work the images can be highly abstracted; the palette is unmistakeable, however. The Tate Gallery and many other public galleries hold his work. Retrospective at Whitechapel Art Gallery with Arts Council tour, 1962. After his death there was a memorial exhibition at Mappin Art Gallery, Sheffield. Vaughan's journals, which have been published, give a graphic insight into his often vulnerable, obsessive and sad private life. Lived in London.

Michael VAUGHAN 1938– Painter and draughtsman of elegant abstracts, and teacher, born in Shipley, Yorkshire. He studied at Bradford College of Art, 1956–60, and Royal Academy Schools, 1960–3, and was one of the group known as the "Bradford Mafia", other members including Norman Stevens, Pete Kaye, David Hockney, John Loker and David Oxtoby. Gained a fellowship in painting at Manchester College of Art, 1963–4, teaching there, 1964–8, also at Hornsey College of Art, 1968–72. Group exhibitions included Young Contemporaries, 1963–4; New Generation, Whitechapel Art Gallery, 1964; British Painting Here and Now, Macy's, New York, 1968; British Painting '74, Arts Council, 1974; and 6 Bradford Artists, Cartwright Hall, Bradford, 1976. Had a series of solo shows at Hanover Gallery from 1968; at l'Uomo e l'Arte, Milan, 1972; and Gimpel Fils, 1979. Later lived and worked in Los Angeles, California, and Beaufort, South Carolina. Arts Council holds examples.

Marc VAUX 1932– Painter, printmaker and teacher, born in Swindon, Wiltshire. Studied at the School of Art there, 1954–7, then at Slade School of Fine Art, 1957–60, winning a Boise Scholarship to travel in latter year. Early in 1960s Vaux appeared in Paris and Tokyo Biennales. He had a solo show at Grabowski Gallery in 1963, another at Hamilton Galleries in 1965, others including Whitechapel Art Gallery in 1973 and Redfern Gallery in 1994. Taught at Bath Academy of Art and Hornsey College of Art for a decade from 1962 and was principal lecturer in painting from 1973 at Central School of Art and Design. Vaux produced geometrical and sometimes Minimal abstracts where were held by Tate Gallery, Arts Council and Gulbenkian Foundation. Lived in London.

Hayward VEAL 1913–1968 Painter and teacher, born in Eaglemont, Victoria, Australia. He studied in Melbourne under A D Colquhoun and Max Meldrum, whose interest in tonal painting was a lasting influence, even though Veal did flirt for a time with abstraction. Veal taught for about a decade in Australia and wrote on art for the Sydney paper *Daily News*. In 1951 he moved to England and while continuing to paint portraits and landscapes established a reputation as a popular art teacher. His *Oil Painting Course* was one of several books. He lived for some time in Reigate, Surrey, before deciding to return with an exhibition to Sydney in 1968, where he died. A number of state galleries in Australia hold his work.

Elizabeth VELLACOTT 1905– Artist, born in Grays, Essex. She studied at Willesden School of Art, 1922–5, then Royal College of Art, 1925–9, where she was influenced by decorative art in Victoria & Albert Museum. Initially she was a designer of fabrics, costumes and theatre sets, concentrating on painting after World War II, during which destruction of her studio cost most of her work prior to 1942. She became known for her meticulous landscape studies in pencil as well as for figurative and imaginative scenes which were stylised in an early Italian manner. Her first show was shared with Gertrude Hermes at The Minories, Colchester, in 1968. A retrospective covering her paintings and drawings, 1942–81, was held at Kettle's Yard, Cambridge, 1981, with a ninetieth birthday show there, 1995. Also showed at New Art Centre. Arts Council holds her work, typical of which was The Expulsion (after Masaccio), exhibited at 1993–4 John Moores Liverpool Exhibition, a figure painting, delicately coloured. Lived in Hemingford Grey, Huntingdon.

David VENABLES 1957– Landscape artist and latterly a photographer who was concerned about "mood and the sense of place" in his work. He studied at Wirral College of Art, 1976–7, then Gwent College of Higher Education, 1977–80. Exhibitions included Williamson Art Gallery, Birkenhead, from 1984; Heswall Library, Wirral, 1986; and Merseyside Artists 3, toured by Walker Art Gallery, Liverpool, 1986–7.

Alex VENESS 1965– Artist, born in Hastings, Sussex, whose work was influenced by cinema clips and photography, as seen in Five RCA Painters, at Paton Gallery, 1994. Veness studied at Chelsea College of Art & Design, 1984–7, and Royal College of Art, 1992–4. Awards included John Minton Travel Award to Barcelona, 1992, and Delfina Studios Award, 1994–6. Also exhibited at La Quiñonera, Mexico City, 1989, and La Agencia there, 1990, prior to postgraduate travel scholarship to the country's Universidad Nacional Autónoma de México in 1991; Atlantis Galleries, 1993; Out of the Nineties, Mall Galleries, 1994; and Wheels on Fire, at Wolverhampton Art Gallery, and New Contemporaries, at Tate Gallery in Liverpool and Camden Arts Centre, both 1996. In 1993 Veness gained a Lloyds Bank commission.

Virginia VENNING 1913– Sculptor in stone, wood and clay for bronze, and watercolourist, born in London. She studied privately in London, Paris and Florence, and sculpture at Regent Street Polytechnic sculpture school, 1931, and Royal Academy Schools, 1934–9. She was a member of SWA and various West Country societies. As a sculptor she carried out commissions for churches, other buildings and gardens in London and West Country; portraits in bronze; and painted watercolours which were mainly landscapes. Showed at RA Summer Exhibitions, SPS and elsewhere. Lived in Shaftesbury, Dorset.

Patrick VENTON 1925–1987 Painter and teacher, born and died in Birmingham, where he studied at the College of Art, 1946–51, then taught part-time for a few years (also taught extra-mural classes for a short time while living in London). His initial success was in the first John Moores Liverpool Exhibition, 1957–8, with his impressive oil on hardboard Still-Life, Kitchen Sink, acquired by the Walker Art Gallery. Venton's was a fine talent that withered due to lack of encouragement. He took part in Six Painters in the late 1950s, which toured from the RBSA galleries, and he had a solo exhibition at Ikon Gallery, Birmingham, in 1966, his last major showing. This had a poor review, and Venton's diffidence, periods of depression and lack of commercial gallery interest meant that he did not show much latterly, although he continued to paint. In his final years Venton and his wife Zena made resin replicas of objects from the British Museum collection, which were sold in its shop. More of chain-smoking Pat Venton's time was spent on the renovation of classic cars. Georges Braque was an early influence on his painting style, as were Vieira da Silva and especially Nicolas de Staël. Venton latterly concentrated on a long series of studio tabletop pictures, the images becoming progressively abstracted.

Joyce VERES 1953– Artist and teacher who graduated from Exeter College of Art and Design, 1973–6, gaining her master's degree, Chelsea School of Art, 1976–7. Went on to become a teacher at Peterhouse Special School, Southport. She showed with Young British Printmakers, 1978; at Dryden Street Gallery, 1980; and MAFA, 1985; her Twelve Monochrome Symbols being included in 1986–7 Walker Art Gallery, Liverpool, touring Merseyside Artists 3. In 1984 she had gained a Merseyside Arts Award.

Norman Welby VERGE 1931– Painter and teacher, born in Whitefish, Montana, America. Verge obtained his bachelor's degree in 1970, studying art at City University and Art Students' League in New York and at Arizona State University and School of Art. As well as showing in America he exhibited at Upper Street Gallery; public libraries in Harrow and Eastbourne, where he taught at the College of Further Education; and at Brighton Museum and Art Gallery. Lived in Willingdon, Sussex.

Charlotte VERITY 1954– Painter and draughtsman, noted for still lifes, born in Germany. She studied at Slade School of Fine Art, 1973–7, winning a Slade Prize in latter year. Also won a Boise Travelling Scholarship in 1978 and a Greater London Arts Association award in 1982. Showed at John Moores Liverpool Exhibition from 1980; Whitechapel Open from same year; and in Still Life; A New Life, Preston and tour, 1985. Showed solo with Anne Berthoud Gallery. Arts Council holds her pencil drawing Scissors. Lived in London.

Colin VERITY 1924– Architect and watercolourist, noted for marine pictures, born in Darwen, Lancashire, who attended Hull School of Architecture, becoming an associate of RIBA in 1965. He was principal architect for Humberside County Council and settled in the county at Beverley. Verity was elected to RSMA in 1975 and shows included Beverley Art Gallery, Francis Iles Gallery in Rochester and Ferens Art Gallery, Hull. National Maritime Museum in Greenwich holds his work.

Simon VERITY 1945– Artist in various media who developed an interest in materials through working with the architect Oliver Hill. He also benefited greatly from Robert Baker's teaching at Wells Cathedral. Verity said that "St Bernard described the mystical union of the soul with God as the 'immersion in the infinite ocean of eternal light and luminous eternity'. To me, rock crystal is a medium capable of conveying something of the nature of transcendental reality to the senses." Verity's work was included in the 1985–6 Piccadilly Gallery show The Brotherhood of Ruralists and Friends.

John VERNEY 1913–1993 Painter, illustrator and writer, born in London, his father being Ralph Verney who was secretary to the Speaker of the House of Commons. His son inherited the title as Sir John Verney in 1959. He was educated at Eton College, Oxford University and the Architectural Association. Went into film-making and served in the Army during World War II, then on demobilisation devoted his time to painting, writing and illustrating, latterly decorating furniture. Exhibited AIA; Leicester, Redfern and New Grafton Galleries and elsewhere, his pictures often of the amusing, mock-naive type. Ministry of Works and London County Council bought his work. Verney illustrated a quantity of books, including series by Gillian Avery and Anthony Buckeridge, and wrote his own, including the entertaining *Going to the Wars*, 1955. He wrote two semi-autobiographical books, *Every Advantage*, 1961, and *Fine Day for a Picnic*, 1968, as well as a further volume of memoirs, *A Dinner of Herbs*, 1966. His amusing diary, *The Dodo-Pad*, appeared for some years. Lived originally in Farnham, Surrey, where he founded the Farnham Trust, to preserve buildings, latterly living in Clare, Suffolk. There was a memorial show at Gainsborough's House, Sudbury, 1994–5.

Joan VERNON-CRYER 1911– Watercolourist, born in Blackburn, Lancashire, She studied at the Technical College, in 1936 at Royal College of Art's painting school under William Rothenstein, teachers including Barnett Freedman. She was elected an associate of RWS in 1970, also exhibiting at RA Summer Exhibition and elsewhere. Her husband was the printmaker Wilfred Fairclough, their son the artist Michael Fairclough. Lived in Kingston upon Thames, Surrey.

Emile Antoine VERPILLEUX 1888–1964 Painter, illustrator and printmaker, born in London. Studied at L'Académie des Beaux-Arts, Antwerp, in London and the Netherlands. Exhibited RA, RBA, NEAC, Goupil Gallery, PS, Paris Salon, in Italy and America. He lived in Sussex for some years. Verpilleux sometimes reversed his initials when signing work. The British Museum, Victoria & Albert Museum, British provincial and some foreign collections hold his work. Later lived in Pembroke, Bermuda.

Nicholas VERRALL 1945– Painter and printmaker noted for his sunlit French scenes. Verrall was born in Northampton and studied at the School of Art there, 1961–6. He became a full-time professional painter in 1970 after two years as a commercial artist and four in picture conservation. Verrall showed at RA Summer Exhibitions from 1976, the year after he won a Royal Horticultural Award for a botanical drawing. Solo shows included Upper Grosvenor Gallery, 1972; Langton Gallery, 1977; and Catto Gallery, 1993. Lord Mayor of London owned his work. Lived in Woking, Surrey.

Virginia VERRAN 1961– Painter, born in Falmouth. She studied at the School of Art there, then Winchester School of Art, completing a postgraduate degree course at Chelsea School of Art in 1984. Verran's pictures could be disturbing images which took something from figuration and abstraction. A museum visit or reading a poem could suggest the basis of a picture. Human frailty was an abiding theme. Verran was a founder-member of City Artists. She also showed with Francis Graham-Dixon Gallery, was included in the Celtic Vision touring exhibition seen in Cornwall, Cardiff and Dublin in 1987–8, and elsewhere. Her oil on canvas Black Painting No. 7 was included in the 1997–8 John Moores Liverpool Exhibition. Had a solo exhibition at Newlyn Art Gallery, 1997. Lived in London.

Eric VERRICO 1932– Artist in pencil, linograph, poster and watercolour and pen and ink, born and lived in London. His surname was "changed to Verrier after the war because of anti-Italian feelings. Verrier was later changed to Houston for business reasons." While still at school, Verrico was taken by his headmaster to Camberwell School of Arts and Crafts. "I really didn't want to go, but I was there, and that was that." Verrico developed into a fine portrait draughtsman during his few student years, his teacher John Minton being "a very strong influence … I never heard a bad word said about him." Hearing that Minton had committed suicide, "I was devastated." Leaving art school at 16 he tried to get a job before joining the Royal Air Force. After National Service, being married and starting a family Verrico rejected art as a way of earning a living, instead managing a television shop, then becoming a motor dealer. Never exhibited, having given up art in 1948, but his work was later shown at the Fine Art Society and included in John Minton and Friends, Michael Parkin Gallery, 1997.

Jack VETTRIANO 1954– Self-taught painter, a Scotsman of Italian descent. He was a mining engineer painting in his spare time until he had two works accepted by RSA in 1988 and chose to paint full-time. A close observer of people, he created figure paintings which owed much to Hollywood films and low life. Also showed at RA Summer Exhibition, The Edinburgh Gallery and in 1993 had a solo exhibition at Catto Gallery. Lived in Edinburgh.

Paule VÉZELAY 1892–1984 Painter, printmaker and writer, born in Clifton, Bristol, as M Watson-Williams; she changed her name in Paris in the 1920s, believing it unrepresentative of her work. Studied at local School of Art, 1909–12; then in London, 1912–14, attended Slade School of Fine Art, London School of Art under George Belcher and John Hassall, and Chelsea Polytechnic School of Art. After exhibiting at NEAC in 1918 and having a first one-man show at Galerie Georges Giroux, Brussels, in 1920, had first one-man exhibition at Dorien Leigh Galleries in London in 1921. Two of her works shown in British pavilion at Venice Biennale in 1924. In 1926 she decided, after a number of visits to Paris, to settle there and it remained her home for much of her life, although ultimately she lived in London. The art Vézelay saw in Paris was so exciting that it affected her own style, which from 1928 was influenced by abstraction. She became deeply involved in the School of Paris and met many of the leading artists, including Picasso, Kandinsky and Gris. Over the years she exhibited in France and elsewhere on the continent; was closely associated with André Masson; made abstract sculptures and collages; and was involved in groups such as Abstraction-Création and Groupe Espace. Retrospective at Grosvenor Gallery in 1968, Zabriskie Gallery, New York in 1980, and Tate Gallery which holds her work, in 1983. England & Co held several Vézelay exhibitions after her death.

David VIBERT 1939– Painter, printmaker and teacher, born in Neath, Glamorgan. He went to Swansea College of Art, 1956–7, and Slade School of Fine Art, 1957–61. After three years teaching in Wales and England Vibert in 1965 studied printmaking at Academia de San Fernando, in Madrid, the following year working at S W Hayter's Atelier 17, in Paris. He then returned to teach art in Wales. Participated in many group shows, in Britain and abroad, having solo exhibitions at Woodstock Gallery, Bristol Arts Centre and Vaughan College, in Leicester. Arts Council, CASW and Galeria El Bosco in Madrid hold his work.

Dilys VIBERT: *see* **Dilys JACKSON**

Andrew VICARI 1938– Figurative painter, draughtsman and teacher, born in Port Talbot, Glamorgan, of Italian parents. Vicari, who described his work as "romantic realism", was the youngest pupil of his year at the Slade School of Fine Art, 1949–51, under William Coldstream, where his tutor was Lucien Freud. This followed a period as a child prodigy and studies at Accademia Brera, Milan. Encouragement from Francis Bacon, Josef Herman and Augustus John was a powerful influence. Vicari had his first solo show at the Obelisk Gallery in 1956. In that year, when he exhibited in illustrious company at Redfern Gallery, David Sylvester wrote of his "images of a remarkable vibrant quality, rich in poetry". Several dozen solo shows followed in London, Paris, New York and Nice. After an exhibition at the Galerie Vendôme, Beirut, in 1975, the Saudi Arabian government commissioned 60 oil paintings – The Triumph of the Bedouin – for the new King Faisal Conference Centre in Riyadh, and to complete them Vicari moved to Monaco, where he had a studio in Monte Carlo. The Majesty of King Faisal, depicting events in his life, painted for the King Faisal Foundation, was unveiled in 1984. Portraiture had become important in Vicari's output, his subjects including

Princess Caroline of Monaco and her father Prince Rainier, Prince Louis de Polignac, Princess Mimosa Parodi Delfino del Drago and many friends. Vicari's Vigonades, a symbolical and satirical series of drawings and paintings, featured enigmatic female figures and touched on the artist's concern with death. Vicari was appointed official painter to Interpol. Following the Gulf War, Vicari began a 215-picture chronicle of the conflict, The Liberation of Kuwait, in a disused factory, amid tight security, using a forklift truck to cope with the biggest canvases. In 1995 he was the first Occidental artist to exhibit in Beijing, China, a trilogy of Mao Tse Tsung, Confucius and Qin Shi Huang, first Emperor of China. Vicari's work is in numerous international public, private and corporate collections, including the Slade.

Richard VICARY 1918– Printmaker and teacher, born in Sutton, Surrey, his mother being Deirdre Vicary, his father the writer Simon Jesty. He attended Medway School of Art, 1936–9, Brighton College of Art, 1946, and Camberwell and Central Schools of Art. Became head of printmaking at Shrewsbury School of Art and published several manuals on the subject. He was a member of RWA and an associate of RE and showed at Whitechapel Art Gallery and elsewhere. Lived at Berwick, Shrewsbury, Shropshire.

Violet VICAT COLE 1886–1955 Painter, born at Caversham, Oxfordshire. She was related to several artists, being the niece of George Vicat Cole and the daughter of Ann Sorel Lavery. She studied with Arthur Cope and on the continent, eventually becoming art mistress at Hastings Grammar School. Exhibited RA, ROI and elsewhere. Hastings Museum and Art Gallery holds her work. Was a member of the Ridley Art Club and East Sussex Art Club. Lived at St Leonards-on-Sea, Sussex.

VICKY 1913–1966 Radical cartoonist named Victor Weisz, born Berlin, attending its Art School. After he moved to settle in England he became noted for his often powerful cartoons in such publications as the *Evening Standard* and *New Statesman*. His books included *Stabs in the Back*, *Vicky's World* and *Let Cowards Flinch*. Exhibited Lefevre Gallery and Modern Art Gallery. Lived in London.

Bob VIGG 1932– Painter of on-the-spot landscapes using a rich palette, and teacher, born in Plymouth, Devon, of Cornish parents, settling in Botallack, St Just, in 1987. Vigg was a mature student of painting at Rolle College, Exmouth, under Alan Cotton and gained a degree in fine art at Exeter University, 1969–74. He taught art at Oliver Goldsmith School, 1975–6, then at Farringdon House, Exeter, 1976–82 leaving to concentrate on his own work. Painted extensively in the West Country notably in West Penwith, with regular trips to France. In 1972 Vigg was made a member of St Ives Society of Artists. Showed in Cornish mixed exhibitions and had a series of solo shows, starting with University of Exeter, 1985, later ones including St Ives Society of Artists from 1994. Vigg was the author of a book on the maritime painter Thomas Luny.

Noel VILLENEUVE 1909–1983 Designer and painter who was born in New York. He was educated in England and France, studying art in London and Paris. Although he showed in Paris before World War II, in London he was known mainly as an interior designer. He died there.

Jean-Luc VILMOUTH 1954– Sculptor, born in Moselle, France. He attended École des Beaux-Arts, Metz, 1971–6, then Royal College of Art, 1976–9, working under Bernard Meadows. Vilmouth showed at Galerie Yvon Lambert, Paris, in 1978–9, in Lisson Gallery, 1979, elsewhere in France and Belgium and in 1980 his abstract work was included in the Royal College of Art's tribute show to Bernard Meadows, 1960–1980. Arts Council holds his compilation of plastic, aluminium, enamel and wood entitled Five Heads, of 1981, bought from Lisson Gallery, 1982. He was included in the Arts Council's 1993–4 touring show Recent British Sculpture. Latterly lived in France.

Ella Doreen VINALL fl. from c.1930– Printmaker, fabric printer and illustrator, born and lived in Acton, west London, daughter of the artist Joseph Vinall. She studied at Slade School of Fine Art under Henry Tonks, 1924–7; with Malcolm Osborne at Royal College of Art, 1927–30; and Central School of Arts and Crafts. She was a member of WIAC, SWA and SGA. Exhibited also at RBA, Walker Art Gallery in Liverpool, RA and elsewhere.

Joseph William Topham VINALL 1873–1953 Artist, teacher and writer, born in Liverpool, father of the artist Ella Doreen Vinall. After education in Burgess Hill, Sussex, Vinall studied at Royal College of Art, under Frank Short and Édouard Lantéri, gaining associate status in 1897, also studying at City and Guilds of London Institute. He was a Royal Exhibitioner and Queen's Prizeman. He became a member of UA and National Society of Art Masters, founding the Woodstock Art Courses. Published a number of instructional books, including *Art and How to Study It*, *Freearm & Industrial Drawing* and *Crayon and Pastel Work for Schools*, and sometimes wrote as T V Allen. Exhibited RA, RP, ROI, in provincial galleries and at Paris Salon. Lived in Ealing, west London.

Pauline VINCENT 1940– Painter, trained at Central School of Art & Design. She travelled widely, used such motifs as carpets, embroideries and gardens and worked freely with a rich palette. Group exhibitions included Proscenium Gallery, 1967; Browse & Darby, 1977; RA Summer Exhibition, 1978; Battersea Open, 1985; and Cleveland Bridge Gallery, Bath, 1991. Had a solo exhibition at Annexe Gallery 1978, then a long series from 1981 with Christopher Hull Gallery.

Paul VINCZE 1907–1994 Sculptor and medallist, born in Galgagyork, Hungary. He studied at State School of Arts and Crafts, Budapest, later privately under the great medallist Ede Talcs and in Rome from 1935–7, having won a travelling scholarship. Although he returned to Hungary, Nazi persecution forced him to leave and in 1938 he moved to England, setting up a studio in London. He was made a British subject in 1948, became an Art Workers' Guild member and a fellow of RBS. Vincze exhibited at RA and widely abroad and his work is represented in national collections and museums around the world, including Ashmolean Museum, Oxford. His awards included a Premio Especial at the International Exhibition, Madrid, in 1951, a silver medal at the Paris Salon, 1964, and the first gold medal of the American Numismatic Association, 1966. Among his output were a prize medal for the Smithsonian Institution, a series for the Shakespeare Birthplace Trust and two medals struck to commemorate the coronation of Queen Elizabeth II in 1953. Died at Magagnosc, France.

Chris VINE 1949– Artist, born in Halifax, Yorkshire, who studied at Bradford College of Art. After a period working in the theatre he went on to become an artist who also undertook freelance publishing commissions. Exhibitions included Drawn to Humour, at Cleveland Art Gallery; The Festival of Humour and Satire, Gabrovo, Bulgaria; Curiouser and Curiouser, Hourglass Gallery, Paris; and Zillah Bell Contemporary Art, Thirsk.

Darrell VINER 1946– Sculptor and teacher, born in Coventry, Warwickshire. He used a wide range of materials and media, concerns central to his work being control, change and transformation. He was involved in the production of computer-generated images and computer-animated film. Viner studied at Hornsey College of Art, 1971–4, then the Slade School of Fine Art, 1974–6. He did extensive part-time teaching and was senior lecturer in sculpture at Portsmouth University, 1980–9. Gained a number of Arts Council, Greater London Arts Association and London Arts Board awards. Among his installations were Semaphore, Chisenhale Gallery, 1990, and a Southampton City Arts commission, 1991. Group appearances included Seven Obsessions, Whitechapel Art Gallery, 1990, and the Arts Council tour Recent British Sculpture, 1993–4. His computer-animated film *Inside Outside* was shown at Coracle Press, 1977, later solo exhibitions including Around, Old Town Hall Art Centre, Havant, 1993. Arts Council holds Viner's work. Lived in London.

Louise VINES 1957– Artist who studied at Camberwell School of Arts and Crafts, 1975–9, then Royal Academy Schools. Showed in Stowells Trophy Exhibition, with local artists in Lambeth and was included in Figurative Painters at Woodlands Art Gallery, 1980.

Paul VINING 1943– Painter, draughtsman and printmaker, musician, writer and teacher, born and lived in London. He studied at Camberwell School of Arts and Crafts, 1960–4, gaining his national diploma; had private vocal tuition with Grayston Burgess and Noel A Noble in the 1960s, and was an associate of the Royal College of Music, 1972. Vining's interest was in early English music; he published reconstructions and wrote articles on it and the nineteenth-century theatre. Was a counter-tenor and choirmaster and directed the Jubilate Singers, 1967–77. After a number of jobs, including Sotheby's, Nature Conservancy Council and Department of Transport, in 1987 he returned to Camberwell College of Arts, including teaching. As a painter he was termed "post-Euston Road" by Francis Hoyland. Mixed shows included Sweet Waters Gallery, Dulwich College and Camden School of Art. Had a solo exhibition, Paintings and Drawings at Camberwell, 1962–1992, at The Tall House, Southwark, 1992.

John VIRTUE 1947– Painter and draughtsman, born in Lancashire. He studied at Slade School of Fine Art, 1965–9. Gained an Arts Council Major Award in 1981 and in 1983 was a major prizewinner in 4th Tolly Cobbold Exhibition. He was included in John Moores Liverpool Exhibition from 1987, other group shows including Nigel Greenwood Gallery in same year and Norwich School of Art, 1988. Showed solo with Lisson Gallery from 1985, having a retrospective Green Haworth: Ten Years 1978–88, London and tour including America, 1988. In 1995 there was an important exhibition at Arnolfini Gallery, Bristol, which toured. From 1971–88 Virtue worked at Oswaldtwistle which was the subject of much of his work, an example being Arts Council's Green Haworth I, of 1979–80. Later lived in South Tawton, Devon. Virtue made many studies in ink and pencil on small prepared boards of a uniform size which he then reduced by selection and combined into bigger panels.

Cor VISSER 1903–1982 Printmaker and painter, born in Spaarndam, Netherlands, who lived more than half his life in East Anglia. He studied at Haarlem Academy of Art where he was taught by the Portuguese artist Samuel Jesserum da Merquita. During World War II, after the Netherlands had fallen to the Germans, Visser was appointed official war artist to the Dutch government in exile in London. Between 1942–5 he was commissioned to make many important portraits which included the reigning monarch, Queen Wilhelmina, members of the Dutch royal family, government ministers and Army officials. Leaflets bearing his portrait of the Queen were dropped by the Royal Air Force for the liberation. After the war Visser returned to Ipswich for the rest of his life, and in 1994 the Museums and Galleries there held a show of his work, which included many charming woodcuts, engravings and lino-cuts. Ipswich, Victoria and Albert Museum and National Portrait Gallery hold examples.

David VOEL: *see* **David MORGAN-JONES**

Lucy VOELCKER 1959– Artist who studied at Architectural Association and Central School of Art. Showed at RA, Ikon Gallery in Birmingham, Christie's and Chicago and Los Angeles Art Fairs. Was included in Six Young British Painters, toured Spain, 1991–2. Contemporary Art Society holds her work.

Karel VOGEL 1897–1961 Sculptor and teacher who studied in Prague, Munich and Vienna, settling in London. Vogel showed at Venice Biennale before World War II, at the Battersea Park show in 1951 and there in 1960 his bronze Boy was lent by Harlow Art Trust. Vogel completed a group for Harlow New Town. In addition to works for State Museum in Prague and Nuremburg City

Museum he created others for schools in Hoddesdon, Albrighton and Moreton Hall, and a figure study adjacent to St Peter's Church, Hammersmith. Taught at Camberwell School of Arts and Crafts.

Andreas VOGT 1945– Artist working in gypsum, marble dust and acrylic, and teacher, born in Zürich, Switzerland. He studied art in Geneva for three years, but did not finish art school. Studied at university in Geneva and Munich, and gained a degree in the history of art, German literature and classical archaeology. Taught history of art and German literature in high school in Geneva, worked for the International Red Cross Committee all over the world and "stopped painting from 1964–86". Paul Klee and Mark Rothko were influences and the myth of Dionysus, Shiva and Nietzsche's writings were important themes in Vogt's work. Exhibitions included Vanessa Devereux Gallery and Connaught Brown, both 1992. Lived in London.

Patricia VOLK 1951– Sculptor, born in Belfast. She studied art as a mature student at Middlesex Polytechnic, 1985–7, then at Bath College of Higher Education, 1987–9, graduating with honours. She did a series of Victim heads, exploring the areas of trust, betrayal, love and death; also looked at the Hero and the idea of the Virgin. Showed in an independent exhibition at ICA in 1989, the year when she also exhibited at Leigh Gallery and Beaux Arts, Bath. Further exhibitions included Bath Society of Artists and West Wharf Gallery, in Cardiff, in 1991. Volk developed her technique over some years, all her pieces being modelled from clay and individually hand-built using coils to create a hollow shell. They were then fired at a high temperature and finished in a variety of materials. Worked in a studio in Bradford-on-Avon, Wiltshire.

Peter VOLLER 1943– Painter and collagist, born in Fleet, Hampshire. He studied at Farnham School of Art, showed at RA and elsewhere and lived in Wrecclesham, Surrey.

Jo VOLLEY 1953– Painter and teacher, born in Grimsby, Lincolnshire. She studied at Slade School of Fine Art, 1972–7, where she was influenced by the work of Sir William Coldstream, Patrick George and Euan Uglow. Won a number of awards including the Boise Travelling Scholarship, which she took in Italy. In 1980 she began teaching part-time at Wimbledon School of Art, in 1986 at the Slade. Volley had a solo show at Slade Gallery, University College, in 1990. Took part in many mixed exhibitions, including Industrial Sponsors, at Gainsborough House, in 1977; British Drawing, at Hayward Gallery, 1982; A Reputation Among Artists, a Norwich School of Art Gallery touring show, in 1986–7; and The Prose of Painting, at Austin/Desmond Fine Art, 1991. Portrait commissions included TRH The Duke and Duchess of York, for the City of London, and the actress Celia Johnson. Volley wrote and devised a tape and slide presentation called *Measured Time* to accompany Euan Uglow's retrospective show at Whitechapel Art Gallery in 1989. University College, City of London Guildhall Collection and Leicestershire Education Authority hold her work. Lived in London.

Nicholas VOLLEY 1950– Figurative painter and draughtsman, often working on a large scale, sometimes rather dark pictures with Kitchen Sink School overtones. He was born in Grimsby, Lincolnshire, attending the School of Art there, 1967–70; Slade School of Fine Art, 1970–5; with a Boise Travelling Scholarship, 1975. Group shows included John Moores Liverpool Exhibition, 1982. Had solo exhibitions with Ian Birksted Gallery, 1981 and 1983, then with Browse & Darby from 1986. Lived for a time in north London.

Sylvia von HARTMANN 1942– Artist, born in Hamburg, Germany. She studied there at the Werkkunstschule, 1961–3, then at Edinburgh College of Art, 1963–5, gaining her diploma, her post-diploma after another year's study. Showed at RA, RSW of which she was made a member in 1983, RSA, Royal Glasgow Institute of the Fine Arts and Scottish Gallery in Edinburgh. Scottish Arts Council holds her work. Lived in Edinburgh.

Martin von HASELBERG: *see* **The KIPPER KIDS**

Richard von MARIENTREU 1902–1991 Painter, born in Grodek in what is now Poland (then part of the Austro-Hungarian Empire). Ryszard Richard Schneider Edler von Marientreu's father was Austrian military governor for the area. Although von Marientreu (pronounced Marientroy) wanted to be a painter, he was sent to the military school in Craców, then the academy in Vienna to continue his training. In 1918, while serving in the Austrian Army, he was badly wounded and had two years in hospital. Against the wishes of his family, von Marientreu left for Vienna and later Prague to study for four years at the Academy of Painting. In 1925 his professor engaged him to paint large frescoes in the cloisters of the Church of Maria Schein, near Karlovy Vary, Czechoslovakia. He was discovered and brought to England by his early patron Marie Ludlow-Symons. Although when he arrived in London in 1933 he could not speak English, introductions to fashionable society soon launched him on a career as a portrait painter. There followed a string of exhibitions in England and abroad. His 1953 exhibition at the RWS Galleries showed three aspects of von Marientreu's output: war canvases and drawings of people in air-raid shelters; his large, powerful and romantic canvases dealing with ancient and mythological themes; and his portraits of notabilities. These – always painted by an immaculate von Marientreu clad in a Savile Row suit – included King George V, the Duke of Edinburgh and Field-Marshal Viscount Montgomery of Alamein. Von Marientreu died in London. He had been naturalized a British citizen after World War II.

Jessica VOORSANGER 1965– Artist in a variety of media, married to the performance artist Patrick Brill, she was also known as Jessica Voorsanger-Brill. Born in New York City, America, she won a scholarship to Brooklyn Museum Art School, New York, 1982–3; attended Tyler School of Art, 1986; then the Rhode Island School of Design. Was a member of the Coalition of Independent Artists, Brooklyn. Voorsanger's work took a sceptical look at media representations of women in subservient roles. Exhibitions included Palazzo Cenci Gallery, Rome, Italy, 1987, Contemporary Art Center, New York, 1990, with solo shows at Freud's Bar and Travellers Bookshop, both 1991. She was included in the Brill family show Relative Values, The Smith Art Gallery & Museum, Stirling, 1993. In 1997, she appeared on the BBC2 Television series *A Date with an Artist*, talking about her early obsession with a Pop idol, David Cassidy, and the Partridge family, seen on American television in the 1970s.

Edward VULLIAMY 1876–1962 Watercolourist, son of French parents, educated at Chigwell and Cambridge University, where he read classics and modern languages, eventually becoming a language lecturer at the University after gaining his master's degree. In World War I served in the British Expeditionary Force in France, in World War II being a special constable. He was honorary keeper of pictures at the Fitzwilliam Museum, resigning in 1955. Showed extensively at Walker's Galleries and NEAC, also at Fine Art Society, Chenil and Cooling Galleries. Lived in Cambridge.

Charles VYSE 1882–1971 Sculptor and potter, born in Stoke-on-Trent, Staffordshire, who studied at Royal College of Art and in Italy. He won a double gold medal; national scholarship; Royal College Scholarship; and a travelling scholarship. Showed at RA and Walker Art Gallery, Liverpool. Was an influential figure in the development of British studio pottery. He was a Chelsea Arts Club member who finally lived in Deal, Kent.

W

Andrew WADDINGTON 1960– Artist who worked mainly on paper, born in Whitchurch, Buckinghamshire. When a boy his family moved to Looe, Cornwall, and he eventually settled near Truro. Waddington attended Falmouth and Dyfed Schools of Art, 1978–82. His pictures drew for inspiration on the Cornish countryside and its animals and had poetic, mystical qualities. Waddington was represented by a typical example – This One Goes Out To The One I Love – in the 1989 Newlyn Orion Galleries exhibition A Century of Art from Cornwall 1889–1989.

Roy WADDINGTON 1917–1981 Draughtsman, painter and teacher, born in Settle, Yorkshire, son of the artist William Waddington. Studied at London University, Slade School of Fine Art under Randolph Schwabe and Tancred Borenius, then at Central School of Art. From early 1940s held a series of teaching posts, latterly being art master at Craig Preparatory School, Westmorland, 1947–9, settling at Staveley, Kendal. Showed with RA, RSA, Lake Artists' Society and Red Rose Guild of Craftsmen in Manchester. He was also a noted calligrapher.

Vera WADDINGTON 1886–1954 Painter and printmaker, born in Wiltshire, who was educated at Slade School of Fine Art, where she gained a number of awards. She was a prolific exhibitor, showing at Carfax and Goupil Galleries, NEAC, Redfern Gallery, SWA and frequently at RA until her last appearance in 1952. She gained an Hon. Mention at the International Print Show in Chicago. Contemporary Art Society and British Museum acquired Miss Waddington's work. Lived at Gerrards Cross, Buckinghamshire, for many years.

Arthur Edward WADE 1895–1989 Painter, who exhibited at RCamA, SWAS and elsewhere in Wales. He was assistant keeper in the department of botany at the National Museum of Wales, Cardiff, which bought his work. Was chairman of SWAS shortly after World War II. Lived in Cardiff.

Dorothy WADE fl. from late 1940s– Designer, painter and teacher, born in Silsden, Yorkshire. Her father was a textile designer and she was on the staff of a fashion college in London. Studied at Leeds College of Art and Bradford Regional College of Art. Exhibited widely, including Beaux Arts Gallery, RBA, WIAC, Leicester Gallery and in the provinces, and had solo shows at Alwin and Woodstock Galleries. Lived in New Malden, Surrey.

Frederick WADE 1948– Artist and lecturer who studied at Wimbledon and School of Art, 1966–8, St Martin's School of Art, 1968–71, Liverpool Polytechnic, 1975–6, then Leicester Polytechnic, 1982–4. He said that his work had much "to do with the pleasure of seeing and of approaching events with a tourist's curiosity" while having "a metaphorical dimension". Showed at Whitechapel Open, at Whitechapel Art Gallery, 1982, Williamson Art Gallery in Birkenhead in 1984 and in 1986–7 was in Merseyside Artists 3, toured by Walker Art Gallery, Liverpool. Solo shows included Riverside Studios, 1981.

Geoffrey WADLOW 1912– Illustrator and cartoonist, born in London, son of an amateur artist. Briefly attended evening classes at Camberwell School of Arts and Crafts under Eric Fraser, started with Unilever as a junior in 1929, then transferred to Lintas advertising agency in 1936, where his colleagues included Keith Vaughan and Felix Kelly. Over the years – including periods with National Fire Service and Royal Air Force in World War II – Wadlow drew for such publications as *Night and Day*, *Punch*, *Lilliput*, *London Opinion* and *Men Only*. He was represented in a show of humorous art which opened in London in 1953, then toured the United Kingdom and America. After retiring from Lintas in 1973 he continued to do freelance work and was included in the Agnew show Beyond the Horizon, in 1988.

Edward WADSWORTH 1889–1949 Painter, mainly in tempera, born in Cleckheaton, Yorkshire. His subjects are still life and landscape, often with a nautical flavour and having a Surrealist element; noted printmaker. Wadsworth studied engineering in Munich, then against family wishes he rejected a career in the mill business and chose to be a painter, studying at Bradford School of Art in 1908 under Charles Stephenson, later that year winning a scholarship to Slade School of Fine Art, 1908–12. Became associated with Wyndham Lewis and Vorticist Group and did work for *Blast* magazine. During World War I Wadsworth served with the Royal Naval Volunteer Reserve; was then engaged in camouflaging allied shipping and produced an outstanding series of dazzle-ship woodcuts. The first show of his woodcuts and drawings was held at the SWE, 1920, a first solo show of paintings following three years later at Leicester Galleries. Wadsworth became a member of Group X in 1920, LG in 1914, NEAC in 1921, Unit One in 1933, and also showed between the wars at Arthur Tooth and Sons, the Mayor Gallery and abroad. He was an extensive traveller on the continent; made murals for the liner *Queen Mary* in 1935; and published a series of books, including *The Black Country*, 1920. Died in London. A memorial show was held at Tate Gallery, which holds his work, in 1951, and at the Venice Biennale, 1952, and a centenary show was held at Bradford City Art Gallery, 1989–90.

Tom WAGHORN 1900–1959 Painter of landscapes and townscapes, mainly in watercolour. Born in London, studied at Battersea School of Art and Chelsea School of Art. Exhibited RA, RBA, RWA, NEAC, UA and elsewhere. Bristol City Art Gallery holds his work. Lived in Richmond, Surrey.

Erich WAGNER 1890–1974 Artist, restorer and writer, born in Vienna, Austria, studying at the Academy of Fine Arts there, 1908–9, and in 1913 in Berlin with Lovis Corinth. After Nazi annexation of Austria in March 1938 Wagner and his Jewish wife left all they owned to flee to England, where they settled in London. Although he mainly worked as a restorer he showed at RA, with LG and elsewhere. In 1986 was included in Art in Exile in Great Britain 1933–45 at Camden Arts Centre.

Faith WAGSTAFF 1910–1992 Artist, especially on paper, trained in architecture, who worked in Marquess of Northampton's office, Islington, then in 1940s with Nancy Nicholson block-printing fabrics. Was noted for her pastel portraits of children and dogs. To earn a living then became a civil servant, but did commissioned work of a topographical type for Canonbury Bookshop and researched and drew two historical maps: *Islington in the days of Elizabeth the First* and *The Pleasure Gardens of Islington*. After retirement encouraged the Alwyne Group of Artists. There was a small memorial show at Canonbury Bookshop, 1992.

John WAIN 1926– Painter, printmaker and teacher, born in Liverpool. Attended Liverpool School of Art, 1946–51, under Martin Bell. Taught for a time in Derbyshire, showed at AIA and elsewhere and lived at Baldrine on the Isle of Wight.

Douglas WAIN-HOBSON 1918– Sculptor and teacher, born and lived in Sheffield, Yorkshire. He studied at Royal College of Art (where he later lectured for a time) under Richard Garbe, 1938–40, then with Frank Dobson, 1946–7. Wain-Hobson won a College gold medal in 1946 and the Prix de Rome the following year. Showed at RA, LG and in Yorkshire.

Beatrice WAINWRIGHT fl. from c.1908–1962 Painter and miniaturist in oil and watercolour. Studied at Leicester School of Art and Heatherley's School of Fine Art. Exhibited widely, including RA, RMS, RSA, Walker Art Gallery, Liverpool, in the provinces, at the Paris Salon and in South America. Lived near Leicester.

Francis WAINWRIGHT 1940– Painter of intricate pictures, notably in egg tempera, and illustrator, born in Yorkshire, who studied at Burslem School of Art. After three years in the Army he moved to Italy, where he continued to study and work on fresco and mosaic restoration; he practised restoration in Florence after the floods of the 1960s. After 16 years in Italy, during which Pietro Annigoni was an influence, Wainwright returned to England in 1976. With his wife Sheila he produced a series of children's books and in 1987 his translation of *Pinocchio* appeared. Showed widely in Britain and internationally and was included in People and Places at Gagliardi Gallery in 1993.

Sora WAINWRIGHT 1921–1998 Painter and teacher, born in Glina, Yugoslavia, where her mother had just arrived from Petrograd, Russia, having fled from Bolshevik revolution. Sora Balevich became the godchild of Queen Maria, was by her given the Serbian first name Zorislava, but was educated at the Smolny Institute, the Tsarist girls' school evacuated from Petrograd. Her artistic precocity was recognised, and she studied icon painting under Pimen Maximovich Sofronov, formerly of the Russian royal icon workshop; pursued fine art at Kolarchev University in Belgrade; and while there she also studied architecture at the Technische Hochschule. In the Austrian town of Lienz, where she ended World War II in a camp with her parents, Sora met and then married one of the liberating Scottish soldiers, Captain Willie Wainwright, travelling with him in Europe and India while he served with the Commonwealth War Graves Commission. In 1957, when he was demobilised, the moved to Nottingham. By then Sora had become an established, widely exhibited painter. Her sole RA Summer Exhibition showing was in that year: a landscape of Beer, Devon. She taught art for a while, then graducated in Slavonic studies from Nottingham University, taught Russian, did technical translating and interpreted for the police.

Andy WAITE 1954– Artist, notable for his still life watercolours which employed a rich palette. He trained in graphic design and worked freelance for several years before becoming a full-time artist in 1989. Solo shows included The Catto Gallery, 1996.

Sarah WAITE 1963– Artist born in Ilkley, Yorkshire, who studied at Bradford College of Art, Central School of Art and Design and Chelsea School of Art, graduating with a first-class honours degree and receiving her master's in painting in 1988. Exhibited in London and was included in Images of the Yorkshire Landscape, organised by Sheeran Lock at Leeds Civic Hall in 1991, where she showed Sharp Haw, 1990, a typical simplified, abstracted scene like a personalised map.

Tessa WAITE 1960– Painter who often used mixed media, and teacher, brought up in Norwich where she received her art education, as well as Canterbury and Cardiff. Her mainly abstract work employed swirling brushmarks and a rich palette, strong in blues and reds. Taught extensively and received, jointly, the WAC Masterclass Award. Also held many residencies, notably at the Mid-Wales Psychiatric Hospital in Talgarth, and made study visits to Japan and India, funded by South East Wales Arts, the British Council and Charles Wallace India Trust. Commissions included a mural and sculpture for Brecon War Memorial Hospital, paintings for the Japanese dance troupe Kikunokai and a book-jacket for Carol Ann Courteney's *Morphine and Dolly Mixtures*. Work is in the collections of CASW, South Glamorgan County Council, many National Health Service trusts and the State of Rajasthan Centre for Arts, India. Exhibited extensively in Wales, at British Council Gallery in India and in 1995 had a solo show at the Museum in Brecon, Powys, where she lived.

Larry WAKEFIELD 1925–1997 Painter in oil, acrylic and watercolour, stage designer, poet and teacher, born in Cheltenham, Gloucestershire as Hilary Edward Larry Wakefield. He studied at Cheltenham College of Art, 1941–4, teachers including Hugh Casson; Göttingen University in Germany, 1947–8; architecture at RWA, Bristol, 1954–6; and at Manchester University for his master's degree, 1974. Teaching appointments included Southampton College of Art, 1956, and Southampton University, 1968–70. Among Wakefield's other engagements were: environmental Colour on the Tyne scheme, for Tyne and Wear Authority, 1964; collaboration with composer Jonathan Harvey on colour projections for his opera *Full Moon* in March, 1967; stage sets for Michael Lawrence's production of *The Flies* by Sartre, 1970; collaboration with the composer Ric Graebner on the opera *Fragmented City*, 1989; and on Graebner's opera based on Racine's *Bérénice*, 1992. In 1983 Wakefield was deputy head of fine art at Southampton Institute of Higher Education, but resigned his lectureship in 1986 to paint full-time. His work was figurative and abstract. "I've been inspired by landscapes, women and cities, and influenced by German Expressionism and English Romanticism." Wakefield had a solo show at Woodstock Gallery, 1968, others including Colin Jellicoe Gallery, from 1975; retrospective at Southampton City Art Gallery, 1979; Art Space Gallery from 1986; Cleveland Bridge Gallery, Bath, 1991; widely abroad; with a post-1979 retrospective at Millais Gallery, Southampton Institute, 1997. Calouste Gulbenkian Foundation and public galleries in Manchester and Southampton, where he lived, hold examples.

Nicole WAKEFIELD: *see* **NICOLE**

Edward WAKEFORD 1914–1973 Painter, artist in collage and teacher who was brought up in the Isle of Man. He studied at Chelsea School of Art and Royal College of Art, then exhibited at London galleries, having solo shows at the Brook Street and Hanover Galleries. In addition he did illustrative work for Shell-Mex and BP and wrote the book *A Prize for Art*. Lived in London for some years, teaching at Chelsea School of Art.

Richard WAKELIN 1921– Architect and sculptor, born in Cardiff. He attended the Welsh School of Architecture there, 1938–41, returning to study there 1946–8, after World War II service in Army. From 1958 he lived in Swansea working as an architect in private practice. He was a member of SWG and of Society of Architect Artists and attended Barry Summer School for some years. Took part in a number of mixed shows, including the WAC/Royal National Eisteddfod exhibition Sculpture for Haverfordwest in 1972 and a year later shared a show with Rosemary Wakelin at West Wales Arts Association, Carmarthen. WAC holds his work.

Shelagh WAKELY 1932– Sculptor and artist in mixed media, born in London, where she lived for many years. Between 1951–62 she studied at Wye College of Agriculture and Chelsea School of Art, taking a research fellowship at Royal College of Art, 1968–71. Then began to make sculpture, having a solo show at Sheila David Gallery in 1975. In the 1970s she was featured in a number of shows at Air Gallery, Serpentine Gallery and appeared in British Council travelling show Graphics at Work at ICA. Also showed LG. In 1979 had solo shows at ICA and Coracle Press, which published her *It is so green outside it is difficult to leave the window*. Arts Council holds her work.

Ineke van der WAL 1954– Versatile artist whose work included allegorical paintings, as in Links of Affinity, Knapp Gallery, 1989. She was born in Ophemert, Netherlands, and moved to Britain in 1972, settling in Pennsylvania, Exeter, Devon. Studied art history at University of Wales, Bangor, 1972–3. She won an Exeter Arts Council Award, 1985, South West Arts Award, 1987, and was South West Arts Fine Art/Photography Award panel member in 1988. Took part in Sixth Annual Brewhouse Open Art Exhibition, Taunton, 1986, and New Art in Exeter, at the Spacex Gallery there, from 1987, as well as participating in solo and two-man exhibitions. These included Brewhouse Arts Centre, 1987, and South Hill Park, Bracknell, 1988.

Peter WALBOURN 1910– Portrait painter, son of the artist Ernest Walbourn, born in Chingford, Essex. He studied at Heatherley's School of Fine Art and at Royal Academy Schools, 1928–32, teachers including Walter Westley Russell, Frederic Whiting and Gerald Brockhurst. Walbourn was elected UA in 1982, also showing with PS, RP and elsewhere. He carried out a lot of commissioned work, including HM Queen Elizabeth The Queen Mother for Middle Temple, Sir Hugh Wontner the Lord Mayor of London and other legal and academic dignitaries. Lived in Sawbridgeworth, Hertfordshire.

Dylan WALDRON 1953– Artist in egg tempera, pencil, watercolour and oil, born in Newcastle-under-Lyme, Staffordshire. He studied at Stourbridge College of Art, on a foundation course, 1971–2, then obtained an honours degree in art and design, Wolverhampton Polytechnic, 1972–6, when he became a full-time artist. Was a member of Leicester Society of Artists, showing at Stamford Artists' Gallery from 1980; Piccadilly Gallery from 1981; RA Summer Exhibitions from 1983; Goldmark Gallery, Uppingham, from 1988; and in 1991 appeared in East Midlands Artist of the Year, first prize winner in drawing and miniature painting. Solo shows included Dudley Art Gallery, 1979, and Birmingham University from the same year; E M Flint Gallery, Walsall, 1980, and Midland Arts Centre from same year; and Alfred East Gallery, Kettering, 1988. Waldron's pictures were usually small, realistic and were mainly interiors and still life. Lived at Slawston, near Market Harborough, Leicestershire.

Jack WALDRON 1923–1984 Sculptor, born in Swansea, South Wales, studied at the School of Art there 1937–8. Waldron was apprenticed to the commercial artist A J Pierson in Swansea until 1940, then he was in the Royal Navy until 1945. After further study, at Swansea College of Art, 1946–9, Waldron had two years doing freelance letter-cutting and industrial design. He then taught sculpture at Stoke-on-Trent College of Art 1951–64, from 1964 becoming senior lecturer in fine art at Stourbridge College of Art. After a first one-man show at Tib Lane Gallery, Manchester, in 1962, Waldron exhibited widely, other one-man exhibitions including Grabowski Gallery, Keele University and the Drian Gallery. Waldron was a finalist in The Unknown Political Prisoner sculpture competition, won by Reg Butler, Tate Gallery, 1953. Waldron carried out many public commissions in England and Wales and his work is in collections of the CASW, Manchester City Art Gallery (Rutherston Collection), Peterhouse College in Cambridge and elsewhere. Was based finally at Stourbridge.

Douglas WALES 1888–1966 Portrait painter whose full name was Arthur Douglas Wales Smith. Born in Darjeeling, India, he served in the Royal Navy for 25 years from 1903, teaching himself to paint. He contributed naval portraits to Kenneth Edwards' study *Men of Action*. Exhibited RA, RP, ROI, Paris Salon and to PS and RSMA, to which he belonged. Lived at Lymington, Hampshire.

Geoffrey WALES 1912–1990 Wood engraver, painter, artist in collage and teacher, born in Margate, Kent. He studied at Thanet School of Art, 1929–33, then at Royal College of Art, 1933–7, where his teachers included Eric Ravilious. Wales adopted the poetic, lyrical and very English style of Ravilious, John Nash and Edward Bawden while being adventurous in technique which gave his work a distinctive quality. Married the painter Marjorie Skeeles. Held a number of teaching posts, finally at Norwich School of Art, 1953–77. Showed at RE and SWE, both of which he was a member, and abroad and was at one time chairman of the Norwich Twenty Group. The Golden Cockerel Press and Folio Society used his work. Lived in Norwich.

Sue WALES 1942– Painter, designer, art editor, illustrator and artist in photography and films. As a child she was encouraged by her grandmother Ethel Fordham, also an artist. Wales studied at Reigate Art School and then in Paris at L'Académie de la Grande Chaumière and Académie Julian. Trained as a graphic designer and returned to England to work as an art editor and illustrator on various magazines. After this she moved into photography and films, where she worked as a set dresser and ultimately as an art director on television commercials. Showed at Clarendon Gallery from 1986 and Tandridge Shows from same year, having her first London show at Anna-Mei Chadwick in 1989. Her work "reflects the centre of my life, my home, my family and garden".

Bettine Christian WALFORD 1905– Painter and draughtsman, notably of watercolours, born in London. She studied with William Wood, at Chelsea Polytechnic, St Martin's and Grosvenor Modern Schools of Art. Exhibited widely, including Goupil Gallery, RA, RBA, NEAC, PS, Paris Salon and in the provinces. She had one-man shows at the French and Kensington Galleries and British Museum bought her work. Lived for many years in London.

Ann Fearon WALKE fl. c.1905–1960 Portrait and figure painter in oil. She studied initially at Cheltenham Ladies' College, then Chelsea School of Art under Augustus John and William Nicholson. Exhibited RA, ROI, UA, on the continent and in America. She did a great deal of ecclesiastical work, including a picture for St Hilary of Poitiers, at Saint Hilary, Cornwall, and an altarpiece for Truro Cathedral. Member of St Ives Society of Artists who lived at Mevagissey, Cornwall.

Allan WALKER 1953– Painter, printmaker, illustrator and landscape architect, born in London. He attended Oxford University, 1972–5, then did postgraduate work at Edinburgh University, 1976–8. He practised as a landscape architect with Exmoor National Park Authority, 1978–83, in 1980 becoming a member of the Institute of Landscape Architects. From 1984 Walker worked as a painter and printmaker. Among his commissions were illustrations for two publications on Middle Eastern insects and portraits and landscapes in Saudi Arabia, both in the mid-1980s. Showed at London Ecology Centre from 1993, in 1994 at Hyundai Gallery in Seoul, South Korea, Stansell Gallery in Taunton and he was an Artist of the Day at Angela Flowers Gallery, chosen by Denis Masi.

Brian WALKER 1926–c.1962 Illustrator in various media. Studied art at West of England College of Art, Bristol, under George Sweet and Rachel Roberts. Exhibited RWA, but his work mainly appeared in magazine form: cartoons and illustrations in publications such as *Punch*, *London Opinion*, *Country Fair* and *Lilliput*, as well the cycling press. Lived at Chew Magna, Somerset.

Edward Donald WALKER 1937– Self-employed marine artist, born in Hull, Yorkshire, who studied at Liverpool College of Art, 1950–3, settling in Lydiate, Merseyside. He was a member of Liverpool Nautical Research Society. Showed at RSMA, Talbot Gallery in Lancaster, Fulmar Gallery in Llandudno, McEwan Gallery in Ballater, Paris Salon and in various galleries in North America. HRH The Princess Royal, HM Juan Carlos of Spain, the politician John Major, Merseyside Maritime Museum and many private collections worldwide hold examples.

Ethel WALKER 1861–1951 Painter, especially of portraits of women, seascapes and flowers, in a style influenced by Impressionism. Born in Edinburgh, she attended the Ridley School of Art and Putney School of Art, in the early 1880s. After a private study trip through Spain and France, where she was impressed by the work of Velazquez and Manet, she studied briefly at the Westminster School of Art with Fred Brown, in 1892, transferring to the Slade School of Fine Art, until 1894, to which she returned several times during the period 1912–22. Also studied part-time at evening classes with Walter Sickert and with James Havard Thomas, the sculptor. Although she had begun exhibiting at RA in 1898 and at the NEAC two years later, she did not have her first one-man show until 1927, at the Redfern Gallery. She became Dame Ethel Walker in 1943. Her work is in many public collections, including the Tate Gallery, which holds a wide range of her pictures. Lived in London.

Ethel WALKER 1941– Artist in oil, watercolour and mixed media, born in Ayrshire, related to the artists James Herald and Dorothy Johnstone. Walker studied at Glasgow School of Art, 1959–64, under Mary Armour and David Donaldson. She admired the work of Francis Cadell, whose verve and colour were influences on her own still lifes, landscapes and interiors, with their angularity and strong tonal contrasts. She was a regular exhibitor at RSW, RSA, Royal Glasgow Institute of the Fine Arts and SSWA. Awards included Anne Redpath Award at SSWA, 1982; *Glasgow Herald* Painting Competition, at Royal Glasgow Institute, 1986; and in 1995 Whyte & Mackay Group Award and Alva Computers Purchase Prize, both at SSWA. Group shows also included Kingfisher Gallery, Fine Art Society and City Art Centre, all in Edinburgh. Later solo shows included Gatehouse Gallery, Glasgow, 1994, and Thackeray Gallery, 1995. Collections included Lillie Art Gallery, Milngavie; Argyllshire County and City of Edinburgh Art Collections; Bank of Scotland and Britoil. Lived at Kilmichael Glassary, By Lochgilphead, Argyll.

Frances WALKER 1930– Painter, draughtsman, printmaker and teacher, born in Kirkcaldy, Fife. She studied at Edinburgh College of Art, then trained as a teacher. Walker was then visiting teacher of art for all schools in Harris and North Uist in the Western Isles. After this Walker taught at Gray's School of Art, Aberdeen, until she retired early in 1986. She then split her work between Aberdeen and the island of Tiree. In addition to a number of solo exhibitions Walker showed with RSA, RSW and RSA, of all of which she was a member. She was featured in Scottish Art in the 20th Century at RWA in 1991.

Harry WALKER 1923–1990 Painter, sculptor in metal and teacher, born in Pollokshaws, Glasgow. He moved to Bath, Somerset, with the Royal Air Force in World War II, settling there and taking up painting and decorating. After night classes and also Bath Academy of Art he became a member of RWA and a technician at West of England College of Art in Bristol. He was so highly thought of there that he went to study at Royal College of Art, obtaining a certificate in bronze casting; while in London also attended Central School of Arts and Crafts. Eventually became a lecturer at Bristol Polytechnic. Was a leading member of Bath Society of Artists. RWA and Bath University hold his work. Although Walker's paintings were originally figurative, notably landscapes, he later turned to more abstract works. Died at his home in Corsham, Wiltshire.

Hazel WALKER 1963– Painter whose work included abstract pictures such as Crossings, oil on paper, at Royal Over-Seas League Open, 1995. She was born at Torphins, Aberdeenshire, and studied at Edinburgh and Cyprus Colleges of Art. She gained a Christian Salvesen Purchase Award, 1987, and a Whyte & Mackay Purchase Award at SSA, 1993. Group shows included Compass Gallery, Glasgow, from 1986; Glasgow Garden Festival, 1988; Loomshop Gallery, Lower Largo, 1993; and Grainstore Gallery, Galway, 1994. Had a solo show at Maclaurin Gallery, Ayr, 1993, later ones including Rubicon Gallery, Dublin 1995. Whyte & Mackay, Christian Salvesen, Paintings in Hospitals Scotland and the Office of Public Works, Ireland, hold examples.

Hirst WALKER 1868–1957 Watercolourist, born in Malton, Yorkshire, who lived finally in the county at Scarborough. After attending King's College School, London, studied art privately. Showed extensively at RBA, also at RA, Goupil Gallery and elsewhere. Victoria & Albert Museum holds Walker's work.

Iain WALKER 1946– Painter, draughtsman and teacher, born in Eton, Berkshire, who grew up in Liverpool, Wiltshire, Singapore and Malaya. Obtained a first-class diploma in art and design with honours at Liverpool College of Art, 1962–7, then studied painting and gained his master's degree with first-class honours from Royal College of Art, 1968–71. Was a senior tutor at City and Guilds of London Art School, 1973–97. Held consultancies with designers and architects, including exhibition work. Exhibited at RA; Walker Art and Bluecoat Galleries, both in Liverpool; Ernst & Young; Fieldborne Gallery; Beaux Arts in Bath, and elsewhere. Public and private collections hold examples.

Jane WALKER 1960– Painter and draughtsman, born in Edinburgh, who studied at Sheffield Polytechnic, 1983–7, and Royal Academy Schools, 1987–90. Mixed exhibitions included Casa de la Cultura, Aguilas, Spain, 1995; and John Moores Liverpool Exhibition, 1995–6, where she was a prizewinner with her oil on canvas House for a Homeless Person. Solo exhibitions included Royal Over-Seas League, 1994, from which she gained a portrait commission award. Lived in London.

John WALKER 1939– Painter, printmaker and teacher, born in Birmingham, attending its College of Art. 1956–60, gained an Abbey Travelling Scholarship and studied at Académie de la Grande Chaumière, Paris, 1961–3. Walker showed at John Moores Exhibition, Liverpool first in 1965; he won a prize then, another in 1974 and in 1976 first prize. In 1967 and 1968 he had solo shows at Axiom Gallery, in the latter year also showing one-man at Hayward Gallery. In 1967–9 Walker was Gregory Fellow at University of Leeds. He now increasingly showed abroad, especially in America; gained a Harkness Fellowship in 1970; and represented Britain at Venice Biennale in 1972. From 1974–8 Walker taught at Royal College of Art, was visiting artist at Columbia University in New York and visiting professor at Yale University, and was artist-in-residence at St Catherine's College, Oxford. In 1979 Walker moved to Australia, becoming dean at Victoria College of Arts, Melbourne, in 1982. In 1970 he had had the first of many shows with Nigel Greenwood, who became his dealer, and had a major show at Hayward Gallery in 1985. Walker's pictures were initially abstract, then in his words were "just this side of abstraction", and while in Australia he developed an interest in primitive ritual. Arts Council, Whitworth Art Gallery in Manchester and other public collections hold his work. Lived in New York and Melbourne.

Julian WALKER 1954– Artist employing mixed media and kinetic devices who studied at St Andrews University, City of

London Polytechnic, Sir John Cass School of Art and Central St Martins College of Art & Design. Exhibited in South Bank Picture Show, at England & Co in the 1992 exhibition Art in Boxes and also in America.

Kathleen WALKER fl. c.1927–1969 Portrait painter, especially of children, designer, printmaker and teacher. Born in Wargrave, Berkshire, she studied at the Royal College of Art, 1920–3, under William Rothenstein and Frank Short, winning a Travelling Scholarship in 1924, having won a British Institution Scholarship the previous year. In 1953 joined the staff of Southover Manor School, Lewes, to teach art. Exhibited RA, NEAC and elsewhere. Work appeared in the *AIA Newsletter/Bulletin.* Lived in London and at Firle, Sussex.

Leonard WALKER 1877–1964 Painter, stained glass window designer and teacher, born in Ealing, Middlesex. He studied at St John's Wood School of Art, later becoming principal there. Walker was made a member of RBA in 1913, RI in 1915, also showing at RA, Walker Art Gallery in Liverpool and Royal Glasgow Institute of the Fine Arts. Among Walker's major stained glass works were ten windows for Hong Kong and Shanghai Bank in Singapore, three memorial windows to the navigator Henry Hudson in St Ethelburga's Church, Bishopsgate, and five sets for Lahore Cathedral, India. Lived in London.

Lily WALKER 1916– Painter, notably in gouache, and teacher, born in Burton upon Trent, Staffordshire. As well as attending Derby Training College she studied at Leicester College of Art. Exhibited at the public galleries in Nottingham and Leicester, where she lived and was a member of the Society of Artists and Sketch Club. Taught art for some years at Wyggeston Grammar School of Girls, Leicester.

Margaret WALKER 1951– Sculptor in a variety of media, born in Birkenhead, Cheshire. She studied at Leicester Polytechnic from 1970 and Brighton Polytechnic from 1972, then settled in London. Exhibitions included Lansdown Gallery, Sussex, 1975; Ikon Gallery in Birmingham, 1979; and The British Art Show, 1980, touring exhibition organised by the Arts Council and selected by critic William Packer. There Walker showed five Untitled abstract works using such materials as paper pulp relief and ceramic.

Nick WALKER 1968– Painter, born in Morecambe, Lancashire, who studied at Preston Polytechnic and Staffordshire University. Group shows included Fuse 95, temporary space, Glasgow, and Royal Over-Seas League Open, both 1995. Had a solo exhibition, Vent, again in temporary spaces around Glasgow, 1994, and Found, in the city's Buddhist Centre, 1995.

Paton WALKER 1905– Painter and draughtsman, full name James A Paton Walker, born in Kilmarnock, Ayrshire, his mother being a commercial artist, Molly Fletcher Wilson. Studied at Ayr Academy and Glasgow University. Member of Hampstead Artists' Council with which he showed, also at St George's Gallery and elsewhere. Lived in London.

Ray WALKER 1945–1984 Painter, notably a muralist, and teacher, born in Liverpool, father a merchant seaman. Despite a poor background, was encouraged by his mother and his art master David Copestake at Hillfoot Hey Grammar School, then attended Liverpool College of Art, 1961–5. Partly supported his studies by playing in a rock band, Liverpool Flintstones, 1959–64, sometimes at the Cavern Club with The Beatles. On the strength of highly imaginative Surrealist work, entered Royal College of Art on a postgraduate scholarship, 1966–9. His diploma show contained pictures mixing realism, fantasy and grotesque eroticism. After a stay in Morocco, Walker lived in squats in Notting Hill. From 1972 until his death lectured at a wide range of colleges and polytechnics. After remarrying, Walker settled in a semi-derelict house in Poplar. Although he had had early success with a solo show at Clytie Jessop Gallery in 1970, Walker's enthusiasm for more socially aware subjects prompted him to concentrate on public murals. In 1973 he had worked with John Bratby on hoardings around Sam Wanamaker's World Centre for Shakespeare Studies. Additionally completed murals for the new Whittington Hospital, Islington, 1977; Bow Mission, 1978; Army recruitment panels for Imperial War Museum, 1981; and Peace Mural, Dalston Junction, commissioned by Greater London Council, 1983–4. There was a memorial show at Royal Festival Hall, 1985, another at Bluecoat Gallery, Liverpool, 1987.

Richard WALKER 1954– Painter, graphic artist, printmaker and muralist, born in Yorkshire, who did a foundation course at Kingston School of Art, 1972–3; a graphic arts degree at Camberwell School of Art, 1973–6; and his master's in printmaking at Chelsea School of Art, 1976–7. After his first show, Walker travelled extensively through America, Europe, the Far East and North Africa. Undertook travel commission for Sinclair, Roche and Temperley (Hong Kong & Singapore), 1991, collaborations including a project with British Telecom and RMJM Architects, 1996, and a mural for One Aldwych restaurant, 1998. His many solo exhibitions included Metropolitan at New Academy Gallery, 1998, where he aptly recorded the speed and razzmatazz of modern city life. British Council, Cleveland City Art Gallery, Customs & Excise, National Theatre and many corporate collections hold examples.

Richard WALKER 1955– Painter who was born in Cumbernauld, Dunbartonshire. Studied at Glasgow School of Art, 1973–7. He showed with Scottish Young Contemporaries, 1984–5, John Moores Liverpool Exhibition from 1985, and Inverclyde Biennial, 1986, gaining first prize. Had solo exhibitions at Glasgow Arts Centre, 1983, and Transmission Gallery, Glasgow, 1986. Man and the elements were notable features of his output. Arts Council holds his work. Lived in Glasgow.

Richard Ian Bentham WALKER 1925– Artist and teacher with a special interest in portraits of musicians, born and lived in

Croydon, Surrey. After Canford School he attended Queen's College, Oxford; Croydon School of Art, 1945–8, with R A Wilson; London University Institute of Education, 1949; and Slade School of Fine Art under William Coldstream. He taught at Croydon Art School, 1948–53, also adult education courses. Walker was a member of UA, SGA and Armed Forces' Art Society. Showed with RA, RP, Paris Salon and elsewhere. His solo exhibitions included Alpine Gallery, 1981. Royal College of Music holds Walker's portrait of the teacher and composer Herbert Howells.

Roy WALKER 1936– Painter, printmaker, creator of hanging constructions and lecturer, born in Welling, Kent. He studied at Gravesend School of Art, 1951–2; Regent Street Polytechnic School of Art, 1952–4; and, after National Service, at the Central School of Arts and Crafts, 1957–60. Walker worked in industry, then in 1966 moved to St Ives, Cornwall. He was a member of RE, Penwith Society of Arts (from 1972 he directed its Print Workshop), Newlyn Society of Artists and Plymouth Society of Artists. He was a visiting lecturer at Falmouth College of Art, Plymouth College of Art/Design and at several colleges/universities in America and Switzerland. Group shows included Marlborough Graphics, 1974; Eye Gallery, Bristol, 1988; Tate Gallery, St Ives, with Porthmeor Printmakers, 1993; and St Ives Now, Collyer-Bristow Gallery, 1996. Solo shows began with Camel Gallery, Wadebridge, 1973, later ones including Annexe Gallery, Truro, 1991, and Galerie de Opmaat, Netherlands, 1993. Victoria & Albert Museum and British Council hold examples.

Winifred WALKER fl. from c.1915–1965 Botanical artist who won many awards in Britain and abroad. She studied at Camden School of Art and showed at RA, SWA, Fine Art Society and elsewhere. Royal Horticultural Society official artist 1929–39 and was artist in residence at the University of California from 1943. Walker was a fellow of the Linnean Society. Among the books which she illustrated were *All the Plants of the Bible* and the fourth edition of Thompson's *The Gardener's Assistant*.

William WALKER 1878–1961 Painter, printmaker and draughtsman, born in Glasgow. Studied art in Glasgow and in several centres on the continent. He exhibited at the RA, RSA and Paris Salon. Lived in Edinburgh.

David WALKER-BARKER 1947– Painter and teacher, born in Ward Green, Yorkshire. Studied at Sheffield College of Art & Design, 1964–8; Goldsmiths' College, 1968–9; and Royal College of Art, 1969–72. Group shows included RA Summer Exhibitions from 1973; Richard Demarco Gallery, Edinburgh, 1976; Summer Show, Serpentine Gallery, 1979; The Alternative Tate, Paton Gallery, 1982; and Coach House Contemporary Art, Kirkby Lonsdale, from 1987. Had a solo show at Mappin Art Gallery, Sheffield, 1974, later ones including Yorkshire Television, Leeds, 1991. Also showed with Hart Gallery. Walker-Barker taught part-time at various colleges and was visual arts fellow at Bradford University in 1979. Arts Council holds his work.

Carol WALKLIN fl. from 1960s– Printmaker, designer and teacher who studied at Beckenham School of Art and Royal College Art, graduating from graphic design school in the 1950s. She worked in publicity for several years, later as a freelance designer doing work for BBC Television, the Print Collectors' Club and the Post Office. Taught relief printmaking with her husband Colin at West Dean College as well as adult education classes. Was elected fellow of RE, 1986. Showed at RA Summer Exhibition, Bankside Gallery and elsewhere, in 1988 being included in four-man show at Woodlands Art Gallery. Lived in Beckenham, Kent.

Brian WALL 1931– Sculptor and teacher, born in London. From 1945–50 worked as a glassblower, then while serving in Royal Air Force attended Luton College of Art, 1951–2. For several years Wall lived in Paris and London. Interested in the work of Ben Nicholson he moved to St Ives in 1954, showed paintings in the Castle Inn there and in the latter 1950s worked part-time as an assistant to Barbara Hepworth. Wall's first sculptures were architectonic in wood, then he opted for steel welded constructions of an abstract nature. Wall returned to London in 1960 and taught at Ealing College of Art, 1961–2 and Central School of Art and Design, 1962–72. Having visited America in the late 1960s, Wall began teaching at the University of California, living and working in Berkeley, becoming professor of art. Wall had many group appearances and one-man shows internationally, especially in Britain and America, notably at the Max Hutchinson Gallery in Houston and New York and the John Berggruen Gallery, San Francisco, in 1983. A Seattle Art Museum show in 1982–3 toured. Arts Council holds his work.

Cynthia WALL 1929– Artist and teacher in oil, watercolour and pastel, married to the artist William Birnie. She was born in London and studied at Glasgow School of Art, 1946–50, teachers including William Armour, David Donaldson, Geoffrey Squire and Kathleen Whyte. Wall taught art in Dunbartonshire for six years, suspended teaching for 18 years while she raised a family, then returned part-time in Renfrewshire, where she had settled in Kilbarchan. She was elected a member of RSW in 1971. Showed continuously there, at RSA, Royal Glasgow Institute of the Fine Arts and at Paisley Art Institute. Solo shows included Open Eye Gallery, Edinburgh, in 1993. Most of Wall's work was still life, with some landscape and figurative subjects.

Tom WALL 1941– Painter and teacher born in London, who aged about 10 years moved to Wales, then attended Newport College of Art, 1956–60. Studied painting and sculpture at Slade School of Fine Art, 1960–3. Subsequent teaching posts included Hereford, Chester and Teesside Colleges of Art. Wall took part in many group shows, including Young Contemporaries, Ferens Art Gallery in Hull, RCamA, SEA, SWG and WAC, which holds his work. In 1966 he shared a show with Arthur Wilson at Arnolfini Gallery, Bristol.

Aidan WALLACE 1903– Painter, born in Elsdon, Northumberland. Studied at Darlington Technical College and became a member of the local Art Club. Showed there and at Laing Art Gallery In Newcastle upon Tyne, where he lived.

Alasdair WALLACE 1967– Artist with Surrealist leanings. He gained an honours degree at Glasgow School of Art, 1987–91. His awards included the 1987 J D Kelly Award, at the School; he also gained three months' study at National College of Art in Dublin and in 1991 the RSA's John Kinross Scholarship. Wallace was a finalist in The Gilchrist Fisher Memorial Fund competition, at Cadogan Contemporary, 1994. Showed at Compass Gallery, Glasgow, from 1991. Also took part in the 1992 Islington and Bath Art Fairs and showed at Cyril Gerber Fine Art, Glasgow. Had a first London exhibition at Rebecca Hossack Gallery, 1995.

André WALLACE 1947– Sculptor of large figures in metal of a populist nature, born in Somerset, where he studied at the College of Art, Liverpool College of Art, Royal Academy Schools and Royal College of Art. He gained the Sainsbury Prize for Sculpture in 1973. As well as making smaller sculptures for interiors Wallace collaborated with architects, developers and councils to produce public pieces such as The Whisper, commissioned by Milton Keynes Development Corporation and sited in 1984 in Silbury Boulevard there. Sites in Newcastle, Telford and London, where he lived, also hold his works.

Anne WALLACE 1960– Painter, born in Buckinghamshire, who did figurative and abstract work. She studied at Amersham College of Art and Design, earning a diploma in textile design, 1978–81, then gained an honours degree in fine art (painting), 1981–4, at Ravensbourne College of Art and Design. Her group show appearances included Hunting Group Art Prizes, finalist, at Mall Galleries, 1984; Ayling Porteous Christmas Exhibition, Chester, 1987; Eva Jekel, 1991; and LG Open, Barbican, 1992. Lived in London.

Bobbie WALLACE 1946– Artist, notably a printmaker, born in New Zealand. Studied at Scottish College of Textiles, Galashiels, 1975–6; gained an honours degree in drawing and painting from Edinburgh College of Art, 1976–80; then obtained a postgraduate diploma in printmaking there, with distinction, 1980–1, the year Wallace received an Andrew Grant Travelling Scholarship. Group shows included Seventh British International Print Bienniale, Bradford (Oxford Gallery Prize), 1982, and Scottish Print Open Three, organised Dundee Printmakers' Workshop, 1983. In 1982 had two solo shows, at Henderson Gallery in Edinburgh and Oxford Gallery, Oxford. Scottish Arts Council holds Wallace's work.

Frank WALLACE 1881–1962 Painter, illustrator, writer and barrister, born in Yorkshire, who attended Eton College and Oxford University. His recreations were shooting and deerstalking, his publications including *Stalks Abroad*, 1908, and *Hunting Winds*, 1949. Harold Frank Wallace was a fellow of the Zoological Society and Royal Geographical Society and showed at Sporting and Greatorex Galleries, London and Scotland, at RSW and RI. He lived in Pelsall, Staffordshire.

Laurence WALLACE 1952– Painter and draughtsman who studied at Hornsey College of Art, 1971–5, then Royal College of Art, 1975–8. He took part in a number of competitions, being a prizewinner in Interior Motives, 1978, also participating in the Spirit of London shows, 1981–3. Wallace's work was remarkable for its analysis of light and shadow in interiors and townscapes, the use of unusual viewpoints and an atmosphere of stillness and absent presence. Mixed shows included Piccadilly and Thumb Galleries from 1978, Business Art Galleries from 1980 and Peterborough Arts Centre, 1983, in the Pacesetters III show. Had a solo show at Royal College of Art in 1977; Thumb Gallery, 1981; Lyric Theatre and Bury Arts Centre both in 1983; and Woodlands Art Gallery, 1984.

Margaret Adeline WALLACE fl. c.1940–1960 Painter and black-and-white artist. Studied at St John's Wood School of Art and in Paris. Showed at UA, SWA, RBA and in Paris. Lived in Windsor, Berkshire.

Paterson WALLACE 1923– Painter, full name A Paterson Wallace, who was born in Montrose, Angus. She studied at Perth Academy, then attended Chelsea School of Art, 1946–9, where her teachers included Ceri Richards and Robert Medley. She illustrated the book *East Anglia from the Sea*, by D and J Hay, and had a number of one-man shows in East Anglia, where she settled at Butley, Suffolk. Was a member of Free Painters and Sculptors and of Ipswich and Woodbridge Art Clubs, in which she was prominent.

Arthur Henry Naunton WALLER 1906–1995 Part-time painter, like his father Canon Arthur Pretyman Waller, born in Waldringfield, Suffolk. Like his father he obtained a Master of Arts degree from Cambridge University and went into the church. He was a member of Ipswich Art Club, the Society of Parson Painters and Norfolk and Norwich Art Circle. He was rector of Frostenden with South Cove from 1946–74, when he retired. Lived finally in Waldringfield.

Arthur Pretyman WALLER 1872–1969 Painter and canon of the Church of England whose son, Arthur Henry Naunton Waller, was also a parson painter in East Anglia. The father was born in Waldringfield, Suffolk, where he later lived. He attended Cambridge University, studying art at Bridgwater Art School. He held a number of church appointments, being rector of Waldringfield with Henley, 1900–48. Exhibited with the Society of Parson Painters, Ipswich Art Club and Norfolk and Norwich Art Circle, 1947–53, which listed him as Canon Arthur Pretyman.

Barbara WALLER 1923– Painter, sculptor and potter, born in Loxwood, Sussex, who specialised in animal subjects. She studied at Farnham School of Art, then at Royal College of Art with Richard Garbe, 1945–7. Showed at RA, WIAC and in the provinces and had two one-man shows with Charles Vyse, with whom she had studied, at Walker's Galleries. Public galleries in Exeter, Nottingham and Liverpool hold her work. Worked for some time in the south of England, then settled in Glasbury-on-Wye, Radnorshire.

Cecil WALLER 1908–1992 Painter who first visited Dorset, which eventually became his home, in 1914, with his mother, a landscape gardener. Attended St John's Wood School of Art, winning a scholarship to the Royal Academy Schools. Made a meagre living painting society portraits, then in 1934 with his wife Amy bought a small chalk cottage at Minchington, in the Cranborne Chase. The area suited his quiet, traditional temperament, and he recorded its landscape, having a particular obsession with light and tone. Rarely exhibited, unable to afford framing or gallery fees. Was including in The Quest for a British Art 1930–55, Salisbury Library & Galleries, Salisbury, 1998.

Grace Marie WALLER 1912– Artist in pastel whose unmarried name was Lawrence, born in Cheshunt, Hertfordshire. She studied art at Tottenham Polytechnic and at Regent Street Polytechnic School of Art, her teachers including Ralph Middleton Todd. Was hon. secretary of Enfield Art Circle, Middlesex, with which she regularly showed, also at Foyles Gallery. Lived in Enfield.

Jonathan WALLER 1956– Painter whose work included large, exuberant figure and flower pictures, born in Stratford-upon-Avon, Warwickshire. He attended Nene College, Northampton, 1979–80; Lanchester Polytechnic, Coventry, 1980–3; and Chelsea School of Art, 1984–5. In 1983–4 was a member of Coventry Artists' Group. Waller's awards included first prize at Midland View 3, 1984; junior painting fellowship, Cardiff, 1985–6; a Mark Rothko Memorial Trust travelling scholarship to America, 1988; and a British Council Grant, working visit to New York, 1990. His many group appearances included Sheffield Open, Mappin Art Gallery, 1983; Fresh Art, Barbican, 1986; The New British Painting, Cincinnati and tour, 1988–90; Connaught Brown, 1991; and Lamont Gallery, 1992. Had a solo show at Nene College, 1984, others including Paton Gallery, 1986–8, and Flowers East from 1990. Contemporary Art Society and Metropolitan Museum, New York, hold his work.

Margaret WALLER 1916– Artist in watercolour, oil and egg tempera, born in Poppleton, Yorkshire, her parents both qualified artists. They encouraged her and taught her watercolour technique. She gained her art teacher's diploma at Liverpool College of Art, studying at Royal Academy Schools, 1937–9, teachers including Walter Westley Russell, Tom Monnington, Francis Jackson and George Clausen. Waller taught for a year after gaining her teaching diploma but preferred freelance painting. Travelled extensively, including France, Italy, Belgium, Madeira and Portugal and had homes in Sark and Guernsey – at St Peter Port – in the Channel Islands. Her output included a decorative altar piece for the Chapel of St John, also large panels for St Stephen's Church, both in Guernsey. Had solo shows in Funchal, Madeira; St Helier, Jersey; St Peter Port, Guernsey; and in Sark. Group shows included RA, RP, SWA, Arts Council, Hesketh Hubbard Art Society, Paris Salon and elsewhere abroad. Also showed with Bluecoat Chambers Society, in Liverpool, of which she was a member.

Mark WALLINGER 1959– Artist with a lifelong interest in racing and thoroughbred horses, the subject of many pictures by him. He formed a group of dealers and collectors which bought a filly named A Real Work of Art; each race was recorded as an artwork, small statues being sold to defray costs of training. Wallinger did a foundation course at Loughton College, 1977–8, then graduated from Chelsea School of Art, 1978–81, gaining his master's degree, 1983–5, from Goldsmiths' College. Group shows included The Koln Show, Cologne, and Australian Sculpture Triennial, National Gallery of Victoria, Melbourne, both 1990; and Young British Artists II, 1993, Saatchi Gallery, which holds his work. Solo shows included Capital, ICA and tour, and Fountain, Anthony Reynolds Gallery, both 1991; and Ikon Gallery, Birmingham, 1995.

Nevile WALLIS 1910–1965 Artist and critic, born and lived in London, son of the writer A F Wallis. Wallis was educated and received his art training at Felsted School, in Essex. He worked as a critic at various times for *Punch, The Observer, The Spectator, The Times* and *The Times Educational Supplement* and wrote several books, including a study of the Victorian artist W P Frith. Exhibited SGA, RI and RSA, work being held by City of Birmingham Museum and Art Gallery.

Jason WALLIS JOHNSTONE 1966– Sculptor, born in Norfolk. After attending Wymondham College, between 1985–92 he was at Great Yarmouth College of Art & Design, Brighton Polytechnic and Royal College of Art, where he obtained his master's degree in sculpture. Wallis Johnstone was in the British Telecom New Contemporaries Touring Exhibition 1990; gained the Robson Millar Award at Malvern Open Drawing, 1992; and was included in Drawing Towards Sculpture at Isis Gallery, Leigh-on-Sea, 1993. He gained a Morris Singer Scholarship in 1992 and was awarded a residency in Bratislava, Slovakia, in 1993.

Kathleen WALNE 1915– Painter, designer and draughtsman, born in Ipswich, Suffolk. She was noted for her watercolours, rich in colour and assuredly designed. Studied at Ipswich Art School. Walne's future husband, Frank Ward, then an art student in London, brought her work to the notice of the Wertheim Gallery's proprietor, Lucy Wertheim, who later recorded in her book *Adventure in Art* how vivid and dynamic the artist's work appeared. Thus it was given a first solo show in 1935, when it was also included in a show of contemporary watercolours at Salford Art Gallery. Salford Art Gallery gave Walne a retrospective in 1986, which partly drew on its own extensive collection of her work. Towner Art Gallery, in Eastbourne, and Auckland City Art Gallery, New Zealand, also hold examples. Walne did not paint for some time while bringing up a family, but then returned to work and had a successful show with her husband at Compendium 2 Gallery, in 1972. Her long association with Lucy Wertheim ended in 1971 when the gallery owner died, having been nursed by Walne. Walne's work was included in Adventure in Art, the touring tribute from Salford Art Gallery, 1991–2, and in David Buckman's monograph on her and her husband, *Mixed*

Palette, published by Sansom & Company in 1997. She lived in Brighton, Sussex.

Josephine WALPOLE 1927– Painter, notably of flowers, writer and gallery owner, born in Cockfield, Suffolk, who studied privately with Stuart Somerville. Between 1964–93 she ran the Deben Gallery in Woodbridge, Suffolk, where she lived, and wrote a number of books, including *Anna: Memorial Tribute to Anna Zinkeisen*, 1978; *Vernon Ward*, 1988; and *Rose in a Suffolk Garden*, 1990. Showed in London and the Suffolk area.

Lois WALPOLE 1952– Maker of baskets, screens and furniture, notable for its use of recycled materials. She was born and lived in London and trained at Bristol Polytechnic, 1971–2; St Martin's School of Art, 1972–5, switching from fine art to craft; then at London College of Furniture, 1981–2. She was a member of the Basketmakers' Association and Contemporary Applied Arts. Walpole gained a huge volume of press coverage for her work. Exhibitions included Whitechapel Art Gallery, 1983; Aspects Gallery, 1984; 2D–3D, at Laing Art Gallery, Newcastle upon Tyne, 1987; Willow to Wire, Piece Hall, Halifax, 1990; Salvaged! Art in a Throwaway World, South Bank Centre, 1991; and Deckchairs, Southern Arts tour, 1993. Contemporary Art Society and Bankfield Museum, Halifax, hold examples.

Sam WALSH 1934–1989 Painter, draughtsman and teacher, born in Enniscorthy, County Wexford, Ireland. He attended Dublin College of Art, 1952–5. Then moved to London, drifting through various jobs for five years, one as a professional guitarist; he also painted, showing at ICA and New Gallery. In 1960 moved to Liverpool, where in 1961 he began to exhibit at Liverpool Academy, being elected a full member in 1966. Walsh did a teacher training course at C F Mott College, 1962–5, while becoming increasingly identified with Pop Artists. He showed widely in north of England and in 1963 his portrait of Francis Bacon appeared at John Moores Exhibition, Liverpool – he was to show a lot there – from which Walker Art Gallery acquired it. In 1968 began teaching full-time at Liverpool College of Art, retiring in 1986, three years after his first serious illness and admission to hospital. Walsh was progressively included in key shows of Liverpool painters, as well as having his own exhibitions; he was in the Liverpool Academy's touring show The Face of Merseyside, in 1976, in 1983 was in the 1st Merseyside Artists Exhibition which toured from Walker Art Gallery, then in 1987 his portrait of Samuel Beckett was shown at National Portrait Gallery. Other portrait subjects included Mick Jagger, J Edgar Hoover and Ivon Hitchens, the painter. A memorial show for Walsh was given at Walker Art Gallery in 1991.

Thomas WALSH 1938– Versatile printmaker, painter and teacher, born in Glasgow, where he studied at the School of Art, 1957–62, Philip Reeves being among his teachers. Glasgow Art Club member. Print Collectors' Club issued his work, which is held by Scottish Arts Council and Glasgow University. Lived in Glasgow.

WALTER: *see* **Walter GOETZ**

Jo WALTER 1950– Painter, draughtsman and teacher, born in Birmingham. Attended Bournville School of Art, 1968–9; University of Leeds fine art department, 1969–74; In 1975 won a Yorkshire Arts Association Bursary, studying at University of Newcastle upon Tyne fine art department, 1975–7. A West Midlands Arts Bursary followed in 1978, enabling Walter to take up a fine art fellowship at Stourbridge College of Art, 1979–81. Teaching included West Glamorgan Institute of Higher Education. Group exhibitions included Hatton Gallery, Newcastle University, 1977; Midland View, Stoke-on-Trent City Art Gallery, 1980; and Wapping Artists Open Studios, 1983. Had a solo show at Midlands Arts Centre in 1978, later ones including Dudley Art Gallery, which holds the artist's work, 1981. Lived for some time in London.

Start WALTER 1920– Painter, photographer and writer, full name Wilfrid Start Walter, son of the Edwardian painter Franz Wilfrid Walter. He was educated in Highgate, north London, where he continued to live. Studied art at Westminster School of Art and Royal Academy Schools. Showed at RA, ROI and Paris Salon. He was a keen fisherman and wrote books about this and various aspects of painting for pleasure. Arts Club member.

Evan WALTERS 1893–1951 Painter, born in Mynydd Bach, near Swansea, who grew up in Llangyfelach, Glamorgan. In 1906 he was apprenticed to a decorating firm in Morriston, from 1910–13 attending Swansea School of Art. Walters worked in America, 1916–19, spending the next 20 years in London, during which time he studied at Regent Street Polytechnic School of Art and Royal Academy Schools. In 1927 Walters had an extremely successful show at Warren Gallery which drew the attention of the press and eminent people in London society and artistic circles. The miner's son's fame and continued triumphs seemed assured, but after this Walters' art seemed to lack firm direction. Half of him wanted freedom from his Welsh roots, the other half hankered for Llangyfelach. From 1939 he worked in both London and Wales, latterly experimenting with a theory which he termed double-vision. However, it is in his studies of mining families and his mother that Walters, master of the transient expression, did his best work. Memorial show held at Glynn Vivian Art Gallery, Swansea, in 1952, and it and National Museum of Wales, Cardiff, holds much of a bequest of over 900 canvases and drawings by Walters.

Allan WALTON 1892–1948 Painter and designer of interiors and fabrics, and teacher, born in Cheadle Hulme, Cheshire. His family owned the Manchester cotton mill John Walton of Colleyhurst, enabling him to attend Harrow School. Abandoned studies in an architect's office to learn to paint under Stanhope Forbes, in Cornwall, then from 1913–16 was at Slade School of Fine Art and in Paris at L'Académie de la Grande Chaumière. After World War I studied with Walter Sickert at Westminster School of Art. In London he began to exhibit and set up as an interior designer, in 1925 designing Marcel Boulestin's first restaurant in Leicester Square. First one-man show at Beaux Arts Gallery in 1928; another followed at Arthur Tooth and Son in 1933; and mixed shows included LG, Wertheim Gallery, Leicester Galleries and Walker Art Gallery, Liverpool. In 1931 with brother Roger set up Allan Walton Textiles, a financially successful firm which pioneered new ground in printed cloth designs, but which closed around 1940. From 1943–5 Walton was director of Glasgow School of Art, then in 1948 was appointed professor of textile design at Royal College of Art but died before he could take it up. As a painter Walton was an exuberant Colourist, depicting his still lifes, landscapes and seascapes with bold brushstrokes. There were several exhibitions at Sally Hunter Fine Art in the mid-1980s. Arts Council and Manchester City Art Gallery hold his work. Lived at Shotley, Suffolk.

Andrew WALTON 1947– Painter, performance artist and teacher, born in Oxford, where he attended the School of Art, 1965–6. This was followed by Cardiff College of Art, 1966–70, at which for a period in the early 1970s he was a lecturer and fellow. Afterwards visited Canada and America and worked in London. Walton took part in the WAC 1969 show Art in Wales Tomorrow; was a member of the 56 Group; and in 1973 participated in Everyday Something Changes, at Chapter Arts Centre, Cardiff. Among his performances was *Anybody's Mortuary Song* at University College, Cardiff, in 1972, in which he was joined by Alan Price and Colin Ainsworth. Produced a series of volumes of drawings, including *The Other Side of the Moon* as well as *Heads*, both published privately in 1974. WAC holds his work.

Barbara WALTON 1955– Painter and draughtsman, born in York, where she did a foundation course at the College of Art, 1975–6, gaining her master's degree in fine art, 1976–81. In 1981–2 obtained postgraduate diploma at Edinburgh College of Art, later studying for master's degree in landscape design at Manchester University. Among her awards was the John Kinross Award, 1981, to study in Florence, and in 1982 the Elizabeth Greenshields Award, to study in Siena. She shared an exhibition at York University, 1982, and showed regularly at Mercury Gallery in London and Edinburgh from 1985, having solo shows from 1988.

Cecile WALTON 1891–1956 Painter, printmaker and illustrator, born in Glasgow, daughter of the artist E A Taylor. Growing up in London she proved early to be a fine draughtsman and flourished in her father's artistic environment. She studied in London, Edinburgh, Paris and Florence, her inclination being to follow the romantic path of Rossetti, Whistler and Jessie M King, although resettlement with her father in Edinburgh broke the link of influences such as the Slade School. Married the artist Eric Robertson after a year's study in Paris from the age of 17, then went to Florence. Back in Scotland she concentrated on watercolour illustrations of fairy tales and portraits. Became a member of the Edinburgh Group. Her career reached its peak in the early 1920s, although her failed marriage with Robertson destroyed her as a painter. The remainder of her life included working with Tyrone Guthrie as a décor artist at the Cambridge Festival Theatre; writing a book on the theatre for children; becoming organiser of BBC *Children's Hour* in Edinburgh in 1933; travels in North Africa; and settling in Kirkcudbright where she found a studio to paint again, although by then the early magic was gone. Exhibited at RSA, RA, RSW and elsewhere.

Constance WALTON 1865–1965 Watercolourist, noted for her flower pictures, born in Glasgow, sister of E A Walton and the designer George Walton. She studied in Paris, was elected RSW and also showed at RSA, Royal Glasgow Institute of the Fine Arts and Walker Art Gallery in Liverpool.

Ian WALTON 1950– Painter and teacher, born in Slough, Buckinghamshire. He studied at Newcastle College of Art, 1969–70, then Canterbury College of Art, 1970–3. Taught at Cyprus College of Art, 1978, and in 1983 was included in Woodlands Art Gallery show British Artists at Cyprus College. Group shows also comprised Pernod Northern Arts, 1969; Northern Young Contemporaries, 1972; Whitechapel Open Exhibition, at Whitechapel Art Gallery, 1976; and Zygos Gallery, Nicosia, 1977.

John WALTON 1915– Artist, illuminator and calligrapher, and teacher, born in Mellis, Suffolk. He studied at Ipswich and Beckenham Schools of Art and Goldsmiths' College School of Art. Held a series of teaching posts from the late 1940s, eventually becoming art director of Oakham School in Rutland, where he lived at Edith Weston. Among his illuminated scrolls was one presented to HM The Queen, in 1967.

John WALTON 1925– Portrait painter and teacher, born in Birkenhead, Cheshire. He studied at Ruskin School of Drawing, Oxford, under Albert Rutherston, 1944–5, then at Slade School of Fine Art, under Randolph Schwabe, 1945–9. Was elected RP in 1976, also showing at RA and Paris Salon. He was principal of Heatherley School of Fine Art. Lived in Radlett, Hertfordshire.

Sylvia WALTON 1915– Painter, commercial artist and teacher, born and lived in London. Studied at Bromley School of Art, 1931–5, then at Royal College of Art, 1935–8, under Percy Hague Jowett. Exhibited LG, SEA and NEAC. Derbyshire Education Committee bought her work.

Tim WALTON 1961– Painter and film-related artist, born in Surrey. He attended Amersham School of Art, 1977–80, then from 1981 was commissioned as special effects, animation and concept artist for many films, including *Superman 3*, *The Last Days of Pompeii*, *The Mission* and *Great Expectations*. While doing this work he continued painting, taking part in group shows at RA, The Art Store, Sue Williams Gallery and elsewhere. His solo shows began in 1986 at Bury Walk Gallery, with another at Ravensdale Gallery in 1988, exhibitions in Munich and Athens and a one-man at John Bonham, Murray Feely Fine Art, 1992.

Margaret WALTY 1952– Watercolour and acrylic miniaturist and illustrator, born in Switzerland. She trained in jewellery at the

École des Arts Decoratifs in Geneva and was largely self-taught as a painter. Created a tiny world painted in jewel colours which featured fairy tales, nursery rhymes, myths and nature studies. After moving to Britain in 1977 she took part in many shows, including RA Summer Exhibition in 1986 and Medici Gallery from 1987. Her solo exhibitions included Gracefield Arts Centre, Dumfries, 1981; The Lion and the Rose, Ontario, Canada, 1982; and Anna-Mei Chadwick from 1989. In 1985 she completed her first book illustration for *The Last Slice of Rainbow*, by Joan Aiken, following it in 1992 with *The Celtic Lunar Zodiac*, by Helena Paterson. She became a founder-member of the Society of Limners in 1986 and in 1987 joined SWA.

WANG Jianan 1955– Painter and ceramist, born in Heilong Jiang, northern China, married to the artist Cai Xiaoli. He graduated from the Engraved Painting Department of the Central Academy of Fine Art of China in 1982. In 1983, after the Cultural Revolution, he established the Zhang Li Art Studio, the first professional studio of its kind in China. The artists worked individually and jointly and won prizes at the 6th National Art Exhibition of China and the Beijing Artists' Association in 1986. Wang won the watercolour prize at the RA Summer Exhibition in London in 1989, having the year before with his wife moved to live in Britain. They evolved a unique technique of watercolour painting based on traditional methods from the Shong Dynasty for painting on silk. The two artists outside China showed widely, including Eastern Art Gallery, 1988; OneOneNine Gallery, 1989; RA and Royal Festival Hall on several occasions; in Hamburg, Tokyo and Hong Kong; and in 1991 Wang had a solo show at Ashmolean Museum, Oxford. In 1992 they shared an exhibition at Gruzelier Modern and Contemporary Art. Central Academy of Fine Art, in China; British Museum; Ashmolean Museum; and Victoria & Albert Museum hold work.

Paul WAPLINGTON 1938– Painter and draughtsman, born in Nottingham, son of a milkman, who at 15 left a school that "I think had the highest Borstal rate in Britain" to earn £1 a week training as a lace curtain draughtsman. He did this for six years, becoming highly skilled, then spent periods in Brussels as a pavement artist, returned to Nottingham and painted landscapes while working on the lace, also painting seascapes and coastal scenes in Devon. In Nottingham his work moved towards Social Realism and he attended life classes at the Society of Artists. For a time Waplington divided his days between his own work and lace draughtsmanship while developing an exhibiting career. The lace discipline, he claimed, helped with design in his pictures, which depicted the lace factory, miners and housing estates with shrewdness and gusto. Had an important solo exhibition at Midland Group, Nottingham, 1978, and was included in 1981–2 Arts Council tour Fragments Against Ruin. Later lived in Portugal.

Catherine WARBURTON 1961– Artist born in Malvern, Worcestershire, who studied for an honours degree in embroidery/fashion textiles at Manchester Polytechnic, 1981–4. Then sold watercolours through open exhibitions around Britain, including RA Summer Exhibition, at several galleries and Leeds Art Fair, 1996. Showed solo at Anna-Mei Chadwick. Her work was reproduced by Canns Down Press and Royle Publications, the greetings card and calendar publisher.

Holly WARBURTON 1957– Film-oriented artist, born in Rochford, Essex. Attended Salisbury College of Art, 1976–7; St Martin's School of Art, gaining a bachelor's degree in fine art, 1977–80; then a master's degree at Royal College of Art, 1981–3. Group exhibitions included Litany To An Embalmed Moment, London Film-makers' Co-op, 1983; The Salon of 1984, ICA, 1984; National Portrait Gallery and Berlin Film Festival, both 1986; Richard Pomeroy Gallery, 1988; Past Rays, Yokohama, Japan, 1989; and Signs of the Times, Museum of Modern Art, Oxford, 1990.

Joan WARBURTON 1920–1996 Painter and draughtsman, born in Edinburgh but brought up in Colchester area, at a finishing school in Belgium and was presented at Court. Studied art in the studio of Oswald Poreau, in Brussels, 1936, then at East Anglian School of Painting, 1937–40. After World War II service, in 1945 married the potter and teacher Peter O'Malley and lived in London where she exhibited in many mixed shows including Leicester Galleries, RA, SEA, WIAC and elsewhere. When her husband retired from Royal College of Art in 1969 they settled in Stoke-by-Nayland, Suffolk. Had early shown solo at The Weekend Gallery, 1948, and Foyles Gallery, 1959; later exhibitions included Parkin Gallery, 1984, and Sally Hunter Fine Art, 1992. Public collections in Derby, Hull and Rugby hold examples.

Stanley WARBURTON 1919– Painter who taught engineering, whose father was a draughtsman. He studied at Manchester's College of Technology, with art tuition at Bury School of Art. Was a leading member of Rochdale and Bury Art Societies and in 1960s and 1970s showed in Lancashire galleries with Colin Hilton's Lancashire Group of Artists. Other venues were MAFA, RBA and widely in the provinces and had a series of solo exhibitions. Public collections in Burnley, Bury, Halifax and Leamington Spa hold examples. Lived in Rochdale, Lancashire.

Archibald WARD fl. from c.1910–1965 Painter, notably in watercolour, printmaker and teacher who studied at Royal College of Art, getting his diploma in 1912. He was principal of Gloucester School of Art, then of its counterpart in Ipswich, Suffolk, where he settled. Ward was remembered by one colleague as a small, severe and "rather uncharismatic" man, by another as a ferocious disciplinarian, "always on the prowl to make sure everyone was where they should be". He was on the committee of the Ipswich Art Club, also showing with RA and RWA. Ipswich Museums and Galleries holds Ward's meticulous watercolour Ipswich Docks, of 1935.

Barry WARD 1937– Sculptor and teacher who settled in Leeds, Yorkshire. He studied at its College of Art and at Slade School of Fine Art. Taught at Leeds College (later at Leeds Metropolitan University), and was included in its 1964 staff show at Leeds City Art Gallery. The Teaching Image, showing Circle No 2, in relief, plaster and paint. Also exhibited at the John Moores Liverpool Exhibition and at AIA Gallery.

Celia WARD 1957– Painter and illustrator, daughter of the artist John Ward. She began painting at 16 and studied part-time at the Royal Academy Schools while reading history at University College. Commissions stemming from an initial showing at the RA Summer Exhibition in 1981 enabled her to paint full-time. Ward illustrated book-jackets for Collins; took part in mixed exhibitions; and had several solo shows at Maas Gallery from 1985, sharing an exhibition at Sally Hunter Fine Art, 1997. Still life; the domestic scene and landscape around her home in Norfolk and her married home in Blackbird Leys, Oxford, where her husband was Anglican priest; backstage scenes at the Royal Opera House from the mid-1990s; and opera at Garsington were favoured subjects.

Dick WARD 1937– Painter, draughtsman and teacher, born in London. He studied at Chelsea School of Art and after teaching at several venues became senior lecturer in painting at Sunderland Polytechnic. Ward's work had a popular, jokey quality, drawing its inspiration from everyday geordie life in the northeast. He took part in many group shows, including AIA; John Moores Exhibition, Liverpool, 1976; Bede Gallery, Jarrow, 1981; Three Painters, Middlesbrough's Cleveland Gallery, 1986; and The Northern Lights, Newcastle Group's 1990 touring show at DLI Museum & Arts Centre, Durham. Arts Council, Sussex University and Nuffield Foundation hold examples. Solo exhibitions included Bede Gallery, 1973 and 1986; Greenwich Theatre Gallery, 1979; Sunderland Arts Centre, 1982; and Gateshead Library, 1988. Had a studio at Cullercoats, Northumberland.

Douglas WARD 1921– Painter and teacher, born in Cleckheaton, Yorkshire, the son of a painter. He was educated in Dewsbury and attended the School of Art there, 1937–40, the Ruskin School of Drawing in Oxford, 1940–1, then after World War II the Slade School of Fine Art, 1946–8. Held a number of teaching posts in Yorkshire, finally being headmaster of Halifax School of Art. Lived for many years at Luddenden Foot, Yorkshire.

Eric WARD 1945– Painter in oil, acrylic and watercolour, born and lived in St Ives, Cornwall. Until 1985 he was a fisherman, then the St Ives harbour-master. He became a Royal National Lifeboat Institution lifeboatman in 1964, then coxswain of the St Ives lifeboat in 1989. He painted from 1987, studying at the St Ives School of Painting under Roy Ray. Ward described his work as "between figurative and abstract. Subject matter is not the most important aspect, but is a vehicle by which the painting surface may be explored." Group shows included Drawn from Life, Penwith Gallery, St Ives, 1988; 100 Years of Cornish Painting, Armada Gallery, Plymouth, 1994; Cassian Gallery, Lincoln, 1995; and Walker Galleries, Harrogate, 1996. Shared shows with John Emanuel at Sims Gallery, St Ives, from 1995. Had a solo exhibition there in 1994, with one previously at Hallam Gallery, 1989. Ward, who was a Chelsea Arts Club member, in 1996 presented a graphic programme on BBC2 Television in the *Video Diaries* series about his life at sea and as a painter.

Frank Clifford WARD 1914– Artist in oil, pastel and watercolour, and teacher, born in Stradbroke, Suffolk, married to the artist Kathleen Walne. He studied at Ipswich School of Art and the Royal College of Art, notable teachers being Percy Horton and Gilbert Spencer. Ward held several teaching posts, including Clapham School of Art while still at Royal College, and was head of the art department at Wilson's School. During war service in Italy his work was purchased by the War Artists' Advisory Committee and it is also in the Garman-Ryan Collection at Walsall Art Gallery. Showed Cooling Galleries, Compendium 2, RA, NEAC and elsewhere. Ward's drawings accompany the text of *The Guns of 6 AGRA* (6 Army Group Royal Artillery), graphically chronicling tough fighting from first action during the landing in Sicily to the final victory in North Italy in 1945. He was an excellent portrait and landscape draughtsman and painter, with a lifelong interest in the techniques of the Renaissance masters. A good selection of Ward's output is illustrated in David Buckman's 1997 monograph on Ward and his wife, *Mixed Palette*, published by Sansom & Company. He lived in Brighton, Sussex.

Gilbert WARD 1935– Sculptor, draughtsman and teacher, born in Yorkshire. He studied fine art at King's College, Durham University and after a number of teaching posts became head of sculpture at Newcastle Polytechnic. Among many commissions throughout Britain by Ward were Scottish and Newcastle Breweries, Darlington Memorial Hospital, BBC, Aberdeen City Council and Newcastle University. His group shows included Young Contemporaries, Mall Galleries; LG; 10 Sculptors at Laing Art Gallery, Newcastle, 1980; Richard Demarco Gallery, Edinburgh, 1988; and The Northern Lights, Newcastle Group show at DLI Museum & Arts Centre, 1990, and tour. Had solo show at York University. Lived near Hexham, Northumberland, and the surrounding landscape was a key reference in Ward's work.

Gordon WARD 1932– Artist and teacher, born in North Walsham, Norfolk, who attended Norwich School of Art, 1949–53, then Slade School of Fine Art, 1955–7, under William Coldstream. Became senior lecturer/head of painting at Gloucestershire College of Art & Design/Gloucestershire College of Arts & Technology. Was a member of RWA, which holds his work, also exhibiting at RA Summer Exhibition and other venues. Lived in Cheltenham, Gloucestershire.

Joan WARD 1925– Sculptor in various materials, born in London, wife of the artist Thomas William Ward. She studied at Bromley School of Art and Royal College of Art, 1945–8, teachers including Frank Dobson and Willi Soukop. Became a member of NS in 1979, also showing at NEAC, RBA, Questors Theatre in Ealing and elsewhere. In 1995 she showed with her husband at Chappel Galleries, Chappel. Lived at Holbrook, Suffolk.

John WARD 1917– Painter, draughtsman, illustrator and teacher, born in Hereford. He studied at the School of Art there, 1933–6, then at Royal College of Art, 1936–9, gaining a drawing prize and in 1947 a travelling scholarship. During World War II Ward served in the Army. Between 1948–52 he was under contract to *Vogue* magazine, combining this with part-time teaching at Wimbledon School of Art. From then on Ward consolidated his reputation as a portrait painter and as a book illustrator. Among his exemplary book illustrations were those for Laurie Lee's *Cider with Rosie*, 1959, and H E Bates' *Autobiography*, 1969–72. Ward painted a number of figure groups; elegant portraits, especially of beautiful young women; and produced notable architectural and landscape watercolours. Showed with Maas Gallery and had a retrospective at Agnew in 1990. Elected RA, 1965. HM The Queen, National Portrait Gallery and RA hold his work. The artist Celia Ward was his daughter. He lived at Bilting, near Ashford, Kent.

Leonard WARD 1887– Watercolourist and printmaker who studied at Birmingham School of Art after initial education at King Edward's Grammar School there. Exhibited extensively at RBSA, of which he was a member, RA, RWS and elsewhere. Lived in Moseley, Birmingham.

Leslie Moffat WARD 1888–1978 Painter and printmaker. Born in Worcester, he studied and settled in Bournemouth, Hampshire. Was a gold medallist, National Competition of School of Art, 1909–10. Became senior assistant at the Southern College of Art, Bournemouth, retiring in 1953. Exhibited from 1915 at the RA; also showed at RI and RE. Had a one-man show at the Red House Art Gallery, Christchurch, Hampshire and at the Eastbourne and Hastings public galleries in 1956. Work in public galleries in Bournemouth, Hastings and Eastbourne.

Louis WARD 1913– Painter, illustrator and teacher, born in Bristol, where he settled in Clifton. He was an ordained parish priest who studied theology at Ripon Hall, Oxford. Also studied full-time at West of England College of Art, Bristol. Taught part-time at Bristol Polytechnic's arts faculty. Showed RWA of which he was a member, in Bristol's Arnolfini Gallery, Arts Council and elsewhere. Did a variety of book and magazine illustration. Member of Bristol Savages club. RWA and Bristol City Art Gallery hold his work.

Martin WARD 1944– Painter and teacher, born in Bexley, Kent. He studied at Bromley College of Art, 1960–2, Ravensbourne College of Art, 1962–4, and Slade School of Fine Art, 1965–7, on a postgraduate fine art course. Ward was treasurer of Young Contemporaries exhibition committee, 1965–7. His teaching experience included Central School of Art and Middlesex Polytechnic. Exhibitions included Young Contemporaries at Tate Gallery and tour, 1967; Greenwich Festival, Artists' Open Studios Event, from 1977; A Sense of Place, at Greenwich Town Hall, 1980; and a solo show that year at Woodlands Art Gallery, when he exhibited abstract works based on an obsession "with a chance image: Two Squares, tilted, with one side congruent". Ward lived in Charlton, southeast London, for some time occupying a Space Studio.

Michael WARD 1954– Painter and teacher who studied at St Albans School of Art, 1971–2, then Wolverhampton Polytechnic, 1972–5. He was a visiting lecturer there and at Bath Academy of Art, Corsham. Group shows included Centaur Gallery from 1975; Middlesex Polytechnic, 1981; and Berry Street Open Studios, 1984. Solo exhibitions included University of Sheffield, 1976 and 1984. Lived for a time in London.

Nicholas WARD 1950– Draughtsman, etcher and teacher, born in Great Yarmouth, Norfolk. He studied at Lowestoft School of Art; St Martin's School of Art, 1968–71, with Peter Coker, James Stroudley and Alan Cooper; and Royal Academy Schools, 1971–4, with Peter Greenham and Denis Lucas. Ward became lecturer in drawing at Great Yarmouth College of Art & Design, 1974–84, resigning to devote more time to personal work, having in 1983 set up a printmaking workshop. From 1984 undertook part-time lecturing at Norfolk Institute of Art & Design and Lowestoft School of Art. In 1992 was elected a fellow of RE. Ward was interested in "the contrast between machinery and nature". Group shows included RA Summer Exhibitions from 1982; British International Miniature Print, 1989; and Department of Transport, Mall Galleries, 1992. Later solo shows included Christchurch Mansion, Ipswich; Bircham Art Gallery, King's Lynn; and Printworks, Colchester, all 1992. British Railways Board and BP Petroleum Development hold examples. Lived in Winterton-on-Sea, Norfolk.

Reginald A WARD 1910– Painter, draughtsman and teacher, born in Stockport, Lancashire. Studied at Manchester and Southport Schools of Art. Exhibited RA, MAFA, RI and widely in north of England. Lived in Southport, Lancashire.

Richard WARD 1957– Painter in acrylic, on canvas and paper, born in Aldeburgh, Suffolk, settling nearby at Aldringham, Leiston. Ward's work swung between figurative and abstract. Among his leading themes were "paintings concerning my HIV-positive status and its emotional, physical and mental effect on me". Ward attended Lowestoft College of Art and Design, 1973–8, studying art and design, industrial ceramics and fine art, gaining his diploma in mural design at Chelsea School of Art, 1983–5. Took part in group shows at Brixton Artists' Collective. The first of many solo shows was held at Regent Gallery, Lowestoft, 1973, later ones including Tudor House Gallery, Aldeburgh, from 1994.

Thomas William WARD 1918– Watercolourist, draughtsman, printmaker and teacher, notable for his pictures of ships and the sea, born in Sheffield, Yorkshire, married to the sculptor Joan Ward. He served at sea in the late 1930s. He studied part-time with Eric Jones in Sheffield, 1937–9, then after World War II military service was at Royal College of Art, 1946–50, winning a Silver Medal in 1949, teachers including Malcolm Osborne and Robert Sargent Austin. Taught at Harrow College of Higher Education.

Was made a member of RE in 1953 and RWS in 1957. Was included in A Survey of Influential East Anglian Artists, Chappel Gallery, Chappel, 1991; a solo show at Chappel in 1995 reviewed five decades of Ward's output. Also exhibited at public galleries in Liverpool, Shipley, Middlesbrough and Wakefield. Victoria & Albert Museum hold his work. Illustrated a number of nautical books and produced *Perspective and Composition*, 1988. Lived in Holbrook, Suffolk.

Vernon WARD 1905–1985 Painter and draughtsman, born and lived in London, who also travelled widely. His father was an art dealer and in the shop Vernon learned to copy all styles of painting. At Henry Tonks' instigation in 1919 aged 14 Ward began three years' study at Slade School of Fine Art. The death of his father when Ward was 21 forced him to seek commercial work to support himself and his mother. His rejection as a serious artist – he was refused election to the ROI – left him bitter. Ward's period costume and flower pictures, landscapes and bird studies were reproduced on chocolate boxes, cards and in *Everybody's* magazine and extensively as prints by The Medici Society and W R Royle, although Ward continued to paint non-commercial work for his own pleasure. His first solo show was at the King Street Galleries in 1976. Others followed there and in the provinces. For most of his life Ward had the use of only one eye, the other having been damaged in an accident. He also suffered a severe nervous breakdown in the 1960s and was latterly crippled by arthritis. Ward died in Twyford Abbey, a nursing home run by the Alexian Brothers. His own memoirs formed much of Josephine Walpole's *Vernon Ward Child of the Edwardian Era*, 1988.

Derek S WARDALE 1952–1990 Painter and teacher who was also a talented musician, brought up in Wallasey, Cheshire, where he attended the Grammar School, 1964–9. He studied art at the local College of Further Education, 1969–71, then from 1971–4 at Hornsey College of Art, where David Tindle was a sympathetic tutor. Wardale's lack of self-confidence is evident in his painting, based on a study of the Pre-Raphaelites (Rossetti was a strong influence) and a painstaking transcription of preparatory photographs which he took of his sitters. His pictures, small in number, were permeated with the idea of death. In the late 1970s and early 1980s Wardale concentrated on teaching at Wirral Metropolitan College, hardly painting at all. In 1984 he had success at the National Portrait Gallery's John Player Awards, recognition repeated there and at the RA, but sterile periods meant that he completed at most three pictures a year. Walker Art Gallery, Liverpool, held a memorial show in 1993.

William WARDEN 1908–1982 Landscape painter in oil and watercolour. Studied at Liverpool City School of Art, 1924–30, and in Sussex under George Graham. Became a member of the Society of Sussex Painters in 1938. Exhibited at RA, NEAC, RBA, with the AEB, Arts Council, Roland, Browse and Delbanco and at the New Grafton Gallery, as well as in the provinces. Hastings Art Gallery has his work, and official purchases include Imperial War Museum, Towner Art Gallery, Eastbourne, Walker Art Gallery, Liverpool and Rye Art Gallery. From the early 1950s Warden concentrated on oils, and regular stays at Agalier, in the Avignon area of France, lightened his palette. Died in Southport, Lancashire, although he lived at Winchelsea Beach, Sussex.

Arthur WARDLE 1864–1949 Painter of birds and animals, born in London, where he died. Wardle studied privately and at the zoo. He was a prolific exhibitor, showing at RA from 1880–1935; he was a member of PS, RI and RBC; and he also showed widely at RBA, ROI and Arthur Tooth and Sons. His first one-man show was at Fine Art Society in 1931. Tate Gallery holds his study Fate, a Chantrey Bequest purchase in 1904. Work also held by Victoria & Albert Museum and Leeds City Art Gallery. Was included in The British Sporting Art Trust's 1983 show at Alpine Gallery.

G Joyce WARDLE 1904–c.1972 Sculptor, ceramist and watercolourist, born in Derby. Miss Wardle studied privately with Frances Wirgman, then at the Southport School of Arts and Crafts, 1939. Exhibited regularly at SWA, of which she was a member, 1951–71, also at RMS and Paris Salon, where she won bronze and silver medals. One-man shows included Atkinson Art Gallery, Southport in Lancashire, where she settled, and SWA.

John Clifford WARDLE 1907– Painter and draughtsman, especially of figures and animals, and teacher. Born in Chesterfield, Derbyshire, where he studied at the School of Art, 1925–30, then at Slade School of Fine Art, 1930–3, with Randolph Schwabe. Member of Bolton Art Circle, having taken up post at Bolton Municipal School of Art in 1945. Exhibited RA, PS and extensively in the north of England. Lived at Haulgh, Lancashire.

Piers WARDLE 1960– Abstract painter, often working on a large scale and producing colourful, complex images, as in his 1991–2 John Moores Exhibition, Liverpool, picture Mitchelson-Morley. Wardle was born in Beckenham, Kent. He studied at Exeter College of Art, 1976–7, and Ruskin School, Oxford, 1977–80. His first major exhibitions were in London at Acme Gallery, 1981, and at Museum of Modern Art, Oxford, in 1982. Other appearances were at Pomeroy Purdy and Bernhard Baron Galleries, and in 1990 he exhibited in Florida at Eastbourne Clark Gallery. Lived in London.

Clare WARDMAN 1960– Gestural abstract painter in whose work subtle colour harmonies and sensual textures were important. She was born in Yorkshire and gained a fine art painting honours degree from Exeter College of Art and Design, 1982. She was at Spacex Studios, Exeter, 1982–6, moving to Edinburgh in 1988. From 1988–90 she was a member of the collective Gallery there; was painter-in-residence, Grizedale, Cumbria, for the first half of 1993; then in 1994–6 managed the Kingfisher Gallery, Edinburgh (having been part-time, 1991–4). Exhibitions included Abstract into Reality, Exeter University, 1983; Visitors 85, Penwith Gallery, St Ives, 1985; Woman 2000, Gatehouse Gallery, Glasgow, 1990; and Scottish Contemporary Painters and Printmakers, Beatrice Royal Gallery, Eastleigh, 1997. Later solo shows included Kingfisher

Gallery, 1997. Scottish Arts Council, Grizedale Society, Bayer Plc, Paintings in Hospitals Scotland and Medical Center at University of Minnesota, America, hold examples.

William WARE 1915– Landscape painter and restorer, born in London. After falling from a ladder, aged three, when he broke his back, William Ware was confined to various hospitals until 16, when he was cured, but at the age of nine he decided to become a painter. He studied at Putney School of Art, gaining a scholarship which took him to Richmond Art School, 1932–7, under Patrick Millard and Albert Houthuesen. Married the artist Eileen Aldridge, their son being the painter Martin Ware. During World War II painted scenes of the London Blitz, a number of pictures being acquired by Imperial War Museum. Set up a gallery in London and gained a reputation as a restorer, doing work for national galleries and museums. Exhibited RA, RP, as well as Leger, Redfern, Upper Grosvenor and Modern Art Galleries. In 1950s completed murals on Greek Shipping Line's *Olympia* and *Arcadia*, holding a one-man show on the maiden voyage of the former. In 1970s painted enthronement of Dr Donald Coggan as archbishop of Canterbury. Lived for many years in London, later in Burwash, Sussex.

Percy WAREHAM 1892– Painter, draughtsman, teacher and writer with a special interest in design and handicrafts, born in Sheffield, Yorkshire. Attended the university there, then Sheffield College of Art, 1909–19, and part-time at the Royal College of Art where his teachers included Beresford Pite and W R Lethaby. Exhibited widely in the north of England, notably with the Sheffield Society of Artists, and in London. Held several art teaching and administrative posts, for about 25 years from 1928 being arts and crafts organiser for West Bromwich Education Committee. Signed work with initials. Lived in Clifton, North Yorkshire.

Lily Florence WARING 1877– Painter and writer, born in Birkenhead, Cheshire. She studied at Cambridge University, where she obtained her Master of Arts degree and was a member of the School of Slavonic and Eastern Studies at London University. Waring's father had been a geographer and she wrote several books on the Balkans. She studied at Manchester School of Art under Richard Glazier, at Cambridge School of Art, where her teachers included John Hookham, and in France. As well as showing widely in France she exhibited in London at RI, RBA, UA and Beaux Arts Gallery, where she had a series of one-man shows, as she did in Cambridge and Birmingham. Lived in Cambridge.

Oliver Byrne WARMAN 1932– Painter in oil of landscapes and gardens, born in London. He was educated at Stowe School, Royal Military College of Science, at Balliol College, Oxford, and studied art at Exeter University. Warman was for some time a regular officer in the Welsh Guards. He was a member of RBA from 1984 and ROI, 1989. Was chief executive of Federation of British Artists and a director of Arts News Agency. He showed at RA Summer Exhibition, RBA, NEAC, ROI, RWA and RSMA as well as The Hann Gallery, Bath. In 1990 had solo exhibition at Bowmoore Gallery. American Embassy, National Westminster Bank and S G Warburg held his work. Lived latterly in Verteillac, France.

Sylvia WARMAN 1922– Portrait sculptor and painter, born in St Leonards-on-Sea, Sussex. She attended classes at Reading University, 1947–54, specialising in portrait sculpture with Albert Carter, winning both the Wells Prize in Fine Art and Owen Ridley Prize. Became a member of SPS and a notable figure in NS, also showing at RA, RWA and at Paris Salon, where she won Bronze and Silver Medals for sculpture. Lived in Caversham, Berkshire.

Byron Winston WARMBY 1902–1978 Painter in oil and watercolour. Studied at Sheffield College of Arts and Crafts, 1920–5, under Henry Hoyland. Exhibited RA, Graves Art Gallery, Sheffield, RBSA and elsewhere in the north of England. Lived in Sheffield, where he was honorary president of the Society of Artists just after World War II.

Dorothy WARNE 1902–1976 Painter of miniatures in watercolour, born at Ealing, Middlesex Studied St John's Wood School of Art, 1923–5. Exhibited RA and RMS. Lived at Richmond, Surrey.

Harold WARNER 1914– Self-taught artist in oil, watercolour and charcoal, born in Colchester, Essex, who spent his career as a bookbinder. His son was the artist Robert Warner. He exhibited in mixed exhibitions at RA, RBA, ROI and Gainsborough's House, Sudbury, having solo shows in Colchester at The Minories and Digby Gallery. Colchester Art Society and the Beecroft Art Gallery, Westcliff-on Sea, have examples. Lived in West Bergholt, Essex.

Howard WARNER 1881–c.1953 Watercolourist and draughtsman who was a surgeon-dentist by profession, born in London. Educated at St Paul's School and London University, he studied art in London and Norwich. Showed at RA, RI and in East Anglia, living in Beccles, Suffolk, where he practised for many years in Northgate and was honorary surgeon to the local hospital. Lived finally in Shenfield, Essex, appearing in the 1953 *Medical Directory*.

Robert WARNER 1947– Painter in watercolour and oil, born in Colchester, Essex, settling nearby at West Bergholt, son of the artist Harold Warner. He studied at Colchester School of Art, 1964–71, under John Nash and Peter Coker. Warner said that from his school days he was interested in Brueghel the Elder. Warner's subjects were "comments on the world at large, the human condition, contemporary goings-on and are sometimes related to history". He was a member of Colchester Art Society and exhibited at RA Summer Exhibition from 1974, Singer & Friedlander/*Sunday Times* Watercolour Competition from 1988, Laing Art Competition from 1990, ROI, NEAC, RI and elsewhere. Held solo exhibitions at Mercury Theatre, Colchester, 1972, 1980 and 1985, and at Minories in the town, 1973. In the 1990 Southend Open Warner won the *Evening Echo* Award for the Most Imaginative Work, in 1993 at the

Essex Open, in Southend, the Laurie Mathews Award for Best Watercolour. Lakeland, Swiss Mountains, Enlightened Ages and Twitchers were among Warner's most notable pictures. Epping Forest District Museum holds work by him.

Robin WARNES 1952– Painter, draughtsman and teacher whose work could include strong abstract tendencies, born in Ipswich, Suffolk, where he became a lecturer at the Suffolk College School of Art and Design. Attended the foundation course at Ipswich School of Art & Design, 1972–4; gained an honours degree in fine art at Canterbury College of Art, 1974–7; then did a postgraduate certificate in painting and drawing at Royal Academy Schools, 1977–80. After in 1979 winning the Creswick Landscape, Richard Jack and Landseer Drawing Prizes, in 1981 he gained the Turner Gold Medal for Landscape Painting in Oil and a David Murray Studentship for Landscape Painting, then in 1990 The Laing Landscape Regional Prize. Residencies included Ipswich Museums Arts in Towns Project, 1989; commissions included the Richard Ellis Drawing Project, Broadgate. Warnes was a prolific exhibitor, mixed shows including Stowells Trophy Exhibition from 1977; RA Summer Exhibition, from 1981; and The John Russell Gallery, Ipswich, from 1988. Later solo exhibitions included Chappel Galleries, Chappel, 1997.

Rose WARNOCK 1959– Painter and muralist, born in Hatfield, Hertfordshire, who studied at Watford School of Art, 1977–9, Birmingham Polytechnic in 1979–82 and Royal College of Art, 1987–9. Showed regularly from mid-1980s, in 1995–6 appearing in John Moores Liverpool Exhibition. In 1994 was commissioned by P&O Group to complete a big mural on the liner *Oriana*. Solo exhibitions included Fischer Fine Art, 1991; Gillian Jason Gallery, 1993; and Jason & Rhodes, 1996. From 1990 Warnock worked in France.

Michael WARRE 1922–1987 Painter, actor, producer, writer and designer, born and lived in London. He was educated at Eton College, where his art teachers included Robin Darwin and Wilfrid Blunt, in the late 1930s. Showed at Leicester Galleries, Kensington Art Gallery, Victoria & Albert Museum and in the provinces. British Council and Brighton Art Gallery hold his work. Warre studied for the theatre at the London Mask Theatre School under John Fernald and made his first stage appearance at the Minack Theatre, Porthcurno, in 1939, which presaged a distinguished acting career in Britain and abroad in which he played major classical and modern roles. He also taught stagecraft, designed scenery and costumes, directed and designed for several theatres and made many television appearances. With Joan Maude he ran a film production company and was involved in various ways in films such as *Henry V*, 1944; *Reach for the Sky*, 1956; and *The Eustace Diamonds*, 1959. Warre wrote *Designing and Making Stage Scenery*, 1965.

Benjamin WARREN 1878–1954 Painter, stained glass artist, designer and teacher, born in Birmingham. He studied at the School of Art there and at Heatherley's School of Fine Art, eventually settling and teaching in Birmingham. Showed at RA, RP, RBA and RBSA.

Charles Wyatt WARREN 1908– Landscape painter who was by profession a local government officer, 1926–68, born and lived in Caernarvon, Wales. He attended the Grammar School there, completed external studies through London University but in art was self-taught. At various times he was a member of Arts Society of Paddington, Caernarvon Art Group, was founder of Caernarvon Art Club and a founder-member and former secretary of NWG. His father, also Charles Wyatt Warren, was a painter and printmaker. Showed RCamA, Denbighshire Art Society, Royal National Eisteddfod, ROI, extensively in Wales and abroad. Had a solo show at London Welsh Association, 1960, some 50 solos following in Britain and North America. Did commissioned work for North Atlantic Treaty Organization, Brussels, and University College of North Wales, Bangor. Gwynedd County Council and CASW hold examples.

Jim WARREN 1960– Artist in various media who studied at Harrow and Central Schools of Art. His group appearances included LG, South Bank Picture Show, Merz Contemporary Art and England & Co's 1990 Art in Boxes. White Space and Crypt Galleries gave him solo shows.

Michael WARREN 1938– Painter and designer, born in Wolverhampton, Staffordshire. He studied at the local College of Art, 1954–8, and started painting full-time, 1972. Warren developed his art in conjunction with active birdwatching; early pictures contained decorative backgrounds to bird subjects, the emphasis gradually giving way to a greater realism while retaining a strong design. Warren studied birds in Britain, America, continental Europe, Africa and the Pacific. He was a member of SWLA, 1971, and a founder-member of the Society for Wildlife Art for the Nation, with work in its collection. His art was used by the Society for the Protection of Birds and lithographs were published by Christies' Contemporary Art. Warren's postage stamp designs were used by the British Post Office and the Marshall Islands and many for conservation stamps by the National Audubon Society, in America. He received extensive commissions from Unicover Corporation in America. Solo exhibitions included Moorland Gallery from 1972; Carl Battaglia Gallery, New York, 1978; Barbican Centre, 1984; and Jane Neville Gallery, 1988. Lived in Winthorpe, Nottinghamshire.

Rebecca WARREN 1965– Conceptual artist, born and worked in London, who gained an honours degree in fine art at Goldsmiths' College, 1989–92; her master's in fine art, Chelsea College of Art, 1992–3; and was artist-in-residence, Oxford University, 1993–4. She took part in a number of collaborations, mainly with Fergal Stapleton, such as The Showroom, 1997. Group exhibitions included Whitworth Young Contemporaries, at Whitworth Gallery, Manchester, 1993; Destroy All Monsters, The Tannery, 1994; Happy Squirrels Club, Bank, Eindhoven, Netherlands, 1996; and Class Vegas, The Embassy, 1997.

Solo shows included Manliness without ostentation …, The Agency, 1995.

John WARREN DAVIS 1919–1998 Sculptor and teacher in wood, bronze, stone and aluminium (in some sources wrongly listed under Davis, in others as Warren-Davis), born in Christchurch, Hampshire. He studied at Westminster School of Art, 1938–9, with Mark Gertler and Bernard Meninsky, then 1949–52 at Brighton College of Art with James Woodford. From 1959–75 he lectured in sculpture at Central School of Art and Design and was a visiting lecturer at Leeds, Portsmouth and Canterbury Polytechnics. Showed with Lords, Molton, Grosvenor and Redfern Galleries and RA Summer Exhibition. Warren Davis "started modelling the figure, moved on to carving under the influence of Brancusi, then to large timber constructions. Later moved back to carving." Arts Council, Contemporary Art Society, National Museum of Wales in Cardiff, Southampton and Leeds and American galleries hold his work. Lived in St Ishmaels, Haverfordwest, Dyfed. Warren Davis' funeral was at Chichester Crematorium, Sussex.

Jonathan WARRENDER 1954– Painter and draughtsman, born in Curry Rivel, Somerset. He attended Camberwell School of Arts and Crafts under Anthony Eyton and Euan Uglow, then worked as a copyist for Sotheby's and Christie's for three years. In 1980 Warrender began his series of bird's-eye views of houses, estates and townscapes. Working on commission, he normally did about two a year only. He would make a series of long walks around the subject, would make notes and sketches of the lie of the land and would supplement this information with an owner's perceptions of the property to be depicted. Having lived in Scotland from the age of 12 Warrender came to paint a number of properties in this area, including Innes House, Elgin; Dunphail House, Forres; Cawdor Castle, Nairn; and The Old Kirk, Altyre, Forres. English properties included The Hall, Castle Rising, King's Lynn; Stowell Park, Cirencester; and Kirby House, Inkpen. Warrender also worked in France and America. In August 1991 he was commissioned by the council of Ayr to paint that town. A show of Warrender's work was held by Deborah Gage (Works of Art) Ltd in 1992. Lived at Pinmore, Girvan, Ayrshire.

David Ross WARRILLOW 1956– Painter and teacher, born in Glasgow, where he settled, studying at the School of Art, 1975–9, David Donaldson and Danny Ferguson being early influences. Taught art in Glasgow Schools, 1980–9, when he began to concentrate on painting. He studied simple, natural forms such as shells, flowers and fruit and painted them in an intense realist way, a follower of Cotan and Melendez of the Spanish seventeenth-century golden age. Later works showed a love for paint and his admiration of Expressionist painters. Mixed exhibitions included Royal Glasgow Institute of the Fine Arts from 1976, Fine Art Society in Glasgow, 1984–9, and RA Summer Exhibitions from 1986. Had a solo show at Glasgow Art Club in 1982, later ones including Kelly Gallery, Glasgow, from 1990, and he also exhibited with Roger Billcliffe Fine Art there. Britoil, Arthur Andersen and Robert Fleming Holdings Ltd have examples.

Richard William WARRINGTON 1868–1953 Painter and stained glass designer who attended Liverpool University's design department under J Herbert McNair, 1900–5, then Liverpool School of Art. Most of his life was spent as a glass designer, including work for Hope Street Unitarian Church. He showed at Walker Art Gallery in Liverpool, where he lived, and it holds paintings and drawings by him.

Mary WARSOP fl. from 1960s– Artist in a variety of media, and teacher, who studied at Watford School of Art, St Martin's School of Art and London University. She lived in Suffolk from 1963 and lectured at Suffolk College until retirement. Had a retrospective at Christchurch Mansion, Ipswich, in 1996. This revealed Warsop's long interest in landscape, drawn from observations in Suffolk, Cornwall and France, works often being made of multiple images, compared and contrasted within a picture.

Celia WASHINGTON 1959– Artist, born in Edinburgh, who studied with Nerina Simi in Florence and at Byam Shaw School. Her pictures could include a strong fantasy element, as in the oil on board Celebration, included in Royal Over-Seas League Open, 1994. Other mixed exhibitions included Originals Gallery, from 1983; Charlotte Lampard Gallery, from 1988; RA Summer Exhibition, 1990; and Angela Flowers Gallery, 1993. Had a series of solo exhibitions at Long & Ryle Art International from 1989. The collections of Crowood Press, Electra Investment Trust and National Star Centre hold examples.

William WASHINGTON 1885–1956 Printmaker, painter and teacher, born in Marple, Cheshire. Initially studied at Ashton-under-Lyne's Heginbottom Art School while working for a lithographic printing firm. Then gained position at Royal College of Art, 1905–9, under Édouard Lantéri. He taught in several art schools, finally becoming acting principal at Hammersmith School of Building and Arts and Crafts in 1949. Exhibited RA, NEAC, RBA of which he was a member, and in Paris. British Museum and Victoria & Albert Museum hold his work. Lived in London.

Tim WASKETT 1967– Artist producing abstract works, such as his Penetrating Blue, oil and carpet on canvas, in Royal Over-Seas League Open, 1995. He was born in Bristol and studied at Bath College of Higher Education, Winchester School of Art and the University of Barcelona, Spain. Group exhibitions included Homage to Kafka, Goldsmiths' Gallery, 1987; Tower Arts Centre, Winchester, 1988; Winchester Gallery, Winchester, 1989; and Five From Winchester, Art Line Gallery, 1989.

George R WATERFIELD 1886–c.1980 Painter, printmaker and illustrator. Studied art in Birmingham, 1902–8, under Sidney Meteyard and Harold Wilson. Exhibited RBSA and at Walker Art Gallery in Liverpool. Lived in Sheldon, Birmingham.

Ken WATERFIELD 1927– Painter in oil and teacher, born in Watford, Hertfordshire, attending the local School of Art, 1940–3. From 1943–5 he was involved in book-jacket design; from 1945–8 was engaged in Army service followed by Colonial Service in Nyasaland to 1960; then taught and was involved in full-time painting from 1972, subjects being abstracts, wildlife, landscape and mythological. Waterfield was made a member of SWLA in 1972. Showed at Hamwic Gallery, Southampton; Westgate Gallery, Winchester; Guildhall, Winchester; and Medici Gallery. Mixed shows included Mall and Tryon Galleries, Ashgate Gallery in Farnham and Ashbarn, Stroud. His main works included At the Flooded Gateway. Lived at Uploders, Bridport, Dorset.

Winifred WATERFIELD fl. c.1935–1955 Watercolourist who studied art in Paris. Exhibited WIAC, Walker's Galleries and in East Anglia. Signed work W W. Lived at Snape, Suffolk.

Billie WATERS 1896–1979 Painter with a strong interest in animals. Born at Richmond, Surrey, she studied at Heatherley's School of Fine Art with Henry Massey, the Grosvenor School of Modern Art with Iain Macnab and for several years from 1926 with Ernest and Dod Procter in Newlyn, which she then visited regularly from the early 1930s. Exhibited RA, Goupil Gallery, SWA, NS, of which she was a member, Leicester Galleries, ROI and Fine Art Society. Member of the Penwith Society of Arts. Lived in London and at Lelant, Cornwall.

Gary WATERS 1953– Painter who studied at Hornsey College of Art, Birmingham Polytechnic and Royal College of Art. Originally he was a photographer. Had a first solo exhibition in Yugoslavia in 1982, then had one-man exhibitions in Cardiff and Halifax and was included in The Self Portrait: a Modern View, which toured from Artsite Gallery, Bath, 1987.

George WATERS 1863–1947 Landscape watercolourist who was by profession a lithographic artist in Belfast, Northern Ireland, with David Allen & Sons, having been born near the city at Holywood. He was a prizewinner at Government School of Design. Waters painted extensively throughout Ireland, was a founder-member of Belfast Art Society and Ulster Society of Painters and a member of Ulster Arts Club, also showing at RHA and Magee's Gallery in Belfast, where he lived for a time. Ulster Museum and other Irish public collections hold examples.

David WATERSON 1870–1954 Printmaker and painter. Exhibited prolifically at RE, of which he was a fellow, and RSA and had work reproduced in *The Studio*. A romantic landscape artist, he lived at Brechin, Angus.

Evelyn WATHERSTON fl. from c.1900–1952 Painter, notably of animals and portraits, born in London, sister of the artist Marjory V Watherston. Studied art in Paris and at the Royal Academy Schools. Exhibited Walker's Galleries especially, SWA, RA, ROI and elsewhere. Huddersfield Art Gallery holds her picture September Ploughing. Member of UA. Lived in Pinner, Middlesex.

Marjory Violet WATHERSTON fl. c.1915–1960 Painter in various media of landscapes, figures and portraits. Born and based in London, she studied art in Paris and at the Royal Academy Schools. Sister of the artist Evelyn Watherston. Exhibited widely, including RA, RI, RP, ROI, in the provinces and at the Paris Salon. Imperial War Museum holds her work, presented by the artist in 1957, shown at the RA in 1917.

Darton WATKINS 1928– Painter, whose full name was Christopher Darton Watkins, notable for precise but atmospheric townscapes, shops and doors. He gained his master's degree from Oxford University, studying at Ruskin School of Art. Among his many exhibitions were Woodstock Gallery, 1962, the year he was awarded 2nd prize, British Open Painting Competition, Arnolfini Gallery, Bristol; Bear Lane Gallery, Oxford, 1964; RA Summer Exhibition, 1967; Seifert-Binder Gallery, Munich, 1980; Anthony Dawson Fine Art, 1990; Gerald Peters Gallery, Santa Fe, New Mexico, 1993; and Original Art Gallery, Båstad, Sweden (Watkins' wife was Swedish), 1996. In 1990 he received a Pollock-Krasner Foundation award "because of the exceptional quality of your work and the extent of your artistic achievement". Watkins was a member of L'Association Internationale des Arts Plastiques, UNESCO. He lived and worked in Tuscany and London.

Denys WATKINS 1945– Artist born in Wellington, New Zealand, whose work included a Surrealist element. He attended Wellington Polytechnic School of Design, then in London Central School of Art and Design and Royal College of Art. Among his awards were British Council Scholarship, 1968–70, and QE II Art Council Award, 1977 and 1983. Group shows included Eight New Zealand Artists, Auckland City Art Gallery, 1977; British International Print Biennale, 1982–6; and Montana Lindauer Award Exhibition, 1988. Had a solo show at Barry Lett Galleries, Auckland, 1972, later ones including Todd Gallery, 1989.

Frank WATKINS 1951– Mixed-media artist, born in Glanaman, South Wales. He attended Newport College of Art, 1970–3, then Cardiff College of Art, 1973–4. He had a strong affinity with artists such as Morandi, Beuys and Dubuffet, his work revealing a notably contemplative and metaphysical nature. Watkins showed with Chapter Arts Centre in Cardiff, Contemporary Art Society and Mostyn Art Gallery, Llandudno. In 1992 had a solo show at Martin Tinney Gallery, Cardiff.

Islwyn WATKINS 1938– Printmaker, teacher, constructions and events artist, born in Tonypandy, Glamorgan. Watkins studied at Cardiff College of Art, 1954–9, then taught in Hertfordshire and Leeds before going to study and teach part-time at the University of Wisconsin, America, 1965–6. After that there were periods of teaching in the Birmingham area, including Birmingham Polytechnic. Watkins participated in many group shows in Wales, London, the English provinces and America, and solo exhibitions included University of Birmingham and New Art Gallery, Rugby. He organised and took part in happenings in London and America. WAC holds his work.

Jesse WATKINS 1899–1980 Sculptor in metal, born at Gravesend, Kent. He was awarded a silver medal by the RBS in 1968. Watkins took part in many mixed shows and had a number of one-man exhibitions in Britain. The Royal Free Hospital and School of Medicine, London, commissioned work from him, which is also in the City Art Gallery, Manchester, at other British locations as well as in Yugoslavia and Norway. Watkins was for some time a sailor and nautical instruments are a theme of his work, which was influenced by that of the American sculptor David Smith. A retrospective was held at Calouste Gulbenkian Gallery, Newcastle upon Tyne, 1970. Lived in New Barnet, Hertfordshire.

Peggy WATKINS 1919– Painter, draughtsman, jeweller in gold and silver and teacher, born in Northampton as Frances Jane Grierson Milligan, daughter of the artist Thomas Vaughan Milligan. She attended Hereford School of Art and Birmingham School of Jewellery and Silversmithing. Watkins was on the full-time staff of Hereford School of Art teaching painting and silve work, later teaching part-time, jewellery and silverwork, at Hereford College of Art. Showed at RA, RSA, RBA and in the provinces, having a solo show at Hereford City Art Gallery, which holds her work. Some of this was signed with her maiden name. Lived in Hereford.

William Arthur WATKINS 1885–1965 Painter, etcher and teacher, born in London, son of the black-and-white artist Arthur Robinson Watkins. Educated at City of London School, where his art master was Herbert Dicksee. Studied at Croydon and Portsmouth Schools of Art but made his career in the National Provincial Bank, retiring in 1946. Was a member of Croydon Art Society and of the Savage Club, a founder-member of Wapping Group of Artists and president of the London Sketch Club, 1961–2. Also elected RI. Ran his own art school in Croydon, where he lived. Contributed to art periodicals, and just after World War II *The Artist* magazine carried a series by him on watercolour painting. Tutor with Galleon Painting Holidays and showed at RA, RBA, Cooling Galleries and elsewhere.

Frank WATKINSON 1925– Artist in wide variety of media and teacher, born and lived in Scarborough, Yorkshire. He studied at the local School of Art, at Anglo-French Art Centre, Goldsmiths' College School of Art and King Edward VII School of Art, Newcastle. He gained his diploma in 1951, his teacher's certificate a year later and joined Royal Drawing Society in 1955. Taught art at Filey County Secondary School and showed in the north of England.

Denys James WATKINS-PITCHFORD 1905–1990 Writer, illustrator, painter, naturalist and teacher, born in Northampton. He studied art in Paris and at the Royal College of Art under William Rothenstein. Became best known as a writer and illustrator of books on natural history and country life under the pen-name B B; he was a fine naturalist and field sportsman. After a period teaching art at Rugby School he chose to concentrate on his own work, which included landscape painting in oil and watercolour but was mainly for the printed page. Although he illustrated the work of others, he produced black-and-white, colour and scraperboard illustrations for several dozen of his own books. *The Little Grey Men* won the Carnegie Medal in 1942. Died in Oxford.

Gill WATKISS 1938– Painter who attended South-West Essex School of Art. Moved to Cornwall in 1959, living and working in and near Penzance. One of the first recognitions of her work was winning the national competition The Small Picture Lives Again, in 1972. Watkiss was noted for her pictures of daily life, of ordinary people and their emotions in a sometimes harsh environment. Edvard Munch and Carel Weight come to mind when looking at a Watkiss picture. She showed widely in Britain in group exhibitions, including Plymouth, Bristol, Taunton, Stroud and in Cornwall at the Wills Lane, New Craftsman and Mid-Cornwall Galleries. Solo exhibitions included Coach-House Gallery, Guernsey, in 1987, and New Grafton Gallery, 1992. In 1990–1 she had a retrospective of 20 years' work at Newlyn Art Gallery, Penzance, which toured. Her work is held by the East and West Ridings of Yorkshire Education Committees, Leicestershire Education Committee and Birmingham University, and Vassar College, of New York, holds several examples.

Arthur WATSON 1951– Printmaker, sculptor and artist in various materials, and administrator, born in Aberdeen. He studied at Gray's School of Art there, graduating in printed textiles, followed by a postgraduate year. Was a founder-member of Peacock Print Workshop and of Artspace in Aberdeen and went on to direct the Workshop. Won a Scottish Arts Council grant in 1976. Among his commissions was a sculpture called Sea Sign for Peterhead Power Station. A sea theme was common in Watson's work. He showed at Venice Biennale in 1990 and had solo exhibitions at Edinburgh Print Workshop, Aberdeen Arts Centre and Compass Gallery in Glasgow. Scottish Arts Council holds his work.

Bill WATSON 1946– Sculptor and teacher, born in Holmes Chapel, Cheshire. He studied at Birmingham College of Art and Design, 1965–6, then Bath Academy of Art in Corsham for sculpture, 1966–9. Won an Arts Council Award in 1978. Taught part-time at West Surrey College of Art from 1975. Watson took part in many mixed shows, including Northern Young Contemporaries, Whitworth Art Gallery in Manchester, 1968; Young Sculptors, RA, 1971; and Southlands College, Roehampton, 1980. He had a solo show at the Project Gallery, Dublin, 1978, another at Woodlands Art Gallery in 1982, where chairs and log trestles were featured. He also showed series of felt tip drawings: the Hallway Drama, Cutlery Carrier and Birdsong Series.

Christine WATSON 1958– Painter and teacher, whose work featured women in classical landscapes. She studied at Winchester School of Art, 1977–80, and Slade School of Fine Art, 1980–2. Showed extensively, including Air Gallery, Peterborough City Art Gallery, Islington Arts Factory, The Orangery at Holland Park and Merz Contemporary Art. In 1991 she shared a three-man show at

Woodlands Art Gallery. Taught at Barnet College and Hendon College and had a London studio.

Clixby WATSON 1906–1964 Painter and illustrator, christened Charles Clixby Watson, who overcame childhood paralysis to study art. Went to St Martin's School of Art, 1920–4, under Robert Swan and Stafford Leake; Goldsmiths' College School of Art, 1926–7, under Stanley Anderson. Exhibited Leicester Galleries and other venues. Did an enormous variety of illustrative work for publications such as *Radio Times*, *Good Housekeeping* and *John Bull*. Lived at Braughing, Hertfordshire.

Dan WATSON 1891–1953 Painter and wood engraver, born in Ashwell, Rutland. He studied at Leicester College of Art, was honorary treasurer for a time of the local Sketch Club and had work bought by the Museum and Art Gallery. He exhibited there, extensively at the Nottingham Art Gallery and Museum and elsewhere in the provinces. Lived in Leicester.

Elizabeth WATSON 1906–1955 Painter and draughtsman who was educated by governesses, at Princess Helena College in Ealing, then in 1922 at a finishing school in Brussels, Belgium, for a year. Refused to be presented as a debutante and until 1927 studied with Henry Tonks at Slade School of Fine Art. She spent several years at L'Académie Moderne, Paris, where the teachers included Léger, Ozenfant and Marchand, and where she met her lifelong friend Quentin Bell. Showed with LG, in 1937 worked on the Paris Peace Exhibition, became secretary of the AIA and joined the Communist Party. During World War II drove for the City of London Ambulance Brigade, married and eventually moved to Essex, raising a family. In the late 1940s she was operated on for a brain tumour, then died. AIA gave her a memorial show in 1956 and in 1994 the Imperial War Museum held a small exhibition of her wartime pictures and published Watson's memoir *Don't Wait for It*.

Fred WATSON 1937– Sculptor in wood and stone and draughtsman, born in Gateshead, County Durham. He studied at King's College, Durham University. Gained a Christie Memorial Prize and Hatton Scholarship. Watson appeared in many group shows in Britain, including Northern Sculptors, at Shipley Art Gallery, Gateshead; Moira Kelly Gallery, 1981; Drawing in Air, Sunderland Arts Centre and tour, 1983–4; Stoneworks, Welsh Sculpture Trust, 1988; and The Northern Lights, Newcastle Group show with tour, DLI Museum & Arts Centre, Durham, 1990. Later solo shows included Moira Kelly, 1980; Gainsborough's House, Sudbury, 1985; and RIBA Sculpture Court, 1989. Contemporary Art Society, Durham University and Milton Keynes Corporation hold Watson's work which gave a classical dignity to everyday objects. Lived in Newcastle upon Tyne, Tyne & Wear.

George Patrick Houston WATSON 1887–1960 Watercolour painter, professionally an architect, born and based in Edinburgh. He studied at the College of Art there. Exhibited RA, RSA, Royal Glasgow Institute of the Fine Arts and elsewhere. Was married to the painter and potter Elizabeth Amour.

John WATSON 1923–1992 Painter, printmaker, muralist, textile designer, ceramist and teacher. He attended Junior School of Art, Manchester, from age 13, 1936–8, then Manchester College of Art, 1939–40, leaving to work with Sir John Gielgud's production of *Macbeth*. He served in Royal Navy, 1941–5, then gained a diploma at Central School of Arts and Crafts, 1946–8. Watson's commissions included a mosaic mural in glass for Buckingham County Council in 1958; textiles for Tamesa Fabrics, 1968; an outdoor mural in Milton Keynes, 1977–8; a painting for Cranfield College, 1979; a ceramic mural for Wolverton Carriage Works in Milton Keynes, 1980–2; and three ceramic murals for schools there, 1983. In Watson's paintings there was a twin allegiance to the English landscape tradition and to that of the German Expressionists. Began showing with Leicester Galleries and LG in 1950s, later at Lumley Cazalet and Mercury Gallery. After a solo show at Leicester Galleries in 1959 he had two in 1960, at Roland, Browse & Delbanco and Robert Erskine's St George's Gallery, where exuberant images from the horse-racing world were shown. Latterly he showed solo with New Academy Gallery, which gave him a memorial show in 1992.

John Bernard WATSON 1924– Painter, commercial artist and sculptor, born in Bradford, Yorkshire. Educated in Colchester, Essex, where he continued to live, then studied art for a time at Ipswich School of Art. Did commercial work for a wide range of publications and exhibited mainly in East Anglia, also in Cornwall.

Leslie Joseph WATSON 1906– Painter and landscape architect, born in Harrogate, Yorkshire, his wife Helen Watson being a painter. He attended Leeds College of Art, 1926–8, then Royal College of Art, 1928–32. Was a member of RSMA, also showing at NEAC, ROI and RA. Lived in Twickenham, Middlesex.

Liz WATSON 1957– Figurative sculptor and teacher, working in such materials as ciment fondu and pigment, born in Uganda. She was educated in Isle of Man, studying at Douglas College of Further Education, 1973–4, then Westminster Hospital, 1975–8. She was at Wimbledon School of Art, 1979–83, attending Sir John Cass College for extended studies in bronze casting in 1990. Had experience of primary school teaching, nursing and worked as a therapeutic masseuse at Westminster Natural Health Centre. Also taught life sculpture at Wandsworth Adult College part-time. Showed from 1981 in Sculpture at Cannizaro, Wimbledon; in 1985 at Littlegarth Gallery, York; and in 1991 in Sculpture at Canterbury.

Lyall WATSON 1908–1994 Painter of bizarre figures, gallery owner, set designer, publisher, muralist and teacher, born in the United Kingdom. He attended Clapham Road Arts School and Goldsmiths' College School of Art, 1926–9, having a first solo exhibition at Piccadilly Arts Club, 1929. From 1930–6 taught physical education and art at Millbank Demonstration School; between 1935–9 was a part-time mural painter, training at City and Guilds Art School. He completed murals in Lambeth Public Library, in restaurants and for Radio London and other venues,

1935–58. In 1938 designed for Ballets Russes, Monte Carlo, in 1950 the pageant *Lambeth Night*. Was founder, Free Painters and Sculptors, 1953, and its chairman for seven years, starting the Woodstock Gallery, 1958, where he participated in many group shows between 1960–85. In 1960 began publishing the *3 Arts Quarterly*. Camden Arts Centre gave him a solo show in 1988.

Mary Spencer WATSON 1913– Sculptor, born in London, daughter of the painter George Spencer Watson. Early on she moved to Langton Matravers, Dorset, where she continued to live and where she was taught to work stone in the quarries at the foot of the Purbeck Hills. In the late 1920s she began studies that lasted about a decade: at Bournemouth School of Art, Slade School of Fine Art, Royal Academy Schools, Central School of Arts and Crafts and with John Skeaping at London Zoo, then finally in Paris, studying woodcarving with Ossip Zadkine. Exhibited RA, NS, Foyles Gallery, New Art Centre, Fine Art Society, Pelter/Sands, Bristol and elsewhere. Commissions include Cheiron Teaching a Young Hero, at Harlow New Town; Musician, at Corfe Castle, Dorset; and an angel in limewood for Guildford Cathedral.

Nigel WATSON fl. from mid-1960s– Sculptor and teacher who studied art and design at Weston-super-Mare School of Art, 1960–3. In 1978 he moved to Devon, where he settled in Ashburton, and taught carving at Plymouth College of Art, The Woodskill Centre in the city, South Dartmoor School and in his own workshop. Late in 1991 he began working in stone and by summer 1992 had carved four figures with which he won an Elm Grant Trust bursary, enabling him to carve in ancient marble quarries in Greece. Showed with Cider Press Centre in Dartington, The Devon Guild of Craftsmen of which he was a member, The Bristol Guild and in 1st RWA Open Sculpture Exhibition, 1993. Commissions included work for Bath University, the American Museum in Bath, Stoke Fleming Church lectern and Knowles Hill School in Newton Abbot.

Sydney Robert WATSON 1892–c.1972 Painter and decorative artist in oil and tempera; etcher. Born in Enfield, Middlesex, Watson studied at the Royal College of Art under Sir Frank Short and W R Lethaby, 1911–15. He exhibited at the RA, NEAC, Manchester City Art Gallery and Nottingham City Museum and Art Gallery. Leicester Museum and Art Gallery holds his work. Lived at Thurcaston, Leicestershire.

William Ferguson WATSON 1895–1966 Painter in oil. Born in Glasgow, Watson studied at Leicester College of Art under Harry Harvey Clarke and exhibited locally. A journalist, he lived in Leicester and was for about 30 years from the early-1930s closely connected with the Leicester Society of Artists.

Alison WATT 1965– Figure and portrait painter, she studied at Glasgow School of Art, 1983–7, graduating with a first-class honours degree in drawing and painting. She completed a post-graduate postgraduate year in 1988, being highly commended. Alison Watt came into national prominence in 1987 when she won the John Player Portrait Award at the National Portrait Gallery with her self-portrait with a teacup on her head. This produced a commission to paint HM Queen Elizabeth The Queen Mother, completed in 1989. Watt was one of the group of outstanding figurative painters who emerged from Glasgow in the 1980s. Her portraits and figure studies were meticulously crafted in the manner of James Cowie or Ingres, cool, quirky and with an underlying mischief. Among her other commissions were work for EMI Records, *The Observer* and *Mirror* Group Newspapers. National Portrait Gallery, BBC and Robert Fleming Holdings hold her work. In 1990 Scottish Gallery, London, held a show of her pictures which toured to Scotland.

Elizabeth Mary WATT 1885–1954 Painter of landscapes, portraits, and figure pictures of a rather twee type, showing some Japanese influence, born in Dundee and educated at Morgan Academy. When her father, a butcher, was made bankrupt and left for America, the family moved to Glasgow, Elizabeth designed for the woven fabric maker Joseph M Saddler, and enrolled as a commercial colourist at Glasgow School of Art, 1905–6, teachers including Maurice Greiffenhagen. A period teaching at Glasgow High School for Girls proved uncongenial, so Watt became a freelance artist. In 1919 she was made a member of the Glasgow Society of Lady Artists, and embarked on a lifetime of steadily successful exhibiting, sometimes with Kate Wylie, also showing at the Royal Glasgow Institute for the Fine Arts and RSA. The Scottish west coast was a favourite subject. For a time shared a studio with Hesse, sister of Benno Schotz, in whose autobiography *Bronze in my Blood* Watt makes a brief appearance.

George Fiddes WATT 1873–1960 Painter, especially of portraits, and printmaker. He was born in Aberdeen, where he eventually died and where he studied at Gray's School of Art; was then at Royal Scottish Academy. He showed at RA, RSA to which he was elected in 1924 and RP of which he was a member. His notable portraits include a number of legal figures, such as Viscount Haldane and Viscount Reading. Tate Gallery holds a portrait of his mother.

Gilbert WATT 1918– Sculptor in a variety of materials, born and lived in Aberdeen, who studied there at Gray's School of Art under T B Huxley-Jones, then at Royal Academy Schools with Maurice Lambert and at British School in Rome, having won Prix de Rome in 1952. Showed in Italy, at RA, RSA, Leicester Galleries, Royal Glasgow Institute of the Fine Arts and elsewhere, also exhibiting solo.

Millar WATT 1895–1975 Cartoonist and painter, full name John Millar Watt, born in Gourock, Clyde. He was educated in Ilford, Essex, and at Cass Art Institute before joining the advertising agency Mather & Crowther, eventually replacing the great poster designer Tom Purvis. He was commissioned in the Army in World War I, afterwards studying at Slade School of Fine Art, meanwhile contributing sports cartoons for the *Daily Chronicle*. After joining the *Daily Sketch*, in 1921 Millar Watt created the prototype of his strip cartoon character POP, the rotund, bald, bespatted figure, sporting top hat, cravat and tailcoat, who *The Times* obituarist said "will go down in newspaper history". POP was syndicated globally, appeared in annuals and was so important to national morale in World War II that Millar Watt was rejected for war work and instead drew POP, now tin-hatted in the Home Guard. King George VI and Winston Churchill were fans. After the war another artist drew POP so that Millar Watt, who had exhibited at RA Summer Exhibitions, could concentrate on landscape painting. Like his artist wife Amy Maulby Biggs, another RA exhibitor who died in 1957, he was a member of Ipswich Art Club. The magazine *Everybody's* commissioned several series of historical illustrations from Millar Watt, who lived in an old house at Lavenham, Suffolk, restored houses and made a study of materials and techniques of the Old Masters. His house included his own copy of Titian's Bacchus and Ariadne. Ipswich Museums and Galleries holds his oil on canvas Higham from Langham.

Thomas WATT 1920–1989 Painter and teacher, born in Perth, Scotland, who studied at Edinburgh College of Art under William Gillies. Later showed at RSA. During World War II, which interrupted Watt's studies for six years, he served with the Royal Indian Navy, being mentioned in dispatches. Won several painting scholarships and awards before becoming senior lecturer and subsequently head of post-diploma studies at Leeds College of Art in 1947. While at Leeds was influenced by American Abstract Expressionism and took part at Leeds City Art Gallery in the Teaching Image exhibition in 1964. Moved to Canterbury in 1965, transforming the Canterbury School of Art into an internationally recognised College before he retired in 1981. Died in North Shields, Tyneside, after one of a series of drawing trips with a local trawler fisherman. The Living Room, Greenwich, gave him a first London exhibition in 1995.

Dorothy WATTS 1905– Watercolourist and designer, born in London. She studied from 1921 at the College of Art in Brighton, Sussex, where she eventually settled, teachers including John Morgan Rendle, E A Sallis Benney and Charles Knight. Watts' early years were spent in fashion work and design for Fleet Street and continental newspapers until after World War II. She also did Christmas card designs for various publishers. Became a member of SWA in 1952, also exhibiting at RI, Britain in Watercolours, RBA and RA. Had solo shows at Rose & Crown, Fletching, 1959, and Langford Hotel, Hove, 1968. Her main works were watercolours of Venice and of Cambridge. Hove Museum & Art Gallery holds her work.

Eleanor WATTS: *see* **Eleanor CAMPBELL-ORDE**

Greg WATTS 1965– Artist with a strong interest in photography, found objects and mixed-media work. he studied at Cambridge College of Arts & Technology, Kingston Polytechnic and University of Florida, in America. As well as showing at Focus Gallery in Florida he appeared in the South Bank Picture Show and in England & Co's 1992 Art in Boxes with works on a small scale.

Joan Alwyn WATTS 1921– Watercolour painter, born in Birmingham, where she studied at College of Art in 1930s. She worked in art and design. Specialised in portrait miniatures, latterly including large watercolour landscapes. Was an associate of RMS, also exhibiting with RBSA, in the provinces and widely in North America, as well as doing commissioned work. Lived in Bridstow, Herefordshire.

Ken WATTS 1932– Self-taught painter, born in London, who lived and worked in South Tyneside from 1959. He was at Northumberland College of Education as an arts technician, 1970–2; painted a mural in Hendon, Sunderland, 1975; worked at Spectro Art Centre, Newcastle, on the development of studios and a gallery, 1976–7; then worked at Bede Gallery, Jarrow, 1978–9; after that in his trade as a setting-out joiner. Won a series of Northern Arts Awards in 1970s, in 1989 gaining first prize in the South Tyneside Open Art Competition. Mixed shows included ROI, 1969; First International Drawing Biennale, Middlesbrough, 1973; Portland Gallery, Manchester, 1976; and Silver Longboat, Darlington, 1989. Solo exhibitions included Serpentine Gallery and Sunderland Arts Centre, both 1975; and Bede Gallery, 1991.

Leonard WATTS 1871–1951 Portrait painter with a strong interest in music. He studied at Royal Academy Schools and was for a time honorary representative of the Association Board of the Royal Academy of Music and Royal College of Music. Watts was elected to RBA in 1893. Also exhibited at RA, ROI, Walker Art Gallery in Liverpool and Royal Glasgow Institute of the Fine Arts. For much of his life he lived in Sussex, latterly in Worthing.

Meryl WATTS 1910– Artist in various media, noted for her colour woodcuts, brought up in Blackheath, southeast London, where she attended the School of Art, teachers including Reginald Brill, James Woodford and William Clause. Showed at RA, widely abroad with British Council and elsewhere. Her woodcut Red Roofs was included in the exhibition The Modern British Artist as Printmaker: 20th Century Images on Paper, Austin/Desmond Contemporary Books, Ascot. British Council and Contemporary Art Society hold examples. Lived for many years at Borth-y-Gest, Porthmadog, Gwynedd.

Michael Richard WATTS 1962– Sculptor and letter-cutter, born in Cossington, Somerset, who moved from Bristol to Harlech, Gwynedd, in 1976, settling in the county at Penrhyndeudraeth. He did a foundation course at Bangor, 1981–2, from 1982–5 gaining an honours degree in fine art from Norwich School of Art. Having won a setting-up grant from WAC, from 1985 Watts was taught letter-cutting and stone-carving by the sculptor Jonah Jones. In spring 1988 he was artist-in-residence for 10 weeks at several schools. Exhibitions included solo show at Oriel y Ddraig, Blaenau Ffestiniog, 1988; International Snow Carving Competition, Savonlinna, Finland, 1990; Journeys, Winchester Gallery, Southern Arts tour, 1992; and Having it Made, Oriel, Cardiff, 1992. In 1991 Watts was engaged on a carved seat wall, Grosvenor Waterside,

Cardiff Bay, Tidemark. This incorporated carved inscriptions of languages connected with the dockland community.

Peter WATTS 1916– Sculptor, born in Chilcompton, Somerset, near where he settled at Wellow. Studied with Clifford Ellis at Bath School of Art, 1937, then was apprenticed to the sculptor Lindsey Clark and studied at City and Guilds of London Art School in period to World War II. He was elected a fellow of RBS in 1970. Did a large amount of commissioned ecclesiastical work, including items for Oban Cathedral, 1951; Bath Abbey, 1959–60; Downside Abbey, 1974; and in America.

Edna WAUGH: *see* **Edna CLARKE HALL**

Nicholas WAYGOOD 1947– Painter and artist in mixed media who did a foundation course at Liverpool Polytechnic, 1974–5, then studied in its department of art and design, 1975–8. Exhibitions included Northern Young Contemporaries, at Whitworth Art Gallery, Manchester, 1977, Tolly Cobbold Eastern Arts 4, 1983–4, and the 1986–7 Merseyside Artists 3 touring exhibition put on by Walker Art Gallery, Liverpool.

Nigel WAYMOUTH 1941– Artist in oil, pencil, watercolour, tempera and acrylic, born in Kasauli, India. He studied at University College and during the 1960s did graphic work for *IT* and *OZ* magazines; decorated London shop-fronts, such as Granny Takes a Trip and Indica; and with Michael English, working as Osiris Posters, produced posters for Jimi Hendrix Experience, The Crazy World of Arthur Brown, Julie Felix and other pop stars. His work was included in The Sixties Art Scene in London, Barbican Art Gallery, 1993, other group appearances including RP, 1976; Fischer Fine Art, from 1977; and St James' Art Group, from 1992. Had a first solo show with Fischer, 1977; Lefevre, 1984; Reid Gallery in Palm Beach, 1985; and Jonathan Clark, 1988. Yale Center for British Art holds his work. Lived in London.

Mark WAYNER 1889–1980 Artist in a range of media, born Mark Weiner in Lomza, Russia, his parents settling in London's East End in 1893. Won a scholarship to Birkbeck College, then attended for half of the third term only at 1909–10 session at Slade School of Fine Art. Began exhibiting in London and in 1932 published *Celebrities in Caricature* with a small publishing house. Lived for some years in Sheffield, Yorkshire, being an associate member of Sheffield Society of Artists, 1950–60. Died in Saffron Walden, Essex. Ben Uri Art Society holds several examples.

Maud Marian WEAR 1873– Painter and miniaturist, born in London, who after private tuition in art went on to Royal Academy Schools, 1896–1901. She was especially noted for her portraits and figure studies. Showed at RA, RMS, NEAC, IS, Paris Salon and widely in provinces. Lived in Blockley, Gloucestershire.

Gillian WEARING 1963– Artist employing a range of media, including cibachrome and video, born in Birmingham. She studied at Chelsea School of Art, graduating in art and design, 1985–7, with an honours degree in fine art from Goldsmiths' College, 1987–90. Awards included BT Young Contemporaries, 1993–4. Selected group exhibitions were Empty Gestures, Diorama Art Centre, 1991; British Art Group Show, Le Musée des Beaux-Arts dans Le Havre, and Instruction, at Marconi Gallery, Milan, both 1992; Not Self Portrait, Karsten Schubert Gallery, 1994; Mobius Strip, Basilico Fine Arts, New York, 1995; and British Art Show 4, 1995–6, with tour. Had a solo show at City Racing, 1993, later ones including Western Security, Hayward Gallery, 1995, and Interim Art, 1996–7. She won the 1997 Turner Prize. Wearing videod herself and others in domestic situations and public places, taking a different look at people's behaviour, attitudes and aspirations.

Tim WEATHERHEAD 1964– Painter, born in Redhill, Surrey. He studied at West Sussex College of Art, 1982–3, then West Surrey College of Art and Design, 1983–7. In 1987 he took up an ICI travel scholarship to Rome, the year his three panels All Roads Lead to Rome were included in John Moores Liverpool Exhibition. Lived for a time in Pulborough, Sussex.

Alexander WEATHERSON 1930– Artist and teacher, born in Mansfield, Nottinghamshire, working in oil, watercolour, printmaking and with objects. He studied at Birmingham College of Art, Royal Academy Schools in 1950s with Bernard Fleetwood-Walker and at Courtauld Institute. Went on to become principal lecturer in fine art at Leeds Polytechnic/Leeds Metropolitan University, 1968–91. Group shows included Redfern Gallery, 1955; Carnegie International in Pittsburgh, America, and Kaplan Gallery, both 1958; John Moores Liverpool Exhibition, 1961; Contemporary Art Society, British Painting in the Sixties, 1963; Richard Demarco Gallery, Edinburgh, 1968; and Arts Spectrum, Alexandra Palace, 1971. Had many solo shows in Britain and abroad, including Gallery One, 1958 and 1961; ICA, 1964; and Leeds City Art Gallery, 1979. Musicological interests sometimes influenced the content of Weatherson's works, obliquely or directly, especially earlier pictures. Arts Council, Contemporary Art Society, the Power Institute in Sydney and several American galleries hold examples. Latterly lived in London, also Le Bourg, Planches, France.

Arthur WEAVER 1918– Painter and teacher, born in London. He studied at Hornsey School of Art, 1933–9, teachers including Russell Reeve and Norman Janes. Showed SWG, SWAS and elsewhere. National Museum of Wales, Cardiff, holds his work. Lived in Risca, Monmouthshire.

Herbert Parsons WEAVER 1872–1945 Architectural painter and teacher, born in Worcester, father of the artist Lydia Weaver. He studied at Royal College of Art, gained gold and silver medals and qualified to teach, eventually becoming headmaster of the School of Art in Shrewsbury, Shropshire, where he settled. Parsons was a keen motorist and specialised in painting old houses abroad. He was a member of RBA, RCamA, Liverpool and Manchester Academies and RWA, also showing at RA and RI.

Peter Malcolm WEAVER 1927– Painter and draughtsman who studied at St Martin's School of Art, 1948–50, and Camberwell School of Arts and Crafts, 1950–1, his teachers including James Bateman and Richard Eurich. Showed at RA and in the provinces. Lived in London.

Boyd WEBB 1947– Sculptor and photographer, born in Christchurch, New Zealand. He studied at the Ilam School of Art, 1968–71, then at Royal College of Art, 1972–5, under Bernard Meadows. Went on to exhibit extensively in Britain and abroad, including Robert Self Gallery, London and Newcastle, 1976–7; Anthony d'Offay, 1981; Centre Georges Pompidou, Paris, and Stedelijk Van Abbemuseum, Eindhoven, both 1983; and Australian Centre of Contemporary Art, Melbourne, 1986. Group show appearances included the Royal College of Art's 1980 tribute to Bernard Meadows, 1960–1980; Fourth Biennale of Sydney, Australia, 1982; Aperto, Venice Biennale, 1986; and in 1992–3 Twelve Stars, Arts Council Gallery, Belfast, and tour. Webb's Homage, 1990, in that show was acquired for European Parliament Collection, and Arts Council holds several examples of his work.

Cecilia WEBB 1888–1957 Sculptor, born at Stamford, Lincolnshire. Daughter of the architect Morpeth Webb. She exhibited RA, RSA, RMS and Paris Salon. A ceramic figure of the Holy Family, 1949, is in Southwell Minster, Nottinghamshire. Lived at Melton Mowbray, Leicestershire.

Clifford WEBB 1895–1972 Wood engraver, etcher and painter. Born in London, Webb studied at Westminster School of Art. In the 1920s he soon established a reputation as one of Britain's most interesting engravers. He specialised in landscapes and animal subjects, illustrating a number of books, notably for the Golden Cockerel Press, and published many children's books. He exhibited at the RA, NEAC, LG, RE, NS and SWE and his work is in the collections of the British Museum and Victoria & Albert Museum. Webb taught drawing at Birmingham School of Art, 1922–6, engraving at St Martin's School of Art and lectured at Westminster School of Art. Lived at Abinger Hammer, Surrey.

Dora WEBB 1887– Miniaturist and sculptor, born in Stamford, Lincolnshire. She studied art privately with Alyn Williams in 1902, two years later at the Grosvenor School of Art with Walter Donne. Exhibited RMS of which she was a member, RA, Walker Art Gallery in Liverpool, at Paris Salon and in the provinces. Her full name was Mahala Theodora Webb and she was the older sister of Cecilia Webb, the sculptor, with whom she lived in Melton Mowbray, Leicestershire.

Geoffrey WEBB 1879–1954 Stained glass and church fittings designer; oil painter on wood. Born at Turnham Green, he studied at Westminster School of Art. Was president of the Guild of Catholic Artists and Craftsmen, 1939–46, and published *The Liturgical Altar*. Signed his work G W above a spider's web. Windows by Webb are at Downside Abbey, Somerset, and at Little Walsingham, Norfolk. Lived at East Grinstead, Sussex.

Geoffrey WEBB 1896–1981 Artist, notably in pastel, fond of landscapes and seascapes, whose full name was Arthur Geoffrey Gascoyne Webb. He was born at Newington, in Kent, and was a self-taught artist who had a chequered career. After education at Wellington College, he entered the Royal Navy in 1914, serving at the battle of Jutland. He also served in the Navy in World War II, and finished with the rank of lieutenant-commander. At other times he taught cricket at several schools; served under the Colonial Office in Nigeria, becoming an expert on Hausa language and customs; was secretary of the Leicestershire County Cricket Club and played for it; and held senior posts in the King George's Fund for Sailors. He painted a lot in East Anglia, and showed at PS, NS, Woodbridge Gallery and elsewhere. Lived finally in Oakham, Rutland.

Gwen Lindsay WEBB 1913–1990 Painter, draughtsman and printmaker, born in London, who attended Berkhamsted School for Girls. She studied at Chelsea School of Art, 1936–9. Was a member of SWLA from 1965 until resignation in 1984. Also exhibited with AEB, SGA and with wildlife shows in the southern English provinces. Ulster Museum and Art Gallery, Belfast, holds her work. Lived in Berkhamsted, Hertfordshire.

Jenny WEBB 1950– Painter, draughtsman and teacher, born in Ealing, west London, who did a pre-diploma course at Berkshire College of Art; an honours degree in fine art, Leeds College of Art; and gained an art teacher's certificate at Goldsmiths' College. Working for Kent Adult Education Service, Webb was head of centre, White Lodge, Folkestone, and head of art for Coastal Region. Showed widely in London and Kent, where she lived with stained glass artist Tyrone Guy. Had a first solo exhibition in Drammen, Norway, in 1991, another at The Waiting Gallery, Ashford, 1996.

John WEBB 1912– Painter chiefly in oil, born and lived in London, who studied at Wimbledon School of Art. Showed at RI, UA, RBA of which he was a member and elsewhere.

Joseph WEBB 1908–1962 Printmaker, muralist and teacher of etching and sculpture, born in Ealing, west London. He studied at Patrick Allan-Fraser School of Art, Hospitalfield, Arbroath. He taught etching at Chiswick School of Art. Webb's prints have an idyllic quality, reminiscent of the work of Samuel Palmer, Graham Sutherland and Robin Tanner. He showed at RA, RE of which he was made an associate in 1930, RSA, RHA and Walker Art Gallery, Liverpool. National Museum of Wales, Cardiff, holds his work. He lived in Wembley, Middlesex, and at Farnham Common, Buckinghamshire.

Kenneth WEBB 1927– Painter in oil and acrylic, muralist and teacher, born in London. Studied at Lydney School of Art, Gloucester College of Art, 1948–52, and University College, Swansea, 1953. From 1953–9 taught at Ulster College of Art. He was a member of NS as well as being an associate of both RUA and RWA. Took part in many group shows in Britain and abroad and was included in Some of the Moderns, The Belgrave Gallery,

1988. Had many solo exhibitions, including David Hendriks Gallery in Dublin, Jersey Art Centre, Verhoff in Washington and Harrods. Arts Council of Northern Ireland holds his work. Lived Latterly at Chagford, Devon.

Marjorie WEBB 1903–1978 Painter, born in Barnes, southwest London, who studied at Central School of Arts and Crafts, later at Farnham College of Art. Until retirement she was mainly a Sunday painter, then had two decades to concentrate on it. All holidays were spent painting, notably the landscapes of Connemara, Kerry and the north of Scotland, and London galleries were regularly visited. Webb greatly admired the work of Anne Redpath. Exhibited at RA, ROI and NEAC and, while living at Petersfield, at the Ash Barn Gallery and the Ashgate Gallery, Farnham. The Ashgate held a show after her death in 1978 and in 1987 Pallant House Gallery, Chichester, put on another. It and Bishop Otter College there hold examples. Webb's work could have a visionary quality. After an operation for cataracts she experimented with new techniques and colour subtleties. Died in West Sussex.

Olive WEBB 1935– Artist, architect and teacher, born in Harrow, Middlesex, who was educated at the North London Collegiate School. She then studied architecture and worked for several London-based architects, later becoming a primary school teacher with special responsibility for art and children's literature. As a mature student, from 1990 Webb gained an honours degree in fine art at the University of Hertfordshire (formerly St Albans School of Art). Webb, as a member of Five Women Artists Plus, took part in several group shows in England and France and had a first solo show at The Heifer Gallery in 1997. This, including acrylics on a fairly large scale, prints and drawings, continued the themes of her degree show: autobiographical pictures using childhood images of menacing rooks, and footballers. The Museum of Football, in Carlisle, holds her work. Lived in Combe Down, Bath, Somerset.

Richard Anthony WEBB 1963– Painter, draughtsman and teacher, born in Portsmouth, Hampshire. He graduated in fine art (painting) from Camberwell School of Art and Crafts, 1982–5, obtaining his master's degree in fine art from Royal College of Art, 1986–8, teachers including Paul Huxley and Ken Kiff. In 1989 he taught at Royal Academy Schools, then from 1991 at Winchester School of Art. Webb said that leading themes in his work were "observation of human idiosyncrasy and inwardness"; influences included "Charles Dickens, Fyodor Dostoyevsky and late Picasso"; his colour was "essentially symbolic and emotional". Webb showed widely in group exhibitions, including Loewe and West, 1988, and Christopher Hull Gallery from that year; Fine Art Society and Agnew, 1990. In 1992 he had a first solo show at Christopher Hull, having shared one at Cadogan Contemporary, 1989. Lived in Southsea, Hampshire.

Richard Kenton WEBB 1959– Painter and teacher. He studied at Chelsea School of Art, 1977–8, then Slade School of Fine Art, 1978–82, winning the Boise Scholarship to Rome, 1982–3. After Royal College of Art, 1983–6, and experience at Cité Internationale des Arts, Paris, 1985, he gained a painting and teaching fellowship in Cheltenham, 1986–7. In 1987 Webb worked in Gloucestershire and lectured part-time at Byam Shaw School of Art, being artist-in-residence at St Stephen's, Oxford, 1988. Webb was included in many mixed shows from around 1980, including Stowells Trophy at RA, 1980; Leicesteshire Schools Exhibition, 1983; Universiade Kobe, Japan, 1985; The Glass of Vision, Chichester Cathedral, 1987; and Bath Contemporary Art Fair, 1988. After a solo show at Chichester Assembly Rooms, 1982, later ones included exhibitions at Benjamin Rhodes Gallery from 1987. Webb's method of painting was compared to the worked and reworked surface of a palimpsest. The work had a symbolic quality and drew on such inspiration as the Bible and Dante's *The Divine Comedy*.

Angela Mary WEBBER 1931– Painter, sculptor, restorer of icons and teacher, born in London. She studied at Hull College of Art, 1949–52. Went on to become freelance equestrian and portrait painter, teaching animal painting. She was a founder of the Society of Sussex Sporting Artists and a member of the Society of Catholic Artists. Showed with Omell Gallery, NEAC, NS and in Saratoga Gallery, Saratoga, in America. Lived in Jevington, Sussex.

Michael WEBBER 1926– Painter, potter, critic and writer, and teacher, born and lived in London. Studied at Northampton School of Art, 1943–6, with Frederick Courtney; at Chelsea School of Art, 1946–8, with Harold Williamson, then at the Central School of Arts and Crafts under Edwin La Dell. Showed at RA, RBA, AIA, Redfern Gallery and Ben Uri Gallery, on whose council he served. For a time ran the Radlett Gallery in Radlett, Hertfordshire. Contributed to many publications as a freelance, notably as art critic of *East Anglian Daily Times*.

Archibald Edward WEBSTER 1899–1991 Painter, born in London, where he lived all his life. Much of his output was views of Islington, where he lived in the same terraced house from 1912. After serving in World War I Webster worked as a baker, on the land and as a clerk before beginning to paint in 1926. He studied at the Working Men's College with Percy Horton and Barnett Freedman and in 1945 gained the Lowes Dickinson Scholarship. Showed at RA, RBA, at Roland, Browse & Delbanco, Leicester and Comedy Galleries, but did not have a solo show until a retrospective at Upper Street Gallery near his home, in 1970. Lord Clark, Lady Epstein and Ivon Hitchens owned his work. Webster's pictures were simple and unsophisticated, but were painted, he said, because of "some bug inside. When I was working, painting was a tonic for my frustration. I get so blooming excited over it!"

Catrin WEBSTER 1966– Painter and teacher, born in Cardiff, who studied at the Slade School of Fine Art, 1986–93, gaining a class one honours degree and postgraduate higher diploma, teachers including Bruce McLean, Paul Richards and John Hoyland. Webster was a teaching fellow at Cardiff University Institute, 1993–4, then was a self-employed artist working part-time at that Institute and Aberystwyth University, also holding workshops and residencies. Awards included Duveen Travel Scholarship, Spain, 1991; WAC travel grants to Italy and Greece, 1996; and British School at Rome Abbey Award in Painting, 1997. She was a member of GOYA (Generating Opportunities for Young Artists in Europe). Group shows included Into the Nineties, Mall Galleries, 1991, and 9th Mostyn Open, Oriel Mostyn, Llandudno, 1997–8. Solo shows included En Plein Air, 1996–8, tour including National Museum of Wales, Cardiff, and Transports, Glynn Vivian Art Gallery, Swansea, 1998. Arts Council, University of Wales in Bangor and other Welsh collections hold examples. Lived in Borth, Cardiganshire.

Harry WEBSTER 1921– Abstract and figurative painter in all media, with some constructions in lead, and teacher, born in Little Aston, Staffordshire. He attended Birmingham School of Arts and Crafts, 1947–52, taught by Bernard Fleetwood-Walker. From 1954–60 Webster taught part-time there, also at Wolverhampton College of Art and Lichfield School of Art. Taught in Somerset, 1960–74, gaining a Goldsmiths' Scholarship to Greece, 1962. From 1975 Webster was based in Suffolk, living finally at Saxmundham, where he taught summer school and private pupils, also giving seminars in early painting techniques at University of East Anglia history of art department. Music was an important influence on Webster's work, and in the 1992 *Aldeburgh Festival Complete Handbook* he contributed illustrations to music by Erik Satie. Group shows included John Moores Liverpool Exhibition; Piccadilly, Louise Hallett, Grabowski and many other galleries including some on the continent; and Birmingham City Art Gallery, which holds his work, as also Somerset and Staffordshire County Councils and the Cambridge Contemporary Art Trust. Solo shows included Halesworth Gallery, Suffolk, 1982–92; Brentwood Art Centre, 1990; and Snape Maltings Concert Hall, Suffolk, 1991.

Herman Armour WEBSTER 1878–1970 Artist who was primarily a printmaker, born in New York, America, his father a banker. Armour studied at Yale University, graduating in 1900 as Bachelor of Philosophy, and led a varied life, at times being a journalist, cattle rancher and miner. Early in the century he studied at Académie Julian, Paris, then volunteered for the French Army, 1914–17, winning the Croix de Guerre, 1916, and American Army, 1917–19. Armour had been elected a member of Société Nationale des Beaux-Arts in 1912, RE in 1914 and was made a knight of the Legion of Honour in 1927. He exhibited at RA, RE, Paris Salon and elsewhere on the continent, among his awards a gold medal for etching at San Francisco International in 1915. Chelsea and Arts Club member who lived for some years in Paris. His work is held in many public collections, including Victoria & Albert Museum.

John Robert WEBSTER 1934–1994 Printmaker, painter and teacher, born in Bridlington, Yorkshire. He attended Leeds College of Art, 1951–5, then again in 1957. He taught at Leeds and at St Asaph, Wales, becoming senior lecturer at St Mary's College, Bangor, 1968–75. Received a diploma in art education at Leeds University Institute, 1975–6, then from 1977 lectured on art education at University College of north Wales in Bangor while being part-time curator of its art gallery from 1982. Showed with Yorkshire Artists, Leeds City Art Gallery, RCamA and NWG in mixed exhibitions and had a number of solo shows, including Fairfield Halls in Croydon and Bangor Art Gallery. Department of the Environment and Welsh National Library, Aberystwyth, hold examples. Lived in Bodorgan, Anglesey, Gwynedd.

John Stuart WEBSTER 1912– Painter and teacher, born in Manchester. After education in the Isle of Man and in Lancashire he attended Liverpool City School of Art under George Marples, 1929–33. Held a number of teaching positions, including Gresham's School. Showed RA, RI and elsewhere. Lived in Holt, Norfolk.

Norman WEBSTER 1924– Printmaker, painter and teacher, born in Southend-on-Sea, Essex, married to the artist Joan Simpson. He attended Tunbridge Wells School of Art, 1940–3, teachers including E Owen Jennings, then Royal College of Art, 1946–9, specialising in engraving, under Robert Austin and Malcolm Osborne, having served in Royal Navy for three years in World War II. Taught printmaking at Leeds Polytechnic. Webster was a member of RWS and RE, also showing with RA, in the provinces and abroad. Ashmolean Museum in Oxford holds his work. Lived in Leeds, Yorkshire.

Walter Ernest WEBSTER 1877–1959 Figure and portrait painter, born in Manchester. Studied at Royal College of Art and Royal Academy Schools. Exhibited RA, ROI, RI, Royal Glasgow Institute of the Fine Arts and Paris Salon, where he won bronze and silver medals before World War I and a gold in 1931. His work was quite widely reproduced and is in the collections of Oldham Art Gallery and Museum, Paisley Museum and Art Gallery and other provincial galleries. Lived in London.

John Dunkin WEDD 1919– Painter and teacher, born in Southbourne, Hampshire. Attended Clifton College, then studied art at Central School of Arts and Crafts at St Martin's School of Art. He showed at John Whibley Gallery and in the provinces. Wrote the book *Pattern and Texture*. Lived at Chiddingstone, Kent, where he organised the local festival.

David WEDGBURY 1937– Painter and draughtsman, born and lived in London, studied at Gravesend School of Art. He went on to work as creative studio manager for a gramophone record company. Wedgbury's mixed shows included Six Blackheath Artists at Greenwich Theatre Gallery, 1969; Blackheath Art Society at Woodlands Art Gallery, 1972; Seen Gallery, 1975; and Who's Who at ICA, 1978. Carried out commissions. His solo shows included Clytie Jessop Gallery, 1970; Nicholas Martine Gallery, 1972; Alexandra Monet Gallery, Brussels, Belgium, 1973; Paideia Gallery, Los Angeles, America, 1978; and Woodlands Art Gallery, 1979, where work had a strongly jokey, Pop Art quality. City of Manchester Art Gallery holds his portrait of the footballer Bobby Charlton. Decca Record Company and London, Manchester and Portsmouth Playboy Clubs also owned examples.

Martin WEDGE 1958– Painter, draughtsman and performance artist whose work included depiction of grotesque figures, reminiscent of Expressionism. Wedge graduated with a degree in fine art, 1980, from Belfast College of Art, gaining his master's in 1982. In 1985 he gained an award from the Arts Council of Ireland to study with Sandro Chia in New York for a year, and in 1986 he was studio assistant there to Brian Wood. Among his street performance and performance/installation works were College of Art, Belfast, 1980–1, and Triskel Arts Centre, Cork, 1992. Took part in numerous group shows, including New North, Tate Gallery and tour, 1990–1; Fenderesky Gallery, Belfast, 1993; and in 1994 Works on Paper and Beyond the Partitions, put on by Belfast's Queen Street Studios, with which he was associated. Solo shows included Triskel Arts Centre, Cork, 1992, and Fenderesky Gallery, 1994.

Francis WEDGWOOD 1898–1959 Artist, particularly noted for his landscapes in oil, 2nd Baron of Barlaston. He was educated at Bedales School and studied at Burslem School of Art, 1920–2, then Slade School of Fine Art, 1922–5, having in World War I served for five years in the Royal Naval Volunteer Reserve and Royal Flying Corps and being wounded. He showed at NEAC from 1927 and RA from 1931, also at Colnaghi.

Geoffrey Heath WEDGWOOD 1900–1977 Printmaker and painter who was noted for his scenes of Liverpool, but who was born in Leek, Staffordshire. After Army service in World War I, Wedgwood studied at Liverpool School of Art, 1919–21, where he won a scholarship to Royal College of Art, studying engraving under Sir Frank Short and being influenced by the more vigorous manner of Job Nixon. Attended the British School in Rome. Won the Rome Prize in engraving in 1925, 10 years later becoming a member of RE. Exhibited there and at RA, NEAC, Fine Art Society, Walker Art Gallery in Liverpool and in America. The Liverpool gallery holds his work, as do British Museum, Victoria & Albert Museum and Art Institute of Chicago. Taught at his old school, the Liverpool Institute, 1932–5, and at Liverpool College of Art, 1935–60. Wedgwood favoured a clean, hard and precise line in his prints. Lived in Roby area of Liverpool.

Fiona WEEDON fl. from 1980s– Painter whose allusive pictures drew on such inspirations as water, surface and depth. She studied at Heatherley's School of Fine Art; St Martin's School of Art; graduated from Kingston School of Art & Design in fine art, winning a Stanley Picker Scholarship; then obtained her master's degree in painting at Chelsea School of Art. Group shows included The Moving Gallery, Rose Gallery, 1990; Stephen Bartley Gallery, 1991; Young Contemporary Painters, Bruton Street Gallery, 1994; and Mall Galleries, 1996. Had a first solo show, Metamorphosis, at Attendi, 1997.

Fritz WEGNER 1924– Freelance artist and illustrator and teacher, born in Vienna, Austria, as James Fritz Wegner. He attended St Martin's School of Art, 1939–42. From 1948 worked as a freelance illustrator and designer. Clients included publishers in Britain and abroad, advertising agencies and the Post Office, for which he designed stamps from 1969. He taught illustration part-time for 25 years at St Martin's. He was a member of Art Workers' Guild and Chartered Society of Designers. Showed with Mel Calman's Cartoon Gallery, one-man and group exhibitions, Bethnal Green Museum and travelling shows. Post Office Museum holds his work. Lived in London.

Morris WEIDMAN 1912–1992 Artist and teacher, born in London, who studied at Camberwell School of Arts and Crafts, 1926–9, and Royal College of Art, 1929–32, then for two years helped the sculptor Bainbridge Copnall on the RIBA building reliefs. Held a number of teaching posts, then after World War II settled in Tunbridge Wells, teaching at the School of Art until he retired. Showed at NEAC and elsewhere, and Ben Uri Art Society holds examples.

Carel WEIGHT 1908–1997 Painter and teacher, born and lived in London, who was partly of German and Swedish descent. Weight was a unique painter of enigmatic, odd dramas in which exotic events can get transplanted to the suburbs, also of some fine portraits. Those of the artist Orovida Pissarro in the Tate Gallery and Ashmolean Museum, Oxford, are notable. Having decided against a career as a singer after some training, Weight studied at Hammersmith School of Art, 1928–30, then Goldsmiths' College School of Art, 1930–3, at both under James Bateman. At Goldsmiths' Weight met his partner for life, Helen Roeder, whom he married in 1990. Weight had his first solo show at Cooling Galleries in 1934. Exhibited at many other venues, including RA from 1931 (he was elected RA in 1965); Leicester Galleries; LG and RBA, of which he was a member. During World War II he served in the Army, being appointed an official war artist in 1945. He painted a mural for the Festival of Britain's Country Pavilion in 1951, another for Manchester Cathedral in 1963. From 1947 he began a long teaching association with the Royal College of Art, becoming professor of painting 1957–73. Weight was regarded with affection by his many students, who included young trend-setters such as David Hockney, although Weight himself was a staid, old-fashioned figure. After his retrospective at the RA in 1982, Weight's work became more fashionable, prices moving up sharply. Another retrospective, which toured, was held at Newport Museum and Art Gallery in 1993. Weight was made Companion of Honour in the 1995 New Year's Honours List.

Georges WEIL 1938– Stylised figurative sculptor, born in Vienna, Austria, who moved to London just before World War II. He studied from 1956–61 in sculpture department at St Martin's School of Art, his teachers being Elisabeth Frink, Eduardo Paolozzi and Anthony Caro. Weil completed portrait sculptures of the statesmen Winston Churchill, Charles de Gaulle and David Ben-Gurion. In 1989 he moved to Israel where in 1992 a major show of his work was held at the Herzlia Museum. He was capable of working on a huge scale, witness a piece for Eilat installed in 1992, but also completed jewellery and sculpture in precious

metals. HM The Queen and the film actress Elizabeth Taylor were among his clients. The Morris Singer Foundry cast Weil's work.

Hanna WEIL 1921– Painter and teacher, born in Munich, Germany. She was educated at North London Collegiate School, attending St Martin's School of Art, 1940–3, where teachers included Vivian Pitchforth and Muriel Pemberton. Went on to teach at Hammersmith School of Arts and Crafts, 1945–8, and St Martin's, 1945–87. Showed with RA, Leicester and Trafford Galleries, in the provinces and abroad. Lived in London.

Harry WEINBERGER 1924– Painter, draughtsman and teacher, born in Berlin, Germany. Left there for England in 1939, settling in London. Studied at Chelsea School of Art under Ceri Richards and privately with Martin Bloch. He was head of painting at Coventry Lanchester Polytechnic until 1983, when he left to paint full-time. He had many solo exhibitions in Britain and Germany including a series with Duncan Campbell Fine Art. Weinberger said that his pictures "present a record almost like a diary". Much of his work was "based on drawings made on journeys. But the subjects I come back to again and again are to do with the sea, seascapes, harbours and ships." Bold designs and rich colours were characteristics of his pictures. Lived in Leamington Spa, Warwickshire.

Mark WEINER: *see* **Mark WAYNER**

Gerald WEIR 1929–c.1972 Painter in oil and watercolour; wood engraver and exhibition designer who worked on the Festival of Britain, in 1951. Born at Rossington, near Doncaster, Weir studied at Liverpool College of Art under N Martin Bell. He exhibited at the Walker Art Gallery, Liverpool. Weir became a lecturer in art at West Cheshire Central College of Further Education. His work is illustrated in Jack Beddington's 1957 selection *Young Artists of Promise*: his 1956 picture Newsvendor. Lived at Lower Bebington, Wirral, Cheshire.

Halcyon WEIR 1912–c.1978 Portrait painter of animals, sculptor, mural painter and collagist. She studied art in Lausanne, Switzerland, then at the Central School of Arts and Crafts under John Farleigh and John Skeaping, 1932–8. Appeared on television discussing crafts for children. Lived at Sunningdale, Berkshire.

Helen Stuart WEIR fl. from c.1915–1969 Painter, born in New York in America. Studied there and in England, France and Germany. Exhibited prolifically at RBA, ROI, SWA of which for a time she was acting president, NEAC and widely abroad. One-man shows included Goupil Gallery. Member of Ridley Art Club and St Ives Society of Artists. Lived in London and St Ives, Cornwall.

Nancy WEIR: *see* **Nancy HUNTLY**

Richard WEISBROD 1906–1991 Self-taught artist in a variety of media, including for a time kinetic sculpture. He was born in Affoltern am Albis, Switzerland, and always longed to paint, but was forced to be a manager of the family silk mill in Switzerland and in England, where he moved to Lancashire in 1932, having begun painting seven years before. He became a member of MAFA and the Manchester Group. His first solo show took place in 1949 at Margo Ingham's Mid-Day Studios in Manchester, followed by ones at Leger Gallery in 1950 and Crane Gallery, Manchester, 1952. After that he had frequent solo shows throughout Europe. Also showed with RA. Colour was important in Weisbrod's work, with a strong basis of powerful drawing. In 1970 Weisbrod married the Manchester painter José Christopherson and they moved to live at Vaud, Switzerland, where they ran the Atelier-Galerie Bois de Chêne. Weisbrod's work is held by many public collections including Manchester City Art Gallery and galleries in Blackburn and Salford.

Ivor WEISS 1919–1986 Artist and designer, born in London, where he studied art at the Northampton Road Polytechnic. During World War II he studied at the Bardi Studio in Cairo, then at the Malta School of Art, where he gained first prize for figure drawing. After the war Weiss continued his studies at Heatherley's School of Fine Art before attending St Martin's School of Art, where he gained his diploma in painting. From 1950–5 he and his wife lived in Alabama in America where they designed and executed murals and mosaics for commercial clients. On returning, Weiss designed and made enamelled jewellery for Harrods and Heal's, a silk scarf for Hardy Amies, stained glass windows for the Stock Exchange in Johannesburg, South Africa, and a mosaic wall for Michelsons Ltd. In his later years Weiss concentrated on painting Jewish life and faces and the life of Tuscany and southern Italy. Mixed shows included RA, RBA, O'Hana Gallery, Whitechapel Art Gallery, The Minories in Colchester and American venues. Later solo shows included Playhouse Gallery, Harlow, 1975; Digby Gallery, Colchester, 1978; and Ben Uri Art Society, 1980, which holds his work.

Hellmuth WEISSENBORN 1898–1982 Painter, printmaker and teacher, born in Leipzig, Germany, his father being an art teacher. Professor Weissenborn studied at Academy for Graphic Art and Book Design, Leipzig, from 1919 after war service, at the same time reading art history, philosophy and anthropology at Leipzig University, gaining his doctorate in 1925. He was appointed to the staff of the Academy as lecturer in 1928. In 1938 he emigrated to London as a freelance artist. From 1941–70 he was visiting teacher at Ravensbourne College of Art, Bromley. In 1943 Weissenborn had his first solo show at Archer Gallery, which led to an order from the Baynard Press, where he met his wife Lesley Macdonald, sister of the artist Frances Macdonald. In 1946 they took over The Acorn Press, founded by Fred Phillips of the Baynard Press in 1927, which had become defunct. This led to the publication of children's books and later limited private press editions of high quality. Showed with LG, Victoria & Albert Museum, in America and Australia and in 1980 had exhibition at Gutenberg Museum, Germany, which surveyed his graphic work, one of many one-man shows. The Museum holds his work. Lived in London.

Victor WEISZ: *see* **VICKY**

Denton WELCH 1915–1948 Writer and artist, born Maurice Denton Welch in Shanghai, China. He was educated at St Michael's, Uckfield, and at Repton, then for four years was at Goldsmiths' College School of Art, a period described in detail in his first published book, *Maiden Voyage*, 1943. He was knocked off his bicycle in 1935 by a motorist, was seriously injured and remained an invalid. This interrupted his artistic career, but he gradually established a name as a writer with such books as *In Youth is Pleasure*, 1945, *Brave and Cruel*, 1948, and *A Voice Through a Cloud*, 1950. *The Denton Welch Journals* were published in 1952. Welch writes with a painter's eye for detail. His pictures, shown at Leicester Galleries and elsewhere, were also detailed, having strong decorative and Neo-Romantic elements. His final years were spent at Crouch, near Sevenoaks, Kent.

Dominic WELCH 1970– Sculptor, notable for carved stone forms of an organic type, such as Egg and Russian Doll, both in the 1996 RWA 2nd Open Sculpture Exhibition, who was born in Taplow, Buckinghamshire. After starting an apprenticeship with Peter Randall-Page in 1989, in 1990 Welch exhibited his first carving, Ammonite, at Spacex Gallery, Exeter. Work carved during the 1991 Stone for Peace Festival in Caen, France, remained on display in the city. During 1992 Welch attended the Aio International Sculpture Symposium in Japan, assisting Randall-Page and other sculptors. Welch won first prize at the Millfield Open in 1994 with On the Wind, the work being bought by the School. In 1995 Welch participated in the International Stone Sculpture Competition in Haulien, Taiwan, and was shortlisted for the Hull Open Sculpture Competition, being commissioned to make a maquette. Lived at Drewsteignton, Exeter, Devon.

Rosemary Sarah WELCH 1946– Painter, notable for her rural scenes featuring horses, she was the daughter of an illustrator of children's books. Was herself a horsewoman with a special interest in heavy horses. She studied under Leonard Fuller at St Ives School of Painting, 1960–3, and later had tuition from Walter Woodington. Was a member of SWA and Society of Equestrian Artists. She showed with St Ives Society of Artists, John Magee in Belfast and in 1991 was included in The Horse at Work at John Davies, Stow-on-the-Wold. Russell-Cotes Art Gallery and Museum, Bournemouth, holds her work. Lived in Lymington, Hampshire.

Tom WELD 1946– Painter, draughtsman and teacher with a special interest in art and its relationship with the land and agriculture. He was born in Beaconsfield, Buckinghamshire, and was untrained. Weld started painting during reading for an English degree at university, after which he combined painting with teaching in many settings, except for several periods of about a year painting full-time. Group shows included Abbot Hall, Kendal; Bridport Art Centre, Dorset; Axminster Festival, Devon; and Yorkshire Moors Festival. Solo shows included St Catherine's College, Oxford; York University; King's Arms Yard, Dorchester, and at the Museum there; and 5 Dryden Street. Lived in North Eggardon, Powerstock, Bridport, Dorset.

Ron WELDON 1925–1994 Painter in watercolour and oil, born in Bournemouth, Hampshire. He attended the Art School there, then Camberwell School of Arts and Crafts, teachers including Martin Bloch, leaving in 1956. Flowers and landscape were Weldon's main subjects. He always painted indoors from drawings taken on the spot, but his pictures in rich colour and lively brushwork well evoke the landscape of Dorset and Somerset, where Weldon died at East Compton. Showed in mixed company at Frances Kyle Gallery, had a series of solo shows in Bath and Wells and was exhibiting at Alpha House Gallery, Sherborne, at the time of his death. He had been divorced from his wife, the novelist Fay Weldon, shortly before this. Paisnel Gallery held an exhibition in 1998.

Antony WELLER 1927– Sculptor working in traditional and modern materials, and teacher, born and lived in London. He studied at Wimbledon School of Art with Freda Skinner and with Maurice Lambert at Royal Academy Schools. Exhibited in RA Summer Exhibition and elsewhere and was a member of Free Painters and Sculptors.

Rudy WELLER 1956– Sculptor, born in London. He studied fine art at Hammersmith, then Chelsea School of Art. Weller's first major commission was the Horses of Helios and the Three Graces for the Criterion Building in London's Haymarket. The work, unveiled in 1992, was cast by The Morris Singer Foundry, in Basingstoke, Hampshire.

Hubert Lindsay WELLINGTON 1879–1967 Landscape painter, teacher and author. Born in Gloucester, and studied at the School of Art there, 1895–8, then at Birmingham School of Art, 1898–9, and the Slade School of Fine Art, 1899–1900. Was married to the illuminator and calligrapher Irene Wellington. He lectured at the National Gallery, 1919–22, was 10 years at the Royal College of Art, principal of Edinburgh College of Art, 1932–42, then lecturer at the Slade, 1947–9. Sometimes signed work H L W. Wellington reviewed for newspapers and magazines and his books included *William Rothenstein*, 1923, and *Jacob Epstein*, 1925. First one-man show at Agnew, 1963. Abbott & Holder had a show of his landscapes, 1996. Wellington also exhibited at NEAC, RA and LG. Tate Gallery holds one of his many early Cotswold scenes, and work is also held by Ashmolean Museum in Oxford and Arts Council. Lived in Henley-on-Thames, Oxfordshire.

Denys George WELLS 1881–1973 Painter in oil and watercolour. Born in Bedford, Wells studied at the Slade School of Fine Art in its heyday, 1897–1903, under Henry Tonks, Philip Wilson Steer and Walter Westley Russell, and throughout his long career – he was still painting at 92 – his work bore the Slade stamp. His wife Ethel modelled for Tonks' picture The Birdcage. Wells' work was regularly exhibited at the RA, NEAC, SBA, Royal Glasgow

Institute of Fine Arts and many galleries in London and the provinces. Wells' work featured his wife, his collection of antiques and the streets of London, where he often painted watercolours, recording the bomb damage of World War II the morning after air raids occurred. The Ministry of Works, Sunderland Museum and Art Gallery and the London County Council bought his pictures. Through the Greater London Council the newspaper magnate Sir Hugh Cudlipp bought a watercolour by Wells of Covent Garden to give to Prince Charles and the Princess of Wales as a wedding present from the people of London. At the request of Queen Mary Wells painted a picture for the Queen's Dolls' House at Windsor and in 1958 he received the Queen's Pension for services to the arts. One-man show at the Mall Galleries in 1972 and at the Medici Galleries in 1986. Lived at New Malden, Surrey.

Douglas WELLS 1875–1963 Watercolourist and architect, born Robert Douglas Wells, who was married to the painter Madeline Wells. He attended Cambridge University and studied at the London School of Art with Frank Brangwyn. After being articled as an architect he became a fellow of the RIBA, having spent some time in Greece at the beginning of the century. He exhibited RA, RBA, of which he was a member, RI, Goupil Gallery and in the provinces. Lived in London.

Edward Francis WELLS 1876–1952 Painter and draughtsman, born in Calcutta, India, where his father was an engineer, moving aged three to Evershot, Dorset. Developed an interest in painting at Clifton College public school, then studied at Slade School of Fine Art, 1893–4; sought admission to St John's Wood Art School; then studied at Royal Academy Schools, gaining the Creswick Prize, 1899. In 1897 had his first acceptance at RA Summer Exhibition, where he showed spasmodically until 1941. After a visit to Italy took a studio in Chelsea and had a successful first solo show in Dorchester. With aristocratic support went on to build a reputation for commissioned portraits, landscapes and figure paintings in an Old Masterish style with a sentimental tinge. Served in the Army in World War I. Exhibited in mixed shows at RI, ROI and RHA, solo exhibitions including Walker's Galleries. From 1945–9 he and his wife showed his work at a dedicated gallery at 162 Sloane Street, Knightsbridge, from 1950 for many years holding frequent exhibitions at the nearby Basil Street Hotel. Died in London.

John WELLS 1907– Painter of landscapes and abstracts, born in London but brought up in Ditchling, Sussex. His father was a doctor and Wells qualified in medicine at University College Hospital, 1925–30. While a medical student he studied in evenings at St Martin's School of Art, 1927–8, on a visit to Cornwall meeting the artists Ben Nicholson and Christopher Wood. After working in a hospital for six years, Wells had a medical practice in the Isles of Scilly, 1936–45, when he moved to Newlyn and began painting full-time in Stanhope Forbes' old studio. Wells had first showed in the *Daily Express* Young Artists Exhibition in 1927; he had his first one-man show at Lefevre Gallery in 1946. In that year he was co-founder of the Crypt Group in St Ives, three years later helping to found the Penwith Society. In 1950–1 he worked briefly with Barbara Hepworth, the sculptor. Won Art Critics' Prize in 1958. Wells showed at the Wills Lane Gallery, St Ives, in many group exhibitions in Britain and abroad and had several one-man shows at Waddington Galleries and Durlacher Gallery, New York. Tate Gallery St Ives held an important one in 1998. Arts Council and Tate Gallery hold his work.

Madeline WELLS fl. from c.1910–1959 Painter, notably in tempera, born in India and married to the painter Douglas Wells. After private education she attended the Westminster School of Art under William Mouat Loudan, the London School of Art with Frank Brangwyn and Central School of Arts and Crafts, where she received instruction in lithography from Ernest Jackson. Exhibited RA, ROI, RI, SWA, extensively at RBA, of which she was a member, and in Paris. Rotherham Museum and Art Gallery holds her work. Lived in London.

Reginald Fairfax WELLS 1877–1951 Sculptor, potter and aircraft maker, he was educated at Norfolk County School and Royal College of Art and was a pupil of the sculptor Édouard Lantéri. Wells was an early protégé of the artists and collectors Charles Ricketts and Charles Haslewood Shannon, whose work they promoted at Fine Art Society and elsewhere. Completed fine busts of both men, but within a few years he fell out of favour. Wells showed at RA, RSA, IS, Royal Glasgow Institute of the Fine Arts and elsewhere. In his maturity Wells became interested in aircraft, and was a member of the Royal Aero Club. Lived near Pulborough, Sussex.

Chris WELSBY fl. from 1970s– Film, installation and video artist who did a foundation course at Central School of Art, 1969–70; gained a first-class honours degree in fine art, Chelsea School of Art, 1970–3; then a higher diploma at Slade School of Fine Art, 1973–5. Group shows included National Film Theatre from 1970; Georges Pompidou Centre, Paris, 1974; Art and the Sea, ICA, 1982; London Film Festival, 1988; and Signs of the Times, Museum of Modern Art, Oxford, 1990. Individual screenings included London Film-makers' Co-op from 1973; Tate Gallery/Midland Group, Nottingham, 1975; Spacex Gallery, Exeter/John Hansard Gallery, Southampton, 1982; and Darkroom Gallery, Cambridge, from 1984. Tate Gallery and National Film Archive both hold works in their film collections; video collections holding works include Arnolfini Gallery, Bristol, and the Museum of the Moving Image.

Alan WELSFORD 1935– Painter, sculptor, film artist and teacher, born in Hainault, Essex. He studied at Walthamstow School of Art, 1956–9, and Slade School of Fine Art, 1959–63. After winning the Rome Prize he spent the following year there at the British School. Welsford went on to be a course leader in fine art at Leicester Polytechnic. As well as taking part in group exhibitions he participated in British and foreign film festivals from the mid-1980s. Welsford made an early mark by winning a prize at 1963 John Moores Exhibitions, Liverpool, the picture

Televised Floodlight Game being bought by Walker Art Gallery there. His canvas Vigilant Resolution was in the 1991–2 show, a complex picture one of a series called in Defence of the Realm, based on submarines. Lived in Broughton Astley, Leicestershire.

Jeremy WELSH 1954– Performance, installation, video and film artist, born in Gateshead, County Durham. He studied at Jacob Kramer College of Art, Leeds; gained an honours degree in fine art at Trent Polytechnic School of Art & Design, Nottingham, 1977; then a postgraduate diploma in fine art (film and video) at Goldsmiths' College, 1982. Events in which he took part included contributions to performances held at The Blue Man, Grantham, 1975–7; performances with Yorkshire-based group Aerschot, 1976–9; Video 84, Montreal, Canada, 1984; The New Pluralism, Tate Gallery, 1986; Waterboy, Café Gallery, and Signs of the Times, Museum of Modern Art, Oxford, both 1990.

Boris WELTMAN 1921– Illustrator, draughtsman and miniaturist, born in London, who studied at Folkestone's Teachers' Training College. He went on to illustrate educational and other books; was a member of RMS, also showing at RA, SM and elsewhere. Lived at Worth, Kent.

Peter WELTON 1933– Artist and teacher, born in Barnetby, Lincolnshire. He was educated at City of Leeds Teacher Training College and King's College, Newcastle, University of Durham, his teachers including Victor Pasmore, Richard Hamilton and Lawrence Gowing. Served in Royal Air Force, 1951–4, then taught from 1961, latterly at Crewe Alsager College, Cheshire. Took part in many group shows, including RA Summer Exhibitions, winning the Purchase Prize in 1984, and Patricia Wells Gallery, Thornbury. His extensive solo shows included Laing Art Gallery, Newcastle, in 1963; University of Durham Gallery, 1976; and Chesil Gallery, Portland, 1985. Laing Art Gallery, Shipley Art Gallery in Gateshead and Newcastle Polytechnic hold his work. Lived in Sandbach, Cheshire.

Sarah WENDEN 1952– Painter, draughtsman and teacher, born in Oxford. She did Voluntary Service Overseas, 1970–1, in Kenya, then gained a degree in town and regional planning at Sheffield University, 1971–4. After working for planning consultants she attended Hornsey College of Art, 1975–6, then Central School of Art & Design, 1976–9, winning the Phoebe Llewellyn-Smith Prize in 1978. Was then at Slade School of Fine Art, 1979–81, gaining a Boise Travelling Scholarship in 1981. Eventually joined the staff of Birmingham Polytechnic as a visiting lecturer, having been a junior fellow at Cardiff College of Art. Showed with Young Contemporaries at ICA, 1980, also in 9 Slade Painters at Seven Dials Gallery. Had a solo show at London University Institute of Education in 1980, another at Woodlands Art Gallery, 1983.

Richard WENTWORTH 1947– Sculptor working in a variety of materials, and teacher. He was born in Samoa and studied at Hornsey College of Art and Royal College of Art, in 1967 working for a short time with Henry Moore. Taught at Goldsmith's College School of Art, 1971–88. Worked in New York on several occasions. Was a prizewinner in Tolly Cobbold Exhibition in 1981. Wentworth employed an element of Surrealism in his work, which had a witty undercurrent and an interest in language and meaning. Ready-made objects were sometimes adapted. Wentworth took part in group exhibitions in London and the provinces, including The Sculpture Show at Hayward Gallery, 1983, showing one-man with Lisson Gallery. Saatchi Collection, Tate Gallery and Arts Council hold his work, which was included in its 1993–4 touring show Recent British Sculpture. A major retrospective was held at Serpentine Gallery in 1994. Lived in London.

Alan WERGE-HARTLEY 1931– Painter and teacher, notable for marine pictures, born in Leeds, Yorkshire, his wife being the designer and jeweller Jeanne Werge-Hartley. He studied at Leeds College of Art, 1947–53, under Maurice de Sausmarez and Edward Pullée, and at Hornsey College of Art, 1972–3. Taught at Portsmouth College of Education and Portsmouth Polytechnic, 1962–90. Showed widely in the Portsmouth area in solo and mixed exhibitions, Portsmouth City Art Gallery holding his work. Lived in Emsworth, Hampshire.

Michael WERNER 1912–1989 Sculptor, painter and teacher, born in Evian, France, who grew up in Graz and Vienna, Austria, where he held the title Baron Werner von Alvensleben. Studied philosophy at the University of Berlin, where he co-founded and ran an anti-Nazi youth movement. When a warrant was issued for his arrest, he escaped to England to study linguistics at Oxford University, leaving two years later for Paris to become a sculptor. There he studied under S W Hayter, of Atelier 17, moved in Surrealist circles and began training as a Freudian analyst, settling in England after two years in 1938. During the war he worked for the BBC Monitoring Service, then as a translator and broadcaster in the Austrian/German department. After the war Werner was involved in the restaurant business, wrote on cookery for the *Daily Mirror* and published two cookery books: *Off the Beaton Track* and *Smashing Dishes*. He was a forceful, demanding teacher, at Bath Academy of Art, 1959; lecturer in sculpture at Bradford College of Art, 1964–8; as lecturer in fine art at Watford School of Art, 1968 until retirement; and in classes at Camden Arts Centre, near where he lived in north London. He was a keen traveller and notable linguist. Werner's sculptures ranged from Surrealist abstractions to depictions of the human form. His monumental figure of the Virgin is on the front of Bartram's Hostel near the Royal Free Hospital. Notable among his portrait heads was that of W H Auden, the poet, shown at RA. From the mid-1980s he took up painting the human form in an Expressionist style. Also exhibited at ICA, with Arts Council, Woburn and Blenheim Palace. Louise Hallett with Annely Juda Fine Art held a seventy-fifth birthday show in 1987, by which time he had had many solo exhibitions. Smithsonian Institution in Washington owns the Auden bust. More of Werner's work is held by County Museum in Los Angeles and there is a mural of 18 panels at Foxford Comprehensive Secondary School, Coventry. Werner remained unmarried, living finally in straitened circumstances. There was a memorial show at Turtle Key Arts Centre,

1996. Mr Norris, of *Mr Norris Changes Trains*, by Christopher Isherwood, was based on Werner.

Marianne von WERTHER 1901–1984 Artist in watercolour and chalk, she was born in Brno, Czechoslovakia, then studied art in Vienna. One-man shows at the Brod Gallery. Participated in mixed exhibitions at the RA, RBA, RI, SGA, NEAC and elsewhere. The South London Art Gallery, Guildhall, London Museum and RWA hold her work. Lived in London.

Karl WESCHKE 1925– Painter and draughtsman, born in Taubenpreskeln, Germany. As a boy he was encouraged to paint by the artist Otto Dix. Taken prisoner of war while serving in the German Air force, Weschke arrived in Britain in 1945. Studied at St Martin's School of Art, 1949. After meeting with members of the David Bomberg-inspired Borough Group in Spain in 1953 and a period in Sweden in 1954–5, Weschke moved to Cornwall in 1955 after becoming acquainted with the artist Bryan Wynter in London. Five years later he settled at Cape Cornwall, St Just, by which time he was a member of the Penwith Society. Weschke went on to win an Arts Council Major Award in 1976; he was a John Moores Liverpool Exhibition prizewinner in 1978; a Southwest Arts Major Award winner in the same year; and two years later he won an Arts Council Purchase Award. Arts Council and Bristol City Art Gallery hold his work, which has Expressionist tendencies and is sometimes sombre, both figurative and landscape. As well as taking part in many British and international group shows, Weschke exhibited regularly in one-man shows. After New Vision Centre Gallery in 1958 venues included Arnolfini Gallery, Bristol, 1964; Newlyn Art Gallery, 1974; Kettle's Yard Gallery, Cambridge, and tour, 1980–1; and Redfern Gallery, 1984.

Frans WESSELMAN 1953– Watercolourist and etcher, born in The Hague, Netherlands. He studied at Groningen College of Art, 1975–8, moving to England in 1979. Became a fellow of RE in 1987. Exhibited solo with Printworks, Colchester; Ombersley Gallery, near Worcester; Gateway Cultural Centre, Shrewsbury; and Silk Top Hat Gallery, Ludlow. Group shows included Catto Gallery, Manor House Gallery, Chipping Norton, RWS and RA. Lived in Church Stretton, Shropshire.

Edward WESSON 1910–1983 Painter in oil but especially watercolour, handling a variety of subjects with an assured wash technique. Born in Blackheath, southeast London, he learned "from reading of the methods of such masters as E W Haslehurst and Adrian Hill – and by bitter experience!" Wesson spent 20 years perfecting his technique before exhibiting, then he was prolific at the RA, NS, RBA, ROI and RI, as well as at provincial galleries. He contributed to *Leisure Painter* and *Artist* magazines and painted posters for British Railways and the National Savings Bank. Lived at Guildford, Surrey, where the Borough collection holds his work.

Alice Moore WEST 1911– Painter in oil who was born in St Albans, Hertfordshire. Educated in Dorset, she studied at Slade School of Fine Art, 1929–33, under Randolph Schwabe and George Charlton. Showed at RA, RBA and Paris Salon. Harrogate Art Gallery holds her work. Lived in London.

Jenny WEST 1957– Painter, draughtsman and sculptor, married to the sculptor Steve West. She studied at North Warwickshire College of Technology and Art, 1973–5; gained an honours degree in fine art from Falmouth School of Art, 1975–8; then was at Royal College of Art, 1978–80. She was artist-in-residence, Whitworth Art Gallery, Manchester, 1984–5. Awards included Yorkshire Arts Association Award, 1982; Manchester Academy Prize for Drawing, 1983; *Manchester Evening News* Prize for Drawing, 1993; and First Prize, Derby Open Exhibition, 1995. West was trained as a sculptor, complex pieces evolving into flat, screen-like objects suspended in space. Early in the 1980s drawing took over from sculpture, and by the time of her solo show at Hart Gallery, 1996, she was producing delicately coloured paintings of architectural fantasies not unlike Renaissance frescoes, layers of paint being eroded with an orbital sander or soaked under a shower, to produce random elements. Mixed shows included British Drawing at Hayward Gallery and LG, both 1982; MAFA from 1983; RA Summer Exhibition, 1991; and Northern Artist, Harewood House, 1993. Other solo shows included Mappin Art Gallery, Sheffield, 1983; Whitworth Art Gallery, 1985; and Lanchester Art Gallery, Coventry University, 1995. Arts Council, Henry Moore Centre at Leeds City Art Gallery, Whitworth and Cooper Gallery in Barnsley, where she lived, hold examples.

Steve WEST 1948– Sculptor, draughtsman and teacher, born in Warrington, Lancashire. He studied at Liverpool College of Art and Design, 1965–9; Royal Academy Schools, 1969–72; and with a Prix de Rome at British School in Rome, 1972–4. A series of awards at the Schools, including first prize for sculptural composition in 1971, was followed by an Exeter Fellowship in Sculpture, 1977, and the South Yorkshire Open Art Exhibition first prize, 1986. In 1992 West was made an associate of RBS. From 1974 he held a number of teaching posts, including Falmouth School of Art, Exeter College of Art and Design and Barnsley College of Art, with a series of visiting lectureships. From the mid-1980s West was a regular exhibitor at European and American art fairs, recent mixed show appearances including MAFA, 1993; Blackheath Gallery, 1994; and Derby Museum and Art Gallery, 1995. In that year had a solo exhibition at Hart Gallery, figurative works with a strong fantasy element. Lived in Barnsley, Yorkshire, with his artist wife Jenny West.

David WESTBY 1948– Sculptor and teacher, was born in Sheffield, Yorkshire. He studied at Sheffield and Falmouth Schools of Art, 1967–71, then Slade School of Fine Art, 1971–3. As a Boise scholar he travelled in Italy in 1973–4. Was Sainsbury artist-in-residence at Eggbuckland School, Plymouth, 1987. Among his commissions was a bronze tactile map adjacent to National Gallery of Scotland, Edinburgh, and a sculpture for entrance of Don Valley Stadium, Sheffield. He was included in the RWA show Artists from Cornwall in 1992. Had solo and two-man exhibitions in

Britain and Italy. People and their historical backgrounds were a key facet of Westby's work. Among part-time lectureships was one from 1986 at Falmouth School of Art and Design. Westby lived and worked in both Italy and Falmouth and in 1994 was included in Falmouth Connections, at Falmouth Art Gallery.

Grace WESTBY 1896– Miniaturist, born at Turramurra, New South Wales, Australia. After private education her art tuition was sporadic and partly private, too; in mid-1920s she had lessons at the National Gallery, and in 1953 attended Chelsea School of Art. Showed at RA and RMS and lived latterly in London.

Julie WESTERMAN 1955– Sculptor and lecturer, born in Leicester, who was later based in Wales. She worked in a variety of materials, including turf, crushed stone, plaster and aluminium. At art school almost all her work was abstract, based on organic forms, but later a personal imagery developed. Between 1971–9 Westerman designed shop interiors, travelled in Europe and worked as a marquee fitter. From 1980–1 she attended Loughborough College of Art and Design for a foundation course, graduated from Chelsea School of Art, 1981–4, in sculpture, then obtained her master's degree in fine art from Birmingham Polytechnic, 1984–5. During the next year she gained a junior fellowship in sculpture at South Glamorgan Institute of Higher Education, in 1986–7 working at Berllanderi Sculpture Workshop, Raglan, Gwent. Conducted a number of workshops and lectured at Ikon Gallery, Birmingham, on The Politics of Art, 1985. Exhibitions included National Garden Festival in Stoke-on-Trent, 1986, and Between the Devil and the Deep Blue Sea, at Stoke's City Art Gallery, 1987.

Anne WESTLEY 1948– Artist and teacher, notably a sculptor and printmaker, born in Kettering, Northamptonshire. She attended Northampton School of Art aged 17, and West of England College of Art, 1965–7, gaining a first-class honours diploma in fine art. Taught from mid-1980s, including Cambridge College of Art, Braintree College, North Essex School of Art in Colchester and Bishop Grosseteste College, Lincoln. Held a series of residencies in schools and participated in print workshops, including Gainsborough's House in Sudbury, Birmingham College of Art and The Minories, Colchester. She was studio assistant and printmaker to Michael Rothenstein, 1983–5. Participated in many group shows, including British School in Rome, 1971; Serpentine Gallery, 1976; RA Summer Exhibitions from 1984; and in 1993 Continuing the Tradition at Chappel Galleries, Chappel. Was elected a member of RE in 1989, becoming a council member in 1991. Solo shows began with Ferens Art Gallery, Hull, in 1971, later ones including Mostyn Art Gallery, Llandudno, and Cheltenham Fringe Festival, both 1986. Gulbenkian Foundation, Ashmolean Museum in Oxford and Eastern Arts Association hold her work.

Sydney Walter WESTOBY 1902–1972 Watercolourist, especially of the Bishop's Stortford area of Hertfordshire, where he lived. Born in London, he was a career civil servant who became deputy director of publications for Her Majesty's Stationery Office. Westoby studied painting privately with Cecil Ross Burnett. He was a keen pencil draughtsman who also completed some fine lettered and illuminated manuscripts. Exhibited RI and locally with Bishop's Stortford Art Society. Latterly suffered from diabetes and when immobile continued painting using a slide projection unit specially constructed for him.

David WESTON 1935– Painter in watercolour, which he specially favoured, oil and acrylic, born in Leicestershire where he settled at Kirby Bellars. A self-taught artist, he went professional in 1969, painting landscape, architecture, interiors, transport and industrial subjects. Had a series of solo shows, including British Transport Museum, Laing Art Gallery in Newcastle, Royal Scottish Museum in Edinburgh, National Railway and Motor Museums and Barbican Centre. Among his most notable pictures were a number of extensive series: Rolls-Royce Fantasia and Histories of the British Steam Locomotive and Motor Car (each 25 canvases) and a History of the English Country House (40 canvases). Anglia Television and Independent Television produced documentaries on Weston. He wrote several books which illustrated his work. Scottish Nuclear Power, Imperial Chemical Industries, British Gas and British Rail as well as museums mentioned hold examples.

Peggy WESTON 1914– Painter in oil who was born in Weymouth, Dorset. Her father was an Army officer, so she was educated partly in the British School in Hong Kong. Student at Goldsmiths' College School of Art. Showed at LG, Goupil Gallery and NEAC. Lived for some time in Brighton, Sussex.

Robert H WESTWATER 1905–1962 Portrait painter and teacher, born in Fife, who studied at Edinburgh College of Art and on the continent, then after a period teaching in London was on the staff of Edinburgh College of Art for a decade, also teaching at Fettes College. He was art critic of *The Scotsman*. Was a member of RP and an associate of RSA, also showing at Royal Glasgow Institute of the Fine Arts. National Gallery of Scotland holds his portrait of the writer Sir Compton Mackenzie. Lived in Edinburgh but died in Southfleet, Kent.

Dennis WESTWOOD 1928– Sculptor. He studied at Wimbledon School of Art and Royal College of Art. Westwood's work was abstract, often on a quite small scale. He took part in many mixed exhibitions, including Young Contemporaries, 1954; AIA Travelling Exhibition, 1957; RSA from 1958; RA from 1960; North East Arts Council Travelling Exhibition, 1967; Gilman's Gallery, Chicago, 1978; International Art Fairs in Basel, Stockholm, Chicago and New York, 1981; Bath Art Fair, 1984; and York Festival, 1988. Among his commissions were a fountain sculpture at Civic Centre, Carlisle, 1965; sculpture for Strathclyde University, 1974; another for Lancaster University, 1979; and for Prudential Assurance Company, 1987. Westwood had a solo show at English-Speaking Union, Edinburgh, 1964, with another at Laing Art Gallery and Museum, in Newcastle upon Tyne, in the same year. Others included Alwin Gallery, 1974, one of several;

South Michigan Art Centre, America, 1978; Jonathan Poole, 1983, the first of several; and Draycott Gallery, 1987.

Maud Llewellyn WETHERED 1898–1990 Sculptor, painter and printmaker, daughter of the artist Vernon Wethered, born in Bury, Sussex. She was educated in Hampstead and studied at the Slade School of Fine Art. Her work was reproduced extensively for the printed page, in such publications as the *London Mercury* literary magazine, *The Studio* and *The Observer*. Showed widely, too, including RA, SWE, Goupil, Redfern and Whitechapel Art Galleries, extensively in the provinces, Australia and America. Lived in London.

Vernon WETHERED 1865–1952 Landscape painter who was born at Clifton, Bristol, where he attended Clifton College, then Oxford University. Studied at Slade School of Fine Art under Fred Brown, 1893–6. Although he spent about a dozen years as a full-time artist, he then concentrated more on business, eventually retiring as a company director. Was the father of artist and sculptor Maud Wethered. He showed extensively at Redfern Gallery and NEAC, also Goupil Gallery, in France and Belgium. Lived in London.

VISCOUNT WEYMOUTH: *see* **Alexander THYNN**

John WHALE 1919– Painter, born in Coventry, Warwickshire. He spent 20 years with the Royal Navy on meteorological duties, including service in the Far East and North Atlantic. After beginning work for British Aircraft Corporation in the Gulf and Saudi Arabia in 1972 Whale began painting, specialising in architecture and marine watercolours, particularly the Arab dhow. After his retirement and return from Saudi Arabia in 1979 he painted for Mathaf Gallery and clients, working from reference material gathered in the Gulf.

Thomas WHALEN 1903–1975 Sculptor, born in Leith, Scotland. During World War I he was a shipwright, carving in his spare time, an interest he pursued when out of work in the 1920s. His talent was spotted and from the late 1920s he was enabled to study for about three years at Edinburgh College of Art. Whalen was the first holder of the Andrew Grant Fellowship and won the RSA Carnegie Travelling Scholarship to the continent. Had first solo show at Cooling Gallery in 1932. Whalen's output was mainly carved reliefs for public buildings. Notable examples were his work for the 1938 Empire Exhibition in Glasgow and reliefs for the Festival of Britain Pavilion of Industry at Kelvingrove in 1951. Whalen was a member of SSA and Royal Glasgow Institute of the Fine Arts and was elected RSA in 1954. His wooden carving Eve is illustrated in Eric Newton's monograph *British Sculpture 1944–1946*. RSA holds his plaster Europa and the Bull, 1943.

Dick WHALL 1939– Conceptualist artist and lecturer, born in Great Yarmouth, Norfolk. After attending Great Yarmouth School of Arts and Crafts, 1956–8, Whall gained his national diploma in design (painting) at Norwich School of Art, 1958–60, continuing his painting studies at Royal Academy Schools, 1960–3, obtaining a postgraduate certificate. Whall lectured at University of Wales Cardiff Institute, 1964–7, after which a number of American and British posts followed, and he was finally head of fine art at Coventry University, 1992–6. He did a large amount of visiting lecturing and external examination at a series of colleges and universities. Between 1989–91 Whall obtained a postgraduate diploma in electronic graphics at Coventry Polytechnic; gained his master's degree in electronic art from Coventry University, 1991–2; obtaining his doctorate there, 1992–6, his project-dissertation topic being Documentum de transmutatio: rhizomatous modelling in hypertext for the digital reformation of art-installation. Whall won over a score of prizes and awards, including the David Murray Scholarship for landscape painting in 1961, repeating his success in 1962 along with the Creswick and Landseer Prizes; a series of Arts Council, West Midlands Arts and Eastern Arts Association and British Council awards followed through the 1970s and 1980s. Whall was a member of the Council for National Academic Awards fine art panel, 1991–2, also of the National Association for Fine Art Education, the British Computer Arts Association and the Printmakers' Council. Took part in numerous mixed shows in Britain and abroad. Had a solo show as Richard Whall at Great Yarmouth Museum and Art Gallery in 1963, later ones including University of Warwick, 1987. Eastern Arts Association, Coventry Polytechnic, Ulster Museum in Belfast and public galleries in Bradford and Leamington Spa, Warwickshire, where he lived, hold Whall's works. His son Andy and daughter Miranda were also artists.

Richard WHALL: *see* **Dick WHALL**

Douglas Feather WHARFE 1919– Painter and commercial artist and draughtsman, born in Haworth, Yorkshire. Educated in Keighley, Yorkshire, where he continued to live and where he attended the School of Art, 1933–40, then Leeds College of Art, 1946–7, with John Frederic Greenwood. He exhibited widely in Yorkshire, including Keighley Art Club.

Christian WHARTON 1937– Watercolourist who was married to the artist Michael Wharton, 1960–72. She studied at St Andrews University, gaining her master's degree with honours, 1958; then attended L'Académie de la Grande Chaumière, Paris, 1959, and studied etching at Regent Street Polytechnic, 1962–4. From 1954 showed at RSA, SSA, SSWA and RSW. Had a joint show with Sir Patrick Nairne at Clarges Gallery, 1983, and solo exhibitions at Barbican Centre, 1990, and The Gallery in Cork Street, 1995, where the theme of large watercolours was water in motion. The Argyll Group, Robert Fleming & Company and Hambros Bank hold examples. Had a studio in Ledburn, Skelmersdale, Lancashire.

Michael WHARTON 1933–1997 Artist and teacher, born in Glasgow, who studied at Slade School of Fine Art, 1955–9. He taught at School of Art in St Albans from 1959–74, and Regent Street Polytechnic, 1958–63. The mystery of movement and its depiction in terms of colour and light was a key feature of

Wharton's work. He had several solo shows at Gilbert Parr Gallery and a touring exhibition in the northeast of England, with a retrospective at The Knapp Gallery, 1994. Surrey, Leicester and Bristol Education Authorities bought examples.

Samuel Ernest WHARTON 1900–c. 1986 Draughtsman and designer in oil and watercolour. Born in Beeston, Wharton studied at Nottingham School of Art under Joseph Else and Arthur Spooner in the 1920s and again in the 1930s, between those times studying with Sydney Meteyard, in 1928–29, at Birmingham School of Art. He exhibited widely, at the RA, RI, RBSA, RSA, and in the provinces, as well as at the Paris Salon 1965–73, where he gained an Hon. Mention for oil painting. He also won a gold medal at Tommaso Campanella Academy, Rome, in 1972. Lived in Coventry, Warwickshire.

Grace WHEATLEY 1888–1970 Painter, sculptor and teacher, born and finally lived in London. She studied at the Slade School of Fine Art under Henry Tonks and Philip Wilson Steer, 1906–8, and in Paris at Atelier Colarossi. Married the painter John Wheatley in 1912. With him she went to South Africa and became senior lecturer in fine art at the University of Cape Town, 1925–37, then they returned to England. Exhibited at RA, British Museum, Tate Gallery, Paris Salon as well as in the provinces, South Africa and Canada. Many provincial galleries hold examples.

John WHEATLEY 1892–1955 Painter, printmaker, draughtsman and teacher. Born in Abergavenny, Monmouth-shire, Wheatley – who was married to the artist Grace Wheatley – studied under Stanhope Forbes, Walter Sickert and at the Slade School of Fine Art, 1912–13. After service in the Artists' Rifles and as an official war artist, 1918–20, Wheatley taught at the Slade School, 1920–5. He was Michaelis Professor of Fine Art, University of Cape Town, 1925–37, director of the National Gallery of South Africa and, 1938–47, director of the Sheffield City Art Galleries. During World War II he was commissioned to paint war portraits. From 1948–50 Wheatley was curator of the National Gallery of British Sports and Pastimes. Wheatley's official career rather overshadowed his abilities as a painter and draughtsman. His first show was with Muirhead Bone at the Grosvenor Galleries, in 1922, and he also exhibited with the RA, NEAC, Leicester Galleries, Cooling Galleries and RHA. His work is held by the Tate Gallery, National Museum of Wales, Cardiff, and other galleries in Britain and South Africa. Lived in London.

Muriel WHEATON 1902–1975 Painter, especially in watercolour, born in Exeter, Devon. She went to school there and attended the local Art School. Also attended the Art School in Christchurch, New Zealand, and St John's Wood School of Art, as well as studying with Robert Kirkland Jamieson, the head of Westminster School of Art. Showed SWA, RBA and RWS, of which she was a member. Lived in Gloucester.

Carol Rosemary WHEELER 1927– Painter, born in London, daughter of the sculptor Sir Charles Wheeler and his artist wife Muriel Wheeler. She studied at Royal Academy Schools, 1946–51, teachers including Henry Rushbury and Philip Connard. Showed at various London venues including RA. She is featured in Charles Wheeler's autobiography *High Relief*, published in 1968, and lived for some years at the family home near Mayfield, Sussex. Her pictures frequently featured horses and circus scenes.

Charles WHEELER 1892–1974 Figure sculptor in bronze, stone and wood, and draughtsman, born in Codsall, Staffordshire. He studied at Wolverhampton School of Art under Robert J Emerson from 1908 and at Royal College of Art, 1912–17, under Édouard Lantéri. He exhibited at RA from 1914. Married the sculptor Muriel Bourne (who exhibited as Muriel Wheeler) in 1918, their daughter being the painter Carol Wheeler. Wheeler was a fellow of RBS and for a time its president. He was president of the RA in 1956–66 and was knighted in 1958. A number of official purchases were made of his work, which includes figures for the Bank of England, 1932; a decorative motif for South Africa House, 1934; and the Jellicoe Memorial and Fountains in Trafalgar Square, 1948. Wheeler was a sculptor in the classical tradition who could produce works of great sensitivity and dignity. Chantrey Bequest acquired his sculpture. His autobiography, *High Relief*, was published in 1968. Lived in London and near Mayfield, Sussex.

David WHEELER 1970– Painter, born in Wakefield, Yorkshire, where he studied at the District College, then Cleveland College of Art & Design and Leeds Metropolitan University. He became painting tutor for the Open College of the Arts, Middlesbrough Art Gallery. Group shows included The Waterlily Foundation Open Exhibition, The Guildhall, Cambridge, and NEAC Open, Mall Galleries, both 1994; and 2nd Summer Open Exhibition, Doncaster Museum & Art Gallery, and Royal Over-Seas League Open, both 1995. The latter included Wheeler's singular oil on canvas portrait of the Pomfret Sisters.

Dorothy M WHEELER 1891–1966 Watercolourist and illustrator who studied at Blackheath School of Art. Her sister Millicent was also an artist. *The Strand Magazine* commissioned her as an illustrator, but she was best known for her illustrations in books by the children's writer Enid Blyton. In 1955 Wheeler's own book *The Three Little Pigs* appeared. Exhibited RA and SWA. Lived in Esher, Surrey.

Geoffrey WHEELER 1929–1995 Technical artist and writer, born in Penn, Buckinghamshire, who joined Great Western Railway's Paddington drawing office in 1945 (he had been accepted as a premium apprentice at Swindon, but the £50 needed was not available). Wheeler trained as a wireless operator in the Royal Navy. Served in ships including HMS *Amethyst*; his first book was an illustrated account of her activities in the Korean War. After working as a steam service engineer, evening classes and two years in a technical publications studio, Wheeler became a freelance artist in 1961, versatile in the subjects handled. He was famous for his cutaway drawings for *Eagle* comic and the BBC's

Blue Peter Annual. Wheeler was an associate member of the Guild of Railway Artists and his work, accurate in the smallest detail, was published in *Railway Magazine*, *Steam Railway* and *Mayfair*. Wheeler's book *Fired by Steam* was first published in 1987. He despatched his cutaway prints of locomotives and traction engines from his windmill home at Bardwell, Suffolk, where he renovated his own Ruston & Hornsby traction engine *Oliver* and ran his own O-gauge railway. Exhibited in the provinces. York Steam Museum and other museums hold examples. In 1996 Bressingham Steam Museum held a memorial show which included his cartoons, contributed to periodicals under the name Crispin. Died in Bury St Edmunds Hospital, Suffolk.

Muriel WHEELER fl. from c.1915–1979 Sculptor and painter, originally Muriel Bourne, who married the sculptor Sir Charles Wheeler. Lady Wheeler came of an artistic family and studied at Wolverhampton School of Art with her future husband and privately. She worked periodically after their marriage, was a model for her husband and features in his autobiography *High Relief*. Was elected a fellow of RBS and was president of SWA and Ridley and St James' Art Societies, exhibiting at RA, NEAC and elsewhere. Her work is illustrated in Eric Newton's monograph *British Sculpture 1944–1946*; her Mother and Child is in Newport Museum and Art Gallery; and a lead bust of Sir Charles by her is the National Portrait Gallery. Lived in London and in Sussex at Five Ashes, near Mayfield.

Nora Constance WHEELER 1892–c.1966 Watercolourist, born at Thrapston, Northamptonshire, she studied art at Hastings School of Art with Vincent Lines and Philip Cole. Exhibited Royal College of Art, RI and extensively in India. Lived at St Leonards-on-Sea, Sussex.

Timothy WHEELER 1941– Painter who also worked extensively in the theatre, mostly opera, engaged in prop-making and other activities, including English National Opera, at Glyndebourne, the Royal Opera House and Royal Court; also worked in films. He studied at Camberwell School of Arts and Crafts, 1959–63. Among his group show appearances were John Moores Exhibition, Liverpool, 1976; LG, 1978; Austin/Desmond Fine Art, 1989; and Catto Gallery, 1991. He was commissioned to paint a portrait of Stella Newton which is in Courtauld Institute collection. Had solo show at RA in 1973; another in Harlow in 1980; and one which featured teddy bears, at Cadogan Gallery, in 1992. Lived in London.

Rowland WHEELWRIGHT 1870–1955 Painter and illustrator, born in Ipswich, Queensland, Australia. After Tonbridge School he attended Herkomer's School at Bushey, Hertfordshire, where he was to live for much of his life. He showed at RA extensively, Paris Salon, RI as well as New Society of Artists and RBA, of both of which he was a member. The Autotype Company published his picture *Joan of Arc Taken Prisoner*. Wheelwright was fond of historical subjects and was also an informed painter of the heavy horse. In later years he favoured pictures of bathers in Cornish coves. Public collections in Preston, Oldham and Cheltenham hold his work.

J Ramsey WHERRETT 1914–1960 Painter in oil, illustrator and designer. Studied at Birmingham College of Art under Bernard Fleetwood-Walker and Harold Holden, 1930–4, and at Leamington Spa School of Art, 1935–7, with Donald Macintyre. Exhibited RA, RBSA, RBA and elsewhere. Wherrett completed a range of work, for industry, for the General Post Office, Imperial Chemical Industries and the Ministry of Labour; decorations for a number of United States Air Force stations; and for publications ranging from *Radio Times* and *Lilliput* to *The Studio* and *Modern Education*. Lived at Woodbridge, Suffolk.

Herbert WHEWELL 1863–1951 Watercolour painter of landscapes, born in Bolton, Lancashire, being educated at the grammar school there. Exhibited RA, RI, Cooling Galleries and, especially, RI and RCamA, being a member of both. Bolton Art Gallery holds his work. Member of the Arts Club and lived in Gomshall, Surrey.

Fred WHICKER 1901–1966 Painter in oil, watercolour and tempera, born in Western Australia. He became a printer at *The Bristol Times and Mirror*, met Gwen Cross during Reginald Bush's evening classes at Bristol Art School and married her in 1931. At first Fred was influenced by his wife's work, althoug he later became more experimental. In Bristol Whicker was a member of New Bristol Arts Club and showed at RWA. He also exhibited figure and landscape paintings at RA, NEAC and ROI. After World War II the Whickers moved to Falmouth, Cornwall, and became members of the St Ives Society of Artists, although life was often economically tough. A joint retrospective was held at Falmouth Art Gallery and the RWA in 1994.

Gwen WHICKER: *see* **Gwen CROSS**

Timothy WHIDBORNE 1927– Painter, notably in tempera, and draughtsman, born in High Wycombe, Buckinghamshire. After initial education at Stowe School he studied extensively in Paris and with Pietro Annigoni in Florence. Exhibited RA and Trafford Gallery, sometimes signing work T W. Lived in London.

Anthony WHISHAW 1930– Painter, draughtsman and teacher, born in London, where he continued to live. He studied at Chelsea School of Art, 1948–52, then Royal College of Art, 1952–5. Whishaw had early success, gaining a travelling scholarship, drawing prize, Abbey Minor Scholarship and Spanish Government Scholarship. In 1960 he had the first of a string of solo shows at Roland, Browse & Delbanco; exhibiting one-man at the ICA in 1971; at Newcastle Polytechnic Art Gallery in 1979; Nicola Jacobs on several occasions in the 1980s; RWA, Bristol, 1993; and Barbican Centre and tour, 1994–5. Showed often at Summer Exhibition at RA and was elected a member of LG in 1978, the year he gained an Arts Council Award. Abbey Premier Scholarship and Lorne Scholarship and a John Moores Exhibition, Liverpool, Minor Painting Prize all followed in the early 1980s. From 1979

Whishaw taught at St Martin's and Chelsea Schools of Art. Over the years Whishaw's work see-sawed between abstraction and figuration, with notable Spanish influences; a sombre palette and Expressionistic tendencies were also present on occasion. Tate Gallery, Graves Art Gallery in Sheffield and a number of other public collections in Britain and abroad hold his work. Elected RA, 1989, RWA, 1992. Was married to the sculptor Jean Gibson.

Hector WHISTLER 1905–1976 Painter, muralist and illustrator, born in Jersey, Channel Islands, cousin of the artist Rex Whistler and glass engraver Laurence Whistler. He attended Victoria College, Jersey, 1915–23; studied architecture at the Architectural Association's school under Sir Howard Robertson; was commissioned in the Army for several years in the mid-1920s; and was at the Slade School of Fine Art under Randolph Schwabe for three terms, 1936–8. After World War II service in the Royal Air Force Whistler lived extensively in Jamaica. Solo exhibitions were held in London and the provinces, in the *Cristoforo Colombo* on the Mediterranean Sea, in Jamaica, New York and Miami. Later ones included The Building Centre, 1957, and Brighton Museum & Art Gallery, 1959. He illustrated Anthony Trollope's *The Prime Minister* for Oxford University Press which holds his work, as do the Chicago Art Institute and The University College of the West Indies. Decorative work included a mural Some Treasure Some Chest for the Anglo-American Ball at the Dorchester Hotel, 1957. Sometimes signed his work R(eginald) H(ector) Whistler, his full name.

Laurence WHISTLER 1912– Glass engraver and writer, younger brother of the artist Rex Whistler. He was educated at Stowe School and Oxford University and served in World War II, being commissioned in the Rifle Brigade. Shows included Agnew, 1969; Marble Hill, Twickenham, 1973; Ashmolean Museum in Oxford and Fine Art Society, 1976; and Kenwood, 1985. He was the first president of the Guild of Glass Engravers, 1975–80, and windows by him include Eastbury, Berkshire (commemorating the writer Edward Thomas and his wife Helen); Ashmansworth, Berkshire (composer Gerald Finzi); and Yalding, Kent (poet Edmund Blunden). Victoria & Albert Museum and Ashmolean Museum, Oxford, hold examples. *Scenes and Signs on Glass*, 1985, was one of a series by him on his art. Among his other books were *Rex Whistler, His Life and His Drawings*, 1948; *The View from this Window* (poems), 1956; the autobiographical *The Initials in the Heart*, 1964; and Rex Whistler's biography, *The Laughter and the Urn*, 1985. Lived at Watlington, Oxfordshire.

Reginald Hector WHISTLER: *see* **Hector WHISTLER**

David WHITAKER 1938– Abstract painter and teacher, born in Blackpool. He attended the School of Art there, 1951–7, then Royal Academy Schools, 1962–6. Teaching experience included Brighton, 1966–80, Ruskin School of Drawing in Oxford, 1975–84, and Wimbledon School of Art also from 1975. In 1973 he spent two months in America on a Mark Rothko Memorial Fellowship, in 1993 a semester in Point Richmond, on an exchange with Judith Foosaner. Showed at Serpentine Gallery, Towner Art Gallery in Eastbourne and elsewhere, in 1994 sharing a three-man exhibition at Morley Gallery. Arts Council holds examples.

Jon WHITAKER 1943– Painter and teacher, born in London, who attended St Albans College of Art, 1959–63. Teaching included Norwich School of Art, where he held a Brinkley Fellowship. From 1982 Whitaker appeared in many group shows, including Wapping Artists Open Studios. Arts Council holds Memory of Trogir, 1983, and The Wanderer II, 1984, by him, figurative pictures with a strong fantasy element.

Rita Elizabeth WHITAKER 1936– Artist stoving enamel on copper and teacher, born in Worthing, Sussex. She studied at the local College of Art and at Regent Street Polytechnic School of Art under Stuart Tresilian. Worked in the jewellery trade, taught art and crafts and finally was a professional artist. She was a member of RMS and SM, also showing at RA, Medici Gallery, Miniature Society of Florida and Georgia Miniature Society, in America. Royal Exchange holds her work. Lived in Newport, Dyfed.

Sheila WHITBY fl. c.1945–1965 Designer in line and watercolour, born and lived in London, who studied at the Slade School of Fine Art, 1948–51, under William Coldstream, Randolph Schwabe, Graham Sutherland and John Piper, then at the Central School of Arts and Crafts, 1951–2, with William Johnstone. She worked mainly for the printed page, appearing in periodicals such as *She*, *Britannia and Eve*, *Woman and Beauty* and for BBC Publications.

Susie WHITCOMBE 1957– Equestrian artist in oil and watercolour, born in London, who studied at Heatherley School of Fine Art under John Walton. On her father's side she was a direct descendant of the watercolourist William Evans. Became a member of Society of Equestrian Artists and had solo shows in London, Tokyo and Melbourne. Lived in West Meon, Hampshire.

Sydney WHITCOMBE 1916– Painter and commercial artist, born in Heaton Chapel, Cheshire. He attended Manchester School of Art, 1934, then studied privately for several years. Exhibited in the Manchester area, where he had a one-man show, and elsewhere. Lived for many years in Richmond, Surrey, then in Ilkley, Yorkshire.

Archie WHITE 1899–1957 Watercolourist and black-and-white artist with a special interest in sailing boats. Born at Copford, Essex, he studied art at the Central School of Arts and Crafts, then eventually returned to live at West Mersea, on the Essex coast. Among his books were *Sailing Ships and Tideways* and *Byways in Essex and Suffolk*. Exhibited RSMA, RBA and RI. Was a contributor to various yachting periodicals.

Arthur WHITE 1865–1953 Landscape and marine painter, and teacher, born in Sheffield. Studied at Sheffield School of Art from 1880 under Henry Archer and J T Cook. Went on to teach in

Sheffield in the closing years of the last century. Exhibited ROI and in the provinces, especially with the St Ives Society of Artists and the Exeter Society of Artists. Lived at Stennack, St Ives, Cornwall.

Caroline WHITE 1952– Painter and teacher, born in London. She studied at St Martin's School of Art in 1969, Bristol Polytechnic faculty of art and design from 1970 and at Chelsea School of Art, 1973. Returned to lecture at Bristol. White was included in the Arts Council's touring exhibition The British Art Show, chosen by William Packer, in 1980. Had a first solo show at Bristol City Art Gallery & Museum in 1975 and exhibited at Festival Gallery, Bath, from 1976, later at Pelter/Sands, Bristol.

Carolyn WHITE 1945– Painter, born in London, who was educated at Eothen School, Caterham, taught by Christine Walker, noted for innovative ideas in art education. Was taught by John Hoyland at Chelsea School of Art, 1963–4, then gained honours degree in painting at Kingston College of Art, taught by Graham Arnold. Showed at RWA, Tish Beere Gallery in Cardiff and elsewhere in mixed exhibitions. Showed solo at Rooksmoor Gallery in Bath from 1987 and in 1994 at The Anderson Gallery, Broadway. In 1992 was artist-in-residence with Glyndebourne Opera.

Charles WHITE 1928–1997 Painter, graphic artist and teacher, born in London. He studied at Sutton and Cheam School of Art, 1943; Newport College of Art, 1944; Sutton and Cheam, 1945; Kingston School of Art, 1946; Slade School of Fine Art, 1949, under William Coldstream, Claude Rogers and F E McWilliam; and in Germany. Held a number of teaching appointments including Newport and Swansea Colleges of Art; Margam College of Further Education; art therapy in mental hospitals and special schools in Wales; extra-mural lecturer at University of Wales; and head of art at Atlantic College/United World College. He was a founder-member of Young Contemporaries, a member of SWG and president of the European Group. His wife was the artist and potter Mary White (Rollinson). Showed with SEA, Royal National Eisteddfod, ICA, Round House, SWE and elsewhere in mixed exhibitions. Had many one-man shows in Britain and in continental Europe, sharing an exhibition with John Goddard at Manor House Fine Arts, Cardiff, in 1995. Charles and Mary White settled in Germany in 1980, and he died at his Rhineland home in the south, an area he often painted. HM The Queen, HRH The Prince of Wales, WAC and Contemporary Art Society hold his work.

Erica WHITE fl. from 1925– Sculptor and painter who was educated at St George's School in Harpenden. She studied at Slade School of Fine Art, where she won a painting prize; Central School of Arts and Crafts, with a sculpture scholarship; and Royal Academy Schools, where she was a bronze and silver medallist. She was elected a fellow of RBS and obtained a Feodora Gleichen Memorial Fund grant. Showed at RA, Royal Glasgow Institute of the Fine Arts and in the English southern provinces. Lived for many years in Bexhill-on-Sea, Sussex.

Ethelbert WHITE 1891–1972 Painter in oil and watercolour, illustrator, wood engraver and poster designer. Born at Isleworth, Middlesex, Berty White and his wife Betty became noted bohemians, travellers by caravan, regular attenders of the Chelsea Arts Ball and singers and collectors of folk songs. He was at St John's Wood Art School, 1911–12, early on becoming friends with advanced painters such as Mark Gertler and C R W Nevinson. White and Nevinson together painted a Futurist version of Hampstead Heath on Fair Day for the 1913 AAA exhibition. White exhibited with the LG and NEAC from 1916. First one-man show at the Paterson and Carfax Gallery in 1921. Illustrated a number of books, including Cyril Beaumont's *Impressions of the Russian Ballet*, Richard Jefferies' *The Story of my Heart* and Henry Thoreau's *Walden*, indicating a love of the countryside which inspired many of his pictures. White was a regular exhibitor at the RA and RWS. Travelled widely in Ireland, France and Spain. Memorial exhibition Fine Art Society, 1979. Lived in London.

Franklin WHITE 1892–1975 Painter, draughtsman and teacher, born at Fulham, near Adelaide, in South Australia. Arriving in England in 1913 on holiday, he was inspired by the National Gallery to paint; attended Heatherley's School of Fine Art, then in 1914 did further study in Paris, being accepted at Slade School of Fine Art in 1915. After war work in Admiralty Aircraft Department, drawing bombed enemy planes, he returned to Slade in 1919, then was invited to join the staff by Henry Tonks. During 1920s and 1930s exhibited at Agnew, Redfern Gallery and NEAC. Retired from Slade in 1957, the following year founding the Samuel Palmer School of Art in Shoreham, Kent, where he had made his home from just after World War I; for some years was assisted by his son Edmund. White was a mainstream artist and fine draughtsman in the Slade tradition, as shown in centenary exhibition at Bourne Gallery, Reigate, 1992. His work is held by British Museum, Victoria & Albert Museum, Ashmolean Museum, Oxford, and other public collections.

Gabriel WHITE 1902–1988 Etcher, painter, administrator and writer, born in Rome. His parents then settled for a time in Switzerland and White did not see England until he was nine; he was then educated at Downside, the Catholic public school, and Oxford University. Worked as a tutor to support himself as an art student under Bernard Meninsky at Westminster School of Art, 1927–30, then studied under Frederick Porter at Central School of Arts and Crafts, 1928–9. At Westminster White met the artist Edward Ardizzone, a lifelong friend, and his sister became White's first wife. White was involved in camouflage work in World War II, attaining the rank of lieutenant-colonel. He was assistant director of art at Arts Council, 1945–58, becoming director in the latter year. In the 1950s White had learned etching under Anthony Gross at Slade School of Fine Art, so that when he retired from the Arts Council in 1970 he continued as a full-time artist, and in 1976 published a book about Ardizzone. Showed LG, Mayor Gallery and Sally Hunter Fine Art, which gave him an etchings memorial show in 1989. Lived in London.

Gwen WHITE 1901–1986 Painter, illustrator, writer and teacher, born in Exeter, Devon, who was married to the stained glass artist C Rupert Moore. She studied at Bournemouth School of Art and the Royal College of Art. Taught part-time at Farnham and St Albans Schools of Art, where her lectures on perspective drawing, archi-tecture and etching were remembered as inspiring. Her *Book of Pictorial Perspective*, published in 1955, was considered a model. White also wrote and illustrated many books for children, such as *A Book of Dolls*, 1956, and *European and American Dolls*, 1966, her work being translated into several languages. She drew for BBC Television programmes and did work for the National Book League. Showed at RA and NEAC. Lived in Radlett, Hertfordshire.

Ianthe WHITE 1901-c.1976 Miniature painter, born in London. She studied at Bristol School of Art with Harry Bush, then exhibited at RMS and SWA both as a member, regularly at latter from 1939–75, SM and elsewhere. Lived latterly at Stonely, Huntingdonshire.

James WHITE and Tim SHEWARD Multi-media artists who began collaborating in 1995. White was born in 1967 and graduated in fine art from the Royal College of Art in 1991. Sheward was born in 1957 and graduated in product design from Kingston Polytechnic in 1989. They participated in group shows including Some of My Best Friends are Geniuses, curated by Jake Chapman for Independent Art Space in 1996. White and Sheward had a solo show at Banner Street, 1996, in 1997 one at Casey Kaplan, New York. Their first solo show at a British commercial gallery was in 1997 at Entwistle. This demonstrated their eye for detail, sense of the ridiculous and interest in the quirks of consumerism and contained sculpture, photo-based work and video.

James Trevor WHITE 1909– Painter and designer, born in Gosport, Hampshire. Studied at Portsmouth School of Art, 1927, then Manchester School of Art, 1933, but was largely self-taught. In this he was encouraged by a collection of modern British pictures. Member of ICA, showed at MAFA and elsewhere. Lived in London.

Jerry WHITE 1952– Painter, born in Sussex, who went to Loughborough College of Art and Royal Academy Schools, 1972–6, winning a Rome Scholarship to study in Italy for a year. After several years in London he moved to Cornwall in 1984, which gave his work a new beginning. He was a member of Newlyn Society of Artists, showed at the Newlyn Art Gallery and the Wolf at the Door Gallery in Penzance. In 1989 his canvas Thinking of You was included in the Newlyn Orion Galleries exhibition A Century of Art in Cornwall 1889–1989. White's work was also in The Edge of Beyond, Belgrave Gallery, 1995.

John WHITE 1932– Painter, illustrator and fashion artist, born in Chipperfield, Hertfordshire. He attended Harrow School of Art from 1945, obtaining his national diploma in 1951. Showed at RA, Young Contemporaries and elsewhere and lived at Herne, Kent.

John WHITE 1933– Marine artist, born in Christchurch, Dorset. He was a member of the British merchant fleet between 1949–55, then in 1955–9 was in the Far East with the Royal Air Force in flying boats. Joined Australia's Merchant Navy in 1960, and after wide experience decided in 1975 to retire from the sea and become a professional artist. After several years exhibiting around Australia, in 1978 returned to England and also showed widely, including RI, Solihull Central Gallery, Sutton Coldfield Gallery, Nevill Gallery in Bath and elsewhere. Lived in Catherine-de-Barnes, West Midlands. Sailing ships were a notable feature of White's work.

John Henry WHITE 1909– Sculptor in wood and metal, born in Newquay, Cornwall. A master mariner who was trained on the HMS *Worcester*, White was a self-taught artist. He showed at RA, RSA and RBS of which he was an associate. Settled in Largs, Ayrshire.

Ken WHITE 1943– Artist in oil and acrylic, born and lived in Swindon, Wiltshire, who attended the local Art School. His training was as a graphic designer, working for the British Council and freelancing in book and magazine illustration. His first mural, 1976, was Golden Lion Bridge, Swindon, used in a national advertising campaign, and this led to dozens more. They included Lethbridge School, Swindon, 1977, for Allied Dunbar; Mercat Murals 3, at Kirkcaldy, 1983, Standard Life; Scarlet Lady, 747 Jumbo Jet, 1986, Virgin, a client for which he worked a lot; Highworth Pool, 1988, Thamesdown Council; and Trompe L'Oeil Mural, Plymouth, 1994, for Plymouth Council. He was a member of Art and Architecture. Exhibited at Roy Miles Gallery 1991.

Laura WHITE 1968– Sculptor and lecturer, born in Worcester, who gained a first-class honours degree in sculpture at Loughborough College of Art and Design, where she was to lecture; gained a diploma in general art and design at Worcester College of Art; did a City and Guilds teacher training, module one; other studies including basic chainsaw techniques. At 26 she became the youngest artist elected to RBS, also belonging to the Loughborough Group, United Abstract Artists, Abstract Art is Beautiful and the International Art Collective. White said that many of her sculptures "lie between being appealing and threatening, vulnerable and frightening, and express feelings and emotions that are questionable, capturing the viewer and drawing them into a conversation with the piece." Residencies included Nottingham Castle and Yorkshire Sculpture Park; commissions Loughborough College for the Blind, 1989, and Hallam University, 1995. Her many group shows included The McHardy Sculpture Company. Had a solo exhibition at Queen Mary's College, Basingstoke, 1992, later ones including Hanover Galleries, Liverpool, 1995.

Noel WHITE fl. from 1960s– Painter and teacher, notably a watercolourist, who studied at Weston-super-Mare School of Art, West of England College of Art in Bristol and at Aarhus University. He became a lecturer at Maidstone College of Art and Design. His work was shown at Towner Art Gallery,

Eastbourne, 1981; The Carved Angel, Dartmouth, 1983; Mishkenot Sha'ananim, Jerusalem, 1985; and at Gallery 47, 1988. Other pictures completed during occupation of a studio in Jerusalem as a guest of the Mishkenot Sha'ananim Foundation in autumn 1985 were included in the three-man show Personal Mythologies at The Herbert Read Gallery, Canterbury College of Art and Design, 1988. Lived at Brightling, Sussex.

Peter WHITE 1929– Painter, artist in stained glass, printmaker and teacher, born in Pinner, Middlesex. Studied at Wimbledon School of Art, 1945–51, then at Royal College of Art, 1951–4, where he concentrated on stained glass. Among White's positions after that were periods working as a printmaker for Michael Rothenstein and Edward Bawden and as a teacher at Cornwall College in Montego Bay, Jamaica. White showed at RA, Young Contemporaries, New Art Centre, Zwemmer and Heal Galleries and elsewhere. Lived for some time in Great Bardfield, Essex.

Peter WHITE 1959– Painter and draughtsman, born in Ayr, Scotland. Studied at Edinburgh College of Art, 1981–5. Awards gained included RSA Latimer Prize, 1987; Marie Curie Foundation Open, where he was joint first prizewinner, 1988, the year he gained a Scottish Arts Council Bursary; and RSA, 1992. White showed extensively in England and Scotland from 1987 in group shows, including RSA Annual Exhibition; Royal Glasgow Institute of the Fine Arts; Royal Over-Seas League; and Discerning Eye, Mall Galleries. In 1993 he had a solo show at Jill George Gallery, muted pictures with a Surrealist tinge. Unilever Plc and Robert Fleming & Company hold his work.

Robert WHITE 1963– Painter and teacher, born in London, who studied at Medway College of Art & Design, Norwich School of Art and Royal Academy Schools. Taught at Kent Institute of Art & Design, 1991, and in 1993 at Southwark College and Camberwell School of Art. Took part in many group exhibitions, including ROI Open, Mall Galleries, from 1988; Acme Open Exhibition, Showroom Gallery, 1992; Eastern Open, King's Lynn Arts Centre, from 1994; and in 1995 The Discerning Eye at the Mall Galleries and Royal Over-Seas Open. Paintings in Hospitals, Norwich School of Art and British and foreign private collections hold examples.

Tom WHITE 1912– Painter and teacher who was born and lived in London. He studied at Wimbledon School of Art with Gerald Cooper, 1926–32, returning to teach there 1936–51 after a further period of study at Royal College of Art, 1932–6, his teachers including Gilbert Spencer. Showed at RA, NS and NEAC. He showed war pictures at National Gallery and Ministry of Information bought his work.

George WHITEBREAD 1930– Artist and teacher who studied at Goldsmiths' College of Art and Royal College of Art. Taught art history at Leeds College of Art and was included in The Teaching Image, the 1964 show of its staff's work at Leeds City Art Gallery, where he showed the wood construction White Relief. Also exhibited at AIA Gallery. Lived for a time in London.

Joan WHITEFORD 1942– Printmaker, born in St John, Cornwall, where she settled at Penzance. Studied at Plymouth College of Art, teachers including William Mann, 1958–63, gaining her national diploma; added her teacher's diploma after another year at Bournemouth College of Art in 1964. Showed with RE, SWA, RA and elsewhere.

Kate WHITEFORD 1952– Painter and draughtsman, born in Glasgow, who studied at the School of Art there, 1969–73. From 1974–6 she studied history of art at Glasgow University, a British Council Scholarship taking her to Rome in 1977. Although her early pictures were abstract in tendency, Whiteford in the 1980s began to incorporate classical and archaeological images in her work. This personal symbolism and her choice of colours created works which impress themselves on the mind. Was artist-in-residence at St Andrews University, 1982–3, the following year holding a similar post at Whitechapel Art Gallery. Whiteford liked to work on a big scale, her 1987 trio of images created with stone chippings on Calton Hill, Edinburgh, being a prime example; they were reminiscent of prehistoric hill carvings, such as the Cerne Abbas Giant. Whiteford had first solo show at Stirling Art Gallery in 1978. Later shows were held at Crawford Centre for the Arts, St Andrews, 1983; Third Eye Centre, Glasgow, 1984; and Riverside Studios, 1986. Scottish National Gallery of Modern Art holds her work. Lived in London.

Margaret della Rovere WHITEHEAD 1903– Painter, modeller and teacher, born in London. Her father was professor of Italian studies at Glasgow University and she attended the School of Art there under Maurice Greiffenhagen, also studying at Bromley School of Art. She went on to hold a series of art teaching posts in Lincoln and Chesterfield, eventually becoming lecturer in art and crafts at the Normal College, Bangor, Caernarvonshire, where she lived. Showed SWA and RCamA both of which she was a member, also NWG, Arts Council and in North America.

Rhonda WHITEHEAD fl. from c.1970– Painter and draughtsman who studied at Royal College of Art, appearing in the Degree Show there, 1971. Other group appearances included RA Summer Exhibition from 1972; 2nd International Drawing Biennial, Middlesbrough, 1975; LG from 1980; St Martin's School of Art, 1981; and Berry Street Open Studios, 1984. Solo shows included Produzenten Galerie, Hamburg, and Electric Gallery, Toronto, both in 1977; Ikon Gallery, Birmingham, 1980; and Paton Gallery, 1984.

William Marlborough WHITEHEAD 1882–1959 Painter, educated in Burnley and at the Royal College of Art. Was a member of the Langham Sketch Club, signing his work W M W. Lived in Leicester.

Brett WHITELEY 1939–1992 Painter, printmaker and sculptor in a variety of materials, born in Sydney, Australia, where he eventually settled. Studied at the Julian Ashton Art School, 1957–9, then an Italian scholarship took him to London. Showed at the Whitechapel Art Gallery and Marlborough Fine Art in 1961 and in that year represented his country at the Young Painters' Convention, Paris, by which time he was a hot property. Whiteley was an artist whose colourful and exciting life was intertwined with his work. Influences on the work were the French poets Rimbaud and Verlaine and the painters Yves Klein and Francis Bacon. He was much affected by travels in the 1960s in America and the Far East. A brilliant draughtsman, sometimes obsessed with certain colours and themes, he could produce febrile, scintillating pictures. There was a series of girls intertwined with the contours of bathtubs; another preoccupied with a number of London murders; and, as a contrast, there were poetic drawings and paintings of Sydney harbour seen from his studio at Lavender Bay. Whiteley continued to show in London, notably at Fischer Fine Art. The Tate Gallery, Museum of Modern Art in New York and many Australian galleries hold examples. Whiteley died in a motel room near Wollongong, south of Sydney, with needles, tablets and a bottle of whisky nearby.

Sue WHITE-OAKES fl. from 1950s– Painter, sculptor, illustrator, photographer and furniture-maker who studied at Central School of Art & Design in 1950s. Worked in industry as a designer of domestic and industrial products in London and Farnham, then moved to Scotland in 1975 as an illustrator and cartographer for Lothian Regional Council and the Forestry Commission. Her own early work was abstract, inspired by machinery. Later she produced a series of aquatic creatures in copper, as shown at Duncan Campbell Contemporary Art, 1993. Had a first solo show at Crystal Palace Gallery, 1962, exhibited at Ashgate Gallery, Farnham, 1967, then showed widely in Scotland and south of England from 1976.

Rachel WHITEREAD 1963– Sculptor, born in London, where she continued to work. She attended Brighton Polytechnic, 1982–5, then Slade School of Fine Art, 1985–7. Gained The Elephant Trust award in 1989. After Whitworth Young Contemporaries in Manchester, 1987, group shows included Slaughterhouse Gallery, 1988, Whitechapel Open in 1989 and South Bank Centre's touring The British Art Show 1990. Solo exhibitions included Carlile Gallery, 1988, and Chisenhale Gallery, 1990. Tomb-like objects created by direct casting and constructed from negative spaces were a key feature of Whiteread's output. She won the Turner Prize in 1993 as her controversial House project (in which she preserved the interior spaces of an East End Victorian terrace house while the structure was demolished) was making her a national celebrity. Had a retrospective at Tate Gallery, Liverpool, 1996–7. In 1997 became the first woman artist to represent Britain with a solo show at the Venice Biennale.

Frederic WHITING 1874–1962 Painter and printmaker, notable for his portraits and equestrian subjects, born in London where he mainly worked. Whiting studied at St John's Wood School of Art, Royal Academy Schools and Académie Julian, Paris. During the civil wars in China, 1900–1, Whiting drew for *The Graphic*, also covering the 1904–5 Russo-Japanese War. Showed at RA, also NPS, RP, RI and RWS, all of which he was a member. Among his foreign awards was a silver medal at Paris Salon in 1926 and a bronze medal at Anglo-German Exhibition, 1913. Walker Art Gallery, Liverpool, holds his work.

Jim WHITING 1951– Sculptor/installations artist, industrial designer and tutor, born in Paris, who lived for a time in Southern Rhodesia, moving to London in 1959. He attended Queen Mary College, London University, 1969–72, gaining a science degree in systems control and electronic engineering; did a foundation course at High Wycombe College of Art, 1972–3; studying sculpture at St Martin's School of Art, 1973–4. In 1974 had a number of jobs, including the Dinner and Dance Band and school teaching, in 1975 starting work as a self-employed industrial designer. In the late 1970s Whiting was a workshop tutor at Architectural Association School of Architecture and was a visiting tutor at Central School of Art's theatre design department. Shows included Bath Festival Ghost Train, 1975; Rotherhithe Festival Insect Train and Whitechapel Open at Whitechapel Art Gallery, both 1976; Hayward Annual at Hayward Gallery, 1979; then latterly his shows were frequently in Germany and Switzerland, including Galerie Klaus Littmann, Basel/Schweiz, 1989. Whiting's work employed a variety of machinery, dummies and other equipment.

Gladys WHITLEY 1886–c.1954 Painter and miniaturist, sometimes working on ivory, born in London. She studied at Heatherley's School of Fine Art under John Crompton, then at Arthur Cope's School. Exhibited RMS of which she was a member, RA, SWA and RI as well as extensively abroad. Lived in Portscatho, Cornwall.

John WHITLOCK: *see* **John Whitlock CODNER**

Kevin WHITNEY 1948– Artist in a wide range of media, including painting, sculpture, murals and prints, and teacher, born in Bletchley, Buckinghamshire. He studied at Ipswich Art School, 1965–7, teachers including Roy Ascott, Tom Phillips and Steve Willats; then at Chelsea Art School, 1967–70, taught by Allen Jones, Howard Hodgkin, Craigie Aitchison, Pat Caulfield, John Hoyland and Miles Murphy. In 1982 Whitney "invented the concept of Official Olympic Artist. I was appointed by the British Olympic Association in May 1983 and subsequently attended the 1984 Los Angeles Olympic Games in that capacity, the first in the history of the modern Olympics and the first for any country worldwide." A team of European artists from five countries attended "the Barcelona Olympic Games in 1992, with myself as art director." The book *British Challenge at the 1984 Olympics*, with paintings by Whitney and text by sports writer Brian Glanville, was published in the same year. Whitney's work then appeared regularly in *The International Olympic Academy Year Report* from 1986. Whitney taught at Chelsea School of Art, 1976–7, gaining his master's degree there, 1977–8. Other teaching appointments included University of Southern California, 1979; Froebel Institute, 1979–80; and Leicester Polytechnic, 1986. He designed sets and costumes for several stage productions and a number of murals, including Aqua Reflective, Kensington Sports Centre, 1994, "the largest indoor mural in the United Kingdom". Took part in many mixed shows and had a string of solo exhibitions, later ones including The International Committee Museum, Lausanne, Switzerland, 1993; and Victoria Art Gallery, Bath, 1995. Lived in London.

Edwin WHITNEY-SMITH 1880–1952 Sculptor, born in Bath, Somerset, who studied art at Bath and Bristol Schools of Art. Exhibited RA, Walker Art Gallery, Liverpool, in the provinces, South America and at the Paris Salon. The RA and public galleries in Liverpool, Preston, Manchester and elsewhere hold his work. He was elected a fellow of the RBS. Arts Club member whose work is held by Tate Gallery. Lived in London.

David WHITTAKER 1964– Self-taught figurative artist, painting in oil, drawing in chinagraph pencil and acrylic gloss. Born in Redruth, Cornwall, he entered the family pub and restaurant business at 16 and during catering college training continued to draw and paint, as he did on his extensive travels on the continent, in Ireland, where for a short time he worked as a pearl fisherman, and in America. Group exhibitions included Peter Blake Gallery, Laguna Beach, California, 1994. Had a solo show at Hyde Park Gallery, 1992, another in 1997 at studio gallery in St Ives, Cornwall, where he had settled. His full name was David Kim Whittaker, and work was signed with a D K W monogram.

Edward WHITTAKER 1948– Abstract painter and teacher who sometimes used unconventional materials, such as oil on hessian with roofing felt in his Untitled, of 1980–1, held by Arts Council. Born in Manchester, Whittaker studied at Chelsea School of Art, 1967–71, then Slade School of Fine Art, 1971–3. He became an associate lecturer at Bath College of Higher Education. Whittaker showed with John Moores Liverpool Exhibition from 1985; The Other Landscape, Southampton City Art Gallery, 1987; Selective Affinities at Woodlands Art Gallery, 1988; and in same year at Harry Zellweger, Basel, Switzerland. He was sometimes known as E S Whittaker. Lived in London.

E S WHITTAKER: *see* **Edward WHITTAKER**

Malcolm WHITTAKER 1937– Painter, artist in mixed media and teacher, born in Hoyland, Barnsley, Yorkshire, where he grew up and settled. His father, grandfather and father-in-law were all miners, but Whittaker had a distaste for the job and his parents encouraged his artistic ambitions. Attended Barnsley College of Art and was admitted to Royal College of Art contemporary with Norman Stevens and David Hockney. Spurned the Pop Art movement, his student works being gritty northern industrial scenes. Taught in schools and colleges in Bradford, Dewbury and Sheffield. Whittaker said that influences and preoccupations in his mature works were "many and varied, cerebral and visual – land surfaces, maps, aerial photographs, geological diagrams, museums, text and book forms … The painting is a new place, a new reality with its own vital presence." Later solo shows included Brunel University, 1992, and Hart Gallery, 1996. Many public collections hold examples, including galleries in Sheffield, Wakefield, Derby, Swansea, Worcester, Barnsley, Leeds and Hull, plus corporate collections.

John WHITTALL 1947– Painter, notably of portraits and still life, born in London. He attended Camberwell School of Arts and Crafts, 1964–9, then Royal Academy Schools under Peter Greenham. From 1972 Whittall was a frequent exhibitor at RA, also showing at National Portrait Gallery, Judd Street Gallery, Mall Galleries, and in 1992 he shared a show at Mistral Galleries. His commissioned portraits of Lord Henry Benson and Sir Kenneth Cork are in the National Portrait Gallery's collection.

Sylvia WHITTALL 1942– Artist in wide variety of media, designer and teacher, born in Blackpool, Lancashire. Was apprenticed to textile design in Manchester in late 1950s, and worked in the field for about nine years. Left to have a family, sat for a teacher's certificate, was an art tutor with Tameside College of Further Education, then after 16 years left to concentrate on own work. Whittall's pictures were mainly figurative and she was especially fascinated by watercolour and large formats. Showed with Colin Jellicoe Gallery in Manchester, the Laing 1992 Exhibition at Salford Art Gallery, MAFA, SWLA, Westminster Gallery and elsewhere. Had a number of solo exhibitions in Manchester area, where she lived at Haughton Green, Denton. Cotman, Bosch and Bacon were cited as influences on her work.

Philip John WHITTEN 1922– Painter and teacher, born in Leyton, Essex. He studied at Hornsey School of Art, 1937–40, where his teachers included Norman Janes and John Charles Moody; at Accrington School of Art, 1941–2; then at the Royal College of Art, 1946–9, with Carel Weight, Edward Bawden and Ruskin Spear. Taught at Eastbourne School of Art, in Sussex, where he lived and was a member of the Society of Artists. Showed in London but principally in Eastbourne, where he had a show at the Towner Art Gallery.

Stephen WHITTLE 1953– Etcher, designer and teacher, born in Leeds, Yorkshire. He studied fine art at Chelsea School of Art and Brighton Polytechnic, obtaining his bachelor's degree there in 1975. Worked in Switzerland and England, finally setting up an etching studio in Skelmersdale, Lancashire. Whittle's subject was the English landscape. His serene, harmonious images stemmed from a deep interest in Transcendental Meditation. From 1979 showed in group exhibitions at Blackheath Gallery and Medici Society, holding solo shows at Drian Gallery and Mentmore Towers, Buckinghamshire. A number of prints were published by Christie's Contemporary Art. London and provincial galleries and others in America, continental Europe and Japan hold his work. Rich colour was a feature.

Michael WHITTLESEA 1938– Painter and illustrator, born in London, who studied at Harrow School of Art. He was elected RWS in 1985, also showing at NEAC and RA. Lived at Hurley, Berkshire.

Leonie WHITTON fl. from 1970s– Painter, artist in mixed media and teacher, born in Huddersfield, Yorkshire. Studied fine art at Newcastle University, then spent two years painting and teaching in Sicily before returning to teach at Falmouth School of Art, becoming senior lecturer in painting. In 1988 was artist-in-residence, teaching at Victoria College, Melbourne, Australia. In 1989 she spent time in America following a decision to relinquish teaching and paint full-time. Mixed shows included Chicago International Art Expo, 1987 and 1989, Cleveland International Drawing Biennale in 1988 and other appearances at Louise Hallett Gallery, Brewhouse Arts Centre in Taunton and A Century of Art in Cornwall 1889–1989, the Newlyn Orion Galleries show in 1989. She held a major solo exhibition in 1988 at Royal Cornwall Museum, Truro. Northern Arts Council holds her work. Lived in Falmouth, Cornwall.

Terry WHYBROW 1932– Artist in acrylic, born in London. He was always interested in painting, studied and practised furniture design until 1980, then decided to paint full-time. Whybrow, notable for his still lifes with apples, said that he was "only interested in the aesthetics of painting (no story to tell)". Exhibited widely in mixed shows through the United Kingdom and America, including Marsden Fine Art and Belgrave Gallery. Had many solo shows in Cornwall, where he lived in St Ives, married to the writer Marion Whybrow, whose books on art in Cornwall included *St Ives 1883–1993*, published in 1994, *The Leach Legacy*, 1996 and a study of Alfred Wallis, Mary Jewels, Bryan Pearce and other Primitives, in 1998.

Ernest Herbert WHYDALE 1886–1952 Painter and etcher, notably of horse and genre subjects, born in Halifax, Yorkshire. He studied at Westminster, Central, Camberwell and Bolt Court Schools after early education in Birmingham and St Leonards-on-Sea showed a talent for art. His teachers included A S Hartrick, George Clausen, Harold Gilman and Walter Bayes. For several years was an accomplished commercial artist. Whydale exhibited at RA from 1910–50, SGA, RE, RSA and Fine Art Society. Victoria & Albert Museum, Fitzwilliam Museum in Cambridge and South London Art Gallery hold his work. Whydale lived in Royston, Hertfordshire, from 1919. He built a studio called Fag's Folly, where he taught and with his brother Arthur promoted amateur theatricals. Painted from a horse-drawn caravan. Manor Gallery, Royston, put on a show of his work in 1970.

Duncan Macgregor WHYTE 1866–1953 Painter, born in Oban, Argyll. Studied art in Glasgow and on the continent. Glasgow Art Gallery and Museum, Kelvingrove, and the New Museum and Art Gallery, Newport, hold his work. Was a member of Glasgow Art Club. Lived at Oban, Argyll.

Geoffrey Earle WICKHAM 1919– Sculptor in a wide range of materials, painter, teacher and critic, born in Wembley, Middlesex. He studied at Willesden School of Art, 1935–8, under Ernest Heber Thompson, then at Royal College of Art, 1946–9, and was for many years principal lecturer in fine art at Sir John Cass School of Art. Wickham was elected a fellow of RBS in 1967 and won its Silver Medal in 1972, showing with AIA, SEA, Leicester and Upper Street Galleries and NEAC. Solo shows included Alwin Gallery, AIA and Arts Theatre Club. From 1982–5 he lived in Japan. After marriage to the potter Gisela Albrecht, Wickham married the artist Akiko Fujikawa. When Wickham's work was shown at Hattingen Art Society, Germany, in 1989 it was strongly influenced by Japan and included rare representational sculpture. Wickham's many commissioned works included City Music, Ludgate Hill, 1962; Winged Form and Emergent Form, both Strand, 1964; Fountainhead, of Motcomb Street, Belgravia, 1971; and Holborn Underground Station mural, 1981. Wrote for magazines including *Arts Review* and *Designed Environment*. Latterly had a studio in Burnham-on-Crouch, Essex.

Mabel Frances WICKHAM 1901–1992 Artist and teacher, born in Fleet, Hampshire, who said that "to me painting is learning to see." Her parents encouraged her talent and from 1919–23 she studied in art department of Clapham High School, including a year's teacher training, then taught art at Lord Digby's School, Sherborne. By the early 1930s opted to teach part-time to develop her own painting, for 14 years attending summer landscape painting courses run by St Clair Marston. Was elected to SWA in 1936, RI in 1938, showed regularly at RA and with local groups such as Sherborne Art Club. Sherborne Town Council commissioned work. On retiring in 1953 Wickham moved to Weymouth, Dorset. She ran her own summer courses and lectured for Workers' Educational Association, Bristol Extra-Mural Department and Portland Bill Observatory; she travelled widely, including the Near East; and attended John Nash's botanical illustration course at Flatford Mill Field Study Centre. Although traditional in her approach, she appreciated the work of Rothko and Matisse. There was a retrospective at Chesil Gallery, Chiswell, 1988, and Wickham shared a show at Dorset County Museum, Dorchester, in 1992.

Helen Cecile WICKS 1925– Painter, born in London, who was educated at St Paul's Girls' School. She attended St Martin's School of Art, 1945–7, under James Bateman and Ruskin Spear. Showed at RP, RA and in the provinces. Lived in London, then in Wembley, Middlesex.

Jan WIELICZKO 1919–1998 Painter, designer and collagist, born in Wilno, Poland. He served in Polish Air Force as a fighter pilot, flying to England where he settled in London. Studied at Slade School of Fine Art from 1946, was influenced by Vladimir Polunin there and, having gained a first prize in 1948, was in 1949 appointed Polunin's assistant in stage design and decorative painting department. Designed scenery for Negro Ballet and painted murals in Rowney House and for Festival of Britain, 1951. Joined Hampstead Artists' Council and was elected to executive committee of AIA. In 1960 set up Centaur Gallery, showing folk art, in Highgate Village. Showed in many mixed exhibitions and had solo shows at Irving Gallery and John Denham Gallery, 1992. Wieliczko's work used a rich palette and had Fauve and Cubist influences.

Stephen M WIENS 1871–1956 Portrait sculptor and painter, of German background and educated partly in that country although born in London. Studied at Royal Academy Schools from 1890 and showed at RA from 1893. In 1920 he changed his name from Siegfried to Stephen. Tate Gallery holds his bronze Girl and Lizard, a Chantrey Purchase in 1907. This was included in Some Chantrey Favourites at RA, 1981. Died in Worthing, Sussex, where he had lived from 1937 and where the Museum & Art Gallery holds several works by him.

Ervin WIESNER 1893–c.1965 Painter, chiefly of portraits, commercial artist and teacher, born in Malacky, Czechoslovakia. He was initially educated in Brno, Czechoslovakia, where he studied art, as he did in Leipzig, Germany, and in Vladivostock, in the Soviet Union. Showed in those places and in Britain at Kelvingrove Gallery in Glasgow, with the London Portrait Society and at Bluecoat Chambers, Liverpool. Among his portraits was one of Czechoslovakia's first president, Thomas Masaryk. Sometimes signed work E W. Died from Parkinson's Disease in Wallasey, Cheshire.

Alfred Kemp WIFFEN 1896–1968 Painter, draughtsman, printmaker, illustrator and teacher, born in Eastwood, Nottinghamshire. After serving in World War I and a period farming in Nottinghamshire he attended Nottingham School of Art under the sculptor Joseph Else. From 1928 taught graphic arts at Liverpool School of Art, retiring in 1961. Exhibited RA, RCamA and Liverpool Academy both of which he was a member and with Deeside Art Group, of which he was president. Nottingham Art Gallery and Museum holds his work. Lived at Hoylake, Cheshire.

Kathleen WIGGLESWORTH 1900– Landscape painter, born in London. She was educated in Sevenoaks, Kent, then as a mature student attended Byam Shaw School of Drawing and Painting, 1948–57, teachers including Peter Greenham and Patrick Phillips. Was elected to NEAC, also showing at RBA, RWA and in elsewhere in the provinces. Lived in Rickmansworth, Hertfordshire.

WILC: *see* **Katerina WILCZYNSKI**

Leslie Arthur WILCOX 1904–1982 Self-taught painter in oil and watercolour, born in London, sea and shipping pictures a speciality. During World War II Wilcox served in the Royal Navy and was for several years a camouflage officer. Exhibited at ROI, RBA, RI and RSW and at provincial venues. Produced work for industrial firms, British Railways and illustrated maritime publications; wrote several books with naval themes. HM The Queen had work by Wilcox on the Royal Yacht *Britannia* and the shipping magnate Aristotle Onassis and businessman Garfield Weston owned his pictures, which are also in public collections, notably the National Maritime Museum, Greenwich, and Government House, Jamaica. Lived at Rustington, Sussex.

Katerina WILCZYNSKI 1894–1978 Painter, draughtsman in ink, printmaker and teacher, born in Poznan, Poland. She grew up in Berlin and studied at academies there and in Leipzig, then freelanced for a time in Paris. In 1930 won the Prix de Rome and and remained there for about a decade, where she sketched many churches later pulled down under Mussolini's town planning schemes. Travelled to London, which was her base, in 1939, from which she travelled extensively to Mediterranean countries, especially Italy and Greece. During World War II showed in war artists' exhibitions at National Gallery and drew many monuments and buildings damaged by enemy action. After the war her work appeared in a string of publications, including *Daphnis and Chloe*, *Homage to Greece* and *The Love Songs of Sappho*. Often signed work WILC. Was noted for her delicate line drawings of literary and artistic figures, such as that of the writer Joyce Cary, held by the National Portrait Gallery; work is also in the Victoria & Albert Museum and in public galleries in Dresden and Cologne. A forceful personality whose life was said to "allow for no generation gap".

David WILD 1931– Painter in oil and watercolour, born and settled in Burnley, Lancashire. Studied at the Art School there, then at Slade School of Fine Art under William Coldstream. After gaining his diploma in 1955 took up an Abbey Major Scholarship to Rome. From 1957 showed extensively through the north of England, including John Moores Liverpool Exhibitions. In 1957 Wild's Standing Nude was included in Jack Beddington's book *Young Artists of Promise*. Wild, who also showed at RA and Woodstock Gallery, was interested in figurative or realist painting, Vermeer and Cézanne being cited as influences. Arts Council, Walker Art Gallery in Liverpool and Manchester City Art Gallery hold examples.

Eveline WILD fl. c.1915–1965 Painter, stained glass designer and miniaturist whose full name was Winifred Eveline Wild, born in Chalfont St Giles, Buckinghamshire. Studied at Central School of Arts and Crafts, her teachers including Noel Rooke and F Ernest Jackson. Showed at RA, RMS, Walker Art Gallery, Liverpool, and Paris Salon. Russell-Cotes Art Gallery in Bournemouth holds her work. Belonged to Bournemouth Arts Club and lived in Boscombe, Hampshire.

Frank Percy WILD 1861–1950 Versatile painter who was born in Leeds, Yorkshire, but was educated partly in France and Germany. Studied at Royal Academy in Antwerp, where he won a silver medal, then in France and Spain. He was elected RBA, also showing at RA, Walker Art Gallery in Liverpool and at New Gallery as well as abroad. He was a Chelsea Arts Club member who settled in Marlow, Buckinghamshire, views of the River Thames being a favourite subject.

Rosina WILD 1898– Painter, born in Gateshead, County Durham, studying with her father Samuel Wild and at the local School of Art. She showed with Gateshead Art Society from its first exhibition in 1948, Artists of the Northern Counties shows and at Shipley Art Gallery, Gateshead, in the 1951 Festival of Britain exhibition.

Samuel WILD 1863–1958 Painter and teacher, born and lived in Gateshead, County Durham, father of the artist Rosina Wild. He studied at Newcastle, Gateshead and South Shields Schools of Art and at Royal College of Art and taught in schools and in part-time classes in the Gateshead area. Showed with Newcastle's Bewick Club, Artists of the Northern Counties, Newcastle Society of Artists and Gateshead Art Club. Shipley Art Gallery in Gateshead holds his watercolour The Avenue, Sheriff Hill, of 1922.

Tony WILD 1941– Artist who employed collage and paint on cardboard, and teacher, born and based in Stoke-on-Trent area, Staffordshire. The parks and products of the Potteries area were frequent subjects. Wild studied at Burslem Art School, 1958–63, later teaching experience including North Staffordshire Polytechnic. Group exhibitions included Northern Young Contemporaries, Whitworth Art Gallery in Manchester, 1962–3; John Moores Liverpool Exhibition at Walker Art Gallery, 1978; Midland View at Midland Group Gallery, Nottingham, 1980; and Summer Show 3 at Serpentine Gallery, 1982. Arts Council holds his work.

Gerald WILDE 1905–1986 Painter, draughtsman and textile designer, born in London. After working in a solicitor's office Wilde attended Chelsea School of Art, 1926–31, and 1932–4, under Percy Hague Jowett and H S Williamson. Following service in the Pioneer Corps in World War II he had his first one-man show at the Hanover Gallery in 1948, also showing with AIA, NEAC, LG and elsewhere. He was early collected by men of perception, such as Sir Edward Marsh, Lord Clark and Peter Watson. Wilde's work is usually abstract, and he employed a unique style of line and colour, as seen in the Tate Gallery's examples: Fata Morgana, of 1949, and Red Composition, of 1952. In 1951 he designed the cover for the catalogue of the Festival of Britain show *Sixty Paintings for '51*. Poor health hindered Wilde's output. An amusing cameo of him is contained in Nicolette Devas' autobiography *Two Flamboyant Fathers*. The ICA gave Wilde a retrospective in 1955 and October Gallery another in 1988. Lived for a time at Cudham, Kent.

Alison WILDING 1948– Sculptor, born in Lancashire. She studied at Nottingham and Ravensbourne Colleges of Art, then at Royal Academy Schools, 1970–3. Wilding showed extensively in mixed shows, including The British Art Show 1979–1984, organised by Arts Council in 1984. Solo exhibitions included Kettle's Yard, Cambridge, 1982, and Salvatore Ala Gallery, New York, 1983. Also showed with Karsten Schubert Ltd, from which Arts Council bought Wilding's Bearing, of 1988. Tate Gallery also holds Wilding's sculpture, which employed unusual combinations of materials, was often small in scale, simple in conception but powerful in its presence. Her abstract works recall those of Brancusi and Barbara Hepworth. In 1992 she was shortlisted for the Turner Prize at the Tate Gallery and in 1993–4 was included in the Arts Council touring show Recent British Sculpture. Lived in London.

Hazel WILDMAN 1943– Artist and teacher, born in Essex, who studied at Walthamstow College of Art, 1962–5, and Royal Academy Schools, 1965–8. She taught part-time at Epsom and Loughborough Colleges of Art, also working at Hayward Gallery. Was included in Summer Show 3 at Serpentine Gallery in 1981, in the same year showing solo at The Minories, Colchester. Wildman liked "the mysterious in art. I don't really like art that has an overt message."

William Ainsworth WILDMAN 1882–1950 Prolific painter and printmaker, born in Manchester, where he studied and in London. Showed at RBA of which he was a member, RA, NEAC, Baillie Gallery, RHA, RWS and elsewhere. Manchester City Art Gallery holds his work. Lived in London.

Reginald Howard WILENSKI 1887–1975 Critic, historian, painter and teacher, born in London. Wilenski attended St Paul's School and Oxford University, was a special lecturer in art history at Bristol University, 1929–30, then at Victoria University in Manchester, 1933–46. Manchester granted him an honorary master's degree in 1938 and he was made a chevalier of the Legion of Honour in 1967. Wilenski was an influential writer, his *The Modern Movement in Art*, 1927, being a key text. Other titles included *French Painting*, 1931, and *Modern French Painters*, 1940. He showed at IS, ROI, RP and Walker Art Gallery in Liverpool. Lived finally at Marlow, Buckinghamshire.

Alec WILES 1924– Painter, cartoonist and sculptor, born in Southampton. Although he attended the School of Art there, 1938–40, Wiles claimed to have been self-taught as a portrait painter and cartoonist. During World War II he served in the Royal Air Force in Egypt, where he taught art for a while. After the war he built up a reputation as a humorous illustrator in such magazines as *Lilliput*, *Punch*, *London Opinion* and *John Bull*. Showed RA, SGA, RP, in the provinces and in America. Finally lived at Twelveheads, Cornwall, where he showed with, and was a member of, the St Ives Society of Artists and the Newlyn and Penwith Societies.

Francis WILES 1889–1956 Figurative sculptor in a range of materials, and teacher, born in Larne, County Antrim, Northern Ireland, who also worked as Frank Wiles. He studied at Belfast College of Art and Dublin's Metropolitan School of Art (where he went on to teach), winning a string of medals in Irish national competitions. Wiles was a keen athlete, enjoying cycling, sailing, swimming and walking. He became a member of RUA (which organised a memorial show at Old Museum, Belfast, 1958), also exhibiting at RHA, RA and RSA. Completed public sculpture around Ireland, including a granite lion for the War Memorial, Newcastle, County Down. Died in Larne, County Antrim, where St Columba's College has sculpture by Wiles. Belfast's Ulster Museum also holds his work.

Frank WILES: *see* **Francis WILES**

Jessica WILKES 1948– Painter and draughtsman, teacher, born in Newcastle upon Tyne, Northumberland. After studying at the local Polytechnic, 1971–5, attended Chelsea School of Art,

1975–6. She won an Arts Council Award in 1977, a year after becoming a professional artist. As well as teaching, including London University and in adult education, she interviewed for the Imperial War Museum. Mixed shows included Peter Stuyvesant Northern Painters & Sculptors, Sunderland Arts Centre, 1974; New Contemporaries, International Art Centre, and John Moores Liverpool Exhibition, both 1976; and Summer Show 1 at Serpentine Gallery, 1982. In 1981 had a solo show at The Gallery, Brixton. Lived in London.

James WILKIE 1890–1957 Artist and teacher from Birmingham who studied at Slade School of Fine Art and was a prize winner, 1913–15. After Army service in France in World War I he returned to the Slade, where he taught from 1919–57. Wilkie was a draughtsman in the Henry Tonks tradition who remains a rather shadowy figure. He was elected to NEAC in 1921, where he was a prolific exhibitor as he was at Redfern and Leicester Galleries, also showing at RA, Fine Art Society, Royal Glasgow Institute of the Fine Arts and elsewhere. The Slade held one of Wilkie's pictures, of a waggon and horses. Lived in London.

John WILKINS 1951– Painter, born in Colchester, Essex, where he studied at the School of Art, 1969–71, then at St Martin's School of Art, 1971–4, and Royal College of Art, 1974–7. Group exhibitions included Simulacra, Riverside Studios, 1982, later ones Ace!, the Arts Council tour, 1996, and John Moores Liverpool Exhibition, 1997–8. He had a first solo exhibition at Cash/Newhouse Gallery, in New York, 1985, later ones including Anthony Reynolds Gallery from 1989, and Harry Zellweger, Basle, 1995.

William Powell WILKINS 1938– Draughtsman, printmaker, teacher and stained glass artist, born in Kersey, Suffolk, son of the writer Vaughan Wilkins. He was brought up in south Wales, attending Swansea College of Art, 1955–7, to study stained glass; Royal College of Art, 1957–60; then evening classes in drawing at Hammersmith School of Art. Among his subsequent positions was teaching art at Malvern College for several years and information officer for the Greater London Council's architects' department. He wrote on architecture for various publications, campaigning against ugliness. Won WAC Bursary, 1971; its Grant, 1978; and an Ingram Merrill Foundation Award, 1980, the year he was first international artist in residence, Artists for the Environment Foundation, Delaware Water Gap National Park, New Jersey. Group shows included Covent Garden Gallery, 1973; Agnew and Roland, Browse & Delbanco, both 1974; elected a member of 56 Group Wales, exhibiting with it extensively, 1975; and Gruenebaum Gallery, New York, 1987. Had a solo show at University College of Wales, Aberystwyth, 1970, later ones including Glynn Vivian Art Gallery, Swansea, 1989, and Piccadilly Gallery, 1991, with frequent shows across America. National Museum of Wales in Cardiff, WAC and University Colleges in Aberystwyth and Swansea hold examples. Lived at Llandeilo, Carmarthenshire.

Derek WILKINSON 1929– Artist in pastel, crayon and colour etching and teacher, born in Halifax, Yorkshire. He attended Blackpool School of Art, 1946–50, then Regional College of Art in Manchester, 1950–1. From 1951–3 did National Service, worked with Metal Box Company from 1953–7, then until 1989 was in department of art and design at Stockport College of Technology, latterly senior lecturer in charge of foundation studies. Wilkinson was a member of MAFA, also taking part in group shows at RA, RBA, Middlesbrough Drawing Biennale and Laing Exhibition. Had a series of solo exhibitions in London, Manchester, Preston, Stockport, Derby, Carlisle, Kendal and Blackpool. Walker Art Gallery in Liverpool and public galleries in Oldham, Salford, Sheffield and Stockport hold examples. Lived in Stockport, Cheshire.

Donald WILKINSON 1937– Artist in various media, born in Keswick, Cumbria. He studied at Carlisle College of Art, 1953–7, and Royal College of Art, 1959–62. Wilkinson was a protégé of Winifred Nicholson, whom he looked after in the last years of her life, holidaying with her in the Hebrides. His group exhibition appearances included Richard Demarco, Edinburgh, 1975; Victoria & Albert Museum, 1979; Invited artist, Ljubljana Print Biennale, 1987; and Anderson O'Day Gallery, 1989. Solo shows included Sheffield University, 1964; Abbot Hall Art Gallery, Kendal, 1987; and he shared a show at Gallery North, Cumbria, 1990. He was noted for light effects achieved in atmospheric landscapes, as in Langstrath after Rain, of 1982, held by Abbot Hall. Arts Council, British Council and other public collections hold his work. Lived in Brampton, near Carlisle, Cumbria.

Evelyn WILKINSON 1893–1968 Painter of flowers, born in Wu-King-Fu, Swatow, China, her father a missionary minister. She attended Edinburgh School of Art and showed at ROI, RA, SWA and RI. Lived for a time in London, her husband being the artist Norman Wilkinson.

Henry WILKINSON 1921– Engraver and teacher, born in Bath, Somerset, son of the artist H R Wilkinson. Initially educated at Peter Symonds' School, in Winchester, he then attended the School of Art there and later the Royal College of Art under Robert Austin and Malcolm Osborne. After World War II he held a number of teaching posts in art schools, including Richmond and Hammersmith, from 1949 joining the City and Guilds of London Art School as instructor in engraving. Exhibited RA, RE and elsewhere. Lived in London and then in Tatsfield, Kent.

Kate Stanley WILKINSON 1883– Landscape painter, born in London, who was married to another landscape painter, Reginald Wilkinson. After private education she studied art privately with Lucy Kemp-Welch, the Slade School of Fine Art and Heatherley's School of Fine Art. She exhibited extensively at ROI, also at SWA, RI, at Society of Sussex Painters, of which she was a member, and at Société des Artistes Français, where she gained an Hon. Mention in 1938. She lived near Tenterden, Kent.

Norman WILKINSON 1878–1971 Oil and watercolour painter, printmaker and poster designer, born in Cambridge.

Although early on he studied figure painting in Paris, further study with the river and coastal painter Louis Grier in Cornwall reinforced Wilkinson's growing belief that he should concentrate on marine subjects, of which he became a master. He also studied art at Portsmouth and Southsea School of Art and later taught there. His career as an illustrator began with a first acceptance by the *Illustrated London News* in 1898, a publication with which he was long associated. He travelled widely abroad, in Europe, the Mediterranean area and in North and South America. In both world wars Wilkinson was important in the development of camouflage techniques, and he presented a big series of pictures concerned with the war at sea to the nation. He showed widely, including the Fine Art Society, RBA, ROI, RI and Walker Art Gallery, Liverpool. Work in many public collections in Britain and abroad. His book *A Brush with Life* was published in 1969. Wilkinson's wife Evelyn was also an an artist.

Ronald Scotthorn WILKINSON 1920–1996 Watercolourist, born in Melton Mowbray, Leicestershire. He studied under H B Hewlett. By profession Wilkinson was a physician who specialised in medico-legal medicine. He completed his medical studies at Radcliffe Infirmary, Oxford, after which he attended postgraduate medical school. Showed with RA Summer Exhibition, Leicester Society of Artists and with Royal Society of Medicine Art Society. Had a solo exhibition with Fine Art Trade Guild in 1984. Lived in London.

Thomas William WILKINSON 1875–1950 Sculptor, mainly of portrait heads, who attended Bradford and Ipswich Schools of Art, being a member of Ipswich Art Club, 1907–49, and an associate of RBS. Exhibited at RA, Paris Salon and elsewhere and lived in Ipswich, Suffolk, for many years.

Maurice Canning WILKS 1910–1984 Landscape and portrait painter, born in Belfast, Northern Ireland, who began night classes at Belfast School of Art, won a scholarship to study full-time and had early success at RHA. Also showed at Victor Waddington Galleries in Dublin, at Oireachtas there, at Anderson & McAuley Gallery in Belfast, widely in North America and at RUA of which he was a member. Ulster Museum, Armagh County Museum and Bangor Town Hall hold examples. Oriel Gallery, Dublin, held a memorial retrospective in 1984.

Stephen WILLATS 1943– Artist, editor and publisher, who was born and continued to work in London. He employed a variety of media such as photographic prints, acrylic paint and Letraset text, mounted on panels. Willats was concerned with people's lives in the modern world, and said: "I am constantly looking for symbols of modern living that are readily identifiable as such and which I can embody in my work as recognisable catalysts that stimulate acts of transformation." By such transformations people "express their self-organisation, and self-identity." Willats attended Ealing School of Art, 1962–3. From 1965 he was editor and publisher of *Control* magazine, from 1972–3 director of The Centre for Behavioural Art, Gallery House. In 1979–80 Willats gained a DAAD Fellowship, West Berlin, and in 1990 was convenor of the symposium Art Creating Society at Museum of Modern Art in Oxford. From 1964's one-man show at Chester Beatty Research Centre Willats had many solo exhibitions in Britain and abroad and was latterly represented by Lisson Gallery. He was constantly putting forward his views in statements and writings in *Control* and other publications; was involved in audio tapes; gave lectures and papers; and produced books and bookworks, some published by Coracle Press. Arts Council, Victoria & Albert Museum and many other public collections in Britain and abroad hold his work.

David WILLETTS 1939– Painter and teacher, born in Birmingham, attending its College of Art, then Royal Academy Schools. Had a solo show at Camden Arts Centre in 1967, later ones including Coracle Press Gallery from 1977. In 1980 Willetts was included in the critic William Packer's selection for the Arts Council touring exhibition The British Art Show. The Arts Council holds Willetts' 1973 acrylic on board On the Return Journey. Lived in Nottingham for some years, teaching at its College of Art.

Suzanne WILLEY 1961– Painter, born in London, where she remained based. She studied at Bath Academy of Art, 1981–4, and Goldsmiths' College School of Art, 1986–8. After appearing in Whitechapel Open in 1987, she was in group exhibitions at Air Gallery and Anderson O'Day in 1988 and in 1990 in LG and Austin/Desmond Fine Art's Christmas exhibition. Willey was interested in found images, such as Hergé's *Tintin* cartoon strip, the basis for her Untitled canvas in 1991–2 John Moores Exhibition, Liverpool. Another Untitled canvas was included in the 1992 Norwich Gallery/Kent Institute of Art and Design South & East show.

Katherine WILLIAM-POWLETT 1911– Watercolourist, born in Fareham, Hampshire. The Honourable Mrs William-Powlett was the daughter of Admiral of the Fleet Baron Keyes, was educated privately and studied painting with Edward Wesson. Was a member of SWA, 1966–85, also Chelsea Art Society, Armed Forces Art Society and Winchester Art Society. Showed with RI, RBA, RSMA and elsewhere, having a series of solo exhibitions at Clarges Gallery from 1970 and at Bladen Gallery, 1977. Signed work K W-P. Lived in London.

Albert WILLIAMS 1923– Painter in oil, notably of flowers, born in Hove Sussex, son of the painter Arthur Williams. Studied with father and at Brighton College of Art. His work appeared on the covers of a number of national magazines such as *Homes and Gardens* and *Woman's Pictorial*, *Woman* and *Woman's Journal*. Showed at RA, with Brighton Arts Club of which he was a member and elsewhere in the provinces. Lived in Brighton.

Alex WILLIAMS fl. from 1970s– Painter, illustrator, printmaker and teacher, studied at St Martin's School of Art. For a period after graduating he taught and ran his own screenprinting business before settling near Hay-on-Wye, Breconshire. In early 1980s worked in California, where his work became known to a wider public, including show business notables. Williams' interest in wildlife subjects lent itself to work for *Country Living* magazine, British Waterfowl Association, the Rare Breeds Survival Trust and National Trust. He illustrated Richard Buckley's award-winning children's book *The Bird Who Couldn't Fly*. Had a solo show at John Noott Twentieth Century, Broadway, 1991.

Andrew WILLIAMS 1954– Painter and administrator, born in Barry, Glamorgan. He studied art and art history at Edinburgh University and Edinburgh College of Art, 1972–7. From 1979–80 Williams supervised the Karolyi Foundation at Vence, in the south of France, and in 1984 he worked in New York. Williams soon established himself as an exhibitor in Britain and abroad and had several shows at 369 Gallery, Edinburgh. In both landscape and in paintings of the figure Williams' work was notable for its sensuous, lush and colourful qualities.

Archie WILLIAMS 1922–1993 Painter, collage artist, draughtsman and teacher, born in Swansea where he first worked as a draughtsman with a firm of reinforced concrete engineers before war service abroad. In 1946 he did a short course at Academy of Art in Florence, then attended Swansea College of Art, 1946–51, remaining for a short period to lecture. For four years from 1952 Williams was a draughtsman with the Whitefriars Stained Glass Studio and then began a series of teaching posts, mainly in the Swansea area. Showed with Swansea Art Society; Howard Roberts Gallery in Cardiff; and in other mixed shows with SWG, SEA and at Royal National Eisteddfod. Glynn Vivian Art Gallery, Swansea, gave Williams a retrospective in 1996. He was noted for his architectural drawings and watercolours. CASW holds his collage Haven.

Aubrey WILLIAMS 1926–1990 Painter, born in Georgetown, British Guiana, now Guyana. His first art education was with the Working People's Art Group, but it took an encounter with the Warrau Indian tribe to decide him to pursue the course he did in painting. Coming to England in 1952 Williams decided against a career in agricultural engineering and attended St Martin's School of Art, 1952–3, having his first one-man show in 1954 at the Archer Gallery. In the mid-1960s he was active in the London-based Caribbean Artists' Movement, he was showing widely in group exhibitions in Britain and abroad and was painting a series of murals. After a while Williams' career tended to be diverted to fringe galleries when he fell out of general favour. Arshile Gorky, the pre-Colombian iconography of Guyana and in the 1970s a series of pictures inspired by the Russian composer Shostakovitch all had their place in Williams' art. Among a series of one-man shows were several in the October Gallery in the 1980s, with a retrospective in Tokyo in 1989, another at Whitechapel Art Gallery, 1998. Was represented in The Other Story, Hayward Gallery and tour, 1989–90. Lived latterly in London and Miami and is represented in Arts Council and other collections.

Barbara Moray WILLIAMS 1911–1975 Wood engraver and decorative watercolourist, born in Petersfield, Hampshire. She studied at Winchester School of Art, 1929–31, and at the Royal College of Art, gaining her diploma in 1934, teachers including Robert Sargent Austin and Malcolm Osborne. She married the artist Magnus A Arnason – after which she sometimes signed work Barbara Arnason – and went to live in Iceland. Exhibited at the RA, RE, NEAC and widely in group shows on the continent, in Scandinavia and North and South America. Had three solo exhibitions in Paris in the mid-1960s.

Bruce WILLIAMS 1962– Painter and sculptor, born in Münster, Germany. He studied at Winchester School of Art and Gwent College of Art and Design. In 1992 Williams' big acrylic on canvas Black Snow was included in Norwich Gallery/Kent Institute of Art and Design's show East & South. This drew on images from national newspapers and the artist's own photographs. Williams was engaged on public art with Artangel Trust, ACGB and Brighton International Festival. His permanent sculpture, Kiss Wall, in Brighton "addressed sexual and racial politics through six public kisses". Lived in Brighton, Sussex.

Catrin WILLIAMS 1966– Painter who, after an arts foundation course at Bangor, gained a bachelor's degree in fine art from Cardiff College of Art, 1989, then became a self-employed artist. In 1990 Williams received a grant to visit Germany, Czechoslovakia and France with the rock group Yr Anhrefn, painting on stage as the group performed. She spent much time running art workshops in Welsh schools, also setting up a project for women in Glasgow as part of its festival of culture. Williams won second prize in the fine art competition at the National Eisteddfod of Wales at Bro Delyn in 1991. Her childhood on a hill farm near Bala, Wales, was an influence on her colourful, vibrant work as were her travels and, latterly, the music of John Cale, a Welshman who lived and worked in New York for several decades, formerly a member of Velvet Underground. Williams worked with the Arad Goch theatre company and had successful exhibitions at Oriel Pendeitch Caernarfon, Stones Bistro in the town, Ancrum Gallery near Jedburgh, Canolfan y Plase, Y Bala and at the National Eisteddfod, Aberystwyth. Lived at Caernarfon, Gwynedd.

Charles WILLIAMS 1965– Painter, born in Evanston, Illinois, America. Graduated in fine art at Maidstone College of Art, 1985–9, then did a postgraduate course at Royal Academy Schools until 1992. Among prizes won were the Academy's silver medal for painting and the Richard Ford Award for study in Spain. He was also a Winsor & Newton Young Artist in Watercolour in 1992. He showed at RA Summer Exhibition, at Mercury Gallery and at the Mall Galleries in the Into the 90s exhibition of postgraduate work. Williams was commissioned by the oil company Chevron to illustrate its 1993 calendar with Britain's native trees and in the same year had a solo show at Cadogan Contemporary. Lived in Maidstone, Kent.

Chester WILLIAMS 1921–1994 Portrait and landscape painter, born in Hollywood, California, America, where he was educated alongside the children of film stars. He arrived in England during World War II to work on camouflage, later attending the Accademia in Venice and in 1954 the Courtauld Institute of Art, by which time he was married to Lucy Halford, who ran a Mayfair public relations agency. For years they ran a mill in Ellingham, Norfolk, as a centre for the arts, notable artists staying there and judging exhibitions. Among Williams' portrait subjects were the writer Rebecca West and the ballerina Svetlana Beriosova. For about five years Williams painted in Oman, effectively court painter to the Sultan. Showed widely abroad. Final two solo shows were at Patrick Seale Gallery in 1983 and at Spink & Son, 1986. Died at Moreton-in-Marsh, Gloucestershire. Memorial exhibition at Cadogan Contemporary, 1996.

Claudia WILLIAMS 1933– Portrait painter who favoured oil, and teacher, born in Purley, Surrey, married to the artist Gwilym Pritchard. Attended Eothen School, Caterham, where the art mistress Christine Walker was an inspiration, then studying under Bernard Meadows at Chelsea School of Art. For a time was a part-time teacher in schools and for Workers' Educational Association. Was a member of RCamA, also exhibiting with Royal National Eisteddfod, NWG and elsewhere; showed with her husband, notably in Bangor at the Arts Festival and at the Art Gallery; and had solo shows at Tegfryn Art Gallery Menai Bridge, living for a time at Llanfaes, Anglesey. Her portraits included the composer William Mathias and the children of the Marquis and Marchioness of Anglesey. WAC, Gwynedd and Cardiff Education Authorities and University College of Wales, Aberystwyth, hold examples.

David WILLIAMS 1943– Painter, printmaker and teacher, born in Torquay, Devon. He attended South Devon College of Art, 1959–64, then Hornsey College of Art, 1965–7. His work included forms derived from architecture, graphs, computer printouts and mass production motifs without being representational. Showed at RA, Camden Arts Centre, Woodlands Art Gallery and Battersea Arts Centre.

David WILLIAMS 1946– Painter, draughtsman, printmaker and teacher, born in London, where he continued to live and teach. He studied at St Martin's School of Art, 1965–9, then Goldsmiths' College School of Art, 1973. Worked for a period for Greenwich Theatre Gallery and taught in Blackheath, southeast London. Among his exhibitions was a solo show at Woodlands Art Gallery, 1980.

Emrys WILLIAMS 1958– Painter, born in Liverpool, who studied at Slade School of Fine Art, 1976–80. From the mid-1970s he won a number of awards, including the Boise Travelling Scholarship and Robert Ross Scholarship, in 1980; Minor Prize at John Moores Exhibition, Liverpool, 1982–3; and third prize at Royal National Eisteddfod, 1985. He gained a Stewart Powell Bowen Fellowship (artist-in-residence at Mostyn Art Gallery, Llandudno, 1983), then in 1985 was artist-in-residence at South Hill Park Art Centre & Wilde Theatre, Bracknell. Took part in many mixed shows, notably in Wales. Had solo shows at Andrew Knight Gallery in Cardiff and Wrexham Arts Centre in 1984; later ones included Lanchester Polytechnic Gallery, Coventry, and Benjamin Rhodes Gallery, 1986; and Glynn Vivian Art Gallery, Swansea, 1996. CASW holds his work.

Emyr Wyn WILLIAMS 1965– Painter whose output included abstract works of great variety, such as his two acrylics on canvas Untitled and Anthraline, in Royal Over-Seas League Opens for 1994 and 1995. Born in Merthyr Tydfil, Glamorganshire, he studied at Howard Gardens Art College, Cardiff, and University of Reading. Won a first prize at Wales Art Fair, 1993. Had a solo show at KF Gallery, Boston, America, 1988; Road to Colour at Cyfarthfa Castle Museum & Art Gallery, Merthyr, 1990; and Geoff Evans Fine Art/Centre Gallery, 1993. Cyfarthfa and the corporate collections of Arthur Andersen & Company and Ernst & Young hold examples. In 1990–1 Williams was commissioned to carry out work for Merthyr's British Rail station.

Enid WILLIAMS 1922– Artist in oil, watercolour and gouache, teacher, born in Stoke-on-Trent, Staffordshire. Her main interest was "in colour and shape relationships rather than in subject-matter". She was a full-time student at Didsbury College, Manchester, 1949–50, then a part-time student at Manchester Regional College of Art, 1958–61. Taught in Manchester area, 1953–82, obtaining an Open University degree in 1973. Williams' mixed shows included Salford, Stockport and Bury Art Galleries; the Ginnel and Colin Jellicoe Galleries, in Manchester; UMIST, Manchester; and Mall Galleries. Had a solo exhibition at Salford Players Theatre, 1978, later ones including Manchester Business School and Memorial Gallery, Lancastrian Hall, Swinton, both 1991. She won the first John Clare Award at Salford Art Gallery, 1984 and Campus Prize, Contemporary Salford, Salford University, 1987. Many private collections in Britain, Japan and South America hold examples. Lived in Worsley, Manchester.

Evelyn WILLIAMS 1929– Sculptor, painter and draughtsman, born and lived in London, married for a time to the painter Michael Fussell. She was educated at Summerhill School, St Martin's School of Art, 1944–7, and Royal College of Art, 1947–50. She gained a first-class diploma there and the E Q Henriques Prize for Drawing. Williams showed widely in group exhibitions, winning a first prize for sculpture in John Moores Liverpool Exhibition, 1961. Other venues included Camden Arts Centre, 1972; ICA, Women's Images of Men, 1980; Tolly Cobbold 5th National Touring Exhibition, 1985; Gimpel Fils, 1987; and Victoria Art Gallery, Bath, 1992. After showing solo at Woodstock Gallery in 1958 Williams was a regular exhibitor. She had a retrospective at Whitechapel Art Gallery in 1972. A fine head and figure draughtsman, Williams completed a series of sculptures of people in prison, powerful and harrowing, as shown at Cleveland Bridge Gallery, Bath, 1991. A University of Warwick show toured, 1994–5. Arts Council, Victoria & Albert Museum and Graves Art Gallery, Sheffield, hold examples.

Ferelith Eccles WILLIAMS: *see* **ECCLES**

Fred WILLIAMS 1927–1982 Painter and printmaker, a major figure in modern Australian art, born in Melbourne. He attended the National Gallery School, 1943–7, and George Bell Art School, 1946–50, then travelled to London and made his living as a framer. While there he attended Chelsea School of Art and Central School part-time, learning etching. His music-hall and London series of paintings and prints are reminiscent of Sickert, Daumier and Goya. In London Williams showed with Australian Artists' Association. Returned to Australia in 1957, initially framing part-time. Moving from the city to Upwey, in the hills near Melbourne, in 1963, he began to develop a strong interest in his native landscape, after 1967 working in the real outback. Gradually he pushed nearer to abstraction, although close inspection proves his pictures to be meticulously constructed records of scenes. Moved to Hawthorn, Melbourne, in 1969, where eventually he died. In 1964 Williams had travelled in Europe on the Helena Rubenstein Travelling Art Scholarship. He became a member of the Commonwealth Art Advisory Board, 1972–4; of the Visual Arts Board of the Australia Council, 1973–6; and was a trustee, Council of the National Gallery of Australia, Canberra, 1975–82. Between 1957–82 Williams had 23 solo commercial shows in Australian galleries and won many prizes. In 1995 Marlborough Fine Art (London) held a major show. National Gallery of Australia, National Gallery of Victoria, all major regional galleries in Australia, Tate Gallery, Metropolitan Museum and Museum of Modern Art in New York and Victoria & Albert Museum hold examples.

Georgina WILLIAMS: *see* **Georgina SAUNDERS**

Gerard WILLIAMS 1959– Artist using a variety of materials such as wood, plasterboard and found objects, born in Manchester. He studied at the Polytechnic there, 1977–8, then graduated with honours from Brighton Polytechnic, 1978–81. Took part in many group shows, including Whitechapel Open at Whitechapel Art Gallery, from 1985; Mario Flecha Gallery, 1987; Tanja Grunert Gallery, Cologne, 1988; and Contemporary Art Center, Athens, 1990. Had solo shows at Interim Art from 1986; Anthony d'Offay Gallery, 1989; and Galleria Franz Paludetta, Turin, 1990. Arts Council holds his work.

Glynn WILLIAMS 1939– Sculptor and teacher, born in Shrewsbury, Shropshire. He attended Wolverhampton College of Art, 1955–60, winning a post-diploma year there in 1961. Having won a Rome Scholarship in sculpture, he attended British School in Rome, 1961–3, and travelled widely in southern Europe. Began to teach, among his appointments being professor of sculpture at Royal College of Art. Showed extensively in group exhibitions throughout Britain and had a series of one-man shows including Bernard Jacobson Gallery. Commissions included Leeds City Council sculpture for Seacroft Civic Centre and British School in Rome garden fountain. Although he was in the 1960s working in a dematerialised style, by the mid-1970s Williams had moved towards a Henry Moore-like organic style. Began carving in stone, taking ancient sculpture as a starting point, and by the early 1990s was slicing and rebuilding his figures. Arts Council holds his work. Retrospective at Margam Park, Port Talbot, 1992, another at Atkinson Gallery, Millfield, Street, 1997. Lived in London.

Graham WILLIAMS 1951– Artist, notably a printmaker, and teacher who studied at Wrexham, 1966–70, Hull, 1970–3, Liverpool, 1974, and Alsager, 1980–1, becoming a teacher at Knowsley Central Tertiary College. His exhibitions included Bluecoat Invitational, Liverpool, 1982, Sheffield Open, and Merseyside Artists touring show, organised by Walker Art Gallery, Liverpool, from 1985, the year he had an etching residency there. Williams also gained a Radio City commission.

Guy WILLIAMS 1920– Painter, printmaker, writer and teacher, born in Mold, Flintshire. He studied at Manchester College of Art, 1937–40, then after the war at Hornsey School of Art, 1946–50. Taught at Parmiter's School. Among a number of instructional books by him were *Pencil Drawing*, *Collecting Pictures* and *Making Mobiles*. He showed at RA Summer Exhibition, SEA, AIA and in the provinces and London County Council held his work. Lived in London.

Harry Hughes WILLIAMS 1892–1953 Prolific painter, illuminator and teacher, born at Pentraeth, Anglesey, son of a farmer, whose family moved to Mynydd Mwyn Farm, Llandrygarn, in 1894. Because he concealed a broken hip after falling from a building when aged 11, Hughes Williams was always disabled. After secondary education at Liverpool's Collegiate School, from 1911–14 Hughes Williams studied at Liverpool City School of Art, won a scholarship to the Royal College of Art and there gained a European travelling scholarship, which the war stopped him taking up. His teachers had included W R Lethaby and W C Penn. Prevented by poor health from war service, Hughes Williams returned to Anglesey, created a studio from a farm granary and began a tough life as a freelance artist, often surviving through commemorative paintings and illuminated addresses. In 1938 Hughes Williams was appointed art master at Llangefni Grammar School, the year he became a full member of RCamA, having first shown there in 1918. Also exhibited at RA; in a Welsh exhibition at Hugo Lang Gallery, Liverpool, 1948; at Paris Salon, 1951; in America and elsewhere in the provinces. Had a solo show at Gladwells Fine Art Dealers, 1949, and was given another at National Library of Wales, Aberystwyth, 1993. Died after a fall at Mynydd Mwyn Farm.

Hubert WILLIAMS 1905–1989 Painter, printmaker and illustrator, his artistic career began when he won first prize in a painting competition to launch the *Children's Newspaper*. Studied at Royal Academy Schools, 1927–32, where he was a Landseer Scholar. Also studied at St Martin's School of Art and Central School of Arts and Crafts. During World War II he was engaged on map drawing. He became a freelance artist noted for his drawings of London buildings and street scenes, work appearing in *The Times*, *The Observer* and *Blue Peter Magazine*. Williams also undertook portraiture and the illustration of children's books. Showed at RA, RP, RI and was for a time a council member of

SGA. Imperial War Museum, Ferens Art Gallery in Hull and many other museums hold his work. Lived in Prestbury, Gloucestershire.

Idris Elgina WILLIAMS: *see* **Idris AERON**

Ivor WILLIAMS 1908–1982 Painter, son of the Welsh painter Christopher Williams. Born in London, studied art at the Central School of Arts and Crafts and the Slade School of Fine Art. Exhibited in mixed shows at the RA, Palser Gallery, SWG, WAC and the Royal National Eisteddfod. One-man shows included David Morgan Ltd, Cardiff, and National Museum of Wales, Turner House, Penarth. While at the Slade Williams won first prize for portrait painting, and he was commissioned to paint a number of portraits and official pictures, such as Field-Marshal Montgomery receiving the freedom of the City of Newport, for Newport City Council, and a portrait of Lord Harlech for the National Library of Wales, Aberystwyth. The National Museum of Wales and CASW own his work. Lived at Llandaff, Cardiff.

Jacqueline WILLIAMS 1962– Painter, a Colourist especially successful in her depictions of interiors. She was born in Lincoln and studied at Gloucester College of Art, 1982–5, then Royal Academy Schools, where she was an outstanding student, 1985–8. She gained the *Antique Collector*'s Prize, 1987; de Segonzac Travel Scholarship, 1988; and the Elizabeth Greenshields Award in 1988 and 1992. She took part in many mixed shows, including London South Bank Picture Show, 1986; Robinson College, Cambridge, 1987; ROI Winsor & Newton finalist, 1987; Ken Howard's Choice, at Arts Club, 1991; NEAC, 1992. She had the first of a series of solo exhibitions at New Grafton Gallery, after graduation, 1989, a sell-out. Cheltenham and Gloucester Building Society and CASW hold her work.

Jan WILLIAMS 1961– Artist born in Birkenhead, Merseyside, who did a foundation course at Wirral College of Art and Design, 1979–80; gained a fine art honours degree at Portsmouth Polytechnic, 1980–3; then took a short course in garden design with John Brookes at Denman's, Fontwell, 1989. Williams created collages using sources as diverse as the beach, car boot sales, rubbish tips, lager cans and dead mosquitoes. She cut and edited her material in order to "arrange the resulting pieces systematically according to colour, tone and subject matter". Her most ambitious project was in 1997, for the refurbished Quay Arts Centre, Newport, Isle of Wight. Group shows included Structure 17, Perpignan, France, 1984; One by Sixteen, Aspex Gallery, Portsmouth, 1989; and Artists of Wirral, Williamson Art Gallery, Birkenhead, 1995. Showed solo with Rebecca Hossack Gallery from 1995.

Jane WILLIAMS 1964– Painter, born in Hitchin, Hertfordshire, who studied at Bedford College of Higher Education and Norwich School of Art. She gained 3rd Prize, South Bank Picture Show, 1992, and GMC Painting Award, Eastern Open, 1995. Other group appearances included Christopher Hull Gallery, 1990; West Wharf Gallery, Cardiff, 1991; Laing Art Competition, Mall Galleries, 1993; Copperfield Road Open Studios/Whitechapel Art Gallery, 1994; and Royal Over-Seas League Open, 1995.

Joan WILLIAMS 1922– Printmaker, watercolourist and teacher, born in Pontypridd, Glamorgan. She studied at High Wycombe School of Art and Royal College of Art and went on to become head of the printmaking department at Maidstone College of Art, having also taught at Medway College of Art and Shusta College, California. She was a member of the Printmakers' Council, RE and RWS. Illustrated books for Oxford University Press. Was an invited artist for a series of exhibitions in contintal Europe, including Ljubljana, Yugoslavia, 1971; Frechen, West Germany, 1972–4; Epinal, France, 1975; and Biella, Italy, 1980. Group exhibitions included RA. Had a solo show with The Richard Bradley Atelier, Norfolk, 1971, later ones including Newport Art Gallery, 1976, and Portland State University, Oregon, 1980. Arts Council, WAC, Department of the Environment and many public galleries in British provinces hold her work. Lived in High Wycombe, Buckinghamshire, and Aylesford, Kent.

Jolán Polatschek WILLIAMS 1908–1988 Landscape artist, painter of abstracts and printmaker, with a delicate sense of colour, who was born in Bielitz, Austria, and initially studied in Vienna, Craców and Munich. After meeting David Jeffrey Williams, founder of the Pit Ponies Protection Society, in 1927, at a meeting led by the Theosophical teacher Krishnamurti, the couple married in 1928 and settled in north London. The works of Rudolph Steiner, mysticism and Theosophy continued to absorb her. Jolán was now able to study at the Central and City & Guilds Schools of Art. She exhibited extensively and internationally, including RA, NEAC, RBA, LG, Leger, Redfern and Whitechapel Galleries, Senefelder Club, SWE and elsewhere. Solo shows included Wertheim, Beaux Arts and Drian Galleries, New Vision Centre and University of Surrey. Her work is in extensive collections in Britain and abroad. John Denham Gallery held a substantial retrospective in 1991.

Kit WILLIAMS fl. from 1970s– Self-taught painter and author, brought up in rural Kent in post-World War II years. Began painting while serving in the Royal Navy. In 1972 one of his pictures was chosen for John Moores Liverpool Exhibition. He subsequently had a series of solo shows in London galleries and several foreign travelling exhibitions. Williams' show at The Bruton Street Gallery in 1994, including works meticulously and luminously painted in oil on gesso panel, showed his love of curious detail and enigma. He was the author of several popular books, notably *Masquerade*. This sold a million copies and clues in its illustrations prompted a treasure hunt for a buried golden hare pendant set with precious stones. The hare's discovery in 1982 ended a two-and-a-half years' search by about two million people.

Kyffin WILLIAMS 1918– Painter and teacher, born in Llangefni, Anglesey, full name John Kyffin Williams. He was educated at Shrewsbury School, from 1936–9 was a land agent in Pwllheli, then in 1941–4 he attended the Slade School Fine Art

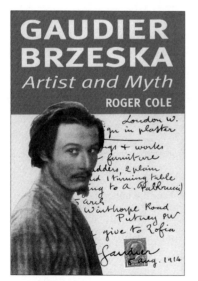

during its evacuation to Oxford. He was senior art master at Highgate School, 1944–73, in 1968 gaining a Winston Churchill Fellowship to record the Welsh in Patagonia. Williams was president of RCamA in 1969–76 and was elected RA in 1974. The artist was especially noted for his palette-knifed Welsh mountainsides, the cottages and the weather, which often gave his pictures a rather dour character. Williams was also a fine portraitist. He exhibited at Colnaghi's from 1948, at the Leicester Galleries, Howard Roberts Gallery in Cardiff, Thackeray Gallery and Tegfryn Art Gallery, Menai Bridge. In 1987 a retrospective exhibition toured from National Museum of Wales, Cardiff. Williams wrote two volumes of autobiography: *Across the Straits*, 1973, and *A Wider Sky*, 1991. His pictures are held by Arts Council, WAC, both the National Museum and National Library of Wales, National Portrait Gallery and elsewhere. Lived in Pwllfanogl, Llanfairpwyll, Gwynedd.

Lois WILLIAMS 1953– Sculptor, maker of objects and teacher, born in Denbigh, north Wales. She abandoned an early intention to become a musician, instead studying at Wrexham Technical College, 1971–2; graduated from Manchester Polytechnic, 1972–5; then did a postgraduate year at Goldsmiths' College, 1975–6. For many years she taught in a secondary school while practising as an artist, dividing her time between Sheffield, Yorkshire, and north Wales. Williams used a wide variety of found objects to create wall- and floor-mounted works. Her Welsh heritage and femininity were both important to the creation of subtle and allusive pieces. Group exhibitions included Northern Young Contemporaries at Whitworth Art Gallery, Manchester, 1975; Sculpture by Women, Ikon Gallery, Birmingham, 1983; Off the Shelf, Rochdale Art Gallery, 1986; New North, Tate Gallery in Liverpool and tour, 1990; and Intimate Portraits, Glynn Vivian Gallery, Swansea, 1955. In 1995–6 a retrospective of her work from 1981 was held at Oriel Mostyn, Llandudno, and Wrexham Library Arts Centre, then was toured.

Lucy Gwendolen WILLIAMS 1870–1955 Sculptor and painter who studied at Wimbledon and Royal Colleges of Art and at Atelier Colarossi, Paris. Among several medals won was a silver at National Eisteddfod in Wales. She travelled in continental Europe and America and was a prolific exhibitor, mixed shows including RA, Walker Art Gallery in Liverpool, RSA, RHA and RCamA, and in 1935 she had a solo exhibition at Brook Street Art Gallery. Public galleries in Cardiff, Leeds and Liverpool acquired statuettes by her, National Library of Wales in Aberystwyth having a representative collection. Lived for a time in London.

Margaret Lindsay WILLIAMS fl. from c.1910–1960 Portrait and decorative artist, born in Cardiff, who attended Cardiff Technical College, where she won a gold medal for art; at Kensington under Sir Arthur Cope; at the Royal Academy Schools, where she gained a string of medals and prizes; then in Italy and the Netherlands. She was a member of RCamA and SWAS, also showing at RA, National Museum of Wales in Cardiff, Walker Art Gallery in Liverpool, Knoedler Gallery, New York, and Corcoran Gallery in Washington. Lived for a time at Dinas Powis, Glamorgan.

Mary WILLIAMS fl. from late 1930s– Painter, born in Ottery St Mary, Devon, where she settled at Sidmouth. She attended Royal Albert Memorial School of Art in Exeter. In 1957 Jack Beddington included her 1938 watercolour Boats on Beer Beach in his book *Young Artists of Promise*. She became a member of RWA and SWA, also exhibiting at RA, RBA and elsewhere, having a solo show at Royal Albert Memorial Museum in Exeter in 1974. It, RWA and Sunderland Art Gallery hold examples.

Michael WILLIAMS 1936– Painter, teacher and editor, born in Patna, India. After reading modern history at Oxford, 1957–60, he studied art history and painting in Paris, 1960–2, then lectured at St Martin's School of Art, 1962–9, becoming head of department there, 1969–71. He moved to Wales in 1971 and in that year began teaching fine art at Goldsmiths' College School of Art, reducing his teaching in 1980 to concentrate on painting. He was a part-time lecturer at Cheltenham and Gloucester College of Higher Education. In the early 1980s Williams was active in the Association of Artists and Designers in Wales as editor of *Link*, in 1985 being elected to the 56 Group. From the second half of the 1980s a WAC travel grant and a Greek government scholarship enabled Williams to paint in Greece. That country and the area where he lived were favourite subjects for oil paintings and watercolours which meticulously depicted the landscape. The resulting pictures were shown in solo exhibitions at Austin/Desmond Fine Art from 1988. Williams showed, too, in mixed exhibitions, including LG, 1964; John Moores Exhibition, Liverpool, 1967; a 56 Group touring show in 1985; and Fine Art Society, 1990.

Morris Meredith WILLIAMS: *see* **MEREDITH WILLIAMS**

Moss WILLIAMS 1894–1975 Painter and sculptor, born in Caernarvon, an area where he spent most of his life. He began painting as a child, contributing to the children's section of the Franco-British Exhibition in 1906. Went on to take part in many group shows, mainly in Wales, including Royal National Eisteddfod, where won two first prizes for sculpture; RCamA; WAC; and Paris Salon, where he gained an Hon. Mention. In 1972 had solo show at Arfon Gallery, Caernarvon. National Library of Wales, Aberystwyth, and Welsh Office hold his work.

Nerys Prys WILLIAMS: *see* **NERYS**

Norah Marguerite WILLIAMS 1906–1988 Illustrator, commercial artist and teacher born in Birmingham. Studied at its School of Arts and Crafts and after several years working for Cadbury Brothers was an occupational therapist with Ipswich and East Suffolk Hospital for almost 35 years from the early 1940s, teaching crafts at Ipswich Civic College, 1960–73. Showed with Art Club in Ipswich, Suffolk, where she lived.

Peter Ernest WILLIAMS 1925– Artist in wide range of media and teacher, born in Bebington, Cheshire, where he continued to live. He studied at Liverpool College of Art and went on to teach in local schools having gained his art teacher's diploma. Showed at Liverpool Academy and elsewhere in the northwest of England and painted murals in churches. Liverpool University holds his work.

Rachel WILLIAMS 1970– Painter, born in Coventry, Warwickshire, who studied at Nuneaton College of Technology and Art, 1990–1, Liverpool John Moores University, 1991–4, and Royal Academy Schools, 1994–7. Group exhibitions included Northern Graduates at New Academy Gallery, 1993; Making a Mark, Mall Galleries, 1995; Premiums, RA from 1996; and John Moores Liverpool Exhibition, 1997–8. Lived in north London.

Richard James WILLIAMS 1876–1964 Illustrator of children's books, painter and teacher, born in Hereford, who attended Cardiff University College; he studied art in Cardiff, Birmingham and London, winning two scholarships and a gold medal. He was a member of RCamA, 1936, and Malvern Art Club, also showing at RI, RBSA, RWA and SWAS. Victoria & Albert Museum, National Museum of Wales in Cardiff and British Museum hold examples. Became headmaster of Worcester School of Arts and Crafts, living in the city.

Robin WILLIAMS 1961– Painter and poet, born in Bangor, Caernarvonshire, who studied at Camberwell School of Arts and Crafts, where he took part in group shows, 1988–91. Was also included in Royal Over-Seas Open, 1994. Poetry Now Publications published his work.

Sarah WILLIAMS 1966– Artist working in a wide range of media and multi-media, born in Plymouth, Devon, aspects of nature being primary inspirations. Williams studied at Plymouth College of Art and Design, 1982–4; graduated from Camberwell School of Art, 1984–7, with further work in 1987–8; then gained her master's degree at Royal College of Art, 1988–90. Among awards was one in 1982–4 to design and create a silver salver for the Lord Mayor's civic collection in London. In 1986 Williams had work experience in the Goldsmiths' Assay Office, and metalwork, jewellery and silversmithing were key features of her art. Showed at London Institute Gallery, 1988, was included in West Tokyo-to-Milan touring exhibition, 1993, and in that year was in Ist RWA Open Sculpture Exhibition. In 1991 Williams set up own workshop in south London.

Sheldon WILLIAMS: *see* **A OSCAR**

Stan WILLIAMS 1948– Painter and teacher, born in New Chapel, Pembrokeshire. He was taught by Aneurin Jones and studied at Swansea Art College, 1966–71. Worked for Urdd (The Welsh League of Youth), 1971–5; taught in Cardigan, 1975–84; and from then taught at Ysgol Dyffrin Teifi. Williams created richly coloured Welsh landscapes and showed with West Wales Arts and in many Eisteddfods, gaining a second prize at Llanrwst in 1989. In 1995 had a solo show at New Library Gallery, Cardigan. The church at Dinas Cross, Pembrokeshire, has a stained glass window by him.

Stephen WILLIAMS fl. from 1970s– Artist and teacher, born and lived in London, who studied at Byam Shaw School of Art with Bill Jacklin, Mike Upton and John Flavin, and at John Moores University with Merilyn Smith. Visiting lectureships included Universities of London, Wolverhampton and Falmouth and Byam Shaw School of Art; State University of New York, America; Poznan Academy of Fine Art, Poland; Tretchikov Academy of Fine and Applied Arts, Russia; and Tasmania University, Australia. In 1982 Williams was co-founder of the Mental Health Art Group at Erconwald Mental Health Centre, from 1986 being a founder and member of the Riverside Artist Group Riverside Studios. Won a series of British Council and Foreign Office Travel Awards. In 1987 Williams was set designer for Sam Dowling's *The Cauldron*, at Tabard Theatre. Curated a series of shows, including International Artists' Centre, Poznan, Poland, 1993, and On the shelf, at Kingsgate Workshops, 1995. Took part in many shows internationally, solo exhibitions including Mario Flecha Gallery, 1988, and Boat Pictures, St John's Studios, 1991. New Museum of Modern Art, New York; Tyler Museum, Oswego; Museum of Modern Art, Lodz; and Power Collection, Museum of Modern Art in Sydney hold examples.

Stephen Lionel WILLIAMS fl. from 1960s– Painter, draughtsman, printmaker and teacher who studied at Liverpool College of Art, 1966–8; Harris College School of Art, 1968–70; and St Katharine's College of Education, Liverpool, 1970–3. As well as teaching in Liverpool he directed the Bridge Arts Centre in Widnes, Cheshire, where he lived. Showed in mixed exhibitions at Mall Galleries and RSA and in northwest of England, having a solo show at Pentagon Gallery, Stoke-on-Trent.

Sybil Charlotte WILLIAMS 1915– Painter, wood engraver and teacher, brought up in Wales. Attended Newport School of Art and Hornsey School of Art. Showed with NEAC, WIAC and South Wales Art Society, signing work S C W. Lived in Pontypool, Monmouthshire.

Thomas Ellis WILLIAMS 1903–1987 Self-taught artist in line, brought up in the Runcorn area of Cheshire, where he continued to live. Showed at NEAC, RCamA and extensively in the north of England. Died in Halton General Hospital.

Vera K WILLIAMS 1912–c.1980 Oil and watercolour painter and miniaturist. Born in Witley, Surrey, she studied art at Godalming Art School, in 1928, with Victor Wyatt Burnand. She wrote on the art of miniature painting and exhibited regularly from the early 1930s for about 40 years, including one-man shows in the late 1930s. Venues included RA, RMS and Leighton House. Lived in London.

David WILLIAMS-ELLIS 1959– Figure and portrait sculptor, born in Ireland, who was educated there and in England. In 1977–8 he studied drawing with Nerina Simi in Florence, being a part-time apprentice with local woodcarvers. In 1978–80 Williams-Ellis studied marble carving at Carrara, in 1981–2 working under Clive

Duncan at Sir John Cass School of Art in London, where he remained based. Williams-Ellis soon established a reputation as a portrait sculptor. Among his subjects were the Countess of Belmore, 1984; William Vestey, 1986; a large bronze eagle for C Hoare and Company in 1986; the Duchess of Abercorn in 1989; and Lord Aberconway, 1991. Showed widely internationally and had a solo show at Cadogan Contemporary, 1991.

Alexander Hardie WILLIAMSON: *see* **Hardie WILLIAMSON**

Anne WILLIAMSON fl. c.1940–1965 Painter who studied at Slade School of Fine Art with Fred Brown and Ambrose McEvoy. She exhibited RA, RBA, RP, NEAC and elsewhere. Lived in London.

Hardie WILLIAMSON 1907–1994 Designer, illustrator, artist and teacher, full name Alexander Hardie Williamson, born in Hull, Yorkshire. When he was a boy his family moved to Edinburgh, where he attended George Heriot's School, then Royal College of Art design school, graduating 1932. During World War II the College was evacuated to Ambleside, where Williamson taught the fabric design course. Although a lifelong asthmatic Williamson was a prolific and hard worker, seeking relaxation in painting and walking in the hilliest parts of Britain. Over 25 years he designed durable, elegant glassware for Ravenshead, responsible for almost 1,650 glasses. His many endpaper and book cover designs for Dent Dutton's *The Children's Illustrated Classics*, produced between 1946–74, embraced almost 100 titles. A good example of Williamson's paintings, the oil on board The Village, of 1932, was offered by the auctioneers Phillips in 1996. Williamson married the artist Susan Plowright in 1939; she died in 1987. Lived finally in Worthing, Sussex.

Harold WILLIAMSON 1898–1972 Painter, draughtsman, etcher and teacher, born Manchester and studied at its School of Art. Exhibited RA, NEAC, Manchester City Art Gallery, Walker Art Gallery, Liverpool, and in America. For a time he was a designer with the fabric and wallpaper firm Arthur Sanderson and Sons. Became painting master at Bournemouth College of Art, 1926–47, then until 1962 was head of the department of fine art at Manchester College of Art and Design. He was illustrated in magazines such as *The Studio* and *Sphere* and his work is in permanent collections in Manchester, Southport and Bournemouth. Belgrave Gallery held a retrospective in 1979. Lived in Sale, Cheshire.

Harold Sandys WILLIAMSON 1892–1978 Painter, designer and teacher, born in Leeds where he studied at the School of Art, 1911–14, and Royal Academy Schools, 1914–15. Became headmaster of Chelsea School of Art, 1930–58, where he employed among his teachers Henry Moore, Graham Sutherland, Ceri Richards and Claude Rogers; students during his time including Prunella Clough, Elizabeth Frink and Patrick Caulfield. Designed posters for General Post Office and London Underground and showed at RA, LG, NEAC and elsewhere. Imperial War Museum and provincial galleries hold his work, which was sympathetic to traditional values while being in tune with Modernism. Died in Norwich, Norfolk.

Lawrie WILLIAMSON 1932– Artist who established himself by painting his memories of Nottinghamshire and Derbyshire colliers at leisure in the 1940s and 1950s, using an Impressionist style. Educated in Derbyshire, Williamson became a Major Exhibitioner at 16; he studied at Nottingham College of Art and Nottingham University and at the Académie des Beaux-Arts, Paris; portraiture with Arthur Spooner, printmaking with S W Hayter and sketched with L S Lowry. Exhibitions included Catto, Portland, Richard Hagen in Broadway and Castle Ashby Gallery. In 1992 Williamson won the Cornelissen prize at ROI for outstanding work; Stanley Grimm prize in 1993 at ROI for the most popular painting; and in 1994 he had his first show at RBSA, of which he was a member.

James WILLIAMSON-BELL 1938– Painter, miniaturist, printmaker and sculptor with a special interest in wildlife art, a full-time artist from 1974. He was a member of RMS and SWLA, of Société des Artistes Français and Bilan de L'Art Contemporain, both based in Paris, and a council member of the Association of Northern Artists. Among his awards was a Paris Salon Gold Medal and two Silver Medals. Showed at RI, RSMA, RE and abroad. Pushkin Museum of Fine Art, Moscow, and other public collections hold examples. He completed commissioned works for Heredities Ltd, publishers and the 1987 British Gas calendar. Lived in Newcastle upon Tyne, Tyne and Wear.

Victor WILLING 1928–1988 Painter and draughtsman, born in Alexandria, Egypt, married to the artist Paula Rego. As a small boy he moved to England where he attended the Royal Grammar School, Guildford, 1940–5, then Slade School of Fine Art, 1949–54. Although Willing had his first solo show in 1955, from 1957–74 he lived in Portugal where he painted little, concentrating mainly on a family business. From 1966 Willing was diagnosed as having multiple sclerosis which prompted him from the late 1960s to paint again in an endeavour to reveal more of his inner self. Settled in London from 1974 he started to have psychoanalysis; he suffered from insomnia and hallucinations. The revelation in drawings and then paintings of his inner visions was the major breakthrough in establishing Willing's personal voice as an artist. His reputation was gradually made, and in 1980 he received the Thorne Scholarship. He was artist-in-residence at Corpus Christi College and Kettle's Yard, Cambridge, in 1982. A retrospective show was held at Whitechapel Art Gallery in 1986, another at Karsten Schubert Ltd, 1993. Lived in London.

Roy WILLINGHAM 1957– Printmaker, painter and teacher, born in Southampton. He graduated in painting and printmaking from Central School of Art and Design and went on to teach life drawing at Sir John Cass School of Art, also being a visiting lecturer at Byam Shaw School of Art. In 1985 he opened Paintworks, an artists' materials and framing shop. Willingham showed regularly with Printmakers' Council and held senior positions in it. Also showed with SWE, RWS and RE. Other mixed exhibition appearances included Whitechapel Open from 1982 and Contemporary Avant-Grade British Printmaking, at Plymouth City Museum and Art Gallery, 1992. In 1985 had a solo show Four Towns, at Stables Theatre Gallery Hastings, and in 1992 one at Duncan Campbell Gallery. Lived in London.

Gary WILLIS 1949– Figurative painter, installation and performance artist, draughtsman, muralist and teacher, born in New South Wales, Australia. He studied at Canberra School of Art, 1970–1; gained his diploma at Phillip Institute of Technology, Melbourne, 1972, in post-object activities and philosophy; obtained a postgraduate art education diploma at Melbourne State College, 1975; and a postgraduate fine art diploma at Phillip Institute, 1980. Held a number of teaching posts in Australia, later ones including Canberra School of Art, 1985, and National Art School, East Sydney, 1986–8. Willis spent periods in London, and was artist-in-residence, Air Gallery, 1984, and Delfina Studios artist-in-residence, 1992–3. Awards included a Commonwealth Scholarship, 1975; Australia Council Theatre Board Grant, 1978; Australia Film Commission Grants, 1979–80; and an Australia Council Visual Arts Board Grant, 1984. Exhibitions included Fire Water, installation-event, UNESCO, Canberra, 1972; Boredom, solo performance-installation, Preston Institute of Technology, Melbourne, 1977; This is it, mural project, Flying Trapeze Cabaret, Melbourne, 1980; Central Journals, an agony in eight fits, large oil on photo works, Reconnaissance Gallery, Melbourne, 1982; London '84, 15 large laminated drawings, Air Gallery Studio, 1984; Identification Specific, paintings on paper, Galleria Pacifico, Amsterdam, and Actors Institute and Hackney Arts Festival, all 1990; and Don Quixote, paintings, drawings and etchings, Corbally Stourton Contemporary Art, 1995. Willis' work is held by many Australian collections, including the National Gallery and National University, both in Canberra; by the Arthur Boyd Collection, London; and Delfina Trust Collection, Spain.

John Christopher Temple WILLIS 1900–1969 Painter, mainly in watercolour. Born in Weymouth, Dorset, he pursued a military career, attaining the rank of major-general. Studied art with Arthur Ackermann and R Talbot Kelly and exhibited at RA, RBA, RI and RSA. Lived at Farnham, Surrey.

John Henry WILLIS 1887–1989 Painter, muralist and teacher, born at Beer Alston, near Tavistock, Devon, who studied at Armstrong College, Durham University; and Royal College of Art. In 1934 Willis was asked to paint a lunette on the theme Barge Day for Laing Art Gallery, Newcastle upon Tyne. He eventually became vice-principal of Hornsey School of Art, where he exhibited, also at RA and as a member of RBA. Willis settled in Paignton, Devon, where in 1951 he founded the Art and Crafts Society, becoming chairman and eventually president. He was also president of Torbay Art Club. Painted a picture of Calstock Viaduct for Tor Abbey.

Lucy WILLIS 1954– Painter, printmaker, draughtsman, teacher and writer, notable for her skilful use of watercolour and depiction of light. She studied at Ruskin School of Drawing and Fine Art, Oxford, 1972–5. In 1976 moved to Greece and set up an etching workshop in affiliation with the Aegean School of Fine Art, returning to England two years later. She established the Moorland House Workshop in Somerset in 1980. In 1988 published her book *Light: How to see it, How to paint it.* The year following she was invited to become artist-in-residence for two weeks at a local compre-hensive school. Willis travelled extensively, as shown in her 1991 exhibition with Chris Beetles Ltd, which included pictures of South India; her first show at that gallery was in 1986. In 1992 Willis gained first prize for her picture Her Majesty's Pleasure in the BP Portrait Award at the National Portrait Gallery. This earned her £10,000 and a further commission of £2,000 with the Gallery.

Patricia Marjorie WILLIS 1914– Painter, notable for her portraits and watercolours, and teacher, born in Kelowna, British Columbia, Canada. Although educated in Canada she studied art at the Byam Shaw School of Drawing and Painting for two periods: 1938–41, then 1952–5. Her teachers included Peter Greenham and Charles Mahoney. From 1957–65 Miss Willis taught at Byam Shaw. Lived in London for some years.

Richard WILLIS 1924– Painter, born in London, who was educated at Harrow School, where he studied art under Maurice Clarke. Then attended Reading University under Anthony Betts. Exhibited RA and RI and lived for some time at Lacock, Wiltshire.

Samuel William Ward WILLIS 1870–1948 Sculptor, born in London. He attended the West London School of Art and then the Royal Academy Schools, 1890–5. He completed a number of public commissions for venues in Britain and abroad and Russell-Cotes Art Gallery and Museum holds his work. Exhibited RA, RSA, Walker Art Gallery, Liverpool, RMS and RBA. Lived in Parkstone, Dorset.

Victor WILLIS fl. from early 1960s– Painter and draughtsman who studied at Camberwell School of Arts and Crafts, 1957–60, City & Guilds of London Art School, Sir John Cass College and Goldsmiths' College, gaining his master's degree in fine art, 1983. His many shows included National Museum of Wales, Cardiff; Camden Arts Centre; NEAC; ROI; Austin/Desmond Fine Art, Sunninghill; and 1983 Goldsmiths' show at Woodlands Art Gallery. For that Willis wrote that he attempted "to visualise and interpret narrative painting. Some of my paintings have a symbolic message which can be read in several ways." In 1993 Willis showed landscapes at Duncan Campbell Contemporary Art. He carried out a commission for British Rail Freight headquarters.

Charles WILLMOTT 1943– Artist in oil, charcoal and pencil, born in Stratford-upon-Avon, Warwickshire. Began painting in the early 1960s and attended Birmingham College of Art. Willmott developed a deep interest in the Orient, to which he travelled. Showed in Singapore, Japan and in England, having a solo exhibition at Phoenix Gallery at Selfridges in 1995. Limited-edition prints of Willmott's work included several of the ballerina Miyako

Yoshida. He was the only son of the artist and metal craftsman Hague Willmott.

John Smith WILLOCK 1887–1976 Artist and teacher, born in Weaste, Lancashire, who was educated at Manchester's Central High School, then by scholarship attended day classes at the School of Art, All Saints, about 1903–4, under Richard Glazier and Henry Cadness. Also was a pupil teacher at Oldham School of Art. With a scholarship Willock trained as a teacher at the Manchester School from 1916, winning a silver medal for design. He also won a three-year scholarship to the Royal College of Art, but the need to support his family prevented his accepting it. Served in France in World War I, afterwards taking up a teaching career, eventually becoming head of the design school at Manchester School/Regional College of Art (he was offered the headship of Salford School of Art). Showed with Society of Modern Painters as a member, also at MAFA, NEAC, IS, Atkinson Art Gallery in Southport, Walker Art Gallery in Liverpool and Ferens Art Gallery, Hull. Manchester City Art Gallery has his work.

Althea WILLOUGHBY 1905–1982 Engraver, born and lived in London, daughter of the painter and illustrator Vera Willoughby and the actor Lewis Willoughby. Studied at Royal College of Art in the 1920s, a fellow-student of the painter Elizabeth Vellacott. Willoughby, who was known to her family as Biddy, led a picaresque life, married twice, but had no children, and was for some time a member of a pre-World War II mystic/New Age-type community. She designed five posters for London Underground and for the Curwen Press, did book illustrating, made some prints and produced a number of vignettes to advertisements which appeared in *Bystander, Eve* and *Vogue*. Shared an exhibition with her mother at the Little Art Room, 1924, and contributed to group shows, including SWE at Redfern Gallery, 1930, and British Art in Industry, 1935.

Esther WILLOUGHBY fl. from early 1920s–1959 Painter and teacher, born in Croydon, Surrey. Studied art in Redhill, then at the Royal College of Art under Gerald Moira and Malcolm Osborne. Married the artist Thomas Moore Smith. Exhibited RA, SWA and in the provinces. Lived at Ferring, Sussex.

Trevor WILLOUGHBY 1926– Painter, illustrator and teacher, born in Hull, Yorkshire. Studied at Belfast Technical College, Hull College of Art and London College of Printing. Teaching experience included St Martin's and Sir John Cass Colleges of Art and Middlesex Polytechnic. Was elected a member of RP in 1970, also showing with RA, RBA, Chenil Gallery and elsewhere. Did magazine and advertising illustration. Lived in London.

Barbara WILLS 1923– Painter, notably a watercolourist, potter and teacher, born in Yorkshire. She attended Sheffield College of Art and Royal College of Art, then taught painting and pottery for many years before moving to Cornwall in 1969. She settled at St Hilary and painted full-time, notably landscapes of the coastline between Mount's Bay and Cudden Point. She was a member of Newlyn Society of Artists and her watercolour Summer Evening, Marazion, was included in the Newlyn Orion Galleries exhibition A Century of Art in Cornwall 1889–1989, held in 1989.

Ferelyth Alison WILLS: *see* **FERELYTH**

Joan WILLS fl.from 1950s– Painter, born in Shrewsbury, Shropshire. As well as private studies with Stanley Grimm and Kenneth Green she attended Sir John Cass College and City and Guilds of London Art School. Was a member of SWA and UA, also exhibiting with NS, RMS and Paris Salon. Lived in London.

Richard Allin WILLS 1939– Painter and teacher, born and lived in Monmouth, Gwent, who studied at Newport College of Art, 1956–61, under Thomas Rathmell. Went on to teach for 25 years in colleges of art, comprehensive and grammar schools. Showed at RA, RWA, RP, UA, Welsh Young Contemporaries, WSW and RWS. Among his portraits was the Duke of Gloucester and a number of commissions were carried out for British Steel, Rank Xerox and HTV. These companies, Contemporary Art Society and Welsh Office own examples. There was a retrospective at St David's Hall, Cardiff, in 1996.

Brian WILLSHER 1930– Sculptor, mainly in wood, of works which mixed geometric abstraction with organic abstraction. He was born and remained based in London. Studied engineering at Woolwich Polytechnic for three years from 1946, then did a number of jobs, eventually qualifying as a dental technician. Began creating first forms from wood in 1956. After a one-man show at Dunn's in Bromley in 1965 and another at Heal's in 1966 his career took off. He was in 1967 given another show at Heal's, showed in Melbourne, Australia, had three works commissioned for Dartington Hall and six for Devon Guild of Craftsmen. Although in 1968 Henry Moore and Herbert Read acclaimed Willsher's work, a tussle with Customs and Excise bureaucrats, who decided to tax his creations as non-sculpture, persuaded Willsher against showing in galleries, and he chose to market his sculptures personally. After a new bout of enthusiasm for bronze sculptures and work at Fiorini Bronze Foundry in 1989 Willsher showed again, with exhibitions at Boundary and Belgrave Galleries in 1990. Shared an exhibition with his son, the painter Daniel Willsher, at Belgrave Gallery, 1997.

Graeme WILLSON 1951– Artist in paint, stained glass and mosaic, and lecturer, born in Yorkshire, where he settled at Ilkley. He studied at Reading University, 1969–73, under Claude Rogers, Terry Frost, John Wonnacott and Keith Critchlow. From 1973–5 Willson held a full-time lectureship at North Lindsey College, South Humberside, then became a freelance painter and visiting lecturer, including Bradford & Ilkley Community College, Chelsea College and Institute of Advanced Architectural Studies at York University. Residencies included Leeds City Art Gallery, 1987 and 1990. Commissions included altarpieces, a ceiling and a mosaic for York Minster, between 1979–94; Provident Finance Group, Bradford, 1989; and a portrait of Sir John Harvey-Jones for

Bradford University, 1991. Among Willson's awards were 1st Prize, Art into Landscape Competition, 1977; RA Award for Painting and Greater London Arts Association Award, both 1983; and Chippendale Award for Painting, 1988. Mixed exhibitions included Serpentine Gallery, 1977; The New Look in English Portraiture, National Portrait Gallery, 1980; Image Space Public, Leeds City Art Gallery, 1986; and Northern Prospects, Harewood House, 1995. Had a solo show at Sloane Street Gallery, 1977; at Cartwright Hall, Bradford, 1980; later ones including University of Leeds, 1989, and Bloomsbury Gallery, 1992. Was a member of Public Art Forum, Art & Architecture, York Art Workers' Association, and an honorary member of Art Workers' Guild. Forbes Collection in New York and Bradford Schools Loan Scheme also hold Willson's work.

WILSON 1903–1972 Painter in oil, pastel draughtsman, illustrator and teacher, born in Cricklewood, full name Helen Wilson. She moved to Scotland when she was six weeks old, studying at Glasgow School of Art under David Forrester Wilson, then on a scholarship at Royal Academy Schools. While there, in the mid-1920s, she won a silver medal for drawing and the Arthur Hacker Prize for a portrait. Later subjects who sat for her included the writer Compton Mackenzie and the psychologist Havelock Ellis; the composer Jean Sibelius declined, claiming that he was too old. After her studies Wilson became an illustrator, working in the museum at the School of Hygiene and Tropical Medicine, producing intricate drawings of insects. Married a doctor, Maurice Rosenfield, who worked at Manor House Hospital. After World War II showed widely; she was vice-president of PS until her death, also exhibiting at RBA, NEAC and at Leicester Galleries. Joined the staff of Heatherley's School of Art. When it closed in 1969 she transferred it to Hampstead, where she lived and was a member of the Choral Society. For a time the school, renamed the Heatherley-Wilson School of Painting, Sculpture and Crafts, operated in her flat. Wilson, remembered as a canny Scot, of strong character with tremendous will-power, eventually founded the Thomas Heatherley Educational Trust, which continues.

Andrew Stout WILSON 1912– Watercolourist who was an engineer by profession, born in Inverness. He was educated at Trinity Academy in Edinburgh, being self-taught as an artist. Showed RSW, RSA, SSA and elsewhere. Lived in Edinburgh, though worked for some time in London, where he also showed.

Anne WILSON 1955– Artist and teacher, born in West Midlands, who studied at Walsall School of Art and Cardiff College of Art. She became head of the visual art department of Kingsway College and produced joint works with Marty St James. Their exhibition at Gallery M in 1994 included cibachromes on canvas and a series of video portraits, the faces comprising, for example, a man silently smoking and another of the sea with sound effects. Selected exhibitions included Hotel, at Air Gallery, 1989; 101 Gallery, Ottawa, Canada, 1991; and Portrait Now, National Portrait Gallery, 1993. They also had work in a number of video festivals around the world.

Arthur WILSON 1927– Painter and teacher, born and lived in London. He was the son of the artist R A Wilson and the father of Richard Wilson. He studied at Chelsea School of Art, 1944–50, gaining his national diploma in design for painting, with a break for Royal Air Force service as a fitter, 1946–8; teachers included Raymond Coxon and Robert Medley. Began part-time teaching in 1952, joined Epsom School of Art & Design in 1965 as a lecturer and was department head of foundation studies, 1982–8. His work showed a strong reference to nature and the sea. Was elected a member of LG in 1967. Mixed shows included Arts Council tour, 1966; Cambridge Arts Festival, 1968; Morley Gallery, 1979; Arts Council exhibition Art and the Sea, with tour, 1981; and ICA, 1982. Had a solo show at University of Surrey, 1968, another at Arnolfini Gallery, Bristol, 1970. Bristol City Art Gallery holds his work.

Avril WILSON 1962– Sculptor, blacksmith and teacher, born in Belfast, Northern Ireland, producing specific site-related work to commission, influences including symbolism, mythology and organic forms. After studying at Ulster Polytechnic, 1980–1, Wilson in 1984 gained a first-class honours degree in three-dimensional design from the Polytechnic in Brighton, Sussex, where she eventually settled, as a member of Red Herring Studios, after obtaining her master's in ceramics from South Glamorgan Institute of Higher Education in 1985. Showed widely in galleries, gardens and elsewhere, in 1996–7 being part of the Sculpture at Goodwood display. Forged steel spandrels by her were in 1993 completed for the centre of Banbury.

Bassett WILSON: *see* **BASSETT**

Ben WILSON 1963– Creator of magical wooden sculptures from found timber in Hadley Woods, north London. Born in Cambridge, Wilson began a foundation course at Middlesex Polytechnic, but then rejected formal art training, deciding to continue with the sculpting he had begun as a child. He created a hut to do this in his mother's garden. Wilson also made his sculptures in schools and gardens in Britain and Australia. He was represented in Art Random, Outsider Art from the Outsider Archive, London, at Kyoto Shoin International, in Japan, 1989, and in Outsiders & Co at England & Co, 1996. Wilson's work is also held by the American Visionary Art Museum, Baltimore.

Chris WILSON 1959– Artist in mixed media, born in Belfast, Northern Ireland. It was said of his works that they were "still and silent … interiors of churches, abbeys, residences, abandoned by all except nature's forces." Wilson gained an honours degree in fine art from Brighton College of Art in 1982, in 1985 obtaining a master's degree from University of Ulster. He contributed to many shows in Ireland, England, Germany, Hong Kong and America. These included Open Futures at Ikon Gallery, Birmingham, 1987; Athena Art Awards, Barbican Centre, 1988; and Arts Council show Shocks to The System, Royal Festival Hall, 1991. Had a solo British Council show in Bucharest in 1992 which toured Romania before travelling to Bulgaria in 1993. Shared a show at Duncan

Campbell Contemporary Art in 1993. Arts Councils of Great Britain, Northern Ireland and Ireland hold his work.

Chrissy WILSON 1948– Painter and graphic artist, born and lived in London, married to the artist Peter Blake. She studied at Sutton School of Art and was employed in studio work. Showed at RA, Fouts & Fowler Gallery and Flowers East and in Japan. Wilson's work, done "to record objects, animals and people", was in the collections of former Arts Council chairman Baron Palumbo and singer Paul McCartney and his wife Linda and that of the screen actress and singer Doris Day.

Cyril WILSON 1911– Painter and teacher, born in High Wycombe, Buckinghamshire. He studied art in Reading and went on to teach at New Abbey College of Art Summer School for many years. Exhibited at SSA as a member, RSW, Royal Glasgow Institute of the Fine Arts, RSA and abroad. One-man shows included Dumfries Arts Festival in 1983 and 1986 and Compass Gallery, Glasgow, in 1988. Two years later he was included in The Compass Contribution at Tramway, Glasgow. Scottish National Gallery of Modern Art and Dundee Art Gallery hold his work. Wilson lived from 1948 near Dumfries, in Scotland, but spent part of each year in Ibiza, off the Spanish coast.

David Forrester WILSON 1873–1950 Painter and teacher, born and lived in Glasgow, where he studied and taught at the School of Art. He was elected RSA in 1933, was a member of Glasgow Art Club, showed extensively at Royal Glasgow Institute of the Fine Arts, also at Baillie Gallery, RSW and Walker Art Gallery in Liverpool. Glasgow Corporation commissioned him to paint a big decorative panel in Glasgow Municipal Buildings banqueting hall.

Douglas WILSON 1936– Painter and teacher, full name George Douglas Wilson, born in Wirral, Cheshire. He studied at Farnham School of Art, then with Percy Horton at Oxford University, 1959–62, where his teachers also included Lawrence Toynbee and Geoffrey Rhoades. He went on to teach, at Wirral College of Art and at Lord Wandsworth College, 1969–74. Exhibited widely, including RBA, RCamA, Liverpool Academy, Thackeray Gallery and elsewhere, his one-man shows including Bluecoat Gallery in Liverpool and Phoenix Gallery, Lavenham. Lived in Newport, Shropshire.

Francis WILSON 1876–1957 Painter in oil of landscapes and portraits. Born in Glasgow, he studied at the School of Art there before a travelling scholarship enabled him to study widely in France and Italy. Exhibited RSA, RSW, Royal Glasgow Institute of the Fine Arts and in Canada. Glasgow Museum and Art Galleries hold his work. Lived in Glasgow, where he was a member of the Art Club.

Frank Avray WILSON 1914– Painter, printmaker, writer and scientist, born in Vacoas, Mauritius. He gained his master's degree in biology at Cambridge University, studying art in France and Norway. In 1956 Wilson helped form the New Vision Centre Gallery, a showplace for abstract and other modern art. Wilson produced some of the most dynamic abstracts of the postwar period in Britain. His work ranged over spikey linear compositions, through others more spare and geometric towards a mature style which comprised images disciplined but energetic. Wilson sought "to create a synthetic vitality, more living than life, the means of supplying our anti-vital, anti-human society with intense symbols". His scientific background was of key importance in understanding his approach to painting, as were his books, which included *Art into Life*, 1958; *Art as Understanding*, 1963; *Nature Regained*, 1977; and *Art as Revelation*, 1981. Had a first solo show at Obelisk Gallery in 1954, later ones including Redfern Gallery, 1995. Also showed at Leicester Galleries and RA; in 1988 he was in Post-War British Abstract Art at Austin/Desmond Fine Art. Public collections in Cleveland, Durham, Leeds, Leicester, Swansea and Wakefield hold his work. Lived in London and Le Tignet, France.

Gerard WILSON 1943– Sculptor, born in Cambridgeshire, who attended Norwich School of Art, 1965, then Brighton Polytechnic, 1966. Had a first solo show at Serpentine Gallery, 1971. In 1980 Wilson was included in the critic William Packer's selection for the Arts Council's touring exhibition The British Art Show.

Helen WILSON: *see* **WILSON**

Helen WILSON 1954– Painter and draughtsman, born in Paisley, Renfrewshire. She was a prizewinning student at Glasgow School of Art and went on to do postgraduate studies at Patrick Allan-Fraser School of Art, Hospitalfield, Arbroath. A travelling scholarship took her to Italy and Yugoslavia. Wilson won the Glasgow Society of Women Artists' Lauder Award in 1979, the Lady Artists' Club Trust Award the year after and in 1988 the RSA's J Murray Thomson Award, four years after she was elected to the Royal Glasgow Institute of the Fine Arts. As well as showing in mixed exhibitions at various locations including National Portrait Gallery, Boundary Gallery and Bath Contemporary Art Fair, Wilson's solo shows included a major tour to Collins Gallery, Glasgow, the MacRobert Arts Centre, Stirling, and Aberdeen Artspace. In 1986 she had a solo show at Sue Rankin Gallery, and two years later was at Compass Gallery in Glasgow and Paisley Museum and Art Galleries. Paisley, the Scottish Arts Council and other Scottish public collections hold her work.

Hugh Cameron WILSON 1885-c.1966 Artist in oil and teacher, born in Glasgow, where he studied at the School of Art with Fra Newbery and Maurice Greiffenhagen. Exhibited Royal Glasgow Institute of the Fine Arts especially, RSA and Walker Art Gallery, Liverpool. His work is held by Glasgow Museum and Art Galleries and Newport Art Gallery, Monmouth. Lived in Glasgow, where he was a member of the Art Club.

Jane and Louise WILSON 1967– Twin sisters who worked together, sometimes appearing in their own work. They believed in breaking down barriers between art and their own lives, employing such means as prints on plywood, video installation and photography. Jane won a degree in fine art at Newcastle Polytechnic, 1986–9, and her master's at Goldsmiths' College, 1990–2. With Louise she won the Barclays Young Artist Award, 1993. Louise gained a degree in fine art at Duncan of Jordanstone College of Art, Dundee, 1986–9, and her master's at Goldsmiths', 1990–2. Group shows included Domestic Violence, Gio Marconi, Milan, and Beyond Belief, Lisson Gallery, both 1994; Speaking of Sofas, Soho House, and General Release, Venice Biennale, both 1995; and British Art Show 4, with tour, 1995–6. Had their own show at Chisenhale and Milch Galleries, both 1995, after AC Projects/Enterprise, New York, and Galerie Krinzinger, Vienna, both 1994.

Kate WILSON 1965– Painter, who studied at Hertfordshire College of Art and Design, 1983–4, graduated with honours degree in fine art from Winchester School of Art, 1984–7, then did post-graduate diploma at Royal Academy Schools, 1988–91. Among her awards were Hampshire Travel Award, 1986, Worshipful Company of Painter-Stainers' Award, 1990, and in 1991 the RA Gold Medal and André de Segonzac Travelling Scholarship. Apart from privately commis- sioned portrait work Wilson did other commissions for Southampton University Chaplaincy and Loreto College, St Albans. Group shows included Art Centre Group, Waterloo, 1987; NEAC in 1991; and Witnesses and Dreamers at Museum of London, 1993. In that year she shared a show at Cadogan Contemporary. After a solo show at Southampton General Hospital in 1987 later ones included The Kepler Gallery in 1992.

Keith WILSON 1965– Artist born in Birmingham who did a foundation course at Bournville College of Art, 1984–5; gained his bachelor's degree in fine art at Ruskin School of Fine Art, Oxford, 1985–8; with a higher diploma at Slade School of Fine Art, 1988–90. Won a Laura Ashley Scholarship in 1989; a Boise Travel Scholarship, 1990; and a LAB Individual Artist Award, 1994. Late in 1995 was an artist-in-residence at Camden Arts Centre, with a subsequent show there. Other exhibitions included Into the Nineties 2, Mall Galleries, 1990; shared show at Diorama Gallery, 1992; Tight at The Tannery, Bermondsey, and Turning Up at The View, Liverpool, both 1994; and shared show at Anna Bornholt Gallery, 1995. Lived in Harrow on the Hill, Middlesex.

Louise WILSON: *see* **Jane and Louise WILSON**

Margaret WILSON fl. from 1960s– Artist, notably a printmaker, who studied at Beckenham School of Art. She showed with Young Contemporaries (work selected for Arts Council tour and two-man show at Irving Gallery), Greenwich Theatre Gallery, Stables Theatre Gallery in Hastings, RA and elsewhere, including Group '77 Printmakers, at Woodlands Art Gallery, 1981. Work in private collections around the world. Taught part-time in schools.

Mark WILSON 1954– Artist, born in Cumbria, who attended Sunderland Polytechnic, gaining an honours degree in drawing and printmaking, 1973–6. His group shows included LYC Gallery, Brampton, 1979; Small Works 5, Newcastle Polytechnic Gallery, 1963; Cork Municipal Art Gallery, Ireland, with tour, 1986–7; and Windmill Holt Gallery, Berwick, 1989. Solo shows included McLaurin Gallery, Alloway, 1981, and Abbot Hall Art Gallery, Kendal, 1983; he had a shared show at Gallery North, Cumbria, 1990. Abbot Hall, Durham University and Pushkin State Museum of Fine Art in Moscow hold his work.

Maurice WILSON 1914– Painter, illustrator and teacher, born in London. He studied at Hastings School of Art under Philip Cole, then at Royal Academy Schools with Walter Westley Russell, Robert Austin and Malcom Osborne. Taught at Bromley School of Art and elsewhere. Animals were an important feature of Wilson's output, which included illustrations for *Radio Times* and a number of books with a series by him, among them *Just Monkeys*, 1937, and *Birds*, 1965. Wilson was a member of SWLA and RI, also exhibiting with RSMA and Dorset Naturalists' Trust at Dorset County Museum, 1982–3. Lived in Bidborough, Kent.

Michael WILSON 1951– Painter and printmaker, born in Liverpool, which remained his home. Studied at Wolver- hampton School of Art and showed in the northwest of England, sharing a show at Allerton Gallery, Liverpool, in 1976.

Muriel WILSON 1892– Watercolourist and printmaker, born in Chicago, in America. Studied art at Crystal Palace and at Central School of Arts and Crafts. Showed at RI, RBA, widely in the provinces and at Paris Salon. Miss Wilson lived in London.

Muriel WILSON 1892–1977 Painter, draughtsman and printmaker. She was the daughter of Sir Francis Samuelson and the wife of the artist Bassett Wilson, had a privileged upbringing and was early found to have an aptitude for watercolours and flower-pieces. Her first recorded show is one with her husband at Walker's Galleries, in 1921, which gained some press notice. In 1920s her reputation grew; a show at Lefevre Gallery led to Contemporary Art Society buying a flower picture which was presented to Leicester City Art Gallery. The Wilsons' competence was transformed from late 1920s when they moved to Paris, made friends among local artists and worked in the studio of André Lhote. Muriel became an expert photographer, tutored by Man Ray. In 1930 the Wilsons travelled to New York and Chicago for shows at Knoedler. Four years later they showed at Lefevre, Darlington Municipal Art Gallery, at Salon des Tuileries in Paris, and also at Galerie Gerbo and L'Association Florence Blumenthal, completing 1934 with an exhibition with the Rhyma Group at Helsingfors, Finland, where they were hailed as pioneers. They continued to show extensively in Paris and travel widely in Europe and elsewhere until World War II. During the war Muriel worked with refugees in France, then with the Motor Transport Corps in England. The Wilsons' late-1930s pictures were looted or destroyed in Paris and Muriel declined to work for about a decade after the war's end. In 1981 Patrick Seale Gallery held a show of both artists' pictures.

Paul WILSON 1956– Abstract artist and teacher who studied at Blackburn College of Technology & Design, 1975, then Gloucestershire College of Art & Design, Cheltenham, 1976, and Chelsea School of Art, 1976–9. Was visiting lecturer at West Sussex College of Art & Design as well as teaching extensively in adult education in London. In 1982 was included in Artists in Adult Education at Woodlands Art Gallery.

Peter WILSON 1940– Painter and printmaker, born in Glasgow, where he attended the School of Art, 1960–4, then was a Byam Shaw Jubilee Scholar, 1964–5. In the latter year Wilson was a John Moores Exhibition, Liverpool, prizewinner. In the three years 1979–81 he gained an East Midlands Arts Award, then in 1982, when he was artist-in- residence at Ferens Art Gallery, Hull, Wilson won an Arts Council Major Award. A Scottish Print Open Purchase Prize was awarded in 1987. Wilson had a busy one-man exhibiting career, his later shows including Usher Gallery, Lincoln, and Waterford Arts Centre, Ireland, in 1987; Mappin Art Gallery, Sheffield, 1988; Leicester Museum and Art Gallery, 1990; and in 1991 a show at The Minories in Colchester and at The Lamont Gallery entitled Under the Surface. Originally Wilson was an abstract painter, but he later favoured narrative pictures; a feeling for intense colour remained. Contemporary Art Society, Arts Council, Scottish Arts Council and many provincial galleries hold his work.

Peter WILSON 1950– Painter and talented draughtsman, born in London. He studied at Goldsmiths' College School of Art, 1978, Camberwell School of Arts and Crafts, 1980–3 and Newcastle University, 1986–8. Wilson's work was concerned with images from daily life as well as dreams and fantasies, as in his charcoal drawing Children in Garden, show in East at Norwich Gallery, 1991. Other notable mixed show appearances were Spirit of London, 1982–4; Northern Young Contemporaries, Whitworth Art Gallery, 1987; Ferens Open, Hull, 1988; and John Moores Liverpool Exhibition, 1989–90. Solo shows included Long Gallery, Newcastle University, and Darlington Arts Centre, 1990. Lived in Gateshead, Tyne and Wear.

Richard WILSON 1953– Installation and sculpture artist, born and lived in London, son of the painter Arthur Wilson. He did a foundation course at London College of Printing, 1970–1, his diploma at Hornsey College of Art, 1971–4, then his master's degree at Reading University, 1974–6. In 1983 with Anne Bean and Paul Burwell founded the Bow Gamelan Ensemble, an orchestra made from scrap which toured the world and released one single and two cassettes. In 1992 Wilson took up a DAAD artist-in-residency in Berlin. Group shows included LG, Camden Arts Centre, 1975; Whitechapel Open, 1976; and Romance Science Endeavour, Portsmouth City Art Gallery, 1981. Showed solo at Coracle Press Gallery from 1976; at Matt's Gallery from 1985; Trigon Biennale, Graz, Austria, 1987; Edge Biennale, Newcastle, and Centre of Contemporary Art, Warsaw, both 1990; and Serpentine Gallery and Gimpel Fils, both 1996. Publications included *12 Pieces*, Coracle Press, 1978; and *The Elements*, Bookworks, 1986. Victoria & Albert Museum, Arts Council, Saatchi Gallery and Centre of Contemporary Art, Warsaw, hold examples.

Robert Arthur WILSON 1884–1979 Painter in oil, tempera and watercolour, printmaker and teacher, born in Monk Wearmouth, County Durham. He was apprenticed to a sign-writer until 21, studying part-time at Sunderland School of Art. A Government National Scholarship took him to the Royal College of Art where he won a scholarship. Then studied at Académie Julian, in Paris, and under Percyval Tudor-Hart, a major influence. Married the painter Stella Louise Wilson and was the father of the artist Arthur Wilson. Taught part-time in Surrey and London art schools. Showed RA, Paris Salon and SGA and had a series of solo exhibitions including Sunderland Art Gallery, notably in 1965. Wrote on tempera and the use of colour and in 1972 privately published his *Memoirs of an Individualist*. British Museum and Victoria & Albert Museum hold his work, which has an honest, art-and-crafts complexion. R A Wilson, as he liked to be known, lived in Bletchingley, Surrey.

Ross WILSON 1957– Painter, draughtsman and teacher who studied at Belfast School of Art and Chelsea College of Art. Living in Country Antrim, he went on to teach in various schools and colleges of art in Northern Ireland. Took part in group shows and had over a dozen solo exhibitions in Belfast, Dublin, Londonderry and Templepatrick from 1980. Wilson was a powerful draughtsman, as shown in Cast No Stones, a big drawing in Salute to Turner, held in 1989; and in Man with Hambletonian, Mount Stewart, in The Broad Perspective, 1990, both Agnew exhibitions.

Scottie WILSON 1890–1972 Primitive artist, born in Glasgow, real name Louis Freeman, also known as Robert Wilson. Wilson liked to keep some mystery about his origins and exact date of birth, of which there are several versions. His parents emigrated from Lithuania and Scottie left school at nine to help his family survive by selling patent medicines in the street. Ran away at 16 and joined the Army, serving in India and South Africa. After a period in Scotland again, he went to Canada from about 1930, where he stayed 14 years, initially running an unsuccessful second-hand furniture business. When his first drawings sold well at the Picture Loan Society, Toronto, in 1943 at a one-man show, he returned to England in 1945 and had a one-man exhibition at the Arcade Gallery in that year. In 1947 was represented in a Surrealist show at the Galerie Maeght, Paris; was also shown in Basle, Switzerland, and in New York. Showed with Brook Street Gallery and Ben Uri Gallery, London. In 1965 designed dinner, tea and coffee services for the Royal Worcester Porcelain Company. Also designed tapestries for the Aubusson workshop in France and for the Edinburgh Weavers' Association. The Tate Gallery, London, Musée d'Art Moderne, Paris, and Museum of Modern Art, New York, hold his work which consisted of coloured drawings, watercolours and decorated plates, with repeated motifs such as faces, birds and fishes. Died in London.

Stanley Reginald WILSON 1890–1973 Versatile and sophisticated printmaker and painter, born and lived in London. He attended Goldsmiths' College School of Art and showed at Connell & Sons, RA, RSA, Royal Glasgow Institute of the Fine Arts and elsewhere. Public galleries in Birmingham and Leeds hold his work, which showed an interest in natural history subjects.

Stella Louise WILSON 1892–1982 Painter in tempera and watercolour, born in London. After Forest Hill School she studied at Camberwell School of Arts and Crafts where she met her future husband, the artist Robert Arthur Wilson. She exhibited RA, RI, SWA of which she was a member, Paris Salon and in the provinces. Lived in Bletchingley, Surrey.

Susan WILSON 1951– Painter and teacher, born in Dunedin, New Zealand. She was expelled from teacher training college for radical political views, studied nursing and worked for two years in a neurosurgical unit. After travels in South America she arrived in England and studied at Camberwell School of Arts and Crafts, 1978–82, then Royal Academy Schools, 1982–6. In the following year she was painting fellow at Cheltenham and Gloucester College of Art and Technology, going on to lecture at Wolverhampton Polytechnic and Royal Academy Schools as a visiting tutor, then becoming a tutor at Chelsea School of Art. Among awards was an Italian Government Scholarship to Venice, 1984; Richard Ford Scholarship to Spain, 1985; and a *Spectator* Competition commendation in 1991. Exhibited widely in group exhibitions, including Whitechapel Open, 1980; John Player Portrait Award from 1984, being a finalist in 1987; Piccadilly Gallery from 1987; and Oriel Mostyn, Llandudno, 1990. Later solo shows included Agnew, 1990, and Cadogan Contemporary, 1991. HRH The Prince of Wales, Contemporary Art Society and National Trust hold her work. Lived in London.

Sylvia WILSON fl. from early 1980s– Abstract artist, born in London, to which she returned to study after periods in Barbados and Australia. Attended Byam Shaw School of Art, 1980–3. Exhibitions included Brixton Art Gallery group show, 1983; Lauderdale House, 1984; and New Moon Group Show at Woodlands Art Gallery, 1986.

Tony WILSON 1944– Printmaker, painter and teacher, born in Birmingham. Studied at the College of Art there, 1960–4, then at Central School of Art & Design, 1964–6. After teaching at Ravensbourne College of Art, 1966–70, from 1974 for many years was on the staff of Camberwell School of Arts and Crafts in charge of printmaking. Mixed shows included Summer Show 2 at Serpentine Gallery and Arts Council's British Painting '74, both 1974. Solo shows included Premises Gallery, 1973.

Vincent WILSON 1933– Painter, printmaker and teacher, born in Mold, Flintshire. He studied at Chester School of Art, 1950–4, and Liverpool College of Art, 1954–5, gaining his teacher's diploma. Taught from 1957, including the Grammar School at Saltash, Cornwall, where he settled. Was a member of RCamA, Newlyn Society of Artists, Penwith Society of Arts and Plymouth Society of Artists. Also took part in group shows at RWA, Royal National Eisteddfod, Thackeray Gallery and WAC. Had a solo exhibition at Exeter University, 1966, followed by others in the West Country and Wales. Plymouth City Art Gallery holds his work.

William WILSON 1905–1972 Printmaker, stained glassdesigner and watercolourist, born in Edinburgh. After apprenticeship to a stained glass studio in Edinburgh Wilson was an outstanding student at Edinburgh College of Art. In 1932 his engraving and etching won an RSA Travelling Scholarship to the continent; two years later he gained an Andrew Grant Fellowship and an RSA Guthrie Award which permitted him to study printmaking at Royal College of Art and stained glass in Germany. In 1937 Wilson opened a stained glass studio in Edinburgh and carried out work for churches and cathedrals in Britain and abroad. Alongside this reputation he painted watercolours, and made prints which established him as possibly Scotland's finest practitioner of that art in the twentieth century. Wilson's work owed a debt to Italian primitive art, yet it has a powerful, often sombre, lyrical quality. He was elected SSA in 1930; was during the 1930s secretary to the Society of Artist Printmakers; became RSW in 1946; and was elected RSA three years later. In his last decade Wilson lost his sight. Scottish National Gallery of Modern Art holds a fine collection of Wilson's graphics and gave him a major reassessment exhibition in 1994.

William Lyons WILSON: *see* **LYONS-WILSON**

Winifred WILSON fl. c.1920–1978 Painter in oil, a farmer by occupation, she studied art privately with Sir John Arnesby Brown. Went on to exhibit widely in the English provinces, and at the RA, ROI, at the Paris Salon and in America. The Graves Art Gallery, Sheffield, holds her work. She was a sister of the painters May and Violet Wilson. Lived at Barlow, near Sheffield.

Hermione WILTSHIRE 1963– Artist in a range of media, born in London, who studied at Central School of Art, 1982–5, then Chelsea School of Art, 1986–7. Awards included GLA Production Awards, 1991, and LAB Production Award, 1994. Group shows included Traces of the Figure, City Museum and Gallery, Stoke-on-Trent, and tour, 1992; Elective Affinities, Tate Gallery in Liverpool, 1993; Summer Exhibition, Gimpel Fils, 1995; and British Art Show 4, 1995–6. Had a solo show at Riverside Studios, 1991; at Lisson Gallery, 1992; and A Pressing Engagement, British Council Window Gallery, Prague, 1994. Arts Council holds her work.

Frederic Charles WINBY 1875–1959 Painter and print-maker. Born in Newport, Monmouthshire, he studied art at the Slade School of Fine Art and at the Académie Julian, Paris. Exhibited RA, RI and in the provinces. Was a member of the Langham Sketch Club. The British Museum holds his work. Lived in London.

Richard WINCER 1951– Sculptor and installation artist and teacher, born in Alvechurch, Worcestershire. He studied at

Stourbridge College of Art, 1970–1, and Goldsmiths' College, 1971–4. Wincer did a variety of jobs, including gardener and biology and pottery technician, then lectured at Leicester Polytechnic. His work was included in Three Artists at Kettle's Yard Gallery in Cambridge, then Summer Show 2 at Serpentine Gallery in 1980 and in 1983 the Arts Council's The Sculpture Show. Lived in London.

Alison WINCKLE 1953– Film, video and performance artist, born in Douglas, Isle of Man, who also taught. She studied at Isle of Man College of Further Education, 1969–71, and Newcastle upon Tyne Polytechnic, 1971–4. She participated in the Arts Council's Film-makers on Tour scheme. Group exhibitions included Performance Week at Battersea Arts Centre, 1976; Hayward Annual, at Hayward Gallery, 1978; and Summer Show 1 at Serpentine Gallery, 1983. Had a solo exhibition at Ceolfrith Arts Centre in Sunderland, 1975, later ones including Acme Gallery, 1979. Lived in London.

Rachel WINDHAM 1916– Painter, born in Bedford into a distinguished and ancient family of philosophers, soldiers and artists. Both parents and her painter aunt Dorothy Dymock encouraged Windham with visits to art galleries and she was inspired by dedicated teachers such as Henry Mansfield Childerstone, a Slade School of Fine Art contemporary of Augustus John and Stanley Spencer. Having taught her for four years, Childerstone prompted her entry to the Slade, where she spent one year, 1937–8, before World War II intervened, which she spent in the Land Army. By now she was an accomplished naturalistic painter of horses, having shown at RA, RBA and NEAC, and she continued to exhibit at county shows and at White City, collecting commissions for horse portraits. By the year 1963, when she was engaged, married and then widowed and alone, living in Wales, Windham was wanting to explore a more creative, contemporary style. After a period of several years working for the Women's Institute and Red Cross and after her mother's death in 1971, Windham again seriously took up full-time painting, working in a Post-Impressionist manner, producing still lifes and landscapes. From the mid-1970s, encouraged by her painter friend Cecily Sash, she adopted asemi-abstract style, eventually moving entirely to non-figuration. William Scott, Patrick Heron and Paul Klee appear to be influences on her simple colour shapes. Had an eightieth birthday show at Oriel 31, Newtown, 1996. Lived in Hay-on-Wye, Herefordshire.

Alan WINDSOR 1931– Artist, writer on art and teacher, born in Fleetwood, Lancashire. Studied art at Regional College of Art in Manchester, 1949–54; Slade School of Fine Art, 1954–6; Paris and Aix Universities, 1956–7; and Courtauld Institute, 1967–9. Windsor became head of the history of art department at Reading University and was the editor of a *Handbook of Modern British Painting* 1900–1980, 1992. Showed at LG, Young Contemporaries, Gimpel Fils and elsewhere. Lived in Farnham, Surrey.

Zalmon WINER: *see* **ZALMON**

David John WINFIELD 1938– Painter and teacher, born and lived in London. Studied at London College of Printing, 1955–8, and Royal College of Art, 1959–62. Victoria & Albert Museum holds his work. Taught at Maidstone College of Art for some years.

Sarah WINFREY 1965– Abstract painter who did a foundation course at Cambridge College of Art and Technology, 1983–4, gaining a fine art honours degree at Leeds Polytechnic, 1984–7. Took part in International Ceramic Summer Workshop, Tokoname, Japan, 1986. Winfrey was part-time visual arts development officer at Peterborough Museum & Art Gallery, 1990–5, as well as holding other posts including secretary of Peterborough Sculpture Trust and project researcher at Glyndebourne Opera. Was artist-in- residence, Tiskarna Gallery, Begunji, Slovenia, 1994. Group shows included Great Bircham Gallery, Norfolk, 1988; David Holmes Gallery, Peterborough, 1993; The John Russell Gallery, Ipswich, 1995; and The Table Studio Group, The Living Room, 1996. Tokoname Museum and Tiskarna Gallery hold examples. Lived in King's Cliffe, Northamptonshire.

Joseph William WINKELMAN 1941– Etcher and relief printmaker, and teacher, born in Keokuk, Iowa, America. He studied at Ruskin School of Drawing, 1968–71, then became a freelance printmaker. From 1972–89 was a part-time tutor. Showed with RE and RWA both of which he was a member, Oxford Gallery, RA and with Wenniger Graphics in Boston. Ashmolean Museum in Oxford, National Museum of Wales in Cardiff, Victoria Art Gallery in Bath and Usher Gallery, Lincoln, hold examples. Lived in Headington, Oxford.

Richard WINKWORTH 1963– Artist, born in Bombay, India, who did a foundation course at the Brassey Institute, 1980–2; graduated in fine art, Brighton University, 1982–5; and gained his master's in printmaking at Chelsea School of Art, 1985–6. Group shows included *Spectator*/Adam & Co Young Professional Artists, Edinburgh and London, 1991–2 (first prize and purchase, 1991); Summer Show, Mercury Gallery, 1994; and L'Age d'Or, Jeremy Hunt Fine Art, 1997. Had a solo show at Sue Williams Gallery, 1993, later ones including Wilson Stephens Fine Art at The Gallery in Cork Street, 1998. The Council of Europe and several corporate collections hold examples.

Gerd WINNER 1936– Notable printmaker who worked in other media, born in Braunschweig, Germany. He attended Hochschule für Bildende Künste, Berlin, and Suomen Taide-akatemian Koulu, Helsinki, 1956–62, studied with W Volkert at Hochschule für Bildende Künste, Berlin, 1961–2, then from 1964 freelanced in Berlin. Between that time and 1969 produced etchings and screenprints with themes such as cars, monsters and lorries. In 1970 stayed in London, granted by the British Council. This was the beginning of an extensive co-operation with Chris Prater and Kelpra Studio. There were several series of screenprints: London Docks, St Katharine's Way, London Transport and Berlin Suite. Marlborough Graphics worked with Winner in 1971 and in 1972 Kelpra Editions produced a series which included Underground and Thames Sunday Afternoon. In 1973–4 Kelpra and Chris Prater published *Making a Print*. After this Winner consolidated his reputation internationally with such projects as Erie Railroad, video-documentation, 1975; three aluminium objects for the school centre Bei der Eich, Goslar-Oker, 1977; and Tokyo project, 1980. Whitworth Art Gallery, Manchester, holds his work. Lived and worked in München and Liebenburg, Germany.

Monica WINNER 1933– Artist in charcoal, oil and mixed media, born and lived in London. She studied at Camden Institute, Sir John Cass College, and Hertfordshire College of Art & Design, 1970–80. As well as Rembrandt, Goya and El Greco, Winner cited the pre-war German Expressionists, David Bomberg and Frank Auerbach as influences. Took part in group shows at Boundary, Square and Mall Galleries and Camden Arts Centre; shared a show with Helen Keats at Ben Uri Art Society, which holds her work, 1987; and had two solo exhibitions: at Crest Gallery, Totteridge, 1986, and Birmingham University, 1992.

Keith WINNETT 1931– Painter and teacher, born and lived in Coventry, Warwickshire, who attended the College of Art there, 1948–54, where his teachers included Paul Harris. During the 1950s held a number of teaching posts, with a special interest in tutoring the mentally disabled, from 1959 becoming full-time at Coventry College of Art after five years part-time there. Showed Zwemmer Gallery, Young Contemporaries, in the Coventry area and in Paris.

Alice Buxton WINNICOTT 1891–1973 Painter and potter who attended Newnham College, Cambridge, having come from an academic background. She studied art with Philip Conway in Richmond, Alfred Collister at Kingston (she was founder of the New Kingston Group), at Wimbledon and with Patrick Millard at St John's Wood, also at Central School of Arts and Crafts. Showed at RA, RCamA and elsewhere. She was the main designer of Claverdon Pottery from the mid-1930s. Later work was signed Claverdon or A Bourne Claverdon. Her pottery in Kent was left to the people who had helped her there. Winnicott's sister, Pauline Taylor, ran the Llanarth Welsh Pony Stud and was cellist with the Dorian Trio, which toured Welsh schools. Winnicott lived latterly at New Quay, Cardiganshire, and is buried in the cemetery there.

Helen Stirling WINSLOW 1890– Painter, notably in tempera, who studied privately in Italy. She was married to the artist Henry Winslow. Exhibited RA, RI, SWA, RBA and elsewhere. Member of the Tempera Society. Lived in London.

Henry WINSLOW 1874–c.1955 Watercolourist, etcher and writer, born in Boston, Massachusetts, America, son of the architect W H Winslow. He was married to the artist Helen Stirling Winslow. Attended École des Beaux-Arts and Whistler's School in Paris, which greatly influenced his style. Architecture, river and port scenes were favourite subjects. Exhibited with RA, RP, Chicago Society of Etchers of which he was a member, Brooklyn Society of Etchers, NEAC and Paris Salon. Winslow's books included *The Etching of Landscapes*, 1914, and a *Book of Poems*, 1953. Gerald M Norman Gallery held a show of Winslow's drawings in 1975. He was an Arts Club member who lived in London but travelled occasionally to New York. The Public Library there holds a lot of his work.

Paul WINSTANLEY 1954– Painter, photographer and teacher, born in Manchester. He studied at Lanchester Polytechnic, Coventry, 1972–3, Cardiff College of Art, 1973–6, and Slade School of Fine Art, 1976–8. He went on to teach at City University. Winstanley was much concerned with urban architecture in his pictures, representationally as in Walkway No.3, in John Moores Liverpool Exhibition, 1989–90; and in a geometrical abstract way as in his series of City Flats pictures held by Arts Council. Winstanley's painting College II, of 1992, was acquired for the European Parliament Collection and was in Twelve Stars, Arts Council Gallery in Belfast and tour, 1992–3.In 1991–2 he was artist-in-residence at Churchill College, Cambridge, followed by his solo shows Paintings, 1991–2, Kettle's Yard, Cambridge and tour, and Driven Landscapes, Camden Arts Centre, 1993. Later one-man exhibitions included Maureen Paley/Interim Art, from 1994; Nathalie Obadia, Paris, and CRG, New York, both from 1995. Lived in London.

Michael WINSTONE 1958– Sculptor, draughtsman and teacher, born in Canada, resident in England from 1962, settling in London. He studied at Portsmouth College of Art and Design, 1977–8, graduated with an honours degree in fine art, 1978–81, then obtained his master's degree from Royal College of Art, 1981–4. He lectured there, also at Kingston, Leeds and Liverpool Universities. Residencies included Grizedale Forest, Cumbria, 1984. Commissions included Gateshead Metropolitan Borough Council, public sculpture, 1985, and Buckmead School, Somerset, sculpture, 1988. Exhibited at Nicholas Treadwell Gallery, Canterbury, 1984; Shipley Art Gallery, Gateshead, 1986; and 1st RWA Open Sculpture Exhibition, 1993. Northern Arts holds examples.

Alexander Charles WINTER 1887–1969 Self-taught painter, born in Bradenham, Norfolk, who finally lived in the county at King's Lynn. Served in World War I, being commissioned in the Royal Air Force when it was formed in 1918, retiring in 1937 as a group captain. Exhibited RSA, NS and Paris Salon, having a solo show at Goupil Gallery. Fermoy Art Gallery, King's Lynn, held his work.

Eric WINTER 1905– Painter and illustrator who studied at Hornsey School of Art, 1921–9, under John Charles Moody. Exhibited at RA and lived in London.

Faith WINTER 1927– Sculptor in a variety of materials, born in Richmond, Surrey, who attended Guildford and Chelsea Schools of Art. She became a member of SPS and an associate of RBS, winning the Feodora Gleichen Memorial Fund award. Showed at RA, RBA and elsewhere, early work under her maiden name

Faith Ashe. Completed a number of commissions, including The Soldiers for the Army at Catterick Camp, Yorkshire, and Sir Arthur "Bomber" Harris outside St Clement Danes Church. Had a studio at Puttenham, Surrey.

Francis WINTER 1901–1996 Watercolourist, printmaker and teacher, born in London, who studied at Hornsey College of Art, 1915–26, teachers including John Henry Willis, John Charles Moody and Frank Swinstead; he also attended the London Day Training College, gaining his art teacher's diploma, teachers including the handwriting specialist Marion Richardson. Winter returned to Hornsey to become a senior lecturer. He was a president of SGA and was latterly an hon. retired fellow of RE. Lived in Aspenden, Buntingford, Hertfordshire.

M E WINTER 1926– Painter and draughtsman, born in Surbiton, Surrey. She studied at Kingston School of Art and the Royal Academy Schools, her teachers including Reginald Brill. Showed at Orleans House, Twickenham, and in other mixed shows. Lived in Hampton Wick, Surrey.

James William WINTERBOTTOM 1924– Painter and teacher, born in Leicester, where he attended the College of Art, 1940–4, then Royal College of Art. Returned to teach at Harrogate School of Art, where he lived. Exhibited RA, Young Contemporaries, Leicester Galleries, NEAC and widely in Yorkshire. Wakefield City Art Gallery and Museum holds his work.

Thom WINTERBURN 1970– Artist, born in Harrogate, Yorkshire, later living in Headingley, Leeds. He studied at Staffordshire Polytechnic, 1988–91. Exhibitions included Czech and Slovak Gallery, Leeds; Bradford Open Print Exhibition; and 1993–4 John Moores, in Liverpool.

David WINTERS 1942– Sculptor in a variety of materials, artist in two dimensions and teacher, born in Belfast, Northern Ireland. He attended the College of Art there, 1961–5, won several awards, then after a year teaching art at Lurgan College, 1965–6, studied at Royal College of Art, 1966–9. He returned to Belfast to teach at Ulster College, but during the 1970s travelled widely, including North America, Mexico, the Far East and Australia on grant and secondment. Exhibitions included Ulster Museum, Whitechapel Art Gallery, Arts Council of Northern Ireland Gallery and Project Gallery in Dublin. Hugh Lane Municipal Gallery of Modern Art in Dublin and Arts Council of Northern Ireland acquired Winters' work.

Denis WIRTH-MILLER 1915– Self-taught painter, born in Folkestone, Kent. Showed at Lefevre, Redfern and Beaux Arts Galleries, Minories in Colchester, Aldeburgh Festival and with Arts Council. HM The Queen, Arts Council and Contemporary Art Society hold examples. Lived in Wivenhoe, Essex.

Derwent WISE 1933– Painter who studied at the department of fine Art, King's College, University of Durham. He took part in many group exhibitions, including RA, RBA, NEAC, RI and The Broad Horizon, at Agnew, 1990. Wise also had solo shows, including University of Newcastle upon Tyne, University of York, the Stonegate Gallery in York and at Queen's Hall Gallery in Hexham. Lived in Northumberland.

Gillian WISE 1936– Artist working in a wide range of techniques, born in London, who between 1972–90 worked as Gillian Wise Ciobotaru. She studied at Wimbledon School of Art, 1954–7, eventually becoming known as one of the six British Constructivists. Gained a UNESCO Fellowship, Prague, Czechoslovakia, 1968; a British Council postgraduate scholarship to the Beaux-Arts, Leningrad, Russia, 1969–70, concentrating on Constructivism at Repin Institute; an Arts Council Award, 1976; and in 1981 a research grant, International Communication Agency, American Embassy. In 1978 Wise was commissioned by the Arts Council to curate the Constructivist section of the Hayward Annual '78 at Hayward Gallery, in which she participated as an artist. Commissioned works included wall screen with Anthony Hill for the Cunard liner *Queen Elizabeth II*, 1968; wall relief, Nottingham University Hospital, 1973–4; relief panel, Unilever House, 1982; and Engineers, 40 computer images on disk for Textum Ars, Paris, 1991. Wise held a large number of positions as research fellow and visiting artist in Britain and America and exhibited widely internationally. She was interested in comparative cultures as they related to the modern art movement, specialised in research into perception of colour in England and America and did much work with geometric forms. Tate Gallery, Victoria & Albert Museum and Contemporary Art Society hold examples. Travelled widely and lived latterly in Paris.

Irene WISE 1950– Painter, illustrator and teacher. She studied at the Froebel Institute, 1970–3, Chelsea School of Art, 1980–3, and the illustration department of Royal College of Art, 1983–7. From 1973–80 she taught in an Inner London Education Authority school. In 1987 she gained the Allen Lane Penguin Book Prize for Design History, the year she gained her master's degree with distinction in illustration and design history. She had shows at Amnesty International, Orleans House Gallery, Association of Illustrators, Glasgow School of Art and elsewhere, and in 1988 shared a show at New Grafton Gallery.

Gillian WISE CIOBOTARU: *see* **Gillian WISE**

Alice WISEMAN 1883– Painter, born in Middleton, Lancashire. After private education she studied with H Carruthers Gould at Heatherley's School of Fine Art. Showed at RA, elsewhere in London and at Paris Salon. Lived in Wimbish, Essex.

David WISEMAN 1949– Painter, draughtsman and teacher, born in Essex. He studied at Colchester School of Art, 1967–9, St Martin's School of Art, 1969–72, and Royal College of Art, 1972–5. From that time he was a visiting lecturer at various colleges, including Winchester, Hull and Cheltenham. Wiseman frequently worked on a large scale. He was originally con cerned with traditional abstract painters' problems: composition, treatment of surface and so on. Later he emphasised the natural environment as his starting point, his pictures being "attempts to find equivalents for certain events or moments in the landscape". This was evident in his solo show which travelled from Brighton Polytechnic Gallery, 1987–8. Wiseman took part in many group exhibitions and his awards included John Minton Award, 1974; Arts Council Award, 1976; and Greater London Arts Association Visual Arts Award, 1978. Other exhibitions included Serpentine Summer Show 1, at Serpentine Gallery, 1980; Peterborough Museum and Art Gallery, 1983; and Centre 181 Gallery, 1985.

Francis WISHART 1951– Painter and printmaker, son of the artists Michael Wishart and Anne Dunn, born in London, named after family friends Francis Wyndham and Francis Bacon. After studying at Slade School of Fine Art, Wishart moved to Paris, where he worked in collaboration with the master printers Lacourière et Frélaut. Wishart showed his work there, also in New York and London, where in 1997 he had an exhibition of monoprints at Michael Parkin Gallery. Work is held by Bibliothèque Nationale, Musée Carnavalet and British Embassy in Paris; Museum of Modern Art and the Metropolitan in New York; and Victoria & Albert Museum.

Michael WISHART 1928–1996 Painter, draughtsman and writer, full name John Michael Wishart, who was married for a time to the artist Anne Dunn, their son being the artist Francis Wishart. Michael studied at Bedales School, then the Central School of Arts and Crafts, under Bernard Meninsky; Anglo-French School where teachers included André Lhote; Cedric Morris' East Anglian School of Painting; and in Paris at Académie Julian. Wishart's hectic social and personal life, his friendship with major writers and painters and life abroad are entertainingly described in his autobiography *High Diver*, 1977. Wishart exhibited in RA Summer Exhibitions, including his portrait of the ballet dancer Rudolf Nureyev, 1968. Had a solo show at Archer Gallery, 1944; series at Leicester and Redfern Galleries; a retrospective at David Paul Gallery, Chichester, 1976; and an exhibition at Parkin Gallery, 1985. Arts Council and Contemporary Art Society hold examples. Lived in Hove, Sussex, but died in London, where he had been born.

Sylvia WISHART 1936– Painter and teacher, born in Stromness, Orkney. Until 1987 was a lecturer at Gray's School of Art, Aberdeen, when she returned to work in Orkney. She took part in extensive group shows, including The Faroe Islands Gallery; RHA; RA; Aberdeen Artists' Society: and Compass Gallery, Glasgow. Solo exhibitions ranged from Alnwick Gallery, Northumberland, through 57 Gallery in Edinburgh, Compass Gallery in 1984 and Pier Arts Centre, Stromness, Orkney, 1981 and 1987. Arts Council, RSA, Aberdeen Art Gallery and Contemporary Art Society hold her work.

Adrian WISZNIEWSKI 1958– Painter and draughtsman, born in Glasgow, of Polish extraction. Wiszniewski (pronounced Vishnevski) studied architecture at Mackintosh School of Architecture in Glasgow, 1975–9; then was at Glasgow School of Art, 1979–83. He won the Haldane Trust Award, Cargill Scholarship and Mark Rothko Memorial Trust Fund Award in the early 1980s and had his first solo exhibition at Compass Gallery in Glasgow in 1984. Air Gallery and Nicola Jacobs shows in London soon followed, as did the acquisition of work by Tate Gallery and Museum of Modern Art in New York. In 1986 Wiszniewski moved to Northumberland and from 1986–7 was artist-in-residence at Walker Art Gallery, Liverpool, his term concluding with a solo show. The artist later moved back to Glasgow. Wiszniewski fast built up an impressive list of appearances in exhibitions in Britain and abroad, many public collections acquiring his often large-scale pictures. As a painter he improvised, one idea leading to another, which gave his works a slightly Surrealist, dreamlike quality, full of allusions, symbolic objects and forms.

Jack Coburn WITHEROP 1906–1984 Painter and engraver of landscapes, river and coastal views and architecture; restorer. He studied at Liverpool School of Art, 1924–30, then went with a scholarship to the Royal College of Art, 1930–3, under Sir William Rothenstein and Malcolm Osborne, having some restoration training with Ernest Tristram. Won a travelling scholarship to Rome, studying there for several months, including restoration at the Vatican studio. After renting a studio in St Ives, Cornwall, 1936–9, he returned to Liverpool at the outbreak of World War II and for five years from 1940 worked for the Air Ministry. In 1945 Witherop began part-time teaching at Liverpool School of Art, from about 1946 being involved in restoration work at Walker Art Gallery. His own work adopted a thicker, looser style than the tight tempera of his St Ives days. In 1968 he stopped painting due to the pressure of restoration work for Walker Art Gallery, Lady Lever and Derby collections. Exhibited at National Gallery, RA and widely elsewhere throughout Britain, in America and South Africa. Work was bought by the Contemporary Art Society, Bradford, Birkenhead, Walker and other galleries.

Isaac WITKIN 1936– Sculptor and teacher, born in Johannesburg, South Africa, where he was initially educated, moving to England in 1957. Studied at St Martin's School of Art, 1957–61, under the influential teacher Anthony Caro. Witkin in 1961–4 was assistant to Henry Moore while developing his own abstract sculpture, mainly in steel but also in stone and wood. Taught at St Martin's 1963–4 and 1966–7; at Bennington College, Vermont, in America, 1965–6, being artist-in-residence there in 1967; then taught at Parsons School of Design, New York, from 1975. Showed at Rowan Gallery, Waddington Galleries and in America and won joint first prize at Paris Biennale in 1965. Arts Council holds his two pieces Night and Vermont III which date from the early 1960s.

Zennor WITNEY 1965– Painter in acrylic also interested in computer-generated art, teacher, born in the New Forest, Hampshire. She was the daughter of the sculptor Greta Berlin and grand-daughter of the artist Sven Berlin. Witney did a foundation course at Winchester School of Art, 1984–5; an honours degree in fine art at West Surrey College of Art and Design, Farnham, 1986–9; and her master's degree at University of South Glamorgan, 1990–2. In 1987 she was a printmaking tutor at Courbertou, France, in 1989–90 being a visiting teacher of printmaking at University of the West of England in Bristol, followed by work as a freelance artist and illustrator. Mixed shows included Young Painters South-East, Metropole Arts Centre, Folkestone, 1988 (work bought by Kent County Library); Arnolfini Gallery in Bristol, 1990; and Cooper's Gallery, Bristol, 1993. Had a solo show at Brewhouse Theatre and Art Centre, Taunton, 1991, and at The Gallery, Bristol, 1993. Lived in Clifton, Bristol.

Edward WOLFE 1897–1982 Portrait, flower and landscape painter, mainly in oil, illustrator and draughtsman in pen and ink and pencil. Born in Johannesburg, South Africa, Wolfe came to England and studied at the Slade School 1916–8, having in his native country worked for periods as a child actor and for a jeweller, during which time he had his first serious art lessons with the British painter George Smithard. Whilst at the Slade was invited by Nina Hamnett to join Roger Fry's Omega Workshops, with which he first exhibited in 1918, the same year that he initially showed with LG. One-man show at Leon Levson's Gallery, Johannesburg, in 1920, having returned in 1919 to paint there; the proceeds helped to fund his return to London, which then became his base, although he was throughout his life to travel in search of the sun. Over the years he painted in places such as France – he was early an admirer of Matisse, who influenced his work – Italy, Morocco, Spain, Tunisia and Mexico. Wolfe became a friend of many notable writers, such as Aldous Huxley, William Plomer and Arnold Bennett, his portraits of the last two being notable (Plomer is in the National Portrait Gallery). In the early 1930s designed sets for C B Cochran. During World War II work included acting as a censor for the BBC at Bristol. Wolfe exhibited extensively in Britain and abroad, mixed and one-man shows, and was elected RA in 1972. There was an Arts Council retrospective in 1967 and in 1997 another, celebrating his centenary, at Paisnel Gallery and James O'Connor, 4 New Burlington Street. Tate Gallery and many other public galleries hold Wolfe's work, which is often rich in colour, suffused in sunlight and highly decorative, but with an underlying strong draughtsmanship.

Erich WOLFSFELD c.1885–1956 Etcher, painter and teacher, born in Krojanke, Germany. He was brought up in Berlin, where he attended the Academy, 1902–13, although had periods away, studying at Académie Julian, Paris, under Jules Lefèbvre, and he learned etching in the studio of Hans Meyer. In 1910 he won the Kaiser Wilhelm Gold Medal for his picture The Archers. Wolfsfeld early showed himself to be an artist in the academic tradition, a fine draughtsman. After Army service in World War I he was in 1920 appointed professor of painting and etching at Berlin Academy. This post he held until 1935, when Nazi pressure forced him out. Between the wars Wolfsfeld established a notable reputation, and he built up a substantial output partly based on extensive travels in Europe and North Africa. He fled Germany in 1939, and just before the war an exhibition of his work was put on at Graves Art Gallery, Sheffield, which led to portrait commissions. His portrait of the sculptor Sir Goscombe John was later acquired by National Portrait Gallery. A number of provincial galleries also hold his work. Wolfsfeld was interned briefly on the Isle of Wight, then settled in London. After the war he continued to travel. He began showing at RA in 1943 and in 1953 Derby Museum and Art Gallery gave him a solo exhibition. In 1977 Belgrave Gallery had an extensive show.

Joan Elizabeth Margaret WOLKERS-RANSOME 1928– Painter, notably of portraits, born in Tunbridge Wells, Kent. Studied at Malvern School of Art with Victor Hume Moody, 1945–50; Royal Academy Schools, teachers including William Dring and Bernard Fleetwood-Walker, 1950–4; and at Amsterdam's Royal Academy, 1954–8. Showed at RA, RP, NEAC and in provincial art galleries. Lived in Exeter, Devon.

Charles WOLLASTON 1914–1992 Painter, potter, printmaker and teacher, born in Frodsham, Cheshire. After Liverpool College Wollaston attended Slade School of Fine Art, 1946–50, teachers including Randolph Schwabe and William Coldstream. Taught for many years at Bognor Regis Training College/College of Education. Was a member of SGA, also showing at RCamA, RP, NEAC and RHA. West Sussex County Council owns a range of his work in various media. Lived in the county at Felpham.

Alfred WOLMARK 1877–1961 Painter and multi-talented designer, born in Warsaw, Poland, travelling to settle in England with his parents as a small boy in 1883. He studied at Royal Academy Schools in the mid-1890s, winning a silver medal for drawing in 1897. Had his first solo show at Bruton Galleries, 1905. He was to build up a wide-ranging appearance in group shows, at RA, 1901–36; AAA, 1908–16; IS, 1911–25; and with 1910–11 first Post-Impressionist exhibition in London, organised by Roger Fry. Soon began to show on continent and in America. Among Wolmark's designing jobs were designs for two Diaghilev ballets, in 1911; stained glass window for St Mary's Church, Slough, in 1915; and decorative pottery for an exhibition in 1916 at Martyn's Gallery. Towards the end of his life he showed extensively in one-man exhibitions at Ben Uri Gallery, which gave him a memorial show in 1961. Fine Art Society had a substantial show in 1970. Work in collections of Tate Gallery, National Portrait Gallery and in many provincial galleries. Died in London.

Garnet WOLSELEY 1884–1967 Painter, born in London, father of the artist John Wolseley. He studied at Slade School of Fine Art, gaining a scholarship in 1901, where he was a prizewinner. Showed at RA, RWA, NEAC and in the provinces. National Museum of Wales holds his work Visions. Wolseley found Celtic pottery vessels which he presented to the British Museum, and he wrote for learned journals on prehistory. Lived in Nettlecombe, Somerset.

John WOLSELEY 1938– Printmaker, painter and teacher, son of the artist Garnet Wolseley. After attending Byam Shaw and St

Martin's Schools of Art Wolseley in 1959–62 worked in Paris with the printmaker S W Hayter, showing at Atelier 17. After a survey trip down the Dordogne river in France in a collapsible dinghy, from 1962–9 Wolseley worked in Birgit Skiöld's print workshop, in 1966 creating 3D works with Noah Morris for Wardour Music Festival. In 1970 Wolseley returned to west of England and started the Nettlecombe Studios artists' and farmers' co-operative, also lecturing at West of England Art College in Bristol. He had had a first solo show at Architectural Association in 1962 with one at Mayor Gallery in 1965. Work in Malta and Gozo in 1968–71 resulted in another exhibition at Mayor. After being included in Florence and Buenos Aires Print Biennales and winning the Kantos Prize for his Cycle of Love etchings Wolseley in 1974–5 spent six months in the Spanish Pyrenees and went on an expedition up the Skrang River, Borneo, moving to Australia in 1976 where he established a new career. He lived all over the continent, latterly in St Kilda, Victoria, and held a number of teaching posts and residencies. His work was always a reflection of the landforms in which he found himself. Notable among his shows was Nomadism: John Wolseley, Twelve Years in Australia, University of Melbourne, 1988. Arts Council, Contemporary Art Society and major Australian galleries hold examples.

Margaret Elizabeth WOLVERSON 1937– Horse and portrait painter, miniaturist and teacher, born in Weston-super-Mare, Somerset, married for a time to the sculptor Martin Wolverson. Studied at Dudley School of Art, 1953–5; Wolverhampton College of Art, 1955–7; and Leicester College of Art, 1957–8, going on to teach at Hornsea Institute of Further Education and Stourbridge College of Art. Exhibitions included RMS of which she was an associate and SM. Ferens Art Gallery in Hull holds her work. Lived in Cheltenham, Gloucestershire.

Martin WOLVERSON 1939– Sculptor in a range of materials and teacher, born in Wolverhampton, Staffordshire, married for a time to the artist Margaret Wolverson. He studied at Wolverhampton College of Art, 1956–60, then Goldsmiths' College, 1960–1, gaining his teacher's certificate. Teaching appointments included Regional College of Art/Hull College of Higher Education. Wolverson was a fellow of RBS, winning its Silver Medal. Exhibited York and Keele Universities, Minories in Colchester and Alwin Gallery. Ferens Art Gallery in Hull and National Coal Board held his work. Lived in Hornsea, Yorkshire.

Jane WOMERSLEY 1954– Artist, notable for untitled constructions from layers of paper, born in Yorkshire. She studied at Beaux-Arts in Marseilles, 1973–4, Manchester Polytechnic, 1974–5, and Chelsea School of Art, 1975–8. Held a fellowship at Gloucester School of Art, 1979–80. Mixed exhibitions included New Contemporaries at ICA, 1978; The Uses of Drawing at Whitechapel Art Gallery, 1979; Cheltenham Art Gallery and Museum, 1980; and Summer Show 3 at Serpentine Gallery, 1981. In that year she had a solo exhibition at Arnolfini Gallery in Bristol. Lived for a time in London.

Ming WONG 1971– Painter and playwright, born in Singapore, who studied there at Raffles Junior College, Nanyang Academy of Fine Arts and LaSalle College of the Arts, then at Slade School of Fine Art. In 1995, his first solo show in 1995, Wayang Sayang, took traditional street opera as its theme and was a sell-out at the Republic's leading contemporary art venue, Substation Gallery. Buyers included Singapore Art Centre and Singapore Art Museum. Group shows included Singapore Art Fair '92, held in Singapore in 1992; and in 1994 Pastel Society of America 22nd Annual Open, New York, and Royal Over-Seas League Open, both 1994. In 1996 the League gave Ming Wong a solo exhibition, Karaoke (The Electric Geisha), an extract from the artist's first full-length play, *Ka-Ra-you-OK?* being performed at the opening.

Ronald WONG 1940– Self-taught artist, notable for aviation subjects, born in Hong Kong, working mainly in oil and acrylic. Wong gained an honours degree in biochemistry at Hatfield Polytechnic, then worked in the Health Service in London, painting spare-time. In 1974 one of Wong's early aviation pictures won the SBAC (Society of British Aerospace Companies) Trophy. Two years later he became a full-time artist. Wong was uncompromising on the need for technical accuracy, combining a dramatic use of light, colour and perspective to achieve a special dynamism and atmosphere. He was a member of the Guild of Aviation Artists and its American equivalent. Worked closely with Royal Air Force and United States Air Force personnel; had pictures at many bases, including Royal Air Force Strike Command. Also painted wildlife, marine and motoring subjects, showing with RSMA and SWLA and Guild of Motoring Artists of which he was also a member. Wong gained the Nockolds Trophy in 1987 and 1993 and the Aviation Painting of the Year Award, 1995. Lived in St Albans, Hertfordshire.

John WONNACOTT 1940– Painter and draughtsman, born in London. He studied at Slade School of Fine Art, 1958–63. Wonnacott participated in a number of prestigious group exhibitions, including Painting and Perception, at MacRobert Arts Centre, Stirling, 1971; British Painting '74, at Hayward Gallery, 1974; British Painting 1952–77, at RA, 1977; Britain Salutes New York, at Marlborough Gallery, New York, 1983; Salute to Turner, Agnew, 1989; and The Pursuit of the Real, British Figurative Painting from Sickert to Bacon, Manchester City Art Gallery and tour, 1990. He showed solo at The Minories, Colchester, 1977; Rochdale Art Gallery and tour, 1978; a series at Marlborough Fine Art from 1980; Scottish National Portrait Gallery, Edinburgh, 1986; and Agnew, 1992. That exhibition included a number of pictures by Wonnacott related to commissions as well as pictures centred on his home in Leigh-on-Sea, Essex. Wonnacott was a realist, able to tackle big-scale subjects such as Whitehills Earth Station, Oxfordshire, or Devonport Dockyard. He said that whether the object of scrutiny was a head or a ship, "my paintings deal with the two-dimensional facts of surface appearance as transmitted from retina to memory." Tate Gallery and Imperial War Museum hold examples.

Winifred WONNACOTT fl. from c.1925–1969 Artist and teacher, she was born of English parents in Belfast, Northern Ireland, later studying craft, sculpture and design at Royal College of Art. At the College she met Charles Tunnicliffe, then in his second year, whom she was soon to marry. She acted as a model for him. In the late 1920s she became a peripatetic teacher in Manchester and then the Macclesfield area, giving up teaching after she and her husband moved to Anglesey just after World War II. Shortly before her death she was collaborating with him on a book, which had to be abandoned.

Alan WOOD 1935– Painter, collagist and teacher, full name John Alan Wood. He was born in Widnes, Lancashire and studied at Liverpool College of Art, 1954–9, then began extensive series of teaching appointments, interspersed with living and working periodically near St Ives in Cornwall and travelling to North America to teach from 1970. Periods as artist-in-residence at University of Cincinnati and teaching at Capilano College, North Vancouver, were included. In addition to extensive group show participations had many one-man exhibitions including New Art Centre; Demarco Gallery, Edinburgh; and University of Cincinnati. Won commissions for a large mural for hall of residence at Leeds University and for government of British Columbia. It holds his work, as do Adelaide and Flinders Universities in Australia, WAC, Tate Gallery and CASW.

Alice WOOD 1968– Artist and illustrator who studied at Bournemouth & Poole College of Art & Design and Camberwell School of Arts and Crafts. Her exhibitions included Association of Illustrators and England & Co, in 1992, in Art in Boxes. For a time Wood assisted the artist Tom Phillips.

Andy WOOD 1947– Artist in watercolour, oil and acrylic, born in Porlock, Somerset, subjects being detailed figurative work, Landscape, architecture, still life and some portraits. He attended Croydon College of Art, 1965–7, then Newport College of Art, 1967–70, gaining his art and design diploma. Between 1970–8 Wood did many jobs to support part-time painting, including school caretaker, theatre electrician, labourer and adventure playground supervisor; then he became a full-time artist. Wood became an associate member of RBA in 1980, in 1981 being made a member of RI. Group exhibitions included Piccadilly Gallery, 1980; Morley Gallery, 1981; Fry Art Museum, Seattle, America, 1986; and Marita Gilliam Gallery, Raleigh, North Carolina, America, 1990. Had a solo show at Westgate Gallery, 1979, later ones included David Hibberd Gallery, Lyme Regis, 1989, and Honiton Festival, 1992. Sultan of Oman, Chelsea Arts Club and Central Carolina Bank hold examples. Lived in Charmouth, Bridport, Dorset.

Bérénice WOOD 1888– Glass painter and decorative artist, daughter of the artist Davidson Knowles. She studied art at Regent Street Polytechnic School of Art and married the painter William T Wood. She was a member of NS 1944–54, also exhibiting at UA and elsewhere. Lived in London.

Charles WOOD 1902– Portrait painter, poster designer and illustrator, whose home was Eastbourne, Sussex, where he attended the School of Art under Arthur Reeve-Fowkes and Oliver Senior. He illustrated for a number of periodicals especially with a nautical theme, including work for the Admiralty. Wrote *How to Draw Portraits* and *Figures in Action*.

Christopher WOOD 1962– Painter in oil, born in Leeds, Yorkshire, who studied at Edinburgh College of Art, 1980–4. After doing odd jobs to support his painting, he went professional in 1987. Was a member of SSWA. There he won the Gatehouse Gallery Award, 1994; the Scottish Arts Club Award and Nancy Graham Memorial Prize, both 1995; and at the Royal Glasgow Institute of the Fine Arts Wood won the James Torrance Memorial Award, 1993, and Army Award, 1994. Also showed at RSA, RSW, SSA and many private galleries, including Thackeray, Cadogan Contemporary, Open Eye in Edinburgh and William Hardie, Glasgow. Had a solo show at The Shore Gallery, Edinburgh, 1987, one at Corpus Christi College, Oxford, 1989, a series at Macaulay Gallery, Stenton, from 1989, and at Vicarage Cottage Gallery, North Shields, from 1992, with one at The Gatehouse Gallery, Glasgow, 1995. Lived in Haddington, East Lothian.

Craig WOOD 1960– Sculptor using modern materials to create abstract, floor-based works, born in Leith, Edinburgh. He attended Dyfed College of Art, Carmarthen, 1984–5, graduating with honours from Goldsmiths' College, 1985–8. Group exhibitions included Monumental Works, The Crypt, 1988; Summer Show, Laure Genillard Gallery, 1990; and Galerie des Archives and Graeme Murray Gallery, Edinburgh, both 1991. Had solo exhibition at The Crypt, 1989, others taking place in 1990 at Laure Genillard, Galerie des Archives and Galerie Etienne Ficheroulle, Brussels.

David WOOD 1933–1996 Painter and printmaker, born in Scotland. He attended Edinburgh College of Art, Sir John Cass College and Slade School of Fine Art. His mixed exhibition appearances included RBA, RSMA, UA, Bloomsbury Workshop, the Meyer Gallery in Ingatestone and Chappel Galleries, Chappel, Essex. For over 20 years Wood lived in East Anglia; he was a member of Colchester Art Society and Ipswich Art Society and was involved in the Gainsborough's House Print Workshop, in Sudbury. Movement and colour were key factors in the work of Wood, who commonly featured people in his pictures. Travelled extensively. His solo exhibitions included The Minories, Colchester; The John Russell Gallery, Ipswich; and Chappel Galleries, Chappel, which gave him a tribute exhibition in 1997. Wood's pictures are in municipal, business and private collections in Britain and abroad. David Wood's grandfather was the artist Frank Wood, his father Watson Wood. For many years he lived at Dedham, Essex, and died of leukemia.

Eleanor WOOD 1955– Watercolourist, printmaker and teacher, born in London, who exploited the natural properties of papers in her works, which included hand-drawn books. The artist studied at Hornsey, Winchester and Chelsea Schools of Art, then settled in the northeast of England where she was active in the Newcastle Group of artists. She showed with the group at Laing Art Gallery, Newcastle; in the 1988 Cleveland Drawing Biennale; in 8 × 8 at Curwen Gallery; and was included in the South Bank Centre 1988–9 touring show The Presence of Painting. Arts Council has several examples of her work. Lived in Darlington, County Durham.

Flora WOOD 1910– Painter, draughtsman and sculptor, born at Portobello, near Edinburgh. After boarding school in England Wood in the mid-1920s spent a winter in Florence, where she underwent academic education at the studio of Mafori Seveni. Returning to Edinburgh, she studied at Edinburgh College of Art with William Gillies and D M Sutherland, followed by a short period of sculpture under Alexander Carrick and further studies in Paris with André Lhote. After marrying Kenneth Maclay, a stockbroker, in 1939, she holidayed abroad including France where she met Picasso, a notable influence. From 1940s showed with RSA and Royal Glasgow Institute of the Fine Arts; also with three bodies of which she was a member: SSA, SSWA and Glasgow Society of Women Artist. Scottish Arts Council sponsored a solo show at Citizen's Theatre, Glasgow, in 1970. Another followed at Lillie Art Gallery, Milngavie, Glasgow, near where she had a studio, in 1979. Further exhibitions included England & Co, 1989. Scottish Arts Council and Kelvingrove Art Gallery, Glasgow, hold her work.

Frank WOOD 1862–1953 Painter and teacher, especially noted for marine subjects, born in Berwick-upon-Tweed, Northumberland. He was the father of the artist Watson Wood and grandfather of David Wood. Studied art at South Kensington Schools and Académie Julian, Paris. Taught as second master at Newcastle School of Art, 1883–9, then as head of Hawick School of Art, 1889–99. Much of Wood's work was done in the northeast of England where he lived and in Edinburgh. Showed at RA, RSA, RSW and elsewhere. In 1995 Mainhill Gallery, Ancrum, held a show of the family's work.

Frank WOOD 1904–1985 Artist who favoured tempera, and teacher, born in Liverpool, who settled with his family in Sunderland, County Durham, 1918. Attended Bede Grammar School, then the local Art School under Richard Ray, eventually opting to teach still life, landscape, pattern construction and textile printing there. Showed at RA, Society of Mural Decorators and Painters in Tempera, RP and with Sunderland Art Club, of which he was chairman. Wood's portrait in tempera on board of his colleague John Summers, with whom he shared sketching holidays, exhibited RP in 1937 and latterly in a private collection, was shown at Sunderland Museum and Art Gallery in 1995.

Gerald Stanley Kent WOOD 1923– Architectural artist, technician and illustrator, and teacher, born in Cambridge. From 1934–9 studied art with Henry John Sylvester Stannard. Wood was a member of the Society of Architectural Illustrators and was qualified to teach in further education. Showed widely, including RA, SGA, Britain in Watercolours, RI, NEAC and elsewhere. The Theatre Museum holds his work. Lived in Luton, Bedfordshire.

Hamilton WOOD: *see* **S E Hamilton WOOD**

Harold WOOD 1918– Versatile and colourful artist, born in Preston, Lancashire, where he studied part-time at Harris Art School, 1935–9. He claimed to be "self-taught in painting"; however, in the five years to World War II he "learned much technical expertise" while working in the decorative art department at Leyland Paint & Varnish. After over six years' wartime service in the Army, including a period in Germany, Wood worked as an illustrator in London. He learned etching for two terms at the Central School of Arts and Crafts, but otherwise "spent all my spare time in the National Gallery". The early Italian masters, Oskar Kokoschka whom he met in 1954, and the writings of John Berger were key influences. For a time Wood was involved in town planning, architectural drawing and model-making, including work for Lancashire County Council, Peterlee New Town and George Wimpey. There was a period restoring furniture in Rye. From 1955 Wood painted full-time, having a notable solo show at Beaux Arts Gallery in 1956. His own family experiences, "a kind of social realism", were key themes, and he gained publicity for a series of oversize portraits of himself and his pregnant pig pictures. As well as mixed shows at Zwemmer and Redfern Galleries and in the provinces, Wood had a solo show at Upper Grosvenor Galleries, 1964, and at Bramante Gallery, Victoria, 1968–70. Eventually Wood worked on commission for the Mathaf Gallery, spending time in Saudi Arabia, reconstructing scenes of the kingdom's history and the story of Abdul Aziz Ibn Saud. He carried out extensive commissions for the writer Wolf Mankowitz and sold to clients in the entertainment world, including Leslie Bricusse, John Mills, Bryan Forbes and Charlton Heston. Completed a mural for Yorkshire High School for Boys, Scarborough, 1959, and Cleveleys Parish Church, 1963. Lived finally at Arlinstown, Ballinghassig, County Cork, Ireland.

James WOOD 1889–1975 Painter, draughtsman, writer and aesthete, born in Southport, Lancashire. From 1908–11 he read history at Cambridge University, then in Paris after studying etching pursued painting with Percyval Tudor-Hart before going to Munich. During World War I was in the Army and Royal Flying Corps, later working on battleship camouflage. Among Wood's writings after World War I were *The Foundations of Aesthetics*, fellow authors being C K Ogden and I A Richards. He also wrote on colour harmony, a favourite topic, and in 1926 published *New World Vistas*, an autobiographical work. From 1930s Wood was a student of Persian Art, which prompted him to learn Persian and to become art adviser to the Persian government. His own paintings were influenced by Kandinsky, and he showed at Leicester and Zwemmer Galleries in solo exhibitions. After 1955 rarely exhibited, but painted several portraits of Cambridge academics. Wood lived in a remote cottage above Llantony, Monmouthshire, from which he continued to monitor artistic developments and where he worked until his death. In 1980 Blond Fine Art held a show of his output. Wood was married to a painter, Elisabeth Robertson, who had previously been the wife of the artist and writer Humphrey Slater.

James Porteous WOOD 1919– Painter, muralist, black-and-white artist and designer, born in Edinburgh. He studied at the College of Art there, 1935–40, teachers including David Young Cameron, and won a travelling scholarship. Became chief designer for Asprey, the Bond Street goldsmiths, silversmiths and jewellers, 1956–80. Showed at RA, RSA, RSW of which he was made a member in 1945, and elsewhere, and had solo exhibitions. Lived latterly in Arisaig, Invernesshire, and sometimes signed work Porteous Wood.

John Barlow WOOD 1862–1949 Watercolour landscapist, born in Etruria, Staffordshire. In 1911 he married Constance Emily Fry, a Quaker, in Ipswich, having lived nearby for some years at Woodbridge, Suffolk. Her brothers Edward Ransome Fry and Robert Douglas Fry were both artists. Wood had worked for Minton's, the potters, on hand-painted ware for a time and from 1885 had shown with Ipswich Art Club, of which he was a member. In 1911 Wood moved to live near Kendal and was an exhibitor with the Lake Artists' Society. He also exhibited at RA, RBA, Walker Art Gallery in Liverpool and with the Royal Glasgow Institute of the Fine Arts. Ipswich Museums and Galleries hold four works by him. He is buried in the Friends' Burial Ground, Kendal.

Karl G WOOD 1888–1958 Watercolourist who lived in Lincolnshire. He worked as an art master, hospital secretary, muralist and organist. Wood cycled all over Britain painting watercolours of buildings and for 20 years set out to record all surviving windmills in Britain, a project which remained unpublished at his death. Wood died at Pluscarde Abbey, Elgin, to which he left 4,000 of his watercolours. These were eventually distributed to record offices and museums. In 1977 Cheltenham Art Gallery and Museums was given over 100 watercolours of Gloucestershire by Wood.

Kenneth WOOD 1921– Artist in pen, watercolour and mixed media, born in London. He studied at Regent Street Polytechnic School of Art, 1940–52, less World War II service including time in the Royal Air Force as a pilot. From 1955 Wood worked both as an architect-designer and as a painter-draughtsman. He completed a relief mural in Guy's Hospital and showed at RA, Royal Exchange, South London Gallery and Waterman's Art Centre in Brentford. Also had a solo show there and at Leatherhead Theatre Gallery and White Rose Gallery, Hampton Court. He was a member of Contemporary Art Society and local art societies. Lived in Teddington, Middlesex.

Lawson WOOD 1878–1957 Illustrator, designer and painter whose work had a strong comic flavour. He was born in London as Clarence Lawson Wood, son of the artist Lawson Pinhorn Wood and grandson of painter and printmaker Lewis John Wood. He studied at Slade School of Fine Art, Heatherley's School of Fine Art and Frank Calderon's School of Animal Painting. For several years from the late 1890s Wood worked as principal artist for the publisher Arthur Pearson. As well as *Pearson's Magazine* he drew for many others including *Boy's Own Paper*, *Illustrated London News* and *The Strand Magazine*. His own books included *The Noo-Zoo Tales*, 1922, and *Meddlesome Monkeys*, 1946. For a while Wood ran a factory producing toys to his own design. Lawson was a member of RI and London Sketch Club and showed prolifically with Walker's Galleries and Brook Street Art Gallery, also RA and elsewhere. Lived finally in Kent.

Lucy WOOD 1969– Artist who gained an honours degree in fine art from Camberwell College, 1992, her master's in arts criticism from City University, 1994. Charles Saatchi, for the Saatchi Collection, bought Wood's early work Can't Play, Won't Play!, a trampoline with a sheet of galss where the canvas should be. That led her to seek other contraptions from children's playgrounds condemned as unsafe. Wood collected them herself in hired trucks. They were refurbished and repainted, with a list of casualties displayed alongside, safety organisations helping her to compile statistics. Examples exhibited in 1998 were Fatal Attraction, a car-shaped climbing frame condemned for trapping children, at Whitechapel Open; and the skeletal tank War Games, from a Romford council estate, shown at East International, Norwich School of Art and Design, Norwich. Wood had a solo show at Auckland Society of Arts, Auckland, New Zealand, 1989. Other mixed exhibitions included Alice, Cornerhouse, Manchester, 1998. Lived and worked in south London.

Olive WOOD fl. c.1930–1973 Painter, draughtsman and portrait miniaturist, born and lived in London, daughter of the miniaturist James Wood. Like him she was a member of RMS, being also a member of SWA and South London Group. Studied at Camberwell School of Arts and Crafts under Herbert Cole and at Clapham School of Art with Leonard Nightingale. Exhibited RA, SWA, South London Group and elsewhere. During World War I Olive Wood served as a driver in the Women's Legion, which was attached to the Army Service Corps. Imperial War Museum holds her work.

Peter Macdonough WOOD 1914–1982 Painter in oil and watercolour, line artist and etcher with special interest in marine subjects. Born at Twickenham, Middlesex, studied art at Southend School of Art, Slade School of Fine Art under Randolph Schwabe and at Hornsey School of Art. Wrote several books on sea and shipping subjects. Exhibited RA, NEAC, RWS and in the provinces. The National Maritime Museum, Greenwich, holds his work. Lived in London.

Porteus WOOD: *see* **James Porteus WOOD**

Rendle WOOD 1894– Painter, born in Plymouth, Devon, full name Robert Sydney Rendle Wood. After Plymouth College of Technology Wood attended the local School of Art under

Frederick Shelley and Edinburgh College of Art with David Foggie. It was probably from Foggie that he acquired his manner of outlining subjects. Wood was a member of NS in which he was active to 1966, St Ives and Plymouth Societies of Artists and the St Mawes Group. Between 1925–30 he was hon. secretary of Ulster Arts Club and worked as fine art manager for the Pollock Gallery, Belfast, also being hon. secretary and a member of Ulster Academy of Arts. He finally lived in St Austell, Cornwall, and is remembered as manager of Widgers, a paint and wallpaper store. Also showed at RWA, RSW, SSA, Walker Art Gallery and elsewhere.

S E Hamilton WOOD 1918– Painter, sculptor and teacher, born in Norwich. He attended the School of Art there, 1936–40, Central School of Arts and Crafts, 1947, and London University Institute of Education. He settled in Norwich and became a prominent member of the Twenty Group there and Norfolk and Norwich Art Circle. Also showed Arts Council and Norwich Castle Museum and Art Gallery and made sculpture for buildings in Norwich. Wrote criticism for the *Eastern Evening News*. He was sometimes just known as Hamilton Wood.

Sidney WOOD 1918– Painter, printmaker and teacher, born in Norwich. Studied at School of Art there, 1936–40, at University of London Institute of Education, 1946, and in same year at Central School of Art. Showed at Mansard Gallery and with Norfolk and Norwich Art Circle, of which he was a member. Shortly after World War II he joined the staff of the City of Norwich School, his old school. Lived in Thorpe, Norfolk.

Susan WOOD 1949– Artist and designer, born in London. She studied at North East London Polytechnic and Sadler's Wells Design School. Shows included Ikon Gallery, Birmingham, 1981; Norwich Castle Museum Gallery, 1982; and in 1983 British Artists at Cyprus College of Art, at Woodlands Art Gallery.

Tom WOOD 1955– Artist in various media, born in Dar es Salaam, Tanganyika. In 1959 he moved to West Yorkshire, studying at Batley School of Art, 1975, Leeds Polytechnic, 1976 and Sheffield School of Art, 1976–8. In 1979 Wood gained a Yorkshire Arts Association Award, one of many awards and prizes won. Others included Elizabeth Greenshields Foundation (Canada) Award, in 1981; Calouste Gulbenkian Foundation Young Printmakers Award, 1983; a second Elizabeth Greenshields Award in 1984; Ninth International Print Biennale prizewinner, 1986; and Hon. Fellowship, Sheffield Polytechnic, 1989. Wood was a prolific exhibitor in group, two-man and solo shows, which included a one-man show at Lister Gallery, Bradford, 1986; one-man exhibition at Dean Clough Contemporary Art Gallery, Halifax, 1987; a one-man show, HRH The Prince of Wales: A Portrait Commission, at Dean Clough and Agnew, 1989; and a solo exhibition at Wakefield Art Gallery, 1990. Wood's work was both figurative and abstract. He said that recurring images were important to him, "a list of odd infatuations – St Michael, fish, branches, heads, dreaming, ladders, vessels, seeds, all with symbolic precedents." Wood's work is held by HRH The Prince of Wales, the National Portrait Gallery Print Collection, Leeds University, London Underground and many provincial galleries.

Victor WOOD 1904–1977 Painter in various media, draughtsman and teacher, born in Dublin as Albert Victor Ormsby Wood into a cultivated family. After attending Aravon School, a private school at Bray, in 1920s entered Metropolitan School of Art in Dublin. For several years worked in stained glass studios of Harry Clarke, sometimes modelling for him. Towards end of 1920s moved to London, married, exhibited at RA and RHA and opened his own art school. After volunteering for the British Army he was badly wounded in the London Blitz and was invalided out. In 1949 moved to Ansty, Sussex, where he lived the life of a reclusive artist, in 1960 moving to Hunstanton, Norfolk, where his eyesight continued to deteriorate, so that he used a jeweller's eyeglass to paint. For many years Wood created highly stylised pictures of women and wrote erotic fiction. Examples were shown in the exhibition A Voyeur in Art at Michael Parkin Gallery, 1992.

Watson WOOD 1900–1985 Painter and printmaker, father of the artist David Wood and son of Frank Wood, with whom he studied at Académie Julian, Paris, in 1920s. On his return Watson attended Edinburgh College of Art and Glasgow School of Art, then set up a studio in Glasgow and was married to a fellow student Alice Sandeman, a member of the Sandeman's port family. Watson was much involved in exhibiting clubs and groups in Scotland, including the New 4 Group, and did a large amount of commissioned work, such as calendars. He was very knowledgeable about Scottish folklore and history, was widely read in Walter Scott, and had clients among Scots settled in North America. In World War II served in the Black Watch, based in Edinburgh. Lived for a time in Benderloch, Argyllshire, and at Strathyre, Perthshire, dying at Comrie. In 1995 Mainhill Gallery, Ancrum, had a show of the Woods' work.

Wilfrid René WOOD 1888–1976 Painter, mostly in watercolour, designer and printmaker, born in Cheadle Hulme, Manchester, his mother an artist. He left the local Grammar School at 16 and was apprenticed to a lithographic printer while training at Manchester School of Art. After study at Central School of Art he served in Army in World War I, then in 1918 attended Slade School of Fine Art under Henry Tonks and Philip Wilson Steer. Based in London, Wood now travelled widely, specialising in architectural subjects. He had his first major London show at Walker's Galleries in 1924. Became involved in poster design for London Underground, Strelizia Reginae being very successful. In 1927 Wood began a series of town exhibitions starting in Oxford, some with his nephew Lawrence G Linnell, and in the late 1930s settled in Barnack, near Stamford, Lincolnshire, marrying the artist Joan Beeby Kingsford. Stamford was to be his subject, although he retained a connection with Manchester, being a member of the Academy for over 40 years and vice-president for over a decade. Wood helped establish the Stamford Arts Centre in

1966 and fund an improved gallery. The residue of his estate was used by Manchester City Art Gallery to buy notable works by modern British artists. In 1988 Stamford Museum and Peterborough Museum and Art Gallery, which hold his work, held a joint show.

William Thomas WOOD 1877–1958 Painter, notable for his atmospheric landscapes of Sussex, born in Ipswich, Suffolk, son of the artist Thomas Wood and married to the painter Bérénice Wood. He studied at Regent Street Polytechnic School of Art and in Italy and was an official war artist in the Balkans in World War I. His style is well captured in the watercolours Downs at Wepham, Arundel, and Burpham, near Arundel, illustrated in *Artists' Country*, by C Geoffrey Holme and G S Sandilands, published 1932. Wood was a member of RWS of which for a time he was vice-president, ROI and NS and was a prolific exhibitor, including RA, Chenil and Goupil Galleries and Walker Art Gallery in Liverpool, having a series of solo shows at Leicester Galleries. He was also a member of the Arts and Chelsea Arts Clubs and is represented in many public collections. Lived in London.

Thomas E WOODARD 1903–1975 Painter who was an engineer by profession. He studied at Regent Street Polytechnic School of Art and Northampton Polytechnic. Helped found the Islington Art Circle, encouraged by Walter Sickert, and the Society of Art in Harlow, where he later lived. Exhibited at RA, public galleries in Bradford and Eastbourne and elsewhere. His wife Florence was also a member of the Islington group.

Ruth WOODBRIDGE 1909–1982 Watercolour painter, mainly of flowers, and teacher, also known as Ruth Law. She was born in Uxbridge, Middlesex, and studied art at Harrow School of Art. Between 1933–44 taught variously at that school and at Watford School of Art and St Albans School of Art. Showed in provinces and at Guernsey Eisteddfod in early 1950s. Lived at Tubney, near Abingdon, Oxford.

Keith WOODCOCK 1940– Aviation and automotive artist working in oil and water media, born in Bradford, Yorkshire. He studied at Salford School of Art; trained in engineering, product and graphic design; then after many years in industry and advertising became a freelance painter in 1982. Woodcock was a member of both the Guild of Aviation Artists and Guild of Motoring Artists. The bulk of his work concentrated on pre-1970 themes and it was featured in many books on aviation and aircraft art. Took part in group shows in Britain, Italy, Germany, France and America. Royal Air Force's Cranwell College and its Hendon Museum, British Aerospace and many other companies and individuals worldwide hold examples. Lived at Bollington, Macclesfield, Cheshire.

David WOODFORD 1938– Artist in oil, watercolour, pencil and other media who said that "as a landscape painter I work directly from the experience of the place, not from an historical sense of art." He attended West Sussex College of Art, 1955–9; Leeds College of Art for teacher training, 1959–60; and Royal Academy Schools, 1965–8, where Charles Mahoney was a notable teacher. Went on to paint professionally. Was a member of RCamA and took part in numerous mixed exhibitions. Solo shows included Waterhouse, Mall and Alpine Club Galleries; Mostyn Gallery, Llandudno; Oriel and Chapter Arts in Cardiff; and Oriel Bangor. Arts Council and National Library of Wales, Aberystwyth, hold examples. Lived at Nant Ffrancon, Bethesda, Bangor, Gwynedd.

James WOODFORD 1893–1976 Sculptor in range of materials, born in Nottingham, where he studied at the School of Art. After service with 11th Sherwood Foresters on the continent in World War I, where he was mentioned in despatches, Woodford attended Royal College of Art. During World War II Woodford was camouflage officer to the Air Ministry. He was elected RA in 1945 and was a fellow of RBS. Woodford was a prolific producer of figurative sculpture. Among his notable works were bronze doors at the RIBA; main doors at Norwich City Hall; stone figures and panels, Huddersfield Library and Art Gallery; statue of Robin Hood in Nottingham; sculpture for Imperial War Graves Commission British cemeteries in Italy; new design of Royal Coat of Arms, 1962; and many coats of arms for government buildings in Britain and abroad. Woodford's output is widely illustrated: in the volume *RBS: Modern British Sculpture*, published 1939; in Arthur T Broadbent's *Sculpture Today in Great Britain 1940–1943*, published 1949; and he was included in Sculpture In Britain Between The Wars, Fine Art Society, 1986. Lived in Twickenham, Middlesex.

Derrick WOODHAM 1940– Abstract sculptor and teacher, born in Blackburn, Lancashire. He attended South-East Essex Technical College and School of Art, 1957–60; Hornsey College of of Art, 1960–2; then Royal College of Art, 1962–5, teachers including Bernard Meadows, Hubert Dalwood and Robert Clatworthy. From 1965–8 was a part-time teacher at Royal College, then held a number of teaching posts in America, from 1980 being professor and director of School of Art, University of Cincinnati, Ohio, where he lived. Among Woodham's awards was the Walter Neurath Prize for Drawing, 1964; Peter Stuyvesant Award and Prix de la Ville de Paris Group Prize, both 1965; and North Jersey Cultural Council Purchase Award, Paramus, 1974. Woodham was a pioneer of Minimal sculpture in Britain and remained preoccupied by geometry. Group shows included The New Generation, Whitechapel Art Gallery, 1965; Sculpture in a City, Arts Council, 1968, with tour; British Sculpture of the 60s, ICA, 1970; and National Sculpture Exhibition, Athens, Georgia, with tour, 1976. Woodham had solo shows at Richard Feigen Gallery in New York from 1966, later exhibitions including Northern Kentucky University, Frankfort, 1984. Arts Council, British Council, Peter Stuyvesant Foundation and Tate Gallery hold examples.

Geoffrey WOODHEAD 1941– Painter and teacher who trained at Bolton and Lancaster Colleges of Art and until 1964 at the Slade School of Fine Art under Keith Vaughan and Claude Rogers. He painted large canvases, pictures intended for public spaces of large buildings, as in North by North West, at Bolton Museum and Art Gallery, 1996. The River Lune, near where he lived, was a key theme. His landscapes used "conventional tools of paint and canvas, loosely designated as Abstract Expressionist, endorsing the importance of colour, compositional elements of the picture and the quality of the pictorial surface." Held a number of part-time lecturing posts, eventually teaching at Kirkham Grammar School, Lancashire, an area where he showed widely.

Helen WOODHOUSE 1950– Figurative artist concerned with the place of women in society whose work embraced found objects, text and paint. Woodhouse completed her degree and postgraduate studies at Newcastle Polytechnic. She held a number of residencies, including Denton High School in Newcastle and Lowick House, Cumbria. In 1990 she created a series of flags for the International Art Festival, Gateshead. Among Woodhouse's exhibitions were Northern Open, at Laing Art Gallery, Newcastle, 1985; Cardiff Polytechnic Gallery, 1988; Art London 89, at Olympia; and Newcastle Group touring show The Northern Lights, 1990, at DLI Museum & Arts Centre, Durham. Northern Arts holds her work.

Walter WOODINGTON 1916– Painter, teacher and curator, born in London where he continued to work. He attended Woolwich Polytechnic School of Art and City and Guilds of London Art School under A R Middleton Todd. He then taught part-time at Woolwich Polytechnic, 1946–60, and was curator of the Royal Academy Schools, 1961–84. Was a member of RBA and RP, also showing at RA, NEAC and New Grafton Gallery, completing town and country house portraits. RA, Zambian government and Unilever Ltd bought his work.

Christine Anne WOODLEY 1949– Watercolourist, designer and illustrator, born in Northampton, who settled in the county at Warkton. Studied at Northampton School of Art, 1967–9, and went on to concentrate on natural history subjects. Showed extensively in the Midlands, at Burghley Horse Trials, Country Landowners' Association game fair and did work for the National Trust.

Gary WOODLEY 1953– Minimalist artist, born in London. He attended Berkshire College of Art, 1970–3, Camberwell School of Arts and Crafts, 1973–6, and Chelsea School of Art, 1977–8. Among Woodley's exhibitions were Amano Gallery, Osaka, Japan, 1981; Galerie Niggendijker, Netherlands, 1988; Mathematics and Modern Art, at Nene College, Northampton, 1990, and in the same year Between Dimensions at Curwen Gallery. Also in 1990 Woodley was Anish Kapoor's choice as Artist of the Day at Flowers East. Arts Council holds Second Homeomorphic Pair, 1980, in plywood and cellulose sealer, and Untitled, 1981, in acrylic and shellac on plywood.

Gary WOODLEY fl. from 1970s– Painter of birds and wildlife subjects, born in Ducklington, Oxfordshire. In 1972 he joined the Boehm of Malvern Ceramic Studios, decorating their productions with studies of animals and birds. He showed with Royal Society for the Protection of Birds around Britain, was a member of SWLA and had solo shows at Regent Gallery, Cheltenham; Wildlife Gallery, Toronto; Brotherton Gallery; and Century Galleries, Henley-on-Thames, 1992. Woodley also illustrated books, including Kenneth Grahame's *The Wind in the Willows*, 1985; and *Where the Windrush Flows*, 1989, collaborating with Mollie Harris.

John WOODMAN 1948– Artist in various media such as graphic design and film, and lecturer, born in London. He studied at London College of Printing, concentrating on typographic design, 1970–3, worked as a graphic designer for London Borough of Lambeth, 1973–5, studied film and photography at Polytechnic of Central London, 1975–6, followed by the same subjects at St Martin's School of Art, 1976–8, and a postgraduate course in experimental media at Slade School of Fine Art, 1978–80. Went on to be senior lecturer in visual communications studies at West Midlands College of Higher Education. For a time was co-editor and designer of *Undercut* magazine. Exhibitions included a joint show, Ritual Landmarks, with Roger Polley, 1983–4, which toured from South Hill Park, Bracknell.

Madge WOODMAN 1910– Painter and draughtsman, born in Hanwell, Middlesex, who attended St Martin's School of Art in mid-1930s. She was a member of SWA and Romsey Art Group and had several solo shows at Mountbatten Gallery, Romsey, from 1972. Lived in Woodfalls, Salisbury, Wiltshire.

Paul Vincent WOODROFFE 1875–1954 Stained glass designer, illustrator, printmaker and painter, born in Madras, India, educated at Stonyhurst, the Roman Catholic public school. At Slade School of Fine Art won a life drawing prize. After working for the stained glass designer Christopher Whall, Woodroffe established his own studio in Chipping Campden and became a member of Art Workers' Guild and British Society of Master Glass Painters. His windows in St Patrick's Cathedral, New York, took over 20 years to finish. Work appeared in *Illustrated London News* and *The Quarto* and many books illustrated included titles by Browning, Housman, Shakespeare and Tennyson. Exhibited at RA, NEAC, Fine Art Society and Baillie Gallery. William Morris Gallery gave him a show in 1982–3. Lived for a time in Bisley, Gloucestershire.

Bill WOODROW 1948– Sculptor, born and lived in London. Studied at Winchester, St Martin's and Chelsea Schools of Art, 1967–72. Although he had a solo show in the latter year, it took Woodrow until the late 1970s to acquire a studio and build up a volume of work towards another. His reputation then grew fast in the 1980s, with a spate of solo exhibitions in Hamburg, London, Banks in Cumbria, Edinburgh, Stuttgart, Paris, Antwerp, Milan, the Museum of Modern Art in Oxford, New York and elsewhere. He showed with Lisson Gallery in London. In 1990 Woodrow held the Point of Entry exhibition in Imperial War Museum, having been invited in 1989 to use its collection as a starting point.

Woodrow created his sculpture from modern domestic and urban scrap materials, such as Twin-tub with Guitar, of 1981, in Tate Gallery. The Arts Council's Crow and Carrion, of the same year, made from the wrecks of umbrellas, is another example. He was included in the Arts Council's 1993–4 exhibition Recent British Sculpture and there was a 1996 Tate show of new and recent work which toured to Darmstadt, Germany.

Gladys WOODRUFF: *see* **Gladys DAWSON**

Brian WOODS 1938– Painter, printmaker and teacher, born in Loughborough, Leicestershire, studying at its College of Art for a diploma with honours, 1963–7. Taught drawing and painting at the College of Art in Rochdale, Lancashire, where he lived, then at Hopwood Hall College full-time for 25 years, accepting early retirement in 1992 when he began full-time painting. Woods shared the first prize for painting with Ian Grant at MAFA in 1986, was elected in 1989 and became its hon. secretary, 1993–5. Group shows included RA Summer Exhibitions, RWA, Bankside Gallery, Castlefield Gallery in Manchester and Harris Art Gallery, Preston. Solo exhibitions included Venice at The Portico Library, Manchester, stemming from an Edward Oldham Trust Travel Bursary. Manchester City Art Gallery and Bury Art Gallery hold examples.

Elsie WOODS 1900–1988 Painter and draughtsman, born in Nottingham, where she was a leading member of the Society of Artists, for long an honorary member after she was no longer able to show. She studied art at Homerton College, Cambridge, 1919–21, and on resuming painting in 1949 had private tuition with the Nottingham artist Edwin Marsh. Showed at RI, RCamA, Nottingham Castle Art Gallery, PS and SWA. Settled eventually in Sheringham, Norfolk, was a member of Norfolk and Norwich Art Circle and exhibited at Norwich Castle Art Gallery.

James Barry WOODS 1947– Painter working mainly in gouache, and illustrator. Born in Heywood, Lancashire, Woods was a self-taught artist who showed at RA, RMS and elsewhere, as well as completing a body of commercial work such as book covers and record sleeve illustrations. Lived in London.

Mary WOODS 1909– Painter, draughtsman, printmaker, teacher and weaver, born in Ilford, Essex. Her full married name was Grace Mary Woods (she was married to the artist Sidney Woods), and her early work was signed with her maiden name Mary Kaye. She studied at West Ham Municipal Art School, 1925–9, under W M Barnes, and Royal College of Art, 1929–32, teachers including Robert Austin and Malcolm Osborne. Teaching experience included several schools, latterly Shortlands House Boys' School, Kent, 1952–4. Was for a time a member of PS, also showing at RA, Catholic Artists' Guild Exhibition, Whitechapel Art Gallery, Senefelder Club and in the provinces. Lived in Orpington, Kent.

Michael WOODS 1933– Artist (latterly mainly a watercolourist), illustrator, potter, teacher and writer, born and finally lived in Norwich, Norfolk. After education at Norwich School and the local School of Art, attended Slade School of Fine Art, under William Coldstream, tutors including Thomas Monnington, Ceri Richards, Anthony Gross, Edward Ardizzone and E H Gombrich. He joined the staff of Charterhouse, 1957, being director of art, 1970–94, also acting as tutor for Open College of the Arts. As a designer, Woods created the historic map of Godalming for The Godalming Trust. The memorial at Dachau Concentration Camp was completed by him for the International Committee. Was an exhibiting member-potter with the British Crafts Centre. Woods illustrated 10 books, including *Roman Crafts*, by Donald Strong and David Brown, and *The Turkoman Carpet*, by George O'Bannon. Wrote and illustrated for *Artist and Illustrator* magazine and was the author of a series of instructional books, later ones including *Starting Landscape Drawing*, 1989, and *The Complete Drawing Course*, 1995. As well as group exhibitions, held solo shows in Godalming, Horsham and Manchester. Portraits included Lord Cawley and His Honour Judge John Bull. Nuffield Foundation, National Trust and City of Norwich hold examples.

Michael WOODS 1952– Artist in various media, photographer and writer. In 1991 with George Melly he published *Paris and the Surrealists*, which prompted him to make assemblages related to Parisian places, examples of which were included in the England & Co show Art in Boxes, 1991. He also took part in Six Surrealist Artists, Crawshaw Gallery; John Bonham, Murray Feely Fine Art's Living British Surrealists; and at Mayor Gallery he showed assemblage art.

Padraic WOODS 1893–1991 Painter and teacher who in his early childhood lived in County Down, Northern Ireland, moved to Belfast and at 15 attended evening school at Belfast School of Art. Became a schoolteacher, but retired in early 1940s to give more time to painting. He became president of Ulster Arts Club and was a member of RUA, also showing at RHA and Dublin Painters' Gallery. Painted widely on the continent and was also known as Patrick J Woods. In 1968 he had a show at Queen's University in Belfast.

Patrick J WOODS: *see* **Padraic WOODS**

Sarah WOODS 1968– She worked for five years as a stockbroker before turning full-time to sculpture, initially largely self-taught. To improve her knowledge she studied at Heatherley's School of Art and worked with sculptor Jonathan Wylder. Exhibitions included Ainscough Contemporary Art.

William L WOODS 1916– Painter, illustrator and teacher, born in Norwich. He studied art at Lowestoft School of Art, 1937–8, then Hornsey School of Art with J C Moody for two periods: 1938–9 and 1946–7. Did book illustration and showed at RA, RWS, ROI and in the provinces, London County Council buying his work. He taught for a time at Berkhamsted School, then for Buckinghamshire Education Committee. Lived at Hemel Hempstead, Hertfordshire.

Christine A WOODSIDE 1946– Painter, printmaker and teacher, born in Aberdeen, who studied at Gray's School of Art there, 1963, winning the David Murray Scholarship for Landscape Painting, 1966, then a post diploma, highly commended, 1968; in that year gained a Hospitalfield Scholarship for painting; in 1969 winning a distinction, Aberdeen College of Education. Began teaching art at Mackie Academy, Stonehaven. 1970. Was elected a member of SSWA, 1986, RSW in 1993. Prizes included a bronze medal at RSA, 1969; Royal Glasgow Institute of the Fine Arts Teachers' Whisky Travel Scholarship, 1995; and RSW May Marshall Brown Award and RSA Saltire Society Purchase Prize, both 1996. Began etching at Dundee Printmakers' Workshop, 1995. Showed widely in Scotland, at Clayton Gallery in Newcastle and Ainscough Contemporary Art. Lived in Perth, where the Museum and Art Gallery holds examples.

Lesley WOODSIDE 1953– Painter and teacher, born and lived in Manchester. She studied at Tameside, Manchester Polytechnic and Chelsea School of Art, gaining her master's degree in 1979, teachers including Bill Clarke. Between 1979–83 lectured at Rochdale and at Manchester Polytechnic, then freelanced as an artist. Showed with Colin Jellicoe Gallery and at the Polytechnic, Manchester, which holds her work, and at Atkinson Art Gallery, Southport. Her work, as in Self Portrait, 1970, could be highly stylized.

Patricia Mariella WOODTHORPE 1928– Painter, notably in egg tempera, and draughtsman, born in London. After education in Berkshire she attended St Martin's School of Art, 1945–6, then Byam Shaw School of Drawing and Painting, 1946–51, her teachers including Peter Greenham. Exhibited RA, RP, NEAC and elsewhere, signing her work M W. Lived in Arundel, Sussex, for a time and later in Beulah, Breconshire.

Derek WOODWARD 1924– Painter and critic, born in Oxford. He studied at Central School of Arts and Crafts and St Martin's School of Art and went on to lecture on exhibition stands and window display. Wrote for *Arts Review* magazine. Exhibited widely in mixed shows in England and on the continent, including Nicholas Treadwell Gallery, 1965, and had a solo show at New Vision Centre Gallery, 1964. Woodward had a keen interest in jazz and classical music.

Ken WOODWARD 1928– Artist, designer and cartoonist and animated film director who studied at Liverpool School of Art. Was involved in animated films as a graphic designer and as a studio manager for Walt Disney Merchandise Studio. He also illustrated children's books. Masks and Surrealism were special interests. Woodward showed in Art in Boxes at England & Co, 1991, other group appearances including Roupell Gallery. Solo exhibitions included Shipley's Bookshop and Comme des Garçons, Tokyo.

Verity WOOKEY 1928– Painter and printmaker who taught part-time and whose work was based on the natural world. She was born in Kingston upon Thames, Surrey. Long resident in East Anglia, she was a member of The Suffolk Group and exhibited at RWS Open Exhibitions; Gainsborough's House, Sudbury; Colchester and Ipswich Art Society shows; Gallery 44 in Aldeburgh; Taplin Gallery, Woodbridge; Clockhouse Society, Snape; and elsewhere. Lived at Martlesham, Woodbridge, Suffolk.

Hal WOOLF 1902–1962 Painter in oil and watercolour of townscapes and landscapes, real name Herman Henry Woolf. His father practised as a dental surgeon in Wimpole Street. Hal was educated at London University, then studied art at Chelsea Polytechnic with Bernard Adams, 1920–2, followed by L'Académie de la Grande Chaumière, Paris. Exhibited extensively at Redfern Gallery, also RA, ROI, LG and was a member of NS, where he also showed, and Chelsea Arts Club. In World War II Woolf was a captain in the Royal Engineers, involved in camouflage. While serving in the Far East he began taking a modest amount of marijuana. In November 1962 Woolf disappeared and was reported missing by his second wife Greta and friends. It eventually emerged that he had been knocked down by a car in Park Lane and taken to St George's Hospital, where after examination and X-ray he was soon released with minor injuries. Woolf was taken into police custody, being in possession of "a dangerous drug", but within 24 hours was returned to hospital, comatose and critically ill. After he died, brain contusion and a skull fracture were revealed by the postmortem. Friends were suspicious about how Woolf had been handled in custody. An inquiry was held in secret, questions were asked in the House of Commons, but no disciplinary action was taken. *The Times* newspaper, in a leader, commented that the case provided "a startling picture of what can happen to an individual citizen in Britain". There was a posthumous exhibition of Woolf's work at the Woodstock Gallery in 1964.

Meg WOOLF: *see* **Meg WOOLF-NELLIST**

Meg WOOLF-NELLIST 1923– Artist in wood and stone and various calligraphic media, and teacher, born in Ramsgate, Kent. She studied at Ravensbourne College of Art, 1939–42, and Brighton College of Art, 1942–3, teachers including Willi Soukop, Carel Weight, Ruskin Spear and Joseph Cribb. Taught for extensive periods from 1943, including being a lecturer in art at Rachel McMillan College of Education, time in Bermuda and in Havering Essex. Originally worked under her maiden name of Woolf, and signed her carvings with a monogram. Showed at AIA, RA, at Roland, Browse and Delbanco, RBA and at Hornchurch Art Gallery. Solo shows included Hove Art Gallery, 1948. Lived in Cranham, Essex.

Dorothy E G WOOLLARD 1886–1986 Printmaker, watercolourist and teacher, born in Bristol. She began painting in her teens in France, then joined Bristol Municipal School of Art, studying etching under Reginald Bush. She remained a lifelong friend of Bush, nursing him in her London flat during his final years, in the 1950s. After Bristol she studied with Frank Short at Royal College of Art under a scholarship. Did map work for the Admiralty in

World War I, then spent a few years in Bristol before moving to London. She was a vigorous, fluent etcher and her pencil drawings were good enough to be published in Black's *Artists' Sketch Books*. Her etchings are well represented in *City Impressions: Bristol Etchers 1910–1935*, published by Redcliffe Press, 1990. Showed at RWA and RE, both of which she was a member, RA, RHA and at Walker Art Gallery in Liverpool. She did a tiny etching for Queen Mary's Dolls' House. After World War II she translated medical books into Braille, then in 1972 moved to Cambridge, dying in a nursing home.

Joan Elizabeth WOOLLARD 1916– Sculptor in clay and teacher, born in Birmingham, where she continued to live. She attended Malvern Girls' College. Later studied at Birmingham College of Art, 1947–52, under Bernard Fleetwood-Walker; at the City and Guilds of London Art School, 1952–4, where her teachers included A R Middleton Todd; and Royal Academy Schools, 1955–6. Showed at RA, NEAC, SGA and RBSA both of which she was a member, and at Paris Salon.

Leslie WOOLLASTON 1900–1976 Self-taught painter in oil of figures and landscapes, born in Birmingham. He was an accomplished creator of popularly pleasing images who exhibited at many venues, including RA, NEAC, ROI, RWA and Paris Salon. Williamson Art Gallery and Museum, Birkenhead, owns his picture Holiday Makers at a River Resort. Lived in London.

Leighton Hall WOOLLATT 1905–1974 Painter and teacher, sculptor, printmaker and mural artist. He was born in Nottingham, son of the artist Edgar Woollatt. Studied at Nottingham College of Art and the Royal Academy Schools, where he won several scholarships and prizes, and Chelsea Polytechnic. Was married to the embroiderer and designer Louisa Woollatt. He taught at various art schools around Britain and exhibited at RA, in Arts Council shows, ROI and in the provinces. During World War II he was an official war artist in Exeter, his war paintings being housed at Exeter Record Office. He completed work on murals in Nottingham, at the Bank of England and elsewhere. Lived in Budleigh Salterton, Devon.

Janet WOOLLEY 1952– Artist and illustrator using montage, acrylic, crayon and photography; teacher. She was born in Plymouth, Devon, did a foundation course at Shrewsbury School of Art, 1968–70; obtained a diploma in art and design (graphic design) at Brighton College of Art & Design, 1970–3; then studied illustration for her master's degree at Royal College of Art, 1973–6, winning a Berger Paint Award & Travel Scholarship Many other awards followed, Benson & Hedges Illustrators Gold, Society of Illustrators in America and Society of Newspaper Design awards among them. Woolley, part-time, was professor of illustration at Central St Martins School of Art, alongside this running a busy graphic art practice, her numerous clients including *The Times, Sunday Times Magazine, The Independent, Radio Times,* Penguin/Puffin Books, *New York Times, Washington Post*, Walt Disney, *Rolling Stone* and Warner Brothers Records. Showed annually with Association of Illustrators and European Illustration in Britain, and in America with the Society of illustration, Communication Arts and the Society of Art Directors. As well as RA Summer Exhibitions, Woolley showed at Portal and Thumb Galleries. Newport Art Gallery holds her work. Lived in London.

Peter WOOLLEY 1923–1981 Illustrator, printmaker, designer and teacher, born in Hemingfield, Yorkshire. Studied at Barnsley School of Art and Sheffield College of Art. Served in Royal Air Force during World War II. Although he showed at Graves Art Gallery, Sheffield, Woolley after marriage in 1952 and teaching in a grammar school, which eventually became a comprehensive school, did no more original work of his own. Lived in Oker, near Matlock, Derbyshire.

Nigel WOOLNER 1940– Architect and artist, born and lived in London, who studied at Regent Street Polytechnic with Geoffrey Wickham, Malcolm Hughes and Sydney Merrills. He became a senior partner in Chapman Taylor Partners. He was a fellow of RIBA and of the Society of Architect Artists. As an artist he completed extensive studies of buildings "in context responding to the sense of place and history" throughout the United Kingdom and continental Europe. "Light is central to all work." Showed at Bedford Park Festival from 1985, at Attendi Gallery, 1996, and elsewhere. Had a solo exhibition at Royal Society of Arts, 1994, at Susie Baynham, 1995, and in Brussels and Vienna.

Frank WOOTTON 1914–1998 Painter in oil and writer, born in Milford, Hampshire. He studied at Eastbourne College of Art under Eric Ravilious and Arthur Reeve-Fowkes, winning a gold medal and travelling scholarship, 1930. In 1939–46 Wootton was an official war artist with the Royal Air Force. Among Wootton's books were *How to Draw Aircraft* and *How to Draw Cars* and several books were published in Britain and America featuring his aviation pictures. Wootton was a president of the Guild of Aviation Artists and vice-president of the Society of Equestrian Artists. Among his awards were the C P Robertson Trophy, Air Ministry, 1979; Royal Aero Club Silver Medal and Companion of Honour, Royal Aeronautical Society, both 1985; and freedom of Guild of Air Pilots and Air Navigators, 1987. Solo exhibitions included Ackermann Gallery, 1964; Tryon Gallery, from 1969; and National Air and Space Museum, Smithsonian Institution, Washington, America, 1983. Imperial War Museum, Royal Air Force, Fleet Air Arm Museum in Yeovilton and other collections hold examples. Lived in Alfriston, Sussex.

Olive WOOTTON fl. from 1950s– Sculptor with a special interest in wildlife subjects, and teacher, who was taught by animal sculptor John Skeaping. Her husband Gordon was also an artist. She taught at Goldsmiths' College School of Art and Royal College of Art. Wootton was an associate of RBS, showed with Young Contemporaries, in RA Summer Exhibitions, SWA, in mixed shows abroad and was included in 1st RWA Open Sculpture Exhibition, 1993. Solo exhibitions included Mason Watts Fine Art, Warwick, 1990. Lived in Scaldwell, Northamptonshire.

Harold WORKMAN 1897–1975 Painter in oil and watercolour of landscapes, townscapes and interiors, born in Oldham, Lancashire, studying at Oldham and Manchester Schools of Art. Oldham's Art Gallery and Museum, Salford Art Gallery and several other provincial collections hold examples. Workman, who was for a time president of UA, was a prolific exhibitor. Venues included RA, NEAC, RBA, RI, ROI, Walker Art Gallery in Liverpool and Royal Glasgow Institute of the Fine Arts. Lived in East Molesey, Surrey.

Neale P WORLEY 1962– Painter, who studied at Amersham College of Further Education, 1978–81. Went to Camberwell School of Arts and Crafts, 1981–4, and Royal Academy Schools, 1986–9. While at the Schools he began showing at RA. In 1990 he was one of three artists selected for a show by New Grafton Gallery as being "the most gifted of the final year graduates" in 1989.

Vincent WOROPAY 1951– Sculptor, draughtsman and teacher, born and lived in London. He studied at Portsmouth School of Art & Design, 1973–4; gained a first-class honours degree in fine art at Brighton Polytechnic, 1974–7; did a higher diploma at Slade School of Fine Art, 1977–9; then won a Rome Scholarship in Sculpture, The British School at Rome, 1979–81. Woropay had extensive teaching experience, visiting lectureships including The Architectural Association; The Bartlett School of Architecture; Slade School of Fine Art; Eton College; Ulster University; and many provincial schools of art. From 1981–91 he lectured at Middlesex Polytechnic, from 1991 being senior lecturer at Wimbledon School of Art. In July 1994 he was artist-in-residence at Lamphey Bishop's Palace, Pembrokeshire. Group shows included LG, 1977; New Contemporaries at ICA from 1978; Portland Clifftop Sculpture Park, 1985; Gillian Jason Gallery, 1991; and Burlington New Gallery, 1994. Woropay had a solo show at Eton College in 1983, later ones including Distant Thunder at Bluecoat Gallery, Liverpool, and Supra Limum, Fabian Carlsson Gallery, both 1988. Commissions included Capo, National Garden Festival at Stoke-on-Trent, 1986; Hand with Kronos, National Garden Festival, Gateshead, 1990; and Rude Block 1 and 2, Romsey Abbey, Hampshire, 1993. Arts Council, National Trust, Contemporary Art Society and Birmingham City Museum and Art Gallery hold examples.

John Raymond WORSDALE 1939– Versatile artist in oil and mixed-media drawings, father of the curator and art critic Godfrey Worsdale and based in Doncaster, Yorkshire. He studied at the School of Art there, 1955–60, majoring in painting and lithography. Group shows included Cooper Art Gallery, Barnsley, 1990–2, and South Yorkshire Gallery, Doncaster, 1991–2. Solo shows included Harlequin Gallery, Greenwich, 1992, and Doncaster Museum and Art Gallery, 1995, which holds his work.

John WORSLEY 1919– Painter and draughtsman, brought up partly in Kenya, then in Sussex where he attended Brighton College. Went to Goldsmiths' College School of Art, 1934–7, studying under James Bateman, Clive Gardiner and Stanley Anderson. The son of a naval officer, Worsley in 1939 joined up and became a midshipman on the armed merchant cruiser *Laurentic*, in which he was sunk off Ulster, but survived to paint a picture of the incident. By this time he was contributing work to the War Artists' Advisory Committee, and after further active service he was appointed as a war artist attached to the commander-in-chief, Mediterranean. Taken prisoner, Worsley ended up as a prisoner of war in Germany and made a valuable record of life in Marlag O camp, managing to bring most of his drawings – with much difficulty – back to England after his release. Worsley thought up the legendary pâpier maché head Albert to facilitate prisoner of war escapes, featured in the film *Albert RN*. During the closing stages of the war Worsley painted portraits of Admiral Sir John Cunningham and Field-Marshal Bernard Montgomery. The only serving sailor to become an official war artist, Worsley made a unique contribution in capturing a record of action and ship life. Imperial War Museum holds his work. From 1966 Worsley made hundreds of sketches of criminal suspects, based on victim accounts, to aid the police; these were often uncannily accurate, and led to arrests. Lived in London.

Leslie WORTH 1923– Artist in watercolour, oil and drawing media, and teacher, born in Bideford, Devon. He studied at Plymouth School of Art, 1938–9; Bideford School of Art, 1940–2; again at Plymouth, 1942–3; and at Royal College of Art, 1943–6, under Gilbert Spencer. He was head of department at Epsom School of Art until 1978, then became a full-time painter. Worth was keeper, RBA, 1987–92, and senior vice-president of RWS in 1985–92, then becoming its president. He carried out a number of watercolour and mural commissions, having solo exhibitions with Agnew and Surrey University. Appeared in mixed exhibitions at Mercury Gallery, Wildenstein and out of London. National Trust, Eton College and public galleries in Aberdeen, Birmingham, Brighton, Rochdale, Southport and Wakefield hold examples. Worth's watercolours were noted for their sureness of touch, economical use of the medium and elegance. Had a first retrospective at Bankside Gallery, 1995. In 1996 Worth's powerful The Buzzard, Derbyshire, won the £15,000 first prize in the Singer & Friedlander/*Sunday Times* Watercolour Competition. Lived in Epsom, Surrey.

Marjan WOUDA 1960– Sculptor, born in Aduard, Netherlands, growing up on the family dairy farm which gave her a fine knowledge of the animals she later sculpted so realistically and feelingly. Arrived in England in 1979, she worked with disturbed adolescents in Wiltshire, then did an art foundation course at Manchester Polytechnic, 1983–4. Gained a first-class honours degree at North East London Polytechnic, 1984–7, specialising in sculpture, then studied fine art (sculpture) at the Polytechnic in Manchester, where she settled, 1987–8, for her master's degree. Mixed exhibitions included MAFA from 1988, of which she was elected a member in 1993, winning a Major Award in 1994; and Het Schaap in de Kunst, Hein Jurgens, Tilburg, Netherlands, in 1994, the year she was also elected an affiliate of RBS. Solo shows included The Green Room, Manchester, 1988, and Raw Clay, Flaxman Gallery,

Stoke-on-Trent, 1990. Wouda's first public sculpture commission was Leigh Pit Pony, for Groundwork Trust, Wigan, 1989; others including two sculptures for London Docklands Development Corporation, 1991; Walsall Working Horse, for Walsall Civic Centre, 1992; and two relief sculptures for the entrance hall of Bury Museum and Art Gallery, 1994. In 1995–8 Chanticleer: Prints and Sculpture by Adrienne Craddock and Marjan Wouda toured the United Kingdom, organised by Sheeran Lock. Lived in Prestwich, Manchester.

Gary WRAGG 1946– Painter, draughtsman and teacher, born in High Wycombe, Buckinghamshire. Studied at School of Art there, 1962–6, then at Camberwell School of Arts and Crafts, 1966–9, and Slade School of Fine Art, 1969–71. In 1968 Wragg won the Rotary Travelling Gift to Italy and Lord Carron Prize, followed by Boise Travelling Scholarship to America and Mexico, 1972. He went on to teach at Camberwell, St Martin's School of Art and Portsmouth Polytechnic, by which time he was appearing widely in group shows. He appeared in British Painting 1952–77 in 1977 at RA; Sydney Biennale, 1982; RA Summer Exhibition; and John Moores Exhibition, Liverpool, 1991–2. After solo studio shows in 1973–5 Wragg gained an Arts Council Major Grant in the latter year, then had solo show at Acme Gallery, 1976. Later shows included Nicola Jacobs, 1982–6, and Goldsmiths' College Gallery, 1990. Wragg's abstract works were often on a large scale and convey energy and intensity. Arts Council holds Big Ear, of 1976. Lived in London.

John WRAGG 1937– Sculptor, painter and teacher, born in York. He studied at the School of Art there, 1953–6, then at Royal College of Art, 1956–60. Taught at Chelsea School of Art, 1961. In 1960 Wragg gained a Sainsbury Award and in 1966 a Sainsbury commission, which resulted in a metal sculpture outside the firm's store in Kings Road, Chelsea. Initially Wragg was a sculptor of mythical figures, such as his Romulus and Remus, at Charterhouse School; then abstract work; then progressed to polychromed resined heads, such as his Rilke series. Had the first of several one-man shows at Hanover Gallery in 1963, later ones including Devizes Museum Gallery and England & Co, 1994. He was featured in British Sculpture in the Twentieth Century, Whitechapel Art Gallery, 1981–2. Gained an Arts Council Major Award in 1977, and the Council holds his work. Lived for some time in Devizes, Wiltshire, and was elected RA in 1991.

Robert WRAITH 1952– Painter, notably of frescoes and portraits, born in London, where he eventually settled. He left Stowe School at 17 and, having misgivings about conventional art schools, studied with Pietro Annigoni in Florence. He held a first solo show at Mall Galleries in 1976, others including Belgrave Gallery in 1979 and King Street Galleries, 1982. Also exhibited in mixed shows including RA, RP, PS, RWS and UA. In 1982 won special commendation in National Portrait Gallery Portrait Award sponsored by Imperial Tobacco. Was commissioned to paint a portrait of Archbishop of Canterbury Dr Robert Runcie.

F Douglas WRAY fl. from c. 1920–1951 Painter mainly of still life, he was married to the artist Marjorie Rodgers. He showed at RA, ROI and RI and lived in London and Middlesex.

Jenny WRAY 1967– Painter and designer, born in 1967, who lived in Willenhall, Staffordshire. She studied at Walsall College of Art, Derbyshire College of Higher Education and Winchester School of Art. She became a textile designer and went on to study for her master's degree in that field at Royal College of Art. Her paintings were drawn from dreams, postcards, natural forms, toys, media images, works of art and visits to museums and galleries, and repeated patterns were a feature of her output. In 1992 she had a show at Walsall Museum & Art Gallery which drew inspiration from the Garman Ryan Collection held there, in which her vibrant sense of colour was well shown. She also conducted workshops and demonstrations.

Marjorie WRAY: *see* **Marjorie RODGERS**

Norman WRAY 1923– Watercolourist and draughtsman, born and lived in Oldham, Lancashire. Wray's father "kept a draper's shop and I began to draw on empty boxes and sheets of white packaging." From 1935 until his marriage in 1955 Wray "lived on Spring Lane, Lees, where Miss Carter wore pink," as depicted by the artist Helen Bradley. Wray began work in local wallpaper mill at 14 and attended classes at Oldham Art School until war service with the Army intervened in 1942. He continued "drawing on the backs of message forms", and when at the end of the war he spent a year in Austria he gained a prize in The Central Mediterranean Force Art Competition. Wray returned to the wallpaper mill until 1957 when he joined the family firm, meanwhile having continued studies at Oldham Art School. He joined Oldham Society of Artists and in 1950 founded the Saddleworth Art Group, showing with it in The Northern Scene at Woodlands Art Gallery, 1973. Showed mainly locally but occasionally in London. Later in life Wray drew and painted on the continent and "did many watercolours in Turkey where my daughter has a flat."

Peter WRAY 1950– Artist, notably a printmaker, and teacher, born in Bishop Auckland, County Durham, who studied at St Mary's College, Strawberry Hill, 1969–72; Goldsmiths' College, 1983–4; and Leeds Polytechnic, 1989–92. Wray became senior lecturer in printmaking at University College of Ripon and York St John, York. He was elected a fellow of RE, 1991. Participated in numerous group shows, including Cleveland Open, Chapel Beck Gallery, Guisborough, 1977; Bankside Gallery (Whatman Prize, 1985, Barcham-Green Prize, 1986); RWA, 1988; British Printmakers, State Commission for Publishing, Moscow, 1989; Curwen Gallery, 1995; and national Print Exhibition, Mall Galleries, 1997. Solo shows included a series at New Academy Gallery from 1994. Cleveland Education Authority, Goldsmiths' College and corporate collections hold examples. Lived in Acomb, York.

Anne WRIGHT 1935– Painter, designer and muralist, born in Nottingham. She studied at the School of Art there, then at Royal

Academy Schools, 1954–9. She twice won the David Murray Landscape Scholarship and a bronze and silver medal for life painting and portrait painting respectively. In group shows appeared at RA Summer Exhibition, RP, Paris Salon, where she won a silver medal, and Chelsea Art Society, of which she was a member. Her portraits included the Bishop of Nottingham and Lord Craigmyle. Large murals were completed for General Dental Council building and headquarters of Sir Robert McAlpine & Sons. Solo shows included Hellenic Exhibition Centre, 1985, and Coach-House Gallery, Guernsey, 1986–91. Travelled extensively and lived in Spain, Morocco and Greece, evident in her landscapes. In 1989 she was made Straker Artist of the Year.

Austin WRIGHT 1911–1997 Sculptor and teacher, born in Chester, but brought up in Cardiff, moving to Yorkshire in 1937. Wright read for a degree in modern languages at Oxford University and trained as a teacher before he became interested in modern art, the paintings of Cézanne and sculpture of Henry Moore. He taught at several places in England before teaching at York Art School, 1949–54. Although at that time he made wood carvings and cast lead sculptures based on the human figure, most of Wright's work was not directly representational. Plant life and the idea of organic growth were key elements in his work, which he produced as a freelance from 1955. In 1957 he won the Ricardo da Silvera Acquisition Prize at São Paulo Biennale and from 1961–4 he was Gregory Fellow in Sculpture at Leeds University. Wright took part in many key group shows in Britain and abroad, had his first of many one-man exhibitions at Roland, Browse & Delbanco in 1956, with major retrospectives at Yorkshire Sculpture Park in 1981 and York City Art Gallery in 1994. Fitzwilliam Museum in Cambridge, National Museum of Wales in Cardiff and many provincial galleries hold examples. Lived in Upper Poppleton, York, and died there at Meadowfields Community Unit.

Bert WRIGHT 1930– Painter who specialised in painting the River Thames, coastal and harbour scenes, also architectural subjects and landscapes. He studied at Nottingham School of Art, 1946–50. He was a member of RSMA and Wapping Group of Artists, also showing with RA and in America. Wright favoured a traditional approach to his subjects. Mullard Electronics, Beecham Group and Standard Chartered Bank were among the firms who commissioned his work, in many private collections. Lived in Ealing, west London.

Bill WRIGHT 1931– Watercolourist, born in Scotland, where he settled at Bellochantuy, Argyll. Wright studied at Glasgow School of Art, 1949–53, under Gilbert Spencer and James Bateman. From 1966–87 he was art adviser to Strathclyde Regional Council. Wright was a member of RSW, SSA and Royal Glasgow Institute of the Fine Arts. Paintings of the sea and shore from Kintyre were strongly represented in his work, widely exhibited in Europe, Egypt, America and India. One-man exhibitions were held at Scottish and Kingfisher Galleries in Edinburgh, at Strathclyde University and at Perth Museum and Art Gallery.

Daphne WRIGHT 1963– Sculptor, born in Ireland, who attended Sligo Regional Technical College, 1981–5; Dublin National College of Art & Design, 1985–7; Newcastle upon Tyne Polytechnic, 1989–91. In 1991–2 was awarded a Cheltenham Fellowship, in 1992–3 a British-Rome Scholarship in Sculpture. In 1993–4 Wright undertook the Diaspora Project, a commission from the Living Arts Project, funded by the Irish Arts Council, and won a Manchester Metropolitan University Fellowship, funded by the Henry Moore Foundation. Mixed shows included Yeats Gallery, Sligo, 1985; The Gymnasium, Goldsmiths', 1991; and Making It at Tate Gallery, Liverpool, 1995. Had a solo show at Cornerhouse, Manchester, 1994; Domestic Shrubbery, a solo travelling show, was at Castlefield, Manchester, 1995.

Edward WRIGHT 1912– Painter, graphic designer and teacher, born in Liverpool, his father being an Ecuadorian diplomat. Studied art at Liverpool School of Art, 1930–1, then at Bartlett School of Architecture, London University, 1933–6, with Albert Richardson. Took part in a number of influential exhibitions in London and North and South America especially devoted to the printed page and architectural themes. Arts Council and the Museum of Modern Art in New York hold his work. Taught at Chelsea School of Art and lived in London for many years.

Elizabeth WRIGHT 1964– Artist, born and lived in London, who gained a bachelor's degree at Birmingham Polytechnic, 1984–7, and master's at Royal College of Art, 1987–90. Group shows included Whitechapel Open at Whitechapel Art Gallery, 1990; The Curator's Egg, Anthony Reynolds Gallery, 1994; and in 1995 On the Edge, Galerie Vaclava, Spaly, Prague, and Venice Biennale (Wright's exhibit was based on the Venice, Milan and Rome telephone directories).

Frank Arnold WRIGHT 1874–1961 Sculptor, born in London, who studied at Royal Academy Schools. He was a fellow of RBS and showed at RA, Royal Glasgow Institute of the Fine Arts and Walker Art Gallery in Liverpool. Lady Violet Charteris, Lady Helen Vincent and the 7th Duke of Rutland were among his subjects. While retaining a studio in the Chiswick area he settled in East Molesey, Surrey.

George WRIGHT 1924–1984 Artist and designer in various media and glass engraver. Born in Croydon, Surrey, Wright was six years at Croydon School of Art from 1944. David Bomberg, Ruskin Spear and Mervyn Peake taught him, and all left a notable impression. He exhibited widely in London, work being bought by the Nuffield Foundation, the London Borough of Hounslow and Courtaulds Ltd. Lived at Richmond, Surrey. Died at Trinity Hospice, Clapham, which has examples of his work.

Gordon Butler WRIGHT 1925– Painter, born in Darlington, County Durham, who attended King's College in Newcastle upon Tyne, studying art at Chichester College of Art, 1943–4, and in Netherlands. Showed at Portal, Grosvenor and Whitgift Galleries and in the provinces. Lived in Harrogate, Yorkshire.

Horace WRIGHT 1888–1960 Watercolourist and draughtsman. Born in Stamford, Lincolnshire, he studied art at the Press Art School under Percy Bradshaw. Exhibited RA, NS, RBA and one-man show at Walker's Galleries. Lived at Edgware, Middlesex.

James WRIGHT fl. from c.1910–1947 Painter, especially of landscapes on the Scottish west coast, where he was born at Ayr. He studied at Glasgow School of Art and was elected RSW in 1920. He frequently showed at RSW, Royal Glasgow Institute of the Fine Arts, RSA and RA, being noted for his robust colour and brushwork. Lived at Garelochhead, Dunbartonshire.

Jennifer WRIGHT 1961– Painter who studied at Ravensbourne College of Art, 1981–4, then Birmingham Polytechnic, 1985–6. She was awarded a Dudley Painting Prize, 1985, a Daler-Rowney Prize, 1987, in 1988–9 gaining a fellowship in painting at Cheltenham School of Art, Cheltenham & Gloucester College of Higher Education. Exhibitions included Dudley Open, 1985, LG at Royal College Gallery, 1987, and Aiding and Abetting at The Gallery at John Jones, 1994.

John WRIGHT 1931– Painter, film-maker, writer and teacher, born in London. As a small boy he was evacuated to Carmarthen. Began teaching in 1955 at Hereford School of Art, subsequently becoming principal of Newport College of Art and Design. He was a founder member of 56 Group and also showed in groups at John Moores Exhibition in Liverpool, Leicester Galleries, SEA, WAC and Royal National Eisteddfod; solo exhibitions included Howard Roberts Gallery in Cardiff, Bear Lane Gallery in Oxford and shows in America. Among his commissioned work was a mural for British Petroleum in London and designs for the publisher Chatto and Windus. Made several films with Spanish subjects, winning a Spanish government documentary film prize in 1972. He was official designer for projects connected with the investiture of HRH The Prince of Wales. WAC, Cambridge University and Glynn Vivian Art Gallery, Swansea, hold his work.

Lawrence WRIGHT 1906–c.1985 Painter, etcher, architect and writer on buildings and environments. Born in Bristol, Wright studied at the Liverpool School of Architecture 1924–29. Before he left he began to exhibit, going on to show at the RA and Walker Art Gallery, Liverpool. The Museum of London holds examples of his work in various media. Publications include *Warm and Snug* and *Perspective in Perspective*. Lived at Alresford, Hampshire.

Lisa WRIGHT 1965– Artist who gained a fine art honours degree at Maidstone College of Art, 1983–7, then her master's in painting at Royal Academy Schools, 1990–3. Wright said that her work "has always been based on familiar spaces, people and objects". She took part in many group exhibitions, including RA Summer Exhibition from 1991; Christopher Hull Gallery from 1992; Raw Gallery from 1993; Royal Over-Seas League from 1994; National Print Exhibition, 1995; and Diverse, at Kent Institute of Art & Design, Canterbury, 1996. Awards included Antique Collectors Prize, 1992; and in 1993 Royal Over-Seas League Travel Scholarship, and Winsor & Newton, W H Patterson and George Isted Prizes. Later solo exhibitions included Sadler's Wells Theatre, 1995. Guinness, Zeneca and other corporate and private collections hold examples. Lived in London.

Mark WRIGHT 1962– Painter, born in Northumberland, who studied at Central School of Art, 1982–5, then Royal College of Art from 1988 for several years. Group shows included Corpus Christi College, Oxford, 1988; Royal College show in Thun, Switzerland, and Into the Nineties, Mall Galleries, 1989; and John Moores Liverpool Exhibition, 1989–90. In 1987 he gained a Northern Arts Award. Lived for a time in London.

Patricia WRIGHT: *see* **Patricia Vaughan DAWSON**

Richard WRIGHT 1960– Painter, born in London, who attended Edinburgh College of Art, 1978–82, Glasgow School of Art, 1993–5, with time at California Institute of the Arts, Los Angeles, in 1994. Group shows included Three Person Show, City Racing, 1992; New Art in Scotland, CCA, Glasgow, 1994; Sugarhiccup, Tramway, Glasgow (where Wright latterly worked), 1996; and About Vision, Museum of Modern Art in Oxford, and tour, 1996–7; and Correspondences, Scottish National Gallery of Modern Art, Edinburgh, 1997–8. In 1994, Wright had solo shows at the California Institute and at Tramway.

Thomas WRIGHT 1899–1962 Sculptor, draughtsman and teacher, son of a craftsman jeweller, who won a scholarship to the Birmingham College of Arts and Crafts. In World War I Wright joined the Royal Flying Corps as a pilot, returning to Birmingham to become a stone carver. He was responsible for commissioned sculptures on many public buildings, although his private work on family themes remained important to him. During World War II Wright served in the Royal Air Force, after which he taught sculpture at Wolverhampton College of Art. A younger sculptor who worked with Wright was John Paddison. RBSA gave Wright a centenary show, featuring some of his private experiments as a carver, many unfinished or only at the sketch-model stage.

Tim WRIGHT 1959– Artist and lecturer, born and lived in London, who did a foundation course at Middlesex Polytechnic, 1978–9; gained a fine art honours degree there, 1979–82; and in 1984–5 completed a part-time foundry/bronze casting course at Hackney College. From 1982–4 Wright was a photographer's assistant and self-employed furniture designer and maker; from 1984–5 was a screenprinter and assistant to the sculptor Julian Opie, making steel sculpture; then in 1985–6 was a sculpture technician at Central School of Art. From 1985 Wright held a number of part-time lectureships, including Croydon and Loughton Colleges, Middlesex and Sunderland Polytechnics, Central and Epsom Schools of Art and Middlesex University. Mixed exhibitions included Camden Annual at Camden Arts Centre, 1984; Crouch End Arts Festival, The Original Gallery,

1985; Displacement, wallmounted constructions and drawings, Pyramid Gallery, 1988; and Painting Show, Wilson Hale Gallery, 1990. Later solo exhibitions included Art Space, 1997, where he showed abstract work.

Isabel WRIGHTSON 1890– Painter and teacher, born in Croydon, Surrey, where she continued to live. Studied at Byam Shaw School of Drawing and Painting and in Newlyn with Stanhope Forbes. For 40 years from just before World War I she was art mistress at Croydon High School for Girls. Showed at RA, ROI, RI and Walker Art Gallery in Liverpool. Queen Mary bought several examples of her work. In retirement lived in Worthing, Sussex.

Julia WROUGHTON 1934– Painter and teacher, born in Bridge of Allan, Stirlingshire. She attended Colchester School of Art to obtain her national diploma in design, 1953–7, teachers including Hugh Cronyn and John O'Connor, then Royal College of Art, 1957–60, with Carel Weight and Colin Hayes. Lived at Inniemore Lodge, Pennyghael, on Isle of Mull, from 1967 running the Inniemore School of Painting. Was a member of RWA, also showing at RA and solo with Torrance Gallery in Edinburgh. Nuffield Foundation holds her work.

Carina WYATT 1963– Abstract artist, born in London. She studied at St Martin's School of Art, 1981–5, then was a guest at Hochschule für Bildende Künste, Braunchsweig, 1986–7. Her exhibitions included Blake Hall, Ongar, 1986; Goethe-Institut, Lagos, Nigeria, 1987, and in that year 3rd Print Biennale, Taiwan. In 1988 Wyatt appeared in Open Print Show at Bankside Gallery. In 1990 was included in Pomeroy Purdy Gallery's Group Painting Show and was John Kirby's choice as Artist of the Day at Flowers East.

Irene WYATT 1903–1987 Painter, born in Acton, west London, daughter of art teacher and designer Lionel Wyatt. In 1921–4 she attended Royal Academy Schools after preliminary training at Hammersmith Art School and Regent Street Polytechnic School of Art. Her teachers included Walter Sickert, Ernest Jackson and Richard Jack. In 1927 she married the sculptor John Smith, but they split in 1938. From the late 1920s Wyatt showed at RA and the Leicester, Goupil and Redfern Galleries and she had two solo exhibitions at Beaux Arts Gallery, 1934–6. During 1938 she toured South Africa, having an exhibition in Johannesburg. In the 1950s Wyatt often visited Spain. As well as a solo show at Hanover Gallery, she had one at Ditchling Gallery, Sussex, in 1962, and at Chenil Gallery in 1987. Piano Nobile Fine Paintings, Richmond, held a retrospective in 1990. From 1971–87 Wyatt lived in Devon, latterly wheelchair-bound and with poor eyesight.

Joyce WYATT 1924– Painter and miniaturist, notable for portraits, born and lived in London. She studied at Hornsey College of Art, 1941–3, teachers including John Charles Moody, and privately with the portrait painters Walter Durac Barnett and Francis Hodge. Wyatt was a member of RMS, PS, SWA and UA. She gained Gold and Silver Medals at Paris Salon, also showing at RA and RBA. Had several solo shows in Scotland and France. Lived latterly at North Stoke, near Wallingford in Oxfordshire.

Leo WYATT 1909–1981 Printmaker and teacher, born in London. He there served an apprenticeship as a commercial engraver, studying under George Taylor Friend at Central School of Arts and Crafts. Won the Goldsmiths', Silversmiths' and Jewellers' Art Council competitions for three years, 1927–9, and concurrently two London County Council evening scholarships. Wyatt subsequently worked in industry in London and the provinces, 1930–47, when he emigrated to South Africa, busy there as a freelance designer and engraver four 14 years. In 1961 he returned to Britain and eventually became visiting lecturer in the faculty of art at Newcastle Polytechnic. His work was in many international exhibitions and was widely reproduced. Solo exhibitions included Calouste Gulbenkian Gallery, Newcastle, 1974; Exe Gallery, Exeter, 1975; and University of Durham, 1978. Victoria & Albert Museum holds his work. Memorial show was held at Oxford Gallery in 1982 and an exhibition of wood engravings at Duncan Campbell Contemporary Art, 1993. Victoria & Albert Museum holds his work. Lived in Newcastle, Tyne and Wear.

William WYATT 1926–1993 Watercolourist and illustrator, born in London, who spent part of his boyhood as a pupil at Sevenoaks School when his school was evacuated there. Encouragement from the art master led to his studying at Woolwich School of Art before serving in the Royal Navy during the latter years of World War II. He worked for leading London studios as an illustrator, then as his reputation as a watercolourist grew he relinquished illustration and showed regularly with RWS. Wyatt specialised in the English landscape, as shown in his memorial exhibition at The Bank Street Gallery, Sevenoaks, 1994.

Charles WYE 1925– Painter and draughtsman, born and lived in London. He was educated partly in Switzerland, also at London University and studied painting with Eva Parnell-Bailey, 1947–53. Showed at UA, NS, RBA, ROI, Artists of Chelsea and in the provinces.

Paul WYETH 1920–1983 Painter and draughtsman notable for portraits, teacher and writer, born and lived in London. He studied at Hammersmith and Willesden Schools of Art and Royal College of Art for periods from 1934–48, his teachers including Douglas I Smart, Alfred Egerton Cooper, Raymond Coxon and Gilbert Spencer. Went on to teach at Hammersmith School of Art. Among several instructional books by Wyeth was *How to Paint in Oils*. He was a member of RP, RBA and Société des Artistes Français, winning Gold and Silver Medals at Paris Salon. Also showed at RA, Wildenstein and Grundy Art Gallery, Blackpool. National Gallery of Victoria, Melbourne, Australia, holds his work. Wyeth finally suffered from cancer.

Barbara WYKEHAM 1923– Painter in gouache, watercolour and oil, born in London, daughter of the writer J B Priestley. Her sister was Sylvia Goaman, partner in the stamp designing firm Michael Goaman. She was taught at Richmond College by the painter Cecil H Birtwhistle and aged 17 was painted by William Coldstream. Attended the Architectural Association School of Architecture to obtain her diploma, worked for among others Hugh Casson and Ove Arup and was elected RIBA. Group exhibitions included Embankment and Christopher Hull Galleries; Petworth House, Sussex; Camden Arts Centre. Kingston Library Gallery; and Chichester Arts Centre. Shared a show with Joan Russell at Christopher Hull. Lived in Stockbridge, Hampshire, and was married to Air Marshal Sir Peter Wykeham.

Vera WYLD fl. from late 1970s– Printmaker, photographer and teacher. She studied fine art at Maidstone College of Art, 1974–8, gaining an honours degree, then did postgraduate work at London University's Institute of Education, 1978–9, a specialist in screenprinting. In 1984–5 she gained a licentiateship and then an associateship of Royal Photographic Society. Taught extensively in Kent. Showed at Maidstone Art College, Rye Art Gallery and Mall Galleries. In 1989 shared three-man show at Woodlands Art Gallery. Showed solo at Associate House, Ashford.

Geoffrey WYLDE 1903– Painter and etcher of portraits and figures; teacher. He was born in Port Elizabeth, Cape Province, South Africa, and studied at the Michaelis School of Fine Art under John Wheatley, 1925–6. During 1927–31 Wylde held a temporary position in the Department of Architecture at Cape Town University, serving from 1931–5 at the Michaelis School as a junior lecturer. Having visited London during that time and become involved with Lucy Wertheim's Twenties Group he emigrated to London in the latter part of the 1930s, although he continued to visit South Africa. From 1950–3 taught at Sir John Cass School of Art, where he completed a series of murals. Showed RA, RP, NEAC and widely in South Africa and handled many portrait commissions. South African National Gallery, Cape Town, holds his work, and Ashmolean Museum, Oxford, his drawing of the novelist Graham Greene. Was a member of PS, UA, Chelsea Arts Club and London Sketch Club.

Jonathan WYLDER 1957– Self-taught sculptor in clay, born in Salisbury, Wiltshire. He was notable for portraits and studies of the female figure; subjects included Alita Sands, the Rhythmic Gymnast Champion, 1992, and Fiona Chadwick, Royal Ballet principal. Showed at Art92, at Business Design Centre in 1992, and had many solo exhibitions in London, the Home Counties, Switzerland, Austria, Hong Kong and America. Ran the Jonathan Wylder Gallery.

Rose WYLIE 1934– Painter and draughtsman, born in Hythe, Kent. She studied at Folkestone School of Art, 1952–6, then at Royal College of Art, 1979–81. Her group show appearances included Hayward Annual, 1982; Cleveland International Drawing Biennale, 1985; Odette Gilbert Gallery, 1988; David Bomberg and Others, at Towner Art Gallery, Eastbourne, 1991; and John Moores Exhibition, Liverpool, 1991–2. She had a solo show at Trinity Arts Centre, Tunbridge Wells, 1985. Although she favoured some type of likeness, Wylie believed that painting should not be merely photographic, being "a transforming process where materials and subject take on new life together". Lived in Newnham, Sittingbourne, Kent.

George WYLLIE 1921– Sculptor using metal who later developed into mixed media, installations, outdoor events, performance and theatre artist, born in Glasgow. He was self-taught and commenced artworks in 1965. Wyllie was an associate of RSA, a former president and then honorary member of SSA, a council member of the Glasgow Group and an honorary doctor of literature, Strathclyde University. Solo shows included Collins Exhibition Hall, Strathclyde University in Glasgow, 1976 and 1981; Serpentine Gallery, 1981; A Day Down a Goldmine, Third Eye Centre, Glasgow, 1982; Worcester Art Museum, Massachusetts, America, 1984; The Paper Boat Installation, World Financial Center, New York, 1990. He completed sculp-ture for General Accident World Headquarters, Perth. Stirling University, Whitworth Art Gallery in Manchester and Kelvingrove Art Gallery, Glasgow, hold examples. Lived in Gourock, Renfrewshire.

Gordon WYLLIE 1930– Painter, teacher and illustrator, born and lived in Greenock, Renfrewshire. Studied at High School there, then Glasgow School of Art, 1949–53, under William Armour, and with Armour's wife Mary and Ian Fleming at Patrick Allan-Fraser School of Art, Hospitalfield, Arbroath, 1953. Became art master at Greenock Academy. Was elected to RSW in 1967, also showing at Compass Gallery in Glasgow, RSA and Royal Glasgow Institute of the Fine Arts. Many solo shows included Compass Gallery, Citizens Theatre in Glasgow and Douglas & Foulis in Edinburgh. Lillie Art Gallery in Milngavie, Paisley Art Gallery and some Scottish local authorities hold examples.

Harold WYLLIE 1880–1973 Marine painter, sculptor and engraver, born in London. Was the son of the marine artist William Lionel Wyllie and married the portrait painter Euphans Hilary Strain. Harold Wyllie was intended for the Navy, but failed his examinations and turned to art. In 1898 he went to New York as a special artist for *The Graphic*, then served in South Africa during the Boer War. For part of World War I he was a pilot with the Royal Flying Corps, then gained a commission in the Army, which he left in 1920 with the rank of lieutenant-colonel. Wyllie was then a student with Frank Short, having prior to the war studied with his father, Thomas Graham Jackson and Edwin Austin Abbey, the American painter. Acknowledged as an expert on shipping matters, Wyllie was in 1932 called on to supervise restoration of the *Implacable*. He listed nautical research as his recreation to the end. He was hon. marine painter to the Royal Yacht Squadron, 1934, and served with the Navy in World War II. Exhibited RA, RI, Leicester Galleries and Royal Glasgow Institute of the Fine Arts. The Imperial War Museum and the National Maritime Museum, Greenwich, hold his work. Lived in Perthshire, Scotland.

Richard WYNDHAM 1896–1948 Painter, printmaker, writer and collector of modern art, full name Guy Richard Charles Wyndham. Dick Wyndham was born into the landed aristocracy and educated at Wellington College and the Royal Military College, Sandhurst. Served in World War I in the Army at the second Battle of Ypres, then Salonika, winning the Military Cross. Bored with the life of a country gentleman at Clouds House, Wiltshire, Wyndham took up art, studying under Harold Speed and Wyndham Lewis. He bought Tickerage Mill, outside Uckfield, Sussex, near his friend Edward Wadsworth, and drove fast cars, flew his own plane and partied with an artistic group. Wyndham showed at Goupil and Leicester Galleries and Tooth, having a first solo exhibition there in 1933, and had work bought by Edward Marsh, Manchester City Art Galleries and galleries in Brighton, Hull, Rochdale and Belfast. Landscapes with water were a noted feature of Wyndham's work. His books included a novel, *Painter's Progress*, 1938, and *The Gentle Savage*, about travels in the Sudan, 1936, celebrated with a show at Tooth in 1937. Wyndham was invalided out of the Army in World War II after a breakdown. Became a foreign correspondent in the Near East and was shot by a sniper in Palestine. His life was recounted by Caroline Dakers in the catalogue of a retrospective show at Henry Wyndham Fine Art, 1993. Wyndham appeared in Wyndham Lewis' novel *The Apes of God* as Richard Whittington.

Sonja WYNDHAM-WEST 1945– Sculptor, painter and teacher. Abstract sculpture used found objects and other materials. Born in London, she attended Wimbledon College of Art, 1960–2. After living abroad, completed an honours degree at Canterbury College of Art, 1985–8. In 1988 was assistant to sculptor Anthony Caro, in 1989 being sculpture fellow at Winchester School of Art. From 1990 taught there, in Hastings and Canterbury. Showed paintings at Nassau Art Gallery, Bahamas, 1980. Had a solo show at Jonathan's, London Stock Exchange, 1982, sharing an exhibition at Stables Theatre Gallery, Hastings, in 1983. Sculpture mixed exhibitions included The Showroom, 1986; Herbert Read Gallery, Canterbury, 1988; and Sculpture at Canterbury, 1991. Solo sculpture shows included Winchester Gallery, Winchester, 1989, with a shared exhibition at Morley Gallery, 1994. Lived in Hastings, Sussex.

Fenton WYNESS 1903–1974 Painter, draughtsman and historian, full name J Fenton Wyness, based in Aberdeen. He studied there at Gray's School of Art, showed locally and at RSA. Wyness was also a fellow of RIBA. The local Art Gallery and Imperial War Museum hold examples. Wyness' residence at 45 Salisbury Terrace in Aberdeen is now commemorated with a plaque.

WYNN 1927– Watercolourist, printmaker and teacher, born in Rangoon, Burma, full name Wynn Pullen. She studied at Harrow School of Art, 1942–5, and taught. Was a member of SGA, Ickenham Art Society and Colne Group, also exhibiting at RSM and RI and had a series of solo shows. London Borough of Hillingdon holds her work. Lived for some time in Ickenham, Middlesex.

Althea WYNNE 1936– Animal and figure sculptor and teacher who trained at Farnham School of Art, Hammersmith College of Art and Royal College of Art. In 1960 she won the Topham Trophy Award and obtained a major commission for London County Council. Then was engaged in teaching, returning to sculpture full-time in 1985, involved in big ceramics for public places in high-fired stoneware. These were shown widely, including the Hannah Peschar Gallery in Ockley, Mall Galleries and Margam Park, Port Talbot. Wynne showed solo at Salisbury Festival and at The Sturkel, Melbury Abbas. Her later public commissions included Rising Doves for Hounslow Council; a Family of Goats in bronze for London Docklands Development Corporation; and the Minster Court Horses, for Prudential Portolio Management Ltd, installed in Mincing Lane in 1991 and cast by The Morris Singer Foundry. She was elected a fellow of RBS in 1994. Lived at Upton Lovell, Warminster, Wiltshire.

David WYNNE 1926– Sculptor, noted for his animal and bird studies, which were mostly modelled and cast, born in Lyndhurst, Hampshire. He was educated at Stowe School, then attended Cambridge University. Studied sculpting with Georg Ehrlich, then in Paris with Wells Bosworth and Paul Landowski. Exhibited widely, including RA, Leicester Galleries and Whitechapel Art Gallery. National Portrait Gallery and Aberdeen Art Gallery hold his work. A retrospective was held at Cannizaro Park, Wimbledon, in 1980, with one celebrating 50 years' work at The Mall Galleries, 1997. Completed many public commissions, including Boy with a Dolphin, on Cheyne Walk, Chelsea, 1974; Girl with a Dolphin, St Katherine-by-the-Tower, 1975; and Five Swimmers Fountain, Elsmsleigh Precinct, Staines, 1980. Wynne's sculpture is noted for its grace and movement and has wide popular appeal. Lived for many years in London.

Nancy WYNNE-JONES 1922– Painter, born in Dolgellau, Merionethshire. She studied at Heatherley's School of Fine Art, at Chelsea School of Art and then St Peter's Loft School of Painting, St Ives, Cornwall. She exhibited with Newlyn Society for about a decade from mid-1950s and had many solo shows, starting with New Vision Centre Gallery in 1962, later ones including Hendriks Gallery, Dublin, 1988, having lived in Ireland for many years. In 1992 she was included in Belgrave Gallery's exhibition British abstract art of the 50s and 60s. Wynne-Jones latterly lived in Kinsale, County Cork, Ireland with her husband the sculptor Conor Fallon, with whom she shared a show at Emmet Gallery, Dublin, in 1977.

John WYNNE-MORGAN 1906– Painter, born in Harrogate, Yorkshire. After private education he studied at Heatherley's School of Fine Art, 1945, then from 1946–50 with Bernard Adams. His work was reproduced extensively in women's magazines and he showed at RP, RA, ROI, NS of which he was a member, RBA and with Chelsea Art Society. Hertfordshire County Council bought his work. Lived in London.

Francis WYNNE THOMAS 1907– Painter and teacher, born in Bromley, Kent. Graduated from Cambridge University and studied at Heatherley's School of Fine Art, where he was taught by Frederic Whiting in 1930–4; in 1949 he was on the staff at Heatherley's. Wynne Thomas's work can be heavily stylised. He showed at RA, RP, UA, RSA, RCamA and elsewhere. Lived in London.

Billy WYNTER 1962– Painter of richly coloured abstracts based on memories of landscape, born in Cornwall, where he settled in West Penwith. He was the son of artist Bryan Wynter. He gained his diploma from Falmouth School of Art, then graduated with honours in fine art from Middlesex Polytechnic. Exhibitions included Wolf at the Door, Penzance, 1990; Rainy Day Gallery, Penzance, 1994; and The Edge of Beyond, Belgrave Gallery, 1995.

Bryan WYNTER 1915–1975 Painter and teacher, born in London. He studied at Westminster School of Art, 1937–8, then Slade School of Fine Art, 1938–40. Shortly after World War II, during which he worked on the land as a conscientious objector, Wynter moved to St Ives, Cornwall, and he remained associated with the St Ives School, living near St Buryan. He had his first one-man show at the Redfern Gallery in 1947 and taught at Bath Academy of Art, Corsham, 1951–6. Was a co-founder of the Crypt Group in 1946, was a member of LG in 1955–61 and of the Penwith Society, 1949–58. At first Wynter was a figurative painter, but in 1956 he painted his first abstract works and in 1960 his initial kinetic picture. Was represented in a number of major international shows and had retrospectives at Falmouth School of Art in 1975 and Hayward Gallery in 1976. Arts Council, Tate Gallery and Victoria & Albert Museum hold his work. His son Billy Wynter was also a painter.

Allan Gairdner WYON 1882–1962 Sculptor and medallist working in a variety of materials, born in London, educated at Highgate Grammar School. Was married to the artist Eileen May Wyon and his father was the medallist Allan Wyon. Studied at Royal Academy Schools under Hamo Thornycroft, winning several medals. Became a member of the Art Workers' Guild and was elected a fellow of the RBS. Exhibited extensively at RA and RMS, also at RSA, RHA, Royal Glasgow Institute of the Fine Arts and at Paris Salon. His works, which often have a religious theme, are in a number of public collections. Wyon completed the carving East Wind in the late 1920s for the head offices of the Underground Railway (later London Transport) at 55 Broadway, Westminster. Was vicar for about 20 years in Newlyn, Cornwall, from the mid-1930s, in his final years living near Cambridge at Great Shelford, dying in King's Lynn, Norfolk, his wife surviving him.

Eileen May WYON 1883– Painter and draughtsman, especially of portraits and figures, who was married to the sculptor Allan Gairdner Wyon. She studied at Dublin Municipal School of Art, in the studio of Sir Arthur Cope and at the Royal Academy Schools. Exhibited RHA, Royal Glasgow Institute of the Fine Arts, UA, St Ives Society of Artists and in Newlyn, Cornwall, where she spent much of her life. Latterly lived at Great Shelford, Cambridgeshire. The church there held her portrait of the vicar. Survived her husband, who died in 1962.

Henry WYSE 1870–1951 Painter, potter, teacher and writer, born in Glasgow. He studied at Dundee and Glasgow Schools of Art and in Paris at Académie Julian and Atelier Colarossi. Went on to teach at Moray House, Edinburgh, where he settled, and became known for a series of instructional books, such as *Modern Methods of Art Instruction* and *Modern Type Display*. Showed at RSA, Royal Glasgow Institute of the Fine Arts, in the English provinces and with Aberdeen and Dundee Art Societies.

X

XENIA: *see* **Xenia BERKELEY**

XI Jian Jun 1962– Artist, born in China, who studied at the Central Academy of Arts and Design, Beijing, then Goldsmiths' College. Group exhibitions included China Art Gallery and National Museum of China, both Beijing in 1985; South Bank Picture Show, Royal Festival Hall, 1988; Whitechapel Open, from 1990; Turkish Pavilion, Venice Biennale, 1994; and University of Essex tour Journeys West, 1995. Solo shows included October Gallery, 1989, and New Signs & New Directions, Venice City Project, Italy, 1993.

Gloria XIMENES 1933– Painter, draughtsman and teacher who studied at St Martin's School of Art, 1959–61, teachers including Joe Tilson and Robin Guthrie, as well as for a short period in Italy. Was a member of Free Painters and Sculptors and local societies in Thames Valley and Weybridge, also showing at NS and WIAC and having several solo exhibitions. Lived in London.

Y

YAIR 1963– Painter, full name Yair Meshoulam, born in Haifa, Israel. He graduated in fine art at Ruskin School of Drawing & Fine Art, Oxford, 1982–5, then gained his master's in painting at Royal College of Art, 1986–8, after which he was a self-employed artist, working part-time at Ben Uri Art Society. He was a member of the Society, of National Association of Artists and of Ridley Art Society. "Colour, mystery, order and the connection of ideas" were important in his output which included the Astronaut Altarpiece, Ezekiel's Chariot and Biblical and St Francis series. Took part in Whitechapel Open at Whitechapel Gallery, from 1989; a two-man show at Ozten Zeki Gallery, 1991; Berlin/London Exchange, organised by the British Council, Bahnof Westend, Berlin, 1994; in the two-man As Above, So Below, at Ben Uri, and showed at Boston Consultancy, Mayfair, both 1995. Held a solo exhibition at studio in Childers Street, Diagrams of Splendour, 1993, another at Ozten Zeki Gallery, 1997. Lived in London.

Brian YALE 1936– Painter, sculptor, designer and teacher, born in Staffordshire, who, after playing in an orchestra during National Service, rejected a musical career in favour of art. Yale attended Stourbridge College of Art, 1952–6, then the Royal College of Art, 1958–62, where he gained a prize and postgraduate scholarship. Lectured at Hornsey College of Art, 1962–8; became an artist/environmental designer in the Greater London Council architect's department, 1968–86; in 1986 was a visiting lecturer, Clemson University, South Carolina; lectured part-time at Sir John Cass College, 1987; and in 1988 became a full-time artist. Commissions included Greater London Council, 1984, to paint the Thames Barrier, to mark its official opening, and a major sculpture for London Docklands Development Corporation, 1988. Took part in many mixed shows, including Young Britain, The New Scene, ICA, for America, 1967; Images of Ourselves, Tate Gallery, 1980; Society of Landscape Painters, from 1989; and Landscape, Woodlands Art Gallery, 1996. Had a solo exhibition at Axiom Gallery, 1966, later ones including Wolseley Fine Arts, 1997. Public collections holding work include Tate Gallery, Arts Council, WAC, Imperial War Museum, British Council, Museum of London and provincial galleries. Yale wrote that he painted landscape "because I believe that is where our strength lies, and I use the realist tradition because I get nearer to achieving my ambition this way." World War I battlefields were a key theme, another the coast around Dungeness, Kent, where he had a cottage.

Pat YALLUP 1929– Watercolourist, gallery owner and teacher, born in Johannesburg, South Africa. Deploring the Apartheid system Yallup emigrated with her family to England after studying at Witwatersrand; after arrival she attended Byam Shaw School of Art, concentrating on portraiture. Much of Yallup's work was abstract, using the wet-into-wet watercolour technique. She started the Sunbury Art Group in Sunbury-on-Thames, 1962; opened Art Centre in Chepstow, 1973; then Old Bell Gallery, also in Chepstow, 1979; the Llandogo Studio and Gallery, near Monmouth, Gwent, where she continued to live, and where she taught, 1981; and Silver Place Gallery, London, 1984, which closed in 1987. Exhibitions included Artists of Fame and Promise at Leicester Galleries, 1963; RI from 1974; and Fine Art Trade Guild from 1986. Had many solo exhibitions. Yallup admired the work of Cézanne and Kandinsky and was influenced by Abstract Symbolism. Was a member of RWS. Unilever, Imperial Chemical Industries and Tarmac hold examples.

Ying Sheng YANG 1961– Strong figurative artist, born in China, who attended the Zhejiang Academy of Art and Nanjing College of Art there, then Wimbledon and Royal Colleges of Art. Among his awards were Fergus Anstruther, 1987; DHL Educational Foundation Scholarship, 1988; and in 1989 the Burston Award and J Andrew Lloyd Scholarship. Mixed shows included Contemporary Chinese Art Retrospective at National Gallery, China, 1988; 4th International Contemporary Art Fair, Olympia, 1989; 3 Ways, Contemporary British Art East Europe tour, 1990; Florence Trust Open Studios Exhibition, 1993; and University of Essex tour Journeys West, 1995. Nanjing and Royal Colleges of Art and Westminster City Council hold examples.

Bruce YARDLEY 1962– Painter of colourful street scenes, still lifes and restaurant interiors, son of the artist John Yardley, he produced his first oils in the 1970s. Trained as an historian at Bristol and Oxford Universities, gaining his doctorate in the late 1980s. Joined the wine trade, first in retailing then as a freelance writer, painting full-time from 1996. Exhibitions included a solo at Catto Gallery, 1998.

Helen YARDLEY 1954– Textile designer, notable for her rugs, born in Plymouth, Devon, creator of bold, unusual abstract designs using singular colour combinations. She did foundation studies at Plymouth College of Art, 1972–3; gained a first-class honours degree in printed and woven textiles at Manchester Polytechnic, 1973–6; and her master's in textiles at Royal College of Art, 1976–8. Exhibited widely, including Aspects Gallery and Crafts Council at ICA, both 1985; Sotheby's Decorative Arts Exhibition, 1988; Great British Design, Tokyo and tour, 1990; and SSWA at RSA, 1995. Numerous commissions included Walt Disney Corporation, 1992; British Telecom, 1993; British Ambassador's

Residence, Jakarta, Indonesia, 1994; Citibank, Brussels, Belgium, 1995; and Home Office, 1996. Victoria & Albert Museum, British Crafts Council and Portsmouth City Museum hold examples. Based in London at A–Z Studios.

John YARDLEY 1933– Painter in oil and watercolour, born in Yorkshire. His work was compared to that of Edward Seago, having a similar deftness in depicting the fleeting scene and light effects in Britain and abroad. Yardley had no formal art training, but began drawing while very young. He began painting in 1953 after completing his National Service and when he retired from banking in 1986 took it up full-time. In 1989 he gained the Catto Gallery Award for work shown at the RWS Open Exhibition and in 1990 was awarded the Watercolour Foundation Prize for work shown at RI and was elected to membership. Had solo shows at Catto Gallery. Lived in Reigate, Surrey.

Annette YARROW 1932– Sculptor, notably of horses, who was born in Southampton and educated at Cheltenham Ladies' College, then as a nurse in Glasgow. With a father who was a tea planter in India and a mother who was a medical practitioner, Yarrow nursed in the sub-continent, becoming matron of a nursing home. After returning to England, although she had no art training she made a sculpture of her son which was so successful that she turned to horses, always her great love, as subjects. In 1973 she was commissioned to produce HRH The Princess Royal on Doublet, which the Princess, gave in first-cast state to the New Zealand Navy. Yarrow's later work comprised many commissions for Asprey's. In 1982 a life-size golden eagle on a globe was erected at Middle Wallop for the Army Air Corps for its twenty-fifth anniversary. Much of Yarrow's sculpting was done in her Hampshire studio, not far from the Basingstoke-based Morris Singer Foundry which cast her pieces.

Catherine YASS 1963– Artist-photographer, born and worked in London, who was interested in the scrutiny of institutions and their inhabitants,sometimes lending them a surreal quality. She graduated from the Slade School of Fine Art, 1982–6; attended Hochschule der Kunst, Berlin, 1984–5; then gained her master's degree at Goldsmiths' College, 1989–90. Group shows included New Contemporaries, ICA, 1984; Madonnas, Diorama Gallery, 1990; Exhibit A, Serpentine Gallery, 1992; and Mélange d'Aoû t, Laure Gennillard Gallery, 1995. Had a solo show at Tavistock Clinic, 1991, others including Spectators, Aspex Gallery, Portsmouth, 1995. Commissions included Starkmann Ltd and Leipzig Bookfair, both 1993; and Salford City Council and Arts Council, both 1994.

Alan YATES 1947– Sculptor in metal and teacher, born in Bishop Auckland, County Durham. He studied art at Bede College, Durham, from 1966, gaining his certificate of education in 1969. He was a member of Society of Designer-Craftsmen and an associate of RBS. Showed at RA, RWA, RSA and widely in the provinces. Durham University's Grey College holds his work. Lived in High Etherley, Bishop Auckland.

Ann YATES 1897–1992 Painter who studied at Laird School of Art in Birkenhead. During World War II she went to live in Llandudno, north Wales, and began exhibiting with RCamA, becoming a member in 1954, a year after being made a member of RI. Also showed at Arlington and Cooling Galleries, RBA and in the provinces. Settled in Dorking, Surrey.

Eric YATES 1919– Sculptor in a variety of materials and painter, notably of marine works, born in Horsham, Sussex. Studied at Southampton University and art part-time at Newton Abbot, Douglas and St Albans Colleges of Art. Was a made a member of Free Painters and Sculptors in 1978 and NS in 1981, also showing at RSMA and RMS. Lived in Emsworth, Hampshire.

Fred YATES 1922– Painter and teacher, born in Urmston, Manchester. His career as an insurance clerk was interrupted by the war, during which he served in the Grenadier Guards, in 1945 returning to Manchester as a painter and decorator. He began to paint Manchester streetlife as an untutored artist, enrolled for a teacher training course at Bournemouth College of Art and in 1950 won a travelling scholarship to Italy. After teaching for about 20 years he moved to Cornwall to paint full-time. While attempting to retain his Primitive style, he added to the Manchester scenes Cornish harbours, images of France and more visionary subjects. Showed at John Moores Exhibition, Liverpool; Compass Gallery, Glasgow; Newlyn Orion Gallery; RA; Redfern Gallery; and in 1992 had a solo show at Thompson's Gallery. Latterly lived in Provence, France.

Hal YATES 1907–1979 Watercolour painter, mainly of landscapes. Born in West Didsbury, Manchester, he studied art privately and part-time at Manchester Art School. Exhibited widely, at RA, RSA, RI, RBA, Paris Salon and in the provinces. Collections holding his work include Whitworth Art Gallery, Manchester; Laing Art Gallery and Museum, Newcastle upon Tyne; and Salford Art Gallery. Lived at Styal, Cheshire.

Harold YATES 1916– Painter, mainly in watercolour, and draughtsman. His father was an amateur artist who worked as a cartoonist for the trade press. Aged 14 Yates attended Portsmouth School of Art for 18 months, where he showed talent for figure work and developed an ambition to be an illustrator. After joining a commercial studio aged 17 he became disillusioned with the disciplines there and painted abstract works in his spare time. Showed with AIA, London Gallery and had a solo show at Foyles Gallery aged 19. While in Army during World War II did documentary work which was bought by War Artists' Advisory Committee, now in Imperial War Museum, at the same time producing pictures with a personal symbolism. After the Army worked as a freelance commercial artist and on the staff of a leading London advertising agency, while continuing to paint part-time. Yates had a solo show at Belgrave Gallery in 1989, a retrospective at Chappel Galleries, Chappel, Essex, in 1992.

Jack YATES 1923– Painter, collagist and artist in other media, photographer and teacher, born in Sheffield,

Yorkshire. He studied at Sheffield College of Arts and Crafts, 1948–9, then worked in a commercial art studio, 1949–50. The female figure was a notable feature of Yates' art, which displayed much wit and a dramatic sense of design. He said that Oskar Kokoschka "opened my eyes". Yates was an influential teacher at Camden Arts Centre, 1965–90, and he went on to teach at Camden School of Art. He was editor of *Kaleidoscope Magazine*, issues 1–8, wrote for *Artist* magazine and with his wife Hanne produced *Collage*, published in Germany in 1981. Arts Council bought his photographic work. Took part in many mixed shows, including LG, 1952; New Art Centre, 1959; RA from 1963; Camden Arts Centre from 1965; Angela Flowers Gallery, 1975; Tate Gallery, 1981; and Knapp Gallery, 1989. Had solo shows at Gallery 60, Colchester, 1963–4, others including Heal's Mansard Gallery, 1965 and 1970; Camden Arts Centre from 1970; Alfred East Gallery in Kettering, 1989; and Jack Yates & Friends, retrospective, Swiss Cottage Library, 1993. Lived in London.

Marie YATES 1940– Artist, born in Lancashire, who described her work as "conceptual, political, feminist" and "non-commercial, dedicated to social change". She studied at Hornsey College of Art; Royal College of Art; University College, London; Middlesex Polytechnic; and Derbyshire College of Higher Education. Yates showed at numerous venues, including British Council, Arts Council and at Arnolfini Gallery, Bristol. Arts Council holds her work Durgan Field Working 1974, comprising 60 black-and-white photographs mounted on board standing on wood blocks, plus a 12-minute tape recording. Lived in London.

Tom YATES 1963– Artist who was born and lived in London. He studied at Hastings School of Art, 1986–7; Chelsea College of Art, 1987–90, and in the mid-1990s did a postgraduate course at Brighton School of Art. Exhibitions included Riverside Open, 1993; Phoenix PILL Gallery, Brighton, 1994; and John Moores Liverpool Exhibition, 1995–6.

Hazel YATES JONES 1939– Artist in watercolour and pen wash, calligrapher, illustrator and teacher, born in Hastings, Sussex. She attended Northampton School of Art, obtaining her national diploma in design, teachers including Frank Cryer; then after teaching she went to West of England College of Art in Bristol, gaining an art teacher's diploma, teachers including Irene Base; followed by studies for a certificate of education at Bristol University. While lecturing at Mander College in Bedford, she completed her bachelor's degree through the Open University. When married she moved to Drimpton, Dorset, where she combined part-time lecturing with freelance work in illustration, graphic design and calligraphy. She showed with Liberty, at Mall Galleries, Hitchin Museum and Bedford Central Library. Among commissioned work was material for Bedfordshire Growers' lorries and packaging, twinning documents for Letchworth and Hitchin and Nelson's Victory at Trafalgar for Bedford School.

John YEADON 1948– Painter and teacher, born in Burnley, Lancashire, who did a pre-diploma course at Burnley College of Art, 1964–6, gained his diploma at Hornsey College of Art, 1966–9, then his master's degree at Royal College of Art, 1969–72. In the latter year Yeadon joined the Communist Party, visited the Soviet Union in 1975, Cuba in 1978 and in 1981 was a guest of the Czech Artists' Fund, with a studio in Prague. Yeadon was a founder-member and was closely involved in the running of the cultural journal *Artery* from 1971. He took a studio with Coventry Artists' Group in 1983 and was its chairman in 1984, settling in the city. Yeadon had extensive teaching experience throughout Britain and was full-time at Coventry Polytechnic from 1974. Group shows included *Morning Star* Rally, Coventry, 1974; the Arts Council's The British Art Show, 1984; Critical Realism, Castle Museum, Nottingham, touring exhibition, 1987–8; and Post-Morality, Kettle's Yard, Cambridge, 1990. Later solo shows included Chronicles & Continuing Tales, The Travails of Blind Bifford Jelly, Ikon Gallery, Birmingham, and tour, 1991–2. Royal College of Art, Arts Council and public galleries in Birmingham and Coventry hold examples. Yeadon was also a keen cellist.

Jack Butler YEATS 1871–1957 Painter and draughtsman. Born in London, son of the Irish portrait painter John Butler Yeats and brother of the poet William Butler Yeats. Studied at Westminster School of Art under Fred Brown. At first worked as a watercolourist and illustrator, much influenced by his idyllic life from the age of eight to sixteen in the northwest of Ireland, described in his book *Sligo*, 1930. He early on showed a precocious talent for drawing and for writing plays. In the early years of the century Yeats' work began to be known through a series of broadsheets, some edited by his brother, issued by the Cuala Press. His plays, similarly Irish and dramatic, had titles such as *The Scourge of the Gulph* and *James Flaunty or the Terror of the Western Seas*. Yeats had a great love of the sea, partly due to his friendship with John Masefield, whom he painted in a rare portrait. Yeats' oil paintings began in 1897, and he did not regularly work in oil until 1905. He had his first exhibition in Dublin in 1899. Then began to show widely, but a series of retrospective exhibition at Victor Waddington's galleries, in Dublin, from 1940 helped to establish his name. Retrospectives at the National Gallery, London, 1942, Dublin, 1945, and the Tate Gallery, 1948, consolidated his reputation. He had been elected RHA in 1915 and was made an Officer of the Legion of Honour in 1949. Yeats began as an illustrator and ended up as an Expressionist, much admired by Oskar Kokoschka, commenting; "People may think what they will of the pictures." Work in many public collections, including the Tate Gallery. Lived in Dublin, Ireland.

YEO Kim Seng 1938– Painter and draughtsman, born in Singapore where he graduated from the Academy of Arts in 1960. During the next four years showed widely in Far East and India, then in 1964 went to Paris to study at École Nationale des Artistes des Beaux-Arts, showing in mixed and one-man exhibitions. During a visit to New York showed at Park South Gallery, then settled in London where he showed at RP, ROI, NEAC and won the first prize at Royal Over-Seas League show in 1971. Had solo show at St Jude's in 1991.

Antonia YEOMAN: *see* **ANTON**

Martin YEOMAN 1953– Painter, mainly of landscape in oil, with an individual palette and poetic sense of place. In 1974 Yeoman was taught by Jane Dowling, and as a result became a guest student with Peter Greenham at Royal Academy Schools, 1975–9. He was a awarded a silver medal for drawing and Richard Ford Landscape Scholarship to Spain. In 1980 Yeoman won the Elizabeth Greenshields Foundation award. He in 1981 and 1983 entered and hung in the Imperial Tobacco Portrait Competition at National Portrait Gallery. Won the Hamerson Purchase Prize in 1984, and was elected to NEAC. Yeoman had a solo show at Highgate Gallery in 1986 and one at New Grafton Gallery in 1990. Mixed show appearances included RA from 1976, Agnew, RBA and RP.

Geoff YEOMANS 1934– Artist and teacher, born in Birkenhead, Cheshire. He studied at Liverpool College of Art, 1955–6, then Birmingham Polytechnic, 1976–7. Yeomans went on to teach at Nuneaton School of Art, 1964–87. He worked extensively with David Berry-Hart and with him formed The Firm, four painters and two sculptors, including Geoff Wilde, Paul Littlehales, Ed Pooley and Mark Compton. Yeomans was featured in the 1992 Norwich Gallery/Kent Institute of Art and Design show East & South with Towards a Greater Definition II (Action Man). Walker Art Gallery in Liverpool holds his oil Outdoor Café Scene.

Richard YEOMANS 1944– Painter and teacher, born in Coventry. He studied painting under Richard Hamilton at the University of Newcastle upon Tyne; trained as an art teacher at Goldsmiths' College; then subsequently completed his master's degree at Birmingham Polytechnic and a doctorate at London University where he researched into the pedagogy of Victor Pasmore and Richard Hamilton. He went on to lecture in painting and art history at Warwick University. After graduation he held many solo shows in the Midlands and participated in numerous group exhibitions in London and the provinces. He travelled widely in the Middle East, writing and lecturing on Islamic art and architecture, inspiration for an exhibition at Woodlands Art Gallery in 1992 which attempted to evoke "the silent Surreality of the desert landscape and monuments".

Laetitia YHAP 1941– Painter, born in St Albans, Hertfordshire, was married for a time to the artist Jeffery Camp. She studied at Camberwell School of Art, 1958–62, then Slade School of Fine Art, 1963–5, having received a Leverhulme Travel Scholarship to Italy in the intervening year. In the 1960s and 1970s showed frequently with Young Contemporaries and with LG, having the first of several solo shows at Piccadilly Gallery in 1968. Also showed Serpentine Gallery in 1979 and Air Gallery in 1984. She was elected a member of LG in 1970 and won a prize four years later in John Moores Exhibition, Liverpool. Yhap lived for many years in Hastings, Sussex, and based much of her work on its beach and fishermen. The supports can be of odd shapes, incorporating driftwood and rope. Tate Gallery and public galleries in Hastings and Hove hold her work. The name Yhap is Chinese, through her father, her mother having been Viennese.

Elaine YHIP 1963– Artist in various media who studied painting at Central School of Art and Design. Early Italian and Flemish painters were strong influences on her work, which was shown in at Royal Festival Hall, Beaumanor Hall in Leicester and in 1990 in England & Co's Art in Boxes.

Frederick YOCUM 1955– Figurative painter, born in Philadelphia, studying at Pennsylvania Academy of Fine Art, 1974–6, then part-time at Heatherley School of Fine Art, 1976–7. He showed in Spirit of London in 1986, Berkeley Square Gallery, 1988, Mostyn Art Gallery in Llandudno, 1989, and was a prizewinner in John Moores Liverpool Exhibition, 1989–90. Had a solo show at Chelmsford Museum in 1983. Lived in London.

Jan YOORS 1922– Sculptor and tapestry designer, son of the stained glass artist and painter Eugène Yoors. Initially educated in Antwerp, Belgium, where part of his art studies were undertaken at the Royal Academy of Fine Arts, 1939–40. Later attended London University and the School of Oriental and African Studies, just after World War II. Showed in London, Brussels and extensively in America. Lived in Purley, Surrey, and in New York.

Alan YOUNG 1941– Painter, especially in watercolour, illustrator, teacher and poet, born in Woking, Surrey, full name Michael Alan Young. He studied at Maidstone College of Art, 1962–5, teachers including John Barnicoat, Brian Wildsmith, Lewin Bassingthwaighte, Peter Coviello, John Plumb, David Hockney and Peter Stroud, then Royal College of Art, 1965–8, where Quentin Blake taught illustration. Became senior lecturer in cultural studies at Kent Institute of Art & Design, Maidstone. Several volumes of poetry included *A Bomb Inside the Hill*, 1971. Illustrated for major magazines in Britain and abroad. Group shows included England & Co, 1991, and Brixton Art Gallery, 1992. Had a solo exhibition at Drew Gallery, Canterbury, 1985, later ones including Trinity Arts Centre, Tunbridge Wells, 1987, and Kent Institute of Art & Design Gallery, 1993. The Welsh border country, the artist's house and Kent pubs were some themes of Young's work. Lived in Tonbridge, Kent.

Brian YOUNG 1934– Painter, stained glass designer and teacher. He studied at St Martin's School of Art, 1951–3, and at Central School of Arts and Crafts, 1957–60, winning awards that enabled him to study on the continent. Taught at Chelsea School of Art and London College of Printing. Showed with Young Contemporaries and at Rowan and Gimpel Fils Galleries. Arts Council bought his abstract oil on canvas Extension I, of 1958. Lived in London.

Donald YOUNG 1924–1990 Painter, draughtsman and teacher, born in London to humble parents who did not encourage his interest in art. In 1940 he gained a State Scholarship to the Central School of Arts and Crafts. Served in the Royal Navy as a radar mechanic, 1942–4, but unable to paint suffered a nervous breakdown and was invalided out. From 1944–6 studied at Chelsea School of Art where he met his future wife, Joyce Parris, also a student there. After declining to complete his Art Teacher's Diploma course at Leicester College, 1948–9, because of the narrowness of the curriculum, Young taught life drawing part-time at Loughborough College of Art, then with his wife returned to London. She now became the breadwinner as a teacher of art and Young was enabled to produce the highly stylised figure paintings which would from then obsess him. In 1958–9 they moved to Beckenham, Kent, and Young developed a new style mixing figurative and abstract concepts. Took part in mixed exhibitions, including Free Painters, Nicholas Treadwell Gallery and elsewhere. Had a solo show at Drian Gallery, 1966; taught adults at Beckenham Arts Centre, 1976–85, where he was reckoned an inspiring teacher; and had further solo exhibitions in Britain and abroad, including Southwark Cathedral, 1971, and Warwick University, 1980. There was a memorial show at Fairfield Halls, Croydon, 1990, and a retrospective at Gothick Dream Fine Art, 1993.

Eileen YOUNG 1896–1986 Painter in watercolour who was a collector of English watercolours, pottery and Chinese ceramics. She studied art under Myles Tonks and exhibited at RA, NEAC, Leicester Galleries, RWS and other London venues. Had several solo exhibitions in the 1940s and 1950s. Her work is owned by the Ashmolean Museum in Oxford; Whitworth Art Gallery, Manchester; Harris Museum and Art Gallery, Preston; and in America by the Mellon Collection. Lived in Guildford, Surrey.

Emily YOUNG 1951– Versatile artist, born in London, who spent most of her youth in Italy and France, her grandmother being the sculptor Kathleen Scott (Lady Kennet, widow of the Polar explorer Robert Falcon Scott). She attended Chelsea and St Martin's Schools of Art. Travelled the world for several years. Went on to found Public Pictures, a community-based mural group, in 1974; worked with The Penguin Café Orchestra from 1975 on record sleeves and stage designs; later turned fully to sculpture, figurative work in a range of stones and marble. She was an associate of RBA and showed at Odette Gilbert and Berkeley Square Galleries, RA Summer Exhibition and Thackeray Gallery, and in 1993 had a solo show at Sue Rankin Gallery. In 1996 was represented in the three-man exhibition Sculpting, at the Fine Art Society, by a series of classical female forms. Lived and worked in Normandy and London.

Florence YOUNG 1919– Painter, draughtsman and miniaturist, born in Preston, Lancashire, self-taught as an artist. She was a member of RMS, SWA and SM and an associate of Société des Artistes Français. Completed much work to commission, especially animal portraits, landscapes and botanical pictures. Showed at Medici and Mall Galleries, Westminster Central Hall, Stowe School and Paris Salon, where her awards included a Silver Medal. Lived in Uxbridge, Middlesex.

Henrietta YOUNG 1951– Painter, notably of portraits, who attended Winchester School of Art. Took part in mixed shows at Salisbury Arts Centre and the Hambledon, Oliver Swann and New Grafton Galleries. Joint shows included New Grafton, 1995, and her solo exhibitions included Hambledon, Oliver Swann and Summerleaze Galleries. Lived in Dorset, but also travelled abroad to paint, including a trip to India.

Jean YOUNG 1914– Painter in oil, born in London, full name Helen Jean Young. She studied while still at School under Otway McCannell at Farnham School of Art; for two years at Regent Street Polytechnic School of Art with Stuart Tresilian; with John Skeaping at London Zoo; and in 1933–8 at Royal Academy Schools, teachers including Walter Russell, F E Jackson and Tom Monnington. She was a medallist for composition at the Schools in 1938. Young specialised in figure compositions, landscapes and birds. She said that Italian, Persian and Indian primitives were key influences, design and colour most important. She was a member of RBA and NEAC. Had a series of solo shows in London, Canterbury and Bath, mixed show appearances including RA, LG and SWLA. Hereford City Museum and Art Gallery holds her work. Lived in Northwood, Middlesex.

Jessie YOUNG 1879– Painter educated at Dulwich High School. She studied at Beckenham School of Art, gaining a scholarship, then in the late 1930s studied watercolour for three years with the landscape painter Louis Burleigh Bruhl. She was especially noted for her flower paintings and exhibited RCamA, BWS of which she was a member, Whitechapel Art Gallery and in the provinces. Lived at King's Langley, Hertfordshire.

John YOUNG 1930– Aviation artist who as a small boy was inspired by seeing Sir Alan Cobham's Flying Circus. He went on to paint a huge range of aircraft from many periods, in a large number of which he had flown, pictures noted for technical accuracy combined with period and location atmosphere. William John Young attended High Wycombe School of Art, 1946–8, then after two years in the Royal Air Force became a painter, illustrating books and working for manufacturers and air forces. Young went freelance in the early 1960s. He showed with the first exhibition of the Society of Aviation Artists; was chairman of the Kronfeld Aviation Art Society; was a founder-member of the Guild of Aviation Artists, and gained its Gold Medal in 1983 and its chairmanship in 1987. Young completed murals for airline offices all over the world; the museums of the Royal New Zealand and Brazilian Air Forces hold examples and the Royal Air Force Museum in Hendon has an extensive collection, a selection on exhibition in the Bomber Command Hall. In 1982, 45 acrylic paintings by Young were reproduced as commemorative postal covers by the Channel Islands.

Lesley YOUNG 1942– Painter, draughtsman, printmaker and teacher, born in Carlisle, Cumberland. She did a foundation year at the local College of Art, then graduated from Newcastle upon Tyne University with an honours degree in fine art in 1966, her teachers including Richard Hamilton, Victor Pasmore and Eduardo Paolozzi. She gained the Annabella Winship Smiles Travelling Scholarship which she used to study etching at Central School of Art. Teaching experience included West Sussex College of Art, Salford College of Technology and Open University and was an art therapist in a psychiatric hospital. Undertook a residency at Chadderton School, Oldham. Young researched landscape painting in Cumbria and women artists and painted portraits of people in everyday surroundings, landscapes and wildlife subjects. Group shows included RA Summer Exhibition from 1975, MAFA, Portland Gallery and the Portico Library in Manchester and was in the 1988 Lancashire South of the Sands touring show, originated at County and Regimental Museum, Preston. Solo exhibitions included Carlisle City Art Gallery, 1985. Manchester City Art Gallery and public galleries in Blackpool, Bolton, Carlisle and Salford hold examples. Lived in Salford, Lancashire.

Monica YOUNG 1929– Potter and artist, born in Paris, France, where she lived until 1940. Studied fine arts at St Martin's and Ealing Schools of Art and at Escuella de Bellas Artes, Barcelona, and earned her living by portrait painting and book illustrating until 1972, when she taught herself to coil large pots. Became a member of the Craftsmen Potters' Association the following year, and began her career in ceramics. Her work was widely shown, venues including Courcoux & Courcoux, Stockbridge; Hannah Peschar Gallery, Ockley; Barbican Centre; Scottish Gallery, Edinburgh; Crafts Council; Contemporary Applied Arts; and provincial public galleries. Department of the Environment and Conoco, Warwick, hold examples. Lived in Richmond, Yorkshire.

Richard YOUNG 1921– Painter and draughtsman, born in Liverpool, although he spent some childhood years in London. His work was substantially home- and interior-oriented, early pictures being in the Kitchen Sink School manner; the paintings of Sickert and Bomberg were influences. Before World War II, in which he served in the Navy as a radio operator, Young did a number of jobs, on demobilisation returning to Liverpool and eventually becoming a self-employed electrician. He studied part-time at Liverpool Art College, his teachers including Arthur Ballard and George Mayer-Marton. In 1979–82 studied further at Liverpool Polytechnic. Took part in many group and solo shows in Liverpool and northwest of England, including regularly at Liverpool Academy. Walker Art Gallery, Liverpool, bought his work. His picture Drawings on the Wall, based on 25 self-portrait drawings from 1948 to 1988, was included in John Moores Exhibition, Liverpool, in 1991–2. Other appearances included Riverside Gallery, 1981; Hayward Annual, 1982, British Drawing; and RA Summer Exhibition, 1986.

Robert YOUNG 1938– Painter and printmaker, born in Vancouver, British Columbia, Canada. Was educated at the University of British Columbia, graduating with an honours degree in art history, and studied art at Vancouver School of Art, 1964–6, after City and Guilds of London Art School, 1962–4. Showed extensively at Redfern Gallery, London, in Germany and in several galleries in Vancouver. Signed work with initials.

Roger YOUNG 1931– Painter, potter and teacher, born and lived in Hove, Sussex. Studied at Brighton College of Art, 1947–53, then went on to teach pottery there. Showed AIA, RA and in Sussex.

Sally YOUNG 1969– Painter whose mixed-media, multiple-image pictures had a hieratic quality. She was born in Belfast and graduated from the University of Ulster there in 1991 with a degree in fine art design. Gained two awards from the Prince's Trust: a Go and See Grant in 1992 and an In Pursuit of Excellence Grant, 1993. Mixed shows included Irish Craft Exhibition in London, 1991; No Access at Ross's Court, Belfast, 1992; and in 1994 Works on Paper and Beyond the Partitions, put on by Queen Street Studios, Belfast, with which she was associated.

Stephen YOUNG 1946– Sculptor, draughtsman and teacher, born in Godalming, Surrey, who studied at Guildford School of Art, 1962–4, and Chelsea School of Art, 1964–8. Went on to teach at Cardiff College of Art. Young was in John Moores Liverpool Exhibition, 1967; Summer Shows at Serpentine Gallery, 1972 and 1980; and in the latter year in The Probity of Art, Oriel, Cardiff. Solo shows included University of Southampton, 1980. WAC holds his work.

Harold YOUNGMAN 1886–1968 Sculptor and teacher, born in Bradford, Yorkshire. Studied at Plymouth School of Art under Frederick Shelley, at the Royal College of Art, 1908–12, with Édouard Lantéri and at the Royal Academy Schools. Taught sculpture at Hornsey School of Art. Exhibited RA, RSA, Royal Glasgow Institute of the Fine Arts and in English provinces. National Museum of Wales, Cardiff, holds his work. Youngman was a fellow of the RBS and the volume *RBS: Modern British Sculpture*, published in 1939, two years after his election, includes typical examples of his expressive carved oak figures: Ishmael and St George. Lived in London.

Nan YOUNGMAN 1906–1995 Artist in oil, watercolour, charcoal and other media, born in Maidstone, Kent, who for most of her career "combined part-time art teaching, children and adults, with my own painting." She was art adviser to Cambridgeshire Education Committee, 1944–56; was the originator of the Pictures for Schools Exhibitions, with a first show at Victoria & Albert Museum, 1947; and made tours abroad for the British Council in connection with art education, starting with West Indies in 1952. Youngman studied at Slade School of Fine Art, 1924–7, under Henry Tonks and Philip Wilson Steer, gaining her diploma; then attended London Day Training College, 1928, under Marion Richardson, 1928, for her art teacher's diploma. She was a member of WIAC, AIA and Cambridge Society of Painters and Sculptors, also exhibiting at RA and LG. Solo exhibitions were at Leicester Galleries, 1953; Zwemmer Gallery, 1962; with a retrospective at the Minories, Colchester, 1971; another at Kettle's Yard, Cambridge; and one at Morley Gallery, 1997. Youngman's main works were oils of south Wales mining valleys, 1950–80, thereafter watercolours of the Norfolk coast. WAC, CASW, public galleries in Manchester and Newport, Whipple Museum in Cambridge and other collections hold examples. Lived at Waterbeach, Cambridgeshire.

LIN Show Yu: *see* **Richard LIN**

Ainslie YULE 1941– Sculptor in a variety of materials, painter and teacher, full name D Ainslie Yule, born at North Berwick, East Lothian. After attending the High School there he studied at Edinburgh College of Art and became Gregory Fellow in sculpture at Leeds University, 1974–5. Went on to lecture in design at Gray's School of Art, Aberdeen, where he lived. Showed at Richard Demarco Gallery, Edinburgh, Serpentine Gallery, LG, Leeds University and abroad. Aberdeen Art Gallery, Leeds City Art Gallery and Scottish Arts Council hold his work.

YUNUS 1943– Sculptor in a wide range of metals and stone, born in India, otherwise known as Ghulam Haider. He studied at St Martin's School of Art under Anthony Caro, and at Hammersmith College of Art and Building. Several themes were covered in his sculptures, texture and reflections being important. He said that "the end result is always organic, and seems to have grown rather than to have been shaped by man." Mixed shows included Alwin Gallery, RA Summer Exhibitions, Royal Glasgow Institute of the Fine Arts, Drian Gallery, New Ashgate Gallery in Farnham, and in Switzerland. Had solo exhibitions at Bear Lane Gallery in Oxford, Primavera Gallery in Cambridge, Commonwealth Institute, Padua in Italy and at Old Gaol, Abingdon. Oxford and Cambridge Universities hold examples. Yunus was an associate of RBS and lived in Weybridge, Surrey

Z

ZALMON 1934– Painter, designer and printmaker, born in Gateshead, County Durham, as Zalmon Winer. He studied art and architecture at Durham University and etching at Central School of Art and Design. Showed at RBA of which he was made an associate in 1984, RA, UA, NS, PS and in Israel. Shipley Art Gallery in Gateshead and Ben Uri Art Society hold examples. Lived in London.

ZERO 1898–1976 Designer, photographer, painter and lecturer, born in Kempen, Germany, real name Hans Schleger, who settled in England in 1932, being naturalised six years later. Studied art at Kunstgewerbeschule, Berlin, 1918–21, and was influenced by Bauhaus ideas. He held down a variety of design jobs in Germany and America in the 1920s before in 1926–9 opening his own studio in New York, adopting the signature Zero. In England he worked as a freelance designer for such clients as London Passenger Transport Board, Ministry of Transport and American Overseas Airlines. From 1953–76 he ran the Hans Schleger and Associates design studio in London. Designed trademarks for Penguin Books, John Lewis Partnership and the Design Centre. He was a visiting lecturer at Chelsea School of Art and Royal College of Art, at the Regional College of Art in Manchester and was visiting associate professor at the Institute of Design, Chicago, 1950–1. He participated in many exhibitions in London and abroad. Victoria & Albert Museum, London Transport Museum and the National Gallery of Australia, Canberra, hold his work. Lived in London.

Partou ZIA 1958– Painter and draughtsman, born in Tehran, Persia. She settled in England in 1970 and obtained an honours degree in history of art from University of Warwick, 1977–80, and an honours degree in fine art from Slade School of Fine Art, 1986–91. Notable teachers included Bernard Cohen, Christopher Le Brun, John Aiken, Prunella Clough, Paula Rego, Bruce McLean and Tess Jaray. Moved to Cornwall in 1993, settling in Newlyn where she was a member of the Society of Artists. In 1996 she obtained a Major Award from South West Arts. Zia said that her pictures were drawn from observation, although "it is often the case that a memory will merge with a place or building I have been preoccupied with." Mixed shows included Young Contemporaries, Whitworth Art Gallery, Manchester, 1989; John Moores Liverpool Exhibition, 1995–6, where she showed a Soutine-like oil on canvas, The Blue House; and Connaught Brown, 1996. In 1996 had a solo show at Saltram House, Plympton.

Elizabeth Rosemary ZIAR 1919– Watercolourist born in St Ives, Cornwall, where she settled in Penzance. Studied at Penzance School of Art, 1936–41, under James Lias, and in 1945 with Leonard Fuller, who ran the St Ives School of Painting. She was a member of Société des Artistes Français, showing at SWA, UA, RBSA and in France, where she won several awards. Had a series of solo exhibitions in south and west of England and in France. Private collections worldwide hold examples.

Archibald ZIEGLER 1903–1971 Painter, draughtsman and teacher, born in London. Studied at Central School of Arts and Crafts and at the Royal College of Art under William Rothenstein, 1927–30. As well as teaching drawing and painting at St Martin's School of Art, Ziegler taught art history at Morley College in London, and for the Workers' Educational Association. Toynbee Hall, in London's East End, had a mural by him. Ziegler had a series of one-man shows in London, including Adams Gallery, 1935; Leger Gallery, 1938; and Ben Uri Gallery, 1950, with a retrospective five years later. Chelsea Arts Club member who lived in London. His daughter was the artist Dahlia Ziegler.

Richard ZIEGLER 1891–1992 Painter of vibrant, colourful works, born and died in Pforzheim, Germany, which awarded him honorary citizenship in 1991 on the occasion of his hundredth birthday. Studied at the Reuchlinin Gymnasium; spent a year in Stratford-upon-Avon; then studied in Geneva, Greifswald and Heidelberg. Ziegler began painting after World War I; he had no formal training, but was notable for experiments with a range of techniques and styles. In the mid-1920s he travelled in Italy and while in Berlin joined the Novembergruppe for about eight years. While living in Paris in 1936 Ziegler decided to emigrate to England. He returned to Germany in 1961, two years later going to Mallorca, returning to Pforzheim in 1990. From 1925–46 Ziegler showed widely in Berlin, Cologne and London. Other shows included Leinster Fine Art, 1981; The Berlin Twenties, Camden Arts Centre and tour, 1983–4; and shows between 1987–91 in Berlin, Chicago, Los Angeles, London, Calw (home of the Ziegler Foundation, where a street is named after him) and Pforzheim.

Kazimierz ZIELENKIEWICZ: *see* **CAZIEL**

Anna ZINKEISEN 1901–1976 Portrait, figure, landscape and mural painter, born in Kilcreggan, Dunbartonshire. Her sister was the artist Doris Zinkeisen. Studied at Royal Academy Schools, where she won several medals. Went on to exhibit widely, including RA, RBA, RHA, ROI, SWA, RSA, Redfern Gallery, in the provinces and abroad. She completed murals on the liners *Queen Mary* and *Queen Elizabeth*. Zinkeisen's pictures are forthrightly realistic. She could be a fine portrait painter, evidenced by her self-portrait in the National Portrait Gallery. Imperial War Museum, City Art Gallery in Bradford, Nottingham City Museum and Art Gallery and collections abroad have examples. Lived in London and in Woodbridge, Suffolk.

Doris ZINKEISEN 1898–1991 Painter, stage-set and costume designer, writer and noted horsewoman, born in Kilcreggan, Dunbartonshire, the sister of Anna Zinkeisen the painter. She studied at Harrow School of Art, then won a scholarship to the Royal Academy Schools. Her first painting was shown at RA in 1918, a portrait of Anna, done when Doris was only 16. She was early on taken up by the impresario Nigel Playfair, which led to a lifelong association with the theatre. She worked with C B Cochran; painted the portraits of many notable actresses, such as Anna Neagle and Evelyn Laye; worked at the Old Vic with Laurence Olivier; created his make-up for the film *Richard III*; and wrote a key book, *Designing for the Stage*. Doris Zinkeisen did murals for the liner *Queen Mary*'s Verandah Grill; won bronze, silver and gold medals at the Paris Salon; and at the end of World War II was the first artist to enter Belsen concentration camp, two of her paintings of it being in the Imperial War Museum. She was a fine horsewoman, winning the Moscow Cup for the Supreme Hack Championship at the International Horse Show in 1934. Doris Zinkeisen's work, which often features horses and carriages in period settings, is noted for its clean draughtsmanship, unique palette and unmistakeable inter-wars stylishness. Her twin daughters were the artists Anne and Janet Grahame Johnstone. Died at Badingham, Suffolk.

Tadeusz ZNICZ-MUSZYNSKI 1921–1988 Painter and teacher, born in Warsaw, Poland. After education there he attended Bologna Unversity after World War II, Kingswood School of Art, 1947–8, and Sir John Cass School of Arts and Crafts, 1948–52. Mixed shows included Free Painters and Sculptors, NS and ROI; solo exhibitions included Grabowski Gallery, Barrett Gallery and shows abroad. He was a member of the Association of Polish Artists in Great Britain and won the Polish Art Council in Great Britain gold medal in 1979. Banco di Roma, London, holds his work. This was sometimes signed Znicz and sometimes Muszynski. Lived in London.

Ernest ZOBOLE 1927– Painter and teacher, born in Rhondda, Glamorgan. He attended Cardiff College of Art, 1948–53, where he and some friends were known as the Rhondda Group. Influences on his work included Marc Chagall and Heinz Koppel, living and teaching in the early 1950s in Dowlais, and like these two artists Zobole brought an often intense personal vision to his work. Scenes of the Rhondda Valley, to which he returned in 1957 after a few years teaching in Anglesey, are commonly in gentle, lyrical colours, nocturnal and dreamlike. Taught for some time at Newport College of Art and was a founder-member of 56 Group. Showed in many group exhibitions, including Howard Roberts Gallery in Cardiff, Dillwyn Gallery in Swansea, SWG, WAC and Royal National Eisteddfod. Solo exhibitions included Piccadilly Gallery. Was included in WAC 1981 landscape show The Dark Hills The Heavy Clouds. WAC, CASW and National Museum of Wales, Cardiff, hold his work.

Israel ZOHAR 1945– Figure and portrait painter, born in Russia, son of a well-known actor. He studied drawing with Abraham Yaskil, 1959; at the Bezalel Academy of Art in Jerusalem, 1967; and classical technique under Ernst Fuchs, 1969. Lectured at The Hebrew University, Jerusalem, 1979. In 1987 Zohar moved to England, settling in north London, having visited on a study tour which included the Netherlands in 1969. There Vermeer and Dutch genre painting made a lasting impression on his work. Had a solo show at Ahura Doron Gallery, Tel-Aviv, 1970; a retrospective in Jerusalem, 1982; another at Musée de L'Athenée, Geneva, 1987; and a solo exhibition at Roy Miles Gallery, 1989. In 1985 Israel Museum bought Zohar's self-portrait of 1980.

Marek ZULAWSKI: *see* **MAREK**

Aleksander ZYW 1905–1995 Painter, born in Lida, Poland, who studied at Warsaw Academy of Fine Arts, 1926–32, then travelled in Dalmatia, Greece and Italy the following year, settling in Paris for five years in 1934. During World War II served with the Polish Army, which brought him to Britain in 1940. He was an official war artist, following the allied campaign into Belgium. Zyw had had his first one-man show at the Art Institute in Warsaw in 1936, a first British solo exhibition taking place at the Scottish Gallery, Edinburgh in 1945. It gave him a retrospective in 1957; others included Zaheta Museum, Warsaw, 1967, and Scottish National Gallery of Modern Art, Edinburgh, 1972 (and tour) and 1986. Zyw took a studio in Edinburgh where he often worked in isolation, broken by occasional trips to Tuscany, Italy, where he finally lived, growing olives. Zyw was a restlessly experimental artist whose output spanned a number of series, each lasting some years. For the last 30 years his output stemmed from careful observation of plants and natural forms. Latterly, when he could not work in oil, he sketched. Tate Gallery holds his work, which is also in several Scottish collections. Died in Castagneto Carducci.

SELECT BIBLIOGRAPHY

This is a selection of sources consulted. Where an artist has written an autobiography I have tried to include it within the entry. Biographies are usually not mentioned there, as in some cases several have been referred to for one artist. Exhibition catalogues and originating galleries are commonly mentioned within an entry to facilitate further research. Some catalogues widely referred to are listed here. I have found national and local newspaper obituaries useful, especially those from *The Independent*, *The Times*, *The Daily Telegraph* and *The Guardian*.

GENERAL REFERENCE WORKS

Adventure in Art, Lucy Wertheim, Ivor Nicholson & Watson Ltd, 1947

Adventures in Monochrome, James Laver, The Studio Publications, no date

Allgemeines Lexicon der bildendun Künstler des XX Jahrhunderts, Hans Vollmer, Seemann, 1953–62

Allgemeines Lexicon der bildendun Künstler von der Antike bis zur Gegenwart, Ulrich Thieme/Felix Becker, Seemann, 1907–50

The Annual Register Vol. 187 – for 1945, M Epstein, Longmans, Green and Co, 1946

Art and Architecture Second Register of Artists and Craftsmen in Architecture, Theo Crosby and Jo Garlick, Art and Architecture Ltd, 1989

Art and Artists of South Africa, Esmé Berman, A A Balkema, 1983

Art at Work in Milton Keynes, Milton Keynes Development Corporation, 1990

Art in a City, John Willett, Methuen & Co Ltd, 1967

Art in Ulster, John Hewitt/Mike Catto, Blackstaff Press Ltd, 1977

Arts Council Collection, Acquisitions 1942–1978, Arts Council of Great Britain, 1979 (and subsequent volumes to 1994)

Arts Review Yearbook & Directory 1974, John Gainsborough, Richard Gainsborough Periodicals Ltd, 1974

Artists and Galleries in Australia and New Zealand, Max Germaine, Lansdowne Editions, 1979

Artists and Galleries of Australia, Max Germaine, Craftsman House, 1990

Artists and the East End, Peter Marcan, Peter Marcan Publications, 1986

Artists at Work, Stanley Casson, George G Harrap & Co Ltd, 1933

Artists Exhibited in Wales 1945–74, Kirstine Brander Dunthorne, Welsh Arts Council, 1975

Artists of Northumbria, Marshall Hall, Marshall Hall Associates, 1982

Artists' Country, G S Sandilands, The Studio Ltd, 1932

The Artist in Wales, David Bell, George G Harrap & Co Ltd, 1957

The Artists of Cumbria, Marshall Hall, Marshall Hall Associates, 1979

The Artist's Guide, Frederick Parkinson, The Artist Publishing Co Ltd, 1951

Avant-Garde British Printmaking 1914–1960, Frances Carey and Antony Griffiths, British Museum Publications, 1990

Britain's Art Colony by the Sea, Denys Val Baker, George Ronald, 1959

British Art Since 1900, Sir John Rothenstein, Phaidon Press Ltd, 1962

British Contemporary Sculpture at Goodwood 1996–97

British Landscape Painters: A History and Gazetteer, Charles Hemming, Gollancz, 1989

British Sculpture 1944–1946, Eric Newton, John Tiranti Ltd, 1947

British Sculpture since 1945, Dennis Farr, Tate Gallery, 1965
British Painting since 1945, Richard Morphet, Tate Gallery, 1965
Catalogue of the National Gallery of Canada, Charles C Hill and Pierre B Landry, Canadian Art, 1988
City Impressions: Bristol Etchers 1910–1935, Sheena Stoddard, Redcliffe Press Ltd,1990
Colours of War, Alan Ross, Jonathan Cape, 1983
A Century of British Painting 1851–1951, Anthony Bertram, The Studio Ltd, 1951
The Challenge of Landscape Painting, Ian Simpson, William Collins Sons & Co Ltd, 1990
Concise Catalogue of British Paintings Volume II British Artists Born in or After 1850, Manchester City Art Gallery, 1978
The Concise Oxford Companion to the Theatre, Phyllis Hartnoll and Peter Found, Oxford University Press, 1992
The Conran Dictionary of Design, Stephen Bayley, Octopus Conran, 1985
Conversations with Painters, Noël Barber, Collins, 1964
Contemporary Artists, St James Press, Chicago and London, various editions
Contemporary British Art, Herbert Read, Penguin Books Ltd, 1951 (and 1964 revision)
Contemporary British Artists, Charlotte Parry-Crooke, Bergstrom + Boyle Books, 1979
Contemporary Designers, Colin Naylor, St James Press, 1990
Crockford's Clerical Directory 1995–6, Church House Publishing, 1996
Debrett's Distinguished People of Today, Debrett's Peerage Ltd, 1990
Debrett's Handbook, Debrett's Peerage Ltd, 1984
The Dictionary of British Artists 1880–1940, J Johnson and A Greutzner, The Antique Collectors' Club, 1988
Dictionary of British Artists Working 1900–1950, Grant M Waters, Eastbourne Fine Art Publications, 1975
Dictionary of British Book Illustrators The Twentieth Century, Brigid Peppin and Lucy Micklethwait, John Murray, 1983
Dictionary of British Equestrian Artists, Sally Mitchell, Antique Collectors' Club, 1985
A Dictionary of British Miniature Painters, Daphne Foskett, Faber and Faber Ltd 1972
A Dictionary of Canadian Artists, Colin S Macdonald, Canadian Publishing Ltd, 1980
Dictionary of Irish Artists: Twentieth Century, Theo Snoddy, Wolfhound Press, 1996
A Dictionary of Modern Painting, Carlton Lake and Robert Maillard, Methuen & Co Ltd, 1958
The Dictionary of National Biography, Oxford University Press, various editions
The Dictionary of Scottish Painters 1600–1960, Paul Harris and Julian Halsby, Canongate Publishing and Phaidon Press in association with Bourne Fine Art Ltd, 1990
Dictionary of Sea Painters, E H H Archibald, Antique Collectors' Club, 1989
Dictionary of South African Biography, C J Beyers, Human Sciences Research Council, 1987
The Dictionary of South African Painters and Sculptors including Namibia, Grania Ogilvie, Everard Read, 1988
A Dictionary of Sporting Artists 1650–1990, Mary Ann Wingfield, Antique Collectors' Club, 1992
The Dictionary of 20th Century British Book Illustrators, Alan Horne, Antique Collectors' Club, 1994
Dictionnaire Critique et Documentaire des Peintres, Sculpteurs, Dessinateurs et Graveurs, E Bénézit, Librairie Gründ, 1976
Le Dictionnaire des Peintres Belges, du XIVe Siecle à Nos Jours, La Renaissance du Livre, 1994
Directory of Playwrights, Directors, Designers, Catherine Itzin, John Offord (Publications) Ltd, 1983

Dudley Metropolitan Borough Public Art Guide, John Bennett, Dudley Metropolitan Borough Council, 1990
An East London Album, Peter Marcan, Peter Marcan Publications, 1992
Encyclopedia of Australian Art, Alan McCulloch/Susan McCulloch, The Herbert Press Ltd, 1994
Encyclopedia of Rock, Phil Hardy and Dave Laing, Macdonald & Co (Publishers) Ltd, 1987
The Euston Road School, Bruce Laughton, Scolar Press, 1986
Everyman's Dictionary of Literary Biography, D C Browning, J M Dent & Sons, 1958
The Eye in the Wind Contemporary Scottish Painting since 1945, Edward Gage, Collins, 1977
Exhibition The Memoirs of Oliver Brown, Evelyn, Adams and Mackay, 1968
50 Artistes de Belgique, Viva Press, 1984
Handbook of Modern British Painting 1900–1980, Alan Windsor, Scolar Press, 1992
Hidden Talents A Dictionary of Neglected Artists Working 1880–1950, Jeremy Wood, Jeremy Wood Fine Art, 1994
A History of British Wood Engraving, Albert Garrett, Midas Books, 1978
A Hundred Years and More, David Jeremiah, Manchester Polytechnic Faculty of Art and Design, 1980
A Hundred Years of British Painting 1851–1951, Hesketh Hubbard, Longmans, Green & Co Ltd, 1951
The Illustrated Guide to Film Directors, David Quinlan, B T Batsford, 1983
Illustrators at Work, Robin Jacques, Studio Books (Longacre Press Ltd), 1963
Image: 1–8, Art and Technics Ltd, 1949–52
The International Who's Who, 1995–6, Europa Publications Ltd, 1995
Jewish Artists The Ben Uri Collection, Walter Schwab and Julia Weiner, Ben Uri Art Society in association with Lund Humphries Publishers Ltd, 1994
Keesing's Contemporary Archives, Vol. No. V, 1943–6, Keesing's Publications Ltd
Liverpool Seen Post-war Artists on Merseyside, Peter Davies, Redcliffe Press Ltd, 1992
Marquis Who's Who in America, Macmillan Directory Division, 1990
The Medical Directory, Cartermill International Ltd, 1996
The Medical Directory, Longman Information and Reference, 1993
Merseyside Painters, People & Places, Walker Art Gallery, Liverpool/Merseyside County Council, 1978
Modern Art in English Churches, Michael Day, A R Mowbray & Co Ltd, 1984
Modern Australian Painting, Donald J Finley, Beaverbrook Newspapers Ltd, 1963
Modern British Sculpture from the Collection, Penelope Curtis, Tate Gallery Publications, 1988
Modern English Painters Lewis to Moore, John Rothenstein, Eyre & Spottiswoode, 1956
Modern English Painters Sickert to Smith, John Rothenstein, Eyre & Spottiswoode, 1952
Modern English Painters Wood to Hockney, John Rothenstein, Macdonald and Jane's, 1974
Modern Masterpieces, Frank Rutter, George Newnes Ltd, no date
Modern Movements in Painting, Charles Marriott, Chapman and Hall, Ltd, 1920
Modern Painting in England, Mary Chamot, Country Life Ltd, 1937
Modern Sculpture, Alan Bowness, Studio Vista Publishers, 1972
Modern Stained Glass in British Churches, Mark Angus, A R Mowbray & Co Ltd, 1984
Motif 1–13, Shenval Press Ltd, 1958–67
North American women artists of the twentieth century: a biographical dictionary, Jules Heller and Nancy G Heller, Garland, 1995
The North West Essex Collection An Introduction, Olive Cook, The Fry Art Gallery Society, 1988

A Northern School Lancashire Artists of the Twentieth Century, Peter Davies, Redcliffe Press Ltd, 1989
Open Air Sculpture in Britain, W J Strachan, A Zwemmer Ltd/Tate Gallery Publications, 1984
The Oxford Companion to the Theatre, Phyllis Hartnoll, Oxford University Press, 1985
The Oxford Companion to Twentieth-Century Art, Harold Osborne, Oxford University Press, 1981
Painting Since 1939, Robin Ironside, The British Council, 1947
A Picture of Flemings A Selection of Scottish Paintings, Bill Smith, Robert Fleming Holdings Ltd, no date
Pitmen Painters: The Ashington Group 1934–1984, William Feaver, Chatto & Windus Ltd, 1988
Poole Pottery, Leslie Hayward, Richard Dennis, 1995
Portal Painters, Eric Lister, Alpine Fine Arts, 1982
Portrait of the Artist Twenty Five Years of British Art, Jorge Lewinski, Carcanet Press Ltd, 1987
Provident Financial Art Collection, Marina Vaizey/John Sheeran, Sheeran Lock, 1995
RBS: Modern British Sculpture, Country Life Ltd, 1939
The Renovation of Kippen Parish Church 1924–1991, R W A Begg, Kippen Church, 1991
RIBA Members '92, RIBA, 1992
Royal Academy Exhibitors 1905–1970, E P Publishing Ltd, 1973
Royal Academy Exhibitors 1971–1989, Charles Baile de Laperriere, Hilmarton Manor Press, 1989
The Royal Glasgow Institute of the Fine Arts 1861–1989, Roger Billcliffe, The Woodend Press, 1992
The Royal Scottish Academy Exhibitors 1826–1990, Charles Baile de Laperriere, Hilmarton Manor Press, 1991
Scottish Painting 1837 to the Present, William Hardie, Studio Vista, 1990
Scottish Watercolours 1740–1940, Julian Halsby, B T Batsford Ltd, 1986
Sculpture Today in Great Britain 1940–1943, Arthur T Broadbent, Alec Tiranti Ltd, 1949
A Short History of English Sculpture, Eric Underwood, Faber and Faber Ltd, 1933
From Sickert to 1948 The Achievement of the Contemporary Art Society, John Russell, Lund Humphries, 1948
The Sixties Art Scene in London, David Mellor, Phaidon Press/Barbican Art Gallery, 1993
The Society of Women Artists Exhibitors 1855–1996, Charles Baile de Laperriere, Hilmarton Manor Press, 1996
St Ives 1883–1993 Portrait of an Art Colony, Marion Whybrow, Antique Collectors' Club, 1994
The Story of the Artists International Association, Lynda Morris and Robert Radford, The Museum of Modern Art Oxford, 1983
Suffolk Artists 1750–1930, Chloë Bennett, Images Publications & Ipswich Borough Council, 1991
Tate Gallery Modern British Paintings, Drawings & Sculpture, Mary Chamot, Dennis Farr & Martin Butlin, The Oldbourne Press, 1964
Technique Anglaise: Current Trends in British Art, Andrew Renton and Liam Gillick, Thames and Hudson One-off Press, 1991
Thirty Years of British Art, Sir Joseph Duveen, Bt., The Studio Ltd, 1930
3 Decades of Private Views at the Drian, Halima Nalecz, Drian Galleries, 1986
The Times Index, Research Publications Ltd, various editions
The Townsend Journals, Andrew Forge, The Tate Gallery, 1976
Twentieth Century British Marine Painting, Denys Brook-Hart, Antique Collectors' Club, 1981

20th Century Painters and Sculptors, Frances Spalding (assistant editor Judith Collins), Antique Collectors' Club, 1990
Twentieth Century Water-colours, Victoria & Albert Museum/Her Majesty's Stationery Office, 1958
Underground Architecture, David Lawrence, Capital Transport Publishing, 1994
Wales on Canvas Fifteen Contemporary Artists, Hywel Harries, Y Lolfa, 1988
War Pictures by British Artists, first and second series, 1942–3: 1 *War at Sea*, Sir Herbert Richmond 2 *Blitz*, J B Morton 3 *RAF*, H E Bates 4 *Army*, Colin Coote; 1 *Women*, Laura Knight 2 *Production*, Cecil Beaton 3 *Soldiers*, William Coldstream 4 *Air Raids*, Stephen Spender
War Through Artists' Eyes, Eric Newton, John Murray, 1945
Water-colour, Percy V Bradshaw, The Studio Ltd, no date
Who Was Who, Adam & Charles Black, various editions
Who Was Who in American Art, Peter Hastings Falk, Sound View Press, 1985
Who's Who, Adam & Charles Black, various editions
Who's Who in American Art 1989–90, R R Bowker, 1989
Who's Who in Art, The Art Trade Press Ltd, various editions
Who's Who in the Theatre, Pitman Publishing, 1972
Women Artists and the Pre-Raphaelite Movement, Jan Marsh and Pamela Gerrish Nunn, Virago, 1989
The Year's Art, A C R Carter, Hutchinson and Co (Publishers) Ltd, various volumes to 1947
Yorkshire Artists A Short Dictionary, Harry Turnbull, Thornton Gallery, 1976
Young Artists of Promise, Jack Beddington, The Studio Ltd, 1957

INDIVIDUAL ARTISTS' BIOGRAPHIES

Ayrton

Michael Ayrton An Illustrated Commentary, Peter Cannon-Brookes, City Museums and Art Gallery, Birmingham, 1977
Michael Ayrton: a biography, Justine Hopkins, André Deutsch, 1994

Ball

A Kind of Madness: The Sculptures of Peter Eugene Ball, Inga Gilbert, Speedwell Books, 1993

Bawden

Edward Bawden, Douglas Percy Bliss, The Pendomer Press, no date
Edward Bawden, Robert Harling, Art and Technics, 1950

Beaton

Cecil Beaton, Hugo Vickers, Weidenfeld and Nicolson, 1985

Blake

Peter Blake, Marina Vaizey, Weidenfeld and Nicolson Ltd, 1986

Bomberg

David Bomberg, William Lipke, Evelyn, Adams & Mackay Ltd, 1967

Bowman

Betty Bowman A More Private View, Sibyl O'Donnell, Bodkin Bookshop & Gallery, 1984

Buhler

Robert Buhler, Colin Hayes, Weidenfeld and Nicolson, 1986

Carr

David Carr The Discovery of an Artist, Bryan Robertson/Ronald Alley, Quartet Books Ltd, 1987

Collins

Cecil Collins: The Quest for Great Happiness, William Anderson, Barrie & Jenkins, 1988

Coward

Out in the Midday Sun The Paintings of Noel Coward, Sheridan Morley, Phaidon/Christie's Ltd, 1988

Cowie

James Cowie, Cordelia Oliver, Edinburgh University Press, 1980

Cripps

Stephen Cripps Pyrotechnic Sculptor, David Toop, Acme Housing Association Ltd/Stephen Cripps Trust, 1992

Dick

Reid Dick, H Granville Fell, A Tiranti, 1945

Dobson

Dobson, T W Earp, A Tiranti, 1945

Eardley

Joan Eardley, William Buchanan, Edinburgh University Press, 1976

Fassett

Kaffe Fassett at the V&A, Knitting and Needlepoint, Sally Harding, Century Hutchinson Ltd, 1988

Fergusson

The Art of J D Fergusson, Margaret Morris, Blackie, 1974

Fisher

Mark Fisher and Margaret Fisher Prout, Vincent Lines, Published privately/distributed by Charles Skilton Ltd, 1966

Freedman

Barnett Freedman, Jonathan Mayne, Pellegrini & Cudahy, no date

Gillies

W G Gillies A Very Still life, W Gordon Smith, Atelier Books, 1991

Guevara

Latin among Lions: Alvaro Guevara, Diana Holman-Hunt, Michael Joseph Ltd, 1974

Hennell

Thomas Hennell: Countryman, Artist and Writer, Michael MacLeod, Cambridge University Press, 1988

Herman

Josef Herman Paintings & Drawings, Edwin Mullins, Evelyn, Adams & Mackay Ltd, 1967

Hitchens

Ivon Hitchens, Peter Khoroche, André Deutsch Ltd, 1990

Hockney

David Hockney, Marco Livingstone, Thames and Hudson, 1987
Portrait of David Hockney, Peter Webb, Chatto & Windus Ltd, 1988

Hodgkins

Frances Hodgkins, Myfanwy Evans, Penguin Books, 1948
Frances Hodgkins Four Vital Years, Arthur R Howell, Rockliff Publishing Corporation Ltd, 1951

Hurry

Paintings and Drawings by Leslie Hurry, Jack Lindsay, The Grey Walls Press, 1950

Hutchinson

Ten Drawings of Gloria by Norman Hutchinson, no publisher, 1963

John

Augustus John, Sir John Rothenstein, Beaverbrook Newspapers Ltd, 1962

Johnstone

William Johnstone, Douglas Hall, Edinburgh University Press, 1980

Jonzen

Karin Jonzen Sculptor, Bachman & Turner, 1976

Keating

The Fake's Progress, Tom Keating, Frank Norman, Geraldine Norman, Arrow Books Ltd, 1978

Kelly

Paintings by Felix Kelly, Herbert Read, Falcon Press Ltd, 1948

Kennington

Eric Kennington Drawing the RAF, Sir Ronald Storrs, Oxford University Press, 1942

Knight

Charles Knight, RWS, ROI, Michael Brockway, F Lewis Publishers Ltd, 1952
Laura Knight, Janet Dunbar, Collins, 1975

Kossowski

Adam Kossowski Murals and Paintings, Benedict Read, Armelle Press, 1990

Lamb

Henry Lamb The Artist and his Friends, Keith Clements, Redcliffe Press Ltd, 1985

Lamba

Sculptures Juginder Lamba, Woburn Fine Arts, 1986

Lewis

The Art of Wyndham Lewis, Charles Handley-Read, Faber and Faber Ltd, 1961

Lowry

L S Lowry, David McLean, The Medici Society Ltd, 1978

MacNeice

Louis MacNeice, Jon Stallworthy, Faber and Faber, 1995

MacTaggart

W MacTaggart, H Harvey Wood, Edinburgh University Press, 1974

Maxwell

John Maxwell, David McClure, Edinburgh University Press, 1976

Meninsky

Bernard Meninsky, John Russell Taylor, Redcliffe Press Ltd, 1990

Mesens

Don't Tell Sybil, An Intimate Memoir of E L T Mesens, George Melly, Heinemann, 1997

Minton

Dance Till the Stars Come Down A Biography of John Minton, Frances Spalding, Hodder and Stoughton, 1991

Moore

Portrait of an Artist Henry Moore, John Read, Whizzard Press/André Deutsch, 1979

Mount

Paul Mount Sculpture a Retrospective Selection, Ronald Gaskell, Nancherrow Studio, 1981

Moynihan

Rodrigo Moynihan, John Ashbery and Richard Shone, Daniel Skira and Partners, 1988

Muncaster

The Wind in the Oak (Life of Claude Muncaster), Martin Muncaster, Robin Garton, 1978

Munnings

The Englishman: A Biography of Sir Alfred Munnings, Reginald Pound, William Heinemann Ltd, 1962

Nash

John Nash The Painter as Illustrator, John Lewis, Potter Books Ltd, 1978
Paul Nash, Sir John Rothenstein, Beaverbrook Newspapers Ltd, 1961

Nicholson

William Nicholson, Lillian Browse, Rupert Hart-Davis, 1956
William Nicholson, Marguerite Steen, Collins, 1943

Pasmore

Victor Pasmore, Clive Bell, Penguin Books, 1945
Victor Pasmore, Jasia Reichardt, Methuen, 1962

Philipson

Robin Philipson, Maurice Lindsay, Edinburgh University Press, 1976

Quanne

Prison Paintings, Michael Quanne, John Berger, John Murray (Publishers) Ltd, 1985

Redpath

Anne Redpath, George Bruce, Edinburgh University Press, 1974

Reid Henry

Highlight the Wild The Art of the Reid Henrys, Bruce Henry, Palaquin Publishing, 1986

Reynolds

Alan Reynolds, J P Hodin, The Redfern Artists Series, no date

Ritchie

Walter Ritchie Sculpture in Brick and Other Materials, Distributed by Peter Dix Associates, 1978

Rocke

Basil Rocke: Artist and Teacher, Rosemary Devonald, Redcliffe Press Ltd, 1989

Rogers

The Affectionate Eye The Life of Claude Rogers, Jenny Pery, Sansom & Company, 1995

Scott

William Scott, Ronald Alley, Methuen, 1963

Seago

Edward Seago: The Other Side of the Canvas, Jean Goodman, William Collins, 1978

Smith

Matthew Smith, Francis Halliday and John Russell, George Allen and Unwin Ltd, 1962

Souza

F N Souza, Edwin Mullins, Anthony Blond Ltd, 1962

Spencer

Stanley Spencer, Elizabeth Rothenstein, Beaverbrook Newspapers Ltd, 1962

Stone

Reynolds Stone, Myfanwy Piper, Art and Technics, 1951

Sutherland

Graham Sutherland: a Biography, Roger Berthoud, 1982

Tabner

Len Tabner 1970–1989, Peter Prendergast, Thos Agnew & Sons Ltd, 1989

Taylor

Leonard Campbell Taylor, RA, His Place in Art, Herbert Furst, F Lewis, Publishers, Ltd, 1945

Underwood

Leon Underwood, Christopher Neve, Thames and Hudson, 1974

Wadsworth

Edward Wadsworth A Painter's Life, Barbara Wadsworth, Michael Russell (Publishing) Ltd, 1989

Welch

The Denton Welch Journals, Jocelyn Brooke, Hamish Hamilton Ltd, 1952

Wells

E F Wells His Art, Life and Times, Anthony H Hull, Alan Sutton Publishing Ltd, 1990

Whistler

Rex Whistler, Laurence Whistler, Art and Technics, 1948

Wilson

It's All Writ Out for You: The Life and Work of Scottie Wilson, George Melly, Thames and Hudson, 1986

Scottie Wilson, Mervyn Levy, Brook Street Gallery, 1966

Yeats

Jack Yeats, T G Rosenthal, Knowledge Publications/Purnell & Sons Ltd, 1966

MIXED/GROUP EXHIBITION CATALOGUES

(numerous annual exhibiting society, public and commercial gallery catalogues not listed here are commonly referred to within artist entries)

no date

The Avant-Garde in Britain 1910–1960, Fine Art Associates

1951

Sixty Paintings for '51, Arts Council/Festival of Britain

1957

Painting and Sculpture, Camberwell School of Arts and Crafts at South London Art Gallery

1960

Sculpture in the Open Air, London County Council, Battersea Park

1962

19 Young Sculptors, Hillfield Gardens, Gloucester

1963

A Painter's Collection (Edward le Bas), Royal College of Art

1963–4

14 Scottish Painters, The Commonwealth Institute/The Arts Council – Scottish Committee, tour

1964

London Group 1914–64, Tate Gallery, and tour
The Teaching Image Work by the Staff of the Leeds College of Art, Leeds City Art Gallery

1966

Contemporary British Sculpture, Arts Council

1967

Outdoor Sculpture, Arts Council
Survey '67: Abstract Painters, Camden Arts Centre

1968

Sculpture in a City, Arts Council
Survey '68: Abstract Sculpture, Camden Arts Centre

1971

The Alistair McAlpine Gift, The Tate Gallery

1972

British Sculptors '72, Royal Academy of Art

1974

British Painting '74, Arts Council
An Element of Landscape, Arts Council

1975–6

British Painting 1900–1960, Sheffield City Art Galleries and tour

1977

British Painting 1952–1977, The Royal Academy of Arts

1977 onwards

The Hayward Annual, Hayward Gallery

1978

Objects and Constructions, The Scottish Arts Council
Painters in Parallel, Scottish Arts Council
A Free Hand, Arts Council
Unit 1, Portsmouth City Museum and Art Gallery

1979–80

The Seven and Five Society 1920–35, Michael Parkin Fine Art Ltd, and tour

1980

British Art Now: An American Perspective, The Solomon R Guggenheim Museum, New York
The Probity of Art, Welsh Arts Council tour
Summer Shows 1,2,3, Serpentine Gallery

1981

British Sculpture in the Twentieth Century, Whitechapel Art Gallery
Contemporary Artists in Camden, Camden Arts Centre plus other venues
The Dark Hills The Heavy Clouds, Welsh Arts Council
Some Chantrey Favourites, Royal Academy of Arts

1981–2

Contemporary Art From Scotland 1981–1982, Scottish Gallery, Edinburgh, and tour
Fragments against Ruin, Arts Council tour

1981–3

Serpentine Summer Shows, Serpentine Gallery

1982

Scottish Art Now, Scottish Arts Council

1983

Have You Seen Sculpture from the Body?, Woodlands Art Gallery
The Sculpture Show, South Bank Centre/Serpentine Gallery
Sculpture in a Country Park, Welsh Sculpture Trust, Margam
Six Artists from the Coast, Laing Art Gallery, Newcastle, and tour
"That's Shell – that is!", Shell Advertising Art, Barbican Art Gallery
Twentieth Century Sporting Art, British Sporting Art Trust at Alpine Club Gallery
Wapping Artists Open Studios

1984

Berry Street Open Studios Exhibition, 8 Berry Street, EC1
The Forgotten Fifties, Graves Art Gallery, Sheffield, and tour
New Vision 56–66, Bede Gallery, Jarrow

1984 onwards

The British Art Show Old Allegiances and New Directions, 1979–1984, Arts Council, 1984, and subsequent shows to *British Art Show 4, 1995–6*

1985

St Ives 1939–64, The Tate Gallery

1985–6

The Brotherhood of Ruralists and Friends, The Piccadilly Gallery

1985 onwards

John Moores Liverpool Exhibition, Walker Art Gallery, Liverpool

1986

Art in Exile in Great Britain 1933–45, Camden Arts Centre
Colour Presentations, Gardner Centre Gallery, University of Sussex, Brighton, and tour
The New English Art Club Centenary Exhibition, Christie's
Sculpture In Britain Between The Wars, The Fine Art Society
Seven Sculptors Working in Wales, Glynn Vivian Art Gallery & Museum, Swansea
Sladey Ladies, Michael Parkin Gallery

1986–7

A Reputation Amongst Artists, Norwich School of Art Gallery tour

1987

British Art in the Twentieth Century The Modern Movement, Royal Academy of Arts
Contemporary Art Society for Wales 50th Anniversary Exhibition, National Museum of Wales, and tour
Peterborough Art '87, Lady Lodge Arts Centre, Peterborough
Royal Academy Exhibitors, Fosse Gallery, Stow-on-the-Wold
The Self Portrait: a Modern View, Artsite Gallery, Bath, and tour

1988

Beyond the Horizon: Artists at Lintas 1930–1950. Thos Agnew & Sons Ltd
Camberwell Artists of the 40s and 50s, The Belgrave Gallery
Cross-Section: British Art in the Twentieth Century, Peter Nahum
A Disquieting Suggestion, John Hansard Gallery, The University of Southampton
Exhibition Road, Painters at the Royal College of Art, Royal College of Art
Lancashire South of the Sands 3. The Contemporary Landscape, County and Regimental Museum, Preston, and tour
The Painters of Camden Town 1905–1920, Christie's
Post-War British Abstract Art, Austin/Desmond Fine Art
Some of the Moderns, The Belgrave Gallery

1988–9

Corsham A Celebration The Bath Academy of Art 1946–72, Michael Parkin Gallery and tour
The Presence of Painting Aspects of British Abstraction 1957–1988, The South Bank Centre tour

1989

A Century of Art in Cornwall 1889–1989, Newlyn Orion, Newlyn
A Century of Printmaking in Britain 1889–1989, Whitworth Art Gallery, Manchester
Complexions, Galerie L'Idee, Zoetermeer/Dean Clough Contemporary Art Gallery, Halifax

Drawn to Paper A Selection of British Drawings and Watercolours 1900–1939, Whitworth Art Gallery, Manchester
An Exhibition of Scottish Painters, Fosse Gallery, Stow-on-the-Wold
The Experience of Painting Eight Modern Artists, The South Bank Centre/Laing Art Gallery, Newcastle upon Tyne tour
Links of Affinity Dutch Contemporary Art in Britain, Knapp Gallery/Glasgow Art Club
Painting the Visible World, Austin/Desmond Fine Art
Portrait of the Artist, The Tate Gallery
Some of the Moderns, The Belgrave Gallery
Spirit in the Mass The Borough Group with Bomberg 1946–1951, Fine Art Associates
Ten Contemporary Scottish Painters, Thackeray Gallery

1989–90

Scottish Art Since 1990, Scottish National Gallery of Modern Art, Edinburgh/Barbican Art Gallery

1990

Artist of the Day, Flowers East
The Birmingham School, Birmingham City Museum and Art Gallery
The British Art Show, South Bank Centre tour
The Broad Horizon, Agnew's
The Compass Contribution Twenty One Years of Contemporary Art 1969–1990, Tramway, Glasgow
Contemporary Artists from Ireland, Austin/Desmond Fine Art
The Fine Art Collections, Pallant House, Chichester, Wildenstein
New North, New Art from the North of Britain, Tate Gallery Liverpool
The Northern Lights Twenty-four Artists from the North East of England, DLI Museum & Arts Centre, Durham, and tour
A Salute to Glasgow, Portland Gallery
Scottish Art 1900–1990, The Scottish Gallery
Some of the Moderns, Belgrave Gallery
The Winners of the Guthrie Award 1920–1989, The Fine Art Society, Glasgow

1990 onwards

Art in Boxes, England & Co

1991

The Birmingham Seven, John Bonham, Murray Feely Fine Art
Danger Artists at Work, City Art Centre, Edinburgh, and tour
East National Open Art Exhibition, Norwich Gallery Norfolk Institute of Art and Design
Eric Gill and the Guild of St Joseph and St Dominic, Hove Museum and Art Gallery, and tour
Images of the Yorkshire Landscape, City of Leeds Civic Hall
Messages from Nowhere, Austin/Desmond & Phipps
Scottish Art in the 20th Century, Royal West of England Academy, Bristol
Sculpture & Sculptors' Drawings, William Jackson Gallery
The Prose of Painting, Austin/Desmond Fine Art
A Survey of Influential East Anglian Artists, Chappel Galleries, Chappel
Westminster School of Art, Sally Hunter Fine Art
Seis Jovenes Pintores Britanicos, Torreon de Lozoya – Segovia, and Spanish tour

1991 onwards

Sculpture at Canterbury, Kent Institute of Art & Design, Canterbury

1991–2 onwards

The Discerning Eye, Mall Galleries/Williamson Gallery, Birkenhead

1992

Artists from Cornwall, Royal West of England Academy
Bluecoat Artists '92, Williamson Art Gallery & Museum, Birkenhead
British Abstract Art of The 50s and 60s, The Belgrave Gallery
East & South National Open Art Exhibition, Norwich Gallery Norfolk Institute of Art and Design/Kent Institute of Art and Design, Canterbury
The Foundations of Behaviour, John Bonham, Murray Feely Fine Art
History and Identity Seven Painters, Norwich Gallery touring exhibition
Somatic States, Norwich Gallery Norfolk Institute of Art and Design
Women Critics Select Women Artists, The Bruton Street Gallery

1992–3

Twelve Stars Selected Works from the European Parliament Collection, Arts Council Gallery, Belfast, and tour

1992 onwards

Young British Artists, Saatchi Gallery

1993

Aberystwyth Artists, Deffett Francis Gallery, Swansea Institute of Higher Education
Contemporary Art From Scotland, Thompson's Gallery (London)
Continuing the Tradition A Survey of Influential East Anglian Artists II, Chappel Galleries, Chappel
(Dis)parities, Herbert Art Gallery & Museum, Coventry
Drawing Towards Sculpture, Isis Gallery & Arts Institute, Leigh-on-Sea
Polish Roots British Soil, City Art Centre, Edinburgh
Recent British Sculpture from the Arts Council Collection, South Bank Centre tour
The Sixties Art Scene in London, Barbican Art Gallery
Through Women's Eyes, City Art Centre, Edinburgh

1993–4

The London Group's 80th Anniversary Open Exhibition, Barbican Centre

1993 onwards

1st Open Sculpture Exhibition, Royal West of England Academy

1994

Aiding and Abetting, The Gallery at John Jones
Beyond the Partitions, Queen Street Studios, Belfast
Falmouth Connections, Falmouth Art Gallery
Made in Greenwich 1974–1994, The Living Room
National Eisteddfod of Wales, Neath and District
New Art in Scotland, Centre for Contemporary Arts, Glasgow

The Northern Art Show, The Mall Galleries
Queen Street Studios Belfast Works on Paper, Queen Street Studios/The Gallery, Dublin Road, Belfast

1994 onwards

Royal Over-Seas League Annual Open Exhibition, Over-Seas House/Edinburgh College of Art

1995

Brilliant! New Art from London, Walker Art Center, Minneapolis
The Edge of Beyond, Belgrave Gallery
Journeys West, University of Essex tour
Making It, Tate Gallery Liverpool
Polish Paper Sculpture, Polish Cultural Institute
Real Art, Southampton City Art Gallery

1996

Colchester Art Society 1946–1996, Chappel Galleries, Chappel
The Deck of Cards, Pallant House, Chichester
Drawing, Fine Art Society
Freezeframe, Lamont Gallery
New Contemporaries, Tate Gallery Liverpool/Camden Arts Centre
Outsiders & Co, England & Co
Sculpting, Fine Art Society
St Ives Now, Collyer-Bristow Gallery
The Table Studio Group, The Living Room
Tenth Anniversary, Cadogan Contemporary

1996–7

About Vision New British Painting in the 1990s, Museum of Modern Art, Oxford
New Territories, Stamford Arts Centre, and tour

1997

Sensation, Young British Artists from the Saatchi Collection, Royal Academy of Arts